RIVERSIDE WEBSTER'S II DICTIONARY

REVISED EDITION

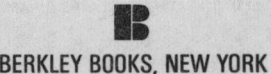

Words are included in this dictionary on the basis of their usage. Words that are known to have current trademark registrations are shown with an initial capital and are also identified as trademarks. No investigation has been made of common-law trademark rights in any word, because such investigation is impracticable. The inclusion of any word in this dictionary is not, however, an expression of the publishers' opinions as to whether or not it is subject to proprietary rights. Indeed, no definition in this dictionary is to be regarded as affecting the validity of any trademark.

Based on *Webster's II New College Dictionary.*

RIVERSIDE WEBSTER'S II DICTIONARY

A Berkley Book / published by arrangement with
Houghton Mifflin Company

PRINTING HISTORY
Houghton Mifflin edition published 1996
Berkley edition / August 1996

The Putnam Berkley World Wide Web site address is
http://www.berkley.com

ISBN: 0-425-15418-1

BERKLEY®
Berkley Books are published by The Berkley Publishing Group,
200 Madison Avenue, New York, New York 10016.
BERKLEY and the "B" design
are trademarks belonging to Berkley Publishing Corporation.

PRINTED IN THE UNITED STATES OF AMERICA

10 9 8 7 6 5 4 3 2

Table of Contents

Abbreviations Used in This Dictionary

Abbreviations in Subject Labels

Abbreviation	Full Form	Abbreviation	Full Form
Anat.	Anatomy	*Meteorol.*	Meteorology
Astron.	Astronomy	*Microbiol.*	Microbiology
Biochem.	Biochemistry	*Mineral.*	Mineralogy
Biol.	Biology	*Mus.*	Music
Bot.	Botany	*Myth.*	Mythology
Brit.	British	*Naut.*	Nautical
Can.	Canadian	*Obs.*	Obsolete
Chem.	Chemistry	*Pathol.*	Pathology
Computer Sci.	Computer Science	*Philos.*	Philosophy
		Physiol.	Physiology
Ecol.	Ecology	*Psychiat.*	Psychiatry
Elect.	Electricity	*Psychoanal.*	Psychoanalysis
Electron.	Electronics	*Psychol.*	Psychology
Engineer.	Engineering	*Rom. Cath. Ch.*	Roman Catholic Church
Geol.	Geology		
Gk. Myth.	Greek Mythology	*Rom. Myth.*	Roman Mythology
Gram.	Grammar		
Ling.	Linguistics	*Scot.*	Scots
Math.	Mathematics	*Theol.*	Theology
Med.	Medicine	*Zool.*	Zoology

Other Abbreviations

Abbreviation	Full Form	Abbreviation	Full Form
abbr.	abbreviation	cg	centigram(s)
A.D.	anno Domini	cm	centimeter(s)
adj.	adjective	*compar.*	comparative
adv.	adverb	*conj.*	conjunction
Amer.	American	cu	cubic
approx.	approximately	D.C.	District of Columbia
B.C.	before Christ		
C	Celsius; centigrade; central	*def. art.*	definite article
		E	east, eastern
c.	circa	EC	east-central
Cap.	capital	esp.	especially
cent.	century	F	Fahrenheit

Abbreviation	Full Form
fl.	flourished
fl oz	fluid ounce
ft	foot, feet
g	gram(s)
gal	gallon(s)
gen.	generally
gr	grain(s)
in.	inch(es)
indef. art.	indefinite article
interj.	interjection
Is.	Island(s)
kg	kilogram(s)
kl	kiloliter(s)
km	kilometer(s)
kph	kilometers per hour
kw	kilowatt(s)
L	liter(s)
lb	pound(s)
m	meter(s)
mg	milligram(s)
min	minute(s)
mm	millimeter(s)
mph	miles per hour
Mt.	Mountain, Mount
Mts.	Mountains
N	north, northern
n.	noun
NC	north-central
NE	northeast
NW	northwest
occas.	occasionally
orig.	origin; originally
oz	ounce(s)
pl.	plural
pl.n.	plural noun

Abbreviation	Full Form
Pop.	population
p.p.	past participle
pref.	prefix
prep.	preposition
prob.	probably
pron.	pronoun
p.t.	past tense
qt	quart(s)
R.	River
rpm	revolutions per minute
S	south, southern
SC	south-central
SE	southeast
sec	second(s)
sing.	singular
St.	Saint
suff.	suffix
superl.	superlative
SW	southwest
U.S.	United States
USSR	Union of Soviet Socialist Republics
usu.	usually
v.	verb
var.	variant
w	watt(s)
W	west, western
WC	west-central
yd	yard(s)

Symbols

&	and
%	percent
†	Regional

Pronunciation Symbols

Symbols	Examples	Symbols	Examples	Symbols	Examples
ă	**pat**	l	**lid, needle** (nēd′l)*	sh	**ship, dish**
ā	**pay**	m	**mum**	t	**tight, stopped**
âr	**care**	n	**no, sudden** (sŭd′n)*	th	**thin**
ä	**father**	ng	**thing**	*th*	**this**
b	**bib**	ŏ	**pot, horrid****	ŭ	**cut**
ch	**church**	ō	**toe, hoarse****	ûr	**urge, term, firm**
d	**deed, milled**	ô	**caught, paw, for****	v	**valve**
ĕ	**pet**	oi	**noise**	w	**with**
ē	**bee**	o͝o	**took**	y	**yes**
f	**fife, phase, rough**	o͞o	**boot**	z	**zebra, xylem**
g	**gag**	ou	**out**	zh	**vision, pleasure, garage**
h	**hat**	p	**pop**	ə	**about, edible, circus**
hw	**which**	r	**roar**	ər	**butter**
ĭ	**pit**	s	**sauce**		
ī	**pie, by**				
îr	**pier**				
j	**judge**				
k	**kick, cat, pique**				

Foreign

œ	*French* **feu**, *German* **schön**
ü	*French* **tu**, *German* **über**
KH	*German* **ich**, *Scottish* **loch**
N	*French* **bon**

Stress

Primary stress (′)	**global** (glō′bəl)
Secondary stress (′)	**globalize** (glō′bə-līz′)

* In English the consonants *l* and *n* often constitute complete syllables by themselves.

** Regional pronunciations of *-or-* vary. In pairs such as **for, four; horse, hoarse;** and **morning, mourning,** the vowel varies between (ô) and (ō). In this Dictionary these vowels are represented as follows: **for** (fôr), **four** (fôr, fōr); **horse** (hôrs), **hoarse** (hôrs, hōrs); and **morning** (môr′nĭng), **mourning** (môr′nĭng, mōr′-). A similar variant occurs in words such as **coral, forest,** and **horrid,** where the pronunciation of *o* before *r* varies between (ô) and (ŏ): **forest** (fôr′ĭst, fŏr′-).

Aa

a *or* **A** (ā) *n., pl.* **a's** *or* **A's. 1.** The first letter of the English alphabet. **2.** A speech sound represented by the letter *a*. **3.** Something with the shape of the letter A. **4.** The first in a series. **5.** The highest grade or rank. **6.** *Mus.* The 6th tone in the scale of C major. **7. A** A human blood type of the ABO group.

a[1] (ə; ā *when stressed*) *indef. art.* **1.** —Used before nouns and noun phrases that denote a single, but unspecified, person or thing <*a* mountain><*a* woman> **2.** —Used before terms, as *few* or *many*, denoting number <*a* hundred animals><just *a* few of the players> **3.** The same <people of *a* kind> **4.** Any <not *a* bite to eat> **5. a.** —Used before a proper name to denote a type or a member of a class <the strength of *a* Hercules> **b.** —Used before a mass noun to indicate a single type or example <*a* dark beer>

a[2] (ə) *prep.* In or for each or every **:** per <twice *a* day><two dollars *a* yard>

†**a**[3] (ə; ā *when stressed*) *v. Regional.* Have <We'd *a* come if it hadn't rained.>

aard•vark (ärd'värk') *n.* A burrowing insectivorous mammal, *Orycteropus afer*, of S Africa, with a stocky, hairy body and a long, tubular snout.

aard•wolf (ärd'wo͝olf') *n.* A hyenalike mammal, *Proteles cristatus*, of S and E Africa, that has gray fur with black stripes and feeds chiefly on termites and insect larvae.

AB (ā'bē') *n.* A human blood type of the ABO group.

a•ba (ə-bä', ä-bä') *n.* A loose-fitting, often sleeveless garment made of woven camel or goat hair, worn by Arabs.

ab•a•ca (ăb'ə-kä') *n.* A Philippine plant, *Musa textilis*, whose leafstalks are the source of Manila hemp.

a•back (ə-băk') *adv.* **—take aback.** To startle **:** dumbfound.

ab•a•cus (ăb'ə-kəs) *n., pl.* **-cus•es** *or* **-ci** (-sī'). A frame holding parallel rods strung with movable beads that is used for manual computation.

a•baft (ə-băft') *adv. Naut.* Toward the stern. **—a•baft'** *prep.*

ab•a•lo•ne (ăb'ə-lō'nē) *n.* A large, edible marine gastropod of the genus *Haliotis*, with an ear-shaped shell.

a•ban•don (ə-băn'dən) *v.* **1.** To desert **:** forsake. **2.** To give up completely **:** surrender. ★ *syns:* DESIST, DISCONTINUE, FORSWEAR, LEAVE, QUIT, RENOUNCE, STOP —*n.* **1.** A complete surrender to feeling or impulse. **2.** Unlimited enthusiasm **:** exuberance. **—a•ban'don•ment** *n.*

a•ban•doned (ə-băn'dənd) *adj.* **1.** Forsaken. **2.** Recklessly unrestrained.

a•base (ə-bās') *v.* **a•based, a•bas•ing.** To lower in rank or prestige **:** humiliate. **—a•base'ment** *n.*

a•bash (ə-băsh') *v.* To embarrass **:** disconcert. **—a•bash'ment** *n.*

a•ba•sia (ə-bā'zhə) *n.* Dysfunction of muscular coordination in walking.

a•bate (ə-bāt') *v.* **a•bat•ed, a•bat•ing.** To decrease in amount, intensity, or degree. **—a•bat'a•ble** *adj.* **—a•bate'ment** *n.*

ab•at•toir (ăb'ə-twär') *n.* A slaughterhouse.

ab•bé (ăb'ā', ă-bā') *n.* The French title of an ecclesiastical figure.

ab•bess (ăb'ĭs) *n.* The superior of a convent.

ab•bey (ăb'ē) *n., pl.* **-beys. 1.** A convent or monastery. **2.** A church that is or once was associated with a monastery or convent.

ab•bot (ăb'ət) *n.* The superior of a monastery.

ab•bre•vi•ate (ə-brē'vē-āt') *v.* **-at•ed, -at•ing. 1.** To shorten. **2.** To shorten (a word or phrase) to a form representing the entire word or phrase. **—ab•bre'vi•a'tion** *n.* **—ab•bre'vi•a'tor** *n.*

ABC (ā'bē'sē') *n., pl.* **ABC's. 1.** *often* **ABC's.** The alphabet. **2. ABC's.** Fundamentals of reading and writing.

ab•di•cate (ăb'dĭ-kāt') *v.* **-cat•ed, -cat•ing.** To relinquish (power or responsibility) formally. **—ab'di•ca•ble** (-kə-bəl) *adj.* **—ab'di•ca'tion** *n.* **—ab'di•ca'tor** *n.*

ab•do•men (ăb'də-mən, ăb-dō'mən) *n.* **1.** The part of the mammalian body that is between the thorax and the pelvis and encloses the viscera. **2.** The major posterior part of an arthropod's body. **—ab•dom'i•nal** (-dŏm'ə-nəl) *adj.* **—ab•dom'i•nal•ly** *adv.*

ab•duct (ăb-dŭkt') *v.* To kidnap. **—ab•duc'tion** *n.* **—ab•duc'tor** *n.*

a•beam (ə-bēm') *adv.* At right angles to a ship's keel.

a•bele (ə-bēl') *n.* A poplar, *Populis alba*, that has leaves with whitish undersides.

a•bed (ə-bĕd') *adv.* In bed.

Ab•er•deen An•gus (ăb'ər-dēn ăng'gəs) *n.* Any of a breed of black, hornless beef cattle orig. developed in Scotland.

ab•er•ra•tion (ăb'ə-rā'shən) *n.* **1.** A departure from the normal, usual, or expected. **2.** Mental disorder. **3.** Blurring or distortion of an image. **—ab•er'rance, ab•er'ran•cy** *n.* **—ab•er'rant** *adj.*

a•bet (ə-bĕt') *v.* **a•bet•ted, a•bet•ting.** To incite, encourage, or assist, esp. in wrongdoing. **—a•bet'ment** *n.* **—a•bet'tor, a•bet'ter** *n.*

a•bey•ance (ə-bā'əns) *n.* The state of being temporarily set aside **:** suspension. ★ *syns:* DORMANCY, INTERMISSION, LATENCY, QUIESCENCE, REMISSION, SUSPENSION **—a•bey'ant** *adj.*

ab•hor (ăb-hôr') *v.* **-horred, -hor•ring.** To consider with horror or disgust **:** loathe. **—ab•hor'rence** *n.* **—ab•hor'rer** *n.*

ab•hor•rent (ăb-hôr'ənt, -hŏr'-) *adj.* Disgusting **:** loathsome. **—ab•hor'rent•ly** *adv.*

a•bide (ə-bīd') *v.* **a•bode** (ə-bōd') *or* **a•bid•ed, a•bid•ing. 1.** To tolerate **:** endure. **2.** To remain **:** stay. **3.** To dwell **:** sojourn. **—abide**

by. To comply with <*abide* by her decision> **—a·bid′ance** *n.* **—a·bid′er** *n.*

a·bid·ing (ə-bī′dĭng) *adj.* Long-lasting **:** enduring <*abiding* love>

a·bil·i·ty (ə-bĭl′ĭ-tē) *n., pl.* **-ties. 1.** Physical or mental power to perform. **2.** A skill or talent. ★ ***syns:*** ADEPTNESS, COMMAND, CRAFT, EXPERTISE, EXPERTNESS, KNACK, KNOW-HOW, MASTERY, PROFICIENCY, SKILL

—ability *or* **-ibility** *suff.* Ability, inclination, or suitability for a specified action or condition <teach*ability*><wear*ability*>

ab in·i·ti·o (ăb′ ĭ-nĭsh′ē-ō′) *adv.* From the beginning.

ab·ject (ăb′jĕkt′, ăb-jĕkt′) *adj.* **1.** Contemptible **:** despicable <an *abject* coward> **2.** Miserable **:** wretched <*abject* poverty> **—ab′ject′ly** *adv.* **—ab·ject′ness, ab·jec′tion** *n.*

ab·jure (ăb-jo͝or′) *v.* **-jured, -jur·ing. 1.** To recant solemnly **:** repudiate. **2.** To renounce under oath **:** forswear. **—ab′ju·ra′tion** *n.* **—ab·jur′er** *n.*

ab·la·tion (ă-blā′shən) *n.* **1.** Surgical removal of a body part. **2.** *Aerospace.* Dissipation of heat generated by atmospheric friction. **—ab·late′** *v.*

ab·la·tive (ăb′lə-tĭv) *adj.* Of or relating to a grammatical case designating separation, direction away from, and sometimes manner or agency, used in some Indo-European languages. **—ab′la·tive** *n.*

a·blaze (ə-blāz′) *adj.* **1.** Being on fire **:** blazing. **2.** Radiantly bright **:** glowing.

a·ble (ā′bəl) *adj.* **a·bler, a·blest. 1.** Having sufficient ability or resources. **2.** Capable or talented. **—a·ble·ness** *n.* **—a′bly** *adv.*

—able *or* **—ible** *suff.* **1.** Capable or worthy of undergoing a specified action <wash*able*> **2.** Inclined or given to a specified state <blam*able*>

a·ble-bod·ied (ā′bəl-bŏd′ēd) *adj.* Physically healthy and strong **:** sound.

able-bodied seaman *or* **able seaman** *n.* A seaman certified for all seaman's duties.

a·bloom (ə-blo͞om′) *adj.* Being in bloom **:** flowering.

ab·lu·tion (ə-blo͞o′shən) *n.* A cleansing of the body.

ABM (ā′bē-ĕm′) *n.* Antiballistic missile.

ab·ne·ga·tion (ăb′nĭ-gā′shən) *n.* Self-denial **:** renunciation.

ab·nor·mal (ăb-nôr′məl) *adj.* Not normal **:** irregular. ★ ***syns:*** ABERRANT, ANOMALOUS, ATYPICAL, DEVIANT, PRETERNATURAL, UNNATURAL **—ab′nor·mal′i·ty** (-măl′ĭ-tē) *n.* **—ab·nor′mal·ly** *adv.*

abnormal psychology *n.* Psychopathology.

a·board (ə-bôrd′, ə-bōrd′) *adv.* On board a passenger vehicle, as a ship, train, or aircraft. **—a·board′** *prep.*

a·bode (ə-bōd′) *n.* A habitation.

a·bol·ish (ə-bŏl′ĭsh) *v.* **1.** To put an end to **:** annul. **2.** To destroy completely **:** annihilate. **—a·bol′ish·a·ble** *adj.* **—a·bol′ish·er** *n.* **—a·bol′ish·ment** *n.*

ab·o·li·tion (ăb′ə-lĭsh′ən) *n.* **1.** An act or the process of abolishing. **2.** *often* **Abolition.** The prohibition of slavery in the U.S. **—ab′o·li′tion·ar′y** *adj.* **—ab·o·li·tion·ism** *n.* **—ab′o·li′tion·ist** *n.*

A-bomb (ā′bŏm′) *n.* An atomic bomb.

a·bom·i·na·ble (ə-bŏm′ə-nə-bəl) *adj.* Utterly loathsome **:** detestable. **—a·bom′i·na·bly** *adv.*

abominable snowman *n.* A hairy humanlike creature allegedly inhabiting the high Himalayas.

a·bom·i·nate (ə-bŏm′ə-nāt′) *v.* **-nat·ed, -nat·ing.** To regard as abominable **:** detest. **—a·bom′i·na′tion** *n.*

ab·o·rig·i·nal (ăb′ə-rĭj′ə-nəl) *adj.* **1.** Being of the earliest of its type **:** indigenous. **2.** Of or relating to aborigines. **—ab′o·rig′i·nal** *n.* **—ab′o·rig′i·nal·ly** *adv.*

ab·o·rig·i·ne (ăb′ə-rĭj′ə-nē) *n.* **1.** An indigenous inhabitant of a region. **2. aborigines.** The flora and fauna native to an area.

a·born·ing (ə-bôr′nĭng, -bōr′-) *adv.* While coming into being or getting started <a poem that died *aborning*>

a·bort (ə-bôrt′) *v.* **1.** To terminate or cause to terminate a pregnancy prematurely. **2.** To terminate (an operation or procedure) before completion. **—a·bort′** *n.*

a·bor·ti·fa·cient (ə-bôr′tə-fā′shənt) *adj.* Causing abortion. **—a·bor′ti·fa′cient** *n.*

a·bor·tion (ə-bôr′shən) *n.* **1.** Induced termination of pregnancy before the fetus can survive. **2.** A miscarriage. **3.** Something malformed. **—a·bor′tive** *adj.* **—a·bor′tive·ly** *adv.* **—a·bor′tive·ness** *n.*

ABO system (ā′bē′ō′) *n.* The antigenic system of human blood, which, by functioning genetically as an allelic unit, produces the 4 human blood groups or types, A, B, AB, and O.

a·bou·li·a (ə-bo͞o′lē-ə, ə-byo͞o′-) *n. var. of* ABULIA.

a·bound (ə-bound′) *v.* **1.** To be plentiful in amount. **2.** To be fully supplied **:** teem.

a·bout (ə-bout′) *adv.* **1.** Approximately <traveled *about* a year> **2.** Here and there. **3.** In the area **:** near. *—prep.* **1.** In reference to **:** concerning. **2.** Close or near to. **3.** Ready <*about* to begin> **4.** On all sides of **:** surrounding.

a·bout-face (ə-bout′fās′, ə-bout′fās′) *n.* A reversal of direction, attitude, or standpoint. **—a·bout′-face′** *v.*

a·bove (ə-bŭv′) *adv.* **1.** In or to a higher place or position. **2.** In an earlier part of a text. *—prep.* **1.** Over or higher than. **2.** Upstream or uphill from. **3.** Superior to. *—adj.* Appearing or stated earlier.

a·bove·board (ə-bŭv′bôrd′, -bōrd′) *adv. & adj.* Without trickery or deceit.

▲ ***word history:*** *Aboveboard* is a compound of *above* and *board.* It is recorded as early as the 17th cent. as a gambler's term. If the gambler's hands were above the board or gaming table then presumably he could not surreptitiously change the cards or indulge in other forms of cheating.

ab•ra•ca•dab•ra (ăb′rə-kə-dăb′rə) *n.* **1.** A magical word once held to avert disease or disaster. **2.** Nonsensical talk **:** gibberish.
a•brade (ə-brād′) *v.* **a•brad•ed, a•brad•ing. 1.** To rub off or wear away by friction **:** erode. **2.** To irritate. **—a•bra′sion** *n.*
a•bra•sive (ə-brā′sĭv, -zĭv) *adj.* **1.** Causing abrasion. **2.** Causing irritation <an *abrasive* voice> *—n.* A substance that abrades. **—a•bra′sive•ly** *adv.* **—a•bra′sive•ness** *n.*
a•breast (ə-brĕst′) *adv. & adj.* **1.** Side by side <lined up four *abreast*> **2.** Up to date with <*abreast* of the news>
a•bridge (ə-brĭj′) *v.* **a•bridged, a•bridg•ing. 1.** To reduce the length of **:** condense <*abridge* a book> **2.** To diminish. **3.** To curtail. **—a•bridg′er** *n.* **—a•bridg′ment, a•bridge′ment** *n.*
a•broach (ə-brōch′) *adj.* **1.** Opened so that a liquid, as wine, can be let out. **2.** Moving about **:** astir.
a•broad (ə-brôd′) *adv. & adj.* **1.** In or to a foreign country. **2.** Covering a large area **:** widely. **3.** Away from one's home.
ab•ro•gate (ăb′rə-gāt′) *v.* **-gat•ed, -gat•ing.** To abolish or annul by authority **:** nullify. **—ab′ro•ga′tion** *n.*
a•brupt (ə-brŭpt′) *adj.* **1.** Unexpected **:** sudden. **2.** Rudely curt **:** brusque. **3.** Steep <an *abrupt* cliff> **—a•brupt′ly** *adv.* **—a•brupt′ness** *n.*
ab•scess (ăb′sĕs′) *n.* A localized collection of pus surrounded by inflammation. **—ab′scess′** *v.*
ab•scis•sa (ăb-sĭs′ə) *n., pl.* **-sas** *or* **-scis•sae** (-sĭs′ē). The coordinate of a point from the *y*–axis measured along a line parallel to the *x*–axis.
ab•scis•sion (ăb-sĭzh′ən) *n.* **1.** An act of cutting off. **2.** The process by which plant parts are shed. **—ab•scise′** (-sīz′) *v.*
ab•scond (ăb-skŏnd′) *v.* To leave quickly and secretly and hide, esp. from the law.
ab•sence (ăb′səns) *n.* **1.** The condition or a period of being away. **2.** Lack <*absence* of curiosity>
ab•sent (ăb′sənt) *adj.* **1.** Not present **:** missing. **2.** Not existent **:** lacking. **3.** Inattentive. *—v.* (ăb-sĕnt′). To keep (oneself) away. **—ab′sen•tee′** *n.* **—ab′sent•ly** *adv.*
ab•sen•tee•ism (ăb′sən-tē′ĭz′əm) *n.* Habitual failure to appear, esp. for work or school.
ab•sent-mind•ed (ăb′sənt-mīn′dĭd) *adj.* **1.** Preoccupied. **2.** Chronically forgetful. **—ab′sent-mind′ed•ly** *adv.* **—ab′sent-mind′ed•ness** *n.*
absent without leave *adj.* Absent without official permission from military duties but without the intention to desert.
ab•sinthe *also* **ab•sinth** (ăb′sĭnth) *n.* A liqueur flavored with anise and wormwood.
ab•so•lute (ăb′sə-lo͞ot′) *adj.* **1.** Perfect in nature or quality **:** complete. **2.** Not mixed **:** pure <*absolute* alcohol> **3. a.** Not limited by restrictions or exceptions **:** unconditional <*absolute* freedom> **b.** Not limited by constitutional provisions or other restraints <an *absolute* ruler> **4.** Positive **:** certain <*absolute* truth> **5.** *Physics.* **a.** Pertaining to measurements derived from basic relationships of space, mass, and time. **b.** Pertaining to absolute temperature. ★ ***syns:*** ABSOLUTISTIC, ARBITRARY, AUTOCRATIC, DESPOTIC, DICTATORIAL, MONOCRATIC, TOTALITARIAN, TYRANNICAL **—ab′so•lute′ly** *adv.* **—ab′so•lute′ness** *n.*
absolute alcohol *n.* Ethyl alcohol with no more than 1% water.
absolute pitch *n.* **1.** The precise pitch of a tone as established by its frequency. **2.** The ability to remember the pitches of tones precisely and reliably.
absolute scale *n.* A scale of temperature with absolute zero as the minimum and scale units equal in magnitude to centigrade degrees.
absolute temperature *n.* Temperature measured on the absolute scale.
absolute value *n.* The numerical value or magnitude of a quantity, as of a negative integer, without regard to its sign.
absolute zero *n.* The temperature at which substances possess no thermal energy, equal to −273.15°C or −459.67°F.
ab•so•lu•tion (ăb′sə-lo͞o′shən) *n. Rom. Cath. Ch.* Formal remission of sin imparted by a priest.
ab•so•lut•ism (ăb′sə-lo͞o′tĭz′əm) *n.* Government in which all power is vested in a single ruler **:** despotism. **—ab′so•lut′ist** *n.* **—ab′so•lut•is′tic** *adj.*
ab•solve (ăb-zŏlv′, -sŏlv′) *v.* **-solved, -solv•ing. 1.** To clear of blame or guilt. **2.** To relieve of an obligation. **—ab•solv′a•ble** *adj.* **—ab•solv′er** *n.*
ab•sorb (ăb-sôrb′, -zôrb′) *v.* **1.** To take in **:** soak in or up. **2.** To assimilate <*absorbed* odd notions in childhood> **3.** *Chem. & Physics.* To retain wholly, without reflection or transmission, what is taken in. **4.** To occupy completely **:** engross. **—ab•sorb′a•bil′i•ty** *n.* **—ab•sorb′a•ble** *adj.* **—ab•sorb′er** *n.* **—ab•sorb′ing•ly** *adv.*
ab•sorb•ent (ăb-sôr′bənt, -zôr′-) *adj.* Capable of absorbing <*absorbent* cotton> **—ab•sorb′en•cy** *n.* **—ab•sorb′ent** *n.*
ab•sorp•tion (ăb-sôrp′shən, -zôrp′-) *n.* **1.** The act or process of absorbing. **2.** Mental concentration. **—ab•sorp′tive** *adj.*
absorption spectrum *n. Physics.* The spectrum of dark lines and bands observed when radiation traverses an absorbing medium.
ab•stain (ăb-stān′) *v.* To refrain from something voluntarily. **—ab•stain′er** *n.* **—ab•sten′tion** *n.*
ab•ste•mi•ous (ăb-stē′mē-əs) *adj.* Consuming food and drink in moderation **:** temperate. **—ab•ste′mi•ous•ly** *adv.* **—ab•ste′mi•ous•ness** *n.*
ab•sti•nence (ăb′stə-nəns) *n.* **1.** Denial of the appetites. **2.** Habitual abstaining from alco-

holic beverages or specified foods. **—ab'sti•nent** *adj.* **—ab'sti•nent•ly** *adv.*

ab•stract (ăb'străkt', ăb-străkt') *adj.* **1.** Considered apart from concrete existence <an *abstract* idea> **2.** Expressed without reference to a specific instance <*abstract* words like "honesty" and "beauty"> **3.** Designating a painting or sculpture whose intellectual and affective content depends solely on intrinsic form : nonobjective. *—n.* (ăb'străkt'). **1.** A summary. **2.** Something abstract, as a term. *—v.* (ăb-străkt'). **1.** To remove. **2.** To steal. **3.** (ăb'străkt') To summarize. **—ab•stract'er** *n.* **—ab•stract'ly** *adv.* **—ab•stract'ness** *n.*

ab•stract•ed (ăb-străk'tĭd) *adj.* Absent-minded : preoccupied. **—ab•stract'ed•ly** *adv.* **—ab•stract'ed•ness** *n.*

abstract expressionism *n.* A school of painting that flourished after World War II until the early 1960's, marked by the exclusion of representational content. **—abstract expressionist** *n.*

ab•strac•tion (ăb-străk'shən) *n.* **1.** The act or process of separating or removing. **2.** An abstract idea. **3.** Preoccupation : absent-mindedness. **4.** An abstract work of art.

ab•struse (ăb-stro͞os') *adj.* Not easily understood : recondite. **—ab•struse'ly** *adv.* **—ab•struse'ness** *n.*

ab•surd (ăb-sûrd', -zûrd') *adj.* Ridiculously incongruous or unreasonable. *—n.* **1.** Existence in a meaningless and irrational universe in which an individual's life has no meaning or purpose. **2.** The literary genre dealing with the theme of an absurd universe. **—ab•surd'i•ty, ab•surd'ness** *n.* **—ab•surd'ly** *adv.*

▲ ***word history:*** *Absurdus* in Latin meant "silly" and "irrational" just as *absurd* does in English, but its literal sense was "out of tune." It was used figuratively outside the realm of music and acoustics to mean "out of harmony with reason."

a•bu•li•a *also* **a•bou•li•a** (ə-bo͞o'lē-ə, ə-byo͞o'-) *n.* Impairment of the ability to act or decide independently. **—a•bu'lic** (-lĭk) *adj.*

a•bun•dant (ə-bŭn'dənt) *adj.* Plentifully supplied : rich <an *abundant* harvest> **—a•bun'dance** *n.* **—a•bun'dant•ly** *adv.*

a•buse (ə-byo͞oz') *v.* **a•bused, a•bus•ing. 1.** To use improperly : misuse. **2.** To harm or injure by maltreatment. **3.** To assail with insults : revile. ★ ***syns:*** MISAPPLY, MISAPPROPRIATE, MISEMPLOY, MISUSE, PERVERT *—n.* (ə-byo͞os'). **1.** Improper use : misuse. **2.** Physical maltreatment. **3.** Coarse or insulting language. **—a•bus'er** *n.* **—a•bu'sive** *adj.* **—a•bu'sive•ly** *adv.* **—a•bu'sive•ness** *n.*

a•but (ə-bŭt') *v.* **a•but•ted, a•but•ting.** To border upon : adjoin. **—a•but'ter** *n.*

a•but•ment (ə-bŭt'mənt) *n.* A structure that supports, as at the end of a bridge.

a•bysm (ə-bĭz'əm) *n.* An abyss.

a•bys•mal (ə-bĭz'məl) *adj.* Immeasurably deep or extreme : profound <*abysmal* ignorance> **—a•bys'mal•ly** *adv.*

a•byss (ə-bĭs') *n.* **1. a.** The primeval chaos. **b.** The bottomless pit : hell. **2.** A yawning gulf. **3.** An immeasurably profound depth or void <vast *abysses* of the galaxies>

Ab•ys•sin•i•an cat (ăb'ĭ-sĭn'ē-ən) *n.* A short-haired cat with a reddish-brown coat tipped with black markings.

Ac *symbol for* ACTINIUM.

a•ca•cia (ə-kā'shə) *n.* A chiefly tropical tree of the genus *Acacia* with compound leaves and tight small yellow or white flower clusters.

ac•a•deme (ăk'ə-dēm') *also* **ac•a•de•mi•a** (-dē'mē-ə) *n.* **1.** The academic environment. **2.** Academic life.

ac•a•dem•ic (ăk'ə-dĕm'ĭk) *adj.* **1.** Of or relating to a school. **2.** Pertaining to liberal or classical rather than technical or vocational education. **3.** Not practical : theoretical. **—ac'a•dem'i•cal•ly** *adv.*

academic freedom *n.* Freedom to pursue and teach relevant knowledge without interference, as from public officials.

ac•a•dem•i•cism (ăk'ə-dĕm'ĭ-sĭz'əm) *also* **a•cad•e•mism** (ə-kăd'ə-mĭz'əm) *n.* Traditional formalism, particularly in art.

a•cad•e•my (ə-kăd'ə-mē) *n., pl.* **-mies. 1.** A school for a special field of study. **2.** A private secondary school. **3.** An association of scholars or artists. **—ac'a•de•mi'cian** (ăk'ə-də-mĭsh'ən) *n.*

a•can•thus (ə-kăn'thəs) *n.* **1.** A plant of the genus *Acanthus,* native to the Mediterranean region, with large thistlelike leaves. **2.** Ornamentation patterned after acanthus leaves.

a cap•pel•la (ä' kə-pĕl'ə) *adv. Mus.* Without instrumental accompaniment <sing *a capella*>

a•cau•date (ā-kô'dāt') *also* **a•cau•dal** (ā-kôd'l) *adj.* Having no tail.

ac•cede (ăk-sēd') *v.* **-ced•ed, -ced•ing. 1.** To give consent : agree. **2.** To come into a public office or dignity. **—ac•ced'ence** *n.*

ac•cel•er•an•do (ä-chĕl'ə-rän'dō, ăk-sĕl'ə-) *adv. Mus.* Gradually quickening in tempo. —Used as a direction. **—ac•cel'er•an•do** *adj. & n.*

ac•cel•er•ate (ăk-sĕl'ə-rāt') *v.* **-at•ed, -at•ing. 1.** To increase the speed of. **2.** To bring about sooner. **—ac•cel•er•a'tion** *n.* **—ac•cel'er•a'tive** *adj.*

ac•cel•er•a•tor (ăk-sĕl'ə-rā'tər) *n.* **1.** A mechanical device, esp. the gas pedal of a vehicle, that increases speed. **2.** *Physics.* A device, such as an electrostatic generator or cyclotron, for accelerating charged particles.

ac•cel•er•om•e•ter (ăk-sĕl'ə-rŏm'ĭ-tər) *n.* A device for measuring acceleration.

ac•cent (ăk'sĕnt') *n.* **1.** Vocal stress or emphasis accorded a particular syllable, word, or phrase. **2.** A characteristic pronunciation <a British *accent*> **3.** A mark or symbol placed over a vowel in certain languages to indicate its quality. *—v.* **1.** To stress the pronunciation of. **2.** To stress : emphasize.

ac•cen•tu•ate (ăk-sĕn'cho͞o-āt') *v.* **-at•ed, -at•ing. 1.** To pronounce with an accent. **2.** To emphasize. **—ac•cen'tu•a'tion** *n.*

ac•cept (ăk-sĕpt′) *v.* **1.** To receive willingly. **2.** To admit to a group or place. **3.** To answer affirmatively <I *accept* your invitation.> **4.** To consent to pay, as by a signed agreement.

ac•cept•a•ble (ăk-sĕp′tə-bəl) *adj.* Adequate : satisfactory <an *acceptable* grade> **—ac•cept′a•bil′i•ty, ac•cept′a•ble•ness** *n.* **—ac•cept′a•bly** *adv.*

ac•cep•tance (ăk-sĕp′təns) *n.* **1. a.** The act or process of accepting. **b.** The state of being accepted or acceptable. **2.** A formal agreement to pay a draft or bill of exchange.

ac•cep•ta•tion (ăk′sĕp-tā′shən) *n.* The usual or accepted meaning, as of a word.

ac•cess (ăk′sĕs′) *n.* **1.** A means of approaching : passage. **2.** The right to enter or use <has *access* to official documents> **3.** A sudden outburst <an *access* of weeping>

ac•ces•si•ble (ăk-sĕs′ə-bəl) *adj.* **1.** Easily approached, entered, or obtainable. **2.** Susceptible <*accessible* to flattery> **—ac•ces′si•bil′i•ty** *n.* **—ac•ces′si•bly** *adv.*

ac•ces•sion (ăk-sĕsh′ən) *n.* **1.** The attainment of rank or dignity. **2. a.** An increase by means of something added. **b.** An addition. **—ac•ces′sion•al** *adj.*

ac•ces•so•ry *also* **ac•ces•sa•ry** (ăk-sĕs′ə-rē) *n., pl.* **-ries. 1.** A supplementary part : adjunct. **2.** Something nonessential but useful or decorative. **3.** One who aids or abets a lawbreaker in the commission of a crime but is not present at the time of the crime. **—ac•ces′so•ry** *adj.*

accessory fruit *n.* A fruit, as the pear, that develops from floral parts and the ovary.

access time *n. Computer Sci.* The time lag between a request for information stored in a computer's memory and its delivery.

ac•ci•dence (ăk′sĭ-dəns, -dĕns′) *n.* The section of morphology dealing with word inflections.

ac•ci•dent (ăk′sĭ-dənt, -dĕnt′) *n.* **1.** An unexpected, undesirable event <a car *accident*> **2.** Something occurring unexpectedly or unintentionally. **3.** A nonessential circumstance or attribute. **4.** Fortune : chance.

ac•ci•den•tal (ăk′sĭ-dĕn′tl) *adj.* **1.** Occurring unexpectedly and unintentionally : by chance. **2.** Not intrinsic : nonessential. ★ ***syns:*** CASUAL, CHANCE, CONTINGENT, FLUKY, FORTUITOUS, INADVERTENT —*n. Mus.* A chromatically altered note not belonging to the key signature. **—ac′ci•den′tal•ly** *adv.*

ac•ci•dent-prone (ăk′sĭ-dənt-prōn′) *adj.* Susceptible to having a greater than average number of accidents.

ac•cip•i•ter (ăk-sĭp′ĭ-tər) *n.* A hawk of the genus *Accipiter,* with a long tail and short wings. **—ac•cip′i•trine′** (-trīn′, -trĭn) *adj.*

ac•claim (ə-klām′) *v.* **1.** To salute or hail : applaud. **2.** To shout approval. **—ac•claim′** *n.* **—ac•claim′er** *n.*

ac•cla•ma•tion (ăk′lə-mā′shən) *n.* **1.** An expression of enthusiastic approval. **2.** An oral vote, esp. an enthusiastic one of approval taken without formal ballot. **—ac•clam′a•to′ry** *adj.*

ac•cli•mate (ə-klī′mĭt, ăk′lə-māt′) *v.* **-mat•ed, -mat•ing.** To accustom or become accustomed to new surroundings or circumstances : adapt. **—ac′cli•ma′tion** *n.*

ac•cli•ma•tize (ə-klī′mə-tīz′) *v.* **-tized, -tiz•ing.** To acclimate. **—ac•cli′ma•tiz′er** *n.* **—ac•cli′ma•ti•za′tion** *n.*

ac•cliv•i•ty (ə-klĭv′ĭ-tē) *n., pl.* **-ties.** An upward slope.

ac•co•lade (ăk′ə-lād′, ăk′ə-läd′) *n.* **1.** An embrace of salutation. **2.** Approval : praise.

ac•com•mo•date (ə-kŏm′ə-dāt′) *v.* **-dat•ed, -dat•ing. 1.** To do a service for : oblige. **2.** To supply with (e.g., lodging). **3.** To have enough space for. **4.** To adapt : adjust. **5.** To reconcile, as differences : settle.

ac•com•mo•dat•ing (ə-kŏm′ə-dā′tĭng) *adj.* Willing to help. **—ac•com′mo•dat′ing•ly** *adv.*

ac•com•mo•da•tion (ə-kŏm′ə-dā′shən) *n.* **1.** The act of accommodating or the state of being accommodated. **2.** Something that fulfills a need : convenience. **3. accommodations.** Lodgings.

ac•com•pa•ni•ment (ə-kŭm′pə-nə-mənt, ə-kŭmp′nə-) *n.* **1.** Something that accompanies : concomitant. **2.** An embellishment : complement. **3.** *Mus.* An instrumental or vocal part that supports a solo part.

ac•com•pa•ny (ə-kŭm′pə-nē, ə-kŭmp′nē) *v.* **-nied, -ny•ing. 1.** To go with as a companion. **2.** To supplement. **3.** *Mus.* To play an accompaniment (for). **—ac•com′pa•nist** *n.*

ac•com•plice (ə-kŏm′plĭs) *n.* One who aids and abets a lawbreaker in a criminal act.

ac•com•plish (ə-kŏm′plĭsh) *v.* To succeed in doing : achieve. ★ ***syns:*** ACHIEVE, ATTAIN, REACH, REALIZE, SCORE **—ac•com′plish•a•ble** *adj.*

ac•com•plished (ə-kŏm′plĭsht) *adj.* **1.** Completed : finished. **2.** Skilled : expert. **3.** Socially adept : poised.

ac•com•plish•ment (ə-kŏm′plĭsh-mənt) *n.* **1.** The act of accomplishing or state of being accomplished. **2.** Something successfully achieved. **3.** Social poise.

ac•cord (ə-kôrd′) *v.* **1.** To cause to conform, agree, or harmonize. **2.** To grant : give. **3.** To be in agreement, unity, or harmony. —*n.* **1.** Agreement : harmony. **2. a.** Settlement of conflicting opinions. **b.** Settlement of points of issue between nations. **—of (one's) own accord.** Voluntarily. **—ac•cor′dance** *n.* **—ac•cor′dant** *adj.* **—ac•cor′dant•ly** *adv.*

ac•cord•ing•ly (ə-kôr′dĭng-lē) *adv.* **1.** Correspondingly. **2.** Consequently : therefore.

according to *prep.* **1.** On the authority of <*according to* informed sources> **2.** In keeping with <*according to* plan> **3.** As determined by <lined up *according to* height>

ac•cor•di•on (ə-kôr′dē-ən) *n.* A portable musical instrument with a small keyboard and free metal reeds that sound when air is forced past them by pleated bellows. **—ac•cor′di•on•ist** *n.*

ac•cost (ə-kôst', ə-kŏst') *v.* To approach and address (another) in a hostile or aggressive manner.
ac•couche•ment (ä'ko͞osh-mäN') *n.* A confinement during childbirth : lying-in.
†**ac•count** (ə-kount') *n.* **1. a.** A narrative or record of events. **b.** A written or oral explanation. **2.** A detailed list. **3.** An exact list of monetary transactions. **4.** A business relationship involving the exchange of money or credit. —*v.* To consider or esteem. —**account for.** To explain. —**on account.** In partial payment for. —**on account of. 1.** Because of. **2.** *Regional.* Because.
ac•count•a•ble (ə-koun'tə-bəl) *adj.* Responsible : answerable. —**ac•count'a•bil'i•ty, ac•count'a•ble•ness** *n.* —**ac•count'a•bly** *adv.*
ac•count•ant (ə-koun'tənt) *n.* An expert in accounting. —**ac•count'an•cy** *n.*
account executive *n.* An advertising executive who manages client accounts.
ac•count•ing (ə-koun'tĭng) *n.* The bookkeeping methods involved in making a financial record of business transactions and in the preparation of statements concerning the assets, liabilities, and operating results of a business.
ac•cou•ter (ə-ko͞o'tər) *v.* To outfit and equip, as for military duty. —**ac•cou'ter•ments** *or* **ac•cou'tre•ments** *pl.n.*
ac•cou•tre (ə-ko͞o'tər) *v. esp. Brit. var. of* ACCOUTER.
ac•cred•it (ə-krĕd'ĭt) *v.* **1.** To attribute to : credit. **2.** To certify as meeting a prescribed standard. —**ac•cred'i•ta'tion** *n.*
ac•cre•tion (ə-krē'shən) *n.* **1.** Growth or increase by gradual external accumulation. **2.** The product of accretion. —**ac•crete'** *v.* —**ac•cre'tion•ar'y, ac•cre'tive** *adj.*
accretion disk *n.* A ring of interstellar material surrounding a celestial object with an intense gravitational field, as a black hole.
ac•crue (ə-kro͞o') *v.* **-crued, -cru•ing. 1.** To come to someone or something as a gain. **2.** To increase by regular growth, as interest on capital. —**ac•cru'al** *n.*
ac•cul•tur•ate (ə-kŭl'chə-rāt') *v.* **-at•ed, -at•ing.** To change or cause to change by the process of acculturation.
ac•cul•tur•a•tion (ə-kŭl'chə-rā'shən) *n.* **1.** Modification of one culture as a result of contact with a different, esp. a more advanced, culture. **2.** The process by which the culture of a society is instilled from infancy onward.
ac•cu•mu•late (ə-kyo͞o'myə-lāt') *v.* **-lat•ed, -lat•ing.** To amass or gather : mount up. —**ac•cu'mu•la•ble** *adj.* —**ac•cu'mu•la'tion** *n.* —**ac•cu'mu•la'tor** *n.*
ac•cu•rate (ăk'yər-ĭt) *adj.* Having no errors : correct. ★ ***syns:*** CORRECT, EXACT, FAITHFUL, PRECISE, PROPER, RIGHT, TRUE, VERACIOUS —**ac'cu•ra•cy, ac'cu•rate•ness** *n.* —**ac'cu•rate•ly** *adv.*
ac•curs•ed (ə-kûr'sĭd, ə-kûrst') *also* **ac•curst** (ə-kûrst') *adj.* **1.** Under a curse : doomed. **2.** Abominable : damnable. —**ac•curs'ed•ly** *adv.*
ac•cu•sa•tion (ăk'yo͞o-zā'shən) *n.* **1.** An act of accusing. **2.** An allegation. **3.** *Law.* A formal charge of a punishable offense brought before a court. ★ ***syns:*** CHARGE, DENOUNCEMENT, DENUNCIATION, IMPUTATION, INCRIMINATION, INDICTMENT.
ac•cu•sa•tive (ə-kyo͞o'zə-tĭv) *adj.* Of or relating to the case of a noun, pronoun, adjective, or participle that is the direct object of a verb or the object of certain prepositions. —*n.* The accusative case.

▲ ***word history:*** The connection between accusation and grammatical case is not immediately evident. The Latin verb *accusare,* the source of English *accuse,* means "to call to account," esp. in the sense of answering a legal charge. *Accusativus* is an adjective derived from *accusare,* and it is the source of English *accusative. Accusativus* at bottom means "pertaining to an accusation," and it seems an odd choice for the name of a grammatical category. But *accusativus,* which has only the grammatical, not the legal meaning in Latin, is a translation of the Greek word *aitiatikē,* which means both "causal" and "accusative," being itself derived from *aitia,* "accusation," "guilt," "cause." Thus the accusative case is the case of something caused or brought about by the verb.

ac•cuse (ə-kyo͞oz') *v.* **-cused, -cus•ing. 1.** To charge with a shortcoming or error. **2.** To bring charges against. —**ac'cu•sa'tion** *n.* —**ac•cus'er** *n.* —**ac•cus'ing•ly** *adv.*
ac•cused (ə-kyo͞ozd') *n.* The defendant or defendants in a criminal case.
ac•cus•tom (ə-kŭs'təm) *v.* To familiarize, as by constant use, practice, or habit.
ac•cus•tomed (ə-kŭs'təmd) *adj.* Usual, characteristic, or normal.
ace (ās) *n.* **1.** A playing card, die, or domino with one spot. **2.** A point scored by one's opponent failing to return a serve in racket games. **3.** A military pilot who has shot down 5 or more enemy planes. **4.** An expert in a given field. —*v.* **aced, ac•ing.** To get the better of : surpass. —**ace in the hole.** A hidden advantage.
†**a•ce•qui•a** (ə-sā'kē-ə, ä-sä'-) *n. SW U.S.* An irrigation canal.
ac•er•ate (ăs'ə-rāt') *also* **ac•er•at•ed** (-rā'tĭd) *adj. Biol.* Pointed at one end like a needle.
ac•er•bate (ăs'ər-bāt') *v.* **-bat•ed, -bat•ing.** To irritate : annoy.
a•cer•bic (ə-sûr'bĭk) *also* **a•cerb** (ə-sûrb') *adj.* Acid or biting, as in taste, manner, or tone. —**a•cer'bi•cal•ly** *adv.* —**a•cer'bi•ty** *n.*
ac•er•ose (ăs'ə-rōs') *adj.* Sharp-pointed and slender, as a pine needle.
a•cet•a•min•o•phen (ə-sē'tə-mĭn'ə-fən) *n.* A crystalline compound used in medicine to relieve pain and fever.
ac•e•tate (ăs'ĭ-tāt') *n.* **1.** A salt or ester of acetic acid. **2.** Cellulose acetate or derivative products.
a•ce•tic (ə-sē'tĭk, ə-sĕt'ĭk) *adj.* Of, relating to, or containing acetic acid or vinegar.

acetic acid *n.* A clear, colorless organic acid with a pungent odor, used in making rubber, plastics, and photographic chemicals.

ac•e•tone (ăs'ĭ-tōn') *n.* A colorless, volatile, highly flammable liquid used as a solvent.

a•cet•y•lene (ə-sĕt'l-ēn', -ĭn) *n.* A colorless, extremely flammable or explosive gas used for metal welding.

a•ce•tyl•sal•i•cyl•ic acid (ə-sēt'l-săl'ĭ-sĭl'ĭk) *n.* Aspirin.

ache (āk) *v.* **ached, ach•ing. 1.** To suffer a dull, steady pain. **2.** *Informal.* To long for something : yearn. **—ach'i•ness** *n.* **—ache** *n.* **—ach'y** *adj.*

a•chieve (ə-chēv') *v.* **a•chieved, a•chiev•ing.** To accomplish or attain by work or effort. **—a•chiev'a•ble** *adj.* **—a•chieve'ment** *n.* **—a•chiev'er** *n.*

A•chil•les (ə-kĭl'ēz) *n. Gk. Myth.* The hero of Homer's *Iliad.*

Achilles' heel *n.* A vulnerable point : weakness.

Achilles jerk *n.* Reflex plantar flexion in response to a blow to the Achilles tendon.

Achilles tendon *n.* The large tendon extending from the heel bone to the calf muscle of the leg.

ach•ro•mat•ic (ăk'rə-măt'ĭk) *adj.* **1.** Designating color, such as a neutral gray, that has zero saturation and therefore no hue. **2.** Refracting light without spectral color separation. **—ach'ro•mat'i•cal•ly** *adv.* **—a•chro'ma•tism, ach'ro•ma•tic'i•ty** *n.*

a•chro•mic (ā-krō'mĭk) *adj.* Colorless.

ac•id (ăs'ĭd) *n.* **1.** *Chem.* Any of a large group of substances that when dissolved in water are capable of turning blue litmus to red, of reacting with a base to form water and a salt, and have a characteristic sour taste. **2.** A sour-tasting substance. **3.** *Slang.* LSD. *—adj.* **1.** *Chem.* Of or relating to an acid. **2.** Sour-tasting. **3.** Biting, sarcastic, or scornful <*acid* prose> **—a•cid'ic** (ə-sĭd'ĭk) *adj.* **—a•cid'i•ty, ac'id•ness** *n.* **—ac'id•ly** *adv.*

ac•id•head (ăs'ĭd-hĕd') *n. Slang.* A user of LSD.

a•cid•i•fy (ə-sĭd'ə-fī') *v.* **-fied, -fy•ing.** To make or become acid. **—a•cid'i•fi'a•ble** *adj.* **—a•cid'i•fi•ca'tion** *n.*

ac•i•do•sis (ăs'ĭ-dō'sĭs) *n.* An abnormal increase in the acidity of the blood. **—ac'i•dot'ic** (ăs'ĭ-dŏt'ĭk) *adj.*

acid precipitation *n.* Precipitation abnormally high in sulfuric and nitric acid content caused by industrial pollution.

acid rain *n.* Acid precipitation falling as rain.

acid rock *n.* Rock music with lyrics suggesting drug-related experiences.

acid test *n.* A decisive test.

a•cid•u•late (ə-sĭj'o͞o-lāt') *v.* **-lat•ed, -lat•ing.** To make or become somewhat acid. **—a•cid'u•la'tion** *n.*

a•cid•u•lous (ə-sĭj'ə-ləs, ə-sĭd'yə-) *adj.* Acid in taste or manner : caustic.

ack-ack (ăk'ăk') *n. Slang.* **1.** An antiaircraft gun. **2.** Antiaircraft fire.

ac•knowl•edge (ăk-nŏl'ĭj) *v.* **-edged, -edg•ing. 1.** To admit the existence, reality, or truth of. **2. a.** To express recognition of <*acknowledged* our presence> **b.** To express gratitude for. **3.** To report the receipt of. ★ *syns:* ADMIT, ALLOW, AVOW, CONCEDE, CONFESS, GRANT *v.* **—ac•knowl'edge•a•ble** *adj.* **—ac•knowl'edg•ment, ac•knowl'edge•ment** *n.*

ac•knowl•edged (ăk-nŏl'ĭjd) *adj.* Commonly recognized or accepted.

a•clin•ic line (ā-klĭn'ĭk) *n.* The magnetic equator.

ac•me (ăk'mē) *n.* The point of attainment : peak.

ac•ne (ăk'nē) *n.* An inflammatory disease of the glands, causing pimples esp. on the face.

ac•o•lyte (ăk'ə-līt') *n.* **1.** One who assists a priest at Mass. **2.** An attendant or follower.

ac•o•nite (ăk'ə-nīt') *n.* **1.** The monkshood. **2.** The dried root of *Aconite napellus* used medicinally.

a•corn (ā'kôrn', ā'kərn) *n.* The nut of the oak tree, usu. set in a woody, cuplike base.

acorn squash *n.* An acorn-shaped squash with a ridged rind and yellow flesh.

a•cot•y•le•don (ā-kŏt'l-ēd'n) *n.* A plant, as a moss or fern, that does not have cotyledons. **—a•cot'y•le'don•ous** *adj.*

a•cous•tic (ə-ko͞o'stĭk) *also* **a•cous•ti•cal** (-stĭ-kəl) *adj.* **1.** Of or relating to sound, the sense of hearing, or the science of sound. **2. a.** Designed to aid in hearing. **b.** Absorbing sound <*acoustic* tile> **—a•cous'ti•cal•ly** *adv.*

a•cous•tics (ə-ko͞o'stĭks) *n.* **1.** (*sing. in number*). The scientific study of sound. **2.** (*pl. in number*). The total effect of sound, esp. in an enclosed space.

ac•quaint (ə-kwānt') *v.* To familiarize or inform <*acquainted* us with the facts>

ac•quain•tance (ə-kwān'təns) *n.* **1.** Knowledge or information : familiarity. **2.** A person whom one knows. **—ac•quain'tance•ship'** *n.*

ac•qui•esce (ăk'wē-ĕs') *v.* **-esced, -esc•ing.** To comply without overt protest. **—ac'qui•es'cence** *n.* **—ac'qui•es'cent** *adj.* **—ac'qui•es'cent•ly** *adv.*

ac•quire (ə-kwīr') *v.* **-quired, -quir•ing. 1.** To secure possession or control of : get. **2.** To come to have <*acquire* immunity> **—ac•quir'a•ble** *adj.* **—ac•quire'ment** *n.*

acquired antibody *n.* An antibody produced by an immune response as compared with one occurring naturally.

acquired immune deficiency syndrome *n.* AIDS.

acquired immunity *n.* Immunity developed during a lifetime.

ac•qui•si•tion (ăk'wĭ-zĭsh'ən) *n.* **1.** The act of acquiring. **2.** Something acquired.

ac•quis•i•tive (ə-kwĭz'ĭ-tĭv) *adj.* Eager to gain and possess : greedy. **—ac•quis'i•tive•ly** *adv.* **—ac•quis'i•tive•ness** *n.*

ac•quit (ə-kwĭt') *v.* **-quit•ted, -quit•ting. 1.** To clear of a charge. **2.** To conduct (oneself). **—ac•quit'tal** *n.* **—ac•quit'ter** *n.*

a•cre (ā′kər) *n.* **1.** —See table at MEASUREMENT. **2. acres.** Landed property : estate.

▲ ***word history:*** The Old English word *æcer,* of which *acre* is the direct descendant, meant simply "field," esp. a field of cultivated land. The word acquired the meaning of "a unit of land measurement" because it was used specifically to mean a field as large as a man could plow in a day. The size of such a field was fixed during medieval times at 4,840 sq yd, which is still the size of a modern acre. Old English *æcer* is descended from the same Indo-European form as Latin *ager* and Greek *agros,* which both mean "field." The Modern English spelling comes from Old French *acre,* an alteration of the Latin form.

a•cre•age (ā′kər-ĭj) *n.* Area of land in acres.

ac•rid (ăk′rĭd) *adj.* **1.** Having a harsh taste or smell. **2.** Acrimonious : caustic. **—a•crid′i•ty** (ə-krĭd′ĭ-tē), **ac′rid•ness** *n.* **—ac′rid•ly** *adv.*

ac•ri•mo•ny (ăk′rə-mō′nē) *n.* Ill-natured animosity, esp. harshness in manner or tone. **—ac′ri•mo′ni•ous** *adj.* **—ac′ri•mo′ni•ous•ly** *adv.* **—ac′ri•mo′ni•ous•ness** *n.*

ac•ro•bat (ăk′rə-băt′) *n.* One skilled in gymnastic feats. **—ac′ro•bat′ic** *adj.* **—ac′ro•bat′i•cal•ly** *adv.*

ac•ro•bat•ics (ăk′rə-băt′ĭks) *n.* (*sing. or pl. in number*). The feats of an acrobat.

ac•ro•meg•a•ly (ăk′rō-mĕg′ə-lē) *n.* Pathological enlargement of the bones of the hands, feet, and face. **—ac′ro•me•gal′ic** *adj. & n.*

ac•ro•nym (ăk′rə-nĭm′) *n.* A word formed from the initial letters or parts of a series of words, as *radar* for *ra*dio *d*etecting *a*nd *r*anging.

ac•ro•pho•bi•a (ăk′rə-fō′bē-ə) *n.* Abnormal fear of heights.

a•crop•o•lis (ə-krŏp′ə-lĭs) *n.* The fortified height or citadel of an ancient Greek city, esp. the Athenian citadel.

a•cross (ə-krôs′, ə-krŏs′) *prep.* **1.** On, at, or from the other side of <*across* the road> **2.** So as to cross <draw a line *across* the paper> —*adv.* From one side to the other <The street was empty and I ran *across.*>

a•cross-the-board (ə-krôs′*th*ə-bôrd′, -bōrd′, ə-krŏs′-) *adj.* **1.** Combining win, place, or show in a single bet on the same contestant. **2.** Including all categories or members.

a•cros•tic (ə-krô′stĭk, ə-krŏs′tĭk) *n.* A poem or series of lines in which certain letters in each line form a name, motto, etc.

a•cryl•ic (ə-krĭl′ĭk) *n.* **1.** Acrylic resin. **2.** Acrylic fiber. **3.** A paint containing acrylic resin.

acrylic fiber *n.* A synthetic fiber polymerized from acrylonitrile.

acrylic resin *n.* A thermoplastic used to produce synthetic rubbers and lightweight plastics.

ac•ry•lo•ni•trile (ăk′rə-lō-nī′trəl, -trēl′, -trīl) *n.* A liquid organic compound used to make acrylic rubber and fibers.

act (ăkt) *n.* **1.** The process of doing : action. **2.** Something done : deed. **2. a.** A theatrical performance that forms part of a longer presentation. **b.** One of the major divisions of a play or opera. **3.** A manifestation of insincerity : pose. **4.** An enactment, as of a legislature. —*v.* **1.** To assume the dramatic role of <*acted* Hamlet> **2.** To conduct oneself : behave. **3.** To take action <We *acted* quickly.> **4.** To behave affectedly : pretend. **5.** To function : serve <a hedge *acting* as a windbreak> **6.** To take effect <hoped the pill would *act*> **—act up.** To misbehave or malfunction. **—act′a•bil′i•ty** *n.* **—act′a•ble** *adj.*

ACTH (ā′sē′tē-āch′) *n.* A pituitary hormone used to stimulate secretion of adrenal cortex hormones, as cortisone : adrenocorticotropic hormone.

ac•tin (ăk′tĭn) *n.* A muscle protein active in muscular contraction.

act•ing (ăk′tĭng) *adj.* Temporarily assuming the authority, duties, or function of another. —*n.* The occupation or performance of an actor.

actinic ray *n.* Photochemically active radiation.

ac•ti•nide (ăk′tə-nīd′) *n.* Any of a series of radioactive elements with atomic numbers ranging from 89 (actinium) through 103 (lawrencium).

ac•ti•nism (ăk′tə-nĭz′əm) *n.* The intrinsic property in radiation that produces photochemical activity. **—ac•tin′ic** *adj.* **—ac•tin′i•cal•ly** *adv.*

ac•tin•i•um (ăk-tĭn′ē-əm) *n. Symbol* **Ac** A highly radioactive metallic element found in uranium ores.

ac•tin•o•gen (ăk-tĭn′ō-jən) *n.* A radioactive element.

ac•ti•no•my•cin (ăk′tə-nō-mī′sĭn) *n.* Any of various red, often toxic antibiotics obtained from soil bacteria.

ac•ti•non (ăk′tə-nŏn′) *n.* A radioactive inert gaseous isotope of radon.

ac•tion (ăk′shən) *n.* **1.** The process of acting or doing. **2.** An act or deed. **3.** A movement or sequence of movements. **4.** *often* **actions.** Behavior : conduct. **5.** The plot of a story or play. **6. a.** The operating parts of a mechanism. **b.** The way such parts operate. **7.** A lawsuit. **8.** Combat. **9.** Significant or exciting activity.

ac•tion•a•ble (ăk′shə-nə-bəl) *adj.* Giving cause for a legal suit or action. **—ac′tion•a•bly** *adv.*

ac•ti•vate (ăk′tə-vāt′) *v.* **-vat•ed, -vat•ing. 1.** To set in motion. **2.** To create or organize (e.g., a military unit). **3.** To purify (sewage) by aeration. **4.** *Chem.* To accelerate a reaction in. **5.** *Physics.* To make (a substance) radioactive. **—ac′ti•va′tion** *n.* **—ac′ti•va′tor** *n.*

ac•tive (ăk′tĭv) *adj.* **1.** In action : moving. **2.** Capable of functioning. **3.** Causing action or change. **4.** Participating <take an *active* role> **5.** In a state of action <an *active* geyser> **6.** Marked by energy : lively. **7.** Expressing action rather than a state of being <an *active* verb such as "run" or "speak"> **—ac′tive•ly** *adv.* **—ac′tive•ness** *n.*

active immunity *n.* Long-lasting immunity to a disease due to antibody production by the organism.
ac·tiv·ism (ăk′tĭv-ĭz′əm) *n.* The practice based on direct action to effect changes in social conditions, government, etc. —**ac′tiv·ist** *n.*
ac·tiv·i·ty (ăk-tĭv′ĭ-tē) *n., pl.* **-ties. 1.** The state of being active. **2.** Energetic action. **3.** A form of supervised action, as in education or recreation.
act of God *n. Law.* An unforeseeable occurrence caused by nature, as a flood.
ac·to·my·o·sin (ăk′tə-mī′ə-sĭn) *n.* A system of actin and myosin that is responsible for muscular expansion and contraction.
ac·tor (ăk′tər) *n.* **1.** A theatrical performer. **2.** A participant.
ac·tress (ăk′trĭs) *n.* A woman who is a theatrical performer.
Acts of the Apostles *pl.n.* (*sing. in number*). —See table at BIBLE.
ac·tu·al (ăk′cho͞o-əl) *adj.* **1.** Existing in fact or reality <*actual,* not ideal, conditions> **2.** Existing or acting at the present moment : current. —**ac′tu·al′i·ty** *n.* —**ac′tu·al·i·za′tion** *n.* —**ac′tu·al·ize′** *v.* —**ac′tu·al·ly** *adv.*
ac·tu·ar·y (ăk′cho͞o-ĕr′ē) *n., pl.* **-ies.** A statistician who computes insurance risks and premiums. —**ac′tu·ar′i·al** *adj.*
ac·tu·ate (ăk′cho͞o-āt′) *v.* **-at·ed, -at·ing. 1.** To put into action or motion. **2.** To stimulate : motivate. —**ac′tu·a′tion** *n.* —**ac′tu·a′tor** *n.*
ac·u·ate (ăk′yo͞o-āt′) *adj.* Pointed at the tip.
a·cu·i·ty (ə-kyo͞o′ĭ-tē) *n.* Perceptual keenness.
a·cu·men (ə-kyo͞o′mən, ăk′yə-) *n.* Accuracy and quickness of judgment.
ac·u·pres·sure (ăk′yə-prĕsh′ər) *n.* Shiatsu.
ac·u·punc·ture (ăk′yo͞o-pŭngk′chər) *n.* A traditional Chinese technique of puncturing the body with fine needles to treat disease or relieve pain.
a·cute (ə-kyo͞ot′) *adj.* **1.** Sharply pointed. **2.** Keenly perceptive or discerning : shrewd. **3.** Sensitive. **4.** Extremely serious or significant : crucial <an *acute* food shortage> **5.** Extremely severe or sharp, as pain. **6.** *Med.* Reaching a crisis rapidly. —Used of a disease. **7.** *Geom.* Describing angles less than 90°. —**a·cute′ly** *adv.* —**a·cute′ness** *n.*
acute accent *n.* A mark indicating: **a.** Primary stress of a spoken sound or syllable. **b.** Sound quality or vowel length.
a·cy·clo·vir (ā-sī′klō-vîr) *n.* A drug used topically to treat herpes simplex infections.
ad (ăd) *n.* An advertisement.
ad·age (ăd′ĭj) *n.* A short maxim : proverb.
a·da·gio (ə-dä′jō, -jē-ō′) *adv.* Slowly. —Used as a musical direction. —*adj.* Slower than andante in tempo. —*n., pl.* **-gios. 1.** An adagio movement in music. **2.** The slow section of a pas de deux in ballet.
Ad·am (ăd′əm) *n.* The first man and progenitor of humankind as described in the Old Testament.
ad·a·mant (ăd′ə-mənt, -mănt′) *n.* A legendary stone thought to be impenetrable. —*adj.* Resolute : unyielding. —**ad′a·mant·ly** *adv.*
ad·a·man·tine (ăd′ə-măn′tēn′, -tīn′, -tĭn′) *adj.* **1.** Made of adamant. **2.** Having the hardness or luster of a diamond. **3.** Unyielding : inflexible <an *adamantine* will>
Ad·am's apple (ăd′əmz) *n.* The projection of the largest laryngeal cartilage at the front of the throat, esp. in men.
a·dapt (ə-dăpt′) *v.* To adjust or become adjusted to a specified use or situation. —**a·dapt′a·bil′i·ty, a·dapt′a·ble·ness** *n.* —**a·dapt′a·ble** *adj.*
ad·ap·ta·tion (ăd′ăp-tā′shən) *n.* **1. a.** The state of being adapted. **b.** The process of adapting. **2.** An adjustment. —**ad′ap·ta′tion·al** *adj.* —**ad′ap·ta′tion·al·ly** *adv.*
a·dapt·er *also* **a·dap·tor** (ə-dăp′tər) *n.* A device used to effect operative compatability between different parts of an apparatus.
a·dap·tive (ə-dăp′tĭv) *adj.* Capable of adapting. —**a·dap′tive·ly** *adv.* —**a·dap′tive·ness** *n.*
adaptive radiation *n.* The evolution of a relatively unspecialized species into several related species characterized by different specializations that fit them for life in various environments.
add (ăd) *v.* **1.** To unite or join so as to increase in size, quantity, or scope : append. **2.** To combine (e.g., a column of figures) to form a sum. **3.** To say or write further. —**add up.** To be reasonable : make sense. —**add up to.** To mean : indicate.
ad·dax (ăd′ăks′) *n.* An antelope, *Addax nasomaculatus,* of Africa, with spirally twisted horns.
add·ed-val·ue tax (ăd′ĭd-văl′yo͞o) *n.* Value-added tax.
ad·dend (ăd′ĕnd′, ə-dĕnd′) *n.* Any of a set of numbers to be added.
ad·den·dum (ə-dĕn′dəm) *n., pl.* **-da** (-də). Something added, esp. a supplement to a book.
add·er¹ (ăd′ər) *n.* One that adds, esp. a computer device that performs arithmetic addition.
ad·der² (ăd′ər) *n.* **1.** Any of various Old World snakes of the family Viperidae. **2.** Any of several nonvenomous snakes of North America.
ad·dict (ə-dĭkt′) *v.* To surrender (oneself) habitually or compulsively to something, as caffeine or alcohol. —*n.* (ăd′ĭkt). One who is addicted, esp. to narcotics. —**ad·dic′tion** *n.* —**ad·dic′tive** *adj.*
ad·di·tion (ə-dĭsh′ən) *n.* **1.** The act or process of adding. **2.** Something added. **3.** The process of combining sets of numbers to find their sum. —**in addition.** As well as : also. —**in addition to.** Besides. —**ad·di′tion·al** *adj.* —**ad·di′tion·al·ly** *adv.*
ad·di·tive (ăd′ĭ-tĭv) *adj.* Involving addition. —*n.* A substance added in smallish amounts to something else to alter it.
ad·dle (ăd′l) *v.* **-dled, -dling. 1.** To make or become confused. **2.** To become rotten, as an egg.

add-on (ăd′ŏn′, -ôn′) *n.* One thing added as a supplement to another, esp. a component that increases the capability of a system.
ad•dress (ə-drĕs′) *v.* **1.** To speak to. **2.** To make a formal speech to. **3.** To mark with a destination <*address* an envelope> **4.** To direct the efforts or attention of (oneself). —*n.* **1.** A spoken or written communication. **2.** A speech. **3.** (*also* ăd′rĕs′). The location of a person or organization. **4.** (*also* ăd′res′). The indication of destination, as on mail or parcels. **5.** *Computer Sci.* A number in information storage or retrieval assigned to a specific memory location. **6.** Skillfulness. —**ad′dress•ee′** *n.*
ad•duce (ə-do͞os′, ə-dyo͞os′, ă-) *v.* **-duced, -duc•ing.** To give or offer as an example or means of proof. ★ ***syns:*** ADVANCE, CITE, LAY, PRESENT
–ade *suff.* **1.** A sweetened beverage <lime*ade*> **2.** The act of <block*ade*>
A•dé•lie penguin (ə-dā′lē) *n.* A common, medium-sized Antarctic penguin, *Pygoscelis adeliae.*
ad•e•nine (ăd′n-ēn′, -ĭn) *n.* A purine derivative that is a constituent of nucleic acid in organs such as the spleen and pancreas.
ad•e•noid (ăd′n-oid′) *n. often* **adenoids.** Lymphoid tissue growths in the nose above the throat. —**ad′e•noid′, ad′e•noi′dal** *adj.*
a•den•o•sine (ə-dĕn′ə-sēn′) *n.* An organic compound that is a structural component of nucleic acids.
adenosine di•phos•phate (dī-fŏs′fāt′) *n.* ADP.
adenosine mon•o•phos•phate (mŏn′ō-fŏs′fāt′) *n.* AMP.
adenosine tri•phos•phate (trī-fŏs′fāt′) *n.* ATP.
a•dept (ə-dĕpt′) *adj.* Highly skilled : expert. —*n.* (ăd′ĕpt′). A highly skilled person. —**a•dept′ly** *adv.* —**a•dept′ness** *n.*
ad•e•quate (ăd′ĭ-kwĭt) *adj.* **1.** Able to fill a requirement. **2.** Barely sufficient or satisfactory. —**ad′e•qua•cy, ad′e•quate•ness** *n.* —**ad′e•quate•ly** *adv.*
à deux (ä′ dœ′) *adj.* Involving 2 individuals, esp. in private <a picnic *à deux*>
ad•here (ăd-hîr′) *v.* **-hered, -her•ing. 1.** To stick fast or together : cling. **2.** To support or be devoted to. **3.** To carry something out without deviation. —**ad•her′ence** *n.* —**ad•her′ent** *adj. & n.*
ad•he•sion (ăd-hē′zhən) *n.* **1.** The act or state of adhering. **2.** An abnormal condition in which bodily tissues are united by fibrous tissue.
ad•he•sive (ăd-hē′sĭv) *adj.* **1.** Tending to adhere : sticky. **2.** Made so as to adhere. —**ad•he′sive** *n.* —**ad•he′sive•ly** *adv.* —**ad•he′sive•ness** *n.*
ad hoc (ăd hŏk′) *adj. & adv.* For a specific case, situation, or purpose <formed an *ad hoc* committee>
ad hom•i•nem (ăd hŏm′ə-nĕm′) *adj. & adv.* Appealing to prejudice or emotion rather than reason <an *ad hominem* debate>
ad•i•a•bat•ic (ăd′ē-ə-băt′ĭk, ī′dī-ə-) *adj.* Of, pertaining to, or designating a reversible thermodynamic process executed at constant entropy. —**ad′i•a•bat′i•cal•ly** *adv.*
a•dieu (ə-do͞o′, ə-dyo͞o′) *interj.* Good-by. —*n., pl.* **a•dieus** *or* **a•dieux** (ə-do͞oz′, ə-dyo͞oz′). A farewell.
ad in•fi•ni•tum (ăd ĭn′fə-nī′təm) *adj. & adv.* Without limit or end : forever.
a•di•os (ä′dē-ōs′, ăd′ē-) *interj.* Good-by.
ad in•ter•im (ăd ĭn′tər-əm) *adj. & adv.* In the meantime.
ad•i•pose (ăd′ə-pōs′) *adj.* Of or pertaining to animal fat : fatty. —**ad′i•pos′i•ty** (-pŏs′ĭ-tē) *n.*
ad•ja•cent (ə-jā′sənt) *adj.* **1.** Close to : nearby <the house and *adjacent* pond> **2.** Next to : adjoining. ★ ***syns:*** ABUTTING, ADJOINING, BORDERING, CONTIGUOUS, JUXTAPOSED, MEETING, TOUCHING —**ad•ja′cen•cy** *n.* —**ad•ja′cent•ly** *adv.*
adjacent angle *n.* Either of 2 angles having a common side and a common vertex.

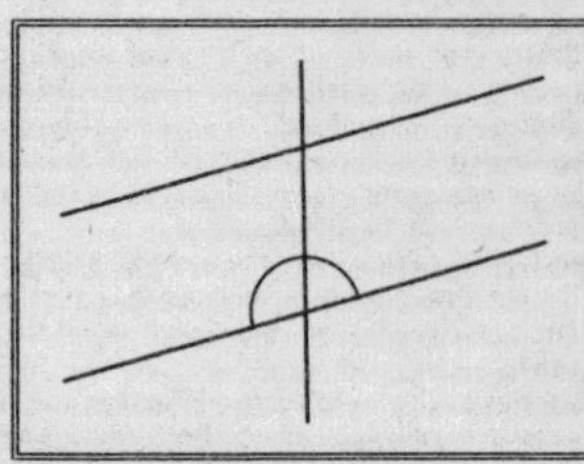

adjacent angle

ad•jec•tive (ăj′ĭk-tĭv) *n.* A word used to describe a noun or limit its meaning. —**ad′jec•ti′val** (-tī′vəl) *adj.* —**ad′jec•ti′val•ly** *adv.*
ad•join (ə-join′) *v.* **1.** To be next to. **2.** To be in or nearly in contact.
ad•join•ing (ə-joi′nĭng) *adj.* Bordering : contiguous.
ad•journ (ə-jûrn′) *v.* **1.** To suspend until a later stated time or indefinitely. **2.** To move from one location to another. —**ad•journ′ment** *n.*
ad•judge (ə-jŭj′) *v.* **-judged, -judg•ing. 1.** To determine by judicial procedure : adjudicate. **2.** To regard or consider.
ad•ju•di•cate (ə-jo͞o′dĭ-kāt′) *v.* **-cat•ed, -cat•ing.** To hear, determine, and settle (a case) by judicial procedure. —**ad•ju′di•ca′tion** *n.* —**ad•ju′di•ca′tive** *adj.* —**ad•ju′di•ca′tor** *n.*
ad•junct (ăj′ŭngkt′) *n.* One connected to another in a dependent or subordinate position.
ad•jure (ə-jo͝or′) *v.* **-jured, -jur•ing.** To command solemnly : ask urgently. —**ad′ju•ra′tion** *n.*
ad•just (ə-jŭst′) *v.* **1.** To alter to match or fit. **2.** To bring into correct relationship. **3.** To conform or adapt. **4.** To make accurate by regulating. **5.** To settle (a claim or debt). ★ ***syns:*** ATTUNE, FIX, REGULATE, SET —**ad•**

just'a·ble *adj.* **—ad·just'er, ad·jus'tor** *n.* **—ad·just'ment** *n.*

ad·ju·tant (ăj'ə-tənt) *n.* **1.** An administrative staff officer who assists a commanding officer. **2.** An assistant. **3.** The marabou. **—ad'ju·tan·cy** *n.*

ad lib (ăd lĭb') *adv.* In an improvisatory manner : spontaneously.

ad-lib (ăd-lĭb') *v.* **-libbed, -lib·bing.** *Informal.* To improvise and deliver extemporaneously. **—ad-lib'** *n. & adj.*

ad·man (ăd'măn') *n. Informal.* A person in the advertising business.

ad·min·is·ter (ăd-mĭn'ĭ-stər) *v.* **1.** To direct : manage. **2. a.** To give as a remedy <*administer* a tranquilizer> **b.** To give (e.g., a sacrament) formally. **3.** To mete out. **4.** To tender (e.g., an oath). **5.** To manage or dispose of (a trust or estate). ★ ***syns:*** ADMINISTRATE, DIRECT, GOVERN, HEAD, MANAGE, RUN, SUPERINTEND **—ad·min'is·trant** *n. & adj.*

ad·min·is·trate (ăd-mĭn'ĭ-strāt') *v.* **-trat·ed, -trat·ing.** To administer.

ad·min·is·tra·tion (ăd-mĭn'ĭ-strā'shən) *n.* **1.** The act of administering. **2.** Management. **3.** *often* **Administration.** The executive branch of a government. **4.** The term of office of an executive officer or body. **5.** *Law.* The managing of a trust or estate. **—ad·min'is·tra'tive** *adj.* **—ad·min'is·tra'tive·ly** *adv.*

ad·min·is·tra·tor (ăd-mĭn'ĭ-strā'tər) *n.* **1.** One who administers : executive. **2.** *Law.* One who administers an estate.

ad·mi·ra·ble (ăd'mər-ə-bəl) *adj.* Worthy of admiration. ★ ***syns:*** COMMENDABLE, ESTIMABLE, LAUDABLE, MERITORIOUS, PRAISEWORTHY **—ad'mi·ra·ble·ness** *n.* **—ad'mir·a·bly** *adv.*

ad·mi·ral (ăd'mər-əl) *n.* **1.** The commander in chief of a fleet or navy. **2.** An Admiral of the Fleet. **3.** A naval officer of the next-to-the-highest rank.

Admiral of the Fleet *n.* The highest rank in the U.S. Navy.

ad·mi·ral·ty (ăd'mər-əl-tē) *n., pl.* **-ties. 1.** A court exercising jurisdiction over maritime cases. **2. Admiralty.** The department of the British government that formerly controlled naval affairs.

†ad·mire (ăd-mīr') *v.* **-mired, -mir·ing. 1.** To regard with wonder and delighted approval. **2.** To have a high opinion of : esteem. **3.** *Regional.* To be pleased. **—ad'mi·ra'tion** (-mə-rā'shən) *n.* **—ad·mir'er** *n.* **—ad·mir'ing·ly** *adv.*

ad·mis·si·ble (ăd-mĭs'ə-bəl) *adj.* Capable of being accepted or allowed. **—ad·mis'si·bil'i·ty, ad·mis'si·ble·ness** *n.*

ad·mis·sion (ăd-mĭsh'ən) *n.* **1.** The act of admitting or the state of being admitted. **2.** A confession of wrongdoing. **3.** The right to enter : access. **4.** An entrance fee. **—ad·mis'sive** *adj.*

ad·mit (ăd-mĭt') *v.* **-mit·ted, -mit·ting. 1.** To allow to enter. **2.** To serve as an entrance. **3.** To accommodate <The room *admits* 45.> **4.** To afford possibility for : allow <a question that *admits* of more than one answer> **5.** To acknowledge or confess <*admit* the truth> **6.** To concede <had to *admit* we were wrong>

ad·mit·tance (ăd-mĭt'ns) *n.* Permission to enter. **—ad·mit'ted·ly** *adv.*

ad·mix·ture (ăd-mĭks'chər) *n.* **1.** A combination, mixture, or blend. **2.** Something added in mixing. **—ad·mix'** *v.*

ad·mon·ish (ăd-mŏn'ĭsh) *v.* **1.** To reprove mildly but seriously. **2.** To warn against something : caution. ★ ***syns:*** REBUKE, REPRIMAND, REPROACH, REPROVE **—ad·mon'ish·er** *n.* **—ad'mo·ni'tion, ad·mon'ish·ment** *n.* **—ad·mon'i·to'ry** *adj.*

ad nau·se·am (ăd nô'zē-əm) *adv.* To a sickening or ridiculous degree <rambled on *ad nauseam*>

ad·noun (ăd'noun') *n.* An adjective used as a noun, as in *the bold and the brave.* **—ad·nom'i·nal** (ăd-nŏm'ə-nəl) *adj.*

a·do (ə-do͞o') *n.* Fuss.

a·do·be (ə-dō'bē) *n.* **1.** A sun-dried brick of clay and straw. **2.** Clay from which these bricks are made. **3.** A structure of adobe.

ad·o·les·cence (ăd'l-ĕs'əns) *n.* The period of physical and psychological development between puberty and maturity. **—ad'o·les'cent** *n. & adj.*

A·don·is (ə-dŏn'ĭs, ə-dō'nĭs) *n.* **1.** *Gk. Myth.* A youth loved by Aphrodite. **2. adonis.** A very handsome young man.

a·dopt (ə-dŏpt') *v.* **1.** To take (a child) into one's family legally and raise as one's own. **2.** To take and follow by choice or assent. **3.** To vote to accept <*adopt* a proposal> **4.** To take up and make one's own, as an idea. **—a·dopt'a·ble** *adj.* **—a·dop'tee** *n.* **—a·dopt'er** *n.* **—a·dop'tion** *n.*

a·dop·tive (ə-dŏp'tĭv) *adj.* Acquired by adoption <*adoptive* parents> **—a·dop'tive·ly** *adv.*

a·dor·a·ble (ə-dôr'ə-bəl, ə-dōr'-) *adj.* **1.** *Informal.* Charming : delightful. **2.** *Archaic.* Worthy of adoration. **—a·dor'a·bil'i·ty, a·dor'a·ble·ness** *n.* **—a·dor'a·bly** *adv.*

a·dore (ə-dôr', ə-dōr') *v.* **a·dored, a·dor·ing. 1.** To worship as divine. **2.** To love or revere deeply. **3.** *Informal.* To like a lot. **—ad'o·ra'tion** *n.* **—a·dor'er** *n.* **— a·dor'ing·ly** *adv.*

a·dorn (ə-dôrn') *v.* **1.** To decorate with or as if with ornaments. **2.** To enhance. **—a·dorn'ment** *n.*

ADP (ā'dē'pē') *n.* An ester that is an adenosine derivative formed in cells and converted to ATP for the storage of energy.

ad rem (ăd rĕm') *adj.* Relevant to the point at issue : pertinent. **—ad rem** *adv.*

a·dre·nal (ə-drē'nəl) *adj.* Of or relating to the adrenal glands or their secretions.

adrenal gland *n.* Either of 2 endocrine glands above each kidney.

A·dren·a·lin (ə-drĕn'ə-lĭn). A trademark for a preparation of adrenaline.

a·dren·a·line (ə-drĕn'ə-lĭn) *n.* Epinephrine.

ad·re·no·cor·ti·co·trop·ic hormone (ə-drē'nō-kôr'tĭ-kō-trŏp'ĭk, -trō'pĭk) *also* **ad·re·**

no•cor•ti•co•tro•phin (-kôr'tĭ-kō-trō'fən) *n.* ACTH.

a•drift (ə-drĭft') *adv. & adj.* **1.** Without being anchored. **2.** Without purpose.

a•droit (ə-droit') *adj.* **1.** Dexterous : deft. **2.** Skillful and adept, esp. in difficult circumstances. **—a•droit'ly** *adv.* **—a•droit'ness** *n.*

ad•sorb (ăd-sôrb', -zôrb') *v.* To collect and hold (gas or vapor) on the surface of a solid. **—ad•sorp'tion** *n.* **—ad•sorp'tive** *adj.*

ad•u•late (ăj'o͞o-lāt') *v.* **-lat•ed, -lat•ing.** To praise excessively or servilely. **—ad'u•la'tion** *n.* **—ad'u•la'tor** *n.* **—ad'u•la•to'ry** (-lə-tôr'ē, -tōr'ē) *adj.*

a•dult (ə-dŭlt', ăd'ŭlt') *n.* One who has attained maturity or legal age. *—adj.* **1.** Mature. **2.** Intended for or befitting mature persons. **—a•dult'hood'** *n.*

a•dul•ter•ate (ə-dŭl'tə-rāt') *v.* **-at•ed, -at•ing.** To make impure, spurious, or inferior by adding improper ingredients. **—a•dul'ter•ant** *n. & adj.* **—a•dul'ter•a'tion** *n.* **—a•dul'ter•a'tor** *n.*

a•dul•ter•y (ə-dŭl'tə-rē, -trē) *n., pl.* **-ries.** Voluntary sexual intercourse between a married person and a partner other than the lawful spouse. **—a•dul'ter•er** *n.* **—a•dul'ter•ess** *n.* **—a•dul'ter•ous** *adj.* **—a•dul'ter•ous•ly** *adv.*

ad•um•brate (ăd'əm-brāt', ə-dŭm'-) *v.* **-brat•ed, -brat•ing. 1.** To give a sketchy outline of. **2.** To give signs of in advance. ★ ***syns:*** FORESHADOW, PREFIGURE, PRESAGE **—ad'um•bra'tion** *n.* **—ad•um'bra•tive** (-brə-tĭv) *adj.*

a•dust (ə-dŭst') *adj.* **1.** Burned. **2.** Melancholy.

▲ ***word history:*** *Adust,* which has etymologically nothing to do with *dust,* acquired the meaning "burned" directly from its Latin source but came to mean "melancholy" through its use in early medical writings. Dryness, heat, and a burnt color of the body and its components, like the blood, certain organs, and the skin, were considered symptoms of a melancholy temperament.

ad va•lo•rem (ăd' və-lôr'əm, -lōr'-) *adj.* According to the value <*ad valorem* taxes on imported goods>

ad•vance (ăd-văns') *v.* **-vanced, -vanc•ing. 1.** To move or cause to move forward. **2.** To propose. **3.** To aid the progress of. **4.** To promote. **5.** To make occur sooner : hasten. **6.** To raise in rate or amount. **7.** To pay (e.g., money) before legally due. *—n.* **1.** The act or process of moving forward. **2.** Progress or improvement. **3.** An increase in price or value. **4. advances.** Personal approaches to gain favor, acquaintance, or an agreement. **5.** Money paid before it is legally due. *—adj.* **1.** Made or given ahead of time : prior. **2.** Going before. **—advance on** (*or* **upon**). To move against. **—in advance. 1.** In front. **2.** Ahead of time. **—ad•vance'ment** *n.*

ad•vanced (ăd-vănst') *adj.* **1.** Highly developed : complex <*advanced* technology> **2.** At a higher level <*advanced* studies> **3.** Progressive <*advanced* ideas> **4.** Far along in course or age <an *advanced* illness><*advanced* years>

ad•van•tage (ăd-văn'tĭj) *n.* **1.** A factor conducive to success. **2.** Profit or benefit : gain. **3.** The first point scored in tennis after deuce. **—take advantage of. 1.** To put to good use. **2.** To exploit. **—ad'van•ta'geous** *adj.* **—ad'van•ta'geous•ly** *adv.* **—ad'van•ta'geous•ness** *n.*

ad•vent (ăd'vĕnt') *n.* **1.** Arrival, esp. of something momentous. **2. Advent. a.** The coming or birth of Christ. **b.** The period of 4 Sundays before Christmas.

ad•ven•ti•tious (ăd'vĕn-tĭsh'əs) *adj.* Acquired by accident : not inherent. **—ad'ven•ti'tious•ly** *adv.* **—ad'ven•ti'tious•ness** *n.*

ad•ven•ture (ăd-vĕn'chər) *n.* **1.** A hazardous undertaking. **2.** An unusual and suspenseful experience. ★ ***syns:*** ENTERPRISE, VENTURE *—v.* **-tured, -tur•ing.** To take risks : dare. **—ad•ven'ture•some** *adj.* **—ad•ven'tur•ous** *adj.* **—ad•ven'tur•ous•ly** *adv.* **—ad•ven'tur•ous•ness** *n.*

ad•ven•tur•er (ăd-vĕn'chər-ər) *n.* **1.** One who adventures. **2.** A soldier of fortune. **3.** One who unscrupulously seeks wealth and social position. **—ad•ven'tur•ess** *n.*

ad•verb (ăd'vûrb') *n.* A word used to modify a verb, an adjective, or another adverb. **—ad•ver'bi•al** *adj.* **—ad•ver'bi•al•ly** *adv.*

ad•ver•sar•i•al (ăd'vər-sâr'ē-əl) *adj.* Characteristic of an adversary : antagonistic.

ad•ver•sar•y (ăd'vər-sĕr'ē) *n., pl.* **-ies.** One who opposes, esp. with animosity.

ad•ver•sa•tive (ăd-vûr'sə-tĭv) *adj.* Expressing antithesis or opposition <the *adversative* conjunction "but"> **—ad•ver'sa•tive** *n.* **—ad•ver'sa•tive•ly** *adv.*

ad•verse (ăd-vûrs', ăd'vûrs') *adj.* **1.** Actively opposed : antagonistic. **2.** Unfavorable : unpropitious. **—ad•verse'ly** *adv.*

ad•ver•si•ty (ăd-vûr'sĭ-tē) *n., pl.* **-ties. 1.** Great affliction or hardship. **2.** A misfortune.

ad•vert (ăd-vûrt') *v.* To allude or refer.

ad•ver•tise (ăd'vər-tīz') *v.* **-tised, -tis•ing. 1.** To call public attention to, esp. to increase sales <*advertise* a new product> **2.** To make generally known. **—ad'ver•tis'er** *n.*

ad•ver•tise•ment (ăd'vər-tīz'mənt, ăd-vûr'tĭs-mənt, -tĭz-) *n.* A notice designed to advertise something.

ad•ver•tis•ing (ăd'vər-tī'zĭng) *n.* **1.** The business of the preparation and distribution of advertisements. **2.** Advertisements as a whole.

ad•vice (ăd-vīs') *n.* Counsel about a course of action : guidance.

ad•vis•a•ble (ăd-vī'zə-bəl) *adj.* Prudent : expedient. **—ad•vis'a•bil'i•ty** *n.* **—ad•vis'a•bly** *adv.*

ad•vise (ăd-vīz') *v.* **-vised, -vis•ing. 1.** To offer advice to. **2.** To suggest or recommend. **3.** To inform or notify. **—ad•vi'see** *n.* **—ad•vis'er, ad•vi'sor** *n.*

ad•vis•ed•ly (ăd-vī'zĭd-lē) *adv.* With consideration : deliberately.

ad•vise•ment (ăd-vīz'mənt) *n.* Careful consideration.

ad•vi•so•ry (ăd-vī'zə-rē) *adj.* **1.** Empowered to advise <an *advisory* council> **2.** Of or containing advice <an *advisory* memo> **—ad•vi′so•ry** *n.*

ad•vo•cate (ăd′və-kāt′) *v.* **-cat•ed, -cat•ing.** To recommend. *—n.* (ăd′və-kĭt, -kāt′). **1.** One who supports or defends a cause. **2.** One who pleads on behalf of another. **—ad′vo•ca′cy** *n.* **—ad′vo•ca′tor** *n.*

adz *or* **adze** (ădz) *n.* A cutting tool with the blade at right angles to the handle, used for dressing wood.

ad•zu•ki bean (ăd-zo͞o′kē) *n.* An Asian plant, *Phaseolus angularis,* widely cultivated for its edible seeds.

a•e•des (ā-ē′dēz) *n., pl.* **aedes.** A mosquito, *Aëdes aegypti,* that transmits yellow fever and dengue.

ae•gis (ē′jĭs) *n.* **1.** Protection. **2.** Sponsorship.

Ae•o•li•an harp (ē-ō′lē-ən, ē-ōl′yən) *n.* A boxlike instrument with stretched strings that sound musically when wind passes over them.

ae•on (ē′ŏn′, ē′ən) *n. var. of* EON.

aer•ate (âr′āt′) *v.* **-at•ed, -at•ing. 1.** To combine or charge (liquid) with a gas, esp. carbon dioxide. **2.** To purify by exposure to air. **3.** To oxygenate (blood). **—aer•a′tion** *n.* **—aer′a′tor** *n.*

aer•i•al (âr′ē-əl, ā-îr′ē-əl) *adj.* **1.** Of, in, or by the air. **2.** Lofty. **3.** Imaginary **:** unsubstantial. **4.** Of or pertaining to aircraft. **5.** *Bot.* Growing in air rather than soil or water. *—n.* (âr′ē-əl). An antenna.

aer•i•al•ist (âr′ē-ə-lĭst) *n.* An acrobat who performs high above the ground, as on a tightrope or trapeze.

aer•ie *also* **aer•y** (âr′ē, ăr′ē, îr′ē) *n., pl.* **-ies.** The nest of a predatory bird, as an eagle, built on a high place.

aer•o•bat•ics (âr′ə-băt′ĭks) *n. (sing. or pl. in number).* Stunt flying.

aer•o•bic (â-rō′bĭk) *adj.* **1.** Living or occurring only in the presence of oxygen <an *aerobic* bacterium> **2.** Of or relating to aerobics. **—aer′obe′** *n.*

aer•o•bics (â-rō′bĭks) *n. (sing. or pl. in number).* Exercises designed to strengthen the cardiopulmonary system.

aer•o•drome (âr′ə-drōm′) *n. esp. Brit. var. of* AIRDROME.

aer•o•dy•nam•ics (âr′ō-dī-năm′ĭks) *n. (sing. in number).* The dynamics of gases, esp. of the atmospheric forces exerted on moving objects. **—aer′o•dy•nam′ic** *adj.*

aer•om•e•ter (â-rŏm′ĭ-tər) *n.* An instrument for determining the weight and density of a gas.

aer•o•nau•tics (âr′ə-nô′tĭks) *n. (sing. in number).* **1.** Design and construction of aircraft. **2.** Aircraft navigation. **—aer′o•naut′** *n.* **—aer′o•nau′tic, aer′o•nau′ti•cal** *adj.* **—aer′o•nau′ti•cal•ly** *adv.*

aer•o•pause (âr′ə-pôz′) *n.* The level of the atmosphere above which aircraft cannot fly.

aer•o•plane (âr′ə-plān′) *n. esp. Brit. var. of* AIRPLANE.

aer•o•shell (âr′ə-shĕl′) *n.* A protective shell for a spacecraft re-entering the atmosphere at high speeds.

aer•o•sol (âr′ə-sôl′, -sŏl′, -sōl′) *n.* **1.** A gaseous suspension of fine particles. **2.** A substance, as an insecticide or detergent, packaged under pressure in a dispenser.

aer•o•space (âr′ə-spās′) *adj.* **1.** Of or designating the earth's atmosphere and the space beyond. **2.** Of or relating to the science or technology of flight.

aes•thete *or* **es•thete** (ĕs′thēt′) *n.* One who has or affects a superior appreciation of the beautiful.

aes•thet•ic *or* **es•thet•ic** (ĕs-thĕt′ĭk) *adj.* **1.** Of aesthetics. **2.** Of or relating to the sense of the beautiful. **3.** Having a love of beauty. **—aes•thet′i•cal•ly** *adv.* **—aes•thet′i•cism′** *n.*

aes•thet•ics *or* **es•thet•ics** (ĕs-thĕt′ĭks) *n. (sing. in number).* The philosophy of beauty and the fine arts.

a•far (ə-fär′) *adv.* Far away **:** far off.

†a•feard *also* **a•feared** (ə-fîrd′) *adj. Regional & Archaic.* Afraid.

af•fa•ble (ăf′ə-bəl) *adj.* **1.** Amiable **:** good-natured. **2.** Gracious **:** gentle. **—af′fa•bil′i•ty** *n.* **—af′fa•bly** *adv.*

af•fair (ə-fâr′) *n.* **1.** A matter or concern. **2. affairs.** Matters of business or public concern. **3.** An occurrence, event, or procedure. **4.** A private matter. **5.** A love affair. **6.** A social gathering.

af•fect[1] (ə-fĕkt′) *v.* **1.** To influence. **2.** To move emotionally. ★ ***syns:*** IMPACT, IMPRESS, INFLUENCE, MOVE, STRIKE, SWAY, TOUCH

af•fect[2] (ə-fĕkt′) *v.* **1.** To simulate or imitate in order to impress **:** pretend. **2.** To like **:** prefer <*affects* flashy clothes> ★ ***syns:*** ASSUME, COUNTERFEIT, FAKE, FEIGN, PRETEND, SIMULATE **—af•fect′er** *n.*

af•fec•ta•tion (ăf′ĕk-tā′shən) *n.* Artificial behavior designed to give a desired impression.

af•fect•ed (ə-fĕk′tĭd) *adj.* Behaving unnaturally to make a particular impression. **—af•fect′ed•ly** *adv.* **—af•fect′ed•ness** *n.*

af•fect•ing (ə-fĕk′tĭng) *adj.* Touching **:** moving <an *affecting* scene of farewell> **—af•fect′ing•ly** *adv.*

af•fec•tion (ə-fĕk′shən) *n.* A fond or tender feeling toward another. **—af•fec′tion•ate** *adj.* **—af•fec′tion•ate•ly** *adv.*

af•fen•pin•scher (ăf′ən-pĭn′chər) *n.* A small dog of European origin, having dark, wiry, shaggy hair and a tufted muzzle.

af•fer•ent (ăf′ər-ənt) *adj.* Directed toward a central section or organ.

af•fi•ance (ə-fī′əns) *v.* **-anced, -anc•ing.** To betroth.

af•fi•da•vit (ăf′ĭ-dā′vĭt) *n.* A written statement made under oath before an official.

af•fil•i•ate (ə-fĭl′ē-āt′) *v.* **-at•ed, -at•ing.** To associate, join, or connect (with). *—n.* (ə-fĭl′ē-ĭt, -āt′). An associate. **—af•fil′i•a′tion** *n.*

af•fin•i•ty (ə-fĭn′ĭ-tē) *n., pl.* **-ties. 1.** A natural attraction **:** liking <an *affinity* for politics> **2.** Relationship **:** kinship.

af•firm (ə-fûrm′) *v.* **1.** To declare positively **:** maintain to be true. **2.** To confirm **:** ratify.

—af•firm'a•ble *adj.* **—af•fir'mant** *adj. & n.* **—af'fir•ma'tion** *n.*

af•fir•ma•tive (ə-fûr'mə-tĭv) *adj.* Affirming that something is true. —*n.* **1.** An affirmative word or phrase. **2.** The side in a debate that supports the proposition being debated. **—af•fir'ma•tive•ly** *adv.*

affirmative action *n.* A policy seeking to redress past discrimination by ensuring equal opportunity.

af•fix (ə-fĭks') *v.* **1.** To attach. **2.** To append. —*n.* (ăf'ĭks'). **1.** Something affixed. **2.** A word element, such as a prefix or suffix, that is attached to a base, stem, or root.

af•fla•tus (ə-flā'təs) *n.* Inspiration.

af•flict (ə-flĭkt') *v.* To inflict physical or mental suffering on. ★ ***syns:*** AGONIZE, CURSE, PLAGUE, RACK, SCOURGE, STRIKE, TORMENT, TORTURE **—af•flic'tion** *n.* **—af•flic'tive** *adj.*

af•flu•ence (ăf'lo͞o-əns) *also* **af•flu•en•cy** (-ən-sē) *n.* **1.** Wealth. **2.** Abundance. **—af'flu•ent** *adj.* **—af'flu•ent•ly** *adv.*

af•ford (ə-fôrd', ə-fōrd') *v.* **1.** To be able to pay for. **2.** To be able to spare <could *afford* 2 days for traveling> **3.** To provide <a tree that *affords* shelter><a book that *affords* pleasure> **—af•ford'a•ble** *adj.*

af•for•est (ə-fôr'ĭst, ə-fŏr'-) *v.* **-est•ed, -est•ing, -ests.** To convert (open land) into forest. **—af•for'es•ta'tion** *n.*

af•fray (ə-frā') *n.* A noisy fight : brawl.

af•front (ə-frŭnt') *v.* **1.** To insult. **2.** To confront. —*n.* A deliberate insult.

af•ghan (ăf'găn', -gən) *n.* **1.** A coverlet knitted or crocheted in colorful geometric designs. **2. Afghan.** A native of Afghanistan.

Afghan hound *n.* A large dog with long, thick hair, a pointed snout, and drooping ears.

af•ghan•i (ăf-găn'ē, -gä'nē) *n.* —See table at CURRENCY.

a•fi•ci•o•na•do (ə-fĭsh'ə-nä'dō, ə-fĭs'ē-, ə-fē'sē-) *n., pl.* **-dos.** An enthusiastic admirer : fan.

a•field (ə-fēld') *adv.* **1.** To or on a field. **2.** Off the usual path or way : astray. **3.** Away from one's environment : abroad.

a•fire (ə-fīr') *adj. & adv.* Burning.

a•flame (ə-flām') *adj. & adv.* Flaming.

af•la•tox•in (ăf'lə-tŏk'sĭn) *n.* A toxic compound that is produced by certain molds and contaminates stored food.

a•float (ə-flōt') *adj. & adv.* **1.** Floating. **2.** At sea. **3.** Flooded. **4.** In circulation.

a•flut•ter (ə-flŭt'ər) *adj.* Filled with nervous excitement.

a•foot (ə-fo͝ot') *adj. & adv.* **1.** On foot. **2.** In the process of happening : astir.

a•fore•men•tioned (ə-fôr'mĕn'shənd, ə-fōr'-) *adj.* Mentioned earlier.

a•fore•said (ə-fôr'sĕd', ə-fōr'-) *adj.* Spoken of before.

a•fore•thought (ə-fôr'thôt', ə-fōr'-) *adj.* Planned beforehand : premeditated.

a•foul of (ə-foul') *prep.* In a snarl : tangled. **—run** (*or* **fall) afoul of.** To have trouble with : come in conflict with.

a•fraid (ə-frād') *adj.* **1.** Fearful : frightened. **2.** Reluctant : hesitant <Are you *afraid* of hard work?> **3.** Regretful <I'm *afraid* I have bad news.> ★ ***syns:*** APPREHENSIVE, FEARFUL, FRIGHTENED, PETRIFIED, SCARED

A-frame (ā'frām) *n.* A structure, as a house, with a steeply angled roof that reaches to the ground.

a•fresh (ə-frĕsh') *adv.* Once more : again.

Af•ri•can-A•mer•i•can (ăf'rĭ-kən-ə-mĕr'ĭ-kən) *adj.* Of or relating to Americans of African ancestry or to their history or culture. **—African American** *n.*

African violet *n.* A plant of the genus *Saintpaulia*, native to Africa, widely cultivated as a house plant and bearing purple, white, or pink flowers.

Af•ri•kaans (ăf'rĭ-käns', -känz') *n.* An official language of the Republic of South Africa that developed from 17th-cent. Dutch.

Af•ri•kan•er (ăf'rĭ-kä'nər) *n.* An Afrikaans-speaking descendant of the Dutch who settled South Africa.

Af•ro (ăf'rō') *n., pl.* **-ros.** A rounded, bushy, tightly curled hair style. —*adj.* **1.** Of or for an Afro hair style. **2.** African in style.

Af•ro-A•mer•i•can (ăf'rō-ə-mĕr'ĭ-kən) *adj.* African-American. **—Af'ro-A•mer'i•can** *n.*

aft (ăft) *adv. & adj.* At, toward, in, or close to the stern of a vessel or rear of an aircraft.

af•ter (ăf'tər) *prep.* **1.** Behind in a place or position. **2.** In quest or pursuit of <seek *after* fame> **3.** Concerning <asked *after* the patient> **4.** At a later time than. **5.** With the same name as. —*conj.* Following the time that. —*adv.* **1.** Afterward <forever *after*> **2.** Behind. —*adj.* **1.** Later. **2.** Nearer the rear, esp. of a ship.

af•ter•birth (ăf'tər-bûrth') *n.* The placenta and membranes ejected from the uterus shortly after childbirth.

af•ter•burn•er (ăf'tər-bûr'nər) *n.* A device that augments the power of a jet engine by injecting extra fuel into the hot exhaust gases.

af•ter•damp (ăf'tər-dămp') *n.* An asphyxiating mixture of gases in a mine after an explosion.

af•ter•deck (ăf'tər-dĕk') *n. Naut.* The part of a ship's deck aft amidships.

af•ter•ef•fect (ăf'tər-ĭ-fĕkt') *n.* A delayed bodily or mental response to a stimulus.

af•ter•glow (ăf'tər-glō') *n.* The light that is emitted or remains after removal of an illumination source.

af•ter•im•age (ăf'tər-ĭm'ĭj) *n.* An image that continues to be seen after a visual stimulus is no longer present.

af•ter•life (ăf'tər-līf') *n.* A life held to follow after death.

af•ter•math (ăf'tər-măth') *n.* **1.** A consequence, esp. of a misfortune or disaster. **2.** A 2nd crop in the same season, esp. of hay.

af•ter•noon (ăf'tər-no͞on') *n.* The day from noon until sunset.

af•ter-shave (ăf'tər-shāv') *n.* A usu. fragrant lotion for the face after shaving.

af·ter·shock (ăf'tər-shŏk') *n.* **1.** A quake of lesser magnitude following a large earthquake. **2.** A subsequent shock or trauma.

af·ter·taste (ăf'tər-tāst') *n.* A taste or feeling that remains after the original stimulus is no longer present.

af·ter·thought (ăf'tər-thôt') *n.* An idea or response that occurs to a person after an event, decision, etc.

af·ter·ward (ăf'tər-wərd) *also* **af·ter·wards** (-wərdz) *adv.* Subsequently.

af·ter·word (ăf'tər-wûrd') *n.* An epilogue to a book or play.

af·ter·world (ăf'tər-wûrld') *n.* A world after death.

Ag *symbol for* SILVER.

a·ga *also* **a·gha** (ä'gə, ăg'a) *n.* An important official of the Ottoman Empire.

a·gain (ə-gĕn') *adv.* **1.** Once more **:** afresh. **2.** To a previous place or position. **3.** Furthermore. **4.** From another standpoint.

a·gainst (ə-gĕnst') *prep.* **1.** In a direction opposite to <swam *against* the current> **2.** So as to hit or touch. **3.** In hostile opposition to <struggle *against* fate> **4.** Contrary to <*against* my wishes>

a·gape[1] (ə-gāp', ə-găp') *adj. & adv.* **1.** With wonder and amazement. **2.** Wide open.

a·ga·pe[2] (ä-gä'pā, ä'gə-pā') *n.* **1.** Christian love. **2.** Love that is spiritual, not sexual.

a·gar (ä'gär', ā'gär') *also* **a·gar-a·gar** (ä'gär-ä'gär', ä'gär-ä'-) *n.* A gelatinous material extracted from certain marine algae, used for gelling foods and as a bacterial culture medium.

ag·a·ric (ăg'-ər-ĭk, ə-găr'ĭk) *n.* A fungus of the family Agaricacae, including the common cultivated mushroom, *Agaricus campestris.*

ag·ate (ăg'ĭt) *n.* **1.** A type of quartz with bands of color. **2.** A playing marble of agate or glass.

a·ga·ve (ə-gä'vē, ə-gä'-) *n.* Any of various fleshy-leaved desert plants of the genus *Agave,* including the century plant.

age (āj) *n.* **1.** The period of existence. **2.** A lifetime. **3.** The time in life when one assumes adult rights and responsibilities **:** legal age. **4.** A distinctive period of life. **5.** The condition of being old. **6.** A geological or historical period. **7.** *Informal.* A long time. ★ ***syns:*** DAY, EPOCH, ERA, PERIOD, TIME —*v.* **aged, ag·ing. 1.** To grow or cause to grow older. **2.** To mature **:** ripen <wine *aging* in casks>

–age *suff.* **1.** Collectively **:** in general <leaf*age*> **2.** Condition **:** state <bond*age*> **3.** Act or result <spoil*age*> **4.** Residence or place of <parson*age*> **5.** Charge or fee <post*age*>

ag·ed (ā'jĭd) *adj.* **1.** Old. **2.** (ājd). Of the age of. **3.** Mature **:** ripened. **—ag'ed·ly** *adv.* **—ag'ed·ness** *n.*

age·ing (ā'jĭng) *n. esp. Brit. var. of* AGING.

age·ism *or* **ag·ism** (ā'jĭz'əm) *n.* Discrimination against the elderly. **—age'ist** *n.*

age·less (āj'lĭs) *adj.* **1.** Not showing the effects of age. **2.** Eternal **:** timeless. **—age'less·ly** *adv.* **—age'less·ness** *n.*

a·gen·cy (ā'jən-sē) *n., pl.* **-cies. 1.** Action **:** power. **2.** A method of action **:** means. **3.** A business that represents or acts on behalf of others. **4.** A governmental department.

a·gen·da (ə-jĕn'də) *n. (sing. in number).* A list of things to do **:** program.

a·gent (ā'jənt) *n.* **1.** One that acts. **2.** One that represents another. **3.** A means by which something is done or caused **:** instrument. **4.** A representative of a governmental department <a CIA *agent*> **5.** A spy.

Agent Orange *n.* A herbicide used in the Vietnam War to defoliate areas of forest.

age-old (āj'ōld') *adj.* Very old.

ag·er·a·tum (ăj'ə-rā'təm) *n.* Any of various plants of the genus *Ageratum,* esp. *A. houstonianum,* bearing violet-blue flower clusters.

ag·gior·na·men·to (ə-jôr'nə-mĕn'tō) *n. pl.* **-tos.** The process of updating an institution or organization.

ag·glom·er·ate (ə-glŏm'ə-rāt') *v.* **-at·ed, -at·ing.** To gather into a rounded mass. —*n.* (ə-glŏm'ər-ĭt). A mass of things clustered together. **—ag·glom'er·a'tion** *n.*

ag·glu·ti·nate (ə-gloo̅t'n-āt') *v.* **-nat·ed, -nat·ing. 1.** To join by adhesion. **2.** To combine (word elements) into a compound. **3.** To cause (e.g., red blood cells) to clump. **—ag·glu'ti·na'tion** *n.* **—ag·glu'ti·na'tive** *adj.*

ag·gran·dize (ə-grăn'dīz', ăg'rən-) *v.* **-dized, -diz·ing. 1.** To increase the scope of **:** extend. **2.** To make greater in power, influence, etc. **3.** To exaggerate. **—ag·gran'dize·ment** *n.* **—ag·gran'diz'er** *n.*

ag·gra·vate (ăg'rə-vāt') *v.* **-vat·ed, -vat·ing. 1.** To make worse. **2.** *Informal.* To annoy. **—ag'gra·vat'ing·ly** *adv.* **—ag'gra·va'tion** *n.* **—ag'gra·va'tor** *n.*

ag·gre·gate (ăg'rə-gĭt', -gāt') *adj.* Gathered into a whole **:** total. —*n.* (ăg'rə-gĭt). A whole considered with reference to its constituent parts. **—ag'gre·gate'** (-gāt') *v.* **—ag'gre·gate·ly** *adv.* **—ag'gre·ga'tion** *n.* **—ag'gre·ga'tive** *adj.* **—ag'gre·ga'tor** *n.*

ag·gres·sion (ə-grĕsh'ən) *n.* **1.** Initiation of usu. hostile action against another **:** attack. **2.** The practice of attacking. **3.** *Psychoanal.* Hostile behavior. **—ag·gres'sor** (-grĕs'ər) *n.*

ag·gres·sive (ə-grĕs'ĭv) *adj.* **1.** Hostile **:** combative. **2.** Energetic and enterprising **:** bold. **—ag·gres'sive·ly** *adv.* **—ag·gres'sive·ness** *n.*

ag·grieve (ə-grēv') *v.* **-grieved, -griev·ing. 1.** To distress. **2.** To treat unjustly.

a·gha (ä'gə, ăg'ə) *n. var. of* AGA.

a·ghast (ə-găst') *adj.* Stricken with horror **:** appalled.

ag·ile (ăj'əl, ăj'īl') *adj.* Moving or able to move with ease and speed **:** nimble. **—ag'ile·ly** *adv.* **—a·gil'i·ty** (ə-jĭl'ĭ-tē), **ag'ile·ness** *n.*

†a·gin (ə-gĭn') *prep. Regional.* Against.

ag·ing (ā'jĭng) *n.* The process of becoming old or mature.

ag·ism (ā'jĭz'əm) *n. var. of* AGEISM.

ag·i·tate (ăj'ĭ-tāt') *v.* **-tat·ed, -tat·ing. 1.** To move with sudden force or violence. **2.** To upset emotionally. **3.** To try to stir up public interest in a cause. **—ag'i·tat'ed·ly** *adv.* **—ag'i·ta'tion** *n.* **—ag'i·ta'tor** *n.*

ag·it·prop (ăj'ĭt-prŏp') *n.* Communist-oriented political propaganda disseminated esp. through the arts.

a·gleam (ə-glēm') *adj. & adv.* Gleaming.

a·glim·mer (ə-glĭm'ər) *adj. & adv.* Glimmering.

a·glit·ter (ə-glĭt'ər) *adj. & adv.* Glittering.

a·glow (ə-glō') *adj. & adv.* Glowing.

ag·nos·tic (ăg-nŏs'tĭk) *n.* One who disclaims any knowledge of God but does not deny the possibility of God's existence. **—ag·nos'tic** *adj.* **—ag·nos'ti·cal·ly** *adv.* **—ag·nos'ti·cism** *n.*

a·go (ə-gō') *adj. & adv.* Earlier than the present time : past.

a·gog (ə-gŏg') *adj.* In a state of excited anticipation. **—a·gog'** *adv.*

ag·o·nize (ăg'ə-nīz') *v.* **-nized, -niz·ing.** To suffer great distress <*agonize* over a decision> **—ag'o·niz'ing·ly** *adv.*

ag·o·ny (ăg'ə-nē) *n., pl.* **-nies. 1.** Intense physical or emotional pain. **2.** A sudden intense emotion <an *agony* of doubt>

ag·o·ra (ä'gə-rä') *n., pl.* **-rot** (-rōt') *or* **-roth** (-rōt'). —See table at CURRENCY.

ag·o·ra·pho·bi·a (ăg'ə-rə-fō'bē-ə) *n.* Abnormal fear of open, esp. public, spaces. **—ag'o·ra·pho'bic** *adj. & n.*

a·gou·ti (ə-go͞ot'ē) *n., pl.* **-tis** *or* **-ties.** A tropical American burrowing rodent of the genus *Dasyprocta,* with grizzled brownish or dark-gray fur.

a·grar·i·an (ə-grâr'ē-ən) *adj.* **1.** Pertaining to land and its ownership. **2.** Pertaining to farming : agricultural. *—n.* One who favors equitable land distribution. **—a·grar'i·an·ism** *n.* **—a·grar'i·an·ly** *adv.*

a·gree (ə-grē') *v.* **a·greed, a·gree·ing. 1.** To grant consent : assent. **2.** To be in accord : match. **3.** To come to an understanding or to terms. **4.** To be appropriate or beneficial. **5.** To correspond in gender, number, case, or person.

a·gree·a·ble (ə-grē'ə-bəl) *adj.* **1.** To one's liking : pleasing. **2.** In accord : suitable. **3.** Ready to consent : willing. **4.** Pleasant and friendly. **—a·gree'a·ble·ness** *n.* **—a·gree'a·bly** *adv.*

a·gree·ment (ə-grē'mənt) *n.* **1.** Harmony of opinion : accord. **2.** A covenant : treaty. **3.** Correspondence in gender, number, case, or person.

ag·ri·busi·ness (ăg'rə-bĭz'nĭs) *n.* Farming engaged in as big business, including the producing, processing, and distributing of farm products.

ag·ri·cul·ture (ăg'rĭ-kŭl'chər) *n.* The science, art, and business of soil cultivation, crop production, and the raising of livestock. **—ag'ri·cul'tur·al** *adj.* **—ag'ri·cul'tur·al·ly** *adv.* **—ag'ri·cul'tur·ist** *n.*

a·gron·o·my (ə-grŏn'ə-mē) *also* **ag·ro·nom·ics** (ăg'rə-nŏm'iks) *n.* The application of the various soil and plant sciences to soil management and crop production. **—ag'ro·nom'ic** (ăg'rə-nŏm'ĭk), **ag'ro·nom'i·cal** *adj.* **—a·gron'o·mist** *n.*

a·ground (ə-ground') *adv. & adj.* Stranded on a reef, shoal, or in shallow water.

a·gue (ā'gyo͞o) *n.* A fever accompanied by chills or shivering.

ah (ä) *interj.* —Used to express surprise, pain, delight, etc.

a·ha (ä-hä') *interj.* —Used to express surprise or triumph.

a·head (ə-hĕd') *adv.* **1.** At or to the front. **2.** In advance : before. **3.** Onward. **—be ahead.** *Informal.* **1.** To be gaining or winning. **2.** To have more than one needs. **—get ahead.** To achieve success.

a·hem (ə-hĕm') *interj.* —Used to attract attention, express doubt, or as a warning.

a·his·tor·i·cal (ā'hĭ-stôr'ĭ-kəl, -stŏr'-) *adj.* Unconcerned with or unrelated to history.

a·hoy (ə-hoi') *interj. Naut.* —Used to hail a ship or attract attention.

aid (ād) *v.* To give help or assistance (to). *—n.* **1.** Assistance. **2.** *also* **aide.** An assistant. **—aid'er** *n.*

aide-de-camp (ād'də-kămp') *n., pl.* **aides-de-camp.** A naval or military officer who acts as a secretary and confidential assistant to a superior officer.

AIDS (ādz) *n.* A severe immunological disorder caused by a retrovirus and resulting in increased susceptibility to opportunistic infections and to certain rare cancers.

ai·grette *or* **ai·gret** (ā-grĕt', ā'grĕt') *n.* A decorative tuft of plumes, esp. of egret feathers.

ail (āl) *v.* **1.** To feel ill. **2.** To make ill or uneasy <What *ails* you?>

ai·lan·thus (ā-lăn'thəs) *n.* A deciduous tree, *Ailanthus altissima,* with compound leaves and malodorous flower clusters.

ai·ler·on (ā'lə-rŏn') *n.* A movable control flap on the trailing edge of an airplane wing.

ail·ment (āl'mənt) *n.* A usu. mild illness.

aim (ām) *v.* **1.** To direct (e.g., a weapon or remark). **2.** To direct a weapon. **3.** To direct one's effort or purpose <*aim* at eliminating racism> *—n.* **1.** The act of aiming. **2.** The direction of something aimed. **3.** Purpose : intention.

aim·less (ām'lĭs) *adj.* Lacking purpose. **—aim'less·ly** *adv.* **—aim'less·ness** *n.*

ain't (ānt). *Nonstandard.* **1.** Am not. **2.** —Used also as a contraction of *is not, are not, has not,* and *have not.*

Ai·nu (ī'no͞o) *n., pl.* **Ainu** *or* **-nus.** A member of an indigenous people inhabiting the northernmost islands of Japan.

ai·o·li (ī-ō'lē) *n.* A rich garlic-flavored mayonnaise.

air (âr) *n.* **1.** The gaseous mixture, mainly nitrogen (approx. 78%) and oxygen (approx. 21%), enveloping the earth. **2.** The sky. **3.** A breeze. **4.** A characteristic impression : appearance <an *air* of superiority> <a house with an *air* of neglect> **5. airs.** Affectation. **6.** *Mus.* A melody : tune. **7.** The airwaves. **8.** The medium through which aircraft travel. ★ *syns:* AMBIANCE, ATMOSPHERE, AURA, FEEL, FEELING, MOOD, SMELL, TONE *—v.* **1.** To expose to the air : ventilate. **2.** To publicly circulate. **—in the air.** Prevalent. **—on**

(or off) the air. Being (or not being) broadcast on radio or television. **—up in the air. 1.** Not decided **:** uncertain. **2.** Excited **:** agitated. **—walk on air.** To feel elated. **—air′less** *adj.* **—air′less•ness** *n.*

air bag *n.* A baglike automotive safety device that inflates upon collision and prevents passengers from pitching forward.

air•borne (âr′bôrn′, -bōrn′) *adj.* **1.** Carried by or through the air <*airborne* viruses> **2.** In flight.

air brake *n.* A brake operated by the power of compressed air.

air•brush *also* **air brush** (âr′brŭsh′) *n.* An atomizer using compressed air to spray liquids, as paint, on a surface. —*v.* To spray with an airbrush.

air•bus (âr′bŭs′) *n.* A usu. short-range large subsonic jet passenger airplane.

air conditioner *n.* An apparatus for regulating, esp. lowering, the temperature and humidity of an enclosed area. **—air′-con•di′tion** *v.* **—air conditioning** *n.*

air•craft (âr′krăft′) *n., pl.* **aircraft.** A machine or device, such as an airplane, helicopter, glider, or dirigible, that is capable of atmospheric flight.

aircraft carrier *n.* A large warship carrying aircraft.

air•drome (âr′drōm′) *n.* An airport.

air•drop (âr′drŏp′) *n.* A delivery, as of supplies, by parachute from airborne aircraft. **—air′drop′** *v.*

air-dry (âr′drī′) *v.* To dry by exposure to the air.

Aire•dale (âr′dāl′) *n.* A large terrier with a wiry tan coat marked with black.

air•field (âr′fēld′) *n.* **1.** An airport having paved runways. **2.** A landing strip.

air•foil (âr′foil′) *n.* An aircraft control part or surface, such as a wing, propeller blade, or rudder, that controls stability, direction, lift, thrust, or propulsion.

air force *n.* The aviation branch of a country's armed forces.

air gun *n.* A gun that is operated by compressed air.

air lane *n.* An established route of travel for aircraft.

air•lift (âr′lĭft′) *n.* Delivery of troops or supplies by aircraft when surface routes are blocked. **—air′lift′** *v.*

air•line (âr′līn′) *n.* **1.** A business organization providing scheduled transport of passengers and freight by air. **2.** The shortest distance between 2 points.

air•lin•er (âr′lī′nər) *n.* A large passenger airplane operated by an airline.

air lock *n.* An airtight chamber between regions of unequal pressure in which air pressure can be regulated.

air mail *also* **air•mail** (âr′māl′) *n.* **1.** The system of transporting mail by air. **2.** Mail transported by air. **—air′mail′** *v. & adj.*

air•man (âr′mən) *n.* **1.** An enlisted person in the U.S. Air Force. **2.** An aviator.

airman basic *n.* An enlisted person of the lowest rank in the U.S. Air Force.

air mass *n.* A large body of air that has approx. the same temperature, pressure, and moisture throughout.

air mile *n.* A unit of distance in air navigation.

air piracy *n.* The hijacking of an airplane in flight. **—air pirate** *n.*

air•plane (âr′plān′) *n.* A vehicle capable of flight, gen. heavier than air, and driven by jet engines or propellers.

air•play (âr′plā′) *n.* The broadcasting of a recording by a radio station.

air pocket *n.* A downward air current that causes an aircraft to lose altitude abruptly.

air•port (âr′pôrt′, -pōrt′) *n.* A permanent facility that provides space for aircraft to take off and land with a control tower, hangars, and accommodations for passengers and cargo.

air•pow•er *or* **air power** (âr′pou′ər) *n.* The strategic strength of a country's air force.

air raid *n.* An attack by enemy aircraft.

air•ship (âr′shĭp′) *n.* A dirigible.

air•sick•ness (âr′sĭk′nĭs) *n.* Nausea resulting from flight in an aircraft. **—air′sick′** *adj.*

air•space (âr′spās′) *n.* The section of the atmosphere above a particular land area, esp. that of a nation.

air speed *n.* The speed of an aircraft relative to the air.

air•strip (âr′strĭp′) *n.* A cleared area serving as a landing strip.

air•tight (âr′tīt′) *adj.* **1.** Impermeable by air or gas <an *airtight* seal> **2.** Unassailable <an *airtight* alibi>

air-to-air missile (âr′tə-âr′) *n.* A guided missile designed to be fired from aircraft at other aircraft.

air-to-sur•face missile (âr′tə-sûr′fĭs) *n.* A guided missile designed to be fired from aircraft at targets on the ground.

air•waves (âr′wāvz′) *pl.n.* The medium used to transmit radio and television signals.

air•way (âr′wā′) *n.* An air lane.

air•wor•thy (âr′wûr′*th*ē) *adj.* Fit to fly <*airworthy* jets> **—air′wor′thi•ness** *n.*

air•y (âr′ē) *adj.* **-i•er, -i•est. 1.** Of or like the air. **2.** Open to the air **:** breezy. **3.** Light as air **:** delicate. **4.** Insubstantial **:** imaginative <*airy* speculations> **5.** Nonchalant <an *airy* disregard for rules> **—air′i•ly** *adv.* **—air′i•ness** *n.*

aisle (īl) *n.* A passageway between rows of seats, as in a church or theater.

aitch (āch) *n.* The letter *h.*

aitch•bone (āch′bōn′) *n.* **1.** The rump bone in cattle. **2.** The cut of beef containing the aitchbone.

▲ ***word history:*** *Aitchbone* is a good example of a folk etymology, which is the refashioning of a word so that it resembles a more familiar, but unrelated, word. The incorrect division between the article and the noun in *a nachebon* resulted in a new noun whose first syllable was unrecognizable. This element was variously interpreted as *each, ash, ice,* and *aitch,* all familiar English words. The bone itself has no physical res[illegible] to the letter H.

a•jar[1] (ə-jär′) *adv. & adj.* Partially opened.
a•jar[2] (ə-jär′) *adv. & adj.* Not in harmony : jarring.
a•kim•bo (ə-kĭm′bō) *adj. & adv.* With hands on hips and elbows bowed outward.
a•kin (ə-kĭn′) *adj.* **1.** Related by blood. **2.** Similar in quality or character. **3.** Linguistically cognate.
Al *symbol for* ALUMINUM.
–al[1] *suff.* Of, pertaining to, or marked by <parent*al*>
–al[2] *suff.* Act : process <retrieva*l*>
à la *also* **a la** (ä′lä, ä′lə, ăl′ə) *prep.* **1.** In the manner or style of <a story *à la* Poe> **2.** According to <*à la* carte>
al•a•bas•ter (ăl′ə-băs′tər) *n.* A dense, translucent, white or tinted fine-grained gypsum.
à la carte (ä′ lä kärt′, ä′lə, ăl′ə) *adv. & adj.* With a separate price for each item on the menu.
a•lac•ri•ty (ə-lăk′rĭ-tē) *n.* **1.** Cheerful eagerness. **2.** Speed : quickness. **—a•lac′ri•tous** *adj.*
à la king (ä′lə kĭng′, ăl′ə) *adj.* Cooked in a cream sauce with green pepper or pimento and mushrooms <turkey *à la king*>
†al•a•me•da (ăl′ə-mē′də, -mā′-) *n. SW U.S.* A promenade or walk, esp. one shaded by cottonwoods.
†al•a•mo (ăl′ə-mō′) *n., pl.* **-mos.** *SW U.S.* A poplar tree, esp. a cottonwood.
à la mode (ä′ lä mōd′, ä′lə, ăl′ə) *adj.* **1.** Fashionable. **2.** Served with ice cream.
a•larm (ə-lärm′) *n.* **1.** A sudden feeling of fear. **2.** A warning of imminent danger. **3.** A device that sounds a warning by a sound or signal. **4.** The sounding mechanism of a clock. **5.** A call to arms. ★ ***syns:*** ALERT, TOCSIN, WARNING —*v.* To fill with alarm : frighten. **—a•larm′a•ble** *adj.*
a•larm•ing (ə-lär′mĭng) *adj.* Frightening. **—a•larm′ing•ly** *adv.*
a•larm•ist (ə-lär′mĭst) *n.* A person who needlessly alarms others. **—a•larm′ism** *n.*
a•las (ə-lăs′) *interj.* —Used to express sadness, regret, or anxiety.
alb (ălb) *n.* A long white linen robe worn as a liturgical vestment.
al•ba•core (ăl′bə-kôr′, -kōr′) *n.* A large marine fish, *Thunnus alalunga,* whose edible flesh is a major source of canned tuna.
al•ba•tross (ăl′bə-trôs′, -trŏs′) *n.* A large, web-footed, long-winged sea bird of the family Diomedeidae, related to the petrel.
al•be•do (ăl-bē′dō) *n., pl.* **-dos.** The reflecting power of a surface, as of a planet.
al•be•it (ôl-bē′ĭt, ăl-) *conj.* Although.
al•bi•no (ăl-bī′nō) *n., pl.* **-nos.** An organism lacking normal pigmentation, as a person having inordinately pale skin, very light hair, and lacking normal eye coloring. **—al′bi•nism** *n.*
al•bum (ăl′bəm) *n.* **1.** A book or binder with blank pages for mounting a collection, as of stamps or photographs. **2. a.** A set of phonograph records stored in one binding. **b.** A recording, esp. a long-playing phonograph record.
al•bu•men (ăl-byōō′mən) *n.* **1.** The white of an egg. **2.** Albumin.
al•bu•min (ăl-byōō′mən) *n.* A simple, water-soluble protein found in egg white, blood serum, milk, and many animal and plant tissues.
al•bu•min•ous (ăl-byōō′mə-nəs) *adj.* Of, resembling, or relating to albumin or albumen.
al•cai•de (ăl-kī′dē) *n.* The commander of a fortress in Spain or Portugal.
al•cal•de (ăl-kăl′dē) *n.* The chief governing or judicial official of a Spanish or Spanish-American town.
al•caz•ar (ăl-kăz′ər, ăl′kə-zär′) *n.* A Spanish fortress or palace.
al•che•my (ăl′kə-mē) *n.* **1.** A medieval chemical philosophy whose chief aim was the conversion of base metals into gold. **2.** An apparently magical power. **—al•chem′i•cal, al•chem′ic** *adj.* **—al•chem′i•cal•ly** *adv.* **—al′che•mist** *n.*
al•co•hol (ăl′kə-hôl′) *n.* **1.** Any of a series of hydroxyl compounds that include ethanol and methanol. **2.** Intoxicating liquor containing alcohol.
al•co•hol•ic (ăl′kə-hô′lĭk, -hŏl′ĭk) *adj.* **1.** Of, relating to, or resulting from alcohol. **2.** Containing or preserved in alcohol. **3.** Suffering from alcoholism. —*n.* A sufferer from alcoholism.
al•co•hol•ism (ăl′kə-hô-lĭz′əm) *n.* **1.** Excessive consumption of and psychophysiological dependence on alcoholic beverages. **2.** A pathological condition caused by this.
al•cove (ăl′kōv′) *n.* A recess or partly enclosed extension of a room : nook.
al•de•hyde (ăl′də-hīd′) *n.* Any of a class of highly reactive organic chemical compounds obtained by oxidation of primary alcohols.
al den•te (ăl dĕn′tē) *adj. & adv.* Cooked enough to be firm but not soft.
al•der (ôl′dər) *n.* Any of various deciduous shrubs or trees of the genus *Alnus,* growing in cool, moist places.
al•der•man (ôl′dər-mən) *n.* A member of a municipal legislature.
Al•der•ney (ôl′dər-nē) *n., pl.* **-neys.** One of a breed of small dairy cattle orig. raised in the Channel Islands.
ale (āl) *n.* A fermented alcoholic beverage similar to but heavier than beer.
a•le•a•to•ry (ā′lē-ə-tôr′ē, -tōr′ē) *adj.* Dependent on chance or luck.
a•lee (ə-lē′) *adv. Naut.* Away from the wind.
a•lem•bic (ə-lĕm′bĭk) *n.* A container formerly used for distilling.
a•lert (ə-lûrt′) *adj.* **1.** Vigilantly attentive : observant. **2.** Mentally perceptive and responsive : quick. **3.** Lively or brisk. ★ ***syns:*** OBSERVANT, OPEN-EYED, VIGILANT, WAKEFUL, WARY, WATCHFUL, WIDE-AWAKE —*n.* **1.** A warning signal of danger or attack. **2.** The time period during which an alert is in effect. —*v.* **1.** To warn. **2.** To inform. **—a•lert′ly** *adv.* **—a•lert′ness** *n.*
A•leut (ə-lōōt′, ăl′ē-ōōt′) *n., pl.* **Aleut** *or* **A•leuts. 1.** A member of a people native to

the Aleutian Islands and coastal areas of SW Alaska. **2.** The language of the Aleut, related to Eskimo. —**A•leu'tian** (ə-lo͞o'shən) *adj. & n.*

al•ex•an•drine *also* **Al•ex•an•drine** (ăl'-ĭg-zăn'drĭn) *n.* A line of verse in iambic hexameter. —**al'ex•an•drine** *adj.*

al•fal•fa (ăl-făl'fə) *n.* A cloverlike plant, *Medicago sativa,* with purple flowers, widely grown for forage.

†**al•for•ja** (ăl-fôr'hə) *n. W U.S.* A leather or canvas saddlebag.

al•fres•co (ăl-frĕs'kō) *adv. & adj.* In the fresh air **:** outdoors.

al•ga (ăl'gə) *n., pl.* **-gae** (-jē). Any of various aquatic, one-celled or multicellular plants without true stems, roots, and leaves but containing chlorophyll. —**al'gal** *adj.*

al•ge•bra (ăl'jə-brə) *n.* A branch of mathematics in which symbols, usu. letters, represent numbers or members of a specified set of numbers and are used to express general relationships that hold for all numbers in the set.

AL•GOL *or* **Al•gol** (ăl'gŏl', -gôl') *n.* A computer language used esp. for solving mathematical and scientific problems.

Al•gon•qui•an (ăl-gŏng'kwē-ən, -kē-ən) *also* **Al•gon•ki•an** (-kē-ən) *n., pl.* **-an** *or* **-ans. 1.** A family of American Indian languages spoken in an area from Labrador to the Carolinas between the Atlantic coast and the Rocky Mountains. **2.** A member of an Algonquian-speaking people. —**Al•gon'qui•an** *adj.*

Al•gon•quin (ăl-gŏng'kwĭn, -kĭn) *also* **Al•gon•kin** (-kĭn) *n., pl.* **-quin** *or* **-quins** *also* **-kin** *or* **-kins. 1.** A member of an American Indian people inhabiting the Ottawa R. valley of Quebec and Ontario. **2.** Their Algonquian language.

al•go•rism (ăl'gə-rĭz'əm) *n.* The Arabic system of numeration.

al•go•ris•tic (ăl'gə-rĭs'tĭk) *adj.* Yielding a precise answer, as a computational system guaranteeing accurate solution.

al•go•rithm (ăl'gə-rĭ*th*'əm) *n. Math.* A mathematical rule or procedure for solving a problem. —**al'go•rith'mic** *adj.*

▲ ***word history:*** *Algorithm* originated as a variant spelling of *algorism.* The spelling was prob. influenced by the word *arithmetic* or its Greek source *arithm,* "number." With the development of sophisticated mechanical computing devices in the 20th cent., however, *algorithm* was adopted as a convenient word for a recursive mathematical procedure, the computer's stock in trade. *Algorithm* has ceased to be used as a variant form of the older word.

algorithmic language *n.* A computer language presenting numerical procedures in standard form.

a•li•as (ā'lē-əs, āl'yəs) *n., pl.* **-as•es.** An assumed name. —*adv.* Otherwise named **:** also known as <Smith, *alias* Jones>

al•i•bi (ăl'ə-bī') *n., pl.* **-bis.** *Law.* **1.** A form of defense by which a defendant attempts to prove that he or she was elsewhere when the crime in question was committed. **2.** *Informal.* An excuse. —**al'i•bi'** *v.*

a•li•en (ā'lē-ən, āl'yən) *adj.* **1.** Owing political allegiance to another country or government **:** foreign. **2.** Not one's own **:** unfamiliar <*alien* culture> **3.** Opposed in character <Stealing is *alien* to my nature.> —*n.* **1.** An unnaturalized resident of a country. **2.** A member of another people, family, region, etc. **3.** An outsider. **4.** *Slang.* A creature from outer space.

al•ien•a•ble (ăl'yə-nə-bəl, ā'lē-ə-) *adj. Law.* Capable of being transferred to a new owner. —**al'ien•a•bil'i•ty** *n.*

al•ien•ate (āl'yə-nāt', ā'lē-ə-) *v.* **-at•ed, -at•ing. 1.** To cause to become indifferent or hostile **:** estrange. **2.** *Law.* To transfer (property) to a new owner. —**al'ien•a'tion** *n.* —**al'ien•a'tor** *n.*

al•ien•ist (āl'yə-nĭst, ā'lē-ə-) *n. Law.* A psychiatrist.

a•light[1] (ə-līt') *v.* **a•light•ed** *or* **a•lit** (ə-lĭt'), **a•light•ing. 1.** To descend and settle, as after flight **:** land. **2.** To dismount.

a•light[2] (ə-līt') *adj. & adv.* **1.** Burning. **2.** Illuminated.

a•lign *also* **a•line** (ə-līn') *v.* **1.** To place in a line. **2.** To ally (oneself) with one side of a cause, dispute, government, etc. **3.** To adjust (e.g., parts of a mechanism) to produce a proper condition or relationship. —**a•lign'er** *n.* —**a•lign'ment** *n.*

a•like (ə-līk') *adj.* Having close resemblance **:** similar. —*adv.* In the same manner or degree. —**a•like'ness** *n.*

al•i•ment (ăl'ə-mənt) *n.* Nourishment **:** food. —**al'i•men'tal** *adj.* —**al'i•men'ta•ry** *adj.* —**al'i•men•ta'tion** *n.*

alimentary canal *n.* The tube of the digestive system extending from the mouth to the anus and including the pharynx, esophagus, stomach, and intestines.

al•i•mo•ny (ăl'ə-mō'nē) *n., pl.* **-nies.** *Law.* A court-ordered allowance for support, usu. given by a man to his former wife after a divorce or legal separation.

a•line (ə-līn) *v. var. of* ALIGN.

A-line (ā'līn') *adj.* Having a fitted top and a flared bottom <an *A-line* gown>

al•i•phat•ic (ăl'ə-făt'ĭk) *adj.* Relating to organic chemical compounds in which the carbon atoms are linked in open chains.

a•lit (ə-lĭt') *v. var. p.t. & p.p. of* ALIGHT[1].

a•live (ə-līv') *adj.* **1.** Having life **:** living. **2.** In existence or effect <keep a dream *alive*> **3.** Full of life **:** lively. ★ ***syns:*** ANIMATE, LIVE, LIVING, VITAL —**alive to.** Sensitive to <*alive to* the dangers of drugs> —**alive with.** Full of <a room *alive with* chatter>. —**a•live'ness** *n.*

a•li•yah (ä-lē'yä, ə-lē'yə) *n.* Immigration of Jewish people into Israel.

a•liz•a•rin (ə-lĭz'ə-rĭn) *also* **a•liz•a•rine** (-ĭn, -ə-rēn') *n.* An orange-red compound used in dyes.

al•ka•li (ăl'kə-lī') *n., pl.* **-lis** *or* **-lies. 1.** A carbonate or hydroxide of an alkali metal, whose aqueous solution is bitter, slippery, caustic, and basic in reactions. 2. Any of various soluble mineral salts present in natural water and arid soils.

al·ka·line (ăl′kə-lĭn, -līn′) *adj.* **1.** Of, relating to, or containing an alkali. **2.** Basic. **—al′ka·lin′i·ty** *n.*

al·ka·lize (ăl′kə-līz′) *also* **al·ka·lin·ize** (-lə-nīz′) *v.* **-lized, -liz·ing** *also* **-ized, -iz·ing.** To make alkaline. **—al′ka·li·za′tion** *or* **al′ka·lin′i·za′tion** *n.*

al·ka·loid (ăl′kə-loid′) *n.* Any of various nitrogen-containing organic bases obtained from plants, including nicotine, quinine, atropine, cocaine, and morphine. **—al′ka·loi′dal** *adj.*

al·ka·lo·sis (ăl′kə-lō′sĭs) *n.* Abnormally high alkali content in the blood and tissues.

al·kyd *or* **al·kyd resin** (ăl′kĭd) *n.* A durable synthetic resin used in paints.

all (ôl) *adj.* **1.** The total entity or extent of <*all* the west><*all* women> **2.** Being the whole number, amount, or quantity of <*all* the guests> **3.** Being the utmost possible <in *all* honesty> **4.** Every <*all* manner of trouble> **5.** Any whatsoever <beyond *all* question> **6.** Nothing but **:** only <*all* work and no play> *—pron.* Each and every one <10 cars raced and *all* crashed.> *—n.* Everything one has <gave our *all* to the cause> *—adv.* **1.** Wholly **:** entirely <*all* confused> **2.** Each **:** apiece <The score was 6 *all.*> **3.** Exclusively <The mail is *all* for me.> **—all but.** Almost. **—all in.** Exhausted. **—all in all.** Everything being taken into account. **—and all.** And everything else <learning to drive *and all*> **—at all. 1.** In any and every way. **2.** To any extent. **—for all.** In spite of.

Al·lah (ăl′ə, ä′lə) *n.* God, esp. in Islam.

all-A·mer·i·can (ôl′ə-mĕr′ĭ-kən) *adj.* **1.** Representative of the best or typical of its kind in the U.S. **2.** Selected as the best amateur in the U.S. at a particular sports position or event. **—all′-A·mer′i·can** *n.*

all-a·round (ôl′ə-round′) *adj. var. of* ALL-ROUND.

al·lay (ə-lā′) *v.* **1.** To relieve or lessen (e.g., grief or pain). **2.** To calm <*allay* one's fears> **—al·lay′er** *n.*

all clear *n.* **1.** A signal indicating that an air raid is over. **2.** An expression used to signify the absence of immediate obstacles or danger.

al·lege (ə-lĕj′) *v.* **-leged, -leg·ing. 1.** To state to be true **:** claim. **2.** To assert without proof. **3.** To cite as an excuse. **—al′le·ga′tion** (ăl′ĭ-gā′shən) *n.* **—al·leg′ed·ly** *adv.* **—al·leg′er** *n.*

al·le·giance (ə-lē′jəns) *n.* Loyalty owed to a sovereign, nation, or cause **:** fidelity.

al·le·go·ry (ăl′ĭ-gôr′ē, -gōr′ē) *n., pl.* **-ries.** A literary, dramatic, or pictorial device in which each character, object, and event symbolically illustrates a moral or religious principle. **—al′le·gor′ic, al′le·gor′i·cal** *adj.* **—al′le·gor′i·cal·ly** *adv.* **—al′le·go′rist** *n.*

al·le·gret·to (ăl′ĭ-grĕt′ō) *adv. Mus.* Faster than andante but slower than allegro.—Used as a direction. **—al′le·gret′to** *adj. & n.*

al·le·gro (ə-lĕg′rō, ə-lā′grō) *adv. Mus.* Faster than allegretto but slower than presto.—Used as a direction. **—al·le′gro** *adj. & n.*

al·lele (ə-lēl′) *n.* Any of a group of possible mutational forms of a gene. **—al·le′lic** (ə-lē′lĭk, ə-lĕl′ĭk) *adj.* **—al·le′lism** *n.*

al·le·lo·morph (ə-lē′lə-môrf′, ə-lĕl′ə-) *n.* An allele. **—al·le′lo·mor′phic** *adj.* **—al·le′lo·mor′phism** *n.*

al·le·lu·ia (ăl′ə-lo͞o′yə) *interj.* Hallelujah.

al·ler·gen (ăl′ər-jən) *n.* Something that causes an allergy. **—al′ler·gen′ic** *adj.*

al·ler·gist (ăl′ər-jĭst) *n.* A physician specializing in treating allergies.

al·ler·gy (ăl′ər-jē) *n., pl.* **-gies. 1.** Abnormal or pathological reaction to environmental substances, as pollens, foods, dust, or microorganisms. **2.** *Informal.* An adverse feeling **:** antipathy. **—al·ler′gic** *adj.*

al·le·vi·ate (ə-lē′vē-āt′) *v.* **-at·ed, -at·ing.** To make less severe **:** ease. **—al·le′vi·a′tion** *n.* **—al·le′vi·a′tive** *adj.* **—al·le′vi·a′tor** *n.*

al·ley (ăl′ē) *n., pl.* **-leys. 1.** A narrow street or passage between or behind buildings. **2.** A bowling alley.

al·ley·way (ăl′ē-wā′) *n.* ALLEY 1.

al·li·ance (ə-lī′əns) *n.* **1. a.** A pact of confederation between nations. **b.** The nations so united. **2.** A union or relationship by kinship, marriage, friendship, etc.

al·li·ga·tor (ăl′ĭ-gā′tər) *n.* Either of 2 large amphibious reptiles, *Alligator mississipiensis* of the SE U.S. or *A. sinensis* of China, with sharp teeth and strong jaws, closely related to the crocodile.

alligator pear *n.* The avocado.

all-im·por·tant (ôl′ĭm-pôr′tnt) *adj.* Very important.

al·lit·er·a·tion (ə-lĭt′ə-rā′shən) *n.* The occurrence in a phrase or line of speech or writing of 2 or more words having the same initial sound; e.g. <"all summer in the sound of the sea" —Whitman> **—al·lit′er·a′tive** *adj.* **—al·lit′er·a′tive·ly** *adv.*

al·lo·cate (ăl′ə-kāt′) *v.* **-cat·ed, -cat·ing.** To allot **:** assign. **—al′lo·ca′tion** *n.*

al·lot (ə-lŏt′) *v.* **-lot·ted, -lot·ting.** To distribute or set aside as a share. ★ ***syns:*** ALLOCATE, ALLOW, APPORTION, ASSIGN, GIVE, PARCEL, PORTION **—al·lot′ment** *n.* **—al·lot′ter** *n.*

all out *adv.* With every possible effort or resource <went *all out*> **—all′-out′** *adj.*

all over *adv.* Over the entire area. **—all′o′ver** *adj.*

al·low (ə-lou′) *v.* **1.** To permit. **2.** To permit to have. **3.** To make a provision for <*allow* time for a shower> **4.** To sanction the presence of **:** let in. **5.** To provide (the needed amount). **6.** To admit **:** concede. **7.** To grant as a discount. **—al·low′a·ble** *adj.* **—al·low′a·bly** *adv.* **—al·low′ed·ly** *adv.*

al·low·ance (ə-lou′əns) *n.* **1.** The act of allowing. **2.** A regular provision of money, food, etc. **3.** A price discount. **4.** Consideration for modifying circumstances <made an *allowance* for mistakes>

al•loy (ăl′oi′, ə-loi′) *n.* **1.** A homogeneous mixture, usu. of 2 or more metals. **2.** Something added that reduces purity or value. **—al•loy′** *v.*

all right *adv.* **1.** Satisfactory <For an old car, it's *all right.*> **2.** Correct <Your conclusions are *all right.*> **3.** Unhurt. **4.** Very well **:** yes. **5.** Certainly <It's a genuine antique, *all right.*>

all-right (ôl′rīt′) *adj. Slang.* **1.** Of sound character **:** dependable. **2.** Good <an *all-right* concert>

all-round (ôl′round′) *also* **all-a•round** (ôl′-ə-round′) *adj.* **1.** Including all aspects. **2.** Versatile.

All Saints' Day *n.* Nov. 1, a Christian feast honoring all the saints.

all•spice (ôl′spīs′) *n.* A tropical American tree, *Pimenta officianalis,* bearing aromatic berries that are used as a spice.

all-star (ôl′stär′) *adj.* Composed entirely of star performers. **—all′-star′** *n.*

all-time (ôl′tīm′) *adj. Informal.* Of all time <an *all-time* attendance record>

all told *adv.* With everything taken into account.

al•lude (ə-lo͞od′) *v.* **-lud•ed, -lud•ing.** To refer to something indirectly. **—al•lu′sion** *n.* **—al•lu′sive** *adj.* **—al•lu′sive•ly** *adv.*

al•lure (ə-lo͝or′) *v.* **-lured, -lur•ing.** To tempt **:** entice. *—n.* The power of attracting. **—al•lure′ment** *n.* **—al•lur′er** *n.* **—al•lur′ing•ly** *adv.*

al•lu•vi•um (ə-lo͞o′vē-əm) *n., pl.* **-vi•ums** *or* **-vi•a** (-vē-ə). Sedimentary material deposited by flowing water, as in a delta or riverbed. **—al•lu′vi•al** *adj.*

al•ly (ə-lī′, ăl′ī′) *v.* **-lied, -ly•ing.** To enter into or unite in a formal relationship, as by a treaty. *—n.* (ăl′ī′, ə-lī′), *pl.* **-lies.** One allied with another.

al•ma ma•ter *also* **Al•ma Ma•ter** (ăl′mə mä′tər, äl′mə) *n.* **1.** The school, college, or university one has attended. **2.** The anthem of such an institution.

al•ma•nac (ôl′mə-năk′, ăl′-) *n.* An annual publication including calendars, weather forecasts, astronomical information, and other useful related tabular information.

al•man•dine (ăl′mən-dēn′) *also* **al•man•dite** (-dīt′) *n.* A deep violet-red garnet used as a gemstone.

al•might•y (ôl-mī′tē) *adj.* Having absolute power **:** omnipotent. *—n.* **the Almighty.** God.

al•mond (ä′mənd, ăm′ənd) *n.* A small tree, *Prunus amygdalus,* bearing pink flowers and oval, edible nuts with soft, light-brown shells.

al•most (ôl′mōst′, ôl-mōst′) *adv.* Very nearly <*almost* finished>

alms (ämz) *pl.n.* Money or goods given in charity.

alms•house (ämz′hous′) *n.* A poorhouse.

al•ni•co (ăl′nĭ-kō′) *n.* A hard, strong alloy of aluminum, cobalt, copper, iron, nickel, and sometimes niobium or tantalum, used to make permanent magnets.

al•oe (ăl′ō) *n.* Any of various fleshy-leaved plants of the genus *Aloe,* native to S Africa.

a•loft (ə-lôft′, ə-lŏft′) *adv.* **1.** In or into a high place. **2.** In or toward a ship's upper rigging.

a•lo•ha (ä-lō′hä′) *interj.* —Used as a greeting or farewell.

a•lone (ə-lōn′) *adj.* **1.** Apart from anything or anyone else **:** solitary. **2.** Excluding anyone else **:** only. **3.** With nothing else added. **4.** Without equal **:** unique. ★ ***syns:*** LONE, LONELY, LONESOME, SOLITARY **—a•lone′** *adv.* **—a•lone′ness** *n.*

a•long (ə-lông′, ə-lŏng′) *adv.* **1.** In a line with **:** following the course of. **2.** With a forward motion <move *along*> **3.** Together <disease *along* with poverty> **4.** As a companion or company <brought the dog *along*> **5.** *Informal.* Advanced to some degree <well *along* in the day> *—prep.* Over, through, or by the course of.

a•long•shore (ə-lông′shôr′, -shōr′, ə-lŏng′-) *adv.* Along the shore.

a•long•side (ə-lông′sīd′, ə-lŏng′-) *adv.* Along, at, or to the side. *—prep.* Side by side with.

a•loof (ə-lo͞of′) *adj.* Distant or reserved in manner or social relations. **—a•loof′ly** *adv.* **—a•loof′ness** *n.*

al•o•pe•cia (ăl′ə-pē′shə, -shē-ə) *n.* Loss of hair. **—al′o•pe′cic** (-pē′sĭk) *adj.*

a•loud (ə-loud′) *adv.* With the voice **:** orally.

alp (ălp) *n.* A high mountain.

al•pac•a (ăl-păk′ə) *n., pl.* **alpaca** *or* **-as. 1.** A domesticated South American mammal, *Lama pacos,* related to the llama, with fine, long, fleecy wool. **2. a.** Its wool. **b.** Cloth made from this wool.

al•pen•horn (ăl′pən-hôrn′) *n.* A long curved wooden horn used by herders in the Alps to call cows to pasture.

alpenhorn

al•pes•trine (ăl-pĕs′trĭn) *adj.* Growing at high altitudes.

al•pha•bet (ăl′fə-bĕt′, -bĭt) *n.* **1.** The letters of a given language, arranged in a traditional order. **2.** Basic or elementary principles.

al•pha•bet•i•cal (ăl′fə-bĕt′ĭ-kəl) *also* **al•pha•bet•ic** (-bĕt′ĭk) *adj.* **1.** Arranged in the traditional order of the letters of a language. **2.** Of or using an alphabet. **—al′pha•bet′i•cal•ly** *adv.*

al•pha•bet•ize (ăl′fə-bĭ-tīz′) *v.* **-ized, -iz•ing.** To put in alphabetical order. **—al′pha•**

bet′i·za′tion (-bĕt′ĭ-zā′shən) *n.* **—al′pha·bet·iz′er** *n.*

alpha decay *n.* The radioactive decay of an atomic nucleus by emission of an alpha particle.

alpha helix *n.* A common structure of proteins, characterized by a single chain of amino acids stabilized by hydrogen bonds.

al·pha·nu·mer·ic (ăl′fə-nōō-mĕr′ĭk, -nyōō-) *adj.* Consisting of both alphabetic and numerical symbols.

alpha particle *n.* A positively charged composite particle, identical with a helium atom nucleus and having 2 protons and 2 neutrons.

alpha ray *n.* A stream of alpha particles.

alpha rhythm *also* **alpha wave** *n.* The most common waveform of the adult human brain, recorded by electroencephalograph, usu. 8 to 13 oscillations per second in subjects at rest.

al·pine (ăl′pīn′, -pĭn) *adj.* **1.** Of or relating to high mountains. **2.** *Biol.* Living or growing above the timberline.

al·pin·ist *also* **Al·pin·ist** (ăl′pə-nĭst) *n.* A mountain climber : mountaineer.

al·read·y (ôl-rĕd′ē) *adv.* Before a specified time : previously.

al·so (ôl′sō) *adv.* In addition : likewise. *—conj.* And in addition.

al·so-ran (ôl′sō-răn′) *n. Informal.* One defeated in an election, race, etc.

al·tar (ôl′tər) *n.* An elevated place or structure before which religious ceremonies may be held or sacrifices offered.

al·ter (ôl′tər) *v.* **1.** To make or become different : change. **2.** To tailor (a garment) for a better fit. **3.** *Informal.* To spay or castrate. **—al′ter·a·ble** *adj.* **—al′ter·a·bly** *adv.* **—al′ter·a′tion** *n.*

al·ter·cate (ôl′tər-kāt′) *v.* **-cat·ed, -cat·ing.** To argue or dispute vehemently. **—al′ter·ca′tion** *n.*

al·ter e·go (ôl′tər ē′gō) *n.* **1.** Another aspect of one's personality. **2.** A constant companion or intimate friend.

al·ter·nate (ôl′tər-nāt′, ăl′-) *v.* **-nat·ed, -nat·ing.** **1.** To happen in successive turns <Day *alternates* with night.> **2.** To change from one condition, action, or place to another regularly <*alternates* between pitcher and catcher> *—adj.* (-nĭt). **1.** Happening successively. **2.** Designating every other one of a series. **3.** Taking the place of another : substitute <an *alternate* method> *—n.* (-nĭt). One who acts in place of another. **—al′ter·nate·ly** *adv.* **—al′ter·na′tion** *n.*

alternating current *n.* An electric current that reverses direction in a circuit at regular intervals.

al·ter·na·tive (ôl-tûr′nə-tĭv, ăl-) *n.* **1.** The choice between possibilities. **2.** One of the possibilities to be chosen. *—adj.* **1.** Allowing a choice. **2.** Unconventional <an *alternative* lifestyle> **—al·ter′na·tive·ly** *adv.*

al·ter·na·tor (ôl′tər-nā′tər, ăl′-) *n.* A generator producing alternating current.

al·though *also* **al·tho** (ôl-*th*ō′) *conj.* Even though.

al·tim·e·ter (ăl-tĭm′ĭ-tər) *n.* An instrument for measuring and indicating altitude, as of an aircraft. **—al·tim′e·try** *n.*

al·ti·tude (ăl′tĭ-tōōd′, -tyōōd′) *n.* **1.** The elevation of an object above a reference level, esp. above sea level or the earth's surface. **2.** *Astron.* The angular distance of a celestial object above the horizon. **3.** *Geom.* **a.** A line segment perpendicular to the base of a figure and extending from the base to the opposite vertex, side, or surface. **b.** The measure of the segment. **—al′ti·tu′di·nal** *adj.*

al·to (ăl′tō) *n., pl.* **-tos.** *Mus.* **1.** The lowest female singing voice : contralto. **2.** A countertenor. **3.** The range between soprano and tenor. **4.** A singer whose voice is within the alto range. **5.** A part written for an alto voice or instrument. **6.** An instrument that is within the alto range.

▲ ***word history:*** *Alto* in Italian means "high." It is applied to the lowest female singing voice because the range of the female alto is the same as that of the highest male singing voice, orig. called the alto.

al·to·geth·er (ôl′tə-gĕ*th*′ər, ôl′tə-gĕ*th*′ər) *adv.* **1.** Completely : entirely. **2.** In all <*Altogether* a dozen gifts arrived.> **3.** As a whole. **—in the altogether.** *Informal.* Nude.

al·tru·ism (ăl′trōō-ĭz′əm) *n.* Selfless regard for the well-being of others. **—al′tru·ist** *n.* **—al′tru·is′tic** *adj.* **—al′tru·is′ti·cal·ly** *adv.*

al·um (ăl′əm) *n.* **1.** Any of various sulfates in which a trivalent metal, such as aluminum, chromium, or iron, is combined with a univalent metal, such as potassium or sodium. **2.** Aluminum potassium sulfate, a compound of this type, used medicinally to stop bleeding.

a·lu·mi·na (ə-lōō′mə-nə) *n.* Any of several forms of aluminum oxide that occur naturally as corundum, in bauxite, and with various impurities as ruby, sapphire, and emery.

al·u·min·i·um (ăl′yə-mĭn′ē-əm) *n. esp. Brit. var. of* ALUMINUM.

a·lu·mi·nize (ə-lōō′mə-nīz′) *v.* **-nized, -niz·ing.** To cover, coat, or treat with aluminum or aluminum paint.

a·lu·mi·nous (ə-lōō′mə-nəs) *adj.* Of, relating to, or having aluminum or alum.

a·lu·mi·num (ə-lōō′mə-nəm) *n. Symbol* **Al** A lightweight, silvery-white, malleable metallic element used for many hard, light, corrosion-resistant alloys.

a·lum·na (ə-lŭm′nə) *n., pl.* **-nae** (-nē′). A woman graduate or former student of a school, college, or university.

a·lum·nus (ə-lŭm′nəs) *n., pl.* **-ni** (-nī′). A male graduate or former student of a school, college, or university.

al·ve·o·late (ăl-vē′ə-lĭt) *adj.* Having alveoli : honeycombed.

al·ve·o·lus (ăl-vē′ə-ləs) *n., pl.* **-li** (-lī′) **1.** A small pit or cavity. **2.** A tooth socket. **3.** A tiny, capillary-rich sac in the lungs where the exchange of oxygen and carbon dioxide takes place. **—al·ve′o·lar** *adj.*

al•ways (ôl′wāz, -wēz, -wĭz) *adv.* **1.** At every instance. **2.** For all time : forever. **3.** At any time.

a•lys•sum (ə-lĭs′əm) *n.* **1.** A plant of the genus *Alyssum,* with dense yellow or white flower clusters. **2.** Sweet alyssum.

Alz•heim•er's disease (älts′hī-mərz, ălts′-) *n.* A disease marked by progressive loss of mental capacity.

am (ăm; *when unstressed* əm) *v. 1st person sing. present tense of* BE.

Am *symbol for* AMERICIUM.

a•mal•gam (ə-măl′gəm) *n.* **1.** An alloy of mercury with other metals, as tin or silver. **2.** A mixture.

a•mal•ga•mate (ə-măl′gə-māt′) *v.* **-mat•ed, -mat•ing.** To mix so as to make a unified whole : blend. **—a•mal′ga•ma′tion** *n.* **—a•mal′ga•ma′tor** *n.*

a•man•dine (ä′mən-dēn′, ăm′ən-) *adj.* Made or garnished with almonds.

am•a•ni•ta (ăm′ə-nī′tə, -nē′-) *n.* Any of various mushrooms of the genus *Amanita,* most of which are highly toxic.

a•man•u•en•sis (ə-măn′yo͞o-ĕn′sĭs) *n., pl.* **-ses** (-sēz′). A secretary.

am•a•ranth (ăm′ə-rănth′) *n.* **1.** A weedy plant of the genus *Amaranthus,* with small greenish or purplish flower clusters. **2.** An imaginary flower that does not fade or die. **—am′a•ran′thine** *adj.*

am•a•ret•to (ăm′ə-rĕt′ō) *n.* An almond-flavored liqueur.

am•a•ryl•lis (ăm′ə-rĭl′ĭs) *n.* A bulbous, tropical plant, *Amaryllis belladonna,* native to S Africa, bearing large, lilylike flowers.

a•mass (ə-măs′) *v.* To accumulate : collect. **—a•mass′a•ble** *adj.* **—a•mass′er** *n.* **—a•mass′ment** *n.*

am•a•teur (ăm′ə-cho͝or′, -ə-tər, -ə-tyo͝or′) *n.* **1.** One who engages in an art, science, or sport for enjoyment rather than money. **2.** One who lacks professional skill. **—am′a•teur′ish** *adj.* **—am′a•teur′ish•ly** *adv.* **—am′a•teur′ism** *n.*

am•a•to•ry (ăm′ə-tôr′ē, -tōr′ē) *adj.* Of, promoting, or expressing love, esp. sexual love.

a•maze (ə-māz′) *v.* **a•mazed, a•maz•ing.** To affect with great surprise or wonder : astonish. **—a•maz′ed•ly** *adv.* **—a•maze′ment** *n.* **—a•maz′ing•ly** *adv.*

Am•a•zon (ăm′ə-zŏn′, -zən) *n.* **1.** *Gk. Myth.* A member of a race of female warriors alleged to have lived in Scythia. **2. amazon.** A tall, athletic woman. **—Am′a•zo′ni•an** (-zō′nē-ən) *adj.*

▲ ***word history:*** The Greeks themselves devised what is probably a folk etymology for *Amazon.* According to Greek legends the Amazons cut off their right breasts to be able to use a bow more easily. The word thus appears to be formed in Greek of the prefix *a-,* "not," and *mazos,* "breast," in reference to the Amazons' mutilated condition. However, it is more likely that the word *Amazon* is a Greek spelling of a non-Greek tribal name.

am•a•zon•ite (ăm′ə-zə-nīt′) *n.* A green variety of microcline, often used as a semiprecious gemstone.

am•bas•sa•dor (ăm-băs′ə-dər) *n.* A diplomat of the highest rank accredited by government as representative in residence to another. **—am•bas′sa•do′ri•al** *adj.* **—am•bas′sa•dor•ship′** *n.*

am•ber (ăm′bər) *n.* A translucent yellow, orange, or brownish-yellow fossil resin, used for making decorative objects, esp. jewelry. **—am′ber** *adj.*

am•ber•gris (ăm′bər-grĭs, -grēs′) *n.* A waxy grayish substance formed in the intestines of sperm whales and used in perfumes as a fixative.

am•ber•jack (ăm′bər-jăk′) *n., pl.* **-jack** *or* **-jacks.** A food and game fish of the genus *Seriola,* of temperate and tropical marine waters.

am•bi•ance *also* **am•bi•ence** (ăm′bē-əns) *n.* The distinctive atmosphere of an environment or setting.

am•bi•dex•trous (ăm′bĭ-dĕk′strəs) *adj.* Using both hands with equal facility. **—am′bi•dex•ter′i•ty** *n.* **—am′bi•dex′trous•ly** *adv.*

am•bi•ent (ăm′bē-ənt) *adj.* Surrounding.

am•big•u•ous (ăm-bĭg′yo͞o-əs) *adj.* **1.** Liable to more than one interpretation. **2.** Uncertain or indefinite <paper of an *ambiguous* hue> ★ ***syns:*** CLOUDY, EQUIVOCAL, NEBULOUS, OBSCURE, SIBYLLINE, UNCERTAIN, UNCLEAR, UNEXPLICIT **—am′bi•gu′i•ty, am•big′u•ous•ness** *n.* **—am•big′u•ous•ly** *adv.*

am•bi•tion (ăm-bĭsh′ən) *n.* **1.** An eager or strong desire to achieve something. **2.** The goal so desired. ★ ***syns:*** DRIVE, ENTERPRISE, INITIATIVE, PUSH

am•bi•tious (ăm-bĭsh′əs) *adj.* **1.** Marked by ambition. **2.** Requiring much effort : challenging. **—am•bi′tious•ly** *adv.*

am•biv•a•lence (ăm-bĭv′ə-ləns) *n.* The existence of mutually conflicting emotions or thoughts about a person, object, or idea. **—am•biv′a•lent** *adj.* **—am•biv′a•lent•ly** *adv.*

am•ble (ăm′bəl) *v.* **-bled, -bling.** To move at a leisurely pace : saunter. **—am′ble** *n.* **—am′bler** *n.*

am•bro•sia (ăm-brō′zhə) *n.* **1.** *Gk. & Rom. Myth.* The food of the gods. **2.** Something with an esp. delightful flavor or fragrance. **—am•bro′sial, am•bro′sian** *adj.*

am•bu•lance (ăm′byə-ləns) *n.* A vehicle equipped for carrying the sick or injured.

am•bu•late (ăm′byə-lāt′) *v.* **-lat•ed, -lat•ing.** To walk or move about. **—am′bu•lant** *adj.* **—am′bu•la•to′ry** *adj.*

am•bus•cade (ăm′bə-skād′, ăm′bə-skād′) *n.* An ambush. **—am′bus•cade** *v.* **—am′bus•cad′er** *n.*

am•bush (ăm′bo͝osh′) *n.* **1.** A surprise attack made from a hiding place. **2.** The hiding place from which an ambush is made. **—am′bush** *v.*

a•me•ba (ə-mē′bə) *n. var. of* AMOEBA.

a•me•lio•rate (ə-mēl'yə-rāt') *v.* **-rat•ed, -rat•ing.** To make or become better : improve. **—a•me'lio•ra'tion** *n.*
a•men (ā-mĕn', ä-) *interj.* —Used at the end of a prayer or a statement to express agreement or approval.
a•me•na•ble (ə-mē'nə-bəl, ə-mĕn'ə-) *adj.* **1.** Obedient : tractable. **2.** Responsible to authority : accountable. **—a•me'na•bly** *adv.*
a•mend (ə-mĕnd') *v.* **1.** To improve. **2.** To correct. **3.** To revise (e.g., a legislative measure) formally by adding, deleting, or rephrasing. **—a•mend'a•ble** *adj.*
a•mend•ment (ə-mĕnd'mənt) *n.* **1.** Improvement. **2.** A correction. **3. a.** A revision. **b.** A formal statement of such a revision.
a•mends (ə-mĕndz') *pl.n.* Reparation for insult, injury, or loss <make *amends*>
a•men•i•ty (ə-mĕn'ĭ-tē, ə-mē'nĭ-) *n., pl.* **-ties.** **1.** Pleasantness : agreeableness. **2.** Something that increases physical or material comfort. **3. amenities.** Social courtesies : civilities.
a•men•or•rhe•a *or* **a•men•or•rhoe•a** (ā-mĕn'ə-rē'ə) *n.* Abnormal suppression or absence of menstruation. **—a•men'or•rhe'ic** *adj.*
am•ent[1] (ăm'ənt, ā'mənt) *n.* A catkin.
a•ment[2] (ā'mĕnt', ā'mənt) *n.* A mentally deficient person.
a•men•tia (ā-mĕn'shə, -sheē-ə) *n.* Subnormal mental development.
Am•er•a•sian (ăm'ə-rā'zhən, -shən) *n.* A person of American and Asian descent. **—Am'er•a'sian** *adj.*
a•merce (ə-mûrs') *v.* **a•merced, a•merc•ing.** To punish, esp. by a fine imposed arbitrarily by a court.
A•mer•i•can (ə-mĕr'ĭ-kən) *n.* **1.** A U.S. citizen. **2.** A native or inhabitant of America or the Americas. **—A•mer'i•can** *adj.* **—A•mer'i•can•i•za'tion** *n.* **—A•mer'i•can•ize'** *v.* **—A•mer'i•can•ness** *n.*
A•mer•i•ca•na (ə-mĕr'ĭ-kā'nə, -kăn'ə, -kā'nə) *pl.n.* A collection of materials relating to American history, geography, or folklore.
American eagle *n.* The bald eagle.
American Indian *n.* A member of any of the aboriginal peoples of North America (except the Eskimos), South America, and the West Indies.
A•mer•i•can•ism (ə-mĕr'ĭ-kə-nĭz'əm) *n.* A custom, language usage, trait, or tradition peculiar to the U.S.
American plan *n.* A hotel plan whereby a guest is charged a fixed daily rate for room, meals, and service.
am•er•i•ci•um (ăm'ə-rĭsh'ē-əm) *n. Symbol* **Am** A white metallic transuranic element of the actinide series.
Am•er•ind (ăm'ə-rĭnd') *also* **Am•er•in•di•an** (ăm'ə-rĭn'dē-ən) *n.* An American Indian or an Eskimo. **—Am'er•in'di•an, Am'er•in'dic** *adj.*
am•e•thyst (ăm'ə-thĭst) *n.* A purple or violet form of transparent quartz or corundum used as a gemstone. **—am'e•thys'tine** *adj.*
a•mi•a•ble (ā'mē-ə-bəl) *adj.* Pleasant and friendly <an *amiable* companion> ★ ***syns:*** AFFABLE, AGREEABLE, COMPLAISANT, CORDIAL, EASY, EASYGOING, GENIAL, GOOD-NATURED **—a'mi•a•bil'i•ty, a'mi•a•ble•ness** *n.* **—a'mi•a•bly** *adv.*
am•i•ca•ble (ăm'ĭ-kə-bəl) *adj.* **1.** Friendly. **2.** Harmonious. **—am'i•ca•bil'i•ty, am'i•ca•ble•ness** *n.* **—am'i•ca•bly** *adv.*
a•mid (ə-mĭd') *also* **a•midst** (ə-mĭdst') *prep.* In the middle of : surrounded by.
a•mid•ships (ə-mĭd'shĭps') *also* **a•mid•ship** (-shĭp') *adv. Naut.* Halfway between the bow and the stern.
a•mi•go (ə-mē'gō) *n., pl.* **-gos.** A friend.
a•mi•no acid (ə-mē'nō, ăm'ə-nō') *n.* Any of a class of nitrogenous organic compounds that are essential components of proteins.
A•mish (ā'mĭsh, ăm'ĭsh) *pl.n.* A sect of Mennonites that settled primarily in SE Pa. in the late 1600's. **—A'mish** *adj.*
a•miss (ə-mĭs') *adj.* Out of proper order or place. *—adv.* In a wrong or improper way.
am•i•ty (ăm'ĭ-tē) *n., pl.* **-ties.** Peaceful relations : friendship.
am•me•ter (ăm'mē'tər) *n.* A device for measuring electric current.
am•mo (ăm'ō) *n.* Ammunition.
am•mo•nia (ə-mōn'yə, ə-mō'nē-ə) *n.* **1.** A colorless, pungent gas widely used to make fertilizers and nitrogen-containing compounds. **2.** A solution of ammonia gas dissolved in water.
am•mo•nite (ăm'ə-nīt') *also* **am•mo•noid** (-noid') *n.* The chambered shell of any of various extinct mollusks of the class *Cephalopoda,* found as fossils.
am•mu•ni•tion (ăm'yə-nĭsh'ən) *n.* **1. a.** Projectiles that can be propelled or discharged from guns. **b.** Nuclear, biological, chemical, or explosive material used as a weapon. **2.** A means of offense or defense.
am•ne•sia (ăm-nē'zhə) *n.* Partial or total loss of memory. **—am•ne'si•ac'** (-zē-ăk', -zhē-ăk'), **am•ne'sic** (-zĭk, -sĭk) *n. & adj.*
am•nes•ty (ăm'nĭ-stē) *n., pl.* **-ties.** A governmental pardon granted to a number of offenders, esp. for political offenses. **—am'nes•ty** *v.*
am•ni•o•cen•te•sis (ăm'nē-ō-sĕn-tē'sĭs) *n., pl.* **-ses** (-sēz'). The surgical removal of an amniotic fluid sample from a pregnant woman, esp. for determining any genetic disorder of the fetus.
am•ni•on (ăm'nē-ən, -ŏn') *n., pl.* **-ni•ons** *or* **-ni•a** (-nē-ə). A membranous sac of watery fluid containing the embryo of a mammal, bird, or reptile. **—am'ni•ot'ic** (-ŏt'ĭk), **am'ni•on'ic** (-ŏn'ĭk) *adj.*
a•moe•ba *also* **a•me•ba** (ə-mē'bə) *n., pl.* **-bas** *or* **-bae** (-bē). Any of various protozoans of the genus *Amoeba* and related genera, found in water, soil, and as internal parasites, consisting essentially of an indefinitely shaped, changeable mass of protoplasm. **—a•moe'bic** *adj.*
a•mok (ə-mŭk', ə-mŏk') *adv. var. of* AMUCK.
a•mong (ə-mŭng') *also* **a•mongst** (ə-mŭngst') *prep.* **1.** Surrounded by : amid. **2.** In the group, number, or class of. **3.** In the com-

pany of <living *among* the poor> **4.** With shares to each of <Divide this *among* you.> **5.** With one another.

a•mon•til•la•do (ə-mŏn'tə-lä'dō) *n., pl.* **-dos.** A pale dry sherry.

a•mor•al (ā-môr'əl, ā-mŏr'əl) *adj.* **1.** Not admitting of moral distinctions or judgments : neither moral nor immoral. **2.** Lacking moral judgment. **—a'mo•ral'i•ty** *n.* **—a•mor'al•ly** *adv.*

am•o•ret•to (ăm'ə-rĕ'ō, ä'mə-) *n., pl.* **-ti** (-tē) *or* **-tos.** A cupid.

am•o•rous (ăm'ər-əs) *adj.* **1.** Feeling or expressing love. **2.** In love. **—am'or•ous•ly** *adv.* **—am'or•ous•ness** *n.*

a•mor•phous (ə-môr'fəs) *adj.* **1.** Lacking definite form : shapeless. **2.** General : vague. **3.** *Chem.* Without distinct crystalline structure. **—a•mor'phous•ness** *n.*

am•or•tize (ăm'ər-tīz', ə-môr'tīz') *v.* **-tized, -tiz•ing.** To liquidate (a debt) by installment payments. **—am'or•ti•za'tion, a•mor'tize•ment** *n.*

A•mos (ā'məs) *n.* —See table at BIBLE.

a•mount (ə-mount') *n.* **1.** The total of 2 or more quantities : aggregate. **2.** A principal plus its interest. —*v.* **1.** To total in number or quantity. **2.** To be equal or tantamount <silence *amounting* to approval>

a•mour (ə-mo͝or') *n.* A love affair, esp. an illicit one.

a•mour-pro•pre (ə-mo͞or'prôp'rə) *n.* Self-respect.

amp (ămp) *n.* **1.** An ampere. **2.** An amplifier, esp. one used to amplify music.

AMP (ā'ĕm-pē') *n.* A mononucleotide found in animal cells, that is reversibly convertible to ADP and ATP.

am•per•age (ăm'pər-ĭj, ăm'pîr'ĭj) *n.* The strength of an electric current as measured in amperes.

am•pere (ăm'pîr') *n.* A unit of electric current equal to a flow of 1 coulomb per second.

am•per•sand (ăm'pər-sănd') *n.* The character or sign (&) that represents *and.*

am•phet•a•mine (ăm-fĕt'ə-mēn', -mĭn) *n.* A colorless volatile liquid used primarily as a central nervous system stimulant.

am•phib•i•an (ăm-fĭb'ē-ən) *n.* **1.** Any of various cold-blooded, smooth-skinned vertebrate of the class Amphibia, such as a frog, that as aquatic larvae breathe by means of gills and metamorphose to an adult form with air-breathing lungs. **2.** An amphibious aircraft or vehicle.

am•phib•i•ous (ăm-fĭb'ē-əs) *adj.* **1.** Capable of living on land and in water. **2.** Capable of operating on land and water <*amphibious* landing craft>

am•phi•bole (ăm'fə-bōl') *n.* Any of a large group of double silicate minerals having mixtures of sodium, calcium, magnesium, iron, and aluminum. **—am'phi•bol'ic** (-bŏl'ĭk) *adj.*

am•phi•the•a•ter (ăm'fə-thē'ə-tər) *n.* A round or oval structure with rows of seats rising gradually outward from a central open space.

am•pho•ra (ăm'fər-ə) *n., pl.* **-rae** (-fə-rē') *or* **-ras.** A 2-handled jar with a narrow neck used by the ancient Greeks and Romans.

am•pi•cil•lin (ăm'pə-sĭl'ən) *n.* An antibiotic related to penicillin.

am•ple (ăm'pəl) *adj.* **-pler, -plest. 1.** Of large size, extent, or capacity. **2.** Generous or abundant. **3.** Sufficient. **—am'ple•ness** *n.* **—am'ply** *adv.*

am•pli•fy (ăm'plə-fī') *v.* **-fied, -fy•ing. 1.** To make larger, louder, or more powerful. **2.** To expand, as by adding details. **—am'pli•fi•ca'tion** *n.* **—am'pli•fi'er** *n.*

am•pli•tude (ăm'plĭ-to͞od', -tyo͞od') *n.* **1.** Greatness of size. **2.** Fullness : plenitude. **3.** Breadth or range, as of intelligence. **4.** *Physics.* The highest value of a periodically varying quantity.

amplitude modulation *n.* The encoding of a carrier wave by variation of its amplitude in accordance with an input signal.

am•poule *also* **am•pule** *or* **am•pul** (ăm'po͞ol', -pyo͞ol') *n.* A small sealed glass container used for a hypodermic injection.

am•pul•la (ăm-po͞ol'ə, -pŭl'ə) *n., pl.* **-pul•lae** (-po͞ol'ē, -pŭl'ē). A nearly round, 2-handled bottle used by the ancient Romans for wine, oil, or perfume.

am•pu•tate (ăm'pyo͞o-tāt') *v.* **-tat•ed, -tat•ing.** To cut off (e.g., a limb), esp. by surgery. **—am'pu•tee'** *n.* **—am'pu•ta'tion** *n.* **—am'pu•ta'tor** *n.*

am•ri•ta (ŭm-rē'tə) *n.* **1.** The ambrosia prepared by the Hindu gods that confers immortality. **2.** The immortality conferred.

a•muck (ə-mŭk') *also* **a•mok** (ə-mŭk', ə-mŏk') *adv.* **1.** In a murderous frenzy <rioters running *amuck*> **2.** In an uncontrolled manner <The disease had run *amuck.*>

am•u•let (ăm'yə-lĭt) *n.* A charm worn as a talisman against evil or injury.

a•muse (ə-myo͞oz') *v.* **a•mused, a•mus•ing.** To occupy in an agreeable pleasing way. ★ *syns:* DISTRACT, DIVERT, ENTERTAIN **—a•mus'a•ble** *adj.* **—a•muse'ment** *n.* **—a•mus'er** *n.*

a•myg•da•line (ə-mĭg'də-lĭn, -līn') *adj.* Of, relating to, or similar to an almond.

am•y•lase (ăm'ə-lās', -lāz') *n.* An enzyme that converts starch to sugar.

an (ən; ăn *when stressed*) *indef. art.* A form of *a.* —Used before words beginning with a vowel or with an unpronounced *h* <*an* emerald><*an* honor>

-an *suff.* **1.** Of, relating to, or like <American> **2.** Believing in or following <Confucian>

an•a•bat•ic (ăn'ə-băt'ĭk) *adj.* Of or relating to rising wind currents.

an•a•bol•ic steroid (ăn'ə-bŏl'ĭk) *n.* A synthetic hormone often used to increase muscle size and strength.

a•nach•ro•nism (ə-năk'rə-nĭz'əm) *n.* **1.** The placement of something as existing or occurring at other than its historical time. **2.** Anything out of its proper place. **—a•nach'ro•**

nis′tic, a•nach′ro•nous *adj.* **—a•nach′ro•nis′ti•cal•ly, a•nach′ro•nous•ly** *adv.*

an•a•co•lu•thon (ăn′ə-kə-lo͞o′thŏn′) *n., pl.* **-thons** *or* **-tha** (-thə). An abrupt change within a sentence to a 2nd grammatical construction inconsistent with the 1st; e.g., *I warned you that if you continue to smoke, what will become of you!* **—an′a•co•lu′thic** *adj.*

an•a•con•da (ăn′ə-kŏn′də) *n.* A large, nonpoisonous arboreal snake, *Eunectes murinus,* of tropical South America, that suffocates its prey in its coils.

an•a•dem (ăn′ə-dĕm′) *n. Archaic.* A garland or wreath for the head.

a•nad•ro•mous (ə-năd′rə-məs) *adj.* Migrating up rivers from the sea to breed in fresh water, as salmon do.

a•nae•mi•a (ə-nē′mē-ə) *n. var. of* ANEMIA.

an•aer•obe (ăn′ə-rōb′, ăn-âr′ōb′) *n.* A microorganism, as a bacterium, able to live in the absence of free oxygen. **—an′aer•o′bic** (ăn′ə-rō′bĭk, -âr-ō′bĭk) *adj.* **—an′aer•o′bic•al•ly** *adv.*

an•aes•the•sia (ăn′ĭs-thē′zhə) *n. var. of* ANESTHESIA.

an•a•gram (ăn′ə-grăm′) *n.* A word or phrase formed by rearranging the letters of another word or phrase, as *leaf* to *flea.*

a•nal (ā′nəl) *adj.* Of, relating to, or near the anus.

an•a•lects (ăn′ə-lĕkts′) *also* **an•a•lec•ta** (ăn′ə-lĕk′tə) *pl.n.* Collected excerpts from literary works. **—an′a•lec′tic** *adj.*

an•al•ge•si•a (ăn′əl-jē′zē-ə, -zhə) *n.* Inability to feel pain although conscious. **—an′al•ge′sic** *n. & adj.*

analog computer *also* **analogue computer** *n.* A computer in which numerical data are represented by measurable quantities such as lengths, electrical signals, or voltage.

a•nal•o•gous (ə-năl′ə-gəs) *adj.* **1.** Corresponding in certain ways. **2.** *Biol.* Similar in function but not in evolutionary origin.

an•a•logue *also* **an•a•log** (ăn′ə-lôg′, -lŏg′) *n.* **1.** One that is analogous. **2.** *Biol.* An analogous organ or structure. *—adj.* Of or being a device in which data are represented by variable measurable physical quantities.

a•nal•o•gy (ə-năl′ə-jē) *n., pl.* **-gies. 1.** Correspondence in some respects between otherwise unlike things. **2.** A logical inference based on the assumption that if 2 things are known to be alike in some respects, then they must be alike in other respects. **3.** *Biol.* Correspondence in function or position between organs of dissimilar evolutionary origin. **—an′a•log′i•cal** *adj.* **—an′a•log′i•cal•ly** *adv.*

a•nal•y•sand (ə-năl′ĭ-sănd′) *n.* One who is being psychoanalyzed.

an•a•lyse (ăn′ə-līz′) *v. esp. Brit. var. of* ANALYZE.

a•nal•y•sis (ə-năl′ĭ-sĭs) *n., pl.* **-ses** (-sēz′). **1.** Separation of an intellectual or substantial whole into its parts for individual study. **2.** *Chem.* **a.** Separation of a substance into its elements to determine their nature (qualitative analysis) or their proportions (quantitative analysis). **b.** A statement of the results of such a study. **3.** Psychoanalysis. **—an′a•lyst** *n.* **—an′a•lyt′ic, an′a•lyt′i•cal** *adj.*

an•a•lyze (ăn′ə-līz′) *v.* **-lyzed, -lyz•ing. 1.** To make a chemical analysis of. **2.** To psychoanalyze. ★ ***syns:*** ANATOMIZE, BREAK DOWN, DISSECT **—an′a•lyz′a•ble** *adj.* **—an′a•ly•za′tion** *n.* **—an′a•lyz′er** *n.*

an•a•pest *also* **an•a•paest** (ăn′ə-pĕst′) *n.* A metrical foot made up of 2 short syllables followed by 1 long one, as in *unaligned.* **—an′a•pes′tic** *adj.*

an•ar•chic (ăn-är′kĭk) *or* **an•ar•chi•cal** (-kĭ-kəl) *adj.* **1.** Of, like, or promoting anarchy. **2.** Lawless. **—an•ar′chi•cal•ly** *adv.*

an•ar•chism (ăn′ər-kĭz′əm) *n.* **1.** The doctrine of the abolishment of all forms of government because they are oppressive and undesirable. **2.** Lawlessness. **—an′ar•chist** *n.* **—an′ar•chis′tic** *adj.*

an•ar•chy (ăn′ər-kē) *n., pl.* **-chies. 1.** Lack of any political authority. **2.** Disorder and confusion. **3.** Absence of any common purpose or standard.

A•na•sa•zi (ä′nə-sä′zē) *n., pl.* **-zi.** A member of an American Indian people of the SW United States whose descendants are the present-day Pueblo peoples.

a•nas•to•mo•sis (ə-năs′tə-mō′sĭs) *n., pl.* **-ses** (-sēz′). **1.** The union or connection of branches as of rivers, leaf veins, or blood vessels. **2.** The surgical connection of separate or severed tubular hollow organs. **—a•nas′to•mot′ic** (-mŏt′ĭk) *adj.*

a•nas•tro•phe (ə-năs′trə-fē) *n.* Inversion of the normal syntactic order of words; e.g., *To church went we.*

a•nath•e•ma (ə-năth′ə-mə) *n., pl.* **-mas. 1.** An ecclesiastical ban, curse, or excommunication. **2.** One that is detested. **—a•nath′e•ma•tize′** *v.*

a•nat•o•mize (ə-năt′ə-mīz′) *v.* **-mized, -miz•ing. 1.** *Biol.* To dissect. **2.** To examine in minute detail **:** analyze.

a•nat•o•my (ə-năt′ə-mē) *n., pl.* **-mies. 1.** The structure of a plant or animal. **2.** The science dealing with the structure of organisms and their elements. **3.** The constituent structure of something. **4.** A detailed analysis. ★ ***syns:*** ARCHITECTURE, CONSTITUTION, FABRIC, MAKE-UP **—an′a•tom′i•cal** (ăn′ə-tŏm′ĭ-kəl) *adj.* **—an′a•tom′i•cal•ly** *adv.* **—a•nat′o•mist** *n.*

—ance *suff.* **1.** State or condition <resembl*ance*> **2.** Action <continu*ance*>

an•ces•tor (ăn′sĕs′tər) *n.* **1.** Someone from whom one is descended **:** forefather. **2.** *Biol.* The organism or type of organism from which later organisms evolved. **3.** A forerunner or predecessor. ★ ***syns:*** ANTECEDENT, FOREBEAR, FOREFATHER, PROGENITOR **—an•ces′tral** *adj.* **—an•ces′tral•ly** *adv.*

an•ces•try (ăn′sĕs′trē) *n., pl.* **-tries. 1.** Ancestral descent. **2.** Ancestors as a group.

an•chor (ăng′kər) *n.* **1.** A heavy object attached to a vessel by a rope or cable and cast overboard to hold the vessel in place either by weight or by flukes. **2.** Something that gives security. **3.** An anchorman or anchorwoman. **—an′chor** *v.*
an•chor•age (ăng′kər-ĭj) *n.* **1.** A place for anchoring. **2.** A fee charged for anchoring. **3.** An anchoring or being anchored.
an•cho•rite (ăng′kə-rīt′) *also* **an•cho•ret** (-rĕt′) *n.* A hermit who has retired into seclusion for religious reasons.
an•chor•man (ăng′kər-măn′) *n.* **1.** *Sports.* The last runner in a relay race. **2.** The narrator or coordinator of a newscast in which several correspondents give reports.
an•chor•wom•an (ăng′kər-wo͝om′ən) *n.* A woman who narrates or coordinates a newscast in which several correspondents give reports.
an•cho•vy (ăn′chō′vē, ăn-chō′vē) *n., pl.* **-vy** *or* **-vies.** A small herringlike marine fish.
an•cient (ān′shənt) *adj.* **1.** Very old. **2.** Of or happening in remote times, esp. before the fall of the Western Roman Empire. —*n.* **1.** A very old person. **2. ancients.** The Greeks and Romans of ancient times. **—an′cient•ly** *adv.* **—an′cient•ness** *n.*
an•cil•lar•y (ăn′sə-lĕr′ē) *adj.* **1.** Subordinate. **2.** Auxiliary : supplementary. **—an′cil•lar′y** *n.*
-ancy *suff.* -ANCE.
and (ənd, ən; ănd *when stressed*) *conj.* **1.** Together or along with : as well as. **2.** Added to : plus. **3.** As a result : in consequence <They invited me *and* here I am.> **4.** —Used between two verbs <go *and* find it><come *and* see>
an•dan•te (än-dän′tā, ăn-dăn′tē) *adv. Mus.* Moderate in tempo. —Used as a direction. **—an•dan′te** *adj. & n.*
an•dan•ti•no (än′dän-tē′nō, ăn′dăn-tē′nō) *adv. Mus.* Slightly faster than andante. **—an′dan•ti′no** *adj. & n.*
and•i•ron (ănd′ī′ərn) *n.* One of a pair of supports for fireplace logs.
and/or *conj.* —Used to indicate that either *and* or *or* may be used for connecting words, phrases, or clauses depending upon the meaning intended.
an•dro•gen (ăn′drə-jən) *n.* A steroid hormone instrumental in the development and maintenance of masculine characteristics. **—an′dro•gen′ic** *adj.*
an•drog•e•nous (ăn-drŏj′ə-nəs) *adj.* Of or relating to production of male offspring.
an•drog•y•nous (ăn-drŏj′ə-nəs) *adj.* Having both female and male characteristics : hermaphroditic. **—an•drog′y•ny** *n.*
an•droid (ăn′droid′) *adj.* Having human features. —*n.* A synthetic person artificially created from biological materials.
an•ec•dote (ăn′ĭk-dōt′) *n.* A short interesting or humorous account of a real or fictitious incident. ★ *syns:* FABLE, STORY, TALE, YARN **—an′ec•do′tal** *adj.*
an•e•cho•ic (ăn′ĭ-kō′ĭk) *adj.* Not having or producing echoes.
a•ne•mi•a *also* **a•nae•mi•a** (ə-nē′mē-ə) *n.* Pathological deficiency in the oxygen-carrying material of the blood. **—a•ne′mic** *adj.*
an•e•mom•e•ter (ăn′ə-mŏm′ĭ-tər) *n.* An instrument for measuring wind force and speed. **—an′e•mo•met′ric** (-mō-mĕt′rĭk) *adj.* **—an′e•mom′e•try** *n.*
a•nem•o•ne (ə-nĕm′ə-nē) *n.* **1.** A plant of the genus *Anemone* of the N Temperate Zone, with white, purple, or red flowers. **2.** The sea anemone.
†a•nent (ə-nĕnt′) *prep.* **1.** Regarding : concerning. **2.** *Regional.* Close to : opposite.
aneroid barometer *n.* A barometer in which atmospheric pressure is indicated by the relative bulges of an elastic metal disk covering a chamber in which there is a partial vacuum.
an•es•the•sia *also* **an•aes•the•sia** (ăn′ĭs-thē′zhə) *n.* Complete or partial loss of physical sensation caused by disease or an anesthetic.
an•es•the•si•ol•o•gy *also* **an•aes•the•si•ol•o•gy** (ăn′ĭs-thē′zē-ŏl′ə-jē) *n.* The medical science of anesthetics, their effects, and use. **—an′es•the′si•ol′o•gist** *n.*
an•es•thet•ic *also* **an•aes•thet•ic** (ăn′ĭs-thĕt′ĭk) *adj.* Inducing anesthesia. —*n.* A substance, as a gas or drug, that induces anesthesia. **—a•nes′the•tist** (ə-nĕs′thĭ-tĭst) *n.* **—a•nes′the•ti•za′tion** *n.* **—a•nes′the•tize′** *v.*
a•new (ə-no͞o′, ə-nyo͞o′) *adv.* **1.** Once more : again. **2.** In a new and different manner or form.
an•gel (ān′jəl) *n.* **1.** *Theol.* One of the immortal beings attendant upon God. **2.** A kind and lovable person. **3.** A financial backer of an enterprise, esp. a dramatic production. **—an•gel′ic** (-jĕl′ĭk), **an•gel′i•cal** *adj.* **—an•gel′i•cal•ly** *adv.*
angel dust *n. Slang.* Phencyclidine.
An•ge•le•no (ăn′jə-lē′nō) *n., pl.* **-nos.** A native or inhabitant of Los Angeles.
an•gel•fish (ān′jəl-fĭsh′) *n.* Any of several brightly colored fishes of the family Chaetodontidae of warm seas, with a laterally compressed body.

angelfish

angel food cake *also* **angel cake** *n.* A white sponge cake made of egg whites, sugar, and flour.

an•gel•i•ca (ăn-jĕl'ĭ-kə) *n.* A plant, *Angelica archangelica,* with aromatic seeds, leaves, stems, and roots that are used medicinally and as flavoring.
an•gel•ol•o•gy (ān'jəl-ŏl'ə-jē) *n.* The branch of theology concerning angels.
angel shark *n.* A shark of the genus *Squatina,* with a broad flat head and body.
an•ger (ăng'gər) *n.* A feeling of great displeasure or hostility : wrath. —**an'ger** *v.*
an•gi•na (ăn-jī'nə) *n.* **1.** A disease, as croup or diphtheria, marked by painful, choking spasms. **2.** Angina pectoris.
angina pec•to•ris (pĕk'tə-rĭs) *n.* Severe paroxysmal chest pain associated with an insufficient supply of blood to the heart.
an•gi•o•gram (ăn'jē-ə-grăm') *n.* An x-ray of the blood vessels, used in diagnosis of the cardiovascular system.
an•gi•o•plas•ty (ăn'jē-ə-plăs'tē) *n., pl.* **-ties.** A surgical procedure that uses a catheter fitted with an inflatable tip to clear blocked arteries.
an•gle[1] (ăng'gəl) *v.* **-gled, -gling. 1.** To fish with a hook and line. **2.** To attempt to get something, esp. by trickery or scheming. —**an'gler** *n.*
an•gle[2] (ăng'gəl) *n.* **1. a.** A flat geometric figure formed by a pair of rays that diverge from a common point. **b.** The rotation required to superimpose either of 2 such lines or angles on the other. **2. a.** The place, position, or direction from which something is seen. **b.** A point of view : aspect. **3.** *Slang.* A scheme. —*v.* **-gled, -gling. 1.** To move or turn at an angle. **2.** To hit at an angle <*angled* the puck into the goal>
An•gle (ăng'gəl) *n.* A member of a Germanic people who migrated to England in the 5th cent. A.D.
angle iron *n.* A length of steel or iron bent at a right angle along its long dimension, used as a support or structural framework.
an•gle•worm (ăng'gəl-wûrm') *n.* A worm, as an earthworm, used as fishing bait.
An•gli•can (ăng'glĭ-kən) *adj.* **1.** Relating to the Church of England or to the churches in other nations that are in communion with it. **2.** Of or relating to England or the English. —**An'gli•can** *n.* —**An'gli•can•ism** *n.*
An•gli•cize (ăng'glĭ-sīz') *v.* **-cized, -ciz•ing.** To make or become English, as in form or style. —**An'gli•ci•za'tion** *n.*
An•glo (ăng'glō) *n., pl.* **-glos.** An English-speaking person, esp. a white North American who is not of Latin descent. —**An'glo** *adj.*
An•glo•phile (ăng'glə-fīl') *n.* One who admires England and its culture.
An•glo•phobe (ăng'glə-fōb') *n.* One who fears or dislikes England or its culture.
An•glo•phone (ăng'lə-fōn') *n.* An English-speaking person, esp. in a country where 2 or more languages are spoken.
An•glo-Sax•on (ăng'glō-săk'sən) *n.* **1.** A member of one of the Germanic peoples (Angles, Saxons, and Jutes) who came to Britain in the 5th and 6th cent. A.D. **2.** Old English. **3.** A person of English ancestry. —**An'glo-Sax'on** *adj.*
An•go•ra (ăng-gôr'ə, -gōr'ə) *n.* **1.** A rabbit, cat, or goat that has long, silky hair. **2. angora.** A yarn made from the hair of an Angora rabbit or goat.
an•gos•tu•ra bark (ăng'gə-stŏŏr'ə, -tyŏŏr'ə) *n.* The bitter, aromatic bark of either of 2 Brazilian trees, *Galipea officinalis* or *Cusparia trifoliata,* used as a tonic and a flavoring agent.
an•gry (ăng'grē) *adj.* **-gri•er, -gri•est. 1.** Feeling or showing anger. **2.** Having a threatening aspect <an *angry* sky> **3.** Inflamed, as a sore. ★ ***syns:*** CHOLERIC, ENRAGED, FURIOUS, INDIGNANT, IRATE, MAD, SEETHING, SORE, WRATHFUL —**an'gri•ly** (-grə-lē) *adv.*
angst (ängkst) *n.* A state of anxiety.
ang•strom *or* **ång•ström** (ăng'strəm) *n.* A unit of length equal to 1 hundred-millionth (10^{-8}) of a centimeter.
an•guish (ăng'gwĭsh) *n.* An agonizing pain of the body or mind : torment. —*v.* To cause or suffer anguish. —**an'guished** *adj.*
an•gu•lar (ăng'gyə-lər) *adj.* **1.** Having or forming an angle or angles. **2.** Measured by an angle or degrees of an arc. **3.** Bony and lean : gaunt. —**an'gu•lar'i•ty** (-lăr'ĭ-tē), **an'gu•lar•ness** *n.* —**an'gu•lar•ly** *adv.*
an•hy•drous (ăn-hī'drəs) *adj.* Without water.
an•il (ăn'ĭl) *n.* The indigo plant or a blue dye obtained from it.
an•ile (ăn'īl', ā'nīl') *adj.* Of or like an old woman. —**a•nil'i•ty** *n.*
an•i•line *also* **an•i•lin** (ăn'ə-lĭn) *n.* A colorless, oily, poisonous liquid used to make rubber, dyes, pharmaceuticals, rocket fuels, and other products.
an•i•ma (ăn'ə-mə) *n.* The inner self : soul.
an•i•mad•vert (ăn'ə-măd-vûrt') *v.* To remark or comment critically, usu. with disapproval. —**an'i•mad•ver'sion** *n.*
an•i•mal (ăn'ə-məl) *n.* **1.** An organism of the kingdom Animalia, distinguished from plants by such characteristics as the power of locomotion and nonphotosynthetic metabolism. **2.** An animal organism other than a human being. **3.** A bestial or brutish person. **4.** Animality. —*adj.* **1.** Of or relating to animals. **2.** Relating to the physical as distinct from the spiritual nature of humans.
an•i•mal•cule (ăn'ə-măl'kyōōl') *n.* A very small or microscopic organism.
an•i•mal•i•ty (ăn'ə-măl'ĭ-tē) *n.* The animal as distinct from the spiritual nature of humans.
an•i•mate (ăn'ə-māt') *v.* **-mat•ed, -mat•ing. 1.** To give life to. **2.** To give interest or zest to. **3.** To design or produce (a cartoon) creating the illusion of motion. —*adj.* (ăn'ə-mĭt). **1.** Having life : alive. **2.** Of or relating to animal life as distinguished from plant life. —**an'i•mat'ed** *adj.* —**an'i•mat'ed•ly** *adv.* —**an'i•ma'tion** *n.* —**an'i•ma'tor, an'i•mat'er** *n.*

animated cartoon *n.* A motion picture consisting of a photographed series of drawings.
a·ni·ma·to (ä'nə-mä'tō) *adv. Mus.* In an animated or lively manner. —Used as a direction. —**a'ni·ma'to** *adj.*
an·i·mism (ăn'ə-mĭz'əm) *n.* The belief that natural phenomena or inanimate objects possess spirits. —**an'i·mist** *n.* —**an'i·mis'·tic** *adj.*
an·i·mos·i·ty (ăn'ə-mŏs'ĭ-tē) *n., pl.* **-ties.** Deep-seated hostility : enmity.
an·i·mus (ăn'ə-məs) *n.* Ill will : animosity.
an·i·on (ăn'ī'ən) *n.* An ion with a negative charge that is attracted to an anode, as in electrolysis.
an·ise (ăn'ĭs) *n.* **1.** A plant, *Pimpinella anisum,* with yellowish-white flower clusters and licorice-flavored seeds. **2.** Aniseed.
an·i·seed (ăn'ĭ-sēd') *n.* The seed of the anise used medicinally and for flavoring.
an·i·sette (ăn'ə-sĕt', -zĕt') *n.* An anise-flavored liqueur.
ankh (ăngk) *n.* An ansate cross.
an·kle (ăng'kəl) *n.* **1.** The joint that connects the foot with the leg. **2.** The slender part of the leg above this joint.
an·kle·bone (ăng'kəl-bōn') *n.* The talus.
an·klet (ăng'klĭt) *n.* **1.** An ornament for the ankle. **2.** A sock reaching just above the ankle.
an·lace (ăn'lĭs) *n.* A 2-edged medieval dagger.
an·nals (ăn'əlz) *pl.n.* **1.** A record of events in the order of their occurrence. **2.** A descriptive account. —**an'nal·ist** *n.*
an·neal (ə-nēl') *v.* **1.** To subject (glass or metal) to heat and slow cooling to toughen and reduce brittleness. **2.** To temper.
an·ne·lid (ăn'ə-lĭd) *also* **an·nel·i·dan** (ə-nĕl'ĭ-dən) *adj.* Of or belonging to the phylum Annelida, which includes worms having cylindrical segmented bodies, as the earthworms. —*n.* An annelid worm.
an·nex (ə-nĕks') *v.* **1.** To append or attach, esp. to a larger entity. **2.** To incorporate (territory) into another country or state. —*n.* (ăn'-ĕks'). A structure added on to a larger one or placed near a main one. —**an'nex·a'tion** *n.*
An·nie Oak·ley (ăn'ē ōk'lē) *n. Slang.* A complimentary admission ticket.
▲ ***word history:*** Annie Oakley was a sharpshooter with Buffalo Bill's show, *The Wild West,* who sometimes used playing cards as targets. Free passes that were punched to prevent their being sold were thought to resemble Annie Oakley's handiwork.
an·ni·hi·late (ə-nī'ə-lāt') *v.* **-lat·ed, -lat·ing.** To destroy all traces of : obliterate. —**an·ni'·hi·la'tion** *n.* —**an·ni'hi·la'tor** *n.*
an·ni·ver·sa·ry (ăn'ə-vûr'sə-rē) *n., pl.* **-ries.** The yearly return of the date of an event that happened in an earlier year.
an·no Dom·i·ni (ăn'ō dŏm'ə-nī', dŏm'ə-nē) *adv.* In a specified year of the Christian era. —Used chiefly in the abbreviated form <A.D. 495>
an·no·tate (ăn'ō-tāt') *v.* **-tat·ed, -tat·ing.** To furnish (a text) with critical commentary or explanatory notes. —**an'no·ta'tion** *n.*
an·nounce (ə-nouns') *v.* **-nounced, -nounc·ing. 1.** To make known publicly. **2.** To proclaim the presence or arrival of. **3.** To act as an announcer. —**an·nounce'ment** *n.*
an·nounc·er (ə-noun'sər) *n.* One who announces, as on a television program or over a public-address system.
an·noy (ə-noi') *v.* To bother or irritate. ★ ***syns:*** AGGRAVATE, BOTHER, BUG, FRET, GALL, IRK, IRRITATE, PEEVE, PROVOKE, RUFFLE, VEX —**an·noy'ing** *adj.* —**an·noy'·ing·ly** *adv.*
an·noy·ance (ə-noi'əns) *n.* **1.** The act of annoying. **2.** A nuisance. **3.** Vexation : irritation.
an·nu·al (ăn'yōō-əl) *adj.* **1.** Recurring, done, or performed every year : yearly <an *annual* checkup> **2.** Determined by a year's time <*annual* precipitation> **3.** *Bot.* Having a life cycle that is completed in a year or season. —*n.* **1.** A yearbook. **2.** An annual plant. —**an'·nu·al·ly** *adv.*
annual ring *n.* A concentric layer of wood, esp. of a tree trunk, indicating a year's growth.

annual ring

an·nu·i·ty (ə-nōō'ĭ-tē, ə-nyōō'-) *n., pl.* **-ties. 1.** The annual payment of an allowance or income. **2.** An investment from which one receives an income for a lifetime or a specified number of years. —**an·nu'i·tant** *n.*
an·nul (ə-nŭl') *v.* **-nulled, -nul·ling.** To declare void or invalid, as a marriage or a law : nullify. —**an·nul'ment** *n.*
an·nu·lar (ăn'yə-lər) *adj.* Shaped like or forming a ring.
an·nun·ci·ate (ə-nŭn'sē-āt') *v.* **-at·ed, -at·ing.** To announce, esp. officially.
an·nun·ci·a·tion (ə-nŭn'sē-ā'shən) *n.* **1.** The act of announcing. **2.** An announcement. **3. Annunciation. a.** The angel Gabriel's announcement of the Incarnation. **b.** The festival, on Mar. 25, that honors this.
an·nus mi·rab·i·lis (ăn'əs mĭ-răb'ə-lĭs) *n.* An extraordinary year.
an·ode (ăn'ōd') *n.* A positively charged electrode, as of an electron tube.
an·o·dize (ăn'ə-dīz') *v.* **-dized, -diz·ing.** To coat (a metallic surface) electrolytically with a protective oxide.

an•o•dyne (ăn'ə-dīn') *adj.* **1.** Capable of relieving pain. **2.** Soothing or comforting <*anodyne* hobbies> **—an'o•dyne'** *n.*
a•noint (ə-noint') *v.* To apply oil, esp. in a religious ceremony.
a•nom•a•ly (ə-nŏm'ə-lē) *n., pl.* **-lies. 1.** Departure from the normal form, order, or rule. **2.** Something irregular or abnormal. **—a•nom'a•lis'tic** *adj.* **—a•nom'a•lis'ti•cal•ly** *adv.* **—a•nom'a•lous** *adj.*
a•non (ə-nŏn') *adv.* **1.** At another time **:** again. **2.** *Archaic.* Soon.
an•o•nym (ăn'ə-nĭm') *n.* **1.** An anonymous person. **2.** A pseudonym.
a•non•y•mous (ə-nŏn'ə-məs) *adj.* **1.** Nameless or unnamed. **2.** Of unknown source. **—an'o•nym'i•ty** (ăn'ə-nĭm'ĭ-tē) *n.* **—a•non'y•mous•ly** *adv.* **—a•non'y•mous•ness** *n.*
a•noph•e•les (ə-nŏf'ə-lēz') *n.* Any of various mosquitoes of the genus *Anopheles,* many of which carry the malaria parasite and transmit the disease to humans.
an•o•rak (ăn'ə-răk') *n.* A heavy, hooded jacket **:** parka.
an•o•rec•tic (ăn'ə-rĕk'tĭk) *or* **an•o•ret•ic** (-rĕt'ĭk) *also* **an•o•rex•ic** (-rĕk'sĭk) *adj.* **1.** Characterized by or causing loss of appetite. **2.** Of or afflicted with anorexia nervosa. **—an'o•rec'tic** *n.*
an•o•rex•i•a (ăn'ə-rĕk'sē-ə) *n.* Loss of appetite, esp. as a result of disease.
anorexia nerv•o•sa (nûr-vō'sə) *n.* A pathological condition that occurs mainly in young women, marked by an abnormal fear of becoming obese.
an•oth•er (ə-nŭ*th*'ər) *adj.* **1.** One more **:** additional <*another* scoop of ice cream> **2.** Distinctly different from the first <tried *another* hair style> **3.** Some other <can do it *another* time> *—pron.* **1.** An additional one. **2.** A different one. **3.** One of an undetermined number or group <by one method or *another*>
an•sate cross (ăn'sāt') *n.* A cross shaped like a T with a loop at the top **:** ankh.
an•swer (ăn'sər) *n.* **1.** A reply, as to a question or demand. **2. a.** A solution or result, as to a puzzle or problem. **b.** The correct solution or response. *—v.* **1.** To respond in words or actions (to). **2.** To respond correctly to. **3.** To serve (e.g., a purpose). **4.** To be liable or accountable. ★ ***syns:*** REJOIN, REPLY, RESPOND, RETORT, RETURN **—an'swer•a•bil'i•ty, an'swer•a•ble•ness** *n.* **—an'swer•a•ble** *adj.* **—an'swer•a•bly** *adv.*
an•swer•ing machine (ăn'sər-ĭng) *n.* An electronic device for answering one's telephone and recording callers' messages.
ant (ănt) *n.* Any of various insects of the family Formicidae, typically having wings only in the males and fertile females and living in highly organized social colonies.
ant– *pref. var. of* ANTI-.
–ant *suff.* **1. a.** Performing, promoting, or causing a specified action <accept*ant*> **b.** Being in a specified state or condition <flip*pant*> **2. a.** One that performs, promotes, or causes a specified action <deodor*ant*> **b.** One that undergoes a specified action <inhal*ant*>
ant•ac•id (ănt-ăs'ĭd) *adj.* Neutralizing acids. **—ant•ac'id** *n.*
an•tag•o•nism (ăn-tăg'ə-nĭz'əm) *n.* Mutual enmity **:** hostility. **—an•tag'o•nist** *n.* **—an•tag'o•nis'tic** *adj.* **—an•tag'o•nis'ti•cal•ly** *adv.*
an•tag•o•nize (ăn-tăg'ə-nīz') *v.* **-nized, -niz•ing.** To incur the antagonism of.
Ant•arc•tic (ănt-ärk'tĭk, -är'tĭk) *adj.* Of or relating to the regions around the South Pole.
Antarctic Circle *n.* A parallel of latitude (66° 33′ S) that marks the limit of the S Frigid Zone.
An•tar•es (ăn-târ'ēz') *n.* The brightest star in the constellation Scorpio.
▲ ***word history:*** The Greek name *Antares* can be interpreted in more than one way: "against Mars," "opposite Mars," or "instead of Mars." Since the planet Mars, which the Greeks called Ares, moves through the sky, it is not always opposite Antares in position. The name *Antares* more likely refers to the star's pronounced red color, which sometimes causes the star to be mistaken for the planet.
an•te (ăn'tē) *n.* **1.** The stake that each poker player must put into the pool before receiving new cards. **2.** *Slang.* A share paid **:** price. **—an'te** *v.*
ant•eat•er (ănt'ē'tər) *n.* A tropical American mammal, *Myrmecophaga tridactyla,* with a long snout and long sticky tongue, that feeds on ants and termites.

anteater

an•te•bel•lum (ăn'tē-bĕl'əm) *adj.* Of or belonging to the period prior to the U.S. Civil War.
an•te•cede (ăn'tĭ-sēd') *v.* **-ced•ed, -ced•ing.** To precede.
an•te•ce•dent (ăn'tĭ-sēd'nt) *adj.* Going before **:** preceding. *—n.* **1.** One that precedes. **2.** An occurrence or event preceding another. **3. antecedents.** One's ancestors. **4.** The word, phrase, or clause to which a pronoun refers, esp. a relative pronoun. **—an'te•ce'dence** *n.* **—an'te•ce'dent•ly** *adv.*
an•te•cham•ber (ăn'tē-chăm'bər) *n.* A room serving as an entryway into a larger room.
an•te•date (ăn'tĭ-dāt') *v.* **-dat•ed, -dat•ing. 1.**

To be of an earlier date than. **2.** To date prior to the true date.

an·te·di·lu·vi·an (ăn′tĭ-də-lo͞o′vē-ən) *adj.* **1.** Of or occurring in the era before the Biblical Flood. **2.** Very old : antiquated. **—an′te·di·lu′vi·an** *n.*

an·te·lope (ăn′tə-lōp′) *n., pl.* **-lope** or **-lopes. 1.** A slender, swift-running, long-horned ruminant of the family Bovidae of Africa and Asia. **2.** An animal, as the pronghorn, similar to an antelope.

an·te·me·rid·i·an (ăn′tē-mə-rĭd′ē-ən) *adj.* Of or occurring in the morning.

an·te me·rid·i·em (ăn′tē mə-rĭd′ē-əm) *adv. & adj.* Before noon. —Used chiefly in the abbreviated form <10:30 A.M.>

an·te·na·tal (ăn′tē-nāt′l) *adj.* Before birth : prenatal.

an·ten·na (ăn-tĕn′ə) *n.* **1.** *pl.* **-ten·nae** (-tĕn′ē). One of the pair of sensory organs on the head of an insect, crustacean, etc. **2.** *pl.* **-nas.** A metallic apparatus for sending and receiving radio waves : aerial. **—an·ten′nal** *adj.*

▲ ***word history:*** The classical Latin word *antenna* meant only "sail yard." The word was used in medieval writings for the sensory organs of insects because medieval naturalists thought that these organs resembled the parts of the yard that project beyond the sail.

an·te·pe·nult (ăn′tē-pē′nŭlt′, -pĭ-nŭlt′) *n.* The 3rd syllable from the end in a word, as *te* in *antepenult.* **—an′te·pe·nul′ti·mate** *adj. & n.*

an·te·ri·or (ăn-tîr′ē-ər) *adj.* **1.** Located in front. **2.** Prior in time : earlier. **—an·te′ri·or·ly** *adv.*

an·te·room (ăn′tē-ro͞om′, -ro͝om′) *n.* **1.** An antechamber. **2.** A waiting room.

an·them (ăn′thəm) *n.* **1.** A hymn of praise or allegiance. **2.** A devotional composition set to words from the Bible.

an·ther (ăn′thər) *n.* The pollen-bearing organ at the end of a stamen that secretes pollen.

ant·hill (ănt′hĭl′) *n.* A mound formed by ants or termites in building a nest.

an·thol·o·gy (ăn-thŏl′ə-jē) *n., pl.* **-gies.** A collection of literary works. **—an·thol′o·gist** *n.* **—an·thol′o·gize′** *v.*

an·thra·cite (ăn′thrə-sīt′) *n.* A hard, clean-burning coal.

an·thrax (ăn′thrăks′) *n.* An infectious, usu. fatal disease of cattle, sheep, and other warm-blooded animals, characterized esp. by malignant ulcers.

an·thro·po·cen·tric (ăn′thrə-pō-sĕn′trĭk) *adj.* Regarding the human being as the central fact or final aim of the universe.

an·thro·poid (ăn′thrə-poid′) *adj.* Resembling a human being, as the apes of the family Pongidae. —*n.* An anthropoid ape, as a gorilla, chimpanzee, or orangutan. **—an′thro·poid′al** *adj.*

an·thro·pol·o·gy (ăn′thrə-pŏl′ə-jē) *n.* The study of the origin and physical, social, and cultural development and behavior of humans. **—an′thro·po·log′ic** (-pə-lŏj′ĭk), **an′thro·po·log′i·cal** *adj.* **—an′thro·po·log′i·cal·ly** *adv.* **—an′thro·pol′o·gist** *n.*

an·thro·po·mor·phism (ăn′thrə-pə-môr′fĭz′əm) *n.* The ascribing of human motivation and characteristics to inanimate objects, animals, or natural phenomena. **—an′thro·po·mor′phic** *adj.* **—an′thro·po·mor′phi·cal·ly** *adv.*

an·thro·po·mor·phous (ăn′thrə-pə-môr′fəs) *adj.* **1.** Having or suggesting human form and appearance. **2.** Anthropomorphic.

an·ti (ăn′tī′, -tē) *n., pl.* **-tis.** *Informal.* One who is opposed or against.

anti– or **ant–** *pref.* **1. a.** In opposition to : against <*anti*clerical> **b.** Counteracting : neutralizing <*anti*body> **2.** Reciprocal <*anti*logarithm>

an·ti·a·bor·tion (ăn′tē-ə-bôr′shən) *adj.* Opposed to abortion. **—an′ti·a·bor′tion·ist** *n.*

an·ti·bal·lis·tic missile (ăn′tĭ-bə-lĭs′tĭk) *n.* A missile designed to destroy a ballistic missile in flight.

an·ti·bi·ot·ic (ăn′tē-bī-ŏt′ĭk) *n.* A substance, as penicillin or streptomycin, produced by organisms such as fungi and bacteria, effective in the suppression or destruction of microorganisms and widely used for prevention and treatment of diseases. **—an′ti·bi·ot′ic** *adj.* **—an′ti·bi·ot′i·cal·ly** *adv.*

an·ti·bod·y (ăn′tĭ-bŏd′ē) *n.* A protein generated in the blood in reaction to foreign proteins or polysaccharides, capable of neutralizing them and producing immunity to certain disease-producing microorganisms.

an·tic (ăn′tĭk) *n.* Often **antics.** A mischievous act or gesture : caper. —*adj.* Ludicrous : far-fetched.

▲ ***word history:*** The source of *antic* is Italian *antico,* which means "ancient." The Italians used *antico* to refer to the grotesque

an′ti·air′craft′ *adj.*
an′ti·al·ler′gic *adj.*
an′ti-A·mer′i·can *adj.*
an′ti·bac·te′ri·al *adj. & n.*
an′ti·busi′ness *adj.*
an′ti·bus′ing *adj.*
an′ti·can′cer *adj.*
an′ti·cler′i·cal *adj.*
an′ti·co·lo′ni·al·ism *n.*
an′ti·crime′ *adj.*
an′ti·dem′o·crat′ic *adj.*
an′ti·de·pres′sant *adj.*
an′ti·de·pres′sive *n.*
an′ti·es·tab′lish·ment *adj.*
an′ti·fem′i·nism *n.*
an′ti·fem′i·nist *adj. & n.*
an′ti-im·pe′ri·al·ism *n.*
an′ti-im·pe′ri·al·ist *adj. & n.*
an′ti-in′tel·lec′tu·al *adj. & n.*
an′ti·la′bor *adj.*
an′ti·ma·lar′i·al *adj. & n.*
an′ti·mi·cro′bi·al *adj. & n.*
an′ti·noise′ *adj.*
an′ti·pol·lu′tion *adj.*
an′ti·pov′er·ty *adj.*
an′ti·slav′er·y *adj.*
an′ti·smog′ *adj.*
an′ti·spas·mod′ic *adj. & n.*
an′ti·sub′ma·rine′ *adj.*
an′ti·tank′ *adj.*
an′ti·ter′ror·ism *n.*
an′ti·ter′ror·ist *adj.*
an′ti·trust′ *adj.*
an′ti·tu′mor *adj.*
an′ti·vi′ral *adj. & n.*
an′ti·war′ *adj.*

designs found on some ancient Roman artifacts. *Antico* is derived from *antiquus*, the same Latin word that is the source of *antique*, which came into English from French. The two words are separate borrowings and the English words *antic* and *antique* do not share any meanings.

an·ti·christ (ăn'tĭ-krīst') *n.* **1.** An enemy of Christ. **2.** A false Christ.

an·tic·i·pate (ăn-tĭs'ə-pāt') *v.* **-pat·ed, -pat·ing. 1.** To foresee. **2.** To look forward to **:** expect. **3.** To act in advance so as to prevent **:** forestall. **—an·tic'i·pa'tion** *n.* **—an·tic'i·pa'tor** *n.* **—an·tic'·i·pa·to'ry** (-pə-tôr'ē, -tōr'ē) *adj.*

an·ti·cli·max (ăn'tē-klī'măks') *n.* **1.** A decline or letdown viewed in disappointing contrast to what has gone before. **2.** A commonplace event that follows a series of significant events. **—an'ti·cli·mac'tic** *adj.* **—an'ti·cli·mac'ti·cal·ly** *adv.*

an·ti·cline (ăn'tĭ-klīn') *n. Geol.* A fold with layers sloping downward on both sides from a common crest. **—an'ti·cli'nal** *adj.*

an·ti·co·ag·u·lant (ăn'tē-kō-ăg'yə-lənt) *n.* A substance that delays or counteracts blood coagulation.

an·ti·cy·clone (ăn'tē-sī'klōn') *n.* A system of winds spiraling outward from a high-pressure center, circling clockwise in the N Hemisphere and counterclockwise in the S Hemisphere. **—an'ti·cy·clon'ic** (-klŏn'ĭk) *adj.*

an·ti·dote (ăn'tĭ-dōt') *n.* **1.** A substance that counteracts the effects of a poison. **2.** Something that counteracts an injurious effect. **—an'ti·dot'al** *adj.*

an·ti·e·lec·tron (ăn'tē-ĭ-lĕk'trŏn') *n.* A positron.

an·ti·freeze (ăn'tĭ-frēz') *n.* A substance, as ethylene glycol, mixed with liquid, esp. water, to lower its freezing point.

an·ti·gen (ăn'tĭ-jən) *n.* A substance that stimulates the production of antibodies. **—an'ti·gen'ic** *adj.* **—an'ti·gen'i·cal·ly** *adv.* **—an'ti·ge·nic'i·ty** *n.*

an·ti·he·ro (ăn'tĭ-hîr'ō) *n.* A fictional protagonist lacking traditional heroic virtues and qualities.

an·ti·his·ta·mine (ăn'tē-hĭs'tə-mēn', -mĭn) *n.* A drug used to relieve symptoms of allergies and colds by interfering with the production of histamines. **—an'ti·his'ta·min'ic** *adj.*

an·ti·knock (ăn'tĭ-nŏk') *n.* A substance added to gasoline that prevents too rapid combustion and reduces engine knock.

an·ti·log (ăn'tē-lôg', -lŏg') *n.* An antilogarithm.

an·ti·log·a·rithm (ăn'tē-lô'gə-rĭth'əm, -lŏg'ə-) *n.* The inverse function of the logarithm of a number; e.g., if $y = \log x$, then $x =$ antilog y.

an·ti·ma·cas·sar (ăn'tē-mə-kăs'ər) *n.* A protective covering for the backs or arms of chairs and sofas.

an·ti·mat·ter (ăn'tĭ-măt'ər) *n.* Antiparticle matter having positron-surrounded nuclei composed of antiprotons and antineutrons.

an·ti·mis·sile missile (ăn'tē-mĭs'əl) *n.* A missile that can intercept and destroy another missile in flight.

an·ti·mo·ny (ăn'tə-mō'nē) *n. Symbol* **Sb** A brittle, blue-white metallic element used in many alloys.

an·ti·neu·tri·no (ăn'tē-nōō-trē'nō, -nyōō-) *n., pl.* **-nos.** The antiparticle of the neutrino.

an·ti·neu·tron (ăn'tē-nōō'trŏn', -nyōō'-) *n.* The antiparticle of the neutron.

an·tin·o·my (ăn-tĭn'ə-mē) *n., pl.* **-mies.** A contradiction, opposition, or conflict.

an·ti·nu·cle·ar (ăn'tē-nōō'klē-ər, -nyōō'-, ăn'tī-) *adj.* Opposing the production or use of nuclear power or nuclear weaponry.

an·ti·ox·i·dant (ăn'tē-ŏk'sĭ-dənt) *n.* A chemical substance that inhibits oxidation.

an·ti·par·ti·cle (ăn'tē-pär'tĭ-kəl) *n.* Either of a pair of atomic particles, such as a positron and electron, that are identical in mass but exactly opposite in electric charge, magnetic properties, and spin.

an·ti·pas·to (ăn'tĭ-pä'stō, -păs'tō) *n., pl.* **-tos** *or* **-ti** (-tē). An appetizer usu. including cheese, smoked meats, fish, and vegetables, served with oil and vinegar.

an·tip·a·thy (ăn-tĭp'ə-thē) *n., pl.* **-thies. 1.** A feeling of aversion, repugnance, or opposition. **2.** An object of aversion. **—an·tip'a·thet'ic, an·tip'a·thet'i·cal** *adj.* **—an·tip'a·thet'i·cal·ly** *adv.*

an·ti·per·son·nel (ăn'tē-pûr'sə-nĕl') *adj.* Designed to injure or kill the military personnel or civilians of an enemy country.

an·ti·per·spi·rant (ăn'tē-pûr'spər-ənt) *n.* A preparation applied to the underarm to reduce excessive perspiration.

an·tiph·o·ny (ăn-tĭf'ə-nē) *n., pl.* **-nies. 1.** Responsive singing or chanting. **2.** One that echoes or answers another. **—an·tiph'o·nal** *adj.* **—an·tiph'o·nal·ly** *adv.*

an·ti·pode (ăn'tĭ-pōd') *n.* A direct opposite. **—an·tip'o·dal** *adj.*

an·tip·o·des (ăn-tĭp'ə-dēz') *pl.n.* **1.** Two places or regions on opposite sides of the earth. **2.** (*sing. or pl. in number*). Any exact opposite of another.

an·ti·pope (ăn'tĭ-pōp') *n.* One claiming to be the pope in opposition to the one chosen canonically.

an·ti·pro·ton (ăn'tē-prō'tŏn') *n.* The antiparticle of the proton.

an·ti·psy·chot·ic (ăn'tē-sī-kŏt'ĭk, ăn'tī-) *adj.* Counteracting the symptoms of psychotic disorders.

an·ti·py·ret·ic (ăn'tē-pī-rĕt'ĭk) *adj.* Reducing fever. —*n.* An antipyretic medication.

an·ti·quar·y (ăn'tĭ-kwĕr'ē) *n., pl.* **-ies.** A student or collector of antiquities.

an·ti·quat·ed (ăn'tĭ-kwā'tĭd) *adj.* Out-of-date **:** obsolete.

an·tique (ăn-tēk') *adj.* **1.** Of ancient times. **2.** Of or typical of an earlier period. **3.** Old-fashioned. —*n.* An object made in an earlier period. —*v.* **-tiqued, -tiqu·ing.** To give the appearance of an antique to. **—an·tique'ly** *adv.* **—an·tique'ness** *n.*

an·tiq·ui·ty (ăn-tĭk'wĭ-tē) *n., pl.* **-ties.** 1. Ancient times. 2. The quality of being ancient. 3. **antiquities.** Something, as statues, from ancient times.

an·ti-Sem·ite (ăn'tē-sĕm'īt') *n.* A person who is prejudiced against Jews. —**an'ti-Se·mit'ic** (-sə-mĭt'ĭk) *adj.* —**an'ti-Sem'i·tism** (-sĕm'ĭ-tĭz'əm) *n.*

an·ti·sep·tic (ăn'tĭ-sĕp'tĭk) *adj.* 1. Destroying or capable of destroying microorganisms that cause disease or decay. 2. Entirely clean. —**an'ti·sep'tic** *n.* —**an'ti·sep'ti·cal·ly** *adv.*

an·ti·so·cial (ăn'tē-sō'shəl) *adj.* 1. Not sociable. 2. Harmful or contrary to the welfare of society <Drug abuse is *antisocial.*>

an·tith·e·sis (ăn-tĭth'ĭ-sĭs) *n., pl.* **-ses** (-sēz'). 1. Direct contrast : opposition. 2. The direct opposite. —**an'ti·thet'i·cal** (ăn'tĭ-thĕt'ĭ-kəl), **an'ti·thet'ic** (-thĕt'-ĭk) *adj.* —**an'ti·thet'i·cal·ly** *adv.*

an·ti·tox·in (ăn'tē-tŏk'sĭn) *n.* 1. An antibody formed in response to and capable of neutralizing a biological poison. 2. An animal serum containing antitoxin.

an·ti·tus·sive (ăn'tē-tŭs'ĭv, ăn'tī-) *adj.* Relieving or suppressing coughing. —**an'ti·tus'·sive** *n.*

an·ti·vi·ral (ăn'tē-vī'rəl, ăn'tī-) *adj.* Destroying or inhibiting the growth and reproduction of viruses <an *antiviral* drug> —**an'ti·vi'ral** *n.*

ant·ler (ănt'lər) *n.* One of the paired, often branched bony growths on the head of a deer. —**ant'lered** *adj.*

ant lion *n.* An insect of the family Myrmeleontidae whose larva digs holes to trap insects, as ants, for food.

an·to·nym (ăn'tə-nĭm') *n.* A word having a sense opposite to that of another word. —**an·ton'y·mous** (ăn-tŏn'ə-məs) *adj.* —**an·ton'·y·my** *n.*

ant·sy (ănt'sē) *adj.* **-si·er, -si·est.** *Slang.* Restless or fidgety.

A·nu·bis (ə-nōō'bĭs) *n. Egypt. Myth.* A jackal-headed god who conducted the dead to judgment.

a·nus (ā'nəs) *n.* The excretory opening of the alimentary canal.

an·vil (ăn'vĭl) *n.* 1. A heavy iron block on which metals are shaped, esp. by hammering. 2. *Anat.* The incus.

anx·i·e·ty (ăng-zī'ĭ-tē) *n., pl.* **-ties.** 1. A state of uneasiness : worry. 2. *Psychiat.* Abnormal fear that lacks a specific cause. ★ ***syns:*** CARE, CONCERN, DISQUIET, DISQUIETUDE, WORRY

anx·ious (ăngk'shəs) *adj.* 1. Uneasy : worried. 2. Eagerly or earnestly desirous. —**anx'·ious·ly** *adv.*

an·y (ĕn'ē) *adj.* 1. One or some, regardless of kind or quantity <Did I get *any* letters?> 2. Of whatever number or amount <Is there *any* cake left?> —*pron.* 1. Any one or ones <Ask *any* of your friends.> 2. Any quantity or part <If *any* of the salad is left, throw it out.> —*adv.* To any degree or extent : at all <I can't eat *any* more.>

an·y·bod·y (ĕn'ē-bŏd'ē, -bŭd'ē) *pron.* Any person : anyone.

an·y·how (ĕn'ē-hou') *adv.* 1. In any case. 2. In any way or by any means.

†**an·y·more** (ĕn'ē-môr', -mōr') *adv.* 1. At present : now. 2. *Regional.* Nowadays.

an·y·one (ĕn'ē-wŭn', -wən) *pron.* Any person : anybody.

an·y·place (ĕn'ē-plās') *adv.* Anywhere.

an·y·thing (ĕn'ē-thĭng') *pron.* Any object, occurrence, or matter whatever.

an·y·time (ĕn'ē-tīm') *adv.* At any time whatever.

an·y·way (ĕn'ē-wā') *adv.* 1. In any case : anyhow. 2. Just the same : nevertheless.

an·y·where (ĕn'ē-hwâr', -wâr') *adv.* 1. To, in, or at any place. 2. To any extent or degree.

A-O·K *also* **A-O·kay** (ā'ō-kā') *adj. & adv. Informal.* Perfectly O.K.

A-one *also* **A-1** (ā'wŭn') *adj. Informal.* Excellent : splendid.

a·or·ta (ā-ôr'tə) *n., pl.* **-tas** *or* **-tae** (-tē). The main trunk of the systemic arteries, carrying blood to all bodily organs except the lungs. —**a·or'tal, a·or'tic** *adj.*

a·pace (ə-pās') *adv.* At a swift pace : rapidly.

A·pach·e (ə-păch'ē) *n., pl.* **-e** *or* **-es.** 1. A member of an American Indian people of the SW United States and N Mexico. 2. Their Athabaskan language.

†**ap·a·re·jo** (ăp'ə-rā'hō, -rā'ō) *n., pl.* **-jos.** *SW U.S.* A packsaddle made of a stuffed leather pad.

a·part (ə-pärt') *adv.* 1. To or in pieces. 2. Separately in time, place, or position. 3. To one side : aside.

a·part·heid (ə-pärt'hīt', -hāt') *n.* A formerly official policy of racial segregation practiced in the Republic of South Africa.

a·part·ment (ə-pärt'mənt) *n.* A room or suite of rooms designed to live in.

ap·a·thy (ăp'ə-thē) *n.* 1. Lack of emotion. 2. Lack of interest : indifference. —**ap'a·thet'·ic** (-thĕt'ĭk) *adj.* —**ap'a·thet'i·cal·ly** *adv.*

ape (āp) *n.* 1. A large tailless primate such as a chimpanzee or gorilla. 2. A monkey. 3. A mimic : imitator. 4. A coarse person. —*v.* **aped, ap·ing.** To mimic : imitate.

ape·man (āp'măn') *n.* An extinct primate held to be intermediate between apes and modern human beings.

a·pé·ri·tif (ā-pĕr'ĭ-tēf') *n.* An alcoholic drink taken before a meal.

ap·er·ture (ăp'ər-chər) *n.* An opening, as a hole : orifice.

a·pex (ā'pĕks') *n., pl.* **apexes** *or* **a·pi·ces** (ā'-pĭ-sēz', ăp'ĭ-). The highest point : peak.

a·pha·sia (ə-fā'zhə) *n.* Loss of the ability to speak or understand speech. —**a·pha'sic** (-zĭk, -sĭk) *adj. & n.*

a·phe·li·on (ə-fē'lē-ən, ə-fēl'yən) *n., pl.* **-li·a** (-lē-ə). The point on a planetary orbit farthest from the sun.

a·phid (ā'fĭd, ăf'ĭd) *n.* A small, soft-bodied insect of the family Aphididae that feeds by sucking sap from plants.

aph•o•rism (ăf'ə-rĭz'əm) *n.* A brief statement of a truth : adage. —**aph'o•ris'tic** (ăf'ə-rĭs'tĭk) *adj.*
aph•ro•dis•i•ac (ăf'rə-dĭz'ē-ăk') *adj.* Stimulating sexual desire. —**aph'ro•dis'i•ac'** *n.*
Aph•ro•di•te (ăf'rə-dī'tē) *n. Gk. Myth.* The goddess of love and beauty.
a•pi•ar•y (ā'pē-ĕr'ē) *n., pl.* **-ies.** A place for keeping bees and beehives. —**a'pi•a•rist** (ā'pē-ə-rĭst) *n.*
a•pi•ces (ā'pĭ-sēz', ăp'ĭ-) *n. var. pl. of* APEX.
a•piece (ə-pēs') *adv.* To or for each one.
ap•ish (ā'pĭsh) *adj.* **1.** Resembling an ape. **2.** Slavishly or foolishly imitative.
a•plomb (ə-plŏm', ə-plŭm') *n.* Self-confidence : assurance.
A•poc•a•lypse (ə-pŏk'ə-lĭps') *n.* **1.** *Bible.* The Book of Revelation. **2. apocalypse.** Great devastation : doom. —**a•poc'a•lyp'tic, a•poc'a•lyp'ti•cal** *adj.*
A•poc•ry•pha (ə-pŏk'rə-fə) *n. (sing. or pl. in number).* **1.** The 14 Biblical books included in the Vulgate but considered uncanonical by Protestants because they are not part of the Hebrew Scriptures; 11 are accepted by the Roman Catholic Church. —See table at BIBLE. **2. apocrypha.** Writings of questionable authenticity.
a•poc•ry•phal (ə-pŏk'rə-fəl) *adj.* **1.** Of questionable authenticity. **2. Apocryphal.** Of or relating to the Apocrypha. —**a•poc'ry•phal•ly** *adv.*
ap•o•gee (ăp'ə-jē) *n.* The point most distant from the earth in a satellite's orbit.

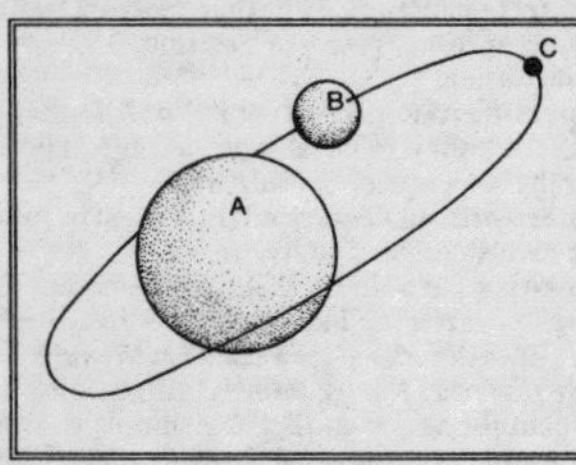

apogee
A. earth, B. satellite, C. point of apogee

a•po•lit•i•cal (ā'pə-lĭt'ĭ-kəl) *adj.* **1.** Having no involvement or interest in politics. **2.** Having no political significance. —**a'po•lit'i•cal•ly** *adv.*
A•pol•lo (ə-pŏl'ō) *n.* **1.** *Gk. Myth.* The god of the sun, prophecy, music, medicine, and poetry. **2. apollo.** A very handsome young man.
a•pol•o•get•ic (ə-pŏl'ə-jĕt'ĭk) *adj.* Making or expressing an apology. —**a•pol'o•get'i•cal•ly** *adv.*
a•pol•o•gize (ə-pŏl'ə-jīz') *v.* **-gized, -giz•ing.** To make an apology. —**a•pol'o•gist** (-jĭst) *n.*
a•pol•o•gy (ə-pŏl'ə-jē) *n., pl.* **-gies. 1.** An expression of regret for an offense or fault. **2.** A formal defense : justification.
ap•o•plex•y (ăp'ə-plĕk'sē) *n.* Sudden loss of consciousness resulting from rupture or blockage of a blood vessel in the brain. —**ap'o•plec'tic** (-plĕk'tĭk) *adj.*
a•port (ə-pôrt', ə-pōrt) *adv. Naut.* Toward or on the port side of a ship.
a•pos•ta•sy (ə-pŏs'tə-sē) *n., pl.* **-sies.** Abandonment of a former allegiance, as to one's religious faith. —**a•pos'tate'** (-tāt', -tĭt) *n. & adj.*
a pos•te•ri•o•ri (ä' pŏ-stîr'ē-ôr'ē, -ōr'ē, -ôr'ī', -ōr'ī', ā') *adj.* Denoting reasoning from facts to general principles : inductive.
a•pos•tle (ə-pŏs'əl) *n.* **1. Apostle.** One of the 12 disciples of Jesus. **2.** A leader or advocate of a new cause.
ap•os•tol•ic (ăp'ə-stŏl'ĭk) *adj.* **1.** Of or relating to the 12 Apostles or their teachings. **2.** Papal.
a•pos•tro•phe[1] (ə-pŏs'trə-fē) *n.* The superscript sign (') used to indicate the omission of one or more letters from a word, the possessive case, and certain plurals, esp. of numbers and letters.
a•pos•tro•phe[2] (ə-pŏs'trə-fē) *n.* The addressing in rhetoric of an absent or imaginary person. —**a•pos'tro•phize'** (-fīz') *v.*
apothecaries' weight *n.* A system of weights used in pharmacy and based on 1 oz equal to 480 grains and 1 lb equal to 12 oz.
a•poth•e•car•y (ə-pŏth'ĭ-kĕr'ē) *n., pl.* **-ries.** A druggist.
ap•o•thegm (ăp'ə-thĕm') *n.* A proverb : maxim.
a•poth•e•o•sis (ə-pŏth'ē-ō'sĭs, ăp'ə-thē'ə-sĭs) *n., pl.* **-ses** (-sēz'). **1.** Elevation to divine stature : deification. **2.** An ideal example.
ap•pall (ə-pôl') *v.* To fill with dismay : horrify. —**ap•pall'ing•ly** *adv.*
ap•pa•loo•sa (ăp'ə-lo͞o'sə) *n.* A saddle horse with a spotted rump.
ap•pa•ra•tus (ăp'ə-rā'təs, -răt'əs) *n., pl.* **-tus** *or* **-tus•es. 1.** Equipment or materials for a specified function or task. **2. a.** A machine. **b.** A group of machines. **3.** A political organization.
ap•par•el (ə-păr'əl) *n.* Clothing : attire. —*v.* **-eled, -el•ing** *or* **-elled, -el•ling.** To dress : clothe.
ap•par•ent (ə-păr'ənt, ə-pâr'-) *adj.* **1.** Easily seen : visible. **2.** Easily perceived : obvious. **3.** Appearing to be true or real : ostensible. —**ap•par'ent•ly** *adv.*
ap•pa•ri•tion (ăp'ə-rĭsh'ən) *n.* A spectral figure : ghost.
ap•peal (ə-pēl') *n.* **1.** An earnest entreaty : plea. **2.** An application, as to a higher authority, for help or a decision. **3.** The power of arousing interest : attraction. **4.** *Law.* The transfer of a case from a lower to a higher court for a new hearing. —*v.* **1.** To make an appeal, as for help. **2.** To have the power of attracting. **3.** *Law.* To transfer or apply to transfer (a case) to a higher court for a new hearing. —**ap•peal'a•ble** *adj.* —**ap•peal'ing•ly** *adv.*

ap•pear (ə-pîr′) *v.* **1.** To come into view. **2.** To look or seem to be. **3.** To be presented or published. **4.** *Law.* To present oneself formally before a court.

ap•pear•ance (ə-pîr′əns) *n.* **1.** The act of appearing. **2.** The way something looks : outward aspect. **3.** A false show : pretense.

ap•pease (ə-pēz′) *v.* **-peased, -peas•ing.** To calm or pacify, esp. by granting demands. **—ap•pease′ment** *n.* **—ap•peas′er** *n.*

ap•pel•lant (ə-pĕl′ənt) *n.* One who appeals a court decision. *—adj.* Appellate.

ap•pel•late (ə-pĕl′ĭt) *adj.* Empowered to hear and review decisions of lower courts.

ap•pel•la•tion (ăp′ə-lā′shən) *n.* A name or title.

ap•pend (ə-pĕnd′) *v.* **1.** To add, esp. as a supplement. **2.** To fix to : attach.

ap•pend•age (ə-pĕn′dĭj) *n.* **1.** Something appended. **2.** *Biol.* A part or organ joined to an axis or trunk.

ap•pen•dec•to•my (ăp′ən-dĕk′tə-mē) *n., pl.* **-mies.** Surgical excision of the vermiform appendix.

ap•pen•di•ci•tis (ə-pĕn′dĭ-sī′tĭs) *n.* Inflammation of the vermiform appendix.

ap•pen•dix (ə-pĕn′dĭks) *n., pl.* **-dix•es** *or* **-di•ces** (-dĭ-sēz′). **1.** Supplementary material, usu. at the end of a written book. **2.** The vermiform appendix.

ap•per•tain (ăp′ər-tān′) *v.* To belong as a function or part : pertain.

ap•pe•stat (ăp′ĭ-stăt′) *n.* The mechanism in the central nervous system that controls food intake.

ap•pe•tite (ăp′ĭ-tīt′) *n.* **1.** A desire for food. **2.** A craving : desire.

ap•pe•tiz•er (ăp′ĭ-tī′zər) *n.* Food or drink served before a meal to whet the appetite.

ap•pe•tiz•ing (ăp′ĭ-tī′zĭng) *adj.* Appealing to the appetite. **—ap′pe•tiz′ing•ly** *adv.*

ap•plaud (ə-plôd′) *v.* To express approval (of), esp. by clapping. **—ap•plaud′er** *n.*

ap•plause (ə-plôz′) *n.* **1.** Approval expressed esp. by clapping. **2.** Commendation : praise.

ap•ple (ăp′əl) *n.* **1.** A tree, *Pyrus malus,* that bears fragrant flowers and edible fruit. **2.** The firm, rounded fruit of the apple tree.

ap•ple•jack (ăp′əl-jăk′) *n.* Liquor distilled from hard cider.

ap•ple•sauce (ăp′əl-sôs′) *n.* **1.** Apples stewed to a pulp. **2.** *Slang.* Nonsense.

ap•pli•ance (ə-plī′əns) *n.* A device, esp. an item of household equipment that is operated by electricity or gas.

ap•pli•ca•ble (ăp′lĭ-kə-bəl, ə-plĭk′ə-) *adj.* Able to be applied : appropriate. **—ap′pli•ca•bil′i•ty** *n.*

ap•pli•cant (ăp′lĭ-kənt) *n.* One who applies, as for a job or admission.

ap•pli•ca•tion (ăp′lĭ-kā′shən) *n.* **1.** The act of applying. **2.** Something applied, esp. to a surface. **3.** A particular use to which something is put. **4.** Usability : relevance. **5.** Careful attention : assiduity. **6. a.** A request, as for aid, employment, or admission. **b.** A form used in making such a request.

ap•pli•ca•tor (ăp′lĭ-kā′tər) *n.* An instrument for applying a substance, as medicine.

ap•plied (ə-plīd′) *adj.* Put into practice : used.

ap•pli•qué (ăp′lĭ-kā′) *n.* A cloth ornament cut out from one material and sewn to a larger piece of another. **—ap′pli•qué′** *v.*

ap•ply (ə-plī′) *v.* **-plied, -ply•ing. 1.** To bring into contact : spread or put on. **2.** To put to a special use. **3.** To give (oneself or one's efforts) to something. **4.** To be relevant. **5.** To submit a request, as for employment. **—ap•pli′er** *n.*

ap•point (ə-point′) *v.* **1.** To name officially for an office or position. **2.** To set or fix by authority. **3.** To furnish : equip <a well-*appointed* office> **—ap•point′ee′** *n.*

ap•point•ive (ə-poin′tĭv) *adj.* Relating to or able to be filled by appointment.

ap•point•ment (ə-point′mənt) *n.* **1.** The act of appointing. **2.** An appointive office or position. **3.** An engagement for a meeting. **4. appointments.** Equipment : furnishings.

ap•por•tion (ə-pôr′shən, ə-pōr′-) *v.* To divide according to a proportion or plan : allot. **—ap•por′tion•ment** *n.*

ap•po•site (ăp′ə-zĭt) *adj.* Appropriate : apt. **—ap′po•site•ly** *adv.* **—ap′po•site•ness** *n.*

ap•po•si•tion (ăp′ə-zĭsh′ən) *n.* A grammatical construction in which a noun or noun phrase is followed by another that is an explanatory equivalent, as *the composer* and *Bach* in *a portrait of the composer Bach.* **—ap′po•si′tion•al** *adj.*

ap•pos•i•tive (ə-pŏz′ĭ-tĭv) *adj.* Of, relating to, or being in apposition. **—ap•pos′i•tive** *n.* **—ap•pos′i•tive•ly** *adv.*

ap•praise (ə-prāz′) *v.* **-praised, -prais•ing.** To assign a value to. **—ap•prais′er** *n.*

ap•pre•cia•ble (ə-prē′shə-bəl) *adj.* Capable of being noticed, estimated, or perceptible. **—ap•pre′cia•bly** *adv.*

ap•pre•ci•ate (ə-prē′shē-āt′) *v.* **-at•ed, -at•ing. 1.** To recognize the value or quality of. **2.** To value highly. **3.** To be aware of : realize. **4.** To feel gratitude for. **5.** To increase in value or price. ★ ***syns:*** CHERISH, ESTEEM, PRIZE, RESPECT, SAVOR, TREASURE, VALUE **—ap•pre′ci•a′tion** *n.* **—ap•pre′ci•a′tor** *n.*

ap•pre•cia•tive (ə-prē′shə-tĭv, -shē-ā′tĭv) *adj.* Capable of or showing appreciation. **—ap•pre′cia•tive•ly** *adv.*

ap•pre•hend (ăp′rĭ-hĕnd′) *v.* **1.** To arrest. **2.** To understand. **3.** To anticipate fearfully. **—ap′pre•hen′sion** *n.*

ap•pre•hen•sive (ăp′rĭ-hĕn′sĭv) *adj.* Fearful or uneasy about the future : anxious. **—ap′pre•hen′sive•ly** *adv.* **—ap′pre•hen′sive•ness** *n.*

ap•pren•tice (ə-prĕn′tĭs) *n.* **1.** One who is learning a trade or occupation under a skilled worker. **2.** A beginner. *—v.* **-ticed, -tic•ing.** To place as an apprentice. **—ap•pren′tice•ship′** *n.*

ap•prise (ə-prīz′) *v.* **-prised, -pris•ing.** To give notice to : inform.

ap•prize (ə-prīz′) *v. esp. Brit. var. of* APPRISE.

ap•proach (ə-prōch′) *v.* **1.** To come near or nearer (to), as in space or time. **2.** To be close to, as in appearance : approximate. 3. To begin to deal with. —*n.* 1. The act of approaching. 2. A means of reaching something : access. 3. A way of dealing with or accomplishing something. —**ap·proach'a·bil'i·ty** *n.* —**ap·proach'a·ble** *adj.*

ap·pro·ba·tion (ăp'rə-bā'shən) *n.* The act of approving, esp. formally : approval.

ap·pro·pri·ate (ə-prō'prē-ĭt) *adj.* Suitable for a particular occasion or use : fitting. —*v.* (-āt') **-at·ed, -at·ing.** 1. To set apart for a particular use. 2. To take or use, often without permission. —**ap·pro'pri·ate·ly** *adv.* —**ap·pro'pri·ate·ness** *n.*

ap·pro·pri·a·tion (ə-prō'prē-ā'shən) *n.* Money that has been set apart by official action for a particular use.

ap·prov·al (ə-pro͞o'vəl) *n.* The act of approving : sanction. —**on approval.** Subject to acceptance or rejection by a prospective buyer.

ap·prove (ə-pro͞ov') *v.* **-proved, -prov·ing.** 1. To regard with favor. 2. To confirm officially : ratify. —**ap·prov'ing·ly** *adv.*

ap·prox·i·mate (ə-prŏk'sə-mĭt) *adj.* Almost exact or accurate. —*v.* (-māt') **-mat·ed, -mat·ing.** To be nearly the same as : approach. —**ap·prox'i·mate·ly** *adv.* —**ap·prox'i·ma'tion** *n.*

ap·pur·te·nance (ə-pûr'tn-əns) *n.* Something that belongs with or to another more important thing : accessory. —**ap·pur'te·nant** *adj.*

ap·ri·cot (ăp'rĭ-kŏt', ā'prĭ-) *n.* A tree, *Prunus armeniaca*, widely cultivated for its edible yellow-orange peachlike fruit.

A·pril (ā'prəl) *n.* The 4th month of the year, having 30 days.

April Fools' Day (fo͞olz) *n.* Apr. 1, marked by the playing of practical jokes.

a pri·o·ri (ä' prē-ôr'ē, -ōr'ē, ā' prī-ôr'ī', -ōr'ī') *adj.* 1. From a cause to an effect : deductive. 2. Based on a hypothesis or theory rather than on experience.

a·pron (ā'prən) *n.* 1. A garment worn over the front of the body to protect the clothes. 2. The paved strip around an airport hangar and terminal building.

▲ ***word history:*** *An apron* was orig. *a napron. Apron* is one of the numerous English words that have either lost or gained an initial *n* because of an incorrect division between the indefinite article and the noun. *Apron* is thus closely related to *napkin* and *napery.*

ap·ro·pos (ăp'rə-pō') *adj.* Relevant : pertinent. —*adv.* 1. Relevantly : pertinently. 2. By the way : incidentally. —*prep.* In the matter of : regarding.

apropos of *prep.* With reference to.

apse (ăps) *n.* A semicircular or polygonal building projection, as of a church.

apt (ăpt) *adj.* 1. Particularly suitable : appropriate. 2. Having a tendency : likely. 3. Quick to understand or learn. —**apt'ly** *adv.* —**apt'ness** *n.*

ap·ti·tude (ăp'tĭ-to͞od', -tyo͞od') *n.* 1. A natural ability or talent. 2. Quickness in understanding or learning. 3. The quality of being suitable : appropriateness.

aq·ua (ăk'wə, ä'kwə) *n., pl.* **aq·uae** (ăk'wē, ä'kwī') *or* **aq·uas.** 1. Water. 2. An aqueous solution. 3. A light bluish green to greenish blue. —**aq'ua** *adj.*

aq·ua·cul·ture (ăk'wə-kŭl'chər, ä'kwə-) *n.* The cultivation of fish or shellfish for food. —**aq'ua·cul'tur·ist** *n.*

Aqua Lung. A trademark for an underwater breathing apparatus.

aq·ua·ma·rine (ăk'wə-mə-rēn', ä'kwə-) *n.* 1. A transparent blue-green gemstone. 2. A pale blue to light greenish blue.

aq·ua·naut (ăk'wə-nôt', ä'kwə-) *n.* One who is trained to live in underwater installations and work in scientific research.

aq·ua·plane (ăk'wə-plān', ä'kwə-) *n.* A board towed by a motorboat and ridden by a person standing on it. —**aq'ua·plane'** *v.*

aqua re·gia (rē'jə, -jē-ə) *n.* A mixture of hydrochloric and nitric acids that can dissolve platinum and gold.

a·quar·i·um (ə-kwâr'ē-əm) *n., pl.* **-i·ums** *or* **-i·a** (-ē-ə). 1. A water-filled container in which to keep and raise aquatic animals and plants. 2. A place in which aquatic animals and plants are kept for public display.

A·quar·i·us (ə-kwâr'ē-əs) *n.* 1. A constellation in the S Hemisphere. 2. a. The 11th sign of the zodiac. b. One born under this sign.

a·quat·ic (ə-kwŏt'ĭk, ə-kwăt'-) *adj.* 1. Living in or on the water. 2. Occurring in or on the water, as sports. —**a·quat'ic** *n.*

aq·ua·tint (ăk'wə-tĭnt', ä'kwə-) *n.* 1. A process of etching capable of producing tonal variations in the resulting print. 2. An etching so made.

a·qua·vit (ä'kwə-vēt') *n.* A Scandinavian liquor flavored with caraway seed.

aqua vi·tae (vī'tē) *n.* 1. Alcohol. 2. Strong liquor such as whiskey.

aq·ue·duct (ăk'wĭ-dŭkt') *n.* 1. A conduit for carrying water from a remote source. 2. A bridgelike structure supporting a conduit or canal over a river or low ground.

a·que·ous (ā'kwē-əs, ăk'wē-) *adj.* Of, like, containing, or dissolved in water : watery.

aqueous humor *n.* A clear fluid in the chamber of the eye between the cornea and lens.

aq·ui·fer (ăk'wə-fər, ä'kwə-) *n.* A layer of underground sand, gravel, or spongy rock in which water collects.

aq·ui·line (ăk'wə-līn', -lĭn) *adj.* 1. Of or like an eagle. 2. Curved or hooked like the beak of an eagle <an *aquiline* nose>

ar (är) *n. var. of* ARE².

-ar *suff.* Of, relating to, or resembling <*polar*>

Ar *symbol for* ARGON.

Ar·ab (ăr'əb) *n.* 1. A native or resident of Arabia. 2. A member of a Semitic people of the Middle East and North Africa. 3. A swift, intelligent graceful horse native to Arabia. —**Ar'ab** *adj.*

ar•a•besque (ăr′ə-bĕsk′) *n.* An intricate design of interwoven leaves, flowers, and geometric forms.
Ar•a•bic (ăr′ə-bĭk) *adj.* Of or relating to Arabs, their language, or their culture. —*n.* The Semitic language of the Arabs.
Arabic numeral *n.* One of the numerical symbols 1, 2, 3, 4, 5, 6, 7, 8, 9, and 0.
ar•a•ble (ăr′ə-bəl) *adj.* Suitable for cultivation by plowing.
a•rach•nid (ə-răk′nĭd) *n.* Any of various arthropods of the class Arachnida, having 4 pairs of legs and including the spiders, scorpions, ticks, and mites.
Ar•a•ma•ic (ăr′ə-mā′ĭk) *n.* A Semitic language used in SW Asia 600 B.C.–A.D. 600.
ar•ba•lest *also* **ar•be•lest** (är′bə-lĭst) *n.* A medieval crossbow.

arbalest

ar•bi•ter (är′bĭ-tər) *n.* One who has the authority to decide.
ar•bi•trage (är′bĭ-träzh′) *n.* The purchase of securities on one market for resale on another to profit from a price discrepancy. —**ar′bi•trage′** *v.* —**ar′bi•tra•geur′** *n.*
ar•bit•ra•ment (är-bĭt′rə-mənt) *n.* **1.** The act of arbitrating. **2.** The judgment of an arbitrator.
ar•bi•trar•y (är′bĭ-trĕr′ē) *adj.* **1.** Based on impulse or whim. **2.** Dictatorial. —**ar′bi•trar′i•ly** *adv.* —**ar′bi•trar′i•ness** *n.*
ar•bi•trate (är′bĭ-trāt′) *v.* **-trat•ed, -trat•ing. 1.** To decide as an arbitrator. **2.** To submit (a dispute) to an arbitrator. **3.** To serve as an arbitrator. —**ar′bi•tra′tion** *n.*
ar•bi•tra•tor (är′bĭ-trā′tər) *n.* One chosen to settle the issue between parties engaged in a dispute or controversy.
ar•bor (är′bər) *n.* A shady garden shelter covered with or formed of climbing plants.
ar•bo•re•al (är-bôr′ē-əl, -bōr′-) *adj.* **1.** Of or resembling a tree. **2.** Living in trees.
ar•bo•re•tum (är′bə-rē′təm) *n., pl.* **-tums** *or* **-ta** (-tə). A place for studying and exhibiting growing trees.
ar•bor•vi•tae (är′bər-vī′tē) *n.* Any of several evergreen shrubs and trees of the genus *Thuja* with small, scalelike leaves.
ar•bu•tus (är-byōō′təs) *n.* Trailing arbutus.
arc (ärk) *n.* **1.** Something with the shape of an arch or curve. **2.** *Geom.* A segment of a curve. **3.** A luminous discharge of electric current across a gap between 2 electrodes. —*v.* **arced, arc•ing** *or* **arcked, arck•ing.** To form an arc.
ARC (ärk) *n.* A combination of symptoms first considered to be a precursor to AIDS, but now thought of as a milder form of the disease.
ar•cade (är-kād′) *n.* **1.** A row of arches supported by columns. **2.** A roofed passageway, esp. one lined with shops.
ar•ca•na (är-kā′nə) *pl.n.* Specialized knowledge or detail that is mysterious to the average person.
ar•cane (är-kān′) *adj.* Mysterious **:** secret.
arch[1] (ärch) *n.* **1.** A curved structure that spans an open space and supports a load. **2.** Something that is similar to an arch in form or function. —*v.* **1.** To provide with an arch. **2.** To form or cause to form an arch.
arch[2] (ärch) *adj.* **1.** Principal **:** chief. **2.** Mischievous **:** roguish. —**arch′ly** *adv.* —**arch′ness** *n.*
ar•chae•ol•o•gy *or* **ar•che•ol•o•gy** (är′kē-ŏl′ə-jē) *n.* The scientific study of material evidence, as buildings and tools, remaining from past human life and culture. —**ar′chae•o•log′i•cal, ar′chae•o•log′ic** *adj.* —**ar′chae•ol′o•gist** *n.*
ar•cha•ic (är-kā′ĭk) *adj.* **1.** Belonging to an earlier time **:** ancient. **2.** Characteristic of language that was once common but is now used chiefly to suggest an earlier style. —**ar•cha′i•cal•ly** *adv.*
ar•cha•ism (är′kē-ĭz′əm, -kā-) *n.* An archaic word or expression.
arch•an•gel (ärk′ān′jəl) *n.* A member of the highest order of angels.
arch•bish•op (ärch-bĭsh′əp) *n.* A bishop of the highest rank. —**arch•bish′op•ric** *n.*
arch•dea•con (ärch-dē′kən) *n.* A church official, chiefly of the Anglican Church, with powers delegated from the bishop.
arch•di•o•cese (ärch-dī′ə-sĭs, -sēs′, -sēz′) *n.* A diocese under jurisdiction of an archbishop. —**arch′di•oc′e•san** (-ŏs′ĭ-sən) *adj.*
arch•duch•ess (ärch-dŭch′ĭs) *n.* **1.** The wife or widow of an archduke. **2.** A royal princess, esp. of imperial Austria.
arch•duke (ärch-dōōk′, -dyōōk′) *n.* A royal prince, esp. of imperial Austria.
arch•en•e•my (ärch′ĕn′ə-mē) *n., pl.* **-mies.** A chief enemy.
ar•che•ol•o•gy (är′kē-ŏl′ə-jē) *n. var. of* ARCHAEOLOGY.
arch•er•y (är′chə-rē) *n.* The sport or practice of shooting with a bow and arrow. —**ar′cher** *n.*
ar•che•type (är′kĭ-tīp′) *n.* An original model on which similar things are patterned **:** prototype. —**ar′che•typ′al, ar′che•typ′ic** (-tĭp′ĭk), **ar′che•typ′i•cal** *adj.*
arch•fiend (ärch-fēnd′) *n.* **1.** A principal fiend. **2.** Satan.
ar•chi•e•pis•co•pal (är′kē-ĭ-pĭs′kə-pəl) *adj.* Relating to an archbishop.

ar•chi•man•drite (är′kə-măn′drīt′) *n.* A cleric in the Greek Orthodox Church ranking below a bishop.

ar•chi•pel•a•go (är′kə-pĕl′ə-gō′) *n., pl.* **-goes** *or* **-gos. 1.** A group of islands. **2.** A sea with a large group of islands.

ar•chi•tect (är′kĭ-tĕkt′) *n.* One who designs and supervises the construction of large structures such as buildings.

ar•chi•tec•ton•ics (är′kĭ-tĕk-tŏn′ĭks) *n. (sing. in number).* **1.** The science of architecture. **2.** The structural design of something, as of a musical composition. **—ar′chi•tec•ton′ic** *adj.*

ar•chi•tec•ture (är′kĭ-tĕk′chər) *n.* **1.** The science or art of designing and erecting structures. **2.** A style or method of construction. **—ar′chi•tec′tur•al** *adj.* **—ar′chi•tec′tur•al•ly** *adv.*

ar•chi•trave (är′kĭ-trāv′) *n.* A horizontal piece supported by the columns of a building in classical architecture.

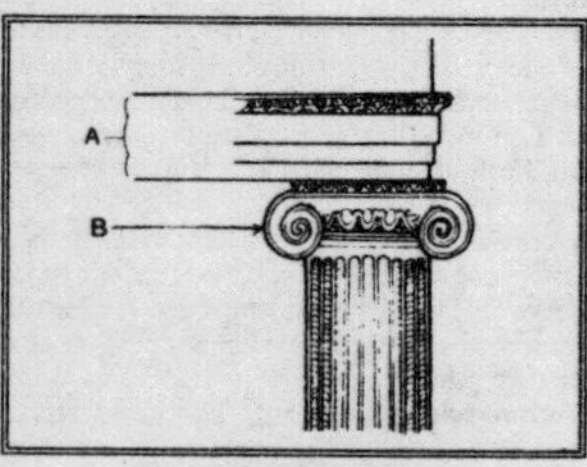

architrave
A column showing
A. the architrave and
B. the volute

ar•chive (är′kīv′) *n. often* **archives. 1.** Public records or documents. **2.** A place where archives are kept. **—ar•chi′val** *adj.* **—ar′chi•vist** (-kə-vĭst, -kī-) *n.*

arch•ri•val (ärch′rī′vəl) *n.* A principal rival.

arch•way (ärch′wā′) *n.* **1.** A passageway under an arch. **2.** An arch over an entrance or passageway.

arcked (ärkt) *v. var. p.t. & p.p. of* ARC.

arck•ing (ärk′ĭng) *v. var. pr.p.* of ARC.

arc lamp *n.* An electric lamp in which a current traverses a gas between 2 incandescent electrodes.

arc•tic (ärk′tĭk, är′tĭk) *adj.* **1.** Exceedingly cold **:** frigid. **2. Arctic.** Of or relating to the region N of the Arctic Circle.

Arctic Circle *n.* The parallel of latitude (66° 33′ N) marking the limit of the N Frigid Zone.

arctic fox *n.* A fox, *Alopex lagopus,* of Arctic regions, with fur that is white or light gray in winter and brown or blue-gray in summer.

–ard *or* **–art** *suff.* One who habitually or excessively is in a specified condition or performs a specified action <drunk*ard*> <brag*gart*>

ar•dent (är′dnt) *adj.* **1.** Marked by warmth of emotion **:** passionate. **2.** Shining **:** glowing. **3.** Hot as fire **:** burning. **—ar′dent•ly** *adv.*

ar•dor (är′dər) *n.* **1.** Warmth of emotion **:** passion. **2.** Intense heat.

ar•du•ous (är′jo͞o-əs) *adj.* Demanding much effort **:** difficult. **—ar′du•ous•ly** *adv.* **—ar′du•ous•ness** *n.*

are[1] (är) *v. 2nd person sing. & 1st, 2nd, & 3rd person pl. present tense of* BE.

are[2] (âr, är) *also* **ar** (är) *n.* A metric unit of area equal to 100 square meters.

ar•e•a (âr′ē-ə) *n.* **1.** A flat space or surface. **2.** A region, as of land. **3.** Range or scope <the *area* of adult education> **4.** The measure of a planar region or of the surface of a solid.

area code *n.* A number given to each telephone area in a country, as in the U.S., used to call another area.

ar•e•a•way (âr′ē-ə-wā′) *n.* A sunken area affording access, light, and air to a basement.

a•re•ca (ə-rē′kə, ăr′ĭ-kə) *n.* Any of various tall palms of the genus *Areca* of SE Asia, bearing white flowers and red or orange egg-shaped nuts.

a•re•na (ə-rē′nə) *n.* **1.** An enclosed space for public entertainment. **2.** A field of interest or activity **:** sphere.

aren't (ärnt, är′ənt). Are not.

ar•gent (är′jənt) *n. Archaic.* Silver.

ar•gen•tite (är′jən-tīt′) *n.* A valuable silver ore that is a lustrous lead-gray color.

ar•gil•la•ceous (är′jə-lā′shəs) *adj.* Of, containing, or resembling clay **:** clayey.

ar•gon (är′gŏn′) *n. Symbol* **Ar** An inert gaseous element constituting approx. 1% of the earth's atmosphere and used in electric light bulbs and fluorescent tubes.

ar•go•sy (är′gə-sē) *n., pl.* **-sies. 1.** A large merchant ship. **2.** A fleet of ships.

ar•got (är′gō′, -gət) *n.* The specialized vocabulary of a particular group, esp. of the underworld.

ar•gu•a•ble (är′gyo͞o-ə-bəl) *adj.* Open to argument. **—ar′gu•a•bly** *adv.*

ar•gue (är′gyo͞o) *v.* **-gued, -gu•ing. 1.** To offer reasons for or against **:** debate. **2.** To try to prove by reasoning **:** maintain. **3.** To engage in a quarrel **:** dispute. **4.** To influence or persuade <*argued* us into staying> ★ ***syns:*** BICKER, CONTEND, DISPUTE, FIGHT, QUARREL, SQUABBLE, WRANGLE **—ar′gu•ment** *n.* **—ar′gu•er** *n.*

†ar•gu•fy (är′gyə-fī′) *v.* **-fied, -fy•ing.** *Regional.* To argue (over) **:** wrangle.

ar•gu•men•ta•tion (är′gyə-mĕn-tā′shən) *n.* The art or process of arguing **:** debate.

ar•gu•men•ta•tive (är′gyə-mĕn′tə-tĭv) *adj.* Given to arguing **:** contentious. **—ar′gu•men′ta•tive•ness** *n.*

ar•gus pheasant (är′gəs) *n.* A large bird, *Argusianus argus,* of S Asia, bearing long tail feathers with brilliantly colored eyelike spots.

ar•gyle *also* **ar•gyll** (är′gīl′) *n.* **1.** A knitting pattern of varicolored diamond-shaped areas. **2.** A sock knit in an argyle pattern.

a•ri•a (är′ē-ə) *n.* A solo vocal piece with accompaniment, as in an opera.

ar•id (ăr′ĭd) *adj.* **1.** Lacking in rainfall **:** dry. **2.** Lacking feeling or interest **:** dull. **—a•rid′i•ty** (ə-rĭd′ĭ-tē) *n.*

Ar•ies (âr′ēz′, âr′ē-ēz′) *n.* **1.** A constellation in the N Hemisphere. **2. a.** The 1st sign of the zodiac. **b.** One born under this sign.

a•right (ə-rīt′) *adv.* Rightly **:** correctly.

a•rise (ə-rīz′) *v.* **a•rose** (ə-rōz′), **a•ris•en** (ə-rĭz′-ən), **a•ris•ing. 1.** To get up. **2.** To move upward **:** ascend. **3.** To come into existence **:** originate.

ar•is•toc•ra•cy (ăr′ĭ-stŏk′rə-sē) *n., pl.* **-cies. 1.** A hereditary privileged ruling class or nobility. **2.** Government by the nobility or by a privileged upper class. **3.** A group or class viewed as superior. **—a•ris′to•crat′** *n.* **—a•ris′to•crat′ic** *adj.* **—a•ris′to•crat′i•cal•ly** *adv.*

a•rith•me•tic (ə-rĭth′mə-tĭk) *n.* The mathematics of real numbers under addition, subtraction, multiplication, and division. **—ar′ith•met′ic** (ăr′ĭth-mĕt′ĭk), **ar′ith•met′i•cal** (-ĭ-kəl) *adj.* **—ar′ith•met′i•cal•ly** *adv.* **—a•rith′me•ti′cian** (-tĭsh′ən) *n.*

ar•ith•met•ic mean (ăr′ĭth-mĕt′ĭk) *n.* The number obtained by dividing the sum of a set of quantities by the number of quantities in the set.

ark (ärk) *n.* **1.** The chest containing the Ten Commandments on stone tablets that was carried by the ancient Hebrews. **2.** The ship that God commanded Noah to build for survival during the Flood.

arm[1] (ärm) *n.* **1.** One of the upper limbs of the human body. **2.** An armlike part. **3.** Force **:** power <the *arm* of the law>

arm[2] (ärm) *n.* **1.** A weapon. **2.** A branch, as the infantry, of a military force. **3. arms.** Heraldic bearings. —*v.* **1.** To equip with weapons. **2.** To prepare for or as if for war. **—armed** *adj.*

ar•ma•da (är-mä′də, -mā′-) *n.* A fleet of warships.

ar•ma•dil•lo (är′mə-dĭl′ō) *n., pl.* **-los.** A burrowing mammal of the family Dasypodidae, with an armorlike covering of jointed, bony plates.

armadillo

Ar•ma•ged•don (är′mə-gĕd′n) *n.* **1.** A final battle between the forces of good and evil. **2.** The time or place of Armageddon.

ar•ma•ment (är′mə-mənt) *n.* **1.** Military weapons and supplies. **2.** *often* **armaments.** The entire military forces and equipment of a country. **3.** The process of arming in preparation for war.

ar•ma•ture (är′mə-chŏŏr′, -chər) *n.* **1. a.** The principal moving part of an electric machine or device, as the rotating part of a dynamo or the vibrating part of a buzzer. **b.** A piece of soft iron connecting the poles of a magnet. **2.** Armor.

arm•chair (ärm′châr′) *n.* A chair that has supports for the arms.

armed forces (ärmd) *pl.n.* The total military forces of a country.

arm•ful (ärm′fŏŏl′) *n., pl.* **-fuls.** The amount that an arm can hold.

arm•hole (ärm′hōl′) *n.* An opening in a garment for the arm.

ar•mi•stice (är′mĭ-stĭs) *n.* A temporary cessation of combat by mutual consent **:** truce.

arm•let (ärm′lĭt) *n.* A band worn on the upper arm, as for ornament.

ar•moire (ärm-wär′) *n.* A large, often ornate cabinet or wardrobe.

ar•mor (är′mər) *n.* **1.** A defensive covering, as chain mail, worn to protect the body. **2.** The armored vehicles of an army. **—ar′mored** *adj.*

ar•mo•ri•al (är-môr′ē-əl, -mōr′-) *adj.* Of, relating to, or bearing coats of arms.

ar•mor•y (är′mə-rē) *n., pl.* **-ies. 1.** A storehouse for weapons. **2.** A weapons factory.

arm•pit (ärm′pĭt′) *n.* The hollow under the arm where it joins the shoulder.

arm•rest (ärm′rĕst′) *n.* A support for the arm, as on a chair.

ar•my (är′mē) *n., pl.* **-mies. 1.** A body of troops organized for warfare. **2.** *often* **Army.** The total military land forces of a country. **3.** A group of people who organize for a specific cause. **4.** A large number, as of people or animals.

army ant *n.* Any of various ants of the subfamily Dorylinae, which form large nomadic colonies.

ar•ni•ca (är′nĭ-kə) *n.* A plant of the genus *Arnica* with yellow flowers from which a tincture is made that is used for sprains and bruises.

a•ro•ma (ə-rō′mə) *n.* **1.** A distinctive usu. pleasant odor **:** fragrance. **2.** An aura. **—ar′o•mat′ic** (ăr′ə-măt′ĭk) *adj.*

a•rose (ə-rōz′) *v. p.t.* of ARISE.

a•round (ə-round′) *adv.* **1.** On or to all sides. **2.** In a circle or circular motion. **3.** In or toward an opposite direction. **4.** From one place to another **:** here and there. **5.** Close at hand **:** nearby. —*prep.* **1.** On all sides of <roses *around* the fountain> **2.** About the circumference of so as to encircle <rode *around* the island in a boat> **3.** Close by **:** near <the suburbs *around* the city> **4.** On or to the farther side of <a store just *around* the corner> **5.** *In-*

formal. At approximately : near <came *around* 7 o'clock>

a•rouse (ə-rouz') *v.* **a•roused, a•rous•ing. 1.** To wake up from or as if from sleep. **2.** To stir up : excite. **—a•rous'al** *n.*

ar•peg•gi•o (är-pĕj'ē-ō', -pĕj'ō) *n., pl.* **-os.** A chord whose tones are sounded in quick succession rather than simultaneously.

ar•raign (ə-rān') *v.* **1.** *Law.* To call before a court to answer an indictment. **2.** To accuse : charge. **—ar•raign'ment** *n.*

ar•range (ə-rānj') *v.* **-ranged, -rang•ing. 1.** To put into a specific order or relation. **2.** To plan or prepare (for). **3.** To agree about : settle. **4.** To reset (music) for instruments or voices different from those for which it was orig. composed. **—ar•range'ment** *n.* **—ar•rang'er** *n.*

ar•rant (ăr'ənt) *adj.* Being completely such : out-and-out <an *arrant* liar>

ar•ras (ăr'əs) *n.* **1.** A tapestry. **2.** A wall hanging of tapestry.

ar•ray (ə-rā') *v.* **1.** To arrange or draw up, as troops in battle order. **2.** To dress or decorate in finery : adorn. —*n.* **1.** An arraying, as of troops. **2.** An impressive group. **3.** Magnificent attire : finery.

ar•rears (ə-rîrz') *pl.n.* **1.** Debts that are overdue. **2.** The condition of not having fulfilled contracted obligations on time <rent in *arrears*> **—ar•rear'age** *n.*

ar•rest (ə-rĕst') *v.* **1.** To check or stop the motion or growth of. **2.** To seize and hold legally. **3.** To engage <*arrested* my attention> —*n.* **1.** The act of arresting. **2.** The condition of being arrested. ★ ***syns:*** APPREHEND, BUST[2], COLLAR, DETAIN, NAB, PICK UP, PINCH, RUN IN, SEIZE

ar•rest•ing (ə-rĕs'tĭng) *adj.* Attracting and holding the attention : striking.

ar•rhyth•mi•a (ə-rĭ*th*'mē-ə) *n.* An irregularity in the force or rhythm of the heartbeat.

ar•ri•ère-pen•sée (ăr'ē-âr'päN-sā') *n.* An ulterior motive.

ar•ri•val (ə-rī'vəl) *n.* **1.** The act of arriving. **2.** One that arrives.

ar•rive (ə-rīv') *v.* **-rived, -riv•ing. 1.** To get to a destination. **2.** To take place <The day of victory has *arrived.*> **3.** To attain recognition or success.

ar•ro•gant (ăr'ə-gənt) *adj.* Overbearing and self-important : haughty. ★ ***syns:*** DISDAINFUL, HAUGHTY, INSOLENT, LOFTY, LORDLY, OVERBEARING, OVERWEENING, PRESUMPTUOUS, PROUD, SUPERCILIOUS, SUPERIOR **—ar'ro•gance** *n.* **—ar'ro•gant•ly** *adv.*

ar•ro•gate (ăr'ə-gāt') *v.* **-gat•ed, -gat•ing.** To claim, take, or assume for oneself without right. **—ar'ro•ga'tion** *n.*

ar•row (ăr'ō) *n.* **1.** A straight, thin shaft for shooting from a bow, usu. with a pointed head at the tip end and feathers at the other end. **2.** A sign or symbol with the shape of an arrow for indicating direction.

ar•row•head (ăr'ō-hĕd') *n.* The pointed tip of an arrow.

ar•row•root (ăr'ō-rōōt', -rŏŏt') *n.* A tropical American plant, *Maranta arundinacea,* with roots from which an edible starch is derived.

ar•roy•o (ə-roi'ō) *n., pl.* **-os.** A channel or gully eroded by a stream.

ar•se•nal (är'sə-nəl) *n.* **1.** A place for storing and manufacturing arms and ammunition. **2.** A supply or stock.

ar•se•nic (är'sə-nĭk) *n. Symbol* **As** A highly poisonous metallic element used in insecticides, weed killers, etc. **—ar•sen'i•cal** (-sĕn'ĭ-kəl) *adj. & n.* **—ar•se'ni•ous** (-sē'nē-əs) *adj.*

ar•son (är'sən) *n.* The crime of maliciously setting fire to property. **—ar'son•ist** *n.*

art[1] (ärt) *n.* **1. a.** Creative or imaginative activity, esp. the expressive arrangement of elements within a medium. **b.** Works, as paintings, that result from this creativity. **2.** A field or category of artistic activity, as literature, music, or ballet. **3.** A nonscientific branch of learning, esp. one of the humanities. **4.** A trade or craft and the methods employed in it. **5.** A practical skill : knack. **6.** The quality of being cunning : artfulness.

art[2] (ərt; ärt *when stressed*) *v. archaic 2nd person sing. present tense of* BE.

—art *suff. var. of* -ARD.

art dec•o (ärt dĕk'ō, är) *n.* A style of decorative art of the 1920's and 1930's marked by the use of geometric designs and bright colors.

ar•te•ri•ole (är-tîr'ē-ōl') *n.* A small terminal branch of an artery, esp. one that unites with a capillary. **—ar•te'ri•o'lar** *adj.*

ar•te•ri•o•scle•ro•sis (är-tîr'ē-ō-sklə-rō'sĭs) *n.* A chronic circulatory disease in which the walls of the arteries thicken and harden. **—ar•te'ri•o•scle•rot'ic** (-rŏt'ĭk) *adj.*

ar•ter•y (är'tə-rē) *n., pl.* **-ies. 1.** A blood vessel that carries blood away from the heart. **2.** A major transportation route from which local routes branch. **—ar•te'ri•al** (-tîr'ē-əl) *adj.*

ar•te•sian well (är-tē'zhən) *n.* A well drilled deep enough to reach water that rises to the surface by internal pressure without pumping.

art•ful (ärt'fəl) *adj.* **1.** Clever : ingenious. **2.** Cunning : crafty. **—art'ful•ly** *adv.* **—art'ful•ness** *n.*

ar•thri•tis (är-thrī'tĭs) *n.* Inflammation of a joint or joints. **—ar•thrit'ic** (-thrĭt'ĭk) *adj.* **—ar•thrit'i•cal•ly** *adv.*

ar•thro•pod (är'thrə-pŏd') *n.* Any of numerous invertebrates of the phylum Arthropoda including insects, crustaceans, arachnids, and myriapods.

ar•ti•choke (är'tĭ-chōk') *n.* A thistlelike plant *Cynara scolymus,* bearing an edible flower head with fleshy scalelike bracts.

ar•ti•cle (är'tĭ-kəl) *n.* **1.** An individual thing : item. **2.** A separate section of a written document. **3.** A nonfictional composition in a publication. **4.** A word, as *a* or *the,* that is used to signal nouns and to specify their applications.

ar•tic•u•lar (är-tĭk'yə-lər) *adj.* Of or relating to an anatomical joint.

ar•tic•u•late (är-tĭk'yə-lĭt) *adj.* **1.** Endowed with the power of speech. **2.** Spoken clearly and distinctly. **3.** Capable of, speaking in, or characterized by clear, effective language. **4.** *Biol.* Jointed **:** segmented. —*v.* (-lāt') **-lat•ed, -lat•ing. 1.** To utter clearly. **2.** To express in words. **3.** To connect by a joint. **—ar•tic'u•late•ly** *adv.* **—ar•tic'u•late•ness** *n.* **—ar•tic'-u•la'tion** *n.* **—ar•tic'u•la•to'ry** *adj.*

ar•ti•fact (är'tə-făkt') *n.* An object, as a tool, produced by human craft, esp. one of historical interest.

ar•ti•fice (är'tə-fĭs) *n.* **1.** A crafty stratagem **:** trick. **2.** Deception **:** trickery. **3.** Cleverness **:** ingenuity.

ar•tif•i•cer (är-tĭf'ĭ-sər) *n.* **1.** A skilled craftsperson. **2.** An inventor.

ar•ti•fi•cial (är'tə-fĭsh'əl) *adj.* **1.** Made by human beings, rather than occurring in nature. **2.** Not natural or genuine **:** pretended. ★ ***syns:*** ERSATZ, MANMADE, SYNTHETIC **—ar'ti•fi'ci•al'i•ty** (-ē-ăl'ĭ-tē) *n.* **—ar'ti•fi'-cial•ly** *adv.*

artificial respiration *n.* A method used to restore normal breathing in an asphyxiated person by rhythmically forcing air into and out of the lungs.

ar•til•ler•y (är-tĭl'ə-rē) *n.* **1.** Large-caliber mounted firing weapons, as cannon. **2.** The army branch specializing in the use of artillery.

ar•ti•san (är'tĭ-zən, -sən) *n.* A manually skilled worker.

art•ist (är'tĭst) *n.* **1.** A practitioner of the fine arts, esp. a painter, sculptor, or musician. **2.** One, esp. a public performer, whose work shows great skill.

ar•tis•tic (är-tĭs'tĭk) *adj.* Showing great skill and artistry. **—ar•tis'ti•cal•ly** *adv.*

art•ist•ry (är'tĭ-strē) *n.* Artistic ability, quality, or craft.

art•less (ärt'lĭs) *adj.* **1.** Without guile or deceit **:** ingenuous. **2.** Free of artificiality **:** natural. **3.** Lacking skill or art **:** crude. **—art'-less•ly** *adv.* **—art'less•ness** *n.*

art nou•veau (är'nōō-vō', ärt') *n.* A style of decorative art of the late 19th and early 20th cent., characterized by the use of flowing, sinuous lines.

art•y (är'tē) *adj.* **-i•er, -i•est.** Affectedly or showily artistic. **—art'i•ly** *adv.* **—art'i•ness** *n.*

ar•um (ăr'əm, âr'-) *n.* A plant of the genus *Arum* bearing small flowers on a clublike spike surrounded by a leaflike part.

-ary *suff.* **1.** Of or pertaining to <bacill*ary*> **2.** One that pertains to or is connected with <bound*ary*>

Ar•y•an (ăr'ē-ən, âr'-) *n.* **1.** A member of the prehistoric people that spoke Indo-European. **2.** In Nazism, a non-Jewish Caucasian, esp. one of Nordic type. **—Ar'y•an** *adj.*

†as (ăz; əz *when unstressed*) *adv.* **1.** To the same degree or extent **:** equally <*as* soft as silk> **2.** For example <fragrant flowers, *as* roses> —*conj.* **1.** To the same degree or extent that <soft *as* silk> **2.** In the same way that <Do *as* I say.> **3.** At the same time that **:** while <The phone rang *as* I sat down to eat.> **4.** Because **:** since <*As* I was sad, I cried.> **5.** That the consequence is <so ambitious *as* to be ruthless> **6.** Though <Stupid *as* he is, he got the job.> —*pron.* **1.** That which **:** who <asked the same question *as* you> **2.** A fact that <He's ashamed, *as* you can see.> **3.** *Regional.* Who or which <Those *as* are willing can help clean up.> —*prep.* In the role, capacity, or function of <This will serve *as* a warning.>

As *symbol for* ARSENIC.

as•a•fet•i•da (ăs'ə-fĕt'ĭ-də) *n.* A malodorous plant resin formerly used medicinally.

as•bes•tos (ăs-bĕs'təs, ăz-) *n.* An incombustible, chemical-resistant fibrous mineral used esp. for fireproofing and electrical insulation.

as•bes•to•sis (ăs'bĕs-tō'sĭs, ăz'-) *n.* Chronic lung inflammation caused by prolonged inhalation of asbestos particles.

as•cend (ə-sĕnd') *v.* **1.** To move upward (along) **:** climb. **2.** To succeed to <*ascended* the throne>

as•cen•dant *also* **as•cen•dent** (ə-sĕn'dənt) *adj.* **1.** Moving upward **:** climbing. **2.** Dominant. —*n.* The condition of being dominant. **—as•cen'dan•cy** *n.*

as•cen•sion (ə-sĕn'shən) *n.* **1.** The act of ascending. **2. Ascension.** The 40th day after Easter, celebrating the ascent of Jesus into heaven.

as•cent (ə-sĕnt') *n.* **1.** The act of moving upward **:** climb. **2.** An upward slope.

as•cer•tain (ăs'ər-tān') *v.* To learn by investigating or examining. **—as'cer•tain'a•ble** *adj.* **—as'cer•tain'ment** *n.*

as•cet•ic (ə-sĕt'ĭk) *n.* One who practices rigid self-denial, esp. as a religious act. **—as•cet'ic** *adj.* **—as•cet'i•cism** *n.*

a•scor•bic acid (ə-skôr'bĭk) *n.* A vitamin found in citrus fruits and leafy green vegetables and used to prevent scurvy **:** vitamin C.

as•cot (ăs'kət, -kŏt') *n.* A wide tie or scarf whose ends are laid flat one over the other.

as•cribe (ə-skrīb') *v.* **-cribed, -crib•ing.** To explain as arising from a particular cause, source, or origin **:** attribute. **—as•crib'a•ble** *adj.* **—as•crip'tion** (ə-skrĭp'shən) *n.*

a•sep•tic (ə-sĕp'tĭk, ā-) *adj.* Free of pathogenic organisms. **—a•sep'sis** *n.*

a•sex•u•al (ā-sĕk'shōō-əl) *adj.* **1.** Having no sex or sex organs **:** sexless. **2.** Of or relating to reproduction without the union of male and female gametes. **—a•sex'u•al'i•ty** (-ăl'ĭ-tē) *n.*

ash[1] (ăsh) *n.* **1.** The solid material remaining when something is burned. **2.** Pulverized particulate matter from a volcano. **3. ashes.** Human remains.

ash[2] (ăsh) *n.* Any of various trees of the genus *Fraxinus,* having compound leaves and yielding strong, durable wood.

a•shamed (ə-shāmd') *adj.* **1.** Feeling shame. **2.** Reluctant through fear of shame <*ashamed* to admit the truth> **—a•sham'ed•ly** *adv.*

ash•en (ăsh'ən) *adj.* Resembling the color of ashes **:** pale.

ash•lar (ăsh′lər) *n.* **1.** A squared building stone. **2.** Masonry of ashlar.

a•shore (ə-shôr′, ə-shōr′) *adv.* To or on the shore.

ash•ram (äsh′rəm) *n.* A religious retreat, esp. of a Hindu philosopher.

ash•tray (ăsh′trā′) *n.* A receptacle for tobacco ashes.

Ash Wednesday *n.* The first day of Lent.

ash•y (ăsh′ē) *adj.* **-i•er, -i•est. 1.** Of or pertaining to ashes. **2.** Of the color of ashes : ashen.

Asian American *n.* A U.S. citizen or resident of Asian descent. **—A′sian-A•mer′i•can** *adj.*

a•side (ə-sīd′) *adv.* **1.** To or toward one side. **2.** Apart. **3.** In reserve **:** away. **—***n.* A line spoken by an actor that other actors on stage are not supposed to hear.

aside from *prep.* **1.** Except for **:** excluding. **2.** In addition to **:** besides.

as if *conj.* **1.** Just as it would be if <It was *as if* he had said nothing.> **2.** That <seemed *as if* we should eat>

as•i•nine (ăs′ə-nīn′) *adj.* Stupid or silly **:** foolish. **—as′i•nin′i•ty** (-nĭn′ĭ-tē) *n.*

ask (ăsk, äsk) *v.* **1.** To put a question to. **2.** To inquire (about). **3.** To request (of). **4.** To demand. **5.** To invite.

a•skance (ə-skăns′) *adv.* **1.** With a sidelong look. **2.** With suspicion or distrust.

a•skew (ə-skyo͞o′) *adv. & adj.* To one side **:** awry.

a•slant (ə-slănt′) *adv. & adj.* At a slant.

a•sleep (ə-slēp′) *adj.* **1.** In or into a condition of sleep. **2.** Inactive. **3.** Numb. **—a•sleep′** *adv.*

a•so•cial (ā-sō′shəl) *adj.* **1.** Shunning the society of others. **2.** Incapable of interacting adequately with others.

as of *prep.* On **:** at **:** from <at home *as of* Dec. 1>

asp (ăsp) *n.* Any of several small venomous African or Eurasian snakes.

as•par•a•gus (ə-spăr′ə-gəs) *n.* A plant, *Asparagus officinalis,* having leaflike stems, scalelike leaves, and succulent, edible young stalks.

as•pect (ăs′pĕkt′) *n.* **1.** Look **:** appearance. **2.** Phase **:** facet. **3.** A position or side facing a given direction.

as•pen (ăs′pən) *n.* Any of several trees of the genus *Populus* with leaves that flutter in even a light breeze.

as•per•i•ty (ă-spĕr′ĭ-tē) *n.* **1.** Roughness **:** harshness. **2.** Ill temper **:** irritability.

as•perse (ə-spûrs′) *v.* **-persed, -pers•ing.** To make false charges or insinuations against **:** malign. **—as•per′sion** *n.*

as•phalt (ăs′fôlt′) *n.* A thick, sticky brownish-black mixture of petroleum tars used in paving and roofing.

as•pho•del (ăs′fə-dĕl′) *n.* Any of several Mediterranean plants of the genera *Asphodeline* and *Asphodelus,* bearing white or yellow flower clusters.

as•phyx•i•a (ăs-fĭk′sē-ə) *n.* Unconsciousness or death caused by a lack of oxygen or an increase of carbon dioxide in the blood. **—as•phyx′i•ant** *n.*

as•phyx•i•ate (ăs-fĭk′sē-āt′) *v.* **-at•ed, -at•ing.** To suffocate. **—as•phyx′i•a′tion** *n.*

as•pic (ăs′pĭk) *n.* A jelly made from meat, fish, or vegetable juices.

as•pi•rant (ăs′pər-ənt, ə-spīr′-) *n.* One who aspires. **—as′pi•rant** *adj.*

as•pi•rate (ăs′pər-ĭt) *n.* **1.** The speech sound represented by the *h* in *happy.* **2.** A speech sound followed by a puff of breath. **—as′pi•rate′** (-pə-rāt′) *v.*

as•pi•ra•tion (ăs′pə-rā′shən) *n.* **1. a.** A strong desire for high achievement or the realization of an ideal. **b.** An object of this desire **:** goal. **2. a.** The pronunciation of an aspirate. **b.** An aspirate. **3.** The removal of a liquid or gas with an aspirator.

as•pi•ra•tor (ăs′pə-rā′tər) *n.* A device that removes liquids or gases from a space by suction.

as•pire (ə-spīr′) *v.* **-pired, -pir•ing.** To have ambition. **—as•pir′ing•ly** *adv.*

as•pi•rin (ăs′pər-ĭn, -prĭn) *n.* **1.** A white crystalline compound derived from salicylic acid and used for the relief of pain and reduction of fever. **2.** A tablet of aspirin.

ass (ăs) *n.* **1.** A hoofed mammal of the genus *Equus* that resembles and is related to the horse, esp. the domesticated donkey. **2.** A foolish or stupid person.

as•sail (ə-sāl′) *v.* **1.** To attack with violence. **2.** To attack verbally. **—as•sail′a•ble** *adj.* **—as•sail′ant** *n.* **—as•sail′er** *n.*

as•sas•sin (ə-săs′ĭn) *n.* A murderer, esp. of a prominent person.

as•sas•si•nate (ə-săs′ə-nāt′) *v.* **-nat•ed, -nat•ing.** To murder, esp. for political reasons. **—as•sas′si•na′tion** *n.*

as•sault (ə-sôlt′) *n.* **1.** A violent verbal or physical attack. **2.** *Law.* An unlawful attempt or threat to do physical injury to another. **—as•sault′** *v.* **—as•sault′er** *n.*

assault rifle *n.* An automatic or semiautomatic rifle designed for use in military attacks.

as•say (ăs′ā′, ă-sā′) *n.* Chemical analysis of a substance, esp. of an ore or drug. **—***v.* (ă-sā′, ăs′ā′). **1.** To subject to a chemical analysis. **2.** To assess **:** evaluate. **3.** To attempt **:** try. **—as•say′er** *n.*

as•sem•blage (ə-sĕm′blĭj) *n.* **1.** The act of assembling. **2.** A collection of people or things. **3.** A sculpture made from miscellaneous objects, as metal scraps, pieces of cloth, string, etc.

as•sem•ble (ə-sĕm′bəl) *v.* **-bled, -bling. 1.** To bring or come together as a group. **2.** To put together the parts of. **—as•sem′bler** *n.*

as•sem•bly (ə-sĕm′blē) *n., pl.* **-blies. 1.** A group of persons gathered together **:** meeting. **2. Assembly.** A lower legislative house. **3. a.** The putting together of parts, as of a machine. **b.** The assembled set of parts. **4.** A signal calling troops to form ranks.

assembly language *n. Computer Sci.* A programming language that is a close approximation of machine code.

assembly line *n.* An arrangement of workers and equipment in which work passes successively from operation to operation to make a completed product.

as•sem•bly•man (ə-sĕm′blē-mən) *n.* A man who is a member of an Assembly.

as•sem•bly•wom•an (ə-sĕm′blē-wo͝om′-ən) *n.* A woman who is a member of an Assembly.

as•sent (ə-sĕnt′) *v.* To express agreement : acquiesce. **—as•sent′** *n.*

as•sert (ə-sûrt′) *v.* **1.** To declare positively : avow. **2.** To defend : maintain. ★ ***syns:*** AFFIRM, AVER, AVOUCH, AVOW, DECLARE, HOLD, MAINTAIN, STATE **—as•ser′tion** *n.* **—as•ser′tive** *adj.* **—as•ser′tive•ly** *adv.* **—as•ser′tive•ness** *n.*

as•sess (ə-sĕs′) *v.* **1.** To assign a value to, esp. for taxation. **2.** To fix the amount of (e.g., a tax). **3.** To subject to a special payment, as a tax. **—as•sess′ment** *n.* **—as•ses′sor** *n.* **—as′ses•so′ri•al** *adj.*

as•set (ăs′ĕt′) *n.* **1.** A valuable possession or quality : resource. **2. assets.** All the property of a person or a business that can be applied to cover liabilities.

as•sev•er•ate (ə-sĕv′ə-rāt′) *v.* **-at•ed, -at•ing.** To state seriously and positively : affirm. **—as•sev′er•a′tion** *n.*

as•sid•u•ous (ə-sĭj′o͞o-əs) *adj.* Constantly attentive : diligent. **—as′si•du′i•ty** (ăs′ĭ-do͞o′-ĭ-tē, -dyo͞o′-) *n.* **—as•sid′u•ous•ly** *adv.* **—as•sid′u•ous•ness** *n.*

as•sign (ə-sīn′) *v.* **1.** To fix : designate <*assign* a day for the test> **2.** To appoint, as to a duty. **3.** To give out : allot. **4.** To attribute : ascribe. **5.** *Law.* To transfer (e.g., property). **—as•sign′a•ble** *adj.* **—as•sign′er** *n.*

as•sig•na•tion (ăs′ĭg-nā′shən) *n.* An arrangement for a tryst between lovers.

as•sign•ment (ə-sīn′mənt) *n.* **1.** The act of assigning. **2.** Something assigned.

as•sim•i•late (ə-sĭm′ə-lāt′) *v.* **-lat•ed, -lat•ing. 1.** *Physiol.* To consume and incorporate into the body : digest. **2.** To take into the mind : understand. **3.** To make or become similar. **4.** To absorb (e.g., a culturally distinct group) into the prevailing culture. **—as•sim′i•la′tion** *n.*

as•sist (ə-sĭst′) *v.* To help : aid. *—n.* **1.** An act of assisting. **2.** A player's maneuver enabling a teammate to put out an opponent, as in baseball, or score a goal, as in hockey. **—as•sis′tance** *n.* **—as•sis′tant** *n.*

as•size (ə-sīz′) *n.* **1.** A judicial inquest. **2. assizes.** A court session held periodically in English and Welsh counties.

as•so•ci•ate (ə-sō′shē-āt′, -sē-) *v.* **-at•ed, -at•ing. 1.** To join in a relationship. **2.** To link in the imagination or mind. *—n.* (-ĭt). **1.** A colleague or partner. **2.** A companion : comrade. **—as•so′ci•ate** (-ĭt, -āt′) *adj.*

as•so•ci•a•tion (ə-sō′sē-ā′shən, -shē-) *n.* **1.** The act of associating. **2.** An organized body of persons : society.

association football *n. esp. Brit.* Soccer.

as•so•ci•a•tive (ə-sō′shē-ā′tĭv, -sē-, -shə-tĭv) *adj.* Of, relating to, or marked by association.

as•so•nance (ăs′ə-nəns) *n.* Repetition of vowel sounds, esp. in poetry.

as•sort (ə-sôrt′) *v.* To separate into groups of a like kind : classify.

as•sort•ed (ə-sôr′tĭd) *adj.* Consisting of different kinds : various.

as•sort•ment (ə-sôrt′mənt) *n.* A collection of various persons or things : variety.

as•suage (ə-swāj′) *v.* **-suaged, -suag•ing. 1.** To make less intense : ease. **2.** To satisfy.

as•sume (ə-so͞om′) *v.* **-sumed, -sum•ing. 1.** To take upon oneself : undertake <*assume* the payments> **2.** To affect : feign <*assumed* an attitude of indifference> **3.** To take for granted without proof : suppose. **—as•sum′a•ble** *adj.* **—as•sum′a•bly** *adv.* **—as•sum′ed•ly** *adv.*

as•sump•tion (ə-sŭmp′shən) *n.* **1.** The act of assuming. **2.** An idea or statement assumed to be true without proof : supposition. **3. Assumption.** *Theol.* The ascent of the Virgin Mary into heaven after her death, celebrated Aug. 15.

as•sur•ance (ə-sho͝or′əns) *n.* **1.** A statement intended to inspire confidence : guarantee. **2. a.** Certainty. **b.** Self-confidence. **3.** Audacity : boldness.

as•sure (ə-sho͝or′) *v.* **-sured, -sur•ing. 1.** To inform confidently. **2.** To cause to feel confident : convince. **3.** To make sure the realization of : ensure.

as•ta•tine (ăs′tə-tēn′, -tĭn) *n. Symbol* **At** A highly unstable radioactive element.

as•ter (ăs′tər) *n.* A plant of the genus *Aster,* with white to bluish, purple, or pink daisy-like flowers.

as•ter•isk (ăs′tə-rĭsk′) *n.* A character (*) used to indicate an omission of letters or words or a reference to a footnote.

a•stern (ə-stûrn′) *adv. & adj.* **1.** Behind a ship or vessel. **2.** Toward the rear of a ship or aircraft.

as•ter•oid (ăs′tə-roid′) *n.* Any of numerous small celestial bodies with orbits lying mainly between Mars and Jupiter. **—as′ter•oid′al** *adj.*

asth•ma (ăz′mə) *n.* An often allergic respiratory disease marked by labored breathing, chest constriction, and coughing. **—asth•mat′ic** (-măt′ĭk) *n. & adj.*

a•stig•ma•tism (ə-stĭg′mə-tĭz′əm) *n.* A defect of a lens, esp. of a lens of the eye, that causes faulty focusing. **—as′tig•mat′ic** (ăs′-tĭg-măt′ĭk) *adj.*

a•stir (ə-stûr′) *adj.* **1.** Being in motion. **2.** Out of bed : awake.

as to *prep.* **1.** Concerning : about <no idea *as to* what he meant> **2.** According to : by <rewarded *as to* talent>

as•ton•ish (ə-stŏn′ĭsh) *v.* To fill with sudden wonder : surprise greatly. —**as•ton'ish•ing•ly** *adv.* —**as•ton'ish•ment** *n.*

as•tound (ə-stound') *v.* To strike with confused wonder.

a•strad•dle (ə-străd'l) *adv. & prep.* In a straddling position : astride.

as•tra•khan (ăs'trə-kăn', -kən) *n.* The curly fur of a young lamb from the region of Astrakhan in SW Russia.

as•tral (ăs'trəl) *adj.* Of, relating to, emanating from, or resembling the stars.

a•stray (ə-strā') *adv.* **1.** Away from the right direction or path. **2.** Away from the morally right or good.

a•stride (ə-strīd') *prep.* With a leg on each side of. —**a•stride'** *adv.*

as•trin•gent (ə-strĭn'jənt) *adj.* Capable of drawing together or constricting tissue : styptic. —*n.* An astringent agent. —**as•trin'gen•cy** *n.*

as•tro•bi•ol•o•gy (ăs'trō-bī-ŏl'ə-jē) *n.* Exobiology.

as•tro•dome (ăs'trə-dōm') *n.* A stadium covered by a dome.

as•tro•dy•nam•ics (ăs'trō-dī-năm'ĭks) *n. (sing. in number).* The dynamics of celestial bodies.

as•tro•labe (ăs'trə-lāb') *n.* An instrument formerly used by mariners to determine the altitude of a celestial body.

as•trol•o•gy (ə-strŏl'ə-jē) *n.* The study of the supposed influence of planets and stars on the course of human affairs. —**as•trol'o•ger** *n.* —**as'tro•log'ic** (ăs'trə-lŏj'ĭk), **as'tro•log'i•cal** *adj.*

as•tro•naut (ăs'trə-nôt') *n.* Someone, esp. a crew member, who travels in a spacecraft.

as•tro•nau•tics (ăs'trə-nô'tĭks) *n. (sing. in number).* The science and technology of the design, construction, and operation of spacecraft. —**as'tro•nau'tic, as'tro•nau'ti•cal** *adj.* —**as'tro•nau'ti•cal•ly** *adv.*

as•tro•nom•i•cal (ăs'trə-nŏm'ĭ-kəl) *or* **as•tro•nom•ic** (-nŏm'ĭk) *adj.* **1.** Of or relating to astronomy. **2.** Unimaginably large : immense. —**as'tro•nom'i•cal•ly** *adv.*

astronomical unit *n.* A unit of distance equal to the average distance between the earth and the sun, about 150 million km or 93 million mi.

as•tron•o•my (ə-strŏn'ə-mē) *n.* The scientific study of the positions, distribution, motion, and composition of celestial bodies. —**as•tron'o•mer** *n.*

as•tro•phys•ics (ăs'trə-fĭz'ĭks) *n. (sing. in number).* The physics of stellar phenomena. —**as'tro•phys'i•cal** *adj.* —**as'tro•phys'i•cist** (-fĭz'ĭ-sĭst) *n.*

As•tro•turf (ăs'trō-tûrf'). A trademark for an artificial grasslike ground covering.

as•tute (ə-sto͞ot', ə-styo͞ot') *adj.* Keen in discernment : shrewd. —**as•tute'ly** *adv.* —**as•tute'ness** *n.*

a•sun•der (ə-sŭn'dər) *adv.* **1.** Into separate parts. **2.** Apart from each other in position.

a•sy•lum (ə-sī'ləm) *n.* **1.** An institution for the care of the sick or needy. **2.** A place of sanctuary. **3.** Governmental protection granted to a foreign political refugee.

a•sym•met•ric (ā'sĭ-mĕt'rĭk) *or* **a•sym•met•ri•cal** (-rĭ-kəl) *adj.* Not symmetrical. —**a•sym'me•try** (ā-sĭm'ĭ-trē) *n.*

as•ymp•tote (ăs'ĭm-tōt', -ĭmp-) *n.* A straight line that is approached but never met by a point on a curve as the point moves an infinite distance from the origin. —**as'ymp•tot'ic** (-tŏt'ĭk), **as'ymp•tot'i•cal** *adj.* —**as'ymp•tot'i•cal•ly** *adv.*

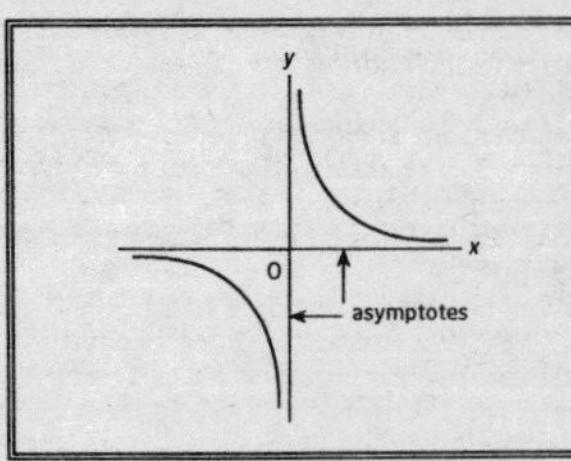

asymptote
Asymptotes of a hyperbola; xy = 1

at[1] (ăt; ət *when unstressed*) *prep.* **1.** Used to indicate position, location, or condition <*at* school><*at* peace> **2.** —Used to indicate direction or aim <smiled *at* him> **3.** —Used to indicate a point in time <*at* dawn> **4.** —Used to indicate manner, means, or reason <angry *at* his arrogance>

at[2] (ät) *n., pl.* **at.** —See table at CURRENCY.

At *symbol for* ASTATINE.

at all *adv.* In any way whatever <can't hear it *at all*>

at•a•vism (ăt'ə-vĭz'əm) *n.* The reappearance in an organism of a hereditary characteristic absent for several generations. —**at'a•vis'tic** (-vĭs'tĭk) *adj.*

ate (āt) *v. p.t. of* EAT.

at•el•ier (ăt'l-yā') *n.* **1.** A workshop. **2.** The studio of an artist.

Ath•a•bas•kan *or* **Ath•a•bas•can** (ăth'ə-băs'kən) *also* **Ath•a•pas•can** (-păs'-) *n.* **1.** A group of related American Indian languages including Navajo, Apache, and languages of NW Canada. **2.** A member of an Athabaskan-speaking people.

a•the•ism (ā'thē-ĭz'əm) *n.* Denial of or disbelief in the existence of God. —**a'the•ist** *n.* —**a'the•is'tic** *adj.*

A•the•na (ə-thē'nə) *also* **A•the•ne** (-nē) *n.* *Gk. Myth.* The goddess of wisdom.

ath•e•nae•um *also* **ath•e•ne•um** (ăth'ə-nē'əm) *n.* A library.

ath•er•o•scle•ro•sis (ăth'ə-rō-sklə-rō'sĭs) *n.* Arteriosclerosis marked by the deposit of plaque containing cholesterol and lipids on the inner walls of the arteries.

a•thirst (ə-thûrst') *adj.* Eager : desirous.

ath•lete (ăth'lēt') *n.* One who participates in competitive sports.

ath•lete's foot *n.* A contagious skin infection caused by a fungus and affecting esp. the feet.

ath•let•ic (ăth-lĕt'ĭk) *adj.* **1.** Of, relating to, or for athletics or athletes. **2.** Physically strong : sturdy. **—ath•let'i•cal•ly** *adv.*

ath•let•ics (ăth-lĕt'ĭks) *n. (sing. or pl. in number).* Activities and exercises that require physical endurance, skill, and strength, esp. competitive sports.

a•thwart (ə-thwôrt') *adv.* From side to side : across. *—prep.* **1.** From one side to the other of : across. **2.** In conflict with : against.

a•tilt (ə-tĭlt') *adj. & adv.* Tilted or inclined upward.

–ation *suff.* **1.** Action : process <strangul*ation*> **2.** The result of an action or process <accultur*ation*>

–ative *suff.* Of, relating to, or associated with <talk*ative*>

at•las (ăt'ləs) *n.* A book of maps.

ATM *n.* An automated teller machine.

at•mos•phere (ăt'mə-sfîr') *n.* **1.** The gaseous mass surrounding a celestial body, esp. the earth. **2.** Environment : surroundings. **3.** *Physics.* A unit of pressure equal to 1.01325×10^5 newtons per sq m. **4.** A predominant feeling : mood. **—at'mos•pher'ic** (-sfĕr'ĭk, -sfîr'-) *adj.* **—at'mos•pher'i•cal•ly** *adv.*

at•mos•pher•ics (ăt'mə-sfĕr'ĭks, -sfîr'-) *n. (sing. in number).* **1.** Electromagnetic radiation produced by natural phenomena such as lightning. **2.** Radio interference caused by this radiation.

at•oll (ăt'ôl', -ŏl', ā'tôl', ā'tŏl') *n.* A coral island that forms a ring and partially or totally encloses a lagoon.

at•om (ăt'əm) *n.* **1.** A very small particle : bit. **2.** *Physics & Chem.* The smallest unit of an element, typically indivisible in chemical reactions except for some removal or exchange of particular electrons.

atom bomb *n.* An atomic bomb.

a•tom•ic (ə-tŏm'ĭk) *adj.* **1.** Of or relating to an atom, atomic bombs, or atomic energy. **2.** Extremely small : infinitesimal.

atomic bomb *n.* A bomb whose great destructive power is from the energy released in the fission of heavy atomic nuclei, as of uranium 235.

atomic clock *n.* A device that keeps precise time by counting the occurrences of something that happens in an atomic or molecular system at regular intervals.

atomic energy *n.* Energy released as a result of reactions involving atomic nuclei.

atomic number *n.* The number of protons in an atomic nucleus of an element.

atomic pile *n.* A nuclear reactor.

atomic weight *n.* The average weight of an atom of an element.

at•om•ize (ăt'ə-mīz') *v.* **-ized, -iz•ing.** To separate into tiny particles.

at•om•iz•er (ăt'ə-mī'zər) *n.* A device for producing a fine spray, as of medicine or perfume.

atom smasher *n. Physics.* A subatomic particle accelerator.

a•ton•al (ā-tō'nəl) *adj. Mus.* Lacking a traditional key or tonality. **—a'to•nal'i•ty** *n.* **—a•ton'al•ly** *adv.*

a•tone (ə-tōn') *v.* **a•toned, a•ton•ing.** To make amends (for).

▲ ***word history:*** The derivation of *atone,* from *at* and *one,* has been obscured somewhat by the fairly recent change in the pronunciation of *one. One* used to be pronounced like *own,* but since the 17th cent. it has been pronounced like *won,* the past tense of *win.* The older pronunciation survives in *alone, lone, lonely,* and *only* in addition to *atone* and its derivatives; the new pronunciation occurs in *once.*

a•tone•ment (ə-tōn'mənt) *n.* Amends made for an injury, wrong, or sin.

a•top (ə-tŏp') *prep.* On top of.

–ator *suff.* One that acts in a particular manner <radi*ator*>

–atory *suff.* **1. a.** Of or pertaining to <perspir*atory*> **b.** Tending to <amend*atory*> **2.** One connected to or with <reform*atory*>

ATP (ā'tē-pē') *n.* A nucleotide obtained from adenosine that supplies energy to cells through its conversion to ADP.

a•tri•um (ā'trē-əm) *n., pl.* **a•tri•a** (ā'trē-ə) *or* **a•tri•ums. 1.** The central court of an ancient Roman house. **2.** A bodily cavity, esp. one of the chambers of the heart.

a•tro•cious (ə-trō'shəs) *adj.* **1.** Exceedingly evil, savage, or cruel. **2.** Extremely bad : abominable. **—a•tro'cious•ly** *adv.* **—a•tro'cious•ness** *n.*

a•troc•i•ty (ə-trŏs'ĭ-tē) *n., pl.* **-ties. 1.** The state or condition of being atrocious. **2.** An atrocious object or act.

at•ro•phy (ăt'rə-fē) *n., pl.* **-phies.** The wasting away of bodily tissues or organs. *—v.* **-phied, -phy•ing.** To undergo or cause to undergo atrophy : wither. **—a•tro'phic** (ā-trō'fĭk) *adj.*

at•ro•pine (ăt'rə-pēn', -pĭn) *n.* A poisonous alkaloid derived from belladonna and related plants and having various medicinal uses, as dilating the pupil of the eye.

at•tach (ə-tăch') *v.* **1.** To fasten or become fastened : affix. **2.** To bind by personal ties, as of loyalty or affection. **3.** *Law.* To seize (property) by legal writ. ★ ***syns:*** AFFIX, CLIP, CONNECT, COUPLE, FASTEN, FIX, SECURE **—at•tach'a•ble** *adj.* **—at•tach'er** *n.*

at•ta•ché (ăt'ə-shā', ă-tă'shā') *n.* An expert in a particular area assigned to the staff of an embassy <a cultural *attaché*>

attaché case *n.* A briefcase that has hinges and flat sides and is similar to a small suitcase.

at•tach•ment (ə-tăch'mənt) *n.* **1.** Something that fastens one thing to another. **2.** A tie of loyalty or affection. **3.** A supplementary part, as of an appliance : accessory. **4.** The seizure of property by legal writ.

at•tack (ə-tăk') *v.* **1.** To set upon with violent physical or verbal force : assail. **2.** To begin work on, esp. with vigor. ★ *syns:* ASSAIL, ASSAULT, BESET, STRIKE —*n.* **1.** The act of attacking : assault. **2.** The onset of disease, esp. when sudden. —**at•tack'er** *n.*

at•tain (ə-tān') *v.* **1.** To achieve, esp. by effort : accomplish. **2.** To arrive at, as in time. —**at•tain'a•bil'i•ty** *n.* —**at•tain'a•ble** *adj.*

at•tain•der (ə-tān'dər) *n. Law.* The loss of all civil rights by a person who has been sentenced to death or outlawry, esp. for treason.

at•tain•ment (ə-tān'mənt) *n.* **1.** The act of attaining. **2.** Something attained.

at•taint (ə-tānt') *v. Law.* To condemn by a sentence of attainder.

at•tar (ăt'ər) *n.* A fragrant essential oil obtained from flowers.

at•tempt (ə-tĕmpt') *v.* To make an effort : try. —**at•tempt'** *n.*

at•tend (ə-tĕnd') *v.* **1.** To be present (at). **2.** To go with : accompany. **3.** To look after : care for. **4.** To pay attention : heed. **5.** To direct or apply oneself.

at•ten•dance (ə-tĕn'dəns) *n.* **1.** The act of attending. **2.** Those that attend a function.

at•ten•dant (ə-tĕn'dənt) *n.* One who attends another to provide a service. —*adj.* Following or accompanying as a result : concomitant <flu and *attendant* miseries>

at•ten•tion (ə-tĕn'shən) *n.* **1.** Mental concentration. **2.** Observation : notice. **3. attentions.** Acts of courtesy, consideration, or gallantry. **4.** A military posture with arms at the side, heels together, and eyes to the front. —**at•ten'tive** *adj.* —**at•ten'tive•ly** *adv.* —**at•ten'tive•ness** *n.*

at•ten•u•ate (ə-tĕn'yo͞o-āt') *v.* **-at•ed, -at•ing. 1.** To make or become fine or thin. **2.** To weaken. —**at•ten'u•a'tion** *n.*

at•test (ə-tĕst') *v.* **1.** To affirm to be genuine by signing one's name as a witness. **2.** To be evidence of. **3.** To give testimony. —**at'tes•ta'tion** *n.*

at•tic (ăt'ĭk) *n.* The room or space directly below the roof of a building.

at•tire (ə-tīr') *v.* **-tired, -tir•ing.** To dress : clothe. —*n.* Dress : clothing.

at•ti•tude (ăt'ĭ-to͞od', -tyo͞od') *n.* **1.** A position of the body or manner of carrying oneself : posture. **2.** A state of feeling or mind about a person or situation. **3.** The orientation of a spacecraft or aircraft relative to a point of reference, as the horizon.

at•ti•tu•di•nize (ăt'i-to͞od'n-īz', -tyo͞od'-) *v.* **-nized, -niz•ing.** To assume an attitude for effect : posture.

at•tor•ney (ə-tûr'nē) *n., pl.* **-neys.** A person, esp. a lawyer, legally appointed to act as agent for another.

attorney general *n., pl.* **attorneys general.** The chief law officer and legal counsel of a state or nation.

at•tract (ə-trăkt') *v.* **1.** To cause to draw near. **2.** To draw to oneself by an appealing quality. **3.** To allure or be alluring. ★ *syns:* ALLURE, APPEAL, DRAW, LURE, MAGNETIZE, PULL —**at•trac'tive** *adj.* —**at•trac'tive•ly** *adv.* —**at•trac'tive•ness** *n.*

at•trac•tion (ə-trăk'shən) *n.* **1.** The act or capability of attracting. **2.** An attractive feature or characteristic. **3.** Something that attracts, as a public entertainment.

at•trib•ute (ə-trĭb'yət) *v.* **-ut•ed, -ut•ing.** To regard or explain as arising or resulting from a source or cause. —*n.* (ăt'rə-byo͞ot'). **1.** A characteristic of a person or thing. **2.** An adjective or term used as an adjective. —**at•trib'ut•a•ble** *adj.* —**at'tri•bu'tion** (at'rə-byo͞o'shən) *n.*

at•trib•u•tive (ə-trĭb'yə-tĭv) *adj.* **1.** Placed directly adjacent to a modified noun without a linking verb <"White" in "white house" is an *attributive* adjective.> **2.** Of or having the nature of an attribution or attribute. —**at•trib'u•tive** *n.* —**at•trib'u•tive•ly** *adv.*

at•trit (ə-trĭt') *v.* **-trit•ted, -trit•ting. 1.** To lose (e.g., personnel) by attrition. **2.** To destroy or kill (e.g., troops).

at•tri•tion (ə-trĭsh'ən) *n.* **1.** An eroding by or as if by friction. **2.** A gradual natural reduction, as in membership or personnel, through retirement, resignation, or death.

at•tune (ə-to͞on', ə-tyo͞on') *v.* **-tuned, -tun•ing.** To bring into accord : harmonize.

a•twit•ter (ə-twĭt'ər) *adj.* Excited.

a•typ•i•cal (ā-tĭp'ĭ-kəl) *adj.* Not typical : uncharacteristic. —**a•typ'i•cal•ly** *adv.*

Au *symbol for* GOLD.

au•burn (ô'bərn) *n.* A reddish brown color. —**au'burn** *adj.*

au cou•rant (ō' ko͞o-räɴ') *adj.* Informed on current affairs : up-to-date.

auc•tion (ôk'shən) *n.* A public sale of items to the highest bidder. —*v.* To sell at auction. —**auc'tion•eer'** *n.*

auction bridge *n.* A variety of the game of bridge in which tricks made in excess of the contract are scored toward game.

auc•to•ri•al (ôk-tôr'ē-əl, -tōr') *adj.* Of or relating to an author.

au•da•cious (ô-dā'shəs) *adj.* **1.** Bold : daring. **2.** Arrogantly impudent : insolent. —**au•da'cious•ly** *adv.* —**au•dac'i•ty** (ô-dăs'ĭ-tē) *n.*

au•di•ble (ô'də-bəl) *adj.* Able to be heard. —**au'di•bil'i•ty** *n.* —**au'di•bly** *adv.*

au•di•ence (ô'dē-əns) *n.* **1.** A body of listeners or spectators. **2.** A formal conference or hearing. **3.** An opportunity to express one's views.

au•di•o (ô'dē-ō') *adj.* Of or relating to sound or sound reproduction. —*n.* **1.** The sound part of television or motion-picture equipment. **2.** The broadcasting or reception of sound.

au•di•o•cas•sette (ô'dē-ō-kə-sĕt') *n.* A cassette containing audiotape.

au•di•ol•o•gy (ô'dē-ŏl'ə-jē) *n.* The study of hearing, esp. of hearing defects and their treatment. —**au'di•o•log'i•cal** (-ə-lŏj'ĭ-kəl) *adj.* —**au'di•ol'o•gist** *n.*

au•di•om•e•ter (ô'dē-ŏm'ĭ-tər) *n.* An instrument for measuring hearing thresholds for pure tones of normally audible frequencies. —**au'di•o•met'ric** (-ə-mĕt'rĭk) —**au'di•om'e•try** *n.*

au·di·o·tape (ô′dē-ō-tāp′) *n.* A magnetic tape recording of sound made for later playback. —*v.* **-taped, -tap·ing.** To record (sound) on magnetic tape.
au·di·o·vis·u·al (ô′dē-ō-vĭzh′o͞o-əl) *adj.* Of, relating to, or involving both hearing and sight.
au·di·o·vis·u·als (ô′dē-ō-vĭzh′o͞o-əlz) *pl.n.* Audiovisual educational materials.
au·dit (ô′dĭt) *n.* An examination or verification of financial records or accounts. —*v.* **1.** To conduct an audit of. **2.** To attend (an academic course) without receiving credit.
au·di·tion (ô-dĭsh′ən) *n.* A hearing, esp. a performance given by an entertainer to demonstrate merit. —*v.* To give or submit to an audition.
au·di·tor (ô′dĭ-tər) *n.* **1.** One who hears; a listener. **2.** One who audits.
au·di·to·ri·um (ô′dĭ-tôr′ē-əm, -tōr′-) *n.* **1.** A room, as in a school, to accommodate an audience. **2.** A building used for public meetings, artistic performances, etc.
au·di·to·ry (ô′dĭ-tôr′ē, -tōr′ē) *adj.* Of or relating to the sense, the organs, or the experience of hearing.
auf Wie·der·seh·en (ouf vē′dər-zān′) *interj.* —Used to express farewell.
au·ger (ô′gər) *n.* A tool used for boring.
▲ ***word history:*** *An auger* was orig. *a nauger.* It is one of the numerous English words that have lost an initial *n* as a result of the incorrect division between the indefinite article and the noun. The Old English word from which *auger* is derived, *nafogār,* is actually a compound word made up of *nafu,* "wheel hub" (related to *navel),* and *gār,* "spear." An *auger* is thus a tool for piercing and boring holes.
aught (ôt) *n.* A zero : cipher.
aug·ment (ôg-mĕnt′) *v.* To make or become greater. —**aug′men·ta′tion** *n.*
au gra·tin (ō grät′n, grăt′n) *adj.* Covered with bread crumbs or grated cheese and oven-browned.
au·gur (ô′gər) *n.* A soothsayer : seer. —*v.* **1.** To predict, esp. from signs : foretell. **2.** To be an omen of : presage.
au·gu·ry (ô′gyə-rē) *n., pl.* **-ries. 1.** The practice of auguring. **2.** An omen : sign.
au·gust (ô-gŭst′) *adj.* Inspiring admiration or awe : majestic. —**au·gust′ly** *adv.*
Au·gust (ô′gəst) *n.* The 8th month of the year, having 31 days.
au jus (ō zhü′) *adj.* Served with the natural juices that accumulate during roasting.
auk (ôk) *n.* Any of several sea birds of the family Alcidae of northern regions with a stocky body and short wings.
aunt (ănt, änt) *n.* **1.** A sister of one's father or mother. **2.** The wife of one's uncle.
au·ra (ôr′ə) *n.* **1.** An emanation. **2.** A distinctive air or quality <a city with an *aura* of romance>
au·ral (ôr′əl) *adj.* Of, relating to, or received through the ear.
au·re·ate (ôr′ē-ĭt) *adj.* **1.** Gold in color. **2.** Marked by an affected and pompous literary style.
au·re·ole (ôr′ē-ōl′) *also* **au·re·o·la** (ô-rē′ə-lə) *n.* A halo.
Au·re·o·my·cin (ôr′ē-ō-mī′sĭn). A trademark for chlortetracycline.
au re·voir (ō′ rə-vwär′) *interj.* —Used to express farewell.
au·ri·cle (ôr′ĭ-kəl) *n.* **1.** *Anat.* **a.** The outer part of the ear. **b.** An atrium of the heart. **2.** *Biol.* An earlike process, part, or appendage.

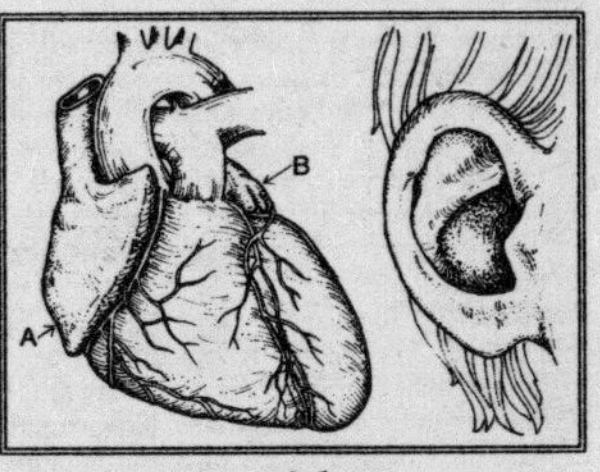

auricle
(Left) *of the heart showing*
A. right auricle, B. left auricle,
and (right) *of the ear*

au·ric·u·lar (ô-rĭk′yə-lər) *adj.* **1.** Aural. **2.** Of or relating to an auricle.
au·rif·er·ous (ô-rĭf′ər-əs) *adj.* Containing gold : gold-bearing.
au·ro·ra (ə-rôr′ə, ə-rōr′ə) *n.* **1.** A brilliant display of flashing and moving lights visible in the night sky, chiefly in polar regions, believed to result from electrically charged particles. **2.** Dawn. —**au·ro′ral** *adj.*
aurora aus·tra·lis (ô-strā′lĭs) *n.* The aurora of the S Hemisphere.
aurora bo·re·al·is (bôr′ē-ăl′ĭs, bōr′-) *n.* The aurora of the N Hemisphere.
aus·cul·ta·tion (ô′skəl-tā′shən) *n.* The act of monitoring sounds originating in bodily organs as an aid to diagnosis.
aus·pice (ô′spĭs) *n., pl.* **aus·pic·es** (ô′spĭ-sēz′, -sĭz). **1. auspices.** Protection and support : patronage. **2.** An omen : portent.
aus·pi·cious (ô-spĭsh′əs) *adj.* **1.** Affording signs of a successful result : favorable. **2.** Prosperous : successful. —**aus·pi′cious·ly** *adv.* —**aus·pi′cious·ness** *n.*
aus·tere (ô-stîr′) *adj.* **1.** Stern, as in manner : severe. **2.** Marked by abstemiousness : ascetic. **3.** Without ornamentation : simple. —**aus·tere′ly** *adv.* —**aus·ter′i·ty** *n.*
aus·tral[1] (ô′strəl) *adj.* Southern.
aus·tral[2] (ous-träl′) *n., pl.* **-tral·es** (-trä′lĕs). A former monetary unit of Argentina.
Aus·tra·loid (ô′strə-loid′) *adj.* Of or being a proposed human racial classification distinguished by dark skin and dark curly hair and including peoples indigenous to Australia and parts of SE Asia. —**Aus′tra·loid′** *n.*

au•tar•chy (ô'tär'kē) *n., pl.* **-chies. 1.** Complete control or power : autocracy. **2.** A country under autarchic rule. **—au•tar'chic, au•tar'chi•cal** *adj.*
au•then•tic (ô-thĕn'tĭk) *adj.* Real : genuine. **—au•then'ti•cal•ly** *adv.* **—au'then•tic'i•ty** (-tis'ĭ-tē) *n.*
au•then•ti•cate (ô-thĕn'tĭ-kāt') *v.* **-cat•ed, -cat•ing.** To prove or be proof of the authenticity of. **—au•then'ti•ca'tion** *n.*
au•thor (ô'thər) *n.* **1.** Someone who writes a literary work. **2.** Someone who creates or originates anything. **—au'thor** *v.* **—au'thor•ship'** *n.*
au•thor•i•tar•i•an (ə-thôr'ĭ-târ'ē-ən, ə-thŏr'-, ô-) *adj.* Favoring or marked by absolute and unquestioning obedience to authority. **—au•thor'i•tar'i•an** *n.* **—au•thor'i•tar'i•an•ism** *n.*
au•thor•i•ta•tive (ə-thôr'ĭ-tā'tĭv, ə-thŏr'-, ô-) *adj.* Being, having, or arising from an authority. **—au•thor'i•ta'tive•ly** *adv.* **—au•thor'i•ta'tive•ness** *n.*
au•thor•i•ty (ə-thôr'ĭ-tē, ə-thŏr'-, ô-) *n., pl.* **-ties. 1. a.** The power to command, determine, influence, or judge. **b.** A person or group with this power. **c. authorities.** Government. **2.** Authorization : right. **3. a.** An accepted source of definitive information. **b.** A quotation or citation from such a source. **4.** An expert in a specific field.
au•thor•ize (ô'thə-rīz') *v.* **-ized, -iz•ing. 1.** To grant legal authority to. **2.** To give permission for : sanction. **3.** To justify. **—au'thor•i•za'tion** *n.*
au•tism (ô'tĭz'əm) *n.* Engrossment in abnormal mental activity, as hallucinations and fantasies, together with withdrawal from external reality. **—au•tis'tic** *adj.*
au•to (ô'tō) *n., pl.* **-tos.** An automobile.
au•to•bahn (ou'tō-bän', ô'tō-) *n.* A superhighway in Germany.
au•to•bi•og•ra•phy (ô'tō-bī-ŏg'rə-fē, -bē-) *n., pl.* **-phies.** The biography of a person written by that person. **—au'to•bi'o•graph'ic, au'to•bi'o•graph'i•cal** *adj.*
au•toch•tho•nous (ô-tŏk'thə-nəs) *adj.* Native to a particular place : indigenous.
au•toc•ra•cy (ô-tŏk'rə-sē) *n., pl.* **-cies.** Government by one person with unlimited power. **—au'to•crat'** (ô'tə-krăt') *n.* **—au'to•crat'ic** *adj.* **—au'to•crat'i•cal•ly** *adv.*
au•to•di•dact (ô'tō-dī'dăkt') *n.* A self-taught person. **—au'to•di•dac'tic** *adj.*
au•to•gi•ro *also* **au•to•gy•ro** (ô'tō-jī'rō) *n., pl.* **-ros.** An aircraft powered by a conventional propeller and provided with lift by a freewheeling horizontal rotor.
au•to•graph (ô'tə-grăf') *n.* **1.** A person's handwritten signature. **2.** A manuscript in the author's handwriting. *—v.* To write one's signature on.
au•to•im•mune (ô'tō-ĭ-myo͞on') *adj.* Of or relating to an immune response by the body against one of its own tissues or types of cells. **—au'to•im•mu'ni•ty** *n.*
au•to•in•tox•i•ca•tion (ô'tō-ĭn-tŏk'sĭ-kā'shən) *n.* Self-poisoning caused by endogenous microorganisms, metabolic wastes, or other toxins in the body.
au•to•mate (ô'tə-māt') *v.* **-mat•ed, -mat•ing.** To operate by or convert to automation.
au•to•mat•ed teller machine (ô'tə-mā'tĭd) *n.* An electronic machine in a public place, connected to a bank's data system and activated by a customer to obtain specified banking services, esp. deposits and cash withdrawals.
au•to•mat•ic (ô'tə-măt'ĭk) *adj.* **1.** Operating or able to operate with little or no external control : self-operating or self-regulating. **2.** Involuntary : reflex. *—n.* A machine or device, esp. a firearm, that is automatic. **—au'to•mat'i•cal•ly** *adv.*
automatic pilot *n.* An automatic steering mechanism, as on an aircraft.
au•to•ma•tion (ô'tə-mā'shən) *n.* **1.** Automatic operation of equipment, a process, or a system. **2.** The techniques and equipment used to achieve automation. **3.** The state of being automatically operated.
au•tom•a•tize (ô-tŏm'ə-tīz') *v.* **-tized, -tiz•ing. 1.** To make automatic. **2.** To automate. **—au•tom'a•ti•za'tion** *n.*
au•tom•a•ton (ô-tŏm'ə-tən, -tŏn') *n., pl.* **-tons** *or* **-ta** (-tə). **1.** A robot. **2.** Someone who behaves mechanically.
au•to•mo•bile (ô'tə-mō-bēl', -mō'bēl') *n.* A self-propelled usu. 4-wheeled passenger vehicle.
au•to•mo•tive (ô'tə-mō'tĭv) *adj.* **1.** Self-propelling. **2.** Of or relating to self-propelled land vehicles, esp. automobiles.
au•to•nom•ic nervous system (ô'tə-nŏm'ĭk) *n.* The part of the vertebrate nervous system that regulates involuntary action, as of the glands, and comprises the sympathetic nervous system and the parasympathetic nervous system.
au•ton•o•mous (ô-tŏn'ə-məs) *adj.* Independent, as of another government : self-governing. **—au•ton'o•mous•ly** *adv.* **—au•ton'o•my** *n.*
au•to•pi•lot (ô'tō-pī'lət) *n.* An automatic pilot.
au•top•sy (ô'tŏp'sē, ô'təp-) *n., pl.* **-sies.** Examination of a body after death to determine the cause of death. **—au'top'sy** *v.*
au•to•stra•da (ou'tō-strä'də, ô'tō-) *n.* An expressway in Italy.
au•tumn (ô'təm) *n.* The season between summer and winter. **—au•tum'nal** (ô-tŭm'nəl) *adj.*
aux•il•ia•ry (ôg-zĭl'yə-rē, -zĭl'ə-) *adj.* **1.** Providing assistance : helping. **2.** Acting in a subsidiary capacity. *—n., pl.* **-ries. 1.** One that acts in an auxiliary capacity. **2.** An auxiliary verb.
auxiliary verb *n.* A verb, as *have, can,* or *will,* that accompanies a main verb and expresses the tense, mood, or voice.
aux•in (ôk'sĭn) *n.* A plant hormone that stimulates growth.
a•vail (ə-vāl') *v.* To be of advantage or use (to). *—n.* Advantage or use <complained to no *avail*>

a•vail•a•ble (ə-vā′lə-bəl) *adj.* 1. Capable of being obtained. 2. Accessible for use : at hand. —**a•vail′a•bil′i•ty** *n.* —**a•vail′a•bly** *adv.*
av•a•lanche (ăv′ə-lănch′) *n.* A mass of material, as snow or rock, that slides down a mountainside.
a•vant-garde (ä′vänt-gärd′) *n.* The leaders in inventing and applying new styles and new techniques in a given field, esp. in the arts. —**a′vant-garde′** *adj.*
av•a•rice (ăv′ər-ĭs) *n.* Greedy desire for wealth : cupidity. —**av′a•ri′cious** *adj.*
a•vast (ə-văst′) *interj. Naut.* —Used as a command to cease or stop.
av•a•tar (ăv′ə-tär′) *n.* An incarnation.
a•vaunt (ə-vônt′) *interj. Archaic.* —Used as a command to go away.
a•venge (ə-vĕnj′) *v.* **a•venged, a•veng•ing.** To take revenge for. ★ ***syns:*** REDRESS, REPAY, REQUITE, VINDICATE. —**a•veng′er** *n.* —**a•veng′ing•ly** *adv.*
av•e•nue (ăv′ə-no͞o′, -nyo͞o′) *n.* 1. A wide street, esp. a thoroughfare lined with trees. 2. A way of achieving something.
a•ver (ə-vûr′) *v.* **a•verred, a•ver•ring.** To state positively : assert. —**a•ver′ment** *n.*
av•er•age (ăv′ər-ĭj, ăv′rĭj) *n.* 1. An arithmetic mean. 2. A usual or typical degree. —*adj.* 1. Of, relating to, or being a mathematical average. 2. Typical : usual. 3. Not exceptional : common. —*v.* **-aged, -ag•ing.** 1. To compute, obtain, or be the average of. 2. To be, do, have, or get typically <a temperature *averaging* 70°>
a•verse (ə-vûrs′) *adj.* Having a feeling of distaste or reluctance <*averse* to discussing personal problems>
a•ver•sion (ə-vûr′zhən, -shən) *n.* 1. A strong dislike. 2. A feeling of distaste for and desire to keep clear of something.
a•vert (ə-vûrt′) *v.* 1. To turn away or aside <*averted* his eyes> 2. To keep from happening : prevent.
a•vi•an (ā′vē-ən) *adj.* Of, relating to, or typical of birds.
a•vi•ar•y (ā′vē-ĕr′ē) *n., pl.* **-ies.** A place, as at a zoo, for keeping and usu. exhibiting live birds. —**a′vi•a•rist** *n.*
a•vi•a•tion (ā′vē-ā′shən, ăv′ē-) *n.* 1. The operation of aircraft. 2. The design, development, and production of aircraft.
a•vi•a•tor (ā′vē-ā′tər, ăv′ē-) *n.* The pilot of an aircraft.
a•vi•a•trix (ā′vē-ā′trĭks, ăv′ē-) *n.* A woman who pilots an aircraft.
av•id (ăv′ĭd) *adj.* 1. Eagerly desirous : greedy. 2. Enthusiastic : ardent. —**a•vid′i•ty** (ə-vĭd′ĭ-tē, ă-vĭd′-) *n.* —**av′id•ly** *adv.*
a•vi•on•ics (ā′vē-ŏn′ĭks, ăv′ē-) *n. (sing. in number).* The science and technology of electronics in conjunction with aeronautics and astronautics. —**a′vi•on′ic** *adj.*
a•vi•ta•min•o•sis (ā-vī′tə-mĭ-nō′sĭs) *n.* A disease, as scurvy, caused by a vitamin deficiency. —**a•vi′ta•min•ot′ic** (-nŏt′ĭk) *adj.*
a•vo (ā′vo͞o) *n., pl.* **a•vos.** —See table at CURRENCY.
av•o•ca•do (ăv′ə-kä′dō, ä′və-) *n., pl.* **-dos.** 1. A tropical American tree, *Persea americana,* grown for its edible fruit. 2. The pear-shaped fruit of the avocado, having a large seed and greenish-yellow pulp.
av•o•ca•tion (ăv′ə-kā′shən) *n.* A usu. pleasurable activity in addition to one's regular work : hobby.
av•o•cet (ăv′ə-sĕt′) *n.* A shore bird of the genus *Recurvirostra,* having long legs and a slender, upturned beak.
a•void (ə-void′) *v.* 1. To stay clear of : shun. 2. To keep from happening : prevent. 3. To refrain from. ★ ***syns:*** BY-PASS, DODGE, DUCK, ELUDE, ESCAPE, ESCHEW, EVADE, SHUN —**a•void′a•ble** *adj.* —**a•void′a•bly** *adv.* —**a•void′ance** *n.*
av•oir•du•pois (ăv′ər-də-poiz′) *n.* 1. Avoirdupois weight. 2. *Informal.* Weight or heaviness, esp. personal weight.
av•oir•du•pois weight (ăv′ər-də-poiz′) *n.* A system of weights and measures based on 1 lb of 16 oz, 7,000 grains or 453.59 g.
a•vouch (ə-vouch′) *v.* 1. To guarantee. 2. To assert : affirm.
a•vow (ə-vou′) *v.* To state openly. —**a•vow′al** *n.* —**a•vow′ed•ly** *adv.*
a•vun•cu•lar (ə-vŭng′kyə-lər) *adj.* Of, relating to, or suggestive of an uncle.
a•wait (ə-wāt′) *v.* 1. To wait (for). 2. To be in store for.
a•wake (ə-wāk′) *v.* **a•woke** (ə-wōk′), **a•waked, a•wak•ing.** 1. To rouse or emerge from sleep : wake up. 2. To stir up : arouse. —*adj.* 1. Not asleep. 2. Alert : watchful.
a•wak•en (ə-wā′kən) *v.* To awake.
a•ward (ə-wôrd′) *v.* 1. To grant as legally due. 2. To bestow for performance or quality. —*n.* 1. A decision, as one made by a judge. 2. Something awarded.
a•ware (ə-wâr′) *adj.* Being mindful or conscious. ★ ***syns:*** COGNIZANT, CONVERSANT, KNOWING, MINDFUL —**a•ware′ness** *n.*
a•wash (ə-wŏsh′, ə-wôsh′) *adj. & adv.* 1. Washed by waves. 2. Flooded. 3. Afloat.
a•way (ə-wā′) *adv.* 1. At or to a long distance <far *away*> 2. In or to another place or direction <ran *away*> 3. From one's possession <gave *away* his record collection> 4. Out of existence <snow melting *away*> 5. Continuously <dogs barking *away*> 6. Without delay <fire *away*> —*adj.* 1. Absent <He's *away* from the office this morning.> 2. At a distance <10 feet *away*>
awe (ô) *n.* A feeling of reverence and dread mingled with wonder. —*v.* **awed, aw•ing.** To fill with awe.
a•wea•ry (ə-wûr′ē) *adj.* Weary : tired.
a•weigh (ə-wā′) *adj. Naut.* Hanging just clear of the bottom, as a ship's anchor.
awe•some (ô′səm) *adj.* 1. Marked by or inspiring awe. 2. *Slang.* Remarkable : outstanding. —**awe′some•ly** *adv.* —**awe′some•ness** *n.*
awe•struck (ô′strŭk′) *also* **awe•strick•en** (ô′strĭk′ən) *adj.* Full of awe.

aw•ful (ô'fəl) *adj.* **1.** Inspiring awe. **2.** Very unpleasant : dreadful. **3.** Great <an *awful* lot of work> —**aw'ful•ly** *adv.*
a•while (ə-hwīl', ə-wīl') *adv.* For a while.
a•whirl (ə-hwûrl, ə-wûrl') *adj.* In a whirl : spinning.
awk•ward (ôk'wərd) *adj.* **1.** Marked by a lack of dexterity and grace : clumsy. **2.** Causing embarrassment and distress. **3.** Difficult to manage or handle : unwieldy. ★ ***syns:*** GAWKY, GRACELESS, INEPT, UNGAINLY —**awk'ward•ly** *adv.* —**awk'ward•ness** *n.*
awl (ôl) *n.* A pointed tool used to make holes, as in leather.
awn (ôn) *n.* One of the slender bristles of the spikelet in many grasses.
awn•ing (ô'nĭng) *n.* A rooflike structure, esp. of canvas, that serves as a shelter, as over a window.
a•woke (ə-wōk') *v. p.t. of* AWAKE.
AWOL (ā'wôl') *adj.* Absent without leave, esp. from military service. —**AWOL** *n.*
a•wry (ə-rī') *adv.* **1.** Askew. **2.** Away from the correct course : amiss.
ax *or* **axe** (ăks) *n.* A tool with a bladed head, used to fell or split lumber.
ax•i•al (ăk'sē-əl) *adj.* Of, relating to, on, around, or along an axis.
ax•il•la (ăk-sĭl'ə) *n., pl.* **-il•lae** (-sĭl'ē). **1.** The armpit. **2.** An analogous structure, as under a bird's wing.
ax•i•om (ăk'sē-əm) *n.* **1.** A statement universally recognized as true : maxim. **2.** A proposition assumed to be true without proof. —**ax'i•o•mat'ic** *adj.* —**ax'i•o•mat'i•cal•ly** *adv.*
ax•is (ăk'sĭs) *n., pl.* **ax•es** (-sēz'). **1.** A straight line around which an object or body rotates or may be thought to rotate. **2.** A line, ray, or line segment serving to orient a space or geometric object, about which the object is symmetrical. **3.** A reference line in a system of coordinates. **4.** *Bot.* The main stem or central part about which plant parts such as leaves are arranged.
axis deer *n.* A deer, *Axis axis,* of C Asia, with a white-spotted brown coat.
ax•le (ăk'səl) *n.* A shaft or spindle on which a wheel or pair of wheels revolves.
ax•le•tree (ăk'səl-trē') *n.* A crossbar or rod having terminal spindles on which the wheels revolve.
Ax•min•ster (ăks'mĭn'stər) *n.* A carpet with stiff jute backing and long, soft cut-wool pile.
ax•o•lotl (ăk'sə-lŏt'l) *n.* Any of several W North American and Mexican salamanders of the genus *Ambystoma.*
ax•on (ăk'sŏn') *also* **ax•one** (-sōn') *n.* The core of a nerve fiber that usu. conducts impulses away from the body of a nerve cell.
a•ya•tol•lah (ī'ə-tō'lə) *n.* A Shiite leader having religious and administrative authority.
aye[1] *also* **ay** (ī) *n.* An affirmative vote or voter. —*adv.* Yes.
aye[2] *also* **ay** (ā) *adv.* Ever : always.
a•zal•ea (ə-zāl'yə) *n.* Any of a group of deciduous or evergreen shrubs of the genus *Rhododendron* grown for their variously colored flowers.
az•i•do•thy•mi•dine (ăz'ĭ-dō-thī'mĭ-dēn', ə-zī'-, ə-zē'-) *n.* AZT.
az•i•muth (ăz'ə-məth) *n.* **1.** The horizontal angular distance from a fixed reference direction to a position, object, or object referent, from a point due S, usu. measured clockwise along the horizon. **2.** The lateral deviation of a projectile or bomb. —**az'i•muth'al** *adj.*
AZT (ā'zē-tē') *n.* An antiviral drug that inhibits replication of the AIDS virus.
Az•tec (ăz'tĕk') *n.* A member of an Indian people of C Mexico whose empire was invaded by Cortés in 1519. —**Az'tec•an** *adj.*
az•ure (ăzh'ər) *n.* A light purplish blue. —**az'•ure** *adj.*

Bb

b *or* **B** (bē) *n., pl.* **b's** *or* **B's. 1.** The 2nd letter of the English alphabet. **2.** A speech sound represented by the letter *b.* **3.** The 7th tone in the scale of C major. **4.** The 2nd-highest grade or rank. **5. B** A human blood type of the ABO group.
B *symbol for* BORON.
Ba *symbol for* BARIUM.
bab•ble (băb'əl) *v.* **-bled, -bling. 1.** To utter indistinct, meaningless sounds. **2.** To talk idly or foolishly : chatter. —**bab'ble** *n.* —**bab'bler** *n.*
babe (bāb) *n.* An infant : baby.
Ba•bel (bā'bəl, băb'əl) *n.* **1.** The site of a tower in the Old Testament where construction was interrupted by a confusion of tongues. **2. babel.** A confusion of voices or sounds.
ba•boon (bă-bo͞on') *n.* A large African monkey of the genus *Papio* or related genera, with a long, doglike muzzle.
ba•bush•ka (bə-bo͝osh'kə) *n.* A woman's head kerchief, usu. folded triangularly.
ba•by (bā'bē) *n., pl.* **-bies. 1.** A very young child : infant. **2.** The smallest or youngest member of a group. **3.** An immature person. —*v.* **-bied, -by•ing.** To treat tenderly and often oversolicitously. ★ ***syns:*** CODDLE, COSSET, INDULGE, MOLLYCODDLE, PAMPER, SPOIL —**ba'by•hood'** *n.* —**ba'by•ish** *adj.*
baby boom *n.* A sudden, large increase in the birthrate, esp. the one in the United States after World War II. —**ba'by-boom'** *adj.* —**ba'by-boom'er** *n.*

baby carriage *n.* A small 4-wheeled carriage for an infant.
baby grand *n.* A small grand piano approx. 5 ft long.
ba•by's-breath *also* **ba•bies'-breath** (bā'bēz-brĕth') *n.* A plant of the genus *Gypsophilos,* bearing numerous small white flowers.
ba•by-sit (bā'bē-sĭt') *v.* To care for children whose parents are not at home. **—baby sitter** *n.*
bac•ca•lau•re•ate (băk'ə-lôr'ē-ĭt) *n.* **1.** The degree of bachelor conferred by colleges and universities. **2.** A commencement address.
bac•ca•rat (bä'kə-rä', băk'ə-) *n.* A gambling game played with cards.
bac•cha•nal (băk'ə-năl', bä'kə-näl', băk'ə-nəl) *n.* **1.** A riotous or drunken festivity. **2.** A participant in a bacchanal : reveler.
bac•cha•na•lia (băk'ə-năl'yə) *n.* A drunken or riotous celebration : orgy. **—bac'cha•na'lian** *adj.*
bach•e•lor (băch'ə-lər, băch'lər) *n.* **1.** A man who is not married. **2.** A person who holds a college degree signifying completion of undergraduate studies.
bach•e•lor's-but•ton (băch'ə-lərz-bŭt'n, băch'lərz-) *n.* The cornflower.
bachelor's degree *n.* A college or university degree signifying completion of the undergraduate curriculum.
ba•cil•lus (bə-sĭl'əs) *n., pl.* **-cil•li** (-sĭl'ī'). Any of various rod-shaped, aerobic bacteria. **—bac'il•lar'y** (băs'ə-lĕr'ē) *adj.*
back (băk) *n.* **1. a.** The part of the vertebrate body nearest the spine. **b.** The analogous part in invertebrates. **2.** The part opposite the front : the rear. **3.** *Football.* A player positioned in the backfield. *—v.* **1.** To move or cause to move backward or in reverse. **2.** To uphold : support. **3.** To form the back of. **—back down** To withdraw from confrontation. **—back off** To retreat, as from a position. **—back up 1.** To accumulate in a clogged state. **2.** To support or corroborate. **3.** *Computer Sci.* To make a backup of. *—adj.* **1.** In or at the back. **2.** Distant : remote. **3.** Of or for a past time or date. **4.** Operating or moving backward. *—adv.* **1.** At, to, or toward the rear. **2.** To, in, or toward a former state, place, or time. **3.** In concealment, reserve, or check. **4.** In reply or return. **—back'less** *adj.*
back•ache (băk'āk') *n.* A back pain.
back•beat (băk'bēt') *n.* A loud, steady beat characteristic of rock music.
back•bite (băk'bīt') *v.* To speak spitefully or nastily about someone who is not present. **—back'bit'er** *n.*
back•board (băk'bôrd', -bōrd') *n.* **1.** A board placed under or behind something to give support. **2.** *Basketball.* The elevated board from which the basket projects.
back•bone (băk'bōn') *n.* **1.** The spine or spinal column of vertebrates. **2.** A main support : mainstay. **3.** Strength and determination of character.
back•drop (băk'drŏp') *n.* **1.** A painted curtain hung across the back of a stage set. **2.** A setting : background.
back•er (băk'ər) *n.* One who gives aid or support.
back•field (băk'fēld') *n. Football.* **1.** The players who are positioned behind the line of scrimmage. **2.** The area in which the backfield lines up.
back•fire (băk'fīr') *n.* An explosion of prematurely ignited fuel or unburned exhaust gases in an internal-combustion engine. *—v.* **1.** To explode in a backfire. **2.** To have a result opposite to that intended.
back•gam•mon (băk'găm'ən) *n.* A board game for 2 persons, played with counters and dice.
back•ground (băk'ground') *n.* **1.** The surface or area against which objects are seen or represented. **2.** Events or conditions surrounding or leading up to something. **3.** A position of relative inconspicuousness. **4.** A person's total experience, education, and knowledge.
back•hand (băk'hănd') *n.* A stroke, as of a tennis racket, made with the back of the hand facing outward and the arm moving forward. *—adj.* Backhanded. **—back'hand'** *v.*
back•hand•ed (băk'hăn'dĭd) *adj.* **1.** Made with or using a backhand. **2.** Indirect : roundabout.
back•hoe (băk'hō') *n.* An excavator with a boom that is drawn backward to the machine.
back•ing (băk'ĭng) *n.* **1.** Something that forms a back. **2. a.** Aid : support. **b.** Those who provide support.
back•lash (băk'lăsh') *n.* **1.** A sudden violent backward whipping motion. **2.** A strong hostile reaction.
back•light (băk'līt') *v.* To light (a subject or scene) from behind. **—back'light'** *n.*
back•log (băk'lôg', -lŏg') *n.* **1.** A reserve supply. **2.** An accumulation, esp. of unfilled orders or unfinished work.
back•pack (băk'păk') *n.* A container for camping supplies mounted on a lightweight frame and worn on the back. *—v.* To hike with a backpack. **—back'pack'er** *n.*
back•ped•al (băk'pĕd'l) *v.* To move backward : retreat or withdraw.
back•rest (băk'rĕst') *n.* A rest for the back.
back•side (băk'sīd') *n.* The buttocks.
back slash *n.* A character (\) used esp. to separate subdirectories in some computer file names.
back•slide (băk'slīd') *v.* To revert to a former, less desirable condition, esp. in religious practice. **—back'slid'er** *n.*
back•space (băk'spās') *v.* To move the carriage of a typewriter or the cursor of a computer terminal back one or more spaces. *—n.* The key used for backspacing.
back•spin (băk'spĭn') *n.* A spin that tends to retard, arrest, or reverse the linear motion of an object, esp. of a ball.
back•stab (băk'stăb') *v.* To attack (someone) unfairly, esp. in an underhand, deceitful manner. **—back'stab'ber** *n.*
back•stage (băk'stāj') *adj.* **1.** Of or occurring in the area behind the performing area in

a theater. 2. Not known to the public : private. **—back'stage'** *adv.*

back·stop (băk'stŏp') *n.* A screen or fence used to prevent a ball from being hit out of a playing area.

back·stretch (băk'strĕch') *n.* The part of a racecourse opposite the homestretch.

back·stroke (băk'strōk') *n.* A swimming stroke executed with the swimmer on his or her back.

back·swept (băk'swĕpt') *adj.* Swept or angled backward.

back talk *n.* An insolent retort.

back-to-back (băk'tə-băk') *adj.* Consecutive.

back·track (băk'trăk') *v.* **1.** To retrace one's steps. **2.** To reverse a policy.

back·up (băk'ŭp') *n.* **1.** A reserve or substitute. **2.** *Computer Sci.* A copy of a program or file stored separately from the original. **3.** An overflow caused by clogging. *—adj.* Auxiliary : standby.

back·ward (băk'wərd) *adv.* **1.** At, to, or toward the back. **2.** With the back leading. **3.** In a reverse manner or order. **4.** Toward a worse condition. **5.** To or toward the past. *—adj.* **1.** Reversed. **2.** Shy : bashful. **3.** Behind others or retarded in development. **—back'ward·ness** *n.* **—back'wards** *adv.*

back·wash (băk'wŏsh', -wôsh') *n.* A backward motion or flow, as of water or air.

back·wa·ter (băk'wô'tər, -wŏt'ər) *n.* A place or situation considered to be backward or stagnant.

back·woods (băk'wŏŏdz', -wŏŏdz') *pl.n.* Heavily wooded, sparsely populated areas. **—back'woods'man** *n.*

ba·con (bā'kən) *n.* The back and sides of a pig salted and smoked.

bac·te·ri·cide (băk-tîr'ĭ-sīd') *n.* A substance that destroys bacteria. **—bac·te'ri·cid'al** *adj.*

bac·te·ri·ol·o·gy (băk-tîr'ē-ŏl'ə-jē) *n.* The scientific study of bacteria. **—bac·te'ri·o·log'ic** (-ə-lŏj'ĭk), **bac·te'ri·o·log'i·cal** *adj.* **—bac·te'ri·ol'o·gist** *n.*

bac·te·ri·o·phage (băk-tîr'ē-ə-fāj') *n.* A viral organism that destroys bacteria.

bac·te·ri·um (băk-tîr'ē-əm) *n., pl.* **-ri·a** (-ē-ə). Any of numerous unicellular microorganisms of various forms that often cause disease. **—bac·te'ri·al** *adj.*

bad (băd) *adj.* **worse** (wûrs), **worst** (wûrst). **1.** Poor : inferior. **2. a.** Evil. **b.** Disobedient or naughty. **3.** Unfavorable<a *bad* review> **4.** Decayed : spoiled <a *bad* apple> **5.** Intense : severe <a *bad* headache> **6.** Invalid <a *bad* check> *—n.* Something bad. *—adv. Informal.* **1.** In a bad manner : badly. **2.** Greatly. **—bad'ly** *adv.* **—bad'ness** *n.*

bade (băd, bād) *v. var. p.t. of* BID.

badge (băj) *n.* An emblem usu. worn as a sign of rank, office, membership, or honor.

badg·er (băj'ər) *n.* A burrowing animal of the family Mustelidae, with long claws on the front feet and a thick, grizzled coat. *—v.* To trouble or harry persistently.

bad·i·nage (băd'n-äzh') *n.* Playful banter.

bad·lands (băd'lăndz') *pl.n.* An area with eroded ridges, peaks, and mesas and sparse vegetation.

bad·min·ton (băd'mĭn'tən) *n.* A court game played with a shuttlecock and light, long-handled rackets.

baf·fle (băf'əl) *v.* **-fled, -fling. 1.** To perplex : puzzle. **2.** To frustrate : stymie. *—n.* A device or partition that stops, alters, or regulates flow, as of a gas, sound, or liquid. **—baf'fle·ment** *n.*

bag (băg) *n.* **1.** A usu. flexible container, as of paper or leather, that can be closed and is used for carrying or storing something. **2.** An amount of game taken at a time. **3.** *Slang.* An area of skill or interest. *—v.* **bagged, bag·ging. 1.** To put into a bag. **2. a.** To bulge or cause to bulge. **b.** To hang loosely. **3.** To gain possesion of, esp. to capture as game. **—bag'ful'** *n.*

bag·a·telle (băg'ə-tĕl') *n.* A trifle.

ba·gel (bā'gəl) *n.* A glazed ring-shaped roll having a chewy texture.

bag·gage (băg'ĭj) *n.* The bags and belongings of a traveler : luggage.

bag·gy (băg'ē) *adj.* **-gi·er,-gi·est.** Hanging loosely : bulging. **—bag'gi·ly** *adv.* **—bag'gi·ness** *n.*

bag·man (băg'mən) *n. Slang.* A person who receives and collects illicit payments, as for racketeers.

bag·pipe (băg'pīp') *n. often* **bagpipes.** A musical instrument with an inflatable bag, a tube with valves, and melody and drone pipes. **—bag'pip'er** *n.*

ba·guette (bă-gĕt') *n.* **1.** A gem cut in the shape of a narrow rectangle. **2.** A long narrow loaf of French bread.

baht (bät) *n., pl.* **bahts** *or* **baht.** —See table at CURRENCY.

bail[1] (bāl) *n.* **1.** Money given to guarantee the appearance for trial of an arrested person. **2.** Temporary release secured by bail. **3.** One that provides bail. *—v.* **1.** To secure the release of by providing bail. **2.** To release (someone) for whom bail has been paid. **3.** *Informal.* To extricate from a difficult situation. **—bail'a·ble** *adj.* **—bail'or, bail'er** *n.*

bail[2] (bāl) *v.* To empty a boat of water by dipping, filling, and emptying a container. **—bail'er** *n.*

bail[3] (bāl) *n.* The arched handle of a container, as a kettle or pail.

bail·iff (bā'lĭf) *n.* **1.** An official who guards prisoners and keeps order in a courtroom. **2.** An assistant to a British sheriff who executes writs and arrests. **3.** An overseer of an estate, esp. in Britain : steward.

bail·i·wick (bā'lə-wĭk') *n.* **1.** The district or office of a bailiff. **2.** One's special sphere or province.

bails·man (bālz'mən) *n.* One who posts bail for another.

bairn (bârn) *n. Scot.* A child.

bait (bāt) *n.* **1.** A lure, as food, used to trap animals or catch fish. **2.** A lure : enticement. *—v.* **1.** To provide (e.g., a hook) with bait. **2.**

To lure : entice. **3.** To set dogs upon (a captive animal), usu. for sport. **4.** To torment with persistent attacks. ★ ***syns:*** BADGER, HECKLE, HECTOR, HOUND, NEEDLE, RIDE, TAUNT —**bait'er** *n.*

bai•za (bī'zä) *n.* —See table at CURRENCY.

baize (bāz) *n.* A coarse feltlike material.

bake (bāk) *v.* **baked, bak•ing. 1.** To cook, esp. in an oven, with dry heat. **2.** To harden and dry in or as if in an oven <*bake* pottery> —*n.* A social gathering at which baked food is served. —**bak'er** *n.*

baker's dozen *n.* A group of 13.

bak•e•ry (bā'kə-rē) *n., pl.* **-ries.** A place where goods such as bread and pastries are prepared or sold.

bake•shop (bāk'shŏp') *n.* A bakery.

baking powder *n.* A powder of baking soda, starch, and an acidic compound used as a leavening agent.

baking soda *n.* Sodium bicarbonate.

bak•sheesh (băk'shēsh', băk-shēsh') *n.* A gratuity : tip.

bal•a•lai•ka (băl'ə-lī'kə) *n.* A 3-stringed musical instrument with a triangular body.

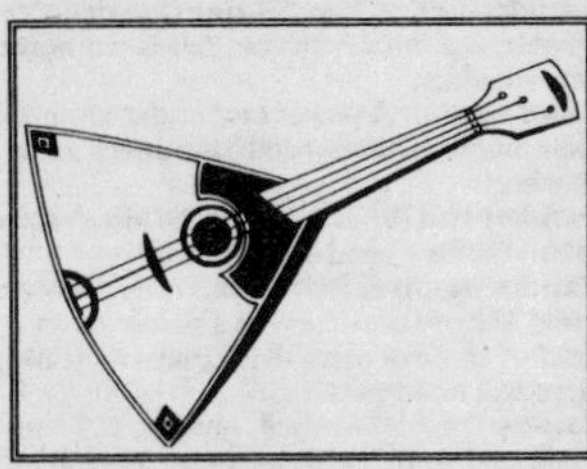

balalaika

bal•ance (băl'əns) *n.* **1.** A device for weighing : scale. **2.** Equilibrium. **3.** A force or influence that tends to produce equilibrium. **4. a.** Agreement of totals in the debit and credit sides of an account. **b.** A difference between these totals. **5.** Something that remains : remainder. ★ ***syns:*** COUNTERPOISE, EQUILIBRIUM, EQUIPOISE, STASIS —*v.* **-anced, -anc•ing. 1.** To weigh in or as if in a balance. **2.** To bring or come into equilibrium. **3.** To counterbalance. **4.** To compute the balance of (an account).

balance wheel *n.* A wheel that regulates rate of movement in a mechanism, as a watch.

bal•bo•a (băl-bō'ə) *n.* —See table at CURRENCY.

bal•brig•gan (băl-brĭg'ən) *n.* A knitted cotton material.

bal•co•ny (băl'kə-nē) *n., pl.* **-nies. 1.** A platform projecting from the wall of a building and surrounded by a railing or parapet. **2.** A gallery projecting over the main floor in a theater or auditorium.

bald (bôld) *adj.* **1.** Lacking hair on the head. **2.** Not having the usual or natural covering. **3.** Undisguised : outright <a *bald* lie> —**bald'ly** *adv.* —**bald'ness** *n.*

bal•da•chin (bôl'də-kĭn, băl'-) *also* **bal•da•chi•no** (băl'də-kē'nō) *n.* A canopy of fabric carried in processions or placed over an altar, throne, or dais.

bald eagle *n.* A North American eagle, *Haliaeetus leucocephalus,* with a dark body and a white head and tail.

bal•der•dash (bôl'dər-dăsh') *n.* Nonsense.

bald-faced (bôld'fāst') *adj.* Blatant : brazen <a *bald-faced* lie>

bald•ing (bôl'dĭng) *adj.* Becoming bald.

bale (bāl) *n.* A large bound bundle or package of raw or finished material. —*v.* **baled, bal•ing.** To wrap in a bale. —**bal'er** *n.*

ba•leen (bə-lēn') *n.* Whalebone.

bale•ful (bāl'fəl) *adj.* **1.** Causing harm : harmful. **2.** Ominous. —**bale'ful•ly** *adv.* —**bale'ful•ness** *n.*

balk (bôk) *v.* **1.** To stop short and refuse to go on. **2.** To check : thwart. **3.** *Baseball.* To make an illegal motion before pitching. —*n.* **1.** A check, hindrance, or defeat. **2.** *Baseball.* An illegal motion made by a pitcher.

balk•y (bô'kē) *adj.* **-i•er, -i•est.** Tending to balk : obstinate. —**balk'i•ness** *n.*

ball[1] (bôl) *n.* **1.** A round or almost round body or mass. **2. a.** A ball used in a game. **b.** A game played with a ball. **3.** A pitched baseball that does not pass through the strike zone and the batter does not swing at. —*v.* To form into a ball.

ball[2] (bôl) *n.* **1.** A formal dance. **2.** *Slang.* A very enjoyable time.

bal•lad (băl'əd) *n.* **1.** A narrative poem, often of folk origin and intended to be sung. **2.** The music for a ballad. **3.** A popular, esp. romantic song. —**bal'lad•eer'** *n.* —**bal'lad•ry** *n.*

bal•last (băl'əst) *n.* **1.** Heavy material put in a vehicle to provide weight and stability. **2.** Coarse gravel or crushed rock that forms a foundation or roadbed. —*v.* To stabilize with ballast.

ball bearing *n.* **1.** A bearing that reduces friction, in which the moving and stationary parts are kept apart by a track containing freely revolving hard balls. **2.** A ball in a ball bearing.

bal•le•ri•na (băl'ə-rē'nə) *n.* A principal ballet dancer in a company.

bal•let (bă-lā', băl'ā') *n.* **1.** An artistic dance form characterized chiefly by a highly formalized technique. **2.** A choreographic presentation, usu. with music, on a narrative or abstract theme. **3.** A company that performs ballet. —**bal•let'ic** *adj.*

bal•let•o•mane (bă-lĕt'ə-măn') *n.* An ardent ballet enthusiast.

ballistic missile *n.* A self-powered projectile that is guided during ascent and assumes a free-falling trajectory during descent.

bal•lis•tics (bə-lĭs'tĭks) *n. (sing. in number).* **1.** The scientific study of the dynamics of projectiles, as bullets. **2.** The study of the flight characteristics of projectiles. —**bal•lis'tic** *adj.*

bal·loon (bə-lo͞on′) *n.* **1.** A bag inflated with a gas, as helium, that causes it to rise and float in the atmosphere. **2.** A toy consisting of an inflatable rubber bag. —*v.* **1.** To expand or cause to expand like a balloon. **2.** To ride in a balloon. **3.** To increase quickly. —**bal·loon′ist** *n.*

balloon tire *n.* A pneumatic tire with a wide tread, inflated to low pressure and designed for maximum cushioning.

bal·lot (băl′ət) *n.* **1.** A paper used to register a vote. **2.** The act or a method of voting. **3.** A list of candidates for office. **4.** The total of votes cast. **5.** The right to vote. —*v.* To cast a ballot : vote.

ball·park (bôl′pärk′) *n.* **1.** A baseball stadium. **2.** **Slang.** The approximately proper range, as of an estimate. —**ball′park′** *adj.*

ball-point pen (bôl′point′) *n.* A pen with a small self-inking ball bearing as its writing point.

ball·room (bôl′ro͞om′, -ro͝om′) *n.* A large room for dancing.

bal·ly·hoo (băl′ē-ho͞o′) *n.* *Informal.* **1.** Sensational or exaggerated advertising. **2.** Noisy talk or uproar. —**bal′ly·hoo′** *v.*

balm (bäm) *n.* **1.** A fragrant oil or ointment used medicinally. **2.** Something that soothes, heals, or comforts.

balm·y (bä′mē) *adj.* **-i·er, -i·est.** **1.** Having the quality of balm : mild and soothing. **2.** *Slang.* Insane : crazy. —**balm′i·ly** *adv.* —**balm′i·ness** *n.*

ba·lo·ney (bə-lō′nē) *n.* **1.** *var. of* BOLOGNA. **2.** *Slang.* Nonsense.

bal·sa (bôl′sə) *n.* A tropical American tree, *Ochroma lagopus,* with extremely light, buoyant wood.

bal·sam (bôl′səm) *n.* **1.** A fragrant resin or ointment obtained from various trees. **2.** A tree that yields balsam, esp. the balsam fir. **3.** A plant of the genus *Impatiens* cultivated for its colorful flowers.

balsam fir *n.* An American evergreen tree, *Abies balsamea,* often used as a Christmas tree.

Bal·ti·more oriole (bôl′tə-môr′, -mŏr′) *n.* An American songbird, *Icterus galbula,* the male of which has brilliant orange, black, and white plumage.

bal·us·ter (băl′ə-stər) *n.* One of the upright posts supporting a handrail.

bal·us·trade (băl′ə-strād′) *n.* A handrail and the balusters that support it.

bam·boo (băm-bo͞o′) *n.* Any of various tall, usually woody tropical grasses of the genus *Bambusa* with hollow, jointed stems.

bam·boo·zle (băm-bo͞o′zəl) *v.* **-zled, -zling.** *Informal.* To deceive : trick.

ban[1] (băn) *v.* **banned, ban·ning.** To forbid : prohibit. —*n.* An official prohibition.

ban[2] (bän) *n., pl.* **ba·ni** (bä′nē). —See table at CURRENCY.

ba·nal (bə-näl′, -năl′, bā′nəl) *adj.* Lacking freshness : trite. —**ba·nal′i·ty** *n.*

ba·nan·a (bə-năn′ə) *n.* A treelike tropical or subtropical plant of the genus *Musa,* esp. *M. sapientum,* with hanging clusters of crescent-shaped edible pulpy fruit.

band[1] (bănd) *n.* **1. a.** A strip used to encircle or bind. **b.** A strip used to trim, finish, or reinforce. **2.** A range of radio wavelengths. —*v.* To encircle, bind, or identify with a band.

band[2] (bănd) *n.* **1.** A group of persons or animals. **2.** A group of musicians who play in an ensemble. —*v.* To form, assemble, or unite in a group.

ban·dage (băn′dĭj) *n.* A strip of material used to dress a wound. —*v.* **-daged, -dag·ing.** To put a bandage on.

ban·dan·na *or* **ban·dan·a** (băn-dăn′ə) *n.* A large brightly colored, usu. patterned handkerchief.

band·box (bănd′bŏks′) *n.* A cylindrical box for carrying articles of apparel.

ban·deau (băn-dō′) *n., pl.* **-deaux** (-dōz′) *or* **-deaus.** **1.** A narrow band, esp. for the hair. **2.** A brassiere.

ban·de·role *or* **ban·de·rol** (băn′də-rōl′) *n.* A narrow forked streamer or flag.

ban·dit (băn′dĭt) *n.* **1.** A robber. **2.** A gangster. —**ban′dit·ry** *n.*

ban·do·leer *or* **ban·do·lier** (băn′də-lîr′) *n.* A belt, esp. for cartridges, that is worn over the shoulder.

band saw *n.* A power saw in the form of a continuous toothed metal band driven around 2 wheels.

band·stand (bănd′stănd′) *n.* An often roofed platform for a band or orchestra.

band·wag·on (bănd′wăg′ən) *n.* **1.** A wagon used to carry musicians in a parade. **2.** *Informal.* A cause or party that gathers increasing approval or support.

ban·dy (băn′dē) *v.* **-died, -dy·ing.** **1.** To toss back and forth. **2.** To exchange casually or frivolously. —*adj.* Curved outward <*bandy* legs>

bane (bān) *n.* **1.** A cause of harm or ruin. **2.** A poison. —**bane′ful** *adj.*

bang[1] (băng) *n.* **1.** A sudden loud noise. **2.** *Slang.* A thrill. —*v.* **1.** To hit or move with a loud noise. **2.** To bump <*banged* her elbow> —*adv.* Exactly : precisely.

bang[2] (băng) *n. often* **bangs.** A fringe of hair cut short, esp. across the forehead.

ban·gle (băng′gəl) *n.* **1.** A rigid bracelet or anklet, esp. one with no clasp. **2.** An ornament that hangs from a necklace.

bang-up (băng′ŭp′) *adj. Informal.* Excellent <a *bang-up* party>

ban·ish (băn′ĭsh) *v.* **1.** To oblige to leave a country : exile. **2.** To drive away : expel. ★ ***syns:*** DEPORT, EXILE, EXPATRIATE, EXPEL, OSTRACIZE —**ban′ish·ment** *n.*

ban·is·ter *also* **ban·nis·ter** (băn′ĭ-stər) *n.* **1.** A baluster. **2.** The handrail of a staircase.

ban·jo (băn′jō) *n., pl.* **-jos** *or* **-joes.** A fretted stringed instrument with a narrow neck, a hollow circular body, and usu. 5 strings. —**ban′jo·ist** *n.*

bank[1] (băngk) *n.* **1.** A piled-up mass, as of earth or snow. **2.** A slope of land adjoining a body of water, as a river. **3.** An elevation of the sea floor. **4.** The sideways slope of a surface on a curve or of a motor vehicle rounding a curve. —*v.* **1.** To border or protect with a bank. **2.** To pile up in a bank. **3.** To cover (a fire) with ashes or fuel for slow burning. **4.** To construct (a curve) with a slope rising to the outside edge. **5.** To tilt (an aircraft) laterally in flight.

bank² (băngk) *n.* **1.** An establishment that performs financial transactions such as receiving, investing, and lending money. **2.** A supply of or storage place for something desired or needed <a blood *bank*> —*v.* **1.** To deposit (money) in a bank. **2.** To transact business with a bank. **3.** To operate a bank. **—bank'er** *n.*

bank³ (băngk) *n.* **1.** A group of things arranged in a row <a *bank* of elevators> **2.** A row of oars.

bank•book (băngk'bo͝ok') *n.* The depositor's book in which a bank enters deposits and withdrawals.

bank holiday *n.* A day on which banks are legally closed.

bank note *n.* A note issued by an authorized bank and acceptable as money.

bank•roll (băngk'rōl') *n. Informal.* A person's ready cash : funds. —*v.* To underwrite the expense of.

bank•rupt (băngk'rŭpt', -rəpt) *n.* A debtor who is judged legally insolvent and whose remaining property is administered for or divided among the creditors. —*adj.* **1.** Financially ruined, esp. legally declared bankrupt. **2.** Utterly lacking : depleted <*bankrupt* of compassion> **—bank'rupt'** *v.* **—bank'rupt'cy** *n.*

ban•ner (băn'ər) *n.* **1.** A piece of cloth attached to a staff and used as a standard by a monarch or commander. **2.** A flag. —*adj.* Unusually good : outstanding.

ban•nock (băn'ək) *n.* A usu. unleavened griddlecake made of oatmeal or barley.

banns (bănz) *pl.n.* An announcement, esp. in church, of a forthcoming marriage.

ban•quet (băng'kwĭt) *n.* **1.** An elaborate feast. **2.** A ceremonial dinner. —*v.* To entertain at or partake of a banquet.

†ban•quette (băng-kĕt') *n.* **1.** A platform lining a trench or parapet wall for guns or gunners. **2.** *S U.S.* A sidewalk. **3.** A long upholstered seat against or built into a wall.

ban•shee (băn'shē) *n.* A female spirit in Gaelic folklore whose wailing warns of a death in a family.

ban•tam (băn'təm) *n.* **1.** One of a breed of small domestic fowl. **2.** A small but aggressive person. **—ban'tam** *adj.*

ban•ter (băn'tər) *n.* Good-humored, teasing conversation. —*v.* To engage or indulge in banter.

Ban•tu (băn'to͞o) *n., pl.* **-tu** *or* **-tus. 1.** A large group of related languages spoken in C, E, and S Africa. **2.** A member of a Bantu-speaking people. **—Ban'tu** *adj.*

ban•yan (băn'yən) *n.* A tropical tree, *Ficus benghalensis,* with many aerial roots that grow downward to form additional trunks.

ban•zai (bän-zī') *n.* A Japanese battle cry or cheer.

ba•o•bab (bā'ə-băb', bou'-) *n.* A tree, *Adansonia digitata,* of tropical Africa, with a trunk up to 30 ft in diameter and hard-shelled fleshy fruit.

baobab

bap•tism (băp'tĭz'əm) *n.* **1.** A Christian sacrament of spiritual rebirth symbolized by the ritual application of water. **2.** An ordeal by which one is initiated. **—bap•tis'mal** *adj.*

Bap•tist (băp'tĭst) *n.* A member of a Protestant denomination that practices voluntary adult baptism by immersion.

bap•tis•ter•y *also* **bap•tis•try** (băp'tĭ-strē) *n.,pl.* **-ies** *also* **-tries.** A place, esp. a part of a church, where the ceremony of baptism is performed.

bap•tize (băp-tīz', băp'tīz') *v.* **-tized, -tiz•ing. 1.** To sprinkle with or immerse in water during baptism. **2.** To initiate. **3.** To christen. **—bap•tiz'er** *n.*

bar (bär) *n.* **1.** A rather long, rigid piece of solid material used esp. as a fastener or support. **2.** A solid block of a substance <a *bar* of soap> **3.** An obstacle : barrier. **4.** A long, narrow marking, as a stripe. **5. a.** The railing in a courtroom enclosing the area where the lawyers and defendants sit. **b.** A system of law courts. **c.** The legal profession. **6.** *Mus.* A vertical line that divides a staff into equal measures. **7. a.** A counter where drinks are served. **b.** A place with such a counter. —*v.* **barred, bar•ring. 1.** To fasten with or as if with bars. **2.** To prohibit : forbid. **3.** To keep out : exclude. —*prep.* Except for : excluding.

barb (bärb) *n.* **1.** A sharp backward-pointing projection, as on an arrow. **2.** A cutting remark. **3.** *Bot.* A hooked bristle or hairlike projection. **—barbed** *adj.*

bar•bar•i•an (bär-bâr'ē-ən) *n.* **1.** A member of a people or culture thought of as being primitive, uncivilized, or savage. **2.** A fierce or cruel person. **3.** A person lacking in culture : boor. **—bar•bar'i•an** *adj.* **—bar•bar'i•an•ism** *n.*

bar•bar•ic (bär-băr'ĭk) *adj.* **1.** Of, relating to, or characteristic of barbarians. **2.** Crude in taste, style, or behavior.

bar•ba•rism (bär'bə-rĭz'əm) *n.* **1.** An act, custom, or trait marked by coarseness or brutality. **2.** A word or form felt to be nonstandard or incorrect in a language.

bar•ba•rous (bär′bər-əs) *adj.* **1.** Uncivilized : primitive. **2.** Cruel : savage. **3.** Uncultured or unrefined, esp. in the use of linguistic forms. —**bar•bar′i•ty** (bär-băr′ĭ-tē) *n.* —**bar′ba•rous•ly** *adv.*

bar•be•cue (bär′bĭ-kyo͞o′) *n.* **1.** A pit or outdoor fireplace for broiling or roasting meat. **2. a.** A whole animal roasted over a fire. **b.** A usu. outdoor social gathering at which food is prepared in this way. —*v.* **-cued, -cu•ing.** To roast (meat) over live coals or an open fire.

barbed wire *n.* Fence wire with barbs at regular intervals.

bar•bel (bär′bəl) *n.* One of the slender, whiskerlike sensory organs on the head of certain fishes, as catfish.

bar•bell (bär′bĕl′) *n.* A bar with weights at each end, lifted for exercise.

bar•ber (bär′bər) *n.* One who cuts hair and shaves or trims beards as an occupation. —**bar′ber** *v.*

bar•ber•ry (bär′bĕr′ē) *n.* A spiny shrub of the genus *Berberis* with small orange or red berries.

bar•ber•shop (bär′bər-shŏp′) *n.* A barber's place of business. —*adj.* Of, consisting of, or relating to the performance of sentimental songs in 4-part harmony.

bar•bi•can (bär′bĭ-kən) *n.* An outdoor defensive fortification.

bar•bi•tal (bär′bĭ-tôl′) *n.* An addictive crystalline compound used as a sedative.

bar•bi•tu•rate (bär-bĭch′ər-ĭt, -ə-rāt′) *n.* A barbituric acid derivative used as a sedative or hypnotic.

bar•bi•tu•ric acid (bär′bĭ-to͝or′ĭk, -tyo͝or′-) *n.* An organic acid used in making barbiturates and some plastics.

bar•ca•role *also* **bar•ca•rolle** (bär′kə-rōl′) *n.* A song of a Venetian gondolier.

bar code *n.* Universal Product Code.

bard (bärd) *n.* An exalted national poet. —**bard′ic** *adj.*

bare (bâr) *adj.* **bar•er, bar•est. 1.** Without clothing : naked. **2.** Exposed to view : unconcealed. **3.** Without addition or decoration : plain. **4.** Just sufficient : mere. ★ *syns:* BALD, NAKED, NUDE —*v.* **bared, bar•ing.** To reveal. —**bare′ness** *n.*

bare•back (bâr′băk′) *adv.* & *adj.* On an animal, as a horse, without a saddle.

bare•faced (bâr′fāst′) *adj.* **1.** Having no covering, esp. no beard, on the face. **2.** Open and brazen <a *barefaced* lie>

bare•foot (bâr′fo͝ot′) *also* **bare•foot•ed** (-fo͝ot′ĭd) *adj.* & *adv.* Without covering on the feet.

bare•hand•ed (bâr′hăn′dĭd) *adj.* & *adv.* **1.** Without covering on the hands. **2.** Without the aid of tools or weapons.

bare•head•ed (bâr′hĕd′ĭd) *adj.* & *adv.* With no covering on the head.

bare•leg•ged (bâr′lĕg′id, -lĕgd′) *adj.* & *adv.* With no covering over the legs.

bare•ly (bâr′lē) *adv.* **1.** By a very little : scarcely <*barely* enough to eat> **2.** In a scanty manner : sparsely.

barf (bärf) *Slang.* To vomit.

bar•gain (bär′gĭn) *n.* **1.** An agreement or contract, esp. one pertaining to the sale and purchase of goods or services. **2.** Something acquired at a price advantageous to the buyer. —*v.* **1.** To negotiate the terms of an agreement. **2.** To reach an agreement. **3.** To exchange : barter.

barge (bärj) *n.* **1.** A flat-bottomed boat towed along a canal or river by other craft and used for transporting freight. **2.** A large pleasure boat. **3.** A power boat used by a naval flag officer. —*v.* **barged, barg•ing. 1.** To transport by barge. **2.** To move clumsily. **3.** To intrude rudely and abruptly <*barged* in on our conversation>

bar•i•tone (băr′ĭ-tōn′) *n.* **1.** A male voice of a range between bass and tenor. **2.** A singer with a baritone voice.

bar•i•um (bâr′ē-əm, băr′-) *n. Symbol* **Ba** A silvery-white metallic element used for deoxidizing copper and in various alloys and rat poison.

bark¹ (bärk) *n.* The harsh, abrupt sound made by a dog. —*v.* **1.** To utter a bark. **2.** To speak gruffly : snap.

bark² (bärk) *n.* The outer covering of the stems, roots, and main trunks of trees and other woody plants. —*v.* **1.** To remove bark from. **2.** To rub off the skin from.

bark³ *also* **barque** (bärk) *n.* A sailing ship with 3 to 5 masts with the after mast fore-and-aft rigged.

bar•keep•er (bär′kē′pər) *also* **bar•keep** (-kēp′) *n.* An owner or manager of a bar selling liquor.

bark•er (bär′kər) *n.* One who stands before the entrance to a show and solicits customers with a loud, colorful sales pitch.

bar•ley (bär′lē) *n.* A cereal grass, *Hordeun vulgare,* bearing seeds used for food and making beer and whiskey.

bar mitz•vah (bär mĭts′və) *n.* **1.** A 13-year-old Jewish boy who assumes the moral and religious duties of an adult. **2.** The ceremony recognizing a bar mitzvah.

barn (bärn) *n.* A building used esp. to store farm products and shelter livestock.

bar•na•cle (bär′nə-kəl) *n.* Any of various marine crustaceans of the order Cirripedia with a hard shell that remain attached to a submerged surface. —**bar′na•cled** *adj.*

barn•storm (bärn′stôrm′) *v.* To travel around, esp. in rural areas, giving dramatic presentations, lecturing, or making political speeches. —**barn′storm′er** *n.*

barn swallow *n.* A widely distributed bird, *Hirundo rustica,* with a deeply forked tail, a dark-blue back, and tan underparts.

barn•yard (bärn′yärd′) *n.* The often fenced yard around a barn.

bar•o•graph (băr′ə-grăf′) *n.* A recording barometer. —**bar′o•graph′ic** *adj.*

ba•rom•e•ter (bə-rŏm′ĭ-tər) *n.* An instrument for measuring atmospheric pressure, used in forecasting the weather. —**bar′o·met′ric** (băr′ə-mĕt′rĭk), **bar′o·met′ri·cal** *adj.* —**ba·rom′e·try** *n.*

bar·on (băr′ən) *n.* A member of the lowest rank of nobility in Great Britain. —**bar′on·age** *n.* —**ba·ro′ni·al** (bə-rō′nē-əl) *adj.* —**bar′o·ny** *n.*

bar·on·ess (băr′ə-nĭs) *n.* **1.** The wife or widow of a baron. **2.** A woman who holds the rank of baron in her own right.

bar·on·et (băr′ə-nĭt, băr′ə-nĕt′) *n.* A man who holds a hereditary title of honor next below a baron. —**bar′on·et·cy** *n.*

ba·roque (bə-rōk′) *adj.* **1.** Of an artistic style characterized by elaborate and ornate forms. **2.** Of a musical style characterized by strict form and elaborate ornamentation. —**ba·roque′** *n.*

barque (bärk) *n. var. of* BARK[3].

bar·racks (băr′əks) *n. (sing. or pl. in number).* A building or group of buildings for housing soldiers.

bar·ra·cu·da (băr′ə-ko͞o′də) *n., pl.* **-da** *or* **-das.** A large, narrow-bodied, chiefly tropical marine fish of the genus *Sphyraena* with very sharp teeth.

barracuda

bar·rage (bə-räzh′) *n.* **1.** A heavy, concentrated discharge of missiles as from small arms. **2.** A concentrated outpouring <a *barrage* of comments> ★ ***syns:*** BOMBARDMENT, BURST, CANNONADE, FUSILLADE, SALVO, SHOWER, STORM, VOLLEY —*v.* **-raged, -rag·ing.** To direct a barrage at.

†**bar·ran·ca** (bə-răng′kə) *n. SW U.S.* A deep ravine : gorge.

bar·ra·try (băr′ə-trē) *n., pl.* **-tries. 1.** *Law.* Persistent incitement of lawsuits. **2.** An unlawful breach of duty by a ship's master or crew that results in injury to the owner of the ship. **3.** The selling or buying of positions in the state or church.

barred (bärd) *adj.* Marked with stripes : striped.

bar·rel (băr′əl) *n.* **1.** A large cask with round flat ends of equal size and sides that bulge. **2.** The amount a barrel will hold. **3.** —See table at MEASUREMENT. **4.** A cylindrical part, as the long tube of a gun. —*v.* **-reled, -rel·ing** *or* **-relled, -rel·ling. 1.** To pack in a barrel. **2.** *Slang.* To move at high speed.

barrel organ *n.* A portable musical instrument similar to a small organ and operated by a hand crank.

bar·ren (băr′ən) *adj.* **1.** Sterile : infertile. **2.** Lacking vegetation <*barren* fields> **3.** Unproductive of results <*barren* efforts> **4.** Utterly lacking : devoid. —**bar′ren·ly** *adv.* —**bar′ren·ness** *n.*

bar·rette (bə-rĕt′, bä-) *n.* A clasp used to hold hair in place.

bar·ri·cade (băr′ĭ-kād′, băr′ĭ-kād′) *n.* A hastily constructed barrier or fortification. —*v.* **-cad·ed, -cad·ing.** To block, confine, or fortify with a barricade.

bar·ri·er (băr′ē-ər) *n.* **1.** A structure, as a fence, built to bar passage. **2.** Something that hinders or restricts <a *barrier* to understanding>

barrier reef *n.* A coral reef parallel to the shore and separated from it by a lagoon too deep for coral growth.

bar·ring (bär′ĭng) *prep.* Apart from the occurrence of : excepting.

bar·ri·o (bär′ē-ō′, băr′-) *n., pl.* **-os.** A chiefly Spanish-speaking neighborhood in a U.S. city.

bar·ris·ter (băr′ĭ-stər) *n.* A British attorney admitted to plead at the bar in the superior courts.

bar·room (bär′ro͞om′, -ro͝om′) *n.* A room or building where alcoholic beverages are sold at a counter or bar.

bar·row[1] (băr′ō) *n.* **1.** A flat, rectangular frame with handles at each end. **2.** A wheelbarrow.

bar·row[2] (băr′ō) *n.* A mound of earth or stones over an ancient burial site.

bar·row[3] (băr′ō) *n.* A pig castrated before reaching sexual maturity.

bar·tend·er (bär′tĕn′dər) *n.* One who serves alcoholic drinks at a bar.

bar·ter (bär′tər) *v.* To trade (e.g., goods) without the exchange of money. —*n.* **1.** The act of bartering. **2.** Something bartered. —**bar′ter·er** *n.*

ba·sal (bā′səl, -zəl) *adj.* **1.** Relating to, located at, or forming a base. **2.** Basic.

basal metabolism *n.* The lowest energy needed to maintain vital functions in an organism at complete rest measured by the heat given off per unit time.

ba·salt (bə-sôlt′, bā′sôlt′) *n.* A dark, dense volcanic rock.

base[1] (bās) *n.* **1.** The lowest part : bottom. **2.** A fundamental principle : basis. **3.** A main constituent. **4.** The point at or from which a process is begun. **5.** One of the 4 corners of a baseball infield. **6.** A central place : headquarters. **7.** A line used as a reference for computations or measurement. **8.** Any of a large class of chemical compounds, including the hydroxides and oxides of metals, that have the ability to turn litmus blue and to react with acids to form salts. **9.** The number that is raised to various powers to generate the principal counting units of a number system. —*adj.* Forming or serving as a base. —*v.* **based, bas·ing. 1.** To form or make a base for. **2.** To establish.

base² (bās) *adj.* **bas·er, bas·est. 1.** Morally bad : contemptible. **2.** Inferior in quality or value. 3. Menial : lowly. **—base'ly** *adv.* **—base'ness** *n.*

base·ball (bās'bôl') *n.* **1.** A game played with a bat and ball by 2 teams on a field with 4 bases laid out in a diamond pattern. **2.** The ball used in baseball.

base·board (bās'bôrd', -bōrd') *n.* A molding that covers the joint between a wall and abutting floor.

base·born (bās'bôrn') *adj.* **1.** Of humble birth. **2.** Of illegitimate birth. **3.** Contemptible : ignoble.

base hit *n. Baseball.* A hit by which the batter reaches base safely.

base·less (bās'lĭs) *adj.* Unfounded : groundless.

base line *n.* **1.** A line serving as a base. **2.** An area within which a baseball player must stay when running between bases.

base·man (bās'mən) *n.* A baseball player assigned to 1st, 2nd, or 3rd base.

base·ment (bās'mənt) *n.* The substructure or foundation of a building.

ba·ses (bā'sēz') *n. pl. of* BASIS.

bash (băsh) *v. Informal.* To strike or smash with a heavy blow. —*n.* **1.** *Informal.* A heavy blow. **2.** *Slang.* A party.

bash·ful (băsh'fəl) *adj.* Socially timid : shy <a *bashful* child> **—bash'ful·ly** *adv.* **—bash'ful·ness** *n.*

ba·sic (bā'sĭk) *adj.* **1.** Of, pertaining to, or forming a base : fundamental. **2.** Of, being, or serving as a starting point. **3.** Of, producing, or resulting from a chemical base. —*n.* A fundamental element or entity <the *basics* of math> **—ba'si·cal·ly** *adv.* **—ba·sic'i·ty** (-sĭs'ĭ-tē') *n.*

BA·SIC (bā'sĭk) *n. Computer Sci.* A common programming language.

bas·il (băz'əl, bā'zəl) *n.* An herb, *Ocimum basilicum*, with aromatic leaves used as seasoning in cooking.

ba·sil·i·ca (bə-sĭl'ĭ-kə, -zĭl'-) *n.* **1.** An oblong church building with a semicircular apse at one end. **2.** A church or cathedral given certain ceremonial rights by the pope.

bas·i·lisk (băs'ə-lĭsk', băz'-) *n.* **1.** A legendary lizardlike serpent with lethal breath and glance. **2.** A tropical American lizard of the genus *Basiliscus*, with an erectile crest.

basilisk

ba·sin (bā'sĭn) *n.* **1.** A round, open container used esp. for holding liquids. **2.** A washbowl : sink. **3.** A region drained by a river system.

ba·sis (bā'sĭs) *n., pl.* **-ses** (-sēz'). **1.** A supporting element : foundation. **2.** The main part. **3.** An essential principle.

bask (băsk) *v.* **1.** To expose oneself to pleasant warmth. **2.** To thrive or take pleasure <*basking* in his wife's praise>

bas·ket (băs'kĭt) *n.* **1.** A container made of woven material, as rushes or twigs. **2.** An open-ended net suspended from a hoop that serves as a goal in basketball. **—bas'ket·ful'** *n.* **—bas'ket·ry** *n.*

bas·ket·ball (băs'kĭt-bôl') *n.* **1.** A game played by 2 teams who attempt to throw a ball through an elevated basket on the opponent's side of the basketball court. **2.** The ball used in basketball.

basket weave *n.* A textile weave with a checkered pattern similar to a woven basket.

bas mitz·vah (bäs mĭts'və) *n. var. of* BAT MITZVAH.

Basque (băsk) *n.* **1.** One of a people of unknown origin living in the W Pyrenees. **2.** The language of the Basques.

bas-re·lief (bä'rĭ-lēf') *n.* Low relief.

bass¹ (băs) *n.* Any of several freshwater or marine food fishes.

bass² (bās) *n.* **1.** A low-pitched tone or sound. **2.** The lowest part in vocal or instrumental part music. **3. a.** A male singing voice of the lowest range. **b.** A singer with a bass voice. **4.** An instrument, esp. a double bass, that sounds in a low register. **—bass** *adj.* **—bass'ist** *n.*

bass clef (bās) *n. Mus.* A clef that designates F below middle C as being on the 4th line above the bottom of the staff.

bass clef

basset hound *n.* A dog with short crooked forelegs and long drooping ears.

bas·si·net (băs'ə-nĕt', băs'ə-nĕt') *n.* A basket on legs, often with a hood at one end, used as an infant's crib.

bas·so (băs'ō) *n., pl.* **-sos** *or* **-si** (-sē). An operatic bass.

bas·soon (bə-sōōn', bă-) *n.* A low-pitched

woodwind instrument with a long wooden body and a double reed. **—bas·soon'ist** *n.*

bass viol (bās) *n. Mus.* A double bass.

bass·wood (băs'wo͝od') *n.* **1.** A North American linden tree, esp. *Tilia americana.* **2.** The soft wood of a basswood.

bast (băst) *n.* Strong plant fiber used to make cordage and textiles.

bas·tard (băs'tərd) *n.* **1.** An illegitimate child. **2.** Something of irregular or inferior origin, kind, or form. **3.** *Slang.* A mean or disagreeable person. **—bas'tard·ly** *adj.* **—bas'tard·y** *n.*

▲ ***word history:*** In Old French *fils de bast* literally meant "child of a packsaddle." The phrase refers to the unsanctified circumstances in which the child was conceived. Travelers used packsaddles as beds—often, no doubt, as impromptu marriage beds. The word *bastard* was formed in Old French from *bast,* "packsaddle," and the pejorative suffix *-ard.*

bas·tard·ize (băs'tər-dīz') *v.* **-ized, -iz·ing.** To lower in quality or value : debase. **—bas'-tard·i·za'tion** *n.*

baste[1] (bāst) *v.* **bast·ed, bast·ing.** To sew with loose running stitches so as to hold in place temporarily.

baste[2] (bāst) *v.* **bast·ed, bast·ing.** To moisten (e.g., meat) periodically with liquid while cooking.

baste[3] (bāst) *v.* **bast·ed, bast·ing. 1.** To beat thoroughly : thrash. **2.** To berate.

bas·tille (bă-stēl') *n.* A prison : jail.

bas·ti·na·do (băs'tə-nā'dō, -nä'-) *also* **bas·ti·nade** (-nād, -näd') *n., pl.* **-does** *also* **-nades. 1.** A beating with a stick, esp. on the soles of the feet. **2.** A stick : cudgel.

bas·tion (băs'chən) *n.* **1.** A projecting part of a fortification. **2.** A bulwark : stronghold <a *bastion* of conservatism>

bat[1] (băt) *n.* **1.** A stout wooden stick : club. **2.** A sharp blow. **3.** A usu. wooden club used to strike a ball, as in baseball or cricket. **—at bat.** Having a turn at batting in baseball. *—v.* **bat·ted, bat·ting. 1.** To hit with or as if with a bat. **2.** To take a turn at bat.

bat[2] (băt) *n.* A nocturnal flying mammal of the order Chiroptera with membranous wings.

bat[3] (băt) *v.* **bat·ted, bat·ting.** To flutter or wink (the eyes).

batch (băch) *n.* **1.** A quantity, as of baked goods, produced or prepared at one time. **2.** An amount needed for one operation. **3.** A group of individuals or objects.

bate (bāt) *v.* **bat·ed, bat·ing.** To lessen the intensity of : moderate.

bath (băth, bäth) *n., pl.* **baths** (bă*th*z, bä*th*z, băths, bäths). **1. a.** The act of washing the body. **b.** The water used for washing the body. **2.** A bathroom. **3.** A bathhouse. **4.** A liquid in which an object is dipped or soaked so as to process it.

bathe (bā*th*) *v.* **bathed, bath·ing. 1.** To take a bath. **2.** To wash in water. **3.** To go swimming. **4.** To apply a liquid to in order to soothe or heal. **5.** To wet : moisten. **6.** To suffuse. **—bath'er** *n.*

bath·house (băth'hous', bäth'-) *n.* **1.** A building equipped with facilities for bathing. **2.** A building equipped with dressing rooms for swimmers.

bathing suit *n.* A swimsuit.

bath·o·lith (băth'ə-lĭth') *n.* Igneous rock that has melted and intruded surrounding strata. **—bath'o·lith'ic** *adj.*

ba·thos (bā'thŏs') *n.* **1.** A ludicrously abrupt shift from an elevated to a commonplace style. **2.** Insincere or overly sentimental pathos. **—ba·thet'ic** (bə-thĕt'ĭk) *adj.*

bath·robe (băth'rōb', bäth'-) *n.* A loose-fitting robe.

bath·room (băth'ro͞om', -ro͝om', bäth'-) *n.* A room with a shower or bathtub and usu. a sink and toilet.

bath·tub (băth'tŭb', bäth'-) *n.* A tub for bathing.

bath·y·scaph (băth'ĭ-skăf') *also* **bath·y·scaphe** (-skăf', -skāf') *n.* A free-diving, self-contained deep-sea research vessel with a crewed observation capsule.

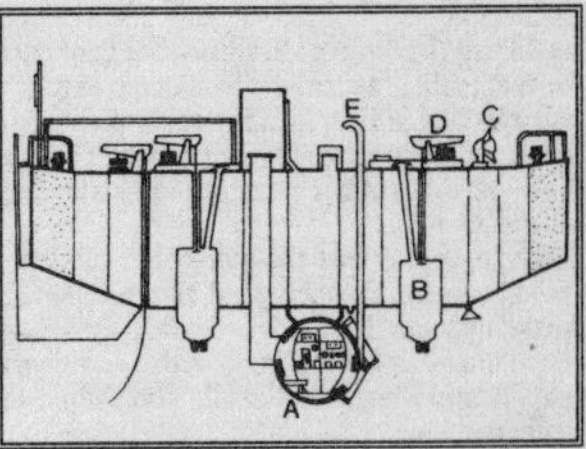

bathyscaph
A. observation capsule, B. pellet ballast hopper, C. propeller, D. release magnet, E. snorkel

bath·y·sphere (băth'ĭ-sfîr') *n.* A crewed deep-diving sphere lowered by cable.

ba·tik (bə-tēk', băt'ĭk) *n.* **1. a.** A method of dyeing textiles in which the parts not to be dyed are covered with removable wax. **b.** A design created by this method. **2.** Fabric dyed by batik.

ba·tiste (bə-tēst', bă-) *n.* A fine, sheer fabric used esp. for clothing.

bat mitz·vah (bät mĭts'və) *n. also* **bas mitz·vah** (bäs). **1.** A 12-to-14-year-old Jewish girl who assumes the religious responsibilities of an adult. **2.** The ceremony confirming a bat mitzvah.

ba·ton (bə-tŏn', băt'n) *n.* A tapered stick, esp. one with which a conductor leads an orchestra or band.

ba·tra·chi·an (bə-trā'kē-ən) *adj.* Of or relating to frogs and toads. *—n.* A frog or toad.

bats·man (băts'mən) *n.* A player at bat, esp. in cricket.

bat•tal•ion (bə-tăl′yən) *n.* **1.** A military unit made up of a headquarters company and 4 infantry companies or a headquarters battery and 4 artillery batteries. **2.** A large body of people, esp. of troops.

bat•ten[1] (băt′n) *n.* A flexible wooden strip for sealing cracks or fastening together parts. —*v.* To secure with or as if with battens.

bat•ten[2] (băt′n) **1.** To become fat. **2.** To thrive and prosper.

bat•ter[1] (băt′ər) *v.* To pound or damage with heavy and repeated blows.

bat•ter[2] (băt′ər) *n.* The baseball or cricket player at bat.

bat•ter[3] (băt′ər) *n.* A thick, beaten mixture, as of flour and liquid, used in cooking.

bat•ter•ing-ram *also* **battering ram** (băt′ər-ĭng-răm′) *n.* An ancient military engine used to batter down walls.

bat•ter•y (băt′ə-rē) *n., pl.* **-ies. 1.** *Law.* The unlawful beating of a person. **2. a.** An artillery emplacement. **b.** A set of heavy guns, as on a warship. **3.** A number of similar things grouped or used together. **4.** The pitcher and catcher on a baseball team. **5.** A device that generates an electric current by chemical reaction.

bat•ting (băt′ĭng) *n.* Rolls or sheets of cotton or wool fiber, as for stuffing mattresses.

bat•tle (băt′l) *n.* **1.** A large-scale military encounter. **2.** An intense competition : struggle. —*v.* **-tled, -tling.** To engage in battle : fight. —**bat′tler** *n.*

bat•tle-ax *or* **bat•tle-axe** (băt′l-ăks′) *n.* A broad-headed ax once used as a weapon.

bat•tle•dore (băt′l-dôr′, -dōr′) *n.* **1.** An early form of badminton played with a flat wooden paddle and a shuttlecock. **2.** The paddle used in battledore.

bat•tle•field (băt′l-fēld′) *n.* A place where a battle is waged.

bat•tle•front (băt′l-frŭnt′) *n.* The area where enemies face one another in battle.

bat•tle•ground (băt′l-ground′) *n.* A battlefield.

bat•tle•ment (băt′l-mənt) *n.* A parapet with indentations that is at the top of a wall and used for defense or decoration.

battle royal *n., pl.* **battles royal. 1.** A battle with more than 2 combatants. **2.** A bitter dispute.

bat•tle•ship (băt′l-shĭp′) *n.* A warship of the largest, most heavily armed and armored class.

bat•ty (băt′ē) *adj.* **-ti•er, -ti•est.** *Slang.* Insane : crazy.

bau•ble (bô′bəl) *n.* A trinket.

baud (bôd) *n.* *Computer Sci.* A unit of speed in data transmission usu. equal to 1 bit per second.

baux•ite (bôk′sīt′) *n.* The principal ore of aluminum.

bawd (bôd) *n.* **1.** A woman who runs a brothel : madam. **2.** A prostitute.

bawd•y (bô′dē) *adj.* **-i•er, -i•est. 1.** Humorously coarse : risqué. **2.** Vulgar : lewd. —**bawd′i•ly** *adv.* —**bawd′i•ness** *n.*

bawl (bôl) *v.* **1.** To cry out loudly : wail. **2.** To shout vehemently.—**bawl out.** *Informal.* To scold severely. —**bawl** *n.* —**bawl′er** *n.*

bay[1] (bā) *n.* A wide inlet of a body of water partially enclosed by land.

bay[2] (bā) *n.* **1.** A compartment or main division of a structure. **2.** A compartment projecting from a wall and containing a bay window.

bay[3] (bā) *adj.* Reddish brown. —*n.* **1.** A reddish brown. **2.** A reddish-brown animal, esp. a horse.

bay[4] (bā) *n.* **1.** A deep, prolonged bark, esp. of hounds. **2.** The position of one cornered and forced to turn and fight. —*v.* To utter a bay.

bay[5] (bā) *n.* LAUREL 1.

bay•ber•ry (bā′bĕr′ē) *n.* An aromatic shrub of the genus *Myrica* bearing waxy gray berries.

bay leaf *n.* The dried leaf of the laurel, used as seasoning in cooking.

bay•o•net (bā′ə-nĭt, -nĕt′, bā′ə-nĕt′) *n.* A blade that attaches to the muzzle end of a rifle. —*v.* **-net•ed, -net•ing** *or* **-net•ted, -net•ting.** To prod or stab with a bayonet.

bay•ou (bī′o͞o, bī′ō) *n.* A marshy, sluggish body of water tributary to a river or lake.

bay rum *n.* An aromatic liquid obtained by distilling the leaves of the bayberry tree, *Pimenta acris,* with rum or synthesized from alcohol, water, and various oils.

bay window *n.* **1.** A large window that projects from the outer wall of a building and forms a bay. **2.** *Slang.* A paunch.

ba•zaar *also* **ba•zar** (bə-zär′) *n.* **1.** A market consisting of a group of shops and stalls lining a street, esp. in the Middle East. **2.** A fair selling articles for charity.

ba•zoo•ka (bə-zo͞o′kə) *n.* A tube-shaped weapon that fires armor-piercing rockets.

BB (bē′bē′) *n.* A shot pellet that measures about .46 cm, or 0.18 in., in diameter.

be (bē) *v.* **was** (wŏz, wŭz; wəz *when unstressed*) *or* **were** (wûr), **being** (bē′ĭng), **been** (bĭn) **1.** To exist <I think, therefore I *am.*> **2.** To occupy a particular position <The book *is* on the desk.> **3.** To take place : occur <The party *is* tomorrow.> **4.** To go. —Used chiefly in the past and perfect tenses <Have you ever *been* to Europe?> **5. a.** To equal in meaning : be identical with <Sunday *is* the first day of the week.> **b.** To symbolize <Food *is* love.> **c.** To belong to a specified class or group <This dog *is* a terrier.> **d.** To have or show a specified quality or characteristic <He *is* intelligent.> **6.** —Used with the past participle of a transitive verb to form the passive voice <The house *was* sold.> **7.** —Used with the present participle of a verb to express continuing action <She *is* cooking dinner.> **8.** —Used with the infinitive of a verb to express intention, obligation, or future action <You *are* to telephone your home immediately>

Be *symbol for* BERYLLIUM.

beach (bēch) *n.* The often sandy or pebbly shore of a body of water. —*v.* To go or drive ashore.

beach buggy *n.* A dune buggy.
beach•comb•er (bēch′kō′mər) *n.* One who lives on what can be found on beaches.
beach flea *n.* Any of various small, jumping crustaceans of the family Orchestiidae, living on sandy beaches near the tide line.
beach•head (bēch′hĕd′) *n.* An area on an enemy shoreline secured by troops in advance of an invading force.
bea•con (bē′kən) *n.* **1.** A signal fire. **2.** A coastal signaling or guiding device. **3.** A radio transmitter that emits a signal as a warning or guide.
bead (bēd) *n.* **1.** A small, often round piece of material pierced for threading or stringing. **2. beads. a.** A necklace made of beads. **b.** A rosary. **3.** A small, round mass, as a drop of moisture. **4.** A narrow projecting strip, as of molding. —*v.* **1.** To ornament with beads. **2.** To form into beads. **—bead′ing** *n.* **—bead′y** *adj.*
bea•dle (bēd′l) *n.* A minor parish official, usu. in an English church, whose duties include ushering.
bea•gle (bē′gəl) *n.* A small, short-legged hound with drooping ears and a smooth coat with white, black, and tan markings.
beak (bēk) *n.* **1.** The bill of a bird. **2.** A part or structure resembling a beak.
beak•er (bē′kər) *n.* **1.** A large, wide-mouthed drinking cup. **2.** A cylindrical glass laboratory vessel with a pouring lip.
beam (bēm) *n.* **1.** A large, oblong length of metal or timber used esp. in construction. **2.** The widest part of a ship. **3.** A radio beam. **4.** A ray of light. —*v.* **1. a.** To emit light **:** shine. **b.** To direct (a radio signal) in a beam. **2.** To smile broadly.
bean (bēn) *n.* **1.** The often edible seed or seed pod of any of various plants of the genus *Phaseolus.* **2.** Any of various plants related to or suggestive of bean plants. **3.** *Slang.* The head. —*v. Slang.* To hit on the head with an object.
bean ball *n. Baseball.* A pitched ball aimed at a batter's head.
bean curd *n.* A cheeselike food made from soybeans.
bean•ie (bē′nē) *n.* A small skullcap.
bean sprouts *pl.n.* The tender edible sprouts of bean seeds, esp. soybean seeds.
bear[1] (bâr) *v.* **bore** (bôr, bōr), **borne** (bôrn) *or* **born, bear•ing. 1.** To support. **2.** To carry. **3.** To endure <couldn't *bear* the tension> **4.** To be equipped with **:** have <*bore* his uncle's name> **5.** To render as testimony <*bore* witness> **6.** To give birth to. **7.** To yield **:** produce <a shrub *bearing* fruit> **8.** To exert force <bring pressure to *bear*> **9.** To move in a particular direction <*bore* left at the intersection> **—bear′a•ble** *adj.* **—bear′a•bly** *adv.* **—bear′er** *n.*
bear[2] (bâr) *n.* **1.** Any of various usu. omnivorous mammals of the family Ursidae with shaggy fur. **2.** A sullen, ill-mannered person. **3.** One that sells commodities or securities with the expectation of a price fall. **—bear′ish** *adj.* **—bear′ish•ness** *n.*
beard (bîrd) *n.* **1.** The hair on a man's chin, cheeks, and throat. **2.** A hairlike growth, as on a goat's chin or certain plants. —*v.* To confront resolutely and boldly.
bear•ing (bâr′ĭng) *n.* **1.** A manner of conducting oneself **:** deportment. **2.** A machine part around which another part turns. **3.** A supporting element. **4.** Relationship with something else **:** connection. **5.** Direction, esp. angular direction as used in navigation. **6. bearings.** Awareness of one's position or situation. **7.** A heraldic emblem.
beast (bēst) *n.* **1.** An animal, esp. a 4-footed animal. **2.** A vile person.
beast•ly (bēst′lē) *adj.* **-li•er, -li•est. 1.** Of, relating to, or like a beast. **2.** Nasty **:** disagreeable. **—beast′li•ness** *n.*
beast of burden *n.* A pack animal.
beat (bēt) *v.* **beat, beat•en** (bēt′n) *or* **beat, beat•ing. 1.** To strike repeatedly. **2.** To shape by beating **:** forge <*beat* silver into a bracelet> **3.** To make by trampling **:** tread. **4.** To defeat. **5.** To surpass. **6.** To throb **:** pulsate. **7.** To mix rapidly <*beat* eggs> **8.** To strike so as to produce a signal or music. **9.** *Informal.* To get ahead of <worked hard and *beat* the deadline> —*n.* **1.** A stroke or blow. **2.** A periodic pulsation **:** throb. **3.** A rhythmic stress, as in music. **4.** A course regularly covered **:** round. —*adj.* Very tired **:** exhausted. **—beat′er** *n.*
be•a•tif•ic (bē′ə-tĭf′ĭk) *adj.* Showing or giving extreme joy or bliss.
be•at•i•fy (bē-ăt′ə-fī′) *v.* **-fied, -fy•ing. 1.** To make extremely happy. **2.** *Rom. Cath. Ch.* To proclaim (a deceased person) to be one of the blessed. **—be•at′i•fi•ca′tion** *n.*
be•at•i•tude (bē-ăt′ĭ-tōōd′, -tyōōd′) *n.* **1.** Supreme blessedness or happiness. **2.** Any of the 9 declarations of blessedness made by Jesus in the Sermon on the Mount.
beat•nik (bēt′nĭk) *n.* A person who acts and dresses unconventionally and disregards established notions of propriety.
beat-up (bēt′ŭp′) *adj. Slang.* Damaged or worn through neglect or heavy use.
beau (bō) *n., pl.* **beaus** *or* **beaux** (bōz). **1.** A suitor. **2.** A dandy **:** fop.
beau geste (bō zhĕst′) *n., pl.* **beaux gestes** *or* **beau gestes** (bō zhĕst′). A gracious or noble gesture.
beau i•de•al (bō′ ī-dē′əl) *n., pl.* **beau i•de•als.** An idealized model.
Beau•jo•lais (bō′zhō-lā′) *n.* A red table wine of French origin.
beau monde (bō mŏnd′, mÔNd′) *n., pl.* **beaux mondes** (bō mÔNd′) *or* **beau mondes** (bō mŏndz′). The world of fashionable society.
beau•te•ous (byōō′tē-əs, -tyəs) *adj.* Beautiful. **—beau′te•ous•ly** *adv.*
beau•ti•cian (byōō-tĭsh′ən) *n.* One who gives cosmetic treatments.
beau•ti•ful (byōō′tə-fəl) *adj.* Marked by beauty. ★ ***syns:*** BEAUTEOUS, COMELY, FAIR, GOOD-LOOKING, GORGEOUS, LOVELY, PRETTY, RAVISHING **—beau′ti•ful•ly** *adv.*

beau•ti•fy (byōō′tə-fī′) *v.* **-fied, -fy•ing.** To make or become beautiful. —**beau′ti•fi•ca′tion** *n.* —**beau′ti•fi′er** *n.*
beau•ty (byōō′tē) *n., pl.* **-ties. 1.** A quality or a combination of qualities that delights the senses or appeals to the mind. **2.** One that is beautiful. **3.** An outstanding or conspicuous example.
beauty mark *n.* A mole or birthmark.
beauty parlor *n.* An establishment providing hairdressing, manicures, facials, etc.
beauty salon *n.* A beauty parlor.
beauty shop *n.* A beauty parlor.
beaux (bō) *n. var. pl. of* BEAU.
beaux-arts (bō-zär′) *pl.n.* The fine arts.
bea•ver (bē′vər) *n.* **1.** A large aquatic rodent of the genus *Castor* with thick fur, a flat paddlelike tail, and chisellike front teeth. **2.** The fur of a beaver.
bea•ver•board (bē′vər-bôrd′, -bōrd′) *n.* A wallboard of compressed wood pulp.
be•bop (bē′bŏp′) *n.* BOP[2].
be•calm (bĭ-käm′) *v.* To make (e.g., a ship) motionless for lack of wind.
be•cause (bĭ-kôz′, -kŭz′) *conj.* For the reason that : since.
because of *prep.* On account of.
beck (bĕk) *n.* **1.** A gesture of beckoning. **2.** A summons.
beck•on (bĕk′ən) *v.* **1.** To signal, as by nodding or waving. **2.** To attract.
be•cloud (bĭ-kloud′) *v.* To darken with or as if with clouds : obscure.
be•come (bĭ-kŭm′) *v.* **1.** To grow or come to be. **2.** To be suitable to : suit.
be•com•ing (bĭ-kŭm′ĭng) *adj.* **1.** Suitable : appropriate. **2.** Attractive. —**be•com′ing•ly** *adv.* —**be•com′ing•ness** *n.*
bed (bĕd) *n.* **1.** A piece of furniture for sleeping. **2.** A plot of cultivated or planted ground. **3.** The bottom of a body of water <a river *bed*> **4.** A horizontal layer, as of rock. **5.** A deposit, as of ore. —*v.* **bed•ded, bed•ding. 1.** To put to bed. **2.** To plant in a bed. **3.** To lay flat or in layers.
be•daub (bĭ-dôb′) *v.* To smear.
be•daz•zle (bĭ-dăz′əl) *v.* To bewilder with intense light. —**be•daz′zle•ment** *n.*
bed•bug (bĕd′bŭg′) *n.* A wingless, bloodsucking insect, *Cimex lectularius,* that infests human dwellings and esp. beds.
bed•clothes (bĕd′klōz′, -klō*thz*′) *pl.n.* Coverings for a bed.
bed•ding (bĕd′ĭng) *n.* **1.** Bedclothes. **2.** A foundation.
be•deck (bĭ-dĕk′) *v.* To deck out : adorn.
be•dev•il (bĭ-dĕv′əl) *v.* **-iled, -il•ing** *or* **-illed, -il•ling. 1.** To torment : plague. **2.** To bewilder : confuse.
be•dew (bĭ-dōō′, -dyōō′) *v.* To moisten with or as if with dew.
bed•fast (bĕd′făst′) *adj.* Bedridden.
bed•fel•low (bĕd′fĕl′ō) *n.* **1.** Someone with whom one shares a bed. **2.** A collaborator, associate, or ally.
be•di•zen (bĭ-dī′zən, -dĭz′ən) *v.* To adorn or dress gaudily.
bed•lam (bĕd′ləm) *n.* **1.** A situation or place of noise and confusion. **2.** *Archaic.* An insane asylum.
Bed•ling•ton terrier (bĕd′lĭng-tən) *n.* A dog orig. bred in England, with a woolly grayish or brownish coat.

Bedlington terrier

Bed•ou•in (bĕd′ōō-ĭn, bĕd′wĭn) *n.* A nomadic Arab of the North African, Arabian, or Syrian deserts.
bed•pan (bĕd′păn′) *n.* A receptacle used as a toilet by a bedridden person.
bed•post (bĕd′pōst′) *n.* A vertical post of a bed.
be•drag•gled (bĭ-drăg′əld) *adj.* **1.** Wet and limp. **2.** Soiled by or as if by dragging in the mud. **3.** Dilapidated.
bed•rid•den (bĕd′rĭd′n) *adj.* Confined to bed by illness or infirmity.
bed•rock (bĕd′rŏk′) *n.* The solid rock underlying the earth's surface.
bed•roll (bĕd′rōl′) *n.* A roll of bedding that can be carried, as by campers.
bed•room (bĕd′rōōm′, -rŏŏm′) *n.* A room for sleeping.
bed•side (bĕd′sīd′) *n.* The place alongside a bed, esp. of a sick person.
bed•sore (bĕd′sôr′, -sōr′) *n.* A skin ulceration on a bedridden person induced by pressure and chafing.
bed•spread (bĕd′sprĕd′) *n.* A decorative outer covering for a bed.
bed•stead (bĕd′stĕd′) *n.* The framework that supports a bed.
bed•time (bĕd′tīm′) *n.* The time at which one goes to bed.
bee (bē) *n.* **1.** Any of various winged, hairy-bodied insects of the order Hymenoptera, characterized by specialized structures for gathering nectar and pollen from flowers. **2.** A gathering at which people work together or compete <a spelling *bee*> <a quilting *bee*>
beech (bēch) *n.* A tree of the genus *Fagus* with light-colored bark, edible nuts, and strong, heavy wood.
beech•nut (bēch′nŭt′) *n.* The nut of a beech tree.
beef (bēf) *n., pl.* **beeves** (bēvz). **1.** A fattened steer, bull, ox, or cow, esp. one for use as meat. **2.** The flesh of a steer, bull, ox, or cow. **3.** *Informal.* Muscle : brawn. **4.** *pl.* **beefs.** *Slang.* A

complaint. —*v. Slang.* To complain. —**beef up.** *Slang.* To make stronger : build up.
beef·cake (bēf′kāk′) *n. Informal.* Photographs of minimally clad, muscular men.
beef·eat·er (bēf′ē′tər) *n.* A yeoman of the royal guard in England.
beef·steak (bēf′stāk′) *n.* A slice of beef suitable for broiling or frying.
beef·y (bē′fē) *adj.* **-i·er, -i·est. 1.** Like beef. **2.** Muscular and heavy in build : brawny. —**beef′i·ness** *n.*
bee·hive (bē′hīv′) *n.* A hive for bees.
bee·keep·er (bē′kē′pər) *n.* One who raises and keeps bees. —**bee′keep′ing** *n.*
bee·line (bē′līn′) *n.* A direct straight route.
been (bĭn) *v. p.p. of* BE.
beep (bēp) *n.* A short, usu. high-pitched sound, as from an electronic device, for signaling or warning. —**beep** *v.* —**beep′er** *n.*
beer (bîr) *n.* An alcoholic beverage brewed from malt and hops.
bees·wax (bēz′wăks′) *n.* The wax bees secrete and use to make honeycombs.
beet (bēt) *n.* A cultivated plant of the genus *Beta* with edible leaves and a fleshy root used as a vegetable or sugar source.
bee·tle[1] (bēt′l) *n.* An insect of the order Coleoptera with modified horny front wings that cover the membranous hind wings when it is not flying.
bee·tle[2] (bēt′l) *adj.* Overhanging : jutting <*beetle* brows> —*v.* **-tled, -tling.** To jut : project.
bee·tle[3] (bēt′l) *n.* A heavy tool for pounding or hammering.
beeves (bēvz) *n. pl. of* BEEF.
be·fall (bĭ-fôl′) *v.* To happen (to).
be·fit (bĭ-fĭt′) *v.* To be appropriate for or suitable to.
be·fog (bĭ-fôg′, -fŏg′) *v.* To obscure with or as if with fog.
be·fore (bĭ-fôr′, -fōr′) *adv.* **1.** In the past : earlier. **2.** In advance : ahead. —*prep.* **1.** Prior to <left *before* dawn> **2.** In front of <stood *before* the judge> **3.** In higher esteem than <put honesty *before* profit> —*conj.* **1.** Prior to the time when <I met you *before.*> **2.** Rather than <would go to jail *before* betraying a fellow soldier>
be·fore·hand (bĭ-fôr′hănd′, -fōr′-) *adv. & adj.* In advance.
be·foul (bĭ-foul′) *v.* To make dirty : sully.
be·friend (bĭ-frĕnd′) *v.* To behave as a friend to.
be·fud·dle (bĭ-fŭd′l) *v.* To confuse.
beg (bĕg) *v.* **begged, beg·ging. 1.** To ask or make a living by asking for charity. **2.** To ask for earnestly : entreat. **3.** To evade <Don't *beg* the question.>
be·gan (bĭ-găn′) *v. p.t. of* BEGIN.
be·get (bĭ-gĕt′) *v.* To father : sire. —**be·get′ter** *n.*
beg·gar (bĕg′ər) *n.* One who begs, esp. for a living. —*v.* To make poor : impoverish. —**beg′gar·y** *n.*
beg·gar·ly (bĕg′ər-lē) *adj.* Of or like a beggar : poor. —**beg′gar·li·ness** *n.*
be·gin (bĭ-gĭn′) *v.* **-gan** (-găn′), **-gun** (-gŭn′), **-gin·ning. 1.** To start doing : commence. **2.** To come into being : arise. **3.** To cause to come into being : originate. ★ ***syns:*** ARISE, COMMENCE, ORIGINATE, START —**be·gin′ner** *n.*
be·gin·ning (bĭ-gĭn′ĭng) *n.* **1.** The time when or place where something begins or is begun. **2.** The initial part of something : commencement. **3.** A source : origin.
be·gone (bĭ-gôn′, -gŏn′) *interj.* —Used as an order of dismissal.
be·go·nia (bĭ-gōn′yə) *n.* Any of various plants of the genus *Begonia* grown for their showy leaves and waxy flowers.
be·grime (bĭ-grīm′) *v.* **-grimed, -grim·ing.** To soil with grime.
be·grudge (bĭ-grŭj′) *v.* **1.** To envy someone the enjoyment or possession of. **2.** To give reluctantly.
be·guile (bĭ-gīl′) *v.* **-guiled, -guil·ing. 1.** To cheat : deceive. **2.** To pass pleasantly : while away. **3.** To charm : delight. —**be·guile′ment** *n.* —**be·guil′er** *n.*
be·guine (bĭ-gēn′) *n.* A ballroom dance based on a native dance of Martinique and St. Lucia.
be·gum (bē′gəm, bā′-) *n.* A Muslim woman of rank.
be·gun (bĭ-gŭn′) *v. p.p. of* BEGIN.
be·half (bĭ-hăf′, -häf′) *n.* Interest, benefit, or support.
be·have (bĭ-hāv′) *v.* **-haved, -hav·ing. 1.** To act, react, or function in a particular manner. **2.** To conduct oneself in a specified and esp. a proper manner.
be·hav·ior (bĭ-hāv′yər) *n.* The way in which someone or something behaves. —**be·hav′ior·al** *adj.*
be·hav·ior·ism (bĭ-hāv′yə-rĭz′əm) *n.* The psychological school holding that observable behavior constitutes the essential or exclusive scientific basis of psychological data and investigation. —**be·hav′ior·ist** *n.* —**be·hav′ior·is′tic** *adj.*
be·head (bĭ-hĕd′) *v.* To decapitate.
be·he·moth (bĭ-hē′məth, bē′ə-) *n.* **1.** An enormous animal described in the Old Testament. **2.** Something of immense size.
be·hest (bĭ-hĕst′) *n.* **1.** An authoritative command. **2.** Insistent prompting.
be·hind (bĭ-hīnd′) *adv.* **1.** In, to, or toward the back. **2.** In the place or condition that is left. **3.** Late. **4.** Slow. —*prep.* **1.** At the back or in the rear of <a garage *behind* the house> **2.** In or to a former place, time, or situation <fears that are now *behind* him> **3.** Later than <*behind* schedule> **4.** Below, as in rank <car sales *behind* last year's> **5.** In support of <Her parents are *behind* her in her efforts.> —*n. Informal.* The buttocks.
be·hind·hand (bĭ-hīnd′hănd′) *adj.* **1.** In arrears. **2.** Behind the times.
be·hold (bĭ-hōld′) *v.* To look at : see. —Often used in the imperative.
be·hold·en (bĭ-hōl′dən) *adj.* Indebted : obliged.

be•hoove (bĭ-hōōv′) *v.* **-hooved, -hoov•ing.** To be proper or necessary for.
beige (bāzh) *n.* A light grayish brown. **—beige** *adj.*
be•ing (bē′ĭng) *n.* **1.** Existence. **2.** One that lives, esp. a person. **3.** One's basic or essential nature : essence.
be•la•bor (bĭ-lā′bər) *v.* **1.** To thrash thoroughly. **2.** To harp on.
be•lat•ed (bĭ-lā′tĭd) *adj.* Tardy : late. **—be•lat′ed•ly** *adv.*
be•lay (bĭ-lā′) *v. Naut.* **1.** To secure (e.g., a rope) around a cleat or pin. **2.** To stop <*Belay* there.>
bel can•to (bĕl kän′tō) *n.* A style of operatic singing characterized by rich tonal lyricism and brilliant vocal technique.
belch (bĕlch) *v.* **1.** To expel stomach gas noisily through the mouth. **2.** To eject violently. **—belch** *n.*
bel•dam *also* **bel•dame** (bĕl′dəm) *n.* An old woman, esp. an ugly one.
be•lea•guer (bĭ-lē′gər) *v.* **1.** To besiege. **2.** To beset : harass.
bel•fry (bĕl′frē) *n., pl.* **-fries. 1.** A bell tower, as on a church. **2.** The part of a belfry where the bells are hung.
be•lie (bĭ-lī′) *v.* **-lied, -ly•ing. 1.** To give a false picture of : misrepresent. **2.** To demonstrate to be false. **3.** To be inconsistent with : contradict. **—be•li′er** *n.*
be•lief (bĭ-lēf′) *n.* **1.** Trust : confidence. **2.** Something, as a tenet, that is believed : conviction. ★ ***syns:*** CONVICTION, FEELING, IDEA, NOTION, OPINION, PERSUASION, POSITION, SENTIMENT, VIEW
be•lieve (bĭ-lēv′) *v.* **-lieved, -liev•ing. 1.** To accept as real or true. **2.** To credit with veracity. **3.** To think : suppose. **4.** To hold religious beliefs. **—be•liev′a•ble** *adj.* **—be•liev′er** *n.*
be•lit•tle (bĭ-lĭt′l) *v.* **-tled, -tling.** To speak or think of as small or unimportant : disparage. **—be•lit′tle•ment** *n.*
bell (bĕl) *n.* **1.** A hollow metal instrument that emits a metallic sound when struck. **2.** Something with the flared shape of a bell. **3.** *Naut.* **a.** A stroke on a bell to mark the hour. **b.** The time indicated by the striking of a bell. *—v.* To furnish with a bell.
bel•la•don•na (bĕl′ə-dŏn′ə) *n.* **1.** A plant, *Atropa belladonna,* with small poisonous black berries. **2.** Atropine.
bell-bot•toms (bĕl′bŏt′əmz) *pl.n.* Trousers with legs that flare out at the bottom. **—bell′-bot′tom** *adj.*
bell•boy (bĕl′boi′) *n.* A hotel employee who assists guests, as by carrying luggage.
belle (bĕl) *n.* An attractive and much-admired girl or woman.
belles-let•tres (bĕl-lĕt′rə) *pl.n. (sing. in number).* Literature regarded for its artistic rather than informative value.
bel•let•rist (bĕl-lĕt′rĭst) *n.* A writer of belles-lettres.
bell•hop (bĕl′hŏp′) *n.* A bellboy.
bel•li•cose (bĕl′ĭ-kōs′) *adj.* Warlike, as in disposition : pugnacious. **—bel′li•cos′i•ty** (-kŏs′ĭ-tē) *n.*
bel•lig•er•ent (bə-lĭj′ər-ənt) *adj.* **1.** Inclined to be aggressive or hostile. **2.** Waging war. ★ ***syns:*** BELLICOSE, COMBATIVE, CONTENTIOUS, HOSTILE, PUGNACIOUS, TRUCULENT **—bel•lig′er•ence** *n.* **—bel•lig′er•ent** *n.* **—bel•lig′er•ent•ly** *adv.*
bell jar *n.* A bell-shaped glass vessel used esp. to establish a controlled atmosphere in scientific experiments.
bel•low (bĕl′ō) *v.* **1.** To make the roar characteristic of a bull. **2.** To shout in a deep powerful voice. **—bel′low** *n.*
bel•lows (bĕl′ōz, -əz) *n. (sing. or pl. in number).* A device with a flexible air chamber that contracts a current of air through a nozzle.

bellows

bell pepper *n.* A pepper plant cultivated for its edible, bell-shaped fruit.
bell•weth•er (bĕl′wĕ*th*′ər) *n.* A leader.
bel•ly (bĕl′ē) *n., pl.* **-lies. 1.** The abdomen. **2.** The underside of an animal's body. **3.** The stomach. *—v.* **-lied, -ly•ing.** To bulge or cause to bulge.
bel•ly•ache (bĕl′ē-āk′) *n.* A pain in the stomach or abdomen. *—v. Slang.* To complain.
bel•ly•but•ton (bĕl′ē-bŭt′n) *n. Informal.* The navel.
belly dance *n.* A dance marked by sinuous movements of the belly. **—bel′ly-dance′** *v.* **—belly dancer** *n.*
bel•ly•ful (bĕl′ē-fo͝ol′) *n. Informal.* An amount exceeding what one can endure.
belly laugh *n.* A deep, jovial laugh.
bel•ly-up (bĕl′ē-ŭp′) *adj. Informal.* Bankrupt.
be•long (bĭ-lông′, -lŏng′) *v.* **1.** To be owned by someone. **2.** To be a part of or in natural association with something. **3.** To be a member of a group. **4.** To have a suitable or appropriate place.
be•long•ings (bĭ-lông′ĭngz, -lŏng′-) *pl.n.* Personal possessions : effects.
be•lov•ed (bĭ-lŭv′ĭd, -lŭvd′) *adj.* Dearly loved. **—be•lov′ed** *n.*
be•low (bĭ-lō′) *adv.* **1.** In or to a lower place or level. **2.** On earth. *—prep.* **1.** Lower than : under. **2.** Inferior to.
belt (bĕlt) *n.* **1.** A band, as of leather, worn around the waist. **2.** A continuous moving

band that transfers motion or conveys material from one wheel or shaft to another. **3.** A geographic region that is distinctive in a specific way. **4.** *Slang.* A powerful hit : punch. **5.** *Slang.* A drink, esp. of hard liquor. —*v.* **1.** To encircle or attach with a belt. **2.** To hit with or as if with a belt.

belt•way (bĕlt'wā') *n.* A highway skirting an urban area.

be•lu•ga (bə-lo͞o'gə) *n* . **1.** A sturgeon, *Huso huso,* of the Black and Caspian seas, whose roe is used for caviar. **2.** A small toothed whale of northern waters that is white when full-grown.

bel•ve•dere (bĕl'vĭ-dîr') *n.* A structure, as an open roofed gallery, located so as to command a view.

be•moan (bĭ-mōn') *v.* To lament : mourn.

be•muse (bĭ-myo͞oz') *v.* **1.** To confuse : bewilder. **2.** To cause to be lost in thought.

bench (bĕnch) *n.* **1.** A long seat for 2 or more persons. **2. a.** The judge's seat in a court of law. **b.** The position or office of a judge. **c.** The judge or judges composing a court. **3.** A craftsman's worktable. —*v.* **1.** To seat on a bench. **2.** To keep out of or remove from a game.

bench mark *also* **bench•mark** (bĕnch'-märk') *n.* **1.** A mark made by a surveyor on a stationary point and used as an elevation reference. **2.** A standard of measurement or evaluation.

bench•warm•er (bĕnch'wôr'mər) *n. Sports.* A substitute player.

bench warrant *n.* A warrant issued by a judge or law court ordering the arrest of an offender.

bend (bĕnd) *v.* **bent** (bĕnt), **bend•ing. 1.** To bring into tension (e.g., a bow). **2.** To assume or cause to assume a different and esp. a curved shape. **3.** To deflect. **4.** To subdue or coerce. **5.** To apply closely : concentrate. **6.** To fasten. **7.** To submit : yield. —*n.* **1.** The act of bending. **2.** Something bent. **3. bends.** *(sing. or pl. in number).* Caisson disease.

bend•er (bĕn'dər) *n. Slang.* A spree.

be•neath (bĭ-nēth') *adv.* **1.** In or to a lower position : below. **2.** Underneath. —*prep.* **1.** Under : below. **2.** Unworthy of.

ben•e•dic•tion (bĕn'ĭ-dĭk'shən) *n.* **1.** A blessing. **2.** The invocation of a divine blessing, usu. at the end of a church service. —**ben'e•dic'to•ry** *adj.*

ben•e•fac•tion (bĕn'ə-făk'shən) *n.* A charitable act or gift.

ben•e•fac•tor (bĕn'ə-făk't ər) *n.* One who gives support or financial aid.

ben•e•fac•tress (bĕn'ə-făk'trĭs) *n.* A woman who gives support or financial aid.

ben•e•fice (bĕn'ə-fĭs) *n.* A church office endowed with fixed capital assets that provide a living.

be•nef•i•cence (bə-nĕf'ĭ-səns) *n.* **1.** The quality of being charitable or kind. **2.** A charitable act or gift. —**be•nef'i•cent** *adj.*

ben•e•fi•cial (bĕn'ə-fĭsh'əl) *adj.* Bringing benefit : helpful. ★ ***syns:*** ADVANTAGEOUS, BENIGNANT, FAVORABLE, GOOD, PROPITIOUS, SALUTARY —**ben'e•fi'cial•ly** *adv.*

ben•e•fi•ci•ar•y (bĕn'ə-fĭsh'ē-ĕr'ē, -fĭsh'ə-rē) *n., pl.* **-ies.** The recipient of a benefit, as income from a will or trust fund.

ben•e•fit (bĕn'ə-fĭt) *n.* **1.** An advantage. **2.** Aid : help. **3.** A payment or series of payments to one in need. **4.** A public performance to raise funds. —*v.* **-fit•ed, -fit•ing** *or* **-fit•ted, -fit•ting. 1.** To be helpful or advantageous to. **2.** To profit.

be•nev•o•lence (bə-nĕv'ə-ləns) *n.* **1.** An inclination to do charitable or kind acts. **2.** A charitable act. —**be•nev'o•lent** *adj.* —**be•nev'o•lent•ly** *adv.*

be•night•ed (bĭ-nī'tĭd) *adj.* **1.** Overtaken by night. **2.** In a state of ignorance. —**be•night'-ed•ly** *adv.* —**be•night'ed•ness** *n.*

be•nign (bĭ-nīn') *adj.* **1.** Having a kind disposition : gentle. **2.** Tending to promote well-being : beneficial. **3.** *Pathol.* Not malignant. —**be•nign'ly** *adv.*

be•nig•nant (bĭ-nĭg'nənt) *adj.* **1.** Favorable : beneficial. **2.** Kindly disposed : gracious. —**be•nig'nant•ly** *adv.*

ben•i•son (bĕn'ĭ-zən) *n.* A benediction : blessing.

ben•ny (bĕn'ē) *n., pl.* **-nies.** *Slang.* An amphetamine tablet.

bent (bĕnt) *adj.* **1.** Not straight : curved or crooked. **2.** Having a fixed purpose : determined. —*n.* A tendency, disposition, or inclination : propensity.

ben•thos (bĕn'thŏs') *n.* **1.** The bottom of a sea or a lake. **2.** The organisms living there. —**ben'thic, ben•thon'ic** *adj.*

bent•wood (bĕnt'wo͝od') *n.* Wood that has been steamed until pliable and then bent and shaped. —**bent'wood'** *adj.*

be•numb (bĭ-nŭm') *v.* **1.** To make numb, esp. by cold. **2.** To make inactive : dull.

Ben•ze•drine (bĕn'zĭ-drēn'). A trademark for a brand of amphetamine.

ben•zene (bĕn'zēn', bĕn-zēn') *n.* A colorless, flammable liquid made from petroleum and used in detergents, insecticides, and motor fuels.

ben•zine (bĕn'zēn', bĕn-zēn') *also* **ben•zin** (bĕn'zĭn) *n.* **1.** Ligroin. **2.** Benzene.

ben•zo•ate (bĕn'zō-āt', -ĭt) *n.* An ester or salt of benzoic acid.

ben•zo•caine (bĕn'zə-kān') *n.* A crystalline ester used as a local anesthetic.

ben•zo•ic acid (bĕn-zō'ĭk) *n.* A white, crystalline, organic acid used to season tobacco and in perfumes, germicides, and dentifrices.

ben•zo•in (bĕn'zō-ĭn, -zoin') *n.* Any of several resins containing benzoic acid, derived as a gum from trees of the genus *Styrax* and used in ointments, perfumes, and medicine.

ben•zol (bĕn'zôl', -zōl') *n.* Benzene.

be•queath (bĭ-kwēth', -kwēth') *v.* **1.** *Law.* To leave or give by will. **2.** To pass on : hand down. —**be•queath'al** *n.* —**be•queath'er** *n.* —**be•queath'ment** *n.*

be•quest (bĭ-kwĕst') *n.* **1.** The act of bequeathing. **2.** Something bequeathed.

be•rate (bĭ-rāt′) *v.* **-rat•ed, -rat•ing.** To scold severely **:** upbraid.
ber•ceuse (bĕr-sœz′) *n., pl.* **-ceuses** (-sœz′). A lullaby.
be•reave (bĭ-rēv′) *v.* **-reaved** *or* **-reft** (-rĕft′), **-reav•ing.** To deprive of (something), esp. a loved one by death. **—be•reaved′** *n. & adj.* **—be•reave′ment** *n.*
be•reft (bĭ-rĕft′) *v. p.t. & p.p. of* BEREAVE. *—adj.* **1.** Lacking or deprived of something <*bereft* of dignity> **2.** Bereaved.
be•ret (bə-rā′, bĕr′ā′) *n.* A soft, round, usu. woolen cap that has no brim.
berg (bûrg) *n.* An iceberg.
ber•ga•mot (bûr′gə-mŏt′) *n.* A small, spiny tree, *Citrus aurantium bergamia,* bearing pear-shaped fruit whose rind yields an aromatic oil that is used in perfumery.
ber•i•ber•i (bĕr′ē-bĕr′ē) *n.* A thiamine-deficiency disease, endemic in E and S Asia and characterized by partial paralysis of the extremities, emaciation, and anemia.
ber•ke•li•um (bər-kē′lē-əm, bûrk′lē-əm) *n. Symbol* **Bk** A synthetic radioactive element.
berm (bûrm) *n.* **1.** A raised bank or path, as along a roadway or canal. **2.** A protective mound or bank of earth.
Bermuda onion *n.* A large, yellow-skinned onion having a mild flavor.
Bermuda shorts *pl.n.* Shorts ending just above the knees.
ber•ry (bĕr′ē) *n., pl.* **-ries. 1.** A usu. fleshy, edible fruit, as the strawberry or raspberry. **2.** *Bot.* A fleshy fruit, as the grape or tomato, that develops from a single ovary but has several or many seeds. **3.** A seed or dried kernel, as that of the coffee plant. *—v.* **-ried, -ry•ing.** To gather berries.
ber•serk (bər-sûrk′, -zûrk′) *adj.* **1.** Destructively or frenziedly violent. **2.** Deranged. **—ber•serk′** *adv.*
berth (bûrth) *n.* **1.** A built-in bed or bunk on a ship or train. **2.** A space at a wharf for a ship to dock. **3.** Sufficient space for a ship to maneuver. **4.** A position of employment, esp. on a ship. *—v.* **1.** To dock (a ship). **2.** To provide with a berth.
ber•yl (bĕr′əl) *n.* A mineral composed chiefly of beryllium, silicon, and oxygen that occurs in hexagonal prisms, is the major source of beryllium, and is used as a gem. **—ber′yl•line** (-ə-lĭn, -līn′) *adj.*
be•ryl•li•um (bə-rĭl′ē-əm) *n. Symbol* **Be** A lightweight, corrosion-resistant, rigid, steel-gray metallic element.
be•seech (bĭ-sēch′) *v.* **-sought** (-sôt′) *or* **-seeched, -seech•ing.** To request earnestly **:** entreat. **—be•seech′er** *n.*
be•seem (bĭ-sēm′) *v. Archaic.* To be suitable for **:** befit.
be•set (bĭ-sĕt′) *v.* **1.** To attack from all sides **:** assail. **2.** To trouble persistently **:** harass <*beset* by doubts>
be•side (bĭ-sīd′) *prep.* **1.** Next to **:** at the side of. **2.** In comparison with. **3.** Except for. **4.** Wide of **:** apart from <*beside* the point> *—adv. Archaic.* In addition to.
be•sides (bĭ-sīdz′) *adv.* **1.** In addition **:** also. **2.** Furthermore **:** moreover. **3.** Else **:** otherwise. *—prep.* **1.** In addition to. **2.** Other than **:** except.
be•siege (bĭ-sēj′) *v.* **1.** To encircle with troops **:** lay siege to. **2.** To crowd around. **3.** To importune or harass, as with requests. **—be•sieg′er** *n.*
be•smear (bĭ-smîr′) *v.* To smear.
be•smirch (bĭ-smûrch′) *v.* To soil **:** sully. **—be•smirch′er** *n.* **—be•smirch′ment** *n.*
be•som (bē′zəm) *n.* A bundle of twigs attached to a handle and used as a broom.
be•sot (bĭ-sŏt′) *v.* **-sot•ted, -sot•ting.** To stupefy or muddle with or as if with liquor.
be•spat•ter (bĭ-spăt′ər) *v.* To soil by splashing, as with mud.
be•speak (bĭ-spēk′) *v.* **1.** To be an indication of **:** signify. **2.** To reserve. **3.** To foretell.
be•spec•ta•cled (bĭ-spĕk′tə-kəld) *adj.* Wearing eyeglasses.
be•sprin•kle (bĭ-sprĭng′kəl) *v.* To sprinkle.
best (bĕst) *adj.* **1.** Exceeding all others in excellence or quality <the *best* chocolate> **2.** Most satisfactory, suitable, useful, or desirable <the *best* procedure> **3.** Greatest **:** largest <spent the *best* part of a day studying> *—adv.* **1.** Most advantageously. **2.** To the greatest extent or degree **:** most. *—n.* **1.** Something that is best. **2.** The best condition, manner, or quality <look your *best*><act your *best*> **3.** One's best efforts <always does her *best*> **4.** One's best clothing. **5.** One's warmest wishes **:** regards. *—v.* To get the better of **:** surpass.
bes•tial (bĕs′chəl, bĕst′yəl) *adj.* **1.** Of, relating to, or like an animal. **2.** Having the manners or qualities of a brute **:** savage. **—bes′ti•al′i•ty** *n.* **—bes′tial•ly** *adv.*
bes•ti•ar•y (bĕs′chē-ĕr′ē, bēs′-) *n., pl.* **-ies.** A medieval collection of allegorical fables about real and imaginary animals, each fable having a moral.
be•stir (bĭ-stûr′) *v.* To cause to become active **:** rouse.
best man *n.* The principal attendant of a bridegroom.
be•stow (bĭ-stō′) *v.* To give or present, esp. as an honor **:** confer. **—be•stow′al** *n.*
be•strew (bĭ-stro͞o′) *v.* To strew.
be•stride (bĭ-strīd′) *v.* **1.** To straddle. **2.** To step over. **3.** To tower over.
best seller *n.* A product, as a book, that is among those sold in the greatest numbers. **—best′-sell′ing** *adj.*
bet (bĕt) *n.* **1.** A wager. **2.** The fact, event, or outcome on which a wager is made. **3.** An object or amount risked in a wager **:** stake. *—v.* **bet** *or* **bet•ted, bet•ting. 1.** To stake (e.g., an amount) in a bet. **2.** To make a bet on (an outcome or a contestant). **3.** To maintain confidently.
be•ta-car•o•tene (bā′tə-kăr′ə-tēn′, bē′-) *n.* One of the isomeric forms of carotene that is widely distributed in nature.
be•take (bĭ-tāk′) *v.* To cause (oneself) to go or move.

beta particle *n.* A high-speed electron or positron, usu. emitted by an atomic nucleus undergoing radioactive decay.
beta ray *n.* A stream of beta particles, esp. a stream of electrons.
beta rhythm *also* **beta wave.** *n.* The second most common waveform observed in electroencephalograms of the adult brain, occuring at a frequency of 13 to 30 oscillations per second and associated with an alert waking state.
be•ta•tron (bā'tə-trŏn', bē'-) *n.* An accelerator capable of raising electrons to energies of up to several hundred million electron volts.
be•tel (bēt'l) *n.* A climbing Asian plant, *Piper betle,* whose leaves are wrapped around the betel nut and chewed for a slightly inebriating effect.
betel nut *also* **be•tel•nut** (bēt'l-nŭt') *n.* The seed of the fruit of the betel palm.
betel palm *n.* A tropical Asian palm cultivated for its seeds.
bête noire (bĕt nwär') *n.* One particularly disliked or to be avoided.
be•think (bĭ-thĭngk') *v.* To remind (oneself) : remember.
be•tide (bĭ-tīd') *v.* To happen to or take place.
be•times (bĭ-tīmz') *adv.* **1.** In good time : early. **2.** *Archaic.* Soon : quickly.
be•to•ken (bĭ-tō'kən) *v.* To be or give a portent or sign of.
be•tray (bĭ-trā') *v.* **1. a.** To be a traitor to or commit treason against. **b.** To be unfaithful or disloyal to. **2.** To make known accidentally. **3.** To reveal : indicate. **4.** To lead astray : deceive. **—be•tray'al** *n.* **—be•tray'er** *n.*
be•troth (bĭ-trōth', -trôth') *v.* To promise to marry. **—be•troth'al** *n.*
be•trothed (bĭ-trōthd', -trôtht') *n.* A person to whom one is engaged to be married.
bet•ter[1] (bĕt'ər) *adj.* **1.** Higher in quality or greater in excellence. **2.** More satisfactory, suitable, useful, or desirable. **3.** Greater : larger. **4.** More healthy than before. *—adv.* **1.** In a more excellent manner. **2.** To a greater degree or extent. **3.** To greater advantage or use. **4.** In excess of : more <*better* than a mile>. *—n.* **1.** Something better. **2.** A superior, as in position, class, or intelligence. *—v.* **1.** To improve. **2.** To surpass : exceed.
bet•ter[2] (bĕt'ər) *n. var. of* BETTOR.
bet•ter•ment (bĕt'ər-mənt) *n.* An improvement.
bet•tor *also* **bet•ter** (bĕt'ər) *n.* One who bets.
be•tween (bĭ-twēn') *prep.* **1.** In the time or position separating. **2. a.** By the combined effect or effort of. **b.** In the combined ownership of <had a controlling interest *between* them> **3.** From one or another of. **—be•tween** *adv.*
be•twixt (bĭ-twĭkst') *prep. & adv. Archaic.* Between.
bev•el (bĕv'əl) *n.* **1. a.** The surface formed when 2 planes meet at an angle other than 90°. **b.** The angle at which these planes meet. **2.** *also* **bevel square.** A rule having an adjustable arm, used to draw or measure angles or to fix a surface at an angle. *—v.* **-eled, -el•ing** *or* **-elled, -el•ling.** To slope or cut to slope at a bevel.
bevel gear *n.* Either of a pair of gears having teeth surfaces cut so that the gear shafts are not parallel.
bev•er•age (bĕv'ər-ij, bĕv'rĭj) *n.* A liquid for drinking, usu. other than water.
bev•y (bĕv'ē) *n., pl.* **-ies. 1.** A group of birds or animals, esp. larks or quail : flock. **2.** An assemblage : group.
be•wail (bĭ-wāl') *v.* To express sorrow or regret over. **—be•wail'er** *n.*
be•ware (bĭ-wâr') *v.* **-wared, -war•ing.** To be cautious (of).
be•whis•kered (bĭ-hwĭs'kərd, -wis'-) *adj.* Having whiskers.
be•wil•der (bĭ-wĭl'dər) *v.* To befuddle or confuse, esp. with conflicting statements or objects. **—be•wil'dered•ly** *adv.* **—be•wil'der•ment** *n.*
be•witch (bĭ-wĭch') *v.* **1.** To place under one's power by or as if by magic. **2.** To captivate totally : fascinate. **—be•witch'er•y** *n.* **—be•witch'ing** *adj.* **—be•witch'ing•ly** *adv.* **—be•witch'ment** *n.*
bey (bā) *n.* **1.** A provincial governor in the Ottoman Empire. **2.** A ruler of the former kingdom of Tunis. **3.** A Turkish title of honor and respect.
be•yond (bē-ŏnd', bĭ-yŏnd') *prep.* **1.** On or onto the far side of : past. **2.** Outside the scope or reach of. **3.** To a degree or amount greater than. **4.** In addition to : besides. **—be•yond'** *adv.*
bez•el (bĕz'əl) *n.* **1.** A slanting surface or bevel on the edge on a cutting tool. **2.** The upper faceted portion of a cut gem. **3.** A groove or flange that holds a beveled edge, as of a gem or watch crystal.
be•zique (bə-zēk') *n.* A card game similar to pinochle using a deck of 64 cards.
Bi *symbol for* BISMUTH.
bi•a•ly (bē-ä'lē) *n., pl.* **-lys.** A baked roll with onion flakes on top.
bi•an•nu•al (bī-ăn'yo͞o-əl) *adj.* Taking place twice each year : semiannual. **—bi•an'nu•al•ly** *adv.*
bi•as (bī'əs) *n.* **1.** A line that cuts diagonally across the grain of fabric. **2.** An inclination or preference that interferes with impartial judgment : prejudice. *—adv.* On a diagonal : aslant. *—v.* **-ased, -as•ing** *or* **-assed, -as•sing.** To cause to have a prejudiced view.
bi•ath•lon (bī-ăth'lən, -lŏn') *n.* An athletic competition that combines events in rifle shooting and cross-country skiing.
bi•ax•i•al (bī-ăk'sē-əl) *adj.* Having 2 axes. **—bi•ax'i•al•ly** *adv.*
bib (bĭb) *n.* A cloth napkin tied under the chin and worn, esp. by children, to protect clothing while eating.
bi•be•lot (bē'bə-lō', bē-blō') *n.* A small ornamental object : trinket.
Bi•ble (bī'bəl) *n.* **1. a.** The sacred book of Christianity, including both the Old Testa-

ment and the New Testament. **b.** The Old Testament, the sacred book of Judaism. —See table p. 69. **2. bible** A book held to be authoritative in its field <the *bible* of Japanese cooking> **—Bib'li•cal, bib'li•cal** (bĭb'lĭ-kəl) *adj.* **—Bib'li•cal•ly, bib'li•cal•ly** *adv.*

Bible Belt *n.* Sections of the U.S., esp. in the South and Middle West, where Protestant fundamentalism is widely practiced.

bib•li•og•ra•phy (bĭb'lē-ŏ g'rə-fē) *n., pl.* **-phies. 1.** A list of the works of an author or publisher. **2.** A list of works or sources of information in print on a particular subject. **3.** A list of works consulted by an author in the preparation of a book or article. **—bib'li•og'ra•pher** *n.* **—bib'li•o•graph'i•cal** (-ə-grăf'ĭ-kəl), **bib'li•o•graph'ic** *adj.* **—bib'li•o•graph'i•cal•ly** *adv.*

bib•li•o•ma•ni•a (bĭb'lē-ə-mā'nē-ə, -mān'yə) *n.* An exaggerated liking for acquiring books. **—bib'li•o•ma'ni•ac'** *n.*

bib•li•o•phile (bĭb'lē-ə-fīl') *also* **bib•li•oph•i•list** (bĭb'lē-ŏf'ə-lĭst) *n.* A book lover or collector.

bib•u•lous (bĭb'yə-ləs) *adj.* Given to or marked by drinking alcoholic beverages. **—bib'u•lous•ly** *adv.*

bi•cam•er•al (bī-kăm'ər-əl) *adj.* Composed of 2 legislative chambers.

bicarbonate of soda *n.* Sodium bicarbonate.

bi•cen•ten•ni•al (bī'sĕn-tĕn'ē-əl) *also* **bi•cen•ten•a•ry** (bī'sĕn-tĕn'ə-rē, bī-sĕn'tə-nĕr'-ē) *adj.* **1.** Happening once very 200 years. **2.** Lasting for 200 years. **3.** Relating to a 200th anniversary or its celebration. **—bi'cen•ten'ni•al** *n.*

bi•ceps (bī'sĕps') *n.* A muscle with 2 points of origin, esp.: **a.** The large muscle at the front of the upper arm. **b.** The large muscle at the back of the thigh. **—bi•cip'i•tal** (-sip'-ĭ-tl) *adj.*

bi•chlo•ride (bī-klôr'īd', -klōr'-) *n.* Dichloride.

bi•chro•mate (bī-krō'māt', -mĭt) *n.* Dichromate.

bick•er (bĭk'ər) *v.* To engage in petty quarreling **:** squabble. **—bick'er** *n.*

bi•con•cave (bī'kŏn-kāv', bī-kŏn'kāv') *adj.* Concave on 2 surfaces. **—bi'con•cav'i•ty** (-kăv'ĭ-tē) *n.*

bi•con•vex (bī'kŏn-vĕks', bī-kŏn'vĕks') *adj.* Convex on 2 surfaces. **—bi'con•vex'i•ty** (-vĕk'sĭ-tē) *n.*

bi•cul•tur•al (bī-kŭl'chər-əl) *adj.* Of or pertaining to 2 distinct cultures in a single nation or geographic region. **—bi•cul'tur•al•ism** *n.*

bi•cus•pid (bī-kŭs'pĭd) *adj.* Having 2 points or cusps, as the crescent moon. —*n.* A bicuspid tooth, esp. a premolar.

bi•cy•cle (bī'sĭk'əl, -sĭ-kəl) *n.* A lightweight vehicle consisting of a metal frame mounted on 2 spoked wheels and having a seat, handlebars for steering, and 2 pedals. —*v.* **-cled, -cling.** To ride or travel on a bicycle. **—bi'cy•clist** *n.*

bid (bĭd) *v.* **bade** (băd, bād) *or* **bid, bid•den** (bĭd'n) *or* **bid, bid•ding. 1.** To command **:** order. **2.** To utter (a salutation). **3.** To invite or send for. **4.** *p.t. & p.p.* **bid.** To state one's intention to take (tricks) in card games. **5.** *p.t. & p.p.* **bid.** To offer (an amount) as a price. **6.** *p.t. & p.p.* **bid.** To offer to pay or accept a specified price. —*n.* **1. a.** An offer of a specified price. **b.** The amount offered. **2.** An invitation. **3. a.** The act of bidding in card games. **b.** The number and suit of tricks or points declared. **c.** A player's turn to bid. **4.** An effort to attain something. **—bid'der** *n.*

bid•da•ble (bĭd'ə-bəl) *adj.* **1.** Capable of being bid. **2.** Obedient **:** tractable.

bid•dy[1] (bĭd'ē) *n., pl.* **-dies.** A hen or young chicken.

bid•dy[2] (bĭd'ē) *n., pl.* **-dies.** *Slang.* A woman, esp. a talkative old one.

bide (bīd) *v.* **bid•ed** *or* **bode** (bōd), **bid•ed, bid•ing. 1.** To remain **:** stay. **2.** To wait **:** tarry. **3.** To await <*bide* one's time>

bi•det (bē-dā') *n.* A low, basinlike bathroom fixture designed to be straddled for bathing the genital and anal areas.

bi•en•ni•al (bī-ĕn'ē-əl) *adj.* **1.** Living or lasting for 2 years. **2.** Occurring every 2nd year. —*n.* **1.** An event that occurs once every 2 years. **2.** *Bot.* A plant that lives only 2 years. **—bi•en'ni•al•ly** *adv.*

bier (bîr) *n.* A platform on which a coffin is placed before burial.

biff (bĭf) *v. Slang.* To punch. **—biff** *n.*

bi•fo•cal (bī-fō'kəl) *adj.* Having 2 different focal lengths.

bifocals *pl.n.* Lenses that correct for both distant and close vision.

bi•fur•cate (bī'fər-kāt', bī-fûr'-) *v.* **-cat•ed, -cat•ing.** To separate or divide into 2 branches or parts. **—bi'fur•cate'** *adj.* **—bi'fur•ca'tion** *n.*

big (bĭg) *adj.* **big•ger, big•gest. 1.** Of considerable size, intensity, quantity, extent, or magnitude **:** large. **2.** Grown-up **:** adult. **3.** Pregnant <*big* with child> **4. a.** Of great significance **:** momentous. **b.** Having or exercising considerable authority or influence **:** powerful. **c.** Conspicuous in position or wealth **:** prominent. **5.** Generous **:** bountiful. **6.** *Informal.* Boastful **:** self-important. ★ ***syns:*** CONSIDERABLE, EXTENSIVE, GOOD, GREAT, HEALTHY, LARGE, SIZABLE, TIDY —*adv.* **1.** In a self-important or boastful way <talk *big*> **2.** With much success. **—big'gish** *adj.* **—big'ness** *n.*

big•a•my (bĭg'ə-mē) *n., pl.* **-mies.** *Law.* Entry into marriage with one person while still legally married to another. **—big'a•mous** *adj.* **—big'a•mist** *n.*

big bang theory *n.* A theory that the universe originated billions of years ago in a violent eruption from a single point of high density and temperature.

Big Dipper *n.* A cluster of 7 stars in the constellation Ursa Major, 4 forming a bowl and 3 the handle of a dipper.

Big•foot (bĭg'fo͝ot') *n.* The Sasquatch.

BOOKS OF THE BIBLE

Books of the Hebrew Scriptures appear as listed in the translation by the Jewish Publication Society of America. Books of the Christian Bible appear as listed in the Jerusalem Bible, a 1966 translation of the 1956 French Roman Catholic version. The Old Testament books shown in italic are considered apocryphal in most Christian churches, but they are accepted as canonical in the Roman Catholic Church, the Eastern Orthodox Churches, and the Armenian and the Ethiopian Oriental Orthodox Churches. The Christian Old Testament parallels the Hebrew Scriptures with the exception of these books.

HEBREW

THE TORAH

Genesis
Exodus
Leviticus
Numbers
Deuteronomy

THE PROPHETS

Joshua
Judges
I Samuel
II Samuel
I Kings
II Kings
Isaiah
Jeremiah
Ezekiel
Hosea
Joel
Amos
Obadiah
Jonah
Micah
Nahum
Habakkuk
Zephaniah
Haggai
Zechariah
Malachi

THE WRITINGS

Psalms
Proverbs
Job
Song of Songs
Ruth
Lamentations
Ecclesiastes
Esther
Daniel
Ezra
Nehemiah
I Chronicles
II Chronicles

CHRISTIAN

OLD TESTAMENT

Genesis
Exodus
Leviticus
Numbers
Deuteronomy
Joshua
Judges
Ruth
I Samuel
II Samuel
I Kings
II Kings
I Chronicles
II Chronicles
Ezra
Nehemiah
Tobit
Judith
Esther
I Maccabees
II Maccabees
Job
Psalms
Proverbs
Ecclesiastes
Song of Songs
(Song of Solomon)
Wisdom of Solomon
Ecclesiasticus
Isaiah
Jeremiah
Lamentations
Baruch
Ezekiel
Daniel
Hosea
Joel
Amos
Obadiah
Jonah
Micah
Nahum
Habakkuk
Zephaniah
Haggai
Zechariah
Malachi

NEW TESTAMENT

Matthew
Mark
Luke
John
Acts of the Apostles
Romans
I Corinthians
II Corinthians
Galatians
Ephesians
Philippians
Colossians
I Thessalonians
II Thessalonians
I Timothy
II Timothy
Titus
Philemon
Hebrews
James
I Peter
II Peter
I John
II John
III John
Jude
Revelation

big·head·ed (bĭg′hĕd′ĭd) *adj.* Conceited : egotistical. —**big′head′ed·ness** *n.*

big-heart·ed (bĭg′här′tĭd) *adj.* Kind : generous. —**big′-heart′ed·ly** *adv.* —**big′-heart′ed·ness** *n.*

big·horn (bĭg′hôrn′) *n.* A sheep, *Ovis canadensis,* of W North American mountains, the male having massive horns.

bight (bīt) *n.* **1.** A loop or slack part in a rope. **2. a.** A curve or bend, esp. in a shoreline. **b.** A wide bay formed by such a curve.

big league *n.* **1.** A major league. **2.** *Informal.* Big time. —**big′-league′** *adj.*

big·mouth (bĭg′mouth′) *n. Informal.* An indiscreet, gossipy, or loud-mouthed person. —**big′mouthed** *adj.*

big-name (bĭg′nām′) *adj.* Well-known and highly popular.

big·ot (bĭg′ət) *n.* One fanatically devoted to one's own group, religion, race, or politics and intolerant of those who differ. —**big′ot·ed** *adj.* —**big′ot·ry** *n.*

big shot *n. Slang.* An influential or important person.

big time *n. Slang.* The most prestigious level of achievement in a competitive profession or field. —**big′-time′** *adj.*

big top *n. Informal.* **1.** The principal tent of a circus. **2.** The circus.

big wheel *n. Slang.* A person of importance or authority.

big·wig (bĭg′wĭg′) *n. Slang.* A big wheel.

bike (bīk) *n. Informal.* **1.** A bicycle. **2.** A motorcycle. —**bike** *v.* —**bik′er** *n.*

bi·ki·ni (bĭ-kē′nē) *n.* **1.** A brief 2-piece bathing suit. **2.** Brief underpants that encircle the hips rather than the waist.

bi·lat·er·al (bī-lăt′ər-əl) *adj.* **1.** Relating to or having 2 sides : 2-sided. **2.** Undertaken by or affecting 2 parties : reciprocal <a *bilateral* trade agreement> —**bi·lat′er·al·ism** *n.* —**bi·lat′er·al·ly** *adv.*

bil·ber·ry (bĭl′bĕr′ē) *n.* Any of several shrubby plants of the genus *Vaccinium,* having edible blue or blackish berries.

bile (bīl) *n.* **1.** A bitter alkaline, brownish-yellow or greenish-yellow liquid secreted by the liver that helps digestion by saponifying fats. **2.** Ill temper : irascibility. —**bil′i·ar′y** (bĭl′ē-ĕr′ē) *adj.*

bilge (bĭlj) *n.* **1.** The lowest inner part of the hull of a ship. **2.** Water that seeps into and collects in the bilge. **3.** *Slang.* Nonsense. —**bilg′y** *adj.*

bi·lin·gual (bī-lĭng′gwəl) *adj.* **1.** Able to speak 2 languages with equal facility. **2.** Relating to or expressed in 2 languages. —**bi·lin′gual** *n.* —**bi·lin′gual·ly** *adv.*

bil·ious (bĭl′yəs) *adj.* **1.** Of, relating to, or containing bile. **2.** Relating to, characterized by or undergoing gastric distress caused by sluggishness of the gallbladder or liver. **3.** Irascible. —**bil′ious·ly** *adv.* —**bil′ious·ness** *n.*

bilk (bĭlk) *v.* To defraud, swindle, or cheat. —*n.* A swindle : hoax. —**bilk′er** *n.*

bill[1] (bĭl) *n.* **1.** An itemized list of fees or charges. **2.** A list of items, as a menu. **3.** An advertising poster or public notice. **4.** A piece of legal paper money. **5.** A commercial note, as a bill of exchange. **6.** A draft of a proposed law. **7.** *Law.* A document presented to a court containing a formal statement of a case, petition, or complaint. —*v.* **1.** To present a statement of charges or costs to. **2.** To enter on a statement of fees or charges. **3.** To advertise by public notice. —**bill′er** *n.*

bill[2] (bĭl) *n.* **1.** The horny beak of a bird. **2.** A beaklike mouth part, as of an octopus. **3.** The visor of a cap. —*v.* To touch beaks together. —**billed** *adj.*

bill·board (bĭl′bôrd′, -bōrd′) *n.* A structure for displaying advertisements.

bil·let (bĭl′ĭt) *n.* **1. a.** Board and lodging for troops, esp. in a civilian building. **b.** A written order directing provision of a billet. **2.** *Informal.* A position of employment : job. —*v.* To lodge or be lodged.

bil·let-doux (bĭl′ā-do͞o′) *n., pl.* **bil·lets-doux** (-do͞o′, -do͞oz′). A love letter.

bill·fold (bĭl′fōld′) *n.* A folding, pocket-sized case for money and personal papers.

bil·liards (bĭl′yərdz) *n. (sing. in number).* A game played on an oblong table with raised, cushioned edges, using a cue to hit 3 small balls. —**bil′liard** *adj.*

bil·lings·gate (bĭl′ĭngz-gāt′, -gĭt) *n.* Foul, abusive language.

bil·lion (bĭl′yən) *n.* **1.** The cardinal number equal to 10^9 : a thousand millions. **2.** *Brit.* The cardinal number equal to 10^{12} : a million millions. —**bil′lion** *adj. & pron.* —**bil′lionth** *n. & adj. & adv.*

bil·lion·aire (bĭl′yə-nâr′) *n.* A person whose wealth amounts to at least 1 billion, as of dollars or pounds.

bill of exchange *n.* A written order for payment of a specified sum of money to a specified person.

bill of fare *n.* A menu.

bill of lading *n.* A receipt issued by a carrier promising delivery of the merchandise listed.

bill of rights *n.* **1.** A formal summary of the rights and liberties guaranteed to a people. **2. Bill of Rights.** The first 10 amendments to the U.S. Constitution.

bil·low (bĭl′ō) *n.* **1.** A large surge or swell of water : wave. **2.** A large surge, as of smoke. —*v.* **1.** To surge in billows. **2.** To swell out. —**bil′low·y** *adj.*

bil·ly club (bĭl′ē) *n.* A short wooden club, used esp. by police officers.

billy goat *n.* A male goat.

bi·lo·bate (bī-lō′bāt′) *adj.* Divided into or having 2 lobes.

bi·met·al·lism (bī-mĕt′l-ĭz′əm) *n.* The use of 2 metals, esp. gold and silver, as the monetary standard of currency.

bi·mod·al (bī-mōd′l) *adj.* Having 2 distinct statistical modes. —**bi′mo·dal′i·ty** *n.*

bi·mo·lec·u·lar (bī′mə-lĕk′yə-lər) *adj.* Relating to, consisting of, or affecting 2 molecules. —**bi′mo·lec′u·lar·ly** *adv.*

bi•month•ly (bī-mŭnth'lē) *adj.* **1.** Occurring every 2 months. **2.** Occurring twice a month : semimonthly. —*n., pl.* **-lies.** A bimonthly publication. —**bi•month'ly** *adv.*
bin (bĭn) *n.* A container or enclosed storage space.
bi•na•ry (bī'nə-rē) *adj.* **1.** Composed of 2 different parts or components. **2.** Of or based on the number 2 or the binary numeration system. **3. a.** Consisting of 2 chemical elements. **b.** Containing 2 different kinds of atoms <a *binary* molecule> —**bi'na•ry** *n.*
binary digit *n.* Either of the digits 0 or 1, used to represent numbers in the binary numeration system.
binary numeration system *n.* A system of numeration based on 2, in which numerals are represented as sums of powers of 2 and in which all numerals can be written with the symbols 0 and 1.
binary star *n.* A system composed of 2 stars orbiting a common center of mass.
bi•na•tion•al (bī-năsh'ə-nəl, -năsh'nəl) *adj.* Of or involving 2 nations.
bin•au•ral (bī-nôr'əl) *adj.* **1.** Of or related to hearing with both ears. **2.** Of or relating to sound transmission from 2 sources with varying acoustics. —**bin•au'ral•ly** *adv.*
bind (bīnd) *v.* **bound** (bound), **bind•ing. 1.** To secure, as with a rope or belt. **2.** To fasten by encircling. **3.** To bandage. **4.** To restrain with or as if with bonds. **5.** To obligate, as with a sense of moral duty. **6.** *Law.* To place under legal obligation by contract or oath. **7.** To cause to stick together in a mass. **8.** To enclose and fasten (pages of a book) between protective covers. **9.** To furnish with a border or edge for reinforcement or ornamentation. **10.** To be tight and uncomfortable <*binds* across the shoulders> **11.** To constipate. —**bind off.** To cast off in knitting. —**bind over.** *Law.* To hold on bail or place under bond. —*n. Informal.* A difficult situation.
bind•er (bīn'dər) *n.* **1.** A notebook cover with rings or clamps for holding paper. **2.** *Law.* A payment or written statement making an agreement legally binding.
bind•er•y (bīn'də-rē) *n., pl.* **-ies.** A place where books are bound.
bind•ing (bīn'dĭng) *n.* **1.** Something that binds or is used as a binder. **2.** The cover that holds together the pages of a book. **3.** A strip over or along the edge of something for reinforcement or ornamentation. —*adj.* **1.** Serving to bind. **2.** Uncomfortably tight. **3.** Obligatory.
bin•dle•stiff (bĭn'dl-stĭf') *n. Slang.* A hobo or migrant worker.
binge (bĭnj) *n. Slang.* **1.** A spree. **2.** A period of uncontrolled self-indulgence.
bin•go (bĭng'gō) *n.* A game of chance in which each player puts markers on a card with numbered squares in accordance with the numbers drawn by a caller.
bin•na•cle (bĭn'ə-kəl) *n.* The nonmagnetic stand that holds a ship's compass.
bin•oc•u•lar (bə-nŏk'yə-lər, bī-) *adj.* Relating to, used by, or involving both eyes simultaneously. —*n. often* **binoculars.** An optical device, as field glasses, designed for use by both eyes simultaneously.

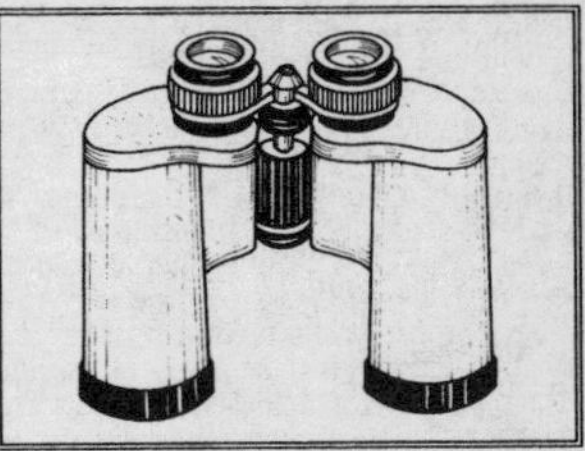

binocular

bi•no•mi•al (bī-nō'mē-əl) *adj.* Composed of or relating to 2 names or terms. —*n.* **1.** *Math.* An expression consisting of 2 terms joined by a plus or minus sign. **2.** *Biol.* A taxonomic name. —**bi•no'mi•al•ly** *adv.*
bi•o (bī'ō) *n., pl.* **-os.** *Informal.* A biography.
bi•o•chem•is•try (bī'ō-kĕm'ĭ-strē) *n.* The chemistry of biological processes and substances. —**bi'o•chem'i•cal** *adj.* —**bi'o•chem'i•cal•ly** *adv.* —**bi'o•chem'ist** *n.*
bi•o•cide (bī'ə-sīd') *n.* A substance capable of destroying living organisms.
bi•o•de•grad•a•ble (bī'ō-dĭ-grā'də-bəl) *adj.* Able to be decomposed by natural processes.
bi•o•di•ver•si•ty (bī'ō-dĭ-vûr'sĭ-tē) *n.* The variety of organisms found within a specified geographic region.
bi•o•feed•back (bī'ō-fēd'băk') *n.* A technique in which a conscious attempt is made to control bodily functions that are considered involuntary, as heartbeat or blood pressure.
bi•o•ge•og•ra•phy (bī'ō-jē-ŏg'rə-fē) *n.* Biological study of the geographic distribution of animals and plants. —**bi'o•ge'o•graph'ic** (-jē'ə-grăf'ĭk), **bi'o•ge'o•graph'i•cal** *adj.* —**bi'o•ge'o•graph'i•cal•ly** *adv.*
bi•og•ra•phy (bī-ŏg'rə-fē, bē-) *n., pl.* **-phies. 1.** A written account of someone's life. **2.** Biographies as a whole. —**bi•og'ra•pher** *n.* —**bi'o•graph'i•cal** (bī'ə-grăf'ĭ-kəl), **bi'o•graph'ic** *adj.* —**bi'o•graph'i•cal•ly** *adv.*
bi•o•haz•ard (bī'ō-hăz'ərd, bī'ō-hăz-) *n.* A biological material, esp. if infective, that threatens humans or their environment.
biological clock *n.* An intrinsic biological mechanism responsible for the periodicity of certain classes of behavior in living organisms.
biological warfare *n.* Warfare in which disease-producing microorganisms or organic biocides are used to destroy human life, livestock, or crops.
bi•ol•o•gy (bī-ŏl'ə-jē) *n.* **1.** The science of living organisms and life processes, including the study of growth, structure, and reproduction.

2. The life processes or characteristic phenomena of a group or category of living organisms. **—bi'o·log'i·cal** (bī'ə-lŏj'ĭ-kəl), **bi'o·log'ic** *adj.* **—bi'o·log'i·cal·ly** *adv.* **—bi·ol'o·gist** *n.*

bi·o·mass (bī'ō-măs') *n.* **1.** The total mass of living matter within a given unit of environmental area. **2.** Plant material, vegetation, or agricultural waste used as a fuel.

bi·ome (bī'ōm') *n.* The entire community of living organisms in a single major ecological region.

bi·o·med·i·cine (bī'ō-mĕd'ĭ-sĭn) *n.* **1.** The study of medicine in relationship to all biological systems. **2.** The branch of medicine that deals with human response to environmental stress. **—bi'o·med'i·cal** *adj.*

bi·on·ics (bī-ŏn'ĭks) *n. (sing. in number).* The application of biological principles to the design and study of engineering systems, esp. electronic systems. **—bi·on'ic** *adj.* **—bi·on'i·cal·ly** *adv.*

bi·o·phys·ics (bī'ō-fĭz'ĭks) *n. (sing. in number).* The physics of biological processes. **—bi'o·phys'i·cal** *adj.* **—bi'o·phys'i·cal·ly** *adv.* **—bi'o·phys'i·cist** *n.*

bi·op·sy (bī'ŏp'sē) *n., pl.* **-sies.** The examination of tissues taken from a living organism, esp. for the presence of disease.

bi·o·re·search (bī'ō-rĭ-sûrch', -rē'sûrch) *n.* Research in the biological sciences.

bi·o·rhythm (bī'ō-rĭ*th*'əm) *n.* **1.** An intrinsically patterned cyclical biological function or process. **2.** The determining factor in a biorhythm.

bi·o·sphere (bī'ə-sfîr') *n.* The part of the earth, its waters, and atmosphere where organisms can live.

bi·o·sta·tis·tics (bī'ō-stə-tĭs'tĭks) *n. (sing. in number).* Application of statistics to biological and medical data. **—bi'o·stat'is·ti'cian** (-stăt'ĭ-stĭsh'ən) *n.*

bi·o·ta (bī-ō'tə) *n.* The animal and plant life of a particular region.

bi·o·tech·nol·o·gy (bī'ō-tĕk-nŏl'ə-jē) *n.* **1.** The use of microorganisms or biological substances to perform industrial processes. **2.** Ergonomics. **—bi'o·tech'no·log'i·cal** (-nə-lŏj'ĭ-kəl) *adj* .

bi·ot·ic (bī-ŏt'ĭk) *adj.* Relating to life or specific life conditions.

bi·o·tin (bī'ə-tĭn) *n.* A colorless crystalline vitamin usu. considered a part of the vitamin B complex and found in egg yolk, liver, milk, and yeast.

bi·o·type (bī'ə-tīp') *n.* A group of organisms with identical genetic but varying physical characteristics.

bi·par·ti·san (bī-pär'tĭ-zən, -sən) *adj.* Consisting of or supported by members of 2 political parties. **—bi·par'ti·san·ship'** *n.*

bi·par·tite (bī-pär'tīt') *adj.* **1.** Having or being composed of 2 parts. **2.** *Bot.* Divided into 2 <*bipartite* leaves>

bi·ped (bī'pĕd') *n.* An animal with 2 feet. **—bi'ped', bi·ped'al** *adj.*

bi·plane (bī'plān') *n.* An aircraft with wings fixed at 2 different levels.

bi·po·lar (bī-pō'lər) *adj.* **1.** Relating to or having 2 poles. **2.** Involving or concerning the earth's poles. **—bi'po·lar'i·ty** *n.*

bi·ra·cial (bī-rā'shəl) *adj.* Of, for, or composed of members of 2 races.

birch (bûrch) *n.* **1.** A deciduous tree of the genus *Betula,* common in the N Hemisphere, with bark separable from the wood in sheets and hard close-grained wood. **2.** A rod from a birch, used as a whip. *—v.* To whip with or as if with a birch rod.

bird (bûrd) *n.* **1.** A member of the class Aves, which includes warm-blooded, egg-laying, feathered vertebrates having forelimbs modified to form wings. **2.** A shuttlecock. *—v.* To observe and identify birds in their natural habitat. **—bird'er** *n.*

bird·brain (bûrd'brān') *n. Slang.* A silly person. **—bird'brained'** *adj.*

bird·ie (bûr'dē) *n.* **1.** A stroke under par for a hole in golf. **2.** A shuttlecock.

bird·lime (bûrd'līm') *n.* A sticky substance smeared on twigs to trap small birds.

bird of paradise *n.* Any of various birds of the family Paradisaeidae, the male of which has brilliant plumage.

bird of prey *n.* A predatory carnivorous bird, as the eagle or hawk **:** raptor.

bird's-eye (bûrdz'ī') *adj.* **1.** Dappled or patterned with spots held to resemble birds' eyes. **2.** Seen from high above or a great distance <a *bird's-eye* view of the terrain>

bird·shot (bûrd'shŏt') *n.* A small lead shot for shotgun shells.

bi·reme (bī'rēm') *n.* An ancient galley with 2 tiers of oars on each side.

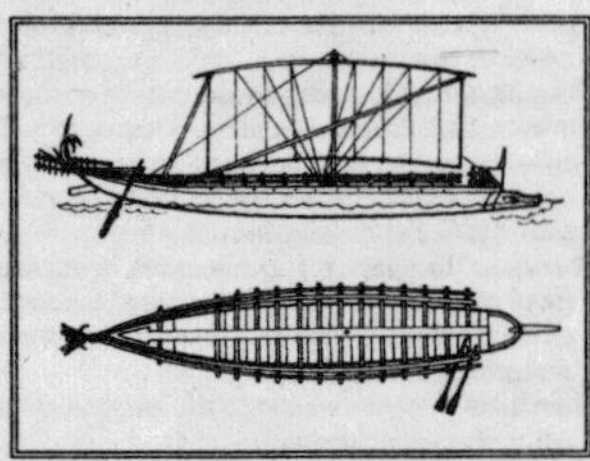

bireme

bi·ret·ta (bə-rĕt'ə) *n.* A square, stiff cap worn by Roman Catholic clergy.

birl·ing (bûr'lĭng) *n.* A game of skill, esp. among lumberjacks, in which 2 competitors try to balance on a floating log while spinning it with their feet. **—birl** *v.*

birr (bîr) *n., pl.* **birr** *or* **birrs.** —See table at CURRENCY.

†birth (bûrth) *n.* **1. a.** The beginning of existence or the fact of being born. **b.** A beginning **:** origin. **2.** The act of bearing young **:** parturition. **3.** Ancestry **:** parentage. *—v. Regional.* To deliver or bear (a baby).

birth control *n.* Control of the number of

children conceived, esp. by planned contraceptive techniques.

birth•day (bûrth′dā′) *n.* The day or anniversary of one's birth.

birth family *n.* A family consisting of one's biological parents and their offspring.

birth•mark (bûrth′märk′) *n.* A blemish or mole on the body since birth : nevus.

birth•place (bûrth′plās′) *n.* A place of birth or origin.

birth•rate (bûrth′rāt′) *n.* The number of births of a specified population per unit of time, esp. per year.

birth•right (bûrth′rīt′) *n.* **1.** A privilege granted to someone by virtue of birth. **2.** A privilege granted to a first-born.

birth•stone (bûrth′stōn′) *n.* A gemstone associated with the month of one's birth.

bis (bĭs) *adv.* Encore : again. —Used esp. as a direction in music.

bis•cuit (bĭs′kĭt) *n.* **1.** A small cake of shortened bread leavened with baking powder or soda. **2.** *esp. Brit.* **a.** A cracker. **b.** A cookie.

bi•sect (bī′sĕkt′, bī-sĕkt′) *v.* **1.** To cut into 2 equal parts. **2.** To split into 2 parts : fork. **—bi′sec′tion** *n.* **—bi′sec′tor** *n.*

bi•sex•u•al (bī-sĕk′sho͞o-əl) *adj.* **1.** Of or relating to both sexes. **2.** *Biol.* Having both male and female organs : hermaphroditic. **3.** Having a sexual interest in members of both sexes. **—bi•sex′u•al** *n.* **—bi•sex′u•al′i•ty** *n.* **—bi•sex′u•al•ly** *adv.*

bish•op (bĭsh′əp) *n.* **1.** A Christian cleric of high rank, usu. governing a diocese. **2.** A chess piece that moves diagonally across unoccupied squares of the same color, with no limit as to number of squares.

bish•op•ric (bĭsh′ə-prĭk) *n.* The rank, office, or diocese of a bishop.

bis•muth (bĭz′məth) *n. Symbol* **Bi** A brittle, white, crystalline metallic element.

bi•son (bī′sən, -zən) *n.* A bovine mammal, *Bison bison,* of W North America, having a dark-brown coat and short, curved horns.

bisque[1] (bĭsk) *n.* **1.** A thick cream soup made from fish, shellfish, or puréed vegetables. **2.** A dessert of ice cream mixed with nuts or crushed macaroons.

bisque[2] (bĭsk) *n.* Clay that has been fired once, but not glazed.

bis•sex•tile (bī-sĕk′stĭl, -stīl′, bĭ-) *adj.* **1.** Of or relating to a leap year. **2.** Of or relating to the extra day falling in a leap year. —*n.* A leap year.

bis•tro (bē′strō, bĭs′trō) *n., pl.* **-tros.** A small nightclub or bar.

bit[1] (bĭt) *n.* **1.** A tiny portion, piece, or amount. **2.** A brief amount of time : moment. **3.** A regularly performed entertainment routine : act. **4.** *Slang.* A particular kind of behavior or activity. **5.** *Informal.* An amount equal to ⅛ of a dollar. ★ ***syns:*** GRAIN, IOTA, JOT, MODICUM, ORT, OUNCE, PARTICLE, SCRAP, SHRED, SMIDGEN, SPECK, TITTLE, WHIT

bit[2] (bĭt) *n.* **1. a.** A threaded, pointed tool designed for drilling and boring. **b.** The sharp part of a tool. **2.** The metal mouthpiece of a horse's bridle.

bit[3] (bĭt) *n. Computer Sci.* **1.** Either of 2 characters, as the binary digits 0 and 1, of a language that has 2 characters only. **2.** A unit of information equivalent to the choice between 2 alternatives having equal likelihood. **3.** A unit of information storage capacity, as of a computer memory.

bitch (bĭch) *n.* **1.** A female canine. **2.** *Slang.* **a.** A mean or spiteful woman. **b.** A promiscuous woman. **3.** A grievance : complaint. **4.** Something difficult or unpleasant. —*v. Slang.* **1.** To complain. **2.** To botch : bungle. **—bitch′er•y** *n.* **—bitch′i•ly** *adv.* **—bitch′i•ness** *n.* **—bitch′y** *adj.*

bite (bīt) *v.* **bit** (bĭt), **bit•ten** (bĭt′n) *or* **bit, bit•ing. 1.** To tear or cut with or as if with the teeth. **2. a.** To pierce the skin of, esp. with or as if with teeth or fangs. **b.** To cut into with a sharp tool. **3.** To eat into : corrode. **4.** To smart or sting or cause to smart or sting. **5.** To take or swallow bait. —*n.* **1. a.** The act or action of biting. **b.** A wound resulting from this. **2. a.** A smarting or stinging sensation. **b.** A sharp, incisive quality. **3.** An amount of food taken into the mouth at one time : mouthful. **4.** *Informal.* A light meal : snack. **5.** The angle at which the upper and lower teeth meet : occlusion. **—bit′er** *n.*

bit•ing (bī′tĭng) *adj.* **1.** Causing a stinging sensation. **2.** Penetrating : incisive.

bit•stock (bĭt′stŏk′) *n.* A handle or brace in which a boring or drilling bit is secured.

bit•ter (bĭt′ər) *adj.* **1.** Having or being a sharp, unpleasant taste. **2.** Causing or manifesting sharp physical or mental pain or discomfort : harsh. **3.** Caused by or exhibiting strong animosity. **4.** Marked by rancor or disappointment. —*v.* To make or become bitter. —*n.* **bitters.** A bitter, usu. alcoholic liquid made with roots or herbs, used esp. in mixed drinks. **—bit′ter•ly** *adv.* **—bit′ter•ness** *n.*

bit•tern (bĭt′ərn) *n.* A wading bird of the genera *Botaurus* and *Ixobrychus,* with mottled plumage and a deep, resonant call.

bit•ter•sweet (bĭt′ər-swēt′) *n.* A North American woody vine, *Celastrus scandens,* bearing orange or yellowish fruits that split open to expose red seeds. —*adj.* **1.** Both bitter and sweet. **2.** Engendering both pain and pleasure.

bi•tu•men (bĭ-to͞o′mən, -tyo͞o′-, bī-) *n.* A mixture of hydrocarbons found in asphalt and tar or distilled from petroleum or coal. **—bi•tu′mi•nous** *adj.*

bituminous coal *n.* A grade of coal that contains a high percentage of bituminous material and burns with a smoky flame.

bi•va•lent (bī-vā′lənt) *adj.* **1.** *Chem.* Having valence 2. **2.** *Biol.* Composed of 2 homologous chromosomes or 2 sets of such chromosomes.

bi•valve (bī′vălv′) *n.* A mollusk, such as an oyster or clam, having a hinged, 2-part shell. **—bi′valve′, bi′valved′** *adj.*

biv•ou•ac (bĭv'o͞o-ăk', bĭv'wăk') *n.* A temporary, usu. open-air, military encampment. —*v.* To camp in a bivouac.
bi•week•ly (bī-wēk'lē) *adj.* **1.** Occurring every 2 weeks. **2.** Occurring twice a week **:** semiweekly. —*n., pl.* **-lies.** A publication issued every 2 weeks. —**bi•week'ly** *adv.*
bi•year•ly (bī-yîr'lē) *adj.* **1.** Occurring every 2 years. **2.** Occurring twice a year **:** semiyearly. —**bi•year'ly** *adv.*
bi•zarre (bĭ-zär') *adj.* Extremely unconventional or far-fetched. —**bi•zarre'ly** *adv.* —**bi•zarre'ness** *n.*
Bk *symbol for* BERKELIUM.
blab (blăb) *v.* **blabbed, blab•bing. 1.** To reveal (secret matters), esp. through indiscreet talk. **2. a.** To chatter indiscreetly. **b.** To gossip. —*n.* **1.** One who blabs. **2.** Lengthy chatter. —**blab'by** *adj.*
blab•ber (blăb'ər) *v.* To blab. —*n.* **1.** Idle chatter. **2.** BLAB 1. —**blab'ber•er** *n.*
blab•ber•mouth (blăb'ər-mouth') *n. Slang.* An indiscreet, gossipy person.
black (blăk) *adj.* **1.** Being of the darkest achromatic visual value **:** absorbing nearly all light of all visible wavelengths. **2.** Having little or no light <a *black* and stormy night> **3.** *often* **Black. a.** Of or belonging to a racial group having brown to black skin, esp. one of African origin. **b.** African-American. **4.** Cheerless and depressing. **5.** Wicked **:** evil <a *black* lie> **6.** Angry **:** sullen. **7.** Soiled **:** dirty. ★ ***syns:*** EBONY, INKY, JET, JETTY, ONYX, PITCH-BLACK, SABLE, SOOTY —*n.* **1.** An achromatic color value of minimum lightness or maximum darkness. **2.** Absence of light **:** darkness. **3.** Black clothing, esp. worn for mourning. **4.** *often* **Black. a.** A member of a racial group having brown to black skin. **b.** African-American. —*v.* To blacken. —**black'ish** *adj.* —**black'ly** *adv.* —**black'ness** *n.*
black-and-blue (blăk'ən-blo͞o') *adj.* Discolored by bruising.
black•ball (blăk'bôl') *n.* **1.** A negative vote preventing an applicant's admission to an organization. **2.** A black ball used as a negative ballot. —**black'ball'** *v.*
black bear *n.* The common North American bear, having a black or dark brown coat.
black belt *n.* **1.** The rank of expert in a martial art, as karate. **2.** A person holding such a rank.
black•ber•ry (blăk'bĕr'ē) *n.* A woody plant of the genus *Rubus,* with usu. thorny stems and black edible berries.
black•bird (blăk'bûrd') *n.* Any of various New World birds of the family Icteridae, as the grackle, of which the male has black or mostly black plumage.
black•board (blăk'bôrd', -bōrd') *n.* A smooth, hard, often dark-colored panel for writing on with chalk **:** chalkboard.
black•bod•y (blăk'bŏd'ē) *n.* A hypothetical body that would totally absorb all incident radiation.
black box *n.* **1.** A device or theoretical construct, esp. an electric circuit, having known or specified performance characteristics but unknown or unspecified constituents and means of operation. **2.** A flight recorder.
black•en (blăk'ən) *v.* **1.** To make or become dark or black. **2.** To defame or sully. —**black'en•er** *n.*
black eye *n.* A discoloration of the flesh around the eye.
black-eyed Su•san (so͞o'zən) *n.* Any of several North American plants of the genus *Rudbeckia,* esp. *R. hirta,* with hairy stems and leaves and flowers that have orange-yellow petals and dark-brown centers.
Black•foot (blăk'fo͝ot') *n., pl.* **-foot** *or* **-feet. 1.** A member of an American Indian people inhabiting the N Great Plains from C Alberta to NW Montana. **2.** Their Algonquian language.
black•guard (blăg'ərd, -ärd') *n.* An unprincipled person **:** scoundrel.
black•head (blăk'hĕd') *n.* A small plug of dried fatty matter capped with dust and epithelial debris that clogs a pore.
black-heart•ed (blăk'här'tĭd) *adj.* Wicked **:** evil.
black hole *n.* A celestial body with a gravitational field so intense that its escape velocity is equal to or exceeds the speed of light.
black humor *n.* Morbid and absurd humor, esp. in its development as a literary genre. —**black humorist** *n.*
black•jack (blăk'jăk') *n.* **1.** A leather-covered bludgeon with a short flexible strap or shaft. **2.** A card game in which each player tries to accumulate cards with a combined point count higher than that of the dealer but not greater than 21.
black letter *n.* A heavy typeface with thick, ornamental serifs.

black letter

black light *n.* Invisible infrared or ultraviolet electromagnetic radiation.
black•list (blăk'lĭst') *n.* A list of organizations or persons that are disapproved of or suspected of disloyalty. —**black'list'** *v.*
black magic *n.* Magic practiced for evil purposes or invoking evil spirits.
black•mail (blăk'māl') *n.* **1.** Extortion, esp. of money, by threatening to expose a past

criminal or discreditable act. **2.** Something, esp. money, extorted in this way. **—black'mail'** *v.* **—black'mail'er** *n.*

▲ ***word history:*** *Blackmail* has nothing to do with the post office. *Black* is used in the figurative sense of "evil" or "wicked." *Mail* is a Scottish word meaning "rent" or "tribute." The term *blackmail* originated in Scotland, where Highland chiefs at one time extorted tribute from Lowlanders and Englishmen on the Scottish border in return for protection from being plundered.

Black Ma•ri•a (mə-rī'ə) *n.* A patrol wagon.

black market *n.* The illegal selling or buying of merchandise in violation of such restrictions as rationing or price control. **—black marketer, black marketeer** *n.*

Black Muslim *n.* A member of the Nation of Islam, an African-American group professing Islamic religious beliefs.

black•out (blăk'out') *n.* **1.** The concealing or extinguishing of lights that might be seen by enemy aircraft crews during an air raid. **2.** Lack of illumination due to an electrical power failure. **3.** A temporary loss of consciousness or memory. **4.** A suppression or stoppage <a news *blackout*>

black pepper *n.* **1.** A peppercorn. **2.** A pungent spice made from ground peppercorns.

Black Power *n.* A movement among African-Americans emphasizing social, economic, and political equality.

black sheep *n.* One considered discreditable by a respectable group or family.

black•smith (blăk'smĭth') *n.* **1.** A person who shapes and forges iron with a hammer and anvil. **2.** A person who makes, repairs, and fits horseshoes.

black•top (blăk'tŏp') *n.* A bituminous material, esp. asphalt, used to surface roads. **—black'top'** *v.*

black widow *n.* A New World spider, *Latrodectus mactans,* of which the extremely venomous female is black with red markings on the underside.

blad•der (blăd'ər) *n.* **1.** Any of various expandable, usu. fluid-storing sacs found in most animals, esp. the urinary bladder. **2.** Something resembling a bladder.

blade (blād) *n.* **1. a.** The cutting part of a weapon or tool. **b.** A sword. **2. a.** A thin, flat part or section <the *blade* of a propeller> **b.** The metal part of an ice skate **:** runner. **3.** *Bot.* The leaf of a grass or similar plant. **4.** A dashing young man.

blah (blä) *Slang. n.* **1.** Nonsense. **2. blahs.** A feeling of dissatisfaction or discomfort. *—adj.* Dull and uninteresting.

blain (blān) *n.* A skin swelling or sore.

blame (blām) *v.* **blamed, blam•ing. 1.** To hold (someone or something) at fault. **2.** To find fault with **:** censure. ★ ***syns:*** CENSURE, CHARGE, CONDEMN, CRITICIZE, DENOUNCE, FAULT, PAN, RAP *—n.* **1.** Responsibility for a fault or error. **2.** Condemnation **:** censure. **—blam'a•ble, blame'a•ble** *adj.* **—blame'less** *adj.* **—blame'less•ness** *n.*

blame•wor•thy (blām'wûr'*th*ē) *adj.* Deserving blame. **—blame'wor'thi•ness** *n.*

blanch (blănch) *also* **blench** (blĕnch) *v.* **1.** To take the color from **:** bleach. **2.** To turn or cause to turn white or pale. **3.** To scald (vegetables).

bland (blănd) *adj.* **1.** Marked by a moderate, undisturbed, or tranquil quality. **2.** Lacking distinctive character **:** insipid. **—bland'ly** *adv.* **—bland'ness** *n.*

blan•dish (blăn'dĭsh) *v.* To coax by wheedling or flattery **:** cajole. **—blan'dish•er** *n.* **—blan'dish•ment** *n.*

blank (blăngk) *adj.* **1.** Bearing no markings, writing, or incisions. **2.** Not filled in **:** incomplete. **3.** Devoid of expression, thought, or feeling **:** vacant. **4.** Appearing dazed or bewildered. **5.** Absolute **:** utter. *—n.* **1.** An empty place **:** void. **2. a.** A space to be filled in on a document. **b.** A document with one or more such spaces. **3.** A cartridge containing powder but no bullet. **4.** An unfinished part or object, as a key form. *—v.* **1.** To obscure. **2.** To prevent (an opponent) from scoring in a sports contest. **—blank'ly** *adv.* **—blank'ness** *n.*

blank check *n.* Carte blanche.

blan•ket (blăng'kĭt) *n.* **1.** A piece of usu. woven material used as a covering, esp. on a bed. **2.** A thick covering layer. *—adj.* Covering or applying to a wide variety of requirements or conditions. **—blank'et** *v.*

blank verse *n.* Verse composed of lines that do not rhyme, usu. in iambic meter.

blare (blâr) *v.* **blared, blar•ing.** To sound or cause to sound loudly and stridently. **—blare** *n.*

blar•ney (blär'nē) *n.* **1.** Flattering talk. **2.** Nonsensical or deceptive talk.

bla•sé (blä-zā', blä'zā) *adj.* **1.** Uninterested because of frequent exposure **:** bored. **2.** Extremely worldly and sophisticated.

blas•pheme (blăs-fēm', blăs'fēm') *v.* **-phemed, -phem•ing.** To speak of or address (something sacred, esp. God) impiously or irreverently. **—blas•phem'er** *n.* **—blas'phe•mous** *adj.* **—blas'phe•mous•ly** *adv.* **—blas'phe•my** *n.*

blast (blăst) *n.* **1.** A strong gust or stream of air or other gas, as steam. **2.** The act of blowing or the sound produced by blowing a wind instrument or whistle. **3.** An explosion or its effect. **4.** A violent verbal assault or outburst. **5.** *Slang.* A wild party or event. *—v.* **1.** To fragment by or as if by an explosion **:** smash. **2.** To blight **:** wither. **3.** *Informal.* To attack or criticize vigorously. **4.** *Slang.* To shoot. **—blast off.** To take off, as a space vehicle. **—blast'er** *n.*

blast•off *also* **blast-off** (blăst'ôf', -ŏf') *n.* A rocket or space vehicle launch.

blas•tu•la (blăs'chə-lə) *n., pl.* **-las** *or* **-lae** (-lē'). An early embryonic form consisting of a hollow cellular sphere. **—blas'tu•lar** *adj.* **—blas'tu•la'tion** *n.*

bla•tant (blāt'nt) *adj.* **1.** Unpleasantly and often vulgarly loud. **2.** Conspicuous, often offensively so : obvious. **—bla′tan•cy** *n.* **—bla′tant•ly** *adv.*

blath•er (blăth′ər) *v.* To talk nonsensically. **—blath′er** *n.* **—blath′er•er** *n.*

blaze[1] (blāz) *n.* **1. a.** A brilliant burst of fire. **b.** A bright, steady light or glare. **2.** A brilliant, striking display. **3.** A sudden outburst <a *blaze* of fury> **4. blazes.** *Slang.* Hell. **—blaze** *v.* **—blaz′ing•ly** *adv.*

blaze[2] (blāz) *n.* **1.** A white or light-colored spot or marking on the face of an animal. **2.** A mark cut or painted on a tree to indicate a trail. —*v.* **blazed, blaz•ing.** To mark (a trail) with blazes.

blaz•er (blā′zər) *n.* A lightweight, informal sports jacket.

bla•zon (blā′zən) *n.* **1.** *Heraldry.* A coat of arms. **2.** An ostentatious display. —*v.* **1.** *Heraldry.* To embellish with or as if with blazons. **2.** To announce : proclaim. **—bla′zon•er** *n.* **—bla′zon•ment** *n.* **—bla′zon•ry** *n.*

bleach (blēch) *v.* **1.** To remove the color from. **2.** To become or cause to become white or colorless. —*n.* A chemical bleaching agent.

bleach•ers (blē′chərz) *pl.n.* An often unroofed open-air grandstand.

bleak (blēk) *adj.* **1.** Exposed to harsh, natural elements : barren. **2.** Cold and harsh : raw. **3. a.** Gloomy and somber : dreary. **b.** Discouraging : depressing. **—bleak′ly** *adv.* **—bleak′ness** *n.*

blear (blîr) *v.* **1.** To blur (the eyes) with or as if with tears. **2.** To blur : dim. **—blear′i•ly** *adv.* **—blear′i•ness** *n.* **—blear′y** *adj.*

bleat (blēt) *n.* The cry of a goat or sheep or a sound similar to this. **—bleat** *v.* **—bleat′er** *n.* **—bleat′ing•ly** *adv.*

bleed (blēd) *v.* **bled** (blĕd), **bleed•ing. 1.** To extract, emit, or lose blood. **2.** To be wounded. **3.** To feel sympathetic grief. **4.** To extract or exude sap or similar fluid. **5.** *Slang.* To obtain money, esp. by extortion. **6.** To become mixed or run, as dyes. **7.** To draw off (liquid or gaseous contents) from : drain. **—bleed′er** *n.*

bleed•ing-heart (blē′dĭng-härt′) *n.* **1.** Any of several plants of the genus *Dicentra* having nodding pink flowers. **2.** A person regarded as excessively sympathetic toward the underprivileged.

bleep (blēp) *n.* A brief high-pitched sound, as from an electronic device. —*v.* **1.** To emit a bleep or bleeps. **2.** To edit out (spoken material) from a broadcast or recording, esp. by replacing with bleeps.

blem•ish (blĕm′ĭsh) *v.* To spoil or impair by a flaw. —*n.* A defect or flaw.

blench[1] (blĕnch) *v.* To recoil out of fear.

blench[2] (blĕnch) *v.* *var. of* BLANCH.

blend (blĕnd) *v.* **blend•ed** *or* **blent** (blĕnt), **blend•ing. 1.** To combine so as to make constituent parts indistinguishable. **2.** To mix (differing varieties or grades) thoroughly so as to obtain a new mixture. **3.** To merge or become merged into one : unite. **—blend** *n.* **—blend′er** *n.*

bless (blĕs) *v.* **blessed** *or* **blest** (blĕst), **bless•ing. 1. a.** To make holy : sanctify. **b.** To make the sign of the cross over. **2.** To call for divine favor upon. **3.** To honor as holy : praise. **4.** To confer well-being or prosperity upon.

bless•ed (blĕs′ĭd) *also* **blest** (blĕst) *adj.* **1.** Worthy of being worshiped or held in veneration : revered. **2.** *Rom. Cath. Ch.* Enjoying the eternal happiness of heaven. —Used as a title for those who have been beatified. **3.** Enjoying or bringing happiness. **4.** *Slang.* —Used as an intensive <without a *blessed* crumb> **—bless′ed•ly** *adv.* **—bless′ed•ness** *n.* **—bless′ing** *n.*

bless•ing (blĕs′ĭng) *n.* **1.** An act of one who blesses. **2.** Something contributing to well-being or prosperity : boon. **3.** Approval. **4.** A short prayer before a meal.

blew (blo͞o) *v.* *p.t. of* BLOW.

blight (blīt) *n.* **1.** Any of several plant diseases. **2. a.** An adverse environmental influence or condition, as drought. **b.** An adverse social or psychological influence or condition. **—blight** *v.*

blight•er (blī′tər) *n.* *esp. Brit.* A worthless fellow.

blimp (blĭmp) *n.* An elongated aircraft with a gas-filled, nonrigid hull.

blind (blīnd) *adj.* **1.** Being without sight. **2.** Of or intended for sightless persons. **3.** Performed by instruments without using sight <*blind* flying> **4.** Unable or unwilling to understand <*blind* to their defects> **5.** Not based on reason or fact <*blind* belief> **6.** Hidden from sight <a *blind* curve><a *blind* seam> **7. a.** Closed at one end <a *blind* passageway> **b.** Without an opening <a *blind* wall> —*n.* **1.** Something that hinders vision or blocks out light. **2.** A shelter for concealment, esp. of hunters. **3.** A subterfuge. —*v.* **1.** To deprive of sight. **2.** To deprive of judgment or perception. **3.** To dazzle. **—blind′ly** *adv.* **—blind′ness** *n.*

blind date *n.* *Informal.* **1.** A date between 2 strangers, often arranged by a 3rd person. **2.** A person on a blind date.

blind•ers (blīn′dərz) *pl.n.* A pair of flaps attached to the bridle of a horse to restrict lateral vision.

blind•fold (blīnd′fōld′) *v.* To cover the eyes with or as if with a cloth or bandage. —*n.* A bandage covering the eyes to prevent seeing. **—blind′fold′** *adj. & adv.*

blind-side (blīnd′sīd′) *v.* **1.** To hit or attack on the blind side. **2.** To take unawares, esp. with harmful results.

bli•ni (blē′nē) *pl.n.* Small pancakes served with caviar, sour cream, and herring.

blink (blĭngk) *v.* **1.** To close and open the eyes rapidly. **2.** To squint. **3.** To twinkle : gleam. —*n.* **1.** The act or action of closing and opening the eyes rapidly. **2.** A quick glimpse. **3.** A flash of light : twinkle. **—on the blink.** Out of order.

blink•er (blĭng′kər) *n.* **1.** A light that signals a message or warning by blinking. **2.** *Slang.* An eye.

blintz (blĭnts) *or* **blin•tze** (blĭn′tsə) *n.* A

thin pancake usu. rolled and stuffed with cottage cheese.
blip (blĭp) *v.* **blipped, blip•ping.** To bleep. —*n.* **1.** The display of a pulse of information, as a spot of light on a radar screen or oscilloscope. **2.** A bleep.
bliss (blĭs) *n.* **1.** Great happiness : joy. **2.** Ecstasy of salvation : spiritual joy. —**bliss'ful** *adj.* —**bliss'ful•ly** *adv.*
blis•ter (blĭs'tər) *n.* **1.** A thin, rounded swelling of the skin containing watery matter. **2.** An air bubble resembling a blister, as on a painted surface. —**blis'ter** *v.*
blis•ter•ing (blĭs'tər-ĭng) *adj.* **1.** Intensely hot. **2.** Severe : extreme.
blithe (blīth, blīth) *adj.* **blith•er, blith•est.** **1.** Filled with gaiety : cheerful. **2.** Carefree : casual. —**blithe'ly** *adv.* —**blithe'ness** *n.* —**blithe'some** *adj.*
blitz (blĭts) *n.* **1.** A blitzkrieg. **2.** An intensive air raid or series of air raids. **3.** An intense campaign. —**blitz** *v.*
blitz•krieg (blĭts'krēg') *n.* **1.** A sudden, swift military offensive. **2.** A swift, concerted effort.
bliz•zard (blĭz'ərd) *n.* A severe storm accompanied by heavy, driving snow.
bloat (blōt) *v.* **1.** To become or cause to become inflated or swollen. **2.** To puff up, as with vanity.
bloat•er (blō'tər) *n.* A lightly smoked and salted herring or mackerel.
blob (blŏb) *n.* **1.** A soft, amorphous mass. **2.** A shapeless splotch or daub, esp. of color.
bloc (blŏk) *n.* A group united for common action <the Eastern *bloc*><the oil *bloc*>
block (blŏk) *n.* **1.** A solid piece, as of wood, with one or more flat sides. **2.** A stand from which auctioned articles are sold. **3.** A pulley or system of pulleys in a frame. **4.** A set of like items, as shares of stock, sold or handled as a unit. **5. a.** An act of hindering or obstructing. **b.** A hindrance or obstacle. **6. a.** A section of a city or town bounded by 4 intersecting streets. **b.** The part of a street bounded by consecutive streets. **7.** *Can.* A group of townships in an unsurveyed area. **8.** Interruption, esp. obstruction of a neural or digestive process. **9.** *Psychol.* The sudden stopping of a thought process with no immediately apparent cause. —*v.* **1.** To support or keep in place with a block. **2.** To shape with or on a block. **3.** To stop or impede movement through : obstruct. —**on the block.** Up for sale, esp. at an auction. —**block'age** *n.* —**block'er** *n.* —**block'ish** *adj.*
block•ade (blŏ-kād') *n.* **1.** Closure of an area, as a harbor, to entrance and exit of traffic. **2.** The forces used in a blockade. —**block'ade'** *v.* —**block•ad'er** *n.*
block and tackle *n.* Pulley blocks and ropes or cables used to hoist heavy objects.
block•bust•er (blŏk'bŭs'tər) *n. Informal.* **1.** A bomb having the capacity to destroy an entire city block. **2.** Something notably effective or successful.
block•bust•ing (blŏk'bŭs'tĭng) *n. Informal.* A real estate practice of inducing homeowners to sell by appealing to the fear that property values will decline because minority groups are about to move into the neighborhood.
block•head (blŏk'hĕd') *n.* A dolt.
block•house (blŏk'hous') *n.* **1.** A military fortification with small openings for observation and firing weapons. **2.** A strongly reinforced building used for observation of missile and weapons tests.
blond (blŏnd) *adj.* **1.** Having pale-colored hair and skin and usu. light eyes. **2.** Of a flaxen or golden color or of any light shade of auburn or brown. —**blond** *n.* —**blond'ish** *adj.* —**blond'ness** *n.*
blonde (blŏnd) *adj.* Blond. —*n.* A blonde woman or girl.
blood (blŭd) *n.* **1. a.** The fluid that is circulated by the heart through the vertebrate vascular system and carries oxygen and nutrients throughout the body and wastes to excretory channels. **b.** A fluid that has similar functions in an invertebrate. **c.** A fluid resembling blood, as the juice of some plants. **2.** Life : lifeblood. **3.** Bloodshed. **4.** Disposition : temperament. **5.** Kinship. **6.** Racial or national ancestry <of Irish *blood*> **7.** A dashing young man : blade. —*adj.* Purebred <a *blood* mare> —**blood'less** *adj.* —**blood'less•ly** *adv.*
blood bank *n.* A place where plasma or whole blood is typed, processed, and stored for future use.
blood bath *n.* A massacre.
blood cell *n.* Any of the cells contained in blood, as an erythrocyte or leukocyte.

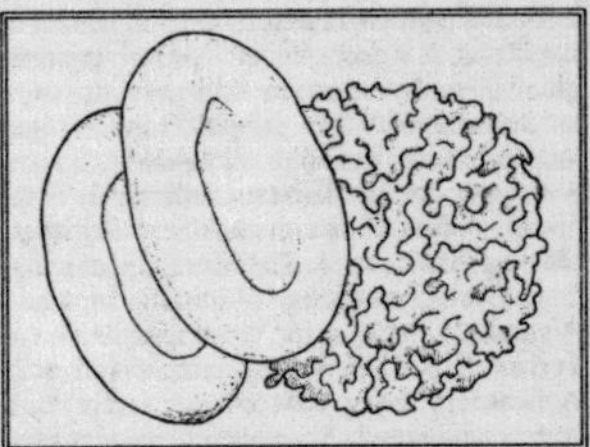

blood cell
(Left) *erythrocytes and* (right) *leukocyte*

blood count *n.* Determination of the number of red and white corpuscles in a specific volume of blood.
blood•cur•dling (blŭd'kûrd'lĭng) *adj.* Causing great horror : terrifying.
blood•ed (blŭd'ĭd) *adj.* **1.** Having blood or a temperament of a certain kind <Reptiles are cold-*blooded.*><hot-*blooded* youth> **2.** Thoroughbred.
blood group *n.* Any of several immunologi-

cally distinct, genetically determined classes of human blood.

blood•hound (blŭd'hound') *n.* **1.** A hound with a smooth coat, drooping ears, and a keen sense of smell. **2.** *Informal.* One who pursues relentlessly.

blood•let•ting (blŭd'lĕt'ĭng) *n.* **1.** Bleeding of a vein as therapy. **2.** Bloodshed.

blood•line (blŭd'līn') *n.* Direct line of descent : pedigree.

blood•mo•bile (blŭd'mə-bēl) *n.* A vehicle equipped for collecting blood from donors for blood banks.

blood poisoning *n.* **1.** Toxemia. **2.** Septicemia.

blood pressure *n.* The pressure of the blood against arterial walls.

blood serum *n.* Blood plasma with the fibrin removed.

blood•shed (blŭd'shĕd') *n.* The shedding of blood, esp. by injuring or killing.

blood•shot (blŭd'shŏt') *adj.* Red and irritated.

blood•stream *also* **bloodstream** (blŭd'strēm') *n.* The blood circulating in the vascular system of a living body.

blood•suck•er (blŭd'sŭk'ər) *n.* **1.** An animal, as a leech, that sucks blood. **2.** *Informal.* A person who clings to or preys upon another : parasite. **—blood'suck'ing** *adj.*

blood•thirst•y (blŭd'thûr'stē) *adj.* Thirsting for or characterized by bloodshed : murderous. **—blood'thirst'i•ly** *adv.* **—blood'thirst'i•ness** *n.*

blood type *n.* Blood group.

blood vessel *n.* A tubular canal through which blood circulates : an artery, vein, or capillary.

blood•y (blŭd'ē) *adj.* **-i•er, -i•est. 1.** Stained with blood. **2.** Of, characteristic of, or containing blood. **3.** Accompanied by or giving rise to bloodshed. **4.** Cruel : bloodthirsty. **5.** —Used as an intensive <a *bloody* idiot> *—adv.* —Used as an intensive <*bloody* well right> *—v.* **-ied, -y•ing.** To stain with or as if with blood. **—blood'i•ly** *adv.* **—blood'i•ness** *n.*

bloom (blo͞om) *n.* **1.** The blossoms of a plant. **2. a.** The state or time of bearing flowers. **b.** A state or time of vigor, freshness, and beauty : prime. **3.** A healthy, rosy complexion. **4.** *Bot.* A powdery layer that coats certain fruits, leaves, and stems. **5.** An excessive planktonic growth in a body of water. *—v.* **1.** To bear flowers. **2.** To shine with health. **3.** To flourish. ★ ***syns:*** BLOSSOM, BURGEON, EFFLORESCE, FLOWER

bloo•mers (blo͞o'mərz) *pl.n.* **1.** Wide, loose trousers gathered at the knee, formerly worn by women and girls for athletics. **2.** Underpants of similar design.

bloop•er (blo͞o'pər) *n.* **1.** *Baseball.* A weak fly ball. **2.** *Informal.* A faux pas.

blos•som (blŏs'əm) *n.* **1.** A flower or mass of flowers, esp. of a plant that bears edible fruit. **2.** The state or time of flowering. *—v.* **1.** To come into flower : bloom. **2.** To develop : flourish.

blot (blŏt) *n.* **1.** A stain : spot. **2.** A moral stigma : disgrace. *—v.* **blot•ted, blot•ting. 1.** To stain or spot. **2.** *Obs.* To disgrace morally. **3.** To cancel or obliterate. **4.** To darken. **5.** To soak up or dry with absorbent material. **6.** To spill or spread in a blot. **7.** To become blotted.

blotch (blŏch) *n.* **1.** A spot : blot. **2.** A discolored area on the skin : blemish. **—blotch** *v.* **—blotch'i•ly** *adv.* **—blotch'i•ness** *n.* **—blotch'y** *adj.*

blot•ter (blŏt'ər) *n.* **1.** A piece or a pad of blotting paper. **2.** A book that contains daily records.

blotting paper *n.* Absorbent paper used to blot up excess ink.

blouse (blous, blouz) *n.* **1.** A loosely fitting shirt extending to or below the waist. **2.** The coat or tunic worn by members of the U.S. Army. *—v.* **bloused, blous•ing.** To hang or cause to hang loose and full.

blow[1] (blō) *v.* **blew** (blo͞o), **blown** (blōn), **blow•ing. 1.** To be in a state of motion, as air. **2.** To move or cause to move by or as if by a current of air. **3. a.** To expel a current of air, as from the mouth. **b.** To expel a current of air, as from a bellows. **4.** To sound or cause to sound by expelling a current of air, as in playing an instrument. **5.** To breathe hard : pant. **6.** To burst or cause to burst. **7.** To burn out or melt, as a fuse. **8.** To spout air and water, as a whale. **9.** To shape or form (e.g., glass) by forcing air or gas through at the end of a pipe. **10.** To free of obstruction by forcing air through <*blow* one's nose> **11.** *Slang.* To spend (money) freely. **12.** *Slang.* To handle ineptly. **13.** *Slang.* To depart in a great hurry <*blew* town> **—blow in.** *Slang.* To arrive. **—blow out. 1.** To extinguish by blowing <*blew out* the candle> **2.** To fail, as an electrical device. **—blow up. 1.** To come into being <A squall *blew up.*> **2.** To fill with air : inflate. **3.** To enlarge (a photographic image or print). **4.** *Slang.* To lose one's temper. *—n.* **1. a.** A blast of air or wind. **b.** A storm. **2.** An act of blowing. **3.** *Slang.* An act of bragging. **—blow'er** *n.*

blow[2] (blō) *n.* **1.** A sudden hard hit, as with the fist or a club. **2.** An unexpected shock. **3.** An unexpected attack.

blow[3] (blō) *n.* A mass of blossoms. *—v.* **blew** (blo͞o), **blown** (blōn), **blow•ing.** To bloom or cause to bloom.

blow-by-blow (blō'bī-blō') *adj.* Describing in great detail.

blow-dry (blō'drī') *v.* T o dry and usu. style (the hair) with a small, hand-held dryer. **—blow'-dry'er** *n.*

blow•fly (blō'flī') *n.* Any of several flies of the family Calliphoridae that deposit their eggs in carrion or in open wounds.

blow•gun (blō'gŭn') *n.* A long narrow pipe through which pellets or darts are blown.

blow•hard (blō'härd') *n.* *Slang.* A braggart.

blow•hole (blō'hōl') *n.* **1.** A nostril on the head of whales and other cetaceans. **2.** A hole in ice to which aquatic mammals, as dolphins, come to breathe.

blow·out (blō'out') *n.* **1.** A sudden bursting, as of a tire. **2.** An abrupt escape of confined gas. **3.** *Slang.* A large party **:** bash.
blow·torch (blō'tôrch') *n.* A usu. portable gas burner that generates a hot flame used to melt and weld soft metals.
blow·up (blō'ŭp') *n.* **1.** An explosion. **2.** A violent outburst of temper. **3.** A photographic enlargement.
blow·y (blō'ē) *adj.* **-i·er, -i·est.** Windy.
blow·zy *also* **blow·sy** (blou'zē) *adj.* **-zi·er, -zi·est** *also* **-si·er, -si·est. 1.** Having a coarse bloated appearance. **2.** Disheveled and frowzy **:** unkempt.
BLT (bē'ĕl-tē') *n.* A bacon, lettuce, and tomato sandwich.
blub·ber[1] (blŭb'ər) *v.* **1.** To sob noisily. **2.** To utter while sobbing. **—blub'ber·er** *n.* **—blub'ber·ing·ly** *adv.*
blub·ber[2] (blŭb'ər) *n.* **1.** The thick fat between the skin and muscle layers of whales and other marine mammals. **2.** Excessive body fat. **—blub'ber·y** *adj.*
bludg·eon (blŭj'ən) *n.* A short, heavy, usu. wooden club that has one end loaded or thicker than the other. *—v.* **1.** To strike with or as if with a bludgeon. **2.** To bully or threaten. **—bludg'eon·er** *n.*
blue (blo͞o) *n.* **1.a.** Any of a group of colors whose hue is that of a clear sky **:** the hue of that portion of the spectrum lying between green and violet. **b.** A pigment of this color. **c.** An object of the color blue. **2.** *often* **Blue.** The Union Army in the Civil War. *—adj.* **blu·er, blu·est. 1.** Of the color blue. **2.** Bluish. **3.** Having a gray or purplish color, as from cold. **4.** *Informal.* Depressed or depressing. **5.** Risqué **:** indecent. *—v.* **blued, blu·ing.** To make or become blue. **—blue'ly** *adv.* **—blue'ness** *n.* **—blu'ish, blue'ish** *adj.*
blue baby *n.* An infant born with bluish skin caused by inadequate oxygenation of the blood.
blue·bell (blo͞o'bĕl') *n.* Any of several plants bearing blue, bell-shaped flowers.
blue·ber·ry (blo͞o'bĕr'ē) *n.* A North American shrub of the genus *Vaccinium,* bearing small, edible berries.
blue·bird (blo͞o'bûrd') *n.* Any of several North American birds of the genus *Sialia,* with blue plumage and in the male of most species a reddish breast.
blue-black (blo͞o'blăk') *adj.* Very dark blue in color.
blue blood *n.* **1.** Aristocratic descent. **2.** A member of the aristocracy. **—blue'-blood'-ed** *adj.*
blue·bot·tle (blo͞o'bŏt'l) *n.* Any of several flies of the genus *Calliphora* that have bright metallic-blue bodies and breed in decaying organic matter.
blue cheese *n.* A semisoft cheese veined with a greenish-blue mold.
blue chip *n.* A stock selling at a high price due to public confidence in its record of consistently steady earnings over the long term. **—blue'-chip'** *adj.*

▲ ***word history:*** Blue chips in poker are usu. the chips with the highest value. It is from this usage that the term *blue chip* is applied to highly regarded stocks.

blue-col·lar (blo͞o'kŏl'ər) *adj.* Of or relating to wage earners whose jobs involve skilled or semiskilled manual labor.
blue·fish (blo͞o'fĭsh') *n.* A voracious food and game fish, *Pomatomus saltatrix,* of temperate and tropical waters of the Atlantic and Indian oceans.
blue·grass (blo͞o'grăs') *n.* **1.** A grass of the genus *Poa,* esp. *P. pratensis,* native to Eurasia but naturalized throughout North America. **2.** Folk music of the S U.S., usu. played on banjos and guitars in rapid tempos with jazzlike improvisation.
blue-green alga (blo͞o'grēn') *n.* An alga of the division Cyanophyta or Myxophyceae, one of the simplest plant forms.
blue·ing (blo͞o'ĭng) *n. var. of* BLUING.
blue jay *n.* A North American bird, *Cyanocitta cristata,* having predominantly blue plumage and a crested head.
blue jeans *pl.n.* Clothes, esp. pants, made of blue denim.
blue law *n.* A law aimed at regulating Sunday commercial activities.
blue·nose (blo͞o'nōz') *n.* A person who is puritanical.
blue·print (blo͞o'prĭnt') *n.* **1.** A photographic reproduction, as of architectural plans or technical drawings, with white lines on a blue background. **2.** A carefully designed and usu. detailed plan of action. **—blue'print'** *v.*
blue ribbon *n.* A first prize. **—blue'rib'-bon** *adj.*
blues (blo͞oz) *pl.n. (sing. or pl. in number).* **1.** A state of depression. **2.** A style of jazz developed from southern African-American secular songs.
blue spruce *n.* An evergreen tree, *Picea pungens,* of the Rocky Mountain region, bearing bluish-green needles.
blue·stock·ing (blo͞o'stŏk'ĭng) *n.* A woman with strong scholarly or literary interests. **—blue'stock'ing** *adj.*

▲ ***word history:*** The term *bluestocking* orig. signified one who was informally and unfashionably dressed in blue worsted rather than black silk stockings. Such informal wear was common at literary and intellectual gatherings in 18th-cent. London, which were scornfully dubbed "bluestocking" societies, and the term *bluestocking* was transferred, sneer and all, to any woman with aspirations to literature and learning.

blu·ets (blo͞o'ĭts) *n. (sing. or pl. in number).* A low-growing plant, *Houstonia caerulea,* of E North America, having small, light-blue flowers with yellow centers.
blue whale *n.* A very large baleen whale, *Sibbaldus musculus,* with a bluish-gray back and ventral throat grooves.
bluff[1] (blŭf) *v.* **1.** To mislead or deceive. **2.** To impress or intimidate by showing more confidence than the facts support. **3.** To engage

in a false display of strength. —**bluff** *n.* —**bluff'a·ble** *adj.* —**bluff'er** *n.*

bluff[2] (blŭf) *n.* A steep headland, promontory, river bank, or cliff. —*adj.* **1.** Having a broad, steep front. **2.** Having a blunt and rough but not unkind manner. —**bluff'ly** *adv.* —**bluff'ness** *n.*

blu·ing *also* **blue·ing** (blo͞o'ĭng) *n.* **1.** A coloring agent for counteracting the yellowing of laundered fabrics. **2.** A rinsing agent for giving a silver tint to graying hair.

blun·der (blŭn'dər) *n.* A mistake usu. caused by ignorance or miscalculation. —*v.* **1.** To move unsteadily or clumsily. **2.** To make a blunder. —**blun'der·er** *n.* —**blun'der·ing·ly** *adv.*

blun·der·buss (blŭn'dər-bŭs') *n.* A short musket with a flaring muzzle, once used to scatter shot at close range.

blunt (blŭnt) *adj.* **1.** Having a dull edge or end. **2.** Abrupt and frank **:** brusque. —*v.* **1.** To make or become blunt. **2.** To make less effective **:** weaken <tried to *blunt* her criticism> —**blunt'ly** *adv.* —**blunt'ness** *n.*

blur (blûr) *v.* **blurred, blur·ring. 1.** To make or become hazy and indistinct **:** obscure. **2.** To smear or stain **:** smudge. **3.** To lessen the perception of **:** dim. —*n.* **1.** A smear or blot **:** smudge. **2.** Something hazy and indistinct. —**blur'ri·ly** *adv.* —**blur'ri·ness** *n.* —**blur'ry** *adj.*

blurb (blûrb) *n.* A brief publicity notice, as on the jacket of a book.

blurt (blûrt) *v.* To speak suddenly and impulsively.

blush (blŭsh) *v.* **1.** To become red in the face esp. from modesty, embarrassment, or shame **:** flush. **2.** To become red or rosy. **3.** To feel ashamed or embarrassed. —**blush** *n.* —**blush'ful** *adj.* —**blush'ing·ly** *adv.*

blush·er (blŭsh'ər) *n.* **1.** One that blushes. **2.** Make-up for giving a rosy tint to the face and esp. the cheekbones.

blush wine *n.* A wine having a slightly pink tinge, similar in style to a dry white wine.

blus·ter (blŭs'tər) *v.* **1.** To blow in violent and noisy gusts, as wind in a storm. **2. a.** To act or speak with noisy threats or boasts. **b.** To bully. —**blus'ter** *n.* —**blus'ter·er** *n.* —**blus'ter·y** *adj.*

bo·a (bō'ə) *n.* **1.** Any of various large, nonvenomous, chiefly tropical snakes of the family Boidae, including the anaconda and boa constrictor, that coil around and suffocate their prey. **2.** A long, fluffy scarf made of soft material such as feathers.

boar (bôr, bōr) *n.* **1.** A male pig. **2.** A wild pig, *Sus scrofa,* of Eurasia and N Africa, that is the ancestor of the domestic hog.

board (bôrd, bōrd) *n.* **1.** A long, flat slab of sawed lumber **:** plank. **2. a.** A flat piece of rigid material, as wood, adapted for a special use. **b.** A flat surface on which a game is played. **3. a.** A table, esp. one set for serving a meal. **b.** Food or meals as a whole <room and *board*> **4.** A table at which official meetings are held. **5.** An organized body of administrators or investigators <*board* of directors> <*board* of inquiry> **6. boards.** A theater stage. **7.** *Naut.* The side of a ship <lee*board*> <over*board*> —**on board.** Aboard. —*v.* **1.** To close or cover with boards. **2.** To furnish or receive meals or lodging or both, in return for pay. **3.** To enter or go aboard (a vehicle or ship). **4.** To come alongside (a ship).

board·er (bôr'dər, bōr'-) *n.* A person who pays a set amount for regular meals or for meals and lodging.

board foot *n., pl.* **board feet.** A unit of cubic measure for lumber, equal to 1 foot square by 1 inch thick.

boarding house *also* **board·ing·house** (bôr'dĭng-hous', bōr'-) *n.* A house where lodging and meals are provided.

board·walk (bôrd'wôk', bōrd'-) *n.* A wooden promenade along a waterfront.

boast (bōst) *v.* **1.** To speak with excessive pride, esp. about one's own accomplishments, abilities, or possessions **:** brag. **2.** To take pride in or be enhanced by the possession of. **3.** To possess <The college *boasts* a new art gallery.> —*n.* **1.** An act of bragging. **2.** A source of pride. —**boast'er** *n.* —**boast·ful** *adj.* —**boast'ful·ly** *adv.* —**boast'ful·ness** *n.*

boat (bōt) *n.* **1.** A rather small, usu. open craft. **2.** A ship. **3.** A boat-shaped dish <a gravy *boat*> —**boat** *v.* —**boat'ing** *n.* —**boat'man** *n.*

boat·er (bō'tər) *n.* **1.** One who boats. **2.** A stiff straw hat with a flat crown.

boat·swain *also* **bo's'n** *or* **bos'n** *or* **bo·sun** (bō'sən) *n.* A petty officer or warrant officer in charge of the deck crew, rigging, cables, and anchors of a ship.

bob[1] (bŏb) *v.* **bobbed, bob·bing. 1.** To move or cause to move up and down. **2.** To curtsey or bow. **3.** To grab for with the teeth <*bob* for apples> —**bob up.** To appear or arise suddenly. —*n.* A quick, jerky movement of the head or body.

bob[2] (bŏb) *n.* **1.** A small, knoblike, hanging object, as a plumb bob. **2.** A fishing float or cork. **3.** A short haircut. —*v.* **bobbed, bob·bing. 1.** To fish with a bob. **2.** To cut short, as hair. —**bob'ber** *n.*

bob[3] (bŏb) *n., pl.* **bob.** *Brit.* A shilling.

bob·bin (bŏb'ĭn) *n.* A spool or reel that holds yarn or thread, as for sewing.

bob·ble (bŏb'əl) *v.* **-bled, -bling. 1.** To bob up and down. **2.** To fumble (e.g., a ball). —*n.* A mistake **:** blunder.

bob·by (bŏb'ē) *n., pl.* **-bies.** *Brit.* A police officer.

bobby pin *n.* A thin, flat, usu. metal hair clip with the ends pressed closely together.

bobby socks *also* **bobby sox** *pl.n. Informal.* Ankle socks.

bob·by·sox·er (bŏb'ē-sŏk'sər) *n. Informal.* A teenage girl.

bob·cat (bŏb'kăt') *n.* A North American wildcat, *Lynx rufus,* having spotted reddish-brown fur, tufted ears, and a very short tail.

bob·o·link (bŏb'ə-lĭngk') *n.* A migratory American songbird, *Dolichonyx oryzivorus,* of which the male has black, white, and yellowish plumage.

bob•sled (bŏb′slĕd′) *n.* **1.** A long racing sled with a steering mechanism to control the front runners. **2. a.** A long sled made of 2 shorter sleds joined in tandem. **b.** Either of these 2 smaller sleds. —**bob′sled′** *v.*

bob•tail (bŏb′tāl′) *n.* **1.** A short or shortened tail. **2.** An animal, as a horse, having a bobtail. —**bob′tailed′** *adj.*

bob•white (bŏb-hwīt′, -wīt′) *n.* A small North American quail, *Colinus virginianus,* having brown plumage with white markings.

boc•cie *or* **boc•ci** *or* **boc•ce** (bŏch′ē) *n.* A game originating in Italy that is played with wooden balls on a long narrow court.

bock beer (bŏk) *n.* A dark strong springtime beer.

bode[1] (bōd) *v.* **bod•ed, bod•ing.** To be a sign or omen of : signify.

bode[2] (bōd) *v. p.t. of* BIDE.

bod•ice (bŏd′ĭs) *n.* **1.** The part of a dress extending from the waist to the shoulder. **2.** *Obs.* A corset.

bod•i•less (bŏd′ē-lĭs) *adj.* Having no form or substance.

bod•i•ly (bŏd′l-ē) *adj.* **1.** Of, relating to, situated in, or exhibited by the body. **2.** Physical rather than mental or spiritual. —*adv.* **1.** In the flesh : in person. **2.** As a complete physical entity.

bod•kin (bŏd′kĭn) *n.* **1.** A small, sharply pointed instrument for making holes in leather or fabric. 2. A blunt needle for pulling ribbon or tape through a series of loops or a hem. 3. *Archaic.* A dagger : stiletto.

bod•y (bŏd′ē) *n., pl.* **-ies. 1. a.** The entire material structure and substance of an organism. **b.** The physical part of a person as opposed to the mental or spiritual aspect. **c.** A corpse or carcass. **d.** A human being : person. **2.** The torso of a human being or an animal. **3.** A bounded aggregate of matter <a *body* of water> **4.** A number of persons, concepts, or things considered as a whole : group <a legislative *body*><a *body* of information> **5.** The center or main part of something. **6. a.** Thickness or substantiality <hair with *body*> **b.** Strength or richness, esp. of flavor.

body bag *n.* A zippered bag, usu. of rubber, for transporting a human corpse.

body building *n.* The technique of developing the musculature of the body through exercise and diet.

body English *n.* The tendency of a person to try to influence the movement of a propelled object, as a ball, by twisting the body toward the goal.

bod•y•guard (bŏd′ē-gärd′) *n.* A usu. armed person or group of persons responsible for the protection of another person.

body language *n.* The postures, gestures, and expressions by which a person communicates nonverbally with others.

body shop *n.* A garage for the repair of automotive vehicular bodies.

body stocking *n.* A tight-fitting, usu. one-piece garment covering the torso, occas. having sleeves and legs.

body suit *n.* A tight-fitting one-piece garment for the torso.

bod•y•surf (bŏd′ē-sûrf′) *v.* To ride flat on a wave without a surfboard. —**bod′y•surf′er** *n.* —**bod′y•surf′ing** *n.*

body•work (bŏd′ē-wûrk′) *n.* The manufacturing or repairing of motor vehicle bodies.

Boer (bōr, bôr, bo͝or) *n.* A South African of Dutch descent. —**Boer** *adj.*

bog (bôg, bŏg) *n.* Soft, waterlogged ground : marsh. —*v.* **bogged, bog•ging.** To sink or cause to sink in or as if in a bog <*bogged* down in regulations> —**bog′gy** *adj.*

bo•gey (bō′gē) *n., pl.* **-geys. 1.** *var. of* BOGY. **2.** One golf stroke over par on a hole. **3.** *Slang.* An unidentified flying aircraft.

bog•ey•man (bo͝og′ē-măn′, bō′gē-, bo͞o′gē-) *n. var. of* BOOGIEMAN.

bog•gle (bŏg′əl) *v.* **-gled, -gling. 1.** To shy away from with or as if with fright or astonishment. **2.** To cause to be overcome, as with fright or astonishment. **3.** To botch.

bo•gus (bō′gəs) *adj.* Counterfeit : fake.

bo•gy *also* **bo•gey** *or* **bo•gie** (bō′gē) *n., pl.* **-gies** *also* **-geys** *or* **-gies. 1.** A hobgoblin. **2.** Something causing annoyance.

Bo•he•mi•an (bō-hē′mē-ən) *n.* **1.** A native or inhabitant of Bohemia. **2.** A Gypsy. **3. bohemian.** One with artistic or literary interests who adopts manners markedly different from those of the majority of society. —**Bo•he′mi•an** *adj.*

A *word history:* The nomadic people called *Bohemians* who roamed Europe from late medieval times had in fact come from the borderlands of India and Iran, not from Bohemia. The Europeans gave them such names as *Bohemian* and *Gypsy* (from *Egyptian*) because they did not know their original homelands. The French word *bohémien* was also used of "social gypsies"—artists and writers who led unconventional lives. Thackeray introduced this sense of the word into English in *Vanity Fair.*

boil[1] (boil) *v.* **1. a.** To vaporize a liquid by the application of heat. **b.** To reach the boiling point or to undergo boiling. **2.** To cook or clean by boiling. **3.** To be agitated like boiling water : churn. **4.** To be stirred up or greatly excited. **5.** To heat to the boiling point. **6.** To form or separate, as sugar, by the process of boiling. —**boil away.** To evaporate by boiling. —**boil down. 1.** To reduce in size or bulk by boiling. **2.** To condense or become condensed : reduce. —**boil over. 1.** To overflow while boiling. **2.** To lose one's temper. —**boil** *n.*

boil[2] (boil) *n.* A painful, localized pus-filled swelling of the skin caused by an infection of bacterial origin.

boil•er (boi′lər) *n.* **1.** A vessel in which a liquid, usu. water, is heated and often vaporized for heating or power. **2.** A container, as a kettle, for boiling liquids. **3.** A storage tank for hot water.

bois•ter•ous (boi'stər-əs, -strəs) *adj.* **1.** Stormy and rough **:** violent. **2.** Loud, noisy, unrestrained, and undisciplined. **—bois'ter•ous•ly** *adv.* **—bois'ter•ous•ness** *n.*

bok choy (bŏk choi') *n. var. of* PAK CHOI.

bold (bōld) *adj.* **1.** Courageous. **2.** Requiring or showing courage. **3.** Unduly forward **:** brazen. **4.** Clear and distinct to the eye **:** conspicuous. **5.** Steep, as a cliff **:** abrupt. **—bold'ly** *adv.* **—bold'ness** *n.*

bold•face (bōld'fās') *n.* Type with heavy, thick lines. **—bold'face'** *v.*

bold-faced (bōld'fāst') *adj.* Impudent.

bole (bōl) *n.* A tree trunk.

bo•le•ro (bō-lâr'ō, bə-) *n., pl.* **-ros. 1.** A very short jacket worn open at the front. **2. a.** A Spanish dance in triple meter. **b.** The music for the bolero.

bo•le•tus (bō-lē'təs) *n., pl.* **-tus•es** *or* **-ti** (-tī'). A fungus of the genus *Boletus,* with an umbrella-shaped cap, of which some species are poisonous and others edible.

bo•li•var (bō-lē'vär', bŏl'ə-vər) *n., pl.* **bo•li•vars** *or* **bo•li•var•es** (bō'lē-vä'räs'). —See table at CURRENCY.

bo•li•vi•a•no (bə-lĭv'ē-ä'nō, bō-) *n., pl.* **-nos.** —See table at CURRENCY.

boll (bōl) *n.* A rounded seedpod or capsule of a plant, as flax or cotton.

bol•lix (bŏl'ĭks) *v. Slang.* To throw into confusion **:** botch.

boll weevil *n.* A small, grayish beetle, *Anthonomus grandis,* whose larvae hatch in and damage cotton bolls.

bo•lo•gna (bə-lō'nē, -nə, -nyə) *also* **ba•lo•ney** *or* **bo•lo•ney** (-nē) *n.* A seasoned smoked sausage made of mixed meats.

bo•lo tie (bō'lō) *n.* A necktie made of a piece of cord fastened with an ornamental clasp or bar.

Bol•she•vik (bōl'shə-vĭk', bŏl'-) *n., pl.* **-viks** *or* **-vi•ki** (-vē'kē). **1.** A member of the extreme left-wing faction of the Communist Party that seized power in Russia in 1917. **2. bolshevik.** An extreme radical. **—Bol'she•vism** *n.* **—Bol'she•vist'** *n. & adj.*

bol•ster (bōl'stər) *n.* A long, narrow cushion or pillow. *—v.* **1.** To support or prop up with or as if with a bolster. **2.** To buoy up <*bolstered* their morale>

bolt[1] (bōlt) *n.* **1.** A threaded metal pin with a head at one end designed to be used with a nut to hold parts together. **2.** A bar that slides into a socket and is used to fasten doors and gates. **3.** A metal bar or rod in a lock mechanism that is thrown or withdrawn by turning the key. **4.** A sliding metal bar used in a breechloading rifle or other breech mechanism. **5.** A short, thick-headed arrow used with a crossbow. **6.** A flash of lightning **:** thunderbolt. **7.** A sudden movement to or away. **8.** A large roll of cloth. *—v.* **1.** To lock with or as if with a bolt. **2.** To eat hurriedly and with little chewing **:** gulp. **3.** To desert or withdraw support from (a political party). **4.** To speak impulsively **:** blurt out. **5.** To move or run suddenly. **6.** To break away from control and run, esp. as a horse. **—bolt'er** *n.*

bolt[2] (bōlt) *v.* To pass through a sieve **:** sift. **—bolt'er** *n.*

bo•lus (bō'ləs) *n.* **1.** A small rounded mass, esp. of chewed food. **2.** A large pill.

bomb (bŏm) *n.* **1. a.** An explosive weapon detonated by impact, proximity to target, or timing device, that is hurled at or dropped on a target. **b.** A weapon that releases destructive material, as smoke or gas, upon detonation. **c.** An atomic bomb. **2.** A portable, manually operated container that ejects a spray, gas, or foam under pressure. **3.** *Slang.* A total failure **:** fiasco. *—v.* **1.** To attack, damage, or destroy with or as if with bombs. **2.** *Slang.* To fail utterly.

bom•bard (bŏm-bärd') *v.* **1.** To attack with bombs, missiles, or shells. **2.** To attack persistently, as with questions. **3.** To irradiate (an atom). **—bom•bard'er** *n.* **—bom•bard'ment** *n.*

bom•bar•dier[1] (bŏm'bər-dîr') *n.* **1.** The aircraft crew member operating the bombing equipment. **2.** A noncommissioned British artillery officer.

bom•bar•dier[2] (bŏm'bər-dîr') *n. Can.* A large enclosed snowmobile.

bom•bast (bŏm'băst') *n.* Flamboyant, pompous writing or speech. **—bom•bas'tic** *adj.* **—bom•bas'ti•cal•ly** *adv.*

bom•ba•zine (bŏm'bə-zēn') *n.* A twilled fabric of silk and worsted or cotton, often dyed black.

bombed (bŏmd) *adj. Slang.* Drunk.

bomb•er (bŏm'ər) *n.* One that bombs, esp. a military aircraft designed to carry and drop bombs.

bomb•shell (bŏm'shĕl') *n.* **1.** A bomb. **2.** A shocking surprise.

bo•na fide (bō'nə fīd', fī'dē, bŏn'ə) *adj.* **1.** Performed or made in good faith **:** sincere. **2.** Authentic **:** genuine.

bo•nan•za (bə-năn'zə) *n.* **1.** A rich mine, vein, or pocket of ore. **2.** A source of great prosperity.

bon•bon (bŏn'bŏn') *n.* A candy coated with chocolate or fondant and having a creamy center.

bond (bŏnd) *n.* **1.** Something, as a cord, that binds or fastens together. **2.** *often* **bonds.** *Archaic.* Captivity **:** confinement. **3.** A uniting force or tie **:** link. **4.** A binding agreement **:** covenant. **5.** The duty, promise, or obligation by which one is bound. **6. a.** An agent that causes objects to cohere <a thermoplastic *bond*> **b.** The union or cohesion brought about by such an agent. **7.** *Law.* **a.** A sum of money paid as bail or surety. **b.** BONDSMAN 2. **8.** A certificate of debt issued by a corporation or government that guarantees payment of the orig. investment plus interest by a specified future date. **9.** The warehousing of taxable goods until the duties or taxes due on them are paid. **10.** An insurance contract in which an agency guarantees payment to an employer in the event of financial loss due to an action of an employee. **11.** A superior grade of white paper, used esp. in business correspondence. —*v.* **1.** To join or hold together securely, as with cement or glue. **2.** To place a guaranteed bond or mortgage on. **3.** To furnish bond or surety for. **4.** To place (e.g., an employee) under bond or guarantee.

bond•age (bŏn′dĭj) *n.* **1.** The condition of a serf or slave : servitude. **2.** The condition of being involuntarily subject to a power, force, or influence.

bond•ser•vant (bŏnd′sûr′vənt) *n.* One obligated to work without wages.

bonds•man (bŏndz′mən) *n.* **1.** *also* **bond•man** (bŏnd′-). A male bondservant. **2.** One who provides surety or bond for another.

bond•wom•an (bŏnd′wo͝om′ən) *n.* A woman bondservant.

bone (bōn) *n.* **1. a.** The dense, semirigid, porous, calcified connective tissue of the skeleton of most vertebrates. **b.** One of the anatomically distinct skeletal structures made of bone. **c.** A piece of bone. **2. bones. a.** The skeleton. **b.** The body. **c.** Mortal remains. **3.** A material, as ivory, resembling bone. **4.** Something made of bone or similar material. —*v.* **boned, bon•ing. 1.** To remove the bones from. **2.** To refresh one's memory. —**bon′i•ness** *n.* —**bon′y** *adj.*

bone-dry (bōn′drī′) *adj.* Without a trace of moisture.

bone•head (bōn′hĕd′) *n. Slang.* A stupid person : dunce. —**bone′head′ed** *adj.* —**bone′-head′ed•ness** *n.*

bone meal *n.* Crushed or ground bones used as plant fertilizer and animal feed.

bon•er (bō′nər) *n. Slang.* A blunder.

bon•fire (bŏn′fīr′) *n.* A large outdoor fire.

bong (bŏng, bông) *n.* A deep ringing sound, as of a bell. —**bong** *v.*

bon•go (bŏng′gō, bông′-) *n., pl.* **-gos** *or* **-goes.** One of a pair of drums played with the hands.

bon•ho•mie (bŏn′ə-mē′) *n.* Geniality.

bo•ni•to (bə-nē′tō) *n., pl.* **-to** *or* **-tos.** One of several marine food and game fishes of the genus *Sarda,* related to the tuna.

bon•kers (bŏng′kərz) *adj. Slang.* Crazy.

bon mot (bôN mō′) *n., pl.* **bons mots** (bôN mō′, mōz′). A clever saying.

bon•net (bŏn′ĭt) *n.* **1.** A hat secured by ribbons tied under the chin. **2.** A feather headdress worn by certain American Indians. **3.** *esp. Brit.* HOOD[1] 2.

bon•ny *also* **bon•nie** (bŏn′ē) *adj.* **-ni•er, -ni•est.** *esp. Scot.* Pleasing or attractive : pretty. —**bon′ni•ness** *n.*

bon•sai (bŏn′sī′, bōn′-) *n., pl.* **-sai. 1.** The craft of growing dwarfed, ornamentally shaped shrubs or trees in small, shallow pots. **2.** A shrub or tree grown by bonsai.

bo•nus (bō′nəs) *n.* Something given or paid in addition to the usual.

bon vi•vant (bŏn′ vē-vänt′, bôN′ vē-väN′) *n., pl.* **bons vi•vants** (bŏn′ vē-vänts′, bôN′ vē-väN′). One who has refined tastes and esp. enjoys excellent food and drink.

bon voy•age (bŏn′ voi-äzh′) *n.* —Used to wish a departing traveler a pleasant journey.

bonze (bŏnz) *n.* A Buddhist monk.

boo (bo͞o) *n., pl.* **boos.** A vocal sound uttered to show contempt or disapproval. —*interj.* —Used to frighten or surprise or to express disapproval. —**boo** *v.*

boob[1] (bo͞ob) *n. Slang.* BOOBY 1.

boob[2] (bo͞ob) *n. Slang.* A woman's breast.

boo-boo (bo͞o′bo͞o) *n., pl.* **-boos.** *Slang.* **1.** A blunder. **2.** A slight physical injury.

boo•by (bo͞o′bē) *n., pl.* **-bies. 1.** *also* **boob** (bo͞ob). A stupid person : dolt. **2.** One of several tropical sea birds of the genus *Sula,* related to the gannets.

booby prize *n.* An insignificant or comical award given to the one with the worst score in a game or contest.

booby trap *n.* A usu. concealed, often explosive device triggered by the movement of an apparently harmless object.

boo•dle (bo͞od′l) *n. Slang.* **1. a.** Money, esp. counterfeit money. **b.** Money taken as a bribe. **2.** Stolen goods : swag.

boog•ie (bo͝og′ē) *v.* **-ied, -ie•ing.** *Slang.* To dance to rock 'n' roll music.

boog•ie•man *also* **boog•y•man** *or* **bog•ey•man** (bo͝og′ē-măn′, bō′gē-, bo͞o′gē-) *n.* A terrifying person or thing : hobgoblin.

boog•ie-woog•ie (bo͝og′ē-wo͝og′ē, bo͞o′gē-wo͞o′gē) *n.* A style of jazz piano marked by a repeated rhythmic and melodic pattern in the bass.

book (bo͝ok) *n.* **1.** A set of pages fastened on one side and enclosed between protective covers. **2.** A printed or written literary work. **3.** A main division of a larger printed or written work. **4. Book.** The Bible. **5. a.** A volume for recording financial transactions. **b. books.** Such records as a whole. **6.** A record of bets placed on a race. —*v.* **1.** To record or list in or as if in a book. **2.** To record charges against (a person) on a police blotter. **3.** To arrange for (e.g., tickets) in advance : reserve. **4.** To hire (e.g., entertainers). —**book′ing** *n.*

book•case (bo͝ok′kās′) *n.* A piece of furniture having shelves for holding books.

book•end *also* **book end** (bo͝ok′ĕnd′) *n.* A support at the end of a row of books that serves to keep them upright.

book•ie (bo͝ok′ē) *n. Slang.* BOOKMAKER 2.

book•ish (bo͝ok′ĭsh) *adj.* **1.** Enjoying books : studious. **2.** Pedantic. —**book′ish•ly** *adv.* —**book′ish•ness** *n.*

book•keep•ing (bo͝ok′kē′pĭng) *n.* The art or practice of recording business accounts and transactions. —**book′keep′er** *n.*

book•let (bo͝ok′lĭt) *n.* A pamphlet.

book•mak•er (bo͝ok′mā′kər) *n.* **1.** One who prints, publishes, or binds books. **2.** One who takes and pays off bets. —**book′mak′ing** *n.*

book•plate (bo͝ok′plāt′) *n.* A label usu. pasted on the inside cover of a book that bears the owner's name.

book value *n.* The financial worth of a business in terms of its account books as opposed to its market value.

book•worm (bo͝ok'wûrm') *n.* **1.** The larva of any of various insects that infest books and feed on the bindings. **2.** One who spends much time studying or reading.

boom[1] (bo͞om) *v.* **1.** To emit a deep, resonant sound. **2.** To grow or develop rapidly : flourish. —*n.* **1.** A booming sound, as of an explosion. **2.** A period of economic prosperity. **3.** A sudden increase, as in wealth.

boom[2] (bo͞om) *n.* **1.** A spar extending from a mast to hold or extend the foot of a sail. **2.** A pole extending upward at an angle from a derrick's mast to support and guide objects being lifted. **3.** A movable arm for maneuvering a microphone.

boom box *n. Slang.* A portable audio system capable of high volume.

boom•er (bo͞o'mər) *n. Informal.* A baby boomer.

boo•mer•ang (bo͞o'mə-răng') *n.* **1.** A flat, curved piece of wood that can be hurled so that it returns to its thrower. **2.** A statement or action that backfires against its originator. —**boo'mer•ang** *v.*

boon[1] (bo͞on) *n.* Something beneficial that is bestowed : favor.

boon[2] (bo͞on) *adj.* Convivial : jolly <a *boon* companion>

boon•docks (bo͞on'dŏks') *pl.n. Slang.* Rural country.

boon•dog•gle (bo͞on'dô'gəl, -dŏg'əl) *n. Informal.* Pointless, wasteful work. —*v.* **-gled, -gling.** To waste time or money on boondoggle. —**boon'dog'gler** *n.*

boon•ies (bo͞o'nēz) *pl.n.* BOONDOCKS.

boor (bo͝or) *n.* A crude, rude person. ★ ***syns:*** BARBARIAN, BOUNDER, CHURL, PHILISTINE, YAHOO —**boor'ish** *adj.* —**boor'ish•ly** *adv.* —**boor'ish•ness** *n.*

boost (bo͞ost) *v.* **1.** To lift by or as if by pushing up from below. **2.** To increase : raise. **3.** To stir up enthusiasm for. —**boost** *n.* —**boost'er** *n.*

booster shot *n.* A supplementary dose of a vaccine to sustain the immune response.

boot[1] (bo͞ot) *n.* **1. a.** A protective piece of footgear covering the foot and part or all of the leg. **b.** Any protective sheath or covering. **2.** *esp. Brit.* The trunk of an automotive vehicle. **3.** A marine or naval recruit in basic training. **4. a.** A kick. **b.** *Slang.* A thrill. **5.** A summary dismissal, as from a job. —*v.* **1.** To put boots on. **2.** To kick. **3.** *Slang.* To dismiss : fire. **4.** *Computer Sci.* To bootstrap.

†**boot**[2] (bo͞ot) *v. Archaic.* To be of help or advantage : avail. —*n.* **1.** *Regional.* Something given in addition. **2.** *Archaic.* Avail : advantage. —**to boot.** In addition.

boot•black (bo͞ot'blăk') *n.* One who cleans and polishes shoes for a living.

boot•ee *also* **boot•ie** (bo͞o'tē) *n.* A soft, usu. knitted baby shoe.

booth (bo͞oth) *n., pl.* **booths** (bo͞o*th*z, bo͞oths). **1.** A small enclosed compartment, as a toll booth or a phone booth. **2.** A seating area in a restaurant having a table and seats whose backs serve as partitions. **3.** A small stand for the sale of goods.

boot•leg (bo͞ot'lĕg') *v.* **-legged, -leg•ging.** To make, transport, or sell (e.g., liquor) illegally. —**boot'leg'ger** *n.*

boot•less (bo͞ot'lĭs) *adj.* Useless. —**boot'less•ly** *adv.* —**boot'less•ness** *n.*

boot•lick (bo͞ot'lĭk') *v.* To treat or behave servilely. —**boot'lick'er** *n.*

boot•strap (bo͞ot'străp') *n.***1.** A loop at the side or the top rear of a boot to help in pulling the boot on. **2.** *Computer Sci.* The portion of a program that, when executed, loads into memory and executes the complete program. —*v.* To establish (a computer program) with a bootstrap.

boo•ty (bo͞o'tē) *n., pl.* **-ties. 1.** Plunder taken from an enemy in wartime. **2.** Goods stolen or seized. **3.** A valuable prize, award, or gain.

booze (bo͞oz) *Slang.* —*n.* Alcoholic drink. —*v.* **boozed, booz•ing.** To consume alcoholic drinks excessively. —**booz'er** *n.* —**booz'y** *adj.*

bop[1] (bŏp) *v.* **bopped, bop•ping.** *Informal.* To strike : hit. —**bop** *n.*

bop[2] (bŏp) *n.* Jazz marked by rhythmic, harmonic complexity and innovations.

bo•rate (bôr'āt', bōr'-) *n.* A boric acid salt.

bo•rax (bôr'ăks', -əks, bōr'-) *n.* Sodium borate, either in hydrated or anhydrous form.

Bor•deaux (bôr-dō') *n., pl.* **Bordeaux** (bôr-dōz'). A red or white wine from the region around Bordeaux.

bor•del•lo (bôr-dĕl'ō) *n., pl.* **-los.** A house of prostitution.

bor•der (bôr'dər) *n.* **1.** A margin or edge. **2.** A decorative strip around an edge. **3.** A geographic or political boundary. —*v.* **1.** To put a border on. **2.** To lie along the border of. **3.** To come near to in character <behavior *bordering on* rudeness>

bor•der•land (bôr'dər-lănd') *n.* **1.** Land on or near a frontier or border. **2.** An indeterminate area or situation.

bor•der•line (bôr'dər-līn') *n.* **1.** A line marking a boundary. **2.** An area between 2 conditions or qualities.

bore[1] (bôr, bōr) *v.* **bored, bor•ing. 1.** To make a hole in or through with or as if with a drill. **2.** To make by drilling or digging. —*n.* **1.** A hole or passage made by drilling. **2.** The inside diameter of a hole, tube, or cylinder. **3.** The caliber of a firearm. **4.** A tool for drilling.

bore[2] (bôr, bōr) *v.* **bored, bor•ing.** To tire with dullness or repetition. ★ ***syns:*** PALL, TIRE, WEARY —**bore** *n.* —**bore'dom** *n.* —**bor'ing•ly** *adv.*

bore[3] (bôr, bōr) *v. p.t. of* BEAR[1].

bo•re•al (bôr'ē-əl, bōr'-) *adj.* Of or located in the north : northern.

boric acid *n.* A crystalline compound used as an antiseptic and a preservative.

born (bôrn) *adj.* **1.** Brought into life or being. **2.** Having a particular talent from birth <a *born* writer> **3.** Derived or resulting from inventions <*born* of necessity>

born-a·gain (bôrn′ə-gĕn′) *adj.* Of, relating to, or being an individual who has made a conversion to Jesus Christ as personal savior <a *born-again* Christian>

borne (bôrn) *v. var. p.p. of* BEAR[1].

bo·ron (bôr′ŏn′, bōr′-) *n. Symbol* **B** A soft, brown nonmetallic element.

bor·ough (bûr′ō, bŭr′ō) *n.* **1.** A self-governing incorporated town, as in some U.S. states. **2.** One of the 5 administrative units of New York City. **3.** *esp. Brit.* **a.** An incorporated town. **b.** A town that sends one or more representatives to Parliament.

bor·row (bŏr′ō, bôr′ō) *v.* **1.** To receive or obtain (something) on loan with the intention of returning it. **2.** To adopt as one's own <*borrowed* another author's ideas>

borscht (bôrsht) *also* **borsch** (bôrsh) *n.* A hot or cold beet soup.

bor·zoi (bôr′zoi′) *n.* A large, slender dog with a silky coat and a narrow head.

bosh (bŏsh) *n. Informal.* Nonsense.

bosk·y (bŏs′kē) *adj.* **-i·er, -i·est.** Thick with trees or bushes : wooded.

bo's'n *or* **bos'n** (bō′sən) *n. vars. of* BOATSWAIN.

bos·om (bo͝oz′əm, bo͞o′zəm) *n.* **1.** The human chest, esp. the female breasts. **2.** The part of a garment covering the chest. **3.** The center : heart.

boss[1] (bôs, bŏs) *n.* **1.** An employer or supervisor. **2.** A politician who controls a party or political machine. *—v.* **1.** To supervise. **2.** To command in a domineering way. **—boss′i·ness** *n. adv.* **—boss′y** *adj.*

boss[2] (bôs, bŏs) *n.* A knoblike circular ornament. *—v.* To decorate with bosses.

Boston cream pie *n.* A cake with custard filling.

Boston terrier *n.* A small dog bred as a cross between a bulldog and a bull terrier.

bo·sun (bō′sən) *n. var. of* BOATSWAIN.

bot·a·ny (bŏt′n-ē) *n.* The science of plants. **—bo·tan′i·cal** (bə-tăn′ĭ-kəl), **bo·tan′ic** *adj.* **—bot′a·nist** *n.*

botch (bŏch) *v.* **1.** To ruin by clumsiness : bungle. **2.** To repair ineptly. ★ ***syns:*** BOLLIX, BUNGLE, FUMBLE, MISHANDLE, MISMANAGE, MUDDLE, MUFF, SPOIL **—botch** *n.*

both (bōth) *adj.* Being two in conjunction : one and the other. *—pron.* The one and the other. *—conj.* —Used with *and* to indicate that each of two things in a phrase or clause is included <*both* parents and children>

both·er (bŏ*th*′ər) *v.* **1.** To annoy or irritate. **2.** To make nervous : fluster. **3.** To take the trouble : concern oneself. *—n.* An annoyance. *—interj.* —Used to express irritation. **—both′er·some** *adj.*

bot·tle (bŏt′l) *n.* **1.** A usu. glass container with a narrow neck. **2.** The quantity that a bottle holds. **3.** Alcoholic drink <turned to the *bottle*> *—v.* **-tled, -tling.** To put in or as if in a bottle. **—bot′tler** *n.*

bot·tle-feed (bŏt′l-fēd′) *v.* To feed (e.g., a baby) with a bottle.

bot·tle·neck (bŏt′l-nĕk′) *n.* **1.** A narrow or obstructed section of a highway or pipeline. **2.** Something that hinders progress or production.

bot·tom (bŏt′əm) *n.* **1.** The deepest or lowest part. **2.** The lowest place or position <at the *bottom* of the class> **3.** The underside. **4.** The supporting part : foundation. **5.** The essence. **6.** The land under a body of water. **7.** *Informal.* The buttocks. *—adj.* Lowest : last. **—bot′tom·less** *adj.*

bottom line *n.* **1.** The lowest line in a financial statement that shows net loss or profit. **2.** The final result : upshot. **3.** The essential point.

bot·u·lism (bŏch′ə-lĭz′əm) *n.* Acute food poisoning caused by bacteria that grow in improperly canned foods.

bou·doir (bo͞o′dwär′, -dwôr′) *n.* A woman's private room.

bouf·fant (bo͞o-fänt′) *adj.* Puffed-out : full <a *bouffant* bridal veil>

bough (bou) *n.* A large tree branch.

bought (bôt) *v. p.t. & p.p. of* BUY.

†**bought·en** (bôt′n) *v. regional var. p.p. of* BUY.

bouil·la·baisse (bo͞o′yə-bās′) *n.* A highly seasoned fish stew made with several kinds of fish and shellfish.

bouil·lon (bo͞o′yŏn′, bo͝ol′-, -yən) *n.* A clear, thin broth usu. of beef or chicken.

boul·der (bōl′dər) *n.* A large, rounded rock.

boul·e·vard (bo͝ol′ə-värd′, bo͞o′lə-) *n.* A wide city street.

bounce (bouns) *v.* **bounced, bounc·ing. 1.** To rebound or cause to rebound. **2.** To bound in a lively manner <*bounced* into the room> **3.** To be returned by a bank as worthless <a check that *bounced*> *—n.* **1.** A bound : rebound. **2.** A spring or leap. **3.** Capacity to bounce : spring. **4.** Vivacity : spirit. **—bounc′i·ly** *adv.* **—bounc′i·ness** *n.* **—bounc′y** *adj.*

bounc·er (boun′sər) *n.* One who ejects disorderly persons from a public place.

bounc·ing (boun′sĭng) *adj.* **1.** Healthy : vigorous. **2.** Lively : spirited.

bound[1] (bound) *v.* **1.** To leap forward : spring. **2.** To advance by leaping. **3.** To bounce. **—bound** *n.*

bound[2] (bound) *n.* **1.** *often* **bounds.** A limit <beyond the *bounds* of credibility> **2. bounds.** The territory on or near limiting lines. *—v.* **1.** To limit. **2.** To border on another area : adjoin. **3.** To demarcate.

bound[3] (bound) *adj.* **1.** Confined by bonds. **2.** Under obligation. **3.** Enclosed in a cover or binding. **4.** Certain <We are *bound* to lose.>

bound[4] (bound) *adj.* On the way <*bound* for Berlin>

bound·a·ry (boun′də-rē, -drē) *n., pl.* **-ries.** Something that marks a limit or border.

bound·er (boun′dər) *n. esp. Brit.* A vulgar, cocksure person.

bound·less (bound′lĭs) *adj.* Without limits : infinite. **—bound′less·ly** *adv.* **—bound′less·ness** *n.*

boun·te·ous (boun′tē-əs) *adj.* Bountiful. **—boun′te·ous·ly** *adv.*

boun·ti·ful (boun'tə-fəl) *adj.* **1.** Giving liberally. **2.** Copious : plentiful. **—boun'ti·ful·ly** *adv.*

boun·ty (boun'tē) *n., pl.* **-ties. 1.** Liberality in giving. **2.** Something liberally given. **3.** A reward, payment, or inducement, esp. one given by a government for the performance of services beneficial to the state.

bounty hunter *n.* One who hunts predatory animals or outlaws for a bounty.

bou·quet (bō-kā', bo͞o-) *n.* **1.** Cut flowers fastened in a bunch. **2.** The fragrance typical of a wine.

bour·bon (bûr'bən) *n.* A whiskey distilled from a fermented mash.

bour·geois (bo͝or-zhwä', bo͝or'zhwä') *n., pl.* **-geois.** A member of the middle class. **—bour·geois** *adj.*

bour·geoi·sie (bo͝or'zhwä-zē') *n.* The middle class as opposed to the nobility or the working class.

bour·geon (bûr'jən) *v. var. of* BURGEON.

bout (bout) *n.* **1.** A match : contest. **2.** A length of time spent in a particular way <a *bout* of drinking><a *bout* of mumps>

bou·tique (bo͞o-tēk') *n.* A small shop selling fashionable clothes and accessories.

bou·ton·niere *also* **bou·ton·nière** (bo͞ot'-n-îr', -yâr') *n.* A flower worn in a buttonhole.

Bou·vier des Flan·dres (bo͞o-vyā' də flăn'-dərz, flăɴ'drə) *n.* A large, rough-coated dog orig. used in Belgium for herding and guarding cattle.

bou·zou·ki (bo͞o-zo͞o'kē, bə-) *n.* A Greek stringed instrument similar to a mandolin.

bo·vine (bō'vīn', -vēn') *adj.* **1.** Of or resembling an ox or cow. **2.** Sluggish : dull.

bow¹ (bō) *n.* **1.** A weapon consisting of a curved stave strung taut from end to end and used to launch arrows. **2.** A rod with horsehair drawn tightly between its ends, used to play the violin, viola, and related stringed instruments. **3.** A knot usu. having 2 loops and 2 ends. **4.** A rainbow. *—v.* **1.** To bend into a bow. **2.** To play (a stringed instrument) with a bow.

bow² (bou) *v.* **1.** To bend (the head, body, or knee) as an expression of greeting, consent, or courtesy. **2.** To comply : submit. **—bow out.** To withdraw : resign. *—n.* The act or an instance of bowing.

bow³ (bou) *n.* The forward part of a boat.

bowd·ler·ize (bōd'lə-rīz', boud'-) *v.* **-ized, -iz·ing.** To expurgate (e.g., a book) prudishly. **—bowd'ler·i·za'tion** *n.*

bow·el (bou'əl, boul) *n.* **1.** An intestine, esp. of a human being. **2.** *often* **bowels.** The digestive tract below the stomach. **3. bowels.** The interior <the *bowels* of the ship>

bow·er (bou'ər) *n.* A shaded, leafy recess : arbor. **—bow'er·y** *adj.*

bow-front (bō'frŭnt') *adj.* Having an outward-curving front, as a bureau.

bow·head (bō'hĕd') *n.* A large-headed whale, *Balaena mysticetus,* of Arctic seas.

bow·ie knife (bō'ē, bo͞o'ē) *n.* A thick-bladed single-edged hunting knife.

bow·knot (bō'nŏt') *n.* **1.** A knot with large, decorative loops. **2.** A bowtie.

bowl¹ (bōl) *n.* **1.** A hemispherical vessel for liquids or food. **2.** A bowl-shaped part, as of a spoon. **3.** A bowl-shaped theater or stadium. **—bowl'ful** *n.*

bowl² (bōl) *n.* **1.** A large wooden ball rolled in certain games. **2.** A roll of the ball, as in bowling. *—v.* **1.** To take part in the game of bowling. **2.** To roll (a ball) in bowling. **—bowl over.** To surprise : astound.

bow·leg (bō'lĕg') *n.* A leg with outward curvature in the region of the knee. **—bow'leg'-ged** *adj.*

bowl·er¹ (bō'lər) *n.* One that bowls.

bowl·er² (bō'lər) *n. esp. Brit.* A derby hat.

bow·line (bō'lĭn, -līn') *n.* A knot with a loop that won't slip.

bowl·ing (bō'lĭng) *n.* **1.** A game played by rolling a ball down a wooden alley in order to knock down a triangular formation of 10 pins. **2.** A similar game, as skittles.

bowling alley *n.* **1.** A smooth, level lane used for bowling. **2.** A place containing bowling alleys.

bow·man (bō'mən) *n.* An archer.

bow·sprit (bou'sprĭt', bō'-) *n.* A spar that extends forward from the stem of a ship.

bow·string (bō'strĭng') *n.* The string tied to either end of an archer's bow.

bow tie (bō) *n.* A small necktie tied in the shape of a bow knot.

box¹ (bŏks) *n.* **1.** A usu. rectangular container, typically having a lid. **2.** The amount that a box holds. **3.** A separated compartment in a theater for the seating of a small group. **4.** *Baseball.* A designated area where the batter, pitcher, or coaches stand. **5.** An awkward situation : predicament. *—v.* To put in or as if in a box.

box² (bŏks) *n.* A blow with the hand. *—v.* **1.** To hit with the hand. **2.** To take part in a boxing match (with).

box³ (bŏks) *n., pl.* **box** or **box·es.** An evergreen tree or shrub of the genus *Buxus,* esp. *B. sempervirens,* having hard, yellowish wood and used for hedges.

box·car (bŏks'kär') *n.* An enclosed railway car used for transporting freight.

box·er¹ (bŏk'sər) *n.* One who boxes, esp. as a profession.

box·er² (bŏk'sər) *n.* A short-haired dog orig. bred in Germany, with a brownish coat and a square muzzle.

boxer shorts *pl.n.* Full-cut undershorts.

box·ing (bŏk'sĭng) *n.* The sport of fighting with the fists, usu. with padded gloves.

box office *n.* A ticket office, as of a stadium or theater.

box spring *n.* A bedspring consisting of a frame enclosed with cloth and containing rows of coil springs.

box·wood (bŏks'wo͝od') *n.* **1.** The box tree. **2.** The hard wood of the box tree.

boy (boi) *n.* A male child or youth. *—interj.* —Used to express mild astonishment, disgust, etc. —**boy'hood'** *n.* —**boy'ish** *adj.* —**boy'ish•ly** *adv.* —**boy'ish•ness** *n.*

boy•cott (boi'kŏt') *v.* To abstain from buying or dealing with as a means of protest. —**boy'cott'** *n.*

boy•friend (boi'frĕnd') *n.* **1.** A favored male companion or sweetheart. **2.** A male friend.

Boy Scout *n.* A member of a worldwide boys' organization that stresses character development and citizenship training.

boy•sen•ber•ry (boi'zən-bĕr'ē) *n.* A prickly bramble hybridized from the loganberry and various blackberries and raspberries, with large, wine-red, edible berries.

Br *symbol for* BROMINE.

bra (brä) *n.* A brassiere. —**bra'less** *adj.*

brace (brās) *n.* **1.** A clamp. **2.** A device, as a supporting beam, that steadies or supports a weight. **3.** *Med.* An appliance used to support a part of the body. **4.** *often* **braces.** A set of bands and wires fixed to teeth to correct crooked alignment. **5.** A symbol, { or }, used to connect several lines of text. **6.** A crank-like handle for securing and turning a bit. **7.** **braces.** *esp. Brit.* Suspenders. **8.** A pair of like things. —*v.* **braced, brac•ing. 1.** To support with or as if with a brace. **2.** To prepare for impact or danger. **3.** To invigorate.

brace•let (brās'lĭt) *n.* An ornamental band encircling the wrist.

brack•en (brăk'ən) *n.* **1.** A fern, *Pteridium aquilinum,* with tough stems. **2.** A growth of bracken.

brack•et (brăk'ĭt) *n.* **1.** An L-shaped fixture, one arm of which is fastened to a vertical surface, the other arm projecting to support a weight, as a shelf. **2.** A small shelf supported by brackets. **3.** Either of a pair of symbols, [ ], used to enclose printed or written material. **4.** A classification or grouping, esp. of taxpayers according to income. —*v.* **1.** To support by means of a bracket. **2.** To set brackets around. **3.** To group together : classify.

brack•ish (brăk'ĭsh) *adj.* Somewhat salty : briny. —**brack'ish•ness** *n.*

bract (brăkt) *n.* A leaflike plant part either on the stalk of a flower cluster or below a flower.

brad (brăd) *n.* A small-headed, tapered nail.

brae (brā) *n. Scot.* A hillside : slope.

brag (brăg) *v.* **bragged, brag•ging.** To talk or assert boastfully. —**brag** *n.* —**brag'ger** *n.*

brag•ga•do•ci•o (brăg'ə-dō'shē-ō') *n., pl.* **-os. 1.** A braggart. **2. a.** Empty boasting. **b.** An arrogant manner : cockiness.

brag•gart (brăg'ərt) *n.* A boastful person.

Brah•ma (brä'mə) *n.* The member of the Hindu triad who created the universe.

Brah•man (brä'mən) *n.* **1.** *also* **Brah•ma** (-mə). The divine reality of the universe in Hinduism, the eternal spirit from which all being originates and to which all returns. **2.** *also* **Brah•min** (-mĭn). A member of the highest Hindu caste. **3.** *also* **Brah•ma** (-mə) *or* **Brah•min** (-mĭn). One of a breed of cattle developed in the S U.S., with a hump between the shoulders and a pendulous dewlap. —**Brah'man•ism'** *n.*

Brah•min (brä'mən) *n.* **1.** A socially and intellectually exclusive person. **2.** *var. of* BRAHMAN 2, 3.

braid (brād) *v.* **1.** To interweave 3 or more strands of : plait. **2.** To decorate with ornamental braid. **3.** To produce by interweaving. —*n.* **1.** A narrow length of material, as hair, that has been braided. **2.** A thin, woven strip of material used for decorating fabrics. —**braid'er** *n.*

Braille *also* **braille** (brāl) *n.* A system of printing for the blind, in which letters and numerals are represented by raised dots.

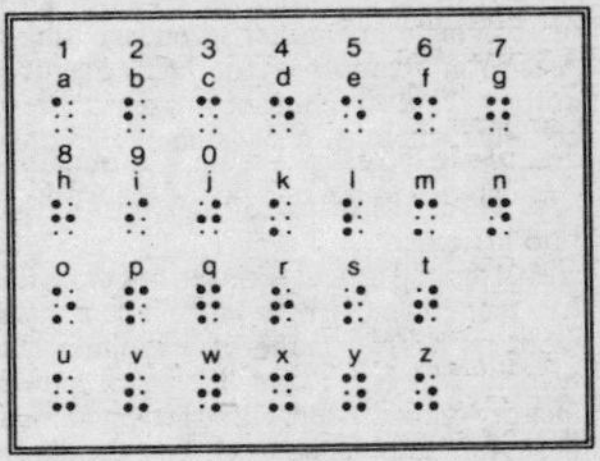

1 2 3 4 5 6 7
a b c d e f g

8 9 0
h i j k l m n

o p q r s t

u v w x y z

Braille

brain (brān) *n.* **1. a.** The large mass of gray nerve tissue enclosed in the cranium of a vertebrate that interprets sensory impulses, coordinates and controls bodily functioning, and is the center of emotion and thought. **b.** A functionally similar portion of the invertebrate nervous system. **2.** **brains.** Intellectual capacity. —*v.* **1.** To smash in the skull of. **2.** *Slang.* To hit on the head. —**brain'i•ness** *n.* —**brain'less** *adj.* —**brain'less•ly** *adv.* —**brain'less•ness** *n.* —**brain'y** *adj.*

brain death *n.* Death as evidenced by the absence of central nervous system activity. —**brain'-dead'** *adj.*

brain•storm (brān'stôrm') *n.* A sudden clever idea. —**brain'storm'** *v.* —**brain'storm'er** *n.*

brain•storm•ing (brān'stôr'mĭng) *n.* A method of problem solving in which all members of a group spontaneously contribute ideas.

brain•wash (brān'wŏsh', -wôsh') *v.* To indoctrinate so as to replace a person's convictions with an opposing set of beliefs.

brain wave *n.* **1.** A rhythmically fluctuating voltage arising from electrical activity in the brain. **2.** A brainstorm.

braise (brāz) *v.* **braised, brais•ing.** To brown (meat or vegetables) in fat and then simmer in a little liquid in a covered pan.

brake[1] (brāk) *n.* A device that slows or stops motion, as of a vehicle. —*v.* **braked, brak•ing. 1.** To slow down with or as if with a brake. **2.** To apply a brake.

brake[2] (brāk) *n.* **1.** A fern, esp. bracken. **2.** An area overgrown with dense bushes : thicket.

brake fluid *n.* Liquid used in a hydraulic brake cylinder.

brake•man (brāk'mən) *n.* A member of a train crew who assists the conductor and inspects the train.

brake shoe *n.* A curved block that presses against and reduces or stops the rotation of a wheel or shaft.

bram•ble (brăm'bəl) *n.* A prickly plant or shrub of the genus *Rubus.*

bran (brăn) *n.* The outer husks of cereals, as wheat, rye, and oats, sifted or bolted from the flour.

branch (brănch) *n.* **1. a.** A secondary woody limb growing out from the trunk of a tree or bush or from another secondary limb. **b.** A similar structure <the *branches* of an antler> **2.** A division of a larger or more complex whole. **3.** A division of a group, as a family or tribe. **4.** A tributary of a river. —*v.* To divide or spread out into or as if into branches.

brand (brănd) *n.* **1. a.** A trademark or distinctive name identifying a product or a manufacturer. **b.** The make of a product thus marked. **2.** A type **:** kind. **3.** A mark showing identity or ownership, burned on an animal's hide. **4.** A mark once burned on the skin of criminals. **5.** A mark of disgrace **:** stigma. **6.** Burning or charred wood. —*v.* To mark with or as if with a brand.

bran•dish (brăn'dĭsh) *v.* To wave or flourish threateningly, as a weapon.

brand-new (brănd'no͞o', -nyo͞o') *adj.* Completely new.

bran•dy (brăn'dē) *n., pl.* **-dies.** An alcoholic liquor distilled from fermented fruit juice or wine. **—bran'dy** *v.*

brash (brăsh) *adj.* **1.** Impetuous **:** rash. **2.** Aggressively self-assertive. **—brash'ly** *adv.* **—brash'ness** *n.*

brass (brăs) *n.* **1.** An alloy of copper and zinc. **2.** Utensils or ornaments made of brass. **3.** *often* **brasses** Wind instruments, as the trumpet and trombone, made of brass. **4.** Effrontery **:** nerve. **—brass'y** *adj.*

bras•se•rie (brăs'ə-re') *n.* A restaurant serving alcoholic drinks, esp. wine or beer.

brass hat *n. Slang.* A high-ranking military officer or civilian official.

bras•siere *or* **bras•sière** (brə-zîr') *n.* A woman's undergarment that supports and contours the breasts.

brat (brăt) *n.* An ill-mannered, spoiled child. **—brat'ty** *adj.*

bra•va•do (brə-vä'dō) *n., pl.* **-does** *or* **-dos. 1.** A pretense of courage. **2.** Defiant, swaggering behavior.

brave (brāv) *adj.* **brav•er, brav•est. 1.** Having or displaying courage **:** valiant. **2.** Having a fine appearance **:** splendid. ★ ***syns:*** AUDACIOUS, BOLD, COURAGEOUS, DAUNTLESS, FEARLESS, GALLANT, GUTSY, HEROIC, INTREPID, METTLESOME, PLUCKY, STOUTHEARTED, UNAFRAID, UNDAUNTED, VALIANT, VALOROUS —*n.* A North American Indian warrior. —*v.* **braved, brav•ing.** To face or endure courageously. **—brave'ly** *adv.* **—brav'er•y**

bra•vo (brä'vō, brä-vō') *interj.* —Used to express approval. **—bra'vo** *n.*

bra•vu•ra (brə-vo͝or'ə, -vyo͝or'ə) *n.* **1.** *Mus.* Brilliant style or technique in performance. **2.** Showy display.

brawl (brôl) *n.* A noisy fight or argument. **—brawl** *v.* **—brawl'er** *n.*

brawn (brôn) *n.* **1.** Strong muscles. **2.** Muscular strength. **—brawn'i•ness** *n.* **—brawn'y** *adj.*

bray (brā) *n.* The loud, harsh sound made by a donkey. **—bray** *v.*

braze (brāz) *v.* **brazed, braz•ing.** To fuse (metals) together by means of a solder with a high melting point.

bra•zen (brā'zən) *adj.* **1.** Made of or like brass. **2.** Having a loud, resonant sound. **3.** Bold **:** impudent. —*v.* To face with bold confidence <*brazen* out the crisis> **—bra'zen•ly** *adv.* **—bra'zen•ness** *n.*

bra•zier (brā'zhər) *n.* A metal container that holds burning coals or charcoal.

Bra•zil nut (brə-zĭl') *n.* A tree, *Bertholletia excelsa,* of South America, that bears pods containing 20 to 30 hard-shelled edible nuts.

breach (brēch) *n.* **1.** A breaking of a law, obligation, or standard. **2.** A gap or rift, esp. in a solid structure. **3.** A disruption of friendly relations **:** estrangement. ★ ***syns:*** BREAK, CLEFT, GAP, HOLE, PERFORATION, RENT, RUPTURE **—breach** *v.*

bread (brĕd) *n.* **1.** A usu. leavened staple food made from a flour or meal mixture that is kneaded and baked. **2.** Food in general. **3.** The necessities of life **:** livelihood. **4.** *Slang.* Money. —*v.* To cover with bread crumbs, as before cooking.

bread•bas•ket (brĕd'băs'kĭt) *n.* **1.** A region serving as a principal source of grain. **2.** *Slang.* The stomach.

bread•board (brĕd'bôrd', -bōrd') *n.* **1.** A board on which bread is sliced. **2.** *Slang.* An experimental model, as of an electronic circuit **:** prototype.

bread•fruit (brĕd'fro͞ot') *n.* A tree, *Artocarpus communis* or *A. incisa* of Polynesia, with deeply lobed leaves and edible fruit.

bread•stuff (brĕd'stŭf') *n.* **1.** Bread. **2.** Flour, meal, or grain used to produce bread.

breadth (brĕdth) *n.* **1.** The measurement from side to side **:** width. **2.** Broad extent or scope. **3.** Freedom from narrowness, as of interests or opinions.

bread•win•ner (brĕd'wĭn'ər) *n.* One whose earnings support a household.

break (brāk) *v.* **broke** (brōk), **bro•ken** (brō'kən), **break•ing. 1.** To reduce to or separate into pieces suddenly **:** smash. **2.** To crack without separating into pieces. **3.** To make or become unusable or inoperative. **4.** To give way **:** collapse. **5.** To make or force a way through, into, or out of. **6.** To part the surface of <*break* ground> **7.** To disrupt the order or unity of <*break* ranks> **8.** To come or bring into notice, esp. suddenly. **9.** To begin suddenly <*broke* into laughter> **10.** To change from one tonal register to another. **11.** To overwhelm : overcome. **12.** To destroy : ruin. **13.** To reduce in rank : demote. **14.** To lessen in force <*break* a fall> **15.** *Informal.* To occur. **—break down.** To undergo a breakdown. **—break in. 1.** To train. **2.** To enter forcibly. **3.** To reduce the newness of (e.g., a new product). **—break off. 1.** To stop suddenly, as in speaking. **2.** To discontinue a relationship. **—break out. 1.** To become affected by a skin eruption. **2.** To escape, as from prison. *—n.* **1.** The act of breaking. **2.** The result of breaking : a crack or fracture. **3.** A disruption in regularity. **4.** A beginning <the *break* of day> **5.** *Informal.* A stroke of luck. **—break'a•ble** *n. & adj.*

break•age (brā'kĭj) *n.* **1.** The act of breaking. **2. a.** A quantity broken. **b.** An allowance for such a loss.

break•down (brāk'doun') *n.* **1.** The act or process of breaking down or the resulting state. **2.** A collapse in mental or physical health. **3.** An analysis, outline, or summary made up of itemized data. **4.** Decomposition or disintegration into elements.

break•er (brā'kər) *n.* **1.** One that breaks. **2.** A wave that breaks into foam.

break•fast (brĕk'fəst) *n.* The first meal of the day. **—break'fast** *v.*

break•front (brāk'frŭnt') *n.* A high, wide cabinet with a central section that projects beyond the end sections.

break-in (brāk'ĭn') *n.* Forcible entry for an illegal purpose, as theft.

break•neck (brāk'nĕk') *adj.* Very fast and dangerous.

break•through (brāk'thro͞o') *n.* **1.** An act of breaking through a restriction or obstacle. **2.** A major achievement or discovery that permits further progress.

break•up (brāk'ŭp') *n.* **1.** A collapse. **2.** Division : dispersion.

break•wa•ter (brāk'wô'tər, -wŏt'ər) *n.* A barrier protecting a shore or harbor from the impact of waves.

bream (brēm) *n., pl.* **bream** *or* **breams.** A European freshwater fish of the genus *Abramis* with a flat body and silvery scales.

breast (brĕst) *n.* **1.** The mammary gland, esp. of the human female. **2.** The front surface of the body from the neck to the abdomen : chest. **3.** The seat of affection. *—v.* To advance boldly against : confront.

breast•bone (brĕst'bōn') *n.* The sternum.

breast-feed (brĕst'fēd') *v.* To feed (a baby) from the breast : nurse.

breast•plate (brĕst'plāt') *n.* A piece of armor plate for covering the breast.

breast stroke *n.* A swimming stroke performed by lying face down in the water, extending the arms in front of the head, then pulling them both back laterally under the surface of the water while doing a frog kick. **—breast'strok'er** *n.*

breast•work (brĕst'wûrk') *n.* A hastily constructed fortification, usu. breast-high.

breath (brĕth) *n.* **1.** The air inhaled and exhaled in respiration. **2.** The act or process of breathing : respiration. **3.** Capacity to breathe. **4.** A single respiration. **5.** A slight stirring of air. **6.** A trace. **7.** A soft-spoken sound : whisper. **—breath'less** *adj.* **—breath'less•ly** *adv.*

breathe (brē*th*) *v.* **breathed, breath•ing. 1.** To inhale and exhale air. **2.** To be alive : live. **3.** To pause to rest or regain breath. **4.** To utter <never *breathed* a word of scandal> **—breath'a•ble** *adj.*

breath•er (brē'*th*ər) *n. Informal.* A short rest period <take a *breather*>

breath•tak•ing (brĕth'tā'kĭng) *adj.* Inspiring awe.

breath•y (brĕth'ē) *adj.* **-i•er, -i•est.** Marked by audible breathing. **—breath'i•ly** *adv.* **—breath'i•ness** *n.*

bred (brĕd) *v. p.t. & p.p.* of BREED.

†breech (brēch) *n.* **1.** The buttocks. **2.** The section of a firearm to the rear of the barrel. **3. breech•es** (brĭch'ĭz). **a.** Knee-length trousers. **b.** Trousers. *—v. Archaic & Regional.* To clothe with breeches.

breech•cloth (brēch'klôth', -klŏth') *n.* A loincloth.

breech delivery *n.* Delivery of a fetus with the feet or buttocks first.

breed (brēd) *v.* **bred** (brĕd), **breed•ing. 1. a.** To produce (offspring). **b.** To reproduce. **2.** To bring about : cause. **3.** To raise or mate (animals). **4.** To bring up : rear. *—n.* **1.** A genetic strain, esp. of a domestic animal developed and maintained by humans. **2.** A kind : type. **—breed'er** *n.*

breeder reactor *n.* A nuclear reactor that generates as well as consumes fissionable material, esp. one that generates more fissionable material than it consumes.

breed•ing (brē'dĭng) *n.* **1.** Line of descent. **2.** Training in social conduct.

breeze (brēz) *n.* **1.** A light current of air. **2.** *Informal.* An easily accomplished task. *—v.* **breezed, breez•ing.** *Informal.* To progress swiftly and effortlessly <*breezed* through the interview> **—breez'i•ly** *adv.* **—breez'i•ness** *n.* **—breez'y** *adj.*

breeze•way (brēz'wā') *n.* A roofed, open-sided passageway connecting 2 structures.

†br'er (brûr, brĕr) *n. S U.S.* BROTHER 1, 2.

breth•ren (brĕ*th*'rən) *n. archaic pl. of* BROTHER.

breve (brĕv, brēv) *n.* **1.** A symbol over a vowel to indicate its short sound. **2.** *Mus.* A single note equivalent to 2 whole notes.

bre•vi•ar•y (brē'vē-ĕr'-ē, brĕv'-ē-) *n., pl.* **-ies.** *Rom. Cath. Ch.* A book containing the daily hymns, offices, and prayers.

brev•i•ty (brĕv'ĭ-tē) *n.* **1.** Brief duration. **2.** Conciseness : terseness.

brew (bro͞o) *v.* **1.** To make (beer or ale) by infusing, boiling, and fermenting malt and hops. **2.** To make (a beverage) by boiling or steeping. **—brew** *n.* **—brew'er** *n.*

brew•er•y (bro͞o'ə-rē, bro͝or'ē) *n., pl.* **-ies.** A place where malt liquors are made.

†**brew•is** (bro͞o′ĭs, bro͞oz) *n. Regional.* A broth.
bri•ar[1] *also* **bri•er** (brī′ər) *n.* **1.** A shrub, *Erica arborea,* of S Europe with a woody root used to make tobacco pipes. **2.** A pipe made from the root of the briar.
bri•ar[2] (brī′ər) *n. var. of* BRIER[1].
bribe (brīb) *n.* Something, as money, offered or given to influence a person to act dishonestly. ★ *syns:* BOODLE, PAYOFF, PAYOLA —*v.* **bribed, brib•ing.** To corrupt or gain influence over by means of a bribe. —**brib′a•ble** *adj.* —**brib′er•y** *n.*
bric-a-brac (brĭk′ə-brăk′) *n.* Small ornamental objects.
brick (brĭk) *n.* A molded rectangular block of clay, baked until hard and used esp. for building. —*v.* To construct or cover with brick.
brick•bat (brĭk′băt′) *n.* **1.** A piece of brick, esp. when thrown as a missile. **2.** An uncomplimentary remark.
brick•lay•er (brĭk′lā′ər) *n.* One skilled in building with bricks. —**brick′lay′ing** *n.*
bri•dal (brīd′l) *adj.* Of or relating to a wedding or a bride. —*n.* A wedding.

▲ ***word history:*** *Bridal* is a compound of two Old English words that mean "bride" and "ale." The compound orig. meant "wedding feast," but by late medieval times was used to refer to the ceremony itself. *Bridal* as an adjective prob. arose from the interpretation of *–al* as the common adjectival suffix.

bride (brīd) *n.* A woman recently married or about to be married.
bride•groom (brīd′gro͞om′, -gro͝om′) *n.* A man recently married or about to be married.
brides•maid (brīdz′mād′) *n.* A woman attendant of the bride at a wedding.
bridge[1] (brĭj) *n.* **1.** A structure that spans and provides passage across an obstacle, as a waterway. **2.** The upper bony ridge of the nose. **3.** *Mus.* A thin, upright piece of wood in some stringed instruments supporting the strings above the sounding board. **4.** A removable or fixed replacement for missing natural teeth. **5.** *Naut.* A platform above the main deck of a ship, from which the ship is controlled. —*v.* **bridged, bridg•ing. 1.** To build a bridge over. **2.** To cross by or as if by a bridge. —**bridge′a•ble** *adj.*
bridge[2] (brĭj) *n.* Any of several games derived from whist and played with 52 cards divided equally among 4 people.
bridge•head (brĭj′hĕd′) *n.* A military position established in enemy territory.
bridge•work (brĭj′wûrk′) *n.* A dental bridge.
bri•dle (brīd′l) *n.* **1.** A harness fitted about a horse's head, used to restrain or guide. **2.** A restraint : check. —*v.* **-dled, -dling. 1.** To put a bridle on. **2.** To restrain with or as if with a bridle. **3.** To show scorn or resentment by tossing the head.
brief (brēf) *adj.* **1.** Short in duration or extent. **2.** Condensed : succinct. —*n.* **1.** A short or summarizing statement, esp. of a legal case. **2. briefs.** Short, tight-fitting underpants. —*v.* To give concise instructions to. —**brief′ly** *adv.* —**brief′ness** *n.*
brief•case (brēf′kās′) *n.* A portable case used for carrying books and papers.
brief•ing (brē′fĭng) *n.* **1.** The act of giving concise preparatory instructions or information. **2.** The information itself.
bri•er[1] *also* **bri•ar** (brī′ər) *n.* A thorny plant or bush. —**bri′er•y** *adj.*
bri•er[2] (brī′ər) *n. var. of* BRIAR[1].
brig (brĭg) *n.* **1.** A 2-masted square-rigged sailing ship. **2.** A ship's prison.
bri•gade (brĭ-gād′) *n.* **1.** A military unit consisting of a large number of troops. **2.** A group of people organized for a specific job or purpose.
brig•a•dier general (brĭg′ə-dîr′) *n., pl.* **brigadier generals.** An officer who ranks below a major general in the U.S. Army, Air Force, and Marine Corps.
brig•and (brĭg′ənd) *n.* One who plunders and robs : bandit. —**brig′and•age** *n.*
brig•an•tine (brĭg′ən-tēn′) *n.* A 2-masted, square-rigged sailing ship with a fore-and-aft mainsail.
bright (brīt) *adj.* **1.** Reflecting or emitting light. **2.** Brilliant : vivid. **3.** Resplendent : splendid. **4.** Intelligent : clever. **5.** Lively : cheerful. ★ *syns:* BRILLIANT, EFFULGENT, INCANDESCENT, LUMINOUS, LUSTROUS, RADIANT, REFULGENT, SHINING —*n.* **brights.** High-beam headlights. —*adv.* In a bright way. —**bright′ly** *adv.* —**bright′ness** *n.*
bright•en (brīt′n) *v.* To make or become bright or brighter.
bril•liant (brĭl′yənt) *adj.* **1.** Very bright : shining. **2.** Brightly vivid in color. **3.** Exceptionally intelligent. **4.** Splendid : magnificent. —*n.* A precious gem finely cut with numerous facets. —**bril′liance, bril′lian•cy** *n.* —**bril′liant•ly** *adv.*
bril•lian•tine (brĭl′yən-tēn′) *n.* An oily, perfumed dressing for the hair.
brim (brĭm) *n.* **1.** The rim of a vessel, as a cup. **2.** A projecting rim <the *brim* of a hat> —*v.* **brimmed, brim•ming. 1.** To fill or be full to the brim. **2.** To overflow. —**brim′ful′** *adj.* —**brim′less** *adj.*
brim•stone (brĭm′stōn′) *n.* Sulfur.
brin•dle (brĭn′dl) *also* **brin•dled** (-dld) *adj.* Grayish or tawny with darker flecks.
brine (brīn) *n.* **1.** Water containing large amounts of salt. **2.** The sea. **3.** Salt water for preserving and pickling foods. —**brin′i•ness** *n.* —**brin′y** *adj.*
bring (brĭng) *v.* **brought** (brôt), **bring•ing. 1.** To take with oneself to a place. **2.** To cause <The rains *brought* mud slides.> **3.** To sell for : fetch. **4.** To persuade : induce. **5.** To lead or force into a specified situation or condition. —**bring about.** To cause to happen. —**bring forth.** To produce. —**bring off.** To carry out successfully. —**bring out. 1.** To expose or reveal. **2.** To produce or publish. —**bring to.** To cause to recover consciousness. —**bring up. 1.** To take care of and rear (a child). **2.** To introduce into discussion : mention. **3.** To vomit.
brink (brĭngk) *n.* **1.** The upper edge, as that of a steep slope. **2.** A verge : rim.

brink•man•ship (brĭngk'mən-shĭp') *n.* A perilous course of action that stops just short of the point of no return.
bri•o (brē'ō) *n.* Vivacity : spirit.
bri•oche (brē-ôsh', -ŏsh') *n.* A soft roll made from butter, eggs, flour, and yeast.
bri•quette *also* **bri•quet** (brĭ-kĕt') *n.* A brick-shaped mass of compressed coal dust or charcoal, used for fuel.
bri•sance (brĭ-zäns', -zäNs') *n.* The shattering effect of a sudden release of energy, as in an explosion. —**bri•sant'** *adj.*
brisk (brĭsk) *adj.* **1.** Vigorous : lively. **2.** Stimulating : invigorating. —**brisk'ly** *adv.* —**brisk'ness** *n.*
bris•ket (brĭs'kĭt) *n.* Meat from the lower chest of an animal.
bris•ling (brĭz'lĭng, brĭs'-) *n.* A small sardine.
bris•tle (brĭs'əl) *n.* A short, stiff, coarse hair. —*v.* **-tled, -tling. 1.** To erect the bristles, as an excited animal. **2.** To react with angry defiance. **3.** To stand on end stiffly. **4.** To be covered or thick with or as if with bristles. —**bris'tly** *adj.*
Bri•tan•nic (brĭ-tăn'ĭk) *adj.* British.
britch•es (brĭch'ĭz) *pl.n.* Breeches.
Brit•i•cism (brĭt'ĭ-sĭz-əm) *n.* A word or idiom peculiar to British English.
Brit•ish (brĭt'ĭsh) *n.* **1.** *(pl. in number).* The people of Great Britain. **2.** British English. —**Brit'ish** *adj.*
British English *n.* The English language as used in England.
British thermal unit *n.* The quantity of heat required to raise the temperature of 1 lb of water by 1°F, gen. defined as 1,054.35 joules.
Brit•on (brĭt'n) *n.* **1.** An inhabitant or native of Britain. **2.** One of a Celtic people of Britain prior to the Roman invasion.
brit•tle (brĭt'l) *adj.* Easily broken : fragile. —**brit'tle•ness** *n.*
broach (brōch) *n.* **1.** A tapered tool used for shaping or enlarging a hole. **2.** A tool for tapping a cask. **3.** *var. of* BROOCH. —*v.* **1.** To introduce (a subject) for discussion. **2.** To tap (e.g., a cask) in order to draw off the contents. —**broach'er** *n.*
broad (brôd) *adj.* **1.** Wide. **2.** Large : spacious. **3.** Clear : bright <*broad* daylight> **4.** General in scope <a *broad* restriction> **5.** Main : essential. **6.** Obvious <a *broad* hint> **7.** Coarse : ribald. —**broad'ly** *adv.* — **broad'ness** *n.*
broad•band (brôd'bănd') *adj.* Of, having, or relating to a wide band of electromagnetic frequencies.
broad•cast (brôd'kăst') *v.* **-cast** *or* **-cast•ed, -cast•ing. 1.** To transmit by television or radio. **2.** To make known widely <*broadcast* gossip> **3.** To throw (seed) about : scatter. —*n.* **1.** Transmission of a radio or television signal. **2.** A radio or television program. —**broad'cast'er** *n.*
broad•cloth (brôd'klôth', -klŏth') *n.* **1.** A densely textured woolen cloth with a lustrous finish. **2.** A closely woven cotton, silk, or synthetic fabric.
broad•en (brôd'n) *v.* To widen.
broad•loom (brôd'lo͞om') *adj.* Woven on a wide loom. —*n.* A broadloom carpet.
broad-mind•ed (brôd'mīn'dĭd) *adj.* Unprejudiced : liberal. —**broad'mind'ed•ly** *adv.* —**broad'-mind'ed•ness** *n.*
broad•side (brôd'sīd') *n.* **1.** The side of a ship above the water line. **2.** Simultaneous discharge of the guns on one side of a warship. **3.** A verbal denunciation or attack.
broad-spec•trum (brôd'spĕk'trəm) *adj.* Having wide effectiveness.
broad•sword (brôd'sôrd', -sōrd') *n.* A sword with a wide, usu. two-edged blade.
bro•cade (brō-kād') *n.* A rich, heavy cloth interwoven with a raised design.
broc•co•li *also* **broc•o•li** (brŏk'ə-lē) *n.* A plant, *Brassica oleracea italica,* with a branched green flower head that is eaten as a vegetable before the buds have opened.
bro•chette (brō-shĕt') *n.* A small skewer.
bro•chure (brō-sho͝or') *n.* A pamphlet.
bro•gan (brō'gən) *n.* A heavy work shoe reaching to the ankle.
brogue (brōg) *n.* **1.** A strong oxford shoe. **2.** A strong dialectal accent, esp. a heavy Irish accent.
broil (broil) *v.* To cook by exposure to direct radiant heat : grill.
broil•er (broi'lər) *n.* **1.** A utensil, as a pan or part of a stove, used for broiling. **2.** A young chicken fit for broiling.
broke (brōk) *adj. Informal.* Completely without money : poor.
bro•ken (brō'kən) *adj.* **1.** Fractured : shattered. **2.** Not upheld : breached <*broken* promises> **3.** Imperfectly spoken. **4.** Subdued : crushed. **5.** Discontinuous : interrupted. **6.** Not functioning : inoperative. —**bro'ken•ly** *adv.*
bro•ken•heart•ed (brō'kən-här'tĭd) *adj.* Crushed by sadness or grief.
bro•ker (brō'kər) *n.* One hired for a fee to negotiate purchases, contracts, or sales.
bro•ker•age (brō'kər-ĭj) *n.* **1.** The business of a broker. **2.** A broker's fee.
bro•me•li•ad (brō-mē'lē-ăd') *n.* Any of various gen. epiphytic tropical American plants usu. having stiff leaves and colorful flowers.
bro•mide (brō'mīd') *n.* **1.** A binary compound of bromine. **2.** Potassium bromide. **3. a.** A trite remark : platitude. **b.** A bore. —**bro•mid'ic** *adj.*

▲ ***word history:*** Several bromine compounds, esp. potassium bromide, have been used medicinally as sedatives. In 1906 Gelett Burgess wrote a book entitled *Are You a Bromide?* in which he used *bromide* to mean a tiresome person of unoriginal thought and trite conversation. *Bromide* was soon after extended to denote the trite remarks made by such persons.

bro•mine (brō'mēn') *n. Symbol* **Br** A heavy, reddish-brown, corrosive, liquid element with irritating fumes.

bron•chi•al (brŏng′kē-əl) *adj.* Of or relating to the bronchi or their extensions.
bron•chi•tis (brŏng-kī′tĭs) *n.* Chronic or acute inflammation of the bronchi. —**bron•chit′ic** (-kĭt′ĭk) *adj.*
bron•chus (brŏng′kəs) *n., pl.* **-chi** (-kī′, -kē′). Either of the main branches of the trachea, each leading to a lung.
bron•co (brŏng′kō) *n., pl.* **-cos.** A small semiwild horse of W North America.
bron•co•bust•er (brŏng′kō-bŭs′tər) *n.* A cowboy who tames broncos.
bron•to•saur (brŏn′tə-sôr′) *also* **bron•to•sau•rus** (-sôr′əs). *n.* A large, herbivorous dinosaur of the genus *Apatosaurus* or *Brontosaurus.*

brontosaur

Bronx cheer (brŏngks) *n. Slang.* RASPBERRY 2.
bronze (brŏnz) *n.* **1.** An alloy of tin and copper. **2.** A work of art made in bronze. **3.** A yellowish to olive brown. —*v.* **bronzed, bronz•ing.** To give a bronze appearance to. —**bronze** *adj.* —**bronz′y** *adj.*
Bronze Age *n.* A period of human culture between the Stone Age and the Iron Age, marked by the use of bronze implements and weapons.
brooch *also* **broach** (brōch, bro͞och) *n.* An ornamental clasp or pin.
brood (bro͞od) *n.* A family of young animals or children, esp. a group of birds hatched at the same time. —*v.* **1.** To sit on and hatch (eggs). **2.** To ponder anxiously **:** worry. ★ *syns:* MOPE, STEW, WORRY
brood•er (bro͞o′dər) *n.* **1.** One that broods. **2.** A heated structure for raising young domestic birds.
brood•mare (bro͞od′mâr′) *n.* A mare used for breeding.
brood•y (bro͞o′dē) *adj.* **-i•er, -i•est. 1.** Moody. **2.** Inclined to sit on eggs to hatch them <a *broody* hen> —**brood′i•ness** *n.*
brook[1] (bro͝ok) *n.* A freshwater stream.
brook[2] (bro͝ok) *v.* To tolerate **:** bear.
brook•let (bro͝ok′lĭt) *n.* A small brook.
brook trout *n.* A freshwater fish, *Salvelinus fontinalis,* of E North America.
broom (bro͞om, bro͝om) *n.* **1.** A brush made of stiff fibers bound together on a long handle. **2.** A shrub of the genus *Cytisus,* with yellow flowers. —**broom′stick** *n.*
broth (brôth, brŏth) *n., pl.* **broths** (brôths, brŏths, brô*th*z, brŏ*th*z). Stock obtained from boiling meat or vegetables.
broth•el (brŏth′əl, brô′*th*əl) *n.* A house of prostitution.
broth•er (brŭ*th*′ər) *n.* **1.** A male having one or both parents in common with another individual. **2.** A fellow man or a male friend. **3.** A lay member of a men's religious order. —**broth′er•li•ness** *n.* —**broth′er•ly** *adj. & adv.*
broth•er•hood (brŭ*th*′ər-ho͝od′) *n.* **1.** The state or quality of being brothers. **2.** An association, as a fraternity, united for a common purpose. **3.** The whole body of persons in a profession or trade.
broth•er-in-law (brŭ*th*′ər-ĭn-lô′) *n., pl.* **broth•ers-in-law. 1.** The brother of one's spouse. **2.** The husband of one's sister. **3.** The husband of the sister of one's spouse.
brougham (bro͞om, bro͞o′əm, brō′əm) *n.* **1.** A light, closed horse-drawn carriage with the driver's seat outside in front. **2.** An automobile with an open seat for the driver.
brought (brôt) *v. p.t. & p.p. of* BRING.
brou•ha•ha (bro͞o′hä-hä′) *n.* A noisy wrangle **:** commotion **:** uproar.
brow (brou) *n.* **1. a.** The ridge over the eyes. **b.** The forehead. **c.** The eyebrow. **2.** The upper part of a steep place.
brow•beat (brou′bēt′) *v.* To intimidate **:** bully. —**brow′beat′er** *n.*
brown (broun) *n.* One of a group of colors between red and yellow. —*adj.* **1.** Of the color brown. **2.** Of dark or tanned complexion. —*v.* To make or become brown. —**brown′ish** *adj.* —**brown′ness** *n.*
brown bear *n.* A very large bear, *Ursus arctos,* with brown to yellowish fur.
brown bread *n.* A bread made of a dark whole-wheat flour.
brown•ie (brou′nē) *n.* **1.** A helpful sprite in folklore. **2. Brownie.** A member of the Girl Scouts from 7 to 9 years of age. **3.** A square or bar of chewy, rich chocolate cake.
brown•out (broun′out′) *n.* A curtailment of electrical power.
brown rice *n.* Unpolished rice that retains the germ and the outer layer.
brown•stone (broun′stōn′) *n.* **1.** A reddish-brown sandstone. **2.** A dwelling faced with brownstone.
brown study *n.* A state of reverie.
brown sugar *n.* Sugar whose crystals retain a coating of dark syrup.
browse (brouz) *v.* **browsed, brows•ing. 1.** To casually inspect goods offered for sale. **2.** To skim through a book. **3.** To graze (on). —**browse** *n.* —**brows′er** *n.*
bru•in (bro͞o′ĭn) *n.* A bear.
bruise (bro͞oz) *v.* **bruised, bruis•ing. 1. a.** To injure without rupturing. **b.** To suffer bruising. **2.** To pound into fragments. **3.** To hurt **:** offend. —*n.* An injury that does not break the skin **:** contusion.

bruis•er (broo͞′zər) *n. Slang.* A large, husky man.
bruit (broo͞t) *v.* To spread news of **:** report.
brunch (brŭnch) *n.* A meal eaten as a combination of lunch and breakfast.
bru•net (broo͞-nĕt′) *adj.* **1.** Of a dark complexion. **2.** Having brown or black eyes and hair. —*n.* A person with brown hair.
bru•nette (broo͞-nĕt′) *adj.* Having brown or dark hair. —*n.* A girl or woman with brown or dark hair.
brunt (brŭnt) *n.* The main shock or impact, esp. of a blow.
brush[1] (brŭsh) *n.* **1.** A device composed of bristles set into a handle, used for cleaning, painting, scrubbing, grooming the hair, etc. **2.** A light touching or grazing. **3.** A brief encounter. **4.** A bushy tail, as of a fox. **5.** A sliding connection completing a circuit between a fixed and a moving conductor. ★ ***syns:*** FLICK, GLANCE, GRAZE, SKIM —*v.* **1.** To use a brush (on). **2.** To remove or apply with or as if with a brush. **3.** To touch or graze in passing. **—brush up.** To renew one's skill.
brush[2] (brŭsh) *n.* **1.** A thicket of bushes. **2.** Small branches broken from trees. **—brush′wood′** *n.* **—brush′y** *adj.*
brush-off (brŭsh′ôf′, -ŏf′) *n. Slang.* A curt dismissal.
brusque *also* **brusk** (brŭsk) *adj.* Rudely abrupt **:** blunt <gave a *brusque* retort> **—brusque′ly** *adv.* **—brusque′ness** *n.*
Brus•sels sprouts (brŭs′əlz) *pl.n.* The budlike, edible heads of a cabbage variety, *Brassica oleracea gemmifera.*
bru•tal (broo͞t′l) *adj.* Savage **:** harsh. **—bru•tal′i•ty** *n.* **—bru′tal•ly** *adv.*
bru•tal•ize (broo͞t′l-īz′) *v.* **-ized, -iz•ing. 1.** To make brutal. **2.** To treat in a brutal way. **—bru′tal•i•za′tion** *n.*
brute (broo͞t) *n.* **1.** A beast. **2.** A brutal person. —*adj.* **1.** Of or pertaining to beasts. **2.** Completely physical or instinctive <*brute* strength> **—brut′ish** *adj.* **—brut′ish•ly** *adv.* **—brut′ish•ness** *n.*
bry•o•phyte (brī′ə-fīt′) *n.* A plant of the division Bryophyta, including the mosses and liverworts.
bub•ble (bŭb′əl) *n.* **1.** A light, thin-walled sphere or hemisphere of liquid holding air or gas. **2.** A small globule of gas, as in a carbonated drink. **3.** A plastic or glass dome. **4.** Something lacking substance or solidity. —*v.* **-bled, -bling.** To form or give off bubbles.
bubble gum *n.* Chewing gum that can be blown into bubbles.
bub•bly (bŭb′lē) *n., pl.* **-blies.** *Informal.* Champagne. —*adj.* **1.** Full of bubbles. **2.** Resembling a bubble.
bu•bo (boo͞′bō, byoo͞′-) *n., pl.* **-boes.** An inflamed swelling of a lymph gland. **—bu•bon′ic** (-bŏn′ĭk) *adj.*
bubonic plague *n.* A highly contagious, usu. fatal epidemic disease marked by chills, fever, and buboes.
buc•ca•neer (bŭk′ə-nîr′) *n.* A pirate.
buck[1] (bŭk) *n.* **1.** A male animal, as a deer or rabbit. **2.** *Informal.* A bold, high-spirited young man. —*v.* **1.** To leap upward arching the back, as a horse. **2.** To butt (against). **3.** To move forward with sudden jerks. **4.** To throw (e.g., a rider) by bucking. **5.** To resist stubbornly. —*adj.* Of the lowest rank <a *buck* sergeant> **—buck** *adj.*
buck[2] (bŭk) *n. Slang.* A dollar.
buck•a•roo *also* **buck•er•oo** (bŭk′ə-roo͞′) *n., pl.* **-roos** *also* **-oos.** A cowboy.
buck•board (bŭk′bôrd′, -bōrd′) *n.* An open 4-wheeled carriage with the seat attached to a flexible board extending from the front to the rear axle.

buckboard

buck•et (bŭk′ĭt) *n.* **1.** A cylindrical vessel used for holding or carrying water, coal, sand, etc. **:** pail. **2.** A similar vessel for holding and conveying material, as the scoop of a steam shovel.
bucket seat *n.* A separate, contoured seat, as in a sports car.
buck•eye (bŭk′ī′) *n.* One of several North American trees of the genus *Aesculus,* with white or reddish flower clusters, compound leaves, and shiny brown nuts.
buck•le[1] (bŭk′əl) *n.* A clasp for fastening ends together. —*v.* **-led, -ling.** To fasten or be fastened with a buckle. **—buckle down.** To apply oneself determinedly.
buck•le[2] (bŭk′əl) *v.* **-led, -ling. 1.** To warp or bend, as under pressure or heat. **2.** To give way **:** collapse. **—buck′le** *n.*
buck•ler (bŭk′lər) *n.* A small circular shield.
buck•ram (bŭk′rəm) *n.* A coarse, stiffened cloth used esp. for binding books.
buck•saw (bŭk′sô′) *n.* A wood-cutting saw set in a deep, usu. H-shaped frame.
buck•shot (bŭk′shŏt′) *n.* A coarse lead shot used for shooting large game animals.
buck•skin (bŭk′skĭn′) *n.* **1.** A soft, grayish-yellow leather. **2. buckskins.** Clothes made from buckskin.
buck•tooth (bŭk′too͞th′) *n.* A large projecting upper front tooth. **—buck′toothed′** *adj.*
buck•wheat (bŭk′hwēt′, -wēt′) *n.* A plant of the genus *Fagopyrum,* native to Asia, with fragrant white flowers and small triangular seeds often used as cereal grain.
bu•col•ic (byoo͞-kŏl′ĭk) *adj.* **1.** Relating to

flocks or shepherds : pastoral. **2.** Rural : rustic. —*n.* A pastoral poem.

bud (bŭd) *n.* **1.** *Bot.* A small swelling on a plant from which a leaf or flower grows. **2.** *Biol.* An asexual reproductive structure. **3.** Something that is still undeveloped. —*v.* **bud•ded, bud•ding. 1.** To put forth buds. **2.** To begin to grow from or as if from a bud. —**bud'der** *n.* —**bud'like'** *adj.*

Bud•dhism (bo͞o'dĭz'əm, bo͝od'ĭz'-) *n.* A religion of E and C Asia based on the doctrines and teachings of Buddha. —**Bud'dhist** *n.* —**Bud•dhis'tic** *adj.*

bud•dle•ia (bŭd'lē-ə, bŭd-lē'ə) *n.* One of several shrubs of the genus *Buddleia,* with purplish or white flower clusters.

bud•dy (bŭd'ē) *n., pl.* **-dies.** *Informal.* A friend.

bud•dy-bud•dy (bŭd'ē-bŭd'ē) *adj. Informal.* Showing or marked by warm friendship.

budge (bŭj) *v.* **budged, budg•ing. 1.** To shift or cause to shift slightly. **2.** To change or cause to change an attitude.

budg•er•i•gar (bŭj'ə-rē-gär') *n.* A small parakeet, *Melopsittacus undulatus,* with blue, green, or yellow plumage.

budg•et (bŭj'ĭt) *n.* **1.** A report of estimated expenditure and income. **2.** The amount of money assigned to a particular purpose. —*v.* **1.** To make a budget. **2.** To allow for in a budget. —**budg'et•ar'y** *adj.*

budg•ie (bŭj'ē) *n. Informal.* A budgerigar.

buff[1] (bŭf) *n.* **1.** A soft, thick leather made chiefly from buffalo, elk, or oxen skins. **2.** A moderate or light yellow. **3.** *Informal.* The bare skin <swam in the *buff*> —*v.* To polish or shine with a buff.

buff[2] (bŭf) *n. Informal.* An enthusiast.

buf•fa•lo (bŭf'ə-lō') *n., pl.* **-loes** *or* **-los** *or* **-lo. 1.** Any of several oxlike Old World mammals of the family Bovidae. **2.** The bison. —*v.* **-loed, -lo•ing** *Slang.* To baffle or confuse.

buff•er[1] (bŭf'ər) *n.* One that buffs.

buff•er[2] (bŭf'ər) *n.* **1.** Something that reduces the shock of impact. **2.** *Chem.* A substance that can stabilize the acidity or alkalinity of a solution by neutralizing, within certain limits, any acid or base that is added. **3.** *Computer Sci.* An area used to store data temporarily.

buf•fet[1] (bə-fā', bo͞o-) *n.* **1.** A large sideboard. **2.** A counter from which food is served. **3.** A meal at which diners serve themselves from dishes displayed on a table.

buf•fet[2] (bŭf'ĭt) *n.* A blow : slap. —*v.* To strike or pound repeatedly : batter.

buf•foon (bə-fo͞on') *n.* A fool : clown. —**buf•foon'er•y** *n.*

bug (bŭg) *n.* **1.** Any of various sucking insects of the order Hemiptera. **2.** Any insect. **3.** A germ or virus. **4.** A defect or problem, as in a system, design, or computer program. **5.** *Slang.* An enthusiast. **6.** A concealed microphone for eavesdropping. —*v.* **bugged, bug•ging. 1.** *Slang.* To bother : annoy. **2.** To hide a microphone in.

bug•a•boo (bŭg'ə-bo͞o') *n., pl.* **-boos.** A source of concern.

bug•bear (bŭg'bâr') *n.* An object or source of dread.

bug•eyed (bŭg'īd') *adj. Slang.* With bulging eyes.

bug•gy (bŭg'ē) *n., pl.* **-gies.** A light, 4-wheeled horse-drawn carriage.

bu•gle (byo͞o'gəl) *n.* A brass wind instrument like a trumpet but without valves. —**bu'gle** *v.* —**bu'gler** *n.*

build (bĭld) *v.* **built** (bĭlt), **build•ing. 1.** To construct. **2.** To give form to : create. **3.** To establish a basis for : found <*built* a case from evidence> —*n.* The physical form of a thing or person. —**build'er** *n.*

build•ing (bĭl'dĭng) *n.* **1.** A usu. roofed and walled structure. **2.** The process or business of constructing buildings.

build-up *also* **build•up** (bĭld'ŭp') *n.* **1.** Gradual increase. **2.** *Informal.* Widely favorable publicity.

built-in (bĭlt'ĭn') *adj.* **1.** Made as an integral part of a larger unit. **2.** Inherent.

bulb (bŭlb) *n.* **1.** *Bot.* A rounded, modified underground stem, as that of a daffodil or onion containing stored food for the shoot within. **2.** A rounded object or part. **3.** A light bulb. —**bul'bous** *adj.*

bulge (bŭlj) *n.* A protuberance. —*v.* **bulged, bulg•ing.** To become or cause to become protuberant. —**bulg'i•ness** *n.*

bul•gur (go͞ol-go͝or', bŭl'gər) *n.* Dried cracked wheat.

bu•lim•i•a (byo͞o-lĭm'ē-ə) *n.* An eating disorder marked by recurrent binge eating and subsequent guilt and depression.

bulk (bŭlk) *n.* **1.** Volume, mass, or size, esp. when large. **2.** The greater part. ★ ***syns:*** AMPLITUDE, MAGNITUDE, MASS, SIZE, VOLUME —**in bulk. 1.** Not packaged. **2.** In large amounts or volume. —*v.* To have or appear to have massive importance or size. —**bulk'i•ness** *n.* —**bulk'y** *adj.*

bulk•head (bŭlk'hĕd') *n.* **1.** An upright partition separating compartments in a ship. **2.** A retaining wall, as in a mine.

bull[1] (bo͝ol) *n.* **1.** The adult male of a bovine animal or certain other large animals. **2.** A person who buys commodities or securities expecting their prices to rise. **3.** *Slang.* A police officer. **4.** *Slang.* Nonsense. —**bull'ish** *adj.* —**bull'ish•ness** *n.*

bull[2] (bo͝ol) *n.* A document from the pope.

†**bull•dog** (bo͝ol'dôg', -dŏg') *n.* A short-haired, heavily built dog with large square jaws. —*v.* *W U.S.* To throw (a steer) by holding its horns and twisting its neck.

bull•doze (bo͝ol'dōz') *v.* **-dozed, -doz•ing. 1.** To clear using a bulldozer. **2.** *Slang.* To coerce : bully.

bull•doz•er (bo͝ol'dō'zər) *n.* A tractor with a large scoop in front for clearing debris and earth.

bul•let (bo͝ol'ĭt) *n.* A usu. metal projectile to be shot from a firearm.

bul•let•proof (bo͝ol'ĭt-pro͞of') *adj.* Impenetrable by bullets. —**bul'let•proof'** *v.*

bul•le•tin (bo͝ol'ĭ-tn, -tĭn) *n.* **1.** A brief report on a matter of public interest. **2.** A regular publication of an organization.

bulletin board *n.* A board for displaying notices.

bull•fight (bo͝ol'fīt') *n.* A spectacle, esp. in Spain, Portugal, and parts of Latin America, in which a bull is engaged and then usu. killed with a sword by a matador. **—bull'fight'er** *n.* **—bull'fight'ing** *n.*

bull•finch (bo͝ol'fĭnch') *n.* A European songbird, *Pyrrhula pyrrhula,* with a short, thick bill and, in the male, a red breast.

bull•frog (bo͝ol'frôg', -frŏg') *n.* A large frog, esp. *Rana catesbeiana,* with a deep, loud croak.

bull•head (bo͝ol'hĕd') *n.* One of several freshwater catfishes of the genus *Ictalurus.*

bull•head•ed (bo͝ol'hĕd'ĭd) *adj.* Extremely obstinate : headstrong. **—bull'head'ed•ly** *adv.* **—bull'head'ed•ness** *n.*

bull•horn (bo͝ol'hôrn') *n.* An electric megaphone used esp. to amplify the voice.

bul•lion (bo͝ol'yən) *n.* Silver or gold ingots.

bul•lock (bo͝ol'ək) *n.* **1.** A castrated bull : steer. **2.** A young bull.

bull•pen (bo͝ol'pĕn') *n.* **1.** *Informal.* A temporary detention room for prisoners. **2.** *Baseball.* A practice area for relief pitchers during a game.

bull session *n. Informal.* A rambling, informal group discussion.

bull's-eye *also* **bull's eye** (bo͝olz'ī') *n.* **1.** The center of a target. **2.** A shot that hits the bull's-eye.

bull terrier *n.* A short-haired dog with a long muzzle and large jaws.

bul•ly (bo͝ol'ē) *n., pl.* **-lies.** One who hurts or intimidates weaker or smaller people. *—v.* **-lied, -ly•ing.** To act like a bully. *—adj. Informal.* First-rate : excellent. *—interj.* —Used to express approval.

bul•rush (bo͝ol'rŭsh') *n.* **1.** A grasslike sedge of the genus *Scirpus* that grows in wet places. **2.** A marsh plant, as a cattail.

bul•wark (bo͝ol'wərk, bŭl'-, -wôrk') *n.* **1.** A defensive wall or rampart. **2.** Something serving as a principal defense.

bum[1] (bŭm) *n.* **1.** A tramp : vagrant. **2.** One who avoids work and tries to live off others. *—v.* **bummed, bum•ming.** *Informal.* **1.** To live as a bum. **2.** To get by begging. **3.** To loaf. *—adj. Slang.* **1.** Worthless. **2.** Disabled.

bum[2] (bŭm) *n. esp. Brit.* The buttocks.

bum•ble (bŭm'bəl) *v.* **-bled, -bling.** To behave or speak in a clumsy or inept manner. **—bum'bler** *n.*

bum•ble•bee (bŭm'bəl-bē') *n.* A large, hairy bee of the genus *Bombus.*

bum•mer (bŭm'ər) *n. Slang.* **1.** A bad reaction to a hallucinogenic drug. **2.** An unpleasant person or situation.

bump (bŭmp) *v.* **1.** To collide forcefully (with). **2.** To move with jerks and jolts. **3.** To displace. **—bump into.** To meet by chance. **—bump off.** *Slang.* To kill. *—n.* **1.** A jolt or knock. **2.** A swelling, usu. caused by a blow. **—bump'y** *adj.*

bump•er[1] (bŭm'pər) *n.* A horizontal metal bar at either end of a car for absorbing the shock of a collision.

bump•er[2] (bŭm'pər) *n.* A glass or cup filled to the brim. *—adj.* Exceptionally full or abundant <a *bumper* harvest>

bump•kin (bŭmp'kĭn, bŭm'-) *n.* An awkward or simple country person.

bump•tious (bŭmp'shəs) *adj.* Obtrusively forward and conceited. **—bump'tious•ly** *adv.* **—bump'tious•ness** *n.*

bun (bŭn) *n.* **1.** A small, usu. sweetened bread roll. **2.** Hair worn in a knot at the back of the head.

bunch (bŭnch) *n.* A cluster or group of similar things. **—bunch** *v.*

bun•co *also* **bun•ko** (bŭng'kō) *n., pl.* **-cos** *also* **-kos.** *Informal.* A confidence game. **—bun'co** *v.*

bun•dle (bŭn'dl) *n.* **1.** A group of things fastened together. **2.** *Slang.* A large amount of money. *—v.* **-dled, -dling. 1.** To make into a bundle. **2.** To dress warmly.

bung (bŭng) *n.* A stopper for a bunghole.

bun•ga•low (bŭng'gə-lō') *n.* A small one-storied house.

bun•gee (bŭn'jē) *n.* An elasticized rubber cord used to fasten, bear weight, or absorb shock.

bung•hole (bŭng'hōl') *n.* The hole for filling or draining a cask or barrel.

bun•gle (bŭng'gəl) *v.* **-gled, -gling.** To do clumsily : botch. **—bun'gler** *n.*

bun•ion (bŭn'yən) *n.* An inflamed swelling on the first joint of the big toe.

bunk[1] (bŭngk) *n.* **1.** A narrow bed built against a wall. **2.** *Informal.* A sleeping place. **—bunk** *v.*

bunk[2] (bŭngk) *n. Slang.* Nonsense.

bunk bed *n.* A double-decker bed.

bun•ker (bŭng'kər) *n.* **1.** A container or compartment for storing fuel, as on a ship. **2.** A sandtrap on a golf course. **3.** An underground fortification.

bunk•house (bŭngk'hous') *n.* Sleeping quarters, as for ranch hands.

bun•kum *also* **bun•combe** (bŭng'kəm) *n.* Empty talk : bunk.

bun•ny (bŭn'ē) *n., pl.* **-nies.** A rabbit.

buns (bŭnz) *pl.n. Slang.* The buttocks.

Bun•sen burner (bŭn'sən) *n.* A small laboratory burner composed of a vertical metal tube connected to a gas source.

bunt (bŭnt) *v.* **1.** To strike with the head : butt. **2.** *Baseball.* To bat (a pitch) with a half swing so that the ball does not reach beyond the infield. *—n.* **1.** The act of bunting. **2.** A bunted ball.

bunt•ing[1] (bŭn'tĭng) *n.* **1.** A light cloth for making flags. **2.** Decorative flags.

bunt•ing[2] (bŭn'tĭng) *n.* One of various short-billed birds of the family Fringillidae.

buoy (bo͞o'ē, boi) *n.* **1.** *Naut.* A floating object moored in water to mark a channel or to warn of danger. **2.** A ring-shaped life preserver. —*v.* **1.** *Naut.* To mark with or as if with a buoy. **2.** To keep afloat. **3.** To lift the spirits of : hearten.

buoy•an•cy (boi′ən-sē, bōō′yən-) *n.* **1.** The ability to float. **2.** The upward force exerted by a fluid on a body in it. **3.** Resilience in recovering from setbacks. **4.** Cheerfulness. **—buoy′ant** *adj.*

bur[1] *also* **burr** (bûr) *n.* **1.** The rough and prickly covering of the seed of certain plants. **2.** *var. of* BURR[1]. —*v. var. of* BURR[1].

bur[2] (bûr) *n. & v. var. of* BURR[2].

bur•ble (bûr′bəl) *n.* **1.** A bubbling sound. **2.** Meaningless sounds : babble. —*vi.* **-bled, -bling. 1.** To gurgle. **2.** To babble : gibber.

bur•den[1] (bûr′dn) *n.* **1.** Something carried. **2.** Something difficult to bear physically or emotionally. **3.** The weight of cargo a vessel can carry. —*v.* To put a burden on : oppress. **—bur′den•some** *adj.*

bur•den[2] (bûr′dn) *n.* **1.** *Mus.* A chorus or refrain. **2.** A recurring central idea.

bur•dock (bûr′dŏk′) *n.* One of several coarse, weedy plants of the genus *Arctium,* with purplish flowers surrounded by bristles.

bu•reau (byŏŏr′ō) *n., pl.* **-reaus** *or* **bu•reaux** (byŏŏr′ōz). **1.** A chest of drawers. **2.** *esp. Brit.* A writing desk with drawers. **3.** A government department. **4.** An agency or business performing a specific service.

bu•reauc•ra•cy (byōō-rŏk′rə-sē) *n., pl.* **-cies. 1. a.** Administration of a government through bureaus and their officials. **b.** The departments and their officials collectively. **2.** An administrative system that is unwieldy and inflexible in its operation. **—bu′reau•crat′** *n.* **—bu′reau•crat′ic** *adj.* **—bu′reau•crat′i•cal•ly** *adv.*

bu•rette *also* **bu•ret** (byōō-rĕt′) *n.* A graduated glass tube with a small bore used for measuring fluids.

burg (bûrg) *n. Informal.* A town or city.

bur•geon *also* **bour•geon** (bûr′jən) *v.* **1. a.** To put forth fresh growth. **b.** To blossom. **2.** To grow rapidly : flourish.

bur•gess (bûr′jĭs) *n.* A citizen of an English borough.

burgh (bûrg) *n.* A Scottish chartered town or borough.

burgh•er (bûr′gər) *n.* **1.** A citizen of a town. **2.** A prosperous, solid citizen.

bur•gla•ry (bûr′glə-rē) *n., pl.* **-ries.** Breaking and entering a building with intent to steal. **—bur′glar** *n.* **—bur•glar′i•ous** *adj.* **—bur′glar•ize′** *v.* **—bur′glar•proof′** *adj.*

bur•gle (bûr′gəl) *v.* **-gled, -gling.** *Informal.* To commit burglary (on).

bur•go•mas•ter (bûr′gə-măs′tər) *n.* The mayor of some European cities.

Bur•gun•dy (bûr′gən-dē) *n., pl.* **-dies. 1.** A red or white wine orig. produced in Burgundy. **2. burgundy.** A purplish red.

bur•i•al (bĕr′ē-əl) *n.* The act or process of burying a dead body.

burl (bûrl) *n.* **1.** A knot on a tree trunk. **2.** Wood marked with burls, used as veneer.

bur•lap (bûr′lăp′) *n.* A coarse cloth made of jute or hemp used esp. in making bags.

bur•lesque (bər-lĕsk′) *n.* **1.** A witty or mocking literary or dramatic imitation. **2.** Vaudeville entertainment marked by low comedy and striptease acts. —*v.* **-lesqued, -lesqu•ing.** To imitate mockingly.

bur•ly (bûr′lē) *adj.* **-li•er, -li•est.** Strong and muscular : husky. **—bur′li•ness** *n.*

burn (bûrn) *v.* **burned** *or* **burnt** (bûrnt), **burn•ing. 1.** To be or cause to be on fire. **2. a.** To destroy or be destroyed by fire. **b.** To alter or become altered by fire or heat. **c.** *Slang.* To execute, esp. to electrocute. **3.** To make or cause by fire or heat <*burned* a hole in the chair> **4.** To use as a fuel. **5.** To give out light or heat. **6.** To look or feel hot. **7.** To sting : smart. **8.** To be excited. ★ *syns:* BLAZE, FLAME, FLARE **—burn out. 1.** To stop burning from lack of fuel. **2.** To wear out or become inoperative as a result of friction or heat. **3.** To become exhausted, esp. from stress. —*n.* **1.** An injury produced by heat or fire. **2.** *Aerospace.* A single firing of a rocket.

burn•er (bûr′nər) *n.* **1.** The part of a stove or lamp where the flame is produced. **2.** A device in which matter is burned.

bur•nish (bûr′nĭsh) *v.* To make glossy by or as if by rubbing. —*n.* A smooth, shiny finish. **—bur′nish•er** *n.*

bur•noose (bər-nōōs′) *n.* A hooded cloak worn esp. by Arabs.

burn•out (bûrn′out′) *n.* **1.** A failure in a device attributable to excessive heat. **2.** *Aerospace.* **a.** The cessation of rocket or jet-engine operation when all fuel is burned up. **b.** The point at which this occurs. **3.** Exhaustion from long-term stress.

burnt (bûrnt) *v. var. p.t. & p.p. of* BURN.

burp (bûrp) *n.* A belch. **—burp** *v.*

burr[1] *also* **bur** (bûr) —*n.* **1.** A rough edge or area remaining from the cutting of material, esp. metal. **2.** A rotary cutting tool that attaches to a drill. —*v.* **1.** To form a rough edge on. **2.** To remove a rough edge from.

burr[2] *also* **bur** (bûr) —*n.* **1.** The trilling of the letter *r,* as in Scottish speech. **2.** A whir or buzz. —*v.* To speak with a burr.

burr[3] (bûr) *n. var. of* BUR[1].

bur•ri•to (bōō-rē′tō, bə-) *n., pl.* **-tos.** A rolled tortilla with a filling, as of beef, beans, or cheese.

bur•ro (bûr′ō, bŏŏr′ō, bŭr′ō) *n., pl.* **-ros.** A small donkey.

bur•row (bûr′ō, bŭr′ō) *n.* A hole made in the ground by a small animal, as a rabbit. —*v.* **1.** To dig a burrow (in). **2.** To progress by or as if by digging. **—bur′row•er** *n.*

bur•sa (bûr′sə) *n., pl.* **-sae** (-sē′) *or* **-sas.** A cavity or sac, esp. one between joints.

bur•sar (bûr′sər, -sär′) *n.* An official in charge of finances, as at a college.

bur•si•tis (bər-sī′tĭs) *n.* Inflammation of a bursa, esp. in the shoulder, elbow, or knee.

burst (bûrst) *v.* **burst, burst•ing. 1.** To come open or force apart violently, esp. from internal pressure. **2.** To be full to the point of breaking open. **3.** To come forth suddenly. **4.** To suddenly give vent to <*burst* into tears> **5.** *Computer Sci.* To detach (a continuous printout) into sheets. —*n.* **1.** The result or act of bursting : explosion. **2.** A sudden outburst.

burst•er (bûr′stər) *n. Computer Sci.* An off-line device used to burst a printout.

bur•y (bĕr′ē) *v.* **-ied, -y•ing. 1.** To conceal by covering with earth. **2.** To place (a corpse) in a grave. **3.** To cover from view : hide. **4.** To absorb. **5.** To put aside : abandon.

bus (bŭs) *n., pl.* **bus•es** *or* **bus•ses.** A large motor coach that carries passengers. —*v.* **bused, bus•ing** *or* **bussed, bus•sing. 1.** To travel or transport in a bus. **2.** To work as a bus boy.

bus boy *n.* A waiter's helper.

bus•by (bŭz′bē) *n., pl.* **-bies.** A tall fur hat worn with a full-dress military uniform.

bush (bo͝osh) *n.* **1.** A low, woody plant with spreading branches. **2.** Rough uncleared land. **3.** A shaggy mass, as of hair. —*v.* To grow like a bush. **—bush′y** *adj.*

bushed (bo͝osht) *adj.* Tired : exhausted.

bush•el (bo͝osh′əl) *n.* —See table at MEASUREMENT.

bush•ing (bo͝osh′ĭng) *n.* A metal lining for reducing friction on moving parts.

bush-league (bo͝osh′lēg′) *adj. Slang.* Inferior. **—bush′-leagu′er** *n.*

Bush•man (bo͝osh′mən) *n.* A San.

bush•mas•ter (bo͝osh′măs′tər) *n.* A large poisonous snake, *Lachesis muta,* of tropical America, with brownish markings.

bush•whack (bo͝osh′hwăk′, -wăk′) *v.* **1.** To travel through or live in woods. **2.** To ambush. **—bush′whack′er** *n.*

busi•ness (bĭz′nĭs) *n.* **1.** One's occupation. **2.** Trade : commerce. **3.** A commercial enterprise. **4.** Volume of trade. **5.** Commercial practice or policy. **6.** One's rightful concern. **7.** An affair or matter <a distressing *business*> ★ ***syns:*** COMMERCE, INDUSTRY, TRADE, TRAFFIC **—bus′i•ness•man** *n.* **—bus′i•ness•per′son** *n.* **—bus′i•ness•wom′an** *n.*

business administration *n.* A college or university course teaching the theories and procedures of business.

business card *n.* A small card printed with a person's name and business affiliation.

bus•ing *also* **bus•sing** (bŭs′ĭng) *n.* The transporting of children by bus to schools outside their neighborhoods, esp. so as to desegregate schools.

bus•kin (bŭs′kĭn) *n.* **1.** A laced halfboot. **2.** Tragic drama.

buss (bŭs) *v.* To kiss. **—buss** *n.*

bust[1] (bŭst) *n.* **1.** A woman's bosom. **2.** A piece of sculpture representing a person's head and torso. **—bust′y** *adj.*

bust[2] (bŭst) *v.* **1.** To break or smash. **2.** To make or become bankrupt. **3.** To reduce the risk of. **4.** To hit. **5.** To arrest. **6.** To break (a horse). —*n.* **1.** A flop. **2.** A financial collapse. **3.** An arrest.

bus•tle[1] (bŭs′əl) *v.* **-tled, -tling.** To hurry busily and briskly. **—bus′tle** *n.*

bus•tle[2] (bŭs′əl) *n.* A pad formerly worn to expand the fullness at the back of a skirt.

bus•y (bĭz′ē) *adj.* **-i•er, -i•est. 1.** Engaged in action : occupied. **2.** Full of activity <a *busy* day> **3.** Prying : nosy. **4.** In use, as a telephone line. **5.** Cluttered with detail to the point of being distracting. —*v.* **-ied, -y•ing.** To make busy. ★ ***syns:*** ENGAGE, ENGROSS, OCCUPY **—bus′i•ly** *adv.*

bus•y•bod•y (bĭz′ē-bŏd′ē) *n., pl.* **-ies.** A prying, meddling person.

bus•y•work (bĭz′ē-wûrk′) *n.* Activity that takes up time but does not necessarily yield productive results.

but (bŭt; *unstressed* bət) *conj.* **1.** On the contrary <caused not success *but* failure> **2.** Contrary to expectation <worked hard *but* accomplished little> **3.** Save : except <everyone *but* me> **4.** Except that. **5.** Without the result that <It never rains *but* it pours.> **6.** Other than <We have no desire *but* to end the conflict.> **7.** That. —Often used after a negative. **8.** That . . . not. —Used after a negative or question. —*prep.* With the exception of : barring. —*n.* An objection or exception <no *buts* about it>

bu•ta•di•ene (byo͞o′tə-dī′ēn′, -dī-ēn′) *n.* A colorless, highly flammable hydrocarbon produced from petroleum.

bu•tane (byo͞o′tān′) *n.* A gas produced from petroleum and used in the manufacture of rubber and as a fuel.

butch•er (bo͝och′ər) *n.* **1.** A person who slaughters animals commercially. **2.** A meat seller. **3.** One who kills brutally. **4.** *Informal.* A bungler. —*v.* **1.** To slaughter or prepare (animals) for market. **2.** To kill barbarously. **3.** To botch. **—butch′er•y** *n.*

but•ler (bŭt′lər) *n.* The head male servant of a household.

butt[1] (bŭt) *v.* To push against with the head or horns. **—butt in (***or* **into).** *Informal.* To meddle in another's affairs. —*n.* A blow or push with the head or horns.

butt[2] (bŭt) *v.* To join end to end.

butt[3] (bŭt) *n.* An object of scorn.

butt[4] (bŭt) *n.* **1.** The thicker or larger end. **2.** A stub or stump. **3.** *Slang.* A cigarette. **4.** *Informal.* The buttocks.

butte (byo͞ot) *n.* An isolated, flat-topped hill rising abruptly from a plain.

but•ter (bŭt′ər) *n.* **1.** A thick, fatty, yellowish substance produced by churning cream. **2.** A substance resembling butter. —*v.* To put butter on. **—butter up.** To flatter. **—but′ter•y** *adj.*

†**butter bean** *n.* **1.** The wax bean. **2.** *Regional.* The lima bean.

but•ter•cup (bŭt′ər-kŭp′) *n.* One of various plants of the genus *Ranunculus,* with shiny, bright-yellow flowers.

but•ter•fat (bŭt′ər-făt′) *n.* The natural fat of milk from which butter is made.

but•ter•fin•gers (bŭt′ər-fĭng′gərz) *n. (used with a sing. verb).* A clumsy person who habitually drops things. **—but′ter•fin′gered** *adj.*

but·ter·fish (bŭt'ər-fĭsh') *n.* A North American marine food fish, *Poronotus triacanthus,* with a flattened body.

but·ter·fly (bŭt'ər-flī') *n.* **1.** One of various insects of the order Lepidoptera, with slender bodies and broad, usu. colorful wings. **2. butterflies.** Mild nausea due to nervous anticipation.

but·ter·milk (bŭt'ər-mĭlk') *n.* The thick, sour liquid remaining after butter has been churned.

but·ter·nut (bŭt'ər-nŭt') *n.* A tree, *Juglans cinerea,* of E North America, bearing egg-shaped edible nuts.

butternut squash *n.* A winter squash with a smooth tan rind and edible orange flesh.

but·ter·scotch (bŭt'ər-skŏch') *n.* A flavoring, candy, or syrup made from butter and brown sugar.

but·tock (bŭt'ək) *n.* **1.** Either of the 2 rounded fleshy parts of the rump. **2. buttocks.** The rear pelvic area : rump.

but·ton (bŭt'n) *n.* **1.** A knob-shaped fastener used to join 2 parts of a garment by fitting through a loop or buttonhole. **2.** An object resembling a button. —*v.* To fasten with buttons. **—but'ton·er** *n.*

but·ton·hole (bŭt'n-hōl') *n.* A slit for a button to pass through. —*v.* **-holed, -hol·ing. 1.** To make a buttonhole (in). **2.** To detain and talk to.

but·ton·hook (bŭt'n-ho͝ok') *n.* A hook for pulling buttons through buttonholes.

but·tress (bŭt'rĭs) *n.* **1.** A supporting structure built against a wall. **2.** A support : prop. —*v.* To support or prop with or as if with a buttress.

bu·tut (bo͞o'to͞ot') *n., pl.* **-tut** *or* **-tuts.** —See table at CURRENCY.

bux·om (bŭk'səm) *adj.* **1.** Healthily plump. **2.** Ample of figure, as a large-bosomed woman. **—bux'om·ness** *n.*

buy (bī) *v.* **bought** (bôt), **buy·ing. 1.** To get by paying money. **2.** To be capable of purchasing. **3.** To bribe. **4.** *Slang.* To believe in <wouldn't *buy* their excuses> **—buy up.** To buy all that is available of. —*n.* **1.** A purchase. **2.** *Informal.* A bargain. **—buy'a·ble** *adj.* **—buy'er** *n.*

buy·out (bī'out') *n.* **1.** The purchase of the entire holdings of an owner. **2.** The purchase of a company or business.

buzz (bŭz) *v.* **1.** To hum like a bee. **2.** To be filled with sound. **3.** To bustle. **4.** To call with a buzzer. **5.** *Informal.* To make a telephone call to. —*n.* **1.** A droning or vibrating sound. **2.** A low murmur. **3.** *Informal.* A telephone call. **4.** *Slang.* A pleasant stimulation, as from alcohol.

buz·zard (bŭz'ərd) *n.* **1.** Any of various North American vultures. **2.** *esp. Brit.* A hawk of the genus *Buteo.*

buzz·er (bŭz'ər) *n.* An electric device that makes a buzzing sound as a signal.

buzz saw *n.* A circular saw.

buzz word *n.* A jargonistic technical word used esp. to impress nonprofessionals.

by (bī) *prep.* **1.** Next to : close to <the light *by* the window> **2.** With the help or use of : through <We came *by* the main road.> **3.** Up to and beyond : past <drove *by* the entrance> **4.** In the period of : during <working *by* night> **5.** Not later than <*by* noon> **6. a.** In the amount of <requests *by* the thousands> **b.** To the extent of <closer *by* a foot> **7. a.** According to. **b.** With respect to. **8.** In the name of <swore *by* my honor> **9.** Through the agency or action of <peace *by* negotiation> **10.** —Used to indicate a succession of specified units of measure <filed out one *by* one> <Little *by* little they made headway.> **11. a.** —Used in multiplication and division <3 *by* 5 is 15> **b.** —Used with measurements <a section 4 *by* 8 feet> —*adv.* **1.** On hand : nearby <stay *by*> **2.** Aside : away <set it *by* for now> **3.** Up to, alongside, and past <The runner raced *by.*> **4.** Into the past <as time goes *by*>

by-and-by (bī'ən-bī') *n.* **1.** A time in the future. **2.** The afterlife.

bye *also* **by** (bī) *n.* **1.** A side issue. **2.** The advantage obtained by a competitor who draws no opponent for a round in a tournament, thus advancing to the next round.

bye-bye (bī'bī') *interj. Informal.* —Used to express farewell.

by·gone (bī'gôn', -gŏn') *adj.* Gone by : past. —*n.* A thing of the past.

by·law (bī'lô') *n.* A rule or law concerning the management of an organization's internal affairs.

by-line *also* **by·line** (bī'līn') *n.* A line above an article in a newspaper or magazine giving the author's name. **—by'-lin'er** *n.*

by-pass *also* **by·pass** (bī'păs'). —*n.* **1.** A way around an obstruction or a congested area. **2.** *Elect.* A shunt. **3. a.** An alternative passage formed surgically between 2 blood vessels. **b.** The operation itself. —*v.* To go around : avoid.

by-path (bī'păth', -päth') *n.* An indirect or minor path.

by-play (bī'plā') *n.* Secondary action or speech going on aside from the main action, esp. on a theater stage.

by-prod·uct (bī'prŏd'əkt) *n.* **1.** Something produced in the course of making the main product. **2.** A secondary result.

by·stand·er (bī'stăn'dər) *n.* A witness to an event.

byte (bīt) *n. Computer Sci.* **1.** A sequence of adjacent binary digits operated on as a unit. **2.** A unit of memory that is used to store 1 alphanumeric character, usu. 8 adjacent bits.

by·way (bī'wā') *n.* **1.** A side road. **2.** A secondary aspect or field of study.

by·word (bī'wûrd') *n.* **1.** A well-known saying. **2.** An object of notoriety.

Byz·an·tine (bĭz'ən-tēn', -tīn', bĭ-zăn'tĭn) *adj.* **1.** Of or relating to the ancient city of Byzantium. **2.** Of or designating the architectural style of Byzantium marked by minarets, domes, round arches, and mosaics. **3. a.** Devious. **b.** Intricate. —*n.* A native or inhabitant of Byzantium.

Cc

c *or* **C** (sē) *n., pl.* **c's** *or* **C's. 1.** The 3rd letter of the English alphabet. **2.** A speech sound represented by the letter *c*. **3.** *Mus.* The 1st tone in the scale of C major. **4.** The 3rd-highest grade in quality or rank. **5. C** The Roman numeral for 100.

C *symbol for* CARBON.

Ca *symbol for* CALCIUM.

cab (kăb) *n.* **1.** A taxicab. **2.** The covered compartment for the driver or operator of a heavy vehicle.

ca•bal (kə-băl′) *n.* **1.** A group of conspirators. **2.** A secret plot. **—ca•bal′** *v.* **—cab′a•lis′tic** *adj.* **—cab′a•lis′ti•cal•ly** *adv.*

†cab•al•le•ro (kăb′ə-lâr′ō, -əl-yâr′ō) *n., pl.* **-ros. 1.** A Spanish gentleman : cavalier. **2.** *SW U.S.* A skilled equestrian.

ca•ban•a *also* **ca•ba•ña** (kə-băn′ə, -băn′yə) *n.* A shelter on a beach or at a swimming pool, used as a bathhouse.

cab•a•ret (kăb′ə-rā′) *n.* A restaurant providing entertainment, as a floor show.

cab•bage (kăb′ĭj) *n.* An edible plant, *Brassica oleracea capitata,* having a large head formed by tightly overlapping leaves.

cab•by *or* **cab•bie** (kăb′ē) *n., pl.* **-bies.** *Informal.* A driver of a taxicab.

cab•er•net (kăb′ər-nā′) *n.* A dry red wine made from the grape variety *Cabernet sauvignon.*

cab•in (kăb′ĭn) *n.* **1.** A small, roughly constructed house. **2. a.** A compartment on a ship used as living quarters. **b.** An enclosed compartment on an airplane for passengers.

cabin boy *n.* A boy who works as a servant on a ship.

cab•i•net (kăb′ə-nĭt) *n.* **1.** An upright cupboardlike repository with shelves, drawers, or compartments, as for the storing or displaying of objects. **2.** *often* **Cabinet.** A body of people appointed by a head of state to act as official advisers and be in charge of the various government departments. **—cab′i•net•ry** *n.*

cab•i•net•mak•er (kăb′ə-nĭt-mā′kər) *n.* A craftsman who makes fine wooden furniture. **—cab′i•net•mak′ing** *n.*

cab•i•net•work (kăb′ə-nĭt-wûrk′) *n.* A cabinetmaker's finished products.

ca•ble (kā′bəl) *n.* **1.** A large-diameter fiber or steel rope. **2.** *Elect.* A bound group of insulated conductors. **3.** A cablegram. **4.** Cable television. —*v.* **-bled, -bling.** To send a cablegram (to).

cable car *n.* A vehicle pulled by an endless cable driven by a stationary engine.

ca•ble•cast (kā′bəl-kăst′) *n.* A cable television telecast. **—ca′ble•cast′** *v.*

ca•ble•gram (kā′bəl-grăm′) *n.* A telegram sent by submarine cable.

cable stitch *n.* A knitting stitch that makes a twisted ropelike pattern.

cable television *also* **cable TV** *n.* A television distribution system in which station signals are picked up by elevated antennas and transmitted via cable to subscribers' receivers.

cab•o•chon (kăb′ə-shŏn′) *n.* A convex-cut, unfaceted gem with a high polish.

ca•boo•dle (kə-bo͞od′l) *n. Informal.* The entire lot or group.

ca•boose (kə-bo͞os′) *n.* The last car of a freight train, having kitchen and sleeping facilities for the train crew.

cab•ri•o•let (kăb′rē-ə-lā′) *n.* **1.** A light, 2-wheeled 1-horse carriage with 2 seats and a folding top. **2.** A coupé with a folding top.

ca•ca•o (kə-kä′ō, -kā′ō) *n., pl.* **-os.** An evergreen tropical American tree, *Theobroma cacao,* bearing reddish-brown seed pods that are used in making chocolate, cocoa, and cocoa butter.

cach•a•lot (kăsh′ə-lŏt′, -lō′) *n.* The sperm whale.

cache (kăsh) *n.* **1.** A hiding place for storing provisions. **2.** A safe place for concealment, as of valuables. **3.** A store of goods in a cache. **—cache** *v.*

ca•chet (kă-shā′) *n.* **1.** A seal on a document or letter. **2.** A mark of distinction.

cack•le (kăk′əl) *v.* **-led, -ling. 1.** To make the shrill cry characteristic of a hen after laying an egg. **2.** To talk or laugh in a shrill, broken way. —*n.* **1.** The act or sound of cackling. **2.** Shrill laughter similar to a hen's cackle. **—cack′ler** *n.*

ca•coph•o•ny (kə-kŏf′ə-nē) *n., pl.* **-nies.** Harsh, discordant sound : dissonance. **—ca•coph′o•nous** *adj.* **—ca•coph′o•nous•ly** *adv.*

cac•tus (kăk′təs) *n., pl.* **-ti** (-tī′) *or* **-tus•es.** Any of a large group of usu. leafless plants of the family Cactaceae, of arid regions, having thick, fleshy, often prickly stems.

cad (kăd) *n.* A man whose behavior is ungentlemanly. **—cad′dish** *adj.*

ca•dav•er (kə-dăv′ər) *n.* A dead body : corpse. **—ca•dav′er•ic** *adj.*

ca•dav•er•ous (kə-dăv′ər-əs) *adj.* Pale and gaunt : corpselike.

cad•die *also* **cad•dy** (kăd′ē) *n., pl.* **-dies.** One hired as an attendant to a golfer, esp. to carry the clubs. **—cad′dy** *v.*

Cad•do•an (kăd′ō-ən) *n.* A family of American Indian languages of the E Great Plains.

cad•dy (kăd′ē) *n., pl.* **-dies.** A small container or chest, esp. for tea.

ca•dence (kād′ns) *also* **ca•den•cy** (kād′n-sē) *n., pl.* **-denc•es** *also* **-den•cies. 1.** Rhythmic, balanced flow or movement as in marching. **2.** Inflection or modulation of the voice. **—ca′denced** *adj.*

ca•den•za (kə-dĕn′zə) *n.* An elaborate virtuosic section for a soloist near the end of a movement of a concerto.

ca•det (kə-dĕt′) *n.* **1.** A student at a military or naval academy. **2.** A younger son or brother. **—ca•det′ship′** *n.*

cadge (kăj) *v.* **cadged, cadg•ing.** *Informal.* To beg or obtain by begging : mooch. **—cadg′er** *n.*

cad•mi•um (kăd'mē-əm) *n. Symbol* **Cd** A soft, bluish-white metallic element used in storage batteries, dental amalgams, and solders. —**cad'mic** *adj.*
cad•re (kăd'rē) *n.* **1.** A nucleus of trained personnel. **2. a.** A tightly knit group, esp. of political activists. **b.** A member of such a group.
ca•du•ce•us (kə-dōō'sē-əs, -dyōō'-) *n., pl.* **-ce•i** (-sē-ī'). **1.** *Gk. Myth.* A winged staff with two serpents entwined around it, carried by the god Hermes. **2.** An insignia used as the symbol of the medical profession.
cae•cum (sē'kəm) *n. var. of* CECUM.
Cae•sar (sē'zər) *n.* **1.** A title of the Roman emperors after Augustus. **2.** *often* **caesar.** A dictator : autocrat.
Cae•sar•e•an *also* **Cae•sar•i•an** (sĭ-zâr'ē-ən) *n.* A Caesarean section.
Caesarean section *also* **caesarean section** *n.* Surgical incision through the abdominal and uterine walls to extract a fetus.
caesar salad *n.* A green salad with a dressing of olive oil, lemon juice, and a raw or coddled egg.
cae•si•um (sē'zē-əm) *n. var. of* CESIUM.
cae•su•ra (sĭ-zhŏŏr'ə, -zŏŏr'ə) *n., pl.* **-ras** *or* **-su•rae** (-zhŏŏr'ē, -zŏŏr'ē). A pause in a line of verse. —**cae•su'ral, cae•su'ric** *adj.*
ca•fé (kă-fā', kə-) *n.* A coffeehouse, restaurant, or bar.
café au lait (ō lā') *n.* Coffee with hot milk.
caf•e•te•ri•a (kăf'ĭ-tîr'ē-ə) *n.* A restaurant in which customers select meals at a counter and carry them on trays to tables.
caf•feine *also* **caf•fein** (kă-fēn', kăf'ēn', -ē-ĭn) *n.* A bitter white alkaloid found in coffee, tea, etc., and used as a stimulant.
caf•tan (kăf'tən, kăf-tăn') *n.* A full-length, often loose-fitting tunic with sleeves, worn chiefly in the Near East.
cage (kāj) *n.* **1. a.** An enclosure with bars or grating for confining birds or animals. **b.** Something resembling a cage. **2.** *Baseball.* **a.** A backstop for batting practice. **b.** A catcher's mask. **3.** *Basketball.* The basket. **4.** The goal in hockey. —*v.* **caged, cag•ing.** To put in or as if in a cage.
ca•gey *also* **ca•gy** (kā'jē) *adj.* **-gi•er, -gi•est. 1.** Wary : careful. **2.** Shrewd. —**ca'gi•ly** *adv.* —**ca'gi•ness** *n.*
ca•hoots (kə-hōōts') *pl.n. Informal.* Questionable collaboration <in *cahoots* with a dishonest attorney>
cai•man *also* **cay•man** (kā'mən, kā-măn', kī-) *n., pl.* **-mans.** A tropical American crocodilian of the genus *Caiman* or related genera, closely related to and resembling the alligator.
cairn (kârn) *n.* A mound of stones erected as a marker or memorial.
cairn•gorm (kârn'gôrm') *n.* A smoky brown or yellow quartz, used as a semiprecious gem.
Cairn terrier *n.* A small dog orig. bred in Scotland, with a rough, shaggy coat.
cais•son (kā'sŏn', -sən) *n.* **1.** A watertight structure in which underwater construction is effected. **2.** A device used to raise a sunken vessel. **3. a.** A large box used to hold ammunition. **b.** A horse-drawn vehicle once used to carry ammunition.
caisson disease *n.* A disorder, esp. in divers, caused by release of nitrogen bubbles in the blood upon too rapid a return from high pressure to atmospheric pressure.
ca•jole (kə-jōl') *v.* **-joled, -jol•ing.** To wheedle : coax. —**ca•jol'er** *n.* —**ca•jol'er•y** *n.* —**ca•jol'ing•ly** *adv.*
Ca•jun (kā'jən) *n.* A member of an ethnic group of S Louisiana descended from French exiles from E Canada.
cake (kāk) *n.* **1.** A sweet baked mixture of flour, liquid, and eggs. **2.** A thin baked or fried portion of batter or other food, as a pancake or a fish cake. **3.** A molded piece, as of soap or ice. —*v.* **caked, cak•ing. 1.** To form into a cake : harden. **2.** To coat : encrust.
cal•a•bash (kăl'ə-băsh') *n.* A large, hard-shelled gourd often used as a utensil.
†**cal•a•boose** (kăl'ə-bōōs') *n. Regional.* A jail.
ca•la•di•um (kə-lā'dē-əm) *n.* Any of various tropical plants of the genus *Caladium,* widely cultivated as potted plants for their showy, variegated foliage.
cal•a•mine (kăl'ə-mīn', -mĭn) *n.* A zinc oxide powder with a small amount of ferric oxide, used in skin lotions and ointments.
ca•lam•i•ty (kə-lăm'ĭ-tē) *n., pl.* **-ties. 1.** A disaster. **2.** Great distress or misfortune. —**ca•lam'i•tous** *adj.* —**ca•lam'i•tous•ly** *adv.* —**ca•lam'i•tous•ness** *n.*
cal•car•e•ous (kăl-kâr'ē-əs) *adj.* Made up of, having, or characteristic of calcium carbonate, calcium, or limestone : chalky.
cal•ces (kăl'sēz') *n. var. pl. of* CALX.
cal•cif•er•ous (kăl-sĭf'ər-əs) *adj.* Forming or having calcium or calcium carbonate.
cal•ci•fy (kăl'sə-fī') *v.* **-fied, -fy•ing.** To make or become stony or chalky. —**cal'ci•fi•ca'tion** *n.*
cal•ci•mine (kăl'sə-mīn') *n.* A white or tinted liquid containing zinc oxide, water, glue, and coloring, used as a wash for walls and ceilings. —**cal'ci•mine'** *v.*
cal•cine (kăl'sīn') *v.* **-cined, -cin•ing.** To treat (a substance) by heating to a high temperature without causing it to melt. —**cal'ci•na'tion** (kăl'sə-nā'shən) *n.*
cal•cite (kăl'sīt') *n.* A common crystalline form of calcium carbonate. —**cal•cit'ic** (-sĭt'ĭk) *adj.*
cal•ci•um (kăl'sē-əm) *n. Symbol* **Ca** A silvery, moderately hard metallic element used in compounds to make plaster, Portland cement, and calcium oxide.
calcium carbonate *n.* A crystalline compound of calcium, carbon, and oxygen that occurs naturally as chalk, limestone, and marble.
calcium oxide *n.* A white, lumpy powder used in making steel, glass, and insecticides and as an industrial alkali : quicklime.
†**cal•cu•late** (kăl'kyə-lāt') *v.* **-lat•ed, -lat•ing. 1.** To compute mathematically : reckon.

2. To estimate : evaluate. 3. *Regional.* To intend : plan <I *calculated* on your help.> —**cal'cu·la·ble** *adj.* —**cal'cu·la·bly** *adv.* —**cal'cu·la'tive** *adj.*

cal·cu·lat·ed (kăl'kyə-lā'tĭd) *adj.* Undertaken with careful estimation of the likely outcome <a *calculated* business venture>

cal·cu·lat·ing (kăl'kyə-lā'tĭng) *adj.* Coldly scheming or shrewd.

cal·cu·la·tion (kăl'kyə-lā'shən) *n.* **1.** The act, process, or result of calculating. **2.** Deliberation : foresight.

cal·cu·la·tor (kăl'kyə-lā'tər) *n.* **1.** One who calculates. **2.** A keyboard machine for the automatic performance of mathematical operations.

cal·cu·lus (kăl'kyə-ləs) *n., pl.* **-li** (-lī') *or* **-lus·es. 1.** *Pathol.* An abnormal concretion in the body, as a kidney stone, usu. of mineral salts. **2.** The mathematics of differential and integral calculus.

cal·de·ra (kăl-dâr'ə, -dîr'ə, kôl-) *n.* A large crater formed by volcanic explosion or by collapse of a volcanic cone.

cal·dron *also* **caul·dron** (kôl'drən) *n.* A large vessel, as a kettle or vat.

▲ ***word history:*** The Latin word *caldaria,* "kettle," has 3 descendants in Modern English. *Caldron,* spelled *caudron,* is the earliest form, borrowed from Norman French. The other forms of *caldaria* came from the central French variant of *caudron. Chaldron,* from Old French *chauderon,* was at first used in English as a synonym of *caldron* meaning "kettle." The 3rd form is *chowder,* from the modern French word *chaudiére,* "pot," meaning "fish stew."

cal·en·dar (kăl'ən-dər) *n.* **1.** Any of various systems of showing time divisions by days, weeks, months, and years. **2.** A table showing these divisions, usu. for a specific year. **3.** A usu. chronological list or schedule. —*v.* To enter on a calendar.

cal·en·der (kăl'ən-dər) *n.* A machine in which paper or cloth is made smooth and glossy by pressing between rollers. —*v.* To press in a calender.

cal·ends (kăl'əndz, kā'ləndz) *n., pl.* **-ends.** The first day of the new moon and first day of the month in the ancient Roman calendar.

ca·len·du·la (kə-lĕn'jə-lə) *n.* A plant of the genus *Calendula,* with orange-yellow flowers.

calf[1] (kăf) *n., pl.* **calves** (kăvz). **1. a.** A young cow or bull. **b.** The young of certain other mammals, as the elephant or whale. **2.** Calfskin.

calf[2] (kăf) *n., pl.* **calves** (kăvz). The back part of the leg between the knee and ankle.

calf·skin (kăf'skĭn') *n.* **1.** The hide of a calf. **2.** Leather made from calfskin.

cal·i·ber (kăl'ə-bər) *n.* **1. a.** The diameter of the inside of a tube. **b.** The diameter of the bore of a firearm. **c.** The diameter of a shell or bullet. **2.** Degree of worth.

cal·i·brate (kăl'ə-brāt') *v.* **-brat·ed, -brat·ing. 1.** To check, standardize, or adjust systematically the graduations of (a measuring instrument). **2.** To determine the caliber of (a tube). —**cal'i·bra'tion** *n.* —**cal'i·bra'tor** *n.*

cal·i·bre (kăl'ə-bər) *n. esp. Brit. var. of* CALIBER.

cal·i·co (kăl'ĭ-kō') *n., pl.* **-coes** *or* **-cos. 1.** A coarse, usu. brightly printed cloth. **2.** An animal, as a cat, having a mottled coat.

California poppy *n.* A plant, *Eschscholtzia californica,* of the North American Pacific Coast, with orange-yellow flowers.

cal·i·for·ni·um (kăl'ə-fôr'nē-əm) *n. Symbol* **Cf** An artificial radioactive element produced in trace quantities by bombarding a curium isotope with helium ions.

cal·i·per *also* **cal·li·per** (kăl'ə-pər) *n. often* **calipers.** An instrument composed of 2 curved hinged legs, used for measuring internal and external dimensions.

ca·liph *also* **ca·lif** (kā'lĭf, kăl'ĭf) *n.* An Islamic leader, the political and religious head of a Muslim state. —**ca'liph·ate'** *n.*

cal·is·then·ics (kăl'ĭs-thĕn'ĭks) *n. (sing. or pl. in number).* Exercises that develop muscular tone and enhance physical well-being. —**cal'is·then'ic** *adj.*

calk (kôk) *v. var. of* CAULK.

call (kôl) *v.* **1.** To cry out loudly : proclaim. **2. a.** To summon <*called* them to supper> **b.** To convene <*call* a meeting of the board> **3.** To telephone. **4.** To designate : name. **5.** To consider : estimate. **6.** To pay a short visit. **7.** To demand payment of (e.g., a loan). **8.** To stop or postpone (a game) officially. **9.** To demand that an opponent show his or her cards in poker. ★ ***syns:*** CONVENE, CONVOKE, MUSTER, SUMMON —*n.* **1. a.** A shout. **b.** The characteristic cry of an animal, esp. a bird. **2.** An invitation or summons. **3.** Demand <a big *call* for 10-speed bikes> **4.** A short visit, esp. as a formality. **5.** A communicating by telephone. —**call for. 1.** To go and get. **2.** To be appropriate for : warrant <This *calls for* a celebration.> —**call off. 1.** To cancel or postpone. **2.** To recall : restrain <*called off* the watchdogs> —**call on (or upon). 1.** To pay a visit to. **2.** To appeal to (someone) to do something. —**call out.** To cause to assemble : summon. —**call up. 1.** To summon into military service. **2.** To remember <*call up* old memories> —**on call. 1.** Available whenever summoned. **2.** Payable on demand. —**call'er** *n.*

cal·la *also* **cal·la lily** (kăl'ə) *n.* A plant of the genus *Zantedeschia,* widely cultivated for its showy, white spathe enclosing a clublike flower stalk.

call·back (kôl'băk') *n.* A recall.

call girl *n.* A prostitute hired by telephone.

cal·lig·ra·phy (kə-lĭg'rə-fē) *n.* **1.** The art of handwriting. **2.** Handwriting : penmanship. —**cal·lig'ra·pher, cal·lig'ra·phist** *n.* —**cal'li·graph'ic** (kăl'ĭ-grăf'ĭk) *adj.*

call·ing (kô'lĭng) *n.* **1.** A strong inner urge or impulse. **2.** An occupation : vocation.

cal·li·o·pe (kə-lī'ə-pē', kăl'ē-ōp') *n.* A keyboard musical instrument fitted with steam whistles.

cal·li·per (kăl'ə-pər) *n. var. of* CALIPER.
call letters *pl.n.* The identifying code letters of a radio or television station.
call loan *n.* A loan repayable on demand.
call number *n.* A library number used to classify a book and indicate its placement on the shelves.
cal·los·i·ty (kă-lŏs'ĭ-tē, kə-) *n., pl.* **-ties. 1.** The state of being calloused. **2.** Hardheartedness. **3.** A callus.
cal·lous (kăl'əs) *adj.* **1.** Having calluses : toughened. **2.** Insensitive : unfeeling. —*v.* To make or become callous.
cal·low (kăl'ō) *adj.* Immature and inexperienced. —**cal'low·ly** *adv.*
cal·lus (kăl'əs) *n.* A thickening of the horny skin layer. —**cal'lus** *v.*
calm (käm) *adj.* **1.** Almost or utterly motionless : undisturbed <a *calm* ocean> **2.** Not excited or agitated <a *calm* manner> ★ ***syns:*** PEACEFUL, PLACID, SERENE, TRANQUIL —*n.* **1.** Absence or cessation of motion. **2.** Serenity : peace. **3.** Little or no wind. —*v.* To make or become calm.
calm·a·tive (kä'mə-tĭv, kăl'mə-) *adj.* Having relaxing or pacifying properties : sedative. —**calm'a·tive** *n.*
cal·o·mel (kăl'ə-mĕl', -məl) *n.* A white, tasteless compound used as a cathartic.
cal·o·rie (kăl'ə-rē) *n.* **1.** The amount of heat required to raise the temperature of 1 g of water by 1°C at 1 atmosphere pressure : small calorie. **2. Calorie. a.** The amount of heat required to raise the temperature of 1 kg of water by 1°C at 1 atmosphere pressure : large calorie. **b.** A unit of energy equal to this amount, used in estimating the energy content of a food when it is oxidized in the body. —**ca·lor'ic** (kə-lôr'ĭk, -lŏr'-), **cal'o·rif'ic** *adj.*
cal·o·rim·e·ter (kăl'ə-rĭm'ĭ-tər) *n.* A device for measuring heat. —**ca·lor'i·met'ric** *adj.* —**cal'o·rim'e·try** *n.*
cal·u·met (kăl'yə-mĕt', kăl'yə-mĕt') *n.* A long-stemmed pipe used by certain North American Indians on ceremonial occasions.
ca·lum·ni·ate (kə-lŭm'nē-āt') *v.* **-at·ed, -at·ing.** To slander. —**ca·lum'ni·a'tion** *n.* —**ca·lum'ni·a'tor** *n.*
cal·um·ny (kăl'əm-nē) *n., pl.* **-nies.** A maliciously false slander. —**ca·lum'ni·ous** *adj.* —**ca·lum'ni·ous·ly** *adv.*
cal·va·dos (kăl'və-dōs') *n.* A French brandy made from apples.
calve (kăv) *v.* **calved, calv·ing.** To give birth to a calf.
calves (kăvz) *n. pl. of* CALF.
Cal·vin·ism (kăl'və-nĭz'əm) *n.* The religious doctrines of John Calvin, emphasizing salvation by God's grace alone. —**Cal'vin·ist** *n.* —**Cal'vin·is'tic** *adj.*
ca·lyp·so (kə-lĭp'sō) *n.* Music that originated in the West Indies and is marked by improvised lyrics on topical subjects.
ca·lyx (kā'lĭks, kăl'ĭks) *n., pl.* **-es** *or* **ca·ly·ces** (kā'lĭ-sēz', kăl'ĭ-). The outer protective covering of a flower, composed of usu. green sepals.
cal·zo·ne (kăl-zō'nē, -zōn') *n.* An Italian turnover of pizza dough with a seasoned filling of cheese or meat.
cam (kăm) *n.* An eccentric wheel that is mounted on a rotating shaft, used to produce variable or reciprocating motion.
ca·ma·ra·de·rie (kä'mə-rä'də-rē, kăm'ə-răd'ə-) *n.* Rapport and good will between friends.
cam·ber (kăm'bər) *n.* **1.** A slightly arched surface, as of a road or a ship's deck. **2.** A setting of automobile wheels closer together at the bottom than at the top. —*v.* To arch or cause to arch slightly.
cam·bi·um (kăm'bē-əm) *n.* A cell layer in vascular plants that produces phloem and xylem. —**cam'bi·al** *adj.*
cam·bric (kām'brĭk) *n.* A finely woven linen or cotton fabric.
cam·cord·er (kăm'kôr'dər) *n.* A lightweight, hand-held video camera that incorporates a videocassette recorder.

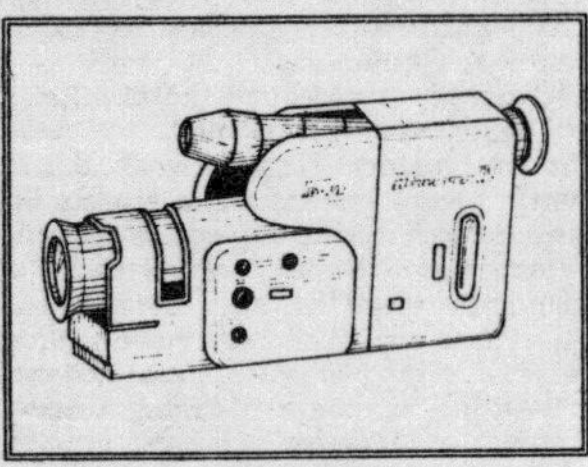

camcorder

came (kām) *v. p.t. of* COME.
cam·el (kăm'əl) *n.* A humped long-necked ruminant mammal of the genus *Camelus,* of N Africa and W Asia, domesticated in desert regions as a beast of burden and source of wool, milk, and meat.
ca·mel·lia (kə-mēl'yə, -mē'lē-ə) *n.* A shrub of the genus *Camellia,* esp. *C. japonica,* with shiny evergreen leaves and showy, variously colored flowers.
camel's hair *also* **camel hair** *n.* **1.** The fine hair of a camel or a substitute for it. **2.** A soft, heavy, usu. light tan cloth made mainly of camel's hair.
Cam·em·bert (kăm'əm-bâr') *n.* A creamy mold-ripened cheese.
cam·e·o (kăm'ē-ō') *n., pl.* **-os. 1.** A gem with a design engraved in relief, usu. of a different hue. **2.** A brief but dramatic appearance of a prominent performer in a single scene on a television show or in a film.
cam·er·a (kăm'ər-ə, kăm'rə) *n.* **1.** A device for taking photographs, gen. composed of a lightproof enclosure with an aperture having a lens through which an image is recorded on a light-sensitive film or plate. **2.** The part of a television transmitting apparatus that receives the primary image on a light-sensitive cathode tube and transforms it into electrical

impulses. **3.** *pl.* **-er•ae** (-ə-rē). A judge's private chamber. **—cam'er•a•man'** *n.* **—cam'er•a•per'son** *n.* **—cam'er•a•wom'an** *n.*

†**ca•mi•sa** (kə-mē'sə) *n. SW U.S.* A shirt or chemise.

cam•i•sole (kăm'ĭ-sōl') *n.* A woman's short, sleeveless undergarment or negligee.

cam•o•mile (kăm'ə-mīl') *n. var. of* CHAMOMILE.

cam•ou•flage (kăm'ə-fläzh', -fläj') *n.* A means of concealment of personnel or materiel, esp. one that makes them appear to be part of the natural surroundings. **—cam'ou•flage'** *v.* **—cam'ou•flag'er** *n.*

camp[1] (kămp) *n.* **1.a.** A place where a group of people, as soldiers, are billeted in temporary shelters such as tents. **b.** The shelters in a campsite or the people who use them. **2.** A recreational area with usu. permanent shelters <a boys' summer *camp*> **3.** A group favorable to a common cause <the liberal *camp*> **—***v.* To shelter or lodge in a camp.

camp[2] (kămp) *Slang.* **—***n.* An affectation or appreciation of manners and taste usu. considered outlandish, vulgar, or banal. **—***v.* To behave in an affected or vulgar way. **—camp** *adj.* **—camp'y** *adj.*

cam•paign (kăm-pān') *n.* **1.** A series of military operations launched to accomplish a given objective within a specific area. **2.** An organized operation or activity to achieve a political, social, or commercial goal. **—cam•paign'** *v.* **—cam•paign'er** *n.*

cam•pa•ni•le (kăm'pə-nē'lē) *n.* A bell tower, esp. one close to but unattached to a building.

cam•pa•nol•o•gy (kăm'pə-nŏl'ə-jē) *n.* The art or study of bell casting and ringing. **—cam'pa•nol'o•gist** *n.*

camp•er (kăm'pər) *n.* **1.** One that camps. **2. a.** A vanlike vehicle equipped as a dwelling for camping or long motor trips. **b.** A portable shelter similar to the top portion of a trailer, made to be set on a pickup truck.

camp•fire (kămp'fīr') *n.* **1.** An outdoor fire in a camp. **2.** A meeting held around such a campfire.

Camp Fire Girl *n.* A member of the Camp Fire Girls, an organization for girls that develops practical skills and provides recreation.

camp follower *n.* **1.** A civilian follower of an army who sells goods or services to it. **2.** One who follows but does not belong to a main body or group.

camp•ground (kămp'ground') *n.* An area used for a camp or camp meeting.

cam•phor (kăm'fər) *n.* A volatile crystalline compound used medicinally and as an insect repellent. **—cam'phor•at'ed** *adj.* **—cam•phor'ic** (-fôr'ĭk, -fŏr'-) *adj.*

camphor tree *n.* An evergreen tree, *Cinnamomum camphora,* indigenous to E Asia, having aromatic wood that is a source of camphor.

camp meeting *n.* An evangelistic meeting held outdoors or in a tent.

camp•site (kămp'sīt') *n.* An area used for camping.

cam•pus (kăm'pəs) *n.* The grounds and buildings of a school, college, or university.

cam•shaft (kăm'shăft') *n.* An engine shaft fitted with a cam or cams.

can[1] (kăn; kən *when unstressed*) *v. p.t.* **could** (kŏŏd). **1.** —Used to indicate: **a.** Mental or physical ability <I *can* see the mountains.> **b.** Possession of a given power, right, or privilege <A citizen *can* vote.> **c.** Possession of a given capacity or skill <They *can* do karate.> **2.** —Used to indicate possibility or probability <*Can* you have the wrong address?> **3.** —Used to request or grant permission <*Can* I have dinner with you?><Yes, you *can.*>

can[2] (kăn) *n.* **1.** A usu. cylindrical metal container. **2.a.** An airtight container, usu. made of tin-coated iron, in which food is preserved. **b.** The contents of such a container. **—***v.* **canned, can•ning. 1.** To preserve in a can or jar. **2.** *Slang.* **a.** To dismiss **:** fire. **b.** To quit <*can* the chitchat> **—can'ner** *n.*

Canada Day *n. Can.* The holiday on July 1 celebrating the anniversary of Canadian Confederation in 1867 **:** Dominion Day.

Canada goose *n.* A wild goose, *Branta canadensis,* of North America, with a black neck and head and grayish plumage.

Ca•na•di•a•na (kə-nā'dē-ăn'ə) *n. Can.* A collection of things relating to Canadian culture, folklore, or history.

Canadian bacon *n.* Cured rolled bacon from the loin of a hog.

Canadian English *n.* The English language as used in Canada.

Canadian French *n.* The French language as used in Canada.

Ca•na•di•an•ize (kə-nā'dē-ə-nīz') *v.* **-ized, -iz•ing.** *Can.* **1.** To assimilate into Canadian culture. **2.** To become Canadian in spirit or methods.

ca•nal (kə-năl') *n.* **1.** An artificial waterway. **2.** *Anat.* A tube **:** duct. **—can'a•li•za'tion** *n.* **—can'a•lize'** *v.*

can•a•pé (kăn'ə-pā', -pē) *n.* A cracker or small piece of bread topped with cheese, meat, or relish.

ca•nard (kə-närd') *n.* A false, unfounded, and misleading story.

ca•nar•y (kə-nâr'ē) *n., pl.* **-ies. 1.** A songbird, *Serinus canaria,* greenish to yellow in color and long bred as a cage bird. **2.** A light to vivid yellow.

ca•nas•ta (kə-năs'tə) *n.* A card game for 2 to 6 players, requiring 2 decks of cards and related to rummy.

can•can (kăn'kăn') *n.* A dance performed by women and marked by high kicks.

can•cel (kăn'səl) *v.* **-celed, -cel•ing** *or* **-celled, -cel•ling. 1.** To cross out with markings such as lines **:** delete. **2.** To annul **:** invalidate <*cancel* an invitation> **3.** To mark or perforate (e.g., a stamp) to indicate it has been used. **4.** To offset **:** equalize. **5. a.** To remove a common factor from a fraction. **b.** To remove a common factor from both members of an equation. **—can'cel·a·ble** *adj.* **—can'cel·er** *n.* **—can'cel·la'tion** *n.*

can·cer (kăn'sər) *n.* **1. a.** Any of various malignant neoplasms that manifest invasiveness and a tendency to metastasize. **b.** The pathological condition marked by such growths. **2.** A spreading evil <a *cancer* of bigotry> **3. Cancer.** A constellation in the N Hemisphere. **4. a. Cancer.** The 4th sign of the zodiac. **b.** One born under this sign. **—can'cer·ous** *adj.*

can·de·la·bra (kăn'dl-ä'brə, -ăb'rə, -ā'brə) *n.* A candelabrum.

can·de·la·brum (kăn'dl-ä'brəm, -ăb'rəm, -ā'brəm) *n., pl.* **-bra** (-brə) *or* **-brums.** A decorative multibranched candlestick.

can·des·cence (kăn-dĕs'əns) *n.* The state of being white hot. **—can·des'cent** *adj.* **—can·des'cent·ly** *adv.*

can·did (kăn'dĭd) *adj.* **1.** Straightforward : frank. **2.** Not posed, as a photograph. **3.** Not prejudiced : impartial. *—n.* An informal photograph. **—can'did·ly** *adv.*

can·di·date (kăn'dĭ-dāt', -dĭt) *n.* One who seeks an office, prize, etc. **—can'di·da·cy** (-də-sē), **can'di·da·ture'** *n.*

can·dle (kăn'dl) *n.* A solid, usu. cylindrical mass of a fatty substance such as tallow or wax, with an axially embedded wick that is burned for illumination. *—v.* **-dled, -dling.** To examine (an egg) for freshness before a light. **—can'dler** *n.*

can·dle·light (kăn'dl-līt') *n.* **1.** Illumination from a candle or candles. **2.** Twilight.

Can·dle·mas (kăn'dl-məs) *n.* A church festival celebrated on Feb. 2 as the feast of the presentation of the infant Jesus in the temple.

can·dle·pins (kăn'dl-pĭnz') *n.* A variation of the game of tenpins using slender bowling pins and a smaller ball.

can·dle·stick (kăn'dl-stĭk') *n.* A holder for securing a candle.

can·dle·wick (kăn'dl-wĭk') *n.* The wick of a candle.

can-do (kăn'dōō') *adj. Informal.* Marked by a willingness to tackle a job and get it done.

can·dor (kăn'dər) *n.* Frankness of expression : straightforwardness.

can·dour (kăn'dər) *n. esp. Brit. var. of* CANDOR.

can·dy (kăn'dē) *n., pl.* **-dies.** A sweet, often rich confection made of sugar or syrup and other ingredients. *—v.* **-died, -dy·ing.** To cook, preserve, saturate, or coat with sugar or syrup.

candy striper *n.* A usu. teenage volunteer nurse's aide.

can·dy·tuft (kăn'dē-tŭft') *n.* Any of various plants of the genus *Iberis,* with white, red, or purplish flower clusters.

cane (kān) *n.* **1. a.** A slender, jointed, woody but usu. flexible stem, as of bamboo or rattan. **b.** A plant having such a stem. **c.** Such stems or strips used for wickerwork. **2.** A stick used for walking or for beating. **3.** Sugar cane. *—v.* **caned, can·ing. 1.** To make, supply, or repair with cane. **2.** To beat with a cane. **—can'er** *n.*

cane·brake (kān'brāk') *n.* A dense cane thicket.

cane sugar *n.* Sucrose obtained from sugar cane.

ca·nine (kā'nīn') *adj.* **1.** Of or relating to a member of the family Canidae, which includes dogs, wolves, and foxes. **2.** Of or designating any of the 4 conical teeth between the incisors and the bicuspids. *—n.* **1.** A canine animal. **2.** A canine tooth.

Ca·nis Ma·jor (kā'nĭs mā'jər, kăn'ĭs) *n.* A constellation in the S Hemisphere.

Canis Mi·nor (mī'nər) *n.* A constellation in the S Hemisphere.

can·is·ter (kăn'ĭ-stər) *n.* **1.** A container for holding dry foods, as flour or tea. **2.** An artillery shell that bursts and scatters the shot it is packed with. **3.** The part of a gas mask that has a filter for removing poison gas from the surrounding air.

can·ker *also* **can·ker sore** (kăng'kər) *n.* An ulcerous sore of the mouth or lips. **—can'ker·ous** *adj.*

can·ker·worm (kăng'kər-wûrm') *n.* The larva of either of 2 moths, *Paleacrita vernata* or *Alsophila pometaria,* that destroys trees.

can·na (kăn'ə) *n.* Any of various tropical plants of the genus *Canna,* with broad leaves and large yellow or red flowers.

can·na·bis (kăn'ə-bĭs) *n.* **1.** The hemp plant. **2.** A euphoriant drug, such as marijuana, derived from the hemp plant.

canned (kănd) *adj.* **1.** Preserved in a can. **2.** *Informal.* Recorded, as laughter, esp. for TV reproduction.

can·ner·y (kăn'ə-rē) *n., pl.* **-ies.** An establishment where foods are canned.

can·ni·bal (kăn'ə-bəl) *n.* **1.** One who eats human flesh. **2.** An animal that feeds on its own kind. **—can'ni·bal·ism** *n.* **—can'ni·bal·is'tic** *adj.*

can·ni·bal·ize (kăn'ə-bə-līz') *v.* **-ized, -iz·ing.** To take usable parts from (e.g., damaged equipment) for the repair of other equipment. **—can'ni·bal·i·za'tion** *n.*

can·no·li (kə-nō'lē, kă-) *n.* A fried pastry roll with a creamy, usu. sweet filling.

can·non (kăn'ən) *n., pl.* **-non** *or* **-nons. 1.** A weapon consisting of a heavy metal tube mounted on wheels or a fixed base, used to fire projectiles. **2.** A heavy firearm larger than 0.60 caliber. **—can'non·eer'** *n.*

can·non·ade (kăn'ə-nād') *v.* **-ad·ed, -ad·ing.** To assault with heavy artillery fire. **—can'non·ade'** *n.*

can·non·ball *also* **can·non ball** (kăn'ən-bôl') *n.* **1.** A round projectile fired from a cannon. **2.** Something that is fast-moving, as a train. **—can'non·ball'** *v.*

can·not (kăn'ŏt', kă-nŏt', kə-) *v.* Can not.

can·ny (kăn'ē) *adj.* **-ni·er, -ni·est. 1.** Careful : shrewd. **2.** Thrifty : frugal. **—can'ni·ly** *adv.* **—can'ni·ness** *n.*

ca·noe (kə-nōō') *n.* A light narrow boat with pointed ends that is moved by paddling. *—v.* **-noed, -noe·ing.** To carry or travel in a canoe. **—ca·noe'ist** *n.*

can•on[1] (kăn'ən) *n.* **1.** A law or body of laws established by a church. **2.** A basis for judgment : criterion. **3.** The Biblical books officially recognized as the Holy Scripture. **4.** *Rom. Cath. Ch.* **a.** *often* **Canon.** The most important part of the Mass, beginning after the Sanctus. **b.** The calendar of accepted saints.

can•on[2] (kăn'ən) *n.* A priest who serves in a cathedral or collegiate church.

ca•ñon (kăn'yən) *n. var. of* CANYON.

ca•non•i•cal (kə-nŏn'ĭ-kəl) *or* **ca•non•ic** (-nŏn'ĭk) *adj.* **1.** Relating to, required by, or obeying canon law. **2.** Orthodox : authoritative. **—ca•non'i•cal•ly** *adv.* **—can'on•ic'i•ty** (kăn'ə-nĭs'ĭ-tē) *n.*

can•on•ize (kăn'ə-nīz') *v.* **-ized, -iz•ing. 1.** To declare officially to be a saint. **2.** To glorify. **—can'on•i•za'tion** *n.*

canon law *n.* The body of officially established rules that the members of a Christian church follow.

can•o•py (kăn'ə-pē) *n., pl.* **-pies. 1.** A cloth covering hanging over something or carried over a dignitary. **2.** A rooflike ornamental structure. **3. a.** The transparent enclosure over the cockpit of an aircraft. **b.** The hemispheric surface of a parachute. **4.** *Ecol.* The uppermost layer in a forest. —*v.* **-pied, -py•ing.** To spread over with or as if with a canopy.

canst (kănst) *v. archaic 2nd person sing. present tense of* CAN[1].

cant[1] (kănt) *n.* **1. a.** Angular deviation from a horizontal or vertical surface or plane. **b.** The tilt caused by such a motion. **2.** A slanted surface or edge. **—cant** *v.*

cant[2] (kănt) *n.* **1.** Whining, affected speech. **2.** Mechanically recited discourse. **3.** Hypocritical and pious language. **4.** The specialized vocabulary of the members of a group : jargon. —*v.* **1.** To whine or plead. **2.** To moralize. **—cant'ing•ly** *adv.*

can't (kănt, känt). Cannot.

can•ta•bi•le (kän-tä'bē-lā', -bi-, kən-) *adv. Mus.* In a lyrical, flowing style. —Used as a direction. **—can•ta'bi•le'** *adj. & n.*

can•ta•loupe *also* **can•ta•loup** (kăn'tl-ōp') *n.* A melon, *Cucumis melo cantalupensis,* with a ribbed, rough rind and aromatic orange flesh.

can•tan•ker•ous (kăn-tăng'kər-əs) *adj.* Bad-tempered and argumentative : disagreeable. **—can•tan'ker•ous•ly** *adv.*

can•ta•ta (kən-tä'tə) *n. Mus.* A composition of choruses, solos, and recitatives.

can•teen (kăn-tēn') *n.* **1. a.** A store for on-base military personnel. **b.** *esp. Brit.* A club for soldiers. **2.** An institutional cafeteria or recreation hall. **3.** A temporary eating place, esp. one set up in an emergency <a Red Cross *canteen*> **4.** A flask for carrying drinking water.

can•ter (kăn'tər) *n.* A gait slower than a gallop but faster than a trot. —*v.* To go or cause to go at a canter.

Canterbury bells *n. (sing. or pl. in number).* A plant, *Campanula medium,* native to Europe, widely cultivated for its violet-blue bell-shaped flowers.

can•ti•cle (kăn'tĭ-kəl) *n.* A liturgical hymn or chant.

can•ti•le•ver (kăn'tl-ē'vər, -ĕv'ər) *n.* A projecting structure, as a beam, supported only at one end. —*v.* To support by, extend outward, or build as a cantilever.

†**can•ti•na** (kăn-tē'nə) *n. SW U.S.* A barroom.

can•tle (kăn'təl) *n.* The rear projecting part of a saddle.

can•to (kăn'tō) *n., pl.* **-tos.** A main division of a long poem.

can•ton (kăn'tən, -tŏn') *n.* A small territorial division of a country, esp. one of the Swiss states. —*v.* **1.** To divide into territorial cantons. **2.** To billet (troops). **—can'ton•al** *adj.*

can•ton•ment (kăn-tōn'mənt, -tŏn'-) *n.* **1.** A group of more or less temporary billets for troops. **2.** Assignment of troops to temporary billets.

can•tor (kăn'tər) *n.* The official soloist or chief singer of the liturgy in a synagogue.

can•vas (kăn'vəs) *n.* **1.** A strong, heavy fabric used esp. for making sails and tents. **2.** A piece of canvas used for an oil painting. **3.** Sailcloth. **4.** Sails as a whole. **5.** The floor of a ring for boxing or wrestling.

can•vas•back (kăn'vəs-băk') *n.* A North American duck, *Aythya valisneria,* with a reddish head and a grayish back.

can•vass (kăn'vəs) *v.* **1.** To scrutinize. **2.a.** To go through (e.g., a neighborhood) to solicit votes, subscriptions, etc. **b.** To make a survey : poll. —*n.* **1.** A thorough examination or detailed discussion. **2.** A solicitation of votes, sales orders, opinions, etc. **—can'vass•er** *n.*

can•yon *also* **ca•ñon** (kăn'yən) *n.* A narrow gorge with steep walls.

cap (kăp) *n.* **1.** A usu. soft close-fitting head covering. **2.** An object like a cap in form, use, or position. **3.a.** A percussion cap. **b.** A small explosive charge for use in a cap pistol. —*v.* **capped, cap•ping. 1.** To put a cap on. **2.** To lie over : cover.

ca•pa•ble (kā'pə-bəl) *adj.* **1.** Having ability or capacity : efficient. **2.** Qualified. **3.** Open or susceptible to <a flaw *capable* of correction> **—ca'pa•bil'i•ty, ca'pa•ble•ness** *n.* **—ca'pa•bly** *adv.*

ca•pa•cious (kə-pā'shəs) *adj.* Roomy.

ca•pac•i•tance (kə-păs'ĭ-təns) *n.* **1.** The ratio of charge to potential on an electrically charged, isolated conductor. **2.** The property of a circuit element that permits it to store charge. **—ca•pac'i•tive** *adj.* **—ca•pac'i•tive•ly** *adv.*

ca•pac•i•tor (kə-păs'ĭ-tər) *n. Elect.* A circuit element composed of 2 metallic plates separated by a dielectric, used to store a charge temporarily.

ca•pac•i•ty (kə-păs'ĭ-tē) *n., pl.* **-ties. 1.** The ability to hold, receive, or contain. **2.** The largest amount that can be contained <a room filled to *capacity*> **3.** The most efficient level or maximum of production. **4.** Ability **:** capability. **5.** Suitability for or receptiveness to specified treatment <the *capacity* of water to freeze> **6.** The role in which a person functions.

cap-a-pie *or* **cap-à-pie** (kăp′ə-pē′) *adv.* From head to foot.

ca•par•i•son (kə-păr′ĭ-sən) *n.* **1.** A usu. ornamental covering for a saddle or harness. **2.** Fancy clothing. **—ca•par′i•son** *v.*

cape[1] (kāp) *n.* A sleeveless garment that fastens at the throat and hangs loosely over the shoulders.

cape[2] (kāp) *n.* **1.** A point of land that projects into water. **2.** A Cape Cod cottage.

Cape Cod cottage *n.* A compact house with 1 or 1½ stories, a gabled roof, and a central chimney.

ca•per[1] (kā′pər) *n.* **1.** A playful leap or hop. **2.** An antic **:** prank. **3.** A criminal undertaking. —*v.* To leap about **:** frolic.

ca•per[2] (kā′pər) *n.* A pickled bud of a Mediterranean shrub, *Capparis spinosa,* used as a condiment.

cap•il•lar•i•ty (kăp′ə-lăr′ĭ-tē) *n., pl.* **-ties.** The attraction or repulsion between surfaces of a liquid and a solid that prevents the surface of the liquid from being flat.

cap•il•lar•y (kăp′ə-lĕr′ē) *adj.* **1.** Relating to or like a hair. **2.** Having a very small inside diameter, as a tube. **3.** *Anat.* In, of, or relating to the capillaries. **4.** *Physics.* Of or relating to capillarity. —*n., pl.* **-ies. 1.** *Anat.* One of the minute blood vessels that connect arteries and veins. **2.** A tube with a small inside diameter.

capillary action *n.* Capillarity.

cap•i•tal[1] (kăp′ĭ-tl) *n.* **1.** A city or town that is the seat of government in a state or nation. **2.** Material wealth in the form of money or property that is used to produce more wealth. **3.a.** The net worth of a business. **b.** The funds contributed to a business by the owners or stockholders. **4.** Capitalists as a group. **5.** An advantage or asset. **6.** A letter, such as A or B, written or printed in a larger size or different form from its corresponding small letter. —*adj.* **1.** Chief **:** principal. **2.** Of or relating to a governmental capital. **3.** First-rate <a *capital* idea> **4.** Very serious <a *capital* error> **5.** Involving death or calling for the death penalty <a *capital* felony> **6.** Relating to monetary capital.

cap•i•tal[2] (kăp′ĭ-tl) *n.* The top part of a column or pillar.

capital goods *pl.n.* Goods used in producing commodities.

cap•i•tal•ism (kăp′ĭ-tl-ĭz′əm) *n.* An economic system characterized by open competition in a free market and by private or corporate ownership of the means of production and distribution.

cap•i•tal•ist (kăp′ĭ-tl-ĭst) *n.* **1.** One who invests capital in business. **2.** A supporter of capitalism. **3.** Someone of great wealth. **—cap′i•tal•is′tic** *adj.* **—cap′i•tal•is′ti•cal•ly** *adv.*

cap•i•tal•ize (kăp′ĭ-tl-īz′) *v.* **-ized, -iz•ing. 1.** To convert into capital. **2.** To supply with capital. **3.** To profit by **:** exploit. **4.** To write or print in capital letters. **—cap′i•tal•i•za′tion** *n.*

capital ship *n.* A warship, as a battleship, of the largest class.

cap•i•ta•tion (kăp′ĭ-tā′shən) *n.* A tax of an equal amount per person.

cap•i•tol (kăp′ĭ-tl) *n.* **1.** The building in which a state legislature meets. **2. Capitol.** The building in which the U.S. Congress meets.

ca•pit•u•late (kə-pĭch′ə-lāt′) *v.* **-lat•ed, -lat•ing. 1.** To surrender under conditional terms. **2.** To cease resisting. **—ca•pit′u•la′tion** *n.* **—ca•pit′u•la′tor** *n.* **—ca•pit′u•la•to′ry** *adj.*

ca•pon (kā′pŏn′, -pən) *n.* A castrated rooster.

cap pistol *n.* A toy pistol with a hammer action that detonates a small charge.

cap•puc•ci•no (kăp′ə-chē′nō, kä′pə-) *n.* Espresso coffee mixed with steamed milk or topped with whipped cream.

ca•price (kə-prēs′) *n.* **1.** A change of mind **:** whim. **2.** A tendency to change one's mind suddenly or impulsively.

ca•pri•cious (kə-prĭsh′əs, -prē′shəs) *adj.* Characterized by or subject to whim. ★ ***syns:*** CHANGEABLE, ERRATIC, FICKLE, INCONSISTENT, INCONSTANT, MERCURIAL, TEMPERAMENTAL, UNPREDICTABLE, UNSTABLE, UNSTEADY, VARIABLE, VOLATILE, WHIMSICAL **—ca•pri′cious•ly** *adv.*

Cap•ri•corn (kăp′rĭ-kôrn′) *n.* **1.** A constellation in the S Hemisphere. **2. a.** The 10th sign of the zodiac. **b.** One born under this sign.

cap•ri•ole (kăp′rē-ōl′) *n.* **1.** An upward leap made by a trained horse without forward motion. **2.** A leap **:** jump. **—cap′ri•ole′** *v.*

cap•size (kăp′sīz′, kăp-sīz′) *v.* **-sized, -siz•ing.** To overturn, as a boat.

cap•stan (kăp′stən, -stăn′) *n.* **1.** *Naut.* A device consisting of a vertical cylinder rotated to hoist weights by winding in a cable. **2.** A small cylindrical pulley that regulates the speed of recorder tape.

cap•su•late (kăp′sə-lāt′, -syŏŏ-, -lĭt) *also* **cap•su•lat•ed** (-lā′tĭd) *adj.* In or formed into a capsule.

cap•sule (kăp′səl, -syōōl) *n.* **1.** A soluble, usu. gelatin container for a dose of oral medicine. **2.** A fibrous, membranous, or fatty envelope, as the sac surrounding the kidney, that encloses an organ or part. **3.** A fruit that contains 2 or more seeds and splits open when dry. **4.** A pressurized modular compartment of an aircraft or spacecraft. **5.** A brief summary. **—cap′su•lar** *adj.* **—cap′sule** *v.*

cap•tain (kăp′tən) *n.* **1.** The leader of a group **:** chief. **2.** The officer who commands a ship. **3.a.** A commissioned officer in the Army, Air Force, or Marine Corps ranking below a major and above a first lieutenant. **b.** A commissioned officer in the Navy ranking below a rear admiral and above a commander. **4.** A prominent figure. —*v.* To direct or command. **—cap′tain•cy** *n.* **—cap′tain•ship′** *n.*

cap•tion (kăp′shən) *n.* **1.** A title or description accompanying an illustration or picture. **2.** A motion-picture subtitle. **3.** A title, as of a document. **—cap′tion** *v.*

cap•tious (kăp′shəs) *adj.* **1.** Tending to criticize. **2.** Deceptive.

cap•ti•vate (kăp′tĭ-vāt′) *v.* **-vat•ed, -vat•ing.** To fascinate : enrapture. **—cap′ti•va′tion** *n.* **—cap′ti•va′tor** *n.*

cap•tive (kăp′tĭv) *n.* A prisoner. *—adj.* **1.** Held as prisoner. **2.** Subjugated, as a nation. **3.** Enraptured. **4.** Obliged to be present <a *captive* audience> **—cap•tiv′i•ty** *n.*

cap•tor (kăp′tər, -tôr′) *n.* One that captures.

cap•ture (kăp′chər) *v.* **-tured, -tur•ing. 1.** To take captive. **2.** To win control or possession of, as in a contest. *—n.* **1.** The act of capturing. **2.** One that is captured.

car (kär) *n.* **1.** An automobile. **2.** A conveyance with wheels that runs along tracks, as a railroad car. **3.** A boxlike enclosure for passengers on a conveyance, as an elevator.

▲ ***word history:*** *Car* was a dying word in English until modern technology revived it. By the middle of the 19th cent. *car* was only a poetic synonym for *chariot,* to which it is related. *Car* sprang to life after the term *motorcar* was adopted late in the 19th cent. for the automobile. *Motorcar* was soon shortened to *car,* which lost all its poetic associations in the brave new era.

car•a•cul (kăr′ə-kəl) *n. var. of* KARAKUL.

ca•rafe (kə-răf′, -räf′) *n.* A glass bottle with a flared lip for serving water or wine.

car•a•mel (kăr′ə-məl, -mĕl′, kär′məl) *n.* **1.** A smooth, chewy candy. **2.** Sugar heated to a brown syrup, used for coloring and sweetening foods.

car•a•pace (kăr′ə-pās′) *n. Zool.* A hard bony outer covering, as the fused dorsal plates of a turtle.

car•at (kăr′ət) *n.* **1.** A unit of weight for precious stones, equal to 200 mg. **2.** *var. of* KARAT.

car•a•van (kăr′ə-văn′) *n.* **1.** A group of travelers journeying together, esp. across a desert. **2.** A file of pack animals or vehicles. **3.** A van. **4.** *esp. Brit.* A house trailer.

car•a•van•sa•ry (kăr′ə-văn′sə-rē) *also* **car•a•van•se•rai** (-rī′) *n., pl.* **-ries** *also* **-rais. 1.** An inn with a large courtyard for accommodating caravans in the Near or Far East. **2.** A large inn.

car•a•vel (kăr′ə-vĕl′) *n.* A small, light sailing ship of the 15th and 16th cent.

car•a•way (kăr′ə-wā′) *n.* A Eurasian plant, *Carum carvi,* with pungent aromatic seeds that are used in cooking.

car•bide (kär′bīd′) *n.* A binary carbon compound composed of carbon and a more electropositive element.

car•bine (kär′bīn′, -bēn′) *n.* A light, short-barreled rifle.

car•bo•hy•drate (kär′bō-hī′drāt′, -bə-) *n.* Any of a group of compounds, including sugars, starches, and cellulose, that are composed of carbon, hydrogen, and oxygen.

car•bol•ic acid (kär-bŏl′ĭk) *n.* PHENOL.

car•bon (kär′bən) *n. Symbol* **C 1.** A nonmetallic element occurring as a powdery noncrystalline solid. **2. a.** A sheet of carbon paper. **b.** A copy made with carbon paper. **—car′bon•i•za′tion** *n.* **—car′bon•ize′** *v.* **—car′bon•ous** *adj.*

carbon 14 *n.* A radioactive carbon isotope used in dating ancient objects that contain carbon.

car•bo•na•ceous (kär′bə-nā′shəs) *adj.* Of, containing, or yielding carbon.

car•bon•ate (kär′bə-nāt′) *v.* **-at•ed, -at•ing.** To charge with carbon dioxide gas, as a beverage. **—car′bon•a′tion** *n.*

carbon black *n.* Any of various divided forms of carbon obtained from the incomplete combustion of gas or oil, used chiefly in rubber and ink.

carbon copy *n.* **1.** A copy, as of a letter, made with carbon paper. **2.** *Informal.* A close copy.

carbon dating *n.* Determination of the approx. age, as of a fossil, by use of the radiation rate of carbon 14.

carbon dioxide *n.* A colorless, odorless, nonflammable gas, produced in respiration, combustion, or organic decomposition.

car•bon•ic acid (kär-bŏn′ĭk) *n.* A weak, unstable acid present only in solutions of carbon dioxide and water.

car•bon•if•er•ous (kär′bə-nĭf′ər-əs) *adj.* Of, producing, or containing carbon or coal.

carbon monoxide *n.* A colorless, odorless, extremely poisonous gas formed by incomplete combustion of carbon or any carbonaceous material.

carbon paper *n.* A lightweight paper coated on one side with a waxy pigment that is transferred onto paper by pressure.

carbon tet•ra•chlo•ride (tĕt′rə-klôr′īd′, -klōr′-) *n.* A poisonous, nonflammable, colorless liquid used in fire extinguishers.

car•boy (kär′boi′) *n.* A large bottle usu. in a protective basket or crate and often used for holding corrosive liquids.

car•bun•cle (kär′bŭng′kəl) *n.* A localized, pus-producing painful skin infection. **—car•bun′cu•lar** (-kyə-lər) *adj.*

car•bu•re•tor (kär′bə-rā′tər, -byə-) *n.* A device in gasoline engines that mixes fuel vapor and air for efficient combustion.

car•cass (kär′kəs) *n.* A dead body, esp. of a slaughtered animal.

car•cin•o•gen (kär-sĭn′ə-jən, kär′sə-nə-jĕn′) *n.* A cancer-causing substance or agent. **—car′ci•no•gen′e•sis** (kär′sə-nə-jĕn′ĭ-sĭs) *n.* **—car′cin•o•gen′ic** *adj.* **—car′ci•no•ge•nic′i•ty** (-jə-nĭs′ĭ-tē) *n.*

car•ci•no•ma (kär′sə-nō′mə) *n., pl.* **-mas** *or* **-ma•ta** (-mə-tə). A malignant tumor derived from skin, mucous membrane, or other tissue that covers an organ or structure. **—car′ci•nom′a•tous** (-nŏm′ə-təs, -nō′mə-) *adj.*

car coat *n.* A knee-length coat.

card[1] (kärd) *n.* **1.** A small piece of stiff paper, cardboard, or plastic, esp.: **a.** A playing card.

b. A postcard. **c.** A greeting card. **d.** A business card. **2. cards.** *(sing. or pl. in number)* A game played with cards. **3.** A program, esp. for a sports event. **4.** *Computer Sci.* A circuit board. **5.** *Informal.* An eccentric or amusing person : character. —*v.* **1.** To attach to or furnish with a card. **2.** To list on a card : catalogue. **3.** *Informal.* To verify the legal age of by checking one's indentification. **—in the cards.** Likely to occur.

card[2] (kärd) *n.* A wire-toothed instrument or machine used to disentangle fibers, as of wool, before spinning or to raise the nap of a fabric. —*v.* To brush or comb out with a card. **—card'er** *n.*

car•da•mom *or* **car•da•mum** (kär'də-məm) *also* **car•da•mon** (-mən) *n.* A tropical Asiatic plant, *Elettaria cardamomum,* having large hairy leaves and capsular fruit with seeds that are used as a spice.

card•board (kärd'bôrd', -bōrd') *n.* A thin stiff pasteboard.

card catalog *n.* An alphabetical listing, esp. of books in a library, with a card for each item.

car•di•ac (kär'dē-ăk') *adj.* Of, near, or relating to the heart <*cardiac* arrest>

cardiac arrest *n.* Sudden cessation of heartbeat and cardiac function, resulting in the loss of effective circulation.

cardiac massage *n.* A procedure employing rhythmic compression of the chest in an effort to restore proper circulation and respiration.

car•di•gan (kär'dĭ-gən) *n.* A sweater or knitted jacket opening down the front.

car•di•nal (kär'dn-əl, kärd'nəl) *adj.* **1.** Being of prime importance. **2.** Of a vivid red color. —*n.* **1.** *Rom. Cath. Ch.* An official appointed by and ranking just below the pope. **2.** Vivid red. **3.** A North American bird, *Richmondena cardinalis,* with a crested head, a short thick bill, and bright red plumage in the male. **4.** A cardinal number. **—car'di•nal•ly** *adv.*

cardinal number *n.* A number, as 7 or 13 or 946, used in counting to indicate quantity but not order.

car•di•o•gram (kär'dē-ə-grăm') *n.* The curve recorded by a cardiograph, used in diagnosis of heart defects.

car•di•o•graph (kär'dē-ə-grăf') *n.* **1.** An instrument for recording the mechanical movements of the heart. **2.** An electrocardiograph. **—car'di•og'ra•phy** (-ŏg'rə-fē) *n.*

car•di•ol•o•gy (kär'dē-ŏl'ə-jē) *n.* The medical study of the heart, its diseases, and their treatment. **—car'di•ol'o•gist** *n.*

car•di•o•pul•mo•nar•y (kär'dē-ō-pool'mə-nĕr'ē) *adj.* Of or relating to the heart and lungs.

cardiopulmonary resuscitation *n.* A procedure used after cardiac arrest in which cardiac massage, mouth-to-mouth resuscitation, and drugs are used to restore breathing.

car•di•o•vas•cu•lar (kär'dē-ō-văs'kyə-lər) *adj.* Of, relating to, or involving the heart and the blood vessels.

card•sharp (kärd'shärp') *n.* An expert cheat at cards. **—card'sharp'ing** *n.*

care (kâr) *n.* **1.** Mental distress : worry. **2.** A source of solicitude or attention. **3.** Caution <take *care*> **4.** Supervision : charge <under a doctor's *care*> ★ ***syns:*** CHARGE, CUSTODY, GUARDIANSHIP, SUPERVISION —*v.* **cared, car•ing. 1.** To be interested or concerned. **2.** To have a liking or inclination. **3.** To give care. **4.** To object : mind.

ca•reen (kə-rēn') *v.* **1.** To lurch while moving rapidly. **2.** To lean (a ship) on one side, as for caulking or repairing.

ca•reer (kə-rîr') *n.* **1.** A chosen profession or occupation. **2.** The general progression of one's life, esp. in one's profession. —*v.* To rush headlong.

care•free (kâr'frē') *adj.* Free from all cares.

care•ful (kâr'fəl) *adj.* **1.** Cautious in thought, speech, or action. **2.** Painstaking : thorough. ★ ***syns:*** CAUTIOUS, CHARY, CIRCUMSPECT, PRUDENT **—care'ful•ly** *adv.*

care•giv•er (kâr'gĭv'ər) *n.* **1.** One who assists a sick or disabled person. **2.** One who attends to the needs of a child or dependent adult. **—care'giv'ing** *adj. & n.*

care•less (kâr'lĭs) *adj.* **1.** Inattentive : negligent. **2.** Inconsiderate : thoughtless. **3.** Indifferent to accuracy or neatness. ★ ***syns:*** MESSY, SLAPDASH, SLIPSHOD, SLOPPY, SLOVENLY, UNTIDY **—care'less•ly** *adv.*

ca•ress (kə-rĕs') *n.* A gentle touch or gesture of affection. —*v.* To stroke or touch affectionately. **—ca•ress'er** *n.*

car•et (kăr'ĭt) *n.* A proofreading symbol used to indicate where material is to be inserted in a printed or written line.

care•tak•er (kâr'tā'kər) *n.* One hired to take charge of goods, property, or another person : custodian.

care•worn (kâr'wôrn', -wōrn') *adj.* Showing signs of worry or care.

car•fare (kär'fâr') *n.* Fare charged a passenger, as on a subway or bus.

car•go (kär'gō) *n., pl.* **-goes** *or* **-gos.** The freight carried by a vehicle, vessel, or aircraft.

car•hop (kär'hŏp') *n.* One who serves customers at a drive-in restaurant.

car•i•bou (kăr'ə-boo') *n., pl.* **-bou** *or* **-bous.** A deer, *Rangifer tarandus,* of New World Arctic regions.

car•i•ca•ture (kăr'ĭ-kə-choor', -chər) *n.* **1.** A usu. pictorial representation in which the subject's distinctive features or characteristics are exaggerated for comic or distorted effect. **2.** An absurdly inferior imitation. **—car'i•ca•ture'** *v.* **—car'i•ca•tur'ist** *n.*

car•ies (kâr'ēz') *n., pl.* **-ies.** Bone or tooth decay.

car•il•lon (kăr'ə-lŏn', -lən) *n.* A stationary set of tuned bells in a tower, usu. played by means of a keyboard.

car•load (kär'lōd') *n.* The load that a car can carry.

car•mine (kär'mĭn, -mīn') *n.* A strong to vivid red color.

car•nage (kär'nĭj) *n.* Massive slaughter.

car•nal (kär′nəl) *adj.* **1.** Of sensual desires and appetites. **2.** Not spiritual : temporal. —**car•nal′i•ty** *n.* —**car′nal•ly** *adv.*

car•na•tion (kär-nā′shən) *n.* A plant, *Dianthus caryophyllus,* widely cultivated for its fragrant white, pink, or red flowers.

car•nel•ian (kär-nēl′yən) *n.* A reddish brown variety of clear chalcedony used as a gemstone.

car•ni•val (kär′nə-vəl) *n.* **1.** The season just before Lent, given to feasting and merrymaking. **2.** A traveling show featuring exhibits and rides.

car•ni•vore (kär′nə-vôr′, -vōr′) *n.* An animal of the order Carnivora, including predominantly flesh-eating mammals.

car•niv•o•rous (kär-nĭv′ər-əs) *adj.* **1.** Belonging or relating to the order Carnivora. **2.** Flesh-eating : predatory. —**car•niv′o•rous•ly** *adv.* —**car•niv′o•rous•ness** *n.*

car•ny *also* **car•ney** (kär′nē) *n., pl.* **-nies** *also* **-neys.** *Slang.* **1.** CARNIVAL 2. **2.** A carnival worker.

car•ob (kăr′əb) *n.* **1.** An evergreen tree, *Ceratonia siliqua,* of the Mediterranean region, with compound leaves and edible pods. **2.** The sweet pulp of the carob pod used as a chocolate substitute.

car•ol (kăr′əl) *v.* **-oled, -ol•ing** *or* **-olled, -ol•ling. 1.** To celebrate in song. **2.** To sing joyously. —*n.* A song of joy, esp. for Christmas. —**car′ol•er** *n.*

car•om (kăr′əm) *n.* **1.** A billiards shot in which the cue ball strikes 2 other balls successively. **2.** A collision followed by a rebound, as a ball bouncing off a wall. —**car′om** *v.*

car•o•tene (kăr′ə-tēn′) *also* **car•o•tin** (-tĭn) *n.* An orange-yellow to red hydrocarbon present in many plants as a pigment and converted to vitamin A by the liver.

ca•rot•id (kə-rŏt′ĭd) *n.* Either of the 2 arteries in the neck that supply blood to the head. —**ca•rot′id** *adj.*

ca•rouse (kə-rouz′) *v.* To engage in rowdy, drunken merrymaking. —**ca•rous′al** *n.* —**ca•rouse′** *n.* —**ca•rous′er** *n.*

car•ou•sel *or* **car•rou•sel** (kăr′ə-sĕl′, -zĕl′) *n.* A merry-go-round.

carp[1] (kärp) *v.* To complain and criticize constantly : nag. —**carp′er** *n.*

carp[2] (kärp) *n.* An edible freshwater fish, *Cyprinus carpio.*

car•pal (kär′pəl) *adj. Anat.* Of, relating to, or near the carpus. —*n.* A carpus bone.

carpal tunnel syndrome *n.* Pain, numbness, and muscular weakness in the thumb, index, and middle fingers, usu. due to inflammation or trauma.

car•pel (kär′pəl) *n. Bot.* The ovule-bearing female flower organ, composed of a modified leaf that forms one or more sections of the pistil. —**car′pel•lar′y** *adj.*

car•pen•ter (kär′pən-tər) *n.* One who builds, finishes, and repairs wooden objects and structures. —**car′pen•ter** *v.* —**car′pen•try** *n.*

car•pet (kär′pĭt) *n.* **1.** A thick, heavy floor covering : rug. **2.** The fabric used for carpets. **3.** A surface like a carpet <a *carpet* of moss> —*v.* To cover with or as if with a carpet. —**on the carpet.** Before a superior for a reprimand.

car•pet•bag (kär′pĭt-băg′) *n.* An old-fashioned traveling bag made of carpet material.

car•pet•bag•ger (kär′pĭt-băg′ər) *n.* A Northerner who was in the South after the Civil War for political or financial gain.

car-pool (kär′po͞ol′) *n.* **1.** An arrangement whereby several commuters share cars and expenses. **2.** A group participating in a carpool. —**car′-pool′** *v.*

car•port (kär′pôrt′, -pōrt′) *n.* A roof projecting from the side of a building, used to shelter a car.

car•pus (kär′pəs) *n., pl.* **-pi** (-pī′). *Anat.* **1.** The wrist. **2.** The bones in the wrist.

car•rel *also* **car•rell** (kăr′əl) *n.* A nook in a library for private study.

car•riage (kăr′ĭj) *n.* **1.** A 4-wheeled usu. horse-drawn vehicle for passengers. **2.** A baby carriage. **3.** A wheeled support or frame for a heavy object, as a cannon. **4.** A machine part for holding or moving another part. **5. a.** The act or process of carrying or transporting. **b.** (kăr′ē-ĭj). The charge for transporting. **6.** Posture : bearing.

carriage trade *n.* Wealthy patrons, as of a business.

car•ri•er (kăr′ē-ər) *n.* **1.** One that transports or conveys. **2.** One that deals in transporting passengers or goods. **3.** *Med.* One that is immune to a pathogen it transmits to others. **4.** An aircraft carrier.

carrier pigeon *n.* A homing pigeon trained to carry messages.

carrier wave *n.* An electromagnetic wave that can be modulated to transmit speech, music, images, or signals.

car•ri•on (kăr′ē-ən) *n.* Dead, rotting flesh.

car•rot (kăr′ət) *n.* The yellow-orange, edible root of a widely cultivated plant, *Daucus carota sativa.*

car•rou•sel (kăr′ə-sĕl′, -zĕl′) *n. var. of* CAROUSEL.

car•ry (kăr′ē) *v.* **-ried, -ry•ing. 1.** To convey : transport <*carry* books><*carry* passengers> **2.** To win over the interest of. **3.** To seize : capture. **4.** To have or keep on one's person. **5.** To involve : imply <The crime *carries* a heavy penalty.> **6.** To behave or conduct (oneself) in a given way. **7.** To sustain : support <Your paycheck *carries* the family.> **8.** To keep in stock : sell. **9.** To cover a range : reach. **10.** To gain support or acceptance for, esp. to secure the adoption of <*carry* a bill> **11.** To win most of the votes of <*carried* the South> **12.** To keep in one's accounts as a debtor. **13.** To place before the public through a mass medium. —**carry away.** To arouse great emotion or enthusiasm in. —**carry on. 1.** To engage in : conduct. **2.** To continue <*carried on* despite difficulties> **3.** To act in an excited, inappropriate, or childish way. —*n., pl.* **-ries. 1.** A portage, as between 2 navigable bodies of water. **2.** The range of a projectile or gun.

car·ry·all (kăr′ē-ôl′) *n.* A large tote bag or pocketbook.

carrying charge *n.* The interest charge on an installment loan.

car·ry-on (kăr′ē-ŏn′) *n.* A piece of luggage compact enough to be carried aboard an airplane.

car·ry·out (kăr′ē-out′) *adj.* Take-out <*carryout* food> —**car′ry·out′** *n.*

car·sick (kär′sĭk′) *adj.* Nauseated from vehicular motion. —**car′sick′ness** *n.*

cart (kärt) *n.* **1.** A 2-wheeled vehicle drawn by an animal. **2.** A small, light vehicle moved by hand <a tea *cart*> —*v.* **1. a.** To transport in a cart. **b.** To lug. **2.** To remove or transport by or as if by force. —**cart′a·ble** *adj.* —**cart′er** *n.*

cart·age (kär′tĭj) *n.* **1.** The act of transporting by cart. **2.** The cost of transporting by cart.

carte blanche (kärt′ blänsh′, blänch′) *n.* Unlimited authority.

car·tel (kär-tĕl′) *n.* An association of independent businesses organized to control prices, production, etc.

car·ti·lage (kär′tl-ĭj) *n.* A tough elastic connective tissue attached to the surfaces of bones near the joints. —**car′ti·lag′i·nous** (-ăj′ə-nəs) *adj.*

car·tog·ra·phy (kär-tŏg′rə-fē) *n.* The art of making maps. —**car·tog′ra·pher** *n.* —**car′to·graph′ic** (-tə-grăf′ĭk), **car′to·graph′i·cal** *adj.*

car·ton (kär′tn) *n.* A container, esp. one made of cardboard.

car·toon (kär-to͞on′) *n.* **1.** A pictorial satire of a current event, often accompanied by a caption : caricature. **2.** A comic strip. **3.** An animated cartoon. **4.** A preliminary full-scale sketch, as for a fresco. —**car·toon′** *v.* —**car·toon′ist** *n.*

car·tridge (kär′trĭj) *n.* **1.** A tubular metal or metal and cardboard case that contains the primer, powder, and bullet or shot pellets of small arms ammunition or shotgun shells. **2.** A removable unit of equipment, as a cassette, designed to fit into a larger piece of equipment.

cart·wheel (kärt′hwēl′, -wēl′) *n.* A sideways handspring with the arms and legs spread like the spokes of a wheel.

carve (kärv) *v.* **carved, carv·ing. 1.** To slice into pieces. **2.** To disjoint, slice, and serve poultry or meat. **3.** To make or form by or as if by cutting. —**carv′er** *n.*

carv·ing (kär′vĭng) *n.* **1.** The cutting of wood, stone, etc., to form a figure or design. **2.** A figure or design formed by carving.

car wash *n.* A place equipped for washing cars.

car·y·at·id (kăr′ē-ăt′ĭd) *n., pl.* **-ids** *or* **-at·i·des** (-ăt′ĭ-dēz′). A supporting column sculptured into a woman's figure.

ca·sa·ba (kə-sä′bə) *n.* A winter melon having a yellow rind and sweet flesh.

cas·cade (kă-skād′) *n.* **1.** A waterfall over steep rocks. **2.** Something resembling a cascade <a *cascade* of ruffles> —*v.* **-cad·ed, -cad·ing.** To drop in or as if in a cascade.

case[1] (kās) *n.* **1.** An instance of the existence or occurrence of something : example. **2. a.** An occurrence of injury or disease. **b.** A client, as of an attorney or physician. **3.** Circumstances : situation. **4.** A set of arguments, reasons, or supporting facts offered in justification. **5.** A question or problem. **6.** *Law.* **a.** An action or suit. **b.** Grounds for an action. **7.** The syntactic relationship of a noun, pronoun, or adjective to the other words of a sentence, indicated in inflected languages by declensional endings and in noninflected languages by position. —*v.* **cased, cas·ing.** *Slang.* To examine with care before acting <*cased* the bank before robbing it>

case[2] (kās) *n.* **1.** A container. **2.** A protective covering. **3.** A set or pair, as of pistols. **4.** The frame or framework of a door or window. **5.** A shallow tray for storing printing type. —*v.* **cased, cas·ing.** To cover or protect with a case.

ca·sein (kā′sēn′, -sē-ĭn) *n.* A milk and cheese protein used in foods and in manufacturing plastics and adhesives.

case·ment (kās′mənt) *n.* **1.** A window sash opening outward by hinges. **2.** A window with casements.

case·work (kās′wûrk′) *n.* Social work treating the problems of a specific case.

cash (kăsh) *n.* **1.** Money in the form of currency. **2.** Payment in money or by check for goods or services. —*v.* To convert into money <*cash* a check>

cash·ew (kăsh′o͞o, kə-sho͞o′) *n.* A tropical American tree, *Anacardium occidentale,* bearing edible kidney-shaped nuts.

cash·ier[1] (kă-shîr′) *n.* **1.** The officer of a business concern or bank in charge of distributing and receiving money. **2.** An employee who handles cash transactions, as in a supermarket.

ca·shier[2] (kă-shîr′) *v.* To dismiss from a position of command or responsibility.

cash·mere (kăzh′mîr′, kăsh′-) *n.* **1.** Fine wool from the Cashmere goat. **2.** A soft fabric made from cashmere.

Cashmere goat *n.* A goat native to the Himalayan regions of India and Tibet and greatly valued for its wool.

cash register *n.* A machine that tabulates and records sales transactions.

cas·ing (kā′sĭng) *n.* An outer cover : case <a shell *casing*>

ca·si·no (kə-sē′nō) *n., pl.* **-nos.** A public room or house, esp. for gambling.

cask (kăsk) *n.* **1.** A barrel. **2.** The quantity a cask will hold.

cas·ket (kăs′kĭt) *n.* **1.** A small chest or case. **2.** A coffin.

casque (kăsk) *n.* A helmet.

cas·sa·va (kə-sä′və) *n.* A tropical American plant of the genus *Manihot,* with a starchy root used as a staple food and the source of tapioca.

cas·se·role (kăs′ə-rōl′) *n.* **1.** A dish in which food is both cooked and served. **2.** Food prepared and served in a casserole.

cas•sette (kə-sĕt′, kă-) *n.* A cartridge for magnetic tape or photographic film.

cas•sia (kăsh′ə) *n.* **1.** Any of various chiefly tropical trees, shrubs, and plants of the genus *Cassia,* with long pods, usu. yellow flowers, and leaves that yield senna. **2.** A tropical Asian tree, *Cinnamomum cassia,* with cinnamonlike bark used as a spice.

cas•sock (kăs′ək) *n.* A long garment worn by members of the clergy.

cast (kăst) *v.* **cast, cast•ing. 1.** To throw forcefully **:** fling. **2.** To shed <a snake *casting* its skin> **3.** To turn or direct, as a glance. **4.** To deposit (a ballot). **5. a.** To give a certain role to. **b.** To choose theatrical performers for. **6.** To form by pouring into a mold. **7.** To compute. —*n.* **1.** The act of casting **:** throw. **2.** A throw of dice. **3.** The performers in a theatrical presentation. **4.** A rigid dressing usu. made of gauze and plaster of Paris, as for a broken bone. **5.** An impression formed in a mold. **6.** A slight trace of color. **7.** Outward form or look. **8.** Something shed, as a snake's skin.

cas•ta•nets (kăs′tə-nĕts′) *pl.n.* A rhythm instrument composed of a pair of ivory or hardwood shells held in the palm of the hand and clapped together with the fingers.

cast•a•way (kăst′ə-wā′) *adj.* **1.** Shipwrecked. **2.** Discarded. —**cast′a•way′** *n.*

caste (kăst) *n.* **1.** One of the 4 major hereditary classes of Hindu society. **2. a.** A social class separated from the others by hereditary, professional, or financial differences. **b.** Social status based on caste.

cas•tel•lat•ed (kăs′tə-lā′tĭd) *adj.* Having turrets and battlements.

cast•er *also* **cas•tor** (kăs′tər) *n.* **1.** A small wheel usu. on a swivel fastened to the underside of an object to facilitate moving. **2.** A bottle or cruet for condiments.

cas•ti•gate (kăs′tĭ-gāt′) *v.* **-gat•ed, -gat•ing.** To criticize or punish severely. —**cas′ti•ga′tion** *n.* —**cas′ti•ga′tor** *n.*

cast•ing (kăs′tĭng) *n.* **1.** Something cast out or off. **2.** Something that has been cast in a mold.

cast iron *n.* A hard, brittle nonmalleable alloy of carbon, iron, and silicon.

cas•tle (kăs′əl) *n.* **1.** A fort or fortified cluster of buildings. **2.** A building similar to a castle. **3.** A rook in the game of chess.

cast-off (kăst′ôf′, -ŏf′) *adj.* Discarded **:** rejected.

cas•tor (kăs′tər) *n. var. of* CASTER.

castor oil *n.* An oil obtained from the seeds of a tropical plant, used as a lubricant and a cathartic.

cas•trate (kăs′trāt′) *v.* **-trat•ed, -trat•ing. 1.** To remove the testicles of **:** geld. **2.** To spay. —**cas•tra′tion** *n.*

ca•stra•to (kă-strä′tō, kə-) *n., pl.* **-ti** (-tē) *or* **-tos.** A male singer castrated before puberty so as to retain a high voice.

ca•su•al (kăzh′o͞o-əl) *adj.* **1.** Occurring by chance. **2.** Nonchalant. **3. a.** Informal. **b.** Suitable for informal use or wear. **4.** Not serious or thorough **:** superficial. —**ca′su•al•ly** *adv.* —**ca′su•al•ness** *n.*

ca•su•al•ty (kăzh′o͞o-əl-tē) *n., pl.* **-ties. 1.** A calamitous accident. **2.** One who is injured or killed in an accident. **3.** One injured, killed, missing in action, or taken prisoner by an enemy.

ca•su•ist•ry (kăzh′o͞o-ĭ-strē) *n.* Subtle but misleading reasoning, esp. about moral principles. —**ca′su•ist** *n.* —**ca′su•is′tic** *adj.* —**ca′su•is′ti•cal•ly** *adv.*

cat (kăt) *n.* **1. a.** A carnivorous mammal, *Felis catus* or *F. domesticus,* domesticated as a rat catcher and pet. **b.** Any other animal of the family Felidae, including the lion, tiger, leopard, or lynx. **2.** *Slang.* A spiteful woman. **3.** *Slang.* A person, esp. a man.

CAT (kăt) *n.* Computerized axial tomography.

ca•tab•o•lism (kə-tăb′ə-lĭz′əm) *n.* Metabolism of complex molecules into simple molecules. —**cat′a•bol′ic** (kăt′ə-bŏl′ĭk) *adj.* —**ca•tab′o•lize′** *v.*

cat•a•clysm (kăt′ə-klĭz′əm) *n.* A sudden and violent upheaval or disaster. —**cat′a•clys′mic, cat′a•clys′mal** *adj.*

cat•a•combs (kăt′ə-kōmz′) *pl.n.* A series of underground passages with recesses for coffins and graves.

cat•a•falque (kăt′ə-fălk′, -fôlk′) *n.* The raised structure on which a coffin stands during a solemn, state funeral.

cat•a•lep•sy (kăt′l-ĕp′sē) *n.* Muscular rigidity and lack of response to stimuli, associated with epilepsy and schizophrenia. —**cat′a•lep′tic** *adj.*

cat•a•logue *also* **cat•a•log** (kăt′l-ôg′, -ŏg′) *n.* **1. a.** A systemized, usu. descriptive list. **b.** A publication containing such a list <a mail-order *catalogue*> **2.** A card catalog. —*v.* **-logued, -logu•ing** *also* **-loged, -log•ing.** To make a catalogue of. —**cat′a•logu′er, cat′a•log′er** *n.*

ca•tal•pa (kə-tăl′pə, -tôl′-) *n.* A chiefly North American tree of the genus *Catalpa,* with large leaves, whitish flower clusters, and long thin pods.

cat•a•lyst (kăt′l-ĭst) *n.* **1.** *Chem.* A substance that alters and esp. increases the rate at which a chemical reaction takes place. **2.** One that precipitates a process or event. —**ca•tal′y•sis** (kə-tăl′ĭ-sĭs) *n.* —**cat′a•lyt′ic** *adj.* —**cat′a•lyt′i•cal•ly** *adv.*

cat•a•lyze (kăt′l-īz′) *v.* **-lyzed, -lyz•ing.** *Chem.* To act as a catalyst in or for. —**cat′a•lyz′er** *n.*

cat•a•ma•ran (kăt′ə-mə-răn′) *n.* A sailboat with 2 parallel hulls.

cat•a•pult (kăt′ə-pŭlt′, -po͝olt′) *n.* **1.** An ancient military device for hurling stones, spears, or other missiles. **2.** A mechanism for launching aircraft from a ship's deck. —**cat′a•pult′** *v.*

cat•a•ract (kăt′ə-răkt′) *n.* **1.** A huge downpour or waterfall. **2.** *Pathol.* Opacity of the lens or capsule of the eye, causing total or partial blindness.

ca·tarrh (kə-tär′) *n.* Mucous-membrane inflammation, esp. of the nose and throat. —**ca·tarrh′al** *adj.*
ca·tas·tro·phe (kə-tăs′trə-fē) *n.* A sudden and terrible disaster **:** calamity. —**cat′a·stroph′ic** (kăt′ə-strŏf′ĭk) *adj.* —**cat′a·stroph′i·cal·ly** *adv.*
cat·a·to·ni·a (kăt′ə-tō′nē-ə) *n.* A schizophrenic disorder marked by stupor, mania, and either rigidity or extreme flexibility of the limbs. —**cat′a·ton′ic** (-tŏn′ĭk) *adj. & n.*
cat·bird (kăt′bûrd′) *n.* A North American songbird, *Dumetalla carolinensis,* with chiefly slate-gray plumage.
catbird seat *n.* A powerful position.
cat·call (kăt′kôl′) *n.* A call or whistle of derision or disapproval. —**cat′call′** *v.*
catch (kăch, kĕch) *v.* **caught** (kôt), **catch·ing. 1.** To seize or capture, esp. after a chase. **2.** To trap or snare. **3.** To take by surprise <*caught* me unaware> **4. a.** To overtake. **b.** To reach in time to board <*caught* the train> **5.** To grasp. **6.** To snatch. **7.** To intercept. **8.** To become entangled. **9.** To fasten. **10.** To take fire **:** kindle. **11.** To become infected by **:** contract. **12.** *Informal.* To see <*caught* the singer's act> ★ ***syns:*** CLUTCH, GRAB, NAB, SEIZE, SNATCH —**catch on.** *Informal.* **1.** To understand. **2.** To become popular. —*n.* **1.** The act of catching. **2.** A fastening or stopping device. **3.** Something caught <a *catch* of fish> **4.** *Informal.* One worth catching. **5.** *Informal.* A tricky or unsuspected condition **:** pitfall. **6.** A game of throwing and catching a ball.
catch·all (kăch′ôl′, kĕch′-) *n.* A container for odds and ends.
catch·er (kăch′ər, kĕch′-) *n.* One that catches, esp. the baseball player whose position is behind home plate.
catch·ing (kăch′ĭng, kĕch′-) *adj.* **1.** Contagious. **2.** Alluring.
Catch-22 (kăch′twĕn-tē-to͞o′, kĕch′-) *n.* A paradox in which seeming alternatives actually cancel each other out, leaving no means of escape from a dilemma.
catch·up (kăch′əp, kĕch′-) *n. var. of* KETCHUP.
catch·y (kăch′ē, kĕch′ē) *adj.* **-i·er, -i·est. 1.** Readily recalled <a *catchy* slogan> **2.** Deceptive **:** tricky.
cat·e·chism (kăt′ĭ-kĭz′əm) *n.* A short book summarizing the basic tenets of a religion in the form of questions and answers. —**cat′e·chist** *n.* —**cat′e·chize′** *v.*
cat·e·gor·i·cal (kăt′ĭ-gôr′ĭ-kəl, -gŏr′-) *or* **cat·e·gor·ic** (-ĭk) *adj.* **1.** Absolute **:** certain. **2.** Of, relating to, or included in a category. —**cat′e·gor′i·cal·ly** *adv.*
cat·e·go·rize (kăt′ĭ-gə-rīz′) *v.* **-rized, -riz·ing.** To place in categories **:** classify. —**cat′e·go·ri·za′tion** *n.*
cat·e·go·ry (kăt′ĭ-gôr′ē, -gōr′ē) *n., pl.* **-ries.** A specifically defined division in a classification system **:** class.
ca·ter (kā′tər) *v.* **1.** To provide food or food service. **2.** To provide something needed or desired. —**ca′ter·er** *n.*
cat·er-cor·nered (kăt′ər-kôr′nərd, kăt′ē-) *also* **cat·er-cor·ner** (-nər) *or* **cat·ty-cor·nered** (kăt′ē-kôr′nərd) *adj.* Diagonal. —**cat′er-cor′nered** *adv.*
cat·er·pil·lar (kăt′ər-pĭl′ər, kăt′ə-) *n.* The wormlike, often brightly colored, hairy or spiny larva of a butterfly or moth.
cat·er·waul (kăt′ər-wôl′) *v.* To make a harsh cry or shriek. —**cat′er·waul′** *n.*
cat·fish (kăt′fĭsh′) *n.* Any of numerous scaleless, chiefly freshwater fishes of the order Siluriformes, with whiskerlike barbels near the mouth.
cat·gut (kăt′gŭt′) *n.* A tough thin cord or thread made from the dried intestines of certain animals, as sheep.
ca·thar·sis (kə-thär′sĭs) *n., pl.* **-ses** (-sēz′). **1.** Purgation, esp. of the bowels. **2.** Emotional or psychological cleansing.
ca·thar·tic (kə-thär′tĭk) *adj.* Purgative. —*n.* A cathartic agent, as a laxative.
ca·the·dral (kə-thē′drəl) *n.* A large or important church, esp. the main church of a bishop's see.
cath·e·ter (kăth′ĭ-tər) *n.* A slender, flexible tube inserted into a bodily duct, as a vein, to expand or maintain an opening. —**cath′e·ter·ize′** *v.*
cath·ode (kăth′ōd′) *n.* **1.** A negatively charged electrode, as of an electron tube. **2.** The positively charged terminal of a primary cell or of a storage battery supplying current. —**ca·thod′ic** (kă-thŏd′ĭk) *adj.*
cath·o·lic (kăth′ə-lĭk, kăth′lĭk) *adj.* **1.** Universal **:** general <*catholic* appeal> **2. Catholic.** Of the Roman Catholic Church. —*n.* **Catholic.** A member of a Catholic church, esp. a Roman Catholic. —**ca·thol′i·cal·ly** (kə-thŏl′ĭ-klē) *adv.*
Ca·thol·i·cism (kə-*th*ŏl′ə-sĭz′əm) *n.* The faith, doctrine, practice, and organization of the Roman Catholic Church.
cat·i·on (kăt′ī′ən) *n.* A positively charged ion that in electrolytes is attracted to a negative electrode. —**cat′i·on′ic** *adj.*
cat·kin (kăt′kĭn′) *n.* A dense cluster of scalelike flowers, as of a birch.
cat·like (căt′līk′) *adj.* Stealthy.
cat·nap (kăt′năp′) *n.* A short nap.
cat·nip (kăt′nĭp′) *n.* A hairy aromatic plant, *Nepeta cataria,* that attracts cats.
cat-o′-nine-tails (kăt′ə-nīn′tālz′) *n.* A whip having 9 knotted cords fastened to a handle.
CAT scan *n.* A cross-sectional picture produced by a CAT scanner.
CAT scanner *n.* A device that produces cross-sectional x-rays of the body using computerized axial tomography.
cat's cradle *n.* A game in which a looped string is transferred from the hands of one player to the next.
cat's-eye (kăts′ī′) *n.* Any of various semiprecious iridescent gems.
cat's-paw *also* **cats·paw** (kăts′pô′) *n.* One used by another as a dupe.
cat·sup (kăt′səp, kăch′əp, kĕch′-) *n. var. of* KETCHUP.

cat·tail (kăt'tāl') *n.* A marsh plant of the genus *Typha,* esp. *T. latifolia,* with long straplike leaves and a dense cylindrical head of minute brown flowers.
cat·tle (kăt'l) *pl.n.* Animals of the genus *Bos,* esp. those of the species *B. taurus,* raised for dairy products and meat.
cat·ty (kăt'ē) *adj.* **-ti·er, -ti·est.** Subtly spiteful or malicious. —**cat'ti·ly** *adv.* —**cat'ti·ness** *n.*
cat·ty-cor·nered (kăt'ē-kôr'nərd) *adj. & adv. var. of* CATER-CORNERED.
cat·walk (kăt'wôk') *n.* A narrow elevated pathway, as on the sides of a bridge.
Cau·ca·sian (kô-kā'zhən, -kăzh'ən) *adj.* Of or being a proposed human racial classification distinguished by light to brown skin color and including peoples indigenous to Europe, N Africa, W Asia, and India. —*n.* **1.** A native or inhabitant of the Caucasus. **2.** A member of the Caucasian racial classification. —**Cau·ca'sian** *adj.*
Cau·ca·soid (kô'kə-soid') *adj.* Of or relating to the Caucasian racial classification. —**Cau'ca·soid'** *n.*
cau·cus (kô'kəs) *n., pl.* **-cus·es** *or* **-cus·ses.** A meeting of the members of a political party to make policy decisions and select candidates. —**cau'cus** *v.*
cau·dal (kôd'l) *adj.* Of or near the tail : posterior. —**cau'dal·ly** *adv.*
caught (kôt) *v. p.t. & p.p. of* CATCH.
caul·dron (kôl'drən) *n. var. of* CALDRON.
cau·li·flow·er (kô'lĭ-flou'ər, kŏl'ĭ-) *n.* A plant, *Brassica oleracea botrytis,* related to the cabbage and broccoli, with an enlarged edible flower head.
caulk *also* **calk** (kôk) *v.* **1.** To pack the seams of (a boat) with oakum or tar to make it watertight. **2.** To seal (pipes) against leakage. —**caulk'er** *n.*
caus·al (kô'zəl) *adj.* **1.** Relating to or being a cause. **2.** Expressing a cause. —**cau·sal'i·ty** (-zăl'ĭ-tē) *n.* —**caus'al·ly** *adv.*
cau·sa·tion (kô-zā'shən) *n.* **1.** The act or process of causing. **2.** Something that effects a cause.
cause (kôz) *n.* **1.** One that produces an effect, result, or consequence. **2.** A motive. **3.** A reason. **4.** A principle or goal. **5.** *Law.* **a.** Grounds for legal action. **b.** A lawsuit. —*v.* **caused, caus·ing.** To be the cause of : bring about. —**caus'er** *n.*
cause cé·lè·bre (kōz' sā-lĕb'rə) *n., pl.* **causes cé·lè·bres** (kōz' sā-lĕb'rə). **1.** A legal case that attracts much attention. **2.** A controversial issue.
cau·se·rie (kōz-rē') *n.* **1.** A chat. **2.** A short, informal piece of writing.
cause·way (kôz'wā') *n.* A raised roadway, as across water.
caus·tic (kô'stĭk) *adj.* **1.** Capable of corroding, burning, or dissolving. **2.** Sharp : sarcastic. —*n.* A caustic substance or material. —**caus'ti·cal·ly** *adv.*
cau·ter·ize (kô'tə-rīz') *v.* **-ized, -iz·ing.** To burn or sear with a cautery. —**cau'ter·i·za'tion** *n.*
cau·ter·y (kô'tə-rē) *n., pl.* **-ies.** A caustic agent or a very hot or cold instrument used to destroy aberrant tissue.
cau·tion (kô'shən) *n.* **1.** Careful forethought. **2.** An admonishment : warning. **3.** *Informal.* One that astonishes. ★ *syns:* CALCULATION, CAREFULNESS, CIRCUMSPECTION, PRECAUTION, WARINESS —*v.* To warn against danger. —**cau'tion·ar'y** *adj.*
cau·tious (kô'shəs) *adj.* Careful : wary.
cav·al·cade (kăv'əl-kād', kăv'əl-kād') *n.* **1.** A procession, esp. of riders or horse-drawn carriages. **2.** A colorful display.
cav·a·lier (kăv'ə-lîr') *n.* **1.** A knight. **2.** A gallant gentleman. **3. Cavalier.** One who supported Charles I of England. —*adj.* **1.** Haughty. **2.** Nonchalant : carefree. —**cav'a·lier'ly** *adv.*
cav·al·ry (kăv'əl-rē) *n., pl.* **-ries.** Troops that fight on horseback or in armored vehicles. —**cav'al·ry·man** *n.*
cave (kāv) *n.* An underground hollow with an opening at the surface. —*v.* **caved, cav·ing.** To hollow out. —**cave in. 1.** To fall in : collapse. **2.** *Informal.* To yield.
ca·ve·at (kā'vē-ăt', kăv'ē-, kä'vē-ät') *n.* A warning or caution.
cave-in (kāv'ĭn') *n.* **1.** An act of caving in. **2.** A place where the ground has caved in.
cave man *n.* **1.** A prehistoric human who lived in caves. **2.** *Informal.* A man who is crude or brutal, esp. toward women.
cav·ern (kăv'ərn) *n.* A large cave. —**cav'ern·ous** *adj.*
cav·i·ar *also* **cav·i·are** (kăv'ē-är') *n.* The roe of a large fish, as a sturgeon, salted and eaten as an appetizer.
cav·il (kăv'əl) *v.* **-iled, -il·ing** *or* **-illed, -il·ling.** To find fault unnecessarily : quibble. —**cav'il** *n.* —**cav'il·er** *n.*
cav·i·ty (kăv'ĭ-tē) *n., pl.* **-ties. 1.** A hole or hollow. **2.** A pitted area in a tooth caused by decay.
ca·vort (kə-vôrt') *v.* To prance about.
caw (kô) *n.* The hoarse, raucous cry of a crow or similar bird. —**caw** *v.*
cay (kē, kā) *n.* An islet of sand or coral.
cayenne pepper *n.* A pungent condiment made from the fruit of a pepper plant, *Capsicum frutescens.*
cay·man (kā'mən, kā-măn', kī-măn') *n. var. of* CAIMAN.
†**cay·use** (kī-yōōs', kī'yōōs') *n. W U.S.* A horse, esp. an Indian pony.
Cb *symbol for* COLUMBIUM.
CB (sē'bē') *n.* Citizens band. —**CB'er** *n.*
Cd *symbol for* CADMIUM.
CD/ROM (sē'dē'rŏm') *n. Computer Sci.* A compact disc that functions as a read-only memory.
Ce *symbol for* CERIUM.
cease (sēs) *v.* **ceased, ceas·ing.** To put or come to an end : stop. —**cease** *n.*
cease-fire (sēs'fīr') *n.* Suspension of hostilities : truce.

cease•less (sēs′lĭs) *adj.* Continual : endless. **—cease′less•ly** *adv.*

ce•cum *also* **cae•cum** (sē′kəm) *n., pl.* **-ca** (-kə). *Anat.* The blind pouch that forms the start of the large intestine. **—ce′cal** (-kəl) *adj.*

ce•dar (sē′dər) *n.* A coniferous evergreen tree of the genus *Cedrus,* with aromatic, often reddish wood.

cede (sēd) *v.* **ced•ed, ced•ing. 1.** To yield or grant, as by treaty. **2.** To transfer or assign, as a title.

ce•di (sā′dē) *n., pl.* **-di** *or* **-dis.** —See table at CURRENCY.

ce•dil•la (sĭ-dĭl′ə) *n.* A mark placed beneath the letter *c,* as in the French word *garçon,* to indicate that the *c* is to be pronounced (s).

ceil•ing (sē′lĭng) *n.* **1.** The upper surface of a room. **2.** A vertical boundary, esp. of atmospheric visibility or operable aircraft altitude. **3.** A maximum limit, esp. as prescribed by law <wage and price *ceilings*>

cel•e•brate (sĕl′ə-brāt′) *v.* **-brat•ed, -brat•ing. 1.** To observe (a day or event) with ceremonies of respect, rejoicing, or festivity. **2.** To perform (a religious ceremony) <*celebrate* Mass> **3.** To praise : extol. ★ ***syns:*** COMMEMORATE, KEEP, OBSERVE, SOLEMNIZE **—cel′e•brant** *n.* **—cel′e•bra′tion** *n.* **—cel′e•bra′tor** *n.*

cel•e•brat•ed (sĕl′ə-brā′tĭd) *adj.* Well-known : famous.

ce•leb•ri•ty (sə-lĕb′rĭ-tē) *n., pl.* **-ties. 1.** A famous person. **2.** Fame : renown. ★ ***syns:*** LUMINARY, NAME, NOTABLE, PERSONAGE

ce•ler•i•ty (sə-lĕr′ĭ-tē) *n.* Speed : swiftness.

cel•er•y (sĕl′ə-rē) *n.* A plant, *Apium graveolens dulce,* grown for its edible stalks.

ce•les•ta (sə-lĕs′tə) *also* **ce•leste** (sə-lĕst′) *n.* A musical instrument with a keyboard and metal plates struck by hammers that produce bell-like tones.

ce•les•tial (sə-lĕs′chəl) *adj.* **1.** Of or relating to the sky. **2.** Heavenly : spiritual.

celestial navigation *n.* Navigation based on the positions of celestial bodies.

celestial sphere *n.* An imaginary sphere of infinite extent with the earth at its center.

cel•i•bate (sĕl′ə-bĭt) *n.* **1.** One who remains unmarried, esp. because of religious vows. **2.** One who is sexually abstinent. **—cel′i•ba•cy** (-bə-sē) *n.* **—cel′i•bate** *adj.*

cell (sĕl) *n.* **1.** A small, confining room, as in a monastery or prison. **2.** The primary organizational unit of a movement <a Communist *cell*> **3.** *Biol.* The smallest unit of an organism that is capable of independent functioning, composed of a membrane enclosing nuclei, cytoplasm, and inanimate matter. **4.** A small, enclosed cavity, as a compartment in a honeycomb. **5.** *Elect.* **a.** A single unit for conversion of chemical energy or heat into electricity, usu. composed of a container with electrodes and an electrolyte. **b.** A solar cell. **6.** *Computer Sci.* A basic storage unit in a computer memory.

cel•lar (sĕl′ər) *n.* **1.** A room for storage, usu. below ground or beneath a building. **2.** A stock of wines.

cell•mate (sĕl′māt′) *n.* One with whom a cell is shared, esp. in a prison.

cel•lo (chĕl′ō) *n., pl.* **-los.** A 4-stringed instrument of the violin family, pitched lower than the viola. **—cel′list** *n.*

cel•lo•phane (sĕl′ə-fān′) *n.* A transparent cellulose material made from wood pulp, used as a moistureproof wrapping.

cel•lu•lar (sĕl′yə-lər) *adj.* **1.** Relating to or resembling a cell. **2.** Made up of cells.

cellular telephone *n.* A mobile radiotelephone that uses a network of short-range transmitters in overlapping zones to connect to telephone lines.

cel•lu•lite (sĕl′yə-līt′) *n.* A fatty deposit, as under the skin around the thighs.

cel•lu•loid (sĕl′yə-loid′) *n.* A flammable plastic material made from cellulose and camphor, used to make photographic film.

cel•lu•lose (sĕl′yə-lōs′, -lōz′) *n.* An amorphous polymer that is the chief constituent of plant tissues and fibers, used to make paper, cellophane, textiles, and explosives. **—cel′lu•lo′sic** *adj.*

Cel•si•us (sĕl′sē-əs, -shəs) *adj.* Of or relating to a temperature scale on which the freezing point of water is 0° and the boiling point is 100° under normal atmospheric pressure.

Celt (kĕlt, sĕlt) *n.* **1.** One of an ancient people of W and C Europe, including the Britons and the Gauls. **2.** A speaker of a Celtic language.

Celt•ic (kĕl′tĭk, sĕl′-) *n.* A group of Indo-European languages, including Welsh and Gaelic. *—adj.* Of or relating to the Celts or the Celtic languages.

cem•ba•lo (chĕm′bə-lō′) *n., pl.* **-los.** A harpsichord. **—cem′ba•list** *n.*

ce•ment (sĭ-mĕnt′) *n.* **1.** A construction adhesive of powdered calcined rock and clay materials that form a paste with water and can be molded or poured to set as a solid mass. **2.** A substance that hardens to function as an adhesive : glue. **3.** A binding element. *—v.* **1.** To join or cover with or as if with cement. **2.** To strengthen.

ce•men•tum (sĭ-mĕn′təm) *n.* A bony substance that covers the root of a tooth.

cem•e•ter•y (sĕm′ĭ-tĕr′ē) *n., pl.* **-ies.** A graveyard.

cen•o•taph (sĕn′ə-tăf′) *n.* A monument built in honor of a dead person whose remains are interred elsewhere.

cen•ser (sĕn′sər) *n.* A vessel for incense, used esp. in a religious ceremony.

cen•sor (sĕn′sər) *n.* **1.** One authorized to examine films and printed materials and suppress what is objectionable. **2.** One of 2 Roman officials overseeing the census. *—v.* To subject to a censor's examination. ★ ***syns:*** BAN, STIFLE, SUPPRESS **—cen•so′ri•al** (-sôr′ē-əl, -sōr′-) *adj.*

cen•so•ri•ous (sĕn-sôr′ē-əs, -sōr′-) *adj.* Tending to or marked by censure : critical.

cen•sor•ship (sĕn′sər-shĭp′) *n.* **1.** The act or process of censoring. **2.** The office of a Roman censor.
cen•sure (sĕn′shər) *n.* **1.** An expression of strong disapproval or criticism. **2.** An official rebuke. —*v.* **-sured, -sur•ing.** To express strong disapproval of : criticize. —**cen′sur•a•ble** *adj.* —**cen′sur•er** *n.*
cen•sus (sĕn′səs) *n.* An official and usu. periodic enumeration of population.
cent (sĕnt) *n.* —See table at CURRENCY.
cen•taur (sĕn′tôr′) *n. Gk. Myth.* One of a race of monsters with a man's head, arms, and trunk and a horse's body and legs.
cen•ta•vo (sĕn-tä′vō) *n., pl.* **-vos.** —See table at CURRENCY.
cen•te•nar•i•an (sĕn′tə-nâr′ē-ən) *n.* A person 100 years old or older.
cen•ten•a•ry (sĕn-tĕn′ə-rē, sĕn′tə-nĕr′ē) *n., pl.* **-ries.** A centennial. —**cen•ten′a•ry** *adj.*
cen•ten•ni•al (sĕn-tĕn′ē-əl) *n.* A 100th anniversary or celebration. —**cen•ten′ni•al** *adj.*
cen•ter (sĕn′tər) *n.* **1.** A point equidistant from all points on the outer boundaries of a body or figure : middle. **2.** A point around which something, as an activity, is concentrated : hub. **3.** A place of origin : heart. **4.** A middle part or position. **5.** A group whose political views are midway between liberal and conservative. **6.** A player who occupies a middle position, as in football. ★ ***syns:*** MIDDLE, MIDPOINT, MIDST —*v.* **1.** To place in or around a center. **2.** To gather at a center : concentrate. **3.** To have a center : focus.
cen•ter•board (sĕn′tər-bôrd′, -bōrd′) *n.* A retractable keellike device, as a flat metal plate, used esp. in sailboats.
cen•ter•fold (sĕn′tər-fōld′) *n.* A magazine center spread, esp. an oversize feature that folds out.
cen•ter•piece (sĕn′tər-pēs′) *n.* An ornamental object or arrangement at the center of a table.
cen•tes•i•mal (sĕn-tĕs′ə-məl) *adj.* Relating to or divided into hundredths.
cen•tes•i•mo (sĕn-tĕs′ə-mō′) *n., pl.* **-mos** *or* **-mi** (-mē). —See table at CURRENCY.
cen•ti•grade (sĕn′tĭ-grād′) *adj.* Celsius.
cen•ti•gram (sĕn′tĭ-grăm′) *n.* One-hundredth (1/100) of a gram.
cen•time (sän′tēm′, sĕn′-) *n.* —See table at CURRENCY.
cen•ti•me•ter (sĕn′tə-mē′tər, sän′-) *n.* —See table at MEASUREMENT.
cen•ti•mo (sĕn′tə-mō′) *n., pl.* **-mos.** —See table at CURRENCY.
cen•ti•pede (sĕn′tə-pēd′) *n.* A flat wormlike arthropod of the class Chilopoda with numerous legs and body segments.
cen•tral (sĕn′trəl) *adj.* **1.** At, in, near, or being a center. **2.** Of primary importance : essential. —*n.* **1.** A telephone exchange. **2.** A telephone operator. —**cen′tral•ly** *adv.*
cen•tral•ize (sĕn′trə-līz′) *v.* **-ized, -iz•ing.** To bring to a center or under a single central authority. —**cen′tral•i•za′tion** *n.*
central nervous system *n.* The part of the vertebrate nervous system consisting of the brain and spinal cord.
cen•tre (sĕn′tər) *n. & v. esp. Brit. var. of* CENTER.
cen•trif•u•gal (sĕn-trĭf′yə-gəl, -trĭf′ə-) *adj.* **1.** Directed or moving away from a center or axis. **2.** Operated by centrifugal force.
centrifugal force *n.* The component of force on a body in curvilinear motion that is directed away from the center of curvature or axis of rotation.
cen•tri•fuge (sĕn′trə-fyōōj′) *n.* A compartment spun about a central axis to separate materials of different density or simulate gravity with centrifugal force.
cen•trip•e•tal (sĕn-trĭp′ĭ-tl) *adj.* Directed or moving toward a center or axis.
centripetal force *n.* The component of force acting on a body in curvilinear motion that is directed toward the center of curvature or axis of rotation.
cen•trist (sĕn′trĭst) *n.* One whose political views are in the center : moderate.
cen•tu•ri•on (sĕn-tŏŏr′ē-ən, -tyŏŏr′-) *n.* An ancient Roman army officer commanding a century.
cen•tu•ry (sĕn′chə-rē) *n., pl.* **-ries. 1.** A period of 100 years. **2.** A subdivision of a legion in the ancient Roman army.
century plant *n.* A fleshy plant of the genus *Agave,* some species of which bloom only once in 10 to 20 years and then die.
ce•phal•ic (sə-făl′ĭk) *adj.* Of or pertaining to the head or skull.
ce•ram•ic (sə-răm′ĭk) *n.* **1.** Any of various hard, brittle materials made by firing a nonmetallic mineral, as clay. **2. a.** An object made of ceramic. **b. ceramics** *(sing. in number).* The art or technique of making articles of ceramic. —**ce•ram′ist** *n.*
ce•re•al (sîr′ē-əl) *n.* **1.** An edible grain, as wheat or corn. **2.** A grass producing grain. **3.** A food prepared from grain.
cer•e•bel•lum (sĕr′ə-bĕl′əm) *n., pl.* **-bel•lums** *or* **-bel•la** (-bĕl′ə). The part of the brain that is responsible for the coordination of voluntary muscular movement. —**cer′e•bel′lar** *adj.*
cer•e•bral (sĕr′ə-brəl, sə-rē′-) *adj.* Of or relating to the brain or cerebrum.
cerebral cortex *n.* The extensive outer layer of gray tissue that covers the cerebrum and is largely responsible for higher nervous functions.
cerebral palsy *n.* Impaired muscle control due to brain damage usu. at or prior to birth.
cer•e•brate (sĕr′ə-brāt′) *v.* **-brat•ed, -brat•ing.** To use the power of reason : think. —**cer′e•bra′tion** *n.*
cer•e•brum (sĕr′ə-brəm, sə-rē′-) *n., pl.* **-brums** *or* **-bra** (-brə). The large rounded brain structure that occupies most of the cranial cavity and is divided into 2 cerebral hemispheres.
cere•cloth (sîr′klôth′, -klŏth′) *n.* Cloth, treated usu. with wax, once used for wrapping corpses.

cere•ment (sîr'mənt) *n.* A cerecloth.
cer•e•mo•ni•al (sĕr'ə-mō'nē-əl) *adj.* Of, relating to, or marked by ceremony. —*n.* **1.** A ceremony. **2.** A set of ceremonies : ritual. —**cer'e•mo'ni•al•ly** *adv.*
cer•e•mo•ni•ous (sĕr'ə-mō'nē-əs) *adj.* **1.** Fond of ceremony and forms. 2. Marked by ceremony : formal. 3. Ceremonial. ★ ***syns:*** COURTLY, FORMAL, POLITE, PUNCTILIOUS —**cer'e•mo'ni•ous•ly** *adv.*
cer•e•mo•ny (sĕr'ə-mō'nē) *n., pl.* **-nies. 1.** A formal act or set of acts performed as prescribed by custom, ritual, or etiquette. **2.** A conventionally polite act. **3.** Strict observance of etiquette or formalities.
ce•re•us (sîr'ē-əs) *n.* A tall tropical American cactus, esp. of the genus *Cereus.*
ce•rise (sə-rēs', -rēz') *n.* A deep purplish red.
ce•ri•um (sîr'ē-əm) *n. Symbol* **Ce** A lustrous, iron-gray, malleable metallic element.
cer•tain (sûr'tn) *adj.* **1.** Without any doubt : indisputable. **2.** Definite : settled. **3.** Sure to happen : inevitable. **4.** Not specified but assumed to be known <a *certain* movie actor> **5.** Appreciable but not specified <a *certain* charm> —*pron.* An indefinite number : some. —**cer'tain•ly** *adv.*
cer•tain•ty (sûr'tn-tē) *n., pl.* **-ties. 1.** Freedom from doubt. **2.** Something, as an established fact, that is certain. ★ ***syns:*** CERTITUDE, CONFIDENCE, CONVICTION, SURENESS, SURETY
cer•tif•i•cate (sər-tĭf'ĭ-kĭt) *n.* **1.** A document testifying to accuracy or truth. **2.** A document certifying fulfillment of requirements, as of a course of study. 3. A document certifying ownership.
certificate of deposit *n.* A bank certificate stating the named person has a specified sum of money on deposit.
cer•ti•fi•ca•tion (sûr'tə-fĭ-kā'shən) *n.* **1.** The act of certifying or state of being certified. **2.** A certified statement.
certified check *n.* A check guaranteed by the bank on which it is drawn to be covered by sufficient funds.
certified public accountant *n.* An accountant who has received a certificate stating he or she has met a state's legal requirements to practice.
cer•ti•fy (sûr'tə-fī') *v.* **-fied, -fy•ing. 1.** To confirm formally : verify. **2.** To guarantee on (a check) that there are sufficient funds on deposit for payment. **3.** To declare legally insane. —**cer'ti•fi'a•ble** *adj.* —**cer'ti•fi'a•bly** *adv.* —**cer'ti•fi'er** *n.*
cer•ti•tude (sûr'tĭ-tōōd', -tyōōd') *n.* Complete assurance.
ce•ru•le•an (sə-rōō'lē-ən) *adj.* Azure.
ce•ru•men (sə-rōō'mən) *n.* Earwax.
cer•vi•cal (sûr'vĭ-kəl) *adj.* Of or relating to a neck or cervix.
cer•vine (sûr'vīn') *adj.* Relating to, resembling, or typical of a deer.
cer•vix (sûr'vĭks) *n., pl.* **-vix•es** or **-vi•ces** (-vĭ-sēz', sər-vī'sēz'). **1.** The neck. **2.** A necklike anatomical structure, as the outer end of the uterus.
Ce•sar•e•an *or* **Ce•sar•i•an** (sĭ-zâr'ē-ən) *adj. vars. of* CAESAREAN.
ce•si•um *also* **cae•si•um** (sē'zē-əm) *n. Symbol* **Cs** A soft, silvery-white metallic element used in photoelectric cells.
ces•sa•tion (sĕ-sā'shən) *n.* The act of ceasing : halt.
ces•sion (sĕsh'ən) *n.* The act of ceding, as of territory, to another.
cess•pool (sĕs'pōōl') *n.* A covered hole or underground pit for sewage.
ce•ta•ce•an (sĭ-tā'shən) *adj.* Of or belonging to the order Cetacea, including aquatic, chiefly marine mammals such as the whale and porpoise. —*n.* An aquatic mammal of the order Cetacea.
Cf *symbol for* CALIFORNIUM.
Cha•blis (shă-blē', shä-, shăb'lē) *n.* A very dry white wine.
cha•dor (chä-dôr') *n.* A loose, usu. black robe worn by Muslim women that covers the body and most of the face.
chafe (chāf) *v.* **chafed, chaf•ing. 1.** To make or become sore or worn by rubbing. **2.** To irritate. **3.** To warm by rubbing. ★ ***syns:*** ABRADE, EXCORIATE, FRET, GALL
cha•fer (chā'fər) *n.* A beetle of the family Scarabaeidae, as the cockchafer.
chaff[1] (chăf) *n.* **1.** Grain husks after being separated from the seed in threshing. **2.** Something trivial or worthless.
chaff[2] (chăf) *v.* To tease good-naturedly. —*n.* Light, good-natured teasing.
chaf•fer (chăf'ər) *v.* To haggle : bargain.
chaf•finch (chăf'ĭnch) *n.* A European songbird, *Fringilla coelebs,* with reddish-brown plumage.
chafing dish *n.* A utensil used for cooking food and keeping it warm at the table.
cha•grin (shə-grĭn') *n.* Lack of mental ease caused by disappointment, humiliation, or failure. —*v.* To cause to experience chagrin.
chain (chān) *n.* **1.** A series of links, often of metal, connected together. **2. chains. a.** Fetters : bonds. **b.** Captivity : bondage. **3.** A series of related things. **4. a.** A measuring instrument for surveying, composed of 100 linked pieces of iron or steel. **b.** A unit of length equal to 66 ft or approx. 20 m. —*v.* **1.** To bind, fasten, or make fast with a chain. **2.** To bind or fetter.
chain gang *n.* A gang of prisoners chained together.
chain letter *n.* A letter directing the recipient to send out multiple copies so that its circulation increases in a geometric progression.
chain mail *n.* Flexible armor of joined metal rings.
chain reaction *n.* **1.** A series of events each of which induces or otherwise influences its successor. **2.** A multistage nuclear or chemical reaction, esp. a self-sustaining series of reactions. —**chain'-re•act'** *v.*
chain saw *n.* A power saw with teeth set on an endless chain.

chain-smoke (chān′smōk′) *v.* To smoke esp. cigarettes in continuing succession.

chain store *n.* One of several retail stores under the same ownership.

chair (châr) *n.* **1.** A seat with a back intended for one person. **2. a.** A position or office of authority, as that of a chairman. **b.** One who holds such a position or office, esp. a chairman. **3.** *Slang.* The electric chair. **4.** A sedan chair. —*v.* To preside over (a meeting).

chair lift *n.* A chair assembly suspended from cables used to carry people, as skiers, up or down slopes.

chair•man (châr′mən) *n.* The presiding officer of a meeting, committee, board, or other organization. —**chair′man•ship′** *n.*

chair•per•son (châr′pûr′sən) *n.* A chairman or chairwoman.

chair•wom•an (châr′wŏŏm′ən) *n.* A woman presiding officer of a meeting, committee, or board.

chaise (shāz) *n.* **1.** A 2-wheeled carriage with a collapsible top. **2.** A post chaise.

chaise longue (shāz lông′) *n., pl.* **chaise longues** *or* **chaises longues** (shāz lông′). A chair with a long seat that can support the sitter's legs.

chal•ced•o•ny (kăl-sĕd′n-ē) *n., pl.* **-nies.** A translucent grayish or milky quartz. —**chal′ce•don′ic** (-sĭ-dŏn′ĭk) *adj.*

chal•co•py•rite (kăl′kə-pī′rīt′) *n.* An important copper ore.

cha•let (shă-lā′) *n.* **1.** A building with balconies and a sloping overhanging roof of the sort that is common in Alpine regions. **2.** A herdsman's hut in the Alps.

chal•ice (chăl′ĭs) *n.* **1.** A drinking goblet. **2.** The cup for the Eucharistic wine.

chalk (chôk) *n.* **1.** A soft mineral derived mainly from fossil seashells. **2.** A piece of chalk used esp. for marking a surface. —*v.* To mark, draw, or write with chalk. —**chalk up.** To credit <*chalked* that *up* to experience> —**chalk′y** *adj.*

chalk•board (chôk′bôrd′, -bōrd′) *n.* A blackboard.

chal•lah (KHä′lə) *n.* A yeast-leavened, usu. braided white egg bread traditionally eaten by Jews on the Sabbath and holidays.

chal•lenge (chăl′ənj) *n.* **1.** An invitation to take part in a sports competition. **2.** A demand for an explanation or justification. **3.** A sentry's order to halt and be identified. **4.** *Law.* A formal objection, esp. to the qualifications of a juror or jury. —*v.* **-lenged, -leng•ing. 1.** To invite to take part in a sports competition. **2.** To question the truth of. **3.** To order to halt and be identified. **4.** *Law.* To object formally to (a juror or jury). —**chal′leng•er** *n.*

chal•lis (shăl′ē) *n.* A light, usu. printed clothing material of wool, cotton, or rayon.

cham•ber (chām′bər) *n.* **1.** A room in a house, esp. a bedroom. **2.** *often* **chambers.** A judge's office. **3.** A hall, esp. for meetings of a legislative body. **4.** A legislative, judicial, or deliberative body. **5.** An enclosed space : cavity. **6.** A compartment at the bore of a gun to hold the charge.

chambered nautilus *n.* A mollusk, *Nautilus pompilius,* having a coiled and partitioned shell lined with a pearly layer.

cham•ber•lain (chām′bər-lĭn) *n.* **1.** A treasurer. **2.** A high-ranking official of a royal court.

cham•ber•maid (chām′bər-mād′) *n.* A maid who cleans bedrooms, as in a hotel.

chamber music *n.* Music composed for performance in a small concert hall by a small group of musicians.

chamber of commerce *n.* An association of merchants and businessmen for the promotion of commercial interests in their community.

cham•bray (shăm′brā′) *n.* A lightweight gingham with white threads across a colored warp.

cha•me•leon (kə-mēl′yən) *n.* An Old World lizard of the family Chamaeleonidae that is able to change color.

cham•fer (chăm′fər) *v.* **1.** To make a bevel on. **2.** To cut a groove in : flute. —*n.* A beveled edge or corner.

cham•ois (shăm′ē) *n., pl.* **cham•ois** (shăm′ēz). **1.** A hoofed mammal, *Rupricapra rupricapra,* of mountainous regions of Europe. **2.** *also* **cham•my** *pl.* **-mies.** Soft leather made from the hide of a chamois, deer, or sheep.

cham•o•mile *or* **cam•o•mile** (kăm′ə-mīl′) *n.* A plant of the genus *Anthemis,* esp. *A. nobilis,* with white flowers.

champ[1] (chămp) *also* **chomp** (chŏmp) *v.* To chew on noisily.

champ[2] (chămp) *n.* A champion.

cham•pagne (shăm-pān′) *n.* A sparkling white wine.

cham•pi•gnon (shăm-pĭn′yən) *n.* An edible mushroom, esp. the common species *Agaricus campestris.*

cham•pi•on (chăm′pē-ən) *n.* **1.** A holder of first place or winner of first prize in a contest. **2.** One who fights for a cause or defends another person. —*v.* To fight for or defend as a champion.

cham•pi•on•ship (chăm′pē-ən-shĭp′) *n.* **1. a.** The title or position of a champion. **b.** A competition or series of competitions held to determine a winner. **2.** Defense or support : advocacy.

chance (chăns) *n.* **1. a.** The unexpected or random element of existence. **b.** This element regarded as a cause of events : luck. **2.** The likelihood of an occurrence : probability. **3.** An opportunity. **4.** A risk : gamble. **5.** A raffle or lottery ticket. **6.** Something that happens unexpectedly or fortuitously. —*v.* **chanced, chanc•ing. 1.** To occur by chance. **2.** To take the risk of. —**chance on** (*or* **upon**). To come upon unexpectedly.

chan•cel (chăn′səl) *n.* The part of a church that includes the choir and altar.

chan•cel•ler•y (chăn′sə-lə-rē, -slə-rē) *n., pl.* **-ies. 1.** The position or rank of a chancellor.

2. The staff or office of an embassy or consulate.

chan•cel•lor (chăn′sə-lər, -slər) *n.* **1.** The chief minister of state in certain European countries. **2.** The president of some U.S. universities. **3.** The presiding judge of a court of chancery or equity in certain states of the U.S. **—chan′cel•lor•ship′** *n.*

chan•cer•y (chăn′sə-rē) *n., pl.* **-ies. 1.** A court with jurisdiction in equity. **2.** An office for the collection and safekeeping of official records. **3.** The office of an embassy or consulate.

chan•cre (shăng′kər) *n.* A dull-red, hard, insensitive lesion that is the first manifestation of syphilis.

chan•croid (shăng′kroid′) *n.* A soft, nonsyphilitic, usu. venereal lesion of the genital region.

chanc•y (chăn′sē) *adj.* **-i•er, -i•est.** Hazardous : risky.

chan•de•lier (shăn′də-lîr′) *n.* A branched light fixture suspended from a ceiling.

chan•dler (chănd′lər) *n.* **1.** A maker or seller of candles. **2.** A dealer in specified supplies and equipment <a ship *chandler*> **—chan′dler•y** *n.*

change (chānj) *v.* **changed, chang•ing. 1.** To make or become different : alter. **2.** To take, put, or use in place of another : exchange. **3.** To replace by another. **4.** To give or receive the equivalent of (money) in smaller denominations or foreign currency. **5.** To put fresh coverings or clothes on <*changed* the bed> ★ ***syns:*** ALTER, MODIFY, MUTATE, TRANSFORM, TURN, VARY —*n.* **1.** The act or result of changing. **2.** Money of lower denominations exchanged for money of higher denominations. **3.** Coins. **4.** A fresh set of clothing. **5.** *Mus.* A pattern in which bells are rung. **—change′a•ble** *adj.* **—change′a•bly** *adv.* **—change′less** *adj.* **—chang′er** *n.*

change•ling (chānj′lĭng) *n.* An infant secretly exchanged for another.

change of life *n.* Menopause.

change•o•ver (chānj′ō′vər) *n.* A conversion from one thing to another.

chan•nel (chăn′əl) *n.* **1.** A streambed. **2.** The deeper navigable part of a river or harbor. **3.** A broad strait. **4.** A passage, as for liquids : duct. **5.** A means of passing, transmitting, or communicating. **6.** *Electron.* A band of frequencies for the transmission and reception of electromagnetic signals, as for television. **7.** A trench or groove. —*v.* **-neled, -nel•ing** *also* **-nelled, -nel•ling. 1.** To form a channel in or through. **2.** To direct or guide along a course. **—chan′nel•i•za′tion** *n.* **—chan′nel•ize′** *v.*

chan•son (shäN-sôN′) *n.* A song, esp. one sung in a cabaret.

chant (chănt) *n.* **1.** A melody, esp. a liturgical melody, in which a number of words or syllables are sung on the same note. **2.** A monotonous rhythmic shout or call. —*v.* **1.** To sing a chant. **2.** To speak or sing in the manner of a chant. **3.** To praise in song.

chan•te•relle (shăn′tə-rĕl′, shän′-) *n.* An edible yellow mushroom, *Cantharellus cibarius,* with a pleasant fruity odor.

chan•teuse (shäN-tœz′) *n.* A woman cabaret singer.

chan•tey (shăn′tē, chăn′-) *n., pl.* **-teys.** A song that is sung by sailors to the rhythm of their work movements.

chan•ti•cleer (chăn′tĭ-klîr′, shăn′-) *n.* A rooster.

chan•try (chăn′trē) *n., pl.* **-tries. 1.** An endowment to cover expenses for the saying of masses and prayers. **2.** A chapel endowed for the saying of masses and prayers.

Cha•nu•kah *or* **Ha•nuk•kah** (KHä′nə-kə, hä′-) *n.* An 8-day Jewish festival commemorating the rededication of the Temple in Jerusalem.

cha•os (kā′ŏs′) *n.* **1.** Total disorder. **2.** *often* **Chaos.** The disordered state existing before the creation of the ordered universe. **—cha•ot′ic** *adj.* **—cha•ot′i•cal•ly** *adv.*

chap[1] (chăp) *v.* **chapped, chap•ping.** To dry and split open, esp. from cold and wind.

chap[2] (chăp) *n. Informal.* A man : fellow.

†cha•pa•re•jos *also* **cha•pa•ra•jos** (shăp′ə-rā′ŏs) *pl.n. SW U.S.* Chaps.

chap•ar•ral (shăp′ə-răl′) *n.* A dense growth of tangled, often thorny shrubs.

chap•book (chăp′bo͝ok′) *n.* A small book containing poems, ballads, stories, or religious tracts.

cha•peau (shă-pō′) *n., pl.* **-peaux** *or* **-peaus** (-pōz′). A hat.

chap•el (chăp′əl) *n.* **1.** A place of worship subordinate to a church, as in a college or hospital. **2.** Religious services held at a chapel. **3.** A place of worship for those not affiliated with an established church.

chap•er•on *also* **chap•er•one** (shăp′ə-rōn′) *n.* An older person, esp. a woman, who supervises young unmarried people. —*v.* **-oned, -on•ing.** To act as a chaperon to or for. **—chap′er•on′age** *n.*

chap•fall•en (chăp′fô′lən, chŏp′-) *adj.* In low spirits : depressed.

chap•lain (chăp′lən) *n.* A member of the clergy attached to a special group, as a military unit. **—chap′lain•cy** *n.*

chap•let (chăp′lĭt) *n.* **1.** A garland for the head. **2.** A string of esp. prayer beads.

chaps (chăps, shăps) *pl.n.* Leather trousers without a seat that are worn over trousers by cowboys.

chap•ter (chăp′tər) *n.* **1.** A division of a book or other writing. **2.** A branch of a group, as a fraternity or religious order.

char[1] (chär) *v.* **charred, char•ring. 1.** To burn partially. **2.** To reduce or be reduced to charcoal by incomplete combustion.

char[2] (chär) *n., pl.* **char** *or* **chars.** A fish of the genus *Salvelinus,* related to the trout.

char[3] (chär) *n.* A charwoman. —*v.* **charred, char•ring.** To work as a charwoman.

char•ac•ter (kăr′ĭk-tər) *n.* **1.** A distinguishing feature : characteristic. **2.** The group of ethical and mental characteristics that mark a person or group. **3.** Moral integrity. **4.** Reputation. **5.** *Informal.* An eccentric person. **6.** A person portrayed in a play or novel. **7.** A symbol, as a letter, in a writing system. ★ ***syns:*** COMPLEXION, DISPOSITION, MAKE-UP, NATURE

char•ac•ter•is•tic (kăr′ĭk-tə-rĭs′tĭk) *adj.* Serving to indicate distinctive character : typical. ★ ***syns:*** DISTINCTIVE, INDIVIDUAL, PECULIAR, TYPICAL, VINTAGE —*n.* A distinguishing feature or attribute. —**char′ac•ter•is′ti•cal•ly** *adv.*

char•ac•ter•ize (kăr′ĭk-tə-rīz′) *v.* **-ized, -iz•ing. 1.** To describe the character or characteristics of. **2.** To be a characteristic of. —**char′ac•ter•i•za′tion** *n.*

cha•rade (shə-rād′) *n.* **1. charades** *(sing. or pl. in number).* A game in which the syllables of words to be guessed are acted out. **2.** A pretense.

char•broil (chär′broil′) *v.* To broil (meat) over charcoal.

char•coal (chär′kōl′) *n.* **1.** A porous carbonaceous material obtained from the destructive distillation of wood and used as a fuel, filter, and absorbent. **2.** A piece of charcoal used for drawing. **3.** A dark gray.

chard (chärd) *n.* A variety of beet, *Beta vulgaris cicla,* with large, succulent leaves that are eaten as a vegetable.

charge (chärj) *v.* **charged, charg•ing. 1.** To entrust with a duty or responsibility. **2.** To order : command. **3.** To accuse. **4.** To ask as a price. **5.** To purchase on credit. **6.** To record an amount owed against. **7.** To rush (at) in or as if in an attack. **8.** To load fully : fill. **9.** To saturate. **10. a.** To cause formation of a net electric charge on or in (a conductor). **b.** To energize (a storage battery). —*n.* **1.** Responsibility : care. **2.** One entrusted to another's care. **3.** A judge's instructions to a jury. **4.** An accusation, esp. a formal indictment. **5.** Price : cost. **6.** A debit to an account. **7.** An attack. **8.** A burden imposed. **9.** A quantity, as of ammunition, needed to fill something. **10. a.** The intrinsic property of matter responsible for all electric phenomena. **b.** A measure of this property. **11.** *Informal.* A pleasant feeling of excitement : thrill. —**charge′a•ble** *adj.*

charge account *n.* A business arrangement by which a customer receives goods or services and pays for them later.

charge card *n.* A credit card.

char•gé d'af•faires (shär-zhā′ də-fâr′) *n., pl.* **char•gés d'af•faires** (-zhā′, -zhāz′). A diplomat temporarily in charge of an embassy or legation.

charg•er (chär′jər) *n.* **1.** A horse ridden in battle : war-horse. **2.** An instrument that recharges electric batteries.

char•i•ot (chăr′ē-ət) *n.* An ancient horse-drawn 2-wheeled vehicle used for war, races, processions, etc. —**char′i•o•teer′** *n.*

cha•ris•ma (kə-rĭz′mə) *n.* An exceptional ability to secure other people's devotion or loyalty. —**char′is•mat′ic** (kăr′ĭz-măt′ĭk) *adj.*

char•i•ta•ble (chăr′ĭ-tə-bəl) *adj.* **1.** Generous in giving to the needy. **2.** Lenient in judging others. —**char′i•ta•bly** *adv.*

char•i•ty (chăr′ĭ-tē) *n., pl.* **-ties. 1.** Help or relief given to the poor. **2.** A fund or institution that helps the poor. **3.** An act or feeling of good will or affection. **4.** Tolerance and leniency in judging others. **5.** *Theol.* **a.** God's love for mankind. **b.** Brotherly love for others.

cha•ri•va•ri *also* **chiv•a•ree** (shĭv′ə-rē′, shĭv′ə-rē′) *n., pl.* **-ris** *also* **-rees.** A noisy mock serenade to newlyweds.

char•la•tan (shär′lə-tən) *n.* One who falsely claims to have expert knowledge or skill : quack. —**char′la•tan•ism** *n.*

Charleston *n.* A quick, lively dance popular in the 1920's.

char•ley horse (chär′lē) *n. Informal.* A muscle cramp in an arm or leg.

charm (chärm) *n.* **1.** The power or ability to please or delight. **2.** A small ornament worn on a chain or bracelet. **3.** Something worn for its purported magical effect, as in bringing luck : amulet. **4.** An act or formula believed to have magical power. —*v.* **1.** To be delightful or pleasing : fascinate. **2.** To effect with or as if with magic : bewitch. ★ ***syns:*** BEWITCH, ENCHANT, ENTHRALL, ENTRANCE, SPELLBIND, WITCH

char•nel *also* **char•nel house** (chär′nəl) *n.* A building or room in which bones or bodies of the dead are placed.

chart (chärt) *n.* **1.** A map. **2.** Something, as a graph or table, that presents information in an easily viewed form. —*v.* **1.** To make a chart of. **2.** To plan in detail.

char•ter (chär′tər) *n.* **1.** An official document granting certain rights and privileges, as to a bank or college. **2.** A document outlining the principles, functions, and organization of a corporate body : constitution. **3.** An authorization from a society to create a local chapter. **4.** The hiring or leasing of a vehicle, as an aircraft. —*v.* **1.** To grant a charter to : establish. **2.** To engage the use of for a fee <*charter* a plane>

charter member *n.* An original member or founder of an organization or group.

char•treuse (shär-trōōz′, -trōōs′, -trœz′) *n.* A light greenish yellow.

char•wom•an (chär′wŏŏm′ən) *n.* A woman hired to do cleaning, as of offices.

char•y (châr′ē) *adj.* **-i•er, -i•est. 1.** Cautious : wary. **2.** Not wasteful, as of time, money, or resources : sparing. —**char′i•ly** *adv.* —**char′i•ness** *n.*

chase¹ (chās) *v.* **chased, chas•ing. 1.** To follow quickly : pursue. **2.** To hunt. **3.** To cause to leave : drive away. **4.** *Informal.* To hasten : rush. —*n.* **1.** The act of chasing : pursuit. **2.** The sport of hunting. **3.** One that is hunted : quarry.

chase² (chās) *n.* A groove : slot. —*v.* **chased, chas•ing.** To ornament by engraving or embossing.

chas•er (chā′sər) *n.* **1.** One that chases. **2.** *Informal.* A drink, as of beer, taken after undiluted liquor.

chasm (kăz'əm) *n.* A deep opening in the earth's surface : gorge. —**chas'mal** *adj.*
chas•sis (shăs'ē, chăs'ē) *n., pl.* **chas•sis** (-ēz). **1.** The framework that supports the body and engine of an automotive vehicle. **2.** The landing gear of an aircraft. **3.** The structure that supports the functioning parts of electronic equipment such as a radio or television set.
chaste (chāst) *adj.* **chast•er, chast•est. 1.** Pure, as in morals : modest. **2.** Not engaging in sexual intercourse : virtuous. **3.** Celibate. **4.** Not ornate in style : simple. ★ ***syns:*** DECENT, MODEST, PURE, VIRTUOUS
chas•ten (chā'sən) *v.* **1.** To punish in order to correct. **2.** To cause to become subdued : restrain. —**chas'ten•er** *n.*
chas•tise (chăs-tīz') *v.* **-tised, -tis•ing. 1.** To punish, esp. by beating. **2.** To scold. —**chas•tis'a•ble** *adj.* —**chas•tise'ment** (chăs-tīz'mənt, chăs'tĭz-) *n.*
chas•ti•ty (chăs'tĭ-tē) *n.* The quality or state of being chaste.
chas•u•ble (chăz'ə-bəl, chăs'-) *n.* A vestment without sleeves worn over the alb by the priest officiating at Mass.
chat (chăt) *v.* **chat•ted, chat•ting.** To converse in a relaxed and informal way. —*n.* A relaxed, informal conversation.
cha•teau *or* **châ•teau** (shă-tō') *n., pl.* **-teaux** (-tōz'). **1.** A castle in France. **2.** A large country house.
chat•e•laine (shăt'l-ān') *n.* **1.** The mistress of a castle or chateau. **2.** A clasp or chain for holding keys, a purse, or a watch.
chat•tel (chăt'l) *n.* **1.** An item of personal, movable property. **2.** A slave.
chat•ter (chăt'ər) *v.* **1.** To make short, meaningless sounds <birds *chattering*> **2.** To talk rapidly and inanely : jabber. **3.** To click or rattle repeatedly. —**chat'ter** *n.*
chat•ter•box (chăt'ər-bŏks') *n.* A very loquacious person.
chat•ty (chăt'ē) *adj.* **-ti•er, -ti•est.** Given to chatting : talkative. —**chat'ti•ly** *adv.* —**chat'ti•ness** *n.*
chauf•feur (shō'fər, shō-fûr') *n.* A person hired to drive an automobile. —**chauf'feur** *v.*
chau•vin•ism (shō'və-nĭz'əm) *n.* **1.** Blind and fanatical patriotism. **2.** Unreasoning belief in the superiority of one's own group <male *chauvinism*> —**chau'vin•ist** *n.* —**chau'vin•is'tic** *adj.* —**chau'vin•is'ti•cal•ly** *adv.*
†**chaw** (chô) *v. Regional.* To chew. —**chaw** *n.*
cheap (chēp) *adj.* **1.** Low in cost : inexpensive. **2.** Requiring little effort to achieve. **3.** Of little value. **4.** Of poor quality : shoddy. **5.** Not worthy of respect. **6.** Stingy. —**cheap** *adv.* —**cheap'ly** *adv.*
cheap•en (chē'pən) *v.* To make or become cheap or cheaper. —**cheap'en•er** *n.*
cheap shot *n.* An unjust action or statement directed esp. at a vulnerable target.
cheap•skate (chēp'skāt') *n. Slang.* A very stingy person.
cheat (chēt) *v.* **1.** To deprive of by trickery or deceit. **2.** To practice trickery or fraud. **3.** To break rules, as of an examination. ★ ***syns:*** BILK, DEFRAUD, GULL, GYP, MULCT, ROOK, SWINDLE, TAKE, VICTIMIZE —*n.* **1.** A fraud or swindle. **2.** One who cheats. —**cheat'er** *n.*
check (chĕk) *n.* **1.** An abrupt stop. **2.** A restraint : control. **3.** A standard for comparing, testing, or verifying. **4.** The act of comparing, testing, or verifying. **5.** A mark to show approval or verification. **6.** A slip or ticket showing identity. **7.** A bill, as at a restaurant. **8.** A written order to a bank to pay money from funds on deposit. **9. a.** A pattern of small squares, as on a chessboard. **b.** A fabric patterned with small squares. **10.** A chess move in which an opponent's king is directly attacked. —*v.* **1.** To arrest the motion of, esp. abruptly : stop. **2.** To hold in restraint : curb. **3.** To test or examine, as for correctness or good condition. **4.** To make a check mark on, as to show that something has been noted. **5.** To deposit for temporary safekeeping <*checked* their luggage> **6.** To correspond item for item : agree. **7.** To mark with a pattern of squares. —**check in.** To register, as at a hotel. —**check out. 1.** To pay for one's lodging and leave, as from a hotel. **2.** To take away after being recorded <*check out* a book from the library>
check•book (chĕk'bo͝ok') *n.* A book that contains blank checks.
check•er (chĕk'ər) *n.* **1. checkers** *(sing. in number).* A game played on a checkerboard by 2 players, each using 12 pieces. **2.** A piece used in the game of checkers. —*v.* **1.** To mark with a pattern of squares. **2.** To cause to undergo frequent changes, as in fortune : vary.
check•er•board (chĕk'ər-bôrd', -bōrd') *n.* A game board divided into 64 squares of 2 alternating colors.
check list *n.* A list in which items can be compared, verified, or identified.
check•mate (chĕk'māt') *v.* **-mat•ed, -mat•ing. 1.** To attack (a chess opponent's king) so that no defense is possible. **2.** To defeat decisively. —**check'mate'** *n.*
check•off (chĕk'ôf', -ŏf') *n.* The authorized deduction of union dues from a member's wages.
check-out (chĕk'out') *n.* **1.** The act, process, or place of checking out, as from a hotel. **2.** A test, as of a machine, for proper functioning.
check•point (chĕk'point') *n.* A place at which vehicular traffic is stopped for inspection, as at a border.
check•room (chĕk'ro͞om', -ro͝om') *n.* A room where items, as clothing or packages, may be left for temporary safekeeping.
check•up (chĕk'ŭp') *n.* A thorough examination, esp. a physical examination.
Ched•dar *also* **ched•dar** (chĕd'ər) *n.* A firm, smooth, usu. yellowish cheese.
cheek (chēk) *n.* **1.** The fleshy part of the face below the eye. **2.** Sauciness.
cheek•bone (chēk'bōn') *n.* A small facial bone below the eye.

cheek•y (chē'kē) *adj.* **-i•er, -i•est.** Impudent. **—cheek'i•ness** *n.*
cheep (chēp) *n.* A faint, high-pitched chirp, as of a young bird. **—cheep'** *v.*
cheer (chîr) *n.* **1.** Good spirits **:** gaiety. **2.** Something providing happiness or joy. **3.** A shout of encouragement or applause. *—v.* **1.** To give courage to **:** hearten. **2.** To fill with happiness. **3.** To encourage or applaud with cheers. **4.** To make or become cheerful <quickly *cheered* up> **—cheer'er** *n.*
cheer•ful (chîr'fəl) *adj.* **1.** In good spirits **:** gay. **2.** Producing a feeling of cheer. ★ ***syns:*** BRIGHT, CHEERY, CHIPPER, HAPPY, LIGHTHEARTED, SUNNY **—cheer'ful•ly** *adv.*
cheer•lead•er (chîr'lē'dər) *n.* Someone who directs the cheering of spectators, as at a football game.
cheer•less (chîr'lĭs) *adj.* Devoid of cheer **:** bleak. **—cheer'less•ly** *adv.*
cheer•y (chîr'ē) *adj.* **-i•er, -i•est. 1.** Bright and cheerful. **2.** Promoting cheer <a *cheery* room> **—cheer'i•ly** *adv.* **—cheer'i•ness** *n.*
cheese (chēz) *n.* A solid food made from the curd of milk, usu. seasoned, pressed into cakes, and aged.
cheese•burg•er (chēz'bûr'gər) *n.* A hamburger topped with a slice of cheese.
cheese•cake (chēz'kāk') *n.* **1.** A cake made with cream cheese or cottage cheese. **2.** *Slang.* Photographs of pretty girls scantily clothed.
cheese•cloth (chēz'klôth', -klŏth') *n.* A coarse, loosely woven cotton gauze.
cheese-par•ing (chēz'pâr'ĭng) *n.* Stinginess **:** parsimony. **—cheese'-par'ing** *adj.*
chees•y (chē'zē) *adj.* **-i•er, -i•est. 1.** Containing or resembling cheese. **2.** *Slang.* Shoddy **:** cheap. **—chees'i•ness** *n.*
chee•tah (chē'tə) *n.* A long-legged, swift-running spotted wildcat, *Acinonyx jubatus,* of Africa and SW Asia.
chef (shĕf) *n.* A cook, esp. a head cook.
chef-d'oeu•vre (shĕ-dœ'vr'ə) *n., pl.* **chefs-d'oeu•vre** (shĕ-). A masterpiece.
che•la (kē'lə) *n., pl.* **-lae** (-lē). A pincer-like claw of a crustacean, as a crab.

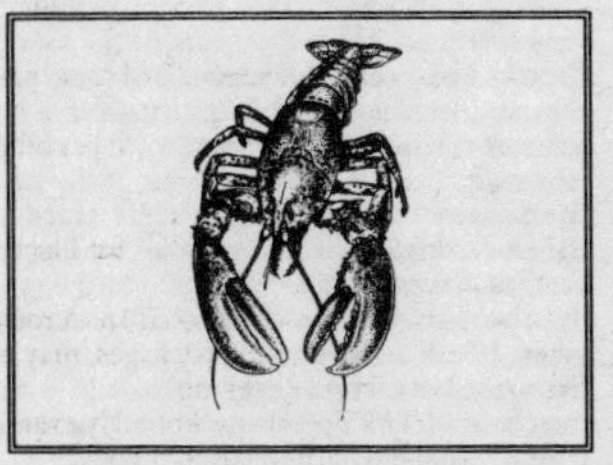

chela
Chelae of a lobster

chem•i•cal (kĕm'ĭ-kəl) *adj.* **1.** Of or relating to chemistry. **2.** Used in or produced by chemistry. *—n.* A substance obtained by or used in a chemical process. **—chem'i•cal•ly** *adv.*
chemical engineering *n.* Engineering that is concerned with the industrial production of chemicals and chemical products. **—chemical engineer** *n.*
chemical warfare *n.* Warfare involving the use of chemicals such as poisons, asphyxiants, and irritants.
che•mise (shə-mēz') *n.* **1.** A woman's loose, shirtlike undergarment. **2.** A loose dress that hangs straight.
chem•ist (kĕm'ĭst) *n.* **1.** A scientist specializing in chemistry. **2.** *esp. Brit.* A pharmacist.
chem•is•try (kĕm'ĭ-strē) *n., pl.* **-tries. 1.** The scientific study of the composition, structure, properties, and reactions of matter. **2.** The composition, structure, properties, and reactions of a substance. **3.** The interrelation of elements in a complex entity. **4.** Mutual attraction **:** rapport.
che•mo (kē'mō, kĕm'ō) *n. Informal.* Chemotherapy.
che•mo•ther•a•py (kē'mō-thĕr'ə-pē, kĕm'-ō-) *n.* Prevention or treatment of disease with chemicals. **—che'mo•ther'a•peu'tic** (-pyōō'-tĭk) *adj.*
chem•ur•gy (kĕm'ər-jē, kĕ-mûr'-) *n.* Industrial development of chemical products from organic raw materials, esp. of agricultural origin. **—chem•ur'gic** (kĭ-mûr'jĭk), **chem•ur'-gi•cal** *adj.*
che•nille (shə-nēl') *n.* **1.** A soft silk, cotton, or worsted yarn with a thick pile. **2.** Fabric made of chenille.
cheque (chĕk) *n. esp. Brit. var. of* CHECK 8.
cheq•uer (chĕk'ər) *n. Brit. var. of* CHECKER.
cher•ish (chĕr'ĭsh) *v.* **1.** To hold dear. **2.** To keep fondly in mind.
Cher•o•kee (chĕr'ə-kē', chĕr'ə-kē') *n., pl.* **-kee** *or* **-kees. 1.** A member of an American Indian people formerly of the S Appalachians, now in NE Oklahoma and W North Carolina. **2.** Their Iroquoian language.
che•root (shə-rōōt', chə-) *n.* A cigar whose ends are square-cut.
cher•ry (chĕr'ē) *n., pl.* **-ries. 1.** Any of several trees of the genus *Prunus* bearing pink or white flowers and rounded edible fruit with a small hard stone. **2.** The fruit or wood of a cherry tree. **3.** A deep or purplish red.
cher•ry•stone (chĕr'ē-stōn') *n.* The quahog clam when half-grown.
chert (chûrt) *n.* **1.** Any of various microscopically crystalline mineral varieties of silica. **2.** A siliceous rock of chalcedonic or opaline silica occurring in limestone.
cher•ub (chĕr'əb) *n., pl.* **cher•u•bim** (chĕr'ə-bĭm, -yə-bĭm) **1.** One of the 2nd order of angels. **2.** A representation of a cherub portrayed as a child with a rosy face and wings. **—che•ru'bic** (chə-rōō'bĭk) *adj.*
chess (chĕs) *n.* A game for 2 players, each with 16 pieces, played on a chessboard.
chess•board (chĕs'bôrd', -bōrd') *n.* A board with 64 squares of alternate colors, used in playing chess and checkers.

chess•man (chĕs′măn′, -mən) *n.* A piece used in chess.
chest (chĕst) *n.* **1.** The part of the body between the neck and abdomen enclosed by the ribs and sternum. **2.** A box with a lid, used esp. for storage. **3.** A piece of furniture with drawers : dresser.
ches•ter•field (chĕs′tər-fēld′) *n.* An overcoat with concealed buttons and a velvet collar.
chest•nut (chĕs′nŭt′, -nət) *n.* **1.** Any of several trees of the genus *Castanea* bearing edible nuts enclosed in a bur. **2.** The nut or wood of a chestnut tree. **3.** A reddish brown. **4.** A stale old joke or story.
chet•rum (chē′trəm, chĕt′rŭm) *n.* —See table at CURRENCY.
chev•a•lier (shĕv′ə-lîr′) *n.* A member of an order of merit or knighthood, as the French Legion of Honor.
chev•i•ot (shĕv′ē-ət) *n.* A coarse woolen fabric used esp. for suits and overcoats.
chev•ron (shĕv′rən) *n.* A sleeve insignia of stripes meeting at an angle, worn to indicate rank, merit, or length of service, as on a police force.
chew (cho͞o) *v.* To grind and crush with the teeth : masticate. —*n.* **1.** An act of chewing. **2.** Something chewed. —**chew′er** *n.*
chewing gum *n.* A sweet preparation of various flavors for chewing, usu. made from chicle.
chew•y (cho͞o′ē) *adj.* **-i•er, -i•est.** Needing much chewing. —**chew′i•ness** *n.*
Chey•enne (shī-ĕn′, -ăn′) *n., pl.* **-enne** *or* **-ennes. 1.** A member of an American Indian people of the W Great Plains, now in Montana and Oklahoma. **2.** Their Algonquian language.
Chi•an•ti (kē-än′tē, -ăn′-) *n.* A dry, usu. red table wine.
chi•ao (jē′ou′) *n., pl.* **chiao.** *var. of* JIAO.
chi•a•ro•scu•ro (kē-är′ə-sko͝or′ō, -skyo͝or′ō) *n., pl.* **-ros.** The use of light and shade in pictorial representation. —**chi•a′ro•scu′rist** *n.*
chic (shēk) *adj.* Smartly stylish : fashionable. —*n.* Stylishness. —**chic′ly** *adv.* —**chic′ness** *n.*
Chi•ca•na (chĭ-kä′nə, shĭ-) *n.* A Mexican-American woman. —**Chi•ca′na** *adj.*
chi•can•er•y (shĭ-kā′nə-rē) *n.* Artful deception : trickery. —**chi•cane′** *n.* & *v.*
Chi•ca•no (chĭ-kä′nō, shĭ-) *n., pl.* **-nos.** An American of Mexican parentage or ancestry. —**Chi•ca′no** *adj.*
chi•chi (shē′shē) *adj.* Showily stylish.
chick (chĭk) *n.* **1. a.** A young chicken. **b.** A young bird. **2.** *Slang.* A young woman.
chick•a•dee (chĭk′ə-dē′) *n.* A small, plump North American bird of the genus *Parus*, with gray plumage and a dark crown.
Chick•a•saw (chĭk′ə-sô′) *n., pl.* **-saw** *or* **-saws. 1.** A member of an American Indian people formerly of NE Mississippi and NW Alabama, now in Oklahoma. **2.** Their Muskogean language.
chick•en (chĭk′ən) *n.* **1.** The common domestic fowl or its young. **2.** The edible flesh of a chicken. **3.** *Slang.* A coward. —*adj. Slang.* Cowardly. —*v. Slang.* To act in a cowardly way <*chickened* out in the end>
chicken feed *n. Slang.* A small sum of money.
chick•en-heart•ed (chĭk′ən-här′tĭd) *adj.* Cowardly : timid.
chicken pox *n.* A contagious viral disease, esp. of children, marked by skin eruptions and mild fever.
chick•pea (chĭk′pē′) *n.* A bushy Old World plant, *Cicer arietenum*, bearing edible pealike seeds.
chick•weed (chĭk′wēd′) *n.* A low, weedy plant, *Stellaria media*, with small white flowers.
chic•le (chĭk′əl) *n.* The coagulated milky juice of a tropical American tree, used as the principal ingredient of chewing gum.
chic•o•ry (chĭk′ə-rē) *n., pl.* **-ries 1.** A plant, *Cichorium intybus*, with blue daisylike flowers and leaves used in salad. **2.** The ground, roasted root of the chicory, used usu. as a coffee substitute.
chide (chīd) *v.* **chid•ed** *or* **chid** (chĭd), **chid•ed** *or* **chid** *or* **chid•den** (chĭd′n), **chid•ing.** To scold : reprove. —**chid′er** *n.*
chief (chēf) *n.* One of highest rank or authority : leader. —*adj.* **1.** Highest in rank or authority. **2.** Most important : principal. —**chief′ly** *adv.*
chief executive *n.* **1. Chief Executive.** The President of the United States. **2.** A principal executive official.
chief executive officer *n.* The highest-ranking executive in a company or organization.
chief of staff *n.* The ranking officer of the U.S. Army, Navy, or Air Force, responsible to the branch secretary and to the President.
chief of state *n.* The formal head of a nation.
chief•tain (chēf′tən) *n.* The leader of a group, esp. a clan or tribe.
chif•fon (shĭ-fŏn′, shĭf′ŏn′) *n.* A sheer fabric.
chif•fo•nier (shĭf′ə-nîr′) *n.* A tall, narrow chest of drawers.
chig•ger (chĭg′ər) *n.* **1.** A mite of the family Trombidiidae that sucks blood and causes intensely irritating itching. **2.** CHIGOE 1.
chi•gnon (shēn′yŏn′, shēn-yŏn′) *n.* A roll of hair worn at the nape of the neck or the back of the head.
chig•oe (chĭg′ō, chē′gō) *n.* **1.** A small tropical flea, *Tunga penetrans*, that burrows under the skin, causing intense irritation and sores. **2.** CHIGGER 1.
Chi•hua•hua (chĭ-wä′wä, -wə) *n.* A tiny dog, orig. bred in Mexico, with a smooth coat and pointed ears.
chil•blain (chĭl′blān′) *n.* An inflammation, as of the hands or feet, caused by exposure to cold. —**chil′blained′** *adj.*
child (chīld) *n., pl.* **chil•dren** (chĭl′drən). **1.** A young person between birth and puberty. **2.** A daughter or son : offspring. **3.** A childish or

immature person. —**child'less** *adj.* —**child'less•ness** *n.*

▲ ***word history:*** The plural of *child* is really a double plural, and neither plural suffix belongs to the original declension of the word. The earliest Old English form *cild* was a neuter noun that formed the plural by adding no suffix, like the Modern English words *sheep* and *deer.* Other neuter nouns, however, formed plurals by suffixing *-ru,* and in later Old English times a new plural, *cildru,* was used for *cild.* This form developed into *childer.* In Old English still another class of nouns formed the plural with the suffix *-an,* which survived in Middle English as *-en.* *Oxen* and *brethren* are modern plurals that show this suffix. In some dialects of Middle English *-en* was the usual plural suffix, and it was added to *childer* to make it conform to other nouns. *Childeren* was prob. pronounced *children,* which became the modern spelling of the plural of *child.*

child abuse *n.* Physical or sexual maltreatment of a child by a parent or other adult.

child•bear•ing (chīld'bâr'ĭng) *n.* Pregnancy and childbirth. —**child'bear'ing** *adj.*

child•birth (chīld'bûrth') *n.* The act or process of giving birth to a child.

child-care *or* **child•care** (chīld'kâr') *adj.* Of or providing care for children, esp. preschoolers. —**child'care'** *n.*

child•hood (chīd'ho͝od') *n.* The period or state of being a child.

child•ish (chīl'dĭsh) *adj.* **1.** Of, relating to, or appropriate for a child. **2.** Marked by or showing lack of maturity **:** immature. ★ ***syns:*** BABYISH, IMMATURE, INFANTILE, JUVENILE, PUERILE —**child'ish•ly** *adv.*

child•like (chīld'līk') *adj.* Like a child, as in ingenuousness.

chil•dren (chĭl'drən) *n. pl. of* CHILD.

child's play *n.* Something that is extremely easy to do.

chil•e con car•ne *also* **chil•i con carne** (chĭl'ē kŏn kär'nē) *n.* A spicy dish made of chili powder or chilis, chopped meat, and usu. beans.

chil•i *also* **chil•e** *or* **chil•li** (chĭl'ē) *n., pl.* **-ies** *also* **-es** *or* **-lies. 1. a.** The very pungent fruit of *Capsicum frutescens,* a variety of red pepper. **b.** A powdered condiment made from dried chili fruits. **2.** Chile con carne.

chili powder *n.* A spicy condiment of ground chilies mixed with seasonings such as cumin and garlic.

chill (chĭl) *n.* **1.** A moderate cold. **2.** A feeling of coldness, often accompanied by shivering. **3.** A dampening of enthusiasm or joy. —*adj.* Chilly. —*v.* **1.** To make or become chilly or cold. **2.** To dispirit **:** discourage. —**chill'ness** *n.*

chill•y (chĭl'ē) *adj.* **-i•er, -i•est. 1.** Moderately but penetratingly cold. **2.** Affected with cold **:** chilled. **3.** Distant **:** unfriendly <a *chilly* greeting> —**chill'i•ness** *n.*

chime (chīm) *n.* **1.** *often* **chimes.** An instrumental set of bells tuned to the musical scale. **2.** The musical sound produced by or as if by a set of bells. —*v.* **chimed, chim•ing. 1.** To emit a harmonious sound when struck. **2.** To act or be in harmony **:** agree. **3.** To make known (e.g., the hour of day) by chiming. —**chime in.** To join in or interrupt a conversation.

chi•me•ra *also* **chi•mae•ra** (kī-mîr'ə, kĭ-) *n.* **1. Chimera.** *Gk. Myth.* A monster with a lion's head, a goat's body, and a serpent's tail. **2.** A foolish fancy.

Chimera

chi•mer•i•cal (kī-mĕr'ĭ-kəl, -mîr'-, kĭ-) *also* **chi•mer•ic** (-mĕr'ĭk, -mîr'-) *adj.* **1.** Imaginary **:** fantastic. **2.** Given to foolish fancies. —**chi•mer'i•cal•ly** *adv.*

chim•ney (chĭm'nē) *n., pl.* **-neys. 1.** A structural passage for the escape of smoke and gases. **2.** A glass tube that encloses a lamp flame.

chimney swift *n.* A swallowlike bird, *Chaetura pelagica,* that often nests in chimneys.

chimp (chĭmp) *n.* A chimpanzee.

chim•pan•zee (chĭm'păn-zē', chĭm-păn'zē) *n.* A gregarious, highly intelligent African ape, *Pan troglodytes.*

chin (chĭn) *n.* The central portion of the lower jaw. —*v.* **chinned, chin•ning.** To pull (oneself) up while grasping an overhead horizontal bar until the chin is level with the bar.

chi•na (chī'nə) *n.* Porcelain ware, esp. high-quality ware.

†**chinch** (chĭnch) *n. Regional.* A bedbug.

chinch bug *n.* An insect, *Blissus leucopterus,* destructive to grains and grasses.

chin•chil•la (chĭn-chĭl'ə) *n.* **1.** A South American rodent, *Chinchilla laniger,* widely raised for its soft pale-gray fur. **2.** A thick woolen fabric used esp. for overcoats.

chine (chīn) *n.* **1.** The backbone **:** spine. **2.** A cut of fish or meat including part of the backbone. **3.** A crest or ridge.

Chinese cabbage *n.* A Chinese plant, *Brassica pekinensis,* bearing a cylindrical head of edible leaves.

Chinese checkers *n.* A game in which players take turns moving marbles from a home point to the opposite point on a board shaped like a 6-pointed star.

chink¹ (chĭngk) *n.* A narrow opening **:** crack. —*v.* To fill chinks in.

chink² (chĭngk) *n.* A short metallic sound, as of coins. —*v.* To make a chink.
chi•no (chē'nō) *n., pl.* **-nos. 1.** A coarse cotton twill. **2. chinos.** Garments, esp. trousers, of chino.
Chi•nook (shĭ-no͝ok', chĭ-) *n., pl.* **-nook** *or* **-nooks. 1.** A member of any of various American Indian peoples of the Columbia River valley in Washington and Oregon. **2.** Any of their languages.
chintz (chĭnts) *n.* A printed and usu. glazed cotton fabric.
chintz•y (chĭnt'sē) *adj.* **-i•er, -i•est. 1.** Of or like chintz. **2.** Cheap : gaudy.
chin-up (chĭn'ŭp') *n.* The act of chinning oneself, esp. as a fitness exercise.
chip (chĭp) *n.* **1.** A small piece cut or broken off. **2.** A mark left when a chip is broken off. **3.** A disk used as a counter in games, as poker. **4.** A thin, crisp piece of food <a potato *chip*> **5.** *Electron.* **a.** A very tiny square of a thin semiconducting material, as silicon, processed to have particular electrical characteristics. **b.** An integrated circuit. —*v.* **chipped, chip•ping. 1.** To break or cut chips from. **2.** To break off in chips. **—chip in.** *Informal.* To contribute.
chip•munk (chĭp'mŭngk') *n.* A squirrellike terrestrial rodent, esp. *Tamias striatus,* of E North America, with a striped back.
chipped beef *n.* Very thinly sliced smoked dried beef.
chip•per (chĭp'ər) *adj. Informal.* Pert : cheerful.
Chip•pe•wa (chĭp'ə-wô', -wä', -wā') *n., pl.* **-wa** *or* **-was.** Ojibwa.
chi•ro•man•cy (kī'rə-măn'sē) *n.* Palmistry. **—chi'ro•man'cer** *n.*
chi•rop•o•dy (kĭ-rŏp'ə-dē, shĭ-) *n.* Podiatry. **—chi•rop'o•dist** *n.*
chi•ro•prac•tic (kī'rə-prăk'tĭk) *n.* A system of therapy in which bodily structures, as the spinal column, are manipulated. **—chi'ro•prac'tor** *n.*
chirp (chûrp) *n.* A high-pitched sound, as that made by a small bird or cricket.
chis•el (chĭz'əl) *n.* A metal tool with a sharp beveled edge used to cut and shape stone, wood, or metal. —*v.* **-eled, el•ing** *or* **-elled, -el•ling. 1.** To use a chisel (on). **2.** *Slang.* **a.** To swindle. **b.** To obtain by swindling. **—chis'el•er** *n.*
chit¹ (chĭt) *n.* A voucher for a small amount owed, as for food or drink.
chit² (chĭt) *n.* A pert girl.
chit•chat (chĭt'chăt') *n.* Trivial or casual conversation : small talk.
chi•tin (kī'tĭn) *n.* A semitransparent horny substance forming the chief component of crustacean shells and insect exoskeletons.
chit•ter•lings *also* **chit•lins** *or* **chit•lings** (chĭt'lĭnz) *pl.n.* Pig intestines prepared as food.
chiv•al•rous (shĭv'əl-rəs) *adj.* **1.** Marked by gallantry and honor. **2.** Of or relating to chivalry. **3.** Marked by courtesy and consideration, esp. toward women.
chiv•al•ry (shĭv'əl-rē) *n., pl.* **-ries. 1.** The qualities, as bravery and courtesy, of the ideal knight. **2.** The institution of knighthood. **3.** A chivalrous act.
chiv•a•ree (shĭv'ə-rē', shĭv'ə-rē') *n. var. of* CHARIVARI.
chive (chīv) *n.* A plant, *Allium schoenoprasum,* with purplish flowers and hollow, grasslike leaves used as a seasoning.
chla•myd•i•a (klə-mĭd'ē-ə) *n.* Any of several common, often asymptomatic, sexually transmitted diseases caused by the microorganism *Chlamydia trachomatis.*
chlo•ral (klôr'əl, klōr'-) *n.* A colorless, mobile oily liquid used to make DDT and chloral hydrate.
chloral hydrate *n.* A colorless crystalline compound used medicinally as a sedative and hypnotic.
chlor•dane (klôr'dān', klōr'-) *also* **chlor•dan** (-dăn') *n.* An odorless viscous liquid used as an insecticide.
chlo•ride (klôr'īd', klōr'-) *n.* A binary compound of chlorine.
chlo•ri•nate (klôr'ə-nāt', klōr'-) *v.* **-nat•ed, -nat•ing.** To treat or combine with chlorine or a chlorine compound. **—chlo'ri•na'tion** *n.* **—chlo'ri•na'tor** *n.*
chlo•rine (klôr'ēn', klōr'-) *n. Symbol* **Cl** A greenish-yellow, highly irritating gaseous element used to purify water and as a disinfectant and bleach.
chlo•rite (klôr'īt', klōr'-) *n.* A gen. green or black secondary mineral often formed by metamorphic alteration of primary dark rock minerals.
chlo•ro•form (klôr'ə-fôrm', klōr'-) *n.* A clear, colorless heavy liquid used in refrigerants and as an anesthetic. —*v.* To use chloroform to anesthetize or kill.
chlo•ro•phyll (klôr'ə-fĭl, klōr'-) *n.* Any of a group of green pigments found in photosynthetic organisms.
chlor•tet•ra•cy•cline (klôr'tĕt-rə-sī'klēn', klōr'-) *n.* An antibiotic obtained from a soil bacterium.
chock (chŏk) *n.* A wedge placed under something, as a wheel, to keep it from moving or to steady it. **—chock** *v.*
chock-a-block (chŏk'ə-blŏk') *adj.* Completely full : jammed.
chock-full (chŏk'fo͝ol', chŭk'-) *adj.* Filled to capacity : stuffed.
choc•o•late (chô'kə-lĭt, chŏk'ə-, chôk'lĭt, chŏk'-) *n.* **1.** Roasted and ground cacao seeds. **2.** A beverage or candy made from chocolate. **3.** A deep brown. **—choc'o•late** *adj.*
Choc•taw (chŏk'tô) *n., pl.* **-taw** *or* **-taws. 1.** A member of an American Indian people formerly of S Mississippi and SW Alabama, now in Mississippi and Oklahoma. **2.** Their Muskogean language.
choice (chois) *n.* **1.** The act of choosing : selection. **2.** The power, opportunity, or right to choose. **3.** One that is chosen. **4.** A variety or number from which to choose. **5.** The best part. ★ *syns:* ELECTION, OPTION, PREFER-

ENCE, SELECTION —*adj.* **1.** Of very fine quality. **2.** Chosen with care.
choir (kwīr) *n.* **1.** A group of singers, esp. one performing church music. **2.** The part of a church used by a choir : chancel.
choir·mas·ter (kwīr'măs'tər) *n.* The director of a choir.
choke (chōk) *v.* **choked, chok·ing. 1.** To stop or interfere with breathing, as by constricting the windpipe : suffocate. **2.** To slow or check the action or growth of. **3.** To obstruct : clog. **4.** To reduce the air intake of (a carburetor) to enrich the fuel mixture. —*n.* **1.** The act of choking. **2.** A device used to choke an internal-combustion engine.
choke·hold (chōk'hōld') *n.* A restraining move in which one person seizes another around the neck in a tight grip.
chok·er (chō'kər) *n.* A necklace that fits closely around the neck.
chol·er (kŏl'ər, kō'lər) *n.* Disposition to anger : irritability.
chol·er·a (kŏl'ər-ə) *n.* An infectious, often fatal epidemic disease marked by watery diarrhea, vomiting, and cramps.
chol·er·ic (kŏl'ə-rĭk, kə-lĕr'ĭk) *adj.* Easily angered : bad-tempered.
cho·les·ter·ol (kə-lĕs'tə-rôl', -rōl') *n.* A white, soapy crystalline substance occurring notably in bile, gallstones, the brain, blood cells, plasma, egg yolk, and seeds.
chomp (chŏmp) *v. var. of* CHAMP[1].
chon (chŏn) *n., pl.* **chon.** —See table at CURRENCY.
chon·drite (kŏn'drīt') *n.* A stone of meteoric origin characterized by chondrules. —**chon·drit'ic** (-drĭt'ĭk) *adj.*
chon·drule (kŏn'dro͞ol') *n.* A small round granule of extraterrestrial origin found embedded in some meteorites.
choose (cho͞oz) *v.* **chose** (chōz), **cho·sen** (chō'zən), **choos·ing. 1.** To pick out : select. **2.** To see fit : desire. ★ ***syns:*** CULL, ELECT, OPT, PICK, SELECT, SINGLE OUT
choos·y *also* **choos·ey** (cho͞o'zē) *adj.* **-i·er, -i·est.** Difficult to please : particular. —**choos'i·ness** *n.*
chop (chŏp) *v.* **chopped, chop·ping. 1.** To cut by striking repeatedly, as with an ax. **2.** To cut into bits : mince. **3.** To hit (a ball) with a short, swift downward stroke. —*n.* **1.** A short, swift downward blow or stroke. **2.** A cut of meat, often from the rib, containing a bone. **3.** A short, irregular motion, as of waves.
chop·house (chŏp'hous') *n.* A restaurant usu. specializing in chops and steaks.
chop·per (chŏp'ər) *n. Slang.* **1.** A helicopter. **2. choppers.** Teeth, esp. false teeth. **3.** A usu. customized motorcycle.
chop·py (chŏp'ē) *adj.* **-pi·er, -pi·est. 1.** Full of short, irregular waves : rough. **2.** Abrupt : jerky. —**chop'pi·ly** *adv.* —**chop'pi·ness** *n.*
chops (chŏps) *pl.n.* The jaws or jowls.
chop·sticks (chŏp'stĭks') *pl.n.* A pair of sticks used esp. in Asia as eating utensils.
chop su·ey (chŏp so͞o'ē) *n.* A dish of meat or chicken with bean sprouts and other vegetables, usu. served with rice.
cho·ral (kôr'əl, kōr'-) *adj.* Of, relating to, sung by, or for a chorus or choir. —**cho'ral·ly** *adv.*
cho·rale *also* **cho·ral** (kə-răl', -räl') *n.* A Protestant hymn, esp. one that has been harmonized, as for the organ.
chord[1] (kôrd, kōrd) *n.* A combination of musical tones sounded at the same time.
chord[2] (kôrd, kōrd) *n.* **1.** A straight line that joins 2 points on a curve. **2.** A string or cord, esp. a cordlike anatomical structure. **3.** *Archaic.* The string of a musical instrument.
▲ ***word history:*** The spelling *chord* for *cord* was introduced in the 16th cent. as etymologically more correct by scholars who knew Latin and Greek. The Greek origin of both words is *khordē*, meaning "gut," "string," "musical note," and "sausage." Both instrument strings and sausage casings were made of animal guts. Latin borrowed the Greek word as *chorda* and used it to mean primarily "instrument string" and "cord, rope." English borrowed the word from French, which had preserved the Latin meanings.
chore (chôr, chōr) *n.* **1.** A daily or routine task. **2.** A burdensome or unpleasant task.
cho·re·a (kô-rē'ə, kō-) *n.* A nervous disorder, esp. of children, marked by irregular and uncontrollable muscle movements.
cho·re·og·ra·phy (kôr'ē-ŏg'rə-fē, kōr'-) *n.* The art of creating and arranging dances, esp. ballets. —**cho're·o·graph'** (-ə-grăf') *v.* —**cho're·og'ra·pher** *n.* —**cho're·o·graph'ic** (-ə-grăf'ĭk) *adj.* —**cho're·o·graph'i·cal·ly** *adv.*
cho·ris·ter (kôr'ĭ-stər, kōr'-, kŏr'-) *n.* One, esp. a boy, who sings in a choir.
chor·tle (chôr'tl) *v.* **-tled, -tling.** To chuckle throatily, esp. in joy or triumph. —**chort'le** *n.* —**chor'tler** *n.*
cho·rus (kôr'əs, kōr'-) *n., pl.* **-rus·es. 1. a.** A group of singers who perform together. **b.** A composition for such a group. **2.** A group of dancers and vocalists who support the soloists, as in a musical comedy. **3.** A group speaking or reciting in unison. **4.** Sounds uttered in concert by many or several. **5.** A repeated part of a song. —*v.* **-rused, -rus·ing** *or* **-russed, -rus·sing.** To utter or sing in chorus. —**cho'ric** *adj.*
chose (chōz) *v. p.t. of* CHOOSE.
cho·sen (chō'zən) *v. p.p. of* CHOOSE. —*adj.* Selected from or preferred above others.
chow[1] (chou) *n.* A heavy-set dog orig. bred in China, with a blackish tongue and a dense coat.
chow[2] (chou) *n. Slang.* Food.
chow-chow (chou'chou') *n.* A relish of chopped vegetables pickled in mustard.
chow·der (chou'dər) *n.* A thick soup often made from fish and usu. having a milk base.
chow mein (chou'mān') *n.* A stew of diced or shredded meat and cooked vegetables served with fried noodles.
chrism (krĭz'əm) *n.* Consecrated oil used for sacramental anointing.

Christ (krīst) *n.* **1.** The Messiah. **2.** Jesus. —**Christ′like′** *adj.*

chris•ten (krĭs′ən) *v.* **1.** To baptize. **2.** To name at baptism. **3.** To dedicate or name (e.g., a ship) ceremonially. —**chris′ten•er** *n.* —**chris′ten•ing** *n.*

Chris•ten•dom (krĭs′ən-dəm) *n.* **1.** Christians as a whole. **2.** The Christian world.

Chris•tian (krĭs′chən) *n.* A believer in Christianity. —*adj.* **1.** Of, pertaining to, or professing belief in Christianity. **2.** Relating to or derived from Jesus or His teachings. **3.** Relating to Christianity or its adherents.

Christian era *n.* The period beginning with the birth of Jesus.

chris•ti•a•ni•a (krĭs′tē-ăn′ē-ə, krĭs′chē-) *n.* A ski turn at high speed in which the body is swung from a crouching position in order to stop or change direction.

Chris•ti•an•i•ty (krĭs′chē-ăn′ĭ-tē) *n.* **1.** The religion founded on the teachings of Jesus Christ. **2.** Christendom. **3.** The quality, state, or fact of being a Christian.

Chris•tian•ize (krĭs′chə-nīz′) *v.* **-ized, -iz•ing.** To adopt or convert to Christianity. —**Chris′tian•i•za′tion** *n.*

Christian name *n.* A name given at birth or baptism.

Christian Science *n.* The church and religious system founded by Mary Baker Eddy, emphasizing healing through spiritual means. —**Christian Scientist** *n.*

Christ•mas (krĭs′məs) *n.* Dec. 25, celebrated by Christians as the anniversary of Christ's birth.

Christ•mas•tide (krĭs′məs-tīd′) *n.* The Christmas season.

chro•mat•ic (krō-măt′ĭk) *adj.* **1.** Of or relating to color. **2.** *Mus.* Proceeding by half steps <a *chromatic* scale> —**chro•mat′i•cal•ly** *adv.* —**chro•mat′i•cism** *n.*

chro•ma•tic•i•ty (krō′mə-tĭs′ĭ-tē) *n.* The aspect of color including consideration of its dominant wavelength and purity.

chro•ma•tog•ra•phy (krō′mə-tŏg′rə-fē) *n.* Separation of complex mixtures by percolation through a selectively adsorbing medium, yielding stratified, sometimes chromatically distinct constituent layers. —**chro•mat′o•graph′ic** (-măt′ə-grăf′ĭk) *adj.* —**chro•mat′o•graph′i•cal•ly** *adv.*

chrome (krōm) *n.* **1.** Chromium. **2.** Something plated with a chromium alloy.

chro•mic (krō′mĭk) *adj.* Of or containing chromium, esp. with valence 3.

chro•mi•um (krō′mē-əm) *n. Symbol* **Cr** A hard, steel-gray metallic element used esp. in steel alloys and stainless steels.

chro•mo•some (krō′mə-sōm′) *n.* A DNA-containing linear body of the cell nuclei that is responsible for determination and transmission of hereditary characteristics. —**chro′mo•so′mal** (-sō′məl) *adj.*

chro•mo•sphere (krō′mə-sfîr′) *n.* **1.** An incandescent, transparent layer of gas that surrounds the photosphere of the sun. **2.** A similar gaseous layer around a star. —**chro′mo•spher′ic** (-sfîr′ĭk, -sfĕr′-) *adj.*

chron•ic (krŏn′ĭk) *adj.* **1.** Of long duration or frequent recurrence. **2.** Habitual **:** inveterate. ★ *syns:* CONTINUING, LINGERING, PERSISTENT, PROLONGED, PROTRACTED —**chron′i•cal•ly** *adv.*

chron•i•cle (krŏn′ĭ-kəl) *n.* **1.** A chronological record of events **:** history. **2. Chronicles** *(sing. in number).* —See table at BIBLE. —*v.* **-cled, -cling.** To record in or as if in a chronicle. —**chron′i•cler** (-klər) *n.*

chron•o•graph (krŏn′ə-grăf′, krō′nə-) *n.* An instrument that shows or graphically records time intervals. —**chron′o•graph′ic** *adj.* —**chron′o•graph′i•cal•ly** *adv.*

chro•nol•o•gy (krə-nŏl′ə-jē) *n., pl.* **-gies. 1.** The science that deals with determining the dates and sequence of events. **2.** Arrangement of events in time. **3.** A chronological table or list. —**chron′o•log′i•cal** (krŏn′ə-lŏj′ĭ-kəl), **chron′o•log′ic** (-ĭk) *adj.* —**chro•nol′o•gist** *n.*

chro•nom•e•ter (krə-nŏm′ĭ-tər) *n.* An extremely accurate timepiece.

chrys•a•lis (krĭs′ə-lĭs) *n.* The pupa of an insect, esp. a moth or butterfly, enclosed in a firm case.

chry•san•the•mum (krĭ-săn′thə-məm) *n.* A plant of the genus *Chrysanthemum* cultivated esp. for its showy flowers.

chub (chŭb) *n., pl.* **chub** *or* **chubs.** A freshwater fish of the family Cyprinidae, related to the carp and minnow.

chub•by (chŭb′ē) *adj.* **-bi•er, -bi•est.** Plump **:** chunky. —**chub′bi•ness** *n.*

chuck[1] (chŭk) *v.* **1.** To squeeze or pat affectionately, esp. under the chin. **2.** To toss **:** throw. **3.** *Informal.* To throw away **:** discard. —**chuck** *n.*

†**chuck**[2] (chŭk) *n.* **1.** A cut of beef extending from the neck to the ribs. **2.** *W U.S.* Food. **3.** A device that holds a tool or work in a machine, as a drill or lathe.

†**chuck•hole** (chŭk′hōl′) *n. Regional.* A rut or pothole in a road.

chuck•le (chŭk′əl) *v.* **-led, -ling.** To laugh quietly or to oneself. —**chuck′le** *n.* —**chuck′ler** *n.*

chuck wagon *n.* A wagon equipped with food and cooking utensils.

chug (chŭg) *n.* The muffled explosive sound made by or as if by a laboring engine. —**chug** *v.*

chuk•ka (chŭk′ə) *n.* An ankle-length usu. suede boot with 2 pairs of eyelets.

chuk•ker *also* **chuk•kar** (chŭk′ər) *n.* A playing period in a polo match.

chum (chŭm) *n.* A close friend **:** pal. —*v.* **chummed, chum•ming.** To be a close friend.

chum•my (chŭm′ē) *adj.* **-mi•er, -mi•est.** *Informal.* Very friendly **:** intimate. —**chum′mi•ly** *adv.* —**chum′mi•ness** *n.*

chump (chŭmp) *n.* A foolish person.

chunk (chŭngk) *n.* **1.** A thick piece. **2.** A large amount.

chunk•y (chŭng′kē) *adj.* **-i•er, -i•est. 1.** Short and thick **:** stocky. **2.** In or containing chunks. —**chunk′i•ness** *n.*

church (chûrch) *n.* **1.** All Christians regarded as a spiritual entity. **2.** A building for public and esp. Christian worship. **3.** A congregation. **4.** A public religious service. **5.** A Christian denomination. **—church'go'er** *n.* **—church'go'ing** *adj. & n.*

church•man (chûrch'mən) *n.* **1.** A clergyman. **2.** A church member.

Church of England *n.* The Anglican church as established in England.

church•war•den (chûrch'wôr'dn) *n.* An elected lay officer who oversees the secular affairs of an Anglican or Episcopal church.

church•yard (chûrch'yärd') *n.* A yard belonging to a church, esp. a cemetery.

churl (chûrl) *n.* **1.** A rude boor. **2.** A miser. **—churl'ish** *adj.* **—churl'ish•ly** *adv.* **—churl'ish•ness** *n.*

churn (chûrn) *n.* A device in which cream or milk is beaten vigorously to make butter. *—v.* **1.** To beat (cream or milk) vigorously in a churn. **2.** To make (butter) by operating a churn. **3.** To move with or produce great agitation. **—churn out.** To produce automatically and in quantity.

chute (sho͞ot) *n.* **1.** An inclined trough, channel, or passage through which something may pass. **2.** *Informal.* A parachute.

chut•ney (chŭt'nē) *n.* A pungent condiment of fruits, spices, and herbs.

chutz•pah (ᴋʜo͝ot'spə) *n. Slang.* Brazenness **:** nerve.

ciao (chou) *interj.* —Used to express greeting or farewell.

ci•ca•da (sĭ-kā'də, -kä'-) *n.* A large insect of the family Cicadidae with a broad head and membranous wings.

cic•a•trix (sĭk'ə-trĭks') *n., pl.* **-tri•ces** (-trī'sēz'). Scar tissue on a flesh wound.

cic•e•ro•ne (sĭs'ə-rō'nē, chē'chə-) *n., pl.* **-nes** *or* **-ni** (-nē). A guide for sightseers.

ci•der (sī'dər) *n.* The juice pressed from fruit, esp. apples, used as vinegar or a fermented or unfermented beverage.

ci•gar (sĭ-gär') *n.* A roll of tobacco leaves used for smoking.

cig•a•rette *also* **cig•a•ret** (sĭg'ə-rĕt', sĭg'ə-rĕt') *n.* A small roll of cut tobacco encased in thin paper for smoking.

cig•a•ril•lo (sĭg'ə-rĭl'ō) *n., pl.* **-los.** A small, narrow cigar.

cil•i•ate (sĭl'ē-ĭt, -āt') *adj.* Having cilia. *—n.* Any of various protozoans of the class Ciliata, having numerous cilia.

cil•i•um (sĭl'ē-əm) *n., pl.* **-i•a** (-ē-ə). **1.** A microscopic hairlike process extending from the surface of a cell and often capable of rhythmical motion. **2.** An eyelash.

cinch (sĭnch) *n.* **1.** A strap for holding a pack or saddle **:** girth. **2.** *Slang.* **a.** A thing easy to do. **b.** A sure thing **:** certainty. *—v.* **1.** To tighten a cinch on. **2.** *Slang.* To make certain of **:** assure.

cin•cho•na (sĭn-kō'nə, sĭng-) *n.* A South American tree of the genus *Cinchona,* whose bark yields quinine.

Cin•co de Ma•yo (sēng'kō də mä'yō) *n.* May 5, a Mexican holiday commemorating the 1862 defeat of French troops at the Battle of Puebla.

cinc•ture (sĭngk'chər) *n.* A girdle **:** belt. **—cinc'ture** *v.*

cin•der (sĭn'dər) *n.* **1.** A piece of partially burned material, as coal, that cannot be burned further. **2.** A fragment of burned, crustlike lava. **3. cinders.** Ashes.

cinder block *n.* A building block made of coal cinders and cement.

cin•e•ast (sĭn'ē-ăst) *also* **cin•é•aste** (sĭn'ā-ăst') *n.* A film enthusiast.

cin•e•ma (sĭn'ə-mə) *n.* **1.** A motion picture. **2.** A motion-picture theater. **3.** Motion pictures in general. **—cin'e•mat'ic** *adj.* **—cin'e•mat'i•cal•ly** *adv.*

cin•e•mat•o•graph (sĭn'ə-măt'ə-grăf') *n.* A movie camera or projector.

cin•e•ma•tog•ra•phy (sĭn'ə-mə-tŏg'rə-fē) *n.* Motion-picture photography. **—cin'e•ma•tog'ra•pher** *n.* **—cin'e•mat'o•graph'ic** (-măt'ə-grăf'ĭk) *adj.*

cin•e•rar•i•a (sĭn'ə-râr'ē-ə) *n.* A tropical plant, *Senecio cruentis,* with flat clusters of variously colored daisylike flowers.

cin•e•rar•i•um (sĭn'ə-râr'ē-əm) *n., pl.* **-i•a** (-ē-ə). A place for keeping the ashes of cremated corpses. **—cin'er•ar'y** (-rĕr'ē) *adj.*

cin•na•bar (sĭn'ə-bär') *n.* A heavy reddish compound, the principal source of mercury.

cin•na•mon (sĭn'ə-mən) *n.* **1.** The aromatic bark of a tropical Asian tree that is used as a spice. **2.** A reddish brown.

cinque•foil (sĭngk'foil', săngk'-) *n.* A plant of the genus *Potentilla,* bearing compound leaves often having 5 lobes.

ci•pher (sī'fər) *n.* **1.** *Math.* The symbol (0) indicating absence of quantity **:** zero. **2.** A nonentity. **3. a.** A system of secret writing **:** code. **b.** The key to a cipher. *—v.* **1.** To calculate arithmetically. **2.** To put in secret writing.

cir•ca (sûr'kə) *prep.* About <*circa* 1776>

cir•ca•di•an (sər-kā'dē-ən, -kăd'ē-, sûr'kə-dī'ən, -dē'-) *adj. Biol.* Exhibiting approx. 24-hour periodicity.

cir•cle (sûr'kəl) *n.* **1.** A plane curve equidistant from a fixed center within it. **2.** A region of a plane bounded by a circle. **3.** Something shaped like a circle. **4.** A group of people who have in common an interest or activity. **5.** A

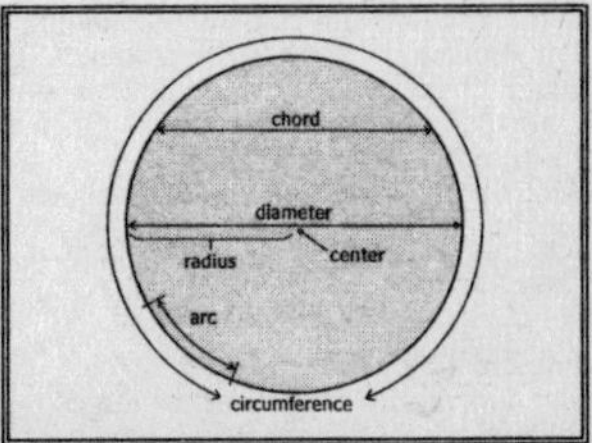

circle

sphere of influence or interest : domain. —*v.* **-cled, -cling. 1.** To make a circle around : enclose. **2.** To move in a circle (around).

cir·clet (sûr′klĭt) *n.* A small circle <a *circlet* of gold>

cir·cuit (sûr′kĭt) *n.* **1. a.** A closed, usu. circular curve. **b.** The region enclosed by a circuit. **2. a.** *Elect.* A closed path through which an electric current flows or may flow. **b.** A configuration of electrically or electromagnetically connected components or devices. **3.** A regular route, as that followed by a judge, around an assigned area or district. **4.** A chain or association, as of theaters or competitive events. —*v.* To make a circuit (of).

circuit board *n. Computer Sci.* An insulated board on which interconnected circuits and components such as microchips are mounted or etched.

circuit breaker *n.* A switch that automatically stops the flow of electric current in an overloaded circuit.

circuit court *n.* The lowest court of record in some U.S. states, occas. holding sessions in different places.

cir·cu·i·tous (sər-kyo͞o′ĭ-təs) *adj.* Indirect : roundabout. —**cir·cu′i·tous·ly** *adv.* —**cir·cu′i·ty, cir·cu′i·tous·ness** *n.*

cir·cuit·ry (sûr′kĭ-trē) *n.* **1.** The plan of an electric circuit. **2.** Electric circuits as a whole.

cir·cu·lar (sûr′kyə-lər) *adj.* **1.** Relating to a circle. **2.** Shaped like a circle : round. **3.** Moving in a circle. **4.** Circuitous. **5.** Self-referential <*circular* reasoning> —*n.* A printed notice or advertisement intended for mass distribution. —**cir′cu·lar′i·ty** (-lăr′ĭ-tē) *n.* —**cir′cu·lar·ly** *adv.*

cir·cu·lar·ize (sûr′kyə-lə-rīz′) *v.* **-ized, -iz·ing.** To publicize with or as if with circulars. —**cir′cu·lar·i·za′tion** *n.*

circular saw *n.* A power saw consisting of a toothed disk rotated at high speed.

cir·cu·late (sûr′kyə-lāt′) *v.* **-lat·ed, -lat·ing. 1.** To move or cause to move in or through a circle or circuit. **2.** To move from person to person or place to place. **3.** To distribute widely : disseminate. —**cir′cu·la′tion** *n.* —**cir′cu·la′tor** *n.* —**cir′cu·la·to′ry** (-lə-tôr′ē, -tōr′ē) *adj.*

cir·cum·cise (sûr′kəm-sīz′) *v.* **-cised, -cis·ing.** To remove the prepuce of (a male) or clitoris of (a female). —**cir′cum·ci′sion** (-sĭzh′ən) *n.*

cir·cum·fer·ence (sər-kŭm′fər-əns) *n.* **1.** The boundary of a circle : perimeter. **2.** The length of the perimeter of a circle. ★ ***syns:*** CIRCUIT, COMPASS, PERIMETER —**cir·cum′fer·en′tial** (-fə-rĕn′shəl) *adj.*

cir·cum·flex (sûr′kəm-flĕks′) *n.* A mark (ˆ) used esp. to indicate a vowel quality.

cir·cum·lo·cu·tion (sûr′kəm-lō-kyo͞o′shən) *n.* The use of an excessive number of words to articulate an idea.

cir·cum·lu·nar (sûr′kəm-lo͞o′nər) *adj.* Surrounding or revolving about the moon.

cir·cum·nav·i·gate (sûr′kəm-năv′ĭ-gāt′) *v.* **-gat·ed, -gat·ing.** To travel completely around, esp. by boat. —**cir′cum·nav′i·ga′tion** *n.* —**cir′cum·nav′i·ga′tor** *n.*

cir·cum·po·lar (sûr′kəm-pō′lər) *adj.* **1.** Located in a polar region. **2.** Designating a star that from a given observer's latitude does not go below the horizon.

cir·cum·scribe (sûr′kəm-skrīb′) *v.* **-scribed, -scrib·ing. 1.** To draw a line around. **2.** To confine within bounds. —**cir′cum·scrip′tion** (-skrĭp′shən) *n.*

cir·cum·so·lar (sûr′kəm-sō′lər) *adj.* Surrounding or revolving about the sun.

cir·cum·spect (sûr′kəm-spĕkt′) *adj.* Aware and heedful of consequences : prudent. —**cir′cum·spec′tion** *n.*

cir·cum·stance (sûr′kəm-stăns′) *n.* **1.** A condition or fact attending and having bearing on an event. **2.** A condition or fact that must be considered in determining a course of action. **3. circumstances.** Financial condition or means. **4.** Ceremony : formalities. **5.** Fate : chance.

cir·cum·stan·tial (sûr′kəm-stăn′shəl) *adj.* **1.** Of, relating to, or dependent on circumstances. **2.** Of no primary significance. **3.** Complete and fully detailed.

circumstantial evidence *n. Law.* Evidence not directly relevant to the facts in dispute but to attendant circumstances from which the occurrence of the facts in dispute might be inferred.

cir·cum·stan·ti·ate (sûr′kəm-stăn′shē-āt′) *v.* **-at·ed, -at·ing.** To provide support or circumstantial evidence of.

cir·cum·ter·res·tri·al (sûr′kəm-tə-rĕs′trē-əl) *adj.* Surrounding or revolving about the earth.

cir·cum·vent (sûr′kəm-vĕnt′, sûr′kəm-vĕnt′) *v.* To avoid or overcome, esp. by ingenuity. —**cir′cum·ven′tion** *n.*

cir·cus (sûr′kəs) *n.* **1.** A public entertainment that features acts by acrobats, clowns, and trained animals. **2.** An arena, often circular and covered by a tent, in which a circus performance is presented.

cirque (sûrk) *n.* A deep, steep basin in a mountain valley.

cir·rho·sis (sĭ-rō′sĭs) *n.* A chronic, ultimately fatal liver disease caused esp. by alcohol abuse or hepatitis. —**cir·rhot′ic** (sĭ-rŏt′ĭk) *adj.*

cir·rus (sîr′əs) *n., pl.* **cir·ri** (sîr′ī′). A high-altitude cloud composed of thin, gen. white fleecy patches.

cis·lu·nar (sĭs-lo͞o′nər) *adj.* Between the earth and the moon.

cis·tern (sĭs′tərn) *n.* A tank for storing water, esp. rainwater.

cit·a·del (sĭt′ə-dəl, -dĕl′) *n.* **1.** A fortress overlooking a city. **2.** A stronghold.

cite (sīt) *v.* **cit·ed, cit·ing. 1.** To quote as an authority or example or as proof. **2.** To mention, esp. in commendation, as for meritorious action. **3.** To summon before a court of law. —**ci·ta′tion** *n.*

cit·i·fy (sĭt′ə-fī′) *v.* **-fied, -fy·ing.** To urbanize. —**cit′i·fi·ca′tion** *n.*

cit·i·zen (sĭt′ĭ-zən) *n.* **1.** A person who owes

loyalty to and is entitled to the protection of a government. 2. A resident of a city or town. —**cit'i•zen•ship'** *n.*
cit•i•zen•ry (sĭt'ĭ-zən-rē) *n., pl.* **-ries.** Citizens as a group.
citizen's band *n.* A radio-frequency band officially set aside for private use.
cit•ric (sĭt'rĭk) *adj.* Of or derived from citrus fruits.
citric acid *n.* A colorless acid that occurs in lemon, lime, and pineapple juices and is used as a flavoring.
cit•rine (sĭt'rĭn, -rēn') *n.* **1.** A pale-yellow quartz. **2.** A pale yellow. —**cit'rine** *adj.*
cit•ron (sĭt'rən) *n.* **1.** A tree, *Citrus medica,* bearing lemonlike fruit with a thick, aromatic rind. **2.** A variety of watermelon, *Citrullus vulgaris citroides,* bearing fruit with a hard rind that is preserved or candied for use esp. in baking.
cit•ro•nel•la (sĭt'rə-nĕl'ə) *n.* An aromatic oil derived from a tropical grass and used esp. in insect repellents.
cit•rus (sĭt'rəs) *n., pl.* **-rus•es** *or* **-rus.** A tree or shrub of the genus *Citrus,* which includes the orange, lemon, lime, and grapefruit. —**cit'rus** *adj.*
cit•y (sĭt'ē) *n., pl.* **-ies. 1.** A place that is larger or more significant than a town. **2.** A U.S. municipality with legal powers granted by state charter. **3.** The residents of a city.
city hall *n.* **1.** The principal administrative building of a city government. **2.** A municipal bureaucracy.
city manager *n.* An administrator appointed by a city council to manage city affairs.
cit•y-state (sĭt'ē-stāt') *n.* An independent state composed of a city and its surrounding territory.
civ•et (sĭv'ĭt) *n.* Any of various catlike mammals of the family Viverridae that secrete a musky fluid used in prefumes.
civ•ic (sĭv'ĭk) *adj.* Of or relating to a city, a citizen, or citizenship. —*n.* **civics** *(sing. in number).* A social science that deals with civic affairs, esp. the rights and duties of citizenship.
civ•il (sĭv'əl) *adj.* **1.** Of or relating to citizens. **2.** Of or relating to the general public as distinct from the military or ecclesiastical. **3.** Of or relating to legal proceedings concerned with the rights of private individuals. **4.** Courteous. —**civ'il•ly** *adv.*
civil defense *n.* The emergency measures to be taken by civilian volunteers in case of a natural disaster, enemy attack, or invasion.
civil disobedience *n.* Refusal to obey civil laws regarded as unjust, usu. by employing methods of passive resistance.
civil engineer *n.* An engineer trained to design and construct public works. —**civil engineering** *n.*
ci•vil•ian (sĭ-vĭl'yən) *n.* A person not serving in a police, firefighting, or military force.
ci•vil•i•ty (sĭ-vĭl'ĭ-tē) *n., pl.* **-ties. 1.** Courtesy : politeness. **2.** A courteous act or expression.
civ•i•li•za•tion (sĭv'ə-lə-zā'shən) *n.* **1.** A relatively advanced stage of social, political, and cultural development. **2.** The culture of a particular people, place, or epoch.
civ•i•lize (sĭv'ə-līz') *v.* **-lized, -liz•ing. 1.** To bring out of a savage or primitive state. **2.** To educate or enlighten : refine. —**civ'i•liz'a•ble** *adj.* —**civ'i•liz'er** *n.*
civil libertarian *n.* One actively concerned with protecting those rights guaranteed to the individual by law.
civil liberty *n.* A fundamental individual right, such as freedom of speech or religion, protected by legal guarantee.
civil rights *pl.n.* Rights guaranteed to an individual by virtue of citizenship.
civil service *n.* The branches of public service that are not legislative, judicial, naval, or military. —**civil servant** *n.*
civil war *n.* A war between opposing factions or regions of the same country.
civ•vies (sĭv'ēz) *pl.n. Slang.* Civilian clothes as opposed to military dress.
Cl *symbol for* CHLORINE.
clab•ber (klăb'ər) *n.* Curdled sour milk. —*v.* To curdle.
clack (klăk) *v.* **1.** To make or cause to make an abrupt sound or series of sounds, as of objects being struck together. **2.** To chatter. —*n.* A clacking sound. —**clack'er** *n.*
clad (klăd) *v. var. p.t. & p.p. of* CLOTHE.
claim (klām) *v.* **1.** To demand or ask for as one's due or one's own. **2.** To state to be true : assert. **3.** To call for : require. —*n.* **1.** A claiming of something as one's rightful due. **2.** A basis for claiming : title or right. **3.** Something claimed. **4.** A statement that something is true : assertion.
claim•ant (klā'mənt) *n.* Someone making a claim.
clair•voy•ance (klâr-voi'əns) *n.* The power to discern what is beyond the range of the human senses. —**clair•voy'ant** *n. & adj.*
clam (klăm) *n.* **1.** Any of various marine and freshwater bivalve mollusks of the class Pelecypoda, many of them edible. **2.** *Informal.* A close-mouthed person. —**clam** *v.*
clam•bake (klăm'bāk') *n.* A gathering at which foods, as clams and corn, are cooked over hot stones.
clam•ber (klăm'bər) *v.* To climb clumsily, esp. on all fours. —**clam'ber•er** *n.*
clam•my (klăm'ē) *adj.* **-mi•er, -mi•est.** Disagreeably damp, sticky, and usu. cold. —**clam'mi•ly** *adv.* —**clam'mi•ness** *n.*
clam•or (klăm'ər) *n.* **1.** A loud outcry or noise. **2.** A vehement demand or protest. —*v.* To make a clamor. —**clam'or•ous** *adj.* —**clam'or•ous•ly** *adv.*
clamp (klămp) *n.* A device for fastening or holding things together. —*v.* To fasten or hold with or as if with a clamp. —**clamp down.** To become stricter.
clam•shell (klăm'shĕl') *n.* **1.** The shell of a

clam. **2.** A dredging bucket consisting of two hinged jaws.

clan (klăn) *n.* **1.** *Scot.* A group of families claiming a common ancestor. **2.** A division of a tribe tracing descent from a common ancestor. **3.** A large group of relatives. —**clan'nish** *adj.* —**clan'nish•ly** *adv.* —**clans'man** *n.* —**clans'wom'an** *n.*

clan•des•tine (klăn-dĕs'tĭn) *adj.* Done in or kept in secrecy.

clang (klăng) *v.* To make or cause to make a loud, resonant metallic sound. —**clang** *n.*

clan•gor (klăng'ər, -gər) *n.* A clang or series of clangs.

clank (klăngk) *n.* A quick, sharp, metallic sound. —**clank** *v.*

clap (klăp) *v.* **clapped, clap•ping. 1.** To strike (the hands) together with a loud sound. **2.** To make a sudden sharp noise. **3.** To applaud. —**clap** *n.*

clap•board (klăb'ərd, klăp'bôrd', -bōrd') *n.* A long board with one edge thicker than the other that is used for surfacing a frame building. —**clap'board** *v.*

clap•per (klăp'ər) *n.* One that claps, esp. the tongue of a bell.

clap•trap (klăp'trăp') *n.* High-flown nonsense.

claque (klăk) *n.* A group of persons hired to applaud at a performance.

clar•et (klăr'ĭt) *n.* A dry red table wine.

clar•i•fy (klăr'ə-fī') *v.* **-fied, -fy•ing.** To make or become clear : elucidate. —**clar'i•fi•ca'tion** *n.*

clar•i•net (klăr'ə-nĕt') *n.* A single-reed woodwind instrument with a cylindrical body and a flaring bell. —**clar'i•net'ist, clar'i•net'tist** *n.*

clar•i•on (klăr'ē-ən) *adj.* Resounding and clear.

clar•i•ty (klăr'ĭ-tē) *n.* The quality or state of being clear.

clash (klăsh) *v.* **1.** To strike together with a harsh, esp. metallic sound. **2.** To be in or come into opposition : conflict. —*n.* **1.** A harsh metallic sound. **2.** A usu. hostile encounter : conflict.

clasp (klăsp) *n.* **1.** A device, as a hook, used to hold parts or objects together. **2. a.** An embrace. **b.** A grip or grasp of the hand. —*v.* **1.** To fasten with a clasp. **2. a.** To embrace. **b.** To grip in or with the hand.

class (klăs) *n.* **1.** A set or group whose members share at least one attribute : kind. **2.** A division based on quality or grade. **3.** A social rank. **4. a.** A group of students graduating at the same time. **b.** A group of students studying the same subject. **5.** *Slang.* High style or quality. ★ ***syns:*** CATEGORY, CLASSIFICATION, ORDER —*v.* To classify.

class action *n.* A lawsuit in which the plaintiffs bring suit on their own behalf and on that of others with the same claim.

clas•sic (klăs'ĭk) *adj.* **1.** Serving as a model of excellence : outstanding. **2.** Of or relating to ancient Greek or Roman literature or art. **3.** Of or in accordance with traditional methods and principles. **4.** Of lasting historical or artistic significance or worth. —*n.* **1.** An artist, author, or work of the highest excellence. **2. classics.** The literature or art of ancient Greece and Rome. **3.** A traditional event.

clas•si•cal (klăs'ĭ-kəl) *adj.* **1.** Of, relating to, or in the style of the ancient Greek and Roman classics. **2.** Of, relating to, or concerned with studies of antiquity. **3.** Of or designating European music of the latter half of the 18th cent. **4.** Standard and authoritative. —**clas'si•cal•ly** *adv.*

clas•si•cism (klăs'ĭ-sĭz'əm) *n.* **1.** The rules and ideals, as of form, simplicity, and proportion, that are the basis of the art and literature of ancient Greece and Rome. **2.** Adherence to traditional rules or principles. **3.** Classical scholarship. —**clas'si•cist** (klăs'ĭ-sĭst) *n.*

classified advertisement *n.* A usu. brief advertisement printed, as in a newspaper, with others of the same category.

clas•si•fy (klăs'ə-fī') *v.* **-fied, -fy•ing. 1.** To assign to or arrange in classes. **2.** To assign to a restricted category for reasons of security. —**clas'si•fi'a•ble** *adj.* —**clas'si•fi•ca'tion** *n.*

class•ism (klăs'ĭz'əm) *n.* Bias based on social or economic class. —**class'ist** *adj. & n.*

class•mate (klăs'māt') *n.* A member of the same class in a school, college, etc.

class•room (klăs'ro͞om') *n.* A room, as in a school, in which classes meet.

class•y (klăs'ē) *adj.* **-i•er, -i•est.** *Slang.* Stylish : elegant.

clas•tic (klăs'tĭk) *adj. Geol.* Made up of fragments.

clat•ter (klăt'ər) *v.* To make, cause to make, or move with a rattling sound. —**clat'ter** *n.*

clause (klôz) *n.* **1.** A group of words containing its own subject and predicate and forming part of a compound or complex sentence. **2.** A distinct part of a document.

claus•tro•pho•bi•a (klô'strə-fō'bē-ə) *n.* A pathological fear of small spaces. —**claus'tro•pho'bic** *adj.*

clav•i•chord (klăv'ĭ-kôrd') *n. Mus.* An early keyboard instrument.

clav•i•cle (klăv'ĭ-kəl) *n.* A bone connecting the sternum and the scapula. —**cla•vic'u•lar** (klə-vĭk'yə-lər) *adj.*

cla•vier (klə-vîr', klā'vē-ər) *n. Mus.* **1.** A keyboard. **2.** An early keyboard instrument, as a harpsichord.

claw (klô) *n.* **1.** A sharp, often curved nail on the toe of an animal. **2.** A clawlike part, as the chela of a lobster. **3.** Something resembling a claw. —*v.* To scratch, grasp, or dig with or as if with claws.

clay (klā) *n.* **1.** A pliable fine-grained earth that hardens when fired, used in making bricks, pottery, and tiles. **2.** Moist earth : mud. **3.** The mortal human body. —**clay'ey** (klā'ē) *adj.*

clay pigeon *n.* A clay disk hurled as a flying target for skeet and trapshooting.

clean (klēn) *adj.* **1.** Free from dirt, impurities, or contamination. **2.** Free from wrongdoing : honorable. 3. Even : regular <a car with *clean* lines> 4. Thorough : complete <a *clean* escape> ★ *syns:* ANTISEPTIC, IMMACULATE, SPOTLESS, STAINLESS —*adv.* In a clean manner. —*v.* To make or become clean. **—clean up. 1.** To dispose of : settle. **2.** *Informal.* To make a large profit, esp. in a short time. **—clean'ly** *adv.*

clean-cut (klēn'kŭt') *adj.* **1.** Clearly outlined or defined. **2.** Trim and neat.

clean•ly (klĕn'lē) *adj.* **-li•er, -li•est.** Habitually clean and neat. **—clean'li•ness** *n.*

clean room *n.* A room that is kept contaminant-free, esp. for the handling of precision parts.

cleanse (klĕnz) *v.* **cleansed, cleans•ing.** To make clean or pure. **—cleans'er** *n.*

clean•up (klēn'ŭp') *n.* The act, process, or result of cleaning up.

clear (klîr) *adj.* **1.** Free from clouds or precipitation : bright. **2.** Free from impediment, restriction, or hindrance. **3.** Easily perceived by the eye, ear, or mind. **4.** Capable of discerning easily. **5.** Free from confusion or doubt. **6.** Free from impurities. **7.** Transparent. **8.** Free from guilt : innocent. **9.** Freed from burden or obligation. —*v.* **1.** To make or become clear. **2.** To rid of impurities or blemishes. **3.** To become free of obstructions. **4.** To free from blame or guilt. **5.** To pass by, under, or over without contact. **6.** To gain (a given amount) as net earnings or profit. **7.** To pass through a clearing-house, as a check. **8.** To make plain or intelligible : explain. **—clear** *adv.* **—clear'ly** *adv.* **—clear'ness** *n.*

clear•ance (klîr'əns) *n.* **1.** The act of clearing. **2.** The amount or distance by which an object clears another. **3.** Permission to proceed.

clear-cut (klîr'kŭt') *adj.* **1.** Sharply defined. **2.** Plain : unambiguous.

clear-head•ed (klîr'hĕd'ĭd) *adj.* Having a clear, orderly mind.

clear•ing (klîr'ĭng) *n.* A tract of land from which trees, brush, and other obstructions have been removed.

clear•ing-house *also* **clear•ing•house** (klîr'ĭng-hous') *n.* An office at which banks settle accounts.

cleat (klēt) *n.* A wood or metal projection that grips, provides support, or prevents slipping.

cleav•age (klē'vĭj) *n.* **1.** The act, process, or result of splitting or cleaving. **2.** A cleft.

cleave[1] (klēv) *v.* **cleft** (klĕft) *or* **cleaved** *or* **clove** (klōv), **cleft** *or* **cleaved** *or* **clo•ven** (klō'vən), **cleav•ing. 1.** To split apart : separate. **2.** To penetrate : pierce.

cleave[2] (klēv) *v.* **cleaved, cleav•ing.** To cling fast : adhere.

cleav•er (klē'vər) *n.* A heavy knife used by butchers.

clef (klĕf) *n.* A symbol that indicates which pitch each line and space represents on a musical staff.

cleft (klĕft) *v. var. p.t. & p.p. of* CLEAVE[1]. —*n.* A crack : fissure.

clem•a•tis (klĕm'ə-tĭs, klə-măt'ĭs) *n.* A plant or vine of the genus *Clematis,* bearing white or variously colored flowers.

clem•ent (klĕm'ənt) *adj.* **1.** Merciful : lenient. **2.** Mild, as weather : temperate. **—clem'en•cy** *n.* **—clem'ent•ly** *adv.*

clench (klĕnch) *v.* **1.** To close or set tightly. **2.** To grip or grasp tightly. **3.** To clinch. **—clench** *n.*

clere•sto•ry (klîr'stôr'ē, -stōr'ē) *n.* A wall with windows that rises above an abutting roofed section of a building or room.

cler•gy (klûr'jē) *n.* The body of persons ordained for religious service.

cler•gy•man (klûr'jē-mən) *n.* A man who is a member of the clergy.

cler•gy•wom•an (klûr'jē-wo͝om'ən) *n.* A woman who is a member of the clergy.

cler•ic (klĕr'ĭk) *n.* A member of the clergy.

cler•i•cal (klĕr'ĭ-kəl) *adj.* **1.** Of or pertaining to clerks or office workers. **2.** Of or typical of the clergy or a member of it.

cler•i•cal•ism (klĕr'ĭ-kə-lĭz'əm) *n.* A policy of supporting the political and secular power of the clergy.

clerk (klûrk; *Brit.* klärk) *n.* **1.** An office worker who performs general business tasks. **2.** An official who performs such tasks as keeping records, as for a court or legislative body. **3.** A salesperson in a store. —*v.* To work as a clerk. **—clerk'ship'** *n.*

†**clev•er** (klĕv'ər) *adj.* **1.** Mentally quick and ingenious : quick-witted. **2.** Showing skill : dexterous. **3.** *Regional.* Handy : suitable. ★ *syns:* ALERT, BRIGHT, INTELLIGENT, KEEN, SHARP, SMART **—clev'er•ly** *adv.*

clev•is (klĕv'ĭs) *n.* A U-shaped metal device for attaching parts.

clew (klo͞o) *n. & v. var. of* CLUE.

cli•ché (klē-shā') *n.* A hackneyed expression or idea.

click (klĭk) *n.* A brief, sharp sound. —*v.* **1.** To make or cause to make a click. **2.** *Informal.* **a.** To be successful. **b.** To function or fit well together.

cli•ent (klī'ənt) *n.* **1.** One who secures the professional services of another. **2.** A customer : patron.

cli•en•tele (klī'ən-tĕl', klē'ən-) *n.* Clients and esp. customers as a whole.

cliff (klĭf) *n.* A steep high face of rock.

cliff•hang•er (klĭf'hăng'ər) *n.* **1.** A serial in which each installment ends in suspense. **2.** A closely matched contest whose outcome is doubtful until the very end.

cli•mac•ter•ic (klī-măk'tər-ĭk, klī'măk-tĕr'ĭk) *n.* **1.** A period of life when physiological changes, esp. menopause, take place. **2.** A critical period or stage.

cli•mac•tic (klī-măk'tĭk) *adj.* Of or being a climax. **—cli•mac'ti•cal•ly** *adv.*

cli•mate (klī'mĭt) *n.* **1.** The average weather conditions of a specified region. **2.** A region with particular weather conditions <a tropical *climate*> **3.** A prevailing atmosphere. **—cli•mat'ic** (-măt'ĭk) *adj.* **—cli•mat'i•cal•ly** *adv.*

cli·ma·tol·o·gy (klī'mə-tŏl'ə-jē) *n.* Meteorological study of climate. —**cli'ma·to·log'i·cal** (-tə-lŏj'ĭ-kəl) *adj.* —**cli'ma·tol'o·gist** *n.*
cli·max (klī'măks') *n.* **1.** The point of greatest intensity or power in a series of events, ideas, or statements. **2.** Orgasm. **3.** The stage at which a community of organisms reaches a stable, self-perpetuating balance. ★ ***syns:*** ACME, APEX, APOGEE, CREST, CROWN, CULMINATION, HEIGHT, PEAK, PINNACLE, SUMMIT, ZENITH —**cli'max** *v.*
climb (klīm) *v.* **1.** To move up or mount, esp. by using the hands and feet **:** ascend. **2.** To go higher, as in rank or fortune **:** rise. **3.** To grow upward. —**climb down.** To descend, esp. by means of the hands and feet. —*n.* **1.** The act of climbing. **2.** A place to be climbed. —**climb'er** *n.*
clime (klīm) *n.* Climate.
clinch (klĭnch) *v.* **1.** To secure or fix, as with a bolt. **2.** To settle definitively <*clinched* the deal> **3.** To hold so as to immobilize. —**clinch** *n.*
clinch·er (klĭn'chər) *n.* One that clinches, esp. a conclusive point, fact, or statement.
cling (klĭng) *v.* **clung** (klŭng), **cling·ing. 1.** To hold tight **:** adhere. **2.** To be emotionally attached. —**cling'er** *n.*
cling·stone (klĭng'stōn') *n.* A fruit, esp. a peach, with pulp that adheres to the stone.
clin·ic (klĭn'ĭk) *n.* **1.** Medical training in which students observe the examination and treatment of patients. **2.** A facility associated with a hospital that treats chiefly outpatients. **3.** A center offering counsel or instruction <a computer *clinic*>
clin·i·cal (klĭn'ĭ-kəl) *adj.* **1.** Of or relating to a clinic. **2.** Of, related to, or involving direct examination and treatment of patients. **3.** Objective **:** dispassionate.
cli·ni·cian (klĭ-nĭsh'ən) *n.* A physician or psychologist who specializes in clinical practice rather than research.
clink[1] (klĭngk) *v.* To make or cause to make a light ringing sound. —**clink** *n.*
clink[2] (klĭngk) *n. Slang.* A jail **:** prison.
clink·er (klĭng'kər) *n.* **1.** Incombustible residue fused into an irregular lump, as that which remains after coal has burned. **2.** *Slang.* An error **:** mistake.
clip[1] (klĭp) *v.* **clipped, clip·ping. 1.** To cut, cut off, or cut out with shears. **2.** To shorten by cutting. **3.** *Informal.* To strike with a sharp blow. **4.** *Slang.* To cheat or overcharge. —*n.* **1.** Something clipped, as a newspaper item. **2.** *Informal.* A sharp blow. **3.** *Informal.* A brisk pace.
clip[2] (klĭp) *n.* **1.** A device that grips or clasps **:** fastener. **2.** A holder for rifle cartridges. —*v.* **clipped, clip·ping. 1.** To grip tightly. **2.** To join (one thing) to another. **3.** To block (an opponent in football) illegally.
clip·board (klĭp'bôrd', -bōrd') *n.* A small writing board with a clip at the top for holding papers or a pad.
clip joint *n. Slang.* A place, as a restaurant, where customers are overcharged.
clip·per (klĭp'ər) *n.* **1.** *often* **clippers.** An implement for clipping or shearing. **2.** A very fast sailing vessel.
clip·ping (klĭp'ĭng) *n.* Something, as a newspaper item, that is clipped off or out.
clique (klēk, klĭk) *n.* An exclusive and usu. small group of people. —**clique** *v.* —**cliqu'ey, cliqu'y** *adj.*
clit·o·ris (klĭt'ər-ĭs, klī'tər-) *n.* A small organ at the upper end of the vulva, homologous with the penis. —**clit'o·ral** *adj.*
cloak (klōk) *n.* **1.** A loose outer garment. **2.** Something that covers or conceals. —*v.* **1.** To cover with or as if with a cloak. **2.** To hide **:** conceal.
cloak-and-dag·ger (klōk'ən-dăg'ər) *adj.* Characterized by or suggesting spying and intrigue.
clob·ber (klŏb'ər) *v. Slang.* **1.** To strike violently and repeatedly. **2.** To defeat decisively.
cloche (klōsh) *n.* A woman's close-fitting, bell-shaped hat.
clock[1] (klŏk) *n.* An instrument other than a watch for measuring or indicating time. —*v.* To time the speed of.
clock[2] (klŏk) *n.* A decorative design on a sock or stocking.
clock·wise (klŏk'wīz') *adv.* In the direction in which the hands of a clock rotate. —**clock'wise'** *adj.*
clock·work (klŏk'wûrk') *n.* The delicate and accurate mechanism of a clock. —**like clockwork** with machinelike precision.
clod (klŏd) *n.* **1.** A lump of clay or earth. **2.** An ignorant or stupid person **:** dolt. —**clod'dish** *adj.*
clod·hop·per (klŏd'hŏp'ər) *n.* **1.** A clumsy country fellow **:** lout. **2.** A large heavy shoe.
clog (klŏg) *n.* **1.** An obstacle or hindrance. **2.** A weight attached, as to the leg of an animal, so as to hinder motion. **3.** A heavy, usu. wooden-soled shoe. —*v.* **clogged, clog·ging. 1.** To make or become obstructed. **2.** To hinder with a clog **:** impede.
cloi·son·né (kloi'zə-nā', klə-wä'-) *n.* Decorative enamelware in which different colors of enamel are poured into areas separated by thin strips of metal.
clois·ter (kloi'stər) *n.* **1.** A covered walk usu. with a colonnade running along the side of a court. **2.** A monastery or convent. —*v.* To confine in or as if in a cloister. —**clois'tral** (-strəl) *adj.*
clomp (klŏmp) *v.* To walk noisily.
clone (klōn) *n.* **1. a.** A group of genetically identical cells descended from a single common ancester. **b.** One or more organisms descended asexually from a single ancestor. **2.** One that is an exact replica of another. —*v.* **cloned, clon·ing.** To duplicate (an organism) asexually. —**clon'al** *adj.*
clop (klŏp) *n.* The sound of a horse's hoofs or a wooden shoe against a pavement. —**clop** *v.*
close (klōs) *adj.* **clos·er, clos·est. 1.** Near, as in time, space, or relation. **2.** With little or no space between elements or parts. **3.** Very short <a *close* haircut> **4.** Nearly even, as a game.

5. Fitting tightly. 6. Much like an original : accurate <a *close* copy> 7. Strict : rigorous <paid *close* attention> 8. Not open : shut. 9. Confined in space. 10. Restricted to specific persons. 11. Hidden from view : secluded. 12. Stingy : miserly. 13. Lacking fresh air : stuffy. —*v.* (klōz) **closed, clos•ing.** 1. To shut or become shut. 2. To stop or fill up. 3. To bring or come to an end : terminate. 4. To bring into contact : join. 5. To discontinue operations, as of a store. 6. To reach an agreement. —**close out.** To dispose of, usu. at a reduced price. —*n.* (klōz). An end : conclusion. —*adv.* (klōs). In a close position : near. —**close'ly** (klōs'lē) *adv.* —**close'ness** (klōs'nĭs) *n.*

close call (klōs) *n.* A narrow escape.

closed circuit *n.* Television with a signal transmitted by wire to a limited number of reception stations.

closed shop *n.* A union shop.

close-fist•ed (klōs'fĭs'tĭd) *adj.* Miserly.

close-knit (klōs'nĭt') *adj.* Closely attached by familial, cultural, or social ties.

close-mouthed (klōs'mou*th*d', -moutht') *adj.* Discreet and circumspect in speaking.

close-out (klōz'out') *n.* A sale in which all of a business's stock is disposed of at reduced prices.

clos•et (klŏz'ĭt) *n.* 1. A small compartment, cabinet, or room for storage. 2. A small private room, as for study. —*v.* To shut up in a private room, as for discussion.

close-up (klōs'ŭp') *n.* 1. A photograph taken at close range. 2. A close examination or view.

clo•sure (klō'zhər) *n.* 1. The act of closing or condition of being closed. 2. Something that closes. 3. Cloture.

clot (klŏt) *n.* A thick or solid mass formed from liquid that has thickened and coagulated. —**clot** *v.*

cloth (klôth, klŏth) *n., pl.* **cloths** (klôths, klô*thz*, klŏths, klŏ*thz*). 1. Material produced by weaving, knitting, or matting natural or synthetic fibers : fabric. 2. A piece of cloth used for a special purpose, as a tablecloth. 3. a. Distinctive professional attire, esp. of the clergy. b. The clergy.

clothe (klō*th*) *v.* **clothed** *or* **clad** (klăd), **cloth•ing.** 1. To put clothes on or provide clothes for : dress. 2. To cover as if with clothes : wrap.

clothes (klōz, klō*thz*) *pl.n.* 1. Wearing apparel : garments. 2. Bedclothes.

clothes•horse (klōz'hôrs', klō*thz*'-) *n.* One excessively concerned with dress.

clothes•pin (klōz'pĭn, klō*thz*'-) *n.* A clip for fastening clothes to a line.

clothes•press *also* **clothes press** (klōz'prĕs', klō*thz*'-) *n.* A chest, closet, or wardrobe for clothes.

cloth•ier (klō*th*'yər, klō'*th*ē-ər) *n.* A manufacturer or seller of clothing or cloth.

cloth•ing (klō'*th*ĭng) *n.* CLOTHES 1.

clo•ture (klō'chər) *n.* A parliamentary procedure, as calling for an immediate vote, by which debate is limited or ended.

cloud (kloud) *n.* 1. a. A visible body of fine drops of water or particles of ice in the air. b. A similar mass, as of smoke or dust in the air. 2. A swarm. 3. Something that looks or seems dark, gloomy, or threatening. —*v.* 1. To cover or become covered with or as if with clouds. 2. To tarnish : sully. —**cloud'i•ness** *n.* —**cloud'y** *adj.*

cloud•burst (kloud'bûrst') *n.* A sudden and very heavy rainstorm.

cloud nine *n. Informal.* A state of great happiness or elation.

†**clout** (klout) *n.* 1. A heavy blow, esp. with the hand. 2. *Informal.* Influence : pull. 3. *Archaic & Regional.* A piece of cloth used for mending : patch. —*v.* 1. To hit heavily, esp. with the hand. 2. *Archaic & Regional.* To bandage or patch.

clove[1] (klōv) *n.* An evergreen tree, *Eugenia aromatica,* whose aromatic buds are dried for use as a spice.

▲ ***word history:*** It may seem odd that garlic and the spice called "clove" in English should share the same name, but *clove*[1] and *clove*[2] are not at all related. *Clove*[2], meaning "bulb section," comes from Old English *clufu,* a noun related to *clēofan,* "to split," the ancestor of *cleave*[1]. *Clove*[1] as a name for the spice is really a misnomer. The full name of the spice in Old French was *clou de girofle,* literally "nail of the clove tree," since the dried flower bud somewhat resembles a small nail. The English gradually shortened the phrase to *clow,* whose modern form is *clove.*

clove[2] (klōv) *n.* A small section of a separable bulb, as that of garlic.

clove[3] (klōv) *v. var. p.t. of* CLEAVE[1].

clo•ven (klō'vən) *v. var. p.p. of* CLEAVE[1].

clo•ver (klō'vər) *n.* A plant of the genus *Trifolium* bearing compound leaves with 3 leaflets and tight flower heads.

clo•ver•leaf (klō'vər-lēf') *n.* An interchange at which highways cross each other on different levels and have curving access and exit ramps so that vehicles may go in any of 4 directions.

clown (kloun) *n.* 1. A comedian who entertains, as at a circus. 2. A coarse, rude person : boor. —*v.* To behave like a clown. —**clown'ish** *adj.* —**clown'ish•ly** *adv.* —**clown'ish•ness** *n.*

cloy (kloi) *v.* To sicken or disgust with too much of something good, esp. of something rich or sweet. —**cloy'ing•ly** *adv.*

club (klŭb) *n.* 1. A heavy stick of wood used as a weapon. 2. A stick used to hit a ball in certain games : bat. 3. One of a suit of playing cards marked with a black figure shaped like a clover leaf. 4. A group of persons organized together for a common purpose. 5. The meeting place of a club. —*v.* **clubbed, club•bing.** 1. To hit or beat with a club. 2. To join or combine for a common purpose.

club•foot (klŭb'fo͝ot') *n.* 1. A congenital deformity of the foot in which the front of the foot is twisted out of position. 2. A foot with clubfoot. —**club'foot'ed** *adj.*

club•house (klŭb'hous') *n.* 1. A building occupied by a club. **2.** The locker rooms for an athletic team.

club sandwich *n.* A sandwich usu. made of 3 slices of bread and meat, tomato, lettuce, and dressing.

club soda *n.* Carbonated water.

cluck (klŭk) *n.* The low, short call of a brooding hen. **—cluck** *v.*

clue *also* **clew** (klo͞o). *—n.* A guide in the solution of a mystery. *—v.* **clued, clue•ing** *or* **clu•ing** *also* **clewed, clew•ing.** To give information <*clued* him in>

clump (klŭmp) *n.* **1.** A thick group, as of trees **:** cluster. **2.** A heavy dull sound. *—v.* **1.** To walk with a clump. **2.** To form or cause to form clumps.

clum•sy (klŭm′zē) *adj.* **-si•er, -si•est. 1.** Lacking dexterity, coordination, or grace. **2.** Not skillful or tactful **:** inept. **—clum′si•ly** *adv.* **—clum′si•ness** *n.*

clung (klŭng) *v. p.t. & p.p. of* CLING.

clunk (klŭngk) *n.* **1.** A dull metallic sound. **2.** A hefty blow. **—clunk** *v.*

clunk•er (clŭng′kər) *n.* **1.** A broken-down car. **2.** A flop **:** failure.

clus•ter (klŭs′tər) *n.* A group **:** bunch. *—v.* To gather or grow in a cluster.

cluster headache *n.* A severe headache that can occur several times daily.

clutch (klŭch) *v.* To seize or attempt to seize and hold tightly. *—n.* **1.** A hand, claw, talon, or paw in the act of seizing. **2.** *often* **clutches.** Power or control. **3.** A device for connecting and disconnecting 2 sections of a rotating shaft or of a shaft and a driving mechanism. **4.** A crucial or tense situation.

clut•ter (klŭt′ər) *n.* A confused disorder. *—v.* To fill so as to hamper movement or lower efficiency **:** litter.

Clydes•dale (klīdz′dāl′) *n.* A large, powerful draft horse.

Cm *symbol for* CURIUM.

co– *pref.* **1.** With **:** together <*co*exist> **2.** Partner **:** associate <*co*star>

Co *symbol for* COBALT.

coach (kōch) *n.* **1.** A closed 4-wheeled carriage. **2.** A closed automobile usu. with 4 doors. **3.** A bus. **4.** A railroad passenger car. **5.** A trainer of athletes or athletic teams. **6.** A private instructor. *—v.* To teach, train, or act as a coach.

coach•man (kōch′mən) *n.* A man who drives a carriage or coach.

co•ad•ju•tor (kō′ə-jo͞o′tər, kō-ăj′ə-tər) *n.* An assistant, esp. to a bishop.

co•ag•u•lant (kō-ăg′yə-lənt) *n.* A substance that causes coagulation.

co•ag•u•late (kō-ăg′yə-lāt′) *v.* **-lat•ed, -lat•ing.** To form a soft, semisolid, or solid mass. **—co•ag′u•la•ble** *adj.* **—co•ag′u•la′tion** *n.* **—co•ag′u•la′tor** *n.*

coal (kōl) *n.* **1.** A natural black carbonaceous solid used as a fuel. **2.** An ember. *—v.* To supply with or take on coal.

co•a•lesce (kō′ə-lĕs′) *v.* **-lesced, -lesc•ing.** To grow or come together into one. **—co′a•les′cence** *n.* **—co′a•les′cent** *adj.*

coal gas *n.* A gas distilled from bituminous coal, used as commercial fuel.

co•a•li•tion (kō′ə-lĭsh′ən) *n.* An alliance, esp. a temporary one. **—co′a•li′tion•ist** *n.*

coal tar *n.* Tar distilled from bituminous coal and used esp. in dyes and drugs.

co-an•chor (kō-ăng′kər) *n.* Either of 2 principle news commentators on a broadcast. **—co-an′chor** *v.*

coarse (kôrs, kōrs) *adj.* **coars•er, coars•est. 1.** Of low or inferior quality. **2.** Lacking refinement. **3.** Consisting of large particles <*coarse* sand> **4.** Harsh. ★ ***syns:*** BOORISH, CHURLISH, CRASS, CRUDE, GROSS, PHILISTINE, RAW, ROUGH, RUDE, TASTELESS, UNCOUTH, VULGAR

coars•en (kôr′sən, kōr′-) *v.* To make or become coarse.

coast (kōst) *n.* **1.** The seashore. **2.** The act of sliding down a slope. *—v.* To move, as down an incline on a sled, without further acceleration. **—coast′al** *adj.*

coast•er (kō′stər) *n.* **1.** One that coasts. **2.** A small disk used to protect a surface.

coaster brake *n.* A brake and clutch operating on the rear wheel and drive mechanism of a bicycle when pedaling is reversed.

coast guard *n.* The military or naval force patrolling a nation's coast.

coast•line (kōst′līn′) *n.* The shape or outline of a coast.

co′ad•min′is•ter *v.*
co•a′gen•cy *n.*
co•a′gent *n.*
co′ap•prove′ *v.*
co′ar•range′ *v.*
co′as•sist′ *v.*
co-au′thor *n. & v.*
co′con•spir′a•tor *n.*
co′con•trib′u•tor *n.*
co′de•fen′dant *n.*
co′de•rive′ *v.*
co′di•rect′ *v.*
co′di•rec′tor *n.*
co′dis•cov′er *v.*
co•ed′i•tor *n.*
co•e′qual *n.*
co′e•qual′i•ty *n.*
co•e′qual•ly *adv.*
co′es•tab′lish *v.*
co′ex•ec′u•tor *n.*
co•fea′ture *n.*
co•fi′nance *v.*
co•found′ *v.*
co•found′er *n.*
co•heir′ *n.*
co•heir′ess *n.*
co′in•hab′it *v.*
co′in•her′i•tor *n.*
co′in•ven′tor *n.*
co′in•ves′ti•ga′tor *n.*
co′in•volve′ *v.*
co•lead′er *n.*
co-oc′cu•py *v.*
co′-oc•cur′ *v.*
co′-oc•cur′rence *n.*
co-own′er *n.*
co•part′ner *n.*
co•part′ner•ship′ *n.*
co•pay′ment *n.*
co′pro•duce′ *v.*
co′pro•duc′tion *n.*
co•pub′lish *v.*
co′re•cip′i•ent *n.*
co•res′i•dence *n.*
co•sov′er•eign *n.*
co•spon′sor *n. & v.*
co•spon′sor•ship′ *n.*
co′trus•tee′ *n.*
co•win′ner *n.*
co′work′er *n.*
co′writ′er *n.*

coat (kōt) *n.* **1.** An outer garment of varying length covering the upper part of the body. **2.** A natural outer covering, as of fur, on an animal. **3.** A layer of covering material. —*v.* To cover with a coat, as of paint. —**coat'ed** *adj.* —**coat'ing** *n.*

coat of arms *n.* Heraldic bearings, as of a family, usu. blazoned on a shield.

coat of mail *n.* An armored garment made of chain mail.

coat•tail (kōt'tāl') *n.* **1.** The loose back part of a coat below the waist. **2. coattails.** The skirts of a formal or dress coat.

coax (kōks) *v.* **1.** To try to persuade by gentle urging. **2.** To obtain by coaxing : wheedle. ★ ***syns:*** BLANDISH, CAJOLE, SOFT-SOAP, SWEET-TALK, WHEEDLE —**coax'er** *n.*

co•ax•i•al (kō-ăk'sē-əl) *adj.* **1.** Having a common axis. **2.** Of or designating a transmission cable composed of a conducting tube enclosed within another separated by insulation.

cob (kŏb) *n.* **1.** A corncob. **2.** A male swan. **3.** A thickset short-legged horse.

co•balt (kō'bôlt') *n.* *Symbol* **Co** A hard, brittle metallic element that resembles nickel and iron.

cob•ble (kŏb'əl) *v.* **-bled, -bling. 1.** To mend or make (boots or shoes). **2.** To make or put together clumsily.

cob•bler[1] (kŏb'lər) *n.* A mender of boots or shoes.

cob•bler[2] (kŏb'lər) *n.* A deep-dish fruit pie with no bottom crust and a thick top crust.

cob•ble•stone (kŏb'əl-stōn') *n.* A naturally rounded stone once used for paving.

CO•BOL *or* **Co•bol** (kō'bôl') *n.* A computer programming language based on English.

co•bra (kō'brə) *n.* A venomous Asian or African snake of the genus *Naja* that is able to expand the skin of the neck into a flattened hood.

cob•web (kŏb'wĕb') *n.* **1. a.** The web spun by a spider to catch its prey. **b.** A single thread of a spider's web. **2.** Something resembling a cobweb, as in intricacy.

co•ca (kō'kə) *n.* **1.** An Andean evergreen shrub of the genus *Erythroxylum* whose leaves contain cocaine. **2.** Dried coca leaves chewed for a stimulating effect and used for extraction of cocaine.

co•caine *also* **co•cain** (kō-kān', kō'kān') *n.* A narcotic alkaloid extracted from coca leaves and used as a local anesthetic and widely as an illegal drug.

coc•cus (kŏk'əs) *n., pl.* **coc•ci** (kŏk'sī'). A bacterium that is spherical in shape.

coc•cyx (kŏk'sĭks) *n., pl.* **coc•cy•ges** (kŏk-sī'jēz, kŏk'sĭ-jēz'). A small bone at the end of the spinal column.

coch•i•neal (kŏch'ə-nēl') *n.* A brilliant red dye made from the dried pulverized bodies of a tropical American scale insect.

coch•le•a (kŏk'lē-ə) *n., pl.* **-le•ae** (-lē-ē'). A spiral tube of the inner ear resembling a snail shell and having nerve endings necessary for hearing. —**coch'le•ar** (-lē-ər) *adj.*

cock (kŏk) *n.* **1. a.** The adult male of the domestic fowl : rooster. **b.** A male bird. **2.** A faucet or valve for regulating the flow of a liquid. **3. a.** The hammer of a firearm. **b.** The position of the hammer when a firearm is ready for firing. —*v.* **1.** To set the hammer of (a firearm) in firing position. **2.** To tilt or turn, esp. to one side. **3.** To raise in preparation for throwing or hitting.

cock•ade (kŏ-kād') *n.* An ornament, as a rosette, usu. worn on a hat as a badge.

cock•a•ma•mie *also* **cock•a•ma•my** (kŏk'ə-mā'mē) *adj. Slang.* **1.** Nearly valueless : trifling. **2.** Nonsensical : ludicrous.

cock•a•tiel *also* **cock•a•teel** (kŏk'ə-tēl') *n.* A crested Australian parrot, *Nymphicus hollandicus,* with gray and yellow plumage.

cock•a•too (kŏk'ə-tōō') *n.* A crested Australian parrot of the genus *Kakatoe.*

cock•a•trice (kŏk'ə-trĭs, -trīs') *n.* A mythical serpent with a lethal glance.

cock•chaf•er (kŏk'chā'fər) *n.* An Old World beetle of the family Scarabaeidae, esp. one that is destructive to plants.

cock•crow (kŏk'krō') *n.* Dawn.

cocked hat *n.* A three-cornered hat.

cock•er•el (kŏk'ər-əl) *n.* A young rooster.

cock•er spaniel (kŏk'ər) *n.* A spaniel with long, drooping ears and a silky coat.

cock•eye (kŏk'ī') *n.* A squinting eye.

cock•eyed (kŏk'īd') *adj.* **1.** Cross-eyed. **2.** *Slang.* **a.** Crooked : awry. **b.** Absurd.

cock•fight (kŏk'fīt') *n.* A fight between gamecocks that are usu. fitted with metal spurs. —**cock'fight'ing** *n.*

cock•le[1] (kŏk'əl) *n.* Any of various bivalve mollusks of the family Cardiidae with shells having radiating ribs.

cock•le[2] (kŏk'əl) *n.* Any of several plants often growing as weeds in grain fields.

cock•le•shell (kŏk'əl-shĕl') *n.* **1.** The shell of a cockle. **2.** A small, light boat.

cock•ney (kŏk'nē) *n., pl.* **-neys. 1.** *often* **Cockney.** A native of London's East End. **2.** The dialect of the cockneys.

cock•pit (kŏk'pĭt') *n.* The space in an aircraft for the pilot and crew.

cock•roach (kŏk'rōch') *n.* Any of various flat-bodied insects of the family Blattidae that are common household pests.

cocks•comb (kŏks'kōm') *n.* The fleshy comb on the head of a rooster.

cock•sure (kŏk'shŏŏr') *adj.* **1.** Absolutely sure. **2.** Overconfident.

cock•tail (kŏk'tāl') *n.* **1.** A mixed alcoholic drink. **2.** An appetizer, as seafood.

cock•y (kŏk'ē) *adj.* **-i•er, -i•est.** Excessively self-confident : conceited. —**cock'i•ly** *adv.* —**cock'i•ness** *n.*

co•co (kō'kō) *n., pl.* **-cos. 1.** The coconut. **2.** The coconut palm.

co•coa (kō'kō) *n.* **1.** A powder made from roasted ground cacao seeds from which much of the fat has been removed. **2.** A hot drink made with cocoa powder, water or milk, and sugar.

▲ ***word history:*** The confusion of *cocoa* with *coco* can be traced to Samuel Johnson's great dictionary, published in 1755. Johnson himself maintained the distinction between the two words in his own writing, but by some editorial or printing error the definitions for *coco* and *cocoa* were printed together under the word *cocoa.* That was unfortunate, because *coco* and *cocoa* are two different words that refer to two different trees. The cacao tree of tropical America produces both cocoa and chocolate. The name *cacao* comes from Nahuatl (Aztec) *cachuatl* and *chocolate* from Nahuatl *xocolatl.* The word *cocoa* is simply a variant spelling of *cacao.* The coconut or coco palm originated in the East Indies. Its name is not a native name but comes from Portuguese *coco,* "goblin," referring to the facelike appearance of the three holes at the bottom of the fruit.

cocoa butter *n.* A yellowish-white, waxy solid obtained from cacao seeds and used esp. in pharmaceuticals and soap.

co•co•nut *also* **co•coa•nut** (kō′kə-nŭt′, -nət) *n.* The fruit of the coconut palm, a large hard-shelled seed enclosing edible white meat and a milky fluid.

coconut palm *n.* A tall palm tree, *Cocos nucifera,* bearing coconuts as fruit.

co•coon (kə-ko͞on′) *n.* The protective silk or fiber pupal case spun by insect larvae.

cod[1] (kŏd) *n., pl.* **cod** or **cods.** An important food fish, *Gadus morhua* or *G. callarias,* of N Atlantic waters.

†**cod**[2] (kŏd) *n.* **1.** *Regional.* A husk or pod. **2.** *Obs.* A bag. **3.** *Archaic.* The scrotum.

co•da (kō′də) *n.* A section that concludes a musical composition.

cod•dle (kŏd′l) *v.* **-dled, -dling. 1.** To cook in simmering water just below the boiling point. **2.** To treat overindulgently.

code (kōd) *n.* **1.** A comprehensive and systematically arranged body of law. **2.** A system of rules of conduct or procedures <an ethical *code*> **3.** A system of signals used in communication. **4.** An arbitrary system of symbols or letters for transmitting esp. secret messages. **—code** *v.*

co•deine (kō′dēn′, -dē-ĭn) *n.* An alkaloid narcotic obtained from opium or morphine and used esp. to relieve pain.

co•dex (kō′dĕks′) *n., pl.* **co•di•ces** (kō′dĭ-sēz′, kŏd′ĭ-). A manuscript volume, esp. a work of the Scriptures or the classics.

cod•fish (kŏd′fĭsh′) *n.* The cod.

codg•er (kŏj′ər) *n. Informal.* An odd or somewhat eccentric fellow.

cod•i•cil (kŏd′ĭ-səl) *n.* A supplement or appendix that modifies a will. **—cod′i•cil′la•ry** (-sĭl′ə-rē) *adj.*

cod•i•fy (kŏd′ə-fī′, kō′də-) *v.* **-fied, -fy•ing.** To arrange systematically. **—cod′i•fi•ca′tion** *n.*

co•ed (kō′ĕd′) *n. Informal.* A woman student at a coeducational college or university. **—co′ed′** *adj.*

co•ed•u•ca•tion (kō′ĕj-o͞o-kā′shən) *n.* The system of education in which both men and women attend the same institution. **—co′ed•u•ca′tion•al** *adj.*

co•ef•fi•cient (kō′ə-fĭsh′ənt) *n.* **1.** A number by which another number or an algebraic term is multiplied **:** factor. **2.** A numerical measure of a physical or chemical property that is constant for a system under given conditions.

coe•len•ter•ate (sĭ-lĕn′tə-rāt′, -tər-ĭt) *n.* An invertebrate animal of the phylum Coelenterata, which includes the jellyfishes, hydras, sea anemones, and corals.

co•erce (kō-ûrs′) *v.* **-erced, -erc•ing. 1.** To compel to a course of action or thought. **2.** To dominate or restrain forcibly. **3.** To bring about by threat or force. **—co•er′cion** *n.* **—co•er′cive** *adj.*

co•e•val (kō-ē′vəl) *adj.* Of or originating in the same period of time. **—co•e′val** *n.*

co•ex•ist (kō′ĭg-zĭst′) *v.* **1.** To exist together or at the same time. **2.** To live peaceably with others in spite of differences. **—co′ex•is′tence** *n.*

co•ex•ten•sive (kō′ĭk-stĕn′sĭv) *adj.* Having the same boundaries, limits, or range. **—co′ex•ten′sive•ly** *adv.*

cof•fee (kô′fē, kŏf′ē) *n.* **1.** A stimulating beverage prepared from the ground beanlike seeds of a tropical tree of the genus *Coffea.* **2.** The seeds from which coffee is made.

coffee cake *n.* A cake made of sweetened yeast dough, often shaped into a ring or braid and containing nuts or raisins.

cof•fee•house (kô′fē-hous′, kŏf′ē-) *n.* A restaurant at which coffee and refreshments are sold.

coffee klatch (klăch, klăch) *n.* A gathering for coffee and casual conversation.

cof•fee•mak•er (kô′fē-mā′kər, kŏf′ē-) *n.* An apparatus used to brew coffee.

cof•fee•pot (kô′fē-pŏt′, kŏf′ē-) *n.* A utensil used for brewing or serving coffee.

coffee shop *n.* A small restaurant serving light meals.

coffee table *n.* A low table that is usu. placed before a sofa.

cof•fer (kô′fər, kŏf′ər) *n.* **1.** A strongbox. **2.** *often* **coffers.** Financial resources.

cof•fer•dam (kô′fər-dăm′, kŏf′ər-) *n.* A temporary enclosure that is pumped dry to expose the bottom of a body of water so that construction may be undertaken.

cof•fin (kô′fĭn, kŏf′ĭn) *n.* A box in which a corpse can be buried.

cog (kŏg) *n.* One of the teeth on the rim of a gear or wheel.

co•gent (kō′jənt) *adj.* Compelling **:** convincing. **—co′gen•cy** (-jən-sē) *n.*

cog•i•tate (kŏj′ĭ-tāt′) *v.* **-tat•ed, -tat•ing.** To ponder or think carefully about. **—cog′i•ta′tion** *n.* **—cog′i•ta′tive** *adj.*

co•gnac (kōn′yăk′, kŏn′-) *n.* A fine brandy, esp. from the vicinity of Cognac in W France.

cog•nate (kŏg′nāt′) *adj.* **1.** Descended from a common ancestor, esp. linguistically akin. **2.** Similar or identical in nature. **—cog′nate′** *n.* **—cog•na′tion** *n.*

cog•ni•tion (kŏg-nĭsh′ən) *n.* **1.** The mental process or faculty of knowing. **2.** Knowledge. —**cog′ni•tive** (kŏg′nĭ-tĭv) *adj.*

cognitive science *n.* The study of the nature of various mental tasks and the processes that enable them to be performed.

cog•ni•zance (kŏg′nĭ-zəns) *n.* **1.** Conscious recognition **:** awareness. **2.** Heed **:** notice. —**cog′ni•zant** *adj.*

cog•no•men (kŏg-nō′mən) *n., pl.* **-mens** *or* **-nom•i•na** (-nŏm′ə-nə). **1.** A surname. **2.** A nickname.

co•gno•scen•te (kŏn′yə-shĕn′tē, kŏg′nə-) *n., pl.* **-ti** (-tē). A connoisseur.

cog railway *n.* A railway designed to climb steep slopes by means of a cogwheel.

cog•wheel (kŏg′hwēl′, -wēl′) *n.* A wheel with cogs.

co•hab•it (kō-hăb′ĭt) *v.* **1.** To live together as spouses. **2.** To live together as lovers when not married. —**co•hab′i•ta′tion** *n.*

co•here (kō-hîr′) *v.* **-hered, -her•ing.** To hold or stick together.

co•her•ent (kō-hîr′ənt, -hĕr′-) *adj.* **1.** Holding or sticking together **:** cohering. **2.** Marked by logical consistency. —**co•her′ence** *n.* —**co•her′ent•ly** *adv.*

co•he•sion (kō-hē′zhən) *n.* **1.** The act, process, quality, or state of cohering. **2.** *Physics.* Mutual attraction by which the elements or particles of a body are held together. —**co•he′sive** *adj.* —**co•he′sive•ly** *adv.* —**co•he′sive•ness** *n.*

co•hort (kō′hôrt′) *n.* **1.** A group of people united in an effort or difficulty. **2.** *Informal.* A companion or associate.

co•ho salmon (kō′hō) *n.* A food and game fish, *Oncorhyncus kisutch,* orig. of Pacific waters.

co•host *or* **co-host** (kō′hōst′) *n.* A joint host, as of a social event. —**co′host′** *v.*

coif (koif) *n.* **1.** A tight-fitting hat. **2.** A coiffure.

coif•feur (kwä-fûr′) *n.* A hairdresser.

coif•feuse (kwä-fûrz′, -fyo͞oz′) *n.* A woman hairdresser.

coif•fure (kwä-fyo͝or′) *n.* A hair style.

coil (koil) *n.* **1.** A series of connected spirals or concentric rings, as of wire. **2.** A spiral or ring. —*v.* To wind in spirals.

coin (koin) *n.* A usu. flat and round piece of metal issued by a government as money. —*v.* **1.** To make (coins) from metal **:** mint. **2.** To invent (a word or expression).

coin•age (koi′nĭj) *n.* **1.** The act or process of coining. **2.** Metal currency **:** coins. **3.** A coined word or expression.

co•in•cide (kō′ĭn-sīd′) *v.* **-cid•ed, -cid•ing. 1.** To be in the same position in space. **2.** To occur at the same time. **3.** To correspond exactly.

co•in•ci•dence (kō-ĭn′sĭ-dəns, -dĕns′) *n.* **1.** Exact correspondence. **2.** A seemingly planned sequence of accidentally occurring events. —**co•in′ci•den′tal, co•in′ci•dent** *adj.* —**co•in′ci•den′tal•ly** *adv.*

co•i•tus (kō′ĭ-təs) *n.* Sexual intercourse, esp. involving vaginal penetration, orgasm, and ejaculation of semen. —**co′i•tal** *adj.*

coitus in•ter•rup•tus (ĭn′tə-rŭp′təs) *n.* Sexual intercourse purposely interrupted by withdrawal of the male prior to ejaculation.

coke (kōk) *n.* The solid carbonaceous residue obtained from bituminous coal after removal of volatile material, used as fuel and in making steel.

co•la¹ (kō′lə) *n.* A carbonated soft drink flavored with an extract from cola nuts.

co•la² (kō′lə) *n. var. pl. of* COLON².

co•la³ *also* **ko•la** (kō′lə) *n.* Either of two African evergreens of the genus *Cola* having nutlike seeds used in carbonated beverages and pharmaceuticals.

col•an•der (kŭl′ən-dər, kŏl′-) *n.* A perforated kitchen utensil for draining food.

cold (kōld) *adj.* **1.** Having a low subnormal temperature. **2.** Feeling uncomfortably chilled. **3.** Lacking warmth of emotion. **4.** *Informal.* Unconscious. ★ ***syns:*** CHILLY, FRIGID, GLACIAL, ICY —*adv.* Totally **:** thoroughly <knew the speech *cold*> —*n.* **1.** A condition of low air temperature. **2.** The sensation of being uncomfortably chilled. **3.** A viral infection of the respiratory passages.

cold-blood•ed (kōld′blŭd′ĭd) *adj.* **1.** Having a body temperature that varies according to the temperature of the surroundings, as reptiles. **2.** Lacking or done without feeling or emotion. —**cold′blood′ed•ly** *adv.*

cold cream *n.* A creamy cosmetic preparation for cleansing and softening the skin.

cold cuts *pl.n.* Assorted sliced cold meats.

cold front *n.* The leading edge of a cold air mass.

cold-heart•ed (kōld′här′tĭd) *adj.* Characterized by lack of sympathy or feeling **:** callous. —**cold′-heart′ed•ly** *adv.*

cold shoulder *n.* Deliberately cold or unfriendly treatment. —**cold′shoul′der** *v.*

cold sore *n.* A small sore on the lips that is caused by a virus and often accompanies a fever or cold.

cold sweat *n.* Simultaneous chill and perspiration, usu. caused by fear or shock.

cold turkey *n. Informal.* Sudden withdrawal from the use of an addictive drug.

cold war *n.* A conflict between nations that stops short of actual warfare.

cole (kōl) *n.* A plant, as the cabbage or rape, of the genus *Brassica.*

cole•slaw *also* **cole slaw** (kōl′slô′) *n.* A salad made of shredded raw cabbage.

col•ic (kŏl′ĭk) *n.* A sharp, sudden pain in the abdomen. —**col′ick•y** *adj.*

col•i•se•um (kŏl′ĭ-sē′əm) *n.* A large amphitheater used esp. for sports events.

co•li•tis (kō-lī′tĭs, kə-) *n.* Inflammation of the mucous membrane of the colon.

col•lab•o•rate (kə-lăb′ə-rāt′) *v.* **-rat•ed, -rat•ing. 1.** To work with others. **2.** To cooperate with an enemy that has invaded one's country. —**col•lab′o•ra′tion** *n.* —**col•lab′o•ra′tor** *n.*

col·lage (kō-läzh′, kə-) *n.* An artistic composition consisting of materials, as cloth or paper, pasted on a surface.

col·lapse (kə-lăps′) *v.* **-lapsed, -laps·ing. 1.** To fall down or in suddenly. **2.** To cease to function, esp. suddenly. **3.** To disintegrate. **4.** To fold together compactly. **—col·lapse′** *n.* **—col·laps′i·ble** *adj.*

col·lar (kŏl′ər) *n.* **1.** The part of a garment that encircles the neck. **2.** A strip or band, as of lace, at the neckline of a garment. **3.** Something that resembles a collar. —*v.* **1.** To seize by or as if by the collar. **2.** *Informal.* To arrest **:** nab.

col·lar·bone (kŏl′ər-bōn′) *n. Anat.* The clavicle.

col·lard (kŏl′ərd) *n. often* **collards.** A smooth-leaved variety of kale, *Brassica oleracea acephala.*

col·late (kə-lāt′, kō-, kŏl′āt′) *v.* **-lat·ed, -lat·ing. 1.** To compare (e.g., texts) carefully. **2.** To assemble in correct sequence.

col·lat·er·al (kə-lăt′ər-əl) *adj.* **1.** Side by side. **2.** Serving to corroborate or support. **3.** Secondary **:** subordinate. **4.** Of or being property used as security for the performance of an obligation. **5.** Descended from a common ancestor but through a different line. —*n.* Property used as security for an obligation, as a loan.

col·la·tion (kə-lā′shən, kŏ-, kō-) *n.* **1.** The act of collating. **2.** A light meal.

col·league (kŏl′ēg′) *n.* A fellow member of a profession, staff, or academic faculty.

col·lect (kə-lĕkt′) *v.* **1.** To bring or gather together in a group **:** assemble. **2.** To accumulate from a number of sources <*collect* coins> **3.** To obtain payment of. —*adj. & adv.* With payment to be made by the receiver. **—col·lect′i·ble, col·lect′a·ble** *adj.* **—col·lec′tion** *n.* **—col·lec′tor** *n.*

col·lect·ed (kə-lĕk′tĭd) *adj.* Composed **:** self-possessed.

col·lec·tive (kə-lĕk′tĭv) *adj.* **1.** Made or formed by collecting. **2.** Of or made by a number of individuals acting as a group <a *collective* plan> —*n.* **1.** A cooperative business or undertaking, usu. under government supervision. **2.** A collective noun.

collective bargaining *n.* Negotiation between the representatives of union workers and their employer.

collective noun *n.* A noun, such as *family* or *public,* denoting a group of persons or things considered as a unit.

col·lec·tiv·ism (kə-lĕk′tə-vĭz′əm) *n.* A system under which ownership and control of the means of producing and distributing goods is in the hands of the people collectively. **—col·lec′tiv·ist** *n.* **—col·lec′tiv·is′tic** *adj.* **—col·lec′tiv·ize′** *v.*

col·leen (kŏ-lēn′, kŏl′ēn′) *n.* An Irish girl.

col·lege (kŏl′ĭj) *n.* **1. a.** A school of higher learning that grants the degree of bachelor. **b.** An undergraduate school or division of a university. **c.** A professional school, often connected with a university <teachers *college*> **d.** The premises of a college. **2.** An assemblage with a common purpose or duties <a *college* of surgeons> **—col·le′giate** (kə-lē′jĭt, -jē-ĭt) *adj.*

col·le·gian (kə-lē′jən, -jē-ən) *n.* A student or recent graduate of college.

col·le·gi·um (kə-lē′jē-əm, -lĕg′ē-) *n., pl.* **-gi·a** (-lē′jē-ə, -lĕg′ē-ə) *or* **-ums.** An executive council of equally empowered members.

col·lide (kə-līd′) *v.* **-lid·ed, -lid·ing. 1.** To come together violently with direct impact. **2.** To be in opposition **:** clash. **—col·li′sion** (-lĭzh′ən) *n.*

col·lie (kŏl′ē) *n.* A large dog with long hair and a long, narrow muzzle, orig. bred in Scotland to herd sheep.

col·lier (kŏl′yər) *n. esp. Brit.* **1.** A coal miner. **2.** A coal ship.

col·lier·y (kŏl′yə-rē) *n., pl.* **-ies.** *esp. Brit.* A coal mine.

col·lin·e·ar (kə-lĭn′ē-ər, kō-) *adj.* **1.** Being on the same line. **2.** COAXIAL 1.

col·lo·cate (kŏl′ə-kāt′) *v.* **-cat·ed, -cat·ing.** To place together in proper order **:** arrange. **—col′lo·ca′tion** *n.*

col·lo·di·on (kə-lō′dē-ən) *n.* A highly flammable syrupy solution of nitrocellulose in alcohol that hardens and is used for surgical dressings and photographic plates.

col·loid (kŏl′oid′) *n.* A suspension of finely divided particles in a continuous medium, as a gaseous, liquid, or solid substance, that do not settle out of the substance and are not readily filtered. **—col·loid′al** *adj.*

col·lo·qui·al (kə-lō′kwē-əl) *adj.* **1.** Characteristic of or appropriate to informal speech and writing. **2.** Relating to conversation. **—col·lo′qui·al·ism** *n.*

col·lo·qui·um (kə-lō′kwē-əm) *n., pl.* **-ums** *or* **-qui·a** (-kwē-ə). A conference or seminar.

col·lo·quy (kŏl′ə-kwē) *n., pl.* **-quies. 1.** A conversation, esp. a formal one. **2.** A written dialogue.

col·lu·sion (kə-lo͞o′zhən) *n.* A secret agreement between 2 or more persons for a deceitful or illegal purpose. **—col·lu′sive** *adj.* **—col·lu′sive·ly** *adv.*

co·logne (kə-lōn′) *n.* Eau de cologne.

co·lon¹ (kō′lən) *n.* **1.** A punctuation mark (:) used after a word introducing a quotation, example, or series. **2.** The sign (:) used between numbers in expressions of time and ratios <2:30 A.M.><1:2>

co·lon² (kō′lən) *n., pl.* **-lons** *or* **-la** (-lə). The part of the large intestine extending from the cecum to the rectum. **—co·lon′ic** (kə-lŏn′ĭk) *adj.*

co·lon³ (kō-lōn′) *n., pl.* **-lons** *or* **-lo·nes** (-lō′nās′). —See table at CURRENCY.

colo·nel (kûr′nəl) *n.* An officer in the U.S. Army, Air Force, or Marine Corps ranking above a lieutenant colonel and below a brigadier general. **—colo′nel·cy** *n.*

▲ ***word history:*** The improbable pronunciation "kernel" for the word spelled *colonel* represents the triumph of popular speech over learned tinkering. The French form actually borrowed in the 16th cent. was *coronel,* from the Italian form *colonello.* The substitution of *r* for *l* in the French form is an example of dissimilation. By this process two similar or identical sounds, like the two *l* sounds in *colonello,* become less alike. In English usage *coronel* was respelled as *colcnel,* with the original *l* restored, but the pronunciation based on this spelling did not win out over "kernel," which was the pronunciation of the older English form.

co·lo·ni·al (kə-lō'nē-əl) *adj.* **1.** Of, relating to, having, or inhabiting colonies. **2.** *often* **Colonial.** Of or relating to the 13 original American colonies. —*n.* An inhabitant of a colony.

co·lo·ni·al·ism (kə-lō'nē-ə-lĭz'əm) *n.* A governmental policy of controlling foreign dependencies. **—co·lo'ni·al·ist** *n.*

col·o·nist (kŏl'ə-nĭst) *n.* **1.** An original founder or settler of a colony. **2.** An inhabitant of a colony.

col·o·nize (kŏl'ə-nīz') *v.* **-nized, -niz·ing. 1.** To found a colony in. **2.** To settle in a colony. **—col'o·ni·za'tion** *n.*

col·on·nade (kŏl'ə-nād') *n.* A row of columns esp. supporting a roof.

colonnade

col·o·ny (kŏl'ə-nē) *n., pl.* **-nies. 1.** A group of settlers in a new land who remain subject to the parent nation. **2.** A region ruled by a distant nation. **3.** A group with similar origins or interests or their living area. **4.** A group of similar organisms that live or grow together <an ant *colony*>

col·o·phon (kŏl'ə-fŏn', -fən) *n.* An inscription, usu. at the end of a book, giving publication facts.

col·or (kŭl'ər) *n.* **1.** The aspect of things that is caused by differing qualities of the light emitted or reflected by them. **2.** A substance, as a dye, pigment, or paint, that gives color. **3.** Skin tone **:** complexion. **4. colors.** A banner or flag, as of a nation or military group. **5.** Outward, often misleading appearance. **6.** Vivid or picturesque detail. —*v.* **1.** To give color to or change the color of. **2.** To give a distinctive quality to. **3.** To distort. **4.** To blush. **—col'or·er** *n.* **—col'or·less** *adj.* **—col'or·less·ly** *adv.*

col·or·a·tion (kŭl'ə-rā'shən) *n.* Arrangement or use of colors.

col·or·a·tu·ra (kŭl'ər-ə-tŏŏr'ə, -tyŏŏr'ə) *n.* **1.** Ornate embellishment in vocal music. **2.** A soprano specializing in coloratura.

color bar *n.* Color line.

col·or·blind (kŭl'ər-blīnd') *adj.* Totally or partially unable to distinguish colors.

col·or-code (kŭl'ər-kōd') *v.* To color, as papers or wires, according to a code to facilitate identification.

col·ored (kŭl'ərd) *adj.* **1.** Having color. **2. a.** Of or belonging to a racial group not considered as white. **b.** Of mixed racial descent. **3.** Biased or distorted, as by incorrect data. **—col'ored** *n.*

col·or·fast (kŭl'ər-făst') *adj.* Having color that will not fade or run with wear or washing. **—col'or·fast'ness** *n.*

col·or·ful (kŭl'ər-fəl) *adj.* **1.** Full of color. **2.** Richly varied **:** vivid. ★ ***syns:*** BRIGHT, GAY, SHOWY, VIVID **—col'or·ful·ly** *adv.*

color line *n.* A social, legal, or economic barrier that separates nonwhite persons from whites.

co·los·sal (kə-lŏs'əl) *adj.* Gigantic in size or degree.

Co·los·sians (kə-lŏsh'ənz, -lŏs'ē-ənz) *pl.n.* *(sing. in number).* —See table at BIBLE.

co·los·sus (kə-lŏs'əs) *n., pl.* **-los·si** (-lŏs'ī') *or* **-sus·es. 1.** A gigantic statue. **2.** Something extremely large or important.

co·los·to·my (kə-lŏs'tə-mē) *n., pl.* **-mies.** Surgical construction of an artificial excretory opening from the colon.

col·our (kŭl'ər) *n. & v. esp. Brit. var. of* COLOR.

colt (kōlt) *n.* A young male horse. **—colt'ish** *adj.* **—colt'ish·ness** *n.*

col·um·bine (kŏl'əm-bīn') *n.* A plant of the genus *Aquilegia,* with variously colored flowers having spurred petals.

co·lum·bi·um (kə-lŭm'bē-əm) *n. Symbol* **Cb** Niobium.

Columbus Day *n.* Oct. 12, a U.S. holiday celebrated officially on the 2nd Monday in Oct. to honor Columbus.

col·umn (kŏl'əm) *n.* **1.** A supporting or decorative pillar used in building. **2.** Something shaped or used like a pillar. **3.** A vertical section of typed or printed lines on a page. **4.** A feature article that appears regularly, as in a newspaper. **5.** A long row, as of troops. **—co·lum'nar** (kə-lŭm'nər) *adj.*

col·um·nist (kŏl'əm-nĭst, -ə-mĭst) *n.* A writer of a magazine or newspaper column.

co·ma (kō'mə) *n., pl.* **-mas.** A deep, prolonged unconsciousness usu. caused by injury, disease, or poison.

Co·man·che (kə-măn'chē) *n., pl.* **-che** *or* **-ches. 1.** A member of an American Indian people formerly of the S Great Plains, now in Oklahoma. **2.** Their Uto-Aztecan language.

co·ma·tose (kō'mə-tōs', kŏm'ə-) *adj.* **1.** Unconscious. **2.** Lethargic **:** torpid.

comb (kōm) *n.* **1.** A thin, toothed strip of material, as plastic, used to arrange or fasten the hair. **2.** Something shaped or used like a comb. **3.** A fleshy crest on the top of the head of a fowl or certain other birds. **4.** A honeycomb.

—*v.* **1.** To dress with or as if with a comb. **2.** To card (e.g., wool). **3.** To search thoroughly.

com•bat (kəm-băt′, kŏm′băt′) *v.* **-bat•ed, -bat•ing** *also* **-bat•ted, -bat•ting. 1.** To fight against in battle. **2.** To oppose or resist vigorously. —*n.* (kŏm′băt′). Fighting, esp. armed conflict **:** battle. —**com•bat′ant** *n.* —**com•bat′ive** *adj.*

combat fatigue *n.* A nervous disorder induced by combat and involving anxiety, depression, and irritability.

comb•er (kō′mər) *n.* **1.** One that combs. **2.** A long, cresting ocean wave.

com•bi•na•tion (kŏm′bə-nā′shən) *n.* **1.** The act or process of combining or state of being combined. **2.** A result of combining **:** aggregate. **3.** A sequence of letters or numbers needed to open certain locks.

com•bine (kəm-bīn′) *v.* **-bined, -bin•ing. 1.** To make or become united **:** merge. **2.** *Chem.* To form a compound. —*n.* (kŏm′bīn′). **1.** A harvesting machine that cuts, threshes, and cleans grain. **2.** A group associated for commercial or political gain.

comb•ings (kō′mĭngz) *pl.n.* Material, as hairs or wool, removed with a comb.

combining form *n.* A word element that joins with other word forms to make compounds, e.g., *co-* in *coexist.*

com•bo (kŏm′bō) *n., pl.* **-bos.** A small band of musicians, esp. jazz musicians.

com•bus•ti•ble (kəm-bŭs′tə-bəl) *adj.* Capable of igniting and burning. —*n.* A combustible substance. —**com•bus′ti•bil′i•ty** *n.* —**com•bus′ti•bly** *adv.*

com•bus•tion (kəm-bŭs′chən) *n.* **1.** The process of burning. **2.** A rapid chemical change, esp. oxidation, that produces light and heat. —**com•bus′tive** (-tĭv) *adj.*

come (kŭm) *v.* **came** (kām), **come, com•ing. 1.** To approach **:** advance. **2.** To arrive. **3.** To reach a certain state, position, or result. **4.** To move into view **:** appear. **5.** To exist at a particular place or point <Spring *comes* before summer.> **6.** To happen <How did you *come* to move here?> **7.** To spring from **:** originate. **8.** To be available <It *comes* in 3 colors.> —**come about.** To take place **:** happen. —**come across. 1.** To find or meet accidentally. **2.** *Slang.* To give or do what is wanted. —**come around** (*or* **round**). **1.** To recover. **2.** To alter one's opinion or standpoint. —**come into.** To inherit. —**come off.** To take place **:** happen. —**come out. 1.** To be revealed. **2.** To make a debut into society. —**come through. 1.** To succeed. **2.** *Informal.* To do what is expected. —**come to.** To recover consciousness. —**come up with.** *Informal.* To produce.

come•back (kŭm′băk′) *n.* **1.** A return to former success or status. **2.** A quick reply.

co•me•di•an (kə-mē′dē-ən) *n.* **1.** A professional entertainer who uses verbal humor or performs comic acts. **2.** An actor in comedy. **3.** A comedy writer. **4.** One who tries to be amusing **:** clown.

co•me•di•enne (kə-mē′dē-ĕn′) *n.* A woman who performs professionally as a comedian.

come•down (kŭm′doun′) *n.* **1.** A decline in level or status. **2.** A source or feeling of disappointment or depression.

com•e•dy (kŏm′ĭ-dē) *n., pl.* **-dies. 1.** An amusing entertainment, as a play or motion picture, in which the characters may be humorous and that ends happily. **2.** A literary composition that has a humorous theme or uses the methods of comedy. **3.** A real-life comic occurrence or situation. —**co•me′dic** (kə-mē′dĭk) *adj.*

come•ly (kŭm′lē) *adj.* **-li•er, -li•est.** Good-looking. —**come′li•ness** *n.*

come-on (kŭm′ŏn′, -ôn′) *n.* Something that entices **:** inducement.

com•er (kŭm′ər) *n.* One that shows promise of achievement.

co•mes•ti•ble (kə-mĕs′tə-bəl) *adj.* Fit to be eaten. —*n.* Something edible.

com•et (kŏm′ĭt) *n.* A celestial body that orbits the sun and has a solid head surrounded by a brilliant cloud and a long, vaporous tail when the head nears the sun.

come•up•pance *also* **come•up•ance** (kŭm-ŭp′əns) *n. Informal.* Justly deserved punishment.

com•fit (kŭm′fĭt, kŏm′-) *n.* A candy.

com•fort (kŭm′fərt) *v.* To console in time of fear or grief. —*n.* **1.** A state of ease or well-being. **2.** Solace. **3.** Help **:** assistance <gave *comfort* to the enemy> **4.** One that brings relief or well-being. **5.** Capacity to give physical ease. —**com′fort•ing•ly** *adv.*

com•fort•a•ble (kŭm′fər-tə-bəl, kŭmf′tə-bəl) *adj.* **1.** Affording comfort. **2.** In a state of comfort. **3.** Adequate <a *comfortable* income> —**com′fort•a•bly** *adv.*

com•fort•er (kŭm′fər-tər) *n.* **1.** One that comforts. **2.** A heavy quilt.

comfort station *n.* A public rest room.

com•fy (kŭm′fē) *adj.* **-fi•er, -fi•est.** *Informal.* Comfortable.

com•ic (kŏm′ĭk) *adj.* **1.** Of or characteristic of comedy. **2.** Comical. —*n.* **1.** One who is comical, esp. a comedian. **2. comics.** *Informal.* Comic strips.

com•i•cal (kŏm′ĭ-kəl) *adj.* Humorous **:** amusing. —**com′i•cal′i•ty, com′i•cal•ness** *n.* —**com′i•cal•ly** *adv.*

comic book *n.* A magazine of comic strips.

comic strip *n.* A narrative series of cartoons.

com•ing (kŭm′ĭng) *adj.* **1.** Approaching. **2.** *Informal.* Showing promise of achievement. —*n.* Advent **:** arrival.

com•i•ty (kŏm′ĭ-tē) *n., pl.* **-ties.** Social courtesy **:** civility.

com•ma (kŏm′ə) *n.* A punctuation mark (,) used to indicate a separation of elements or ideas in a sentence.

com•mand (kə-mănd′) *v.* **1.** To give orders (to). **2.** To rule (over). **3.** To dominate by position **:** overlook. ★ *syns:* BID, CHARGE, DIRECT, ENJOIN, INSTRUCT, ORDER, REQUIRE, TELL —*n.* **1.** The act of commanding. **2.** An authoritative order. **3.** A signal that activates a device, as a computer. **4.** Controlling power **:** mastery. **5. a.** A military unit, post, or district under the control of one officer. **b.** A group of officers authorized to command.

com•man•dant (kŏm'ən-dănt') *n.* A military commander.

com•man•deer (kŏm'ən-dîr') *v.* To confiscate esp. for military or public use.

com•mand•er (kə-măn'dər) *n.* **1.** One who commands **:** leader. **2.** An officer in the U.S. Navy who ranks above a lieutenant commander and below a captain.

commander in chief *n., pl.* **commanders in chief.** The supreme military commander of a nation's armed forces.

com•mand•ing (kə-măn'dĭng) *adj.* Dominating, as by size or position.

com•mand•ment (kə-mănd'mənt) *n.* **1.** An order **:** command. **2.** *often* **Commandment.** One of the Ten Commandments.

command module *n.* The part of a spacecraft that houses the astronauts and the controls.

com•man•do (kə-măn'dō) *n., pl.* **-dos** *or* **-does.** A member of a small military force trained to make quick surprise raids.

com•mem•o•rate (kə-mĕm'ə-rāt') *v.* **-rat•ed, -rat•ing. 1.** To honor the memory of, esp. ceremonially. **2.** To be a memorial to, as a holiday. **—com•mem'o•ra'tion** *n.* **—com•mem'o•ra•tive** (-ər-ə-tĭv, -ə-rā'-) *adj. & n.* **—com•mem'o•ra'tor** *n.*

com•mence (kə-mĕns') *v.* **-menced, -menc•ing.** To start **:** begin.

com•mence•ment (kə-mĕns'mənt) *n.* **1.** A beginning. **2.** A graduation ceremony.

com•mend (kə-mĕnd') *v.* **1.** To praise **:** applaud. **2.** To recommend. **3.** To entrust to another. **—com•mend'a•ble** *adj.* **—com•mend'a•bly** *adv.* **—com'men•da'tion** (kŏm'ən-dā'shən) *n.*

com•men•da•to•ry (kə-mĕn'də-tôr'ē, -tōr'ē) *adj.* Serving to praise.

com•men•sal (kə-mĕn'səl) *adj.* **1.** Of or relating to those who normally eat at the same table. **2.** *Biol.* Of or marked by commensalism. **—com•men'sal** *n.*

com•men•sal•ism (kə-mĕn'sə-lĭz'əm) *n.* *Biol.* A relationship in which two or more organisms live in close attachment or partnership and in which one may benefit but neither is parasitic on the other.

com•men•su•ra•ble (kə-mĕn'sər-ə-bəl, -shər-) *adj.* Measurable by a common standard or unit. **—com•men'su•ra•bil'i•ty** *n.* **—com•men'su•ra•bly** *adv.*

com•men•su•rate (kə-mĕn'sər-ĭt, -shər-) *adj.* **1.** Equal in size, extent, or duration. **2.** Proportionate <a salary *commensurate* with experience> **3.** Commensurable. **—com•men'su•ra'tion** *n.*

com•ment (kŏm'ĕnt') *n.* **1.** A statement of observation, analysis, or criticism. **2.** An expression of opinion. **—com'ment'** *v.*

com•men•tar•y (kŏm'ən-tĕr'ē) *n., pl.* **-ies.** A series of comments that explain or interpret. ★ *syns:* ANNOTATION, EXEGESIS, INTERPRETATION, NOTE

com•men•tate (kŏm'ən-tāt') *v.* **-tat•ed, -tat•ing.** To comment on or act as a commentator.

com•men•ta•tor (kŏm'ən-tā'tər) *n.* One who reports and analyzes news on radio or television.

com•merce (kŏm'ərs) *n.* The buying and selling of goods **:** business.

com•mer•cial (kə-mûr'shəl) *adj.* **1.** Of, relating to, or engaged in commerce. **2.** Designed for profit. **3.** Supported by advertising <*commercial* TV> *—n.* An advertisement on television or radio. **—com•mer'cial•ism** *n.* **—com•mer'cial•ist** *n.* **—com•mer'cial•is'tic** *adj.*

commercial bank *n.* A bank whose primary functions are to take demand deposits and negotiate short-term loans.

com•mer•cial•ize (kə-mûr'shə-līz') *v.* **-ized, -iz•ing.** To make commercial, esp. for gain. **—com•mer'cial•i•za'tion** *n.*

com•min•gle (kə-mĭng'gəl) *v.* **-gled, -gling.** To mix together **:** blend.

com•mis•er•ate (kə-mĭz'ə-rāt') *v.* **-at•ed, -at•ing.** To feel or display sympathy (for). **—com•mis'er•a'tion** *n.* **—com•mis'er•a'tive** *adj.* **—com•mis'er•a'tor** *n.*

com•mis•sar (kŏm'ĭ-sär') *n.* An official of the Communist Party whose duties include political indoctrination and enforcement of party loyalty.

com•mis•sar•i•at (kŏm'ĭ-sâr'ē-ət) *n.* An army department providing food and other supplies.

com•mis•sar•y (kŏm'ĭ-sĕr'ē) *n., pl.* **-ies.** A store for food and supplies, esp. on a military base.

com•mis•sion (kə-mĭsh'ən) *n.* **1. a.** Official permission to carry out a task. **b.** The permission so granted. **c.** The task so consigned. **d.** A document conferring such permission. **2.** A group authorized to carry out certain functions or tasks. **3.** A perpetration <*commission* of a felony> **4.** An allowance to a salesperson or agent for his or her services. **5.** A certificate conferring the rank of a commissioned officer. *—v.* **1.** To give a commission to. **2.** To put in an order for. **—in commission.** In use or in working condition. **—out of commission.** Not in use or in usable condition.

commissioned officer *n.* A military officer who ranks above a warrant officer or an enlisted man or woman.

com•mis•sion•er (kə-mĭsh'ə-nər) *n.* **1.** A member of a commission. **2.** A governmental department official. **3.** An administrative official in a professional sport.

com•mit (kə-mĭt') *v.* **-mit•ted, -mit•ting. 1.** To be responsible for <*commit* murder> **2.** To entrust **:** consign. **3.** To place officially in custody or confinement. **4.** To pledge or obligate (oneself). **—com•mit'ment, com•mit'tal** *n.* **—com•mit'ta•ble** *adj.*

com•mit•tee (kə-mĭt'ē) *n.* A group delegated

to perform a particular function or task. —**com•mit'tee•man** *n.* —**com•mit'tee•wom'an** *n.*

com•mix (kə-mĭks', kŏ-) *v.* **-mixed, -mix•ing.** To mix or cause to mix together : blend. —**com•mix'ture** *n.*

com•mode (kə-mōd') *n.* **1.** A low bureau or cabinet. **2.** A movable washstand. **3.** A toilet.

com•mo•di•ous (kə-mō'dē-əs) *adj.* Capacious : roomy.

com•mod•i•ty (kə-mŏd'ĭ-tē) *n., pl.* **-ties. 1.** Something useful. **2.** A transportable item of commerce or trade, esp. a mining or agricultural product.

com•mo•dore (kŏm'ə-dôr', -dōr') *n.* **1.** Formerly, a naval officer ranking below a rear admiral. **2. a.** The senior captain of a merchant fleet or naval squadron. **b.** The highest-ranking officer of a yacht club.

com•mon (kŏm'ən) *adj.* **1.** Shared by all : mutual. **2.** Relating to the entire community : public. **3.** Widespread : general. **4. a.** Ordinary : usual. **b.** Most widely known. **5.** Standard or average. **6.** Unrefined : vulgar. ★ ***syns:*** COMMUNAL, GENERAL, JOINT, MUTUAL, PUBLIC —*n.* **1.** An area of land shared by an entire community. **2. Commons.** The House of Commons. —**com'mon•ly** *adv.*

common carrier *n.* One that transports passengers or goods for a fee.

common denominator *n.* **1.** A number into which all the denominators of a set of fractions may be evenly divided. **2.** A commonly shared characteristic or theme.

com•mon•er (kŏm'ə-nər) *n.* A person not of the nobility.

Common Era *n.* The period coinciding with the Christian era.

common fraction *n.* A fraction whose denominator and numerator are both whole numbers.

common ground *n.* A foundation for mutual understanding.

common law *n.* An unwritten system of law based on judicial decisions, usages, and customs. —**com'mon-law'** *adj.*

common market *n.* An economic association of nations.

common multiple *n.* A number that is a multiple of each of 2 or more given quantities.

com•mon•place (kŏm'ən-plās') *adj.* Common : ordinary. —*n.* Something ordinary, esp. a trite remark.

common sense *n.* The native ability to make sound judgments.

com•mon•weal (kŏm'ən-wēl') *n.* **1.** The public good or welfare. **2.** *Archaic.* A commonwealth.

com•mon•wealth (kŏm'ən-wĕlth') *n.* **1.** The people of a state or nation. **2.** A state or nation governed by the people : republic. **3.** A federation of autonomous states.

Commonwealth Day *n.* Victoria Day.

Commonwealth of Nations. An association including the United Kingdom, its dependencies, and many former colonies.

com•mo•tion (kə-mō'shən) *n.* Turbulent or violent motion : tumult.

com•mu•nal (kə-myōō'nəl, kŏm'yə-nəl) *adj.* **1.** Of or relating to a community or commune. **2.** Public. —**com'mu•nal'i•ty** (-năl'ĭ-tē) *n.* —**com•mu'nal•ly** *adv.*

com•mune[1] (kə-myōōn') *v.* **-muned, -mun•ing.** To communicate privately <*commune* with nature>

com•mune[2] (kŏm'yōōn') *n.* **1.** The smallest local political unit of some European countries. **2. a.** A small, often rural community whose members share work and income and often own property collectively. **b.** The members of a commune.

com•mu•ni•ca•ble (kə-myōō'nĭ-kə-bəl) *adj.* **1.** Capable of being transmitted. **2.** Talkative. —**com•mu'ni•ca•bil'i•ty** *n.* —**com•mu'ni•ca•bly** *adv.*

com•mu•ni•cant (kə-myōō'nĭ-kənt) *n.* **1.** One who receives Communion. **2.** One who communicates.

com•mu•ni•cate (kə-myōō'nĭ-kāt') *v.* **-cat•ed, -cat•ing. 1.** To make known : disclose. **2.** To transmit, as a disease. **3.** To have an exchange, as of ideas. **4.** To receive Communion. —**com•mu'ni•ca'tor** *n.*

com•mu•ni•ca•tion (kə-myōō'nĭ-kā'shən) *n.* **1.** The act of communicating. **2.** The exchange of ideas, messages, or information. **3.** A message. **4. communications. a.** A system for communicating. **b.** The art and technology of communicating. —**com•mu'ni•ca'tive** *adj.*

com•mun•ion (kə-myōōn'yən) *n.* **1.** An act or instance of sharing or exchanging, as of feelings or thoughts. **2. a.** A spiritual or religious fellowship. **b.** A Christian denomination. **3. Communion.** The Eucharist or its consecrated elements.

com•mu•ni•qué (kə-myōō'nĭ-kā', -myōō'nĭ-kā') *n.* An official message.

com•mu•nism (kŏm'yə-nĭz'əm) *n.* **1.** An economic system in which production and goods are commonly owned. **2. Communism. a.** A one-party system of government in which the state plans and controls the economy. **b.** The Marxist-Leninist version of Communist doctrine. —**com'mu•nist** *n.* —**com'mu•nis'tic** *adj.* —**com'mu•nis'ti•cal•ly** *adv.*

com•mu•ni•ty (kə-myōō'nĭ-tē) *n., pl.* **-ties. 1. a.** A group of people residing in the same region and under the same government. **b.** The region in which they reside. **2.** A class or group with common interests. **3.** Likeness or identity. **4.** Society in general.

community college *n.* An often government-funded 2-year college without residential facilities.

community property *n.* Property owned jointly by a married couple.

com•mu•nize (kŏm'yə-nīz') *v.* **-nized, -niz•ing. 1.** To subject to public ownership or control. **2.** To convert to communistic principles or practices. —**com'mu•ni•za'tion** *n.*

com•mu•ta•tion (kŏm′yə-tā′shən) *n.* **1.** An exchange or substitution. **2.** *Law.* A reduction of a penalty to one less severe. **3.** The travel of a commuter.
com•mu•ta•tive (kŏm′yə-tā′tĭv, kə-myōō′tə-tĭv) *adj.* **1.** Relating to, involving, or marked by substitution or exchange. **2.** Independent of order, as a logical or mathematical operation combining objects 2 at a time. **—com•mu′ta•tiv′i•ty** (kə-myōō′tə-tĭv′ĭ-tē) *n.*
com•mu•ta•tor (kŏm′yə-tā′tər) *n.* A switching device used in electric motors or generators to provide a flow of current in a desired direction through a desired path.
com•mute (kə-myōōt′) *v.* **-mut•ed, -mut•ing. 1.** To substitute **:** exchange. **2.** To reduce (a penalty or payment) in severity. **3.** To travel as a commuter. *—n. Informal.* The trip made by a commuter.
com•mut•er (kə-myōō′tər) *n.* One who travels regularly between 2 places, as city and suburb.
com•pact[1] (kəm-păkt′, kŏm-, kŏm′păkt′) *adj.* **1.** Solidly united or packed together. **2.** Grouped within a small space. **3.** Expressed concisely. *—v.* (kəm-păkt′). To compress together. *—n.* (kŏm′păkt′). **1.** A small case for cosmetics. **2.** A small automobile. **—com•pact′er** *n.* **—com•pact′ly** *adv.*
com•pact[2] (kŏm′păkt′) *n.* An agreement or covenant.
com•pact disc (kŏm′păkt′) *or* **compact disk** *n.* A small optical disk on which data or music is encoded.
com•pac•tor (kəm-păk′tər, kŏm′păk′-) *n.* A device for compressing trash into small packages for disposal.
†com•pa•dre (kəm-pä′drā) *n. SW U.S.* A close friend or associate.
com•pan•ion (kəm-păn′yən) *n.* **1.** One who accompanies another. **2.** One hired to live or travel with another. **3.** One of a matched pair or set **:** mate. **—com•pan′ion•ship′** *n.*
com•pan•ion•a•ble (kəm-păn′yə-nə-bəl) *adj.* Friendly **:** sociable. **—com•pan′ion•a•bly** *adv.*
com•pan•ion•way (kəm-păn′yən-wā′) *n.* A staircase from a ship's deck to the area or cabins below.
com•pa•ny (kŭm′pə-nē) *n., pl.* **-nies. 1.** A group of people. **2.** People assembled socially. **3.** A guest or guests. **4.** Companionable association. **5.** A commercial enterprise. **6.** A group of theatrical performers. **7.** A subdivision of a batallion or regiment. **8.** A ship's crew and officers.
com•pa•ra•ble (kŏm′pər-ə-bəl) *adj.* **1.** Able to be compared. **2.** Worthy of comparison. **3.** Like or equivalent. **—com′pa•ra•bil′i•ty** *n.* **—com′pa•ra•bly** *adv.*
com•par•a•tive (kəm-păr′ə-tĭv) *adj.* **1.** Of or based on comparison. **2.** Estimated by comparison **:** relative <a *comparative* newcomer> **3.** Indicating a degree of comparison of adjectives and adverbs higher than positive and lower than superlative. *—n.* **1.** The comparative degree of an adjective or adverb. **2.** A comparative adjective or adverb. **—com•par′a•tive•ly** *adv.*
com•pare (kəm-pâr′) *v.* **-pared, -par•ing. 1.** To represent as similar or equal **:** liken. **2.** To examine so as to note the likenesses or differences of. **3.** To form the positive, comparative, or superlative degree of (an adjective or adverb). *—n.* Comparison <cuisine beyond *compare*>
com•par•i•son (kəm-păr′ĭ-sən) *n.* **1.** The act of comparing. **2.** Similarity **:** likeness. **3.** The modification of an adjective or adverb to indicate the positive, comparative, or superlative degree.
com•part•ment (kəm-pärt′mənt) *n.* One of the spaces or sections into which an area or container is subdivided. **—com′part•men′tal** (kŏm′pärt-mĕn′tl) *adj.*
com•part•men•tal•ize (kŏm′pärt-mĕn′tl-īz′, kəm-pärt′-) *v.* **-ized, -iz•ing.** To separate into distinct areas or categories. **—com′part•men′tal•i•za′tion** *n.*
com•pass (kŭm′pəs, kŏm′-) *n.* **1.** A device for determining geographic direction, esp. a magnetic needle mounted or suspended horizontally and free to pivot until aligned with the earth's magnetic field. **2.** *often* **compasses.** A hinged V-shaped device for drawing circles or circular arcs. **3.** An enclosing boundary **:** circumference. **4.** An enclosed space or area. **5.** A range or scope **:** extent. *—v.* **1.** To go around **:** circle. **2.** To shut in on all sides **:** encircle. **3.** To accomplish or gain. **4.** To plot **:** scheme.
com•pas•sion (kəm-păsh′ən) *n.* Actively sympathetic concern for the suffering of another **:** mercy. **—com•pas′sion•ate** *adj.*
com•pat•i•ble (kəm-păt′ə-bəl) *adj.* Capable of living or functioning harmoniously with others. *—n. Computer Sci.* A device that can be used with or substituted for another. **—com•pat′i•bil′i•ty, com•pat′i•ble•ness** *n.* **—com•pat′i•bly** *adv.*
com•pa•tri•ot (kəm-pā′trē-ət, -ŏt′) *n.* A person from one's own country.
com•peer (kəm-pîr′, kŏm′pîr′) *n.* An equal or peer.
com•pel (kəm-pĕl′) *v.* **-pelled, -pel•ling.** To constrain **:** force.
com•pen•di•um (kəm-pĕn′dē-əm) *n., pl.* **-ums** *or* **-di•a** (-dē-ə). A short, detailed summary.
com•pen•sate (kŏm′pən-sāt′) *v.* **-sat•ed, -sat•ing. 1.** To make up for **:** offset. **2.** To make payment or reparation to **:** reimburse. **—com′pen•sa′tion** *n.* **—com•pen′sa•to′ry** (kəm-pĕn′sə-tôr′ē, -tōr′ē) *adj.*
com•pete (kəm-pēt′) *v.* **-pet•ed, -pet•ing.** To contend with another **:** vie.
com•pe•tent (kŏm′pĭ-tənt) *adj.* **1.** Qualified **:** capable. **2.** Adequate for a specified purpose. **3.** Legally qualified to perform an act. **—com′pe•tence, com′pe•ten•cy** *n.*
com•pe•ti•tion (kŏm′pĭ-tĭsh′ən) *n.* **1.** The act of competing **:** rivalry. **2.** A test of skill **:** contest. **—com•pet′i•tive** *adj.*
com•pet•i•tor (kəm-pĕt′ĭ-tər) *n.* One who

competes against another, as in business or sports : rival.

com•pile (kəm-pīl′) *v.* **-piled, -pil•ing. 1.** To gather into a single book. **2.** To put together from materials gathered from a number of sources. **3.** *Computer Sci.* To convert to machine language. **—com′pi•la′tion** (kŏm′pə-lā′shən) *n.* **—com•pil′er** *n.*

com•pla•cen•cy (kəm-plā′sən-sē) *also* **com•pla•cence** (-səns) *n.* **1.** Gratification. **2.** Smug self-satisfaction. **—com•pla′cent** *adj.* **—com•pla′cent•ly** *adv.*

com•plain (kəm-plān′) *v.* **1.** To express feelings of dissatisfaction, pain, or resentment. **2.** To make a formal charge. ★ ***syns:*** BEEF, BELLYACHE, GRIPE, GROUSE, KICK, WHINE **—com•plain′er** *n.*

com•plain•ant (kəm-plā′nənt) *n.* One who files a formal charge, as in a court of law : plaintiff.

com•plaint (kəm-plānt′) *n.* **1.** An expression of dissatisfaction, pain, or resentment. **2.** A reason or cause for complaining : grievance. **3.** An illness. **4.** *Law.* A plaintiff's formal charge.

com•plai•sance (kəm-plā′səns) *n.* Willingness to comply. **—com•plai′sant** *adj.*

com•pleat (kəm-plēt′) *adj.* Highly proficient or knowledgeable <was the *compleat* chess player>

†com•plect•ed (kəm-plĕk′tĭd) *adj. Regional.* Marked by or having a particular facial complexion <dark-*complected*>

com•ple•ment (kŏm′plə-mənt) *n.* **1.** Something that completes, perfects, or makes up a whole. **2.** The number or quantity required to make up a whole. **3.** Either of a pair of angles whose measures add up to 90°. **4.** A word or group of words used to complete a predicate. —*v.* (kŏm′plə-mĕnt′). To make complete or be a complement to. **—com′ple•men′ta•ry** (-tə-rē, -trē) *adj.*

com•plete (kəm-plēt′) *adj.* **1.** Having all necessary or normal parts : whole. **2.** At an end : concluded. **3.** Thorough <a *complete* success> ★ ***syns:*** ENTIRE, FULL, INTACT, INTEGRAL, PERFECT, WHOLE —*v.* **-plet•ed, -plet•ing. 1.** To make complete. **2.** To end. **—com•ple′tion** *n.*

com•plex (kəm-plĕks′, kŏm′plĕks′) *adj.* **1.** Consisting of composite parts. **2.** Intricate <a *complex* problem> ★ ***syns:*** BYZANTINE, COMPLICATED, CONVOLUTED, ELABORATE, INTRICATE, INVOLUTE, INVOLVED, KNOTTY, LABYRINTHINE —*n.* (kŏm′plĕks′). **1.** A whole composed of interconnected or intricate parts. **2.** A group of repressed memories, emotions, and desires that influences one's behavior and personality. **—com•plex′i•ty** *n.* **—com•plex′ly** *adv.*

complex fraction *n.* A fraction in which the numerator or denominator is expressed as a fraction.

com•plex•ion (kəm-plĕk′shən) *n.* **1.** The natural color and appearance of the skin, esp. of the face. **2.** General appearance or character. **—com•plex′ioned** *adj.*

complex number *n.* A number of the form $a + bi$, where a and b are real numbers and $i^2 = -1$.

complex sentence *n.* A sentence consisting of an independent clause and at least one other independent or dependent clause.

com•pli•ance (kəm-plī′əns) *n. also* **com•pli•an•cy** (-ən-sē) *n.* **1.** Acquiescence to a rule, request, demand, etc. **2.** A tendency or disposition to yield to others. **—com•pli′ant** *adj.* **—com•pli′ant•ly** *adv.*

com•pli•cate (kŏm′plĭ-kāt′) *v.* **-cat•ed, -cat•ing.** To make or become complex. **—com′pli•ca′tion** *n.*

com•plic•it (kəm-plĭs′ĭt) *adj.* Having complicity.

com•plic•i•ty (kəm-plĭs′ĭ-tē) *n.* Involvement as an accomplice in a crime or wrongdoing.

com•pli•ment (kŏm′plə-mənt) *n.* **1.** An expression of admiration or praise. **2. compliments.** Good wishes : regards <*compliments* to the chef> **—com′pli•ment** *v.*

com•pli•men•ta•ry (kŏm′plə-mĕn′tə-rē, -trē) *adj.* **1.** Expressing a compliment <*complimentary* reviews> **2.** Given free as a favor or courtesy <*complimentary* tickets> **—com′pli•men′ta•ri•ly** *adv.*

com•ply (kəm-plī′) *v.* **-plied, -ply•ing.** To agree or yield, as to a wish or command. **—com•pli′er** *n.*

com•po•nent (kəm-pō′nənt) *n.* A constituent element. **—com•po′nent** *adj.*

com•port (kəm-pôrt′, -pōrt′) *v.* **1.** To conduct (oneself) in a given way. **2.** To be appropriate : harmonize.

com•port•ment (kəm-pôrt′mənt, -pōrt′-) *n.* Deportment : bearing.

com•pose (kəm-pōz′) *v.* **-posed, -pos•ing. 1.** To make up : constitute. **2.** To make by combining elements or parts. **3.** To create or produce (e.g., a song or poem). **4.** To make tranquil or calm. **5.** To adjust or settle. **6.** To set or arrange (e.g., type). **—com•pos′ed•ly** *adv.* **—com•pos′er** *n.*

com•pos•ite (kəm-pŏz′ĭt) *adj.* **1.** Made up of distinct components : compound. **2.** Of, belonging to, or typical of the Compositae, a large plant family characterized by flower heads consisting of many small, densely clustered flowers that appear to be a single bloom. —*n.* **1.** A compound. **2.** A composite plant. **—com•pos′ite•ly** *adv.*

com•po•si•tion (kŏm′pə-zĭsh′ən) *n.* **1.** The act or product of composing, esp. an artistic or literary work. **2.** Make-up : constitution. **3.** The unified arrangement of artistic parts. **4.** A short essay, as for school. **5.** The setting of printing type. **—com′po•si′tion•al** *adj.*

com•pos•i•tor (kəm-pŏz′ĭ-tər) *n.* A typesetter.

com•post (kŏm′pōst′) *n.* A fertilizer consisting of decayed organic matter. **—com′post** *v.*

com•po•sure (kəm-pō′zhər) *n.* Calm self-possession.

com•pote (kŏm′pōt′) *n.* **1.** Fruit cooked or stewed in syrup. **2.** A stemmed dish used for holding fruit, candy, etc.

com•pound[1] (kŏm′pound′) *n.* **1.** A combination of 2 or more parts, elements, or ingredients. **2.** A solid or hyphenated word composed of 2 or more words or word elements. **3.** A substance consisting of atoms of 2 or more different elements in definite proportions and usu. having properties unlike those of its constituent elements. —*v.* (kŏm-pound′, kəm-). **1.** To combine. **2.** To produce by combining. **3.** To compute (interest) on both the principal and accrued interest. **4.** To increase <Illness *compounded* our woes.> —*adj.* (kŏm′pound′, kŏm-pound′). Made up of 2 or more parts. **—com•pound′a•ble** *adj.*

com•pound[2] (kŏm′pound) *n.* A group of buildings enclosed by a wall or fence.

compound eye *n.* The eye of most insects and some crustaceans, composed of many light-sensitive elements, each with its own refractive system that forms a portion of an image.

compound fracture *n.* A fracture in which broken bone lacerates soft tissue.

compound interest *n.* Interest computed on both the principal and accrued unpaid interest.

compound sentence *n.* A sentence formed of 2 or more independent clauses.

com•pre•hend (kŏm′prĭ-hĕnd′) *v.* **1.** To perceive or understand. **2.** To include : comprise. **—com′pre•hen′sion** *n.*

com•pre•hen•si•ble (kŏm′prĭ-hĕn′sə-bəl) *adj.* Able to be understood. **—com′pre•hen′si•bil′i•ty** *n.* **—com′pre•hen′si•bly** *adv.*

com•pre•hen•sive (kŏm′prĭ-hĕn′sĭv) *adj.* Broad in scope or content.

com•press (kəm-prĕs′) *v.* To press together or condense. —*n.* (kŏm′prĕs′). A soft pad applied to control bleeding or reduce pain. **—com•press′i•bil′i•ty** *n.* **—com•press′i•ble** *adj.* **—com•pres′sion** *n.*

compressed air *n.* Air under greater than atmospheric pressure.

com•pres•sor (kəm-prĕs′ər) *n.* Something that compresses, esp. a machine for compressing gases.

com•prise (kəm-prīz′) *v.* **-prised, -pris•ing. 1.** To be made up of : consist of. **2.** To include : contain. **—com•pris′a•ble** *adj.*

com•pro•mise (kŏm′prə-mīz′) *n.* **1.** A settlement of differences between opposing sides in which each side makes concessions. **2.** Something combining the qualities of different things. —*v.* **-mised, -mis•ing. 1.** To settle by or accept concessions. **2.** To expose to suspicion, danger, or disrepute. **3.** To make a compromise. **—com′pro•mis′er** *n.*

comp•trol•ler (kən-trō′lər) *n. var. of* CONTROLLER 2.

com•pul•sion (kəm-pŭl′shən) *n.* **1.** The act of compelling or state of being compelled. **2.** An irresistible impulse to act irrationally. **—com•pul′sive** *adj.*

com•pul•so•ry (kəm-pŭl′sə-rē) *adj.* **1.** Using or exerting compulsion : coercive. **2.** Mandatory. ★ ***syns:*** IMPERATIVE, MANDATORY, NECESSARY, OBLIGATORY, REQUIRED, REQUISITE **—com•pul′so•ri•ly** *adv.*

com•punc•tion (kəm-pŭngk′shən) *n.* Disquietude caused by a sense of guilt.

com•pute (kəm-pyo͞ot′) *v.* **-put•ed, -put•ing. 1.** To determine by mathematics, esp. by numerical methods. **2.** To use a computer. **—com•put′a•bil′i•ty** *n.* **—com•put′a•ble** *adj.* **—com′pu•ta′tion** *n.*

com•put•er (kəm-pyo͞o′tər) *n.* One that computes, esp. a programmable high-speed electronic machine that performs mathematical or logical calculations and processes, retrieves, and stores information.

computer graphics *n. (sing. or pl. in number).* Visual computer output, as on a display screen or printer.

com•put•er•ize (kəm-pyo͞o′tə-rīz′) *v.* **-ized, -iz•ing. 1.** To process or store (data) with or in a computer or computer system. **2.** To furnish with a computer or computer system. **—com•put′er•i•za′tion** *n.*

computerized axial tomography *n.* Tomography in which computer analysis of a series of cross-sectional scans made along a single axis of a structure is used to construct a three-dimensional image.

computer language *n.* Any of various codes that are used to provide data and instructions to computers.

computer virus *n.* A computer program designed to copy itself into the other programs stored in a computer with either a benign or negative effect.

com•rade (kŏm′răd′, -rəd) *n.* **1.** A companion, friend, or associate. **2.** *often* **Comrade.** A fellow member, esp. of the Communist Party. **—com′rade•ship′** *n.*

Com•sat (kŏm′săt′). A trademark for a communications satellite.

con[1] (kŏn) *adv.* Against <argue pro and *con*> —*n.* An argument or opinion against something.

con[2] (kŏn) *v.* **conned, con•ning.** To examine or study carefully, esp. to memorize.

con[3] (kŏn) *Slang.* —*v.* **conned, con•ning.** To swindle : dupe. —*n.* A swindle.

con[4] (kŏn) *n. Slang.* A convict.

con bri•o (kŏn brē′ō, kōn) *adv. Mus.* With vigor. —Used as a direction.

con•cat•e•nate (kŏn-kăt′n-āt′, kən-) *v.* **-nat•ed, -nat•ing.** To connect in a series or chain. **—con•cat′e•nate** (-ĭt, -āt′) *adj.* **—con•cat′e•na′tion** *n.*

con•cave (kŏn-kāv′, kŏn′kāv′) *adj.* Curved or rounded inward like the inner surface of a ball. **—con•cav′i•ty** (-kăv′ĭ-tē), **con•cave′ness** *n.*

con•ceal (kən-sēl′) *v.* To keep from sight or disclosure. **—con•ceal′a•ble** *adj.*

con•cede (kən-sēd′) *v.* **-ced•ed, -ced•ing. 1.** To acknowledge as true or real : admit. **2.** To grant, as a privilege. **3.** To yield. **—con•ced′er** *n.*

†con•ceit (kən-sēt′) *n.* **1.** An exaggerated opinion of oneself : vanity. **2.** An imaginative or witty idea. **3.** An elaborate metaphor. —*v. Regional.* To imagine.

†**con•ceit•ed** (kən-sē′tĭd) *adj.* **1.** Unduly proud of oneself **:** vain. **2.** *Regional.* Inclined to be whimsical.
con•ceive (kən-sēv′) *v.* **-ceived, -ceiv•ing. 1.** To become pregnant (with). **2.** To create in the mind **:** devise. **3.** To believe or think <couldn't *conceive* the news to be true> **—con•ceiv′a•bil′i•ty** *n.* **—con•ceiv′a•ble** *adj.* **—con•ceiv′a•bly** *adv.* **—con•ceiv′er** *n.*
con•cen•trate (kŏn′sən-trāt′) *v.* **-trat•ed, -trat•ing. 1.** To draw toward a common center **:** focus. **2.** To direct one's attention. **3.** *Chem.* To increase the concentration of (a mixture or solution). *—n. Chem.* A product of concentration. **—con′cen•tra′tive** *adj.* **—con′cen•tra′tor** *n.*
con•cen•tra•tion (kŏn′sən-trā′shən) *n.* **1. a.** The act of concentrating, esp. of paying close attention. **b.** The state of being concentrated. **2.** Something concentrated. **3.** *Chem.* The amount of a particular substance in a specified amount of another substance.
concentration camp *n.* A camp for confinement of prisoners of war and political dissidents.
con•cen•tric (kən-sĕn′trĭk) *also* **con•cen•tri•cal** (-trĭ-kəl) *adj.* Having a common center. **—con•cen′tri•cal•ly** *adv.* **—con′cen•tric′i•ty** (-trĭs′ĭ-tē) *n.*
con•cept (kŏn′sĕpt′) *n.* **1.** A general understanding, esp. one derived from particular instances or occurrences. **2.** A thought. **—con•cep′tu•al** *adj.*
con•cep•tion (kən-sĕp′shən) *n.* **1.** The formation of a zygote capable of developing into a new organism. **2.** The ability to form mental concepts. **3.** Something, as a thought or plan, conceived in the mind.
con•cep•tu•al•ize (kən-sĕp′cho͞o-ə-līz′) *v.* **-ized, -iz•ing.** To form concepts (of). **—con•cep′tu•al•i•za′tion** *n.*
con•cern (kən-sûrn′) *v.* **1.** To relate or pertain to **:** affect. **2.** To engage the attention of. **3.** To cause uneasiness in **:** trouble. *—n.* **1.** Something interesting or important. **2.** Sincere regard. **3.** Uneasiness **:** worry. **4.** A business enterprise.
con•cern•ing (kən-sûr′nĭng) *prep.* In regard to **:** about.
con•cert (kŏn′sûrt′, -sərt) *n.* **1.** A musical performance for an audience. **2.** Agreement in feeling, purpose, or action. *—v.* (kən-sûrt′). **1.** To plan by mutual agreement. **2.** To act together in harmony.
con•cert•ed (kən-sûr′tĭd) *adj.* Achieved or planned together <a *concerted* effort>
con•cer•ti•na (kŏn′sər-tē′nə) *n.* A small accordion with bellows and buttons instead of keys.
con•cert•mas•ter (kŏn′sərt-măs′tər) *n.* The first violinist and assistant conductor of a symphony orchestra.
con•cer•to (kən-chĕr′tō) *n., pl.* **-tos** *or* **-ti** (-tē). An orchestral composition featuring one or more solo instruments.
con•ces•sion (kən-sĕsh′ən) *n.* **1.** The act of conceding. **2.** Something conceded. **3.** Something, as a tract of land, granted esp. by a government to be used for a particular purpose. **4.** The privilege of running a subsidiary business on certain premises.
con•ces•sion•aire (kən-sĕsh′ə-nâr′) *n.* The holder or operator of a concession.
con•ces•sive (kən-sĕs′ĭv) *adj.* Like or containing a concession.
conch (kŏngk, kŏnch) *n., pl.* **conchs** (kŏngks) *or* **conch•es** (kŏn′chĭz). Any of various tropical marine mollusks of the genus *Strombus* and other genera, with large spiral shells and edible flesh.

conch

con•chol•o•gy (kŏng-kŏl′ə-jē) *n.* The study of shells and mollusks. **—con′cho•log′i•cal** (-kə-lŏj′ĭ-kəl) *adj.* **—con•chol′o•gist** *n.*
con•cierge (kôɴ-syârzh′) *n.* A building custodian esp. in France who attends the door and acts as janitor.
con•cil•i•ate (kən-sĭl′ē-āt′) *v.* **-at•ed, -at•ing. 1.** To placate **:** appease. **2.** To gain the friendship of. **3.** To reconcile. **—con•cil′•i•a′•tion** *n.* **—con•cil′i•a′tor** *n.* **—con•cil′i•a•to′-ry** *adj.*
con•cise (kən-sīs′) *adj.* Short and to the point <a *concise* report>
con•ci•sion (kən-sĭzh′ən) *n.* The state or quality of being concise.
con•clave (kŏn′klāv′, kŏng′-) *n.* A private or secret meeting, esp. one in which Roman Catholic cardinals elect a new pope.
con•clude (kən-klo͞od′) *v.* **-clud•ed, -clud•ing. 1.** To come or bring to an end **:** close. **2.** To bring about (a settlement or agreement). **3.** To arrive at a decision (about). **4.** To determine **:** resolve. **—con•clu′sion** *n.*
con•clu•sive (kən-klo͞o′sĭv) *adj.* Serving to end doubt or uncertainty **:** decisive.
con•coct (kən-kŏkt′) *v.* **1.** To prepare by combining ingredients, as in cookery. **2.** To invent **:** contrive. **—con•coct′er, con•coc′tor** *n.* **—con•coc′tion** *n.*
con•com•i•tant (kən-kŏm′ĭ-tənt) *adj.* Accompanying. *—n.* Something that accompanies. **—con•com′i•tance** *n.* **—con•com′i•tant•ly** *adv.*
con•cord (kŏn′kôrd′, kŏng′-) *n.* **1.** Harmony **:** accord. **2.** A formal agreement **:** treaty.
con•cor•dance (kən-kôr′dns) *n.* **1.** A condition of agreement **:** harmony. **2.** An alphabeti-

cal index of the major words in a text or the works of an author, giving the passages in which they occur.

con•cor•dant (kən-kôr′dnt) *adj.* Harmonious. **—con•cor′dant•ly** *adv.*

con•cor•dat (kən-kôr′dăt′) *n.* A formal agreement : covenant.

con•course (kŏn′kôrs′, -kōrs′, kŏng′-) *n.* **1.** A large crowd. **2. a.** A large open space, as in an airport, for the passage of crowds. **b.** A broad thoroughfare.

con•cres•cence (kən-krĕs′əns) *n.* The growing together of related parts, as of the anatomy.

con•crete (kŏn-krēt′, kŏn′krēt′) *adj.* **1.** Of or pertaining to an actual specific thing or instance <*concrete* facts> **2.** Tangible : real. **3.** Coalesced into one mass : solid. **4.** Made of concrete. *—n.* (kŏn′krēt′, kŏn-krēt′). **1.** A building material made by mixing water with cement, gravel, and sand. **2.** A mass that is formed by the coalescence of particles or elements. *—v.* (kŏn′krēt′, kŏn-krēt′) **-cret•ed, -cret•ing. 1.** To coalesce into a solid mass. **2.** To build or cover with concrete.

con•cre•tion (kən-krē′shən) *n.* **1.** The act or process of concreting : coalescence. **2.** A solid mass. **3.** *Pathol.* CALCULUS 1.

con•cu•bine (kŏng′kyə-bīn′, kŏn′-) *n.* A woman who lives with a man without being legally married to him. **—con•cu′bin•age** (kŏn-kyōō′bə-nĭj, kən-) *n.*

con•cu•pis•cence (kŏn-kyōō′pĭ-səns) *n.* Strong sexual desire : lust. **—con•cu′pis•cent** *adj.*

con•cur (kən-kûr′) *v.* **-curred, -cur•ring. 1.** To have or express the same opinion : agree. **2.** To cooperate. **3.** To coincide. **—con•cur′rence** *n.*

con•cur•rent (kən-kûr′ənt) *adj.* **1.** Occurring at the same time. **2.** Acting together. **3.** *Law.* Having equal authority.

con•cuss (kən-kŭs′) *v.* To injure by concussion.

con•cus•sion (kən-kŭsh′ən) *n.* **1.** A violent jolt : shock. **2.** An injury of a soft bodily structure, esp. the brain, that results from a severe blow. **—con•cus′sive** (-kŭs′ĭv) *adj.* **—con•cus′sive•ly** *adv.*

con•demn (kən-dĕm′) *v.* **1.** To express strong disapproval of : denounce. **2. a.** To find guilty. **b.** To pronounce judgment against : sentence. **3.** To declare officially unfit for use. **4.** To declare appropriated by law for public use. **—con•demn′a•ble** *adj.* **—con′dem•na′tion** *n.* **—con•dem′na•to′ry** *adj.* **—con•demn′er** *n.*

con•den•sate (kŏn′dən-sāt′, -dĕn-, kən-dĕn′sāt′) *n.* A product of condensation.

con•dense (kən-dĕns′) *v.* **-densed, -dens•ing. 1.** To make or become more compact : concentrate. **2.** To make concise : abridge <*condense* three articles into one> **3.** To form a liquid from (e.g., a vapor). **4.** To undergo condensation. **—con•dens′a•bil′i•ty** *n.* **—con•dens′a•ble, con•dens′i•ble** *adj.* **—con′den•sa′tion** (kŏn′dĕn-sā′shən) *n.* **—con•dens′er** *n.*

condensed milk *n.* Sweetened evaporated milk.

con•de•scend (kŏn′dĭ-sĕnd′) *v.* **1.** To agree to do something one considers beneath one's dignity or rank : deign. **2.** To deal with or treat others in a patronizing way. **—con′de•scend′er** *n.* **—con′de•scend′ing** *adj.* **—con′de•scend′ing•ly** *adv.* **—con′de•scen′sion** *n.*

con•di•ment (kŏn′də-mənt) *n.* A seasoning for food.

con•di•tion (kən-dĭsh′ən) *n.* **1.** Mode or state of being. **2.** A state of health or fitness. **3.** *Informal.* A disease or ailment. **4.** A requirement : prerequisite. **5.** Something that restricts or modifies : qualification. **6.** *often* **conditions.** Existing circumstances <poor sailing *conditions*> ★ ***syns:*** MODE, POSTURE, SITUATION, STATE, STATUS *—v.* **1.** To make conditional. **2.** To make fit. **3.** To accustom (a person) to : adapt. **4.** *Psychol.* To cause to respond in a given manner to a given stimulus.

con•di•tion•al (kən-dĭsh′ə-nəl) *adj.* **1.** Imposing, based on, or including a condition or conditions. **2.** Stating or implying a grammatical condition. *—n.* A mood, tense, clause, or word expressing a grammatical condition. **—con•di′tion•al′i•ty** (-dĭsh′ə-năl′ĭ-tē) *n.*

con•di•tioned (kən-dĭsh′ənd) *adj.* **1.** Subject to or dependent on conditions. **2.** Prepared for a specific action or process. **3.** *Psychol.* Displaying or trained to display a modified or new response.

con•di•tion•er (kən-dĭsh′ə-nər) *n.* **1.** One that conditions. **2.** An additive or application that improves the quality or usability of a substance.

con•do (kŏn′dō) *n. Informal.* CONDOMINIUM 2.

con•dole (kən-dōl′) *v.* **-doled, -dol•ing.** To express sorrow or sympathy. **—con•do′la•to′ry** *adj.* **—con•do′lence** *n.* **—con•dol′er** *n.*

con•dom (kŏm′dəm) *n.* A thin rubber sheath designed to cover the penis during sexual intercourse to prevent conception or the spread of disease.

con•do•min•i•um (kŏn′də-mĭn′ē-əm) *n.* **1.** Joint rule or sovereignty. **2. a.** A residential structure, as an apartment building, in which the units are owned individually. **b.** An apartment in such a structure.

con•done (kən-dōn′) *v.* **-doned, -don•ing.** To overlook, disregard, or forgive (an offense). **—con•don′er** *n.*

con•dor (kŏn′dôr′, -dər) *n.* A very large New World vulture, *Vultur gryphus,* of the Andes, or *Gymnogyps californianus,* of the Calif. mountains.

con•duce (kən-dōōs′, -dyōōs′) *v.* **-duced, -duc•ing.** To lead to a specific result : contribute. **—con•du′cive** *adj.*

con•duct (kən-dŭkt′) *v.* **1.** To direct the course of : control <*conduct* an experiment> <*conduct* a meeting> **2.** To guide or lead. **3.** To serve as a medium for conveying : transmit <Some plastics *conduct* light.> **4.** To behave or act in a given way. *—n.* (kŏn′dŭkt′).

1. The way one behaves. 2. Management : control. —**con•duct′i•bil′i•ty** *n.* —**con•duct′i•ble** *adj.* —**con•duc′tion** *n.*
con•duc•tance (kən-dŭk′təns) *n.* A measure of a material's capacity for conducting electricity.
con•duc•tive (kən-dŭk′tĭv) *adj.* Exhibiting the power or ability to transmit or conduct. —**con′duc•tiv′i•ty** *n.*
con•duc•tor (kən-dŭk′tər) *n.* **1.** One who conducts, esp: **a.** The person in charge of a public conveyance, as a streetcar or railroad train. **b.** The director of a musical ensemble, as an orchestra. **2.** *Physics.* A substance or medium that conducts heat, light, or sound.
con•duit (kŏn′dĭt, -do͞o-ĭt) *n.* **1.** A channel or pipe for conveying fluids, as water. **2.** A tube or duct through which electric wires or cable pass. **3.** A means of communicating.
cone (kōn) *n.* **1.** A surface formed by a straight line that passes through a fixed point and moves along the intersection with a fixed curve. **2.** The figure formed by a cone, bound by its vertex and a plane that intersects above or below the vertex. **3.** A scaly cylindrical or rounded structure bearing seeds <a pine *cone*> **4.** A photoreceptor in the retina of the eye. **5.** A cone-shaped wafer for holding ice cream.

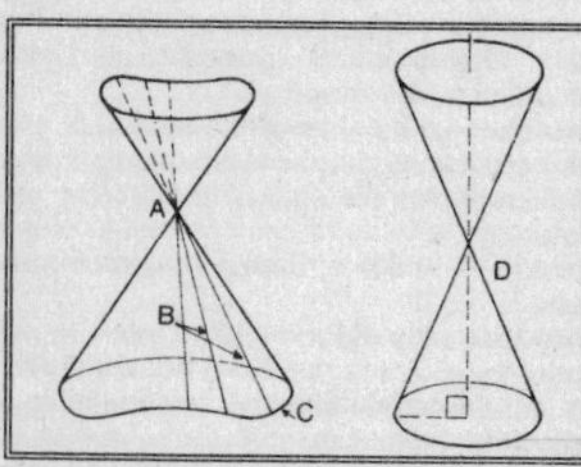

cone
A. vertex, B. elements, C. directrix, D. right circular cone

co•ney (kō′nē, kŭn′ē) *n. var. of* CONY.
con•fab•u•late (kən-făb′yə-lāt′) *v.* **-lat•ed, -lat•ing.** To converse informally : chat. —**con•fab′u•la′tion** *n.* —**con•fab′u•la′tor** *n.* —**con•fab′u•la•to′ry** *adj.*
con•fec•tion (kən-fĕk′shən) *n.* A sweet preparation, as candy.
con•fec•tion•er (kən-fĕk′shə-nər) *n.* A maker or seller of confections.
con•fec•tion•er•y (kən-fĕk′shə-nĕr′ē) *n., pl.* **-ies. 1.** Candies and confections as a whole. **2.** *also* **con•fec•tion•ar•y.** A confectioner's shop.
con•fed•er•a•cy (kən-fĕd′ər-ə-sē) *n., pl.* **-cies. 1. a.** A political alliance persons, parties, or states : league. **b. Confederacy.** The 11 S states that seceded from the U.S. during the Civil War. **2.** A conspiracy.
con•fed•er•ate (kən-fĕd′ər-ĭt) *n.* **1.** A member of a confederacy : ally. **2.** An accomplice. **3.** A supporter of the Confederacy. —*v.* (ə-rāt′) **-at•ed, -at•ing.** To join together in a confederacy.
con•fed•er•a•tion (kən-fĕd′ə-rā′shən) *n.* **1.** The act of confederating or condition of being confederated. **2.** A confederacy.
con•fer (kən-fûr′) *v.* **-ferred, -fer•ring. 1.** To bestow or award. **2.** To hold a conference : consult together. —**con•fer′ment** *n.* —**con•fer′ra•ble** *adj.* —**con•fer′ral** *n.* —**con•fer′rer** *n.*
con•fer•ence (kŏn′fər-əns, -frəns) *n.* **1.** A meeting for discussion. **2.** An association of athletic teams.
con•fess (kən-fĕs′) *v.* **1.** To acknowledge or disclose one's wrongdoing or fault. **2.** To acknowledge belief in. **3.** To disclose (one's sins) to God or a priest for absolution. —**con•fess′ed•ly** (-ĭd-lē) *adv.*
con•fes•sion (kən-fĕsh′ən) *n.* **1.** An act of confessing. **2.** Something confessed. **3.** A formal admission of guilt. **4.** Disclosure of one's sins to a priest for absolution. **5.** A church or religious group adhering to a particular creed.
con•fes•sion•al (kən-fĕsh′ə-nəl) *n.* A small stall in which a priest hears confessions.
con•fes•sor *also* **con•fess•er** (kən-fĕs′ər) *n.* **1.** A priest to whom sins are confessed. **2.** A person who confesses.
con•fet•ti (kən-fĕt′ē) *pl.n.* (*sing. in number*). Small pieces or streamers of colored paper strewn about on festive occasions.
con•fi•dant (kŏn′fĭ-dănt′, -dänt′, kŏn′fĭ-dănt′, -dänt′) *n.* One to whom private matters are confided.
con•fide (kən-fīd′) *v.* **-fid•ed, -fid•ing. 1.** To tell confidentially. **2.** To entrust to another. —**con•fid′er** *n.* —**con•fid′ing** *adj.* —**con•fid′ing•ly** *adv.*
con•fi•dence (kŏn′fĭ-dəns) *n.* **1.** Reliance or trust. **2.** A trusting relationship. **3.** A feeling of self-assurance. **4.** The assurance that someone will keep a secret. **5.** A secret. ★ ***syns:*** BELIEF, FAITH, RELIANCE, TRUST —**con′fi•dent** *adj.*
confidence game *n.* A swindle brought about by gaining the victim's confidence.
confidence man *n.* One who swindles by using a confidence game.
con•fi•den•tial (kŏn′fĭ-dĕn′shəl) *adj.* **1.** Disclosed in secret. **2.** Entrusted with another's confidence. —**con′fi•den′ti•al′i•ty** *n.* —**con′fi•den′tial•ly** *adv.*
con•fig•u•ra•tion (kən-fĭg′yə-rā′shən) *n.* Arrangement of elements or parts. —**con•fig′u•ra′tion•al•ly** *adv.* —**con•fig′u•ra′tive** (-rā′tĭv), **con•fig′u•ra′tion•al** *adj.*
con•fine (kən-fīn′) *v.* **-fined, -fin•ing. 1.** To keep within bounds : limit or restrict. **2.** To put in prison. —*n.* **confines** (kŏn′fīnz′). The limits of an area : borders. —**con•fin′a•ble, con•fine′a•ble** *adj.* —**con•fine′ment** *n.* —**con•fin′er** *n.*
con•firm (kən-fûrm′) *v.* **1.** To support or establish the validity of : corroborate. **2.** To make stronger : establish. **3.** To ratify for-

mally. **4.** To administer the rite of confirmation to. ★ ***syns:*** ATTEST, AUTHENTICATE, BACK, BEAR OUT, CORROBORATE, SUBSTANTIATE, VALIDATE, VERIFY, WARRANT —**con·firm'a·ble** *adj.* —**con·fir'ma·to'ry, con·fir'ma·tive** *adj.*

con·fir·ma·tion (kŏn'fər-mā'shən) *n.* **1.** An act of confirming. **2.** Something that verifies. **3.** A rite admitting a person to full membership in a church or synagogue.

con·fis·cate (kŏn'fĭ-skāt') *v.* **-cat·ed, -cat·ing. 1.** To appropriate (private property) for the public treasury. **2.** To appropriate or seize by or as if by authority. —**con'fis·ca'tion** *n.* —**con'fis·ca'tor** *n.*

con·fla·gra·tion (kŏn'flə-grā'shən) *n.* A large, destructive fire.

con·flate (kən-flāt') *v.* **-flat·ed, -flat·ing.** To combine (e.g., 2 variant texts) into a whole. —**con·fla'tion** *n.*

con·flict (kŏn'flĭkt') *n.* **1.** Prolonged open warfare. **2.** A state of disharmony : clash. ★ ***syns:*** BELLIGERENCY, HOSTILITIES, STRIFE, WAR, WARFARE —*v.* (kən-flĭkt'). To be opposed : differ. —**con·flic'tive** *adj.*

conflict of interest *n.* A conflict between the public obligations and private interests of a public official.

con·flu·ence (kŏn'flo͞o-əns) *n.* **1. a.** A flowing together of 2 or more streams. **b.** The point of juncture of such streams. **2.** An assembly. —**con·flu'ent** *adj. & n.*

con·flux (kŏn'flŭks') *n.* A confluence.

con·form (kən-fôrm') *v.* **1.** To make or become similar in form or character : correspond. **2.** To act or be in compliance. **3.** To act in accordance with prevailing modes or customs. —**con·form'a·bil'i·ty** *n.* —**con·form'a·ble** *adj.* —**con·form'a·bly** *adv.* —**con·form'er** *n.* —**con·form'ist** *n.*

con·for·mance (kən-fôr'məns) *n.* Conformity.

con·for·ma·tion (kŏn'fər-mā'shən) *n.* The shape, structure, or arrangement of something.

con·for·mi·ty (kən-fôr'mĭ-tē) *n., pl.* **-ties. 1.** Correspondence in form or character : agreement. **2.** Action in agreement with prevailing modes or customs.

con·found (kən-found', kŏn-) *v.* **1.** To bewilder or perplex. **2.** To mistake (one thing) for another <*confound* truths and lies> —**con·found'er** *n.*

con·fra·ter·ni·ty (kŏn'frə-tûr'nĭ-tē) *n., pl.* **-ties.** A group united in a common profession or for a common purpose.

con·frere (kŏn'frâr') *n.* An associate : colleague.

con·front (kən-frŭnt') *v.* **1.** To come face to face with, esp. with defiance or hostility. **2.** To come up against : encounter. —**con'fron·ta'tion** (kŏn'frən-tā'shən) *n.* —**con'fron·ta'tion·al** *adj.*

Con·fu·cian·ism (kən-fyo͞o'shə-nĭz'əm) *n.* The ethical principles based on the teachings of Confucius. —**Con·fu'cian** *n. & adj.* —**Con·fu'cian·ist** *n.*

con·fuse (kən-fyo͞oz') *v.* **-fused, -fus·ing. 1.** To bewilder : mislead. **2.** To mix up : jumble. **3.** To fail to differentiate from something else <*confuse* wealth with happiness> **4.** To make unclear : blur. ★ ***syns:*** DISORDER, JUMBLE, SCRAMBLE, SNARL —**con·fus'ed·ly** (-fyo͞o'zĭd-lē) *adv.* —**con·fus'ing·ly** *adv.* —**con·fu'sion** *n.*

con·fute (kən-fyo͞ot') *v.* **-fut·ed, -fut·ing.** To disprove decisively : refute. —**con·fut'a·ble** *adj.* —**con'fu·ta'tion** (kŏn'-) *n.* —**con·fu'ta·tive** *adj.*

con·ga (kŏng'gə) *n.* **1.** A dance of Latin-American origin in which the dancers form a long, winding line. **2.** Music for the conga. —**con'ga** *v.*

con game *n. Slang.* A confidence game.

con·geal (kən-jēl') *v.* **1.** To solidify, as by freezing. **2.** To jell : coagulate. —**con·geal'a·ble** *adj.* —**con·geal'ment** *n.*

con·gen·ial (kən-jēn'yəl) *adj.* **1.** Having the same temperament, habits, or tastes : sympathetic. **2.** Friendly : sociable. **3.** Agreeably suited to one's needs or nature. —**con·ge'ni·al'i·ty** (-jē'nē-ăl'ĭ-tē), **con·gen'ial·ness** *n.* —**con·gen'ial·ly** *adv.*

con·gen·i·tal (kən-jĕn'ĭ-tl) *adj.* **1.** Existing from the time of birth but not hereditary. **2.** Being such as if by nature <a *congenital* liar> —**con·gen'i·tal·ly** *adv.*

con·ger (kŏng'gər) *n.* A large, scaleless marine eel of the family Congridae, esp. *Conger oceanicus,* of Atlantic waters.

con·ge·ries (kŏn'jə-rēz', kən-jîr'ēz') *n.* (*sing. in number*). A collection of things.

con·gest (kən-jĕst') *v.* **1.** To overfill : clog. **2.** *Pathol.* To cause excessive blood accumulation in (an organ or vessel). —**con·ges'tion** *n.* —**con·ges'tive** *adj.*

con·glom·er·ate (kən-glŏm'ə-rāt') *v.* **-at·ed, -at·ing.** To form or cause to form into a mass of adhering material. —*n.* (-ər-ĭt). **1.** An adhering mass : cluster. **2.** *Geol.* Pebbles and gravel embedded in a cementing material such as hardened clay. **3.** A business enterprise consisting of many widely diversified companies. —**con·glom'er·ate** (-ər-ĭt) *adj.* —**con·glom'er·a'tion** *n.*

con·grat·u·late (kən-grăch'ə-lāt') *v.* **-lat·ed, -lat·ing.** To praise or acknowledge the good fortune or achievement of. —**con·grat'u·la'tion** *n.* —**con·grat'u·la'tor** *n.* —**con·grat'u·la·to'ry** (-lə-tôr'ē, -tōr'ē) *adj.*

con·gre·gate (kŏng'grĭ-gāt') *v.* **-gat·ed, -gat·ing.** To come or bring together in a crowd : assemble. —**con'gre·ga'tor** *n.*

con·gre·ga·tion (kŏng'grĭ-gā'shən) *n.* **1.** An act of congregating. **2.** An assembly. **3.** A group of people gathered for religious worship, esp. on a regular basis.

con·gre·ga·tion·al (kŏng'grĭ-gā'shə-nəl) *adj.* **1.** Of or relating to a congregation. **2. Congregational.** Of or relating to a Protestant denomination in which each individual member church is autonomous. —**con'gre·ga'tion·al·ism** *n.* —**con'gre·ga'tion·al·ist** *n.*

con·gress (kŏng'grĭs) *n.* **1.** A formal meeting

or assembly to discuss problems. **2.** The legislature of a nation, esp. of a republic. **3. Congress.** The national legislative body of the U.S., consisting of the Senate and the House of Representatives. **—con•gres'sion•al** *adj.* **—con•gres'sion•al•ly** *adv.*

con•gress•man (kŏng'grĭs-mən) *n.* A member of the U.S. Congress, esp. of the House of Representatives.

con•gress•wom•an (kŏng'grĭs-wo͝om'ən) *n.* A woman member of the U.S. Congress, esp. of the House of Representatives.

con•gru•ent (kŏng'gro͞o-ənt, kən-gro͞o'ənt) *adj.* **1.** Corresponding **:** congruous. **2.** *Math.* Having the same size and shape <*congruent* triangles> **—con•gru'ence** *n.* **—con'gru•ent•ly** *adv.*

con•gru•ous (kŏng'gro͞o-əs) *adj.* **1.** Corresponding in nature or kind **:** harmonious. **2.** *Math.* Congruent.

con•ic (kŏn'ĭk) *also* **con•i•cal** (-ĭ-kəl) *adj.* **1.** Shaped like a cone. **2.** Relating to a cone.

con•i•fer (kŏn'ə-fər, kō'nə-) *n.* A usu. evergreen cone-bearing tree, as a fir or pine. **—co•nif'er•ous** (kō-nĭf'ər-əs, kə-) *adj.*

con•jec•ture (kən-jĕk'chər) *n.* Inference based on incomplete or inconclusive evidence. **—con•jec'tur•a•ble** *adj.* **—con•jec'tur•al** *adj.* **—con•jec'ture** *v.*

con•join (kən-join') *v.* To join or become joined together **:** unite. **—con•joint'** *adj.*

con•ju•gal (kŏn'jo͝o-gəl, -jə-) *adj.* Of or relating to marriage or the relationship between spouses. **—con'ju•gal•ly** *adv.*

con•ju•gate (kŏn'jə-gāt') *v.* **-gat•ed, -gat•ing.** To inflect a word, esp. a verb. *—adj.* (-gĭt, -gāt'). Joined together, esp. in pairs **:** coupled. **—con'ju•gate'ly** *adv.* **—con'ju•ga'tive** *adj.* **—con'ju•ga'tor** *n.*

con•ju•ga•tion (kŏn'jə-gā'shən) *n.* **1.** A verb inflection. **2.** A schematic presentation of the full set of inflected forms of a verb. **—con'ju•ga'tion•al** *adj.*

con•junct (kən-jŭngkt', kŏn'jŭngkt') *adj.* Joined together **:** combined.

con•junc•tion (kən-jŭngk'shən) *n.* **1.** A combination or association. **2.** The simultaneous occurrence of 2 conditions, events, etc. **3.** A word, as *and* or *but*, that connects other words in a sentence.

con•junc•ti•va (kŏn'jŭngk-tī'və) *n., pl.* **-vas** *or* **-vae** (-vē'). The mucous membrane lining the inner surface of the eyelid and the surface of the eyeball. **—con'junc•ti'val** *adj.*

con•junc•tive (kən-jŭngk'tĭv) *adj.* **1.** Connective **:** joining. **2.** Joined together **:** combined. **3.** Of or used as a conjunction. *—n.* A conjunctive word.

con•junc•ti•vi•tis (kən-jŭngk'tə-vī'tĭs) *n.* *Pathol.* Inflammation of the conjunctiva, often highly contagious.

con•junc•ture (kən-jŭngk'chər) *n.* **1.** A set of circumstances. **2.** A critical set of circumstances **:** crisis.

con•jure (kŏn'jər, kən-jo͝or') *v.* **-jured, -jur•ing. 1.** To call on or entreat solemnly, esp. by an oath. **2.** To summon (a spirit) by sorcery. **3.** To cause or effect by or as if by magic. **4.** To call to mind <sights *conjuring* up past travels> **—con'ju•ra'tion** *n.* **—con'jur•er, con'ju•ror** *n.*

conk (kŏngk, kôngk) *v. Slang.* **1.** To strike, esp. on the head. **2.** To fail abruptly <The oven *conked* out.> **3.** To fall asleep <*conked* out after dinner>

con man *n. Slang.* A confidence man.

con•nect (kə-nĕkt') *v.* **1.** To join or become joined **:** unite. **2.** To think of as related **:** associate. **—con•nect'ed•ly** *adv.* **—con•nec'tor, con•nect'er** *n.*

con•nec•tion (kə-nĕk'shən) *n.* **1.** Junction **:** union. **2.** A link or bond. **3.** An association or relationship. **4.** Logical ordering of words or ideas **:** coherence. **5.** The relation of a word or idea to its context. **6.** A person with whom one is associated, as by kinship or business. **7.** The meeting of various means of transportation for the transfer of passengers.

con•nec•tive (kə-nĕk'tĭv) *adj.* Serving or tending to connect. *—n.* Something that connects, esp. a connecting word, as a conjunction. **—con'nec•tiv'i•ty** *n.*

connect time *n. Computer Sci.* The elapsed time during which a user of a remote terminal is connected with a timesharing system.

con•nex•ion (kə-nĕk'shən) *n. esp. Brit. var. of* CONNECTION.

conning tower *n.* **1.** The pilothouse of a warship. **2.** An enclosed, raised observation post on a submarine, often used as a means of entrance and exit.

con•nip•tion (kə-nĭp'shən) *n. Informal.* A fit of anger or other violent emotion.

con•nive (kə-nīv') *v.* **-nived, -niv•ing. 1.** To pretend ignorance of a known wrong, thus implying sanction. **2.** To cooperate secretly. **3.** To conspire. **—con•niv'ance** *n.* **—con•niv'er** *n.* **—con•niv'er•y** *n.*

con•nois•seur (kŏn'ə-sûr') *n.* An astute judge in matters of art or taste **:** expert. **—con'nois•seur'ship'** *n.*

con•no•ta•tion (kŏn'ə-tā'shən) *n.* A figurative meaning of a word in addition to the literal meaning. **—con'no•ta'tive** *adj.*

con•note (kə-nōt') *v.* **-not•ed, -not•ing. 1.** To suggest in addition to literal meaning. **2.** To involve as a condition <Lying often *connotes* guilt.>

con•nu•bi•al (kə-no͞o'bē-əl, -nyo͞o'-) *adj.* Conjugal. **—con•nu'bi•al•ly** *adv.*

con•quer (kŏng'kər) *v.* **1.** To subdue or defeat, esp. by force of arms. **2.** To overcome or surmount. **—con'quer•or** *n.*

con•quest (kŏn'kwĕst', kŏng'-) *n.* **1.** The act or process of conquering. **2.** Something conquered.

con•quis•ta•dor (kŏn-kwĭs'tə-dôr', kông-kēs'-) *n., pl.* **-dors** *or* **-do•res** (-dôr'ās, -ēz). A conqueror, esp. one of the 16th-cent. Spanish conquerors of Mexico and Peru.

con•san•guin•e•ous (kŏn'săng-gwĭn'ē-əs) *adj.* Having blood relationship. **—con'san•guin'i•ty** *n.*

con•science (kŏn'shəns) *n.* **1.** The faculty of

recognizing the difference between right and wrong with regard to one's own behavior. 2. Conformity to one's own sense of proper conduct.

con•sci•en•tious (kŏn'shē-ĕn'shəs) *adj.* **1.** Honest : scrupulous. **2.** Painstaking.

conscientious objector *n.* One whose religious and moral principles prohibit participation in military service.

con•scious (kŏn'shəs) *adj.* **1. a.** Aware of one's own existence, sensations, and environment. **b.** Capable of thought, will, or perception. **c.** Awake. **2.** Subjectively perceived <*conscious* regret> **3.** Deliberate <a *conscious* affront>

con•script (kŏn'skrĭpt') *n.* One who is drafted : draftee. —*v.* (kən-skrĭpt'). To compulsorily enroll, esp. in the armed services : draft. —**con•scrip'tion** *n.*

con•se•crate (kŏn'sĭ-krāt') *v.* **-crat•ed, -crat•ing. 1.** To set apart or declare as holy. **2.** *Theol.* To change (the Eucharistic elements) into the body and blood of Jesus. **3.** To induct (a priest) into an order of bishops. **4.** To dedicate to a specific goal. —**con'se•cra'tion** *n.* —**con'se•cra'tor** *n.*

con•sec•u•tive (kən-sĕk'yə-tĭv) *adj.* Successively following without interruption : continuous. —**con•sec'u•tive•ly** *adv.* —**con•sec'u•tive•ness** *n.*

con•sen•sus (kən-sĕn'səs) *n.* **1.** Collective opinion. **2.** General accord.

con•sent (kən-sĕnt') *v.* To give assent : agree. —*n.* Agreement and acceptance, as to an act. —**con•sent'er** *n.*

con•se•quence (kŏn'sĭ-kwĕns', -kwəns) *n.* **1.** An effect or result. **2.** Distinction or importance.

con•se•quent (kŏn'sĭ-kwĕnt', -kwənt) *adj.* Following as a natural effect or result. —**con'se•quent'ly** *adv.*

con•se•quen•tial (kŏn'sĭ-kwĕn'shəl) *adj.* **1.** Of consequence : significant. **2.** Arrogant or self-important : pompous.

con•ser•va•tion (kŏn'sər-vā'shən) *n.* **1.** The act or process of conserving : saving. **2.** Controlled use and protection of natural resources, as forests. —**con'ser•va'tion•al** *adj.* —**con'ser•va'tion•ist** *n.*

con•serv•a•tive (kən-sûr'və-tĭv) *adj.* **1.** Favoring traditional views and values : tending to oppose change. **2.** Moderate : cautious. **3.** Traditional in style or manner. **4.** Tending to conserve : preservative. —*n.* **1.** A conservative person. **2.** A supporter of a conservative political party. —**con•serv'a•tive•ly** *adv.* —**con•serv'a•tive•ness** *n.* —**con•ser'va•tism** *n.*

con•ser•va•tor (kən-sûr'və-tər, kŏn'sər-vā'tər) *n.* **1.** A person in charge of maintaining or restoring valuable items. **2.** *Law.* A guardian.

con•serv•a•to•ry (kən-sûr'və-tôr'ē, -tōr'ē) *n., pl.* **-ries. 1.** A greenhouse. **2.** A school of music or dramatic art.

con•serve (kən-sûrv') *v.* **-served, -serv•ing. 1. a.** To save from loss or depletion. **b.** To avoid wasting. **2.** To preserve (fruits) with sugar. —*n.* (kŏn'sûrv'). A jam of fruits stewed in sugar. —**con•serv'a•ble** *adj.* —**con•serv'er** *n.*

con•sid•er (kən-sĭd'ər) *v.* **1.** To think about seriously. **2.** To regard as : deem. **3.** To judge : believe. —**con•sid'ered** *adj.*

con•sid•er•a•ble (kən-sĭd'ər-ə-bəl) *adj.* **1.** Large in amount, extent, or degree. **2.** Worthy of consideration : important. —**con•sid'er•a•bly** *adv.*

con•sid•er•ate (kən-sĭd'ər-ĭt) *adj.* Mindful of the needs or feelings of others. —**con•sid'er•ate•ly** *adv.*

con•sid•er•a•tion (kən-sĭd'ə-rā'shən) *n.* **1.** Careful deliberation. **2.** Something to be considered in making a decision or judgment. **3.** Mindful regard for others. **4.** Payment : recompense.

con•sid•er•ing (kən-sĭd'ər-ĭng) *prep.* In view of <spry *considering* your age>

con•sign (kən-sīn') *v.* **1.** To entrust to the care of another. **2.** To deliver (e.g., goods or merchandise) for custody or sale. —**con•sign'a•ble** *adj.* —**con'sign•ee'** *n.* —**con•sig'nor, con•sign'er** *n.*

con•sign•ment (kən-sīn'mənt) *n.* **1.** The act of consigning. **2.** Something consigned.

con•sist (kən-sĭst') *v.* **1.** To be made up or composed <Mud *consists* of soil and water.> **2.** To be inherent : have a basis.

con•sis•ten•cy (kən-sĭs'tən-sē) *n., pl.* **-cies. 1.** Agreement among things or parts. **2.** Compatibility or agreement among successive acts, ideas, or events. **3.** Degree of texture, density, or viscosity. —**con•sis'tent** *adj.* —**con•sis'tent•ly** *adv.*

con•sis•to•ry (kən-sĭs'tə-rē) *n., pl.* **-ries.** *Rom. Cath. Ch.* A solemn assembly of cardinals with the pope presiding.

con•sole[1] (kən-sōl') *v.* **-soled, -sol•ing.** To solace : comfort. —**con•sol'a•ble** *adj.* —**con'so•la'tion** *n.* —**con•sol'er** *n.* —**con•sol'ing•ly** *adv.*

con•sole[2] (kŏn'sōl') *n.* **1.** The desklike section of an organ that contains the keyboard, stops, and pedals. **2.** A radio or television cabinet designed to stand on the floor. **3.** A control panel.

con•sol•i•date (kən-sŏl'ĭ-dāt') *v.* **-dat•ed, -dat•ing. 1.** To form into a compact mass. **2.** To unite or become united into one system or body : combine. —**con•sol'i•da'tion** *n.* —**con•sol'i•da'tor** *n.*

con•som•mé (kŏn'sə-mā', kŏn'sə-mā') *n.* A clear soup of meat or vegetable stock.

con•so•nance (kŏn'sə-nəns) *n.* Harmony : agreement.

con•so•nant (kŏn'sə-nənt) *adj.* **1.** Being in agreement or accord. **2.** Corresponding or harmonious in sound. —*n.* **1.** A speech sound produced by partially or completely obstructing the flow of air from the mouth. **2.** A letter of the alphabet representing a consonant, as *b, m, s, t,* etc. —**con'so•nan'tal** *adj.* —**con'so•nan'tal•ly** *adv.* —**con'so•nant•ly** *adv.*

con•sort (kŏn′sôrt′) *n.* A spouse, esp. the spouse of a monarch. —*v.* (kən-sôrt′). **1.** To keep or unite in company : associate. **2.** To be in accord.

con•sor•ti•um (kən-sôr′tē-əm, -shē-) *n., pl.* **-ti•a** (-tē-ə, -shē-ə). An association of financial institutions or capitalists, esp. in international finance.

con•spic•u•ous (kən-spĭk′yo͞o-əs) *adj.* **1.** Obvious : noticeable. **2.** Notable : remarkable. —**con•spic′u•ous•ly** *adv.* —**con•spic′u•ous•ness** *n.*

con•spir•a•cy (kən-spîr′ə-sē) *n., pl.* **-cies. 1.** The act of conspiring. **2.** A group of conspirators.

con•spire (kən-spīr′) *v.* **-spired, -spir•ing. 1.** To plan together in secret to commit a wrongful act. **2.** To act or work together. —**con•spir′a•tor** *n.*

con•sta•ble (kŏn′stə-bəl, kŭn′-) *n.* **1.** A peace officer. **2.** *esp. Brit.* A police officer.

con•stab•u•lar•y (kən-stăb′yə-lĕr′ē) *n., pl.* **-ies. 1.** Constables in general. **2.** An armed police unit organized along military lines.

con•stant (kŏn′stənt) *adj.* **1.** Recurring continually : persistent. **2.** Invariable : uniform. **3.** Steadfast : faithful. —*n.* Something that is unchanging. —**con′stan•cy** *n.* —**con′stant•ly** *adv.*

con•stel•la•tion (kŏn′stə-lā′shən) *n.* Any of 88 stellar groups named after and thought to resemble various mythological characters, inanimate objects, and animals.

con•ster•na•tion (kŏn′stər-nā′shən) *n.* Sudden amazement, confusion, or dismay.

con•sti•pa•tion (kŏn′stə-pā′shən) *n.* Difficult or infrequent evacuation of the bowels. —**con′sti•pate′** *v.*

con•stit•u•en•cy (kən-stĭch′o͞o-ən-sē) *n., pl.* **-cies. 1.** The body of voters represented by an elected legislator. **2.** The district so represented.

con•stit•u•ent (kən-stĭch′o͞o-ənt) *adj.* **1.** Component. **2.** Having power to elect or designate. **3.** Empowered to make or amend a constitution. —*n.* **1.** A member of a group represented by an elected official. **2.** A component part.

con•sti•tute (kŏn′stĭ-to͞ot,′ -tyo͞ot′) *v.* **-tut•ed, -tut•ing. 1.** To make up : compose. **2.** To set up : establish or enact. **3.** To designate, as for an office : appoint.

con•sti•tu•tion (kŏn′stĭ-to͞o′shən, -tyo͞o′-) *n.* **1. a.** Composition : structure. **b.** A person's physical make-up. **2. a.** The fundamental laws of an institution, as a nation. **b.** The document containing such laws.

con•sti•tu•tion•al (kŏn′stĭ-to͞o′shə-nəl, -tyo͞o′-) *adj.* **1.** Essential : basic <a *constitutional* reluctance to lie> **2.** Consistent with, contained in, or operating under a constitution. —*n.* A regular walk for one's health. —**con′sti•tu′tion•al′i•ty** *n.* —**con′sti•tu′tion•al•ly** *adv.*

con•strain (kən-strān′) *v.* **1.** To oblige : compel. **2.** To keep confined. **3.** To check : restrain. —**con•strained′** *adj.* —**con•strain′ed•ly** *adv.*

con•straint (kən-strānt′) *n.* **1.** Threat or use of force : compulsion. **2.** A restriction. **3.** The quality or state of being restrained. **4.** Embarrassed reserve.

con•strict (kən-strĭkt′) *v.* To contract or compress : squeeze. —**con•stric′tion** *n.* —**con•stric′tive** *adj.* —**con•stric′tive•ly** *adv.* —**con•stric′tor** *n.*

con•struct (kən-strŭkt′) *v.* To make, build, or create. —**con•struct′i•ble** *adj.* —**con•struc′tor, con•struct′er** *n.*

con•struc•tion (kən-strŭk′shən) *n.* **1.** The act, process, or work of building. **2.** Something built. **3.** Arrangement of words in a meaningful clause or sentence. —**con•struc′tion•al** *adj.*

construction paper *n.* A heavy paper in a variety of colors, used in artwork.

con•struc•tive (kən-strŭk′tĭv) *adj.* **1.** Helpful : useful. **2.** Of or relating to construction. —**con•struc′tive•ly** *adv.* —**con•struc′tive•ness** *n.*

con•strue (kən-stro͞o′) *v.* **-strued, -stru•ing. 1.** To interpret <*construed* their smiles as approval> **2.** To translate, esp. aloud. **3.** To analyze the grammatical structure of.

con•sul (kŏn′səl) *n.* **1.** An official appointed to reside in a foreign city and represent his or her government's citizens and commercial interests there. **2.** A chief magistrate of the ancient Roman Republic. —**con′su•lar** *adj.* —**con′sul•ship′** *n.*

con•sul•ate (kŏn′sə-lĭt) *n.* The premises occupied by a consul.

con•sult (kən-sŭlt′) *v.* **1.** To seek information or advice from. **2.** To confer. —**con•sult′ant** *n.* —**con′sul•ta′tion** *n.*

con•sume (kən-so͞om′) *v.* **-sumed, -sum•ing. 1.** To eat or drink up : ingest. **2.** To expend (e.g., fuel) : use up. **3.** To squander : waste. **4.** To destroy completely, as by fire. **5.** To engross : absorb. —**con•sum′a•ble** *adj. & n.*

con•sum•er (kən-so͞o′mər) *n.* **1.** One that consumes. **2.** A buyer of goods or services.

con•sum•er•ism (kən-so͞o′mə-rĭz′əm) *n.* The protection of the rights of consumers.

con•sum•mate (kŏn′sə-māt′) *v.* **-mat•ed, -mat•ing. 1.** To complete : conclude. **2.** To complete (a marriage) with the initial act of sexual intercourse. —*adj.* (kən-sŭm′ĭt, kŏn′sə-mət). **1.** Perfect. **2.** Highly skilled. **3.** Utter : complete. —**con•sum′mate•ly** *adv.* —**con′sum•ma′tion** *n.*

con•sump•tion (kən-sŭmp′shən) *n.* **1. a.** The act of consuming. **b.** A quantity consumed. **2.** The using of consumer goods and services. **3.** *Pathol.* A wasting of tissue. **4.** Tuberculosis.

con•sump•tive (kən-sŭmp′tĭv) *adj.* **1.** Tending to waste or destroy. **2.** Afflicted with consumption. —*n.* One afflicted with consumption.

con•tact (kŏn′tăkt′) *n.* **1.** The touching of 2 objects or surfaces. **2.** The state of being in communication. **3.** A useful connection. **4.** A connection between 2 electric conductors. **5.** *Informal.* A contact lens. —*v.* **1.** To come or bring into contact. **2.** To communicate with. —*adj.* **1.** Sustaining or making contact. **2.** Caused or transmitted by touching. —**con•tac'tu•al** *adj.*

contact lens *n.* A thin lens worn over the cornea of the eye.

con•ta•gion (kən-tā'jən) *n.* **1. a.** Disease transmission by contact. **b.** A disease transmitted by contact. **2.** The tendency to spread, as of an influence or emotion. —**con•ta'gious** *adj.* —**con•ta'gious•ly** *adv.* —**con•ta'gious•ness** *n.*

con•tain (kən-tān') *v.* **1.** To have within : enclose. **2.** To include : comprise. **3.** To be capable of holding. **4.** To keep back : restrain. —**con•tain'a•ble** *adj.* —**con•tain'ment** *n.*

con•tain•er (kən-tā'nər) *n.* A receptacle for holding or carrying.

con•tain•er•ize (kən-tā'nə-rīz') *v.* **-ized, -iz•ing.** To ship (cargo) in large, standardized containers for ease in handling.

container ship *n.* A ship designed to carry cargo in standardized containers.

con•tam•i•nate (kən-tăm'ə-nāt') *v.* **-nat•ed, -nat•ing.** To pollute by contact or mixture. —**con•tam'i•nant** *n.* —**con•tam'i•na'tion** *n.* —**con•tam'i•na'tive** *adj.* —**con•tam'i•na'tor** *n.*

con•temn (kən-tĕm') *v.* To view as contemptible : abhor.

con•tem•plate (kŏn'təm-plāt') *v.* **-plat•ed, -plat•ing.** **1.** To look at, ponder, or consider pensively. **2.** To consider as possible : intend. —**con'tem•pla'tion** *n.* —**con•tem'pla•tive** (kən-tĕm'plə-tĭv) *adj.* & *n.* —**con'tem•pla'tor** *n.*

con•tem•po•ra•ne•ous (kən-tĕm'pə-rā'nē-əs) *adj.* Contemporary. —**con•tem'po•ra'ne•ous•ly** *adv.* —**con•tem'po•ra'ne•ous•ness** *n.*

con•tem•po•rar•y (kən-tĕm'pə-rĕr'ē) *adj.* **1.** Belonging to the same period of time. **2.** Modern : current. —**con•tem'po•rar'y** *n.*

con•tempt (kən-tĕmpt') *n.* **1. a.** Bitter scorn or disdain. **b.** The state of being scorned or despised. **2.** *Law.* Willful disobedience or open disrespect.

con•tempt•i•ble (kən-tĕmp'tə-bəl) *adj.* Despicable. —**con•tempt'i•bil'i•ty** *n.* —**con•tempt'i•bly** *adv.*

con•temp•tu•ous (kən-tĕmp'cho͞o-əs) *adj.* Scornful. —**con•temp'tu•ous•ly** *adv.* —**con•temp'tu•ous•ness** *n.*

con•tend (kən-tĕnd') *v.* **1.** To fight, vie, or dispute. **2.** To assert or maintain. —**con•tend'er** *n.*

con•tent[1] (kŏn'tĕnt') *n.* **1.** *often* **contents.** Something contained in a receptacle. **2.** *often* **contents.** Subject matter of a document, book, etc. **3.** Meaning or significance, as of an artistic work. **4.** The proportion of a given substance, as alcohol.

con•tent[2] (kən-tĕnt') *adj.* Contented. —*v.* To make satisfied : gratify. —*n.* Satisfaction : contentment.

con•tent•ed (kən-tĕn'tĭd) *adj.* Satisfied : happy. —**con•tent'ed•ly** *adv.* —**con•tent'ed•ness** *n.*

con•ten•tion (kən-tĕn'shən) *n.* **1.** Controversy. **2.** Rivalry : competition. **3.** An assertion. —**con•ten'tious** *adj.* —**con•ten'tious•ly** *adv.* —**con•ten'tious•ness** *n.*

con•tent•ment (kən-tĕnt'mənt) *n.* Satisfaction : happiness.

con•ter•mi•nous (kən-tûr'mə-nəs) *also* **co•ter•mi•nous** (kō-) *adj.* CONTIGUOUS 1. —**con•ter'mi•nous•ly** *adv.*

con•test (kŏn'tĕst') *n.* **1.** A fight. **2.** A competition. —*v.* (kən-tĕst', kŏn'tĕst'). **1.** To compete or strive (for). **2.** To challenge : dispute <*contest* a will> ★ ***syns:*** BUCK, CHALLENGE, COMBAT, DISPUTE, FIGHT, OPPOSE, RESIST —**con•test'a•ble** *adj.* —**con•tes'tant** *n.* —**con•test'er** *n.*

con•text (kŏn'tĕkst') *n.* **1.** The explanatory words and ideas surrounding a particular word or statement in a discourse. **2.** The circumstances in which an event occurs. —**con•tex'tu•al** (kən-tĕks'cho͞o-əl) *adj.* —**con•tex'tu•al•ly** *adv.*

con•tig•u•ous (kən-tĭg'yo͞o-əs) *adj.* **1.** Sharing a common boundary. **2.** Adjacent to : nearby. —**con'ti•gu'i•ty** (kŏn'tĭ-gyo͞o'ĭ-tē), **con•tig'u•ous•ness** *n.* —**con•tig'u•ous•ly** *adv.*

con•ti•nence (kŏn'tə-nəns) *n.* **1.** Self-control, esp. with regard to passions and desires. **2.** The ability to control excretory functions. —**con'ti•nent** *adj.*

con•ti•nent (kŏn'tə-nənt) *n.* **1.** One of the 7 principal land masses of the globe. **2. the Continent.** The European mainland.

con•ti•nen•tal (kŏn'tə-nĕn'tl) *adj.* **1.** Of, relating to, or resembling a continent. **2.** *often* **Continental.** Relating to the European mainland. **3. Continental.** Of or relating to the American colonies during and immediately after the Revolutionary War. —**Con'ti•nen'tal** *n.*

continental divide *n.* A divide that separates continental river systems flowing in opposite directions.

con•tin•gen•cy (kən-tĭn'jən-sē) *n., pl.* **-cies.** A possible or fortuitous event.

con•tin•gent (kən-tĭn'jənt) *adj.* **1.** Likely to happen but not certain : possible. **2.** Dependent on condition. **3.** Fortuitous. —*n.* **1.** A share or quota, as of troops. **2.** A representative group.

con•tin•u•a (kən-tĭn'yo͞o-ə) *n. var. pl. of* CONTINUUM.

con•tin•u•al (kən-tĭn'yo͞o-əl) *adj.* **1.** Recurring regularly and frequently. **2.** Continuous in time : incessant <*continual* worry> —**con•tin'u•al•ly** *adv.*

con•tin•u•a•tion (kən-tĭn'yo͞o-ā'shən) *n.* **1.** The act or fact of continuing or the state of being continued. **2.** A supplement or sequel. **3.** Resumption after interruption.

con•tin•ue (kən-tĭn'yo͞o) *v.* **-ued, -u•ing.** **1.** To go on : persist. **2.** To last : endure. **3.** To remain in the same state, capacity, or place.

4. To resume. **5.** To extend. **6.** To cause to remain or last. **7.** *Law.* To adjourn or postpone (a judicial proceeding). **—con·tin′u·ance** *n.* **—con·tin′u·er** *n.*

continuing education *n.* Education courses designed esp. for part-time, adult students.

con·ti·nu·i·ty (kŏn′tə-no͞o′ĭ-tē, -nyo͞o′-) *n., pl.* **-ties. 1.** The quality or state of being continuous. **2.** An uninterrupted succession or unbroken course.

con·tin·u·ous (kən-tĭn′yo͞o-əs) *adj.* Uninterrupted in time, sequence, substance, or extent. ★ ***syns:*** CEASELESS, CONSTANT, CONTINUAL, ENDLESS, ETERNAL, EVERLASTING, INCESSANT, NONSTOP, PERPETUAL, RELENTLESS, ROUND-THE-CLOCK, TIMELESS, UNCEASING, UNREMITTING **—con·tin′u·ous·ly** *adv.* **—con·tin′u·ous·ness** *n.*

con·tin·u·um (kən-tĭn′yo͞o-əm) *n., pl.* **-u·a** (-yo͞o-ə) *or* **-ums.** A continuous extent, succession, or whole no part of which can be distinguished from adjacent parts except by arbitrary partition.

con·tort (kən-tôrt′) *v.* To twist severely out of shape **:** wrench. **—con·tor′tion** *n.*

con·tor·tion·ist *n.* An acrobat who exhibits extraordinary bodily positions.

con·tour (kŏn′to͝or′) *n.* **1.** The outline of a figure, body, or mass. **2.** *often* **contours.** A surface, esp. of a curving form. *—adj.* Following the contour or form of something <a *contour* seat> **—con′tour′** *v.*

con·tra·band (kŏn′trə-bănd′) *n.* **1.** Goods barred from import or export. **2.** Smuggling or smuggled goods.

con·tra·bass (kŏn′trə-bās′) *n.* A double bass. **—con′tra·bass′ist** *n.*

con·tra·bas·soon (kŏn′trə-bə-so͞on′, -bă-) *n.* The largest and lowest-pitched of the double-reed wind musical instruments.

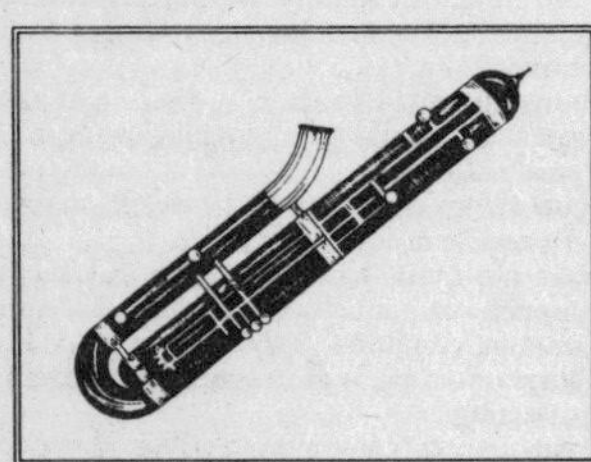

contrabassoon

con·tra·cep·tion (kŏn′trə-sĕp′shən) *n.* Prevention of conception. **—con′tra·cep′tive** *adj. & n.*

con·tract (kŏn′trăkt′) *n.* A formal agreement between 2 or more parties **:** covenant. *—v.* (kən-trăkt′, kŏn′trăkt′). **1.** To enter into or settle by contract. **2.** To become afflicted with (a disease). **3.** To draw together **:** shrink. **4.** To shorten (a word or phrase) by omitting some of the letters or sounds. ★ ***syns:*** CATCH, DEVELOP, GET, TAKE **—con·tract′i·bil′i·ty** *n.* **—con·tract′i·ble** *adj.* **—con·trac′tion** *n.* **—con′trac′tor** *n.*

con·trac·tile (kən-trăk′təl, -tīl′) *adj.* Able to contract or causing contraction.

con·trac·tu·al (kən-trăk′cho͞o-əl) *adj.* Of, relating to, or like a contract. **—con·trac′tu·al·ly** *adv.*

con·tra·dict (kŏn′trə-dĭkt′) *v.* **1.** To assert or express the opposite of. **2.** To deny the statement of <*contradicted* the police officer> **3.** To be inconsistent with. **—con′tra·dict′a·ble** *adj.* **—con′tra·dict′er, con′tra·dic′tor** *n.* **—con′tra·dic′tion** *n.* **—con′tra·dic′to·ry** *adj.*

con·trail (kŏn′trāl′) *n.* A visible trail of water droplets or ice crystals produced in the wake of an aircraft at high altitudes.

con·tra·in·di·cate (kŏn′trə-ĭn′dĭ-kāt′) *v.* To indicate the inadvisability of (e.g., use of certain drugs).

con·tral·to (kən-trăl′tō) *n., pl.* **-tos.** *Mus.* **1.** The lowest female voice or singing part. **2.** A woman having a contralto voice.

con·trap·tion (kən-trăp′shən) *n. Informal.* A mechanical contrivance **:** gadget.

con·tra·pun·tal (kŏn′trə-pŭn′tl) *adj. Mus.* Of, relating to, or incorporating counterpoint. **—con′tra·pun′tal·ly** *adv.*

con·tra·ri·e·ty (kŏn′trə-rī′ĭ-tē) *n., pl.* **-ties. 1.** The quality or state of being contrary. **2.** Something that is contrary.

con·trar·i·wise (kŏn′trĕr′ē-wīz′) *adv.* In a contrary manner or direction.

con·trar·y (kŏn′trĕr′ē) *adj.* **1.** Completely opposite, as in direction or character. **2.** Unfavorable **:** adverse. **3.** (*also* kən-trâr′ē). Recalcitrant **:** willful. **4.** Counter **:** opposed. ★ ***syns:*** BALKY, DIFFICULT, FROWARD, IMPOSSIBLE, ORNERY, PERVERSE, WAYWARD *—n., pl.* **-ies.** The opposite. *—adv.* Contrariwise. **—con′trar′i·ly** *adv.* **—con′trar′i·ness** *n.*

con·trast (kən-trăst′) *v.* **1.** To put in opposition in order to point out differences. **2.** To show differences when compared. *—n.* (kŏn′trăst′). **1.** Notable dissimilarity between things compared. **2.** Something markedly dissimilar to something else. **—con·trast′a·ble** *adj.*

con·tra·vene (kŏn′trə-vēn′) *v.* **-vened, -ven·ing. 1.** To act or be contrary to **:** violate. **2.** To oppose in argument.

con·tre·temps (kŏn′trə-täN′, kôN′trə-täN′) *n., pl.* **-temps** (-täNz′, -täNz′). An embarrassing or inopportune occurrence.

con·trib·ute (kən-trĭb′yo͞ot) *v.* **-ut·ed, -ut·ing. 1.** To give or supply in common with others. **2.** To act as a determining factor. **3.** To submit for publication. **—con′tri·bu′tion** *n.* **—con·trib′u·tive** *adj.* **—con·trib′u·tive·ly** *adv.* **—con·trib′u·tor** *n.* **—con·trib′u·to′ry** *adj.*

con·trite (kən-trīt′, kŏn′trīt′) *adj.* Penitant **:** repentant. **—con·trite′ly** *adv.* **—con·tri′tion** (-trĭsh′ən) *n.*

con·triv·ance (kən-trī′vəns) *n.* Something

that is contrived, as a mechanical device or clever plan.

con•trive (kən-trīv′) *v.* **-trived, -triv•ing. 1.** To plan or devise. **2.** To bring about by artifice **:** scheme. **3.** To invent or fabricate. **—con•triv′er** *n.*

con•trol (kən-trōl′) *v.* **-trolled, -trol•ling. 1.** To exercise dominating influence or authority over **:** direct. **2.** To regulate or verify (an experiment) by systematic comparison. *—n.* **1.** Authority or ability to regulate, dominate, or direct. **2.** A check or restraint. **3.** A standard of comparison for checking experimental results. **4.** *often* **controls.** A set of instruments for operating a machine or vehicle. **5.** An organization to direct a space flight. **—con•trol′la•ble** *adj.*

con•trol•ler (kən-trō′lər) *n.* **1.** One that controls, esp. a device that automatically regulates a machine. **2.** *also* **comp•trol•ler.** A business executive or government official who is in charge of financial affairs.

con•tro•ver•sy (kŏn′trə-vûr′sē) *n., pl.* **-sies. 1.** An often public dispute marked by the expression of opposing views. **2.** An argument. **—con′tro•ver′sial** (-vûr′shəl, -sē-əl) *adj.* **—con′tro•ver′sial•ly** *adv.*

con•tro•vert (kŏn′trə-vûrt′) *v.* To deny or contradict. **—con′tro•vert′i•ble** *adj.*

con•tu•ma•cious (kŏn′tə-mā′shəs) *adj.* Obstinately disobedient or insubordinate **:** recalcitrant. **—con′tu•ma•cy** (-mə-sē) *n.*

con•tu•me•ly (kŏn′to͞o-mə-lē, -tyo͞o-, -təm-lē) *n., pl.* **-lies.** Rude treatment **:** insolence. **—con′tu•me′li•ous** *adj.*

con•tuse (kən-to͞oz′, -tyo͞oz′) *v.* **-tused, -tus•ing.** To bruise. **—con•tu′sion** *n.*

co•nun•drum (kə-nŭn′drəm) *n.* **1.** A riddle. **2.** A complicated problem.

con•ur•ba•tion (kŏn′ər-bā′shən) *n.* A metropolitan area.

con•va•lesce (kŏn′və-lĕs′) *v.* **-lesced, -lesc•ing.** To return to health after illness **:** recuperate. **—con′va•les′cence** *n.* **—con′va•les′cent** *adj. & n.*

con•vec•tion (kən-vĕk′shən) *n.* Heat transfer by the actual movement of a heated liquid or gas between regions of unequal density. **—con•vec′tion•al** *adj.*

con•vene (kən-vēn′) *v.* **-vened, -ven•ing.** To assemble or convoke formally. **—con•ven′a•ble** *adj.* **—con•ven′er** *n.*

con•ven•ience (kən-vēn′yəns) *n.* **1.** The quality of being suitable or useful. **2.** Material comfort or advantage. **3.** Something that saves time and effort.

convenience store *n.* A small retail store that is open long hours and that typically sells staple groceries and snacks.

con•ven•ient (kən-vēn′yənt) *adj.* **1.** Suited or favorable to a person's needs, comfort, or purpose. **2.** Within easy reach **:** handy. ★ ***syns:*** APPROPRIATE, FIT, GOOD, PROPER, SUITABLE, TAILOR-MADE **—con•ven′ient•ly** *adv.*

con•vent (kŏn′vənt, -vĕnt′) *n.* A community or the premises of a religious order, esp. of nuns. **—con•ven′tu•al** *adj.*

con•ven•ti•cle (kən-vĕn′tĭ-kəl) *n.* A meeting or assembly, esp. a secret one for religious worship.

con•ven•tion (kən-vĕn′shən) *n.* **1. a.** A formal assembly or meeting, as of a political party. **b.** The body of persons at such an assembly. **2.** A compact or agreement, esp. an international one. **3.** General custom or usage. **4.** An accepted or fixed practice.

con•ven•tion•al (kən-vĕn′shə-nəl) *adj.* **1.** Conforming to established practice or custom. **2.** Ordinary **:** commonplace. **3.** Using means other than nuclear energy <*conventional* weapons> **—con•ven′tion•al′i•ty** *n.* **—con•ven′tion•al•ly** *adv.*

con•ven•tion•al•ize (kən-vĕn′shə-nə-līz′) *v.* **-ized, -iz•ing.** To make conventional. **—con•ven′tion•al•i•za′tion** *n.*

con•verge (kən-vûrj′) *v.* **-verged, -verg•ing.** To approach a common point or result **:** meet. **—con•ver′gence, con•ver′gen•cy** *n.* **—con•ver′gent** *adj.*

con•ver•sant (kən-vûr′-sənt, kŏn′vər-) *adj.* Familiar, as by study <*conversant* with American literature>

con•ver•sa•tion (kŏn′vər-sā′shən) *n.* An informal talk or discussion. **—con′ver•sa′tion•al** *adj.* **—con′ver•sa′tion•al•ist** *n.* **—con′ver•sa′tion•al•ly** *adv.*

con•verse[1] (kən-vûrs′) *v.* **-versed, -vers•ing. 1.** To participate in a conversation. **2.** *Computer Sci.* To interact with a computer online. *—n.* (kŏn′vûrs′). Conversation.

con•verse[2] (kən-vûrs′, kŏn′vûrs′) *adj.* Reversed **:** contrary. *—n.* (kŏn′vûrs′). Reverse **:** opposite. **—con•verse′ly** *adv.*

con•ver•sion (kən-vûr′zhən, -shən) *n.* **1.** The act of converting or state of being converted. **2.** Adoption of a new religion or belief. **3.** Unlawful appropriation of property. **4.** A score of extra points after a touchdown in football.

con•vert (kən-vûrt′) *v.* **1.** To change into another form, substance, state, or product **:** transform. **2.** To induce or be induced to adopt a new religion or belief. **3.** To adapt to a new or different use or purpose. **4.** To exchange for something of equal value. **5.** *Law.* To misappropriate (another's property). *—n.* (kŏn′vûrt′). One who has undergone conversion, esp. to a new religion. **—con•vert′er, con•ver′tor** *n.*

con•vert•i•ble (kən-vûr′tə-bəl) *adj.* **1.** Able to be converted. **2.** Having a top that can be folded back or removed, as a car. **—con•vert′i•ble** *n.*

con•vex (kŏn-vĕks′, kŏn′vĕks′) *adj.* Curved or rounded outward like the outer surface of a ball. **—con•vex′i•ty** *n.*

con•vey (kən-vā′) *v.* **1.** To transport **:** carry. **2.** To transmit **:** conduct. **3.** To make known **:** communicate. **—con•vey′a•ble** *adj.* **—con•vey′er, con•vey′or** *n.*

con•vey•ance (kən-vā′əns) *n.* **1.** The act of conveying. **2.** A means of conveying **:** vehicle. **3.** *Law.* Transfer of title to property or a document effecting it.

con•vict (kən-vĭkt′) *v.* To find or prove

(someone) guilty. —*n.* (kŏn′vĭkt′). A convicted person.
con•vic•tion (kən-vĭk′shən) *n.* **1.** The act of convicting or state of being convicted. **2.** A strong opinion or belief.
con•vince (kən-vĭns′) *v.* **-vinced, -vinc•ing.** To cause to believe firmly : persuade. —**con•vinc′ing•ly** *adv.*
con•viv•i•al (kən-vĭv′ē-əl) *adj.* **1.** Sociable. **2.** Festive. —**con•viv′i•al′i•ty** (-ăl′ĭ-tē) *n.* —**con•viv′i•al•ly** *adv.*
con•vo•ca•tion (kŏn′və-kā′shən) *n.* **1.** The act of convoking. **2.** A formal or ceremonial assembly, as of clergy.
con•voke (kən-vōk′) *v.* **-voked, -vok•ing.** To cause to assemble or convene formally. —**con•vok′er** *n.*
con•vo•lut•ed (kŏn′və-lōō′tĭd) *adj.* **1.** Coiled : twisted. **2.** Intricate : complex.
con•vo•lu•tion (kŏn′və-lōō′shən) *n.* **1.** A convoluted formation or configuration. **2.** A convex fold of the brain's surface.
con•voy (kŏn′voi′, kən-voi′) *v.* To accompany for protection : escort. —*n.* (kŏn′voi′). **1.** A protective armed escort, as for ships or vehicles. **2.** A group, as of vehicles, traveling together.
con•vulse (kən-vŭls′) *v.* **-vulsed, -vuls•ing.** **1.** To shake or agitate violently. **2.** To cause to experience convulsions. —**con•vul′sive** *adj.* —**con•vul′sive•ly** *adv.*
con•vul•sion (kən-vŭl′shən) *n.* **1.** An intense paroxysmal involuntary muscular contraction. **2.** A fit, as of uncontrollable laughter. **3.** A violent turmoil.
co•ny *also* **co•ney** (kō′nē, kŭn′ē) *n., pl.* **-nies** *also* **-neys** **1. a.** A rabbit, esp. the Old World species *Oryctolagus cuniculus.* **b.** A similar animal. **2.** Rabbit fur.
coo (kōō) *n., pl.* **coos.** **1.** The soft murmuring sound that a dove or pigeon makes. **2.** A sound resembling a coo. —**coo** *v.*
cook (kŏŏk) *v.* **1.** To apply heat to food before eating. **2.** To prepare or treat by heating. —**cook up.** *Informal.* To fabricate : concoct <*cook up* a scheme> —*n.* One who prepares food.
cook•book (kŏŏk′bŏŏk′) *n.* A book of recipes and directions for cooking.
cook•er (kŏŏk′ər) *n.* One that cooks, esp. a utensil or an appliance for cooking.
cook•er•y (kŏŏk′ə-rē) *n., pl.* **-ies.** The preparation of food.
cook•ie *or* **cook•y** (kŏŏk′ē) *n., pl.* **-ies.** A sweet, usu. small, flat cake.
cook•out (kŏŏk′out′) *n.* A meal cooked and served outdoors.
cool (kōōl) *adj.* **1.** Somewhat cold <*cool* fall nights> **2.** Affording or allowing relief from heat. **3.** Controlled : calm. **4.** Indifferent : unenthusiastic <a *cool* handshake> **5.** Impudent : audacious. **6.** *Slang.* Superb : first-rate. —*v.* To make or become cool. —*n.* **1.** Moderate cold or something cool. **2.** *Slang.* Composure <lost my *cool*> —**cool′ly** *adv.* —**cool′ness** *n.*
cool•ant (kōō′lənt) *n.* A cooling agent, esp. a fluid that circulates through a machine or bathes some of its parts.
cool•er (kōō′lər) *n.* **1.** A container or device for cooling. **2.** *Slang.* A jail.
coo•lie (kōō′lē) *n.* An unskilled laborer of the Far East.
coon (kōōn) *n. Informal.* A raccoon.
coon•skin (kōōn′skĭn′) *n.* **1.** The skin of a raccoon, used as fur. **2.** Something, as a hat, made of coonskin.
coop (kōōp) *n.* An enclosure or cage. —*v.* To keep in or as if in a coop.
co-op (kō′ŏp′, kō-ŏp′) *n.* A cooperative.
coo•per (kōō′pər) *n.* One who makes or repairs barrels. —**coo′per•age** *n.*
co•op•er•ate (kō-ŏp′ə-rāt′) *v.* To act or work together toward a common purpose or end. —**co•op′er•a′tion** *n.* —**co•op′er•a′tor** *n.*
co•op•er•a•tive (kō-ŏp′ər-ə-tĭv, -ŏp′rə-, -ə-rā′-tĭv) *adj.* **1.** Done in cooperation with others. **2.** Characterized by willingness to cooperate. **3.** Engaged in joint economic activity. —*n.* An enterprise owned jointly by those who use its facilities or services. —**co•op′er•a•tive•ly** *adv.* —**co•op′er•a•tive•ness** *n.*
co-opt (kō-ŏpt′) *v.* **1.** To elect as a fellow member of a group. **2.** To pre-empt : appropriate. **3.** To win over (e.g., a minority) by assimilating into an established group.
co•or•di•nate (kō-ôr′dn-āt, -ĭt′) *n.* **1.** One that is equal in rank, importance, or degree. **2.** *Math.* Any of a set of numbers that gives the location of a point. —*adj.* (-ĭt, -āt′). **1.** Of equal rank, importance, or degree. **2.** Of or involving coordination. **3.** Of or based on coordinates. —*v.* (-āt′) **-nat•ed, -nat•ing.** **1.** To place in proper position or order : adjust. **2.** To work together in a common action or effort. —**co•or′di•nate•ly** *adv.* —**co•or′di•na′tor** *n.*
co•or•di•na•tion (kō-ôr′dn-ā′shən) *n.* **1.** The act of coordinating or state of being coordinate. **2.** Organized muscular action in executing complex movements.
coot (kōōt) *n.* **1.** A short-billed, dark-gray aquatic bird of the genus *Fulica.* **2.** *Informal.* An eccentric person.
coo•tie (kōō′tē) *n. Slang.* A body louse.
cop (kŏp) *n. Informal.* A police officer. —*v.* **copped, cop•ping.** *Slang.* **1.** To pilfer : steal. **2.** To capture : seize. —**cop out.** *Slang.* **1.** To be noncommittal. **2.** To renege.
cope[1] (kōp) *v.* **coped, cop•ing.** To struggle or contend, esp. successfully.
cope[2] (kōp) *n.* A long capelike ecclesiastical garment.
cop•i•er (kŏp′ē-ər) *n.* One that copies, esp. a machine for making copies.
co•pi•lot (kō′pī′lət) *n.* The associate pilot of an aircraft.
cop•ing (kō′pĭng) *n.* The top part of a wall.
co•pi•ous (kō′pē-əs) *adj.* Large in quantity : abundant. —**co′pi•ous•ly** *adv.*
cop-out (kŏp′out′) *n. Slang.* **1.** An act of copping out. **2.** An excuse for copping out.
cop•per (kŏp′ər) *n.* **1.** *Symbol* **Cu** A reddish-brown metallic element that is a very good

conductor of heat and electricity. **2.** Something made of copper, as a coin.

cop•per•as (kŏp'ər-əs) *n.* A greenish, crystalline ferrous sulfate used in purifying water and making fertilizers.

cop•per•head (kŏp'ər-hĕd') *n.* A venomous snake, *Agkistrodon contortrix* or *Ancistron contortrix,* of the E U.S., with reddish-brown markings.

cop•ra (kŏp'rə) *n.* Dried coconut meat from which coconut oil is obtained.

copse (kŏps) *n.* A thicket.

cop•ter (kŏp'tər) *n.* A helicopter.

cop•u•la (kŏp'yə-lə) *n., pl.* **-las.** A linking verb. **—cop'u•la'tive** *adj.*

cop•u•late (kŏp'yə-lāt') *v.* **-lat•ed, -lat•ing.** To have sexual intercourse. **—cop'u•la'tion** *n.*

cop•y (kŏp'ē) *n., pl.* **-ies. 1.** A reproduction of an original. **2.** One of a number of printed texts having the same contents. **3.** Matter to be set in type. ★ ***syns:*** DUPLICATE, FACSIMILE, REPLICA, REPRODUCTION —*v.* **-ied, -y•ing. 1.** To make a copy (of). **2.** To imitate. **—cop'y•ist** *n.*

copy desk *n.* The desk where newspaper copy is edited.

cop•y-ed•it (kŏp'ē-ĕd'ĭt) *v.* To correct and edit (e.g., a manuscript) for publication. **—copy editor** *n.*

cop•y•right (kŏp'ē-rīt') *n.* The sole right to sell, publish, or distribute a literary or artistic work. *—adj.* Protected by copyright. *—v.* To protect by copyright.

cop•y•writ•er (kŏp'ē-rī'tər) *n.* A writer of copy, esp. in advertising.

coq au vin (kōk' ō văN', kŏk') *n.* Chicken cooked in wine.

co•quette (kō-kĕt') *n.* A woman who flirts. **—co•quet'tish** *adj.* **—co•quet'tish•ly** *adv.* **—co•quet'tish•ness** *n.*

cor•a•cle (kôr'ə-kəl, kŏr'-) *n.* A small round boat made of a wicker or wood frame covered with waterproof material.

cor•al (kôr'əl, kŏr'-) *n.* **1.** A hard rocklike material formed by the skeletons of marine polyps and often used for jewelry. **2.** A pinkish orange.

coral reef *n.* A marine ridge or mound made chiefly of compacted coral.

coral snake *n.* A venomous snake of the genus *Micrurus,* of tropical America, brightly banded with red, black, and yellow.

cor•bel (kôr'bəl, -bĕl') *n.* A bracket, as of stone or brick, projecting from the face of a wall to support an arch or cornice.

cord (kôrd) *n.* **1.** A heavy string of twisted strands. **2.** A thin insulated electric cable used to connect an appliance with an electrical outlet. **3.** A ribbed fabric, as corduroy. **4.** A cubic measure used for cut fuel wood, equal to a stack measuring 4 by 4 by 8 ft. **—cord** *v.* **—cord'er** *n.*

cord•age (kôr'dĭj) *n.* Ropes, esp. ropes in the rigging of a ship.

cor•date (kôr'dāt') *adj.* With a heart-shaped outline <a *cordate* leaf>

cord•ed (kôr'dĭd) *adj.* **1.** Fastened with cords. **2.** Ribbed, as corduroy. **3.** Stacked in cords, as firewood.

cor•dial (kôr'jəl) *adj.* Warm : heartfelt. *—n.* **1.** A stimulant. **2.** A liqueur. **—cor'dial'i•ty** (-jăl'ĭ-tē, -jē-ăl'-, -dē-ăl'-), **cor'dial•ness** *n.* **—cor'dial•ly** *adv.*

▲ ***word history:*** *Cordial* had its origin as a medical term, and in early use the word's derivation from Latin *cor,* "heart," was not forgotten. The first recorded use of *cordial* in English is in Chaucer's *Canterbury Tales,* where it indicates a medicine. Such cordials were supposed to achieve a beneficial effect by stimulating the heart. The heart in medieval physiology was also considered the locus of feelings and affections; from this association the adjective *cordial* meaning "hearty" or "heartfelt" arose.

cor•dil•le•ra (kôr'dĭl-yâr'ə, kôr-dĭl'ər-ə) *n.* A mountain chain.

cord•ite (kôr'dīt') *n.* A smokeless gunpowder.

cord•less (kôrd'lĭs) *adj.* **1.** Without a cord. **2.** Operated by battery.

cor•do•ba (kôr'də-bə, -və) *n.* —See table at CURRENCY.

cor•don (kôr'dn) *n.* **1.** An encircling line, as of people or ships. **2.** An ornamental braid. *—v.* To encircle with a cordon.

cor•do•van (kôr'də-vən) *n.* A fine, soft leather orig. made in Spain.

cor•du•roy (kôr'də-roi', kôr'də-roi') *n.* **1.** A heavy ribbed cotton cloth. **2. corduroys.** Corduroy trousers.

core (kôr, kōr) *n.* **1.** The inedible, seed-bearing central part of certain fruits, as the pear. **2.** The inmost part of something. **3.** The most important part. **4.** An internal computer memory. **5.** The part of a nuclear reactor where fission occurs.

co•re•spon•dent (kō'rĭ-spŏn'dənt) *n. Law.* A person named as having committed adultery with the defendant in a divorce case.

cor•gi (kôr'gē) *n.* A Welsh corgi.

co•ri•an•der (kôr'ē-ăn'dər, kōr'-) *n.* An herb, *Coriandrum sativum,* cultivated for its aromatic seeds.

Co•rin•thi•an (kə-rĭn'thē-ən) *adj.* Of or relating to ancient Corinth. *—n.* **1.** A native or inhabitant of Corinth. **2. Corinthians** *(sing. in number).* —See table at BIBLE.

cork (kôrk) *n.* **1.** The light, elastic bark of the cork oak, used esp. for bottle stoppers. **2.** A stopper made of cork. *—v.* To stop with a cork. **—cork'y** *adj.*

cork•age (kôr'kĭj) *n.* A fee paid at a restaurant for the consumption of a bottle of liquor not bought on the premises.

cork oak *n.* An evergreen oak tree, *Quercus suber,* of S Europe.

cork•screw (kôrk'skrōō') *n.* A pointed metal spiral attached to a handle, used for drawing corks from bottles. *—adj.* Like a corkscrew : spiral.

corm (kôrm) *n.* An underground stem, as that of the gladiolus, similar to a bulb.

cor•mo•rant (kôr′mər-ənt) *n.* A large aquatic bird of the genus *Phalacrocorax,* with dark plumage and a hooked bill.

corn¹ (kôrn) *n.* **1. a.** An American cereal plant, *Zea mays,* bearing kernels on large ears. **b.** The kernels of this plant, used for food or fodder. **2.** *esp. Brit.* Grain, esp. wheat. **3.** *Slang.* Something that is corny. —*v.* To pickle in brine.

corn² (kôrn) *n.* A hard growth of skin, esp. on or near a toe.

corn•ball (kôrn′bôl′) *adj. Slang.* Corny.

corn bread *also* **corn•bread** (kôrn′brĕd′) *n.* Bread made from cornmeal.

corn chip *n. often* **corn chips.** A crisp snack made from cornmeal batter.

corn•cob (kôrn′kŏb′) *n.* The woody core on which kernels of corn grow.

corn•crib (kôrn′krĭb′) *n.* A structure for drying and storing corn.

cor•ne•a (kôr′nē-ə) *n.* The transparent membrane covering the iris and the pupil of the eyeball. —**cor′ne•al** *adj.*

cor•ner (kôr′nər) *n.* **1. a.** The place where 2 surfaces or lines meet and form an angle. **b.** The angle so formed. **2.** A place where 2 streets come together. **3.** A position from which retreat or escape is impossible. **4.** A region : quarter. **5.** Control of the available supply of a commodity so as to raise its price. —*v.* **1.** To drive into a corner. **2.** To form a corner in (a commodity). **3.** To turn, as at a corner.

cor•ner•back *also* **corner back** (kôr′nər-băk′) *n. Football.* Either of 2 defensive halfbacks stationed a short distance behind the linebackers and near the sidelines.

cor•ner•stone *also* **corner stone** (kôr′nər-stōn′) *n.* **1.** A stone forming part of the corner of a building, esp. one laid with a special ceremony. **2.** The main part : basis.

cor•net (kôr-nĕt′) *n.* A 3-valved brass band instrument resembling a trumpet. —**cor•net′ist, cor•net′tist** *n.*

corn•flow•er (kôrn′flou′ər) *n.* A garden plant, *Centaurea cyanus,* with blue, white, or pink flowers.

cor•nice (kôr′nĭs) *n.* A horizontal projecting part that crowns the wall of a building.

corn•meal *also* **corn meal** (kôrn′mēl′) *n.* Coarse meal made from corn.

†**corn pone** (pōn) *n. S U.S.* Corn bread made without milk or eggs.

corn•row (kôrn′rō′) *v.* To style (hair) by dividing into sections and braiding closely in rows. —**corn′row′** *n.*

corn snow *n.* Coarse granules of snow formed by alternate freezing and melting.

corn•stalk *also* **corn stalk** (kôrn′stôk′) *n.* A stalk of corn.

corn•starch (kôrn′stärch′) *n.* A starch made from corn and used in cooking as a thickener.

corn syrup *n.* A sweet syrup made from cornstarch.

cor•nu•co•pi•a (kôr′nə-kō′pē-ə) *n.* **1.** A goat's horn depicted as overflowing with fruit, flowers, and corn, signifying prosperity. **2.** An abundance.

corn•y (kôr′nē) *adj.* **-i•er, -i•est.** *Slang.* Trite or mawkishly sentimental. —**corn′i•ly** *adv.* —**corn′i•ness** *n.*

co•rol•la (kə-rŏl′ə, -rō′lə) *n. Bot.* The petals of a flower.

cor•ol•lar•y (kôr′ə-lĕr′-ē, kŏr′-) *n., pl.* **-ies. 1.** A deduction from an already proven proposition. **2.** A result : consequence.

co•ro•na (kə-rō′nə) *n., pl.* **-nas** *or* **-nae** (-nē). A colored circle of light around the sun or moon, esp. the halo visible around the sun during a total eclipse.

cor•o•nar•y (kôr′ə-nĕr-ē, kŏr′-) *adj.* Of or designating either of 2 arteries that supply blood to the heart muscle. —*n., pl.* **-ies.** *Informal.* A coronary thrombosis.

coronary thrombosis *n.* Occlusion of a coronary artery by a blood clot, often causing destruction of heart muscle.

cor•o•na•tion (kôr′ə-nā′shən, kŏr′-) *n.* The crowning of a monarch.

cor•o•ner (kôr′ə-nər, kŏr′-) *n.* A public official who determines the cause of deaths not due to natural causes.

cor•o•net (kôr′ə-nĕt′, kŏr′-) *n.* **1.** A small crown worn by nobility. **2.** A headband.

cor•po•ra (kôr′pər-ə) *n. pl. of* CORPUS.

cor•po•ral¹ (kôr′pər-əl) *adj.* Of the body : physical. —**cor′po•ral′i•ty** *n.*

cor•po•ral² (kôr′pər-əl, -prəl) *n.* A noncommissioned officer ranking above a private first class and below a sergeant.

cor•po•rate (kôr′pər-ĭt, -prĭt) *adj.* **1.** Of or being a corporation. **2.** Combined into one body : joint <*corporate* action>

cor•po•ra•tion (kôr′pə-rā′shən) *n.* A group of persons authorized to act as an entity having privileges and liabilities distinct from those of its members.

cor•po•re•al (kôr-pôr′ē-əl, -pōr′-) *adj.* **1.** Of, relating to, or typical of the body. **2.** Of a material nature : physical.

corps (kôr, kōr) *n., pl.* **corps** (kôrz, kōrz). **1.** A branch or section of the armed forces with a specialized function. **2.** A body of persons associated under common direction <the press *corps*>

corpse (kôrps) *n.* A dead body.

cor•pu•lence (kôr′pyə-ləns) *n.* Excessive fatness. —**cor′pu•lent** *adj.*

cor•pus (kôr′pəs) *n., pl.* **-po•ra** (-pər-ə). **1.** A body, esp. a corpse. **2.** A body of writings on a specific subject.

cor•pus•cle (kôr′pə-səl, -pŭs′əl) *n.* **1.** A living cell, esp. one, as in blood, capable of free movement in a matrix or fluid. **2.** A minute particle. —**cor•pus′cu•lar** *adj.*

corpus de•lic•ti (də-lĭk′tī′) *n.* **1.** *Law.* The material evidence establishing that a crime has been committed. **2.** The body of a murder victim.

cor•rade (kə-răd′) *v.* **-rad•ed, -rad•ing.** To wear away or be worn away by abrasion. —**cor•ra′sion** *n.* —**cor•ra′sive** *adj.*

cor•ral (kə-răl′) *n.* An enclosure for confining or capturing animals. —*v.* **-ralled, -ral•ling. 1.** To drive into or confine in a corral. **2.** *Informal.* To take possession of.

cor•rect (kə-rĕkt′) *v.* **1.** To make right. **2.** To mark the errors of. **3.** To reprove or discipline. ★ ***syns:*** AMEND, EMEND, MEND, RECTIFY, REMEDY, RIGHT —*adj.* **1.** Free from error : accurate. **2.** Conforming to conventions. —**cor•rect′a•ble, cor•rect′i•ble** *adj.* —**cor•rec′tion** *n.* —**cor•rec′tion•al** *adj.* —**cor•rec′tive** *adj. & n.* —**cor•rect′ly** *adv.* —**cor•rect′ness** *n.*

cor•re•late (kôr′ə-lāt′, kŏr′-) *v.* **-lat•ed, -lat•ing.** To connect or be connected by causal, complementary, or parallel relation. —**cor′re•late** *n. & adj.* —**cor′re•la′tion** *n.* —**cor′re•la′tion•al** *adj.*

cor•rel•a•tive (kə-rĕl′ə-tĭv) *adj.* **1.** Reciprocally related. **2.** Indicating a reciprocal grammatical relationship <the *correlative* conjunctions *either . . . or*> —**cor•rel′a•tive** *n.* —**cor•rel′a•tive•ly** *adv.*

cor•re•spond (kôr′ĭ-spŏnd′, kŏr′-) *v.* **1.** To be consistent, compatible, or harmonious. **2.** To be equal or similar. **3.** To communicate by letter. —**cor′re•spond′ing•ly** *adv.*

cor•re•spon•dence (kôr′ĭ-spŏn′dəns, kŏr′-) *n.* **1.** Agreement between things. **2.** Similarity. **3. a.** Communication by letters. **b.** The letters exchanged.

cor•re•spon•dent (kôr′ĭ-spŏn′dənt, kŏr′-) *n.* **1.** A person who communicates by letter with another. **2.** A reporter, as for a newspaper, who supplies news, often from remote locations. **3.** Something that corresponds. —*adj.* Corresponding.

cor•ri•dor (kôr′ĭ-dər, -dôr′, kŏr′-) *n.* **1.** A long, narrow hall, often with rooms opening onto it. **2.** A tract of land forming a passageway through a foreign country.

cor•ri•gen•dum (kôr′ə-jĕn′dəm, kŏr′-) *n., pl.* **-da** (-də). **1.** A typesetting error to be corrected. **2. corrigenda.** A list of errors in a book printed on a separate page with their corrections.

cor•ri•gi•ble (kôr′ĭ-jə-bəl, kŏr′-) *adj.* Capable of being corrected.

cor•rob•o•rate (kə-rŏb′ə-rāt′) *v.* **-rat•ed, -rat•ing.** To attest the truth of. —**cor•rob′o•ra′tion** *n.* —**cor•rob′o•ra′tive** *adj.* —**cor•rob′o•ra′tor** *n.*

cor•rode (kə-rōd′) *v.* **-rod•ed, -rod•ing.** To eat away or be eaten away gradually, esp. by chemical action. —**cor•rod′i•ble, cor•ro′si•ble** (-rō′sə-bəl) *adj.* —**cor•ro′sion** *n.* —**cor•ro′sive** *adj. & n.*

cor•ru•gate (kôr′ə-gāt′, kŏr′-) *v.* **-gat•ed, -gat•ing.** To form into folds or ridges and grooves. —**cor′ru•ga′tion** *n.*

corrugated iron *n.* Sheet iron, usu. galvanized, shaped in parallel grooves and ridges for strength.

cor•rupt (kə-rŭpt′) *adj.* **1.** Evil : depraved. **2.** Open to bribery : dishonest <a *corrupt* politician> **3.** Rotting : putrid. ★ ***syns:*** CROOKED, DISHONEST, VENAL —*v.* To make or become corrupt. —**cor•rupt′er, cor•rup′tor** *n.* —**cor•rupt′i•bil′i•ty, cor•rupt′i•ble•ness** *n.* —**cor•rupt′i•ble** *adj.* —**cor•rupt′i•bly** *adv.* —**cor•rup′tion** *n.* —**cor•rupt′ly** *adv.* —**cor•rupt′ness** *n.*

cor•sage (kôr-säzh′) *n.* A small bunch of flowers worn by a woman.

cor•sair (kôr′sâr′) *n.* **1.** A fast-moving pirate ship. **2.** A pirate.

cor•set (kôr′sĭt) *n.* A stiffened undergarment worn on the torso to give shape to the waist and hips. —**cor′se•tière′** *n.*

cor•tege (kôr-tĕzh′) *n.* **1.** A retinue, as for a distinguished person. **2.** A ceremonial procession, esp. a funeral procession.

cor•tex (kôr′tĕks′) *n., pl.* **-ti•ces** (-tĭ-sēz′) *or* **-tex•es. 1.** *Anat.* The outer layer of an organ or part. **2.** *Bot.* An outer layer of plant tissue. —**cor′ti•cal** (-tĭ-kəl) *adj.*

cor•ti•sone (kôr′tĭ-sōn′, -zōn′) *n.* A hormone produced by the adrenal cortex and used in the treatment of rheumatoid arthritis, allergies, and gout.

co•run•dum (kə-rŭn′dəm) *n.* A very hard mineral, aluminum oxide, that occurs in gem varieties, as ruby and sapphire, and in a common form used esp. in abrasives.

cor•us•cate (kôr′ə-skāt′, kŏr′-) *v.* **-cat•ed, -cat•ing.** To flash : sparkle. —**cor′us•ca′tion** *n.*

cor•vette (kôr-vĕt′) *n.* **1.** A lightly armed warship smaller than a destroyer. **2.** An obsolete warship smaller than a frigate.

cor•ymb (kôr′ĭmb, -ĭm, kŏr′-) *n.* A usu. flat-topped flower cluster.

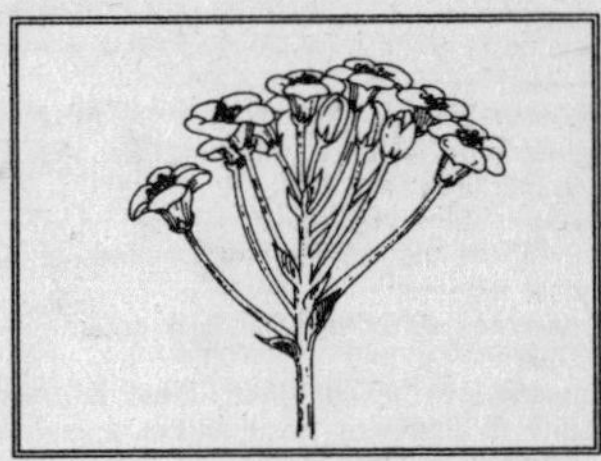

corymb

co•ry•za (kə-rī′zə) *n.* An acute inflammation of the upper respiratory tract : head cold.

cosh (kŏsh) *esp. Brit.* —*n.* A blackjack. —*v.* To hit with a cosh.

co•sign (kō-sīn′) *v.* To sign (a document) jointly with another or others.

co•sig•na•to•ry (kō-sĭg′nə-tôr′ē, -tōr′ē) *n., pl.* **-ries.** One who cosigns.

cos lettuce *n.* Romaine.

cos•met•ic (kŏz-mĕt′ĭk) *n.* A preparation, as rouge, designed to beautify the body, esp. the face. —*adj.* **1.** Serving to beautify the body. **2.** Superficial : insignificant. —**cos•met′i•cal•ly** *adv.*

cos•me•tol•o•gy (kŏz′mĭ-tŏl′ə-jē) *n.* The study of cosmetics or the art of their use. —**cos′me•tol′o•gist** *n.*

cos•mic (kŏz'mĭk) *adj.* **1.** Of or relating to the cosmos. **2.** Vast. **—cos'mi•cal•ly** *adv.*
cosmic ray *n.* A stream of radiation of extraterrestrial origin, mainly of protons, alpha particles, and other atomic nuclei, that enters the atmosphere and produces secondary radiation.
cos•mog•o•ny (kŏz-mŏg'ə-nē) *n.* **1.** The origin of the universe. **2.** A theory of the evolution of the universe.
cos•mog•ra•phy (kŏz-mŏg'rə-fē) *n., pl.* **-phies. 1.** The study of the features of nature. **2.** A description of the world.
cos•mol•o•gy (kŏz-mŏl'ə-jē) *n.* The study of the origin and structure of the universe.
cos•mo•naut (kŏz'mə-nôt') *n.* A Russian or Soviet astronaut.
cos•mo•pol•i•tan (kŏz'mə-pŏl'ĭ-tn) *adj.* **1.** Common to or representative of many parts of the world. **2.** At home anywhere in the world. *—n.* A cosmopolite.
cos•mop•o•lite (kŏz-mŏp'ə-līt') *n.* A cosmopolitan person.
cos•mos (kŏz'məs, -mŏs') *n.* **1.** The universe regarded as a systematically arranged whole. **2.** An orderly harmonious system. **3.** A tall American garden plant of the genus *Cosmos,* esp. *C. bipinnatus,* having variously colored daisylike flowers.
Cos•sack (kŏs'ăk') *n.* A member of a people of S Ukraine and European Russia, famous as horsemen. **—Cos'sack'** *adj.*
cos•set (kŏs'ĭt) *v.* To pamper.
cost (kôst) *n.* **1.** The amount paid or asked for a purchase. **2.** Loss : sacrifice. ★ ***syns:*** CHARGE, PRICE, TAB *—v.* To have as a price. **—cost'less** *adj.*
co•star *also* **co-star** (kō'stär') *n.* An actor given equal billing in a play or film. *—v.* To present or act as a costar.
cost-ef•fec•tive (kôst'ĭ-fĕk'tĭv) *adj.* Economical as regards the cost for goods or services received.
cos•tive (kŏs'tĭv) *adj.* Having or causing constipation.
cost•ly (kôst'lē) *adj.* **-li•er, -li•est. 1.** Expensive. **2.** Involving great sacrifice or loss. **—cost'li•ness** *n.*
cost of living *n.* **1.** The average cost of the basic necessities of life, as food, housing, and clothes. **2.** The cost of necessary goods and services as defined by an established standard.
cost-plus (kôst'plŭs', kŏst'-) *n.* The cost of production plus a specified profit margin. **—cost'-plus'** *adj.*
cos•tume (kŏs'to͞om', -tyo͞om') *n.* **1.** Clothes typical of one country or period. **2.** A set of clothes appropriate for a particular season or occasion. **3.** Clothes worn by one playing a part or dressing up in disguise. **—cos'tum•er** *n.*
co•sy (kō'zē) *adj. & n. var. of* COZY.
cot (kŏt) *n.* A small, often collapsible bed.
†**cote** (kōt) *n.* **1.** A small shelter for sheep or birds. **2.** *Regional.* A cottage.
co•te•rie (kō'tə-rē) *n.* A close circle of people who have similar interests.
co•ter•mi•nous (kō-tûr'mə-nəs) *adj. var. of* CONTERMINOUS.
co•til•lion (kō-tĭl'yən, kə-) *n.* **1.** A lively group dance with intricate steps. **2.** A formal ball, esp. one for debutantes.
cot•tage (kŏt'ĭj) *n.* A small house, esp. one in the country. **—cot'tag•er** *n.*
cottage cheese *n.* A soft, white cheese made from soured skim milk.
cottage industry *n.* A small-scale, usu. manufacturing business carried on at home.
cotter pin *n.* A metal pin fastened in place by bending apart its 2 ends after insertion in a hole.
cot•ton (kŏt'n) *n.* **1.** A plant or shrub of the genus *Gossypium,* grown in warm climates for the fiber surrounding its seeds. **2.** The soft, white, fibrous substance around cottonseeds, used primarily in making textiles. **3.** Cloth or thread made of cotton. *—v. Informal.* To become friendly <doesn't *cotton* to strangers> **—cot'ton•y** *adj.*
cotton candy *n.* Spun sugar.
cot•ton•mouth (kŏt'n-mouth') *n.* The water moccasin.
cot•ton•seed (kŏt'n-sēd') *n.* The seed of the cotton plant, yielding oil and meal.
cot•ton•tail (kŏt'n-tāl') *n.* A New World rabbit of the genus *Sylvilagus,* with a brownish or grayish coat and a tail having a white underside.
cot•ton•wood (kŏt'n-wo͝od') *n.* A poplar with seeds covered by cottony hair.
cot•y•le•don (kŏt'l-ēd'n) *n. Bot.* A leaf of a plant embryo, one of the first to appear from a sprouting seed. **—cot'y•le'don•al, cot'y•le'do•nous** *adj.*
couch (kouch) *n.* A sofa or bed on which one may recline or sit. *—v.* To phrase in a certain form <*couched* the complaint tactfully>
couch•ant (kou'chənt) *adj. Heraldry.* Lying down with the head up.
cou•gar (ko͞o'gər) *n.* The mountain lion.
cough (kôf, kŏf) *v.* **1.** To eject air from the lungs suddenly and loudly. **2.** To make a noise similar to that of coughing. **3.** To expel by coughing. **—cough** *n.*
could (ko͝od) *v. p.t. of* CAN.
could•n't (ko͝od'nt). Could not.
†**cou•lee** (ko͞o'lē) *n. W U.S.* A deep gully or ravine formed by rain or melting snow.
cou•lomb (ko͞o'lŏm', -lōm') *n.* An electrical charge equal to the electricity transferred by a steady current of 1 ampere in 1 sec.
coun•cil (koun'səl) *n.* **1.** A group of people called together for discussion or consultation. **2.** An official legislative or administrative body. **—coun'cil•man** *n.* **—coun'cil•or, coun'cil•lor** *n.* **—coun'cil•wom'an** *n.*
coun•sel (koun'səl) *n.* **1.** Deliberation or consultation. **2.** Advice : guidance. **3.** A plan or action. **4.** A personal opinion <keep one's own *counsel*> **5.** *pl.* **counsel.** A lawyer or group of lawyers, esp. when conducting a case in court. *—v.* **-seled, -sel•ing** *also* **-selled, -sel•ling. 1.** To give counsel (to). **2.** To recommend.

coun•sel•or *also* **coun•sel•lor** (koun′sə-lər, -slər) *n.* **1.** An adviser. **2.** A lawyer.

count[1] (kount) *v.* **1.** To name or indicate one by one in order to find the total number. **2.** To recite numbers in order. **3.** To take account of in a reckoning. **4.** To believe to be : deem. **5.** To have a specified importance. **—count on.** To rely on. *—n.* **1.** The act of counting. **2.** A number obtained by counting. **3.** *Law.* A particular charge in an indictment. **—count′a•ble** *adj.*

count[2] (kount) *n.* A nobleman in certain European countries, corresponding in rank to an English earl.

count•down (kount′doun′) *n.* The act of counting in descending order to indicate the time remaining before an event, as the launching of a rocket.

coun•te•nance (koun′tə-nəns) *n.* **1.** A person's face, esp. the expression of the face. **2.** Approval : favor. *—v.* **-nanced, -nanc•ing.** To condone : approve.

coun•ter[1] (koun′tər) *adj.* In an opposite direction : contrary. *—v.* **1.** To move or act in opposition (to). **2.** To offer in response. **3.** To meet (a blow) with another blow. *—n.* **1.** An opposite. **2.** An answering blow. *—adv.* In an opposing direction or manner.

count•er[2] (koun′tər) *n.* **1.** A level surface on which business is transacted or food served. **2.** A small piece, as of ivory, used for reckoning or for keeping a place in games. **3.** A token or imitation coin.

count•er[3] (koun′tər) *n.* One that counts, esp. an electrical device.

counter– *pref.* **1.** Contrary : opposite <*counter*clockwise> **2.** Retaliatory : in return <*counter*attack>

coun•ter•act (koun′tər-ăkt′) *v.* To oppose and make ineffective by contrary action. **—coun′ter•ac′tion** *n.*

coun•ter•at•tack (koun′tər-ə-tăk′) *n.* An attack made in opposition to another attack. **—coun′ter•at•tack′** *v.*

coun•ter•bal•ance (koun′tər-băl′əns) *n.* **1.** A force or influence that balances another. **2.** A weight balancing another. **—coun′ter•bal′ance** *v.*

coun•ter•claim (koun′tər-klām′) *n.* An opposing claim to offset another, esp. in a lawsuit. **—coun′ter•claim′** *v.*

coun•ter•clock•wise (koun′tər-klŏk′wīz′) *adj. & adv.* In a direction opposite to that in which the hands of a clock move.

coun•ter•cul•ture (koun′tər-kŭl′chər) *n.* A culture, esp. of the young, with values in opposition to those of traditional society.

coun•ter•es•pi•o•nage (koun′tər-ĕs′pē-ə-näzh′, -nĭj) *n.* Espionage intended to discover and counteract enemy espionage.

coun•ter•feit (koun′tər-fĭt) *v.* **1.** To copy, with the intent to deceive : forge. **2.** To make a show of : feign. *—adj.* **1.** Made in imitation of the genuine so as to deceive : forged. **2.** Pretended : feigned. ★ ***syns:*** BOGUS, ERSATZ, FAKE, FALSE, FRAUDULENT, PHONY, SHAM, SPURIOUS **—coun′ter•feit** *n.* **—coun′ter•feit•er** *n.*

coun•ter•foil (koun′tər-foil′) *n.* The portion of a paper, as a check or ticket, kept by the issuer as a record of the transaction.

coun•ter•in•sur•gen•cy (koun′tər-ĭn-sûr′-jən-sē) *n.* Military and political activity intended to deal with insurgents.

coun•ter•in•tel•li•gence (koun′tər-ĭn-tĕl′-ə-jəns) *n.* An intelligence agency whose duties are to keep valuable information from an enemy, to prevent subversion and sabotage, and to gather political and military data.

coun•ter•ir•ri•tant (koun′tər-ĭr′ĭ-tənt) *n.* An additional irritation that takes attention away from another.

coun•ter•man (koun′tər-măn′, -mən) *n.* One who serves at a counter.

coun•ter•mand (koun′tər-mănd′) *v.* **1.** To reverse (an order). **2.** To recall by a contrary order.

coun•ter•of•fen•sive (koun′tər-ə-fĕn′sĭv) *n.* A military offensive undertaken to stop an enemy attack.

coun•ter•pane (koun′tər-pān′) *n.* A bedspread.

coun′ter•ac′cu•sa′tion *n.*
coun′ter•as•sur′ance *n.*
coun′ter•a′gent *n.*
coun′ter•ar′gu•ment *n.*
coun′ter•as•sault′ *n.*
coun′ter•bid′ *n. & v.*
coun′ter•block•ade′ *n.*
coun′ter•blow′ *n.*
coun′ter•charge′ *n. & v.*
coun′ter•check′ *n.*
coun′ter•com•plaint′ *n.*
coun′ter•coup′ *n.*
coun′ter•cry′ *n.*
coun′ter•cur′rent *n.*
coun′ter•de•mand′ *n.*
coun′ter•dem′on•stra′tion *n.*
coun′ter•de•ploy′ment *n.*
coun′ter•ev′i•dence *n.*
coun′ter•fire′ *n.*
coun′ter•flow′ *n.*
coun′ter•force′ *n.*
coun′ter•fugue′ *n.*
coun′ter•gov′ern•ment *n.*
coun′ter•in•fla′tion•ar′y *adj.*
coun′ter•in′flu•ence *n.*
coun′ter•leg′is•la′tion *n.*
coun′ter•march′ *n.*
coun′ter•meas′ure *n.*
coun′ter•move′ *n.*
coun′ter•of′fer *n.*
coun′ter•plan′ *n.*
coun′ter•plea′ *n.*
coun′ter•plot′ *n. & v.*
coun′ter•po•si′tion *n.*
coun′ter•pres′sure *n.*
coun′ter•prop′a•gan′da *n.*
coun′ter•pro•pos′al *n.*
coun′ter•ques′tion *n.*
coun′ter•re•ac′tion *n.*
coun′ter•res′o•lu′tion *n.*
coun′ter•seal′ *n.*
coun′ter•state′ment *n.*
coun′ter•step′ *n.*
coun′ter•strike′ *n. & v.*
coun′ter•stroke′ *n.*
coun′ter•sug•ges′tion *n.*
coun′ter•suit′ *n.*
coun′ter•sur•veil′lance *n.*
coun′ter•tac′tic(s) *n.*
coun′ter•ter′ror *n.*
coun′ter•ter′ror•ism *n.*
coun′ter•threat′ *n.*
coun′ter•thrust′ *n.*
coun′ter•vi′o•lence *n.*

coun·ter·part (koun'tər-pärt') *n.* One that corresponds very closely to another, as in function or appearance.
coun·ter·point (koun'tər-point') *n.* **1.** *Mus.* The combination of 2 or more melodies into a harmonic relationship while retaining their linear character. **2.** A contrasting but matching element : foil.
coun·ter·poise (koun'tər-poiz') *n.* **1.** A counterbalancing weight or influence. **2.** The state of being balanced : equilibrium. **—coun'ter·poise'** *v.*
coun·ter·pro·duc·tive (koun'tər-prə-dŭk'tĭv) *adj.* Tending to obstruct rather than aid the achievement of a goal.
coun·ter·rev·o·lu·tion (koun'tər-rĕv'ə-lōō'shən) *n.* A movement arising to restore the system overthrown by a revolution.
coun·ter·sign (koun'tər-sīn') *v.* To add a confirming signature to (a previously signed document). *—n.* **1.** A confirming signature added to a previously signed document. **2.** A secret sign or signal given by a person who wishes to pass a guard.
coun·ter·sink (koun'tər-sĭngk') *n.* **1.** A hole with the top part enlarged so that the head of a screw or bolt will lie flush with or below the surface. **2.** A tool for making a countersink. **—coun'ter·sink** *v.*
coun·ter·spy (koun'tər-spī') *n.* A spy engaged in counterespionage.
coun·ter·ten·or (koun'tər-tĕn'ər) *n.* An adult male with a very high voice, higher than a tenor.
coun·ter·vail (koun'tər-văl', koun'tər-văl') *v.* **-vailed, -vail·ing.** To counteract.
coun·ter·weight (koun'tər-wāt') *n.* A counterbalance.
count·ess (koun'tĭs) *n.* **1.** The wife or widow of an earl or count. **2.** A woman with either rank in her own right.
count·ing·house *also* **counting house** (koun'tĭng-hous') *n.* An office in which a firm's bookkeeping and correspondence are carried out.
count·less (kount'lĭs) *adj.* Too many to be counted : infinite.
coun·tri·fied *also* **coun·try·fied** (kŭn'trĭ-fīd') *adj.* **1.** Typical of country life : rural. **2.** Unsophisticated.
coun·try (kŭn'trē) *n., pl.* **-tries. 1.** An area or region. **2.** An area away from cities and towns. **3. a.** A state or nation. **b.** The territory of a state or nation. **4.** The land of one's origin or citizenship.
country club *n.* A club with facilities for social and sports activities.
coun·try-dance (kŭn'trē-dăns') *n.* An English folk dance in which dancers face each other, usu. in lines.
coun·try·man (kŭn'trē-mən) *n.* A person from one's own country : compatriot.
country music *n.* Popular music derived from folk music of the rural U.S., esp. the S or SW U.S.
coun·try·side (kŭn'trē-sīd') *n.* A rural area or its inhabitants.
coun·try·wom·an (kŭn'trē-wŏŏm'ən) *n.* A woman from one's own country : compatriot.
coun·ty (koun'tē) *n., pl.* **-ties.** An administrative district of a country or state.
coup (kōō) *n.* **1.** A brilliant sudden move : masterstroke. **2.** A coup d'état.
coup d'é·tat (kōō' dā-tä') *n., pl.* **coups d'état** (kōō' dā-tä'). The sudden, violent overthrow of a government.
cou·pé (kōō-pā') *also* **coupe** (kōōp) *n.* A closed automobile with 2 doors.
cou·ple (kŭp'əl) *n.* **1.** A pair. **2.** Something joining 2 things together. **3.** *(sing. or pl. in number).* Two people closely associated, esp. a man and woman who are married. **4.** A few : some. ★ ***syns:*** BRACE, DOUBLET, PAIR *—v.* **-pled, -pling. 1.** To join together. **2.** To form pairs. **3.** To copulate. **—cou'pler** *n.*
cou·plet (kŭp'lĭt) *n.* Two successive rhyming lines of poetry.
cou·pon (kōō'pŏn', kyōō'-) *n.* **1.** A detachable certificate on a bond to be presented for payment of interest due. **2.** A certificate that entitles the bearer to a discount, refund, or gift. **3.** Part of an advertisement to be cut out and filled in when sending away for something.
cour·age (kûr'ĭj, kŭr'-) *n.* The ability to face danger without fear. **—cou·ra'geous** *adj.* **—cou·ra'geous·ly** *adv.*
cou·reur de bois (kōō-rōōr'də bwä') *n. Can.* A French or Métis woodsman of the Canadian North.
cou·ri·er (kŏŏr'ē-ər, kûr'-) *n.* **1.** A messenger, esp. one in the diplomatic service. **2.** A person who assists travelers with their arrangements.
course (kôrs, kōrs) *n.* **1.** Progress or the direction of progress. **2.** The path over which something moves. **3.** Duration <in the *course* of a week> **4.** A way of acting or behaving. **5.** A series : sequence <a *course* of treatment> **6. a.** A complete series of studies. **b.** A unit of such a series. **7.** A portion of a meal served at one time <the soup *course*> *—v.* **coursed, cours·ing. 1.** To move rapidly (over or through). **2.** To hunt (game) with dogs. **3.** To flow <tears *coursing* down one's cheeks> **—of course.** Certainly.
cours·er (kôr'sər, kōr'-) *n.* A swift or spirited horse.
court (kôrt, kōrt) *n.* **1.** A courtyard. **2.** A short street, esp. one with buildings on 3 sides. **3.** The residence of a monarch. **4.** The attendants and family of a monarch. **5.** A monarch's council and advisers. **6. a.** A judge or judges whose task it is to try cases of law. **b.** A place where trials are held. **7.** An open area marked off for playing a game. *—v.* **1.** To try to gain the favor of. **2.** To woo. **3.** To behave so as to attract <*court* disaster>
cour·te·ous (kûr'tē-əs) *adj.* Considerate toward others : polite. ★ ***syns:*** CIVIL, GENTEEL, MANNERLY, POLITE **—cour'te·ous·ly** *adv.* **—cour'te·ous·ness** *n.*
cour·te·san (kôr'tĭ-zən, kōr'-) *n.* A prosti-

tute, esp. one associating with high-ranking or wealthy men.

cour•te•sy (kûr′tĭ-sē) *n., pl.* **-sies. 1.** Courteous behavior. **2.** A polite remark or gesture.

court•house (kôrt′hous′, kōrt′-) *n.* A building for holding courts of law.

court•i•er (kôr′tē-ər, kōr′-) *n.* An attendant at a royal court.

court•ly (kôrt′lē, kōrt′-) *adj.* **-li•er, -li•est. 1.** Suitable for a royal court. **2.** Dignified in manner : refined. **—court′li•ness** *n.*

court-mar•tial (kôrt′mär′shəl, kōrt′-) *n., pl.* **courts-mar•tial. 1.** A military or naval court for trial of crimes against military or naval law. **2.** A trial by court-martial. **—court′-mar′tial** *v.*

court•room (kôrt′rōōm′, -rŏŏm′, kōrt′-) *n.* A room in which a law court is held.

court•ship (kôrt′shĭp′, kōrt′-) *n.* The time or act of courting.

court•yard (kôrt′yärd′, kōrt′-) *n.* An open space enclosed by walls, within or adjoining a large building.

cous•cous (kōōs′kōōs′) *n.* A North African dish of steamed crushed grain.

cous•in (kŭz′ĭn) *n.* **1.** A child of one's uncle or aunt. **2.** A relative. **3.** A member of a culturally similar race or nation <our Canadian *cousins*>

cou•ture (kōō-tŏŏr′) *n.* **1.** The business of a couturier. **2.** Fashion designers as a group.

cou•tu•ri•er (kōō-tŏŏr′ē-ər, -ē-ā′) *n.* One who designs, makes, and sells fashionable women's clothing.

cove (kōv) *n.* A small inlet or bay.

cov•en (kŭv′ən, kō′vən) *n.* An assembly of 13 witches.

cov•e•nant (kŭv′ə-nənt) *n.* A binding agreement : compact. **—cov′e•nant** *v.*

cov•er (kŭv′ər) *v.* **1.** To place something on or over. **2.** To clothe. **3.** To serve as a covering for. **4.** To extend over <a park *covering* many acres> **5.** To conceal **:** hide. **6.** To insure. **7.** To be sufficient to meet the cost of. **8.** To treat of **:** include. **9.** To traverse. **10.** To aim a firearm at. **11.** To report the details of <*cover* the election> **12.** *Informal.* To act as a replacement during another's absence. *—n.* **1.** Something that covers. **2.** A position offering protection from attack. **3.** Something that disguises or conceals. **4.** A table setting for one person. **5.** A mailing envelope.

cov•er•age (kŭv′ər-ĭj) *n.* **1.** The extent to which something is covered. **2.** All the risks covered by an insurance policy.

cov•er•alls (kŭv′ər-ôlz′) *pl.n.* A one-piece protective outer garment.

cover charge *n.* A fixed amount added to the bill, as at a restaurant or nightclub.

cover crop *n.* A crop planted to prevent erosion and provide humus.

cover girl *n.* A model whose picture appears on magazine covers.

cov•er•let (kŭv′ər-lĭt) *n.* A bedspread.

cover letter *n.* A letter sent with an enclosure as an explanation.

†**cov•er•lid** (kŭv′ər-lĭd′) *n. Regional.* A coverlet.

cov•ert (kŭv′ərt, kō′vərt) *adj.* **1.** Covered over. **2.** Secret **:** clandestine. *—n.* **1.** A sheltered place. **2.** A thicket providing cover for game. **—cov′ert•ly** *adv.*

cov•er-up *also* **cov•er•up** (kŭv′ər-ŭp′) *n.* An attempt to conceal scandal or crime.

cov•et (kŭv′ĭt) *v.* **1.** To desire enviously (that which belongs to another). **2.** To crave. **—cov′et•ous** *adj.* **—cov′et•ous•ly** *adv.* **—cov′et•ous•ness** *n.*

cov•ey (kŭv′ē) *n., pl.* **-eys.** A small flock of birds, esp. quail or partridges.

cow[1] (kou) *n.* **1.** The mature female of cattle of the genus *Bos* or of certain other large animals. **2.** A domesticated bovine animal.

cow[2] (kou) *v.* To intimidate.

cow•ard (kou′ərd) *n.* One who shows ignoble fear in the face of pain or danger. **—cow′ard•ice** *n.*

cow•ard•ly (kou′ərd-lē) *adj.* Ignobly lacking in courage. ★ ***syns:*** CHICKEN, CHICKEN-HEARTED, CRAVEN, DASTARDLY, FAINT-HEARTED, GUTLESS, LILY-LIVERED, PUSILLANIMOUS, YELLOW, YELLOW-BELLIED **—cow′ard•li•ness** *n.* **—cow′ard•ly** *adv.*

cow•bird (kou′bûrd′) *n.* A blackbird of the genus *Molothrus* that lays its eggs in the nests of other birds.

cow•boy (kou′boi′) *n.* A hired man, esp. in the American West, who tends cattle, typically on horseback.

cow•er (kou′ər) *v.* To cringe from fear.

cow•girl (kou′gûrl′) *n.* A hired woman, esp. in the American West, who tends cattle, typically on horseback.

cow•hand (kou′hănd′) *n.* A cowboy or cowgirl.

cow•herd (kou′hûrd′) *n.* A person who herds cattle.

cow•hide (kou′hīd′) *n.* **1. a.** The hide of a cow. **b.** Leather made from cowhide. **2.** A coarse, heavy, usu. braided leather whip.

cowl (koul) *n.* **1.** The hood or hooded robe worn esp. by a monk. **2.** The top portion at the front of a car to which the windshield and dashboard are attached.

cow•lick (kou′lĭk′) *n.* A tuft of hair that cannot be combed to lie flat.

cowl•ing (kou′lĭng) *n.* A detachable metal covering for an airplane engine.

cow•poke (kou′pōk′) *n.* A cowhand.

cow•pox (kou′pŏks′) *n.* A mild skin disease of cows caused by a virus that gives humans immunity to smallpox.

cow•punch•er (kou′pŭn′chər) *n.* A cowhand.

cow•ry *also* **cow•rie** (kou′rē) *n., pl.* **-ries.** Any of numerous mollusks of the family Cypraeidae of tropical waters, with glossy, often brightly colored shells.

cow•slip (kou′slĭp′) *n.* **1.** An Old World primrose, *Primula veris,* with pale-yellow flowers. **2.** The marsh marigold.

cox (kŏks) *Informal. —n.* A coxswain. *—v.* To act as coxswain (for).

cox•comb (kŏks'kōm') *n.* A conceited foolish person : fop.
cox•swain (kŏk'sən, -swān') *n.* The person who steers a racing shell or boat.
coy (koi) *adj.* **1.** Shy, esp. flirtatiously so. **2.** Annoyingly unforthcoming. —**coy'ly** *adv.* —**coy'ness** *n.*
coy•dog (kī'dôg', -dŏg', koi'-) *n.* A hybrid offspring of a coyote and a feral dog.
coy•o•te (kī-ō'tē, kī'ōt') *n.* A wolflike carnivorous animal, *Canis latrans,* native to North America.
coy•pu (koi'po͞o) *n., pl.* **-pus.** A large beaverlike South American rodent, *Myocaster coypu.*
coz•en (kŭz'ən) *v.* To cheat : defraud. —**coz'en•age** *n.*
co•zy *also* **co•sy** (kō'zē) *adj.* **-zi•er, -zi•est** *also* **-si•er, -si•est.** Warm and comfortable : snug. —*n., pl.* **-zies** *also* **-sies.** A covering placed over a teapot to keep the tea hot. —**co'zi•ly** *adv.* —**co'zi•ness** *n.*
CPR (sē'pē-är') *n.* Cardiopulmonary resuscitation.
Cr *symbol for* CHROMIUM.
crab[1] (krăb) *n.* **1.** Any of numerous chiefly marine crustaceans with a short, broad shell, 4 pairs of legs, and a pair of pincers. **2.** The crab louse.
crab[2] (krăb) *n. Informal.* A peevish, ill-tempered person. —**crab** *v.* —**crab'by** *adj.*
crab apple *n.* Any of several trees of the genus *Pyrus,* with small, sour fruit.
crab•bed (krăb'ĭd) *adj.* **1.** Irritable : morose. 2. Difficult to read. —**crab'bed•ly** *adv.* —**crab'bed•ness** *n.*
crab•grass (krăb'grăs') *n.* A coarse, weedy creeping grass of the genus *Digitaria.*
crab louse *n.* A body louse, *Phthirus pubis,* that gen. infests the pubic region.
crack (krăk) *v.* **1.** To break or cause to break apart with a snap. **2.** To break or cause to break without completely separating into parts. 3. To change sharply in tone. —Used of a voice. **4.** To strike with a sudden sharp sound. 5. To break open <*crack* a safe> **6.** To solve. 7. *Informal.* To tell (a joke). **8.** To reduce (petroleum) to simpler compounds by heating. —**crack down.** *Informal.* To act to restrain or restrict. —**crack up.** *Informal.* **1.** To damage or wreck. **2.** To have a physical or mental breakdown. **3.** To experience or cause considerable amusement. —*n.* **1.** A sudden sharp noise. **2.** A narrow opening or break : fissure. **3.** A sudden, sharp blow. **4.** A cracking of the voice. **5.** An attempt : try. **6.** A witty remark. **7.** *Slang.* Chemically purified, potent cocaine usu. smoked through a glass pipe. —*adj.* Highly proficient : first-rate.
crack•down (krăk'doun') *n.* An act or example of cracking down.
crack•er (krăk'ər) *n.* **1.** A dry, thin, crisp biscuit or wafer. **2.** A firecracker.
crack•er•jack (krăk'ər-jăk') *adj. Slang.* Of excellent quality : fine. —**crack'er•jack'** *n.*
crack•le (krăk'əl) *v.* **-led, -ling. 1.** To make or cause to make a series of sharp snapping sounds. **2.** To become covered with a network of small cracks. —**crack'le** *n.* —**crack'ly** *adj.*
crack•pot (krăk'pŏt') *n.* A bizarre or eccentric person.
crack•up (krăk'ŭp') *n. Informal.* **1.** A crash or wreck, as of an aircraft. **2.** A physical or mental breakdown.
cra•dle (krād'l) *n.* **1.** A small, low bed for an infant, often on rockers. **2.** A place of origin. **3.** The support for a telephone receiver. **4.** A frame attached to a scythe for catching grain as it is cut. —*v.* **-dled, -dling.** To place gently in or as if in a cradle.
craft (krăft) *n.* **1.** A special skill or ability. **2.** Cunning : guile. **3. a.** An occupation, esp. one that demands manual skill. **b.** The members of such an occupation or trade. **4.** *pl.* **craft.** An aircraft, boat, or ship.
crafts•man (krăfts'mən) *n.* A skilled worker : artisan. —**crafts'man•ship'** *n.* —**crafts'per•son** *n.*
crafts•wom•an (krăfts'wo͝om'ən) *n.* A woman skilled in a craft : artisan.
craft•y (krăf'tē) *adj.* **-i•er, -i•est.** Marked by devious cunning : sly : shrewd. —**craft'i•ly** *adv.* —**craft'i•ness** *n.*
crag (krăg) *n.* A steep cliff or projecting mass of rock. —**crag'gy** *adj.*
cram (krăm) *v.* **crammed, cram•ming. 1.** To force or stuff. 2. To pack in tightly. 3. To eat greedily. **4.** *Informal.* To prepare hastily for an examination.
cramp[1] (krămp) *n.* **1.** A painful involuntary contraction of a muscle usu. resulting from strain or cold. **2. cramps.** Sharp abdominal spasms and pains.
cramp[2] (krămp) *n.* Anything that restrains or compresses, as a clamp. —*v.* **1.** To restrain from free action : hamper. **2.** To turn (the wheels of a car) sharply.
cran•ber•ry (krăn'bĕr'ē) *n.* A trailing North American shrub, *Vaccinium macrocarpon,* growing in damp ground and bearing edible, tart red berries.
crane (krān) *n.* **1.** A large wading bird of the family Cruidae, with very long legs and neck. **2.** A machine for lifting and moving heavy objects. —*v.* **craned, cran•ing.** To strain or stretch (the neck).
cra•ni•um (krā'nē-əm) *n., pl.* **-ums** *or* **-ni•a** (-nē-ə). The skull, esp. the part that encloses the brain. —**cra'ni•al** *adj.*
crank[1] (krăngk) *n.* **1.** A handle attached at right angles to a shaft and turned in order to transmit rotary motion. **2.** *Informal.* An ill-tempered or eccentric person. —*v.* To operate or start by a crank. —**crank out** To produce rapidly and mechanically.
†**crank**[2] (krăngk) *adj. Regional.* 1. Lively. **2.** Overconfident.
crank•case (krăngk'kās') *n.* The housing of a crankshaft.
crank•shaft (krăngk'shăft') *n.* A shaft driven by a crank.
crank•y (krăng'kē) *adj.* **-i•er, -i•est. 1.** Pee-

vish : grouchy. **2.** Eccentric : odd. **—crank'i•ly** *adv.* **—crank'i•ness** *n.*

cran•ny (krăn'ē) *n., pl.* **-nies.** A crevice.

crape (krāp) *n.* Crepe.

craps (krăps) *n. (sing. or pl. in number).* A gambling game played with dice.

crap•shoot•er (krăp'sho͞o'tər) *n.* A person who plays craps.

crash[1] (krăsh) *v.* **1.** To break noisily : smash. **2.** To cause or undergo damage on impact. **3.** To make a sudden loud noise. **4.** To collapse suddenly, as a business. **5.** *Informal.* To get into (e.g., a party) without invitation. *—n.* **1.** A loud, sudden sound. **2.** A collision : wreck. **3.** A sudden failure, esp. of a business. *—adj. Informal.* Intensive <a *crash* diet>

crash[2] (krăsh) *n.* A coarse cotton material used for draperies and towels.

crash helmet *n.* A padded, protective helmet, as worn by motorcyclists.

crash-land (krăsh'lănd') *v.* To land an aircraft in an emergency, often without the use of the landing gear.

crass (krăs) *adj.* Coarse and unrefined : gross. **—crass'ly** *adv.* **—crass'ness** *n.*

crate (krāt) *n.* A container, as a slatted wooden box. *—v.* **crat•ed, crat•ing.** To pack in a crate.

cra•ter (krā'tər) *n.* **1.** A cavity at the mouth of a volcano. **2.** A hole in the ground made by an explosion or a falling meteorite.

cra•vat (krə-văt') *n.* A necktie.

crave (krāv) *v.* **craved, crav•ing. 1.** To desire intensely : long for. **2.** To ask for earnestly : beg.

cra•ven (krā'vən) *adj.* Cowardly. **—cra'ven** *n.* **—cra'ven•ly** *adv.*

crav•ing (krā'vĭng) *n.* An overwhelming longing : yearning.

craw (krô) *n.* **1.** The crop of a bird. **2.** An animal's stomach.

craw•fish (krô'fĭsh') *n.* A crayfish.

crawl (krôl) *v.* **1.** To move slowly by drawing the body along the ground. **2.** To move on hands and knees. **3.** To advance slowly <the hours *crawled* by> **4.** To feel as if covered with crawling creatures. ★ ***syns:*** CREEP, SLIDE, SNAKE, WORM *—n.* **1.** A slow pace. **2.** A swimming stroke performed face down consisting of alternating overarm strokes and a flutter kick.

cray•fish (krā'fĭsh') *n.* Any of various small, lobsterlike freshwater crustaceans of the genera *Cambarus* and *Astacus.*

cray•on (krā'ŏn', -ən) *n.* A colored stick, as of wax or charcoal, used for drawing. **—cray'on'** *v.*

craze (krāz) *v.* **crazed, craz•ing.** To make or become insane. *—n.* Something popular for a short time : fad.

cra•zy (krā'zē) *adj.* **-zi•er, -zi•est. 1.** Mad : insane. **2.** *Informal.* Very enthusiastic. **3.** *Informal.* Very impractical. **—cra'zi•ly** *adv.* **—cra'zi•ness** *n.*

crazy bone *n.* The funny bone.

crazy quilt *n.* A patchwork quilt of pieces arranged in no definite pattern.

creak (krēk) *v.* To make a squeaking noise. **—creak** *n.* **—creak'i•ly** *adv.* **—creak'i•ness** *n.* **—creak'y** *adj.*

cream (krēm) *n.* **1.** The yellowish fatty component of unhomogenized milk. **2.** A yellowish white. **3.** A substance resembling or containing cream, as certain cosmetics or foods. **4.** The finest part. *—v.* To beat into a creamy consistency. **—cream'i•ness** *n.* **—cream'y** *adj.*

cream cheese *n.* A soft cheese made from milk enriched with cream.

cream•er (krē'mər) *n.* A small pitcher.

cream•er•y (krē'mə-rē) *n., pl.* **-ies.** A place where dairy products are made or sold.

crease (krēs) *n.* A mark made by folding and pressing. **—crease** *v.*

cre•ate (krē-āt') *v.* **-at•ed, -at•ing. 1.** To bring into being. **2.** To give rise to.

cre•a•tion (krē-ā'shən) *n.* **1.** The act of creating. **2.** Something that is created. **3.** All things in the world.

cre•a•tion•ism (krē-ā'shə-nĭz'əm) *n.* The position that the Biblical account of creation is literally true. **—cre•a'tion•ist** *n.*

cre•a•tive (krē-ā'tĭv) *adj.* Inventive : imaginative. **—cre•a'tive•ly** *adv.* **—cre'a•tiv'i•ty, cre•a'tive•ness** *n.*

cre•a•tor (krē-ā'tər) *n.* **1.** One that creates. **2. Creator.** God.

crea•ture (krē'chər) *n.* **1.** A living being. **2.** A human being.

crèche (krĕsh) *n.* A representation of the stable scene of Jesus's birth.

cre•dence (krēd'ns) *n.* Acceptance as true : belief.

cre•den•tial (krĭ-dĕn'shəl) *n.* Something that is a basis for credit or confidence.

cre•den•za (krĭ-dĕn'zə) *n.* A usu. legless cabinet or sideboard.

cred•i•ble (krĕd'ə-bəl) *adj.* **1.** Plausible : believable. **2.** Deserving confidence. **—cred'i•bil'i•ty** *n.* **—cred'i•bly** *adv.*

cred•it (krĕd'ĭt) *n.* **1.** Belief in the truth of something : trust. **2.** A favorable reputation. **3.** A source of distinction. **4.** Praise. **5.** Official certification that a student has completed a course. **6.** Financial trustworthiness. **7.** Time given for payment of goods sold on trust. **8.** An accounting entry of payment received. **9.** The balance of a bank account that is in the holder's favor. *—v.* **1.** To believe in. **2.** To give credit to <*credited* me with the invention>

cred•it•a•ble (krĕd'ĭ-tə-bəl) *adj.* Meriting praise. **—cred'it•a•bly** *adv.*

credit card *n.* A card authorizing purchases on credit.

cred•i•tor (krĕd'ĭ-tər) *n.* A person to whom money is owed.

credit union *n.* A cooperative organization that makes low-interest loans to its members.

cred•it•wor•thy (krĕd'ĭt-wûr'thē) *adj.* Having a favorable credit rating.

cre•do (krē'dō, krā'-) *n., pl.* **-dos.** A creed.

cred•u•lous (krĕj'ə-ləs) *adj.* Gullible. **—cre•**

du'li•ty (krĭ-dōō'lĭ-tē, -dyōō-), **cred'u•lous•ness** *n.* —**cred'u•lous•ly** *adv.*

Cree (krē) *n., pl.* **Cree** *or* **Crees. 1.** A member of an American Indian people living from E Canada to Alberta. **2.** Their Algonquian language.

creed (krēd) *n.* **1.** A statement of religious belief, esp. one authorized by a church. **2.** A system of principles or opinions.

creek (krēk, krĭk) *n.* A small stream. —**up the creek.** In a difficult position.

Creek (krēk) *n., pl.* **Creek** *or* **Creeks. 1.** A member of an American Indian people formerly of Alabama, Georgia, and NW Florida, now chiefly in Oklahoma. **2.** Their Muskogean language.

creel (krēl) *n.* A wickerwork basket for holding fish.

creep (krēp) *v.* **crept** (krĕpt), **creep•ing. 1.** To move with the body close to the ground : crawl. **2.** To move cautiously or stealthily : sneak. **3.** *Bot.* To grow along a surface, clinging by means of tendrils. **4.** To feel as if covered with creeping creatures. —*n.* **1.** *Slang.* An annoying or repulsive person. **2. creeps.** *Informal.* A feeling of fear or repugnance. —**creep'er** *n.* —**creep'y** *adj.*

cre•mate (krē'māt', krĭ-māt') *v.* **-mat•ed, -mat•ing.** To incinerate (a corpse). —**cre•ma'tion** *n.*

cre•ma•to•ri•um (krē'mə-tôr'ē-əm, -tōr'-) *n., pl.* **-ums** *or* **-ri•a.** A crematory.

cre•ma•to•ry (krē'mə-tôr'ē, -tōr'ē, krĕm'ə-) *n., pl.* **-ries.** A place where corpses are cremated.

crème de la crème (krĕm'də lä krĕm') *n.* **1.** The very best. **2.** The social elite.

crème de menthe (krĕm'də mäNt ') *n.* A green or white mint-flavored liqueur.

cren•e•lat•ed (krĕn'ə-lā'tĭd) *adj.* Having battlements. —**cren'e•la'tion** *n.*

Cre•ole (krē'ōl') *n.* **1.** A person of European ancestry born in Spanish America or the West Indies. **2. a.** One descended from the orig. French settlers of S U.S. **b.** The French dialect of these people. **3.** A person of mixed black and European, esp. French or Spanish ancestry.

cre•o•sote (krē'ə-sōt') *n.* An oily liquid obtained by distilling coal tar and used as a wood preservative.

crepe *also* **crêpe** (krāp) *n.* A thin, soft crinkled fabric of silk or other fiber.

crêpe de Chine (krāp'də shēn') *n.* A silk crepe.

crêpe su•zette (krāp'sōō-zĕt') *n.* A thin dessert pancake usu. rolled with orange sauce and often served with a flaming brandy or liqueur sauce.

crept (krĕpt) *v. p.t. & p.p.* of CREEP.

cre•pus•cu•lar (krĭ-pŭs'kyə-lər) *adj.* **1.** Of or resembling twilight. **2.** *Zool.* Becoming active at twilight.

cres•cen•do (krə-shĕn'dō, -sĕn'-) *adv. Mus.* Gradually increasing in loudness. —**cres•cen'do** *adj. & n.*

cres•cent (krĕs'ənt) *n.* **1.** The shape of the moon in its first or last quarter with concave and convex edges. **2.** Anything with the shape of a crescent. —**cres'cent** *adj.*

cress (krĕs) *n.* Any of various related plants, as those of the genera *Cardamine* or *Arabis,* with sharp-tasting edible leaves.

crest (krĕst) *n.* **1.** A ridge or tuft on the head of a bird or animal. **2.** *Heraldry.* A device set above the escutcheon on a coat or arms. **3.** The highest point, as of a wave or mountain top. —*v.* **1.** To reach the crest of. **2.** To rise to a crest.

crest•fall•en (krĕst'fô'lən) *adj.* Dispirited : depressed.

cre•tin (krēt'n) *n.* **1.** A person afflicted with cretinism. **2.** *Slang.* An idiot : dolt.

cre•tin•ism (krēt'n-ĭz'əm) *n.* A congenital condition due to a deficiency of thyroid hormone during prenatal development and marked in childhood by dwarfed stature, mental retardation, and subnormal metabolic rate.

cre•tonne (krĭ-tŏn', krē'tŏn') *n.* A strong, colorfully printed cotton or linen cloth.

cre•vasse (krə-văs') *n.* A deep crack, esp. in a glacier.

crev•ice (krĕv'ĭs) *n.* A narrow crack.

crew[1] (krōō) *n.* **1.** A group of people working together. **2.** The persons who operate an aircraft, ship, etc. **3.** A team of rowers. —**crew** *v.*

crew[2] (krōō) *v. var. p.t. & p.p. of* CROW[2].

crew cut *n.* A closely cropped haircut.

crew•el (krōō'əl) *n.* Slackly twisted worsted yarn used in embroidery.

crib (krĭb) *n.* **1.** A small bed with high sides, for a child. **2.** A small building or bin for grain storage. **3.** A trough or rack for fodder : manger. **4.** *Informal.* **a.** Plagiarism. **b.** A petty theft. **c.** PONY 2. —*v.* **cribbed, crib•bing. 1.** To confine. **2.** *Informal.* **a.** To plagiarize. **b.** To steal. **3.** *Informal.* To use a crib for schoolwork. —**crib'ber** *n.*

crib•bage (krĭb'ĭj) *n.* A card game usu. played by 2 players and scored on a board.

crib death *n.* Sudden infant death syndrome.

crick[1] (krĭk) *n.* A painful muscle spasm.

†**crick**[2] (krĭk) *n. Regional.* A creek.

crick•et[1] (krĭk'ĭt) *n.* Any of various leaping insects of the family Gryllidae, the male of the species producing a shrill, chirping sound by rubbing the front wings together.

crick•et[2] (krĭk'ĭt) *n.* An outdoor game played with bats, a ball, and wickets by 2 teams of 11 players each. —**crick'et•er** *n.*

cri•er (krī'ər) *n.* One who calls out public proclamations.

crime (krīm) *n.* An offense committed against the law.

crim•i•nal (krĭm'ə-nəl) *adj.* **1.** Of or involving a crime. **2.** Relating to the administration of penal laws. **3.** Guilty of crime. ★ ***syns:*** ILLEGAL, ILLEGITIMATE, ILLICIT, LAWLESS, UNLAWFUL, WRONGFUL —*n.* A person who has committed a crime. —**crim'i•nal'i•ty** *n.* —**crim'i•nal•ly** *adv.*

criminal law *n.* Law dealing with crime and its punishment.
crim•i•nol•o•gy (krĭm'ə-nŏl'ə-jē) *n.* The scientific study of crime and criminal behavior. —**crim'i•nol'o•gist** *n.*
crimp (krĭmp) *v.* **1.** To cause to become crinkled : corrugate. **2.** To cause (hair) to form tight curls. —*n.* Something, as a hair curl, that has been produced by crimping.
crim•son (krĭm'zən, -sən) *n.* A deep red. —*v.* To make or become crimson.
cringe (krĭnj) *v.* **cringed, cring•ing.** To recoil in fear : cower.
crin•kle (krĭng'kəl) *v.* **-kled, -kling.** To wrinkle. —**crin'kle** *n.* —**crin'kly** *adj.*
crin•o•line (krĭn'ə-lĭn) *n.* A coarse fabric used for lining and stiffening garments.
crip•ple (krĭp'əl) *n.* One that is lame or partially disabled. —*v.* **-pled, -pling.** To disable or impair.
cri•sis (krī'sĭs) *n., pl.* **-ses** (-sēz'). **1.** A decisive or crucial moment. **2.** A sudden change for better or worse in the course of an acute illness.
crisp (krĭsp) *adj.* **1.** Easily broken : brittle <*crisp* bacon> **2.** Fresh and firm <*crisp* lettuce> **3.** Brisk : bracing. **4.** Curly. —*n. esp. Brit.* A potato chip. —*v.* To make or become crisp. —**crisp'ly** *adv.* —**crisp'ness** *n.* —**crisp'y** *adj.*
crisp•er (krĭs'pər) *n.* A compartment in a refrigerator used to keep vegetables fresh.
criss•cross (krĭs'krôs', -krŏs') *v.* **1.** To mark with crossed lines. **2.** To move back and forth. —*n.* A pattern of crossed lines. —**criss'cross'** *adj. & adv.*
cri•te•ri•on (krī-tîr'ē-ən) *n., pl.* **-te•ri•a** (-tîr'ē-ə) *or* **-ons.** A standard or rule by which something can be judged.
crit•ic (krĭt'ĭk) *n.* **1.** One who forms and expresses judgments of the merits, faults, etc., of a matter. **2.** One who expresses judgments of artistic or literary works. **3.** One inclined to find fault.
crit•i•cal (krĭt'ĭ-kəl) *adj.* **1.** Tending to judge adversely. **2.** Marked by exact and careful judgment and evaluation. **3.** Of or relating to critics or criticism. **4.** Of or forming a crisis : crucial. ★ ***syns:*** ACUTE, CRUCIAL, DESPERATE, DIRE —**crit'i•cal•ly** *adv.*
critical mass *n.* The smallest mass of a fissionable material that will sustain a nuclear chain reaction.
crit•i•cism (krĭt'ĭ-sĭz'əm) *n.* **1.** The act of criticizing, esp. adversely : censure. **2. a.** The judgments of a critic. **b.** A review expressing such judgments.
crit•i•cize (krĭt'ĭ-sīz') *v.* **-cized, -ciz•ing. 1.** To analyze and evaluate. **2.** To judge adversely.
cri•tique (krĭ-tēk') *n.* A critical analysis or review. —**cri•tique'** *v.*
†**crit•ter** (krĭt'ər) *n. Regional.* **1.** A domestic animal. **2.** A living creature.
croak (krōk) *n.* A hoarse, rasping cry, as that of a frog. —*v.* **1.** To utter a croak. **2.** *Slang.* To die. —**croak'i•ly** *adv.*
cro•chet (krō-shā') *n.* Needlework done by looping thread or wool with a hooked needle. —*v.* **-cheted** (-shād'), **-chet•ing** (-shā'ĭng). To make (crochet).
crock (krŏk) *n.* An earthenware pot or jar. —**crock'er•y** *n.*
crocked (krŏkt) *adj. Slang.* Intoxicated.
croc•o•dile (krŏk'ə-dīl') *n.* Any of various aquatic reptiles of the genus *Crocodylus,* of tropical regions, with thick armorlike skin and long jaws.
crocodile tears *pl.n.* Insincere grief.
croc•o•dil•i•an (krŏk'ə-dĭl'ē-ən, -dĭl'yən) *n.* Any of various reptiles of the order Crocodylia, including the alligators, crocodiles, and caimans. —**croc'o•dil'i•an** *adj.*
cro•cus (krō'kəs) *n., pl.* **-es.** A plant of the genus *Crocus,* widely cultivated in gardens and bearing variously colored flowers.
croft (krôft, krŏft) *n. Brit. & Scot.* A small farm, esp. a tenant farm. —**croft'er** *n.*
crois•sant (krwä-säɴ') *n.* A rich crescent-shaped roll, often of puff pastry.
crone (krōn) *n.* **1.** An old woman. **2.** A hag.
cro•ny (krō'nē) *n., pl.* **-nies.** A close friend.
crook (kro͝ok) *n.* **1.** A bent or curved object, as a shepherd's staff. **2.** A bend or curve. **3.** *Informal.* A person who lives by dishonest means. —*v.* To bend or curve.
crook•ed (kro͝ok'ĭd) *adj.* **1.** Not straight : bent. **2.** *Informal.* Dishonest. —**crook'ed•ly** *adv.* —**crook'ed•ness** *n.*
crook•neck (kro͝ok'nĕk') *n.* A squash with a long curved neck and yellow flesh.
croon (kro͞on) *v.* **1.** To sing in a low, soft voice. **2.** To sing popular songs in a sentimental way. —**croon'** *n.* —**croon'er** *n.*
crop (krŏp) *n.* **1. a.** Agricultural produce that can be harvested. **b.** The yield at a harvest. **2.** A short haircut. **3.** A riding whip. **4.** *Zool.* A pouch in a bird's esophagus where food is partially digested. —*v.* **cropped, crop•ping. 1.** To cut off the top of (a plant). **2.** To cut very short : trim. **3.** To harvest. **4.** To appear unexpectedly.
crop-dust•ing (krŏp'dŭs'tĭng) *n.* The spraying of crops with pesticide, usu. from an airplane. —**crop'-dust'** *v.*
crop•per[1] (krŏp'ər) *n.* A sharecropper.
crop•per[2] (krŏp'ər) *n.* **1.** A heavy fall : tumble. **2.** A fiasco.
cro•quet (krō-kā') *n.* An outdoor game in which the players drive wooden balls through hoops using long-handled mallets.
cro•quette (krō-kĕt') *n.* A small patty or roll of minced food fried in deep fat.
cro•sier *also* **cro•zier** (krō'zhər) *n.* A staff carried by bishops and abbots.
cross (krôs, krŏs) *n.* **1.** A structure consisting of an upright post and a crossbar. **2.** A representation of the cross on which Jesus was crucified. **3.** A medal with the shape of a cross. **4.** A mark formed by the intersection of 2 lines. **5.** *Biol.* **a.** A plant or animal produced by crossbreeding. **b.** The process of crossbreeding. —*v.* **1.** To go or pass across. **2.** To intersect. **3.** To make a line across. **4.** To put cross-

wise. **5.** To interfere with **:** thwart. **6.** To crossbreed. *—adj.* **1.** Intersecting. **2.** Opposing **:** contrary. **3.** Ill-tempered **:** irritable. **4.** Crossbred. **—cross'ly** *adv.* **—cross'ness** *n.*

cross•bar (krôs'bär', krŏs'-) *n.* A horizontal bar, stripe, or line.

cross•bones (krôs'bōnz', krŏs'-) *n.* Two bones placed crosswise, usu. beneath a skull, symbolizing death or danger.

cross•bow (krôs'bō', krŏs'-) *n.* A powerful bow fixed crosswise on a wooden stock.

cross•breed (krôs'brēd', krŏs'-) *v.* To produce (a hybrid) by the mating of individuals of different breeds or varieties. **—cross'-breed'** *n.*

cross-coun•try (krôs'kŭn'trē, krŏs'-) *adj.* **1.** Moving across open countryside. **2.** Extending across a country. **—cross'-coun'try** *adv.*

cross•cur•rent (krôs'kûr'ənt, -kŭr'-, krŏs'-) *n.* **1.** A current flowing counter to another. **2.** A conflicting tendency.

cross•cut (krôs'kŭt', krŏs'-) *v.* To run or cut across or crosswise. *—adj.* **1.** Used or suitable for cutting crosswise. **2.** Cut on the bias or across the grain. *—n.* A cut or course that goes crosswise.

cross-dress (krôs'drĕs', krŏs'-) *v.* To dress in the clothing characteristic of the opposite sex. **—cross'-dress'er** *n.* **—cross'-dress'ing** *n.*

cross-ex•am•ine (krôs'ĭg-zăm'ĭn, krŏs'-) *v.* To question closely, esp. in order to check answers to previous questioning. **—cross'-ex•am'i•na'tion** *n.*

cross-eye (krôs'ī', krŏs'ī') *n.* Strabismus in which the eye turns toward the nose. **—cross'-eyed'** *adj.*

cross-file (krôs'fīl', krŏs'-) *v.* To register as a candidate in the primaries of more than one political party. **—cross'-fil'er** *n.*

cross•fire (krôs'fīr', krŏs'-) *n.* **1.** Crossing lines of gunfire from 2 opposing positions. **2.** A rapid, often acrimonious discussion.

cross•hatch (krôs'hăch', krŏs'-) *v.* To mark or shade with 2 or more sets of intersecting parallel lines.

cross•ing (krô'sĭng, krŏs'ĭng) *n.* **1.** An intersection, as of 2 streets. **2.** The place for crossing something, as a river or highway.

cross-leg•ged (krôs'lĕg'ĭd, -lĕgd', krŏs'-) *adv.* & *adj.* **1.** With the legs or ankles crossed and the knees far apart. **2.** With one leg lying over and across the other leg.

cross matching *n.* The process in which the compatibility of blood is tested before a blood transfusion.

cross•patch (krôs'păch', krŏs'-) *n. Informal.* An ill-tempered, grumpy person.

cross•piece (krôs'pēs', krŏs'-) *n.* A transverse part of a structure.

cross-pur•pose (krôs'pûr'pəs, krŏs'-) *n.* An opposing or conflicting purpose.

cross-re•fer (krôs'rĭ-fûr', krŏs'-) *v.* To refer from one part or passage to another. **—cross'-ref'er•ence** *n.*

cross•road (krôs'rōd', krŏs'-) *n.* **1.** A road intersecting another. **2.** *often* **crossroads.** An intersection of 2 or more roads.

cross section *n.* **1.** A section cut across an object. **2.** A sample meant to represent the nature of the whole.

cross-town (krôs'toun', krŏs'-) *adj.* Extending across a town or city <a *cross-town* subway line> **—cross'-town'** *adv.*

cross•walk (krôs'wôk', krŏs'-) *n.* A lane marked off for pedestrians to use when crossing a street.

cross•wind (krôs'wĭnd', krŏs'-) *n.* A wind blowing at right angles to one's direction of travel.

cross•wise (krôs'wīz', krŏs'-) *also* **cross•ways** (-wāz') *adv.* Across. *—adj.* Crossing.

cross•word puzzle (krôs'wûrd', krŏs'-) *n.* A puzzle in which a pattern of numbered squares is to be filled with words in answer to correspondingly numbered clues.

crotch (krŏch) *n.* The angle or region of the angle formed by the junction of 2 parts, as legs or branches.

crotch•et (krŏch'ĭt) *n.* A peculiar whim. **—crotch'et•y** *adj.*

crouch (krouch) *v.* **1.** To bend over close to the ground. **2.** To cower. **—crouch** *n.*

croup (kro͞op) *n.* Laryngitis, esp. in children, marked by a harsh cough and difficulty in breathing. **—croup'y** *adj.*

crou•pi•er (kro͞o'pē-ər, -pē-ā') *n.* One who collects and pays bets at a gaming table.

crou•ton (kro͞o'tŏn', kro͞o-tŏn') *n.* A small crisp piece of fried bread or toast.

crow[1] (krō) *n.* A large, black bird of the genus *Corvus* with a raucous call.

crow[2] (krō) *v.* **1.** *p.t.* & *p.p.* **crowed** *or* **crew** (kro͞o). To utter the shrill cry of a rooster. **2.** To exult, esp. over another's misfortune. **3.** To make an inarticulate noise expressing pleasure. *—n.* The shrill cry of a cock.

Crow (krō) *n., pl.* **Crow** *or* **Crows. 1.** A member of an American Indian people of the N Great Plains. **2.** Their Siouan language.

crow•bar (krō'bär') *n.* A metal bar, usu. with a chisel-shaped end, used as a lever.

crowd (kroud) *n.* **1.** A large number of people or things gathered closely together. **2.** A particular social group. *—v.* **1.** To congregate in numbers. **2.** To press close. **3.** To stuff tightly **:** cram.

crown (kroun) *n.* **1.** An ornamental circlet or head covering, often made of precious metal and jewels, and worn by royalty. **2.** The power of a sovereign. **3.** A reward or honor for achievement. **4.** Something like a crown. **5.** A former British coin. **6.** The highest part of the head. **7.** The highest point **:** summit. **8.** The part of a tooth that projects beyond the gum line. *—v.* **1.** To put a crown upon. **2.** To enthrone. **3.** To honor or reward <*crowned* their efforts with success> **4.** To surmount **:** top. **5.** To put the finishing touch on **:** cap.

Crown corporation *n. Can.* A government-owned company.

crow's-foot (krōz'fo͝ot') *n., pl.* **-feet.** Any of the wrinkles at the outer corner of the eye.

crow's-nest (krōz'nĕst') *n. Naut.* A small, partly enclosed lookout platform near the top of a ship's mast.
cro•zier (krō'zhər) *n. var. of* CROSIER.
cru•ces (kro͞o'sēz) *n. var. pl. of* CRUX.
cru•cial (kro͞o'shəl) *adj.* **1.** Critical : decisive. **2.** Difficult : severe.
cru•ci•ble (kro͞o'sə-bəl) *n.* A vessel used for melting materials at high temperatures.
cru•ci•fix (kro͞o'sə-fĭks') *n.* A representation of Jesus on the cross.
cru•ci•fix•ion (kro͞o'sə-fĭk'shən) *n.* **1.** The act of putting to death on a cross. **2. Crucifixion.** The crucifying of Jesus.
cru•ci•form (kro͞o'sə-fôrm') *adj.* In the shape of a cross.
cru•ci•fy (kro͞o'sə-fī') *v.* **-fied, -fy•ing. 1.** To put to death by nailing or binding to a cross. **2.** To treat unfairly or cruelly : torment <was *crucified* by the media>
†**crud** (krŭd) *n.* **1.** *Slang.* **a.** A coating of filth. **b.** One that is disgusting. **2.** *Regional.* A milk curd. **—crud'dy** *adj.*
crude (kro͞od) *adj.* **crud•er, crud•est. 1.** Not refined : raw. **2.** Lacking refinement or tact. **3.** Not carefully made : rough. *—n.* Unrefined petroleum. **—crude'ly** *adv.* **—cru'di•ty, crude'ness** *n.*
crude oil *n.* Petroleum.
cru•di•tés (kro͞o'dĭ-tā') *pl.n.* Raw vegetables, often served with a dip.
cru•el (kro͞o'əl) *adj.* **-el•er, -el•est** *or* **-el•ler, -el•lest. 1.** Inflicting suffering. **2.** Painful. **—cru'el•ly** *adv.* **—cru'el•ty** *n.*
cru•et (kro͞o'ĭt) *n.* A small, usu. glass bottle for holding oil or vinegar.
cruise (kro͞oz) *v.* **cruised, cruis•ing. 1.** To sail about, as for pleasure. **2.** To move leisurely about the streets. **3.** To travel at a speed providing maximum operating efficiency. **—cruise** *n.*
cruise missile *n.* A medium-range low-flying guided missile that can be launched from land, air, or sea.
cruis•er (kro͞o'zər) *n.* **1.** A fast warship of medium tonnage. **2.** A motorboat equipped with living facilities. **3.** A squad car.
crul•ler (krŭl'ər) *n.* A small, sweet cake fried in deep fat.
crumb (krŭm) *n.* **1.** A small fragment, as of bread. **2.** A small scrap. *—v.* **1.** To crumble. **2.** To cover with crumbs : bread.
crum•ble (krŭm'bəl) *v.* **-bled, -bling.** To break into small pieces. **—crum'bly** *adj.*
crum•my *also* **crumb•y** (krŭm'ē) *adj.* **-mi•er, -mi•est** *also* **-i•er, -i•est.** *Slang.* **1.** Wretched : miserable. **2.** Shabby : worthless.
crum•pet (krŭm'pĭt) *n. esp. Brit.* A light, soft bread similar to a muffin, baked on a griddle and often toasted.
crum•ple (krŭm'pəl) *v.* **-pled, -pling. 1.** To crush together : rumple. **2.** To collapse.
crunch (krŭnch) *v.* **1.** To bite with a crackling noise. **2.** To grind or crush noisily. *—n.* **1.** The sound or act of crunching. **2.** A critical situation. **—crunch'y** *adj.*
cru•sade (kro͞o-sād') *n.* **1.** *often* **Crusade.** Any of the medieval Christian military expeditions to capture the Holy Land from the Muslims. **2.** A vigorous campaign to promote a cause. *—v.* **-sad•ed, -sad•ing.** To take part in a crusade. **—cru•sad'er** *n.*
crush (krŭsh) *v.* **1.** To squeeze between opposing forces so as to damage or injure. **2.** To extract by pressing. **3.** To embrace violently. **4.** To break or grind into small bits. **5.** To put down : suppress. *—n.* **1.** The act of crushing. **2.** A large, closely packed crowd. **3.** *Informal.* An infatuation.
crust (krŭst) *n.* **1.** The hard, outside surface area of bread. **2.** A piece of old dry bread. **3.** A hard surface layer. **4.** The shell of a pie, usu. made of pastry. *—v.* To cover or become covered with a crust.
crus•ta•cean (krŭ-stā'shən) *n.* Any of various chiefly aquatic arthropods of the class *Crustacea,* including lobsters and crabs, with a segmented body and paired, jointed limbs.
crust•y (krŭs'tē) *adj.* **-i•er, -i•est. 1.** Like or with a crust. **2.** Brusque. **—crust'i•ly** *adv.*
crutch (krŭch) *n.* **1.** A support usu. designed to fit under the armpit and used as an aid in walking. **2.** Any support or prop.
crux (krŭks, kro͝oks) *n., pl.* **-es** *or* **cru•ces** (kro͞o'sēz) **1.** A crucial or vital moment. **2.** The basic feature. **3.** A difficult problem.
cru•zei•ro (kro͞o-zâr'ō, -ro͞o) *n., pl.* **-ros.** A former monetary unit of Brazil.
cry (krī) *v.* **cried, cry•ing. 1.** To shed tears. **2.** To call loudly. **3.** To utter a characteristic call or sound. —Used of an animal. **4.** To proclaim publicly. ★ ***syns:*** BAWL, HOWL, KEEN, SOB, WAIL, WEEP *—n., pl.* **cries. 1.** A loud emotional utterance. **2.** A fit of weeping. **3.** A plea : entreaty. **4.** The characteristic call of an animal.
cry•ba•by (krī'bā'bē) *n.* One who complains or cries often.
crypt (krĭpt) *n.* An underground vault, esp. one used for burying the dead.
cryp•tic (krĭp'tĭk) *adj.* Enigmatic.
cryp•to•gram (krĭp'tə-grăm') *n.* A coded message.
cryp•tog•ra•phy (krĭp-tŏg'rə-fē) *n.* The writing and deciphering of messages in secret code. **—cryp•tog'ra•pher** *n.*
crys•tal (krĭs'təl) *n.* **1. a.** A 3-dimensional structure made up of atoms, molecules, or ions arranged in basic units that are repeated throughout the structure. **b.** The basic unit of such a structure. **c.** Something having such a structure. **2.** A clear, high-quality glass. **—crys'tal•line** *adj.*
crystal ball *n.* A glass globe for foretelling the future.
crystal gazing *n.* Divination by looking into a crystal ball. **—crystal gazer** *n.*
crys•tal•lize (krĭs'tə-līz') *v.* **-lized, -liz•ing. 1.** To assume or cause to assume a crystalline structure. **2.** To assume or cause to assume a definite or fixed shape. **—crys'tal•li•za'tion** *n.*
Cs *symbol for* CESIUM.
Cu *symbol for* COPPER.

cub (kŭb) *n.* **1.** A young beast of certain animals, as the lion or wolf. **2.** A youth or novice, esp. in newspaper reporting.
cub•by•hole (kŭb'ē-hōl') *n.* A small enclosed space, as a cupboard.
cube (kyo͞ob) *n.* **1.** *Math.* A regular solid with 6 congruent square faces. **2.** Something gen. shaped like a cube. **3.** *Math.* The 3rd power of a number <8 is the *cube* of 2> —*v.* **cubed, cub•ing. 1.** To raise (a number) to the 3rd power. **2.** To cut or shape into cubes.
cube root *n.* A number whose cube is equal to a specified number.
cu•bic (kyo͞o'bĭk) *adj.* **1.** Having the form of a cube. **2. a.** Having 3 dimensions. **b.** Having the volume of a cube whose edge is a specified unit <a *cubic* yard>
cu•bi•cle (kyo͞o'bĭ-kəl) *n.* A small partitioned compartment.
cub•ism (kyo͞o'bĭz'əm) *n.* A style of art in which the subject matter is portrayed by geometric forms, esp. cubes. —**cub'ist** *n.*
cu•bit (kyo͞o'bĭt) *n.* An ancient unit of length equal to approx. 17 to 22 in.
Cub Scout *n.* A member of the Boy Scouts aged 8 to 10 years.
cuck•old (kŭk'əld, ko͝ok'-) *n.* A man whose wife is unfaithful. —**cuck'old** *v.*
cuck•oo (ko͞o'ko͞o, ko͝ok'o͞o) *n., pl.* **-oos.** A grayish European bird, *Cuculus canorus,* that lays its eggs in other birds' nests and has a characteristic 2-note call. —*n.* **1.** The characteristic call of the cuckoo. **2.** A fool. —*adj.* Silly.
cuckoo clock *n.* A wall clock with a mechanical cuckoo that indicates intervals of time by a cuckoo call.
cu•cum•ber (kyo͞o'kŭm'bər) *n.* A vine, *Cucumis sativus,* grown for its edible fruit, with a green rind and white flesh.
cud (kŭd) *n.* Food brought up into the mouth of ruminants from the first stomach and chewed again.
cud•dle (kŭd'l) *v.* **-dled, -dling. 1.** To hold close and fondle. **2.** To lie close : snuggle. —**cud'dle** *n.* —**cud'dly** *adj.*
cudg•el (kŭj'əl) *n.* A short, thick stick. —**cudg'el** *v.*
cue[1] (kyo͞o) *n.* A long, tapered rod for propelling the ball in pool and billiards.
cue[2] (kyo͞o) *n.* **1.** A word or signal for an actor to enter or begin speaking. **2.** A reminder : hint. —**cue** *v.*
cue[3] (kyo͞o) *n.* The letter *q.*
cue ball *n.* A white ball that the player strikes with the cue in pool and billiards.
†**cues•ta** (kwĕs'tə) *n. SW U.S.* A ridge with a cliff on one side and a gentle slope on the other.
cuff[1] (kŭf) *n.* **1.** A lower end of a sleeve. **2.** The turned-up fold of a trouser leg.
cuff[2] (kŭf) *v.* To slap : strike. —**cuff** *n.*
cuff links *n.* Linked buttons for fastening the cuffs of a shirt.
cui•rass (kwĭ-răs') *n.* Armor for protecting the back and breast.
cui•sine (kwĭ-zēn') *n.* **1.** A characteristic style of cooking or preparing food. **2.** The food prepared.
cul-de-sac (kŭl'dĭ-săk', ko͝ol'-) *n.* A street closed at one end.
cu•li•nar•y (kyo͞o'lə-nĕr'ē, kŭl'ə-) *adj.* Of or relating to cookery.
cull (kŭl) *v.* **1.** To select. **2.** To collect : gather. —**cull'er** *n.*
cul•mi•nate (kŭl'mə-nāt') *v.* **-nat•ed, -nat•ing.** To rise to the highest point. —**cul'mi•na'tion** *n.*
cu•lottes (ko͞o-lŏts', kyo͞o-) *pl.n.* A woman's full trousers made to look like a skirt.
cul•pa•ble (kŭl'pə-bəl) *adj.* Deserving blame. —**cul'pa•bil'i•ty** *n.*
cul•prit (kŭl'prĭt) *n.* One guilty of a crime.
cult (kŭlt) *n.* **1.** A system of religious worship. **2. a.** Obsessive and faddish devotion to a principle or person. **b.** A group of persons sharing such devotion : sect. —**cult'ic** *adj.* —**cult'ish** *adj.* —**cult'ist** *n.*
cul•ti•vate (kŭl'tə-vāt') *v.* **-vat•ed, -vat•ing. 1.** To prepare and improve (land), as by fertilizing or plowing, for growing crops. **2.** To grow (a plant or crop). **3.** To improve and refine, as by education. **4.** To seek the acquaintance or good will of. —**cul'ti•va•ble, cul'ti•vat'a•ble** *adj.* —**cul'ti•va'tion** *n.* —**cul'ti•va'tor** *n.*
cul•ture (kŭl'chər) *n.* **1.** A particular form of civilization, esp. the beliefs, customs, arts, and institutions of a society at a given time. **2.** Refinement in intellectual and artistic taste. **3.** The act of developing the intellectual faculties through education. **4.** Cultivation of soil ; tillage. **5.** *Biol.* A growth of microorganisms, as bacteria, in a nutrient medium. —**cul'tur•al** *adj.* —**cul'ture** *v.* —**cul'tured** *adj.*
culture shock *n.* A condition of anxiety and disorientation that can affect someone suddenly exposed to a new culture.
cul•vert (kŭl'vərt) *n.* A sewer or drain crossing under a road or railroad.
cum (ko͝om, kŭm) *prep.* Together with : plus <a bedroom-*cum*-study>
cum•ber (kŭm'bər) *v.* To burden. —**cum'ber•some** *adj.* —**cum'ber•some•ly** *adv.* —**cum'brous** *adj.*
cum•in (kŭm'ĭn, ko͞o'mĭn, kyo͞o'-) *n.* A plant, *Cuminum cyminum,* with aromatic seeds used as a condiment.
cum lau•de (ko͝om lou'də, lou'dē, kŭm lô'dē) *adv. & adj.* With honor. —Used as a mark of high academic attainment.
cum•mer•bund (kŭm'ər-bŭnd') *n.* A wide sash worn as an accessory to men's formal dress.
cu•mu•la•tive (kyo͞om'yə-lā'tĭv, -lə-tĭv) *adj.* Increasing with successive additions. —**cu'mu•la'tive•ly** *adv.*
cu•mu•lo•nim•bus (kyo͞om'yə-lō-nĭm'bəs) *n., pl.* **-bus•es** *or* **-bi** (-bī'). A very dense, vertically developed cumulus, usu. producing heavy rains or thunderstorms.
cu•mu•lus (kyo͞om'yə-ləs) *n., pl.* **-li** (-lī'). A large white, fluffy cloud with a flat base and rounded outlines on top.

cu•ne•i•form (kyōō'nē-ə-fôrm', kyōō-nē'-) *adj.* Wedge-shaped, as the characters used in ancient Assyrian and Babylonian writing. —*n.* Cuneiform writing.

†**cun•ning** (kŭn'ĭng) *adj.* **1.** Crafty : sly. **2.** Contrived with ingenuity. **3.** *Regional.* Pretty : cute. —*n.* **1.** Craftiness : guile. **2.** Skill : dexterity. —**cun'ning•ly** *adv.*

cup (kŭp) *n.* **1.** A small, bowl-shaped container, usu. having a handle, used for drinking. **2.** The contents of a cup. **3.** —See table at MEASUREMENT. **4.** Something like a cup. —*v.* **cupped, cup•ping.** To shape like a cup. —**cup'ful'** *n.*

cup•board (kŭb'ərd) *n.* A storage closet.

cup•cake (kŭp'kāk') *n.* A small cake baked in a cup-shaped mold.

Cu•pid (kyōō'pĭd) *n.* **1.** *Rom. Myth.* The god of love. **2. cupid.** A representation of a winged boy with a bow and arrow used as a symbol of love.

cu•pid•i•ty (kyōō-pĭd'ĭ-tē) *n.* Excessive desire for material gain : avarice.

cu•po•la (kyōō'pə-lə) *n.* A small structure, usu. a dome, on top of a roof or building.

cu•pro•nick•el (kōō'prō-nĭk'əl, kyōō'-) *n.* An alloy of copper and nickel used in coins.

cur (kûr) *n.* **1.** A dog of mixed bread : mongrel. **2.** A contemptible person.

cu•rate (kyŏŏr'ĭt) *n.* A cleric who assists a vicar or rector. —**cu'ra•cy** *n.*

cu•ra•tive (kyŏŏr'ə-tĭv) *adj.* Having the ability to cure. —**cu'ra•tive** *n.* —**cur'a•tive•ly** *adv.*

cu•ra•tor (kyōō-rā'tər, kyŏŏr'ā-tər) *n.* One in charge of an institution such as a museum. —**cu'ra•tor'i•al** *adj.*

curb (kûrb) *n.* **1.** A check or restraint. **2.** A raised stone or concrete edging along the side of a street. **3.** A strap or chain on a bit used to restrain a horse. —*v.* **1.** To control or restrain. **2.** To lead (a dog) into the gutter to defecate.

curb•ing (kûr'bĭng) *n.* **1.** The material for constructing a curb. **2.** A curb.

curb•stone (kûrb'stōn') *n.* The stone or stones forming a curb.

curd (kûrd) *n.* The coagulated part of milk used for making cheese.

cur•dle (kûr'dl) *v.* **-dled, -dling.** To change into curd.

cure (kyŏŏr) *n.* **1.** Recovery from illness. **2.** A course of medical treatment for restoring health. **3.** A remedy. ★ ***syns:*** ELIXIR, NOSTRUM, REMEDY —*v.* **cured, cur•ing. 1.** To restore to health. **2.** To rid of (e.g., an ailment). **3.** To process (e.g., meat), as by smoking or salting. —**cur'a•ble** *adj.* —**cure'less** *adj.* —**cur'er** *n.*

cure-all (kyŏŏr'ôl') *n.* A remedy for all evils or diseases.

cu•ret•tage (kyŏŏr'ĭ-täzh') *n.* Surgical scraping and cleaning of a bodily cavity.

cur•few (kûr'fyōō) *n.* **1.** An order enjoining specified segments of the population to leave the streets at a certain hour. **2.** The signal announcing curfew.

▲ ***word history:*** A *curfew* was orig. a medieval regulation requiring that fires be put out or covered at a certain hour at night. The rule was probably instituted as a public safety measure to minimize the risk of a general conflagration. A bell was rung at the prescribed hour, and the word *curfew* has been extended to denote both the bell and the hour in addition to the regulation.

cu•ri•a *also* **Cu•ri•a** (kyŏŏr'ē-ə) *n.* The official body that governs the Roman Catholic Church.

cu•rie (kyŏŏr'ē, kyōō-rē') *n.* A unit of radioactivity equal to the radioactivity of a sample of an element in which 3.7 x 10^{10} nuclear disintegrations occur each sec.

cu•ri•o (kyŏŏr'ē-ō') *n., pl.* **-os.** An unusual or strange object.

cu•ri•ous (kyŏŏr'ē-əs) *adj.* **1.** Eager to acquire knowledge. **2.** Inquisitive : prying. **3.** Strange : singular. —**cu'ri•os'i•ty** *n.* —**cu'ri•ous•ly** *adv.* —**cu'ri•ous•ness** *n.*

cu•ri•um (kyŏŏr'ē-əm) *n. Symbol* **Cm** A metallic synthetic radioactive element.

curl (kûrl) *v.* **1.** To form into ringlets. **2.** To curve or coil : wind. **3.** To play the game of curling. —*n.* **1.** Something shaped like a coil. **2.** A ringlet of hair. —**curl'er** *n.* —**curl'i•ness** *n.* —**curl'y** *adj.*

cur•lew (kûrl'yōō, kûr'lōō) *n.* A brownish, long-legged shore bird of the genus *Numenius,* with a downward-curving bill.

curl•i•cue (kûr'lĭ-kyōō') *n.* A fancy flourish or curve.

curl•ing (kûr'lĭng) *n.* A game played on ice, in which 2 teams slide heavy, rounded stones toward a target.

cur•mudg•eon (kər-mŭj'ən) *n.* A quarrelsome and ill-tempered person.

cur•rant (kûr'ənt, kŭr'-) *n.* **1.** Any of various usu. prickly shrubs of the genus *Ribes,* having clusters of black or red fruit used for jellies. **2.** A small seedless raisin.

cur•ren•cy (kûr'ən-sē, kŭr'-) *n., pl.* **-cies. 1.** Money in circulation as a medium of exchange. —See table pp. 172–3. **2.** General use or acceptance.

cur•rent (kûr'ənt, kŭr'-) *adj.* **1.** Occurring in or belonging to the present. **2.** In widespread or general use. —*n.* **1.** Continuous flow, as of air or water. **2.** The swiftest part of a moving body of gas or liquid. **3. a.** A flow of electric charge. **b.** The rate of electric charge. —**cur'rent•ly** *adv.*

cur•ric•u•lum (kə-rĭk'yə-ləm) *n., pl.* **-la** (-lə) *or* **-lums.** A course of study offered by a school. —**cur•ric'u•lar** *adj.*

cur•ric•u•lum vi•tae (kə-rĭk'yə-ləm vī'tē, kə-rĭk'ə-ləm wē'tī') *n.* A résumé.

cur•ry[1] (kûr'ē, kŭr'ē) *v.* **-ried, -ry•ing. 1.** To groom (a horse) using a currycomb. **2.** To prepare (tanned leather). —**curry favor.** To seek or gain favor by flattery.

cur•ry[2] (kûr'ē, kŭr'ē) *n., pl.* **-ries. 1.** Curry powder. **2.** A dish or sauce heavily spiced with curry powder and often served with rice. —**cur'ry** *v.*

CURRENCY TABLE: LISTED BY BASIC UNIT (BOLD) AND SUBUNIT

UNIT	COUNTRY
afghani	Afghanistan
agora	Israel
at	Laos
avo	Macao
baht	Thailand
baiza	Oman
balboa	Panama
ban	Romania
birr	Ethiopia
bolivar	Venezuela
boliviano	Bolivia
butut	Gambia
cedi	Ghana
cent	Antigua and Barbuda
	Australia
	Bahamas
	Barbados
	Belize
	Brunei
	Canada
	Cayman Islands
	Cyprus
	Dominica
	Ethiopia
	Fiji
	Grenada
	Guyana
	Hong Kong
	Jamaica
	Kenya
	Kiribati
	Liberia
	Malta
	Mauritius
	Namibia
	Nauru
	Netherlands
	Netherlands Antilles
	New Zealand
	Saint Kitts-Nevis
	Saint Lucia
	Saint Vincent and the Grenadines
	Seychelles
	Sierra Leone
	Singapore
	Solomon Islands
	Somalia
	South Africa
	Sri Lanka
	Suriname
	Swaziland
	Taiwan
	Tanzania
	Trinidad and Tobago
	Tuvalu
	Uganda
	United States
	Zimbabwe
centavo	Argentina
	Bolivia
	Brazil
	Cape Verde
	Colombia
	Cuba
	Dominican Republic
	Ecuador
	El Salvador
	Guatemala
	Guinea-Bissau
	Honduras
	Mexico
	Mozambique
	Nicaragua
	Philippines
	Portugal
	São Tomé and Príncipe
centesimo	Chile
	Italy
	Panama
	San Marino
	Uruguay
	Vatican City
centime	Algeria
	Belgium
	Benin
	Burkina Faso
	Burundi
	Cameroon
	Central African Republic
	Chad
	Comoros
	Congo
	Djibouti
	Equatorial Guinea
	France
	Gabon
	Guinea
	Haiti
	Ivory Coast
	Liechtenstein
	Luxembourg
	Madagascar
	Mali
	Monaco
	Morocco
	Niger
	Rwanda
	Senegal
	Switzerland
	Togo
	Vanuatu
centimo	Andorra
	Costa Rica
	Paraguay
	Peru
	Spain
	Venezuela
chetrum	Bhutan
chon	North Korea
	South Korea
colon	Costa Rica
	El Salvador
cordoba	Nicaragua
dalasi	Gambia
deutsche mark	Germany
dinar	Algeria
	Bahrain
	Iraq
	Jordan
	Kuwait
	Libya
	Tunisia
	Yemen
	Yugoslavia
dinar	Iran
dirham	Morocco
	United Arab Emirates
dirham	Libya
	Qatar
dobra	São Tomé and Príncipe
dollar	Antigua and Barbuda
	Australia
	Bahamas
	Barbados
	Belize
	Brunei
	Canada
	Cayman Islands
	Dominica
	Fiji
	Grenada
	Guyana
	Hong Kong
	Jamaica
	Kiribati
	Liberia
	Nauru
	New Zealand
	Saint Kitts-Nevis
	Saint Lucia
	Saint Vincent and the Grenadines
	Singapore
	Solomon Islands
	Taiwan
	Trinidad and Tobago
	Tuvalu
	United States
	Zimbabwe
dong	Vietnam
drachma	Greece
escudo	Cape Verde
	Portugal
eyrir	Iceland
fillér	Hungary

CURRENCY TABLE: LISTED BY BASIC UNIT (BOLD) AND SUBUNIT *(Continued)*

UNIT	COUNTRY
fils	Bahrain
	Iraq
	Jordan
	Kuwait
	United Arab Emirates
	Yemen
forint	Hungary
franc	Belgium
	Benin
	Burkina Faso
	Burundi
	Cameroon
	Central African Republic
	Chad
	Comoros
	Congo
	Djibouti
	Equatorial Guinea
	France
	Gabon
	Guinea
	Ivory Coast
	Liechtenstein
	Luxembourg
	Madagascar
	Mali
	Monaco
	Niger
	Rwanda
	Senegal
	Switzerland
	Togo
gourde	Haiti
groschen	Austria
grosz	Poland
guarani	Paraguay
guilder	Netherlands
	Netherlands Antilles
	Suriname
halala	Saudi Arabia
haler	Czech Republic
	Slovakia
hao	Vietnam
jiao	China
khoum	Mauritania
kina	Papua New Guinea
kip	Laos
kobo	Nigeria
kopeck	Russia
koruna	Czech Republic
	Slovakia
krona	Iceland
	Sweden
krone	Denmark
	Norway
kurus	Turkey
kwacha	Malawi
	Zambia
kwanza	Angola
kyat	Burma
laree	Maldives
lek	Albania
lempira	Honduras
leone	Sierra Leone
lepton	Greece
leu	Romania
lev	Bulgaria
likuta	Zaire
lilangeni	Swaziland
lira	Italy
	Malta
	San Marino
	Turkey
	Vatican City
loti	Lesotho
lwei	Angola
markka	Finland
metical	Mozambique
millime	Tunisia
mongo	Mongolia
naira	Nigeria
ngultrum	Bhutan
ngwee	Zambia
nuevo sol	Peru
öre	Denmark
	Norway
	Sweden
ouguiya	Mauritania
pa'anga	Tonga
paisa	Bangladesh
	India
	Nepal
	Pakistan
para	Yugoslavia
pataca	Macao
penni	Finland
penny	Ireland
	United Kingdom
peseta	Andorra
	Spain
pesewa	Ghana
peso	Argentina
	Chile
	Colombia
	Cuba
	Dominican Republic
	Guinea-Bissau
	Mexico
	Philippines
	Uruguay
pfennig	Germany
piaster	Egypt
	Lebanon
	Sudan
	Syria
pound	Cyprus
	Egypt
	Ireland
	Lebanon
	Sudan
	Syria
	United Kingdom
pul	Afghanistan
pula	Botswana
pya	Burma
qindarka	Albania
quetzal	Guatemala
rand	Namibia
	South Africa
real	Brazil
rial	Iran
riel	Cambodia
ringgit	Malaysia
riyal	Qatar
	Saudi Arabia
riyal-omani	Oman
ruble	Russia
rufiyaa	Maldives
rupee	India
	Mauritius
	Nepal
	Pakistan
	Seychelles
	Sri Lanka
rupiah	Indonesia
satang	Thailand
schilling	Austria
sen	Cambodia
	Indonesia
	Japan
	Malaysia
sene	Western Samoa
seniti	Tonga
sente	Lesotho
shekel	Israel
shilling	Kenya
	Somalia
	Tanzania
	Uganda
stotinka	Bulgaria
sucre	Ecuador
taka	Bangladesh
tala	Western Samoa
tambala	Malawi
thebe	Botswana
toea	Papua New Guinea
tugrik	Mongolia
vatu	Vanuatu
won	North Korea
	South Korea
yen	Japan
yuan	China
zaire	Zaire
zloty	Poland

cur•ry•comb (kûr'ē-kōm', kŭr'-) *n.* A metal comb used to groom horses.
curry powder *n.* A powder of blended spices, as coriander, cumin, and turmeric.
curse (kûrs) *n.* **1.** A prayer for harm to befall someone or something. **2.** The harm resulting from an invocation. **3.** A profane oath. **4.** Something bringing or causing harm **:** scourge. —*v.* **cursed** *or* **curst** (kûrst), **curs•ing. 1.** To call evil down on. **2.** To swear (at). **3.** To bring evil upon.
cur•sive (kûr'sĭv) *adj.* Written with the letters joined together. —**cur'sive•ly** *adv.*
cur•sor (kûr'sər) *n.* A visual indicator on a video display terminal showing the user's position on the screen.
cur•so•ry (kûr'sə-rē) *adj.* Not thorough **:** hasty. —**cur'so•ri•ly** *adv.*
curt (kûrt) *adj.* Rudely short **:** abrupt. —**curt'ly** *adv.* —**curt'ness** *n.*
cur•tail (kər-tāl') *v.* To shorten. —**cur•tail'ment** *n.*
cur•tain (kûr'tn) *n.* Hanging material that can be drawn back, esp. in a window, used to decorate, shade, or screen. —**cur'tain** *v.*
curt•sy (kûrt'sē) *n., pl.* **-sies.** A respectful gesture made by bending the knees with one foot forward and lowering the body.
cur•va•ceous (kûr-vā'shəs) *adj.* Voluptuous in figure. —**cur•va'ceous•ness** *n.*
cur•va•ture (kûr'və-chŏŏr', -chər) *n.* An example or measure of curving.
curve (kûrv) *n.* **1.** A bend without angles or straight parts. **2.** Something in the form of a curve. —*v.* **curved, curv•ing.** To form or move in the shape of a curve.
cur•vi•lin•e•ar (kûr'və-lĭn'ē-ər) *adj.* Made up of curved lines.
cush•ion (kŏŏsh'ən) *n.* **1.** A pillow or pad with a soft filling. **2.** Something soft and resilient that prevents injury. **3.** The soft, felt rim around a billiard table. —*v.* **1.** To provide a cushion for. **2.** To soften or lessen the shock of.
cush•y (kŏŏsh'ē) *adj.* **-i•er, -i•est.** *Slang.* Making few demands **:** easy <a *cushy* job>
cusp (kŭsp) *n.* A pointed end, as of a tooth.
cus•pid (kŭs'pĭd) *n.* A canine tooth.
cus•pi•dor (kŭs'pĭ-dôr') *n.* A spittoon.
cuss (kŭs) *v. Informal.* To curse (at). —*n.* **1.** A curse. **2.** A perverse creature.
cuss•ed (kŭs'ĭd) *adj. Informal.* Vexatious **:** perverse. —**cuss'ed•ness** *n.*
cus•tard (kŭs'tərd) *n.* A sauce or dessert made from milk, eggs, sugar, and flavoring.
cus•to•di•an (kŭ-stō'dē-ən) *n.* **1.** One who has custody or care of something. **2.** A janitor. —**cus•to'di•an•ship'** *n.*
cus•to•dy (kŭs'tə-dē) *n., pl.* **-dies. 1.** The act or right of guarding, esp. as granted by a court. **2.** Detention under guard, esp. by the police. —**cus•to'di•al** *adj.*
cus•tom (kŭs'təm) *n.* **1.** An accepted practice or convention followed by tradition. **2.** A habitual course of action of an individual. **3. customs** *(sing. in number).* Taxes on imported goods. **4.** Business patronage, as of a store. —*adj.* **1.** Made-to-order. **2.** Selling made-to-order goods.
cus•tom•ar•y (kŭs'tə-mĕr'ē) *adj.* **1.** Commonly practiced or used **:** habitual. **2.** Based on custom or tradition. —**cus'tom•ar'i•ly** *adv.*
cus•tom-built (kŭs'təm-bĭlt') *adj.* Built to individual order.
cus•tom•er (kŭs'tə-mər) *n.* **1.** A person who buys, esp. on a regular basis. **2.** A person with whom one must deal.
cus•tom•house *also* **cus•tom house** (kŭs'təm-hous') *n.* An office where customs are paid and ships are cleared for leaving or entering the country.
cut (kŭt) *v.* **cut, cut•ting. 1.** To penetrate with a sharp edge. **2.** To divide into parts using a sharp-edged instrument <*cut* the material> **3.** To leave out as if by cutting **:** omit. **4.** To sever the outer edges of **:** shorten. **5.** To reap. **6.** To have (a new tooth) grow through the gums. **7.** *Informal.* To stop <*cut* the foolishness> **8.** To reduce the size, extent, or strength of <*cut* the labor force> **9.** *Informal.* To fail purposely to attend <*cut* classes> ★ ***syns:*** GASH, INCISE, PIERCE, SLASH, SLIT —**cut in. 1.** To interrupt. **2.** To interrupt a dancing couple and take one of the pair as one's partner. —**cut out. 1.** To put an end to **:** stop. **2.** *Informal.* To depart suddenly. —**cut up.** *Informal.* To fool around **:** clown. —*n.* **1.** The act or result of incising or separating. **2.** A part that has been cut from a meat carcass <a *cut* of beef> **3.** A reduction <a budget *cut*> **4.** The manner in which a thing, esp. a piece of clothing, is cut. **5.** A wounding remark. **6.** An excavated passage or channel. **7.** *Informal.* A share, as of profits. **8.** *Informal.* An unauthorized absence, as from school. **9.a.** An engraved surface for printing. **b.** A print made from such a surface.
cut-and-dried (kŭt'n-drīd') *adj.* According to a plan or formula **:** routine.
cu•ta•ne•ous (kyōō-tā'nē-əs) *adj.* Of or relating to the skin.
cut•back (kŭt'băk') *n.* A reduction.
cute (kyōōt) *adj.* **cut•er, cut•est. 1.** Delightfully attractive. **2.** Clever **:** shrewd.
cute•sy (kyōōt'sē) *adj.* **-si•er, -si•est.** *Slang.* Obviously contrived to charm.
cut glass *n.* Glassware shaped or decorated using cutting instruments.
cu•ti•cle (kyōō'tĭ-kəl) *n.* **1.** The epidermis. **2.** Hardened skin, as at the base of a toenail or fingernail.
cut•lass (kŭt'ləs) *n.* A short, thick, curved sword.
cut•ler•y (kŭt'lə-rē) *n.* **1.** Cutting tools. **2.** Implements used as tableware.
cut•let (kŭt'lĭt) *n.* A thin slice of meat, as lamb or veal.
cut•off (kŭt'ôf', -ŏf') *n.* **1.** A short cut or bypass. **2.** A device for shutting off a flow, as of electricity or water.
cut-offs *also* **cut•offs** (kŭt'ôfs', -ŏfs') *pl.n.* Pants, as blue jeans, made into shorts by cutting off part of the legs.

cut•out (kŭt′out′) *n.* Something cut out or prepared for cutting out.
cut-rate (kŭt′rāt′) *adj.* On sale or sold at a lower price.
cut•ter (kŭt′ər) *n.* **1.** One that cuts. **2.** *Naut.* **a.** A ship's boat used to carry pasengers and provisions. **b.** A small, armed Coast Guard powerboat. **3.** A light sleigh.
cut•throat (kŭt′thrōt′) *n.* **1.** A murderer. **2.** A ruthless, unprincipled person. —*adj.* **1.** Murderous **:** brutal. **2.** Merciless or relentless in competition.
cut•ting (kŭt′ĭng) *adj.* **1.** Sharply penetrating. **2.** Bitterly sarcastic. —*n.* A shoot removed from a plant to form new roots and grow into a new plant.
cut•tle•bone (kŭt′l-bōn′) *n.* The chalky internal shell of the cuttlefish, used as a calcium supplement for caged birds.
cut•tle•fish (kŭt′l-fĭsh′) *n.* A squidlike marine mollusk of the genus *Sepia,* having 10 arms and a chalky internal shell and secreting a dark, inky fluid.
cut•up (kŭt′ŭp′) *n. Informal.* A mischievous person.
–cy *suff.* **1.** State **:** condition **:** quality <accuracy> **2.** Rank **:** office <captaincy>
cy•a•nide (sī′ə-nīd′) *also* **cy•a•nid** (-nĭd) *n.* Any of a large group of salts and esters, esp. the highly poisonous salts potassium cyanide and sodium cyanide.
cy•ber•net•ics (sī′bər-nĕt′ĭks) *n. (sing. in number).* The scientific study of the control processes in mechanical, electronic, and biological systems.
cy•ber•space (sī′bər-spās′) *n.* The continuum of computer networks and bulletin board systems in which on-line communication takes place.
cyc•la•mate (sĭk′lə-māt′, sī′klə-) *n.* A salt of cyclamic acid, having a sweet taste.
cyc•la•men (sĭk′lə-mən, sī′klə-) *n.* Any of several plants of the genus *Cyclaneri,* with pink, white, or red flowers.
cyc•la•mic acid (sĭk′lə-mĭk, sī′klə-). A sour-sweet chemical compound of carbon, hydrogen, oxygen, nitrogen, and sulfur.
cy•cle (sī′kəl) *n.* **1.** A time interval in which an event occurs repeatedly. **2.** A recurring sequence of events. **3.** A series of poems or musical works on a single theme. **4.** A motorcycle or bicycle. —*v.* **-cled, -cling.** To ride a motorcycle or bicycle. **—cy′clic** (sī′klĭk, sĭk′lĭk), **cy′cli•cal** *adj.*
cy•clist (sī′klĭst) *n.* A person who rides a cycle.
cy•clom•e•ter (sī-klŏm′ĭ-tər) *n.* A device that records the revolutions of a wheel for measuring the distance traveled.
cy•clone (sī′klōn′) *n. Meteorol.* A storm or system of winds that rotates about a low-pressure center and is usu. accompanied by stormy and destructive weather. **—cy•clon′ic** (-klŏn′ĭk) *adj.*
cy•clo•spor•ine (sī′klə-spôr′ēn, -ĭn, -spōr′-) *n.* An immunosuppressive drug used mainly to prevent the rejection of transplanted organs.
cy•clo•tron (sī′klə-trŏn′) *n.* A device that accelerates charged subatomic particles in a spiral path by an alternating electric field in a constant magnetic field.
cyg•net (sĭg′nĭt) *n.* A young swan.
cyl•in•der (sĭl′ən-dər) *n.* **1.** *Math.* **a.** A surface that contains all the lines that intersect a given plane curve and that are parallel to a given line. **b.** A solid bounded by a surface of this kind and by 2 parallel planes, esp. when the given curve is a circle and the given line is perpendicular to the plane of the circle. **2.** An object in the shape of a cylinder. **3.** A piston chamber in an engine. **4.** The chamber of a revolver that holds the cartridges. **—cy•lin′dri•cal** (sə-lĭn′drĭ-kəl) *adj.* **—cy•lin′dri•cal•ly** *adv.*

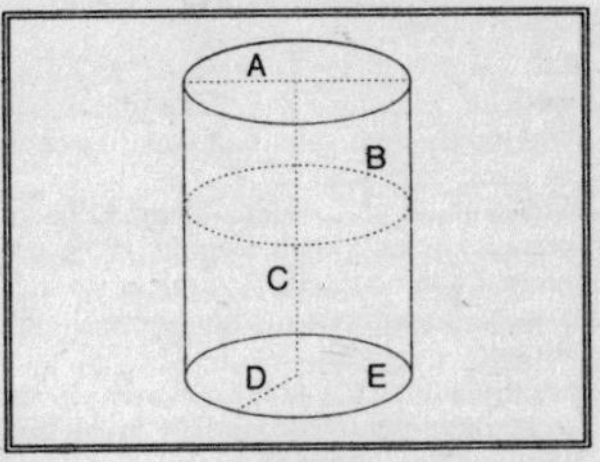

cylinder
A. diameter,
B. circumference,
C. altitude
D. radius, E. base

cym•bal (sĭm′bəl) *n. Mus.* A concave brass plate sounded by being struck against another or by being hit with a drumstick.
cyn•ic (sĭn′ĭk) *n.* One who believes all human action has selfish motives. **—cyn′i•cal** *adj.* **—cyn′i•cism** *n.*
cy•no•sure (sī′nə-shŏŏr′, sĭn′ə-) *n.* A focal point of admiration and interest.
▲ ***word history:*** A cynosure attracts attention for a compelling reason. The word *cynosure* is derived from Greek *kunosoura,* the Greek name for the constellation now known as Ursa Minor. In ancient times this constellation was used in navigation because it is located near the N celestial pole. *Cynosure* was orig. borrowed into English as the name of the same constellation but was also used figuratively to mean a guide or center of attention.
cy•press (sī′prəs) *n.* An evergreen tree of the genus *Cupressus,* growing in warm climates and bearing small, scalelike needles.
cyst (sĭst) *n.* A sac in the body, esp. an abnormal, membranous one containing fluid. **—cys′tic** *adj.*
cystic fibrosis *n.* A hereditary disease of mucous glands throughout the body, usu. de-

veloping in childhood and resulting in disorders of the pancreas and lungs.
cys•ti•tis (sĭ-stī'tĭs) *n.* Inflammation of the bladder.
cy•tol•o•gy (sī-tŏl'ə-jē) *n.* The scientific study of the structure, formation, and function of cells. **—cy'to•log'i•cal** (-tə-lŏj'ĭ-kəl), **cy'to•log'ic** *adj.* **—cy•tol'o•gist** *n.*
cy•to•plasm (sī'tə-plăz'əm) *n.* The protoplasm outside a cell nucleus. **—cy'to•plas'mic** *adj.*
czar *also* **tsar** *or* **tzar** (zär) *n.* **1.** A former emperor of Russia. **2.** An autocrat. **3.** *Informal.* One having authority.
cza•ri•na (zä-rē'nə) *n.* A czar's wife.
czar•ism (zär'ĭz'əm) *n.* The Russsian system of government under the czars. **—czar'ist** *n.*

Dd

d *or* **D** (dē) *n., pl.* **d's** or **D's. 1.** The 4th letter of the English alphabet. **2.** A speech sound represented by the letter *d.* **3.** *Mus.* The 2nd tone in the scale of C major. **4.** The lowest passing academic grade. **5. D** The Roman numeral for 500.
dab (dăb) *v.* **dabbed, dab•bing. 1.** To apply with light, short strokes. **2.** To touch quickly and lightly **:** pat. *—n.* **1.** A small amount. **2.** A quick, light pat.
dab•ble (dăb'əl) *v.* **-bled, -bling. 1.** To splatter with or as if with a liquid. **2.** To splash playfully in water. **3.** To work at something casually or without serious purpose. **—dab'bler** *n.*
dace (dās) *n., pl.* **dace** *or* **dac•es.** A small freshwater fish of the family Cyprinidae, resembling the minnow.
da•cha (dä'chə) *n.* A Russian house in the country.
dachs•hund (däks'ho͝ont', däks'ho͝ond') *n.* A small dog with a long body, very short legs, and drooping ears.
Da•cron (dā'krŏn', dăk'rŏn'). A trademark for a synthetic textile fiber.
dac•tyl (dăk'təl) *n.* A metrical foot of 1 stressed syllable followed by 2 unstressed syllables. **—dac•tyl'ic** (-tĭl'ĭk) *adj.*
dad (dăd) *n. Informal.* Father.
Da•da (dä'dä) *also* **Da•da•ism** (-ĭz'əm) *n.* A literary and artistic movement marked by the abolition of traditional aesthetic and cultural forms and a technique of comic derision. **—Da'da•ist** *n.* **—Da'da•is'tic** *adj.*
dad•dy (dăd'ē) *n., pl.* **-dies.** *Informal.* Father.
daddy long•legs (lông'lĕgz', lŏng'-) *n.* An arachnid of the order Phalangida, with a rounded body and long, thin legs.
daf•fo•dil (dăf'ə-dĭl') *n.* A bulbous plant, *Narcissus pseudo-narcissus,* having usu. yellow flowers with a trumpet-shaped center.
daf•fy (dăf'ē) *adj.* **-fi•er, -fi•est.** *Informal.* **1.** Silly **:** zany. **2.** Crazy.
daft (dăft) *adj.* **1.** Crazy **:** insane. **2.** Foolish **:** stupid. **—daft'ly** *adv.* **—daft'ness** *n.*
dag•ger (dăg'ər) *n.* **1.** A short, pointed, sharp-edged weapon used for stabbing. **2.** A reference mark (†) used in printing.
da•guerre•o•type (də-gâr'ə-tīp') *n.* An early photograph with the image produced on a light-sensitive silver-coated plate.
dahl•ia (dăl'yə, dăl'-, dāl'-) *n.* A plant of the genus *Dahlia,* with tuberous roots and variously colored flowers.
dai•ly (dā'lē) *adj.* Of, relating to, happening, or published every day. *—adv.* **1.** Every day. **2.** Once a day. *—n., pl.* **-lies.** A daily publication, esp. a newspaper.
daily double *n.* A bet won by selecting the winners of 2 specified races on 1 day.
dain•ty (dān'tē) *adj.* **-ti•er, -ti•est. 1.** Delicately beautiful **:** exquisite. **2.** Choice **:** delicious. **3.** Having or showing refined taste **:** discriminating. **4.** Excessively fastidious. *—n., pl.* **-ties.** A delicacy. **—dain'ti•ly** *adv.* **—dain'ti•ness** *n.*
dai•qui•ri (dī'kə-rē, dăk'ə-) *n., pl.* **-ris.** A drink made with rum and lime juice.
dair•y (dâr'ē) *n., pl.* **-ies. 1.** A commercial establishment for processing and selling milk and milk products. **2.** A dairy farm. **—dair'y•maid'** *n.* **—dair'y•man** *n.*
dairy farm *n.* A farm where milk and milk products are produced.
dair•y•ing (dâr'ē-ĭng) *n.* The business of running a dairy.
da•is (dā'ĭs, dās) *n.* A raised platform, as in a lecture hall, for speakers and guests of honor.
dai•sy (dā'zē) *n., pl.* **-sies. 1.** A plant having rayed flowers, esp. *Chrysanthemum leucanthemum,* with white rays and a yellow center. **2.** A low-growing plant, *Bellis perennis,* having pink or white rayed flowers.

▲ ***word history:*** The name *daisy,* a compound word meaning "day's eye," was orig. applied to the European plant *Bellis perennis,* which in the U.S. is called the English daisy. The term *day's eye* is particularly appropriate for this plant because it folds its petals at night and opens them in the morning with the sun.

Da•ko•ta (də-kō'tə) *n., pl.* **-ta** *or* **-tas. 1.** A Sioux, esp. a member of the eastern branch. **2.** The Siouan language of the Dakota. **—Da•ko'tan** *adj. & n.*
da•la•si (dä-lä'sē) *n., pl.* **-si.** —See table at CURRENCY.
dale (dāl) *n.* A valley.

dal•ly (dăl'ē) *v.* **-lied, -ly•ing. 1.** To flirt. **2.** To waste time : dawdle. **—dal'li•ance** *n.*

Dal•ma•tian (dăl-mā'shən) *n.* **1.** A native or inhabitant of Dalmatia. **2.** A dog having a short, smooth white coat with black spots.

dam[1] (dăm) *n.* A barrier constructed across a waterway for controlling or raising the level of the water. *—v.* **dammed, dam•ming. 1.** To construct a dam across. **2.** To restrain : check.

dam[2] (dăm) *n.* The female parent of a quadruped.

dam•age (dăm'ĭj) *n.* **1.** Impairment of the worth or usefulness of persons or property : harm. **2. damages.** *Law.* Compensation to be paid for loss or injury. **—dam'age** *v.* **—dam'age•a•ble** *adj.* **—dam'ag•ing•ly** *adv.*

dam•ask (dăm'əsk) *n.* **1.** A rich reversible patterned fabric, as of silk or linen. **2.** A fine table linen. **—dam'ask** *adj.*

dame (dām) *n.* **1.** A married woman : matron. **2.** *Slang.* A woman.

damn (dăm) *v.* **1.** To pronounce an adverse judgment on. **2.** To condemn to eternal punishment. **3.** To swear at. *—adj. & adv. Informal.* —Used as an intensive <a *damn* fool> <*Damn* right I will> *—n. Informal.* A bit : jot <wasn't worth a *damn*> **—dam•na'tion** *n.*

dam•na•ble (dăm'nə-bəl) *adj.* Deserving blame : odious. **—dam'na•bly** *adv.*

damp (dămp) *adj.* Somewhat wet : moist. *—n.* **1.** Humidity : moisture. **2.** A foul or poisonous gas, esp. in a mine. *—v.* **1.** To moisten. **2.** To extinguish (e.g., a fire) by cutting off air. **3.** To check : restrain. **4.** *Physics.* To decrease the amplitude of. **—damp'ish** *adj.* **—damp'ly** *adv.*

damp•en (dăm'pən) *v.* **1.** To moisten. **2.** To depress (e.g., the spirits). **—damp'en•er** *n.*

damp•er (dăm'pər) *n.* **1.** One that depresses or restrains. **2.** An adjustable plate, as in a flue, to control the draft.

dam•sel (dăm'zəl) *n.* A maiden.

dam•sel•fly (dăm'zəl-flī') *n.* A slender-bodied insect of the order Odonata that is related to the dragonfly.

dam•son (dăm'zən) *n.* A Eurasian tree, *Prunus institia,* bearing dark-purple fruit.

dance (dăns) *v.* **danced, danc•ing. 1.** To move rhythmically to music, using improvised or prescribed gestures and steps. **2.** To leap or skip about. **3.** To bob up and down. *—n.* **1.** A series of rhythmic gestures and steps, usu. to music. **2.** A party or gathering for dancing. **3.** A single round of dancing. **4.** The art of dancing. **—danc'er** *n.*

D and C *n.* Dilation and curettage.

dan•de•li•on (dăn'dl-ī'ən) *n.* A plant, *Taraxacum officinale,* widely naturalized as a weed in North America and having yellow flowers and notched leaves used in salads.

dan•der (dăn'dər) *n. Informal.* Temper.

dan•dle (dăn'dl) *v.* **-dled, -dling.** To move (e.g., a child) up and down on the knees or in the arms. **—dan'dler** *n.*

dan•druff (dăn'drəf) *n.* A scaly scurf formed on and shed from the scalp.

dan•dy (dăn'dē) *n., pl.* **-dies. 1.** One who affects exaggerated elegance. **2.** *Informal.* Something excellent or agreeable. **—dan'di•fy'** *v.* **—dan'dy** *adj.* **—dan'dy•ish** *adj.* **—dan'dy•ism** *n.*

Dane (dān) *n.* A native or inhabitant of Denmark.

dan•ger (dān'jər) *n.* **1.** Exposure to possible risk, injury, or harm. **2.** A source or instance of risk, injury, or harm. ★ ***syns:*** HAZARD, JEOPARDY, PERIL, RISK

dan•ger•ous (dān'jər-əs) *adj.* **1.** Involving or full of danger. **2.** Able or apt to cause harm. **—dan'ger•ous•ly** *adv.* **—dan'ger•ous•ness** *n.*

dan•gle (dăng'gəl) *v.* **-gled, -gling. 1.** To hang or cause to hang loosely and swing back and forth. **2.** To lack clear grammatical relation in a sentence <a *dangling* participle>

Dan•iel (dăn'yəl) *n.* —See table at BIBLE.

Dan•ish (dā'nĭsh) *adj.* Of Denmark, the Danes, or the Danish language. *—n.* **1.** The Germanic language of the Danes. **2.** *pl.* **-ish** *or* **-ish•es.** A Danish pastry.

Danish pastry *n.* A sweet buttery pastry made with raised dough.

dank (dăngk) *adj.* Uncomfortably humid and cool. **—dank'ly** *adv.* **—dank'ness** *n.*

dan•seur (däN-sœr') *n., pl.* **-seurs** (-sœr'). A man who is a ballet dancer.

dan•seuse (däN-sœz') *n., pl.* **-seuses** (-sœz'). A woman who is a ballet dancer.

dap•per (dăp'ər) *adj.* **1.** Neatly or stylishly dressed : trim. **2.** Alert and active : jaunty.

dap•ple (dăp'əl) *v.* **-pled, -pling.** To mark with spots of a different color : mottle.

dare (dâr) *v.* **dared, dar•ing. 1.** To have the courage necessary for. **2.** To challenge (another) to do something requiring courage. **3.** To confront bravely. ★ ***syns:*** BRAVE, CHALLENGE, DEFY, FACE *—n.* A challenge.

dare•dev•il (dâr'dĕv'əl) *n.* One who is daringly bold. **—dare'dev'il** *adj.*

dar•ing (dâr'ĭng) *adj.* Fearlessly bold. **—dar'ing** *n.* **—dar'ing•ly** *adv.*

dark (därk) *adj.* **1.** Having little or no light. **2.** Not light in color. **3.** Dismal : gloomy. **4.** Difficult to comprehend : obscure. **5.** Unenlightened : ignorant <a *dark* period in history> **6.** Wicked : sinister. ★ ***syns:*** DIM, DUSKY, MURKY, OBSCURE, TENEBROUS *—n.* **1.** Absence of light. **2.** Night or nightfall. **—in the dark. 1.** In secret. **2.** In a state of ignorance. **—dark'ish** *adj.* **—dark'ly** *adv.* **—dark'ness** *n.*

Dark Ages *pl.n.* The early part of the Middle Ages.

dark•en (där'kən) *v.* **1.** To make or become dark or darker. **2.** To make or become sad or gloomy. **3.** To tarnish : stain.

dark horse *n.* A little-known contestant whose chances of winning are uncertain.

dark•room (därk'ro͞om', -ro͝om') *n.* A darkened or specially illuminated room for processing photographic materials.

dark star *n.* A star normally obscured or too faint for direct visual observation.

dar•ling (där'lĭng) *n.* **1.** A much-loved person. **2.** A favorite. —*adj.* **1.** Very dear **:** beloved. **2.** *Informal.* Charming **:** adorable.

darn (därn) *v.* To mend by weaving stitches across a hole (in). —**darn** *n.*

dar•nel (där′nəl) *n.* An Old World grass of the genus *Lolium.*

darning needle *n.* **1.** A long needle with a large eye. **2.** *Informal.* A dragonfly.

dart (därt) *n.* **1.** A slender, pointed missile either thrown or shot. **2. darts** *(sing. in number).* The game of throwing darts at a target. **3.** Something shaped like a dart. **4.** A sudden, rapid movement. **5.** A tapered tuck to adjust the fit of a garment. —*v.* To move or thrust suddenly.

dart•er (där′tər) *n.* **1.** One that darts. **2.** A small, often brightly colored freshwater fish of the family Percidae, indigenous to E North America.

Dar•win•ism (där′wə-nĭz′əm) *n.* A theory of biological evolution that states that species of animals and plants develop through natural selection.

dash (dăsh) *v.* **1.** To break **:** smash. **2.** To knock, throw, or thrust violently. **3.** To splash. **4.** To perform or finish hastily. **5.** To move quickly **:** rush. **6.** To destroy **:** ruin. —*n.* **1.** A swift, harsh blow or stroke. **2.** A splash. **3.** A small amount <a *dash* of pepper> **4.** A sudden movement **:** rush. **5.** A short race on foot. **6.** Vigor **:** vitality. **7.** A punctuation mark (—) used in writing or printing. **8.** A dashboard. —**dash′er** *n.*

dash•board (dăsh′bôrd′, -bōrd′) *n.* A panel under the windshield of a motor vehicle where the instruments, dials, and controls are located.

da•shi•ki (də-shē′kē) *n., pl.* **-kis.** A loose, often brightly colored African tunic.

dash•ing (dăsh′ĭng) *adj.* **1.** Audacious and gallant. **2.** Splendidly elegant.

das•tard (dăs′tərd) *n.* A base coward. —**das′tard•li•ness** *n.* —**das′tard•ly** *adj.*

da•ta (dā′tə, dăt′ə, dä′tə) *pl.n. (sing. or pl. in number).* **1.** Information, esp. information organized for analysis. **2.** Numerical information that is used for computer processing. **3.** *pl. of* DATUM.

data bank *n.* A data base.

da•ta•base *also* **data base** (dā′tə-bās′, dăt′ə-) *n.* A collection of data arranged for ease of retrieval, as by a computer.

data processing *n.* **1.** Preparation of information for computer processing. **2.** Storage or processing of raw data by a computer. —**data processor** *n.*

date[1] (dāt) *n.* **1.** Time stated in terms of the day, month, and year. **2.** The day of the month. **3.** A particular point or period in time at which something occurred or existed or is to occur. **4.** Duration of something. **5.** The time or historical period to which something belongs. **6. a.** A social appointment. **b.** A person's companion on a date. —*v.* **dat•ed, dat•ing. 1.** To mark or provide with a date <*date* a letter> **2.** To ascertain the date of. **3.** To reveal the age of. **4.** To have origin in a particular time in the past <a vase *dating* from 400 B.C.> **5.** To go on dates (with).

date[2] (dāt) *n.* The oblong edible fruit of the date palm.

dat•ed (dā′tĭd) *adj.* **1.** Showing or marked with a date. **2.** Old-fashioned.

date•less (dāt′lĭs) *adj.* **1.** Having no date. **2.** Without limits **:** endless. **3.** Too old to be dated. **4.** Timeless **:** eternal.

date•line (dāt′līn′) *n.* A phrase at the beginning of a printed article giving the date and its place of origin.

date palm *n.* A tropical tree, *Phoenix dactylifera,* having featherlike leaves and bearing clusters of dates.

da•tive (dā′tĭv) *adj.* Of or being a grammatical case in Latin, Russian, and certain other languages that marks the indirect object. —*n.* The dative case.

da•tum (dā′təm, dăt′əm, dä′təm) *n., pl.* **-ta** (-tə). One piece of information **:** fact.

daub (dôb) *v.* **1.** To cover, coat, or smear with an adhesive substance, as plaster. **2.** To paint unskillfully. —*n.* **1.** A soft adhesive coating material. **2.** A crude painting. —**daub′er** *n.* —**daub′ing•ly** *adv.*

daugh•ter (dô′tər) *n.* **1.** A female offspring. **2.** A female descendant. **3.** A woman considered as if in a relationship of child to parent <a *daughter* of the nation> —**daugh′ter•ly** *adj.*

daugh•ter-in-law (dô′tər-ĭn-lô′) *n., pl.* **daugh•ters-in-law.** One's son's wife.

daunt (dônt) *v.* **1.** To drain the courage of **:** intimidate. **2.** To dishearten.

daunt•less (dônt′lĭs) *adj.* Fearless.

dau•phin (dô′fĭn) *n.* The eldest son of a king of France.

dav•en•port (dăv′ən-pôrt′, -pōrt′) *n.* A large couch or sofa.

dav•it (dăv′ĭt, dā′vĭt) *n.* A small crane used esp. for lifting small boats.

daw•dle (dôd′l) *v.* **-dled, -dling. 1.** To take more time than is needed. **2.** To waste time. —**daw′dler** *n.*

dawn (dôn) *n.* **1.** The first appearance of the morning daylight. **2.** A beginning. ★ ***syns:*** AURORA, COCKCROW, DAYBREAK, MORN, MORNING, SUNRISE, SUNUP —*v.* **1.** To begin to grow light in the morning. **2.** To emerge. **3.** To begin to be understood.

day (dā) *n.* **1.** The period of light between dawn and nightfall. **2.** The 24-hour period of a single rotation of the earth on its axis. **3.** The part of a day set aside for work. **4.** A period of activity or prominence in one's lifetime. **5.** A specified period of time **:** era <in *days* of old> **6.** The issue at hand <carried the *day*>

day•bed (dā′bĕd′) *n.* A sofa that can be converted into a bed.

day•book (dā′bo͝ok′) *n.* A diary or private journal.

day•break (dā′brāk′) *n.* DAWN 1.

day care *n.* Provision of daytime supervision, training, and medical services, esp. for infants and preschool children.

day•dream (dā'drēm') *n.* A dreamlike fantasy. **—day'dream** *v.*
day•light (dā'līt') *n.* **1.** The light of day. **2.** Daybreak. **3.** Daytime. **4.** Understanding or insight into what was once obscure. **5. daylights.** *Slang.* Mental stability **:** wits.
day•light-sav•ing time (dā'līt-sā'vĭng) *n.* Time that is usu. one hour ahead of standard time to provide more daylight at the end of the working day.
day lily *n.* A perennial garden plant with yellow, orange, or purplish lilylike flowers.
Day of Atonement *n.* Yom Kippur.
days (dāz) *adv.* Regularly or habitually in the daytime <worked *days*>
day•time (dā'tīm') *n.* The time between dawn and dark **:** day.
day-to-day (dā'tə-dā') *adj.* **1.** Happening on a daily or routine basis. **2.** Of or marked by planning or thought only for the present with little regard for the future.
daze (dāz) *v.* **dazed, daz•ing. 1.** To stun, as with a heavy blow or shock **:** stupefy. **2.** To dazzle, as with intense light. ★ ***syns:*** BEDAZZLE, BLIND, DAZZLE **—daze** *n.*
daz•zle (dăz'əl) *v.* **-zled, -zling. 1.** To overpower or be overpowered with intense light. **2.** To bewilder or overwhelm with a spectacular display. **—daz'zle** *n.*
D-day (dē'dā') *n.* A day on which an operation or military offensive is launched.
DDT (dē'dē-tē') *n.* A colorless contact insecticide that is toxic to humans and animals when ingested or absorbed.
de– *pref.* **1.** Do or make the opposite of **:** reverse <*de*criminalize> **2.** Remove or remove from <*de*throne>
dea•con (dē'kən) *n.* **1.** A cleric ranking immediately below a priest in the Anglican, Eastern Orthodox, and Roman Catholic churches. **2.** A lay assistant to a Protestant minister. **—dea'con•ess** *n.* **—dea'con•ry** *n.*
de•ac•ti•vate (dē-ăk'tə-vāt') *v.* **1.** To make inactive. **2.** To remove from active military status. **—de•ac'ti•va'tion** *n.*
dead (dĕd) *adj.* **1.** No longer living. **2.** Having no capacity to live **:** inanimate. **3.** Lacking feeling or sensitivity. **4. a.** No longer in use or existence <a *dead* language> **b.** Dormant <a *dead* volcano> **5.** Unproductive <*dead* capital> **6.** Quiet **:** dull. **7.** Worn-out **:** weary. **8.** No longer having significance or relevance <a *dead* issue> **9.** Having the physical look of death. **10.** Exact **:** unerring. **11.** Drained of electric charge, as a battery. **12.** Lacking bounce or elasticity. **13.** Not circulating **:** stagnant. **14. a.** Sudden **:** abrupt <a *dead* stop> **b.** Complete <*dead* silence> *—n.* The period of greatest intensity, as of cold or darkness. *—adv.* **1.** Altogether **:** absolutely. **2.** Directly <*dead* ahead> **—dead'ness** *n.*
dead•beat (dĕd'bēt') *n. Slang.* A person who does not pay incurred debts.
dead bolt *n.* A bolt on a lock that is moved by turning the key or knob without activation of a spring.
dead•en (dĕd'n) *v.* **1.** To make less intense, sensitive, or vigorous. **2.** To make soundproof. **—dead'en•er** *n.*
dead end *n.* **1.** An end of a passage that affords no outlet. **2.** A point beyond which no progress can be made **:** impasse. **—dead'-end'** *adj.*
dead•eye (dĕd'ī') *n.* **1.** *Naut.* A flat disk through which lanyards are passed to fasten the shrouds. **2.** *Slang.* A sharpshooter.

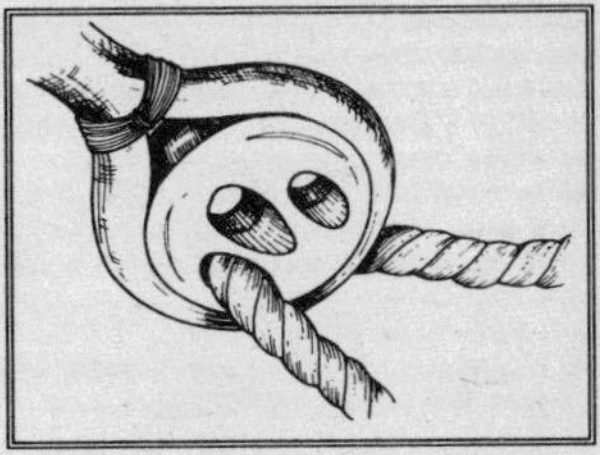

deadeye

dead heat *n.* A contest in which 2 or more entrants finish at the same time **:** tie.
dead•line (dĕd'līn') *n.* A time limit before which something must be finished.
dead•lock (dĕd'lŏk') *n.* A stoppage resulting from the uncompromising positions of opposing forces. **—dead'lock'** *v.*
dead•ly (dĕd'lē) *adj.* **-li•er, -li•est. 1.** Causing or tending to cause death. **2.** Like death. **3.** Implacable <*deadly* enemies> **4.** Destructive in effect <gave the play a *deadly* review> **5.** Utter <*deadly* earnestness> **6.** Extreme <under *deadly* strain> **7.** *Informal.* Dull and boring. ★ ***syns:*** FATAL, LETHAL, MORTAL *—adv.* **1.** So as to resemble death. **2.** To an extreme <I'm *deadly* serious.> **—dead'li•ness** *n.*
dead•pan (dĕd'păn') *adj. & adv. Informal.* With an expressionless face or manner.
dead reckoning *n.* The determination of the position of an aircraft or ship without astronomical observations, as by computations of the course and distance traveled from a known position.
dead•wood (dĕd'wŏŏd') *n.* **1.** Dead wood on a tree. **2.** One that is burdensome or superfluous.
deaf (dĕf) *adj.* **1.** Partially or totally incapable of hearing. **2.** Unwilling or refusing to listen **:** heedless. **—deaf'ness** *n.*
deaf•en (dĕf'ən) *v.* To make deaf.
deaf-mute (dĕf'myōōt') *n.* A person who cannot speak or hear.
deal[1] (dēl) *v.* **dealt** (dĕlt), **deal•ing. 1.** To apportion **:** distribute. **2.** To administer **:** deliver <*dealt* a blow to the chin> **3.** To give out (playing cards) among players of a game. **4.** To be concerned <a report *dealing* with poverty> **5.** To behave in a particular manner toward another or others. **6.** To take action in response to something <*dealt* with all

complaints> **7.** To conduct business **:** trade. —*n.* **1.** The act of apportioning or distributing. **2. a.** Cards distributed in a card game **:** hand. **b.** The turn or right of a player to deal cards. **3.** An undetermined quantity, extent, or degree <spent a great *deal* of time> **4.** *Informal.* **a.** A business transaction. **b.** A favorable bargain or sale. **5.** *Informal.* Treatment received <a raw *deal*> **—deal'er** *n.*

deal[2] (dēl) *n.* Pine or fir wood or boards.

deal•er•ship (dē'lər-shĭp') *n.* A franchise to sell an item in a certain area.

deal•ing (dē'lĭng) *n.* **1. dealings.** Transactions with others, usu. in business. **2.** A way of acting in relation to others.

dean (dēn) *n.* **1.** An administrator in a college, university, or high school. **2.** The head of the body of canons governing a cathedral or collegiate church. **3.** The senior member of a body or group **:** doyen.

dear (dîr) *adj.* **1. a.** Loved and cherished <my *dear* parents> **b.** Greatly valued **:** precious. **2.** High-priced **:** costly. —*n.* A greatly loved person. —*adv.* **1.** Fondly or affectionately. **2.** At a high price. **—dear'ly** *adv.*

dearth (dûrth) *n.* Scarcity **:** lack.

death (dĕth) *n.* **1.** The cessation of life. **2.** The state of being dead. **3.** Termination or extinction <the *death* of slavery> **4.** The cause of dying. **5.** A manner of dying <a martyr's *death*> **6. a.** Bloodshed. **b.** Execution. **—death'like'** *adj.*

death•bed (dĕth'bĕd') *n.* **1.** The bed on which a person dies. **2.** The last hours before death.

death•blow (dĕth'blō') *n.* A blow or event that is fatal.

death cup *n.* A poisonous mushroom, *Amanita phalloides.*

death•less (dĕth'lĭs) *adj.* Not subject to death **:** immortal.

death•ly (dĕth'lē) *adj.* **1.** Of, resembling, or typical of death. **2.** Causing death **:** fatal. —*adv.* **1.** In the manner of death. **2.** Very **:** extremely <*deathly* pale>

death rate *n.* The ratio of deaths to population in a specified community.

death row (rō) *n.* The part of a prison for housing inmates who have received the death penalty.

death's-head (dĕths'hĕd') *n.* The human skull symbolizing mortality or death.

death•trap (dĕth'trăp') *n.* **1.** An unsafe structure. **2.** A perilous situation.

death•watch (dĕth'wŏch') *n.* A watch kept with a dying or dead person.

deb (dĕb) *n. Informal.* A debutante.

de•ba•cle (dĭ-bä'kəl, -băk'əl) *n.* A sudden, calamitous downfall, collapse, or failure.

de•bar (dē-bär') *v.* To forbid, shut out, or bar. **—de•bar'ment** *n.*

de•bark (dĭ-bärk') *v.* To disembark.

de•base (dĭ-bās') *v.* To lower in quality, character, or value **:** demean. **—de•base'ment** *n.* **—de•bas'er** *n.*

de•bate (dĭ-bāt') *v.* **-bat•ed, -bat•ing. 1.** To consider **:** deliberate <*debating* whether to go> **2.** To argue opposing points. **3.** To discuss or argue (e.g., a question) formally. **—de•bate'** *n.* **—de•bat'a•ble** *adj.* **—de•bat'a•bly** *adv.* **—de•bat'er** *n.*

de•bauch (dĭ-bôch') *v.* To lead away from virtue **:** corrupt. **—de•bauch'er•y** *n.*

de•ben•ture (dĭ-bĕn'chər) *n.* A certificate or voucher acknowledging a debt.

de•bil•i•tate (dĭ-bĭl'ĭ-tāt') *v.* **-tat•ed, -tat•ing.** To make weak or feeble. **—de•bil'i•ta'tion** *n.* **—de•bil'i•ta'tive** *adj.*

de•bil•i•ty (dĭ-bĭl'ĭ-tē) *n.* Abnormal bodily weakness.

deb•it (dĕb'ĭt) *n.* An item of debt as recorded in an account. —*v.* **1.** To enter in a ledger as a debit. **2.** To charge with a debt.

deb•o•nair (dĕb'ə-nâr') *adj.* **1.** Suave **:** urbane. **2.** Affable **:** genial. **3.** Jaunty **:** nonchalant. **—deb'o•nair'ly** *adv.*

de•bouch (dĭ-bouch', -bo͞osh') *v.* To march or issue into the open.

de•brief (dē-brēf') *v.* To interrogate in order to obtain intelligence gathered, esp. on a military mission.

de•bris *also* **dé•bris** (də-brē', dā'brē') *n.* **1.** Scattered remains **:** ruins. **2.** Discarded waste **:** litter.

debt (dĕt) *n.* **1.** Something owed, as money or goods. **2.** The condition of indebtedness.

▲ ***word history:*** The pronunciation of *debt* represents the orig. pronunciation of the word, which was borrowed from French *dette.* Medieval writers knew that *dette* was derived from Latin *debitum,* and in the 15th cent. the spelling *debt* first appeared. This form was promoted as more correct by the language reformers of the 16th cent. and is now the only acceptable spelling.

debt•or (dĕt'ər) *n.* One who owes a debt to another.

de•bug (dē-bŭg') *v.* **1.** To find and remove a concealed electronic listening device from. **2.** To correct malfunctioning elements in (e.g., a computer program).

de•bunk (dē-bŭngk') *v. Informal.* To expose the fallacy or fraudulence of.

de•but *also* **dé•but** (dā-byo͞o', dĭ-, dā'byo͞o') *n.* **1.** A first public appearance. **2.** The formal presentation of a young woman to society. **3.** The beginning of a course of action, as a career. **—de•but'** *v.*

deb•u•tante *also* **dé•bu•tante** (dĕb'yo͞o-tänt', dā'byo͞o-) *n.* A young woman who is making her debut.

deca– *or* **dec–** *also* **deka–** *or* **dek–** *pref.* Ten <*deca*gram>

dec•ade (dĕk'ād', dĕ-kād') *n.* A period of 10 years.

dec•a•dence (dĕk'ə-dəns, dĭ-kād'ns) *n.* A process, period, or condition of decline or deterioration, as in art or morals. **—dec'a•dent** *adj.* **—dec'a•dent•ly** *adv.*

de•caf (dē'kăf') *n. Informal.* Decaffeinated coffee. **—de'caf'** *adj.*

de•caf•fein•at•ed (dē-căf'ə-nā'tĭd) *adj.* Having the caffeine removed.

dec•a•gon (dĕk'ə-gŏn') *n.* A polygon with 10 angles and 10 sides.

dec•a•gram (dĕk'ə-grăm') *n.* A metric unit of mass equal to 10 grams.
de•cal (dē'kăl', dĭ-kăl') *n.* A picture or design transferred by decalcomania.
de•cal•co•ma•ni•a (dē-kăl'kə-mā'nē-ə) *n.* **1.** The process of transferring designs or pictures printed on special paper to material such as glass or metal. **2.** Decal.
dec•a•li•ter (dĕk'ə-lē'tər) *n.* A metric unit of volume equal to 10 liters.
Dec•a•logue *or* **Dec•a•log** (dĕk'ə-lôg', -lŏg') *n.* The Ten Commandments.
dec•a•me•ter (dĕk'ə-mē'tər) *n.* A metric unit of length equal to 10 meters.
de•camp (dĭ-kămp') *v.* **1.** To leave a camping ground. **2.** To depart suddenly.
de•cant (dĭ-kănt') *v.* To pour off (e.g., wine) without disturbing the sediment.
de•cant•er (dĭ-kăn'tər) *n.* An ornamental bottle for serving liquids, as wine.
de•cap•i•tate (dĭ-kăp'ĭ-tāt') *v.* **-tat•ed, -tat•ing.** To cut off the head of : behead. **—de•cap'i•ta'tion** *n.* **—de•cap'i•ta'tor** *n.*
de•cath•lon (dĭ-kăth'lən, -lŏn') *n.* An athletic contest with 10 different track and field events.
de•cay (dĭ-kā') *v.* **1.** To rot. **2.** To decline in quality or quantity : deteriorate. **3.** *Physics.* To disintegrate or diminish by radioactive decomposition. ★ ***syns:*** DECOMPOSE, DETERIORATE, MOLDER, PUTREFY, ROT, SPOIL, TURN **—de•cay'** *n.*
de•cease (dĭ-sēs') *v.* **-ceased, -ceas•ing.** To die. **—de•cease'** *n.* **—de•ceased'** *n.*
de•ce•dent (dĭ-sēd'nt) *n.* A deceased person.
de•ceit (dĭ-sēt') *n.* **1.** Deception. **2.** A trick : stratagem. **—de•ceit'ful** *adj.* **—de•ceit'ful•ly** *adv.* **—de•ceit'ful•ness** *n.*
de•ceive (dĭ-sēv') *v.* **-ceived, -ceiv•ing.** To mislead or delude. ★ ***syns:*** DELUDE, DUPE, FOOL, HOODWINK, MISLEAD **—de•ceiv'a•ble** *adj.* **—de•ceiv'er** *n.*
de•cel•er•ate (dē-sĕl'ə-rāt') *v.* **-at•ed, -at•ing.** To decrease in velocity. **—de•cel'er•a'tion** *n.* **—de•cel'er•a'tor** *n.*
De•cem•ber (dĭ-sĕm'bər) *n.* The 12th month of the year, having 31 days.
de•cen•ni•al (dĭ-sĕn'ē-əl) *adj.* **1.** Lasting for 10 years. **2.** Happening once every 10 years. **—de•cen'ni•al** *n.*
de•cent (dē'sənt) *adj.* **1.** Marked by conformity to recognized standards of propriety or morality. **2.** Meeting accepted standards : adequate <a *decent* income> **3.** Kind or obliging. **4.** Properly or modestly clothed. **—de'cen•cy** *n.* **—de'cent•ly** *adv.*
de•cen•tral•ize (dē-sĕn'trə-līz') *v.* **-ized, -iz•ing. 1.** To distribute the administrative functions of (a central authority) among several local authorities. **2.** To redistribute a concentration of (e.g., population) over a wider area. **—de•cen'tral•i•za'tion** *n.*
de•cep•tion (dĭ-sĕp'shən) *n.* **1.** The use of deceit. **2.** The state or fact of being deceived. **3.** A ruse.
de•cep•tive (dĭ-sĕp'tĭv) *adj.* Intended or tending to mislead or deceive. **—de•cep'tive•ly** *adv.* **—de•cep'tive•ness** *n.*
de•ci•bel (dĕs'ə-bəl, -bĕl') *n.* A unit for expressing relative difference in sounds.
de•cide (dĭ-sīd') *v.* **-cid•ed, -cid•ing. 1.** To settle or conclude. **2.** To determine or influence the settlement of. **3.** To make up or cause to make up one's mind. ★ ***syns:*** CONCLUDE, DETERMINE, RESOLVE, SETTLE **—de•cid'a•ble** *adj.* **—de•cid'er** *n.*
de•cid•ed (dĭ-sī'dĭd) *adj.* **1.** Definite : unquestionable. **2.** Resolute. **—de•cid'ed•ly** *adv.* **—de•cid'ed•ness** *n.*
de•cid•u•ous (dĭ-sĭj'o͞o-əs) *adj.* **1.** Falling off or shed usu. at the end of a particular season or stage of growth. **2.** Shedding leaves at the end of the growing season.
dec•i•gram (dĕs'ĭ-grăm') *n.* One-tenth (1/10) of a gram.
dec•i•liter (dĕs'ə-lē'tər) *n.* One-tenth (1/10) of a liter.
de•cil•lion (dĭ-sĭl'yən) *n.* **1.** The cardinal number equal to 10^{33}. **2.** *esp. Brit.* The cardinal number equal to 10^{60}. **—de•cil'lionth** *adj. & n.*
dec•i•mal (dĕs'ə-məl) *n.* **1.** A linear group of natural numbers that represents a fraction, every decimal place indicating a multiple of a power of 10, e.g., .3 = 3/10, .03 = 3/100, .003 = 3/1000. **2.** A number with a decimal point. *—adj.* **1.** Expressed or capable of being expressed as a decimal. **2. a.** Based on 10. **b.** Ordered or numbered by 10's. **—dec'i•mal•ly** *adv.*
decimal point *n.* A period placed to the left of a decimal to indicate where the place values change from positive to negative powers of 10.
dec•i•mate (dĕs'ə-māt') *v.* **-mat•ed, -mat•ing. 1.** To destroy or kill a large proportion of. **2.** To select by lot and kill one in every 10 of. **—dec'i•ma'tion** *n.*
dec•i•me•ter (dĕs'ə-mē'tər) *n.* One-tenth (1/10) of a meter.
de•ci•pher (dĭ-sī'fər) *v.* **1.** To decode. **2.** To interpret or read (something ambiguous or indistinct). **—de•ci'pher•a•ble** *adj.*
de•ci•sion (dĭ-sĭzh'ən) *n.* **1.** A final choice : judgment. **2.** Resoluteness.
de•ci•sive (dĭ-sī'sĭv) *adj.* **1.** Conclusive. **2.** Marked by firm determination : resolute. **3.** Unquestionable <a *decisive* victory> **—de•ci'sive•ly** *adv.* **—de•ci'sive•ness** *n.*
deck[1] (dĕk) *n.* **1. a.** A horizontal platform that extends between the sides of a ship. **b.** A platform similar to a ship's deck. **2.** A set of playing cards. *—v.* **1.** To furnish with a deck. **2.** To knock down, as by punching.
deck[2] (dĕk) *v.* To array or adorn.
deck hand *n.* A member of a ship's crew assigned to work on deck.
de•claim (dĭ-klām') *v.* To speak or deliver loudly or dramatically. **—dec'la•ma'tion** (dĕk'lə-mā'shən) *n.* **—de•clam'a•to'ry** (-klăm'ə-tôr'ē, -tōr'ē) *adj.*
de•clare (dĭ-klâr') *v.* **-clared, -clar•ing. 1.** To state formally or officially. **2.** To state em-

phatically : affirm. **3.** To reveal : show. **4.** To make a full statement of (e.g., dutiable goods). **—dec′la•ra′tion** *n.* **—de•clar′a•tive** *adj.* **—de•clar′er** *n.*

de•clas•si•fy (dē-klăs′ə-fī′) *v.* To remove the security classification of (a document). **—de•clas′si•fi•ca′tion** *n.*

de•clen•sion (dĭ-klĕn′shən) *n.* **1.** Inflection of nouns, pronouns, and adjectives. **2.** A slope : descent. **3.** A decrease or decline : deterioration. **—de•clen′sion•al** *adj.*

de•cline (dĭ-klīn′) *v.* **-clined, -clin•ing. 1.** To refuse or reject (something). **2.** To slope downward : descend. **3.** To deteriorate little by little, as from disease. **4.** To wane. **5.** To give the inflected forms of. **—de•clin′a•ble** *adj.* **—dec′li•na′tion** *n.* **—dec′li•na′tion•al** *adj.* **—de•cline′** *n.* **—de•clin′er** *n.*

de•cliv•i•ty (dĭ-klĭv′ĭ-tē) *n., pl.* **-ties.** A steep descending slope.

de•code (dē-kōd′) *v.* To convert (a coded message) into plain text. **—de•cod′er** *n.*

dé•colle•tage (dā′kôl-täzh′) *n.* A low or plunging neckline on a garment.

dé•colle•té (dā′kôl-tā′) *adj.* Having a low or plunging neckline.

de•com•pose (dē′kəm-pōz′) *v.* **1.** To separate or break down into component parts. **2.** To decay or cause to decay. **—de′com•pos′a•ble** *adj.* **—de′com•pos′er** *n.* **—de•com′po•si′tion** (dē-kŏm′pə-zĭsh′ən) *n.*

de•com•press (dē′kəm-prĕs′) *v.* **1.** To relieve of pressure. **2.** To bring (a person working in compressed air) back to normal air pressure. **—de′com•pres′sion** *n.*

de•con•gest (dē′kən-jĕst′) *v.* To relieve the congestion of (e.g., sinuses). **—de′con•ges′tion** *n.* **—de′con•ges′tive** *adj.*

de•con•ges•tant (dē′kən-jĕs′tənt) *n.* An agent that alleviates congestion, as of the sinuses.

de•con•struc•tion (dē′kən-strŭk′shən) *n.* A theory of literary criticism that questions traditional assumptions about the meaning of texts. **—de′con•struct′** *v.* **—de′con•struc′tion•ist** *n. & adj.*

de•con•tam•i•nate (dē′kən-tăm′ə-nāt′) *v.* To free of contamination.

de•con•trol (dē′kən-trōl′) *v.* To free from control, esp. from governmental control.

dé•cor *or* **de•cor** (dā′kôr′, dā-kôr′) *n.* An interior decorative arrangement.

dec•o•rate (dĕk′ə-rāt′) *v.* **-rat•ed, -rat•ing. 1.** To furnish or adorn with fashionable or beautiful things. **2.** To bestow an emblem of honor on.

dec•o•ra•tion (dĕk′ə-rā′shən) *n.* **1.** The act or art of decorating. **2.** An ornament. **3.** An emblem of honor, as a medal.

dec•o•ra•tive (dĕk′ər-ə-tĭv, -ə-rā′-) *adj.* Serving to decorate : ornamental.

dec•o•ra•tor (dĕk′ə-rā′tər) *n.* One who decorates, esp. an interior decorator.

dec•o•rous (dĕk′ər-əs, dĭ-kôr′-, -kōr′-) *adj.* Marked by decorum : seemly.

de•co•rum (dĭ-kôr′əm, -kōr′-) *n.* Conformity to accepted conventions of behavior : propriety.

de•cou•page *also* **dé•cou•page** (dā′ko͞o-päzh′) *n.* The technique of decorating a surface with cutouts, as of paper.

de•coy (dē′koi′, dĭ-koi′) *n.* **1.** An artificial animal used to lure game. **2.** A means to trap, mislead, or lure into danger. **—de•coy′** *v.* **—de•coy′er** *n.*

de•crease (dĭ-krēs′) *v.* **-creased, -creas•ing.** To grow or cause to grow gradually less : reduce. ★ ***syns:*** ABATE, DIMINISH, DWINDLE, LESSEN, REDUCE, TAPER *—n.* (dē′krēs′). The act or process of decreasing or the resulting state : decline.

de•cree (dĭ-krē′) *n.* **1.** An authoritative order having legal force. **2.** A judicial judgment. *—v.* **-creed, -cree•ing.** To establish, ordain, or decide by decree.

dec•re•ment (dĕk′rə-mənt) *n.* **1.** A gradual decrease. **2.** The amount lost by gradual waste or diminution. **—dec′re•ment′al** *adj.*

de•crep•it (dĭ-krĕp′ĭt) *adj.* Broken down or worn out, as from long use or old age. **—de•crep′it•ly** *adv.* **—de•crep′i•tude′** *n.*

de•cre•scen•do (dē′krə-shĕn′dō, dā′-) *adv.* *Mus.* Gradually decreasing in force or loudness. **—de′cre•scen′do** *n. & adj.*

de•crim•i•nal•ize (dē-krĭm′ə-nə-līz′) *v.* **-ized, -iz•ing.** To remove the criminal classification of.

de•cry (dĭ-krī′) *v.* To belittle or disparage openly : denounce. **—de•cri′er** *n.*

ded•i•cate (dĕd′ĭ-kāt′) *v.* **-cat•ed, -cat•ing. 1.** To set apart for a special use. **2.** To commit (oneself) to a particular course of action. **3.** To address or inscribe (e.g., a literary work) to someone. **—ded′i•ca′tion** *n.* **—ded′i•ca•to′ry** (-kə-tôr′ē, -tōr′ē) *adj.*

de•duce (dĭ-do͞os′, -dyo͞os′) *v.* **-duced, -duc•ing.** To come to (a conclusion) by reasoning. **—de•duc′i•ble** *adj.*

▲ ***word history:*** *Deduce* and *deduct* were both borrowed in the early 16th cent. from Latin *deducere,* "to lead or bring away." *Deducere* also meant "to subtract" in classical Latin and developed the sense "to derive a logical conclusion from" in Medieval Latin. In English *deduce* and *deduct* were at first used interchangeably with both meanings of the Latin word, but gradually *deduce* was restricted to "derive" and *deduct* was used primarily to mean "subtract." *Deduction,* however, still serves as the noun for both.

de•duct (dĭ-dŭkt′) *v.* To subtract. **—de•duct′i•ble** *adj.*

de•duc•tion (dĭ-dŭk′shən) *n.* **1.** Subtraction. **2.** An amount that is or may be deducted. **3. a.** The act or process of deducing. **b.** A conclusion arrived at by this process. **—de•duc′tive** *adj.* **—de•duc′tive•ly** *adv.*

deed (dēd) *n.* **1.** Something performed : act. **2.** An exploit : feat. **3.** Performance or action in general. **4.** A legal document, esp. one relating to the transference of property. *—v.* To transfer or convey by deed.

deem (dēm) *v.* To consider or judge.

deep (dēp) *adj.* **1.** Extending far downward below a surface. **2.** Extending far backward from front to rear or far inward from an outer surface. **3.** Coming from or penetrating to a depth. **4.** Far distant in time or space. **5.** Very learned **:** wise. **6.** Hard to understand **:** recondite. **7.** Extreme **:** intense. **8.** Rich and vivid in shade <*deep* green> **9.** Low in pitch **:** resonant. ★ ***syns:*** ABSTRUSE, ESOTERIC, HEAVY, PROFOUND, RECONDITE —*n.* **1.** A deep place in land or in a body of water, esp. in the ocean. **2.** The most extreme or intense part, as of the night or winter. **3.** The ocean. —*adv.* **1.** To a great depth **:** deeply <feelings ran *deep*> **2.** Advanced in time **:** late. **—deep′ly** *adv.* **—deep′ness** *n.*

deep•en (dē′pən) *v.* To make or become deep or deeper.

deep-freeze (dēp′frēz′) *v.* To quick-freeze.

deep-fry (dēp′frī′) *v.* To fry in a deep pan.

deep-root•ed (dēp′ro͞o′tĭd, -ro͝ot′ĭd) *adj.* Firmly implanted.

deep-sea (dēp′sē′) *adj.* Of, pertaining to, or occurring in deep parts of the sea.

deep-seat•ed (dēp′sē′tĭd) *adj.* Deeply rooted **:** ingrained.

deep-six (dēp′sĭks′) *v. Slang.* **1.** To throw overboard. **2.** To toss out **:** get rid of.

deer (dîr) *n., pl.* **deer.** A hoofed ruminant mammal of the family Cervidae, the males of which have deciduous antlers.

deer fly *n.* Any of various blood-sucking flies of the genus *Chrysops.*

deer•skin (dîr′skĭn′) *n.* Leather made from the hide of a deer.

de-es•ca•late (dē-ĕs′kə-lāt′) *v.* To decrease the scope or intensity of (e.g., a war).

de•face (dĭ-fās′) *v.* To mar or spoil the surface or appearance of **:** disfigure.

de fac•to (dĭ făk′tō, dā) *adv.* In actuality or fact **:** really. —*adj.* **1.** Actual. **2.** Actually exercising authority.

de•fal•cate (dĭ-făl′kāt′, -fôl′-, dĕf′əl-kāt′) *v.* **-cat•ed, -cat•ing.** To misuse funds **:** embezzle. **—de•fal′ca′tor** *n.*

de•fame (dĭ-fām′) *v.* **-famed, -fam•ing.** To libel or slander. **—def′a•ma′tion** (dĕf′ə-mā′shən) *n.* **—de•fam′a•to′ry** (dĭ-făm′ə-tôr′ē, -tōr′ē) *adj.* **—de•fam′er** *n.*

de•fault (dĭ-fôlt′) *n.* **1.** Failure to fulfill an obligation or perform a task. **2.** Failure to make a required appearance in court. **3.** Failure to complete or participate in a competition. **—de•fault′** *v.* **—de•fault′er** *n.*

de•feat (dĭ-fēt′) *v.* **1.** To win a victory over **:** beat. **2.** To thwart the success of <*defeated* our plans> ★ ***syns:*** BEAT, BEST, CLOBBER, CONQUER, DRUB, LICK, OVERCOME, ROUT, SHELLAC, SUBDUE, THRASH, TRIM, TRIUMPH, TROUNCE, VANQUISH, WHIP, WORST —*n.* The act of defeating or state of being defeated. **—de•feat′er** *n.*

de•feat•ism (dĭ-fē′tĭz′əm) *n.* Expectation or acceptance of defeat. **—de•feat′ist** *n.*

def•e•cate (dĕf′ĭ-kāt′) *v.* **-cat•ed, -cat•ing.** To void feces from the bowels. **—def′e•ca′tion** *n.* **—def′e•ca′tor** *n.*

de•fect (dē′fĕkt′, dĭ-fĕkt′) *n.* **1.** A lack of something desirable or necessary. **2.** A fault or imperfection. ★ ***syns:*** BLEMISH, FAULT, FLAW, IMPERFECTION —*v.* (dĭ-fĕkt′). To desert a country, party, or previously espoused cause. **—de•fec′tion** *n.* **—de•fec′tor** *n.*

de•fec•tive (dĭ-fĕk′tĭv) *adj.* Having a defect **:** faulty. **—de•fec′tive** *n.*

de•fence (dĭ-fĕns′) *n. esp. Brit. var. of* DEFENSE.

de•fend (dĭ-fĕnd′) *v.* **1.** To protect from danger, attack, or harm. **2.** To maintain or support **:** justify. **3.** *Law.* **a.** To represent (a defendant) in a criminal or civil case. **b.** To contest (an action or claim). ★ ***syns:*** GUARD, PROTECT, SAFEGUARD, SECURE, SHIELD **—de•fend′a•ble** *adj.* **—de•fend′er** *n.*

de•fen•dant (dĭ-fĕn′dənt) *n.* A person against whom a legal action is brought.

de•fense (dĭ-fĕns′) *n.* **1.** The act of defending **:** protection. **2.** Something that protects or defends. **3.** An argument that supports or justifies. **4.** A sports team or group of players attempting to keep the opposition from scoring. **5.** A defendant with his or her legal counsel. **—de•fense′less** *adj.* **—de•fen′si•ble** *adj.* **—de•fen′sive** *adj. & n.*

defense mechanism *n. Psychoanal.* A usu. unconscious mental mechanism that protects a person from shame, anxiety, or loss of self-esteem.

de•fer[1] (dĭ-fûr′) *v.* **-ferred, -fer•ring.** To put off until a future time **:** postpone. **—de•fer′ment, de•fer′ral** *n.* **—de•fer′ra•ble** *adj.* **—de•fer′rer** *n.*

de•fer[2] (dĭ-fûr′) *v.* **-ferred, -fer•ring.** To comply with or submit to the wishes, opinion, or decision of another. **—de•fer′rer** *n.*

def•er•ence (dĕf′ər-əns) *n.* Courteous respect for another's opinion, wishes, or judgment. **—def′er•en′tial** *adj.*

de•fi•ance (dĭ-fī′əns) *n.* **1.** Bold resistance to an opposing force or authority. **2.** Deliberately provocative behavior.

de•fi•ant (dĭ-fī′ənt) *adj.* Marked by defiance. **—de•fi′ant•ly** *adv.*

deficiency disease *n.* A disease, as scurvy, caused by a diet lacking in specific vitamins and minerals.

de•fi•cient (dĭ-fĭsh′ənt) *adj.* **1.** Lacking an essential quality or element. **2.** Inadequate in amount or degree **:** insufficient. **—de•fi′cien•cy** *n.* **—de•fi′cient•ly** *adv.*

def•i•cit (dĕf′ĭ-sĭt) *n.* **1.** The amount by which a sum of money is short of the required amount. **2.** Inadequacy **:** insufficiency.

de•file[1] (dĭ-fīl′) *v.* **-filed, -fil•ing. 1.** To make dirty **:** pollute. **2.** To corrupt. **3.** To profane or sully (e.g., a reputation). **4.** To desecrate. **5.** To violate the chastity of **:** ravish. **—de•file′ment** *n.* **—de•fil′er** *n.*

de•file[2] (dĭ-fīl′) *v.* **-filed, -fil•ing.** To march in single file or in columns. —*n.* A narrow gorge or pass.

de•fine (dĭ-fīn′) *v.* **-fined, -fin•ing. 1.** To state the specific meaning of (a word). **2.** To describe the nature of **:** explain. **3.** To delineate. **4.** To specify. **—de•fin′a•ble** *adj.* **—de•fin′er** *n.* **—def′i•ni′tion** (dĕf′ə-nĭsh′ən) *n.*

def·i·nite (dĕf′ə-nĭt) *adj.* **1.** Having specified bounds. **2.** Certain : sure <a *definite* success> **3.** Precise and explicit. **4.** Serving to designate a person or thing that is or can be immediately identified <"The" is the *definite* article.> ★ *syns:* CATEGORICAL, CLEAR-CUT, DECIDED, EXPLICIT, EXPRESS, POSITIVE, PRECISE, SPECIFIC, UNAMBIGUOUS, UNEQUIVOCAL —**def′i·nite·ly** *adv.*

de·fin·i·tive (dĭ-fĭn′ĭ-tĭv) *adj.* **1.** Precisely outlining or defining. **2.** Determining finally : decisive. **3.** Being complete and authoritative, as a biographical work.

de·flate (dĭ-flāt′) *v.* **-flat·ed, -flat·ing. 1. a.** To release contained gas or air from. **b.** To collapse through such a release. **2.** To reduce or lessen in importance or magnitude. **3.** To reduce (currency) in value or amount, effecting a decline in prices. —**de·fla′tion** *n.* —**de·fla′tion·ar′y** *adj.*

de·flect (dĭ-flĕkt′) *v.* To turn aside or cause to turn aside : swerve. —**de·flect′a·ble** *adj.* —**de·flec′tion** *n.* —**de·flec′tive** *adj.* —**de·flec′tor** *n.*

de·flow·er (dē-flou′ər) *v.* To destroy the virginity of : ravish.

de·fog (dē-fôg′, -fŏg′) *v.* To remove fog from. —**de·fog′ger** *n.*

de·fo·li·ant (dē-fō′lē-ənt) *n.* A chemical dusted or sprayed on plants or trees to cause the leaves to fall off.

de·fo·li·ate (dē-fō′lē-āt′) *v.* **-at·ed, -at·ing.** To strip of leaves, esp. by the use of a defoliant. —**de·fo′li·a′tion** *n.*

de·for·est (dē-fôr′ĭst, -fŏr′-) *v.* To clear of trees or forests. —**de·for′es·ta′tion** *n.*

de·form (dĭ-fôrm′) *v.* **1.** To spoil the natural form of : misshape. **2.** To mar the appearance of : disfigure <a face *deformed* by anger> —**de·form′a·ble** *adj.* —**de′for·ma′tion** (dē′fôr-mā′shən, dĕf′ər-) *n.*

de·for·mi·ty (dĭ-fôr′mĭ-tē) *n., pl.* **-ties. 1.** The state of being deformed. **2.** A bodily malformation.

de·fraud (dĭ-frôd′) *v.* To swindle : cheat. —**de·fraud′er** *n.*

de·fray (dĭ-frā′) *v.* To pay or provide for payment of <*defray* expenses> —**de·fray′a·ble** *adj.* —**de·fray′al** *n.*

de·frost (dē-frôst′, -frŏst′) *v.* **1.** To free or become free from ice or frost. **2.** To cause to thaw out. —**de·frost′er** *n.*

deft (dĕft) *adj.* Dexterous : skillful. —**deft′ly** *adv.* —**deft′ness** *n.*

de·funct (dĭ-fŭngkt′) *adj.* Having ceased to live or exist. —**de·func′tive** *adj.* —**de·funct′ness** *n.*

de·fuse (dē-fyo͞oz′) *v.* **1.** To remove the fuse or detonator from. **2.** To make less dangerous, tense, or hostile.

de·fy (dĭ-fī′) *v.* **-fied, -fy·ing. 1.** To face up to : challenge. **2.** To withstand or resist successfully. **3.** To dare or challenge to perform something thought to be impossible. —**de·fi′er** *n.*

de·gas (dē-găs′) *v.* To remove gas from.

de·gauss (dē-gous′) *v.* To neutralize the magnetic field of.

de·gen·er·ate (dĭ-jĕn′ə-rāt′) *v.* To decline in value, quality, or desirability : deteriorate. —*adj.* (-ər-ĭt). Morally depraved or sexually deviant. —*n.* (-ər-ĭt). A degenerate person : pervert. —**de·gen′er·a·cy** *n.* —**de·gen′er·ate·ly** *adv.* —**de·gen′er·a′tion** *n.* —**de·gen′er·a·tive** *adj.*

de·grade (dĭ-grād′) *v.* **1.** To reduce in grade, rank, or status : demote. **2.** To corrupt : debase. —**de·grad′able** *adj.* —**deg′ra·da′tion** (dĕg′rə-dā′shən) *n.*

de·gree (dĭ-grē′) *n.* **1.** One of a series of stages or steps. **2.** Relative rank, dignity, or position. **3.** Relative amount or intensity <a high *degree* of competence> **4.** Relative extent or condition <improved to a great *degree*> **5.** A unit on a temperature scale. **6.** A unit of arc or angular measure equal to 1/360 of a complete revolution. **7.** An academic title awarded to a person who has completed a given course of study or conferred as an honor. **8.** A classification according to seriousness, as of a crime. **9.** One of the grammatical forms used in the comparison of adjectives and adverbs. **10.** *Mus.* A note or tone of a musical scale.

de·horn (dē-hôrn′) *v.* To remove the horns from (an animal).

de·hu·man·ize (dē-hyo͞o′mə-nīz′) *v.* To deprive of human qualities, esp. to make routine and mechanical.

de·hu·mid·i·fy (dē′hyo͞o-mĭd′ə-fī′) *v.* To remove atmospheric moisture from. —**de′hu·mid′i·fi′er** *n.*

de·hy·drate (dē-hī′drāt′) *v.* To lose or cause to lose water or moisture.

de·ice (dē-īs′) *v.* To rid or keep free of ice. —**de·ic′er** *n.*

de·i·fy (dē′ə-fī′) *v.* **-fied, -fy·ing. 1.** To raise to divine rank. **2.** To worship or revere as a god. —**de′i·fi·ca′tion** *n.*

deign (dān) *v.* To deem barely worthy of one's dignity : condescend.

de·in·sti·tu·tion·al·ize (dē-ĭn′stĭ-to͞o′shə-nə-līz′, -tyo͞o′-) *v.* **1.** To remove the institutional nature from. **2.** To release (e.g., a mental health patient) from an institution.

de·ism (dē′ĭz′əm) *n.* A system of thought that affirms the existence of God but denies the validity of revelation. —**de′ist** *n.*

de·i·ty (dē′ĭ-tē) *n., pl.* **-ties. 1.** A god or goddess. **2.** The nature or state of a god. **3. Deity.** God.

de·ject (dĭ-jĕkt′) *v.* To lower the spirits of : dishearten. —**de·jec′tion** *n.* —**de·ject′ed·ly** *adv.* —**de·ject′ed·ness** *n.*

de ju·re (dē jo͝or′ē, dā yo͝or′ā) *adv. & adj.* By law : by right.

dek– *or* **deka–** *pref. var. of* DECA–.

deke (dēk) *v.* **deked, dek·ing.** *Hockey.* To fake a movement or shot in order to outmaneuver an opposing player.

Del·a·ware (dĕl′ə-wâr′) *n., pl.* **-ware** *or* **-wares. 1.** A member of an American Indian people formerly of the Delaware and lower Hudson river valleys, now chiefly in Oklahoma. **2.** Their Algonquian language.

de·lay (dĭ-lā′) *v.* **1.** To postpone until a later

time : defer. **2.** To cause to be detained or late. **3.** To waste time : procrastinate. ★ ***syns:*** DETAIN, RETARD, SLOW —*n.* **1.** The act of delaying or the state of being delayed. **2.** The time period in which someone is delayed. —**de•lay′er** *n.*

de•le (dē′lē) *n.* A mark indicating that something is to be deleted from typeset material. —**de′le** *v.*

de•lec•ta•ble (dĭ-lĕk′tə-bəl) *adj.* **1.** Exceedingly pleasant : delightful. **2.** Savory : delicious. —**de•lec′ta•bil′i•ty** *n.*

de•lec•ta•tion (dē′lĕk-tā′shən) *n.* Pleasure : enjoyment.

del•e•gate (dĕl′ĭ-gāt′, -gĭt) *n.* **1.** A person empowered to act as representative for another : agent or deputy. **2.** A member of the lower legislative house of Md., Va., and W.Va. —*v.* (-gāt′) **-gat•ed, -gat•ing. 1.** To empower and send as one's delegate. **2.** To commit or entrust to another.

del•e•ga•tion (dĕl′ĭ-gā′shən) *n.* **1.** The act of delegating or state of being delegated. **2.** A person or group of persons empowered to represent another or others.

de•lete (dĭ-lēt′) *v.* **-let•ed, -let•ing.** To remove or cancel : omit. —**de•le′tion** *n.*

del•e•te•ri•ous (dĕl′ĭ-tîr′ē-əs) *adj.* Having an injurious effect : harmful. —**del′e•te′ri•ous•ly** *adv.* —**del′e•te′ri•ous•ness** *n.*

delft (dĕlft) *or* **delft•ware** (dĕlft′wâr′) *n.* **1.** A style of glazed, usu. blue and white earthenware. **2.** Pottery that resembles delft.

del•i (dĕl′ē) *n.* A delicatessen.

de•lib•er•ate (dĭ-lĭb′ər-ĭt) *adj.* **1. a.** Planned in advance : premeditated. **b.** Said or done intentionally. **2.** Careful and thorough in deciding or determining. **3.** Leisurely or slow in motion or manner. —*v.* (-ə-rāt′) **-at•ed, -at•ing.** To consider carefully, as by weighing alternatives. —**de•lib′er•ate•ly** *adv.* —**de•lib′er•ate•ness** *n.* —**de•lib′er•a′tion** *n.* —**de•lib′er•a•tive** *adj.* —**de•lib′er•a•tive•ly** *adv.*

del•i•ca•cy (dĕl′ĭ-kə-sē) *n., pl.* **-cies. 1.** The state or quality of being delicate. **2.** A select or choice food.

del•i•cate (dĕl′ĭ-kĭt) *adj.* **1.** Pleasing to the senses, esp. in a subtle way <a *delicate* fragrance> **2.** Exquisitely fine <*delicate* embroidery> **3.** Frail in constitution. **4.** Easily damaged or broken. **5.** Marked by sensitivity or discrimination. **6. a.** Considerate. **b.** Concerned with propriety. **c.** Squeamish or fastidious. **7.** Requiring tactful treatment. **8.** Fine or soft in touch or skill. **9.** Keenly accurate in response or reaction. **10.** Very subtle in difference. ★ ***syns:*** CHOICE, DAINTY, ELEGANT, EXQUISITE, FINE —**del′i•cate•ly** *adv.*

del•i•ca•tes•sen (dĕl′ĭ-kə-tĕs′ən) *n.* A store that sells cooked or prepared foods.

de•li•cious (dĭ-lĭsh′əs) *adj.* **1.** Highly pleasing to the senses, esp. of taste. **2.** Very pleasant : delightful. ★ ***syns:*** DELECTABLE, HEAVENLY, LUSCIOUS, SAVORY, SCRUMPTIOUS, TASTY, TOOTHSOME, YUMMY —**de•li′cious•ly** *adv.* —**de•li′cious•ness** *n.*

de•light (dĭ-līt′) *n.* **1.** Great joy or pleasure. **2.** Something that affords delight. —*v.* To take or give great pleasure or joy. —**de•light′ful** *adj.* —**de•light′ful•ly** *adv.*

de•light•ed (dĭ-lī′tĭd) *adj.* Filled with delight. —**de•light′ed•ly** *adv.* —**de•light′ed•ness** *n.*

de•lim•it (dĭ-lĭm′ĭt) *v.* To fix the limits of : demarcate. —**de•lim′i•ta′tion** *n.*

de•lim•it•er (dĭ-lĭm′ĭ-tər) *n. Computer Sci.* A character marking the beginning or end of a unit of data.

de•lin•e•ate (dĭ-lĭn′ē-āt′) *v.* **-at•ed, -at•ing. 1.** To draw or trace the outline of : sketch. **2.** To represent in words or gestures : portray. —**de•lin′e•a′tion** *n.*

de•lin•quent (dĭ-lĭng′kwənt) *adj.* **1.** Failing to do what is required by law or obligation. **2.** Being behind in payment. —**de•lin′quen•cy** *n.* —**de•lin′quent** *n.* —**de•lin′quent•ly** *adv.*

del•i•quesce (dĕl′ĭ-kwĕs′) *v.* **-quesced, -quesc•ing. 1.** *Chem.* To become liquid by absorbing atmospheric moisture. **2.** To melt. —**del′i•ques′cent** *adj.*

de•lir•i•um (dĭ-lîr′ē-əm) *n.* **1.** A temporary mental disturbance resulting from high fever, intoxication, or shock and marked by confusion, tremors, hallucinations, and incoherent speech. **2.** Uncontrolled emotion, esp. excitement. —**de•lir′i•ous** *adj.* —**de•lir′i•ous•ly** *adv.* —**de•lir′i•ous•ness** *n.*

delirium tre•mens (trē′mənz, trĕm′ənz) *n.* An acute delirium caused by chronic and excessive use of alcohol.

de•liv•er (dĭ-lĭv′ər) *v.* **1.** To set free : liberate. **2.** To assist in the birth of. **3.** To surrender to another : hand over. **4.** To take to the intended recipient <*deliver* mail> **5.** To send to an intended goal or target. **6.** To give or utter. **7.** To do what is desired or expected <*deliver* on a pledge> —**de•liv′er•a•ble** *adj.* —**de•liv′er•ance** *n.* —**de•liv′er•er** *n.*

de•liv•er•y (dĭ-lĭv′ə-rē) *n., pl.* **-ies. 1.** The act of delivering or conveying. **2.** Something delivered. **3.** The act or process of giving birth : parturition. **4. a.** A way of speaking or singing. **b.** Utterance. **5.** The manner or act of throwing.

dell (dĕl) *n.* A small, secluded, usu. wooded valley.

del•phin•i•um (dĕl-fĭn′ē-əm) *n.* A plant of the genus *Delphinium,* bearing spikes of variously colored spurred flowers.

del•ta (dĕl′tə) *n.* A usu. triangular alluvial deposit at the mouth of a river.

delta ray *n.* An electron ejected from matter by ionizing radiation.

delta wing *n.* An aircraft with swept-back wings.

de•lude (dĭ-lo͞od′) *v.* **-lud•ed, -lud•ing.** To cause to be deceived.

del•uge (dĕl′yo͞oj) *n.* **1. a.** A great flood. **b.** A heavy downpour. **2.** Something overwhelming. —*v.* **-uged, -ug•ing.** To swamp with or as if with water.

de•lu•sion (dĭ-lo͞o′zhən) *n.* **1. a.** The act or process of deluding. **b.** The state of being deluded. **2.** A false conviction held contrary to invalidating facts, characteristic of some mental disorders. **—de•lu'sion•al** *adj.* **—de•lu'sive** *adj.*

de luxe *also* **de•luxe** (dĭ-lo͝oks', lŭks') *adj.* Highly luxurious or elegant.

delve (dĕlv) *v.* **delved, delv•ing.** To search carefully and laboriously.

de•mag•net•ize (dē-măg'nĭ-tīz') *v.* To rid of magnetic properties. **—de•mag'net•i•za'tion** *n.*

dem•a•gogue *also* **dem•a•gog** (dĕm'ə-gôg',-gŏg') *n.* A leader who comes to power by appealing to the prejudices and emotions of the people. **—dem'a•gogu'er•y, dem'a•gog'y** (-gŏj'ē, -gô'jē, -gŏg'ē) *n.*

de•mand (dĭ-mănd') *v.* **1.** To ask for firmly **:** command. **2.** To claim or assert as due or just. **3.** To require **:** need. —*n.* **1.** The act of demanding. **2.** Something demanded. **3. a.** The state of being desired or sought after. **b.** An urgent requirement, claim, or need. **4. a.** The ability and desire to purchase something. **b.** The quantity of goods wanted at a given price.

de•mand•ing (dĭ-măn'dĭng) *adj.* Needing constant attention or effort.

de•mar•cate (dĭ-mär'kāt', dē'mär-kāt') *v.* **-cat•ed, -cat•ing. 1.** To set the boundaries of **:** delimit. **2.** To separate as if by boundaries. **—de'mar•ca'tion** *n.*

de•mean[1] (dĭ-mēn') *v.* To conduct or behave (oneself) in a particular manner.

de•mean[2] (dĭ-mēn') *v.* **1.** To debase or degrade. **2.** To humble (oneself).

de•mean•or (dĭ-mē'nər) *n.* One's conduct toward others **:** deportment.

de•ment•ed (dĭ-mĕn'tĭd) *adj.* Insane.

de•men•tia (dĭ-mĕn'shə) *n.* Irreversible deterioration of intellectual faculties.

de•mer•it (dĭ-mĕr'ĭt) *n.* **1.** A defect **:** fault. **2.** A mark against one's record, esp. for bad conduct.

de•mesne (dĭ-mān', -mēn') *n.* **1.** The grounds of an estate. **2.** A large piece of landed property **:** estate. **3.** A region or territory. **4.** A domain **:** realm.

dem•i•god (dĕm'ē-gŏd') *n.* A mythological semidivine being, esp. the offspring of a god and a mortal.

dem•i•john (dĕm'ē-jŏn') *n.* A large, narrow-necked glass or earthenware bottle usu. enclosed in a wicker case.

de•mil•i•ta•rize (dē-mĭl'ĭ-tə-rīz') *v.* To free from military control, forces, or installations. **—de•mil'i•ta•ri•za'tion** *n.*

dem•i•mon•daine (dĕm'ē-mŏn-dān') *n.* A woman who belongs to the demimonde.

dem•i•monde (dĕm'ē-mŏnd') *n.* **1.** A class comprising women who are supported by wealthy lovers or protectors. **2.** A group living on the edge of respectability.

de•mise (dĭ-mīz') *n.* **1.** Death. **2.** The transfer of an estate by will or lease.

dem•i•tasse (dĕm'ē-tăs', -täs') *n.* **1.** A small cup of strong coffee. **2.** The cup used to serve demitasse.

dem•o (dĕm'ō) *n., pl.* **-os.** *Informal.* **1.** A demonstration. **2.** A product used for demonstration purposes.

de•mo•bi•lize (dē-mō'bə-līz') *v.* **1.** To release from military service. **2.** To disband.

de•moc•ra•cy (dĭ-mŏk'rə-sē) *n., pl.* **-cies. 1.** Government exercised either directly by the people or through elected representatives. **2.** A political or social unit based on democratic rule. **3.** Rule by the majority. **4.** The principles of social equality and respect for the individual within a community.

dem•o•crat (dĕm'ə-krăt') *n.* **1.** One who advocates democracy. **2. Democrat.** One belonging to the Democratic Party.

dem•o•crat•ic (dĕm'ə-krăt'ĭk) *adj.* **1.** Of, marked by, or advocating democracy. **2.** Relating to, encompassing, or promoting the people's interests. **3.** Believing in or practicing social equality. **4. Democratic.** Of or relating to the Democratic Party. **—dem'o•crat'i•cal•ly** *adv.* **—de•moc'ra•tize'** *v.*

Democratic Party *n.* One of the 2 major political parties in the U.S.

dé•mo•dé (dā'mō-dā') *adj.* Out-of-date.

de•mog•ra•phy (dĭ-mŏg'rə-fē) *n.* The study of the characteristics of human population, as size, growth, and vital statistics. **—dem'o•graph'ic** (dĕm'ə-grăf'ĭk) *adj.* **—dem'o•graph'i•cal•ly** *adv.*

de•mol•ish (dĭ-mŏl'ĭsh) *v.* **1.** To tear down **:** raze. **2.** To do away with **:** end.

dem•o•li•tion (dĕm'ə-lĭsh'ən) *n.* The act or process of demolishing, esp. destruction by the use of explosives.

de•mon (dē'mən) *n.* **1.** An evil being **:** devil. **2.** A persistently vexatious person, force, or drive. **3.** One who zealously undertakes an activity <a *demon* for work> **—de•mon'ic** (dĭ-mŏn'ĭk) *adj.* **—de•mon'i•cal•ly** *adv.*

de•mon•e•tize (dĭ-mŏn'ĭ-tīz', -mŭn'-) *v.* **1.** To divest (e.g., a unit of currency) of monetary value. **2.** To stop using (a metal) as a monetary standard.

de•mo•ni•ac (dĭ-mō'nē-ăk') *also* **de•mo•ni•a•cal** (dē'mə-nī'ə-kəl) *adj.* **1.** Arising or appearing to arise from possession by a demon. **2.** Of, resembling, or suggestive of a demon **:** fiendish.

de•mon•ize (dē'mə-nīz') *v.* **-ized, -iz•ing. 1.** To turn into or as if into a demon. **2.** To represent as evil. **—de'mon•i•za'tion** *n.*

de•mon•ol•o•gy (dē'mə-nŏl'ə-jē) *n.* The study of or belief in demons.

de•mon•stra•ble (dĭ-mŏn'strə-bəl) *adj.* **1.** Capable of being demonstrated. **2.** Obvious or apparent. **—de•mon'stra•bil'i•ty** *n.* **—de•mon'stra•bly** *adv.*

dem•on•strate (dĕm'ən-strāt') *v.* **-strat•ed, -strat•ing. 1.** To prove or show by evidence or reasoning. **2.** To show or reveal <*demonstrates* talent> **3.** To explain, esp. by using examples. **4.** To make a public protest <students *demonstrating* against nuclear weapons> **—dem'on•stra'tion** *n.* **—dem'on•stra'tor** *n.*

de•mon•stra•tive (dĭ-mŏn'strə-tĭv) *adj.* **1.** Serving to manifest or prove. **2.** Involving or marked by demonstration. **3.** Given to or marked by the open expression of emotion, esp. affection. **4.** Specifying the person or thing referred to <a *demonstrative* pronoun> —*n.* A demonstrative adjective or pronoun. **—de•mon'stra•tive•ly** *adv.* **—de•mon'stra•tive•ness** *n.*

de•mor•al•ize (dĭ-môr'ə-līz', -mŏr'-) *v.* **1.** To undermine the confidence or morale of **:** discourage. **2.** To corrupt **:** degrade. **—de•mor'al•i•za'tion** *n.* **—de•mor'al•iz'er** *n.*

de•mote (dĭ-mōt') *v.* **-mot•ed, -mot•ing.** To reduce in grade, rank, or position. **—de•mo'tion** *n.*

de•mul•cent (dĭ-mŭl'sənt) *adj.* Soothing. —*n.* A soothing ointment used esp. on irritated mucous surfaces.

de•mur (dĭ-mûr') *v.* **-murred, -mur•ring.** To take issue **:** object. **—de•mur'ral** *n.*

de•mure (dĭ-myŏŏr') *adj.* **-mur•er, -mur•est. 1.** Modest and reserved. **2.** Feigning modesty **:** coy. **—de•mure'ly** *adv.*

de•mur•rer (dĭ-mûr'ər, -mŭr'-) *n. Law.* A plea to dismiss a lawsuit on the grounds that the plaintiff's statements are insufficient to sustain the claim.

den (dĕn) *n.* **1.** A wild animal's shelter **:** lair. **2.** A small and esp. squalid abode. **3.** A small, private room for relaxation or study. **4.** A place in which a secret or illicit activity is carried on <an opium *den*>

de•na•ture (dē-nā'chər) *v.* **-tured, -tur•ing.** To change the nature or natural qualities of, esp. to make unfit for consumption. **—de•na'tur•ant** *n.* **—de•na'tur•a'tion** *n.*

den•drite (dĕn'drīt') *n.* The branching portion of a nerve cell that carries impulses toward the cell body.

den•drol•o•gy (dĕn-drŏl'ə-jē) *n.* The botanical study of trees.

den•gue (dĕng'gē, -gā') *n.* An infectious tropical disease transmitted by mosquitoes, characterized by fever and severe joint pains.

de•ni•al (dĭ-nī'əl) *n.* **1.** A refusal to comply with a request. **2.** A refusal to acknowledge the truth of a statement. **3.** A repudiation **:** disavowal. **4.** Self-denial **:** abstinence.

den•ier (dĕn'yər) *n.* A measure of fineness for nylon, rayon, and silk yarns.

den•i•grate (dĕn'ĭ-grāt') *v.* **-grat•ed, -grat•ing.** To defame **:** slander.

den•im (dĕn'əm) *n.* **1.** A coarse twilled cloth used for jeans, overalls, and work clothes. **2. denims.** Denim garments.

den•i•zen (dĕn'ĭ-zən) *n.* **1.** An inhabitant. **2.** A habitué.

de•nom•i•nate (dĭ-nŏm'ə-nāt') *v.* To give a name to **:** designate.

de•nom•i•na•tion (dĭ-nŏm'ə-nā'shən) *n.* **1.** The act of naming. **2.** The name of a class or group **:** classification. **3.** A class of units having specified values, as in a system of currency or weights. **4.** An organized body of similar religious congregations. **—de•nom'i•na'tion•al** *adj.*

de•nom•i•na•tor (dĭ-nŏm'ə-nā'tər) *n.* **1.** The numeral below the line in a fraction. **2.** A common trait or characteristic.

de•note (dĭ-nōt') *v.* **-not•ed, -not•ing. 1.** To indicate or reveal **:** mark. **2.** To serve as a name or symbol for **:** signify. **3.** To refer to specifically **:** mean explicitly. **—de'no•ta'tion** *n.* **—de•no'ta•tive** *adj.*

dé•noue•ment *also* **de•noue•ment** (dā'nōō-mäN') *n.* The outcome of the plot of a literary work, as a play or novel.

de•nounce (dĭ-nouns') *v.* **-nounced, -nounc•ing. 1.** To condemn openly, esp. as evil **:** censure. **2.** To accuse officially or formally. **3.** To announce formally the ending of (e.g., a treaty). **—de•nounc'er** *n.*

dense (dĕns) *adj.* **dens•er, dens•est. 1.** Crowded closely together **:** compact. **2.** Thick or impenetrable <*dense* smoke> **3.** Slow to understand **:** stupid. **—dense'ly** *adv.* **—dense'ness** *n.*

den•si•ty (dĕn'sĭ-tē) *n., pl.* **-ties. 1.** The quality or state of being dense. **2.** The amount or quantity of something per unit measure, as of length, area, or volume.

dent (dĕnt) *n.* **1.** A small surface depression made by pressure or a blow. **2.** Meaningful progress **:** headway. **—dent** *v.*

den•tal (dĕn'tl) *adj.* Of or relating to the teeth or to dentistry.

dental floss *n.* A strong thread used to clean between teeth.

dental hygienist *n.* A licensed dental professional who provides preventive dental services, as cleaning.

den•ti•frice (dĕn'tə-frĭs) *n.* A paste or powder for cleaning the teeth.

den•tine (dĕn'tēn', dĕn-tēn') *also* **den•tin** (dĕn'tĭn) *n.* The calcareous part of a tooth, beneath the enamel, containing the pulp chamber and root canals.

den•tist (dĕn'tĭst) *n.* Someone whose profession is the diagnosis, treatment, and prevention of diseases of the teeth and gums. **—den'tist•ry** *n.*

den•ti•tion (dĕn-tĭsh'ən) *n.* The kind, number, and arrangement of teeth, as in a human being.

den•ture (dĕn'chər) *n.* A set of artificial teeth.

de•nude (dĭ-nōōd', -nyōōd') *v.* **-nud•ed, -nud•ing.** To remove all covering from. **—den'u•da'tion** (dĕn'yōō-dā'shən) *n.*

de•nun•ci•a•tion (dĭ-nŭn'sē-ā'shən, -shē-) *n.* The act of denouncing, esp. a public censure.

de•ny (dĭ-nī') *v.* **-nied, -ny•ing. 1.** To contradict or declare untrue. **2.** To reject as untrue. **3.** To refuse to acknowledge or recognize. **4.** To refuse to grant **:** withhold.

de•o•dor•ant (dē-ō'dər-ənt) *n.* A substance used to prevent, mask, or destroy unpleasant odors.

de•o•dor•ize (dē-ō'də-rīz') *v.* **-ized, -iz•ing.** To disguise or absorb the odor of. **—de•o'dor•iz'er** *n.*

de•ox•y•ri•bo•nu•cle•ic acid (dē-ŏk'sē-rī'bō-nōō-klē'ĭk, -nyōō-) *n.* DNA.

de•part (dĭ-pärt') *v.* **1.** To go away (from) **:** leave. **2.** To deviate. **3.** To die.

de•part•ment (dĭ-pärt′mənt) *n.* **1.** A specialized division of a large organization, as a government, business, or college. **2.** *Informal.* A sphere of special knowledge or activity. —**de′part•men′tal** *adj.*

de•part•men•tal•ize (dē′pärt-mĕn′tl-īz′) *v.* **-ized, -iz•ing.** To organize into departments. —**de′part•men′tal•i•za′tion** *n.*

department store *n.* A retail store organized into departments and offering a wide variety of goods.

de•par•ture (dĭ-pär′chər) *n.* **1.** The act of going away. **2.** The act of starting out, as on a trip or a new course of action. **3.** A divergence : deviation.

de•pend (dĭ-pĕnd′) *v.* **1.** To place trust : rely. **2.** To be determined, contingent, or dependent. **3.** To hang down.

de•pend•a•ble (dĭ-pĕn′də-bəl) *adj.* Capable of being depended on : reliable. —**de•pend′a•bil′i•ty** *n.*

de•pend•ence *also* **de•pend•ance** (dĭ-pĕn′dəns) *n.* **1.** The state or quality of being dependent. **2.** The state of being influenced, determined, or controlled by something else. **3.** Trust : reliance.

de•pend•en•cy *also* **de•pend•an•cy** (dĭ-pĕn′dən-sē) *n., pl.* **-cies. 1.** Dependence. **2.** A territory under the authority and control of another country from which it is geographically separated.

de•pend•ent *also* **de•pend•ant** (dĭ-pĕn′dənt) *adj.* **1.** Determined by or contingent on something or someone else. **2.** Subordinate. **3.** Depending on or needing the aid of another for support. **4.** Hanging down. —*n.* One, as a child, who relies on another for support. —**de•pend′ent•ly** *adv.*

de•pict (dĭ-pĭkt′) *v.* **1.** To represent in a picture or sculpture. **2.** To represent in words : describe. —**de•pic′tion** *n.*

de•pil•a•to•ry (dĭ-pĭl′ə-tôr′ē, -tōr′ē) *n., pl.* **-ries.** A cream or liquid used to remove unwanted body hair.

de•plane (dē-plān′) *v.* To disembark from an aircraft.

de•plete (dĭ-plēt′) *v.* **-plet•ed, -plet•ing.** To use up, empty, or exhaust. —**de•ple′tion** *n.*

de•plor•a•ble (dĭ-plôr′ə-bəl, -plōr′-) *adj.* **1.** Grievous : lamentable. **2.** Very bad : wretched. —**de•plor′a•bly** *adv.*

de•plore (dĭ-plôr′, -plōr′) *v.* **-plored, -plor•ing. 1.** To express or feel great disapproval of : censure. **2.** To express or feel great regret about.

de•ploy (dĭ-ploi′) *v.* To spread out (e.g., troops) to form an extended front. —**de•ploy′ment** *n.*

de•po•lar•ize (dē-pō′lə-rīz′) *v.* To counteract or eliminate the polarization of.

de•po•lit•i•cize (dē′pə-lĭt′ĭ-sīz′) *v.* To remove the political aspect or status from.

de•po•nent (dĭ-pō′nənt) *n.* A person who testifies under oath, esp. in writing.

de•pop•u•late (dē-pŏp′yə-lāt′) *v.* To lower greatly the population of, as by disease or massacre. —**de•pop′u•la′tion** *n.*

de•port (dĭ-pôrt′, -pōrt′) *v.* **1.** To banish from a country. **2.** To behave or conduct (oneself) in a specified manner. —**de′por•ta′tion** *n.* —**de′port•ee′** *n.*

de•port•ment (dĭ-pôrt′mənt, -pōrt′-) *n.* Behavior : demeanor.

de•pose (dĭ-pōz′) *v.* **-posed, -posing. 1.** To remove from office or a powerful position. **2.** To testify under oath, esp. in writing. —**de•pos′a•ble** *adj.* —**de•pos′al** *n.*

de•pos•it (dĭ-pŏz′ĭt) *v.* **1.** To entrust (money) to a bank. **2.** To set or lay down : place. **3.** To put down (e.g., layers of sediment) by a natural process. **4.** To give as partial payment or security. —**de•pos′it** *n.* —**de•pos′i•tor** *n.*

dep•o•si•tion (dĕp′ə-zĭsh′ən) *n.* **1.** The act of deposing, as from office. **2.** The act of depositing. **3.** Testimony given under oath, esp. in writing. **4.** A deposit.

de•pos•i•to•ry (dĭ-pŏz′ĭ-tôr′ē, -tōr′ē) *n., pl.* **-ries.** A place where something is deposited for safekeeping : repository.

de•pot (dē′pō) *n.* **1.** A station. **2.** A warehouse. **3.** A place where military materials are stored or troops are assembled.

de•prave (dĭ-prāv′) *v.* **-praved, -prav•ing.** To debase morally : corrupt. —**de•praved′** *adj.* —**de•prav′i•ty** (-prăv′ĭ-tē) *n.*

dep•re•cate (dĕp′rĭ-kāt′) *v.* **-cat•ed, -cat•ing. 1.** To show disapproval of. **2.** To belittle : depreciate. —**dep′re•ca′tion** *n.* —**dep′re•ca′tor** *n.* —**dep′re•ca•to′ry** *adj.*

de•pre•ci•ate (dĭ-prē′shē-āt′) *v.* **-at•ed, -at•ing. 1.** To diminish or become diminished in value or price. **2.** To disparage. ★ ***syns:*** CHEAPEN, DEVALUATE, DEVALUE, DOWNGRADE, LOWER —**de•pre′ci•a′tion** *n.* —**de•pre′cia•to′ry** *adj.*

dep•re•da•tion (dĕp′rĭ-dā′shən) *n.* The act of destroying or marauding.

de•press (dĭ-prĕs′) *v.* **1.** To lower in spirits : sadden. **2.** To press down : lower. **3.** To diminish in price or value. **4.** To diminish the activity or force of. —**de•pres′sor** *n.*

de•pres•sant (dĭ-prĕs′ənt) *adj.* Serving to lower the rate of vital physiological activities. —*n.* A depressant agent : sedative.

de•pressed (dĭ-prĕst′) *adj.* **1.** Low in spirits : dejected. **2.** Suffering from psychological depression. **3.** Suffering from social and economic hardship. ★ ***syns:*** BACKWARD, DISADVANTAGED, IMPOVERISHED, UNDERPRIVILEGED.

de•pres•sion (dĭ-prĕsh′ən) *n.* **1.** The act of depressing or state of being depressed. **2.** An emotional disorder characterized by an inability to concentrate, insomnia, and feelings of guilt and dejection. **3.** A sunken or depressed area : hollow. **4.** A period of severe economic decline. —**de•pres′sive** *adj.*

de•pres•sur•ize (dē-prĕsh′ə-rīz′) *v.* **-ized, -iz•ing.** To release from pressure. —**de•pres′sur•i•za′tion** *n.*

de•prive (dĭ-prīv′) *v.* **-prived, -priv•ing. 1.** To take something away from. **2.** To keep from possessing or enjoying : deny. —**dep′ri•va′tion** (dĕp′rə-vā′shən) *n.*

depth (dĕpth) *n.* **1.** The quality or state of being deep. **2.** The extent, measurement, or dimension downward, inward, or backward. **3.** *often* **depths.** A deep part or place. **4.** The most profound or extreme stage or part. **5.** Mental complexity : profundity. **6.** The range of one's comprehension.

depth charge *n.* An explosive device designed to detonate underwater.

dep•u•ta•tion (dĕp'yə-tā'shən) *n.* **1.** DELEGATION 2. **2.** The act of deputing or the state of being deputed.

de•pute (dĭ-pyōōt') *v.* **-put•ed, -put•ing.** To delegate.

dep•u•tize (dĕp'yə-tīz') *v.* **-tized, -tiz•ing.** To appoint as a deputy.

dep•u•ty (dĕp'yə-tē) *n., pl.* **-ties. 1.** A person designated or authorized to act for or assist another. **2.** A representative in a legislative body in certain countries.

de•rail (dē-rāl') *v.* To run or cause to run off the rails. **—de•rail'ment** *n.*

de•rail•leur (dĭ-rā'lər) *n.* A device for shifting gears on a bicycle by moving the chain between sprocket wheels of different sizes.

derailleur

de•range (dĭ-rānj') *v.* **-ranged, -rang•ing. 1.** To disturb the arrangement or normal condition of : disarrange. **2.** To make insane. **—de•range'ment** *n.*

der•by (dûr'bē; *Brit.* där'-) *n., pl.* **-bies. 1.** One of various annual horse races, esp. for 3-year-olds. **2.** A race open to all contestants. **3.** A stiff felt hat with a round crown and narrow, curved brim.

der•e•lict (dĕr'ə-lĭkt) *adj.* **1.** Negligent : remiss. **2.** Abandoned by an owner or guardian. *—n.* **1.** Abandoned property, esp. a ship abandoned at sea. **2.** A vagrant.

der•e•lic•tion (dĕr'ə-lĭk'shən) *n.* **1.** Willful neglect, as of responsibility. **2.** Abandonment.

de•ride (dĭ-rīd') *v.* **-rid•ed, -rid•ing.** To laugh at or ridicule contemptuously. **—de•ri'sion** (-rĭzh'ən) *n.* **—de•ri'sive** *adj.* **—de•ri'sive•ly** *adv.* **—di•ri'so•ry** *adj.*

de ri•gueur (də rē-gûr') *adj.* Required or prescribed by custom, manners, or fashion : socially obligatory.

der•i•va•tion (dĕr'ə-vā'shən) *n.* **1.** The act or process of deriving. **2.** The source of something : origin. **3.** Etymology. **4.** The process by which new words are formed from existing words, chiefly by the addition of affixes to roots, stems, or words.

de•riv•a•tive (dĭ-rĭv'ə-tĭv) *adj.* Obtained by derivation. *—n.* **1.** Something derived. **2.** A word formed by derivation.

de•rive (dĭ-rīv') *v.* **-rived, -riv•ing. 1.** To obtain or receive from a source. **2.** To arrive at by reasoning : deduce. **3.** To trace the development or origin of (e.g., a word). **4.** To produce (a compound) from other substances by chemical reaction.

der•mal (dûr'məl) *also* **der•mic** (-mĭk) *adj.* Of or relating to the skin.

der•ma•ti•tis (dûr'mə-tī'tĭs) *n.* Skin inflammation.

der•ma•tol•o•gy (dûr'mə-tŏl'ə-jē) *n.* The medical study of skin physiology and pathology. **—der'ma•tol'o•gist** *n.*

der•o•gate (dĕr'ə-gāt') *v.* **-gat•ed, -gat•ing. 1.** To take away : detract. **2.** To disparage. **—der'o•ga'tion** *n.*

de•rog•a•to•ry (dĭ-rŏg'ə-tôr'ē, -tōr'ē) *adj.* **1.** Tending to belittle : disparaging. **2.** Detracting. **—de•rog'a•to'ri•ly** *adv.*

der•rick (dĕr'ĭk) *n.* **1.** A machine for lifting and moving heavy objects : crane. **2.** A framework over a drilled hole, as an oil well, used to support boring equipment.

der•ri•ère *also* **der•ri•ere** (dĕr'ē-âr') *n.* The buttocks.

der•ring-do (dĕr'ĭng-dōō') *n.* Daring action or spirit : daring.

der•rin•ger (dĕr'ĭn-jər) *n.* A short-barreled, pocket-sized pistol.

der•vish (dûr'vĭsh) *n.* A member of a Muslim religious order that engages in whirling dances and ecstatic devotion.

DES (dē'ē-ĕs') *n.* Diethylstilbestrol.

de•sal•i•nate (dē-săl'ə-nāt') *v.* **-nat•ed, -nat•ing.** To desalinize.

de•sal•i•nize (dē-săl'ə-nīz') *v.* **-nized, -niz•ing.** To remove (salt) from sea or saline water. **—de•sal'i•ni•za'tion** *n.*

de•salt (dē-sôlt') *v.* To desalinize.

des•cant (dĕs'kănt') *v.* **1.** To discourse at length. **2.** To play or sing part music.

de•scend (dĭ-sĕnd') *v.* **1.** To move, come, or go from a higher to a lower level. **2.** To slope. **3. a.** To come down from a source : derive. **b.** To pass through inheritance. **4.** To arrive or attack suddenly.

de•scen•dant (dĭ-sĕn'dənt) *n.* **1.** An individual descended from another. **2.** Something derived from an earlier form or prototype. ★ *syns:* CHILD, OFFSPRING, SCION *—adj. var. of* DESCENDENT.

de•scen•dent *also* **de•scen•dant** (dĭ-sĕn'dənt) *adj.* **1.** Moving downward : descending. **2.** Descending from an ancestor.

de•scent (dĭ-sĕnt') *n.* **1.** The act or an instance of descending. **2.** A slope. **3.** Ancestry. **4.** A lowering or decline, as in status or level. **5.** A sudden onslaught.

de•scram•ble (dē-skrăm'bəl) *v.* **-bled, -bling.** To decode.

de•scribe (dĭ-skrīb') *v.* **-scribed, -scrib•ing.**

1. To give an account of in words. 2. To trace or draw the outline of (e.g., a circle). ★ *syns:* NARRATE, RECITE, RECOUNT, RELATE, REPORT —**de•scrib'a•ble** *adj.* —**de•scrib'er** *n.*

de•scrip•tion (dĭ-skrĭp'shən) *n.* **1.** The act, process, or technique of describing. **2.** A statement or account that describes. **3.** A kind : type. —**de•scrip'tive** *adj.*

de•scry (dĭ-skrī') *v.* **-scried, -scry•ing. 1.** To catch sight of : discern. **2.** To discover by investigation or close observation. —**de•scri'er** *n.*

des•e•crate (dĕs'ĭ-krāt') *v.* **-crat•ed, -crat•ing.** To violate the sanctity of : profane. —**des'e•cra'tion** *n.*

de•seg•re•gate (dē-sĕg'rĭ-gāt') *v.* To abolish segregation, esp. racial segregation, in. —**de•seg're•ga'tion** *n.*

de•sen•si•tize (dē-sĕn'sĭ-tīz') *v.* To make insensitive or less sensitive, as to pain. —**de•sen'si•tiz'er** *n.*

des•ert¹ (dĕz'ərt) *n.* A dry, barren region that can support little or no vegetation.

de•sert² (dĭ-zûrt') *n.* **1.** *often* **deserts.** Something, esp. a punishment, that is warranted or merited. **2.** The fact or state of deserving reward or punishment.

de•sert³ (dĭ-zûrt') *v.* **1.** To abandon, esp. when most needed. **2.** To abandon (e.g., a military post) in violation of orders. —**de•sert'er** *n.* —**de•ser'tion** *n.*

de•sert•i•fi•ca•tion (dĭ-zûr'tə-fĭ-kā'shən) *n.* The transformation of arable or habitable land to desert.

de•serve (dĭ-zûrv') *v.* **-served, -serv•ing.** To be worthy of : merit.

des•ic•cant (dĕs'ĭ-kənt) *n.* An agent, as silica gel, used to absorb moisture.

des•ic•cate (dĕs'ĭ-kāt') *v.* **-cat•ed, -cat•ing.** To dry out completely : dehydrate. —**des'ic•ca'tion** *n.* —**des'ic•ca'tive** *adj.*

de•sid•er•a•tum (dĭ-sĭd'ə-rä'təm, -rā'-) *n., pl.* **-ta** (-tə). A necessary and desired thing.

de•sign (dĭ-zīn') *v.* **1.** To think up : invent. **2.** To form a plan for <*design* a new marketing strategy> **3.** To have as a goal or intention. **4.** To plan by making preliminary sketches or outlines. —*n.* **1.** A drawing or sketch. **2.** The order or arrangement of the components and details of something in accordance with a plan. **3. a.** A decorative or artistic work. **b.** The art of creating designs. **4.** A plan : project. **5.** A well-thought-out purpose : intention. ★ *syns:* BLUEPRINT, IDEA, LAYOUT, PLAN, SCHEMA, SCHEME, STRATEGY —**de•sign'ed•ly** *adv.* —**de•sign'er** *n.*

des•ig•nate (dĕz'ĭg-nāt') *v.* **-nat•ed, -nat•ing. 1.** To point out : specify. **2.** To give a name or title to : characterize. **3.** To appoint or select, as for an office. —**des'ig•nate** (-nĭt) *adj.* —**des'ig•na'tion** *n.*

de•sign•ing (dĭ-zī'nĭng) *adj.* Crafty : conniving. —**de•sign'ing•ly** *adv.*

de•sir•a•ble (dĭ-zīr'ə-bəl) *adj.* **1.** Attractive, pleasing, or valuable. **2.** Worth wanting : advisable <a *desirable* tax reform> —**de•sir'a•bil'i•ty, de•sir'a•ble•ness** *n.*

de•sire (dĭ-zīr') *v.* **-sired, -sir•ing. 1.** To hope or wish for ardently : crave. **2.** To ask for : request. ★ *syns:* ACHE, CRAVE, HANKER, LONG, WISH, YEARN —*n.* **1.** A strong wish or longing : craving. **2.** A request or petition. **3.** Something desired. **4.** Sexual appetite : passion. —**de•sir'er** *n.*

de•sir•ous (dĭ-zīr'əs) *adj.* Desiring.

de•sist (dĭ-zĭst', -sĭst') *v.* To cease doing something : stop.

desk (dĕsk) *n.* **1.** A piece of furniture usu. with drawers or compartments and a level top for writing. **2.** A table, counter, or booth where specified services are performed. **3.** A department of a large organization in charge of a specified operation.

desk•top (dĕsk'tŏp') *adj.* **1.** Designed for use on a desk. **2.** Small enough to fit conveniently in an individual workspace.

desktop publishing *n. Computer Sci.* The design and production of publications, such as newsletters, using microcomputers with graphics capability.

des•o•late (dĕs'ə-lĭt) *adj.* **1.** Having no inhabitants : deserted. **2.** Made uninhabitable or useless. **3.** Dismal : dreary. **4.** Forlorn : forsaken. —*v.* (-lāt') **-lat•ed, -lat•ing.** To make desolate. —**des'o•late•ly** *adv.*

des•o•la•tion (dĕs'ə-lā'shən) *n.* **1.** The act of desolating. **2.** The state of being desolate : devastation. **3.** A wasteland. **4.** Loneliness or sadness : misery.

de•spair (dĭ-spâr') *n.* **1.** Complete absence of hope. **2.** Something destroying all hope. —*v.* To abandon all purpose or hope.

des•patch (dĭ-spăch') *n.* & *v. var. of* DISPATCH.

des•per•a•do (dĕs'pə-rä'dō, -rā'-) *n., pl.* **-does** *or* **-dos.** A brazen, dangerous outlaw or criminal.

des•per•ate (dĕs'pər-ĭt, -prĭt) *adj.* **1.** Rash or violent out of despair. **2.** Almost hopeless : grave. **3.** Overpowering : intense.

des•per•a•tion (dĕs'pə-rā'shən) *n.* **1.** The state of being desperate. **2.** Rashness arising out of despair.

des•pi•ca•ble (dĕs'pĭ-kə-bəl, dĭ-spĭk'ə-) *adj.* Deserving scorn or contempt : vile. —**des'pi•ca•bly** *adv.*

de•spise (dĭ-spīz') *v.* **-spised, -spis•ing. 1.** To regard with scorn or contempt : disdain. **2.** To regard as trivial or worthless. ★ *syns:* ABHOR, CONTEMN, DISDAIN, SCORN

de•spite (dĭ-spīt') *prep.* In spite of : notwithstanding.

de•spoil (dĭ-spoil') *v.* To strip of property or possessions by force : pillage. —**de•spoil'er** *n.* —**de•spoil'ment** *n.*

de•spo•li•a•tion (dĭ-spō'lē-ā'shən) *n.* The act of despoiling or the state of being despoiled.

de•spond (dĭ-spŏnd') *v.* To become discouraged. —*n.* A state of despondency.

de•spon•den•cy (dĭ-spŏn'dən-sē) *n.* Depression of spirits from loss of hope. —**de•spon'dent** *adj.*

des•pot (dĕs'pət) *n.* **1.** An absolute ruler. **2.** A person who wields power oppressively.

—**des•pot'ic** (dĭ-spŏt'ĭk) *adj.* —**des•pot'i•cal•ly** *adv.* —**des'pot•ism** *n.*

des•sert (dĭ-zûrt') *n.* A usu. sweet food, as pastry, served as the final course of a meal.

des•ti•na•tion (dĕs'tə-nā'shən) *n.* **1.** The place to which someone is going or something is sent. **2.** The purpose for which something is created or intended.

des•tine (dĕs'tĭn) *v.* **-tined, -tin•ing. 1.** To determine in advance : preordain. **2.** To assign for a specific end, use, or purpose. **3.** To be bound for a specified destination.

des•ti•ny (dĕs'tə-nē) *n., pl.* **-nies. 1.** The inevitable lot to which a person or thing is destined : fate. **2.** A predetermined or inevitable course of events.

des•ti•tute (dĕs'tĭ-to͞ot', -tyo͞ot') *adj.* **1.** Utterly devoid. **2.** Utterly impoverished : indigent. —**des'ti•tu'tion** *n.*

de•stroy (dĭ-stroi') *v.* **1.** To ruin thoroughly : spoil. **2.** To tear down or break up : raze. **3.** To kill.

de•stroy•er (dĭ-stroi'ər) *n.* **1.** One that destroys. **2.** A small, highly maneuverable warship.

de•struct (dĭ-strŭkt') *n.* The deliberate destruction of a space vehicle, missile, or rocket after launching.

de•struc•ti•ble (dĭ-strŭk'tə-bəl) *adj.* Capable of being destroyed.

de•struc•tion (dĭ-strŭk'shən) *n.* **1.** The act of destroying or the state of being destroyed. **2.** A cause or means of destroying. —**de•struc'tive** *adj.* —**de•struc'tive•ly** *adv.* —**de•struc'tive•ness** *n.*

des•ue•tude (dĕs'wĭ-to͞od', -tyo͞od') *n.* A state of disuse.

des•ul•to•ry (dĕs'əl-tôr'ē, -tōr'ē) *adj.* **1.** Marked by lack of continuity : disconnected. **2.** Aimless.

de•tach (dĭ-tăch') *v.* **1.** To disconnect : separate. **2.** To extricate oneself : withdraw. ★ ***syns:*** DISCONNECT, DISENGAGE, UNCOUPLE, UNFASTEN —**de•tach'a•ble** *adj.*

de•tached (dĭ-tăcht') *adj.* **1.** Standing apart : separate. **2.** Not emotionally involved : indifferent. **3.** Impartial.

de•tach•ment (dĭ-tăch'mənt) *n.* **1. a.** The act or process of separating. **b.** The state of being separate. **2.** Indifference : aloofness. **3.** Impartiality. **4. a.** The dispatch of military personnel or equipment from a larger unit for special duty. **b.** A permanent military unit, usu. smaller than a platoon, organized for special duties.

de•tail (dĭ-tāl', dē'tāl') *n.* **1.** An individual part : particular. **2.** Particulars considered separately and in relation to a whole. **3.** Military personnel selected for a particular duty. —*v.* **1.** To report in detail. **2.** To name or state explicitly. **3.** To select and dispatch for a particular duty.

de•tain (dĭ-tān') *v.* **1.** To hold back : delay. **2.** To hold in custody : confine.

de•tect (dĭ-tĕkt') *v.* To find out or discover the nature, existence, or fact of. —**de•tect'a•ble, de•tect'i•ble** *adj.* —**de•tec'tion** *n.* —**de•tec'tor** *n.*

de•tec•tive (dĭ-tĕk'tĭv) *n.* A person, often a police officer, whose work is investigating and trying to solve crimes.

de•tent (dĭ-tĕnt') *n.* A pawl.

dé•tente (dā-täɴt', -tänt') *n.* A relaxation or reduction of tension, as between nations.

de•ten•tion (dĭ-tĕn'shən) *n.* **1.** The act of detaining or state of being detained. **2.** A period of temporary custody that precedes disposition by a court. **3.** A forced delay.

de•ter (dĭ-tûr') *v.* **-terred, -ter•ring.** To discourage or prevent from acting, as by intimidation. —**de•ter'ment** *n.*

de•ter•gent (dĭ-tûr'jənt) *n.* Any of various usu. synthetic cleaning agents that are chemically different from soap.

de•te•ri•o•rate (dĭ-tîr'ē-ə-rāt') *v.* **-rat•ed, -rat•ing.** To worsen : degenerate.

de•ter•mi•nant (dĭ-tûr'mə-nənt) *n.* Something that influences or determines.

de•ter•mi•nate (dĭ-tûr'mə-nĭt) *adj.* **1.** Precisely defined. **2.** Conclusively settled.

de•ter•mine (dĭ-tûr'mĭn) *v.* **-mined, -min•ing. 1.** To decide or settle authoritatively or conclusively. **2.** To limit in scope or extent : fix the limits of. **3.** To be the determinant of : regulate <Need will *determine* expenditures.> **4.** To reach a decision, as after consideration or calculation. **5.** To ascertain the extent, position, quality, or nature of something. ★ ***syns:*** BOUND, DELIMIT, DEMARCATE, LIMIT —**de•ter'mi•na•ble** *adj.* —**de•ter'mi•na•bly** *adv.* —**de•ter'mi•na'tion** *n.*

de•ter•mined (dĭ-tûr'mĭnd) *adj.* **1.** Firm : resolute. **2.** Decided or resolved. —**de•ter'mined•ly** *adv.*

de•ter•rent (dĭ-tûr'ənt, -tŭr'-) *n.* Something that deters. —*adj.* Serving to deter. —**de•ter'rence** *n.*

de•test (dĭ-tĕst') *v.* To dislike strongly : abhor. —**de•test'a•ble** *adj.* —**de•test'a•bly** *adv.* —**de'tes•ta'tion** *n.*

de•throne (dē-thrōn') *v.* **-throned, -thron•ing.** To depose (e.g., a king).

det•o•nate (dĕt'n-āt') *v.* **-nat•ed, -nat•ing.** To explode violently.

det•o•na•tor (dĕt'n-ā'tər) *n.* A device, as a fuse or percussion cap, used to detonate an explosive.

de•tour (dē'to͝or', dĭ-to͝or') *n.* **1.** A road used temporarily instead of a main road. **2.** A deviation from a direct course of action. —*v.* To take or cause to take a detour.

de•tox (dē-tŏks') *Informal. v.* To detoxify. —*n.* (dē'tŏks'). A place where patients are detoxified.

de•tox•i•fy (dē-tŏk'sə-fī') *v.* **-fied, -fy•ing. 1.** To remove poison or the effects of a poison from. **2.** To treat (a person) for alcohol or drug dependence. —**de•tox'i•fi•ca'tion** *n.*

de•tract (dĭ-trăkt') *v.* **1.** To take away : diminish. **2.** To distract. —**de•trac'tion** *n.* —**de•trac'tive** *adj.* —**de•trac'tor** *n.*

de•train (dē-trān') *v.* To leave or cause to leave a railroad train.

det•ri•ment (dĕt'rə-mənt) *n.* **1.** Damage, injury, or loss. **2.** Something that causes damage, injury, or loss. **—det'ri•men'tal** *adj.* **—det'ri•men'tal•ly** *adv.*

de•tri•tus (dĭ-trī'təs) *n.* **1.** Loose fragments, esp. those formed by the disintegration of rocks. **2.** Debris.

deuce[1] (do͞os, dyo͞os) *n.* **1.** A playing card or side of a die with 2 figures or spots. **2.** A tie in which each side has 40 points.

deuce[2] (do͞os, dyo͞os) *n.* The devil. —Used as a mild oath.

de•us ex ma•chi•na (dā'əs ĕks mä'kə-nə, -nä', măk'ə-nə) *n.* A character, device, or event suddenly introduced into a literary work to resolve a difficulty.

deu•te•ri•um (do͞o-tîr'ē-əm, dyo͞o-) *n.* An isotope of hydrogen that contains one more neutron in its nucleus than hydrogen does.

Deu•ter•on•o•my (do͞o'tə-rŏn'ə-mē, dyo͞o'-) *n.* —See table at BIBLE.

deut•sche mark (doi'chə märk') *n.* —See table at CURRENCY.

de•val•u•ate (dē-văl'yo͞o-āt') *v.* **-at•ed, -at•ing. 1.** To lessen or annul the value of. **2.** To lower the exchange value of (currency) by lowering its gold equivalency. **—de•val'u•a'tion** *n.*

de•val•ue (dē-văl'yo͞o) *v.* To devaluate.

dev•as•tate (dĕv'ə-stāt') *v.* **-tat•ed, -tat•ing. 1.** To destroy **:** ruin. **2.** To overwhelm **:** overpower. **—dev'as•ta'tion** *n.*

de•vel•op (dĭ-vĕl'əp) *v.* **1.** To realize the possibilities of. **2.** To grow, unfold, or expand gradually. **3.** To make more available or effective. **4.** To elaborate or enlarge. **5.** To acquire gradually. **6.** To process (a photosensitive material) to make the latent image visible. **7.** To progress from earlier to later stages of maturation. **—de•vel'op•er** *n.* **—de•vel'op•ment** *n.* **—de•vel'op•men'tal** *adj.*

de•vi•ant (dē'vē-ənt) *adj.* Deviating from a norm, esp. from an accepted standard. **—de'vi•ance** *n.* **—de'vi•ant** *n.*

de•vi•ate (dē'vē-āt') *v.* **-at•ed, -at•ing.** To turn or cause to turn away from a specified course or prescribed behavior. —*n.* (-ĭt). A deviant person. **—de'vi•a'tion** *n.*

de•vice (dĭ-vīs') *n.* **1.** Something constructed for a specific purpose, esp. a machine. **2.** A plan or scheme **:** stratagem. **3.** An emblem or motto, esp. in heraldry.

dev•il (dĕv'əl) *n.* **1.** *often* **Devil.** The major spirit of evil, ruler of Hell, and foe of God **:** Satan. **2.** A subordinate evil spirit **:** demon. **3.** A wicked or malevolent person. **4.** A person **:** individual <you lucky *devil*> **5.** An energetic, daring, or clever person. **6.** A printer's apprentice. —*v.* **-iled, -il•ing** *or* **-illed, -il•ling. 1.** To annoy, torment, or harass. **2.** To season (food) highly.

dev•il•ish (dĕv'ə-lĭsh) *adj.* **1.** Of, resembling, or characteristic of a devil **:** fiendish. **2.** *Informal.* Extreme **:** excessive.

dev•il-may-care (dĕv'əl-mā-kâr') *adj.* **1.** Reckless. **2.** Rakish and carefree.

dev•il•ment (dĕv'əl-mənt) *n.* Mischief.

devil's advocate *n.* A person who opposes an argument with which he or she may not disagree, as for the sake of argument or to determine its validity.

dev•il•try (dĕv'əl-trē) *also* **dev•il•ry** (-əl-rē) *n., pl.* **-tries** *also* **-ries.** Wanton or reckless mischief.

de•vi•ous (dē'vē-əs) *adj.* **1.** Wandering from a direct or straight course. **2.** Straying from a proper way **:** erring. **3.** Not straightforward **:** shifty. **—de'vi•ous•ness** *n.*

de•vise (dĭ-vīz') *v.* **-vised, -vis•ing. 1.** To form or arrange mentally **:** contrive <*devise* a plan> **2.** *Law.* To give or transmit (real property) by will. —*n. Law.* **1.** The act of giving or transmitting real property by will. **2.** A will or clause in a will that devises real property.

de•vi•tal•ize (dē-vīt'l-īz') *v.* To reduce or destroy the vitality of.

de•void (dĭ-void') *adj.* Utterly lacking.

de•voir (dəv-wär', dĕv'wär') *n.* **1.** *often* **devoirs.** An act or expression of respect or courtesy **:** civility. **2.** Responsibility or duty.

de•volve (dĭ-vŏlv') *v.* **-volved, -volv•ing.** To hand down or delegate to another.

de•vote (dĭ-vōt') *v.* **-vot•ed, -vot•ing. 1.** To give or apply (one's time, attention, or self) completely. **2.** To consecrate **:** hallow. **3.** To set aside for a special use <money *devoted* to research>

de•vot•ed (dĭ-vō'tĭd) *adj.* **1.** Showing ardent attachment or loyalty. **2.** Affectionate. **—de•vot'ed•ly** *adv.*

dev•o•tee (dĕv'ə-tē', -tā') *n.* A zealous enthusiast or supporter.

de•vo•tion (dĭ-vō'shən) *n.* **1.** Ardent attachment or loyalty. **2.** Religious zeal **:** piety. **3.** *often* **devotions.** An act of religious observance, esp. private prayer.

de•vour (dĭ-vour') *v.* **1.** To eat up ravenously. **2.** To destroy or waste. **3.** To take in enthusiastically <*devour* a spy novel> **4.** To engulf. **—de•vour'er** *n.*

de•vout (dĭ-vout') *adj.* **1.** Extremely religious **:** pious. **2.** Displaying piety or reverence. **3.** Showing sincerity **:** earnest. **—de•vout'ly** *adv.* **—de•vout'ness** *n.*

dew (do͞o, dyo͞o) *n.* **1.** Moisture condensed from the atmosphere onto cool surfaces, usu. at night. **2.** Something moist, refreshing, or pure. **—dew'y** *adj.*

dew•ber•ry (do͞o'bĕr'ē, dyo͞o'-) *n.* A trailing form of the blackberry.

dew•claw (do͞o'klô', dyo͞o'-) *n.* A vestigial digit on the foot of some mammals.

dew•lap (do͞o'lăp', dyo͞o'-) *n.* A loose fold of skin that hangs from the neck of certain animals, as cattle.

dew point *n.* The temperature at which dew condenses from the air.

dex•ter•i•ty (dĕk-stĕr'ĭ-tē) *n.* **1.** Proficiency in using the body or hands **:** adroitness. **2.** Mental agility **:** cleverness.

dex•ter•ous (dĕk'stər-əs, -strəs) *also* **dex•trous** (-strəs) *adj.* **1.** Skillful or adroit in using the hands, body, or mind. **2.** Performed with dexterity. ★ ***syns:*** ADROIT, DEFT, FAC-

ILE, NIMBLE, SLICK —**dex′ter•ous•ly** *adv.* —**dex′ter•ous•ness** *n.*

dex•trose (dĕk′strōs′) *n.* A sugar found in plant and animal tissue and derived synthetically from starch.

di•a•be•tes (dī′ə-bē′tĭs, -tēz) *n.* Any of several metabolic disorders marked by excessive discharge of urine, esp. diabetes mellitus. —**di′a•bet′ic** (-bĕt′ĭk) *adj. & n.*

diabetes mel•li•tus (mə-lī′təs, mĕl′ĭ-) *n.* A chronic disease of pancreatic origin, marked by insulin deficiency, excess sugar in the blood and urine, weakness, and emaciation.

di•a•bol•ic (dī′ə-bŏl′ĭk) *also* **di•a•bol•i•cal** (-ĭ-kəl) *adj.* Exceedingly wicked : fiendish. —**di′a•bol′i•cal•ly** *adv.*

di•a•crit•ic (dī′ə-krĭt′ĭk) *n.* A mark, as a circumflex, added to a letter to indicate a special phonetic value or to distinguish words otherwise graphically identical. —**di′a•crit′i•cal, di′a•crit′ic** *adj.*

Di•a de la Ra•za (dē′ä dĕ lä rä′sä) *n.* Oct. 12, celebrated in many Spanish-speaking areas in honor of Christopher Columbus.

di•a•dem (dī′ə-dĕm′) *n.* A headband or crown worn esp. as an emblem of royalty.

di•aer•e•sis (dī-ĕr′ĭ-sĭs) *n. var. of* DIERESIS.

di•ag•no•sis (dī′əg-nō′sĭs) *n., pl.* **-ses** (-sēz′). **1.** Identification, as of a disease, by analysis and examination. **2.** The result of diagnosis. —**di′ag•nose′** *v.* —**di′ag•nos′tic** (-nŏs′tĭk) *adj.* —**di′ag•nos•ti′cian** *n.*

di•ag•o•nal (dī-ăg′ə-nəl) *adj.* **1.** *Math.* Joining 2 opposite corners of a polygon that are not adjacent. **2.** Slanting. —*n.* A diagonal plane or line. —**di•ag′o•nal•ly** *adv.*

di•a•gram (dī′ə-grăm′) *n.* A plan, sketch, drawing, or outline designed to explain, demonstrate, or clarify the relationship among parts of a whole or to illustrate how something works. —**di′a•gram′** *v.* —**di′a•gram•mat′ic** (-grə-măt′ĭk), **di′a•gram•mat′i•cal** *adj.* —**di′a•gram•mat′i•cal•ly** *adv.*

di•al (dī′əl) *n.* **1.** A graduated, usu. circular face on which a measurement, as speed, is indicated by a moving pointer. **2. a.** A rotatable disk with numbers and letters that electronically establishes a connection with the number to which a telephone call is made. **b.** The control that selects the station to which a radio or television receiver is tuned. **3. a.** A clock face. **b.** A sundial. —*v.* **-aled, -al•ing** *or* **-alled, -al•ling. 1.** To select or indicate by manipulating a dial. **2.** To call on a telephone.

di•a•lect (dī′ə-lĕkt′) *n.* A regional form of a language. —**di′a•lec′tal** *adj.*

di•a•lec•tic (dī′ə-lĕk′tĭk) *n. often* **dialectics** (*sing. in number*). A system of argument or exposition in which the conflict between contradictory facts or ideas is resolved. —**di′a•lec′ti•cal, di′a•lec′tic** *adj.*

di•a•logue *also* **di•a•log** (dī′ə-lôg′, -lŏg′) *n.* **1.** A conversation between 2 or more persons. **2.** A conversational passage in a literary work.

di•al•y•sis (dī-ăl′ĭ-sĭs) *n., pl.* **-ses** (-sēz′). Separation of smaller substances from larger molecules or crystalloid from colloidal particles in a solution by diffusion through semipermeable membranes.

di•am•e•ter (dī-ăm′ĭ-tər) *n.* **1. a.** *Math.* A straight line segment that passes through the center of a circle or sphere with both of its ends on the boundary. **b.** The measure of a diameter. **2.** Thickness or width.

di•a•met•ri•cal (dī′ə-mĕt′rĭ-kəl) *also* **di•a•met•ric** (-rĭk) *adj.* **1.** Of, relating to, or along a diameter. **2.** Being exactly opposite : contrary. —**di′a•met′ri•cal•ly** *adv.*

dia•mond (dī′mənd, dī′ə-) *n.* **1.** A very hard, highly refractive colorless or white crystalline form of carbon used as a gemstone and as an industrial abrasive. **2.** A lozenge or rhombus. **3. a.** A playing card with a red, lozenge-shaped figure. **b. diamonds** *(sing. or pl. in number).* The suit comprising cards marked with this figure. **4.** *Baseball.* **a.** An infield. **b.** The entire playing field.

dia•mond•back (dī′mənd-băk′, dī′ə-) *n.* A large, venomous rattlesnake of the genus *Crotalus,* of the S and W U.S. and Mexico.

di•an•thus (dī-ăn′thəs) *n.* A plant of the genus *Dianthus,* including carnations and pinks.

di•a•pa•son (dī′ə-pā′zən, -sən) *n.* **1.** The full range of an instrument or voice. **2.** Either of 2 principal stops on a pipe organ that form the tonal basis for the entire scale.

di•a•per (dī′ə-pər, dī′pər) *n.* A folded piece of absorbent material placed between a baby's legs and fastened at the waist to serve as underpants. —*v.* To put a diaper on.

di•aph•a•nous (dī-ăf′ə-nəs) *adj.* **1.** Of such fine texture as to be transparent or translucent. **2.** Delicate in form. **3.** Vague or insubstantial <*diaphanous* fantasies> —**di•aph′a•nous•ly** *adv.*

di•a•phragm (dī′ə-frăm′) *n.* **1. a.** *Anat.* A muscular membranous partition separating the abdominal and thoracic cavities. **b.** A membranous part that separates or divides. **2.** A thin disk, esp. in a microphone, whose vibrations transform sound waves into electric signals or electric signals into sound waves. **3.** A contraceptive device consisting of a usu. rubber disklike cap that covers the uterine cervix.

di•ar•rhe•a *also* **di•ar•rhoe•a** (dī′ə-rē′ə) *n.* Excessively frequent, loose bowel movements.

di•a•ry (dī′ə-rē) *n., pl.* **-ries. 1.** A daily record, esp. a personal record of events, experiences, and observations : journal. **2.** A book for keeping a diary. —**di′a•rist** *n.*

di•as•to•le (dī-ăs′tə-lē) *n. Physiol.* Normal rhythmic dilatation and relaxation of the heart cavities during which they are filled with blood. —**di′a•stol′ic** (-ə-stŏl′ĭk) *adj.*

di•as•tro•phism (dī-ăs′trə-fĭz′əm) *n.* The process by which the major features of the earth's crust, as mountains and continents, are formed.

di•a•ther•my (dī′ə-thûr′mē) *n.* The therapeutic induction of heat in bodily tissues by high-frequency electromagnetic waves. **—di'a·ther'mic** *adj.*

di·a·tom (dī'ə-tŏm') *n.* Any of various tiny planktonic algae of the class Bacillariophyceae, with siliceous cell walls consisting of 2 overlapping symmetrical parts.

di·a·tom·ic (dī'ə-tŏm'ĭk) *adj.* Having 2 atoms in a molecule.

di·a·ton·ic (dī'ə-tŏn'ĭk) *adj.* Of or relating to a standard major or minor musical scale with 8 tones and no chromatic deviations.

di·a·tribe (dī'ə-trīb') *n.* A bitter, often abusive criticism or denunciation.

dib·ble (dĭb'əl) *n.* A pointed garden tool used to make holes in soil, esp. for planting seedlings or bulbs. **—dib'ble** *v.*

dice (dīs) *n., pl.* **dice. 1. a.** *pl. of* DIE[2] 2. **b.** A game of chance using dice. **2.** *pl. also* **dic·es.** A small cube, as of food. *—v.* **diced, dic·ing. 1.** To play or gamble with dice. **2.** To cut (food) into small cubes. **—dic'er** *n.*

di·chlo·ride (dī-klôr'īd', -klōr'-) *n.* A binary chemical compound containing 2 chloride atoms per molecule.

di·chot·o·my (dī-kŏt'ə-mē) *n., pl.* **-mies.** Division into 2 usu. contradictory parts or opinions. **—di·chot'o·mous** *adj.*

di·chro·mate (dī-krō'māt', dī'krō-) *n.* A chemical compound with 2 chromium atoms per anion.

dick (dĭk) *n. Slang.* A detective.

dick·er (dĭk'ər) *v.* To haggle or bargain.

dick·ey *also* **dick·ie** *or* **dick·y** (dĭk'ē) *n., pl.* **-eys** *also* **-ies. 1.** A woman's blouse front worn under a suit jacket or low-necked garment. **2.** A man's detachable shirt front. **3.** A small bird.

di·cot·y·le·don (dī-kŏt'l-ēd'n) *n.* A plant of the subclass Dicotyledonae, marked by a pair of seed leaves appearing at germination. **—di·cot'y·le'don·ous** *adj.*

dic·tate (dĭk'tāt', dĭk-tāt') *v.* **-tat·ed, -tat·ing. 1.** To speak or read aloud for another to transcribe or record. **2.** To issue or command authoritatively. *—n.* (dĭk'tāt'). A directive, command, or guiding principle. **—dic·ta'tion** *n.*

dic·ta·tor (dĭk'tā'tər, dĭk-tā'-) *n.* **1. a.** A ruler with absolute authority and supreme governmental jurisdiction. **b.** A tyrant. **2.** One who dictates. **—dic·ta'tor·ship'** *n.*

dic·ta·to·ri·al (dĭk'tə-tôr'ē-əl, -tōr-) *adj.* **1.** Tending to dictate **:** domineering. **2.** Relating to or characteristic of a dictator **:** autocratic. ★ ***syns:*** BOSSY, DOGMATIC, IMPERIOUS, MASTERFUL, OVERBEARING, PEREMPTORY **—dic'ta·to'ri·al·ly** *adv.*

dic·tion (dĭk'shən) *n.* **1.** Selection and usage of words in writing or speaking. **2.** Enunciation.

dic·tion·ar·y (dĭk'shə-nĕr'ē) *n., pl.* **-ies.** A reference book containing an explanatory alphabetical list of words with definitions, pronunciations, and often other information, such as synonym lists.

dic·tum (dĭk'təm) *n., pl.* **-ta** (tə) *or* **-tums. 1.** A dogmatic and authoritative statement. **2.** A popular saying **:** maxim.

did (dĭd) *v. p.t. of* DO.

di·dac·tic (dī-dăk'tĭk) *also* **di·dac·ti·cal** (-tĭ-kəl) *adj.* **1.** Intended to instruct. **2.** Morally instructive. **3.** Inclined to teach or moralize excessively.

did·dle (dĭd'l) *v.* **-dled, -dling. 1.** To swindle **:** cheat. **2.** To waste time.

did·n't (dĭd'nt). Did not.

di·do (dī'dō) *n., pl.* **-dos** *or* **-does.** *Informal.* A mischievous antic **:** caper.

die[1] (dī) *v.* **died, dy·ing. 1.** To stop living **:** expire. **2.** To lose vitality or force **:** subside. **3.** To cease existing, esp. by degrees **:** fade. **4.** *Informal.* To desire intensely <*dying* to buy a house> **5.** To cease operation **:** stop <The engine suddenly *died.*> ★ ***syns:*** CROAK, DECEASE, DEPART, EXPIRE, GO, PASS, PERISH, SUCCUMB

die[2] (dī) *n.* **1.** *pl.* **dies.** A device used to shape material by stamping or punching. **2.** *pl.* **dice** (dīs). A small cube marked on each side with from 1 to 6 dots, usu. used in pairs in games.

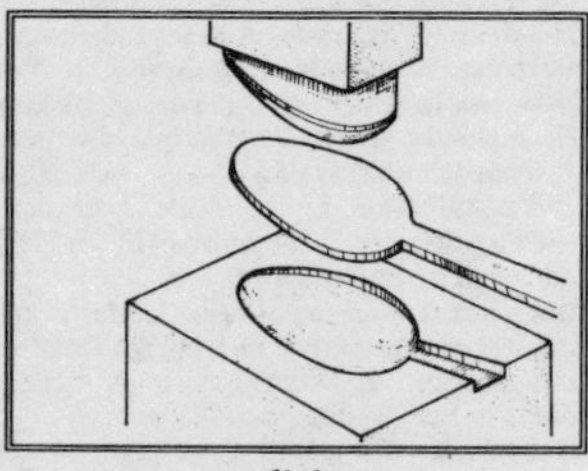

die[2]

die·hard (dī'härd') *n.* One who tenaciously resists change or refuses to abandon a position. **—die'hard'** *adj.*

diel·drin (dēl'drĭn) *n.* A persistent and highly toxic insecticide.

di·e·lec·tric (dī'ĭ-lĕk'trĭk) *n.* A nonconductor of electricity.

di·er·e·sis *also* **di·aer·e·sis** (dī-ĕr'ĭ-sĭs) *n., pl.* **-ses** (-sēz'). A mark (¨) over a vowel to indicate that it is to be pronounced in a separate syllable.

die·sel (dē'zəl, -səl) *n.* **1.** A diesel engine. **2.** A vehicle driven by a diesel engine.

diesel engine *n.* An internal-combustion engine in which an air-fuel mixture is ignited by heat generated from high compression in the cylinder.

di·et[1] (dī'ĭt) *n.* **1.** Food and drink usu. or habitually consumed. **2.** A regulated selection of foods, esp. as medically prescribed. **3.** Something taken or provided regularly <a *diet* of horror movies> *—v.* To eat or cause to eat according to a prescribed regimen. **—di'e·tar'y** *adj.* **—di'et·er** *n.*

di·et[2] (dī'ĭt) *n.* A legislature **:** assembly.

di·e·tet·ics (dī'ĭ-tĕt'ĭks) *n. (sing. in number).* The study of diet and its relationship to health and hygiene. **—di′e·tet′ic** *adj.* **—di′e·ti′tian, di′e·ti′cian** *n.*

di·eth·yl·stil·bes·trol (dī-ĕth′əl-stĭl-bĕs′trôl′, -trōl′) *n.* A synthetic estrogen formerly used to treat menstrual disorders.

dif·fer (dĭf′ər) *v.* **1.** To be dissimilar. **2.** To have a different opinion **:** disagree.

dif·fer·ence (dĭf′ər-əns, dĭf′rəns) *n.* **1.** The quality, state, or degree of being different. **2.** A disagreement or controversy or the cause of one. **3.** *Math.* The amount by which a number or quantity is greater or less than another.

dif·fer·ent (dĭf′ər-ənt, dĭf′rənt) *adj.* **1.** Having dissimilarities **:** unlike. **2.** Separate, distinct, or varied. **3.** Differing from others **:** unusual. ★ ***syns:*** DISPARATE, DISSIMILAR, UNLIKE **—dif′fer·ent·ly** *adv.*

dif·fer·en·tial (dĭf′ə-rĕn′shəl) *adj.* Of, relating to, or showing a difference. —*n.* **1.** The degree or amount to which similar things differ. **2.** A differential gear.

differential calculus *n.* The mathematics of the variation of a function with respect to changes in independent variables.

differential gear *n.* An arrangement of gears used on the powered axle of automotive vehicles to allow different rates of wheel rotation, as on curves.

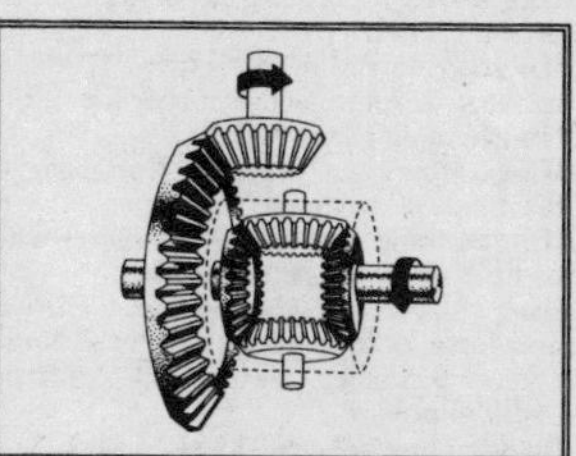

differential gear

dif·fer·en·ti·ate (dĭf′ə-rĕn′shē-āt′) *v.* **-at·ed, -at·ing. 1.** To distinguish, state, or show the difference. **2.** To make or become different. **—dif′fer·en′ti·a′tion** *n.*

dif·fi·cult (dĭf′ĭ-kŭlt′, -kəlt) *adj.* **1.** Hard to do, achieve, understand, or master. **2.** Hard to please or satisfy. ★ ***syns:*** HARD, KNOTTY, TOUGH

dif·fi·cul·ty (dĭf′ĭ-kŭl′tē, -kəl-tē) *n., pl.* **-ties. 1.** The state or quality of being difficult. **2.** Something requiring great effort. **3.** A cause of trouble or worry. **4.** Conflicts or problems <emotional *difficulties*><financial *difficulties*>

dif·fi·dent (dĭf′ĭ-dənt) *adj.* Shy **:** timid. **—dif′fi·dence** *n.* **—dif′fi·dent·ly** *adv.*

dif·frac·tion (dĭ-frăk′shən) *n.* The deflection of radiation, esp. a beam of light as it passes an obstacle or aperture.

dif·fuse (dĭ-fyōōz′) *v.* **-fused, -fus·ing.** To pour out and cause to spread freely. —*adj.* (-fyōōs′). **1.** Widely scattered. **2.** Wordy **:** verbose. **—dif·fu′sion** *n.*

dig (dĭg) *v.* **dug** (dŭg), **dig·ging. 1.** To turn over, break up, or remove (e.g., earth), as with a shovel. **2.** To make (a hole) by or as if by digging. **3.** To learn by investigation or research <*dug* up the facts> **4.** To prod against <*dug* me in the back> **5.** *Slang.* To understand, appreciate, or enjoy. —*n.* **1.** A poke **:** nudge. **2.** A gibe or taunt. **3.** An archaeological excavation. **—dig in. 1.** *Informal.* **a.** To begin to work intensively. **b.** To begin to eat. **2.** To entrench oneself.

di·gest (dĭ-jĕst′, dī-) *v.* **1.** To transform (food) into an assimilable state, as by chemical and muscular action in the alimentary canal. **2.** To assimilate mentally. **3.** To organize, usu. by classifying or summarizing. —*n.* (dī′jĕst′). A systematic arrangement of condensed material **:** synopsis. **—di·gest′i·bil′i·ty** *n.* **—di·gest′i·ble** *adj.* **—di·ges′tion** *n.* **—di·ges′tive** *adj.*

digestive tract *n.* The alimentary canal.

dig·it (dĭj′ĭt) *n.* **1.** A finger or toe. **2.** Any of the Arabic numerals 0 through 9.

dig·i·tal (dĭj′ĭ-təl) *adj.* **1.** Of, like, or involving a digit, esp. a finger. **2.** Expressed in digits, esp. for computer use. **3.** Giving a reading in digits <a *digital* watch>

digital computer *n.* A computer that uses data represented as digits, usu. in the binary numeration system, to perform operations.

dig·i·tal·is (dĭj′ĭ-tăl′ĭs) *n.* **1.** A plant of the genus *Digitalis,* which includes the foxgloves. **2.** A drug prepared from digitalis, used as a cardiac stimulant.

dig·i·tate (dĭj′ĭ-tāt′) *adj.* **1.** Having digits or fingerlike parts. **2.** *Bot.* Having radiating fingerlike leaflets or lobes. **—dig′i·tate′ly** *adv.*

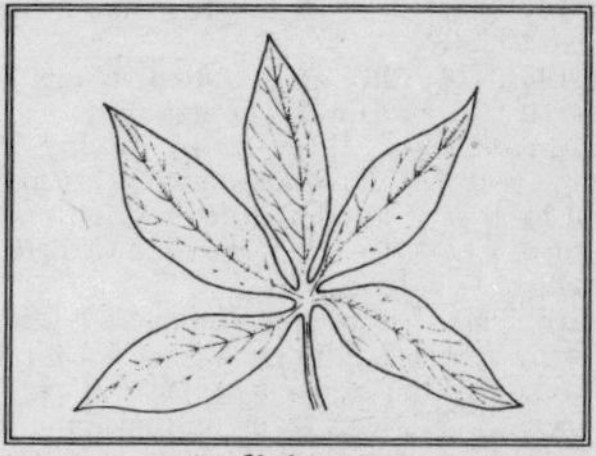

digitate
Digitate leaves

dig·ni·fied (dĭg′nə-fīd′) *adj.* Possessing or showing dignity **:** poised.

dig·ni·fy (dĭg′nə-fī′) *v.* **-fied, -fy·ing.** To give dignity or distinction to.

dig·ni·tar·y (dĭg′nĭ-tĕr′ē) *n., pl.* **-ies.** A high-ranking, influential person **:** notable. ★ ***syns:*** BIG SHOT, BIG WHEEL, BIGWIG, EMINENCE, LEADER, LION, LUMINARY, NABOB, NOTABILITY, NOTABLE, PERSONAGE, PERSONALITY, SOMEBODY, SOMEONE, VIP

dig•ni•ty (dĭg'nĭ-tē) *n., pl.* **-ties. 1.** The state of being esteemed or honored. **2.** Poise or formal reserve in appearance and demeanor. **3.** A high rank or office.

di•graph (dī'grăf') *n.* A pair of letters, as the *ea* in *seat,* that represents a single sound. **—di•graph'ic** *adj.*

di•gress (dĭ-grĕs', dī-) *v.* To wander or turn away from the main subject in a discourse. **—di•gres'sion** *n.* **—di•gres'sive** *adj.* **—di•gres'sive•ly** *adv.*

dik-dik (dĭk'dĭk') *n.* A very small African antelope of the genus *Madoqua.*

dike (dīk) *n.* An embankment, esp. of earth, built to control flood waters : levee.

di•lap•i•dat•ed (dĭ-lăp'ĭ-dā'tĭd) *adj.* In a state of disrepair or decay. **—di•lap'i•da'tion** *n.*

di•late (dī-lāt', dī'lāt') *v.* **-lat•ed, -lat•ing.** To make or become enlarged : expand. **—di•lat'a•ble** *adj.* **—di•la'tion, dil'a•ta'tion** (dĭl'ə-tā'shən) *n.* **—di•la'tor** *n.*

dilation and curettage *n.* A surgical procedure in which the uterine lining is scraped for diagnostic or therapeutic purposes.

dil•a•to•ry (dĭl'ə-tôr'ē, -tōr'ē) *adj.* **1.** Tending to cause or causing delay. **2.** Marked by procrastination. **—dil'a•to'ri•ly** *adv.*

di•lem•ma (dĭ-lĕm'ə) *n.* **1.** A choice between evenly balanced alternatives. **2.** A predicament defying satisfactory solution.

dil•et•tante (dĭl'ĭ-tänt', dĭl'ĭ-tänt', -tän'tē) *n., pl.* **-tantes** *or* **-tan•ti** (-tän'tē). One whose interest in something, as art, is superficial and amateurish. **—dil'et•tan'tism** *n.*

dil•i•gent (dĭl'ə-jənt) *adj.* Marked by persevering, painstaking effort : assiduous. **—dil'i•gence** *n.* **—dil'i•gent•ly** *adv.*

dill (dĭl) *n.* An aromatic herb, *Anethum graveolens,* bearing aromatic leaves and seeds used as seasoning.

dil•ly (dĭl'ē) *n., pl.* **-lies.** *Slang.* One that is extraordinary.

dil•ly•dal•ly (dĭl'ē-dăl'ē) *v.* **-lied, -ly•ing.** To waste time by dawdling or hesitating.

di•lute (dĭ-lo͞ot', dī-) *v.* **-lut•ed, -lut•ing.** To thin or reduce the concentration or strength of by or as if by admixture. ★ ***syns:*** CUT, THIN, WEAKEN —*adj.* Reduced in strength : diluted. **—di•lu'tion** *n.*

dim (dĭm) *adj.* **dim•mer, dim•mest. 1.** Minimally lighted. **2.** Faint : indistinct. **3.** Dull. **4.** Lacking sharp perception or clarity of understanding. **5.** Negative or pessimistic. —*v.* **dimmed, dim•ming. 1.** To make or become dim. **2.** To reduce the light of. **—dim'ly** *adv.* **—dim'ness** *n.*

dime (dīm) *n.* A U.S. coin worth 10 cents.

di•men•sion (dĭ-mĕn'shən) *n.* **1.** A measure of extension, esp. height, width, or length. **2.** *often* **dimensions.** Scope or magnitude : extent. **—di•men'sion•al** *adj.* **—di•men'sion•al'i•ty** (-shə-năl'ĭ-tē) *n.*

di•min•ish (dĭ-mĭn'ĭsh) *v.* **1.** To make or become less or smaller. **2.** To detract from the prestige of : belittle. **3.** To taper. **—di•min'ish•a•ble** *adj.* **—di•min'ish•ment** *n.* **—dim'i•nu'tion** *n.*

di•min•u•en•do (dĭ-mĭn'yo͞o-ĕn'dō) *adv.* Decrescendo. **—di•min'u•en'do** *adj. & n.*

di•min•u•tive (dĭ-mĭn'yə-tĭv) *adj.* **1.** Very small : tiny. **2.** Designating certain suffixes that denote smallness of size, familiarity, youth, or affection, as *-ling* in *duckling.* **—di•min'u•tive** *n.*

dim•i•ty (dĭm'ĭ-tē) *n., pl.* **-ties.** A thin, usu. corded cotton fabric.

dim•mer (dĭm'ər) *n.* A device that reduces the intensity of an electric light.

dim•ple (dĭm'pəl) *n.* **1.** A small depression in the flesh, as in the cheek. **2.** A slight surface depression. —*v.* **-pled, -pling.** To form or produce dimples (in).

dim•wit (dĭm'wĭt') *n. Slang.* A stupid person. **—dim'wit'ted** *adj.* **—dim'wit'ted•ly** *adv.* **—dim'wit'ted•ness** *n.*

din (dĭn) *n.* Loud, confused, continuous, and harsh noise.

di•nar (dĭ-när') *n.* —See table at CURRENCY.

dine (dīn) *v.* **dined, din•ing. 1.** To eat dinner. **2.** To give dinner to <*dined* the prospective clients in lavish style>

din•er (dī'nər) *n.* **1.** One that dines. **2.** A dining car on a train. **3.** A restaurant usu. shaped like a railroad car.

di•nette (dī-nĕt') *n.* A nook or small room for informal meals.

ding-a-ling (dĭng'ə-lĭng') *n. Informal.* A silly person : nitwit.

din•ghy (dĭng'ē) *n., pl.* **-ghies. 1.** A small rowboat. **2.** An inflatable rubber life raft.

din•gle (dĭng'gəl) *n.* A dell.

din•go (dĭng'gō) *n., pl.* **-goes.** A wild dog, *Canis dingo,* of Australia.

din•gus (dĭng'əs) *n. Slang.* An object whose name is forgotten or unknown.

din•gy (dĭn'jē) *adj.* **-gi•er, -gi•est. 1.** Dirty and discolored, as from smoke : grimy. **2.** Squalid : dreary. **3.** Shabby or worn. **—din'gi•ly** *adv.* **—din'gi•ness** *n.*

din•ky (dĭng'kē) *adj.* **-ki•er, -ki•est.** *Informal.* Small or insignificant.

din•ner (dĭn'ər) *n.* **1.** The main meal of the day. **2.** A formal meal or banquet.

din•ner•ware (dĭn'ər-wâr') *n.* **1.** Tableware other than cutlery and flatware used in serving a meal. **2.** A set of dishes.

di•no•saur (dī'nə-sôr') *n.* Any of various extinct, often gigantic reptiles of the orders Saurischia and Ornithischia.

dint (dĭnt) *n.* **1.** Effort : force <won by *dint* of sheer perseverance> **2.** A dent.

di•o•cese (dī'ə-sĭs, -sēs', -sēz') *n.* The district or territory under the jurisdiction of a bishop. **—di•oc'e•san** (-ŏs'ĭ-sən) *adj. & n.*

di•ode (dī'ōd') *n.* **1.** A vacuum tube having 2 electrodes, a cathode, and an anode. **2.** A 2-terminal semiconductor device used mainly as a rectifier.

di•o•ram•a (dī'ə-răm'ə, -rä'mə) *n.* A 3-dimensional scene in miniature.

di•ox•in (dī-ŏk'sĭn) *n.* Any of several carcinogenic or teratogenic hydrocarbons that occur as impurities in petroleum-derived herbicides.

dip (dĭp) *v.* **dipped, dip•ping. 1.** To plunge briefly into a liquid. **2.** To scoop up : ladle. **3.** To lower and then immediately raise (e.g., a flag) in salute. **4.** To lower or drop suddenly : duck. **5.** To appear to sink <The sun *dipped* below the horizon.> **6.** To incline downward : slope. **7.** To investigate a subject superficially : dabble. **8.** To take money from <*dipped* into their savings account> —*n.* **1.** An act of dipping, esp. a brief plunge into water. **2.** A liquid into which something is dipped. **3.** A quantity obtained by dipping. **4.** A downward course : drop <a *dip* in sales> **5.** *Slang.* A silly person.

diph•the•ri•a (dĭf-thîr'ē-ə, dĭp-) *n.* An acute febrile contagious disease caused by a bacillus and characterized by formation of false membranes in the throat and other air passages, causing respiratory difficulty.

diph•thong (dĭf'thông', -thŏng', dĭp'-) *n.* A single speech sound that begins with one vowel sound and moves to another in the same syllable, as *oi* in the word *oil.*

di•plo•ma (dĭ-plō'mə) *n.* A document issued by an educational institution showing that a person has earned a degree or finished a course of study.

di•plo•ma•cy (dĭ-plō'mə-sē) *n.* **1.** The practice or art of conducting international negotiations. **2.** Tact and skill in dealing with people.

dip•lo•mat (dĭp'lə-măt') *n.* A person adroit at or employed in diplomacy. **—dip'lo•mat'ic** *adj.*

dip•per (dĭp'ər) *n.* **1.** One that dips. **2.** A container for dipping, esp. a long-handled cup for dipping water. **3. Dipper. a.** The Big Dipper. **b.** The Little Dipper.

dip•py (dĭp'ē) *adj.* **-pi•er, -pi•est.** Silly.

dip•so•ma•ni•a (dĭp'sə-mā'nē-ə, -mān'yə) *n.* An insatiable craving for alcohol. **—dip'so•ma'ni•ac'** (-mā'nē-ăk') *n. & adj.*

dip•tych (dĭp'tĭk) *n.* A pair of carved or painted panels hinged together.

diptych

dire (dīr) *adj.* **dir•er, dir•est. 1.** Having or warning of terrible consequences : disastrous. **2.** Requiring urgent remedial action. **—dire'ful** *adj.* **—dire'ful•ly** *adv.*

di•rect (dĭ-rĕkt', dī-) *v.* **1.** To regulate the affairs of : manage. **2.** To take authoritative charge of : control. **3.** To order : command. **4. a.** To guide (someone) toward a goal. **b.** To show the way to. **5.** To cause to move in a direct course. **6.** To address (e.g., a letter) to a destination. **7.** To instruct or supervise the performance of a work. —*adj.* **1.** Moving or lying in a straight line. **2.** Forthright : straightforward <a *direct* question> **3.** With nothing intervening : immediate <*direct* contact> **4.** By action of voters rather than through representatives or delegates. **5.** Without compromise : absolute <*direct* opposites> **6.** Of unbroken descent : lineal. **7.** Consisting of a person's exact words <a *direct* quote> —*adv.* Straight : directly. **—di•rect'ness** *n.*

direct current *n.* An electric current that flows only in one direction.

di•rec•tion (dĭ-rĕk'shən, dī-) *n.* **1.** The act of directing. **2.** *often* **directions.** Instructions for doing something. **3.** An order or command. **4.** The line or path along which something travels, lies, or points. **5.** A trend. **—di•rec'tion•al** *adj.*

di•rec•tive (dĭ-rĕk'tĭv, dī-) *n.* An authoritative order or instruction.

di•rect•ly (dĭ-rĕkt'lē, dī-) *adv.* **1.** In a direct line. **2.** At once : immediately.

direct mail *n.* Advertising circulars or other printed matter sent directly through the mail to prospective customers or contributors. **—di•rect'-mail'** *adj.*

di•rec•tor (dĭ-rĕk'tər, dī-) *n.* **1.** One that directs : manager. **2.** One who guides or supervises the performers in a theatrical production. **3.** One of a group of persons who supervise the affairs of an institution or corporation. **—di•rec'tor•ship'** *n.*

di•rec•tor•ate (dĭ-rĕk'tər-ĭt, dī-) *n.* **1.** The position or office of a director. **2.** A body of directors.

di•rec•to•ry (dĭ-rĕk'tə-rē, dī-) *n., pl.* **-ries. 1.** A book that lists data, as names and addresses, concerning a specific group of persons or organizations. **2.** *Computer Sci.* A listing of the files contained in a storage device.

dirge (dûrj) *n.* A slow, mournful musical composition.

dir•ham (də-răm') *n.* —See table at CURRENCY.

dir•i•gi•ble (dîr'ə-jə-bəl, dĭ-rĭj'ə-) *n.* An airship.

dirk (dûrk) *n.* A dagger.

dirn•dl (dûrn'dəl) *n.* A full-skirted dress with a gathered waistband.

dirt (dûrt) *n.* **1.** Earth or soil. **2.** A soiling substance, as grime. **3.** Profane or obscene language. **4.** Hateful or scandalous gossip.

dirt bike *n.* A lightweight motorbike for use on rough surfaces, as dirt roads or trails.

dirt-cheap (dûrt'chēp') *adj. & adv.* Extremely cheap.

dirt•y (dûr'tē) *adj.* **-i•er, -i•est. 1.** Not clean : grimy. **2.** Lackluster in color. **3.** Menacing : hostile <gave me a *dirty* look> **4.** Rough or stormy, as weather. **5.** Unsportsmanlike. **6.** Indecent, obscene, or scandalous. ★ ***syns:*** BLACK, FILTHY, GRIMY, GRUBBY, SOILED,

UNCLEAN —*v.* **-ied, -y•ing.** To make or become soiled. **—dirt'i•ness** *n.*
dirty tricks *pl.n. Informal.* **1.** Covert intelligence operations. **2.** Unethical behavior, esp. in politics.
dis– *pref.* **1.** Not <*dis*similar> **2. a.** Absence of <*dis*interest> **b.** Opposite of <*dis*favor>
dis•a•ble (dĭs-ā'bəl) *v.* **-bled, -bling. 1.** To incapacitate or make powerless. **2.** To disqualify legally. ★ ***syns:*** CRIPPLE, IMMOBILIZE, INCAPACITATE, KNOCK OUT, PARALYZE **—dis'a•bil'i•ty** (-ə-bĭl'ĭ-tē) *n.*
dis•a•buse (dĭs'ə-byo͞oz') *v.* To free from a misconception or delusion.
dis•ad•van•tage (dĭs'əd-văn'tĭj) *n.* **1. a.** A handicap. **b.** An unfavorable circumstance. **2.** Damage or loss : detriment. **—dis•ad'van•ta'geous** (-ăd'vən-tā'jəs) *adj.*
dis•ad•van•taged (dĭs'əd-văn'tĭjd) *adj.* Suffering socioeconomic disadvantage.
dis•af•fect (dĭs'ə-fĕkt') *v.* To cause to be discontented, disloyal, or resentful : estrange. **—dis'af•fect'ed** *adj.* **—dis'af•fect'ed•ly** *adv.* **—dis'af•fec'tion** *n.*
dis•a•gree (dĭs'ə-grē') *v.* **1.** To fail to agree. **2.** To have a different opinion. **3.** To argue : quarrel. **4.** To cause adverse effects. **—dis'a•gree'ment** *n.*
dis•a•gree•a•ble (dĭs'ə-grē'ə-bəl) *adj.* **1.** Unpleasant or offensive. **2.** Quarrelsome : belligerent. **—dis'a•gree'a•ble•ness** *n.* **—dis'a•gree'a•bly** *adv.*
dis•al•low (dĭs'ə-lou') *v.* To reject or refuse to allow. **—dis'al•low'ance** *n.*
dis•ap•pear (dĭs'ə-pîr') *v.* **1.** To drop from sight : vanish. **2.** To cease to exist. **—dis'ap•pear'ance** *n.*
dis•ap•point (dĭs'ə-point') *v.* To fail to satisfy the expectations, desires, or hopes of. **—dis'ap•point'ment** *n.*
dis•ap•pro•ba•tion (dĭs-ăp'rə-bā'shən) *n.* Moral disapproval : condemnation.
dis•ap•prove (dĭs'ə-pro͞ov') *v.* **1.** To condemn. **2.** To refuse to approve : reject. **—dis'ap•prov'al** *n.*
dis•arm (dĭs-ärm') *v.* **1.** To divest of weapons. **2.** To make harmless. **3.** To win the trust of. **4.** To reduce or abolish armed forces. **—dis•arm'a•ment** *n.*
dis•ar•range (dĭs'ə-rānj') *v.* To disturb the order of. **—dis'ar•range'ment** *n.*
dis•ar•ray (dĭs'ə-rā') *n.* **1.** A state of disorder or confusion. **2.** Disorderly dress. —*v.* To upset or throw into turmoil.
dis•as•sem•ble (dĭs'ə-sĕm'bəl) *v.* To take apart.
dis•as•so•ci•ate (dĭs'ə-sō'shē-āt', -sē-) *v.* To dissociate. **—dis'as•so'ci•a'tion** *n.*
dis•as•ter (dĭ-zăs'tər) *n.* A grave occurrence having ruinous results. ★ ***syns:*** CALAMITY, CATACLYSM, CATASTROPHE, TRAGEDY **—dis•as'trous** *adj.* **—dis•as'trous•ly** *adv.*
dis•a•vow (dĭs'ə-vou') *v.* To deny or disclaim any knowledge of or responsibility for. **—dis'a•vow'al** *n.*
dis•band (dĭs-bănd') *v.* To break up : disperse. **—dis•band'ment** *n.*
dis•bar (dĭs-bär') *v.* To prohibit (a lawyer) from practicing law. **—dis•bar'ment** *n.*
dis•be•lieve (dĭs'bĭ-lēv') *v.* To refuse to believe (in) : reject or deny. **—dis'be•lief'** *n.* **—dis'be•liev'er** *n.*
dis•burse (dĭs-bûrs') *v.* **-bursed, -burs•ing.** To pay out. **—dis•burse'ment, dis•bur'sal** *n.* **—dis•burs'er** *n.*
disc (dĭsk) *n.* **1.** *also* **disk.** *Informal.* A phonograph record. **2.** *var. of* DISK.
dis•card (dĭs-kärd') *v.* **1.** To get rid of : junk. **2. a.** To throw out (a playing card) from one's hand. **b.** To play (a card other than a trump) from a suit unlike the card led. —*n.* (dĭs'kärd'). **1.** The act of discarding. **2.** One that is discarded.
disc brake *also* **disk brake** *n.* A brake whose retarding friction is generated between stationary pads and a rotating disk.
dis•cern (dĭ-sûrn', -zûrn') *v.* **1.** To perceive (something hidden or obscure) : detect. **2.** To perceive as separate and distinct : discriminate. **3.** To comprehend mentally. **—dis•cern'er** *n.* **—dis•cern'i•ble** *adj.* **—dis•cern'ment** *n.*
dis•cern•ing (dĭ-sûr'nĭng, -zûr'-) *adj.* Showing insight and judgment : perceptive. **—dis•cern'ing•ly** *adv.*
dis•charge (dĭs-chärj') *v.* **1.** To relieve of a burden, load, or contents : unload. **2. a.** To release, as from confinement or duty. **b.** To dismiss from employment. **3.** To send or pour forth. **4.** To shoot or fire. **5.** To perform the obligations or requirements of (e.g., an office). **6.** To comply with the terms of (e.g., a promise or debt). **7.** To undergo or cause electrical discharge. —*n.* (dĭs'chärj', dĭs-chärj'). **1.** The act of discharging or condition of being discharged. **2.** Something discharging or discharged.
dis•ci•ple (dĭ-sī'pəl) *n.* **1.** A person who believes in and helps disseminate the teachings of a master. **2.** *often* **Disciple.** One of Jesus's followers.
dis•ci•pli•nar•i•an (dĭs'ə-plə-nâr'ē-ən) *n.* A believer in or enforcer of stern discipline.
dis•ci•pline (dĭs'ə-plĭn) *n.* **1. a.** Training intended to elicit a specified pattern of behavior or character. **b.** Behavior that results from such training. **2.** A condition of order based on obedience to authority. **3.** Punishment meant to correct or train. **4.** A set of methods or rules of conduct. **5.** A specific branch of knowledge or of teaching. —*v.* **-plined, -plin•ing. 1.** To train or develop by teaching and control. **2.** To penalize. **3.** To impose order on. **—dis'ci•pli•na'ry** *adj.*
disc jockey *also* **disk jockey** *n.* A radio announcer whose chief purpose is presenting and playing phonograph records.
dis•claim (dĭs-klām') *v.* To deny a claim to or association with : disavow. **—dis•claim'er** *n.*
dis•close (dĭs-klōz') *v.* To make known or open to view : expose. **—dis•clo'sure** *n.*
dis•co (dĭs'kō') *n., pl.* **-cos.** A discotheque.
dis•col•or (dĭs-kŭl'ər) *v.* To make or become different in color.

dis·com·fit (dĭs-kŭm′fĭt) *v.* **1.** To thwart. **2.** To make upset or uneasy : disconcert. **—dis·com′fi·ture′** *n.*

dis·com·fort (dĭs-kŭm′fərt) *n.* **1.** Physical or mental distress. **2.** An annoyance or inconvenience. *—v.* To make uncomfortable.

dis·com·mode (dĭs′kə-mōd′) *v.* **-mod·ed, -mod·ing.** To inconvenience.

dis·com·pose (dĭs′kəm-pōz′) *v.* **1.** To disrupt the composure or tranquillity of. **2.** To disorder. **—dis′com·po′sure** *n.*

dis·con·cert (dĭs′kən-sûrt′) *v.* To upset : discompose. **—dis′con·cert′ing·ly** *adv.*

dis·con·nect (dĭs′kə-nĕkt′) *v.* To interrupt or break the connection of or between. **—dis′con·nec′tion** *n.*

dis·con·nect·ed (dĭs′kə-nĕk′tĭd) *adj.* **1.** Not connected. **2.** Incoherent.

dis·con·so·late (dĭs-kŏn′sə-lĭt) *adj.* **1.** Beyond consolation : utterly dejected. **2.** Cheerless : gloomy <a *disconsolate* landscape> **—dis·con′so·late·ly** *adv.*

dis·con·tent (dĭs′kən-tĕnt′) *n.* Lack of contentment : dissatisfaction. **—dis′con·tent′ed** *adj.* **—dis′con·tent′ed·ly** *adv.*

dis·con·tin·ue (dĭs′kən-tĭn′yo͞o) *v.* **1.** To bring or come to an end : terminate. **2.** To stop trying, taking, or using : abandon. **—dis′con·tin′u·ance, dis′con·tin′u·a′tion** *n.*

dis·con·tin·u·ous (dĭs′kən-tĭn′yo͞o-əs) *adj.* Marked by gaps or interruptions. **—dis·con′ti·nu′i·ty** *n.*

dis·cord (dĭs′kôrd′) *n.* **1.** Lack of accord or harmony : dissension. **2.** A harsh or confused mingling of sounds. **3.** An unpleasant combination of musical sounds : dissonance. **—dis·cor′dant** *adj.*

dis·co·theque *also* **dis·co·thèque** (dĭs′kə-tĕk′, dĭs′kə-tĕk′) *n.* A nightclub featuring dancing to recorded or sometimes live music.

dis·count (dĭs′kount′, dĭs-kount′) *v.* **1.** To subtract or deduct, as from a price. **2.** To purchase, sell, or loan money on (a commercial paper, as a bill or note) after deducting the interest. **3.** To disregard or doubt (e.g., a rumor) as being unreliable or exaggerated. **4.** To make allowance for. **5.** To underestimate the significance of : minimize. *—n.* (dĭs′kount′). **1.** A reduction from a standard price or the full amount of a debt. **2.** The rate of interest discounted. **3.** The act or an example of discounting a commercial paper. **—dis′count′a·ble** *adj.*

dis·coun·te·nance (dĭs-koun′tə-nəns) *v.* **1.** To treat or regard with disfavor. **2.** To make uneasy : disconcert.

discount store *n.* A store that sells goods below the manufacturer's suggested retail price.

dis·cour·age (dĭ-skûr′ĭj, -skŭr′-) *v.* **-aged, -ag·ing. 1.** To deprive of enthusiasm : dishearten. **2.** To deter : dissuade. **3.** To try to prevent by expressing doubts or objections. ★ *syns:* DISHEARTEN, DISPIRIT **—dis·cour′age·ment** *n.* **—dis·cour′ag·ing·ly** *adv.*

dis·course (dĭs′kôrs′, -kōrs′) *n.* **1.** Spoken or written expression. **2.** A conversation. **3.** A formal and lengthy written or spoken discussion of a subject. *—v.* (dĭ-skôrs′, -skōrs′) **-coursed, -cours·ing. 1.** To write or speak formally and extensively. **2.** To converse : talk. **—dis·cours′er** *n.*

dis·cour·te·ous (dĭs-kûr′tē-əs) *adj.* Lacking courteous manners : rude. **—dis·cour′te·ous·ly** *adv.* **—dis·cour′te·sy** *n.*

dis·cov·er (dĭ-skŭv′ər) *v.* **1.** To gain knowledge of through observation or study. **2.** To find, learn of, or observe for the first time. **—dis·cov′er·a·ble** *adj.* **—dis·cov′er·er** *n.* **—dis·cov′er·y** *n.*

dis·cred·it (dĭs-krĕd′ĭt) *v.* **1.** To mar the reputation of : disgrace. **2.** To cause to be doubted. **3.** To refuse to believe. *—n.* **1.** Tarnish to or loss of one's reputation. **2.** Loss of credibility : doubt. **—dis·cred′it·a·ble** *adj.* **—dis·cred′it·a·bly** *adv.*

dis·creet (dĭ-skrēt′) *adj.* **1.** Having or displaying caution and self-restraint : prudent. **2.** Not ostentatious : modest. **—dis·creet′ly** *adv.* **—dis·creet′ness** *n.*

dis·crep·an·cy (dĭ-skrĕp′ən-sē) *also* **dis·crep·ance** (-əns) *n., pl.* **-cies** *also* **-anc·es. 1.** Disagreement, as between facts : inconsistency. **2.** An instance of discrepancy. **—dis·crep′ant** *adj.*

dis·crete (dĭ-skrēt′) *adj.* **1.** Constituting a separate thing : distinct. **2.** Made up of unconnected distinct parts.

dis·cre·tion (dĭ-skrĕsh′ən) *n.* **1.** The quality of being discreet : circumspection. **2.** Freedom or power to act or judge on one's own. **—dis·cre′tion·ar′y** *adj.*

dis·crim·i·nate (dĭ-skrĭm′ə-nāt′) *v.* **-nat·ed, -nat·ing. 1.** To distinguish between things : differentiate. **2.** To act prejudicially. **—dis·crim′i·nate·ly** *adv.* **—dis·crim′i·na′tion** *n.* **—dis·crim′i·na′tive** *adj.*

dis·crim·i·nat·ing (dĭ-skrĭm′ə-nā′tĭng) *adj.* **1.** Recognizing or making fine distinctions : perceptive. **2.** Fussy.

dis·crim·i·na·to·ry (dĭ-skrĭm′ə-nə-tôr′ē, -tōr′ē) *adj.* **1.** Displaying or marked by prejudice : biased. **2.** Discriminating. **—dis·crim′i·na·to′ri·ly** *adv.*

dis·cur·sive (dĭ-skûr′sĭv) *adj.* Covering a wide field of subjects : digressive. **—dis·cur′sive·ly** *adv.* **—dis·cur′sive·ness** *n.*

dis·cus (dĭs′kəs) *n.* **1.** A disk, typically wooden, that is hurled for distance in athletic competitions. **2.** A small, brilliantly colored disk-shaped South American freshwater fish, *Symphysodon discus.*

dis·cuss (dĭ-skŭs′) *v.* **1.** To talk over : speak about. **2.** To consider or examine (a subject) through discourse. **—dis·cuss′i·ble** *adj.* **—dis·cus′sion** *n.*

dis·cus·sant (dĭ-skŭs′ənt) *n.* A participant in a discussion.

dis·dain (dĭs-dān′) *v.* **1.** To treat contemptuously : despise. **2.** To reject scornfully. *—n.* Scornful aloofness. **—dis·dain′ful** *adj.* **—dis·dain′ful·ly** *adv.*

dis·ease (dĭ-zēz′) *n.* A condition of an organism that impairs normal physiological functioning. **—dis•eased′** *adj.*

dis•em•bark (dĭs′ĕm-bärk′) *v.* To go or cause to go ashore from a ship.

dis•em•bod•y (dĭs′ĕm-bŏd′ē) *v.* **1.** To free (the soul or spirit) from the body. **2.** To divest of material form or existence. **—dis′em•bod′i•ment** *n.*

dis•em•bow•el (dĭs′ĕm-bou′əl) *v.* To eviscerate. **—dis′em•bow′el•ment** *n.*

dis•en•chant (dĭs′ĕn-chănt′) *v.* To divest of illusions or false beliefs.

dis•en•cum•ber (dĭs′ĕn-kŭm′bər) *v.* To relieve of burdens or hardships.

dis•en•fran•chise (dĭs′ĕn-frăn′chīz′) *v.* To disfranchise.

dis•en•gage (dĭs′ĕn-gāj′) *v.* To release from something that holds fast, joins, or entangles. **—dis′en•gage′ment** *n.*

dis•en•tan•gle (dĭs′ĕn-tăng′gəl) *v.* To untangle. **—dis′en•tan′gle•ment** *n.*

dis•e•qui•lib•ri•um (dĭs-ē′kwə-lĭb′rē-əm, -ĕk′wə-) *n.* Lack or loss of equilibrium or stability.

dis•es•teem (dĭs′ĭ-stēm′) *v.* To regard with disfavor. —*n.* Lack of esteem.

dis•fa•vor (dĭs-fā′vər) *n.* **1.** Disapproval. **2.** The state of being regarded with disapproval. **—dis•fa′vor** *v.*

dis•fig•ure (dĭs-fĭg′yər) *v.* To mar or ruin the shape or appearance of **:** deform. **—dis•fig′ure•ment** *n.*

dis•fran•chise (dĭs-frăn′chīz′) *v.* To deprive of a franchise, privilege, or right of citizenship, esp. of the right to vote. **—dis•fran′chise′ment** *n.*

dis•gorge (dĭs-gôrj′) *v.* **1.** To regurgitate **:** vomit. **2.** To spew forth violently.

dis•grace (dĭs-grās′) *n.* **1.** The state of being strongly and generally disapproved **:** shame. **2.** Something that brings dishonor, disrespect, or disfavor. ★ ***syns:*** DISCREDIT, DISHONOR, DISREPUTE, IGNOMINY, OBLOQUY, OPPROBRIUM, SHAME **—dis•grace′** *v.* **—dis•grace′ful** *adj.* **—dis•grace′ful•ly** *adv.* **—dis•grace′ful•ness** *n.*

dis•grun•tle (dĭs-grŭn′tl) *v.* **-tled, -tling.** To make irritable or upset.

dis•guise (dĭs-gīz′) *v.* **-guised, -guis•ing. 1.** To change the appearance or character of to prevent recognition. **2.** To hide or obscure by dissembling **:** misrepresent. —*n.* **1.** Clothes and often make-up worn to prevent recognition. **2.** A pretense that conceals the truth.

dis•gust (dĭs-gŭst′) *v.* **1.** To arouse nausea in **:** sicken. **2.** To offend the moral sense of **:** repel. **3.** To cause to become impatient or annoyed. —*n.* Profound aversion or repugnance. **—dis•gust′ed•ly** *adv.* **—dis•gust′ing•ly** *adv.*

dish (dĭsh) *n.* **1. a.** An open, gen. shallow container for holding or serving food. **b.** The amount a dish holds. **2. a.** The food served in a dish. **b.** A particular variety or way of preparing food. **3.** Something that resembles a dish, esp. in being concave in shape. —*v.* **1.** To serve (food) in or as if in a dish. **2.** To hollow out **:** make concave.

dis•ha•bille (dĭs′ə-bēl′) *n.* The state of being casually or carelessly dressed.

dis•har•mo•ny (dĭs-här′mə-nē) *n.* Lack of harmony **:** discord.

dish•cloth (dĭsh′klôth′, -klŏth′) *n.* A cloth used for washing dishes.

dis•heart•en (dĭs-här′tn) *v.* To discourage, demoralize, or dispirit.

di•shev•el (dĭ-shĕv′əl) *v.* **-eled, -el•ing** *or* **-elled, -el•ling.** To disorder or disarrange (e.g., the hair). **—di•shev′el•ment** *n.*

dis•hon•est (dĭs-ŏn′ĭst) *adj.* **1.** Tending to lie, cheat, or deceive. **2.** Arising from, gained by, or showing falseness or fraud. **—dis•hon′est•ly** *adv.* **—dis•hon′es•ty** *n.*

dis•hon•or (dĭs-ŏn′ər) *n.* **1.** Loss of honor **:** disgrace. **2.** Something that causes loss of honor. **3.** Failure to pay a commercial obligation, as a bill or note. —*v.* **1.** To bring shame or disgrace on. **2.** To fail to pay (e.g., a note). **—dis•hon′or•a•ble** *adj.*

dish•rag (dĭsh′răg′) *n.* A dishcloth.

dish•ware (dĭsh′wâr′) *n.* Dishes in which food is served.

dish•wash•er (dĭsh′wŏsh′ər, -wô′shər) *n.* One that washes dishes.

dis•il•lu•sion (dĭs′ĭ-lo͞o′zhən) *v.* To disenchant. **—dis′il•lu′sion** *n.*

dis•in•cline (dĭs′ĭn-klīn′) *v.* To be or cause to be reluctant or unwilling.

dis•in•fect (dĭs′ĭn-fĕkt′) *v.* To cleanse of harmful microorganisms. **—dis′in•fec′tant** *n. & adj.* **—dis′in•fec′tion** *n.*

dis•in•gen•u•ous (dĭs′ĭn-jĕn′yo͞o-əs) *adj.* Not candid **:** crafty. **—dis′in•gen′u•ous•ly** *adv.* **—dis′in•gen′u•ous•ness** *n.*

dis•in•her•it (dĭs′ĭn-hĕr′ĭt) *v.* To exclude or prevent from inheritance.

dis•in•te•grate (dĭs-ĭn′tĭ-grāt′) *v.* **1.** To separate into components **:** fragment. **2.** To undergo a change in structure, as an atomic nucleus. **—dis•in′te•gra′tion** *n.* **—dis•in′te•gra′tor** *n.*

dis•in•ter (dĭs′ĭn-tûr′) *v.* **1.** To exhume (a corpse). **2.** To disclose, uncover, or expose.

dis•in•ter•est•ed (dĭs-ĭn′trĭ-stĭd, -tə-rĕs′tĭd) *adj.* **1.** Unbiased **:** impartial. **2.** Not interested **:** indifferent. **—dis•in′ter•est** *n.* **—dis•in′ter•est•ed•ly** *adv.*

dis•in•vest•ment (dĭs′ĭn-vĕst′mənt) *n.* Reduction or consumption of capital investment.

dis•join (dĭs-join′) *v.* To disconnect.

dis•joint (dĭs-joint′) *v.* **1.** To disconnect or separate at the joints. **2.** To destroy the orderly arrangement of.

dis•joint•ed (dĭs-join′tĭd) *adj.* **1.** Separated at the joints. **2.** Lacking unity or order **:** incoherent <a *disjointed* lecture> **—dis•joint′ed•ly** *adv.*

disk *also* **disc** (dĭsk) *n.* **1.** A thin, flat, round plate. **2.** Something resembling a disk. **3.** *var. of* DISC 1. **4.** *Computer Sci.* A magnetic disk.

disk drive *n. Computer Sci.* A device that reads data stored on a magnetic or optical disk and writes data onto the disk for storage.

disk•ette (dĭ-skĕt′) *n.* A floppy disk.
disk pack *n.* A computer storage device consisting of several magnetic disks that can be used and stored as a unit.

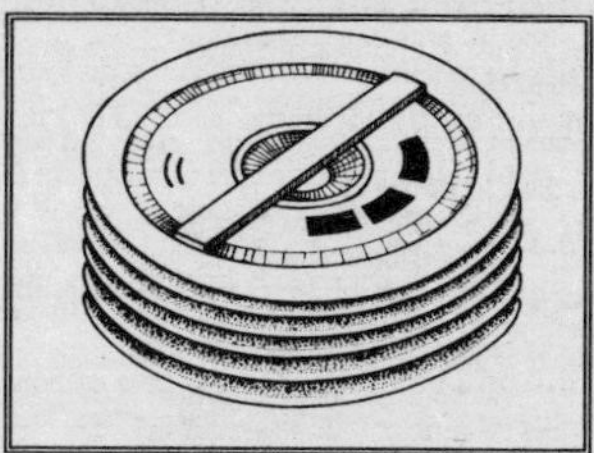

disk pack

dis•like (dĭs-līk′) *v.* To regard with disapproval or distaste. **—dis•like′** *n.*
dis•lo•cate (dĭs′lō-kāt′, dĭs-lō′kāt′) *v.* **1.** To put out of normal position, esp. to displace (a bone) from a socket or joint. **2.** To throw into disorder **:** disrupt.
dis•lodge (dĭs-lŏj′) *v.* To remove or drive out from a dwelling or position.
dis•loy•al (dĭs-loi′əl) *adj.* Being untrue to duty or obligation **:** faithless. **—dis•loy′al•ly** *adv.* **—dis•loy′al•ty** *n.*
dis•mal (dĭz′məl) *adj.* **1.** Causing gloom or depression **:** dreary <*dismal* rain and fog> **2.** Characterized by a lack of hope **:** dejected. **3.** Causing dread or dismay **:** dire. **4.** Without substance or interest. **—dis′mal•ly** *adv.* **—dis′mal•ness** *n.*

▲ ***word history:*** The word *dismal* was orig. a noun phrase—*dis mal*—meaning "evil days," from Latin *dies mali.* In the medieval calendar two days each month were considered unlucky. A *dismal day* was one of these unlucky days. By the 16th cent. the phrase *dismal day* had become so common that *dismal* was interpreted as an adjective and came to mean "unlucky" and "causing dread." In more recent times these senses have been weakened to "depressing" and "gloomy."

dis•man•tle (dĭs-măn′tl) *v.* **-tled, -tling. 1.** To divest of equipment or furnishings. **2.** To tear down or take apart. **—dis•man′tle•ment** *n.*
dis•may (dĭs-mā′) *v.* **1.** To cause fear or apprehension in **:** daunt. **2.** To discourage or trouble greatly. **—dis•may′** *n.*
dis•mem•ber (dĭs-mĕm′bər) *v.* **1.** To cut or tear off the limbs of. **2.** To separate into parts. **—dis•mem′ber•ment** *n.*
dis•miss (dĭs-mĭs′) *v.* **1.** To discharge, as from a job. **2.** To permit or direct to leave. **3.** To rid one's mind of **:** dispel. **4.** To refuse to accept **:** repudiate. **5.** *Law.* To disallow or reject further judicial hearing on (a claim or action). **—dis•miss′al** *n.* **—dis•miss′i•ble** *adj.*
dis•mis•sive (dĭs-mĭs′ĭv) *adj.* **1.** Serving to dismiss. **2.** Showing indifference or disregard.
dis•mount (dĭs-mount′) *v.* **1.** To get down from (e.g., a horse). **2.** To unseat (a rider) from a horse. **3.** To remove from a mounting, setting, or support. **4.** To take apart **:** disassemble. **—dis′mount′** *n.*
dis•o•bey (dĭs′ə-bā′) *v.* To fail or refuse to obey. **—dis′o•be′di•ence** (-bē′dē-əns) *n.* **—dis′o•be′di•ent** *adj.*
dis•o•blige (dĭs′ə-blīj′) *v.* **1.** To neglect or refuse to act in accord with the wishes of. **2.** To offend, as by slighting. **3.** To inconvenience. **—dis′o•blig′ing•ly** *adv.*
dis•or•der (dĭs-ôr′dər) *n.* **1.** Lack of order **:** confusion. **2.** A breach of civil peace **:** public disturbance. **3.** An illness **:** ailment. *—v.* To throw into confusion.
dis•or•der•ly (dĭs-ôr′dər-lē) *adj.* **1.** Lacking regular order **:** untidy. **2.** Not disciplined **:** unruly. **3.** Disturbing the public peace or decorum. ★ ***syns:*** RIOTOUS, ROWDY, UNRULY **—dis•or′der•li•ness** *n.*
dis•or•gan•ize (dĭs-ôr′gə-nīz′) *v.* To break up the organization, structure, or unity of.
dis•o•ri•ent (dĭs-ôr′ē-ĕnt′, -ōr′-) *v.* To cause to lose a sense of direction, location, or awareness **:** confuse.
dis•own (dĭs-ōn′) *v.* To disclaim as one's own **:** repudiate.
dis•par•age (dĭ-spăr′ĭj) *v.* **-aged, -ag•ing. 1.** To speak of in a belittling manner **:** decry. **2.** To reduce in rank or esteem. **—dis•par′age•ment** *n.* **—dis•par′ag•ing•ly** *adv.*
dis•pa•rate (dĭs′pər-ĭt, dĭ-spăr′-) *adj.* Completely distinct in kind or quality. **—dis′pa•rate•ly** *adv.* **—dis•par′i•ty** *n.*
dis•pas•sion•ate (dĭs-păsh′ə-nĭt) *adj.* Unaffected by emotion or bias. **—dis•pas′sion** *n.* **—dis•pas′sion•ate•ly** *adv.*
dis•patch *also* **des•patch** (dĭ-spăch′) *v.* **1.** To send off to a particular destination or on specific business. **2.** To deal with promptly. **3.** To kill summarily. *—n.* **1.** The act of dispatching. **2.** Speed in movement or performance. **3.** A message. **4.** An item sent to a news organization, as by a correspondent. **—dis•patch′er** *n.*
dis•pel (dĭ-spĕl′) *v.* **-pelled, -pel•ling. 1.** To rid one's mind of <*dispel* all fears> **2.** To cause to separate **:** scatter.
dis•pen•sa•ble (dĭ-spĕn′sə-bəl) *adj.* Capable of being dispensed with.
dis•pen•sa•ry (dĭ-spĕn′sə-rē) *n., pl.* **-ries.** A place where medical supplies and preparations are dispensed.
dis•pen•sa•tion (dĭs′pən-sā′shən, -pĕn-) *n.* **1.** The act of dispensing. **2.** Something dispensed. **3.** A system by which something is dispensed. **4.** Exemption or release from rule or obligation. **5.** Divine ordering of worldly affairs. **6.** A religious system or code of commands.
dis•pense (dĭ-spĕns′) *v.* **-pensed, -pens•ing. 1.** To distribute in portions. **2.** To prepare and give out (medicines). **3.** To administer (e.g., laws). **4.** To release or exempt. **—dispense with. 1.** To forgo. **2.** To get rid of. **—dis•pen′ser** *n.*

dis·perse (dĭ-spûrs′) *v.* **-persed, -pers·ing. 1.** To break up **:** scatter. **2.** To vanish or cause to vanish **:** dispel. **3.** To disseminate (e.g., knowledge). **—dis·pers′i·ble** *adj.* **—dis·per′sion, dis·per′sal** *n.*

di·spir·it (dĭ-spĭr′ĭt) *v.* To deprive of spirit **:** discourage. **—di·spir′it·ed·ly** *adv.*

dis·place (dĭs-plās′) *v.* **1.** To change the place or position of **:** remove. **2.** To take the place of. **3.** To discharge from an office. **4.** To cause a physical displacement of.

displaced person *n.* One who has been driven from his or her homeland by war.

dis·place·ment (dĭs-plās′mənt) *n.* **1.** The act of displacing or the state of being displaced. **2. a.** The volume or weight of fluid displaced by a floating body. **b.** The measure of the distance that a body has been moved through space.

dis·play (dĭ-splā′) *v.* **1.** To put forth for viewing **:** exhibit. **2.** To make noticeable <*displayed* their fear> **3.** To spread out **:** unfurl. —*n.* **1.** The act of displaying. **2.** Something displayed. **3.** *Computer Sci.* A device that gives information in a visual form, as on a cathode-ray tube.

dis·please (dĭs-plēz′) *v.* To incur the disapproval or dislike of **:** offend. **—dis·pleas′ing·ly** *adv.* **—dis·plea′sure** *n.*

dis·port (dĭ-spôrt′, -pōrt′) *v.* To entertain (oneself) **:** play.

dis·pos·al (dĭs-pō′zəl) *n.* **1.** Order **:** arrangement. **2.** The act of getting rid of or throwing away. **3.** An apparatus or device for disposing of something. **4.** Management **:** administration. **5.** The transference of something by gift or sale. **6.** The freedom to use something.

dis·pose (dĭ-spōz′) *v.* **-posed, -pos·ing. 1.** To arrange. **2.** To make willing or receptive **:** incline. **—dispose of. 1.** To attend to **:** settle. **2.** To transfer or part with, as by selling. **3.** To get rid of. **—dis·pos′a·ble** *adj. & n.*

dis·po·si·tion (dĭs′pə-zĭsh′ən) *n.* **1.** Temperament. **2.** Habitual inclination or tendency. **3.** Distribution or arrangement. **4.** A final settlement, as of property. **5.** An act of disposing.

dis·pos·sess (dĭs′pə-zĕs′) *v.* To deprive of the ownership or occupancy of land, possessions, or property. **—dis′pos·ses′sion** *n.*

dis·praise (dĭs-prāz′) *v.* To disparage. —*n.* Strong disapproval.

dis·pro·por·tion (dĭs′prə-pôr′shən, -pōr′-) *n.* Absence of proper proportion **:** disparity. **—dis′pro·por′tion·al, dis′pro·por′tion·ate** *adj.*

dis·prove (dĭs-pro͞ov′) *v.* To show to be false, invalid, or erroneous. ★ ***syns:*** BELIE, CONFUTE, DISCREDIT, REBUT, REFUTE **—dis·proof′** *n.*

dis·pu·ta·tion (dĭs′pyo͞o-tā′shən) *n.* **1.** A debate **:** argument. **2.** A dispute.

dis·pu·ta·tious (dĭs′pyo͞o-tā′shəs) *adj.* Argumentative. **—dis′pu·ta′tious·ly** *adv.*

dis·pute (dĭ-spyo͞ot′) *v.* **-put·ed, -put·ing. 1.** To debate **:** argue. **2.** To question the validity or truth of. **3.** To strive against **:** resist. **4.** To quarrel. —*n.* **1.** A verbal controversy **:** debate. **2.** A quarrel. **—dis·put′a·ble** *adj.* **—dis·put′a·bly** *adv.* **—dis·pu′tant, dis·put′er** *n.*

dis·qual·i·fy (dĭs-kwŏl′ə-fī′) *v.* **1.** To make unqualified, unfit, or ineligible. **2.** To declare unqualified, unfit, or ineligible. **—dis·qual′i·fi·ca′tion** *n.*

dis·qui·et (dĭs-kwī′ĭt) *v.* To trouble **:** disturb. —*n.* Disquietude. **—dis·qui′et·ing** *adj.* **—dis·qui′et·ing·ly** *adv.*

dis·qui·e·tude (dĭs-kwī′ĭ-to͞od′, -tyo͞od′) *n.* A state of uneasiness **:** anxiety.

dis·qui·si·tion (dĭs′kwĭ-zĭsh′ən) *n.* A formal, often written discourse.

dis·re·gard (dĭs′rĭ-gärd′) *v.* **1.** To ignore. **2.** To treat without proper attention **:** neglect. **—dis′re·gard** *n.* **—dis′re·gard′ful** *adj.*

†dis·re·mem·ber (dĭs′rĭ-mĕm′bər) *v.* *Regional.* To fail to remember **:** forget.

dis·re·pair (dĭs′rĭ-pâr′) *n.* The state of being neglected or in need of repair.

dis·rep·u·ta·ble (dĭs-rĕp′yə-tə-bəl) *adj.* Not respectable. **—dis·rep′u·ta·bly** *adv.*

dis·re·pute (dĭs′rĭ-pyo͞ot′) *n.* Loss of reputation **:** disgrace.

dis·re·spect (dĭs′rĭ-spĕkt′) *n.* Lack of respect or courteous regard. **—dis′re·spect′ful** *adj.* **—dis′re·spect′ful·ly** *adv.*

dis·robe (dĭs-rōb′) *v.* To undress.

dis·rupt (dĭs-rŭpt′) *v.* **1.** To throw into disorder or confusion. **2.** To break up **:** interrupt. **—dis·rup′tion** *n.* **—dis·rup′tive** *adj.*

dis·sat·is·fy (dĭs-săt′ĭs-fī′) *v.* To fail to satisfy **:** disappoint. **—dis·sat′is·fac′tion** *n.* **—dis·sat′is·fied′** *adj.*

dis·sect (dĭ-sĕkt′, dī-, dī′sĕkt′) *v.* **1.** To cut apart (tissue) for study or examination. **2.** To analyze closely or thoroughly. **—dis·sec′tion** *n.*

dis·sect·ed (dĭ-sĕk′tĭd, dī-) *adj.* *Bot.* Divided into numerous narrow segments or lobes.

dissected
Dissected leaves

dis·sem·ble (dĭ-sĕm′bəl) *v.* **-bled, -bling. 1.** To conceal the true nature of. **2.** To make a pretense of **:** simulate.

dis·sem·i·nate (dĭ-sĕm′ə-nāt′) *v.* **-nat·ed, -nat·ing.** To scatter or spread widely <*disseminate* rumors> **—dis·sem′i·na′tion** *n.* **—dis·sem′i·na′tor** *n.*

dis•sen•sion (dĭ-sĕn′shən) *n.* Difference of opinion : discord.
dis•sent (dĭ-sĕnt′) *v.* **1.** To differ in opinion : disagree. **2.** To withhold approval or assent. —*n.* **1.** Disagreement. **2.** Religious nonconformity. —**dis•sent′er** *n.*
dis•ser•ta•tion (dĭs′ər-tā′shən) *n.* A formal discourse, esp. a doctoral thesis.
dis•serv•ice (dĭs-sûr′vĭs) *n.* Injury : harm.
dis•sev•er (dĭ-sĕv′ər) *v.* To sever.
dis•si•dent (dĭs′ĭ-dənt) *adj.* Strongly and openly dissenting, esp. in opinion or belief. —**dis′si•dence** *n.* —**dis′si•dent** *n.*
dis•sim•i•lar (dĭ-sĭm′ə-lər) *adj.* Different or distinct : unlike. —**dis•sim′i•lar′i•ty** *n.*
dis•si•mil•i•tude (dĭs′ə-mĭl′ĭ-to͞od′, -tyo͞od′) *n.* Lack of resemblance.
dis•sim•u•late (dĭ-sĭm′yə-lāt′) *v.* To dissemble.
dis•si•pate (dĭs′ə-pāt′) *v.* **-pat•ed, -pat•ing. 1.** To drive away or dispel : scatter. **2.** To squander or waste. **3.** To vanish by dispersion. **4.** To indulge in pleasure recklessly : carouse. **5.** To lose (e.g., heat) irreversibly. —**dis′si•pa′tion** *n.*
dis•so•ci•ate (dĭ-sō′shē-āt′, -sē-) *v.* **-at•ed, -at•ing.** To separate or become separated from association with another : disconnect. —**dis•so′ci•a′tion** *n.*
dis•so•lute (dĭs′ə-lo͞ot′) *adj.* Lacking moral restraint : profligate. —**dis′so•lute′ly** *adv.* —**dis′so•lute′ness** *n.*
dis•so•lu•tion (dĭs′ə-lo͞o′shən) *n.* **1.** Disintegration into component parts : decomposition. **2.** Death. **3.** *Law.* Annulment or termination of a legal bond, tie, or contract. **4.** Formal adjournment or dismissal of a legislature or assembly.
dis•solve (dĭ-zŏlv′) *v.* **-solved, -solv•ing. 1.** To pass or cause to pass into solution <*dissolve* sugar in water> **2.** To melt. **3.** To cause to disappear : dispel. **4.** To separate into component parts : disintegrate. **5.** To bring to an end : terminate. **6.** To break down emotionally. —**dis•solv′a•ble** *adj.*
dis•so•nance (dĭs′ə-nəns) *n.* **1.** A harsh or unpleasant combination of sounds : discord. **2.** Lack of agreement : conflict. —**dis′so•nant** *adj.* —**dis′so•nant•ly** *adv.*
dis•suade (dĭ-swād′) *v.* **-suad•ed, -suad•ing.** To sway or try to sway from a course of action by persuasion. —**dis•sua′sion** *n.* —**dis•sua′sive** *adj.*
dis•taff (dĭs′tăf′) *n.* **1.** A stick holding flax or wool from which thread is drawn and spun by hand. **2.** Women as a group.
dis•tal (dĭs′təl) *adj. Anat.* Located far from the place of origin or attachment.
dis•tance (dĭs′təns) *n.* **1.** Spatial or chronological separation. **2.** The length of a path, esp. a straight line segment, that joins 2 points. **3.** The space that separates any 2 specified instants in time. **4. a.** The degree of difference separating 2 things in relationship. **b.** The degree of progress between 2 points in a course. **5.** Aloofness. **6.** The whole way <went the *distance*> —*v.* **-tanced, -tanc•ing.** To outdo.
dis•tant (dĭs′tənt) *adj.* **1.** Apart or separate in time or space. **2.** Far removed <the *distant* past> **3.** Coming from, located at, or going to a distance. **4.** Remotely related. **5.** Reserved : aloof. —**dis′tant•ly** *adv.*
dis•taste (dĭs-tāst′) *n.* Aversion : dislike. —**dis•taste′ful** *adj.* —**dis•taste′ful•ly** *adv.* —**dis•taste′ful•ness** *n.*
dis•tem•per (dĭs-tĕm′pər) *n.* An infectious, often fatal virus disease of certain mammals, as dogs and cats.
dis•tend (dĭ-stĕnd′) *v.* To expand by or as if by internal pressure : swell. —**dis•ten′si•ble** *adj.* —**dis•ten′tion, dis•ten′sion** *n.*
dis•til (dĭ-stĭl′) *v. esp. Brit. var. of* DISTILL.
dis•till (dĭ-stĭl′) *v.* **1.** To subject to or obtain by distillation. **2.** To separate from. **3.** To give off in drops. —**dis•till′er** *n.* —**dis•till′er•y** *n.*
dis•til•late (dĭs′tə-lāt′, -lĭt, dĭ-stĭl′ĭt) *n.* The substance condensed from vapor in distillation.
dis•til•la•tion (dĭs′tə-lā′shən) *n.* Any of various heat-dependent processes used to purify or separate a fraction of a relatively complex mixture or substance, esp. the vaporization of a liquid mixture with subsequent cooling to condensation.
dis•tinct (dĭ-stĭngkt′) *adj.* **1.** Distinguished from all others : individual. **2.** Easily recognized : clear. **3.** Unquestionable : decided. —**dis•tinct′ly** *adv.* —**dis•tinct′ness** *n.*
dis•tinc•tion (dĭ-stĭngk′shən) *n.* **1.** The act of distinguishing. **2.** A difference. **3.** A distinguishing attribute or factor. **4.** Excellence or eminence : virtue. **5.** Honor.
dis•tinc•tive (dĭ-stĭngk′tĭv) *adj.* **1.** Serving to identify or set apart : distinguishing. **2.** Typical : characteristic. —**dis•tinc′tive•ly** *adv.* —**dis•tinc′tive•ness** *n.*
dis•tin•guish (dĭ-stĭng′gwĭsh) *v.* **1.** To recognize as being different. **2.** To perceive clearly : discern. **3.** To discriminate. **4.** To make noticeable or different : set apart. **5.** To make well known. —**dis•tin′guish•a•ble** *adj.* —**dis•tin′guish•a•bly** *adv.*
dis•tin•guished (dĭ-stĭng′gwĭsht) *adj.* **1.** Marked by excellence : eminent. **2.** Dignified in appearance or deportment.
dis•tort (dĭ-stôrt′) *v.* **1.** To twist out of proper shape or condition : contort. **2.** To give an inaccurate and misleading account of : misrepresent. **3.** To reproduce inaccurately. —**dis•tor′tion** *n.*
dis•tract (dĭ-străkt′) *v.* **1.** To cause to turn away from a focus of attention : divert. **2.** To cause to feel conflicting emotions : disturb. —**dis•trac′tion** *n.*
dis•trait (dĭ-strā′) *adj.* Absent-minded or inattentive, esp. because of anxiety.
dis•traught (dĭ-strôt′) *adj.* **1.** Anxious : worried. **2.** Crazed : insane.
dis•tress (dĭ-strĕs′) *v.* To cause anxiety or misery to : trouble greatly. —*n.* **1.** Anxiety or suffering. **2.** Severe mental or physical strain. **3.** The state of needing immediate help. ★ ***syns:*** AFFLICTION, AGONY, AN-

GUISH, HURT, MISERY, PAIN, WOE —**dis•tress'ing•ly** *adv.*
dis•trib•ute (dĭ-strĭb'yōōt) *v.* **-ut•ed, -ut•ing. 1.** To divide and dispense in portions. **2.** To deliver or give out. **3.** To supply (goods) to retailers. **4.** To classify. —**dis'tri•bu'tion** *n.* —**dis•trib'u•tive** *adj.*
dis•trib•u•tor (dĭ-strĭb'yə-tər) *n.* **1.** One that distributes, esp. a wholesaler. **2.** A device that directs electric current to the spark plugs of a gasoline engine.
dis•trict (dĭs'trĭkt) *n.* **1.** An administrative or political division of a territory. **2.** A distinctive area <the theater *district*>
district attorney *n.* The prosecuting officer of a designated judicial district.
dis•trust (dĭs-trŭst') *n.* Lack of trust. ★ ***syns:*** DOUBT, DOUBTFULNESS, MISTRUST, SUSPICION —*v.* To doubt : suspect. —**dis•trust'ful** *adj.* —**dis•trust'ful•ly** *adv.*
dis•turb (dĭ-stûrb') *v.* **1.** To trouble or upset the tranquillity of. **2.** To unsettle mentally or emotionally. **3.** To interfere with : interrupt. **4.** To disarrange. —**dis•tur'bance** *n.* —**dis•turb'er** *n.*
dis•u•nite (dĭs'yōō-nīt') *v.* To make or become separate or divided.
dis•u•ni•ty (dĭs-yōō'nĭ-tē) *n.* Discord.
dis•use (dĭs-yōōs') *n.* The state of being no longer in use : desuetude.
ditch (dĭch) *n.* A trench or furrow dug in the ground. —*v.* **1.** To dig or make a ditch in. **2.** To surround with a ditch. **3.** *Slang.* To throw away : discard. **4.** To bring (a disabled aircraft) down on water.
dith•er (dĭ*th*'ər) *n.* A state of indecision or nervousness.
dit•to (dĭt'ō) *n., pl.* **-tos. 1.** The same as stated above or before. —Used to avoid repetition of a word. **2.** One of a pair of marks (″) used as a substitute for the word *ditto.* **3.** A copy or duplicate. —*adv.* As before.
dit•ty (dĭt'ē) *n., pl.* **-ties.** A simple song.
di•u•ret•ic (dī'ə-rĕt'ĭk) *adj.* Causing an increased urine discharge. —**di'u•ret'ic** *n.*
di•ur•nal (dī-ûr'nəl) *adj.* **1.** Relating to or happening in a day or each day : daily. **2.** Active or occurring during the daytime.
di•va (dē'və) *n., pl.* **-vas** *or* **-ve** (-vā'). A prima donna.
di•van (dī'văn', dĭ-văn') *n.* A long backless and armless couch.
dive (dīv) *v.* **dived** *or* **dove** (dōv), **dived, div•ing. 1.** To plunge headfirst into water, esp. as a sport. **2.** To go or cause to go underwater : submerge. **3.** To fall sharply : plummet. **4.** To rush headlong <*dove* into the crowd> **5.** To plunge, as into an activity. —*n.* **1.** An act or instance of diving. **2.** A sudden drop or fall. **3.** *Slang.* A cheap, disreputable bar. —**div'er** *n.*
di•verge (dĭ-vûrj', dī-) *v.* **-verged, -verg•ing. 1.** To go or move in different directions from a common point : branch out. **2.** To differ, as in opinion or manner. **3.** To turn aside from a set course or norm : deviate. —**di•ver'gence** *n.* —**di•ver'gent** *adj.*
di•vers (dī'vərz) *adj.* Various : several.
di•verse (dĭ-vûrs', dī-, dī'vûrs') *adj.* **1.** Unlike in kind : distinct. **2.** Having diversity in form : varied. —**di•verse'ness** *n.*
di•ver•si•fy (dĭ-vûr'sə-fī', dī-) *v.* **-fied, -fy•ing. 1.** To give variety to : vary. **2.** To spread out activities or investments, esp. in business. —**di•ver'si•fi•ca'tion** *n.*
di•ver•sion (dĭ-vûr'zhən, -shən, dī-) *n.* **1.** The act of diverting : deviation. **2.** Something that relaxes or entertains : recreation. —**di•ver'sion•ar'y** *adj.*
di•ver•si•ty (dĭ-vûr'sĭ-tē, dī-) *n., pl.* **-ties. 1.** Difference. **2.** Variety.
di•vert (dĭ-vûrt', dī-) *v.* **1.** To turn away from a purpose or direction : deflect. **2.** To distract. **3.** To entertain.
di•vest (dĭ-vĕst', dī-) *v.* **1.** To strip, as of clothing. **2.** To deprive, as of property.
di•ves•ti•ture (dĭ-vĕs'tĭ-chər, -chŏŏr', dī-) *n.* **1.** An act of divesting. **2.** The sale, liquidation, or spinoff of a corporate division or subsidiary.
di•vide (dĭ-vīd') *v.* **-vid•ed, -vid•ing. 1.** To separate or become separated into parts : split. **2.** To classify : group. **3.** To separate into opposing factions : disunite. **4.** To cause to be cut off : keep apart <a wall *dividing* a city> **5.** To apportion among a number : distribute. **6.** *Math.* To perform the operation of division on (a number). **7.** To branch out, as a river. —*n.* A watershed. —**di•vid'a•ble** *adj.*
div•i•dend (dĭv'ĭ-dĕnd') *n.* **1.** *Math.* A number that is to be divided. **2.** A share of profits paid to a stockholder. **3.** *Informal.* A share of a surplus : bonus.
di•vid•er (dĭ-vī'dər) *n.* **1.** One that divides. **2. dividers.** COMPASS 2.
div•i•na•tion (dĭv'ə-nā'shən) *n.* **1.** The art of foretelling the future or the unknown through supernatural means. **2.** A presentiment.
di•vine¹ (dĭ-vīn') *adj.* **-vin•er, -vin•est. 1.** Of, relating to, or being a deity. **2.** Emanating from or devoted to a deity. **3.** *Informal.* Supremely pleasing. —*n.* A clergyman. —**di•vine'ly** *adv.* —**di•vine'ness** *n.*
di•vine² (dĭ-vīn') *v.* **-vined, -vin•ing. 1.** To foretell : prophesy. **2.** To infer : guess.
divining rod *n.* A forked branch or stick that allegedly indicates the location of subterranean water or minerals by bending downward when held over a source.
di•vin•i•ty (dĭ-vĭn'ĭ-tē) *n., pl.* **-ties. 1.** The condition or quality of being divine. **2. Divinity.** God. **3.** Theology.
di•vis•i•ble (dĭ-vĭz'ə-bəl) *adj.* Capable of being divided, esp. of being divided evenly with no remainder. —**di•vis'i•bil'i•ty** *n.*
di•vi•sion (dĭ-vĭzh'ən) *n.* **1.** The act of dividing or state of being divided. **2.** Something that serves to separate or divide. **3.** A group or section into which something is divided. **4.** A self-contained tactical military unit capable of independent combat operations. **5.** *Math.* The process of determining how many times one quantity is contained in another. —**di•vi'sion•al** *adj.*

di•vi•sive (dĭ-vī′sĭv) *adj.* Creating dissension or disunity. **—di•vi′sive•ness** *n.*
di•vi•sor (dĭ-vī′zər) *n. Math.* The number by which a dividend is to be divided.
di•vorce (dĭ-vôrs′, -vōrs′) *n.* **1.** The legal termination of a marriage. **2.** The complete separation of things. **—di•vorce′** *v.* **—di•vor•cé** *n.* **—di•vor•cée** *n.*
div•ot (dĭv′ət) *n.* A piece of turf torn up by a golf club in hitting the ball.
di•vulge (dĭ-vŭlj′) *v.* **-vulged, -vulg•ing.** To reveal or make known : disclose.
div•vy (dĭv′ē) *v.* **-vied, -vy•ing.** *Slang.* To divide <*divvied* up the loot>
diz•zy (dĭz′ē) *adj.* **-zi•er, -zi•est. 1.** Experiencing a whirling sensation. **2.** Producing or tending to produce giddiness or vertigo. **3.** *Informal.* Silly : foolish. **—diz′zi•ly** *adv.* **—diz′zi•ness** *n.* **—diz′zy** *v.*
DNA (dē′ĕn-ā′) *n.* A nucleic acid having a very complicated structure and forming the main constituent of the chromosomes of living cells : deoxyribonucleic acid.
do (do͞o) *v.* **did** (dĭd), **done** (dŭn), **do•ing, does** (dŭz). **1.** To perform : accomplish. **2.** To carry out the requirements of : fulfill. **3.** To create, compose, or make. **4.** To bring about : effect <The treatment *did* some good.> **5.** To put forth : exert <*did* our best to help> **6.** To attend to : deal with <have to *do* the marketing> **7.** To render or give <*do* honor to the war dead> **8.** To work at for a living <What do you *do*?> **9.** To work out the details of : solve <*did* the puzzle quickly> **10. a.** To present or perform (e.g., a play) : stage. **b.** To have the role of : play. **11.** To tour. **12.** To be sufficient or convenient : suffice. **13.** *Informal.* To serve in prison <*did* time> **14.** *Slang.* To swindle : cheat <*did* them out of their savings> **15.** To behave or conduct oneself : act. **16.** To set or style (the hair). **17.** To get by : fare <not *doing* well> **18.** *Slang.* To partake of : use <didn't *do* drugs> **19.** —Used as a substitute for an antecedent verb <earned as much as you *did*> **20.** —Used as an auxiliary: **a.** With a simple infinitive to indicate the tense in questions, negative statements, and inverted phrases <*Do* you hear it?><I *did* not play well.> **b.** As a means of emphasis <I *do* want you to come.><*Do* be quick.> **—do away with. 1.** To make an end of : eliminate. **2. a.** To destroy. **b.** To kill. **—do in.** *Slang.* **1.** To tire completely : exhaust. **2.** To kill. **—do up. 1.** To adorn or dress lavishly. **2.** To wrap and tie (a package). *—n., pl.* **do's** *or* **dos. 1.** Commotion : ado. **2.** An entertainment : party. **3.** A statement of what should be done <*do*'s and don'ts> **—do′a•ble** *adj.*
Do•ber•man pin•scher (dō′bər-mən pĭn′shər) *n.* A medium-sized, short-haired dog orig. bred in Germany.
do•bra (dō′brə) *n.* —See table at CURRENCY.
dob•son fly (dŏb′sən) *n.* An insect, *Corydalus cornutus,* with 4 many-veined wings.
doc (dŏk) *n. Informal.* Doctor.
do•cent (dō′sənt, dō-sĕnt′) *n.* A teacher or lecturer at certain universities.
doc•ile (dŏs′əl, -īl′) *adj.* Easily taught, trained, or controlled : tractable. **—do•cil′i•ty** (dŏ-sĭl′ĭ-tē, dō-) *n.*
dock[1] (dŏk) *n.* **1. a.** A landing pier for ships or boats. **b.** A loading platform for trucks or trains. **2.** A pier or wharf. *—v.* **1.** To maneuver or come into a dock. **2.** *Aerospace.* To couple (e.g., 2 or more spacecraft) in space.
dock[2] (dŏk) *v.* **1.** To clip or cut off (e.g., an animal's tail). **2.** To deduct or withhold a part of (a salary).
dock[3] (dŏk) *n.* An enclosure where the defendant sits or stands in a criminal court.
dock[4] (dŏk) *n.* A weedy plant of the genus *Rumex,* with small flower clusters.
dock•age (dŏk′ĭj) *n.* **1.** A charge for docking privileges. **2.** Facilities for docking.
dock•et (dŏk′ĭt) *n.* **1.** A calender of cases awaiting adjudication. **2.** An agenda. **—dock′et** *v.*
dock•yard (dŏk′yärd′) *n.* A shipyard.
doc•tor (dŏk′tər) *n.* **1.** A person trained and licensed to practice the healing arts, as medicine or surgery. **2.** A person holding the highest degree given by a university. *—v.* **1. a.** To administer medical treatment to. **b.** To practice medicine. **2.** To repair, esp. in a haphazard way. **3.** To tamper with so as to deceive <*doctored* the coroner's report> **4.** To modify or alter for a desired end. **—doc′tor•al** *adj.*
doc•tor•ate (dŏk′tər-ĭt) *n.* The degree, status, or title of an academic doctor.
doc•tri•naire (dŏk′trə-nâr′) *n.* One dogmatically attached to a theory or practice.
doc•trine (dŏk′trĭn) *n.* **1.** Something taught as a body of principles. **2.** A dogma. **—doc′trin•al** *adj.*
doc•u•dra•ma (dŏk′yə-drä′mə, -drăm′ə) *n.* A television or movie dramatization based on fact.
doc•u•ment (dŏk′yə-mənt) *n.* An official paper that can be used to furnish evidence or information. *—v.* (-mĕnt′). To prove with, support by, or provide by documents. **—doc′u•men•ta′tion** *n.*
doc•u•men•ta•ry (dŏk′yə-mĕn′tə-rē) *adj.* **1.** Of, relating to, or based on documents. **2.** Presented in factual but artistic form. **—doc′u•men′ta•ry** *n.*
dod•der[1] (dŏd′ər) *v.* To tremble or move unsteadily, as from age : totter.
dod•der[2] (dŏd′ər) *n.* A parasitic twining vine of the genus *Cuscuta.*
dodge (dŏj) *v.* **dodged, dodg•ing. 1.** To avoid (e.g., a blow) by moving quickly out of the way. **2.** To evade, esp. by stratagem. **3.** To shift suddenly. **—dodge** *n.*
dodg•er (dŏj′ər) *n.* **1.** One who dodges or evades. **2.** A dishonest or shifty person : trickster. **3.** A small printed handbill.
do•do (dō′dō) *n., pl.* **-does** *or* **-dos. 1.** An extinct flightless bird, *Raphus cucullatus,* once found on the island of Mauritius. **2.** *Informal.* One who is entirely out-of-date : fogy. **3.** *Informal.* A stupid person.

doe (dō) *n., pl.* **does** *or* **doe. 1.** A mature female deer. **2.** A female of various mammals, as the hare or kangaroo.
do·er (do͞o′ər) *n.* One who does something, esp. an active, energetic person.
does (dŭz) *v. 3rd person sing. present tense of* DO.
doe·skin (dō′skĭn′) *n.* **1.** Leather made from the skin of a doe, deer, or goat. **2.** A fine, soft, smooth woolen fabric.
does·n't (dŭz′ənt). Does not.
doff (dôf, dŏf) *v.* **1.** To take off (clothing). **2.** To tip or remove (one's hat) in greeting. **3.** To throw away **:** discard.
dog (dôg, dŏg) *n.* **1.** A domesticated carnivorous mammal, *Canis familiaris,* raised in a wide variety of breeds and held to have orig. derived from several wild species. **2.** Any of various animals of the family Canidae, as the dingo. **3.** *Informal.* A fellow <you witty *dog*> **4.** *Slang.* **a.** An uninteresting or unattractive person. **b.** A hopelessly inferior product or creation. **c.** A contemptible person. **5. dogs.** *Slang.* The feet. **6.** Any of various hooked or U-shaped metallic devices used for gripping or holding heavy objects. —*adv.* Completely <*dog*-weary> —*v.* **dogged, dog·ging. 1.** To track or trail relentlessly. **2.** To hold or fasten with a mechanical dog.
dog·cart (dôg′kärt′, dŏg′-) *n.* A vehicle drawn by one horse and accommodating two persons seated back to back.
dog days *pl.n.* The hot, sultry period between mid-July and Sept.
doge (dōj) *n.* The chief magistrate of the former republics of Venice and Genoa.
dog-ear (dôg′îr′, dŏg′-) *n.* The turned-down corner of a page of a book. **—dog′-ear** *v.* **—dog′-eared′** *adj.*
dog-eat-dog (dôg′ēt-dôg′, dŏg′ēt-dŏg′) *adj.* Ruthlessly acquisitive or competitive.
dog·fight (dôg′fīt′, dŏg′-) *n.* An aerial battle between fighter planes.
dog·fish (dôg′fĭsh′, dŏg′-) *n.* A small shark, chiefly of the family Squalidae of Atlantic and Pacific coastal waters.
dog·ged (dô′gĭd, dŏg′ĭd) *adj.* Stubbornly unyielding **:** tenacious. **—dog′ged·ly** *adv.* **—dog′ged·ness** *n.*
dog·ger·el (dô′gər-əl, dŏg′ər-) *n.* Loose, irregular verse, esp. of an inferior nature.
dog·gy *or* **dog·gie** (dô′gē, dŏg′ē) *n., pl.* **-gies.** A dog, esp. a small one.
doggy bag *or* **doggie bag** *n.* A bag for leftover food taken home from a restaurant.
dog·house (dôg′hous′, dŏg′-) *n.* A dog shelter.
†do·gie (dō′gē) *n. W U.S.* A stray or motherless calf.
dog·leg (dôg′lĕg′, dŏg′-) *n.* **1.** A sharp bend, esp. in a road. **2.** A golf hole with a sharply angled fairway. **—dog′leg′** *v.*
dog·ma (dôg′mə, dŏg′-) *n.* **1.** A system of doctrines proclaimed true by a religious sect. **2.** A principle, belief, or idea, esp. one considered to be absolute truth.
dog·mat·ic (dôg-măt′ĭk, dŏg-) *adj.* Characterized by an authoritative assertion of unproved or unprovable principles. **—dog·mat′i·cal·ly** *adv.*
dog·ma·tism (dôg′mə-tĭz′əm, dŏg′-) *n.* Dogmatic assertion of belief or opinion.
dog·nap (dôg′năp′) *v.* **-naped, -nap·ing** *or* **-napped, -nap·ping.** To steal (a dog), esp. for sale to a research laboratory. **—dog′nap′er, dog′nap′per** *n.*
do-good·er (do͞o′go͝od′ər) *n. Informal.* An earnest but naive supporter of philanthropic or humanitarian reforms.
dog paddle *n.* A swimming stroke in which the arms paddle and the legs kick up and down. **—dog′-pad′dle** *v.*
dogtooth violet *n.* A plant, *Erythronium americanum,* of North America, bearing lily-like yellow flowers.
†dog·trot (dôg′trŏt′, dŏg′-) *n.* **1.** An easy, steady trot. **2.** *Regional.* A roofed passage between 2 parts of a structure.
dog·wood (dôg′wo͝od′, dŏg′-) *n.* A tree, *Cornus florida* of E North America, bearing small greenish flowers surrounded by petallike white or pink bracts.
doi·ly (doi′lē) *n., pl.* **-lies.** A small, ornamental mat, usu. of lace or linen.
do·ings (do͞o′ĭngz) *pl.n.* Events or activities, esp. social activities.
do-it-your·self (do͞o′ĭt-yər-sĕlf′) *adj. Informal.* Designed to be done or used without professional help.
do·jo (dō′jō) *n.* A school for training in Japanese arts of self-defense.
dol·ce vi·ta (dōl′chā vē′tä) *n.* A sensual and self-indulgent life.
dol·drums (dōl′drəmz′, dôl′-, dŏl′-) *pl.n.* **1.** The ocean regions near the equator where there is little or no wind. **2.** A period or condition of depression or inactivity.
dole (dōl) *n.* **1. a.** The distribution of goods, esp. of money, food, or clothing, as charity. **b.** Something so distributed. **2.** *esp. Brit.* The governmental distribution of relief payments to the unemployed. —*v.* **doled, dol·ing. 1.** To distribute or dispense as charity. **2.** To distribute sparingly <*dole* out food>
dole·ful (dōl′fəl) *adj.* Filled with or expressing grief **:** sad. **—dole′ful·ly** *adv.* **—dole′ful·ness** *n.*
doll (dŏl) *n.* **1.** A child's toy representing a human being. **2.** *Slang.* **a.** An attractive person. **b.** A woman. —*v. Slang.* To dress elegantly, as for a special occasion.
dol·lar (dŏl′ər) *n.* —See table at CURRENCY.
dol·lop (dŏl′əp) *n.* A lump, portion, or helping <a *dollop* of whipped cream>
dol·ly (dŏl′ē) *n., pl.* **-lies. 1.** A doll. **2.** A low platform that moves on small wheels or rollers, used for moving heavy loads. **3.** A wheeled apparatus for moving a motion-picture or television camera about the set.
dol·men (dōl′mən, dŏl′-) *n.* A prehistoric structure made up of 2 or more upright stones supporting a horizontal stone.
do·lo·mite (dō′lə-mīt′, dŏl′ə-) *n.* A gray, pink,

or white mineral consisting mainly of calcium and magnesium.

do·lor·ous (dŏ'lə-rəs, dŏl'-) *adj.* Marked by or expressive of grief or pain. **—do'lor·ous·ly** *adv.* **—do'lor·ous·ness** *n.*

dol·phin (dŏl'fĭn, dôl'-) *n.* **1.** Any of various marine mammals, chiefly of the family Delphinidae, that are related to the whales but are gen. smaller and have a beaklike snout. **2.** Either of 2 iridescently colored marine fishes, *Coryphaena hippurus* or *C. equisetis.*

dolt (dōlt) *n.* A dull, stupid person : clod.

-dom *suff.* **1.** State : condition <star*dom*> **2. a.** Domain : position : rank <duke*dom*> **b.** A group having a specified position, office, or character <official*dom*>

do·main (dō-mān') *n.* **1.** A territory over which rule or control is exercised. **2.** A sphere of activity or interest : field.

dome (dōm) *n.* **1.** A hemispherical vault or roof. **2.** Something suggesting a dome.

do·mes·tic (də-mĕs'tĭk) *adj.* **1.** Of or relating to a home, household, or family life. **2.** Enjoying or interested in home life and household affairs. **3.** Tame : domesticated <*domestic* animals> **4.** Of or relating to the policies or affairs within a country. **5.** Indigenous to or produced in a particular country. *—n.* A household servant. **—do·mes'ti·cal·ly** *adv.* **—do'mes·tic'i·ty** *n.*

do·mes·ti·cate (də-mĕs'tĭ-kāt') *v.* **-cat·ed, -cat·ing.** To train or adapt to live with and be of use to human beings. **—do·mes'ti·ca'tion** *n.*

dom·i·cile (dŏm'ĭ-sīl', -səl, dō'mĭ-) *n.* A dwelling place : home. **—dom'i·cile'** *v.* **—dom'i·cil'i·ar'y** (-sĭl'ē-ĕr'ē) *adj.*

dom·i·nant (dŏm'ə-nənt) *adj.* **1.** Having the most control or influence. **2.** Most prominent. **3.** *Genetics* Producing a particular characteristic even when paired with an unlike gene for the same characteristic. **—dom'i·nance** *n.* **—dom'i·nant·ly** *adv.*

dom·i·nate (dŏm'ə-nāt') *v.* **-nat·ed, -nat·ing. 1.** To influence, control, or rule by superior power or authority. **2.** To occupy the most prominent position in or over. **—dom'i·na'tion** *n.* **—dom'i·na'tor** *n.*

dom·i·neer (dŏm'ə-nîr') *v.* **1.** To rule over arbitrarily or arrogantly : tyrannize. **2.** To be bossy or overbearing.

do·min·ion (də-mĭn'yən) *n.* **1.** Supreme authority or control : sovereignty. **2.** A territory or sphere of control or influence : realm.

Dominion Day *n. Can.* Canada Day.

dom·i·no[1] (dŏm'ə-nō') *n., pl.* **-noes** *or* **-nos. 1. a.** A masquerade costume consisting of a cloak with a hood and a mask worn over the top half of the face. **b.** The mask itself. **2.** A person wearing a domino.

dom·i·no[2] (dŏm'ə-nō') *n., pl.* **-noes** *or* **-nos. 1.** A small, rectangular block whose face is divided into halves, each half being blank or marked from 1 to 6 dots. **2. dominoes** *or* **dominos** *(sing. in number).* A game played with a set of gen. 28 dominoes.

don[1] (dŏn) *n.* **1. Don.** Sir. —Used as a courtesy title with a man's given name in Spanish-speaking countries. **2.** A Spanish gentleman. **3.** A head, tutor, or fellow at an English university. **4.** A Mafia leader.

don[2] (dŏn) *v.* **donned, don·ning.** To put on : dress in <*donned* a new suit>

do·ña (dōn'yə) *n.* **1. Doña.** Lady. —Used as a courtesy title with a woman's given name in Spanish-speaking countries. **2.** A Spanish gentlewoman.

do·nate (dō'nāt', dō-nāt') *v.* **-nat·ed, -nat·ing.** To present as a gift to a fund or cause. **—do·na'tion** *n.* **—do'na'tor** *n.*

done (dŭn) *adj.* **1.** Completely finished : through. **2.** Cooked adequately. **3.** Socially acceptable <not *done* in public>

dong (dông, dŏng) *n.* —See table at CURRENCY.

Don Juan (dŏn wŏn', jo͞o'ən) *n.* A man obsessed with seducing women : libertine.

don·key (dŏng'kē, dŭng'-, dông'-) *n., pl.* **-keys. 1.** The domesticated ass, prob. descended from the wild ass *Equus asinus.* **2.** *Informal.* A stubborn or stupid person.

don·nish (dŏn'ĭsh) *adj.* Of, resembling, or characteristic of a university don : pedantic.

don·ny·brook (dŏn'ē-bro͝ok') *n.* A brawl.

do·nor (dō'nər) *n.* A person who gives, donates, or contributes, as to a fund or cause.

Don Qui·xo·te (dŏn'kē-hō'tē, kwĭk'sət) *n.* An impractical idealist.

don't (dōnt). Do not.

do·nut (dō'nŭt', -nət) *n. var. of* DOUGHNUT.

doo·dad (do͞o'dăd') *n. Informal.* A nameless or unnamed gadget or article.

doo·dle (do͞od'l) *v.* **-dled, -dling.** To scribble aimlessly, esp. when preoccupied. **—doo'dle** *n.*

doom (do͞om) *n.* **1.** A decision or judgment, esp. an official condemnation to a severe penalty. **2.** Destiny or fate, esp. a ruinous or tragic fate. **3.** Inevitable destruction or ruin : annihilation. *—v.* **1.** To condemn. **2.** To destine, esp. to an unhappy end.

▲ ***word history:*** The semantics of *doom* illustrates the process of pejoration, by which a word of a good or neutral connotation acquires an evil one. *Doom* is related to the verb *do* and basically means "something set up" and specif. "a law, statute." Even by Old English times, however, *doom* meant "judgment," esp. an adverse judgment, condemnation, or punishment.

dooms·day (do͞omz'dā') *n.* **1.** Judgment Day. **2.** A dreaded day of judgment or reckoning.

door (dôr, dōr) *n.* **1.** A movable panel for closing off an entrance. **2.** An entrance or passage. **3.** A means of access.

door·bell (dôr'bĕl', dōr'-) *n.* A bell rung at an outer door as a signal.

door·jamb (dôr'jăm', dōr'-) *n.* Either of the 2 vertical pieces that frame a doorway and support the lintel.

door·knob (dôr'nŏb', dōr'-) *n.* A knob that when turned opens a door.

door·man (dôr'măn', -mən, dōr'-) *n.* An attendant at the entrance of a building.

door·mat (dôr′măt′, dōr′-) *n.* A mat outside a door, used to wipe wet or dirty shoes.
door·step (dôr′stĕp′, dōr′-) *n.* A step that leads to a door.
door·way (dôr′wā′, dōr′-) *n.* An entrance to a room or building.
door·yard (dôr′yärd′, dōr′-) *n.* A yard adjacent to the door of a house.
doo·zy *or* **doo·zie** (do͞o′zē) *n.* , *pl.* **-zies.** *Slang.* Something extraordinary or bizarre.
do·pa (dō′pə) *n.* An amino acid that is used to treat Parkinson's disease.
dope (dōp) *n.* **1.** One of various chiefly liquid preparations added to produce desired properties **:** additive. **2.** *Informal.* A narcotic, esp. one that is addictive. **3.** *Slang.* A stupid person. **4.** *Slang.* Facts and details **:** information. —*v.* **doped, dop·ing. 1.** To treat with an additive. **2.** *Informal.* To administer a drug to, esp. in secret **:** drug. **3.** *Informal.* To figure out.
dope·ster (dōp′stər) *n.* One who analyzes and predicts future events, esp. in sports.
dop·ey *also* **dop·y** (dō′pē) *adj.* **-i·er, -i·est.** *Slang.* **1.** Dazed or sluggish as if drugged. **2.** Stupid or foolish.
dorm (dôrm) *n. Informal.* A dormitory.
dor·mant (dôr′mənt) *adj.* **1.** Asleep or inactive. **2.** *Biol.* Being in a relatively inactive or resting condition in which some processes are slowed down or suspended. **—dor′man·cy** *n.*
dor·mer (dôr′mər) *n.* A window set in a small gable projecting from a roof.
dor·mi·to·ry (dôr′mĭ-tôr′ē, -tōr′ē) *n., pl.* **-ries. 1.** A large room providing sleeping quarters for a number of people. **2.** A building for housing a number of people.
dor·mouse (dôr′mous′) *n.* Any of various squirrellike rodents of the family Gliridae.
†dor·nick (dôr′nĭk) *n. Regional.* A small chunk of rock **:** stone.
dor·sal (dôr′səl) *adj. Anat.* Of, relating to, or located on or near the back.
do·ry (dôr′ē, dōr′ē) *n., pl.* **-ries.** A small, narrow, flat-bottomed fishing boat with high sides and a sharp prow.
DOS (dŏs, dôs) *n. Computer Sci.* An operating system that resides on a disk.
dose (dōs) *n.* **1.** A specified amount of a therapeutic agent prescribed to be taken at one time or at stated intervals. **2.** *Med.* The amount of radiation administered to a certain bodily part. **—dos′age** *n.* **—dose** *v.*
do·sim·e·ter (dō-sĭm′ĭ-tər) *n.* A device that measures and indicates the amount of x-rays or radioactivity absorbed.
dos·si·er (dŏs′ē-ā′, dô′sē-ā′) *n.* A collection of documents or papers giving detailed information about a person or subject.
dot (dŏt) *n.* **1.** A small speck **:** spot. **2.** A small round mark made by or as if by a writing implement. **3.** A precise moment in time. —*v.* **dot·ted, dot·ting.** To mark or cover with or as if with dots.
dot·age (dō′tĭj) *n.* Senility.
dot·ard (dō′tərd) *n.* A senile person.
dote (dōt) *v.* **dot·ed, dot·ing. 1.** To show excessive fondness or love. **2.** To show mental deterioration, esp. as a result of senility. **—dot′er** *n.*
dot matrix *n. Computer Sci.* A dense grid of dots used to form characters or designs, as by some computer printers.
dou·ble (dŭb′əl) *adj.* **1.** Twice as much in size, power, quantity, or amount. **2.** Composed of two like parts <*double* doors> **3.** Composed of two unlike parts **:** dual <a *double* meaning> **4.** Accommodating or designed for two. **5. a.** Acting two parts. **b.** Marked by duplicity **:** deceitful. **6.** *Bot.* Having more than the usual number of petals. —*adv.* **1.** Two together <riding *double*> **2.** In two <bent *double*> —*n.* **1.** Something or someone that resembles another **:** duplicate. **2.** An understudy. **3.** A sharp turn in running **:** reversal. **4. doubles.** A match between two pairs of players, as in tennis. **5.** *Baseball* A hit in which the batter reaches 2nd base. **6.** A bid doubling one's opponent's bid in bridge. —*v.* **-bled, -bling. 1.** To make or become twice as great. **2.** To fold in two <*double* the blanket> **3.** *Baseball.* To hit a double. **4.** To challenge (an opponent's bid) with a double in bridge. **5.** To reverse direction <*double* back over the trail> **6.** To serve an additional purpose <My bed *doubles* as a couch.> **—dou′bly** *adv.*
double agent *n.* A spy who pretends to work for a government while actually working for another.
double bass *n.* The largest and lowest-pitched member of the violin family.
dou·ble-breast·ed (dŭb′əl-brĕs′tĭd) *adj.* Fastened by lapping one half over the other and usu. having a double row of buttons with a single row of buttonholes.
dou·ble-cross (dŭb′əl-krôs′, -krŏs′) *v. Slang.* To betray. **—dou′ble-cross′** *n.*
dou·ble-deal·ing (dŭb′əl-dē′lĭng) *adj.* Marked by duplicity **:** treacherous. —*n.* Deceit. **—dou′ble-deal′er** *n.*
dou·ble-deck·er (dŭb′əl-dĕk′ər) *n.* **1.** A vehicle, as a bus, with 2 decks for passengers. **2.** Two beds built one above the other. **3.** A sandwich with 3 slices of bread and 2 layers of filling.
double dipping *n.* The practice of holding a salaried governmental position while receiving a pension from another.
dou·ble-en·ten·dre (dŭb′əl-än-tän′drə, do͞o′blän-täɴ′drə) *n.* A word or expression having a double meaning, esp. when the 2nd meaning is risqué.
dou·ble-head·er (dŭb′əl-hĕd′ər) *n.* Two games played consecutively on the same day.
dou·ble-joint·ed (dŭb′l-join′tĭd) *adj.* Having flexible joints permitting connected parts to be bent at unusual angles.
double knit *n.* A jerseylike knitted fabric having a double thickness and interlocking stitches.
double play *n. Baseball.* A play in which two players are put out.
dou·ble·speak (dŭb′əl-spēk′) *n.* DOUBLE TALK 2.

dou•blet (dŭb′lĭt) *n.* **1.** A close-fitting jacket worn by men between the 15th and 17th cent. **2. a.** A pair of similar things. **b.** One of a pair.
double take *n.* A delayed reaction to something unusual.
double talk *n.* **1.** Meaningless speech consisting of nonsense syllables mixed with intelligible words : gibberish. **2.** Evasive or ambiguous language.
dou•ble•think (dŭb′əl-thĭngk′) *n.* Simultaneous belief in 2 contradictory ideas or points of view.
▲ ***word history:*** *Doublethink* was coined by George Orwell in his novel *Nineteen Eighty-four,* published in 1949. It is rare that an invented word gains sufficient currency to be included in a dictionary.
dou•bloon (dŭ-blo͞on′) *n.* An obsolete Spanish gold coin.
doubt (dout) *v.* **1.** To be uncertain or unsure about. **2.** To tend to distrust : disbelieve. —*n.* **1.** A lack of certainty or conviction. **2.** An uncertain state of affairs. ★ ***syns:*** DOUBTFULNESS, DUBIETY, QUESTION, SKEPTICISM, UNCERTAINTY —**doubt′er** *n.*
doubt•ful (dout′fəl) *adj.* **1.** Not sure : uncertain. **2.** Experiencing or exhibiting doubt <*doubtful* about the future> **3.** Of uncertain outcome : undecided. **4.** Equivocal in nature or character : questionable <a *doubtful* past> —**doubt′ful•ly** *adv.* —**doubt′ful•ness** *n.*
doubt•less (dout′lĭs) *adj.* Assured : positive. —*adv.* **1.** Certainly. **2.** Probably. —**doubt′less•ly** *adv.*
douche (do͞osh) *n.* **1.** A stream of liquid or air applied to a part or cavity of the body in order to cleanse or medicate. **2.** A device for application of a douche. —**douche** *v.*
dough (dō) *n.* **1.** A thick, soft mixture of flour or meal, liquids, and other ingredients that is baked, esp. to make bread or pastry. **2.** A doughlike pasty mass. **3.** *Slang.* Money. —**dough′y** *adj.*
dough•boy (dō′boi′) *n.* An American infantryman in World War I.
dough•nut *also* **do•nut** (dō′nŭt′, -nət) *n.* A small, usu. ring-shaped cake made of rich, light dough that is deep-fried.
dough•ty (dou′tē) *adj.* **-ti•er, -ti•est.** Marked by valor : courageous.
Doug•las fir (dŭg′ləs) *n.* An evergreen timber tree, *Pseudotsuga taxifolia,* of NW North America.
dour (do͝or, dour) *adj.* **1.** Stern and forbidding. **2.** Morose and gloomy : ill-humored.
douse (dous) *v.* **doused, dous•ing. 1.** To plunge into liquid : immerse. **2.** To drench. **3.** To extinguish.
dove[1] (dŭv) *n.* **1.** Any of various birds of the family Columbidae, which includes the pigeons. **2.** An advocate of peace and conciliatory measures as opposed to armed conflict. —**dov′ish** *adj.*
dove[2] (dōv) *v. var. p.t. of* DIVE.
dove•tail (dŭv′tāl′) *n.* A fan-shaped tenon that when fitted into a corresponding mortise forms a tight interlocking joint. —*v.* **1.** To cut into or join by means of dovetails. **2.** To connect or combine precisely and harmoniously.
dow•a•ger (dou′ə-jər) *n.* **1.** A widow who holds a title or property from her dead husband. **2.** An elderly woman of high social position.
dow•dy (dou′dē) *adj.* **-di•er, -di•est. 1.** Not neat : shabby. **2.** Old-fashioned.
dow•el (dou′əl) *n.* A round wooden pin that fits tightly into a corresponding hole to fasten together 2 pieces. —**dow′el** *v.*
dow•er (dou′ər) *n.* **1.** The part of or interest in a deceased man's real estate allotted by law to his widow for her lifetime. **2.** A dowry. —*v.* To give a dower to : endow.
down[1] (doun) *adv.* **1. a.** From a higher to a lower place <climb *down*> **b.** From an upright position to a horizontal position <knocked all the pins *down*> **2.** In or to a lower position, point, or state <sit *down*> **3.** From earlier times or people. **4.** In partial payment at the time of purchase. **5.** Earnestly or energetically. **6.** In writing. **7.** To the source <tracked the gossip *down*> —*adj.* **1. a.** Directed or moving downward <the *down* staircase> **b.** In a low or lower position <The blinds are *down.*> **2. a.** Sick <*down* with the flu> **b.** Low in spirits : dejected. **3.** Completed : finished <5 *down,* 5 to go> —*prep.* In a descending direction along, into, upon, or through. —*n.* **1.** A movement downward : descent. **2.** *Football.* Any of a series of plays during which a team must advance at least 10 yds. to retain possession of the ball. —*v.* **1.** To bring, strike, put, or throw down. **2.** To gulp.
down[2] (doun) *n.* **1.** Fine, soft, fluffy feathers, as on a young bird. **2.** A soft, fine substance like down <peach *down*>
down[3] (doun) *n. often* **downs.** An expanse of grassy upland used for grazing.
down•beat (doun′bēt′) *n.* The downward hand movement made by a conductor to indicate the first beat of a musical measure.
down•cast (doun′kăst′) *adj.* **1.** Directed downward <*downcast* eyes> **2.** Low in spirits : dejected.
down•er (dou′nər) *n. Slang.* **1.** A depressant or sedative drug, as a barbiturate or tranquilizer. **2.** One that is depressing.
down•fall (doun′fôl′) *n.* **1. a.** A sudden loss of wealth, position, or happiness : ruin. **b.** Something that causes a downfall. **2.** A fall of rain or snow, esp. when heavy or unexpected. —**down′fall′en** *adj.*
down•grade (doun′grād′) *n.* **1.** A downward slope or grade, as in a road. **2.** A downward turn or trend. —*v.* To lower in rank, reputation, or importance.
down•heart•ed (doun′här′tĭd) *adj.* Low in spirits : downcast.
down•hill (doun′hĭl′) *adv.* Toward the bottom of a hill. —**down′hill′** *adj.*
down-home (doun′hōm′) *adj.* Of, pertaining to, or typical of the rural S U.S. or its people, as in naturalness or informality.
down•load (doun′lōd′) *v.* **1.** To unload. **2.**

Computer Sci. To transfer (data or programs) from a central computer to a peripheral computer or device.

down payment *n.* A partial payment made at the time of purchase.

down·play (doun′plā′) *v.* To minimize the significance of.

down·pour (doun′pôr′, -pōr′) *n.* A heavy rainfall.

down·right (doun′rīt′) *adj.* **1.** Out-and-out : complete. **2.** Straightforward : candid. —*adv.* Thoroughly.

down·scale (doun′skāl′) *adj.* Of or for low-income consumers. —*v.* To reduce in scale : scale down.

down·shift (doun′shĭft′) *v.* To shift into a lower automotive gear.

down·size (doun′sīz′) *v.* To make in a smaller size.

down·stage (doun′stāj′) *adv. & adj.* Toward or at the front of a theater stage.

down·stairs (doun′stârz′) *adv.* **1.** Down the stairs. **2.** To or on a lower floor. —*n.* (-stârz′) *(sing. in number).* The lower or main floor. —**down′stairs′** *adj.*

down·stream (doun′strēm′) *adv. & adj.* In the direction of a stream's current.

down·swing (doun′swĭng′) *n.* **1.** A swing downward. **2.** A downward trend.

Down syndrome (doun) *or* **Down's syndrome** (dounz) *n.* A congenital disorder marked by mild to moderate mental retardation and short stature.

down·time (doun′tīm′) *n.* A period of time when something, as a machine or a factory, is inactive.

down-to-earth (doun′tə-ûrth′) *adj.* Sensible : practical.

down·town (doun′toun′) *n.* The lower part and esp. the business center of a city or town. —*adv.* (-toun′). To, toward, or in the downtown. —**down′town′** *adj.*

down·trod·den (doun′trŏd′n) *adj.* Subjected to oppression.

down·turn (doun′tûrn′) *n.* A decline, esp. in business or financial affairs.

down under *n. Informal.* Australia or New Zealand.

down·ward (doun′wərd) *also* **down·wards** (-wərdz) *adv.* From a higher to a lower place, point, level, or condition. —**down′ward** *adj.*

down·wind (doun′wĭnd′) *adv. & adj.* In the direction toward which the wind blows : leeward.

dow·ry (dou′rē) *n., pl.* **-ries.** Money or property brought by a bride to her husband at marriage.

dowse (douz) *v.* **dowsed, dows·ing.** To use a divining rod to find underground water or minerals. —**dows′er** *n.*

dox·ol·o·gy (dŏk-sŏl′ə-jē) *n., pl.* **-gies.** A hymn or verse in praise of God.

doy·en (doi-ĕn′, doi′ən, dwä-yăN′) *n.* The eldest or senior male member of a group.

doy·enne (doi-ĕn′, dwä-yĕn′) *n.* The eldest or senior female member of a group.

doze (dōz) *v.* **dozed, doz·ing.** To sleep lightly : nap. —**doze** *n.*

doz·en (dŭz′ən) *n.* **1.** *pl.* **dozen.** A set of 12. **2.** *pl.* **dozens.** An indefinite number. —**doz′en** *adj.* —**doz′enth** *adj.*

drab (drăb) *adj.* **drab·ber, drab·best. 1. a.** Of a light, dull brown color. **b.** Of an olive brown : khaki-colored. **2.** Commonplace : dull. —**drab′ness** *n.*

dra·cae·na (drə-sē′nə) *n.* Any of several tropical plants of the genera *Dracaena* and *Cordyline,* some species of which are widely grown as house plants for their decorative foliage.

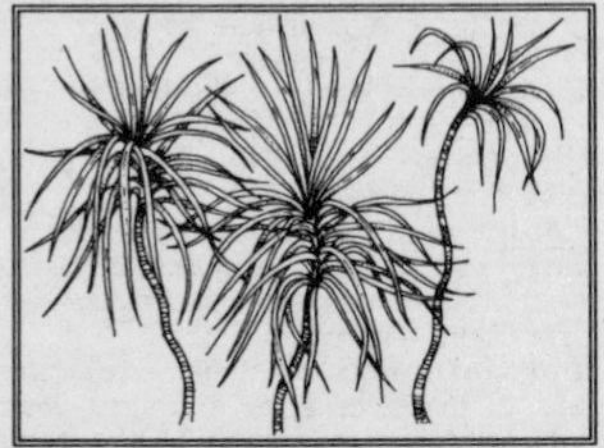

dracaena

drach·ma (drăk′mə) *n., pl.* **-mas** *or* **-mae** (-mē). **1.** —See table at CURRENCY. **2.** A silver coin of ancient Greece.

dra·co·ni·an (drā-kō′nē-ən, drə-) *adj.* Exceedingly harsh : very severe <*draconian* budget cuts>

draft (drăft, dräft) *n.* **1. a.** A current of air. **b.** A device in a flue that controls the circulation of air. **2.** The act of pulling or drawing a load. **3.** A preliminary sketch, outline, or version. **4. a.** Compulsory assignment to military service. **b.** The group of people assigned. **5. a.** A gulp, drink, or inhalation of something. **b.** The amount taken in. **6.** A document for the transfer of money. **7.** The depth of a ship's keel below the water line, esp. when loaded. —*v.* **1. a.** To select for a specific duty. **b.** To conscript for military service. **2.** To work up a tentative plan for or sketch of. —*adj.* **1.** Used for drawing heavy loads <*draft* horses> **2.** Drawn from a keg or tap <*draft* beer> —**draft·ee′** *n.*

drafts·man (drăfts′mən, dräfts′-) *n.* A person who draws designs or plans, as of machinery. —**drafts′man·ship′** *n.*

draft·y (drăf′tē, dräf′-) *adj.* **-i·er, -i·est.** Being exposed to or having drafts of air. —**draft′i·ness** *n.*

drag (drăg) *v.* **dragged, drag·ging. 1.** To draw along, pull, or haul by force. **2.** To trail or cause to trail along the ground. **3.** To search or dredge the bottom of (a body of water), as with a hook or net. **4.** To move or cause to move with great reluctance or difficulty. **5.** To pass or proceed slowly <Time *dragged.*> **6.** To prolong boringly <*dragged* out the lecture> **7.** *Slang.* To draw on a cigarette, pipe, or cigar **:** puff. —*n.* **1.** The act of dragging. **2.** Something, as a harrow, dragged along on the ground. **3.** Something that slows or stops motion, as a brake on a fishing reel. **4.** The retarding force exerted on a moving body by a fluid medium, as air or water. **5.** *Slang.* Someone or something esp. bothersome. **6.** *Slang.* A puff on a cigarette, pipe, or cigar. **7.** *Slang.* A street. **8.** *Slang.* Clothing of either sex worn by a member of the opposite sex. **—drag′ger** *n.*

drag•net (drăg′nĕt′) *n.* **1.** A trawling net. **2.** A system of search in which all available resources are used.

drag•o•man (drăg′ə-mən) *n., pl.* **-mans** or **-men.** An interpreter in countries where Arabic, Turkish, or Persian is spoken.

drag•on (drăg′ən) *n.* An imaginary giant reptile of story and legend usu. represented as a winged, fire-breathing monster.

drag•on•fly (drăg′ən-flī′) *n.* Any of various large insects of the order Odonata, with 2 pairs of narrow, net-veined wings and a long, slender body.

dra•goon (drə-go͞on′, dră-) *n.* A heavily armed mounted soldier of the 17th and 18th cent. —*v.* To coerce.

drain (drān) *v.* **1.** To draw off (a liquid) gradually <*drained* water from the pool> **2. a.** To cause liquid to go out from **:** empty <*drained* the pool> **b.** To draw off the surface water of. **3.** To use up completely **:** exhaust. —*n.* **1.** A means, as a pipe or channel, of draining liquid. **2.** The act or process of draining. **3.** Something that drains or exhausts. **—drain′er** *n.*

drain•age (drā′nĭj) *n.* **1.** The act, process, or a way of draining. **2.** A natural or artificial system of drains. **3.** Something that is drained off.

drain•pipe (drān′pīp′) *n.* A pipe for carrying off rainwater or sewage.

drake (drāk) *n.* A male duck.

dram (drăm) *n.* **1.** —See table at MEASUREMENT. **2. a.** A small drink, as of a liqueur. **b.** A small amount **:** bit.

dra•ma (drä′mə, drăm′ə) *n.* **1.** A play in prose or verse, esp. one recounting a serious story. **2.** Dramatic art of a particular kind or period <Shakespearean *drama*> **3.** A succession of events with the dramatic progression or emotional content typical of a play. **—dra•mat′ic** (drə-măt′ĭk) *adj.* **—dra•mat′i•cal•ly** *adv.* **—dram′a•tist** *n.*

dram•a•tize (drăm′ə-tīz′, drä′mə-) *v.* **-tized, -tiz•ing. 1.** To adapt for presentation as a drama. **2.** To present or regard in a dramatic or melodramatic manner. **—dram′a•ti•za′tion** *n.*

drank (drăngk) *v. p.t. of* DRINK.

drape (drāp) *v.* **draped, drap•ing. 1.** To cover or hang with cloth in loose folds <*draped* the sculpture> **2.** To arrange or hang in loose, graceful folds. **3.** To stretch or cause to stretch out loosely <*draped* my arms over the railing> —*n.* **1.** *often* **drapes.** A drapery **:** curtain. **2.** The manner in which cloth hangs or falls.

drap•er (drā′pər) *n. esp. Brit.* One who deals in dry goods and cloth.

drap•er•y (drā′pə-rē) *n., pl.* **-ies. 1.** Cloth or clothing gracefully arranged in loose folds. **2.** *often* **draperies.** Curtains, usu. of heavy fabric, that hang straight in loose folds. **3.** *esp. Brit.* The business of a draper.

dras•tic (drăs′tĭk) *adj.* Extremely harsh or severe. **—dras′ti•cal•ly** *adv.*

draught (drăft) *n., v., & adj. esp. Brit. var. of* DRAFT.

draughts (drăfts, dräfts) *n. (sing. in number). esp. Brit.* The game of checkers.

draw (drô) *v.* **drew** (dro͞o), **drawn** (drôn), **draw•ing. 1. a.** To move or cause to move in a specified direction or to a specified position, as by leading <*drew* us into the dining room> **b.** To pull or move so as to cover or uncover <*draw* the curtains> **2.** To pull or take out (e.g., a weapon) for use <*draw* a gun> **3. a.** To earn or bring in <savings *drawing* interest> **b.** To withdraw (money). **4.** To take in (air) **:** inhale. **5.** To describe (a line or figure), as with a pen **:** sketch. **6.** To elicit in response **:** evoke <*drew* applause from the audience> **7.** To receive in return for services or efforts <*drew* daily wages> **8.** To get by chance or in a chance drawing. **9.** To attract. **10.** To devise or formulate from evidence at hand <*drew* the wrong conclusion> **11.** To eviscerate. **12.** To displace (a given depth of water) in floating. **13.** To provoke <*drawing* enemy fire> **14.** To end (a contest) undecided or tied. **15.** To compose or write in a set form <*draw up* a legal document> **16.** To change the shape of. **17.** To take (cards) from a dealer or central stack. **18.** To move or cause to move steadily <The holiday was *drawing* near.> —*n.* **1.** The act or result of drawing. **2.** A tied contest. **3.** Something that attracts interest or attendance. **—draw on** (*or* **upon**). To use as a source. **—draw out. 1.** To cause to converse freely and easily. **2.** To prolong.

draw•back (drô′băk′) *n.* An undesirable feature **:** disadvantage.

draw•bridge (drô′brĭj′) *n.* A bridge that can be lowered, raised, or turned aside.

draw•er (drô′ər) *n.* **1.** One who draws. **2.** (*also* drôr). A sliding boxlike compartment in furniture. **3.** **drawers.** Underpants.

draw•ing (drô′ĭng) *n.* **1.** The act of one that draws. **2.** A selection of lots, as at a raffle. **3. a.** The art of representing forms and figures on a surface by means of lines. **b.** A portrayal or representation made by drawing.

drawing card *n.* One that attracts interest or attendance.

drawing room *n.* A living room or parlor in a private house.

drawl (drôl) *v.* To speak with drawn-out vowels. **—drawl** *n.*

drawn (drôn) *v. p.p.* of DRAW.

draw•string (drô′strĭng′) *n.* A cord or string run through a casing or hem and pulled to close or tighten an opening.

dray (drā) *n.* A low, heavy cart without sides, used for haulage.

dread (drĕd) *n.* **1.** Great fear : terror. **2.** Nervous or fearful anticipation. —*v.* **1.** To be in great fear of. **2.** To anticipate with alarm, anxiety, or reluctance. —*adj.* **1.** Causing fear : terrifying. **2.** Inspiring awe.

dread•ful (drĕd′fəl) *adj.* **1. a.** Causing fear or dread. **b.** Inspiring awe. **2.** Extremely disagreeable or distasteful. —**dread′ful•ly** *adv.* —**dread′ful•ness** *n.*

dread•locks (drĕd′lŏks′) *pl.n.* Hair that has formed long matted clumps due to lack of washing and combing.

dread•nought (drĕd′nôt′) *n.* A heavily armed battleship.

dream (drēm) *n.* **1.** A series of mental images, thoughts, and emotions occurring in certain stages of sleep. **2.** A daydream. **3.** A state of abstraction : trance. **4.** A hope or aspiration. **5.** One that is esp. lovely or pleasant. —*v.* **dreamed** *or* **dreamt** (drĕmt), **dream•ing. 1.** To have a dream (of). **2.** To daydream. **3.** To consider possible. —**dream•er** *n.* —**dream′y** *adj.*

dream•world (drēm′wûrld′) *n.* A realm of illusion or fantasy.

drear (drîr) *adj.* Dreary.

drea•ry (drîr′ē) *adj.* **-ri•er, -ri•est. 1.** Bleak and gloomy <*dreary* weather> **2.** Monotonous : dull <*dreary* chores> —**drear′i•ly** *adv.* —**drear′i•ness** *n.*

dredge[1] (drĕj) *n.* **1.** A machine used to remove sand or mud, esp. from the bottom of a body of water. **2.** A boat or barge equipped with a dredge. —*v.* **dredged, dredg•ing. 1.** To clean, deepen, or widen with a dredge. **2.** To bring up : unearth <*dredged* up old regrets> —**dredg′er** *n.*

dredge[2] (drĕj) *v.* **dredged, dredg•ing.** To coat (food) by sprinkling with a powder, as flour or sugar.

dregs (drĕgz) *pl.n.* **1.** The sediment of a liquid. **2.** The least desirable part.

drei•del *also* **drei•dl** (drād′l) *n.* A small spinning top used in games played at Chanukah.

drench (drĕnch) *v.* To wet completely.

dress (drĕs) *n.* **1.** A one-piece, outer garment for women and girls. **2.** Clothing. —*v.* **1.** To put clothes on <*dress* the baby> **2.** To decorate or arrange a display in <*dress* a store window> **3.** To groom (the hair). **4.** To apply healing materials to (a wound). **5.** To prepare for use <*dress* lumber> **6.** To make ready for sale or cooking. **7.** To wear formal clothes. —**dress down.** To reprimand.

dres•sage (drə-säzh′, drĕ-) *n.* Guidance of a horse through a series of intricate maneuvers by almost imperceptible movements of the hands, legs, and weight.

dress•er[1] (drĕs′ər) *n.* One that dresses or assists in dressing.

dress•er[2] (drĕs′ər) *n.* A chest of drawers for clothing, usu. with a mirror above it.

dress•ing (drĕs′ĭng) *n.* **1.** Medicine or bandages applied to a wound. **2.** A sauce, as for salads. **3.** A stuffing, as for fowl.

dressing gown *n.* A lounging robe.

dress•mak•er (drĕs′mā′kər) *n.* A maker of women's dresses. —**dress′mak′ing** *n.*

dress rehearsal *n.* A final rehearsal.

dress•y (drĕs′ē) *adj.* **-i•er, -i•est. 1.** Elegant or showy in dress or appearance. **2.** Smart or stylish : chic. —**dress′i•ness** *n.*

drew (dro͞o) *v.* *p.t. of* DRAW.

drib•ble (drĭb′əl) *v.* **-bled, -bling. 1.** To drip or cause to drip : trickle. **2.** To slobber : drool. **3.** To move (a ball) by bouncing or kicking repeatedly, as in basketball or soccer. —*n.* **1.** A trickle or drip. **2.** A small quantity. **3.** The act of dribbling a ball.

drib•let (drĭb′lĭt) *n.* **1.** A tiny falling drop of liquid. **2.** A very small amount.

dri•er[1] (drī′ər) *n.* **1.** A substance added to varnish, paint, or ink to expedite drying. **2.** *var. of* DRYER.

dri•er[2] (drī′ər) *adj. compar. of* DRY.

dri•est (drī′ĭst) *adj. superl. of* DRY.

†drift (drĭft) *v.* **1.** To be or cause to be borne along by or as if by currents of air or water. **2.** To move about aimlessly : wander. **3.** To accumulate or cause to accumulate in piles <wind *drifting* the snow> **4.** *W U.S.* To drive (livestock) slowly or far afield, esp. for grazing. —*n.* **1.** The act or state of drifting. **2.** Something moving along on a current of air or water. **3.** A mass of material, as sand or snow, deposited by air or water currents. **4.** A general meaning or direction. —**drift′er** *n.*

drift•wood (drĭft′wo͝od′) *n.* Wood floating in or washed ashore by water.

drill[1] (drĭl) *n.* **1.** Any of several tools used for boring. **2.** Ordered and repetitive instruction as a means of teaching or training. **3.** A specific exercise meant to develop a skill or familiarize someone with a procedure <a fire *drill*> —*v.* **1.** To make (a hole) with a drill. **2.** To train by continuous repetition.

drill[2] (drĭl) *n.* **1.** A furrow in which seeds are planted. **2.** An implement or machine for planting seeds in holes or furrows.

drill[3] (drĭl) *n.* Long-wearing cotton or linen twill, gen. used for work clothes.

drill•mas•ter (drĭl′măs′tər) *n.* A noncommissioned officer who instructs recruits in military drill.

drink (drĭngk) *v.* **drank** (drăngk), **drunk** (drŭngk), **drink•ing. 1.** To take in and swallow (liquid). **2.** To absorb (moisture or liquid). **3.** To make or join in a toast <*drank* to success> **4.** To take in through the intellect or senses. **5.** To use alcoholic beverages, esp. immoderately. —*n.* **1.** A liquid suitable for drinking : beverage. **2.** An alcoholic beverage. **3.** An amount of liquid swallowed <a *drink* of water> —**drink′a•ble** *adj.* —**drink′er** *n.*

drip (drĭp) *v.* **dripped, drip•ping. 1.** To fall or let fall in drops. **2.** To shed drops. —*n.* **1.** The process of dripping. **2.** Liquid or moisture that falls in drops. **3.** *Slang.* A boring or dull person.

drip-dry (drĭp′drī′) *adj.* Made of a fabric that will not wrinkle when hung dripping wet. —**drip′-dry′** *v.*

drive (drīv) *v.* **drove** (drōv), **driv·en** (drĭv′ən), **driv·ing. 1.** To propel, push, force, or press onward. **2.** To repulse by authority or force. **3.** To force into a particular act or state. **4.** To penetrate or force to penetrate. **5. a.** To control, guide, and direct (a vehicle). **b.** To operate or be conveyed in a vehicle. **6.** To supply the motivating force to : spur. **7.** To impress or project energetically and convincingly. **8.** To hit (a ball) hard in a game. **9.** To rush, dash, or advance violently <a *driving* sleet> —*n.* **1.** The act of driving. **2.** A road for vehicles. **3.** A trip in a vehicle. **4.** The means or apparatus by which motion is transmitted to a machine. **5.** An organized movement or campaign to accomplish something. **6.** Initiative, energy, or aggressiveness. **7.** *Psychoanal.* A driving tendency or instinct, esp. of sexual or aggressive origin. **8.** A full-scale military offensive. **9.** A hard-hit ball in a game. **10.** The act of rounding up and driving cattle, as to new pastures.

drive-in (drīv′ĭn′) *adj.* Permitting customers to remain in their vehicles while being served. —**drive′-in′** *n.*

driv·el (drĭv′əl) *v.* **-eled, -el·ing** *or* **-elled, -el·ling. 1.** To drool : slobber. **2.** To talk nonsensically. —**driv′el** *n.*

driv·er (drī′vər) *n.* **1.** One that drives, esp. a chauffeur. **2.** A wooden-headed golf club used for making long shots from the tee.

drive-up (drīv′ŭp′) *adj.* Drive-in.

drive·way (drīv′wā′) *n.* A private road connecting a building, as a house or garage, with the street.

driz·zle (drĭz′əl) *v.* **-zled, -zling.** To rain gently in fine mistlike drops. —**driz′zle** *n.* —**driz′zly** *adj.*

drogue (drōg) *n.* **1.** A sea anchor. **2.** A funnel- or cone-shaped device towed behind an aircraft as a target. **3.** A parachute used to decelerate a fast-moving object, as a spacecraft, or to pull a larger parachute from its storage pack.

droll (drōl) *adj.* Whimsically comical or amusingly odd. —**droll′er·y** *n.*

drom·e·dar·y (drŏm′ĭ-dĕr′ē, drŭm′-) *n., pl.* **-ies.** A one-humped camel, *Camelus dromedarius,* widely used in N Africa and W Asia as a beast of burden.

drone[1] (drōn) *n.* **1.** A male bee, esp. a honey bee, that is stingless, performs no work, and produces no honey. **2.** A person who lives off others. **3.** An unmanned aircraft operated by remote control.

drone[2] (drōn) *v.* **droned, dron·ing. 1.** To make a low, dull, continuous humming sound. **2.** To speak in a monotonous tone. —**drone** *n.*

drool (dro͞ol) *v.* **1.** To let saliva dribble from the mouth. **2.** *Informal.* To make an exaggerated show of desire. **3.** *Informal* To speak nonsensically. —**drool** *n.*

droop (dro͞op) *v.* **1.** To hang or bend downward : sag. **2.** To become weak or depressed <Our spirits *drooped.*> —**droop** *n.* —**droop′i·ness** *n.* —**droop′y** *adj.*

drop (drŏp) *n.* **1.** A tiny rounded or pear-shaped mass of liquid. **2.** A minute quantity of a substance. **3. drops.** Liquid medicine administered in drops. **4.** A small amount : bit <not a *drop* of compassion> **5.** Something, as an earring, shaped or hanging like a drop. **6.** The act of falling : descent. **7.** A swift decrease or decline, as in quality, quantity, or intensity. **8. a.** The vertical distance from a higher to a lower level. **b.** The distance through which something drops or falls. **9.** A sheer incline, as the face of a cliff. **10.** A delivery by parachute. **11.** Something arranged to fall or be lowered. **12.** A slot through which something is deposited in a receptacle. **13.** A central place where something, as mail, is brought and subsequently distributed. —*v.* **dropped, drop·ping. 1.** To fall or allow to fall <a petal *dropping* from the flower><*dropped* her handkerchief> **2.** To become or cause to become less, as in number, intensity, or volume. **3.** To descend from one level to another. **4.** To fall into a state of exhaustion or death. **5.** To pass into a given state or condition <*dropped* into a light sleep> **6.** To bring down <*dropped* the deer with a single shot> **7.** To mention casually. **8.** To write (e.g., a note) at one's leisure. **9.** To cease consideration or treatment of <*dropped* the charges for lack of evidence> **10.** To terminate an association or relationship with. **11.** To leave unfinished <*dropped* what we were doing to help them> **12.** To leave out (e.g., a letter) in speaking or writing. **13.** To leave at a particular place : deposit. —**drop behind.** To fall behind. —**drop by** (or **in**). To stop in for an informal visit. —**drop out. 1.** To withdraw from school without graduating. **2.** To withdraw from conventional society, esp. because of disillusionment with its values.

drop kick *n.* A kick made by dropping a football to the ground and kicking it when it starts to rebound. —**drop′-kick′** *v.*

drop·let (drŏp′lĭt) *n.* A small drop.

drop-off (drŏp′ôf′, -ŏf′) *n.* **1.** A steep slope. **2.** A noticeable decrease, as in attendance or sales.

drop·out (drŏp′out′) *n.* One who drops out, as from school.

drop·per (drŏp′ər) *n.* A short, thin tube with a suction bulb at one end for drawing in and releasing liquid in drops.

drop·sy (drŏp′sē) *n.* A diseased condition in which abnormally large amounts of fluid collect in body tissues and cavities.

dross (drôs, drŏs) *n.* **1.** The impurity that forms on the surface of molten metal. **2.** Inferior, trivial, or worthless matter.

drought (drout) *also* **drouth** (drouth) *n.* **1.** A long period with no rain. **2.** A shortage.

drove[1] (drōv) *v. p.t. of* DRIVE.

drove[2] (drōv) *n.* **1.** A flock or herd being driven in a body. **2.** A crowd : throng.

drov·er (drō′vər) *n.* One who drives cattle or sheep.

drown (droun) *v.* **1.** To kill or die by submerging and suffocating in a liquid. **2.** To drench with or as if with a liquid. **3.** To deaden one's awareness of as if by immersion. **4.** To cause (a sound) to be overpowered by making a louder sound.

drowse (drouz) *v.* **drowsed, drows•ing.** To doze. —**drowse** *n.*

drows•y (drou'zē) *adj.* **-i•er, -i•est. 1.** Sleepy. **2.** Inducing sleepiness. —**drows'i•ly** *adv.* —**drows'i•ness** *n.*

drub (drŭb) *v.* **drubbed, drub•bing. 1.** To hit harshly with or as if with a stick **:** thrash. **2.** To defeat completely **:** trounce.

drudge (drŭj) *n.* A person who does hard, tiresome, or menial tasks. —**drudge** *v.* —**drudg'er•y** *n.*

drug (drŭg) *n.* **1.** A substance used therapeutically in the treatment of disease or illness. **2.** A narcotic, esp. one that is addictive. —*v.* **drugged, drug•ging. 1.** To administer a drug to. **2.** To mix or poison (food or drink) with drugs. **3.** To make dull or sleepy with or as if with a drug.

drug•gist (drŭg'ĭst) *n.* A pharmacist.

drug•store (drŭg'stôr', -stōr') *n.* A store where drugs, medical supplies, and other articles are sold.

dru•id *also* **Dru•id** (dro͞o'ĭd) *n.* A member of a priesthood of the Celtic religion of ancient Britain and Gaul.

drum (drŭm) *n.* **1.** A musical percussion instrument consisting of a hollow cylinder with a membrane stretched across one or both ends that is played by beating with the hands or with sticks. **2.** The sound made by striking a drum. **3.** Something, as a large oil container, shaped like a drum. —*v.* **drummed, drum•ming. 1.** To play a drum. **2.** To tap or thump rhythmically or incessantly. **3.** To instill by continual repetition **:** inculcate. **4.** To dismiss or expel in disgrace. —**drum up. 1.** To bring about through persistent effort. **2.** To invent **:** devise.

drum•beat (drŭm'bēt') *n.* The sound produced by striking a drum.

drum•lin (drŭm'lĭn) *n.* A rounded hill of glacial drift.

drum major *n.* A male leader of a marching band.

drum ma•jor•ette (mā'jə-rĕt') *n.* A female leader of a marching band.

drum•mer (drŭm'ər) *n.* **1.** A person who plays a drum, as in a band. **2.** A traveling sales representative.

drum•stick (drŭm'stĭk') *n.* **1.** A stick for playing a drum. **2.** The lower part of a fowl's leg.

drunk (drŭngk) *adj.* **1.** Intoxicated with alcohol to the point of impairment of physical and mental faculties. **2.** Caused or influenced by intoxication. **3.** Overwhelmed by strong feeling or emotion. —*n.* **1.** A drunkard. **2.** A drinking spree.

drunk•ard (drŭng'kərd) *n.* A person who is drunk habitually.

drunk•en (drŭng'kən) *adj.* **1.** DRUNK 1. **2.** Habitually drunk. **3.** Of, relating to, or caused by intoxication. —**drunk'en•ly** *adv.* —**drunk'en•ness** *n.*

drupe (dro͞op) *n.* A fleshy fruit, as the plum, usu. having a single hard stone.

dry (drī) *adj.* **dri•er, dri•est** *also* **dry•er, dry•est. 1.** Free from moisture or liquid. **2.** Having or marked by little or no rain <*dry* desert regions> **3.** Not under water. **4.** Not liquid **:** solid <*dry* foods> **5.** Requiring or desiring drink **:** thirsty. **6.** Marked by the absence of natural or normal moisture. **7.** Eaten without garnish, as butter or jelly. **8.** Humorous or sarcastic in a shrewd, impersonal way. **9.** Wearisome and dull. **10.** Not sweet. —Used of wines. **11.** *Informal.* Prohibiting or opposed to the sale or consumption of alcoholic beverages. —*v.* **dried, dry•ing.** To make or become dry. —**dry'ly** *adv.* —**dry'ness** *n.*

dry•ad (drī'əd, -ăd') *n.* A wood nymph.

dry cell *n.* A sealed electric cell having a paste electrolyte.

dry-clean (drī'klēn') *v.* To cleanse (clothing or fabrics) with chemical solvents rather than water. —**dry cleaning** *n.*

dry dock *n.* A basin-shaped dock from which water can be emptied, used for building and repairing ships.

dry•er *also* **dri•er** (drī'ər) *n.* An appliance for removing moisture, as by heating.

dry goods *pl.n.* Clothing, sewing articles, and textiles as distinguished esp. from foodstuffs and hardware.

dry ice *n.* Solidified carbon dioxide.

dry measure *n.* A system of units for measuring solids such as grains, fruits, and vegetables by volume.

dry rot *n.* A fungous disease of timber that causes it to become brittle and crumble.

dry run *n.* A trial exercise **:** rehearsal.

D.T.'s (dē-tēz') *pl.n.* Delirium tremens.

du•al (do͞o'əl, dyo͞o'-) *adj.* **1.** Made up of 2 parts **:** double <*dual* carburetors> **2.** Having a double purpose or character. —**du'al•ism, du•al'i•ty** (-ăl'ĭ-tē) *n.*

dub[1] (dŭb) *v.* **dubbed, dub•bing. 1.** To confer knighthood on. **2.** To nickname.

dub[2] (dŭb) *v.* **dubbed, dub•bing. 1.** To insert a new sound track, often a synchronized translation of the original dialogue, into (a film). **2.** To insert (sound) into a film or tape. —**dub** *n.* —**dub'ber** *n.*

du•bi•e•ty (do͞o-bī'ĭ-tē, dyo͞o-) *n., pl.* **-ties. 1.** The quality or state of being dubious. **2.** An uncertainty.

du•bi•ous (do͞o'bē-əs, dyo͞o'-) *adj.* **1.** Causing doubt **:** equivocal. **2.** Reluctant to agree **:** skeptical. **3. a.** Questionable as to quality or validity. **b.** Verging on impropriety. **4.** Not yet decided. —**du'bi•ous•ly** *adv.*

du•cal (do͞o'kəl, dyo͞o'-) *adj.* Of or relating to a duke or dukedom.

duc•at (dŭk'ət) *n.* Any of various gold coins formerly used in Europe.

duch•ess (dŭch'ĭs) *n.* **1.** The wife of a duke. **2.** A woman holding title to a duchy in her own right.

duch•y (dŭch'ē) *n., pl.* **-ies.** The rank or domain of a duke or duchess.

duck[1] (dŭk) *n.* **1.** Any of various wild or domesticated aquatic birds of the family Anatidae, with a broad, flat bill, short legs, and webbed feet. **2.** The flesh of a duck used as food. **3.** *Slang.* A person, esp. one thought of as peculiar.

duck² (dŭk) *v.* **1.** To lower (the head and body) quickly, esp. to avoid being hit or observed. **2.** To evade (e.g., one's obligations) : shirk. **3.** To push suddenly under water.

duck³ (dŭk) *n.* **1.** A strong cotton or linen cloth, lighter than canvas. **2. ducks.** Clothing made of duck, esp. white trousers.

duck•bill (dŭk'bĭl') *n.* The platypus.

duck•ling (dŭk'lĭng) *n.* A young duck.

duck•pin (dŭk'pĭn') *n.* **1.** A bowling pin shorter and fatter than a tenpin. **2. duckpins** *(sing. in number).* A bowling game played with duckpins and small balls.

duck soup *n. Slang.* Something easy to accomplish.

duck•y (dŭk'ē) *adj.* **-i•er, -i•est.** *Slang.* Satisfactory : fine.

duct (dŭkt) *n.* **1.** A tube through which something flows. **2.** *Anat.* A bodily passage, esp. one carrying a secretion. **3.** *Elect.* A pipe or tube for carrying wires or cables. **—duct'less** *adj.*

duc•tile (dŭk'tĭl) *adj.* **1.** Able to be drawn into a fine strand or wire <a *ductile* metal> **2.** Easily influenced or persuaded : docile. **—duc•til'i•ty** (-tĭl'ĭ-tē) *n.*

ductless gland *n.* An endocrine gland.

dud (dŭd) *n. Informal.* **1.** A bomb, shell, or explosive round that fails to detonate. **2.** One that turns out to be a failure. **3. duds. a.** Clothing. **b.** Personal belongings.

dude (do͞od, dyo͞od) *n.* **1.** *Informal.* A city person who vacations on a ranch. **2.** *Informal.* A man who is a very stylish dresser. **3.** *Slang.* A guy : fellow.

dude ranch *n.* A vacation resort modeled after a western ranch.

dudg•eon (dŭj'ən) *n.* A sullen, angry, or indignant mood <high *dudgeon*>

due (do͞o, dyo͞o) *adj.* **1.** Payable at once or on demand. **2.** Owing <$40 still *due*> **3.** Proper : fitting <*due* respect> **4.** Meeting special requirements : sufficient. **5.** Scheduled or expected to occur <*due* at noon> *—n.* **1.** Something that is deserved or owed. **2. dues.** A fee or charge for membership, as in a club. *—adv.* Directly <*due* north>

du•el (do͞o'əl, dyo͞o'-) *n.* **1.** A formal combat between 2 people, usu. fought to resolve a point of honor. **2.** A struggle that resembles a duel. **—du'el** *v.* **—du'el•ist** *n.*

du•en•de (do͞o-ĕn'dā) *n.* Unusual power to attract or charm.

due process *n.* An established course esp. of judicial proceedings designed to protect the legal rights of the individual.

du•et (do͞o-ĕt', dyo͞o-) *n.* **1.** A musical composition for 2 instruments or voices. **2.** The 2 performers of such a composition.

due to *prep.* Because of.

duf•fel bag (dŭf'əl) *n.* A large canvas or duck bag for carrying personal belongings.

duf•fer (dŭf'ər) *n. Informal.* An inept, incompetent, or stupid person.

dug (dŭg) *v. p.t. & p.p. of* DIG.

dug•out (dŭg'out') *n.* **1.** A boat made by hollowing out a log. **2.** A rough shelter dug into the ground, used esp. in combat for protection from artillery. **3.** *Baseball.* Either of 2 usu. sunken shelters at the side of a field for the players.

duke (do͞ok, dyo͞ok) *n.* **1.** A member of the highest level of the British peerage, ranking above a marquis. **2.** A ruler of an independent European duchy. **3. dukes.** *Slang.* The fists. **—duke'dom** *n.*

dul•cet (dŭl'sĭt) *adj.* **1.** Melodious. **2.** Having an agreeable soothing quality.

dul•ci•mer (dŭl'sə-mər) *n.* A musical instrument with wire strings played with 2 small hammers or by plucking.

dull (dŭl) *adj.* **1.** Stupid. **2.** Insensitive. **3.** Dispirited : dejected. **4.** Not brisk or rapid : sluggish. **5.** Having a blunt edge or point : not sharp. **6.** Not intensely or acutely felt. **7.** Arousing no interest or curiosity : unexciting. **8.** Not vivid or bright : drab. **9.** Overcast : cloudy. **10.** Not clear or resonant. ★ ***syns:*** COLORLESS, DRAB, DRY, FLAT, LACKLUSTER, LIFELESS, PEDESTRIAN, PROSAIC, UNINSPIRED *—v.* To make or become dull. **—dull'ish** *adj.* **—dull'ness** *n.* **—dul'ly** *adv.*

dull•ard (dŭl'ərd) *n.* One who is mentally dull or slow.

du•ly (do͞o'lē, dyo͞o'-) *adv.* **1.** In a proper manner : rightfully. **2.** Punctually.

dumb (dŭm) *adj.* **1.** Unable to speak : mute. **2.** Temporarily speechless, as from shock. **3.** *Informal.* Stupid. **—dumb'ly** *adv.* **—dumb'ness** *n.*

dumb•bell (dŭm'bĕl') *n.* **1.** A weight consisting of a short bar with a metal ball or disk at each end that is lifted for exercise. **2.** *Slang.* DUMMY 2.

dumb•wait•er (dŭm'wā'tər) *n.* A small elevator used to convey goods, as food or dishes, from one floor to another.

dum•dum (dum'dum') *n.* A soft-nosed bullet designed to expand on contact.

dum•found *or* **dumb•found** (dŭm'found') *v.* To confound with amazement.

dum•my (dŭm'ē) *n., pl.* **-mies. 1.** A model of a real object, as a human figure, used as a practical substitute. **2.** A stupid person : dullard. **3.** A person or agency secretly in the service of another. **4. a.** The partner who exposes his or her hand to be played by the declarer in bridge. **b.** The hand thus exposed.

dump (dŭmp) *v.* **1.** To release, throw down, or discard in a mass. **2. a.** To empty (material) out of a container or vehicle. **b.** To empty out (a container or vehicle). **3.** To get rid of by or as if by dumping. **4.** To place (goods) on the market, esp. in a foreign country, in large quantities and at a low price. **5.** *Computer Sci.* To reproduce (data stored internally) onto an external storage medium, as a printout. *—n.* **1.** A place where garbage or trash is

dumped. **2.** A military storage place. **3.** *Slang.* A disreputable place.
dump•ling (dŭmp'lĭng) *n.* **1.** A small ball of dough cooked in soup or stew. **2.** Sweetened dough wrapped around fruit, as an apple, baked and served as dessert.
dumps (dŭmps) *pl.n. Informal.* Low, gloomy spirits : depression.
Dump•ster (dŭmp'stər). A trademark for a large container designed for receiving, transporting, and dumping waste materials.
dump truck *n.* A heavy-duty truck with a bed that tilts to dump loose material.
dump•y (dŭm'pē) *adj.* **-i•er, -i•est. 1.** Short and plump : squat. **2.** Run-down : shabby. **—dump'i•ness** *n.*
dun[1] (dŭn) *v.* **dunned, dun•ning.** To ask (a debtor) persistently for payment.
dun[2] (dŭn) *n.* A brownish gray to dull grayish brown. **—dun** *adj.*
dunce (dŭns) *n.* A slow-witted or stupid person.

▲ ***word history:*** The word *dunce* comes from the name of John *Duns* Scotus, an eminent 13th-cent. scholastic theologian. In the early 16th cent. the humanist scholars of classical Greek and Latin and the religious reformers criticized the *Dunses,* or followers of Scotus, for their resistance to the new learning and theology. By the end of the 16th cent. *dunse* or *dunce* acquired its meaning of "a stupid person."

dune (do͞on, dyo͞on) *n.* A ridge or hill of sand blown or drifted by the wind.
dune buggy *n.* A small, light, 4-wheeled vehicle equipped with oversized tires for driving on sand dunes.
dung (dŭng) *n.* The excrement of animals : manure.
dun•ga•ree (dŭng'gə-rē') *n.* **1.** A sturdy, coarse denim fabric, esp. blue denim. **2. dungarees.** Pants or overalls made from dungaree.
dun•geon (dŭn'jən) *n.* A dark, underground prison chamber.
dung•hill (dŭng'hĭl') *n.* A pile of dung.
dunk (dŭngk) *v.* **1.** To dip (e.g., a doughnut) into a liquid before eating. **2.** To submerge (someone) playfully, as in a swimming pool. **3.** *Basketball.* To slam (a ball) through the basket.
du•o (do͞o'ō, dyo͞o'ō) *n., pl.* **-os. 1.** A duet. **2.** Two people or objects in close association : pair.
du•o•de•num (do͞o'ə-dē'nəm, dyo͞o'-, do͞o-ŏd'n-əm, dyo͞o-) *n., pl.* **-de•na** (-dē'nə) *or* **-de•nums.** The beginning portion of the small intestine, extending from the lower end of the stomach to the jejunum. **—du'o•de'nal** *adj.*
dupe (do͞op, dyo͞op) *n.* **1.** A person who is easily manipulated or deceived. **2.** One who is the tool of another person or power. *—v.* **duped, dup•ing.** To deceive or trick.
du•ple (do͞o'pəl, dyo͞o'-) *adj. Mus.* Having 2 or a multiple of 2 beats to the measure.
du•plex (do͞o'plĕks', dyo͞o'-) *adj.* Double. *—n.* **1.** An apartment with rooms on 2 adjoining floors. **2.** A 2-family house.
du•pli•cate (do͞o'plĭ-kĭt, dyo͞o'-) *adj.* **1.** Being identical with another. **2.** Existing in or consisting of 2 corresponding parts. *—n.* **1.** Either of 2 things that are identical. **2.** An exact copy of an original. *—v.* (-kāt') **-cat•ed, -cat•ing. 1.** To make an exact copy of <*duplicate* a key> **2.** To do or perform again : repeat. **—du'pli•ca'tion** *n.*
du•pli•ca•tor (do͞o'plĭ-kā'tər, dyo͞o'-) *n.* A machine that makes copies of written or printed material.
du•plic•i•ty (do͞o-plĭs'ĭ-tē, dyo͞o-) *n., pl.* **-ties.** Deliberate deception.
du•ra•ble (do͝or'ə-bəl, dyo͝or'-) *adj.* Capable of withstanding wear or decay <a *durable* fabric> **—du'ra•bil'i•ty** *n.*
du•rance (do͝or'əns, dyo͝or'-) *n.* Imprisonment, esp. for a long time.
du•ra•tion (do͞o-rā'shən, dyo͞o-) *n.* The period of time during which something exists or lasts.
du•ress (do͞o-rĕs', dyo͞o-) *n.* **1.** Compulsion by threat. **2.** *Law.* **a.** Coercion illegally applied. **b.** Forced restraint.
dur•ing (do͝or'ĭng, dyo͝or'-) *prep.* **1.** Throughout the course or duration of. **2.** Within the time of.
dusk (dŭsk) *n.* The time of evening immediately before darkness.
dusk•y (dŭs'kē) *adj.* **-i•er, -i•est. 1.** Marked by dim or inadequate light : shadowy. **2.** Somewhat dark in color, as skin. **—dusk'i•ness** *n.*
dust (dŭst) *n.* **1.** Fine, dry particles of matter. **2. a.** Earth, esp. when considered as a place of interment. **b.** The surface of the ground. **3.** Something worthless. **4.** A debased or scorned condition. *—v.* **1.** To remove dust from by wiping, brushing, or beating. **2.** To sprinkle or cover with powdered material. **—dust'y** *adj.*
dust bowl *n.* A region marked by insufficient rainfall and dust storms.
dust•er (dŭs'tər) *n.* **1.** One that dusts. **2.** A brush or cloth used for removing dust. **3.** A loose, lightweight coat or smock.
dust•pan (dŭst'păn') *n.* A short-handled pan for swept-up refuse.
dust storm *n.* A severe windstorm that sweeps clouds of dust across an arid region.
Dutch (dŭch) *n.* **1.** The people of the Netherlands. **2.** The Germanic language of the Netherlands. **—Dutch** *adj.* **—Dutch'man** *n.* **—Dutch'wom'an** *n.*
Dutch door *n.* A door divided in half horizontally so that either part can be opened or closed.
Dutch•man's-breech•es (dŭch'mənz-brĭch'ĭz) *n.* A woodland plant, *Dicentra cucullaria,* of E North America, bearing yellowish-white 2-spurred flowers.
Dutch oven *n.* A large, usu. cast-iron pot or kettle with a tight lid.
Dutch treat *n. Informal.* An outing for which each person pays his or her own way.
du•te•ous (do͞o'tē-əs, dyo͞o'-) *adj.* Dutiful or obedient. **—du'te•ous•ly** *adv.*

du·ti·a·ble (do͞o′tē-ə-bəl, dyo͞o′-) *adj.* Subject to import tax.

du·ti·ful (do͞o′tĭ-fəl, dyo͞o′-) *adj.* **1.** Careful to perform duties. **2.** Imbued with or expressing a sense of duty. **—du′ti·ful·ly** *adv.* **—du′ti·ful·ness** *n.*

du·ty (do͞o′tē, dyo͞o′-) *n., pl.* **-ties. 1.** Something that a person ought to or must do. **2.** Moral obligation. **3.** A service, action, or task assigned to one, esp. in military service. **4.** A government tax, esp. on imports.

dwarf (dwôrf) *n., pl.* **dwarfs** *or* **dwarves** (dwôrvz). A person, animal, or plant whose size is very much smaller than normal. *—v.* **1.** To stunt the natural growth of. **2.** To cause to seem small by comparison. **—dwarf′ish** *adj.* **—dwarf′ish·ness** *n.*

dweeb (dwēb) *n. Slang.* **1.** A subservient person **:** flunky. **2.** A despised person.

dwell (dwĕl) *v.* **dwelt** (dwĕlt) *or* **dwelled, dwell·ing. 1.** To live as an inhabitant **:** reside. **2.** To continue in a given place or condition. **3. a.** To focus one's attention.**b.** To treat of at length **:** expatiate. **—dwell′er** *n.*

dwell·ing (dwĕl′ĭng) *n.* A residence.

dwin·dle (dwĭn′dəl) *v.* **-dled, -dling.** To waste away **:** diminish.

Dy *symbol for* DYSPROSIUM.

dyb·buk (dĭb′ək) *n.* A wandering soul believed in Jewish folklore to enter and control the body of a living person.

dye (dī) *n.* **1.** An agent used to color or stain materials. **2.** A color imparted by a dye. *—v.* **dyed, dye·ing.** To color with or become colored by a dye. **—dy′er** *n.*

dyed-in-the-wool (dīd′ĭn-*th*ə-wo͝ol′) *adj.* Thoroughgoing **:** out-and-out.

dye·stuff (dī′stŭf′) *n.* DYE 1.

dy·ing (dī′ĭng) *adj.* **1.** About to die. **2.** Drawing to an end <a *dying* day> **3.** Uttered or done immediately before death.

dy·nam·ic (dī-năm′ĭk) *adj.* **1.** Energetic **:** vigorous <a *dynamic* leader> **2.** Marked by or tending to produce progress <*dynamic* social reforms> **3.** Of energy, motion, or force in relation to force. **—dy·nam′i·cal·ly** *adv.*

dy·nam·ics (dī-năm′ĭks) *n.* The branch of physics that deals with force, energy, and motion and the relationship between them.

dy·na·mite (dī′nə-mīt′) *n.* A powerful explosive composed of nitroglycerin or ammonium nitrate combined with an absorbent material and usu. packaged in sticks. *—v.* **-mit·ed, -mit·ing.** To blow up with or as if with dynamite.

dy·na·mo (dī′nə-mō′) *n., pl.* **-mos. 1.** An electric generator, esp. one that produces direct current. **2.** *Informal.* A highly energetic and enthusiastic person.

dy·na·mom·e·ter (dī′nə-mŏm′ĭ-tər) *n.* An instrument for measuring mechanical power or force.

dy·nas·ty (dī′nə-stē) *n., pl.* **-ties. 1.** A succession of rulers from the same line or family. **2.** A family or group that maintains great power, wealth, or position for many years. **—dy·nas′tic** (dī-năs′tĭk) *adj.*

dys·en·ter·y (dĭs′ən-tĕr′ē) *n.* An infection of the lower intestines that produces pain, fever, and severe diarrhea.

dys·func·tion (dĭs-fŭngk′shən) *n.* Abnormal or impaired functioning, esp. of a bodily system or organ. **—dys·func′tion·al** *adj.*

dys·lex·i·a (dĭs-lĕk′sē-ə) *n.* Impairment of the ability to read. **—dys·lex′ic** *adj.*

dys·pep·sia (dĭs-pĕp′shə, -sē-ə) *n.* Indigestion. **—dys·pep′tic** *adj.*

dys·pro·si·um (dĭs-prō′zē-əm) *n. Symbol* **Dy** A soft, silvery metallic element used in nuclear research.

dys·pla·sia (dĭs-plā′zhə, -zhē-ə) *n.* Abnormal development of tissues, organs, or cells. **—dys·plas′tic** (-plăs′tĭk) *adj.*

dys·tro·phy (dĭs′trə-fē) *n.* Atrophy of muscle tissue, esp. muscular dystrophy.

Ee

e *or* **E** (ē) *n., pl.* **e's** *or* **E's. 1.** The 5th letter of the English alphabet. **2.** A speech sound represented by the letter *e.* **3.** Something shaped like the letter E. **4.** *Mus.* The 3rd tone in the scale of C major. **5.** A grade indicating that a student's work is failing.

each (ēch) *adj.* Being one of two or more considered separately **:** every. *—pron.* Every one of two or more **:** each one. *—adv.* For or to each one **:** apiece.

each other *pron.* Each the other. —Used to indicate a reciprocal relationship or action <looking out for *each other*>

ea·ger (ē′gər) *adj.* Marked by enthusiastic interest or desire <*eager* to start> ★ *syns:* AGOG, ANXIOUS, ARDENT, ATHIRST, AVID, IMPATIENT, KEEN, RARING, THIRSTY **—ea′ger·ly** *adv.* **—ea′ger·ness** *n.*

ea·gle (ē′gəl) *n.* **1.** A large bird of prey of the family Accipitridae, having a powerful bill, broad strong wings, and soaring flight. **2.** A former U.S. gold coin having a face value of $10. **3.** A score of 2 under par on a hole in golf.

ea·gle-eyed (ē′gəl-īd′) *adj.* Having exceptionally keen vision.

ea·glet (ē′glĭt) *n.* A young eagle.

-ean *suff. var. of* -IAN.

ear[1] (îr) *n.* **1.** The hearing organ in vertebrates, esp. the outer part. **2.** The sense of hearing. **3.** Keenness of hearing. **4.** Attention **:** heed <give *ear* to these appeals> **5.** Something resembling the external ear <the *ears* of a vase> **—all ears.** Listening closely. **—by ear.** Without reference to a musical score. **—ear'less** *adj.*

ear² (îr) *n.* The spike of a cereal plant, as corn, that bears the seeds.

ear·ache (îr'āk') *n.* An ache in the ear.

ear·drum (îr'drŭm') *n. Anat.* The tympanic membrane.

eared (îrd) *adj.* **1.** Having ears or earlike projections. **2.** Having a specified kind or number of ears <floppy-*eared*>

eared seal *n.* Any of various seals of the family Otariidae, including the fur seals and sea lions, having external ears and hind flippers that can be turned forward for walking on land.

eared seal
earless seal (left), *eared seal* (right)

ear·ful (îr'fo͝ol') *n.* **1.** A flow of gossip or information. **2.** A scolding.

earl (ûrl) *n.* A British nobleman who ranks above a viscount and below a marquis. **—earl'dom** *n.*

earless seal *n.* Any of various seals of the family Phocidae, including the hair seals, marked by short fore flippers, reduced hind flippers specialized for swimming, and the absence of external ears.

ear·lobe (îr'lōb') *n.* The fleshy tissue at the lower part of the external ear.

ear·ly (ûr'lē) *adj.* **-li·er, -li·est. 1.** Of, pertaining to, or occurring near the beginning of a series, time period, or course of events. **2.** Belonging to a remote time period **:** primitive <*early* mammals> **3.** Taking place or appearing before the usual or expected time <an *early* frost> **4.** Taking place in the near future. *—adv.* **-li·er, -li·est. 1.** Near the beginning of a series, time period, or course of events. **2.** Far back in time. **3.** Before the usual or expected time. **—ear'li·ness** *n.*

early bird *n.* **1.** An early riser. **2.** One who arrives early.

early on *adv.* At or during an early stage.

ear·mark (îr'märk') *n.* An identifying mark or characteristic. *—v.* **1.** To put an identifying mark on <*earmark* cattle> **2.** To reserve for a certain purpose **:** designate <*earmark* funds for research>

ear·muff (îr'mŭf') *n.* Either of a pair of ear coverings connected by an adjustable band and worn to protect against the cold.

earn (ûrn) *v.* **1.** To receive in return for work or services. **2.** To acquire as a result of one's efforts <*earn* high marks> **3.** To produce as a profit or return <investments that *earn* interest> ★ ***syns:*** DESERVE, GAIN, GET, MERIT, RATE, WIN **—earn'er** *n.*

ear·nest¹ (ûr'nĭst) *adj.* **1.** Characterized by or showing deep sincerity **:** serious. **2.** Important **:** grave. **—in earnest.** With serious intent. **—ear'nest·ly** *adv.* **—ear'nest·ness** *n.*

ear·nest² (ûr'nĭst) *n.* **1.** Money paid in advance to bind an agreement. **2.** A token **:** promise.

earn·ings (ûr'nĭngz) *pl.n.* Something earned, as salary or profits.

ear·phone (îr'fōn') *n.* A device that converts electric signals, as from a radio, to audible sound and fits over or in the ear.

ear·plug (îr'plŭg') *n.* **1.** A soft plug fitted into the ear canal to keep out water or sound. **2.** An earphone that fits into the ear.

ear·ring (îr'rĭng, îr'ĭng) *n.* A piece of jewelry worn on the lobe of the ear.

ear·shot (îr'shŏt') *n.* The distance within which sound can be heard.

ear·split·ting (îr'splĭt'ĭng) *adj.* So loud and shrill as to hurt the ears.

earth (ûrth) *n.* **1. Earth.** The planet 3rd in order from the sun, on which human beings live. **2.** The land surface of the world **:** ground. **3.** Soil **:** dirt. **—down to earth.** Realistic **:** sensible.

earth·en (ûr'thən, -*th*ən) *adj.* **1.** Made of earth. **2.** Worldly.

earth·en·ware (ûr'thən-wâr', -*th*ən-) *n.* Ware, as dishes or pots, made from porous baked clay.

earth·ling (ûrth'lĭng) *n.* An inhabitant of the earth **:** human being.

earth·ly (ûrth'lē) *adj.* **1.** Of or pertaining to this earth. **2. a.** Not heavenly or divine **:** secular. **b.** Terrestrial. **3.** Possible **:** conceivable <no *earthly* excuse> ★ ***syns:*** MUNDANE, SECULAR, TEMPORAL, TERRESTRIAL, WORLDLY **—earth'li·ness** *n.*

earth·mov·er (ûrth'mo͞o'vər) *n.* A machine, such as a bulldozer, used for digging or pushing earth. **—earth'mov'ing** *adj.*

earth·quake (ûrth'kwāk') *n.* A sudden movement of the earth's crust caused by stress accumulated along geologic faults or volcanic activity.

earth science *n.* Any of several geologic sciences concerned with the origin, structure, and physical phenomena of the earth.

earth·shak·ing (ûrth'shā'kĭng) *adj.* Of enormous importance.

earth station *n.* An on-ground terminal linked to a spacecraft or satellite by an antenna and associated electronic equipment for the purpose of transmitting or receiving messages, tracking, or control.

earth·ward (ûrth'wərd) *adj. & adv.* To or toward the earth. **—earth'wards** *adv.*

earth•work (ûrth'wûrk') *n.* An earthen embankment or military fortification.
earth•worm (ûrth'wûrm') *n.* Any of various annelid worms of the class Oligochaeta that burrow into soil.
earth•y (ûr'thē) *adj.* **-i•er, -i•est. 1.** Consisting of or like earth or soil. **2.** Crude and natural : unrefined <*earthy* humor> **—earth'i•ness** *n.*
ear•wax (îr'wăks') *n.* The waxy secretion from the external-ear canal.
ear•wig (îr'wĭg') *n.* Any of various insects of the order Dermaptera, with pincerlike appendages at the rear of the body.
ease (ēz) *n.* **1.** Freedom from worry, pain, or agitation. **2.** Freedom from embarrassment or awkwardness : naturalness. **3.** Freedom from difficulty or great effort. *—v.* **eased, eas•ing. 1.** To free or become free from pain, worry, or trouble. **2.** To make or become less troublesome or difficult. **3.** To lessen the strain, pressure, or tension of : loosen. **4.** To move into place carefully <*eased* the boat into the slip>
ea•sel (ē'zəl) *n.* A frame to support an artist's canvas or a picture.
ease•ment (ēz'mənt) *n.* **1.** The act of easing or the condition of being eased. **2.** *Law.* A right afforded a person to make limited use of another's real property.
east (ēst) *n.* **1. a.** The direction of the earth's axial rotation. **b.** The mariner's compass point 90° clockwise from north. **2.** *often* **East. a.** Asia and the nearby islands of the Indian and Pacific oceans. **b.** The Eastern part of the U.S. **c.** The Eastern part of Canada, usu. Ont., Que., and the Atlantic Provinces. *—adj.* **1.** To, toward, of, or in the east. **2.** Coming from the east. *—adv.* In, from, or toward the east. **—east'er•ly** *adj. & adv.* **—east'ward** *adj. & adv.* **—east'wards** *adv.*
Eas•ter (ē'stər) *n.* A Christian festival celebrating Christ's resurrection.

▲ ***word history:*** The word *Easter,* although the name of a Christian festival, had its origins in pagan times. *Eastre* or *Eostre,* the Old English spelling of *Easter,* was orig. the name of a Germanic goddess who was worshiped at a festival at the spring equinox. Her name is closely related to Latin *aurora* and Greek *reros,* both of which mean "dawn."

east•ern (ē'stərn) *adj.* **1.** Of, in, or toward the east. **2.** Coming from the east. **3. Eastern. a.** Of, relating to, or characteristic of Eastern regions. **b.** Of or designating the Eastern Orthodox Church. **—east'ern•er, East'ern•er** *n.*
Eastern Orthodox Church *n.* Any of the Christian churches in communion with the patriarch of Constantinople.
eas•y (ē'zē) *adj.* **-i•er, -i•est. 1.** Capable of being accomplished with ease : not difficult. **2.** Free from worry, anxiety, or pain. **3.** Relaxed : easygoing. **4.** Not strict : lenient. **5.** Not hurried or forced : moderate. **6.** Readily obtainable <*easy* loans> ★ ***syns:*** EFFORTLESS, FACILE, READY, SIMPLE, SMOOTH *—adv. Informal.* In an easy manner : easily. **—eas'i•ly** *adv.* **—eas'i•ness** *n.*
eas•y•go•ing (ē'zē-gō'ĭng) *adj.* Without worry, concern, or haste : carefree.
eat (ēt) *v.* **ate** (āt), **eat•en** (ēt'n), **eat•ing. 1.** To take (food) into the mouth and swallow. **2.** To consume or destroy as if by eating. **3.** To erode or corrode. **—eat (one's) words.** To take back something one has said. **—eat'a•ble** *adj.* **—eat'er** *n.*
eat•er•y (ē'tə-rē) *n., pl.* **-ies.** *Informal.* A restaurant.
eau de co•logne (ō' də kə-lōn') *n.* A scented liquid consisting of alcohol and various fragrant oils.
eaves (ēvz) *pl.n.* The overhanging lower edge of a roof.
eaves•drop (ēvz'drŏp') *v.* To listen secretly to a private conversation. **—eaves'drop'per** *n.*

▲ ***word history:*** The *eavesdrop* of a building is the space of ground where water falls from the eaves. An *eavesdropper* was orig. someone who stood in the eavesdrop in order to overhear private conversations taking place inside. The noun *eavesdrop* did not survive Old English times, but *eavesdropper* and *eavesdropping,* which was a legal offense, were preserved in legal texts. The modern verb *eavesdrop* is prob. derived from *eavesdropper.*

ebb (ĕb) *n.* **1.** Ebb tide. **2.** A time of decline. *—v.* **1.** To recede, as the tide does. **2.** To decline : diminish.
ebb tide *n.* The period of a tide between high water and a succeeding low water.
eb•o•nite (ĕb'ə-nīt') *n.* A hard, usu. black rubber.
eb•o•ny (ĕb'ə-nē) *n., pl.* **-nies.** The hard, dark-colored wood of a tropical Asian tree, *Diospyros ebenum.* *—adj.* **1.** Resembling ebony. **2.** Black.
e•bul•lient (ĭ-bŏŏl'yənt, ĭ-bŭl'-) *adj.* **1.** Filled with excitement or lively enthusiasm : exuberant. **2.** Boiling : bubbling. **—e•bul'lience** *n.* **—e•bul'lient•ly** *adv.*
eb•ul•li•tion (ĕb'ə-lĭsh'ən) *n.* **1.** The process or state of boiling or bubbling. **2.** A sudden outpouring, as of emotion.
ec•cen•tric (ĭk-sĕn'trĭk) *adj.* **1.** Departing from an established pattern, as of behavior : unconventional. **2.** Deviating from a circular path or form. **3.** Not at or in the geometric center. **4.** Having different centers <*eccentric* circles> *—n.* **1.** An odd or unconventional person. **2.** A disk or wheel with its axis of revolution displaced from its center so that it is able to impart reciprocating motion. **—ec•cen'tri•cal•ly** *adv.* **—ec'cen•tric'i•ty** (ĕk'sĕn-trĭs'ĭ-tē) *n.*
Ec•cle•si•as•tes (ĭ-klē'zē-ăs'tēz') *pl.n. (sing. in number)* —See table at BIBLE.
ec•cle•si•as•tic (ĭ-klē'zē-ăs'tĭk) *adj.* Ecclesiastical. *—n.* A clergyman : cleric.
ec•cle•si•as•ti•cal (ĭ-klē'zē-ăs'tĭ-kəl) *adj.* Of or relating to a church, esp. as an institution. **—ec•cle'si•as'ti•cal•ly** *adv.*
ech•e•lon (ĕsh'ə-lŏn') *n.* **1.** A steplike formation, as of military aircraft or naval vessels.

2. A level of command or authority, as in a hierarchy.
e•chi•no•derm (ĭ-kī'nə-dûrm') *n.* Any of various gen. spiny marine invertebrates having an internal calcareous skeleton, including starfishes and sea urchins.
ech•o (ĕk'ō) *n., pl.* **-oes. 1. a.** Repetition of a sound caused by sound waves reflecting from a surface. **b.** A sound made in this way. **2.** A repetition or imitation. **3.** *Electron.* A reflected wave that is received by radio or radar. ★ ***syns:*** REPERCUSSION, REVERBERATION —*v.* **-oed, -o•ing. 1.** To repeat or be repeated by or as if by an echo. **2.** To repeat or imitate <*echoing* the accepted opinion>
é•clair (ā-klâr', ā'klâr') *n.* A light, tube-shaped pastry filled with cream or custard and often iced with chocolate.
é•clat (ā-klä') *n.* **1.** Great brilliance, as of performance or achievement. **2.** Conspicuous success or acclaim.
ec•lec•tic (ĭ-klĕk'tĭk) *adj.* Consisting of components from diverse sources or styles. —**ec•lec'tic** *n.* —**e•clec'ti•cal•ly** *adv.*
e•clipse (ĭ-klĭps') *n.* **1.** The complete or partial blocking of a celestial body by another. **2.** A fall into obscurity **:** decline. —*v.* **e•clipsed, e•clips•ing. 1.** To cause an eclipse of. **2.** To surpass **:** outshine.
e•clip•tic (ĭ-klĭp'tĭk) *n.* The apparent path of the sun among the stars in one year.
ec•logue (ĕk'lôg', -lŏg') *n.* A pastoral poem in the form of a dialogue.
ec•o•cide (ek'ō-sīd', ē'kō-) *n.* Deliberate destruction of the natural environment, as by pollutants.
e•col•o•gy (ĭ-kŏl'ə-jē) *n.* **1.** The science of the interaction and relationships between living organisms and their environments. **2.** The interaction between living organisms and their environment. —**ec'o•log'i•cal** (ĕk'ə-lŏj'ĭ-kəl, ē'kə-), **ec'o•log'ic** *adj.* —**ec'o•log'i•cal•ly** *adv.* —**e•col'o•gist** *n.*
e•con•o•met•rics (ĭ-kŏn'ə-mĕt'rĭks) *n. (sing. in number).* Application of mathematical and statistical techniques to economics.
ec•o•nom•ic (ĕk'ə-nŏm'ĭk, ē'kə-) *adj.* **1.** Of or relating to the development, production, and management of material wealth. **2.** Of or relating to the necessities of life **:** utilitarian.
ec•o•nom•i•cal (ĕk'ə-nŏm'ĭ-kəl, ē'kə-) *adj.* **1.** Not wasteful in managing funds or resources **:** frugal. **2.** Operating efficiently. —**ec'o•nom'i•cal•ly** *adv.*
ec•o•nom•ics (ĕk'ə-nŏm'ĭks, ē'kə-) *n. (sing. in number).* The science dealing with the production, distribution, and consumption of commodities. —**e•con'o•mist** (ĭ-kŏn'ə-mĭst) *n.*
e•con•o•mize (ĭ-kŏn'ə-mīz') *v.* **-mized, -miz•ing.** To reduce expenses **:** be thrifty. —**e•con'o•miz'er** *n.*
e•con•o•my (ĭ-kŏn'ə-mē) *n., pl.* **-mies. 1.** Careful or thrifty management of resources. **2.** A reduction in expenses. **3.** A system for the management of resources and production of goods and services <a farm-based *economy*>
ec•o•sys•tem (ĕk'ō-sĭs'təm) *n.* An ecological community and its environment interacting and functioning as a unit.
ec•ru (ĕk'rōō, ā'krōō) *n.* A light yellowish brown.
ec•sta•sy (ĕk'stə-sē) *n., pl.* **-sies.** Intense joy or delight **:** rapture. —**ec•stat'ic** (ĕk-stăt'ĭk) *adj.* —**ec•stat'i•cal•ly** *adv.*
ec•u•men•i•cal (ĕk'yə-mĕn'ĭ-kəl) *adj.* **1.** Worldwide **:** universal. **2.** Of or providing unity among Christian churches or religions. —**ec'u•men'i•cal•ly** *adv.* —**ec'u•me•nism** (-mə-nĭz'əm) *n.*
ec•ze•ma (ĕk'sə-mə, ĭg-zē'-) *n.* A noncontagious skin inflammation marked by itching and scaly patches. —**ec•zem'a•tous** (ĕg-zĕm'ə-təs, -zē'mə-) *adj.*
—ed *suff.* **1.** —Used to form the past tense and past participle of regular verbs <lift*ed*> **2.** Characterized by **:** having <kindheart*ed*>
E•dam (ē'dəm, ē'dăm') *n.* A mild, yellow Dutch cheese usu. pressed into balls.
ed•dy (ĕd'ē) *n., pl.* **-dies.** A current, as of air or water, moving against the direction of the main current, esp. in a circular motion. —**ed'dy** *v.*
e•del•weiss (ā'dəl-vīs', -wīs') *n.* An Alpine plant, *Leontopodium alpinum,* with whitish, downy leaves and small flowers.
e•de•ma (ĭ-dē'mə) *n.* An abnormal accumulation of serous fluid in the tissues. —**e•dem'a•tous** (ĭ-dĕm'ə-təs) *adj.*
E•den (ēd'n) *n.* **1.** In the Bible, the first home of Adam and Eve. **2.** A place or state of ultimate happiness **:** paradise.
edge (ĕj) *n.* **1.** The usu. thin, sharpened side of a cutting blade. **2.** Keenness **:** zest. **3.** The line or area where something begins or ends <the *edge* of a table> <at the *edge* of despair> **4.** An advantage. —*v.* **edged, edg•ing. 1.** To put an edge or border on. **2.** To sharpen. **3.** To move gradually <*edged* away from the snarling dog> —**on edge.** Highly tense or nervous.
edge•wise (ĕj'wīz') *also* **edge•ways** (-wāz') *adv.* With the edge foremost.
edg•ing (ĕj'ĭng) *n.* Something forming or serving as an edge or border.
edg•y (ĕj'ē) *adj.* **-i•er, -i•est. 1.** Feeling or showing nervous tension. **2.** Having a sharp edge. ★ ***syns:*** FIDGETY, JITTERY, JUMPY, NERVOUS, RESTIVE, RESTLESS, SKITTISH, TENSE, UNEASY, UPTIGHT —**edg'i•ness** *n.*
ed•i•ble (ĕd'ə-bəl) *adj.* Safe or fit to be eaten. —**ed'i•bil'i•ty** *n.* —**ed'i•ble** *n.*
e•dict (ē'dĭkt') *n.* A formal proclamation, command, or decree.
ed•i•fice (ĕd'ə-fĭs) *n.* A building, esp. a large one.
ed•i•fy (ĕd'ə-fī') *v.* **-fied, -fy•ing.** To instruct so as to promote intellectual or esp. moral improvement **:** enlighten. —**ed'i•fi•ca'tion** *n.* —**ed'i•fi'er** *n.*
ed•it (ĕd'ĭt) *v.* **1.** To prepare for publication, as by adapting or correcting. **2.** To prepare an

edition of <*edit* a collection of letters> **3.** To put together the parts of (e.g., a film) by cutting, combining, and splicing. **4.** To delete <*edit* out a dull passage> **—ed'i•tor** *n.* **—ed'i•tor•ship'** *n.*

▲ ***word history:*** The verb *edit* was derived in English from the noun *editor* and not vice versa as one would expect. The process by which *edit* was formed is called back-formation. By this process a syllable thought to be an affix is removed from what is incorrectly considered to be a base word, and the base becomes a new word in its own right. *Editor* can thus be analyzed as a verb, *edit,* plus the noun suffix *-or.* The English word *editor,* however, was borrowed from Latin *editor* and is recorded 150 years earlier than the verb *edit.*

e•di•tion (ĭ-dĭsh'ən) *n.* **1.** The form in which a book is published. **2.** The entire number of copies, as of a book, printed at one time. **3.** A single copy of a publication. **4.** One similar to an original : version.

ed•i•to•ri•al (ĕd'ĭ-tôr'ē-əl, -tōr'-) *n.* An article in a publication expressing the opinion of a publisher or an editor. *—adj.* **1.** Of or relating to an editor or an editor's work. **2.** Of, expressed in, or being an editorial. **—ed'i•to'ri•al•ly** *adv.*

ed•i•to•ri•al•ize (ĕd'ĭ-tôr'ē-ə-līz', -tōr'-) *v.* **-ized, -iz•ing. 1.** To express an opinion in or as if in an editorial. **2.** To present opinion as if it were factual reporting. **—ed'i•to'ri•al•iz'er** *n.*

ed•u•ca•ble (ĕj'ə-kə-bəl) *adj.* Capable of being educated.

ed•u•cate (ĕj'ə-kāt') *v.* **-cat•ed, -cat•ing. 1.** To provide with training or schooling : teach. **2.** To promote or supervise the mental or moral growth of. **—ed'u•ca'tor** *n.*

ed•u•ca•tion (ĕj'ə-kā'shən) *n.* **1.** The process of educating or of being educated. **2.** The knowledge obtained through learning. **3.** The field of teaching and learning : pedagogy. **—ed'u•ca'tion•al** *adj.* **—ed'u•ca'tion•al•ly** *adv.*

e•duce (ĭ-do͞os', ĭ-dyo͞os') *v.* **e•duced, e•duc•ing. 1.** To evoke : elicit. **2.** To conclude from given facts : deduce.

—ee *suff.* **1.** One that receives or benefits from a specified action <address*ee*> **b.** One that possesses a specified thing <mortgag*ee*> **2.** One that performs a specified action <absent*ee*>

eel (ēl) *n., pl.* **eel** *or* **eels.** Any of various smooth-skinned, snakelike marine or freshwater fishes of the order Anguilliformes or Apodes.

—eer *suff.* One engaged in or concerned with <ballad*eer*>

e'er (âr) *adv.* Ever.

ee•rie *or* **ee•ry** (îr'ē) *adj.* **-ri•er, -ri•est.** Suggesting the supernatural or ghostly : uncanny <an *eerie* wailing sound> **—ee'ri•ly** *adv.* **—ee'ri•ness** *n.*

ef•face (ĭ-fās') *v.* **-faced, -fac•ing. 1.** To wipe out : erase. **2.** To make indistinct. **3.** To conduct (oneself) inconspicuously. **—ef•face'ment** *n.* **—ef•fac'er** *n.*

ef•fect (ĭ-fĕkt') *n.* **1.** Something brought about by a cause : result. **2.** The power or capacity to obtain a desired result : influence. **3.** The way in which something acts on an object <the drying *effect* of strong sunlight> **4.** Something that produces an intended impression <vivid lighting *effects*> **5.** The state of being in force <laws now in *effect*> **6.** Basic meaning : purport <words to that *effect*> **7. effects.** Belongings : possessions. ★ ***syns:*** CONSEQUENCE, FRUIT, ISSUE, OUTCOME, RESULT, SEQUEL, UPSHOT *—v.* **1.** To bring into existence. **2.** To bring about. **—take effect.** To become operative. **—ef•fect'er** *n.*

ef•fec•tive (ĭ-fĕk'tĭv) *adj.* **1.** Producing an expected effect. **2.** Producing or designed to produce a desired effect. **3.** In effect : operative. ★ ***syns:*** EFFECTUAL, EFFICACIOUS, EFFICIENT, PRODUCTIVE **—ef•fec'tive•ly** *adv.* **—ef•fec'tive•ness** *n.*

ef•fec•tu•al (ĭ-fĕk'cho͞o-əl) *adj.* Producing a desired effect. **—ef•fec'tu•al•ly** *adv.*

ef•fec•tu•ate (ĭ-fĕk'cho͞o-āt') *v.* **-at•ed, -at•ing.** To bring about : effect.

ef•fem•i•nate (ĭ-fĕm'ə-nĭt) *adj.* Having qualities more often associated with women than with men. **—ef•fem'i•na•cy** *n.* **—ef•fem'i•nate•ly** *adv.*

ef•fer•ent (ĕf'ər-ənt) *adj.* Directed outward from a central organ or part. **—ef'fer•ent** *n.* **—ef'fer•ent•ly** *adv.*

ef•fer•vesce (ĕf'ər-vĕs') *v.* **-vesced, -vesc•ing. 1.** To give off small bubbles as gas comes out of a liquid. **2.** To show high spirits. **—ef'fer•ves'cence** *n.* **—ef'fer•ves'cent** *adj.* **—ef'fer•ves'cent•ly** *adv.*

ef•fete (ĭ-fēt') *adj.* **1.** Exhausted of force or effectiveness : worn-out. **2.** Decadent. **—ef•fete'ly** *adv.* **—ef•fete'ness** *n.*

ef•fi•ca•cious (ĕf'ĭ-kā'shəs) *adj.* Producing a desired effect <an *efficacious* drug> **—ef'fi•ca'cious•ly** *adv.*

ef•fi•cient (ĭ-fĭsh'ənt) *adj.* **1.** Acting effectively with a minimum of waste or effort. **2.** Exhibiting a high ratio of output to input. **—ef•fi'cien•cy** *n.*

ef•fi•gy (ĕf'ə-jē) *n., pl.* **-gies.** A sculptured or painted representation, esp. a crude image or dummy of a hated person.

ef•flo•resce (ĕf'lə-rĕs') *v.* **-resced, -resc•ing.** To bloom : blossom.

ef•flo•res•cence (ĕf'lə-rĕs'əns) *n.* **1.** A time or condition of flowering. **2.** A gradual process of development. **3.** The highest point. **—ef'flo•res'cent** *adj.*

ef•flu•ence (ĕf'lo͞o-əns) *n.* **1.** An act or instance of flowing out. **2.** Something that flows out or forth : emanation. **—ef'flu•ent** *adj. & n.*

ef•flu•vi•um (ĭ-flo͞o'vē-əm) *n., pl.* **-vi•a** (-vē-ə) *or* **-vi•ums.** An often foul-smelling outflow or vapor. **—ef•flu'vi•al** *adj.*

ef•fort (ĕf'ərt) *n.* **1.** Exertion of physical or mental energy. **2.** A difficult exertion. **3.** A usu. earnest attempt. **4.** Something done through exertion : achievement. **5.** *Physics.* Force applied against inertia. ★ ***syns:*** EXERTION, PAINS, STRAIN, STRUGGLE, TROUBLE —**ef'fort·ful** *adj.* —**ef'fort·less** *adj.*

ef·fron·ter·y (ĭ-frŭn'tə-rē) *n., pl.* **-ies.** Shameless boldness : audacity.

ef·ful·gent (ĭ-fo͝ol'jənt, ĭ-fŭl'-) *adj.* Shining brilliantly. —**ef·ful'gence** *n.*

ef·fu·sion (ĭ-fyo͞o'zhən) *n.* **1.** An act or instance of pouring forth. **2.** An excessive or unrestrained outpouring of feeling, as in speech. —**ef·fuse'** (ĭ-fyo͞oz') *v.* —**ef·fu'sive** *adj.* —**ef·fu'sive·ly** *adv.*

eft (ĕft) *n.* A newt.

e·gal·i·tar·i·an (ĭ-găl'ĭ-târ'ē-ən) *adj.* Advocating equal rights for all human beings. —**e·gal'i·tar'i·an** *n.* —**e·gal'i·tar'i·an·ism** *n.*

egg[1] (ĕg) *n.* **1.** A female gamete : ovum. **2.** The hard-shelled ovum of a bird, esp. one produced by a chicken, used as food.

egg[2] (ĕg) *v.* To urge or incite to action <Some onlookers *egged* the fighters on.>

egg-and-dart (ĕg'ən-därt') *n.* A decorative molding alternating egg-shaped figures with anchor, dart, or tongue-shaped figures.

egg·beat·er (ĕg'bē'tər) *n.* A kitchen device with rotating blades for whipping, beating, or mixing.

egg·head (ĕg'hĕd') *n. Slang.* An intellectual.

egg·nog (ĕg'nŏg') *n.* A drink of beaten eggs, sugar, and milk or cream, often mixed with liquor.

egg·plant (ĕg'plănt') *n.* A tropical Old World plant, *Solanum melongena,* cultivated for its purple-skinned, ovoid, edible fruit.

egg roll *n.* A deep-fried cylindrical case made of egg dough filled with minced vegetables and sometimes meat.

egg·shell (ĕg'shĕl') *n.* The thin, brittle outer covering of an egg.

e·gis (ē'jĭs) *n. var. of* AEGIS.

eg·lan·tine (ĕg'lən-tīn', -tēn') *n.* The sweetbrier.

e·go (ē'gō, ĕg'ō) *n.* **1.** The self, esp. as distinct from the external world. **2.** *Psychoanal.* The conscious personality component that most directly controls behavior and is most in touch with reality. **3.** Self-love : egotism.

e·go·cen·tric (ē'gō-sĕn'trĭk, ĕg'ō-) *adj.* **1.** Thinking, observing, or judging things in relation to the self. **2.** Self-centered : selfish. —**e'go·cen'tric** *n.* —**e'go·cen·tric'i·ty** (-trĭs'ĭ-tē) *n.*

e·go·ism (ē'gō-ĭz'əm, ĕg'ō-) *n.* **1.** The ethical doctrine that self-interest is the proper motive for all human conduct. **2.** Egotism : conceit. —**e'go·ist** *n.* —**e'go·is'tic, e'go·is'ti·cal** *adj.* —**e'go·is'ti·cal·ly** *adv.*

e·go·ma·ni·a (ē'gō-mā'nē-ə, -mān'yə, ĕg'ō-) *n.* Obsession with the self. —**e'go·ma'ni·ac'** (-nē-ăk') *n.* —**e'go·ma·ni'a·cal** (-mə-nī'ə-kəl) *adj.*

e·go·tism (ē'gə-tĭz'əm, ĕg'ə-) *n.* **1.** The tendency to refer to oneself excessively or boastfully. **2.** Self-importance : conceit. —**e'go·tist** *n.* —**e'go·tis'tic, e'go·tis'ti·cal** *adj.* —**e'go·tis'ti·cal·ly** *adv.*

ego trip *n. Slang.* Something that gratifies the ego. —**e'go-trip'** *v.*

e·gre·gious (ĭ-grē'jəs, -jē-əs) *adj.* Outstandingly bad : flagrant. —**e·gre'gious·ly** *adv.* —**e·gre'gious·ness** *n.*

e·gress (ē'grĕs') *n.* **1.** The act of going out : emergence. **2.** A means of going out : exit.

e·gret (ē'grĭt, ĕg'rĭt) *n.* Any of several usu. white wading birds, esp. *Casmerodius alba,* having long, drooping plumes.

ei·der (ī'dər) *n.* A sea duck of the genus *Somateria,* of N regions, having soft, commercially valuable down.

ei·der·down (ī'dər-doun') *n.* **1.** The down of the eider duck. **2.** A quilt stuffed with eiderdown.

eight (āt) *n.* **1.** The cardinal number equal to 7 + 1. **2.** The 8th in a set or sequence. —**eight** *adj. & pron.* —**eighth** *n. & adj. & adv.*

eight ball *n.* The black pool ball with the number 8. —**behind the eight ball.** *Slang.* In a disadvantageous position.

eight·een (ā-tēn') *n.* **1.** The cardinal number equal to 17 + 1. **2.** The 18th in a set or sequence. —**eight·een'** *adj. & pron.* —**eight·eenth'** *n. & adj. & adv.*

eight·y (ā'tē) *n.* The cardinal number equal to 8 × 10. —**eight'i·eth** *n. & adj. & adv.* —**eight'y** *adj. & pron.*

ein·stein·i·um (īn-stī'nē-əm) *n. Symbol* **Es** A metallic element produced by nuclear bombardment.

ei·ther (ē'*th*ər, ī'*th*ər) *pron.* One or the other. —*conj.* —Used before the first of two or more alternatives linked by *or* <*Either* we go now or we stay here all day.> —*adj.* **1.** One or the other <Use *either* tool.> **2.** One and the other : each <repairs on *either* side of the road> —*adv.* Also : likewise <If you don't diet, I won't *either.*>

e·jac·u·late (ĭ-jăk'yə-lāt') *v.* **-lat·ed, -lat·ing. 1.** To discharge (e.g., semen) abruptly. **2.** To utter suddenly and energetically : exclaim. —**e·jac'u·la'tion** *n.* —**e·jac'u·la·to'ry** (-lə-tôr'ē, -tōr'ē) *adj.*

e·ject (ĭ-jĕkt') *v.* To drive or throw off or out forcefully : expel. —**e·jec'tion** *n.* —**e·jec'tor** *n.*

e·jec·ta (ĭ-jĕk'tə) *pl.n.* Ejected matter.

eke (ēk) *v.* **eked, ek·ing.** To earn or supplement with great effort <*eke* out an income with night work>

e·kis·tics (ĭ-kĭs'tĭks) *n. (sing. in number).* The science that deals with human settlements, including community design and planning. —**e·kis'tic** *adj.*

ek·pwe·le (ĕk-pwē'lē) *n.* A former monetary unit of Equatorial Guinea.

e·lab·o·rate (ĭ-lăb'ər-ĭt) *adj.* **1.** Planned or done with attention to numerous details or parts. **2.** Very complex : intricate. —*v.* (-ə-rāt') **-rat·ed, -rat·ing. 1.** To work out with careful detail. **2.** To express in greater detail : provide further information. —**e·lab'o·rate·ly** *adv.* —**e·lab'o·rate·ness** *n.* —**e·lab'o·ra'tion** (-ə-rā'shən) *n.*

é•lan (ā-läɴ', ā-län') *n.* **1.** Enthusiasm **:** vigor. **2.** Spirit and style **:** flair.

e•land (ē'lənd, ē'lănd') *n.* A large African antelope, *Taurotragus oryx* or *T. derbianus,* with a tan coat and spirally twisted horns.

e•lapse (ĭ-lăps') *v.* **e•lapsed, e•laps•ing.** To pass <Much time has *elapsed.*>

e•las•tic (ĭ-lăs'tĭk) *adj.* **1.** *Physics.* Returning to an initial or prior state or form after deformation. **2.** Adapting to changing circumstances **:** flexible. **3.** Resilient **:** springy. —*n.* **1.** Something made of elastic. **2.** A rubber band. —**e•las'ti•cal•ly** *adv.* —**e•las•tic'i•ty** (ĭ-lă-stĭs'ĭ-tē, ē'lă-) *n.*

e•late (ĭ-lāt') *v.* **e•lat•ed, e•lat•ing.** To raise the spirits of. ★ ***syns:*** BUOY, ELEVATE, EXALT, EXHILARATE, INSPIRE, INSPIRIT, UPLIFT —**e•lat'ed•ly** *adv.* —**e•lat'ed•ness** *n.* —**e•la'tion** *n.*

el•bow (ĕl'bō') *n.* **1.** The joint of the arm between the upper arm and forearm. **2.** Something with a bend resembling an elbow. —*v.* **1.** To jostle or shove aside with the elbow. **2.** To make (one's way) by pushing with the elbow or elbows.

el•bow•room (ĕl'bō-ro͞om', -ro͝om') *n.* Ample room to move about or function in.

eld•er[1] (ĕl'dər) *adj.* Older. —*n.* **1.** An older person, esp. one who is an influential member of a family, community, or tribe. **2.** A governing official of a church. —**el'der•ship'** *n.*

el•der[2] (ĕl'dər) *n.* Any of various shrubs of the genus *Sambucus,* bearing small white flower clusters and red or blackish berries.

el•der•ber•ry (ĕl'dər-bĕr'ē) *n.* The edible fruit of an elder used to make wine or jelly.

eld•er•ly (ĕl'dər-lē) *adj.* **1.** Approaching old age. **2.** Of or characteristic of older persons. —**el'der•li•ness** *n.*

eld•est (ĕl'dĭst) *adj.* Greatest in age.

El Do•ra•do (ĕl' də-rä'dō) *n.* A legendary place of great wealth or opportunity.

e•lect (ĭ-lĕkt') *v.* **1.** To choose by vote, as for an office. **2.** To choose **:** pick. **3.** To decide <*elected* to sell the property> —*adj.* **1.** Singled out on purpose. **2.** Elected but not yet installed <the mayor-*elect*> —*n.* **1.** One chosen or selected, esp. for spiritual salvation. **2.** *(pl. in number).* An exclusive or privileged group.

e•lec•tion (ĭ-lĕk'shən) *n.* **1.** The act or power of electing. **2.** The fact of being elected. **3.** Predestined salvation.

e•lec•tion•eer (ĭ-lĕk'shə-nîr') *v.* To work actively for a political candidate.

e•lec•tive (ĭ-lĕk'tĭv) *adj.* **1.** Filled or selected by election <an *elective* post> **2.** Empowered to elect. **3.** Optional <*elective* courses> —*n.* An optional academic course. —**e•lec'tive•ly** *adv.*

e•lec•tor (ĭ-lĕk'tər) *n.* **1.** A qualified voter. **2.** A member of the U.S. electoral college. —**e•lec'tor•al** *adj.*

electoral college *n.* A group of electors chosen to elect the U.S. President and Vice President.

e•lec•tor•ate (ĭ-lĕk'tər-ĭt) *n.* A body of qualified voters.

e•lec•tric (ĭ-lĕk'trĭk) *or* **e•lec•tri•cal** (-trĭ-kəl) *adj.* **1.** Of, relating to, or operated by electricity. **2.** Emotionally exciting **:** thrilling. **3.** Charged with emotion **:** tense. —**e•lec'tri•cal•ly** *adv.*

electrical storm *n.* A thunderstorm.

electric chair *n.* A chair for electrocuting condemned prisoners.

electric eye *n.* A photoelectric cell.

electric field *n.* A region of space marked by the presence of a detectable electric intensity at every point.

e•lec•tri•cian (ĭ-lĕk-trĭsh'ən, ē'lĕk-) *n.* One whose work is the installation or maintenance of electric equipment.

e•lec•tric•i•ty (ĭ-lĕk-trĭs'ĭ-tē, ē'lĕk-) *n.* **1.** A property of matter that causes bodies to attract or repel each other and is responsible for such phenomena as lightning. **2.** Electric current as a power source. **3.** Emotional excitement or tension.

▲ ***word history:*** The effects of electricity have been observed since ancient times, when it was noticed that amber when rubbed attracts small bits of straw and wood. When this electromagnetic effect was first examined in the early 17th cent., the words *electric* and *electricity* were coined from Greek *ēlektron,* "amber."

e•lec•tri•fy (ĭ-lĕk'trə-fī') *v.* **-fied, -fy•ing. 1.** To give an electric charge to. **2.** To equip (e.g., a building) for the use of electricity. **3.** To excite greatly **:** thrill. —**e•lec'tri•fi•ca'tion** *n.* —**e•lec'tri•fi'er** *n.*

e•lec•tro•car•di•o•gram (ĭ-lĕk'trō-kär'dē-ə-grăm') *n.* The tracing made by an electrocardiograph.

e•lec•tro•car•di•o•graph (ĭ-lĕk'trō-kär'dē-ə-grăf') *n.* An instrument that records the electrical activity of the heart. —**e•lec'tro•car'di•o•graph'ic** (-grăf'ĭk) *adj.* —**e•lec'tro•car'di•og'ra•phy** (-ŏg'rə-fē) *n.*

e•lec•tro•chem•is•try (ĭ-lĕk'trō-kĕm'ĭ-strē) *n.* The study of phenomena that involve electricity and chemistry. —**e•lec'tro•chem'i•cal** (-ĭ-kəl) *adj.*

e•lec•tro•cute (ĭ-lĕk'trə-kyo͞ot') *v.* **-cut•ed, -cut•ing. 1.** To kill with electricity. **2.** To execute (a condemned prisoner) by electricity. —**e•lec'tro•cu'tion** *n.*

e•lec•trode (ĭ-lĕk'trōd') *n.* A conductor that transfers electric charges into or out of another conducting medium or that influences the flow of current in another conducting medium.

e•lec•tro•dy•nam•ics (ĭ-lĕk'trō-dī-năm'ĭks) *n. (sing. in number).* The physics of the interactions of electric, magnetic, and mechanical phenomena. —**e•lec'tro•dy•nam'ic** *adj.*

e•lec•tro•en•ceph•a•lo•gram (ĭ-lĕk'trō-ĕn-sĕf'ə-lə-grăm') *n.* A tracing of the electrical activity of the brain made by an electroencephalograph.

e•lec•tro•en•ceph•a•lo•graph (ĭ-lĕk'trō-ĕn-sĕf'ə-lə-grăf') *n.* An instrument for recording

the electrical activity of the brain. **—e·lec′tro·en·ceph′a·log′ra·phy** (-lŏg′rə-fē) *n.*
e·lec·trol·o·gist (ĭ-lĕk-trŏl′ə-jĭst, ē′lĕk-) *n.* One who removes hair or blemishes from the body by the use of an electric current.
e·lec·trol·y·sis (ĭ-lĕk-trŏl′ĭ-sĭs, ē′lĕk-) *n.* **1.** A chemical change produced in an electrolyte by an electric current. **2.** Destruction of tissue, esp. hair roots, by an electric current.
e·lec·tro·lyte (ĭ-lĕk′trə-līt′) *n.* A substance that breaks apart into ions when dissolved or melted, thus becoming electrically conductive. **—e·lec′tro·lyt′ic** (-lĭt′ĭk) *adj.* **—e·lec′tro·lyt′i·cal·ly** *adv.*
e·lec·tro·mag·net (ĭ-lĕk′trō-măg′nĭt) *n.* A magnet made of a soft iron core wound with a coil of wire that magnetizes the core when a current passes through it.
e·lec·tro·mag·net·ic (ĭ-lĕk′trō-măg-nĕt′ĭk) *adj.* Of, caused by, or relating to electromagnetism. **—e·lec′tro·mag·net′i·cal·ly** *adv.*
e·lec·tro·mag·net·ism (ĭ-lĕk′trō-măg′nĭ-tĭz′əm) *n.* **1.** Magnetism arising from electric charge in motion. **2.** The physics of electricity and magnetism.
e·lec·trom·e·ter (ĭ-lĕk-trŏm′ĭ-tər, ē′lĕk-) *n.* An instrument for detecting or measuring electric charge and potential differences.
e·lec·tro·mo·tive (ĭ-lĕk′trō-mō′tĭv) *adj.* Of, relating to, or tending to produce electric current.
electromotive force *n.* **1.** A force that tends to produce an electric current. **2.** The energy per unit of charge that is converted into electrical form by a device such as a battery or generator.
e·lec·tron (ĭ-lĕk′trŏn′) *n.* A subatomic particle with a negative electric charge.
e·lec·tron·ic (ĭ-lĕk-trŏn′ĭk, ē′lĕk-) *adj.* **1.** Of or involving electrons. **2.** Of, based on, or operated by the controlled flow of charge carriers, esp. electrons. **3.** Of or relating to electronics. **—e·lec·tron′i·cal·ly** *adv.*
electronic mail *n. Computer Sci.* Messages sent and received electronically via telecommunication links between users of different computer systems or terminals.
e·lec·tron·ics (ĭ-lĕk-trŏn′ĭks, ē′lĕk-) *n. (sing. in number).* The science and technology of electronic phenomena and devices.
electron microscope *n.* A microscope that uses an electron beam to produce magnified images, esp. of very small objects.
electron tube *n.* A sealed enclosure, either highly evacuated or containing a controlled quantity of gas, in which electrons act as the principal carriers of current between at least 2 electrodes.
e·lec·tro·plate (ĭ-lĕk′trə-plāt′) *v.* To coat with a thin layer of metal by electrolysis.
e·lec·tro·stat·ic (ĭ-lĕk′trō-stăt′ĭk) *adj.* **1.** Of or relating to static electric charges. **2.** Of or relating to electrostatics.
e·lec·tro·stat·ics (ĭ-lĕk′trō-stăt′ĭks) *n. (sing. in number).* The physics of static electric charges.
e·lec·tro·type (ĭ-lĕk′trə-tīp′) *n.* A duplicate metal plate used in printing, made by electroplating a mold of the original plate. **—e·lec′tro·type′** *v.*
el·ee·mos·y·nar·y (ĕl′ə-mŏs′ə-nĕr′ē, ĕl′ē-ə-) *adj.* Of, relating to, or contributed as charity.
el·e·gance (ĕl′ĭ-gəns) *n.* **1.** Grace and refinement in appearance, movement, or manners. **2.** Tasteful richness in decoration or presentation. **3.** Something refined and graceful. **—el′e·gant** *adj.*
el·e·gi·ac (ĕl′ə-jī′ək, ĭ-lē′jē-ăk′) *adj.* **1.** Of or relating to an elegy. **2.** Expressing sorrow **:** mournful. **—el′e·gi′ac·al·ly** *adv.*
el·e·gy (ĕl′ə-jē) *n., pl.* **-gies.** A poem expressing sorrow for one who is dead. **—el′e·gist** *n.*
el·e·ment (el′ə-mənt) *n.* **1.** A fundamental part. **2. elements.** The basic principles <the *elements* of biology> **3.** *Math.* A member of a set. **4.** *Chem. & Physics.* A substance composed of atoms having an identical number of protons in each nucleus and not separable into less complex substances by chemical means. **5. elements.** The forces of the weather <exposed to the *elements*> **6.** A native or congenial environment. ★ ***syns:*** COMPONENT, CONSTITUENT, FACTOR, INGREDIENT, PART
el·e·men·tal (ĕl′ə-mĕn′tl) *adj.* **1.** Of, relating to, or being an element. **2.** Fundamental **:** essential. **3.** Constituting or like a force of nature in power or effect.
el·e·men·ta·ry (ĕl′ə-mĕn′tə-rē, -trē) *adj.* **1.** Fundamental, essential, or irreducible. **2.** Of or introducing fundamental principles <an *elementary* textbook>
elementary particle *n.* A particle of matter or energy that is thought not to be divisible into smaller particles.
elementary school *n.* A school for the first 6 to 8 grades.
el·e·phant (ĕl′ə-fənt) *n.* Either of 2 very large mammals, *Elephas maximus,* of SC Asia, or *Loxodonta africana,* of Africa, with a long, flexible trunk and curved tusks.
el·e·phan·ti·a·sis (ĕl′ə-fən-tī′ə-sĭs) *n.* Enlargement and hardening of tissues, esp. of the lower body, resulting from the blockage of lymph ducts by parasitic worms.
el·e·phan·tine (ĕl′ə-făn′tēn′, -tīn′, ĕl′ə-fən-) *adj.* **1.** Enormous in size **:** gigantic. **2.** Heavy-footed **:** ponderous.
el·e·vate (ĕl′ə-vāt′) *v.* **-vat·ed, -vat·ing. 1.** To lift up **:** raise. **2.** To promote to a higher rank. **3.** To raise to a higher moral, cultural, or intellectual level. **4.** To lift the spirits of **:** elate. ★ ***syns:*** BOOST, HOIST, LIFT, PICK UP, RAISE, UPLIFT
el·e·va·tion (ĕl′ə-vā′shən) *n.* **1.** The act of elevating or state of being elevated. **2.** An elevated place or position. **3.** The height to which something is elevated, as above sea level.
el·e·va·tor (ĕl′ə-vā′tər) *n.* **1.** A platform or enclosure raised and lowered to carry freight or people. **2.** A grain elevator. **3.** A movable surface on an aircraft that produces upward or downward motion.

e·lev·en (ĭ-lĕv′ən) *n.* **1.** The cardinal number equal to 10 + 1. **2.** The 11th in a set or sequence. **3.** Something, esp. a football team, with 11 members. **—e·lev′en** *adj. & pron.* **—e·lev′enth** *n. & adj. & adv.*

elf (ĕlf) *n., pl.* **elves** (ĕlvz). A small, often mischievous imaginary creature. **—elf′in** *adj.* **—elf′ish** *adj.*

e·lic·it (ĭ-lĭs′ĭt) *v.* To bring out or call forth : evoke.

e·lide (ĭ-līd′) *v.* **e·lid·ed, e·lid·ing.** To omit, esp. to slur over (a speech sound) in pronunciation. **—e·li′sion** (ĭ-lĭzh′ən) *n.*

el·i·gi·ble (ĕl′ĭ-jə-bəl) *adj.* **1.** Qualified, as for an office. **2.** Desirable and suited to be chosen, esp. for marriage. **—el′i·gi·bil′i·ty** *n.* **—el′i·gi·ble** *n.*

e·lim·i·nate (ĭ-lĭm′ə-nāt′) *v.* **-nat·ed, -nat·ing. 1.** To get rid of : remove <*eliminate* an injustice> **2.** To leave out : omit. **3.** *Physiol.* To excrete as waste. ★ ***syns:*** ERADICATE, LIQUIDATE, PURGE, REMOVE **—e·lim′i·na′tion** *n.* **—e·lim′i·na′tive, e·lim′i·na·to′ry** (-nə-tôr′ē, -tōr′ē) *adj.* **—e·lim′i·na′tor** *n.*

e·lite *or* **é·lite** (ĭ-lēt′, ā-lēt′) *n.* **1.** *(pl. in number).* **a.** The best or most skilled members of a group. **b.** A small but powerful group. **2.** A typewriter type size providing 12 characters to the inch. **—e·lite′** *adj.*

e·lit·ism *or* **é·lit·ism** (ĭ-lē′tĭz′əm, ā-lē′-) *n.* Rule or domination by or belief in an elite. **—e·lit′ist** *n.*

e·lix·ir (ĭ-lĭk′sər) *n.* **1.** A sweetened aromatic solution of alcohol and water used as a vehicle for medicine. **2.** A medicine regarded as a cure-all : panacea.

elk (ĕlk) *n., pl.* **elks** *or* **elk. 1.** The wapiti. **2.** A large deer, *Alces alces,* of N Eurasia.

elk·hound (ĕlk′hound′) *n.* A hunting dog, orig. bred in Scandinavia, with grayish fur and a tail curled up over the back.

ell[1] (ĕl) *n.* A wing of a building at right angles to the main structure.

ell[2] (ĕl) *n.* A former English linear measure, esp. for cloth, equal to 45 in.

el·lipse (ĭ-lĭps′) *n.* A closed plane curve that is oval in shape.

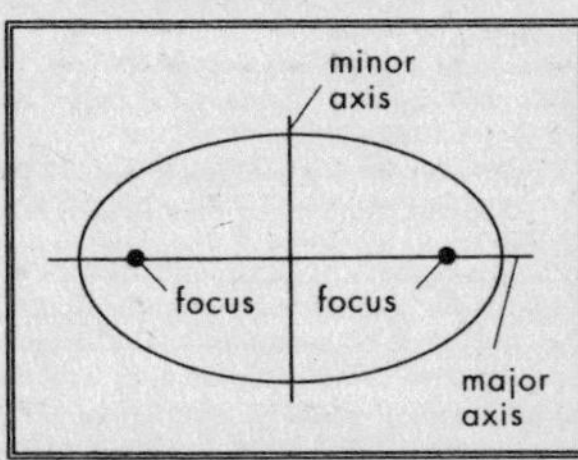

ellipse

el·lip·sis (ĭ-lĭp′sĭs) *n., pl.* **-ses** (-sēz′). **1.** The omission of a word or phrase implied by the context. **2.** A series of marks (e.g., . . . or ***) indicating an omission.

el·lip·soid (ĭ-lĭp′soid′) *n.* A geometric surface whose plane sections are ellipses or circles. **—el·lip′soid′, el′lip·soid′al** (-soid′l) *adj.*

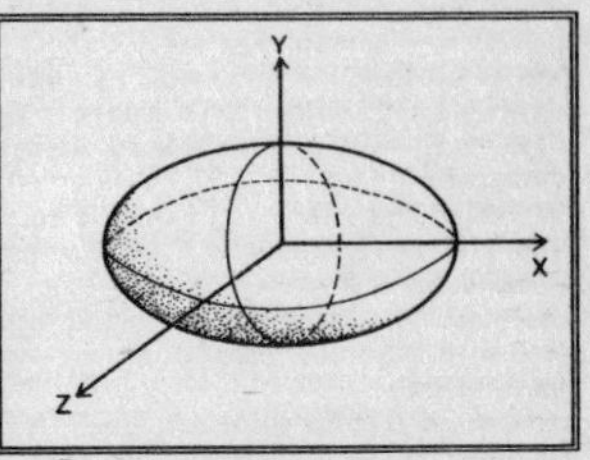

ellipsoid

el·lip·tic (ĭ-lĭp′tĭk) *or* **el·lip·ti·cal** (-tĭ-kəl) *adj.* **1.** Of, relating to, or shaped like an ellipse. **2.** Of, relating to, or marked by ellipsis.

elm (ĕlm) *n.* Any of various deciduous shade trees of the genus *Ulmus,* with arching branches.

el·o·cu·tion (ĕl′ə-kyōō′shən) *n.* The art of public speaking. **—el′o·cu′tion·ar′y** (-shə-nĕr′ē) *adj.* **—el′o·cu′tion·ist** *n.*

e·lon·gate (ĭ-lông′gāt′, ĭ-lŏng′-) *v.* **-gat·ed, -gat·ing.** To make or become longer : lengthen. **—e·lon′ga′tion** *n.*

e·lope (ĭ-lōp′) *v.* **e·loped, e·lop·ing.** To run away, esp. in order to get married. **—e·lope′ment** *n.* **—e·lop′er** *n.*

el·o·quent (ĕl′ə-kwənt) *adj.* **1.** Speaking or spoken fluently and persuasively. **2.** Vividly or movingly expressive <an *eloquent* gesture> **—el′o·quence** *n.* **—el′o·quent·ly** *adv.*

else (ĕls) *adj.* **1.** Different : other <anybody *else*> **2.** More : additional <Do you need anything *else*?> *—adv.* **1.** Differently : besides <How *else* could I have answered?> **2.** Otherwise <Step high, or *else* you will trip.>

else·where (ĕls′hwâr′, -wâr′) *adv.* To or in another or different place.

e·lu·ci·date (ĭ-lōō′sĭ-dāt′) *v.* **-dat·ed, -dat·ing.** To make clear : clarify. **—e·lu′ci·da′tion** *n.* **—e·lu′ci·da′tor** *n.*

e·lude (ĭ-lōōd′) *v.* **e·lud·ed, e·lud·ing. 1.** To avoid being captured by : evade. **2.** To escape the understanding of.

e·lu·sive (ĭ-lōō′sĭv, -zĭv) *adj.* Tending to elude. **—e·lu′sive·ly** *adv.* **—e·lu′sive·ness** *n.*

el·ver (ĕl′vər) *n.* A young eel.

elves (ĕlvz) *n. pl. of* ELF.

E·ly·si·um (ĭ-lĭz′ē-əm, ĭ-lĭzh′-) *n.* A place of ideal happiness : paradise. **—E·ly′sian** (ĭ-lĭzh′ən) *adj.*

em (ĕm) *n.* **1.** A unit of measure for printed matter that is equal to the width of the letter M. **2.** A pica.

′em (əm) *pron. Informal.* Them.

e·ma·ci·ate (ĭ-mā′shē-āt′) *v.* **-at·ed, -at·ing.**

To become or cause to become abnormally thin. —**e·ma′ci·a′tion** *n.*

E-mail (ē′māl′) *n.* Electronic mail.

em·a·nate (ĕm′ə-nāt′) *v.* **-nat·ed, -nat·ing.** To come or send forth, as from a source : issue or emit. —**em′a·na′tion** *n.*

e·man·ci·pate (ĭ-măn′sə-pāt′) *v.* **-pat·ed, -pat·ing.** To set free : liberate. —**e·man′ci·pa′tion** *n.* —**e·man′ci·pa′tor** *n.*

e·mas·cu·late (ĭ-măs′kyə-lāt′) *v.* **-lat·ed, -lat·ing. 1.** To castrate. **2.** To deprive of vigor : enervate. —**e·mas′cu·la′tion** *n.* —**e·mas′cu·la′tor** *n.*

em·balm (ĕm-bäm′) *v.* To treat (a corpse) with preservatives in order to prevent decay. —**em·balm′er** *n.*

em·bank (ĕm-băngk′) *v.* To support or protect with a bank of earth or stone. —**em·bank′ment** *n.*

em·bar·go (ĕm-bär′gō) *n., pl.* **-goes.** A prohibition on trade, esp. a government order forbidding the entry or departure of merchant ships. —**em·bar′go** *v.*

em·bark (ĕm-bärk′) *v.* **1.** To board or cause to board a vessel or aircraft. **2.** To set out on a venture. —**em′bar·ka′tion** *n.*

em·bar·rass (ĕm-băr′əs) *v.* **1.** To cause to feel self-conscious or ill at ease : disconcert. **2.** To burden with financial difficulties. **3.** To impede : hinder. ★ ***syns:*** ABASH, CONFUSE, DISCOMFORT, DISCONCERT, FAZE, MORTIFY —**em·bar′rass·ing·ly** *adv.* —**em·bar′rass·ment** *n.*

em·bas·sy (ĕm′bə-sē) *n., pl.* **-sies. 1.** The position or function of an ambassador. **2.** A mission led by an ambassador. **3.** An ambassador and his or her staff. **4.** The headquarters of an ambassador.

em·bat·tle (ĕm-băt′l) *v.* To prepare for battle.

em·bed (ĕm-bĕd′) *v.* To fix or become fixed tightly in a surrounding mass.

em·bel·lish (ĕm-bĕl′ĭsh) *v.* **1.** To make beautiful by ornamentation : adorn. **2.** To add fanciful details to <*embellished* the account> —**em·bel′lish·ment** *n.*

em·ber (ĕm′bər) *n.* **1.** A piece of glowing coal or wood, as in a dying fire. **2. embers.** The smoldering ashes of a dying fire.

em·bez·zle (ĕm-bĕz′əl) *v.* **-zled, -zling.** To take (e.g., money) fraudulently in violation of a trust. —**em·bez′zle·ment** *n.* —**em·bez′zler** *n.*

em·bit·ter (ĕm-bĭt′ər) *v.* **1.** To make bitter. **2.** To arouse bitter feelings in. —**em·bit′ter·ment** *n.*

em·bla·zon (ĕm-blā′zən) *v.* **1.** To ornament brightly or colorfully. **2.** To make illustrious : extol.

em·blem (ĕm′bləm) *n.* **1.** Something that represents or suggests something else : symbol. **2.** A distinctive design or device. —**em′blem·at′ic** (-blə-măt′ĭk), **em′blem·at′i·cal** *adj.*

em·bod·y (ĕm-bŏd′ē) *v.* **-ied, -y·ing. 1.** To give bodily form to (e.g., an abstraction). **2.** To personify. **3.** To make part of a system or whole. ★ ***syns:*** INCARNATE, MANIFEST, PERSONIFY —**em·bod′i·ment** *n.*

em·bold·en (ĕm-bōl′dən) *v.* To impart courage to : encourage.

em·bo·lism (ĕm′bə-lĭz′əm) *n.* The obstruction of a blood vessel, as by an air bubble or a detached clot.

em·bon·point (äN′bôN-pwăN′) *n.* Plumpness : corpulence.

em·boss (ĕm-bôs′, -bŏs′) *v.* **1.** To shape or decorate in relief. **2.** To raise the surface of <*emboss* type>

em·bou·chure (äm′bo͞o-sho͝or′) *n.* **1.** The mouthpiece of a wind instrument. **2.** The way in which the lips are applied to an embouchure to produce a musical tone.

em·bow·er (ĕm-bou′ər) *v.* To enclose in or as if in a bower.

em·brace (ĕm-brās′) *v.* **-braced, -brac·ing. 1.** To clasp in the arms : hug. **2.** To encircle. **3.** To include : encompass. **4.** To take up willingly <*embraced* the cause> —*n.* The act of embracing : hug.

em·bra·sure (ĕm-brā′zhər) *n.* A usu. flared opening in a wall for a door, window, or gun.

em·bro·cate (ĕm′brə-kāt′) *v.* **-cat·ed, -cat·ing.** To moisten and rub with a liquid medicine. —**em′bro·ca′tion** *n.*

em·broi·der (ĕm-broi′dər) *v.* **1.** To decorate (fabric) with needlework. **2.** To add fictitious details (to). —**em·broi′der·er** *n.*

em·broi·der·y (ĕm-broi′də-rē) *n., pl.* **-ies. 1.** The act or art of embroidering. **2.** Embroidered fabric. **3.** Fanciful details.

em·broil (ĕm-broil′) *v.* **1.** To involve in contention or hostile actions. **2.** To throw into confusion. —**em·broil′ment** *n.*

em·bry·o (ĕm′brē-ō′) *n., pl.* **-os. 1.** An organism in its early developmental stage, esp. before birth or germination. **2.** A rudimentary stage <talent in *embryo*> —**em′bry·on′ic** (-ŏn′ĭk) *adj.*

em·bry·ol·o·gy (ĕm′brē-ŏl′ə-jē) *n.* The science concerned with the formation and growth of embryos. —**em′bry·o·log′ic** (-ə-lŏj′ĭk), **em′bry·o·log′i·cal** *adj.* —**em′bry·ol′o·gist** *n.*

em·cee (ĕm′sē′) *n. Informal.* A master of ceremonies. —**em′cee′** *v.*

e·mend (ĭ-mĕnd′) *v.* To correct and improve by textual editing. —**e′men·da′tion** *n.* —**e·mend′er** *n.*

em·er·ald (ĕm′ər-əld, ĕm′rəld) *n.* **1.** A bright-green transparent form of beryl used as a gemstone. **2.** A bright green.

e·merge (ĭ-mûrj′) *v.* **e·merged, e·merg·ing. 1.** To rise or come into view : appear. **2.** To come into existence. **3.** To become evident. —**e·mer′gence** *n.* —**e·mer′gent** *adj.*

e·mer·gen·cy (ĭ-mûr′jən-sē) *n., pl.* **-cies.** An unexpected situation that requires prompt action.

e·mer·i·tus (ĭ-mĕr′ĭ-təs) *adj.* Retired but retaining the title held immediately before retirement <president *emeritus*> —**e·mer′i·tus** *n.*

em·er·y (ĕm′ə-rē, ĕm′rē) *n.* A grainy, impure corundum used for polishing and grinding.

e•met•ic (ĭ-mĕt'ĭk) *adj.* Inducing vomiting. **—e•met'ic** *n.*
em•i•grate (ĕm'ĭ-grāt') *v.* **-grat•ed, -grat•ing.** To leave a native country or region to settle elsewhere. **—em'i•grant** *n.* **—em'i•gra'tion** *n.*
é•mi•gré (ĕm'ĭ-grā') *n.* One who emigrates, esp. for political reasons.
em•i•nence (ĕm'ə-nəns) *n.* **1.** Great distinction or superiority. **2.** A high-ranking person. **3.** A rise of ground **:** hill.
em•i•nent (ĕm'ə-nənt) *adj.* **1.** Standing out **:** prominent. **2.** Outstanding, as in attainments **:** distinguished <an *eminent* scientist> **—em'i•nent•ly** *adv.*
eminent domain *n. Law.* The right of a government to take private property for public use.
e•mir (ĕ-mîr') *n.* A prince, chieftain, or governor in some parts of the Middle East and Africa.
e•mir•ate (ĭ-mîr'ĭt, -āt') *n.* **1.** The office of an emir. **2.** The nation or territory ruled by an emir.
em•is•sar•y (ĕm'ĭ-sĕr'ē) *n., pl.* **-ies.** A messenger or agent.
e•mit (ĭ-mĭt') *v.* **e•mit•ted, e•mit•ting. 1.** To send or give out <*emit* radiation> **2.** To express **:** utter. **3.** To put (e.g., money) into circulation. **—e•mis'sion** *n.*
e•mol•lient (ĭ-mŏl'yənt) *adj.* Soothing and softening, esp. to the skin. **—e•mol'lient** *n.*
e•mol•u•ment (ĭ-mŏl'yə-mənt) *n.* Compensation, as a salary, from a post of employment.
e•mote (ĭ-mōt') *v.* **e•mot•ed, e•mot•ing.** To express emotion theatrically.
e•mo•tion (ĭ-mō'shən) *n.* **1.** Strong feeling. **2.** A particular feeling, as love or hate.
e•mo•tion•al (ĭ-mō'shə-nəl) *adj.* **1.** Of or relating to emotion. **2.** Easily stirred by emotion. **3.** Marked by or stirring the emotions. **—e•mo'tion•al'i•ty** (-năl'ĭ-tē) *n.* **—e•mo'tion•al•ly** *adv.*
em•pa•thize (ĕm'pə-thīz') *v.* **-thized, -thiz•ing.** To feel empathy.
em•pa•thy (ĕm'pə-thē) *n.* Identification with and understanding of the thoughts or feelings of another. **—em'pa•thet'ic** (-thĕt'ĭk), **em•path'ic** (-păth'ĭk) *adj.*
em•pen•nage (ĕm'pə-nĭj) *n.* The tail of an aircraft.
em•per•or (ĕm'pər-ər) *n.* The ruler of an empire.
em•pha•sis (ĕm'fə-sĭs) *n., pl.* **-ses** (-sēz'). **1.** Special weight or significance <an *emphasis* on promptness> **2.** Stress given, as to a syllable or word.
em•pha•size (ĕm'fə-sīz') *v.* **-sized, -siz•ing.** To place emphasis on **:** stress.
em•phat•ic (ĕm-făt'ĭk) *adj.* Expressed or carried out with emphasis. **—em•phat'i•cal•ly** *adv.*
em•phy•se•ma (ĕm'fĭ-sē'mə) *n.* A pulmonary disease in which the lungs lose their elasticity, resulting in labored breathing and susceptibility to infection.
em•pire (ĕm'pīr') *n.* **1.** A group of territories or nations ruled by a single supreme authority. **2.** Imperial dominion.
em•pir•i•cal (ĕm-pîr'ĭ-kəl) *also* **em•pir•ic** (-pîr'ĭk) *adj.* Relying on or gained from observation or experiment rather than theory <*empirical* knowledge> **—em•pir'i•cal•ly** *adv.*
em•pir•i•cism (ĕm-pîr'ĭ-sĭz'əm) *n.* **1.** The belief that experience, esp. of the senses, is the single source of knowledge. **2.** The use of empirical methods in science. **—em•pir'i•cist** *n.*
em•place•ment (ĕm-plās'mənt) *n.* **1.** A platform or mounting for guns or military equipment. **2.** Placement.
em•ploy (ĕm-ploi') *v.* **1.** To put to service or use. **2.** To apply or devote (e.g., time) to an activity. **3.** To provide with gainful work. **—***n.* Employment. **—em•ploy'a•ble** *adj.* **—em•ploy'er** *n.*
em•ploy•ee *also* **em•ploy•e** (ĕm-ploi'ē, ĕm'ploi-ē') *n.* A person who works for another for compensation.
em•ploy•ment (ĕm-ploi'mənt) *n.* **1.** The act of employing or state of being employed. **2.** An occupation or activity.
em•po•ri•um (ĕm-pôr'ē-əm, -pōr'-) *n., pl.* **-ri•ums** *or* **-ri•a** (-ē-ə) A large store carrying a great variety of goods.
em•pow•er (ĕm-pou'ər) *v.* To authorize.
em•press (ĕm'prĭs) *n.* **1.** A woman who rules an empire. **2.** An emperor's wife or widow.
emp•ty (ĕmp'tē) *adj.* **-ti•er, -ti•est. 1.** Containing nothing. **2.** Without occupants **:** vacant. **3.** Lacking force or substance <*empty* promises> **—***v.* **-tied, -ty•ing. 1.** To make or become empty. **2.** To flow or pour out **:** discharge. **—***n., pl.* **-ties.** An empty container. **—emp'ti•ly** *adv.* **—emp'ti•ness** *n.*
emp•ty-hand•ed (ĕmp'tē-hăn'dĭd) *adj.* Bringing or taking away nothing.
em•py•re•an (ĕm'pī-rē'ən) *n.* **1.** The highest part of heaven. **2.** The sky.
e•mu (ē'myoo͞) *n.* A large, flightless Australian bird, *Dromiceius novaehollandia,* related and similar to the ostrich.
em•u•late (ĕm'yə-lāt') *v.* **-lat•ed, -lat•ing.** To strive to equal or better, esp. by imitating. **—em'u•la'tion** *n.* **—em'u•lous** (-ləs) *adj.*
e•mul•si•fy (ĭ-mŭl'sə-fī') *v.* **-fied, -fy•ing.** To make into an emulsion. **—e•mul'si•fi•ca'tion** *n.* **—e•mul'si•fi'er** *n.*
e•mul•sion (ĭ-mŭl'shən) *n.* **1.** *Chem.* A suspension of small droplets of one liquid in a second liquid with which the first will not mix. **2.** A light-sensitive coating on photographic film, paper, or glass. **—e•mul'sive** *adj.*
en (ĕn) *n.* A space equal to half the width of an em.
-en[1] *suff.* **1.** To make or become <deaf*en*> <short*en*> **2.** To cause or come to have <strength*en*>
-en[2] *suff.* Of or resembling <earth*en*>
en•a•ble (ĕn-ā'bəl) *v.* **-bled, -bling. 1.** To supply with the means, knowledge, or opportunity. **2.** To give legal power to.
en•act (ĕn-ăkt') *v.* **1.** To make (e.g., a legisla-

tive bill) into law. **2.** To act out <*enact* a drama> **—en•act′ment** *n.*

e•nam•el (ĭ-năm′əl) *n.* **1.** A decorative or protective vitreous, usu. opaque coating baked on a surface, as of pottery. **2.** A paint that forms a hard, glossy surface. **3.** The hard, calcareous covering on the exposed portion of a tooth. *—v.* **-eled, -el•ing** *or* **-elled, -el•ling.** To coat, inlay, or decorate with enamel.

e•nam•el•ware (ĭ-năm′əl-wâr′) *n.* Utensils, esp. kitchen utensils, made of metal coated with enamel.

en•am•or (ĭ-năm′ər) *v.* To imbue with love : captivate.

en•am•our (ĭ-năm′ər) *v. esp. Brit. var. of* ENAMOR.

en bloc (äɴ blŏk′) *adv.* As a unit.

en•camp (ĕn-kămp′) *v.* To set up or stay in a camp. **—en•camp′ment** *n.*

en•cap•su•late (ĕn-kăp′sə-lāt′) *v.* **-lat•ed, -lat•ing.** To enclose or become enclosed in or as if in a capsule. **—en•cap′su•la′tion** *n.*

en•case (ĕn-kās′) *v.* To enclose in or as if in a case. **—en•case′ment** *n.*

–ence *or* **–ency** *suff.* **1.** Condition or quality <depend*ence*> **2.** Action <emerg*ence*> <insurg*ency*>

en•ceph•a•li•tis (ĕn-sĕf′ə-lī′tĭs) *n.* Inflammation of the brain. **—en•ceph′a•lit′ic** (-lĭt′ĭk) *adj.*

en•chain (ĕn-chān′) *v.* To put in chains.

en•chant (ĕn-chănt′) *v.* **1.** To cast a spell over : bewitch. **2.** To delight greatly : enrapture. **—en•chant′ment** *n.*

en•chi•la•da (ĕn′chə-lä′də) *n.* A rolled tortilla filled with meat or cheese and served with chili sauce.

en•ci•pher (ĕn-sī′fər) *v.* To encode. **—en•ci′pher•er** *n.* **—en•ci′pher•ment** *n.*

en•cir•cle (ĕn-sûr′kəl) *v.* **1.** To make a circle around : surround. **2.** To move or go around. **—en•cir′cle•ment** *n.*

en•clave (ĕn′klāv′, ŏn′-) *n.* **1.** A country or part of a country lying inside the boundaries of another. **2.** A cultural group living within a larger group.

en•close (ĕn-klōz′) *v.* **1.** To surround on all sides : close in. **2.** To insert in the same envelope or package with something else. **—en•clo′sure** *n.*

en•code (ĕn-kōd′) *v.* **-cod•ed, -cod•ing. 1.** To put (e.g., a message) into code. **2.** *Computer Sci.* To convert into machine language. **—en•cod′er** *n.*

en•co•mi•um (ĕn-kō′mē-əm) *n., pl.* **-mi•ums** *or* **-mi•a** (-mē-ə). High praise.

en•com•pass (ĕn-kŭm′pəs, -kŏm′-) *v.* **1.** To surround. **2.** To envelop : enclose. **3.** To include : comprise.

en•core (ŏn′kôr′, -kōr′) *n.* **1.** An audience's demand for an additional performance. **2.** A performance in response to an encore. *—v.* **-cored, -cor•ing.** To demand an encore of.

en•coun•ter (ĕn-koun′tər) *n.* **1.** An unplanned or unexpected meeting. **2.** A hostile or violent meeting : clash. *—v.* **1.** To meet or come upon, esp. unexpectedly. **2.** To confront in a hostile situation.

encounter group *n.* A usu. unstructured therapy group in which individuals try to increase their sensitivity and responsiveness, reveal their feelings, and relate to others openly and intimately, as by touching or speaking freely.

en•cour•age (ĕn-kûr′ĭj, -kŭr′-) *v.* **-aged, -ag•ing. 1.** To inspire with courage or hope. **2.** To support : foster. **—en•cour′age•ment** *n.* **—en•cour′ag•ing•ly** *adv.*

en•croach (ĕn-krōch′) *v.* To intrude gradually upon the rights or possessions of another <trees that *encroached* upon his neighbor's land> **—en•croach′er** *n.* **—en•croach′ment** *n.*

en•crust (ĕn-krŭst′) *v.* To cover with or as if with a crust. **—en′crust•a′tion** (ĕn′krŭ-stā′shən) *n.*

en•crypt (ĕn-krĭpt′) *v.* **1.** To put into code or cipher. **2.** *Computer Sci.* To scramble (data) to prevent unauthorized access. **—en•cryp′tion** *n.*

en•cum•ber (ĕn-kŭm′bər) *v.* **1.** To weigh down unduly : burden. **2.** To hinder : impede. **—en•cum′brance** (-brəns) *n.*

–ency *suff. var. of* -ENCE.

en•cyc•li•cal (ĕn-sĭk′lĭ-kəl) *n.* A papal letter to the church bishops.

en•cy•clo•pe•di•a *or* **en•cy•clo•pae•di•a** (ĕn-sī′klə-pē′dē-ə) *n.* A comprehensive reference work with articles on a broad range of subjects. **—en•cy′clo•pe′dic** *adj.*

en•cyst (ĕn-sĭst′) *v.* To enclose in or as if in a cyst. **—en•cyst′ment** *n.*

end (ĕnd) *n.* **1.** A part lying at a boundary : extremity. **2.** The point at which something ceases : conclusion. **3.** A result : outcome. **4.** An ultimate extent : limit <at the *end* of her patience> **5.** A goal : purpose. **6.** A share of responsibility <your *end* of the job> **7.** A remnant : remainder. **8.** *Football.* Either of the players in the outermost position on the line of scrimmage. *—v.* **1.** To come or bring to an end : finish. **2.** To form the end of. **3.** To ruin : destroy. ★ ***syns:*** CLOSE, COMPLETE, CONCLUDE, FINISH, TERMINATE

en•dan•ger (ĕn-dān′jər) *v.* To expose to danger : imperil. **—en•dan′ger•ment** *n.*

en•dan•gered (ĕn-dān′jərd) *adj.* Threatened with extinction <an *endangered* species of salmon>

en•dear (ĕn-dîr′) *v.* To make beloved. **—en•dear′ing•ly** *adv.*

en•dear•ment (ĕn-dîr′mənt) *n.* An expression of affection.

en•deav•or (ĕn-dĕv′ər) *n.* A concerted effort : try. **—en•deav′or** *v.*

en•deav•our (ĕn-dĕv′ər) *n.* & *v. esp. Brit. var. of* ENDEAVOR.

en•dem•ic (ĕn-dĕm′ĭk) *adj.* Widespread in or peculiar to a particular area or people.

end•ing (ĕn′dĭng) *n.* **1.** A conclusion : termination. **2.** A suffix.

en•dive (ĕn′dīv′, ŏn′dēv′) *n.* **1.** A plant, *Cichorium endivia,* with crisp succulent leaves used in salads. **2.** A plant, *Cichorium intybus,* related to the endive and bearing a pointed cluster of whitish leaves used in salads.

end•less (ĕnd′lĭs) *adj.* **1.** Having or appearing to have no end or limit : infinite. **2.** Interminable : incessant <an *endless* sermon> **3.** Having the ends joined : continuous <an *endless* belt> **—end′less•ly** *adv.* **—end′less•ness** *n.*

end•most (ĕnd′mōst′) *adj.* At or closest to the end.

en•do•crine (ĕn′də-krĭn, -krēn′, -krīn′) *adj.* Of or relating to a ductless gland, as the thyroid or adrenal, whose internal secretions go directly into the bloodstream. **—en′do•crine** *n.*

en•do•cri•nol•o•gy (ĕn′də-krə-nŏl′ə-jē) *n.* The physiology or study of the endocrine glands. **—en′do•cri•nol′o•gist** *n.*

en•do•don•tics (ĕn′dō-dŏn′tĭks) *n. (sing. in number).* The branch of dentistry that deals with diseases of the tooth root, dental pulp, and surrounding tissue. **—en′do•don′tic** *adj.* **—en′do•don′tist** *n.*

en•dog•e•nous (ĕn-dŏj′ə-nəs) *adj.* Originating or produced from within.

en•do•me•tri•o•sis (ĕn′dō-mē′trē-ō′sĭs) *n.* A usu. painful condition marked by the abnormal occurrence of endometrial tissue outside the uterus.

en•do•me•tri•um (ĕn′dō-mē′trē-əm) *n., pl.* **-tri•a** (-trē-ə). The glandular mucous membrane that lines the uterus. **—en′do•me′tri•al** *adj.*

en•dor•phin (ĕn-dôr′fĭn) *n.* Any of a group of hormones with tranquilizing and pain-killing capabilities that are secreted by the brain.

en•dorse (ĕn-dôrs′) *v.* **-dorsed, -dors•ing. 1.** To write one's signature on the back of (e.g., a check) as evidence that ownership has been legally transferred. **2.** To approve of publicly : support. **—en′dor•see′** *n.* **—en•dorse′ment** *n.*

en•do•scope (ĕn′də-skōp′) *n.* An instrument for examining a bodily canal or hollow organ. **—en′do•scop′ic** (-skŏp′ĭk) *adj.* **—en•dos′co•py** (-dŏs′kə-pē) *n.*

en•do•ther•mic (ĕn′də-thûr′mĭk) *also* **en•do•ther•mal** (-məl) *adj.* Marked by or causing heat absorption.

en•dow (ĕn-dou′) *v.* **1.** To supply with income or income-producing property. **2.** To equip with a quality or talent. **—en•dow′ment** *n.*

en•due (ĕn-do͞o′, -dyo͞o′) *v.* **-dued, -du•ing.** To provide with a quality or power.

en•dur•ance (ĕn-do͝or′əns, -dyo͝or′-) *n.* **1.** The capacity to withstand stress. **2.** Perseverance.

en•dure (ĕn-do͝or′, -dyo͝or′) *v.* **-dured, -dur•ing. 1.** To carry on through : undergo successfully. **2.** To tolerate : bear. **3.** To continue in existence. **—en•dur′a•ble** *adj.*

end•wise (ĕnd′wīz′) *also* **end•ways** (-wāz′) *adv.* **1.** On end. **2.** With the end forward. **3.** Lengthwise.

en•e•ma (ĕn′ə-mə) *n.* **1.** The injection of a liquid into the rectum, esp. for cleansing. **2.** The liquid injected as an enema.

en•e•my (ĕn′ə-mē) *n., pl.* **-mies. 1.** One who seeks to harm another : foe. **2.** A hostile force or power.

en•er•get•ic (ĕn′ər-jĕt′ĭk) *adj.* Possessing or exhibiting energy. ★ ***syns:*** DYNAMIC, FORCEFUL, KINETIC, PEPPY, SPRIGHTLY, VIGOROUS **—en′er•get′i•cal•ly** *adv.*

en•er•gize (ĕn′ər-jīz′) *v.* **-gized, -giz•ing.** To give energy to. **—en′er•giz′er** *n.*

en•er•gy (ĕn′ər-jē) *n., pl.* **-gies. 1.** Capacity for working or acting : vigor. **2.** Strength : force. **3.** Vitality of expression. **4.** *Physics.* The work that a physical system is capable of doing. **5.** Usable heat or electric power.

en•er•vate (ĕn′ər-vāt′) *v.* **-vat•ed, -vat•ing.** To deprive of vitality : weaken. **—en′er•va′tion** *n.*

en•fant ter•ri•ble (äɴ-fäɴ′ tĕ-rē′blə) *n., pl.* **en•fants ter•ri•bles** (äɴ-fäɴ′ tĕ-rē′blə). One whose unconventional behavior and ideas cause embarrassment or dismay.

en•fee•ble (ĕn-fē′bəl) *v.* **-bled, -bling.** To weaken. **—en•fee′ble•ment** *n.*

en•fi•lade (ĕn′fə-lād′, -läd′) *n.* The firing of guns so as to sweep the length of an enemy target.

en•fold (ĕn-fōld′) *v.* **1.** To envelop. **2.** To enclose. **3.** To embrace.

en•force (ĕn-fôrs′, -fōrs′) *v.* **1.** To compel observance of <*enforce* traffic laws> **2.** To bring about by force or firmness <*enforce* silence> **—en•force′a•ble** *adj.* **—en•force′ment** *n.* **—en•forc′er** *n.*

en•fran•chise (ĕn-frăn′chīz′) *v.* **1.** To endow with civil rights, esp. the right to vote. **2.** To free : emancipate. **3.** To give a franchise to. **—en•fran′chise′ment** *n.*

en•gage (ĕn-gāj′) *v.* **-gaged, -gag•ing. 1.** To employ : hire. **2.** To secure and hold : engross <*engaged* her interest> **3.** To pledge or promise, esp. to marry. **4.** To enter into conflict (with) <We have *engaged* the enemy.> **5.** To interlock : mesh. **6.** To participate or induce to participate <*engage* in a discussion>

en•gage•ment (ĕn-gāj′mənt) *n.* **1.** Betrothal. **2.** A promise, esp. to meet someone : appointment. **3.** Employment. **4.** A battle.

en•gag•ing (ĕn-gā′jĭng) *adj.* Attractive : charming. **—en•gag′ing•ly** *adv.*

en•gen•der (ĕn-jĕn′dər) *v.* **1.** To give rise to. **2.** To procreate : propagate.

en•gine (ĕn′jən) *n.* **1.** A machine that turns energy into mechanical motion. **2.** A mechanical device or instrument <*engines* of destruction> **3.** A locomotive.

en•gi•neer (ĕn′jə-nîr′) *n.* **1.** One trained or engaged in a branch of engineering. **2.** One who operates an engine, esp. a locomotive. —*v.* **1.** To plan and manage as an engineer. **2.** To plan or accomplish with skill.

en•gi•neer•ing (ĕn′jə-nîr′ĭng) *n.* **1.** The application of scientific principles to practical ends. **2.** The design and construction of large-scale or complex structures such as bridges, roads, and tunnels.

Eng•lish (ĭng′glĭsh) *adj.* Of, relating to, or characteristic of England, its people, or their language. —*n.* **1.** The people of England. **2.** The Germanic language of England, the U.S., and other countries that are or were formerly under English influence or control. —**Eng′lish•man** *n.* —**Eng′lish•wom′-an** *n.*

English Canada *n.* The part of Canada where English is the predominant language.

English Canadian *n.* A Canadian whose first language is English.

English horn *n.* A woodwind instrument larger than an oboe and pitched lower.

en•gorge (ĕn-gôrj′) *v.* **1.** To devour greedily. **2.** To gorge : glut. **3.** To fill to excess, as with blood. —**en•gorge′ment** *n.*

en•graft (ĕn-grăft′) *v.* To graft (a scion) onto or into another plant.

en•grave (ĕn-grāv′) *v.* **-graved, -grav•ing. 1.** To carve or cut into a surface <*engrave* words on a tombstone> **2. a.** To carve, cut, or etch (e.g., a design) into a printing surface. **b.** To print from a surface made by such a process. —**en•grav′er** *n.*

en•grav•ing (ĕn-grā′vĭng) *n.* **1.** The art or technique of one that engraves. **2.** An engraved printing plate. **3.** A print made from an engraved plate.

en•gross (ĕn-grōs′) *v.* **1.** To occupy the full attention of : absorb. **2.** To copy in a large, clear hand. —**en•gross′ing•ly** *adv.*

en•gulf (ĕn-gŭlf′) *v.* **1.** To enclose completely. **2.** To swallow up by or as if by flowing over.

en•hance (ĕn-hăns′) *v.* **-hanced, -hanc•ing.** To make greater, as in beauty or value : heighten. —**en•hance′ment** *n.*

e•nig•ma (ĭ-nĭg′mə) *n.* One that baffles the understanding.

en•ig•mat•ic (ĕn′ĭg-măt′ĭk) *adj.* Being an enigma. —**en′ig•mat′i•cal•ly** *adv.*

en•jamb•ment *or* **en•jambe•ment** (ĕn-jăm′mənt) *n.* Continuation of a sentence from one line or couplet of a poem to the next so that closely related words fall on different lines.

en•join (ĕn-join′) *v.* **1.** To direct with emphasis and authority : command. **2.** To forbid, esp. by legal action. —**en•join′der** *n.*

en•joy (ĕn-joi′) *v.* **1.** To get pleasure from : relish <*enjoyed* the puppet show> **2.** To have the benefit or use of <*enjoying* a successful career> —**en•joy′a•ble** *adj.* —**en•joy′a•bly** *adv.* —**en•joy′ment** *n.*

en•large (ĕn-lärj′) *v.* **-larged, -larg•ing. 1.** To make or become larger <*enlarged* the photograph> **2.** To speak or write in greater detail <*enlarged* on the topic> —**en•large′ment** *n.* —**en•larg′er** *n.*

en•light•en (ĕn-līt′n) *v.* **1.** To provide with spiritual or intellectual understanding. **2.** To inform. —**en•light′en•ment** *n.* —**en•light′-en•er** *n.*

en•list (ĕn-lĭst′) *v.* **1.** To enroll for service in the armed forces. **2.** To secure the help of <*enlist* the guests for dishwashing> —**en•list′ment** *n.*

enlisted man *n.* A man who has enlisted in the armed forces without an officer's commission or warrant.

enlisted woman *n.* A woman who has enlisted in the armed forces without an officer's commission or warrant.

en•liv•en (ĕn-lī′vən) *v.* To make livelier : animate. —**en•liv′en•ment** *n.*

en masse (ŏn măs′) *adv.* All together.

en•mesh (ĕn-mĕsh′) *v.* To catch in or as if in a mesh : entangle.

en•mi•ty (ĕn′mĭ-tē) *n., pl.* **-ties.** Deep hatred, as between enemies.

en•no•ble (ĕn-nō′bəl) *v.* **-bled, -bling. 1.** To make noble : exalt. **2.** To raise in rank to the nobility. —**en•no′ble•ment** *n.*

en•nui (ŏn-wē′, ŏn′wē) *n.* Boredom.

e•nor•mi•ty (ĭ-nôr′mĭ-tē) *n., pl.* **-ties. 1.** Excessive wickedness. **2.** A monstrous offense or crime : outrage.

e•nor•mous (ĭ-nôr′məs) *adj.* Very great in size or degree : immense. —**e•nor′mous•ly** *adv.* —**e•nor′mous•ness** *n.*

e•nough (ĭ-nŭf′) *adj.* Sufficient to satisfy need or desire. —*pron.* An adequate quantity <*enough* for everyone> —*adv.* **1.** To a satisfactory degree. **2.** Tolerably : rather <felt well *enough*>

en•plane (ĕn-plān′) *v.* To board an aircraft.

en•quire (ĕn-kwīr′) *v. var. of* INQUIRE.

en•rage (ĕn-rāj′) *v.* To put into a rage.

en•rap•ture (ĕn-răp′chər) *v.* **-tured, -tur•ing.** To fill with rapture : delight.

en•rich (ĕn-rĭch′) *v.* **1.** To make rich or richer. **2.** To make fuller or more meaningful <metaphors that *enrich* the poem> —**en•rich′-ment** *n.*

en•roll *also* **en•rol** (ĕn-rōl′) *v.* **-rolled, -roll•ing. 1.** To enter the name of on a roll, register, or record. **2.** To place one's name on a roll, register, or record. —**en•roll′ment, en•rol′ment** *n.*

en route (ŏn ro͞ot′, ĕn) *adv. & adj.* On the way.

en•sconce (ĕn-skŏns′) *v.* **-sconced, -sconc•ing. 1.** To settle (oneself) securely. **2.** To put in a safe or concealed place.

en•sem•ble (ŏn-sŏm′bəl) *n.* A group of complementary parts contributing to a single effect, esp.: **a.** A coordinated outfit of clothing. **b.** A group of persons, as musicians, performing together. **c.** Music for 2 or more performers.

en•shrine (ĕn-shrīn′) *v.* **-shrined, -shrin•ing. 1.** To place in or as if in a shrine. **2.** To hold sacred : cherish. —**en•shrine′ment** *n.*

en•shroud (ĕn-shroud′) *v.* To cover with or as if with a shroud : obscure.

en•sign (ĕn′sən) *n.* **1.** (*also* ĕn′sīn′). A flag or banner, esp. one displayed on a ship or aircraft. **2.** A commissioned officer of the lowest rank in the U.S. Navy or Coast Guard. **3.** (*also* ĕn′sīn′). A badge or token.

en•si•lage (ĕn′sə-lĭj) *n.* **1.** The process of storing and fermenting green fodder in a silo. **2.** Fodder that has been stored : silage. —**en•sile′** (ĕn-sīl′) *v.*

en·slave (ĕn-slāv′) *v.* To make a slave of : subjugate. **—en·slave′ment** *n.*

en·snare (ĕn-snâr′) *v.* To catch in or as if in a snare : trap.

en·sue (ĕn-so͞o′) *v.* **-sued, -su·ing.** To follow as a result or consequence.

en·sure (ĕn-sho͝or′) *v.* **-sured, -sur·ing.** To make certain of : insure.

—ent *suff.* **1. a.** Performing or causing a specified action <absorb*ent*> **b.** Being in a specified state <bival*ent*> **2.** One that performs or causes a specified action <refer*ent*>

en·tail (ĕn-tāl′) *v.* **1.** To have or require as a necessary accompaniment or result. **2.** To limit the inheritance of (property) to a certain line of heirs. **—en·tail′ment** *n.*

en·tan·gle (ĕn-tăng′gəl) *v.* **1.** To tangle : snarl. **2.** To complicate : confuse. **—en·tan′gle·ment** *n.*

en·tente (ŏn-tŏnt′) *n.* **1.** An agreement between governments for cooperative action. **2.** The parties to an entente.

en·ter (ĕn′tər) *v.* **1.** To go or come into. **2.** To pierce : penetrate. **3.** To start : begin. **4.** To become a member (of) or participant (in). **5.** To enroll or inscribe. **6.** *Law.* **a.** To place formally on record. **b.** To go upon or into in order to take possession.

en·ter·i·tis (ĕn′tə-rī′tĭs) *n.* Intestinal inflammation.

en·ter·prise (ĕn′tər-prīz′) *n.* **1.** An undertaking, esp. a large or risky one. **2.** A business organization. **3.** Readiness to venture : initiative.

en·ter·pris·ing (ĕn′tər-prī′zĭng) *adj.* Exhibiting initiative, imagination, and readiness to venture. **—en′ter·pris′ing·ly** *adv.*

en·ter·tain (ĕn′tər-tān′) *v.* **1.** To hold the attention of : amuse. **2.** To receive as a guest : offer hospitality (to). **3.** To hold in mind : consider. **—en′ter·tain′er** *n.* **—en′ter·tain′ment** *n.*

en·thrall (ĕn-thrôl′) *v.* **1.** To enslave. **2.** To fascinate : captivate. **—en·thrall′ment** *n.*

en·throne (ĕn-thrōn′) *v.* **-throned, -thron·ing. 1.** To seat on a throne. **2.** To raise to a high position : exalt. **—en·throne′ment** *n.*

en·thuse (ĕn-tho͞oz′) *v.* **-thused, -thus·ing.** *Informal.* To make or become enthusiastic.

en·thu·si·asm (ĕn-tho͞o′zē-ăz′əm) *n.* **1. a.** Intense feeling for a subject or cause. **b.** Eagerness : zeal. **2.** Something inspiring. **—en·thu′si·ast′** *n.* **—en·thu′si·as′tic** *adj.* **—en·thu′si·as′ti·cal·ly** *adv.*

en·tice (ĕn-tīs′) *v.* **-ticed, -tic·ing.** To attract by arousing desire or hope : lure. **—en·tice′ment** *n.* **—en·tic′er** *n.* **—en·tic′ing·ly** *adv.*

en·tire (ĕn-tīr′) *adj.* **1.** Having no part left out : whole. **2.** Unlimited : complete <my *entire* attention> **—en·tire′ly** *adv.*

en·tire·ty (ĕn-tī′rə-tē) *n., pl.* **-ties. 1.** The state of being entire : completeness. **2.** The entire amount.

en·ti·tle (ĕn-tīt′l) *v.* **1.** To give a name or title to. **2.** To furnish with a right <a ticket *entitling* the bearer to admission> **—en·ti′tle·ment** *n.*

entitlement program *n.* A government program that guarantees benefits to all members of a particular group.

en·ti·ty (ĕn′tĭ-tē) *n., pl.* **-ties. 1.** The fact of existence. **2.** Something that exists separately : thing.

en·tomb (ĕn-to͞om′) *v.* To place in or as if in a tomb : bury. **—en·tomb′ment** *n.*

en·to·mol·o·gy (ĕn′tə-mŏl′ə-jē) *n.* The scientific study of insects. **—en′to·mo·log′ic** (-mə-lŏj′ĭk), **en′to·mo·log′i·cal** *adj.* **—en′to·mol′o·gist** *n.*

en·tou·rage (ŏn′to͞o-räzh′) *n.* A group of attendants or associates : retinue.

en·tr'acte (ŏn′trăkt′, äɴ-träkt′) *n.* **1.** An interval between 2 acts of a play. **2.** An entertainment offered during an entr'acte.

en·trails (ĕn′trālz′, -trəlz) *pl.n.* Internal organs : viscera.

en·train (ĕn-trān′) *v.* To put or go on board a train. **—en·train′ment** *n.*

en·trance[1] (ĕn′trəns) *n.* **1.** The act of entering. **2.** A place or means for entering. **3.** The right to enter : admission.

en·trance[2] (ĕn-trăns′) *v.* **-tranced, -tranc·ing.** To fascinate : enchant. **—en·trance′ment** *n.* **—en·tranc′ing·ly** *adv.*

en·trant (ĕn′trənt) *n.* One who enters a competition.

en·trap (ĕn-trăp′) *v.* To catch in or as if in a trap. **—en·trap′ment** *n.*

en·treat (ĕn-trēt′) *v.* To make an earnest request (of) : implore.

en·treat·y (ĕn-trē′tē) *n., pl.* **-ies.** An earnest request : plea.

en·tre·chat (ŏn′trə-shä′) *n.* A leap during which a ballet dancer crosses the feet repeatedly.

en·trée *or* **en·tree** (ŏn′trā′, ŏn-trā′) *n.* **1. a.** The right to enter. **b.** Permission to enter. **2.** The main course of a meal.

en·trench (ĕn-trĕnch′) *v.* **1.** To provide with or dig a trench, as for defense. **2.** To fix or seat firmly. **3.** To encroach. **—en·trench′ment** *n.*

en·tre·pre·neur (ŏn′trə-prə-nûr′) *n.* One who launches or manages a business venture, often assuming risks. **—en′tre·pre·neu′ri·al** (-no͝or′ē-əl, -nyo͝or′-, -nûr′-) *adj.*

en·tro·py (ĕn′trə-pē) *n.* **1.** A measure of a system's capacity to undergo spontaneous change. **2.** A measure of the disorder or randomness in a system.

en·trust (ĕn-trŭst′) *v.* **1.** To give over to another for care or performance <*entrusted* the task to an aide> **2.** To give as a trust to (someone).

en·try (ĕn′trē) *n., pl.* **-tries. 1.** An act or the right of entering. **2.** A place for entering. **3. a.** The act of entering an item, as in a record, list, or reference work. **b.** The item entered <a dictionary *entry*> **4.** One entered in a competition.

en·twine (ĕn-twīn′) *v.* To twine around or together.

e·nu·mer·ate (ĭ-no͞o′mə-rāt′, ĭ-nyo͞o′-) *v.* **1.** To name or count of one by one : list. **2.** To count. —**e•nu'mer•a'tion** *n.* —**e•nu'mer•a'-tor** *n.*

e•nun•ci•ate (ĭ-nŭn'sē-āt', -shē-) *v.* **-at•ed, -at•ing. 1.** To pronounce, esp. with clarity. **2.** To announce : proclaim. —**e•nun'ci•a'-tion** *n.*

en•u•re•sis (ĕn'yə-rē'sĭs) *n.* Involuntary urination.

en•vel•op (ĕn-vĕl'əp) *v.* To enclose entirely with or as if with a covering. —**en•vel'op•ment** *n.*

en•ve•lope (ĕn'və-lōp', ŏn'-) *n.* **1.** Something that covers or encloses. **2.** A flat paper container, esp. for a letter. **3.** The gas-filled bag of a balloon.

en•ven•om (ĕn-vĕn'əm) *v.* **1.** To make poisonous. **2.** To embitter.

en•vi•a•ble (ĕn'vē-ə-bəl) *adj.* Highly desirable. —**en'vi•a•bly** *adv.*

en•vi•ous (ĕn'vē-əs) *adj.* Feeling, showing, or marked by envy. —**en'vi•ous•ly** *adv.* —**en'-vi•ous•ness** *n.*

en•vi•ron•ment (ĕn-vī'rən-mənt) *n.* **1.** Surroundings. **2.** The combination of external physical conditions affecting the growth and development of organisms. —**en•vi'ron•men'tal** *adj.* —**en•vi'ron•men'tal•ly** *adv.*

en•vi•ron•men•tal•ist (ĕn-vī'rən-mĕn'tl-ĭst) *n.* One who seeks to preserve the natural environment. —**en•vi'ron•men'tal•ism** *n.*

en•vi•rons (ĕn-vī'rənz) *pl.n.* A surrounding area, esp. of a city.

en•vis•age (ĕn-vĭz'ĭj) *v.* **-aged, -ag•ing.** To have or form a mental image of.

en•voi *also* **en•voy** (ĕn'voi', ŏn'-) *n.* A short closing passage of a poem or book.

en•voy (ĕn'voi', ŏn'-) *n.* **1.** A messenger or agent. **2.** A governmental representative dispatched on a special diplomatic mission.

en•vy (ĕn'vē) *n., pl.* **-vies. 1.** Discontented desire for someone else's possessions or advantages. **2.** An object of such feelings. ★ ***syns:*** COVETOUSNESS, ENVIOUSNESS, JEALOUSY —*v.* **-vied, -vy•ing.** To feel envy because of or toward.

en•zyme (ĕn'zīm') *n.* Any of numerous proteins produced by living organisms and functioning as biochemical catalysts in animals and plants. —**en'zy•mat'ic** (ĕn'zə-măt'ĭk) *adj.*

e•o•li•an (ē-ō'lē-ən) *adj.* Of, caused by, or transmitted by the wind.

e•on *also* **ae•on** (ē'ŏn', ē'ən) *n.* An indefinitely long period of time : age.

–eous *suff.* Having the nature of : resembling <gas*eous*>

ep•au•let *also* **ep•au•lette** (ĕp'ə-lĕt', ĕp'ə-lĕt') *n.* A shoulder ornament, as on a military uniform.

é•pée *also* **e•pee** (ā-pā') *n.* A fencing sword with a bowl-shaped guard and a long blade lacking a cutting edge.

e•pergne (ĭ-pûrn', ā-pûrn') *n.* A centerpiece with extended arms or branches supporting holders, as for flowers or fruit, used esp. on a dinner table.

e•phed•rine (ĭ-fĕd'rĭn) *n.* A white, odorless crystalline alkaloid used to treat allergies and asthma.

e•phem•er•al (ĭ-fĕm'ər-əl) *adj.* Lasting but a short time. —**e•phem'er•al•ly** *adv.*

ep•ic (ĕp'ĭk) *n.* **1.** A long narrative poem celebrating the feats of heroes. **2.** A long narrative work, as a novel, that resembles an epic. —**ep'ic** *adj.*

ep•i•can•thic fold (ĕp'ĭ-kăn'thĭk) *n.* A fold of skin of the upper eyelid tending to cover the inner corner of the eye.

ep•i•cen•ter (ĕp'ĭ-sĕn'tər) *n.* The part of the earth's surface directly above the origin of an earthquake.

ep•i•cure (ĕp'ĭ-kyŏŏr') *n.* One with refined tastes, esp. in food and wine.

ep•i•cu•re•an (ĕp'ĭ-kyŏŏ-rē'ən) *adj.* **1.** Devoted to pleasure. **2.** Suited to the tastes of an epicure <an *epicurean* banquet> —**ep'i•cu•re'an** *n.*

ep•i•dem•ic (ĕp'ĭ-dĕm'ĭk) *adj.* **1.** Affecting many individuals at the same time <Cholera was *epidemic.*> **2.** Widely prevalent <*epidemic* anxiety> —*n.* **1.** An epidemic outbreak of contagious disease. **2.** A rapid spread or increase in occurrence <an *epidemic* of robberies>

ep•i•der•mis (ĕp'ĭ-dûr'mĭs) *n.* The protective outer layer of the skin. —**ep'i•der'mal** *adj.*

ep•i•du•ral (ĕp'ĭ-dŏŏr'əl, -dyŏŏr'-) *adj.* Located on or over the dura mater. —*n.* An injection, esp. of an anesthetic, into the epidural space of the spine.

ep•i•glot•tis (ĕp'ĭ-glŏt'ĭs) *n.* The elastic cartilage at the base of the tongue that folds over the glottis to protect the trachea during the act of swallowing. —**ep'i•glot'tal** (-glŏt'l) *adj.*

ep•i•gram (ĕp'ĭ-grăm') *n.* A terse witty poem or saying. —**ep'i•gram•mat'ic** (-grə-măt'ĭk) *adj.*

ep•i•graph (ĕp'ĭ-grăf') *n.* **1.** An inscription. **2.** A quotation placed at the beginning of a literary work.

e•pig•ra•phy (ĭ-pĭg'rə-fē) *n.* The study of inscriptions. —**e•pig'ra•pher** *n.*

ep•i•lep•sy (ĕp'ə-lĕp'sē) *n.* A nervous disorder marked by usu. recurring attacks of convulsions and loss of consciousness. —**ep'i•lep'tic** *n. & adj.*

ep•i•logue *also* **ep•i•log** (ĕp'ə-lôg', -lŏg') *n.* **1.** A speech given by an actor to the audience at the end of a play. **2.** An additional chapter placed at the end of a novel.

ep•i•neph•rine *also* **ep•i•neph•rin** (ĕp'ə-nĕf'rĭn) *n.* An adrenal hormone that raises the blood pressure and quickens the pulse, used in synthesized form as a cardiovascular stimulant.

E•piph•a•ny (ĭ-pĭf'ə-nē) *n., pl.* **-nies.** A Christian festival held on Jan. 6, celebrating the revealing of Christ to the Gentiles as represented by the Magi.

ep•i•phyte (ĕp'ə-fīt') *n.* A plant that grows on another plant on which it depends for mechanical support but not for nutrients. —**ep'i•phyt'ic** (-fĭt'ĭk) *adj.*

e·pis·co·pa·cy (ĭ-pĭs′kə-pə-sē) *n., pl.* **-cies. 1.** Bishops as a group : episcopate. **2.** Church government by bishops.

e·pis·co·pal (ĭ-pĭs′kə-pəl) *adj.* **1.** Of or relating to a bishop. **2.** Governed by bishops. **3. Episcopal.** Of or relating to the Protestant Episcopal Church.

E·pis·co·pa·li·an (ĭ-pĭs′kə-pā′lē-ən, -pāl′-yən) *n.* A member of the Protestant Episcopal Church. **—E·pis′co·pa′li·an** *n.*

e·pis·co·pate (ĭ-pĭs′kə-pĭt, -pāt′) *n.* **1.** The position, term, or rank of a bishop. **2.** The jurisdiction of a bishop : diocese. **3.** Bishops as a group.

ep·i·sode (ĕp′ĭ-sōd′) *n.* **1.** An incident : occurrence. **2.** A part of a narrative that forms a unit and often a coherent story in itself. **—ep′i·sod′ic** (-sŏd′ĭk) *adj.*

e·pis·tle (ĭ-pĭs′əl) *n.* **1.** A letter. **2. Epistle.** One of the letters in the New Testament. **—e·pis′to·lar′y** (-tə-lĕr′ē) *adj.*

ep·i·taph (ĕp′ĭ-tăf′) *n.* An inscription, as on a gravestone, in memory of a deceased person.

ep·i·the·li·um (ĕp′ə-thē′lē-əm) *n., pl.* **-li·ums** *or* **-li·a** (-lē-ə). The thin membranous tissue forming the covering of the outer bodily surface and most of the internal surfaces and organs. **—ep′i·the′li·al, ep′i·the′li·oid′** *adj.*

ep·i·thet (ĕp′ə-thĕt′) *n.* **1.** A term used to characterize a person or thing. **2.** An abusive word or phrase.

e·pit·o·me (ĭ-pĭt′ə-mē) *n.* **1.** A summary, as of a book. **2.** A perfect example.

e·pit·o·mize (ĭ-pĭt′ə-mīz′) *v.* **-mized, -miz·ing. 1.** To make an epitome of : sum up. **2.** To be a perfect example of : embody.

ep·och (ĕp′ək, ĕp′ŏk′) *n.* **1.** A historical period : era. **2.** An event marking the beginning of a new era. **—ep′och·al** *adj.* **—ep′och·al·ly** *adv.*

ep·ox·y (ĕp′ŏk′sē, ĭ-pŏk′-) *n., pl.* **-ies.** A durable, corrosion-resistant resin used esp. in surface coatings and glues. **—ep′ox′y** *v.*

Ep·som salts (ĕp′səm) *pl.n.* Hydrated magnesium sulfate, used as a cathartic.

eq·ua·ble (ĕk′wə-bəl, ē′kwə-) *adj.* **1. a.** Steady : unvarying. **b.** Free from extremes. **2.** Not easily disturbed : serene <an *equable* temperament> **—eq′ua·bil′i·ty, eq′ua·ble·ness** *n.* **—eq′ua·bly** *adv.*

e·qual (ē′kwəl) *adj.* **1.** Of the same measure, quantity, or value as another. **2.** Possessing the same privileges or rights <*equal* before the law> **3.** Having the necessary strength or ability <*equal* to the task> *—n.* One equal to another. *—v.* **e·qualed, e·qual·ing** *or* **e·qualled, e·qual·ling. 1.** To be equal to. **2.** To do or achieve something equal to : match. **—e·qual′i·ty** (ĭ-kwŏl′ĭ-tē) *n.* **—e′qual·ly** *adv.*

e·qual·ize (ē′kwə-līz′) *v.* **-ized, -iz·ing.** To make or become equal or uniform. **—e′qual·i·za′tion** *n.* **—e′qual·iz′er** *n.*

e·qua·nim·i·ty (ē′kwə-nĭm′ĭ-tē, ĕk′wə-) *n.* Calmness : composure.

e·quate (ĭ-kwāt′) *v.* **e·quat·ed, e·quat·ing.** To make or consider as equal.

e·qua·tion (ĭ-kwā′zhən, -shən) *n.* **1.** The act of equating or state of being equated. **2.** A mathematical statement that 2 expressions are equal. **—e·qua′tion·al** *adj.*

e·qua·tor (ĭ-kwā′tər) *n.* An imaginary great circle around the earth, the plane of which is perpendicular to the axis of rotation and that is everywhere equidistant from the poles. **—e′qua·to′ri·al** (ē′kwə-tôr′ē-əl, -tōr′-, ĕk′-wə-) *adj.*

eq·uer·ry (ĕk′wə-rē) *n., pl.* **-ries. 1.** An officer charged with the supervision of the horses belonging to a royal or noble household. **2.** A personal attendant to a member of the British royal family.

e·ques·tri·an (ĭ-kwĕs′trē-ən) *adj.* **1.** Of or relating to horsemanship. **2.** Representing a subject on horseback. *—n.* One who rides or performs on a horse. **—e·ques′tri·enne′** (-trē-ĕn′) *n.*

e·qui·an·gu·lar (ē′kwē-ăng′gyə-lər, ĕk′wē-) *adj.* Having all angles equal.

e·qui·dis·tant (ē′kwə-dĭs′tənt, ĕk′wə-) *adj.* Equally distant. **—e′qui·dis′tance** *n.*

e·qui·lat·er·al (ē′kwə-lăt′ər-əl, ĕk′wə-) *adj.* Having all sides or faces equal. **—e′qui·lat′er·al** *n.*

e·qui·lib·ri·um (ē′kwə-lĭb′rē-əm, ĕk′wə-) *n.* Balance between opposing forces or influences.

e·quine (ē′kwīn′, ĕk′wīn′) *adj.* Of, relating to, or typical of a horse. **—e′quine′** *n.*

e·qui·nox (ē′kwə-nŏks′, ĕk′wə-) *n.* Either of the 2 times a year when the sun crosses the celestial equator and day and night are approx. the same in length. **—e′qui·noc′tial** (-nŏk′shəl) *adj.*

e·quip (ĭ-kwĭp′) *v.* **e·quipped, e·quip·ping.** To furnish with what is needed <*equipped* themselves for a long hike>

eq·ui·page (ĕk′wə-pĭj) *n.* A carriage equipped with horses and attendants.

e·quip·ment (ĭ-kwĭp′mənt) *n.* **1.** The act of equipping or state of being equipped. **2.** Things with which one is equipped.

e·qui·poise (ē′kwə-poiz′, ĕk′wə-) *n.* **1.** Equilibrium : balance. **2.** A counterbalance.

eq·ui·ta·ble (ĕk′wĭ-tə-bəl) *adj.* Impartial in judgment or treatment : just. **—eq′ui·ta·ble·ness** *n.* **—eq′ui·ta·bly** *adv.*

eq·ui·ta·tion (ĕk′wĭ-tā′shən) *n.* The act or art of riding horses.

eq·ui·ty (ĕk′wĭ-tē) *n., pl.* **-ties. 1.** The quality of being just or impartial : fairness. **2.** The value of property beyond a mortgage or liability. **3.** *Law.* **a.** A system of jurisprudence supplementing the common law. **b.** Justice applied in circumstances not covered by law.

e·quiv·a·lent (ĭ-kwĭv′ə-lənt) *adj.* Equal or virtually equal, as in meaning or effect. **—e·quiv′a·lence, e·quiv′a·len·cy** *n.* **—e·quiv′a·lent** *n.* **—e·quiv′a·lent·ly** *adv.*

e·quiv·o·cal (ĭ-kwĭv′ə-kəl) *adj.* **1.** Deliberately ambiguous or misleading. **2.** Questionable : dubious. **—e·quiv′o·cal·ly** *adv.*

e·quiv·o·cate (ĭ-kwĭv′ə-kāt′) *v.* **-cat·ed, -cat·ing.** To use vague or intentionally evasive language. ★ *syns:* HEDGE, PUSSYFOOT, WAFFLE —**e•quiv'o•ca'tion** *n.* —**e•quiv'o•ca'tor** *n.*

Er *symbol for* ERBIUM.

–er[1] *suff.* **1. a.** One that does something specified <build*er*> **b.** One that undergoes something specified <broil*er*> **c.** One that has or contains <six-foot*er*> **2. a.** One associated with <bank*er*> **b.** One living in or coming from <London*er*>

–er[2] *suff.* —Used to form the comparative degree of adjectives and adverbs <old*er*> <quick*er*>

e•ra (îr'ə, ĕr'ə) *n.* **1.** A time period reckoned from a specific date. **2.** A time period distinguished by a certain characteristic <the gaslight *era*>

e•rad•i•cate (ĭ-răd'ĭ-kāt') *v.* **-cat•ed, -cat•ing.** To remove by or as if by uprooting : eliminate. —**e•rad'i•ca•ble** *adj.* —**e•rad'i•ca'tion** *n.* —**e•rad'i•ca'tor** *n.*

e•rase (ĭ-rās') *v.* **e•rased, e•ras•ing. 1.** To remove (e.g., something written) by or as if by rubbing or scraping. **2.** To obliterate. —**e•ras'a•ble** *adj.* —**e•ras'er** *n.* —**e•ra'sure** *n.*

er•bi•um (ûr'bē-əm) *n. Symbol* **Er** A soft, malleable silvery rare-earth element.

ere (âr) *prep.* Previous to : before. —*conj.* **1.** Before. **2.** Rather than.

e•rect (ĭ-rĕkt') *adj.* **1.** Directed upward : upright. **2.** *Physiol.* Stiff : rigid. —*v.* **1.** To construct : build. **2.** To raise upright <*erect* a tent pole> **3.** To set up : establish. —**e•rect'ly** *adv.* —**e•rect'ness** *n.* —**e•rec'tor** *n.*

e•rec•tile (ĭ-rĕk'təl, -tīl') *adj.* Of, relating to, or being vascular tissue capable of filling with blood and becoming rigid. —**e•rec•til'i•ty** (-tĭl'ĭ-tē) *n.*

e•rec•tion (ĭ-rĕk'shən) *n.* **1.** The act of erecting : construction. **2.** The state of erectile tissue when filled with blood.

ere•long (âr-lông', -lŏng') *adv.* Before long.

er•e•mite (ĕr'ə-mīt') *n.* A hermit.

erg (ûrg) *n.* A unit of energy or work.

er•go (ûr'gō, âr'-) *conj. & adv.* Therefore : consequently.

er•go•nom•ics (ûr'gə-nŏm'ĭks) *n. (sing. in number).* The applied science of equipment design intended to reduce operator fatigue and discomfort. —**er'go•nom'ic, er'go•no•met'ric** *adj.*

er•gos•ter•ol (ûr-gŏs'tə-sôl', -rōl') *n.* A steroid alcohol synthesized by yeast from sugars and converted under ultraviolet radiation to vitamin D.

er•got (ûr'gət, -gŏt') *n.* **1. a.** A disease of rye and other cereal plants. **b.** Any of various fungi of the genus *Claviceps* that cause this disease. **2.** A drug or medicine made from dried ergot fungi.

er•mine (ûr'mĭn) *n.* **1.** A weasel, *Mustela erminea,* with brownish fur that becomes white in its winter phase. **2.** The white fur of the ermine.

e•rode (ĭ-rōd') *v.* **e•rod•ed, e•rod•ing. 1.** To wear away or become worn away by or as if by rubbing or abrading <a river *eroding* its banks> **2.** To eat away : corrode.

e•rog•e•nous (ĭ-rŏj'ə-nəs) *adj.* Responsive to sexual stimulation.

e•ro•sion (ĭ-rō'zhən) *n.* The process of eroding or state of being eroded. —**e•ro'sion•al** *adj.*

e•ro•sive (ĭ-rō'sĭv) *adj.* Tending to cause erosion. —**e•ro'sive•ness** *n.*

e•rot•ic (ĭ-rŏt'ĭk) *adj.* Of or promoting sexual desire : amatory. —**e•rot'i•cal•ly** *adv.* —**e•rot'i•cism** *n.*

e•rot•i•ca (ĭ-rŏt'ĭ-kə) *pl.n. (sing. or pl. in number).* Literature or art with an erotic quality or theme.

err (ûr, ĕr) *v.* **1.** To make a mistake. **2.** To sin.

er•rand (ĕr'ənd) *n.* A short trip undertaken to perform a specified task, usu. for another.

er•rant (ĕr'ənt) *adj.* **1.** Traveling about, esp. in search of adventure. **2.** Straying from the proper or customary. **3.** Moving aimlessly. —**er'rant** *n.* —**er'rant•ry** *n.*

er•rat•ic (ĭ-răt'ĭk) *adj.* **1.** Lacking a fixed course : wandering. **2.** Irregular : inconsistent. **3.** Eccentric. —**er•rat'i•cal•ly** *adv.*

er•ra•tum (ĭ-rä'təm, ĭ-rā'-) *n., pl.* **-ta** (-tə). An error in printing or writing.

er•ro•ne•ous (ĭ-rō'nē-əs) *adj.* Containing an error : mistaken. —**er•ro'ne•ous•ly** *adv.* —**er•ro'ne•ous•ness** *n.*

er•ror (ĕr'ər) *n.* **1.** Something that unintentionally deviates from what is correct or true : mistake. **2.** The state of being mistaken or wrong. **3.** *Baseball.* A misplay in fielding or throwing.

er•satz (ĕr'zäts', ĕr-zäts') *adj.* Being a usu. inferior substitute : artificial.

erst (ûrst) *adv. Archaic.* Formerly.

erst•while (ûrst'hwīl', -wīl') *adj.* Former. —**erst'while'** *adv.*

e•ruct (ĭ-rŭkt') *v.* To belch. —**e•ruc'ta'tion** *n.*

er•u•dite (ĕr'yə-dīt', ĕr'ə-) *adj.* Deeply learned : scholarly.

er•u•di•tion (ĕr'yə-dĭsh'ən, ĕr'ə-) *n.* Deep learning : scholarship.

e•rupt (ĭ-rŭpt') *v.* **1.** To emerge or force out violently from limits : explode <Lava *erupted* from the volcano.> **2.** To become suddenly and violently active. **3.** To break out in a skin rash. —**e•rup'tion** *n.* —**e•rup'tive** *adj.*

–ery *suff.* **1.** A place for <bak*ery*> **2.** A collection <fin*ery*> **3.** A condition <slav*ery*> **4.** Act : practice <brib*ery*> **5.** Characteristics or qualities of <snobb*ery*>

er•y•sip•e•las (ĕr'ĭ-sĭp'ə-ləs, îr'-) *n.* An acute, inflammatory skin disease caused by a streptococcus.

e•ryth•ro•cyte (ĭ-rĭth'rə-sīt') *n.* One of the disk-shaped blood cells that contains hemoglobin and is responsible for the red color of blood.

e•ryth•ro•my•cin (ĭ-rĭth'rə-mī'sĭn) *n.* An antibiotic obtained from a strain of fungus and effective against many bacteria.

Es *symbol for* EINSTEINIUM.

–es[1] *suff. var. of* –s[1].

—es[2] *suff. var. of* –s[2].

es•ca•late (ĕs′kə-lāt′) *v.* **-lat•ed, -lat•ing.** To enlarge, increase, or intensify <*escalate* a conflict> **—es′ca•la′tion** *n.*

es•ca•la•tor (ĕs′kə-lā′tər) *n.* A moving stairway consisting of steps attached to an endless belt.

es•cal•lop (ĭ-skŏl′əp, ĭ-skăl′-) *n. & v. var. of* SCALLOP.

es•ca•pade (ĕs′kə-pād′) *n.* A playful or reckless adventure.

es•cape (ĭ-skāp′) *v.* **-caped, -cap•ing. 1.** To break free (from). **2.** To avoid capture or harm. **3.** To succeed in avoiding <*escape* punishment> **4.** To elude the memory of. **5.** To issue involuntarily (from) **:** leak out. *—n.* **1.** An act, instance, or means of escaping. **2.** Leakage. **3.** Temporary freedom from unpleasant realities **:** diversion. **—es•cap′ee′** *n.* **—es•cap′er** *n.*

es•cape•ment (ĭ-skāp′mənt) *n.* **1.** A mechanism used esp. in timepieces to control the wheel movement and provide energy impulses to a pendulum or balance. **2.** A mechanism, as in a typewriter, that controls the lateral movement of the carriage. **3.** An escape or means of escape.

escapement
A. escape wheel spindle, B. escape wheel, C. lever

escape velocity *n.* The minimum velocity that a body, as a rocket, must attain to overcome the gravitational attraction of another body, as the earth.

escape wheel *n.* The rotating notched wheel in an escapement.

es•cap•ism (ĭ-skā′pĭz′əm) *n.* The avoidance of unpleasant realities in fantasy or entertainment. **—es•cap′ist** *n. & adj.*

es•ca•role (ĕs′kə-rōl′) *n.* Endive.

es•carp•ment (ĭ-skärp′mənt) *n.* **1.** A steep slope or long cliff formed by erosion or faulting. **2.** A steep slope in front of a fortification.

—escence *suff.* The process of giving off light in a specified way <fluor*escence*>

—escent *suff.* **1.** Giving off light in a specified way <phosphor*escent*> **2.** Beginning to be **:** becoming <sen*escent*>

es•chew (ĕs-cho͞o′) *v.* To avoid <*eschew* evil> **—es•chew′al** *n.*

es•cort (ĕs′kôrt′) *n.* **1.** One or more persons or vehicles accompanying another to guide, protect, or pay honor. **2.** A man who accompanies a woman. *—v.* (ĭ-skôrt′). To go with as an escort.

es•cri•toire (ĕs′krĭ-twär′) *n.* A writing desk.

es•crow (ĕs′krō′, ĭ-skrō′) *n.* Money or property put into the custody of a 3rd party until specified conditions are met.

es•cu•do (ĭ-sko͞o′dō) *n., pl.* **-dos.** —See table at CURRENCY.

es•cutch•eon (ĭ-skŭch′ən) *n.* **1.** A shield with an emblem bearing a coat of arms. **2.** A protective plate, as for a keyhole.

—ese *suff.* **1.** Of, characteristic of, or originating in a specified place <Vietnam*ese*> **2.** Native or inhabitant of <Taiwan*ese*> **3.** Language or style of <Chin*ese*> <journal*ese*>

Es•ki•mo (ĕs′kə-mō′) *n., pl.* **-mo** *or* **-mos.** A member of a people native to Arctic North America, Greenland, and NE Siberia. **—Es′ki•mo′** *adj.*

Eskimo dog *n.* A large dog orig. bred in Greenland and Labrador with a thick coat and bushy tail.

e•soph•a•gus (ĭ-sŏf′ə-gəs) *n., pl.* **-gi** (-jī′). A muscular, membranous tube for the passage of food from the pharynx to the stomach. **—e•soph′a•ge′al** (ĭ-sŏf′ə-jē′əl) *adj.*

es•o•ter•ic (ĕs′ə-tĕr′ĭk) *adj.* **1.** Meant for or understood only by a particular and often small group <*esoteric* poetry> **2.** Private **:** confidential. **—es′o•ter′i•cal•ly** *adv.*

ESP (ē′ĕs-pē′) *n.* Extrasensory perception.

es•pa•drille (ĕs′pə-drĭl′) *n.* A shoe with a canvas upper and a flexible sole.

es•pal•ier (ĭ-spăl′yər, -yā′) *n.* A tree or shrub trained to grow in a flat plane against a surface. **—es•pal′ier** *v.*

es•pe•cial (ĭ-spĕsh′əl) *adj.* Being above or apart from others **:** exceptional. **—es•pe′cial•ly** *adv.*

Es•pe•ran•to (ĕs′pə-rän′tō, -răn′-) *n.* An artificial language with a vocabulary based on words that are the same in many European languages.

es•pi•o•nage (ĕs′pē-ə-näzh′, -nĭj) *n.* The act or practice of spying to obtain secret intelligence.

es•pla•nade (ĕs′plə-näd′, -nād′) *n.* A flat, open area, esp. along a shoreline.

es•pou•sal (ĭ-spou′zəl) *n.* **1.** The act of supporting <his *espousal* of the immigrants′ cause> **2.** A wedding.

es•pouse (ĭ-spouz′) *v.* **-poused, -pous•ing. 1.** To marry. **2.** To give support to.

es•pres•so (ĕ-sprĕs′ō) *n., pl.* **-sos.** Strong coffee made by forcing steam through darkly roasted, powdered coffee beans.

es•prit (ĕ-sprē′) *n.* **1.** Mental liveliness **:** wit. **2.** Spirit.

es•prit de corps (ĕ-sprē′ də kôr′) *n.* A spirit of enthusiasm and devotion to a common cause among a group.

es•py (ĭ-spī′) *v.* **-pied, -py•ing.** To catch a view of **:** glimpse.

—esque *suff.* Resembling <Lincoln*esque*>

es•quire (ĕs′kwīr′, ĭ-skwīr′) *n.* **1.** A candidate for knighthood who served as the attendant of a knight. **2.** A member of the English gentry ranking below a knight. **3. Esquire.** —Used as a title of courtesy usu. after the full name of a person, esp. an attorney <John Doe, *Esq.*>

—ess *suff.* Female <lion*ess*>

es•say (ĕ-sā′, ĕs′ā′) *v.* To make an attempt at : try. —*n.* **1.** An attempt : endeavor. **2.** (ĕs′ā′). A short literary composition expressing the author's viewpoint on a subject. **—es•say′er** *n.* **—es′say′ist** *n.*

es•sence (ĕs′əns) *n.* **1.** The properties of a thing that make it what it is : fundamental nature. **2.** The most important element. **3.** A concentrate of a substance. **4.** A perfume. ★ ***syns:*** BEING, ESSENTIALITY, NATURE, PITH, QUINTESSENCE, TEXTURE

es•sen•tial (ĭ-sĕn′shəl) *adj.* **1.** Of, containing, or being an essence. **2.** Indispensable : necessary. **—es•sen′tial** *n.* **—es•sen′ti•al′i•ty** (-shē-ăl′ĭ-tē), **es•sen′tial•ness** *n.* **—es•sen′tial•ly** *adv.*

—est¹ *suff.* —Used to form the superlative degree of adjectives and adverbs <old*est*> <quick*est*>

—est² *suff.* —Used to form the archaic 2nd person present sing. of verbs <know*est*>

es•tab•lish (ĭ-stăb′lĭsh) *v.* **1.** To set in a secure position. **2.** To found : create. **3.** To cause to be recognized or accepted <*establish* a reputation> **4.** To prove.

es•tab•lish•ment (ĭ-stăb′lĭsh-mənt) *n.* **1. a.** The act or process of establishing. **b.** The state of being established. **2.** A place of business or residence, including its staff and possessions. **3.** An organized group. **4.** A group of people who control a field of activity or rule a society or government.

es•tate (ĭ-stāt′) *n.* **1.** An extensive tract of land containing a large house. **2.** All of a person's possessions, esp. those left after death. **3.** A stage or condition of life <a pauper's *estate*>

es•teem (ĭ-stēm′) *v.* **1.** To regard with respect : prize. **2.** To regard as : consider. —*n.* High regard : respect.

es•ter (ĕs′tər) *n.* Any of a large group of organic compounds formed when an acid and an alcohol interact.

es•thete (ĕs′thēt′) *n. var. of* AESTHETE.

es•thet•ic (ĕs-thĕt′ĭk) *adj. var. of* AESTHETIC.

es•thet•ics (ĕs-thĕt′ĭks) *n. var. of* AESTHETICS.

es•ti•ma•ble (ĕs′tə-mə-bəl) *adj.* Deserving of esteem : admirable.

es•ti•mate (ĕs′tə-māt′) *v.* **-mat•ed, -mat•ing. 1.** To calculate the approx. amount or extent of. **2.** To evaluate. —*n.* (-mĭt). **1.** A rough or preliminary calculation, as of work to be done. **2.** An opinion : judgment.

es•trange (ĭ-strānj′) *v.* **-tranged, -trang•ing.** To make unfriendly, unsympathetic, or distant. ★ ***syns:*** ALIENATE, DISAFFECT **—es•trange′ment** *n.*

es•tro•gen (ĕs′trə-jən) *n.* Any of several steroid hormones that regulate female reproductive functions and secondary sex characteristics. **—es′tro•gen′ic** (-jĕn′ĭk) *adj.* **—es′tro•gen′i•cal•ly** *adv.*

es•trus (ĕs′trəs) *n.* The state of sexual excitement in most female mammals that immediately precedes ovulation : heat. **—es′trous** *adj.*

es•tu•ar•y (ĕs′cho͞o-ĕr′ē) *n., pl.* **-ies.** The wide lower course of a river into which the tides flow.

é•ta•gère *also* **e•ta•gere** (ā′tä-zhâr′) *n.* A piece of furniture with open shelves for ornaments : whatnot.

et cet•er•a *also* **et•cet•er•a** (ĕt sĕt′ər-ə, -sĕt′rə) And other things of the same kind : and so forth.

etch (ĕch) *v.* **1. a.** To cut into the surface of (e.g., glass) by the action of acid. **b.** To produce (e.g., a pattern) by etching. **2.** To impress deeply <words *etched* in my memory> **—etch′er** *n.*

etch•ing (ĕch′ĭng) *n.* **1.** The process or art of etching. **2. a.** A design etched on a plate. **3.** An impression made from such a plate.

e•ter•nal (ĭ-tûr′nəl) *adj.* **1.** Without beginning or end : everlasting. **2.** Meant to last indefinitely <an *eternal* flame> **3.** Seemingly endless or unvarying. **—e′ter•nal** *n.* **—e′ter•nal′i•ty** (ē′tər-năl′ĭ-tē), **e•ter′nal•ness** *n.* **—e•ter′nal•ly** *adv.*

e•ter•ni•ty (ĭ-tûr′nĭ-tē) *n., pl.* **-ties. 1.** All time without beginning or end. **2.** The quality of being eternal. **3.** Immortality. **4.** A seemingly endless time.

—eth¹ *suff.* —Used to form the archaic 3rd person present sing. of verbs <know*eth*>

—eth² *suff. var. of* -TH².

eth•ane (ĕth′ān′) *n.* A colorless, odorless gas that occurs as a constituent of natural gas and is used for fuel and refrigeration.

eth•a•nol (ĕth′ə-nôl′, -nōl′) *n.* Alcohol 1.

e•ther (ē′thər) *n.* **1.** A volatile, highly flammable liquid compound used as a solvent and an anesthetic. **2.** The heavens. **3.** A massless substance once thought to fill space.

e•the•re•al (ĭ-thîr′ē-əl) *adj.* **1.** Light and insubstantial. **2.** Highly refined : delicate. **3.** Heavenly. **—e•the′re•al•ly** *adv.* **—e•the′re•al•ness** *n.*

eth•ic (ĕth′ĭk) *n.* **1.** A principle of right or good conduct. **2.** A system of moral values. **3. ethics** *(sing. in number).* The branch of philosophy dealing with the rules of right conduct.

eth•i•cal (ĕth′ĭ-kəl) *adj.* **1.** Of or relating to ethics. **2.** Conforming to accepted principles of right and wrong, esp. those governing the conduct of a profession, as medicine. **—eth′i•cal•ly** *adv.*

eth•nic (ĕth′nĭk) *adj.* Of or relating to a racial, national, or cultural group. —*n. Informal.* A member of an ethnic group, esp. within a larger community. **—eth•nic′i•ty** (-nĭs′ĭ-tē) *n.*

eth•no•cen•trism (ĕth′nō-sĕn′trĭz′əm) *n.* Belief in the superiority of one's own ethnic group. **—eth'no·cen'tric** *adj.* **—eth'no·cen'tri·cal·ly** *adv.*

eth·nol·o·gy (ĕth-nŏl'ə-jē) *n.* The anthropological study of the origins and characteristics of racial and cultural groups. **—eth'no·log'ic** (-nə-lŏj'ĭk), **eth'no·log'i·cal** *adj.* **—eth·nol'o·gist** *n.*

e·thol·o·gy (ē-thŏl'ə-jē) *n.* **1.** The scientific study of animal behavior. **2.** The study of human ethos. **—e'tho·log'i·cal** (ē'thə-lŏj'ĭ-kəl, ĕth'ə-) *adj.* **—e·thol'o·gist** *n.*

e·thos (ē'thŏs') *n.* The character, system of values, and attitudes peculiar to a people or culture.

eth·yl (ĕth'əl) *n.* An organic radical occurring in ether and alcohol.

ethyl alcohol *n.* Alcohol 1.

eth·yl·ene (ĕth'ə-lēn') *n.* A colorless, flammable gas obtained from natural gas and petroleum and used as a fuel.

ethylene glycol *n.* A colorless syrupy alcohol used as an antifreeze.

e·ti·ol·o·gy (ē'tē-ŏl'ə-jē) *n.* **1.** The study of causes or origins. **2.** The cause, esp. of a disease. **—e'ti·o·log'ic** (-ə-lŏj'ĭk), **e'ti·o·log'i·cal** *adj.* **—e'ti·o·log'i·cal·ly** *adv.* **—e'ti·ol'o·gist** *n.*

et·i·quette (ĕt'ĭ-kĕt', -kĭt) *n.* The prescribed forms and practices of correct behavior.

E·trus·can (ĭ-trŭs'kən) *n.* **1.** An inhabitant of Etruria, an ancient country in WC Italy. **2.** The language of the Etruscans. **—E·trus'can** *adj.*

—ette *suff.* **1.** Small <din*ette*> **2.** Female <usher*ette*>

é·tude *also* **e·tude** (ā'to͞od', ā'-tyo͞od') *n.* A musical piece for the development of a player's technique.

et·y·mol·o·gy (ĕt'ə-mŏl'ə-jē) *n., pl.* **-gies. 1.** The history of a word as shown by determining its earliest use and recording its changes in form and meaning. **2.** The branch of linguistics that deals with etymologies. **—et'y·mo·log'i·cal** (-mə-lŏj'ĭ-kəl) *adj.* **—et'y·mol'o·gist** *n.*

et·y·mon (ĕt'ə-mŏn') *n., pl.* **-mons** *or* **-ma** (-mə) **1.** An earlier form of a word in the same language or in an ancestor language. **2.** A foreign word from which a particular loan-word is derived.

Eu *symbol for* EUROPIUM.

eu·ca·lyp·tus (yo͞o'kə-lĭp'təs) *n., pl.* **-tus·es** *or* **-ti** (-tī') A tall native Australian tree of the genus *Eucalyptus,* with aromatic leaves that yield an oil used medicinally.

Eu·cha·rist (yo͞o'kər-ĭst) *n.* **1.** The Christian sacrament of Communion. **2.** The consecrated bread and wine of the Eucharist. **—Eu'cha·ris'tic** *adj.*

eu·chre (yo͞o'kər) *n.* A card game in which the winning side must take 3 of 5 tricks. *—v.* **-chred, -chring.** *Informal.* To cheat : trick.

eu·gen·ics (yo͞o-jĕn'ĭks) *n.* *(sing. in number).* The study of and methods for improving a species genetically. **—eu·gen'ic** *adj.* **—eu·gen'i·cist** (-ĭ-sĭst) *n.*

eu·lo·gize (yo͞o'lə-jīz') *v.* **-gized, -giz·ing.** To write or deliver a eulogy for. **—eu'lo·gist, eu'lo·giz'er** *n.*

eu·lo·gy (yo͞o'lə-jē) *n., pl.* **-gies. 1.** A speech honoring a person or thing. **2.** High praise. **—eu'lo·gis'tic** *adj.*

eu·nuch (yo͞o'nək) *n.* A castrated man.

eu·phe·mism (yo͞o'fə-mĭz'əm) *n.* A less direct term used in place of one considered offensive. **—eu'phe·mis'tic** *adj.* **—eu'phe·mis'ti·cal·ly** *adv.*

eu·pho·ny (yo͞o'fə-nē) *n., pl.* **-nies.** Agreeable sound, esp. of spoken words. **—eu·pho'ni·ous** (-fō'nē-əs) *adj.* **—eu·pho'ni·ous·ly** *adv.*

eu·pho·ri·a (yo͞o-fôr'ē-ə, -fōr'-) *n.* A strong feeling of elation or well-being. **—eu·phor'ic** (-fôr'ĭk, -fōr'-) *adj.*

eu·phor·i·ant (yo͞o-fôr'ē-ənt, -fōr'-) *n.* A drug that induces euphoria. **—eu·phor'i·ant** *adj.*

eu·re·ka (yo͞o-rē'kə) *interj.* —Used to express triumph upon a discovery.

Eu·ro·cen·tric (yo͝or'ō-sĕn'trĭk) *adj.* Centered or focused on Europe and Europeans. **—Eu'ro·cen'trism** *n.*

Eu·ro·dol·lar (yo͝or'ō-dŏl'ər) *n.* A U.S. dollar deposited in a foreign bank, esp. in Europe.

European plan *n.* A hotel plan in which rates cover only the cost of the room.

eu·ro·pi·um (yo͞o-rō'pē-əm) *n.* *Symbol* **Eu** A soft, silvery-white rare-earth element used in nuclear research.

Eu·sta·chian tube (yo͞o-stā'shən, -shē-ən, -stā'kē-ən) *n.* A narrow tube between the middle ear and the pharynx that equalizes air pressure on both sides of the eardrum.

eu·tha·na·sia (yo͞o'thə-nā'zhə, -shə) *n.* The act or practice of killing a suffering individual, esp. painlessly, for reasons considered merciful.

eu·then·ics (yo͞o-thĕn'ĭks) *n.* *(sing. in number).* The study of the improvement of human functioning and well-being by improvement of living conditions. **—eu·then'ist** *n.*

e·vac·u·ate (ĭ-văk'yo͞o-āt') *v.* **-at·ed, -at·ing. 1. a.** To remove the contents of. **b.** To create a vacuum in (a container). **2.** To expel waste matter from (the bowels). **3.** To depart from (e.g., a threatened place) : vacate. **—e·vac'u·a'tion** *n.* **—e·vac'u·a'tor** *n.*

e·vac·u·ee (ĭ-văk'yo͞o-ē') *n.* One evacuated from a hazardous place.

e·vade (ĭ-vād') *v.* **e·vad·ed, e·vad·ing.** To elude or avoid by cunning. **—e·vad'er** *n.*

e·val·u·ate (ĭ-văl'yo͞o-āt') *v.* **-at·ed, -at·ing. 1.** To determine the value of. **2.** To examine carefully : appraise. **—e·val'u·a'tion** *n.* **—e·val'u·a'tor** *n.*

ev·a·nesce (ĕv'ə-nĕs') *v.* **-nesced, -nesc·ing.** To disappear like vapor : fade away.

ev·a·nes·cent (ĕv'ə-nĕs'ənt) *adj.* Vanishing or passing quickly : fleeting. **—ev'a·nes'cence** *n.* **—ev'a·nes'cent·ly** *adv.*

e·van·gel·i·cal (ē'văn-jĕl'ĭ-kəl) *also* **e·van·gel·ic** (-jĕl'ĭk) *adj.* **1.** Of, relating to, or according to the Christian gospel, esp. the 4 Gospels of the New Testament. **2.** Of or being a Protestant group that stresses the authority of the gospel and salvation by faith in Christ. **3.** Zealous in preaching or proselytizing. —**e'van·gel'i·cal·ism** *n.* —**e'van·gel'i·cal·ly** *adv.*

e·van·gel·ism (ĭ-văn'jə-lĭz'əm) *n.* **1.** Zealous preaching and spreading of the gospel. **2.** Zeal for a cause.

e·van·gel·ist (ĭ-văn'jə-lĭst) *n.* **1.** *often* **Evangelist.** An author of one of the four New Testament Gospels. **2.** A zealous Protestant preacher or missionary. —**e·van'gel·is'tic** *adj.* —**e·van'gel·is'ti·cal·ly** *adv.*

e·van·gel·ize (ĭ-văn'jə-līz') *v.* **-ized, -iz·ing. 1.** To preach the gospel (to). **2.** To convert to Christianity.

e·vap·o·rate (ĭ-văp'ə-rāt') *v.* **-rat·ed, -rat·ing. 1.** To change into vapor. **2.** To concentrate (e.g., milk) by removing moisture. **3.** To disappear : vanish. —**e·vap'o·ra'tion** *n.* —**e·vap'o·ra'tive** *adj.* —**e·vap'o·ra'tor** *n.*

e·va·sion (ĭ-vā'zhən) *n.* An act or means of evading.

e·va·sive (ĭ-vā'sĭv) *adj.* **1.** Marked by evasion <*evasive* action> **2.** Intentionally vague : equivocal. —**e·va'sive·ly** *adv.* —**e·va'sive·ness** *n.*

eve (ēv) *n.* **1.** The evening or day preceding a special day. **2.** The period just before a certain event. **3.** Evening.

Eve (ēv). In the Bible, the first woman and the wife of Adam.

e·ven (ē'vən) *adj.* **1.** Having a horizontal surface : flat <an *even* road> **2.** Having no irregularities : smooth. **3.** On the same plane or line : level. **4.** Equally matched : balanced <an *even* contest> **5.** Equal in amount or extent. **6.** Neither owing nor being owed. **7.** Fully revenged <getting *even*> **8.** Exactly divisible by 2. **9.** Exact <an *even* dozen> —*adv.* **1.** To a higher extent or degree. —Used as an intensive <an *even* worse insult> **2.** At that time : just. **3.** Notwithstanding <*Even* with his bad knee, he walks quickly.> **4.** Indeed. —Used as an intensive <looked sad, *even* depressed> —*v.* To make or become even. —**e'ven·ly** *adv.* —**e'ven·ness** *n.*

e·ven·hand·ed (ē'vən-hăn'dĭd) *adj.* Fair : impartial. —**e'ven·hand'ed·ly** *adv.* —**e'ven·hand'ed·ness** *n.*

eve·ning (ēv'nĭng) *n.* Late afternoon and early night.

evening star *n.* A bright planet, esp. Venus, seen in the W shortly after sunset.

e·ven·song (ē'vən-sông', -sŏng') *n.* **1.** A vesper service. **2.** Evening prayer.

e·vent (ĭ-vĕnt') *n.* **1.** An occurrence, esp. a significant one <a literary *event*> **2.** An item in a sports program. **3.** A final result : outcome. —**e·vent'ful** *adj.* —**e·vent'ful·ly** *adv.* —**e·vent'ful·ness** *n.*

e·ven·tide (ē'vən-tīd') *n.* Evening.

e·ven·tu·al (ĭ-vĕn'cho͞o-əl) *adj.* Happening or expected to happen at an unspecified future time : ultimate <his *eventual* return> —**e·ven'tu·al·ly** *adv.*

e·ven·tu·al·i·ty (ĭ-vĕn'cho͞o-ăl'ĭ-tē) *n., pl.* **-ties.** Something that may take place : possibility.

e·ven·tu·ate (ĭ-vĕn'cho͞o-āt') *v.* **-at·ed, -at·ing.** To result eventually.

ev·er (ĕv'ər) *adv.* **1.** At all times : always <*ever* attentive> **2.** At any time <Have you *ever* traveled abroad?> **3.** In any possible way or case.

ev·er·glade (ĕv'ər-glād') *n.* A tract of low, swampy land.

ev·er·green (ĕv'ər-grēn') *adj.* Having green foliage throughout the year. —*n.* An evergreen tree or plant.

ev·er·last·ing (ĕv'ər-lăs'tĭng) *adj.* Lasting forever or for a long time : eternal. —*n.* **1.** Eternity. **2.** A plant, esp. a strawflower, that keeps its form and color long after it is dry. —**ev'er·last'ing·ly** *adv.*

ev·er·more (ĕv'ər-môr', -mōr') *adv. Archaic.* Forever.

eve·ry (ĕv'rē) *adj.* **1.** Each with no exception <*every* day of the week> **2.** Each of a particular succession of objects or intervals <*every* 3 hours> **3.** All possible : utmost <given *every* opportunity>

eve·ry·bod·y (ĕv'rē-bŏd'ē) *pron.* Every person : everyone.

eve·ry·day (ĕv'rē-dā') *adj.* **1.** Suitable for routine occasions. **2.** Common : ordinary.

eve·ry·one (ĕv'rē-wŭn') *pron.* Every person : everybody.

eve·ry·place (ĕv'rē-plās') *adv.* Everywhere.

eve·ry·thing (ĕv'rē-thĭng') *pron.* All factors or things that exist or are pertinent.

eve·ry·where (ĕv'rē-hwâr', -wâr') *adv.* In all places.

e·vict (ĭ-vĭkt') *v.* To put (e.g., a tenant) out by legal process. —**e·vic'tion** *n.* —**e·vic'tor** *n.*

ev·i·dence (ĕv'ĭ-dəns) *n.* **1.** Facts or signs on which a conclusion can be based <fossil *evidence* of climatic change> **2.** An indication. —*v.* **-denced, -denc·ing.** To indicate clearly. —**in evidence.** Clearly present : evident.

ev·i·dent (ĕv'ĭ-dənt) *adj.* Easily seen or understood : obvious. —**ev'i·dent·ly** *adv.*

e·vil (ē'vəl) *adj.* **1.** Morally wrong or bad : wicked. **2.** Causing harm : injurious. —*n.* **1.** Something morally bad : wickedness. **2.** A cause of suffering or injury <social *evils*> —**e'vil·ly** *adv.* —**e'vil·ness** *n.*

▲ ***word history:*** The word *evil* is ult. related to the words *up* and *over* and to the prefix *hypo–*, "under, beneath." The basic sense of *evil,* which is now lost, was therefore probably "exceeding proper bounds" or "overreaching," and the word did not signify merely the absence of good.

e·vil·do·er (ē'vəl-do͞o'ər) *n.* A perpetrator of evil. —**e'vil·do'ing** *n.*

e·vil·mind·ed (ē'vəl-mīn'dĭd) *adj.* Having evil thoughts or intentions. —**e'vil·mind'ed·ly** *adv.* —**e'vil·mind'ed·ness** *n.*

e·vince (ĭ-vĭns') *v.* **e·vinced, e·vinc·ing.** To demonstrate : manifest.

e·vis·cer·ate (ĭ-vĭs'ə-rāt') *v.* **-at·ed, -at·ing. 1.** To remove the entrails of. **2.** To remove a critical or vital part of. —**e·vis'cer·a'tion** *n.*

e•voke (ĭ-vōk′) *v.* **e•voked, e•vok•ing. 1.** To call forth : summon <*evoked* dark spirits> **2.** To call to mind <*evoke* childhood memories> **—ev′o•ca′tion** (ĕv′ə-kā′shən) *n.* **—e•voc′a•tive** (ĭ-vŏk′ə-tĭv) *adj.* **—e•voc′a•tive•ly** *adv.*

ev•o•lu•tion (ĕv′ə-lōō′shən) *n.* **1.** A gradual process of change or development. **2.** *Biol.* The theory that existing species of plants and animals have developed from previously existing species through a process of gradual change. **—ev′o•lu′tion•ar′y** (-shə-nĕr′ē) *adj.* **—ev′o•lu′tion•ism** *n.* **—ev′o•lu′tion•ist** *n.*

e•volve (ĭ-vŏlv′) *v.* **e•volved, e•volv•ing. 1.** To change or develop gradually. **2.** *Biol.* To develop by evolutionary processes. **3.** To work out : develop <*evolve* a system> **—e•volve′ment** *n.*

ewe (yōō) *n.* A female sheep.

ew•er (yōō′ər) *n.* A wide-mouthed jug or pitcher.

ex[1] (ĕks) *n.* The letter x.

ex[2] (ĕks) *n.* *Slang.* A former spouse.

ex– *pref.* Former <*ex*-governor>

ex•ac•er•bate (ĭg-zăs′ər-bāt′, ĭk-săs′-) *v.* **-bat•ed, -bat•ing.** To make worse or more severe : aggravate <*exacerbate* tensions> **—ex•ac′er•bat′ing•ly** *adv.* **—ex•ac′er•ba′tion** *n.*

ex•act (ĭg-zăkt′) *adj.* Strictly accurate : precise. —*v.* **1.** To demand and obtain by or as if by force : extort. **2.** To call for or require <*exact* a great effort> **—ex•ac′tion** *n.* **—ex•act′ly** *adv.* **—ex•act′ness** *n.*

ex•act•ing (ĭg-zăk′tĭng) *adj.* **1.** Making severe demands. **2.** Requiring much care and accuracy. **—ex•act′ing•ly** *adv.*

ex•act•i•tude (ĭg-zăk′tĭ-tōōd′, -tyōōd′) *n.* The quality of being exact.

ex•ag•ger•ate (ĭg-zăj′ə-rāt′) *v.* **-at•ed, -at•ing.** To represent as greater than is actually the case : overstate. **—ex•ag′ger•a′tion** *n.* **—ex•ag′ger•a′tive, ex•ag′ger•a•to′ry** (-ər-ə-tôr′ē, -tōr′ē) *adj.* **—ex•ag′ger•a′tor** *n.*

ex•alt (ĭg-zôlt′) *v.* **1.** To raise to a high rank or position : elevate. **2.** To praise highly : glorify. **3.** To fill with pride or joy : elate. **—ex′al•ta′tion** *n.*

ex•am (ĭg-zăm′) *n.* An examination.

ex•am•i•na•tion (ĭg-zăm′ə-nā′shən) *n.* **1.** The act of examining or state of being examined. **2.** A test of knowledge or skill.

ex•am•ine (ĭg-zăm′ĭn) *v.* **-ined, -in•ing. 1.** To inspect closely : observe carefully. **2.** To determine the knowledge or skills of by questioning. **3.** To question formally. **—ex•am′in•ee′** *n.* **—ex•am′in•er** *n.*

ex•am•ple (ĭg-zăm′pəl) *n.* **1.** One that is representative of a group : sample. **2.** One worthy of imitation : model. **3.** A case or punishment serving as a precedent or warning. **4.** An illustrative problem or exercise.

ex•as•per•ate (ĭg-zăs′pə-rāt′) *v.* **-at•ed, -at•ing.** To make angry or frustrated : irritate. **—ex•as′per•at′ing•ly** *adv.* **—ex•as′per•a′tion** *n.*

ex•ca•vate (ĕk′skə-vāt′) *v.* **-vat•ed, -vat•ing. 1.** To hollow or dig out. **2.** To remove (e.g., soil) by digging. **3.** To expose by digging. **—ex′ca•va′tion** *n.* **—ex′ca•va′tor** *n.*

ex•ceed (ĭk-sēd′) *v.* **1.** To surpass. **2.** To go beyond the limits of.

ex•ceed•ing•ly (ĭk-sē′dĭng-lē) *adv.* To an extraordinary degree : extremely <*exceedingly* careful>

ex•cel (ĭk-sĕl′) *v.* **-celled, -cel•ling.** To be greater or do better than (others) : surpass.

ex•cel•lence (ĕk′sə-ləns) *n.* **1.** The quality of being excellent : superiority. **2.** An excellent quality or capacity. **3. Excellence.** Excellency.

Ex•cel•len•cy (ĕk′sə-lən-sē) *n., pl.* **-cies.** —Used as a form of address or title for high officials, as ambassadors or bishops.

ex•cel•lent (ĕk′sə-lənt) *adj.* Exceptionally good : fine. ★ ***syns:*** CAPITAL, DANDY, FINE, FIRST-CLASS, FIRST-RATE, GREAT, SPLENDID, SUPER, SUPERB, SUPERIOR, TERRIFIC **—ex′cel•lent•ly** *adv.*

ex•cel•si•or (ĭk-sĕl′sē-ər) *n.* Fine curved wood shavings used esp. for packing.

ex•cept (ĭk-sĕpt′) *prep.* Not including : but. —*conj.* **1.** Were it not that : only. **2.** Otherwise than. **3.** *Archaic.* Unless. —*v.* **1.** To leave out : exclude. **2.** To object.

ex•cept•ing (ĭk-sĕp′tĭng) *prep.* Except.

ex•cep•tion (ĭk-sĕp′shən) *n.* **1.** The act of excepting. **2.** One that is excepted, esp. a case not conforming to a rule. **3.** A criticism or objection.

ex•cep•tion•a•ble (ĭk-sĕp′shə-nə-bəl) *adj.* Open to objection. **—ex•cep′tion•a•bil′i•ty** *n.* **—ex•cep′tion•a•bly** *adv.*

ex•cep•tion•al (ĭk-sĕp′shə-nəl) *adj.* **1.** Being an exception : unusual. **2.** Well above average. **—ex•cep′tion•al•ly** *adv.*

ex•cerpt (ĕk′sûrpt′) *n.* A passage, as from a book : extract. —*v.* (ĭk-sûrpt′, ĭg-zûrpt′) To select and take out an excerpt from.

ex•cess (ĭk-sĕs′, ĕk′sĕs′) *n.* **1.** An amount beyond what is required or appropriate. **2.** The state of exceeding what is required or appropriate <talking to *excess*> **3.** Overindulgence : intemperance. ★ ***syns:*** GLUT, OVERAGE, OVERSTOCK, OVERSUPPLY, SUPERFLUITY, SURPLUS —*adj.* Exceeding what is required or appropriate.

ex•ces•sive (ĭk-sĕs′ĭv) *adj.* Exceding what is necessary, usual, or proper. **—ex•ces′sive•ly** *adv.* **—ex•cess′ive•ness** *n.*

ex•change (ĭks-chānj′) *v.* **-changed, -chang•ing. 1.** To give in return for something else : trade <*exchange* recipes> **2.** To turn in (merchandise) for a replacement. —*n.* **1.** An act of exchanging. **2.** A place where things are exchanged, esp. a marketplace for securities or commodities. **3.** A central office that makes connections between individual telephones. **—ex•change′a•ble** *adj.*

ex•cheq•uer (ĭks-chĕk′ər, ĕks′chĕk′ər) *n.* **1. Exchequer.** The British governmental department charged with the collection and care of the national revenue. **2.** A treasury, esp. of a nation or organization. **3.** Financial resources : funds.

▲ ***word history:*** The Exchequer got its name from the checkered cloth, resembling a chessboard, that covered the counting tables of the Norman and Angevin kings of England. The word *exchequer* is derived from the Old French word *eschequier,* "chessboard." The *x* in *exchequer* is an etymological phantom. Many Old French words beginning with *es–* come from Latin words beginning with *ex–,* but *eschequier* is derived from Latin *scaccus,* "check in chess," which is ult. from Persian *shāh,* "king," the king being the most important piece in chess. When other English words like *exchange* (from Old French *eschangier* and Vulgar Latin *excambiare*) were respelled to reflect their Latin origins, *exchequer* was erroneously altered in the same manner.

ex•cise¹ (ĕk′sīz′) *n.* An internal tax on the production, sale, or consumption of a commodity, as tobacco, within a country.

ex•cise² (ĭk-sīz′) *v.* **-cised, -cis•ing.** To remove by or as if by cutting, esp. surgically. **—ex•ci′sion** (-sĭzh′ən) *n.*

ex•cit•a•ble (ĭk-sī′tə-bəl) *adj.* Easily excited. **—ex•cit′a•bil′i•ty, ex•cit′a•ble•ness** *n.* **—ex•cit′a•bly** *adv.*

ex•cite (ĭk-sīt′) *v.* **-cit•ed, -cit•ing. 1.** To rouse to action or motion **:** stimulate. **2.** To stir up strong feeling in **:** provoke. **3.** To elicit **:** induce <*excited* their interest> **—ex′ci•ta′tion** (ĕk′sĭ-tā′shən) *n.* **—ex•cit′ed•ly** *adv.* **—ex•cite′ment** *n.* **—ex•cit′ing•ly** *adv.*

ex•claim (ĭk-sklām′) *v.* To cry out or utter suddenly, as from emotion.

ex•cla•ma•tion (ĕks′klə-mā′shən) *n.* A sudden, forceful utterance. **—ex•clam′a•to′ry** (ĭk-sklăm′ə-tôr′ē, -tōr′ē) *adj.*

exclamation point *n.* A punctuation mark (!) used after an exclamation or interjection.

ex•clude (ĭk-sklōōd′) *v.* **-clud•ed, -clud•ing. 1.** To keep out **:** bar. **2.** To omit from consideration **:** disregard. **3.** To put out **:** expel. **—ex•clu′sion** *n.*

ex•clu•sive (ĭk-sklōō′sĭv) *adj.* **1.** Not shared with others <*exclusive* control> **2.** Excluding certain or most people, as from membership. **3.** For the wealthy **:** expensive <*exclusive* shops> **4.** Complete **:** undivided. **—ex•clu′sive•ly** *adv.* **—ex•clu′sive•ness, ex′clu•siv′i•ty** *n.*

exclusive of *prep.* Not including **:** besides.

ex•com•mu•ni•cate (ĕks′kə-myōō′nĭ-kāt′) *v.* To deprive of the right of church membership by ecclesiastical authority. **—ex′com•mu′ni•ca′tion** *n.*

ex•co•ri•ate (ĭk-skôr′ē-āt′, -skōr′-) *v.* **-at•ed, -at•ing. 1.** To wear off or tear the skin of **:** abrade. **2.** To censure harshly **:** upbraid. **—ex•co′ri•a′tion** *n.*

ex•cre•ment (ĕk′skrə-mənt) *n.* Bodily waste, esp. feces. **—ex′cre•men′tal** *adj.*

ex•cres•cence (ĭk-skrĕs′əns) *n.* An abnormal outgrowth, esp. on the body. **—ex•cres′cent** *adj.*

ex•cre•ta (ĭk-skrē′tə) *pl.n.* Expelled waste matter, as sweat, urine, or feces.

ex•crete (ĭk-skrēt′) *v.* **-cret•ed, -cret•ing.** To eliminate (waste matter) from the body. **—ex•cre′tion** *n.* **—ex′cre•to′ry** (ĕk′skrĭ-tôr′ē, -tōr′ē) *adj.*

ex•cru•ci•at•ing (ĭk-skrōō′shē-ā′tĭng) *adj.* Intensely painful **:** agonizing. **—ex•cru′ci•at′ing•ly** *adv.*

ex•cul•pate (ĕk′skəl-pāt′, ĭk-skŭl′-) *v.* **-pat•ed, -pat•ing.** To clear of wrongdoing. **—ex′cul•pa′tion** *n.* **—ex•cul′pa•to′ry** (ĭk-skŭl′pə-tôr′ē, -tōr′ē) *adj.*

ex•cur•sion (ĭk-skûr′zhən) *n.* **1.** A usu. short journey made for pleasure **:** outing. **2.** A trip at a special reduced fare. **3.** A digression. **—ex•cur′sion•ist** *n.*

ex•cur•sive (ĭk-skûr′sĭv) *adj.* Given to or marked by digression **:** rambling. **—ex•cur′sive•ly** *adv.* **—ex•cur′sive•ness** *n.*

ex•cuse (ĭk-skyōōz′) *v.* **-cused, -cus•ing. 1.** To forgive **:** pardon. **2.** To make allowance for **:** overlook. **3.** To apologize for. **4.** To justify. **5.** To release from a duty **:** exempt. **6.** To allow to leave **:** release. —*n.* (-skyōōs′) **1.** An explanation to elicit forgiveness. **2.** A ground or reason for being excused. **3.** *Informal.* An inferior example <a poor *excuse* for a sailboat> **—ex•cus′a•ble** *adj.* **—ex•cus′a•bly** *adv.*

ex•e•cra•ble (ĕk′sĭ-krə-bəl) *adj.* **1.** Deserving execration **:** detestable. **2.** Very bad **:** vile. **—ex′e•cra•bly** *adv.*

ex•e•crate (ĕk′sĭ-krāt′) *v.* **-crat•ed, -crat•ing.** To feel or express detestation for **:** abhor. **—ex′e•cra′tion** *n.* **—ex′e•cra′tor** *n.*

ex•e•cute (ĕk′sĭ-kyōōt′) *v.* **-cut•ed, -cut•ing. 1.** To put into effect **:** carry out. **2.** To make valid, as by signing <*execute* a deed> **3.** To carry out what is called for in <*execute* a will> **4.** To put to death by legal authority. **5.** *Computer Sci.* To run (a program or instruction). **—ex′e•cu′tion** *n.*

ex•e•cu•tion•er (ĕk′sĭ-kyōō′shə-nər) *n.* One who puts others to death by legal authority.

ex•ec•u•tive (ĭg-zĕk′yə-tĭv) *n.* **1.** An administrator or manager in an organization. **2.** The branch of government responsible for putting the laws of a country into effect. —*adj.* **1.** Of or responsible for the carrying out of plans or policies. **2.** Of or relating to the branch of government that puts laws into effect.

Executive Council *n. Can.* The cabinet of a provincial government.

ex•ec•u•tor (ĭg-zĕk′yə-tər) *n.* A person appointed to carry out a will.

ex•ec•u•trix (ĭg-zĕk′yə-trĭks′) *n., pl.* **-trix•es** *or* **-tri•ces** (-trī′sēz′). A woman appointed to carry out a will.

ex•e•ge•sis (ĕk′sə-jē′sĭs) *n., pl.* **-ses** (-sēz′). Explanation or interpretation of a text. **—ex′e•get′ic** (-jĕt′ĭk), **ex′e•get′i•cal** *adj.*

ex•em•plar (ĭg-zĕm′plär′, -plər) *n.* **1.** One worthy of imitation **:** model. **2.** A typical example.

ex•em•pla•ry (ĭg-zĕm′plə-rē) *adj.* **1.** Serving as a model. **2.** Worthy of imitation **:** commendable.

ex•em•pli•fy (ĭg-zĕm′plə-fī′) *v.* **-fied, -fy•ing. 1.** To illustrate by giving examples. **2.** To be an example of. **—ex•em′pli•fi•ca′tion** *n.*

ex•empt (ĭg-zĕmpt′) *v.* To release from an obligation or duty to which others are subject. —**ex•empt′** *adj.* —**ex•empt′i•ble** *adj.* —**ex•emp′tion** *n.*

ex•er•cise (ĕk′sər-sīz′) *n.* **1.** An act of using <the *exercise* of caution> **2.** Physical or mental activity that develops fitness. **3.** Something done to maintain or inprove a skill <a piano *exercise*> **4. exercises.** A public ceremony <commencement *exercises*> —*v.* **-cised, -cis•ing. 1.** To put into operation : use. **2.** To bring to bear : exert. **3.** To subject to physical or mental activity so as to develop fitness. **4.** To worry or upset. —**ex′er•cis′er** *n.*

ex•ert (ĭg-zûrt′) *v.* **1.** To bring to bear : exercise. **2.** To put (oneself) to a strenuous effort. —**ex•er′tion** *n.*

ex•hale (ĕks-hāl′, ĕk-sāl′) *v.* **-haled, -hal•ing. 1.** To breathe out. **2.** To emit (e.g., vapor). —**ex′ha•la′tion** (ĕks′hə-lā′shən, ĕk′sə-) *n.*

ex•haust (ĭg-zôst′) *v.* **1.** To let out or release (a liquid or gas). **2.** To use up : consume <*exhausted* the food supply> **3.** To use up the energy of : wear out. **4.** To develop or consider completely <*exhaust* a subject> —*n.* **1. a.** The escape of gases, as from an engine. **b.** The gases released. **2.** A device that releases or expels waste gases. —**ex•haust′i•bil′i•ty** *n.* —**ex•haust′i•ble** *adj.* —**ex•haus′tion** (-zôs′chən) *n.*

ex•haus•tive (ĭg-zô′stĭv) *adj.* **1.** Tending to exhaust. **2.** Thorough : comprehensive <an *exhaustive* analysis> —**ex•haus′tive•ly** *adv.* —**ex•haus′tive•ness** *n.*

ex•hib•it (ĭg-zĭb′ĭt) *v.* **1.** To display, esp. for public view. **2.** To introduce (documents or evidence) in a court of law. —*n.* **1.** An act of exhibiting. **2.** Something exhibited. —**ex′hi•bi′tion** (ĕk′sə-bĭsh′ən) *n.* —**ex•hib′i•tor** *n.*

ex•hi•bi•tion•ism (ĕk′sə-bĭsh′ə-nĭz′əm) *n.* The practice of deliberately attracting undue attention to oneself. —**ex′hi•bi′tion•ist** *n.* —**ex′hi•bi′tion•is′tic** *adj.*

ex•hil•a•rate (ĭg-zĭl′ə-rāt′) *v.* **-rat•ed, -rat•ing. 1.** To make cheerful : elate. **2.** To refresh : invigorate. —**ex•hil′a•ra′tion** *n.* —**ex•hil′a•ra′tive** *adj.*

ex•hort (ĭg-zôrt′) *v.* To urge or incite by strong appeal, advice, or argument. —**ex′hor•ta′tion** (ĕk′sôr-tā′shən, ĕg′zôr-) *n.* —**ex•hor′ta•tive** *adj.*

ex•hume (ĭg-zyo͞om′, ĕks-hyo͞om′) *v.* **-humed, -hum•ing.** To remove from a grave : disinter. —**ex′hu•ma′tion** (ĕks′hyo͞o-mā′shən) *n.*

ex•i•gen•cy (ĕk′sə-jən-sē, ĕg′zə-) *n., pl.* **-cies. 1.** The quality of requiring immediate attention or effort : urgency. **2.** An emergency. **3.** *often* **exigencies.** Pressing needs. —**ex′i•gence** *n.* —**ex′i•gent** *adj.*

ex•ig•u•ous (ĭg-zĭg′yo͞o-əs, ĭk-sĭg′-) *adj.* Extremely meager : scanty. —**ex′i•gu′i•ty** (ĕk′sĭ-gyo͞o′ĭ-tē) *n.* —**ex•ig′u•ous•ly** *adv.*

ex•ile (ĕg′zīl′, ĕk′sīl′) *n.* **1.** Forced or self-imposed removal from one's native country : banishment. **2.** One who has left or been driven from his or her country. —*v.* **-iled, -il•ing.** To send into exile : banish.

ex•ist (ĭg-zĭst′) *v.* **1.** To have being or actuality. **2.** To have life : live. **3.** To occur.

ex•is•tence (ĭg-zĭs′təns) *n.* **1.** The fact or state of existing, living, or occurring. **2.** Manner of existing <a day-to-day *existence*> —**ex•is′tent** *adj.*

ex•is•ten•tial (ĕg′zĭ-stĕn′shəl, ĕk′sĭ-) *adj.* **1.** Of or relating to existence. **2.** Based on experience. **3.** Of or relating to existentialism. —**ex′is•ten′tial•ly** *adv.*

ex•is•ten•tial•ism (ĕg′zĭ-stĕn′shə-lĭz′əm, ĕk′sĭ-) *n.* A philosophy that emphasizes the absence of supernatural authority and the freedom and responsibility of the individual in a universe that lacks essential meaning. —**ex′is•ten′tial•ist** *n.*

ex•it (ĕg′zĭt, ĕk′sĭt) *n.* **1.** The act of going away or out. **2.** A passage or way out. **3.** A departure from the stage, as in a play. —**ex′it** *v.*

ex•o•bi•ol•o•gy (ĕk′sō-bī-ŏl′ə-jē) *n.* The search for and study of extraterrestrial life. —**ex′o•bi•ol′o•gist** *n.*

ex•o•dus (ĕk′sə-dəs) *n.* **1.** A departure of a large number of people. **2. Exodus.** —See table at BIBLE.

ex of•fi•ci•o (ĕks′ ə-fĭsh′ē-ō′) *adj. & adv.* Because of office or position.

ex•og•e•nous (ĕk-sŏj′ə-nəs) *n. Biol.* Derived from external causes.

ex•on•er•ate (ĭg-zŏn′ə-rāt′) *v.* **-at•ed, -at•ing.** To clear of blame. —**ex•on′er•a′tion** *n.* —**ex•on′er•a′tor** *n.*

ex•or•bi•tant (ĭg-zôr′bĭ-tənt) *adj.* Exceeding appropriate or usual limits or bounds : immoderate. —**ex•or′bi•tance** *n.* —**ex•or′bi•tant•ly** *adv.*

ex•or•cise (ĕk′sôr-sīz′, -sər-) *v.* **-cised, -cis•ing. 1.** To expel (an evil spirit) by or as if by enacting a ritual. **2.** To free from evil spirits. —**ex′or•cis′er** *n.* —**ex′or•cism** *n.* —**ex′or•cist** *n.*

ex•o•ther•mic (ĕk′sō-thûr′mĭk) *also* **ex•o•ther•mal** (-məl) *adj.* Releasing rather than absorbing heat.

ex•ot•ic (ĭg-zŏt′ĭk) *adj.* **1.** Of or from another part of the world : foreign. **2.** Intriguingly different. —**ex•ot′ic** *n.* —**ex•ot′i•cal•ly** *adv.*

ex•pand (ĭk-spănd′) *v.* **1.** To make or become greater in size, scope, or range. **2.** To open up or out : unfold. **3.** To speak or write at greater length : enlarge. —**ex•pand′a•ble** *adj.* —**ex•pand′er** *n.*

ex•panse (ĭk-spăns′) *n.* A wide, open extent <the *expanse* of sky>

ex•pan•sion (ĭk-spăn′shən) *n.* **1.** The act or process of expanding or state of being expanded. **2.** An expanded part.

ex•pan•sive (ĭk-spăn′sĭv) *adj.* **1.** Capable of expanding or inclined to expand. **2.** Comprehensive : broad. **3.** Open and generous : outgoing. —**ex•pan′sive•ly** *adv.* —**ex•pan′sive•ness** *n.*

ex par•te (ĕks pär′tē) *adj. & adv. Law.* From only one side or point of view.

ex·pa·ti·ate (ĭk-spā′shē-āt′) *v.* **-at·ed, -at·ing.** To talk or write at length : elaborate. **—ex·pa′ti·a′tion** *n.*

ex·pa·tri·ate (ĕks-pā′trē-āt′) *v.* **-at·ed, -at·ing. 1.** To send into exile. **2.** To leave one's country and reside in another. *—n.* (-ĭt, -āt′). An expatriated person. **—ex·pa′tri·a′tion** *n.*

ex·pect (ĭk-spĕkt′) *v.* **1.** To look forward to : believe to be probable <*expecting* rain> **2.** To consider due <*expect* civility> **3.** *Informal.* To presume : suppose. **—ex·pect′er** *n.*

ex·pec·tan·cy (ĭk-spĕk′tən-sē) *n., pl.* **-cies. 1.** Expectation. **2.** An expected amount <a life *expectancy* of 76 years>

ex·pec·tant (ĭk-spĕk′tənt) *adj.* **1.** Expecting. **2.** Pregnant. **—ex·pec′tant·ly** *adv.*

ex·pec·ta·tion (ĕk′spĕk-tā′shən) *n.* **1.** The act or state of expecting. **2.** Eager anticipation for something coming. **3. a. expectations.** Something expected. **b.** Future prospects.

ex·pec·to·rant (ĭk-spĕk′tər-ənt) *adj.* Promoting expulsion of mucus from the respiratory tract. *—n.* An expectorant medication.

ex·pec·to·rate (ĭk-spĕk′tə-rāt′) *v.* **-rat·ed, -rat·ing.** To spit. **—ex·pec′to·ra′tion** *n.*

ex·pe·di·ence (ĭk-spē′dē-əns) *n.* Expediency.

ex·pe·di·en·cy (ĭk-spē′dē-ən-sē) *n., pl.* **-cies. 1.** Suitableness : fitness. **2.** The use of self-serving means. **3.** An expedient.

ex·pe·di·ent (ĭk-spē′dē-ənt) *adj.* **1.** Appropriate to a given purpose. **2.** Promoting narrow or selfish interests. *—n.* A means to an end, esp. one disregarding the welfare of others. **—ex·pe′di·ent·ly** *adv.*

ex·pe·dite (ĕk′spĭ-dīt′) *v.* **-dit·ed, -dit·ing. 1.** To speed up : facilitate. **2.** To perform efficiently. **—ex′pe·dit′er, ex′pe·di′tor** *n.*

ex·pe·di·tion (ĕk′spĭ-dĭsh′ən) *n.* **1. a.** A journey of some length or difficulty for a definite purpose. **b.** The group undertaking such a journey. **2.** Speed in performing : promptness.

ex·pe·di·tion·ar·y (ĕk′spĭ-dĭsh′ə-nĕr′ē) *adj.* Of, relating to, or being an expedition, esp. a military one.

ex·pe·di·tious (ĕk′spĭ-dĭsh′əs) *adj.* Acting or done with efficiency and promptness. **—ex′pe·di′tious·ly** *adv.* **—ex′pe·di′tious·ness** *n.*

ex·pel (ĭk-spĕl′) *v.* **-pelled, -pel·ling. 1.** To drive or force out. **2.** To dismiss, as from a school. **—ex·pel′la·ble** *adj.* **—ex·pel′ler** *n.*

ex·pend (ĭk-spĕnd′) *v.* **1.** To spend. **2.** To use up : consume.

ex·pend·a·ble (ĭk-spĕn′də-bəl) *adj.* Subject to being used up or sacrificed if needed : nonessential.

ex·pen·di·ture (ĭk-spĕn′də-chər) *n.* **1.** The act or process of expending. **2.** An amount spent.

ex·pense (ĭk-spĕns′) *n.* **1. a.** Something paid out or given up to attain an end. **b.** Sacrifice <at the *expense* of his pride> **2. expenses. a.** Charges incurred by an employee while at work. **b.** *Informal.* Reimbursement for such charges. **3.** Something necessitating the spending of money.

ex·pen·sive (ĭk-spĕn′sĭv) *adj.* High-priced. ★ *syns:* COSTLY, DEAR, HIGH

ex·pe·ri·ence (ĭk-spîr′ē- əns) *n.* **1.** Something done, seen, or taken part in <her *experiences* as a nurse> **2.** The events lived through by an individual or group. **3. a.** Participation or observation leading to knowledge or skill. **b.** The knowledge or skill acquired <a worker with extensive *experience*> *—v.* **-enced, -enc·ing.** To participate in personally : undergo. **—ex·pe′ri·en′tial** *adj.*

ex·pe·ri·enced (ĭk-spîr′ē-ənst) *adj.* Knowledgeable through experience.

ex·per·i·ment (ĭk-spĕr′ə-mənt) *n.* A test performed to demonstrate a truth, examine a hypothesis, or learn about something not yet known. *—v.* (-mĕnt′) To conduct an experiment. **—ex·per′i·men′tal** *adj.* **—ex·per′i·men′tal·ly** *adv.* **—ex·per′i·men·ta′tion** *n.* **—ex·per′i·ment′er** *n.*

ex·pert (ĕk′spûrt′) *n.* A person with great knowledge, skill, or experience in a specific subject. *—adj.* (ĭk-spûrt′, ĕk′spûrt′). Having or showing great skill or knowledge. **—ex·pert′ly** *adv.* **—ex·pert′ness** *n.*

ex·per·tise (ĕk′spər-tēz′) *n.* Specialized knowledge, skill, or ability.

ex·pi·ate (ĕk′spē-āt′) *v.* **-at·ed, -at·ing.** To make amends for : atone. **—ex′pi·a′tion** *n.* **—ex′pi·a′tor** *n.* **—ex′pi·a·to′ry** (-ə-tôr′ē, -tōr′ē) *adj.*

ex·pire (ĭk-spīr′) *v.* **-pired, -pir·ing. 1.** To come to an end. **2.** To die. **3.** To breathe out : exhale. **—ex′pi·ra′tion** *n.*

ex·plain (ĭk-splān′) *v.* **1.** To make understandable : clarify. **2.** To give the reason for : account for. **—ex·plain′a·ble** *adj.* **—ex·plain′er** *n.* **—ex′pla·na′tion** (ĕk′splə-nā′shən) *n.* **—ex·plan′a·to·ry** (-splăn′ə-tôr′ē, -tōr′ē) *adj.*

ex·ple·tive (ĕks′plĭ-tĭv) *n.* An often profane or obscene exclamation.

ex·pli·ca·ble (ĕk′splĭ-kə-bəl, ĭk-splĭk′ə-) *adj.* Capable of being explained.

ex·pli·cate (ĕk′splĭ-kāt′) *v.* **-cat·ed, -cat·ing.** To make clearer the meaning of : explain in detail. **—ex′pli·ca′tion** *n.* **—ex′pli·ca′tive** *adj.* **—ex′pli·ca′tor** *n.*

ex·plic·it (ĭk-splĭs′ĭt) *adj.* Clearly expressed or defined : specific <*explicit* instructions> **—ex·plic′it·ly** *adv.* **—ex·plic′it·ness** *n.*

ex·plode (ĭk-splōd′) *v.* **-plod·ed, -plod·ing. 1.** To release or cause to release energy violently and suddenly : burst. **2.** To break out suddenly : burst forth. **3.** To increase rapidly and without control. **4.** To show to be false : refute. **—ex·plod′er** *n.*

ex·ploit (ĕk′sploit′) *n.* A notable deed or act. *—v.* (ĭk-sploit′). **1.** To use to best advantage. **2.** To make use of selfishly or unethically <*exploiting* low-paid farm workers> **—ex·ploit′a·ble** *adj.* **—ex′ploi·ta′tion** *n.* **—ex·ploit′a·tive** *adj.* **—ex·ploit′er** *n.*

ex·plore (ĭk-splôr′, -splōr′) *v.* **-plored, -plor·ing. 1.** To investigate in a systematic way : examine. **2.** To search into or range over for the purpose of discovery. —**ex′plo•ra′tion** (ĕk′splə-rā′shən) *n.* —**ex•plor′a•to′ry** (-ə-tôr′ē, -tōr′ē) *adj.* —**ex•plor′er** *n.*

ex•plo•sion (ĭk-splō′zhən) *n.* **1. a.** A sudden, violent release of energy. **b.** A loud, sharp sound made by this. **2.** A sudden outburst, as of emotion. **3.** A rapid, uncontrolled increase.

ex•plo•sive (ĭk-splō′sĭv) *adj.* **1.** Of or relating to an explosion. **2.** Likely to explode. —*n.* A substance, esp. a chemical preparation, that explodes. —**ex•plo′sive•ly** *adv.* —**ex•plo′sive•ness** *n.*

ex•po•nent (ĭk-spō′nənt) *n.* **1.** One who represents, advocates, or speaks for a cause or group. **2.** *Math.* A number or symbol, as 4 in $(x + y)^4$, that indicates the number of times an expression is used as a factor. —**ex′po•nen′tial** (ĕk′spə-nĕn′shəl) *adj.* —**ex′po•nen′tial•ly** *adv.*

ex•port (ĭk-spôrt′, -spōrt′, ĕk′spôrt′, -spōrt′) *v.* To send or transport abroad for sale or trade. —*n.* (ĕk′spôrt′, -spōrt′). **1.** An act of exporting. **2.** A commodity exported. —**ex•port′a•ble** *adj.* —**ex′por•ta′tion** *n.* —**ex•port′er** *n.*

ex•pose (ĭk-spōz′) *v.* **-posed, -pos•ing. 1.** To lay bare **:** uncover. **2.** To lay open, as to something harmful <*exposed* himself to a lawsuit> **3.** To make known **:** reveal. **4.** To subject (e.g., a photographic film) to light. —**ex•pos′er** *n.*

ex•po•sé (ĕk′spō-zā′) *n.* An exposure of something discreditable.

ex•po•si•tion (ĕk′spə-zĭsh′ən) *n.* **1.** A statement of meaning or intent. **2.** Writing or speech that explains or gives information. **3.** A public exhibition. —**ex•pos′i•tor** (ĭk-spŏz′ĭ-tər) *n.* —**ex•pos′i•to′ry** (-tôr′ē, -tōr′ē) *adj.*

ex post fac•to (ĕks′ pōst făk′tō) *adj.* Enacted, formulated, or done after the fact **:** retroactive <*ex post facto* laws>

ex•pos•tu•late (ĭk-spŏs′chə-lāt′) *v.* **-lat•ed, -lat•ing.** To reason earnestly in an effort to dissuade or correct someone. —**ex•pos′tu•la′tion** *n.* —**ex•pos′tu•la′tor** *n.* —**ex•pos′tu•la•to′ry** (-lə-tôr′ē, -tōr′ē) *adj.*

ex•po•sure (ĭk-spō′zhər) *n.* **1.** An act of exposing or the state of being exposed. **2.** A position with respect to direction <a northern *exposure*> **3. a.** The act of exposing a sensitized photographic film or plate. **b.** The film or plate exposed.

ex•pound (ĭk-spound′) *v.* **1.** To present a detailed statement (of). **2.** To explain at length. —**ex•pound′er** *n.*

ex•press (ĭk-sprĕs′) *v.* **1.** To make known in words <*express* an opinion> **2.** To communicate, as by gesture **:** show. **3.** To represent **:** symbolize. **4.** To press out, as juice from fruit. **5.** To send by fast transportation. —*adj.* **1.** Clearly stated **:** explicit. **2.** Sent rapidly and directly <an *express* parcel> **3.** Direct and with few or no local stops <an *express* bus> —*adv.* By express transport. —*n.* An express vehicle or transport system. —**ex•press′i•ble** *adj.* —**ex•press′ly** *adv.*

ex•pres•sion (ĭk-sprĕsh′ən) *n.* **1.** An act of expressing. **2.** Communication, esp. in words **:** utterance. **3.** Something that expresses. **4.** A particular phrase or word <a regional *expression* like "you-all"> **5.** A manner of expressing oneself, esp. in speech or performance. **6.** A facial aspect or look conveying feeling <an astonished *expression*> **7.** *Math.* A symbol or group of symbols representing a quantity or formula. —**ex•pres′sion•less** *adj.*

ex•pres•sion•ism (ĭk-sprĕsh′ə-nĭz′əm) *n.* A movement in the fine arts that emphasizes subjective expression of the artist's inner experiences. —**ex•pres′sion•ist** *n.* —**ex•pres′sion•is′tic** *adj.*

ex•pres•sive (ĭk-sprĕs′ĭv) *adj.* **1.** Of or relating to expression <*expressive* power> **2.** Serving or tending to express <a tone *expressive* of regret> **3.** Full of expression **:** significant. —**ex•pres′sive•ly** *adv.* —**ex•pres′sive•ness** *n.*

ex•press•way (ĭk-sprĕs′wā′) *n.* A multilane highway designed for high-speed travel.

ex•pro•pri•ate (ĕk-sprō′prē-āt′) *v.* **-at•ed, -at•ing. 1.** To acquire or take (another's property), esp. for public use. **2.** To deprive of possession. —**ex•pro′pri•a′tion** *n.* —**ex•pro′pri•a′tor** *n.*

ex•pul•sion (ĭk-spŭl′shən) *n.* The act of expelling or state of being expelled.

ex•punge (ĭk-spŭnj′) *v.* **-punged, -pung•ing.** To remove or delete **:** erase. —**ex•pung′er** *n.*

ex•pur•gate (ĕk′spər-gāt′) *v.* **-gat•ed, -gat•ing.** To remove objectionable material from, esp. before publication. —**ex′pur•ga′tion** *n.* —**ex′pur•ga′tor** *n.*

ex•qui•site (ĕk′skwĭ-zĭt, ĭk-skwĭz′ĭt) *adj.* **1.** Intricately or delicately beautiful in design or execution <an *exquisite* miniature portrait> **2.** Acutely refined or appreciative <*exquisite* taste> **3.** Intense **:** keen. **4.** Excellent **:** flawless. —**ex′qui•site•ly** *adv.* —**ex′qui•site•ness** *n.*

ex•tant (ĕk′stənt, ĭk-stănt′) *adj.* Still in existence **:** not lost or destroyed <*extant* writings>

ex•tem•po•ra•ne•ous (ĭk-stĕm′pə-rā′nē-əs) *adj.* Acting or done without preparation or practice beforehand **:** impromptu. —**ex•tem′po•ra′ne•ous•ly** *adv.* —**ex•tem′po•ra′ne•ous•ness** *n.*

ex•tem•po•re (ĭk-stĕm′pə-rē) *adj.* Extemporaneous. —*adv.* Extemporaneously.

ex•tem•po•rize (ĭk-stĕm′pə-rīz′) *v.* **-rized, -riz•ing.** To perform extemporaneously **:** improvise. —**ex•tem′po•ri•za′tion** *n.* —**ex•tem′po•riz′er** *n.*

ex•tend (ĭk-stĕnd′) *v.* **1.** To stretch to full length **:** spread out. **2.** To make longer, wider, or broader <*extend* boundaries><*extending* individual rights> **3.** To reach **:** stretch <Her property *extends* to the river.> **4.** To prolong <*extend* a deadline> **5.** To exert to full capacity. **6.** To offer <*extend* congratulations> —**ex•tend′i•bil′i•ty, ex•ten′si•bil′i•ty** *n.* —**ex•tend′i•ble, ex•ten′si•ble** *adj.*

extended family *n.* A family unit making up one household that consists of parents, children, and other close relatives.

ex•tend•er (ĕk-stĕn′dər) *n.* A substance added to another to modify, dilute, or adulterate.

ex•ten•sion (ĭk-stĕn′shən) *n.* **1.** The act of extending or state of being extended. **2.** An added part.

ex•ten•sive (ĭk-stĕn′sĭv) *adj.* Great in extent : large or broad. —**ex•ten′sive•ly** *adv.* —**ex•ten′sive•ness** *n.*

ex•tent (ĭk-stĕnt′) *n.* **1.** The area over or length to which a thing extends : size. **2.** The degree to which a thing extends. **3.** An expanse.

ex•ten•u•ate (ĭk-stĕn′yo͞o-āt′) *v.* **-at•ed, -at•ing.** To minimize or try to minimize the seriousness of : excuse. —**ex•ten′u•a′tion** *n.* —**ex•ten′u•a′tor** *n.*

ex•te•ri•or (ĭk-stîr′ē-ər) *adj.* External : outer. —*n.* An exterior surface or part.

ex•ter•mi•nate (ĭk-stûr′mə-nāt′) *v.* **-nat•ed, -nat•ing.** To destroy completely : annihilate. —**ex•ter′mi•na′tion** *n.* —**ex•ter′mi•na′tor** *n.*

ex•tern *or* **ex•terne** (ĕk′stûrn′) *n.* A person associated with but not officially residing in an institution, as a hospital.

ex•ter•nal (ĭk-stûr′nəl) *adj.* **1.** Of, for, or on the outside : exterior. **2.** Acting or coming from the outside <*external* influences on a country> **3.** Apparent from outside. **4.** Of or relating to foreign countries. —*n.* **externals.** External circumstances or appearances. —**ex•ter′nal•ly** *adv.*

ex•tinct (ĭk-stĭngkt′) *adj.* **1.** No longer existing <*extinct* reptiles> **2.** Not active <an *extinct* volcano> **3.** Extinguished. —**ex•tinc′tion** *n.*

ex•tin•guish (ĭk-stĭng′gwĭsh) *v.* **1.** To put out (e.g., a fire). **2.** To put an end to : destroy. ★ *syns:* DOUSE, QUENCH, SNUFF —**ex•tin′guish•a•ble** *adj.* —**ex•tin′guish•er** *n.*

ex•tir•pate (ĕk′stər-pāt′) *v.* **-pat•ed, -pat•ing.** **1.** To root out : uproot. **2.** To destroy : exterminate. —**ex′tir•pa′tion** *n.* —**ex′tir•pa′tive** *adj.* —**ex′tir•pa′tor** *n.*

ex•tol *also* **ex•toll** (ĭk-stōl′) *v.* **-tolled, -tol•ling.** To praise highly. —**ex•tol′ler** *n.* —**ex•tol′ment** *n.*

ex•tort (ĭk-stôrt′) *v.* To obtain by coercive means, as threats or intimidation. —**ex•tor′tion** *n.* —**ex•tor′tion•ate** (-shə-nĭt) *adj.* —**ex•tor′tion•ist** *n.*

ex•tra (ĕk′strə) *adj.* Being beyond what is expected or usual : additional. —*adv.* Exceptionally : unusually. —*n.* **1.** Something additional : accessory. **2.** An extra edition of a newspaper. **3.** A performer hired to play a minor film part.

ex•tract (ĭk-străkt′) *v.* **1.** To draw out, esp. forcibly <*extract* a tooth> **2.** To obtain in spite of resistance <*extract* a confession> **3.** To obtain by chemical or mechanical action. **4.** To remove for separate consideration : excerpt. **5.** *Math.* To determine (a root). —*n.* (ĕk′străkt′). **1.** A passage taken from a longer work : excerpt. **2.** A concentrated substance : essence <maple *extract*> —**ex•tract′a•ble, ex•tract′i•ble** *adj.* —**ex•trac′tor** *n.*

ex•trac•tion (ĭk-străk′shən) *n.* **1.** The act or process of extracting. **2.** Something obtained by extracting : extract. **3.** Origin : ancestry <of German *extraction*>

ex•tra•cur•ric•u•lar (ĕk′strə-kə-rĭk′yə-lər) *adj.* **1.** Outside a school's curriculum. **2.** Outside the usual duties of a job.

ex•tra•dite (ĕk′strə-dīt′) *v.* **-dit•ed, -dit•ing.** To surrender to or obtain by extradition. —**ex′tra•dit′a•ble** *adj.*

ex•tra•di•tion (ĕk′strə-dĭsh′ən) *n.* Legal surrender of an alleged criminal to the jurisdiction of another state, country, or government for trial.

ex•tra•dos (ĕk′strə-dŏs′, -dō′, -dŏs′) *n., pl.* **-dos** (-dōz′) *or* **-dos•es.** The upper or exterior curve of an arch.

ex•tra•ga•lac•tic (ĕk′strə-gə-lăk′tĭk) *adj.* Situated or coming from beyond the galaxy.

ex•tra•mar•i•tal (ĕk′strə-măr′ĭ-tl) *adj.* Adulterous.

ex•tra•mu•ral (ĕk′strə-myo͝or′əl) *adj.* **1.** Occurring outside the walls or boundaries, as of a community. **2.** Involving teams from different schools.

ex•tra•ne•ous (ĭk-strā′nē-əs) *adj.* **1.** Coming from the outside : foreign. **2.** Not vital or essential. —**ex•tra′ne•ous•ly** *adv.* —**ex•tra′ne•ous•ness** *n.*

ex•tra•or•di•naire (ĕk′strə-ôr′dn-âr′, -dē-nâr′) *adj.* Extraordinary <a jazz singer *extraordinaire*>

ex•traor•di•nar•y (ĭk-strôr′dn-ĕr′ē, ĕk′strə-ôr′-) *adj.* Beyond what is common or usual : remarkable. —**ex•traor′di•nar′i•ly** (-nâr′ə-lē) *adv.*

ex•trap•o•late (ĭk-străp′ə-lāt′) *v.* **-lat•ed, -lat•ing.** To infer (unknown information) by projecting or extending known information. —**ex•trap′o•la′tion** *n.* —**ex•trap′o•la′tive** *adj.* —**ex•trap′o•la′tor** *n.*

ex•tra•sen•so•ry (ĕk′strə-sĕn′sə-rē) *adj.* Being beyond the range of the known senses.

ex•tra•ter•res•tri•al (ĕk′strə-tə-rĕs′trē-əl) *adj.* Originating or occurring outside the earth or its atmosphere. —**ex′tra•ter•res′tri•al** *n.*

ex•tra•ter•ri•to•ri•al (ĕk′strə-tĕr′ĭ-tôr′ē-əl, -tōr′-) *adj.* **1.** Situated outside territorial limits. **2.** Of or pertaining to extraterritoriality.

ex•tra•ter•ri•to•ri•al•i•ty (ĕk′strə-tĕr′ĭ-tôr′ē-ăl′ĭ-tē, -tōr-) *n.* Exemption from local legal jurisdiction, as that extended to foreign diplomats.

ex•trav•a•gant (ĭk-străv′ə-gənt) *adj.* **1.** Given to imprudent or lavish spending : wasteful. **2.** Excessive : unrestrained <*extravagant* requests> —**ex•trav′a•gance** *n.* —**ex•trav′a•gant•ly** *adv.*

ex•trav•a•gan•za (ĭk-străv′ə-găn′zə) *n.* A lavish, showy entertainment.

ex•tra•ve•hic•u•lar (ĕk′strə-vē-hĭk′yə-lər) *adj.* Done or occurring outside a vehicle, esp. a spacecraft in flight <*extravehicular* activity>

ex•treme (ĭk-strēm′) *adj.* **1.** Farthest from a center : outermost <the *extreme* edge of the continent> **2.** Final : last. **3.** Of the highest or utmost degree <*extreme* poverty><an *extreme* nationalist> **4.** Severe : drastic. —*n.* **1.** The highest or utmost degree. **2.** Either of the 2 ends of a scale or range <the *extremes* of flood and drought> **3.** An extreme condition. **4.** A drastic measure. —**ex•treme'ly** *adv.* —**ex•treme'ness** *n.*

ex•trem•ist (ĭk-strē'mĭst) *n.* One who advocates or resorts to extreme measures, esp. in politics. —**ex•trem'ism** *n.*

ex•trem•i•ty (ĭk-strĕm'ĭ-tē) *n., pl.* **-ties. 1.** The farthest point or portion. **2.** The utmost degree. **3.** Extreme distress or peril. **4.** An extreme measure. **5.** A bodily limb or appendage.

ex•tri•cate (ĕk'strĭ-kāt') *v.* **-cat•ed, -cat•ing.** To free from difficulty or entanglement : disengage. —**ex'tri•ca'tion** *n.*

ex•trin•sic (ĭk-strĭn'sĭk, -zĭk) *adj.* **1.** Not inherent : extraneous. **2.** Coming from the outside : external. —**ex•trin'si•cal•ly** *adv.*

ex•tro•vert *also* **ex•tra•vert** (ĕk'strə-vûrt') *n.* One who is socially outgoing and communicative. —**ex'tro•ver'sion** *n.*

ex•trude (ĭk-stro͞od') *v.* **-trud•ed, -trud•ing. 1.** To thrust or push out <A spider *extrudes* filaments.> **2.** To shape (e.g., plastic) by forcing through a die. **3.** To project or protrude. —**ex•tru'sion** *n.* —**ex•tru'sive** *adj.*

ex•u•ber•ant (ĭg-zo͞o'bər-ənt) *adj.* **1.** Full of unrestrained high spirits : ebullient. **2.** Plentiful : abundant. —**ex•u'ber•ance** *n.* —**ex•u'ber•ant•ly** *adv.*

ex•ude (ĭg-zo͞od') *v.* **-ud•ed, -ud•ing. 1.** To ooze forth. **2.** To give off : radiate <*exuding* charm> —**ex'u•da'tion** (ĕks'yo͞o-dā'shən) *n.* —**ex'u•date'** *n.*

ex•ult (ĭg-zŭlt') *v.* To rejoice greatly : be jubilant. —**ex•ul'tant** *adj.* —**ex•ul'tant•ly** *adv.* —**ex'ul•ta'tion** (ĕk'səl-tā'shən, ĕg'zəl-) *n.*

ex•urb (ĕk'sûrb) *or* **ex•ur•bi•a** (ĕk-sûr'bē-ə, ĕg-zûr'-) *n.* An often wealthy residential area outside the suburbs of a city. —**ex•ur'ban** *adj.* —**ex•ur'ban•ite'** *n.*

-ey *suff. var. of* -Y[1].

eye (ī) *n.* **1.** An organ of sight or of light sensitivity. **2.** The faculty of seeing : vision. **3.** A look : gaze. **4.** The ability to perceive, judge, or discriminate. **5.** A point of view. **6.** Something suggesting an eye <the *eye* of a needle> —*v.* **eyed, eye•ing** *or* **ey•ing.** To watch closely : look at. —**see eye to eye.** To be in complete agreement.

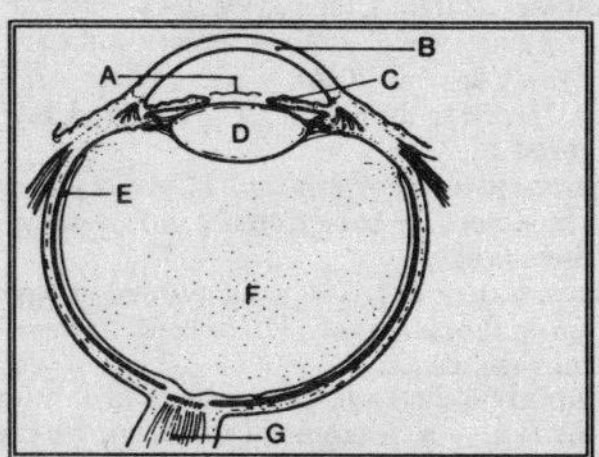

eye
A. pupil, B. cornea, C. iris, D. lens, E. retina, F. vitreous humor, G. optic nerve

eye•ball (ī'bôl') *n.* The part of the eye enclosed by the socket and eyelids and connected at the rear to the optic nerve.

eye•brow (ī'brou') *n.* **1.** The bony ridge over the eye. **2.** The short hairs covering the eyebrow.

eye•drop•per (ī'drŏp'pər) *n.* A dropper for administering liquid eye medicines.

eye•ful (ī'fo͝ol') *n.* **1.** A complete or satisfying view. **2.** An impressive sight.

eye•glass (ī'glăs') *n.* **1.** A lens, as a monocle, used to improve vision. **2. eyeglasses.** Corrective lenses set in a frame.

eye•lash (ī'lăsh') *n.* **1.** A row of hairs fringing the eyelid. **2.** A single hair of an eyelash.

eye•let (ī'lĭt) *n.* **1.** A small hole or perforation for a cord or hook to fit through in closing a fastening. **2.** A metal ring reinforcing an eyelet.

eye•lid (ī'lĭd') *n.* Either of 2 folds of skin and muscle that open and close over an eye.

eye•lin•er (ī'lī'nər) *n.* Make-up used to outline the eyes.

eye opener *n.* A startling revelation.

eye•piece (ī'pēs') *n.* The lens or lens group of an optical instrument closest to the eye : ocular.

eye shadow *n.* A colored cosmetic applied to the eyelids.

eye•sight (ī'sīt') *n.* **1.** The faculty of sight : vision. **2.** Range of vision.

eye•sore (ī'sôr', ī'sōr') *n.* Something ugly.

eye•stalk (ī'stôk') *n.* A movable stalklike structure bearing at its tip one of the eyes of a crab or similar crustacean.

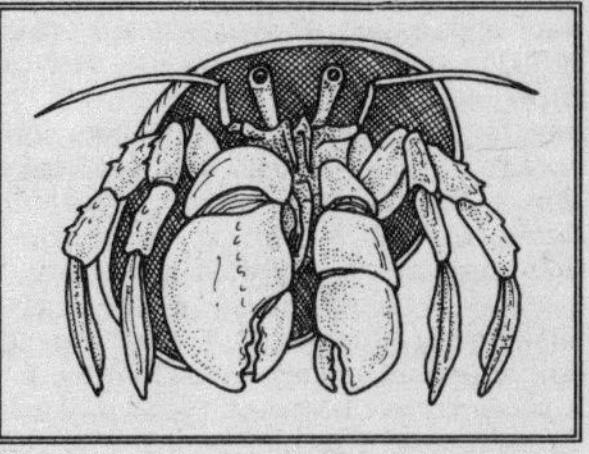

eyestalk

eye•strain (ī'strān') *n.* Fatigue in an eye muscle, marked by symptoms such as pain and headache.

eye•tooth (ī'to͞oth') *n.* A canine of the upper jaw.

eye•wash (ī'wŏsh', ī'wôsh') *n.* **1.** A medicated liquid used for washing the eyes. **2.** Meaningless or deceptive language.

eye•wit•ness (ī'wĭt'nəs) *n.* A person who has personally seen something and can testify to it firsthand.

ey•rir (ā'rîr') *n., pl.* **au•rar** (ou'rär', œ'-). —See table at CURRENCY.

E•ze•ki•el (ĭ-zē'kē-əl). —See table at BIBLE.

Ff

f *or* **F** (ĕf) *n., pl.* **f's** *or* **F's. 1.** The 6th letter of the English alphabet. **2.** A speech sound represented by the letter *f.* **3.** *Mus.* The 4th tone in the scale of C major. **4.** A failing grade.

F *symbol for* FLUORINE.

fa•ble (fā'bəl) *n.* **1.** A fictitious story making a moral point and often using animal characters. **2.** A legend. **3.** A falsehood : lie. **—fab'u•list** (făb'yə-lĭst) *n.*

fa•bled (fā'bəld) *adj.* **1.** Renowned through fables : legendary. **2.** Fictitious.

fab•ric (făb'rĭk) *n.* **1.** A complex underlying structure <the *fabric* of civilization> **2.** Cloth produced esp. by knitting, weaving, or felting fibers.

fab•ri•cate (făb'rĭ-kāt') *v.* **-cat•ed, -cat•ing. 1.** To construct by combining or assembling : make. **2.** To make up in order to deceive <*fabricate* excuses> **—fab'ri•ca'tion** *n.* **—fab'ri•ca'tor** *n.*

fab•u•lous (făb'yə-ləs) *adj.* **1.** Like a fable or myth : legendary. **2.** Told of or celebrated in fables. **3.** Hardly believable : astonishing. **4.** *Informal.* Very pleasing or successful. ★ *syns:* AMAZING, ASTONISHING, FANTASTIC, INCREDIBLE, MARVELOUS, MIRACULOUS, PHENOMENAL, PRODIGIOUS, STUPENDOUS, UNBELIEVABLE, WONDERFUL, WONDROUS **—fab'u•lous•ly** *adv.* **—fab'u•lous•ness** *n.*

fa•çade *also* **fa•cade** (fə-säd') *n.* **1.** The face of a building. **2.** An artificial or deceptive outward appearance. ★ *syns:* CLOAK, FACE, FRONT, GUISE, MASK, PRETENSE, PUT-ON, SHOW, VENEER, WINDOW-DRESSING

face (fās) *n.* **1.** The surface of the front of the head from ear to ear and from forehead to chin. **2.** The expression of the features of the countenance. **3.** A contorted facial expression : grimace. **4.** Outward appearance. **5.** Standing in the eyes of others : prestige. **6.** Impudence : effrontery. **7.** The most significant or prominent surface of an object. **8. a.** A planar surface bounding a solid. **b.** Any of the surfaces of a rock or crystal. **9.** Appearance and geologic surface features of an area of land : topography. —*v.* **faced, fac•ing. 1.** To occupy a position with the face forward. **2.** To front on. **3. a.** To confront with awareness. **b.** To overcome by confronting boldly or bravely. **4.** To be certain to encounter <An unskilled youth *faces* a tough life.> **5. a.** To furnish with a cover or surface of a different material. **b.** To line or trim the edge of, esp. with contrasting material. **—face off.** To start play, as in hockey or lacrosse, by releasing the puck or ball between 2 opponents. **—face up to.** To recognize the existence of and confront bravely. **—face'less** *adj.*

face card *n.* A king, queen, or jack of a deck of playing cards.

face•lift•ing (fās'lĭf'tĭng) *also* **face-lift** (-lĭft') *n.* **1.** Plastic surgery for tightening facial tissues. **2.** A renovation, as of a building. **—face'-lift'** *v.*

face•mask (fās'măsk') *n.* A protective or disguising cover for the face, often enveloping the entire head.

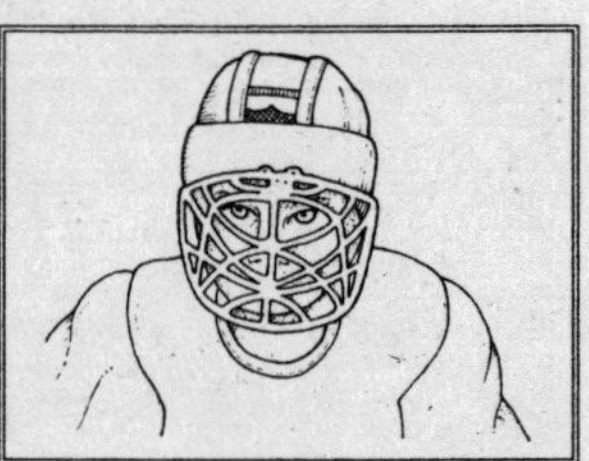

facemask

face-off (fās'ôf', -ŏf') *n.* **1.** A method of starting play, as in ice hockey or lacrosse, by releasing the puck or ball between 2 opposing players. **2.** A confrontation.

face-sav•er (fās'sā'vər) *n.* Something that preserves one's dignity or self-esteem. **—face'-sav'ing** *n. & adj.*

fac•et (făs'ĭt) *n.* **1.** One of the flat surfaces cut on a gemstone. **2.** A small smooth surface on a tooth or bone. **3.** An aspect : phase <several *facets* to the problem> **—fac'et•ed, fac'et•ted** *adj.*

fa•ce•tious (fə-sē'shəs) *adj.* Playfully jocular : humorous. **—fa•ce'tious•ly** *adv.* **—fa•ce'tious•ness** *n.*

face value *n.* **1.** The value printed or written on the face, as of a bill or bond. **2.** Apparent significance.

fa•cial (fā'shəl) *adj.* Of or having to do with the face. —*n.* A cosmetic treatment for the face. **—fa'cial•ly** *adv.*

fac•ile (făs'əl) *adj.* **1.** Carried out with little effort : easy. **2.** Working, performing, or speaking effortlessly : fluent. **3.** Arrived at without due care, effort, or examination : superficial. **—fac'ile•ly** *adv.*

fa·cil·i·tate (fə-sĭl′ĭ-tāt′) *v.* **-tat·ed, -tat·ing.** To make easier. —**fa·cil′i·ta′tion** *n.* —**fa·cil′i·ta′tor** *n.*

fa·cil·i·ty (fə-sĭl′ĭ-tē) *n., pl.* **-ties. 1.** Ease in moving, performing, or doing : aptitude. **2.** *often* **facilities.** Something that facilitates an action or process. **3.** Something created to serve a particular function <a new health *facility*>

fac·ing (fā′sĭng) *n.* **1.** A piece of cloth sewn to a garment as decoration or lining. **2.** An outer protective or decorative layer applied to a surface.

fac·sim·i·le (făk-sĭm′ə-lē) *n.* **1.** An exact copy, as of a document. **2. a.** An electronic method of transmitting images or printed matter. **b.** An image so transmitted.

fact (făkt) *n.* **1. a.** Something put forth as objectively real. **b.** Something objectively verified. **2.** Something with real, demonstrable existence : actuality. **3.** A crime <an accessory before the *fact*>

fac·tion (făk′shən) *n.* **1.** A group of persons forming a cohesive, usu. contentious minority within a larger group. **2.** Conflict within an organization or state : discord. —**fac′tion·al** *adj.* —**fac′tion·al·ism** *n.*

fac·tious (făk′shəs) *adj.* **1.** Produced or marked by faction. **2.** Creating faction : divisive. —**fac′tious·ly** *adv.*

fac·ti·tious (făk-tĭsh′əs) *adj.* **1.** Produced artificially. **2.** Lacking authenticity or genuineness : sham. —**fac·ti′tious·ly** *adv.*

fac·tor (făk′tər) *n.* **1.** One who acts for someone else : agent. **2.** One that actively contributes to an accomplishment, result, or process. **3.** *Math.* One of 2 or more quantities that when multiplied together yield a given product <2 and 8 are *factors* of 16.> **4.** A gene. —*v. Math.* To determine or indicate explicitly the factors of.

fac·to·ry (făk′tə-rē) *n., pl.* **-ries.** A place where goods are manufactured : plant.

fac·to·tum (făk-tō′təm) *n.* An employee or assistant with a wide range of duties.

fac·tu·al (făk′cho͞o-əl) *adj.* **1.** Of the nature of fact : real. **2.** Containing facts.

fac·ul·ty (făk′əl-tē) *n., pl.* **-ties. 1.** An inherent ability or power. **2.** Any of the powers or capacities of the human mind. **3.** The ability to act. **4. a.** A division or branch of learning at a college or university <the *faculty* of medicine> **b.** The instructors within such a division. **c.** A body of instructors.

fad (făd) *n.* A transitory fashion adopted with wide enthusiasm. —**fad′dish** *adj.* —**fad′dish·ness** *n.* —**fad′dist** *n.*

fade (fād) *v.* **fad·ed, fad·ing. 1.** To lose or cause to lose brightness, brilliance, or loudness gradually : dim. **2.** To lose freshness : wither. **3.** To lose vitality or strength : wane. **4.** To disappear gradually : vanish. ★ ***syns:*** DECLINE, DETERIORATE, FAIL, FLAG, LANGUISH, WANE, WEAKEN —**fade′less** *adj.* —**fade′less·ly** *adv.*

fa·er·ie *also* **fa·er·y** (fā′ə-rē, fâr′ē) *n., pl.* **-ies.** *Archaic.* **1.** A fairy. **2.** The land of the fairies. —**fa′er·ie** *adj.*

fag¹ (făg) *n.* A drudge : menial. —*v.* **fagged, fag·ging.** To work to the point of exhaustion.

fag² (făg) *n. Slang.* A cigarette.

fag end *n.* **1.** The frayed end of a cloth or rope. **2. a.** A remnant. **b.** The last part.

fag·ot *also* **fag·got** (făg′ət) *n.* A bundle of twigs, sticks, or branches tied together.

fag·ot·ing *also* **fag·goting** (făg′ə-tĭng) *n.* A method of decorating cloth by pulling out horizontal threads and tying the remaining vertical threads into hourglass-shaped bunches.

Fahr·en·heit (făr′ən-hīt′) *adj.* Of or relating to a temperature scale that registers the freezing point of water as 32° F and the boiling point of water as 212° F at 1 atmosphere of pressure.

fa·ience *also* **fa·ïence** (fī-äns′, -äɴs′, fā-) *n.* Earthenware decorated with colorful opaque glazes.

fail (fāl) *v.* **1.** To prove so deficient as to be totally ineffective. **2.** To be unsuccessful. **3.** To give or receive an academic grade below the acceptable minimum. **4.** To weaken, decline, or cease to function properly. **5.** To disappoint or prove undependable. **6.** To omit or neglect.

fail·ing (fā′lĭng) *n.* A minor fault or defect. —*prep.* In the absence of : without.

faille (fīl) *n.* A ribbed fabric of silk, cotton, or rayon.

fail-safe (fāl′sāf′) *adj.* **1.** Able to compensate automatically for a mechanical failure. **2.** Acting according to predetermined conditions to stop a military attack. **3.** Guaranteed not to fail. —**fail′-safe′** *v.* & *n.*

fail·ure (fāl′yər) *n.* **1.** The state or fact of failing. **2.** One that has failed.

fain (fān) *Archaic.* —*adv.* Happily : gladly. —*adj.* **1.** Ready : willing. **2.** Pleased : happy. **3.** Required by circumstances.

faint (fānt) *adj.* **1.** Having little strength or vigor : feeble. **2.** Lacking clarity or brightness : dim. **3.** Likely to swoon <felt *faint*> —*n.* A sudden, usu. brief loss of consciousness. —*v.* To fall into a swoon. —**faint′ly** *adv.* —**faint′ness** *n.*

faint-heart·ed (fānt′här′tĭd) *adj.* Lacking courage or conviction : timid or cowardly. —**faint-heart′ed·ness** *n.*

†**fair¹** (fâr) *adj.* **1.** Visually pleasing : lovely. **2.** Of light color, as hair or skin. **3.** Sunny and clear. **4.** Free of blemishes : clean. **5.** Favorable : promising. **6. a.** Impartial <a *fair* judge> **b.** Just <a *fair* decision> **7.** In accordance with rules or standards <*fair* tactics> **8.** Moderately good. ★ ***syns:*** DISPASSIONATE, EQUITABLE, FAIR-MINDED, IMPARTIAL, JUST, OBJECTIVE, UNBIASED, UNPREJUDICED —*adv.* **1.** In a proper or legal way <played *fair*> **2.** Directly : straight. —*v.* **1.** To join so as to be smooth or regular. **2.** *Regional.* To become clear. —**fair′ly** *adv.* —**fair′ness** *n.*

fair² (fâr) *n.* **1.** A gathering for the buying and selling of goods and merchandise : market. **2.** A competitive exhibition, as of farm prod-

ucts or manufactured goods. **3.** A fund-raising event, as for a charity.
fair-haired (fâr′hârd′) *adj.* **1.** Having light-colored hair. **2.** Favorite.
fair-mind•ed (fâr′mīn′dĭd) *adj.* Just and impartial. **—fair′-mind′ed•ness** *n.*
fair-trade agreement (fâr′trād′) *n.* A commercial agreement under which distributors sell a product at no less than a minimum price set by the manufacturer.
fair•way (fâr′wā′) *n.* The part of a golf course covered with short grass and extending from the tee to the putting green.
fair•y (fâr′ē) *n., pl.* **-ies.** A tiny imaginary being in human form depicted as being mischievous and having magical powers.
fair•y•land (fâr′ē-lănd′) *n.* **1.** The land of the fairies. **2.** An enchanting place.
fairy tale *n.* **1.** A fictitious tale of fanciful creatures, usu. for children. **2.** A fanciful explanation or story.
fait ac•com•pli (fā′tä-kôN-plē′, fĕt′ä-) *pl.* **faits ac•com•plis** (fā′tä-kôN-plē′, -plēz′, fĕt′-ä-). An accomplished and presumably irreversible deed or fact.
faith (fāth) *n.* **1.** Belief in the truth, value, or trustworthiness of someone or something. **2.** Loyalty or allegiance. **3. a.** Belief and trust in God. **b.** Religious conviction. **c.** A system of religious beliefs.
faith•ful (fāth′fəl) *adj.* **1.** Supportive : loyal. **2.** Worthy of trust or belief. **3.** Consistent with fact. ★ ***syns:*** CONSTANT, FAST, FIRM, LOYAL, RESOLUTE, STAUNCH, STEADFAST, STEADY, TRUE **—faith′ful•ly** *adv.* **—faith′-ful•ness** *n.*
faith•less (fāth′lĭs) *adj.* **1.** Not true to duty or obligation : DISLOYAL. **2.** Lacking religious faith. **3.** Unworthy of trust or belief. ★ ***syns:*** DISLOYAL, FALSE, FALSE-HEARTED, PERFIDIOUS, TRAITOROUS, TREACHEROUS, UNFAITHFUL, UNTRUE **—faith′less•ly** *adv.* **—faith′less•ness** *n.*
fake (fāk) *adj.* Having a false or misleading appearance : fraudulent. *—n.* **1.** One that is not genuine or authentic : sham. **2.** A brief feint intended to mislead one's opponent in certain sports. *—v.* **faked, fak•ing. 1.** To fabricate and present as genuine : counterfeit. **2.** To feign : simulate. **3.** To perform a fake in certain sports. **—fak′er** *n.* **—fak′er•y** *n.*
fa•kir (fə-kîr′) *n.* A Hindu or Muslim religious mendicant, esp. one performing feats of endurance or magic.
fal•con (făl′kən, fôl′-, fô′kən) *n.* A bird of prey of the family Falconidae, having a short curved beak and long pointed wings. **—fal′-con•er** *n.* **—fal′con•ry** *n.*
fall (fôl) *v.* **fell** (fĕl), **fall•en** (fô′lən), **fall•ing. 1.** To drop down freely under the influence of gravity. **2.** To come down from an erect position, esp. suddenly : collapse. **3.** To be severely wounded or killed in battle. **4.** To hang down, as hair. **5.** To assume an expression of disquiet or disappointment <The child's face *fell.*> **6. a.** To be overthrown or conquered. **b.** To suffer ruin or failure. **7.** To slope downward. **8.** To lessen or diminish. **9.** To decline in rank, status, or importance. **10.** To act immorally : err or sin. **11.** To pass into a specific state or situation <*fall* silent><*fall* in love> **12.** To come as if by descending <Night *fell* quickly.> **13.** To happen at a given time or place. **14.** To be allotted or assigned <The worst job *fell* to me.> **15.** To be within the scope or range of something. **16.** To come to rest by chance <My gaze *fell* on the tree.> ★ ***syns:*** DROP, PITCH, PLUNGE, SPILL, SPRAWL, TOPPLE, TUMBLE **—fall back.** To give ground : retreat. **—fall back on (*or* upon).** To resort to. **—fall for.** *Informal.* **1.** To fall in love with. **2.** To be deceived by. **—fall in.** To take one's place in a military formation. **—fall off.** To become less : decrease. **—fall on (*or* upon).** To attack without warning. **—fall out.** To quarrel. **—fall through.** To collapse or fail. *—n.* **1.** An act of falling. **2.** Something that has fallen <a *fall* of snow> **3. a.** An amount that has fallen. **b.** The distance that something falls. **4.** *often* **Fall.** Autumn. **5. falls** *(sing. or pl. in number).* A waterfall. **6.** A hanging article of dress, as a veil or hairpiece. **7.** An overthrow : collapse <the *fall* of a monarchy> **8.** A reduction or decline. **9.** A moral lapse or loss of innocence.
fal•la•cious (fə-lā′shəs) *adj.* **1.** Containing or based on fundamental errors in reasoning. **2.** Misleading : deceptive.
fal•la•cy (făl′ə-sē) *n., pl.* **-cies. 1.** A false notion. **2.** A statement or argument based on a false or invalid inference.
fall•back (fôl′băk′) *n.* **1.** A mechanism for carrying out programmed instructions despite malfunction or failure of the primary device. **2.** Something to which one can retreat or resort.
fall guy *n. Slang.* **1.** A scapegoat. **2.** A gullible victim : dupe.
fal•li•ble (făl′ə-bəl) *adj.* **1.** Capable of making an error. **2.** Apt to be erroneous. **—fal′li•bil′i•ty** *n.* **—fal′li•bly** *adv.*
fall•ing-out (fô′lĭng-out′) *n., pl.* **fall•ings-out** *or* **fall•ing-outs.** A disagreement : quarrel.
falling star *n.* An object, as a meteoroid, often visible as a result of being ignited by atmospheric friction.
fall•off (fôl′ôf′, -ŏf′) *n.* A decrease.
Fal•lo•pi•an tube (fə-lō′pē-ən) *n.* Either of 2 slender ducts through which ova pass from the ovaries to the uterus in the female reproductive system of human beings and higher mammals.
fall•out (fôl′out′) *n.* **1. a.** Slow descent through the atmosphere of minute particles of radioactive debris after a nuclear explosion. **b.** The radioactive debris itself. **2.** An incidental result or side effect.
fal•low (făl′ō) *adj.* **1.** Plowed but left unsown during a growing season. **2.** Marked by inactivity <talents lying *fallow*> **—fal′low** *n.* & *v.* **—fal′low•ness** *n.*
fallow deer *n.* Either of 2 Eurasian deer,

Dama dama or *D. mesopotamica,* having a yellowish coat spotted with white in summer and broad antlers in the male.
false (fôls) *adj.* **fals•er, fals•est. 1.** Being contrary to truth or fact. **2.** Deliberately untrue or deceptive. **3.** Unfaithful : treacherous. **4.** Not real or natural : artificial. **5.** *Mus.* Of incorrect pitch. —*adv.* In a faithless manner. **—false'ly** *adv.* **—false'ness** *n.* **—fal'si•ty** *n.*
false-heart•ed (fôls'här'tĭd) *adj.* Deceitful or disloyal.
false•hood (fôls'ho͝od') *n.* **1.** Inaccuracy. **2.** The act of lying. **3.** A lie.
fal•set•to (fôl-sĕt'ō) *n., pl.* **-tos. 1.** A male singing voice marked by artificially produced tones in an upper register. **2.** A man who sings falsetto. **—fal•set'to** *adv.*
fal•si•fy (fôl'sə-fī') *v.* **-fied, -fy•ing. 1.** To give an untruthful account of. **2. a.** To make false by altering or adding to. **b.** To counterfeit : forge. **—fal'si•fi•ca'tion** *n.* **—fal'si•fi'er** *n.*
fal•ter (fôl'tər) *v.* **1.** To waver : hesitate. **2.** To speak hesitatingly : stammer. **3.** To move, operate, or perform ineptly or unsteadily. —*n.* **1.** Unsteadiness in action or speech. **2.** A faltering sound. **—fal'ter•er** *n.* **—fal'ter•ing•ly** *adv.*
fame (fām) *n.* **1.** Great renown. **2.** Public esteem. **—famed** *adj.*
fa•mil•iar (fə-mĭl'yər) *adj.* **1.** Encountered frequently : common. **2.** Having good knowledge of something. **3.** Of established friendship : intimate. **4.** Informal <lectured in a *familiar* style> **5.** Taking undue liberties : presumptuous. —*n.* **1.** A close friend or associate. **2.** A spirit, often taking animal form, believed to serve esp. a witch. **—fa•mil'iar•ly'** *adv.*
fa•mil•i•ar•i•ty (fə-mĭl'ē-ăr'ĭ-tē) *n., pl.* **-ties. 1.** Acquaintance with or knowledge of something. **2.** Established friendship. **3.** Undue liberty : impropriety.
fa•mil•iar•ize (fə-mĭl'yə-rīz') *v.* **-ized, -iz•ing. 1.** To make familiar, known, or recognized. **2.** To make acquainted with. **—fa•mil'iar•i•za'tion** *n.*
fam•i•ly (făm'ə-lē, făm'lē) *n., pl.* **-lies. 1.** A social unit consisting esp. of a man and woman and their offspring. **2.** A group of people sharing common ancestry. **3.** All the members of a household. **4.** A group of like things : class. **5.** *Biol.* A taxonomic category below an order and above a genus. **—fa•mil'ial** (fə-mĭl'yəl) *adj.*
family tree *n.* **1.** A genealogical diagram of a family. **2.** The ancestors and descendants of a family.
fam•ine (făm'ĭn) *n.* **1.** A drastic, wide-ranging food shortage. **2.** A drastic shortage : dearth. **3.** Severe hunger : starvation.
fam•ish (făm'ĭsh) *v.* To starve or cause to starve. **—fam'ished** *adj.*
fa•mous (fā'məs) *adj.* **1.** Well-known. **2.** *Informal.* Excellent. ★ ***syns:*** CELEBRATED, DISTINGUISHED, EMINENT, FAMED, ILLUSTRIOUS, NOTED, PRE-EMINENT, PROMINENT, RENOWNED **—fa'mous•ly** *adv.*
fan¹ (făn) *n.* **1.** A device for creating a current of air, as a hand-held usu. wedge-shaped, lightweight implement or a machine that rotates thin, rigid vanes. **2.** Something that is similar to an open fan. —*v.* **fanned, fan•ning. 1.** To direct movement of a current of air upon. **2.** To stir up by or as if by fanning. **3.** To spread like a fan. **4.** *Baseball.* To strike out.
fan² (făn) *n. Informal.* An ardent devotee.
fa•nat•ic (fə-năt'ĭk) *n.* One having excessive zeal for and irrational attachment to a cause or position. **—fa•nat'ic, fa•nat'i•cal** *adj.* **—fa•nat'i•cism** *n.*
fan•ci•er (făn'sē-ər) *n.* One having a special enthusiasm for or interest in something, esp. breeding a certain plant or animal <a rose *fancier*><a cat *fancier*>
fan•ci•ful (făn'sĭ-fəl) *adj.* **1.** Created in the fancy : unreal. **2.** Tending to indulge in fancy. **3.** Exhibiting invention or whimsy in design : imaginative. **—fan'ci•ful•ly** *adv.* **—fan'ci•ful•ness** *n.*
fan•cy (făn'sē) *n., pl.* **-cies. 1. a.** Imagination, esp. of a fantastic or whimsical nature. **b.** An image created by the mind. **2.** A capricious notion. **3.** Capricious inclination or liking. **4.** Critical sensibility : taste. ★ ***syns:*** CAPRICE, CONCEIT, HUMOR, IMPULSE, NOTION, VAGARY, WHIM, WHIMSY —*adj.* **-ci•er, -ci•est. 1.** Highly decorated. **2.** Arising in the fancy : capricous. **3.** Skillfully executed. **4.** Of superior grade : fine. **5.** Excessive : exorbitant. —*v.* **-cied, -cy•ing. 1.** To visualize : imagine. **2.** To take a fancy to : like. **3.** To suppose : guess. —*interj.* —Used to express surprise. **—fan'ci•ly** *adv.* **—fan'ci•ness** *n.*
fancy dress *n.* A masquerade costume. **—fan'cy-dress'** *adj.*
fan•cy-free (făn'sē-frē') *adj.* **1.** Carefree. **2.** Not in love : unattached.
fan•cy•work (făn'sē-wûrk') *n.* Decorative needlework.
fan•dan•go (făn-dăng'gō) *n., pl.* **-gos. 1.** An animated Spanish or Spanish-American dance. **2.** Music for a fandango.
fan•fare (făn'fâr') *n.* **1.** A loud trumpet flourish. **2.** A spectacular public display.
fang (făng) *n.* **1.** One of the hollow, grooved teeth with which a poisonous snake injects

fang
(Left) *of a cat and* (right) *of a snake*

its venom. **2.** A long, pointed tooth of a carnivore. **—fanged** *adj.*

fan•jet (făn′jĕt′) *n.* An aircraft equipped with turbojet engines.

fan mail *n.* Mail sent to a public figure by admirers.

fan•tail (făn′tāl′) *n.* **1.** A fanlike tail or end. **2.** Something, as a bird or fish, having a fanlike tail. **—fan′tailed′** *adj.*

fan•ta•sia (făn-tā′zhə, -zhē-ə, făn′tə-zē′ə) *n. Mus.* A composition structured according to the composer's fancy.

fan•ta•size (făn′tə-sīz′) *v.* **-sized, -siz•ing.** To imagine or indulge in fantasies.

fan•tas•tic (făn-tăs′tĭk) *adj.* **1.** Existing only in the fancy **:** unreal. **2. a.** Extravagant. **b.** Bizarre. **3.** Capricious or fancifully eccentric. **4.** *Informal.* Superb **:** wonderful. **—fan•tas′ti•cal•ly** *adv.*

fan•ta•sy (făn′tə-sē, -zē) *n., pl.* **-sies. 1.** Creative imagination. **2.** A creation of the fancy. **3.** A capricious or fantastic idea **:** conceit. **4.** Fiction marked by highly fanciful or supernatural elements. **5.** *Psychol.* An imagined event fulfilling a wish. **6.** *Mus.* A fantasia.

fan•zine (făn′zēn) *n.* An amateur-produced fan magazine.

far (fär) *adv.* **1. a.** To, at, or from a considerable distance. **b.** To a considerable degree **:** much. **2.** To or at a specific distance, degree, or position. **3.** Not at all **:** anything but. **4.** To an advanced point or stage <a student who will go *far*> *—adj.* **1.** At considerable distance. **2.** More distant. **3.** Extensive or lengthy. **4.** Of an extreme nature <the *far* right> ★ ***syns:*** DISTANT, FARAWAY, FAR-OFF, REMOTE, REMOVED **—by far.** To a considerable degree. **—far and away.** By a great margin. **—far and wide.** Everywhere. **—so far. 1.** Up to the present moment. **2.** To a limited degree.

far•ad (făr′əd,-ăd′) *n.* A unit of capacitance equal to that of a capacitor that acquires a charge of 1 coulomb when a potential difference of 1 volt is applied.

far•a•way (făr′ə-wā′) *adj.* **1.** Very distant **:** remote. **2.** Dreamy <a *faraway* look>

farce (färs) *n.* **1.** A theater piece marked by humorous characterizations and improbable plots. **2.** A ludicrous show **:** mockery. **3.** A seasoned stuffing. **—far′ci•cal** *adj.*

fare (fâr) *v.* **fared, far•ing. 1.** To get along. **2.** To turn out **:** go. **3.** To feed on **:** eat. *—n.* **1.** A transportation charge, as for a bus. **2.** A passenger transported for a fee. **3.** Food and drink **:** diet <peasant *fare*> **—far′er** *n.*

fare-thee-well (fâr′thē-wĕl′) *n.* **1.** Perfection. **2.** The most extreme degree.

fare•well (fâr-wĕl′) *interj.* —Used to say good-by. *—n.* **1.** A good-by. **2.** A departure. **—fare′well′** *adj.*

far-fetched (fär′fĕcht′) *adj.* Highly improbable.

far-flung (fär′flŭng′) *adj.* **1.** Widely distributed. **2.** Distant **:** remote.

fa•ri•na (fə-rē′nə) *n.* Fine meal prepared from cereal grain or other plant products, used as a cooked cereal or in puddings.

far•i•na•ceous (făr′ə-nā′shəs) *adj.* **1.** Made from, rich in, or composed of starch. **2.** Powdery or mealy in texture.

farm (färm) *n.* **1.** Land cultivated for agricultural production. **2. a.** Land used for the breeding and raising of domestic animals. **b.** An area of water used for the breeding and raising of a particular type of aquatic animals <a trout *farm*> **3.** *Baseball.* A farm team. *—v.* **1.** To raise livestock or crops as a business. **2.** To use (land or a body of water) for this purpose. **—farm out. 1.** To send (work) from a central point to be done elsewhere. **2.** *Baseball.* To assign (a player) to a minor-league team. **—farm′er** *n.*

farmer cheese *n.* A cheese like cottage cheese but drier and firmer in texture.

farm•house (färm′hous′) *n.* A farm dwelling.

farm•land (färm′lănd′, -lənd) *n.* Land suitable for agricultural production.

farm•stead (färm′stĕd′) *n.* A farm, including its land and buildings.

farm team *n. Baseball.* A minor-league team affiliated with a major-league team for training recruits and maintaining temporarily unneeded players.

farm•yard (färm′yärd′) *n.* An area surrounded by or near farm buildings.

far-off (fär′ôf′, -ŏf′) *adj.* Remote **:** distant.

far-out (fär′out′) *adj. Slang.* Very unconventional.

far•ra•go (fə-rä′gō, -rā′-) *n., pl.* **-goes.** A medley **:** conglomeration.

far-reach•ing (fär′rē′chĭng) *adj.* Having a wide range, influence, or effect.

far•row (făr′ō) *n.* A litter of pigs. *—v.* To produce a farrow.

far•see•ing (fär′sē′ĭng) *adj.* **1.** FAR-SIGHTED 2. **2.** Keen-sighted.

far-sight•ed (fär′sī′tĭd) *adj.* **1.** Able to see objects at a distance better than those that are nearby. **2.** Planning prudently for the future **:** foresighted. **—far-sight′ed•ly** *adv.* **—far-sight′ed•ness** *n.*

far•ther (fär′*th*ər) *adv.* **1.** To or at a greater distance. **2.** In addition. **3.** To a greater extent or degree. *—adj.* **1.** More distant or remote. **2.** Additional.

far•ther•most (fär′*th*ər-mōst′) *adj.* Farthest.

far•thest (fär′*th*ĭst) *adj.* Most distant. *—adv.* To or at the most distant point in space or time.

far•thing (fär′*th*ĭng) *n.* **1.** A former British coin worth ¼ of a penny. **2.** Something of little worth.

far•thin•gale (fär′*th*ĭng-gāl′) *n.* A support, as a hoop, worn by 16th- and 17th-cent. women to make skirts swell out.

fas•ci•nate (făs′ə-nāt′) *v.* **-nat•ed, -nat•ing. 1.** To attract intensely and irresistibly. **2.** To hold motionless **:** spellbind. **—fas′ci•nat′ing•ly** *adv.* **—fas′ci•na′tion** *n.* **—fas′ci•na′tor** *n.*

fas•cism (făsh′ĭz′əm) *n.* A governmental system marked by a centralized dictatorship, stringent socioeconomic controls, and often belligerent nationalism. —**fas'cist** *n.* —**fas·cis'tic** (fə-shĭs'tĭk) *adj.*

fash·ion (făsh'ən) *n.* **1.** The aspect or configuration of something. **2.** Kind : variety. **3.** Manner of performing : way. **4.** Current style or custom. **5.** A piece of clothing in the current style. —*v.* **1.** To make into a given form or shape. **2.** To make fitting : adapt. —**fash'ion·a·ble** *adj.* —**fash'ion·a·ble·ness** *n.* —**fash'ion·a·bly** *adv.*

fast[1] (făst) *adj.* **1.** Rapid : swift. **2.** Performed quickly. **3.** Ahead of the actual time <a *fast* watch> **4.** Suited to rapid travel, as an expressway lane. **5. a.** Dissipated : wild. **b.** Flouting conventional sexual standards. **6.** Resistant <acid-*fast*> **7.** Securely fixed or fastened. **8.** Tightly shut : secure. **9.** Constant and loyal, as friends. **10.** Resistant to fading <*fast* dyes> **11.** Deep and undisturbed <in a *fast* sleep> **12.** Designed for or compatible with a short exposure time <*fast* camera film> —*adv.* **1.** Securely : tightly. **2.** Deeply : soundly <*fast* asleep> **3.** Quickly : rapidly. **4.** In a dissipated, immoderate way <living *fast*> —**fast'ness** *n.*

fast[2] (făst) *v.* To eat sparingly or abstain from all or certain foods. —**fast** *n.*

fast·back (făst'băk') *n.* A car with a downward curving slope from roof to rear.

fast-breed·er reactor (făst'brē'dər) *n.* A breeder reactor that requires high-energy neutrons to produce fissionable material.

fas·ten (făs'ən) *v.* **1.** To join or become joined to something else : connect. **2. a.** To fix securely. **b.** To close or shut. **3.** To focus steadily. —**fas'ten·er** *n.*

fast-food (făst'fo͞od') *adj.* Specializing in foods prepared and served quickly.

fast-for·ward (făst-fôr'wərd) *n.* A function on a tape recorder or player that permits rapid advancement of the tape. —**fast-for'ward** *v.*

fas·tid·i·ous (fă-stĭd'ē-əs, fə-) *adj.* **1.** Meticulously attentive to details. **2.** Difficult to please : exacting. —**fas·tid'i·ous·ly** *adv.* —**fas·tid'i·ous·ness** *n.*

fast-talk (făst'tôk') *v.* To affect or influence, esp. by glib, deceptive talk. —**fast'-talk'er** *n.*

fast-track (făst-trăk) *adj.* High-powered and aggressive <a *fast-track* career> —**fast track** *n.*

fat (făt) *n.* **1. a.** Any of various soft solid or semisolid organic compounds that are energy-rich and occur widely in animal tissue and in the nuts, seeds, and fruits of plants. **b.** The tissue that contains a high proportion of such substances. **2.** Obesity : corpulence. **3.** The most desirable part. **4.** Unnecessary excess. —*adj.* **fat·ter, fat·test. 1.** Having much or too much flesh or fat. **2.** Greasy : oily. **3.** Abounding in desirable elements. **4.** Fertile or productive : rich. **5.** Abundant : ample <a *fat* paycheck> **6.** Thick : large. ★ ***syns:*** CORPULENT, FLESHY, GROSS, OBESE, OVERWEIGHT, PORCINE, PORTLY, STOUT, WEIGHTY —*v.* **fat·ted, fat·ting.** To make or become fat. —**fat'ness** *n.* —**fat'ti·ness** *n.* —**fat'ty** *adj.*

fa·tal (fāt'l) *adj.* **1.** Causing death : deadly. **2.** Causing ruin : disastrous. **3.** Decisively important : fateful. **4.** Affecting one's destiny. —**fa·tal'ly** *adv.*

▲ ***word history:*** The Latin adjective *fatalis,* the source of English *fatal,* meant primarily "destined by fate," but in later Latin it also took on the malign senses of the noun *fatum,* "fate," from which it is derived, and meant "deadly, destructive." English adopted *fatal* with its neutral Latin meaning, though the pejorative sense, "causing ruin or death," has now supplanted the more neutral sense "destined."

fa·tal·ism (fāt'l-ĭz'əm) *n.* The belief that events are predetermined by fate and cannot be altered. —**fa'tal·ist** *n.* —**fa'tal·is'tic** *adj.* —**fa'tal·is'ti·cal·ly** *adv.*

fa·tal·i·ty (fā-tăl'ĭ-tē, fə-) *n., pl.* **-ties. 1.** Death by accident or disaster. **2.** A deadly effect : deadliness. **3.** The quality or state of being doomed to disaster.

fat·back (făt'băk') *n.* The strip of salt-cured fat taken from the upper part of a pork side.

fat cat *n. Slang.* **1.** A wealthy, powerful person. **2.** A rich person who contributes heavily to a political campaign.

fate (fāt) *n.* **1.** The power or force held to predetermine events. **2.** Fortune : lot. **3.** A final result. **4.** Unfortunate destiny : doom. ★ ***syns:*** DESTINY, KISMET, LOT, PORTION, PREDESTINATION

fat·ed (fā'tĭd) *adj.* **1.** Controlled by fate. **2.** Doomed.

fate·ful (fāt'fəl) *adj.* **1.** Decisively significant. **2.** Governed by fate. **3.** Portentous : ominous. **4.** Bringing disaster or death. —**fate'ful·ly** *adv.* —**fate'ful·ness** *n.*

fa·ther (fä'*th*ər) *n.* **1. a.** A male parent. **b.** A child's male ancestor : forefather. **2.** An originator. **3. Father.** GOD. **4. Father.** A priest. —Used esp. as a title. **5.** *often* **Father.** One of the authoritative early Christian writers who formulated doctrines and codified observances. **6.** A venerable elderly man. **7.** A prominent citizen <the city *fathers*> —*v.* **1.** To beget. **2.** To act or serve as a father (to). —**fa'ther·hood'** *n.* —**fa'ther·less** *adj.* —**fa'ther·li·ness** *n.* —**fa'ther·ly** *adj.*

fa·ther-in-law (fä'*th*ər-ĭn-lô') *n., pl.* **fa·thers-in-law.** The father of one's spouse.

fa·ther·land (fä'*th*ər-lănd') *n.* **1.** One's native land. **2.** The native land of one's ancestors.

fath·om (făth'əm) *n., pl.* **-oms** *or* **-om.** A unit of length equal to 6 ft or approx. 1.83 m, used chiefly in measuring marine depths. —*v.* **1.** To determine the depth of : sound. **2.** To understand fully. —**fath'om·a·ble** *adj.*

fath·om·less (făth'əm-lĭs) *adj.* **1.** Too deep to be measured. **2.** Too difficult to understand.

fa·tigue (fə-tēg') *n.* **1.** Extreme weariness from prolonged exertion or stress. **2.** Manual labor assigned to military personnel. **3. fa-**

tigues. Military clothes for heavy work and field duty. —*v.* **-tigued, -tigu•ing.** To make or become tired out : exhaust. —**fat'i•ga•ble** (făt'ĭ-gə-bəl) *adj.*

fat•ten (făt'n) *v.* **1.** To make or become fat. **2.** To increase the amount of.

fatty acid *n.* Any of a class of organic acids obtained from decomposing fat, esp. those of a commercially valuable subgroup derived from animals and plants.

fa•tu•i•ty (fə-to͞o'ĭ-tē, -tyo͞o'-) *n.* Stupidity : absurdity.

fat•u•ous (făch'o͞o-əs) *adj.* Complacently foolish : silly. —**fat'u•ous•ly** *adv.* —**fat'u•ous•ness** *n.*

fau•bourg (fō'bo͝org', fō-bo͝or') *n.* **1.** A suburb, esp. of a French city. **2.** A metropolitan district or quarter in New Orleans.

fau•cet (fô'sĭt) *n.* A fixture for drawing liquid, as from a pipe or cask.

fault (fôlt) *n.* **1.** A defect or impairment : weakness. **2.** A mistake or minor offense. **3.** Responsibility for a mistake or offense : culpability. **4.** *Geol.* A fracture in the earth's crust in which adjoining surfaces are shifted in a direction parallel to the plane of the fracture. **5.** A bad service, as in tennis. —*v.* **1.** To criticize. **2.** To produce a geologic fault (in). **3.** To commit a fault or error. —**fault'i•ly** *adv.* —**fault'less** *adj.* —**fault'less•ly** *adv.* —**fault'y** *adj.*

fault•find•er (fôlt'fīn'dər) *n.* A petty critic. —**fault'find'ing** *n. & adj.*

faun (fôn) *n. Rom. Myth.* A rural deity represented as part goat and part man.

fau•na (fô'nə) *n., pl.* **-nas** *or* **-nae** (-nē'). Animals as a group, esp. of a given time or region. —**fau'nal** *adj.*

Faust (foust) *n.* A legendary German magician who sold his soul to the devil for power and worldly experience.

fau•vism (fō'vĭz'əm) *n.* An art movement marked by the use of flamboyant colors and bold, often distorted forms.

faux (fō) *adj.* Artificial : fake <*faux* pearls>

faux pas (fō pä') *n.,pl.* **faux pas** (fō päz'). A social blunder.

fa•vor (fā'vər) *n.* **1.** A kind or friendly attitude. **2.** A kind act. **3.** An indulgence : privilege. **4. a.** Friendly regard and approval shown esp. by a superior : partiality. **b.** The condition of being held in this regard. **5.** Approval or support : sanction. **6. favors.** Sexual privileges, esp. as granted by a woman. **7.** A token of love or remembrance. **8.** A small gift given to guests at a party. **9.** Advantage : benefit <decided in our *favor*> —*v.* **1.** To oblige kindly. **2.** To like or prefer. **3.** To approve or support. **4.** To facilitate or help. **5.** To look like : resemble. **6.** To treat carefully <*favor* a sore leg> —**fa'vor•er** *n.* —**fa'vor•ing•ly** *adv.*

fa•vor•a•ble (fā'vər-ə-bəl, fāv'rə-) *adj.* **1.** Advantageous : beneficial. **2.** Promising : encouraging. **3.** Approving. —**fa'vor•a•ble•ness** *n.* —**fa'vor•a•bly** *adv.*

fa•vor•ite (fā'vər-ĭt, fāv'rĭt) *n.* **1.** One that is preferred above all others. **2.** One esp. indulged by a superior. **3.** A contestant considered to be the most likely winner. —**fa'vor•ite** *adj.*

favorite son *n.* One favored by his own state delegates for nomination at a national political convention.

fa•vor•it•ism (fā'vər-ĭ-tĭz'əm, fāv'rə-) *n.* A display of often unjust partiality : bias.

fa•vour (fā'vər) *n. & v. esp. Brit. var. of* FAVOR.

fawn[1] (fôn) *n.* **1.** A young deer less than a year old. **2.** A light grayish brown.

fawn[2] (fôn) *v.* **1.** To display slavish affection. **2.** To seek favor by flattery. —**fawn'er** *n.* —**fawn'ing•ly** *adv.*

fax (făks) *n.* FACSIMILE 2. —*v.* To transmit (printed matter or an image) by electronic means.

fay (fā) *n.* A fairy or elf.

faze (fāz) *v.* **fazed, faz•ing.** To disconcert : discompose.

Fe *symbol for* IRON.

fe•al•ty (fē'əl-tē) *n., pl.* **-ties. 1.** Loyalty and allegiance owed to a feudal lord. **2.** Faithfulness.

fear (fîr) *n.* **1. a.** Alarm and agitation caused by expectation or realization of danger. **b.** An example of this feeling. **2.** Reverence : awe. **3.** A state of dread or apprehension <living in *fear*> —*v.* **1.** To be frightened (of). **2.** To be apprehensive (about). **3.** To be in awe of : revere <*fear* God> **4.** To suspect <I *fear* you are mistaken.> —**fear'er** *n.* —**fear'ful** *adj.* —**fear'ful•ly** *adv.* —**fear'ful•ness** *n.* —**fear'less** *adj.* —**fear'less•ly** *adv.* —**fear'less•ness** *n.*

fear•some (fîr'səm) *adj.* **1.** Causing or able to cause fear. **2.** Timid. —**fear'some•ly** *adv.* —**fear'some•ness** *n.*

fea•si•ble (fē'zə-bəl) *adj.* **1.** Able to be accomplished : possible. **2.** Appropriate : suitable. **3.** Likely. —**fea'si•bil'i•ty, fea'si•ble•ness** *n.* —**fea'si•bly** *adv.*

feast (fēst) *n.* **1.** A periodic religious festival. **2.** A large elaborate meal, usu. for many people : banquet. —*v.* **1.** To give a feast for. **2.** To provide with pleasure : delight. **3.** To eat heartily or with pleasure. —**feast'er** *n.*

feat (fēt) *n.* A notable achievement or exploit. ★ ***syns:*** ACHIEVEMENT, EXPLOIT, GEST, MASTERSTROKE, STUNT, TOUR DE FORCE

feath•er (fĕ*th*'ər) *n.* **1.** One of the light hollow-shafted structures that form the external covering of birds. **2. feathers.** Plumage. **3. feathers.** Clothing, esp. finery. **4.** Character : nature. —*v.* **1.** To cover, adorn, or line with feathers. **2.** To fit (an arrow) with a feather. **3.** To turn (an oar blade) horizontal to the surface of the water between strokes. **4.** To alter the pitch of (a propeller) so the blades are parallel with the line of flight. —**a feather in (one's) cap.** A creditable achievement. —**in fine feather.** In an excellent mood or condition. —**feath'er•i•ness** *n.* —**feath'er•less** *adj.* —**feath'er•y** *n.*

feather bed *n.* **1.** A mattress stuffed with feathers. **2.** A bed with a feather mattress.

feath•er•bed•ding (fĕth′ər-bĕd′ĭng) *n.* The practice of requiring an employer to limit production or employ more workers than needed because of safety regulations or union rules. **—feath′er•bed′** *v.*

feath•er•edge (fĕ*th*′ər-ĕj′) *n.* A thin fragile edge, esp. of a board.

feath•er•stitch (fĕ*th*′ər-stĭch′) *n.* An embroidery stitch that produces a decorative zigzag line. **—feath′er•stitch′** *v.*

feath•er•weight (fĕ*th*′ər-wāt′) *n.* **1.** A boxer weighing from 119 to 126 lb. **2.** One of little weight, size, or significance.

fea•ture (fē′chər) *n.* **1. a.** The shape or appearance of the face. **b. features.** The face or its parts. **2.** A conspicuous or distinctive characteristic. **3.** The main film presentation at a theater. **4.** A prominent article in a newspaper or magazine. **5.** A special sales attraction or inducement. *—v.* **-tured, -tur•ing. 1.** To give special attention to **:** publicize. **2.** To have as a characteristic. **3.** To depict the features of.

feb•ri•fuge (fĕb′rə-fyo͞oj′) *n.* A fever-reducing agent.

feb•rile (fĕb′rəl, fē′brəl) *adj.* Of or marked by a fever **:** feverish.

Feb•ru•ar•y (fĕb′ro͞o-ĕr′ē, fĕb′yo͞o-) *n., pl.* **-ies** *or* **-ys.** The 2nd month of the year, having 28 days, 29 in leap years.

fe•ces (fē′sēz) *pl.n.* Bodily waste excreted from the bowels **:** excrement. **—fe′cal** (-kəl) *adj.*

feck•less (fĕk′lĭs) *adj.* **1.** Ineffective **:** weak. **2.** Careless and irresponsible. **—feck′less•ly** *adv.* **—feck′less•ness** *n.*

fe•cund (fē′kənd, fĕk′ənd) *adj.* Productive or fruitful. **—fe•cun′di•ty** *n.*

fe•cun•date (fē′kən-dāt′, fĕk′ən-) *v.* **-dat•ed, -dat•ing.** To fertilize.

fed (fĕd) *v. p.t. & p.p. of* FEED.

fed•er•al (fĕd′ər-əl) *adj.* **1.** Of or designating government in which individual states retain certain controlling powers and are united under a central authority. **2. a.** *often* **Federal.** Of or pertaining to the U.S. central government. **b. Federal.** *Can.* Of or pertaining to the central government of Canada. **3. Federal.** Of or supporting the Union in the American Civil War. *—n.* **Federal.** A soldier or supporter of the Union during the American Civil War. **—fed′er•al•ly** *adv.*

fed•er•al•ism (fĕd′ər-ə-lĭz′əm) *n.* **1.** The doctrine or organizational system of federal government. **2.** Advocacy of this system. **—fed′er•al•ist** *n.*

fed•er•al•ize (fĕd′ər-ə-līz′) *v.* **-ized, -iz•ing. 1.** To join in a federal union. **2.** To put under the control of a federal government. **—fed′er•al•i•za′tion** *n.*

fed•er•ate (fĕd′ə-rāt′) *v.* **-at•ed, -at•ing.** To unite or join, as in a league or federal union. **—fed′e•ra′tion** *n.*

fe•do•ra (fĭ-dôr′ə, -dōr′ə) *n.* A felt hat with a low crown creased lengthwise and a brim that can be turned up or down.

fed up *adj.* Extremely annoyed or disgusted.

fee (fē) *n.* **1.** A fixed charge <tuition *fees*> **2.** A charge for professional service <a lawyer's *fee*> **3.** *Law.* An inherited estate in land. **4.** A fief.

fee•ble (fē′bəl) *adj.* **-bler, -blest. 1.** Without strength **:** weak. **2.** Lacking force **:** ineffective or inadequate. **—fee′ble•ness** *n.* **—fee′bly** *adv.*

fee•ble-mind•ed (fē′bəl-mīn′dĭd) *adj.* Intellectually subnormal. **—fee′ble-mind′ed•ness** *n.*

feed (fēd) *v.* **fed** (fĕd), **feed•ing. 1.** To supply with food or provide as food. **2.** To consume food. **3.** To supply for consumption or use. *—n.* **1.** Food for animals **:** fodder. **2.** *Informal.* A meal. **3. a.** Material fed into a machine. **b.** A device that supplies such material <a paper *feed*> **—feed′er** *n.*

feed•back (fēd′băk′) *n.* **1.** Return of a portion of the output of a process or system to the input. **2. a.** Return of data about the result of a process, esp. for correction or control. **b.** The data so returned.

feed•lot (fēd′lŏt′) *n.* A place where livestock are fattened for market.

feed•stock (fēd′stŏk′) *n.* The raw materials required for an industrial process.

feed•stuff (fēd′stŭf′) *n.* FEED 1.

feel (fēl) *v.* **felt** (fĕlt), **feel•ing. 1. a.** To perceive through the sense of touch. **b.** To perceive as a physical sensation <*feel* a dull pain><*feel* the heat> **2. a.** To touch. **b.** To examine by touching. **3. a.** To undergo the experience of. **b.** To be aware of **:** sense. **c.** To suffer from emotionally. **4.** To believe **:** consider. **5.** To have compassion or pity. *—n.* **1.** Perception by touching <the *feel* of velvet> **2.** The sense of touch. **3.** The nature, state, or quality of something perceived through or as if through touch <the *feel* of a new sports car>

feel•er (fē′lər) *n.* **1.** An exploratory remark or suggestion. **2.** A sensory or tactile organ, as an antenna, tentacle, or barbel.

feel•ing (fē′lĭng) *n.* **1. a.** The sensation involving tactile perception. **b.** A sensation perceived by touch. **c.** A physical sensation. **2. a.** Emotion, esp. compassion or sympathy. **b. feelings.** Sensibilities <You hurt my *feelings.*> **3. a.** A mental awareness. **b.** A distinct mood or impression. **4. a.** Opinion **:** belief. **b.** Sentiment. **5.** Intuitive cognition **:** hunch. **6.** Emotional and intuitive awareness. **7.** An aptitude **:** bent. *—adj.* **1. a.** Exhibiting emotional sensitivity. **b.** Easily moved emotionally. **2.** Expressing sympathy. **—feel′ing•ly** *adv.*

feet (fēt) *n. pl. of* FOOT.

feign (fān) *v.* **1.** To give a false appearance (of). **2.** To dissemble **:** pretend.

feint (fānt) *n.* A misleading movement intended to draw defensive action away from the real target. **—feint** *v.*

†**feist** (fīst) *n. Regional.* A small mongrel dog.

†**feist•y** (fī′stē) *adj.* **-i•er, -i•est. 1.** *Regional.* Touchy **:** quarrelsome. **2.** Spirited **:** plucky.

feld•spar (fĕld′spär′, fĕl′-) *n.* Any of a large

group of minerals consisting largely of silicates that occur principally in igneus, plutonic, and some metamorphic rocks.

fe·lic·i·tate (fĭ-lĭs'ĭ-tāt') *v.* **-tat·ed, -tat·ing.** To wish happiness to : congratulate. —**fe·lic'i·ta'tion** *n.* —**fe·lic'i·ta'tor** *n.*

fe·lic·i·tous (fĭ-lĭs'ĭ-təs) *adj.* **1.** Well-chosen : apt. **2.** Agreeable in manner or style. —**fe·lic'i·tous·ly** *adv.* —**fe·lic'i·tous·ness** *n.*

fe·lic·i·ty (fĭ-lĭs'ĭ-tē) *n., pl.* **-ties. 1.** Blissful happiness. **2.** A cause of bliss. **3.** An apt style or manner of expression or an instance of it.

fe·line (fē'līn') *adj.* **1.** Of or relating to the family Felidae, including wild and domestic cats and related animals such as lions and tigers. **2.** Like a cat, as in stealth or agility. —**fe'line'** *n.* —**fe'line'ly** *adv.* —**fe'line'ness, fe·lin'i·ty** (fĭ-lĭn'ĭ-tē) *n.*

fell[1] (fĕl) *v.* **1.** To cut or knock down. **2.** To kill. **3.** To sew or finish (a seam) with the raw edges turned under and stitched down. —**fell'a·ble** *adj.* —**fell'er** *n.*

fell[2] (fĕl) *adj.* **1.** Fierce and cruel. **2.** Lethal. —**fell'ness** *n.*

fell[3] (fĕl) *n.* An animal's hide : pelt.

fell[4] (fĕl) *v. p.t. of* FALL.

fel·lah (fĕl'ə) *n., pl.* **-lahs** *or* **fel·la·hin** (fĕl'ə-hēn') *or* **-la·heen.** A peasant or agricultural laborer in Arab countries.

fel·low (fĕl'ō) *n.* **1.** A man or boy. **2.** *Informal.* A boyfriend. **3.** A comrade : associate. **4.** An equal : peer. **5.** One of a pair : counterpart. **6.** A member of a scientific or literary society. **7.** A recipient of a stipend for graduate study. —*adj.* Sharing certain characteristics, interests, or pursuits.

fel·low·ship (fĕl'ō-shĭp') *n.* **1.** Friendly relationship : companionship. **2.** A union of peers or friends : fraternity. **3. a.** A graduate scholarship or grant. **b.** A foundation awarding such scholarships or grants.

fel·on[1] (fĕl'ən) *n.* A perpetrator of a felony.

fel·on[2] (fĕl'ən) *n.* A festering inflammation near the end of a finger or toe.

fel·o·ny (fĕl'ə-nē) *n., pl.* **-nies.** A serious crime, as murder, rape, or burglary, punishable by a severe sentence. —**fe·lo'ni·ous** *adj.* —**fe·lo'ni·ous·ly** *adv.* —**fe·lo'ni·ous·ness** *n.*

felt[1] (fĕlt) *n.* **1.** A fabric made of matted, pressed animal fibers, as fur or wool. **2.** A fabric or material resembling felt. —*v.* **1.** To make into or become like felt. **2.** To press or mat together.

felt[2] (fĕlt) *v. p.t. & p.p. of* FEEL.

fe·male (fē'māl') *adj.* **1. a.** Of, relating to, typical of, or designating the sex that produces ova or bears young. **b.** Consisting of members of the female sex. **c.** Suitable to the female sex : feminine. **2.** *Bot.* **a.** Relating to or designating an organ, as a pistil, that produces seeds or spores after fertilization. **b.** Having pistils but not stamens. **3.** Having a hollow part designed to receive a projecting part, as a plug or prong. —**fe'male'** *n.* —**fe'male'ness** *n.*

▲ ***word history:*** The word *female* is unrelated to the word *male. Female* is a respelling of *femelle,* which is ult. from Latin *femella,* a diminutive of *femina,* "woman." After its adoption into English from French in the 15th cent., *femelle* was used primarily as an adjective. This circumstance led to the respelling of the word as *femal,* where *-al* was regarded as the adjectival suffix. The spelling *femal,* as well as the word's obvious correlation with the word *male,* suggested an etymological association with the word *male.* This error has been preserved in the now standard modern spelling *female.*

fem·i·nine (fĕm'ə-nĭn) *adj.* **1.** Of or designating the female sex. **2.** Characterized by or possessing qualities gen. attributed to women. **3.** Of or designating the class of words or grammatical forms referring chiefly to females. —*n.* **1.** The feminine gender. **2.** A word or form of the feminine gender. —**fem'i·nine·ly** *adv.* —**fem'i·nin'i·ty** *n.*

fem·i·nism (fĕm'ə-nĭz'əm) *n.* **1.** Advocacy of the political and socioeconomic equality of men and women. **2.** The movement supporting feminism. —**fem'i·nist** *n.* —**fem'i·nis'tic** *adj.*

femme fa·tale (fĕm' fə-tăl', -täl', făm') *n., pl.* **femmes fa·tales** (fĕm' fə-tăl', -tălz', -täl', -tälz', făm'). A charming or seductive woman.

fe·mur (fē'mər) *n., pl.* **-murs** *or* **fem·o·ra** (fĕm'ər-ə). **1.** The bone of the vertebrate lower or hind limb, located between the pelvis and knee in humans. **2.** The human thigh. —**fem'o·ral** (fĕm'ər-əl) *adj.*

fen (fĕn) *n.* Low, marshy land : bog.

fence (fĕns) *n.* **1.** A structure that functions as a boundary or barrier, usu. constructed of posts, boards, wire, or rails. **2.** *Slang.* **a.** A recipient and seller of stolen goods. **b.** A place where such goods are sold. —*v.* **fenced, fenc·ing. 1.** To surround, close in, or separate by or as if by a fence. **2.** To engage in the art or sport of fencing. **3.** To be evasive : hedge. **4.** *Slang.* To receive and sell stolen goods. —**on the fence.** *Informal.* Undecided or neutral. —**fenc'er** *n.*

fenc·ing (fĕn'sĭng) *n.* **1.** The art or sport of using a foil, épée, or saber. **2.** Material used in building fences.

fend (fĕnd) *v.* **1.** To keep or ward off. **2.** To manage without help.

fend·er (fĕn'dər) *n.* A protective device, as a guard over the wheel of a vehicle or a fireplace screen.

fen·es·tra·tion (fĕn'ə-strā'shən) *n.* Design and position of windows and doors in a building.

fen·nel (fĕn'əl) *n.* A native Eurasian plant, *Foeniculum vulgare,* with an edible stalk and aromatic seeds used as flavoring.

fe·ral (fîr'əl, fĕr'-) *adj.* **1. a.** Existing in an untamed state. **b.** Having returned to a wild state from domestication. **2.** Of or like a wild animal : savage.

fer-de-lance (fĕr'də-lăns') *n.* A venomous tropical American snake, *Bothrops atrox,* with brown and gray markings.

fer·ment (fûr'mĕnt') *n.* **1.** Something, as a

yeast, mold, or enzyme, that causes fermentation. **2.** Great agitation or unrest. —*v.* (fər-mĕnt′). **1.** To undergo or subject to fermentation. **2.** To agitate **:** excite. **—fer•ment′a•bil′i•ty** *n.* **—fer•ment′a•ble** *adj.* **—fer•ment′er** *n.*

fer•men•ta•tion (fûr′mĕn-tā′shən) *n.* **1.** Chemical decomposition of complex organic compounds into simpler substances, esp. the process by which yeasts convert sugar to carbon dioxide and alcohol in the absence of oxygen. **2.** Great agitation **:** commotion.

fer•mi•um (fûr′mē-əm) *n. Symbol* **Fm** A synthetic metallic radioactive element.

fern (fûrn) *n.* Any of numerous flowerless and seedless plants of the class Filicinae that have fronds with divided leaflets and reproduce by spores. **—fern′y** *adj.*

fe•ro•cious (fə-rō′shəs) *adj.* **1.** Very fierce and cruel, as a wild animal. **2.** Extremely intense <a *ferocious* storm> **—fe•ro′cious•ly** *adv.* **—fe•ro′cious•ness, fe•roc′i•ty** (fə-rŏs′ĭ-tē) *n.*

fer•ret (fĕr′ĭt) *n.* **1.** A domesticated, usu. albino form of the Old World polecat, often trained to hunt rodents or rabbits. **2.** A related North American mammal, *Mustela nigripes,* with yellowish fur. —*v.* **1.** To hunt with ferrets. **2.** To drive out **:** expel. **3.** To uncover and bring forward by searching, as a secret. **4.** To search intensively. **—fer′ret•er** *n.*

fer•ric (fĕr′ĭk) *adj.* Of, pertaining to, or containing iron, esp. with valence 3.

ferric oxide *n.* A dark compound occurring as hematite ore and rust.

Fer•ris wheel *also* **fer•ris wheel** (fĕr′ĭs) *n.* A large upright, power-driven wheel with suspended compartments in which passengers ride for amusement.

fer•ro•mag•net•ic (fĕr′ō-măg-nĕt′ĭk) *adj.* Relating to or typical of substances, as iron and nickel, that are readily magnetized. **—fer′ro•mag′ne•tism** *n.*

fer•rous (fĕr′əs) *adj.* Of, pertaining to, or containing iron, esp. with valence 2.

fer•rule (fĕr′əl, -o͞ol′) *n.* A ring or cap at or near the end of a wooden handle or cane to reinforce it or prevent splitting.

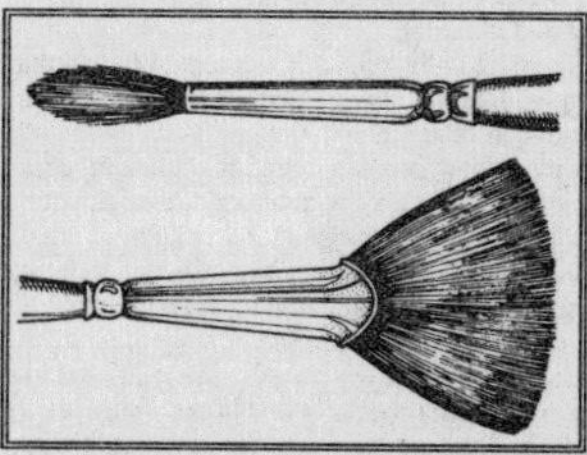

ferrule

fer•ry (fĕr′ē) *v.* **-ried, -ry•ing. 1.** To move or carry by boat across a body of water. **2.** To cross on or as if on a ferry. **3.** To carry from one point to another, esp by aircraft <*ferried* supplies to the troops on the front line> —*n., pl.* **-ries. 1.** A ferryboat. **2.** The embarkation point for a ferryboat. **3.** The transporting of something, esp. an aircraft, under its own power to its end user.

fer•ry•boat (fĕr′ē-bōt′) *n.* A boat used to transport passengers or goods.

fer•tile (fûr′tl) *adj.* **1.** *Biol.* **a.** Able to reproduce. **b.** Able to initiate, sustain, or support reproduction. **2.** Rich in material required to maintain plant growth <*fertile* farm land> **3.** Characterized by great productivity **:** prolific <a *fertile* intellect> ★ ***syns:*** FECUND, FRUITFUL, PRODUCTIVE, PROLIFIC, RICH **—fer′tile•ly** *adv.* **—fer•til′i•ty, fer′tile•ness** *n.*

fer•til•ize (fûr′tl-īz′) *v.* **-ized, -iz•ing. 1.** To begin biological reproduction esp. by supplying with sperm or pollen. **2.** To make fertile, as by adding fertilizer. **—fer′til•iz′a•ble** *adj.* **—fer′til•i•za′tion** *n.*

fer•til•iz•er (fûr′tl-ī′zər) *n.* One that fertilizes, esp. a material such as manure, compost, or a chemical compound added to increase soil fertility.

fer•ule (fĕr′əl, -o͞ol′) *n.* A baton, stick, or cane used to punish children.

fer•vent (fûr′vənt) *adj.* **1.** Ardent **:** passionate. **2.** Very hot. **—fer′ven•cy, fer′vent•ness** *n.* **—fer′vent•ly** *adv.*

fer•vid (fûr′vĭd) *adj.* **1.** Intensely fervent **:** impassioned. **2.** Very hot. **—fer′vid•ly** *adv.* **—fer′vid•ness** *n.*

fer•vor (fûr′vər) *n.* **1.** Emotional intensity **:** ardor. **2.** Intense heat.

fer•vour (fûr′vər) *n. esp. Brit. var. of* FERVOR.

fes•cue (fĕs′kyo͞o) *n.* Any of various grasses of the genus *Festuca,* often cultivated as pasturage.

fes•tal (fĕs′təl) *adj.* FESTIVE 1. **—fes′tal•ly** *adv.*

fes•ter (fĕs′tər) *v.* **1.** To generate pus **:** suppurate. **2.** To be or become a source of resentment or irritation **:** rankle.

fes•ti•val (fĕs′tə-vəl) *n.* **1.** A regularly recurring occasion of religious feasting or special ceremonies. **2.** A season or series of related cultural events <an art *festival*> **3.** Conviviality **:** revelry.

fes•tive (fĕs′tĭv) *adj.* **1.** Of, relating, or appropriate to a feast or festival. **2.** Merry **:** joyous. **—fes′tive•ly** *adv.* **—fes′tive•ness** *n.*

fes•tiv•i•ty (fĕ-stĭv′ĭ-tē) *n., pl.* **-ties. 1.** A joyous celebration **:** festival. **2. festivities.** The proceedings or events of a festival. **3.** The gaiety of a festival.

fes•toon (fĕ-sto͞on′) *n.* **1.** A string or garland hung in a loop between 2 points. **2.** An ornamental festoon, as in sculpture. —*v.* **1.** To decorate with or as if with festoons. **2.** To make festoons. **—fes•toon′er•y** *n.*

fet•a (fĕt′ə, fē′tə) *n.* A white semisoft Greek cheese made usu. of goat's or ewe's milk and preserved in brine.

fe•tal *also* **foe•tal** (fēt′l) *adj.* Of, relating to, or like a fetus.

fetal position *n.* A bodily position at rest in which the spine is curved, the head is bowed forward, and the arms and legs are drawn in toward the chest.

fetch (fĕch) *v.* **1.** To go after and return with. **2.** To cause to come forth, as tears. **3.** To bring as a price : sell for. **4.** To strike (a blow). **—fetch'er** *n.*

fetch•ing (fĕch'ĭng) *adj. Informal.* Very attractive. **—fetch'ing•ly** *adv.*

fete *also* **fête** (fāt, fĕt) *n.* **1.** A feast or festival. **2.** An elaborate outdoor entertainment. —*v.* **fet•ed, fet•ing.** To honor with a fete.

fet•id (fĕt'ĭd, fē'tĭd) *adj.* Malodorous. **—fet'id•ly** *adv.* **—fet'id•ness** *n.*

fet•ish (fĕt'ĭsh) *n.* **1.** An object believed to have magical powers, esp. of protection. **2.** An object of unreasonably obsessive attention or regard <made a *fetish* of cleanliness> **3.** A nonsexual object that arouses or gratifies sexual desire. **—fet'ish•ism** *n.* **—fet'ish•ist** *n.* **—fet'ish•is'tic** *adj.*

fet•lock (fĕt'lŏk') *n.* A projection above and behind the hoof of a horse or related animal marked by a tuft of hair.

fe•tol•o•gy (fē-tŏl'ə-jē) *n.* Medical study of a fetus. **—fe•tol'o•gist** *n.*

fe•tos•co•py (fē-tŏs'kə-pē) *n.* Examination of a fetus in the uterus by insertion of a fiber-optic device into the amniotic cavity. **—fe'to•scope'** (fē'tə-skōp') *n.*

fet•ter (fĕt'ər) *n.* **1.** A shackle or chain attached to the ankles, used as a restraint. **2. fetters.** A restriction : restraint. —*v.* **1.** To put fetters on : shackle. **2.** To restrict the freedom of.

fet•tle (fĕt'l) *n.* Condition : emotional state <in fine *fettle*>

fet•tuc•ci•ne (fĕt'ə-chē'nē) *n.* Narrow strips of pasta.

fe•tus *also* **foe•tus** (fē'təs) *n.* The unborn young of a mammal from the time the major features of its body have appeared; esp. in humans, the unborn young after the 8th week of development.

feud (fyo͞od) *n.* A bitter, prolonged quarrel, as between families. **—feud** *v.*

feu•dal (fyo͞od'l) *adj.* Of, relating to, or characteristic of feudalism. **—feu'dal•ize'** *v.* **—feu'dal•ly** *adv.*

feu•dal•ism (fyo͞od'l-ĭz'əm) *n.* A medieval European political and economic system based on vassalage. **—feu'dal•ist** *n.* **—feu'dal•is'tic** *adj.*

feu•da•to•ry (fyo͞o'də-tôr'ē, -tōr'ē) *n., pl.* **-ries. 1.** One who holds a feudal fee : vassal. **2.** A feudal fee. —*adj.* Owing feudal homage or allegiance.

fe•ver (fē'vər) *n.* **1.** Abnormally high body temperature. **2.** A disease characterized by an abnormally high body temperature. **3.** Heightened activity or emotion. **4.** A craze. **—fe'ver•ish** *adj.* **—fe'ver•ish•ly** *adv.* **—fe'ver•ish•ness** *n.*

fever blister *n.* A cold sore.

few (fyo͞o) *adj.* Amounting to or made up of a small number. —*n. (pl. in number).* **1.** An indefinitely small number <Only a *few* remained.> **2.** A select or limited group <the discerning *few*> —*pron. (pl. in number).* A small number.

fey (fā) *adj.* **1.** Having visionary power : clairvoyant. **2.** Seemingly spellbound.

fez (fĕz) *n., pl.* **fez•zes.** A man's felt cap shaped like a flat-topped cone, usu. red with a black tassel hanging from the crown.

fi•an•cé (fē'än-sā', fē-än'sā') *n.* A man engaged to be married.

fi•an•cée (fē'än-sā', fē-än'sā') *n.* A woman engaged to be married.

fi•as•co (fē-ăs'kō, -äs'-) *n., pl.* **-coes** *or* **-cos.** A total failure.

fi•at (fē'ät', fī'ăt', -ət) *n.* An authoritative and often arbitrary decree.

fib (fĭb) *n.* A trivial lie. —*v.* **fibbed, fib•bing.** To tell a fib. **—fib'ber** *n.*

fi•ber (fī'bər) *n.* **1.** A slender, elongated structure, as of plant or animal tissue or of synthetic material. **2.** A group of fibers that form a single substance, as muscle or flax. **3.** Internal strength : character. **—fi'brous** (fī'brəs) *adj.*

fi•ber•board (fī'bər-bôrd', -bōrd') *n.* A building material made of plant fibers, as wood, compressed into rigid sheets.

Fi•ber•glas (fī'bər-glăs'). A trademark for a type of fiber glass.

fiber glass *n.* A material composed of glass fibers in resin.

fiber optics *n. (sing. in number).* The optics of light transmission through very fine, flexible glass rods by internal reflection. **—fi'ber-op'tic** *adj.*

fi•ber•scope (fī'bər-skōp') *n.* A flexible fiber-optic instrument used to view otherwise inaccessible objects.

fi•bre (fī'bər) *n. esp. Brit. var. of* FIBER.

fi•bril (fī'brəl, fĭb'rəl) *n.* A small, slender fiber. **—fi'bril•lar** *adj.*

fib•ril•la•tion (fĭb'rə-lā'shən, fī'brə-) *n.* Rapid irregular contractions of the muscle fibers of the cardiac ventricles.

fi•brin (fī'brĭn) *n.* An insoluble protein formed from fibrinogen in blood clotting.

fi•brin•o•gen (fī-brĭn'ə-jən) *n.* A blood plasma protein that is converted to fibrin in blood clotting.

fi•broid (fī'broid') *adj.* Resembling or made up of fibrous tissue. —*n.* A benign tumor of smooth muscle.

fi•bro•ma (fī-brō'mə) *n., pl.* **-mas** *or* **-ma•ta** (-mə-tə). A benign, usu. enclosed tumor of primarily fibrous tissue.

fi•bro•vas•cu•lar (fī'brō-văs'kyə-lər) *adj.* Having both fibrous and vascular tissue, as in the woody tissue of plants.

fib•u•la (fĭb'yə-lə) *n., pl.* **-lae** (-lē') *or* **-las.** The smaller outer vertebrate bone of the lower limb or hind leg, in humans between the knee and ankle.

–fic *suff.* Causing : making <sopori*fic*>

–fication *suff.* Production : making <grati*fication*>

fiche (fēsh) *n.* A microfiche.

fi·chu (fĭsh′o͞o, fē′sho͞o) *n.* A woman's lightweight triangular scarf, worn over the shoulders and fastened loosely in front.

fick·le (fĭk′əl) *adj.* Erratically changeable : capricious. —**fick′le·ness** *n.*

fic·tion (fĭk′shən) *n.* **1.** A creation of the imagination. **2. a.** A literary work whose content is produced by the imagination and is not necessarily based on fact. **b.** The category of literature comprising works of this kind, including novels, short stories, and plays. —**fic′tion·al** *adj.*

fic·ti·tious (fĭk-tĭsh′əs) *adj.* **1.** Imaginary : nonexistent. **2.** Deliberately deceptive : false <a *fictitious* address> —**fic·ti′tious·ly** *adv.* —**fic·ti′tious·ness** *n.*

fic·tive (fĭk′tĭv) *adj.* **1.** Relating to or being fiction : fictional. **2.** Not genuine : sham.

fid·dle (fĭd′l) *n. Informal.* A violin. —*v.* **-dled, -dling. 1.** *Informal.* To play the violin. **2. a.** To fidget. **b.** To putter. **3.** To tinker or tamper with. —**fid′dler** *n.*

fiddler crab *n.* A burrowing crab of the genus *Uca,* the male having a greatly enlarged anterior claw.

fid·dle·sticks (fĭd′l-stĭks′) *interj.* —Used to express mild annoyance.

fi·del·i·ty (fĭ-dĕl′ĭ-tē, fī-) *n., pl.* **-ties. 1.** Loyalty : faithfulness. **2.** Exact correspondence to truth or fact : accuracy. **3.** The degree to which an electronic system reproduces distortion-free sound.

fidg·et (fĭj′ĭt) *v.* To move or cause to move nervously or restlessly. —*n.* **fidgets.** Nervousness or restlessness. —**fidg′et·er** *n.* —**fidg′et·i·ness** *n.* —**fidg′et·y** *adj.*

fi·du·ci·ar·y (fĭ-do͞o′shē-ĕr′ē, -dyo͞o′-, fī-) *adj.* **1.** Relating to or involving the holding of something in trust. **2.** Held in trust. —*n., pl.* **-ies.** A fiduciary agent : trustee.

fie (fī) *interj.* —Used to express disgust or unpleasant surprise.

fief (fēf) *n.* A feudal estate in land : fee.

fief·dom (fēf′dəm) *n.* **1.** The estate of a feudal lord. **2.** Something over which one person or group exercises control.

field (fēld) *n.* **1.** A broad, level, open expanse of land. **2.** A cultivated expanse of land devoted to the growing of a given crop. **3.** A formation of land that contains a specified natural resource <a natural gas *field*> **4.** An airport or airfield. **5.** A background area, as on a flag or painting. **6. a.** An area in which a sports event takes place : stadium. **b.** All the contestants or participants in an event. **7. a.** An area of activity, knowledge, or interest. **b.** One's profession or employment. **c.** A setting of practical activity or application. **8.** A battle or battlefield. **9.** *Physics.* A region of space marked by a physical property, as electromagnetic force, with a determinable value at each point in the region. —*v.* **1.** To retrieve (a ball) and perform the required maneuver, esp. in baseball. **2.** To place (a sports team) in a contest. **3.** To respond to <*fielded* some tough questions> —**field′er** *n.*

field day *n.* **1.** A day for a given outdoor activity, as athletic competition, nature study, etc. **2.** *Informal.* A time of great pleasure, activity, or opportunity.

field event *n.* A throwing and jumping event of a track meet.

field glass *n. often* **field glasses.** A portable binocular instrument for viewing distant objects.

field hockey *n.* HOCKEY 2.

field magnet *n.* A magnet that supplies a magnetic field in an electrical device such as a generator or motor.

field marshal *n.* A European army officer usu. ranking just below the commander-in-chief.

field mouse *n.* A small mouse, as of the genera *Apodemus* or *Microtus,* inhabiting fields and meadows.

field of force *n.* A spatial region throughout which the force of a single agent, as an electric current, is operative.

field-test (fēld′tĕst′) *v.* To test in natural operating conditions. —**field test** *n.*

field trip *n.* A group excursion for firsthand observation, as to a museum, woods, or historical place.

fiend (fēnd) *n.* **1.** An evil spirit : demon. **2.** A diabolically evil person. **3.** *Informal.* An addict <a dope *fiend*> **4.** One totally engrossed in something <a sports *fiend*> —**fiend′ish** *adj.* —**fiend′ish·ly** *adv.* —**fiend′ish·ness** *n.*

fierce (fîrs) *adj.* **fierc·er, fierc·est. 1.** Savage and violent in nature : ferocious. **2.** Extremely severe : terrible <a *fierce* hurricane> **3.** Very ardent or intense <*fierce* dedication> **4.** *Informal.* Very difficult or disagreeable <a *fierce* exam> —**fierce′ly** *adv.* —**fierce′ness** *n.*

fier·y (fīr′ē, fī′ə-rē) *adj.* **-i·er, -i·est. 1. a.** Consisting of or containing fire. **b.** Blazing or glowing. **2.** Hot and inflamed <a *fiery* sunburn> **3. a.** Full of spirit or intense emotion. **b.** Volatile : tempestuous <a *fiery* temper> —**fier′i·ness** *n.*

fi·es·ta (fē-ĕs′tə) *n.* A festival or religious holiday.

fife (fīf) *n.* A small musical instrument like a flute but having a higher range.

fif·teen (fĭf-tēn′) *n.* **1.** The cardinal number equal to 14 + 1. **2.** The 15th in a set or sequence. —**fif·teen′** *adj. & pron.* —**fif·teenth′** *n. & adj. & adv.*

fifth (fĭfth) *n.* **1.** The ordinal number matching the number 5 in a series. **2.** One of 5 equal parts. **3.** ⅕ of a gallon or ⅘ of a quart of liquor. **4. Fifth.** The Fifth Amendment. —**fifth** *adj. & adv.*

Fifth Amendment *n.* An amendment to the U.S. Constitution, ratified in 1791, stating that no one may be forced to testify as a witness against himself or herself.

fifth column *n.* A secret organization that operates inside a country to further an enemy's military and political aims. —**fifth columnist** *n.*

fifth wheel *n.* One that is superfluous.

fif·ty (fĭf′tē) *n.* The cardinal number equal to

5 × 10. **—fif'ti•eth** *n. & adj. & adv.* **—fif'ty** *adj. & pron.*

fif•ty-fif•ty (fĭf'tē-fĭf'tē) *adj. Informal.* Divided in 2 equal portions <a *fifty-fifty* split> **—fif'ty-fif'ty** *adv.*

fig (fĭg) *n.* **1.** A tree or shrub of the genus *Ficus,* native to the Mediterranean region, bearing sweet pear-shaped, edible fruit. **2.** A trivial amount <didn't care a *fig*>

fight (fīt) *v.* **fought** (fôt), **fight•ing. 1.** To take part in combat. **2.** To contend (with) : struggle. **3.** To argue : quarrel. **4.** To participate in boxing or wrestling (against). **5.** To try to prevent or oppose (e.g., a cold). **6.** To wage (a battle). **7.** To make (one's way) by or as if by combat. *—n.* **1.** A battle. **2.** A conflict or struggle. **3.** A boxing or wrestling match. **4.** Tendency or power to fight <The *fight* had all gone out of them.>

fight•er (fī'tər) *n.* **1.** One that fights. **2.** A boxer or wrestler. **3.** A fast, maneuverable aircraft used in combat.

fig•ment (fĭg'mənt) *n.* An invention or fabrication.

fig•u•ra•tive (fĭg'yər-ə-tĭv) *adj.* **1.** Based on or using a figure of speech : metaphorical. **2.** Represented by a figure or symbol : emblematic. **—fig'ur•a•tive•ly** *adv.*

fig•ure (fĭg'yər) *n.* **1.** A written or printed symbol representing something other than a letter, esp. a numeral. **2. figures.** Mathematical calculations. **3.** An amount shown in numbers. **4.** Outline, form, or silhouette. **5.** Human shape or form. **6.** An individual, esp. a famous person. **7.** The impression a person makes <a pathetic *figure*> **8. a.** A diagram. **b.** A design or pattern. **9.** A group of dance steps. **10.** A figure of speech. *—v.* **-ured, -ur•ing. 1.** To compute. **2.** To represent : depict. **3.** To ornament with a design. **4.** *Informal.* **a.** To believe <didn't *figure* that it would happen> **b.** To interpret or regard <*figured* them for liars and cheats> **5.** To be a part of or have importance.

figure eight *n.* A figure, as an ice-skating maneuver, shaped like an 8.

fig•ure•head (fĭg'yər-hĕd') *n.* **1.** A person with nominal leadership but no actual authority. **2.** A carved figure on a ship's prow.

figure of speech *n.* An expression, as a metaphor or hyperbole, in which words are used in a nonliteral way for a forceful, dramatic, or illuminating effect.

fig•u•rine (fĭg'yə-rēn') *n.* A small molded or sculptured figure : statuette.

fil•a•ment (fĭl'ə-mənt) *n.* **1.** A thin, finely spun thread, fiber, or wire. **2.** A fine wire enclosed in an electric lamp bulb and heated electrically to incandescence. **—fil'a•men'ta•ry** *adj.* **—fil'a•men'tous** *adj.*

fil•bert (fĭl'bərt) *n.* The edible nut of a Eurasian hazel, *Corylus maxima.*

filch (fĭlch) *v.* To steal. **—filch'er** *n.*

file[1] (fīl) *n.* **1.** A receptacle that keeps loose objects, esp. papers, in proper order. **2.** A collection of objects arranged in or as if in a file. **3.** A line of persons, animals, or things each behind the other. *—v.* **filed, fil•ing. 1.** To arrange or keep in order. **2.** To enter (e.g., a document) on public official record. **3.** To send (copy) to a publication. **4.** To move in a line.

▲ ***word history:*** The various senses of the noun *file*[1] are derived from 2 different French words that ult. have the same etymology. French *file,* "line of soldiers," is the source of English *file* meaning "line." French *fil,* "thread," is the source of English *file* meaning "a receptacle for papers or documents." This sense developed in English from the practice of keeping papers in order by threading them on string or wire. The word has been extended to various filing systems of all kinds. Both French words, *fil* and *file,* are derived from Latin *filum,* "thread."

file[2] (fīl) *n.* A steel tool with hardened ridged surfaces, used in smoothing, polishing, boring, or grinding down. *—v.* **filed, fil•ing.** To smooth, polish, grind, or remove with or as if with a file.

file clerk *n.* An employee who maintains the files and records of an office.

fi•let[1] (fĭ-lā', fĭl'ā') *n.* Net or lace with a pattern of squares.

fi•let[2] (fĭ-lā', fĭl'ā') *n. & v. var. of* FILLET 2.

fi•let mi•gnon (fĭl'ā mēn-yŏɴ', fĭ-lā') *n.* A small, tender cut of beef from the loin.

fil•i•al (fĭl'ē-əl) *adj.* Of, relating to, or appropriate for a son or daughter <a *filial* duty to one's parents>

fil•i•bus•ter (fĭl'ə-bŭs'tər) *n.* Use of obstructionist tactics, as prolonged speechmaking, to prevent or hinder legislative action. **—fil'i•bus'ter** *v.* **—fil'i•bus'ter•er** *n.*

fil•i•gree (fĭl'ə-grē') *n.* Intricate lacelike ornamental work from silver or gold fine twisted wire. **—fil'i•gree'** *v. & adj.*

fil•ing (fī'lĭng) *n. often* **filings.** A shaving scraped off with a file.

Fil•i•pi•no (fĭl'ə-pē'nō) *n., pl.* **-nos. 1.** A native or inhabitant of the Philippines. **2.** The official language of the Philippines. **—Fil'i•pi'no** *adj.*

fill (fĭl) *v.* **1.** To put into or hold as much as possible. **2.** To stop up (e.g., an opening). **3.** To satisfy completely : fulfill <*fill* all requirements> **4.** To supply the materials for <*fill* a prescription> **5.** To supply (an empty space) with material, as writing. **6.** To put someone into (e.g., a vacant position). **7.** To hold or discharge the duties of (e.g., a position). **—fill in.** To act as a substitute. *—n.* **1.** A full amount <ate my *fill*> **2.** A built-up piece of land or the material, as earth or gravel, used for it.

fill•er (fĭl'ər) *n.* **1.** Something added to augment size or weight or to fill space. **2.** A material used to fill pores, cracks, or holes in a surface before it is finished.

fil•lér (fĭl'âr') *n.* —See table at CURRENCY.

fil•let (fĭl'ĭt) *n.* **1.** A narrow strip of material, as ribbon. **2.** *also* **fi•let** (fĭ-lā', fĭl'ā'). A boneless piece of fish or meat. *—v.* **1.** To bind or ornament with or as if with a fillet. **2.** *also* **fi•**

let (fĭ-lā′, fĭl′ā′). To slice, bone, or make into fillets.

fill•ing (fĭl′ĭng) *n.* **1.** Something used to fill a space, container, or cavity. **2.** An edible mixture used to fill sandwiches, cakes, or pastries. **3.** The horizontal threads crossing the warp in weaving : weft.

filling station *n.* A retail establishment at which vehicles are serviced, esp. with gasoline, oil, air, and water.

fil•lip (fĭl′əp) *n.* **1.** A light blow or gesture made with a snap of the fingers. **2.** Something that arouses or excites. **—fil′lip** *v.*

fil•ly (fĭl′ē) *n., pl.* **-lies.** A young female horse.

film (fĭlm) *n.* **1.** A thin skin or membranous coating. **2.** A thin coating <a *film* of dust> **3.** A photosensitive strip or sheet of flexible cellulose material used to make photographic negatives or transparencies. **4. a.** A movie. **b.** Movies as a whole. —*v.* **1.** To cover with or as if with a film. **2.** To make a movie of. **—film′y** *adj.*

film•dom (fĭlm′dəm) *n.* The movie industry.

film•go•er (fĭlm′gō′ər) *n.* One who frequently goes to see movies.

film•mak•ing (fĭlm′mā′kĭng) *n.* The making of movies. **—film′mak′er** *n.*

fil•mog•ra•phy (fĭl-mŏg′rə-fē) *n., pl.* **-phies.** Writings, as lists or books, about films or film figures.

film•strip (fĭlm′strĭp′) *n.* A strip of film with graphic matter, as photographs, for still projection on a screen.

fils (fĭls) *n., pl.* **fils.** —See table at CURRENCY.

fil•ter (fĭl′tər) *n.* **1.** A device containing a porous substance through which a liquid or gas can be passed to separate out suspended matter. **2.** A device for passing waves or oscillations of certain frequencies while blocking others. —*v.* **1.** To put (liquid or gas) through a filter. **2.** To remove by putting through a filter. **—fil′ter•a•bil′i•ty** *n.* **—fil′ter•a•ble, fil′tra•ble** *adj.*

filth (fĭlth) *n.* **1.** Dirty or foul matter or refuse. **2.** Foulness : corruption. **3.** Something considered offensive, esp. obscenity.

filth•y (fĭl′thē) *adj.* **-i•er, -i•est. 1.** Covered with or full of filth. **2.** Obscene. **3.** So objectionable as to elicit despisal. ★ ***syns:*** ABHORRENT, CONTEMPTIBLE, DESPICABLE, DISGUSTING, FOUL, LOATHSOME, MEAN, NASTY, ODIOUS, REPUGNANT, ROTTEN, SHABBY, SORRY, VILE, WRETCHED **—filth′i•ly** *adv.* **—filth′i•ness** *n.*

fil•trate (fĭl′trāt′) *v.* **-trat•ed, -trat•ing.** To pass or cause to pass through a filter. —*n.* The portion of matter that passes through the filter. **—fil•tra′tion** *n.*

fin[1] (fĭn) *n.* **1.** A thin, membranous appendage that extends from the body of a fish or other aquatic animal, used esp. for swimming and balancing. **2.** Something like a fin. **3.** FLIPPER 2.

fin[2] (fĭn) *n. Slang.* A 5–dollar bill.

fi•na•gle (fĭ-nā′gəl) *v.* **-gled, -gling.** *Informal.* To obtain or achieve by questionable or wily methods : wangle. **—fi•na′gler** *n.*

fi•nal (fī′nəl) *adj.* **1.** Occurring at or forming the end : concluding. **2.** Of, relating to, or constituting the last element in a series, process, etc. **3.** Definitive and decisive : unalterable. —*n.* **1.** The last or one of the last of a series of athletic contests. **2.** A final academic examination. **—fi•nal′i•ty** (fī-năl′ə-tē, fĭ-) *n.* **—fi′nal•ly** *adv.*

fi•na•le (fĭ-năl′ē, -nä′lē) *n.* The concluding part, esp. of a musical composition.

fi•nal•ist (fī′nə-lĭst) *n.* A competitor in the final part of a contest.

fi•nal•ize (fī′nə-līz′) *v.* **-ized, -iz•ing.** To put into final form : complete. **—fi′nal•i•za′tion** *n.* **—fi′nal•iz′er** *n.*

fi•nance (fĭ-năns′, fī-, fī′năns′) *n.* **1.** The management of monetary affairs. **2. finances.** Monetary resources : funds. —*v.* **-nanced, -nanc•ing. 1.** To supply the funds or capital for. **2.** To supply funds to. **3.** To sell or provide on credit. **—fi•nan′cial** *adj.* **—fi•nan′cial•ly** *adv.*

fin•an•cier (fĭn′ən-sîr′, fī-năn′-, fĭ′nən-) *n.* An expert in large-scale financial affairs.

finch (fĭnch) *n.* A relatively small bird of the family Fringillidae, as a goldfinch, grosbeak, or canary, having a short stout bill.

find (fīnd) *v.* **found** (found), **find•ing. 1.** To come upon, as after a search or often by accident. **2.** To attain : achieve. **3.** To ascertain : determine. **4.** To regard : consider <*found* the house charming> **5.** To regain : recover. **6.** To assert as a conclusion or verdict. ★ ***syns:*** LOCATE, PINPOINT, SPOT —*n.* **1.** An act of finding. **2.** Something found, esp. a valuable discovery.

find•er (fīn′dər) *n.* **1.** One that finds. **2.** A device on a camera that indicates what will be in the photograph.

fin de siè•cle (făN′ də sē-ĕk′lə) *adj.* Of or typical of the artistic climate of the latter part of the 19th cent.

find•ing (fīn′dĭng) *n.* **1.** Something found or discovered. **2.** *often* **findings.** The conclusion reached after investigation or examination.

fine[1] (fīn) *adj.* **fin•er, fin•est. 1.** Superior, as in quality or skill <*fine* porcelain><a *fine* musician> **2.** Very pleasant and enjoyable. **3.** Very sharp, as a knife edge. **4. a.** Consisting of tiny particles <*fine* dust> **b.** Very thin in texture or diameter. **5.** Subtle <a *fine* distinction> **6.** Marked by refined manners : elegant. **7.** Clear and unclouded. **8.** *Informal.* Being in good health. —*adv. Informal.* Very well <The children are doing *fine.*> **—fine′ly** *adv.* **—fine′ness** *n.*

fine[2] (fīn) *n.* A sum of money imposed as a penalty for an offense. **—fine** *v.*

fine art *n.* Art, as music, painting, and sculpture, created for aesthetic pleasure.

fine print *n.* The portion of a document that contains qualifications or restrictions in small type or obscure language.

fin•er•y (fī′nə-rē) *n., pl.* **-ies.** Elaborate clothes and jewels.

fi•nesse (fĭ-nĕs′) *n.* **1.** Fineness and delicacy

of performance or workmanship. **2.** Skillful handling of a situation.

fine-tune (fīn'to͞on', -tyo͞on') *v.* To make small adjustments in for optimal performance or effectiveness.

fin•ger (fĭng'gər) *n.* **1.** Any of the 5 digits of the hand. **2.** A glove part covering a finger. **3.** Something, as a peninsula, that resembles a finger. —*v.* **1.** To touch with the fingers : handle. **2.** *Mus.* To use the fingers in playing an instrument.

fin•ger•board (fĭng'gər-bôrd', -bōrd') *n.* A strip of wood on the neck of a stringed instrument against which the strings are pressed by the fingers in playing.

finger bowl *n.* A small bowl of water used for rinsing the fingers at the table.

fin•ger•ing (fĭng'gər-ĭng) *n. Mus.* **1.** The act or technique of using the fingers in playing an instrument. **2.** Marking that indicates which fingers are to be used.

fin•ger•ling (fĭng'gər-lĭng) *n.* A young fish.

fin•ger•nail (fĭng'gər-nāl') *n.* The thin, transparent plate covering the dorsal surface of the tip of each finger.

fin•ger•print (fĭng'gər-prĭnt') *n.* A pattern formed by the ridges of the skin on the tips of the fingers and thumbs, used esp. as a means of identification. —**fin'ger•print'** *v.*

finger tip *also* **fin•ger•tip** (fĭng'gər-tĭp') *n.* The extreme end of a finger.

fin•i•al (fĭn'ē-əl) *n.* An ornamental projecting or terminating part, as on a lamp.

fin•ick•y (fĭn'ĭ-kē) *adj.* Hard to please : choosy. —**fin'ick•i•ness** *n.*

fi•nis (fĭn'ĭs, fī'nĭs) *n.* The end.

fin•ish (fĭn'ĭsh) *v.* **1.** To reach the end (of) <*finish* a road race> **2.** To bring to an end : conclude. **3.** To consume all of : use up <*finish* a cake> **4. a.** To destroy or kill. **b.** To wear out completely. **5.** To give (a surface) a particular texture. —*n.* **1.** The final part : end <a close *finish* in the horse race> **2.** Surface treatment or texture. **3.** Smoothness of execution : perfection. **4.** Refinement in speech, manners, or behavior : polish. —**fin'ish•er** *n.*

fi•nite (fī'nīt') *adj.* **1.** Having limits or bounds. **2.** Being neither infinite nor infinitesimal. —**fi'nite•ly** *adv.* —**fi'nite•ness** *n.*

fink (fĭngk) *n. Slang.* **1.** A hired strikebreaker. **2.** An informer. **3.** An undesirable person. —**fink** *v.*

fin•nan had•die (fĭn'ən hăd'ē) *n.* Smoked haddock.

fin•ny (fĭn'ē) *adj.* **-ni•er, -ni•est. 1.** Having or suggesting fins. **2.** Of, relating to, or typical of fish.

fiord (fyôrd, fyōrd) *n. var. of* FJORD.

fir (fûr) *n.* **1.** An evergreen tree of the genus *Abies,* having flat needles and erect cones. **2.** The wood of a fir.

fire (fīr) *n.* **1. a.** A chemical reaction, esp. the burning of a combustible substance with oxygen that releases heat and light. **b.** A fire distinguished by magnitude, destructive power, or utility <a field *fire*><a stove *fire*> **2.** Great enthusiasm : fervor. **3.** Discharge of firearms. —*v.* **fired, fir•ing. 1.** To cause to ignite or become ignited. **2.** To maintain or tend a fire (in). **3.** To bake in a kiln <*fire* a vase> **4.** To arouse the emotions of. **5.** To discharge (a firearm, explosive, or projectile). **6.** *Informal.* To project or throw suddenly and forcefully. **7.** To let go from a job : dismiss. —**fire'less** *adj.* —**fire'proof'** *adj. & v.*

fire alarm *n.* A device used to signal the outbreak of a fire.

fire ant *n.* Any of a genus of ants of the S United States and tropical America that inflict a painful sting.

fire•arm (fīr'ärm') *n.* A weapon for firing a missile, esp. a pistol or rifle using an explosive charge.

fire•ball (fīr'bôl') *n.* **1.** A ball of fire. **2.** A particularly bright meteor. **3.** A very bright, intensely hot ball-shaped cloud of dust, gas, and vapor caused by a nuclear explosion. **4.** A very energetic person.

fire•base (fīr'bās') *n.* A military site from which fire is directed against the enemy.

fire•bomb (fīr'bŏm') *n.* A bomb designed to start a fire. —**fire'bomb'** *v.*

fire•box (fīr'bŏks') *n.* **1.** A box containing a fire alarm. **2.** A chamber, as a steam locomotive furnace, in which fuel is burned.

fire•brand (fīr'brănd') *n.* **1.** A piece of burning wood. **2.** One who agitates or stirs up trouble or conflict.

fire•break (fīr'brāk') *n.* A strip of land that is cleared to stop the spread of a fire.

fire•brick (fīr'brĭk') *n.* A highly heat-resistant brick esp. of fire clay, used to line fireplaces and furnaces.

fire•bug (fīr'bŭg') *n. Informal.* A pyromaniac : arsonist.

fire clay *n.* The heat-resistant clay used esp. for firebricks.

fire•crack•er (fīr'krăk'ər) *n.* A small explosive charge and a fuse in a heavy paper casing, exploded to entertain.

fire•damp (fīr'dămp') *n.* A gas, mainly methane, occurring naturally in coal mines and forming explosive mixtures with air.

fire•dog (fīr'dôg', -dŏg') *n.* An andiron.

fire engine *n.* A large motor vehicle that carries firefighters and extinguishing equipment to a fire.

fire escape *n.* A structure or device for emergency exit from a building.

fire•fight (fīr'fīt') *n.* An exchange of gunfire, as between infantry units.

fire•fight•er (fīr'fī'tər) *n.* One who fights fires as an occupation.

fire•fly (fīr'flī') *n.* A night-flying beetle of the family Lampyridae, having an abdominal organ that gives off a flashing light.

fire•house (fīr'hous') *n.* A fire station.

fire irons *pl.n.* Equipment, including tongs, a shovel, and a poker, used to tend a fire.

fire•light (fīr'līt') *n.* The light from a fire, as in a fireplace.

fire•man (fīr'mən) *n.* **1.** A firefighter. **2.** One who tends fires : stoker.

fire•place (fīr′plās′) *n.* An open recess at the base of a chimney for a fire : hearth.
fire•plug (fīr′plŭg′) *n.* A hydrant.
fire•pow•er (fīr′pou′ər) *n.* The capacity, as of a weapon, military unit, or ship, for discharging fire.
fire•side (fīr′sīd′) *n.* **1.** The area around a fireplace or hearth. **2.** HOME 1.
fire station *n.* A building housing fire equipment and firefighters.
fire tower *n.* A tower where a lookout for forest fires is stationed.
fire•trap (fīr′trăp′) *n.* A building susceptible to fire or hard to escape from if there is a fire.
fire wall *n.* A fireproof wall used as a barrier to forestall the spread of a fire in buildings and machinery.
fire•wa•ter (fīr′wô′tər, -wŏt′ər) *n. Slang.* Strong liquor, esp. whiskey.
fire•wood (fīr′wo͝od′) *n.* Wood burned in a fireplace or for fuel.
fire•works (fīr′wûrks′) *pl.n.* Explosives and combustibles used to generate colored lights, smoke, and noise for entertainment.
firing line *n.* **1.** The line of positions from which guns are fired at targets. **2.** The often vulnerable forefront of an activity or pursuit.
firm[1] (fûrm) *adj.* **1.** Not yielding to pressure : solid. **2.** Marked by the tone and resiliency of healthy tissue <*firm* muscles> **3.** Securely fastened or fixed in place. **4.** Indicating resolution or determination. **5.** Constant and steadfast. **6. a.** Fixed : definite <a *firm* deal> **b.** Unfluctuating : steady <*firm* prices> **7.** Strong and sure <a *firm* grip> —*adv.* Unwaveringly : resolutely. —*v.* To make or become firm. —**firm′ly** *adv.* —**firm′ness** *n.*
firm[2] (fûrm) *n.* A business partnership of 2 or more persons.
fir•ma•ment (fûr′mə-mənt) *n.* The expanse of the heavens : sky.
firm•ware (fûrm′wâr′) *n. Computer Sci.* Programming instructions that are stored in the read-only memory unit of a computer.
firn (fîrn) *n.* Snow partially consolidated by thawing and freezing but not yet converted to glacial ice.
first (fûrst) *adj.* **1.** Corresponding in order to the number 1. **2.** Coming before all others. **3.** Taking place or acting prior to all others : earliest. **4.** Ranking above all others in importance or quality : foremost. —*adv.* **1.** Before or above all others in time, order, rank, or importance. **2.** For the first time. **3.** Preferably : rather. —*n.* **1.** The ordinal number matching the number 1 in a series. **2.** The first in a set or sequence. **3.** The one coming, taking place, or ranking before or above all others. **4.** The beginning <from the *first*><at *first*> **5.** The transmission gear producing the lowest drive speeds in an automotive vehicle. —**first′ly** *adv.*
first aid *n.* Emergency care given to sick or injured persons.
first-born (fûrst′bôrn′) *adj.* First in order of birth : eldest. —**first′-born′** *n.*
first class *n.* **1.** The highest or best of a particular group. **2.** A class of mail including letters, postcards, and packages sealed against inspection. —**first′-class′** *adj. & adv.*
first cousin *n.* COUSIN 1.
first-de•gree burn (fûrst′dĭ-grē′) *n.* A mild burn causing redness of the skin.
first•hand (fûrst′hănd′) *adj.* Coming or received from the original source <*firsthand* information> —**first′hand′** *adv.*
first lieutenant *n.* A military officer who ranks above a 2nd lieutenant and below a captain.
first mate *n.* A ship's officer who ranks just below the captain.
first person *n.* A category of linguistic forms, as verbs or pronouns, indicating the speaker or writer of the sentence in which they are used.
first-rate (fûrst′rāt′) *adj.* Foremost in quality, rank, or importance. —**first′rate′** *adv.*
first-string (fûrst′strĭng′) *adj.* Being a regular member, as of a team, rather than a substitute.
firth (fûrth) *n. esp. Scot.* A narrow inlet of the sea : fjord.
fis•cal (fĭs′kəl) *adj.* **1.** Of or relating to the treasury or finances of a nation or branch of government. **2.** Of or relating to finances. —**fis′cal•ly** *adv.*
fiscal year *n.* A 12-month period for which an organization plans the use of its funds.
fish (fĭsh) *n., pl.* **fish** *or* **fish•es. 1.** Any of numerous cold-blooded aquatic vertebrates having fins, gills for breathing, and usu. scales. **2.** The flesh of a fish used as food. —*v.* **1.** To try to catch fish. **2.** To seek by feeling one's way : grope. **3.** To try to get something slyly or indirectly. **4.** To pull or draw forth. —**fish′ing** *n.*
fish and chips *pl.n.* Fried fillets of fish and French-fried potatoes.
fish•bowl (fĭsh′bōl′) *n.* **1.** A usu. transparent bowl for keeping live fish. **2.** Lack of privacy.
fish•er•man (fĭsh′ər-mən) *n.* **1.** One who fishes commercially or for sport. **2.** A commercial fishing vessel.
fish•er•y (fĭsh′ə-rē) *n., pl.* **-ies. 1.** The business or occupation of catching, processing, or selling fish. **2.** A place for catching fish. **3.** A fish hatchery.
fish•eye (fĭsh′ī′) *adj.* Of or being a camera lens that covers an angle of about 180°.
fish•hook (fĭsh′ho͝ok′) *n.* A usu. barbed metal hook used to catch fish.
fishing rod *n.* A rod of wood, steel, or fiber glass with a line and often a reel, used to catch fish.
fish•meal (fĭsh′mēl′) *n.* Pulverized dried fish or fish parts used as fertilizer and animal feed.
fish story *n. Informal.* An exaggerated, boastful story that is probably not true.
fish•tail (fĭsh′tāl′) *v.* To swing the tail of an aircraft or the rear end of a motor vehicle from side to side while moving forward.
fish•wife (fĭsh′wīf′) *n.* A coarse, shrewish woman.
fish•y (fĭsh′ē) *adj.* **-i•er, -i•est. 1.** Resembling

fish, as in taste or odor. **2.** Inspiring suspicion <a *fishy* excuse> **—fish'i•ly** *adv.* **—fish'i•ness** *n.*

fis•sile (fĭs'əl, -īl') *adj.* **1.** Capable of being split. **2.** *Physics.* Fissionable. **—fis•sil'i•ty** (fĭ-sĭl'ĭ-tē) *n.*

fis•sion (fĭsh'ən) *n.* **1.** The act or process of splitting into parts. **2.** *Physics.* A reaction in which an atomic nucleus splits into fragments whose mass does not quite equal the mass of the original nucleus and hundreds of millions of electron volts of energy are generated. **—fis'sion•a•ble** *adj.*

fis•sure (fĭsh'ər) *n.* A narrow crack or opening, as in a rock face. **—fis'sure** *v.*

fist (fĭst) *n.* **1.** A tightly closed hand with the fingers bent into the palm. **2.** INDEX 2.

fist•fight (fĭst'fīt') *n.* A fight using the fists.

fist•ful (fĭst'fo͝ol') *n.* A handful.

fist•i•cuffs (fĭs'tĭ-kŭfs') *pl.n.* **1.** A fight involving use of the fists. **2.** Boxing.

fis•tu•la (fĭs'cho͞o-lə, -chə-) *n., pl.* **-las** *or* **-lae** (-lē'). An abnormal passage leading from an abscess, cavity, or hollow organ to the body surface or to another hollow organ. **—fis'tu•lous** *adj.*

fit[1] (fĭt) *v.* **fit•ted** *or* **fit, fit•ting. 1.** To be the correct size and shape (for). **2.** To be appropriate (to). **3.** To be or make suitable. **4.** To equip or outfit, as a vessel. **5.** To provide a place or time for <The dentist can *fit* you in at 2:00 p.m.> **6.** To belong. *—adj.* **fit•ter, fit•test. 1.** Suited, adapted, or adequate for a particular circumstance or purpose. **2.** Appropriate : proper. **3.** Physically healthy. *—n.* **1.** The quality, state, or way of being fitted. **2.** The way in which a garment fits. **—fit'ly** *adv.* **—fit'ness** *n.* **—fit'ter** *n.*

fit[2] (fĭt) *n.* **1.** *Med.* **a.** A sudden, violent appearance of a disease <a *fit* of malaria> **b.** A convulsion. **2.** A sudden emotional outburst. **3.** A sudden period of activity.

fitch (fĭch) *n.* The fur of the Old World polecat.

fit•ful (fĭt'fəl) *adj.* Irregular : intermittent <*fitful* sleep> **—fit'ful•ly** *adv.* **—fit'ful•ness** *n.*

fit•ting (fĭt'ĭng) *adj.* Suitable to the circumstances. *—n.* **1.** The act of trying on clothes for alteration. **2.** A detachable part for a machine or apparatus. **—fit'ting•ly** *adv.* **—fit'ting•ness** *n.*

five (fīv) *n.* **1.** The cardinal number equal to 4 + 1. **2.** The 5th in a set or sequence. **3.** Something having 5 parts, units, or members. **—five** *adj. & pron.*

five-pins (fīv'pĭnz') *n. Can.* A bowling game in which the ball is rolled down an alley in order to knock down the 5 pins at the end of the alley.

†fix (fĭks) *v.* **1.** To fasten or place securely. **2.** *Chem.* To make a substance nonvolatile or solid. **3.** *Biol.* To convert (nitrogen) into stable compounds that can be assimilated. **4.** To treat (a photographic image) with a chemical preservative. **5.** To direct steadily <*fixed* her eyes on the screen> **6.** To specify <*fix* a time to meet> **7.** To ascribe : assign <*fixed* the blame on us> **8.** To set right : adjust. **9.** To repair. **10.** To make ready : prepare <*fix* dinner> **11.** *Informal.* To get even with. **12.** To influence or arrange the outcome of illegally. **13.** To spay or castrate (an animal). **14.** *Regional.* To intend <was *fixing* to go home> *—n.* **1.** A difficult or embarrassing situation or position. **2.** The position of a ship, aircraft, etc., as determined by observations or radio. **3.** An example of connivance to prearrange a result. **4.** *Slang.* An injection of a narcotic. **—fix'a•ble** *adj.* **—fix'er** *n.*

fix•a•tion (fĭk-sā'shən) *n.* A strong, often unhealthy attachment or preoccupation. **—fix'ate'** *v.*

fix•a•tive (fĭk'sə-tĭv) *n.* Something used to fix, protect, preserve, or stabilize.

fixed (fĭkst) *adj.* **1.** Set firmly in position : stationary. **2.** Not changing or varying : constant. **3.** Firmly, often dogmatically held in the mind <*fixed* notions> **4.** *Chem.* **a.** Nonvolatile, as certain oils. **b.** Being in a stable combined form. **5.** Illegally prearranged. **—fix'ed•ly** *adv.* **—fix'ed•ness** *n.*

fix•ings (fĭk'sĭngz) *pl.n. Informal.* Accessories : trimmings.

fix•i•ty (fĭk'sĭ-tē) *n., pl.* **-ties.** The quality or state of being fixed : stability.

fix•ture (fĭks'chər) *n.* **1.** Something fixed or installed as a part of a larger system <plumbing *fixtures*> **2.** One regarded as permanently established or fixed, as in a certain place <a *fixture* of Paris society>

fizz (fĭz) *v.* To make a hissing or bubbling sound. *—n.* **1.** A fizzing sound. **2.** Tiny gas bubbles : effervescence.

fiz•zle (fĭz'əl) *v.* **-zled, -zling. 1.** To make a hiss or sputter, esp. when going out. **2.** To fail or die out, esp. after a positive beginning. *—n.* A fiasco.

fjord *or* **fiord** (fyôrd, fyōrd) *n.* A long, narrow, often deep inlet from the sea with steep cliffs on either side.

flab (flăb) *n.* Loose, flaccid body tissue.

flab•ber•gast (flăb'ər-găst') *v.* To amaze : astound.

flab•by (flăb'ē) *adj.* **-bi•er, -bi•est. 1.** Flaccid. **2.** Lacking force or vitality : ineffectual. **—flab'bi•ness** *n.*

flac•cid (flăk'sĭd, flăs'ĭd) *adj.* Lacking firmness or resilience. **—flac•cid'i•ty** *n.* **—flac'cid•ly** *adv.*

flack (flăk) *n.* A press agent. **—flack** *v.* **—flack'er•y** *n.*

flac•on (flăk'ən, -ŏn') *n.* A small stoppered often decorative bottle.

flag[1] (flăg) *n.* **1.** A piece of cloth having a distinctive size, color, and design, used for a symbol, standard, signal, etc. **2.** Something suggestive of a flag in appearance or function. *—v.* **flagged, flag•ging. 1.** To mark with a flag for identification or ornamentation. **2.** To signal with or as if with a flag.

flag[2] (flăg) *n.* A plant, as an iris or cattail, with long blade-shaped leaves.

flag[3] (flăg) *v.* **flagged, flag•ging. 1.** To hang

limply : droop. **2.** To lessen in strength or vigor : weaken.

flag⁴ (flăg) *n.* Flagstone or a slab of flagstone. **—flag** *v.*

flag·el·late (flăj′ə-lāt′) *v.* **-lat·ed, -lat·ing.** To punish by flogging : scourge. **—flag′el·la′tion** *n.*

fla·gel·lum (flə-jĕl′əm) *n., pl.* **-gel·la** (-jĕl′ə). **1.** *Biol.* A whiplike extension of certain cells or unicellular organisms that serves in locomotion. **2.** A whip.

flag officer *n.* A U.S. Navy or Coast Guard officer holding the rank of rear admiral, vice admiral, or admiral.

flag·on (flăg′ən) *n.* A container with a handle, and often a lid, used for holding wines or liquors.

flag·pole (flăg′pōl′) *n.* A pole on which a flag is raised.

fla·grant (flā′grənt) *adj.* Conspicuously bad or offensive : outrageous. **—fla′gran·cy, fla′grance** *n.* **—fla′grant·ly** *adv.*

flag·ship (flăg′shĭp′) *n.* **1.** A ship that carries a fleet or squadron commander and his flag. **2.** The chief one of a related group.

flag·staff (flăg′stăf′) *n.* A flagpole.

flag·stone (flăg′stōn′) *n.* A flat, fine-grained, hard, evenly layered stone split into slabs for paving.

flail (flāl) *n.* A device for threshing grain by hand. —*v.* **1.** To beat or strike with or as if with a flail. **2.** To thrash about.

flair (flâr) *n.* **1.** Talent or aptitude : knack. **2.** Distinctive style.

flak (flăk) *n.* **1. a.** Antiaircraft artillery. **b.** The bursting shells fired from such artillery. **2.** *Informal.* **a.** Excessive or abusive criticism. **b.** Dissension.

flake (flāk) *n.* **1.** A flat, thin piece or layer. **2.** *Slang.* An eccentric : oddball. —*v.* **flaked, flak·ing.** To form into or separate in flakes. **—flak′i·ly** *adv.* **—flak′i·ness** *n.* **—flak′y** *adj.*

flam·boy·ant (flăm-boi′ənt) *adj.* **1.** Elaborately showy : ornate. **2.** Rich and vivid in color. **—flam·boy′ance, flam·boy′an·cy** *n.* **—flam·boy′ant·ly** *adv.*

flame (flām) *n.* **1.** The often bright, tongue-shaped zone of burning gases and fine suspended matter that forms in combustion. **2.** Active, blazing combustion. **3.** Something resembling a flame in appearance, motion, or intensity. **4.** Violent passion. **5.** A sweetheart. **—flame** *v.*

fla·men·co (flə-mĕng′kō) *n.* **1.** A dance of the Andalusian Gypsies marked by strong, often improvised rhythms. **2.** Music for the flamenco.

flame·out (flām′out′) *n.* In-flight combustion failure of a jet aircraft engine.

flame thrower *n.* A weapon that shoots ignited incendiary fuel, as napalm.

fla·min·go (flə-mĭng′gō) *n., pl.* **-gos** *or* **-goes.** A large tropical wading bird of the family Phoenicopteridae, having pinkish plumage, long legs, and a long neck.

flam·ma·ble (flăm′ə-bəl) *adj.* Igniting easily and burning rapidly : inflammable. **—flam′ma·bil′i·ty** *n.* **—flam′ma·ble** *n.*

flange (flănj) *n.* A projecting rim or edge used to strengthen or guide an object or attach it to another object.

flank (flăngk) *n.* **1. a.** The fleshy part of the body between the last rib and the hip. **b.** A cut of meat from this part of an animal. **2.** A lateral part <the *flank* of a mountain> **3.** The right or left side of a military formation or bastion. —*v.* **1.** To guard the flank of. **2.** To attack or menace the flank of (enemy troops). **3.** To be situated at the flank of. **4.** To put something on each side of. **—flank′er** *n.*

flan·nel (flăn′əl) *n.* **1.** A woven fabric with a nap, made of wool or a wool and cotton or synthetic blend. **2. flannels.** Trousers or undergarments made of flannel. **—flan′nel·ly** *adj.*

flan·nel·ette (flăn′ə-lĕt′) *n.* Cotton flannel.

flap (flăp) *n.* **1.** A loose, flat piece affixed at only one side, as on an envelope. **2.** The act or sound of waving or fluttering. **3.** A control section of the rear edge of an aircraft wing that increases lift or drag. **4.** A striking with something flat : slap. **5.** *Slang.* Agitation : commotion. —*v.* **flapped, flap·ping. 1.** To move up and down, as arms or wings. **2.** To move or sway loosely : flutter. **3.** To hit with something flat.

flap·doo·dle (flăp′do͞od′l) *n. Slang.* Nonsense.

flap·jack (flăp′jăk′) *n.* A pancake.

flap·pa·ble (flăp′ə-bəl) *adj. Slang.* Easily excited or upset.

flap·per (flăp′ər) *n.* **1.** One that flaps. **2.** *Informal.* A young woman of the 1920's whose dress and behavior were ostentatiously unconventional.

flare (flâr) *v.* **flared, flar·ing. 1.** To flame up or burn with a bright light. **2.** To erupt or intensify suddenly, as an emotion or activity. **3.** To spread or open outward <a *flared* skirt> —*n.* **1.** A sudden, brief, intense blaze of light. **2.** A signaling or illuminating device that produces a bright light. **3.** An eruption of emotion or activity. **4.** An expanding outward.

flare-up (flâr′ŭp′) *n.* An outburst or eruption, as of flame or strong emotion.

flash (flăsh) *v.* **1.** To burst or cause to burst into or as if into flame. **2.** To appear or occur briefly or suddenly. **3.** To emit light intermittently : sparkle. **4.** To cause (light) to burst forth intermittently. **5.** To proceed rapidly. **6.** To signal with beams of light. **7.** To communicate or display (information) very quickly. **8.** To flaunt. —*n.* **1.** A short, sudden burst of light. **2.** A sudden perception <a *flash* of insight> **3.** An instant <did it in a *flash*> **4.** A short, important news transmission or dispatch. **5.** A device, as a flash bulb, that produces instantaneous illumination.

flash·back (flăsh′băk′) *n.* The interruption of a story, motion picture, etc., to show or tell about an earlier incident.

flash bulb *n.* A glass bulb full of shredded magnesium or aluminum foil that when electrically ignited produces a very brief flash of light for photography.

flash card *n.* A card printed with words or numbers and briefly displayed as part of a learning drill.

flash•cube (flăsh′kyo͞ob′) *n.* A rotating cube containing 4 flash bulbs.

flash flood *n.* A sudden, violent flood after a heavy rain.

flash gun *n.* A portable photographic device that holds and electrically triggers a flash bulb.

flash lamp *n.* An electric lamp used in photography to produce a very brief high-intensity light.

flash•light (flăsh′līt′) *n.* A small, portable lamp usu. powered by batteries.

flash point *n.* **1.** The lowest temperature at which the vapor of a combustible liquid will ignite. **2.** The brink of crisis.

flash•y (flăsh′ē) *adj.* **-i•er, -i•est. 1.** Superficially or briefly brilliant. **2.** Tastelessly showy **:** gaudy. **—flash′i•ly** *adv.* **—flash′i•ness** *n.*

flask (flăsk) *n.* **1.** A small, flat, bottlelike container usu. with a cap. **2.** A long-necked bottle used in laboratories.

flat[1] (flăt) *adj.* **flat•ter, flat•test. 1. a.** Having a horizontal surface with no curvature or tilt. **b.** Having a smooth, even surface, as a board. **2.** Low and shallow, as a box. **3.** Lying prostrate **:** prone. **4.** Absolute **:** unequivocal <a *flat* denial> **5.** Unvarying, as a fixed rate or fee. **6.** Uninteresting **:** dull. **7.** Lacking flavor or zest. **8.** Deflated <a *flat* tire> **9.** *Mus.* **a.** Being below the correct pitch. **b.** Being a semitone lower than the corresponding natural key. *—adv.* **1.** Level with the ground **:** horizontally. **2.** So as to be flat. **3.** Directly **:** completely <went *flat* against the rules> **4.** *Mus.* Below the correct pitch. *—n.* **1.** A flat surface or part. **2.** *often* **flats.** A stretch of level land. **3.** A shallow container for a number of seeds or immature plants. **4.** A flat tire. **5.** A shoe with a flat heel. **6.** *Mus.* **a.** A sign (♭) attached to a note to indicate that its pitch is a semitone lower than usual. **b.** A note lowered a semitone. *—v.* **flat•ted, flat•ting. 1.** To make flat **:** flatten. **2.** *Mus.* **a.** To lower (a note) a semitone. **b.** To sing or play below the correct pitch. **—flat′ly** *adv.* **—flat′ness** *n.*

flat[2] (flăt) *n.* An apartment entirely on one floor of a building.

flat•bed (flăt′bĕd′) *n.* A truck that has a shallow rear platform without sides.

flat•boat (flăt′bōt′) *n.* A boat with a flat bottom and square ends for the transport of freight on inland waterways.

flat•car (flăt′kär′) *n.* A roofless, sideless railroad freight car.

flat•fish (flăt′fĭsh′) *n.* A chiefly marine fish of the order Pleuronectiformes or Heterosomata, as a flounder or sole, having a compressed body with both eyes on the upper side.

flat•foot (flăt′fo͝ot′) *n.* **1.** *pl.* **-feet** (-fēt′). A condition in which the arch of the foot is broken down so that all of the sole touches the ground. **2.** *pl.* **-foots.** *Slang.* A police officer. **—flat′-foot′ed** *adj.*

flat•i•ron (flăt′ī′ərn) *n.* An externally heated device used to press clothes.

flat out *adv.* **1.** In a direct, blunt way. **2.** At top speed.

flat-out (flăt′out′) *adj.* Thoroughgoing **:** out-and-out.

flat•ten (flăt′n) *v.* **1.** To make or become flat. **2.** To knock down. **—flat′ten•er** *n.*

flat•ter (flăt′ər) *v.* **1.** To compliment (someone) extravagantly, esp. to win favor. **2.** To gratify the vanity of. **3. a.** To portray favorably. **b.** To show off to advantage. ★ ***syns:*** ADULATE, BLANDISH, SOFT-SOAP, SWEET-TALK. **—flat′ter•er** *n.* **—flat′ter•ing** *adj.* **—flat′ter•ing•ly** *adv.*

flat•ter•y (flăt′ə-rē) *n.* Excessive often insincere praise.

flat•top (flăt′tŏp′) *n.* **1.** *Informal.* An aircraft carrier. **2.** A very short haircut with a flattish, brushlike crown.

flat•u•lent (flăch′ə-lənt) *adj.* **1.** Causing or having excessive gas in the digestive tract. **2.** Pompous **:** self-important. **—flat′u•lence** *n.* **—flat′u•lent•ly** *adv.*

flat•ware (flăt′wâr′) *n.* **1.** Tableware that is relatively flat and fashioned usu. of a single piece, as plates. **2.** Table utensils, as knives, forks, and spoons.

flat•worm (flăt′wûrm′) *n.* Any of various flat-bodied worms, as the tapeworm.

flaunt (flônt) *v.* To display ostentatiously **:** show off <*flaunting* her diamonds> **—flaunt′er** *n.* **—flaunt′ing•ly** *adv.*

flau•tist (flô′tĭst, flou′-) *n.* A flutist.

fla•vor (flā′vər) *n.* **1.** Distinctive taste. **2.** A distinctive, characteristic quality <the *flavor* of Paris> **3.** A flavoring. *—v.* To impart flavor to. **—fla′vor•ful** *adj.* **—fla′vor•less** *adj.* **—fla′vor•some** *adj.*

fla•vor•ing (flā′vər-ĭng) *n.* A substance, as an extract or spice, that imparts flavor.

fla•vour (flā′vər) *n. esp. Brit. var. of* FLAVOR.

flaw (flô) *n.* **1.** An imperfect or defective part, as a crack or blemish. **2.** An intangible defect <a character *flaw*> **—flaw** *v.* **—flaw′less** *adj.* **—flaw′less•ly** *adv.* **—flaw′less•ness** *n.*

flax (flăks) *n.* A plant of the genus *Linum,* with blue flowers, seeds that yield linseed oil, and slender stems from which a fine textile fiber is derived.

flax•en (flăk′sən) *adj.* **1.** Made of or suggesting flax. **2.** Pale yellow, as flax fiber.

flay (flā) *v.* **1.** To strip off the skin of (e.g., an animal). **2.** To scold or criticize harshly.

flea (flē) *n.* A small, wingless, bloodsucking jumping insect of the order Siphonaptera, parasitic on warm-blooded animals.

flea-bit•ten (flē′bĭt′n) *adj.* **1.** Covered with fleas or their bites. **2.** *Informal.* Shabby <a *flea-bitten* hotel>

flea market *n.* A market where antiques and used household goods are sold.

fleck (flĕk) *n.* **1.** A tiny spot or mark. **2.** A small flake or bit. —*v.* To mark with flecks : spot : speckle.

fledg•ling *also* **fledge•ling** (flĕj′lĭng) *n.* **1.** A young bird with newly acquired flight feathers. **2.** A person who is young and inexperienced.

flee (flē) *v.* **fled** (flĕd), **flee•ing. 1.** To run away (from). **2.** To pass swiftly away : vanish. —**fle′er** *n.*

fleece (flēs) *n.* **1.** A coat of wool, as of a sheep or alpaca. **2.** A soft, woolly covering or mass. —*v.* **fleeced, fleec•ing. 1.** To shear the fleece from. **2.** To defraud : swindle. **3.** To cover with or as if with fleece. —**fleec′er** *n.* —**fleec′i•ly** *adv.* —**fleec′i•ness** *n.* —**fleec′y** *adj.*

fleet[1] (flēt) *n.* **1.** A number of warships operating together under a single command. **2.** A number of vehicles, as taxicabs or fishing boats, operated as a unit.

fleet[2] (flēt) *adj.* Moving rapidly or nimbly. —**fleet′ly** *adv.* —**fleet′ness** *n.*

fleet•ing (flē′tĭng) *adj.* Passing quickly : ephemeral. —**fleet′ing•ly** *adv.*

Flem•ish (flĕm′ĭsh) *adj.* Of Flanders or the Flemings. —*n.* **1.** The Germanic language of the Flemings. **2.** The Flemings.

flesh (flĕsh) *n.* **1.** Soft bodily tissue, esp. skeletal muscle. **2.** The meat of animals as distinguished from the edible tissue of fish or fowl. **3.** The pulpy part of a fruit or vegetable. **4.** The carnal body as distinguished from the mind or soul. **5.** Humanity in general. **6.** One's family : kin. —*v.* To fill out (a framework or structure).

flesh and blood *n.* **1.** Human nature or physical existence, together with its weaknesses. **2.** FLESH 6.

flesh•ly (flĕsh′lē) *adj.* **-li•er, -li•est. 1.** Of or relating to the body : corporeal. **2.** Of or relating to carnal desires : sensual. **3.** Not spiritual : worldly. —**flesh′li•ness** *n.*

flesh•pot (flĕsh′pŏt′) *n.* **1.** A place in which physical gratification is obtained. **2.** Physical well-being and gratification.

flesh•y (flĕsh′ē) *adj.* **-i•er, -i•est. 1.** Of, relating to, or suggestive of flesh. **2.** Corpulent : plump. **3.** Juicy and pulpy, as fruit. —**flesh′i•ness** *n.*

fleur-de-lis (flûr′də-lē′, flo͝or′-) *n., pl.* **fleurs-de-lis** (flûr′də-lēz′, flo͝or′-). A heraldic emblem and artistic design consisting of a stylized 3-petaled iris, once used as the armorial emblem of French sovereigns.

flew (flo͞o) *v. p.t. of* FLY[1].

flex (flĕks) *v.* **1.** To bend, esp. repeatedly. **2.** To contract (a muscle).

flex•i•ble (flĕk′sə-bəl) *adj.* **1.** Able to be bent or flexed : pliable. **2.** Responsive or adaptable to change. **3.** Easily persuaded. —**flex′i•bil′i•ty** *n.* —**flex′i•bly** *adv.*

flex•time (flĕks′tīm′) *n.* A plan that allows employees to set their own work schedules within a wide range of hours.

flex•ure (flĕk′shər) *n.* **1.** A bend or turn. **2.** An act of bending.

flick[1] (flĭk) *n.* A light, quick blow, jerk, or touch or the sound accompanying it. —*v.* **1.** To touch or hit with a flick. **2.** To cause to move with a light snap <*flicked* the light switch off>

flick[2] (flĭk) *n. Informal.* A movie.

flick•er[1] (flĭk′ər) *v.* **1.** To flutter <shadows *flickering* on the wall> **2.** To burn unsteadily, as a candle : gutter. —*n.* **1.** A wavering light. **2.** A brief sensation <a *flicker* of understanding>

flick•er[2] (flĭk′ər) *n.* A large North American woodpecker of the genus *Colaptes,* with a brownish back and a spotted breast.

flied (flīd) *v. p.t. & p.p. of* FLY[1] 7.

fli•er *also* **fly•er** (flī′ər) *n.* **1.** One that flies, esp. an aircraft pilot. **2.** A daring or speculative venture. **3.** A printed advertisement for mass distribution.

flight[1] (flīt) *n.* **1.** The act or process of flying. **2.** A scheduled airline run or trip. **3.** A group flying together. **4.** Rapid passage or movement, as of time. **5.** An extraordinary effort or display. **6.** A series of stairs leading from one floor to another.

flight[2] (flīt) *n.* An act or an instance of fleeing <unlawful *flight* to escape arrest>

flight attendant *n.* One employed to assist passengers in an aircraft.

flight bag *n.* A lightweight, flexible piece of luggage with zippered outside pockets.

flight•less (flīt′lĭs) *adj.* Incapable of flying <*flightless* birds>

flight recorder *n.* A device, as on certain aircraft, that documents preflight checks, in-flight procedures, and the landing.

flight•y (flī′tē) *adj.* **-i•er, -i•est. 1.** Inclined to act capriciously : fickle. **2.** Marked by irresponsible behavior. **3.** Easily excited : skittish. —**flight′i•ness** *n.*

flim•flam (flĭm′flăm′) *n. Informal.* **1.** Nonsense. **2.** A swindle. —**flim′flam′** *v.*

flim•sy (flĭm′zē) *adj.* **-si•er, -si•est. 1.** Lacking substance or strength <*flimsy* lace><a *flimsy* chair> **2.** Unconvincing : implausible <a *flimsy* excuse> —**flim′si•ly** *adv.* —**flim′si•ness** *n.*

flinch (flĭnch) *v.* **1.** To wince, as from pain. **2.** To draw away : retreat. —**flinch** *n.* —**flinch′er** *n.*

fling (flĭng) *v.* **flung** (flŭng), **fling•ing. 1.** To throw violently. **2.** To throw (oneself) into an activity energetically. **3.** To toss aside : discard <*fling* caution to the winds> —*n.* **1.** An act of flinging : throw. **2.** A spree. **3.** *Informal.* A brief attempt or effort <took a *fling* at skiing>

flint (flĭnt) *n.* **1.** A hard quartz that sparks when struck with steel. **2.** A spark-producing alloy used in cigarette lighters to ignite the fuel. —**flint′y** *adj.*

flint•lock (flĭnt′lŏk′) *n.* **1.** A gunlock in which a flint strikes a metal plate, thus producing sparks that ignite the charge. **2.** An obsolete firearm equipped with a flintlock.

flip (flĭp) *v.* **flipped, flip•ping. 1.** To throw or toss with a light brisk motion. **2.** To toss in the air, imparting a spin. 3. a. To turn over, esp. with a quick motion. b. To turn through : leaf. 4. To flick. 5. To move or operate (e.g., a lever or switch). 6. To turn a somersault. 7. *Slang.* a. To go crazy. b. To react in a strong usu. enthusiastic manner. —*adj.* **flip·per, flip·pest.** *Informal.* 1. Disrespectful : impudent. 2. Unconcerned : indifferent. —**flip** *n.*

flip chart *n.* A chart with sheets that can be flipped over to present information sequentially.

flip-flop (flĭp′flŏp′) *n.* 1. The movement or sound of repeated flapping <the *flip-flop* of sandals on a stone floor> 2. A backward somersault. 3. *Informal.* A reversal, as of opinion. —**flip′-flop′** *v.*

flip·pant (flĭp′ənt) *adj.* Marked by disrespect, impudence, or indifference. —**flip′pan·cy** *n.* —**flip′pant·ly** *adv.*

flip·per (flĭp′ər) *n.* 1. A wide, flat limb, as of a seal, adapted esp. for swimming. 2. A paddlelike rubber shoe used in swimming and skin diving.

flip side *n.* The reverse side.

flirt (flûrt) *v.* 1. To make playfully romantic or sexual overtures. 2. To act so as to attract or provoke : trifle <*flirt* with death> 3. To move abruptly : jerk. —*n.* 1. One who flirts. 2. An abrupt, jerky movement. —**flir·ta′tion** *n.* —**flir·ta′tious** *adj.* —**flir·ta′tious·ness** *n.*

flit (flĭt) *v.* **flit·ted, flit·ting.** To move quickly or abruptly : dart. —**flit′ter** *n.*

flitch (flĭch) *n.* A salted and cured side of bacon.

flit·ter (flĭt′ər) *v.* To flutter.

fliv·ver (flĭv′ər) *n.* An old or cheap car.

float (flōt) *v.* 1. a. To be or cause to be suspended within or on the surface of a fluid. b. To be or cause to be suspended in space. 2. To drift randomly from place to place. 3. To move lightly and easily. 4. To offer (a security) for sale. 5. To arrange for (e.g., a loan). —*n.* 1. Something that floats, as a raft. 2. A floating object, as a cork, on a fishing line. 3. A large, flat vehicle carrying a parade exhibit. 4. A milkshake with ice cream floating in it. —**float′a·ble** *adj.* —**float′er** *n.*

floating rib *n.* One of the 4 lower ribs that, unlike the other ribs, are not attached at the front.

flock (flŏk) *n.* 1. A group of animals living, traveling, or feeding together. 2. A group led by a single person, esp. the members of a church. 3. A large number. —*v.* To travel or gather in or as if in a flock.

floe (flō) *n.* A flat mass of floating ice or a segment separated from it.

flog (flŏg, flôg) *v.* **flogged, flog·ging.** To beat with a whip or stick. —**flog′ger** *n.*

flood (flŭd) *n.* 1. An overflow of water onto land that is normally dry. 2. A large outpouring <a *flood* of mail> 3. **Flood.** The great deluge described in the Old Testament. —*v.* 1. To inundate with or as if with a flood. 2. To fill abundantly or excessively <*flood* the market>

flood·gate (flŭd′gāt′) *n.* A gate for controlling the flow from a large body of water.

flood·light (flŭd′līt′) *n.* An electric lamp that produces a broad and intensely bright beam of light. —**flood′light′** *v.*

flood tide *n.* 1. The incoming tide. 2. A high point : climax.

floor (flôr, flōr) *n.* 1. The lower surface of a room on which one stands. 2. The ground surface <the ocean *floor*><the *floor* of a forest> 3. The lower part of a room, used for conducting business <the *floor* of the senate> 4. The right to speak to a meeting or assembly, as granted under parliamentary rules. 5. a. A story of a building. b. The occupants of such a story. —*v.* 1. To provide or furnish with a floor. 2. To knock down. 3. To overwhelm : stun.

floor exercise *n.* A competitive gymnastics event consisting of tumbling maneuvers performed on a mat.

floor show *n.* A series of nightclub acts.

floor·walk·er (flôr′wô′kər, flōr′-) *n.* A department store employee who is in charge of salespeople and aids customers.

flop (flŏp) *v.* **flopped, flop·ping.** 1. To fall down or cause to fall down heavily : plop. 2. To move about in a clumsy or relaxed way. 3. *Informal.* To fail completely. 4. *Slang.* To go to bed. —**flop** *n.*

flop·house (flŏp′hous′) *n.* A cheap hotel.

flop·py (flŏp′ē) *adj.* **-pi·er, -pi·est.** Loose and flexible <a *floppy* hat> —**flop′pi·ly** *adv.* —**flop′pi·ness** *n.*

floppy disk *n. Computer Sci.* A flexible plastic disk coated with magnetic material used to store computer data.

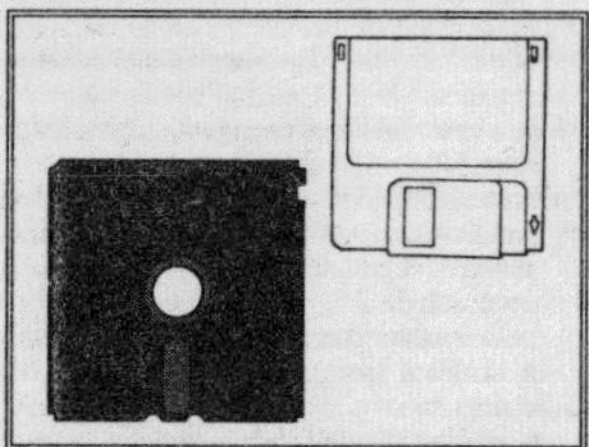

floppy disk
5¼ inch and 3½ inch floppy disks

flo·ra (flôr′ə, flōr′ə) *n., pl.* **-ras** *or* **flo·rae** (flôr′ē′, flōr′ē′). Plants as a whole, esp. those of a specific region or season.

flo·ral (flôr′əl, flōr′-) *adj.* Of or relating to flowers. —**flo′ral·ly** *adv.*

flo·res·cence (flô-rĕs′əns, flə-) *n.* A state or time of blossoming. —**flo·res′cent** *adj.*

flor·id (flôr′ĭd, flŏr′-) *adj.* 1. Flushed with rosy color. 2. Ornate. —**flo·rid′i·ty, flor′id·ness** *n.* —**flor′id·ly** *adv.*

flo·rin (flôr′ĭn, flŏr′-) *n.* 1. A guilder. 2. A former British coin worth 2 shillings.

flo•rist (flôr′ĭst, flōr′-, flŏr′-) *n.* One whose business is the cultivation or sale of flowers and ornamental plants.
floss (flôs, flŏs) *n.* **1.** Short or waste silk fibers. **2.** A soft, loosely twisted embroidery thread. **3.** A soft, silky, fibrous substance, as the tassel on corn. **4.** Dental floss. —*v.* **1.** To clean between (teeth) with dental floss. **2.** To use dental floss.
floss•y (flô′sē, flŏs′ē) *adj.* **-i•er, -i•est. 1.** Made of or resembling floss. **2.** *Slang.* Ostentatiously stylish. —**floss′i•ness** *n.*
flo•ta•tion (flō-tā′shən) *n.* The act or state of floating.
flo•til•la (flō-tĭl′ə) *n.* **1.** A fleet of small ships. **2.** A group resembling a small fleet.
flot•sam (flŏt′səm) *n.* Wreckage remaining afloat after a ship has sunk.
flounce[1] (flouns) *n.* A strip of gathered material attached along the upper edge to another surface, as on a garment or curtain.
flounce[2] (flouns) *v.* **flounced, flounc•ing.** To move with exaggerated, jerky movements <*flounced* out of the house angrily> —**flounce** *n.*
floun•der[1] (floun′dər) *v.* **1.** To struggle clumsily, as to obtain footing. **2.** To act or speak in a clumsy, confused way.
floun•der[2] (floun′dər) *n.* Any of various edible marine flatfishes of the families Bothidae and Pleuronectidae.
flour (flour) *n.* **1.** A soft, fine, powderlike substance produced by grinding grain, esp. wheat. **2.** A soft, fine powder like flour. —*v.* To coat with flour. —**flour′y** *adj.*

▲ ***word history:*** The word *flour* is simply a specialized use of the word *flower* in its medieval spelling. The *flower* of wheat or any other grain is the finest part of the meal that is left after the bran has been sifted out. The distinction in spelling between *flour* and *flower* did not become standard until the 19th cent.

flour•ish (flûr′ĭsh, flŭr′-) *v.* **1.** To grow abundantly **:** thrive. **2.** To do well **:** succeed and prosper. **3.** To brandish. —*n.* **1.** An added decorative touch, esp. in handwriting **:** embellishment. **2.** A dramatic act or gesture. **3.** A musical fanfare.
flout (flout) *v.* To have or show contempt for **:** scorn. —**flout′ing•ly** *adv.*
flow (flō) *v.* **1.** To move or come forth freely like a fluid. **2.** To circulate, as blood. **3.** To move or proceed steadily and easily. **4.** To rise. —Used of the tide. **5.** To derive. **6.** To be plentiful **:** abound. **7.** To hang in a loose, graceful way. —**flow** *n.*
flow chart *n.* A chart or diagram of the sequence and progress of a series of operations for a specific project.
flow•er (flou′ər) *n.* **1.** The part of a seed-bearing plant that contains specialized male and female organs, as stamens and a pistil, and produces seeds and usu. colorful blossoms. **2.** A plant cultivated for its blossoms. **3.** The period of highest development **:** peak. **4.** The best example or representative. —*v.* **1.** To produce flowers. **2.** To develop fully. —**flow′er•less** *adj.*
flow•er•pot (flou′ər-pŏt′) *n.* A pot, often of earthenware, in which plants are grown.
flow•er•y (flou′ə-rē) *adj.* **-i•er, -i•est. 1.** Full of, covered with, or suggestive of flowers. **2.** Full of high-sounding, ornate expressions. —**flow′er•i•ness** *n.*
flown (flōn) *v. p.p. of* FLY[1].
flu (flo͞o) *n. Informal.* Influenza.
flub (flŭb) *v.* **flubbed, flub•bing.** To bungle **:** botch. —**flub** *n.*
fluc•tu•ate (flŭk′cho͞o-āt′) *v.* **-at•ed, -at•ing. 1.** To shift irregularly **:** waver. **2.** To undulate. —**fluc′tu•a′tion** *n.*
flue (flo͞o) *n.* A conduit or passage through which air, gas, steam, or smoke can flow <a chimney *flue*>
flu•ent (flo͞o′ənt) *adj.* **1.** Having facility in language use. **2.** Flowing smoothly and naturally **:** polished <*fluent* verse> **3.** Flowing or capable of flowing **:** fluid. —**flu′en•cy** *n.* —**flu′ent•ly** *adv.*
fluff (flŭf) *n.* **1.** Light down **:** fuzz. **2.** Something that resembles fluff in consistency or appearance. **3.** Something unimportant. **4.** *Informal.* A mistake or memory lapse, esp. by an actor or announcer. —*v.* **1.** To make or become fluffy. **2.** *Informal.* To misread or forget (one's lines).
fluff•y (flŭf′ē) *adj.* **-i•er, -i•est. 1.** Of, like, or covered with fluff. **2.** Light and airy **:** soft. —**fluff′i•ly** *adv.* —**fluff′i•ness** *n.*
flu•id (flo͞o′ĭd) *n.* A substance, as water or air, that flows readily and tends to assume the shape of its container. —*adj.* **1.** Flowing readily, as a liquid. **2.** Smooth and effortless. **3.** Easily changed or tending to change **:** adaptable. **4.** Convertible into cash <*fluid* assets> —**flu•id′i•ty, flu′id•ness** *n.* —**flu′id•ly** *adv.*
fluid ounce *n.* —See table at MEASUREMENT.
fluke[1] (flo͞ok) *n.* A flatfish, esp. a flounder of the genus *Paralichthys.*
fluke[2] (flo͞ok) *n.* **1.** The triangular fastening blade of an anchor. **2.** A barb or barbed head, as on an arrow or harpoon. **3.** One of the 2 lobes of a whale's tail.
fluke[3] (flo͞ok) *n.* An unexpected stroke of good fortune. —**fluk′y** *adj.*
flume (flo͞om) *n.* **1.** A narrow gorge, usu. with a stream running through it. **2.** An artificial channel to carry a stream of water.
flung (flŭng) *v. p.t. & p.p. of* FLING.
flunk (flŭngk) *v. Informal.* **1.** To fail, esp. in an examination or course. **2.** To give a failing grade to.
flun•ky *also* **flun•key** (flŭng′kē) *n., pl.* **-kies** *also* **-keys. 1.** An obsequious person **:** toady. **2.** One who does menial work.
flu•o•res•cence (flo͞o′ə-rĕs′əns, flo͝o-rĕs′-) *n.* **1.** Emission of electromagnetic radiation, esp. of visible light, caused by absorption of incident radiation and persisting only as long as the stimulating radiation continues. **2.** The radiation emitted. —**flu′o•resce′** *v.* —**flu′o•res′cent** *adj.*

fluorescent lamp *n.* An electric lamp consisting of a glass tube whose inner wall is coated with a material that fluoresces under the influence of ultraviolet radiation, produced within the tube usu. by means of collisions between free electrons and mercury atoms.

fluor•i•date (flo͝or'ĭ-dāt', flôr'-, flōr'-) *v.* **-dat•ed, -dat•ing.** To add a fluorine compound to (e.g., a water supply) to prevent tooth decay. **—fluor'i•da'tion** *n.*

flu•o•ride (flo͞o'ə-rīd', flo͝or'īd', flôr'-, flōr'-) *n.* A binary compound of fluorine with another element or a radical.

flu•o•rine (flo͞o'ə-rēn', -rĭn, flo͝or'ēn', -ĭn, flôr'-, flōr'-) *n. Symbol* **F** A pale-yellow, corrosive, poisonous gaseous element.

fluor•o•scope (flo͝or'ə-skōp', flôr'-, flōr'-, flo͞o'ər-ə-) *n.* A fluorescent screen on which the inner structure of an optically opaque object, as the human body, may be viewed by transmission of x-rays through the object. **—fluor'o•scope'** *v.* **—fluor'o•scop'ic** (-skŏp'-ĭk) *adj.* **—fluo•ros'co•py** (flo͞o-rŏs'kə-pē) *n.*

flur•ry (flûr'ē, flŭr'ē) *n., pl.* **-ries. 1.** A sudden gust of wind. **2.** A brief, light fall of snow. **3.** A sudden burst of activity or excitement. **—flur'ry** *v.*

flush[1] (flŭsh) *v.* **1.** To flow and spread out suddenly and abundantly. **2.** To blush or cause to blush. **3.** To glow, esp. with a reddish color. **4.** To clean or wash out with a brief, rapid gush of water. **5.** To excite or elate, as with pride. —*n.* **1.** A brief, copious flow, as of water. **2.** A reddish tinge or glow : blush. **3.** Animation or exhilaration. **4.** Freshness or vigor <the *flush* of youth> —*adj.* **1.** Having a reddish color. **2.** Abundant : plentiful. **3.** Affluent : prosperous. **4. a.** Having surfaces in the same plane : even. **b.** Arranged with adjacent sides, surfaces, or edges close together. **c.** Having margins aligned with no indentations. **5.** Direct and accurate, as a blow. —*adv.* **1.** So as to be in one plane, even, or aligned with a margin. **2.** Squarely : solidly.

flush[2] (flŭsh) *n.* A hand in certain card games, as poker, in which all the cards are of the same suit.

flush[3] (flŭsh) *v.* To cause (e.g., a game bird) to fly from cover.

flus•ter (flŭs'tər) *v.* To make or become nervous or upset. **—flus'ter** *n.*

flute (flo͞ot) *n.* **1.** A high-pitched tubular woodwind instrument with finger holes and keys. **2.** One of the long, parallel decorative grooves on the shaft of a column. **3.** A grooved pleat, as in cloth. **—flut'ed** *adj.* **—flut'ing** *n.*

flut•ist (flo͞o'tĭst) *n.* A flute player.

flut•ter (flŭt'ər) *v.* **1.** To flap or wave rapidly and irregularly. **2.** To fly with a light, quick beating of the wings. **3.** To beat rapidly or erratically, as one's heart. **4.** To move about in a restless or excited way. **—flut'ter** *n.* **—flut'ter•y** *adj.*

flutter kick *n.* A swimming kick in which the legs are moved up and down in rapid strokes without bending the knees.

flux (flŭks) *n.* **1. a.** An act of flowing. **b.** A continued flow : flood. **2.** A state of constant change or fluctuation. **3.** A substance applied in soldering to facilitate flowing and prevent oxide formation. —*v.* **1.** To fuse : melt. **2.** To apply a flux to.

fly[1] (flī) *v.* **flew** (flo͞o), **flown** (flōn), **fly•ing. 1. a.** To move through the air by means of wings or winglike parts. **b.** To travel by air. **c.** To pilot (an aircraft). **2.** To rise, float, or cause to float in the air <pennants *flying*> **3.** To try to escape : flee. **4.** To rush : hasten. **5.** To pass by swiftly. **6.** To react explosively <*flew* into a rage> **7.** *p.t. & p.p.* **flied.** To hit a fly ball. —*n., pl.* **flies. 1.** A fold of cloth covering the fastening on a garment, esp. trousers. **2.** A cloth flap covering an entrance, as of a tent. **3.** A fly ball. **4. flies.** The area directly over the stage of a theater, used esp. for lighting equipment. **—on the fly. 1.** In a great hurry. **2.** In the air. **—fly'a•ble** *adj.*

fly[2] (flī) *n., pl.* **flies. 1.** Any of numerous winged insects of the order Diptera, esp. one of the family Muscidae, which includes the housefly and the tsetse. **2.** A fishing lure simulating a fly.

fly ball *n.* A baseball batted in a high arc.

fly•blown (flī'blōn') *adj.* Contaminated : spoiled.

fly-by-night (flī'bī-nīt') *adj.* **1.** Unstable : unreliable. **2.** Temporary : transitory.

fly•catch•er (flī'kăch'ər, -kĕch'-) *n.* Any of various birds of the New World family Tyrannidae or the Old World family Muscicapidae that catch flying insects.

fly•er (flī'ər) *n. var. of* FLIER.

flying boat *n.* A seaplane that is kept afloat by its hull rather than by pontoons.

flying buttress *n.* A projecting arched structure that braces part of a main wall.

flying fish *n.* A marine fish of the family Exocoetidae, having winglike fins that sustain short, gliding flights over the water.

flying saucer *n.* An unidentified flying object usu. reported and described as a luminous disk in the sky.

flying squirrel *n.* A squirrel of the genera *Pteromys, Glaucomys,* and related genera, with membranes between the forelegs and hind legs enabling it to glide through the air.

fly•leaf (flī'lēf') *n.* A blank leaf at the beginning or end of a book.

fly•pa•per (flī'pā'pər) *n.* Paper that is coated with a sticky, occas. poisonous substance to catch flies.

fly•speck (flī'spĕk') *n.* **1.** A tiny, dark speck or stain made by fly excrement. **2.** Something minute or insignificant.

fly•weight (flī'wāt') *n.* A boxer weighing 112 lb or less.

fly•wheel (flī'hwēl', -wēl') *n.* A rotating wheel with a heavy rim that regulates the speed of a machine shaft.

Fm *symbol for* FERMIUM.

foal (fōl) *n.* The young of an equine animal, as a horse, esp. one under a year old. —*v.* To give birth to a foal.

foam (fōm) *n.* **1.** A mass of bubbles formed in or on the surface of a liquid : froth. **2.** A light, firm, spongy material, as rubber, used esp. for insulation and upholstery. —*v.* To form or cause to form foam. —**foam'i•ness** *n.* —**foam'y** *adj.*
fob[1] (fŏb) *n.* **1.** A short ribbon or chain attached to a pocket watch. **2.** An ornament or seal worn on a fob.
fob[2] (fŏb) *v.* **1.** To dispose of by fraud or deceit. **2.** To put off by evasion or excuse.
focal length *n.* The distance of a focus from a lens or mirror.
fo'c's'le (fōk'səl) *n. var. of* FORECASTLE.
fo•cus (fō'kəs) *n., pl.* **-cus•es** *or* **-ci** (-sī'). **1.** A point in an optical system to which rays of light or other radiation converge or from which they appear to diverge. **2. a.** Focal length. **b.** The distinctness or clarity with which an optical system renders an image. **c.** Adjustment for distinctness or clarity. **3.** A center of interest or activity. —*v.* **-cused, -cus•ing** *or* **-cussed, -cus•sing. 1. a.** To produce a clear image of (e.g., photographed material). **b.** To adjust (a lens) to produce a clear image. **2.** To concentrate : direct. **3.** To converge or cause to converge at a focus. —**fo'cal** *adj.* —**fo'cal•ly** *adv.*
fod•der (fŏd'ər) *n.* Coarse feed for livestock, as chopped stalks of corn and hay.
foe (fō) *n.* **1.** An enemy, esp. in wartime. **2.** An opponent : adversary.
foe•tal (fēt'l) *adj. var. of* FETAL.
foe•tus (fē'təs) *n. var. of* FETUS.
fog (fôg, fŏg) *n.* **1.** Cloudlike masses of condensed water vapor lying close to the ground and obscuring visibility. **2.** Mental confusion or bewilderment. —*v.* **fogged, fog•ging.** To obscure or be obscured with or as if with fog. —**fog'gi•ly** *adv.* —**fog'gi•ness** *n.* —**fog'gy** *adj.*
fog•horn (fôg'hôrn', fŏg'-) *n.* A warning horn sounded in a fog or in darkness.
fo•gy *also* **fo•gey** (fō'gē) *n., pl.* **-gies** *also* **-geys.** A person with old-fashioned attitudes. —**fo'gy•ish** *adj.*
foi•ble (foi'bəl) *n.* A minor character weakness or failing.
foil[1] (foil) *v.* To keep from being successful : thwart.
foil[2] (foil) *n.* **1.** A thin, flexible sheet of metal. **2.** One that by strong contrast intensifies another's characteristics.
foil[3] (foil) *n.* A fencing sword with a light, thin, flexible blade and a blunt point.
foist (foist) *v.* To pass off (something inferior or false) as valuable or genuine.
fold[1] (fōld) *v.* **1.** To double or become doubled so that one part lies on another <*fold* paper> **2.** To bring (e.g., wings) from an extended to a closed position. **3.** To place together and intertwine <*fold* one's arms> **4.** To clasp, envelop, or wrap. **5.** To mix in (a cooking ingredient) by very gently turning one part over another. **6.** *Informal.* **a.** To give in : yield. **b.** To fail financially. —*n.* **1.** A part, as a line, layer, pleat, or crease, formed by folding. **2.** A folded piece or edge. —**fold'a•ble** *adj.*
fold[2] (fōld) *n.* **1. a.** An enclosure for domestic animals, esp. sheep. **b.** A flock of sheep. **2. a.** A group of people united by common beliefs. **b.** A church and its members.
fold•er (fōl'dər) *n.* **1.** One that folds. **2.** A printed booklet or circular consisting of one or several folded sheets of paper. **3.** A folded sheet of heavy paper or cardboard used for loose papers.
fol•de•rol (fŏl'də-rŏl') *n.* **1.** Nonsense. **2.** A pretty but useless trinket.
fo•li•age (fō'lē-ĭj) *n.* The leaves of growing plants and trees.
fo•li•o (fō'lē-ō') *n., pl.* **-os. 1.** A large sheet of paper folded once in the middle, making 2 leaves or 4 pages of a book or manuscript. **2.** A book consisting of folios. **3.** A page number in a book.
folk (fōk) *n., pl.* **folk** *or* **folks. 1.** An ethnic group, as a tribe or nation. **2.** People of a specified kind or group <rich *folk*> **3. folks.** *Informal.* One's relatives or family. **4. folks.** *Informal.* People in general. —*adj.* Of, pertaining to, or originating among the common people <a *folk* story>
folk etymology *n.* A change in form of a word or phrase so that it resembles a more familiar term mistakenly taken to be analogous, as *sparrowgrass* for *asparagus.*
folk•lore (fōk'lôr', -lōr') *n.* The traditional beliefs, practices, and legends of a people handed down orally. —**folk'lor'ist** *n.*
folk music *n.* Music that originates among the common people of a nation or region, traditionally transmitted orally.
folk singer *n.* One who sings folk songs. —**folk singing** *n.*
folk song *n.* A song that is part of the folk music of a people or region and that is marked by simplicity and directness of the feelings expressed.
folk•sy (fōk'sē) *adj.* **-si•er, -si•est.** *Informal.* **1.** Marked by informality of manner or style. **2.** Congenial : friendly. —**folk'si•ly** *adv.* —**folk'si•ness** *n.*
folk•way (fōk'wā') *n.* A traditional way of acting or thinking shared by the members of a cultural group.
fol•li•cle (fŏl'ĭ-kəl) *n.* **1.** A tiny anatomical cavity or sac <a hair *follicle*> **2.** A structure in an ovary containing ova.
fol•low (fŏl'ō) *v.* **1.** To come or go after. **2.** To chase : pursue. **3.** To attend : accompany. **4.** To go along the course of. **5.** To comply with : obey. **6.** To come after in time, order, or position. **7.** To engage in (e.g., a trade). **8.** To ensue : result. **9.** To pay attention to. **10.** To grasp the meaning or logic of : understand.
fol•low•er (fŏl'ō-ər) *n.* **1.** One that follows, esp. a pursuer. **2. a.** An attendant. **b.** A subordinate. **3.** An adherent of the methods or teachings of another.
fol•low•ing (fŏl'ō-ĭng) *adj.* **1.** Coming next, as in time : succeeding. **2.** Listed or mentioned next. —*n.* A group of admirers, disciples, or attendants.
fol•low-up (fŏl'ō-ŭp') *n.* The act of repeat-

ing or supplementing previous action, as by a letter or visit.

fol·ly (fŏl′ē) *n., pl.* **-lies. 1.** Lack of good sense and judgment. **2.** An act or instance of foolishness. **3.** An inordinately costly and often unprofitable undertaking.

fo·ment (fō-mĕnt′) *v.* **1.** To stir up : incite. **2.** To treat therapeutically with heat and moisture. **—fo·ment′** *n.* **—fo′men·ta′tion** *n.* **—fo·ment′er** *n.*

fond (fŏnd) *adj.* **1.** Affectionate : loving <a *fond* smile> **2.** Having a liking or affection <*fond* of music> **3.** Immoderately affectionate : doting. **4.** Deeply felt : cherished <*fond* memories> **—fond′ly** *adv.* **—fond′ness** *n.*

▲ ***word history:*** *Fond* is an example of a word that has undergone *melioration,* or a shift in connotation from bad to neutral or good. *Fond* was originally *fonned,* meaning "insipid or tasteless" and "foolish." It later meant "foolishly affectionate, doting" but even the mild reproach conveyed by this sense was lost, and *fond* now means only "having a strong liking for." The verb *fon,* of which *fond* was orig. a past participle, is very likely the same word as the word *fun.*

fon·dant (fŏn′dənt) *n.* **1.** A sweet, creamy sugar paste used in candies and icings. **2.** A candy containing fondant.

fon·dle (fŏn′dl) *v.* **-dled, -dling.** To stroke, handle, or caress affectionately.

fon·due (fŏn-do͞o′) *n.* A hot dish of melted cheese usu. flavored with wine.

font[1] (fŏnt) *n.* **1.** A basin in a church that holds baptismal or holy water. **2.** A source of abundance : fount.

font[2] (fŏnt) *n.* A full set of printing type of the same size and typeface.

food (fo͞od) *n.* **1.** A substance, usu. of plant or animal origin, taken in and assimilated by an organism to maintain life and growth : nourishment. **2.** A specified kind of nourishment <dog *food*><breakfast *food*> **3.** Nourishment in solid form <hearty *food* and drink> **4.** Something that sustains, nourishes, or provides <*food* for thought>

food chain *n.* An ecological community of plants and animals in which each kind uses the kind usu. next below it as food.

food poisoning *n.* Poisoning marked by vomiting, diarrhea, and prostration and caused by eating food contaminated by natural toxins or bacteria.

food processor *n.* An appliance with interchangeable blades that processes food, as by slicing or shredding, at high speed.

food stamp *n.* A stamp issued by the government and sold or given to low-income persons to be redeemed for food.

food·stuff (fo͞od′stŭf′) *n.* Something that can be used as food.

food web *n.* A complex of interrelated food chains in an ecological community.

fool (fo͞ol) *n.* **1.** One deficient in good sense or judgment. **2.** A court jester. **3.** One who can easily be tricked : dupe. —*v.* **1.** To dupe. **2.** To take by surprise. **3.** To speak or act in jest : joke. **4.** *Informal.* To amuse oneself : play <just *fooling* around> **5.** To toy or tamper with.

fool·er·y (fo͞o′lə-rē) *n., pl.* **-ies.** Foolish speech or behavior : nonsense.

fool·har·dy (fo͞ol′här′dē) *adj.* **-di·er, -di·est.** Unwisely daring : rash. **—fool′har′di·ly** *adv.* **—fool′har′di·ness** *n.*

fool·ish (fo͞o′lĭsh) *adj.* **1.** Lacking or resulting from a lack of good sense or judgment : unwise. **2.** Ridiculous : absurd. **—fool′ish·ly** *adv.* **—fool′ish·ness** *n.*

fool·proof (fo͞ol′pro͞of′) *adj.* Affording no opportunity for misuse, error, or failure.

fools·cap (fo͞olz′kăp′) *n.* A sheet of paper approx. 13 x 16 in.

foot (fo͝ot) *n., pl.* **feet** (fēt). **1.** The lower extremity of the vertebrate leg that is in direct contact with the ground. **2.** Something like a foot in function or position <the *foot* of a hill> **3.** A unit of poetic meter that consists of a group of syllables. **4.** —See table at MEASUREMENT. **5.** The end, as of a bed, that is opposite the head. **6.** The lowest rank or part. —*v.* **1.** To go on foot : walk. **2.** To dance. **3.** To add up <*foot* up the bill> **4.** *Informal.* To pay <*foot* the bill> **—on foot.** Walking rather than riding. **—foot′less** *adj.*

foot·age (fo͝ot′ĭj) *n.* **1.** Length or extent expressed in feet. **2.** A segment of motion-picture film or videotape <news *footage*>

foot·ball (fo͝ot′bôl′) *n.* **1. a.** A game played by 2 11-member teams on a long rectangular field with goals at either end. **b.** *Can.* A similar game played by 2 12-member teams. **c.** The inflated oval ball used in either of these games. **2.** *esp. Brit.* Rugby or soccer.

foot·board (fo͝ot′bôrd′, -bōrd′) *n.* **1.** A board or small platform on which to rest or support the feet. **2.** An upright board that forms the foot of a bedstead.

foot·bridge (fo͝ot′brĭj′) *n.* A bridge for pedestrians.

foot·ed (fo͝ot′ĭd) *adj.* **1.** Having a foot or feet <a *footed* vase><a *footed* animal> **2.** Having a particular kind or number of feet <web-*footed*>

foot·fall (fo͝ot′fôl′) *n.* **1.** A footstep. **2.** The sound of a footstep.

foot·hill (fo͝ot′hĭl′) *n.* A low hill at or near the foot of a mountain.

foot·hold (fo͝ot′hōld′) *n.* **1.** A place that provides support for the foot, as in climbing. **2.** A position providing a base for advancement.

foot·ing (fo͝ot′ĭng) *n.* **1.** Secure placement of the feet. **2. a.** A basis : foundation. **b.** A basis for social or business dealings with others : standing.

foot·lights (fo͝ot′līts′) *pl.n.* **1.** Lights in a row along the front of a stage floor. **2.** The theater regarded as a profession.

foot·lock·er (fo͝ot′lŏk′ər) *n.* A small trunk for personal belongings kept esp. at the foot of a bed.

foot·loose (fo͝ot′lo͞os′) *adj.* Free to do as one pleases.

foot·man (fo͝ot′mən) *n.* A male household

servant who attends the door, waits on table, and runs errands.

foot•note (fo͝ot′nōt′) *n.* **1.** A note of reference, explanation, or comment usu. at the bottom of a page. **2.** A commentary. **—foot′note′** *v.*

foot•path (fo͝ot′păth′, -päth′) *n.* A usu. narrow path for persons on foot.

foot•print (fo͝ot′prĭnt′) *n.* An outline of the foot on a surface.

foot•sore (fo͝ot′sôr′, -sōr′) *adj.* Having tired or sore feet, as from walking.

foot•step (fo͝ot′stĕp′) *n.* **1.** A step with the foot. **2.** The distance covered by a footstep <a *footstep* away> **3.** The sound of a footstep. **4.** A footprint. **5.** A step up or down.

foot•stool (fo͝ot′sto͞ol′) *n.* A low stool for the feet.

foot•wear (fo͝ot′wâr′) *n.* Coverings, as shoes or boots, for the feet.

foot•work (fo͝ot′wûrk′) *n.* The way in which one uses the feet, as in boxing.

fop (fŏp) *n.* A man preoccupied with his clothes **:** dandy. **—fop′per•y** *n.* **—fop′pish** *adj.* **—fop′pish•ness** *n.*

for (fôr; fər *when unstressed*) *prep.* **1.** —Used to indicate the object, recipient, or aim of an act or activity <studied *for* the exam><a gift *for* you><ran *for* President> **2.** —Used to indicate a destination <headed *for* town> **3.** As a result of <jump *for* joy> **4.** —Used to indicate amount, extent, or duration <a check *for* $10><walked *for* miles> **5.** Considering the usual nature or character of <cold *for* July> **6.** In spite of <unhappy *for* all their wealth> **7. a.** On behalf of <spoke *for* everyone> **b.** In favor of <Are you *for* or against the plan?> **8.** As equal to <paid $30 *for* the fare> **9.** As against <ounce *for* ounce> **10.** As being <took it *for* granted> **11.** —Used to indicate appropriateness or responsibility <It's not *for* me to say.> *—conj.* Because; since.

fo•ra (fôr′ə, fōr′ə) *n. var. pl. of* FORUM.

for•age (fôr′ĭj, fŏr′-) *n.* **1.** Food for domestic animals, esp. that gathered by grazing. **2.** A search for provisions or food. *—v.* **-aged, -ag•ing. 1.** To search for provisions or food. **2.** To make a raid **:** plunder. **3.** To wander or rummage through, esp. in search of provisions. **—for′ag•er** *n.*

for•ay (fôr′ā′, fŏr′ā′) *n.* **1.** A raid. **2.** A 1st attempt or venture. **—for′ay′** *v.*

for•bear[1] (fôr-bâr′) *v.* **-bore** (-bôr′, -bōr′), **-borne** (-bôrn′, -bōrn′), **-bear•ing. 1.** To desist or refrain from. **2.** To be patient or tolerant. **—for•bear′ance** *n.*

for•bear[2] (fôr′bâr′, fōr′-) *n. var. of* FOREBEAR.

for•bid (fər-bĭd′, fôr-) *v.* **-bade** (-băd′, -bād′) *or* **-bad** (-băd′), **-bid•den** (-bĭd′n) *or* **-bid, -bid•ding. 1.** To order (someone) not to do something. **2.** To prohibit, esp. by law. **3.** To prevent **:** preclude. ★ ***syns:*** BAN, DISALLOW, ENJOIN, INTERDICT, OUTLAW, PROHIBIT, PROSCRIBE

for•bid•ding (fər-bĭd′ĭng, fôr-) *adj.* Tending to discourage or repel.

force (fôrs, fōrs) *n.* **1. a.** Energy or strength **:** power. **b.** The use of such power. **2.** Intellectual vigor or influence. **3.** A group organized or available for a certain purpose. **4.** *Physics.* A vector quantity that tends to produce an acceleration of a body in the direction of its application. *—v.* **forced, forc•ing. 1.** To compel to act. **2.** To get by coercion. **3.** To produce with effort <*force* a smile> **4.** To move (something) against resistance **:** push. **5.** To open or break down by force. **6.** To inflict or impose, as one's will. **7.** To cause rapid growth by artificial means <*force* lilies> **—in force. 1.** In large numbers. **2.** In effect. **—force′a•ble** *adj.* **—force′ful** *adj.* **—force′ful•ly** *adv.* **—forc′er** *n.*

force•meat (fôrs′mēt′, fōrs′-) *n.* Finely ground meat, fish, or poultry usu. used in stuffing.

for•ceps (fôr′səps) *n. (pl. in number).* An instrument that resembles a pair of tongs and is used for grasping, manipulating, or extracting, esp. in surgery.

forc•i•ble (fôr′sə-bəl, fōr′-) *adj.* **1.** Achieved or accomplished by force. **2.** Marked by force. **—forc′i•bly** *adv.*

ford (fôrd, fōrd) *n.* A shallow part of a body of water where a crossing can be made without a boat. *—v.* To cross at a ford.

fore (fôr, fōr) *adj. & adv.* In, at, or toward the front **:** forward. *—n.* The front. *—interj.* —Used by a golfer to warn others that a ball is about to be hit their way.

fore-and-aft (fôr′ən-ăft′, fōr′-) *adj.* Parallel with a ship's keel.

fore•arm[1] (fôr-ärm′, fōr-) *v.* To arm or prepare in advance, as for a conflict.

fore•arm[2] (fôr′ärm′, fōr′-) *n.* The arm between the wrist and elbow.

fore•bear *also* **for•bear** (fôr′bâr′, fōr′-) *n.* An ancestor.

fore•bode (fôr-bōd′, fōr-) *v.* **1.** To give an indication or warning of. **2.** To have a premonition of (future bad fortune). **—fore•bod′ing** *n.* **—fore•bod′ing•ly** *adv.*

fore•cast (fôr′kăst′, fōr′-) *v.* **1.** To estimate in advance, esp. to predict (the weather). **2.** To be an indication of **:** foreshadow. **—fore′cast′** *n.* **—fore′cast′er** *n.*

fore•cas•tle (fōk′səl, fôr′kăs′əl, fōr′-) *also* **fo′c′s′le** (fōk′səl) *n.* **1.** The section of a ship's upper deck situated forward of the foremast. **2.** Housing for the crew at the bow of a merchant ship.

fore•check (for′chek′, for′-) *v. Hockey.* To check an opponent in his zone.

fore•close (fôr-klōz′, fōr-) *v.* **1.** To terminate (a mortgage) and take legal possession of the mortgaged property. **2.** To exclude **:** debar. **—fore•clo′sure** *n.*

fore•fa•ther (fôr′fä′*th*ər, fōr′-) *n.* An ancestor.

fore•fin•ger (fôr′fĭng′gər, fōr′-) *n.* The finger next to the thumb.

fore•foot (fôr′fo͝ot′, fōr′-) *n.* A front foot of an animal.

fore•front (fôr′frŭnt′, fōr′-) *n.* The foremost part **:** vanguard.

fore·go[1] (fôr-gō′, fōr-) *v.* To go before : precede.

fore·go[2] (fôr-gō′, fōr-) *v. var. of* FORGO.

fore·go·ing (fôr-gō′ĭng, fōr-, fôr′gō′ĭng, fōr′-) *adj.* Just before : previous.

fore·gone (fôr′gôn′, -gŏn′, fōr′-) *adj.* Known in advance : inevitable.

fore·ground (fôr′ground′, fōr′-) *n.* **1.** The part of a picture or view depicted as nearest to the viewer. **2.** The forefront.

fore·hand (fôr′hănd′, fōr′-) *n.* A stroke, as in tennis, made with the hand moving palm forward. **—fore′hand′** *adj. & adv.*

fore·head (fôr′ĭd, fŏr′-, fôr′hĕd′, fōr′-) *n.* The part of the head or face above the eyes.

for·eign (fôr′ĭn, fŏr′-) *adj.* **1.** Situated outside one's native country <*foreign* cities> **2.** Of, from, by, or for a country other than one's own <*foreign* languages> **3.** Carried on or involved with other nations <*foreign* trade> **4.** Occurring abnormally in the body, esp. introduced from the outside. **5.** Not relevant : extraneous. **—for′eign·ness** *n.*

for·eign·er (fôr′ə-nər, fŏr′-) *n.* Someone from a foreign country : alien.

fore·knowl·edge (fôr-nŏl′ĭj, fōr-) *n.* Prior knowledge of something : prescience.

fore·leg (fôr′lĕg′, fōr′-) *n.* One of an animal's front legs.

fore·limb (fôr′lĭm′, fōr′-) *n.* A front appendage, as an arm, wing, foreleg, or flipper.

fore·lock (fôr′lŏk′, fōr′-) *n.* A lock of hair growing from the forehead.

fore·man (fôr′mən, fōr′-) *n.* **1.** One who supervises a group of workers. **2.** The spokesperson for a jury.

fore·mast (fôr′məst, -măst′, fōr′-) *n. Naut.* The forward mast of a sailing vessel.

fore·most (fôr′mōst′, fōr′-) *adj. & adv.* First in time, rank, or position.

fore·noon (fôr′no͞on′, fōr′-) *n.* The time between sunrise and noon.

fo·ren·sic (fə-rĕn′sĭk, -zĭk) *adj.* Of, relating to, or used in legal proceedings or formal debate. **—fo·ren′si·cal·ly** *adv.*

fo·ren·sics (fə-rĕn′sĭks, -zĭks) *n. (sing. in number).* The art or study of formal debate.

fore·or·dain (fôr′ôr-dān′, fōr′-) *v.* To decree or ordain beforehand : predestine.

fore·part (fôr′pärt′, fōr′-) *n.* **1.** The first or earliest part. **2.** An anterior part.

fore·quar·ter (fôr′kwôr′tər, fōr′-) *n.* The section including the foreleg and shoulder of an animal or side of meat.

fore·run·ner (fôr′rŭn′ər, fōr′-) *n.* **1.** One that precedes. **2.** One that indicates the approach of others : harbinger.

fore·sail (fôr′səl, -sāl′, fōr′-) *n. Naut.* The principal square sail on the foremast of a square-rigged vessel.

fore·see (fôr-sē′, fōr-) *v.* To know or see beforehand <*foresaw* the outcome> **—fore·see′a·ble** *adj.* **—fore·se′er** *n.*

fore·shad·ow (fôr-shăd′ō, fōr-) *v.* To indicate or warn of beforehand.

fore·shore (fôr′shôr′, fōr′shōr′) *n.* The part of a shore covered at high tide.

fore·short·en (fôr-shôr′tn, fōr-) *v.* To shorten certain lines in (e.g., a figure or design) in order to give the illusion of depth.

fore·sight (fôr′sīt′, fōr′-) *n.* **1.** The act or power of foreseeing. **2.** The act of looking forward. **3.** Concern for the future : prudence. **—fore′sight′ed** *adj.* **—fore′sight′ed·ly** *adv.* **—fore′sight′ed·ness** *n.*

fore·skin (fôr′skĭn′, fōr′-) *n.* The loose fold of skin that covers the glans of the penis.

for·est (fôr′ĭst, fŏr′-) *n.* **1.** A large, thick growth of trees. **2.** Something resembling a forest, as in density or quantity. **—for′est·ed** *adj.* **—for′est·land′** *n.*

fore·stall (fôr-stôl′, fōr-) *v.* To delay or prevent by taking measures against in advance. **—fore·stall′er** *n.*

forest ranger *n.* An officer in charge of managing or protecting a public forest or section of a public forest.

for·est·ry (fôr′ĭ-strē, fŏr′-) *n.* The science and art of developing, maintaining, and managing forests. **—for′est·er** *n.*

fore·taste (fôr′tāst′, fōr′-) *n.* An advance sample or indication. **—fore·taste′** *v.*

fore·tell (fôr-tĕl′, fōr-) *v.* To tell of beforehand : predict. **—fore·tell′er** *n.*

fore·thought (fôr′thôt′, fōr′-) *n.* Prior thought, preparation, or planning.

fore·to·ken (fôr-tō′kən, fōr-) *v.* To indicate beforehand. **—fore′to′ken** *n.*

for·ev·er (fôr-ĕv′ər, fər-) *adv.* **1.** For eternity. **2.** Without cease : incessantly.

for·ev·er·more (fôr-ĕv′ər-môr′, -mōr′, fər-) *adv.* Forever.

fore·warn (fôr-wôrn′, fōr-) *v.* To warn ahead of time.

fore·wom·an (fôr′wo͝om′ən, fōr′-) *n.* **1.** A woman who serves as the leader of a work crew, as in a factory. **2.** A woman who chairs and speaks for a jury.

fore·word (fôr′wûrd′, -wərd, fōr′-) *n.* An introductory statement, esp. in a book.

for·feit (fôr′fĭt) *n.* **1.** Something given up as punishment : penalty. **2.** Something that is placed in escrow and redeemed after the payment of a fine. **3.** A forfeiture. —*v.* To lose or give up as a forfeit. **—for′feit·a·ble** *adj.* **—for′feit·er** *n.*

for·fei·ture (fôr′fĭ-cho͝or′, -chər) *n.* **1.** The act of forfeiting. **2.** Something forfeited : penalty.

for·gath·er (fôr-găth′ər, fōr-) *v.* To come together : convene.

forge[1] (fôrj, fōrj) *n.* A hearth or furnace where metals are heated and wrought : smithy. —*v.* **forged, forg·ing. 1.** To shape (metal) by heating and beating or hammering. **2.** To give shape to <*forge* a peace treaty> **3.** To make or reproduce esp. for deceptive purposes <*forge* a signature> **—forg′er** *n.* **—for′ger·y** *n.*

forge[2] (fôrj, fōrj) *v.* **forged, forg·ing. 1.** To advance slowly but surely. **2.** To advance quickly and abruptly.

for·get (fər-gĕt′, fôr-) *v.* **-got** (-gŏt′), **-got·ten** (-gŏt′n) *or* **-got, -get·ting. 1.** To be unable to remember. **2.** To fail to attend to : neglect. **3.**

To fail to become aware of at the right time <*forgot* about the rent> **—forget (oneself).** To lose one's reserve or self-restraint. **—for·get'ful** *adj.* **—for·get'ful·ly** *adv.* **—for·get'ful·ness** *n.* **—for·get'ta·ble** *adj.*

for·get-me-not (fər-gĕt'mē-nŏt', fôr-) *n.* A low-growing plant of the genus *Myosotis,* with small blue flower clusters.

for·give (fər-gĭv', fôr-) *v.* **-gave** (-gāv'), **-giv·en** (-gĭv'ən), **-giv·ing. 1.** To pardon or absolve. **2.** To stop being angry about or resentful against. **3.** To relieve from payment of. **—for·giv'a·ble** *adj.* **—for·give'ness** *n.* **—for·giv'er** *n.*

for·go *also* **fore·go** (fôr-gō', fōr-) *v.* **-went** (-wĕnt'), **-gone** (-gôn', -gŏn'), **-go·ing.** To give up or let go : relinquish. **—for·go'er** *n.*

fo·rint (fôr'ĭnt') *n.* —See table at CURRENCY.

fork (fôrk) *n.* **1.** A utensil with 2 or more tines for serving or eating food. **2.** A pronged implement used esp. for digging. **3. a.** A separation into 2 or more parts or branches. **b.** The place where this occurs <a *fork* in the road> **c.** Any of the branches <the left *fork*> *—v.* **1.** To lift or carry with a fork. **2.** To give the shape of a fork to. **3.** To divide into 2 or more branches. **4.** *Informal.* To hand over : pay.

forked (fôrkt, fôr'kĭd) *adj.* Shaped like or having a fork.

fork lift *n.* An industrial vehicle with a pronged platform that lifts and carries heavy loads.

fork lift

for·lorn (fôr-lôrn', fər-) *adj.* **1.** Abandoned : deserted. **2.** Pitiful. **3.** Almost hopeless. **—for·lorn'ly** *adv.* **—for·lorn'ness** *n.*

form (fôrm) *n.* **1.** The shape and structure of something. **2.** A body, esp. of a person : figure. **3.** The basic nature of something. **4.** The mode in which something exists : variety <a *form* of plant life> **5.** Procedure as established by custom or regulation. **6.** Manners as determined by etiquette or custom. **7.** Performance according to established criteria. **8.** Fitness, as of an animal, with regard to training or health. **9.** A fixed order of words, as in a ceremony : formula. **10.** A document with blanks into which required information is to be inserted. **11.** Manner or style in musical or literary composition. **12.** The design or structure of a work of art <symphonic *form*> **13.** A model from which a mold can be made. **14.** A grade in a British school or in some U.S. private schools. *—v.* **1.** To shape or become shaped. **2.** To assume or shape into a given form. **3.** To develop by instruction. **4.** To come to have. **5.** To constitute or be a part of. **6.** To conceive in the mind <*form* an opinion> **7.** To put in order : arrange.

-form *suff.* Having the form of <cruci*form*>

for·mal (fôr'məl) *adj.* **1.** Of or relating to the outward aspect of something. **2.** Relating to the essential form of something <a *formal* precept> **3.** Following or based on accepted conventions. **4.** Marked by strict observation of forms. **5.** Stiff or cold <a *formal* demeanor> **6.** Outwardly correct but lacking in substance <a purely *formal* leave-taking> **—for'mal·ly** *adv.*

for·mal·de·hyde (fôr-măl'də-hīd') *n.* A colorless gaseous compound used in water solution as a preservative and disinfectant.

for·mal·ism (fôr'mə-lĭz'əm) *n.* FORMALITY 2. **—for'mal·ist** *n.*

for·mal·i·ty (fôr-măl'ĭ-tē) *n., pl.* **-ties. 1.** The quality or state of being formal. **2.** Rigorous observance of established forms or rules. **3.** An established form or rule.

for·mal·ize (fôr'mə-līz') *v.* **-ized, -iz·ing. 1.** To give a definite structure or shape to. **2.** To make formal. **3.** To give formal approval to. **—for'mal·i·za'tion** *n.*

for·mat (fôr'măt') *n.* **1.** A general plan of organization and arrangement. **2.** The form or layout of a publication. *—v.* **-mat·ted, -mat·ting.** *Computer Sci.* To produce (e.g., data) in a specified form.

for·ma·tion (fôr-mā'shən) *n.* **1.** The act or process of forming. **2.** Something formed. **3.** The way in which something is formed : shape. **4.** A given arrangement, as of troops.

for·ma·tive (fôr'mə-tĭv) *adj.* **1.** Forming or capable of forming. **2.** Of or pertaining to formation, growth, or development.

for·mer (fôr'mər) *adj.* **1.** Taking place earlier in time. **2.** Preceding in order or place. **3.** Being the 1st mentioned of 2.

for·mer·ly (fôr'mər-lē) *adv.* Previously.

form·fit·ting (fôrm'fĭt'ĭng) *adj.* Conforming closely to the contours of the body.

For·mi·ca (fôr-mī'kə). A trademark for any of various high-pressure laminated plastic materials, used esp. for chemical- and heat-resistant surfaces.

for·mi·da·ble (fôr'mĭ-də-bəl, fôr-mĭd'ə-bəl) *adj.* **1.** Inspiring dread, fear, or awe. **2.** Difficult to undertake or overcome. **—for'mi·da·bly** *adv.*

form·less (fôrm'lĭs) *adj.* Lacking definite form or shape. **—form'less·ly** *adv.* **—form'less·ness** *n.*

form letter *n.* A usu. impersonal letter in a standardized format, sent to different people or to large numbers of people.

for·mu·la (fôr'myə-lə) *n., pl.* **-las** *or* **-lae** (-lē'). **1.** An established form of words or rules for use in a ceremony or procedure. **2.** *Chem.* A symbolic representation of the composition or composition and structure of a chemical compound. 3. *Math.* A statement, esp. an equation, of a logical relation. 4. A recipe. 5. A nutritious liquid food for an infant. —**for′mu·la′ic** (-lā′ĭk) *adj.*

for·mu·late (fôr′myə-lāt′) *v.* **-lat·ed, -lat·ing. 1.** To state as a formula. **2.** To express in an orderly and systematic way. **3.** To devise : invent. **4.** To prepare according to a particular formula. —**for′mu·la′tion** *n.* —**form′u·la′tor** *n.*

for·ni·ca·tion (fôr′nĭ-kā′shən) *n.* Sexual intercourse between partners who are not married to each other. —**for′ni·cate′** *v.* —**for′ni·ca′tor** *n.*

for·sake (fôr-sāk′, fər-) *v.* **-sook** (-so͝ok′), **-sak·en** (-sā′kən), **-sak·ing. 1.** To give up : forswear. **2.** To abandon or desert.

for·sooth (fôr-so͞oth′, fər-) *adv. Archaic.* In truth : certainly.

for·swear (fôr-swâr′, fōr-) *v.* **-swore** (-swôr′, -swōr′), **-sworn** (-swôrn′, -swōrn′), **-swear·ing. 1.** To renounce : forsake. **2.** To swear falsely : perjure oneself.

for·syth·i·a (fôr-sĭth′ē-ə, fər-) *n.* An Asian shrub of the genus *Forsythia,* widely cultivated for its early-blooming yellow flowers.

fort (fôrt, fōrt) *n.* A fortified structure or area, esp. a permanent army post.

for·te[1] (fôr′tā′, fôrt, fōrt) *n.* An activity in which one excels.

for·te[2] (fôr′tā′) *adv. Mus.* Loudly. —Used as a direction. —**for′te′** *adj.*

forth (fôrth, fōrth) *adv.* **1.** Out into plain sight <come *forth*> **2.** Onward or forward <from this time *forth*>

forth·com·ing (fôrth-kŭm′ĭng, fōrth-) *adj.* **1.** About to appear or occur. **2.** Readily available.

forth·right (fôrth′rīt′, fōrth′-) *adj.* Straightforward : direct. —**forth′right′ly** *adv.* —**forth′right′ness** *n.*

forth·with (fôrth-wĭth′, -wĭ*th*′, fōrth-) *adv.* At once : promptly.

for·ti·fy (fôr′tə-fī′) *v.* **-fied, -fy·ing. 1.** To strengthen and secure (a position) militarily. **2.** To give physical strength to : invigorate. **3.** To strengthen morally or mentally : encourage. **4.** To enrich (a substance), as by adding vitamins. —**for′ti·fi·ca′tion** *n.* —**for′ti·fi′er** *n.*

for·tis·si·mo (fôr-tĭs′ə-mō′) *adv. Mus.* Very loudly. —Used as a direction. —**for·tis′si·mo′** *adj.*

for·ti·tude (fôr′tĭ-to͞od′, -tyo͞od′) *n.* Strength of mind allowing a person to withstand pain or adversity courageously.

fort·night (fôrt′nīt′) *n.* A period of 2 weeks. —**fort′night′ly** *adj. & adv.*

FOR·TRAN (fôr′trăn′) *n. Computer Sci.* A programming language for problems expressible in algebraic terms.

for·tress (fôr′trĭs) *n.* A fortified place, esp. one that includes a town.

for·tu·i·tous (fôr-to͞o′ĭ-təs, -tyo͞o′-) *adj.* Occurring by accident or chance : not planned. —**for·tu′i·tous·ly** *adv.*

for·tu·i·ty (fôr-to͞o′ĭ-tē, -tyo͞o′-) *n., pl.* **-ties. 1.** A fortuitous occurrence. **2.** The quality or state of being fortuitous.

for·tu·nate (fôr′chə-nĭt) *adj.* **1.** Bringing or brought by good fortune : auspicious. **2.** Having good fortune ★ ***syns:*** HAPPY, LUCKY, PROVIDENTIAL —**for′tu·nate·ly** *adv.*

for·tune (fôr′chən) *n.* **1.** A hypothetical force that controls the events of life : chance. **2.** Good or bad luck : fate. **3.** Success, esp. when resulting from luck. **4. a.** Wealth. **b.** A large amount of money.

fortune hunter *n.* One who seeks wealth, esp. through marriage.

for·tune·tell·er (fôr′chən-tĕl′ər) *n.* One who claims to be able to predict the future. —**for′tune·tell′ing** *n. & adj.*

for·ty (fôr′tē) *n., pl.* **-ties.** The cardinal number equal to 4 × 10. —**for′ti·eth** *n. & adj. & adv.* —**for′ty** *adj. & pron.*

for·ty-five (fôr′tē-fīv′) *n.* **1.** A.45-caliber pistol. **2.** A phonograph record played at 45 revolutions a minute.

for·ty-nin·er (fôr′tē-nī′nər) *n.* A person in the 1849 California gold rush.

forty winks *n. (sing. or pl. in number). Informal.* A brief nap.

fo·rum (fôr′əm, fōr′-) *n., pl.* **-rums** *or* **fo·ra** (fôr′ə, fōr′ə). **1.** A public square or marketplace in ancient Rome. **2.** A public meeting place or medium for open discussion. **3.** A court of law : tribunal. **4.** A public program involving panel discussion and audience participation.

for·ward (fôr′wərd) *adj.* **1.** At, in, near, belonging to, or situated in the front. **2.** Going, tending to go, or moving frontward. **3.** Lacking restraint : presumptuous. **4.** Well developed, esp. technologically, economically, or politically. **5.** Intellectually or socially advanced : precocious. —*adv.* **1.** *also* **for·wards** (-wərdz). To or toward the front : frontward. **2.** In, into, or toward the future <looking *forward* to the weekend> **3.** Out into view : forth. —*n.* A player in the front line of offense or defense, as in basketball. —*v.* **1.** To send forward to a subsequent destination or address. **2.** To help to advance. —**for′ward·ly** *adv.* —**for′ward·ness** *n.*

for·ward·er (fôr′wər-dər) *n.* One that forwards, esp. an agent who facilitates the passage of received goods to their destination.

for·went (fôr-wĕnt′, fōr-) *v. p.t. of* FORGO.

fos·sil (fŏs′əl) *n.* **1.** The remains or a trace of an animal or plant of a past geologic age embedded in the earth's crust. **2.** One that is outdated or antiquated. —**fos′sil·i·za′tion** *n.* —**fos′si·lize′** *v.*

fos·ter (fô′stər, fŏs′tər) *v.* **1.** To bring up : nurture. **2.** To cultivate and encourage. —*adj.* Giving or receiving parental care though not related through blood or legal ties <*foster* parents><a *foster* child>

fought (fôt) *v. p.t. & p.p. of* FIGHT.

foul (foul) *adj.* **1.** Offensive to the senses, esp. to the sense of smell : repulsive. **2.** Rotten, as spoiled meat. **3.** Very dirty : filthy. **4.** Morally detestable. **5.** Vulgar or obscene. **6.** Unpleasant <*foul* weather> **7.** Not fair **:** dishonorable. **8. a.** Designating the limiting lines of a playing area. **b.** Contrary to the rules of a sport or game. **9.** Entangled or twisted, as an anchor or rope. —*n.* **1. a.** A batted baseball that touches the ground outside fair territory. **b.** An infraction of the rules of play in a sport or game. **2.** A collision or entanglement. —*adv.* In a foul way. —*v.* **1.** To make or become foul **:** dirty. **2.** To dishonor. **3.** To obstruct **:** clog. **4.** To entangle or become entangled. **5.** To make or hit a foul. **—foul up.** *Slang.* To blunder or cause to blunder. **—foul'ly** *adv.* **—foul'ness** *n.*

fou•lard (fo͞o-lärd') *n.* A lightweight silk or silk and cotton twill or plain-woven fabric usu. having a small printed design.

foul-mouthed (foul'mou*th*d', -moutht') *adj.* Using vulgar or obscene language.

foul play *n.* Unfair or treacherous behavior, esp. when it involves violence.

foul-up (foul'ŭp') *n. Informal.* **1.** Confusion due to mismanagement. **2.** A mechanical problem.

found[1] (found) *v.* **1.** To establish (e.g., a college), often with funds to permit continuation and maintenance. **2.** To establish the basis of. **—found'er** *n.*

found[2] (found) *v.* **1.** To melt (metal) and pour into a mold. **2.** To make by founding metal. **—found'er** *n.*

found[3] (found) *v. p.t. & p.p. of* FIND.

foun•da•tion (foun-dā'shən) *n.* **1.** The act of founding or state of being founded. **2.** The basis on which something stands or is supported. **3. a.** An endowment fund. **b.** An institution supported by an endowment. **4.** A cosmetic base for make-up. **5.** A corset. **—foun•da'tion•al** *adj.*

foun•der (foun'dər) *v.* **1.** To go or cause to go lame. —Used of a horse. **2.** To break down **:** fail. **3.** *Naut.* To sink, as a ship.

found•ling (found'lĭng) *n.* An abandoned child of unknown parents.

foun•dry (foun'drē) *n., pl.* **-dries.** An establishment where metal is founded.

fount (fount) *n.* **1.** A fountain. **2.** An abundant source.

foun•tain (foun'tən) *n.* **1.** A natural spring of water. **2. a.** An artificially created stream of water. **b.** The device or structure from which such a stream springs. **3.** A point of origin **:** source. **4.** A soda fountain.

foun•tain•head (foun'tən-hĕd') *n.* **1.** A spring that is the source of a stream. **2.** A main origin or source.

fountain pen *n.* A pen with a reservoir of ink that feeds the writing point.

four (fôr, fōr) *n.* **1.** The cardinal number equal to 3 + 1. **2.** The 4th in a set or sequence. **3.** Something having 4 parts, units, or members. **—four** *adj. & pron.*

four-flush (fôr'flŭsh', fōr'-) *v. Slang.* To bluff. **—four'-flush'er** *n.*

four•fold (fôr'fōld', fōr'-) *adj.* **1.** Having 4 parts or aspects. **2.** Being 4 times as many or as much. **—four'fold'** *adv.*

Four-H Club (fôr'āch', fōr'-) *n.* A youth organization that offers instruction in modern agriculture.

four-in-hand (fôr'ĭn-hănd', fōr'-) *n.* **1.** A team of 4 horses. **2.** A horse-drawn vehicle driven by one person. **3.** A necktie that is tied in a slipknot, the ends being left hanging and overlapping.

four-o'clock (fôr'ə-klŏk', fōr'-) *n.* A plant of the genus *Mirabilis,* esp. *M. jalapa,* widely cultivated for its tubular flowers that open in the late afternoon.

four-post•er (fôr'pō'stər, fōr'-) *n.* A bed having tall corner posts orig. intended to support a canopy or curtains.

four•score (fôr'skôr', fōr'skōr') *adj.* Being 4 times 20 **:** 80.

four•some (fôr'səm, fōr'-) *n.* **1.** A group of 4 persons, esp. of 2 couples. **2.** The players in a golf match played by 4 persons.

four•square (fôr'skwâr', fōr'-) *adj.* **1.** Having a square shape. **2.** Unwavering **:** firm. **3.** Forthright. **—four'square'** *adv.*

four•teen (fôr-tēn', fōr-) *n.* **1.** The cardinal number equal to 13 + 1. **2.** The 14th in a set or sequence. **3.** Something having 14 parts, units, or members. **—four•teen'** *adj. & pron.* **—four•teenth'** *n. & adj. & adv.*

fourth (fôrth, fōrth) *n.* **1.** The ordinal number matching the number 4 in a series. **2.** One of 4 equal parts. **3.** The 4th forward gear of a motor vehicle. **—fourth** *adj. & adv.*

fourth estate *n.* Journalists collectively.

Fourth of July *n.* Independence Day.

Fourth World *n.* The least-developed or poorest countries of the Third World.

four-wheel (fôr'hwēl', -wēl', fōr'-) *adj.* Of or designating an automotive drive mechanism in which all 4 wheels are linked to the source of driving power.

fowl (foul) *n., pl.* **fowl** *or* **fowls. 1.** A bird of the order Galliformes, used as food or hunted as game, esp. the common domesticated chicken, *Gallus gallus.* **2.** The edible flesh of a fowl. —*v.* To hunt or trap wild fowl. **—fowl'er** *n.*

fox (fŏks) *n.* **1.** A carnivorous mammal of the genus *Vulpes* or related genera, having a pointed snout, upright ears, and a long, bushy tail. **2.** The fur of a fox. **3.** A sly or crafty person. —*v.* To outwit **:** trick.

Fox (fŏks) *n., pl.* **Fox** *or* **-es. 1.** A member of an American Indian people formerly of the upper Midwest, now in Iowa and Oklahoma. **2.** Their Algonquian language.

foxed (fŏkst) *adj.* Stained with yellowish-brown spots, as an old book or print.

fox•glove (fŏks'glŭv') *n.* A native European plant of the genus *Digitalis,* esp. *D. purpurea,* having a tall spike of tubular, pinkish-purple flowers and leaves that are the source of the medicinal drug digitalis.

fox•hole (fŏks'hōl') *n.* A shallow pit dug by a soldier for refuge against enemy fire.

fox•hound (fŏks'hound') *n.* A dog bred and developed for fox hunting.

fox terrier *n.* A small dog, orig. bred in England, having a wiry or smooth white coat with dark markings.

fox trot *n.* **1.** A ballroom dance in 4/4 or 2/4 time. **2.** The music for a foxtrot. —**fox'-trot'** *v.*

fox•y (fŏk'sē) *adj.* **-i•er, -i•est.** Like a fox, as in slyness or cleverness. —**fox'i•ly** *adv.* —**fox'i•ness** *n.*

foy•er (foi'ər, foi'ā') *n.* **1.** The lobby of a public building, as a hotel. **2.** A vestibule or entrance hall.

Fr *symbol for* FRANCIUM.

fra•cas (frā'kəs) *n.* A disorderly uproar.

frac•tal (frăk'təl) *n.* A geometric pattern that is repeated at ever smaller scales to produce irregular shapes that cannot be represented by classical geometry.

frac•tion (frăk'shən) *n.* **1.** A small part : bit. **2.** A disconnected piece : fragment. **3.** *Math.* A quotient of 2 quantities shown as a numerator over a denominator. **4.** *Chem.* A component of a compound, separated by distillation or crystallization. —**frac'tion•al** *adj.*

frac•tious (frăk'shəs) *adj.* **1.** Apt to cause trouble : unruly. **2.** Irritable. —**frac'tious•ly** *adv.* —**frac'tious•ness** *n.*

frac•ture (frăk'chər) *n.* **1. a.** The act or process of breaking. **b.** The state of being broken. **2.** A break or crack, as in bone. —**frac'-ture** *v.*

frag•ile (frăj'əl, -īl') *adj.* **1.** Easily damaged or broken. **2.** Tenuous : flimsy <a *fragile* claim to the estate> —**frag'ile•ly** *adv.* —**fra•gil'-i•ty** (frə-jĭl'ĭ-tē) *n.*

frag•ment (frăg'mənt) *n.* **1.** A part detached or broken off. **2.** Something unfinished or incomplete <knew *fragments* of the plan> —*v.* (frăg'mĕnt'). To break into fragments. —**frag'-men•ta'tion** *n.*

frag•men•tar•y (frăg'mən-tĕr'ē) *adj.* In pieces. —**frag'men•tar'i•ly** (-târ'ə-lē) *adv.* —**frag'men•tar'i•ness** *n.*

fra•grant (frā'grənt) *adj.* Having a pleasant, esp. sweet odor. —**fra'grance** *n.* —**fra'-grant•ly** *adv.*

frail (frāl) *adj.* **1.** Delicate <a *frail* child> **2.** Easily damaged. **3.** Not substantial : slight. —**frail'ly** *adv.* —**frail'ness** *n.*

frail•ty (frāl'tē) *n., pl.* **-ties. 1.** The quality or state of being frail. **2.** A fault caused by moral weakness.

frak•tur (fräk-to͝or') *n.* A style of letter formerly used in German manuscripts and printing.

frame (frām) *v.* **framed, fram•ing. 1.** To construct from various parts : build. **2.** To conceive or design. **3.** To adjust or arrange for a given purpose <a question *framed* to draw a negative response> **4.** To put into words. **5.** To provide with or as if with a frame : enclose. **6.** *Slang.* To rig events or evidence so as to make (a person) seem guilty. —*n.* **1.** Something made up of parts fitted and joined together, as: **a.** A skeletal structure <the *frame* of a building> **b.** An open structure <a picture *frame*> **c.** A machine built on or using a frame. **d.** The human body. **3.** General structure : system <the *frame* of national government> **4.** One exposure on a roll of movie film. **5.** *Slang.* A frame-up. **6.** A round of play in some games, such as bowling. —**fram'er** *n.*

frame-up (frām'ŭp') *n. Slang.* A scheme to incriminate an innocent person.

frame•work (frām'wûrk') *n.* **1.** A supporting or enclosing structure. **2.** A basic system or arrangement, as of ideas.

franc (frăngk) *n.* —See table at CURRENCY.

fran•chise (frăn'chīz') *n.* **1.** A privilege granted to a person or group by a government. **2.** Constitutional or statutory right to vote. **3.** Authorization to sell a manufacturer's products. **4.** The limit or territory within which a privilege or immunity is authorized. —**fran'-chise'** *v.* —**fran'chi•see'** *n.* —**fran'chis'er** *n.*

fran•ci•um (frăn'sē-əm) *n. Symbol* **Fr** An unstable radioactive metallic element.

Fran•co-A•mer•i•can (frăng'kō-ə-mĕr'ĭ-kən) *n.* An American of French descent, esp. a French-Canadian. —**Fran'co-A•mer'i•can** *adj.*

fran•gi•ble (frăn'jə-bəl) *adj.* Breakable. —**fran'gi•bil'i•ty, fran'gi•ble•ness** *n.*

frank (frăngk) *adj.* Sincere and open : straightforward <a *frank* discussion about finances> —*v.* **1.** To mark (mail) officially so that it can be sent free of postage. **2.** To send (mail) without charge. —*n.* **1.** A signature or mark on mail indicating that it can be sent without charge. **2.** The right of sending mail free. —**frank'ly** *adv.* —**frank'ness** *n.*

Frank•en•stein (frăng'kən-stīn') *n.* **1.** A creation or agency that destroys its creator. **2.** A monster resembling a man.

frank•furt•er (frăngk'fər-tər) *n.* A smoked sausage, as of beef or beef and pork.

frank•in•cense (frăng'kĭn-sĕns') *n.* An aromatic gum resin obtained from African and Asian trees of the genus *Boswellia* and burned as incense.

Franklin stove *n.* A cast-iron stove shaped like a fireplace but utilizing metal baffles to increase its energy efficiency.

fran•tic (frăn'tĭk) *adj.* Emotionally distraught, as from worry or fear. —**fran'ti•cal•ly, fran'tic•ly** *adv.*

frap•pé (fră-pā', frăp) *n.* **1.** A frozen, often fruit-flavored mixture that is similar to sherbet. **2.** A beverage, as a liqueur, poured over shaved ice. **3.** A milk shake containing ice cream.

fra•ter•nal (frə-tûr'nəl) *adj.* **1. a.** Of or relating to brothers. **b.** Exhibiting comradeship. **2.** Of or being a fraternity. **3.** *Biol.* Of or relating to a twin or twins that developed from separately fertilized ova. —**fra•ter'nal•ism** *n.* —**fra•ter'nal•ly** *adv.*

fra•ter•ni•ty (frə-tûr'nĭ-tē) *n., pl.* **-ties. 1.** A group of persons united by similar interests, backgrounds, or occupations. **2.** A social organization of male college students, usu. designated by Greek letters. **3.** The quality or state of being brothers.

frat•er•nize (frăt'ər-nīz') *v.* **-nized, -niz•ing.**

1. To associate with others in a friendly or brotherly way. 2. To associate with the enemy, often in violation of military law. —**frat′er·ni·za′tion** *n.* —**frat′er·niz′er** *n.*

frat·ri·cide (frăt′rĭ-sīd′) *n.* **1.** The act of murdering one's brother or sister. **2.** One who has murdered a brother or sister. —**frat′ri·cid′al** *adj.*

fraud (frôd) *n.* **1.** A deliberate deception perpetrated for unlawful or unfair gain. **2.** A trick or swindle. **3. a.** One who defrauds : cheat. **b.** An impostor.

fraud·u·lent (frô′jə-lənt) *adj.* Marked by, being, or done by fraud. —**fraud′u·lence** *n.* —**fraud′u·lent·ly** *adv.*

fraught (frôt) *adj.* Filled or charged <a mission *fraught* with danger>

fray[1] (frā) *n.* **1.** A scuffle or brawl. **2.** A heated contest or dispute.

fray[2] (frā) *v.* **1.** To wear away, unravel, or tatter (fabric edges) by rubbing. **2.** To irritate or strain (e.g., one's nerves).

fraz·zle (frăz′əl) *v.* **-zled, -zling.** *Informal.* **1.** To tatter or wear out : fray. **2.** To fatigue completely. —**fraz′zle** *n.*

freak (frēk) *n.* **1.** A person, animal, thing, or occurrence that is markedly abnormal or unusual. **2.** A sudden whim : caprice. **3.** *Slang.* **a.** A drug user or addict. **b.** A fan or enthusiast <a jogging *freak*> —**freak out.** *Slang.* **1.** To experience or cause to experience hallucinations or paranoia induced by a drug. **2.** To make or become highly agitated or excited. —**freak′i·ly** *adv.* —**freak′ish** *adj.* —**freak′ish·ly** *adv.* —**freak′ish·ness** *n.* —**freak′y** *adj.*

freck·le (frĕk′əl) *n.* A small, often sun-induced precipitation of pigment in the skin. —**freck′le** *v.* —**freck′ly** *adj.*

free (frē) *adj.* **fre·er, fre·est.** **1.** Not imprisoned or constrained. **2.** Not under necessity or obligation. **3. a.** Politically independent <a *free* nation> **b.** Possessing political and civil liberties <a *free* citizenry> **4. a.** Not affected by a specified circumstance or condition. **b.** Exempt <tax-*free*> **5.** Not literal <a *free* translation from the French> **6.** Costing nothing. **7. a.** Not being occupied or used. **b.** Unobstructed : clear <a *free* lane> **8.** Frank : open. **9.** Too familiar : forward. **10.** Lavish or liberal, as with money. —*adv.* **1.** In a free way. **2.** Without charge. —*v.* **freed, free·ing.** **1.** To set at liberty. **2.** To release or rid <*freed* from tyranny> **3.** To untangle or clear. ★ ***syns:*** EMANCIPATE, LIBERATE, MANUMIT, RELEASE —**free′ly** *adv.* —**free′ness** *n.*

free·bie *also* **free·bee** (frē′bē) *n.* *Slang.* Something given or received without cost.

free·board (frē′bôrd′, -bōrd′) *n.* *Naut.* The vertical distance between the water line and the uppermost full deck.

free·boot·er (frē′bo͞o′tər) *n.* One who plunders, esp. a pirate.

free·born (frē′bôrn′) *adj.* **1.** Born as a free person and not a slave. **2.** Of or appropriate to a freeborn person.

freed·man (frēd′mən) *n.* A man freed from slavery.

free·dom (frē′dəm) *n.* **1.** The state of being free of constraints. **2. a.** Political independence. **b.** Possession of political and civil rights. **3.** Free will. **4.** Facility as of movement. **5.** Frankness or boldness of expression. **6.** Unrestricted access or use.

Free·dom·ite (frē′də-mīt′) *n.* *Can.* A member of the Dukhobor sect, the Sons of Freedom.

freed·wom·an (frēd′wo͝om′ən) *n.* A woman who has been freed from slavery.

free-for-all (frē′fər-ôl′) *n.* A competition or brawl in which many participate.

free·form (frē′fôrm′) *adj.* Having a usu. flowing asymmetrical shape or outline <*freeform* sculpture> —**free′form′** *adv.*

free·hand (frē′hănd′) *adj.* Done or drawn without the use of mechanical aids <*freehand* sketches> —**free′hand′** *adv.*

free·hold (frē′hōld′) *n.* **1.** An estate held in fee or for life. **2.** The tenure by which a freehold is held. —**free′hold′er** *n.*

free·lance *n.* One, esp. a writer or artist, who sells his or her services to employers as those services are needed. —**free′lance′** *v.* & *adj.*

free·load (frē′lōd′) *v.* *Slang.* To take advantage of the hospitality or generosity of others : sponge. —**free′load′er** *n.*

free love *n.* The practice of living in a sexual relationship without marriage or formal obligations.

free·man (frē′mən) *n.* **1.** A person not in slavery or bondage. **2.** One possessing all the rights and privileges of a citizen.

Free·ma·son (frē′mā′sən) *n.* A member of an international fraternal charitable organization officially called Free and Accepted Masons. —**Free′ma′son·ry** *n.*

fre·er (frē′ər) *adj.* *compar. of* FREE.

free speech *n.* The right to express any opinion in public without censorship or restraint.

fre·est (frē′ĭst) *adj.* *superl. of* FREE.

free·stand·ing (frē′stăn′dĭng) *adj.* Standing unsupported or without attachment.

free·stone (frē′stōn′) *n.* **1.** A stone, as limestone, that can be cut without splitting or shattering. **2.** A fruit, as a peach, with a stone that does not cling to the pulp.

free·think·er (frē′thĭngk′ər) *n.* One who has rejected dogma and authority, esp. in his or her religious thinking. —**free′think′ing** *adj.* & *n.*

free trade *n.* Tariff-free trade between nations or states.

free verse *n.* Verse marked by an unconventional metrical or stanzaic pattern and either an irregular rhyme or no rhyme.

free·way (frē′wā′) *n.* A multilane highway : expressway.

free·wheel (frē′hwēl′, -wēl′) *v.* To live or move freely, aimlessly, or irresponsibly.

free will *n.* **1.** The ability or discretion to choose freely. **2.** The belief that a human being's choices are or can be made freely, without external constraint.

freeze (frēz) *v.* **froze** (frōz), **fro·zen** (frō′zən),

freez•ing. 1. a. To change or cause to change from liquid to solid by losing heat. **b.** To acquire a surface of ice from cold. **2.** To preserve (e.g., food) by cooling to an extremely low temperature. **3.** To make or become nonfunctional through the formation of ice or frost. **4.** To injure or be injured by cold. **5. a.** To be at the temperature at which ice forms. **b.** To feel uncomfortably cold. **6.** To make or become rigid **:** solidify. **7.** To become incapable of acting through shyness or fear. **8.** To be or become icily formal. **9.** To fix (wages or prices) at a given level. **10.** To prohibit further use or manufacture of. *—n.* **1.** An act of freezing or the state of being frozen. **2.** A cold snap.

freeze-dry (frēz′drī′) *v.* To preserve (foodstuffs) by freezing and then drying in a vacuum. **—freeze′-dried′** *adj.*

freez•er (frē′zər) *n.* One that freezes, esp. a thermally insulated room or cabinet for freezing and storing perishable food.

freight (frāt) *n.* **1.** Goods transported by a vehicle or vessel **:** cargo. **2. a.** Commercial transportation of goods. **b.** The fee for such transportation. **3.** A train transporting goods only. *—v.* **1.** To carry as cargo. **2.** To load with cargo.

freight•er (frā′tər) *n.* A vehicle, esp. a ship, that carries freight.

French (frĕnch) *n.* **1.** The language of France. **2.** (*pl. in number*). The people of France. **—French** *adj.* **—French′man** *n.* **—French′wom′an** *n.*

French Canada *n.* The part of Canada where French is the predominant language.

French Canadian *n.* A Canadian whose first language is French.

French dressing *n.* **1.** A seasoned oil and vinegar salad dressing. **2.** A commercially prepared creamy dressing, usu. pinkish or orange and often sweet.

French fries *pl.n.* Thin strips of potatoes that are French-fried.

French-fry (frĕnch′frī′) *v.* To fry (e.g., potato strips) in deep fat.

French horn *n.* A brass wind instrument that flares from a narrow mouthpiece to a wide bell.

fre•net•ic (frə-nĕt′ĭk) *adj.* Wildly excited **:** frenzied. **—fre•net′i•cal•ly** *adv.*

fren•zy (frĕn′zē) *n., pl.* **-zies. 1.** A state of wild excitement or violent agitation. **2.** Temporary insanity or delirium. **—fren′zied** *adj.* **—fren′zied•ly** *adv.*

fre•quen•cy (frē′kwən-sē) *n., pl.* **-cies. 1.** The number of times a given event occurs within a specific interval, esp.: **a.** The number of complete cycles of a wave occuring per unit of time. **b.** The number of complete vibrations or oscillations that a body undergoes in a unit of time. **2.** The fact or state of occurring frequently.

frequency modulation *n.* Variation of a transmitting radio wave's frequency in accordance with an input signal.

fre•quent (frē′kwənt) *adj.* Happening or appearing often or at close intervals. *—v.* (frē-kwĕnt′, frē′kwənt). To visit (a place) often. **—fre•quent′er** *n.* **—fre′quent•ly** *adv.* **—fre′quent•ness** *n.*

fres•co (frĕs′kō) *n., pl.* **-coes** *or* **-cos. 1.** The art of painting on fresh plaster with water-based paint. **2.** A painting executed in fresco.

fresh (frĕsh) *adj.* **1.** Recently produced, made, or harvested. **2.** Not preserved, as by freezing. **3.** Not saline <*fresh* water> **4.** New **:** additional <*fresh* evidence> **5.** Different <a *fresh* approach to the problem> **6.** Not soiled <*fresh* linen> **7.** Clear <still *fresh* in my mind> **8.** Having just arrived <*fresh* from the country> **9.** Refreshed **:** revived. **10.** Invigorating <*fresh* mountain air> **11.** Brisk <a *fresh* breeze> **12.** *Informal.* Impudent. **—fresh′ly** *adv.* **—fresh′ness** *n.*

fresh•en (frĕsh′ən) *v.* **1.** To make or become fresh. **2.** To increase in strength. —Used of the wind. **—fresh′en•er** *n.*

fresh•et (frĕsh′ĭt) *n.* The overflow of a stream as a result of heavy rain or a thaw.

fresh•man (frĕsh′mən) *n.* **1.** A student in the first year of high school or college. **2.** A beginner **:** novice.

fresh•wa•ter (frĕsh′wô′tər, -wŏt′ər) *adj.* **1.** Of, relating to, living in, or consisting of water that is not saline. **2.** Accustomed to navigating inland waters only <a *freshwater* sailor>

fret[1] (frĕt) *v.* **fret•ted, fret•ting. 1.** To be or cause to be anxious or irritated. **2.** To wear or be worn away **:** erode. **3.** To make by erosion. **4.** To ripple (water). *—n.* **1.** Agitation **:** worry. **2.** Erosion.

fret[2] (frĕt) *n.* A ridge set across the fingerboard of a stringed instrument, as a guitar.

fret[3] (frĕt) *n.* An ornamental design, as within a border, composed of repeated symmetric figures. **—fret** *v.*

fret•ful (frĕt′fəl) *adj.* Irritable. **—fret′ful•ly** *adv.* **—fret′ful•ness** *n.*

fret saw *n.* A long, narrow-bladed saw with fine teeth, used in making ornamental work in thin wood or metal.

fret•work (frĕt′wûrk′) *n.* **1.** Decorative work consisting of frets. **2.** Ornamental openwork or 3-dimensional fretwork.

fri•a•ble (frī′ə-bəl) *adj.* Easily crumbled **:** brittle. **—fri′a•bil′i•ty, fri′a•ble•ness** *n.*

fri•ar (frī′ər) *n.* A member of a usu. mendicant Roman Catholic order.

fri•ar•y (frī′ə-rē) *n., pl.* **-ies.** A monastery of friars.

fric•as•see (frĭk′ə-sē′, frĭk′ə-sē′) *n.* Pieces of meat or poultry stewed in gravy. **—fric′as•see′** *v.*

fric•tion (frĭk′shən) *n.* **1.** The rubbing of a surface or object against another. **2.** A conflict **:** clash. **3.** *Physics.* A force that retards or resists the relative motion of 2 touching objects. **—fric′tion•al** *adj.* **—fric′tion•less** *adj.*

friction match *n.* A match that ignites when struck on an abrasive surface.

friction tape *n.* A strong adhesive tape used esp. to insulate electrical conductors.

Fri·day (frī′dē, -dā′) *n.* The 6th day of the week.

friend (frĕnd) *n.* **1.** Someone whom one knows and likes. **2.** A supporter or patron of a cause or group. **3. Friend.** A member of the Society of Friends : Quaker. **—friend′less** *adj.* **—friend′ship′** *n.*

friend·ly (frĕnd′lē) *adj.* **-li·er, -li·est. 1.** Of, relating to, or appropriate to a friend. **2.** Likely to support, favor, or help. **3.** Comforting : warm. ★ ***syns:*** AMIABLE, AMICABLE, CHUMMY, CONGENIAL, CONVIVIAL, WARM-HEARTED **—friend′li·ness** *n.*

fri·er (frī′ər) *n. var. of* FRYER.

frieze (frēz) *n.* A decorative, often sculptured horizontal band along the upper part of a building or a wall in a room.

frig·ate (frĭg′ĭt) *n.* **1.** A square-rigged warship of the 17th to mid-19th cent. **2.** A medium-sized U.S. warship.

fright (frīt) *n.* **1.** Sudden and intense fear : alarm. **2.** *Informal.* Something very unsightly or strange.

fright·en (frīt′n) *v.* **1.** To fill with fear. **2.** To force or drive by arousing fear <was *frightened* into telling the truth> ★ ***syns:*** ALARM, PANIC, SCARE, STARTLE, TERRIFY, TERRORIZE **—fright′en·ing·ly** *adv.*

fright·ful (frīt′fəl) *adj.* **1.** Causing shock or disgust. **2.** Producing or causing fright : terrifying. **3.** *Informal.* **a.** Awful : extreme. **b.** Disagreeable : unpleasant. **—fright′ful·ly** *adv.* **—fright′ful·ness** *n.*

frig·id (frĭj′ĭd) *adj.* **1.** Very cold. **2.** Lacking emotional warmth. **3.** Sexually unresponsive. **—fri·gid′i·ty, frig′id·ness** *n.* **—frig′id·ly** *adv.*

†**fri·jol** (frē-hōl′, frē′hōl′) *also* **fri·jo·le** (frē-hō′lē) *n., pl.* **fri·jo·les** (frē-hō′lēz, frē′hō′-) *SW U.S.* A cultivated bean used for food.

frill (frĭl) *n.* **1.** A decorative ruffled, pleated, or gathered border or edging. **2.** *Informal.* A superfluous item. **—frill′y** *adj.*

fringe (frĭnj) *n.* **1.** A border or edging that consists of hanging threads, cords, strips, or loops. **2.** Something like a fringe. **3.** A peripheral part <on the *fringes* of the crowd> **—fringe** *v.*

fringe benefit *n.* A benefit, as medical insurance, given to an employee in addition to salary or wages.

frip·per·y (frĭp′ə-rē) *n., pl.* **-ies. 1.** Showy and often cheap finery. **2.** An ostentatious or pretentious display.

Fris·bee (frĭz′bē). A trademark for a disk-shaped plastic toy that players throw and catch.

frisk (frĭsk) *v.* **1.** To skip or leap about : frolic. **2.** To search (a person) by running the hands quickly over clothing.

frisk·y (frĭs′kē) *adj.* **-i·er, -i·est.** Lively and playful : frolicsome. **—frisk′i·ly** *adv.* **—frisk′i·ness** *n.*

frit·ter[1] (frĭt′ər) *v.* To squander or reduce (e.g., money or time) bit by bit.

frit·ter[2] (frĭt′ər) *n.* A small fried cake of batter often containing fruit, vegetables, or fish.

friv·o·lous (frĭv′ə-ləs) *adj.* **1.** Trivial : insignificant. **2.** Devoid of seriousness : silly. **—fri·vol′i·ty** (-vŏl′ĭ-tē), **friv′o·lous·ness** *n.* **—friv′o·lous·ly** *adv.*

frizz (frĭz) *v.* To form or be formed into small, tight curls. **—frizz** *n.* **—friz′zi·ly** *adv.* **—friz′zi·ness** *n.* **—friz′zy** *adj.*

friz·zle[1] (frĭz′əl) *v.* **-zled, -zling. 1.** To fry until curled and crisp. **2.** To fry with a sizzling noise.

friz·zle[2] (frĭz′əl) *v.* **-zled, -zling.** To frizz or cause to frizz. **—friz′zle** *n.*

fro (frō) *adv.* Away : back <running to and *fro*>

frock (frŏk) *n.* **1.** A girl's or woman's dress. **2.** A smock <an artist's *frock*> **3.** A robe worn by monks, friars, and clerics.

frock coat *n.* A man's dress coat with knee-length skirts.

frog (frôg, frŏg) *n.* **1.** A tailless, mainly aquatic amphibian of the order Salientia, and esp. of the family Ranidae, with a smooth, moist skin, webbed feet, and long hind legs adapted for jumping. **2.** A decorative loop of braid or cord for fastening the front of a garment. **3.** An arrangement of intersecting railroad tracks that allows wheels to cross the junction. **4.** A spiked or perforated holder for flower stems. **5.** *Informal.* Hoarseness in the throat.

frog·man (frôg′măn′, -mən, frŏg′-) *n.* A swimmer supplied with equipment, as breathing apparatus, that permits the performance of underwater maneuvers, esp. military observation and demolition.

frol·ic (frŏl′ĭk) *n.* **1.** Merriment : gaiety. **2.** Playful, carefree activity. *—v.* **-icked, -ick·ing. 1.** To romp about playfully. **2.** To make merry : have fun. **—frol′ick·er** *n.* **—frol′ic·some** *adj.*

from (frŭm, frŏm; frəm *when unstressed) prep.* **1. a.** —Used to indicate a particular time or place as a starting point <*from* 7 o'clock on><ran home *from* the store> **b.** —Used to indicate a specific point as the first of two limits <*from* grades 6 to 8> **2.** —Used to indicate a source, cause, agent, or instrument <a letter *from* home><take a book *from* the library> **3.** —Used to indicate separation, removal, or exclusion <keep me *from* making an error><freedom *from* want> **4.** —Used to indicate differentiation <know right *from* wrong>

frond (frŏnd) *n.* A leaf, as of a fern, usu. divided into smaller leaflets.

front (frŭnt) *n.* **1.** The forward surface or part, as of a structure. **2.** The area or position directly before or ahead. **3.** A position of leadership or superiority. **4.** The forehead. **5.** Bearing : demeanor <put up a brave *front*> **6.** A feigned manner or appearance. **7.** Land bordering a body of water or a street. **8.** An area of major combat. **9.** A field of activity <the economic *front*> **10.** *Meteorol.* The boundary between 2 air masses of different temperatures. **11.** An apparently respectable person, group, or business used as a cover for illegal or secret activities. *—adj.* In, of, or facing the front. *—v.* **1.** To look out on : face. **2.** To serve as a front for. **3.** To oppose. **—fron'tal** *adj.* **—fron'tal•ly** *adv.*

front•age (frŭn'tĭj) *n.* **1. a.** The front part of a piece of property, as a building or lot. **b.** The measured extent of such frontage. **2.** Land adjacent to a building, street, etc.

fron•tier (frŭn-tîr', frŏn-) *n.* **1.** An international border or the area along it. **2.** A region that marks the point of farthest settlement in a territory. **3.** An undeveloped field for research or discovery. **—fron•tiers'man** *n.* **—fron•tiers'wom•an** *n.*

▲ ***word history:*** *Frontier* and *front* are both derived from Latin *frons,* "forehead, front, façade." *Frontier* was borrowed into English from French in the 15th cent. with the meaning "borderland," the region of a country that fronts on another country. The use of *frontier* to mean "a region at the edge of a settled area" is a special American development. The edge of the settled country was where unlimited cheap land was available to pioneers willing to live the hard but independent life there. This sense of *frontier* has also been extended to other areas of achievement and conquest.

fron•tis•piece (frŭn'tĭ-spēs') *n.* An illustration usu. facing or immediately preceding the title page of a book or periodical.

front-run•ner (frŭnt'rŭn'ər) *n.* A leading contender in a competition, as a race.

front•ward (frŭnt'wərd) *adj. & adv.* At or toward the front. **—front'wards** *adv.*

frost (frôst, frŏst) *n.* **1.** A deposit of tiny ice crystals formed from frozen water vapor. **2.** The atmospheric conditions when the temperature is below the freezing point. *—v.* **1.** To cover or become covered with or as if with frost. **2.** To kill or injure by frost. **3.** To cover (glass or metal) with a rough or speckled surface. **4.** To decorate (e.g., a cake) with icing. **—frost'i•ly** *adv.* **—frost'i•ness** *n.* **—frost'y** *adj.*

frost•bite (frôst'bīt', frŏst'-) *n.* Local bodily tissue destruction resulting from freezing. **—frost'bite'** *v.*

frost heave *n.* An uplifting of a surface caused by freezing beneath the surface.

frost•ing (frô'stĭng, frŏs'tĭng) *n.* **1.** Icing. **2.** A frosted surface on glass or metal.

froth (frôth, frŏth) *n.* **1.** A mass of bubbles on or in a liquid : foam. **2.** A salivary foam, as of an animal, resulting from exhaustion or disease. **3.** Something insubstantial or trivial. *—v.* To expel or exude froth. **—froth'i•ly** *adv.* **—froth'i•ness** *n.* **—froth'y** *adj.*

frou-frou (fro͞o'fro͞o) *n.* **1.** A rustling sound, as of a silk skirt. **2.** Fussy or frilly dress or decoration.

fro•ward (frō'wərd, frō'ərd) *adj.* Obstinate. **—fro'ward•ness** *n.*

frown (froun) *v.* **1.** To wrinkle the brow, as in displeasure or thought. **2.** To regard with distaste or disapproval. **—frown** *n.* **—frown'-ing•ly** *adv.*

frow•zy *also* **frow•sy** (frou'zē) *adj.* **-zi•er, -zi•est** *also* **-si•er, -si•est** Appearing unkempt or slovenly. **—frow'zi•ly** *adv.* **—frow'zi•ness** *n.*

froze (frōz) *v. p.t. of* FREEZE.

fro•zen (frō'zən) *adj.* **1.** Covered with, surrounded by, or made into ice. **2.** Extremely cold. **3.** Preserved by freezing. **4.** Immobilized, as by fear. **5.** Coldly reserved : unfriendly. **6. a.** Kept at a fixed level, as wages. **b.** Not available for withdrawal, sale, or liquidation.

fruc•ti•fy (frŭk'tə-fī', fro͝ok'-) *v.* **-fied, -fy•ing. 1.** To bear fruit. **2.** To make fruitful. **—fruc'ti•fi•ca'tion** *n.*

fruc•tose (frŭk'tōs', fro͝ok'-, fro͞ok'-) *n.* A very sweet sugar occurring in honey and many fruits.

fru•gal (fro͞o'gəl) *adj.* Economical : thrifty. **—fru•gal'i•ty** (-găl'ĭ-tē), **fru'gal•ness** *n.* **—fru'gal•ly** *adv.*

fruit (fro͞ot) *n., pl.* **fruit** *or* **fruits. 1. a.** The ripened, seed-bearing part of a flowering plant, as a pod or berry. **b.** A fleshy and edible plant part of this kind, as an apple or plum. **2.** The fertile, often spore-bearing structure of a plant that does not bear seeds. **3.** Outcome : result <the *fruit* of our labors> *—v.* To produce or cause to produce fruit. **—fruit'age** *n.* **—fruit'ful** *adj.* **—fruit'less** *adj.*

fruit bat *n.* Any of various tropical and subtropical Old World fruit-eating bats of the family Pteropodidae.

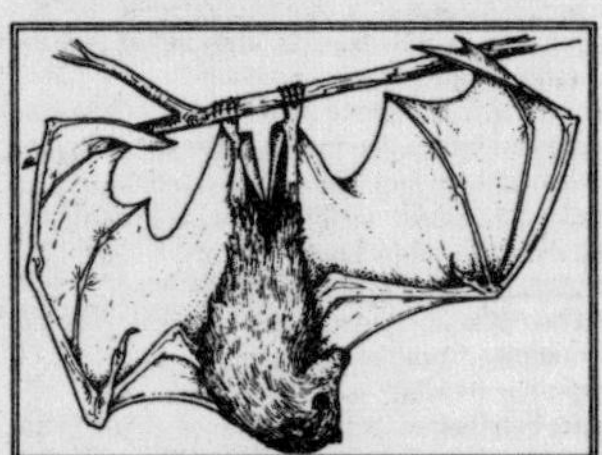

fruit bat

fruit•cake (fro͞ot'kāk') *n.* **1.** A heavy, spiced cake containing nuts and candied or dried fruits. **2.** *Slang.* An eccentric person.

fruit fly *n.* A small fly of the family Drosophilidae, with larvae that feed on ripening or fermenting fruit.

fru•i•tion (fro͞o-ĭsh'ən) *n.* **1.** Achievement of something worked for or desired : accomplishment. **2.** The state of bearing fruit.

fruit•y (fro͞o'tē) *adj.* **-i•er,-i•est. 1.** Tasting of fruit. **2.** Overly sweet or sentimental. **3.** *Slang.* Eccentric. **—fruit'i•ness** *n.*

frump•y (frŭmpē) *adj.* **-i•er, -i•est. 1.** Unfashionable : dowdy. **2.** Dull : staid. **—frump** *n.* **—frump'i•ness** *n.*

frus•trate (frŭs'trāt') *v.* **-trat•ed, -trat•ing. 1.** To prevent from attaining a goal or fulfilling a desire : thwart. **2.** To prevent the fruition of : nullify. **—frus'trat'ing•ly** *adv.* **—frus•tra'-tion** *n.*

fry[1] (frī) *v.* **fried, fry•ing.** To cook over direct heat, esp. in hot fat or oil. —*n., pl.* **fries. 1.** A dish of fried food. **2.** A social gathering at which fried food is served.

fry[2] (frī) *n., pl.* **fry. 1.** A small fish, esp. a recently hatched one. **2.** Members of a class or group <the young *fry*>

fry•er *also* **fri•er** (frī'ər) *n.* **1.** One that fries. **2.** A fairly small young chicken suitable for frying.

fry•ing pan (frī'ĭng) *n.* A shallow, long-handled pan used for frying food.

fuch•sia (fyo͞o'shə) *n.* **1.** A chiefly tropical plant of the genus *Fuchsia,* widely grown for its drooping purplish, reddish, or white flowers. **2.** A strong, vivid purplish red. —**fuch'sia** *adj.*

fud•dle (fŭd'l) *v.* **-dled, -dling.** To make confused **:** befuddle.

fud•dy-dud•dy (fŭd'ē-dŭd'ē) *n., pl.* **-dies.** A fussy or old-fashioned person.

fudge (fŭj) *n.* **1.** A soft, rich candy containing sugar, butter, and flavoring, as chocolate. **2.** Nonsense. —*v.* **fudged, fudg•ing. 1.** To falsify. **2.** To avoid taking a stand **:** evade.

fu•el (fyo͞o'əl) *n.* Matter consumed to generate energy, esp.: **a.** A material such as wood, coal, or oil burned to generate heat. **b.** A fissionable substance used in a nuclear reactor. —*v.* **-eled, -el•ing** *or* **-elled, -el•ling. 1.** To take in or provide with fuel. **2.** To stimulate <comments that *fuel* an argument> —**fu'el•er** *n.*

fuel cell *n.* A device in which the chemical energy of a fuel is continuously converted to electricity.

fuel rod *n.* A protective metal tube containing pellets of fuel for a nuclear reactor.

fu•gi•tive (fyo͞o'jĭ-tĭv) *adj.* **1.** Running or trying to run away or escape, as from the law. **2.** Vanishing quickly **:** fleeting <a *fugitive* hope> —*n.* One who flees.

fugue (fyo͞og) *n.* **1.** *Mus.* A musical composition in which the theme is elaborately repeated by different voices or instruments. **2.** A psychological disturbance in which actions are not remembered after return to a normal state.

–ful *suff.* **1. a.** Full of <event*ful*> **b.** Characterized by <boast*ful*> **c.** Tending, given, or able to <mourn*ful*> **2.** A quantity that fills <cup*ful*>

ful•crum (fo͝ol'krəm, fŭl'-) *n., pl.* **-crums** *or* **-cra** (-krə). The point or support on which a lever turns.

ful•fill *also* **ful•fil** (fo͝ol-fĭl') *v.* **-filled, -fill•ing. 1.** To convert into actuality **:** effect. **2.** To carry out (e.g., an order). **3.** To satisfy (e.g., requirements). —**ful•fill'er** *n.* —**ful•fill'ment, ful•fil'ment** *n.*

full[1] (fo͝ol) *adj.* **1.** Containing all that is possible or normal **:** filled. **2.** Complete in every detail <a *full* account> **3.** Of maximum degree <*full* speed> **4.** Having many or a great deal <*full* of flaws> **5.** Completely qualified, empowered, or accepted <a *full* member> **6. a.** Rounded in shape <a *full* figure> **b.** Having much fabric **:** wide <a *full* skirt> **7.** Satiated, esp. with food or drink. **8.** Having body and depth **:** rich. **9.** Completely preoccupied, as with thoughts. —*adv.* **1.** Entirely <*full*-grown> **2.** Directly <a blow *full* on the chin> —*n.* The complete or maximum size, amount, or state of development. —**full'ness, ful'ness** *n.*

full[2] (fo͝ol) *v.* To increase the bulk and weight of (woolen cloth) by shrinking and beating or pressing. —**full'er** *n.*

full•back (fo͝ol'băk') *n.* A backfield player stationed behind the halfbacks in football, field hockey, soccer, and rugby.

full-blood•ed (fo͝ol'blŭd'ĭd) *adj.* **1.** Of unmixed blood **:** purebred. **2.** Vigorous.

full-blown (fo͝ol'blōn') *adj.* **1.** In full bloom. **2.** Fully developed **:** mature.

full-bod•ied (fo͝ol'bŏd'ēd) *adj.* Having richness and intensity of flavor, as a wine.

full dress *n.* Attire appropriate for ceremonial or formal occasions.

full-fledged (fo͝ol'flĕjd') *adj.* **1.** With developed adult plumage. **2.** Having full rank or status <a *full-fledged* member>

full moon *n.* The phase of the moon when visible as a fully illuminated disk.

full-scale (fo͝ol'skāl') *adj.* **1.** Of the actual size. **2.** Utilizing all resources.

full tilt *adv.* At high or top speed.

ful•ly (fo͝ol'ē) *adv.* **1.** Completely or totally <*fully* satisfied> **2.** At least <*Fully* half the team were sick.>

ful•mi•nate (fo͝ol'mə-nāt', fŭl'-) *v.* **-nat•ed, -nat•ing. 1.** To condemn or denounce severely. **2.** To explode. —**ful'mi•na'tion** *n.* —**ful'mi•na'tor** *n.*

ful•some (fo͝ol'səm) *adj.* Offensively insincere or excessive <*fulsome* flattery> —**ful'some•ly** *adv.* —**ful'some•ness** *n.*

fum•ble (fŭm'bəl) *v.* **-bled, -bling. 1.** To handle idly or nervously. **2.** To grope clumsily or uncertainly **:** blunder. **3.** To drop or mishandle a baseball or football. —*n.* **1.** The act or an instance of fumbling. **2.** A fumbled ball. —**fum'bler** *n.*

fume (fyo͞om) *n. often* **fumes.** A usu. irritating or disagreeable smoke, gas, or vapor. —*v.* **fumed, fum•ing. 1.** To treat with or subject to fumes. **2.** To emit fumes. **3.** To feel or show anger or distress.

fu•mi•gate (fyo͞o'mĭ-gāt') *v.* **-gat•ed, -gat•ing.** To subject to fumes, usu. so as to exterminate vermin or insects. —**fu'mi•ga'tion** *n.* —**fu'mi•ga'tor** *n.*

fun (fŭn) *n.* **1.** Enjoyment or amusement **:** pleasure. **2.** Playful, often noisy activity.

func•tion (fŭngk'shən) *n.* **1. a.** The characteristic or proper activity of a person or thing. **b.** The special purpose for which something exists. **2.** Specific duty, occupation, or role. **3.** An official ceremony or formal social occasion. **4.** Something closely related to or dependent on something else. **5.** *Math.* A rule of correspondence between 2 sets such that there is a unique element in 1 set assigned to each element in the other. —*v.* To serve or perform a function. —**func′tion•less** *adj.*

func•tion•al (fŭngk′shə-nəl) *adj.* **1.** Of or relating to a function. **2.** Designed for a particular function or use : practical. **3.** Able to perform : operative. **4.** *Pathol.* Affecting function but not the structure of an organism. —**func′tion•al•ly** *adv.*

functional illiterate *n.* One with some education but below minimum literacy standard.

func•tion•ar•y (fŭngk′shə-nĕr′ē) *n., pl.* **-ies.** One, esp. an official, who performs a certain function.

function word *n.* A word, as a preposition or conjunction, primarily indicating grammatical function.

fund (fŭnd) *n.* **1.** A source of supply : stock. **2. a.** A sum of money put aside for a particular purpose. **b. funds.** Available money. —*v.* **1.** To make long-term arrangements for paying off (a debt). **2.** To furnish a fund for.

fun•da•men•tal (fŭn′də-mĕn′tl) *adj.* **1. a.** Essential : basic. **b.** Of major significance : central. **2.** Serving as the primary origin. —**fun′da•men′tal** *n.* —**fun′da•men′tal•ly** *adv.*

fun•da•men•tal•ism (fŭn′də-mĕn′tl-ĭz′əm) *n.* **1.** A Protestant religious movement that emphasizes a belief in the literal truth of the Bible. **2.** A movement marked by rigid adherence to basic principles. —**fun′da•men′tal•ist** *n.* —**fun′da•men′tal•ist′ic** *adj.*

fund•rais•er (fŭnd′rā′zər) *n.* **1.** One who raises funds, as for an organization or a campaign. **2.** A social function, as a dinner, for raising funds. —**fund′-rais′ing** *adj.*

fu•ner•al (fyōō′nər-əl) *n.* The service or ceremonies held in conjunction with the burial or cremation of a dead person.

fu•ner•ar•y (fyōō′nə-rĕr′ē) *adj.* Of or appropriate for a funeral or burial.

fu•ne•re•al (fyōō-nîr′ē-əl) *adj.* **1.** Of or befitting a funeral. **2.** Sorrowful : mournful. —**fu•ne′re•al•ly** *adv.*

fun•gi•cide (fŭn′jĭ-sīd′, fŭng′gĭ-) *n.* A substance that kills or inhibits fungi.

fun•gus (fŭng′gəs) *n., pl.* **fun•gi** (fŭn′jī′) *or* **-gus•es.** Any of numerous spore-bearing plants, including the yeasts, molds, mildews, and mushrooms, that have no chlorophyll. —**fun′gous, fun′gal** *adj.*

fu•nic•u•lar (fyōō-nĭk′yə-lər, fə-) *n.* A cable railway on a mountain, esp. one with ascending and descending cars that counterbalance one another.

funk (fŭngk) *n.* **1.** Cowardly fright or panic. **2.** A state of depression.

funk•y (fŭng′kē) *adj.* **-i•er, -i•est.** *Slang.* **1.** Having an earthy quality that is characteristic of the blues <*funky* jazz> **2.** Outlandishly and often humorously vulgar <*funky* clothes> —**funk′i•ness** *n.*

fun•nel (fŭn′əl) *n.* **1.** A cone-shaped utensil with a tube used to channel a substance into a container. **2.** A flue or shaft for ventilation or smoke. —*v.* **-neled, -nel•ing** *or* **-nelled, -nel•ling** To pass or cause to pass through or as if through a funnel.

fun•ny (fŭn′ē) *adj.* **-ni•er, -ni•est. 1.** Evoking amusement or laughter. **2.** Odd : strange <something *funny* going on> —*n., pl.* **-nies.** *Informal.* **1.** A joke. **2. funnies.** Comic strips. —**fun′ni•ly** *adv.* —**fun′ni•ness** *n.*

funny bone *n. Informal.* The point near the elbow where pressure on a nerve may produce a tingling sensation.

fur (fûr) *n.* **1. a.** The thick coat of soft hair covering the body of a mammal, as a fox or beaver. **b.** The dressed pelts of fur-bearing animals used esp. for apparel. **2.** A coating suggestive of fur. —**furred** *adj.* —**fur′ri•ness** *n.* —**fur′ry** *adj.*

fur•be•low (fûr′bə-lō′) *n.* **1.** A ruffle on clothing. **2.** A piece of showy trimming or ornamentation.

fur•bish (fûr′bĭsh) *v.* **1.** To brighten, as by rubbing : polish. **2.** To renovate.

fu•ri•ous (fyŏŏr′ē-əs) *adj.* **1.** Full of, showing, or marked by rage. **2.** Marked by violent activity <worked at a *furious* pace> —**fu′ri•ous•ly** *adv.*

furl (fûrl) *v.* **1.** To fold or roll up and secure (a flag or sail) to something, as a pole or mast. **2.** To curl or fold. —**furl** *n.*

fur•long (fûr′lông′, -lŏng′) *n.* A unit of distance or length equal to approx. 201 m or 220 yd.

▲ ***word history:*** Since Old English times the word *furlong* has been used to indicate a unit of length, literally "a furrow's length." A *furlong* was orig. defined as the length of a furrow in a square field of 10 acres, but as the size of an acre varied during medieval times so did the length of a furrow. *Furlong* was also used to denote 1/8 of both a Roman and an English mile. A *furlong way,* first recorded in Chaucer's poetry, was a measure of time—the length of time it took to walk 1/8 of a mile.

fur•lough (fûr′lō) *n.* A leave of absence from duty granted esp. to personnel of the armed forces. —**fur′lough** *v.*

fur•nace (fûr′nĭs) *n.* An enclosure in which a fuel is consumed, usu. by burning, to produce heat.

fur•nish (fûr′nĭsh) *v.* **1.** To outfit or equip. **2.** To give : supply <*furnish* an example> —**fur′nish•er** *n.*

fur•nish•ings (fûr′nĭ-shĭngz) *pl.n.* **1.** Furniture and other movable equipment, as for a home. **2.** Apparel and accessories.

fur•ni•ture (fûr′nə-chər) *n.* Movable articles, as chairs and tables, that are necessary or useful esp. for a room.

fu•ror (fyŏŏr′ôr′, -ōr′) *n.* **1.** Violent anger : rage. **2.** Great excitement. **3.** An uproar.

fur•ri•er (fûr′ē-ər) *n.* One who dresses, designs, sells, or repairs furs. —**fur′ri•er•y** *n.*

fur•ring (fûr′ĭng) *n.* Wood or metal strips applied to a wall or floor to make a level surface or air space.

fur•row (fûr′ō, fŭr′ō) *n.* **1.** A long, narrow trench made in the earth by a plow or other tool. **2.** A deep wrinkle in the skin, esp. of the forehead. —**fur′row** *v.*

fur•ther (fûr′*th*ər) *adj.* **1.** More distant in degree, time, or space <was *further* from the truth><the *further* street light> **2.** Additional. —*adv.* **1.** To a greater extent : more. **2.** In addition : furthermore. **3.** At or to a more distant point in time or space. —*v.* To help forward : advance. —**fur′ther•ance** *n.* —**fur′ther•er** *n.*

fur•ther•more (fûr′*th*ər-môr′, -mōr′) *adv.* In addition : besides.

fur•ther•most (fûr′*th*ər-mōst′) *adj.* Being most distant : farthest.

fur•thest (fûr′*th*ĭst) *adj.* Most distant in degree, time, or space. —*adv.* **1.** To the greatest degree or extent. **2.** At or to the most distant point in time or space.

fur•tive (fûr′tĭv) *adj.* **1.** Stealthy : surreptitious. **2.** Shifty : sly. —**fur′tive•ly** *adv.* —**fur′tive•ness** *n.*

fu•ry (fyo͝or′ē) *n., pl.* **-ries. 1.** Violent anger. **2.** Turbulence. **3.** An angry or spiteful woman. ★ ***syns:*** IRE, RAGE, WRATH

furze (fûrz) *n.* Gorse.

fuse[1] (fyo͞oz) *n.* **1.** A length of readily combustible material that can be ignited to carry a flame to detonate an explosive. **2.** *var. of* FUZE.

fuse[2] (fyo͞oz) *v.* **fused, fus•ing. 1.** To reduce to a liquid or plastic state by heating : melt. **2.** To blend or bring together by or as if by melting : mix. —*n.* An electrical circuit safety device that melts when the circuit is overloaded and thus opens the circuit. —**fu′si•bil′i•ty** *n.* —**fus′i•ble** *adj.*

fu•see *also* **fu•zee** (fyo͞o-zē′) *n.* **1.** A large-headed friction match that is difficult to blow out. **2.** A colored signal flare.

fu•se•lage (fyo͞o′sə-läzh′, -zə-) *n.* The central section of an aircraft, to which the wings and tail assembly are joined.

fu•sil•lade (fyo͞o′sə-läd′, -lād′, -zə-) *n.* A rapid or simultaneous discharge of a number of firearms.

fu•sion (fyo͞o′zhən) *n.* **1.** The act or procedure of liquefying by heat. **2.** A blend or mixture produced by fusion. **3.** A nuclear reaction in which nuclei combine to form more massive nuclei, with the release of huge amounts of energy.

fuss (fŭs) *n.* **1.** Unnecessarily nervous or futile activity : commotion. **2.** Unnecessary worry or concern. **3.** A complaint : objection. **4.** A quarrel. —**fuss** *v.* —**fuss′er** *n.*

fuss-budg•et (fŭs′bŭj′ĭt) *n.* One who fusses over trifles.

fuss•y (fŭs′ē) *adj.* **-i•er, -i•est. 1.** Easily upset. **2.** Frequently complaining. **3. a.** Hard to please : fastidious. **b.** Meticulous. **4. a.** Requiring careful attention <*fussy* work> **b.** Unnecessarily detailed <a *fussy* dress> —**fuss′i•ly** *adv.* —**fuss′i•ness** *n.*

fus•tian (fŭs′chən) *n.* **1.** A sturdy cotton cloth. **2.** Pompous, pretentious language.

fus•ty (fŭs′tē) *adj.* **-ti•er, -ti•est. 1.** Smelling of mold or decay. **2.** Old-fashioned. —**fus′ti•ly** *adv.* —**fus′ti•ness** *n.*

fu•tile (fyo͞ot′l, fyo͞o′tīl′) *adj.* Without useful result : ineffectual. ★ ***syns:*** FRUITLESS, UNAVAILING, USELESS, VAIN —**fu′tile•ly** *adv.* —**fu•til′i•ty** *n.*

fu•ton (fo͞o′tŏn) *n.* A pad usu. of tufted cotton batting used on a floor or on a raised frame as a bed.

fu•ture (fyo͞o′chər) *n.* **1.** The time yet to come. **2.** Something that will take place in time yet to be. **3.** A prospective condition, esp. with regard to advancement or success. **4.** The future tense or a verb form in the future tense. —*adj.* That is to be.

future tense *n.* A verb tense expressing future time.

fu•tur•ism (fyo͞o′chə-rĭz′əm) *n.* An artistic movement marked by the depiction of the energetic and dynamic quality of contemporary life. —**fu′tur•ist** *n.* —**fu′tur•is′tic** *adj.*

fu•tu•ri•ty (fyo͞o-to͝or′ĭ-tē, -tyo͝or′-, -cho͝or′-) *n., pl.* **-ties. 1.** FUTURE 1. **2.** The state or quality of being of or in the future. **3.** A future possibility or event.

fuze *also* **fuse** (fyo͞oz) *n.* A mechanical, electrical, or electronic device for detonating an explosive, as a grenade or bomb.

fu•zee (fyo͞o-zē′) *n. var. of* FUSEE.

fuzz[1] (fŭz) *n.* A mass of fine, light fibers, particles, or hairs : down <peach *fuzz*>

fuzz[2] (fŭz) *n. Slang.* The police.

fuzz•y (fŭz′ē) *adj.* **-i•er, -i•est. 1.** Covered with fuzz. **2.** Of or like fuzz. **3. a.** Blurred : indistinct. **b.** Not clearly worked out : confused. —**fuzz′i•ly** *adv.* —**fuzz′i•ness** *n.*

-fy *suff.* Cause to become <paci*fy*>

Gg

g *or* **G** (jē) *n., pl.* **g's** *or* **G's. 1.** The 7th letter of the English alphabet. **2.** A speech sound represented by the letter *g*. **3.** *Mus.* The 5th tone in the scale of C major. **4.** *Slang.* $1,000. **5. G.** A unit of force equal to the gravity exerted on a body at rest.

Ga *symbol for* GALLIUM.

gab (găb) *v.* **gabbed, gab•bing.** *Informal.* To chat idly. —**gab** *n.* —**gab′ber** *n.*

gab•ar•dine (găb′ər-dēn′) *n.* **1.** A firm cotton, wool, or rayon twill with a smooth surface and slanting ribs. **2.** GABERDINE 1, 2.

gab•ble (găb′əl) *v.* **-bled, -bling.** To speak or utter incoherently or rapidly : jabber. —**gab′ble** *n.*

gab•by (găb′ē) *adj.* **-bi•er, -bi•est.** *Informal.* Inclined to talk too much : garrulous. —**gab′bi•ness** *n.*

gab•er•dine (găb′ər-dēn′) *n.* **1.** A long, coarse cloak or frock worn esp. by Jews in the Middle Ages. **2.** *esp. Brit.* A loose smock worn by laborers. **3.** GABARDINE 1.

gab•fest (găb′fĕst′) *n. Slang.* An informal gathering during which news and gossip are exchanged.

ga•ble (gā′bəl) *n.* The triangular wall section formed by the two slopes of a roof. —**ga′bled** *adj.*

Ga•bri•el (gā′brē-əl) *n.* An archangel described in the Bible who acts as God's messenger.

gad (găd) *v.* **gad•ded, gad•ding.** To wander about restlessly and with little or no purpose : rove. —**gad′der** *n.*

gad•a•bout (găd′ə-bout′) *n.* Someone who goes about seeking fun or excitement.

gad•fly (găd′flī′) *n.* **1.** A fly, esp. of the family Tabanidae, that bites or annoys livestock. **2.** A critical but often constructively provocative person.

gadg•et (găj′ĭt) *n. Informal.* A usu. small mechanical device : contrivance. ★ ***syns:*** CONTRAPTION, CONTRIVANCE, DOODAD, GIMMICK —**gadg′et•ry** *n.*

gad•o•lin•i•um (găd′l-ĭn′ē-əm) *n. Symbol* **Gd** A silvery-white, malleable, ductile metallic element.

Gael (gāl) *n.* A Gaelic-speaking Celt of Scotland, Ireland, or the Isle of Man.

Gael•ic (gā′lĭk) *n.* A branch of the Celtic languages. —**Gael′ic** *adj.*

gaff (găf) *n.* **1.** An iron hook used for landing large fish. **2.** A spar on the top edge of a fore-and-aft sail. **3.** *Slang.* Harsh treatment : abuse. —**gaff** *v.*

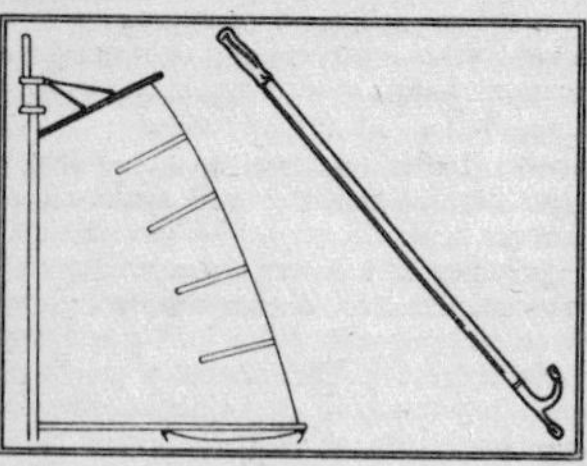

gaff

gaffe (găf) *n.* A clumsy social blunder.

†**gaf•fer** (găf′ər) *n.* **1.** *Regional.* **a.** An old man. **b.** A rustic. **2.** A lighting electrician on a film or television set.

gag (găg) *n.* **1.** Something forced into or over the mouth esp. to prevent speech or outcry. **2.** An obstacle to free speech. **3. a.** A practical joke. **b.** A humorous remark : joke. —*v.* **gagged, gag•ging. 1.** To prevent from speaking or crying out by using a gag. **2.** To prevent from speaking out. **3.** To block off : obstruct. **4.** To retch or cause to retch. **5.** To make jokes.

ga•ga (gä′gä′) *adj. Slang.* **1.** Silly : crazy. **2.** Totally ethusiastic or infatuated.

gage[1] (gāj) *n.* **1.** Something deposited as security against an obligation : pledge. **2.** Something, as a glove, thrown down as a challenge to fight.

gage[2] (gāj) *n. var. of* GAUGE.

gag•gle (găg′əl) *n.* **1.** A flock of geese. **2.** A cluster : group.

gag•ster (găg′stər) *n.* **1.** A standup comedian. **2.** One who tells or plays jokes.

gai•e•ty (gā′ĭ-tē) *n., pl.* **-ties. 1.** A state of joyful exuberance : merriment. **2.** Festive activity. ★ ***syns:*** FESTIVITY, FUN, MERRYMAKING, REVEL, REVELRY

gai•ly (gā′lē) *adv.* In a gay manner.

gain (gān) *v.* **1.** To acquire possession of : earn. **2.** To win, as in a competition <*gained* 1st prize in the race> **3.** To develop an increase in <*gained* speed> **4.** To come to : reach <*gained* the top of the hill> **5.** To secure as profit. **6.** To improve : progress. —*n.* **1.** Advantage : profit. **2.** An increase. **3.** An acquisition. —**gain′er** *n.*

gain•ful (gān′fəl) *adj.* Producing gain : profitable. —**gain′ful•ly** *adv.*

gain•say (gān-sā′) *v.* To dispute : deny. —**gain•say′er** *n.*

gait (gāt) *n.* **1.** A way of moving on foot. **2.** The order of foot movements, as a canter or gallop, by which a horse can move.

gai•ter (gā′tər) *n.* **1.** A leg covering that extends from the knee to the instep. **2.** A spat. **3.** An ankle-high shoe with elastic sides. **4.** An overshoe with a fabric top.

gal (găl) *n. Informal.* A girl.

ga•la (gā′lə, găl′ə, gä′lə) *n.* A festive celebration. —**ga′la** *adj.*

ga•lac•tose (gə-lăk′tōs′) *n.* A simple sugar typically occurring in lactose.

Ga•la•tians (gə-lā′shənz) *n. (sing. in number).* —See table at BIBLE.

gal•ax•y (găl′ək-sē) *n., pl.* **-ies. 1. a.** Any of numerous large-scale aggregates of stars, gas, and dust, containing an average of 100 billion solar masses and ranging in diameter from 1,500 to 300,000 light-years. **b.** *often* **Galaxy.** The Milky Way. **2.** A brilliant or distinguished assembly. —**ga•lac′tic** (gə-lăk′tĭk) *adj.*

gale (gāl) *n.* **1.** A very powerful wind. **2.** An outburst, as of hilarity.

ga•le•na (gə-lē′nə) *n.* A gray mineral that is the principal ore of lead.

gall[1] (gôl) *n.* **1. a.** Liver bile. **b.** The gallbladder. **2.** Bitterness of feeling : animosity. **3.** Something bitter to undergo. **4.** Impudence : brazenness.

gall[2] (gôl) *n.* A skin sore caused by chafing. —*v.* **1.** To make or become sore by chafing.

2. To irritate : annoy. **—gall'ing** *adj.* **—gall'ing·ly** *adv.*
gall³ (gôl) *n.* An abnormal swelling of plant tissue caused by insects or disease organisms.
gal·lant (găl'ənt) *adj.* **1.** Showy in appearance or dress : dashing. **2.** Stately : majestic. **3.** Spirited and courageous. **4.** (*also* gə-lănt', -länt'). Courteous and attentive to women : chivalrous. *—n.* (gə-lănt', -länt', găl'ənt). **1.** A fashionable young man. **2.** A man who is courteous and attentive to women. **—gal'lant·ly** *adv.*
gal·lant·ry (găl'ən-trē) *n., pl.* **-ries. 1.** Noteworthy courage. **2.** Courteous attentiveness to women. **3.** A gallant act.
gall·blad·der *also* **gall bladder** (gôl'blăd'ər) *n.* A small sac under the right lobe of the liver in which bile is stored.
gal·le·on (găl'ē-ən, găl'yən) *n.* A large 3-masted sailing ship used for trading and warfare in the 15th and 16th cent.
†gal·ler·y (găl'ə-rē, găl'rē) *n., pl.* **-ies. 1.** A long outdoor balcony, esp. one with a roof. **2.** A long narrow passageway, as a corridor. **3.** *Regional.* A porch : verandah. **4.** The balcony of an auditorium, theater, or church. **5.** A group of spectators, as at a golf tournament. **6. a.** A building or room in which works of art are displayed. **b.** An organization that sells works of art. **7.** An underground passageway.
gal·ley (găl'ē) *n., pl.* **-leys. 1.** A medieval ship propelled by sails and oars. **2.** The kitchen of a ship or airliner. **3. a.** A long tray used by printers to hold set type. **b.** A printer's proof taken from composed type in order to detect and correct errors.

galley

Gal·lic (găl'ĭk) *adj.* Of or pertaining to Gaul or France.
†gal·li·gas·kins (găl'ĭ-găs'kĭnz) *pl.n.* **1.** Full-length, loosely fitting hose or breeches worn in the 16th and 17th cent. **2.** Loose breeches. **3.** *Regional.* Leggings.
gal·li·mau·fry (găl'ə-mô'frē) *n., pl.* **-fries.** A hodgepodge.
gal·li·nule (găl'ə-no͞ol', -nyo͞ol') *n.* A wading bird of the genera *Gallinula, Porphyrio,* or *Porphyrula,* with dark iridescent plumage.
gal·li·um (găl'ē-əm) *n. Symbol* **Ga** A rare silvery metallic element used in semiconductor technology and as a component of various low-melting alloys.
gal·li·vant (găl'ə-vănt') *v.* To wander about in search of amusement or pleasure.
gal·lon (găl'ən) *n.* —See table at MEASUREMENT.
gal·lop (găl'əp) *n.* **1.** A horse's 3-beat gait that is faster than a canter. **2.** A fast running pace. **—gal'lop** *v.*
gal·lows (găl'ōz) *n., pl.* **-lows** *or* **-lows·es. 1.** A framework usu. with 2 upright beams and a crossbeam from which condemned persons are hanged. **2.** Execution on a gallows or by hanging.
gall·stone (gôl'stōn') *n.* A small, hard concretion of chloresterol crystals that forms in the gallbladder or in a bile duct.
gal·lus·es (găl'ə-sĭz) *pl.n. Informal.* Suspenders for trousers.
ga·lore (gə-lôr', -lōr') *adj. Informal.* In abundance : plentiful.
ga·losh (gə-lŏsh') *n.* A high waterproof overshoe.
gal·va·nism (găl'və-nĭz'əm) *n.* Direct-current electricity, esp. when produced chemically. **—gal·van'ic** (-văn'ĭk) *adj.*
gal·va·nize (găl'və-nīz') *v.* **-nized, -niz·ing. 1.** To stimulate or shock with or as if with an electric current. **2.** To arouse to awareness or action : provoke. **3.** To coat (iron or steel) with rust-resistant zinc. **—gal'va·ni·za'tion** *n.* **—gal'va·niz'er** *n.*
gal·va·nom·e·ter (găl'və-nŏm'ĭ-tər) *n.* A device for detecting or measuring small electric currents. **—gal'va·no·met'ric** (-nō-mĕt'rĭk) *adj.*
gam·bit (găm'bĭt) *n.* **1.** A chess opening in which a piece is sacrificed for a favorable position. **2.** A carefully planned maneuver.
gam·ble (găm'bəl) *v.* **-bled, -bling. 1. a.** To bet (e.g., money) on an uncertain outcome, as of a contest. **b.** To play a game of chance. **2.** To take a chance : speculate. **3.** To expose to risk : venture. *—n.* **1.** A bet : wager. **2.** An undertaking of uncertain outcome. **—gam'bler** *n.*
gam·bol (găm'bəl) *v.* **-boled, bol·ing** *or* **-bolled, -bol·ling.** To frisk about : frolic. **—gam'bol** *n.*
gam·brel roof (găm'brəl) *n.* A roof with 2 slopes on each side, the lower slope steeper than the upper.
game¹ (gām) *n.* **1.** A way of diverting oneself : amusement. **2. a.** A competitive activity governed by specific rules. **b.** A single contest of a game. **c.** The number of points required to win a game. **3.** A calculated way of doing something : scheme. **4.** Animals, birds, or fish hunted for food or sport. **5.** An object of ridicule or scorn. **6.** *Informal.* A way of earning a living : occupation. *—v.* **gamed, gam·ing.** To gamble. *—adj.* **gam·er, gam·est.** Courageous : plucky. **—game'ly** *adv.* **—game'ness** *n.*
game² (gām) *adj.* **gam·er, gam·est.** Lame <a *game* knee>
game·cock (gām'kŏk') *n.* A rooster bred and trained for cockfighting.

game•keep•er (gām'kē'pər) *n.* Someone in charge of protecting and maintaining wildlife on a private preserve.
game plan *n.* **1.** The strategy devised before or used during a sports event. **2.** A strategy for reaching an objective.
games•man•ship (gāmz'mən-shĭp') *n.* Skill at winning games by dubious means but without breaking the rules.
game•some (gām'səm) *adj.* Frolicsome **:** playful. **—game'some•ly** *adv.* **—game'some•ness** *n.*
game•ster (gām'stər) *n.* A gambler, esp. a habitual one.
gam•ete (găm'ēt', gə-mēt') *n.* A germ cell, esp. a mature sperm or egg.
game theory *n.* Mathematical analysis of abstract models of strategic competition aimed at determining the best strategy.
gam•in (găm'ĭn) *n.* An often impudent boy who roams the streets **:** urchin.
ga•mine (gă-mēn') *n.* **1.** A girl who roams about the streets **:** urchin. **2.** A girl with impish appeal.
gam•ma globulin (găm'ə) *n.* A protein fraction of blood serum containing antibodies and used to treat infectious diseases.
gamma ray *n.* Electromagnetic radiation emitted by radioactive decay and having energies from ten thousand to ten million electron volts.
†**gam•mer** (găm'ər) *n. Regional.* An elderly woman.
gam•mon[1] (găm'ən) *n. esp. Brit.* Misleading talk **:** hocus-pocus. **—gam'mon** *v.*
gam•mon[2] (găm'ən) *n.* **1.** A cured ham. **2.** The lower part of a side of bacon.
gam•ut (găm'ət) *n.* The complete range or extent.
gam•y (gā'mē) *adj.* **-i•er, -i•est. 1.** Having the strong flavor of game, esp. when slightly spoiled. **2.** Showing resolute spirit **:** plucky. **3. a.** Disreputable. **b.** Scandalous. **—gam'i•ness** *n.*
gan•der (găn'dər) *n.* **1.** A male goose. **2.** *Slang.* A quick look **:** glance.
gang (găng) *n.* **1.** A group of persons who work together or socialize regularly. **2.** A group of criminals or adolescent hoodlums. **3.** A set, as of matched tools. *—v.* To group together in or as a gang. **—gang up on.** *Informal.* To attack as a group.
gang•land (găng'lănd') *n.* Organized crime.
gan•gling (găng'glĭng) *adj.* Tall and thin **:** lanky.
gan•gli•on (găng'glē-ən) *n., pl.* **-gli•a** (-glē-ə) *or* **-ons.** A compact group of nerve cells usu. located outside the brain or spinal cord. **—gan'gli•on'ic** (-ŏn'ĭk) *adj.*
gang•plank (găng'plăngk') *n.* A movable board or ramp used to board or leave a ship.
▲ ***word history:*** The element *gang–* in *gangplank* and *gangway* is the same as the word *gang,* but it preserves an older meaning of that word. *Gang* in Old and Middle English denoted the action of walking, with specific applications such as "way, passage," and "journey." A *gangplank* thus provides passage between a ship and a landing place. *Gangway* denotes a gangplank as well as various other kinds of passageways, such as aisles. *Gang* is related to the Old English verb *gangan,* "to walk, go," which has now been replaced by the verb *go.*
gang•plow (găng'plou') *n.* A plow equipped with several blades that make parallel furrows.
gan•grene (găng'grēn', găng-grēn') *n.* Death and decay of bodily tissue caused esp. by failure of blood supply. **—gan'grene** *v.* **—gan'gre•nous** (-grə-nəs) *adj.*
gang•ster (găng'stər) *n.* A member of a criminal gang **:** racketeer.
gang•way (găng'wā') *n.* **1.** A passageway, as through an obstructed area. **2.** A gangplank.
gan•net (găn'ĭt) *n.* A large sea bird, *Morus bassanus,* of rocky coastal regions, with white plumage and black wing tips.
gant•let (gônt'lĭt, gănt'-) *n. var. of* GAUNTLET.
gan•try (găn'trē) *n., pl.* **-tries.** A framelike support, esp. a movable vertical structure with platforms used in assembling or servicing rockets before they are launched.
gaol (jāl) *n. & v. esp. Brit. var. of* JAIL.
gap (găp) *n.* **1.** An opening, as in a wall **:** cleft. **2.** A pass through mountains. **3.** An empty space. **—gap** *v.*
gape (gāp, găp) *v.* **gaped, gap•ing. 1. a.** To open the mouth wide. **b.** To yawn. **2.** To stare in amazement with the mouth open. **3.** To become widely opened or separated. **—gape** *n.* **—gap'er** *n.*
gar (gär) *n.* A fish of the genus *Lepisosteus,* having a long snout and an elongated body covered with bony plates.
ga•rage (gə-räzh', -räj') *n.* **1.** A structure in which motor vehicles can be parked. **2.** A business place where motor vehicles are repaired and serviced. **—ga•rage'** *v.*
garage sale *n.* A sale of clothing or used household goods held at the seller's home.
garb (gärb) *n.* **1.** Clothing. **2.** A particular way of dressing. *—v.* To clothe **:** dress.
gar•bage (gär'bĭj) *n.* **1.** Food wastes. **2.** Unwanted or worthless material **:** trash.
gar•ban•zo (gär-bän'zō) *n., pl.* **-zos.** The chickpea.
gar•ble (gär'bəl) *v.* **-bled, -bling.** To distort or scramble so as to be unintelligible <*garbles* his words><*garbled* the message> **—gar'ble** *n.* **—gar'bler** *n.*
gar•çon (gär-sôɴ') *n., pl.* **-çons** (-sôɴ'). A waiter in a restaurant.
gar•den (gär'dn) *n.* **1.** A plot of land for growing flowers, vegetables, or fruit. **2.** A parklike public area, esp. one with flowers, plants, or animals on display. **3.** A fertile, well-cultivated region. *—v.* To work in or make into a garden. **—gar'den•er** *n.*
gar•de•nia (gär-dēn'yə) *n.* A shrub, *Gardenia jasminoides,* with glossy evergreen leaves and fragrant white flowers.

gar•den-va•ri•e•ty (gär′dn-və-rī′ĭ-tē) *adj.* Commonplace **:** familiar.
gar•gan•tu•an *also* **Gar•gan•tu•an** (gär-găn′cho͞o-ən) *adj.* Of immense size **:** enormous.
gar•gle (gär′gəl) *v.* **-gled, -gling.** To force exhaled air through a liquid held in the back of the mouth so as to cleanse or medicate the mouth or throat. **—gar′gle** *n.*
gar•goyle (gär′goil′) *n.* A projecting roof spout carved to represent a grotesque human or animal figure.
gar•ish (gâr′ĭsh) *adj.* Too bright and showy **:** gaudy <a *garish* costume> **—gar′ish•ly** *adv.* **—gar′ish•ness** *n.*
gar•land (gär′lənd) *n.* A chain, wreath, or crown of flowers or leaves. —*v.* To embellish with or form into a garland.
gar•lic (gär′lĭk) *n.* A plant, *Allium sativum,* related to the onion, having a bulb with a strong odor and flavor used as a seasoning. **—gar′lick•y** *adj.*
gar•ment (gär′mənt) *n.* An article of clothing. **—gar′ment** *v.*
gar•ner (gär′nər) *v.* **1.** To gather and store. **2.** To amass **:** accumulate.
gar•net (gär′nĭt) *n.* **1.** A usu. dark-red silicate mineral used as a gemstone and abrasive. **2.** A dark red.
gar•nish (gär′nĭsh) *v.* **1.** To embellish **:** decorate. **2.** To add decorative or flavorful touches to (food or drink). **—gar′nish** *n.*
gar•nish•ee (gär′nĭ-shē′) *v.* **-eed, -ee•ing.** *Law.* To attach (e.g., a debtor's pay) by garnishment. **—gar′nish•ee′** *n.*
gar•nish•ment (gär′nĭsh-mənt) *n.* A legal proceeding in which property belonging to a debtor is turned over to a creditor.
gar•ni•ture (gär′nĭ-chər) *n.* Something that garnishes **:** embellishment.
gar•ret (găr′ĭt) *n.* An attic.
gar•ri•son (găr′ĭ-sən) *n.* **1.** A military installation, esp. a permanent one. **2.** The troops stationed at a garrison. —*v.* To assign to or occupy as a garrison.
gar•rote *or* **gar•rotte** (gə-rŏt′, -rōt′) *n.* **1. a.** A method of execution by strangulation with an iron collar. **b.** The collar used. **2.** Strangulation, esp. so as to commit robbery. **—gar•rote′** *v.* **—gar•rot′er** *n.*
gar•ru•lous (găr′ə-ləs, -yə-) *adj.* Talkative, esp. excessively so **:** chatty. **—gar•ru′li•ty** (gə-ro͞o′lĭ-tē), **gar′ru•lous•ness** *n.*
gar•ter (gär′tər) *n.* A strap or band worn to hold up hose.
garter snake *n.* A nonvenomous North American snake of the genus *Thamnophis,* with longitudinal stripes.
gas (găs) *n., pl.* **gas•es** *or* **gas•ses. 1.** A substance capable of expanding to fill a container completely and taking on the shape of the container. **2.** A gas used as fuel. **3.** Gasoline. **4.** A gas that is used to produce a poisonous, irritating, or asphyxiating atmosphere. **—gas** *v.* **—gas′e•ous** (găs′ē-əs, găsh′əs) *adj.* **—gas′sy** *adj.*
gash (găsh) *n.* A long, deep cut. **—gash** *v.*
gas•ket (găs′kĭt) *n.* A seal, as of rubber, used between matched machine parts or around pipe joints to prevent the escape of a gas or fluid.
gas•kin (găs′kĭn) *n.* The part of the hind leg of a horse or related animal between the stifle and the hock.

gaskin

gas•light (găs′līt′) *n.* **1.** Light produced by burning illuminating gas. **2.** A gas burner or lamp.
gas mask *n.* A respirator covering the face and having a chemical air filter to protect against poisonous gases.
gas•o•hol (găs′ə-hôl) *n.* A fuel blended from ethanol and unleaded gasoline.
gas•o•line *also* **gas•o•lene** (găs′ə-lēn′, găs′-ə-lēn′) *n.* A highly flammable mixture of liquid hydrocarbons derived chiefly from crude petroleum and used esp. as a fuel and a solvent.
gasp (găsp) *v.* **1.** To inhale sharply with emotion, as shock. **2.** To make violent or labored attempts to breathe. **—gasp** *n.*
gas•tric (găs′trĭk) *adj.* Of or relating to the stomach.
gastric juice *n.* The acidic digestive fluid secreted by the stomach glands.
gas•tri•tis (gă-strī′tĭs) *n.* Inflammation of the stomach.
gas•tro•en•ter•i•tis (găs′trō-ĕn′tə-rī′tĭs) *n.* Inflammation of the mucous membrane of the stomach and intestines.
gas•tro•en•ter•ol•o•gy (găs′trō-ĕn′tə-rŏl′-ə-jē) *n.* Medical study of the stomach and intestines. **—gas′tro•en′ter•ol′o•gist** *n.*
gas•tro•in•tes•ti•nal (găs′trō-ĭn-tĕs′tə-nəl) *adj.* Of or relating to the stomach and intestines.
gas•trol•o•gy (gă-strŏl′ə-jē) *n.* The medical study of the stomach and its diseases. **—gas′-tro•log′i•cal** (găs′trə-lŏj′ĭ-kəl), **gas′tro•log′ic** *adj.* **—gas′tro•log′i•cal•ly** *adv.* **—gas•trol′o•gist** *n.*
gas•tron•o•my (gă-strŏn′ə-mē) *n.* The art of good eating. **—gas′tro•nome′** (găs′trə-nōm′) *n.* **—gas′tro•nom′ic** (-nŏm′ĭk), **gas′tro•nom′-i•cal** *adj.*
gas•tro•pod (găs′trə-pŏd′) *n.* A mollusk of the class Gastropoda, as a snail, slug, or lim-

pet, with a single shell and a broad, muscular organ of locomotion.

gas·works (găs′wûrks′) *n.* (*sing. or pl. in number*). A factory where gas is manufactured.

gate[1] (gāt) *n.* **1. a.** An opening in a wall or fence. **b.** An often hinged structure that closes or blocks a gate. **2.** A device for controlling the passage of water or gas through a dam or conduit. **3.** The total admission receipts or number in attendance at a public performance.

†**gate**[2] (gāt) *n. Regional.* A particular way of acting or doing **:** manner.

gate·crash·er (gāt′krăsh′ər) *n. Slang.* One who gains admittance without invitation or enters without paying.

gate·fold (gāt′fōld′) *n.* A folded insert in a publication whose full size exceeds that of the regular page.

gate·keep·er (gāt′kē′pər) *n.* One in charge of a gate.

gate·post (gāt′pōst′) *n.* An upright post on or against which a gate is hung or closed.

gate·way (gāt′wā′) *n.* **1.** An opening, as in a fence, for a gate. **2.** A way of access.

gath·er (găth′ər) *v.* **1.** To come or bring together. **2.** To accumulate **:** amass. **3.** To harvest **:** pick. **4.** To increase gradually <*gather* velocity> **5.** To pull (cloth) along a thread into small folds. **6.** To summon up **:** muster <*gathered* his wits> **7.** To draw about or close to something. **8.** To conclude **:** infer. ★ *syns:* CALL, CONVENE, CONVOKE, MUSTER, SUMMON —*n.* A small fold or pucker made in cloth by gathering. —**gath′er·er** *n.* —**gath′er·ing** *n.*

gauche (gōsh) *adj.* Socially awkward. —**gauche′ly** *adv.* —**gauche′ness** *n.*

gau·che·rie (gō′shə-rē′) *n.* A gauche act.

gau·cho (gou′chō) *n., pl.* **-chos.** A South American cowboy.

gaud (gôd) *n.* A gaudy ornament.

gaud·y (gô′dē) *adj.* **-i·er, -i·est.** Too highly ornamented to be in good taste. ★ *syns:* CHINTZY, FLASHY, GARISH, GLARING, LOUD, MERETRICIOUS, TACKY, TAWDRY. —**gaud′i·ly** *adv.* —**gaud′i·ness** *n.*

gauge *also* **gage** (gāj) *n.* **1. a.** A standard, system, or scale of measurement. **b.** A standard dimension, quantity, or capacity. **2.** An instrument for measuring, registering, or testing. **3.** A means of estimating or evaluating. **4.** The distance between the 2 rails of a railroad. **5.** The diameter of a shotgun barrel. —*v.* **gauged, gaug·ing** *also* **gaged, gag·ing. 1.** To measure. **2.** To ascertain the capacity, volume, or contents of. **3.** To evaluate **:** estimate. —**gaug′er** *n.*

†**gaum** (gôm) *v. Regional.* To smudge or smear.

gaunt (gônt) *adj.* **1.** Thin and bony **:** haggard. **2.** Desolate **:** bleak. —**gaunt′ly** *adv.* —**gaunt′ness** *n.*

gaunt·let[1] *also* **gant·let** (gônt′lĭt, gänt′-) *n.* **1.** A glove that protects the hand. **2.** A challenge to fight.

gaunt·let[2] *also* **gant·let** (gônt′lĭt, gänt′-) *n.* **1.** A form of punishment in which two lines of persons facing each other and armed with sticks or clubs beat the person forced to run between them. **2.** A severe trial **:** ordeal.

gauze (gôz) *n.* A loosely woven, often transparent fabric used esp. for surgical bandages and curtains. —**gauz′i·ly** *adv.* —**gauz′i·ness** *n.* —**gauz′y** *adj.*

ga·vage (gə-väzh′) *n.* Introduction of material into the stomach via a tube.

gave (gāv) *v. p.t. of* GIVE.

gav·el (găv′əl) *n.* The mallet used by a presiding officer or auctioneer. —**gav′el** *v.*

ga·votte (gə-vŏt′) *n.* A French peasant dance similar to the minuet.

gawk (gôk) *v.* To stare stupidly **:** gape.

gawk·y (gô′kē) *adj.* **-i·er, -i·est.** Clumsy **:** awkward. —**gawk′i·ness** *n.*

gay (gā) *adj.* **1.** Merry. **2.** Bright and lively, esp. in color. **3.** Inclined to social pleasures. **4.** Homosexual. —*n.* A homosexual.

gaze (gāz) *v.* **gazed, gaz·ing.** To look intently or steadily. ★ *syns:* GAPE, GAWK, GOGGLE, OGLE, PEER, STARE —**gaze** *n.* —**gaz′er** *n.*

ga·ze·bo (gə-zē′bō, -zā′-) *n., pl.* **-bos.** A summerhouse.

ga·zelle (gə-zĕl′) *n.* A slender, graceful, swift-running horned mammal of the genus *Gazella* or related genera.

ga·zette (gə-zĕt′) *n.* **1.** A newspaper. **2.** An official journal. —*v. esp. Brit.* To announce or publish in a gazette.

gaz·et·teer (găz′ĭ-tîr′) *n.* A dictionary or index of geographic terms.

gaz·pa·cho (gə-spä′cho, gəz-pä′-) *n.* A chilled soup of uncooked tomatoes, onions, green peppers, and herbs.

Gd *symbol for* GADOLINIUM.

Ge *symbol for* GERMANIUM.

ge·an·ti·cline (jē-ăn′tĭ-klīn′) *n.* A large upward fold of the earth's crust. —**ge·an′ti·cli′nal** *adj.*

gear (gîr) *n.* **1.a.** A toothed wheel that meshes with another toothed part to transmit motion. **b.** A transmission configuration for a given ratio of engine to axle torque in a motor vehicle. **2.** An assembly of parts that performs a particular function <landing *gear*> **3.** Equipment <tennis *gear*> —*v.* **1. a.** To provide with or connect by gears. **b.** To put into gear. **2.** To adjust or adapt.

gear·box (gîr′bŏks′) *n.* TRANSMISSION 3.

gear·shift (gîr′shĭft′) *n.* A mechanism used to shift from one transmission gear to another.

gear·wheel (gîr′hwēl′, -wēl′) *n.* A wheel configured with a toothed rim.

geck·o (gĕk′ō) *n., pl.* **-os** *or* **-oes.** Any of various usu. small lizards of the family Gekkonidae, of warm regions, having toes with adhesive pads enabling them to climb on vertical surfaces.

geese (gēs) *n. pl. of* GOOSE.

gee·zer (gē′zər) *n. Slang.* An old man.

ge·fil·te fish (gĕ-fĭl′tə) *n.* Chopped fish mixed with crumbs, eggs, and seasoning, cooked in a broth and served chilled in balls or oval-shaped cakes.

Gei•ger counter (gī'gər) *n.* An instrument used to detect, measure, and record nuclear radiation and cosmic rays.

gei•sha (gā'shə) *n., pl.* **-sha** *or* **-shas.** One of a class of professional women in Japan trained to entertain men, as by singing, dancing, or talking amusingly.

gel (jĕl) *n.* A jellylike mixture formed when the particles of a colloid become relatively large.

gel•a•tin *also* **gel•a•tine** (jĕl'ə-tən) *n.* **1.** A transparent, brittle protein derived from boiled animal tissues and used in foods, drugs, and photographic film. **2.** A jelly made with gelatin, used esp. as a salad base or dessert. **—ge•lat'i•nous** (jə-lăt'n-əs) *adj.*

geld (gĕld) *v.* To castrate (e.g., a horse).

geld•ing (gĕl'dĭng) *n.* A gelded animal, esp. a horse.

gel•id (jĕl'ĭd) *adj.* Very cold : frigid. **—ge•lid'•i•ty** (jə-lĭd'ĭ-tē) *n.*

gel•ig•nite (jĕl'ĭg-nīt') *n.* An explosive mixture of nitroglycerin, guncotton, wood pulp, and potassium nitrate.

gem (jĕm) *n.* **1.** A precious or semiprecious stone, esp. one that has been cut and polished. **2.** One that is highly valued.

Gem•i•ni (jĕm'ə-nī', -nē') *n.* **1.** *Astron.* A constellation in the N Hemisphere. **2. a.** The 3rd sign of the zodiac. **b.** One born under this sign.

gem•ol•o•gy *or* **gem•mol•o•gy** (jĕ-mŏl'ə-jē) *n.* The study of gems. **—gem'o•log'i•cal** *adj.* **—gem•ol'o•gist** *n.*

gem•stone (jĕm'stōn') *n.* A precious or semiprecious stone that can be used in jewelry after being cut and polished.

ge•müt•lich (gə-müt'lĭkh) *adj.* Congenial : friendly.

gen•darme (zhän'därm') *n.* A policeman in France.

gen•dar•me•rie *also* **gen•dar•mer•y** (zhän-där'mə-rē) *n.* A group of gendarmes.

gen•der (jĕn'dər) *n.* **1.** Any of 2 or more grammatical categories, as masculine or feminine, into which words are divided and that determine agreement with and selection of modifiers or grammatical forms. **2.** Sex classification.

gene (jēn) *n.* A functional hereditary unit located at a particular point on a chromosome that controls or acts in the transmission of hereditary characteristics.

ge•ne•al•o•gy (jē'nē-ŏl'ə-jē, -ăl'-, jĕn'ē-) *n., pl.* **-gies. 1.** A record or account of the descent of a family, group, or person from an ancestor. **2.** Direct descent from a progenitor : pedigree. **3.** The study of ancestry. **—ge'ne•a•log'•i•cal** (-ə-lŏj'ĭ-kəl) *adj.* **—ge'ne•a•log'i•cal•ly** *adv.* **—ge'ne•al'o•gist** *n.*

gene pool *n.* The collective genetic information contained within a population of sexually reproducing organisms.

gen•er•a (jĕn'ər-ə) *n. pl. of* GENUS.

gen•er•al (jĕn'ər-əl) *adj.* **1.** Of, relating to, or involving the whole or every member of a group or class. **2.** Affecting or typical of most : prevalent. **3.** Not specialized or restricted. **4.** Being usu. the case. **5.** Not detailed or precise. **6.** Not limited : diversified. **7.** Being superior in rank <a *general* manager> ★ ***syns:*** BROAD, COMPREHENSIVE, EXPANSIVE, EXTENSIVE, INCLUSIVE, OVERALL, SWEEPING, WIDESPREAD. *—n.* An officer in the U.S. Army, Air Force, or Marine Corps ranking above a colonel. **—gen'er•al•ly** *adv.*

▲ ***word history:*** The Latin adjective *generalis,* the ult. ancestor of the English word *general,* meant literally "pertaining to the whole genus (kind or class)." The English noun *general* meaning "a military officer" preserves something of the Latin sense. It orig. designated a general officer, the commander of the general, or entire, army. Since such an officer was of a very high rank, the term *general* was also prefixed to the titles of other officers to indicate superiority of rank and command.

general assembly *n.* **1.** A legislative body. **2. General Assembly.** The chief deliberative body of the United Nations.

gen•er•al•is•si•mo (jĕn'ər-ə-lĭs'ə-mō') *n., pl.* **-mos.** A commander in chief in certain countries.

gen•er•al•i•ty (jĕn'ə-răl'ĭ-tē) *n., pl.* **-ties. 1.** The quality or state of being general. **2.** An inexact, inadequate, or vague statement or idea. **3.** The greatest portion : majority.

gen•er•al•ize (jĕn'ər-ə-līz') *v.* **-ized, -iz•ing. 1.** To make general rather than specific. **2.** To form a general conclusion (from). **3.** To think or speak in generalities. **—gen'er•al•i•za'•tion** *n.*

general practitioner *n.* A physician who treats a variety of medical problems rather than specializing.

general relativity *n.* The theory of gravitation propounded by Albert Einstein, extending the special theory of relativity to accelerated frames of reference and introducing the principle that gravitational forces cannot be distinguished from those caused by inertia.

gen•er•al•ship (jĕn'ər-əl-shĭp') *n.* **1.** The office or rank of a general. **2.** Leadership or skill displayed by a military commander of high rank. **3.** Skillful management.

general staff *n.* A group of officers charged with assisting the commander of a division or larger unit in planning and supervising military operations.

general store *n.* A retail store that sells a wide variety of merchandise but is not subdivided into departments.

gen•er•ate (jĕn'ə-rāt') *v.* **-at•ed, -at•ing.** To bring into existence, esp. by a physical or chemical process : create. **—gen'er•a'tive** (-ər-ā'tĭv, -ə-rə-tĭv) *adj.*

gen•er•a•tion (jĕn'ə-rā'shən) *n.* **1.** The act or process of generating : production. **2.** A group of individuals having a common ancestor and constituting a single stage of descent. **3.** The average time interval between the birth of parents and the birth of their offspring. —**gen′er·a′tion·al** *adj.*

gen·er·a·tor (jĕn′ə-rā′tər) *n.* One that generates, esp. a machine to change mechanical energy into electrical energy.

ge·ner·ic (jĭ-nĕr′ĭk) *adj.* **1.** Of, relating to, or indicating an entire class or group : general. **2.** Of or relating to a biological genus. **3.** Not bearing a trademark or trade name. —**ge·ner′i·cal·ly** *adv.*

gen·er·ous (jĕn′ər-əs) *adj.* **1.** Having or showing willingness to give or share freely. **2.** Lacking pettiness or meanness : magnanimous. **3.** Abundant : copious. ★ ***syns:*** BIG, MAGNANIMOUS, UNSELFISH —**gen′er·os′i·ty** (-ə-rŏs′ĭ-tē) *n.* —**gen′er·ous·ly** *adv.*

gen·e·sis (jĕn′ĭ-sĭs) *n., pl.* **-ses** (-sēz′). **1.** A coming into existence : origin. **2. Genesis.** —See table at BIBLE.

ge·net·ic (jə-nĕt′ĭk) *adj.* **1.** Of or relating to origin or development. **2.** Of or relating to genetics. —**ge·net′i·cal·ly** *adv.*

genetic code *n.* The information coded within the nucleotide sequences of RNA and DNA that specifies the amino acid sequence in the synthesis of proteins and on which heredity is based. —**genetic coding** *n.*

ge·net·ics (jə-nĕt′ĭks) *n.* (*sing. in number*). The biological study of heredity, esp. the study of hereditary transmission and variation. —**ge·net′i·cist** (-ĭ-sĭst) *n.*

gen·ial (jēn′yəl) *adj.* **1.** Cheerful, friendly, and good-humored : gracious. **2.** Favorable to health or growth. —**ge′ni·al′i·ty** (jē′nē-ăl′ĭ-tē) *n.* —**gen′ial·ly** *adv.*

ge·nie (jē′nē) *n.* A supernatural creature capable of assuming human form.

gen·i·tal (jĕn′ĭ-təl) *adj.* **1.** Of or pertaining to biological reproduction. **2.** Of the genitalia. —*n.* **genitals.** The genitalia.

gen·i·ta·lia (jĕn′ĭ-tāl′yə) *pl.n.* The reproductive organs, esp. the external sex organs.

gen·i·tive (jĕn′ĭ-tĭv) *adj.* Of, relating to, or designating a grammatical case that marks possession or source. —*n.* The genitive case. —**gen′i·ti′val** (-tī′vəl) *adj.*

gen·i·to·u·ri·nar·y (jĕn′ĭ-tō-yŏŏr′ə-nĕr′ē) *adj.* Relating to the genital and urinary organs or their functions.

gen·ius (jēn′yəs) *n.* **1.** Exceptional intellectual ability or creative power. **2.** A person of genius. **3.** A strong inclination or natural talent. **4.** A distinctive or prevailing spirit, as of a place, person, or time. **5.** A person with influence over another. **6.** *pl.* **ge·ni·i** (jē′nē-ī′). The guardian spirit of a person or place.

gen·o·cide (jĕn′ə-sīd′) *n.* The systematic annihilation of a political, racial, or cultural group. —**gen′o·cid′al** *adj.*

ge·nome (jē′nōm′) *n.* A complete haploid set of chromosomes with its associated genes. —**ge·nom′ic** (-nŏm′ĭk) *adj.*

gen·re (zhän′rə) *n.* **1.** A style of painting in which scenes of everyday life are depicted. **2.** A particular type or category, esp. of literary work.

gens (jĕnz) *n., pl.* **gen·tes** (jĕn′tēz′) A Roman clan that includes families of the same name that have descended through the male line.

gent (jĕnt) *n. Informal.* A man : fellow.

gen·teel (jĕn-tēl′) *adj.* **1.** Refined : polite. **2.** Elegant : fashionable. **3.** Artificially or prudishly refined. —**gen·teel′ly** *adv.* —**gen·teel′ness** *n.*

gen·tian (jĕn′shən) *n.* A plant of the genus *Gentiana,* with deep-blue flowers.

gen·tile (jĕn′tīl′) *n.* **1. Gentile.** Someone, esp. a Christian, who is not a Jew. **2.** A pagan : heathen.

gen·til·i·ty (jĕn-tĭl′ĭ-tē) *n.* **1.** The quality of being genteel. **2.** The condition of being born to the gentry.

gen·tle (jĕn′tl) *adj.* **-tler, -tlest. 1.** Amiable : kindly. **2.** Not harsh, severe, or violent. **3.** Easily handled or managed : docile. **4.** Not steep or sudden : gradual. **5.** Of or from a family of high social standing : well-born. ★ ***syns:*** MILD, SOFT, SOFTHEARTED, TENDER, TENDERHEARTED. —**gen′tle** *v.* —**gen′tle·ness** *n.* —**gen′tly** *adv.*

gen·tle·folk (jĕn′tl-fōk′) *also* **gen·tle·folks** (-fōks′) *pl.n.* Well-bred persons of good family background.

gen·tle·man (jĕn′tl-mən) *n.* **1.** A man of gentle or noble birth. **2.** A well-bred or polite man. **3.** A man spoken of in a polite way. —**gen′tle·man·ly** *adj.*

gen·tle·wom·an (jĕn′tl-wŏŏm′ən) *n.* **1.** A woman of gentle or noble birth. **2.** A well-bred or polite woman. **3.** A woman attendant to a lady of rank.

gen·tri·fi·ca·tion (jĕn′trə-fĭ-kā′shən) *n.* The restoration of deteriorated urban property by the middle classes, often resulting in displacement of lower-income people. —**gen′tri·fy′** *v.*

gen·try (jĕn′trē) *n.* **1.** People of gentle birth and high social standing : aristocracy. **2.** An English social class next below the nobility in rank.

gen·u·flect (jĕn′yə-flĕkt′) *v.* To bend one knee, as in worship. —**gen′u·flec′tion** *n.*

gen·u·ine (jĕn′yōō-ĭn) *adj.* **1.** Real : authentic. **2.** Not hypocritical : sincere. —**gen′u·ine·ly** *adv.* —**gen′u·ine·ness** *n.*

ge·nus (jē′nəs) *n., pl.* **gen·er·a** (jĕn′ər-ə). **1.** A category of related plants or animals usu. including several species. **2.** A kind or class having common attributes.

ge·o·cen·tric (jē′ō-sĕn′trĭk) *adj.* **1.** Of, relating to, or measured from the center of the earth. **2.** Having the earth as a center. —**ge′o·cen′tri·cal·ly** *adv.*

ge·o·chro·nol·o·gy (jē′ō-krə-nŏl′ə-jē) *n.* The chronology of the earth's history as governed by geologic data. —**ge′o·chron′o·log′ic** (-krŏn′ə-lŏj′ĭk), **ge′o·chron′o·log′i·cal** (-ĭ-kəl) *adj.*

ge·ode (jē′ōd′) *n.* A hollow, usu. spheroidal rock with crystals lining the cavity.

ge·o·des·ic (jē′ə-dĕs′ĭk) *adj.* Made of lightweight straight elements that form interlocking polygons <a *geodesic* dome>

ge·od·e·sy (jē-ŏd′ĭ-sē) *n.* The geologic science of the size and shape of the earth. —**ge·**

od′e•sist (-sĭst) *n.* —**ge′o•det′ic** (jē′ə-dĕt′ĭk) *adj.*

ge•og•ra•phy (jē-ŏg′rə-fē) *n., pl.* **-phies. 1.** The science dealing with the earth's natural features, climate, resources, and population. **2.** The natural features of an area. **3.** A book on geography. —**ge•og′ra•pher** *n.* —**ge′o•graph′ic** (-ə-grăf′ĭk), **ge′o•graph′i•cal** *adj.* —**ge′o•graph′i•cal•ly** *adv.*

ge•ol•o•gy (jē-ŏl′ə-jē) *n., pl.* **-gies. 1.** The science dealing with the origin, history, and structure of the earth. **2.** The structure of a particular area of the earth's surface. —**ge′o•log′ic** (jē′ə-lŏj′ĭk), **ge′o•log′i•cal** *adj.* —**ge′o•log′i•cal•ly** *adv.* —**ge•ol′o•gist** *n.*

ge•o•mag•ne•tism (jē′ō-măg′nĭ-tĭz′əm) *n.* The magnetism of the earth. —**ge′o•mag•net′ic** (-măg-nĕt′ĭk) *adj.*

geometric progression *n.* A sequence of numbers, as 5, 25, 125, 625, in which each term is the product of a constant factor and the preceding term.

ge•om•e•try (jē-ŏm′ĭ-trē) *n., pl.* **-tries.** The mathematical study of the properties, measurement, and relationships of points, lines, angles, surfaces, and solids. —**ge′o•met′ric** (-ə-mĕt′rĭk), **ge′o•met′ri•cal** *adj.*

ge•o•mor•phol•o•gy (jē′ō-môr-fŏl′ə-jē) *n.* The geologic study of the configuration and evolution of land forms. —**ge′o•mor′pho•log′ic** (-môr′fə-lŏj′ĭk), **ge′o•mor′pho•log′i•cal** *adj.* —**ge′o•mor′pho•log′i•cal•ly** *adv.* —**ge′o•mor•phol′o•gist** *n.*

ge•o•phys•ics (jē′ō-fĭz′ĭks) *n. (sing. in number).* The physics of geologic phenomena. —**ge′o•phys′i•cal** *adj.* —**ge′o•phys′i•cist** *n.*

ge•o•pol•i•tics (jē′ō-pŏl′ĭ-tĭks) *n. (sing. in number).* The study of the relationship between geography and politics. —**ge′o•po•lit′i•cal** (-pə-lĭt′ĭ-kəl) *adj.*

ge•o•sci•ence (jē′ō-sī′əns) *n.* A science, as geology or geochemistry, that deals with the earth.

ge•o•sta•tion•ar•y (jē′ō-stā′shə-nĕr′ē) *adj.* Of or being a satellite that travels above the earth's equator at a speed matching that of the earth's rotation, thus remaining stationary in relation to the earth.

ge•o•syn•chro•nous (jē′ō-sĭng′krə-nəs, -sĭn′-) *adj.* Geostationary. —**ge′o•syn′chro•nous•ly** *adv.*

ge•o•syn•cline (jē′ō-sĭn′klīn′) *n.* An extensive depression in the earth's crust in which a succession of sedimentary strata has accumulated. —**ge′o•syn•cli′nal** *adj.*

ge•o•ther•mal (jē′ō-thûr′məl) *also* **ge•o•ther•mic** (-mĭk) *adj.* Of or relating to the internal heat of the earth.

ge•ra•ni•um (jĭ-rā′nē-əm) *n.* **1.** A widely cultivated plant of the genus *Geranium,* with rounded leaves and clusters of red, pink, or white flowers. **2.** A plant of the genus *Pelargonium,* with divided leaves and pink or purplish flowers.

▲ ***word history:*** The word *geranium* refers to plants of 2 different but related genera. One genus is called *Geranium,* which is ult. from Greek *geranos,* "crane." The genus is so named because the fruits of the plants that belong to it are similar in shape to the bill of the crane. The popular name for these plants is *cranesbill.* The plant commonly called the *geranium* in English belongs to the genus *Pelargonium,* from *pelargos,* the Greek word for "stork." The name for this genus also alludes to the shape of its fruit, which resembles the bill of a stork.

ger•bil (jûr′bĭl) *n.* A mouselike rodent of the genus *Gerbillus* or related genera, of desert regions of Africa and Asia Minor, having long hind legs and a long tail.

ger•i•at•rics (jĕr′ē-ăt′rĭks) *n. (sing. in number).* The medical study of the physiology and pathology of old age. —**ger′i•at′ric** *adj.* —**ger′i•a•tri′cian** (-ə-trĭsh′ən) *n.*

germ (jûrm) *n.* **1.** A small organic structure or cell from which a new organism may develop. **2.** An origin from which something larger or more complex may develop. **3.** A microorganism, esp. a pathogen.

Ger•man (jûr′mən) *n.* **1.** A native or inhabitant of Germany. **2.** The Germanic language of Germany. —**Ger′man** *adj.*

ger•mane (jər-mān′) *adj.* Relevant.

Ger•man•ic (jûr-măn′ĭk) *n.* A branch of the Indo-European language family that comprises English, German, Dutch, Afrikaans, Flemish, the Scandinavian languages, etc. —**Ger•man′ic** *adj.*

ger•ma•ni•um (jər-mā′nē-əm) *n. Symbol* **Ge** A brittle, crystalline, gray-white element widely used as a semiconductor and alloying agent.

German measles *n.* A contagious viral disease capable of causing defects in infants born to mothers infected during the first trimester of pregnancy.

German shepherd *n.* A large dog often trained to help the police and the blind.

germ cell *n.* A cell, as an egg or sperm cell, having reproduction as its primary function.

ger•mi•cide (jûr′mĭ-sīd′) *n.* A germ-killing agent. —**ger′mi•ci′dal** *adj.*

ger•mi•nal (jûr′mə-nəl) *adj.* **1.** Of or relating to a germ cell. **2.** Of or in the earliest stage of development.

ger•mi•nate (jûr′mə-nāt′) *v.* **-nat•ed, -nat•ing.** To begin to grow **:** sprout. —**ger′mi•na′tion** *n.*

germ plasm *n.* **1.** The cytoplasm of a germ cell. **2.** Germ cells as a whole. **3.** Hereditary material **:** genes.

ger•on•tol•o•gy (jĕr′ən-tŏl′ə-jē) *n.* The study of the physiological and pathological phenomena associated with aging. —**ge•ron′to•log′i•cal** (jə-rŏn′tl-ŏj′ĭ-kəl), **ge•ron′to•log′ic** *adj.* —**ger′on•tol′o•gist** *n.*

ger•ry•man•der (jĕr′ē-măn′dər, gĕr′-) *v.* To divide (an area) into voting districts in order to give an unfair advantage to one political party. —**ger′ry•man′der** *n.*

ger•und (jĕr′ənd) *n.* A verbal form that functions as a noun.

gest (jĕst) *n.* A notable feat.

Ge•sta•po (gə-stä′pō, -shtä′-) *n.* The secret police of Nazi Germany.

ges•ta•tion (jĕ-stā′shən) *n.* The carrying of developing offspring in the uterus **:** pregnancy. **—ges′tate** (jĕs′tāt′) *v.* **—ges•ta′tion•al** *adj.*

ges•tic•u•late (jĕ-stĭk′yə-lāt′) *v.* **-lat•ed, -lat•ing.** To make gestures, esp. while talking. **—ges•tic′u•la′tion** *n.*

ges•ture (jĕs′chər) *n.* **1.** A motion of the limbs or body to express or emphasize a thought or feeling. **2.** The use of gestures. **3.** Something said or done as an often formal sign of attitude or intent. **—ges′ture** *v.* **—ges′tur•er** *n.*

Ge•sund•heit (gə-zo͝ont′hīt′) *interj.* —Used to wish good health to a person who has just sneezed.

get (gĕt) *v.* **got** (gŏt), **got** *or* **got•ten** (gŏt′n), **get•ting. 1.** To come into possession of, as by earning, receiving, winning, or buying **:** acquire or obtain. **2.** To go after and obtain **:** fetch. **3.** To make contact with, as by telephone. **4.** To acquire involuntarily **:** catch <*got* a cold> **5.** To ascertain by calculation. **6.** To have <She's *got* a large house.> **7.** To understand. **8.** To perceive by hearing **:** hear. **9.** To cause to be in a particular position or condition <tried to *get* the door open> **10.** To cause to come or go. **11.** To prevail upon **:** persuade <*got* her to consent> **12.** To seize **:** capture. **13.** To kill, esp. in revenge. **14.** To hit **:** strike. **15.** To elicit an emotional response from. **16.** To annoy **:** irritate. **17.** To have as an obligation <He has *got* to be reasonable.> **18.** To become <He *got* mad when he heard the news.> **19.** To come or go <*got* home early><had to *get* out of town> **20.** To leave immediately. **21.** To be able <never *got* to go to Europe> **22.** To receive as retribution **:** incur. **—get along. 1.** To be on friendly terms. **2.** To manage with reasonable success. **—get by. 1.** To survive **:** manage. **2.** To be successful with the minimum possible effort. **—get over.** To recover from. **—get′ter** *n.*

get•a•way (gĕt′ə-wā′) *n.* **1.** The act or an instance of escaping. **2.** A start, as of a race.

get-to•geth•er (gĕt′tə-gĕ*th*′ər) *n. Informal.* A small party.

get-up (gĕt′ŭp′) *n.* A costume **:** outfit.

gew•gaw (gyo͞o′gô′) *n.* A bauble **:** trinket.

gey•ser (gī′zər) *n.* A natural hot spring that intermittently ejects steam and hot water.

ghast•ly (găst′lē) *adj.* **-li•er, -li•est. 1.** Shocking **:** dreadful. **2.** Suggestive of a ghost **:** deathly pale. **3.** Very unpleasant. ★ ***syns:*** GRIM, GRISLY, GRUESOME, HIDEOUS, HORRIBLE, HORRID, MACABRE **—ghast′li•ness** *n.*

▲ ***word history:*** The words *ghastly* and *ghost* are related, but the former is not derived from the latter. *Ghastly* is formed from the Middle English verb *gasten,* which meant "to frighten, terrify." *Ghost* is the modern descendent of Old English *gāst,* which meant "spirit, soul, spiritual being." Both *ghastly* and *ghost* are derived from a prehistoric Germanic root, *gaist–*. The presence of the *h* in the modern spelling of both words is a relatively recent development. It was introduced into *ghost* in the 15th cent., perhaps from the influence of Flemish *gheest,* "ghost," and appeared in *ghastly* in the 16th cent., prob. as a result of the semantic association of the two English words.

ghat (gôt, gät) *n.* A broad flight of steps down to the bank of a river.

gher•kin (gûr′kĭn) *n.* A small cucumber, esp. one suitable for pickling.

ghet•to (gĕt′ō) *n., pl.* **-tos** *or* **-toes.** A section of a city in which a minority group lives because of economic or social pressure.

ghet•to•ize (gĕt′ō-īz′) *v.* **-ized, -iz•ing.** To set apart in or as if in a ghetto. **—ghet′to•i•za′tion** *n.*

ghost (gōst) *n.* **1.** The spirit of a dead person, believed to appear to or haunt living persons **:** specter. **2.** A slight trace **:** suggestion <a *ghost* of a frown on his face> **3.** A false, usu. faint, secondary telvision or photographic image. **4.** *Informal.* A ghostwriter. —*v.* To write as a ghostwriter. **—ghost′ly** *adj.*

ghost•writ•er (gōst′rī′tər) *n.* A person hired to write for and give credit of authorship to another. **—ghost′write′** *v.*

ghoul (go͞ol) *n.* A legendary evil spirit that plunders graves and feeds on corpses. **—ghoul′ish** *adj.* **—ghoul′ish•ly** *adv.* **—ghoul′ish•ness** *n.*

GI (jē′ī′) *n., pl.* **GIs** *or* **GI's.** An enlisted person in the U.S. armed forces. —*adj.* **1.** Of, relating to, or characteristic of a GI. **2.** In conformity with military procedures or regulations. **3.** Issued by an official U.S. military supply department.

gi•ant (jī′ənt) *n.* **1.** An enormous legendary humanlike being of extraordinary strength. **2.** One of great power, size, or importance. —*adj.* Huge **:** enormous. ★ ***syns:*** COLOSSAL, ELEPHANTINE, ENORMOUS, GARGANTUAN, GIGANTIC, HERCULEAN, HUGE, IMMENSE, JUMBO, MAMMOTH, MASSIVE, MIGHTY, MONSTROUS, MONUMENTAL, MOUNTAINOUS, STUPENDOUS, TITANIC, TREMENDOUS, VAST **—gi′ant•ess** *n.*

gib•ber (jĭb′ər) *v.* To chatter unintelligibly. **—gib′ber** *n.*

gib•ber•ish (jĭb′ər-ĭsh) *n.* Unintelligible or meaningless speech.

gib•bet (jĭb′ĭt) *n.* A gallows. —*v.* **-bet•ed, -bet•ing** *or* **-bet•ted, -bet•ting.** To hang or execute by hanging on a gibbet.

gib•bon (gĭb′ən) *n.* A tropical Asian ape of the genera *Hylobates* or *Symphalangus,* with a slender body and long arms.

gib•bous (gĭb′əs) *adj.* More than half but not entirely illuminated. —Used of the moon or a planet. **—gib′bous•ly** *adv.* **—gib′bous•ness** *n.*

gibe (jīb) *v.* **gibed, gib•ing.** To make taunting remarks **:** ridicule. **—gibe** *n.* **—gib′er** *n.*

gib•let (jĭb′lĭt) *n. often* **giblets.** The heart, liver, or gizzard of a fowl.

Gib•son (gĭb′sən) *n.* A dry martini with a small pickled onion.

gid•dy (gĭd′ē) *adj.* **-di•er, -di•est. 1. a.** Dizzy.

b. Causing or capable of causing dizziness. 2. Frivolous and silly : flighty. ★ ***syns:*** BIRDBRAINED, DIZZY, FLIGHTY, FRIVOLOUS, GAGA, HAREBRAINED, LIGHTHEADED, SCATTERBRAINED, SILLY, SKITTISH —**gid′di•ly** *adv.* —**gid′di•ness** *n.*

gift (gĭft) *n.* **1.** Something that is given : present. **2.** The power or act of giving. **3.** A special aptitude or ability : talent.

gift•ed (gĭf′tĭd) *adj.* Endowed with a special aptitude or ability : talented.

gig[1] (gĭg) *n.* **1.** A light 2-wheeled carriage. **2.** A long, light ship's boat.

gig[2] (gĭg) *n.* A spear with prongs used for fishing. —**gig** *v.*

gig[3] (gĭg) *n. Slang.* A job, esp. an engagement for a jazz musician.

gig[4] (gĭg) *n. Slang.* A demerit, esp. one assigned as punishment to military personnel. —**gig** *v.*

gig•a•byte (jĭg′ə-bīt′, gĭg′-) *n. Computer Sci.* A unit of information equal to 2^{30} bytes or 1,024 megabytes.

gi•gan•tic (jī-găn′tĭk) *adj.* Of extraordinary size : huge. —**gi•gan′ti•cal•ly** *adv.*

gig•gle (gĭg′əl) *v.* **-gled, -gling.** To laugh with repeated short sounds. —**gig′gle** *n.* —**gig′gler** *n.* —**gig′gly** *adj.*

gig•o•lo (jĭg′ə-lō′, zhĭg′-) *n., pl.* **-los.** A man who is supported by a woman, esp. one who is paid to be an escort or dancing partner.

Gi•la monster (hē′lə) *n.* A venomous lizard, *Heloderma suspectum,* of the SW U.S.

gild (gĭld) *v.* **gild•ed** *or* **gilt** (gĭlt), **gild•ing. 1.** To coat with or as if with a thin layer of gold. **2.** To make deceptively attractive : embellish. —**gild′er** *n.*

gill[1] (gĭl) *n.* An organ, as of fishes and various aquatic invertebrates, for taking oxygen from water.

gill[2] (jĭl) *n.* —See table at MEASUREMENT.

gilt (gĭlt) *v. p.t. & p.p. of* GILD —*adj.* Covered with or of the color of gold. —*n.* A thin layer of gold or a gold-colored substance applied to a surface.

gilt-edged (gĭlt′ĕjd′) *adj.* Of the best quality or highest value.

gim•bal (gĭm′bəl, jĭm′-) *n. often* **gimbals.** A device that keeps an object supported on it, as a ship's compass, level.

gim•crack (jĭm′krăk′) *n.* A cheap and showy object of little or no value.

gim•let (gĭm′lĭt) *n.* A small hand boring tool with a screw tip and a cross handle.

gim•mick (gĭm′ĭk) *n. Informal.* **1.** A tricky device, esp. when used dishonestly or secretly. **2.** A significant feature that is obscured or misrepresented. **3.** A clever new stratagem. **4.** A gadget : contrivance. —**gim′mick•ry** *n.* —**gim′mick•y** *adj.*

gimp (gĭmp) *n. Slang.* A limping walk. —**gimp** *v.* —**gimp′y** *adj.*

gin[1] (jĭn) *n.* A clear alcoholic liquor that is distilled from grain and flavored with juniper berries.

gin[2] (jĭn) *n.* **1.** A machine that separates seeds from cotton fibers. **2.** A snare : trap. —*v.* **ginned, gin•ning.** To remove the seeds from (cotton) with a gin.

gin•ger (jĭn′jər) *n.* **1.** A tropical Asian plant, *Zingiber officinale,* with a pungent aromatic rootstock used esp. as a spice. **2.** *Informal.* Vigor : vivacity. —**gin′ger•y** *adj.*

ginger ale *n.* A sweet carbonated soft drink flavored with ginger.

gin•ger•bread (jĭn′jər-brĕd′) *n.* **1.** A molasses cake or cookie flavored with ginger. **2.** Lavish or superfluous ornamentation, esp. in architecture.

gin•ger•ly (jĭn′jər-lē) *adv.* Cautiously. —**gin′ger•li•ness** *n.* —**gin′ger•ly** *adj.*

gin•ger•snap (jĭn′jər-snăp′) *n.* A brittle molasses cookie spiced with ginger.

ging•ham (gĭng′əm) *n.* A cotton fabric with a woven pattern.

gin•gi•vi•tis (jĭn′jə-vī′tĭs) *n.* Inflammation of the gums.

gink•go *also* **ging•ko** (gĭng′kō) *n., pl.* **-goes** *also* **-koes.** A widely planted Chinese shade tree, *Ginkgo biloba,* with fan-shaped leaves and yellowish fruit.

gin rummy *n.* A variety of the game rummy.

gin•seng (jĭn′sĕng′) *n.* A Chinese herb, *Panax schinseng,* with an aromatic root believed to have medicinal properties.

Gip•sy (jĭp′sē) *n. & adj. var. of* GYPSY.

gi•raffe (jĭ-răf′) *n.* An African mammal, *Giraffa camelopardis,* with an extremely long neck and legs.

gir•an•dole (jĭr′ən-dōl′) *n.* A branched candleholder, sometimes backed by a mirror.

gird (gûrd) *v.* **gird•ed** *or* **girt** (gûrt), **gird•ing. 1.** To encircle or attach with or as if with a belt. **2.** To surround. **3.** To prepare, as for action : brace.

gird•er (gûr′dər) *n.* A strong horizontal beam that is a main support in building.

gir•dle (gûr′dl) *n.* **1.** Something, as a belt or sash, that is worn around the waist. **2.** A supporting undergarment worn by women over the waist and hips. —**gir′dle** *v.*

girl (gûrl) *n.* A female child or youth. —**girl′hood′** *n.* —**girl′ish** *adj.* —**girl′ish•ly** *adv.* —**girl′ish•ness** *n.*

▲ ***word history:*** In Modern English *girl* is the ordinary word denoting a female child. In Middle English times, however, from the 13th to the 15th cent., *girl* indicated a child or youth of either sex. Nothing is known of the history of *girl* before its appearance in English, and it appears that no related forms exist in any other language.

girl Friday *n.* A woman employee who is responsible for a great variety of tasks.

girl•friend (gûrl′frĕnd′) *n.* **1.** A female friend. **2.** A favored female companion or sweetheart.

Girl Scout *n.* A member of a girls' organization that stresses character development and citizenship training.

girt (gûrt) *v. var. p.t. & p.p. of* GIRD.

girth (gûrth) *n.* **1.** Distance around something : circumference. **2.** A strap encircling an animal's body to secure something, as a saddle, on its back.

gis•mo *also* **giz•mo** (gĭz′mō) *n., pl.* **-mos.** *Slang.* A device or part whose name is forgotten or unknown : gadget.

gist (jĭst) *n.* The central idea of a matter : essence.

give (gĭv) *v.* **gave** (gāv), **giv•en** (gĭv′ən), **giv•ing. 1. a.** To make a present of. **b.** To deliver in exchange : pay. **2.** To place in the keeping or possession of. **3.** To convey <*Give* her my love.> **4.** To bestow, esp. formally : grant. **5.** To cause to have or be subject to. **6.** To bring forth : produce. **7.** To furnish : provide. **8.** To administer. **9.** To accord or relinquish to another : yield. **10.** To donate : contribute. **11.** To submit for consideration or acceptance : proffer. **12.** To cause to take place, esp. for entertainment. **13.** To apply : devote. **14.** To yield, as to pressure : collapse. **—give away. 1.** To present (a bride) to the bridegroom at a wedding ceremony. **2.** To betray. **—give in.** To surrender : submit. **—give out. 1.** To break down. **2.** To become used up : run out. **—give up. 1.** To surrender. **2.** To leave off : stop. **3.** To part with : relinquish. **4.** To abandon hope for. —*n. Informal.* The quality of being resilient : elasticity. **—giv′er** *n.*

give-and-take (gĭv′ən-tāk′) *n.* A lively exchange, as of conversation or opinions.

give•a•way (gĭv′ə-wā′) *n. Informal.* **1.** Something, as a premium, that is given away free. **2.** Something that betrays, esp. unintentionally.

giv•en (gĭv′ən) *adj.* **1.** Specified <on a *given* day> **2.** Granted as a supposition. **3.** Tending : inclined <*given* to lying> **—giv′en** *n.*

given name *n.* A name given at birth or baptism.

giz•mo (gĭz′mō) *n. var. of* GISMO.

giz•zard (gĭz′ərd) *n.* A muscular enlargement of the digestive tract of a bird.

gla•brous (glā′brəs) *adj.* Having no hair or down : smooth. **—gla′brous•ness** *n.*

gla•cé (glă-sā′) *adj.* **1.** Having a glazed surface. **2.** Coated with a sugar glaze. —*v.* **1.** To glaze. **2.** To candy.

gla•cial (glā′shəl) *adj.* **1.** Of or pertaining to glaciers. **2.** Of, relating to, or being a period in the past when glaciers covered much of the earth's surface. **3.** Extremely cold. **—gla′cial•ly** *adv.*

gla•ci•ate (glā′shē-āt′, -sē-) *v.* **-at•ed, -at•ing. 1.** To subject to the action of glaciers. **2.** To freeze. **—gla′ci•a′tion** *n.*

gla•cier (glā′shər) *n.* A very large mass of ice formed from compacted snow and slowly moving down a slope.

gla•ci•ol•o•gy (glā′shē-ŏl′ə-jē, -sē-) *n.* The scientific study of glaciers.

glad[1] (glăd) *adj.* **glad•der, glad•dest. 1.** Experiencing, displaying, or affording joy and pleasure : happy. **2.** Willing <*glad* to help> **3.** Grateful <*glad* for his help> ★ ***syns:*** CHEERFUL, CHEERY, FESTIVE, GAY, JOYFUL, JOYOUS **—glad′ly** *adv.* **—glad′ness** *n.*

glad[2] (glăd) *n. Informal.* A gladiolus.

glad•den (glăd′n) *v.* To make glad.

glade (glād) *n.* A clearing in a forest.

glad hand *n.* A hearty, effusive, often insincere greeting. **—glad′-hand′** *v.*

glad•i•a•tor (glăd′ē-ā′tər) *n.* **1.** A man who entertained the public by fighting to the death in ancient Rome. **2.** A person engaged in an intense controversy or struggle. **—glad′i•a•to′ri•al** (-ə-tôr′ē-əl, -tōr′-) *adj.*

glad•i•o•lus (glăd′ē-ō′ləs) *n., pl.* **-li** (-lī′, -lē′) *or* **-lus•es.** A plant of the genus *Gladiolus* that is widely cultivated for its spike of variously colored flowers.

glad•some (glăd′səm) *adj.* Showing or giving cheer : joyful. **—glad′some•ly** *adv.* **—glad′some•ness** *n.*

Gladstone bag *n.* A piece of hand luggage composed of 2 hinged compartments.

glam•or•ize *also* **glam•our•ize** (glăm′ə-rīz′) *v.* **-ized, -iz•ing. 1.** To make glamorous. **2.** To treat or portray in a romantic way : idealize.

glam•our *also* **glam•or** (glăm′ər) *n.* A compellingly romantic and exciting attractiveness. **—glam′or•ous, glam′our•ous** *adj.*

glance (glăns) *v.* **glanced, glanc•ing. 1.** To give a brief or hasty look. **2.** To strike a surface at an angle and be deflected. **3.** To shine : glitter. —*n.* **1.** A brief or hasty look. **2.** A light, brief touch : brush. **3.** A gleam.

gland (glănd) *n.* An organ or structure that secretes a substance, esp. one that extracts specific substances from the blood and alters them for subsequent secretion. **—glan′du•lar** (glăn′jə-lər) *adj.*

glans (glănz) *n.* A small mass of erectile tissue at the tip of the penis or clitoris.

glare[1] (glâr) *v.* **glared, glar•ing. 1.** To stare angrily or fiercely. **2.** To shine intensely and dazzlingly. —*n.* **1.** An angry or fierce stare. **2.** An intense and dazzling light.

glare[2] (glâr) *n.* A sheet of glassy and very slippery ice.

glar•ing (glâr′ĭng) *adj.* **1.** Staring angrily or fiercely. **2.** Intensely bright : dazzling. **3.** Gaudy : garish **4.** Obtrusively conspicuous : fragrant. **—glar′ing•ly** *adv.*

glass (glăs) *n.* **1.** Any of a large class of gen. transparent or translucent materials that harden from the molten state without crystallizing and becoming true solids. **2.** Something, as a container for drinking, made of glass. **3. glasses.** A device with a pair of lenses used as an aid to vision. **4.** A glassful. **5.** Glassware. **—glass** *adj.* **—glass′y** *adj.*

glass blowing *n.* The process or art of shaping objects from molten glass by blowing air into them through a tube. **—glass blower** *n.*

glass•ful (glăs′fo͝ol′) *n.* The amount a glass will hold.

glass•ware (glăs′wâr′) *n.* Objects made of glass.

glau•co•ma (glou-kō′mə, glô-) *n.* An eye disease characterized by abnormally high pressure within the eyeball and partial or complete loss of vision.

glaze (glāz) *n.* **1.** A thin, smooth coating, as

on ceramics. **2.** A thin, glassy coating of ice. —*v.* **glazed, glaz•ing. 1.** To fit with glass <*glaze* a window> **2.** To apply glaze to. **3.** To become glassy. —**glaz'er** *n.*

gla•zier (glā'zhər) *n.* Someone who fits glass, esp. in windows.

gleam (glēm) *n.* **1.** A brief beam of light. **2.** A subdued glow of light. **3.** A faint indication : trace <a *gleam* of intelligence> —*v.* **1.** To appear briefly : flash. **2.** To glow in a subdued or faint way.

glean (glēn) *v.* **1.** To gather (grain left behind by reapers). **2.** To collect bit by bit. —**glean'er** *n.* —**glean'ings** *pl.n.*

glee (glē) *n.* **1.** Boisterous merriment : joy. **2.** An unaccompanied song for 3 or more usu. male voices. —**glee'ful** *adj.* —**glee'ful•ly** *adv.*

glee club *n.* A singing group that performs usu. short pieces of choral music.

glen (glĕn) *n.* A valley.

Glen•gar•ry (glĕn-găr'ē) *n., pl.* **-ries.** A Scottish woolen cap creased lengthwise with short ribbons at the back.

glib (glĭb) *adj.* **glib•ber, glib•best.** Speaking or spoken easily and fluently but often superficially or insincerely. —**glib'ly** *adv.* —**glib'ness** *n.*

glide (glīd) *v.* **glid•ed, glid•ing. 1.** To move or pass smoothly and with little effort. **2.** To move silently and furtively. **3.** To fly without propelling power. —*n.* **1.** A smooth, effortless motion. **2.** An act of flying without propelling power.

glid•er (glī'dər) *n.* **1.** One that glides. **2.** A light aircraft without an engine that is designed to glide after being towed aloft. **3.** A swinging couch that is suspended in a vertical frame.

glim•mer (glĭm'ər) *n.* **1.** A dim unsteady light. **2.** A faint indication : suggestion. —*v.* **1.** To give off a dim unsteady light. **2.** To appear faintly.

glimpse (glĭmps) *n.* A hurried momentary look. —*v.* **glimpsed, glimps•ing.** To get a glimpse of.

glint (glĭnt) *n.* A brief flash of light : sparkle. —**glint** *v.*

glis•sade (glĭ-säd', -sād') *n.* **1.** A gliding ballet step. **2.** A controlled slide, in either a standing or a sitting position, used in descending a steep icy or snowy incline. —**glis•sade'** *v.* —**glis•sad'er** *n.*

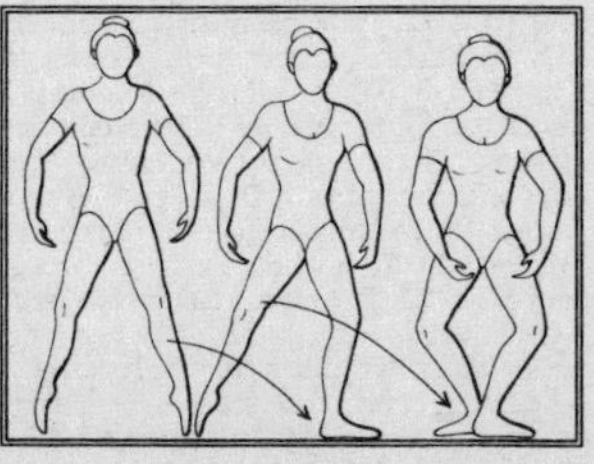

glissade

glis•san•do (glĭ-sän'dō) *n., pl.* **-di** (-dē) *or* **-dos.** A rapid slide through a series of consecutive musical tones.

glis•ten (glĭs'ən) *v.* To shine softly with reflected light. —**glis'ten** *n.*

glis•ter (glĭs'tər) *v.* To glisten. —*n.* Glitter : brilliance.

glitch (glĭch) *n.* **1.** A minor malfunction or mishap. **2.** *Electron.* A false signal caused by an unwanted surge of power.

glit•ter (glĭt'ər) *n.* **1.** Sparkling light. **2.** Showy or brilliant attractiveness. **3.** Small bits of light-reflecting material used for decoration. —*v.* **1.** To sparkle brilliantly. **2.** To be brilliantly but often deceptively attractive. —**glit'ter•y** *adj.*

glitz (glĭts) *n. Slang.* Excessive showiness : flashiness. —**glitz'y** *adj.*

gloam•ing (glō'mĭng) *n.* Twilight.

gloat (glōt) *v.* To feel, express, or observe with great, often malicious pleasure or self-satisfaction. —**gloat'er** *n.*

glob (glŏb) *n.* **1.** A drop. **2.** A large rounded mass.

glob•al (glō'bəl) *adj.* **1.** Spherical. **2.** Worldwide. **3.** Comprehensive. —**glob'al•ize** *v.* —**glob'al•ly** *adv.*

globe (glōb) *n.* **1.** A spherical object, as a representation of the earth. **2.** The earth. **3.** Something, as a fishbowl, shaped like a globe.

globe•trot•ter (glōb'trŏt'ər) *n.* One who travels extensively. —**globe'trot'ting** *n.*

glob•ule (glŏb'yo͞ol) *n.* A tiny, spherical mass. —**glob'u•lar** (-yə-lər) *adj.*

glob•u•lin (glŏb'yə-lĭn) *n.* Any of a class of simple proteins found widely in blood, milk, muscle, tissue, and plant seeds.

glock•en•spiel (glŏk'ən-spēl', -shpēl') *n.* A musical percussion instrument consisting of a series of metal bars tuned to the chromatic scale and played with 2 light hammers.

gloom (glo͞om) *n.* **1.** Partial or total darkness. **2.** An atmosphere of depression. **3.** Depression or melancholy. —**gloom'i•ly** *adv.* —**gloom'i•ness** *n.* —**gloom'y** *adj.*

glop (glŏp) *n. Slang.* **1.** A messy mixture, as of food. **2.** Something considered worthless <wrote terrible *glop*>

glo•ri•fy (glôr'ə-fī', glōr'-) *v.* **-fied, -fy•ing. 1.** To give glory to, as through worship : exalt. **2.** To make glorious by exaggerating the excellence of. **3.** To give high praise to : extol. —**glo'ri•fi•ca'tion** *n.*

glo•ri•ous (glôr'ē-əs, glōr'-) *adj.* **1.** Having or deserving glory : illustrious. **2.** Bringing glory. **3.** Magnificent : resplendent. **4.** *Informal.* Delightful. —**glo'ri•ous•ly** *adv.*

glo•ry (glôr'ē, glōr'ē) *n., pl.* **-ries. 1. a.** Great distinction : renown. **b.** Something that brings glory. **2.** Adoration and praise offered in worship. **3.** Magnificence : splendor. **4.** A wonderful asset. **5.** The height of achievement, triumph, or prosperity. —*v.* **-ried, -ry•ing.** To rejoice jubilantly : exult.

gloss[1] (glôs, glŏs) *n.* **1.** A shine on a surface :

luster. **2.** A superficially or deceptively attractive appearance. —*v.* To treat superficially in an attempt to excuse or ignore <tried to *gloss* over the hostility between them>

gloss[2] (glôs, glŏs) *n.* **1.** A note that explains or translates a difficult expression. **2.** A commentary that accompanies a text. **3.** A glossary. —*v.* To provide with glosses.

glos•sa•ry (glô'sə-rē, glŏs'ə-) *n., pl.* **-ries.** A list of words with their definitions.

glos•so•la•li•a (glô'sə-lā'lē-ə, glŏs'ə-) *n.* Fabricated and nonmeaningful speech, esp. the speech associated with a trance state or certain schizophrenic syndromes.

gloss•y (glô'sē, glŏs'ē) *adj.* **-i•er, -i•est. 1.** Having a smooth, shiny, lustrous surface. **2.** Superficially attractive **:** showy. —*n., pl.* **-ies.** A photographic print on smooth, shiny paper. —**gloss'i•ly** *adv.* —**gloss'i•ness** *n.*

glot•tis (glŏt'ĭs) *n., pl.* **-tis•es** *or* **-ti•des** (-ĭ-dēz'). The opening between the vocal cords at the upper part of the larynx. —**glot'tal** (glŏt'l) *adj.*

glove (glŭv) *n.* **1.** A covering for the hand with a separate section for each finger. **2.** An oversized padded leather covering for the hand, as that used in baseball, boxing, or hockey. —**gloved** *adj.*

glow (glō) *v.* **1.** To shine hotly and steadily, esp. without a flame. **2.** To have a bright, warm ruddy color. **3.** To blush. **4.** To be elated or exuberant <*glowing* with parental pride> —*n.* **1.** A light produced by a heated substance. **2.** Warmth or brilliance of color, esp. redness. **3.** A warm feeling of emotion. **4.** A feeling of warmth. —**glow'ing•ly** *adv.*

glow•er (glou'ər) *v.* To look angrily or sullenly **:** glare. —**glow'er** *n.* —**glow'er•ing•ly** *adv.*

glow•worm (glō'wûrm') *n.* The luminous larva or grublike female of an insect, esp. a firefly.

glox•in•i•a (glŏk-sĭn'ē-ə) *n.* A tropical South America plant of the genus *Sinningia,* esp. *S. speciosa,* cultivated as a house plant for its variously colored flowers.

gloze (glōz) *v.* **glozed, gloz•ing.** To underplay or minimize **:** gloss.

glu•cose (glo͞o'kōs') *n.* **1.** Dextrose. **2.** A colorless to yellowish syrupy mixture of dextrose, maltose, and dextrins with approx. 20% water, used esp. in confectionery.

glue (glo͞o) *n.* Any of various adhesive substances used to stick things together. —*v.* **glued, glu•ing.** To stick or fasten with or as if with glue. —**glu'ey** *adj.* —**glu'i•ness** *n.*

glum (glŭm) *adj.* **glum•mer, glum•mest.** Moody and sullen **:** morose. —**glum'ly** *adv.* —**glum'ness** *n.*

glut (glŭt) *v.* **glut•ted, glut•ting. 1.** To fill beyond capacity, esp. with food **:** satiate. **2.** To provide with a supply that exceeds demand. —*n.* An oversupply.

glu•ten (glo͞ot'n) *n.* A mixture of plant proteins used as an adhesive and as a substitute for flour. —**glu'ten•ous** *adj.*

glu•ti•nous (glo͞ot'n-əs) *adj.* Resembling glue **:** sticky.

glut•ton (glŭt'n) *n.* Someone who eats immoderately. —**glut'ton•ous** *adj.* —**glut'ton•ous•ly** *adv.* —**glut'ton•y** *n.*

glyc•er•in (glĭs'ər-ĭn) *n.* Glycerol.

glyc•er•ol (glĭs'ə-rôl', -rōl', -rŏl') *n.* A sweet, syrupy liquid, derived from fats and oils and used as a solvent, antifreeze, lubricant, and sweetener.

gly•co•gen (glī'kə-jən) *n.* A white powder that is the principal animal storage carbohydrate, chiefly in the liver.

gly•co•side (glī'kə-sīd') *n.* Any of a group of organic compounds, occurring abundantly in plants, that produce sugars and related substances on hydrolysis. —**gly'co•sid'ic** (-sĭd'ĭk) *adj.*

G-man (jē'măn') *n.* An FBI agent.

gnarl (närl) *n.* A hard protruding knot on a tree. —**gnarled** *adj.*

gnash (năsh) *v.* To strike or grind (the teeth) together, as in pain or rage.

gnat (năt) *n.* A small, winged insect, esp. one that bites.

gnaw (nô) *v.* **1.** To bite or chew persistently (on). **2.** To wear away, consume, or produce by gnawing. **3.** To afflict or trouble, as if by gnawing. —**gnaw'er** *n.*

gneiss (nīs) *n.* A banded, granitelike metamorphic rock with the minerals arranged in layers.

gnome (nōm) *n.* One of a fabled race of dwarflike creatures who live underground and guard treasure or precious metals. —**gnom'ish** *adj.*

gnu (no͞o, nyo͞o) *n.* Either of 2 large bearded African antelopes, *Connochaetes gnou* or *C. taurinus,* with curved horns.

go (gō) *v.* **went** (wĕnt), **gone** (gôn, gŏn), **go•ing. 1.** To move along **:** proceed <*going* too fast> **2.** To move away from **:** leave. **3.** To be expecting, intending, or about to do something <is *going* to eat out tonight> **4.** To follow a particular course of action <*go* swimming> **5.** To function correctly <The car won't *go.*> **6.** To be, come to be, or continue in a certain state or condition <*goes* barefoot at home><*go* crazy> **7.** To belong <clothes that *go* in the closet> **8.** To extend <bookcases *going* from floor to ceiling> **9.** To lead <a path that *goes* to town> **10.** To be allotted. **11.** To serve <It *goes* to show that practice makes perfect.> **12.** To be compatible **:** harmonize. **13.** To die. **14.** To come apart, as under pressure **:** break. **15.** To fail <His hearing is *going.*> **16.** To be used up <Our money *went* fast.> **17.** To be abolished or discarded <Luxuries will have to *go.*> **18.** To pass, as time **:** elapse. **19.** To turn out **:** fare <How is your job *going?*> **20.** To hold out **:** endure <*go* without food> **21.** To pass as a result of being sold <*went* at a low price> **22.** To be as a general rule <quiet, as children *go*> **23.** To be capable of entering or being held <a sweater that won't *go* in the drawer> **24.** To wager **:** bid. **25.** To furnish **:** provide <*went* bail for his client>

26. To participate to the extent of <*went* halves> **27.** To pass to someone, as by will <furniture that *went* to relatives> *—n., pl.* **goes.** *Informal.* **1.** An attempt : try. **2.** A turn, as in a game. **3.** Vitality : energy. *—adj. Informal.* Functioning properly and ready for action. **—go back on. 1.** To abandon. **2.** To betray. **3.** To fail to keep. **—go for. 1.** To try to obtain. **2.** *Informal.* To having a liking for : enjoy. **—go in for.** *Informal.* To enjoy participating in or partaking of. **—go off. 1.** To take place : happen. **2.** To explode. **—go on. 1.** To proceed. **2.** To continue to exist. **3.** To take place : happen. **—go out.** To become extinguished. **—go over.** To gain acceptance or approval : succeed. **—go places.** To be on the road to success. **—go (someone) one better.** To surpass : outdo. **—go under.** To suffer destruction or defeat : fail.

goad (gōd) *n.* **1.** A pointed stick for prodding an animal. **2.** Something that urges : stimulus. **—goad** *v.*

go-a•head (gō'ə-hĕd') *n. Informal.* Permission to proceed.

goal (gōl) *n.* **1.** A purpose : objective. **2.** The finish line of a race. **3. a.** A structure or area into which participants in certain sports must direct play in order to score. **b.** The score awarded for this.

goal•ie (gō'lē) *n.* A goalkeeper.

goal•keep•er (gōl'kē'pər) *n.* The player who defends the goal, as in soccer and hockey.

goal post *also* **goal•post** (gōl'pōst') *n.* One of a pair of posts with or without a crossbar forming the goal in various games.

goat (gōt) *n.* **1.** A horned, bearded ruminant mammal of the genus *Capra,* orig. of mountainous regions and now widely domesticated. **2.** A lecher. **3.** A scapegoat. **—goat'ish** *adj.*

goat•ee (gō-tē') *n.* A pointed chin beard.

goat•herd (gōt'hûrd') *n.* One who herds and tends goats.

goat•skin (gōt'skĭn') *n.* **1.** The skin of a goat used for leather. **2.** Something, as a container for wine, made from goatskin.

gob[1] (gŏb) *n.* A mass : lump.

gob[2] (gŏb) *n. Slang.* A sailor.

gob•bet (gŏb'ĭt) *n.* **1.** A chunk or piece, esp. of raw meat. **2.** A lump : mass.

gob•ble[1] (gŏb'əl) *v.* **-bled, -bling. 1.** To eat up greedily. **2.** To take greedily : grab.

gob•ble[2] (gŏb'əl) *v.* **-bled, -bling.** To make the gutteral, chortling sound of a male turkey. **—gob'ble** *n.*

gob•ble•dy•gook *also* **gob•ble•de•gook** (gŏb'əl-dē-go͝ok') *n.* Wordy and often unintelligible jargon.

gob•bler (gŏb'lər) *n.* A male turkey.

Go•be•lin (gō'bə-lĭn) *n.* A tapestry noted for rich pictorial design.

go-be•tween (gō'bĭ-twēn') *n.* Someone who acts as an intermediary between 2 parties.

gob•let (gŏb'lĭt) *n.* A drinking glass with a stem and base.

gob•lin (gŏb'lĭn) *n.* A grotesque elfin creature thought to work mischief or evil.

go-by (gō'bī') *n. Informal.* An intentional slight : snub.

god (gŏd) *n.* **1. God.** A being worshiped by monotheists as the perfect, omnipotent, omniscient originator and ruler of the universe. **2.** A being of supernatural powers and attributes that is worshiped by a people. **3.** Someone or something considered to be extremely valuable or important. **—god'like'** *adj.*

god•child (gŏd'chīld') *n.* A person for whom another serves as sponsor at baptism.

god•daugh•ter (gŏd'dô'tər) *n.* A female godchild.

god•dess (gŏd'ĭs) *n.* **1.** A female deity. **2.** A woman of exceptional beauty, charm, or grace.

god•fa•ther (gŏd'fä'*th*ər) *n.* A man who sponsors a person at baptism.

god•for•sak•en (gŏd'fər-sā'kən) *adj.* Located in a dismal or remote area.

god•head (gŏd'hĕd') *n.* **1.** Divinity : godhood. **2. Godhead. a.** God. **b.** The divine and essential nature of God.

god•hood (gŏd'ho͝od') *n.* The quality or state of being a god : divinity.

god•less (gŏd'lĭs) *adj.* Not recognizing a god. **—god'less•ness** *n.*

god•ly (gŏd'lē) *adj.* **-li•er, -li•est. 1.** Devout : pious. **2.** Divine. **—god'li•ness** *n.*

god•moth•er (gŏd'mŭ*th*'ər) *n.* A woman who sponsors a person at baptism.

god•par•ent (gŏd'pâr'ənt, -păr'-) *n.* A godfather or godmother.

god•send (gŏd'sĕnd') *n.* Something needed or wanted that comes unexpectedly, as if from God.

god•son (gŏd'sŭn') *n.* A male godchild.

go-get•ter (gō'gĕt'ər) *n. Informal.* An enterprising, energetic person.

gog•gle (gŏg'əl) *v.* **-gled, -gling.** To stare or gaze with bulging eyes. *—n.* **1.** A stare or leer. **2. goggles.** A pair of usu. tinted protective eyeglasses that fit close against the face.

go-go (gō'gō') *adj.* **1.** Of, for, or employed to perform in a discotheque <a *go-go* dancer> **2.** Very enterprising.

go•ing (gō'ĭng) *n.* **1.** Departure. **2.** The condition of the ground, as for walking. **3.** *Informal.* Progress toward an objective. *—adj.* **1.** Working : running. **2.** Flourishing. **3.** Prevailing : current.

go•ings-on (gō'ĭngz-ŏn') *pl.n. Informal.* Behavior or proceedings, esp. when looked upon with disapproval.

goi•ter (goi'tər) *n.* An abnormal enlargement of the thyroid gland, visible as a swelling at the front of the neck.

gold (gōld) *n.* **1.** *Symbol* **Au** A soft, yellow, highly malleable and ductile metallic element that is used esp. in coins and jewelry. **2.** Coins made of gold. **3.** Money. **4.** A moderate to vivid yellow. **—gold** *adj.*

gold•brick (gōld'brĭk') *also* **gold•brick•er** (-brĭk'ər) *n. Slang.* Someone who avoids work : shirker. **—gold'brick'** *v.*

gold digger *n. Slang.* A woman who seeks money and gifts from men.

gold•en (gōl′dən) *adj.* **1.** Made of, relating to, or containing gold. **2.** Having the color of gold. **3.** Blond. **4.** Rich **:** splendid <a *golden* voice> **5.** Lustrous **:** shining <the *golden* sun> **6.** Marked by prosperity **:** flourishing. **7.** Advantageous **:** favorable <a *golden* opportunity> **8.** Having a promising future <*golden* youth>

gold•en•rod (gōl′dən-rŏd′) *n.* A North American plant of the genus *Solidago* with branching clusters of small yellow flowers.

gold•eye (gōld′ī′) *n.* A food and game fish, *Amphiodon alosoides,* found in NW Canada.

gold-filled (gōld′fĭld′) *adj.* Made of a hard base metal with an outer layer of gold.

gold•finch (gōld′fĭnch′) *n.* A small New World bird of the genus *Spinus,* esp. *S. tristis,* the male of which has yellow plumage with a black forehead, wings, and tail.

gold•fish (gōld′fĭsh′) *n.* A reddish or brass-colored freshwater fish, *Carassius auratus,* often kept in aquariums and ornamental pools.

gold leaf *n.* Gold beaten into extremely thin sheets used esp. for gilding.

gold•smith (gōld′smĭth′) *n.* One who fashions or deals in objects made of gold.

go•lem (gō′ləm) *n.* In Jewish folklore, an artificially created human being supernaturally endowed with life.

golf (gŏlf, gôlf) *n.* A game played with a small hard ball and various clubs on a course with 9 or 18 holes. **—golf** *v.* **—golf′er** *n.*

Go•li•ath (gə-lī′əth) *—n.* **1.** Philistine giant killed by David in the Bible. **2.** One of colossal power or achievement.

go•nad (gō′năd′) *n.* An organ that produces gametes **:** testis or ovary. **—go•nad′al, go•nad′ic** *adj.*

go•nad•o•trop•ic (gō-năd′ə-trŏp′ĭk, -trō′pĭk) *also* **go•nad•o•troph•ic** (-trŏf′ĭk, trō′fĭk) *adj.* Acting on or stimulating the gonads, as a hormone.

go•nad•o•tro•pin (gō-năd′ə-trō′pĭn, -trŏp′ĭn) *also* **go•nad•o•tro•phin** (-trō′fĭn, -trō′pĭn) *n.* A gonadotropic substance.

gon•do•la (gŏn′dl-ə, gŏn-dō′lə) *n.* **1.** A long, narrow boat propelled with a single oar and used on the canals of Venice. **2.** A railroad freight car with low sides. **3.** A cabin suspended under a balloon or dirigible. **4.** An enclosed car suspended from a cable used for transporting passengers, as up and down a ski slope.

gondola
(Left) *a Venetian gondola and* (right) *a cable gondola*

gon•do•lier (gŏn′dl-îr′) *n.* Someone who propels a gondola.

gone (gôn, gŏn) *v. p.p. of* GO *—adj.* **1.** Bygone **:** past. **2.** Dead. **3.** Ruined **:** lost. **4.** Engrossed **:** absorbed. **5.** Used up **:** exhausted. **6.** *Slang.* Infatuated.

gon•er (gô′nər, gŏn′ər) *n. Slang.* One that is doomed or ruined.

gon•fa•lon (gŏn′fə-lŏn′, -lən) *n.* A banner hung from a crosspiece.

gong (gông, gŏng) *n.* A metal disk that produces a loud, sonorous tone. **—gong** *v.*

gon•o•coc•cus (gŏn′ə-kŏk′əs) *n., pl.* **-coc•ci** (-kŏk′sī′, -kŏk′ī′). A bacterium, *Neisseria gonorrhoeae,* causing gonorrhea. **—gon′o•coc′cal** (-kŏk′əl), **gon′o•coc′cic** (-kŏk′ĭk, -kŏk′sĭk) *adj.*

gon•or•rhe•a (gŏn′ə-rē′ə) *n.* An infectious bacterial disease of the genitourinary tract that is transmitted chiefly by sexual intercourse. **—gon′or•rhe′al** *adj.*

goo (go͞o) *n. Informal.* **1.** A sticky substance. **2.** Sentimental drivel. **—goo′ey** *adj.*

†goo•ber (go͞o′bər) *n. Regional.* A peanut.

good (go͝od) *adj.* **bet•ter** (bĕt′ər), **best** (bĕst). **1.** Having desirable or favorable qualities. **2. a.** Suitable **:** appropriate. **b.** Convenient. **3.** Whole **:** sound. **4.** Superior to the average **:** satisfactory <*good* treatment> **5.** Discriminating <has very *good* taste> **6.** Salutary **:** beneficial <*good* restful sleep> **7.** Competent **:** skilled <a *good* musician> **8. a.** Sure **:** safe <a *good* investment> **b.** Valid or sound <a *good* excuse> **c.** Genuine **:** real. **9. a.** Ample **:** considerable <a *good* hem> **b.** Bountiful <*good* farmland> **10.** Full <a *good* 10 miles> **11.** Pleasant **:** enjoyable <a *good* time> **12. a.** Virtuous **:** upright. **b.** Benevolent **:** cheerful. **c.** Loyal **:** staunch. **13 a.** Well-behaved <Try to be *good.*> **b.** Socially correct **:** proper. *—n.* **1.** Something that is good. **2.** Welfare **:** benefit <for his own *good*> **3.** Goodness. **4. goods. a.** Wares **:** merchandise. **b.** Personal belongings. **5. goods.** Fabric **:** cloth. *—adv. Informal.* Well. **—as good as.** Nearly **:** almost. **—for good.** Permanently **:** forever.

good-by *or* **good-bye** (go͝od-bī′) *interj.* —Used to express farewell. *—n., pl.* **-bys** *or* **-byes.** An expression of farewell.

good-for-noth•ing (go͝od′fər-nŭth′ĭng) *n.* One of little worth or usefulness. **—good′-for-noth′ing** *adj.*

Good Friday *n.* The Friday before Easter, commemorating Christ's crucifixion.

good•heart•ed (go͝od′här′tĭd) *adj.* Having a kind, generous disposition. **—good′heart′ed•ness** *n.*

good-hu•mored (go͝od′hyo͞o′mərd) *adj.* Showing or marked by good humor **:** amiable. **—good′-hu′mored•ly** *adv.* **—good′-hu′mored•ness** *n.*

good-look•ing (go͝od′lo͝ok′ĭng) *adj.* Of pleasing appearance **:** handsome.

good·ly (go͝od′lē) *adj.* **-li·er, -li·est. 1.** Pleasing in appearance. **2.** Rather large : considerable.
good-na·tured (go͝od′nā′chərd) *adj.* Easygoing, cheerful, and affable in nature. **—good′-na′tured·ly** *adv.* **—good′-na′tured·ness** *n.*
good·ness (go͝od′nĭs) *n.* The condition or quality of being good : virtue, benevolence, or excellence.
good will *also* **good·will** (go͝od′wĭl′) *n.* **1.** Benevolence. **2.** Cheerful willingness. **3.** A good relationship, as of a business with its customers.
good·y (go͝od′ē) *n., pl.* **-ies.** *Informal.* Something attractive or desirable, esp. something good to eat. *—interj.* —Used to express delight.
good·y-good·y (go͝od′ē-go͝od′ē) *adj.* Affectedly good : prudish. **—good′y-good′y** *n.*
goof (go͞of) *Slang.* *—n.* **1.** A stupid or foolish person. **2.** A mistake : blunder. *—v.* **1.** To blunder. **2.** To spend time doing trivial things <*goofed* off all afternoon>
goof·ball (go͞of′bôl′) *n. Slang.* **1.** A foolish or goofy person. **2.** A barbiturate or tranquilizer in pill form. **—goof′ball** *adj.*
goof-off (go͞of′ôf′, -ŏf) *n.* One who shuns work or responsibility : shirker.
goof·y (go͞o′fē) *adj.* **-i·er, -i·est.** *Slang.* Silly : ridiculous. **—goof′i·ly** *adv.* **—goof′i·ness** *n.*
goo·gol (go͞o′gôl′) *n.* The number 10 raised to the power 100 (10^{100}).
gook (go͝ok) *n. Slang.* A dirty, sludgy, or slimy substance.
goon (go͞on) *n. Slang.* **1.** A thug hired to intimidate or injure opponents. **2.** A stupid person.
goose (go͞os) *n., pl.* **geese** (gēs). **1.** A large water bird of the family Anatidae that is related to the ducks and swans. **2.** A female goose. **3.** *Informal.* A silly person.
goose·ber·ry (go͞os′bĕr′ē, go͞oz′-) *n.* The edible greenish berry of a spiny shrub, *Ribers grossularia.*
goose bumps *pl.n.* Goose flesh.
goose flesh *n.* Momentary roughness of skin caused esp. by fear or cold.
goose pimples *pl.n.* Goose flesh.
go·pher (gō′fər) *n.* A burrowing North American rodent of the family Geomyidae, having external cheek pouches.
gore[1] (gôr, gōr) *v.* **gored, gor·ing.** To stab or pierce with a horn or tusk.
gore[2] (gôr, gōr) *n.* A tapering piece of cloth, as in a skirt or sail. **—gore** *v.*
gore[3] (gôr, gōr) *n.* Blood.
gorge (gôrj) *n.* **1.** A deep, narrow ravine. **2.** The throat. **3.** A mass that obstructs a passage. *—v.* **gorged, gorg·ing. 1.** To devour greedily. **2.** To fill to capacity : satiate. **—gorg′er** *n.*
gor·geous (gôr′jəs) *adj.* Dazzlingly beautiful : magnificent. **—gor′geous·ly** *adv.* **—gor′geous·ness** *n.*
Gor·gon·zo·la (gôr′gən-zō′lə) *n.* A pungent, blue-veined Italian cheese.
go·ril·la (gə-rĭl′ə) *n.* A large African ape, *Gorilla gorilla,* with a stocky body and dark, coarse hair.
gor·man·dize (gôr′mən-dīz′) *v.* **-dized, -diz·ing.** To eat greedily : gorge. **—gor′man·diz′er** *n.*
gorse (gôrs) *n.* A spiny shrub, *Ulex europaeus,* bearing fragrant yellow flowers.
gor·y (gôr′ē, gōr′ē) *adj.* **-i·er, -i·est. 1.** Covered or stained with blood : bloody. **2.** Marked by much bloodshed or violence.
gos·hawk (gŏs′hôk′) *n.* A large hawk, *Accipiter gentilis,* with broad, rounded wings.
gos·ling (gŏz′lĭng) *n.* A young goose.
gos·pel (gŏs′pəl) *n.* **1.** *often* **Gospel.** The teachings of Christ and the Apostles. **2. Gospel.** Any of the 1st 4 books of the New Testament. **3.** Something accepted as absolute truth. **4.** Gospel music.

▲ ***word history:*** The ancestor of *gospel* is the Old English compound *gōdspel,* literally "good tidings." It originated as a loan translation of Latin *evangelium,* a borrowing of Greek *euangelion,* which in Christian contexts meant "good tidings," specifically the good news of the kingdom of God brought by Jesus.

gospel music *n.* American religious music associated with evangelism and based on simple folk melodies blended with rhythmic and melodic elements of spirituals and jazz.
gos·sa·mer (gŏs′ə-mər) *n.* **1.** A fine film of cobwebs floating in the air. **2.** A sheer, gauzy fabric. **3.** Something delicate, light, or flimsy. **—gos′sa·mer** *adj.*
gos·sip (gŏs′əp) *n.* **1.** Rumor or talk of a personal or sensational nature. **2.** Someone who habitually spreads sensational or intimate facts. *—v.* To engage in or spread gossip. **—gos′sip·er** *n.* **—gos′sip·y** *adj.*

▲ ***word history:*** *Gossip* was orig. a compound of *god* and *sib,* meaning "godparent." At first denoting only the relationship of godparent to godchild, *gossip* was later used to indicate the relationship of godparent to parent and the relationship between the godparents of the same child. *Gossip* thus designated a relationship among peers as much as one between generations, and from the extended senses the meaning "friend" evolved. The derogatory use of *gossip* to mean a person who engages in idle chatter and rumor-spreading appeared in the 16th cent., but the use of *gossip* to mean the conversation of a gossip is not recorded until the early 18th cent.

got (gŏt) *v. p.t. & p.p. of* GET.
Goth (gŏth) *n.* A member of a Germanic people who invaded the Roman Empire early in the Christian era.
Goth·ic (gŏth′ĭk) *adj.* **1.** Of or pertaining to the Goths. **2.** Of or relating to an architectural style prevalent in W Europe from the 12th through the 15th cent. **3.** *often* **gothic.** Of or relating to a style of fiction emphasizing the grotesque, mysterious, and desolate. *—n.* **1.** The extinct Germanic language of the Goths. **2.** Gothic architecture.

got·ten (gŏt'n) *v. var. p.p. of* GET.
Gou·da (gou'də, gōō'-) *n.* A mild, close-textured cheese made from milk.
gouge (gouj) *n.* **1.** A chisel with a rounded, scooplike blade. **2.** A groove or hole made with or as if with a gouge. —*v.* **gouged, goug·ing. 1.** To make a groove or hole in with or as if with a gouge. **2.** To exact exorbitant prices from. —**goug'er** *n.*
gou·lash (gōō'läsh, -lăsh) *n.* A beef or veal stew seasoned chiefly with paprika.
gou·ra·mi (gōō-rä'mē, gōōr'ə-) *n., pl.* **-mis.** Any of various freshwater fishes of the family Anabantidae of SE Asia, many species of which are popular in home aquariums.
gourd (gôrd, gōrd, gŏŏrd) *n.* **1.** A vine of the family Cucurbitaceae that is related to the pumpkin, squash, and cucumber and bears inedible fruit with a hard rind. **2.** The dried, hollowed-out shell of a gourd, used esp. as a drinking utensil.
gourde (gŏŏrd) *n.* —See table at CURRENCY.
gour·mand (gŏŏr'mənd, -mänd') *n.* A person who enjoys eating well and heartily and often to excess.
gour·met (gŏŏr-mā', gŏŏr'mā') *n.* Someone who understands and appreciates fine food and drink **:** epicure.
gout (gout) *n.* A disturbance of the uric-acid metabolism marked by painful inflammation of the joints. —**gout'y** *adj.*
gov·ern (gŭv'ərn) *v.* **1.** To guide **:** control. **2.** To direct or manage the public policy and affairs of **:** rule. **3.** To regulate **:** determine. **4.** To restrain. —**gov'ern·a·ble** *adj.* —**gov'er·nance** *n.*
gov·ern·ess (gŭv'ər-nĭs) *n.* A woman who educates and trains a child, esp. in a private household.
gov·ern·ment (gŭv'ərn-mənt) *n.* **1.** The administration of the public policy and affairs of an area **:** rule. **2.** A system or policy by which a political unit is governed. **3.** A governing organization **:** body. **4.** The agency or organization through which a governing body exercises authority and performs its functions. —**gov'ern·men'tal** *adj.* —**gov'ern·men'tal·ly** *adv.*
gov·er·nor (gŭv'ər-nər) *n.* **1.** One who governs, as the chief executive of a U.S. state or an official appointed to exercise political authority over a territory. **2.** A device that automatically regulates the speed of a machine. —**gov'er·nor·ship'** *n.*
gown (goun) *n.* **1.** A loose, flowing garment, as a nightgown. **2.** A woman's dress, esp. a formal one. **3.** A distinctive official robe, esp. one worn by a scholar, judge, or clergyman.
grab (grăb) *v.* **grabbed, grab·bing. 1.** To take suddenly **:** snatch. **2.** *Slang.* To capture the attention of. —**grab** *n.* —**grab'ber** *n.* —**grab'by** *adj.*
grab bag *n.* **1.** A container full of articles, such as party gifts, to be drawn unseen. **2.** A miscellaneous assortment.
gra·ben (grä'bən) *n.* A depression of the earth's crust between 2 parallel faults.
grace (grās) *n.* **1.** Seemingly effortless beauty, ease, and charm of movement, form, or proportion. **2.** A charming or pleasing quality or characteristic. **3.** Skill at avoiding an improper, inept, or clumsy course. **4.** Good will **:** favor. **5.** A temporary exemption, as from paying a debt **:** reprieve. **6. a.** Divine love and protection given to mankind by God. **b.** A virtue granted by God. **7.** A short prayer said at mealtime. **8.** —Used as a title of courtesy for a duke, duchess, or archbishop. —*v.* **graced, grac·ing. 1.** To favor **:** honor. **2.** To embellish. —**grace'ful** *adj.* —**grace'ful·ly** *adv.* —**grace'ful·ness** *n.* —**grace'less** *adj.* —**grace'less·ly** *adv.* —**grace'less·ness** *n.*
gra·cious (grā'shəs) *adj.* **1.** Marked by courtesy and kindness. **2.** Compassionate **:** merciful. **3.** Marked by good taste and elegance. ★ *syns:* AFFABLE, CONGENIAL, CORDIAL, GENIAL, SOCIABLE —**gra'cious·ly** *adv.* —**gra'cious·ness** *n.*
grack·le (grăk'əl) *n.* Any of several New World blackbirds of the family Icteridae with iridescent blackish plumage.
grad (grăd) *n. Informal.* A graduate.
gra·da·tion (grā-dā'shən) *n.* **1. a.** A series of successive steps or stages. **b.** A step or stage in such a series. **c.** Advancement by such a series. **2.** The act of grading. —**gra·da'tion·al** *adj.*
grade (grād) *n.* **1.** A stage or degree in a process or series. **2.** A position in a scale, as of quality. **3.** A group of persons or things falling in the same specified position or rank **:** class. **4.** A class at an elementary school. **5.** A mark indicating the quality of a student's work. **6.** A military, naval, or civil-service rank. **7.** The degree to which something, as a road, slopes. **8.** A slope. —*v.* **grad·ed, grad·ing. 1.** To arrange in grades **:** rank or sort. **2.** To evaluate. **3.** To give an academic grade to. **4.** To level to a desired gradient <*grade* a road>
grade school *n.* An elementary school. —**grade'-school'er** *n.*
gra·di·ent (grā'dē-ənt) *n.* A slope or degree of slope.
grad·u·al (grăj'ōō-əl) *adj.* Occurring or progressing in degrees or even, continuous stages. —**grad'u·al·ly** *adv.* —**grad'u·al·ness** *n.*
grad·u·al·ism (grăj'ōō-ə-lĭz'əm) *n.* The policy of or belief in advancing toward a goal by gradual, often slow stages.
grad·u·ate (grăj'ōō-āt') *v.* **-at·ed, -at·ing. 1.** To grant or be granted an academic degree or diploma. **2.** To divide into steps, categories, or grades. **3.** To mark with intervals for use in measurement. —*n.* (-ĭt). **1.** One who has received an academic degree or diploma. **2.** A container marked with lines for measuring contents. —*adj.* (-ĭt). **1.** Possessing an academic degree or diploma. **2.** Of or relating to studies beyond a bachelor's degree.
grad·u·a·tion (grăj'ōō-ā'shən) *n.* **1.** Conferral or receipt of an academic degree or diploma. **2.** A commencement ceremony. **3.** A mark on a graduated scale.

graf•fi•to (grə-fē'tō) *n., pl.* **-ti** (-tē). A drawing or inscription, as one made on a wall in a public place.

graft¹ (grăft) *v.* **1.** To insert (a shoot from one plant) into another living plant so that the 2 grow together as a single plant. **2.** To transplant or implant (tissue) into a bodily part. —*n.* **1. a.** A shoot grafted onto another living plant. **b.** The point of union of such plant parts. **2.** Material, esp. tissue or an organ, used in surgical grafting. —**graft'er** *n.*

graft² (grăft) *n.* **1.** The act of using one's public position unscrupulously for money or advantage. **2.** Money or advantage gained by graft. —**graft** *v.* —**graft'er** *n.*

gra•ham (grā'əm) *n.* Whole-wheat flour.

Grail (grāl) *n.* The legendary cup or chalice used by Christ at the Last Supper and later searched for by knights.

grain (grān) *n.* **1. a.** A small, hard seed or fruit of a cereal grass, as wheat. **b.** The seeds or fruits of such plants as a group. **2.** Cereal grasses as a group. **3.** A small hard particle <a *grain* of sand> **4.** A very small amount. **5.** —See table at MEASUREMENT. **6.** The arrangement or pattern of the constituents of material such as wood and leather. **7.** Texture. **8.** Basic nature : disposition.

grain alcohol *n.* ALCOHOL *1.*

grain elevator *n.* A tall building used for storing and discharging grain.

grain•y (grā'nē) *adj.* **-i•er, -i•est. 1.** Made of or like grain : granular. **2.** Resembling the grain of wood. —**grain'i•ness** *n.*

gram (grăm) *n.* —See table at MEASUREMENT.

gram•mar (grăm'ər) *n.* **1.** The study of the classes of words, their relations to each other, and their arrangement into sentences. **2.** The system of rules implicit in a language, regarded as a mechanism for generating sentences. **3. a.** The syntactic and inflectional rules of a language. **b.** Writing or speech evaluated with reference to conformity to such rules. —**gram•mar'i•an** (grə-mâr'ē-ən) *n.* —**gram•mat'i•cal** (-măt'ĭ-kəl) *adj.* —**gram•mat'i•cal•ly** *adv.*

grammar school *n.* **1.** An elementary school. **2.** *esp. Brit.* A secondary or preparatory school.

gram•o•phone (grăm'ə-fōn') *n.* A phonograph.

gran•a•ry (grăn'ə-rē, grā'nə-) *n., pl.* **-ries.** A building in which grain is stored.

grand (grănd) *adj.* **1.** Large in size, scope, or extent. **2.** Splendid : magnificent. **3.** Of higher rank or greater importance : chief. **4.** Stately : regal. **5.** Lofty : admirable. **6.** Complete : inclusive <the *grand* total> ★ *syns:* BARONIAL, GRANDIOSE, IMPOSING, LORDLY, MAGNIFICENT, MAJESTIC, NOBLE, PRINCELY, REGAL, ROYAL, STATELY —*n.* **1.** A grand piano. **2.** *Slang.* $1,000. —**grand'ly** *adv.* —**grand'ness** *n.*

gran•dam (grăn'dăm') *also* **gran•dame** (-dām') *n.* An old woman.

grand•child (grănd'chīld', grăn'-) *n.* A child of one's son or daughter.

grand•daugh•ter (grăn'dô'tər) *n.* A daughter of one's son or daughter.

grande dame (grän'däm', gräɴ däm') *n.* A usu. elderly woman of high social position or majestic manner.

gran•dee (grăn-dē') *n.* A nobleman of the highest rank in Portugal or Spain.

gran•deur (grăn'jər, -jŏŏr') *n.* The condition or quality of being grand : splendor.

grand•fa•ther (grănd'fä'*th*ər, grăn'-) *n.* **1.** The father of one's mother or father. **2.** An ancestor.

grandfather clock *n.* A pendulum clock in a tall narrow cabinet.

gran•dil•o•quence (grăn-dĭl'ə-kwəns) *n.* Pompous or bombastic speech or expression. —**gran•dil'o•quent** *adj.*

gran•di•ose (grăn'dē-ōs', grăn'dē-ōs') *adj.* **1.** Grand and impressive. **2.** Affectedly splendid or grand : pompous. —**gran'di•ose'ly** *adv.* —**gran'di•os'i•ty** (-ŏs'ĭ-tē) *n.*

grand jury *n.* A jury convened in private to evaluate criminal accusations against persons and to determine whether the evidence warrants indictment.

grand mal (grănd'măl', grän', grän mäl') *n.* A form of epilepsy marked by severe seizures.

grand•moth•er (grănd'mŭ*th*'ər, grăn'-) *n.* **1.** The mother of one's father or mother. **2.** A female ancestor.

grand opera *n.* A drama with the complete text set to music.

grand•par•ent (grănd'pâr'ənt, -păr'-, grăn'-) *n.* A parent of one's mother or father.

grand piano *n.* A piano with the strings strung in a horizontal frame.

Grand Prix (gräɴ'prē') *n., pl.* **Grand Prix** (prēz', prē') Any of several competitive international road races for sports cars of specific engine size.

grand slam *n.* **1.** The taking of all the tricks in the game of bridge. **2.** *Baseball.* A home run hit when 3 runners are on base.

grand•son (grănd'sŭn', grăn'-) *n.* A son of one's son or daughter.

grand•stand (grănd'stănd', grăn'-) *n.* A usu. roofed stand for spectators, as at a sports event.

grange (grānj) *n.* **1. Grange.** An association of farmers in the U.S. **2.** *esp. Brit.* A farm with its residence and other buildings.

gran•ite (grăn'ĭt) *n.* A coarse-grained, hard igneous rock that consists chiefly of quartz, orthoclase, and mica and is used for building. —**gra•nit'ic** (grə-nĭt'ĭk) *adj.*

gran•ite•ware (grăn'ĭt-wâr') *n.* Enameled iron utensils.

†**gran•ny** *or* **gran•nie** (grăn'ē) *n., pl.* **-nies. 1.** A grandmother. **2.** A fussy person. **3.** *S U.S.* A midwife.

granny knot *n.* A knot resembling a square knot but with the second tie crossed incorrectly.

granny knot

gra•no•la (grə-nō'lə) *n.* Rolled oats mixed, as with dried fruit and seeds, and eaten esp. as a snack.

grant (grănt) *v.* **1.** To consent to : allow. **2.** To bestow : give. **3.** To admit as being true : acknowledge. —*n.* **1.** The act of granting. **2. a.** Something granted. **b.** A giving of funds for a specific purpose. **3.** *Law.* **a.** A transfer of property by deed. **b.** The instrument by which property is transferred. **c.** Property thus transferred. —**grant•ee'** *n.* —**grant'er, gran'tor** *n.*

grants•man•ship (grănts'mən-shĭp') *n.* The technique of obtaining grants, as to subsidize research.

gran•u•lar (grăn'yə-lər) *adj.* **1.** Composed or seeming to be composed of granules. **2.** Grainy. —**gran'u•lar'i•ty** *n.*

gran•u•late (grăn'yə-lāt') *v.* **-lat•ed, -lat•ing. 1.** To form into granules or crystals. **2.** To make or become rough and grainy. —**gran'u•la'tion** *n.*

gran•ule (grăn'yo͞ol) *n.* A small grain or particle : pellet.

grape (grāp) *n.* Any of numerous woody vines of the genus *Vitis,* bearing clusters of fleshy, smooth-skinned, purple, red, or green fruit, eaten raw or dried and widely used in winemaking.

grape•fruit (grāp'fro͞ot') *n.* A tropical or semitropical tree, *Citrus paradisi,* cultivated for its large round edible fruit, with a yellow rind and juicy, acidic pulp.

grape hyacinth *n.* Any of various plants of the genus *Muscari,* with narrow leaves and rounded, usu. blue flowers in dense terminal clusters.

grape•shot (grāp'shŏt') *n.* A cluster of small iron balls formerly used as a cannon charge.

grape sugar *n.* Dextrose from grapes.

grape•vine (grāp'vīn') *n.* **1.** A vine that produces grapes. **2.** An informal means of transmitting rumor or information.

graph (grăf) *n.* A drawing or diagram that shows a relationship between sets of things. —**graph** *v.*

graph•ic (grăf'ĭk) *also* **graph•i•cal** (-ĭ-kəl) *adj.* **1.** Written, drawn, printed, or engraved. **2.** Vividly set forth or described. **3.** Of or relating to the graphic arts. —**graph'i•cal•ly** *adv.*

graphic arts *pl.n.* The arts, as painting, drawing, and engraving, of representation, writing, or printing on 2-dimensional surfaces.

graph•ics (grăf'ĭks) *n. (sing. or pl. in number).* **1.** The making of drawings or blueprints, as in engineering or architecture, in accordance with the rules of mathematics. **2.** The graphic arts.

graph•ite (grăf'īt') *n.* A soft form of carbon used in lead pencils, lubricants, paints, and coatings. —**gra•phit'ic** (gră-fĭt'ĭk) *adj.*

graph•ol•o•gy (gră-fŏl'ə-jē) *n.* The study of handwriting, esp. for the purpose of analyzing personality or character. —**graph•ol'o•gist** *n.*

grap•nel (grăp'nəl) *n.* A small anchor with 3 or more flukes.

grap•ple (grăp'əl) *n.* **1.** An implement with hooks used to hold an enemy ship alongside for boarding. **2.** A grapnel. **3.** Hand-to-hand combat. —*v.* **-pled, -pling. 1.** To seize, fasten, or drag with or as if with a grapple. **2.** To seize firmly with the hands. **3.** To try to come to grips : struggle. **4.** To wrestle. —**grap'pler** *n.*

grappling iron *also* **grappling hook** *n.* GRAPPLE 1.

grasp (grăsp) *v.* **1. a.** To seize and grip tightly. **b.** To make a motion of grasping : clutch. **2.** To comprehend : understand. —*n.* **1.** A firm hold : grip. **2.** The power to seize and hold. **3.** Comprehension. **4.** An embrace.

grasp•ing (grăs'pĭng) *adj.* Excessively eager to acquire material possessions : greedy. —**grasp'ing•ly** *adv.* —**grasp'ing•ness** *n.*

grass (grăs) *n.* **1. a.** Any of numerous plants of the family Graminae with narrow leaves and jointed stems. **b.** These plants as a group. **2.** Ground, as a lawn, covered with grass. **3.** *Slang.* Marijuana. —**grass'i•ness** *n.* —**grass'like'** *adj.* —**grass'y** *adj.*

grass•hop•per (grăs'hŏp'ər) *n.* Any of various related jumping insects of the families Locustidae (or Acrididae) and Tettigoniidae with long hind legs.

grass•land (grăs'lănd') *n.* An area, such as a prairie, that is covered with grass or grasslike vegetation.

grass•roots (grăs'ro͞ots', -ro͝ots') *pl.n. (sing. or pl. in number).* People or society at a local level rather than at the center of a political organization. —**grass'roots'** *adj.*

grass widow *n.* A woman who is separated or divorced from her husband.

grate[1] (grāt) *v.* **grat•ed, grat•ing. 1.** To fragment, shred, or pulverize by rubbing against a rough surface. **2.** To make or cause to make a rasping sound. **3.** To annoy : irritate. —*n.* A rasping noise. —**grat'er** *n.* —**grat'ing** *adj.* —**grat'ing•ly** *adv.*

grate[2] (grāt) *n.* **1.** A framework of bars used to block an opening. **2.** An iron frame similar to a grate that is used to hold burning fuel, as in a fireplace.

grate•ful (grāt'fəl) *adj.* **1.** Thankful : appreciative. **2.** Expressing gratitude. —**grate'ful•ly** *adv.* —**grate'ful•ness** *n.*

grat•i•fy (grăt'ə-fī') *v.* **-fied, -fy•ing. 1.** To give or be a source of pleasure to. **2.** To fulfill the desires of **:** indulge. **—grat'i•fi•ca'tion** *n.* **—grat'i•fi'er** *n.*

grat•ing (grā'tĭng) *n.* GRATE[2] 1.

grat•is (grăt'ĭs, grā'tĭs) *adv. & adj.* Without charge **:** free.

grat•i•tude (grăt'ĭ-to͞od', -tyo͞od') *n.* The state of being grateful **:** thankfulness.

gra•tu•i•tous (grə-to͞o'ĭ-təs, -tyo͞o'-) *adj.* **1.** Given or done without payment **:** free. **2.** Unjustified **:** unwarranted. **—gra•tu'i•tous•ly** *adv.* **—gra•tu'i•tous•ness** *n.*

gra•tu•i•ty (grə-to͞o'ĭ-tē, -tyo͞o'-) *n., pl.* **-ties.** A tip for service.

grau•pel (grou'pəl) *n.* Precipitation consisting of snow pellets.

gra•va•men (grə-vā'mən) *n., pl.* **-mens** *or* **-vam•i•na** (-văm'ə-nə). *Law.* The part of a charge or accusation that weighs most heavily against the accused.

grave[1] (grāv) *n.* **1.** An excavation in the ground for the burial of a corpse. **2.** A place of burial <a watery *grave*>

grave[2] (grāv) *adj.* **grav•er, grav•est. 1.** Very serious **:** important. **2.** Bringing or threatening great danger or harm **:** critical. **3.** Solemn **:** dignified. **4.** Somber. **5.** (*also* gräv). Of, being, or written with the mark (`), as the *è* in *Sèvres.* **—grave'ly** *adv.* **—grave'ness** *n.*

grave[3] (grāv) *v.* **graved, grav•en** (grā'vən) *or* **graved, grav•ing.** To carve or sculpt **:** engrave. **—grav'er** *n.*

grav•el (grăv'əl) *n.* Loose rock fragments.

grav•el•ly (grăv'ə-lē) *adj.* **1.** Of, full of, or covered with gravel. **2.** Having a harsh rasping sound <a *gravelly* voice>

grave•stone (grāv'stōn') *n.* A stone marker on a grave **:** tombstone.

grave•yard (grāv'yärd') *n.* An area set aside as a burial ground **:** cemetery.

graveyard shift *n.* **1.** A work shift that begins late at night, as at midnight. **2.** The workers on a graveyard shift.

grav•id (grăv'ĭd) *adj.* Pregnant.

gra•vim•e•ter (gră-vĭm'ĭ-tər, grā'və-mē'-) *n.* An instrument for determining specific gravity. **—gra•vim'e•try** (-vĭm'ĭ-trē) *n.*

grav•i•tate (grăv'ĭ-tāt') *v.* **-tat•ed, -tat•ing. 1.** To move under the force of gravity. **2.** To be drawn as if by an irresistible force.

grav•i•ta•tion (grăv'ĭ-tā'shən) *n.* The attraction or force of attraction that tends to draw material objects together. **—grav'i•ta'tion•al** *adj.* **—grav'i•ta'tion•al•ly** *adv.* **—grav'i•ta'tive** *adj.*

grav•i•ty (grăv'ĭ-tē) *n.* **1.** The attractive central gravitational force exerted by a celestial body such as the earth. **2.** Weight. **3.** Seriousness. **4.** Importance.

gra•vure (grə-vyo͝or') *n.* **1.** A method of printing with etched plates or cylinders. **2.** Photogravure.

gra•vy (grā'vē) *n., pl.* **-vies. 1. a.** The juices from cooked meat. **b.** A sauce made by seasoning and thickening these juices. **2.** *Slang.* Something desirable, as money, that is unexpectedly or easily gained.

gray *also* **grey** (grā) *adj.* **1.** Of or relating to a neutral color shading between black and white. **2.** Dismal **:** gloomy <a *gray* day> **3.** Having gray hair. *—n.* **1.** A neutral color shading between black and white. **2.** An object or animal of the color gray. **—gray'ish** *adj.* **—gray'ness** *n.*

gray•beard (grā'bîrd') *n.* An old man.

gray•ling (grā'lĭng) *n., pl.* **-ling** *or* **-lings.** Any of several freshwater food and game fishes of the genus *Thymallus,* with a small mouth and a large dorsal fin.

gray matter *n.* The brownish-gray nerve tissue of the brain and spinal cord, consisting principally of nerve cells and fibers.

gray whale *n.* A baleen whale of N Pacific waters having grayish-black coloring with white blotches.

graze[1] (grāz) *v.* **grazed, graz•ing. 1.** To feed on growing grasses and herbage. **2.** To put (livestock) out to graze. **—graz'er** *n.*

graze[2] (grāz) *v.* **grazed, graz•ing. 1.** To touch lightly in passing. **2.** To scratch slightly **:** abrade. **—graze** *n.*

gra•zier (grā'zhər) *n.* One who grazes cattle.

grease (grēs) *n.* **1.** Melted or soft animal fat. **2.** An oily substance, esp. lubricant. *—v.* (grēs, grēz) **greased, greas•ing.** To coat, smear, or lubricate with grease. **—greas'i•ness** *n.* **—greas'y** *adj.*

grease paint *also* **grease•paint** (grēs'pānt') *n.* Theatrical make-up.

great (grāt) *adj.* **1.** Large in size **:** big. **2.** Superior **:** outstanding <a *great* painting> **3.** Large in quantity or number **:** numerous. **4.** Eminent **:** renowned <a *great* novelist> **5.** *Informal.* Very good **:** first-rate <a *great* performance> **6.** Being a generation removed from the relative specified <a *great*-uncle> *—n.* One that is great. **—great'ly** *adv.* **—great'ness** *n.*

great ape *n.* Any of a family of apes including chimpanzees, gorillas, and orangutans.

great•coat (grāt'kōt') *n.* An overcoat.

Great Dane *n.* A massive and powerful dog with a smooth, short coat.

great•heart•ed (grāt'här'tĭd) *adj.* **1.** Noble or courageous. **2.** Magnanimous **:** generous. **—great'heart'ed•ly** *adv.* **—great'heart'ed•ness** *n.*

Great Power *n.* A nation with great influence in international affairs.

grebe (grēb) *n.* Any of various diving birds of the family Podicipedidae with lobed, fleshy membranes along each toe and a pointed bill.

greed (grēd) *n.* A desire to acquire more than one needs or deserves **:** avarice.

greed•y (grē'dē) *adj.* **-i•er, -i•est. 1.** Excessively eager to acquire or possess something, esp. in quantity. ★ ***syns:*** ACQUISITIVE, AVARICIOUS, AVID, COVETOUS, DESIROUS, GRABBY, GRASPING, HUNGRY, RAPACIOUS **2.** Wanting to eat or drink more than one can reasonably consume. ★ ***syns:*** GLUTTONOUS, HOGGISH, PIGGISH, RAVENOUS, VORACIOUS

3. Extremely desirous. **—greed'i•ly** *adv.* **—greed'i•ness** *n.*

Greek (grēk) *n.* **1.** A native or inhabitant of Greece. **2.** The ancient or modern language of Greece. **—Greek** *adj.*

green (grēn) *n.* **1. a.** Any of a group of colors whose hue is that of growing grass. **b.** The hue of the visible spectrum lying between yellow and blue. **2. greens.** Leafy plants or plant parts. **3.** A grassy lawn or plot, esp. the closely mowed area of grass at the end of a golf fairway. *—adj.* **1.** Of the color green. **2.** Covered with green foliage or growth. **3.** Made with green or leafy vegetables <a *green* salad> **4.** Not ripe **:** immature. **5.** Lacking experience. *—v.* To become green. **—green'ish** *adj.* **—green'ness** *n.*

green•back (grēn'băk') *n.* A note of U.S. currency.

green bean *n.* The string bean.

green•belt (grēn'bĕlt') *n.* An area of recreational parks, farmland, or uncultivated land surrounding a community.

green card *n.* An official document issued by the U.S. government to aliens, allowing them to work legally in the United States.

green•er•y (grē'nə-rē) *n., pl.* **-ies.** Green plants or foliage.

green-eyed (grēn'īd') *adj.* Jealous.

green•gro•cer (grēn'grō'sər) *n. esp. Brit.* A retailer of fresh fruit and vegetables. **—green'gro'cer•y** *n.*

green•horn (grēn'hôrn') *n.* An inexperienced person, esp. one easily fooled.

green•house (grēn'hous') *n.* A glass-enclosed structure in which plants requiring an even temperature can be cultivated.

greenhouse effect *n.* The phenomenon whereby the earth's atmosphere traps solar radiation, caused by gases such as carbon dioxide and methane that allow incoming sunlight to pass through but absorb heat radiated back from the earth's surface.

green manure *n.* A growing crop, as a clover or grass, plowed under the soil to enhance fertility.

green pepper *n.* The unripened green fruit of various pepper plants.

green•room (grēn'rōōm', -rŏŏm') *n.* A room or lounge in a theater or concert hall for performers to use when off stage.

green•sward (grēn'swôrd') *n.* Turf that is covered with green grass.

green thumb *n.* An unusual skill at growing plants.

Green•wich time (grĭn'ĭj, -ĭch, grĕn'-) *n.* The time at the meridian at Greenwich, England (0° longitude), used to calculate standard time in most of the world.

green•wood (grēn'wŏŏd') *n.* A forest when the foliage is green.

greet (grēt) *v.* **1.** To address in a friendly way **:** welcome. **2.** To receive with a specified reaction. **3.** To be perceived by <A fascinating spectacle *greeted* his eyes.> **—greet'er** *n.*

greet•ing (grē'tĭng) *n.* A gesture or word of salutation on meeting.

greeting card *n.* A folded card bearing a message, as of greeting or congratulations.

gre•gar•i•ous (grĭ-gâr'ē-əs) *adj.* **1.** Tending to form or move in groups. **2.** Enjoying the company of others **:** sociable. **—gre•gar'i•ous•ly** *adv.* **—gre•gar'i•ous•ness** *n.*

Gre•go•ri•an calendar (grĭ-gôr'ē-ən, -gōr'-) *n.* The calendar, sponsored (1582) by Pope Gregory XIII, that is in use in most of the world.

grem•lin (grĕm'lĭn) *n.* A mischievous elf to whom mechanical malfunctions, esp. in aircrafts, are attributed.

gre•nade (grə-nād') *n.* A small bomb detonated by a fuse and thrown by hand or fired from a rifle equipped with a launcher.

gren•a•dier (grĕn'ə-dîr') *n.* A member of a regiment formerly armed with grenades.

gren•a•dine (grĕn'ə-dēn', grĕn'ə-dēn') *n.* A syrup made from pomegranates or red currants and used esp. in mixed drinks.

grew (grōō) *v. p.t. of* GROW.

grey (grā) *n. & adj. var. of* GRAY.

grey•hound (grā'hound') *n.* A slender, swift-running dog with long legs.

grid (grĭd) *n.* **1.** A framework of bars **:** grate. **2.** A pattern of lines forming squares, used as a reference for locating points on a map, chart, aerial photograph, etc. **3.** A conducting plate in a storage battery. **4.** A network or coil of fine wires located between the plate and filament in an electron tube. **5.** A football field.

grid•dle (grĭd'l) *n.* A flat metal surface used for cooking.

grid•dle•cake (grĭd'l-kāk') *n.* A pancake.

grid•i•ron (grĭd'ī'ərn) *n.* **1.** A flat framework of metal bars used for broiling. **2.** A framework or network suggestive of a gridiron. **3.** A football field.

grid•lock (grĭd'lŏk') *n.* A traffic jam in which no vehicular movement is possible. **—grid'lock'** *v.* **—grid'locked'** *adj.*

grief (grēf) *n.* **1.** Deep sadness, as that caused by bereavement **:** sorrow. **2.** A cause of grief.

griev•ance (grē'vəns) *n.* **1.** Something considered to afford just cause for complaint or protest. **2.** A complaint of unfair treatment, esp. by an employee.

grieve (grēv) *v.* **grieved, griev•ing.** To feel or cause to feel grief.

griev•ous (grē'vəs) *adj.* **1.** Causing grief, anguish, or pain. **2.** Grave **:** dire. **—griev'ous•ly** *adv.* **—griev'ous•ness** *n.*

grif•fin *also* **grif•fon** *or* **gryph•on** (grĭf'ĭn) *n.* A fabulous beast with a lion's body and an eagle's head and wings.

gri•gri *also* **gris-gris** (grē'grē) *n.* An African charm, fetish, or amulet.

grill (grĭl) *n.* **1.** A cooking utensil with parallel metal bars **:** gridiron. **2.** Food cooked on a grill. **3.** A restaurant, as in a hotel, where grilled foods are a specialty. **4.** *var. of* GRILLE. *—v.* **1.** To broil on a grill. **2.** *Informal.* To question closely and relentlessly.

grille *also* **grill** (grĭl) *n.* A metal grating used as a screen, divider, or barrier.

grim (grĭm) *adj.* **grim•mer, grim•mest. 1.**

Unyielding : relentless. 2. Forbidding in appearance. 3. Grisly : ghastly. 4. Gloomy : dismal. —**grim'ly** *adv.* —**grim'ness** *n.*

grim•ace (grĭm'əs, grĭ-mās') *n.* A facial expression of pain, disapproval, or disgust. —**grim'ace** *v.*

grime (grīm) *n.* Black dirt or soot, usu. clinging to or ingrained in a surface. —**grim'i•ness** *n.* —**grim'y** *adj.*

grin (grĭn) *v.* **grinned, grin•ning.** To smile broadly. —**grin** *n.*

grind (grīnd) *v.* **ground** (ground), **grind•ing. 1.** To reduce to fine particles. **2.** To sharpen, shape, or refine by friction <*grind* a knife> **3.** To press or rub together : gnash <*grinds* his teeth> **4.** To move with noisy friction <a car *grinding* to a halt> **5.** To bear down on harshly : oppress. **6.** To produce or operate by or as if by turning a crank <*ground* out a book a year> **7.** *Informal.* To study or work hard : drudge. —*n.* **1.** *Informal.* Laborious work, routine, or study. **2.** Someone who studies or works excessively. —**grind'ing•ly** *adv.*

grind•er (grīn'dər) *n.* **1.** One that grinds. **2.** A molar. **3. grinders.** *Informal.* The teeth. **4.** HERO 4.

grind•stone (grīnd'stōn') *n.* A stone disk that revolves on an axle for grinding, polishing, or sharpening.

grip (grĭp) *n.* **1. a.** A firm hold : grasp. **b.** Power and strength in holding firmly. **2.** Understanding : mastery. **3.** A device to be grasped and held : handle. **4.** A suitcase. —*v.* **gripped, grip•ping. 1.** To grasp and keep a firm hold on. **2.** To attract and keep the attention or interest of. —**grip'ping•ly** *adv.*

gripe (grīp) *v.* **griped, grip•ing. 1.** To suffer or cause to suffer sharp bowel pains. **2.** *Informal.* To annoy : vex. **3.** *Informal.* To complain petulantly : grumble. —*n.* **1.** *Informal.* A complaint. **2.** *often* **gripes.** A sharp, repeated bowel pain.

grippe (grĭp) *n.* Influenza. —**grip'py** *adj.*

gris-gris (grē'grē) *n. var. of* GRIGRI.

gris•ly (grĭz'lē) *adj.* **-li•er, -li•est.** Ghastly : gruesome.

grist (grĭst) *n.* **1.** Grain ready to be ground. **2.** Ground grain.

gris•tle (grĭs'əl) *n.* Cartilage. —**gris'tly** *adj.*

grist•mill (grĭst'mĭl') *n.* A mill for grinding grain.

grit (grĭt) *n.* **1.** Tiny rough granules, as of sand. **2.** *Informal.* Great courage and fortitude. **3. Grit.** *Can.* A member of the Liberal Party of Canada. —*v.* **grit•ted, grit•ting.** To clamp (the teeth) together. —**grit'ty** *adj.*

grits (grĭts) *pl.n.* Coarsely ground grain.

griz•zled (grĭz'əld) *adj.* Grizzly.

griz•zly (grĭz'lē) *adj.* **-zli•er, -zli•est.** Flecked or mixed with gray. —*n., pl.* **-zlies.** A grizzly bear.

grizzly bear *n.* A large grayish bear, *Ursus horribilis,* of W North America.

groan (grōn) *v.* To utter a deep, prolonged sound indicative of pain, grief, or vexation. —**groan** *n.* —**groan'ing•ly** *adv.*

groat (grōt) *n.* A British coin worth 4 pence, used from the 14th to the 17th cent.

gro•cer (grō'sər) *n.* A storekeeper who sells groceries.

gro•cer•y (grō'sə-rē) *n., pl.* **-ies. 1.** A store in which food and household staples are sold. **2. groceries.** The goods sold in a grocery.

grog (grŏg) *n.* Alcoholic liquor, esp. rum, diluted with water.

grog•gy (grŏg'ē) *adj.* **-gi•er, -gi•est.** Weak, unsteady on the feet, and dazed. —**grog'gi•ly** *adv.* —**grog'gi•ness** *n.*

groin (groin) *n.* **1. a.** The crease where the thigh meets the abdomen. **b.** The area of this crease. **2.** The curved edge of a building formed by 2 intersecting vaults.

grom•met (grŏm'ĭt) *n.* A reinforced eyelet through which something, as a fastener, may be passed.

groom (gro͞om, gro͝om) *n.* **1.** A male servant, esp. one who takes care of horses. **2.** A bridegroom. —*v.* **1.** To make trim and neat. **2.** To clean and brush (an animal). **3.** To prepare for a particular position.

grooms•man (gro͞omz'mən, gro͝omz'-) *n.* A bridegroom's attendant at his wedding.

groove (gro͞ov) *n.* **1.** A long, narrow channel or furrow. **2.** A humdrum, fixed routine. —**groove** *v.*

groov•y (gro͞o'vē) *adj.* **-i•er, -i•est.** *Slang.* Delightful : wonderful.

grope (grōp) *v.* **groped, grop•ing. 1.** To reach or feel about uncertainly in or as if in search. **2.** To look for uncertainly or blindly <*grope* for a reason> —**grope** *n.* —**grop'ing•ly** *adv.*

gros•beak (grōs'bēk') *n.* Any of several often colorful birds of the genera *Hesperiphona, Pinicola,* and related genera, with a thick, rounded bill.

gro•schen (grō'shən) *n., pl.* **-schen.** —See table at CURRENCY.

gros•grain (grō'grān') *n.* A heavy, horizontally ribbed silk or rayon fabric.

gross (grōs) *adj.* **1.** Exclusive of deductions : total <*gross* yearly profits> **2.** Glaringly obvious : egregious. **3.** Lacking refinement or delicacy : coarse. **4.** Obscene : vulgar. **5.** Overweight : corpulent. **6.** General : broad. —*n.* **1.** *pl.* **gross•es.** An entire amount exclusive of deductions : total. **2.** *pl.* **gross.** A group of 12 dozen or 144 items. —*v.* To earn as a total before deductions. —**gross'ly** *adv.* —**gross'ness** *n.*

gross national product *n.* The total market value of all the goods and services produced by a nation during a year.

grosz (grôsh) *n., pl.* **gro•szy** (grô'shē). —See table at CURRENCY.

gro•tesque (grō-tĕsk') *adj.* **1.** Ludicrously incongruous or distorted. **2.** Outlandish : bizarre. —**gro•tesque'** *n.* —**gro•tesque'ly** *adv.* —**gro•tesque'ness** *n.*

gro•tes•que•ry *also* **gro•tes•que•rie** (grō-tĕs'kə-rē) *n., pl.* **-ries. 1.** The state of being grotesque. **2.** Something grotesque.

grot•to (grŏt'ō) *n., pl.* **-toes** *or* **-tos. 1.** A cave. **2.** A cavelike excavation or structure.

grouch (grouch) *n.* **1.** A spell of grumbling or sulking. **2.** A habitually irritable or complaining person. **—grouch** *v.* **—grouch'i•ly** *adv.* **—grouch'i•ness** *n.* **—grouch'y** *adj.*

ground[1] (ground) *n.* **1.** The surface of the earth. **2.** Earth : soil. **3.** An area of land set aside for a particular purpose. **4. grounds.** The land surrounding a building. **5.** A basis for an argument, belief, or action. **6.** A background. **7. grounds.** Sediment at the bottom of a liquid, esp. coffee : dregs. **8.** A conducting body, as the earth, used as a return for electric currents and as an arbitrary zero of potential. *—v.* **1.** To place or set on the ground. **2.** To provide a basis or reason for. **3.** To instruct in basic principles. **4.** To prevent (an aircraft, pilot, or crew) from flying. **5.** To connect (an electric current) to a ground. **6.** To run or cause to run aground. **—ground'less** *adj.* **—ground'less•ly** *adv.* **—ground'less•ness** *n.*

ground[2] (ground) *v. p.t. & p.p. of* GRIND.

ground•break•ing (ground'brā'kĭng) *n.* The act of breaking ground to begin a construction project. *—adj.* Highly original <a *groundbreaking* technology>

ground cloth *n.* A ground sheet.

ground cover *n.* Low-growing plants that form a dense, extensive growth and tend to prevent soil erosion.

ground crew *n.* A team of technicians and mechanics who maintain and service aircraft or spacecraft on the ground.

ground-ef•fect machine (ground'ĭ-fĕkt') *n.* A vehicle designed for traveling over land or water by means of an air cushion.

ground•er (groun'dər) *n.* A batted baseball that bounces or rolls along the ground.

ground glass *n.* Glass that has been ground or etched to create a roughened, nontransparent surface.

ground hog *also* **ground•hog** (ground'hôg', -hŏg') *n.* A woodchuck.

ground•ling (ground'lĭng) *n.* **1.** One with uncultivated tastes. **2.** A spectator in the cheaper part of an Elizabethan theater.

ground•mass (ground'măs') *n.* The fine-grained crystalline base of porphyritic rock in which larger crystals are embedded.

ground rule *n.* **1.** A rule in sports that modifies play on a particular field, course, or court. **2.** A basic rule.

ground sheet *also* **ground•sheet** (ground'shēt') *n.* **1.** A waterproof cover for protecting an area of ground, as a baseball field. **2.** A waterproof sheet laid under camp bedding to protect against dampness.

ground squirrel *n.* A rodent of the genus *Citellus* (or *Spermophilus*), related to and resembling the chipmunk.

ground swell *n.* **1.** A deep broad swell in the ocean often caused by a distant earthquake. **2.** A strong, rapid growth : surge.

ground water *also* **ground•wa•ter** (ground'wô'tər, -wŏt'ər) *n.* Water under the surface of the earth that feeds springs and wells.

ground•work (ground'wûrk') *n.* A basis : foundation.

group (gro͞op) *n.* A number of individuals or objects collected, situated, or classified together. *—v.* To place or be in a group.

grou•per (gro͞o'pər) *n.* A large fish of the genera *Epinephelus, Mycteroperca,* or related genera, indigenous to warm seas.

group•ie (gro͞o'pē) *n. Slang.* A fan, esp. a young woman, who follows a rock group around on tours.

group therapy *n.* Psychotherapy involving sessions guided by a therapist and attended by several patients who discuss their emotional problems with each other.

grouse[1] (grous) *n., pl.* **grouse.** Any of various plump game birds of the family Tetraonidae with brownish plumage.

grouse[2] (grous) *v.* **groused, grous•ing.** To grumble : complain. **—grouse** *n.*

grout (grout) *n.* A material, as mortar, used to fill cracks in masonry or spaces between tiles. **—grout** *v.* **—grout'er** *n.*

grove (grōv) *n.* A small stand of trees usu. lacking undergrowth.

grov•el (grŭv'əl, grŏv'-) *v.* **-eled, el•ing** *or* **-elled, -el•ling. 1.** To lie or creep in a prostrate position, as from fear. **2.** To behave in a servile way : cringe. **—grov'el•er** *n.* **—grov'el•ing•ly** *adv.*

grow (grō) *v.* **grew** (gro͞o), **grown** (grōn), **grow•ing. 1.** To spring up, develop, and reach maturity. **2.** To be capable of developing : flourish. **3.** To expand : increase. **4.** To come into existence : spring forth. **5.** To come together by or as if by growth. **6.** To become. **7.** To raise : cultivate. **—grow up.** To become an adult. **—grow'er** *n.*

growl (groul) *n.* A deep guttural, threatening sound, as of a dog. **—growl** *v.* **—growl'er** *n.*

grown-up (grōn'ŭp') *adj.* Of or characteristic of adults : mature. **—grown'-up'** *n.*

growth (grōth) *n.* **1. a.** The process of growing. **b.** A stage attained in the process of growing. **2.** An increase, as in size or amount. **3.** Something that has increased or developed <a *growth* of weeds> **4.** An abnormal formation of bodily tissue, as a tumor.

grub (grŭb) *v.* **grubbed, grub•bing. 1.** To clear of roots by digging. **2.** To dig up by the roots. **3. a.** To search laboriously as if by digging : rummage. **b.** To work hard : drudge. *—n.* **1.** The thick, wormlike larva of certain insects, as beetles. **2.** *Slang.* Food. **3.** A drudge. **—grub'ber** *n.*

grub•by (grŭb'ē) *adj.* **-bi•er, -bi•est.** Unkempt : sloppy **—grub'bi•ly** *adv.* **—grub'bi•ness** *n.*

grub•stake (grŭb'stāk') *n.* Funds or materials supplied to a mining prospector or business entrepreneur for a share of future profits. **—grub'stake'** *v.*

grudge (grŭj) *v.* **grudged, grudg•ing.** To give or allow reluctantly : begrudge. *—n.* A feeling of ill will or deep resentment. **—grudg'er** *n.* **—grudg'ing•ly** *adv.*

gru•el (gro͞o'əl) *n.* A thin porridge.

gru•el•ing *also* **gru•el•ling** (grōō'ə-lĭng) *adj.* Extremely tiring : exhausting. —**gru'el•ing•ly** *adv.*

grue•some (grōō'səm) *adj.* Causing horror or repugnance : grisly. —**grue'some•ly** *adv.* —**grue'some•ness** *n.*

gruff (grŭf) *adj.* **1.** Brusque and unfriendly in manner. **2.** Harsh in sound : hoarse. ★ ***syns:*** BLUFF, BLUNT, BRUSQUE, CURT. —**gruff'ly** *adv.* —**gruff'ness** *n.*

grum•ble (grŭm'bəl) *v.* **-bled, -bling.** To mutter discontentedly. —**grum'ble** *n.* —**grum'bler** *n.* —**grum'bly** *adj.*

grump•y (grŭm'pē) *adj.* **-i•er, -i•est.** Irritable and moody : cranky. —**grump** *n.* —**grump'i•ly** *adv.* —**grump'i•ness** *n.*

grunge (grŭnj) *n. Slang.* **1.** Filth : dirt. **2.** One that is dirty, inferior, or obnoxious.

grun•gy (grŭn'jē) *adj.* **-gi•er, -gi•est.** *Slang.* Being in a dirty, run-down, or inferior condition.

grun•ion (grŭn'yən) *n.* A small fish, *Leuresthes tenuis,* of Calif. coastal waters that spawns inshore at approx. full moon.

grunt (grŭnt) *n.* A low, guttural sound, as of a pig. —**grunt** *v.*

gryph•on (grĭf'ən) *n. var. of* GRIFFIN.

G-suit (jē'sōōt') *n.* A flight garment designed to counteract the effects of high acceleration by exerting pressure on parts of the body below the chest.

gua•ca•mo•le (gwä'kə-mō'lē) *n.* A thick paste of mashed and seasoned avocado, served as a dip.

gua•nine (gwä'nēn') *n.* A purine that is a constituent of both ribonucleic and deoxyribonucleic acids.

gua•no (gwä'nō) *n.* A substance that consists mainly of the excrement of sea birds and is used as a fertilizer.

gua•ra•ni (gwä'rə-nē') *n., pl.* **-ni** *or* **-nis.** —See table at CURRENCY.

guar•an•tee (găr'ən-tē') *n.* **1.** A promise or assurance, esp. as to the durability or quality of a product. **2.** GUARANTY 1. **3.** A guarantor. **4.** Something held or given as security : pledge. —*v.* **-teed, -tee•ing. 1.** To assume responsibility for the default or debt of. **2.** To undertake to accomplish, continue, or perform. **3.** To furnish security for. **4.** To give a guarantee for.

guar•an•tor (găr'ən-tər, -tôr') *n.* One who gives a guarantee or guaranty.

guar•an•ty (găr'ən-tē) *n., pl.* **-ties. 1.** An undertaking to pay another's debts or fulfill another's obligations in the event of default. **2.** Something that guarantees. **3.** A guarantor.

guard (gärd) *v.* **1.** To shield from danger or harm : protect. **2.** To watch over or keep watch at, esp. to prevent escape, violence, or indiscretion. **3.** To take precautions <*guard* against error> —*n.* **1.** A person or group on sentinel duty. **2.** The duty or act of protecting : watchful care. **3.** A defensive position, as in fencing. **4.** One of the 2 football players on either side of the center. **5.** One of the 2 basketball players stationed near the middle of the court. **6.** An apparatus or device that protects against damage, harm, or loss.

guard•house (gärd'hous') *n.* **1.** A building that serves as headquarters for a military guard. **2.** A military jail.

guard•i•an (gär'dē-ən) *n.* **1.** One that guards, protects, or defends. **2.** One who is legally responsible for the person or property of another. —**guard'i•an•ship'** *n.*

guard•rail (gärd'rāl') *n.* A protective rail, as on a highway.

guard•room (gärd'rōōm', -rŏŏm') *n.* **1.** A room used by guards on duty. **2.** A room for confining military prisoners.

guards•man (gärdz'mən) *n.* **1.** A member of the U.S. National Guard. **2.** *esp. Brit.* A soldier in a household guard regiment.

gua•va (gwä'və) *n.* A tropical American tree, *Psidium guajava,* bearing edible yellow-skinned fruit.

gu•ber•na•to•ri•al (gōō'bər-nə-tôr'ē-əl, -tōr'-, gyōō'-) *adj.* Of a governor.

gue•non (gə-nōn') *n.* Any of various African monkeys of the genus *Cercopithecus,* with long hind legs and a long tail.

guenon

guer•don (gûr'dn) *n.* A reward : requital.

Guern•sey (gûrn'zē) *n., pl.* **-seys.** One of a breed of brown-and-white dairy cattle.

guer•ril•la *or* **gue•ril•la** (gə-rĭl'ə) *n.* A member of an irregular military force that is capable of great speed and mobility.

guess (gĕs) *v.* **1.** To make a judgment (about) on the basis of insufficient evidence. **2.** To come to a correct conclusion about, esp. by chance. **3.** To suppose : believe. —**guess** *n.* —**guess'er** *n.*

guess•work (gĕs'wûrk') *n.* An answer or result obtained by guessing.

guest (gĕst) *n.* **1.** The recipient of hospitality at the table or home of another. **2.** A customer at a commercial establishment, as a hotel or restaurant. **3.** A visiting participant in a program or presentation.

guff (gŭf) *n. Slang.* **1.** Nonsense : baloney. **2.** Back talk.

guf•faw (gə-fô') *n.* A loud or coarse burst of laughter. —**guf•faw'** *v.*

guid•ance (gīd'ns) *n.* **1.** An act or instance of guiding. **2.** Counseling, as on emotional difficulties : advice.

guide (gīd) *n.* **1.** One who directs or leads another, as in a course of action. **2.** Someone employed to indicate and explain points of interest, as in a foreign city. **3.** Something, as a sign or mark, that serves to indicate or direct. **4.** A device on a machine that acts as an indicator or regulator. —*v.* **guid•ed, guid•ing. 1.** To show the way to : conduct. **2.** To manage the course of : direct. ★ ***syns:*** CONDUCT, DIRECT, ESCORT, LEAD, PILOT, SHEPHERD, SHOW, STEER, USHER —**guid'a•ble** *adj.* —**guid'er** *n.*

guide•book (gīd'bo͝ok') *n.* A handbook of information, esp. for travelers.

guided missile *n.* A missile whose course can be controlled while in flight.

guide•line (gīd'līn') *n.* A statement or outline of procedure or policy.

guide•post (gīd'pōst') *n.* A signpost.

guide•word (gīd'wûrd') *n.* A word or term at the top of a page of a reference book, as a dictionary, indicating the first or last entry on the page.

gui•don (gī'dŏn', gīd'n) *n.* A standard, as a small flag, carried by a military unit.

guild (gĭld) *n.* An association of persons of the same occupation or trade, esp. a medieval society of artisans or merchants.

guil•der (gĭl'dər) *n.* —See table at CURRENCY.

guile (gīl) *n.* Crafty cunning : deceitfulness. —**guile'ful** *adj.* —**guile'ful•ly** *adv.* —**guile'ful•ness** *n.* —**guile'less** *adj.* —**guile'less•ly** *adv.* —**guile'less•ness** *n.*

guil•lo•tine (gĭl'ə-tēn', gē'ə-) *n.* A machine for beheading condemned prisoners. —**guil'lo•tine'** *v.*

guilt (gĭlt) *n.* **1.** The fact of being responsible for wrongdoing or a crime. **2.** A feeling of responsibility for having done something wrong. —**guilt'less** *adj.* —**guilt'less•ly** *adv.* —**guilt'less•ness** *n.*

guilt•y (gĭl'tē) *adj.* **-i•er, -i•est. 1.** Responsible for or chargeable with a reprehensible act. **2.** Burdened with, prompted by, or showing a feeling of guilt. —**guilt'i•ly** *adv.* —**guilt'i•ness** *n.*

guin•ea (gĭn'ē) *n.* **1.** A former British gold coin worth 1 pound and 5 pence. **2.** The sum of 1 pound and 5 pence.

guinea fowl *n.* A widely domesticated pheasantlike bird, *Numida meleagris*, having blackish plumage spotted with white.

guinea hen *n.* **1.** A female guinea fowl. **2.** A guinea fowl.

guinea pig *n.* Any of various almost tailless rodents of the genus *Cavia* that are often used for biological experimentation.

guise (gīz) *n.* **1.** Outward and esp. false appearance : semblance. **2.** A mode or form of dress : garb.

gui•tar (gĭ-tär') *n.* A musical instrument usu. with 6 strings that is played by strumming or plucking. —**gui•tar'ist** *n.*

gulch (gŭlch) *n.* A gully : ravine.

gul•den (go͞ol'dən, go͞ol'-) *n., pl.* **-dens** *or* **-den.** A guilder.

gulf (gŭlf) *n.* **1.** A large area of an ocean or sea partially enclosed by land. **2.** A chasm : abyss. **3.** A separation : gap.

gulf•weed (gŭlf'wēd') *n.* Any of several brownish seaweeds of the genus *Sargassum* of tropical Atlantic waters that have rounded air bladders and often form dense floating masses.

gull[1] (gŭl) *n.* Any of various usu. gray and white aquatic birds of the subfamily Larinae with long wings and webbed feet.

gull[2] (gŭl) *n.* A gullible person : dupe. —*v.* To dupe : cheat.

gul•let (gŭl'ĭt) *n.* **1.** The esophagus. **2.** The throat.

gul•li•ble (gŭl'ə-bəl) *adj.* Easily cheated, deceived, or duped. —**gul'li•bil'i•ty** *n.* —**gul'li•bly** *adv.*

gul•ly (gŭl'ē) *n., pl.* **-lies.** A channel or ditch cut in the earth by running water, esp. after a downpour.

gulp (gŭlp) *v.* **1.** To swallow rapidly or greedily. **2.** To gasp or choke, as in nervousness. **3.** To stifle by or as if by swallowing. —*n.* **1.** An act of gulping. **2.** A large mouthful <a *gulp* of hot tea>

gum[1] (gŭm) *n.* **1.** Any of various viscous plant substances that dry into water-soluble, noncrystalline, brittle solids. **2.** A tree that yields gum. **3.** Chewing gum. —*v.* **gummed, gum•ming.** To cover, smear, seal, clog, or fix in place with or as if with gum. —**gum'my** *adj.*

gum[2] (gŭm) *n.* The firm connective tissue surrounding the bases of the teeth.

gum arabic *n.* A gum exuded by various African trees and used esp. in the preparation of pills, emulsions, mucilage, and candies.

gum•bo (gŭm'bō) *n., pl.* **-bos.** A stew or soup containing okra.

gum•boil (gŭm'boil') *n.* A boil or abscess on the gum.

gum•drop (gŭm'drŏp') *n.* A firm jellylike sugar-coated candy made with gum arabic or gelatin.

gump•tion (gŭmp'shən) *n. Informal.* Initiative : enterprise.

gum•shoe (gŭm'sho͞o') *n. Slang.* A detective. —**gum'shoe'** *v.*

gun (gŭn) *n.* **1.** A weapon made of a metal tube that fires a projectile at high velocity. **2.** A cannon. **3.** A portable firearm. **4. a.** A device that sprays forcibly. **b.** A device that shoots a projectile <a dart *gun*> **5.** A discharge of a gun. **6.** A throttle. —*v.* **gunned, gun•ning. 1.** To shoot. **2.** To open the throttle of in order to accelerate. —**gun for.** To try to catch, ruin, or acquire.

gun•boat (gŭn'bōt') *n.* A small lightly armed vessel.

gun•cot•ton (gŭn'kŏt'n) *n.* Nitrocellulose.

gun•fight (gŭn'fīt') *n.* A battle with guns. —**gun'fight'er** *n.*

gun•fire (gŭn'fīr') *n.* The firing of guns.

gung ho (gŭng'hō') *adj. Slang.* Extremely enthusiastic.

gunk (gŭngk) *n. Informal.* A filthy, slimy, or greasy substance. —**gunk'y** *adj.*

gun·lock (gŭn′lŏk′) *n.* A device for igniting the charge in a firearm.

gun·man (gŭn′mən) *n.* A man, esp. a criminal, who is armed with a gun.

gun·met·al (gŭn′mĕt′l) *n.* **1.** An alloy of copper with 10% tin. **2.** Metal used for guns. **3.** A dark gray.

gun·nel (gŭn′əl) *n. var. of* GUNWALE.

gun·ner (gŭn′ər) *n.* **1.** A soldier, sailor, or airman who aims or fires a gun. **2.** Someone who hunts with a gun.

gun·ner·y (gŭn′ə-rē) *n.* **1.** The science of the construction and operation of guns. **2.** The use of guns.

gunnery sergeant *n.* A noncommissioned U.S. Marine officer ranking above a staff sergeant and below a master sergeant.

gun·ny (gŭn′ē) *n.* A coarse fabric made of jute or hemp used esp. for making sacks.

gunny sack *n.* A sack made of gunny.

gun·pow·der (gŭn′pou′dər) *n.* An explosive powder used in blasting and in guns.

gun·shot (gŭn′shŏt′) *n.* **1.** Shot or a shot fired from a gun. **2.** The range of a gun.

gun-shy (gŭn′shī′) *adj.* **1.** Afraid of loud noises, as gunfire. **2.** Very wary : distrustful.

gun·sling·er (gŭn′slĭng′ər) *n.* A gunman.

gun·smith (gŭn′smĭth′) *n.* Someone who makes or repairs firearms.

gun·wale *also* **gun·nel** (gŭn′əl) *n.* The upper edge of a ship's side.

gup·py (gŭp′ē) *n., pl.* **-pies.** A small tropical freshwater fish, *Poecilia reticulata* or *Lebistes reticulatus*, popular in home aquariums.

gur·gle (gûr′gəl) *v.* **-gled, -gling. 1.** To flow in a broken, uneven current making low sounds. **2.** To make a sound resembling that of gurgling water. **—gur′gle** *n.* **—gur′gling·ly** *adv.*

Gur·kha (go͝or′kə) *n.* A soldier from Nepal serving in the British or Indian armies.

gur·ney (gûr′nē) *n., pl.* **-neys.** A metal stretcher with wheeled legs, used for transporting patients.

gu·ru (go͞o′ro͞o′, go͞o-ro͞o′) *n.* **1.** A spiritual teacher in Hinduism. **2.** A mentor.

gush (gŭsh) *v.* **1.** To flow forth plentifully or violently : spout. **2.** To be overly sentimental or enthusiastic. **—gush** *n.* **—gush′y** *adj.*

gush·er (gŭsh′ər) *n.* **1.** One that gushes. **2.** An oil well with a plentiful natural flow.

gus·set (gŭs′ĭt) *n.* A triangular insert, as in a sleeve, for strengthening or enlarging.

gus·sy (gŭs′ē) *v.* **-sied, -sy·ing.** To dress up : decorate.

gust (gŭst) *n.* **1.** A violent, abrupt rush of wind. **2.** A sudden outburst, as of emotion. —*v.* To blow in gusts. **—gust′i·ly** *adv.* **—gust′i·ness** *n.* **—gust′y** *adj.*

gus·ta·to·ry (gŭs′tə-tôr′ē, -tōr′ē) *adj.* Of, pertaining to, or associated with the sense of taste.

gus·to (gŭs′tō) *n.* Hearty enjoyment : zest.

gut (gŭt) *n.* **1. a.** The alimentary canal. **b.** One of its parts, as the intestines. **2. guts.** The bowels : entrails. **3. guts.** The essential inner parts of something. **4. guts.** *Informal.* Fortitude : courage. —*v.* **gut·ted, gut·ting. 1.** To disembowel : eviscerate. **2.** To destroy the interior of.

gut·less (gŭt′lĭs) *adj. Informal.* Lacking courage : cowardly. **—gut′less·ness** *n.*

guts·y (gŭt′sē) *adj.* **-i·er, -i·est.** *Informal.* Courageous.

gut·ter (gŭt′ər) *n.* A channel for draining off water. —*v.* **1.** To melt away rapidly. —Used of a candle. **2.** To flicker.

gut·ter·snipe (gŭt′ər-snīp′) *n.* **1.** A street urchin. **2.** One who is of the lowest class.

gut·tur·al (gŭt′ər-əl) *adj.* Of, relating to, produced in, or sounded in the throat. **—gut′tur·al** *n.* **—gut′tur·al·ly** *adv.*

guy[1] (gī) *n.* A rope, cord, or cable fastened to something to steady, guide, or hold it. —*v.* To steady, guide, or hold with a guy.

guy[2] (gī) *n. Informal.* **1.** A man : fellow. **2. guys.** Persons of either sex. —*v.* To make fun of : mock.

guz·zle (gŭz′əl) *v.* **-zled, -zling.** To drink greedily, excessively, and esp. habitually. **—guz′zler** *n.*

gym (jĭm) *n. Informal.* A gymnasium.

gym·na·si·um (jĭm-nā′zē-əm) *n., pl.* **-ums** *or* **-si·a** (-zē-ə, -zhə). **1.** A room or building equipped for indoor sports, as gymnastics. **2.** (gĭm-nä′zē-o͝om′). A high school in various C European countries that prepares students to enter the university.

gym·nas·tics (jĭm-năs′tĭks) *n. (sing. or pl. in number).* Body-building exercises, esp. those performed with special apparatus in a gymnasium. **—gym′nast′** *n.* **—gym·nas′tic** *adj.*

gym·no·sperm (jĭm′nə-spûrm′) *n.* A plant of the class Gymnospermae, including the coniferous trees and other plants bearing seeds not enclosed within an ovary.

gy·ne·col·o·gy (gī′nĭ-kŏl′ə-jē, jĭn′ĭ-) *n.* The branch of medicine dealing with the diseases, reproductive physiology, and endocrinology of women. **—gy′ne·co·log′i·cal** (-kə-lŏj′ĭ-kəl), **gy′ne·co·log′ic** *adj.* **—gy′ne·col′o·gist** *n.*

gyp (jĭp) *Informal.* —*v.* **gypped, gyp·ping.** To cheat, swindle, or defraud. —*n.* **1.** A swindle. **2.** A swindler. **—gyp′per** *n.*

gyp·sum (jĭp′səm) *n.* A white mineral that is used to make plaster of Paris, gypsum plaster, and plasterboard.

Gyp·sy *also* **Gip·sy** (jĭp′sē) *n., pl.* **-sies. 1.** One of a nomadic people orig. from N India and now living mainly in Europe and the U.S. **2. gypsy.** One inclined to a nomadic way of life.

gypsy moth *n.* A moth, *Pothetria dispar,* whose hairy caterpillars are very destructive to trees.

gy·rate (jī′rāt′) *v.* **-rat·ed, -rat·ing. 1.** To revolve around a center or axis. **2.** To move in a circular or spiral path. **—gy·ra′tion** *n.* **—gy′ra′tor** *n.* **—gy′ra·to′ry** (-rə-tôr′ē, -tōr′ē) *adj.*

gyr•fal•con (jûr′făl′kən, -fôl′-, -fô′kən) *n.* A falcon, *Falco rusticolus,* of N regions, with color phases ranging from black to white.
gy•ro (jī′rō) *n., pl.* **-ros. 1.** A gyroscope. **2.** A gyrocompass.
gy•ro•com•pass (jī′rō-kŭm′pəs, -kŏm′-) *n.* A navigational instrument in which a gyroscope maintains a pointer's N–S orientation.
gy•ro•scope (jī′rə-skōp′) *n.* A spinning disk or wheel whose spin axis maintains its angular orientation when not subjected to external torques. **—gy′ro•scop′ic** (-skŏp′ĭk) *adj.*

Hh

h *or* **H** (āch) *n., pl.* **h's** *or* **H's. 1.** The 8th letter of the English alphabet. **2.** A speech sound represented by the letter *h.* **3.** Something with the shape of the letter H.
H *symbol for* HYDROGEN.
Ha•bak•kuk (hăb′ə-kŭk′, hə-băk′ək) *n.* —See table at BIBLE.
ha•be•as cor•pus (hā′bē-əs kôr′pəs) *n. Law.* A writ issued to bring a person before a judge or court in order to release that person from unlawful detention or restraint.
hab•er•dash•er (hăb′ər-dăsh′ər) *n.* One who deals in men's furnishings, as shirts and socks.
hab•er•dash•er•y (hăb′ər-dăsh′ə-rē) *n., pl.* **-ies. 1.** Goods sold by a haberdasher. **2.** The shop of a haberdasher.
ha•bil•i•ment (hə-bĭl′ə-mənt) *n.* **1.** *often* **habiliments.** Attire, esp. that characteristic of an office, rank, or occasion. **2. habiliments.** Equipment : trappings.
hab•it (hăb′ĭt) *n.* **1.** An often involuntary pattern of behavior acquired by frequent repetition. **2.** Usual practice or manner. **3.** An addiction. **4.** Distinctive dress or costume <a monk's *habit*><a riding *habit*> ★ ***syns:*** CHARACTERISTIC, PATTERN, TRAIT
hab•it•a•ble (hăb′ĭ-tə-bəl) *adj.* Fit for use as a dwelling place. **—hab′it•a•bil′i•ty, hab′it•a•ble•ness** *n.* **—hab′it•a•bly** *adv.*
hab•i•tat (hăb′ĭ-tăt′) *n.* **1.** The environment in which an animal or plant lives. **2.** The place where one can usually be found.
hab•i•ta•tion (hăb′ĭ-tā′shən) *n.* **1.** The act of inhabiting or state of being inhabited. **2. a.** Natural surroundings. **b.** A place to live in.
hab•it-form•ing (hăb′ĭt-fôr′mĭng) *adj.* **1.** Tending to cause physiological addiction. **2.** Tending to become habitual.
ha•bit•u•al (hə-bĭch′o͞o-əl) *adj.* **1.** Practiced by or acting according to habit. **2.** Persisting in an ingrained habit : inveterate. **3.** Usual : customary. **—ha•bit′u•al•ly** *adv.* **—ha•bit′u•al•ness** *n.*
ha•bit•u•ate (hə-bĭch′o͞o-āt′) *v.* **-at•ed, -at•ing.** To accustom by frequent exposure or repetition. **—ha•bit′u•a′tion** *n.*
hab•i•tude (hăb′ĭ-to͞od′, -tyo͞od′) *n.* A person's habitual manner or behavior.
ha•bit•u•é (hə-bĭch′o͞o-ā′, hə-bĭch′o͞o-ā′) *n.* One who frequents a particular place.
ha•ci•en•da (hä′sē-ĕn′də, ä′sē-) *n.* **1.** A large estate, plantation, or ranch in Spanish-speaking countries. **2.** The main house of a hacienda.
hack[1] (hăk) *v.* **1.** To cut or chop with irregular, heavy blows. **2.** To cough harshly. **3.** *Informal.* To manage successfully. **4.** To use a computer expertly or enthusiastically. *—n.* **1.** A blow or notch made by hacking. **2.** A tool, as a hoe, used for hacking. **3.** A rough, dry cough. **—hack′er** *n.*
hack[2] (hăk) *n.* **1.** HACKNEY 1. **2.** A decrepit or overworked horse. **3.** A vehicle, as a coach or carriage, for hire. **4.** One hired to do routine work, esp. writing by formula. **5. a.** A taxicab. **b.** A taxicab driver. *—v.* **1.** To drive a taxicab. **2.** To do routine writing for hire. *—adj.* **1.** By or for a hack. **2.** Hackneyed.
hack•er (hăk′ər) *n.* **1. a.** A computer buff. **b.** One who illegally gains access to another's electronic system. **2.** An enthusiastic amateur at a sport.
hack•ie (hăk′ē) *n. Slang.* A taxi driver.
hack•le (hăk′əl) *n.* **1.** One of the long, slender, often glossy feathers on the neck of a bird, esp. of a rooster. **2. hackles. a.** The hairs at the back of the neck, esp. of a dog, that can rise and bristle with anger or fear. **b.** Temper : dander.
hack•ney (hăk′nē) *n., pl.* **-neys. 1.** A horse for ordinary driving or riding. **2.** A carriage or coach available for hire. *—v.* To overuse to the point of triteness.
hack•neyed (hăk′nēd) *adj.* Grown stale through overuse : banal.
hack•saw (hăk′sô′) *n.* A fine- toothed saw in a frame, used for cutting metal.
had (hăd) *v. p.t. & p.p. of* HAVE.
had•dock (hăd′ək) *n., pl.* **-dock** *or* **-docks.** A food fish, *Melanogrammus aeglefinus,* of N Atlantic waters.
Ha•des (hā′dēz) *n.* **1.** *Gk. Myth.* The abode of the dead. **2.** *often* **hades.** Hell.
hadj (hăj) *n. var. of* HAJ.
had•n't (hăd′nt). Had not.
haf•ni•um (hăf′nē-əm) *n. Symbol* **Hf** A silvery metallic element used esp. in nuclear reactor control rods.
haft (hăft) *n.* A hilt or handle, as of a weapon or tool.
hag (hăg) *n.* **1.** A repulsively ugly old woman. **2.** A witch. **—hag′gish** *adj.*
Hag•ga•dah (hə-gä′də, -gô′-) *n., pl.* **-doth** (-dōt′, -dôth′). Traditional Jewish literature, esp. the nonlegal part of the Talmud.

Hag•ga•i (hăg'ē-ī', hăg'ī') *n.* —See table at BIBLE.

hag•gard (hăg'ərd) *adj.* Worn- out and exhausted : gaunt. ★ *syns:* CAREWORN, GAUNT, WAN, WORN —**hag'gard•ly** *adv.* —**hag'gard•ness** *n.*

hag•gle (hăg'əl) *v.* **-gled, -gling.** To argue in an attempt to bargain or come to terms. —**hag'gle** *n.* —**hag'gler** *n.*

hag•i•og•ra•phy (hăg'ē-ŏg'rə-fē, hā'jē-) *n., pl.* **-phies. 1.** Biography of saints or revered persons. **2.** An idealizing biography. —**hag'i•og'ra•pher** *n.* —**hag'i•o•graph'ic** (-ə-grăf'ĭk), **hag'i•o•graph'i•cal** *adj.*

Hai•da (hī'də) *n., pl.* **-da** *or* **-das. 1.** A member of an American Indian people inhabiting the coastal islands of W British Columbia and S Alaska. **2.** Their language.

hai•ku (hī'ko͞o) *n., pl.* **-ku.** An unrhymed Japanese lyric poem having a fixed 3-line 17-syllable form.

hail[1] (hāl) *n.* **1. a.** Precipitation of small, hard pellets of ice and snow. **b.** A hailstone. **2.** Something giving the effect of hail. —*v.* **1.** To fall as hail. **2.** To pour down like hail.

hail[2] (hāl) *v.* **1. a.** To call to in greeting or welcome. **b.** To acclaim with enthusiasm. **2.** To signal in order to catch the attention of <*hail* a taxi> —**hail from.** To come or originate from. —*n.* **1.** A greeting or expression of approval or acclaim. **2.** Earshot. —*interj.* —Used to express a greeting or commendation. —**hail'er** *n.*

hail•stone (hāl'stōn') *n.* A hard pellet of snow and ice that forms hail.

hail•storm (hāl'stôrm') *n.* A storm in which there is precipitation of hail.

hair (hâr) *n.* **1. a.** One of the fine, threadlike strands that grow from the skin of mammals or on a plant or insect. **b.** A covering of such strands, as on an animal or the human head. **2.** A very small distance or slender margin. —**haired** *adj.* —**hair'less** *adj.*

hair•breadth (hâr'brĕdth') *adj.* Extremely close or narrow <a *hairbreadth* getaway> —*n. var. of* HAIRSBREADTH.

hair•brush (hâr'brŭsh') *n.* A brush for the hair.

hair•cloth (hâr'klôth', -klŏth') *n.* A wiry fabric made esp. from horsehair.

hair•cut (hâr'kŭt') *n.* **1.** A shortening, trimming, or shaping of the hair by cutting. **2.** The style in which hair is cut.

hair•do (hâr'do͞o') *n., pl.* **-dos.** A coiffure.

hair•dress•er (hâr'drĕs'ər) *n.* One who cuts or styles hair. —**hair'dress'ing** *n.*

hair•line (hâr'līn') *n.* **1.** The outline of hair growing on the head, esp. at the forehead. **2.** A very slender line.

hair piece *also* **hair•piece** (hâr'pēs') *n.* A covering or bunch of human or artificial hair used to conceal baldness or shape or supplement a hairdo.

hair•pin (hâr'pĭn') *n.* A slender, U-shaped pin for holding the hair in place. —*adj.* Doubled back in a U <a *hairpin* curve>

hair-rais•ing (hâr'rā'zĭng) *adj.* Very exciting or horrifying. —**hair'-rais'er** *n.*

hairs•breadth (hârz'brĕdth') *also* **hair•breadth** (hâr'brĕdth') *n.* A small space, extent, or margin.

hair•split•ting (hâr'splĭt'ĭng) *n.* The act or process of making petty distinctions. —**hair'split'ter** *n.*

hair•spring (hâr'sprĭng') *n.* A fine coiled spring alternately wound and unwound by the balance wheel of a timepiece.

hair•style (hâr'stīl') *n.* A way of wearing the hair : hairdo. —**hair'styl'ing** *n.* —**hair'styl'ist** *n.*

hair trigger *n.* A gun trigger set to react to the slightest pressure.

hair-trig•ger (hâr'trĭg'ər) *adj.* Reacting immediately to the smallest provocation.

hair•y (hâr'ē) *adj.* **-i•er, -i•est. 1.** Covered with or as if with hair. **2.** Of or suggestive of hair. **3.** *Slang.* Causing anxiety, as from difficulty or danger. —**hair'i•ness** *n.*

haj *or* **hajj** *also* **hadj** (hăj) *n.* A pilgrimage to Mecca made during Ramadan.

hake (hāk) *n., pl.* **hake** *or* **hakes.** A marine food fish of the genera *Merluccius* and *Urophycis,* resembling the cod.

ha•la•la (hə-lä'lə) *n., pl.* **halala** *or* **-las.** —See table at CURRENCY.

hal•berd (hăl'bərd) *n.* A medieval weapon consisting of both an axlike blade and a steel spike on the end of a long pole.

hal•cy•on (hăl'sē-ən) *adj.* **1.** Calm and tranquil. **2.** Prosperous.

hale[1] (hāl) *adj.* **hal•er, hal•est.** Not infirm : healthy and robust. —**hale'ness** *n.*

hale[2] (hāl) *v.* **haled, hal•ing.** To force to go <*haled* us into court>

ha•ler (hä'lər, -lĕr') *n., pl.* **-lers** *or* **-le•ru** (-lə-ro͞o'). —See table at CURRENCY.

half (hăf, häf) *n., pl.* **halves** (hăvz, hävz). **1.** Either of 2 equal parts composing a whole. **2.** A part of something approx. equivalent to what remains. **3.** Either of the 2 playing periods that make up a game, as in football. —*adj.* **1.** Being one of 2 equal parts. **2.** Being nearly a half. **3.** Being partial or incomplete <a *half* smile> —**half** *adv.*

half•back (hăf'băk', häf'-) *n.* **1.** *Football.* Either of the 2 players who, along with the fullback and quarterback, make up the offensive backfield. **2.** A player positioned behind the front line in various sports.

half-baked (hăf'bākt', häf'-) *adj.* **1.** Not fully baked. **2.** *Informal.* **a.** Not sufficiently thought out. **b.** Lacking common sense.

half boot *n.* A low boot whose top comes to just above the ankle.

half-breed (hăf'brēd', häf'-) *n.* A person of mixed racial descent. —**half'-breed'** *adj.*

half brother *n.* A brother related through only one parent.

half-caste (hăf'kăst', häf'-) *n.* A person of mixed racial descent : half-breed. —**half'-caste'** *adj.*

half•cocked (hăf'kŏkt', häf'-) *adj. Informal.* Not well thought out : ill-conceived. —**half'-cocked'** *adv.*

half•heart•ed (hăf'här'tĭd, häf'-) *adj.* Lacking interest, spirit, or enthusiasm. —**half′heart′ed·ly** *adv.* —**half′heart′ed·ness** *n.*

half-life (hăf′līf′, häf′-) *n. Physics.* The time required for half of something to undergo a specific process, esp. for half the nuclei in a sample of radioactive material to undergo decay.

half-mast (hăf′măst′, häf′-) *n.* The position approx. halfway up a pole at which a flag is flown to symbolize mourning or to signal distress. —**half′-mast′** *v.*

half-moon (hăf′mo͞on′, häf′-) *n.* **1.** The moon with just half its disk visibly lighted. **2.** Something crescent-shaped. —**half′moon′** *adj.*

half·pen·ny (hā′pə-nē, hāp′nē) *n., pl.* **half·pence** (hā′pəns) *or* **half·pen·nies.** A British coin worth one half of a penny.

half sister *n.* A sister related through only one parent.

half sole *n.* A shoe or boot sole extending from the arch to the toe.

half step *n. Mus.* A semitone.

half-track (hăf′trăk′, häf′-) *n.* A lightly armored military vehicle propelled by continuous rear treads.

half-truth (hăf′tro͞oth′, häf′-) *n.* A statement usu. meant to deceive by mixing truth and falsehood.

half·way (hăf′wā′, häf′-) *adj.* **1.** In the middle between 2 points or states. **2.** Partial. —**half′way′** *adv.*

halfway house *n.* **1.** A stopping place, as an inn, at the midpoint of a journey. **2.** A rehabilitation center where people who have left an institution are helped to readjust to the outside world.

half-wit (hăf′wĭt′, häf′-) *n.* **1.** A mentally deficient person. **2.** A stupid or silly person. —**half′-wit′ted** *adj.* —**half′-wit′ted·ly** *adv.* —**half′-wit′ted·ness** *n.*

hal·i·but (hăl′ə-bət, hŏl′-) *n., pl.* **-but** *or* **-buts.** Any of several large, edible flatfishes of the genus *Hippoglossus* and related genera, of N Atlantic or Pacific waters.

hal·ite (hăl′īt′, hā′līt′) *n.* Salt in large crystals or masses **:** rock salt.

hal·i·to·sis (hăl′ĭ-tō′sĭs) *n.* A condition marked by bad-smelling breath.

hall (hôl) *n.* **1. a.** A corridor **:** passageway. **b.** A large vestibule or lobby. **2. a.** A large public building used esp. for meetings and entertainment. **b.** A large room for such events. **3.** A school, college, or university building. **4. a.** The main residence on a large estate. **b.** The main dwelling of a medieval king or nobleman.

hal·le·lu·jah (hăl′ə-lo͞o′yə) *interj.* —Used to express praise, joy, or thanksgiving. —*n.* The exclamation of "hallelujah."

hall·mark (hôl′märk′) *n.* **1.** A mark stamped on an article, esp. of gold or silver, to indicate purity, quality, or origin. **2.** An indication of quality or superiority. **3.** A distinctive characteristic.

hal·low (hăl′ō) *v.* **1.** To sanctify **:** consecrate. **2.** To honor **:** revere.

Hal·low·een *also* **Hal·low·e′en** (hăl′ō-ēn′, hŏl′-) *n.* Oct. 31, the eve of All Saints' Day, celebrated esp. by children.

hal·lu·ci·na·tion (hə-lo͞o′sə-nā′shən) *n.* **1. a.** An illusion of perceiving something that is nonexistent. **b.** Something, as an image or vision, perceived in a hallucination. **2.** A delusion. —**hal·lu′ci·nate′** *v.* —**hal·lu′ci·na′tion·al** *adj.* —**hal·lu′ci·na′tive** *adj.* —**hal·lu′ci·na·to′ry** *adj.*

hal·lu·ci·no·gen (hə-lo͞o′sə-nə-jən) *n.* An agent or substance, esp. a drug, that causes hallucination. —**hal·lu′ci·no·gen′ic** *adj.*

hall·way (hôl′wā′) *n.* HALL 1.

ha·lo (hā′lō) *n., pl.* **-los** *or* **-loes. 1.** A circular band of colored light around a shining body, as the sun or moon. **2.** A circle of light around the head, as in a depiction of a saint. **3.** An aura of glory. —**ha′lo** *v.*

hal·o·gen (hăl′ə-jən) *n.* One of a set of 5 physically and chemically similar nonmetallic elements including fluorine, chlorine, bromine, iodine, and astatine. —**ha·log′e·nous** (hə-lŏj′ə-nəs) *adj.*

halt[1] (hôlt) *n.* **1.** An esp. temporary suspension of movement or progress. **2.** A stop. —*v.* To come or bring to a halt.

halt[2] (hôlt) *v.* **1.** To hesitate. **2.** To walk with a limp. —*adj. Archaic.* Lame.

hal·ter (hôl′tər) *n.* **1.** A rope or leather strap fitted around the neck or head of an animal, as a horse, to hitch or lead it. **2.** A noose for hanging a condemned person. **3.** A woman's bodice tied behind the neck and across the back. —*v.* **1.** To fit (an animal) with a halter. **2.** To control with or as if with a halter **:** restrain.

halt·ing (hôl′tĭng) *adj.* **1.** Lame **:** hobbling. **2.** Defective. **3.** Hesitant.

halve (hăv, häv) *v.* **halved, halv·ing. 1.** To divide into 2 equal portions. **2.** To decrease by half. **3.** *Informal.* To apportion or share equally.

halves (hăvz, hävz) *n. pl. of* HALF.

hal·yard (hăl′yərd) *n.* A rope for hoisting or lowering a sail, flag, or yard.

ham (hăm) *n.* **1.** A cut of meat from the thigh of a hog. **2.** The back of the knee or thigh. **3.** *Slang.* A performer who acts with unnecessary exaggeration. **4.** *Informal.* An amateur radio operator. —*v.* **hammed, ham·ming.** To overact or exaggerate.

ham·burg·er (hăm′bûr′gər) *also* **ham·burg** (-bûrg′) *n.* **1. a.** Ground beef. **b.** A cooked patty of ground beef. **2.** A roll or bun containing a hamburger.

ham·let (hăm′lĭt) *n.* A small, usu. rural village or town.

ham·mer (hăm′ər) *n.* **1.** A hand tool with a heavy head, used to strike or pound forcibly. **2.** A tool or device like a hammer in function or shape, esp.: **a.** The part of a gun that strikes the firing pin or percussion cap, causing it to go off. **b.** Any of the padded wooden pieces that strike the strings of a piano. —*v.* **1.** To strike or pound forcibly. **2.** To flatten or shape with or as if with a hammer. **3.** To keep at something continuously

<*hammer* away at the problem> —**ham′·mer·er** *n.*
ham·mer·head (hăm′ər-hĕd′) *n.* **1.** The heavy striking head of a hammer. **2.** A large predatory shark of the genus *Sphyrna,* whose eyes are set in long fleshy projections at the sides of the head.
hammer lock *also* **ham·mer·lock** (hăm′ər-lŏk′) *n.* A wrestling hold in which the opponent's arm is pulled behind the back and twisted upward.
ham·mer·toe (hăm′ər-tō′) *n.* A malformed toe that is bent downward.
ham·mock (hăm′ək) *n.* A hanging bed or couch of strong fabric or heavy netting suspended between 2 supports, as trees.

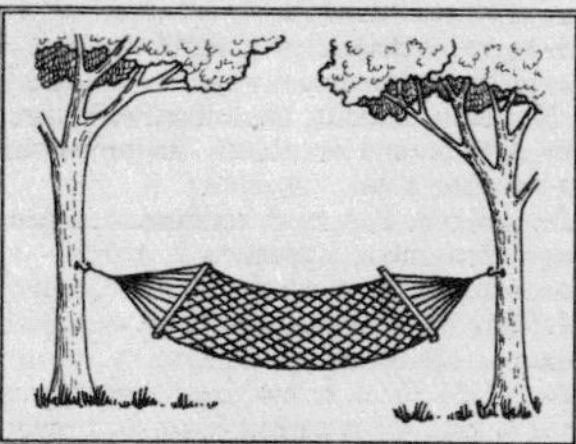

hammock

ham·per¹ (hăm′pər) *v.* To restrict or impede the movement or progress of.
ham·per² (hăm′pər) *n.* A large, usu. covered receptacle.
ham·ster (hăm′stər) *n.* Any of several rodents of the family Cricetidae, esp. *Mesocricetus auratus,* with large cheek pouches and a short tail, often kept as a pet.
ham·string (hăm′strĭng′) *n.* **1.** Either of 2 large tendons at the back of the human knee. **2.** The large tendon at the back of the hind leg of a 4-footed animal. —*v.* **1.** To cripple by severing the hamstring. **2.** To make ineffectual : frustrate.
hand (hănd) *n.* **1.** The part of the arm below the wrist, consisting of the palm, 4 fingers, and an opposable thumb and used esp. for grasping. **2.** A unit of length equal to 4 in., or 10.16 cm, used esp. to indicate the height of a horse. **3.** Something shaped or functioning like the human hand. **4.** A pointer on a circular dial, as of a clock, meter, or gauge. **5.** Lateral direction <at your left *hand*> **6.** A style or sample of handwriting. **7.** A burst of applause. **8.** Assistance : aid. **9. a.** The cards dealt to or held by a player. **b.** A round of play <a *hand* of bridge> **10.** A laborer, worker, or employee. **11.** A member of a group or crew, as of a ship. **12. a.** A participant. **b.** A specialist in a given activity. **13.** Ability : skill. **14.** *often* **hands. a.** Possession : keeping. **b.** Control : dominion. **15.** A source, esp. of information <got the story at first *hand*> **16.** A promise, esp. to marry. —*v.* **1.** To give or convey with or as if with the hand. **2.** To help or direct with the hands. —**hand down. 1.** To pass on, as from parent to offspring. **2.** To deliver (a verdict) officially. —**hand out. 1.** To give out : distribute. **2.** To administer (e.g., punishment). —**hands down. 1.** With ease : effortlessly. **2.** Without any dispute.
hand·bag (hănd′băg′) *n.* A small bag for carrying money and small personal articles : pocketbook.
hand·ball (hănd′bôl′) *n.* **1.** A court game in which the players hit a small rubber ball against a wall with their hands. **2.** The ball used in handball.
hand·bill (hănd′bĭl′) *n.* A hand-distributed printed sheet or leaflet.
hand·book (hănd′bo͝ok′) *n.* A reference book or manual giving information or instruction on a specific subject.
hand·car (hănd′kär′) *n.* A small open railroad car propelled by either a small motor or a hand pump.
hand·clasp (hănd′klăsp′) *n.* A handshake.
hand·craft (hănd′krăft′) *v.* To fashion by hand. —*n. var. of* HANDICRAFT.
hand·cuff (hănd′kŭf′) *n. often* **handcuffs.** A pair of circular metal shackles chained together that can be fastened around the wrists. —*v.* **1.** To shackle with handcuffs. **2.** To make ineffective.
hand·ed (hăn′dĭd) *adj.* **1.** Using or designed for one hand in preference to the other <right-*handed*> **2.** Requiring a certain number of people, as certain card games.
hand·ful (hănd′fo͝ol′) *n., pl.* **-fuls. 1.** The amount or number that can be held in the hand. **2.** A small, undesignated amount or number. **3.** *Informal.* One hard to control or manage easily.
hand·gun (hănd′gŭn′) *n.* A gun that can be grasped and fired with one hand : pistol.
hand·i·cap (hăn′dē-kăp′) *n.* **1. a.** A competition in which advantages or penalties are given to individual contestants to equalize the odds. **b.** Such an advantage or penalty. **2.** A physiological or mental disability that increases the difficulty of normal achievement. **3.** An impediment : obstacle. —*v.* **-capped, -cap·ping. 1.** To give a handicap to (e.g., a competitor). **2.** To hinder : impede.
hand·i·capped (hăn′dē-kăpt′) *adj.* Physically or mentally disabled.
hand·i·craft (hăn′dē-krăft′) *also* **hand·craft** (hănd′krăft′) *n.* **1.** Skill with the hands. **2. a.** A trade, craft, or occupation requiring manual skillfulness. **b.** Skilled work produced by hand.
hand·i·work (hăn′dē-wûrk′) *n.* **1.** Work accomplished by hand. **2.** Work performed by a single individual. **3.** The result of one's actions or efforts.
hand·ker·chief (hăng′kər-chĭf, -chēf′) *n.* **1.** A small piece of usu. square cloth used esp. to wipe the face or blow the nose. **2.** A kerchief or scarf.
han·dle (hăn′dl) *v.* **-dled, -dling. 1.** To touch, pick up, manipulate, or hold with the hands.

2. To administer to or represent : manage <*handle* a prizefighter> **3.** To sell or deal in. ★ *syns:* MANIPULATE, PLY, WIELD —*n.* **1.** A part that is held or controlled with the hand. 2. *Slang.* A person's name or identifying term. —**han'dler** *n.*

han•dle•bar (hăn'dl-bär') *n.* *often* **handlebars.** A curved bar for steering, as on a bicycle, with a handle at either end.

hand•made (hănd'mād') *adj.* Made or prepared by hand or a hand operation.

hand•maid (hănd'mād') *also* **hand•maid•en** (-mād'n) *n.* A woman attendant or servant.

hand-me-down (hănd'mē-doun') *n.* Something, as clothing, used by a person after being outgrown or discarded by another. —**hand'-me-down'** *adj.*

hand•out (hănd'out') *n.* **1.** Food, clothing, or cash given to the needy. **2.** A leaflet or folder distributed free of charge : flyer. **3.** A press release, esp. for publicity.

hand-pick (hănd'pĭk') *v.* To select personally and with care.

hand•rail (hănd'rāl') *n.* A narrow supportive rail gripped with the hand.

hand•set (hănd'sĕt') *n.* A telephone transmitter and receiver combined in a single unit.

hand•shake (hănd'shāk') *n.* The clasping of hands by 2 people, as in greeting, farewell, or agreement.

hands-off (hăndz'ôf', -ŏf') *adj.* Characterized by noninterference.

hand•some (hăn'səm) *adj.* **-som•er, -som•est. 1.** Very attractive and often striking in appearance. **2.** Liberal : generous <a *handsome* salary> —**hand'some•ly** *adv.* —**hand'some•ness** *n.*

hands-on (hăndz'ŏn', -ôn') *adj.* Not theoretical : applied <*hands-on* learning>

hand•spring (hănd'sprĭng') *n.* An acrobatic feat in which the body flips entirely forward or backward, landing first on the hands, then on the feet.

hand•stand (hănd'stănd') *n.* The act of supporting the body on the hands with the feet balanced in the air.

hand-to-hand (hănd'tə-hănd') *adj.* At close quarters, as in fighting.

hand-to-mouth (hănd'tə-mouth') *adj.* Having or providing barely enough for subsistence.

hand•work (hănd'wûrk') *n.* Work accomplished by hand.

hand•writ•ing (hănd'rī'tĭng) *n.* **1.** Writing performed with the hand. **2.** The style of writing of an individual.

hand•y (hăn'dē) *adj.* **-i•er, -i•est. 1.** Manually adept. **2.** Easy to reach : accessible. **3. a.** Easy to use. **b.** Useful. —**hand'i•ly** *adv.* —**hand'i•ness** *n.*

hand•y•man (hăn'dē-măn') *n.* One who does various odd jobs.

hang (hăng) *v.* **hung** (hŭng), **hang•ing. 1.** To attach or be attached from above, unsupported from below. **2.** To suspend or be fastened so as to swing freely on the point of suspension <*hang* a door> **3.** *p.t. & p.p.* **hanged** *or* **hung.** To put to death or die by suspension by the neck. **4.** To remain stationary in space : hover. **5. a.** To furnish or decorate by suspending hangings about <*hung* the mantelpiece with holly> **b.** To fasten or attach to a wall <*hang* a picture> **6. a.** To let droop downward <*hang* one's head> **b.** To fit the body in easy lines. **7.** To cause (a jury) to be deadlocked. —**hang around.** *Informal.* **1.** To linger or loiter aimlessly. **2.** To associate. —**hang in.** *Informal.* To persevere. —**hang on. 1.** To cling firmly to something. **2.** To persist : persevere. **3.** To keep a telephone connection open. —**hang out.** *Slang.* To spend one's time in a particular place. —**hang up. 1.** To hamper : impede. **2.** To complete a telephone conversation by replacing the receiver on its cradle. —*n.* **1.** The manner in which something hangs. **2.** Particular meaning or import. **3.** *Informal.* The proper way of using or doing something.

han•gar (hăng'ər) *n.* A building for sheltering and repairing aircraft.

hang•dog (hăng'dôg', -dŏg') *adj.* **1.** Disgraced or guilty. **2.** Downcast : abject.

hang•er (hăng'ər) *n.* **1.** A person who hangs something. **2.** A frame, hook, or strap on which something can be hung or to which something hangs.

hang•er-on (hăng'ər-ŏn', -ôn') *n., pl.* **hang•ers-on.** A sycophant : parasite.

hang glider *n.* A kite-shaped device from which a rider hangs suspended in a harness while gliding through the air. —**hang gliding** *n.*

hang•ing (hăng'ĭng) *n.* **1.** Execution by suspending by the neck, esp. on a gallows. **2.** *often* **hangings.** Something hung, as curtains or tapestries.

hang•man (hăng'mən) *n.* One employed to execute condemned persons by hanging.

hang•nail (hăng'nāl') *n.* A small bit of dead skin hanging loose at the side or bottom of a fingernail.

hang•out (hăng'out') *n.* A frequently visited place : haunt.

hang•o•ver (hăng'ō'vər) *n.* **1.** Disagreeable aftereffects of excessive alcohol consumption. **2.** One that remains from an earlier time : vestige.

hang-up (hăng'ŭp') *n.* *Informal.* **1.** An emotional or psychological problem or inhibition. **2.** An impediment or obstacle.

hank (hăngk) *n.* A coil or loop, as of hair or yarn.

han•ker (hăng'kər) *v.* To have a craving : yearn. —**han'ker•er** *n.* —**han'ker•ing** *n.*

han•kie *also* **han•ky** (hăng'kē) *n., pl.* **-kies.** *Informal.* A handkerchief.

han•ky-pan•ky (hăng'kē-păng'kē) *n.* *Slang.* **1.** Devious or dubious activity. **2.** Foolish talk or action.

han•som (hăn'səm) *n.* A 2-wheeled horse-drawn carriage with the driver's seat elevated in back.

Ha•nuk•kah *or* **Ha•nu•kah** (KHä'nə-kə, hä'-) *n. vars. of* CHANUKAH.
hao (hou) *n., pl.* **hao.** —See table at CURRENCY.
hao•le (hou'lē, -lā) *n.* A person, esp. a white person, who is not a native Hawaiian.
hap (hăp) *n.* **1.** Luck : chance. **2.** An event : happening.
hap•haz•ard (hăp-hăz'ərd) *adj.* Marked by chance : hit-or-miss. —**hap•haz'ard•ly** *adv.* —**hap•haz'ard•ness** *n.*
hap•less (hăp'lĭs) *adj.* Unlucky : unfortunate. —**hap'less•ly** *adv.* —**hap'less•ness** *n.*
hap•loid (hăp'loid') *adj.* Having the number of chromosomes in the normal germ cell, which is half the number in the normal body cell. —**hap'loid'** *n.*
hap•ly (hăp'lē) *adv.* By chance.
hap•pen (hăp'ən) *v.* **1.** To come to pass : occur. **2.** To occur by chance. **3.** To discover something by chance. **4.** To appear or turn up by chance.
hap•pen•ing (hăp'ə-nĭng) *n.* **1.** An event, esp. an important one. **2.** An often spontaneously staged event or performance.
hap•pen•stance (hăp'ən-stăns') *n.* A chance event.
hap•py (hăp'ē) *adj.* **-pi•er, -pi•est. 1.** Fortunate. **2.** Having, displaying, or marked by pleasure or joy. **3.** Fitting : appropriate. **4.** Pleased and willing. **5.** Unduly enthusiastic or concerned <money-*happy*> —**hap'pi•ly** *adv.* —**hap'pi•ness** *n.*
hap•py-go-luck•y (hăp'ē-gō-lŭk'ē) *adj.* Carefree.
happy hour *n.* The part of the day when a bar offers drinks at lower prices.
ha•ra-ki•ri (hä'rə-kîr'ē, hăr'ə-) *n.* Ritual suicide by disembowelment.
ha•rangue (hə-răng') *n.* **1.** A long, bombastic speech. **2.** A tirade. —**ha•rangue'** *v.* —**ha•rangu'er** *n.*
ha•rass (hə-răs', hăr'əs) *v.* **1.** To annoy or disturb persistently. **2.** To make exhausted. **3.** To wear out (an enemy) by frequent attacks. —**ha•rass'er** *n.* —**ha•rass'ment** *n.*
har•bin•ger (här'bən-jər) *n.* A precursor : herald.
har•bor (här'bər) *n.* **1.** A sheltered anchorage for ships. **2.** A place of shelter : refuge. —*v.* **1.** To provide with shelter. **2.** To entertain (a thought or feeling). —**har'bor•age** *n.* —**har'bor •er** *n.*
hard (härd) *adj.* **1.** Firmly resistant to pressure <a *hard* shell> **2.** Physically or mentally strong : toughened. **3.** Difficult to perform, comprehend, or endure. **4.** Forceful : intense <a *hard* punch in the nose> **5.** Energetic : diligent. **6.** Severe : harsh. **7.** Callous : unsympathetic. **8.** Oppressive : unjust. **9.** Real : factual. **10.** High in alcoholic content. **11.** Containing salts that hinder the lathering of soap <*hard* water> **12.** Backed by bullion : stable <*hard* currency> **13.** Physically addictive and detrimental <Heroin is a *hard* drug.> —**hard up.** *Informal.* Short of cash. —**hard** *adv.* —**hard'ness** *n.*
hard•back (härd'băk') *adj.* Bound between cardboard, cloth, or leather rather than paper covers. —**hard'back'** *n.*
hard•ball (härd'bôl') *n.* **1.** Baseball. **2.** *Informal.* The use of any means, however ruthless, to attain an objective.
hard-bit•ten (härd'bĭt'n) *adj.* Seasoned or toughened by hard experience.
hard-boiled (härd'boild') *adj.* **1.** Cooked solid by boiling in the shell. **2.** *Informal.* Callous : unsympathetic.
hard•bound (härd'bound') *adj.* Hardback.
hard copy *n.* Readable printed copy of the output of a computer.
hard-core *also* **hard•core** (härd'kôr') *adj.* **1.** Obstinately resistant to change : inveterate <a *hard-core* offender> **2.** Regarded as constituting a stubborn social problem <*hard-core* unemployment> **3.** Extremely explicit. —Used of pornography.
hard•cov•er (härd'kŭv'ər) *adj.* Hardback.
hard disk *n.* A rigid magnetic disk fixed permanently within a drive unit and used for storing computer data.
hard•en (här'dn) *v.* **1.** To make or become hard or harder. **2.** To make or become physically or mentally tough. **3.** To make or become callous or unsympathetic. ★ ***syns:*** CAKE, CONCRETE, CONGEAL, DRY, PETRIFY, SET, SOLIDIFY —**hard'en•er** *n.*
hard hat *n.* **1. a.** A rigid head covering worn for protection by construction workers. **b.** *Informal.* A construction worker. **2.** *Informal.* An aggressively patriotic and politically conservative person. —**hard'hat'** *adj.*
hard•head•ed (härd'hĕd'ĭd) *adj.* **1.** Willfully stubborn. **2.** Coldly practical or realistic. —**hard'head'ed•ly** *adv.* —**hard'head'ed•ness** *n.*
hard•heart•ed (härd'här'tĭd) *adj.* Unfeeling : heartless. —**hard'heart'ed•ly** *adv.* —**hard'heart'ed•ness** *n.*
har•di•hood (här'dē-hŏŏd') *n.* **1. a.** Unwavering courage. **b.** Audacious boldness. **2.** Vitality : vigor.
hard landing *n.* A landing by impact of a spacecraft lacking devices, as retrorockets, to slow it down.
hard line *n.* An inflexible position, as on an issue. —**hard'-line', hard'line'** *adj.* —**hard'lin'er** *n.*
hard•ly (härd'lē) *adv.* **1.** By a very little : just. **2.** Almost certainly not.
hard-nosed (härd'nōzd') *adj.* Stubborn : hard-headed.
hard palate *n.* The fairly hard, bony forward part of the palate forming the roof of the mouth.
hard•pan (härd'păn') *n.* A compact layer of hard clay or subsoil.
hard rock *n.* Rock music that features harsh, amplified sound and electronic distortion, modulations, and feedback.
hard sell *n. Informal.* A sales or advertising method involving aggressive, high-pressure promotion.
hard-shell (härd'shĕl') *also* **hard-shelled**

(-shĕld′) *adj.* **1.** Having a thick or hardened shell. **2.** Uncompromising : inflexible.

hard•ship (härd′shĭp′) *n.* **1.** Extreme privation : suffering. **2.** A source of privation or suffering.

hard•tack (härd′tăk′) *n.* A hard biscuit made with flour and water.

hard•top (härd′tŏp′) *n.* A car with a rigid top designed to suggest a convertible.

hard•ware (härd′wâr′) *n.* **1.** Metal ware, as machine parts, tools, and utensils. **2. a.** The mechanical and electronic components of a computer or spacecraft. **b.** The physical apparatus involved in an industrial, technological, or military operation or system.

hard-wired (härd′wīrd′) *adj. Computer Sci.* Of or implemented through permanently connected logic circuitry and therefore not subject to change by programming.

hard•wood (härd′wo͝od′) *n.* **1.** The wood of a broad-leaved flowering tree as distinguished from that of a tree with needles and cones. **2.** The tree itself.

har•dy (här′dē) *adj.* **-di•er, -di•est. 1.** Stalwart and robust. **2.** Able to survive very unfavorable conditions, as cold weather <*hardy* perennial plants> **3.** Courageous : intrepid. **4.** Boldly daring : audacious. **—har′di•ly** *adv.* **—har′di•ness** *n.*

hare (hâr) *n.* Any of various mammals of the family Leporidae, esp. of the genus *Lepus,* related to the rabbits but with longer ears and legs.

hare•brained (hâr′brānd′) *adj.* Silly : foolish <a *harebrained* notion>

hare•lip (hâr′lĭp′) *n.* A congenital condition in which the upper lip is split. **—hare′lipped′** *adj.*

har•em (hâr′əm, hăr′-) *n.* **1.** A house or rooms for the women of a Muslim household. **2.** The women living in a harem.

hark (härk) *v.* To listen closely. **—hark back.** To return to an earlier subject or circumstance.

har•le•quin (här′lə-kwĭn, -kĭn) *n.* A clown : jester. *—adj.* Patterned with vividly colored diamond shapes.

har•lot (här′lət) *n.* A prostitute. **—har′lot•ry** (-lə-trē) *n.*

harm (härm) *n.* **1.** Physical or emotional injury or damage. **2.** Hurt : wickedness. *—v.* To cause harm to : hurt. ★ *syns:* DAMAGE, DETRIMENT, HURT, INJURY **—harm′ful** *adj.* **—harm′ful•ly** *adv.* **—harm′ful•ness** *n.* **—harm′less** *adj.* **—harm′less•ly** *adv.* **—harm′less•ness** *n.*

har•mon•ic (här-mŏn′ĭk) *adj.* **1.** Of or relating to musical harmony or harmonics. **2.** Marked by musical harmony : harmonious. *—n.* **1.** A higher tone in a complex musical tone. **2. harmonics** (*sing. in number).* The study of the physical characteristics of musical sound. **—har•mon′i•cal•ly** *adv.*

har•mon•i•ca (här-mŏn′ĭ-kə) *n.* A small, rectangular musical instrument consisting of a series of tuned metal reeds vibrated by the player's breath.

har•mo•ni•ous (här-mō′nē-əs) *adj.* **1.** Characterized by accord and agreement. **2.** Having components agreeably combined. **3.** Pleasing to the ear : melodious. **—har•mo′ni•ous•ly** *adv.*

har•mo•ni•um (här-mō′nē-əm) *n.* A keyboard wind instrument with free metal reeds actuated by a bellows.

har•mo•ny (här′mə-nē) *n., pl.* **-nies. 1.** Accord or agreement, as of feeling or opinion. **2.** An agreeable combination of component parts. **3.** The combination of musical tones into chords and progressions of chords. ★ *syns:* CONCORD, RAPPORT, UNITY **—har′mo•ni•za′tion** *n.* **—har′mo•nize′** *v.* **—har′mo•niz′er** *n.*

har•ness (här′nĭs) *n.* **1.** The straps and tackle other than a yoke by which a draft animal pulls an implement or vehicle. **2.** Something resembling a harness. *—v.* **1.** To equip (e.g., a draft animal) with a harness. **2.** To control and utilize <*harness* water power> **—har′ness•er** *n.*

harp (härp) *n.* A musical instrument consisting of a triangular upright frame with strings plucked with the fingers. *—v.* To play a harp. **—harp on (***or* **upon).** To write or talk about excessively and tiresomely. **—harp′ist** *n.*

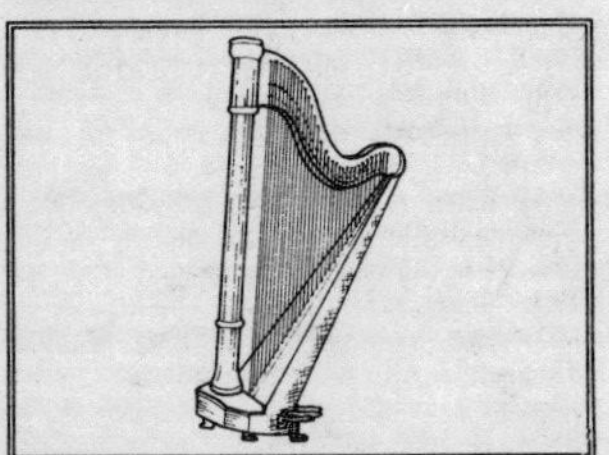

harp

har•poon (här-po͞on′) *n.* A spear with a barbed head used in hunting whales and large fish. **—har•poon′** *v.*

harp•si•chord (härp′sĭ-kôrd′) *n.* A pianolike keyboard instrument whose strings are plucked by means of quills or leather plectrums. **—harp′si•chord′ist** *n.*

har•py (här′pē) *n., pl.* **-pies. 1.** A shrewish or vicious woman. **2.** A predatory person.

har•ri•dan (hăr′ĭ-dn) *n.* A mean, scolding woman : shrew.

har•ri•er[1] (hăr′ē-ər) *n.* **1.** One that harries. **2.** A slender, narrow-winged hawk of the genus *Circus* that preys on small animals.

har•ri•er[2] (hăr′ē-ər) *n.* **1.** One of a breed of small hounds orig. trained to hunt rabbits. **2.** A cross-country runner.

har•row (hăr′ō) *n.* An implement with sharp teeth or upright disks for breaking up and smoothing soil. *—v.* **1.** To pulverize (soil) with a harrow. **2.** To distress greatly.

har•ry (hăr'ē) *v.* **-ried, -ry•ing. 1.** To raid : pillage. **2.** To harass.
harsh (härsh) *adj.* **1.** Disagreeable, esp. to the ear. **2.** Extremely severe. **—harsh'ly** *adv.* **—harsh'ness** *n.*
hart (härt) *n., pl.* **harts** *or* **hart.** A fully grown male deer.
har•um-scar•um (hâr'əm-skâr'ə m, hăr'əm-skăr'əm) *adj.* Irresponsible : reckless. **—har'um-scar'um** *adv.*
har•vest (här'vĭst) *n.* **1.** The act or process of gathering a crop. **2. a.** A ripe crop. **b.** The season for gathering crops. **3.** The result of an action. *—v.* **1.** To reap (a crop). **2.** To acquire as if by gathering. **—har'vest•er** *n.*
has (hăz) *v. 3rd person sing. present tense of* HAVE.
has-been (hăz'bĭn') *n. Informal.* A person who is no longer successful, useful, effective, or popular.
hash[1] (hăsh) *n.* **1.** A usu. fried or baked mixture of chopped meat and potatoes. **2.** A haphazard mixture : hodgepodge. *—v.* **1.** To chop up into small pieces. **2.** *Informal.* To make a mess of. **b.** To discuss carefully : review.
hash[2] (hăsh) *n. Slang.* Hashish.
hash•ish (hăsh'ēsh', -ĭsh) *n.* A dry, resinous extract prepared from the hemp plant and used as a mild narcotic.
Ha•sid *or* **Has•sid** *also* **Chas•sid** (KHä'-sĭd) *n., pl.* **-si•dim** (-sē'dĭm). A member of a Jewish movement of popular mysticism founded in E Europe about 1750. **—Ha•si'dic** *adj.* **—Ha•si'dism** *n.*
has•n't (hăz'ənt). Has not.
hasp (hăsp) *n.* A hinged fastener for a door that is passed over a staple and secured by a pin, bolt, or padlock.
has•sle (hăs'əl) *n. Slang.* **1.** An argument or trivial quarrel. **2.** Bother : nuisance. **—has'sle** *v.*
has•sock (hăs'ək) *n.* A thick, firm cushion used esp. as a footstool.
haste (hāst) *n.* **1.** Swiftness of motion or action. **2.** Excessive eagerness to act. **3.** Rash or precipitate action. **—make haste.** To hurry : hasten.
has•ten (hā'sən) *v.* To move or cause to move rapidly.
hast•y (hā'stē) *adj.* **-i•er, -i•est. 1.** Swift : rapid. **2.** Made or done too quickly and impulsively. **—hast'i•ly** *adv.* **—hast'i•ness** *n.*
hat (hăt) *n.* A covering for the head, esp. one with a crown and brim.
hat•box (hăt'bŏks') *n.* A usu. round box for storing or carrying a hat.
hatch[1] (hăch) *n.* **1.** A small door or opening, as in a ship's deck or the roof or floor of a building. **2.** A hatchway.
hatch[2] (hăch) *v.* **1.** To come or cause to come forth from an egg. **2.** To cause (an egg) to produce young by incubation. **3.** To devise or contrive (e.g., a secret plot). **—hatch** *n.* **—hatch'er•y** *n.*
hatch[3] (hăch) *v.* To give an effect of shading by etching or drawing fine crossed or parallel lines on. **—hatch** *n.*
hatch•back (hăch'băk') *n.* An automobile with a sloping back and an upward-opening rear hatch.
hatch•et (hăch'ĭt) *n.* **1.** A small ax with a short handle. **2.** A tomahawk.
hatchet job *n. Slang.* A usu. malicious verbal attack.
hatchet man *n. Slang.* **1.** One hired to kill. **2.** One hired to carry out a disagreeable task or unscrupulous order.
hatch•ling (hăch'lĭng) *n.* A newly hatched bird, amphibian, fish, or reptile.
hatch•way (hăch'wā') *n.* A hatch leading to a hold, compartment, or cellar.
hate (hāt) *v.* **hat•ed, hat•ing. 1.** To feel animosity or hostility toward : detest. **2.** To have distaste for <*hates* waiting in line> ★ ***syns:*** ABOMINATE, DESPISE, DETEST, EXECRATE, LOATHE *—n.* **1.** Intense hatred. **2.** An object or target of hatred. **—hate'ful** *adj.* **—hate'ful•ly** *adv.* **—hate'ful•ness** *n.* **—hat'er** *n.*
ha•tred (hā'trĭd) *n.* Deep-seated antagonism or enmity : violent ill will.
hat•ter (hăt'ər) *n.* One who makes, sells, or repairs hats.
hau•berk (hô'bərk) *n.* A long coat of mail.
haugh•ty (hô'tē) *adj.* **-ti•er, -ti•est.** Arrogantly proud : lordly. **—haugh'ti•ly** *adv.* **—haugh'ti•ness** *n.*
haul (hôl) *v.* **1.** To pull, drag, or carry. **2.** To cart or truck. *—n.* **1.** The act of hauling. **2.** The distance over which someone travels or something is transported. **3.** Something hauled. **4.** An amount acquired or collected at one time <a *haul* of sardines>
haul•age (hô'lĭj) *n.* **1.** The act or process of hauling. **2.** A charge for hauling.
haunch (hônch, hŏnch) *n.* **1.** The human and animal hip, buttock, and upper thigh. **2.** The loin and leg of a 4-footed animal : hindquarters.
†**haunt** (hônt, hŏnt) *v.* **1.** To appear to or visit in the form of an apparition, as a ghost. **2.** To visit frequently. **3.** To linger in the mind : obsess. *—n.* **1.** A place often visited. **2.** (hănt). *Regional.* A supernatural being, esp. a ghost. **—haunt'ing** *adj.*
haute cou•ture (ōt' ko͞o-to͝or') *n.* **1.** The designers who create exclusive fashions for women. **2.** The high-fashion clothing created by these designers.
haute cui•sine (ōt' kwĭ-zēn') *n.* Artfully prepared, often elaborate cuisine.
have (hăv) *v.* **had, hav•ing, has. 1.** To own as a material possession or as a characteristic, quality, or function. **2.** To maintain a relation to. **3.** To be obliged : must. **4.** To entertain in one's mind. **5. a.** To gain an advantage over. **b.** *Informal.* To deceive or trick. **6.** To engage in sexual relations with. **7.** To store in a given place. **8.** To choose or accept. **9.** To take a portion of. **10.** To contain, consist of, or be made of. **11.** To show or exercise <*have* compassion> **12.** To permit to take place. **13. a.** To cause to be. **b.** To cause to be done. **c.** To persuade or compel. **14.** To undergo the experience of. **15.** To be-

get or bear (offspring). **16.** To possess competence in. **17.** To welcome as a guest. **18.** —Used with a past participle to form the following tenses indicating completed action: **a.** Present perfect < *has* left> **b.** Past perfect <*had* left> **c.** Future perfect <will *have* left> —*n.* One having material wealth. **—have at.** To make an attack on. **—have had it.** To have tolerated all one can. **—have it in for.** To have a grudge against. **—have it out.** To settle something, esp. by dispute. **—have to do with.** To associate, deal, or be concerned with.

ha•ven (hā'vən) *n.* **1.** A harbor or anchorage : port. **2.** A place of refuge : sanctuary.

have-not (hăv'nŏt') *n.* One who is poor or has very limited material wealth.

have•n't (hăv'ənt). Have not.

hav•er•sack (hăv'ər-săk') *n.* A bag for supplies, carried over the shoulder.

hav•oc (hăv'ək) *n.* **1.** Widespread destruction. **2.** Confusion : chaos. **—cry havoc.** To sound an alarm.

haw[1] (hô) *n.* An utterance used by a speaker who is groping for words. —*v.* To hesitate in speaking.

haw[2] (hô) *n.* **1.** A hawthorn tree or shrub. **2.** The fruit of a hawthorn.

Hawaiian guitar *n.* An electric guitar with 6 to 8 steel strings that are plucked while being pressed with a steel bar.

hawk[1] (hôk) *n.* **1.** Any of various predatory birds of the order Falconiformes and esp. of the genera *Accipiter* and *Buteo,* with a short, hooked bill and strong claws for seizing small prey. **2. a.** One who advocates a warlike foreign policy. **b.** One with an aggressive or pugnacious attitude. **—hawk'ish** *adj.* **—hawk'ish•ly** *adv.* **—hawk'ish•ness** *n.*

hawk[2] (hôk) *v.* To peddle (goods) by calling out. **—hawk'er** *n.*

hawk-eyed (hôk'īd') *adj.* Having keen eyesight.

haw•ser (hô'zər) *n.* A heavy rope or cable for towing or mooring a ship.

haw•thorn (hô'thôrn') *n.* A thorny tree or shrub of the genus *Crataegus,* bearing white or pink flowers and red fruit.

hay (hā) *n.* Forage plants, as grass or alfalfa, cut and dried for animal food. —*v.* To prepare herbage for hay.

hay•cock (hā'kŏk') *n. esp. Brit.* A conical mound of hay.

hay fever *n.* An acute, severe irritation of the upper respiratory tract and the eyes, caused by an allergy to certain airborne pollens, esp. of ragweed.

hay•loft (hā'lôft',-lŏft') *n.* A loft in a barn or stable for storing hay.

hay•seed (hā'sēd') *n.* **1.** Grass seed or bits of chaff that fall from hay. **2.** *Slang.* A yokel : hick.

hay•stack (hā'stăk') *n.* A large stack of hay stored outdoors.

hay•wire (hā'wīr') *adj. Informal.* **1.** Not functioning properly : out of order. **2.** Emotionally upset or out of control.

haz•ard (hăz'ərd) *n.* **1.** A chance event : accident. **2.** A chance or source of danger : risk. **3.** An obstacle, as a sand trap or pond, on a golf course. —*v.* To take a chance on : venture. **—haz'ard•ous** *adj.*

haze[1] (hāz) *n.* **1.** A foglike mixture of dust, smoke, and vapor suspended in the air. **2.** A vague or confused state of mind.

†**haze**[2] (hāz) *v.* **hazed, haz•ing. 1.** To harass with silly, disagreeable, or demeaning tasks. **2.** *Regional.* To drive (e.g., cattle) with saddle horses. **—haz'er** *n.*

ha•zel (hā'zəl) *n.* **1.** A shrub or small tree of the genus *Corylus,* bearing edible brown nuts with smooth shells. **2.** A yellowish or light brown. **—ha'zel** *adj.*

ha•zel•nut (hā'zəl-nŭt') *n.* The edible nut of a hazel.

haz•y (hā'zē) *adj.* **-i•er, -i•est. 1.** Marked by haze or mist. **2.** Not clear : vague. **—haz'i•ly** *adv.* **—haz'i•ness** *n.*

H-bomb (āch'bŏm') *n.* A hydrogen bomb.

he (hē) *pron.* **1.** The male that is neither the speaker nor the hearer. **2.** —Used to refer to a person whose sex is not specified <*He* who laughs last, laughs best.>

He *symbol for* HELIUM.

head (hĕd) *n.* **1.** The uppermost or forwardmost bodily extremity, containing the brain, the principal nerve centers, and the eyes, ears, nose, and mouth. **2 a.** Mind, intellect, or intelligence. **b.** Ability or aptitude. **3.** Calmness : self-control. **4.** Complete freedom to act or choose. **5.** *often* **heads** *(sing. in number).* The obverse side of a coin. **6. a.** An individual : person. **b.** *pl.* **head.** One animal, as within a herd. **7.** One in charge of something : leader. **8.** The first or foremost position. **9.** A critical point : crisis. **10.** A projecting or striking part of something, as a weapon. **11. a.** The higher or upper part of something. **b.** The most important end <the *head* of the table> **12.** Either of 2 interchangeable ends, as of a drum. **13.** Pressure, as of a gas or liquid. **14.** A rounded, compact mass of leaves, as of lettuce, or flowers, as of a daisy or clover. **15.** *Computer Sci.* A device that reads data from and writes data to a magnetic disk or tape drive. **16.** *Slang.* One who uses drugs habitually. —*adj.* **1.** Of chief importance. **2.** At the front or top. **3.** Coming from in front <a *head* wind> —*v.* **1.** To be in charge of. **2.** To be in the first or foremost position of. **3.** To aim or turn in a given direction. **4.** To set out or proceed. **—over (one's) head. 1.** Beyond one's power to manage or comprehend. **2.** To one of higher rank <went *over my head* to the boss> **—head'ed** *adj.* **—head'less** *adj.*

head•ache (hĕd'āk') *n.* **1.** An ache in the head. **2.** *Informal.* An annoying or bothersome problem. **—head'ach'y** *adj.*

head•band (hĕd'bănd') *n.* A band worn on or around the head.

head•board (hĕd'bôrd', -bōrd') *n.* A board or frame that stands at the head of a bed.

head cold *n.* Coryza.

head•dress (hĕd′drĕs′) *n.* An ornamental covering for the head.

head•first (hĕd′fûrst′) *adv.* **1.** With the head foremost **:** headlong. **2.** Impetuously **:** recklessly. **—head′first′** *adj.*

head•gear (hĕd′gîr′) *n.* A decorative or protective covering, as a hat or helmet, for the head.

head-hunt•ing (hĕd′hŭn′tĭng) *n.* **1.** The custom of severing and preserving human heads as trophies. **2.** *Slang.* The business of recruiting executive personnel for a company or corporation. **—head′-hunt′er** *n.*

head•ing (hĕd′ĭng) *n.* **1.** Something, as a title, that stands at the head, as of a page or chapter. **2.** The direction in which a ship or aircraft is moving **:** course.

head•land (hĕd′lənd, -lănd′) *n.* A high ridge of land or rock jutting out into a body of water.

head•light (hĕd′līt′) *n.* A light mounted on the front of an automotive vehicle.

head•line (hĕd′līn′) *n.* The caption or title of a newspaper article or story printed in large type. —*v.* **-lined, -lin•ing. 1.** To provide (e.g., a newspaper article) with a headline. **2.** To serve or present as the star performer. **—head′lin′er** *n.*

head•lock (hĕd′lŏk′) *n.* A wrestling hold in which the head of a wrestler is locked under the arm of another.

head•long (hĕd′lông′, -lŏng′) *adv.* **1.** With the head foremost **:** headfirst. **2. a.** At breakneck speed. **b.** Rashly **:** impetuously. **—head′long′** *adj.*

head•mas•ter (hĕd′măs′tər) *n.* A man who is a school principal, esp. of a private school.

head•mis•tress (hĕd′mĭs′trĭs) *n.* A woman who is a school principal, esp. of a private school.

head-on (hĕd′ŏn′, -ôn′) *adj.* **1.** Having the front end first in position or contact <a *head-on* collision> **2.** Unwavering **:** direct. **—head′-on′** *adv.*

head•phone (hĕd′fōn′) *n.* An earphone held over the ear by a headband.

head•piece (hĕd′pēs′) *n.* **1.** A helmet or cap that protects the head. **2.** A headset.

head•quar•ters (hĕd′kwôr′tərz) *pl.n. (sing. or pl. in number).* **1.** The official center of command, as of a military unit. **2.** An administrative center.

head•rest (hĕd′rĕst′) *n.* **1.** A support for the head, as on a chair back. **2.** A padded cushion at the top of the back of an automobile seat, esp. to prevent whiplash injury.

head•set (hĕd′sĕt′) *n.* A pair of headphones on a headband.

head•stall (hĕd′stôl′) *n.* The part of a horse's bridle that fits over the head.

head•stand (hĕd′stănd′) *n.* The act of supporting the body on the top of the head esp. with the help of the forearms.

head start *n.* An early start that gives an advantage, as to competitors in a race.

head•stone (hĕd′stōn′) *n.* A memorial stone marker at the head of a grave.

head•strong (hĕd′strông′, -strŏng′) *adj.* Rashlywillful **:** obstinate.

head•wait•er (hĕd′wā′tər) *n.* A waiter in charge of a restaurant or dining-room staff.

head•wa•ters (hĕd′wô′tərz, -wŏt′ərz) *pl.n.* The waters that form the source of a river.

head•way (hĕd′wā′) *n.* **1.** Forward movement. **2.** Progress toward a goal. **3.** Clearance beneath an arch or ceiling.

head wind *n.* A wind blowing in the direction directly opposite to the course of an aircraft or ship.

head•work (hĕd′wûrk′) *n.* Work involving mental effort. **—head′work′er** *n.*

head•y (hĕd′ē) *adj.* **-i•er, -i•est. 1.** Tending to intoxicate. **2.** Headstrong. **—head′i•ly** *adv.* **—head′i•ness** *n.*

heal (hēl) *v.* **1.** To restore to sound health. **2.** To set right **:** remedy. **—heal′a•ble** *adj.* **—heal′er** *n.*

health (hĕlth) *n.* **1.** The overall condition or functioning of an organism at a particular time. **2.** Optimal mental and physical soundness and well-being. **3.** A desire for someone's well-being, often expressed as a toast. **—health′ful** *adj.* **—health′ful•ly** *adv.* **—health′ful•ness** *n.*

health food *n.* A food considered to be very beneficial to a person's health.

health maintenance organization *n.* An HMO.

health•y (hĕl′thē) *adj.* **-i•er, -i•est. 1.** In a state of good health. **2.** Promoting good health. **3.** Characteristic of good health. **4.** Quite large <a *healthy* raise> **—health′i•ly** *adv.* **—health′i•ness** *n.*

heap (hēp) *n.* **1.** A disorderly or haphazard assortment of things **:** pile. **2.** *often* **heaps.** *Informal.* A great many. —*v.* **1.** To put, pile, or rise in a heap. **2.** To fill to excess. **3.** To bestow lavishly.

hear (hîr) *v.* **heard** (hûrd), **hear•ing. 1.** To perceive by the ear. **2.** To listen to with careful attention. **3.** To get as information by hearing. **4.** To listen to in order to examine officially or formally, as in a court of law. **—hear′er** *n.*

hear•ing (hîr′ĭng) *n.* **1.** The sense by which sound is detected and perceived. **2.** Range within which sounds can be perceived. **3.** An opportunity to be heard. **4.** *Law.* **a.** A preliminary examination of an accused person. **b.** A usu. investigatory session for listening to argument or testimony.

hearing aid *n.* A small electronic amplifying device used to enhance the hearing of partially deaf persons.

heark•en (här′kən) *v.* To listen closely.

hear•say (hîr′sā′) *n.* Information heard from another person **:** rumor.

hearse (hûrs) *n.* A vehicle for taking a dead body to a church or graveyard.

heart (härt) *n.* **1.** The hollow, muscular organ in vertebrates that receives blood from the veins and pumps it into the arteries by regular, rhythmic contraction. **2.** The heart considered as an emotional center, as: **a.**

Mood or disposition. **b.** Compassion : concern. **c.** Affection : love. **d.** Resolute courage. **3.** The most central and essential part : basis <the *heart* of the controversy> **4. a.** Any of a suit of playing cards marked with a conventionalized red heart-shaped design. **b. hearts** *(sing. in number).* A card game in which the object is either to avoid hearts when taking tricks or to take all the hearts. ★ ***syns:*** CORE, ESSENCE, GIST, KERNEL, MARROW, MEAT, NITTY-GRITTY, NUB, PITH, QUINTESSENCE, ROOT, SOUL, STUFF **—by heart.** By memory <learned it *by heart*> **—with all (one's) heart. 1.** With great sincerity or devotion. **2.** Very willingly.

heart•ache (härt'āk') *n.* Emotional sorrow or grief.

heart attack *n.* An acute episode of impaired or interrupted heart functioning.

heart•beat (härt'bēt') *n.* **1.** A single complete cycle of contraction and relaxation of the heart. **2.** Vital force.

heart•break (härt'brāk') *n.* Great sorrow or disappointment. **—heart'break'ing** *adj.* **—heart'break'ing•ly** *adv.*

heart•bro•ken (härt'brō'kən) *adj.* Suffering from or indicating heartbreak. **—heart'bro'ken•ly** *adv.*

heart•burn (härt'bûrn') *n.* A feeling of burning in the stomach and esophagus, usu. caused by excess acid in the stomach.

heart•en (här'tn) *v.* To impart courage to : encourage.

heart•felt (härt'fĕlt') *adj.* Deeply felt : earnest and sincere.

hearth (härth) *n.* **1. a.** The floor of a fireplace. **b.** The paved area in front of a fireplace. **2.** The fireside as a symbol of family life or the home. **3.** *Metallurgy.* The lowest part of a refinery furnace, in which a metal or ore is treated by exposure to heat.

hearth•stone (härth'stōn') *n.* **1.** Stone used in building a hearth. **2.** The home : domestic life.

heart•land (härt'lănd') *n.* An important central region, esp. one regarded as vital to a nation's economy or defense.

heart•less (härt'lĭs) *adj.* Lacking compassion : pitiless. **—heart'less•ly** *adv.* **—heart'less•ness** *n.*

heart-rend•ing (härt'rĕn'dĭng) *adj.* **1.** Causing great distress or suffering. **2.** Evoking deep sympathy.

heart•sick (härt'sĭk') *adj.* Profoundly dejected. **—heart'sick'ness** *n.*

heart•strings (härt'strĭngz') *pl.n.* The deepest feelings, as of pity or affection.

heart•throb (härt'thrŏb') *n.* **1.** A pulsation of the heart. **2. a.** Tender emotion. **b.** A loved one : sweetheart.

heart-to-heart (härt'tə-härt') *adj.* Forthright : frank.

heart•warm•ing (härt'wôr'mĭng) *adj.* Eliciting feelings of warm sympathy.

heart•wood (härt'wŏŏd') *n.* The inner, older, no longer active central wood of a tree or woody plant.

heart•y (här'tē) *adj.* **-i•er, -i•est. 1.** Expressed with or marked by exuberant warmth. **2.** Thorough : unequivocal. **3.** Full of health and vigor. **4.** Nourishing : substantial. **—heart'i•ly** *adv.* **—heart'i•ness** *n.*

heat (hēt) *n.* **1.** A form of energy that can be transmitted through a solid or fluid medium by conduction, through a fluid medium by convection, and through space as infrared radiation. **2.** The physiological sensation of being warm. **3. a.** Warmth provided for a building or room. **b.** Intense or excessive warmth. **4.** Estrus. **5.** Intensity of emotion. **6.** *Slang.* **a.** Pressure : stress. **b.** Heightening of police activity in pursuing criminals. **c.** The police. **7. a.** One of several rounds in a competition. **b.** A preliminary race to determine final contenders. *—v.* **1.** To make or become warm or hot. **2.** To make or become excited. **—heat'er** *n.*

heat•ed (hē'tĭd) *adj.* Angry : vehement <a *heated* argument> **—heat'ed•ly** *adv.*

heat exhaustion *n.* A reaction to intense heat, marked by weakness, nausea, dizziness, and profuse sweating.

heath (hēth) *n.* **1.** An open, uncultivated stretch of land covered with low-growing shrubs and plants. **2.** An Old World, usu. low-growing shrub of the genus *Erica,* with small evergreen leaves and small flowers.

hea•then (hē'*th*ən) *n., pl.* **-thens** *or* **-then. 1.** A member of a people or nation that does not recognize the God of Judaism, Christianity, or Islam. **2.** An uncivilized, unenlightened, or irreligious person. **—hea'then** *adj.* **—hea'then•dom** *n.* **—hea'then•ish** *adj.* **—hea'then•ism** *n.*

heath•er (hĕ*th*'ər) *n.* **1.** A low-growing Eurasian shrub, *Calluna vulgaris,* that grows in dense masses and has small evergreen leaves and small pinkish-purple flower clusters. **2.** HEATH 2. **—heath'er** *adj.* **—heath'er•y** *adj.*

heat lightning *n.* Sporadic flashes of light unaccompanied by thunder.

heat stroke *n.* Illness caused by prolonged exposure to intense heat and marked by hot dry skin, high fever, rapid pulse, and in severe cases collapse.

heave (hēv) *v.* **heaved, heav•ing. 1.** To raise or lift, esp. forcibly. **2.** To throw : hurl. **3.** *p.t. & p.p.* **hove** (hōv). *Naut.* **a.** To pull, push, or haul, as by a rope. **b.** To pull into or come to be in a specified position <The barge *hove* alongside.> **4.** To utter (e.g., a sigh) with effort. **5.** To rise or be forced upward : bulge. **6.** *Informal.* To retch or vomit. *—n.* **1.** The act or effort of heaving. **2.** *Informal.* An act of throwing. **3.** An act of gagging or vomiting. **4. heaves** *(sing. or pl. in number).* A disease of horses affecting the lungs and marked by coughing and difficult breathing. **—heav'er** *n.*

heav•en (hĕv'ən) *n.* **1.** *often* **heavens.** The sky as it appears from the earth. **2.** The realm of God, the angels, and the blessed souls of the dead. **3. Heaven.** God. **4.** A place or state of blissful happiness. **—heav'en•li•ness** *n.*

—heav'en·ly *adj.* **—heav'en·ward** *adv. & adj.* **—heav'en·wards** *adv.*

heav·y (hĕv'ē) *adj.* **-i·er, -i·est. 1.** Having great weight. **2.** Having high density or specific gravity. **3. a.** Large, as in number or quantity <*heavy* snowfall><*heavy* traffic> **b.** Intense or concentrated <*heavy* fighting> **4.** Very thick or dense <*heavy* jungle growth> **5. a.** Forceful **:** powerful <a *heavy* blow> **b.** Rough and violent, as stormy weather. **6.** Partaking or involved to a great or excessive degree <a *heavy* smoker><a *heavy* gambler> **7. a.** Of great seriousness or significance **:** grave. **b.** Sorrowful or painful, as bad news. **8. a.** Hard to do **:** arduous. **b.** Hard to bear **:** oppressive <*heavy* taxation> **9. a.** Substantial **:** hearty. **b.** Not rapidly or easily digested. **10.** Having large or coarse facial or bodily features. **11.** Burdened with care or sadness <a *heavy* heart> **12.** Lacking vivacity or grace **:** clumsy or dull. **13. a.** Loaded down <trees *heavy* with fruit> **b.** Indicating weariness or sleepiness <*heavy* eyelids> **14.** Involving large-scale manufacturing, esp. of basic products such as steel. **15.** Bearing weighty arms or armor, as cavalry. **16.** *Slang.* Of great profundity. *—adv.* In a heavy manner. *—n., pl.* **-vies. 1.** A villain in a novel or drama. **2.** A wicked person. **3.** *Slang.* An important or influential person. **—heav'i·ly** *adv.* **—heav'i·ness** *n.*

heav·y-du·ty (hĕv'ē-do͞o'tē, -dyo͞o'-) *adj.* Designed for hard use or wear.

heav·y-hand·ed (hĕv'ē-hăn'dĭd) *adj.* **1.** Ungainly **:** clumsy. **2.** Tyrannical. **3.** Not tactful. **—heav'y-hand'ed·ly** *adv.* **—heav'y-hand'ed·ness** *n.*

heav·y-heart·ed (hĕv'ē-här'tĭd) *adj.* Melancholy **:** depressed. **—heav'y-heart'ed·ly** *adv.* **—heav'y-heart'ed·ness** *n.*

heavy metal *n.* **1.** A metal with a specific gravity greater than about 5.0. **2.** Very loud, brash rock music.

heav·y·set (hĕv'ē-sĕt') *adj.* Having a heavy, thickset build.

heavy water *n.* An isotopic variety of water, esp. deuterium oxide, used as a moderator in certain nuclear reactors.

heav·y·weight (hĕv'ē-wāt') *n.* **1.** One of above average weight. **2.** A competitor in the heaviest class, esp. a boxer weighing more than 175 lb. or 81 kg. **3.** *Informal.* One of great power or importance **:** VIP.

heb·e·tude (hĕb'ĭ-to͞od', -tyo͞od') *n.* Mental lethargy. **—heb'e·tu'di·nous** *adj.*

He·bra·ic (hĭ-brā'ĭk) *also* **He·bra·i·cal** (-ĭ-kəl) *adj.* Of, pertaining to, or characteristic of the Hebrews or their language or culture. **—He'bra'ist** (hē'brā'ĭst) *n.*

He·brew (hē'bro͞o) *n.* **1.** A member of a Semitic people claiming descent from Abraham, Isaac, and Jacob. **2.** The ancient and modern forms of the language of the Hebrews. **3. Hebrews.** *(sing. in number).* —See table at BIBLE. **—He'brew** *adj.*

heck·le (hĕk'əl) *v.* **-led, -ling.** To badger persistently, as with questions, comments, or gibes. **—heck'ler** *n.*

hec·tare (hĕk'târ') *n.* —See table at MEASUREMENT.

hec·tic (hĕk'tĭk) *adj.* **1.** Intensely active, rushed, or chaotic. **2. a.** Marked by a persistent and fluctuating fever, as in tuberculosis. **b.** Feverish **:** flushed.

hec·to·gram (hĕk'tə-grăm') *n.* A metric unit of mass equal to 100 grams.

hec·to·li·ter (hĕk'tə-lē'tər) *n.* A metric unit of volume equal to 100 liters.

hec·to·me·ter (hĕk'tə-mē'tər) *n.* A metric unit of length equal to 100 meters.

hec·tor (hĕk'tər) *n.* A bully. *—v.* **1.** To frighten or bully **:** intimidate. **2.** To swagger.

▲ ***word history:*** The word *hector,* which is both a noun meaning "a bully" and a verb meaning "to intimidate," is derived from *Hector,* the name of the Trojan hero who figures so largely in the *Iliad.* In the 17th cent. the name of this hero was used as a generic term for a swaggering braggart or bully. The behavior of such persons is denoted by the verb *hector,* which appeared at the same time as the noun.

he'd (hēd). **1.** He had. **2.** He would.

hedge (hĕj) *n.* **1.** A boundary or fence of shrubs or low-growing trees. **2.** A means of protection, esp. against financial loss. **3.** A deliberately ambiguous statement. *—v.* **hedged, hedg·ing. 1.** To bound or fence with or as if with a hedge. **2.** To hinder or encumber. **3.** To limit financial risk by a counterbalancing transaction <*hedge* a bet> **4.** To equivocate. **—hedg'er** *n.*

hedge·hog (hĕj'hôg', -hŏg') *n.* **1.** Any of several small Old World mammals of the family Erinaceidae, bearing dense, erectile spines on the back and rolling into a ball in self-defense. **2.** A porcupine.

hedge·hop (hĕj'hŏp') *v.* To fly an airplane close to the ground, as in spraying crops. **—hedge'hop'per** *n.*

hedge·row (hĕj'rō') *n.* A row of bushes, shrubs, or trees forming a hedge.

he·don·ism (hēd'n-ĭz'əm) *n.* **1.** A way of life devoted to the pursuit of pleasure. **2.** The philosophy that pleasure is the principal good in life. **—he'don·ist** *n.* **—he'don·is'tic** *adj.*

heed (hēd) *v.* To pay close attention (to). *—n.* Close attention. **—heed'ful** *adj.* **—heed'ful·ly** *adv.* **—heed'ful·ness** *n.* **—heed'less** *adj.* **—heed'less·ly** *adv.* **—heed'less·ness** *n.*

hee·haw (hē'hô') *n.* **1.** The braying sound made by a donkey. **2.** A noisy laugh **:** guffaw. **—hee'haw'** *v.*

heel[1] (hēl) *n.* **1. a.** The rounded back part of the human foot under and behind the ankle. **b.** An analogous part in other vertebrates. **2.** The part, as of a shoe, covering or supporting the heel. **3.** A lower, rearward, or bottom part. **4.** Either end of a loaf of bread. **5.** A cad. *—v.* **1.** To provide with a heel. **2.** *Slang.* To supply esp. with money. **3.** To follow along at one's heels. **—on** (*or* **upon**) **the heels of.** Directly following in time or space. **—heel'less** *adj.*

heel[2] (hēl) *v.* To list or cause to list to one side **:** tilt. **—heel** *n.*

heft (hĕft) *n. Informal.* Weight : bulk. —*v.* **1.** To find or estimate the weight of by lifting. **2.** To lift up : hoist.

heft·y (hĕf′tē) *adj.* **-i·er, -i·est. 1.** Heavy : bulky. **2.** Powerful : robust. **3.** Sizable.

he·gem·o·ny (hĭ-jĕm′ə-nē, hĕj′ə-mō′nē) *n.* Dominance, esp. of one nation over others.

he·gi·ra *also* **he·ji·ra** (hĭ-jī′rə, hĕj′ər-ə) *n.* A journey esp. to flee danger or privation.

heif·er (hĕf′ər) *n.* A young cow, esp. one that has not had a calf.

height (hīt) *n.* **1.** The highest point : summit. **2. a.** The highest degree : zenith. **b.** The point of greatest intensity. **3. a.** The distance from the base to the apex of something upright. **b.** Elevation above a specified level : altitude. **4.** Measurement from head to foot. **5.** An elevation of ground.

height·en (hīt′n) *v.* **1.** To increase in quantity or degree. **2.** To raise or be raised.

Heim·lich maneuver (hīm′lĭKH′, -lĭk′) *n.* A maneuver for dislodging food from a choking person's trachea in which the closed fist is placed below the rib cage to force air from the lungs upward.

hei·nous (hā′nəs) *adj.* Abominably wicked. —**hei′nous·ly** *adv.* —**hei′nous·ness** *n.*

heir (âr) *n.* One who inherits or is entitled to inherit another's property or title.

heir apparent *n., pl.* **heirs apparent.** An heir who is legally assured of the right to inherit provided he or she outlives an ancestor.

heir·ess (âr′ĭs) *n.* A woman who is an heir, esp. to a fortune.

heir·loom (âr′lo͞om′) *n.* **1.** A valued family possession handed on from generation to generation. **2.** An item of personal property acquired by legal inheritance.

heir presumptive *n., pl.* **heirs presumptive.** An heir who could lose the right to inherit through the birth of a closer relative.

heist (hīst) *Slang.* —*v.* To steal or steal from. —*n.* A theft.

he·ji·ra (hĭ-jī′rə, hĕj′ər-ə) *n. var. of* HEGIRA.

held (hĕld) *v. p.t. & p.p. of* HOLD[1].

hel·i·cal (hĕl′ĭ-kəl) *adj.* Of or having the shape of a helix. —**hel′i·cal·ly** *adv.*

hel·i·ces (hĕl′ĭ-sēz′, hē′lĭ-) *n. var. pl. of* HELIX.

hel·i·cop·ter (hĕl′ĭ-kŏp′tər) *n.* An aircraft supported in the air by horizontal rotors turning on an approx. vertical central axis.

he·li·o·cen·tric (hē′lē-ō-sĕn′trĭk) *also* **he·li·o·cen·tri·cal** (-trĭ-kəl) *adj.* Pertaining to or having the sun as a center. —**he′li·o·cen·tric′i·ty** (-trĭs′ĭ-tē) *n.*

he·li·o·graph (hē′lē-ə-grăf′) *n.* A signaling device using sunlight reflected from a movable mirror to transmit code. —**he′li·o·graph′** *v.* —**he′li·o·graph′ic** *adj.*

he·li·o·trope (hē′lē-ə-trōp′, hēl′yə-) *n.* A cultivated American plant of the genus *Heliotropium,* esp. *H. arborescens,* with small, very fragrant purplish or white flowers.

hel·i·port (hĕl′ə-pôrt′, -pōrt′) *n.* A level area where helicopters land and take off.

he·li·um (hē′lē-əm) *n. Symbol* **He** An extremely light, nonflammable, inert gaseous element.

he·lix (hē′lĭks) *n., pl.* **he·lix·es** *or* **hel·i·ces** (hĕl′ĭ-sēz′, hē′lĭ-). **1.** A three-dimensional curve that lies on a cylinder or cone, so that its angle to a plane perpendicular to the axis is constant. **2.** A spiral shape or structure.

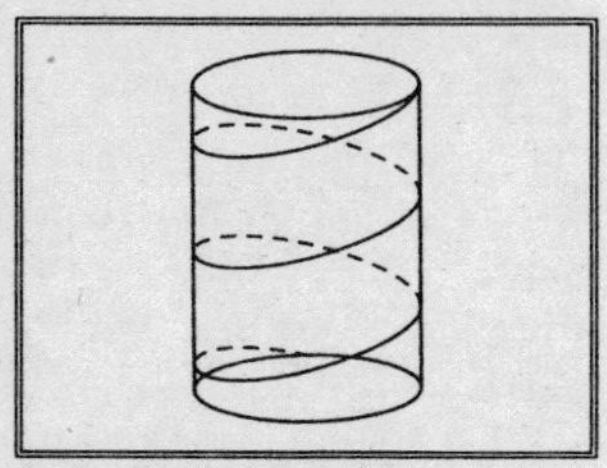

helix
Cylindrical model

hell (hĕl) *n.* **1.** The underworld abode of the dead. **2.** *often* **Hell.** The abode of the devil and souls condemned to eternal punishment. **3.** A place or condition of evil, torment or destruction. **4. a.** Great distress : anguish. **b.** A cause of trouble or misery. —**hell′ish** *adj.* —**hell′ish·ly** *adv.*

he'll (hēl). **1.** He will. **2.** He shall.

hell-bent (hĕl′bĕnt′) *adj.* Obstinately determined. —**hell′-bent′** *adv.*

hell·cat (hĕl′kăt′) *n.* **1.** A shrewish, malevolent woman. **2.** A fiendish person.

hel·le·bore (hĕl′ə-bôr′, -bōr′) *n.* Any of various North American plants of the genus *Veratrum,* esp. *V. viride,* bearing white or greenish flowers and yielding a toxic alkaloid used in medicine.

Hel·lene (hĕl′ēn′) *also* **Hel·le·ni·an** (hə-lē′nē-ən) *n.* A Greek.

Hel·len·ic (hə-lĕn′ĭk) *adj.* Of or pertaining to the ancient Greeks or their culture.

Hel·le·nism (hĕl′ə-nĭz′əm) *n.* **1.** Ancient Greek civilization and culture. **2.** Devotion to or adoption of Greek thought, style, or cultural customs. —**Hel′le·nist** *n.* —**Hel′le·nis′tic** *adj.*

†**hell·er** (hĕl′ər) *n. Regional.* One who behaves wildly or rashly.

hell-for-leath·er (hĕl′fər-lĕth′ər) *adv. & adj. Informal.* At breakneck speed.

hell·gram·mite (hĕl′grə-mīt′) *n.* The brownish aquatic larva of the dobson fly, used esp. as fishing bait.

hell·hole (hĕl′hōl′) *n.* A place of extreme squalor or wretchedness.

hel·lion (hĕl′yən) *n. Informal.* A devilish or vexatious person.

hel·lo (hĕ-lō′, hə-) *also* **hul·lo** (hə-). —*interj.* —Used esp. as a greeting or to answer the telephone. —*n., pl.* **-loes.** A greeting or call of "hello."

helm (hĕlm) *n.* **1.** A tiller or wheel for steering a ship. **2.** A position of control or command.

hel·met (hĕl′mĭt) *n.* A protective metal, leather, or plastic covering for the head.

helms·man (hĕlmz′mən) *n.* One at the helm of a ship.

hel·ot (hĕl′ət, hē′lət) *n.* A serf **:** slave. **—hel′·ot·ry** *n.*

help (hĕlp) *v.* **1.** To give aid (to) **:** assist. **2.** To contribute to the progress of **:** advance. **3.** To give relief to **:** alleviate. **4.** To benefit (someone) by making improvements. **5.** To have the power to change or prevent. **6.** To keep from **:** escape. **7.** To wait on, as in a store. *—n.* **1.** Assistance. **2.** Relief. **3.** One that assists. **4. a.** One hired to help. **b.** Such workers in general. **—help′er** *n.* **—help′ful** *adj.* **—help′ful·ly** *adv.* **—help′ful·ness** *n.* **—help′less** *adj.* **—help′less·ly** *adv.* **—help′less·ness** *n.*

help·ing (hĕl′pĭng) *n.* A single serving of food.

help·mate (hĕlp′māt′) *n.* A helper and companion, esp. a spouse.

help·meet (hĕlp′mēt′) *n.* A helpmate.

▲ ***word history:*** The word *helpmeet* owes its existence to a misreading of a passage in the King James Bible. In Genesis 2:18 God promises Adam to "make him an help meet for him," that is, a helper suitable for him. The words *help meet* were even in the 17th cent. misread as one word, and since the "help" turned out to be Eve, the new compound was interpreted as meaning "spouse." *Helpmate* is an alteration of *helpmeet* that substitutes *mate,* "spouse," for the now unintelligible *meet* of *helpmeet.*

hel·ter-skel·ter (hĕl′tər-skĕl′tər) *adv.* **1.** In confused or disorderly haste. **2.** In an aimless, haphazard way. *—adj.* **1.** Rushed and confused. **2.** Aimless **:** haphazard. *—n.* Great confusion.

helve (hĕlv) *n.* A handle of a tool such as an ax, chisel, or hammer.

Hel·ve·tian (hĕl-vē′shən) *adj. & n.* Swiss.

hem[1] (hĕm) *n.* An edge of cloth folded under and stitched down. *—v.* **hemmed, hem·ming. 1.** To fold under and stitch down the edge of. **2.** To surround and confine. **—hem′·mer** *n.*

hem[2] (hĕm) *n.* A short sound made in clearing the throat used esp. to attract attention or fill a pause in speech. *—v.* **hemmed, hem·ming.** To utter a hem.

he-man (hē′măn′) *n. Informal.* A man marked by strength and virility.

hem·a·tite (hĕm′ə-tīt′, hē′mə-) *n.* A reddish mineral that is the main ore of iron and consists of a compound of iron and oxygen.

he·ma·tol·o·gy (hē′mə-tŏl′ə-jē) *n.* The biological science that deals with the blood and blood-generating organs. **—he′ma·tol′o·gist** *n.*

heme (hēm) *n.* The iron-containing deep-red pigment of hemoglobin.

hemisphere (hĕm′ĭ-sfîr′) *n.* **1. a.** Either half of a sphere that is divided by a plane passing through its center. **b.** Either symmetrical half of an approx. spherical shape. **2.** Either the N or S half of the earth divided by the equator or the E or W half divided by a geographic meridian. **—hem′i·spher′ic, hem′i·spher′i·cal** *adj.*

hem·lock (hĕm′lŏk′) *n.* **1. a.** An evergreen tree of the genus *Tsuga,* of North America and E Asia, having flat needles and small cones. **b.** The wood of a hemlock. **2. a.** Any of several poisonous plants of the genera *Conium* and *Cicuta,* with compound leaves and small whitish flowers. **b.** A poison obtained from the hemlock plant.

he·mo·di·al·y·sis (hē′mō-dī-ăl′ĭ-sĭs) *n., pl.* **-ses** (-sēz′). The removal esp. of metabolic waste products from the bloodstream by dialysis.

he·mo·glo·bin (hē′mə-glō′bĭn) *n.* A protein in the red blood cells of vertebrates that contains iron and carries oxygen to bodily tissues.

he·mo·phil·i·a (hē′mə-fĭl′ē-ə) *n.* An inherited blood disease marked by severe, protracted, sometimes spontaneous bleeding. **—he′mo·phil′i·ac′** *n.*

hem·or·rhage (hĕm′ər-ĭj) *n.* Bleeding, esp. abnormally severe or copious bleeding. **—hem′or·rhage** *v.*

hem·or·rhoid (hĕm′ə-roid′) *n.* **1.** A painful mass of dilated veins in swollen anal tissue. **2. hemorrhoids.** The pathological condition in which hemorrhoids occur.

he·mo·stat (hē′mə-stăt′) *n.* **1.** An agent, as a chemical, that stops bleeding. **2.** A clamplike surgical instrument for preventing or reducing bleeding. **—he′mo·stat′ic** *adj.*

hemp (hĕmp) *n.* **1.** A tall Asian plant, *Cannabis sativa,* whose stems yield a fiber used to make cordage. **2.** The fiber of the hemp. **3.** A narcotic, as hashish, derived from hemp. **—hemp′en** *adj.*

hem·stitch (hĕm′stĭch′) *n.* A decorative stitch, made by pulling out several parallel threads and tying the remaining threads together in even bunches to form designs. **—hem′stitch′** *v.*

hen (hĕn) *n.* A female bird, esp. a full-grown female domestic fowl.

hence (hĕns) *adv.* **1.** For this reason **:** consequently. **2.** From now <3 days *hence*> **3.** Away from this place.

hence·forth (hĕns′fôrth′) *also* **hence·for·ward** (hĕns-fôr′wərd) *adv.* From this time or point on.

hench·man (hĕnch′mən) *n.* **1.** A loyal follower. **2.** One who supports a political figure chiefly for personal gain.

hen·na (hĕn′ə) *n.* **1. a.** An Asian and N African tree or shrub, *Lawsonia inermis,* bearing fragrant white or reddish flowers. **b.** A brownish-red dyestuff derived from henna leaves and used esp. as a cosmetic dye. **2.** A strong reddish brown. *—v.* To treat or dye (e.g., hair) with henna.

hen·peck (hĕn′pĕk′) *v. Informal.* To subject (one's husband) to chronic nagging.

hep (hĕp) *adj. var. of* HIP[2].
hep•a•rin (hĕp'ər-ĭn) *n.* An organic compound found esp. in liver tissue that is used medically to slow or prevent blood clotting.
he•pat•ic (hĭ-păt'ĭk) *adj.* Of, like, acting on, or affecting the liver.
he•pat•i•ca (hĭ-păt'ĭ-kə) *n.* A forest plant of the genus *Hepatica,* esp. *H. americana,* of E North America, with 3-lobed leaves and white or lavender flowers.
hep•a•ti•tis (hĕp'ə-tī'tĭs) *n.* Inflammation of the liver marked by jaundice and caused by infectious or toxic agents.
her (hûr; hər, ər *when unstressed*) *pron. objective case of* SHE. —Used: **1.** As the direct object of a verb <We saw *her* at the park.> **2.** As the indirect object of a verb <We mailed *her* the records.> **3.** As the object of a preposition <That car belongs to *her.*> *—adj.* —Used as a modifier before a noun <*her* hat><*her* achievements>
her•ald (hĕr'əld) *n.* **1.** A messenger who announces important news. **2.** One that comes before as a sign of what is to follow **:** harbinger. **3.** An official whose duty it once was to make royal proclamations. *—v.* To announce **:** proclaim.
he•ral•dic (hə-răl'dĭk) *adj.* Of or pertaining to heralds or heraldry.
her•ald•ry (hĕr'əl-drē) *n., pl.* **-ries. 1.** The art or practice of tracing genealogies and devising and granting coats of arms. **2.** An armorial badge, emblem, or device. **3.** Heraldic pageantry.
herb (ûrb, hûrb) *n.* **1.** A soft-stemmed plant that usu. withers and dies each year. **2.** An often pleasant-smelling plant used in medicine or cooking. **—herb'al** *adj. & n.*
her•ba•ceous (hûr-bā'shəs, ûr-) *adj.* **1.** Of, like, or consisting of herbs. **2.** Green and leaflike.
herb•age (ûr'bĭj, hûr'-) *n.* **1.** Grass or leafy vegetation used esp. for grazing. **2.** The fleshy, often edible parts of plants.
herb•al•ist (hûr'bə-lĭst, ûr'-) *n.* One who gathers, grows, or uses herbs, esp. medicinal herbs.
her•bar•i•um (hûr-bâr'ē-əm, ûr-) *n., pl.* **-i•ums** *or* **-i•a** (-ē-ə). **1.** A collection of dried plant specimens esp. for scientific study. **2.** A place housing a herbarium.
her•bi•cide (hûr'bĭ-sīd', ûr'-) *n.* A chemical agent used to kill plants, esp. weeds. **—her'bi•cid'al** *adj.*
her•bi•vore (hûr'bə-vôr', -vōr', ûr-) *n.* A herbivorous animal.
her•biv•o•rous (hûr-bĭv'ər-əs, ûr-) *adj.* Feeding chiefly on plants. **—her•biv'o•rous•ly** *adv.*
her•cu•le•an (hûr'kyə-lē'ən, hûr-kyo͞o'lē-) *adj.* Of unusual size, force, or difficulty.
herd (hûrd) *n.* **1.** A number of animals of the same kind kept or staying together as a group. **2.** A large crowd of people. *—v.* **1.** To assemble in a herd. **2.** To gather, keep, drive, or lead in or as if in a herd. **—herd'er** *n.* **—herds'man** *n.*
here (hîr) *adv.* **1.** In or at this place <Let's skate *here.*> **2.** At the present time **:** now <Let's take a vote *here.*> **3.** At or on this point or detail <*Here* we disagree.> **4.** To or toward this place <Bring it *here.*>
here•a•bout (hîr'ə-bout') *also* **here•a•bouts** (-bouts') *adv.* Near or around here.
here•af•ter (hîr-ăf'tər) *adv.* **1.** From now on. **2.** In the future or the afterlife. *—n.* Existence after death **:** afterlife.
here•by (hîr-bī', hîr'bī') *adv.* By means of this.
he•red•i•tar•y (hə-rĕd'ĭ-tĕr'ē) *adj.* **1. a.** Passing from an ancestor to a legal heir. **b.** Having an inherited title or possession. **2.** Transmitted or transmissible by genetic inheritance. **3.** Of long-standing tradition. **—he•red'i•tar'i•ly** *adv.*
he•red•i•ty (hə-rĕd'ĭ-tē) *n.* **1.** The genetic passage of physical traits from parent to offspring. **2.** The set of physical traits passed to an organism through heredity.
here•in (hîr-ĭn') *adv.* In or into this.
here•of (hîr-ŭv', -ŏv') *adv.* Relating to or concerning this.
here•on (hîr-ŏn', -ôn') *adv.* Hereupon.
her•e•sy (hĕr'ĭ-sē) *n., pl.* **-sies. 1.** An opinion or doctrine in conflict with orthodox religious beliefs. **2. a.** Dissent from accepted or dominant opinion, doctrine, or theory. **b.** Adherence to such dissent.
her•e•tic (hĕr'ĭ-tĭk) *n.* A dissenter from orthodox beliefs, esp. religious beliefs. **—he•ret'i•cal** (hə-rĕt'ĭ-kəl) *adj.*
here•to (hîr-to͞o') *adv.* To this document, matter, or proposition.
here•to•fore (hîr'tə-fôr', -fōr') *adv.* Up to the present time.
here•un•to (hîr-ŭn'to͞o, hîr'ŭn-to͞o') *adv.* Hereto.
here•up•on (hîr'ə-pŏn', -pôn') *adv.* Immediately following this.
here•with (hîr-wĭth', -wĭth') *adv.* **1.** Together with this. **2.** Hereby.
her•i•ta•ble (hĕr'ĭ-tə-bəl) *adj.* Capable of being inherited.
her•i•tage (hĕr'ĭ-tĭj) *n.* **1.** Property passed down by inheritance. **2.** Something handed on from past generations **:** legacy.
her•maph•ro•dite (hər-măf'rə-dīt') *n.* A person, animal, or plant that has both male and female reproductive organs. **—her•maph'ro•dit'ic** (-dĭt'ĭk) *adj.*
her•met•ic (hər-mĕt'ĭk) *also* **her•met•i•cal** (-ĭ-kəl) *adj.* **1.** Tightly sealed so that air cannot enter or escape **:** airtight. **2.** Resistant to or proof against outside influences. **—her•met'i•cal•ly** *adv.*

▲ ***word history:*** An airtight seal is called a *hermetic* seal by a roundabout chain of circumstances. *Hermetic* is an adjective derived from the name *Hermes* Trismegistus, the Greek name for the Egyptian god Thoth, who was regarded as the originator of the science of alchemy. The adjective *hermetic,* beginning in the 17th cent., meant "pertaining to alchemy" and the occult sciences in general.

Alchemy, and later chemistry, was itself variously known as the *hermetic* art, philosophy, or science. A *hermetic* seal was a kind of seal used by alchemists that involved melting closed an opening in a glass vessel. Since the resulting seal was airtight, any airtight seal has come to be called *hermetic.*

her•mit (hûr′mĭt) *n.* One who lives as a recluse, esp. for religious reasons.

her•mit•age (hûr′mĭ-tĭj) *n.* **1.** The dwelling place of a hermit. **2.** A secluded retreat **:** hideaway.

her•ni•a (hûr′nē-ə) *n., pl.* **-ni•as** *or* **-ni•ae** (-nē-ē′). Protrusion of a body part, as the intestine, through the abnormally weakened wall that usu. contains it **:** rupture. **—her′ni•al** *adj.*

he•ro (hîr′ō) *n., pl.* **-roes. 1.** A figure in mythology and legend renowned for great strength, courage, and daring. **2.** A man celebrated for special achievements and attributes. **3.** The leading male character in a story or play. **4.** *Slang.* A long split sandwich roll containing a variety of fillings. **—he•ro′ic** *adj.* **—he•ro′i•cal•ly** *adv.*

heroic couplet *n.* A rhymed couplet in iambic pentameter.

her•o•in (hĕr′ō-ĭn) *n.* A highly addictive narcotic obtained from morphine.

her•o•ine (hĕr′ō-ĭn) *n.* **1.** A woman renowned for her courage and daring. **2.** A woman celebrated for her special achievements and attributes. **3.** The leading female character in a story or play.

her•o•ism (hĕr′ō-ĭz′əm) *n.* **1.** Heroic behavior. **2.** Heroic attributes, esp. courage.

her•on (hĕr′ən) *n.* A bird of the family Ardeidae, with a long pointed bill, long legs, and a long neck.

her•pes (hûr′pēz′) *n.* A viral disease that causes small blisters on the skin or mucous membrane. **—her•pet′ic** (-pĕt′ĭk) *adj.*

herpes sim•plex (sĭm′plĕks′) *n.* Either of two recurrent viral diseases marked by the eruption of blisters on the mouth and face or on the genitals.

her•pe•tol•o•gy (hûr′pĭ-tŏl′ə-jē) *n.* The scientific study of reptiles and amphibians. **—her′pe•to•log′ic** (-tə-lŏj′ĭk), **her′pe•to•log′i•cal** *adj.* **—her′pe•to•log′i•cal•ly** *adv.* **—her′pe•tol′o•gist** *n.*

her•ring (hĕr′ĭng) *n., pl.* **-ring** *or* **-rings.** A valuable food fish of the family Clupeidae, esp. *Clupea harengus,* of Atlantic and Pacific waters.

her•ring•bone (hĕr′ĭng-bōn′) *n.* **1.** A pattern consisting of rows of short slanted parallel lines with adjacent rows slanting in opposite directions. **2.** A fabric with a herringbone pattern.

hers (hûrz) *pron.* —Used to indicate the one or ones belonging to her <If your car won't start, take *hers.*>

her•self (hər-sĕlf′) *pron.* **1.** That one identical with her. —Used: **a.** Reflexively as the direct or indirect object of a verb or as the object of a preposition <She burned *herself.*> **b.** For emphasis <She *herself* couldn't be sure.> **c.** In an absolute construction <In debt *herself,* she was unable to contribute.> **2.** Her normal condition or state <She isn't *herself* today.>

hertz (hûrts) *n.* A unit of frequency equal to 1 cycle per sec.

he's (hēz). **1.** He has. **2.** He is.

hes•i•tant (hĕz′ĭ-tənt) *adj.* Given to hesitating. **—hes′i•tan•cy** *n.*

hes•i•tate (hĕz′ĭ-tāt′) *v.* **-tat•ed, -tat•ing. 1.** To pause in doubt before acting, speaking, or deciding **:** waver. **2.** To be unwilling <Don't *hesitate* to ask for money.> **3.** To falter in speech. ★ ***syns:*** FALTER, HALT, PAUSE, SHILLY-SHALLY, STAGGER, VACILLATE, WAVER **—hes′i•tat′ing•ly** *adv.* **—hes′i•ta′tion** *n.*

het•er•o•dox (hĕt′ər-ə-dŏks′) *adj.* **1.** Not in accord with established beliefs, esp. at variance with religious doctrine. **2.** Holding unorthodox or unconventional opinions. **—het′er•o•dox′y** *n.*

het•er•o•ge•ne•ous (hĕt′ər-ə-jē′nē-əs, -jēn′yəs) *also* **het•er•og•e•nous** (-ə-rŏj′ə-nəs) *adj.* Consisting of dissimilar parts, elements, or ingredients. **—het′er•o•ge•ne′i•ty** (-rō-jə-nē′ĭ-tē) *n.* **—het′er•o•ge′ne•ous•ly** *adv.*

het•er•o•sex•u•al (hĕt′ə-rō-sĕk′shōō-əl) *adj.* **1.** Of, relating to, or marked by sexual attraction to the opposite sex. **2.** Involving different sexes. **—het′er•o•sex′u•al** *n.* **—het′er•o•sex′u•al′i•ty** (-ăl′ĭ-tē) *n.*

hew (hyōō) *v.* **hewed, hewn** (hyōōn) *or* **hewed, hew•ing. 1.** To make or give shape to with or as if with an ax. **2.** To fell with an ax. **3.** To adhere strictly <*hew* to the rule> **—hew′er** *n.*

hex (hĕks) *n.* **1.** A malevolent curse. **2.** One held to bring bad luck **:** jinx. —*v.* **1.** To put under an evil spell. **2.** To jinx.

hex•a•dec•i•mal (hĕk′sə-dĕs′ə-məl) *adj.* Of or based on the number 16.

hex•a•gon (hĕk′sə-gŏn′) *n.* A 6-sided polygon. **—hex•ag′o•nal** (-săg′ə-nəl) *adj.* **—hex•ag′o•nal•ly** *adv.*

hex•am•e•ter (hĕk-săm′ĭ-tər) *n.* A line of verse with 6 metrical feet.

hey•day (hā′dā′) *n.* A time of maximum power, prosperity, or popularity **:** peak.

Hf *symbol for* HAFNIUM.

Hg *symbol for* MERCURY.

hi•a•tus (hī-ā′təs) *n.* A slight break or lapse in space, time, or continuity **:** break.

hi•ba•chi (hĭ-bä′chē) *n., pl.* **-chis.** A portable charcoal brazier esp. for grilling food.

hi•ber•nate (hī′bər-nāt′) *v.* **-nat•ed, -nat•ing.** To spend the winter in an inactive sleeplike state. **—hi′ber•na′tion** *n.* **—hi′ber•na′tor** *n.*

▲ ***word history:*** The English word *hibernate* is ult. derived from Latin *hibernus,* "wintry." *Hibernus* descends from the Indo-European root *ghiem–,* from which the Sanskrit word *himrā–,* "snow," is also derived. *Himalaya* is a Sanskrit compound of *himrā–,* "snow," and *ālaya,* "abode, place," and means "the place of snow."

hi·bis·cus (hī-bĭs′kəs, hĭ-) *n.* A chiefly tropical plant, shrub, or tree of the genus *Hibiscus,* bearing large, colorful flowers.

hic·cup *also* **hic·cough** (hĭk′ŭp) *n.* **1.** A spasm of the diaphragm that occurs on inhalation and closes the glottis, producing a short, sharp sound. **2. hiccups.** An attack of such spasms. **—hic′cup** *v.*

hick (hĭk) *n. Informal.* An awkward, unsophisticated country person.

hick·o·ry (hĭk′ə-rē) *n., pl.* **-ries.** A chiefly North American deciduous tree of the genus *Carya,* having smooth or shaggy bark, hard edible nuts, and heavy, tough wood.

hi·dal·go (hĭ-dăl′gō) *n., pl.* **-goes.** A member of the lesser nobility in Spain.

hide[1] (hīd) *v.* **hid** (hĭd), **hid·den** (hĭd′n) *or* **hid, hid·ing. 1.** To put, keep, or remain out of sight. **2.** To keep from being disclosed <tried to *hide* the truth> **3.** To obscure from sight. **4.** To seek shelter or protection. ★ ***syns:*** BURY, CACHE, CONCEAL, ENSCONCE, PLANT, SECRETE, STASH **—hid′er** *n.*

hide[2] (hīd) *n.* The skin of an animal.

hide-and-seek (hīd′n-sēk′) *n.* A game in which one player tries to find and catch others who are hiding.

hide·a·way (hīd′ə-wā′) *n.* **1.** A place of concealment. **2.** An isolated retreat.

hide·bound (hīd′bound′) *adj.* Obstinately narrow-minded or inflexible.

hid·e·ous (hĭd′ē-əs) *adj.* **1.** Physically repulsive. **2.** Morally offensive. **—hid′e·ous·ly** *adv.* **—hid′e·ous·ness** *n.*

hide-out (hīd′out′) *n.* HIDEAWAY 1.

hie (hī) *v.* **hied, hie·ing** *or* **hy·ing.** To make haste : hurry.

hi·er·ar·chy (hī′ə-rär′kē, hī′rär′-) *n., pl.* **-chies. 1.** An authoritative body, esp. of clergy, organized according to rank. **2.** A graded or ranked series of persons or things. **—hi′er·ar′chi·cal, hi′er·ar′chic** *adj.* **—hi′er·ar′chi·cal·ly** *adv.*

hi·er·o·glyph·ic (hī′ər-ə-glĭf′ĭk, hī′rə-) *n.* **1.** A pictorial symbol used in a writing system, esp. that of ancient Egypt. **2. hieroglyphics.** Symbols or writing difficult to decipher. **—hi′er·o·glyph′i·cal·ly** *adv.*

hi-fi (hī′fī′) *n., pl.* **-fis. 1.** High fidelity. **2.** Electronic equipment for reproducing high-fidelity sound.

hig·gle·dy-pig·gle·dy (hĭg′əl-dē-pĭg′əl-dē) *adv.* In total confusion.

high (hī) *adj.* **1.** Extending relatively far upward : tall or lofty. **2.** Being at or near a peak or climax <*high* noon> **3.** Long past in time. **4.** Having a shrill or piercing tone. **5.** Far from the equator <*high* latitudes> **6.** Very important or serious. **7.** Having an exalted or noble quality or character. **8.** Above average, as in quantity, magnitude, or degree. **9.** Expensive. **10.** Elated. **11.** *Informal.* Intoxicated, as by alcohol or drugs. **12.** Advanced in development or complexity. *—n.* **1.** A high place, level, or degree. **2.** The transmission gear of a motor vehicle producing the greatest speed. **3.** A center of high barometric pressure. **4.** *Informal.* **a.** Intoxication. **b.** Great elation. *—adv.* **1.** At, in, or to a high position or degree. **2.** In luxury <living *high*> **—high′ly** *adv.*

high·ball (hī′bôl′) *n.* A mixed drink usu. served in a tall glass.

high beam *n.* A high-intensity headlight on a vehicle.

high·born (hī′bôrn′) *adj.* Of noble or aristocratic birth.

high·boy (hī′boi′) *n.* A tall chest of drawers mounted on a base with 4 legs.

high·bred (hī′brĕd′) *adj.* **1.** Highborn. **2.** Of or from superior breeding stock.

high·brow (hī′brou′) *n. Informal.* One of superior knowledge or culture. **—high′brow′, high′browed′** *adj.*

high·chair (hī′châr′) *n.* A very young child's feeding chair that has long legs.

high·er-up (hī′ər-ŭp′, hī′ər-ŭp′) *n. Informal.* A superior in rank or status.

high·fa·lu·tin (hī′fə-lo͞ot′n) *adj. Informal.* Pretentious or grandiose.

high fashion *n.* **1.** Haute couture. **2.** The newest in fashion or design.

high fidelity *n.* Minimally distorted electronic sound reproduction, as on records or tape. **—high′-fi·del′i·ty** *adj.*

high-flown (hī′flōn′) *adj.* **1.** Exalted. **2.** Highly pretentious or inflated.

high frequency *n.* A radio frequency between 3 and 30 megahertz.

high·hand·ed (hī′hăn′dĭd) *adj.* Overbearing in manner. **—high′hand′ed·ly** *adv.* **—high′hand′ed·ness** *n.*

high-hat (hī′hăt′) *adj. Slang.* Supercilious : patronizing. **—high′-hat′** *v. & n.*

high jinks *or* **hi·jinks** (hī′jĭnks′) *pl.n.* Playful, often noisy and rowdy activity.

high jump *n.* A jump for height in a track and field contest.

high jump

high·land (hī′lənd) *n.* **1.** Land elevated above a surrounding area. **2. highlands.** A hilly or mountainous region.

high·light (hī′līt′) *n.* A significant event or detail. *—v.* **1.** To emphasize. **2.** To be the major event or detail of.

high-mind·ed (hī′mīn′dĭd) *adj.* Characterized by noble principles or behavior. **—high′-mind′ed·ness** *n.*

high·ness (hī′nĭs) *n.* **1.** The quality or state

of being high or tall. 2. **Highness.** A title used for royalty.
high-pres·sure (hī′prĕsh′ər) *Informal.* —*adj.* Using or involving aggressive and insistent sales methods. —*v.* To try to persuade by using high-pressure techniques.
high relief *n.* Sculptural relief with modeled forms that project from the background by at least half their depth.
high-rise (hī′rīz′) *n.* An elevator-equipped multistory building.
high·road (hī′rōd′) *n.* **1.** *esp. Brit.* A main road. **2.** A direct or guaranteed way.
high school *n.* A secondary school of grades 9 or 10 through 12. —**high′-school′er** *n.*
high seas *pl.n.* The waters of an ocean or sea beyond the limits of a nation's territorial jurisdiction.
high-sound·ing (hī′soun′dĭng) *adj.* Pompous : bombastic.
high-spir·it·ed (hī′spĭr′ĭ-tĭd) *adj.* **1.** Unbroken in spirit : proud. **2.** Exuberant. —**high′-spir′it·ed·ly** *adv.*
high·stick·ing (hī′stĭk′ĭng) *n. Hockey.* An offense in which a player carries the stick above the shoulders.
high-strung (hī′strŭng′) *adj.* Highly nervous and excitable : temperamental.
high·tail (hī′tāl′) *v. Slang.* To withdraw hastily <*hightail* it for cover>
high tech (tĕk) *n.* **1.** A style of interior design incorporating industrial materials or motifs. **2.** High technology.
high technology *n.* Technology involving highly advanced or specialized systems or devices.
high-ten·sion (hī′tĕn′shən) *adj.* Having or using high voltage.
high-test (hī′tĕst′) *adj.* Of or relating to gasoline with a high octane number.
high tide *n.* The highest level reached by the tide.
high-toned (hī′tōnd′) *adj.* **1.** Of superior intellectual, moral, or social quality. **2.** *Informal.* Pretentious.
high·way (hī′wā′) *n.* A main public road, esp. one connecting towns and cities.
high·way·man (hī′wā′mən) *n.* A robber who waylays travelers on a road.
hi·jack (hī′jăk′) *v. Informal.* **1.** To steal (goods) by stopping a vehicle along the road. **2.** To seize control of (a vehicle, esp. an airplane in flight) so as to force it to an alternative destination. —**hi′jack′er** *n.*
hi·jinks (hī′jĭnks) *pl.n. var. of* HIGH JINKS.
hike (hīk) *v.* **hiked, hik·ing. 1.** To take a lengthy walk. **2.** To raise in amount. **3. a.** To go up, esp. to be caught up. **b.** To pull up (e.g., clothing) with a sudden motion. —**hike** *n.* —**hik′er** *n.*
hi·lar·i·ous (hĭ-lâr′ē-əs, -lăr′-) *adj.* Provoking or marked by boisterous laughter. —**hi·lar′i·ous·ly** *adv.* —**hi·lar′i·ty** *n.*
hill (hĭl) *n.* **1.** A usu. rounded natural land elevation smaller than a mountain. **2.** A small pile or mound, as of soil. —**hill′i·ness** *n.* —**hill′y** *adj.*
hill·bil·ly (hĭl′bĭl′ē) *n., pl.* **-lies.** *Informal.* One from an isolated rural region.
hill·ock (hĭl′ək) *n.* A low or small hill.
hill·side (hĭl′sīd′) *n.* The side of a hill.
hill·top (hĭl′tŏp′) *n.* The top of a hill.
hilt (hĭlt) *n.* A handle, esp. of a sword or dagger. —**to the hilt.** Fully : completely.
him (hĭm) *pron. objective case of* HE. —Used: **1.** As the direct object of a verb <We saw *him* at the park.> **2.** As the indirect object of a verb <We mailed *him* the records.> **3.** As the object of a preposition <That car belongs to *him.*>
him·self (hĭm-sĕlf′) *pron.* **1.** That one identical with him. —Used: **a.** Reflexively as the direct or indirect object of a verb or as the object of a preposition <He burned *himself.*> **b.** For emphasis <He *himself* couldn't be sure.> **c.** In an absolute construction <In debt *himself,* he was unable to contribute.> **2.** His normal condition or state <He isn't *himself* today.>
hind¹ (hīnd) *adj.* Rear or posterior <a dog's *hind* legs>
hind² (hīnd) *n.* The female of the European red deer.
hin·der (hĭn′dər) *v.* **1.** To interfere with the action of. **2.** To obstruct the progress of. —**hin′der·er** *n.*
Hin·di (hĭn′dē) *n.* The literary and official language of N India. —**Hin′di** *adj.*
hind·most (hīnd′mōst′) *adj.* Farthest to the back or rear.
hind·quar·ter (hīnd′kwôr′tər) *n.* **1.** The hind part of a side of meat. **2.** *often* **hindquarters.** The rump or haunches of a quadruped.
hin·drance (hĭn′drəns) *n.* **1.** The action of hindering or state of being hindered. **2.** An obstacle : impediment.
hind·sight (hīnd′sīt′) *n.* Comprehension of the meaning of an event that was lacking when it happened.
Hin·du (hĭn′dōō) *n.* **1.** One of a people native to India, esp. N India. **2.** A believer in Hinduism. —**Hin′du** *adj.*
Hin·du·ism (hĭn′dōō-ĭz′əm) *n.* A complex body of religious, philosophical, and cultural beliefs and practices of India.
hinge (hĭnj) *n.* **1.** A jointed device that permits a part, as a door or gate, to turn or swing on a stationary frame. **2.** A part or structure similar to a hinge. —*v.* **hinged, hing·ing. 1.** To affix by or provide with a hinge. **2.** To be contingent.
hint (hĭnt) *n.* **1.** A slight or indirect indication : clue. **2.** A very small amount : trace. —*v.* **1.** To make known by a hint. **2.** To offer a hint. —**hint′er** *n.*
hin·ter·land (hĭn′tər-lănd′) *n.* **1.** An inland area. **2.** A region far from cities.
hip¹ (hĭp) *n.* **1.** The part of the body between the waist and thigh that projects outward over the hipbone. **2.** The hip joint.
hip² (hĭp) *also* **hep** (hĕp) *adj.* **hip·per, hip·pest** *also* **hep·per, hep·pest.** *Slang.* **1.** Informed and up-to-date. **2.** Aware : alert.

hip³ (hĭp) *n.* The berrylike, often bright-red seed case of a rose.
hip•bone (hĭp′bōn′) *n.* A large, flat bone forming a lateral half of the pelvis.
hip joint *n.* The joint between the hipbone and the thighbone.
hip•pie *also* **hip•py** (hĭp′ē) *n., pl.* **-pies.** *Informal.* A usu. young person who adopts unconventional beliefs or practices.
hip•po (hĭp′ō) *n., pl.* **-pos.** A hippopotamus.
hip•po•drome (hĭp′ə-drōm′) *n.* An arena used esp. for horse shows.
hip•po•pot•a•mus (hĭp′ə-pŏt′ə-məs) *n., pl.* **-mus•es** *or* **-mi** (-mī′). A large, thick-skinned, short-legged African aquatic mammal, *Hippopotamus amphibius,* with a broad widemouthed muzzle.
hip roof *n.* A roof having sloping edges and sides.
hire (hīr) *v.* **hired, hir•ing.** To pay for the services or use of. —*n.* **1.** Money paid for services or for the use of something. **2.** The act of hiring or the state or fact of being hired. —**hir′er** *n.*
hire•ling (hīr′lĭng) *n.* A hired person motivated solely by the pay.
hir•sute (hûr′so͞ot′, hîr′-) *adj.* Covered with hair : hairy. —**hir′sute′ness** *n.*
his (hĭz) *adj.* —Used to indicate that the male previously referred to is the possessor or the agent or recipient of an action <*his* hat><*his* accomplishments> —*pron. (sing. or pl. in number).* That or those belonging to him <The idea for the fund raiser was *his.*><The cats are *his.*>
His•pan•ic (hĭ-spăn′ĭk) *adj.* Of or relating to Spain or Spanish-speaking Latin America. —*n.* **1.** A Spanish-speaking person. **2.** A Hispanic American.
Hispanic American *n.* **1.** A U.S. citizen or resident of Hispanic descent. **2.** A Spanish American. —**His•pan′ic-A•mer′i•can** *adj.*
hiss (hĭs) *n.* **1.** A sound resembling a sustained *s.* **2.** Disapproval or contempt expressed by a hiss. —*v.* **1.** To emit a hiss. **2.** To denounce by hissing. —**hiss′er** *n.*
his•ta•mine (hĭs′tə-mēn′, -mĭn) *n.* A white crystalline compound that occurs in plant and animal tissue and is believed to cause allergic reactions. —**his′ta•min′ic** (-mĭn′ĭk) *adj.*
his•tol•o•gy (hĭ-stŏl′ə-jē) *n.* The scientific study of the minute structure of animal and plant tissues as seen through a microscope. —**his′to•log′i•cal** (hĭs′tə-lŏj′ĭ-kəl) *adj.* —**his•tol′o•gist** *n.*
his•to•ri•an (hĭ-stôr′ē-ən, -stŏr′-) *n.* A specialist in the writing or study of history.
his•tor•ic (hĭ-stôr′ĭk, -stŏr′-) *adj.* **1.** Significant or renowned in history. **2.** Historical.
his•tor•i•cal (hĭ-stôr′ĭ-kəl, -stŏr′-) *adj.* **1.** Of, relating to, or taking place in history. **2.** Relating to, concerned with, or based on past events. **3.** Historic. —**his•tor′i•cal•ly** *adv.* —**his•tor′i•cal•ness** *n.*
his•to•ric•i•ty (hĭs′tə-rĭs′ĭ-tē) *n.* Historical authenticity.
his•to•ri•og•ra•phy (hĭ-stôr′ē-ŏg′rə-fē, -stŏr′-) *n.* **1.** The principles or techniques of historical research. **2.** The usu. official writing of history. **3.** Literature dealing with history. —**his•to′ri•og′ra•pher** *n.* —**his•to′ri•o•graph′ic** (-ē-ə-grăf′ĭk), **his•to′ri•o•graph′i•cal** *adj.*
his•to•ry (hĭs′tə-rē) *n., pl.* **-ries. 1.** A narrative of events : story. **2.** A chronological record of events, as of the life of a people. **3.** The branch of knowledge concerned with the recording and explanation of historical events. **4.** The recorded events of the past. **5.** A past of particular interest.
his•tri•on•ic (hĭs′trē-ŏn′ĭk) *adj.* **1.** Of or having to do with actors or acting. **2.** Unduly dramatic or emotional : affected. —**his′tri•on′i•cal•ly** *adv.*
his•tri•on•ics (hĭs′trē-ŏn′ĭks) *n.* **1.** *(sing. in number).* Theatrical arts. **2.** *(pl. in number).* Unduly dramatic emotional display calculated for effect.
hit (hĭt) *v.* **hit, hit•ting. 1. a.** To deal a blow (to) : strike. **b.** To come or cause to come against forcefully. **2.** To have an adverse effect on. **3.** To arrive at : reach. **4.** To come upon : discover. **5.** To make an appeal to <*hit* her for a loan> **6.** To drive (e.g., a ball) with a blow. **7.** *Baseball.* To bat successfully. ★ ***syns:*** BASH, BELT, BOP, CLIP, CLOBBER, CLOUT, KNOCK, PASTE, SLAM, SLOG, SLUG, SMACK, SMASH, SMITE, SOCK, STRIKE, SWAT, WALLOP, WHACK, WHAM —*n.* **1. a.** A blow. **b.** A collision. **2.** A shot, blow, or throw that succeeds. **3.** A great success. **4.** *Baseball.* A base hit. —**hit it off.** To get along well together. —**hit the road.** To set out : depart. —**hit′ter** *n.*
hit-and-run (hĭt′n-rŭn′) *adj.* Of or indicating a driver who fails to stop after hitting a pedestrian or another vehicle.
hitch (hĭch) *v.* **1.** To catch or tie, esp. with a hook or knot. **2.** To connect : attach. **3.** *Informal.* To unite in marriage. **4.** To lift up by tugging or jerking. **5.** *Informal.* To hitchhike. —*n.* **1.** A temporary knot for fastening. **2.** A short tug : jerk. **3.** A difficulty or delay. **4.** A period of service, esp. military service.
hitch•hike (hĭch′hīk′) *v.* To travel by obtaining rides from passing drivers. —**hitch′hik′er** *n.*
hith•er (hĭ*th*′ər) *adv.* To this place : here. —*adj.* Being on the near side : nearer.
hith•er•to (hĭ*th*′ər-to͞o′) *adv.* Up to now.
hit-or-miss (hĭt′ər-mĭs′) *adj.* Having no definite pattern or purpose : random.
HIV (āch′ī-vē′) *n.* A retrovirus that causes AIDS.
hive (hīv) *n.* **1.** A natural or manmade structure in which bees, esp. honeybees, live. **2.** A colony of bees housed in a hive. **3.** A crowded place full of busy people.
hives (hīvz) *pl.n. (sing. or pl. in number).* An allergic condition marked by itching welts.
HMO (āch′ĕm-ō′) *n.* A corporation providing curative and preventive medicine within certain limits to enrolled members.

Hmong (hmông) *n., pl.* **Hmong** *or* **Hmongs.** **1.** A member of a people inhabiting parts of S China, Vietnam, Laos, and Thailand. **2.** The language of the Hmong.
Ho *symbol for* HOLMIUM.
hoa•gie (hō′gē) *n.* HERO 4.
hoar (hôr, hōr) *adj.* Hoary. —*n.* Hoarfrost.
hoard (hôrd, hōrd) *n.* A hidden stockpile : cache. —*v.* To amass a hoard (of). ★ ***syns:*** LAY UP, SQUIRREL, STASH, STOCKPILE —**hoard′er** *n.*
hoar•frost (hôr′frôst′, -frŏst′, hōr′-) *n.* A deposit of ice crystals forming on a cold surface exposed to moist air.
hoarse (hôrs, hōrs) *adj.* **hoars•er, hoars•est.** **1.** Having a harsh, grating sound. **2.** Having a grating voice. —**hoarse′ly** *adv.* —**hoarse′ness** *n.*
hoar•y (hôr′ē, hōr′ē) *adj.* **-i•er, -i•est.** **1.** Grayish or white <a *hoary* beard> **2.** Very old : aged. —**hoar′i•ness** *n.*
hoax (hōks) *n.* A trick or fraud intended to deceive. —**hoax** *v.* —**hoax′er** *n.*
hob[1] (hŏb) *n.* A projection at the side or back of the inside of a fireplace, used for keeping things warm.
hob[2] (hŏb) *n.* An elf or hobgoblin.
hob•ble (hŏb′əl) *v.* **-bled, -bling.** **1.** To limp or cause to limp along. **2.** To fetter (an animal). **3.** To hinder the progress of : hamper. —*n.* **1.** A hobbling walk or gait. **2.** A device, as a rope or strap, for hobbling an animal. —**hob′bler** *n.*
hob•by (hŏb′ē) *n., pl.* **-bies.** An activity engaged in primarily for pleasure : pastime. —**hob′by•ist** *n.*

▲ ***word history:*** *Hobby* is a shortened form of *hobbyhorse,* which orig. denoted a small horse. *Hobbyhorse* developed other senses denoting representations of horses, such as a toy horse for children to ride. It is this last sense that led to the development of the modern meaning of the word *hobby.* A person with a hobby was thought to pursue a favorite pastime or obsession with the zeal of a child riding a hobbyhorse.

hob•by•horse (hŏb′ē-hôrs′) *n.* **1.** A child's toy consisting of a long stick, usu. with an imitation horse's head at one end. **2.** A rocking horse. **3.** A favorite subject or topic.
hob•gob•lin (hŏb′gŏb′lĭn) *n.* **1.** A goblin or elf. **2.** A bugbear : bugaboo.
hob•nail (hŏb′nāl′) *n.* A short, broad-headed nail used on shoe or boot soles for traction or to prevent wear.
hob•nob (hŏb′nŏb′) *v.* **-nobbed, -nob•bing.** To be on familiar terms <*hobnobs* with the jet set>
ho•bo (hō′bō) *n., pl.* **-boes** *or* **-bos.** A vagrant or migrant person : tramp.
hock[1] (hŏk) *n.* The joint or area in the hind leg of a quadruped, as a horse or hog, that corresponds to the human ankle.
hock[2] (hŏk) *Informal.* —*v.* To pawn. —*n.* The state of being pawned.
hock•ey (hŏk′ē) *n.* **1.** A game played on ice by 2 teams of skaters whose object is to drive a puck into the opponents' goal with curved sticks. **2.** A kind of hockey played on a field with a ball rather than a puck.
ho•cus-po•cus (hō′kəs-pō′kəs) *n.* **1.** Nonsense words or phrases used by sorcerers. **2.** A sleight-of-hand trick. **3.** Chicanery.
hod (hŏd) *n.* **1.** A V-shaped, long-handled trough held over the shoulder for carrying loads, as bricks or mortar. **2.** A pail for carrying coal.
hodge•podge (hŏj′pŏj′) *n.* A jumbled or random mixture.
hoe (hō) *n.* A long-handled tool with a flat blade, used to weed, cultivate, and loosen the soil. —**hoe** *v.* —**ho′er** *n.*
hoe•cake (hō′kāk′) *n.* A thin cake made of cornmeal.
hoe-down (hō′doun′) *n.* **1.** A square dance. **2.** A party featuring hoe-downs.
hog (hôg, hŏg) *n.* **1.** Any of various mammals of the family Suidae, which includes both the domesticated pig and wild species, as the boar and the wart hog. **2.** A greedy, selfish, or dirty person. —*v.* **hogged, hog•ging.** To take selfishly. —**hog′gish** *adj.* —**hog′gish•ly** *adv.* —**hog′gish•ness** *n.*
ho•gan (hō′gän′, -gən) *n.* A Navajo dwelling usu. built of logs and mud.
hogs•head (hôgz′hĕd′, hŏgz′-) *n.* **1.** A large barrel or cask, esp. one that holds from 63 to 140 gal. **2.** Any of several U.S. measures of liquid volume, esp. one equal to 63 gal.
hog-tie *also* **hog•tie** (hôg′tī′, hŏg′-) *v.* **1.** To tie together the feet or legs of. **2.** To hamper : impede.
hog•wash (hôg′wŏsh′, -wôsh′, hŏg′-) *n.* **1.** Swill fed to hogs. **2.** False or ridiculous talk or writing.
hoi pol•loi (hoi′ pə-loi′) *n.* The common people : masses.
hoist (hoist) *v.* To raise or haul up : lift. —*n.* **1.** An apparatus, as a crane or winch, for hoisting. **2.** The act of hoisting : pull or lift. —**hoist′er** *n.*
hoke (hōk) *v.* **hoked, hok•ing.** *Slang.* To give a false or misleading quality to.
hold[1] (hōld) *v.* **held** (hĕld), **hold•ing.** **1.** To take or have and keep in or as if in one's grasp : possess. **2.** To bear : support. **3.** To keep or put in a particular place, position, or relationship. **4.** To receive or be able to receive as contents : contain. **5.** To have or keep in one's possession : own. **6.** To keep back : control or restrain. **7.** To capture the interest or attention of. **8.** To retain or defend by force. **9.** To stop or delay the movement or progress of. **10.** To occupy (a position, as political office). **11.** To bind : obligate <*held* him to his word> **12.** To keep in the memory. **13. a.** To believe : judge. **b.** To state positively : affirm. **14.** To cause to take place <*hold* a meeting> <*hold* a party> **15.** To maintain a grasp or grip. **16.** To remain unyielding or securely fixed <The rope *held.*> **17.** To be valid <Our theory *holds.*> —*n.* **1.** The act or a means of holding : grasp or grip. **2.** A strong influence or power : control. **3.** Something held or used for

support. **4.** A cell for prisoners. **5.** *Archaic.* A stronghold. **6.** A temporary halt or delay. **—hold forth.** To talk at great length. **—hold out. 1.** To last. **2.** To continue to work or resist. **3.** To refuse to reach or satisfy an agreement. **—hold over. 1.** To put off : postpone. **2.** To cause to continue longer than planned. **—hold up. 1.** To last : endure. **2.** To rob, esp. at gunpoint. **—hold with.** To be in accord with. **—hold'er** *n.*

hold[2] (hōld) *n.* The cargo storage area inside an aircraft or ship.

hold•ing (hōl'dĭng) *n.* **1.** Rented or leased land. **2.** *often* **holdings.** Property, as land, money, or stocks, that is legally owned.

holding pattern *n.* A usu. circular course flown by an aircraft awaiting clearance to land at an airport.

hold•out (hōld'out') *n.* One who refuses to agree or cooperate.

hold•o•ver (hōld'ō'vər) *n.* One that remains from an earlier time, as an officeholder.

hold•up (hōld'ŭp') *n.* **1.** A delay. **2.** An armed robbery.

hole (hōl) *n.* **1.** An opening in a solid : space or gap. **2.** A hollow place, as a depression or cave. **3.** An animal's habitation : burrow. **4.** An ugly, wretched place. **5.** A fault, error, or omission <*holes* in one's thinking> **6.** A troublesome situation. **7. a.** The small, cup-lined depression into which the ball must be hit in golf. **b.** One of the divisions of a golf course, from the tee to the hole. **—hole up.** To hide, take shelter, or seclude oneself in or as if in a hole. **—hole** *v.*

hol•i•day (hŏl'ĭ-dā') *n.* **1.** A day free from work, esp. one set aside by law to commemorate a special person or event. **2.** A day set aside for religious observance. **3.** *esp. Brit.* A vacation.

ho•li•ness (hō'lē-nĭs) *n.* **1.** Sanctity : sacredness. **2. Holiness.** —Used as a title of address for the pope.

ho•lism (hō'lĭz'əm) *n.* A theory or belief emphasizing the importance of the whole and the interdependence of its parts. **—ho'list** *n.* **—ho•lis'tic** *adj.* **—ho•lis'ti•cal•ly** *adv.*

hol•lan•daise sauce (hŏl'ən-dāz') *n.* A rich, creamy sauce of butter, egg yolks, and lemon juice or vinegar.

hol•ler[1] (hŏl'ər) *v.* To shout : yell. **—hol'ler** *n.*

†hol•ler[2] (hŏl'ər) *adj. & n. & v. Regional. var. of* HOLLOW.

hol•low (hŏl'ō) *adj.* **1.** Having a space or cavity within. **2.** Rounded like the inside of a bowl : concave or sunken. **3.** Lacking substance or significance. **4.** Deep-toned and echoing. *—n.* **1.** An opening, space, or cavity within something. **2.** A small valley. **3.** An emptiness : void. *—v.* To make hollow. **—hol'low•ly** *adv.* **—hol'low•ness** *n.*

hol•ly (hŏl'ē) *n., pl.* **-lies.** A tree or shrub of the genus *Ilex,* typically bearing glossy, spiny-edged leaves and bright-red berries.

hol•ly•hock (hŏl'ē-hŏk') *n.* A plant, *Althaea rosea,* widely cultivated for its tall spikes of large, variously colored flowers.

hol•mi•um (hōl'mē-əm) *n. Symbol* **Ho** A malleable rare-earth element.

hol•o•caust (hŏl'ə-kôst', hō'lə-) *n.* **1.** Widespread or complete destruction, esp. by fire. **2. Holocaust.** The genocide of European Jews and other groups by the Nazis during World War II.

hol•o•gram (hŏl'ə-grăm', hō'lə-) *n.* A photographic image in 3 dimensions made without the use of a camera lens by a reflected laser beam of light on photographic film.

hol•o•graph (hŏl'ə-grăf', hō'lə-) *n.* A document, as a letter or will, handwritten by the person who signed it. **—hol'o•graph'ic, hol'o•graph'i•cal** *adj.*

ho•log•ra•phy (hō-lŏg'rə-fē) *n.* The process of producing or using a hologram. **—ho'lo•graph'** (hō'lə-grăf') *v.* **—ho•log'ra•pher** *n.* **—ho'lo•graph'ic** *adj.*

Hol•stein (hōl'stīn') *n.* One of a breed of black-and-white dairy cattle.

hol•ster (hōl'stər) *n.* A leather case shaped to hold a pistol. **—hol'stered** *adj.*

ho•ly (hō'lē) *adj.* **-li•er, -li•est. 1.** Belonging to, derived from, or associated with a divine power : sacred. **2.** Regarded with or deserving of worship or veneration : revered. **3.** Spiritually perfect : saintly. ★ ***syns:*** BLESSED, HALLOWED, SACRED, SACROSANCT, SANCTIFIED

Holy Communion *n.* COMMUNION 3.

Holy Ghost *n.* The 3rd person of the Christian Trinity.

Holy Spirit *n.* The Holy Ghost.

holy war *n.* A war declared for a religious or high moral purpose.

hom•age (ŏm'ĭj, hŏm'-) *n.* Great respect or honor, esp. when expressed publicly.

hom•burg (hŏm'bûrg') *n.* A felt hat with a high, dented crown and a stiff, slightly rolled brim.

home (hōm) *n.* **1. a.** A place where one lives : residence. **b.** An apartment or house. **2.** A household. **3.** A place of origin. **4.** A habitat, as of an animal or plant. **5.** The goal in a game, as baseball. **6.** An institution for those who need help or care. ★ ***syns:*** ABODE, DIGS, DWELLING, HABITATION, HOUSE, LODGINGS, PAD, PLACE *—adv.* **1.** At or toward home. **2.** At the center of a target. **3.** To the heart or center. *—v.* **homed, hom•ing. 1.** To return home. **2.** To be guided to a target electronically.

home•bod•y (hōm'bŏd'ē) *n.* A person whose life is centered around the home.

home•boy (hōm'boi') *n. Slang.* **1.** A male friend from one's home town or neighborhood. **2.** A fellow male gang member.

home•com•ing (hōm'kŭm'ĭng) *n.* **1.** A return to one's home. **2.** A yearly celebration for visiting college alumni.

home economics *n.* The principles and practice of managing a household.

home•land (hōm'lănd') *n.* One's native land.

home•less (hōm'lĭs) *adj.* Having no home or refuge.

home•ly (hōm'lē) *adj.* **-li•er, -li•est. 1.** Peculiar to the home or everyday life <*homely* chores> **2.** Not pretentious or complex <*homely* proverbs> **3.** Physically unattractive : plain. **—home'li•ness** *n.*

home•made (hōm'mād') *adj.* Made in the home or by one's own hands.

home•mak•er (hōm'mā'kər) *n.* One who runs a household, esp. as a wife and mother. **—home'mak'ing** *n. & adj.*

ho•me•op•a•thy (hō'mē-ŏp'ə-thē) *n.* A system of medical treatment based on the use of small quantities of drugs that in large amounts produce symptoms resembling the disease being treated. **—ho'me•o•path'** (-ə-păth') *n.* **—ho'me•o•path'ic** *adj.*

ho•me•o•sta•sis (hō'mē-ō-stā'sĭs) *n.* A state of equilibrium between different but interrelated functions or elements, as in an organism or group. **—ho'me•o•stat'ic** (-stăt'ĭk) *adj.*

home plate *n. Baseball.* A slab at one of the corners of a diamond that a base runner must touch in order to score.

hom•er (hō'mər) *n.* A home run.

home run *n. Baseball.* A hit that enables the batter to make a complete circuit of the bases and score a run.

home•sick (hōm'sĭk') *adj.* Yearning for home and family. **—home'sick'ness** *n.*

home•spun (hōm'spŭn') *adj.* **1.** Spun or woven at home. **2.** Made of a loosely woven, coarse woolen cloth. **3.** Simple and plain : homely <*homespun* wisdom>

home•stead (hōm'stĕd') *n.* **1.** A family's house, esp. a farmhouse, with adjacent buildings and land. **2.** A tract of land granted, as under the Homestead Act, to a settler who cleared, cultivated, and lived on it. **—home'stead'** *v.*

home•stead•er (hōm'stĕd'ər) *n.* **1.** A person who has settled land as a homestead. **2.** *Can.* A person who has been given a federal grant of a homestead.

home•stretch (hōm'strĕch') *n.* **1.** The section of a racecourse between the last turn and the finish line. **2.** The final stages of a venture.

home•ward (hōm'wərd) *adj. & adv.* To or toward home. **—home'wards** *adv.*

home•work (hōm'wûrk') *n.* **1.** Work, as school assignments, to be done at home. **2.** Preparatory work.

home•y *also* **hom•y** (hō'mē) *adj.* **-i•er, -i•est.** Suggestive of home, as in coziness or intimacy. **—hom'ey•ness** *n.*

hom•i•cide (hŏm'ĭ-sīd', hō'mĭ-) *n.* **1.** A killing of one person by another. **2.** A person who kills another. **—hom'i•cid'al** *adj.*

hom•i•let•ics (hŏm'ə-lĕt'ĭks) *n. (sing. in number).* The art of preaching sermons. **—hom'i•let'ic** *adj.*

hom•i•ly (hŏm'ə-lē) *n., pl.* **-lies. 1.** A sermon delivered to a congregation. **2.** A tiresomely moralizing lecture or reprimand.

homing pigeon *n.* A pigeon trained to fly back to its home roost.

hom•i•nid (hŏm'ə-nĭd) *n.* A primate of the family Hominidae, of which *Homo sapiens* is the only extant species. **—hom'i•nid** *adj.*

hom•i•ny (hŏm'ə-nē) *n.* Hulled and dried kernels of corn, often ground into a coarse white meal and boiled.

ho•mo•ge•ne•ous (hō'mə-jē'nē-əs, -jēn'yəs) *adj.* **1.** Of the same or similar nature or kind. **2.** Of uniform make-up or structure. **—ho'mo•ge•ne'i•ty** (-jə-nē'ĭ-tē) *n.* **—ho'mo•ge'ne•ous•ly** *adv.* **—ho'mo•ge'ne•ous•ness** *n.*

ho•mog•e•nize (hō-mŏj'ə-nīz', hə-) *v.* **-nized, -niz•ing. 1.** To make homogeneous. **2. a.** To disperse particles evenly throughout a fluid. **b.** To make uniform in consistency, esp. to make (milk) homogeneous by emulsifying the fat content. **—ho•mog'e•ni•za'tion** *n.* **—ho•mog'e•niz'er** *n.*

hom•o•graph (hŏm'ə-grăf', hō'mə-) *n.* One of 2 or more words having the same spelling but differing in origin, meaning, and sometimes pronunciation.

ho•mol•o•gous (hō-mŏl'ə-gəs, hə-) *adj.* Similar and related in structure, function, or evolutionary origin. **—hom'o•logue'** (hŏm'ə-lôg', hō'mə-), **hom'o•log'** *n.* **—ho•mol'o•gy** *n.*

hom•o•nym (hŏm'ə-nĭm', hō'mə-) *n.* One of 2 or more words having the same sound and often the same spelling but differing in meaning and origin.

ho•mo•pho•bi•a (hō'mə-fō'bē-ə) *n.* Aversion to gay or homosexual people. **—ho'mo•phobe'** *n.* **—ho'mo•pho'bic** *adj.*

hom•o•phone (hŏm'ə-fōn', hō'mə-) *n.* One of 2 or more words having the same sound but differing in spelling, origin, and meaning.

Ho•mo sa•pi•ens (hō'mō sā'pē-ĕnz', -ənz) *n.* The human race.

ho•mo•sex•u•al (hō'mə-sĕk'shōō-əl, -mō-) *adj.* Of or relating to sexual attraction toward others of the same sex. **—ho'mo•sex'u•al** *n.* **—ho'mo•sex'u•al'i•ty** *n.*

hom•y (hō'mē) *adj. var. of* HOMEY.

hon•cho (hŏn'chō) *n., pl.* **-chos.** *Slang.* One who is in charge : boss or manager.

hone (hōn) *n.* A fine-grained stone for sharpening cutting tools, as knives or razors. —*v.* **honed, hon•ing. 1.** To sharpen on a hone. **2.** To perfect.

hon•est (ŏn'ĭst) *adj.* **1.** Not deceptive : truthful. **2.** Not fraudulent : genuine. **3.** Of good repute. **4.** Frank : sincere. **5.** Without affectation. **—hon'est•ly** *adv.*

hon•es•ty (ŏn'ĭ-stē) *n.* The quality or state of being honest. ★ ***syns:*** INCORRUPTIBILITY, INCORRUPTIBLENESS, INTEGRITY, RECTITUDE, UPRIGHTNESS

hon•ey (hŭn'ē) *n., pl.* **-eys. 1.** A sweet, sticky substance made by honeybees from the nectar of flowers and used as food. **2.** Sweetness. **3.** *Informal.* Darling : dear. **—hon'eyed, hon'ied** *adj.*

hon•ey•bee (hŭn'ē-bē') *n.* Any of various bees of the genus *Apis,* esp. *A. mellifera,* living in highly organized colonies and producing honey.

hon•ey•comb (hŭn'ē-kōm') *n.* A wax structure with many small, hexagonal cells fabricated by honeybees to hold honey and eggs. —*v.* To fill with openings or spaces like those in a honeycomb.

hon•ey•dew (hŭn′ē-do͞o′, -dyo͞o′) *n.* A sweetish, sticky substance deposited on plant leaves by certain insects, esp. aphids.

honeydew melon *n.* A smooth-skinned, whitish melon, *Cucumis melo,* with sweet green flesh.

hon•ey•moon (hŭn′ē-mo͞on′) *n.* **1.** A trip or holiday taken by a newly married couple. **2.** An early period of harmony, as in a relationship. —**hon′ey•moon′** *v.* —**hon′ey•moon′er** *n.*

hon•ey•suck•le (hŭn′ē-sŭk′əl) *n.* A shrub or vine of the genus *Lonicera,* bearing tubular, often highly fragrant flowers.

honk (hôngk, hŏngk) *n.* **1.** The loud, harsh, resonant cry of a goose. **2.** A sound resembling a honk, as that of an automobile horn. —**honk** *v.* —**honk′er** *n.*

hon•ky-tonk (hông′kē-tôngk′, hŏng′kē-tŏngk′) *n.* A cheap, noisy bar or nightclub.

hon•or (ŏn′ər) *n.* **1.** Esteem **:** respect. **2. a.** Recognition or distinction. **b.** A symbol or gesture of recognition or distinction. **3.** Privilege. **4. a.** Reputation. **b.** A source or cause of credit. **5. Honor.** A person of superior status. —Used esp. as a title for mayors and judges. **6.** Personal integrity. —*v.* **1.** To hold in or treat with honor. **2.** To confer honor or distinction upon. **3.** To accept as valid <*honor* a credit card> —**hon′or•ee′** *n.*

hon•or•a•ble (ŏn′ər-ə-bəl) *adj.* **1.** Deserving honor. **2.** Conferring or accompanied by honor. **3.** Marked by integrity. **4.** Illustrious. **5. Honorable.** —Used as a title of respect for a high- ranking person. —**hon′or•a•ble•ness** *n.* —**hon′or•a•bly** *adv.*

hon•o•rar•i•um (ŏn′ə-râr′ē-əm) *n., pl.* **-i•ums** *or* **-i•a** (-ē-ə). A payment made for services for which a fee is not required by law or custom.

hon•or•ar•y (ŏn′ə-rĕr′ē) *adj.* **1.** Conferred or held as an honor without the usual prerequisites <an *honorary* doctorate> **2.** Unpaid **:** voluntary <*honorary* chairman>

hon•or•if•ic (ŏn′ə-rĭf′ĭk) *adj.* Giving or conveying respect or honor.

hon•our (ŏn′ər) *n. & v. esp. Brit. var. of* HONOR.

hood¹ (ho͝od) *n.* **1.** A covering for the head and neck, often attached to a garment. **2.** Something shaped or functioning like a hood, as the hinged metal covering of an automobile engine. —**hood′ed** *adj.*

hood² (ho͝od) *n. Slang.* A hoodlum.

–hood *suff.* **1.** Quality or state <child*hood*> **2.** A group sharing a given quality or state <brother*hood*>

hood•lum (ho͝od′ləm, ho͝od′-) *n.* **1.** A ruffian or gangster. **2.** A tough, wild, or destructive young man.

hoo•doo (ho͞o′do͞o) *n.* **1.** Voodoo. **2. a.** Misfortune. **b.** One thought to bring misfortune. —**hoo′doo** *v.*

hood•wink (ho͝od′wĭngk′) *v.* To deceive by trickery.

hoo•ey (ho͞o′ē) *n. Slang.* Nonsense.

hoof (ho͝of, ho͞of) *n., pl.* **hooves** (ho͝ovz, ho͞ovz) *or* **hoofs. 1.** The horny covering of the toes or lower part of the foot of a mammal of the orders Perissodactyla and Artiodactyla, as a horse, ox, or deer. **2.** The foot of a hoofed mammal, esp. of a horse. —*v. Slang.* **1.** To dance. **2.** To walk. —**hoofed** (ho͝oft, ho͞oft) *adj.*

hook (ho͝ok) *n.* **1.** A curved or bent object or part, often of metal, used to catch, drag, suspend, attach, or fasten something. **2.** Something shaped like a hook. **3.** A thrown or struck ball, as in golf, that moves in a curving direction. **4.** A short, swinging punch delivered with the arm bent and rigid. —*v.* **1.** To catch or make fast with or as if with a hook. **2.** *Slang.* To cause to become dependent or addicted. **3.** *Slang.* To steal. **4.** To bend **:** curve. —**hook up. 1.** To connect (an electric or electronic device) to a source of power. **2.** To form a tie or association.

hoo•kah (ho͝ok′ə) *n.* A smoking pipe with a long tube passing through a container of water that cools the smoke as it is drawn through.

hook•er (ho͝ok′ər) *n. Slang.* A prostitute.

hook•up (ho͝ok′ŭp′) *n.* An arrangement or linkage of parts or devices acting as a unit, as in an electronic system.

hook•worm (ho͝ok′wûrm′) *n.* A parasitic intestinal worm of the family Ancylostomatidae, with hooked mouth parts.

hook•y (ho͝ok′ē) *n. Informal* Truancy <play *hooky*>

hoo•li•gan (ho͞o′lĭ-gən) *n. Informal.* A hoodlum **:** tough. —**hoo′li•gan•ism** *n.*

hoop (ho͞op, ho͝op) *n.* **1.** A circular piece of wood or metal used esp. to hold together the staves of a cask or barrel. **2.** A circular or ringlike object. **3.** A circle of pliable material for expanding a skirt. **4.** *Basketball. Informal.* The basket.

hoop•la (ho͞op′lä′, ho͝op′-) *n. Slang.* **1.** Noisy commotion. **2.** Exaggerated or misleading publicity.

hoose•gow (ho͞os′gou′) *n. Slang.* A jail.

Hoo•sier (ho͞o′zhər) *n. Informal.* A native or resident of Indiana.

hoot (ho͞ot) *v.* **1.** To make the deep, hollow cry of an owl. **2.** To make a loud cry, esp. in derision. —**hoot** *n.* —**hoot′er** *n.*

hoo•te•nan•ny (ho͞ot′n-ăn′ē) *n., pl.* **-nies.** An informal gathering at which folk singers perform.

hooves (ho͝ovz, ho͞ovz) *n. var. pl. of* HOOF.

hop¹ (hŏp) *v.* **hopped, hop•ping. 1.** To move with a light springing motion. **2.** To make a short quick leap on one foot. **3.** To move as if by hopping <*hop* aboard> —*n.* **1.** A light, springy leap. **2.** *Informal.* A dance. **3.** A quick trip, esp. by air.

hop² (hŏp) *n.* **1.** A vine of the genus *Humulus,* esp. *H. lupulus,* with lobed leaves and green flowers resembling pine cones. **2. hops.** The dried flowers of the hop plant, yielding an oil used in brewing beer.

hope (hōp) *v.* **hoped, hop•ing.** To want or wish for with a feeling of confident expectation. —*n.* **1.** A wish or desire accompanied by expectation of its fulfillment. **2.** Something wished. **3.** One that gives cause for hope. —**hope'ful** *adj.* & *n.* —**hope'ful•ly** *adv.* —**hope'ful•ness** *n.* —**hope'less** *adj.* —**hope'less•ly** *adv.* —**hope'less•ness** *n.*

Ho•pi (hō'pē) *n., pl.* **-pi** *or* **-pis. 1.** A member of a Pueblo people of NE Arizona. **2.** Their Uto-Aztecan language.

hop•per (hŏp'ər) *n.* **1.** One that hops, esp. a hopping insect. **2.** A receptacle in which materials, as coal, grain, or ashes, are held in readiness for unloading or dispensing.

hop•scotch (hŏp'skŏch') *n.* A child's game in which a player throws an object, as a stone, into areas of a figure drawn on the ground and then hops through the areas to retrieve the object.

horde (hôrd, hōrd) *n.* A large crowd.

hore•hound (hôr'hound', hōr'-) *n.* An aromatic Eurasian plant, *Marrubium vulgare,* with leaves that yield a bitter extract used as flavoring esp. in candy.

ho•ri•zon (hə-rī'zən) *n.* **1.** The line along which the earth and sky appear to meet. **2.** Range or limit of knowledge, experience, or interest.

hor•i•zon•tal (hôr'ĭ-zŏn'tl, hŏr'-) *adj.* Parallel to the horizon. —**hor'i•zon'tal** *n.* —**hor'i•zon'tal•ly** *adv.*

hor•mone (hôr'mōn') *n.* A product of living cells that is carried, as by the bloodstream, to other cells, which it stimulates by chemical action. —**hor•mon'al** *adj.*

horn (hôrn) *n.* **1.** One of the bony, curved, usu. permanent projections on the heads of certain hoofed mammals, as cattle or antelopes. **2.** Something that resembles a horn. **3.** The hard, smooth substance forming the outer covering of the horns, as of cattle. **4.** A brass wind instrument, esp. a French horn. **5.** A signaling device that produces a loud sound <a car *horn*> —**horn in.** To join in without being invited : intrude. —**horn'less** *adj.* —**horn'y** *adj.*

horned toad *n.* A short-tailed lizard of the genus *Phrynosoma,* of W North America and Central America, with hornlike projections on the head and a flattened, spiny body.

hor•net (hôr'nĭt) *n.* Any of various large stinging wasps, esp. of the genera *Vespa* and *Vespula,* that build large, papery nests.

horn of plenty *n.* A cornucopia.

horn•pipe (hôrn'pīp') *n.* An animated, vigorous British folk dance.

horn•pout (hôrn'pout') *n.* A freshwater catfish, *Ictalurus nebulosus* or *Ameiurus nebulosus* , with a large head bearing barbels.

†**horn•swog•gle** (hôrn'swŏg'əl) *v.* **-gled, -gling.** *Regional.* To bamboozle : deceive.

ho•rol•o•gy (hə-rŏl'ə-jē) *n.* **1.** The science of measuring time. **2.** The art of making timepieces. —**hor'o•log'i•cal** (hôr'ə-lŏj'ĭ-kəl, hŏr'-) *adj.* —**ho•rol'o•gist** *n.*

hor•o•scope (hôr'ə-skōp', hŏr'-) *n.* **1.** A chart of the relative positions of the planets and signs of the zodiac at a given moment, as that of a person's birth, used by astrologers esp. to foretell future events. **2.** A forecast based on a horoscope.

hor•ren•dous (hô-rĕn'dəs, hə-) *adj.* Dreadful. —**hor•ren'dous•ly** *adv.*

hor•ri•ble (hôr'ə-bəl, hŏr'-) *adj.* **1.** Arousing or marked by horror. **2.** Extremely disagreeable : offensive <a *horrible* taste> —**hor'ri•bly** *adv.*

hor•rid (hôr'ĭd, hŏr'-) *adj.* **1.** HORRIBLE 1. **2.** HORRIBLE 2. —**hor'rid•ly** *adv.*

hor•rif•ic (hô-rĭf'ĭk, hŏ-) *adj.* Terrifying. —**hor•rif'i•cal•ly** *adv.*

hor•ri•fy (hôr'ə-fī', hŏr'-) *v.* **-fied, -fy•ing. 1.** To cause to experience a feeling of horror. **2.** To shock or dismay <We were *horrified* by the expense.>

hor•ror (hôr'ər, hŏr'-) *n.* **1.** An intense and painful feeling of revulsion, terror, or dread. **2.** Intense dislike : loathing. **3.** One that causes a feeling of horror. **4.** *Informal.* Something unpleasant or ugly <That tie is a *horror!*>

hors de com•bat (ôr' də kôN-bä') *adj.* & *adv.* Out of action : incapacitated.

hors d'oeuvre (ôr dûrv') *n., pl.* **hors d'oeuvres** (ôr dûrvz') *or* **hors d'oeuvre.** An appetizer served before a meal.

horse (hôrs) *n.* **1.** A large, hoofed quadruped mammal, *Equus caballus,* with a long mane and tail, used for riding and for pulling vehicles or carrying loads. **2.** A supporting frame or device consisting of a crossbar and 4 legs. **3.** A piece of gymnastic equipment used esp. for vaulting.

horse•back (hôrs'băk') *adv.* On the back of a horse <ride *horseback*>

horse chestnut *n.* Any of several Eurasian trees of the genus *Aesculus,* esp. *A. hippocastanum,* with spikes of white flowers and shiny nuts enclosed in a spiny bur.

horse•flesh (hôrs'flĕsh') *n.* Horses as a group, esp. for driving, riding, or racing.

horse•fly (hôrs'flī') *n.* A large fly of the family Tabanidae, the female of which sucks the blood of various mammals.

horse•hair (hôrs'hâr') *n.* **1.** The hair from a horse's mane or tail. **2.** Stiff cloth made of horsehair.

horse•hide (hôrs'hīd') *n.* **1.** The hide of a horse. **2.** *Informal.* A baseball.

horse•laugh (hôrs'lăf', -läf') *n.* A loud, raucous laugh.

horse•man (hôrs'mən) *n.* A man who rides a horse or breeds and raises horses. —**horse'man•ship'** *n.*

horse•play (hôrs'plā') *n.* Rowdy, boisterous play.

horse•pow•er (hôrs'pou'ər) *n.* A unit of power equal to 745.7 watts or 33,000 ft-lb per min.

horse•rad•ish (hôrs'răd'ĭsh) *n.* A Eurasian plant, *Armoracia rusticana* or *A. lapathifolia,* with a pungent white root used as a condiment.

horse sense *n. Informal.* Native good judgment **:** common sense.

horse•shoe (hôrs′sho͞o′, hôrsh′-) *n.* **1.** A protective U-shaped iron plate nailed to the rim of a horse's hoof. **2. horseshoes** *(sing. in number).* A game whose object is to encircle a stake with tossed horseshoes.

horseshoe crab *n.* A marine arthropod of the class Merostomata, of E North America, with a rounded body and a stiff pointed tail.

horse•tail (hôrs′tāl′) *n.* A nonflowering, narrow-leaved plant of the genus *Equisetum,* having a jointed, hollow stem.

horse•whip (hôrs′hwĭp′, -wĭp′) *n.* A whip for controlling a horse. **—horse′whip′** *v.*

horse•wom•an (hôrs′wo͝om′ən) *n.* A woman who rides a horse or breeds and raises horses.

hors•y *also* **hors•ey** (hôr′sē) *adj.* **-i•er, -i•est. 1.** Of or resembling a horse. **2.** Relating to or interested in horses and racing.

hor•ta•to•ry (hôr′tə-tôr′ē, -tōr′ē) *adj.* Marked by or given to exhortation.

hor•ti•cul•ture (hôr′tĭ-kŭl′chər) *n.* The science or art of raising and tending plants, esp. garden plants. **—hor′ti•cul′tur•al** *adj.* **—hor′ti•cul′tur•ist** *n.*

ho•san•na (hō-zăn′ə) *interj.* —Used to praise or glorify God.

hose (hōz) *n.* **1.** *pl.* **hose.** Stockings and socks. **2.** *pl.* **hos•es.** A flexible tube for carrying fluids or gases under pressure. —*v.* **hosed, hos•ing.** To water, wash, or squirt with a hose.

Ho•se•a (hō-zē′ə, -zā′ə) *n.* —See table at BIBLE.

ho•sier•y (hō′zhə-rē) *n.* Stockings and socks.

hos•pice (hŏs′pĭs) *n.* **1.** A shelter or lodging for travelers or the needy. **2.** An establishment caring for the physical and emotional needs of terminally ill patients.

hos•pi•ta•ble (hŏs′pĭ-tə-bəl, hŏ-spĭt′ə-bəl) *adj.* **1.** Treating guests with warmth and generosity. **2.** Not narrow-minded **:** receptive. **—hos′pi•ta•bly** *adv.*

hos•pi•tal (hŏs′pĭ-təl, -pĭt′l) *n.* An institution where the sick and injured receive medical, surgical, and emergency care.

hos•pi•tal•i•ty (hŏs′pĭ-tăl′ĭ-tē) *n., pl.* **-ties.** Hospitable reception, treatment, or inclination.

hos•pi•tal•ize (hŏs′pĭt′l-īz′) *v.* **-ized, -iz•ing.** To admit to a hospital for care or treatment. **—hos′pi•tal•i•za′tion** *n.*

host[1] (hōst) *n.* **1.** One who receives and entertains guests. **2.** *Biol.* A living organism, as an animal or plant, on or in which a parasite lives. **—host** *v.*

host[2] (hōst) *n.* **1.** An army. **2.** A large number **:** multitude.

host[3] *also* **Host** (hōst) *n.* The consecrated bread of the Eucharist.

hos•tage (hŏs′tĭj) *n.* A person held as security pending the fulfillment of certain terms.

hos•tel (hŏs′təl) *n.* **1.** A supervised, low-priced lodging esp. for young travelers. **2.** An inn or hotel. **—hos′tel•er** *n.*

hos•tel•ry (hŏs′təl-rē) *n., pl.* **-ries.** A lodging, as an inn or hotel.

host•ess (hō′stĭs) *n.* **1.** A woman who receives and entertains guests. **2.** A woman who greets patrons, as in a restaurant.

hos•tile (hŏs′təl, -tīl′) *adj.* **1.** Of or relating to an enemy. **2.** Experiencing or expressing antagonism. **—hos′tile•ly** *adv.*

hos•til•i•ty (hŏ-stĭl′ĭ-tē) *n., pl.* **-ties. 1.** Deep-seated hatred or oppositon **:** antagonism. **2. a.** A hostile act or incident. **b. hostilities.** Open warfare.

hos•tler (hŏs′lər) *n.* One who stables and cares for horses, as at an inn.

hot (hŏt) *adj.* **hot•ter, hot•test. 1.** Marked by or giving off great heat. **b.** Being at or marked by a high temperature. **2.** Abnormally, uncomfortably, or undesirably warm. **3.** Very pungent. **4. a.** Electrically charged <a *hot* wire> **b.** Radioactive, esp. to a hazardous degree. **5.** Marked by emotional warmth **:** ardent. **6.** *Slang.* Recently and unlawfully acquired <a *hot* car> **7.** *Informal.* **a.** Newly produced or obtained <*hot* news> **b.** Arousing intense interest <a *hot* topic> **8.** *Slang.* Having or marked by exceptional skill. **—hot** *adv.* **—hot′ly** *adv.* **—hot′ness** *n.*

hot air *n. Slang.* Vain or idle talk.

hot•bed (hŏt′bĕd′) *n.* **1.** A glass-covered, heated bed of soil used esp. for raising seedlings. **2.** An environment conducive to rapid and excessive growth, esp. of something negative <a *hotbed* of rumors>

hot-blood•ed (hŏt′blŭd′ĭd) *adj.* Easily excited **:** passionate. **—hot′-blood′ed•ly** *adv.* **—hot′-blood′ed•ness** *n.*

hot•box (hŏt′bŏks′) *n.* An overheated axle or journal bearing, as on a railway car.

hot cake *n.* A pancake.

hot dog *n.* A heated frankfurter usu. served in a long roll.

ho•tel (hō-tĕl′) *n.* A public establishment providing lodging and often meals, entertainment, and other services.

hot flash *n.* A transient vasomotor symptom of menopause involving dilation of the skin capillaries and the sensation of heat.

hot•foot (hŏt′fo͝ot′) *v.* To hasten.

hot•head•ed (hŏt′hĕd′ĭd) *adj.* **1.** Having a fiery temper. **2.** Recklessly impulsive. **—hot′head′** *n.* **—hot′head′ed•ly** *adv.* **—hot′head′ed•ness** *n.*

hot•house (hŏt′hous′) *n.* A heated greenhouse for raising plants.

hot line *n.* A direct communications line for use in a crisis.

hot plate *n.* A portable, often electric appliance for heating or cooking food.

hot potato *n.* An issue or problem that entails embarrassing or unpleasant consequences for anyone handling it.

hot rod *n.* An automobile rebuilt or modified for greater power and speed. **—hot rod•der** *n.*

hot seat *n. Slang.* **1.** The electric chair. **2.** A position of difficulty or stress.

hot•shot (hŏt′shŏt′) *n. Slang.* One who ostentatiously displays skill or expertise.

hot tub *n.* A large tub filled with hot water for bathing or soaking.
hot-wire (hŏt'wīr') *v. Informal.* To start the engine of (e.g., an automobile) without a key, as by short-circuiting the ignition system.
hound (hound) *n.* **1.** Any of several kinds of long-eared dogs orig. bred and used for hunting. **2.** A devotee. —*v.* **1.** To pursue without letup. **2.** To nag constantly.
hour (our) *n.* **1.** One of the 24 parts of a day. **2.** The time of day as indicated on a timepiece. **3. a.** A customary time <lunch *hour*> **b. hours.** A specific period of time <office *hours*>
hour·glass (our'glăs') *n.* A 2-chambered glass instrument with a narrow connecting neck that measures the passage of an hour by the trickling of sand or mercury from one chamber to the other.
hou·ri (ho͝or'ē) *n., pl.* **-ris.** One of the beautiful young maidens of the Koranic paradise.
hour·ly (our'lē) *adj.* **1. a.** Done or occurring every hour. **b.** Recurring frequently. **2.** By the hour <*hourly* wages> —**hour'ly** *adv.*
house (hous) *n., pl.* **hous·es** (hou'zĭz). **1. a.** A residential building occupied by one or more families. **b.** A household. **2. a.** A building used for a given purpose, as entertainment. **b.** The audience or patrons of such a place. **3.** A business firm. **4.** A legislative body. —*v.* (houz) **housed, hous·ing. 1.** To provide with lodgings or work space. **2.** To shelter or store. **3.** To serve as shelter for : contain.
house·boat (hous'bōt') *n.* A barge equipped for use as a home.
house·break·ing (hous'brā'kĭng) *n.* The act of breaking into another's house for the purpose of committing a felony. —**house'-break'er** *n.*
house·bro·ken (hous'brō'kən) *adj.* Trained, as a dog, in habits of excretion appropriate to indoor living.
house·coat (hous'kōt') *n.* A woman's often long-skirted robe for wear at home.
house·fly (hous'flī') *n.* A common fly, *Musca domestica,* that is found in and around human dwellings and is a carrier of a wide variety of diseases.
house·hold (hous'hōld') *n.* A unit comprising a family and others who share the same living space. —*adj.* **1.** Domestic. **2.** Commonplace. —**house'hold'er** *n.*
house·hus·band (hous'hŭz'bənd) *n.* A husband who manages the household while his wife earns the family income.
house·keep·er (hous'kē'pər) *n.* One employed to direct or perform the domestic tasks in a household. —**house'keep'ing** *n.*
house·maid (hous'mād') *n.* A woman employed to do housework.
house·moth·er (hous'mŭ*th*'ər) *n.* A woman who supervises a residence, as a dormitory, for young people.
house·warm·ing (hous'wôr'mĭng) *n.* A party to celebrate the recent occupancy of a residence.
house·wife (hous'wīf') *n.* **1.** A married woman who manages the affairs of a household. **2.** (hŭz'ĭf). A small container for sewing equipment, as needles and thread. —**house'wife'li·ness** *n.* —**house'wife'ly** *adj.* —**house'wif'er·y** *n.*
house·work (hous'wûrk') *n.* Household tasks, esp. cleaning.
hous·ing (hou'zĭng) *n.* **1.** Habitations for people. **2.** A dwelling place. **3.** Something that covers, protects, or supports.
hove (hōv) *v. Naut. p.t. & p.p. of* HEAVE.
hov·el (hŭv'əl, hŏv'-) *n.* A small, wretchedly squalid dwelling : hut.
hov·er (hŭv'ər, hŏv'-) *v.* **1.** To fly, soar, or float suspended in the air. **2.** To remain or linger close by. **3.** To waver : vacillate. —**hov'-er·er** *n.* —**hov'er·ing·ly** *adv.*
how (hou) *adv.* **1.** In what manner or way <*How* do you spell it?> **2.** In what condition or state <*How* is your mother?> **3.** To what extent, degree, or amount <*How* efficient is she?> **4.** For what reason <*How* can you be so sad?> **5.** With what meaning <*How* should we interpret that remark?> —*conj.* **1.** In what manner or state <don't know *how* they did it> **2.** In whatever way : however <do it *how* you like> —**how come.** *Informal.* For what reason : why <*How come* we can't go?>
how·dah (hou'də) *n.* A usu. canopied seat on the back of an elephant or camel.
†**how·dy** (hou'dē) *interj. Regional.* —Used to express greeting.
how·ev·er (hou-ev'ər) *adv.* **1.** By whatever manner or means. **2.** To whatever extent or degree. —*conj.* Nevertheless.
how·it·zer (hou'ĭt-sər) *n.* A short cannon that fires shells at a high angle.
howl (houl) *v.* **1.** To utter a long, loud, plaintive sound characteristic of wolves. **2.** To cry loudly : wail. —**howl** *n.*
howl·er (hou'lər) *n.* **1.** One that howls. **2.** An absurd or amusing mistake.
how·so·ev·er (hou'sō-ev'ər) *adv.* **1.** To whatever extent or degree. **2.** By whatever means.
hoy·den (hoid'n) *n.* A lively, boisterous, or saucy girl or young woman.
hua·ra·che (wə-rä'chē, hə-) *n.* A flat-heeled sandal with woven leather strips on the upper part.
hub (hŭb) *n.* **1. a.** The center of a wheel. **b.** The center of a fan or propeller. **2.** A focus of activity.
hub·bub (hŭb'ŭb') *n.* Noisy uproar or confusion : tumult.
hub·cap (hŭb'kăp') *n.* A removable metal cap fitting over the hub of an automobile wheel.
hu·bris (hyo͞o'brĭs) *n.* Excessive self-confidence : arrogance. —**hu·bris'tic** *adj.*
huck·le·ber·ry (hŭk'əl-bĕr'ē) *n.* A New World shrub of the genus *Gaylussacia,* related to the blueberries and bearing glossy, blackish, many-seeded edible berries.
huck·ster (hŭk'stər) *n.* **1.** One that peddles goods : hawker. **2.** *Slang.* An advertising copywriter.
hud·dle (hŭd'l) *n.* **1.** A closely packed group or crowd. **2.** *Football.* A brief gathering of

teammates to prepare signals for the next play. 3. A private meeting or conference. —*v.* **-dled, -dling. 1.** To consult : confer.
2. To consult : confer.

hue (hyōō) *n.* **1.** The characteristic of color that allows it to be categorized on a scale running from red through yellow, green, and blue to violet. **2.** A particular color : shade. **3.** Color <sunset *hues*> —**hued** *adj.*

hue and cry *n.* A vehement public outcry or protest.

huff (hŭf) *n.* A fit of ill temper or resentment. —*v.* To breathe heavily, as from exertion. —**huff′i·ly** *adv.* —**huff′i·ness** *n.* —**huf′fy** *adj.*

hug (hŭg) *v.* **hugged, hug·ging. 1.** To clasp closely : embrace. **2.** To cling, keep, or stay close to. —**hug** *n.* —**hug′ga·ble** *adj.* —**hug′ger** *n.*

huge (hyōōj) *adj.* **hug·er, hug·est.** Of great size, quantity, or extent : immense. —**huge′ly** *adv.* —**huge′ness** *n.*

Hu·gue·not (hyōō′gə-nŏt′) *n.* A French Protestant of the 16th and 17th cent.

hu·la (hōō′lə) *n.* A Hawaiian dance marked by undulating movements of the hips, arms, and hands.

hulk (hŭlk) *n.* **1.** A heavy, bulky ship. **2.** An old, dilapidated ship. **3.** One that is massive, unwieldy, or awkward. —*v.* To bulk : loom.

hulk·ing (hŭl′kĭng) *adj.* Unwieldy or bulky : massive.

hull (hŭl) *n.* **1. a.** The cluster of leaflets at the stem end of certain fruits. **b.** The outer husk or pod of certain seeds, nuts, and fruits. **2.** The framework of a ship. **3.** The external casing of a rocket, guided missile, or spaceship. —*v.* To remove the hulls from <*hull* strawberries>

hul·la·ba·loo (hŭl′ə-bə-lōō′) *n.* Great uproar or noisy excitement.

hul·lo (hə-lō′) *interj. & n. var. of* HELLO.

hum (hŭm) *v.* **hummed, hum·ming. 1.** To emit or produce a continuous low-pitched sound : drone. **2.** To be full of or alive with activity. **3.** To sing with the lips closed. —**hum** *n.* —**hum′mer** *n.*

hu·man (hyōō′mən) *adj.* **1.** Of or typical of human beings. **2.** Having human qualities or form. **3.** Composed of people <made a *human* blockade> —*n.* A human being. —**hu′man·ly** *adv.* —**hu′man·ness** *n.*

human being *n.* **1.** A member of the genus *Homo* and esp. of the species *H. sapiens.* **2.** A person.

hu·mane (hyōō-mān′) *adj.* **1.** Compassionate : merciful. **2.** Emphasizing human values and concerns. —**hu·mane′ly** *adv.* —**hu·mane′ness** *n.*

hu·man·ism (hyōō′mə-nĭz′əm) *n.* **1.** A philosophy or attitude centered chiefly on the values, interests, and potential of human beings. **2.** *often* **Humanism.** The shift to secular concerns that resulted from the study of the Greek and Roman classics during the Renaissance. —**hu′man·ist** *n.* —**hu′man·is′tic** *adj.*

hu·man·i·tar·i·an (hyōō-măn′ĭ-târ′ē-ən) *n.* One promoting human welfare, esp. through philanthropy. —**hu·man′i·tar′i·an** *adj.* —**hu·man′i·tar′i·an·ism** *n.*

hu·man·i·ty (hyōō-măn′ĭ-tē) *n., pl.* **-ties. 1.** Human beings as a group : humankind. **2.** The quality, state, or fact of being human. **3.** The quality of being humane : kindness. **4. humanities.** The cultural as distinguished from the scientific branches of learning.

hu·man·ize (hyōō′mə-nīz′) *v.* **-ized, -iz·ing. 1.** To endow with human form or qualities. **2.** To make humane. —**hu′man·i·za′tion** *n.*

hu·man·kind (hyōō′mən-kīnd′) *n.* Human beings as a group : the human race.

hu·man·oid (hyōō′mə-noid′) *adj.* Nearly human, as in appearance. —*n.* An android.

hum·ble (hŭm′bəl) *adj.* **-bler, -blest. 1.** Marked by modesty or meekness. **2.** Respectfully deferential. **3.** Lowly and unpretentious. —*v.* **-bled, -bling. 1.** To make humble. **2.** To lower in status or condition. **3.** To humiliate. —**hum′ble·ness** *n.* —**hum′bler** *n.* —**hum′bly** *adv.*

hum·bug (hŭm′bŭg′) *n.* **1.** A fraud : hoax. **2.** Foolish talk. —*v.* **-bugged, -bug·ging.** To deceive. —**hum′bug′ger·y** *n.*

hum·din·ger (hŭm′dĭng′ər) *n. Slang.* One that is markedly superior.

hum·drum (hŭm′drŭm′) *adj.* Monotonous : boring.

hu·mer·us (hyōō′mər-əs) *n., pl.* **-mer·i** (-mə-rī′). The long bone of the upper arm in humans. —**hu′mer·al** *adj.*

hu·mid (hyōō′mĭd) *adj.* Marked by a large amount of moisture : damp.

hu·mid·i·fy (hyōō-mĭd′ə-fī′) *v.* **-fied, -fy·ing.** To make humid. —**hu·mid′i·fi′er** *n.*

hu·mid·i·ty (hyōō-mĭd′ĭ-tē) *n.* **1.** Dampness. **2.** The amount of moisture in the atmosphere.

hu·mi·dor (hyōō′mĭ-dôr′) *n.* A container for cigars in which the air is kept humidified by a special device.

hu·mil·i·ate (hyōō-mĭl′ē-āt′) *v.* **-at·ed, -at·ing.** To injure the dignity or pride of : humble. —**hu·mil′i·at′ing·ly** *adv.* —**hu·mil′i·a′tion** *n.*

hu·mil·i·ty (hyōō-mĭl′ĭ-tē) *n.* The quality or state of being humble.

hum·ming·bird (hŭm′ĭng-bûrd′) *n.* A very small New World bird of the family Trochil-

hummingbird

idae, with brilliant plumage and a long, slender bill.

hum•mock (hŭm'ək) *n.* A low, rounded hill or mound, as of earth or snow. —**hum'mock•y** *adj.*

hum•mus (ho͝om'əs, hŭm'-) *n.* A thick dip or spread made of mashed chickpeas, tahini, oil, lemon juice, and garlic.

hu•mor (hyo͞o'mər) *n.* **1.** The quality of being funny or comical. **2.** The ability to perceive, enjoy, or express what is funny or comical. **3. a.** A state of mind or feeling : mood. **b.** Characteristic disposition : temperament. **4.** A sudden whim : caprice. **5.** *Physiol.* A bodily fluid, as blood or lymph. —*v.* To indulge the wishes or mood of. —**hu'mor•ist** *n.* —**hu'mor•less** *adj.* —**hu'mor•less•ly** *adv.* —**hu'mor•less•ness** *n.* —**hu'mor•ous** *adj.* —**hu'mor•ous•ly** *adv.* —**hu'mor•ous•ness** *n.*

hu•mour (hyo͞o'mər) *n. & v. esp. Brit. var. of* HUMOR.

hump (hŭmp) *n.* **1.** A rounded lump or protuberance, as on the back of a camel. **2.** HUMPBACK 1. —**over the hump.** Past the critical or most difficult stage.

hump•back (hŭmp'băk') *n.* **1.** An abnormal condition in which the back has a hump or curvature. **2.** A person with a humpback. —**hump'backed'** *adj.*

hu•mus (hyo͞o'məs) *n.* The dark-colored organic part of soil consisting of decayed plant and animal matter.

Hun (hŭn) *n.* **1.** One of a nomadic Mongolian people who invaded Europe in the 5th cent. A.D. **2.** *often* **hun.** A barbarous person.

hunch (hŭnch) *n.* An intuitive feeling. —*v.* **1.** To bend or draw up into a hump. **2.** To push or thrust oneself forward.

hunch•back (hŭnch'băk') *n.* **1.** A person whose back is hunched due to abnormal curvature of the upper spine. **2.** An abnormally humped back. —**hunch'backed'** *adj.*

hun•dred (hŭn'drĭd) *n., pl.* **-dreds** *or* **-dred.** The cardinal number equal to 10×10 or 10^2. —**hun'dred** *adj. & pron.* —**hun'dredth** *n. & adj. & adv.*

hun•dred•weight (hŭn'drĭd-wāt') *n., pl.* **-weight** *or* **-weights. 1.** A unit of weight equal to approx. 45.36 kg or 100 lb. **2.** *esp. Brit.* A unit of weight equal to approx. 50.8 kg or 112 lb.

hung (hŭng) *v. p.t. & p.p. of* HANG.

hun•ger (hŭng'gər) *n.* **1.** A strong need or desire for food. **2.** A strong craving <a *hunger* for praise> —**hun'ger** *v.* —**hun'gri•ly** *adv.* —**hun'gry** *adj.*

hunk (hŭngk) *n. Informal.* A large piece.

†**hun•ker** (hŭng'kər) *v.* To crouch close to the ground : squat. —*n.* **hunkers.** *Regional.* The haunches.

hun•ky-do•ry (hŭng'kē-dôr'ē, -dōr'ē) *adj. Slang.* Generally satisfactory : fine.

hunt (hŭnt) *v.* **1. a.** To pursue (game) for food or sport. **b.** To make a search (for) : seek. **2.** To chase and try to capture (e.g., a criminal). **3.** To travel over or through in search of prey. —*n.* **1.** The act or sport of hunting. **2. a.** A hunting expedition. **b.** The participants in a hunting expedition. —**hunt'er** *n.* —**hunt'ress** *n.*

hunts•man (hŭnts'mən) *n.* One who hunts, esp. one who has charge of the hounds for a hunt.

hur•dle (hûr'dl) *n.* **1.** A movable barrier to be jumped over in a race. **2.** An obstacle to be overcome. —*v.* **-dled, -dling. 1.** To leap over (a barrier). **2.** To surmount (an obstacle). —**hur'dler** *n.*

hur•dy-gur•dy (hûr'dē-gûr'dē, hûr'dē-gûr'-) *n., pl.* **-dies.** A musical instrument, as a barrel organ, played by turning a crank.

hurl (hûrl) *v.* **1.** To throw forcefully : fling. **2.** To utter with intensity. **3.** *Baseball.* To pitch. **4.** To move very rapidly : hurtle. —**hurl** *n.* —**hurl'er** *n.*

hur•ly-bur•ly (hûr'lē-bûr'lē) *n., pl.* **-lies.** Uproar : turmoil.

hur•rah (ho͝o-rä', -rô') *interj.* —Used to express pleasure, approval, or exultation. —**hur•rah'** *n. & v.*

hur•ri•cane (hûr'ĭ-kān', hŭr'-) *n.* A severe tropical cyclone with winds exceeding 75 mph.

hur•ry (hûr'ē, hŭr'ē) *v.* **-ried, -ry•ing. 1.** To move or cause to move speedily or hastily. **2.** To act or urge to act with excessive haste : rush. —*n., pl.* **-ries. 1.** The act of hurrying. **2.** A condition of urgency : rush. —**hur'ried•ly** *adv.* —**hur'ried•ness** *n.*

hurt (hûrt) *v.* **hurt, hurt•ing. 1.** To experience or cause to experience physical pain or emotional distress. **2.** To cause harm to : damage. **3.** To offend. —*n.* **1.** A bodily pain or injury. **2.** Mental suffering. **3.** Damage : harm. —**hurt'ful** *adj.*

hur•tle (hûr'tl) *v.* **-tled, -tling. 1.** To move very swiftly, esp. with a rushing sound. **2.** To hurl or fling forcefully.

hus•band (hŭz'bənd) *n.* A man who is married. —*v.* To use or manage wisely.

hus•band•man (hŭz'bənd-mən) *n.* One engaged in farming : farmer.

hus•band•ry (hŭz'bən-drē) *n.* **1.** Agriculture. **2.** Wise management of resources.

hush (hŭsh) *v.* **1.** To make or become quiet. **2.** To make or become calm. **3.** To keep secret : suppress. —*n.* Silence.

hush-hush (hŭsh'hŭsh') *adj. Informal.* Confidential : secret.

hush•pup•py (hŭsh'pŭp'ē) *n.* A small round cornmeal fritter fried in deep fat.

husk (hŭsk) *n.* **1.** The dry or leaflike outer envelope of certain vegetables, fruits, and seeds. **2.** An often worthless external layer or shell. —*v.* To remove the husk from <*husk* corn> —**husk'er** *n.*

husk•y[1] (hŭs'kē) *adj.* **-i•er, -i•est.** Having a hoarse or grating sound. —**husk'i•ly** *adv.* —**husk'i•ness** *n.*

husk•y[2] (hŭs'kē) *adj.* **-i•er, -i•est.** Strong and ruggedly built. —**husk'i•ness** *n.*

hus•ky[3] (hŭs'kē) *n., pl.* **-kies.** A thick-coated Arctic dog used esp. to pull sleds.

hus•sar (hŏŏ-zär', -sär') *n.* A member of the light cavalry in some European armies.
hus•sy (hŭz'ē, hŭs'ē) *n., pl.* **-sies. 1.** An impertinent or mischievous girl. **2.** A brazen or immoral woman.
hus•tings (hŭs'tĭngz) *pl.n. (sing. or pl. in number).* **1.** A political campaign. **2.** A place for political campaign speeches.
hus•tle (hŭs'əl) *v.* **-tled, -tling. 1.** To push roughly : jostle. **2.** To move or urge hurriedly along. **3.** To work quickly and busily. **4.** *Slang.* To make energetic efforts to solicit business or make money. **—hus'tle** *n.* **—hus'tler** *n.*
hut (hŭt) *n.* A small, often crudely built and temporary dwelling : shack.
hutch (hŭch) *n.* **1.** A pen for small animals. **2.** A low cupboard with drawers and usu. open shelving on top. **3.** A shack : hut.
huz•za *also* **huz•zah** (hə-zä') *Archaic. interj.* —Used to express joy, approval, or exultation. **—huz•za'** *n.*
hy•a•cinth (hī'ə-sĭnth) *n.* A bulbous plant of the genus *Hyacinthus,* bearing a cluster of variously colored, highly fragrant bell-shaped flowers.
hy•brid (hī'brĭd) *n.* **1.** An offspring of genetically dissimilar animals or plants, as members of different varieties, species, or breeds. **2.** Something of mixed origin or make-up. **—hy'brid** *adj.*
hy•brid•ize (hī'brĭ-dīz') *v.* **-ized, -iz•ing.** To produce or cause to produce hybrids : crossbreed. **—hy'brid•i•za'tion** *n.*
hy•dra (hī'drə) *n., pl.* **-dras** *or* **-drae** (-drē). Any of various small freshwater polyps of the genus *Hydra,* with a tubular body and at one end an oral opening surrounded by tentacles.

hydra

hy•dran•gea (hī-drān'jə, -drăn'-) *n.* A shrub or tree of the genus *Hydrangea,* bearing large, flat-topped or rounded white, pink, or blue flower clusters.
hy•drant (hī'drənt) *n.* A standing pipe with a valve and spout for drawing water from a water main : fireplug.
hy•drate (hī'drāt') *n.* A chemical compound formed by the combination of water with another substance in definite proportions. —*v.* **-drat•ed, -drat•ing.** To form a hydrate. **—hy•dra'tion** *n.*
hy•drau•lic (hī-drô'lĭk) *adj.* **1.** Of, involving, moved by, or operated by a pressurized liquid, esp. water. **2.** Of or pertaining to hydraulics. **3.** Hardening under water, as Portland cement.
hy•drau•lics (hī-drô'lĭks) *n. (sing. in number).* The scientific study and technological application of the behavior of fluids.
hy•dro•car•bon (hī'drə-kär'bən) *n.* An organic compound, as methane, that contains only hydrogen and carbon.
hy•dro•ceph•a•lus (hī'drō-sĕf'ə-ləs) *also* **hy•dro•ceph•a•ly** (-lē) *n.* An abnormal accumulation of fluid in the cerebral ventricles that causes skull enlargement and brain atrophy. **—hy'dro•ce•phal'ic** (-sə-făl'ĭk) *adj.*
hy•dro•chlo•ric acid (hī'drə-klôr'ĭk, -klōr'-) *n.* A colorless, fuming, poisonous solution of hydrogen chloride in water.
hy•dro•dy•nam•ics (hī'drō-dī-năm'ĭks) *n. (sing. in number).* The science of the characteristics of fluids in motion, esp. fluids that cannot be compressed.
hy•dro•e•lec•tric (hī'drō-ĭ-lĕk'trĭk) *adj.* Of, pertaining to, or using electricity produced by the power of running water. **—hy'dro•e•lec•tric'i•ty** (-trĭs'ĭ-tē) *n.*
hy•dro•foil (hī'drə-foil') *n.* **1.** A winglike blade attached to the hull of a boat below the water line to raise it clear of the water for fuel-efficient operation at high speed. **2.** A boat having hydrofoils.
hy•dro•gen (hī'drə-jən) *n. Symbol* **H** A colorless, highly flammable gas that is the lightest of the chemical elements. **—hy•drog'e•nous** (-drŏj'ə-nəs) *adj.*
hy•dro•gen•ate (hī'drə-jə-nāt', hī-drŏj'ə-) *v.* **-at•ed, -at•ing. 1.** To treat or combine chemically with hydrogen. **2.** To treat (a liquid vegetable oil) with hydrogen and convert it to a solid fat. **—hy'dro•gen•a'tion** *n.*
hydrogen bomb *n.* An extremely destructive bomb whose explosive power is obtained from the rapid release of atomic energy in the fusion of hydrogen and lithium nuclei.
hydrogen peroxide *n.* A colorless, unstable, strongly oxidizing liquid compound used esp. in solution as an antiseptic.
hy•drol•y•sis (hī-drŏl'ĭ-sĭs) *n.* Decomposition of a chemical compound by reaction with the elements of water. **—hy'dro•lize'** (hī'drə-līz') *v.* **—hy'dro•lyt'ic** (-lĭt'ĭk) *adj.*
hy•drom•e•ter (hī-drŏm'ĭ-tər) *n.* An instrument for measuring the specific gravity of a fluid.
hy•dro•pho•bi•a (hī'drə-fō'bē-ə) *n.* **1.** Pathological fear of water. **2.** Rabies. **—hy'dro•pho'bic** *adj.*
hy•dro•plane (hī'drə-plān') *n.* **1.** A seaplane. **2.** A speedboat designed so that the prow and much of the hull lift out of the water and skim the surface at high speeds. **—hy'dro•plane** *v.*
hy•dro•pon•ics (hī'drə-pŏn'ĭks) *n. (sing. in number).* The cultivation of plants in a water and mineral solution. **—hy'dro•pon'ic** *adj.* **—hy'dro•pon'i•cal•ly** *adv.*
hy•dro•stat•ics (hī'drə-stăt'ĭks) *n. (sing. in*

number). The science of the characteristics of fluids at rest, esp. fluids that cannot be compressed. —**hy'dro•stat'ic, hy'dro•stat'i•cal** *adj.*

hy•dro•ther•a•py (hī'drə-thĕr'ə-pē) *n.* The use of water in the treatment of disease or disability.

hy•drous (hī'drəs) *adj.* Containing water, esp. when chemically combined.

hy•drox•ide (hī-drŏk'sīd') *n.* A chemical compound of an element or radical joined to an oxygen-and-hydrogen group.

hy•e•na (hī-ē'nə) *n.* Any of several carnivorous mammals of the genera *Hyaena* or *Crocuta,* of Africa and Asia, with coarse hair and powerful jaws.

hy•giene (hī'jēn') *n.* **1.** The science concerned with maintenance of sound health and prevention of disease. **2.** Conditions and practices that contribute to disease prevention. —**hy'gi•en'ic** (-jē-ĕn'ĭk) *adj.* —**hy'gi•en'i•cal•ly** *adv.* —**hy•gien'ist** *n.*

hy•grom•e•ter (hī-grŏm'ĭ-tər) *n.* An instrument that measures the amount of moisture in the air. —**hy•grom'e•try** *n.*

hy•ing (hī'ĭng) *v. var. pres. p. of* HIE.

hy•men (hī'mən) *n.* A thin membrane partly closing the external vaginal orifice.

hy•me•ne•al (hī'mə-nē'əl) *adj.* Of or relating to a nuptial ceremony or marriage.

hymn (hĭm) *n.* A song of praise or thanksgiving, esp. to God. —**hymn** *v.*

hym•nal (hĭm'nəl) *n.* A book of hymns.

hype (hīp) *n. Slang.* **1.** Something intended to deceive. **2.** Exaggerated advertising or promotion. —**hype** *v.*

hyper– *pref.* **1.** Over **:** above <*hyper*sonic> **2.** Excessive **:** excessively <*hyper*sensitive>

hy•per•ac•tive (hī'pər-ăk'tĭv) *adj.* Excessively or abnormally active. —**hy'per•ac•tiv'i•ty** *n.*

hy•per•bo•la (hī-pûr'bə-lə) *n.* A plane curve that has 2 branches and is composed of the set of all points such that the difference of their distances from the 2 fixed points is a constant.

hy•per•bo•le (hī-pûr'bə-lē) *n.* Exaggeration used as a figure of speech.

hy•per•bol•ic (hī'pər-bŏl'ĭk) *or* **hy•per•bol•i•cal** (-ĭ-kəl) *adj.* **1.** Of or marked by hyperbole. **2.** Of or shaped like a hyperbola.

hy•per•crit•i•cal (hī'pər-krĭt'ĭ-kəl) *adj.* Overcritical. —**hy'per•crit'i•cal•ly** *adv.*

hy•per•sen•si•tive (hī'pər-sĕn'sĭ-tĭv) *adj.* Abnormally or excessively sensitive. —**hy'per•sen'si•tive•ness, hy'per•sen'si•tiv'i•ty** *n.*

hy•per•son•ic (hī'pər-sŏn'ĭk) *adj.* Of or relating to speed equal to or exceeding 5 times the speed of sound. —**hy'per•son'i•cal•ly** *adv.*

hy•per•ten•sion (hī'pər-tĕn'shən) *n.* A condition of abnormally high blood pressure. —**hy'per•ten'sive** *adj. & n.*

hy•per•text (hī'pər-tĕkst') *n.* A computer-based text retrieval system that provides access to information supplementing a particular text.

hy•per•thy•roid•ism (hī'pər-thī'roi-dĭz'əm) *n.* Abnormally excessive activity of the

hy'per•ac'cu•ra•cy *n.*
hy'per•ac'cu•rate *adj.*
hy'per•a•cute' *adj.*
hy'per•ag•gres'sive *adj.*
hy'per•a•lert' *adj.*
hy'per•al'tru•ism *n.*
hy'per•a•ware' *adj.*
hy'per•a•ware'ness *n.*
hy'per•cau'tious *adj.*
hy'per•civ'i•lized' *adj.*
hy'per•con'cen•tra'tion *n.*
hy'per•con'fi•dence *n.*
hy'per•con'fi•dent *adj.*
hy'per•con•form'ist *adj. & n.*
hy'per•con•form'i•ty *n.*
hy'per•con'sci•en'tious *adj.*
hy'per•con•ser'va•tive *adj. & n.*
hy'per•de•vel'oped *adj.*
hy'per•de•vel'op•ment *n.*
hy'per•dis•ten'tion *n.*
hy'per•e•mo'tive *adj.*
hy'per•en'er•get'ic *adj.*
hy'per•en•thu'si•asm *n.*
hy'per•en•thu'si•as'tic *adj.*
hy'per•ex•cit'a•bil'i•ty *n.*
hy'per•ex•cit'a•ble *adj.*
hy'per•ex•cit'ed *adj.*
hy'per•ex•cite'ment *n.*
hy'per•ex•cre'tion *n.*
hy'per•fem'i•nine *adj.*
hy'per•flex'ion *n.*
hy'per•func'tion•al *adj.*
hy'per•in•fla'tion *n.*
hy'per•in•fla'tion•ar'y *adj.*
hy'per•in'tel•lec'tu•al *adj. & n.*
hy'per•in•tel'li•gence *n.*
hy'per•in•tel'li•gent *adj.*
hy'per•mas'cu•line *adj.*
hy'per•met'a•bol'ic *adj.*
hy'per•me•tab'o•lism *n.*
hy'per•mil'i•tant *adj.*
hy'per•mod'ern *adj.*
hy'per•mod'ern•ist *adj. & n.*
hy'per•mo•der'ni•ty *n.*
hy'per•mo'tile *adj.*
hy'per•mo•til'i•ty *n.*
hy'per•mu'ta•ble *adj.*
hy'per•neu•rot'ic *adj. & n.*
hy'per•nu•tri'tion *n.*
hy'per•or'tho•dox' *adj.*
hy'per•ox'y•gen•ate' *v.*
hy'per•pa'tri•ot'ic *adj.*
hy'per•phys'i•cal *adj.*
hy'per•pig'men•ta'tion *n.*
hy'per•pig'ment•ed *adj.*
hy'per•pro•duc'tion *n.*
hy'per•pur'ist *adj. & n.*
hy'per•rad'i•cal *adj. & n.*
hy'per•ra'tion•al *adj.*
hy'per•re•ac'tive *adj.*
hy'per•re'ac•tiv'i•ty *n.*
hy'per•re'al•ism *n.*
hy'per•re'al•ist *adj. & n.*
hy'per•re'al•is'tic *adj.*
hy'per•res'o•nance *n.*
hy'per•res'o•nant *adj.*
hy'per•re•spon'sive *adj.*
hy'per•ro•man'tic *adj. & n.*
hy'per•sa'line' *adj.*
hy'per•sa•lin'i•ty *n.*
hy'per•sal'i•va'tion *n.*
hy'per•scru'pu•lous *adj.*
hy'per•se•cre'tion *n.*
hy'per•sen'si•bil'i•ty *n.*
hy'per•sen'si•tize' *v.*
hy'per•sen'ti•men'tal *adj.*
hy'per•so•phis'ti•cat'ed *adj.*
hy'per•spec'u•la•tive *adj.*
hy'per•stat'ic *adj.*
hy'per•sus•cep'ti•ble *adj.*
hy'per•sus•pi'cious *adj.*
hy'per•tech'ni•cal *adj.*
hy'per•tense' *adj.*
hy'per•ther'mal *adj.*
hy'per•tox'ic *adj.*
hy'per•tox•ic'i•ty *n.*
hy'per•var'i•a•bil'i•ty *n.*
hy'per•var'i•a•ble *adj.*
hy'per•vas'cu•lar'i•ty *n.*
hy'per•vig'i•lance *n.*
hy'per•vig'i•lant *adj.*
hy'per•vir'u•lent *adj.*
hy'per•vis'cous *adj.*

thyroid gland or the resulting physical condition.

hy•per•tro•phy (hī-pûr′trə-fē) *n.* Abnormal overdevelopment of tissue or a bodily organ. —**hy′per•troph′ic** (-trŏf′ĭk) *adj.* —**hy•per′tro•phy** *v.*

hy•per•ven•ti•la•tion (hī′pər-vĕn′tl-ā′shən) *n.* Fast or deep respiration resulting in abnormally low levels of carbon dioxide in the blood. —**hy′per•ven′ti•late** *v.*

hy•phen (hī′fən) *n.* A punctuation mark (-) used to connect or divide words or syllables. —**hy′phen** *v.*

hy•phen•ate (hī′fə-nāt′) *v.* **-at•ed, -at•ing.** To join or separate with a hyphen. —**hy′phen•a′tion** *n.*

hyp•no•sis (hĭp-nō′sĭs) *n., pl.* **-ses** (-sēz′). An induced sleeplike state in which the subject readily accepts the hypnotist's suggestions.

hyp•not•ic (hĭp-nŏt′ĭk) *adj.* **1.** Of or pertaining to hypnosis or hypnotism. **2.** Inducing or tending to induce sleep or a sleeplike state. —*n.* An agent, esp. a drug, that induces sleep. —**hyp•not′i•cal•ly** *adv.*

hyp•no•tism (hĭp′nə-tĭz′əm) *n.* **1.** The theory or practice of inducing hypnosis. **2.** Hypnosis. —**hyp′no•tist** *n.*

hyp•no•tize (hĭp′nə-tīz′) *v.* **-tized, -tiz•ing.** **1.** To practice hypnotism on. **2.** To fascinate **:** mesmerize. —**hyp′no•tiz′a•ble** *adj.* —**hyp′no•ti•za′tion** *n.*

hy•po (hī′pō) *n., pl.* **-pos.** *Informal.* A hypodermic needle, syringe, or injection.

hypo– *or* **hyp–** *pref.* **1.** Below **:** beneath **:** under <*hypo*dermic> **2.** Lower than normal <*hypo*thermia>

hy•po•al•ler•gen•ic (hī′pō-ăl′ər-jĕn′ĭk) *adj.* Having a decreased tendency to provoke an allergic reaction.

hy•po•chon•dri•a (hī′pə-kŏn′drē-ə) *n.* Mental depression accompanied by an abnormal preoccupation with imaginary physical ailments. —**hy′po•chon′dri•ac′** (-ăk′) *n. & adj.* —**hy′po•chon•dri′a•cal** (-kən-drī′ə-kəl) *adj.*

hy•poc•ri•sy (hĭ-pŏk′rĭ-sē) *n., pl.* **-sies.** The feigning of qualities and beliefs that one does not actually possess or hold, esp. a pretense of piety or moral superiority. —**hyp′o•crite′** (hĭp′ə-krĭt′) *n.* —**hyp′o•crit′i•cal** *adj.* —**hyp′o•crit′i•cal•ly** *adv.*

hy•po•der•mic (hī′pə-dûr′mĭ k) *adj.* Injected or used for injection under the skin. —*n.* **1.** A hypodermic injection. **2.** A hypodermic syringe or needle.

hypodermic needle *n.* **1.** A slender, hollow needle for use with a hypodermic syringe. **2.** A hypodermic syringe.

hypodermic syringe *n.* A syringe fitted with a hypodermic needle and used for injecting a substance, as a drug, under the skin.

hy•po•gly•ce•mi•a (hī′pō-glī -sē′mē-ə) *n.* An abnormally low level of glucose in the blood. —**hy′po•gly•ce′mic** *adj.*

hy•pot•e•nuse (hī-pŏt′n-o͞os′, -yo͞os′) *n.* The longest side of a triangle that contains a right angle.

hy•poth•e•sis (hī-pŏth′ĭ-sĭs) *n., pl.* **-ses** (-sēz′). **1.** A theory that explains a set of facts and can be tested by further investigation. **2.** An assumption used as a basis for investigation or argument. —**hy′po•thet′i•cal** (hī′pə-thĕt′ĭ-kəl) *adj.* —**hy′po•thet′i•cal•ly** *adv.*

hy•poth•e•size (hī-pŏth′ĭ-sīz′) *v.* **-sized, -siz•ing.** To set forth as a hypothesis.

hy•po•thy•roid•ism (hī′pō-thī′roi-dĭz′əm) *n.* Abnormally deficient activity of the thyroid gland or the resulting pathological condition.

hys•sop (hĭs′əp) *n.* A woody Asian plant, *Hyssopus officinalis,* bearing spikes of small blue flowers and aromatic leaves used as a condiment and in perfumery.

hys•ter•ec•to•my (hĭs′tə-rĕk′tə-mē) *n., pl.* **-mies.** Partial or complete surgical removal of the uterus.

hys•ter•i•a (hĭ-stĕr′ē-ə, -stîr′-) *n.* **1.** A neurosis marked by physical symptoms, as paralysis, without apparent organic cause. **2.** Excessive or uncontrollable emotion.

hys•ter•ic (hĭ-stĕr′ĭk) *n.* **1.** One suffering from hysteria. **2. hysterics** *(sing. or pl. in number).* **a.** A fit of uncontrollable laughing and crying. **b.** An attack of hysteria.

hys•ter•i•cal (hĭ-stĕr′ĭ-kəl) *adj.* **1.** Of, marked by, or caused by hysteria. **2.** Having or tending to have hysterics. **3.** *Informal.* Extremely funny. —**hys•ter′i•cal•ly** *adv.*

Ii

i *or* **I** (ī) *n., pl.* **i's** *or* **I's. 1.** The 9th letter of the English alphabet. **2.** A speech sound represented by the letter *i.* **3.** Something with the shape of the letter I. **4.** The Roman numeral for 1.

I[1] (ī) *pron.* The one who is speaking or writing. —*n., pl.* **I's.** The self **:** ego.

I[2] *symbol for* IODINE.

–ial *suff.* Of or marked by <baron*ial*>

i•amb (ī′ămb′) *also* **i•am•bus** (ī-ăm′bəs) *n.* A metrical foot made up of a short or unstressed syllable followed by a long or stressed syllable. —**i•am′bic** *adj. & n.*

–ian *suff.* **1.** Of, belonging to, or like <Washington*ian*> **2.** One skilled in, belonging to, or like <politic*ian*>

i•at•ro•gen•ic (ī-ăt′rə-jĕn′ĭk) *adj.* Induced by a physician's activity or manner. —Used of a disease. —**i•at′ro•gen′i•cal•ly** *adv.*

i•bex (ī′bĕks′) *n.* An Old World mountain goat, *Capra ibex,* with long, curving horns.

–ibility *suff. var. of* -ABILITY.
i•bis (ī'bĭs) *n.* A long-billed wading bird of the family Threskiornithidae.
–ible *suff. var. of* -ABLE.
i•bu•pro•fen (ī'byōō-prō'fən) *n.* An anti-inflammatory medication used esp. to treat arthritis and as a pain reliever.
–ic *suff.* **1.** Of, relating to, or marked by <Gael*ic*> **2.** Having a relatively high valence <sulfur*ic* acid>
ice (īs) *n.* **1.** Water that has frozen solid. **2.** A dessert of flavored and sweetened crushed ice. **3.** *Informal.* Extreme coldness of manner. —*v.* **iced, ic•ing. 1.** To form ice : freeze. **2.** To coat with ice. **3.** To cool or chill. **4.** To cover or decorate (e.g., a cake) with icing. —**ic'i•ly** *adv.* —**ic'i•ness** *n.* —**ic'y** *adj.*
ice age *n.* A cold period characterized by extensive glaciation.
ice bag *n.* A small waterproof bag used as an ice pack.
ice•berg (īs'bûrg') *n.* A mass of floating ice broken away from a glacier.
ice•boat (īs'bōt') *n.* **1.** A vehicle with runners and usu. a sail, for use on ice. **2.** An icebreaker.
ice•bound (īs'bound') *adj.* Locked in or covered by ice.
ice•box (īs'bŏks') *n.* A refrigerator.
ice•break•er (īs'brā'kər) *n.* **1.** A sturdy ship for breaking a way through icebound waters. **2.** A pier or dock apron forming a buffer against floating ice.
ice cap *n.* An extensive, perennial, usu. level cover of ice and snow.
ice cream *n.* A smooth, sweet, cold food made of milk products and flavorings.
ice hockey *n.* HOCKEY 1.
ice•house (īs'hous') *n.* A place where ice is stored.
ice milk *n.* A food similar to ice cream but containing less butterfat.
ice pack *n.* **1.** A floating mass of compacted ice. **2.** A folded cloth or bag filled with ice and applied to sore body parts.
ice pick *n.* A pointed tool for chipping or breaking ice.
ice skate *n.* A shoe with a runner fixed to it for skating on ice. —**ice'-skate'** *v.*
ice storm *n.* A storm in which precipitation freezes on contact.
ice water *n.* Iced or chilled water.
ich•thy•ol•o•gy (ĭk'thē-ŏl'ə-jē) *n.* The zoological study of fishes. —**ich'thy•o•log'ic** (-ə-lŏj'ĭk), **ich'thy•o•log'i•cal** *adj.* —**ich'thy•ol'o•gist** *n.*
i•ci•cle (ī'sĭ-kəl) *n.* A hanging spike of ice made by dripping water that freezes.
ic•ing (ī'sĭng) *n.* A sweet glaze for coating cakes and cookies.
i•con (ī'kŏn') *n.* **1.** *also* **i•kon** An image, esp. a picture of a sacred Christian personage painted on a wooden panel. **2.** *Computer Sci.* A picture on a screen that represents a specific command.
i•con•o•clast (ī-kŏn'ə-klăst') *n.* **1.** One who destroys or opposes the use of sacred images. **2.** One who attacks traditional beliefs or institutions. —**i•con'o•clasm** *n.* —**i•con'o•clas'tic** *adj.*
–ics *suff.* **1.** Science : art : study : knowledge : skill <aerodynam*ics*> **2.** Activities or practices of <mechan*ics*>
id (ĭd) *n.* *Psychoanal.* The part of the psyche associated with instinctual needs and drives and providing psychic energy.
I'd (īd). **1.** I had. **2.** I should. **3.** I would.
i•de•a (ī-dē'ə) *n.* **1.** Something existing in the mind, such as an image or thought. **2.** An opinion : belief. **3.** A plan : design. **4.** Meaning : purport.
i•de•al (ī-dē'əl, ī-dēl') *n.* **1.** A conception or standard of perfection. **2.** One considered a perfect model. **3.** An ultimate objective : goal. **4.** An honorable principle or motive. ★ *syns:* EXAMPLE, EXEMPLAR, MODEL, STANDARD —*adj.* **1.** Embodying an ideal : perfect. **2.** Existing only in the mind : imaginary. —**i•de'al•ly** *adv.*
i•de•al•ism (ī-dē'ə-lĭz'əm) *n.* **1.** The practice of seeing things in ideal form. **2.** Pursuit of high-minded or worthy goals. **3.** A philosophical system holding that reality consists of ideas or perceptions. —**i•de'al•ist** *n.* —**i'de•al•is'tic** *adj.*
i•de•al•ize (ī-dē'ə-līz') *v.* **-ized, -iz•ing.** To envision or represent as ideal. —**i•de'al•i•za'tion** *n.*
i•dem (ī'dĕm') *pron.* —Used to indicate a previously mentioned reference.
i•den•ti•cal (ī-dĕn'tĭ-kəl) *adj.* **1.** Being the same. **2.** Exactly equal and alike. **3.** Of or designating a twin or twins developed from the same ovum. —**i•den'ti•cal•ly** *adv.*
i•den•ti•fi•ca•tion (ī-dĕn'tə-fĭ-kā'shən) *n.* **1.** The act of identifying or state of being identified. **2.** Proof of identity.
i•den•ti•fy (ī-dĕn'tə-fī') *v.* **-fied, -fy•ing. 1.** To find out the identity of. **2.** To regard as the same or similar : equate. **3.** To associate (oneself) closely with an individual or group. —**i•den'ti•fi'a•ble** *adj.*
i•den•ti•ty (ī-dĕn'tĭ-tē) *n., pl.* **-ties. 1.** The condition or fact of being a certain person or thing and recognizable as such. **2.** The condition or fact of being the same as something else : sameness.
id•e•o•gram (ĭd'ē-ə-grăm', ī'dē-) *also* **id•e•o•graph** (-grăf) *n.* **1.** A symbol used in a writing system to represent an idea or thing without expressing a particular word or phrase for it, as Chinese characters. **2.** A graphic symbol, as $ or %.
i•de•o•logue (ī'dē-ə-lôg', -lŏg', ĭd'ē-) *n.* An advocate of a particular ideology.
i•de•ol•o•gy (ī'dē-ŏl'ə-jē, ĭd'ē-) *n., pl.* **-gies.** A body of ideas characteristic of a person, group, culture, or political party. —**i'de•o•log'i•cal** (-ə-lŏj'ĭ-kəl) *adj.*
ides (īdz) *n. (sing. in number).* The 15th day of Mar., May, Jul., or Oct. or the 13th day of the other months in the ancient Roman calendar.
id•i•o•cy (ĭd'ē-ə-sē) *n., pl.* **-cies. 1.** The con-

dition of profound mental retardation. **2.** Something extremely foolish or stupid.

id·i·om (ĭd'ē-əm) *n.* **1.** An expression having a meaning that cannot be understood from the individual meanings of its component words. **2.** The way of speaking or putting words together peculiar to a language. **3.** A kind of language or vocabulary. **—id'i·o·mat'·ic** (-ə-măt'ĭk) *adj.* **—id'i·o·mat'i·cal·ly** *adv.*

▲ ***word history:*** *Idiom,* like *idiot,* is derived ult. from Greek *idios,* "private." Greek *idiōma* meant basically any peculiarity or unique feature, but esp. a peculiarity of language or literary style. In English the word *idiom* was used to mean "language" in general, then "dialect," and finally to denote a peculiarity of expression, phrase, or grammatical construction in a particular language.

id·i·op·a·thy (ĭd'ē-ŏp'ə-thē) *n.* A disease without a known cause. **—id'i·o·path'ic** (-ə-păth'ĭk) *adj.*

id·i·o·syn·cra·sy (ĭd'ē-ō-sĭng'krə-sē) *n., pl.* **-sies.** A peculiarity, esp. in behavior : eccentricity. **—id'i·o·syn·crat'ic** (-sĭn-krăt'ĭk) *adj.* **—id'i·o·syn·crat'i·cal·ly** *adv.*

id·i·ot (ĭd'ē-ət) *n.* **1.** *Obs.* A person of profound mental retardation, generally unable to learn connected speech or guard against common dangers. **2.** A foolish or stupid person. **—id'i·ot'ic** (-ŏt'ĭk) *adj.* **—id'i·ot'i·cal·ly** *adv.*

▲ ***word history:*** The development of the pejorative senses of *idiot* occurred in ancient Greek, although the meaning "a mentally deficient person" is a more modern refinement. Greek *idiōtēs,* the source of *idiot,* is derived from *idios,* "private," and orig. meant a private citizen in contrast to a public official. The use of *idiōtēs* was extended to other pairs of opposites such as layman/professional, layman/priest, common person/distinguished person, and unskilled worker/craftsman. A person of no special status, knowledge, or skill was *idiōtēs,* and the term became one of abuse.

i·dle (īd'l) *adj.* **i·dler, i·dlest. 1.** Doing nothing : unoccupied. **2.** Not working : unemployed. **3.** Lazy. **4.** Unfounded : groundless <*idle* talk> *—v.* **i·dled, i·dling. 1.** To pass time unproductively. **2.** To move lazily. **3.** To run at a slow speed or out of gear. **4.** To render unemployed or inactive. **—i'dle·ness** *n.* **—i'dler** *n.* **—i'dly** *adv.*

i·dol (īd'l) *n.* **1.** An image that is worshiped. **2.** One that is blindly adored.

i·dol·a·try (ī-dŏl'ə-trē) *n.* **1.** The worship of idols. **2.** Blind adoration. **—i·dol'a·ter** *n.* **—i·dol'a·trous** *adj.*

i·dol·ize (īd'l-īz') *v.* **-ized, -iz·ing. 1.** To regard with excessive admiration or devotion. **2.** To worship as an idol. **—i'dol·i·za'tion** *n.* **—i'dol·iz'er** *n.*

i·dyll *also* **i·dyl** (īd'l) *n.* **1.** A poem about country life. **2.** A scene, event, or condition of rural simplicity and happiness. **3.** A romantic interlude. **—i·dyl'lic** (ī-dĭl'ĭk) *adj.* **—i·dyl'li·cal·ly** *adv.*

—ie *suff. var. of* -Y³.

if (ĭf) *conj.* **1.** In the event that <*If* the cat's hungry, feed it.> **2.** On condition that <They will work only *if* they are paid in advance.> **3.** Although possibly <a funny *if* tactless reply> **4.** Whether <I wonder *if* she could be right?>

if·fy (ĭf'ē) *adj. Informal.* Marked by doubt, uncertainty, or chance.

ig·loo (ĭg'lo͞o) *n.* A dome-shaped Eskimo dwelling built of blocks of ice.

ig·ne·ous (ĭg'nē-əs) *adj.* **1.** Of fire. **2.** Formed by solidification from a molten state <*igneous* rock>

ig·nite (ĭg-nīt') *v.* **-nit·ed, -nit·ing.** To start or cause to start to burn.

ig·ni·tion (ĭg-nĭsh'ən) *n.* **1.** An act of igniting. **2.** A system or device for igniting the fuel mixture in an engine.

ig·no·ble (ĭg-nō'bəl) *adj.* **1.** Dishonorable in character or purpose : base. **2.** Not belonging to the nobility. **—ig·no'bly** *adv.*

ig·no·min·i·ous (ĭg'nə-mĭn'ē-əs) *adj.* **1.** Marked by or deserving shame or disgrace : dishonorable. **2.** Deeply embarrassing : humiliating. **—ig'no·min'y** *n.*

ig·no·ra·mus (ĭg'nə-rā'məs) *n.* An ignorant person.

ig·no·rant (ĭg'nər-ənt) *adj.* **1.** Lacking or displaying a lack of education or knowledge. **2.** Not aware : uninformed. ★ ***syns:*** OBLIVIOUS, UNAWARE, UNCONSCIOUS, UNWITTING **—ig'no·rance** *n.*

ig·nore (ĭg-nôr', -nōr') *v.* **-nored, -nor·ing.** To pay no attention to : disregard. **—ig·nor'a·ble** *adj.*

i·gua·na (ĭ-gwä'nə) *n.* A large tropical American lizard of the family Iguanidae.

i·kon (ī'kŏn') *n. var. of* ICON.

il·e·i·tis (ĭl'ē-ī'tĭs) *n.* Inflammation of the ileum.

il·e·um (ĭl'ē-əm) *n., pl.* **-e·a** (-ē-ə). The lower part of the small intestine between the jejunum and the cecum.

ilk (ĭlk) *n.* Sort : kind.

ill (ĭl) *adj.* **worse** (wûrs), **worst** (wûrst). **1.** Not healthy : sick. **2.** Unsound : bad <*ill* health> **3.** Hostile : unfriendly. **4.** Not favorable <*ill* omens> **5.** Not up to standards <*ill* treatment> *—adv.* **worse, worst. 1.** In an ill manner : not well. **2.** With difficulty : scarcely. *—n.* **1.** Evil. **2.** Trouble or harm. **3.** Something causing suffering <persistent social *ills*>

I'll (īl). **1.** I will. **2.** I shall.

ill-ad·vised (ĭl'əd-vīzd') *adj.* Done without careful thought or good advice.

ill-bred (ĭl'brĕd') *adj.* Badly brought up : ill-mannered.

il·le·gal (ĭ-lē'gəl) *adj.* Forbidden by law or official rules. ★ ***syns:*** ILLICIT, UNLAWFUL **—il'le·gal'i·ty** *n.* **—il·le'gal·ly** *adv.*

il·leg·i·ble (ĭ-lĕj'ə-bəl) *adj.* Not legible. **—il·leg'i·bil'i·ty** *n.* **—il·leg'i·bly** *adv.*

il·le·git·i·mate (ĭl'ə-jĭt'ə-mĭt) *adj.* **1.** Against the law : illegal. **2.** Born out of wedlock. **3.** Illogical. **—il'le·git'i·ma·cy** *n.* **—il'le·git'i·mate·ly** *adv.*

ill-fat•ed (ĭl′fā′tĭd) *adj.* **1.** Destined for misfortune. **2.** Unlucky.

ill-fa•vored (ĭl′fā′vərd) *adj.* **1.** Unattractive : ugly. **2.** Objectionable : offensive.

ill-found•ed (ĭl′foun′dĭd) *adj.* Having no factual basis.

ill-got•ten (ĭl′gŏt′n) *adj.* Obtained in a dishonest way.

ill-hu•mored (ĭl′hyōō′mərd) *adj.* Irritable : surly. —**ill′-hu′mored•ly** *adv.*

il•lib•er•al (ĭ-lĭb′ər-əl) *adj.* Narrow-minded : prejudiced.

il•lic•it (ĭ-lĭs′ĭt) *adj.* Forbidden by custom or law : unlawful. —**il•lic′it•ly** *adv.*

il•lit•er•ate (ĭ-lĭt′ər-ĭt) *adj.* **1.** Unable to read and write. **2.** Not educated. —**il•lit′er•a•cy** (-ə-sē) *n.* —**il•lit′er•ate** *n.*

ill-man•nered (ĭl′măn′ərd) *adj.* Lacking or showing a lack of good manners : rude.

ill-na•tured (ĭl′nā′chərd) *adj.* Disagreeable in disposition : surly.

ill•ness (ĭl′nĭs) *n.* A sickness.

il•log•i•cal (ĭ-lŏj′ĭ-kəl) *adj.* Contrary to the principles of logic. —**il•log′i•cal′i•ty** (-kăl′ĭ-tē) *n.* —**il•log′i•cal•ly** *adv.*

ill-starred (ĭl′stärd′) *adj.* Ill-fated.

ill-tem•pered (ĭl′tĕm′pərd) *adj.* Having or showing a bad temper.

ill-treat (ĭl′trēt′) *v.* To maltreat. —**ill′-treat′ment** *n.*

il•lu•mi•nate (ĭ-lōō′mə-nāt′) *v.* **-nat•ed, -nat•ing. 1.** To supply or brighten with light. **2.** To make understandable : clarify. **3.** To provide with understanding : enlighten. **4.** To decorate (e.g., a manuscript) with pictures or designs. —**il•lu′mi•na′tion** *n.* —**il•lu′mi•na′tor** *n.*

il•lu•mine (ĭ-lōō′mĭn) *v.* **-mined, -min•ing.** To illuminate.

ill-use (ĭl′yōōz′) *v.* To maltreat. —**ill′-us′age** (ĭl′yōō′sĭj) *n.* —**ill′-use′** (ĭl′yōōs′) *n.*

il•lu•sion (ĭ-lōō′zhən) *n.* **1.** A mistaken perception of reality. **2.** A false belief : misconception. —**il•lu′sive, il•lu′so•ry** *adj.*

il•lus•trate (ĭl′ə-strāt′, ĭ-lŭs′trāt′) *v.* **-trat•ed, -trat•ing. 1.a.** To clarify, esp. by the use of examples. **b.** To clarify by serving as an example or comparison. **2.** To provide (a publication) with explanatory or decorative features. —**il′lus•tra′tor** *n.*

il•lus•tra•tion (ĭl′ə-strā′shən) *n.* **1.** The act of illustrating or state of being illustrated. **2.** An example used to illustrate. **3.** A picture, diagram, or chart in a text.

il•lus•tra•tive (ĭ-lŭs′trə-tĭv, ĭl′ə-strā′tĭv) *adj.* Serving to illustrate.

il•lus•tri•ous (ĭ-lŭs′trē-əs) *adj.* Celebrated : renowned. —**il•lus′tri•ous•ness** *n.*

ill will *n.* Unfriendly feeling : enmity.

I'm (īm). I am.

im•age (ĭm′ĭj) *n.* **1.** A reproduction of the form of someone or something, esp. a sculptured likeness. **2.** An optically formed representation of an object, esp. one made by a mirror or lens. **3. a.** A mental picture of something absent or imaginary. **b.** A figure of speech. **4.** One closely resembling another <the *image* of her mother> **5.** A personification. **6.** The impression made on the public, as by a famous person : reputation. —*v.* **-aged, -ag•ing. 1.** To make a likeness of. **2.** To reflect. **3.** To picture in the mind : imagine. **4.** To describe or depict vividly.

im•age•ry (ĭm′ĭj-rē) *n., pl.* **-ries. 1.** Mental pictures. **2.** Vivid figures of speech conveying mental pictures.

i•mag•in•a•ble (ĭ-măj′ə-nə-bəl) *adj.* Capable of being conceived of by the imagination. —**i•mag′in•a•bly** *adv.*

i•mag•i•nar•y (ĭ-măj′ə-nĕr′ē) *adj.* Existing only in the imagination.

imaginary number *n.* A number whose square is negative.

imaginary unit *n.* The positive square root of −1.

i•mag•i•na•tion (ĭ-măj′ə-nā′shən) *n.* **1.** The mental power of forming images of unreal or absent objects. **2.** Such power used creatively. **3.** Resourcefulness. —**i•mag′i•na•tive** *adj.* —**i•mag′i•na•tive•ly** *adv.*

i•mag•ine (ĭ-măj′ĭn) *v.* **-ined, -in•ing. 1.** To form a mental picture of. **2.** To suppose : think <I *imagine* it's late.>

i•ma•go (ĭ-mā′gō, ĭ-mä′-) *n., pl.* **-goes** *or* **-gi•nes** (gə-nēz′) An insect in its sexually mature adult stage.

i•mam (ĭ-mäm′) *n.* **1.** A prayer leader in a mosque. **2.** A Muslim scholar. **3. Imam.** Any of various religious and temporal leaders claiming descent from Muhammad.

im•bal•ance (ĭm-băl′əns) *n.* A lack of balance, as in proportion.

im•be•cile (ĭm′bə-sĭl, -səl) *n.* **1.** *Obs.* A person of moderate to severe mental retardation. **2.** A stupid or silly person. —**im′be•cile, im′be•cil′ic** (-sĭl′ĭk) *adj.* —**im′be•cil′i•ty** (-sĭl′ĭ-tē) *n.*

im•bed (ĭm-bĕd′) *v. var. of* EMBED.

im•bibe (ĭm-bīb′) *v.* **-bibed, -bib•ing. 1.** To drink. **2.** To take in : absorb. —**im•bib′er** *n.*

im•bri•cate (ĭm′brĭ-kāt′) *adj.* With edges overlapping in a regular arrangement, as roof tiles or fish scales.

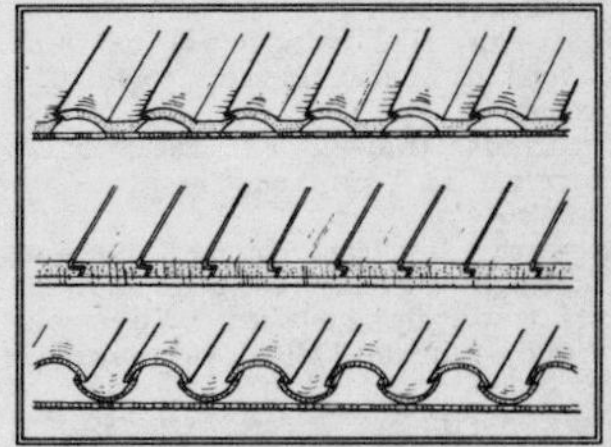

imbricate
Three styles of imbricate roofing: (top) Spanish, (middle) English, (bottom) mission

im•bro•glio (ĭm-brōl′yō) *n., pl.* **-glios. 1.** A complicated situation or disagreement. **2.** A confused heap : tangle.

im•bue (ĭm-byo͞o′) *v.* **-bued, -bu•ing. 1.** To saturate, as with a stain or dye. **2.** To permeate or pervade : instill <a poem *imbued* with revolutionary spirit>

im•i•ta•ble (ĭm′ĭ-tə-bəl) *adj.* Capable or worthy of imitation.

im•i•tate (ĭm′ĭ-tāt′) *v.* **-tat•ed, -tat•ing. 1. a.** To copy the actions or appearance of (another). **b.** To adopt the style of : model oneself after. **2.** To duplicate : reproduce. **3.** To appear like : resemble. ★ ***syns:*** APE, BURLESQUE, MIMIC, MOCK, PARODY —**im′i•ta′tor** *n.*

im•i•ta•tion (ĭm′ĭ-tā′shən) *n.* **1.** An act of imitating. **2.** Something copied from an original.

im•i•ta•tive (ĭm′ĭ-tā′tĭv) *adj.* **1.** Of, marked by, or inclined to imitation. **2.** Not original : derivative.

im•mac•u•late (ĭ-măk′yə-lĭt) *adj.* **1.** Free from sin, stain, or fault : pure. **2.** Impeccably clean. —**im•mac′u•late•ly** *adv.*

im•ma•nent (ĭm′ə-nənt) *adj.* **1.** Existing within : inherent. **2.** Restricted to the mind : subjective. —**im′ma•nence, im′ma•nen•cy** *n.* —**im′ma•nent•ly** *adv.*

im•ma•te•ri•al (ĭm′ə-tîr′ē-əl) *adj.* **1.** Lacking material body or form. **2.** Of no importance or relevance. —**im′ma•te′ri•al•ly** *adv.* —**im′ma•te′ri•al•ness** *n.*

im•ma•ture (ĭm′ə-tyo͝or′, -to͝or′, -cho͝or′) *adj.* **1.** Not fully grown : undeveloped. **2.** Suggesting a lack of maturity. —**im′ma•ture′ly** *adv.* —**im′ma•tur′i•ty** *n.*

im•meas•ur•a•ble (ĭ-mĕzh′ər-ə-bəl) *adj.* **1.** Not capable of being measured. **2.** Very large or great. —**im•meas′ur•a•bly** *adv.*

im•me•di•a•cy (ĭ-mē′dē-ə-sē) *n., pl.* **-cies. 1.** The quality of being immediate : directness. **2.** Something of urgent importance.

im•me•di•ate (ĭ-mē′dē-ĭt) *adj.* **1.** Acting or happening without an intervening object, agent, or cause. **2.** Directly perceived. **3.** Occurring at once : instant. **4.** Close in time, location, or relation <our *immediate* surroundings> **5.** Present <*immediate* needs> —**im•me′di•ate•ly** *adv.*

im•me•mo•ri•al (ĭm′ə-môr′ē-əl, -mōr′-) *adj.* Beyond the limits of memory, tradition, or records.

im•mense (ĭ-mĕns′) *adj.* Exceptionally large : huge. —**im•mense′ly** *adv.* —**im•men′si•ty** *n.*

im•merse (ĭ-mûrs′) *v.* **-mersed, -mers•ing. 1.** To put into a liquid : submerge. **2.** To baptize by submerging in water. **3.** To engross : absorb. —**im•mers′i•ble** *adj.* —**im•mer′sion** *n.*

im•mesh (ĭ-mĕsh′) *v. var. of* ENMESH.

im•mi•grant (ĭm′ĭ-grənt) *n.* One who leaves one country to settle in another.

im•mi•grate (ĭm′ĭ-grāt′) *v.* **-grat•ed, -grat•ing.** To leave one country and settle in another. —**im′mi•gra′tion** *n.*

im•mi•nent (ĭm′ə-nənt) *adj.* About to happen : impending. —**im′mi•nence** *n.*

im•mo•bile (ĭ-mō′bəl, -bēl′, -bīl′) *adj.* **1.** Not moving : motionless. **2.** Not capable of moving : fixed. —**im′mo•bil′i•ty** *n.*

im•mo•bi•lize (ĭ-mō′bə-līz′) *v.* **-lized, -liz•ing.** To render immobile. —**im•mo′bi•li•za′tion** *n.*

im•mod•er•ate (ĭ-mŏd′ər-ĭt) *adj.* Exceeding normal bounds : extreme. —**im•mod′er•ate•ly** *adv.*

im•mod•est (ĭ-mŏd′ĭst) *adj.* **1.** Lacking modesty : indecent. **2.** Boastful. —**im•mod′est•ly** *adv.* —**im•mod′es•ty** *n.*

im•mo•late (ĭm′ə-lāt′) *v.* **-lat•ed, -lat•ing. 1.** To kill as a sacrifice. **2.** To destroy completely. —**im′mo•la′tion** *n.* —**im′mo•la′tor** *n.*

im•mor•al (ĭ-môr′əl, ĭ-mŏr′-) *adj.* Not moral. —**im•mor′al•ly** *adv.*

im•mo•ral•i•ty (ĭm′ô-răl′ĭ-tē, ĭm′ə-) *n., pl.* **-ties. 1.** Lack of morality. **2.** An immoral act or practice.

im•mor•tal (ĭ-môr′tl) *adj.* **1.** Exempt from death. **2.** Lasting forever, as in fame. —*n.* **1.** One not subject to death. **2.** A person of lasting fame. —**im′mor•tal′i•ty** *n.* —**im•mor′tal•ly** *adv.*

im•mor•tal•ize (ĭ-môr′tl-īz′) *v.* **-ized, -iz•ing.** To make immortal.

im•mov•a•ble (ĭ-mo͞o′və-bəl) *adj.* **1.** Not capable of moving or of being moved. **2.** Adhering closely to a position or principle : steadfast. —**im•mov′a•bly** *adv.*

im•mune (ĭ-myo͞on′) *adj.* **1.** Exempt. **2.** Not affected or responsive. **3.** Resistant, as to a disease. —**im•mu′ni•ty** *n.*

immune response *n.* An integrated bodily response to an antigen, esp. one mediated by lymphocytes.

immune system *n.* The integrated body system of organs, tissues, cells, and cell products such as antibodies that differentiates self from nonself and neutralizes potentially pathogenic organisms or substances.

im•mu•nize (ĭm′yə-nīz′) *v.* **-nized, -niz•ing.** To make immune. —**im′mu•ni•za′tion** *n.*

im•mu•no•de•fi•cien•cy (ĭm′yə-nō-dĭ-fĭsh′ən-sē, ĭ-myo͞o′-) *n., pl.* **-cies.** An inability to develop a normal immune response. —**im′mu•no•de•fi′cient** *adj.*

im•mu•nol•o•gy (ĭm′yə-nŏl′ə-jē) *n.* The study of immunity to diseases. —**im′mu•no•log′ic** (-nə-lŏj′ĭk), **im′mu•no•log′i•cal** *adj.* —**im′mu•no•log′i•cal•ly** *adv.*

im•mu•no•sup•pres•sion (ĭm′yə-nō-sə-prĕsh′ən, ĭ-myo͞o′-) *n.* Suppression of the immune response, as by drugs or radiation. —**im′mu•no•sup•pres′sant** (-prĕs′ənt) *n.* —**im′mu•no•sup•pres′sive** *adj.*

im•mure (ĭ-myo͝or′) *v.* **-mured, -mur•ing. 1.** To confine by or as if by walls : jail. **2.** To build into a wall.

im•mu•ta•ble (ĭ-myo͞o′tə-bəl) *adj.* Unchanging or unchangeable. —**im•mu′ta•bil′i•ty** *n.* —**im•mu′ta•bly** *adv.*

imp (ĭmp) *n.* **1.** A mischievous child. **2.** A little demon.

im•pact (ĭm′păkt′) *n.* **1. a.** A collision. **b.** The impetus or force produced by a collision. **2.** An initial, usu. strong effect. —*v.* (ĭm-păkt′). **1.** To pack firmly together. **2.** To strike or affect forcefully.

im•pact•ed (ĭm-păk′tĭd) *adj.* **1.** Wedged together at the broken ends <an *impacted* bone> **2.** Wedged inside the gum in such a way that normal eruption is prevented <an *impacted* wisdom tooth>

im•pair (ĭm-pâr′) *v.* To diminish in strength, value, quantity, or quality : harm. —**im•pair′ment** *n.*

im•pa•la (ĭm-pä′lə, -păl′ə) *n.* A large African antelope, *Aepyceros melampus,* the male of which has slender curved horns.

im•pale (ĭm-pāl′) *v.* **-paled, -pal•ing. 1.** To pierce with a sharp stake or point. **2.** To kill by thus piercing. —**im•pale′ment** *n.*

im•pal•pa•ble (ĭm-păl′pə-bəl) *adj.* **1.** Not perceptible to touch : intangible. **2.** Not easily distinguished : elusive. —**im•pal′pa•bil′i•ty** *n.* —**im•pal′pa•bly** *adv.*

im•pan•el (ĭm-păn′əl) *v.* **-eled, -el•ing** *or* **-elled, -el•ling.** To enter the names of (a jury) on a panel or list.

im•part (ĭm-pärt′) *v.* **1.** To grant : bestow <*impart* wisdom> **2.** To make known : communicate <*impart* the bad news>

im•par•tial (ĭm-pär′shəl) *adj.* Not partial : unbiased. —**im•par′ti•al′i•ty** (-shē-ăl′ĭ-tē) *n.* —**im•par′tial•ly** *adv.*

im•pass•a•ble (ĭm-păs′ə-bəl) *adj.* Impossible to travel over or across.

im•passe (ĭm′păs′) *n.* **1.** A road or passage having no exit. **2.** A difficult situation with no apparent way out. **3.** A deadlock.

im•pas•sioned (ĭm-păsh′ənd) *adj.* Filled with passion.

im•pas•sive (ĭm-păs′ĭv) *adj.* **1.** Unemotional : stolid. **2.** Showing no emotion : expressionless. —**im•pas′sive•ly** *adv.*

im•pa•tient (ĭm-pā′shənt) *adj.* **1.** Unwilling to wait or tolerate delay : restless. **2.** Expressing or caused by irritation at having to wait <an *impatient* oath> **3.** Restlessly eager <*impatient* to depart> **4.** Intolerant <*impatient* of weakness> —**im•pa′tience** *n.* —**im•pa′tient•ly** *adv.*

im•peach (ĭm-pēch′) *v.* **1.** To charge with misconduct in public office before a proper court of justice. **2.** To make an accusation against : challenge <*impeached* the witness's honesty> —**im•peach′a•ble** *adj.* —**im•peach′er** *n.* —**im•peach′ment** *n.*

im•pec•ca•ble (ĭm-pĕk′ə-bəl) *adj.* **1.** Having no flaws : perfect. **2.** Not capable of sin. —**im•pec′ca•bly** *adv.*

im•pe•cu•ni•ous (ĭm′pĭ-kyo͞o′nē-əs) *adj.* Having no money : penniless. —**im′pe•cu′ni•ous•ness** *n.*

im•ped•ance (ĭm-pēd′ns) *n.* A measure of the total opposition to the flow of an electric current, esp. in an alternating-current circuit.

im•pede (ĭm-pēd′) *v.* **-ped•ed, -ped•ing.** To obstruct or slow down the progress of.

im•ped•i•ment (ĭm-pĕd′ə-mənt) *n.* **1.** One that stands in the way : obstruction. **2.** Something that impedes, esp. an organic speech defect.

im•ped•i•men•ta (ĭm-pĕd′ə-mĕn′tə) *pl.n.* Things that impede or encumber.

im•pel (ĭm-pĕl′) *v.* **-pelled, -pel•ling. 1.** To spur to action : provoke. **2.** To drive forward : propel. —**im•pel′ler** *n.*

im•pend (ĭm-pĕnd′) *v.* **1.** To hover threateningly. **2.** To be about to happen.

im•pen•e•tra•ble (ĭm-pĕn′ĭ-trə-bəl) *adj.* **1.** Not capable of being penetrated. **2.** Not capable of being seen through or understood : unfathomable. —**im•pen′e•tra•bil′i•ty** *n.* —**im•pen′e•tra•bly** *adv.*

im•pen•i•tent (ĭm-pĕn′ĭ-tənt) *adj.* Not sorry : unrepentant. —**im•pen′i•tence** *n.*

im•per•a•tive (ĭm-pĕr′ə-tĭv) *adj.* **1.** Expressing a command or request <an *imperative* verb form> **2.** Empowered to command or control. **3.** Compulsory. —**im•per′a•tive** *n.* —**im•per′a•tive•ly** *adv.*

im•per•cep•ti•ble (ĭm′pər-sĕp′tə-bəl) *adj.* **1.** Not perceptible by the mind or senses. **2.** Extremely small or slight. ★ ***syns:*** IMPALPABLE, INDISTINGUISHABLE, INSENSIBLE, INTANGIBLE, UNAPPRECIABLE, UNNOTICEABLE —**im′per•cep′ti•bly** *adv.*

im•per•fect (ĭm-pûr′fĭkt) *adj.* **1.** Not perfect. **2.** Of or being a verb tense that shows an uncompleted or continuous action or condition. ★ ***syns:*** DEFECTIVE, FAULTY —*n.* **1.** The imperfect tense. **2.** A verb in the imperfect tense. —**im•per′fect•ly** *adv.*

im•per•fec•tion (ĭm′pər-fĕk′shən) *n.* **1.** The quality or condition of being imperfect. **2.** A defect.

im•pe•ri•al[1] (ĭm-pîr′ē-əl) *adj.* **1.** Of or relating to an empire or emperor. **2.** Designating a nation or government having dependent colonies. **3.** Majestic : regal. —**im•pe′ri•al•ly** *adv.*

im•pe•ri•al[2] (ĭm-pîr′ē-əl) *n.* A pointed beard on the lower lip and chin.

im•pe•ri•al•ism (ĭm-pîr′ē-ə-lĭz′əm) *n.* The national policy or practice of acquiring foreign territories or establishing dominance over other nations. —**im•pe′ri•al•ist** *n.* —**im•pe′ri•al•is′tic** *adj.*

imperial moth *n.* A large New World moth, *Eacles imperialis,* with yellow wings

imperial moth

having purplish or brownish markings.

im·per·il (ĭm-pĕr'əl) *v.* **-iled, -il·ing** *or* **-illed, -il·ling.** To put in peril : endanger.

im·pe·ri·ous (ĭm-pîr'ē-əs) *adj.* **1.** Commanding : domineering. **2.** Urgent. **—im·pe'ri·ous·ly** *adv.* **—im·pe'ri·ous·ness** *n.*

im·per·ish·a·ble (ĭm-pĕr'ĭ-shə -bəl) *adj.* Not perishable. **—im·per'ish·a·bly** *adv.*

im·per·ma·nent (ĭm-pûr'mə-nənt) *adj.* Not permanent : temporary. **—im·per'ma·nence** *n.* **—im·per'ma·nent·ly** *adv.*

im·per·me·a·ble (ĭm-pûr'mē-ə-bəl) *adj.* Not permeable. **—im·per'me·a·bil'i·ty** *n.* **—im·per'me·a·bly** *adv.*

im·per·mis·si·ble (ĭm'pər-mĭs'ə-bəl) *adj.* Not permissible.

im·per·son·al (ĭm-pûr'sə-nəl) *adj.* **1.** Having no personal reference or connection <an *impersonal* comment> **2.** Showing no emotion or personality <an *impersonal* tone> **—im·per'son·al·ly** *adv.*

im·per·son·ate (ĭm-pûr'sə-nāt') *v.* **-at·ed, -at·ing.** To assume the chararacter or manner of. **—im·per'son·a'tion** *n.* **—im·per'son·a'tor** *n.*

im·per·ti·nent (ĭm-pûr'tn-ənt) *adj.* **1.** Improperly bold or disrespectful : impudent. **2.** Not pertinent : irrelevant. **—im·per'ti·nence** *n.* **—im·per'ti·nent·ly** *adv.*

im·per·turb·a·ble (ĭm'pər-tûr'bə-bəl) *adj.* Unshakably calm. **—im'per·turb'a·bil'i·ty** *n.* **—im'per·turb'a·bly** *adv.*

im·per·vi·ous (ĭm-pûr'vē-əs) *adj.* **1.** Incapable of being penetrated <material *impervious* to water> **2.** Incapable of being affected <*impervious* to our pleas> **—im·per'vi·ous·ly** *adv.* **—im·per'vi·ous·ness** *n.*

im·pe·ti·go (ĭm'pĭ-tī'gō) *n.* A contagious skin disease marked by pustules.

im·pet·u·ous (ĭm-pĕch'o͞o-əs) *adj.* Marked by sudden action or emotion : impulsive <*impetuous* haste> **—im·pet'u·os'i·ty** (-ŏs'ĭ-tē) *n.* **—im·pet'u·ous·ly** *adv.*

im·pe·tus (ĭm'pĭ-təs) *n.* **1. a.** A driving force : impulse. **b.** An incitement : stimulus. **2.** Momentum.

im·pi·e·ty (ĭm-pī'ĭ-tē) *n., pl.* **-ties. 1.** The quality of being impious : irreverence. **2.** An impious act.

im·pinge (ĭm-pĭnj') *v.* **-pinged, -ping·ing. 1.** To make impact : strike : collide. **2.** To encroach<next-door neighbors *impinging* on our privacy> **—im·pinge'ment** *n.*

im·pi·ous (ĭm'pē-əs, ĭm-pī'-) *adj.* **1.** Not pious : irreverent. **2.** Disrespectful : discourteous. **—im'pi·ous·ly** *adv.*

imp·ish (ĭm'pĭsh) *adj.* Mischievous. **—imp'ish·ly** *adv.* **—imp'ish·ness** *n.*

im·pla·ca·ble (ĭm-plăk'ə-bəl, -plā'kə-) *adj.* Not capable of being placated or appeased <*implacable* rage> **—im·pla'ca·bil'i·ty** *n.* **—im·pla'ca·bly** *adv.*

im·plant (ĭm-plănt') *v.* **1.** To set in firmly. **2.** To fix in the mind : instill. **3.** To insert surgically. **—im'plant'** *n.* **—im'plan·ta'tion** *n.*

im·plau·si·ble (ĭm-plô'zə-bəl) *adj.* Difficult to believe : unlikely. **—im·plau'si·bil'i·ty** *n.* **—im·plau'si·bly** *adv.*

im·ple·ment (ĭm'plə-mənt) *n.* A utensil or tool. —*v.* (-mĕnt'). **1.** To put into effect : carry out. **2.** To furnish with implements. **—im'ple·men·ta'tion** *n.*

im·pli·cate (ĭm'plĭ-kāt') *v.* **-cat·ed, -cat·ing. 1.** To involve, esp. in illegal activity. **2.** To imply.

im·pli·ca·tion (ĭm'plĭ-kā'shən) *n.* **1.** The act of implicating or state of being implicated. **2.** The act of implying : indirect expression. **3.** Something implied.

im·plic·it (ĭm-plĭs'ĭt) *adj.* **1.** Contained in the nature of someone or something but not readily apparent. **2.** Understood but not directly expressed <an *implicit* assumption> **3.** Complete : absolute. ★ ***syns:*** IMPLIED, TACIT, UNDERSTOOD, UNSPOKEN **—im·plic'it·ly** *adv.*

im·plode (ĭm-plōd') *v.* **-plod·ed, -plod·ing.** To collapse violently : burst inward. **—im·plo'sion** *n.*

im·plore (ĭm-plôr', -plōr') *v.* **-plored, -plor·ing.** To appeal urgently to : entreat. **—im·plor'er** *n.* **—im·plor'ing·ly** *adv.*

im·ply (ĭm-plī') *v.* **-plied, -ply·ing. 1.** To involve by logical necessity : entail. **2.** To express indirectly : suggest.

im·po·lite (ĭm'pə-līt') *adj.* Rude.

im·pol·i·tic (ĭm-pŏl'ĭ-tĭk) *adj.* **1.** Not expedient : imprudent. **2.** Tactless.

im·pon·der·a·ble (ĭm-pŏn'dər-ə-bəl) *adj.* Incapable of being weighed or evaluated precisely. **—im·pon'der·a·ble** *n.*

im·port (ĭm-pôrt', -pōrt', ĭm'pôrt', -pōrt') *v.* **1.** To bring in (goods) from a foreign country for trade or sale. **2.** *Computer Sci.* To transfer (e.g., a file) from one database to another. **3.** To mean : signify. **4.** To be significant. —*n.* (ĭm'pôrt', -pōrt'). **1.** Something imported. **2.** Meaning. **3.** Significance : importance. **—im·port'er** *n.*

im·por·tance (ĭm-pôr'tns) *n.* The quality of being important : significance.

im·por·tant (ĭm-pôr'tnt) *adj.* **1.** Likely to determine or influence events : significent. **2.** Having fame or authority : prominent <*important* people> ★ ***syns:*** BIG, CONSEQUENTIAL, MOMENTOUS, SIGNIFICANT, WEIGHTY **—im·por'tant·ly** *adv.*

im·por·ta·tion (ĭm'pôr-tā'shən, -pōr-) *n.* **1.** The act or business of importing goods. **2.** Something imported.

im·por·tu·nate (ĭm-pôr'chə-nĭt) *adj.* Persistent in pressing demands or requests. **—im·por'tu·nate·ly** *adv.*

im·por·tune (ĭm'pôr-to͞on', -tyo͞on', ĭm-pôr'chən) *v.* **-tuned, -tun·ing.** To press with repeated requests. **—im'por·tun'er** *n.* **—im'por·tu'ni·ty** *n.*

im·pose (ĭm-pōz') *v.* **-posed, -pos·ing. 1.** To enact or apply as compulsory. **2.** To obtrude or force (e.g., oneself) upon another or others. **3.** To take unfair advantage <*imposed* on her kindness> **4.** To pass off <*impose* a fraud on the public> **—im'po·si'tion** (-pə-zĭsh'ən) *n.*

im·pos·ing (ĭm-pō′zĭng) *adj.* Awesome : impressive. **—im·pos′ing·ly** *adv.*

im·pos·si·ble (ĭm-pŏs′ə-bəl) *adj.* **1.** Not capable of existing or taking place. **2.** Unlikely to happen or be done. **3.** Unacceptable. **4.** Difficult to tolerate or deal with. **—im·pos′si·bil′i·ty** *n.* **—im·pos′si·bly** *adv.*

im·post (ĭm′pōst′) *n.* A tax or duty.

im·pos·tor (ĭm-pŏs′tər) *n.* One who assumes a false identity. ★ *syns:* CHARLATAN, FAKE, FRAUD, PHONY, PRETENDER, QUACK

im·pos·ture (ĭm-pŏs′chər) *n.* Deception by the assumption of a false identity.

im·po·tent (ĭm′pə-tənt) *adj.* **1.** Without strength or vigor : weak. **2.** Having no power : ineffectual. **3.** Incapable of sexual intercourse. —Used of males. **—im′po·tence, im′po·ten·cy** *n.* **—im′po·tent·ly** *adv.*

im·pound (ĭm-pound′) *v.* **1.** To confine in or as if in a pound <*impound* stray dogs> **2.** To seize and keep in legal custody. **3.** To hold (water) in a reservoir. **—im·pound′ment** *n.*

im·pov·er·ish (ĭm-pŏv′ər-ĭsh, -pŏv′rĭsh) *v.* **1.** To make poor. **2.** To deprive of natural richness or fertility. **—im·pov′er·ish·ment** *n.*

im·prac·ti·ca·ble (ĭm-prăk′tĭ-kə-bəl) *adj.* Incapable of being done or put into practice. **—im·prac′ti·ca·bly** *adv.*

im·prac·ti·cal (ĭm-prăk′tĭ-kəl) *adj.* **1.** Unwise to put into effect : not sensible or prudent. **2.** Unable to deal with practical or financial matters efficiently. **—im·prac′ti·cal′i·ty** *n.*

im·pre·cise (ĭm′prĭ-sīs′) *adj.* Not precise.

im·preg·na·ble (ĭm-prĕg′nə-bəl) *adj.* Incapable of being successfully attacked : unconquerable. **—im·preg′na·bil′i·ty** *n.*

im·preg·nate (ĭm-prĕg′nāt′) *v.* **-nat·ed, -nat·ing. 1.** To make pregnant. **2.** To fertilize (e.g., an ovum). **3.** To fill throughout : saturate. **—im′preg·na′tion** *n.* **—im·preg′na′tor** *n.*

im·pre·sa·ri·o (ĭm′prĭ-sär′ē-ō′, -sâr′-) *n., pl.* **-os.** A theatrical manager or producer, esp. the director of an opera company.

im·press[1] (ĭm-prĕs′) *v.* **1.** To apply or produce with pressure. **2.** To stamp or mark with or as if with pressure. **3.** To fix firmly in the mind. **4.** To affect strongly and usu. favorably. —*n.* (ĭm′prĕs′). **1.** The act of impressing. **2.** A mark made by impressing. **3.** A stamp or seal for impressing. **—im·press′i·ble** *adj.*

im·press[2] (ĭm-prĕs′) *v.* **1.** To force to serve in a military force. **2.** To confiscate (property). **—im·press′ment** *n.*

im·pres·sion (ĭm-prĕsh′ən) *n.* **1.** A mark or design made on a surface by pressure. **2.** An effect or feeling retained in the mind as a result of experience. **3.** An indistinct notion or recollection. **4.** A satiric or humorous imitation of a famous personality done esp. by an entertainer. **5.** The copies of a publication printed at one time.

im·pres·sion·a·ble (ĭm-prĕsh′ə-nə-bəl) *adj.* Easily influenced : suggestible.

im·pres·sion·ism (ĭm-prĕsh′ə-nĭz′əm) *n.* A style of late 19th-cent. painting in which the immediate appearance of scenes is depicted with unmixed primary colors applied in small strokes to simulate reflected light. **—im·pres′sion·ist** *n.* **—im·pres′sion·ist′ic** *adj.*

im·pres·sive (ĭm-prĕs′ĭv) *adj.* Making a strong impression : striking. **—im·pres′sive·ly** *adv.* **—im·pres′sive·ness** *n.*

im·pri·ma·tur (ĭm′prə-mä′to͝or′) *n.* **1.** Official permission to print or publish. **2.** Official approval or authorization.

im·print (ĭm-prĭnt′, ĭm′prĭnt′) *v.* **1. a.** To make or impress (a mark or design) on a surface. **b.** To make or stamp a mark on. **2.** To fix firmly in the mind. —*n.* (ĭm′prĭnt′). **1.** A mark or design made by imprinting. **2.** A lasting influence or effect. **3.** A publisher's name, often with the date and place of publication, printed at the bottom of a title page.

im·pris·on (ĭm-prĭz′ən) *v.* To put in prison. **—im·pris′on·ment** *n.*

im·prob·a·ble (ĭm-prŏb′ə-bəl) *adj.* Not likely to occur or be true. **—im·prob′a·bil′i·ty** *n.* **—im·prob′a·bly** *adv.*

im·promp·tu (ĭm-prŏmp′to͞o, -tyo͞o) *adj.* Devised or performed without prior planning or preparation : extemporaneous. **—im·promp′tu** *adv.*

im·prop·er (ĭm-prŏp′ər) *adj.* **1.** Not suited to circumstances or needs : unsuitable. **2.** Lacking propriety : indecorous. **3.** Incorrect. **—im·prop′er·ly** *adv.*

improper fraction *n.* A fraction having a numerator larger than or the same as the denominator.

im·pro·pri·e·ty (ĭm′prə-prī′ĭ-tē) *n., pl.* **-ties. 1.** The quality or state of being improper. **2.** An improper act or remark.

im·prove (ĭm-pro͞ov′) *v.* **-proved, -prov·ing. 1.** To make or become better. **2.** To increase (e.g., land) in productivity or value. **—im·prov′a·ble** *adj.*

im·prove·ment (ĭm-pro͞ov′mənt) *n.* **1.** The act or process of improving or the condition of being improved. **2.** A change that improves.

im·prov·i·dent (ĭm-prŏv′ĭ-dənt) *adj.* Not providing for the future. **—im·prov′i·dence** *n.* **—im·prov′i·dent·ly** *adv.*

im·pro·vise (ĭm′prə-vīz′) *v.* **-vised, -vis·ing. 1.** To make up, compose, or perform without preparation. **2.** To make from available materials <*improvise* a costume from sheets> **—im·prov′i·sa′tion** (ĭm-prŏv′ĭ-zā′shən, ĭm′prə-vĭ-) *n.* **—im·prov′i·sa·to′ry** *adj.* **—im′pro·vis′er** *n.*

im·pru·dent (ĭm-pro͞od′nt) *adj.* Not prudent : unwise. **—im·pru′dence** *n.* **—im·pru′dent·ly** *adv.*

im·pu·dent (ĭm′pyə-dənt) *adj.* Marked by rude boldness or disrespect. ★ *syns:* AUDACIOUS, BOLD, BOLD-FACED, BRAZEN, CHEEKY, FORWARD, FRESH, IMPERTINENT, INSOLENT, SASSY, SAUCY **—im′pu·dence** *n.* **—im′pu·dent·ly** *adv.*

im·pugn (ĭm-pyo͞on′) *v.* To attack as false : cast doubt on.

im·pulse (ĭm′pŭls′) *n.* **1.** A driving force or the motion produced by it. **2.** A sudden spontaneous urge. **3.** A motivating force. **4.** A general tendency. **5.** *Physiol.* A transfer of energy from one neuron to another.

im•pul•sive (ĭm-pŭl′sĭv) *adj.* **1.** Acting on impulse rather than thought. **2.** Resulting from impulse : uncalculated <an *impulsive* gesture> **3.** Setting objects in motion. **—im•pul′sive•ly** *adv.* **—im•pul′sive•ness** *n.*

im•pu•ni•ty (ĭm-pyo͞o′nĭ-tē) *n.* Exemption from punishment.

im•pure (ĭm-pyo͝or′) *adj.* **1.** Not pure : unclean. **2.** Unchaste or obscene. **3.** Mixed with another substance : adulterated. **4.** Deriving from more than one source or style. **—im•pure′ly** *adv.* **—im•pu′ri•ty** *n.*

im•pute (ĭm-pyo͞ot′) *v.* **-put•ed, -put•ing.** To attribute (e.g., a mistake) to another : charge. **—im′pu•ta′tion** *n.*

in (ĭn) *prep.* **1.** Within the bounds of <walking *in* the park> **2.** Into. **3.** To a condition of <divided *in* 2><*in* love> **4.** Having the activity or function of <*in* business> **5.** During. **6.** Wearing <a man *in* shorts> **7.** Having the arrangement or style of <hanging *in* pleats><a letter *in* verse> **8.** By means of. **9.** With reference to <4 feet *in* height> **10.** Out of <picked 1 *in* 4> *—adv.* **1.** To the inside <walked *in*> **2.** To a goal or place <drove *in* from the country> **3.** So as to be included or contained. **4.** So as to be fashionable. *—adj.* **1.** Incoming <the *in* bus> **2.** Available or at home. **3.** Having power <the *in* party> **4.** Fashionable or fashion-minded <the *in* crowd> *—n.* **1.** One in office or power. **2.** Influence. **—in for.** Guaranteed to get or have.

In *symbol for* INDIUM.

in– *pref.* Not <*in*congruous>

in ab•sen•tia (ĭn′ăb-sĕn′shə, -shē-ə) *adv.* In absence.

in•ac•ces•si•ble (ĭn′ăk-sĕs′ə-bəl) *adj.* Not accessible : unreachable. **—in′ac•ces′si•bil′i•ty** *n.* **—in′ac•ces′si•bly** *adv.*

in•ac•tion (ĭn-ăk′shən) *n.* Lack of action.

in•ac•ti•vate (ĭn-ăk′tə-vāt′) *v.* **-vat•ed, -vat•ing.** To make inactive. **—in•ac′ti•va′tion** *n.*

in•ac•tive (ĭn-ăk′tĭv) *adj.* **1.** Not active or inclined to be active. **2.** Out of current use or service. ★ ***syns:*** DORMANT, IDLE, INERT, INOPERATIVE **—in•ac′tive•ly** *adv.* **—in′ac•tiv′i•ty, in•ac′tive•ness** *n.*

in•ad•e•quate (ĭn-ăd′ĭ-kwĭt) *adj.* Not adequate. **—in•ad′e•qua•cy** *n.* **—in•ad′e•quate•ly** *adv.*

in•ad•ver•tent (ĭn′əd-vûr′tnt) *adj.* **1.** Unintentional : accidental. **2.** Inattentive. **—in′ad•ver′tence** *n.* **—in′ad•ver′tent•ly** *adv.*

in•al•ien•a•ble (ĭn-āl′yə-nə-bəl) *adj.* Not capable of being given up or transferred <*inalienable* rights> **—in•al′ien•a•bil′i•ty** *n.* **—in•al′ien•a•bly** *adv.*

in•ane (ĭn-ān′) *adj.* Without sense or substance : silly <an *inane* comment> **—in•ane′ly** *adv.* **—in•an′i•ty** (ĭn-ăn′ĭ-tē) *n.*

in•an•i•mate (ĭn-ăn′ə-mĭt) *adj.* **1.** Not having the qualities of living organisms. **2.** Unanimated : lifeless. **—in•an′i•mate•ly** *adv.* **—in•an′i•mate•ness** *n.*

in•a•ni•tion (ĭn′ə-nĭsh′ən) *n.* Exhaustion, esp. from malnourishment.

in•ap•pre•cia•ble (ĭn′ə-prē′shə-bəl) *adj.* Too small to be significant : negligible. **—in′ap•pre′cia•bly** *adv.*

in•ar•tic•u•late (ĭn′är-tĭk′yə-lĭt) *adj.* **1.** Not uttering or forming intelligible words or syllables <an *inarticulate* cry> **2.** Unable to speak : speechless. **3.** Unable to speak clearly or effectively. **4.** Unexpressed <*inarticulate* sorrow> **—in′ar•tic′u•late•ly** *adv.* **—in′ar•tic′u•late•ness** *n.*

---

in′a•bil′i•ty *n.*
in′ac•cept′a•ble *adj.*
in•ac′cu•ra•cy *n.*
in•ac′cu•rate *adj.*
in•ac′tion *n.*
in′ad•mis′si•bil′i•ty *n.*
in′ad•mis′si•ble *adj.*
in′ad•vis′a•bil′i•ty *n.*
in′ad•vis′a•ble *adj.*
in•ap′pli•ca•ble *adj.*
in•ap′po•site *adj.*
in′ap•pre′cia•tive *adj.*
in′ap•proach′a•ble *adj.*
in′ap•pro′pri•ate *adj.*
in•apt′ *adj.*
in•ap′ti•tude′ *n.*
in′ar•tis′tic *adj.*
in′at•ten′tion *n.*
in′at•ten′tive *adj.*
in•au′di•ble *adj.*
in•au′di•bly *adv.*
in′aus•pi′cious *adj.*
in•ca′pa•bil′i•ty *n.*
in•ca′pa•ble *adj.*
in′ci•vil′i•ty *n.*
in′com•mu′ni•ca•ble *adj.*
in•com′pre•hen′si•ble *adj.*
in′com•pre•hen′sion *n.*
in′con•ceiv′a•bil′i•ty *n.*
in′con•ceiv′a•ble *adj.*
in′con•clu′sive *adj.*
in′con•sec′u•tive *adj.*
in′con•sis′ten•cy *n.*
in′con•sis′tent *adj.*
in•con′so•nant *adj.*
in′con•ver′sant *adj.*
in′co•or′di•na′tion *n.*
in′cor•po′re•al *adj.*
in′cor•rect′ *adj.*
in•cur′a•ble *adj.*
in′de•fen′si•ble *adj.*
in•def′i•nite *adj.*
in′de•struc′ti•ble *adj.*
in′de•ter′min•a•ble *adj.*
in′dis•cern′i•ble *adj.*
in′dis•cov′er•a•ble *adj.*
in′dis•tin′guish•a•ble *adj.*
in•duc′tile *adj.*
in•ed′i•ble *adj.*
in•ed′u•ca•ble *adj.*
in′ef•fec′tive *adj.*
in′ef•fec′tu•al *adj.*
in•ef′fi•ca′cious *adj.*
in•ef′fi•ca•cy *n.*
in′e•las′tic *adj.*
in′e•las•tic′i•ty *n.*
in•el′i•gi•bil′i•ty *n.*
in•el′i•gi•ble *adj.*
in•eq′ui•ta•ble *adj.*
in•eq′ui•ty *n.*
in′e•rad′i•ca•ble *adj.*
in′ex•pe′di•ent *adj.*
in′ex•pen′sive *adj.*
in′ex•pres′sive *adj.*
in′ex•tin′guish•a•ble *adj.*
in•fea′si•ble *adj.*
in•fer′tile *adj.*
in′fer•til′i•ty *n.*
in•fran′gi•ble *adj.*
in′har•mo′ni•ous *adj.*
in•hos′pi•ta•ble *adj.*
in′ju•di′cious *adj.*
in′of•fen′sive *adj.*
in′sa•lu′bri•ous *adj.*
in•san′i•tar•y *adj.*
in•sen′si•tive *adj.*
in•sen′si•tiv′i•ty *n.*
in′sig•nif′i•cant *adj.*
in′so•bri′e•ty *n.*
in′sup•press′i•ble *adj.*
in′sus•cep′ti•ble *adj.*

in·as·much as (ĭn′əz-mŭch′) *conj.* Because of the fact that : since.

in·au·gu·ral (ĭn-ô′gyər-əl) *adj.* **1.** Of or for an inauguration. **2.** Initial : opening. —*n.* **1.** An inauguration. **2.** An inaugural speech.

in·au·gu·rate (ĭn-ô′gyə-rāt′) *v.* **-rat·ed, -rat·ing. 1.** To put into office with a formal ceremony : install. **2.** To begin officially. **3.** To begin use of formally : dedicate. **—in·au′gu·ra′tion** *n.* **—in·au′gu·ra′tor** *n.*

in between *adv. & prep.* Between.

in-be·tween (ĭn′bĭ-twēn′) *adj.* Intermediate <a vague *in-between* statement> —*n.* An intermediate or intermediary.

in·board (ĭn′bôrd′, -bōrd′) *adj.* **1.** Within a ship's hull. **2.** Close to or near the fuselage of an aircraft <the *inboard* engines> **—in′·board′** *adv.*

in·born (ĭn′bôrn′) *adj.* **1.** Possessed at birth : natural. **2.** Hereditary : inherent.

in·bound (ĭn′bound′) *adj.* Incoming.

in·bred (ĭn′brĕd′) *adj.* **1.** Produced by inbreeding. **2.** Deep-seated : innate.

in·breed (ĭn′brēd′, ĭn-brēd′) *v.* To produce by repeatedly breeding closely related individuals.

In·ca (ĭng′kə) *n., pl.* **-ca** *or* **-cas. 1.** One of an Indian people who ruled Peru before the Spanish conquest in the 16th cent. **2.** A ruler of the Inca empire. **—In′can** *adj. & n.*

in·cal·cu·la·ble (ĭn-kăl′kyə-lə-bəl) *adj.* **1.** Not calculable : indeterminate. **2.** Unpredictable. **—in·cal′cu·la·bly** *adv.*

in·can·des·cent (ĭn′kən-dĕs′ənt) *adj.* **1.** Giving off visible light when heated. **2.** Shining brightly. **3.** Ardently emotional or intense. **—in′can·des′cence** *n.*

incandescent lamp *n.* A lamp in which a filament is heated to incandescence by an electric current.

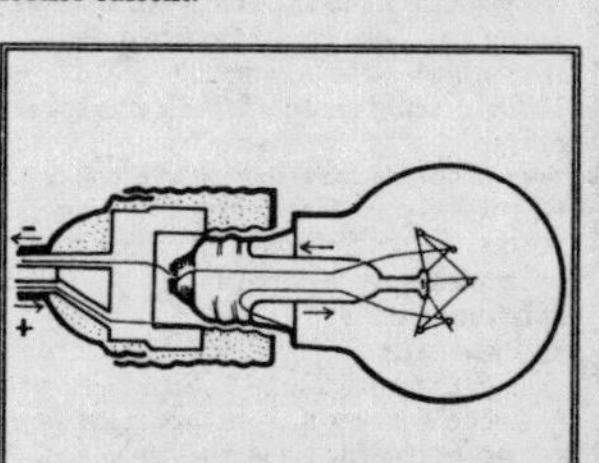

incandescent lamp

in·can·ta·tion (ĭn′kăn-tā′shən) *n.* **1.** A recitation of magic charms or spells. **2.** A magic formula for chanting or reciting.

in·ca·pac·i·tate (ĭn′kə-păs′ĭ-tāt′) *v.* **-tat·ed, -tat·ing. 1.** To render incapable : disable. **2.** *Law.* To disqualify. **—in′ca·pac′i·ta′tion** *n.*

in·ca·pac·i·ty (ĭn′kə-păs′ĭ-tē) *n., pl.* **-ties. 1.** Inadequate ability or strength. **2.** A defect : disability. **3.** *Law.* A disqualification.

in·car·cer·ate (ĭn-kär′sə-rāt′) *v.* **-at·ed, -at·ing. 1.** To put in jail. **2.** To confine. **—in·car′·cer·a′tion** *n.*

in·car·nate (ĭn-kär′nĭt, -nāt′) *adj.* **1.** Having a bodily form and nature. **2.** Embodied : personified <beauty *incarnate*> —*v.* (-nāt′) **-nat·ed, -nat·ing. 1.** To give bodily form to. **2.** To personify : embody.

in·car·na·tion (ĭn′kär-nā′shən) *n.* **1.** The act of incarnating or state of being incarnated. **2. Incarnation.** *Theol.* The embodiment of God in the human form of Jesus. **3.** One regarded as personifying a given abstract quality or idea.

in·case (ĭn-kās′) *v. var. of* ENCASE.

in·cen·di·ar·y (ĭn-sĕn′dē-ĕr′ē) *adj.* **1.** Causing or capable of causing fires <an *incendiary* bomb> **2.** Of or relating to arson. **3.** Tending to inflame : inflammatory. **—in·cen′di·ar·y** *n.*

in·cense[1] (ĭn-sĕns′) *v.* **-censed, -cens·ing.** To make angry : infuriate.

in·cense[2] (ĭn′sĕns′) *n.* **1.** A substance, as a gum or wood, burned to produce a pleasant odor. **2.** The smoke or odor produced.

in·cen·tive (ĭn-sĕn′tĭv) *n.* Something inciting one to action or effort : stimulus.

in·cep·tion (ĭn-sĕp′shən) *n.* A beginning : origin. **—in·cep′tive** *adj.*

in·cer·ti·tude (ĭn-sûr′tĭ-to͞od′, -tyo͞od′) *n.* **1.** Uncertainty. **2.** Lack of confidence. **3.** Instability : insecurity.

in·ces·sant (ĭn-sĕs′ənt) *adj.* Occurring without interruption : continuous. **—in·ces′·sant·ly** *adv.*

in·cest (ĭn′sĕst′) *n.* Sexual intercourse between persons so closely related that their marriage is forbidden by law or custom. **—in·ces′tu·ous** (ĭn-sĕs′cho͞o-əs) *adj.* **—in·ces′tu·ous·ly** *adv.*

inch (ĭnch) *n.* —See table at MEASUREMENT. —*v.* To move slowly or by small amounts.

▲ ***word history:*** The Latin word *uncia,* meaning "a 1/12 part," was borrowed into English twice. *Uncia* was borrowed into Old English as *ynce,* denoting a linear measure of 1/12 of a foot. The word remains in Modern English as *inch. Uncia* also developed into Old French *unce,* a unit of troy weight equal to 1/12 of a pound. It was borrowed into Middle English and survives in Modern English as *ounce.*

in·cho·ate (ĭn-kō′ĭt) *adj.* In an early stage : incipient. **—in·cho′ate·ly** *adv.* **—in·cho′ate·ness** *n.*

inch·worm (ĭnch′wûrm′) *n.* A measuring worm.

in·ci·dence (ĭn′sĭ-dəns) *n.* **1.** The extent or rate of occurrence <the reduced *incidence* of polio> **2.** The striking of a surface, as by radiation.

in·ci·dent (ĭn′sĭ-dənt) *n.* **1.** A usu. minor event : occurrence. **2.** An event that disrupts normal procedure or causes a crisis. —*adj.* **1.** Tending to occur, esp. along with something else <summer heat and *incident* thunderstorms> **2.** Striking a surface <*incident* radiation>

in•ci•den•tal (ĭn'sĭ-dĕn'tl) *adj.* **1.** Occurring or likely to occur at the same time or as a result. **2.** Subordinate : minor <*incidental* expenses> —*n.* A minor attendant circumstance, item, or expense. —**in'ci•den'tal•ly** *adv.*

in•cin•er•ate (ĭn-sĭn'ə-rāt') *v.* **-at•ed, -at•ing.** To burn up. —**in•cin'er•a'tion** *n.*

in•cin•er•a•tor (ĭn-sĭn'ə-rā'tər) *n.* One that incinerates, esp. a furnace for burning waste.

in•cip•i•ent (ĭn-sĭp'ē-ənt) *adj.* Just beginning to appear or occur. —**in•cip'i•ence** *n.* —**in•cip'i•ent•ly** *adv.*

in•cise (ĭn-sīz') *v.* **-cised, -cis•ing. 1.** To make or cut into with a sharp tool. **2.** To carve (e.g., writing) into a surface : engrave.

in•ci•sion (ĭn-sĭzh'ən) *n.* **1.** The act of incising. **2.** A cut or notch, esp. a surgical cut.

in•ci•sive (ĭn-sī'sĭv) *adj.* **1.** Having or suggesting sharp intellect : penetrating. **2.** Cogent and effective : telling <an *incisive* summary> ★ ***syns:*** ACUTE, BITING, PENETRATING, PERCEPTIVE, SHARP, SHREWD, TRENCHANT —**in•ci'sive•ly** *adv.* —**in•ci'sive•ness** *n.*

in•ci•sor (ĭn-sī'zər) *n.* A cutting tooth at the front of the mouth.

in•cite (ĭn-sīt') *v.* **-cit•ed, -cit•ing.** To provoke to action : goad. —**in•cite'ment** *n.* —**in•cit'er** *n.*

in•clem•ent (ĭn-klĕm'ənt) *adj.* **1.** Stormy or rainy <*inclement* weather> **2.** Showing no mercy. —**in•clem'en•cy** *n.*

in•cli•na•tion (ĭn'klə-nā'shən) *n.* **1.** An attitude : disposition. **2.** A tendency to act or think in a certain way : propensity. **3.** A preference. **4.** A bow or tilt. **5.** A slope.

in•cline (ĭn-klīn') *v.* **-clined, -clin•ing. 1.** To deviate or cause to deviate from the horizontal or vertical : slant. **2.** To dispose or be disposed <Experience *inclined* her to be cautious.> **3.** To bow or nod. —*n.* (ĭn'klīn'). An inclined surface.

in•close (ĭn-klōz') *v. var. of* ENCLOSE.

in•clude (ĭn-klōōd') *v.* **-clud•ed, -clud•ing. 1.** To have as a part or member : contain. **2.** To put into a group or total. —**in•clu'sion** *n.* —**in•clu'sive** *adj.* —**in•clu'sive•ly** *adv.*

in•cog•ni•to (ĭn-kŏg'nĭ-tō, ĭn'kŏg-nē'tō) *adv.* *& adj.* With one's identity hidden.

in•co•her•ent (ĭn'kō-hîr'ənt) *adj.* **1.** Lacking order, connection, or harmony. **2.** Unable to think or speak clearly or consecutively. —**in'co•her'ence** *n.* —**in'co•her'ent•ly** *adv.*

in•com•bus•ti•ble (ĭn'kəm-bŭs'tə-bəl) *adj.* Incapable of burning. —**in'com•bus'ti•ble** *n.*

in•come (ĭn'kŭm') *n.* Money or its equivalent received in return for work, from a business, or as profit from investments.

income tax *n.* A tax on income earned by an individual or business.

in•com•ing (ĭn'kŭm'ĭng) *adj.* Coming in or soon to come in.

in•com•men•su•rate (ĭn'kə-mĕn'sər-ĭt, -shər-) *adj.* **1.** Not commensurate : disproportionate. **2.** Inadequate : insufficient. —**in'com•men'su•rate•ly** *adv.*

in•com•mode (ĭn'kə-mōd') *v.* **-mod•ed, -mod•ing.** To inconvenience : disturb.

in•com•mu•ni•ca•do (ĭn'kə-myōō'nĭ-kä'dō) *adv. & adj.* Without being able to communicate with others.

in•com•pa•ra•ble (ĭn-kŏm'pər-ə-bəl) *adj.* **1.** Incapable of being compared. **2.** Without rival : unique. —**in•com'pa•ra•bly** *adv.*

in•com•pat•i•ble (ĭn'kəm-păt'ə-bəl) *adj.* **1.** Not suited for combination or association <*incompatible* colors><*incompatible* roommates> **2.** Inconsistent. —**in'com•pat'i•bil'i•ty** *n.* —**in'com•pat'i•bly** *adv.*

in•com•pe•tent (ĭn-kŏm'pĭ-tənt) *adj.* Not competent. —**in•com'pe•tence, in•com'pe•ten•cy** *n.* —**in•com'pe•tent** *n.*

in•com•plete (ĭn'kəm-plēt') *adj.* Not complete. —**in'com•plete'ly** *adv.* —**in'com•plete'ness** *n.*

in•com•press•i•ble (ĭn'kəm-prĕs'ə-bəl) *adj.* Not capable of being compressed. —**in'com•press'i•bil'i•ty** *n.*

in•con•gru•ent (ĭn-kŏng'grōō-ənt, ĭn'kŏn-grōō'ənt) *adj.* **1.** Not congruent. **2.** Incongruous. —**in'con•gru'ence** *n.* —**in'con•gru'ent•ly** *adv.*

in•con•gru•ous (ĭn-kŏng'grōō-əs) *adj.* **1.** Not corresponding : disagreeing. **2.** Made up of diverse or discordant elements. **3.** Unsuited to the surroundings or setting <an *incongruous* costume> —**in'con•gru'i•ty** *n.* —**in•con'gru•ous•ly** *adv.*

in•con•se•quen•tial (ĭn-kŏn'sĭ-kwĕn'shəl) *adj.* Without importance : insignificant. —**in•con'se•quen'ti•al'i•ty** (-shē-ăl'ĭ-tē) *n.*

in•con•sid•er•a•ble (ĭn'kən-sĭd'ər-ə-bəl) *adj.* Unimportant : trivial. —**in'con•sid'er•a•bly** *adv.*

in•con•sid•er•ate (ĭn'kən-sĭd'ər-ĭt) *adj.* Not considerate : thoughtless. —**in'con•sid'er•ate•ly** *adv.* —**in'con•sid'er•ate•ness** *n.*

in•con•sol•a•ble (ĭn'kən-sō'lə-bəl) *adj.* Incapable of being consoled. —**in'con•sol'a•bly** *adv.*

in•con•spic•u•ous (ĭn'kən-spĭk'yōō-əs) *adj.* Not readily seen or noticed. ★ ***syns:*** OBSCURE, UNNOTICEABLE, UNOBTRUSIVE —**in'con•spic'u•ous•ly** *adv.* —**in'con•spic'u•ous•ness** *n.*

in•con•stant (ĭn-kŏn'stənt) *adj.* **1.** Likely to change : unpredictable. **2.** Faithless : fickle. —**in•con'stan•cy** *n.* —**in•con'stant•ly** *adv.*

in•con•test•a•ble (ĭn'kən-tĕs'tə-bəl) *adj.* Not capable of being challenged or doubted : unquestionable. —**in'con•test'a•bil'i•ty** *n.* —**in'con•test'a•bly** *adv.*

in•con•ti•nent (ĭn-kŏn'tə-nənt) *adj.* **1.** Not restrained : uncontrolled. **2.** Unable to contain or restrain something specified. **3.** Incapable of controlling the excretory functions. —**in•con'ti•nence** *n.* —**in•con'ti•nent•ly** *adv.*

in•con•tro•vert•i•ble (ĭn-kŏn'trə-vûr'tə-bəl) *adj.* Unquestionable : indisputable. —**in•con'tro•vert'i•bly** *adv.*

in•con•ven•ience (ĭn'kən-vēn'yəns) *n.* **1.** The quality or state of being inconvenient. **2.**

Something inconvenient. —*v.* **-ienced, -ienc•ing.** To cause inconvenience to : bother.

in•con•ven•ient (ĭn'kən-vēn'yənt) *adj.* Not convenient : causing trouble or difficulty. —**in'con•ven'ient•ly** *adv.*

in•cor•po•rate (ĭn-kôr'pə-rāt') *v.* **-rat•ed, -rat•ing. 1.** To combine into a unified whole : unite. **2.** To form or cause to form a legal corporation. **3.** To give a physical form to : embody. —**in•cor'po•ra'tion** *n.* —**in•cor'po•ra'tor** *n.*

in•cor•po•re•al (ĭn'kôr-pôr'ē-əl, -pōr'-) *adj.* Without material form or substance. —**in'cor•po're•al•ly** *adv.*

in•cor•ri•gi•ble (ĭn-kôr'ə-jə-bəl, -kŏr'-) *adj.* Incapable of being reformed or corrected <an *incorrigible* criminal> —**in•cor'ri•gi•bil'i•ty** *n.* —**in•cor'ri•gi•ble** *n.* —**in•cor'ri•gi•bly** *adv.*

in•cor•rupt•i•ble (ĭn'kə-rŭp'tə-bəl) *adj.* **1.** Not capable of being corrupted morally. **2.** Not subject to decay. —**in'cor•rupt'i•bil'i•ty** *n.* —**in'cor•rupt'i•bly** *adv.*

in•crease (ĭn-krēs') *v.* **-creased, -creas•ing. 1.** To make or become greater or larger. **2.** To have offspring : reproduce. ★ ***syns:*** AMPLIFY, AUGMENT, ENLARGE, EXPAND, EXTEND, GROW, MAGNIFY, MOUNT, MULTIPLY, SNOWBALL, SWELL —*n.* (ĭn'krēs'). **1.** The act of increasing. **2.** The amount or rate of increasing. —**in•creas'ing•ly** *adv.*

in•cred•i•ble (ĭn-krĕd'ə-bəl) *adj.* **1.** Too unlikely to be believed : unbelievable. **2.** Extraordinary : astonishing. —**in•cred'i•bil'i•ty** *n.* —**in•cred'i•bly** *adv.*

in•cred•u•lous (ĭn-krĕj'ə-ləs) *adj.* **1.** Skeptical : disbelieving. **2.** Expressive of disbelief. —**in'cre•du'li•ty** (ĭn'krĭ-dōō'lĭ-tē, -dyōō'-) *n.* —**in•cred'u•lous•ly** *adv.*

in•cre•ment (ĭn'krə-mənt) *n.* **1.** An increase. **2.** Something gained or added, esp. one of a series of regular additions. —**in'cre•men'tal** *adj.*

in•crim•i•nate (ĭn-krĭm'ə-nāt') *v.* **-nat•ed, -nat•ing.** To involve in or charge with a wrongful act, as a crime. —**in•crim'i•na'tion** *n.* —**in•crim'i•na•to'ry** (-nə-tôr'ē, -tōr'ē) *adj.*

in•crust (ĭn-krŭst') *v. var. of* ENCRUST.

in•cu•bate (ĭn'kyə-bāt', ĭng'-) *v.* **-bat•ed, -bat•ing. 1.** To warm and hatch (eggs), as by bodily heat. **2.** To maintain (e.g., a bacterial culture) in favorable conditions for growth. —**in'cu•ba'tion** *n.*

in•cu•ba•tor (ĭn'kyə-bā'tər, ĭng'-) *n.* **1.** A cabinet in which a desired temperature can be maintained, used for bacterial culture. **2.** An enclosure for maintaining a premature infant in a controlled environment. **3.** A temperature-controlled enclosure for hatching eggs artificially.

in•cu•bus (ĭn'kyə-bəs, ĭng'-) *n., pl.* **-bus•es** *or* **-bi** (-bī'). **1.** An evil spirit believed to seize or harm women as they sleep. **2.** A nightmare. **3.** A nightmarish burden.

in•cu•des (ĭng-kyōō'dēz) *n. pl. of* INCUS.

in•cul•cate (ĭn-kŭl'kāt') *v.* **-cat•ed, -cat•ing.** To impress on the mind by frequent repetition or instruction. —**in'cul•ca'tion** *n.* —**in•cul'ca'tor** *n.*

in•cul•pate (ĭn-kŭl'pāt') *v.* **-pat•ed, -pat•ing.** To incriminate.

in•cum•bent (ĭn-kŭm'bənt) *adj.* **1.** Lying or resting on something else. **2.** Imposed as an obligation : obligatory. **3.** Currently in office <the *incumbent* governor> —*n.* One who is currently in office. —**in•cum'ben•cy** *n.* —**in•cum'bent•ly** *adv.*

in•cu•nab•u•lum (ĭn'kyə-năb'yə-ləm, ĭng'-) *n., pl.* **-la** (-lə). A book printed before 1501.

in•cur (ĭn-kûr') *v.* **-curred, -cur•ring.** To become liable or subject to, esp. because of one's own actions. —**in•cur'rence** *n.*

in•cu•ri•ous (ĭn-kyŏŏr'ē-əs) *adj.* Lacking interest or curiosity : detached.

in•cur•sion (ĭn-kûr'zhən) *n.* A sudden hostile intrusion into another's territory.

in•cus (ĭng'kəs) *n., pl.* **in•cu•des** (ĭng-kyōō'dēz). An anvil-shaped bone in the middle ear of mammals.

in•debt•ed (ĭn-dĕt'ĭd) *adj.* Obligated to another, as for money or a favor : beholden. —**in•debt'ed•ness** *n.*

in•de•cent (ĭn-dē'sənt) *adj.* **1.** Offensive to good taste : improper. **2.** Morally offensive : immodest. —**in•de'cen•cy** *n.* —**in•de'cent•ly** *adv.*

in•de•ci•pher•a•ble (ĭn'dĭ-sī'fər-ə-bəl) *adj.* Not capable of being deciphered or interpreted.

in•de•ci•sion (ĭn'dĭ-sĭzh'ən) *n.* Inability to make up one's mind : irresolution.

in•de•ci•sive (ĭn'dĭ-sī'sĭv) *adj.* **1.** Without a clear-cut result : inconclusive. **2.** Marked by indecision : irresolute. —**in'de•ci'sive•ly** *adv.* —**in'de•ci'sive•ness** *n.*

in•dec•o•rous (ĭn-dĕk'ər-əs) *adj.* Lacking good taste or propriety. —**in•dec'o•rous•ly** *adv.* —**in•dec'o•rous•ness** *n.*

in•deed (ĭn-dēd') *adv.* **1.** Without doubt : certainly. **2.** In reality : in fact. **3.** Admittedly. —*interj.* —Used to express surprise, irony, or disbelief.

in•de•fat•i•ga•ble (ĭn'dĭ-făt'ĭ-gə-bəl) *adj.* Tireless. —**in•de•fat'i•ga•bly** *adv.*

in•de•fin•a•ble (ĭn'dĭ-fī'nə-bəl) *adj.* Not capable of being defined or precisely described <an *indefinable* charm> —**in'de•fin'a•ble•ness** *n.* —**in'de•fin'a•bly** *adv.*

in•def•i•nite (ĭn-dĕf'ə-nĭt) *adj.* **1.** Not decided or specified <an *indefinite* date> **2.** Vague : unclear. **3.** Lacking fixed limits. ★ ***syns:*** OPEN, UNCERTAIN, UNDECIDED, UNDETERMINED, UNRESOLVED, UNSETTLED, UNSURE, VAGUE —**in•def'i•nite•ly** *adv.* —**in•def'i•nite•ness** *n.*

in•del•i•ble (ĭn-dĕl'ə-bəl) *adj.* **1.** Not able to be erased or washed away : permanent <an *indelible* memory> **2.** Making marks that are hard to erase or wash away <an *indelible* pen> —**in•del'i•bly** *adv.*

in•del•i•cate (ĭn-dĕl'ĭ-kĭt) *adj.* **1.** Lacking in propriety : coarse. **2.** Lacking sensitivity : tactless. —**in•del'i•ca•cy** *n.* —**in•del'i•cate•ly** *adv.*

in•dem•ni•fy (ĭn-dĕm′nə-fī′) *v.* **-fied, -fy•ing. 1.** To protect against loss or damage **:** insure. **2.** To make compensation to for loss or damage. **—in•dem′ni•fi•ca′tion** *n.* **—in•dem′ni•fi′er** *n.*

in•dem•ni•ty (ĭn-dĕm′nĭ-tē) *n., pl.* **-ties. 1.** Security against damage or loss **:** insurance. **2.** A legal exemption from liability for damages. **3.** Compensation for damage or loss.

in•dent[1] (ĭn-dĕnt′) *v.* **1.** To set (e.g., the first line of a paragraph) in from the margin. **2.** To make notches in **:** serrate. *—n.* An indentation.

in•dent[2] (ĭn-dĕnt′) *v.* **1.** To make a dent or depression in. **2.** To impress **:** stamp.

in•den•ta•tion (ĭn′dĕn-tā′shən) *n.* **1.** The act of indenting or state of being indented. **2.** The blank space between a margin and the beginning of an indented line. **3.** A recess in a coastline or border. **4.** A notch in an edge.

in•den•ture (ĭn-dĕn′chər) *n.* **1.** A legal deed or contract. **2.** *often* **indentures.** A contract obligating one party to work for another for a specified period of time. *—v.* **-tured, -tur•ing.** To bind into the service of another.

in•de•pend•ence (ĭn′dĭ-pĕn′dəns) *n.* The quality or state of being independent.

Independence Day *n.* July 4, a U.S. legal holiday commemorating the adoption of the Declaration of Independence in 1776.

in•de•pend•ent (ĭn′dĭ-pĕn′dənt) *adj.* **1.** Politically self-governing. **2.** Free from the control of others **:** self-reliant. **3. a.** Not affiliated with a larger group or system. **b.** Not committed to a political party or faction <an *independent* candidate> **4.** Not relying on others, esp. for financial support. **5.** Providing or being enough income to enable one to live without working. *—n.* One that is independent, esp. a candidate or voter not committed to a political party. **—in′de•pend′ent•ly** *adv.*

in-depth (ĭn′dĕpth′) *adj.* Thorough **:** detailed <an *in-depth* analysis>

in•de•scrib•a•ble (ĭn′dĭ-skrī′bə-bəl) *adj.* **1.** Incapable of being described. **2.** Exceeding description. **—in′de•scrib′a•bly** *adv.*

in•de•ter•mi•nate (ĭn′dĭ-tûr′mə-nĭt) *adj.* **1.** Not determined. **2.** Incapable of being determined. **3.** Unclear or imprecise **:** vague. **—in′de•ter′mi•na•cy** *n.* **—in′de•ter′mi•nate•ly** *adv.*

in•dex (ĭn′dĕks′) *n., pl.* **-dex•es** *or* **-di•ces** (-dĭ-sēz′). **1.** A list or catalogue for aiding reference, esp. an alphabetized listing in a printed work that gives the pages on which various names, places, and subjects are mentioned. **2.** Something serving to guide or point out, esp. a printed character calling attention to a paragraph or section. **3.** Something that measures or indicates **:** sign. **4.** A pointer, as in a scientific instrument. **5. a.** *Math.* A small number just above and to the left of a radical sign indicating what root is to be extracted. **b.** Any number or symbol indicating an operation to be performed on an expression. **6.** A number or scale indicating change in magnitude, as of prices, relative to the magnitude at some specified point usu. taken as 100 <the cost-of-living *index*> *—v.* **1.** To provide with or enter in an index. **2.** To indicate **:** signal. **3.** To adjust through indexation.

in•dex•a•tion (ĭn′dĕk-sā′shən) *n.* The linkage of economic factors, as wages or prices, to a cost-of-living index so they rise and fall within the rate of inflation.

index finger *n.* The finger next to the thumb.

index of refraction *n.* The ratio of the speed of light in a vacuum to the speed of light in a medium under consideration.

In•di•an (ĭn′dē-ən) *n.* **1.** A native or inhabitant of India. **2.** An American Indian. **—In′di•an** *adj.*

Indian corn *n.* The American corn plant or its ripened ears.

Indian meal *n.* Cornmeal.

Indian pipe *n.* A waxy white woodland plant, *Monotropa uniflora,* with a single nodding flower.

Indian summer *n.* A period of mild weather in late autumn.

India paper *n.* **1.** A thin, uncoated, delicate paper used esp. for taking impressions of engravings. **2.** A thin, strong opaque printing paper used esp. for Bibles.

in•di•cate (ĭn′dĭ-kāt′) *v.* **-cat•ed, -cat•ing. 1.** To point out **:** show <*indicate* the quickest route> **2.** To serve as a sign or symptom of **:** signify. **3.** To suggest the advisability of **:** call for. **4.** To express briefly. **—in′di•ca′tion** *n.* **—in′di•ca′tor** *n.*

in•dic•a•tive (ĭn-dĭk′ə-tĭv) *adj.* **1.** Serving to indicate. **2.** Of or being a verb mood used to express actions and conditions that are objective facts. *—n.* **1.** The indicative mood. **2.** A verb in the indicative mood.

in•di•ces (ĭn′dĭ-sēz′) *n. var. pl. of* INDEX.

in•dict (ĭn-dīt′) *v.* **1.** To accuse of an offense **:** charge. **2.** To make a formal accusation against by the findings of a grand jury. **—in•dict′a•ble** *adj.* **—in•dict′er, in•dic′tor** *n.* **—in•dict′ment** *n.*

in•dif•fer•ent (ĭn-dĭf′ər-ənt) *adj.* **1.** Not mattering **:** unimportant. **2.** Having no marked feeling or preference **:** impartial. **3.** Uninterested **:** apathetic. **4.** Neither good nor bad **:** mediocre. **5.** Neither right nor wrong. **—in•dif′fer•ence** *n.* **—in•dif′fer•ent•ly** *adv.*

in•dig•e•nous (ĭn-dĭj′ə-nəs) *adj.* Living or occurring naturally in an area **:** native.

in•di•gent (ĭn′də-jənt) *adj.* Impoverished **:** needy. **—in′di•gence** *n.*

in•di•gest•i•ble (ĭn′dĭ-jĕs′tə-bəl, -dī-) *adj.* Impossible or difficult to digest. **—in′di•gest′i•bil′i•ty** *n.* **—in′di•gest′i•bly** *adv.*

in•di•ges•tion (ĭn′dĭ-jĕs′chən, -dī-) *n.* Difficulty or discomfort in digesting food.

in•dig•nant (ĭn-dĭg′nənt) *adj.* Marked by or filled with indignation. **—in•dig′nant•ly** *adv.*

in•dig•na•tion (ĭn′dĭg-nā′shən) *n.* Anger aroused by injustice or unworthiness.

in•dig•ni•ty (ĭn-dĭg′nĭ-tē) *n., pl.* **-ties. 1.** Humiliating treatment. **2.** Something that offends one's pride **:** affront.

in·di·go (ĭn'dĭ-gō') *n., pl.* **-gos** *or* **-goes. 1.** A blue dye obtained from a plant or produced synthetically. **2.** A dark blue.

indigo bunting *n.* A small North American bird, *Passerina cyanea,* the male of which has deep-blue plumage.

indigo snake *n.* A nonvenomous bluish-black snake, *Drymarchon corais,* of the S U.S. and N Mexico.

in·di·rect (ĭn'də-rĕkt', -dī-) *adj.* **1.** Not taking a direct course **:** roundabout. **2.** Not straight to the point or forthright **:** devious. **3.** Not immediate or intended **:** secondary <*indirect* results> **—in'di·rec'tion** *n.* **—in·di·rect'ly** *adv.*

in·dis·creet (ĭn'dĭ-skrēt') *adj.* Lacking discretion. **—in'dis·creet'ly** *adv.* **—in'dis·cre'tion** (-skrĕsh'ən) *n.*

in·dis·crim·i·nate (ĭn'dĭ-skrĭm'ə-nĭt) *adj.* **1.** Lacking discrimination. **2.** Haphazard **:** random. **3.** Not sorted out **:** confused. **—in'dis·crim'i·nate·ly** *adv.*

in·dis·pen·sa·ble (ĭn'dĭ-spĕn'sə-bəl) *adj.* Absolutely necessary **:** essential. **—in'dis·pen'sa·bil'i·ty** *n.* **—in'dis·pen'sa·ble** *n.* **—in'dis·pen'sa·bly** *adv.*

in·dis·posed (ĭn'dĭ-spōzd') *adj.* **1.** Mildly ill. **2.** Not inclined **:** averse. **—in·dis'po·si'tion** (-dĭs'pə-zĭsh'ən) *n.*

in·dis·put·a·ble (ĭn'dĭ-spyōō'tə-bəl) *adj.* Beyond dispute **:** undeniable. **—in'dis·put'a·ble·ness** *n.* **—in'dis·put'a·bly** *adv.*

in·dis·sol·u·ble (ĭn'dĭ-sŏl'yə-bəl) *adj.* **1.** Impossible to break or undo. **2.** Incapable of being dissolved or decomposed.

in·dis·tinct (ĭn'dĭ-stĭngkt') *adj.* **1.** Not clearly outlined **:** blurred. **2.** Vague, faint, or dim **:** unclear. **—in'dis·tinct'ly** *adv.* **—in'dis·tinct'ness** *n.*

in·dite (ĭn-dīt') *v.* **-dit·ed, -dit·ing. 1.** To write **:** compose. **2.** To put down in writing. **—in·dit'er** *n.*

in·di·um (ĭn'dē-əm) *n. Symbol* **In** A soft, silvery-white metallic element used for mirrors and transistor compounds.

in·di·vid·u·al (ĭn'də-vĭj'ōō-əl) *adj.* **1.** Of, for, or relating to a single human being. **2.** Existing as a distinct entity **:** separate. **3.** Having individuality **:** unlike others <an *individual* style of dancing> **—*n.*** A single person or organism, as opposed to a group. **—in'di·vid'u·al·ly** *adv.*

in·di·vid·u·al·ism (ĭn'də-vĭj'ōō-ə-lĭz'əm) *n.* **1.** Individuality. **2.** Assertion of the self. **3. a.** The theory that one should have freedom in one's economic pursuits and should succeed by one's own initiative. **b.** The doctrine that the interests of the individual should have preference over the interests of the state or social group.

in·di·vid·u·al·ist (ĭn'də-vĭj'ōō-ə-lĭst) *n.* **1.** One who thinks or acts in an independent way. **2.** One advocating individualism. **—in'di·vid'u·al·is'tic** *adj.*

in·di·vid·u·al·i·ty (ĭn'də-vĭj'ōō-ăl'ĭ-tē) *n.* **1.** The quality of being individual **:** distinctness. **2.** The aggregate of characteristics that distinguish one person from others.

in·di·vid·u·al·ize (ĭn'də-vĭj'ōō-ə-līz') *v.* **-ized, -iz·ing. 1.** To give individuality to. **2.** To consider individually. **3.** To modify to suit a specific individual.

in·di·vis·i·ble (ĭn'də-vĭz'ə-bəl) *adj.* Not able to be divided.

in·doc·tri·nate (ĭn-dŏk'trə-nāt') *v.* **-nat·ed, -nat·ing. 1.** To instruct in a doctrine. **2.** To train to accept a system of thought uncritically. **—in·doc'tri·na'tion** *n.*

In·do-Eu·ro·pe·an (ĭn'dō-yŏŏr'ə-pē'ən) *n.* A family of languages comprising most of the languages of Europe and parts of S Asia. **—In'do-Eu'ro·pe'an** *adj.*

in·do·lent (ĭn'də-lənt) *adj.* Disinclined to exert oneself **:** lazy. **—in'do·lence** *n.*

in·dom·i·ta·ble (ĭn-dŏm'ĭ-tə-bəl) *adj.* Incapable of being subdued or defeated. **—in·dom'i·ta·bly** *adv.*

in·door (ĭn'dôr', -dōr') *adj.* Of or within the inside of a building.

in·doors (ĭn-dôrz', -dōrz') *adv.* In or into a building.

in·dorse (ĭn-dôrs') *v. var. of* ENDORSE.

in·du·bi·ta·ble (ĭn-dōō'bĭ-tə-bəl, -dyōō'-) *adj.* Too evident to be doubted **:** unquestionable. **—in·du'bi·ta·bly** *adv.*

in·duce (ĭn-dōōs', -dyōōs') *v.* **-duced, -duc·ing. 1.** To move by persuasion or influence **:** prevail upon. **2.** To cause to occur **:** bring on <*induce* childbirth> **3.** To infer by inductive reasoning. **—in·duc'er** *n.*

in·duce·ment (ĭn-dōōs'mənt, -dyōōs'-) *n.* **1.** The act of inducing. **2.** Something that induces **:** motive or incentive.

in·duct (ĭn-dŭkt') *v.* **1.** To place formally in office **:** install. **2.** To admit as a new member **:** initiate. **3.** To summon into military service **:** draft. **—in'duc·tee'** *n.*

in·duc·tance (ĭn-dŭk'təns) *n.* A circuit element, usu. a conducting coil, in which electromagnetic induction generates electromotive force.

in·duc·tion (ĭn-dŭk'shən) *n.* **1.** The act of inducting or of being inducted. **2.** Reasoning in which conclusions are drawn from particular instances or facts. **3. a.** The generation of electromotive force in a closed circuit by a magnetic field that changes with time. **b.** The production of an electric charge in an uncharged body by bringing a charged body close to it.

in·duc·tive (ĭn-dŭk'tĭv) *adj.* **1.** Of, relating to, or using induction <*inductive* reasoning> **2.** *Elect.* Of or resulting from inductance. **—in·duc'tive·ly** *adv.* **—in·duc'tive·ness** *n.*

in·dulge (ĭn-dŭlj') *v.* **-dulged, -dulg·ing. 1.** To give in to the desires of, esp. to excess **:** pamper. **2.** To yield to **:** gratify <*indulge* a craving> **3.** To allow (oneself) a special pleasure. **—in·dulg'er** *n.*

in·dul·gence (ĭn-dŭl'jəns) *n.* **1.** The act of indulging or state of being indulgent. **2.** Something indulged in. **3.** Something given as a favor. **4.** Lenient treatment **:** tolerance. **5.** *Rom.*

Cath. Ch. The remission of punishment still due for a sin that has been sacramentally absolved.

in•dul•gent (ĭn-dŭl′jənt) *adj.* Showing, marked by, or inclined to indulgence : lenient. **—in•dul′gent•ly** *adv.*

in•dus•tri•al (ĭn-dŭs′trē-əl) *adj.* **1.** Of, relating to, or used in industry. **2.** Characterized by highly developed industries. **—in•dus′tri•al•ly** *adv.*

in•dus•tri•al•ism (ĭn-dŭs′trē-ə-lĭz′əm) *n.* A system in which industries are dominant. **—in•dus′tri•al•ist** *n.*

in•dus•tri•al•ize (ĭn-dŭs′trē-ə-līz′) *v.* **-ized, -iz•ing.** To become or cause to be industrial. **—in•dus′tri•al•i•za′tion** *n.*

in•dus•tri•ous (ĭn-dŭs′trē-əs) *adj.* Hardworking : diligent. **—in•dus′tri•ous•ly** *adv.* **—in•dus′tri•ous•ness** *n.*

in•dus•try (ĭn′də-strē) *n., pl.* **-tries. 1.** The commercial production and sale of goods and services. **2.** A branch of manufacture and trade <the electronics *industry*> **3.** Industrial management as distinguished from labor. **4.** Diligence.

–ine *suff.* Of or resembling <serpent*ine*>

in•e•bri•ate (ĭn-ē′brē-āt′) *v.* **-at•ed, -at•ing.** To make drunk : intoxicate. *—n.* (-ĭt). An intoxicated person. **—in•e′bri•ant** *adj. & n.* **—in•e′bri•a′tion** *n.*

in•ef•fa•ble (ĭn-ĕf′ə-bəl) *adj.* Beyond expression : indescribable or unutterable. **—in•ef′fa•bly** *adv.*

in•ef•face•a•ble (ĭn′ĭ-fā′sə-bəl) *adj.* Not effaceable : indelible.

in•ef•fi•cient (ĭn′ĭ-fĭsh′ənt) *adj.* **1.** Not producing the desired effect. **2.** Wasteful of time, energy, or materials. **—in′ef•fi′cien•cy** *n.* **—in′ef•fi′cient•ly** *adv.*

in•el•e•gant (ĭn-ĕl′ĭ-gənt) *adj.* **1.** Lacking elegance. **2.** Unrefined : crude. **—in•el′e•gance** *n.*

in•e•luc•ta•ble (ĭn′ĭ-lŭk′tə-bəl) *adj.* Not capable of being avoided or overcome : inescapable. **—in′e•luc′ta•bly** *adv.*

in•ept (ĭn-ĕpt′) *adj.* **1.** Not suitable : inappropriate. **2.** Awkward or incompetent : bungling. **—in•ep′ti•tude, in•ept′ness** *n.* **—in•ept′ly** *adv.*

in•e•qual•i•ty (ĭn′ĭ-kwŏl′ĭ-tē) *n., pl.* **-ties. 1.** The condition or an instance of being unequal. **2.** Social or economic disparity. **3.** Lack of regularity : unevenness. **4.** Variability : changeability. **5.** *Math.* An algebraic statement that a quantity is greater than or less than another quantity.

in•eq•ui•ta•ble (ĭn-ĕk′wĭ-tə-bəl) *adj.* Not equitable : unfair. **—in•eq′ui•ta•bly** *adv.*

in•eq•ui•ty (ĭn-ĕk′wĭ-tē) *n., pl.* **-ties. 1.** Injustice : unfairness. **2.** An example of injustice.

in•er•ran•cy (ĭn-ĕr′ən-sē) *n.* Freedom from error or untruths : infallibility.

in•ert (ĭn-ûrt′) *adj.* **1.** Not able to move or act. **2.** Slow to move or act : sluggish. **3.** Displaying no chemical activity <an *inert* gas> **—in•ert′ly** *adv.* **—in•ert′ness** *n.*

in•er•tia (ĭn-ûr′shə) *n.* **1.** The tendency of a body to remain at rest or to stay in motion unless acted upon by an external force. **2.** Resistance to motion or change. **—in•er′tial** *adj.* **—in•er′tial•ly** *adv.*

in•es•cap•a•ble (ĭn′ĭ-skā′pə-bəl) *adj.* Incapable of being escaped or avoided. **—in′es•cap′a•bly** *adv.*

in•es•ti•ma•ble (ĭn-ĕs′tə-mə-bəl) *adj.* **1.** Incapable of being estimated or calculated. **2.** Of a value too great to be estimated. **—in•es′ti•ma•bly** *adv.*

in•ev•i•ta•ble (ĭn-ĕv′ĭ-tə-bəl) *adj.* Not able to be avoided or prevented. **—in•ev′i•ta•bil′i•ty** *n.* **—in•ev′i•ta•bly** *adv.*

in•ex•act (ĭn′ĭg-zăkt′) *adj.* **1.** Not true, accurate, or precise. **2.** Not rigorous. **—in′ex•act′ly** *adv.*

in•ex•cus•a•ble (ĭn′ĭk-skyo͞o′zə-bəl) *adj.* Not capable of being excused or justified **—in′ex•cus′a•bly** *adv.*

in•ex•haust•i•ble (ĭn′ĭg-zô′stə-bəl) *adj.* **1.** Incapable of being used up. **2.** Tireless. **—in′ex•haust′i•bly** *adv.*

in•ex•o•ra•ble (ĭn-ĕk′sər-ə-bəl) *adj.* Not capable of being moved by entreaty : unyielding. **—in•ex′o•ra•bly** *adv.*

in•ex•pe•ri•ence (ĭn′ĭk-spîr′ē-əns) *n.* Lack of experience.

in•ex•pe•ri•enced (ĭn′ĭk-spîr′ē-ənst) *adj.* Lacking experience. ★ ***syns:*** GREEN, RAW, UNPRACTICED, UNSEASONED, UNTRIED

in•ex•pert (ĭn-ĕk′spûrt′) *adj.* Not expert : unskilled. **—in•ex′pert′ly** *adv.*

in•ex•pli•ca•ble (ĭn-ĕk′splĭ-kə-bəl, ĭn′ĭk-splĭk′ə-) *adj.* Not capable of being explained. **—in•ex′pli•ca•bly** *adv.*

in•ex•press•i•ble (ĭn′ĭk-sprĕs′ə-bəl) *adj.* Incapable of being expressed. **—in′ex•press′i•bly** *adv.*

in ex•tre•mis (in′ĕk-strē′mĭs) *adv.* At the point of death.

in•ex•tri•ca•ble (ĭn-ĕk′strĭ-kə-bəl) *adj.* **1.** Not capable of being untied or untangled. **2.** Too complex to resolve. **—in•ex′tri•ca•bly** *adv.*

in•fal•li•ble (ĭn-făl′ə-bəl) *adj.* **1.** Not capable of making mistakes <an *infallible* leader> **2.** Not capable of failing : certain <an *infallible* method> **—in•fal′li•bil′i•ty** *n.* **—in•fal′li•bly** *adv.*

in•fa•mous (ĭn′fə-məs) *adj.* **1.** Having a bad reputation : notorious. **2.** Shocking or disgraceful. **—in′fa•mous•ly** *adv.*

in•fa•my (ĭn′fə-mē) *n., pl.* **-mies. 1.** Evil notoriety or reputation. **2.** The state of being infamous. **3.** A disgraceful, publicly known act.

in•fan•cy (ĭn′fən-sē) *n., pl.* **-cies. 1.** The condition or time of being an infant. **2.** An early stage of existence. **3.** *Law.* Minority.

in•fant (ĭn′fənt) *n.* **1.** A child in the earliest age : baby. **2.** *Law.* A minor.

in•fan•ti•cide (ĭn-făn′tĭ-sīd′) *n.* **1.** The killing of an infant. **2.** One who kills an infant.

in•fan•tile (ĭn′fən-tīl′, -tĭl) *adj.* **1.** Of or relating to infants or infancy. **2.** Immature : childish.

infantile paralysis *n.* Poliomyelitis.

in•fan•try (ĭn′fən-trē) *n., pl.* **-tries.** The branch of an army made up of soldiers who are trained to fight on foot. **—in′fan•try•man** *n.*

in•farct (ĭn′färkt′, ĭn-färkt′) *n. Med.* An area of dead tissue caused by an insufficient supply of blood. **—in•farct′ed** *adj.* **—in•farc′tion** *n.*

in•fat•u•ate (ĭn-făch′o͞o-āt′) *v.* **-at•ed, -at•ing.** To arouse an extravagant or foolish love in. **—in•fat′u•at′ed** *adj.* **—in•fat′u•a′tion** *n.*

in•fect (ĭn-fĕkt′) *v.* **1.** To contaminate with disease-causing microorganisms. **2.** To transmit a disease to. **3.** To affect as if by contagion <a panic that *infected* the whole town> **—in•fec′tive** *adj.*

in•fec•tion (ĭn-fĕk′shən) *n.* **1.** Invasion of a bodily part by disease-causing microorganisms. **2.** The condition resulting from such an invasion. **3.** An infectious disease.

in•fec•tious (ĭn-fĕk′shəs) *adj.* **1.** Able to cause infection. **2.** Transmitted by infection. **3.** Readily communicated <an *infectious* grin> **—in•fec′tious•ly** *adv.*

in•fe•lic•i•tous (ĭn′fĭ-lĭs′ĭ-təs) *adj.* **1.** Not happy : unfortunate. **2.** Not apt, as in expression. **—in′fe•lic′i•ty** *n.* **—in′fe•lic′i•tous•ly** *adv.*

in•fer (ĭn-fûr′) *v.* **-ferred, -fer•ring. 1.** To conclude by reasoning : deduce. **2.** To have as a logical consequence. **3.** To lead to as a result or conclusion. **—in•fer′a•ble** *adj.*

in•fer•ence (ĭn′fər-əns) *n.* **1.** The act or process of inferring <reasoning by *inference*> **2.** Something inferred, as a conclusion. **—in′fer•en′tial** *adj.*

in•fe•ri•or (ĭn-fîr′ē-ər) *adj.* **1.** Located under or below : lower. **2.** Low or lower in order, rank, or quality. **—in•fe′ri•or** *n.* **—in•fe′ri•or′i•ty** (-ôr′ĭ-tē , -ŏr′-) *n.*

in•fer•nal (ĭn-fûr′nəl) *adj.* **1.** Of, like, or relating to hell. **2.** Damnable : abominable. **—in•fer′nal•ly** *adv.*

in•fer•no (ĭn-fûr′nō) *n., pl.* **-nos.** A place or condition suggestive of hell.

in•fest (ĭn-fĕst′) *v.* To spread in or over in numbers large enough to be harmful or offensive. **—in′fes•ta′tion** *n.*

in•fi•del (ĭn′fĭ-dəl, -dĕl′) *n.* **1.** One who has no religion. **2.** An unbeliever in a religion, esp. Christianity or Islam.

in•fi•del•i•ty (ĭn′fĭ-dĕl′ĭ-tē) *n., pl.* **-ties. 1.** Lack of fidelity : disloyalty. **2.** Lack of religious belief. **3.** Sexual unfaithfulness, esp. to one's spouse.

in•field (ĭn′fēld′) *n. Baseball.* The part of a playing field within the base lines. **—in′field′er** *n.*

in•fight•ing (ĭn′fī′tĭng) *n.* **1.** Close-range fighting. **2.** Contention among members of a group. **—in′fight′er** *n.*

in•fil•trate (ĭn-fĭl′trāt′, ĭn′fĭl-) *v.* **-trat•ed, -trat•ing. 1.** To pass or cause to pass into something through pores or small openings. **2.** To pass or enter gradually or stealthily <*infiltrate* spies into enemy territory> **—in′fil•tra′tion** *n.*

in•fi•nite (ĭn′fə-nĭt) *adj.* **1.** Without boundaries or limits : unlimited <an *infinite* distance><*infinite* caution> **2.** Immeasurably great or large. **3.** *Math.* **a.** Greater in value than any specified number, however large. **b.** Having a measure that is infinite. **—in′fi•nite** *n.* **—in′fi•nite•ly** *adv.*

in•fin•i•tes•i•mal (ĭn-fĭn′ĭ-tĕs′ə-məl) *adj.* Immeasurably small : minute. **—in•fin′i•tes′i•mal•ly** *adv.*

in•fin•i•tive (ĭn-fĭn′ĭ-tĭv) *n.* A verb form that is not inflected and in English is usu. preceded by *to* or an auxiliary verb.

in•fin•i•tude (ĭn-fĭn′ĭ-to͞od′, -tyo͞od′) *n.* **1.** The state of being infinite. **2.** An immeasurably large number or extent.

in•fin•i•ty (ĭn-fĭn′ĭ-tē) *n., pl.* **-ties. 1.** The quality or state of being infinite. **2.** Unbounded space, time, or amount. **3.** An indefinitely large number.

in•firm (ĭn-fûrm′) *adj.* **1.** Physically weak, esp. from age : feeble. **2.** Not sound or valid.

in•fir•ma•ry (ĭn-fûr′mə-rē) *n., pl.* **-ries.** An institution for the care of the sick or disabled.

in•fir•mi•ty (ĭn-fûr′mĭ-tē) *n., pl.* **-ties. 1.** Physical weakness, esp. from age : feebleness. **2.** A disease : ailment. **3.** A weakness of character : foible.

in•flame (ĭn-flām′) *v.* **1.** To set on fire : kindle. **2.** To arouse to strong or excessive feeling. **3.** To intensify. **4.** To produce or affect with inflammation.

in•flam•ma•ble (ĭn-flăm′ə-bəl) *adj.* **1.** Tending to catch fire easily : flammable. **2.** Easily excited, esp. to anger or outrage.

▲ ***word history:*** Hydrogen was once called the *inflammable* gas not because it does not burn but because it is so easily ignited. *Inflammable* is derived ultimately from the Latin prefix *in-*, "in," and the noun *flamma*, "flame." There is another prefix *in-*, however, which English also borrowed from Latin, that means "not," and the word *inflammable* can be misunderstood as meaning "not capable of burning." In order to eliminate possibly dangerous confusion about the combustibility of various materials, safety officials in the 20th cent. have adopted the word *flammable,* which had a brief life in the early 19th cent. to mean "able to burn." Materials that do not burn are unambiguously labeled *nonflammable.*

in•flam•ma•tion (ĭn′flə-mā′shən) *n.* Localized redness, swelling, heat, and pain in response to an injury or infection.

in•flam•ma•to•ry (ĭn-flăm′ə-tôr′ē, -tōr′ē) *adj.* **1.** Characterized by or causing inflammation. **2.** Arousing strong or uncontrolled feeling <an *inflammatory* harangue>

in•flate (ĭn-flāt′) *v.* **-flat•ed, -flat•ing. 1.** To fill and expand with a gas. **2.** To increase unsoundly : puff up <successes that *inflated* our hopes> **3.** To raise (e.g., prices) abnormally. **—in•flat′a•ble** *adj.*

in•fla•tion (ĭn-flā′shən) *n.* **1.** The act of inflating or state of being inflated. **2.** A sharp rise in the prices of goods and serv-ices. —**in•fla'tion•ar'y** *adj.*

in•flect (ĭn-flĕkt') *v.* **1.** To turn : veer. **2.** To vary the tone or pitch of (the voice), esp. in speaking. **3.** To change the form of (a word) to indicate number, tense, person, etc. —**in•flec'tive** *adj.*

in•flec•tion (ĭn-flĕk'shən) *n.* **1.** A change in pitch or tone of voice. **2. a.** A change in the form of a word to indicate number, tense, person, etc. **b.** A word derived by such a change <"Gives" and "gave" are *inflections* of "give."> —**in•flec'tion•al** *adj.* —**in•flec'tion•al•ly** *adv.*

in•flex•i•ble (ĭn-flĕk'sə-bəl) *adj.* **1.** Not flexible : rigid. **2.** Not subject to change : unalterable. **3.** Unyielding. ★ ***syns:*** IMMUTABLE, INVARIABLE, IRONBOUND, IRONCLAD, STIFF, UNCHANGEABLE —**in•flex'i•bil'i•ty** *n.* —**in•flex'i•bly** *adv.*

in•flict (ĭn-flĭkt') *v.* **1.** To cause to be suffered <*inflict* a wound><*inflict* punishment> **2.** To afflict. —**in•flict'er, in•flic'tor** *n.* —**in•flic'tion** *n.*

in•flo•res•cence (ĭn'flə-rĕs'əns) *n.* A characteristic arrangement of flowers on a stalk. —**in'flo•res'cent** *adj.*

in•flow (ĭn'flō') *n.* An influx.

in•flu•ence (ĭn'flōō-əns) *n.* **1.** The power to produce effects, esp. indirectly or through an intermediary. **2.** The condition of being affected <under the *influence* of drugs> **3.** One exercising indirect power to sway or affect. —*v.* **-enced, -enc•ing. 1.** To exert influence over : affect. **2.** To modify. —**in'flu•en'tial** (-ĕn'shəl) *adj.*

in•flu•en•za (ĭn'flōō-ĕn'zə) *n.* An acute infectious viral disease marked by respiratory inflammation, fever, muscular pain, and often intestinal discomfort.

in•flux (ĭn'flŭks') *n.* A stream of people or things coming in.

in•fo (ĭn'fō) *n. Informal.* Information.

in•fold (ĭn-fōld') *v.* **1.** To fold inward. **2.** *var. of* ENFOLD.

in•form (ĭn-fôrm') *v.* **1.** To give information to : tell. **2.** To disclose often incriminating information <*inform* against an accomplice> **3.** To give a special quality or character to : imbue.

in•for•mal (ĭn-fôr'məl) *adj.* **1.** Not following a prescribed form or pattern <an *informal* debate> **2.** Characterized by lack of formality. **3.** Of or for ordinary use or communication : casual <*informal* language> ★ ***syns:*** CASUAL, EASY, EASYGOING, RELAXED —**in'for•mal'i•ty** *n.* —**in•for'mal•ly** *adv.*

in•form•ant (ĭn-fôr'mənt) *n.* One who discloses or furnishes information.

in•for•ma•tion (ĭn'fər-mā'shən) *n.* **1.** The act of informing or state of being informed. **2.** Facts learned, as about current or past events : data. —**in'for•ma'tion•al** *adj.*

in•for•ma•tive (ĭn-fôr'mə-tĭv) *adj.* Providing information : instructive.

in•formed (ĭn-fôrmd') *adj.* Having or based on information.

in•form•er (ĭn-fôr'mər) *n.* **1.** An informant. **2.** One who informs against others.

in•frac•tion (ĭn-frăk'shən) *n.* A violation of a rule.

in•fra•red (ĭn'frə-rĕd') *adj.* Of, being, or using electromagnetic radiation with wavelengths longer than those of visible light and shorter than those of microwaves.

in•fra•son•ic (ĭn'frə-sŏn'ĭk) *adj.* Producing or using waves or vibrations with frequencies below that of audible sound.

in•fra•struc•ture (ĭn'frə-strŭk'chər) *n.* **1.** An underlying base or foundation. **2.** The basic facilities needed for the functioning of a system.

in•fre•quent (ĭn-frē'kwənt) *adj.* **1.** Not frequent : rare. **2.** Rarely occurring or appearing. ★ ***syns:*** OCCASIONAL, RARE, SCARCE, SPORADIC —**in•fre'quen•cy** *n.* —**in•fre'quent•ly** *adv.*

in•fringe (ĭn-frĭnj') *v.* **-fringed, -fring•ing. 1.** To break (e.g., a law) : violate. **2.** To encroach : trespass. —**in•fringe'ment** *n.*

in•fu•ri•ate (ĭn-fyŏŏr'ē-āt') *v.* **-at•ed, -at•ing.** To make very angry : enrage. —**in•fu'ri•at'ing•ly** *adv.* —**in•fu'ri•a'tion** *n.*

in•fuse (ĭn-fyōōz') *v.* **-fused, -fus•ing. 1.** To introduce : inject <*infuse* new enthusiasm into the campaign> **2.** To imbue : fill <*infused* us with pride> **3.** To steep without boiling, as tea. —**in•fu'sion** *n.*

in•fus•i•ble (ĭn-fyōō'zə-bəl) *adj.* Not able to be fused or melted.

–ing[1] *suff.* —Used to form the present participle of verbs and participial adjectives <see*ing*><charm*ing*>

–ing[2] *suff.* **1.** An action : activity <danc*ing*> <berry*ing*> **2.** The result of an action or process <an oil paint*ing*> **3.** Something used in an action or process <stuff*ing*>

in•gen•ious (ĭn-jēn'yəs) *adj.* **1.** Showing great skill in creating or devising : creative. **2.** Original and imaginative <an *ingenious* plan for escape> —**in•gen'ious•ly** *adv.* —**in•gen'ious•ness** *n.*

in•gé•nue (ăn'zhə-nōō') *n.* **1.** An artless, innocent young woman. **2.** An actress playing such a young woman.

in•ge•nu•i•ty (ĭn'jə-nōō'ĭ-tē, -nyōō'-) *n., pl.* **-ties.** Inventive skill : cleverness.

in•gen•u•ous (ĭn-jĕn'yōō-əs) *adj.* **1.** Lacking sophistication : artless. **2.** Straightforward : frank. —**in•gen'u•ous•ly** *adv.* —**in•gen'u•ous•ness** *n.*

in•gest (ĭn-jĕst') *v.* To take in by or as if by swallowing. —**in•ges'tion** *n.*

in•gle•nook (ĭng'gəl-nŏŏk') *n.* **1.** A corner or recess beside a fireplace. **2.** A bench in an inglenook.

in•glo•ri•ous (ĭn-glôr'ē-əs, -glōr'-) *adj.* **1.** Not glorious. **2.** Dishonorable : ignominious. —**in•glo'ri•ous•ly** *adv.*

in•got (ĭng'gət) *n.* A mass of metal shaped in a bar or block.

in•grain (ĭn-grān') *v.* To impress deeply into the mind or nature : imbue. —*n.* Yarn or fiber dyed before being spun or woven.

in·grained (ĭn-grānd′) *adj.* **1.** Worked deeply into the texture or fiber. **2.** Firmly established : deep-seated.
in·grate (ĭn′grāt′) *n.* One who is ungrateful.
in·gra·ti·ate (ĭn-grā′shē-āt′) *v.* **-at·ed, -at·ing.** To gain favor with deliberately. **—in·gra′ti·at′ing·ly** *adv.* **—in·gra′ti·a′tion** *n.*
in·grat·i·tude (ĭn-grăt′ĭ-to͞od′, -tyo͞od′) *n.* Lack of gratitude.
in·gre·di·ent (ĭn-grē′dē-ənt) *n.* An element in a mixture or compound.
in·gress (ĭn′grĕs′) *n.* **1.** A going in or entering. **2.** Permission to enter.
in-group (ĭn′gro͞op′) *n.* A clique.
in·grown (ĭn′grōn′) *adj.* Grown abnormally into the flesh.
in·gui·nal (ĭng′gwə-nəl) *adj.* Of or located in the groin.
in·hab·it (ĭn-hăb′ĭt) *v.* To reside in. **—in·hab′it·a·ble** *adj.*
in·hab·i·tant (ĭn-hăb′ĭ-tənt) *n.* A permanent resident.
in·ha·lant (ĭn-hā′lənt) *n.* Something that is inhaled, as a medicine.
in·ha·la·tor (ĭn′hə-lā′tər) *n.* A device that discharges a vapor to ease breathing by inspiration.
in·hale (ĭn-hāl′) *v.* **-haled, -hal·ing.** To breathe in or take in by breathing. **—in′ha·la′tion** (-hə-lā′shən) *n.*
in·hal·er (ĭn-hā′lər) *n.* **1.** One that inhales. **2.** An inhalator. **3.** A respirator.
in·here (ĭn-hîr′) *v.* **-hered, -her·ing.** To be inherent or innate.
in·her·ent (ĭn-hîr′ənt, -hĕr′-) *adj.* Existing as an essential element or feature : intrinsic. **—in·her′ent·ly** *adv.*
in·her·it (ĭn-hĕr′ĭt) *v.* **1.** To receive (property) from a person by legal succession or will. **2.** *Biol.* To receive from one's parents by genetic transmission. **—in·her′it·a·ble** *adj.* **—in·her′i·tor** *n.*
in·her·i·tance (ĭn-hĕr′ĭ-təns) *n.* **1.** The act of inheriting. **2.** Something inherited or to be inherited. **3.** A heritage : legacy.
in·hib·it (ĭn-hĭb′ĭt) *v.* **1.** To hold back : restrain. **2.** To prevent the full expression of : suppress. **3.** To forbid : prohibit. **—in·hib′it·a·ble** *adj.* **—in·hib′i·tor, in·hib′it·er** *n.* **—in·hib′i·tive, in·hib′i·to′ry** (-tôr′ē, -tōr′ē) *adj.*
in·hi·bi·tion (ĭn′hĭ-bĭsh′ən, ĭn′ĭ-) *n.* **1.** The act of inhibiting or state of being inhibited. **2.** The self-imposed suppression of a feeling, need, or drive.
in-house (ĭn′hous′) *adj.* Being or coming from within an organization <an *in-house* publication>
in·hu·man (ĭn-hyo͞o′mən) *adj.* **1.** Lacking kindness, pity, or emotional warmth. **2.** Not suited to human beings <a vast hall of *inhuman* dimensions> **3.** Monstrous. **—in·hu′man·ly** *adv.*
in·hu·mane (ĭn′hyo͞o-mān′) *adj.* Lacking pity or compassion : cruel. **—in′hu·mane′ly** *adv.*
in·hu·man·i·ty (ĭn′hyo͞o-măn′ĭ-tē) *n., pl.* **-ties. 1.** Lack of pity or compassion. **2.** An inhumane or cruel act.
in·im·i·cal (ĭn-ĭm′ĭ-kəl) *adj.* **1.** Harmful : injurious <living habits *inimical* to health> **2.** Hostile : malign. **—in·im′i·cal·ly** *adv.*
in·im·i·ta·ble (ĭn-ĭm′ĭ-tə-bəl) *adj.* Incapable of being imitated : matchless. **—in·im′i·ta·bly** *adv.*
in·iq·ui·ty (ĭ-nĭk′wĭ-tē) *n., pl.* **-ties. 1.** Wickedness : sinfulness. **2.** A grossly immoral act : sin. **—in·iq′ui·tous** *adj.*
in·i·tial (ĭ-nĭsh′əl) *adj.* Of, being, or happening at the beginning. *—n.* The first letter of a name or a word. *—v.* **-tialed, -tial·ing** *also* **-tialled, -tial·ling.** To sign or mark with initials. **—in·i′tial·ly** *adv.*
in·i·tial·ize (ĭ-nĭsh′ə-līz′) *v.* **-ized, -iz·ing.** *Computer Sci.* To set to a starting position or value. **—in·i′tial·i·za′tion** *n.*
in·i·ti·ate (ĭ-nĭsh′ē-āt′) *v.* **-at·ed, -at·ing. 1.** To cause to begin : start or launch. **2.** To introduce (someone) to a new interest or activity. **3.** To admit into membership, as with a ceremony. *—n.* (-ĭt). **1.** One who has been initiated. **2.** A beginner : novice. **—in·i′ti·a′tion** *n.* **—in·i′ti·a′tor** *n.* **—in·i′ti·a·to′ry** (-ə-tôr′ē, -tōr′ē) *adj.*
in·i·ti·a·tive (ĭ-nĭsh′ē-ə-tĭv, ĭ-nĭsh′ə-) *n.* **1.** The ability to originate or follow through with a plan of action or task : enterprise. **2.** The act or role of taking the first or leading step <seized the *initiative* and attacked> **3.** A procedure by which citizens propose a law by petition and have it submitted to be voted on by the electorate.
in·ject (ĭn-jĕkt′) *v.* **1. a.** To force or drive (a liquid or gas) into something <*inject* fuel into an engine cylinder> **b.** To introduce (liquid medicine, serum, etc.) into the body, as with a hypodermic syringe. **2.** To introduce, as into conversation <*inject* a word of warning> **3.** To put into an orbit, trajectory, or stream. **—in·jec′tion** *n.*
in·junc·tion (ĭn-jŭngk′shən) *n.* **1.** A command or order. **2.** *Law.* A court order forbidding or calling for a certain action. **—in·junc′tive** *adj.*
in·jure (ĭn′jər) *v.* **-jured, -jur·ing. 1.** To cause physical harm to : hurt. **2.** To damage : impair. **3.** To commit an injustice or offense against : wrong.
in·ju·ri·ous (ĭn-jo͝or′ē-əs) *adj.* Causing or apt to cause injury : harmful. **—in·ju′ri·ous·ly** *adv.*
in·ju·ry (ĭn′jə-rē) *n., pl.* **-ries. 1.** An act of injuring or harming. **2.** A wound or other damage suffered. **3.** Injustice.
in·jus·tice (ĭn-jŭs′tĭs) *n.* **1.** Violation of justice or another's rights : unfairness. **2.** An unjust act : wrong.
ink (ĭngk) *n.* A usu. dark-colored liquid or paste used esp. for writing or printing. *—v.* To supply or mark with ink. **—ink′y** *adj.*
ink·horn (ĭngk′hôrn′) *n.* A small container made esp. of horn to hold ink.
ink·ling (ĭngk′lĭng) *n.* **1.** A slight suggestion : hint. **2.** A vague notion or idea.

ink•stand (ĭngk′stănd′) *n.* **1.** A stand for holding ink and writing implements. **2.** An inkwell.
ink•well (ĭngk′wĕl′) *n.* A small reservoir for holding ink.
inky cap *n.* A mushroom of the genus *Coprinus,* with gills that dissolve into a dark liquid on maturing.

inky cap

in•laid (ĭn′lād′) *adj.* **1.** Set into a surface in a decorative design. **2.** Ornamented with a pattern set into a surface.
in•land (ĭn′lənd) *adj.* **1.** Of or situated in the interior of a country. **2.** Operating within a country **:** domestic. *—adv.* In or toward the interior. *—n.* The interior of a country. **—in′land′er** *n.*
in-law (ĭn′lô′) *n.* A relative by marriage.
in•lay (ĭn′lā′, ĭn-lā′) *v.* To set (e.g., wooden pieces) into a surface in a decorative design. *—n.* (ĭn′lā′). **1.** Material or a design set into a surface. **2.** A solid dental filling, as of gold, cemented in place.
in•let (ĭn′lĕt′, -lĭt) *n.* **1.** A recess, as a bay or cove, along a coastline. **2.** A narrow passage of water, as between 2 islands. **3.** A drainage passageway.
in•mate (ĭn′māt′) *n.* **1.** A resident in a dwelling or building. **2.** One confined to an institution.
in me•mo•ri•am (ĭn′mə-môr′ē-əm, -mōr′-) *prep.* In memory of. —Used to honor the dead.
inn (ĭn) *n.* **1.** A lodging house **:** hotel. **2.** A tavern.
in•nards (ĭn′ərdz) *pl.n. Informal.* **1.** Internal organs **:** viscera. **2.** The inner parts, as of a structure.
in•nate (ĭ-nāt′, ĭn′āt′) *adj.* **1.** Having at birth **:** inborn. **2.** Having as an essential characteristic **:** inherent <the *innate* strength of steel> **—in•nate′ly** *adv.*
in•ner (ĭn′ər) *adj.* **1.** Situated farther inside <an *inner* compartment> **2.** More hidden **:** deeper <an *inner* meaning> **3.** Of or relating to the mind or spirit <the *inner* person> **4.** More exclusive or influential <*inner* circles>
inner city *n.* The usu. older central part of a city, esp. when crowded, neglected, and decaying. **—in′ner-cit′y** *adj.*
inner ear *n.* The part of the vertebrate ear including the semicircular canals, vestibule, and cochlea.
in•ner•most (ĭn′ər-mōst′) *adj.* **1.** Farthest within. **2.** Most intimate <*innermost* thoughts>
inner tube *n.* An inflatable rubber tube placed inside a tire.
in•ning (ĭn′ĭng) *n.* One of 9 divisions of a regulation baseball game in which each team has a turn at bat.
inn•keep•er (ĭn′kē′pər) *n.* The manager or owner of an inn.
in•no•cent (ĭn′ə-sənt) *adj.* **1.** Free from sin or wrongdoing **:** sinless. **2.** Not guilty legally of a given crime. **3.** Harmless **:** innocuous. **4.** Not experienced **:** naive. **5.** Guileless **:** artless. **—in′no•cence** *n.* **—in′no•cent** *n.* **—in′no•cent•ly** *adv.*
in•noc•u•ous (ĭ-nŏk′yo͞o-əs) *adj.* **1.** Having no ill effect **:** harmless. **2.** Lacking distinction **:** insipid. **—in•noc′u•ous•ly** *adv.* **—in•noc′u•ous•ness** *n.*
in•no•vate (ĭn′ə-vāt′) *v.* **-vat•ed, -vat•ing.** To begin something new **:** introduce. **—in′no•va′tive** *adj.* **—in′no•va′tor** *n.*
in•no•va•tion (ĭn′ə-vā′shən) *n.* **1.** The act of innovating. **2.** Something that is new or unusual.
in•nu•en•do (ĭn′yo͞o-ĕn′dō) *n., pl.* **-does.** An indirect, usu. disparaging implication **:** insinuation.
in•nu•mer•a•ble (ĭ-no͞o′mər-ə-bəl, ĭ-nyo͞o′-) *adj.* Countless **:** numberless.
in•oc•u•late (ĭ-nŏk′yə-lāt′) *v.* **-lat•ed, -lat•ing.** To introduce a disease virus or other causative agent into so as to immunize, treat, or test. **—in•oc′u•la′tion** *n.*
in•oc•u•lum (ĭ-nŏk′yə-ləm) *n., pl.* **-la** (-lə) *or* **-lums.** The material used in an inoculation.
in•op•er•a•ble (ĭn-ŏp′ər-ə-bəl, -ŏp′rə-) *adj.* **1.** Not operable. **2.** Incapable of being treated by surgery.
in•op•er•a•tive (ĭn-ŏp′ər-ə-tĭv, -ŏp′rə-) *adj.* **1.** Not working. **2.** Not effective.
in•op•por•tune (ĭn-ŏp′ər-to͞on′, -tyo͞on′) *adj.* Untimely **:** ill-timed. **—in•op′por•tune′ly** *adv.* **—in•op′por•tune′ness** *n.*
in•or•di•nate (ĭn-ôr′dn-ĭt) *adj.* **1.** Exceeding normal limits. **2.** Not regulated **:** disorderly. **—in•or′di•nate•ly** *adv.*
in•or•gan•ic (ĭn′ôr-găn′ĭk) *adj.* **1.** Not composed of or involving living organisms or their remains or products. **2.** Mineral.
in•pa•tient (ĭn′pā′shənt) *n.* A patient admitted to a hospital.
in•put (ĭn′po͝ot′) *n.* **1.** Something or an amount put in. **2.** Energy or power for driving a machine. **3.** Information put into a communications or computer system. **4.** Contribution to a common effort. **—in′put′** *v.*
in•quest (ĭn′kwĕst′) *n.* **1.** A judicial inquiry, esp. into the cause of a death. **2.** An investigation **:** inquiry.
in•quire (ĭn-kwīr′) *v.* **-quired, -quir•ing. 1.** To ask (a question). **2.** To request information <*inquire* about mortgage rates> **3.** To

make a study : investigate. —**in•quir'er** *n.* —**in•quir'ing•ly** *adv.*

in•quir•y (ĭn-kwīr'ē, ĭn'kwə-rē) *n., pl.* **-ies. 1.** The act of inquiring. **2.** A question or request for information. **3.** A close examination : investigation.

in•qui•si•tion (ĭn'kwĭ-zĭsh'ən) *n.* **1.** An official investigation. **2. Inquisition.** *Rom. Cath. Ch.* A tribunal formerly established to seek out and punish heretics. **3.** An investigation or interrogation that violates individual rights. —**in•quis'i•tor** *n.* —**in•quis'i•to'ri•al** *adj.*

in•quis•i•tive (ĭn-kwĭz'ĭ-tĭv) *adj.* **1.** Unduly curious. **2.** Inquiring : probing <an *inquisitive* mind> —**in•quis'i•tive•ly** *adv.* —**in•quis'i•tive•ness** *n.*

in re (ĭn rā', rē') *prep.* In regard to.

in•road (ĭn'rōd') *n.* **1.** A hostile intrusion : raid. **2.** An advance, often at the expense of another.

in•rush (ĭn'rŭsh') *n.* A sudden rushing in.

in•sane (ĭn-sān') *adj.* **1.** Afflicted with a serious mental disorder impairing a person's ability to function. **2.** Typical of, used by, or for the insane. **3.** Very foolish or irrational : absurd. ★ ***syns:*** BATTY, CRAZY, GAGA, LOONY, LUNATIC, MAD, NUTS, SCREWY —**in•sane'ly** *adv.* —**in•san'i•ty** (-săn'ĭ-tē) *n.*

in•sa•tia•ble (ĭn-sā'shə-bəl, -shē-ə-) *adj.* Incapable of being satisfied <an *insatiable* appetite>

in•scribe (ĭn-skrīb') *v.* **-scribed, -scrib•ing. 1.** To write, print, or cut (letters or words) on a surface. **2.** To mark (a surface) with words or letters. **3.** To enter (a name) in a register : enroll. **4.** To write a short signed message on (a gift). **5.** To enclose (e.g., a polygon) in another geometric figure so that every vertex of the enclosed figure touches the enclosing figure. —**in•scrib'er** *n.* —**in•scrip'tion** (-skrĭp'shən) *n.*

in•scru•ta•ble (ĭn-skrōō'tə-bəl) *adj.* Difficult to understand or interpret : enigmatic. —**in•scru'ta•bil'i•ty, in•scru'ta•ble•ness** *n.* —**in•scru'ta•bly** *adv.*

in•seam (ĭn'sēm') *n.* The inside seam of a pant leg.

in•sect (ĭn'sĕkt') *n.* Any of numerous small, usu. winged invertebrate animals of the class Insecta, with 3 pairs of legs, a segmented body, and usu. 2 pairs of wings.

in•sec•ti•cide (ĭn-sĕk'tĭ-sīd') *n.* A substance for killing insects.

in•sec•tiv•o•rous (ĭn'sĕk-tĭv'ər-əs) *adj.* Feeding on insects.

in•se•cure (ĭn'sĭ-kyŏŏr') *adj.* **1.** Not adequately protected or guarded : unsafe. **2.** Unstable <*insecure* footing> **3.** Not self-confident. —**in'se•cure'ly** *adv.* —**in'se•cu'ri•ty** *n.*

in•sem•i•nate (ĭn-sĕm'ə-nāt') *v.* **-nat•ed, -nat•ing. 1.** To sow seed in. **2.** To introduce semen into the uterus of. —**in•sem'i•na'tion** *n.* —**in•sem'i•na'tor** *n.*

in•sen•sate (ĭn-sĕn'sāt', -sĭt) *adj.* **1.** Inanimate. **2.** Unconscious. **3.** Without sensibility : callous or brutal.

in•sen•si•ble (ĭn-sĕn'sə-bəl) *adj.* **1.** Imperceptible : inappreciable. **2.** Unconscious. **3. a.** Unresponsive : unaffected <*insensible* to heat> **b.** Unaware : unmindful. —**in•sen'si•bil'i•ty** *n.* —**in•sen'si•bly** *adv.*

in•sen•tient (ĭn-sĕn'shənt) *adj.* Devoid of consciousness or sensation. —**in•sen'tience** *n.*

in•sep•a•ra•ble (ĭn-sĕp'ər-ə-bəl) *adj.* Incapable of being separated. —**in•sep'a•ra•bil'i•ty** *n.* —**in•sep'a•ra•bly** *adv.*

in•sert (ĭn-sûrt') *v.* **1.** To put or thrust in <*inserted* the coin in the slot> **2.** To interpolate. —*n.* (ĭn'sûrt'). Something inserted or to be inserted. —**in•ser'tion** *n.*

in•set (ĭn-sĕt', ĭn'sĕt') *v.* To set in : insert. —**in'set'** *n.*

in•shore (ĭn'shôr', -shōr') *adj.* Close to or moving toward a shore. —**in'shore'***adv.*

in•side (ĭn-sīd', ĭn'sīd') *n.* **1.** An interior part. **2.** An inside side or surface. **3. insides.** *Informal.* The internal organs or parts. **4.** *Slang.* A position of special power or influence. —*adv.* (ĭn-sīd'). Into or in the interior : within. —*prep.* (ĭn-sīd'). **1.** Within <*inside* a box>. **2.** Into <going *inside* the house> —**in'side'** *adj.*

in•sid•er (ĭn-sī'dər) *n.* One who has special knowledge of or access to confidential information.

in•sid•i•ous (ĭn-sĭd'ē-əs) *adj.* **1.** Working or spreading harmfully in a stealthy way. **2.** Designed to entrap : treacherous. **3.** Attractive but harmful : seductive. —**in•sid'i•ous•ly** *adv.* —**in•sid'i•ous•ness** *n.*

in•sight (ĭn'sīt') *n.* **1.** The ability to perceive the true or hidden nature of things. **2.** A perceptive observation. —**in•sight'ful** *adj.* —**in•sight'ful•ly** *adv.*

in•sig•ni•a (ĭn-sĭg'nē-ə) *n., pl.* **-nia** *or* **-ni•as. 1.** A badge of office or rank. **2.** A distinguishing sign.

in•sin•cere (ĭn'sĭn-sîr') *adj.* Hypocritical. —**in'sin•cere'ly** *adv.* —**in'sin•cer'i•ty** *n.*

in•sin•u•ate (ĭn-sĭn'yōō-āt') *v.* **-at•ed, -at•ing. 1. a.** To introduce (e.g., a suspicion) slyly. **b.** To introduce (oneself) by sly and ingenious means. **2.** To hint. —**in•sin'u•at'ing•ly** *adv.* —**in•sin'u•a'tion** *n.*

in•sip•id (ĭn-sĭp'ĭd) *adj.* **1.** Lacking flavor : tasteless. **2.** Lacking interest : dull. —**in•sip'id•ly** *adv.* —**in•sip'id•ness** *n.*

in•sist (ĭn-sĭst') *v.* **1.** To be firm in a course or demand <*insisted* on getting his way> **2.** To assert strongly <*insisted* they were innocent> —**in•sis'tence** *n.* —**in•sis'tent** *adj.* —**in•sis'tent•ly** *adv.*

in si•tu (ĭn sī'tōō, sĭt'ōō) *adj. & adv.* In the original place.

in•so•far (ĭn'sō-fär') *adv.* To such an extent.

in•sole (ĭn'sōl') *n.* **1.** The inside sole of a shoe. **2.** A strip of material put inside a shoe for protection or comfort.

in•so•lent (ĭn'sə-lənt) *adj.* Disrespectfully or presumptuously arrogant : impertinent. —**in'so•lence** *n.* —**in'so•lent•ly** *adv.*

in•sol•u•ble (ĭn-sŏl′yə-bəl) *adj.* **1.** Not capable of being dissolved. **2.** Not capable of being solved. —**in•sol′u•bil′i•ty, in•sol′u•ble•ness** *n.* —**in•sol′u•bly** *adv.*

in•sol•vent (ĭn-sŏl′vənt) *adj.* Not able to meet debts : bankrupt. —**in•sol′ven•cy** *n.* —**in•sol′vent** *n.*

in•som•ni•a (ĭn-sŏm′nē-ə) *n.* Chronic sleeplessness. —**in•som′ni•ac′** *adj. & n.*

in•so•much as (ĭn′sō-mŭch′) *conj.* **1.** To such an extent as. **2.** Inasmuch as : since.

in•sou•ci•ant (ĭn-so͞o′sē-ənt) *adj.* Cheerfully nonchalant. —**in•sou′ci•ance** *n.*

in•spect (ĭn-spĕkt′) *v.* **1.** To examine carefully, esp. for flaws. **2.** To review officially <*inspect* the troops> —**in•spec′tion** *n.* —**in•spec′tor** *n.*

in•spi•ra•tion (ĭn′spə-rā′shən) *n.* **1. a.** Stimulation of the intellect or emotions to a high level. **b.** The condition of being so stimulated. **2.** One that moves the intellect or emotions or prompts action. **3.** A sudden creative idea or act. **4.** Inhalation. —**in′spi•ra′tion•al** *adj.* —**in′spi•ra′tion•al•ly** *adv.*

in•spire (ĭn-spīr′) *v.* **-spired, -spir•ing. 1.** To guide or affect by divine influence. **2.** To fill with high emotion : exalt. **3.** To stimulate to creativity or action. **4.** To elicit : arouse. **5.** To inhale. —**in•spir′er** *n.* —**in•spir′ing•ly** *adv.*

in•spir•it (ĭn-spĭr′ĭt) *v.* To animate.

in•sta•bil•i•ty (ĭn′stə-bĭl′ĭ-tē) *n., pl.* **-ties.** Lack of stability.

in•stall *also* **in•stal** (ĭn-stôl′) *v.* **-stalled, -stall•ing. 1.** To place in position for use. **2.** To induct into an office or position. **3.** To settle : ensconce. —**in′stal•la′tion** *n.* —**in•stall′er** *n.*

in•stall•ment *also* **in•stal•ment** (ĭn-stôl′mənt) *n.* **1.** One of several successive payments, as of a debt. **2.** A part of something issued at intervals, as a serialized literary work.

in•stance (ĭn′stəns) *n.* **1.** An illustrative case : example. **2.** An occasion <in the first *instance*> **3.** A prompting : request <interceded at the *instance* of a friend> —*v.* **-stanced, -stanc•ing. 1.** To cite as an example. **2.** To illustrate : exemplify.

in•stant (ĭn′stənt) *n.* **1.** A very short time : moment. **2.** A specific point in time. —*adj.* **1.** Immediate. **2.** Designed for quick preparation < *instant* soup> **3.** Urgent.

in•stan•ta•ne•ous (ĭn′stən-tā′nē-əs) *adj.* **1.** Happening or completed instantly or without delay. **2.** Present or happening at a given instant <*instantaneous* velocity> —**in′stan•ta′ne•ous•ly** *adv.*

in•stan•ter (ĭn-stăn′tər) *adv.* Instantly.

in•stant•ly (ĭn′stənt-lē) *adv.* At once : immediately.

in•stead (ĭn-stĕd′) *adv.* In place of that just mentioned <were going to fly, but drove *instead*>

instead of *prep.* In place of : rather than.

in•step (ĭn′stĕp′) *n.* The arched middle portion of the foot.

in•sti•gate (ĭn′stĭ-gāt′) *v.* **-gat•ed, -gat•ing. 1.** To urge forward. **2.** To stir up : foment. —**in′sti•ga′tion** *n.* —**in′sti•ga′tor** *n.*

in•still *also* **in•stil** (ĭn-stĭl′) *v.* **-stilled, -still•ing. 1.** To impart by gradual instruction or effort : implant. **2.** To pour in by drops. —**in′stil•la′tion** *n.* —**in•still′er** *n.*

in•stinct (ĭn′stĭngkt′) *n.* **1.** The innate, complex, and normally adaptive aspect of animal behavior. **2.** A strong impulse or motivation. **3.** A natural talent : aptitude. —**in•stinc′tive** *adj.* —**in•stinc′tive•ly** *adv.* —**in•stinc′tu•al** (-cho͞o-əl) *adj.*

in•sti•tute (ĭn′stĭ-to͞ot′, -tyo͞ot′) *v.* **-tut•ed, -tut•ing. 1.** To establish : found. **2.** To begin : initiate. —*n.* **1.** Something instituted, esp. a law or precept. **2.** An organization established to promote or further a cause. **3.** An educational institution. **4.** A short series of classes : seminar.

in•sti•tu•tion (ĭn′stĭ-to͞o′shən, -tyo͞o′-) *n.* **1.** The act of instituting. **2.** An important cultural or societal custom or practice. **3.** A permanent feature : fixture. **4. a.** An organization, esp. one dedicated to public service. **b.** The buildings of such an organization. **5.** A place of confinement. —**in′sti•tu′tion•al** *adj.* —**in′sti•tu′tion•al•ize′** *v.* —**in′sti•tu′tion•al•ly** *adv.*

in•struct (ĭn-strŭkt′) *v.* **1.** To impart knowledge or skill to : teach. **2.** To direct : order. —**in•struc′tive** *adj.*

in•struc•tion (ĭn-strŭk′shən) *n.* **1.** The act or profession of instructing. **2. a.** Imparted knowledge. **b.** A lesson. **3.** An order or direction. —**in•struc′tion•al** *adj.*

in•struc•tor (ĭn-strŭk′tər) *n.* A person who instructs, esp. a low-ranking college teacher. —**in•struc′tor•ship′** *n.*

in•stru•ment (ĭn′strə-mənt) *n.* **1.** A means by which something is accomplished : agency. **2.** A person controlled by another : dupe. **3.** A mechanical tool or implement. **4.** A device for recording, indicating, or measuring, esp. in a control system. **5.** A device used by a musician in producing music. **6.** A legal document. —*v.* To supply with instruments.

in•stru•men•tal (ĭn′strə-mĕn′tl) *adj.* **1.** Acting as a means. **2.** Performed on or composed for musical instruments. —**in′stru•men′tal•ly** *adv.*

in•stru•men•tal•ist (ĭn′strə-mĕn′tl-ĭst) *n.* A player of a musical instrument.

in•stru•men•tal•i•ty (ĭn′strə-mĕn-tăl′ĭ-tē) *n., pl.* **-ties.** Means : agency.

in•stru•men•ta•tion (ĭn′strə-mĕn-tā′shən) *n.* **1.** The use of instruments. **2.** Instrumentality. **3.** The study and practice of arranging music for instruments.

in•sub•or•di•nate (ĭn′sə-bôr′dn-ĭt) *adj.* Not obeying orders. —**in′sub•or′di•nate•ly** *adv.* —**in′sub•or′di•na′tion** *n.*

in•sub•stan•tial (ĭn′səb-stăn′shəl) *adj.* **1.** Lacking substance : unreal. **2.** Not solid : flimsy. —**in′sub•stan′ti•al′i•ty** *n.*

in•suf•fer•a•ble (ĭn-sŭf′ər-ə-bəl) *adj.* Not able to be endured : intolerable. —**in•suf′fer•a•ble•ness** *n.* —**in•suf′fer•a•bly** *adv.*

in•suf•fi•cient (ĭn′sə-fĭsh′ənt) *adj.* Not

enough : inadequate. **—in′suf•fi′cien•cy** *n.* **—in′suf•fi′cient•ly** *adv.*

in•su•lar (ĭn′sə-lər, ĭns′yə-) *adj.* **1.** Of or being an island. **2.** Typical or suggestive of the isolated life of an island. **3.** Narrow-minded. **—in′su•lar′i•ty** *n.*

in•su•late (ĭn′sə-lāt′, ĭns′yə-) *v.* **-lat•ed, -lat•ing. 1.** To set apart : isolate. **2.** To stop the passage of heat, electricity, or sound into or out of, esp. by interposing material that acts as a barrier. **—in′su•la′tion** *n.* **—in′su•la′tor** *n.*

in•su•lin (ĭn′sə-lĭn, ĭns′yə-) *n.* **1.** A hormone in the pancreas that regulates the metabolism of carbohydrates by controlling blood glucose levels. **2.** A preparation derived from the pancreas of the pig or the ox used in the treatment of diabetes.

in•sult (ĭn-sŭlt′) *v.* To speak to or treat insolently or contemptuously : affront. *—n.* (ĭn′sŭlt′). An insolent or contemptuous act or remark.

in•su•per•a•ble (ĭn-sōō′pər-ə-bəl) *adj.* Not able to be overcome : insurmountable. **—in•su′per•a•bly** *adv.*

in•sup•port•a•ble (ĭn′sə-pôr′tə-bəl, -pōr′-) *adj.* **1.** Unendurable : intolerable. **2.** Unjustifiable <*insupportable* claims>

in•sur•ance (ĭn-shŏŏr′əns) *n.* **1.** The act or business of insuring or state of being insured. **2.** A contract binding a company to compensate a party for future specified losses in return for continuing payments. **3.** The total amount to be paid in case of loss <bought $100,000 of life *insurance*> **4.** A protective or compensatory measure.

in•sure (ĭn-shŏŏr′) *v.* **-sured, -sur•ing. 1.** To cover with insurance. **2.** To make certain or sure. **—in•sur′a•ble** *adj.* **—in•sur′er** *n.*

in•sured (ĭn-shŏŏrd′) *n.* Someone covered by insurance.

in•sur•gent (ĭn-sûr′jənt) *adj.* Rising in insurrection against established authority : rebelling. **—in•sur′gence, in•sur′gen•cy** *n.* **—in•sur′gent** *n.*

in•sur•mount•a•ble (ĭn′sər-moun′tə-bəl) *adj.* Insuperable <*insurmountable* difficulties> **—in′sur•mount′a•bly** *adv.*

in•sur•rec•tion (ĭn′sə-rĕk′shən) *n.* An open revolt against established authority. **—in′sur•rec′tion•ist** *n.*

in•tact (ĭn-tăkt′) *adj.* **1.** Not damaged in any way. **2.** Whole. **—in•tact′ness** *n.*

in•ta•glio (ĭn-tăl′yō, -täl′-) *n., pl.* **-glios.** An engraved figure or design depressed below the surface of hard metal or stone.

in•take (ĭn′tāk′) *n.* **1.** An opening through which a fluid is admitted. **2. a.** The act of taking in. **b.** Something taken in.

in•tan•gi•ble (ĭn-tăn′jə-bəl) *adj.* **1.** Incapable of being touched. **2.** Incapable of being perceived. **3.** Not readily defined or measured <such *intangible* factors as morale> **—in•tan′gi•bil′i•ty, in•tan′gi•ble•ness** *n.* **—in•tan′gi•ble** *n.* **—in•tan′gi•bly** *adv.*

in•te•ger (ĭn′tĭ-jər) *n.* Any member of the set (. . . –2, –1, 0, +1, +2, . . .), expressible as the sum or difference of two natural numbers.

in•te•gral (ĭn′tĭ-grəl, ĭn-tĕg′rəl) *adj.* **1.** Essential for completeness : constituent. **2.** Entire : whole. **3.** *Math.* Expressed or expressible as integers. *—n.* An entire unit : whole.

in•te•grate (ĭn′tĭ-grāt′) *v.* **-grat•ed, -grat•ing. 1.** To make into a whole by bringing parts together : unify. **2.** To join (e.g., parts) together : unite. **3.** To open to people of all races or ethnic groups. **—in′te•gra′tion** *n.* **—in′te•gra′tive** *adj.*

integrated circuit *n.* A tiny wafer of material on which a complex of electronic components and their interconnections is etched or imprinted. **—integrated circuitry** *n.*

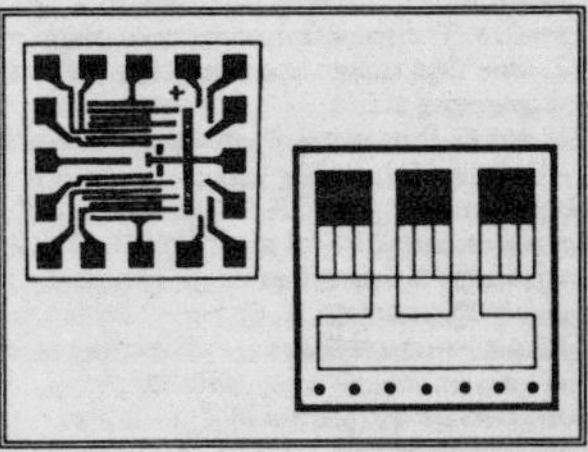

integrated circuit

in•teg•ri•ty (ĭn-tĕg′rĭ-tē) *n.* **1.** Strict adherence to a standard of value or conduct. **2.** Personal honesty and independence. **3.** Completeness : unity. **4.** Soundness.

in•teg•u•ment (ĭn-tĕg′yə-mənt) *n.* An outer covering or coat, as an animal's skin, a shell, or a seed coat.

in•tel•lect (ĭn′tl-ĕkt′) *n.* **1. a.** The capacity for understanding and knowledge. **b.** The ability to think abstractly or profoundly. **2.** A person of notable intellect.

in•tel•lec•tu•al (ĭn′tl-ĕk′chōō -əl) *adj.* **1.** Of, relating to, or engaging the intellect. **2.** Given to use of the intellect : inclined to rational or creative thought. **—in′tel•lec′tu•al** *n.* **—in′tel•lec′tu•al′i•ty** (-ăl′ĭ-tē) *n.* **—in′tel•lec′tu•al•ly** *adv.*

in•tel•lec•tu•al•ize (ĭn′tl-ĕk′chōō-ə-līz′) *v.* **-ized, -iz•ing.** To examine rationally or objectively, esp. so as to avoid emotional involvement. **—in′tel•lec′tu•al•i•za′tion** *n.* **—in′tel•lec′tu•al•iz′er** *n.*

in•tel•li•gence (ĭn-tĕl′ə-jəns) *n.* **1.** The capacity to learn and to solve problems and difficulties. **2.** Superior mental powers. **3.** News : information. **4. a.** Secret information, esp. about an enemy. **b.** The gathering of this information.

intelligence quotient *n.* The ratio of tested mental age to chronological age, usu. expressed as a quotient multiplied by 100.

in•tel•li•gent (ĭn-tĕl′ə-jənt) *adj.* Having or showing intelligence. **—in•tel′li•gent•ly** *adv.*

in·tel·li·gent·si·a (ĭn-tĕl′ə-jĕnt′sē-ə, -gĕnt′-) *n.* The intellectual elite of a society.

in·tel·li·gi·ble (ĭn-tĕl′ə-jə-bəl) *adj.* Capable of being understood. **—in·tel′li·gi·bil′i·ty** *n.* **—in·tel′li·gi·bly** *adv.*

in·tem·per·ance (ĭn-tĕm′pər-əns) *n.* Lack of temperance, esp. in drinking alcoholic beverages. **—in·tem′per·ate** *adj.* **—in·tem′per·ate·ly** *adv.*

in·tend (ĭn-tĕnd′) *v.* **1.** To have in mind as a purpose : plan. **2.** To design for a particular use. **3.** To signify : mean.

in·tend·ed (ĭn-tĕn′dĭd) *adj.* **1.** Intentional : deliberate. **2.** Proposed : prospective. —*n. Informal.* One's fiancé or fiancée.

in·tense (ĭn-tĕns′) *adj.* **1.** Extreme in degree, strength, or effect <an *intense* storm> **2.** Marked by great concentration or strain <an *intense* gaze> **3.** Deep : profound. ★ ***syns:*** DESPERATE, FIERCE, FURIOUS, TERRIBLE, VEHEMENT, VIOLENT **—in·tense′ly** *adv.* **—in·tense′ness** *n.*

in·ten·si·fy (ĭn-tĕn′sə-fī′) *v.* **-fied, -fy·ing.** To make or become more intense. **—in·ten′si·fi·ca′tion** *n.*

in·ten·si·ty (ĭn-tĕn′sĭ-tē) *n., pl.* **-ties. 1.** Exceptionally great effect, concentration, or force. **2.** Degree : strength.

in·ten·sive (ĭn-tĕn′sĭv) *adj.* **1.** Concentrated and forceful <*intensive* study> **2.** Characterized by a full application of all resources <*intensive* hospital care> **3.** Adding emphasis. —*n.* A linguistic element, as the adverbs *extremely* or *awfully*, that adds emphasis. **—in·ten′sive·ly** *adv.*

in·tent (ĭn-tĕnt′) *n.* **1.** Purpose : aim. **2.** The state of mind with which an act is committed. **3.** Meaning : significance. —*adj.* **1.** Concentrated : intense. **2.** Fixed on a purpose <*intent* on leaving> **—in·tent′ly** *adv.* **—in·tent′ness** *n.*

in·ten·tion (ĭn-tĕn′shən) *n.* **1.** A plan of action : design. **2.** An aim that guides action : object. **3.** Significance : import. ★ ***syns:*** AIM, DESIGN, END, GOAL, INTENT, OBJECT, PURPOSE, TARGET, VIEW

in·ten·tion·al (ĭn-tĕn′shə-nəl) *adj.* Deliberately done : intended. **—in·ten′tion·al′i·ty** (-năl′ĭ-tē) *n.* **—in·ten′tion·al·ly** *adv.*

in·ter (ĭn-tûr′) *v.* **-terred, -ter·ring.** To put into a grave : bury. **—in·ter′ment** *n.*

inter– *pref.* **1.** Between or among <*inter*collegiate> **2.** Mutually : together <*inter*relate>

in·ter·act (ĭn′tər-ăkt′) *v.* To act on each other. **—in′ter·ac′tion** *n.*

in·ter·ac·tive (ĭn′tər-ăk′tĭv) *adj.* **1.** Acting on each other. **2.** *Computer Sci.* Of a two-way electronic or communications system in which response is direct and continual. **3.** Of a form of television entertainment in which the viewer can affect events on the screen. **—in′ter·ac′tive·ly** *adv.*

in·ter·breed (ĭn′tər-brēd′) *v.* **1.** To breed with another kind or species. **2.** To inbreed.

in·ter·ca·late (ĭn-tûr′kə-lāt′) *v.* **-lat·ed, -lat·ing** To insert (e.g., an extra day) in a calendar. **—in·ter′ca·lar′y** *adj.* **—in·ter′ca·la′tion** *n.*

in·ter·cede (ĭn′tər-sēd′) *v.* **-ced·ed, -ced·ing. 1.** To argue on another's behalf. **2.** To mediate. **—in′ter·ced′er** *n.*

in·ter·cept (ĭn′tər-sĕpt′) *v.* **1.** To interrupt the course of, esp. by seizing <*intercept* a message><*intercept* a football pass> **2.** To intersect. **3.** *Math.* To cut off or bound part of (e.g., a line). **—in′ter·cept′** *n.* **—in′ter·cep′tion** *n.*

in′ter-Af′ri·can *adj.*
in′ter·a′gen·cy *adj.*
in′ter-A·mer′i·can *adj.*
in′ter-A′sian *adj.*
in′ter·bor′ough *adj.*
in′ter·branch′ *adj.*
in′ter·bron′chi·al *adj.*
in′ter·cam′pus *adj.*
in′ter·cap′il·lar′y *adj.*
in′ter-Car′ib·be′an *adj.*
in′ter·cel′lu·lar *adj.*
in′ter·cer′e·bral *adj.*
in′ter·chro′mo·so′mal *adj.*
in′ter·church′ *adj.*
in′ter·cit′y *adj.*
in′ter·clan′ *adj.*
in′ter·class′ *adj.*
in′ter·coast′al *adj.*
in′ter·co·lo′ni·al *adj.*
in′ter·com·mu′nal *adj.*
in′ter·com·mu′ni·ty *adj.*
in′ter·cor′po·rate *adj.*
in′ter·cor·pus′cu·lar *adj.*
in′ter·coun′ty *adj.*
in′ter·cul′tur·al *adj.*
in′ter·de·pend′ence *n.*
in′ter·de·pend′en·cy *n.*
in′ter·de·pend′ent *adj.*
in′ter·di′a·lec′tal *adj.*
in′ter·di·vi′sion·al *adj.*
in′ter·do·min′ion *adj.*
in′ter·dor′sal *adj.*
in′ter·eth′nic *adj.*
in′ter-Eu′ro·pe′an *adj.*
in′ter·fac′ul·ty *adj.*
in′ter·fam′i·ly *adj.*
in′ter·gang′ *adj.*
in′ter·gen′er·a′tion·al *adj.*
in′ter·glan′du·lar *adj.*
in′ter·gov′ern·men′tal *adj.*
in′ter·group′ *adj.*
in′ter·is′land *adj.*
in′ter·lam′i·nar *adj.*
in′ter·lay′er·ing *n.*
in′ter·li′brar′y *adj.*
in′ter·lob′u·lar *adj.*
in′ter·mem′bra·nous *adj.*
in′ter·mesh′ *v.*
in′ter·min′is·te′ri·al *adj.*
in′ter·mi·tot′ic *adj.*
in′ter·mo′lar *adj.*
in′ter·moun′tain *adj.*
in′ter·mu·nic′i·pal *adj.*
in′ter·mus′cu·lar *adj.*
in′ter·na′sal *adj.*
in′ter·nu′cle·ar *adj.*
in′ter·o′ce·an′ic *adj.*
in′ter·of′fice *adj.*
in′ter·op′tic *adj.*
in′ter·or′bit·al *adj.*
in′ter·pa·ro′chi·al *adj.*
in′ter·par′ty *adj.*
in′ter·pol′li·nate′ *v.*
in′ter·pro·fes′sion·al *adj.*
in′ter·pro·vin′cial *adj.*
in′ter·pul′mo·nar′y *adj.*
in′ter·re′gion·al *adj.*
in′ter·re·lig′ious *adj.*
in′ter·re′nal *adj.*
in′ter·sec′tion·al *adj.*
in′ter·sex′u·al *adj.*
in′ter·so′cial *adj.*
in′ter·so·ci′e·tal *adj.*
in′ter·spi′nal *adj.*
in′ter·tan′gle *v.*
in′ter·tar′sal *adj.*
in′ter·ter′ri·to′ri·al *adj.*
in′ter·tex′tu·al *adj.*
in′ter·tid′al *adj.*
in′ter·trib′al *adj.*
in′ter·u′ni·ver′si·ty *adj.*
in′ter·val′ley *adj.*
in′ter·var′si·ty *adj.*
in′ter·vas′cu·lar *adj.*
in′ter·ven·tric′u·lar *adj.*
in′ter·word′ *adj.*
in′ter·zo′nal *adj.*

in·ter·cep·tor *also* **in·ter·cept·er** (ĭn'tər-sĕp'tər) *n.* **1.** One that intercepts. **2.** A fighter plane that intercepts enemy aircraft.

in·ter·ces·sion (ĭn'tər-sĕsh'ən) *n.* **1.** Entreaty in favor of another. **2.** Mediation. —**in'ter·ces'sion·al** *adj.* —**in'ter·ces'sor** *n.* —**in'ter·ces'so·ry** *adj.*

in·ter·change (ĭn'tər-chānj') *v.* **1.** To switch each of (2 things) into the other's place. **2.** To exchange. —*n.* (ĭn'tər-chānj') **1.** An exchange. **2.** A highway intersection that allows traffic to move between roads without crossing traffic streams. —**in'ter·change'a·ble** *adj.* —**in'ter·change'a·bly** *adv.* —**in'ter·chang'er** *n.*

in·ter·col·le·giate (ĭn'tər-kə-lē'jĭt, -jē-ĭt) *adj.* Involving or representing 2 or more colleges.

in·ter·com (ĭn'tər-kŏm') *n.* A 2-way communication system, as between parts of a house.

in·ter·com·mu·ni·cate (ĭn'tər-kə-myōō'nĭ-kāt') *v.* **1.** To communicate with each other. **2.** To be connected, as rooms. —**in'ter·com·mu'ni·ca'tion** *n.* —**in'ter·com·mu'ni·ca'tive** *adj.*

in·ter·con·nect (ĭn'tər-kə-nĕkt') *v.* To connect or be connected with each other. —**in'ter·con·nec'tion** *n.*

in·ter·con·ti·nen·tal (ĭn'tər-kŏn'tə-nĕn'tl) *adj.* Extending or occurring between or among continents.

in·ter·course (ĭn'tər-kôrs', -kōrs') *n.* **1.** Exchange between persons or groups : communication. **2.** Sexual intercourse.

in·ter·dict (ĭn'tər-dĭkt') *v.* To prohibit or forbid, esp. by official decree. —*n.* (ĭn'tər-dĭkt'). A prohibition. —**in'ter·dic'tion** *n.* —**in'ter·dic'tor** *n.* —**in'ter·dic'to·ry** *adj.*

in·ter·est (ĭn'trĭst, -tər-ĭst) *n.* **1. a.** Concern and curiosity about something. **b.** Something that arouses such feelings. **2.** Regard for one's advantage : self-interest. **3.** A claim or legal share in something. **4. a.** A charge for a loan, usu. a percentage of the amount borrowed. **b.** Return on invested capital <*interest* on a bank deposit> —*v.* **1.** To stimulate the curiosity and attention of. **2.** To cause to become concerned or involved with.

in·ter·est·ed (ĭn'trĭ-stĭd, -tər-ĭ-stĭd, -tə-rĕs'tĭd) *adj.* **1.** Feeling or displaying interest <*interested* in architecture> **2.** Having a claim or share. **3.** Influenced by self- interest. —**in'ter·est·ed·ly** *adv.*

interest group *n.* A group of persons strongly supporting a particular cause, such as an item of legislation.

in·ter·est·ing (ĭn'trĭ-stĭng, -tər-ĭ-stĭng, -tə-rĕs'tĭng) *adj.* Stimulating interest. —**in'ter·est·ing·ly** *adv.*

in·ter·face (ĭn'tər-fās') *n.* **1.** A surface that forms a common boundary between adjacent areas, strata, or substances. **2. a.** A point at which independent systems interact. **b.** A system by which this is done. **c.** *Computer Sci.* The point of interaction or communication between a computer and another entity, as a printer. —**in'ter·face'** *v.* —**in'ter·fa'cial** *adj.*

in·ter·fere (ĭn'tər-fîr') *v.* **-fered, -fer·ing. 1.** To come between so as to impede : hinder. **2.** To obstruct illegally the movement of an opposing player in some sports. **3.** To intrude in the affairs of others : meddle. **4.** To prevent clear reception of broadcast signals. —**in'ter·fer'ence** *n.*

in·ter·fer·on (ĭn'tər-fîr'ŏn') *n.* A protein produced in cells that acts to prevent duplication of infectious viral forms.

in·ter·ga·lac·tic (ĭn'tər-gə-lăk'tĭk) *adj.* Between galaxies.

in·ter·im (ĭn'tər-ĭm) *n.* An intervening period. —*adj.* Temporary.

in·te·ri·or (ĭn-tîr'ē-ər) *adj.* **1.** Of or in the inside : inner. **2.** Away from a coast or border : inland. —*n.* **1.** The inner part or area : inside. **2.** A person's spiritual or mental being. **3.** A representation of the inside of a room or structure, as in a painting. **4.** The inland part of a country or region.

interior decorator *n.* One who plans the layout, furnishings, and decoration of architectural interiors. —**interior decoration** *n.*

in·ter·ject (ĭn'tər-jĕkt') *v.* To insert between other parts or elements. —**in'ter·jec'tor** *n.* —**in'ter·jec'to·ry** *adj.*

in·ter·jec·tion (ĭn'tər-jĕk'shən) *n.* **1.** An exclamation. **2.** A word used exclamatorily to express emotion that is capable of standing alone grammatically, as *Heavens!* or *Oh!* —**in'ter·jec'tion·al** *adj.*

in·ter·lace (ĭn'tər-lās') *v.* **-laced, -lac·ing. 1.** To lace together : interweave. **2.** To intersperse.

in·ter·lard (ĭn'tər-lärd') *v.* To insert at intervals : intersperse.

in·ter·lin·e·ar (ĭn'tər-lĭn'ē-ər) *adj.* Inserted between lines of a text <an *interlinear* translation>

in·ter·lock (ĭn'tər-lŏk') *v.* To join closely, as by hooking or overlapping.

in·ter·loc·u·tor (ĭn'tər-lŏk'yə-tər) *n.* One who takes part in a conversation.

in·ter·loc·u·to·ry (ĭn'tər-lŏk'yə-tôr'ē, -tōr'ē) *adj.* Pronounced during a legal action and temporarily in effect <an *interlocutory* decree>

in·ter·lope (ĭn'tər-lōp', ĭn'tər-lōp') *v.* **-loped, -lop·ing. 1.** To violate the rights of others. **2.** To interfere : meddle. —**in'ter·lop'er** *n.*

in·ter·lude (ĭn'tər-lōōd') *n.* **1.** An intervening event or period of time. **2.** An entertainment presented between the acts of a play. **3.** A short musical piece between parts of a longer composition.

in·ter·mar·ry (ĭn'tər-măr'ē) *v.* **1.** To marry a member of another group. **2.** To become connected by the marriages of members <The tribes *intermarried.*> **3.** To marry within one's family, clan, or tribe. —**in'ter·mar'riage** *n.*

in·ter·me·di·ar·y (ĭn'tər-mē'dē-ĕr'ē) *n., pl.* **-ies. 1.** A mediator : go-between. **2.** An agent

: means. **3.** An intermediate stage. —*adj.* **1.** Acting as a mediator. **2.** Intermediate.

in•ter•me•di•ate (ĭn'tər-mē'dē-ĭt) *adj.* Located or occurring in the middle or between 2 extremes. —**in'ter•me'di•a•cy** *n.* —**in'ter•me'di•ate** *n.* —**in'ter•me'di•ate•ly** *adv.*

in•ter•mez•zo (ĭn'tər-mĕt'sō, -mĕd'zō) *n., pl.* **-zos** *or* **-zi** (-sē, -zē). **1.** *Mus.* A short movement separating sections of a longer composition. **b.** A short instrumental composition. **2.** A brief entr'acte.

in•ter•mi•na•ble (ĭn-tûr'mə-nə-bəl) *adj.* Boringly protracted <an *interminable* lecture> —**in•ter'mi•na•bly** *adv.*

in•ter•min•gle (ĭn'tər-mĭng'gəl) *v.* To blend or become mixed together.

in•ter•mis•sion (ĭn'tər-mĭsh'ən) *n.* A temporary suspension or pause, esp. between the parts of a performance, as of a play.

in•ter•mit•tent (ĭn'tər-mĭt'nt) *adj.* Starting and stopping at intervals. ★ ***syns:*** FITFUL, OCCASIONAL, PERIODIC, SPORADIC —**in'•ter•mit'tent•ly** *adv.*

in•ter•mix (ĭn'tər-mĭks') *v.* To intermingle. —**in'ter•mix'ture** *n.*

in•tern *also* **in•terne** (ĭn'tûrn') *n.* **1.** An advanced student or recent graduate who undergoes supervised practical training, esp. at a hospital. **2.** One who is interned or confined. —*v.* **1.** To serve as an intern. **2.** (ĭn-tûrn'). To confine, esp. during wartime. —**in•tern'ment** *n.* —**in'tern•ship'** *n.*

in•ter•nal (ĭn-tûr'nəl) *adj.* **1.** Inner : interior. **2.** Coming from or residing within : inherent. **3.** Within the body. **4.** Of or pertaining to a country's domestic affairs. —**in•ter'nal•ly** *adv.*

internal-combustion engine *n.* An engine, as in an automobile, in which fuel is burned inside the engine.

in•ter•nal•ize (ĭn-tûr'nə-līz') *v.* **-ized, -iz•ing.** To make internal, personal, or subjective. —**in•ter'nal•i•za'tion** *n.*

internal medicine *n.* Medical study and treatment of nonsurgical diseases.

in•ter•na•tion•al (ĭn'tər-năsh'ə-nəl) *adj.* Of, pertaining to, or involving 2 or more nations. —**in'ter•na'tion•al•ly** *adv.*

in•ter•na•tion•al•ism (ĭn'tər-năsh'ə-nə-lĭz'-əm) *n.* A policy of cooperation among nations, esp. in politics and economy. —**in'ter•na'tion•al•ist** *n.*

in•ter•na•tion•al•ize (ĭn'tər-năsh'ən-ə-līz') *v.* To place under international control. —**in'•ter•na'tion•al•i•za'tion** *n.*

international law *n.* A body of rules considered binding between nations.

in•terne (ĭn'tûrn') *n.* & *v. var. of* INTERN.

in•ter•nec•ine (ĭn'tər-nĕs'ēn', -īn', -ĭn, -nē'-sīn') *adj.* **1.** Mutually destructive. **2.** Of or pertaining to struggle within a group.

in•tern•ee (ĭn'tûr-nē') *n.* A person who is interned or confined.

In•ter•net (ĭn'tər-nĕt') *n.* A matrix of networks that connects different kinds of computers around the world.

in•ter•nist (ĭn'tûr'nĭst, ĭn-tûr'-) *n.* A physician specializing in internal medicine.

in•ter•per•son•al (ĭn'tər-pûr'sə-nəl) *adj.* Between persons <*interpersonal* relationships> —**in'ter•per'son•al•ly** *adv.*

in•ter•plan•e•tar•y (ĭn'tər-plăn'ĭ-tĕr'ē) *adj.* Between planets.

in•ter•play (ĭn'tər-plā') *n.* Action and reaction : interaction. —**in'ter•play'***v.*

in•ter•po•late (ĭn-tûr'pə-lāt') *v.* **-lat•ed, -lat•ing.** **1.** To insert between other things or elements. **2.** To change (a text) by introducing additional material. —**in•ter'po•la'tion** *n.* —**in•ter'po•la'tor** *n.*

in•ter•pose (ĭn'tər-pōz') *v.* **1.** To insert between parts. **2.** To introduce (e.g., a comment) into a conversation or speech. **3.** To put (oneself) in : intrude. **4.** To intervene. —**in'ter•pos'er** *n.* —**in'ter•po•si'tion** (-pə-zĭsh'ən) *n.*

in•ter•pret (ĭn-tûr'prĭt) *v.* **1.** To clarify the meaning of by explaining or restating. **2.** To represent or delineate the meaning of, esp. by artistic performance <an actress *interpreting* a role> **3.** To translate. —**in•ter'•pret•a•ble** *adj.* —**in•ter'pre•ta'tion** *n.* —**in•ter'pret•er** *n.*

in•ter•pre•ta•tive (ĭn-tûr'prĭ-tā'tĭv) *also* **in•ter•pre•tive** (-prĭ-tĭv) *adj.* Of or based on interpreting : explanatory. —**in•ter'pre•ta'•tive•ly** *adv.*

in•ter•ra•cial (ĭn'tər-rā'shəl) *adj.* Between different races.

in•ter•reg•num (ĭn'tər-rĕg'nəm) *n., pl.* **-nums** *or* **-na** (-nə). **1.** A period of time between 2 successive reigns. **2.** A lapse in continuity. —**in'ter•reg'nal** *adj.*

in•ter•re•late (ĭn'tər-rĭ-lāt') *v.* To put into or have a mutual relationship. —**in'ter•re•la'•tion** *n.* —**in'ter•re•la'tion•ship'** *n.*

in•ter•ro•gate (ĭn-tĕr'ə-gāt') *v.* **-gat•ed, -gat•ing.** **1.** To question formally. **2.** To send out a signal to (e.g., a computer) for triggering an appropriate response. —**in•ter'ro•ga'tion** *n.* —**in•ter'ro•ga'tor** *n.*

in•ter•rog•a•tive (ĭn'tə-rŏg'ə-tĭv) *adj.* **1.** Being, suggesting, or asking a question. **2.** Used to ask a question <an *interrogative* pronoun> —**in'ter•rog'a•tive** *n.* —**in'ter•rog'a•tive•ly** *adv.*

in•ter•rog•a•to•ry (ĭn'tə-rŏg'ə-tôr'ē, -tōr'ē) *adj.* Interrogative.

in•ter•rupt (ĭn'tə-rŭpt') *v.* **1.** To break the progress or continuity of. **2.** To impede or stop by breaking in on. **3.** To break in while someone else is speaking or performing. —**in'ter•rupt'er** *n.* —**in'ter•rup'tion** *n.* —**in'ter•rup'tive** *adj.*

in•ter•scho•las•tic (ĭn'tər-skə-lăs'tĭk) *adj.* Occurring or conducted between or among schools.

in•ter•sect (ĭn'tər-sĕkt') *v.* **1.** To cut through or across. **2.** To form an intersection (with).

in•ter•sec•tion (ĭn'tər-sĕk'shən) *n.* **1.** The act or point of intersecting. **2.** A place where streets or roads intersect. **3.** *Math.* The point or locus of points common to 2 or more geometric elements.

in·ter·sperse (ĭn′tər-spûrs′) *v.* **-spersed, -spers·ing. 1.** To scatter among other things. **2.** To provide with things distributed at intervals. **—in′ter·sper′sion** *n.*

in·ter·state (ĭn′tər-stāt′) *adj.* Between or connecting 2 or more states. *—n.* An interstate highway.

in·ter·stel·lar (ĭn′tər-stĕl′ər) *adj.* Between the stars.

in·ter·stice (ĭn-tûr′stĭs) *n., pl.* **-sti·ces** (-stĭ-sēz′, -sĭz). A small space between things : opening <the *interstices* of a net> **—in′ter·sti′tial** (in′tər-stĭsh′əl) *adj.*

in·ter·twine (ĭn′tər-twīn′) *v.* To twine together. **—in′ter·twine′ment** *n.*

in·ter·ur·ban (ĭn′tər-ûr′bən) *adj.* Situated between or connecting urban areas.

in·ter·val (ĭn′tər-vəl) *n.* **1.** A space between 2 points or objects. **2.** A period of time between 2 events or moments. **3.** The differences in pitch between 2 musical tones. **4.** *Math.* A set containing all the numbers between a pair of given numbers.

†in·ter·vale (ĭn′tər-văl′) *n. Regional.* A tract of low-lying land, esp. along a river.

in·ter·vene (ĭn′tər-vēn′) *v.* **-vened, -ven·ing. 1.** To appear, come, or lie between things, esp. as an unrelated or disruptive circumstance. **2.** To enter or come between so as to modify <The police *intervened* to break up the fight.> **3.** To interfere, often with force, in a foreign dispute or conflict. **—in′ter·ven′tion** (-vĕn′shən) *n.*

in·ter·view (ĭn′tər-vyo͞o′) *n.* **1.** A formal personal meeting, esp. one arranged for formal discussion or to evaluate an applicant. **2.** A conversation, as one conducted by a reporter, to elicit information. **—in′ter·view′** *v.* **—in′ter·view′er** *n.*

in·ter·weave (ĭn′tər-wēv′) *v.* **1.** To weave together. **2.** To blend together : intertwine.

in·tes·tate (ĭn-tĕs′tāt′, -tĭt) *adj.* **1.** Not having made a legal will. **2.** Not disposed of by a will. **—in·tes′ta·cy** (-tə-sē) *n.*

in·tes·tine (ĭn-tĕs′tĭn) *n. often* **intestines.** The part of the alimentary canal from the stomach to the anus. **—in·tes′ti·nal** *adj.* **—in·tes′ti·nal·ly** *adv.*

in·ti (ĭn′tē) *n.* A former monetary unit of Peru.

in·ti·mate[1] (ĭn′tə-mĭt) *adj.* **1.** Characterized by very close association or familiarity. **2.** Essential : fundamental. **3.** Affording privacy and informality <an *intimate* café> **4.** Very personal. *—n.* An intimate friend. **—in′ti·ma·cy, in′ti·mate·ness** *n.* **—in′ti·mate·ly** *adv.*

in·ti·mate[2] (ĭn′tə-māt′) *v.* **-mat·ed, -mat·ing.** To communicate indirectly : imply artfully. **—in′ti·mat′er** *n.* **—in′ti·ma′tion** *n.*

in·tim·i·date (ĭn-tĭm′ĭ-dāt′) *v.* **-dat·ed, -dat·ing. 1.** To make fearful : frighten. **2.** To discourage, coerce, or suppress by or as if by threatening. **—in·tim′i·da′tion** *n.* **—in·tim′i·da′tor** *n.*

in·to (ĭn′to͞o) *prep.* **1.** To the inside of. **2.** To the activity or occupation of <went *into* medicine> **3.** To the condition of. **4.** So as to be in <enter *into* an agreement> **5.** To a point in the course of <lasted *into* the next week> **6.** Against <ran *into* a wall> **7.** *Informal.* Interested in : involved with <a friend who is *into* yoga>

in·tol·er·a·ble (ĭn-tŏl′ər-ə-bəl) *adj.* **1.** Not tolerable : unbearable. **2.** Inordinate : excessive. **—in·tol′er·a·bly** *adv.*

in·tol·er·ant (ĭn-tŏl′ər-ənt) *adj.* **1.** Not tolerant, as of opposing views : bigoted. **2.** Not able to endure <*intolerant* of hot weather> **—in·tol′er·ance** *n.* **—in·tol′er·ant·ly** *adv.*

in·to·na·tion (ĭn′tō-nā′shən) *n.* **1.** The act of intoning. **2.** A manner of speaking or producing tones. **3.** The ranging of pitch in speech, esp. as an element of meaning.

in·tone (ĭn-tōn′) *v.* **-toned, -ton·ing. 1.** To recite in a chanting voice. **2.** To utter in a monotone. **—in·ton′er** *n.*

in to·to (ĭn tō′tō) *adv.* Totally : in full.

in·tox·i·cate (ĭn-tŏk′sĭ-kāt′) *v.* **-cat·ed, -cat·ing. 1.** To stimulate or stupefy, esp. with alcohol. **2.** To excite : exhilarate. **—in·tox′i·cant** (-kənt) *n.* **—in·tox′i·ca′tion** *n.*

intra– *pref.* Within <*intra*mural>

in·tra·cel·lu·lar (ĭn′trə-sĕl′yə-lər) *adj.* Within a cell or cells.

in·tra·cos·tal (ĭn′trə-kŏs′tl) *adj.* On the inner surface of a rib or ribs.

in·tra·cra·ni·al (ĭn′trə-krā′nē-əl) *adj.* Within the skull.

in·trac·ta·ble (ĭn-trăk′tə-bəl) *adj.* **1.** Hard to manage : obstinate. **2.** Difficult to treat or cure <an *intractable* virus>

in·tra·dos (ĭn′trə-dŏs′, -dō′, -ĭn-trā′dŏs′, -dōs′) *n., pl.* **-dos** (-dōz′) *or* **-dos·es** (-dŏs′ĭz) The inner curve of an arch.

intrados

in·tra·mu·ral (ĭn′trə-myo͝or′əl) *adj.* Carried on or being within a school or other institution <*intramural* sports>

in·tra·mus·cu·lar (ĭn′trə-mŭs′kyə-lər) *adj.* Within a muscle.

in·tran·si·gent (ĭn-trăn′sə-jənt) *adj.* Not willing to moderate a position : uncompromising. **—in·tran′si·gence, in·tran′si·gen·cy** *n.* **—in·tran′si·gent** *n.*

in·tran·si·tive (ĭn-trăn′sĭ-tĭv) *adj.* Not needing a direct object to complete its meaning. —Used of a verb. *—n.* An intransitive verb or verb construction. —**in•tran'si•tive•ly** *adv.* —**in•tran'si•tive•ness** *n.*

in•tra•oc•u•lar (ĭn'trə-ŏk'yə-lər) *adj.* Within the eyeball.

in•tra•state (ĭn'trə-stāt') *adj.* Within a state.

in•tra•u•ter•ine (ĭn'trə-yōō'tər-ĭn, -tə-rīn') *adj.* Within the uterus.

intrauterine device *n.* A metal or plastic loop, ring, or spiral inserted into the uterus as a contraceptive.

in•tra•ve•nous (ĭn'trə-vē'nəs) *adj.* Within a vein. —**in'tra•ve'nous•ly** *adv.*

in•trep•id (ĭn-trĕp'ĭd) *adj.* Outstandingly courageous : fearless. —**in•trep'id•ly** *adv.* —**in•trep'id•ness** *n.*

in•tri•cate (ĭn'trĭ-kĭt) *adj.* **1.** Having many elaborately arranged parts or elements : complex. **2.** Difficult to solve or comprehend. —**in'tri•ca•cy** (-kə-sē) *n.* —**in'tri•cate•ly** *adv.*

in•trigue (ĭn'trēg', ĭn-trēg') *n.* **1. a.** A furtive maneuver or plan : plot. **b.** Involvement in such plots. **2.** A clandestine love affair. —*v.* (ĭn-trēg') **-trigued, -trigu•ing. 1.** To engage in intrigues : plot. **2.** To effect by scheming. **3.** To stimulate the interest or curiosity of. —**in•trigu'er** *n.*

in•trin•sic (ĭn-trĭn'sĭk) *adj.* Of or relating to the fundamental nature of a thing : inherent. —**in•trin'si•cal•ly** *adv.*

in•tro•duce (ĭn'trə-dōōs', -dyōōs') *v.* **-duced, -duc•ing. 1.** To present (a person) by name to another : make acquainted. **2.** To bring into use or practice for the first time <*introduce* reforms> **3.** To bring in and establish in a new environment. **4.** To insert or inject. **5.** To bring to another's notice. **6.** To begin : preface. ★ ***syns:*** INAUGURATE, INITIATE, INSTITUTE, LAUNCH, ORIGINATE —**in'tro•duc'er** *n.* —**in'tro•duc'tion** (-dŭk'shən) *n.* —**in'tro•duc'to•ry** *adj.*

in•tro•it *also* **In•tro•it** (in'trō'ĭt, -troit', ĭn-trō'ĭt) *n.* **1.** A psalm or hymn sung at the beginning of a service. **2.** *Rom. Cath. Ch.* The beginning of the proper of the Mass.

in•tro•mit (ĭn'trə-mĭt') *v.* **-mit•ted, -mit•ting.** To cause or allow to enter : admit. —**in'tro•mis'sion** *n.* —**in'tro•mit'tent** *adj.* —**in'tro•mit'ter** *n.*

in•tro•spec•tion (ĭn'trə-spĕk'shən) *n.* Examination of one's thoughts and feelings. —**in'tro•spect'** *v.* —**in'tro•spec'tive** *adj.* —**in'tro•spec'tive•ly** *adv.*

in•tro•vert (ĭn'trə-vûrt') *n.* One who is chiefly concerned with one's own mental life rather than with friends and social activities. —**in'tro•ver'sion** *n.* —**in'tro•ver'sive** *adj.* —**in'tro•vert'ed** *adj.*

in•trude (ĭn-trōōd') *v.* **-trud•ed, -trud•ing. 1.** To push or thrust in. **2.** To put or come in without being asked or wanted. **3.** To appear inappropriately. —**in•trud'er** *n.* —**in•tru'sion** *n.* —**in•tru'sive** *adj.* —**in•tru'sive•ly** *adv.*

in•trust (ĭn-trŭst') *v. var. of* ENTRUST.

in•tu•it (ĭn-tōō'ĭt, -tyōō'-) *v.* To understand or sense through intuition.

in•tu•i•tion (ĭn'tōō-ĭsh'ən, -tyōō-) *n.* **1. a.** The capacity of knowing without the use of rational processes. **b.** Knowledge acquired in this way. **2.** Keen insight. —**in•tu'i•tive** *adj.* —**in•tu'i•tive•ly** *adv.*

In•u•it (ĭn'yōō-ĭt) *n., pl.* **-it** *or* **-its. 1.** A member of an Eskimo people, esp. of Arctic Canada or Greenland. **2.** Their language.

in•un•date (ĭn'ən-dāt') *v.* **-dat•ed, -dat•ing. 1.** To cover with water : overflow. **2.** To overwhelm with or as if with a flood : swamp. —**in'un•da'tion** *n.*

in•ure (ĭn-yŏŏr') *v.* **-ured, -ur•ing.** To make accustomed to something usu. undesirable : harden. —**in•ure'ment** *n.*

in u•ter•o (ĭn yōō'tə-rō) *adv. & adj.* In the uterus.

in•vade (ĭn-vād') *v.* **-vad•ed, -vad•ing. 1.** To go into by force so as to conquer or pillage. **2.** To enter and overrun harmfully. **3.** To encroach upon : violate. —**in•vad'er** *n.*

in•va•lid[1] (ĭn'və-lĭd) *n.* A chronically sick or disabled person. —*adj.* Disabled by disease or injury.

in•val•id[2] (ĭn-văl'ĭd) *adj.* **1.** Not factually or legally valid. **2.** Falsely reasoned : unsound. —**in'va•lid'i•ty** (-və-lĭd'ĭ-tē) *n.* —**in•val'id•ly** *adv.*

in•val•i•date (ĭn-văl'ĭ-dāt') *v.* **-dat•ed, -dat•ing.** To make invalid : nullify. —**in•val'i•da'tion** *n.* —**in•val'i•da'tor** *n.*

in•val•u•a•ble (ĭn-văl'yōō-ə-bəl) *adj.* **1.** Of great value : priceless. **2.** Of great help or use <his *invaluable* assistance> —**in•val'u•a•ble•ness** *n.* —**in•val'u•a•bly** *adv.*

in•var•i•a•ble (ĭn-vâr'ē-ə-bəl) *adj.* Not changing : constant. —**in•var'i•a•bly** *adv.*

in•va•sion (ĭn-vā'zhən) *n.* The act of invading.

in•va•sive (ĭn-vā'sĭv) *adj.* **1.** Invading. **2.** Tending to spread rapidly and harmfully. —**in•va'sive•ness** *n.*

in•vec•tive (ĭn-vĕk'tĭv) *n.* Vituperative or denunciatory language.

in•veigh (ĭn-vā') *v.* To protest angrily : rail. —**in•veigh'er** *n.*

in•vei•gle (ĭn-vā'gəl, -vē'-) *v.* **-gled, -gling. 1.** To win over by guile or persuasion. **2.** To obtain by cajolery. —**in•vei'gle•ment** *n.* —**in•vei'gler** *n.*

in•vent (ĭn-vĕnt') *v.* **1.** To produce or devise first : originate. **2.** To make up : concoct <*invent* an excuse> ★ ***syns:*** CONCOCT, CONTRIVE, COOK UP, DEVISE, DREAM UP, FABRICATE, FORMULATE, HATCH, MAKE UP —**in•ven'tor** *n.*

in•ven•tion (ĭn-vĕn'shən) *n.* **1.** The act of inventing. **2.** A new method, process, or device evolved from study and testing. **3.** Something made up, esp. a falsehood. **4.** Skill in inventing : inventiveness.

in•ven•tive (ĭn-vĕn'tĭv) *adj.* **1.** Of or marked by invention. **2.** Having or showing skill in inventing : creative. —**in•ven'tive•ly** *adv.* —**in•ven'tive•ness** *n.*

in•ven•to•ry (ĭn'vən-tôr'ē, -tōr'ē) *n., pl.* **-ries. 1. a.** A list of items, esp. a periodic detailed enumeration of goods or possessions. **b.** The process of making an inventory. **c.** The items listed in an inventory. **2.** A supply : stock. **—in'ven·to'ry** *v.*

in·ver·ness *also* **In·ver·ness** (ĭn'vər-nĕs') *n.* A loose overcoat with a detachable cape.

in·verse (ĭn-vûrs', ĭn'vûrs') *adj.* **1.** Reversed in order or sequence. **2.** Opposite in effects or nature. **3.** Inverted. *—n.* Something opposite : reverse. **—in·verse'ly** *adv.*

in·ver·sion (ĭn-vûr'zhən, -shən) *n.* **1.** The act of inverting or the state of being inverted. **2.** An interchange of position, esp. of adjacent objects in a sequence. **3.** A state in which the temperature of the air increases with increasing altitude and keeps the surface air and pollutants down.

in·vert (ĭn-vûrt') *v.* **1.** To turn upside down or inside out. **2.** To reverse the position, order, or condition of. **—in·vert'er** *n.* **—in·vert'i·ble** *adj.*

in·ver·tase (ĭn-vûr'tās', ĭn'vər-tās', -tāz') *n.* An enzyme that catalyzes the conversion of sucrose to glucose and fructose.

in·ver·te·brate (ĭn-vûr'tə-brĭt, -brāt') *adj.* Lacking a backbone or spinal column. **—in·ver'te·brate** *n.*

in·vest (ĭn-vĕst') *v.* **1.** To put (money) into something, as stocks or property, in order to obtain profit or interest. **2.** To utilize for future benefit <*invested* her time wisely> **3.** To furnish with authority or power. **4.** To place in office : install. **5.** To envelop : shroud. **—in·ves'tor** *n.*

in·ves·ti·gate (ĭn-vĕs'tĭ-gāt') *v.* **-gat·ed, -gat·ing.** To make a systematic inquiry (into) : examine deeply. **—in·ves'ti·ga'tion** *n.* **—in·ves'ti·ga'tive** *adj.* **—in·ves'ti·ga'tor** *n.*

in·ves·ti·ture (ĭn-vĕs'tə-chŏŏr', -chər) *n.* The act or ceremony of installing someone in a high office.

in·vest·ment (ĭn-vĕst'mənt) *n.* **1.** The act of investing. **2.** An amount invested. **3.** A possession acquired and kept for future benefit. **4.** Investiture.

in·vet·er·ate (ĭn-vĕt'ər-ĭt) *adj.* **1.** Solidly fixed or established : deep-rooted. **2.** Continuing or persisting in a habit <an *inveterate* skeptic> **—in·vet'er·a·cy, in·vet'er·ate·ness** *n.* **—in·vet'er·ate·ly** *adv.*

in·vid·i·ous (ĭn-vĭd'ē-əs) *adj.* Tending to cause animosity or imply a slight <an *invidious* comparison> **—in·vid'i·ous·ly** *adv.* **—in·vid'i·ous·ness** *n.*

in·vig·o·rate (ĭn-vĭg'ə-rāt') *v.* **-rat·ed, -rat·ing.** To impart strength or vitality to : refresh : animate. **—in·vig'o·rat'ing·ly** *adv.* **—in·vig'o·ra'tion** *n.*

in·vin·ci·ble (ĭn-vĭn'sə-bəl) *adj.* Incapable of being overcome or defeated. ★ *syns:* IMPREGNABLE, INDOMITABLE, INSUPERABLE, UNCONQUERABLE **—in·vin'ci·bil'i·ty** *n.* **—in·vin'ci·bly** *adv.*

in·vi·o·la·ble (ĭn-vī'ə-lə-bəl) *adj.* **1.** Secure from violation or profanation. **2.** Safe from trespass or assault. **—in·vi'o·la·bil'i·ty** *n.* **—in·vi'o·la·bly** *adv.*

in·vi·o·late (ĭn-vī'ə-lĭt) *adj.* Not violated : intact. **—in·vi'o·late·ly** *adv.* **—in·vi'o·late·ness** *n.*

in·vis·i·ble (ĭn-vĭz'ə-bəl) *adj.* **1.** Not visible. **2.** Not open to view : hidden. **3.** Imperceptible. **—in·vis'i·bil'i·ty** *n.* **—in·vis'i·bly** *adv.*

in·vi·ta·tion (ĭn'vĭ-tā'shən) *n.* **1.** The act of inviting. **2.** A request for someone's presence or participation. **3.** An enticement or attraction.

in·vite (ĭn-vīt') *v.* **-vit·ed, -vit·ing. 1.** To request the presence or participation of. **2.** To ask formally. **3.** To welcome <*invite* questions from the audience> **4.** To bring on : provoke <only *inviting* trouble> **5.** To tempt : entice. *—n.* (ĭn'vīt'). *Informal.* An invitation.

in·vit·ing (ĭn-vī'tĭng) *adj.* Attractive : tempting. **—in·vit'ing·ly** *adv.* **—in·vit'ing·ness** *n.*

in vi·tro (ĭn vē'trō) *adj. & adv.* In an artificial environment outside the living organism <*in vitro* fertilization>

in vi·vo *adj. & adv.* Within a living organism.

in·vo·ca·tion (ĭn'və-kā'shən) *n.* **1.** An appeal to a higher power for aid. **2.** A prayer used in invoking, esp. at the opening of a service or ceremony.

in·voice (ĭn'vois') *n.* **1.** An itemized list of goods shipped or services rendered, detailing the costs : bill. **2.** A consignment of goods. **—in'voice'** *v.*

in·voke (ĭn-vōk') *v.* **-voked, -vok·ing. 1.** To call on for aid, support, or inspiration <*invoke* the Muse> **2.** To appeal to for justification : cite. **3.** To call for earnestly : solicit. **4.** To conjure. **5.** To resort to : implement <*invoked* martial law> **—in·vok'er** *n.*

in·vol·un·tar·y (ĭn-vŏl'ən-tĕr'ē) *adj.* **1.** Not done willingly or by conscious choice. **2.** Not subject to conscious control <*involuntary* muscles> **—in·vol'un·tar'i·ly** *adv.* **—in·vol'un·tar'i·ness** *n.*

in·vo·lute (ĭn'və-lōōt') *adj.* **1.** Intricate : complex. **2.** Having margins or whorls rolled inward.

in·vo·lu·tion (ĭn'və-lōō'shən) *n.* **1.** Complexity : intricacy. **2.** Something complex or intricate, as a complicated grammatical construction.

in·volve (ĭn-vŏlv') *v.* **-volved, -volv·ing. 1.** To contain as a part. **2.** To have as a consequence : entail. **3.** To make a participant of : draw in. **4.** To engross : absorb. **5.** To make intricate : complicate. **—in·volve'ment** *n.*

in·vul·ner·a·ble (ĭn-vŭl'nər-ə-bəl) *adj.* **1.** Immune to attack : impregnable. **2.** Not able to be damaged or wounded. **—in·vul'ner·a·bil'i·ty** *n.* **—in·vul'ner·a·bly** *adv.*

in·ward (ĭn'wərd) *adj.* **1.** Situated or located inside : inner. **2.** Moving or facing toward the interior. **3.** Of or existing in the mind. *—adv.* *also* **in·wards** (-wərdz). **1.** Toward the center, inside, or interior. **2.** Toward the mind or the self. **—in'ward·ness** *n.*

in•ward•ly (ĭn′wərd-lē) *adv.* **1.** On or in the inside : within. **2.** To oneself : privately <*inwardly* laughing>
i•o•dide (ī′ə-dīd′) *n.* A chemical compound composed of iodine and another element or radical.
i•o•dine (ī′ə-dīn′, -dĭn, -dēn′) *n.* **1.** *Symbol* **I** A lustrous, gray, corrosive, poisonous element. **2.** A solution of iodine, alcohol, and sodium iodide or potassium iodide, used as an antiseptic.
i•o•dize (ī′ə-dīz′) *v.* **-dized, -diz•ing.** To treat or combine with iodine or an iodide.
i•on (ī′ən, ī′ŏn′) *n.* An atom, group of atoms, or molecule that has acquired a net electric charge by gaining or losing electrons from a neutral configuration.
–ion *suff.* An act, a condition, or the outcome of an act <creat*ion*><sedat*ion*>
i•on•ize (ī′ə-nīz′) *v.* **-ized, -iz•ing.** To convert completely or partially into ions. **—i′o•ni•za′tion** *n.*
i•on•o•sphere (ī-ŏn′ə-sfîr′) *n.* A region of the earth's atmosphere consisting of free electrons and ionized gases extending from approx. 30 to 250 mi or 50 to 400 km. **—i•on′o•spher′ic** (-sfîr′ĭk,-sfĕr′-) *adj.*
i•o•ta (ī-ō′tə) *n.* A very small amount : bit.
IOU (ī′ō-yōō′) *n., pl.* **IOU's** *or* **IOUs.** A promise to pay a debt.
–ious *suff.* Having or full of <bil*ious*>
ip•e•cac (ĭp′ĭ-kăk′) *n.* A South American shrub, *Cephaelis ipecacuanha,* with roots used medicinally to induce vomiting.
ip•so fac•to (ĭp′sō făk′tō) *adv.* By that very fact.
Ir *symbol for* IRIDIUM.
i•ras•ci•ble (ĭ-răs′ə-bəl, ī-răs′-) *adj.* Easily angered : hot-tempered. **—i•ras′ci•bil′i•ty, i•ras′ci•ble•ness** *n.* **—i•ras′ci•bly** *adv.*
i•rate (ī-rāt′, ī′rāt′) *adj.* Very angry : enraged. **—i•rate′ly** *adv.*
ire (īr) *n.* Anger : rage. **—ire′ful** *adj.* **—ire′ful•ly** *adv.* **—ire′ful•ness** *n.*
i•ren•ic (ī-rĕn′ĭk, ī-rē′nĭk) *adj.* Promoting peace : conciliatory. **—i•ren′i•cal•ly**
ir•i•des•cent (ĭr′ĭ-dĕs′ənt) *adj.* Producing an array of rainbowlike colors. **—ir′i•des′cence** *n.*
i•rid•i•um (ĭ-rĭd′ē-əm, ī-rĭd′-) *n.* *Symbol* **Ir** A hard, brittle, highly corrosion-resistant, yellow metallic element.
i•ris (ī′rĭs) *n., pl.* **i•ris•es** *or* **i•ri•des** (ī′rĭ-dēz′, ĭr′ĭ -). **1.** The pigmented part of the eye that regulates the size of the pupil by expanding and contracting around it. **2.** A plant of the genus *Iris,* with narrow sword- shaped leaves and showy flowers.
Irish setter *n.* A large, slender dog having a silky reddish-brown coat.
irk (ûrk) *v.* To cause irritation or annoyance : vex. **—irk′some** *adj.* **—irk′some•ly** *adv.* **—irk′some•ness** *n.*
i•ron (ī′ərn) *n.* **1.** *Symbol* **Fe** A hard, gray, brittle metallic element, used alloyed in many important building materials. **2.** Great strength or hardness. **3.** Any of various tools made of iron alloy or similar metal. **4.** A golf club with a metal head. **5.** A device with a weighted flat bottom used when heated for pressing wrinkles from fabric. **6. irons.** Metal restraints for the wrists or ankles : shackles. —*v.* To press with an iron. **—iron out.** To settle through compromise : work out. **—i′ron•er** *n.* **—i′ron•ing** *n.*
Iron Age *n.* The gen. prehistoric period succeeding the Bronze Age, marked by the introduction of iron metallurgy, in Europe beginning around the 8th cent. B.C.
i•ron•bound (ī′ərn-bound′) *adj.* Rigid : unyielding.
i•ron•clad (ī′ərn-klăd′) *adj.* **1.** Sheathed with protective iron plates. **2.** Rigid : fixed <an *ironclad* law>
Iron Curtain *n.* The political and idealogical barrier existing between the Soviet bloc and W Europe from 1945 to 1990.
i•ron•ic (ī-rŏn′ĭk) *also* **i•ron•i•cal** (-ĭ-kəl) *adj.* **1.** Marked by or constituting irony. **2.** Given to using irony. **—i•ron′i•cal•ly** *adv.*
iron lung *n.* A tank enclosing the entire body except the head and assisting respiration by alternately increasing and decreasing air pressure.
i•ron•stone (ī′ərn-stōn′) *n.* **1.** An iron ore mixed with silica and clay. **2.** A heavy, hard white pottery.
i•ron•ware (ī′ərn-wâr′) *n.* Products made of iron.
i•ron•work (ī′ərn-wûrk′) *n.* Work in iron, as railings and gates.
i•ron•works (ī′ərn-wûrks′) *n. (sing. or pl. in number).* A place for smelting iron or manufacturing iron products.
i•ro•ny (ī′rə-nē) *n., pl.* **-nies. 1.** The use of words to suggest the opposite of what they literally mean. **2.** Incongruity between what might be expected to happen and what actually happens.
Ir•o•quoi•an (ĭr′ə-kwoi′ən) *n.* **1.** A family of American Indian languages of E North America. **2.** A member of an Iroquoian-speaking people. **—Ir′o•quoi′an** *adj.*
Ir•o•quois (ĭr′ə-kwoi′) *n., pl.* **-quois** (-kwoi′, -kwoiz′). **1.** A member of an American Indian confederacy of New York State composed of the Mohawk, Oneida, Onondaga, Cayuga, Seneca, and later the Tuscarora peoples. **2.** Any of their languages.
ir•ra•di•ate (ĭ-rā′dē-āt′) *v.* **-at•ed, -at•ing. 1.** To treat with or expose to radiation. **2.** To send forth as if in rays : radiate. **—ir•ra′di•a′tion** *n.* **—ir•ra′di•a′tor** *n.*
ir•ra•tion•al (ĭ-răsh′ə-nəl) *adj.* **1.** Not capable of reasoning. **2.** Having lost mental clarity : incoherent. **3.** Contrary to reason : illogical. **4.** *Math.* Not expressible as an integer or a quotient of integers. **—ir•ra′tion•al′i•ty** *n.* **—ir•ra′tion•al•ly** *adv.*
ir•rec•on•cil•a•ble (ĭ-rĕk′ən-sī′lə-bəl, ĭ-rĕk′ən-sī′-) *adj.* Not capable of being reconciled. **—ir•rec′on•cil′•a•bil′i•ty** *n.* **—ir•rec′on•cil′a•bly** *adv.*
ir•re•cov•er•a•ble (ĭr′ĭ-kŭv′ər-ə-bəl) *adj.* Not

capable of being recovered : irreparable. —**ir'·re·cov'er·a·ble·ness** *n.* —**ir're·cov'er·a·bly** *adv.*

ir·re·deem·a·ble (ĭr'ĭ-dē'mə-bəl) *adj.* **1.** Not capable of being bought back or turned in for exchange. **2.** Not convertible into coin. **3.** Not able to be saved or reformed.

ir·re·den·tist (ĭr'ĭ-dĕn'tĭst) *n.* An advocate of the recovery of territory that one's nation has lost. —**ir're·den'tism** *n.* —**ir're·den'tist** *adj.*

ir·re·duc·i·ble (ĭr'ĭ-do͞o'sə-bəl, -dyo͞o'-) *adj.* Not capable of being reduced, as to a smaller amount. —**ir're·duc'i·bil'i·ty** *n.* —**ir're·duc'i·bly** *adv.*

ir·ref·u·ta·ble (ĭ-rĕf'yə-tə-bəl, ĭr'ĭ-fyo͞o'tə-bəl) *adj.* Not able to be disproved <*irrefutable* evidence> —**ir·ref'u·ta·bil'i·ty** *n.* —**ir·ref'u·ta·bly** *adv.*

ir·reg·u·lar (ĭ-rĕg'yə-lər) *adj.* **1.** Not according to rule or general practice. **2.** Not straight, uniform, or orderly. **3.** Unconventional. **4.** Uneven <an *irregular* pulse> **5.** Not up to standard : imperfect. **6.** Not following a standard pattern of grammatical inflections <The verb "be" is *irregular.*> —*n.* **1.** One that is irregular. **2.** A guerrilla. —**ir·reg'u·lar'i·ty** (-lăr'ĭ-tē) *n.* —**ir·reg'u·lar·ly** *adv.*

ir·rel·e·vant (ĭ-rĕl'ə-vənt) *adj.* Not relating to the subject at hand : not pertinent. ★ *syns:* EXTRANEOUS, IMMATERIAL, INAPPLICABLE. —**ir·rel'e·vance, ir·rel'e·van·cy** *n.* —**ir·rel'e·vant·ly** *adv.*

ir·re·lig·ious (ĭr'ĭ-lĭj'əs) *adj.* Indifferent or opposed to religion. —**ir're·lig'ious·ly** *adv.* —**ir're·lig'ious·ness, ir're·lig'ion** *n.*

ir·re·me·di·a·ble (ĭr'ĭ-mē'dē-ə-bəl) *adj.* Beyond correction or repair : hopeless. —**ir're·me'di·a·bly** *adv.*

ir·re·mis·si·ble (ĭr'ĭ-mĭs'ə-bəl) *adj.* Not pardonable. —**ir're·mis'si·bil'i·ty** *n.*

ir·re·mov·a·ble (ĭr'ĭ-mo͞o'və-bəl) *adj.* Not removable. —**ir're·mov'a·bly** *adv.*

ir·rep·a·ra·ble (ĭ-rĕp'ər-ə-bəl) *adj.* Not able to be repaired or set right again. —**ir·rep'a·ra·bil'i·ty** *n.* —**ir·rep'a·ra·bly** *adv.*

ir·re·place·a·ble (ĭr'ĭ-plā'sə-bəl) *adj.* Not able to be replaced.

ir·re·press·i·ble (ĭr'ĭ-prĕs'ə-bəl) *adj.* Impossible to hold back or restrain. —**ir're·press'i·bil'i·ty** *n.* —**ir're·press'i·bly** *adv.*

ir·re·proach·a·ble (ĭr'ĭ-prō'chə-bəl) *adj.* Beyond reproach : impeccable. —**ir're·proach'a·ble·ness** *n.* —**ir're·proach'a·bly** *adv.*

ir·re·sist·i·ble (ĭr'ĭ-zĭs'tə-bəl) *adj.* **1.** Impossible to resist. **2.** Highly appealing. —**ir're·sist'i·bil'i·ty** *n.* —**ir're·sist'i·bly** *adv.*

ir·res·o·lute (ĭ-rĕz'ə-lo͞ot') *adj.* Lacking in resolution : indecisive. —**ir·res'o·lute'ly** *adv.* —**ir·res'o·lute'ness** *n.*

ir·re·spec·tive (ĭr'ĭ-spĕk'tĭv) *adj.* Regardless <*irrespective* of race or nationality>

ir·re·spon·si·ble (ĭr'ĭ-spŏn'sə-bəl) *adj.* **1.** Not accountable. **2.** Not fit to assume responsibility. **3.** Showing no sense of responsibility <*irresponsible* behavior> ★ *syns:* FECKLESS, INCAUTIOUS, RECKLESS —**ir're·spon'si·bil'i·ty** *n.* —**ir're·spon'si·bly** *adv.*

ir·re·triev·a·ble (ĭr'ĭ-trē'və-bəl) *adj.* Impossible to retrieve or recover.

ir·rev·er·ence (ĭ-rĕv'ər-əns) *n.* **1.** Lack of reverence : disrespect. **2.** A disrespectful action or remark. —**ir·rev'er·ent** *adj.* —**ir·rev'er·ent·ly** *adv.*

ir·re·vers·i·ble (ĭr'ĭ-vûr'sə-bəl) *adj.* Impossible to reverse. —**ir're·vers'i·bil'i·ty** *n.* —**ir're·vers'i·bly** *adv.*

ir·rev·o·ca·ble (ĭ-rĕv'ə-kə-bəl) *adj.* Not able to be revoked : irreversible. —**ir·rev'o·ca·bil'i·ty** *n.* —**ir·rev'o·ca·bly** *adv.*

ir·ri·ga·ble (ĭr'ĭ-gə-bəl) *adj.* Able to be irrigated.

ir·ri·gate (ĭr'ĭ-gāt') *v.* **-gat·ed, -gat·ing. 1.** To supply (land or crops) with water artificially, as with ditches or pipes. **2.** To wash out (e.g., a bodily wound) with water or a medicated fluid. —**ir'ri·ga'tion** *n.* —**ir'ri·ga'tion·al** *adj.* —**ir'ri·ga'tor** *n.*

ir·ri·ta·ble (ĭr'ĭ-tə-bəl) *adj.* **1.** Easily annoyed or irritated. **2.** Ill- tempered. **3.** Abnormally sensitive or responsive to stimuli. ★ *syns:* CANTANKEROUS, CRANKY, CROSS, GROUCHY, GRUMPY, ILL-TEMPERED, IRASCIBLE, PEEVISH, QUERULOUS, SURLY, TESTY —**ir'ri·ta·bil'i·ty, ir'ri·ta·ble·ness** *n.* —**ir'ri·ta·bly** *adv.*

ir·ri·tate (ĭr'ĭ-tāt') *v.* **-tat·ed, -tat·ing. 1.** To make angry : annoy or bother. **2.** To provoke. **3.** To chafe or inflame. —**ir'ri·tant** *adj. & n.* —**ir'ri·tat'ing·ly** *adv.* —**ir'ri·ta'tion** *n.* —**ir'ri·ta'tor** *n.*

ir·rupt (ĭ-rŭpt') *v.* To rush or burst in : invade. —**ir·rup'tion** *n.* —**ir·rup'tive** *adj.* —**ir·rup'tive·ly** *adv.*

is (ĭz) *v. 3rd person sing. present tense of* BE.

I·sa·iah (ī-zā'ə, ī-zī'ə) *n.* —See table at BIBLE.

–ish *suff.* **1.** Of or characteristic of <Dan*ish*> **2.** Having the usu. undesirable qualities of <child*ish*> **3.** Somewhat : rather <yellow*ish*> **4.** Approximately <fiv*ish*>

i·sin·glass (ī'zĭng-glăs', ī'zən-) *n.* A transparent gelatin made from the air bladder of certain fishes.

Is·lam (ĭs'ləm, ĭz'-, ĭ-slăm') *n.* **1.** A monotheistic religion based on the teachings of Muhammad. **2. a.** The peoples or nations that practice Islam. **b.** Islamic civilization. —**Is·lam'ic** (-lăm'ĭk, -lä'mĭk) *adj.*

is·land (ī'lənd) *n.* **1.** A land mass, esp. one smaller than a continent, completely surrounded by water. **2.** Something like an island, esp. in being isolated. —**is'land·er** *n.*

isle (īl) *n.* An island, esp. one that is small.

is·let (ī'lĭt) *n.* A little island.

ism (ĭz'əm) *n. Informal.* A particular doctrine or theory.

–ism *suff.* **1.** A practice or policy <terror*ism*> **2.** Typical behavior or quality <hero*ism*> **3.** A condition <pauper*ism*> **4.** A distinctive usage or characteristic <American*ism*> **5.** A system of principles : doctrine <pacif*ism*>

is·n't (ĭz'ənt). Is not.

i·so·bar (ī'sə-bär') *n.* A line on a map connecting points of equal pressure. **—i'so·bar'ic** (-bär'ĭk, -băr'-) *adj.*

i·so·late (ī'sə-lāt') *v.* **-lat·ed, -lat·ing. 1.** To set apart from others or the rest : put by itself. **2.** To place in quarantine. **—i'so·la'tion** *n.* **—i'so·la'tor** *n.*

i·so·la·tion·ism (ī'sə-lā'shə-nĭz'əm) *n.* A national policy of avoiding economic or political entanglements with other countries. **—i'so·la'tion·ist** *n.*

i·so·mer (ī'sə-mər) *n.* A compound that has the same kinds and numbers of atoms as another compound but differs in chemical or physical properties because of the arrangement or linkage of the atoms. **—i'so·mer'ic** *adj.*

i·so·met·ric (ī'sə-mĕt'rĭk) *also* **i·so·met·ri·cal** (-rĭ-kəl) *adj.* **1.** Of equal size or dimensions. **2.** *Physiol.* Involving muscle contraction against resistance in which the length of the muscle remains the same <an *isometric* exercise> *—n.* **1.** A line connecting isometric points. **2. isometrics.** *(sing. in number).* Isometric exercise.

i·so·morph (ī'sə-môrf') *n.* One of 2 or more organisms or objects showing close similarity in form or structure. **—i'so·mor'phic** *adj.* **—i'so·mor'phism** *n.*

i·so·oc·tane (ī'sō-ŏk'tān') *n.* A highly flammable liquid used to determine the octane numbers of fuels.

i·so·pro·pyl alcohol (i'sə-prō'pəl) *n.* A clear, colorless, mobile flammable liquid used in antifreeze compounds, solvents, lotions, and cosmetics.

i·sos·ce·les (ī-sŏs'ə-lēz') *adj.* Having 2 equal sides <an *isosceles* triangle>

i·so·therm (ī'sə-thûrm') *n.* A line on a map linking points having the same temperature. **—i'so·ther'mal** *adj.*

i·so·tope (ī'sə-tōp') *n.* One of a set of atoms that contain in their nuclei the same number of protons but different numbers of neutrons. **—i'so·top'ic** (-tŏp'ĭk) *adj.* **—i'so·top'i·cal·ly** *adv.*

i·so·trop·ic (ī'sə-trŏp'ĭk) *adj.* Being the same in all directions. **—i·sot'ro·py** (ī-sŏt'rə-pē), **i·sot'ro·pism** (-pĭz'əm) *n.*

Is·ra·el (ĭz'rē-əl) *n.* **1.** The descendants of Jacob in the Bible. **2.** The Hebrew people.

Is·rae·li (ĭz-rā'lē) *adj.* Of or pertaining to the state of Israel or its inhabitants. **—Is·rae'li** *n.*

Is·ra·el·ite (ĭz'rē-ə-līt') *n.* A Hebrew. **—Is'ra·el·lite'** *adj.*

is·sue (ĭsh'o͞o) *n.* **1.** An act of flowing, going, or giving out. **2.** Something published or offered, as a stamp or a copy of a periodical. **3.** A final result : outcome. **4.** Something proceeding from a source <the *issue* of a creative mind> **5.** Offspring. **6.** A point of debate or discussion or dispute. **7.** A culmination. **8.** An outlet. **9.** *Pathol.* A discharge, as of pus or blood. *—v.* **-sued, -su·ing. 1.** To go or come out. **2.** To come or put forth. **3.** To distribute : give out <*issue* weapons> **4.** To be born or descended. **5.** To result. **6.** To publish or be published. **7.** To circulate. **—take issue.** To disagree. **—is'su·ance** *n.* **—is'su·er** *n.*

—ist *suff.* **1.** One that makes, operates, plays, or is connected with <novel*ist*> **2.** A specialist in a given art, science, or skill <biolo*gist*> **3.** An adherent or advocate of a given doctrine or theory <anarch*ist*> **4.** One characterized by a given trait or quality <romanti*cist*>

isth·mus (ĭs'məs) *n.* **1.** A narrow strip of land connecting 2 larger land masses. **2.** *Anat.* **a.** A narrow strip of tissue joining 2 larger organs. **b.** A narrow passage between 2 larger cavities. **—isth'mi·an** *adj.*

it (ĭt) *pron.* **1.** That one previously mentioned. —Used to refer to a nonhuman entity, an animal or human being of unknown sex, a group of persons, or an abstraction. **2.** —Used as the subject of an impersonal verb <*It* is snowing.> **3.** —Used to refer to a general state of affairs <couldn't stand *it* any longer> *—n.* A player in a game who tries to catch or find the others.

I·tal·ian·ate (ĭ-tăl'yə-nāt', -nĭt) *adj.* Italian in character.

i·tal·ic (ĭ-tăl'ĭk, ī-tăl'-) *adj.* Of or being a style of printing type in which the letters slant to the right. *—n. often* **italics.** Italic typeface or print.

i·tal·i·cize (ĭ-tăl'ĭ-sīz', ī-tăl'-) *v.* **-cized, -ciz·ing.** To print in italics. **—i·tal'i·ci·za'tion** *n.*

itch (ĭch) *n.* **1.** A skin sensation prompting a desire to scratch. **2.** A contagious skin disease characterized by intense irritation, eruption, and itching. **3.** A restless craving <an *itch* to see the world> **—itch** *v.* **—itch'i·ness** *n.* **—itch'y** *adj.*

—ite *suff.* **1.** A native or resident of <Manhattan*ite*> **2.** An adherent of <Trotsky*ite*> **3.** A mineral : rock <tek*tite*> **4.** A commercial product <ebon*ite*>

i·tem (ī'təm) *n.* **1.** A separately specified article or unit in a series or list. **2.** A clause in a document. **3.** A piece of information : detail. **4.** A short article, as in a newspaper or magazine.

i·tem·ize (ī'tə-mīz') *v.* **-ized, -iz·ing.** To detail item by item : list. **—i'tem·i·za'tion** *n.* **—i'tem·iz'er** *n.*

it·er·ate (ĭt'ə-rāt') *v.* **-at·ed, -at·ing.** To say or do again : repeat. **—it'er·a'tion** *n.*

i·tin·er·ant (ī-tĭn'ər-ənt, ĭ-tĭn'-) *adj.* Traveling from place to place <an *itinerant* peddler> **—i·tin'er·ant** *n.*

i·tin·er·ar·y (ī-tĭn'ə-rĕr'ē, ĭ-tĭn'-) *n., pl.* **-ies. 1.** A route or scheduled route of a journey. **2.** A travelers' record of a journey. **3.** A guidebook.

it'll (ĭt'l). **1.** It will. **2.** It shall.

its (ĭts) *adj.* Of it. —Used to indicate possession or the agent or recipient of an action <a dog wagging *its* tail>

it's (ĭts). **1.** It is. **2.** It has.

it·self (ĭt-sĕlf') *pron.* The one identical with it. —Used reflexively, for emphasis, and in certain idiomatic constructions <turns *itself* off> <in the machine *itself*><acting *itself* again>

it•ty-bit•ty (ĭt'ē-bĭt'ē) *also* **it•sy-bit•sy** (ĭt'sē-bĭt'sē) *adj. Informal.* Extremely small.

–ity *suff.* A condition or quality <abnormal*ity*>

–ium *suff.* Chemical element or group <californ*ium*>

I've (īv). I have.

–ive *suff.* Acting or inclined to act in a specified way <prevent*ive*>

i•vied (ī'vēd) *adj.* Covered or overgrown with ivy.

i•vo•ry (ī'və-rē, īv'rē) *n., pl.* **-ries. 1.** The hard, smooth, yellowish-white material that forms the tusks of elephants and certain other animals. **2.** A substance similar to ivory. **3.** An object made of ivory. **4.** A yellowish white. **—i'vo•ry** *adj.*

ivory tower *n.* A place or attitude of retreat, esp. preoccupation with remote, lofty, or intellectual considerations rather than mundane affairs.

i•vy (ī'vē) *n., pl.* **i•vies. 1.** A climbing or trailing plant of the genus *Hedera,* esp. *H. helix,* with lobed evergreen leaves. **2.** Any of various similar plants.

–ization *suff.* The action, process, or result of doing something specified <colon*ization*>

–ize *suff.* **1.** To cause to be or to resemble <dramat*ize*><human*ize*> **2.** To become <material*ize*> **3.** To treat as <idol*ize*> **4.** To affect with <anesthet*ize*> **5.** To subject to <tyrann*ize*> **6.** To treat according to <pasteur*ize*> **7.** To engage in <botan*ize*>

Jj

j *or* **J** (jā) *n., pl.* **j's** *or* **J's. 1.** The 10th letter of the English alphabet. **2.** A speech sound represented by the letter *j.* **3.** Something with the shape of the letter J.

jab (jăb) *v.* **jabbed, jab•bing. 1.** To thrust or poke sharply. **2.** To hit with short punches. *—n.* A quick thrust or punch.

jab•ber (jăb'ər) *v.* To speak quickly or unintelligibly. **—jab'ber** *n.* **—jab'ber•er** *n.*

jab•ber•wock•y (jăb'ər-wŏk'ē) *n.* Nonsensical speech that appears to make sense.

jab•ot (zhă-bō', jă-) *n.* A decorative frill down the front of a shirt or dress.

jac•a•ran•da (jăk'ə-răn'də) *n.* **1.** A tropical American tree of the genus *Jacaranda,* with compound leaves and pale-purple flowers. **2.** The hard, brown wood of the jacaranda.

jack (jăk) *n.* **1.** *often* **Jack.** A man : fellow. **2.** A playing card ranking below a queen and bearing a representation of a knave. **3.** A device for lifting heavy objects. **4.** The male of certain animals, esp. the ass. **5. a. jacks** *(sing. or pl. in number).* A game played with a set of 6-pronged metal pieces and a ball. **b.** One of the metal pieces in the game of jacks. **6.** A socket into which a plug is inserted to make an electric circuit. **7.** A small flag on a ship, usu. indicating nationality. *—v.* **1.** To raise by means of a jack. **2.** To raise <*jacked* prices up>

jack•al (jăk'əl, -ôl') *n.* A doglike mammal of the genus *Canis,* of Asia and Africa.

jack•a•napes (jăk'ə-nāps') *n.* An impudent person.

jack•ass (jăk'ăs') *n.* **1.** A male donkey or ass. **2.** A stupid person.

jack•boot (jăk'bōōt') *n.* A stout military boot reaching above the knee.

jack•daw (jăk'dô') *n.* An Old World bird, *Corvus monedula,* resembling the crow.

jack•et (jăk'ĭt) *n.* **1.** A short coat. **2.** An outer covering, as of a book.

jack•ham•mer (jăk'hăm'ər) *n.* A pneumatic tool for breaking pavement and drilling rock.

jack-in-the-box (jăk'ĭn-thə-bŏks') *n.* A small box from which a puppet springs up when the lid is released.

jack-in-the-pul•pit (jăk'ĭn-*th*ə-pōōl'pĭt, -pŭl'-) *n.* A plant, *Arisaema triphyllum,* of E North America, with a leaflike spathe enclosing a clublike spadix.

jack•knife (jăk'nīf') *n.* **1.** A large pocketknife. **2.** A dive executed by bending at the waist in midair and touching the feet with the hands before straightening out. *—v.* To bend or form an acute angle.

jack-of-all-trades (jăk'əv-ôl'trādz') *n., pl.* **jacks-of-all-trades.** A person who is handy at many kinds of work.

jack-o'-lan•tern (jăk'ə-lăn'tərn) *n.* A hollowed-out pumpkin cut to look like a face and used as a lantern.

jack•pot (jăk'pŏt') *n.* The cumulative stakes in certain games, as poker.

jack rabbit *n.* A large long-legged hare of the genus *Lepus* of W North America.

jack rabbit

jack•screw (jăk′skrōō′) *n.* A lifting jack operated by a screw.
Ja•cob's ladder (jā′kəbz) *n.* A plant of the genus *Polemonium,* with blue flowers and paired ladderlike leaflets.
Ja•cuz•zi (jə-kōōz′zē, jă-). A trademark for a device that swirls the water in a pool or bath.
jade[1] (jād) *n.* A hard, usu. green gemstone.
jade[2] (jād) *n.* **1.** A worn-out broken-down horse. **2.** A disreputable woman. —*v.* **jad•ed, jad•ing.** To tire or become tired.
jad•ed (jā′dĭd) *adj.* **1.** Worn- out : fatigued. **2.** Made dull by excess : sated. —**jad′ed•ly** *adv.* —**jad′ed•ness** *n.*
jag[1] (jăg) *n.* A sharp projection.
jag[2] (jăg) *n. Slang.* A binge or spree.
jag•ged (jăg′ĭd) *adj.* Having sharp or ragged projections. —**jag′ged•ly** *adv.* —**jag′ged•ness** *n.*
jag•uar (jăg′wär′, -yōō-är′) *n.* A large feline mammal, *Panthera onca,* of tropical America, with a tawny coat and black spots.
jai a•lai (hī′ lī′, hī′ ə-lī′, hī′ ə-lī′) *n.* A game like handball in which players catch and propel a ball using a hand-shaped basket strapped to the wrist.

jai alai

jail (jāl) *n.* A prison, esp. for temporary incarceration. —*v.* To detain in custody. ★ ***syns:*** IMMURE, IMPRISON, INCARCERATE, INTERN
jail•bird (jāl′bûrd′) *n. Informal.* A prisoner or former prisoner.
jail•break (jāl′brāk′) *n.* An escape from jail, usu. forcibly.
jail•er *also* **jail•or** (jā′lər) *n.* A person in charge of a jail.
†**jakes** (jāks) *n. (sing. in number) Regional.* A privy.
ja•la•pe•ño (hä′lə-pān′yō) *n., pl.* **-ños.** A cultivated pepper, *Capsicum annuum,* having a pungent green or red fruit used in cooking.
ja•lop•y (jə-lŏp′ē) *n., pl.* **-ies.** An old, rundown vehicle, esp. a car.
ja•lou•sie (jăl′ə-sē) *n.* A blind, window, or door with adjustable horizontal slats.
jam[1] (jăm) *v.* **jammed, jam•ming. 1.** To press or wedge into a tight position. **2.** To apply suddenly, as car brakes. **3.** To lock in an unworkable position. **4.** To crowd into and block. **5.** To clog or block. **6.** To crush. **7.** *Electron.* To make (broadcast signals) unintelligible by electronic means. **8.** *Mus.* To take part in a jazz session. —*n.* **1.** The act of jamming or state of being jammed. **2.** A congestion, as of traffic. **3.** *Informal.* A difficult situation.
jam[2] (jăm) *n.* A preserve of fruit boiled to a pulp with sugar.
jamb (jăm) *n.* The vertical side piece of a door or window frame.
jam•ba•lay•a (jŭm′bə-lī′ə) *n.* A Creole dish of oysters, shrimp, and chicken or ham cooked with rice.
jam•bo•ree (jăm′bə-rē′) *n.* **1.** A large, festive gathering. **2.** A large assembly, as of Boy Scouts.
James (jāmz) *n.* —See table at BIBLE.
jam session *n.* Improvisation by a group of jazz musicians.
jan•gle (jăng′gəl) *v.* **-gled, -gling. 1.** To make or cause to make a harsh, usu. metallic sound. **2.** To jar (the nerves). —**jan′gle** *n.* —**jan′gler** *n.*
jan•i•tor (jăn′ĭ-tər) *n.* A person who attends to cleaning and repairs in a building. —**jan′i•to′ri•al** *adj.*
Jan•u•ar•y (jăn′yōō-ĕr′ē) *n., pl.* **-ies.** The first month of the year, having 31 days.
ja•pan (jə-păn′) *n.* A black varnish producing a hard, shiny finish. —**ja•pan′** *v.*
Japanese beetle *n.* A brown and green beetle, *Popillia japonica,* that is very damaging to plants.
jape (jāp) *v.* **japed, jap•ing.** To joke. —**jape** *n.* —**jap′er** *n.* —**jap′er•y** *n.*
jar[1] (jär) *n.* A cylindrical vessel with a wide mouth.
jar[2] (jär) *v.* **jarred, jar•ring. 1.** To make a discordant sound. **2.** To have a disturbing effect : grate. **3.** To jolt. **4.** To clash. —*n.* **1.** A jolt. **2.** A harsh sound.
jar•di•nière (jär′dn-îr′, zhär′dē-nyâr′) *n.* An ornamental pot or stand for plants.
jar•gon (jär′gən) *n.* **1.** Unintelligible talk. **2.** The specialized language of a trade or profession <sales *jargon*> —**jar′gon•is′tic** *adj.*
jas•mine (jăz′mĭn) *also* **jes•sa•mine** (jĕs′ə-mĭn) *n.* A vine or shrub, esp. *Jasminum officinalis* of Asia and *Gelsemium sempervirens* of SE U.S., with fragrant white or yellow flowers.
jas•per (jăs′pər) *n.* An opaque variety of quartz, usu. reddish, yellow, or brown.
ja•to (jā′tō) *n.* A takeoff assisted by an auxiliary rocket or jet.
jaun•dice (jôn′dĭs, jän′-) *n. Pathol.* Yellowish staining of the eyes, skin, and bodily fluids by bile pigment.
jaun•diced (jôn′dĭst, jän′-) *adj.* **1.** Affected with jaundice. **2.** Showing prejudice or malice.
jaunt (jônt, jänt) *n.* A short trip for pleasure. —**jaunt** *v.*
jaun•ty (jôn′tē, jän′-) *adj.* **-ti•er, -ti•est. 1.** Stylish : dapper. **2.** Buoyantly carefree and self-confident : sprightly. —**jaun′ti•ly** *adv.* —**jaun′ti•ness** *n.*
ja•va (jăv′ə, jä′və) *n. Informal.* Coffee.

jave•lin (jăv′lən, jăv′ə-) *n.* **1.** A light spear thrown as a weapon. **2.** A spear used in competitions of distance throwing.
jaw (jô) *n.* **1.** Either of 2 bony structures that hold the teeth and frame the mouth. **2.** Either of 2 hinged parts in a mechanical device. —*v. Slang.* To talk, esp. excessively.
jaw•bone (jô′bōn′) *n.* A bone of the jaw, esp. the lower jaw. —*v.* To try to persuade by using one's influence.
jaw•break•er (jô′brā′kər) *n.* **1.** A hard piece of candy. **2.** *Slang.* A word that is hard to pronounce.
jay[1] (jā) *n.* The letter j.
jay[2] (jā) *n.* A crested bird of the genera *Garrulus, Cyanocitta,* and *Aphelocoma,* related to the crows and often having a loud, harsh call.
Jay•cee (jā′sē′) *n.* A member of a junior chamber of commerce.
jay•walk (jā′wôk′) *v.* To cross a street carelessly without obeying traffic regulations. **—jay′walk′er** *n.*
jazz (jăz) *n.* **1.** A kind of music first played by black musicians in S U.S., having a strong rhythmic structure with frequent syncopation and often involving solo and ensemble improvisations. **2.** *Slang.* **a.** Pretentious talk <all that legal *jazz*> **b.** Nonsense. —*v.* **1.** To play in a jazz style. **2.** *Slang.* To lie or exaggerate (to) <Don't *jazz* me.> **—jazz up.** *Informal.* To make more interesting **:** enliven. **—jazz′er** *n.* **—jazz′y** *adj.*
jeal•ous (jĕl′əs) *adj.* **1.** Resentful or bitter in rivalry **:** envious. **2.** Inclined to suspect rivalry. **3.** Vigilant in guarding. **4.** Arising from feelings of envy or bitterness. **5.** Intolerant of infidelity. **—jeal′ous•ly** *adv.* **—jeal′ous•ness, jeal′ous•y** *n.*
jean (jēn) *n.* **1.** A strong, heavy cotton. **2. jeans.** Pants made of jean or denim.
Jeep (jēp) *n.* A trademark for a civilian motor vehicle.
jeer (jîr) *v.* To shout derisively **:** scoff. **—jeer** *n.* **—jeer′er** *n.* **—jeer′ing•ly** *adv.*
Je•ho•vah (jĭ-hō′və) *n.* God, esp in Christian translations of the Old Testament.
je•june (jĭ-jo͞on′) *adj.* **1.** Insubstantial. **2.** Lacking interest **:** dull. **3.** Immature.
je•ju•num (jĭ-jo͞o′nəm) *n., pl.* **-na** (-nə). The part of the small intestine between the duodenum and the ileum.
jell (jĕl) *v.* **1.** To become or cause to become gelatinous. **2.** To take shape or cause to take shape <a plan that finally *jelled*>
jel•ly (jĕl′ē) *n., pl.* **-lies. 1.** A soft, semisolid food with a somewhat elastic consistency, made by the setting of a liquid containing pectin or gelatin. **2.** Something like jelly. **—jel′ly** *v.*
jel•ly•bean (jĕl′ē-bēn′) *n.* A small ovoid candy with a hardened sugar coating.
jel•ly•fish (jĕl′ē-fĭsh′) *n.* **1.** A usu. free-swimming marine coelenterate of the class Scyphozoa, having a gelatinous, tentacled, often bell-shaped medusoid stage as the dominant or only phase of its life cycle. **2.** *Informal.* A spineless weakling.
jel•ly•roll (jĕl′ē-rōl′) *n.* A thin sheet of sponge cake layered with jelly and then rolled up.
jeop•ard•ize (jĕp′ər-dīz′) *v.* **-ized, -iz•ing.** To expose to loss or danger.
jeop•ard•y (jĕp′ər-dē) *n.* Exposure to loss or danger **:** peril.

▲ ***word history:*** The word *jeopardy* illustrates the human tendency to anticipate the worst in an uncertain situation. The French source of jeopardy, *jeu parti,* literally "divided game," orig. denoted a chess problem, and came to mean a position in any game for which the chances of either winning or losing were even. In English *jeopardy* retained the senses of the French word but extended them to mean "an uncertain or undecided situation." By Chaucer's time, the late 14th cent., *jeopardy* had acquired its modern sense of "peril."

jer•bo•a (jər-bō′ə) *n.* Any of various small, leaping rodents, with long hind legs, of the family Dipodidae, of Asia and Africa.

jerboa

jer•e•mi•ad (jĕr′ə-mī′əd) *n.* A prolonged complaint or a tale of woe.
Jer•e•mi•ah (jĕr′ĕ-mī′ə) *n.* —See table at BIBLE.
jerk[1] (jûrk) *v.* **1.** To give a sharp pull or twist to. **2.** To make quick abrupt movements. —*n.* **1.** A sudden movement, as a pull or tug. **2.** A sudden spasmodic, muscular movement. **3.** *Slang.* A foolish or annoying person. ★ ***syns:*** SNAP, TUG, WRENCH, YANK **—jerk′i•ly** *adv.* **—jerk′i•ness** *n.* **—jerk′y** *adj.*
jerk[2] (jûrk) *v.* To cut (meat) into long strips and cure by drying or smoking.
jer•kin (jûr′kĭn) *n.* A short, close-fitting jacket, usu. sleeveless.
jerk•wa•ter (jûrk′wô′tər, -wŏt′ər) *adj. Informal.* Of little importance.
jerk•y (jûr′kē) *n.* Meat cured by jerking.
jer•ry-build (jĕr′ē-bĭld′) *v.* To build shoddily and cheaply. **—jer′ry•build′er** *n.*
jer•sey (jûr′zē) *n., pl.* **-seys. 1.** A soft knitted fabric. **2.** A knitted sweater, shirt, or jacket. **3.** *often* **Jersey.** A breed of fawn-colored dairy cattle yielding milk rich in butter fat.
jess (jĕs) *n.* A short strap fastened around the leg of a hawk or falcon, to which a leash may be attached. —*v.* To fasten jesses on. **—jessed** (jĕst) *adj.*

jes•sa•mine (jĕs'ə-mĭn) *n. var. of* JASMINE.
jest (jĕst) *n.* **1.** An act or remark intended to cause laughter. **2.** A playful mood <said only in *jest*> —*v.* **1.** To speak or act playfully. **2.** To make witty remarks.
jest•er (jĕs'tər) *n.* One given to jesting, esp. a fool at a medieval royal court.
Jes•u•it (jĕzh'o͞o-ĭt, jĕz'yo͞o-) *n.* A member of the Society of Jesus, a Roman Catholic order founded by Ignatius Loyola in 1534.
jet[1] (jĕt) *n.* **1.** A hard, black mineral that takes a high polish, used in jewelry. **2.** A deep black. —**jet** *adj.* —**jet'ty** *adj.*
jet[2] (jĕt) *n.* **1. a.** A gushing stream of liquid or gas emitted through a narrow opening forcefully. **b.** A nozzle for emitting such a stream. **2.** A jet airplane. —*v.* **jet•ted, jet•ting. 1.** To squirt. **2.** To travel by jet airplane. **3.** To move quickly.
jet airplane *n.* An airplane driven by jet propulsion.
je•té (zhə-tā') *n.* A leap in ballet.
jet engine *n.* **1.** An engine that develops thrust by the ejection of a gaseous jet of combustion products. **2.** An airplane engine equipped to consume atmospheric oxygen.
jet lag *n.* The psychological and physiological disruption of body rhythms resulting from high-speed air travel across several time zones.
jet-pro•pelled (jĕt'prə-pĕld') *adj.* Driven by jet propulsion.
jet propulsion *n.* Propulsion provided by the rearward expulsion of matter in a jet stream, esp. propulsion by jet engines.
jet•sam (jĕt'səm) *n.* **1.** Cargo jettisoned from a vessel in distress. **2.** Discarded cargo and equipment washed ashore.
jet set *n.* An international group of well-to-do people who go from one fashionable place to another for pleasure. —**jet setter** *n.*
jet stream *n.* **1.** A wind near the troposphere, gen. moving from a westerly direction at speeds often exceeding 250 mph or 400 kph. **2.** A high-speed stream : jet.
jet•ti•son (jĕt'ĭ-sən, -zən) *v.* **1.** To throw (cargo) overboard. **2.** To discard as useless or burdensome <*jettisoned* the diet plan>
jet•ty (jĕt'ē) *n., pl.* **-ties. 1.** A wall built out into a body of water to protect a harbor or influence the current. **2.** A pier.
Jew (jo͞o) *n.* **1.** A person whose religion is Judaism. **2.** A descendant of the ancient Hebrew people.
jew•el (jo͞o'əl) *n.* **1.** An expensive ornament for personal adornment made of precious metal set with gems. **2.** A gem. **3.** A small gem or gem substitute used as a bearing in a watch. **4.** One that is highly esteemed or valued. —*v.* **-eled, -el•ing** *or* **-elled, -el•ling.** To adorn or furnish with jewels. —**jew'el•ry** *n.*
jew•el•er *also* **jew•el•ler** (jo͞o'ə-lər) *n.* A person who makes or deals in jewelry.
Jew•ish (jo͞o'ĭsh) *adj.* Of, relating to, or typical of the Jews, their customs, or their religion. —**Jew'ish•ness** *n.*
Jew•ry (jo͞o'rē) *n.* The Jewish people as a group.
jew's-harp (jo͞oz'härp') *n.* A small musical instrument consisting of a U-shaped frame, held in the mouth, with a springy metal piece attached, that is plucked to produce twanging sounds.
jiao (jyou) *also* **chiao** (chyou) *n., pl.* **jiao** *also* **chiao.** —See table at CURRENCY.
jib[1] (jĭb) *n. Naut.* A triangular sail set forward of the foremast.
jib[2] (jĭb) *v.* **jibbed, jib•bing.** To stop short : balk.
jibe[1] (jīb) *v.* **jibed, jib•ing.** To shift (a fore-and-aft sail) from one side of a vessel to the other so as to change tack.
jibe[2] (jīb) *v.* **jibed, jib•ing.** *Informal.* To be in accord : agree.
jif•fy (jĭf'ē) *also* **jiff** (jĭf) *n., pl.* **-fies** *also* **jiffs.** *Informal.* A very short time.
jig (jĭg) *n.* **1. a.** Any of various lively dances in triple time. **b.** The music for a jig. **2.** A device used to guide a tool. —*v.* **jigged, jig•ging. 1.** To dance a jig. **2.** To jerk up and down. **3.** To operate a jig.
jig•ger (jĭg'ər) *n.* **1.** A small measure for liquor, usu. holding 1½ oz. **2.** A gadget or device whose name eludes one.
jig•gle (jĭg'əl) *v.* **-gled, -gling.** To jerk lightly up and down. —**jig'gle** *n.*
jig•saw (jĭg'sô') *n.* A saw with a narrow vertical blade, for cutting curves.
jigsaw puzzle *n.* A puzzle consisting of a mass of irregularly shaped pieces that form a picture when fitted together.
ji•had (jĭ-häd') *n.* A Muslim holy war against infidels.
jil•lion (jĭl'yən) *n. Informal.* A large, indeterminate number.
jilt (jĭlt) *v.* To discard (a lover). —*n.* A woman who discards a lover.
Jim Crow *n. Slang.* Systematic discrimination against African-American people. —**Jim'-Crow'** *adj.* —**Jim'-Crow'ism** *n.*
jim•my (jĭm'ē) *n., pl.* **-mies.** A short crowbar, esp. one used by a burglar. —*v.* **-mied, -my•ing.** To force open with or as if with a jimmy.
jim•son•weed (jĭm'sən-wēd') *n.* A coarse, foul-smelling, poisonous plant, *Datura stramonium,* with large, trumpet-shaped purplish or white flowers.
jin•gle (jĭng'gəl) *v.* **-gled, -gling.** To make or cause to make a metallic clinking noise. —*n.* **1.** A jingling sound. **2.** A short, catchy rhyme or tune.
jin•go•ism (jĭng'gō-ĭz'əm) *n.* Extreme nationalism marked esp. by a belligerent foreign policy. —**jin'go, jin'go•ist** *n.* —**jin'go•is'tic** *adj.*
jin•ni (jĭn'ē, jĭ-nē') *n., pl.* **jinn** (jĭn). A spirit with supernatural powers for good or evil in Muslim legend.
jin•rik•sha (jĭn-rĭk'shô') *n.* A ricksha.
jinx (jĭngks) *n. Informal.* **1.** One thought to bring bad luck. **2.** A period of bad luck. —*v.* To bring bad luck to.

jit•ney (jĭt′nē) *n., pl.* **-neys.** *Informal.* A small bus carrying passengers for a low fare.

jit•ter (jĭt′ər) *v.* **-tered, -ter•ing.** To be nervous : fidget. —*n.* Nervous agitation <Exams give me the *jitters.*> —**jit′ter•y** *adj.*

jit•ter•bug (jĭt′ər-bŭg′) *n.* **1.** A lively dance with various 2-step patterns and acrobatic maneuvers. **2.** One who performs this dance. —**jit′ter•bug′** *v.*

jive (jīv) *n. Slang.* **1.** Jazz or swing music. **2.** The specialized speech of jazz musicians and fans. **3.** Foolish or glib talk.

job (jŏb) *n.* **1.** A piece of work : task. **2.** Regular work done for payment. **3.** A specific piece of work to be done for a fee <a remodeling *job*> **4.** The position in which one is employed. **5.** A responsibility. —*v.* **jobbed, job•bing. 1.** To do odd jobs or piecework. **2.** To deal in (goods) as a jobber. **3.** To subcontract (work). —**job′less** *adj.* —**job′less•ness** *n.*

Job (jōb) *n.* —See table at BIBLE.

job action *n.* A workers' strike or slowdown to protest a company decision or to win demands.

job•ber (jŏb′ər) *n.* **1.** One who buys goods in bulk and sells them to retailers. **2.** One who does piecework.

job control language *n. Computer Sci.* A language used for communicating with a computer's operating system.

job•hold•er (jŏb′hōl′dər) *n.* A person with a regular job.

job lot *n.* A miscellaneous assortment of items sold as one lot.

job•name (jŏb′nām′) *n. Computer Sci.* A code assigned to a specific job instruction in a computer program for user reference.

jock (jŏk) *n. Slang.* A male athlete, esp. in college.

jock•ey (jŏk′ē) *n., pl.* **-eys.** A rider in horse races, esp. a professional. —*v.* **1.** To ride as jockey. **2.** To maneuver for advantage or position.

jo•cose (jō-kōs′) *adj.* **1.** Given to joking : playful. **2.** Marked by joking : humorous. —**jo•cose′ly** *adv.* —**jo•cose′ness, jo•cos′i•ty** (-kŏs′ĭ-tē) *n.*

joc•u•lar (jŏk′yə-lər) *adj.* Marked by joking : playful : facetious. —**joc′u•lar′i•ty** (-lăr′ĭ-tē) *n.* —**joc′u•lar•ly** *adv.*

joc•und (jŏk′ənd, jō′kənd) *adj.* Merry : cheerful. —**jo•cun′di•ty** (jō-kŭn′dĭ-tē) *n.* —**joc′und•ly** *adv.*

jodh•purs (jŏd′pərz) *pl.n.* Wide-hipped riding breeches fitting tightly at the knees and ankles.

Jo•el (jō′əl) *n.* —See table at BIBLE.

jog[1] (jŏg) *v.* **jogged, jog•ging. 1.** To move or shake slightly. **2.** To stir to activity <*jog* one's memory> **3.** To move or ride at a slow steady trot, esp. for sport or exercise. —*n.* **1.** A slight shake or nudge. **2.** A slow steady pace. —**jog′ger** *n.*

jog[2] (jŏg) *n.* **1.** A projecting or indented part in a surface or line. **2.** An abrupt shift in direction.

jog•gle (jŏg′əl) *v.* **-gled, -gling.** To shake slightly. —**jog′gle** *n.*

john (jŏn) *n. Slang.* **1.** A toilet. **2.** A prostitute's client.

John (jŏn) *n.* —See table at BIBLE.

John Doe (dō′) *n. Law.* A fictitious or unidentified person.

John Han•cock (hăn′kŏk′) *n. Informal.* A person's signature.

john•ny•cake (jŏn′ē-kāk′) *n.* A thin, flat cornmeal bread.

John•ny-come-late•ly (jŏn′ē-kŭm-lāt′lē) *n., pl.* **-lies.** *Informal.* A latecomer, esp. a recent adherent to a cause or fashion.

joie de vi•vre (zhwä də vē′vrə) *n.* Lively enjoyment of life.

join (join) *v.* **1.** To put or come together. **2.** To bring or put into close association. **3.** To become a member of. **4.** *Math.* To connect (points), as with a straight line. **5.** To participate. ★ ***syns:*** CONNECT, LINK, UNITE —*n.* A joint : junction.

join•er (joi′nər) *n.* **1.** *esp. Brit.* A carpenter, esp. a cabinetmaker. **2.** *Informal.* One given to joining clubs and organizations.

joint (joint) *n.* **1.** A place where 2 or more things are joined. **2.** A point of connection between bones. **3.** A cut of meat that can be roasted. **4.** *Slang.* **a.** A shabby or disreputable gathering place. **b.** An establishment <ate at a fancy *joint*> **5.** *Slang.* A marijuana cigarette. —*adj.* **1.** Undertaken or shared by 2 or more <a *joint* tax return> **2.** Marked by cooperation <a *joint* effort> —*v.* **1.** To provide with a joint. **2.** To cut (meat) into joints. —**joint′ly** *adv.*

joint-stock company (joint′stŏk′) *n.* a business whose capital is held in transferable shares of stock by its joint owners.

join•ture (join′chər) *n. Law.* **1.** An arrangement by which a husband sets aside property to be used for the support of his wife after his death. **2.** The property itself.

joint venture *n.* A partnership or conglomerate, often formed to share risk or expertise.

joist (joist) *n.* One of the parallel beams set from wall to wall to support a floor.

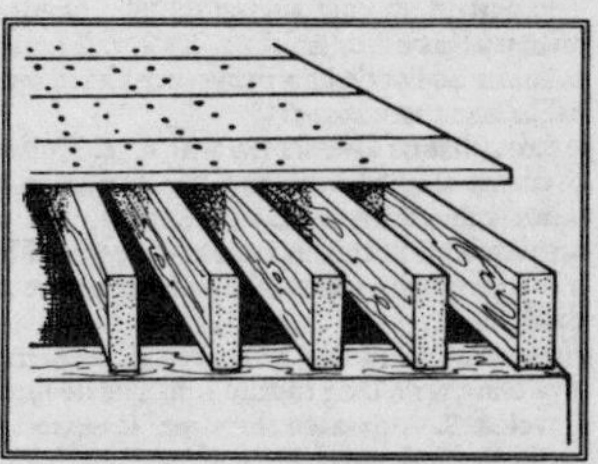

joist

joke (jōk) *n.* **1.** Something said to cause laughter, esp. a brief story with a punch line. **2.** A mischievous trick. **3.** A ridiculous situation.

4. An object of amusement. ★ ***syns:*** GAG, JAPE, JEST, QUIP, WITTICISM —*v.* **joked, jok•ing. 1.** To play or tell jokes. **2.** To speak facetiously. —**jok'ing•ly** *adv.*

jok•er (jō'kər) *n.* **1.** One who jokes. **2.** An extra playing card, printed with a jester, used in certain games as a wild card. **3.** A clause in a document or legislative bill that changes or voids its purport. ★ ***syns:*** CARD, CLOWN, COMEDIAN, COMIC, HUMORIST, JESTER, WAG, WIT, ZANY

jol•li•fi•ca•tion (jŏl'ə-fĭ-kā'shən) *n.* Festivity : revelry.

jol•ly (jŏl'ē) *adj.* **-li•er, -li•est. 1.** Full of good humor : merry. **2.** Enjoyable. —*adv. esp. Brit.* Very <a *jolly* good swimmer> —**jol'li•ty** *n.* —**jol'ly** *v.*

jolt (jōlt) *v.* **1.** To shake or knock about. **2.** To move in a bumpy manner. **3.** To startle. —*n.* **1.** A sudden jarring or jerking. **2.** A sudden shock.

Jo•nah (jō'nə) *n.* —See table at BIBLE.

jon•quil (jŏng'kwĭl, jŏn'-) *n.* A widely grown plant, *Narcissus jonquilla,* with long, narrow leaves and yellow flowers.

josh (jŏsh) *v.* **1.** To tease. **2.** To joke.

Josh•u•a (jŏsh'o͞o-ə) *n.* —See table at BIBLE.

joss (jŏs) *n.* A Chinese idol or image.

joss stick *n.* A stick of incense.

jos•tle (jŏs'əl) *v.* **-tled, -tling. 1.** To come into contact (with). **2.** To make one's way by pushing or shoving. **3.** To contend for a favorable position. —**jos'tle** *n.*

jot (jŏt) *n.* A tiny bit : iota. —*v.* **jot•ted, jot•ting.** To make a brief note of <*jot* down a phone number>

joule (jo͞ol, joul) *n.* A unit of energy equal to the work done by a force of 1 newton acting through a distance of 1 m.

jounce (jouns) *v.* **jounced, jounc•ing.** To bump : jolt. —**jounce** *n.* —**jounc'y** *adj.*

jour•nal (jûr'nəl) *n.* **1.** A personal daily record of experiences and observations : diary. **2.** An official record of daily proceedings, as of a legislative body. **3.** A book in which daily financial transactions are recorded. **4.** A newspaper. **5.** A periodical containing articles of specialized interest <a medical *journal*> **6.** The part of an axle supported by a bearing.

jour•nal•ese (jûr'nə-lēz', -lēs') *n.* The vocabulary and style of writing considered typical of most newspapers.

jour•nal•ism (jûr'nə-lĭz'əm) *n.* **1.** Collection, writing, editing, and dissemination of news through the media. **2.** Material written for publication in the media. —**jour'nal•ist** *n.* —**jour'nal•is'tic** *adj.* —**jour'nal•is'ti•cal•ly** *adv.*

jour•ney (jûr'nē) *n., pl.* **-neys. 1. a.** A trip, esp. one over a long distance. **b.** The distance traveled. **2.** A passage from one stage to another. —*v.* to travel.

jour•ney•man (jûr'nē-mən) *n.* **1.** One who has served an apprenticeship at a trade and works in another's employ. **2.** An experienced, capable worker.

▲ ***word history:*** A *journeyman,* a skilled craftsman, is not an itinerant worker. *Journeyman* preserves an older sense of the word *journey* that reveals its origins. A *journeyman* was orig. a daily worker, one who worked for another for daily wages. He was distinguished from an apprentice, who was learning the trade, and a master artisan, who was in business for himself. *Journey* is derived from Old French *journee,* which meant "day," "day's work," and "day's travel." *Journee* is descended from Latin *diurnus,* "daily," from *dies,* "day." *Journee* in the sense "day's travel" developed in English into the word *journey,* "a trip."

joust (joust, jŭst, jo͞ost) *n.* A combat with lances between 2 knights on horseback, esp. as part of a medieval tournament. —*v.* To engage in a joust.

Jove (jōv) *interj.* —Used to express surprise or emphasis <by *Jove!*>

jo•vi•al (jō'vē-əl) *adj.* Good- humored : jolly. —**jo'vi•al'i•ty** (-ăl'ĭ-tē) *n.*

jowl[1] (joul) *n.* **1.** The lower jaw. **2.** The cheek.

jowl[2] (joul) *n.* **1.** Loose, flabby flesh under the lower jaw. **2.** A similar part, as a dewlap or wattle. —**jowl'y** *adj.*

joy (joi) *n.* **1.** Great happiness : delight. **2.** A source of happiness. —**joy'ful** *adj.* —**joy'ful•ly** *adv.* —**joy'ful•ness** *n.* —**joy'less** *adj.* —**joy'less•ly** *adv.* —**joy'less•ness** *n.*

joy•ous (joi'əs) *adj.* Causing or feeling joy. —**joy'ous•ly** *adv.* —**joy'ous•ness** *n.*

joy ride *n.* A reckless ride at high speed, often in a stolen vehicle.

joy•stick (joi'stĭk') *n. Slang.* **1.** The control stick of an airplane. **2.** A manual control lever, as for a computer monitor.

ju•bi•lant (jo͞o'bə-lənt) *adj.* **1.** Exultingly joyful. **2.** Expressing joy. —**ju'bi•lance** *n.* —**ju'bi•lant•ly** *adv.*

ju•bi•la•tion (jo͞o'bə-lā'shən) *n.* **1.** Exultation. **2.** A happy celebration.

ju•bi•lee (jo͞o'bə-lē') *n.* **1.** A special anniversary, such as a 25th or 50th anniversary. **2.** A time of celebration.

Ju•da•ic (jo͞o-dā'ĭk) *also* **Ju•da•i•cal** (-ĭ-kəl) *adj.* Of or relating to Judaism or Jews. —**Ju•da'i•cal•ly** *adv.*

Ju•da•ism (jo͞o'dē-ĭz'əm) *n.* The monotheistic religion of the Jewish people.

Ju•das (jo͞o'dəs) *n.* One who betrays under the guise of friendship.

Jude (jo͞od) *n.* —See table at BIBLE.

judge (jŭj) *v.* **judged, judg•ing. 1.** *Law.* To pass judgment (on) in a court. **2.** To decide authoritatively after deliberation. **3.** To form an evaluation of. **4.** To have as an assumption : suppose. ★ ***syns:*** ADJUDGE, ADJUDICATE, ARBITRATE, DECIDE, DECREE, DETERMINE, REFEREE, RULE, UMPIRE —*n.* **1.** *Law.* A public official authorized to decide cases brought before a court. **2.** An arbiter designated to decide a competition or contest. **3.** One who can give an authoritative opinion : connoisseur. **4. Judges.** *(sing. in number).* —See table at BIBLE. —**judge'ship'** *n.*

judg•ment *also* **judge•ment** (jŭj'mənt) *n.*

1. The ability to make a decision or form an opinion. **2.** An authoritative opinion. **3.** An estimate. **4.** A decision reached after consideration, esp. the decision of an arbiter in a contest. **5.** *Law.* A determination of a court. —**judg·ment'al** *adj.*

Judgment Day *n.* In Christian doctrine, the day when God judges all human beings.

ju·di·ca·ture (jo͞o'dĭ-kə-cho͝or', -chər) *n.* **1.** The administration of justice. **2.** Law courts or judges as a whole.

ju·di·cial (jo͞o-dĭsh'əl) *adj.* **1.** Of, relating to, or befitting courts of law or the administration of justice. **2.** Decreed or enforced by a court of law. —**ju·di'cial·ly** *adv.*

ju·di·ci·ar·y (jo͞o-dĭsh'ē-ĕr'ē) *n., pl.* **-ies. 1.** The judicial branch of government. **2. a.** A system of courts of law. **b.** Judges of these courts.

ju·di·cious (jo͞o-dĭsh'əs) *adj.* Having or exercising sound judgment. —**ju·di'cious·ly** *adv.* —**ju·di'cious·ness** *n.*

Ju·dith (jo͞o'dĭth) *n.* —See table at BIBLE.

ju·do (jo͞o'dō) *n.* A form of self-defense developed from jujitsu that emphasizes principles of balance and leverage, often used as a method of physical training.

jug (jŭg) *n.* **1.** A small pitcher. **2.** A container for liquids with a narrow neck, a handle, and usu. a stopper. **3.** *Slang.* A jail.

jug·ger·naut (jŭg'ər-nôt') *n.* A massive and destructive force or object.

jug·gle (jŭg'əl) *v.* **-gled, -gling. 1.** To keep (several objects) in motion in the air at one time by alternately throwing and catching. **2.** To keep (several activities) in progress at one time. **3.** To manipulate so as to deceive <*juggled* the figures> —**jug'gler** *n.*

jug·u·lar (jŭg'yə-lər) *adj.* Of or situated in the region of the neck or throat. —*n.* A jugular vein.

jugular vein *n.* Any of various large veins of the neck.

juice (jo͞os) *n.* **1. a.** A natural fluid in plant or animal tissue. **b.** A bodily secretion. **2.** *Slang.* **a.** Electric current. **b.** Fuel for an engine. —*v.* **juiced, juic·ing.** To extract the juice from. —**juice up.** To add energy, power, or excitement to.

juic·er (jo͞o'sər) *n.* A device for extracting juice from fruit.

juic·y (jo͞o'sē) *adj.* **-i·er, -i·est. 1.** Full of juice. **2. a.** Interesting. **b.** Racy **:** titillating <*juicy* gossip> —**juic'i·ness** *n.*

ju·jit·su *also* **ju·jut·su** (jo͞o-jĭt'so͞o) *n.* A Japanese martial art using holds, throws, and stunning blows to subdue an opponent.

juke box (jo͞ok) *n.* A coin-operated automatic record player equipped with push buttons for the selection of records.

ju·lep (jo͞o'lәp) *n.* A mint julep.

Jul·ian calendar (jo͞ol'yən) *n.* A calendar introduced by Julius Caesar in Rome in 46 B.C. that established the 12-month year of 365 days with a leap year every 4 years, eventually replaced by the Gregorian calendar.

ju·li·enne (jo͞o'lē-ĕn') *adj.* Cut into strips. —Used of vegetables.

Ju·ly (jo͞o-lī', jo͞o-) *n.* The 7th month of the year, with 31 days.

jum·ble (jŭm'bəl) *v.* **-bled, -bling. 1.** To mix in a confused mass. **2.** To muddle **:** confuse. —**jum'ble** *n.*

jum·bo (jŭm'bō) *n., pl.* **-bos.** An exceptionally large person, animal, or object. —*adj.* Larger than average <*jumbo* shrimp>

jump (jŭmp) *v.* **1.** To spring into the air by a muscular effort of the legs and feet. **2.** To move suddenly <*jumped* out of the car> **3.** To move involuntarily, as in surprise. **4.** To leap over or cause to leap over. **5.** To make a sudden verbal attack **:** lash out. **6.** To arrive at hastily <*jump* to conclusions> **7.** To react eagerly so as to seize <*jump* at the bargain> **8.** To rise or increase suddenly. **9.** To skip <The typewriter *jumped* a space.> **10.** To take (an opponent's piece) in checkers by moving over it with one's own. **11.** *Computer Sci.* To move from one set of instructions in a program to another further behind or further ahead. —**jump bail.** To forfeit one's bail by absconding. —*n.* **1.** A leap. **2.** A barrier to be jumped. **3.** A sudden, involuntary movement. **4.** A sudden, sharp rise, as in salary.

jump·er[1] (jŭm'pər) *n.* **1.** One that jumps. **2.** A short length of wire used temporarily to bypass or complete a circuit.

jum·per[2] (jŭm'pər) *n.* **1.** A sleeveless dress worn usu. over a blouse. **2.** A loose protective garment worn over other clothes. **3.** *often* **jumpers.** A child's pants attached to a biblike bodice.

jumping jack *n.* **1.** A puppet that can be made to dance by pulling on the strings attached to its limbs. **2.** A physical exercise performed by jumping to a position with legs spread wide and hands touching overhead and then back to a standing position with arms at the sides.

jump shot *n. Basketball.* A shot made by a player at the highest point of a jump.

jump-start (jŭmp'stärt') *v.* To start (an automobile) by connecting a jumper cable from its battery to that of another car or by pushing the automobile and suddenly releasing the clutch. —**jump'-start'** *n.*

jump suit *n.* **1.** A parachutist's uniform. **2.** A usu. loose one-piece garment consisting of a shirt and trousers.

jump·y (jŭm'pē) *adj.* **-i·er, -i·est.** Jittery **:** nervous. —**jump'i·ness** *n.*

jun·co (jŭng'kō) *n., pl.* **-cos.** A North American finch of the genus *Junco,* having mainly gray plumage.

junc·tion (jŭngk'shən) *n.* **1.** The process of joining or the state of being joined. **2.** The place where 2 things meet, esp. the place where 2 roads or railways join.

junc·ture (jŭngk'chər) *n.* **1.** The point at which 2 things join **:** junction. **2.** A point in time, esp. a critical one.

June (jo͞on) *n.* The 6th month of the year, having 30 days.

June beetle *or* **June bug** *n.* Any of various North American beetles of the subfamily Melolonthinae, with larvae that live in the soil and often destroy crops.

jun•gle (jŭng′gəl) *n.* **1.** Land covered by dense tropical vegetation. **2.** A dense thicket or growth. **3.** An environment marked by ruthless struggling to survive.

jungle gym *n.* A structure of poles and bars for children to climb and play on.

jun•ior (jo͞on′yər) *adj.* **1.** Younger. —Used to distinguish the son from the father of the same name. **2.** Intended for or including young people. **3.** Of lower rank or shorter period of tenure <the *junior* partner> **4.** Of or relating to the 3rd year of a U.S. high school or college. —*n.* **1.** One younger than another. **2.** One lower in rank or period of service. **3.** A 3rd-year student in a U.S. high school or college.

junior college *n.* An educational institution offering a 2-year course gen. equivalent to the first 2 years of a 4- year undergraduate course.

junior high school *n.* A U.S. school that gen. includes the 7th, 8th, and sometimes 9th grades.

ju•ni•per (jo͞o′nə-pər) *n.* An evergreen tree or shrub of the genus *Juniperus,* having scale-like, often prickly foliage, fragrant wood, and bluish- gray berries.

junk[1] (jŭngk) *n.* **1.** Discarded materials such as glass, paper, rags, and metal that can be used for other purposes. **2.** *Informal.* Something fit to be discarded **:** trash. **3.** *Informal.* Nonsense. **4.** *Slang.* Heroin. —*v.* To throw away as useless.

junk[2] (jŭngk) *n.* A Chinese flat-bottomed ship with battened sails.

junk bond *n.* A corporate bond having a high yield and high risk.

jun•ket (jŭng′kĭt) *n.* **1.** A custardlike dessert of flavored milk set with rennet. **2.** A party, banquet, or outing. **3.** A trip taken by an official and paid for with public funds. —**jun′ket** *v.* —**jun′ket•er** *n.*

▲ ***word history:*** The transitional stage between the meanings "a food" and "a trip" for *junket* is found in the meaning "picnic." The most recent sense, "a trip taken by a public official at public expense," developed in the U.S. and has acquired decidedly negative connotations.

junk food *n.* Food with little nutritional value in proportion to the number of calories it contains.

junk•ie *also* **junk•y** (jŭng′kē) *n., pl.* **-ies.** *Slang.* **1.** A drug addict, esp. one using heroin. **2.** One with a consuming interest in something <a soap opera *junkie*>

junk mail *n.* Mail of little interest to its recipient, usu. advertisements mailed in bulk.

junk•yard (jŭngk′yärd′) *n.* An area used for storing junk, as scrap metal, that can be resold.

Ju•no•esque (jo͞o′nō-ĕsk′) *adj.* Having a stately bearing and regal beauty.

jun•ta (ho͝on′tə, ho͞on′-, jŭn′-) *n.* A group of persons, esp. military officers, in power following a coup d'état.

Ju•pi•ter (jo͞o′pĭ-tər) *n.* The 5th planet from the sun and the largest in the solar system.

ju•rid•i•cal (jo͝o-rĭd′ĭ-kəl) *also* **ju•rid•ic** (-ĭk) *adj.* Of or relating to the administration of the law.

ju•ris•dic•tion (jo͝or-ĭs-dĭk′shən) *n.* **1.** The right or power to interpret and apply the law. **2.** Authority or control. **3.** The territorial range over which an authority extends. —**ju′ris•dic′tion•al** *adj.*

ju•ris•pru•dence (jo͝or′ĭs-pro͞od′ns) *n.* **1.** The science or philosophy of law. **2.** A division or department of law.

ju•rist (jo͝or′ĭst) *n.* An expert in the law.

ju•ris•tic (jo͝o-rĭs′tĭk) *also* **ju•ris•ti•cal** (-tĭ-kəl) *adj.* **1.** Of or relating to jurisprudence or a jurist. **2.** Of or relating to legality or law.

ju•ror (jo͝or′ər, -ôr′) *n.* One who serves on a jury.

ju•ry (jo͝or′ē) *n., pl.* **-ries. 1.** A group of people called by law and sworn to hear evidence in a case and give a verdict. **2.** A committee to select winners in a contest.

just (jŭst) *adj.* **1.** Fair in one's dealings and actions <a *just* king> **2.** Morally right. **3.** Deserved **:** merited <*just* deserts> **4.** Legitimate. **5.** Proper **:** fitting <*just* proportions> **6.** Based on sound reason. —*adv.* (jəst, jĭst; jŭst *when stressed).* **1.** Exactly. **2.** A very short time before <*just* left> **3.** By a narrow margin **:** barely <*just* missed the bus> **4.** Only a little distance <*just* down the street> **5.** Merely **:** simply <I *just* said it in jest> **6.** Really <*just* lovely> —**just the same.** Nevertheless. —**just′ly** *adv.* —**just′ness** *n.*

jus•tice (jŭs′tĭs) *n.* **1.** The principle of ideal or moral rightness. **2.** The upholding of what is right **:** fairness. **3.** The administration of law. **4.** A judge.

justice of the peace *n.* A local magistrate empowered to try minor cases, administer oaths, and perform marriages.

jus•ti•fy (jŭs′tə-fī′) *v.* **-fied, -fy•ing. 1.** To show to be right or valid. **2.** To pronounce free from blame or guilt. **3.** To adjust or space (lines) to the proper length in printing. —**jus′ti•fi′a•ble** *adj.* —**jus′ti•fi′a•bly** *adv.* —**jus′ti•fi•ca′tion** *n.*

jut (jŭt) *v.* **jut•ted, jut•ting.** To protrude **:** project. —**jut** *n.*

jute (jo͞ot) *n.* Either of 2 Asian plants, *Corchorus capsularis* or *C. olitorius,* yielding a strong, coarse fiber used to make sacking and rope.

Jute (jo͞ot) *n.* A member of a Germanic people who migrated to Britain in the 5th and 6th cent. A.D.

ju•ve•nile (jo͞o′və-nəl, -nīl′) *adj.* **1.** Not yet adult **:** young. **2.** Childish **:** immature. **3.** Intended or suitable for children or young people. —*n.* **1.** A young person. **2.** An actor who plays youthful roles. **3.** A children's book. —**ju′ve•nile•ness** *n.*

jux•ta•pose (jŭk′stə-pōz′) *v.* To put side by side. —**jux′ta•posed** *adj.* —**jux′ta•po•si′tion** *n.*

Kk

k *or* **K** (kā) *n., pl.* **k's** *or* **K's. 1.** The 11th letter of the English alphabet. **2.** A speech sound represented by the letter *k.* **3.** *Computer Sci.* A unit of storage capacity equal to 1024 bytes.

K *symbol for* POTASSIUM.

ka•bob (kə-bŏb′) *n.* Shish kebab.

ka•bu•ki (kä-bo͞o′kē, kə-) *n.* Traditional Japanese drama in which dances and songs are performed in a stylized manner.

ka•chi•na (kə-chē′nə) *n.* **1.** A deified ancestral spirit of the Pueblo peoples. **2.** A carved doll resembling such a spirit.

Kad•dish (kä′dĭsh) *n.* A Jewish prayer recited at the daily service and by mourners after the death of a relative.

kaf•fee klatsch (kô′fē klăch′, kä′fē klăch′) *n.* A coffee klatch.

Kai•ser (kī′zər) *n.* An emperor, esp. a German emperor from 1871–1918.

kale (kāl) *n.* A cabbage, *Brassica oleracea acephala,* with crinkled leaves not forming a tight head.

ka•lei•do•scope (kə-lī′də-skōp′) *n.* **1.** A tubular instrument rotated to produce successive symmetric designs by means of mirrors reflecting the changing patterns made by bits of loose colored glass at the end of the tube. **2.** A series of continuously changing colors. **3.** A series of changing events or phases. **—ka•lei′do•scop′ic** (-skŏp′ĭk), **ka•lei′do•scop′i•cal** *adj.* **—ka•lei′do•scop′i•cal•ly** *adv.*

ka•mi•ka•ze (kä′mĭ-kä′zē) *n.* **1.** A Japanese pilot in World War II who was trained to make a suicidal crash on a target. **2.** An aircraft loaded with explosives used in a suicide attack.

kan•ga•roo (kăng′gə-ro͞o′) *n., pl.* **-roo** *or* **-roos.** Any of various herbivorous marsupials of the family Macropodidae, of Australia, with short forelegs, large hind limbs adapted for jumping, and a long tail.

kangaroo court *n.* An illegal, self-appointed court, esp. one marked by dishonesty or incompetence.

ka•o•lin *also* **ka•o•line** (kā′ə-lĭn) *n.* A fine clay used in ceramics.

ka•pok (kā′pŏk′) *n.* A silky fiber derived from the fruit of the silk-cotton tree and used for insulation and as padding in mattresses, pillows, and life preservers.

ka•put (kä-po͝ot′) *adj. Informal.* **1.** Destroyed : wrecked. **2.** Out of order.

kar•a•kul *or* **car•a•cul** (kăr′ə-kəl) *n.* One of a breed of C Asian sheep with a pelt that is curly and shiny in the young but coarse and wiry in the adult.

kar•a•o•ke (kăr′ē-ō′kē) *n.* An audiovisual system that plays an accompaniment to a song performed by following the words on a video screen.

kar•at *or* **car•at** (kăr′ət) *n.* A unit of measure for the fineness of gold, equal to 1/24 of the total amount of pure gold in an alloy.

ka•ra•te (kə-rä′tē, kä-rä′tā) *n.* A Japanese art of self-defense in which sharp blows and kicks are administered to pressure-sensitive points of an opponent's body.

kar•ma (kär′mə, kûr′mə) *n.* **1.** The total effect of one's conduct, believed in Buddhism and Hinduism to determine one's destiny in a future life. **2.** Fate. **3.** *Informal.* Aura or atmosphere. **—kar′mic** (-mĭk) *adj.*

karst (kärst) *n.* An area of irregular limestone where erosion has produced sinkholes, caverns, and underground streams.

kart (kärt) *n.* A miniature racing car.

ka•ty•did (kā′tē-dĭd′) *n.* Any of various green insects related to the grasshoppers and the crickets, with specialized organs on the wings of the male that make a shrill sound when rubbed together.

kay (kā) *n.* The letter *k.*

kay•ak (kī′ăk′) *n.* A watertight Eskimo canoe having a light frame covered with skins except for an opening in the center.

kay•o (kā′ō, kā′ō′) *n., pl.* **-os.** *Slang.* A knockout in boxing. **—kay′o** *v.*

ka•zoo (kə-zo͞o′) *n., pl.* **-zoos.** A toy musical instrument with a paper membrane that produces buzzing tones when a player hums or sings into the mouthpiece.

ke•bab *also* **ke•bob** (kə-bŏb′) *n.* Shish kebab.

kedge (kĕj) *n.* A small anchor.

keel[1] (kēl) *n.* **1. a.** The main structural member of a ship, running lengthwise along the center line from stern to bow, to which the frames are attached. **b.** A similar structure in an aircraft. **2.** Something that resembles a ship's keel in shape or function, as the breastbone of a bird. —*v.* To capsize. **—keel over. 1.** To fall over suddenly. **2.** To faint.

†**keel**[2] (kēl) *v. Regional.* To make cool.

keel•haul (kēl′hôl′) *v.* To drag under the keel of a ship as a punishment.

keel•son (kēl′sən, kĕl′-) *n. Naut.* A timber fastened above and parallel to the keel to give additional strength.

keen[1] (kēn) *adj.* **1.** Having a sharp edge or point. **2.** Intellectually acute. **3.** Highly sensitive <a *keen* sense of smell> **4.** Strong : intense <a *keen* winter wind> **5.** Pungent. **6.** Enthusiastic. **7.** *Slang.* Great : wonderful. **—keen′ly** *adv.* **—keen′ness** *n.*

keen[2] (kēn) *n.* A wailing lament for the dead. **—keen** *v.*

keep (kēp) *v.* **kept** (kĕpt), **keep•ing. 1.** To retain possession of. **2.** To have as a supply. **3.** To provide with maintenance and support <*kept* a large family on a small income> **4.** To store customarily <*kept* the bread knife in the drawer> **5.** To tend : manage. **6.** To continue or cause to continue in a given state or course of action. **7.** To detain : confine. **8.** To refrain from divulging <*keep* secrets> **9.** To adhere to. **10.** To celebrate. **11.** To remain fresh or unspoiled. ★ *syns:* RESERVE, RE-

TAIN, WITHHOLD —**keep down.** To prevent from succeeding. —**keep up. 1.** To maintain in good condition. **2.** To persevere in. **3.** To continue without interruption. —*n.* **1.** Care : custody. **2.** A means of support <earn one's *keep*> **3.** A castle's stronghold. **4.** A jail. —**for keeps. 1.** Forever : permanently <gave it to me *for keeps*> —**keep at it.** To persevere. —**keep (one's) nose clean.** To keep out of trouble. —**keep'er** *n.*

keep•sake (kēp'sāk') *n.* A memento.

keg (kĕg) *n.* A small barrel.

kelp (kĕlp) *n.* Any of various large brown seaweeds of the order Laminariales.

kel•pie[1] *also* **kel•py** (kĕl'pē) *n., pl.* **-pies.** *Scot.* A legendary malevolent water spirit.

kel•pie[2] (kĕl'pē) *n.* A sheep dog orig. bred in Australia.

Kel•vin (kĕl'vĭn) *adj.* Designating or relating to a temperature scale whose zero point is approx. −273.16°C.

†**ken** (kĕn) *v.* **kenned** *or* **kent, ken•ning. 1.** *Scot.* To know (a person or thing). **2.** *Regional.* To recognize. —*n.* **1.** Range of understanding. **2.** Range of vision.

ken•do (kĕn'dō) *n.* The Japanese art of fencing with bamboo sticks.

kendo

ken•nel (kĕn'əl) *n.* **1.** A shelter for a dog. **2.** A place where dogs are bred, boarded, or trained. —**ken'nel** *v.*

ke•no (kē'nō) *n.* A game of chance resembling lotto in which balls rather than counters are used.

Kentucky bluegrass *n. Bot.* Bluegrass.

kep•i (kā'pē, kĕp'ē) *n., pl.* **-is.** A military visored cap with a flat round top.

kept (kĕpt) *v. p.t. & p.p. of* KEEP.

ker•a•tin (kĕr'ə-tən) *n.* A strong, fibrous protein that is the basic substance of nails, hair, horns, and hoofs. —**ke•rat'i•nous** (kə-răt'n-əs) *adj.*

kerb (kûrb) *n. esp. Brit. var. of* CURB 2.

ker•chief (kûr'chĭf) *n.* **1.** A piece of cloth worn over the head or around the neck : scarf. **2.** A handkerchief.

ker•nel (kûr'nəl) *n.* **1.** A grain or seed, as of a cereal plant, enclosed in a hard husk. **2.** The inner, usu. edible part of a nut. **3.** The central, most important part.

ker•o•sene *also* **ker•o•sine** (kĕr'ə-sēn', kĕr'ə-sēn') *n.* A thin oil distilled from petroleum and used as a fuel and solvent.

kes•trel (kĕs'trəl) *n.* **1.** A small European falcon, *Falco tinnunculus*, with gray and brown plumage. **2.** The North American sparrow hawk.

ketch (kĕch) *n.* A fore-and-aft-rigged sailing vessel with 2 masts.

ketch•up (kĕch'əp, kăch'-) *or* **catch•up** (kăch'əp, kĕch'-) *also* **cat•sup** (kăt'səp, kăch'-əp, kĕch'-) *n.* A spicy, thick, smooth sauce, esp. one made from tomatoes.

ket•tle (kĕt'l) *n.* **1.** A metal pot, usu. with a lid, for boiling or stewing. **2.** A teakettle.

ket•tle•drum (kĕt'l-drŭm') *n.* A large copper or brass hemispherical drum with a parchment head that can be tuned by adjusting the tension.

key[1] (kē) *n., pl.* **keys. 1. a.** A usu. metal notched device for opening or closing a lock. **b.** A device resembling a key, as for winding a clock. **2.** A means of access, control, or possession. **3. a.** A crucial element. **b.** A solution to a test. **c.** A code or table for solving or explaining. **4. a.** A button or lever pressed to operate a machine. **b.** A lever pressed by a finger in playing a musical instrument, as a piano. **5.** *Mus.* A tonal system consisting of 7 tones in fixed relationship to a tonic. **6.** The pitch of a voice. **9.** A characteristic level of intensity or tone. —*v.* **1.** To regulate the musical pitch of. **2.** To bring into harmony : adjust. **3.** To supply an explanatory key for. —*adj.* Of crucial importance. —**key up.** To make nervous.

key[2] (kē) *n., pl.* **keys.** A reef or low island.

key•board (kē'bôrd', -bōrd') *n.* A series of keys, as on a piano, typewriter, or word processor. —*v.* **1.** To set by means of a keyed typesetting machine. **2.** To generate (e.g., documents) by means of a word processor.

key•card (kē'kärd') *n.* A plastic card with a magnetically coded strip that is scanned to operate a mechanism such as an automated teller machine.

key club *n.* A private club serving liquor and offering entertainment.

key•hole (kē'hōl') *n.* A hole into which a key is inserted.

key•note (kē'nōt') *n.* **1.** *Mus.* The tonic of a key. **2.** A central idea. —*v.* **1.** T give the keynote of. **2.** To give the keynote address at.

keynote address *n.* An opening speech, as at a political convention, outlining the issues for discussion.

key•pad (kē'păd') *n.* A computer input device having numeric and function keys.

key•punch (kē'pŭnch') *n.* A machine with a keyboard used to punch holes in tapes or cards for data-processing systems. —**key'punch'** *v.* —**key'punch'er** *n.*

key signature *n. Mus.* The group of sharps or flats at the right of the clef on a staff identifying the key.

key•stone (kē'stōn') *n.* **1.** The wedge-shaped stone at the top of an arch that locks its parts together. **2.** A central supporting element.

key•stroke (kē'strōk') *n.* A stroke of a key, as of a typewriter or word processor.
khak•i (kăk'ē, kä'kē) *n., pl.* **-is. 1.** A yellowish brown. **2. a.** A sturdy cloth of the color khaki. **b. khakis.** A uniform of khaki cloth. **—khak'i** *adj.*
khan (kän, kăn) *n.* **1.** A chieftain or man of importance in India and some C Asian countries. **2.** A medieval Turkish, Mongolian, or Tartar ruler. **—khan'ate'***n.*
khe•dive (kə-dēv') *n.* A Turkish viceroy ruling Egypt from 1867–1914.
Khmer (kmâr) *n., pl.* **Khmer** *or* **Khmers. 1.** A member of a people of Cambodia. **2.** The official language of Cambodia.
khoum (ko͞om, ko͝om) *n.* —See table at CURRENCY.
kib•butz (kĭ-bo͞ots') *n., pl.* **-but•zim** (-bo͞ot'-sēm'). An Israeli collective farm.
kib•itz (kĭb'ĭts, kĭ-bĭts) *n. Informal.* To look on and offer unwanted, usu. meddlesome advice to others. **—kib'itz•er** *n.*
ki•bosh (kī'bŏsh') *n.* A check or restraint.
kick (kĭk) *v.* **1.** To strike or strike out with the foot. **2.** *Sports.* **a.** To strike a ball with the foot. **b.** To propel (a ball) by striking it with the foot. **3.** To recoil, as a firearm when fired. **4.** *Informal.* To protest vigorously **:** object. **—kick around.** *Informal.* **1.** To treat badly. **2.** To move from place to place. **3.** To consider (an idea). **—kick in.** *Slang.* **1.** To contribute (one's share). **2.** To die. **—kick off. 1.** To begin or resume play in a sport with a kickoff. **2.** To begin. *n.* **1. a.** A blow with the foot. **b.** The thrusting motion of the legs in swimming. **2.** The recoil of a firearm. **3.** *Slang.* A complaint. **4.** *Slang.* Pleasurable stimulation. **5.** *Slang.* A temporary enthusiasm. **—kick the bucket.** *Slang.* To die. **—kick upstairs.** *Informal.* To promote to a higher yet less desirable position.
kick•back (kĭk'băk') *n.* **1.** *Slang.* A secret payment to a person who is in a position to influence a source of income. **2.** A very strong reaction **:** repercussion.
kick•er (kĭk'ər) *n.* **1.** One that kicks. **2.** *Informal.* A sudden surprising turn of events.
kick•off (kĭk'ôf', -ŏf') *n.* **1.** A kick, as in football or soccer, that begins play. **2.** A beginning.
kick•stand (kĭk'stănd') *n.* A swiveling metal bar for holding a 2-wheeled vehicle upright when not in use.
kick•y (kĭk'ē) *adj.* **-i•er, -i•est.** *Slang.* Providing excitement by being unusual or unconventional.
kid (kĭd) *n.* **1.** A young goat. **2.** Leather made from the skin of a young goat. **3.** *Informal.* A child. —*v.* **kid•ded, kid•ding.** *Informal.* **1.** To mock playfully **:** tease. **2.** To deceive for fun **:** fool. **—kid'der** *n.*
kid•dy *also* **kid•die** (kĭd'ē) *n., pl.* **-dies.** *Slang.* A small child.
kid•nap (kĭd'năp') *v.* **-naped, -nap•ing** *or* **-napped, -nap•ping.** To seize and hold (a person) unlawfully, often for ransom. ★ ***syns:*** ABDUCT, CARRY OFF, SNATCH, SPIRIT **—kid'nap'er** *n.*
kid•ney (kĭd'nē) *n., pl.* **-neys.** Either of a pair of organs located in the abdominal cavity of vertebrates close to the back that function to keep proper water balance in the body and excrete wastes in the form of urine.
kidney bean *n.* A bean, *Phaseolus vulgaris,* grown for its edible seeds.
kid•vid (kĭd'vĭd') *n. Slang.* Television programs for children.
kiel•ba•sa (kĕl-bä'sə, kĭl-, kēl-) *n.* A smoked Polish sausage.
Ki•ku•yu (kĭ-ko͞o'yo͞o) *n., pl.* **-yu** *or* **-yus. 1.** A member of a people of central and S Kenya. **2.** Their Bantu language.
kill (kĭl) *v.* **1.** To cause the death of. **2.** To pass (time) in aimless activity. **3.** To cause extreme pain to. **4.** To delete. **5.** To thwart passage of <*kill* a legislative bill> ★ ***syns:*** DESTROY, DISPATCH, FINISH, SLAY, ZAP —*n.* **1.** An act of killing. **2.** An animal killed, esp. in hunting. **—kill'er** *n.*
kill•deer (kĭl'dîr') *n., pl.* **killdeer** *or* **-deers.** A New World bird, *Charadrius vociferus,* having a distinctive cry.
killer whale *n.* A black and white predatory whale, *Orcinus orca,* inhabiting cold seas.
kill•ing (kĭl'ĭng) *n.* **1.** A murder. **2.** A sudden large profit. —*adj.* **1.** Fatal. **2.** Exhausting. **3.** *Informal.* Extremely funny.
kill•joy (kĭl'joi') *n.* One who spoils the fun of others.
kiln (kĭl, kĭln) *n.* An oven for hardening or drying a substance, esp. one for firing ceramics.
ki•lo (kē'lō) *n., pl.* **-los.** A kilogram.
kil•o•bit (kĭl'ə-bĭt') *n.* 1,000 binary digits.
kil•o•byte (kĭl'ə-bīt') *n.* A unit of computer memory equal to 1,024 (2^{10}) bytes.
ki•lo•cy•cle (kĭl'ə-sī'kəl) *n.* **1.** A unit equal to 1,000 cycles. **2.** A kilohertz.
kil•o•gram (kĭl'ə-grăm') *n.* —See table at MEASUREMENT.
kil•o•hertz (kĭl'ə-hûrts') *n.* 1,000 hertz.
kil•o•li•ter (kĭl'ə-lē'tər) *n.* A metric unit of volume equal to 1,000 liters.
kil•o•me•ter (kĭl'ə-mē'tər, kĭ-lŏm'ĭ-tər) *n.* —See table at MEASUREMENT. **—kil'o•met'ric** (-mĕt'rĭk) *adj.*
kil•o•ton (kĭl'ə-tŭn') *n.* **1.** 1,000 tons. **2.** An explosive force equal to that of 1,000 tons of TNT.
kil•o•watt (kĭl'ə-wŏt') *n.* 1,000 watts.
kil•o•watt-hour (kĭl'ə-wŏt'our') *n.* A unit of electric power consumption equal to the power of 1 kilowatt acting for 1 hour.
kilt (kĭlt) *n.* A knee-length wool skirt with deep pleats, usu. of tartan, worn esp. by men in the Scottish Highlands.
kil•ter (kĭl'tər) *n.* Good condition <The TV was out of *kilter.*>
ki•mo•no (kə-mō'nə, -nō) *n., pl.* **-nos. 1.** A long, loose, Japanese robe with wide sleeves and a broad sash. **2.** A loose robe worn chiefly by women.

kin (kĭn) *n.* One's relatives.
ki•na (kē'nə) *n., pl.* **-na** *or* **-nas.** —See table at CURRENCY.
kind[1] (kīnd) *adj.* Warm-hearted, friendly, or generous in nature. ★ ***syns:*** BENIGN, GOODHEARTED, KINDHEARTED, KINDLY —**kind'ness** *n.*

▲ ***word history:*** *Kind*[1] is a word that has undergone *melioration.* By this process a word with neutral connotations develops favorable ones. The Old English ancestor of *kind, gecynde,* meant "natural, inborn, inherent," and was used of such fearsome things as death and thunder. In the 13th cent., however, *kind* was used to mean "well-born," and "of a good nature." These senses have passed from standard English, but the derived sense "possessing all the (good) qualities usu. attributed to those of good birth" underlies the modern meanings of *kind.*

kind[2] (kīnd) *n.* **1.** A category of related individuals. **2.** A specific type. ★ ***syns:*** BREED, FEATHER, ILK, LOT, SORT, SPECIES, STRIPE, TYPE, VARIETY —**in kind. 1.** With goods or produce rather than money. **2.** In the same manner. —**kind of.** *Informal.* Rather < *kind of* tired.>
kin•der•gar•ten (kĭn'dər-gär'tn) *n.* A school or class for children from 4 to 6 years of age.
kin•der•gart•ner (kĭn'dər-gärt'nər) *n.* **1.** A child who attends kindergarten. **2.** A kindergarten teacher.
kind•heart•ed (kīnd'här'tĭd) *adj.* Having or proceeding from a kind nature. —**kind'heart'ed•ly** *adv.* —**kind'heart'ed•ness** *n.*
kin•dle (kĭnd'l) *v.* **-dled, -dling. 1.** To ignite. **2.** To catch fire. **3.** To stir up : arouse.
kin•dling (kĭnd'lĭng) *n.* Easily ignited material used to start a fire.
kind•ly (kīnd'lē) *adj.* **-li•er, -li•est.** Of a kind or helpful nature. —*adv.* **1.** Out of kindness <*kindly* overlooked their errors> **2.** In a kind way <spoke *kindly* to us> **3.** Pleasantly : agreeably <The sun shone *kindly.*> **4.** In an accommodating way <Would you *kindly* be seated?> —**kind'li•ness** *n.*
kin•dred (kĭn'drĭd) *n.* A person's relatives. —*adj.* Having a similar nature. —**kin'dred•ness** *n.*
kine (kīn) *n. archaic var. pl. of* COW[1].
kin•e•mat•ics (kĭn'ə-măt'ĭks) *n. (sing. in number).* The study of motion apart from the effects of mass and force. —**kin'e•mat'ic, kin'e•mat'i•cal** *adj.* —**kin'e•mat'i•cal•ly** *adv.*
kin•e•scope (kĭn'ə-skōp') *n.* **1.** A cathode-ray tube in a television receiver that translates received electrical signals into a visible picture on a luminescent screen. **2.** A film of a television broadcast.
ki•net•ic (kĭ-nĕt'ĭk) *adj.* Of, pertaining to, or produced by motion.
kinetic energy *n.* The energy possessed by a body because of its motion.
ki•net•ics (kĭ-nĕt'ĭks) *n. (sing. in number).* The science that deals with all aspects of motion, encompassing both kinematics and dynamics.
kin•folk (kĭn'fōk') *also* **kins•folk** (kĭnz'fōk') *or* **kin•folks** (kĭn'fōks') *pl.n.* One's relatives : kindred.
king (kĭng) *n.* **1.** A man who is a monarch. **2.** The most powerful or eminent, as of a group or place. **3.** A playing card with a figure of a king on it. **4. a.** The principal chess piece, capable of being moved one square in any direction. **b.** A piece in checkers that has reached the opponent's side of the board. **5. Kings** *(sing. in number).* —See table at BIBLE. —**king'ship'** *n.*
king•bolt (kĭng'bōlt') *n.* A vertical bolt used to join the body of a vehicle to the front axle and usu. acting as a pivot.
king crab *n.* A large crab, *Paralithodes camtschatica,* inhabiting the coastal waters of Japan, Alaska, and Siberia.
king•dom (kĭng'dəm) *n.* **1.** A land ruled by a king or queen. **2.** An area in which one thing dominates <the *kingdom* of the imagination> **3.** The highest taxonomic division into which natural organisms and objects are classified <the animal *kingdom*><the plant *kingdom*>
king•fish•er (kĭng'fĭsh'ər) *n.* Any of various crested birds of the family Alcedinidae that feed on fish.
King James Bible *n.* An English translation of the Bible published in 1611.
king•ly (kĭng'lē) *adj.* **-li•er, -li•est. 1.** Having the rank or status of king. **2.** Pertaining to or suitable for a king : regal. —*adv.* Royally. —**king'li•ness** *n.*
king•pin (kĭng'pĭn') *n.* **1.** The foremost pin in an arrangement of bowling pins. **2.** The most important or essential person or thing. **3.** A kingbolt.
king-size (kĭng'sīz') *also* **king-sized** (-sīzd') *adj.* Larger than the standard or usual size <a *king-size* bed>
kink (kĭngk) *n.* **1.** A tight twist or curl. **2.** A muscle cramp. **3.** A slight difficulty or flaw. **4.** A mental quirk. —*v.* To form a kink (in).
kink•a•jou (kĭng'kə-jo͞o') *n.* A tropical American arboreal mammal, *Potos flavus,* with brown fur and a long prehensile tail.
kink•y (kĭng'kē) *adj.* **1.** Tightly curled : frizzy. **2.** Marked by or engaging in eccentric or deviant sexual practices. —**kink'i•ly** *adv.* —**kink'i•ness** *n.*
kins•folk (kĭnz'fōk') *pl.n. var. of* KINFOLK.
kin•ship (kĭn'shĭp') *n.* The state or quality of being kin.
kins•man (kĭnz'mən) *n.* A male relative.
kins•wom•an (kĭnz'wo͝om'ən) *n.* A female relative.
ki•osk (kē-ŏsk', kē'ŏsk') *n.* A small structure used as a refreshment booth or newsstand.
Ki•o•wa (kī'ə-wô', -wä', -wā') *n., pl.* **-wa** *or* **-was. 1.** A member of an American Indian people formerly of the S Great Plains, now chiefly in SW Oklahoma. **2.** Their language.
kip (kĭp) *n., pl.* **kip.** —See table at CURRENCY.

kip·per (kĭp′ər) *n.* A salted and smoked herring. —*v.* To cure (fish) by salting and smoking.
kirk (kûrk) *n. Scot.* A church.
kirsch (kîrsh) *n.* A colorless brandy made from fermented cherry juice.
kir·tle (kûr′tl) *n.* A woman's long dress or skirt.
kis·met (kĭz′mĕt′, -mĭt) *n.* Fate.
kiss (kĭs) *v.* **1.** To touch or caress with the lips as a sign of passion, affection, or greeting. **2.** To touch lightly. —*n.* **1. a.** A touch or caress with the lips. **b.** A light touch. **2.** A small piece of candy.
kiss·er (kĭs′ər) *n.* **1.** One who kisses. **2.** *Slang.* The human mouth. **3.** *Slang.* The human face.
kit (kĭt) *n.* **1.** A set of articles used for a particular purpose <a survival *kit*> **2.** A set of parts to be assembled <a stereo *kit*> **3.** A receptacle, as a box, bag, or knapsack.
kitch·en (kĭch′ən) *n.* A place where food is prepared or cooked.
kitch·en·ette (kĭch′ə-nĕt′) *n.* A small kitchen.
kitchen police *n.* **1.** Enlisted military personnel assigned to perform kitchen work. **2.** The work of the kitchen police.
kitch·en·ware (kĭch′ən-wâr′) *n.* Utensils for kitchen use.
kite (kīt) *n.* **1.** A light framework covered with plastic, cloth, or paper designed to fly in a steady breeze at the end of a long string. **2.** Any of various predatory birds of the subfamilies Milvinae and Elaninae, having a long, usu. forked tail.
kith and kin (kĭth) *n.* Friends and neighbors.
kitsch (kĭch) *n.* **1.** Sentimental, often pretentious bad taste, esp. in the arts. **2.** Something that exemplifies kitsch. —**kitsch′y** *adj.*
kit·ten (kĭt′n) *n.* A young cat.
kit·ten·ish (kĭt′n-ĭsh) *adj.* Playful and coy. —**kit′ten·ish·ly** *adv.*
kit·ty[1] (kĭt′ē) *n., pl.* **-ties.** A pool of money.
kit·ty[2] (kĭt′ē) *n., pl.* **-ties.** *Informal.* A cat, esp. a kitten.
kit·ty-cor·nered (kĭt′ē-kôr′nərd) *adj.* Catercornered.
ki·wi (kē′wē) *n.* **1.** A flightless bird of the genus *Apteryx,* native to New Zealand, with vestigial wings and a long slender bill. **2.** A vine, *Actinidia chinensis,* native to Asia, yielding edible fruit with a fuzzy skin.

kiwi

klep·to·ma·ni·a (klĕp′tə-mā′nē-ə) *n.* Obsessive desire to steal, esp. without economic motive. —**klep′to·ma′ni·ac′** *n.*
klieg light (klēg) *n.* A powerful lamp used esp. in making movies.
klutz (klŭts) *n. Slang.* A stupid or clumsy person. —**klutz′i·ness** *n.* —**klutz′y** *adj.*
knack (năk) *n.* **1.** A clever way of doing something. **2.** A natural talent.
knack·wurst *also* **knock·wurst** (nŏk′wûrst′, -wŏŏrst′) *n.* A short, thick, heavily seasoned sausage.
†**knap** (năp) *n. Regional.* The crest of a hill.
knap·sack (năp′săk′) *n.* A supply or equipment bag, as of canvas or nylon, worn on the back.
knave (nāv) *n.* **1.** A rogue. **2.** JACK 2. —**knav′er·y** *n.* —**knav′ish** *adj.* —**knav′ish·ly** *adv.* —**knav′ish·ness** *n.*
knead (nēd) *v.* **1.** To work and press into a uniform mass. **2.** To shape by or as if by kneading. —**knead′er** *n.*
knee (nē) *n. Anat.* The joint or region of the human leg that is the articulation for the tibia, fibula, and patella. —*v.* **kneed, knee·ing.** To push or strike with the knee.
knee·cap (nē′kăp′) *n.* The patella.
kneel (nēl) *v.* **knelt** (nĕlt) *or* **kneeled, kneel·ing.** To rest or go down on bent knees.
knell (nĕl) *v.* **1.** To sound a bell, esp. for a funeral **:** toll. **2.** To announce, signal, or summon by or as if by tolling. —*n.* **1.** An act or instance of knelling **:** toll. **2.** A signal of disaster.
Knes·set (knĕs′ĕt′) *n.* The Israeli parliament.
knew (no͞o, nyo͞o) *v. p.t. of* KNOW.
knick·ers (nĭk′ərz) *pl.n.* Full breeches gathered and banded below the knee.
knick·knack (nĭk′năk′) *n.* A trinket.
knife (nīf) *n., pl.* **knives** (nīvz). **1.** A cutting instrument having a sharp blade and a handle. **2.** A cutting edge **:** blade. —*v.* **knifed, knif·ing. 1.** To use a knife on, esp. to cut, stab, or wound. **2.** *Informal.* To hurt or betray in an underhand way.
knight (nīt) *n.* **1.** A usu. high-born medieval gentleman-soldier serving a monarch. **2.** The holder of a nonhereditary honor conferred by a monarch in recognition of services to the country. **3.** A member of any of various fraternal orders or societies. **4.** A chess piece usu. in the shape of a horse's head. —*v.* To make (a person) a knight. —**knight′hood′** *n.* —**knight′ly** *adj.*
knish (knĭsh) *n.* Dough stuffed with potato, meat, or cheese, and baked or fried.
knit (nĭt) *v.* **knit** *or* **knit·ted, knit·ting. 1.** To make by intertwining thread or yarn in a set of connected loops. **2.** To join securely. **3.** To draw (the brow) together in wrinkles **:** furrow. —**knit** *n.*
knitting needle *n.* A long, thin, pointed rod for knitting.
knit·wear (nĭt′wâr′) *n.* Knitted garments.
knob (nŏb) *n.* **1. a.** A rounded protuberance.

b. A rounded handle. 2. A prominent rounded hill. —**knobbed** *adj.* —**knob'by** *adj.*

knock (nŏk) *v.* 1. To strike with a hard blow. 2. To produce by hitting. 3. *Slang.* To criticize : disparage. 4. To collide. 5. To make the clanking noise of a defective engine. —**knock around (***or* **about).** *Informal.* 1. To be rough or brutal with. 2. To wander from place to place. 3. To discuss. —**knock back.** *Informal.* To drink quickly. —**knock down.** 1. To declare sold at an auction. 2. *Informal.* To reduce in price. —**knock off.** 1. *Informal.* To stop. 2. *Informal.* To make or accomplish hastily. 3. *Informal.* To deduct. 4. *Slang.* To kill. —**knock out.** 1. To render unconscious. 2. To make useless or inoperative. 3. *Slang.* To amaze. —**knock** *n.*

knock•down (nŏk'doun') *adj.* 1. Forceful enough to overwhelm <a *knockdown* punch> 2. Designed to be easily assembled or disassembled <*knockdown* furniture> —**knock'down'** *n.*

knock•er (nŏk'ər) *n.* One that knocks, as a fixture for knocking on a door.

knock-knee (nŏk'nē') *n.* A condition in which one or both knees turn inward abnormally. —**knock'-kneed'** *adj.*

knock•out (nŏk'out') *n.* 1. The act of knocking out or the state of being knocked out. 2. *Slang.* Something that is exceptionally attractive.

knock•wurst (nŏk'wûrst', -wo͝orst') *n. var. of* KNACKWURST.

knoll (nōl) *n.* A small mound : hillock.

knot (nŏt) *n.* 1. **a.** A compact interlacing, as of string or cord. **b.** A fastening made by tying together lengths of material, as string. 2. A unifying bond, esp. of marriage. 3. A tight group or cluster. 4. A difficulty. 5. **a.** A hard node on a tree trunk from which a branch grows. **b.** A dark spot in wood marking such a node. 6. A protuberant growth in living tissue. 7. *Naut.* A unit of speed, 1 nautical mph, approx. 1.15 statute mph. —*v.* **knot•ted, knot•ting.** 1. To tie in or fasten with a knot. 2. To entangle. —**knot'ti•ness** *n.* —**knot'ty** *adj.*

knot•hole (nŏt'hōl') *n.* A hole in lumber where a knot used to be.

know (nō) *v.* **knew** (no͞o, nyo͞o), **known** (nōn), **know•ing.** 1. To perceive directly with the mind or senses. 2. To believe to be true. 3. To have understanding or experience of <*know* yacht racing> 4. To be subjected to <a person who had *known* no pain> 5. To recognize or be familiar with. ★ *syns:* APPREHEND, COMPREHEND, FATHOM, GRASP, UNDERSTAND —*n.* Knowledge. —**in the know.** Privy to confidential or special information. —**know'a•ble** *adj.*

know-how (nō'hou') *n. Informal.* Special knowledge and skill.

know•ing (nō'ĭng) *adj.* 1. Having knowledge or comprehension. 2. Clever : shrewd. 3. Suggestive of private knowledge <a *knowing* smile> 4. Deliberate : conscious. —**know'ing•ly** *adv.* —**know'ing•ness** *n.*

knowl•edge (nŏl'ĭj) *n.* 1. The fact or state of knowing. 2. Understanding acquired through experience. 3. The total or range of what has been perceived or learned. 4. Erudition : learning. ★ *syns:* EDUCATION, ERUDITION, INSTRUCTION, LEARNING, SCHOLARSHIP —**know'ledge•a•ble** *adj.* —**know'ledge•a•bly** *adv.*

knuck•le (nŭk'əl) *n.* A joint of a finger, esp. one connecting a finger to the hand. —*v.* **-led, -ling.** To press or hit with the knuckles. —**knuckle down.** To set to work earnestly. —**knuckle under.** To give in : yield.

knuck•le•bone (nŭk'əl-bōn') *n.* A knobbed bone, as of a joint or knuckle.

knuck•le•head (nŭk'əl-hĕd') *n.* A stupid person.

knurl (nûrl) *n.* 1. A protuberance, as a knob or knot. 2. One of a set of small ridges, as along the edge of an object such as a thumbscrew. —**knurl'y** *adj.*

ko•a•la (kō-ä'lə) *n.* An Australian arboreal marsupial, *Phascolarctos cinereus,* with thick grayish fur.

ko•bo (kô'bô') *n, pl.* **-bo.** —See table at CURRENCY.

kohl•ra•bi (kōl-rä'bē, -răb'ē) *n., pl.* **-bies.** A plant, *Brassica caulorapa,* with a thickened stem eaten as a vegetable.

ko•la (kō'lə) *n. var. of* COLA[3].

kook (ko͞ok) *n. Slang.* An eccentric person. —**kook'i•ness** *n.* —**kook'y** *adj.*

kook•a•bur•ra (ko͝ok'ə-bûr'ə, -bŭr'ə) *n.* A large kingfisher, *Dacelo novaeguineae* or *D. gigas,* native to Australia, with a raucous call similar to laughter.

ko•peck (kō'pĕk') *n.* —See table at CURRENCY.

Ko•ran (kô-răn', -rän', kō-) *n.* The sacred text of Islam, considered by Muslims to contain the revelations made to Muhammad by Allah. —**Ko•ran'ic** *adj.*

ko•ru•na (kôr'ə-nä') *n.* —See table at CURRENCY.

ko•sher (kō'shər) *adj.* 1. Fit to eat according to Jewish dietary laws. 2. *Slang.* Permissible : proper.

kow•tow (kou'tou', kō'-) *v.* To show servile deference.

Kr *symbol for* KRYPTON.

kraal (kräl) *n. So. Afr.* 1. A native village. 2. An enclosure for livestock.

Krem•lin (krĕm'lən) *n.* 1. The citadel of Moscow. 2. The government of the former Soviet Union.

Krem•lin•ol•o•gy (krĕm'lə-nŏl'ə-jē) *n.* Study of the policies of the former Soviet government. —**Krem'lin•o•log'i•cal** (-nə-lŏj'ĭ-kəl) *adj.* —**Krem'lin•ol'o•gist** *n.*

Krish•na (krĭsh'nə) *n.* The 8th and principal avatar of Vishnu, often represented as a handsome young man playing a flute.

kro•na[1] (krō'nə) *n., pl.* **-nur** (-nər). —See table at CURRENCY.

kro•na[2] (krō'nə) *n., pl.* **-nor** (-nôr', -nər). —See table at CURRENCY.

kro•ne (krō′nə) *n., pl.* **-ner** (-nər). —See table at CURRENCY.

ku•chen (ko͞o′kən, -KHən) *n.* A yeast-raised coffee cake.

kryp•ton (krĭp′tŏn′) *n. Symbol* **Kr** A white, inert gaseous element used mainly in fluorescent lamps.

ku•dos (kyo͞o′dŏs′, -dōs′) *n.* Acclaim or prestige resulting from notable achievement or high position.

▲ ***word history:*** The word *kudos* is etymologically a singular form, a modern borrowing of Greek *kudos,* "glory, renown." In very recent times, however, *kudos* has been reanalyzed as a plural form and consequently a new singular *kudo* sometimes occurs. Certain features of *kudos* predispose it to this kind of treatment. In the first place, it is an unfamiliar word, drawn from the vocabulary of Homer by academic and learned persons. In their usage it did not often occur as the subject of a sentence, where the verb could provide a clue to whether *kudos* was singular or plural. Secondly, *kudos* has no recorded plural in English. A person unfamiliar with Homeric Greek who saw the form *kudos* in an English publication would be likely to interpret it as the regular plural of a noun ending in *o,* like *typos* for *typo* and *altos* for *alto.* Once *kudos* was treated as a plural, the linguistic pressure to supply a singular would have been very strong. Although the form *kudo* has not achieved general acceptance and the construction "kudos are" is often considered incorrect, the linguistic processes in the development of *kudo/kudos* as the singular and plural forms of an English noun are highly productive and have been going on in English and other languages since prehistoric times. The development of the singular *pea* from the earlier singular form *pease* is an example of the same kind of reanalysis.

kud•zu (ko͝od′zo͞o) *n.* A fast-growing Japanese vine, *Pueraria lobata,* with clusters of reddish- purple flowers, grown for fodder and for containment of erosion.

kudzu

Ku Klux Klan (ko͞o′ klŭks klăn′, kyo͞o′) *n.* A U.S. secret society dedicated to legal and de facto segregation of blacks.

ku•lak (ko͞o-lăk′, -läk′) *n.* A prosperous peasant in czarist Russia.

kum•quat (kŭm′kwŏt′) *n.* A tree or shrub of the genus *Fortunella,* bearing a small edible fruit.

kung fu (ko͝ong′fo͞o′, go͝ong′-) *n.* A Chinese art of self-defense similar to karate.

Kurd (kûrd, ko͝ord) *n.* A member of a people inhabiting the transnational region of Kurdistan.

ku•rus (kə-ro͞osh′, ko͞o-) *n., pl.* **-rus.** —See table at CURRENCY.

kwa•cha (kwä′chə) *n.* —See table at CURRENCY.

kwan•za (kwän′zə) *n., pl.* **-za** *or* **-zas.** —See table at CURRENCY.

Kwan•za (kwän′zə) *n.* An African-American cultural festival celebrated from Dec. 26 to Jan. 1.

kwash•i•or•kor (kwăsh′ē-ôr′kôr, kwä′shē-) *n.* Severe malnutrition esp. in children, characterized by anemia, potbelly, depigmentation of the skin, and loss of hair.

kyat (chät) *n.* —See table at CURRENCY.

Ll

l *or* **L** (ĕl) *n., pl.* **l's** *or* **L's. 1.** The 12th letter of the English alphabet. **2.** A speech sound represented by the letter *l.* **3.** Something with the shape of the letter L. **4.** The Roman numeral for 50.

†**la** (lä) *interj. Chiefly Regional.* —Used to indicate surprise.

La *symbol for* LANTHANUM.

lab (lăb) *n.* A laboratory.

la•bel (lā′bəl) *n.* **1.** Something, as a slip of paper, that serves to describe or identify. **2.** A descriptive or identifying term. —*v.* **-beled, -bel•ing** *or* **-belled, -bel•ling. 1.** To affix a label to. **2.** To describe or identify with a label.

la•bi•al (lā′bē-əl) *adj.* Of or pertaining to the lips or labia.

la•bile (lā′bīl′, -bəl) *adj.* **1.** Open to change **:** adaptable. **2.** Constantly undergoing or likely to undergo chemical change **:** unstable.

la•bi•um (lā′bē-əm) *n., pl.* **-bi•a** (-bē-ə). Any of the folds of tissue surrounding the vulva.

la•bor (lā′bər) *n.* **1.** Physical or mental exertion **:** work. **2.** A particular task. **3. a.** Those who do work for wages. **b.** Trade unions or their officials. **4.** The physical efforts involved in childbirth. ★ ***syns:*** DRUDGERY, MOIL, SWEAT, TOIL, TRAVAIL, WORK —*v.* **1.** To work. **2.** To strive or treat painstakingly, exhaustively, or laboriously. **3.** To proceed with great effort. **4.** To suffer from a disadvantage or burden <*labored* under a major handicap> **—la'bor·er** *n.*

lab·o·ra·to·ry (lăb'rə-tôr'ē, -tōr'ē) *n., pl.* **-ries. 1.** A place equipped for scientific analysis, experimentation, research, or testing. **2.** A place where chemicals and drugs are produced.

Labor Day *n.* The first Monday in Sept., a legal holiday in the U.S. and Canada in recognition of working people.

la·bored (lā'bərd) *adj.* Done without natural ease **:** strained.

la·bo·ri·ous (lə-bôr'ē-əs, -bōr'-) *adj.* Done, produced with, or requiring much work or effort. **—la·bo'ri·ous·ly** *adv.* **—la·bo'ri·ous·ness** *n.*

la·bor·sav·ing (lā'bər-sā'vĭng) *adj.* Designed to conserve or diminish labor.

labor union *n.* An organization of workers formed to promote the members' interests with respect to wages and working conditions.

la·bour (lā'bər) *n., v., & adj. esp. Brit. var. of* LABOR.

la·bur·num (lə-bûr'nəm) *n.* A tree or shrub of the genus *Laburnum,* esp. *L. anagyroides,* with drooping yellow flower clusters.

lab·y·rinth (lăb'ə-rĭnth') *n.* An intricate structure of winding, interconnecting passages **:** maze. **—lab'y·rin'thine'** (-rĭn'thĭn, -thēn') *adj.*

lac (lăk) *n.* The resinous secretion of an Asian insect used to make shellac.

lac·co·lith (lăk'ə-lĭth') *n.* A mass of igneous rock intruded between layers of sedimentary rock, causing uplift.

lace (lās) *n.* **1.** A string or cord used to pull together 2 edges. **2.** A delicate fabric of fine threads woven in an open weblike pattern. —*v.* **laced, lac·ing. 1.** To tie or be tied with a lace. **2.** To intertwine. **3.** To add a small amount of liquor to. **—lac'y** *adj.*

lac·er·ate (lăs'ə-rāt') *v.* **-at·ed, -at·ing.** To tear or rip. **—lac'er·a'tion** *n.*

lace·wing (lās'wĭng') *n.* Any of various greenish or brownish insects of the families Chrysopidae and Hemerobiidae, with 4 gauzy wings, threadlike antennae, and larvae that feed on insect pests such as aphids.

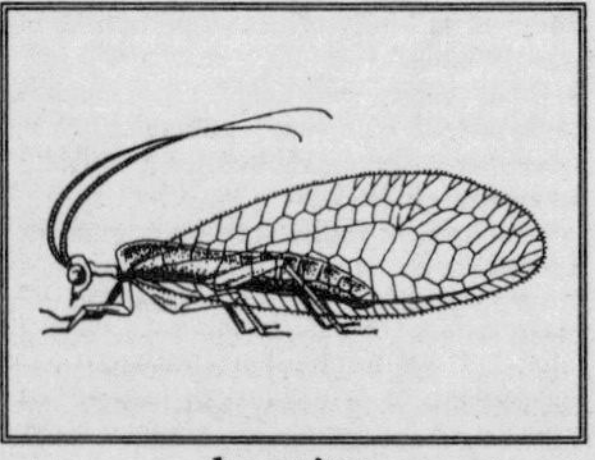

lacewing

lach·ry·mal *also* **lac·ri·mal** (lăk'rə-məl) *adj.* Of or relating to tears or the tear-producing glands.

lach·ry·mose (lăk'rə-mōs') *adj.* **1.** Tearful. **2.** Sorrowful. **—lach'ry·mose'ly** *adv.*

lack (lăk) *n.* An absence or deficiency **:** need. —*v.* **1.** To be without or have little of. **2.** To be deficient (in).

lack·a·dai·si·cal (lăk'ə-dā'zĭ-kəl) *adj.* Lacking spirit, life, or interest. **—lack'a·dai'si·cal·ly** *adv.*

lack·ey (lăk'ē) *n., pl.* **-eys. 1.** A uniformed male servant. **2.** An obsequious follower **:** toady.

lack·lus·ter (lăk'lŭs'tər) *adj.* Lacking vitality **:** dull.

la·con·ic (lə-kŏn'ĭk) *adj.* Using few words **:** terse. **—la·con'i·cal·ly** *adv.*

lac·quer (lăk'ər) *n.* A clear or colored synthetic or resinous surface coating that is dissolved in a solvent and dries to leave a glossy finish. **—lac'quer** *v.*

lac·ri·mal (lăk'rə-məl) *adj. var. of* LACHRYMAL.

la·crosse (lə-krôs', -krŏs') *n.* A game played on a field by 2 teams with long-handled rackets and a hard rubber ball.

lac·tate (lăk'tāt') *v.* **-tat·ed, -tat·ing.** To secrete milk. **—lac·ta'tion** *n.*

lac·te·al (lăk'tē-əl) *n.* Of, producing, or like milk.

lac·tic (lăk'tĭk) *adj.* Of, relating to, or obtained from milk.

lactic acid *n.* A syrupy liquid that is present in sour milk, molasses, various fruits, and wines.

lac·tose (lăk'tōs') *n.* A white crystalline sugar that is found in milk.

la·cu·na (lə-kyōō'nə, -kōō'-) *n., pl.* **-nae** (-nē) *or* **-nas.** A missing part or empty space **:** gap.

lad (lăd) *n.* **1.** A boy. **2.** A young man.

lad·der (lăd'ər) *n.* A framework of 2 long parallel side pieces crossed by equally spaced rungs for climbing.

lad·die (lăd'ē) *n.* A lad.

lad·en (lād'n) *adj.* **1.** Weighed down with a load **:** heavy. **2.** Burdened **:** oppressed.

lad·ing (lā'dĭng) *n.* Freight **:** cargo.

la·dle (lād'l) *n.* A spoon with a deep bowl and a long handle that is used for taking up and serving liquids. **—la'dle** *v.*

la·dy (lā'dē) *n., pl.* **-dies. 1.** A woman of breeding, cultivation, and often high social position. **2.** The female head of a household. **3.** A woman. **4. Lady.** *Brit.* The general feminine title of rank and esp. of nobility.

▲ ***word history:*** The word *lady* was not orig. an honorific title, but it did designate a woman of some social importance, at least within her own household. The Old English form of *lady, hlæfdige,* denoted the mistress of a household, esp. one who had authority over servants and other dependents. The word is ult. a compound of *hlāf,* "bread," and *dīg-,* a root meaning basically "to knead," which is related to *dough* and *diary.* As the "bread kneader" of the household a lady was in a position of some authority and dominance.

la•dy•bug (lā'dē-bŭg') *also* **la•dy•bird** (-bûrd') *n.* Any of numerous small, reddish black-spotted beetles of the family Coccinellidae.

la•dy•fin•ger (lā'dē-fĭng'gər) *n.* A small, oval sponge cake shaped like a finger.

lady in waiting *n., pl.* **ladies in waiting.** A lady appointed to wait on a princess or queen.

la•dy•like (lā'dē-līk') *adj.* **1.** Characteristic of a lady **:** well-bred. **2.** Appropriate for or becoming to a lady.

la•dy•ship (lā'dē-shĭp') *n. often* **Ladyship.** —Used as a form of address for a woman holding the rank of lady.

la•dy's-slip•per (lā'dēz-slĭp'ər) *n.* Any of various orchids of the genus *Cypripedium,* bearing flowers with a pouchlike lip.

lag (lăg) *v.* **lagged, lag•ging. 1.** To fail to keep up **:** straggle. **2.** To weaken gradually **:** slacken. —*n.* **1.** The act, process, or state of lagging. **2. a.** The amount or duration of lagging. **b.** An interval, as between events.

la•ger (lä'gər) *n.* A kind of beer that is stored to allow sedimentation.

lag•gard (lăg'ərd) *n.* One that lags.

la•gniappe (lăn-yăp', lăn'yăp') *n.* Something, as a small gift, that is given free or as a bonus.

la•goon (lə-go͞on') *n.* A shallow body of water, esp. one separated from the ocean by sandbars or coral reefs.

la•ic (lā'ĭk) *also* **la•i•cal** (-ĭ-kəl) *adj.* Of or relating to the laity **:** secular.

laid (lād) *v. p.t. & p.p. of* LAY[1].

laid•back (lād'băk') *adj. Informal.* Casual or relaxed in atmosphere or character.

lain (lān) *v. p.p. of* LIE[1].

lair (lâr) *n.* **1.** The dwelling of a wild animal **:** den. **2.** A refuge or hideaway.

laird (lârd) *n. Scot.* A landed estate owner.

lais•sez faire (lĕs'ā fâr') *n.* An economic doctrine that opposes government regulation of or interference in matters of commerce. —**lais'sez-faire'ism** *n.*

la•i•ty (lā'ĭ-tē) *n.* **1.** Laypeople as distinguished from clergy. **2.** Nonprofessionals.

lake (lāk) *n.* **1.** A large inland body of fresh or salt water. **2.** A pool of liquid.

La•ko•ta (lə-kō'tə) *n., pl.* **-ta** *or* **-tas.** Teton.

lam (lăm) *Slang.* —*v.* **lammed, lam•ming.** To run away in haste. —*n.* Flight, esp. from the law <on the *lam*>

la•ma (lä'mə) *n.* A Buddhist monk of Tibet or Mongolia.

la•ma•ser•y (lä'mə-sĕr'ē) *n., pl.* **-ies.** A monastery of lamas.

La•maze (lə-mäz') *adj.* Pertaining to or being a method of childbirth in which the mother is prepared physically and psychologically to give birth without using drugs.

lamb (lăm) *n.* **1. a.** A young sheep. **b.** The flesh of a lamb used as meat. **2.** A sweet, gentle person.

lam•baste (lăm-bāst') *v.* **-bast•ed, -bast•ing.** *Slang.* **1.** To beat **:** thrash. **2.** To berate.

lam•bent (lăm'bənt) *adj.* **1.** Flickering gently. **2.** Radiant **:** glowing. **3.** Marked by brilliance <*lambent* wit> —**lam'ben•cy** *n.* —**lam'bent•ly** *adv.*

lamb•skin (lăm'skĭn') *n.* A lamb's hide or leather made from it.

lame (lām) *adj.* **lam•er, lam•est. 1.** Disabled in a limb, esp. so as to impair free movement. **2.** Weak **:** unsatisfactory. —*v.* **lamed, lam•ing.** To make lame. —**lame'ly** *adv.* —**lame'ness** *n.*

la•mé (lă-mā', lä-) *n.* A brocaded fabric with metallic threads in the filling.

lame•brain (lām'brān') *n.* A stupid person **:** ninny. —**lame'brained'** *adj.*

lame duck *n.* An elected officeholder who has been defeated for re-election but continues in office until the inauguration of his or her successor.

la•mel•la (lə-mĕl'ə) *n., pl.* **-mel•lae** (-mĕl'ē) *or* **-las.** A thin layer, scale, or plate.

la•ment (lə-mĕnt') *v.* **1.** To express sorrow or regret (over) **:** mourn. **2.** To weep **:** wail. —*n.* **1.** An expression of sorrow or regret. **2.** An elegy **:** dirge. —**lam'en•ta•ble** *adj.* —**lam'en•ta•bly** *adv.*

lam•en•ta•tion (lăm'ən-tā'shən) *n.* **1.** An act or instance of lamenting. **2. Lamentations** *(sing. in number).* —See table at BIBLE.

lam•i•na (lăm'ə-nə) *n., pl.* **-nae** (-nē') *or* **-nas.** A thin plate or layer. —**lam'i•nar, lam'i•nal** *adj.*

lam•i•nate (lăm'ə-nāt') *v.* **-nat•ed, -nat•ing. 1.** To press or form into a thin plate or sheet. **2.** To split into thin layers. **3.** To make by joining several layers. —**lam'i•na'tion** *n.* —**lam'i•nate** (-nĭt, -nāt') *n. & adj.* —**lam'i•na'tor** *n.*

lamp (lămp) *n.* **1. a.** A device that generates heat, light, or therapeutic radiation. **b.** A vessel holding oil or alcohol burned through a wick for illumination. **2.** A device similar to a lamp that produces heat.

lamp•black (lămp'blăk') *n.* A black pigment composed of fine soot.

lamp•light•er (lămp'lī'tər) *n.* Someone hired to light gas-burning street lights.

lam•poon (lăm-po͞on') *n.* A broad satirical piece, esp. one that ridicules a person, group, or institution. —**lam•poon'** *v.* —**lam•poon'er•y** *n.*

lamp•post (lămp'pōst') *n.* A post to which a street lamp is attached.

lam•prey (lăm'prē) *n., pl.* **-preys.** Any of various primitive eellike fishes of the family Petromyzontidae with a jawless sucking mouth and a rasping tongue.

LAN (lăn) *n. Computer Sci.* A system that links together electronic office equipment, such as computers, and forms a network within an office or a building **:** a local area network.

la•nai (lə-nī', lä-) *n.* A verandah **:** porch.

lance (lăns) *n.* **1.** A spear with a sharp metal head. **2.** An implement similar to a lance, esp. a lancet. —*v.* **lanced, lanc•ing. 1.** To pierce with a lance. **2.** To make a surgical incision in.

lance corporal *n.* An enlisted man in the U.S. Marine Corps who ranks above a private first class and below a corporal.

lanc•er (lăn′sər) *n.* A cavalry soldier equipped with a lance.

lan•cet (lăn′sĭt) *n.* A surgical knife with a pointed and usu. double-edged blade.

land (lănd) *n.* **1.** The solid part of the surface of the earth. **2.** A particular region : area. **3.** The people of a nation. **4.** A nation : country. **5.** Real estate : property. —*v.* **1.** To set down or settle on land, esp. after traveling by water or air. **2.** To arrive or cause to arrive at a destination. **3.** To alight or cause to alight. **4.** To catch by or as if by fishing <*landed* a new job>

lan•dau (lăn′dô′, -dou′) *n.* **1.** A 4-wheeled closed carriage with a roof in 2 sections that can be lowered or detached. **2.** A style of automobile with a similar roof.

land•ed (lăn′dĭd) *adj.* Owning land <*landed* gentry>

landed immigrant *n. Can.* A person granted legal status as an immigrant who will eventually be eligible for citizenship.

land•er (lăn′dər) *n.* A space vehicle designed to land on a celestial body.

land•fall (lănd′fôl′) *n.* **1.** The sighting of or reaching land, as after a sea voyage. **2.** The land that is first sighted or reached.

land•fill (lănd′fĭl′) *n.* **1.** A method of waste disposal in which garbage and trash are buried in low-lying ground. **2.** Land built up by landfill.

land grant *n.* A grant of land made by a government esp. for railroads, highways, or state colleges.

land•hold•er (lănd′hōl′dər) *n.* Someone who owns land. —**land′hold′ing** *n.*

land•ing (lăn′dĭng) *n.* **1.** The act of coming to land or rest, esp. after a voyage or flight. **2.** A place for loading and discharging passengers and cargo. **3.** A level area at the top or bottom of a staircase.

landing gear *n.* The structure that supports the weight of an aircraft.

land•la•dy (lănd′lā′dē) *n.* A woman who owns and rents land, buildings, or dwelling units.

land•locked (lănd′lŏkt′) *adj.* **1.** Completely or almost completely surrounded by land. **2.** Confined to inland waters <*landlocked* salmon>

land•lord (lănd′lôrd′) *n.* **1.** One who owns and rents land, buildings, or dwelling units. **2.** An innkeeper. —**land′la′dy** *n.*

land•lub•ber (lănd′lŭb′ər) *n.* One not familiar with the sea or seamanship.

land•mark (lănd′märk′) *n.* **1.** A marker that indicates a boundary line. **2.** A prominent feature on land that serves to identify or guide. **3.** A historically significant event, structure, or site.

land•mass (lănd′măs′) *n.* A large land area.

land•own•er (lănd′ō′nər) *n.* A landholder.

land•scape (lănd′skāp′) *n.* **1.** A view or vista of natural scenery on land. **2.** A representation, esp. a painting, that depicts a landscape. —*v.* **-scaped, -scap•ing.** To beautify or improve (a section of ground) by contouring the land and planting flowers, shrubs, or trees. —**land′scap′er** *n.*

land•slide (lănd′slīd′) *n.* **1.** The fall or slide down a steep slope of a mass of earth or rock. **2.** A great victory, esp. in a political contest.

land•ward (lănd′wərd) *adj. & adv.* To or toward land. —**land′wards** *adv.*

lane (lān) *n.* **1.** A narrow path or road, often bordered by fences. **2.** A narrow lengthwise division, as of a road : strip <a shipping *lane*>

lan•guage (lăng′gwĭj) *n.* **1.** The sounds, words, and combinations of words that constitute a system for the expression and communication of thoughts and feelings among a number of people, as those with a shared history or set of traditions. **2.** A nonverbal method of communication. **3.** A particular style or form of utterance. **4.** *Computer Sci.* A system of symbols and rules used for communication with or between computers. ★ *syns:* DIALECT, SPEECH, TONGUE, VERNACULAR

lan•guid (lăng′gwĭd) *adj.* **1.** Lacking in vitality or energy : weak. **2.** Lacking in spirit : listless. **3.** Sluggish : slow. —**lan′guid•ly** *adv.* —**lan′guid•ness** *n.*

lan•guish (lăng′gwĭsh) *v.* **1.** To become languid : weaken. **2.** To become depressed : pine. **3.** To assume a sad air, esp. in order to gain sympathy. —**lan′guish•er** *n.* —**lan′guish•ment** *n.*

lan•guor (lăng′gər, lăng′ər) *n.* **1.** Lack of energy : weakness. **2.** Languid indolence. —**lan′guor•ous** *adj.*

lank (lăngk) *adj.* **1.** Lean : slender. **2.** Long, straight, and limp <*lank* hair> —**lank′ly** *adv.* —**lank′ness** *n.*

lank•y (lăng′kē) *adj.* **-i•er, -i•est.** Tall, thin, and ungraceful. —**lank′i•ness** *n.*

lan•o•lin (lăn′ə-lĭn) *n.* A fatty substance obtained from sheep's wool and used esp. in soaps and ointments.

la•nose (lā′nōs′) *adj.* Woolly.

lan•ta•na (lăn-tä′nə, -tăn′ə) *n.* Any of various aromatic, chiefly tropical shrubs of the genus *Lantana,* bearing small variously colored flowers in dense clusters.

lan•tern (lăn′tərn) *n.* **1.** A usu. portable light with transparent or translucent sides. **2.** The chamber in a lighthouse where the light is located.

lan•tha•nide (lăn′thə-nīd′) *n.* A rare-earth element.

lan•tha•num (lăn′thə-nəm) *n. Symbol* **La** A soft, silvery-white metallic element.

lan•yard (lăn′yərd) *n.* **1.** A rope used for securing something on ships. **2.** A cord worn around the neck to hold something, as a knife or whistle.

lap[1] (lăp) *n.* **1.** The front of a seated person from the lower trunk to the knees. **2.** The portion of a garment that covers the lap. **3.** Responsibility : control <dumped her problems in my *lap*>

lap[2] (lăp) *v.* **lapped, lap•ping. 1.** To fold, wind, or wrap over or around something. **2.** To lay or extend so as to overlap. —*n.* **1.** A part that overlaps another. **2.** The amount by which one part overlaps another. **3.** One complete circuit, as around a racetrack. **4.** A single segment, as of a journey.

lap[3] (lăp) *v.* **lapped, lap•ping. 1.** To take up (food or drink) with the tongue. **2.** To wash with a gentle slapping sound <waves *lapping* against the dock> **—lap up.** To take in eagerly **:** devour < *lapping* up compliments> —*n.* The act, process, or sound of lapping.

lap•a•ro•scope (lăp′ər-ə-skōp′) *n.* A slender tubular endoscope inserted through an incision in the abdominal wall to examine the abdominal or pelvic cavities. **—lap′a•ros′co•py** (lăp′ə-rŏs′kə-pē) *n.*

lap•board (lăp′bôrd′, -bōrd′) *n.* A flat board that rests on the lap as a substitute for a table or desk.

lap dog *n.* A small dog that is easily held in the lap.

la•pel (lə-pĕl′) *n.* The part of a garment, esp. a coat, that is an extension of the collar and folds back.

lap•i•dar•y (lăp′ĭ-dĕr′ē) *n., pl.* **-ies.** A cutter and polisher of precious stones. —*adj.* **1.** Of or pertaining to precious stones or the work of a lapidary. **2.** Concise and polished <*lapidary* prose>

lap•in (lăp′ĭn) *n.* Rabbit fur, esp. when sheared and dyed.

lap•is laz•u•li (lăp′ĭs lăz′yə-lē, lăzh′ə-) *n.* An opaque, blue semiprecious stone.

lap•pet (lăp′ĭt) *n.* A decorative flap or loose fold on a garment or headdress.

lapse (lăps) *v.* **lapsed, laps•ing. 1.** To fall to a less desirable state. **2.** To pass **:** elapse. **3.** To be no longer in force, as through disuse or the passage of time. —*n.* **1.** A minor failure or error. **2.** A fall to a less desirable state. **3.** An interval of passing time. **4.** The ending of a privilege or right through disuse, neglect, or death.

lap•top (lăp′tŏp′) *n.* A microcomputer small enough to use on one's lap.

laptop

lap•wing (lăp′wĭng′) *n.* An Old World narrow-crested bird of the genus *Vanellus,* related to the plovers.

lar•board (lär′bərd) *n. Naut.* PORT[2].

lar•ce•ny (lär′sə-nē) *n., pl.* **-nies.** The crime of theft. **—lar′ce•nous** *adj.*

larch (lärch) *n.* A coniferous tree of the genus *Larix,* with deciduous needles and durable wood.

lard (lärd) *n.* The white solid or semisolid rendered fat of a hog. —*v.* **1.** To insert strips of fat into (meat) before cooking. **2.** To enrich (e.g., writing) with additions.

lar•der (lär′dər) *n.* A place, as a room, where foods, as meat, are stored.

lar•ee (lâr′ē) *n.* —See table at CURRENCY.

large (lärj) *adj.* **larg•er, larg•est. 1.** Greater than average in size or amount **:** big. **2.** Greater than average in scope, breadth, or capacity. **—at large. 1.** Not confined **:** free. **2.** As a whole **:** generally. **3.** Not representing a particular nation, state, or district. **—large′ly** *adv.* **—large′ness** *n.*

large calorie *n.* CALORIE 2.

large intestine *n.* The portion of the intestine from the end of the small intestine to the anus.

large-scale (lärj′skāl′) *adj.* **1.** Large **:** extensive. **2.** Drawn to show detail <a *large-scale* map>

lar•gess *also* **lar•gesse** (lär-zhĕs′, -jĕs′, lär′jĕs′) *n.* **1.** Generosity in giving. **2.** A liberal gift.

lar•go (lär′gō) *adv. Mus.* In a slow and solemn manner. —Used as a direction. **—lar′go** *adj.* & *n.*

lar•i•at (lăr′ē-ət) *n.* A long rope with a running noose at one end **:** lasso.

lark[1] (lärk) *n.* **1.** Any of various chiefly Old World birds of the family Alaudidae, having a melodious song. **2.** A bird similar to the lark, as a meadowlark.

lark[2] (lärk) *n.* **1.** A carefree adventure. **2.** A playful prank. —*v.* To engage in fun or playful pranks.

lark•spur (lärk′spûr′) *n.* Any of various plants of the genus *Delphinium,* with spurred, often blue or purplish flowers.

†**lar•rup** (lăr′əp) *v. Regional.* To beat **:** flog. **—lar′rup** *n.*

lar•va (lär′və) *n., pl.* **-vae** (-vē). **1.** The wingless, often wormlike form of a newly hatched insect. **2.** A newly hatched animal, as a tadpole, that differs markedly from the adult. **—lar′val** *adj.*

lar•yn•gi•tis (lăr′ən-jī′tĭs) *n.* Inflammation of the larynx.

lar•ynx (lăr′ĭngks) *n., pl.* **la•ryn•ges** (lə-rĭn′jēz′) *or* **lar•ynx•es.** The upper portion of the respiratory tract between the pharynx and the trachea that contains the vocal cords. **—la•ryn′ge•al** (lə-rĭn′jē-əl, -jəl, lăr′ən-jē′əl) *adj.*

la•sa•gna *also* **la•sa•gne** (lə-zän′yə) *n.* Wide flat noodles, usu. baked with a sauce of meat, tomatoes, and cheese.

las•car (lăs′kər) *n.* An East Indian sailor.

las•civ•i•ous (lə-sĭv′ē-əs) *adj.* Lustful **:** lewd. **—las•civ′i•ous•ly** *adv.* **—las•civ′i•ous•ness** *n.*

la•ser (lā′zər) *n.* A device that converts incident electromagnetic radiation of mixed frequencies to discrete frequencies of highly amplified and coherent visible radiation.

laser printer *n.* A printer that uses a laser to make an image on a rotating drum and electrostatically transfers the image to paper.

lash[1] (lăsh) *n.* **1.** A stroke with or as if with a whip. **2.** A whip. **3.** An eyelash. —*v.* **1.** To strike with or as if with a lash **:** whip. **2.** To move rapidly back and forth. **3.** To attack verbally. —**lash'er** *n.*

lash[2] (lăsh) *v.* To hold securely in place with a cord, rope, or chain.

lass (lăs) *n.* A young woman **:** girl.

lass•ie (lăs'ē) *n.* A lass.

las•si•tude (lăs'ĭ-to͞od', -tyo͞od') *n.* Exhaustion, listless weakness, or torpor.

las•so (lăs'ō, lă-so͞o') *n., pl.* **-sos** *or* **-soes.** A long rope or leather thong with a running noose used esp. to catch horses and cattle. —**las'so** *v.*

last[1] (lăst) *adj.* **1.** Being, coming, or placed after all the rest **:** final. **2.** Being most recent **:** latest. **3.** Conclusive **:** authoritative. **4.** Least likely or expected <the *last* person to criticize> —*adv.* **1.** After all others in chronology or sequence. **2.** Most recently. **3.** At the end **:** finally. —*n.* **1.** The one that is last. **2.** The end. —**at last.** Finally. —**last'ly** *adv.*

last[2] (lăst) *v.* **1.** To continue to exist or operate. **2.** To be adequate (for).

last[3] (lăst) *n.* A foot-shaped block or form on which shoes are made or repaired.

last rites *pl.n.* Rites performed in connection with a death or burial.

latch (lăch) *n.* A fastening, as for a gate or door, that usu. consists of a movable bar that fits into a slot or notch. —*v.* To close with or as if with a latch. —**latch on to (***or* **onto).** *Informal.* **1.** To cling to. **2.** To get hold of **:** obtain.

latch•et (lăch'ĭt) *n.* A leather strap or thong for fastening a shoe or sandal.

latch•key (lăch'kē') *n.* A key for opening a latch, esp. one on an outside door or gate.

latch•string (lăch'strĭng') *n.* A cord fastened to a latch and often passed through a hole in the door so that the latch can be lifted from the outside.

late (lāt) *adj.* **lat•er, lat•est. 1.** Coming, happening, or staying after the proper or usual time. **2.** Being or happening toward the end or close. **3.** Of a time just past **:** recent. **4.** Having recently died <his *late* father> —*adv.* **lat•er, lat•est. 1.** After the proper or usual time. **2.** At or into an advanced point or period of time. **3.** Recently. ★ ***syns:*** BELATED, OVERDUE, TARDY —**late'ness** *n.*

late•ly (lāt'lē) *adv.* Not long ago **:** recently.

la•tent (lāt'nt) *adj.* Present but not evident or active. —**la'ten•cy** *n.*

lat•er•al (lăt'ər-əl) *adj.* On, toward, or from the side. —*n. Football.* A usu. underhand pass that is thrown sideways or backward. —**lat'er•al•ly** *adv.*

la•tex (lā'tĕks') *n.* **1.** The usu. milky, viscous sap of certain plants, as the rubber tree. **2.** A water emulsion of rubber or plastic globules used esp. in paints.

lath (lăth) *n., pl.* **laths** (lă*th*z, lăths). **1.** A narrow, thin strip of wood or metal used esp. as a supporting structure for plaster. **2.** A building material, as a sheet of metal mesh, used esp. as a support for plaster.

lathe (lā*th*) *n.* A machine on which a piece of material is held while it is spun and shaped by a tool. —**lathe** *v.*

lath•er (lă*th*'ər) *n.* **1.** A foam or froth, esp. that formed by soap or detergent and water. **2.** Froth formed by sweating, esp. by a horse. **3.** A dither **:** agitation. —*v.* **1.** To produce lather. **2.** To cover with lather. —**lath'er•er** *n.* —**lath'er•y** *adj.*

Lat•in (lăt'n) *n.* **1.** The language of ancient Rome. **2.** A member of a people speaking a Romance language. —**Lat'in** *adj.*

La•ti•na (lə-tē'nə, lă-) *n.* A Latino woman or girl.

Lat•in-A•mer•i•can (lăt'n-ə-mĕr'ĭ-kən) *adj.* Of or designating Western Hemisphere nations south of the United States that have Spanish, Portuguese, or French as their official languages. —**Latin American** *n.*

La•ti•no (lə-tē'nō, lă-) *n., pl.* **-nos. 1.** A Spanish-speaking Latin American. **2.** A person of Spanish-speaking heritage, esp. in the United States.

lat•i•tude (lăt'ĭ-to͞od', -tyo͞od') *n.* **1. a.** The angular distance N or S of the earth's equator measured along a meridian. **b.** A region of the earth indicated by its latitude. **2.** Freedom from limitations **:** leeway. —**lat'i•tu'di•nal** *adj.*

lat•i•tu•di•nar•i•an (lăt'ĭ-to͞od'n-âr'ē-ən, -tyo͞od'-) *adj.* Tolerant, as toward the religious beliefs and behavior of others. —**lat'i•tu'di•nar'i•an** *n.*

la•trine (lə-trēn') *n.* A toilet, as in a barracks.

lat•ter (lăt'ər) *adj.* **1.** Of or being the second of 2 persons or things mentioned. **2.** Closer to the end. —**lat'ter•ly** *adv.*

lat•ter-day (lăt'ər-dā') *adj.* Of the present time or a time not long past.

lat•tice (lăt'ĭs) *n.* **1.** A framework of interwoven strips, as of wood or metal. **2.** A structure, as a window or gate, that has a lattice.

lat•tice•work (lăt'ĭs-wûrk') *n.* **1.** An object, a structure, or material resembling a lattice. **2.** A structure made of lattices.

laud (lôd) *v.* To praise **:** acclaim. —**laud** *n.* —**laud'a•ble** *adj.* —**laud'a•bly** *adv.*

lau•da•num (lôd'n-əm) *n.* A tincture of opium, formerly used as a drug.

lau•da•to•ry (lô'də-tôr'ē, -tōr'ē) *adj.* Of, pertaining to, or expressing praise.

laugh (lăf, läf) *v.* **1.** To express mirth, joy, or derision with a smile and usu. unarticulated sounds. **2.** To feel or show amusement or derision. —*n.* **1.** The sound or act of laughing. **2.** Something that is amusing or ridiculous **:** joke. —**laugh'a•ble** *adj.* —**laugh'a•bly** *adj.* —**laugh'ing•ly** *adv.*

laugh•ing•stock (lăf'ĭng-stŏk', lä'fĭng-) *n.* An object of jokes or ridicule **:** butt.

laugh•ter (lăf′tər, läf′-) *n.* The act of or sound produced by laughing.
launch[1] (lônch) *v.* **1.** To set in motion with force : propel. **2.** To put (a boat) into the water. **3.** To put into operation : initiate. **—launch** *n.* **—launch′er** *n.*
launch[2] (lônch) *n.* **1.** A large ship's boat. **2.** A large open motorboat.
launching pad *also* **launch pad** *n.* A base or platform from which a spacecraft or rocket is launched.
laun•der (lôn′dər) *v.* To wash or wash and iron (e.g., clothes). **—laun′der•er** *n.* **—laun′dress** *n.*
Laun•dro•mat (lôn′drə-măt′). A trademark for a commercial self-service laundry.
laun•dry (lôn′drē) *n., pl.* **-dries. 1.** Clothes or linens that are to be or that have been laundered. **2.** A place where laundering is done. **—laun′dry•man′** *n.*
lau•re•ate (lôr′ē-ĭt, lŏr′-) *n.* One honored for accomplishment, as in science.
lau•rel (lôr′əl, lŏr′-) *n.* **1. a.** A shrub or tree, *Laurus nobilis,* native to the Mediterranean region, with aromatic evergreen leaves and small, blackish berries. **b.** A shrub or tree, as the mountain laurel, that is similar to the laurel. **2.** *often* **laurels. a.** A wreath of laurel leaves. **b.** Glory : honor.
la•va (lä′və, lăv′ə) *n.* **1.** Molten rock from a volcano. **2.** Rock that is formed when lava cools and hardens.
la•va•bo (lə-vä′bō, -vā′-) *n., pl.* **-boes.** A washbowl and water tank with a spout that are fastened to a wall.
la•vage (lə-väzh′) *n.* A washing out, esp. of a hollow bodily organ.
lav•a•liere (lăv′ə-lîr′) *also* **la•val•lière** (lä′-väl-yâr′) *n.* A pendant that is worn on a chain around the neck.
lav•a•to•ry (lăv′ə-tôr′ē, -tōr′ē) *n., pl.* **-ries. 1.** A permanently installed washbowl with running water. **2.** A bathroom.
lave (lāv) *v.* **laved, lav•ing.** To wash.
lav•en•der (lăv′ən-dər) *n.* **1.** An aromatic Old World plant of the genus *Lavandula,* bearing small fragrant purplish flower clusters. **2.** A light purple. **—lav′en•der** *adj.*
lav•ish (lăv′ĭsh) *adj.* **1.** Giving or spending profusely. **2.** Marked by or produced with extravagance : luxurious. *—v.* To give or expend unstintingly. **—lav′ish•er** *n.* **—lav′ish•ly** *adv.* **—lav′ish•ness** *n.*
†**law** (lô) *n.* **1. a.** A rule of action or conduct established by authority, society, or custom. **b.** A body of such rules. **c.** The control that ensues when such rules are enforced. **2. a.** The study and science of laws : jurisprudence. **b.** The profession of a lawyer. **3.** The body of precepts that express the divine will as set forth in the Old Testament. **4.** A formulation of a relationship that holds between or among phenomena for all cases in which the specified conditions are met. **5.** A code of ethics or behavior. ★ ***syns:*** AXIOM, FUNDAMENTAL, PRINCIPLE, THEOREM *—v. Regional.* To litigate.
law-a•bid•ing (lô′ə-bī′dĭng) *adj.* Acting in accordance with the law.
law•break•er (lô′brā′kər) *n.* Someone who breaks the law.
law•ful (lô′fəl) *adj.* **1.** Allowed by law. **2.** Recognized by law. **—law′ful•ly** *adv.* **—law′ful•ness** *n.*
law•giv•er (lô′gĭv′ər) *n.* A legislator.
law•less (lô′lĭs) *adj.* **1.** Without laws. **2.** Unrestrained by law : disobedient. **—law′less•ly** *adv.* **—law′less•ness** *n.*
law•mak•er (lô′mā′kər) *n.* One who makes laws : legislator. **—law′mak′ing** *n.*
lawn[1] (lôn) *n.* Ground covered with grass that is mowed regularly.
▲ ***word history:*** The word *lawn*[1], which now denotes a carefully kept ornamental plot of closely mown grass, originated as a variant spelling of *laund,* a word now obsolete that meant "a woodland glade." *Laund* was borrowed from Old French *lande.* It is likely that *lande* entered Old French from a Celtic source, but the ultimate origin of *lande* is Germanic, and the word is cognate with—that is, has the same ancestor as—English *land.*
lawn[2] (lôn) *n.* A very fine, thin cotton or linen fabric. **—lawn′y** *adj.*
law•ren•ci•um (lô-rĕn′sē-əm, lō-) *n. Symbol* **Lw** A synthetic radioactive element.
law•suit (lô′so͞ot′) *n.* A case before a court of law.
law•yer (lô′yər, loi′ər) *n.* A person who is trained and qualified to give legal advice to clients and represent them in court.
lax (lăks) *adj.* **1. a.** Careless : negligent. **b.** Not strict : lenient. **2.** Not tense : slack. **—lax′i•ty, lax′ness** *n.* **—lax′ly** *adv.*
lax•a•tive (lăk′sə-tĭv) *n.* A substance, esp. a drug, that stimulates evacuation of the bowels. **—lax′a•tive** *adj.*
lay[1] (lā) *v.* **laid** (lād), **lay•ing. 1.** To place on a surface. **2.** To knock down. **3.** To allay : calm. **4.** To produce and deposit (eggs). **5.** To bet : wager. **6.** To spread over a surface. **7.** To bring to a given condition. **8.** To set or place in position. **9.** To prepare : devise <*lay* plans> **10.** To impose, esp. as a burden or punishment. **11.** To put forth : submit. **—lay away.** To set aside for future delivery or use. **—lay off. 1.** To dismiss (a worker) from a job, esp. temporarily. **2.** *Slang.* To cease : stop. *—n.* The manner, location, or appearance of something relative to something else.
lay[2] (lā) *adj.* **1.** Of, pertaining to, or belonging to the laity. **2.** Nonprofessional.
lay[3] (lā) *n.* A ballad.
lay[4] (lā) *v. p.t. of* LIE[1].
lay•a•way (lā′ə-wā′) *n.* A payment plan in which merchandise is reserved with a down payment until the balance is paid in full.
lay•er (lā′ər) *n.* **1.** One that lays. **2.** A single thickness, coating, or sheet that lies over or under another.
lay•er•ing (lā′ər-ĭng) *n.* The process of rooting branches, twigs, or stems still attached to a parent plant, as by placing a specially treated part in moist soil.

lay•ette (lā-ĕt′) *n.* A set of clothing and equipment for a newborn child.
lay•man (lā′mən) *n.* **1.** Someone who is not a member of the clergy. **2.** Someone who does not belong to a particular profession or specialty. **—lay′wom′an** *n.*
lay•off (lā′ôf′, -ŏf′) *n.* **1.** The temporary dismissal of an employee. **2.** A period of temporary suspension, rest, or inactivity.
lay•out (lā′out′) *n.* **1.** An arrangement **:** plan. **2.** A set, as of tools **:** outfit.
lay•per•son (lā′pûr′sən) *n.* A layman or laywoman. **—lay′peo′ple** *n.*
lay•wom•an (lā′wo͝om′ən) *n.* **1.** A woman who is not a cleric. **2.** A woman who is a nonprofessional.
laze (lāz) *v.* **lazed, laz•ing.** To be lazy **:** take it easy.
la•zy (lā′zē) *adj.* **-zi•er, -zi•est. 1.** Disposed to be idle. **2.** Moving slowly **:** sluggish. ★ ***syns:*** IDLE, INDOLENT, SHIFTLESS, SLOTHFUL **—la′zi•ly** *adv.* **—la′zi•ness** *n.*
la•zy•bones (lā′zē-bōnz′) *pl.n. (sing. or pl. in number). Slang.* A lazy person.
lazy Su•san (so͞o′zən) *n.* A revolving tray for food or condiments.
lea (lē, lā) *n.* A meadow **:** grassland.
leach (lēch) *v.* **1.** To pass (a liquid) through a substance so as to remove soluble materials. **2.** To be washed or washed out by leaching. **—leach′a•ble** *adj.*
lead[1] (lēd) *v.* **led** (lĕd), **lead•ing. 1.** To conduct along a way **:** guide. **2.** To be ahead or at the head of <*led* the procession> **3.** To live **:** pursue <*lead* a happy life> **4.** To tend toward a given result <practice that *led* to success> **5.** To direct the performance or activity of <*lead* an orchestra> **6.** To make the beginning play, as in a game or contest. **—lead off. 1.** To start **:** begin. **2.** To be the first player at bat in an inning. **—lead on.** To entice **:** lure. *—n.* **1.** The front, foremost, or winning position. **2.** A margin of advantage or superiority. **3.** A clue. **4.** Leadership. **5.** An example. **6. a.** A principal role, esp. in a play. **b.** A person playing such a role. **7.** The beginning play in a game. **8. a.** The prerogative of making the initial play in a card game. **b.** The suit or card played. **9.** A leash. **—lead′er** *n.* **—lead′er•ship′** *n.* **—lead′ing** *adj.*
lead[2] (lĕd) *n.* **1.** *Symbol* **Pb** A soft, heavy dull-gray metallic element, used in solder, bullets, and paints. **2.** A plumb bob suspended by a line for making soundings, as in the ocean. **3.** A thin metal strip used in printing to separate lines of type. **4.** A thin usu. graphitic stick used as the writing substance in a pencil. *—v.* **1.** To line, cover, weight, fill, or treat with lead. **2.** To provide space between (lines of printing type) with leads. **3.** To secure (window glass) with lead. **—lead′ing** *n.*
lead•en (lĕd′n) *adj.* **1.** Made of or containing lead. **2.** Of the color of lead **:** dark gray. **3.** Heavy **:** oppressive. **4.** Weighted down **:** burdened. **—lead′en•ness** *n.*
lead•off (lēd′ôf′, -ŏf′) *n.* **1.** An opening move or play. **2.** One that leads off.
lead poisoning (lĕd) *n.* Acute or chronic poisoning caused by the absorption of lead or any of its salts into the system.
lead-time (lēd′tīm′) *n.* The time between the decision to begin a project and its completion.
leaf (lēf) *n., pl.* **leaves** (lēvz). **1.** A usu. green, flat vascular plant structure that is attached to a stem and functions as a main organ of photosynthesis and transpiration. **2.** Something that resembles a leaf, as a page of a book. **3.** Foliage. **4.** A removable or hinged section, as of a table top. *—v.* **1.** To put forth leaves. **2.** To turn the pages of a magazine or book. **—leaf′less** *adj.* **—leaf′y** *adj.*
leaf•age (lē′fĭj) *n.* Leaves **:** foliage.
leaf•hop•per (lēf′hŏp′ər) *n.* Any of numerous insects of the family Cicadellidae that suck juices from plants.
leaf•let (lēf′lĭt) *n.* **1.** A segment of a compound leaf. **2.** A printed handbill **:** flier.
leaf mold *n.* Humus or compost made up of organic matter, as of decomposed leaves.
leaf•stalk (lēf′stôk′) *n.* The stalk by which a leaf is attached to a stem **:** petiole.
league[1] (lēg) *n.* **1.** An association, as of states or persons, for common action **:** alliance. **2.** *Informal.* A level, as of competition **:** class. **—league** *v.*
league[2] (lēg) *n.* A unit of distance equal to 3 mi or approx. 4.8 km.
leak (lēk) *v.* **1.** To escape or pass through a breach or flaw. **2.** To allow to escape or pass through a breach or flaw. **3.** To make or become publicly known through a breach of secrecy. *—n.* **1. a.** An opening, as a hole or crack, through which something can escape or pass. **b.** An escape or passage through a leak. **2.** A disclosure of confidential information. **—leak′age** *n.* **—leak′i•ness** *n.* **—leak′y** *adj.*
lean[1] (lēn) *v.* **1.** To bend or slant away from a perpendicular position **:** incline. **2.** To incline the weight of the body for support. **3.** To rely for help or support. **4.** To have a tendency **:** be inclined. **—lean** *n.*
lean[2] (lēn) *adj.* **1.** Not fat or fleshy **:** thin. **2.** Having little or no fat <*lean* beef> **3.** Not productive, plentiful, or satisfying. **—lean′ly** *adv.* **—lean′ness** *n.*
lean•ing (lē′nĭng) *n.* An inclination.
lean-to (lēn′to͞o′) *n., pl.* **-tos. 1.** A structure with a single sloping roof, usu. built against and supported by an outside wall. **2.** A shelter or shed resembling a lean-to.
leap (lēp) *v.* **leaped** *or* **leapt** (lĕpt, lēpt), **leap•ing. 1.** To move from the ground with a spring of the legs **:** jump. **2.** To jump over. *—n.* A jump. **—leap′er** *n.*
leap•frog (lēp′frôg′, -frŏg′) *n.* A game in which one player leaps over another who is kneeling or bending over. **—leap′frog′** *v.*
leap year *n.* A year in the Gregorian calendar with 366 days, Feb. 29 being the extra day.
learn (lûrn) *v.* **learned** *or* **learnt** (lûrnt), **learn•ing. 1.** To acquire knowledge, understanding, or mastery (of) by study or experi-

ence. **2.** To memorize. **3.** To become informed of : discover. —**learn'er** *n.*

learn•ed (lûr'nĭd) *adj.* Erudite : scholarly. —**learn'ed•ly** *adv.* —**learn'ed•ness** *n.*

▲ ***word history:*** The adjective *learned* is the same word as the past participle of the verb *learn.* Since Old English times *learn* has always meant "to gain knowledge," but in Middle English times it also meant "to teach," although this sense is no longer current in standard Modern English. In Middle English the past participle *learned* has the sense "taught," and it has survived as an adjective, esp. with the meaning "erudite."

learn•ing (lûr'nĭng) *n.* Knowledge and esp. erudition.

lease (lēs) *n.* A contract for the use or occupation of real estate usu. for a given period in exchange for rent. —*v.* **leased, leas•ing. 1.** To grant by lease. **2.** To use or occupy under a lease.

lease•hold (lēs'hōld') *n.* **1.** Possession by lease. **2.** Property held by lease. —**lease'hold'er** *n.*

leash (lēsh) *n.* **1.** A chain, rope, or strap for leading or holding an animal in check. **2.** Control : restraint. —**leash** *v.*

least (lēst) **1.** Lowest in rank or importance. **2.** Smallest in degree or size. —*adv.* In or to the smallest degree. —*n.* One that is least. —**at least.** In any event.

least common denominator *n.* Lowest common denominator.

least common multiple *n.* The smallest quantity exactly divisible by each of 2 or more other numbers; e.g., 12 is the least common multiple of 2, 3, 4, and 6.

†**least•ways** (lēst'wāz') *adv. Regional.* At least.

least•wise (lēst'wīz') *adj. Informal.* At least : anyway.

leath•er (lĕth'ər) *n.* The hide of an animal dressed for use. —**leather** *adj.* —**leath'er•y** *adj.*

leath•er•neck (lĕth'ər-nĕk') *n. Slang.* A U.S. Marine.

leave[1] (lēv) *v.* **left** (lĕft), **leav•ing. 1.** To go away (from). **2. a.** To permit or cause to remain. **b.** To deliver. **3.** To have as a remainder. **4.** To refrain from interfering with. **5.** To bequeath. **6.** To forsake : abandon. —**leave out.** To omit.

leave[2] (lēv) *n.* **1.** Permission. **2.** Official permission for absence from duty. **3.** Formal farewell.

leave[3] (lēv) *v.* **leaved, leav•ing.** To put forth foliage : leaf.

leaved (lēvd) *adj.* **1.** Bearing a leaf or leaves. **2.** Having a given number or kind of leaves <4-*leaved*> <serrate-*leaved*>

leav•en (lĕv'ən) *n.* **1.** A fermenting substance, as yeast, used to cause batters and doughs to rise. **2.** Something that enlivens or lightens. —*v.* **1.** To add a fermenting agent to (dough). **2.** To enliven or lighten.

leav•en•ing (lĕv'ə-nĭng) *n.* An agent that produces fermentation : leaven.

leaves (lēvz) *n. pl. of* LEAF.

leave-tak•ing (lēv'tā'kĭng) *n.* An exchange of good-bys : farewell.

leav•ings (lē'vĭngz) *pl.n.* Bits left over : remnants.

lech•er•y (lĕch'ə-rē) *n.* **1.** Excessive indulgence in sexual activity. **2.** Lasciviousness : prurience. —**lech'er** *n.* —**lech'er•ous** *adj.* —**lech'er•ous•ly** *adv.*

lec•i•thin (lĕs'ə-thĭn) *n.* Any of a group of phosphorus-containing compounds found in all plant and animal tissues, derived commercially from egg yolks, soybeans, and corn, and used in the production of foods, pharmaceuticals, cosmetics, and plastics.

lec•tern (lĕk'tərn) *n.* A tall desk, often with a slanted top, that serves as a support for the books or notes of a standing speaker.

lec•tor (lĕk'tər) *n.* One who reads aloud the lessons in a church service.

lec•ture (lĕk'chər) *n.* **1.** A speech delivered before an audience or class, esp. to provide information or instruction. **2.** A reprimand. —**lec'ture** *v.* —**lec'tur•er** *n.*

led (lĕd) *v. p.t. & p.p. of* LEAD[1].

le•der•ho•sen (lā'dər-hō'zən) *pl.n.* Leather shorts worn by men and boys, esp. in Bavaria.

ledge (lĕj) *n* **1.** A horizontal projection forming a shelf, as on a wall or cliff. **2.** An underwater ridge of rock.

ledg•er (lĕj'ər) *n.* A book in which sums of money received and paid out, as by a business, are recorded.

lee (lē) *n.* **1.** The side, as of a ship, that is away from the wind. **2.** Shelter : cover.

leech (lēch) *n.* **1.** Any of various chiefly aquatic bloodsucking annelid worms of the family Hirudinea, esp. *Hirudo medicinalis,* once used by physicians to bleed their patients. **2.** One who preys on or lives off others : parasite.

leek (lēk) *n.* A plant, *Allium porrum,* related to the onion, with a slender, edible bulb.

leer (lîr) *n.* A sly, suggestive, or cunning look. —**leer** *v.*

leer•y (lîr'ē) *adj.* **-i•er, -i•est.** *Informal.* Distrustful : wary. —**leer'i•ly** *adv.* —**leer'i•ness** *n.*

lees (lēz) *pl.n.* Dregs.

lee•ward (lē'wərd, lo͞o'ərd) *adj.* Facing or located away from the wind. —*n.* The lee side. —**lee'ward** *adv.*

lee•way (lē'wā') *n.* **1.** The drift of a ship or plane away from the correct course. **2.** A permitted margin of variation or freedom.

left[1] (lĕft) *adj.* **1.** Of, at, or located on the side of the body that faces north when the subject is facing east. **2.** *often* **Left.** Of or belonging to the political Left. —*n.* **1. a.** The direction or position that is toward or on the left side. **b.** The left side or hand. **2.** *often* **Left.** The persons and groups seeking egalitarian political goals through reform or revolution. —*adv.* On or toward the left.

left[2] (lĕft) *v. p.t. & p.p. of* LEAVE[1].

left field *n.* The part of a baseball outfield that is to the left as viewed from home plate. —**left fielder** *n.*

left-hand (lĕft′hănd′) *adj.* **1.** Of or located on the left. **2.** Left-handed.

left-hand•ed (lĕft′hăn′dĭd) *adj.* **1.** Using the left hand more easily than the right. **2.** Done with the left hand. **3.** Clumsy : awkward. **4.** Counterclockwise. —*adv.* With the left hand. —**left′-hand′ed•ly** *adv.* —**left′-hand′ed•ness** *n.*

left•ism *also* **Left•ism** (lĕf′tĭz′əm) *n.* The ideology of the Left. —**left′ist** *n.*

left•o•ver (lĕft′ō′vər) *n. often* **leftovers.** An unused portion, esp. of food : remnant.

leg (lĕg) *n.* **1.** A limb or appendage of an animal, used esp. for locomotion and support. **2.** Something that resembles the leg of an animal in shape or function <a piano *leg*> **3.** The part of a garment that covers the leg. **4.** A stage of a trip. —*v.* **legged, leg•ging.** *Informal.* To go on foot.

leg•a•cy (lĕg′ə-sē) *n., pl.* **-cies. 1.** Something bequeathed by will : bequest. **2.** Something handed down from one who has gone before or from the past.

le•gal (lē′gəl) *adj.* **1.** Of or pertaining to law or lawyers. **2. a.** Based on or authorized by law : lawful. **b.** Established by law : statutory. —**le•gal′i•ty** *n.* —**le′gal•i•za′tion** *n.* —**le′gal•ize′** *v.* —**le′gal•ly** *adv.*

le•gal•ism (lē′gə-lĭz′əm) *n.* Literal and usu. too strict adherence to the letter of the law. —**le′gal•ist** *n.* —**le′gal•is′tic** *adj.*

le•gal-size (lē′gəl-sīz′) *adj.* Being a sheet of paper that measures approx. 8½ by 14 inches.

leg•ate (lĕg′ĭt) *n.* An official envoy, esp. of the pope. —**leg′ate•ship′** *n.*

leg•a•tee (lĕg′ə-tē′) *n.* One who inherits a legacy.

le•ga•tion (lĭ-gā′shən) *n.* **1.** A diplomatic mission in a foreign country headed by a minister. **2.** The premises occupied by a minister to a foreign government.

le•ga•to (lĭ-gä′tō) *adv. Mus.* Smoothly and with successive notes connected. —Used as a direction. —**le•ga′to** *adj.* & *n.*

leg•end (lĕj′ənd) *n.* **1.** A story handed down from the past, esp. one that is widely believed but unverifiable. **2.** An inscription or title on an object, as a coin. **3.** An explanatory caption for an illustration.

▲ ***word history:*** The word *legend* is derived from Latin *legenda,* a participial form derived from the verb *legere,* "to read." In Medieval Latin *legenda* was used to mean "something to be read" and esp. the narrative of a saint's life. These biographies were considered to be important as both historical records and moral examples. The word *legenda* was borrowed into English as *legend* in the 14th cent. It is likely that the utterly incredible exploits and events recounted in some legends led to the development of the sense "unverified popular tale, myth" for the English word.

leg•en•dar•y (lĕj′ən-dĕr′ē) *adj.* Of, based on, or of the nature of a legend.

leg•er•de•main (lĕj′ər-də-mān′) *n.* Sleight of hand.

leg•ged (lĕg′ĭd, lĕgd) *adj.* Having a given kind or number of legs <long-*legged*>

leg•gings (lĕg′ĭngz) *pl.n.* A leg covering.

leg•gy (lĕg′ē) *adj.* **-gi•er, -gi•est. 1.** Having very long legs. **2.** Having long, attractive legs. —**leg′gi•ness** *n.*

leg•horn (lĕg′hôrn′, -ərn) *n.* **1.** A hat of finely plaited straw. **2.** *often* **Leghorn.** A domestic fowl orig. bred in Mediterranean regions and raised esp. for producing eggs.

leg•i•ble (lĕj′ə-bəl) *adj.* Capable of being read. —**leg′i•bil′i•ty** *n.* —**leg′i•bly** *adv.*

le•gion (lē′jən) *n.* **1.** A Roman army unit that consisted of from 3,000 to 6,000 infantrymen. **2.** A great number : multitude. —*adj.* Constituting a great number : numerous. —**le′gion•ar′y** (-jə-nĕr′ē) *n.* & *adj.* —**le′gion•naire′** (-jə-nâr′) *n.*

leg•is•late (lĕj′ĭ-slāt′) *v.* **-lat•ed, -lat•ing. 1.** To pass laws. **2.** To enact into law. **3.** To bring about by or as if by legislating. —**leg′is•la′tor** *n.*

leg•is•la•tion (lĕj′ĭ-slā′shən) *n.* **1.** The act or process of passing laws : lawmaking. **2.** A law or group of laws proposed or enacted by a legislature.

leg•is•la•tive (lĕj′ĭ-slā′tĭv) *adj.* **1.** Of or pertaining to legislation or a legislature. **2.** Having the power to legislate.

Legislative Assembly *n. Can.* The elected governing body in most provinces.

leg•is•la•ture (lĕj′ĭ-slā′chər) *n.* An officially selected body of persons with the power and responsibility to make and change laws.

le•git (lə-jĭt′) *adj. Slang.* Legitimate.

le•git•i•mate (lə-jĭt′ə-mĭt) *adj.* **1.** In accordance with the law : lawful. **2.** In accordance with accepted standards or rules. **3.** Reasonable : sensible. **4.** Genuine : real. **5.** Born of legally married parents. —*v.* (-māt′) **-mat•ed, -mat•ing. 1.** To establish as or declare to be legitimate. **2.** To authorize. —**le•git′i•ma•cy** *n.* —**le•git′i•mate•ly** *adv.*

le•git•i•mize (lə-jĭt′ə-mīz′) *v.* **-mized, -miz•ing.** To legitimate. —**le•git′i•mi•za′tion** *n.*

leg•ume (lĕg′yo͞om′, lə-gyo͞om′) *n.* **1.** A plant of the family Leguminosae, as a bean or pea, bearing pods that split when mature. **2.** The pod or seeds of a legume used as food. —**le•gu′mi•nous** *adj.*

leg•work (lĕg′wûrk′) *n. Informal.* A task, as gathering information, that involves physical activity.

lei¹ (lā, lā′ē) *n.* A wreath of flowers, esp. one worn around the neck.

lei² (lā) *n. pl. of* LEU.

lei•sure (lē′zhər, lĕzh′ər) *n.* **1.** Time during which one is free from work or duties. **2.** Effortless ease. —**lei′sure•ly** *adj.* & *adv.*

leit•mo•tif *also* **leit•mo•tiv** (līt′mō-tēf′) *n.* Something, as a dominant theme in a novel, that is repeated over and over.

lek (lĕk) *n.* —See table at CURRENCY.

LEM (lĕm) *n.* A lunar excursion module.

lem•ming (lĕm′ĭng) *n.* A rodent of the genus *Lemmus* and related genera, of N regions, as *L. lemmus,* noted for its periodic mass migrations.

lem•on (lĕm′ən) *n.* **1.** A tree, *Citrus limonia,* cultivated for its yellow acidic juicy fruit. **2.** *Informal.* Something, as a television set or automobile, that proves to be defective or unsatisfactory.

lem•on•ade (lĕm′ə-nād′) *n.* A sweetened beverage of lemon juice and water.

lem•pi•ra (lĕm-pîr′ə) *n.* —See table at CURRENCY.

le•mur (lē′mər) *n.* Any of several arboreal primates of the family Lemuridae with soft fur, large eyes, and a long tail.

lemur

lend (lĕnd) *v.* **lent** (lĕnt), **lend•ing. 1.** To allow the temporary use of. **2.** To give out (money) for temporary use, usu. at interest. **3.** To furnish **:** provide. **4.** To offer (oneself) **:** accommodate. **—lend′er** *n.*

length (lĕngkth, lĕngth) *n.* **1.a.** The longest dimension of something. **b.** The measure of something on its longest dimension. **2.** A measured dimension or distance. **3.** Extent or duration. **4.** A measure of something used as a unit to estimate distances <an arm's *length*> **—length′y** *adj.*

length•en (lĕngk′thən, lĕng′-) *v.* To make or become longer.

length•wise (lĕngkth′wīz′, lĕngth′-) *adv. & adj.* Of or along the direction of the length **:** longitudinally.

le•ni•ent (lē′nē-ənt, lēn′yənt) *adj.* **1.** Inclined to be forgiving and mild **:** merciful. **2.** Not demanding **:** tolerant. **—le′ni•en•cy, le′ni•ence** *n.* **—le′ni•ent•ly** *adv.*

len•i•tive (lĕn′ĭ-tĭv) *adj.* Capable of easing pain or discomfort. **—len′i•tive** *n.*

lens (lĕnz) *n.* **1.** A curved piece of transparent material, as glass, that is used to refract light rays so that they converge or diverge to form an image. **2.** A combination of 2 or more lenses for forming an image for viewing or photographing. **3.** A transparent structure in the eye that focuses light rays entering through the pupil to form an image on the retina.

lent (lĕnt) *v. p.t. & p.p. of* LEND.

Lent (lĕnt) *n.* A 40-day period of fasting and penitence observed by many Christians from Ash Wednesday until Easter. **—Lent′en** *adj.*

▲ ***word history:*** The word *Lent* is derived from the Old English word *lencten,* which denoted both the season of spring and the ecclesiastical season. *Lencten* is ult. derived from the same root as the adjective *long.* The meaning "spring" probably arose because spring is the time of year when the days grow longer. The ecclesiastical sense developed from the fact that Lent partially coincides with spring.

len•til (lĕn′təl) *n.* A leguminous Old World plant, *Lens esculenta,* bearing pods that contain edible seeds.

Le•o (lē′ō) *n.* **1.** A constellation in the N Hemisphere. **2. a.** The 5th sign of the zodiac. **b.** One born under this sign.

le•one (lē-ōn′) *n.* —See table at CURRENCY.

le•o•nine (lē′ə-nīn′) *adj.* Of, pertaining to, or resembling a lion.

leop•ard (lĕp′ərd) *n.* A large feline mammal, *Panthera pardus,* of Africa and Asia, with a tawny coat with dark rosettelike markings.

le•o•tard (lē′ə-tärd′) *n.* A snug-fitting garment worn esp. by dancers.

lep•er (lĕp′ər) *n.* **1.** Someone suffering from leprosy. **2.** An outcast.

lep•re•chaun (lĕp′rĭ-kôn′, -kŏn′) *n.* A mischief-making elf of Irish folklore.

lep•ro•sy (lĕp′rə-sē) *n.* A chronic infectious bacterial disease marked by the progressive destruction of tissue. **—lep′rous** *adj.*

lep•ton (lĕp′tŏn′) *n., pl.* **-ta** (-tə). —See table at CURRENCY.

les•bi•an (lĕz′bē-ən) *n.* A woman who is a homosexual. **—les′bi•an** *adj.* **—les′bi•an•ism′** *n.*

lese maj•es•ty *also* **lèse ma•jes•té** (lĕz′-măj′ĭ-stē) *n.* An offense or crime against the ruler or supreme power of a state.

le•sion (lē′zhən) *n.* **1.** A wound **:** injury. **2.** A well-defined bodily area in which tissue has changed in a way that is characteristic of a disease.

less (lĕs) *adj.* **1.** Smaller. **2.** Of lower importance, degree, or rank. —*adv.* To a smaller extent, degree, or frequency. —*n.* A smaller amount. —*prep.* Subtracting **:** minus.

–less *suff.* Without **:** lacking <blame*less*> <wing*less*>

les•see (lĕ-sē′) *n.* One holding property under a lease.

less•en (lĕs′ən) *v.* To decrease or cause to decrease.

less•er (lĕs′ər) *adj.* Not as great in size or significance <a *lesser* benefit>

les•son (lĕs′ən) *n.* **1.** Something that is to be or has been learned. **2. a.** A period of instruction **:** class. **b.** A reading or exercise used to instruct. **3.** An edifying example. **4.** A passage from sacred writings that is read as part of a religious service.

les•sor (lĕs′ôr′, lĕ-sôr′) *n.* One who lets property by a lease.

lest (lĕst) *conj.* For fear that.

let[1] (lĕt) *v.* **let, let•ting. 1.** To give permission to **:** allow <wouldn't *let* him drive> **2.** To cause to **:** make <*Let* me hear from you soon.> **3.** To rent **:** lease. **—let down.** To disappoint. **—let on.** To allow to be known : reveal. **—let up. 1.** To become less : diminish. **2.** To be or become less strict or demanding.

let[2] (lĕt) *n.* **1.** An obstruction : obstacle. **2.** An invalid stroke in a net game, as tennis, that must be replayed.

let•down (lĕt′doun′) *n.* **1.** A decrease, as in effort or energy. **2.** A disappointment.

le•thal (lē′thəl) *adj.* Of, causing, or capable of causing death. **—le′thal•ly** *adv.*

leth•ar•gy (lĕth′ər-jē) *n.* **1.** Drowsiness. **2.** Indifference : apathy. **—le•thar′gic** (lə-thär′jĭk) *adj.* **—le•thar′gi•cal•ly** *adv.*

let's (lĕts). Let us.

Lett (lĕt) *n. & adj.* Latvian.

let•ter (lĕt′ər) *n.* **1.** A written symbol that represents a speech sound and constitutes an alphabetical unit. **2.** A printed or written communication sent to a recipient. **3.** The literal sense of something <the *letter* of the law> **4. letters. a.** Literature. **b.** Learning. *—v.* To mark or write with letters : inscribe. **—let′ter•er** *n.*

let•ter•head (lĕt′ər-hĕd′) *n.* **1.** A heading on a sheet of letter paper, usu. a name and address. **2.** Stationery printed or engraved with a letterhead.

let•ter-per•fect (lĕt′ər-pûr′fĭkt) *adj.* Absolutely correct : flawless.

let•ter•press (lĕt′ər-prĕs′) *n.* Printing in which a raised inked surface is pressed directly on paper.

let•ter-qual•i•ty (lĕt′ər-kwŏl′ĭ-tē) *adj.* Of or producing printed characters similar in clarity to those produced by a typewriter.

letters patent *pl.n.* A document granting a patentee exclusive right to the enjoyment or possession of an invention.

let•tuce (lĕt′əs) *n.* A plant of the genus *Lactuca,* esp. *L. sativa,* grown for its edible leaves that are used esp. in salads.

let•up (lĕt′ŭp′) *n.* **1.** Reduction, as in force or intensity : slowdown. **2.** A pause.

le•u (lē′o͞o) *n., pl.* **lei** (lā). —See table at CURRENCY.

leu•ke•mi•a (lo͞o-kē′mē-ə) *n.* Any of a group of usu. fatal diseases in which white blood cells proliferate in uncontrolled numbers. **—leu•ke′mic** *adj.*

leu•ko•cyte *also* **leu•co•cyte** (lo͞o′kə-sīt′) *n.* A white or colorless nucleated blood cell.

lev (lĕf) *n., pl.* **lev•a** (lĕv′ə). —See table at CURRENCY.

lev•ee[1] (lĕv′ē) *n.* An embankment built to prevent a body of water, esp. a river, from overflowing.

lev•ee[2] (lĕv′ē, lə-vē′, -vā′) *n.* **1.** A reception once held by a monarch or other high-ranking personage upon arising from bed. **2.** A formal reception, as at a court.

lev•el (lĕv′əl) *n.* **1.** Relative position, height, or rank on a scale. **2.** A standard elevation from which other heights and depths are measured. **3. a.** A horizontal line or plane at right angles to the plumb. **b.** The position or height of such a line or plane <ankle *level*> **4.** A flat, horizontal surface. **5.** A flat tract of land. **6.** A device for determining whether a surface is horizontal. *—adj.* **1.** Having no irregularities, roughness, or indentations. **2.** Horizontal. **3.** Of the same position, height, or rank as another. **4.** Consistent : uniform. **5.** Steady and reasonable in judgment. *—v.* **-eled, -el•ing** *or* **-elled, -el•ling. 1.** To make or become level or flat. **2.** To tear or knock down : raze. **3.** To equalize. **4.** To direct : aim. **—lev′el•er** *n.* **—lev′el•ly** *adv.* **—lev′el•ness** *n.*

lev•el•head•ed (lĕv′əl-hĕd′ĭd) *adj.* Having or showing common sense and good judgment : sensible. **—lev′el•head′ed•ness** *n.*

lev•er (lĕv′ər, lē′vər) *n.* **1.** A simple machine with a rigid body, usu. a metal bar, pivoted on a fixed fulcrum. **2.** A projecting handle for operating or adjusting a mechanism. **3.** A bar that is used to dislodge or pry something.

lev•er•age (lĕv′ər-ĭj, lē′vər-) *n.* **1. a.** The action of a lever. **b.** The mechanical advantage of a lever. **2.** Power to act effectively.

le•vi•a•than (lə-vī′ə-thən) *n.* **1.** A very large sea creature. **2.** Something of enormous size.

Le•vi's (lē′vīz′). A trademark for heavy denim trousers.

lev•i•tate (lĕv′ĭ-tāt′) *v.* **-tat•ed, -tat•ing.** To rise or raise in the air in apparent defiance of gravity. **—lev′i•ta′tion** *n.*

Le•vit•i•cus (lə-vĭt′ĭ-kəs) *n.* —See table at BIBLE.

lev•i•ty (lĕv′ĭ-tē) *n.* Lack of seriousness : frivolity.

lev•y (lĕv′ē) *v.* **-ied, -y•ing. 1.** To collect or impose (e.g., a tax). **2.** To draft for military service. **3.** To carry on (a war). **4.** To confiscate property to satisfy a legal claim. *—n.* **1.** The act or process of levying. **2.** An amount, as of money or property, levied. **3.** Troops that have been drafted for military service. **—lev′i•er** *n.*

lewd (lo͞od) *adj.* **1.** Preoccupied with sex : lustful. **2.** Indecent : obscene. **—lewd′ly** *adv.* **—lewd′ness** *n.*

▲ ***word history:*** A thousand years ago it was no disgrace to be a *lewd* person. The word *lewd,* from Old English *læwede,* orig. meant "lay, not belonging to the clergy." Each subsequent sense of *lewd* that developed, however, had a worse connotation than the preceding one. During Middle English times the word *lewd* ran the gamut of senses from "lay" through "unlearned," "low-class," "ignorant, ill-mannered," and "wicked" to "lascivious." The last sense is the only one that survives in Modern English.

lex•i•cog•ra•phy (lĕk′sĭ-kŏg′rə-fē) *n.* The work or process of writing, compiling, or editing dictionaries. **—lex′i•cog′ra•pher** *n.* **—lex′i•co•graph′ic** (-kə-grăf′ĭk), **lex′i•co•graph′i•cal** *adj.*

lex•i•con (lĕk′sĭ-kŏn′) *n.* **1.** A dictionary. **2.** A vocabulary, as of an individual or group. **—lex′i•cal** *adj.*

Li *symbol for* LITHIUM.

li•a•bil•i•ty (lī′ə-bĭl′ĭ-tē) *n., pl.* **-ties. 1.** The state of being liable. **2.** Something owed to another : debt. **3.** A handicap : disadvantage. **4.** A tendency : likelihood.

li•a•ble (lī'ə-bəl) *adj.* **1.** Legally obligated : responsible. **2.** Subject. **3.** Apt : likely <*liable* to be angry>

li•ai•son (lē'ā-zŏn', lē-ā'zŏn', lē'ə-) *n.* **1.** Communication, as between different units of an organization. **2.** A channel or means of communication. **3.** A close relationship : connection. **4.** An adulterous sexual relationship.

li•an•a (lē-ä'nə, -ăn'ə) *n.* Any climbing, woody, usu. tropical vine.

li•ar (lī'ər) *n.* Someone who tells lies.

lib (lĭb) *n. Informal.* Liberation.

li•ba•tion (lī-bā'shən) *n.* **1. a.** The act of pouring out a liquid as a religious offering. **b.** The liquid poured. **2.** *Informal.* A drink, esp. an alcoholic drink.

li•bel (lī'bəl) *n.* **1.** A written, printed, oral, or pictorial statement that damages by defaming a person's character or reputation. **2.** The act or tort of publishing or uttering a libel. —*v.* **-beled, -bel•ing** *or* **-belled, -bel•ling.** To make or publish a libel about. **—li'bel•ous** *adj.*

lib•er•al (lĭb'ər-əl, lĭb'rəl) *adj.* **1.** Generous. **2.** Abundant : ample. **3.** Not literal : loose. **4.** Of, pertaining to, or based on the liberal arts. **5.** Respectful of the ideas or behavior of others : tolerant. **6.** Favoring democratic reform and the use of governmental resources to effect social progress. **7. Liberal.** Of or belonging to a political party that advocates liberal views, esp. in the U.S., Great Britain, and Canada. —*n.* Someone who holds liberal opinions or ideas. **—lib'er•al•ism** *n.* **—lib'er•al'i•ty** (lĭb'ə-răl'ĭ-tē) *n.* **—lib'er•al•ize'** *v.* **—lib'er•al•ly** *adv.*

liberal arts *pl.n.* Academic disciplines, as languages, history, and philosophy, that provide general cultural information.

lib•er•ate (lĭb'ə-rāt') *v.* **-at•ed, -at•ing.** To set free, as from oppression, confinement, or foreign control. **—lib'er•a'tion** *n.* **—lib'er•a'tor** *n.*

lib•er•tar•i•an (lĭb'ər-târ'ē-ən) *n.* **1.** A believer in freedom of thought and action. **2.** A believer in free will.

lib•er•tine (lĭb'ər-tēn') *n.* A morally unrestrained, dissolute person. **—lib'er•tine'** *adj.* **—lib'er•tin•ism** *n.*

lib•er•ty (lĭb'ər-tē) *n., pl.* **-ties. 1.** The state of being free : freedom. **2.** Permission : authorization. **3.** *often* **liberties.** A disrespectful course of action, esp. unwarranted familiarity. **4.** An authorized leave from naval duty. ★ ***syns:*** FREEDOM, LATITUDE, LEEWAY, LICENSE

li•bi•do (lĭ-bē'dō, -bī'-) *n., pl.* **-dos. 1.** Psychic energy that is associated with instinctual biological drives. **2.** Sexual desire. **—li•bid'i•nal** (lə-bĭd'n-əl) *adj.* **—li•bid'i•nous** (-əs) *adj.*

Li•bra (lī'brə, lē'-) *n.* **1.** A constellation in the S Hemisphere. **2. a.** The 7th sign of the zodiac. **b.** One born under this sign.

li•brar•i•an (lī-brâr'ē-ən) *n.* Someone who specializes in library work.

li•brar•y (lī'brĕr'ē) *n., pl.* **-ies. 1.** A place in which literary and artistic materials, as books and periodicals, are kept for reading, reference, or borrowing. **2.** A collection of reading materials.

li•bret•to (lĭ-brĕt'ō) *n., pl.* **-bret•tos** *or* **-bret•ti** (-brĕt'ē). **1.** The text of a dramatic musical work, esp. of an opera. **2.** A book containing a libretto. **—li•bret'tist** *n.*

lice (līs) *n. pl. of* LOUSE.

li•cence (lī'səns) *n. esp. Brit. var. of* LICENSE.

li•cense (lī'səns) *n.* **1. a.** Permission, esp. legal permission to operate or own a specified thing. **b.** Proof, usu. in the form of a document, card, plate, or tag, that a license has been granted. **2.** Latitude of action, esp. when used without restraint. —*v.* **-censed, -cens•ing.** To grant a license to or for. **—li'cens•ee'** *n.* **—li'cens•er** *n.*

li•cen•ti•ate (lī-sĕn'shē-ĭt) *n.* A person who is granted a license by an authorized body to practice a specified profession.

li•cen•tious (lī-sĕn'shəs) *adj.* Lacking in moral restraint : immoral. **—li•cen'tious•ly** *adv.* **—li•cen'tious•ness** *n.*

li•chee (lē'chē) *n. var. of* LITCHI.

li•chen (lī'kən) *n.* Any of numerous plants consisting of a fungus, usu. of the class Ascomycetes, closely combined with certain of the green or blue-green algae to form a crustlike, scaly, or branching growth on rocks and tree trunks. **—li'chened** *adj.* **—li'chen•ous** *adj.*

lic•it (lĭs'ĭt) *adj.* Lawful.

lick (lĭk) *v.* **1.** To pass the tongue along. **2.** To move unsteadily over like a tongue. **3.** *Slang.* **a.** To thrash. **b.** To defeat. —*n.* **1.** An act or process of licking. **2.** A small quantity : bit. **3.** An exposed salt deposit that is licked by animals. **4.** A blow.

lick•e•ty-split (lĭk'ĭ-tē-splĭt') *adv. Informal.* Very rapidly.

lick•spit•tle (lĭk'spĭt'l) *n.* A fawning underling : toady.

lic•o•rice (lĭk'ər-ĭs, -ĭsh) *n.* **1.** A plant, *Glycyrrhiza glabra,* with blue flowers and a sweet root used esp. to flavor medicines and candy. **2.** A confection made from or flavored with licorice root.

lid (lĭd) *n.* **1.** A hinged or removable cover for a container. **2.** An eyelid. **3.** *Slang.* A hat. **—lid'ded** *adj.* **—lid'less** *adj.*

lie[1] (lī) *v.* **lay** (lā), **lain** (lān), **ly•ing. 1.** To be in, remain in, or take a horizontal or recumbent position : recline. **2.** To be or stay in a particular condition. **3.** To be located. **4.** To extend. —*n.* The position in which something is located or situated.

lie[2] (lī) *n.* An untrue statement made deliberately : falsehood. ★ ***syns:*** CANARD, FALSEHOOD, FALSITY, FIB, PREVARICATION, STORY, TALE, UNTRUTH —*v.* **lied, ly•ing. 1.** To tell a lie. **2.** To give a false impression.

lied (lēd, lēt) *n., pl.* **lie•der** (lē'dər). A German art song.

lief (lēf) *adv.* Willingly : readily.

liege (lēj) *n.* **1.** A feudal lord. **2.** A vassal. —*adj.* Faithful : loyal.

lien (lēn, lē'ən) *n.* The legal right to take and hold or sell the property of another to satisfy an obligation or debt.

lieu (lo͞o) *n. Archaic.* Place : stead. **—in lieu of.** In place of.

lieu•ten•ant (lo͞o-tĕn'ənt) *n.* **1.** An officer in the U.S. Army, Air Force, and Marine Corps ranking below a captain. **2.** An officer in the U.S. Navy ranking above an ensign and below a lieutenant commander. **3.** An officer ranking below a captain in a police or fire department. **4.** Someone authorized to act in place of another : deputy. **—lieu•ten'an•cy** *n.*

lieutenant colonel *n.* An officer in the U.S. Army, Air Force, and Marine Corps ranking above a major and below a colonel.

lieutenant commander *n.* An officer in the U.S. Navy ranking above a lieutenant and below a commander.

lieutenant general *n.* An officer in the U.S. Army, Air Force, and Marine Corps ranking above a major and below a general.

lieutenant governor *n.* **1.** An elected official ranking just below the governor of a U.S. state. **2.** *Can.* The nonelective chief of government of a province.

life (līf) *n., pl.* **lives** (līvz). **1.** The property or quality by which living organisms are distinguished from dead organisms or inanimate matter, esp. as shown in the ability to grow, carry on metabolism, respond to stimuli, and reproduce. **2.** Living organisms as a whole <animal *life*> **3.** A human being. **4.** The period of time between an organism's birth or inception and its death : lifetime. **5.** A biography. **6.** Animate and esp. human activities. **7.** A manner of living. **8.** Animation : vitality. ★ *syns:* DURATION, EXISTENCE, LIFETIME, TERM **—life'less** *adj.* **—life'like'** *adj.*

life•blood (līf'blŭd') *n.* An indispensable source of vitality or life.

life•boat (līf'bōt') *n.* A boat used esp. for rescue at sea.

life•guard (līf'gärd') *n.* An expert swimmer hired to safeguard other swimmers, as at a beach.

life line *also* **life•line** (līf'līn') *n.* **1.** A line to which a drowning or falling victim may cling. **2.** A means or route for transporting indispensable supplies. **3.** A source of salvation in a crisis.

life•long (līf'lông', -lŏng') *adj.* Continuing throughout a lifetime.

life preserver *n.* A buoyant device, as one in the shape of a ring, used to keep a person afloat in water.

lif•er (lī'fər) *n. Slang.* **1.** A prisoner serving a life sentence. **2.** A career military officer or enlisted person.

life raft *n.* A raft usu. of wood or inflatable material used by people who have been forced into water by emergency.

life•sav•er (līf'sā'vər) *n.* **1.** One that saves a life. **2.** A lifeguard. **3.** A life preserver shaped like a ring. **4.** One that provides help in a crisis or emergency. **—life'sav'ing** *n. & adj.*

life•style *also* **life-style** *or* **life style** (līf'stīl') *n.* A way of life that reflects an individual's preferences or values.

life•time (līf'tīm') *n.* The period during which an individual lives or exists.

life•work (līf'wûrk') *n.* The primary work of a person's lifetime.

lift (lĭft) *v.* **1. a.** To elevate : raise. **b.** To rise : ascend. **2.** To bring to an end : stop. **3.** To repay (a debt). **—lift off.** To begin flight, as a spacecraft. *—n.* **1.** The act or process of lifting. **2.** Force or power available for lifting <the *lift* of a derrick> **3.** A load. **4.** The extent or height to which something is lifted. **5.** An elevation of spirits. **6.** A device or machine designed to pick up, raise, or carry something. **7.** *esp. Brit.* An elevator. **8.** A ride in a vehicle along the way to a destination. **9.** The component of the total aerodynamic force acting on an airfoil or aircraft that is exerted in an upward direction opposing the pull of gravity. **—lift'er** *n.*

lift•off (lĭft'ôf', -ŏf') *n.* The vertical takeoff or moment of takeoff of an aircraft and esp. of a rocket.

lig•a•ment (lĭg'ə-mənt) *n.* A band of tough, fibrous tissue joining bones or cartilages or holding a body organ in place. **—lig'a•men'tous** *adj.*

li•gate (lī'gāt') *v.* **-gat•ed, -gat•ing.** To tie or bind with a ligature.

lig•a•ture (lĭg'ə-cho͝or', -chər) *n.* **1.** Something, as a cord or wire, that ties or binds. **2.** A thread used in surgery for tying blood vessels. **3.** A printing character, as *fi,* that combines 2 or more letters.

light[1] (līt) *n.* **1.** Electromagnetic radiation that can be perceived by the normal, unaided human eye and has wavelengths between 3,900 and 7,700 angstroms. **2.** Brightness. **3.** A source of light, as an electric lamp. **4.** The illumination from a source of light. **5.** Daylight. **6.** Daybreak : dawn. **7.** A source of fire, as a match. **8.** A way of looking at or considering something. **9.** Enlightenment : understanding. **10.** A prominent person. **11.** A device, esp. a traffic signal, that uses light as a warning. *—adj.* **1.** Not dark : bright. **2.** Mixed with white : pale <a *light* green> *—v.* **light•ed** *or* **lit** (lĭt), **light•ing.** **1.** To set or be set on fire : ignite. **2.** To provide with or cause to give out light : illuminate. **—light'ness** *n.*

light[2] (līt) *adj.* **1.** Not heavy. **2.** Of less force, quantity, intensity, or volume than usual or normal <a *light* tap on the arm><*light* snow> **3.** Intended as entertainment : not profound. **4.** Free from worries, cares, or troubles <a *light* spirit> **5.** Frivolous : trivial. **6.** Requiring little exertion or effort <*light* office duties> **7.** Agile : nimble. **8.** Dizzy. *—adv.* **1.** In a light manner : lightly. **2.** With little luggage <traveling *light*> *—v.* **light•ed** *or* **lit** (lĭt), **light•ing.** **1.** To come to rest : settle, alight, or land. **2.** To come unexpectedly. **—light out.** To leave hastily. **—light'ly** *adv.* **—light'ness** *n.*

light bulb *n.* An incandescent lamp or its glass housing.
light•en[1] (līt'n) *v.* To make or become light or lighter : brighten. —**light'en•er** *n.*
light•en[2] (līt'n) *v.* **1.** To make or become less heavy. **2.** To make or become less troublesome, oppressive, or severe.
light•er[1] (lī'tər) *n.* A mechanical device used to light a cigarette, cigar, or pipe.
light•er[2] (lī'tər) *n.* A barge used esp. to load and unload a cargo ship.
light•face (līt'fās') *n.* A typeface with thin, light lines. —**light'faced'** *adj.*
light-fin•gered (līt'fĭng'gərd) *adj.* Skilled at petty thievery.
light•head•ed (līt'hĕd'ĭd) *adj.* **1.** Dizzy. **2.** Not serious : frivolous.
light•heart•ed (līt'här'tĭd) *adj.* Free from trouble, anxiety, or care : cheerful. —**light'heart'ed•ly** *adv.* —**light'heart'ed•ness** *n.*
light•house (līt'hous') *n.* A structure with a powerful light to guide sailors.
light•ning (līt'nĭng) *n.* The flash of light that accompanies a high-tension natural electric discharge in the atmosphere. —*adj.* Very fast or sudden.
lightning bug *n.* A firefly.
lightning rod *n.* A grounded metal rod positioned high on a structure to protect it from lightning.
light opera *n.* An operetta.
lights (līts) *pl.n.* The lungs, esp. the lungs of an animal used for food.
light•ship (līt'shĭp') *n.* A ship with a powerful light or horn that is anchored in dangerous waters to warn other vessels.
light show *n.* A display of colored lights in kaleidoscopic patterns, often accompanied by film loops and slides.
light•weight (līt'wāt') *n.* **1.** One that weighs relatively little. **2.** A boxer or wrestler whose weight is between 127 and 135 lb. **3.** Someone of little consequence. —**light'weight'** *adj.*
light-year *also* **light year** (līt'yîr') *n.* A measure equal to the distance light travels in a year, approx. 5.88 trillion mi, or 9.46 trillion km.
lig•ne•ous (lĭg'nē-əs) *adj.* WOODY 1, 2.
lig•ni•fy (lĭg'nə-fī') *v.* **-fied, -fy•ing.** To make or become woody or woodlike.
lig•nite (lĭg'nīt') *n.* A low- grade, brownish-black soft coal.
lig•ro•in (lĭg'rō-ĭn) *n.* A volatile, flammable fraction of petroleum obtained by distillation and used as a solvent.
lik•a•ble *also* **like•a•ble** (lī'kə-bəl) *adj.* Capable of being liked : pleasing.
†**like[1]** (līk) *v.* **liked, lik•ing. 1.** To find attractive or pleasant : enjoy < *likes* apples> **2.** To want : wish <Do as you *like.*> **3.** To be fond of. **4.** *Regional.* To be pleasing to. ★ ***syns:*** ENJOY, RELISH, SAVOR —*n.* Something one enjoys : preference.
like[2] (līk) *prep.* **1.** Similar or similarly to. **2.** Characteristic of. **3.** Disposed to <feels *like* quitting> **4.** Such as <artists *like* painters and sculptors> —*adj.* Being the same or almost the same : similar. ★ ***syns:*** ALIKE, ANALOGOUS, COMPARABLE, EQUIVALENT, PARALLEL, UNIFORM —*n.* Something similar or related. —*conj.* In the same way that : as <can't cook *like* she does>
–like *suff.* Resembling : characteristic of <child*like*><shell-*like*>
like•li•hood (līk'lē-ho͝od') *n.* Probability.
like•ly (līk'lē) *adj.* **-li•er, -li•est. 1.** Probable : apt <*likely* to fail> **2.** Believable : credible <a *likely* explanation> **3.** Apt to succeed or yield a desired result : promising <a *likely* theory> —*adv.* Probably.
like-mind•ed (līk'mīn'dĭd) *adj.* Of the same mind or way of thinking.
lik•en (lī'kən) *v.* To see or describe as being like : compare.
like•ness (līk'nĭs) *n.* **1.** Resemblance. **2.** Appearance : semblance. **3.** A copy : image.
like•wise (līk'wīz') *adv.* **1.** In a similar way. **2.** As well : also.
lik•ing (lī'kĭng) *n.* **1.** A feeling of approval or fondness. **2.** Preference : taste.
li•ku•ta (lē-ko͞o'tä) *n., pl.* **ma•ku•ta** (mä-). —See table at CURRENCY.
li•lac (lī'lək, -lŏk', -lăk') *n.* **1.** A shrub, *Syringa vulgaris,* widely grown for its large fragrant purplish or white flower clusters. **2.** A pale purple. —**li'lac** *adj.*
li•lan•ge•ni (lĭ-läng'gĕ-nē) *n.* —See table at CURRENCY.
Lil•li•pu•tian *also* **lil•li•pu•tian** (lĭl'ə-pyo͞o'shən) *n.* A very small being or person. —*adj.* Tiny : diminutive.
lilt (lĭlt) *n.* **1.** A light, cheerful tune or song. **2.** A rhythmical way of speaking.
lil•y (lĭl'ē) *n., pl.* **-ies. 1.** Any of various plants of the genus *Lilium,* often bearing trumpet-shaped flowers. **2.** A plant similar or related to the lily, as the water lily.
lil•y-liv•ered (lĭl'ē-lĭv'ərd) *adj.* Timid : cowardly.
lily of the valley *n., pl.* **lilies of the valley.** A widely cultivated plant, *Convallaria majalis,* bearing fragrant, bell-shaped white flowers on a leafless raceme.
li•ma bean (lī'mə) *n.* Any of several varieties of a tropical American plant, *Phaseolus limensis,* bearing flat pods with light-green edible seeds.
limb (lĭm) *n.* **1.** A large bough of a tree : branch. **2.** An animal's jointed appendage used for locomotion or grasping, as an arm, leg, wing, or flipper.
lim•ber (lĭm'bər) *adj.* **1.** Bending easily : pliable. **2.** Moving nimbly and easily : agile. —*v.* To make or become limber. —**lim'ber•ly** *adv.* —**lim'ber•ness** *n.*
lim•bo (lĭm'bō) *n., pl.* **-bos. 1.** *often* **Limbo.** *Theol.* The abode of souls kept from entering Heaven by such circumstances as failure to be baptized. **2.** A place or condition of oblivion or neglect.
Lim•burg•er (lĭm'bûr'gər) *n.* A soft white cheese with a very strong odor and flavor.
lime[1] (līm) *n.* A spiny tree, *Citrus aurantifo-*

lia, native to Asia, with evergreen leaves, fragrant white flowers, and edible egg-shaped fruit, with a green rind and acid juice.

lime² (līm) *n.* Any of several Old World linden trees.

lime³ (līm) *n.* **1.** Calcium oxide. **2.** Birdlime. —*v.* **limed, lim•ing.** To treat or mark with lime. —**lim'y** *adj.*

lime•ade (lī-mād') *n.* A sweetened beverage of lime juice and water.

lime•kiln (līm'kĭl', -kĭln') *n.* A furnace for reducing naturally occurring forms of calcium carbonate to lime.

lime•light (līm'līt') *n.* **1.** A stage light in which lime is heated to incandescence producing brilliant illumination. **2.** A focus of public attention.

lim•er•ick (lĭm'ər-ĭk) *n.* A humorous verse of 5 lines usu. with the rhyme scheme *aabba.*

lime•stone (līm'stōn') *n.* A form of sedimentary rock that is composed mainly of calcium carbonate and is used in building and in making lime and cement.

lim•it (lĭm'ĭt) *n.* **1.** The point beyond which something may not or cannot proceed. **2. a.** A boundary. **b. limits.** Bounds. **3.** The greatest or smallest amount or number. —*v.* To place a limit on **:** confine or restrict. —**lim'i•ta'tion** *n.* —**lim'it•less** *adj.* —**lim'it•less•ly** *adv.*

lim•it•ed (lĭm'ĭ-tĭd) *adj.* **1.** Restricted or confined within limits. **2.** Of or indicating trains or buses that make few stops and provide fast service.

limn (lĭm) *v.* **limned, limn•ing** (lĭm'nĭng). **1.** To describe. **2.** To depict by drawing or painting. —**limn'er** (lĭm'nər) *n.*

lim•o (lĭm'ō) *n., pl.* **lim•os.** *Informal.* A limousine.

lim•ou•sine (lĭm'ə-zēn', lĭm'ə-zēn') *n.* **1.** A luxurious large automobile, often driven by a chauffeur. **2.** A small bus used to carry passengers esp. to airports and hotels.

limp (lĭmp) *v.* **1.** To walk lamely. **2.** To proceed in an unsteady or unpredictable way. —*n.* A jerky, irregular, or awkward gait. —*adj.* **1.** Lacking or having lost rigidity **:** flabby. **2.** Not firm or strong **:** weak. —**limp'ly** *adv.* —**limp'ness** *n.*

lim•pet (lĭm'pĭt) *n.* Any of numerous marine gastropod mollusks, esp. of the families Acmaeidae and Patellidae, that have a conical shell and adhere to tidal rocks.

lim•pid (lĭm'pĭd) *adj.* Transparently clear. —**lim•pid'i•ty** *n.* —**lim'pid•ly** *adv.*

lin•age (lī'nĭj) *n.* The number of lines in a piece of printed or written matter.

linch•pin (lĭnch'pĭn') *n.* A locking pin inserted through a shaft, as of an axle, to keep a wheel from slipping off.

lin•den (lĭn'dən) *n.* Any of various shade trees of the genus *Tilia,* having heart-shaped leaves and yellow flowers.

line¹ (līn) *n.* **1.** A path taken by a point that is free to move <a straight *line*> <a *curved line*> **2.** A thin, continuous mark, as that made by a pen applied to a surface. **3. a.** A boundary **:** border. **b.** A limit. **4.** A contour. **5.** A cable, string, rope, cord, or wire. **6.** An electric cable. **7.** A telephone connection. **8.** A transportation system. **9. a.** A course of action, behavior, or thought. **b.** A course taken by something in motion. **10.** A general manner or method. **11.** Alignment. **12.** An occupation or trade. **13.** A group arranged in a sequence, row, or series. **14.** A horizontal row of written or printed words. **15.** A brief letter **:** note. **16. lines.** The dialogue of a dramatic work. **17.** *Football.* **a.** A line of scrimmage. **b.** The linemen. ★ ***syns:*** COLUMN, FILE, QUEUE, RANK, ROW, STRING —*v.* **lined, lin•ing. 1.** To incise or mark with lines. **2.** To place in or form a line (along). —**line up. 1.** To align. **2.** To secure and make available <*lined up* a group to help>

line² (līn) *v.* **lined, lin•ing. 1.** To cover the inner surface of. **2.** To fill generously, as with money or food.

lin•e•age (lĭn'ē-ĭj) *n.* Direct descent from an ancestor **:** ancestry.

lin•e•al (lĭn'ē-əl) *adj.* **1.** Belonging to, consisting of, or being in a direct line of descent from an ancestor. **2.** Linear.

lin•e•a•ment (lĭn'ē-ə-mənt) *n.* A distinctive contour, shape, or feature of the body and esp. of the face.

lin•e•ar (lĭn'ē-ər) *adj.* **1.** Of, pertaining to, consisting of, or resembling a line. **2.** Long and narrow.

linear perspective *n.* A technique in painting and drawing in which parallel lines con-

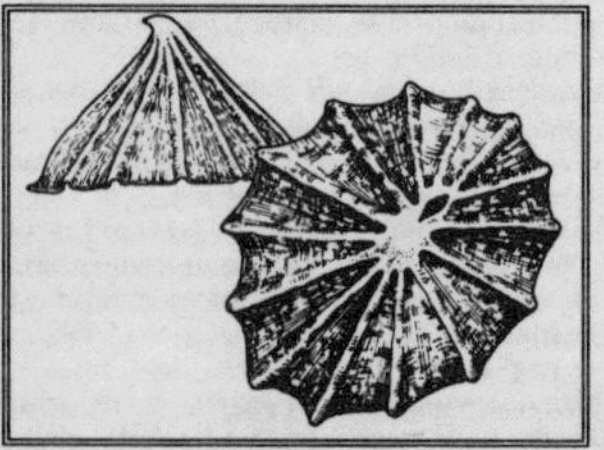

limpet

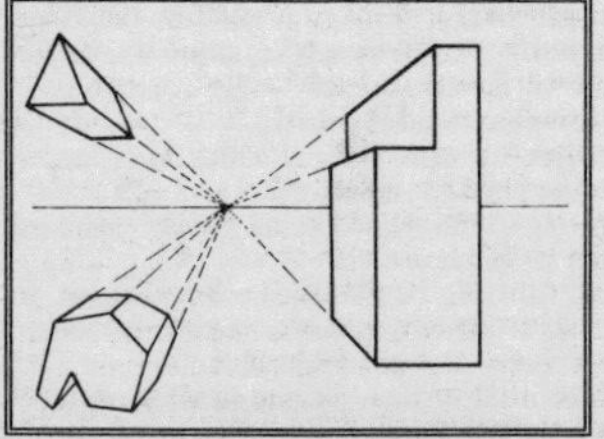

linear perspective

verge so as to give the illusion of depth and distance.

line·back·er (līn′băk′ər) *n. Football.* One of the defensive players positioned immediately behind the line of scrimmage.

line drive *n. Baseball.* A hard-hit ball whose path approximates a straight line nearly parallel with the ground.

line·man (līn′mən) *n.* **1.** Someone who installs or repairs electric power or communication lines. **2.** A player on the forward line of a team, esp. in football.

lin·en (lĭn′ən) *n.* **1.** Thread, yarn, or fabric made of flax. **2.** *often* **linens.** Household articles, as sheets, made of linen or similar fabric. **—lin′en** *adj.*

line of scrimmage *n. Football.* An imaginary line across the field where the ball is positioned for each play.

line printer *n.* A high-speed printer that prints each line of type as a unit instead of printing each character individually.

lin·er¹ (lī′nər) *n.* A ship or airplane that carries passengers on a regular route.

lin·er² (lī′nər) *n.* One that lines or serves as a lining.

line score *n. Baseball.* A record of the runs, hits, and errors of each inning of a game.

lines·man (līnz′mən) *n.* **1.** *Football.* An official who marks the downs. **2.** An official in a court game, as tennis, who calls shots that fall out of bounds. **3.** LINEMAN 1.

line-up *also* **line·up** (līn′ŭp′) *n.* **1.** A line of persons, esp. suspects, formed for inspection or identification. **2.** The members of a team who take part in a game.

ling (lĭng) *n., pl.* **ling** *or* **lings.** Any of various marine food fishes related to or resembling the cod.

lin·ger (lĭng′gər) *v.* **1.** To stay as if reluctant to leave : tarry. **2.** To persist. **3.** To be slow in acting : procrastinate. **—lin′ger·er** *n.* **—lin′ger·ing·ly** *adv.*

lin·ge·rie (län′zhə-rē′, län′zhə-rā′) *n.* Women's underwear.

lin·go (lĭng′gō) *n., pl.* **-goes.** Language that is unfamiliar or unintelligible.

lin·gua fran·ca (lĭng′gwə frăng′kə) *n.* A language used for communication between persons who speak different languages.

lin·guist (lĭng′gwĭst) *n.* **1.** A fluent speaker of several languages. **2.** One who specializes in linguistics.

lin·guis·tics (lĭng-gwĭs′tĭks) *n. (sing. in number).* The study of the nature and structure of human speech. **—lin·guis′tic** *adj.* **—lin·guis′ti·cal·ly** *adv.*

lin·i·ment (lĭn′ə-mənt) *n.* A liquid medicine applied to the skin.

lin·ing (lī′nĭng) *n.* Material used to cover or coat an inside surface.

link (lĭngk) *n.* **1.** One of the rings forming a chain. **2.** Something that is like a link <a sausage *link*>. **3.** A bond : tie. **4.** A cuff link. —*v.* To connect or become connected by or as if by a link or links.

link·age (lĭng′kĭj) *n.* **1. a.** The act or process of linking. **b.** The state of being linked. **2.** A system of connecting structures.

links (lĭngks) *pl.n.* A golf course.

lin·net (lĭn′ĭt) *n.* A small Old World songbird, *Acanthis cannabina.*

li·no·le·um (lĭ-nō′lē-əm) *n.* A floor and counter-top covering consisting of a surface of hardened linseed oil and a filler, as powdered cork, on a canvas or burlap backing.

lin·seed (lĭn′sēd′) *n.* The seeds of flax, which are the source of an oil used in paints and varnishes.

lin·sey-wool·sey (lĭn′zē-wo͝ol′zē) *n.* A linen or cotton fabric woven with wool.

lint (lĭnt) *n.* **1.** Fine bits of fiber and fluff : fuzz. **2.** Downy material scraped from linen and used to dress wounds.

lin·tel (lĭn′tl) *n.* A horizontal beam across the top of a door or window that supports the weight of the structure above it.

li·on (lī′ən) *n.* **1.** A large carnivorous feline mammal, *Panthera leo,* of Africa and India, with a short tawny coat and a long, heavy mane in the male. **2.** A person of great importance or prestige. **—li′on·ess** *n.*

li·on·heart·ed (lī′ən-här′tĭd) *adj.* Extremely courageous.

li·on·ize (lī′ə-nīz′) *v.* **-ized, -iz·ing.** To treat (a person) as a celebrity.

lip (lĭp) *n.* **1. a.** *Anat.* Either of the 2 fleshy, muscular folds that surround the opening of the mouth. **b.** A part or structure that resembles a lip. **2.** A rim or margin, as of a bell, vessel, or crater. **3.** *Slang.* Impudent talk.

lip·o·suc·tion (lĭp′ō-sŭk′shən, lī′pō-) *n.* A surgical procedure that uses suction to remove excess fat from an area of the body.

lip reading *n.* A technique for interpreting unheard speech by watching a speaker's lip and facial movements. **—lip′-read′** *v.* **—lip reader** *n.*

lip service *n.* An expression of acquiescence or allegiance that is not acted upon.

lip·stick (lĭp′stĭk′) *n.* A stick of waxy lip coloring enclosed in a cylindrical case.

lip-synch *also* **lip-sync** (lĭp′sĭngk′) *v.* **-synched, -synch·ing** *also* **-synced, -sync·ing.** To move the lips in synchronization with recorded speech or song.

liq·ue·fy *also* **liq·ui·fy** (lĭk′wə-fī′) *v.* **-fied, -fy·ing.** To make or become liquid. **—liq′ue·fac′tion** *n.* **—liq′ue·fi′er** *n.*

li·queur (lĭ-kûr′, -kyo͝or′) *n.* A sweet alcoholic beverage flavored with aromatic ingredients : cordial.

liq·uid (lĭk′wĭd) *n.* A substance that flows readily and is difficult to compress. —*adj.* **1.** Of or being a liquid. **2.** Liquefied, esp.: **a.** Melted by heating <*liquid* butter> **b.** Condensed by cooling <*liquid* nitrogen> **3.** Easily converted into or being cash <*liquid* assets> **4.** Shining and clear <*liquid* eyes> **5.** Flowing readily. **—li·quid′i·ty** *n.*

liq·ui·date (lĭk′wĭ-dāt′) *v.* **-dat·ed, -dat·ing.** **1.** To repay (e.g., a debt) : settle. **2.** To close down (e.g., a business firm) by settling accounts and dividing up assets. **3.** To put an end to, esp. to kill. **—liq′ui•da′tion** *n.* **—liq′ui•da′tor** *n.*

liq•uid-crys•tal display (lĭk′wĭd-krĭs′təl) *n.* An alphanumeric display in which a normally transparent liquid forms opaque patterns when an electric field is applied.

liq•uor (lĭk′ər) *n.* **1.** A distilled alcoholic beverage. **2.** A liquid solution or substance.

li•ra (lîr′ə, lē′rə) *n., pl.* **li•re** (lîr′ā, lē′rā) *or* **li•ras.** —See table at CURRENCY.

li•sen•te (lē-sĕn′tā) *n. pl. of* SENTE.

lisle (līl) *n.* A fine, tightly twisted strong cotton thread.

lisp (lĭsp) *n.* A speech defect or mannerism marked by the pronunciation of *s* and *z* as (th) and (*th*). **—lisp** *v.* **—lisp′er** *n.*

lis•some (lĭs′əm) *adj.* Supple : lithe. **—lis′some•ly** *adv.* **—lis′some•ness** *n.*

list[1] (lĭst) *n.* **1.** A series of numbers or words, as the names of persons. **2.** A catalogue : index. —*v.* **1.** To itemize. **2.** To enter on a list : register.

list[2] (lĭst) *n.* A tilt to one side, as of a ship. —*v.* To tilt or cause to tilt.

list[3] (lĭst) *v. Archaic.* To listen or listen to.

lis•ten (lĭs′ən) *v.* **1.** To try to hear. **2.** To pay heed. **—lis′ten•er** *n.*

list•ing (lĭs′tĭng) *n.* **1.** A list. **2.** Something that is entered in a list.

list•less (lĭst′lĭs) *adj.* Lacking energy, spirit, or enthusiasm : lethargic. **—list′less•ly** *adv.* **—list′less•ness** *n.*

list price *n.* An advertised or published price that is often subject to discount.

lists (lĭsts) *pl.n.* **1.** An arena for tournaments, esp. jousting. **2.** A place of combat. **3.** An area of controversy.

lit (lĭt) *v. var. p.t. & p.p. of* LIGHT.

lit•a•ny (lĭt′n-ē) *n., pl.* **-nies. 1.** A prayer in which phrases recited by a leader alternate with answers from a congregation. **2.** A repetitive recital or list.

li•tchi *also* **li•chee** (lē′chē) *n.* **1.** A Chinese tree, *Litchi chinensis,* bearing edible fruit. **2.** The fruit of the litchi tree.

li•ter (lē′tər) *n.* —See table at MEASUREMENT.

lit•er•al (lĭt′ər-əl) *adj.* **1.** Conforming to or in accordance with the exact meaning of a word. **2.** Word for word : verbatim. **3.** Concerned primarily with facts : prosaic. **4.** Without embellishment or exaggeration. **—lit′er•al•ly** *adv.* **—lit′er•al•ness** *n.*

lit•er•al•ism (lĭt′ər-ə-lĭz′əm) *n.* **1.** Adherence to the explicit sense of a given doctrine or text. **2.** Literal portrayal : realism. **—lit′er•al•ist** *n.* **—lit′er•al•is′tic** *adj.*

lit•er•ar•y (lĭt′ə-rĕr′ē) *adj.* **1.** Of or pertaining to literature. **2.** Appropriate to or used in literature. **3.** Knowledgeable in literature. **—lit′er•ar′i•ly** *adv.*

lit•er•ate (lĭt′ər-ĭt) *adj.* **1.** Having the ability to read and write. **2.** Having or showing skill in using words. **3.** Knowledgeable : educated. **—lit′er•a•cy** *n.* **—lit′er•ate** *n.*

lit•er•a•ti (lĭt′ə-rä′tē) *pl.n.* The intelligentsia, esp. distinguished writers.

lit•er•a•tim (lĭt′ə-rā′tĭm, -rä′-) *adv.* Letter for letter : literally.

lit•er•a•ture (lĭt′ər-ə-cho͝or′, -chər) *n.* **1.** Writing of lasting value and excellence. **2.** Written works in verse or prose. **3.** Printed matter, as circulars for a political campaign.

lithe (līth, līth) *adj.* **lith•er, lith•est.** Bending easily : resilient : supple. **—lithe′ly** *adv.* **—lithe′ness** *n.*

lithe•some (līth′səm, līth′-) *adj.* Lithe.

lith•i•um (lĭth′ē-əm) *n. Symbol* **Li** A soft, silvery-white metallic element.

li•thog•ra•phy (lĭ-thŏg′rə-fē) *n.* A printing process in which a flat surface, as stone or sheet aluminum, is treated so that the ink adheres only to the portions that are to be printed. **—lith′o•graph′** (lĭth′ə-grăf′) *n.* & *v.* **—li•thog′ra•pher** *n.* **—lith′o•graph′ic, lith′o•graph′i•cal** *adj.*

li•thol•o•gy (lĭ-thŏl′ə-jē) *n.* The microscopic study, description, and classification of rocks. **—li•thol′o•gist** *n.*

lith•o•sphere (lĭth′ə-sfîr′) *n.* The solid outer part of the earth.

lit•i•gate (lĭt′ĭ-gāt′) *v.* **-gat•ed, -gat•ing.** To engage in or make the subject of legal proceedings. **—lit′i•gant** *n.* **—lit′i•ga′tion** *n.* **—lit′i•ga′tor** *n.*

li•ti•gious (lĭ-tĭj′əs) *adj.* **1.** Of or pertaining to litigation. **2.** Given to engaging in litigation. **—li•ti′gious•ness** *n.*

lit•mus (lĭt′məs) *n.* A blue powder obtained from certain lichens that changes to red with increasing acidity and to blue with increasing alkalinity.

litmus paper *n.* White paper treated with litmus and used as an acid-base indicator.

li•tre (lī′tər) *n. esp. Brit. var. of* LITER.

lit•ter (lĭt′ər) *n.* **1.** A couch, often with a canopy, that is mounted on shafts and used to carry a single passenger. **2.** A stretcher for carrying a sick or wounded person. **3.** Material, as straw, that is used as bedding for animals. **4.** The young produced at one birth by a multiparous mammal. **5.** An accumulation of waste material : rubbish. —*v.* **1.** To give birth to a litter. **2.** To scatter litter (about). **—lit′ter•er** *n.*

lit•ter•bug (lĭt′ər-bŭg′) *n. Informal.* One who litters a public area, as a park.

lit•tle (lĭt′l) *adj.* **lit•tler** *or* **less** (lĕs), **lit•tlest** *or* **least** (lēst) . **1.** Not large : small. **2.** Not very much <*little* time><*little* money> **3.** Not significant : unimportant. **4.** Narrow : petty. ★ ***syns:*** BANTAM, PETITE, SMALL —*adv.* **less, least.** Not much : hardly. —*n.* **1.** A small quantity or amount. **2.** A short distance or time. **—lit′tle•ness** *n.*

Little Dipper *n.* Ursa Minor.

lit•to•ral (lĭt′ər-əl) *adj.* Of, relating to, or existing on a shore. —*n.* A shore.

lit•ur•gy (lĭt′ər-jē) *n., pl.* **-gies.** A prescribed rite for a public religious service : ritual. **—li•tur′gi•cal** (lĭ-tûr′jĭ-kəl) *adj.* **—li•tur′gi•cal•ly** *adv.*

liv•a•ble *also* **live•a•ble** (lĭv′ə-bəl) *adj.* **1.** Suitable to live with or in. **2.** Bearable.

live[1] (lĭv) *v.* **lived, liv•ing. 1.** To be or continue to be alive. **2.** To reside. **3.** To pass (one's life). **4.** To subsist. **5.** To remain in human memory. **—live down.** To live so as to overcome the shame, effect, or remembrance of over time.

live[2] (līv) *adj.* **1.** Having life : living. **2.** Broadcast during actual performance <a *live* talk show> **3.** Of current interest <a *live* topic> **4.** Burning : glowing <a *live* coal> **5.** Not exploded but capable of exploding <*live* ammunition> **6.** Carrying electric current <a *live* circuit>

live-in (lĭv′ĭn′) *adj.* Residing in the place at which one is employed.

live•li•hood (līv′lē-ho͝od′) *n.* A means of subsistence or support.

live•long (lĭv′lông′, -lŏng′) *adj.* Entire : whole <complained the *livelong* day>

live•ly (līv′lē) *adj.* **-li•er, -li•est. 1.** Full of life : vigorous <a *lively* youngster> **2.** Spirited : animated <a *lively* discussion> **3.** Intense : keen <did a *lively* business in clothing> **4.** Bouncing easily on impact : resilient. **—live′li•ness** *n.*

liv•en (lī′vən) *v.* To become or cause to become lively or livelier.

liv•er[1] (lĭv′ər) *n.* A large glandular organ of vertebrates that secretes bile and acts in metabolism and in blood formation.

liv•er[2] (lĭv′ər) *n.* One with a specified lifestyle <a high *liver*>

liv•er•ish (lĭv′ər-ĭsh) *adj.* **1.** Resembling liver, esp. in color. **2.** Having a liver disorder : bilious. **3.** Irritable : peevish.

liv•er•wort (lĭv′ər-wûrt′, -wôrt′) *n.* One of numerous green nonflowering plants of the class Hepaticae, related to the mosses.

liv•er•wurst (lĭv′ər-wûrst′, -wo͝orst′) *n.* A kind of sausage made primarily of liver.

liv•er•y (lĭv′ə-rē, lĭv′rē) *n., pl.* **-ies. 1.** A distinctive uniform worn by male household servants. **2. a.** The care and boarding of horses for a fee. **b.** The hiring out of horses and vehicles. **—liv′er•ied** *adj.*

liv•er•y•man (lĭv′ə-rē-mən, lĭv′rē-) *n.* A keeper or employee of a livery stable.

lives (līvz) *n. pl. of* LIFE.

live•stock (līv′stŏk′) *n.* Farm animals, as cattle, raised for human use or profit.

live wire (līv) *n. Informal.* An alert, energetic person.

liv•id (lĭv′ĭd) *adj.* **1.** Discolored from a bruise. **2.** Pale : ashen. **3.** Very angry.

liv•ing (lĭv′ĭng) *adj.* **1.** Being alive. **2.** Full of vitality and life. **3.** True to life : natural <the photograph's *living* colors> **—*n.* 1.** The condition of maintaining life. **2.** A style of life. **3.** A livelihood. ★ ***syns:*** KEEP, LIVELIHOOD, MAINTENANCE, SUBSISTENCE, SUPPORT, SUSTENANCE.

living room *n.* A room in a household for the general use of the occupants.

living wage *n.* A wage sufficient to provide minimally satisfactory living conditions.

living will *n.* A will in which the signer requests not to be kept alive by medical life-support systems in the event of a terminal illness.

liz•ard (lĭz′ərd) *n.* One of numerous reptiles of the suborder Sauria (or Lacertilia) typically with an elongated scaly body, 4 legs, and a tapering tail.

lla•ma (lä′mə) *n.* A South American ruminant, *Lama peruana,* related to the camel and raised for its soft, fleecy wool.

lo (lō) *interj.* —Used to show surprise or attract attention.

load (lōd) *n.* **1.** A mass or weight that is lifted or supported. **2.** Something conveyed, as by a vehicle, person, or animal. **3.** A share, as of work, that is allotted or required. **4.** Something, as a heavy responsibility, that oppresses : burden. **5.** *often* **loads.** *Informal.* A great amount or number. **—*v.* 1.** To place a load in or on. **2.** To take on or receive a load. **3.** To oppress : burden. **4.** To charge with ammunition <*load* a gun> **5.** To insert into (a holder or magazine). **6.** To provide in abundance. **—load′er** *n.* **—load′ing** *n.*

load•ed (lō′dĭd) *adj.* **1.** Intended to trap or trick <a *loaded* question> **2.** *Slang.* Drunk. **3.** *Slang.* Rich : wealthy.

loaf[1] (lōf) *n., pl.* **loaves** (lōvz). A shaped mass of food, esp. bread.

loaf[2] (lōf) *v.* To spend time idling : laze. **—loaf′er** *n.*

loam (lōm) *n.* Soil that consists chiefly of sand, clay, silt, and decayed plant matter. **—loam′y** *adj.*

loan (lōn) *n.* **1.** Money lent at interest. **2.** Something borrowed for temporary use. **—*v.*** To lend.

loan shark *n. Informal.* A usurer, esp. one who is financed and supported by gangsters. **—loan′shark′ing** *n.*

loan-word *also* **loan•word** (lōn′wûrd′) *n.* A word, as *sombrero,* adopted from one language for use in another.

loath (lōth, lō*th*) *adj.* Averse : reluctant.

loathe (lō*th*) *v.* **loathed, loath•ing.** To dislike intensely : abhor.

loath•ing (lō′*th*ĭng) *n.* Intense dislike : abhorrence.

loath•some (lō*th*′səm, lōth′-) *adj.* Arousing loathing : disgusting. **—loath′some•ly** *adv.* **—loathe′some•ness** *n.*

loaves (lōvz) *n. pl. of* LOAF[1].

lob (lŏb) *v.* **lobbed, lob•bing.** To hit, throw, or propel (e.g., a ball) in a high arc. **—lob** *n.* **—lob′ber** *n.*

lob•by (lŏb′ē) *n., pl.* **-bies. 1.** A foyer or waiting room, as in a hotel or theater. **2.** A group of private persons trying to influence legislators. **—*v.*** **-bied, -by•ing.** To try to influence (legislators), esp. in favor of a special interest. **—lob′by•ist** *n.*

lobe (lōb) *n.* A rounded projecting anatomical part or division, as the fleshy lower part of the ear. **—lo′bar** *adj.* **—lobed** *adj.*

†lob•lol•ly (lŏb′lŏl′ē) *n., pl.* **-lies.** *Regional.* **1.** A mudhole : mire. **2.** A lout.

†lo•bo (lō′bō) *n., pl.* **-bos.** *W U.S.* The gray or timber wolf, *Canis lupus.*

lo•bot•o•my (lō-bŏt′ə-mē, lə-) *n., pl.* **-mies.** Surgical severance of one or more cerebral nerve tracts.

lob•ster (lŏb′stər) *n.* **1.** Any of several large, edible marine crustaceans of the genus *Homarus,* with 5 pairs of legs, the first pair being large and clawlike. **2.** Any of several crustaceans related to the lobster.

lob•ule (lŏb′yo͞ol) *n.* **1.** A small lobe. **2.** A subdivision or section of a lobe. **—lob′u•lar** (-yə-lər) *adj.*

lo•cal (lō′kəl) *adj.* **1.** Of, pertaining to, being in, or serving a particular area or place. **2.** Making numerous stops en route <a *local* bus> **3.** Confined to a small part of the body <a *local* anesthetic> *—n.* **1.** A local public conveyance, as a train. **2.** A local branch or chapter of an organization, esp. of a labor union. **—lo′cal•ly** *adv.*

lo•cale (lō-kăl′, -käl′) *n.* **1.** A locality at which a particular event takes place. **2.** The setting or scene, as of a novel.

lo•cal•i•ty (lō-kăl′ĭ-tē) *n., pl.* **-ties.** A specific place, neighborhood, or district.

lo•cal•ize (lō′kə-līz′) *v.* **-ized, -iz•ing.** To confine or be confined to a specific locality. **—lo′cal•i•za′tion** *n.*

lo•cate (lō′kāt′, lō-kāt′) *v.* **-cat•ed, -cat•ing. 1.** To specify or determine the place, position, or boundaries of. **2.** To look for and find. **3.** To establish or become established **:** settle. **—lo′ca′tor** *n.*

lo•ca•tion (lō-kā′shən) *n.* **1.** An act or process of locating. **2.** A place where something is or can be located. **3.** A site outside a motion-picture or television studio at which a movie is shot.

loch (lŏkh, lŏk) *n. Scot.* **1.** A lake. **2.** An arm of the sea.

lo•ci (lō′sī′) *n. pl. of* LOCUS.

lock[1] (lŏk) *n.* **1.** A device that is used, as on a door, to secure or fasten and is operated by a key or combination. **2.** A portion of a waterway closed off with gates to raise or lower boats by changing the level of the water. **3.** A mechanism by which the charge of ammunition in a firearm is exploded. **4.** Any of several wrestling holds. *—v.* **1.** To fasten or be fastened with a lock. **2.** To keep in or out by means of a lock. **3.** To entangle or become entangled **:** interlock.

lock[2] (lŏk) *n.* **1.** A strand, tuft, or curl of hair. **2. locks.** The hair of the head.

lock•er (lŏk′ər) *n.* **1.** An enclosure, esp. in a public place, that can be locked and is used for storage, as of clothing and valuables. **2.** A flat trunk for storage. **3.** A refrigerated storage compartment.

lock•et (lŏk′ĭt) *n.* A small ornamental case for a picture or keepsake, that is often worn as a pendant on a necklace.

lock•jaw (lŏk′jô′) *n.* **1.** Tetanus. **2.** A symptom of tetanus in which a spasm of the jaw muscles locks the jaws closed.

lock•nut *also* **lock nut** (lôk′nŭt′) *n.* A usu. thin nut screwed down on another nut to keep it from loosening.

lock•out (lŏk′out′) *n.* The shutdown of a workplace by an employer during a labor dispute.

lock•smith (lŏk′smĭth′) *n.* Someone who makes or repairs locks.

lock step *n.* A way of marching in which the marchers follow each other closely.

lock•up (lŏk′ŭp′) *n. Informal.* A jail, esp. one in which accused persons are held prior to court hearings.

lo•co (lō′kō) *adj. Slang.* Insane **:** crazy.

lo•co•mo•tion (lō′kə-mō′shən) *n.* The act of moving or ability to move from place to place.

lo•co•mo•tive (lō′kə-mō′tĭv) *n.* A self-propelled electric or diesel-powered vehicle that travels on rails and moves railroad cars. *—adj.* **1.** Of or involved in locomotion. **2.** Of or pertaining to a locomotive.

lo•co•mo•tor (lō′kə-mō′tər) *adj.* Of locomotion **:** LOCOMOTIVE 1.

lo•co•weed (lō′kō-wēd′) *n.* A plant of the genera *Oxytropis* and *Astragalus,* of the W and C U.S., that is poisonous to livestock.

lo•cus (lō′kəs) *n., pl.* **-ci** (-sī′). **1.** A locality **:** place. **2.** *Geom.* The configuration or set of all points satisfying specified conditions.

lo•cust (lō′kəst) *n.* **1.** Any of numerous grasshoppers of the family Locustidae that often travel in swarms and damage vegetation. **2.** A cicada. **3.** A tree, *Robinia pseudoacacia,* with feathery leaves, fragrant white flower clusters, and hard, durable wood.

lo•cu•tion (lō-kyo͞o′shən) *n.* **1.** A particular expression or word considered stylistically. **2.** Style of speech **:** phraseology.

lode (lōd) *n.* A deposit of mineral ore.

lode•star (lōd′stär′) *n.* A star, esp. the North Star, used as a reference point.

lode•stone (lōd′stōn′) *n.* **1.** A magnetized piece of magnetite. **2.** A strong attraction.

lodge (lŏj) *n.* **1.** An often rustic house, as a cabin, used as a temporary or seasonal dwelling or shelter. **2.** An inn. **3.** The den of an animal such as the beaver. **4. a.** A local chapter of a fraternal organization. **b.** The meeting hall of such a chapter. *—v.* **lodged, lodg•ing. 1.** To provide with quarters. **2.** To live in rented accommodations. **3.** To file **:** register <*lodge* a charge> **4.** To vest (e.g., authority). **5.** To force, fix, or implant. **6.** To be or become embedded.

lodg•er (lŏj′ər) *n.* Someone who rents a room in another's house.

lodg•ing (lŏj′ĭng) *n.* **1.** A place to sleep or live. **2. lodgings.** Rented living quarters.

lodg•ment *also* **lodge•ment** (lŏj′mənt) *n.* **1.** An act of lodging or the state of being lodged. **2.** A place for lodging. **3.** An accumulation or deposit.

lo•ess (lō′əs, lĕs, lo͞os) *n.* A fine-grained calcareous clay or silt thought to be deposited as dust blown by the wind.

loft (lôft, lŏft) *n.* **1.** A large, usu. unpartitioned floor of an industrial or commercial building, as a warehouse. **2.** An attic. **3.** A gallery, as in a church <a choir *loft*> *—v.* To throw or strike (e.g., a ball) in a high arc.

loft•y (lôf′tē, lŏf′-) *adj.* **-i•er, -i•est. 1.** Imposingly high : towering. **2.** Elevated : noble. **3.** Arrogant : overbearing. **—loft′i•ly** *adv.* **—loft′i•ness** *n.*

log[1] (lôg, lŏg) *n.* **1.** A trunk or section of a trunk of a felled or fallen tree. **2.** A mechanism for determing a ship's speed. **3. a.** A record of a ship's or aircraft's speed or progress. **b.** The book in which this record is kept. *—v.* **logged, log•ging. 1.** To cut down trees for timber. **2. a.** To enter in a log. **b.** To travel (a specified distance or time). **—log in** (*or* **on**). To enter into a computer the command to begin a session. **—log out** (*or* **off**). To enter into a computer the command to end a session. **—log′ger** *n.*

log[2] (lôg, lŏg) *n.* Logarithm.

lo•gan•ber•ry (lō′gən-bĕr′ē) *n.* A prickly plant, *Rubus loganobaccus,* cultivated for its edible acidic red fruit.

log•a•rithm (lô′gə-rĭth′əm, lŏg′ə-) *n.* The exponent indicating the power to which a base number must be raised to produce a given number. **—log′a•rith′mic** *adj.*

loge (lōzh) *n.* **1.** A small compartment, esp. a theater box. **2.** The forward rows of a theater mezzanine.

log•ger•head (lô′gər-hĕd′, lŏg′ər-) *n.* A marine turtle, *Caretta caretta,* with a large beaked head. **—at loggerheads.** In a state of contention : at odds.

log•gi•a (lô′jē-ə, lŏj′ē-ə) *n.* **1.** A roofed but open gallery or arcade along the front or side of a building, often at an upper level. **2.** An open balcony in a theater.

log•ic (lŏj′ĭk) *n.* **1.** The scientific study of the principles of reasoning, esp. of the method and validity of deductive reasoning. **2.** Valid reasoning. **3.** A particular system or method of reasoning. **—lo•gi′cian** (lō-jĭsh′ən) *n.*

log•i•cal (lŏj′ĭ-kəl) *adj.* **1.** Of, relating to, or in accordance with logic. **2.** Marked by consistency of reasoning. **3.** Reasonable. **4.** Capable of reasoning rationally. ★ ***syns:*** CONSEQUENT, INTELLIGENT, RATIONAL, REASONABLE, SENSIBLE **—log′i•cal•ly** *adv.*

lo•gis•tics (lō-jĭs′tĭks) *n. (sing. or pl. in number).* The methods of procuring, distributing, maintaining, and replacing materiel and personnel, as in a military operation. **—lo•gis′-tic** *adj.*

log•jam (lôg′jăm′, lŏg′-) *n.* **1.** A mass of floating logs jammed immovably together in a waterway, as a river. **2.** A deadlock.

lo•go (lō′gō, lô′-, lŏg′ō) *n.* A logotype.

lo•go•type (lō′gə-tīp′, lô′-, lŏg′ə-) *n.* A distinctive identifying symbol, as of a company or publication.

log•roll•ing *or* **log-roll•ing** (lôg′rō′lĭng, lŏg′-) *n.* The exchanging of votes among legislators to assure the success of projects of interest to each one. **—log′roll′er** *n.*

lo•gy (lō′gē) *adj.* **-gi•er, -gi•est.** Marked by sluggishness : lethargic. **—lo′gi•ness** *n.*

loin (loin) *n.* **1. a.** The region of the body between the ribs and pelvis. **b.** A cut of meat from this part of an animal. **2. loins. a.** The area of the thighs and groin. **b.** The reproductive organs.

loin•cloth (loin′klôth′, -klŏth′) *n.* A cloth worn as a garment around the loins.

loi•ter (loi′tər) *v.* **1.** To remain in a place for no apparent reason : linger. **2.** To dawdle : delay. **—loi′ter•er** *n.*

loll (lŏl) *v.* **1.** To move, stand, sit, or rest in an indolent manner. **2.** To droop or hang loosely. **—loll′ing•ly** *adv.*

lol•li•pop *also* **lol•ly•pop** (lŏl′ē-pŏp′) *n.* A piece of hard candy on a stick.

lone (lōn) *adj.* **1.** Single : solitary <a *lone* horseman> **2.** Isolated : unfrequented <the *lone* prairie> **3.** Being the only one : sole <the *lone* concert hall in the city>

lone•ly (lōn′lē) *adj.* **-li•er, -li•est. 1.** Being without companions : lone. **2.** Devoid of people : unfrequented. **3. a.** Dejected because of being alone. **b.** Producing such dejection. **—lone′li•ness** *n.*

lon•er (lō′nər) *n. Informal.* Someone who avoids the company of others.

lone•some (lōn′səm) *adj.* **1.** Dejected because of lack of companionship. **2.** Unfrequented : remote. **—lone′some•ly** *adv.* **—lone′some•ness** *n.*

long[1] (lông, lŏng) *adj.* **1. a.** Of considerable length. **b.** Tall. **2.** Of considerable duration. **b.** Too protracted : tedious. **3.** Of a specified length or duration <a foot *long*><a year *long*> **4.** Far-reaching <a *long* view of the situation> **5.** Having much or too much of something <*long* on optimism> **6.** Being a speech sound or syllable of comparatively great duration. ★ ***syns:*** EXTENDED, LENGTHY *—adv.* **1.** For or during an extended period of time. **2.** For or throughout a given period <worked all day *long*> *—n.* A long time.

long[2] (lông, lŏng) *v.* To have a strong persistent wish or desire : yearn. **—long′ing** *n.* **—long•ing•ly** *adv.*

long•boat (lông′bōt′, lŏng′-) *n.* The longest boat carried by a sailing ship.

long•bow (lông′bō′, lŏng′-) *n.* A wooden bow approx. 5 to 6 ft long.

long distance *n.* Telephone communication with a distant point. **—long′-dis′tance** *adj. & adv.*

lon•gev•i•ty (lŏn-jĕv′ĭ-tē) *n.* **1.** Long life. **2.** Long continuance or duration.

long•hair (lông′hâr′, lŏng′-) *n.* An enthusiast of the arts and esp. of classical music.

long•hand (lông′hănd′, lŏng′-) *n.* Cursive handwriting.

long•horn (lông′hôrn′, lŏng′-) *n.* One of a breed of long-horned cattle formerly raised in the SW U.S.

long•house *n.* A long communal dwelling, esp. of the Iroquois.

lon•gi•tu•di•nal (lŏn′jĭ-to͞od′n-əl, -tyo͞od′-) *adj.* **1.** Of or relating to length. **2.** Running or placed lengthwise. **3.** Of or relating to longitude. **—lon′gi•tu′di•nal•ly** *adv.*

lon•gi•tude (lŏn′jĭ-to͞od′, -tyo͞od′) *n.* Angular distance E and W of the prime meridian at Greenwich, England.

long-lived (lông′līvd′, -lĭvd′, lŏng′-) *adj.* Existing or living for a long time.
long-play·ing (lông′plā′ĭng, lŏng′-) *adj.* Pertaining to or being a phonograph record turning at 33⅓ rpm.
long-range (lông′rānj′, lŏng′-) *adj.* **1.** Involving or requiring an extended time span. **2.** Of, appropriate for, or covering great distances <a *long-range* bomber>
long·shore·man (lông′shôr′mən, -shōr′-, lŏng′-) *n.* A dock laborer who loads and unloads cargo.
long-stand·ing (lông′stăn′dĭng, lŏng′-) *adj.* Having endured for a long time.
long-suf·fer·ing (lông′sŭf′ər-ĭng, lŏng′-) *adj.* Patiently bearing difficulties or wrongs. **—long′-suf′fer·ing·ly** *adv.*
long-term (lông′tûrm′, lŏng′-) *adj.* Involving or in effect for a number of years.
long ton *n.* —See table at MEASUREMENT.
long-wind·ed (lông′wĭn′dĭd, lŏng′-) *adj.* Tiresomely talkative. **—long′-wind′ed·ly** *adv.* **—long′-wind′ed·ness** *n.*
look (lo͝ok) *v.* **1.** To use the power of sight : see. **2.** To direct one's gaze or attention. **3.** To appear to be : seem <*looks* unhappy> **4.** To face in a certain direction : point. **5.** To have an appearance that accords with <*looks* his age> **—look after.** To take care of. **—look for. 1.** To search for. **2.** To expect. **—look out.** To be on guard : be vigilant. **—look up. 1.** To search for and find, as in a reference book. **2.** To find and make a call on : visit. **3.** *Informal.* To improve. *—n.* **1.** The action of looking : gaze. **2.** Aspect : appearance. **3. looks.** Personal appearance. **—look′er** *n.*
looking glass *n.* A mirror.
look·out (lo͝ok′out′) *n.* **1.** Someone who has been assigned to keep watch, as on a ship. **2.** The act of keeping watch. **3.** A place commanding a wide view for observation. **4.** A matter of worry or concern.
look-see (lo͝ok′sē′) *n. Informal.* A survey.
loom[1] (lo͞om) *v.* **1.** To appear or come into view as a massive or indistinct image. **2.** To seem to be imminent and threatening.
loom[2] (lo͞om) *n.* A machine for interweaving thread or yarn to produce cloth.
loon[1] (lo͞on) *n.* Any of several diving birds of the genus *Gavia,* having a laughlike cry.
loon[2] (lo͞on) *n.* A foolish or crazy person.
loon·y (lo͞o′nē) *adj.* **-i·er, -i·est.** *Informal.* Foolish or crazy. **—loon′y** *n.*
loony bin *n. Informal.* An insane asylum.
loop (lo͞op) *n.* **1.** An approx. circular or oval length of line, as thread, folded over and joined at the ends. **2.** A loop-shaped pattern, figure, or path. *—v.* **1.** To make or form into a loop. **2.** To join, fasten, or encircle with a loop.
loop·hole (lo͞op′hōl′) *n.* **1.** A small hole or slit in a wall through which small arms may be fired. **2.** A means of escape or evasion.
loose (lo͞os) *adj.* **loos·er, loos·est. 1.** Not tightly fastened. **2.** Not confined. **3.** Not taut : slack. **4.** Not tight-fitting. **5.** Not bound, bundled, stapled, or gathered together. **6.** Not exact or strict <a *loose* translation> **7.** Showing a lack of restraint or responsibility. **8.** Not compact or dense in structure. **9.** Sexually unrestrained : immoral. *—adv.* In a loose manner. *—v.* **loosed, loos·ing. 1.** To release. **2.** To make or become loose : undo. **3.** To make less tight or compact : loosen. **4.** To slacken : relax. **5.** To discharge (a missile). **—loose′ly** *adv.* **—loose′ness** *n.*
loos·en (lo͞o′sən) *v.* **1.** To make or become loose or looser. **2.** To allow or cause to become less restrained or strict.
loot (lo͞ot) *n.* **1.** Valuables plundered in time of war. **2.** Goods that have been stolen. *—v.* To plunder : steal. **—loot′er** *n.*
lop (lŏp) *v.* **lopped, lop·ping. 1.** To remove branches or twigs from : trim. **2.** To cut off, esp. with a single blow.
lope (lōp) *v.* **loped, lop·ing.** To run with a steady, easy gait. **—lope** *n.* **—lop′er** *n.*
lop·sid·ed (lŏp′sī′dĭd) *adj.* **1.** Heavier, higher, or larger on one side than on the other. **2.** Tilting to one side. **—lop′sid′ed·ly** *adv.* **—lop′sid′ed·ness** *n.*
lo·qua·cious (lō-kwā′shəs) *adj.* Too talkative. **—lo·qua′cious·ly** *adv.* **—lo·quac′i·ty** (-kwăs′ĭ-tē) *n.*
lord (lôrd) *n.* **1.** A man with dominion and power over others. **2.** The owner of a feudal estate. **3. Lord.** *esp. Brit.* The general masculine title of rank and esp. of nobility. **4. Lord. a.** God. **b.** Jesus. *—v.* To behave in a domineering, haughty, or patronizing manner <*lording* it over the new workers>

▲ ***word history:*** The actual as well as the symbolic importance of bread as a basic foodstuff is exhibited by the word *lord. Lord* is derived from a compound formed in very early Old English times from the words *hlāf,* "bread," and *weard,* "ward, guardian." *Lord,* therefore, literally means "guardian of the bread." Since such a position was the dominant one in a household, *lord* came to denote a man of authority and rank in society at large.

lord·ly (lôrd′lē) *adj.* **-li·er, -li·est. 1.** Of, relating to, or typical of a lord. **2.** Noble : grand. **3.** Pretentiously overbearing : haughty. **—lord′li·ness** *n.*
lord·ship (lôrd′shĭp′) *n.* **1.** *often* **Lordship.** —Used as a form of address for a man holding the title of lord. **2.** The authority or position of a lord.
Lord's Supper *n.* The Eucharist.
lore (lôr, lōr) *n.* **1.** Traditional fact or belief. **2.** Knowledge, as that gained through experience or education.
lor·gnette (lôrn-yĕt′) *n.* A pair of eyeglasses or opera glasses with a short handle.
lorn (lôrn) *adj.* Forlorn : bereft.
lor·ry (lôr′ē, lŏr′ē) *n., pl.* **-ries.** *esp. Brit.* A motor truck.
lose (lo͞oz) *v.* **lost** (lôst, lŏst), **los·ing. 1.** To fail to find in a customary place : mislay. **2.** To fail to sustain or keep. **3.** To be deprived of <*lost* his job> **4.** To fail to win <afraid they'll *lose* the game> **5.** To fail to use : waste

<*lose* an opportunity> **6.** To get rid of <wants to *lose* weight> **7.** To stray from <*lost* her way> **—los'er** *n.*

loss (lôs, lŏs) *n.* **1.** The damage or suffering that is caused by losing. **2.** One that is lost. **3. losses.** Killed, wounded, or captured persons, esp. soldiers : casualties.

loss leader *n.* An article sold at or below cost to attract customers.

lost (lôst, lŏst) *adj.* **1.** Unable to find one's way. **2.** Not won or used. **3.** No longer practiced or possessed : gone. **4.** Unable to function : helpless. **5.** Absorbed : engrossed.

lot (lŏt) *n.* **1.** An object used in making a choice or determination by chance. **2.** The use of lots for choice or determination. **3.** Fate : fortune. **4.** A group of people or things : set. **5.** A large amount, extent, or number. **6.** A piece of land with designated boundaries : plot.

lo•ti (lō'tē) *n., pl.* **loti.** —See table at CURRENCY.

lo•tion (lō'shən) *n.* A liquid medicine or cosmetic for external application.

lot•ter•y (lŏt'ə-rē) *n., pl.* **-ies. 1.** A contest in which winners are selected by a chance drawing. **2.** An event or activity whose outcome depends on chance.

lo•tus (lō'təs) *n.* **1. a.** An aquatic plant, *Nelumbo nucifera,* with fragrant pinkish flowers and large leaves. **b.** One of several plants similar or related to the lotus, as certain water lilies. **2.** A fruit described in Homer's *Odyssey* that produced a dreamy, indolent state in those who ate it.

loud (loud) *adj.* **1.** Marked by high volume and intensity of sound. **2.** Producing a loud sound : noisy. **3.** Gaudy, as in color : flashy. **—loud, loud'ly** *adv.* **—loud'ness** *n.*

loud•mouth (loud'mouth') *n.* Someone who tends to talk loudly, irritatingly, and often indiscreetly. **—loud'mouthed'** (-mou*th*d', -moutht') *adj.*

loud•speak•er (loud'spē'kər) *n.* A device that converts electric signals to audible sound and projects it.

lounge (lounj) *v.* **lounged, loung•ing.** To move or act in a relaxed, lazy manner. —*n.* **1.** A waiting room, as in a hotel or theater. **2.** A long couch. **—loung'er** *n.*

lour (lou'ər) *v. & n. var. of* LOWER[1].

louse (lous) *n.* **1.** *pl.* **lice** (līs). One of numerous small, flat-bodied, wingless biting or sucking insects of the family Anoplura, many of which live as parasites on various animals, including human beings. **2.** *pl.* **lous•es.** *Slang.* A mean or contemptible person. —*v.* **loused, lous•ing.** *Slang.* To bungle <*loused* up everything>

louse•wort (lous'wûrt', -wôrt') *n.* A plant of the genus *Pedicularis,* with irregular, variously colored flower clusters.

lous•y (lou'zē) *adj.* **-i•er, -i•est. 1.** Lice-infested. **2.** *Slang.* **a.** Mean : contemptible. **b.** Inferior : poor. **3.** *Slang.* Abundantly supplied <*lousy* with jewelry> **—lous'i•ly** *adv.* **—lous'i•ness** *n.*

lout (lout) *n.* An awkward, stupid fellow : oaf. **—lout'ish** *adj.*

lou•ver *also* **lou•vre** (lōō'vər) *n.* **1.** A framed opening in a wall fitted with movable slanted slats that let air in but keep precipitation out. **2.** One of the slats used in a louver. **—lou'vered** *adj.*

love (lŭv) *n.* **1.** Intense affection. **2.** A feeling of attraction resulting from sexual desire. **3.** Enthusiasm or fondness <*love* of music> **4.** A beloved person. **5.** A score of zero in tennis. —*v.* **loved, lov•ing. 1.** To feel love for. **2.** To enjoy enthusiastically <*loves* skating> ★ *syns:* ADORE, CHERISH **—lov'a•ble** *adj.* **—love'less** *adj.*

love•bird (lŭv'bûrd') *n.* Any of various Old World parrots, esp. of the genus *Agapornis,* often kept as a pet.

love•lorn (lŭv'lôrn') *adj.* Bereft of love or a lover. **—love'lorn'ness** *n.*

love•ly (lŭv'lē) *adj.* **-li•er, -li•est. 1.** Beautiful <a *lovely* face> **2.** Enjoyable : delightful. **—love'li•ness** *n.* **—love'ly** *n.*

love•mak•ing (lŭv'mā'kĭng) *n.* **1.** Sexual activity and esp. sexual intercourse. **2.** Courtship.

lov•er (lŭv'ər) *n.* **1.** One who loves another, esp. sexually. **2.** A devotee <an animal *lover*> **3.** A sexual partner.

love seat *n.* A small sofa that seats two.

love•sick (lŭv'sĭk') *adj.* **1.** Yearning with love. **2.** Showing or expressing a lover's yearning. **—love'sick'ness** *n.*

lov•ing (lŭv'ĭng) *adj.* Feeling or expressing love : affectionate. **—lov'ing•ly** *adv.*

loving cup *n.* A large, ornamental cup with 2 or more handles that is often given as an award or trophy.

low[1] (lō) *adj.* **1.** Not high or tall <a *low* cabinet> **2. a.** Of less than usual depth <*low* water> **b.** Being below a normal surface or level. **3.** Less than average, as in amount, degree, or intensity <a *low* price> **4. a.** *Mus.* Being a sound produced by a relatively small frequency of vibrations <the *low* notes of a tuba> **b.** Not loud <a *low* whisper> **5.** Of humble social status. **6.** Morally blameworthy. **7.** Vulgar : coarse. **8.** Sad : dejected. **9.** Near the equator. **10.** Adverse : unfavorable <a *low* opinion> —*n.* **1.** A low position, level, or degree. **2.** A region of depressed barometric pressure. **3.** The gear adjustment in an automotive transmission that produces the smallest output speed for a given engine speed. **—low** *adv.* **—low'ness** *n.*

low[2] (lō) *v.* To moo. **—low** *n.*

low beam *n.* A low-intensity vehicular headlight.

low•brow (lō'brou') *n.* *Informal.* One who lacks cultivation. **—low'brow'** *adj.*

low•down (lō'doun') *n.* *Slang.* The full facts : whole truth.

low-down (lō'doun') *adj.* **1.** Despicable : mean. **2.** Emotionally depressed.

low•er[1] *also* **lour** (lou'ər) *v.* **1.** To look angry : frown. **2.** To grow dark or threatening, as the sky. **—low'er** *n.*

low•er² (lō′ər) *adj.* **1.** Being below, as in rank or position. **2.** Being or denoting the larger and usu. more representative house of a bicameral legislature. —*v.* **1.** To let, bring, or move down. **2.** To reduce, as in value, amount, or quality : diminish.

low•er-case (lō′ər-kās′) *adj.* Of, relating to, or being small letters as distinguished from capitals. —**lower case** *n.*

lower class *n.* The group in society that ranks below the middle class and is of low social and economic status. —**low′er-class′** *adj.*

lowest common denominator *n.* The least common multiple of the denominators of a set of fractions.

lowest common multiple *n.* Least common multiple.

low frequency *n.* A radio-wave frequency in the range between 30 and 300 kilohertz.

low-key (lō′kē′) *also* **low-keyed** (-kēd′) *adj.* Restrained : subdued.

low•land (lō′lənd) *n.* Land that is low and usu. level in relation to the surrounding countryside.

low•ly (lō′lē) *adj.* **-li•er, -li•est. 1.** Low in position or rank. **2.** Meek : humble. —**low′li•ness** *n.*

low profile *n.* An unobtrusive mode of behavior or lifestyle.

low relief *n.* Sculptural relief that projects very little from the background.

low-rise (lō′rīz′) *adj.* Having few stories and often no elevators <a *low-rise* apartment building>

low-ten•sion (lō′tĕn′shən) *adj.* **1.** Of or at low potential or voltage. **2.** Operating at low voltage.

low tide *n.* The lowest ebb tide.

lox¹ (lŏks) *n.* Smoked salmon.

lox² (lŏks) *n.* Liquid oxygen.

loy•al (loi′əl) *adj.* **1.** Firm in allegiance to one's country and government. **2.** Faithful to a person, ideal, or cause. —**loy′al•ly** *adv.* —**loy′al•ty** *n.*

loy•al•ist (loi′ə-lĭst) *n.* Someone who is loyal to a government or political party, esp. during a revolt.

loz•enge (lŏz′ənj) *n.* **1.** A figure shaped like a diamond. **2.** A small medicated candy with the shape of a lozenge.

LSD (ĕl′ĕs-dē′) *n.* A powerful drug that induces hallucinations.

Lu *symbol for* LUTETIUM.

lu•au (lo͞o-ou′) *n.* A Hawaiian feast.

lub•ber (lŭb′ər) *n.* **1.** An awkward fellow. **2.** An inexperienced sailor.

lu•bri•cant (lo͞o′brĭ-kənt) *n.* A material, as grease or machine oil, that is applied to moving parts to reduce friction.

lu•bri•cate (lo͞o′brĭ-kāt′) *v.* **-cat•ed, -cat•ing.** To apply a lubricant to. —**lu′bri•ca′tion** *n.* —**lu′bri•ca′tor** *n.*

lu•bri•cous (lo͞o′brĭ-kəs) *also* **lu•bri•cious** (lo͞o-brĭsh′əs) *adj.* **1.** Slippery. **2. a.** Lewd : wanton. **b.** Salacious. **3.** Shifty : tricky. —**lu•bric′i•ty** (-brĭs′ĭ-tē) *n.*

lu•cid (lo͞o′sĭd) *adj.* **1.** Readily understood. **2.** Mentally clear : rational. **3.** Translucent. —**lu•cid′i•ty** (-sĭd′ĭ-tē), **lu′cid•ness** *n.* —**lu′cid•ly** *adv.*

Lu•ci•fer (lo͞o′sə-fər) *n.* The devil : Satan.

Lu•cite (lo͞o′sīt′). A trademark for a transparent thermoplastic acrylic resin.

luck (lŭk) *n.* **1.** The random occurrence of good or adverse fortune : chance. **2.** Good fortune. —*v.* To find or attain something advantageous or desirable by chance <*lucked* out when she bought the antique> —**luck′less** *adj.*

luck•y (lŭk′ē) *adj.* **-i•er, -i•est.** Having, believed to bring, or resulting from good luck. —**luck′i•ly** *adv.* —**luck′i•ness** *n.*

lu•cra•tive (lo͞o′krə-tĭv) *adj.* Producing wealth or profits. —**lu′cra•tive•ly** *adv.*

lu•cre (lo͞o′kər) *n.* **1.** Money. **2.** Profit.

lu•cu•brate (lo͞o′kyə-brāt′) *v.* **-brat•ed, -brat•ing.** To study laboriously.

lu•di•crous (lo͞o′dĭ-krəs) *adj.* Laughable because of obvious absurdity or incongruousness. —**lu′di•crous•ly** *adv.* —**lu′di•crous•ness** *n.*

luff (lŭf) *v.* **1.** To steer a sailing vessel nearer into the wind. **2.** To flap. —Used of a sail.

lug¹ (lŭg) *n.* An earlike handle or projection, as on a machine, used as a hold.

lug² (lŭg) *v.* **lugged, lug•ging. 1.** To drag : haul. **2.** To carry with difficulty.

luge (lo͞ozh) *n.* A sled similar to a toboggan that is ridden in a supine position.

lug•gage (lŭg′ĭj) *n.* Baggage, esp. suitcases.

lug nut *n.* A heavy rounded nut that fits over a bolt.

lu•gu•bri•ous (lo͞o-go͞o′brē-əs, -gyo͞o′-) *adj.* Mournful or gloomy, esp. exaggeratedly so. —**lu•gu′bri•ous•ly** *adv.* —**lu•gu′bri•ous•ness** *n.*

Luke (lo͝ok) *n.* —See table at BIBLE.

luke•warm (lo͝ok′wôrm′) *adj.* **1.** Mildly warm : tepid. **2.** Unenthusiastic : halfhearted. —**luke′warm′ly** *adv.*

lull (lŭl) *v.* **1.** To cause to rest or sleep : soothe. **2.** To cause to have a false sense of safety. —*n.* A temporary period of calm or inactivity.

lul•la•by (lŭl′ə-bī′) *n., pl.* **-bies.** A soothing song to lull a child to sleep.

lum•ba•go (lŭm-bā′gō) *n.* Painful inflammatory rheumatism of the muscles and tendons of the lumbar region.

lum•bar (lŭm′bər, -bär′) *adj.* Of or situated in the part of the back and sides between the lowest ribs and the pelvis.

lum•ber¹ (lŭm′bər) *n.* **1.** Timber, esp. when sawed into boards and planks. **2.** *esp. Brit.* Miscellaneous stored items. —*v.* To cut and prepare timber for market.

lum•ber² (lŭm′bər) *v.* To walk or move clumsily, heavily, or noisily.

lum•ber•jack (lŭm′bər-jăk′) *n.* One who fells trees and prepares them for the sawmill.

lum•ber•yard (lŭm′bər-yärd′) *n.* A commercial establishment where lumber is stored and sold.

lu•men (lo͞o′mən) *n., pl.* **-mens** *or* **-mi•na** (-mə-nə). *Anat.* The inner open space or cavity of a tubular organ. —**lu′men•al, lu′min•al** *adj.*

lu•mi•nar•y (lo͞o′mə-nĕr′ē) *n., pl.* **-ies. 1.** An object, esp. a celestial body, that is a source of light. **2.** A celebrity.

lu•mi•nes•cence (lo͞o′mə-nĕs′əns) *n.* The production, as in fluorescence, of light without heat. —**lu′mi•nes′cent** *adj.*

lu•mi•nous (lo͞o′mə-nəs) *adj.* **1.** Emitting light. **2.** Lighted : illuminated. **3. a.** Well-expressed : clear. **b.** Inspiring. —**lu′mi•nos′i•ty** (-nŏs′ĭ-tē) *n.* —**lu′mi•nous•ly** *adv.*

lum•mox (lŭm′əks) *n.* A clumsy oaf : lout.

lump[1] (lŭmp) *n.* **1.** An irregularly shaped piece or mass. **2.** A small cube, as of sugar. **3.** A swelling or small palpable mass. **4. lumps.** Punishment. —*adj.* Undivided : unbroken <a *lump* sum> —*v.* **1.** To put or consider together indiscriminately. **2.** To form or cause to form lumps. —**lump′i•ness** *n.* —**lump′y** *adj.*

lump[2] (lŭmp) *v. Informal.* To put up with : tolerate <like it or *lump* it>

lump•ec•to•my (lŭm-pĕk′tə-mē) *n., pl.* **-mies.** Surgical excision of a tumor from the breast.

lu•na•cy (lo͞o′nə-sē) *n., pl.* **-cies. 1.** Insanity. **2.** Great folly.

luna moth *n.* A large, pale-green North American moth, *Actias luna,* with a long projection on each hind wing.

lu•nar (lo͞o′nər) *adj.* Of, relating to, caused by, or affecting the moon.

lunar excursion module *n.* A spacecraft designed to transport astronauts from a command module orbiting the moon to the lunar surface and back.

lu•na•tic (lo͞o′nə-tĭk) *adj.* **1.** Insane. **2.** Of or used for the insane. **3.** Wildly foolish <*lunatic* ideas> —**lu′na•tic** *n.*

lunch (lŭnch) *n.* **1.** A meal eaten at midday. **2.** Food for lunch. —**lunch** *v.*

lunch•eon (lŭn′chən) *n.* A lunch, esp. a formal one.

lunch•eon•ette (lŭn′chə-nĕt′) *n.* A restaurant at which light lunches are served.

lung (lŭng) *n.* A saclike, usu. paired organ in the chest of most vertebrates that removes carbon dioxide from the blood and provides it with oxygen.

lunge (lŭnj) *n.* **1.** A sudden pass or thrust, as with a fencing foil. **2.** A sudden forward movement : plunge. —*v.* **lunged, lung•ing.** To move with a lunge.

lu•pine (lo͞o′pĭn) *n.* A plant of the genus *Lupinus,* bearing long spikes of variously colored flowers.

lu•pus (lo͞o′pəs) *n.* Any of several diseases of the skin and mucous membranes.

lurch[1] (lûrch) *v.* **1.** To walk with a stagger. **2.** To pitch or roll suddenly or erratically, as a ship. —**lurch** *n.*

lurch[2] (lûrch) *n.* A losing position in cribbage. —**in the lurch.** In a difficult position.

lure (lo͝or) *n.* **1.** Something attractive or appealing : enticement. **2.** An artificial bait to catch fish. —*v.* **lured, lur•ing.** To attract or entice with the prospect of reward or pleasure.

lu•rid (lo͝or′ĭd) *adj.* **1.** Horrifying : gruesome. **2.** Sensational. **3.** Glowing with the glare of fire through a haze. —**lu′rid•ly** *adv.* —**lu′rid•ness** *n.*

lurk (lûrk) *v.* **1.** To lie concealed, as in ambush. **2.** To move furtively.

lus•cious (lŭsh′əs) *adj.* **1.** Pleasant to smell or taste : delicious. **2.** Appealing to the senses. —**lus′cious•ly** *adv.* —**lus′cious•ness** *n.*

lush[1] (lŭsh) *adj.* **1.** Covered with luxuriant growth or vegetation <a *lush* green lawn> **2.** Sumptuous : opulent. —**lush′ly** *adv.* —**lush′ness** *n.*

lush[2] (lŭsh) *n. Slang.* An alcoholic.

lust (lŭst) *n.* **1.** Intense and often excessive or unrestrained sexual desire. **2.** An intense desire. —**lust′ful** *adj.* —**lust′ful•ly** *adv.*

▲ ***word history:*** The noun *lust* preserves the same form it had in Old English, but its meaning is now quite different. It orig. was a word of neutral connotations, meaning simply "pleasure." In theological usage it was used to refer to pleasures and desires, esp. sexual desire, that were considered sinful. In this context *lust* was a term of opprobrium and reproach. This disapproval has carried over to the most recent sense of *lust,* "an overwhelming desire or craving." The meaning "pleasure" is now obsolete.

lus•ter (lŭs′tər) *n.* **1.** A soft and esp. reflected light : sheen or shine. **2.** Brilliance or radiance : brightness. **3.** Splendor : glory. —**lus′trous** (-trəs) *adj.* —**lus′ter•less** *adj.*

lus•tre (lŭs′tər) *n. esp. Brit. var. of* LUSTER.

lust•y (lŭs′tē) *adj.* **-i•er, -i•est. 1.** Full of vitality : vigorous. **2.** *Archaic.* Merry. —**lust′i•ly** *adv.* —**lust′i•ness** *n.*

lute (lo͞ot) *n.* A musical stringed instrument with a fretted fingerboard, a pear-shaped body, and usu. a bent neck.

lu•te•ti•um *also* **lu•te•ci•um** (lo͞o-tē′shē-əm, -shəm) *n. Symbol* **Lu** A silvery rare-earth element.

Lu•ther•an (lo͞o′thər-ən) *n.* A member of a branch of the Protestant Church that adheres to the teachings of Martin Luther. —**Lu′ther•an** *adj.* —**Lu′ther•an•ism** *n.*

lux•u•ri•ant (lŭg-zho͝or′ē-ənt, lŭk-sho͝or′-) *adj.* **1.** Growing or yielding abundantly : lush. **2.** Very elaborate : ornate <patches of *luxuriant* prose> —**lux•u′ri•ance** *n.* —**lux•u′ri•ant•ly** *adv.*

lux•u•ri•ate (lŭg-zho͝or′ē-āt′, lŭk-sho͝or′-) *v.* **-at•ed, -at•ing. 1.** To take pleasure : revel. **2.** To grow abundantly.

lux•u•ri•ous (lŭg-zho͝or′ē-əs, lŭk-sho͝or′-) *adj.* **1.** Fond of or inclined to luxury. **2.** Marked by luxury : sumptuous. ★ ***syns:*** LAVISH, LUSH, LUXURIANT, OPULENT, PLUSH, RICH —**lux•u′ri•ous•ly** *adv.*

lux•u•ry (lŭg′zhə-rē, lŭk′shə-) *n., pl.* **-ries. 1.** Something, esp. something that is expensive or hard to obtain, that provides comfort, pleasure, or enjoyment but is not absolutely essential. **2.** Sumptuous surroundings or living.

Lw *symbol for* LAWRENCIUM.

lwei (lwā) *n., pl.* **lwei.** —See table at CURRENCY.

–ly[1] *suff.* **1.** Like **:** resembling **:** having the characteristics of <father*ly*> **2.** Recurring at a specified interval of <hour*ly*>

–ly[2] *suff.* **1.** In a specified manner <gradual*ly*> **2.** With respect to <part*ly*>

ly•ce•um (lī-sē′əm) *n.* **1.** A hall in which public programs such as lectures and concerts are presented. **2.** An organization that sponsors public programs such as lectures and concerts.

lye (lī) *n.* **1.** The powerfully alkaline solution yielded by leaching wood ashes. **2.** Potassium hydroxide. **3.** Sodium hydroxide.

ly•ing-in (lī′ĭng-ĭn′) *n.* Confinement of a woman in childbirth.

Lyme disease (līm) *n.* An inflammatory disease that is caused by a spirochete transmitted by ticks.

lymph (lĭmf) *n.* A clear, transparent, watery liquid that contains chiefly white blood cells and some red blood cells and circulates through the system to bathe the tissues, carries fat from the intestines, and supplies lymphocytes to the blood. **—lym•phat′ic** (lĭm-făt′ĭk) *adj. & n.*

lymph node *n.* A roundish body of lymphoid tissue that supplies lymphocytes to the heart and blood vessels and purifies the lymph.

lym•pho•cyte (lĭm′fə-sīt′) *n.* A white blood cell formed in lymphoid tissue and constituting 22–28% of all leukocytes.

lym•phoid (lĭm′foid′) *adj.* Of or relating to lymph or lymphatic tissue.

lynch (lĭnch) *v.* To execute, esp. by hanging, without due process of law.

lynx (lĭngks) *n.* A wildcat of the genus *Lynx*, esp. *L. canadensis*, with thick soft fur, a short tail, and tufted ears.

lyre (līr) *n.* An ancient stringed instrument related to the harp.

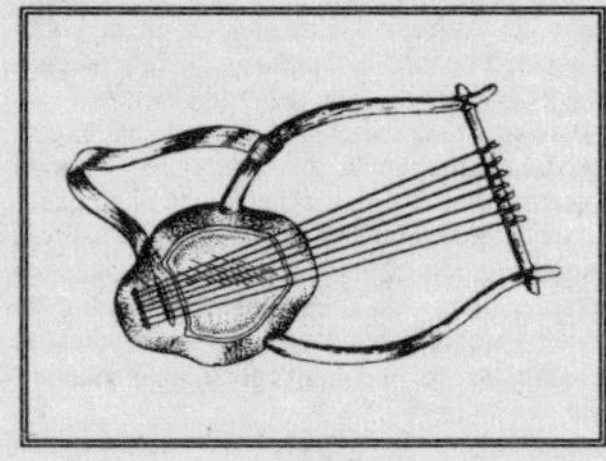

lyre

lyr•ic (lĭr′ĭk) *adj.* **1.** Expressing feeling, esp. deep personal emotion, in an affecting and direct way. **2.** Appropriate for singing. —*n.* **1.** A lyric poem. **2.** *often* **lyrics.** The words of a song. **—lyr′i•cal** *adj.* **—lyr′i•cal•ly** *adv.* **—lyr′i•cism** (-sĭz′əm) *n.*

lyr•i•cist (lĭr′ĭ-sĭst) *n.* Someone who writes song lyrics.

ly•ser•gic acid di•eth•yl•am•ide (lĭ-sûr′jĭk, lī-; dī′ĕth-əl-ăm′īd′) *n.* LSD.

Mm

m *or* **M** (ĕm) *n., pl.* **m's** *or* **M's. 1.** The 13th letter of the English alphabet. **2.** A speech sound represented by the letter *m.* **3.** Something with the shape of the letter M. **4.** The Roman numeral for 1,000.

ma (mä, mô) *n. Informal.* Mother.

ma'am (măm) *n.* Madam.

mac (măk) *n. esp. Brit.* A raincoat.

ma•ca•bre (mə-kä′brə, -bər) *adj.* Suggestive of the horror of death **:** gruesome <a *macabre* story of revenge>

mac•ad•am (mə-kăd′əm) *n.* A road pavement consisting of layers of compacted broken stone, now usu. cemented with asphalt or tar. **—mac•ad′am•ize′** *v.*

ma•caque (mə-kăk′, -käk′) *n.* A short-tailed monkey of the genus *Macaca* of SE Asia, Japan, Gibraltar, and N Africa.

mac•a•ro•ni (măk′ə-rō′nē) *n.* Dried pasta, usu. in the shape of hollow tubes.

mac•a•roon (măk′ə-ro͞on′, măk′ə-ro͞on′) *n.* A cookie made with sugar, egg whites, and ground almonds or coconut.

ma•caw (mə-kô′) *n.* Any of various tropical American parrots of the genera *Ara* and *Anodorhynchus,* with long tails, powerful curved bills, and usu. brilliant plumage.

Mac•ca•bees (măk′ə-bēz′) *pl.n.* (*sing. in number*). —See table at BIBLE.

mace[1] (mās) *n.* **1.** A heavy club with a flanged or spiked metal head, used in medieval times for crushing armor. **2.** A ceremonial staff carried or displayed as a symbol of authority.

mace[2] (mās) *n.* A spice made from the bright-red covering that partly encloses the nutmeg kernel.

mac•er•ate (măs′ə-rāt′) *v.* **-at•ed, -at•ing. 1.** To make soft so as to separate into constituents by soaking in a liquid. **2.** To cause to become thin, usu. by starvation. **—mac′er•a′tion** *n.*

Mach (mäk) *n.* Mach number.

ma•chet•e (mə-shĕt'ē, -chĕt'ē) *n.* A large heavy knife with a broad blade, used as a weapon and for cutting vegetation.

Mach•i•a•vel•li•an•ism (măk'ē-ə-vĕl'ē-ə-nĭz'əm, -vĕl'ə-) *n.* The doctrine of Machiavelli that denies the relevance of morality in political affairs.

mach•i•nate (măk'ə-nāt', măsh'-) *v.* **-nat•ed, -nat•ing.** To plot. **—mach'i•na'tion** *n.* **—mach'i•na'tor** *n.*

ma•chine (mə-shēn') *n.* **1. a.** A system or device built to use energy in performing a task <a sewing *machine*> **b.** Any of several simple devices, as an inclined plane, lever, or screw, that act on an applied force so as to change its magnitude or direction or both. **2.** A device or system, as a computer, that performs or helps in performing a human task. **3.** One who acts mechanically or rigidly. **4.** An organized group whose members are under the control of one or more leaders. *—v.* **-chined, -chin•ing.** To shape by machine.

machine gun *n.* An automatic rapid-fire gun, often mounted, that uses small-arms ammunition. **—ma•chine'-gun'** *v.* **—machine gunner** *n.*

machine language *n. Computer Sci.* A set of coded instructions that a computer can use directly without further translation.

ma•chin•er•y (mə-shē'nə-rē, -shēn'rē) *n., pl.* **-ies. 1.** Machines or machine parts as a whole. **2.** The operating parts of a machine. **3.** A system of related elements that functions in a definable way.

ma•chin•ist (mə-shē'nĭst) *n.* A person skilled in the use of machine tools.

ma•chis•mo (mä-chēz'mō) *n.* An exaggerated sense of masculinity stressing aggressiveness, virility, and courage.

Mach number *n.* The ratio of an object's speed to the speed of sound in the surrounding atmosphere.

ma•cho (mä'chō') *adj.* Marked by machismo. *—n., pl.* **-chos. 1.** Machismo. **2.** A man who exhibits machismo.

mack•er•el (măk'ər-əl, măk'rəl) *n., pl.* **-el** *or* **-els.** An Atlantic food fish, *Scomber scombrus,* with dark wavy bars on the back and a silvery belly.

mack•i•naw (măk'ə-nô') *n.* A short double-breasted coat of thick, usu. plaid woolen material.

mack•in•tosh *also* **mac•in•tosh** (măk'ĭn-tŏsh') *n. esp. Brit.* **1.** A raincoat. **2.** A lightweight waterproof fabric orig. of rubberized cotton.

mac•ra•mé (măk'rə-mā') *n.* Lacework made of rough cords or strings woven and knotted into a pattern.

mac•ro (măk'rō') *n., pl.* **-ros.** A single instruction in computer programming language that represents a series of instructions in machine language.

mac•ro•bi•ot•ics (măk'rō-bī-ŏt'ĭks) *n. (sing. in number).* A method believed by its adherents to promote longevity, chiefly by means of a diet consisting mainly of whole grains, vegetable, and fish. **—mac'ro•bi•ot'ic** *adj.*

mac•ro•code (măk'rə-kōd') *n.* A coding system in which single codes generate several sets of computer instructions.

mac•ro•cosm (măk'rō-kŏz'əm) *n.* **1.** The entire world **:** universe. **2.** A system reflecting on a large scale one of its component parts or systems. **—mac'ro•cos'mic** *adj.*

mac•ro•in•struc•tion (măk'rō-ĭn-strŭk'-shən) *n.* A macro.

ma•cron (mā'krŏn', -krən) *n.* A diacritical mark, as the (ā) in *take,* placed over a vowel to indicate a long sound or phonetic value in pronunciation.

mac•ro•phage (măk'rə-fāj') *n.* A large phagocytic cell.

mac•ro•scop•ic (măk'rə-skŏp'ĭk) *also* **mac•ro•scop•i•cal** (-ĭ-kəl) *adj.* Large enough to be seen with the unaided eye.

mad (măd) *adj.* **mad•der, mad•dest. 1.** Afflicted with a mental disorder **:** insane. **2.** *Informal.* Very enthusiastic <*mad* about baseball> **3.** Angry **:** resentful. **4.** Lacking restraint or reason **:** foolish. **5.** Marked by frantic confusion or excitement <a *mad* dash for the exit> **6.** Boisterously happy **:** hilarious <a *mad* time at the party> **7.** Rabid. **—mad'ly** *adv.* **—mad'man'** *n.* **—mad'ness** *n.* **—mad'wom'an** *n.*

Mad•am (măd'əm) *n.* **1.** *pl.* **Mes•dames** (mā-dăm'). **a.** —Used as a courtesy title in addressing a woman. **b.** —Used formerly as a courtesy title before a given name but now used only before a surname or a title indicating rank or office <*Madam* Justice> **2. madam.** The mistress of a household. **3. madam.** A woman manager of a brothel.

Ma•dame (mə-dăm', măd'əm) *n., pl.* **Mes•dames** (mā-dăm') —Used as a French courtesy title for a married woman.

mad•cap (măd'kăp') *n.* A rash, impulsive person. *—adj.* Impulsive **:** wild.

mad•den (măd'n) *v.* **1.** To drive mad **:** derange. **2.** To make angry **:** infuriate. **—mad'den•ing•ly** *adv.*

mad•der (măd'ər) *n.* **1. a.** A plant of the genus *Rubia,* esp. *R. tinctoria,* with small yellow flowers and a red fleshy root. **b.** The root of this plant, once an important source of dye. **2.** A red dye derived from the madder root.

mad•ding (măd'ĭng) *adj. Archaic.* Frenzied <the *madding* crowd>

made (mād) *v. p.t. & p.p. of* MAKE.

Ma•dei•ra (mə-dîr'ə) *n.* A fortified dessert wine.

Mad•e•moi•selle (măd'ə-mə-zĕl', măd'-mwə-zĕl') *n., pl.* **Mad•e•moi•selles** (-zĕlz') *or* **Mes•de•moi•selles** (mād'mwä-zĕl') **1.** —Used as a French courtesy title for a young girl or unmarried woman. **2. mademoiselle.** A French governess.

made-to-or•der (mād'tə-ôr'dər) *adj.* **1.** Custom-made. **2.** Highly suitable.

made-up (mād'ŭp') *adj.* **1.** Invented **:** fabricated <a *made-up* alibi> **2.** Marked by the application of make-up <*made-up* lips>

mad•house (măd'hous') *n.* **1.** Formerly, an insane asylum. **2.** *Informal.* A place of great confusion and disorder.

Madison Avenue *n.* The American advertising industry.

ma•dras (măd'rəs, mə-drăs', -dräs') *n.* A fine-textured cotton cloth usu. having a striped or plaid design.

mad•ri•gal (măd'rĭ-gəl) *n.* A musical composition for 2 or more unaccompanied voices that was developed during the early Renaissance.

mael•strom (māl'strəm) *n.* **1.** An extraordinarily violent whirlpool. **2.** A situation resembling a maelstrom in turmoil <a *maelstrom* of scandal>

maes•tro (mīs'trō) *n., pl.* **-tros** *or* **-tri** (-trē). A master in an art, esp. a famous conductor or composer of music.

Ma•fi•a (mä'fē-ə) *n.* **1.** A secret terrorist organization in Sicily. **2.** An alleged international criminal organization.

Ma•fi•o•so (mä'fē-ō'sō) *n., pl.* **-si** (-sē'). A member of the Mafia.

mag•a•zine (măg'ə-zēn', măg'ə-zēn') *n.* **1.** A place for storage, esp. of ammunition. **2.** A periodical containing written matter, as articles, and usu. illustrations and advertising. **3. a.** A compartment for holding the cartridges in a firearm. **b.** A compartment in a camera for holding rolls or cartridges of film.

▲ ***word history:*** The use of *magazine* to mean "a periodical publication" is a specialized development of the original, more general meaning "storehouse." *Magazine* was at one time used in book titles to mean a storehouse of information on a special topic, equivalent to the use of *encyclopedia* today. The word was also used in titles of periodical publications that contained a storehouse of miscellaneous literary works, articles on various topics, and other features. From the latter use the word *magazine* became a generic term for all such publications.

ma•gen•ta (mə-jĕn'tə) *n.* A vivid purplish red.

mag•got (măg'ət) *n.* The legless soft-bodied larva of any of various insects of the order Diptera, often found in decaying matter. **—mag'got•y** *adj.*

Ma•gi (mā'jī') *pl.n.* The 3 wise men of the East who traveled to Bethlehem to worship the infant Jesus.

mag•ic (măj'ĭk) *n.* **1.** The art that purports to control or forecast natural events or forces by invoking the supernatural. **2.** Exercise of sleight of hand or conjuring for entertainment. **3.** A mysterious quality of enchantment <the *magic* of exotic lands> ★ ***syns:*** CONJURATION, SORCERY, WITCHCRAFT, WITCHING, WIZARDRY **—mag'ic, mag'i•cal** *adj.* **—mag'i•cal•ly** *adv.* **—ma•gi'cian** (mə-jĭsh'ən) *n.*

mag•is•te•ri•al (măj'ĭ-stîr'ē-əl) *adj.* **1.** Of, relating to, or typical of a master or teacher : authoritative. **2.** Overbearing : dogmatic. **3.** Of or relating to a magistrate or his or her official functions.

mag•is•trate (măj'ĭ-strāt', -strĭt) *n.* **1.** A civil officer empowered to administer and enforce law. **2.** A minor official with limited judicial authority, as a justice of the peace.

mag•ma (măg'mə, mäg'-) *n., pl.* **-ma•ta** (-mä'tə) *or* **-mas.** *Geol.* Molten matter beneath the earth's crust that often cools and hardens to form igneous rock.

mag•nan•i•mous (măg-năn'ə-məs) *adj.* Noble of heart and mind, esp. generous in forgiving. **—mag'na•nim'i•ty** (-nə-nĭm'ĭ-tē) *n.* **—mag•nan'i•mous•ly** *adv.* **—mag•nan'i•mous•ness** *n.*

mag•nate (măg'nāt') *n.* A person of influence or power, esp. in business or industry : tycoon <an oil *magnate*>

mag•ne•sia (măg-nē'zhə, -shə) *n.* A white, powdery compound that is an oxide of magnesium and is used esp. as a laxative.

mag•ne•si•um (măg-nē'zē-əm, -zhəm) *n.* *Symbol* **Mg** A light, moderately hard, silvery metallic element.

mag•net (măg'nĭt) *n.* **1.** An object that is surrounded by a magnetic field and attracts iron or steel. **2.** An electromagnet. **3.** One that exerts attraction. **—mag'net•ism** *n.*

mag•net•ic (măg-nĕt'ĭk) *adj.* **1.** Of or pertaining to magnets or magnetism. **2.** Having the properties of a magnet. **3.** Capable of being magnetized. **4.** Having an unusual ability or power to attract <a *magnetic* personality> **—mag•net'i•cal•ly** *adv.*

magnetic disk *n. Computer Sci.* **1.** A memory device covered with a magnetic coating on which information is stored by magnetization of microscopically small needles. **2.** A floppy disk. **3.** A hard disk.

magnetic equator *n.* A line joining all points on the earth's surface where a magnetic needle balances horizontally without dipping.

magnetic field *n.* A detectable force that exists at every point in the region around a magnet or electric current.

magnetic north *n.* The direction of the earth's magnetic field to which the N-seeking pole of a magnetic needle points when free from local magnetic influence.

magnetic recording *n.* The recording of a signal, as sound or television images, on a magnetizable surface for storage and subsequent retrieval.

magnetic resonance im•ag•ing (ĭm'ĭ-jĭng) *n.* The use of nuclear magnetic resonance to produce images of atoms and molecules in solids, esp. human tissues and organs.

magnetic tape *n.* A plastic tape having a magnetizable coating for use in magnetic recording.

mag•net•ite (măg'nĭ-tīt') *n.* A mineral form of black iron oxide that is an important iron ore.

mag•net•ize (măg'nĭ-tīz') *v.* **-ized, -iz•ing. 1.** To make magnetic. **2.** To attract, charm, or influence <a speaker who *magnetized* the audience> **—mag′net·iz′a·ble** *adj.* **—mag′net·i·za′tion** *n.* **—mag′net·iz′er** *n.*

mag·ne·to (măg-nē′tō) *n., pl.* **-tos.** A small alternator that works by means of permanent magnets, used to generate the electricity for the spark in some engines.

mag·ne·tom·e·ter (măg′nĭ-tŏm′ĭ-tər) *n.* An instrument for comparing the intensity and direction of magnetic fields.

mag·ne·to·sphere (măg-nē′tə-sfîr′) *n.* A region surrounding the earth, extending from about 500 to several thousand km above the surface, in which charged particles are trapped and their behavior dominated by the earth's magnetic field.

mag·nif·i·cent (măg-nĭf′ĭ-sənt) *adj.* **1.** Lavish **:** grand. **2.** Noble in thought or deed **:** exalted. **3.** Outstanding of its kind **:** superlative <a *magnificent* painting> **—mag·nif′i·cence** *n.* **—mag·nif′i·cent·ly** *adv.*

mag·ni·fy (măg′nə-fī′) *v.* **-fied, -fy·ing. 1.** To make larger in size **:** enlarge. **2.** To cause to appear greater or seem more important **:** exaggerate. **3.** To make (an object) appear larger than it really is, esp. by means of a lens. **4.** To praise or glorify. **—mag′ni·fi·ca′tion** *n.* **—mag′ni·fi′er** *n.*

mag·nil·o·quent (măg-nĭl′ə-kwənt) *adj.* Lofty and extravagant in speech **:** grandiloquent. **—mag·nil′o·quence** *n.* **—mag·nil′o·quent·ly** *adv.*

mag·ni·tude (măg′nĭ-to͞od′, -tyo͞od′) *n.* **1.** Greatness in size, extent, or significance. **2.** Size **:** quantity. **3.** *Astron.* The relative brightness of a celestial body expressed on a numerical scale.

mag·no·lia (măg-nōl′yə) *n.* Any of various trees and shrubs of the genus *Magnolia,* many of which are cultivated for their white, pink, purple, or yellow flowers.

mag·num (măg′nəm) *n.* A bottle for wine or liquor holding approx. 2/5 gal.

mag·num o·pus (măg′nəm ō′pəs) *n.* A literary or artistic masterpiece, esp. an artist's, writer's, or composer's greatest single work.

mag·pie (măg′pī′) *n.* Any of various birds of the family Corvidae, found worldwide and noted for their chattering call.

ma·guey (mə-gā′, măg′wā) *n., pl.* **-gueys. 1.** Any of various agaves or related plants. **2.** The fiber obtained from a maguey.

Mag·yar (măg′yär′, mäg′-) *n.* A member of the chief ethnic group of Hungary. **—Mag′yar′** *adj.*

ma·ha·ra·jah *or* **ma·ha·ra·ja** (mä′hə-rä′jə, -zhə) *n.* A king or prince in India ranking above a rajah.

ma·ha·ra·ni *or* **ma·ha·ra·nee** (mä′hə-rä′nē) *n.* **1.** The wife of a maharajah. **2.** A princess in India ranking above a rani.

ma·ha·ri·shi (mä′hə-rē′shē, mə-här′ə-shē) *n.* A Hindu teacher of spiritual knowledge.

ma·hat·ma (mə-hät′mə, -hăt′-) *n.* A person venerated in India and Tibet for great knowledge and love of humanity.

mah·jong *also* **mah·jongg** (mä′zhŏng′, -zhông′) *n.* A Chinese game usu. played by 4 persons with rectangular tiles bearing various designs.

ma·hog·a·ny (mə-hŏg′ə-nē) *n., pl.* **-nies. 1.** Any of various tropical American trees of the genus *Swietenia,* prized for their hard, reddish-brown wood. **2.** The wood of a mahogany, esp. of *S. mahogani,* used for making furniture.

ma·hout (mə-hout′) *n.* The keeper and driver of an elephant.

maid (mād) *n.* **1.** A girl or an unmarried woman. **2.** A woman servant.

maid·en (mād′n) *n.* MAID 1. *—adj.* **1.** Of, relating to, or suitable for a maiden. **2.** Being an unmarried woman <a *maiden* aunt> **3.** Earliest or first <a *maiden* flight> **—maid′en·hood′** *n.*

maid·en·hair (mād′n-hâr′) *n.* A fern of the genus *Adiantum,* with dark stems and light-green feathery fronds.

maiden name *n.* A woman's family name if different from her married name.

maid of honor *n., pl.* **maids of honor.** An unmarried woman who is the chief attendant of a bride.

maid·ser·vant (mād′sûr′vənt) *n.* A woman servant.

mail[1] (māl) *n.* **1. a.** Material, as letters, handled by a postal system. **b.** Mail processed for distribution from a post office at a specified time <the morning *mail*> **2.** *often* **mails.** A nation's system for transporting mail. *—v.* To send by mail. **—mail′er** *n.*

▲ ***word history:*** The word *mail*[1], which denotes the material handled by the post office, is a survivor of the days when the few letters and dispatches that were exchanged were carried by horsemen in their traveling bags. In Middle English times the word *mail* meant simply "bag," esp. one used by a traveler for provisions. Such bags were used to carry letters, and the word *mail* eventually came to designate the contents rather than the container.

mail[2] (māl) *n.* Armor made of connected metal rings, overlapping scales, or loops of chain. **—mailed** *adj.*

mail·box (māl′bŏks′) *n.* **1.** A public container where mail is deposited for collection. **2.** A private box for incoming mail.

mail drop *n.* **1.** A receptacle or slot for mail delivery. **2.** An address at which one receives mail but does not reside.

mail·man (māl′măn′, -mən) *n.* One who delivers mail.

mail order *n.* An order for goods received and often filled by mail.

maim (mām) *v.* **1.** To disable or disfigure, usu. by depriving of the use of a limb or bodily member **:** cripple. **2.** To make imperfect or defective **:** impair.

main (mān) *adj.* Being most important **:** chief. *—n.* **1.** The principal or most important part or point. **2.** A large pipe, duct, conduit, or conductor used to carry water, oil, gas, or electricity. **3.** Physical power <might and *main*> —**main'ly** *adv.*

main•frame (mān'frām') *n.* A large, powerful computer, often serving several connected terminals.

main•land (mān'lănd', -lənd) *n.* The chief land mass of a country, territory, or continent.

main•line (mān'līn') *v. Slang.* To inject a narcotic drug directly into a vein.

main•mast (mān'məst) *n.* The principal mast of a sailing vessel.

main•sail (mān'səl) *n.* The principal sail of a sailing vessel.

main•spring (mān'spring') *n.* **1.** The principal spring in a mechanism, esp. a clock or watch. **2.** A motivating cause.

main•stay (mān'stā') *n.* **1.** A strong rope that supports the mainmast of a sailing vessel. **2.** A main support.

main•stream (mān'strēm') *n.* The chief direction or trend of an action or line of thought. —**main'stream'** *adj. & v.*

main street *n.* **1.** The principal street of a small town or city. **2. Main Street.** The smug, materialistic, and provincial culture of a small town.

main•tain (mān-tān') *v.* **1.** To carry on : continue <*maintain* a sound economy> **2.** To keep in a desirable condition <*maintain* bridges> **3.** To provide for <*maintain* a large family> **4.** To defend, as against attack or danger. **5.** To declare : assert. —**main•tain'a•ble** *adj.* —**main'te•nance** (-tə-nəns) *n.*

maî•tre d' (mā'trə dē', mā'tər) *n., pl.* **maî•tre d's** (dēz'). *Informal.* A maître d'hôtel.

maî•tre d'hô•tel (mā'trə dō-tĕl') *n., pl.* **maî•tres d'hô•tel** (mā'trə dō-tĕl'). **1.** A headwaiter. **2.** A major-domo.

maize (māz) *n.* Corn.

maj•es•ty (măj'ĭ-stē) *n., pl.* **-ties. 1.** The authority, greatness, and dignity of a sovereign. **2. Majesty.** —Used as a title in speaking of or to a sovereign <Your royal *Majesty*> **3.** A quality of stateliness or grandeur. —**ma•jes'tic** (mə-jĕs'tĭk) *adj.* —**ma•jes'ti•cal•ly** *adv.*

ma•jol•i•ca (mə-jŏl'ĭ-kə, -yŏl'-) *n.* Tin-glazed earthenware often richly decorated and colored, esp. an earthenware of this type made in Italy.

ma•jor (mā'jər) *adj.* **1.** Greater in importance, rank, or stature <a *major* breakthrough in virus research> **2.** Demanding great attention : serious <a *major* accident> **3.** *Mus.* Designating a scale or mode with half steps between the 3rd and 4th and the 7th and 8th degrees. —*n.* **1.** An officer in the U.S. Army, Air Force, or Marine Corps ranking above a captain and below a lieutenant colonel. **2. a.** A field or subject selected as an academic specialization. **b.** A student specializing in a particular major. —*v.* To be a student in an academic major.

ma•jor-do•mo (mā'jər-dō'mō) *n., pl.* **-mos. 1.** The chief steward or butler in the household of a sovereign or noble. **2.** A steward or butler.

ma•jor•ette (mā'jə-rĕt') *n.* A drum majorette.

major general *n.* An officer in the U.S. Army, Air Force, or Marine Corps ranking above a brigadier general and below a lieutenant general.

ma•jor•i•ty (mə-jôr'ĭ-tē, -jŏr'-) *n., pl.* **-ties. 1.** The greater number or part of something. **2.** The excess of a greater number over a smaller number : margin <won by a *majority* of 5,000 votes> **3.** The status of having reached the legal age of responsibility.

ma•jor-med•i•cal (mā'jər-mĕd'ĭ-kəl) *adj.* Of, pertaining to, or being an insurance plan that pays for most of the medical bills incurred during a major illness.

make (māk) *v.* **made** (mād), **mak•ing. 1. a.** To cause to happen or exist. **b.** To bring into being : create or fashion <*make* a blouse> **2. a.** To cause to be or become <*made* our feelings known> **b.** To cause to assume a specified function or role <*made* me boss> **3.** To compel <*made* us go> **4.** To carry out, engage in, or perform <*made* an attempt> **5. a.** To formulate in the mind <*make* plans> **b.** To arrive at <*make* decisions> **6.** To acquire, gain, or earn <*make* friends><*make* money> **7.** To achieve : attain. **8.** To set in order : prepare. **9.** To provide <*make* room> **10. a.** To grow or develop into <*made* a good doctor> **b.** To be capable of being made into <Oak *makes* sturdy furniture.> **11.** To amount to in importance <*makes* a big difference> **12.** To institute or establish : enact <*make* new laws> —*n.* **1.** An act or process of making. **2.** The manner or style in which something is made. **3.** A particular line of manufactured goods : brand <a famous *make* of shoe> —**make believe.** To pretend. —**make do.** To manage with whatever is available. —**make fun of.** To mock : ridicule. —**make good. 1.** To carry out : fulfill <*made good* our vow> **2.** To repay : idemnify <*make good* one's obligations> **3.** To succeed <*make good* in the leading role> —**make light of.** To treat as unimportant <*made light of* our fears> —**make out. 1.** To see, esp. with difficulty. **2.** To comprehend <couldn't *make out* what he meant> **3.** To fill in (e.g., a document). **4.** *Slang.* To fare <*made out* poorly in politics> —**make up. 1.** To invent : fabricate <*made up* an alibi> **2.** To compensate for a transgression or omission. **3.** To come to a reconciliation after a misunderstanding or argument. **4.** To decide <*make up* your mind.> **5.** To apply cosmetics. —**make way. 1.** To provide room for passage. **2.** To make progress. —**mak'er** *n.*

make-be•lieve (māk'bĭ-lēv') *n.* Playful pretense. —**make'-be•lieve'** *adj.*

make•shift (māk'shĭft') *n.* Something used as a temporary substitute. —**make'shift'** *adj.*

make-up *also* **make•up** (māk'ŭp') *n.* **1.** The manner in which something is put together : construction. **2.** The qualities of temperament constituting a personality. **3.** Cosmetics, as eye shadow or lipstick, applied to the face.

make-work (māk'wûrk') *n.* Work that consumes time but is not productive.

ma•ku•ta (mä-ko͞o'tä) *n. pl. of* LIKUTA.

Mal•a•chi (măl'ə-kī') *n.* —See table at BIBLE.

mal•a•chite (măl'ə-kīt') *n.* A green mineral carbonate of copper used as an ore of copper and for ornamental stoneware.

mal•ad•just•ed (măl'ə-jŭs'tĭd) *adj.* Poorly adjusted, as to one's environment or circumstances. **—mal'ad•just'ment** *n.*

mal•a•droit (măl'ə-droit') *adj.* Marked by lack of dexterity : awkward. **—mal'a•droit'ly** *adv.* **—mal'a•droit'ness** *n.*

mal•a•dy (măl'ə-dē) *n., pl.* **-dies.** A disease or disorder : sickness.

Mal•a•gas•y (măl'ə-găs'ē) *n., pl.* **-y** *or* **-ies.** A native or inhabitant of Madagascar. **—Mal'a•gas'y** *adj.*

mal•aise (mə-lāz', mă-) *n.* A vague feeling of ill-being.

ma•la•mute (mä'lə-myo͞ot', măl'ə-) *n.* A powerful dog, orig. bred in Alaska as a sled dog, with a thick gray, black, or white coat and a bushy tail.

mal•a•prop•ism (măl'ə-prŏp-ĭz'əm) *n.* Ludicrous misuse of a word.

mal•a•pro•pos (măl'ăp-rə-pō') *adj.* Inappropriate. **—mal'a•pro•pos'** *adv.*

ma•lar•i•a (mə-lâr'ē-ə) *n.* An infectious disease transmitted by the bite of the infected female anopheles mosquito and marked by cycles of chills, fever, and sweating. **—ma•lar'i•al** *adj.*

ma•lar•key *also* **ma•lar•ky** (mə-lär'kē) *n. Slang.* Nonsense.

Mal•a•thi•on (măl'ə-thī'ŏn'). A trademark for an organic compound used as an insecticide.

mal•con•tent (măl'kən-tĕnt') *adj.* Unhappy with existing circumstances : discontented. **—mal'con•tent'** *n.*

mal de mer (măl' də mâr') *n.* Seasickness.

male (māl) *adj.* **1.** Of, relating to, or being the sex that has organs to produce spermatozoa for fertilizing ova. **2.** Of, relating to, or typical of the male sex : masculine. **3.** Designed to fit into a matching socket or opening. *—n.* An individual of the male sex. **—male'ness** *n.*

mal•e•dic•tion (măl'ĭ-dĭk'shən) *n.* A curse.

mal•e•fac•tor (măl'ə-făk'tər) *n.* **1.** One who has committed a crime : criminal. **2.** An evildoer. **—mal'e•fac'tion** *n.*

ma•lef•ic (mə-lĕf'ĭk) *adj.* **1.** Having a malignant influence : sinister. **2.** Malicious.

ma•lef•i•cence (mə-lĕf'ə-səns) *n.* **1.** Evil or harm. **2.** The quality or state of being malefic. **—ma•lef'i•cent** *adj.*

ma•lev•o•lent (mə-lĕv'ə-lənt) *adj.* **1.** Having or exhibiting ill will or spite : malicious. **2.** Having an evil influence. ★ ***syns:*** EVIL, MALICIOUS, MALIGN, MALIGNANT, MEAN, NASTY, POISONOUS, SPITEFUL, VENOMOUS, VICIOUS, WICKED **—ma•lev'o•lence** *n.* **—ma•lev'o•lent•ly** *adv.*

mal•fea•sance (măl-fē'zəns) *n. Law.* Misconduct, esp. by a public official.

mal•for•ma•tion (măl'fôr-mā'shən) *n.* An abnormal form or structure. **—mal•formed'** *adj.*

mal•func•tion (măl-fŭngk'shən) *v.* To fail to function properly. **—mal•func'tion** *n.*

mal•ice (măl'ĭs) *n.* **1.** The desire to harm others : ill will. **2.** *Law.* Intent to commit an unlawful act or injure another without just cause or reason. **—ma•li'cious** (mə-lĭsh'əs) *adj.* **—ma•li'cious•ly** *adv.*

ma•lign (mə-līn') *v.* To speak evil of. *—adj.* **1.** Evil in nature, intent, or influence. **2.** Strongly suggestive of evil, menace, or harm. ★ ***syns:*** BALEFUL, SINISTER **—ma•lign'er** *n.*

ma•lig•nant (mə-lĭg'nənt) *adj.* **1.** Exhibiting intense malevolence. **2.** Extremely harmful : pernicious. **3.** *Pathol.* **a.** Designating an abnormal growth that tends to spread. **b.** Life-threatening : virulent. **—ma•lig'nan•cy** *n.* **—ma•lig'nant•ly** *adv.* **—ma•lig'ni•ty** *n.*

ma•lin•ger (mə-lĭng'gər) *v.* To pretend to be ill or injured in order to avoid responsibility or work. **—ma•lin'ger•er** *n.*

mall (môl, măl) *n.* **1.** A shaded public promenade or walk. **2. a.** A street lined with shops and closed to vehicles. **b.** A shopping center. **c.** A large concourse affording access to shops, businesses, and restaurants. **3.** A center strip dividing a highway.

mal•lard (măl'ərd) *n., pl.* **mallard** *or* **-lards.** A wild duck, *Anas platyrhynchos,* the male of which has a green head and neck.

mal•le•a•ble (măl'ē-ə-bəl) *adj.* **1.** Capable of being shaped, bent, or drawn out, as by hammering. **2.** Capable of being altered or influenced : tractable. ★ ***syns:*** DUCTILE, FLEXIBLE, MOLDABLE, PLASTIC, PLIABLE, PLIANT, SUPPLE, WORKABLE **—mal'le•a•bil'i•ty, mal'le•a•ble•ness** *n.* **—mal'le•a•bly** *adv.*

mal•let (măl'ĭt) *n.* **1. a.** A hammer with a cylindrical wooden head and a short handle. **b.** A tool with a large head for striking a surface without damaging it. **2.** A long-handled implement for striking a ball, as in croquet and polo.

mal•le•us (măl'ē-əs) *n., pl.* **-le•i** (-ē-ī', -ē-ē'). *Anat.* The largest of 3 small bones in the middle ear.

mal•low (măl'ō) *n.* A plant of the widely distributed genus *Malva,* bearing pink or white flowers.

mal•nour•ished (măl-nûr'ĭsht) *adj.* Improperly nourished.

mal•nu•tri•tion (măl'no͞o-trĭsh'ən, -nyo͞o-) *n.* Faulty and esp. insufficient nutrition.

mal•oc•clu•sion (măl'ə-klo͞o'zhən) *n.* Failure of the upper and lower teeth to meet properly.

mal•o•dor (măl-ō'dər) *n.* A bad odor. **—mal•o'dor•ous** *adj.* **—mal•o'dor•ous•ly** *adv.* **—mal•o'dor•ous•ness** *n.*

mal•prac•tice (măl-prăk'tĭs) *n.* **1.** Improper or negligent treatment by a physician that results in injury or damage to the patient. **2.** Improper or unethical conduct on the part of one, as a lawyer, rendering professional services.

malt (môlt) *n.* **1.** Grain, usu. barley, that has sprouted, used chiefly in brewing and distilling. **2.** An alcoholic beverage brewed from malt. **—malt'y** *adj.*

malt•ed milk (môl'tĭd) *n.* **1.** A powder consisting of dried milk, a malt extract, and wheat flour. **2.** A drink made of malted milk powder mixed with milk and usu. flavoring and ice cream.

malt liquor *n.* Fermented beer or ale made with malt.

mal•tose (môl'tōs', -tōz') *n.* A sugar found in malt.

mal•treat (măl-trēt') *v.* To treat abusively and harshly. **—mal•treat'ment** *n.*

ma•ma *also* **mam•ma** (mä'mə, mə-mä') *n.* Mother.

mam•ba (mäm'bə) *n.* A venomous tropical African snake of the genus *Dendraspis,* esp. *D. angusticeps,* a black or green tree snake.

mam•bo (mäm'bō) *n., pl.* **-bos.** A dance of Latin-American origin that resembles the rumba.

mam•mal (măm'əl) *n.* A member of the group of vertebrate animals, including humans, the females of which secrete milk for nourishing their young. **—mam•ma'li•an** (mă-mā'lē-ən) *adj. & n.*

mam•mal•o•gy (mă-măl'ə-jē, -mŏl'-) *n.* The branch of zoology that deals with mammals. **—mam•mal'o•gist** *n.*

mam•ma•ry (măm'ər-ē) *adj.* Of, relating to, or being a mammary gland.

mammary gland *n.* A milk-producing organ in female mammals that consists of clusters of small cavities with ducts terminating in a nipple.

mam•mo•gram (măm'ə-grăm') *n.* An x-ray image produced by mammography.

mam•mog•ra•phy (mă-mŏg'rə-fē) *n., pl.* **-phies.** X-ray examination of the breasts for detection of tumors.

mam•mon (măm'ən) *n. often* **Mammon.** Riches considered as an evil influence or an object of worship.

mam•moth (măm'əth) *n.* An extinct elephant of the genus *Mammuthus,* once found throughout the N Hemisphere. *—adj.* Of great size : enormous.

man (măn) *n., pl.* **men** (mĕn). **1.** An adult male human being. **2.** A human being, regardless of sex. **3.** The human race : mankind. **4.** *Informal.* **a.** A husband. **b.** A male lover or sweetheart. **5.** A male servant or subordinate. **6.** One of the pieces used in a board game, as chess. **7.** *often* **Man.** *Slang.* **a.** A policeman. **b.** A man, esp. a white man, in a position of power or authority. *—v.* **manned, man•ning. 1.** To supply with men, as for defense or support. **2.** To be stationed at esp. in order to operate <*man* the guns>

man•a•cle (măn'ə-kəl) *n.* **1.** One of a pair of handcuffs. **2.** A fetter : restraint. **—man'a•cle** *v.*

man•age (măn'ĭj) *v.* **-aged, -ag•ing. 1.** To direct or control the use of. **2. a.** To exert control over. **b.** To make submissive. **3.** To succeed in accomplishing one's purpose : get along. **4.** To direct or administer (e.g., a business). **—man'age•a•bil'i•ty** *n.* **—man'age•a•ble** *adj.* **—man'age•a•bly** *adv.*

man•age•ment (măn'ĭj-mənt) *n.* **1.** The act, practice, or process of managing. **2.** Those who manage an organization. **3.** Executive skill.

man•ag•er (măn'ĭ-jər) *n.* **1.** One who manages a business or enterprise. **2.** One who directs an athlete or team. **—man'a•ge'ri•al** *adj.* **—man'ag•er•ship'** *n.*

ma•ña•na (mä-nyä'nä) *adv.* **1.** Tomorrow. **2.** At an indefinite time in the future.

man•a•tee (măn'ə-tē') *n.* An aquatic mammal of the genus *Trichechus* found in Atlantic coastal waters of the tropical Americas and Africa.

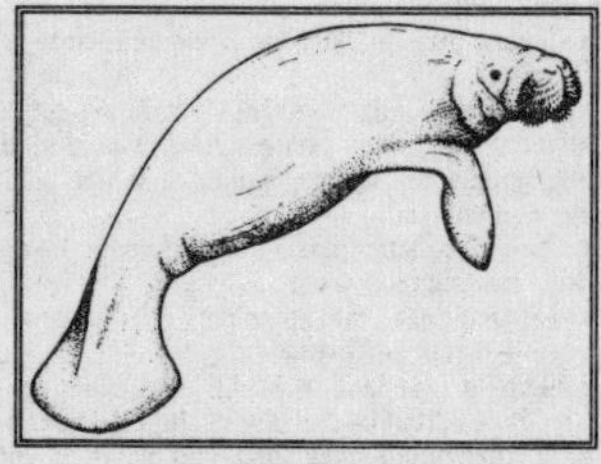

manatee

Man•dan (măn'dăn') *n., pl.* **-dan** *or* **-dans. 1.** A member of an American Indian people of North Dakota. **2.** Their Siouan language.

man•da•rin (măn'də-rĭn) *n.* A member of any of the 9 ranks of high public officials in imperial China.

man•date (măn'dāt') *n.* **1.** An authoritative command. **2.** An instruction given by an electorate to a representative. **3. a.** Control over a territory granted by the League of Nations to one of its member nations. **b.** A territory under mandate. **—man'date'** *v.*

man•da•to•ry (măn'də-tôr'ē, -tōr'ē) *adj.* **1.** Of, relating to, having the nature of, or containing a mandate. **2.** Obligatory.

man•di•ble (măn'də-bəl) *n.* **1.** A jaw of a vertebrate, esp. a lower jaw. **2.** Either of the parts of a bird's beak. **—man•dib'u•lar** (-dĭb'yə-lər) *adj.*

man•do•lin (măn'dl-ĭn', măn'dl-ĭn') *n.* A stringed musical instrument with a pear-shaped body and a fretted neck.

man•drake (măn'drāk') *n.* A Eurasian plant, *Mandragora officinarum,* bearing purplish flowers and a branched root thought to look like the human body.

man•drel *or* **man•dril** (măn'drəl) *n.* **1.** A spindle or shaft used to hold material that is being shaped on a lathe. **2.** A rotary shaft on which a working tool is mounted.

man•drill (măn′drĭl) *n.* A large fierce baboon, *Mandrillus sphinx,* of W Africa.

mane (mān) *n.* The long hair growing from the neck and head of certain animals, as a horse.

man-eat•er (măn′ē′tər) *n.* **1.** An animal that feeds on human flesh. **2.** A cannibal.

ma•nège *also* **ma•nege** (mă-nĕzh′) *n.* The art and practice of training a horse in classical riding maneuvers and exercises.

ma•neu•ver (mə-no͞o′vər, -nyo͞o′-) *n.* **1. a.** A tactical or strategic movement, as of troops or warships. **b.** *often* **maneuvers.** A military training exercise simulating combat. **2. a.** A physical movement or way of doing something requiring dexterity and skill. **b.** A controlled change in the course or position of a vehicle, as an aircraft or automobile. **3.** A calculated and skillful move **:** stratagem. **—ma•neu′ver** *v.* **—ma•neu′ver•a•bil′i•ty** *n.* **—ma•neu′ver•a•ble** *adj.*

man Friday *n.* An efficient, faithful male aide or employee.

man•ful (măn′fəl) *adj.* Courageous **:** resolute. **—man′ful•ly** *adv.* **—man′ful•ness** *n.*

man•ga•nese (măng′gə-nēz′, -nēs′) *n. Symbol* **Mn** A gray-white, brittle metallic element used to strengthen steel alloys.

mange (mānj) *n.* A contagious skin disease of mammals marked by itching and hair loss. **—mang′y** *adj.*

man•ger (mān′jər) *n.* A trough holding livestock feed.

man•gle[1] (măng′gəl) *v.* **-gled, -gling. 1.** To disfigure or mutilate by battering, cutting, or tearing. **2.** To spoil or ruin through ineptitude or ignorance <*mangled* the concerto> **—man′gler** *n.*

man•gle[2] (măng′gəl) *n.* A machine that presses laundry by running it between heated rollers.

man•go (măng′gō) *n., pl.* **-goes** *or* **-gos.** A tropical evergreen tree, *Mangifera indica,* cultivated for its sweet, juicy fruit.

man•grove (măn′grōv′, măng′grōv′) *n.* Any of various tropical evergreen trees or shrubs of the genus *Rhizophora,* having stiltlike roots and stems and forming dense thickets along tidal shores.

man•han•dle (măn′hăn′dəl) *v.* To handle roughly.

Man•hat•tan (măn-hăt′n, mən-) *n.* A cocktail of sweet vermouth and whiskey.

man•hole (măn′hōl′) *n.* A hole through which one may enter a sewer, conduit, or drain.

man•hood (măn′ho͝od′) *n.* **1.** The state or condition of being an adult male. **2.** The composite of qualities, as courage, determination, and vigor, often attributed to a man. **3.** Men as a group.

man-hour (măn′our′) *n.* An industrial unit of production equal to the work of one person in one hr.

man•hunt (măn′hŭnt′) *n.* An extensive organized search for a person, as a criminal fugitive.

ma•ni•a (mā′nē-ə, mān′yə) *n.* **1.** Inordinately intense enthusiasm **:** craze. **2.** A symptom of manic-depressive illness marked by intense excitement and physical overactivity.

—mania *suff.* An intense or unreasonable desire or enthusiasm for <ballleto*mania*>

ma•ni•ac (mā′nē-ăk′) *n.* **1.** An insane person. **2.** One with an excessive enthusiasm for something. **—ma′ni•ac′, ma•ni′a•cal** (mə-nī′ə-kəl) *adj.*

man•ic (măn′ĭk) *adj.* Of, pertaining to, or marked by mania.

man•ic-de•pres•sive (măn′ĭk-dĭ-prĕs′ĭv) *adj.* Characterized by or afflicted with alternating periods of manic excitation and depression. **—man′ic-de•pres′sive** *n.*

man•i•cot•ti (măn′ĭ-kŏt′ē) *n.* Tubular pasta filled with meat or ricotta cheese, usu. served hot with a tomato sauce.

man•i•cure (măn′ĭ-kyo͝or′) *n.* A cosmetic treatment for the hands and fingernails. —*v.* **-cured, -cur•ing. 1.** To shape, clean, and often polish the fingernails of. **2.** To trim or clip evenly or closely. **—man′i•cur′ist** *n.*

man•i•fest (măn′ə-fĕst′) *adj.* Clearly apparent **:** obvious. —*v.* To reveal **:** display. —*n.* A list of passengers or cargo. **—man′i•fest•ly** *adv.*

man•i•fes•ta•tion (măn′ə-fĕ-stā′shən) *n.* **1.** The act or process of manifesting **:** demonstration. **2.** An indication of the existence or presence of something.

man•i•fes•to (măn′ə-fĕs′tō) *n., pl.* **-toes** *or* **-tos.** A public declaration of intentions or principles, esp. of a political nature.

man•i•fold (măn′ə-fōld′) *adj.* **1.** Of many kinds **:** multiple. **2.** Having many parts, forms, or aspects. —*n.* A pipe with several openings for making a number of connections. —*v.* **1.** To make numerous copies of. **2.** To multiply.

man•i•kin *or* **man•ni•kin** (măn′ĭ-kĭn) *n.* **1.** A man short in stature. **2.** A mannequin.

Manila hemp *n.* The fiber of the abaca, used to make rope, paper, and cordage.

Manila paper *n.* Strong, usu. buff-colored paper or thin cardboard orig. manufactured from Manila hemp.

man•i•oc (măn′ē-ŏk′) *n.* CASSAVA.

ma•nip•u•late (mə-nĭp′yə-lāt′) *v.* **-lat•ed, -lat•ing. 1.** To control or operate with dexterity **:** handle. **2.** To manage or influence shrewdly and often deviously <*manipulated* the news> **—ma•nip′u•la′tion** *n.* **—ma•nip′u•la′tive** *adj.* **—ma•nip′u•la′tor** *n.*

man•kind (măn′kīnd′, -kīnd′) *n.* **1.** The human race. **2.** Men as opposed to women.

man•like (măn′līk′) *adj.* **1.** Resembling a human being. **2.** Belonging to or befitting a man.

man•ly (măn′lē) *adj.* **-li•er, -li•est. 1.** Having qualities traditionally attributed to a man. **2.** Of a man **:** masculine. —*adv.* In a manly way. **—man′li•ness** *n.*

man-made (măn′mād′) *adj.* Made by human beings.

man•na (măn′ə) *n.* **1.** Food miraculously provided for the Israelites during their flight from

Egypt. **2.** Something valuable that one receives unexpectedly.

manned (mănd) *adj.* Conveying or operated by a human being <a *manned* space station>

man•ne•quin (măn'ĭ-kĭn) *n.* **1.** A life-size model of the human body, used to fit or display clothes **:** dummy. **2.** One who models clothes.

man•ner (măn'ər) *n.* **1. a.** A way of doing something <danced in a graceful manner>. **b.** The way in which a thing is done or takes place. **2.** Characteristic bearing or behavior <a dignified *manner*> **3. manners. a.** Socially correct behavior. **b.** The customs of a society or period, esp. as the subject of a literary work. **4.** Kind **:** sort. ★ ***syns:*** MANNERS, DECORUM, ETIQUETTE, PROPRIETIES

man•nered (măn'ərd) *adj.* **1.** Having manners of a specific kind <an ill-*mannered* boor> **2.** Affected or artificial <*mannered* writing>

man•ner•ism (măn'ə-rĭz'əm) *n.* **1.** A distinctive behavioral trait **:** idiosyncrasy. **2.** Exaggerated or affected style or manner.

man•ner•ly (măn'ər-lē) *adj.* Having good manners **:** polite. **—man'ner•li•ness** *n.*

man•ni•kin (măn'ĭ-kĭn) *n. var. of* MANIKIN.

man•nish (măn'ĭsh) *adj.* **1.** Of or befitting a man. **2.** Resembling a man. **—man'nish•ly** *adv.* **—man'nish•ness** *n.*

ma•noeu•vre (mə-no͞o'vər, -nyo͞o'-) *n. & v. esp. Brit. var. of* MANEUVER.

man-of-war (măn'ə-wôr') *n., pl.* **men-of-war** (mĕn'-). **1.** A warship. **2.** The Portuguese man-of-war.

ma•nom•e•ter (mə-nŏm'ĭ-tər) *n.* An instrument that measures and indicates the pressure of liquids and gases. **—man'o•met'ric** (măn'ə-mĕt'rĭk) *adj.*

man•or (măn'ər) *n.* **1.** The estate of a medieval lord in W Europe. **2.** A landed estate. **3.** The principal house of an estate. **—ma•no'ri•al** (mă-nôr'ē-əl, -nōr'-) *adj.*

man•pow•er (măn'pou'ər) *n.* **1.** Human physical power. **2.** Power in terms of the workers available to a particular group or needed for a specific task.

man•qué (mäɴ-kā') *adj.* Frustrated **:** unfulfilled <a writer *manqué*>

man•sard (măn'särd') *n.* A roof with 2 slopes on all 4 sides, the lower slope being nearly vertical and the upper nearly horizontal.

manse (măns) *n.* **1.** *esp Scot.* A clergyman's house and land. **2.** A Presbyterian minister's house.

man•ser•vant (măn'sûr'vənt) *n., pl.* **men•ser•vants.** A male servant.

man•sion (măn'shən) *n.* A large, imposing house.

man-sized (măn'sīzd') *also* **man-size** (-sīz') *adj. Informal.* Quite large <a *man-sized* sandwich>

man•slaugh•ter (măn'slô'tər) *n. Law.* The unlawful killing of one human being by another without express or implied intent to do injury.

man•slay•er (măn'slā'ər) *n.* One that kills a human being.

man•sue•tude (măn'swĭ-to͞od', -tyo͞od') *n.* Gentleness **:** mildness.

man•ta (măn'tə) *n.* **1.** A rough-textured cotton fabric or blanket made and used in Latin America and the SW U.S. **2.** *also* **manta ray.** Any of several fishes of the family Mobulidae, having large, very flat bodies with winglike pectoral fins.

man•teau (măn-tō') *n.* A loose cloak.

man•tel *also* **man•tle** (măn'təl) *n.* **1.** An ornamental facing surrounding a fireplace. **2.** A shelf over a fireplace.

man•tel•piece (măn'təl-pēs') *n.* MANTEL 2.

man•til•la (măn-tē'yə, -tē'ə, -tĭl'ə) *n.* A usu. lace scarf worn over the head and shoulders by women esp. in Spain and Latin America.

man•tis (măn'tĭs) *n., pl.* **tis•es** *or* **-tes** (-tēz'). Any of various chiefly tropical insects of the family Mantidae, usu. pale-green and with forelimbs often folded as if in prayer.

man•tis•sa (măn-tĭs'ə) *n. Math.* The fractional part of a logarithm to the base 10.

man•tle (măn'təl) *n.* **1.** A loose sleeveless coat **:** cloak. **2.** Something that conceals or covers <a *mantel* of snow> **3.** *var. of* MANTEL. **4.** A device in gas lamps consisting of a sheath of threads that gives off brilliant illumination when heated by a flame. **—***v.* **-tled, -tling.** To cover with or as if with a mantle.

man•tra (măn'trə) *n.* A sacred Hindu verbal formula repeated in prayer, meditation, or incantation.

man•u•al (măn'yo͞o-əl) *adj.* **1.** Of, relating to, or done by the hands <*manual* skill> **2.** Operated by hand <a *manual* gearshift> **3.** Employing or requiring physical energy <*manual* work> **—***n.* **1.** A small reference book, esp. one providing instructions. **2.** An organ keyboard. **3.** Prescribed movements in the handling of a weapon, esp. a rifle. **—man'u•al•ly** *adv.*

man•u•fac•to•ry (măn'yə-făk'tə-rē) *n., pl.* **-ries.** A factory.

man•u•fac•ture (măn'yə-făk'chər) *v.* **-tured, -tur•ing. 1.** To make from raw materials, esp. with the use of industrial machines. **2.** To concoct **:** fabricate <*manufacture* an alibi> **—***n.* **1.** The act, craft, or process of manufacturing. **2.** A manufactured product. **3.** An industry. **—man'u•fac'tur•er** *n.*

man•u•mit (măn'yə-mĭt') *v.* **-mit•ted, -mit•ting.** To emancipate.

ma•nure (mə-no͝or', -nyo͝or') *n.* Fertilizer, esp. animal dung or compost. **—***v.* **-nured, -nur•ing.** To apply manure to.

man•u•script (măn'yə-skrĭpt') *n.* **1.** A typewritten or handwritten composition, as a book or document. **2.** Handwriting.

Manx (măngks) *n., pl.* **Manx. 1.** The people of the Isle of Man. **2.** The extinct Celtic language of the Manx. **—Manx** *adj.* **—Manx'man** *n.* **—Manx'wom'an** *n.*

man•y (mĕn'ē) *adj.* **more** (môr, mōr), **most** (mōst). Amounting to or consisting of a large indefinite number. ★ ***syns:*** LEGION, MULTITUDINOUS, MYRIAD, NUMEROUS, VOLUMINOUS **—***n. (pl. in number).* A large indefinite

number of persons or things. —*pron. (pl. in number).* A large number of persons or things.
man•y•fold (mĕn′ē-fōld′) *adv.* By many times.
Mao•ism (mou′ĭz′əm) *n.* Marxism-Leninism developed in China mainly by Mao Zedong. —**Mao′ist** *n.*
Mao•ri (mou′rē) *n., pl.* **Maori** *or* **-ris.** A member of a Polynesian people of New Zealand. —**Mao′ri** *adj.*
map (măp) *n.* A usu. plane-surface representation of a region of the earth or sky. —*v.* **mapped, map•ping. 1.** To make a map of. **2.** To plan, esp. in detail **:** delineate <*mapped* out a new sales technique> —**map′mak′er** *n.* —**map′per** *n.*
ma•ple (mā′pəl) *n.* **1.** A tall deciduous tree or shrub of the genus *Acer,* with lobed leaves and winged seeds borne in pairs. **2.** The hard close-grained wood of a maple, used esp. for furniture and flooring.
maple sugar *n.* Sugar made by boiling down maple syrup.
maple syrup *n.* A sweet syrup made from the sap of the sugar maple.
mar (mär) *v.* **marred, mar•ring. 1.** To deface or damage. **2.** To spoil **:** ruin.
mar•a•bou (măr′ə-bo͞o′) *n.* **1.** Any of several large Old World storks of the genus *Leptoptilus.* **2.** The soft down of the marabou, used esp. for trimming women's garments.
ma•ra•ca (mə-rä′kə) *n.* A percussion instrument having a hollow, gourdlike rattle containing dried beans or pebbles.

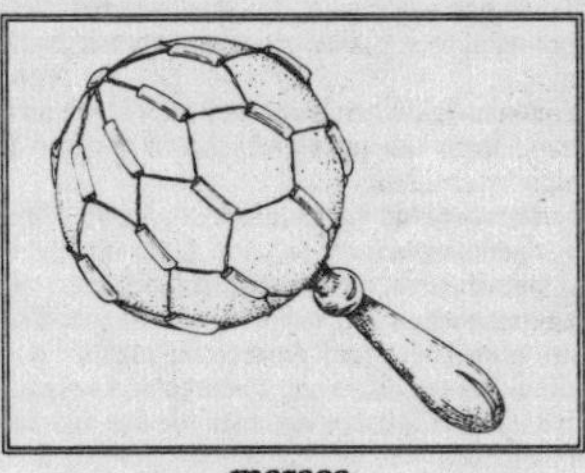

maraca

mar•a•schi•no (măr′ə-skē′nō, -shē′nō) *n., pl.* **-nos.** A cherry preserved in a real or imitation cherry cordial.
mar•a•thon (măr′ə-thŏn′) *n.* **1.** A cross-country footrace of 26 mi, 385 yds. **2.** A long-distance race <a swimming *marathon*> **3.** A contest of endurance.
ma•raud (mə-rôd′) *v.* To raid for plunder **:** pillage. —**ma•raud′er** *n.*
mar•ble (mär′bəl) *n.* **1.** A limestone, often irregularly colored by impurities, used for architectural and ornamental purposes. **2.** A piece or sculpture of marble. **3. a.** A small hard ball, usu. of glass, used in children's games. **b. marbles** (*sing. in number*). Any of various games played with marbles. **4. marbles.** *Slang.* Common sense or sanity <lost their *marbles*> —**mar′ble** *v.* —**mar′bly** *adj.*
mar•bling (mär′bling) *n.* A streaking or veinlike marking of fat in a cut of meat.
march[1] (märch) *v.* **1.** To move or cause to move in or as if in a military formation. **2.** To walk in a determined and forceful manner. **3.** To advance steadily <time *marching* on> —*n.* **1.** The act of marching. **2.** Forward movement **:** progression <the *march* of history> **3.** A measured pace used in marching. **4.** The distance covered by marching <3 days' *march* from here> **5.** A musical composition with regularly accented rhythm suitable to accompany marching.
march[2] (märch) *n.* The border or boundary of a country or area of land **:** frontier.
March (märch) *n.* The 3rd month of the year, having 31 days.
mar•chion•ess (mär′shə-nĭs) *n.* **1.** The wife or widow of a marquis. **2.** A peeress holding the rank of marquis in her own right.
Mar•di gras (mär′dē grä′) *n.* The Tuesday before Ash Wednesday, often celebrated with carnivals and parades of costumed merrymakers.
mare[1] (mâr) *n.* A female of the equine species, esp. a female horse.
ma•re[2] (mä′rā) *n., pl.* **-ri•a** (-rē-ə). *Astron.* One of the large, dark areas on the surface of the moon or Mars.
mar•ga•rine (mär′jər-ĭn) *n.* A butter substitute that is a blend of hydrogenated vegetable oils and other ingredients, as emulsifiers and vitamins.

▲ ***word history:*** Margarine is a relatively new substance, the product of modern chemistry. Both the substance and its name originated in France in the 19th cent. The substance was orig. made from a combination of animal fats, one of which was called *margaric acid* (*acide margarique* in French). The adjective *margaric* or *margarique* is derived from Greek *margaron,* "pearl," and was applied to the compound in question because its crystals had a pearly sheen. Margarine is naturally white; it is colored yellow in imitation of the natural yellow color of butter.

mar•gin (mär′jən) *n.* **1.** An edge **:** border. **2.** The blank space bordering the printed or written area on a page. **3.** An amount allowed beyond the necessary <a *margin* for error> **4.** A measure, quantity, or degree of difference <won by a slim *margin*> —**mar′gin•al** *adj.* —**mar′gin•al•ly** *adv.*
mar•gi•na•li•a (mär′jə-nā′lē-ə) *pl.n.* Notes in the margin of a book.
mar•gue•rite (mär′gə-rēt′, -gyə-) *n.* A plant, *Chrysanthemum frutescens,* with white or pale-yellow flowers similar to those of the daisy.
ma•ri•a•chi (mä′rē-ä′chē) *n.* **1.** A Mexican street band. **2. a.** The music performed by a mariachi. **b.** A musician playing in a mariachi.
mar•i•gold (măr′ə-gōld′, mâr′-) *n.* Any of

various plants of the genus *Tagetes,* native to tropical America, widely cultivated for their orange or yellow flowers.

mar•i•jua•na *or* **mar•i•hua•na** (măr'ə-wä'-nə) *n.* **1.** Hemp. **2.** The dried flower clusters and leaves of the hemp plant, esp. when taken to induce euphoria.

ma•rim•ba (mə-rĭm'bə) *n.* A large xylophone with resonant tubes under the wooden bars.

ma•ri•na (mə-rē'nə) *n.* A boat basin with facilities, as docks, moorings, and supplies, for small boats.

mar•i•nade (măr'ə-năd') *n.* A liquid mixture, usu. of vinegar or wine and oil with various herbs and spices, for soaking meat, fowl, or fish before cooking.

mar•i•nate (măr'ə-nāt') *v.* **-nat•ed, -nat•ing.** To soak (e.g., meat) in a marinade.

ma•rine (mə-rēn') *adj.* **1. a.** Of or pertaining to the sea, sea navigation, or shipping or to maritime affairs. **b.** Native to or formed by the sea <*marine* organisms> **2.** Of or pertaining to marines. —*n.* **1.** The naval or mercantile ships or shipping fleet of a country. **2. a.** A soldier serving on a ship or at a naval installation. **b. Marine.** A member of the Marine Corps.

Marine Corps *n.* A branch of the U.S. armed forces comprising mainly amphibious troops under the authority of the Secretary of the Navy.

mar•i•ner (măr'ə-nər) *n.* A sailor.

mar•i•o•nette (măr'ē-ə-nĕt') *n.* A jointed wooden figure, as of a person, manipulated from above by attached wires or strings.

mar•i•tal (măr'ĭ-tl) *adj.* Of or pertaining to marriage : conjugal. —**mar'i•tal•ly** *adv.*

mar•i•time (măr'ĭ-tīm') *adj.* **1.** Located on or close to the sea. **2.** Of or concerned with shipping or navigation.

mar•jo•ram (mär'jər-əm) *n.* **1.** An aromatic plant, *Majorana hortensis,* with leaves used as seasoning. **2.** A plant, *Origanum vulgare,* similar to the marjoram.

mark[1] (märk) *n.* **1.** A visible trace or sign, as a scratch, dent, or stain. **2.** A punctuation mark. **3. a.** An academic grade. **b.** *often* **marks.** An appraisal <got high *marks* for leadership> **4.** Something, as a label or stamp, placed on an article to signify ownership, manufacture, or origin. **5.** A recognized standard of quality : norm. **6.** Importance : significance. **7.** A target. **8.** An objective : goal. **9.** A characteristic <responsibility as a *mark* of maturity> **10.** A lasting impression. **11.** *Slang.* The intended victim of a swindler : dupe <an easy *mark*> **12.** Something used to indicate position. —*v.* **1.** To make a mark (on). **2.** To show by a mark <*marked* my answer in the space provided> **3.** To heed : note <*mark* my words> **4.** To be a feature of : characterize. **5.** To grade (scholastic work). —**mark down.** To mark for sale at a lower price. —**mark up.** To mark for sale at a higher price. —**mark'er** *n.*

mark[2] (märk) *n.* A deutsche mark.

Mark (märk) *n.* —See table at BIBLE.

mark•down (märk'doun') *n.* **1.** A price reduction. **2.** The amount by which a price is reduced.

marked (märkt) *adj.* **1.** Having a clearly defined character : noticeable. **2.** Singled out, as for attack. —**mark'ed•ly** *adv.*

mar•ket (mär'kĭt) *n.* **1. a.** A public gathering for purchasing and selling merchandise. **b.** A place where such a gathering takes place. **2.** A store or shop that sells a particular type of goods <a fish *market*> **3. a.** A geographic region regarded as a place for sales <seafood for the domestic *market*> **b.** A catogory of a population considered as buyers <the teen *market*> **4.** Demand <no *market* for used stockings> —*v.* **1.** To sell or offer for sale. **2.** To buy food and household supplies. —**mar'ket•a•bil'i•ty** *n.* —**mar'ket•a•ble** *adj.*

mar•ket•place (mär'kĭt-plās') *n.* **1.** A place, as a public square, where a market is held. **2.** The business world.

mark•ka (mär'kä') *n., pl.* **-kaa** (-kä'). —See table at CURRENCY.

marks•man (märks'mən) *n.* One skilled at firing a gun or other weapon.

mark•up (märk'ŭp') *n.* **1.** A price rise. **2.** The difference between the cost of an item and its selling price.

marl (märl) *n.* A mixture of clays, carbonates of calcium and magnesium, and remnants of shells, forming a loam used as fertilizer.

mar•lin (mär'lĭn) *n.* Any of several large marine game fish of the genus *Makaira.*

mar•line•spike (mär'lĭn-spīk') *also* **mar•ling•spike** (-lĭng-) *n. Naut.* A pointed metal tool used to separate strands of rope in splicing.

mar•ma•lade (mär'mə-lād') *n.* A preserve made from the pulp and rind of fruits <orange *marmalade*>

mar•mo•re•al (mär-môr'ē-əl, -mōr'-) *also* **mar•mo•re•an** (-ē-ən) *adj.* Like marble, as in smoothness, whiteness, or hardness.

mar•mo•set (mär'mə-sĕt') *n.* Any of various small tropical American monkeys of the genera *Callithrix, Cebuella, Saguinus,* and *Leontideus,* with soft, dense fur and tufted ears.

mar•mot (mär'mət) *n.* Any of various short-legged rodents of the genus *Marmota,* found throughout the N Hemisphere.

ma•roon[1] (mə-ro͞on') *v.* **1.** To put (a person) ashore on a deserted island or isolated coast. **2.** To abandon or isolate (a person) with small chance of escape or rescue.

ma•roon[2] (mə-ro͞on') *n.* A dark purplish red.

mar•plot (mär'plŏt') *n.* A meddler whose interference jeopardizes the success of an undertaking.

mar•quee (mär-kē') *n.* **1.** A large tent used esp. for outdoor gatherings. **2.** A rooflike structure projecting over an entrance to a building, as a theater.

mar•quess (mär'kwĭs) *n. esp. Brit. var. of* MARQUIS.

mar•que•try (mär'kə-trē) *n.* An inlay, as of

wood or ivory, used chiefly for decorating furniture.

mar·quis (mär′kwis, mär-kē′) *n.* A nobleman ranking below a duke and above an earl or count.

mar·quise (mär-kēz′) *n., pl.* **-quises** (-kēz′, -kē′zĭz). A marchioness.

mar·qui·sette (mär′kĭ-zĕt′, -kwĭ-) *n.* A fine fabric used for clothing, curtains, and mosquito nets.

mar·riage (măr′ĭj) *n.* **1.** The state of being married : wedlock. **2.** The act of marrying or the ceremony of being married. **3.** Close union <a *marriage* of minds> ★ ***syns:*** NUPTIALS, WEDDING —**mar′riage·a·bil′i·ty** *n.* —**mar′riage·a·ble** *adj.*

mar·row (măr′ō) *n.* **1.** The soft material that fills bone cavities. **2.** The principal or essential part : core.

mar·ry (măr′ē) *v.* **-ried, -ry·ing. 1.** To take as a husband or wife. **2.** To unite in matrimony. **3.** To become closely united.

Mars (märz) *n.* The 4th planet from the sun.

marsh (märsh) *n.* An area of wet, low-lying land : bog. —**marsh′y** *adj.*

mar·shal (mär′shəl) *n.* **1.** The highest-ranking military officer of some countries. **2. a.** A federal or municipal officer in the U.S. who executes court orders. **b.** The head of a fire or police department in the U.S. **3.** One in charge of a parade or ceremony. **4.** A high official in a royal court. —*v.* **-shaled, -shal·ing** *or* **-shalled, -shal·ling. 1.** To arrange or assemble in methodical order : organize. **2.** To guide (a person) ceremoniously : usher.

marsh·land (märsh′lănd′) *n.* A marshy tract of land.

marsh·mal·low (märsh′mĕl′ō, -măl′ō) *n.* A soft white candy with a spongy texture.

marsh mallow *n.* A plant, *Althaea officinalis,* of E North America, with a mucilaginous root used in confectionery.

marsh marigold *n.* A plant of the genus *Caltha,* esp. *C. palustris,* bearing bright yellow flowers.

mar·su·pi·al (mär-so͞o′pē-əl) *n.* A mammal of the order Marsupialia, including the kangaroo, opossum, bandicoot, and wombat, found esp. in Australia.

mart (märt) *n.* A trading center : market.

mar·ten (mär′tn) *n., pl.* **marten** *or* **-tens. 1.** Any of various carnivores of the genus *Martes,* of N wooded areas. **2.** The fur of the marten.

mar·tial (mär′shəl) *adj.* **1.** Of, relating to, or like war. **2.** Of, relating to, or associated with the armed services.

martial art *n.* Any of several Oriental arts of self-defense or combat, as karate or judo, usu. practiced as sport.

martial law *n.* Temporary rule by military authorities imposed on a civilian population esp. in time of war or when civil authority is unable to maintain public safety.

Mar·tian (mär′shən) *adj.* Of or relating to the planet Mars. —*n.* A hypothetical inhabitant of the planet Mars.

mar·tin (märt′n) *n.* A bird that resembles and is closely related to the swallows.

mar·ti·net (mär′tn-ĕt′) *n.* A stern disciplinarian.

mar·ti·ni (mär-tē′nē) *n., pl.* **-nis.** A cocktail of gin or vodka and dry vermouth.

Martin Luther King Day *n.* The 3rd Monday in Jan., observed in the United States in commemoration of the birthday of Martin Luther King, Jr.

mar·tyr (mär′tər) *n.* **1.** One who chooses to die rather than renounce religious principles. **2.** One who makes great sacrifices to advance a belief, cause, or principle. **3.** One who endures great suffering. —**mar′tyr** *v.* —**mar′tyr·dom** *n.*

mar·vel (mär′vəl) *n.* **1.** One that evokes surprise, admiration, or wonder. **2.** Strong surprise : astonishment. ★ ***syns:*** MIRACLE, PHENOMENON, PRODIGY, SENSATION, WONDER, WONDERMENT —*v.* **-veled, -vel·ing** *or* **-velled, -vel·ling.** To be filled with wonder or astonishment.

mar·vel·ous (mär′və-ləs) *adj.* **1.** Causing astonishment : wondrous. **2.** Of the highest or best kind : first-rate. —**mar′vel·ous·ly** *adv.* —**mar′vel·ous·ness** *n.*

Marx·ism (märk′sĭz′əm) *n.* The system of thought developed by Karl Marx. —**Marx′ist** *n.*

mar·zi·pan (mär′zə-păn′, märt′sə-pän′) *n.* A confection of ground almonds, egg whites, and sugar.

mas·car·a (măs-kăr′ə) *n.* A cosmetic for coloring or darkening the eyelashes and eyebrows.

mas·cot (măs′kŏt′, -kət) *n.* One that is thought to bring good luck.

mas·cu·line (măs′kyə-lĭn) *adj.* **1.** Of or relating to men or boys : male. **2.** Suggestive or typical of a man. **3.** Of, relating to, or being the gender of nouns classified as male. —*n.* **1.** The masculine gender. **2.** A word or word form belonging to the masculine gender. —**mas′cu·lin′i·ty** *n.*

ma·ser (mā′zər) *n.* Any of several devices that are similar to the laser but operate with microwaves rather than light.

mash (măsh) *n.* **1.** A mixture of crushed grain that ferments and is used to distill alcohol or spirits. **2.** A mixture of ground grains for feeding livestock. **3.** A soft pulpy mass. —*v.* **1.** To convert into a soft pulpy mass <*mash* potatoes> **2.** To grind or crush. —**mash′er** *n.*

mask (măsk, mäsk) *n.* **1.** A covering worn over the face to disguise or protect. **2.** A figure of a head worn by actors in Greek and Roman drama to identify a trait. **3.** A mold of a face, esp. one made after death. **4.** The face or facial markings of an animal, as a fox. **5.** A disguise or concealment <a *mask* of concern> —*v.* **1.** To cover for concealment or protection. **2.** To put a mask on for disguise. **3.** To conceal one's true personality, character, or motives.

mas·o·chism (măs′ə-kĭz′əm) *n.* **1.** Abnormal sexual excitement marked by pleasure in being subjected to physical pain or abuse. **2.** Derivation of pleasure from being dominated or mistreated. **—mas'o•chist** *n.* **—mas'o•chis'tic** *adj.*

ma•son (mā'sən) *n.* **1.** A person who works with stone or brick. **2. Mason.** A Freemason.

Ma•son•ic (mə-sŏn'ĭk) *adj.* Of or relating to Freemasons or Freemasonry.

ma•son•ry (mā'sən-rē) *n., pl.* **-ries. 1.** The trade of a mason. **2.** Stonework or brickwork. **3. Masonry.** Freemasonry.

masque (măsk) *n.* **1.** A popular 16th- and early 17th-cent. English dramatic entertainment based on a mythological or allegorical theme. **2.** A masquerade.

mas•quer•ade (măs'kə-rād') *n.* **1. a.** A costume party at which masks are worn. **b.** A costume for such a party. **2.** A disguise or pretense. —*v.* **ad•ed, -ad•ing. 1.** To wear a mask or disguise. **2.** To go about as if in disguise <a spy *masquerading* as a teacher> **—mas'quer•ad'er** *n.*

mass (măs) *n.* **1.** A body or quantity of matter of nonspecific shape. **2.** A large, nonspecific number or amount. **3.** The major part : majority. **4.** Physical bulk or volume. **5.** *Physics.* The measure of a body's resistance to acceleration. **6. masses.** The common people. —*v.* To gather or form into a mass.

Mass *or* **mass** (măs) *n.* **1. a.** Celebration of the Eucharist in Roman Catholic and some Protestant churches. **b.** A service including this celebration. **2.** A musical setting of certain parts of the Mass.

mas•sa•cre (măs'ə-kər) *n.* **1.** The savage killing of a considerable number of people. ★ ***syns:*** BLOOD BATH, BLOODLETTING, BLOODSHED, BUTCHERY, CARNAGE, POGROM, SLAUGHTER **—mas'sa•cre** *v.*

mas•sage (mə-säzh') *n.* A body rub given to improve circulation and relax muscles. **—mas•sage'** *v.*

mas•seur (mă-sûr') *n.* A man whose occupation is giving massages.

mas•seuse (mă-sœz') *n.* A woman whose occupation is giving massages.

mas•sif (mă-sēf') *n.* A large mountain mass or compact group of connected mountains forming a part of a range.

mas•sive (măs'ĭv) *adj.* **1.** Consisting of or constituting a large mass : bulky. **2.** Large or imposing in degree, scope, or intensity <a *massive* project> **—mas'sive•ly** *adv.* **—mas'sive•ness** *n.*

mass medium *n., pl.* **mass media.** A medium, as television, radio, or newspapers, of public communication.

mass-pro•duce (măs'prə-do͞os', -dyo͞os') *v.* To manufacture in large quantities. **—mass production** *n.*

mast (măst) *n.* **1.** An upright pole that supports the sails and running rigging of a sailing vessel. **2.** An upright pole.

mas•tec•to•my (mă-stĕk'tə-mē) *n., pl.* **-mies.** Surgical removal of a breast.

mas•ter (măs'tər) *n.* **1.** One with control or authority over another or others. **2.** The captain of a merchant ship. **3.** A male teacher or tutor. **4.** Someone of great learning, skill, or ability : expert. **5. a.** A master's degree. **b.** One holding such a degree. **6. Master.** —Used as a courtesy title in speaking of or to a boy not old enough to be addressed as Mister. **7.** An original from which copies can be made. —*v.* **1.** To make oneself a master of <*mastered* the game> **2.** To overcome (e.g., an addiction) : defeat. **—mas'ter•ship'** *n.*

mas•ter•ful (măs'tər-fəl) *adj.* **1.** Given to playing the master : domineering. **2.** Having or showing mastery : expert <a *masterful* piano technique> **—mas'ter•ful•ly** *adv.*

master key *n.* A key that opens different locks whose keys are not the same.

mas•ter•ly (măs'tər-lē) *adj.* Having or showing the skill of a master. **—mas'ter•li•ness** *n.* **—mas'ter•ly** *adv.*

mas•ter•mind (măs'tər-mīnd') *n.* Someone who plans or directs an undertaking. **—mas'ter•mind'** *v.*

master of ceremonies *n.* The host of a formal event or a program of varied entertainment.

mas•ter•piece (măs'tər-pēs') *n.* An extraordinary and ingenious work. ★ ***syns:*** CHEF-D'OEUVRE, MAGNUM OPUS, MASTERWORK, TOUR DE FORCE

master plan *n.* A plan giving complete instruction or guidance.

master's degree (măs'tərz) *n.* An academic degree conferred upon those who complete at least one year of study beyond the bachelor's degree.

master sergeant *n.* A noncommissioned officer of the next-to-highest rank in the U.S. Army, Air Force, and Marine Corps.

mas•ter•stroke (măs'tər-strōk') *n.* A masterly act, achievement, or action.

mas•ter•work (măs'tər-wûrk') *n.* A masterpiece.

mas•ter•y (măs'tə-rē) *n.* **1.** Consummate skill or knowledge. **2.** The status of a master or ruler <*mastery* of the skies>

mast•head (măst'hĕd') *n.* **1.** The top of a ship's mast. **2.** The listing in a publication, as a newspaper, of its staff and operations.

mas•tic (măs'tĭk) *n.* A pastelike cement.

mas•ti•cate (măs'tĭ-kāt') *v.* **-cat•ed, -cat•ing.** To chew (food). **—mas'ti•ca'tion** *n.*

mas•tiff (măs'tĭf) *n.* A large dog with a short fawn-colored coat.

mas•ti•tis (mă-stī'tĭs) *n.* Inflammation of the breast or udder.

mas•to•don (măs'tə-dŏn') *n.* Any of several extinct mammals of the genus *Mammut,* resembling the elephant.

mas•toid (măs'toid') *n.* The rear portion of the temporal bone behind the ear. **—mas'toid'** *adj.*

mas•tur•ba•tion (măs'tər-bā'shən) *n.* The act of exciting the genitals, usu. to orgasm, by means, as manual contact, other than sexual intercourse. **—mas'tur•bate'** *v.* **—mas'tur•ba'tor** *n.*

mat[1] (măt) *n.* **1.** A flat, often coarse piece of

material, as one used for wiping the feet. **2.** A thick floor pad used in athletic events, as wrestling or tumbling. **3.** A dense or tangled mass. —*v.* **mat•ted, mat•ting.** To form into a dense or tangled mass.

mat[2] (măt) *n.* **1.** A border around a picture serving as a frame or creating a contrast between the picture and a frame. **2.** *also* **matte.** A dull finish. —*adj. also* **matte.** Having a dull finish. —**mat** *v.*

mat•a•dor (măt'ə-dôr') *n.* A bullfighter who performs the final passes and kills the bull.

match[1] (măch) *n.* **1.** One similar or identical to another. **2.** One that harmonizes with another. **3.** An athletic game or contest between 2 or more <a tennis *match*> **4.** A marriage. —*v.* **1.** To be similar or identical. **2.** To harmonize with <a tie that *matches* a shirt> **3.** To place in opposition or competition **:** pit <*match* wits> **4.** To do as well as or better than **:** equal. **5.** To provide with an adversary or competitor. **6.** To correspond to <a photograph *matching* the description> **7.** To marry.

match[2] (măch) *n.* A narrow strip, as of wood, that is coated on one end with a compound easily ignitable by friction.

match•book (măch'bo͝ok') *n.* A small folder containing rows of safety matches.

match•less (măch'lĭs) *adj.* Without match or equal **:** peerless. —**match'less•ly** *adv.* —**match'less•ness** *n.*

match•mak•er (măch'mā'kər) *n.* One who arranges marriages.

mate[1] (māt) *n.* **1.** One of a matched pair. **2.** A spouse. **3.** The male or female of a pair of animals or birds. **4.** A companion or associate. **5. a.** An officer on a merchant ship who ranks below the captain. **b.** A U.S. Navy petty officer who is an assistant to a warrant officer. —*v.* **mat•ed, mat•ing. 1.** To join closely or fit together. **2.** To pair or bring together as mates.

mate[2] (māt) *n.* A checkmate. —**mate** *v.*

ma•té (mä'tā') *n.* A beverage, popular in South America, made from the dried leaves of an evergreen tree.

ma•te•ri•al (mə-tîr'ē-əl) *n.* **1.** The substance of which a thing is or can be made. **2.** *often* **materials.** Something, as a tool, needed for making something or carrying out a task. **3.** Fabric **:** cloth. —*adj.* **1.** Of, relating to, or existing in the form of matter. **2.** Of or relating to the body **:** bodily <*material* necessities> **3.** Physical as opposed to spiritual or intellectual. **4.** Substantial <a *material* difference> **5.** Important **:** relevant <*material* evidence> —**ma•te'ri•al•ly** *adv.*

ma•te•ri•al•ism (mə-tîr'ē-əl-ĭz'əm) *n.* **1.** *Philos.* The theory that physical matter is the only reality and that everything, including thought, feeling, mind, and will, is explainable in terms of matter. **2.** A great or excessive concern with material as opposed to spiritual or intellectual things. —**ma•te'ri•al•ist** *n.* —**ma•te'ri•al•is'tic** *adj.* —**ma•te'ri•al•is'ti•cal•ly** *adv.*

ma•te•ri•al•ize (mə-tîr'ē-ə-līz') *v.* **-ized, -iz•ing. 1.** To take or cause to take material form. **2.** To appear as if from nowhere. —**ma•te'ri•al•i•za'tion** *n.*

ma•te•ri•el *or* **ma•té•ri•el** (mə-tîr'ē-ĕl') *n.* **1.** The equipment and supplies, as guns and ammunition, of a military force. **2.** An organization's equipment and supplies.

ma•ter•nal (mə-tûr'nəl) *adj.* **1.** Of or relating to a mother or motherhood. **2.** Inherited from or related through a mother <*maternal* grandparents>

ma•ter•ni•ty (mə-tûr'nĭ-tē) *n.* **1.** The state of being a mother. **2.** The feelings associated with motherhood. **3.** A hospital facility for the prenatal and postnatal care of babies and their mothers.

math (măth) *n.* Mathematics.

math•e•mat•ics (măth'ə-măt'ĭks) *n.* *(sing. in number).* The study of numbers, their form, arrangement, and associated relationships, using rigorously defined literal, numerical, and operational symbols. —**math'e•mat'i•cal** *adj.* —**math'e•mat'i•cal•ly** *adv.* —**math'e•ma•ti'cian** (-mə-tĭsh'ən) *n.*

mat•i•nee *or* **mat•i•née** (măt'n-ā') *n.* A daytime dramatic or musical performance.

ma•tri•arch (mā'trē-ärk') *n.* A woman ruler of a clan, family, or tribe. —**ma'tri•ar'chal** *adj.* —**ma'tri•ar'chy** *n.*

mat•ri•cide (măt'rĭ-sīd', mā'trĭ-) *n.* **1.** The act of murdering one's own mother. **2.** One who has committed matricide. —**mat'ri•cid'al** (-sīd'l) *adj.*

ma•tric•u•late (mə-trĭk'yə-lāt') *v.* **-lat•ed, -lat•ing.** To admit or be admitted into a group, esp. into a college or university. —**ma•tric'u•la'tion** *n.*

mat•ri•lin•e•al (măt'rə-lĭn'ē-əl) *adj.* Based on or tracing ancestral descent through the maternal line. —**mat'ri•lin'e•al•ly** *adv.*

mat•ri•mo•ny (măt'rə-mō'nē) *n.* Marriage. —**mat'ri•mo'ni•al** *adj.* —**mat'ri•mo'ni•al•ly** *adv.*

ma•trix (mā'trĭks) *n., pl.* **ma•tri•ces** (mā'trĭ-sēz', măt'rĭ-) *or* **ma•trix•es. 1.** Something, as a substance, within which something else originates, develops, or is contained. **2.** A die or mold.

ma•tron (mā'trən) *n.* **1.** A married woman, esp. a mature woman of dignity and social position. **2.** A woman supervisor in a public institution, as a prison. —**ma'tron•li•ness** *n.* —**ma'tron•ly** *adj. & adv.*

matte (măt) *n. & adj. var. of* MAT[2].

mat•ter (măt'ər) *n.* **1. a.** Something that occupies space and displays the properties of inertia and gravitation when at rest as well as in motion. **b.** MATERIAL 1. **2.** A subject of concern, interest, feeling, or action <refused to discuss the *matter*> **3.** Trouble or difficulty <What's the *matter* with her?> **4.** An approximate quantity, amount, or extent <just a *matter* of hours> **5.** Something printed or written. **6.** Something sent by mail. —*v.* To be of significance or importance. —**no matter.** Regardless of <wanted it *no matter* what the cost>

mat•ter-of-fact (măt'ər-əv-făkt') *adj.* Relating to or adhering to facts. —**mat'ter-of-fact'ly** *adv.*
Mat•thew (măth'yo͞o) *n.* —See table at BIBLE.
mat•tock (măt'ək) *n.* A digging implement with the blade at right angles to the handle.

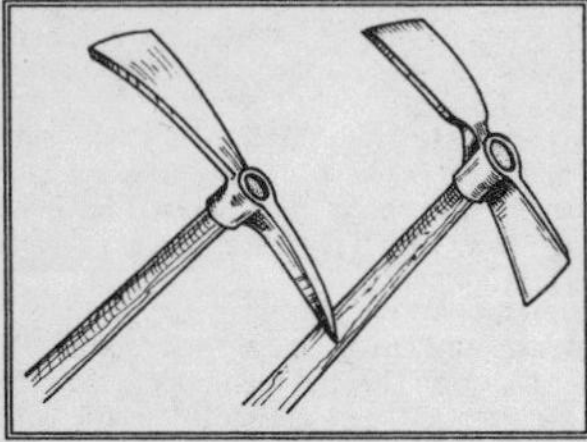

mattock

mat•tress (măt'rĭs) *n.* **1.** A cloth case filled with soft material used on or as a bed. **2.** An inflatable pad used on or as a bed.
mat•u•rate (măch'ə-rāt') *v.* **-rat•ed, -rat•ing.** To mature. —**mat'u•ra'tion** *n.*
ma•ture (mə-tyo͝or', -to͝or', -cho͝or') *adj.* **-tur•er, -tur•est. 1.** Having attained full growth or development. **2.** Having reached a desired stage, esp. after processing <a *mature* brandy> **3.** Having the characteristics associated with an adult. **4.** Carefully thought out <a *mature* decision> **5.** Due and payable <a *mature* bond> ★ ***syns:*** ADULT, BIG, DEVELOPED, FULL-BLOWN, FULL-FLEDGED, FULL-GROWN, GROWN, GROWN-UP, RIPE, RIPENED —*v.* **-tured, -tur•ing.** To make or become mature. —**ma•ture'ly** *adv.* —**ma•tu'ri•ty** *n.*
mat•zo (mät'sə) *n., pl.* **-zoth** (-sōth', -sōt', -sōs') *or* **-zos** (-səz, -səs, -sōz'). Unleavened bread, eaten esp. during Passover.
matzo ball *n.* A small dumpling made from matzo meal.
maud•lin (môd'lĭn) *adj.* Effusively or tearfully sentimental.
maul (môl) *n.* A heavy hammer with a long handle, used to drive stakes or piles. —*v.* **1.** To injure or damage by or as if by beating or bruising. **2.** To handle roughly.
maun•der (môn'dər) *v.* To speak or wander about in a confused or aimless manner.
mau•so•le•um (mô'sə-lē'əm, zə-) *n., pl.* **-le•ums** *or* **-le•a** (-lē'ə). A large and stately tomb.
mauve (mōv, môv) *n.* A moderate reddish or grayish purple.
ma•ven *also* **ma•vin** (mā'vən) *n.* An expert <a cooking *maven*>
mav•er•ick (măv'ər-ĭk, măv'rĭk) *n.* **1.** An unbranded or orphaned range calf or colt. **2.** A person who refuses to abide by the policies or views of a group.
maw (mô) *n.* **1.** The mouth, gullet, or stomach of a hungry or ferocious animal. **2.** A gaping opening.
mawk•ish (mô'kĭsh) *adj.* Excessively and disgustingly sentimental. —**mawk'ish•ly** *adv.* —**mawk'ish•ness** *n.*
max•i (măk'sē) *n.* An ankle- or floor-length garment, as a skirt or coat.
max•il•la (măk-sĭl'ə) *n., pl.* **-il•lae** (-sĭl'ē) *or* **-las.** Either of a pair of bones forming the upper jaw. —**max'il•lar'y** (măk'-sə-lĕr'ē) *adj.*
max•im (măk'sĭm) *n.* A concise saying.
max•i•mal (măk'sə-məl) *adj.* **1.** Of or being a maximum. **2.** Being the greatest or highest possible. —**max'i•mal•ly** *adv.*
max•i•mize (măk'sə-mīz') *v.* **-mized, -miz•ing. 1.** To increase to the maximum. **2.** To assign the highest importance to.
max•i•mum (măk'sə-məm) *n., pl.* **-mums** *or* **-ma** (-mə). **1.** The greatest or greatest possible number, measure, quantity, or degree. **2.** An upper limit permitted by authority. —**max'i•mum** *adj.*
may (mā) *v. p.t.* **might** (mīt). **1.** To be allowed or permitted to <You *may* borrow the car.> **2.** —Used to indicate a measure of likelihood or possibility <It *may* snow tonight.> **3.** —Used to express a desire or wish, purpose, contingency, or result.
May (mā) *n.* The 5th month of the year, having 31 days.
Ma•ya (mä'yə) *n., pl.* **-yas** *or* **-ya.** A member of an Indian people of S Mexico and Central America. —**Ma'ya** *adj.* —**Ma'yan** *n. & adj.*
May apple *n.* A plant, *Podophyllum peltatum,* of E North America, bearing a single nodding white flower, edible yellow fruit, and poisonous roots, leaves, and seeds.
may•be (mā'bē) *adv.* Perhaps.
May Day *n.* May 1, marked by the celebration of spring and in some places as a holiday honoring the labor force.
may•flow•er (mā'flou'ər) *n.* Any of a wide variety of plants, as the trailing arbutus, that blossom in May.
may•hem (mā'hĕm', mā'əm) *n.* **1.** *Law.* The willfull crippling or maiming of a person. **2.** Wanton violence or damage.
may•n't (mā'ənt, mānt). May not.
may•o (mā'ō) *n. Slang.* Mayonnaise.
may•on•naise (mā'ə-nāz') *n.* A dressing made of beaten raw egg yolk, oil, lemon juice or vinegar, and seasonings.
may•or (mā'ər, mâr) *n.* The chief magistrate of a town, city, borough, or municipal corporation. —**may'or•al** *adj.* —**may'or•al•ty, may'or•ship'** *n.*
may•pole (mā'pōl') *n.* A pole hung with streamers around which May Day merrymakers dance.
†**maze** (māz) *n.* A complicated, usu. confusing network of passageways or pathways : labyrinth. —*v.* **mazed, mazing.** *Regional.* To stupefy : daze. —**maz'y** *adj.*
ma•zur•ka (mə-zûr'kə, -zo͝or'-) *n.* **1.** A lively Polish dance similar to the polka. **2.** Music for a mazurka, written in 3/4 or 3/8 time.
MC (ĕm'sē') *n.* A master of ceremonies.
Md *symbol for* MENDELEVIUM.
me (mē) *pron. The objective case of* I.

—Used: **1.** As the direct object of a verb <They helped *me.*> **2.** As the indirect object of a verb <They offered *me* money.> **3.** As the object of a preposition <This memorandum is addressed to *me.*>

mead (mēd) *n.* An alcoholic beverage made from fermented honey.

mead•ow (mĕd'ō) *n.* A tract of grassland.

mead•ow•lark (mĕd'ō-lärk') *n.* Any of several songbirds of the genus *Sturnella,* of North America.

mea•ger *also* **mea•gre** (mē'gər) *adj.* **1.** Lean : thin. **2.** Deficient in quantity <a *meager* income> **3.** Deficient in richness, fertility, or vigor. ★ ***syns:*** EXIGUOUS, MEASLY, POOR, PUNY, SCANT, SCANTY, SKIMPY, SPARE, SPARSE, STINGY —**mea'ger•ly** *adv.* —**mea'ger•ness** *n.*

meal[1] (mēl) *n.* **1.** The coarsely ground edible seed of a grain. **2.** A granular substance made by grinding. —**meal'y** *adj.*

meal[2] (mēl) *n.* **1.** The food served and eaten at one time. **2.** The time or occasion of eating a meal.

meal ticket *n. Slang.* One that is a source of financial support.

meal•time (mēl'tīm') *n.* The usual time set aside for eating a meal.

meal•y•bug (mē'lē-bŭg') *n.* Any of various insects of the genus *Pseudococcus,* some of which are harmful to plants, esp. citrus trees.

meal•y-mouthed (mē'lē-mouthd', -moutht') *adj.* Unwilling to speak simply and directly : evasive.

mean[1] (mēn) *v.* **meant** (mĕnt), **mean•ing. 1. a.** To convey or be intended to convey the sense of : denote. **b.** To be a symbol of : signify. **2.** To have as a purpose : intend. **3.** To be likely to result in <Freezing rain *means* slippery roads.> **4.** To be of a specified significance or importance <Wealth *meant* little to them.>

mean[2] (mēn) *adj.* **1.** Low, as in grade or quality : inferior. **2.** Marked by pettiness and ill will : malicious <a *mean* remark> **3.** Dishonorable : base <a *mean* purpose> **4.** Parsimonious : stingy. **5.** *Slang.* Difficult to cope with <*mean* weather for driving> —**mean'ly** *adv.* —**mean'ness** *n.*

mean[3] (mēn) *n.* **1.** A middle point between 2 extremes. **2.** *Math.* **a.** A number that represents an entire set of numbers, determined for the set in any of several ways : average. **b.** An arithmetic mean. **3. means.** Something, as a method, by which an end is achieved. **4. means.** Wealth, as money or property. —*adj.* Occupying a middle position between 2 extremes.

me•an•der (mē-ăn'dər) *v.* **1.** To take a winding course. **2.** To wander about without fixed direction. —**me•an'der** *n.*

mean•ing (mē'nĭng) *n.* **1. a.** Something signified by a word : denotation or connotation. **b.** Something one wishes to convey, esp. through language. **2.** Something intended : purpose. 3. Importance : significance. ★ ***syns:*** ACCEPTION, IMPORT, INTENT, MESSAGE, PURPORT, SENSE, SIGNIFICANCE, SIGNIFICATION, VALUE —**mean'ing•ful** *adj.* —**mean'ing•less** *adj.*

mean•time (mēn'tīm') *n.* The period between occurrences : interval. —*adv.* Meanwhile.

mean•while (mēn'hwīl', -wīl') *n.* Meantime. —*adv.* **1.** During or in the intervening time. **2.** At the same time.

mea•sles (mē'zəlz) *n. (sing. in number).* An acute, contagious viral disease, usu. occurring in childhood, characterized by the eruption of red spots.

mea•sly (mēz'lē) *adj.* **-sli•er, -sli•est.** *Slang.* Despicably small : meager.

meas•ure (mĕzh'ər) *n.* **1.** The act, process, or result of determining the dimensions, capacity, or amount of something. **2.** Something, as a ruler, used in determining measures. **3. a.** A unit used in expressing measures. **b.** A system of such units. **4.** A basis for comparison : criterion. **5.** An appropriate or sufficient extent, amount, or degree. **6.** Limit : bounds <wealth knowing no *measure*> **7.** *often* **measures.** An action taken as a means to an end : expedient. **8.** A bill or enactment of a legislature. **9.** The notes and rests between 2 successive bars on a musical staff. —*v.* **-ured, -ur•ing. 1.** To determine the measurements of. **2.** To have a particular measurement. **3.** To estimate by comparison or evaluation : appraise. **4.** To consider carefully <*measure* one's words> **5.** To serve as a measure of <An altimeter *measures* altitude.> —**measure up. 1.** To live up to certain standards. **2.** To be the equal of. —**meas'ur•a•ble** *adj.* —**meas'ura•bly** *adv.* —**meas'ur•er** *n.*

meas•ure•ment (mĕzh'ər-mənt) *n.* **1.** The act or process of measuring. **2.** A dimension, capacity, or amount determined by measuring.

measuring worm *n.* A geometrid caterpillar that moves in alternate contractions and expansions suggestive of measuring.

meat (mēt) *n.* **1.** The flesh of an animal used as food. **2.** The edible, fleshy inner part <pecan *meats*> **3.** The essential part : core. **4.** Nourishment : food. —**meat'i•ness** *n.* —**meat'y** *adj.*

meat•ball (mēt'bôl') *n.* A small ball of often spiced ground or chopped meat.

mec•ca (mĕk'ə) *n.* A place that is the center of an activity or interest.

me•chan•ic (mĭ-kăn'ĭk) *n.* A person who is skilled in repairing, building, or using machines or tools.

me•chan•i•cal (mĭ-kăn'ĭ-kəl) *adj.* **1. a.** Of or relating to machines or tools. **b.** Of or relating to mechanics. **2.** Performed, produced, or operated by or as if by a machine. —**me•chan'i•cal•ly** *adv.*

mechanical drawing *n.* **1.** Drafting. **2.** A drawing, as an architect's plans, that is made with instruments.

mechanical engineering *n.* The branch of engineering that encompasses the generation and application of heat and mechani-

MEASUREMENT TABLE

U.S. CUSTOMARY SYSTEM

UNIT	RELATION TO OTHER U.S. CUSTOMARY UNITS	METRIC EQUIVALENT
LENGTH		
inch	1/12 foot	2.54 centimeters
foot	12 inches or 1/3 yard	0.30 meter
yard	36 inches or 3 feet	0.91 meter
rod	16½ feet or 5½ yards	5.03 meters
furlong	220 yards or 1/8 mile	0.20 kilometer
mile (statute)	5,280 feet or 1,760 yards	1.61 kilometers
mile (nautical)	6,076 feet or 2,025 yards	1.852 kilometers
VOLUME OR CAPACITY (LIQUID MEASURE)		
fluid ounce	1/16 pint	29.574 milliliters
gill	4 fluid ounces	0.12 liter
cup	8 fluid ounces	0.24 liter
pint	16 fluid ounces	0.47 liter
quart	2 pints or 1/4 gallon	0.95 liter
gallon	128 fluid ounces or 8 pints	3.79 liters
barrel		
(wine)	31½ gallons	119.24 liters
(beer)	36 gallons	136.27 liters
(oil)	42 gallons	158.99 liters
VOLUME OR CAPACITY (DRY MEASURE)		
cup	½ pint	0.275 liter
pint	2 cups or ½ quart	0.55 liter
quart	4 cups or 2 pints	1.10 liters
peck	8 quarts or 1/4 bushel	8.81 liters
bushel	4 pecks	35.239 liters
WEIGHT		
grain	1/7000 pound	64.799 milligrams
dram	1/16 ounce	1.772 grams
ounce	16 drams	28.350 grams
pound	16 ounces	453.6 grams
ton (short)	2,000 pounds	907.18 kilograms
ton (long)	2,240 pounds	1,016.0 kilograms
GEOGRAPHIC AREA		
acre	43,560 square feet or 4,840 square yards	4,047 square meters

cal power and the production, design, and use of machines and tools. **—mechanical engineer** *n.*

me•chan•ics (mĭ-kăn′ĭks) *n. (sing. or pl. in number).* **1.** The scientific study and analysis of the action of forces on matter and systems composed of matter. **2.** The design, operation, construction, and application of machinery or mechanical structures. **3.** The technical side of an activity <the *mechanics* of baseball>

mech•a•nism (mĕk′ə-nĭz′əm) *n.* **1. a.** A mechanical apparatus **:** machine. **b.** The arrangement of connected machine parts. **2.** A system of interacting parts <the *mechanism* of the brain> **3.** A means or process by which something is done or brought into being.

mech•a•nis•tic (mĕk′ə-nĭs′tĭk) *adj.* **1.** Mechanically determined. **2.** Mechanical. **—mech′a•nis′ti•cal•ly** *adv.*

mech•a•nize (mĕk′ə-nīz′) *v.* **-nized, -niz•ing. 1.** To equip with machines or machinery <*mechanize* a factory> **2.** To equip (a military unit) with motor vehicles, as tanks and trucks. **3.** To make mechanical, automatic, or unspontaneous. **—mech′a•ni•za′tion** *n.*

med•al (mĕd′l) *n.* **1.** A flat piece of metal stamped with a commemorative design or inscription, often presented as an award. **2.** A piece of metal stamped with a religious symbol.

med•al•ist (mĕd′l-ĭst) *n.* **1.** A designer, collector, or maker of medals. **2.** One who is awarded or receives a medal.

me•dal•lion (mə-dăl′yən) *n.* **1.** A large medal.

MEASUREMENT TABLE *(Continued)*

CONVERSION BETWEEN METRIC AND U.S. CUSTOMARY UNITS

WHEN YOU KNOW	MULTIPLY BY	TO FIND
FROM METRIC TO U.S. CUSTOMARY		
millimeters	0.04	inches
centimeters	0.39	inches
meters	3.28	feet
	1.09	yards
kilometers	0.62	miles
milliliters	0.03	fluid ounces
liters	1.06	quarts
	0.26	gallons
cubic meters	35.31	cubic feet
grams	0.035	ounces
kilograms	2.20	pounds
metric ton (1,000 kg)	1.10	short ton
square centimeters	0.16	square inches
square meters	1.20	square yards
square kilometers	0.39	square miles
hectares	2.47	acres
FROM U.S. CUSTOMARY TO METRIC		
inches	2.54	centimeters
feet	30.48	centimeters
yards	0.91	meters
miles	1.61	kilometers
fluid ounces	29.57	milliliters
cups	0.24	liters
pints	0.47	liters
quarts	0.95	liters
gallons	3.79	liters
cubic feet	0.028	cubic meters
ounces	28.35	grams
pounds	0.45	kilograms
short tons (2,000 lbs)	0.91	metric tons
square inches	6.45	square centimeters
square feet	0.09	square meters
square yards	0.84	square meters
square miles	2.59	square kilometers
acres	0.40	hectares

TEMPERATURE CONVERSION BETWEEN CELSIUS AND FAHRENHEIT

°C = (°F − 32) ÷ 1.8
°F = (°C × 1.8) + 32

2. An emblem of registration for a taxicab. 3. Something resembling a large medal, as: **a.** An oval or circular design used in decoration. **b.** A painting set in an oval frame **c.** A circular portion of food.

med•dle (mĕd′l) *v.* **-dled, -dling.** To intrude in other people's business or affairs. **—med′dler** *n.* **—med′dle•some** *adj.*

me•di•a (mē′dē-ə) *n. var. pl. of* MEDIUM.

me•di•ae•val (mē′dē-ē′vəl, mĕ-dē′vəl) *adj. var. of* MEDIEVAL.

me•di•al (mē′dē-əl) *adj.* **1.** Occurring in the middle. **2.** Average or mean **:** ordinary.

me•di•an (mē′dē-ən) *n.* **1.** Something that lies halfway between 2 extremes. **2.** A number in a set that has the property of having half the other numbers greater than it and half less than it. *—adj.* **1.** Relating to, situated in, or directed toward the middle **:** medial. **2.** Of, relating to, or constituting the median of a set of numbers.

median strip *n.* A strip dividing opposing highway traffic lanes.

me•di•ate (mē′dē-āt′) *v.* **-at•ed, -at•ing. 1.** To help opposing sides in a dispute come to an agreement. **2.** To bring about (e.g., a settlement) by acting as an intermediary. **—me′di•a′tion** *n.* **—me′di•a′tor** *n.*

med•ic (mĕd′ĭk) *n. Informal.* **1.** A surgeon or physician. **2.** A medical student or intern. **3.** A military medical corpsman.

med•i•ca•ble (mĕd′ĭ-kə-bəl) *adj.* Potentially responsive to treatment with medicine <a *medicable* disease>

Med•i•caid *also* **med•i•caid** (mĕd′ĭ-kād′) *n.* A program jointly funded by the states and

MEASUREMENT TABLE *(Continued)*

BRITISH IMPERIAL SYSTEM

UNIT	RELATION TO OTHER BRITISH IMPERIAL UNITS	CONVERSION TO U.S. CUSTOMARY UNITS	CONVERSION TO METRIC UNITS
VOLUME OR CAPACITY (LIQUID MEASURE)			
pint	½ quart	1.20 pints	0.57 liter
quart	2 pints ¼ gallon	1.20 quarts	1.14 liters
gallon	8 pints 4 quarts	1.20 gallons	4.55 liters
VOLUME OR CAPACITY (DRY MEASURE)			
peck	¼ bushel	1.03 pecks	9.09 liters
bushel	4 pecks	1.03 bushels	36.37 liters

METRIC PREFIXES

A multiple of a unit in the metric system is formed by adding a prefix to its name. The prefixes change the magnitude of the unit by orders of ten. Those for 10^9 to 10^{-9} are given below.

PREFIX	SYMBOL	MULTIPLYING FACTOR
giga-	G	10^9 = 1,000,000,000
mega-	M	10^6 = 1,000,000
kilo-	k	10^3 = 1,000
hecto-	h	10^2 = 100
deca-	da	10 = 10
deci-	d	10^{-1} = 0.1
centi-	c	10^{-2} = 0.01
milli-	m	10^{-3} = 0.001
micro-	μ	10^{-6} = 0.000,001
nano-	n	10^{-9} = 0.000,000,001

the federal government that provides medical aid for people who are unable to pay their own medical expenses.

med•i•cal (mĕd′ĭ-kəl) *adj.* Of or relating to the study or practice of medicine. **—med′i•cal•ly** *adv.*

medical examiner *n.* A physician officially authorized by a governmental unit, as a county, to ascertain the cause of death.

me•dic•a•ment (mĭ-dĭk′ə-mənt, mĕd′ĭ-kə-) *n.* An agent that promotes recovery from injury or illness **:** medicine.

Med•i•care *also* **med•i•care** (mĕd′ĭ-kâr′) *n.* A program under the Social Security Administration that provides medical care, esp. for the elderly.

med•i•cate (mĕd′ĭ-kāt′) *v.* **-cat•ed, -cat•ing. 1.** To treat with medicine. **2.** To add a medicinal substance to. **—med′i•ca′tion** *n.*

me•dic•i•nal (mə-dĭs′ə-nəl) *adj.* Of, relating to, or having the properties of medicine.

med•i•cine (mĕd′ĭ-sĭn) *n.* **1.** The science of diagnosing, treating, curing, or preventing disease or damage to the body or mind. **2.** The practice of medicine. **3.** An agent, as a drug, for treating injury or disease.

medicine ball *n.* A large heavy ball used for conditioning exercises.

medicine man *n.* A shaman, esp. a Native American shaman.

med•i•co (mĕd′ĭ-kō′) *n., pl.* **-cos.** *Informal.* **1.** A physician. **2.** A medical student.

me•di•e•val *also* **me•di•ae•val** (mē′dē-ē′vəl, mĕ-dē′vəl) *adj.* Of or relating to the Middle Ages. **—me′di•e′val•ism** *n.* **—me′di•e′val•ist** *n.* **—me′di•e′val•ly** *adv.*

me•di•o•cre (mē′dē-ō′kər) *adj.* Of moderate or low quality **:** undistinguished. **—me′di•oc′ri•ty** (-ŏk′rĭ-tē) *n.*

med•i•tate (mĕd′ĭ-tāt′) *v.* **-tat•ed, -tat•ing. 1.** To think deeply and quietly **:** ponder. **2.** To consider at length **:** contemplate. **—med′i•ta′tion** *n.* **—med′i•ta′tive** *adj.*

me•di•um (mē′dē-əm) *n., pl.* **-di•a** (-dē-ə) *or*

-ums. 1. a. Something that occupies a position midway between extremes. **b.** A middle condition or position. **2.** Something through which energy is transmitted. **3.** A means by which something is accomplished, conveyed, or transferred <money as a *medium* of exchange> **4.** *pl.* **media.** A means of communicating information or ideas, as publishing or television. **5.** *pl.* **mediums.** A person believed to have the power to communicate with the spirits of the dead. **6.** *pl.* **media.** An environment in which something, as a plant or animal, can live or thrive. **7.** An artistic technique or means of expression. **8.** A substance in which something is kept, preserved, or mixed. *—adj.* Intermediate in amount, degree, position, or quality.

med•ley (mĕd'lē) *n., pl.* **-leys. 1.** A jumbled mixture. **2.** A piece of music consisting of a series of melodies from various sources.

Mé•doc (mā-dôk', -dŏk') *n.* A red Bordeaux wine.

me•dul•la (mə-dŭl'ə) *n., pl.* **-las** *or* **-dul•lae** (-dŭl'ē) **1.** *Anat.* The core of certain vertebrate structures, as bone marrow. **2.** The medulla oblongata.

medulla ob•lon•ga•ta (ŏb'lông-gä'tə) *n., pl.* **medulla ob•lon•ga•tas** (-təz) *or* **medullae ob•lon•ga•tae** (-tē). A mass of nerve tissue at the base of the brain that controls bodily functions, as breathing and circulation.

me•du•soid (mə-dōō'soid', -dyōō'-) *adj.* Having the shape of a jellyfish. **—me•du'soid'** *n.*

meed (mēd) *n. Archaic.* **1.** A merited wage or reward. **2.** A fitting recompense.

meek (mēk) *adj.* **1.** Showing patience and humility **:** gentle. **2.** Easily imposed on **:** submissive. **—meek'ly** *adv.* **—meek'ness** *n.*

meer•schaum (mîr'shəm, -shôm') *n.* A tobacco pipe made of a tough, compact, usu. white mineral.

meet[1] (mēt) *v.* **met** (mĕt), **meet•ing. 1.** To come upon **:** encounter. **2.** To be present at the arrival of <*met* the bus> **3.** To be introduced to. **4.** To connect (with) **:** join. **5.** To form a group **:** assemble. **6.** To come together in order to confer or have a discussion. **7.** To satisfy (e.g., a need) **:** fulfill <*met* all the conditions> **8.** To perceive through the senses. **9.** To pay **:** settle. **10.** To deal with **:** cope. **11.** To come together <Let's *meet* for lunch.> **12.** To fight **:** oppose. *—n.* A meeting, esp. for athletic competition.

meet[2] (mēt) *adj.* Appropriate **:** fitting.

meet•ing (mēt'ĭng) *n.* **1.** The act or process of coming together **:** encounter. **2.** An assembly of people.

meg•a•buck (mĕg'ə-bŭk') *n. Slang.* One million dollars.

meg•a•byte (mĕg'ə-bīt') *n.* A unit of computer memory equal to 1,048,576 (2^{20}) bytes.

meg•a•cy•cle (mĕg'ə-sī'kəl) *n. Physics.* **1.** One million cycles. **2.** Megahertz.

me•ga•death (mĕg'ə-dĕth') *n.* One million deaths. —Used as a unit in reference to nuclear warfare.

meg•a•hertz (mĕg'ə-hûrtz') *n., pl.* **-hertz.** *Physics.* One million cycles per sec, used esp. as a radio-frequency unit.

meg•a•lith (mĕg'ə-lĭth') *n.* A huge stone used in the building of prehistoric monuments. **—meg'a•lith'ic** *adj.*

meg•a•lo•ma•ni•a (mĕg'ə-lō-mā'nē-ə, -mān'yə) *n.* A psychopathological condition marked by fantasies of power, wealth, or omnipotence. **—meg'a•lo•ma'ni•ac'** (-mā'nē-ăk') *n.* **—meg'a•lo•ma•ni'a•cal** (-mə-nī'ə-kəl) *adj.*

meg•a•lop•o•lis (mĕg'ə-lŏp'ə-lĭs) *n.* An extremely large urban complex.

meg•a•phone (mĕg'ə-fōn') *n.* A funnel-shaped device used to direct and amplify the voice.

meg•a•ton (mĕg'ə-tŭn') *n.* A unit of explosive force equal to that of 1 million metric tons of TNT.

meg•a•watt (mĕg'ə-wŏt') *n.* A unit of electrical power equal to 1 million watts.

mei•o•sis (mī-ō'sĭs) *n., pl.* **-ses** (-sēz'). *Biol.* Cell division that reduces the chromosomes of reproductive cells to half the normal number. **—mei•ot'ic** (-ŏt'ĭk) *adj.*

mel•an•cho•li•a (mĕl'ən-kō'lē-ə) *n.* A mental disorder marked by feelings of dejection and usu. by withdrawal.

mel•an•chol•ic (mĕl'ən-kŏl'ĭk) *adj.* **1.** Afflicted with or subject to melancholy. **2.** Of or relating to melancholia.

mel•an•chol•y (mĕl'ən-kŏl'ē) *n.* Depression of spirits **:** gloom. *—adj.* **1.** Sad **:** depressed. **2.** Tending to cause melancholy.

mé•lange *also* **me•lange** (mā-läNzh') *n.* A mixture.

mel•a•nin (mĕl'ə-nĭn) *n.* A dark pigment found in the skin, retina, and hair.

mel•a•nism (mĕl'ə-nĭz'əm) *n.* Abnormally dark pigmentation, as of the skin, resulting esp. from sunburn.

mel•a•no•ma (mĕl'ə-nō'mə) *n., pl.* **-mas** *or* **-ma•ta** (-mə-tə). A dark-colored malignant mole or tumor.

Mel•ba toast (mĕl'bə) *n.* Crisp, thinly sliced toast.

meld[1] (mĕld) *v.* To announce or show (a card or combination of cards) for a score in a card game. *—n.* A card or combination of cards declared for a score.

meld[2] (mĕld) *v.* To merge or cause to merge **:** blend.

me•lee *also* **mê•lée** (mā'lā', mā-lā') *n.* **1.** Confused hand-to-hand fighting **:** free-for-all. **2.** A confused and tumultuous mingling, as of a crowd.

mel•io•rate (mēl'yə-rāt', mē'lē-ə-) *v.* **-rat•ed, -rat•ing.** To improve or cause to improve. **—mel'io•ra'tion** *n.* **—mel'io•ra'tive** *adj. & n.*

mel•lif•lu•ous (mə-lĭf'lōō-əs) *adj.* Flowing smoothly and sweetly. **—mel•lif'lu•ous•ly** *adv.* **—mel•lif'lu•ous•ness** *n.*

mel•low (mĕl'ō) *adj.* **1.** Soft and sweet **:** fully ripened. **2.** Rich and full-flavored **:** properly aged <a *mellow* brandy> **3.** Having or showing the gentleness characteristic of maturity. **4.** Relaxed and good-humored **:** genial. **5.** Soft and resonant <a *mellow* tone> —*v.* To make or become mellow. **—mel'low•ly** *adv.* **—mel'low•ness** *n.*

me•lo•di•ous (mə-lō'dē-əs) *adj.* **1.** Of, pertaining to, or producing melody. **2.** Pleasant to listen to. **—me•lo'di•ous•ly** *adv.*

mel•o•dra•ma (mĕl'ə-drä'mə, -drăm'ə) *n.* **1.** A dramatic presentation marked by suspense, sensational episodes, and romantic sentiment. **2.** Behavior or events having the characteristics of a melodrama. **—mel'o•dra•mat'ic** (-drə-măt'ĭk) *adj.* **—mel'o•dra•mat'i•cal•ly** *adv.*

mel•o•dra•mat•ics (mĕl'ə-drə-măt'ĭks) *n.* *(sing. or pl. in number).* **1.** A melodrama. **2.** Melodramatic behavior.

mel•o•dy (mĕl'ə-dē) *n., pl.* **-dies. 1.** A succession and esp. a pleasing succession of musical tones **:** tune. **2.** Musical sounds. **—me•lod'ic** (mə-lŏd'ĭk) *adj.* **—me•lod'i•cal•ly** *adv.*

mel•on (mĕl'ən) *n.* Any of several large fruits, as a cantaloupe or watermelon, that grow on a vine and have a hard rind and juicy flesh.

melt (mĕlt) *v.* **1.** To change or be changed from a solid to a liquid by or as a result of heat or pressure. **2.** To dissolve <sugar *melting* in water> **3.** To disappear **:** vanish <inhibitions that gradually *melted*> **4.** To pass or merge imperceptibly <*melted* into the crowd> **5.** To make or become gentle or mild **:** soften.

melt•down (mĕlt'doun') *n.* Severe overheating of a nuclear-reactor core, resulting in escape of radiation.

melting pot *n.* **1.** A container for melting something. **2.** A place where immigrants of different races or cultures form an integrated society.

mem•ber (mĕm'bər) *n.* **1.** A distinct part of a whole. **2.** A part, as an organ or limb, of a person, animal, or plant. **3.** A person belonging to a group or organization.

mem•ber•ship (mĕm'bər-shĭp') *n.* **1.** The state of being a member. **2.** The total number of members in a group.

mem•brane (mĕm'brān') *n.* A thin pliable layer of tissue covering surfaces or separating or connecting regions, structures, or organs of an animal or plant. **—mem'bra•nous** (-brə-nəs) *adj.*

me•men•to (mə-mĕn'tō) *n., pl.* **-tos** *or* **-toes.** A keepsake **:** souvenir.

mem•o (mĕm'ō) *n., pl.* **-os.** A memorandum.

mem•oir (mĕm'wär', -wôr') *n.* **1.** An account based on personal experience. **2. a.** *often* **memoirs.** An autobiography. **b.** A biography or biographical sketch. **3. a.** A report, esp. on a scholarly or scientific subject. **b. memoirs.** A record of the proceedings of a learned society.

mem•o•ra•bil•i•a (mĕm'ər-ə-bĭl'ē-ə, -bĭl'yə) *pl.n.* Things that are worth remembering or keeping.

mem•o•ra•ble (mĕm'ər-ə-bəl) *adj.* Worth remembering or noting **:** remarkable. **—mem'o•ra•bly** *adv.*

mem•o•ran•dum (mĕm'ə-răn'dəm) *n., pl.* **-dums** *or* **-da** (-də). **1.** A brief informal note written esp. as a reminder. **2.** A written, informal communication, as from one office to another within an organization.

me•mo•ri•al (mə-môr'ē-əl, -mōr'-) *n.* **1.** Something, esp. a monument, designed or established to perpetuate remembrance, as of a person. **2.** A statement of facts addressed to a government or legislature. —*adj.* Serving to perpetuate remembrance. **—me•mo'ri•al•ize'** *v.*

Memorial Day *n.* A U.S. holiday celebrated on the last Monday in May in honor of members of the armed forces killed in war.

mem•o•rize (mĕm'ə-rīz') *v.* **-rized, -riz•ing.** To commit to memory. **—mem'o•ri•za'tion** *n.* **—mem'o•riz'er** *n.*

mem•o•ry (mĕm'ə-rē) *n., pl.* **-ries. 1.** The mental faculty of storing past experiences and recalling them at will. **2.** The act or an instance of remembering **:** recollection. **3.** All that a person can remember. **4.** Something remembered. **5.** The time period within which something is remembered. **6.** A unit of a computer that stores data for retrieval.

men (mĕn) *n. pl. of* MAN.

men•ace (mĕn'ĭs) *n.* **1. a.** A threat <the *menace* of war> **b.** Something that poses a threat **:** danger. **2.** An annoying person. **—men'ace** *v.* **—men'ac•ing•ly** *adv.*

mé•nage (mā-näzh') *n.* **1.** A household. **2.** Household management.

me•nag•er•ie (mə-năj'ə-rē, năzh'-) *n.* An exhibition of live wild animals.

me•nar•che (mə-när'kē) *n.* The beginning of menstruation, esp. the 1st occurrence.

mend (mĕnd) *v.* **1.** To repair **:** fix. **2.** To correct **:** reform <*mended* their ways> **3.** To get better **:** heal. —*n.* **1.** The act of mending. **2.** A mended place.

men•da•cious (mĕn-dā'shəs) *adj.* Prone to or marked by lying or deceit **:** untruthful. **—men•da'cious•ly** *adv.* **—men•dac'i•ty** (-dăs'ĭ-tē) *n.*

men•de•le•vi•um (mĕn'də-lē'vē-əm) *n.* *Symbol* **Md** A radioactive transuranium element of the actinide series.

men•di•cant (mĕn'dĭ-kənt) *adj.* Practicing begging. —*n.* **1.** A beggar. **2.** A member of a mendicant order of friars.

men•folk (mĕn'fōk') *or* **men•folks** (-fōks') *pl.n.* **1.** Men as a group. **2.** The male members of a family or community.

men•ha•den (mĕn-hād'n) *n., pl.* **menhaden** *or* **-dens.** An inedible fish, *Brevoortia tyrannus*, of American Atlantic and Gulf waters, used esp. as bait.

me•ni•al (mē'nē-əl, mēn'yəl) *adj.* **1.** Of, relating to, or appropriate to a household servant. **2.** Requiring little skill or responsibility **:** lowly. —*n.* A servant, esp. a household servant. **—me'ni•al•ly** *adv.*

men•in•gi•tis (mĕn'ĭn-jī'tĭs) *n.* Inflammation of the membranes that enclose the brain and spinal cord.

me•ninx (mē'nĭngks) *n., pl.* **me•nin•ges** (mə-nĭn'jēz'). One of the membranes that enclose the spinal cord and brain. —**men'in·ge'al** (mĕn'ĭn-jē'əl) *adj.*

me·nis·cus (mə-nĭs'kəs) *n., pl.* **-nis·ci** (-nĭs'ī') *or* **-cus·es. 1.** An object shaped like a crescent. **2.** A concavo-convex lens. **3.** The curved upper surface of a nonturbulent liquid standing in a container.

men·o·pause (mĕn'ə-pôz') *n.* The time at which menstruation ceases. —**men'o·paus'al** *adj.*

me·no·rah (mə-nôr'ə, -nōr'ə) *n. Judaism.* A nine-branched candelabrum used in celebration of Chanukah.

men·ses (mĕn'sēz') *pl.n.* Blood and dead cell debris discharged from the uterus through the vagina by women who are not pregnant at approx. monthly intervals between puberty and menopause.

men·stru·ate (mĕn'strōō-āt') *v.* **-at·ed, -at·ing.** To discharge the menses. —**men'stru·al** *adj.* —**men'stru·a'tion** *n.*

men·su·ra·tion (mĕn'sə-rā'shən, -shə-) *n.* The act, process, or art of measuring. —**men'su·ra·ble** *adj.*

-ment *suff.* **1.** Action : process <appease*ment*> **2.** Result of an action or process <advance*ment*> **3.** Means or agent of an action or process <adorn*ment*>

men·tal (mĕn'tl) *adj.* **1.** Of or relating to the mind : intellectual. **2. a.** Of, relating to, or affected by mental disorder. **b.** Intended for the care of the mentally ill <a *mental* ward> —**men'tal·ly** *adv.*

mental age *n.* A measure used in psychological testing that expresses a person's level of mental development relative to the age at which that level is average.

mental deficiency *n.* Subnormal intellectual development or functioning resulting from congenital causes, brain injury, or disease and marked by impaired learning ability.

men·tal·i·ty (mĕn-tăl'ĭ-tē) *n., pl.* **-ties. 1.** Intellectual capability or power. **2.** A way of thinking : attitude.

mental retardation *n.* Mental deficiency.

men·thol (mĕn'thôl') *n.* A white organic compound obtained from peppermint oil. —**men'tho·lat'ed** (-thə-lā'tĭd) *adj.*

men·tion (mĕn'shən) *v.* To refer to, esp. casually or incidentally : cite. —**men'tion** *n.* —**men'tion·a·ble** *adj.*

men·tor (mĕn'tôr', -tər) *n.* A person looked upon for wise advice and guidance.

men·u (mĕn'yōō, mān'-) *n.* **1.** A list of the food and drink available, as at a restaurant. **2.** The dishes available or served at a meal. **3.** *Computer Sci.* A list in a screen display of available program options and commands. **4.** A list of options.

me·ow (mē-ou') *n.* The cry of a cat. —**me·ow'** *v.*

me·phi·tis (mə-fī'tĭs) *n.* **1.** A sickening smell : stench. **2.** An evil-smelling gas emitted from the earth. —**me·phit'ic** *adj.*

mer·can·tile (mûr'kən-tēl', -tīl') *adj.* Of or relating to trade or merchants.

mer·ce·nar·y (mûr'sə-nĕr'ē) *adj.* **1.** Concerned only with making money and obtaining material gain. **2.** Paid to serve in a foreign army. —**mer'ce·nar'y** *n.*

mer·cer (mûr'sər) *n. esp. Brit.* A textile dealer.

mer·cer·ize (mûr'sə-rīz') *v.* **-ized, -iz·ing.** To treat (cotton thread) with sodium hydroxide so as to shrink the fibers and increase color absorption and luster.

mer·chan·dise (mûr'chən-dīz', -dīs') *n.* Goods or commodities that may be bought and sold. —*v.* (-dīz') **-dised, -dis·ing.** To buy and sell (goods or commodities). —**mer'chan·dis'er** *n.*

mer·chant (mûr'chənt) *n.* **1.** One who buys and sells goods for profit. **2.** One who runs a retail business : storekeeper.

mer·chant·man (mûr'chənt-mən) *n.* A commercial ship.

merchant marine *n.* **1.** A nation's commercial ships. **2.** The personnel of the merchant marine.

merchant ship *n.* A merchantman.

mer·cu·ri·al (mər-kyŏŏr'ē-əl) *adj.* **1.** Being rapidly changeable in character <a *mercurial* disposition> **2.** Containing or caused by the action of the element mercury. —**mer·cu'ri·al·ly** *adv.*

mer·cu·ric (mər-kyŏŏr'ĭk) *adj.* Of, relating to, or containing mercury with a valence of +2.

mer·cu·rous (mər-kyŏŏr'əs, mûr'kyə-rəs) *adj. Chem.* Relating to or containing mercury with a valence of +1.

mer·cu·ry (mûr'kyə-rē) *n., pl.* **-ries. 1.** *Symbol* **Hg** A silvery-white liquid metallic element commonly used in thermometers and barometers. **2. Mercury.** The smallest planet in the solar system and the one closest to the sun.

mer·cy (mûr'sē) *n., pl.* **-cies. 1.** Kind and compassionate treatment : clemency. **2.** A disposition to be benevolent and forgiving. **3.** Something to be thankful for <a *mercy* no one was hurt> —**mer'ci·ful** *adj.* —**mer'ci·ful·ly** *adv.* —**mer'ci·less** *adj.* —**mer'ci·less·ly** *adv.*

mere (mîr) *adj. superl.* **mer·est. 1.** Being no more than what is stated <a *mere* whim of mine> **2.** Unadulterated : pure. —**mere'ly** *adv.*

mer·e·tri·cious (mĕr'ĭ-trĭsh'əs) *adj.* **1.** Attractive in a tawdry manner. **2.** Based on error or pretense : spurious. —**mer'e·tri'cious·ly** *adv.* —**mer'e·tri'cious·ness** *n.*

mer·gan·ser (mər-găn'sər) *n.* A duck of the genus *Mergus,* having a narrow, slightly hooked bill and usu. a crested head.

merge (mûrj) *v.* **merged, merg·ing.** To bring or come together so as to form one.

merg·er (mûr'jər) *n.* The union of 2 or more groups, as corporations.

me·rid·i·an (mə-rĭd'ē-ən) *n.* **1. a.** A great circle on the earth's surface passing through the N and S poles. **b.** Either half of such a circle lying between the poles. **2.** The highest point or stage : apex. —**me·rid'i·an** *adj.*

me•ringue (mə-răng′) *n.* A mixture of baked stiffly beaten egg whites and sugar, often used as a topping for cakes or pies.

me•ri•no (mə-rē′nō) *n., pl.* **-nos. 1. a.** A sheep orig. bred in Spain. **b.** The fine wool of the merino. **2.** A soft lightweight fabric orig. made of merino wool.

mer•it (mĕr′ĭt) *n.* **1.** A usu. high level of superiority : worth <a painting of *merit*> **2.** A praiseworthy or blameworthy feature, action, or quality. **3. merits.** The factual substance of a disputed issue and esp. of legal case. ★ ***syns:*** CALIBER, QUALITY, STATURE, VALUE, VIRTUE, WORTH —*v.* To deserve : earn.

mer•i•toc•ra•cy (mĕr′ĭ-tŏk′rə-sē) *n., pl.* **-cies. 1.** A system in which advancement is based on achievement or ability. **2.** Leadership by talented achievers.

mer•i•to•ri•ous (mĕr′ĭ-tôr′ē-əs, -tōr′-) *adj.* Deserving praise : admirable. —**mer′i•to′ri•ous•ly** *adv.*

mer•maid (mûr′mād′) *n.* A legendary sea creature with the upper body of a woman and the tail of a fish. —**mer′man′** *n.*

mer•ri•ment (mĕr′ĭ-mənt) *n.* **1.** Mirthful delight : amusement. **2.** Lighthearted celebration : festivity.

mer•ry (mĕr′ē) *adj.* **-ri•er, -ri•est. 1.** Full of gaiety : high-spirited. **2.** Marked by or offering festivity. **3.** Delightful : entertaining. **4.** Brisk <a *merry* pace> ★ ***syns:*** FESTIVE, GALA, GLAD, GLADSOME, HAPPY, JOYFUL, JOYOUS —**mer′ri•ly** *adv.* —**mer′ri•ness** *n.*

mer•ry-go-round (mĕr′ē-gō-round′) *n.* **1.** A revolving circular platform with seats, often in the form of horses, on which people ride for amusement. **2.** A busy round : whirl <a *merry-go-round* of appointments>

mer•ry•mak•ing (mĕr′ē-mā′kĭng) *n.* **1.** Participation in festivity : revelry. **2.** A festivity. —**mer′ry•mak′er** *n.*

me•sa (mā′sə) *n.* A flat-topped hill or small plateau with steep sides.

més•al•liance (mā′zăl-yäɴs′, mā′zə-lī′əns) *n.* A marriage with a person of inferior social position.

mes•cal (mĕ-skăl′) *n.* **1.** A cactus, *Lophophora williamsii,* of Mexico and SW U.S., having buttonlike outgrowths that are dried and chewed as a drug by certain Indian tribes. **2.** A Mexican liquor distilled from the fermented juice of certain species of agave.

mes•ca•line (mĕs′kə-lēn′) *n.* An alkaloid hallucinogenic drug.

Mes•dames (mā-dăm′) *n. pl. of* MADAME *or* MADAM.

Mes•de•moi•selles (mā′də-mə-zĕl′, măd′-mwə-) *n. pl. of* MADEMOISELLE.

mesh (mĕsh) *n.* **1. a.** One of the open spaces in a thread, cord, or wire network. **b.** *often* **meshes.** The threads, cords, or wires surrounding these spaces. **2.** A network. **3.** A fabric with an open network of interlacing threads. **4.** Something that entraps or snares <the *meshes* of politics> **5. a.** The engagement of gear teeth. **b.** The state of being so engaged. —*v.* **1.** To ensnare : entangle. **2.** To engage or interlock <gears *meshing*> **3.** To fit together effectively : harmonize.

mes•mer•ize (mĕz′mə-rīz′, mĕs′-) *v.* **-ized, -iz•ing. 1.** To hypnotize. **2.** To enthrall. —**mes•mer′ic** (-mĕr′ĭk) *adj.* —**mes′mer•ism** *n.* —**mes′mer•iz′er** *n.*

mes•on (mĕz′ŏn′, mē′zŏn′, mĕs′ŏn′, mē′sŏn′) *n.* Any of a family of subatomic particles that consist solely of a quark and an antiquark.

mes•o•sphere (mĕz′ə-sfîr′, mĕs′-) *n.* The atmospheric layer above the stratosphere.

mes•quite (mĕ-skēt′, mə-) *n.* A shrub or small tree of the genus *Prosopis,* esp. *P. juliflora,* of the SW U.S. and Mexico, whose pods are used as forage.

mess (mĕs) *n.* **1.** A disorderly accumulation : jumble. **2.** A cluttered, untidy, or dirty state. **3.** A confused, disturbed, or troublesome state : chaos. **4. a.** A serving of food. **b.** A group of persons, usu. in the military, who regularly eat meals together. **c.** A meal eaten by such a group. —*v.* **1.** To make untidy, dirty, or disorderly. **2.** To handle or manage badly : bungle. **3.** *Slang.* To manhandle. **4.** To meddle.

mes•sage (mĕs′ĭj) *n.* **1.** A communication transmitted from one person or group to another. **2.** A basic theme or idea <I get the *message.*>

Mes•sei•gneurs (mā′sān-yœr′) *n. pl. of* MONSEIGNEUR.

mes•sen•ger (mĕs′ən-jər) *n.* A person who carries messages or does errands.

messenger RNA *n.* An ribonucleic acid that carries genetic information necessary for protein synthesis in cells.

Mes•si•ah (mə-sī′ə) *n.* **1. a.** The anticipated deliverer and king of the Jews. **b.** Jesus Christ. **2. messiah.** A liberator or deliverer. —**Mes′si•an′ic** (mĕs′ē-ăn′ĭk) *adj.*

Mes•sieurs (mā-syœ′) *n. pl. of* MONSIEUR.

mess•mate (mĕs′māt′) *n.* One with whom one eats regularly.

mess•y (mĕs′ē) *adj.* **-i•er, -i•est. 1.** Marked by dirt or disorder. **2.** Lacking precision and neatness. **3.** Unpleasantly difficult to resolve or settle <a *messy* divorce case> ★ ***syns:*** DISHEVELED, MUSSY, SLIPSHOD, SLOPPY, SLOVENLY, UNKEMPT, UNTIDY —**mess′i•ly** *adv.* —**mess′i•ness** *n.*

mes•ti•za (mĕ-stē′zə) *n.* A woman of mixed European and American Indian ancestry.

mes•ti•zo (mĕ-stē′zō) *n., pl.* **-zos** *or* **-zoes.** A person, esp. a man, of mixed European and American Indian ancestry.

met (mĕt) *v. p.t. & p.p. of* MEET[1].

me•tab•o•lism (mə-tăb′ə-lĭz′əm) *n.* **1.** The complex of chemical and physical processes involved in the maintenance of life. **2.** The use or functioning of a substance or class of substances within a living body. —**met′a•bol′ic** (mĕt′ə-bŏl′ĭk) *adj.* —**me•tab′o•lize′** *v.*

me•tab•o•lite (mə-tăb′ə-līt′) *n.* An organic compound produced by metabolism.

met•a•car•pus (mĕt′ə-kär′pəs) *n.* The part of the hand or forefoot that contains the 5 bones extending from the bones of the fingers or toes to the wrist or ankle.

met•a•gal•ax•y (mĕt'ə-găl'ək-sē) *n.* The universe.

met•al (mĕt'l) *n.* **1.** One of a category of usu. whitish, lustrous electropositive elements that are typically ductile and malleable. **2.** An alloy of 2 or more metallic elements. **3.** Strength of character. **—me•tal'lic** *adj.* **—me•tal'i•cal•ly** *adv.*

met•al•lur•gy (mĕt'l-ûr'jē) *n.* The science and technology of metals and their properties. **—met'al•lur'gic, met'al•lur'gi•cal** *adj.* **—met'al•lur'gist** *n.*

met•a•mor•phism (mĕt'ə-môr'fĭz'əm) *n.* *Geol.* An alteration in the texture, composition, or structure of rock produced by great heat or pressure. **—met'a•mor'phic** *adj.*

met•a•mor•pho•sis (mĕt'ə-môr'fə-sĭs) *n., pl.* **-ses** (-sēz'). **1.** A transformation, as by supernatural means. **2.** A marked alteration in appearance, condition, character, or function. **3.** *Biol.* Change in the structure and habits of an animal during normal growth, usu. in the postembryonic stage. **—met'a•mor'phose'** (-fōz', -fōs') *v.*

met•a•phor (mĕt'ə-fôr', -fər) *n.* A figure of speech in which a term is transferred from the object it ordinarily designates to an object it may designate only by implicit comparison or analogy, as in the phrase *evening of life.* **—met'a•phor'i•cal** *adj.* **—met'a•phor'i•cal•ly** *adv.*

met•a•phys•ics (mĕt'ə-fĭz'ĭks) *n. (sing. in number).* The branch of philosophy that methodically investigates the nature of 1st principles and problems of ultimate reality. **—met'a•phys'i•cal** *adj.* **—met'a•phy•si'cian** (-fĭ-zĭsh'ən) *n.*

me•tas•ta•sis (mə-tăs'tə-sĭs) *n., pl.* **-ses** (-sēz'). *Pathol.* Transference of a disease-producing agency, as malignant cells, from one site to another elsewhere in the body. **—me•tas'ta•size'** *v.* **—met'a•stat'ic** (mĕt'ə-stăt'ĭk) *adj.*

met•a•tar•sus (mĕt'ə-tär'səs) *n., pl.* **-si** (-sī'). **1.** The part of the human foot that forms the instep and consists of the 5 bones between the toes and the ankle. **2.** A part of the hind foot of a 4-legged animal that corresponds to the metatarsus. **—met'a•tar'sal** *adj.*

mete[1] (mēt) *v.* **met•ed, met•ing.** To distribute by or as if by measure **:** dole.

mete[2] (mēt) *n.* A boundary.

me•te•or (mē'tē-ər, -ôr') *n.* **1.** The incandescent trail or streak that is seen in the sky when a meteoroid is made luminous by friction with the earth's atmosphere. **2.** A meteoroid.

me•te•or•ic (mē'tē-ôr'ĭk, -ŏr'-) *adj.* **1.** Of, relating to, or produced by a meteor. **2.** Like a meteor in speed, brilliance, or briefness <a *meteoric* career>

me•te•or•ite (mē'tē-ə-rīt') *n.* The metallic or stony remains of a meteoroid that reaches the earth after burning incompletely in the atmosphere.

me•te•or•oid (mē'tē-ə-roid') *n.* One of a large number of celestial bodies of various size that appear as meteors when they enter the earth's atmosphere.

me•te•or•ol•o•gy (mē'tē-ə-rŏl'ə-jē) *n.* The science concerned with atmospheric phenomena, esp. weather and weather conditions. **—me'te•or•o•log'i•cal** (-ər-ə-lŏj'ĭkəl), **me'te•or•o•log'ic** *adj.* **—me'te•or•ol'o•gist** *n.*

me•ter[1] (mē'tər) *n.* The measured rhythm typical of verse or music.

me•ter[2] (mē'tər) *n.* —See table at MEASUREMENT.

me•ter[3] (mē'tər) *n.* **1.** A device for measuring or recording various values, as speed or the rate of flow of a liquid. **2.** A postage meter. **3.** A parking meter. —*v.* To measure or control with a meter.

-meter *suff.* Measuring device <anemom*eter*>

me•ter-kil•o•gram-sec•ond system (mē'tər-kĭl'ə- grăm-sĕk'ənd) *n.* A system of units for mechanics, using the meter, the kilogram, and the second as fundamental units of length, mass, and time.

meter maid *n.* A woman member of a police department who writes tickets for violations of parking regulations.

meth•a•done hydrochloride (mĕth'ə-dōn') *n.* A synthetic narcotic used in treating heroin addiction.

meth•am•phet•a•mine (mĕth'ăm-fĕt'ə-mēn', -mĭn) *n.* A derivative of amphetamine used in the form of its crystalline hydrochloride as a stimulant.

meth•ane (mĕth'ān') *n.* A colorless, odorless, flammable gas that is the chief component of natural gas and is used esp. as a fuel.

meth•a•nol (mĕth'ə-nôl', -nōl') *n.* A colorless, poisonous, flammable alcohol used as an antifreeze, fuel, general solvent, and denaturant for ethyl alcohol.

meth•a•qua•lone (mĕth'ə-kwā'lōn') *n.* A potentially habit-forming sedative and hypnotic drug.

me•thinks (mĭ-thĭngks') *v. p.t.* **me•thought** (-thôt'). *Archaic.* It seems to me.

▲ ***word history:*** The archaic form *methinks* is strictly speaking not one word but two: the pronoun *me* and the obsolete verb *think,* meaning "to seem." The obsolete verb is related to but not the same as the current verb *think,* meaning "to have in mind." *Methinks* is an impersonal construction, that is, one without an expressed subject. In *methinks, me* is a dative form of the pronoun *I* functioning as the indirect object of *thinks,* and *thinks* is the 3rd person singular form of the verb.

meth•od (mĕth'əd) *n.* **1.** A manner, means, or process for accomplishing something. **2.** Systematic arrangement **:** order. ★ ***syns:*** FASHION, MANNER, MODE, SYSTEM, WAY **—me•thod'i•cal** (mə-thŏd'ĭ-kəl), **me•thod'ic** *adj.* **—me•thod'i•cal•ly** *adv.*

Meth•od•ist (mĕth'ə-dĭst) *n.* A member of a Protestant Christian denomination whose

theology developed from the teachings of John and Charles Wesley. —**Meth'od•ism** *n.* —**Meth'od•ist** *adj.*
meth•od•ol•o•gy (mĕth'ə-dŏl'ə-jē) *n., pl.* **-gies.** **1.** A system of methods and principles used in a specific branch of knowledge. **2.** The branch of logic that deals with the general principles of the formation of knowledge. —**meth'od•o•log'i•cal** (-də-lŏj'ĭ-kəl) *adj.*
meth•yl (mĕth'əl) *n.* An organic radical derived from methane and occurring in many organic compounds.
methyl alcohol *n.* Methanol.
met•i•cal (mĕt'ĭ-kăl', mĕt'ĭ-käl') *n.* —See table at CURRENCY.
me•tic•u•lous (mə-tĭk'yə-ləs) *adj.* **1.** Very careful : precise. **2.** Excessively concerned with details : nit-picking. —**me•tic'u•lous•ly** *adv.* —**me•tic'u•lous•ness** *n.*
mé•tier (mā-tyā') *n.* A sphere of activity to which one is esp. suited.
Mé•tis *also* **Me•tis** (mā'tē, mā-tē', mā-tēs') *n., pl.* **Métis.** *Can.* A person of mixed European, usu. French-Canadian, and American Indian ancestry. —**Mé'tisse** *n.*
me•tre (mē'tər) *n. esp. Brit. var. of* METER.
met•ric (mĕt'rĭk) *adj.* Of or relating to the metric system.
met•ri•cal (mĕt'rĭ-kəl) *adj.* **1.** Of, relating to, or composed in rhythmic meter. **2.** Of or relating to measurement.
met•ri•ca•tion (mĕt'rĭ-kā'shən) *n.* Conversion to or adoption of the metric system.
metric system *n.* A decimal system of weights and measures based on the meter as a unit of length and the kilogram as a unit of mass.
metric ton *n.* A unit of mass equal to 1,000 kgs.
met•ri•fy (mĕt'rə-fī') *v.* **-fied, -fy•ing.** To convert to or adopt the metric system. —**met'ri•fi•ca'tion** *n.*
met•ro (mĕt'rō) *n., pl.* **-ros.** **1.** A subway system. **2.** *also* **Mét•ro.** *Can.* The subway system in Montreal.
met•ro•nome (mĕt'rə-nōm') *n.* A device for marking time by means of a series of clicks

metronome

at precise intervals. —**met'ro•nom'ic** (mĕt'rə-nŏm'ĭk) *adj.*
me•trop•o•lis (mə-trŏp'ə-lĭs) *n.* **1.** A major city. **2.** A city regarded as the center of a specific activity <a great entertainment *metropolis*> —**met'ro•pol'i•tan** (mĕt'rə-pŏl'ĭ-tn) *adj.*
-metry *suff.* Process or science of measuring <iso*metry*>
met•tle (mĕt'l) *n.* **1.** Quality or strength of character. **2.** Courage : spirit. —**met'tle•some** *adj.*
mew[1] (myōō) *n.* **1.** A secret place : hideaway. **2. mews.** A small street with living quarters converted from stables. —*v.* **mewed, mew•ing.** To confine in or as if in a cage.
mew[2] (myōō) *v.* To meow. —**mew** *n.*
mez•za•nine (mĕz'ə-nēn', mĕz'ə-nēn') *n.* **1.** A partial story between 2 main stories of a building. **2.** The lowest balcony in a theater, esp. the first few rows.
mez•zo-so•pran•o (mĕt'sō-sə-prăn'ō, -prä'nō, mĕd'zō-) *n.* **1.** A woman's voice with a range between soprano and contralto. **2.** A woman with this voice.
Mg *symbol for* MAGNESIUM.
MIA (ĕm'ī-ā') *n.* A serviceman who is reported missing in action whose death cannot be confirmed.
mi•as•ma (mī-ăz'mə, mē-) *n., pl.* **-mas** *or* **-ma•ta** (-mə-tə). **1.** A poisonous atmosphere once believed to rise from swamps and cause disease. **2.** A harmful influence. —**mi•as'mal, mi•as'mic** *adj.*
mi•ca (mī'kə) *n.* One of a group of silicate minerals that are similar in physical structure and chemical composition and that split easily into thin transparent or translucent sheets. —**mi•ca'ceous** (-kā'shəs) *adj.*
Mi•cah (mī'kə) *n.* —See table at BIBLE.
mice (mīs) *n. pl. of* MOUSE.
mi•cra (mī'krə) *n. var. pl. of* MICRON.
mi•crobe (mī'krōb') *n.* A microorganism. —**mi•cro'bi•al, mi•cro'bic** *adj.*
mi•cro•bi•ol•o•gy (mī'krō-bī-ŏl'ə-jē) *n.* The scientific study of microorganisms and their effects on other forms of life. —**mi'cro•bi'o•log'i•cal** (-ə-lŏj'ĭ-kəl) *adj.* —**mi'cro•bi•ol'o•gist** *n.*
mi•cro•bus (mī'krō-bŭs') *n.* A small bus that resembles a station wagon.
mi•cro•ceph•a•ly (mī'krō-sĕf'ə-lē) *n.* Abnormal smallness of the head, often associated with pathological mental conditions. —**mi'cro•ce•phal'ic** (-sə-făl'ĭk) *n. & adj.*
mi•cro•chip (mī'krə-chĭp') *n.* CHIP 5a.
mi•cro•cir•cuit (mī'krō-sûr'kĭt) *n.* An electronic circuit that consists of components of very small size. —**mi'cro•cir'cuit•ry** (-kĭ-trē) *n.*
mi•cro•cline (mī'krō-klīn') *n.* A mineral of the feldspar group.
mi•cro•com•put•er (mī'krō-kəm-pyōō'tər) *n.* A computer using a microprocessor.
mi•cro•cosm (mī'krō-kŏz'əm) *n.* A diminutive world, esp. a system that is analogous to a larger one in configuration, constitution, or development. —**mi'cro•cos'mic, mi'cro•cos'mi•cal** *adj.*
mi•cro•e•lec•tron•ics (mī'krō-ĭ-lĕk-trŏn'-

ĭks) *n. (sing. in number).* A branch of electronics dealing with miniature components. —**mi′cro•e•lec•tron′ic** *adj.*

mi•cro•fiche (mī′krō-fēsh′) *n., pl.* **microfiche** *or* **-fich•es.** A microfilm sheet containing rows of written or printed pages in reduced form.

mi•cro•film (mī′krō-fĭlm′) *n.* **1.** A film on which printed matter is photographed in greatly reduced size. **2.** A reproduction on microfilm. —**mi′cro•film′** *v.*

mi•cro•groove (mī′krō-gro͞ov′) *n.* A long-playing phonograph record.

mi•crom•e•ter (mī-krŏm′ĭ-tər) *n.* An instrument for measuring minute distances, esp. by the use of a finely threaded screw.

mi•cron (mī′krŏn′) *n., pl.* **-crons** *or* **-cra** (-krə). A unit of length equal to one-millionth (10^{-6}) of a meter.

mi•cro•or•gan•ism (mī′krō-ôr′gə-nĭz′əm) *n.* An organism, as a bacterium or a protozoan, too small to be seen without the aid of a microscope.

mi•cro•phone (mī′krə-fōn′) *n.* An instrument that converts acoustical waves into electric signals, usu. fed into a recorder, amplifier, or broadcasting transmitter. —**mi′cro•phon′ic** (-fŏn′ĭk) *adj.*

mi•cro•proc•es•sor (mī′krō-prŏs′ĕs-ər) *n. Computer Sci.* A semiconductor processing unit contained on an integrated-circuit chip.

mi•cro•scope (mī′krə-skōp′) *n.* An optical instrument that produces magnified images of very small objects, esp. of objects too small to be seen with the unaided eye. —**mi•cros′co•py** (-krŏs′kə-pē) *n.*

mi•cro•scop•ic (mī′krə-skŏp′ĭk) *also* **mi•cro•scop•i•cal** (-ĭ-kəl) *adj.* **1.** Too small to be seen by the unaided eye but large enough to be studied under a microscope. **2.** Of, relating to, or entailing the use of a microscope. —**mi′cro•scop′i•cal•ly** *adv.*

mi•cro•sec•ond (mī′krō-sĕk′ənd) *n.* One-millionth (10^{-6}) of a sec.

mi•cro•sur•ger•y (mī′krō-sûr′jə-rē) *n.* Surgery on minute living structures, as by means of microscopes and lasers. —**mi′cro•sur′gi•cal** (-jĭ-kəl) *adj.*

mi•cro•wave (mī′krə-wāv′) *n.* An electromagnetic wave with a wavelength ranging approx. from 1 mm to 1 m.

microwave oven *n.* An oven in which microwaves heat and cook food.

mid (mĭd) *adj.* Being in the middle or center **:** central.

mid•air (mĭd-âr′) *n.* A region or point in the air above the surface of the ground.

mid•day (mĭd′dā′) *n.* Noon.

mid•den (mĭd′n) *n.* A dunghill or refuse heap, esp. of a primitive habitation.

mid•dle (mĭd′l) *adj.* **1.** Being equally distant from extremes or limits **:** central. **2.** Being at neither one extreme nor the other. **3. Middle.** Designating or constituting a period, as in the development of a language, between earlier and later stages. —*n.* **1.** An area or point equidistant between extremes **:** center. **2.** Something intermediate between extremes **:** mean. **3.** The waist. ★ ***syns:*** CENTRAL, INTERMEDIATE, MEAN, MEDIAL, MEDIAN, MID, MIDDLE-OF-THE-ROAD, MIDWAY —**mid′dle•most′** *adj.*

middle age *n.* The period of human life between about 40 and 60. —**mid′dle-aged′** *adj.*

Middle Ages *pl.n.* The period of European history extending approx. from A.D. 476 to 1453.

Middle America *n.* The part of the U.S. middle class that is of average income and education and conservative attitudes and values. —**Middle American** *n. & adj.*

mid•dle•brow (mĭd′l-brou′) *n. Informal.* A moderately cultured person. —**mid′dle•brow′** *adj.*

middle class *n.* The social class occupying a socioeconomic position intermediate between the lower and upper classes. —**mid′dle-class′** *adj.*

middle ear *n.* The space between the tympanic membrane and the inner ear through which sound waves are carried by the malleus, incus, and stapes.

mid•dle•man (mĭd′l-măn′) *n.* A go-between, esp. one who buys goods from producers for resale at a profit to retailers or consumers.

middle-of-the-road (mĭd′l-əv-thə-rōd′) *adj.* Pursuing or advocating a course of action that avoids extremes, esp. in politics.

middle school *n.* A school that usu. includes grades 5 through 8.

mid•dle•weight (mĭd′l-wāt′) *n.* A boxer weighing between 147 and 160 lbs.

†**mid•dling** (mĭd′lĭng) *adj.* **1.** Of medium quality, degree, size, or condition. **2.** Less than excellent **:** mediocre. —*n. often* **middlings.** *SE U.S.* Pork or bacon cut from between the ham and shoulder of a pig. —**mid′dling** *adv.*

mid•dy (mĭd′ē) *n., pl.* **-dies. 1.** *Informal.* A midshipman. **2.** A loose blouse with a sailor collar worn by women or children.

midge (mĭj) *n.* Any of various small, gnatlike flies of the family Chironomidae.

midg•et (mĭj′ĭt) *n.* **1.** An unusually small person. **2.** Something very small of its class.

mid•i (mĭd′ē) *n.* A skirt, dress, or coat extending to the calf.

mid•land (mĭd′lənd) *n.* The middle or interior part of a region or country.

mid•most (mĭd′mōst′) *adj.* **1.** Located in the exact middle **:** middlemost. **2.** Located nearest the middle. —**mid′most′** *adv.*

mid•night (mĭd′nīt′) *n.* The middle of the night **:** 12 o'clock.

midnight sun *n.* The sun at midnight during the summer in the Arctic or Antarctic Circle.

mid•point (mĭd′point′) *n.* A point near or at the middle.

mid•riff (mĭd′rĭf′) *n.* **1.** The diaphragm. **2.** The part of the human torso from the chest to the waist.

mid•ship•man (mĭd′shĭp′mən, mĭd-shĭp′mən) *n.* A student training to be a commissioned naval officer.

midst (mĭdst) *n.* **1.** The middle part or position : center. **2.** The condition of being surrounded or enveloped. **3.** A position among others in a group <a guest in our *midst*> —*prep.* Amid : among.
mid•stream (mĭd′strēm′) *n.* The middle of a stream.
mid•sum•mer (mĭd′sŭm′ər) *n.* **1.** The middle of the summer. **2.** The summer solstice.
mid•term (mĭd′tûrm′) *n.* **1.** The middle of a term, esp. an academic term. **2.** An examination given in the middle of an academic term.
mid•town (mĭd′toun′) *n.* A central portion of a city. —**mid′town′** *adj.*
mid•way (mĭd′wā′) *n.* The area of an amusement park, fair, or carnival where amusements, as side shows, are located. —*adv. & adj.* In the middle of the distance or way : halfway.
mid•week (mĭd′wēk′) *n.* The middle of the week. —**mid′week′ly** *adj. & adv.*
mid•wife (mĭd′wīf′) *n.* A woman who assists other women in childbirth. —**mid′wife′ry** *n.*
mid•win•ter (mĭd′wĭn′tər) *n.* **1.** The middle of the winter. **2.** The winter solstice.
mid•year (mĭd′yîr′) *n.* **1.** The middle of a year. **2.** An examination given in the middle of an academic year. —**mid′year′** *adj.*
mien (mēn) *n.* **1.** A person's bearing or manner : demeanor. **2.** Appearance.
miff (mĭf) *v.* To cause to be displeased.
might[1] (mīt) *n.* **1.** Force : power. **2.** Physical strength.
might[2] (mīt) *v.* —Used to indicate a present condition contrary to fact; a possibility or probability weaker than *may*; possibility, probability, or permission in the past; or a greater degree of politeness than *may, should,* or *ought.*
might•y (mī′tē) *adj.* **-i•er, -i•est. 1.** Having or showing great power : strong. **2.** Awesome or imposing : great. —*adv. Informal.* Exceedingly : very. —**might′i•ly** *adv.* —**might′i•ness** *n.*
mi•gnon•ette (mĭn′yə-nĕt′) *n.* A garden plant, *Reseda odorata,* with small, fragrant greenish flowers.
mi•graine (mī′grān′) *n.* Severe, recurrent headache, often accompanied by nausea.
mi•grant (mī′grənt) *n.* One that migrates, esp. from one region to another in search of seasonal work. —**mi′grant** *adj.*
mi•grate (mī′grāt′) *v.* **-grat•ed, -grat•ing. 1.** To move from a country or area and settle in another. **2.** To move periodically from one climate or region to another. —**mi•gra′tion** *n.* —**mi•gra′tion•al** *adj.* —**mi′gra•to′ry** (-grə-tôr′ē, -tōr′ē) *adj.*
mi•ka•do (mĭ-kä′dō) *n., pl.* **-dos.** An emperor of Japan.
mike (mīk) *n. Informal.* A microphone.
mil (mĭl) *n.* A unit of length equal to one-thousandth (10^{-3}) of an in.
milch (mĭlch) *adj.* Giving milk <*milch* cows>
mild (mīld) *adj.* **1.** Gentle in manner, disposition, or behavior. **2.** Not extreme : moderate. **3.** Not sharp, bitter, or strong, as in taste. —**mild′ly** *adv.* —**mild′ness** *n.*
mil•dew (mĭl′do͞o′, -dyo͞o′) *n.* A superficial white or grayish coating formed by fungi on organic materials, as paint, fabric, paper, or leather. —**mil′dew′** *v.* —**mil′dew′y** *adj.*
mile (mīl) *n.* **1.** —See table at MEASUREMENT. **2.** A nautical mile.
mile•age (mī′lĭj) *n.* **1.** Distance traveled, measured, or expressed in miles. **2.** Service, use, or wear expressed in miles traveled. **3.** Money allowed for travel expenses at a specified rate per mile.
mile•post (mīl′pōst′) *n.* A post that indicates distance in miles to a given place.
mile•stone (mīl′stōn′) *n.* **1.** A stone marker used as a milepost. **2.** An important point in progress or development.
mi•lieu (mēl-yœ′) *n.* Environment.
mil•i•tant (mĭl′ĭ-tənt) *adj.* **1.** Engaged in combat. **2.** Working aggressively for a cause. —**mil′i•tan•cy** *n.* —**mil′i•tant** *n.*
mil•i•ta•rism (mĭl′ĭ-tə-rĭz′əm) *n.* **1.** The predominance of the professional military class in state affairs. **2.** A policy in which military preparedness is of primary importance. —**mil′i•ta•rist** *n.* —**mil′i•ta•ris′tic** *adj.* —**mil′i•ta•ris′ti•cal•ly** *adv.*
mil•i•ta•rize (mĭl′ĭ-tə-rīz′) *v.* **-rized, -riz•ing. 1.** To train or equip for war. **2.** To impart militarism to.
mil•i•tar•y (mĭl′ĭ-tĕr′ē) *adj.* **1.** Of or relating to armed forces, soldiers, or war. **2.** Characteristic of or appropriate to a soldier or the armed forces. —*n.* **1.** The armed forces of a nation. **2.** Members of the military. —**mil′i•tar′i•ly** (-târ′ə-lē) *adv.*
mil•i•tate (mĭl′ĭ-tāt′) *v.* **-tat•ed, -tat•ing.** To have influence or force.
mi•li•tia (mĭ-lĭsh′ə) *n.* A reserve military force that is on call for service only in an emergency. —**mi•li′tia•man** *n.*
milk (mĭlk) *n.* **1.** A whitish liquid produced by the mammary glands of all mature female mammals to feed their young. **2.** A liquid, as the sap of some plants, like milk. —*v.* **1.** To draw the milk from (a female mammal). **2.** To extract as if by milking. —**milk′i•ness** *n.* —**milk′y** *adj.*
milk glass *n.* An opaque or translucent glass orig. of a whitish color.
milk•maid (mĭlk′mād′) *n.* A woman or girl who milks cows.
milk•man (mĭlk′măn′) *n.* A man who delivers or sells milk.
milk of magnesia *n.* A liquid suspension of magnesium hydroxide used as a laxative and antacid.
milk shake *n.* A drink made of milk, flavoring, and usu. ice cream thoroughly shaken or blended.
milk•sop (mĭlk′sŏp′) *n.* A man lacking in manly qualities.
milk tooth *n.* One of the set of temporary 1st teeth of a young mammal.

milk•weed (mĭlk'wēd') *n.* A plant of the genus *Asclepias,* esp. *A. syriaca,* having milky juice and pointed pods that open to release seeds with downy tufts.

Milky Way *n.* The galaxy in which the solar system is located, visible at night as a luminous band.

mill[1] (mĭl) *n.* **1.** A building with machinery for grinding grain into meal or flour. **2.** A device for crushing or grinding <a pepper *mill*> **3.** A building with machinery for processing materials **:** factory. —*v.* **1.** To crush or grind in or as if in a mill. **2.** To process or produce in a mill. **3.** To move around in a disorderly or confused mass.

mill[2] (mĭl) *n.* A monetary unit equal to 1/1000 of a U.S. dollar or 1/10 of a cent.

mill•dam (mĭl'dăm') *n.* A dam constructed to create a millpond.

mil•len•ni•um (mĭ-lĕn'ē-əm) *n., pl.* **-ums** *or* **-ni•a** (-ē-ə). **1.** A period of 1,000 years. **2.** The 1,000-year reign of Christ on earth mentioned in the New Testament. **3.** A period of prosperity, happiness, justice, and peace. —**mil•len'ni•al** *adj.*

mill•er (mĭl'ər) *n.* **1.** Someone who operates, owns, or works in a mill, esp. a grain mill. **2.** Any of various moths whose wings are covered with a powdery substance.

mil•let (mĭl'ĭt) *n.* A grass, *Panicum miliaceum,* grown for its edible white seeds.

mil•liard (mĭl'yərd, -yärd', mĭl'ē-ärd') *n. esp. Brit.* A billion.

mil•li•gram (mĭl'ĭ-grăm') *n.* —See table at MEASUREMENT.

mil•li•li•ter (mĭl'ə-lē'tər) *n.* —See table at MEASUREMENT.

mil•lime (mĭl'ĭm, -ēm) *n.* —See table at CURRENCY.

mil•li•me•ter (mĭl'ə-mē'tər) *n.* —See table at MEASUREMENT.

mil•li•ner (mĭl'ə-nər) *n.* Someone who makes, designs, or sells women's hats.

mil•li•ner•y (mĭl'ə-nĕr'ē) *n.* **1.** Articles, esp. women's hats, sold by a milliner. **2.** The profession or business of a milliner.

†**mill•ing** (mĭl'ĭng) *n.* **1.** The act or process of grinding, esp. of grinding grain into meal or flour. **2.** The ridged edge of a coin. **3.** *W U.S.* The process of halting a cattle stampede by turning the lead animals in a wide arc so that they form the center of a gradually tightening spiral.

mil•lion (mĭl'yən) *n.* **1.** The cardinal number equal to 1,000 × 1,000 or 10^6. **2.** *often* **millions.** A large unspecified number. —**mil'lion** *adj.* —**mil'lionth** *n. & adj. & adv.*

mil•lion•aire (mĭl'yə-nâr') *n.* Someone whose wealth amounts to 1,000,000 or more units of currency, as dollars.

mil•li•pede (mĭl'ə-pēd') *n.* An arthropod of the class Diplopoda, having a wormlike body with legs attached in double pairs to most body segments.

mil•li•sec•ond (mĭl'ĭ-sĕk'ənd) *n.* A unit of time equal to 1/1000 (10^{-3}) sec.

mill•pond (mĭl'pŏnd') *n.* A pond created by constructing a dam to produce a waterfall for operating a mill.

mill•race (mĭl'rās') *n.* **1.** A fast-moving current of water that powers a mill wheel. **2.** A canal in which a millrace flows.

mill•stone (mĭl'stōn') *n.* One of a pair of large cylindrical stones for grinding grain.

mill•stream (mĭl'strēm') *n.* **1.** A stream whose flow is used to operate a mill. **2.** A millrace.

milt (mĭlt) *n.* **1.** Fish sperm, including the seminal fluid. **2.** The reproductive glands of male fishes when filled with milt.

mime (mīm) *n.* **1. a.** The art of pantomime. **b.** A performer or performance in pantomime. **2.** A mimic. —*v.* **mimed, mim•ing. 1.** To imitate **:** mimic. **2.** To portray or act in pantomime. —**mim'er** *n.*

mim•e•o•graph (mĭm'ē-ə-grăf') *n.* A machine that makes duplicates of written, drawn, or typed material from a stencil that is fitted around an inked drum. —**mim'e•o•graph'** *v.*

mi•me•sis (mĭ-mē'sĭs, mī-) *n.* The act or process of mimicking **:** imitation.

mi•met•ic (mĭ-mĕt'ĭk, mī-) *adj.* Of, relating to, or using mimicry.

mim•ic (mĭm'ĭk) *v.* **-icked, -ick•ing. 1.** To imitate closely, as in speech or behavior **:** ape. **2.** To imitate so as to ridicule. **3.** To resemble closely **:** simulate. —**mim'ic** *n.* —**mim'ick•er** *n.*

mim•ic•ry (mĭm'ĭ-krē) *n., pl.* **-ries. 1.** The act, art, or practice of mimicking. **2.** A resemblance of one organism to another or to a natural object, as for protection from predators.

mi•mo•sa (mĭ-mō'sə, -zə) *n.* Any of various mostly tropical shrubs or trees of the genus *Mimosa,* with ball-like clusters of small flowers.

min•a•ret (mĭn'ə-rĕt') *n.* A tall, slender tower that is attached to a mosque.

min•a•to•ry (mĭn'ə-tôr'ē, -tōr'ē) *adj.* Conveying a menace **:** threatening.

mince (mĭns) *v.* **minced, minc•ing. 1.** To chop or cut into small pieces. **2.** To refrain from using, as for the sake of politeness. —**minc'ing•ly** *adv.*

mince•meat (mĭns'mēt') *n.* Spiced finely chopped raisins, apples, and sometimes meat, used esp. for a pie filling.

†**mind** (mīnd) *n.* **1.** The part of a human being that governs thought, perception, feeling, will, memory, and imagination. **2.** Recollection **:** memory. **3.** Direction of an individual's thoughts **:** attention. **4.** Point of view **:** opinion. **5.** Desire **:** purpose. **6. a.** Intellectual capacity **:** intelligence. **b.** A person considered with respect to intellectual ability. **7.** Normal mental or emotional function **:** sanity. —*v.* **1.** To occupy oneself with <*minding* my own business> **2.** To obey. **3.** To take charge of **:** tend <*minded* the children> **4.** To be cautious or careful. **5.** To be concerned (about) **:** object (to). **6.** *Regional.* **a.** To put (a person)

in mind of something : remind. **b.** To bring (an object or idea) to mind : remember. **7.** *Regional.* To have in mind as a goal or purpose : intend.

mind-blowing (mīnd′blō′ing) *adj. Slang.* **1.** Producing hallucinatory effects : psychedelic. **2.** Affecting the mind or emotions with overwhelming intensity.

mind-bog·gling (mīnd′bŏg′lĭng) *adj. Informal.* Overwhelming.

mind·ed (mīn′dĭd) *adj.* **1.** Disposed : inclined. **2.** Having a specified kind of mind <broad-*minded*>

mind·ful (mīnd′fəl) *adj.* Keeping in mind : heedful. **—mind′ful·ness** *n.*

mind·less (mīnd′lĭs) *adj.* **1.** Lacking intelligence, good sense, or purpose. **2.** Heedless. **—mind′less·ness** *n.*

mind·set (mīnd′sĕt′) *n.* A fixed mental attitude that predetermines one's responses to and interpretations of situations.

mine¹ (mīn) *n.* **1.** An underground or inground excavation from which minerals, as metals or coal, can be extracted. **2.** A mineral or ore deposit. **3.** A source from which an abundant supply can be obtained. **4. a.** A tunnel dug under an enemy position. **b.** An explosive device, as one floating in the water or buried in the ground, that is detonated by a time fuse or contact. **—***v.* **mined, min·ing. 1.** To extract from or as if from a mine. **2.** To dig a mine (in). **3.** To lay explosive mines in. **4.** To undermine : subvert. **—min′er** *n.*

mine² (mīn) *pron.* The one or ones belonging to me.

min·er·al (mĭn′ər-əl) *n.* **1.** A natural solid inorganic substance, as silver, quartz, or diamond, having a definite chemical composition and characteristic crystalline structure and being neither animal nor vegetable in origin. **2. a.** A mixture of inorganic compounds, as granite. **b.** An organic derivative, as coal. **3.** An ore. **—min′er·al** *adj.* **—min′er·al·ize′** *v.*

min·er·al·o·gy (mĭn′ə-rŏl′ə-jē, -răl′-) *n.* The scientific study of minerals. **—min′er·a·log′i·cal** (-ər-ə-lŏj′ĭ-kəl) *adj.* **—min′er·al′o·gist** *n.*

mineral oil *n.* A light oil distilled from petroleum, esp. one used as a laxative.

mineral water *n.* Water that contains dissolved minerals or gases.

min·e·stro·ne (mĭn′ĭ-strō′nē) *n.* A thick vegetable soup containing beans and pasta.

mine sweeper *n.* A ship that is designed for the detection, removal, or neutralization of underwater explosive mines.

min·gle (mĭng′gəl) *v.* **-gled, -gling.** To bring or come together in close association : mix. **—min′gler** *n.*

min·i (mĭn′ē) *n.* Something smaller than others of its kind.

min·i·a·ture (mĭn′ē-ə-choor′, mĭn′ə-, -chər) *n.* **1. a.** A model or copy in greatly reduced size. **b.** Something very small of its class. **2.** A very small painting. **—***adj.* On a small or greatly reduced scale.

▲ ***word history:*** The idea of smallness was not orig. part of the meaning of *miniature. Miniature* is derived from Latin *minium,* "red lead," a compound of lead used as a pigment. In medieval times chapter headings and other important divisions of a text were distinguished by being written in red, while the rest of the book was written in black. The Latin verb *miniare,* derived from *minium,* meant "to color red." *Miniatura,* the past participle, denoted the process of writing in red. Sections of a manuscript were also marked off with large ornate initial capital letters, which often were decorated with small paintings. *Miniatura* was used to denote these paintings as well. Since the paintings were necessarily very small, *miniatura* came to denote a small painting or a small object of any kind.

min·i·a·tur·ize (mĭn′ē-ə-chə-rīz′, mĭn′ə-) *v.* **-ized, -iz·ing.** To plan or make on a greatly reduced scale. **—min′i·a·tur′i·za′tion** *n.*

min·i·bike (mĭn′ē-bīk′) *n.* A small motorcycle for one passenger.

min·i·bus (mĭn′ē-bŭs′) *n.* A small bus.

min·i·car (mĭn′ē-kär′) *n.* A small car.

min·i·com·put·er (mĭn′ē-kəm-pyoo′tər) *n.* A small computer with more memory than a microcomputer.

min·im (mĭn′ĭm) *n.* A unit of fluid measure equal to 1/60 fl dr.

min·i·mal (mĭn′ə-məl) *adj.* Of or being a minimum. **—min′i·mal·ly** *adv.*

minimal art *n.* A kind of abstract art that consists mainly of geometric forms and shapes. **—minimal artist** *n.*

min·i·mal·ism (mĭn′ə-mə-lĭz′əm) *n.* Use of the fewest and barest elements, as in the arts, literature, or design. **—min′i·mal·ist** *adj. & n.*

min·i·mize (mĭn′ə-mīz′) *v.* **-mized, -miz·ing. 1.** To reduce to a minimum. **2.** To think of or represent as of minimum value or importance.

min·i·mum (mĭn′ə-məm) *n., pl.* **-mums** *or* **-ma** (-mə). **1.** The least possible degree or quantity. **2.** The lowest number, quantity, or degree permitted, reached, or recorded. **—min′i·mum** *adj.*

min·ion (mĭn′yən) *n.* **1.** A usu. servile dependent or follower. **2.** Someone who is much favored. **3.** A subordinate, as in an organization.

min·i·skirt (mĭn′ē-skûrt′) *n.* A very short skirt.

min·is·ter (mĭn′ĭ-stər) *n.* **1.** A pastor of a church, esp. a Protestant church : clergyman. **2.** A high officer of state who heads a governmental division. **3.** A diplomat who ranks next below an ambassador. **4.** An agent for another. **—***v.* To attend to the needs of others. **—min′is·te′ri·al** (-stîr′ē-əl) *adj.* **—min′is·trant** (-strənt) *adj. & n.* **—min′is·tra′tion** *n.*

min·is·try (mĭn′ĭ-strē) *n., pl.* **-tries. 1.** The act of serving : ministration. **2. a.** Ministers of religion : clergy. **b.** The position, duties, or term of service of a minister. **3. a.** A department of government headed by a minister. **b.** The position, duties, or term of office of a minister of government. **c.** Governmental ministers as a group.

min•i•van (mĭn'ē-văn') *n.* A small passenger van having usu. removable rear seats for cargo.

mink (mĭngk) *n., pl.* **mink** *or* **minks.** A semiaquatic weasellike carnivore of the genus *Mustela,* esp. *M. vison,* with soft, thick, lustrous fur.

min•now (mĭn'ō) *n., pl.* **minnow** *or* **-nows.** A small freshwater fish of the family Cyprinidae, often used as bait.

mi•nor (mī'nər) *adj.* **1.** Lesser in amount, size, degree, or importance. **2.** Not legally of age. **3.** *Mus.* **a.** Having a half step between the 2nd and 3rd and 5th and 6th degrees <a *minor* scale> **b.** Based on a minor scale <a *minor* key> —*n.* **1.** One not yet of legal age. **2.** An academic subject secondary in importance to a major. —*v.* To study an academic minor.

mi•nor•i•ty (mĭ-nôr'ĭ-tē, -nŏr'-, mī-) *n., pl.* **-ties. 1.** The smaller in number of 2 groups that form a whole. **2.** A population segment that differs, as in religion, race, or sex, from the larger group to which it belongs. **3.** The state or period of being under legal age.

min•ster (mĭn'stər) *n.* **1.** A church belonging to a monastery. **2.** A large, important church.

min•strel (mĭn'strəl) *n.* **1.** A medieval traveling musician. **2.** A performer, often made up in imitation of a black, in a variety show featuring songs, jokes, and comic skits.

mint[1] (mĭnt) *n.* **1.** A place where coins are manufactured, esp. by a government. **2.** An enormous amount, esp. of money. —*v.* **1.** To manufacture (coins). **2.** To make up : invent. —*adj.* Undamaged as if newly minted. **—mint'age** *n.*

mint[2] (mĭnt) *n.* A plant of the genus *Mentha,* with aromatic foliage used for flavoring. **—mint'y** *adj.*

mint julep *n.* An iced and sweetened drink made of bourbon and mint leaves.

min•u•end (mĭn'yo͞o-ĕnd') *n.* A quantity from which another is to be subtracted.

min•u•et (mĭn'yo͞o-ĕt') *n.* A slow, stately pattern dance or the music for it.

mi•nus (mī'nəs) *prep.* **1.** *Math.* Reduced by the subtraction of : less <9 *minus* 4 equals 5.> **2.** *Informal.* Lacking : without <came *minus* her coat> —*adj.* **1.** *Math.* Less than zero : negative <a *minus* value> **2.** Slightly lower or less than <a mark of A *minus*> —*n.* **1.** The minus sign. **2.** A negative number, quantity, or quality.

min•us•cule (mĭn'ə-skyo͞ol', mĭ-nŭs'kyo͞ol') *adj.* Very small : tiny. —*n.* A lower-case letter.

minus sign *n.* A sign (–) used to indicate subtraction or a negative quantity.

min•ute[1] (mĭn'ĭt) *n.* **1. a.** A unit of time equal to 1/60 hour or 60 sec. **b.** A unit of angular measurement equal to 1/60 degree or 60 sec. **2. a.** A short interval of time. **b.** A particular moment in time. **3. minutes.** An official record of transactions or proceedings, esp. of a meeting.

mi•nute[2] (mī-no͞ot', -nyo͞ot', mĭ-) *adj.* **-nut•er, -nut•est. 1.** Extremely small : tiny. **2.** Of little significance : trifling. **3.** Characterized by careful examination of details. **—mi•nute'ly** *adv.*

minute hand *n.* The long hand that indicates the minutes on a timepiece.

min•ute•man *or* **Min•ute•man** (mĭn'ĭt-măn') *n.* A Revolutionary War militiaman pledged to be ready to fight at a minute's notice.

mi•nu•ti•a (mĭ-no͞o'shē-ə, -nyo͞o'-, -shə) *n., pl.* **-ti•ae** (-shē-ē'). A minor detail.

minx (mĭngks) *n.* A high-spirited or impudent girl or woman.

mir•a•cle (mĭr'ə-kəl) *n.* **1.** An event that seems impossible to explain by natural laws and so is regarded as supernatural in origin or as an act of God. **2.** One that excites admiration or awe : wonder. **—mi•rac'u•lous** (mĭ-răk'yə-ləs) *adj.*

mi•rage (mĭ-räzh') *n.* **1.** An optical illusion, caused by atmospheric conditions, in which nonexistent bodies of water, often with inverted reflections of faraway objects, are seen. **2.** Something illusory and impossible to attain.

mire (mīr) *n.* Deep, heavy mud or soil. —*v.* **mired, mir•ing.** To stick or cause to stick in or as if in mire. **—mir'y** *adj.*

mir•ror (mĭr'ər) *n.* **1.** A surface, as of glass, that reflects undiffused light to form an image of an object. **2.** Something that gives a true representation of something else. —*v.* To reflect in or as if in a mirror.

mirth (mûrth) *n.* Gaiety and merriment expressed by laughter. **—mirth'ful** *adj.* **—mirth'ful•ly** *adv.* **—mirth'ful•ness** *n.* **—mirth'less** *adj.* **—mirth'less•ly** *adv.*

mis– *pref.* **1.** Bad : badly : wrong : wrongly <*mis*conduct> **2.** Failure : lack <*mis*fire>

mis'a•dapt' *v.*
mis•add' *v.*
mis'ad•dress' *v.*
mis'ad•just' *v.*
mis'ad•min'is•ter *v.*
mis'ad•min'is•tra'tion *n.*
mis'ad•vise' *v.*
mis•aim' *v.*
mis'a•lign' *v.*
mis'a•lign'ment *n.*
mis•al'lo•cate' *v.*
mis•al'lo•ca'tion *n.*
mis•al'pha•bet•ize' *v.*
mis'a•nal'y•sis *n.*
mis•an'a•lyze' *v.*
mis•ap'pli•ca'tion *n.*
mis'ap•ply' *v.*
mis'ap•prais'al *n.*
mis'ar•tic'u•late' *v.*
mis'ar•tic'u•la'tion *n.*
mis'as•sem'ble *v.*
mis'as•sump'tion *n.*
mis'at•trib'ute *v.*
mis•at'tri•bu'tion *n.*
mis•au'thor•i•za'tion *n.*
mis•au'thor•ize' *v.*
mis•bal'ance *v.*
mis'be•have' *v.*
mis'be•hav'ior *n.*
mis'be•lief' *n.*
mis•bill' *v.*
mis•build' *v.*
mis•cal'cu•late' *v.*

mis·ad·ven·ture (mĭs′əd-vĕn′chər) *n.* A mishap : misfortune.
mis·al·li·ance (mĭs′ə-lī′əns) *n.* An inappropriate alliance, esp. a mésalliance.
mis·an·thrope (mĭs′ən-thrōp′, mĭz′-) *n.* Someone who scorns or hates humanity. **—mis′an·throp′ic** (-thrŏp′ĭk) *adj.* **—mis·an′thro·py** (-ăn′thrə-pē) *n.*
mis·ap·pre·hend (mĭs-ăp′rĭ-hĕnd′) *v.* To understand incorrectly : misunderstand. **—mis·ap′pre·hen′sion** (-hĕn′shən) *n.*
mis·ap·pro·pri·ate (mĭs′ə-prō′prē-āt′) *v.* **1.** To appropriate wrongly. **2.** To appropriate dishonestly for one's own use. **—mis′ap·pro′pri·a′tion** *n.*
mis·be·got·ten (mĭs′bĭ-gŏt′n) *adj.* Unlawfully begotten, esp. illegitimate.
mis·car·riage (mĭs-kăr′ĭj) *n.* **1.** Failure to achieve a proper or desired result. **2.** Premature expulsion of a nonviable fetus from the uterus.
mis·car·ry (mĭs-kăr′ē) *v.* **1.** To go wrong : fail. **2.** To undergo a miscarriage : abort.
mis·cast (mĭs-kăst′) *v.* To cast (e.g., an actor) in an inappropriate role.
mis·ce·ge·na·tion (mĭs′ĭ-jə-nā′shən, mĭ-sĕj′ə-) *n.* Marriage or cohabitation between persons of different races, esp. between white and nonwhite persons.
mis·cel·la·ne·ous (mĭs′ə-lā′nē-əs) *adj.* Consisting of a variety of elements, parts, or characteristics. **—mis′cel·la′ne·ous·ly** *adv.* **—mis′cel·la′ne·ous·ness** *n.*
mis·cel·la·ny (mĭs′ə-lā′nē) *n., pl.* **-nies. 1.** A collection of various elements, items, or ingredients. **2.** A collection of a variety of literary works.
mis·chance (mĭs-chăns′) *n.* **1.** Bad luck. **2.** An unfortunate occurrence : mishap.
mis·chief (mĭs′chĭf) *n.* **1. a.** Behavior that causes annoyance or harm. **b.** A cause of annoyance or harm. **2.** A tendency to misbehave : mischievousness. **3.** Injury caused by a specific human agency.
mis·chie·vous (mĭs′chə-vəs) *adj.* **1.** Tending to behave in a playful way. **2.** Annoying or harmful. **3.** Causing injury. **—mis′chie·vous·ly** *adv.*
mis·ci·ble (mĭs′ə-bəl) *adj. Chem.* Capable of being mixed. **—mis′ci·bil′i·ty** *n.*
mis·con·ceive (mĭs′kən-sēv′) *v.* To mistake the meaning of. **—mis′con·ceiv′er** *n.* **—mis′con·cep′tion** (-sĕp′shən) *n.*
mis·con·duct (mĭs-kŏn′dŭkt′) *n.* **1.** Improper behavior or conduct. **2.** Bad or dishonest management, as by elected officials.
mis·count (mĭs-kount′) *v.* To count incorrectly. —*n.* (mĭs′kount′). An incorrect count.
mis·cre·ant (mĭs′krē-ənt) *n.* Someone who engages in evil or criminal acts. **—mis′cre·ant** *adj.*

mis·cal′cu·la′tion *n.*
mis·cat′a·log′ *v.*
mis·chan′nel *v.*
mis·charge′ *v.*
mis·claim′ *v.*
mis·clas′si·fi·ca′tion *n.*
mis·clas′si·fy *v.*
mis·code′ *v.*
mis·com′pre·hen′sion *n.*
mis·com′pu·ta′tion *n.*
mis′com·pute′ *v.*
mis′con·nect′ *v.*
mis′con·nec′tion *n.*
mis′con·struc′tion *n.*
mis′con·strue′ *v.*
mis·cop′y *v.*
mis·cut′ *v.*
mis·date′ *v.*
mis′de·clare′ *v.*
mis′de·fine′ *v.*
mis′de·liv′er *v.*
mis′de·liv′er·y *n.*
mis′de·scribe′ *v.*
mis′de·scrip′tion *n.*
mis′de·vel′op *v.*
mis·di′ag·nose′ *v.*
mis·di′ag·no′sis *n.*
mis·di′al *v.*
mis′di·vi′sion *n.*
mis·draw′ *v.*
mis·ed′u·cate′ *v.*
mis·ed′u·ca′tion *n.*
mis·em′pha·sis *n.*
mis·em′pha·size′ *v.*
mis′em·ploy′ *v.*
mis′em·ploy′ment *n.*
mis·es′ti·mate′ *v.*
mis·es′ti·ma′tion *n.*
mis′e·val′u·ate′ *v.*
mis′e·val′u·a′tion *n.*
mis·fash′ion *v.*
mis·file′ *v.*
mis·fo′cus *v.*
mis·form′ *v.*
mis′for·ma′tion *n.*
mis·func′tion *v.*
mis·gauge′ *v.*
mis·gov′ern *v.*
mis·gov′ern·ment *n.*
mis·grade′ *v.*
mis·hear′ *v.*
mis′i·den′ti·fi·ca′tion *n.*
mis′i·den′ti·fy *v.*
mis′in·fer′ *v.*
mis·in′fer·ence *n.*
mis′in·form′ *v.*
mis·in′for·ma′tion *n.*
mis′in·struct′ *v.*
mis′in·struc′tion *n.*
mis·la′bel *v.*
mis·lo′cate′ *v.*
mis′lo·ca′tion *n.*
mis·make′ *v.*
mis·man′age *v.*
mis·man′age·ment *n.*
mis·mark′ *v.*
mis·match′ *v.*
mis′match′ *n.*
mis·meas′ure *v.*
mis′meas′ure *n.*
mis·nav′i·gate′ *v.*
mis·nav′i·ga′tion *n.*
mis·num′ber *v.*
mis·or′der *v.*
mis·o′ri·ent *v.*
mis·o′ri·en·ta′tion *n.*
mis·pack′age *v.*
mis·page′ *v.*
mis·pag′i·na′tion *n.*
mis′per·ceive′ *v.*
mis′per·cep′tion *n.*
mis′per·form′ *v.*
mis′po·si′tion *v.*
mis′pre·scribe′ *v.*
mis·print′ *v.*
mis′print′ *n.*
mis′pro·nounce′ *v.*
mis′pro·nun′ci·a′tion *n.*
mis′quo·ta′tion *n.*
mis·quote′ *v.*
mis·rec′ol·lec′tion *n.*
mis·reg′is·ter *v.*
mis·reg′is·tra′tion *n.*
mis·reg′u·late′ *v.*
mis′re·mem′ber *v.*
mis′re·port′ *v.*
mis·route′ *v.*
mis·ship′ *v.*
mis·ship′ment *n.*
mis·sing′ *v.*
mis·sort′ *v.*
mis·space′ *v.*
mis·style′ *v.*
mis·teach′ *v.*
mis·throw′ *v.*
mis·time′ *v.*
mis·ti′tle *v.*
mis·trans′late′ *v.*
mis′trans·la′tion *n.*
mis·type′ *v.*
mis·write′ *v.*

mis•cue (mĭs-kyōō′) *n.* A mistake **:** error. **—mis•cue′** *v.*

mis•deed (mĭs-dēd′) *n.* An improper or wrong act.

mis•de•mean•or (mĭs′dĭ-mē′nər) *n.* **1.** A misdeed. **2.** *Law.* An offense less serious than a felony.

mis•di•rect (mĭs′dĭ-rĕkt′, -dī-) *v.* To give an incorrect direction to. **—mis′di•rec′tion** *n.*

mis•do•ing (mĭs-dōō′ĭng) *n.* Wrongful acts. **—mis•do′er** *n.*

mise en scène (mēz′äɴ sĕn′) *n.* **1.** The arrangement of properties and performers on a stage. **2.** A physical environment.

mi•ser (mī′zər) *n.* A greedy, grasping person, esp. one who hoards money. **—mi′ser•li•ness** *n.* **—mi′ser•ly** *adj.*

mis•er•a•ble (mĭz′ər-ə-bəl, mĭz′rə-) *adj.* **1.** Very unhappy or uncomfortable **:** wretched. **2.** Causing unhappiness or discomfort. **3.** Very poor **:** squalid. **4.** Very inadequate **:** inferior. **—mis′er•a•ble•ness** *n.* **—mis′er•a•bly** *adv.*

mis•er•y (mĭz′ə-rē) *n., pl.* **-ies. 1.** A state of suffering, as that caused by poverty **:** wretchedness. **2.** A source or cause of suffering **:** affliction. **3.** Emotional distress.

mis•fea•sance (mĭs-fē′zəns) *n. Law.* Improper and unlawful execution of an act that in itself is lawful and proper.

mis•fire (mĭs-fīr′) *v.* **1.** To fail to fire, explode, or ignite. **2.** To fail to achieve a desired result. **—mis′fire′** *n.*

mis•fit (mĭs′fĭt′, mĭs-fĭt′) *n.* **1.** An improper fit. **2.** Someone who is badly adjusted to his or her environment.

mis•for•tune (mĭs-fôr′chən) *n.* **1.** Bad fortune. **2.** An unfortunate occurrence or condition.

mis•giv•ing (mĭs-gĭv′ĭng) *n. often* **misgivings.** A feeling of concern or doubt.

mis•guide (mĭs-gīd′) *v.* To give mistaken guidance to **:** misdirect. **—mis•guid′ance** *n.* **—mis•guid′ed•ly** *adv.*

mis•han•dle (mĭs-hăn′dl) *v.* **1.** To handle roughly or clumsily. **2.** To manage badly or inefficiently.

mis•hap (mĭs′hăp′, mĭs-hăp′) *n.* An unfortunate accident.

mish•mash (mĭsh′măsh′) *n.* A random mixture **:** hodgepodge.

mis•in•ter•pret (mĭs′ĭn-tûr′prĭt) *v.* To understand or explain incorrectly. **—mis′in•ter′pre•ta′tion** *n.*

mis•judge (mĭs-jŭj′) *v.* To err in judging. **—mis•judg′ment** *n.*

mis•lay (mĭs-lā′) *v.* To put in a place one cannot remember **:** lose.

mis•lead (mĭs-lēd′) *v.* **1.** To lead in a wrong direction. **2.** To lead into wrongdoing or error, often by purposefully deceiving.

mis•like (mĭs-līk′) *v.* To dislike. **—mis•like′** *n.*

mis•name (mĭs-nām′) *v.* To call by an incorrect name.

mis•no•mer (mĭs-nō′mər) *n.* An inappropriate or wrong name.

mi•sog•a•my (mĭ-sŏg′ə-mē) *n.* Hatred of marriage. **—mi•sog′a•mist** *n.*

mi•sog•y•ny (mĭ-sŏj′ə-nē) *n.* Hatred of women. **—mi•sog′y•nist** *n.*

mis•place (mĭs-plās′) *v.* **1. a.** To put in an incorrect place. **b.** To mislay. **2.** To place on a wrong object <*misplaced* confidence> **—mis•place′ment** *n.*

mis•play (mĭs′plā′) *n.* A mistaken or inept play, esp. in a game. **—mis•play′** *v.*

mis•read (mĭs-rēd′) *v.* **1.** To read incorrectly. **2.** To misinterpret.

mis•rep•re•sent (mĭs-rĕp′rĭ-zĕnt′) *v.* To represent falsely, wrongly, or misleadingly. **—mis•rep′re•sen•ta′tion** *n.*

mis•rule (mĭs-rōōl′) *v.* To misgovern. **—mis•rule′** *n.*

miss[1] (mĭs) *v.* **1.** To fail to reach, hit, or make contact with. **2.** To fail to understand or perceive. **3.** To fail to accomplish or obtain. **4.** To fail to perform or attend. **5.** To omit. **6.** To avoid. **7.** To feel or regret the absence or loss of. **8.** To misfire. *—n.* **1.** A failure to reach, hit, or succeed. **2.** A misfire.

miss[2] (mĭs) *n.* **1. Miss.** —Used as a courtesy title before the name of an unmarried girl or woman. **2.** A young unmarried woman.

mis•sal (mĭs′əl) *n. Rom. Cath. Ch.* A book containing the prayers and responses used in the Mass throughout the year.

mis•shape (mĭs-shāp′) *v.* To deform **:** distort. **—mis•shap′en** *adj.*

mis•sile (mĭs′əl, -īl′) *n.* **1.** An object, as a rock, that is projected or thrown at a target **:** projectile. **2.** A guided missile. **3.** A ballistic missile. **—mis′sile•ry** *n.*

miss•ing (mĭs′ĭng) *adj.* **1.** Absent. **2.** Lost. **3.** Lacking.

mis•sion (mĭsh′ən) *n.* **1. a.** A body of envoys to a foreign country. **b.** A permanent diplomatic office in a foreign country. **2. a.** A body of missionaries sent out by a church. **b.** The place where the ministry of such a body is exercised. **3.** An assignment to be carried out **:** task. ★ ***syns:*** COMMISSION, ERRAND, OFFICE, TASK

mis•sion•ar•y (mĭsh′ə-nĕr′ē) *n., pl.* **-ies.** One sent out to do religious or charitable work. **—mis′sion•ar′y** *adj.*

mis•sive (mĭs′ĭv) *n.* A written message.

mis•speak (mĭs-spēk′) *v.* To speak mistakenly, inappropriately, or rashly.

mis•spell (mĭs-spĕl′) *v.* To spell incorrectly. **—mis•spell′ing** *n.*

mis•spend (mĭs-spĕnd′) *v.* To squander.

mis•state (mĭs-stāt′) *v.* To state falsely or incorrectly. **—mis•state′ment** *n.*

mis•step (mĭs-stĕp′) *n.* **1.** A wrong step. **2.** A mistake, as in behavior **:** blunder.

mist (mĭst) *n.* **1.** A mass of tiny water droplets in the air. **2.** Water vapor that condenses on a surface and clouds it. **3.** Something that dims or conceals. *—v.* To be, make, or become misty.

mis•take (mĭ-stāk′) *n.* **1.** A wrong statement, decision, or action **:** error. **2.** A misunderstanding. **—mis•tak'a•ble** *adj.* **—mis•tak'a•bly** *adv.* **—mis•take'** *v.*

mis•tak•en (mĭ-stā'kən) *adj.* **1.** Having a wrong opinion, perception, or understanding. **2.** Based on error : wrong. **3.** Misunderstood. **—mis•tak'en•ly** *adv.*

Mis•ter (mĭs'tər) *n.* **1.** —Used as a title of courtesy before a man's name. **2. mister.** *Informal.* Used as a form of address without a name in speaking to a man.

mis•tle•toe (mĭs'əl-tō') *n.* A parasitic plant, *Viscum album,* that grows on trees and has evergreen leaves and white berries.

mis•treat (mĭs-trēt') *v.* To treat wrongly or badly : abuse. **—mis•treat'ment** *n.*

mis•tress (mĭs'trĭs) *n.* **1.** A woman in a position of control, authority, or ownership. **2.** A country enjoying supremacy <*mistress* of the hemisphere> **3.** A woman who cohabits with a man who is not her husband. **4. Mistress.** —Used formerly as a title of courtesy when speaking to a woman.

mis•tri•al (mĭs-trī'əl, -trīl') *n.* A trial that is invalid because of procedural error.

mis•trust (mĭs-trŭst') *n.* A lack of trust : doubt. —*v.* To have no trust in : doubt or suspect. **—mis•trust'ful** *adj.* **—mis•trust'ful•ly** *adv.*

mist•y (mĭs'tē) *adj.* **-i•er, -i•est. 1.** Consisting of, marked by, or resembling mist. **2.** Clouded or obscured by or as if by mist : dim. **—mist'i•ly** *adv.* **—mist'i•ness** *n.*

mis•un•der•stand (mĭs'ŭn-dər-stănd') *v.* To fail to understand correctly.

mis•un•der•stand•ing (mĭs'ŭn-dər-stăn'dĭng) *n.* **1.** A misinterpretation. **2.** A quarrel : disagreement.

mis•use (mĭs-yo͞oz') *v.* **1.** To use improperly or wrongly. **2.** To mistreat : abuse. —*n.* (-yo͞os'). **1.** Improper or wrong use. **2.** Mistreatment : abuse. **—mis•us'age** *n.*

mite[1] (mīt) *n.* Any of various small, often parasitic arachnids.

mite[2] (mīt) *n.* **1.** A very small amount of money. **2. a.** A very small object or creature. **b.** A tiny amount : bit.

mi•ter (mī'tər) *n.* **1.** A tall, pointed headdress worn esp. by bishops. **2.** A joint made by fitting together 2 beveled surfaces to form a right angle. —*v.* To fit together with or meet in a miter joint.

mit•i•gate (mĭt'ĭ-gāt') *v.* **-gat•ed, -gat•ing.** To make or become less intense, severe, or painful. **—mit'i•ga'tion** *n.* **—mit'i•ga'tive** *adj.* **—mit'i•ga'tor** *n.*

mi•to•sis (mī-tō'sĭs) *n.* **1.** The process in which the chromosomes of a cell duplicate themselves and separate into 2 identical groups just before cell division. **—mi•tot'ic** (-tŏt'ĭk) *adj.*

mitt (mĭt) *n.* **1.** A woman's glove that does not fully cover the fingers. **2.** A baseball glove, as that used by a catcher.

mit•ten (mĭt'n) *n.* A covering for the hand with one section for the thumb alone.

mix (mĭks) *v.* **1.** To combine or blend into a single mass. **2.** To make, create, or form by combining constituent parts **3.** To bring or come together : join. **4.** To crossbreed. **5.** To associate. **6.** To confuse <*mixed* up the instructions> **7.** To be or become involved <didn't *mix* in politics> —*n.* Something formed by mixing, esp. a packaged mixture of baking ingredients. **—mix'a•ble** *adj.*

mixed number *n.* A number, as 7½, that represents the sum of an integer and a fraction.

mix•ture (mĭks'chər) *n.* **1.** Something made by mixing. **2.** A combination of diverse qualities or elements. **3. a.** The act or process of mixing. **b.** The state of being mixed. **4.** *Chem.* A composition of substances not bound to each other.

mix-up (mĭks'ŭp') *n.* A state of confusion : muddle.

miz•zen *also* **miz•en** (mĭz'ən) *n.* **1.** A fore-and-aft sail set on the mizzenmast. **2.** A mizzenmast.

miz•zen•mast *also* **miz•en•mast** (mĭz'ən-məst, -măst') *n.* The 3rd mast aft on sailing ships with 3 or more masts.

Mn *symbol for* MANGANESE.

mne•mon•ic (nĭ-mŏn'ĭk) *adj.* Aiding or designed to aid the memory. —*n.* A mnemonic device, as a rhyme or formula.

Mo *symbol for* MOLYBDENUM.

moan (mōn) *n.* A low, sustained sound, esp. of pain or sorrow. **—moan** *v.*

moat (mōt) *n.* A wide, deep, usu. water-filled ditch surrounding a castle.

mob (mŏb) *n.* **1.** A large, unruly crowd. **2.** The mass of common people : rabble. **3.** *Informal.* A gang of criminals. —*v.* **mobbed, mob•bing. 1.** To crowd around and annoy or jostle. **2.** To crowd into <passengers *mobbing* the railroad station>

▲ ***word history:*** Every age has its linguistic fads and ephemeral coinages; occasionally some of them survive and become part of the standard vocabulary. In the 17th and 18th cent. the abbreviation of long words or phrases to one or two syllables had a vogue that was much deplored by the self-appointed literary watchdogs of the day. *Mob* is one such abbreviation that caught on. It is short for *mobile,* which was used in the early 17th cent. to denote "the masses." In this usage *mobile* was itself a shortening of the Latin phrase *mobile vulgus,* "the excitable populace." The note of contempt orig. inherent in English *mob* was also found in the Latin phrase.

mo•bile (mō'bəl, -bēl', -bīl') *adj.* **1.** Capable of being moved or of moving. **2.** Changing readily in mood, expression, or appearance. **3.** Enjoying or affording opportunity for a change from one social status to another. —*n.* (mō'bēl'). A sculpture consisting of parts that move, esp. in response to air currents. **—mo•bil'i•ty** (-bĭl'ĭ-tē) *n.*

mobile home *n.* A trailer serving as a permanent home.

mobile telephone *also* **mobile phone** *n.* A portable radiotelephone, esp. one in an automobile.

mo•bi•lize (mō'bə-līz') *v.* **-lized, -liz•ing. 1.** To put into motion. **2.** To assemble and prepare for war. **3.** To organize for action or use. ★ ***syns:*** MARSHAL, MUSTER, ORGANIZE, RALLY **—mo'bi•li•za'tion** *n.*

mob•ster (mŏb'stər) *n.* A member of a gang of criminals.

moc•ca•sin (mŏk'ə-sĭn) *n.* A soft leather shoe or slipper.

mo•cha (mō'kə) *n.* **1.** A rich coffee of high quality. **2.** A flavoring made of coffee, often with chocolate or cocoa.

mock (mŏk) *v.* **1.** To treat with ridicule or scorn **:** deride. **2.** To imitate in derision or sport. *—adj.* False **:** sham. **—mock'er** *n.* **—mock'ing•ly** *adv.*

mock•er•y (mŏk'ə-rē) *n., pl.* **-ies. 1.** Scornful derision or ridicule. **2.** An object of scorn or ridicule. **3.** A false, derisive, or impudent imitation. **4.** Something ludicrously unsuitable or futile. ★ ***syns:*** CARICATURE, FARCE, PARODY, SHAM, TRAVESTY

mock-he•ro•ic (mŏk'hĭ-rō'ĭk) *n.* A satirical imitation or burlesque of the heroic manner or style.

mock•ing•bird (mŏk'ĭng-bûrd') *n.* A songbird, *Mimus polyglottos,* that is common in the S U.S. and often mimics the songs of other birds.

mock orange *n.* Any of several deciduous shrubs of the genus *Philadelphus,* bearing white, usu. fragrant flowers.

mock•up *also* **mock-up** (mŏk'ŭp') *n.* An often full-sized model of a structure, as an airplane, used for study, demonstration, or testing.

mod (mŏd) *n.* A modern and unconventionally fashionable style of dress. *—adj.* Modern, esp. unconventional in dress.

mode (mōd) *n.* **1. a.** A way or method of doing something **:** manner. **b.** A particular variety, form, or manner. **2.** The value occurring most frequently in a set of data. **3.** The current or preferred fashion or style in dress. **—mod'al** (mōd'l) *adj.*

mod•el (mŏd'l) *n.* **1.** A miniature representation of an object. **2.** A pattern on which something not yet produced will be based. **3.** A design or type. **4.** One serving as an example to be emulated or imitated. **5. a.** One who poses for a photographer or artist. **b.** One who models clothes. *—v.* **-eled, -el•ing** *or* **-elled, -el•ling. 1.** To construct or plan, esp. after a pattern. **2.** To display (clothing) by wearing. **3.** To serve or work as a model. *—adj.* **1.** Serving as or used as a model. **2.** Worthy of imitation <a *model* student> **—mod'el•er** *n.*

mo•dem (mō'dĕm') *n.* A device that converts data from one form to another, as from a digital computer to a telephone.

mod•er•ate (mŏd'ər-ĭt) *adj.* **1.** Not extreme or excessive. **2.** Temperate. **3. a.** Of average extent or quality. **b.** Mediocre. **4.** Opposed to extreme political measures or views. *—n.* Someone who holds moderate political views or opinions. *—v.* (-ə-rāt') **-at•ed, -at•ing. 1.** To make or become less extreme or intense. **2.** To preside over as a moderator. **—mod'er•a'tion** *n.*

mod•er•a•tor (mŏd'ə-rā'tər) *n.* **1.** One that moderates. **2.** A person who presides over a discussion or meeting.

mod•ern (mŏd'ərn) *adj.* **1.** Of, relating to, or typical of the recent past or the present. **2.** Advanced, as in style **:** up-to-date. **—mod'ern** *n.* **—mo•der'ni•ty** (mə-dûr'nĭ-tē) *n.* **—mod'ern•ly** *adv.*

mod•ern•ize (mŏd'ər-nīz') *v.* **-ized, -iz•ing.** To make or become modern, as in appearance or style. ★ ***syns:*** REFURBISH, REJUVENATE, RENOVATE, RESTORE, REVAMP, UPDATE **—mod'ern•i•za'tion** *n.*

mod•ern•ism (mŏd'ər-nĭz'əm) *n.* A theory, practice, or belief characteristic of modern times. **—mod'ern•ist'ic** *adj.*

mod•est (mŏd'ĭst) *adj.* **1.** Having or showing a lack of conceit or vanity. **2.** Retiring or reserved **:** diffident. **3.** Observing conventional proprieties in behavior, speech, and dress. **4.** Of moderate amount or size. ★ ***syns:*** DEMURE, DIFFIDENT, SELF-EFFACING, SHY, TIMID **—mod'es•ty** *n.*

mod•i•cum (mŏd'ĭ-kəm) *n.* A small amount.

mod•i•fy (mŏd'ə-fī') *v.* **-fied, -fy•ing. 1.** To alter **:** change. **2.** To make or become less extreme **:** moderate. **3.** To limit or qualify the meaning of (e.g., a word or phrase). **—mod'i•fi'a•ble** *adj.* **—mod'i•fi•ca'tion** *n.* **—mod'i•fi'er** *n.*

mod•ish (mō'dĭsh) *adj.* Fashionable **:** stylish <a *modish* dress> **—mod'ish•ly** *adv.* **—mod'ish•ness** *n.*

mo•diste (mō-dēst') *n.* One who makes, designs, or sells fashionable clothing for women.

mod•u•late (mŏj'ə-lāt', mŏd'yə-) *v.* **-lat•ed, -lat•ing. 1.** To soften **:** temper. **2.** To vary the tone or intensity of. **3.** *Mus.* To pass from one key or tonality to another by a chord progression. **4.** *Electron.* To vary the frequency, amplitude, or phase of (a carrier wave). **—mod'u•la'tion** *n.* **—mod'u•la'tive, mod'u•la•to'ry** (-lə-tôr'ē, -tōr'ē) *adj.* **—mod'u•la'tor** *n.*

mod•ule (mŏj'o͞ol, mŏd'yo͞ol) *n.* **1.** One of a series of a standardized units or components that function together in a system. **2.** *Electron.* A self-contained assembly of electronic components and circuitry. **3.** A self-contained unit of a spacecraft for performing a particular task. **—mod'u•lar** (-ə-lər) *adj.*

mo•dus op•er•an•di (mō'dəs ŏp'ə-răn'dē, -dī') *n.* A method of working or operating.

modus vi•ven•di (vĭ-vĕn'dē, -dī') *n.* A way of life.

mo•gul (mō'gəl) *n.* A very powerful or important person.

mo•hair (mō'hâr') *n.* A fabric or yarn made of the silky hair of the Angora goat.

Mo•ham•med•an (mō-hăm'ĭ-dən) *adj. & n. var. of* MUHAMMADAN. **—Mo•ham'med•an•ism** *n.*

Mo•hawk (mō'hôk') *n., pl.* **-hawk** *or* **-hawks. 1.** A member of an American Indian people formerly of NE New York, now in S

Ontario and extreme N New York. **2.** Their Iroquoian language.
Mohs scale (mōz) *n.* A scale for classifying the relative hardness of minerals that ranges from 1 for the softest to 15 for the hardest.
moi·e·ty (moi'ĭ-tē) *n., pl.* **-ties. 1.** A half. **2.** A portion : part.
moil (moil) *v.* To toil : drudge. —**moil** *n.*
moi·ré (mwä-rā') *n.* Fabric, esp. silk, with a wavy pattern.

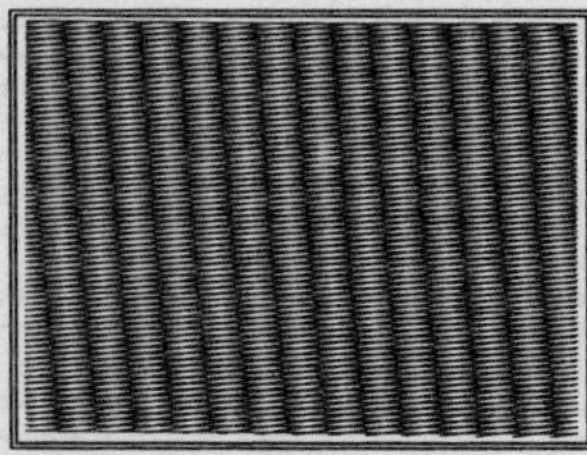

moiré

moist (moist) *adj.* Slightly wet : damp. —**moist'ly** *adv.* —**moist'ness** *n.*
mois·ten (moi'sən) To make or become moist. —**mois'ten·er** *n.*
mois·ture (mois'chər) *n.* Dampness, esp. that caused by water present in the air as vapor. —**mois'tur·ize'** *v.* —**mois'tur·iz'er** *n.*
mois·ture·proof (mois'chər-pro͞of') *adj.* Impervious to moisture.
mo·lar (mō'lər) *n.* A tooth located behind the bicuspids that has a broad surface for grinding food. —**mo'lar** *adj.*
mo·las·ses (mə-lăs'ĭz) *n.* A dark, thick syrup produced in refining sugar.
mold¹ (mōld) *n.* **1.** A hollow form in which a liquid or plastic substance can be shaped. **2.** A frame around or on which something can be shaped or formed. **3.** Something shaped on or made in a mold. **4.** General shape : form. **5.** Distinctive character or type. —*v.* To shape or form in or as if in a mold. —**mold'a·ble** *adj.*
mold² (mōld) *n.* **1.** A growth of fungus often producing disintegration of organic matter. **2.** A fungus that forms mold. —*v.* To become moldy.
mold³ (mōld) *n.* Loose soil that is rich in decayed plant and animal material.
mold·board (môld'bôrd', -bōrd') *n.* The curved plate of a plow that turns over the soil.
mold·er (mōl'dər) *v.* To crumble or cause to crumble : disintegrate.
mold·ing (mōl'dĭng) *n.* **1.** Something that is molded. **2.** The act or process of shaping or forming in a mold. **3.** An ornamental strip used to decorate a surface.
mold·y (mōl'dē) *adj.* **-i·er, -i·est. 1.** Of, like, or covered with mold. **2.** Damp or musty, as from decay. —**mold'i·ness** *n.*
mole¹ (mōl) *n.* A small, usu. slightly raised and dark growth on the human skin.
mole² (mōl) *n.* A small, burrowing mammal with a narrow snout, minute eyes, and silky fur.
mole³ (mōl) *n.* A massive stone wall used as a breakwater.
mo·lec·u·lar (mə-lĕk'yə-lər) *adj.* Of, relating to, or caused by molecules.
molecular biology *n.* The branch of biology in which the structure and development of biological systems are studied in terms of their molecular constituents. —**molecular biologist** *n.*
mol·e·cule (mŏl'ĭ-kyo͞ol') *n.* The simplest structural unit that has the characteristic physical and chemical properties of a compound.
mole·hill (mōl'hĭl') *n.* A small mound of earth dug up by a mole.
mole·skin (mōl'skĭn') *n.* **1.** The fur of the mole. **2.** A sturdy napped cotton fabric used esp. to make clothing.
mo·lest (mə-lĕst') *v.* **1.** To bother or annoy. **2.** To accost sexually. —**mo'les·ta'tion** (mō'lĕ-stā'shən) *n.* —**mo·lest'er** *n.*
moll (mŏl) *n. Slang.* The girl friend of a gangster.
mol·li·fy (mŏl'ə-fī') *v.* **-fied, -fy·ing. 1.** To soothe the temper of : placate. **2.** To soften. **3.** To make less intense. —**mol'li·fi·ca'tion** *n.*
mol·lusk *also* **mol·lusc** (mŏl'əsk) *n.* Any of various members of the phylum Mollusca, largely marine invertebrates, including the edible shellfish.
mol·ly·cod·dle (mŏl'ē-kŏd'l) *n.* A pampered boy or man. —*v.* To spoil by pampering : coddle.
Mol·o·tov cocktail (mŏl'ə-tôf', mō'lə-) *n.* A makeshift incendiary bomb consisting of a breakable container full of flammable liquid and fitted with a rag wick that is ignited just before the bomb is thrown.
molt (mōlt) *v.* To shed an external covering, as horns, feathers, or skin, which is replaced periodically by new growth. —*n.* The act of molting.
mol·ten (mōl'tn) *adj.* Liquefied by heat : melted and often glowing.
mo·lyb·de·num (mə-lĭb'də-nəm) *n. Symbol* **Mo** A hard gray metallic element used to strengthen steel alloys.
mom (mŏm) *n. Informal.* Mother.
mo·ment (mō'mənt) *n.* **1.** A brief interval of time : instant. **2.** A particular point in time, esp. the present. **3.** A time of excellence or importance. **4.** Importance. ★ ***syns:*** FLASH, INSTANT, JIFFY, MINUTE, SECOND, TRICE
mo·men·tar·i·ly (mō'mən-târ'ə-lē) *adv.* **1.** For only a moment. **2.** Very soon. **3.** From moment to moment.
mo·men·tar·y (mō'mən-tĕr'ē) *adj.* **1. a.** Lasting only a moment. **b.** Ephemeral. **2.** Present or occurring at every moment.
mo·men·tous (mō-mĕn'təs) *adj.* Of great importance : significant. —**mo·men'tous·ly** *adv.* —**mo·men'tous·ness** *n.*
mo·men·tum (mō-mĕn'təm) *n., pl.* **-ta** (-tə) *or* **-tums. 1.** The product of a body's mass and

linear velocity. **2.** Speed or force of motion : impetus.

mon•arch (mŏn′ərk, -ärk′) *n.* **1.** A usu. hereditary sovereign of a kingdom or empire, as a king or queen. **2.** One of great power or sovereign position. **3.** A very large orange and black butterfly, *Danaus plexippus.* **—mo•nar′chic** (mə-när′kĭk), **mo•nar′chi•cal** *adj.*

mon•ar•chism (mŏn′ər-kĭz′əm) *n.* Belief in or advocacy of monarchic government. **—mon′ar•chist** (-kĭst) *n.* **—mon′ar•chis′tic** *adj.*

mon•ar•chy (mŏn′ər-kē) *n., pl.* **-chies. 1.** Government by a monarch. **2.** A state or nation ruled by a monarch.

mon•as•ter•y (mŏn′ə-stĕr′ē) *n., pl.* **-ies.** A residence of a community of persons under religious vows, esp. monks. **—mon′as•te′ri•al** (-stîr′ē-əl, -stĕr′-) *adj.*

mo•nas•tic (mə-năs′tĭk) *adj.* Of, relating to, or typical of monasteries or monks or life in monasteries.

mo•nas•ti•cism (mə-năs′tĭ-sĭz′əm) *n.* The monastic life or system.

mon•au•ral (mŏn-ôr′əl, mō-nôr′-) *adj.* Of or relating to a system of transmitting, recording, or reproducing sound by techniques in which one or more sources are channeled into a single carrier.

Mon•day (mŭn′dē, -dā′) *n.* The 2nd day of the week.

mon•e•tar•y (mŏn′ĭ-tĕr′ē, mŭn′-) *adj.* Of or relating to money or the means by which it is circulated. **—mon′e•tar′i•ly** *adv.*

mon•ey (mŭn′ē) *n., pl.* **-eys** *or* **-ies. 1. a.** Something, as paper or metal currency, that is officially established as being exchangeable for goods and services. **b.** Currency officially issued by a government. **2.** Wealth considered in terms of its monetary value.

mon•eyed *also* **mon•ied** (mŭn′ēd) *adj.* **1.** Having ample money : wealthy. **2.** Composed of or arising from money.

mon•ey•lend•er (mŭn′ē-lĕn′dər) *n.* Someone whose business is lending money at interest.

mon•ey•mak•ing (mŭn′ē-mā′kĭng) *n.* The acquisition of money. *—adj.* **1.** Engaged in or successful at moneymaking. **2.** Producing profit : lucrative. **—mon′ey•mak′er** *n.*

money market *n.* **1.** The trade in short-term, low-risk securities, such as certificates of deposit and U.S. Treasury notes. **2.** A mutual fund that sells its shares in order to purchase short-term securities.

money order *n.* An order, usu. issued by a bank or post office, for the payment of a stated amount of money to the payee named on the order.

mon•ger (mŭng′gər, mŏng′-) *n.* **1.** A dealer. **2.** A person who disseminates or stirs up something undesirable.

mon•go (mŏng′gō) *n., pl.* **-go.** —See table at CURRENCY.

Mon•gol (mŏng′gəl, -gōl′, mŏn′-) *n.* **1.** A member of any of the traditionally nomadic peoples of Mongolia. **2.** A native of Mongolia. **3.** A member of the Mongoloid racial division. **—Mon′gol** *adj.*

Mon•go•li•an (mŏng-gō′lē-ən, -gōl′yən, mŏn-) *n.* **1.** A native or inhabitant of Mongolia. **2.** A member of the Mongoloid racial division. **—Mon•go′li•an** *adj.*

mon•gol•ism (mŏng′gə-lĭz′əm, mŏn′-) *n.* Down syndrome.

Mon•gol•oid (mŏng′gə-loid′, mŏn′-) *adj.* **1.** Of or designating a purported human racial classification distinguished by yellowish-brown skin and straight black hair and including peoples indigenous to central and eastern Asia. **2. mongoloid.** Of or affected with Down syndrome. **—Mon′gol•oid′** *n.*

mon•goose (mŏng′go͞os′, mŏn′-) *n., pl.* **-goos•es.** A chiefly African or Asian carnivorous mammal, esp. of the genus *Herpestes,* that has the ability to kill venomous snakes.

mon•grel (mŭng′grəl, mŏng′-) *n.* An animal or plant, esp. a dog, that results from interbreeding.

mon•ied (mŭn′ēd) *adj. var. of* MONEYED.

mon•ies (mŭn′ēz) *n. var. pl. of* MONEY.

mon•i•ker *or* **mon•ick•er** (mŏn′ĭ-kər) *n. Slang.* A person's name.

mo•nism (mō′nĭz′əm, mŏn′ĭz′-) *n.* A metaphysical theory that reality is a unified whole. **—mo′nist** *n.*

mo•ni•tion (mō-nĭsh′ən, mə-) *n.* A caution or warning.

mon•i•tor (mŏn′ĭ-tər) *n.* **1.** A student who is assigned to aid a teacher. **2. a.** A device for recording or controlling an activity or process. **b.** A screen on which the picture being picked up by a camera is checked or viewed. **c.** A device that accepts video signals from a computer and displays information on a screen. *—v.* **1.** To check (the transmission quality of a signal) by a receiver. **2.** To test for radiation intensity. **3.** To track by or as if by an electronic device. **4.** To check by means of a receiver for significant content. **5.** To keep watch over : supervise <*monitor* the history test> **—mon′i•to′ri•al** (-tôr′ē-əl, -tōr′-) *adj.*

mon•i•to•ry (mŏn′ĭ-tôr′ē, -tōr′ē) *adj.* Giving a caution or warning.

monk (mŭngk) *n.* A man who belongs to a religious brotherhood and lives in a monastery. **—monk′ish** *adj.* **—monk′ish•ly** *adv.* **—monk′ish•ness** *n.*

mon•key (mŭng′kē) *n., pl.* **-keys.** A member of the order Primates, excluding man, esp. one of the long-tailed smaller species as distinguished from the larger apes. *—v. Informal.* **1.** To play mischievously or idly : fool. **2.** To tamper.

mon•key•shine (mŭng′kē-shīn′) *n. often* **monkeyshines.** *Slang.* A prank.

monkey wrench *n.* A wrench that has one adjustable jaw.

monk's cloth *n.* A heavy cotton cloth in a coarse basket weave.

monks•hood (mŭngks′ho͝od′) *n.* A usu. poisonous plant of the genus *Aconitum,* having variously colored hooded flowers.

mon•o[1] (mŏn′ō) *n.* Mononucleosis.

mon·o² (mŏn′ō) *adj.* Monaural.
mon·o·chro·mat·ic (mŏn′ə-krō-măt′ĭk) *adj.* Of, consisting of, or having one color. —**mon′o·chro·mat′i·cal·ly** *adv.*
mon·o·cle (mŏn′ə-kəl) *n.* An eyeglass for one eye.
mon·o·cot·y·le·don (mŏn′ə-kŏt′l-ēd′n) *n.* Any of various plants of the Monocotyledonae, a major division of angiosperms, marked by a single embryonic seed leaf appearing at germination. —**mon′o·cot′y·le′don·ous** *adj.*
mo·noc·u·lar (mŏ-nŏk′yə-lər, mə-) *adj.* **1.** Of, relating to, or having one eye. **2.** Adapted to the use of only one eye.
mon·o·cul·ture (mŏn′ə-kŭl′chər) *n.* **1.** The cultivation of a single crop in an area or region. **2.** A single homogeneous society or culture. —**mon′o·cul′tur·al** *adj.*
mon·o·dy (mŏn′ə-dē) *n., pl.* **-dies.** A dirge or elegy. —**mo·nod′ic** (mə-nŏd′ĭk) *adj.* —**mon′o·dist** (-dĭst) *n.*
mon·o·fil·a·ment (mŏn′ə-fĭl′ə-mənt) *n.* A single strand of untwisted synthetic fiber used esp. for fishing line.
mo·nog·a·my (mə-nŏg′ə-mē) *n.* Marriage with only one person at a time. —**mo·nog′a·mist** *n.* —**mo·nog′a·mous** *adj.*
mon·o·gram (mŏn′ə-grăm′) *n.* A design consisting of one or more of the initials of a name. —*v.* **-grammed, -gram·ming** *or* **-gramed, -gram·ing.** To mark with a monogram.
mon·o·graph (mŏn′ə-grăf′) *n.* A scholarly treatise on a particular and usu. limited subject. —**mon′o·graph′ic** *adj.*
mon·o·lin·gual (mŏn′ə-lĭng′gwəl) *adj.* Using or knowing only one language.
mon·o·lith (mŏn′ə-lĭth′) *n.* **1.** A single large stone, as one used in architecture or sculpture. **2.** Something, as a large organization, that constitutes a uniform single unit. —**mon′o·lith′ic** *adj.*
mon·o·logue *also* **mon·o·log** (mŏn′ə-lôg′, -lŏg′) *n.* **1.** A long speech by one person that often precludes conversation. **2.** A soliloquy. **3.** A continuous series of jokes and stories delivered by a comedian. —**mo·nol′o·gist** (mə-nŏl′ə-jĭst, mŏn′ə-lô′gĭst, -lŏg′ĭst) *n.*
mon·o·ma·ni·a (mŏn′ə-mā′nē-ə, -mān′yə) *n.* **1.** Pathological obsession with a single idea. **2.** An intense concentration on one subject. —**mon′o·ma′ni·ac′** *n.* —**mon′o·ma·ni′a·cal** (-mə-nī′ə-kəl) *adj.*
mon·o·mer (mŏn′ə-mər) *n. Chem.* A molecule that can be chemically bound as a unit of a polymer. —**mon′o·mer′ic** (-mĕr′ĭk) *adj.*
mo·no·mi·al (mŏ-nō′mē-əl, mə-) *n.* An algebraic expression having only one term. —**mo·no′mi·al** *adj.*
mon·o·nu·cle·ar (mŏn′ō-nōō′klē-ər, -nyōō′-) *adj.* Having a single nucleus.
mon·o·nu·cle·o·sis (mŏn′ō-nōō′klē-ō′sĭs, -nyōō′-) *n.* An infectious disease marked by the presence of an abnormally large number of mononuclear leukocytes in the bloodstream.
mon·o·nu·cle·o·tide (mŏn′ō-nōō′klē-ə-tīd′, -nyōō′-) *n.* A nucleotide containing one molecule each of a phosphoric acid, a pentose, and either a purine or pyrimidine base.
mon·o·phon·ic (mŏn′ə-fŏn′ĭk) *adj.* Monaural.
mon·o·plane (mŏn′ə-plān′) *n.* An airplane with a single pair of wings.
mo·nop·o·ly (mə-nŏp′ə-lē) *n., pl.* **-lies. 1.** Exclusive control, as of a commodity or service, by one group. **2.** A company, person, or group having a monopoly. **3.** A commodity or service controlled by one group. —**mo·nop′o·list** *n.* —**mo·nop′o·lis′tic** *adj.* —**mo·nop′o·li·za′tion** *n.* —**mo·nop′o·lize′** *v.*
mon·o·rail (mŏn′ə-rāl′) *n.* **1.** A single rail on which a wheeled vehicle can travel. **2.** A vehicle that travels on a monorail.
mon·o·so·di·um glu·ta·mate (mŏn′ə-sō′dē-əm glōō′tə-māt′) *n.* Sodium glutamate.
mon·o·syl·la·ble (mŏn′ə-sĭl′ə-bəl) *n.* A word consisting of one syllable. —**mon′o·syl·lab′ic** (-sĭ-lăb′ĭk) *adj.* —**mon′o·syl·lab′i·cal·ly** *adv.*
mon·o·the·ism (mŏn′ə-thē-ĭz′əm) *n.* The belief or doctrine that there is only one God. —**mon′o·the′ist** *n.* —**mon′o·the·is′tic** *adj.*
mon·o·tone (mŏn′ə-tōn′) *n.* A succession of sounds, syllables, or words in a single unvarying tone or pitch.
mo·not·o·nous (mə-nŏt′n-əs) *adj.* **1.** Sounded or uttered in a single unvarying tone or pitch. **2.** Lacking in variety **:** repetitiously dull. —**mo·not′o·nous·ly** *adv.* —**mo·not′o·ny** *n.*
mon·o·un·sat·u·rat·ed (mŏn′ō-ŭn-săch′ə-rā′tĭd) *adj.* Being an unsaturated fat composed esp. of fatty acids having only one double bond in the carbon chain.
mon·ox·ide (mə-nŏk′sīd′) *n.* An oxide in which each molecule contains 1 oxygen atom.
Mon·sei·gneur (mōɴ′sān-yœr′) *n., pl.* **Mes·sei·gneurs** (mā′sān-yœr′). A French title of honor or respect given to dignitaries, as princes.
Mon·sieur (mə-syœ′) *n., pl.* **Mes·sieurs** (mā-syœ′). —Used as a courtesy title with the name of a Frenchman.
Mon·si·gnor (mŏn-sēn′yər) *n., pl.* **Mon·si·gnors** *or* **Mon·si·gno·ri** (mŏn′sēn-yôr′ē, -yōr′ē). A title given to certain Roman Catholic prelates.
mon·soon (mŏn-sōōn′) *n.* A wind system that affects the climate of a large area and reverses direction seasonally, esp. the one that produces wet and dry seasons in India and S Asia.
mon·ster (mŏn′stər) *n.* **1.** A structurally abnormal or grotesquely deformed animal or plant. **2.** An animal, plant, or object of frightening or strange shape. **3.** An extremely vicious or wicked person. —**mon·stros′i·ty** (-strŏs′ĭ-tē) *n.* —**mon′strous** *adj.* —**mon′strous·ly** *adv.* —**mon′strous·ness** *n.*
mon·strance (mŏn′strəns) *n.* A receptacle in which the consecrated Host is held and displayed.
mon·tage (mŏn-täzh′, mōɴ-) *n.* **1.** An artistic composition, esp. a composite photograph,

made by combining and arranging several separate or different components. **2.** A rapid sequence of thematically related short scenes or images in a motion picture or television program.

month (mŭnth) *n.* **1.** One of the 12 divisions of a year. **2. a.** A period of 4 weeks. **b.** A period of 30 days.

month·ly (mŭnth'lē) *adj.* **1.** Occurring or payable each month. **2.** Continuing for a month. —*n., pl.* **-lies.** A publication issued once a month. —**month'ly** *adv.*

mon·u·ment (mŏn'yə-mənt) *n.* **1.** A structure, as a statue, built as a memorial to an event or person. **2.** A place, area, or region set aside as public property by a government, as for its historical or aesthetic significance.

mon·u·men·tal (mŏn'yə-mĕn'tl) *adj.* **1.** Of, similar to, or serving as a monument. **2.** Impressively large **:** massive. **3.** Very important. **4.** Enormous <*monumental* arrogance> —**mon'u·men'tal·ly** *adv.*

moo (mo͞o) *v.* To emit the deep, bellowing sound made by a cow. —**moo** *n.*

mooch (mo͞och) *v. Slang.* To get by wheedling or coaxing **:** beg. —**mooch'er** *n.*

mood[1] (mo͞od) *n.* **1.** A temporary state of emotion or mind **:** feeling. **2.** Prevailing spirit **:** disposition.

mood[2] (mo͞od) *n.* A verb form or set of verb forms inflected to indicate whether the action or state expressed is viewed as fact, possibility, or command.

mood·y (mo͞o'dē) *adj.* **-i·er, -i·est. 1.** Given to moods, esp. of gloom **:** temperamental. **2.** Morose **:** gloomy. —**mood'i·ly** *adv.* —**mood'i·ness** *n.*

moon (mo͞on) *n.* **1.** The natural satellite of the earth. **2.** A natural satellite that revolves around a planet. **3.** Moonlight. —*v.* To pass time in romantic reverie.

moon·beam (mo͞on'bēm') *n.* A ray of moonlight.

moon·light (mo͞on'līt') *n.* The light of the moon. —*v. Informal.* To work at a job supplementary to one's regular one. —**moon'light'er** *n.*

moon·lit (mo͞on'lĭt') *adj.* Illuminated by moonlight.

moon·scape (mo͞on'skāp') *n.* **1.** A view or picture of the moon's surface. **2.** A desolate landscape.

moon·shine (mo͞on'shīn') *n.* **1.** Moonlight. **2.** *Informal.* Vacuous or inane talk. **3.** *Slang.* Illegally distilled whiskey.

moon shot *n.* The launching of a spacecraft to the moon.

moon·stone (mo͞on'stōn') *n.* A translucent form of feldspar with a pearly luster that is used as a gem.

moon·struck (mo͞on'strŭk') *adj.* **1.** Mentally unbalanced. **2.** Filled with romantic sentiment.

moor[1] (mo͝or) *v.* To make fast by means of lines, cables, or anchors. —**moor'age** *n.*

moor[2] (mo͝or) *n.* A broad expanse of open land, often with boggy areas and patches of low shrubs, as heather.

Moor (mo͝or) *n.* One of a N African people who invaded and conquered Spain in the 8th cent. —**Moor'ish** *adj.*

moor·ing (mo͝or'ĭng) *n.* **1.** A place where a ship or aircraft can be moored. **2.** *often* **moorings.** A stabilizing element.

moose (mo͞os) *n., pl.* **moose.** A very large North American deer, *Alces americana,* with a broad pendulous muzzle.

moot (mo͞ot) *v.* **1.** To bring up as a subject for debate or discussion. **2.** To debate or discuss. —*adj.* **1.** Open to debate **:** arguable. **2.** Having no legal significance.

mop (mŏp) *n.* A cleaning implement used esp. for floors and consisting of absorbent material attached to a handle. —*v.* **mopped, mop·ping.** To clean or wash with or as if with a mop. —**mop up.** To complete a task or action.

mope (mōp) *v.* **moped, mop·ing. 1.** To be apathetic or dejected. **2.** To move in a leisurely manner **:** dawdle. —**mop'er** *n.*

mo·ped (mō'pĕd') *n.* A motorbike that can be pedaled.

mop·pet (mŏp'ĭt) *n.* A child.

mop-up (mŏp'ŭp') *n.* The act or process of completing a task or action.

mo·raine (mə-rān') *n.* Debris, as boulders and stones, deposited by a glacier.

mor·al (môr'əl, mŏr'-) *adj.* **1.** Of or pertaining to the principles of right and wrong. **2.** In accordance with standards of right conduct **:** virtuous. **3.** Arising from the inner sense of right and wrong. **4.** Psychological rather than physical or concrete <*moral* support> **5.** Likely but not proved <a *moral* certainty> —*n.* **1.** The principle or lesson taught by a story, event, or experience. **2. morals.** Conduct, esp. sexual conduct, with regard to standards of right and wrong. —**mor'al·ly** *adv.*

mo·rale (mə-răl') *n.* **1.** The state of mind of an individual with respect to the tasks he or she is expected to perform. **2.** Esprit de corps.

mor·al·ist (môr'ə-lĭst, mŏr'-) *n.* **1.** Someone who is concerned with moral principles and questions. **2.** Someone who wishes to regulate the morals of others. —**mor'al·ism** *n.* —**mor'a·lis'tic** *adj.* —**mor'al·is'ti·cal·ly** *adv.*

mo·ral·i·ty (mə-răl'ĭ-tē, mô-) *n., pl.* **-ties. 1.** The quality of being virtuous. **2.** Moral behavior **:** virtue.

mor·al·ize (môr'ə-līz', mŏr'-) *v.* **-ized, -iz·ing.** To think, discuss, or judge in terms of morality. —**mor'al·i·za'tion** *n.* —**mor'al·iz'er** *n.*

mo·rass (mə-răs', mô-) *n.* **1.** A marsh or bog. **2.** Something that hinders, engulfs, or overwhelms.

mor·a·to·ri·um (môr'ə-tôr'ē-əm, -tōr'-, mŏr'-) *n., pl.* **-ums** *or* **-to·ri·a** (-tôr'ē-ə, -tōr'-). A temporary pause in activity.

mo·ray (môr'ā, mə-rā') *n.* Any of various often voracious marine eels of the family Muraenidae, of chiefly tropical waters.

mor•bid (môr′bĭd) *adj.* **1.** Of, pertaining to, or caused by disease. **2.** Preoccupied with unwholesome feelings or matters. **3.** Gruesome : grisly. ★ ***syns:*** MACABRE, SICK, SICKLY, UNHEALTHY, UNWHOLESOME —**mor•bid′i•ty** (-bĭd′ĭ-tē), **mor′bid•ness** *n.* —**mor′bid•ly** *adv.*

mor•da•cious (môr-dā′shəs) *adj.* **1.** Prone to biting. **2.** Sarcastic, as in manner : caustic. —**mor•da′cious•ly** *adv.* —**mor•dac′i•ty** (-dăs′ĭ-tē) *n.*

mor•dant (môr′dnt) *adj.* **1.** Biting : caustic. **2.** Incisive : trenchant. —**mor′dan•cy** *n.* —**mor′dant•ly** *adv.*

more (môr, mōr) *adj.* **1.** Greater, as in number, size, or degree. **2.** Additional : supplementary. —*n.* An additional or larger quantity, number, degree, or amount. —*adv.* **1.** In or to a greater extent or degree. **2.** In addition. —*pron.* Additional things or persons <*More* were bought at the same shop.>

mo•rel (mə-rĕl′, mô-) *n.* Any of several edible mushrooms, esp. *Morchella esculenta,* with a spongelike cap.

more•o•ver (môr-ō′vər, mōr-, môr′ō′vər, mōr′-) *adv.* Furthermore : besides.

mo•res (môr′āz′, mōr′-, -ēz′) *pl.n.* **1.** The moral customs and rules of a social group. **2.** Manners : habits.

Mor•gan (môr′gən) *n.* A saddle and trotting horse orig. bred in America.

morgue (môrg) *n.* **1.** A place in which the bodies of persons found dead are kept until claimed or identified. **2.** A file of old issues and reference materials in a newspaper or magazine office.

mor•i•bund (môr′ə-bŭnd′, mŏr′-) *adj.* Approaching death. —**mor′i•bun′di•ty** *n.*

Mor•mon (môr′mən) *n.* A member of the Church of Jesus Christ of Latter-day Saints, founded by Joseph Smith in 1830. —**Mor′mon•ism** *n.*

morn (môrn) *n.* Morning.

morn•ing (môr′nĭng) *n.* The early part of the day, from midnight to noon or from sunrise to noon.

morn•ing-glo•ry (môr′nĭng-glôr′ē, -glōr′ē) *n.* A usu. twining plant of the genus *Ipomoea,* with funnel-shaped flowers that close late in the day.

morning star *n.* A planet, esp. Venus, seen in the E just before or at sunrise.

mo•roc•co (mə-rŏk′ō) *n.* A soft, grainy-textured leather made of goatskin.

mo•ron (môr′ŏn′, mōr′-) *n.* **1.** A mentally retarded person whose intelligence is equal to that of a child between 7 and 12 years of age. **2.** A very stupid person. —**mo•ron′ic** (mə-rŏn′ĭk) *adj.* —**mo•ron′i•cal•ly** *adv.*

mo•rose (mə-rōs′, mô-) *adj.* **1.** Sullen in disposition. **2.** Gloomy. —**mo•rose′ly** *adv.* —**mo•rose′ness** *n.*

mor•pheme (môr′fēm′) *n.* A meaningful linguistic unit that cannot be divided into smaller meaningful parts. —**mor•phem′ic** *adj.* —**mor•phem′i•cal•ly** *adv.*

mor•phi•a (môr′fē-ə) *n.* Morphine.

mor•phine (môr′fēn′) *n.* An addictive narcotic drug derived from opium and used as a sedative and anesthetic.

mor•phol•o•gy (môr-fŏl′ə-jē) *n.* **1.** The study of the form and structure of living organisms. **2.** The study of word formation in a language. —**mor′pho•log′i•cal** (môr′fə-lŏj′ĭ-kəl), **mor′pho•log′ic** *adj.* —**mor•phol′o•gist** *n.*

mor•ris (môr′ĭs, mŏr′-) *n.* An English folk dance performed by costumed dancers.

Morris chair *n.* An easy chair with removable cushions and an adjustable back.

mor•row (môr′ō, mŏr′ō) *n.* The day after a specified day.

Morse code *n.* A code, used esp. in telegraphy, consisting of short and long sounds or dots and dashes.

mor•sel (môr′səl) *n.* **1.** A small piece, esp. of food. **2.** A tasty delicacy.

†mor•tal (môr′tl) *adj.* **1.** Subject to death <Human beings are *mortal.*> **2.** Causing death : fatal. **3.** Of or characteristic of human beings <a *mortal* weakness> **4.** Unrelentingly hostile : implacable <*mortal* enemies> **5.** Extreme : dire <in *mortal* terror> **6.** *Rom. Cath. Ch.* Causing eternal damnation <a *mortal* sin> —*n.* A human being. —*adv. Regional.* Extremely : very. —**mor′tal•ly** *adv.*

mor•tal•i•ty (môr-tăl′ĭ-tē) *n., pl.* **-ties. 1.** The state of being mortal. **2.** Death rate.

mor•tar (môr′tər) *n.* **1.** A vessel in which substances can be crushed or ground with a pestle. **2.** A muzzle-loading cannon for firing shells at short ranges and in high trajectories. **3.** A mix, as of cement with sand and water, that is used in masonry.

mor•tar•board (môr′tər-bôrd′, -bōrd′) *n.* **1.** A square board for holding mortar. **2.** An academic cap topped by a flat square.

mort•gage (môr′gĭj) *n.* **1.** A temporary transfer of property to a creditor as security for the repayment of a debt. **2.** A contract or deed defining the terms of a mortgage. —*v.* **-gaged, -gag•ing.** To pledge or convey by means of a mortgage. —**mort′ga•gee′** *n.* —**mort′ga•gor** *n.*

mor•ti•cian (môr-tĭsh′ən) *n.* An undertaker.

mor•ti•fy (môr′tə-fī′) *v.* **-fied, -fy•ing. 1.** To humiliate. **2.** To discipline (e.g., the body) through pain or self-denial. **3.** To become gangrenous. —**mor′ti•fi•ca′tion** *n.* —**mor′ti•fy′ing•ly** *adv.*

mor•tise (môr′tĭs) *n.* A usu. rectangular hole in a piece of wood that receives a tenon of another piece to form a joint.

mor•tu•ar•y (môr′chōō-ĕr′ē) *n., pl.* **-ies.** A place where dead bodies are kept until burial or cremation.

mo•sa•ic (mō-zā′ĭk) *n.* **1.** A decorative design on a surface made by inlaying small pieces, as of colored glass or tile, in cement. **2.** A miscellany : patchwork. —**mo•sa′ic** *adj.*

mo•sey (mō′zē) *v. Informal.* To move along slowly : amble.

Mos•lem (mŏz′ləm, mŏs′-) *n. & adj. var. of* MUSLIM.

mosque (mŏsk) *n.* A Muslim house of worship.
mos•qui•to (mə-skē'tō) *n., pl.* **-toes** *or* **-tos.** Any of various winged insects of the family Culicidae, of which the females suck the blood of animals.
mosquito net *n.* A fine net or screen for keeping out mosquitoes.
moss (môs, mŏs) *n.* Any of various small green bryophytes of the class Musci that often form a dense, matlike growth. **—moss'i•ness** *n.* **—moss'y** *adj.*
moss•back (môs'băk', mŏs'-) *n. Slang.* A very conservative or old-fashioned person.
moss rose *n.* A variety of rose, *Rosa centifolia muscosa,* bearing fragrant pink flowers with a mossy flower stalk and calyx.
most (mōst) *adj.* **1.** Greatest <the *most* talent> **2.** The greatest part of <*most* women> *—n.* The greatest amount, quantity, or degree <the *most* I've ever seen> *—pron.* The largest part or number <*Most* left early.> *—adv.* **1.** In or to the highest degree <*most* beautiful><*most* impatiently> **2.** In or to a high degree **:** very <a *most* meticulous worker>
most•ly (mōst'lē) *adv.* For the most part **:** mainly.
mot (mō) *n.* A short, witty saying.
mote (mōt) *n.* A particle, as of dust.
mo•tel (mō-tĕl') *n.* A hotel for motorists, with rooms usu. opening directly onto a parking area.
mo•tet (mō-tĕt') *n.* A polyphonic choral composition, often based on a religious text and usu. sung without accompaniment.
moth (môth, mŏth) *n., pl.* **moths** (mô*th*z, mŏ*th*z, môths, mŏths). **1.** Any of numerous insects of the order Lepidoptera, gen. distinguished from butterflies by their nocturnal activity, stout bodies, and featherlike antennae. **2.** The clothes moth. **—moth'proof'** *adj. & v.*
moth•ball (môth'bôl', mŏth'-) *n.* **1.** A ball, as of camphor, used to repel moths from clothing. **2. mothballs.** Protective and usu. long-term storage <battleships put into *mothballs*>
moth-eat•en (môth'ēt'n, mŏth'-) *adj.* **1.** Eaten away by moths <a *moth-eaten* blanket> **2. a.** Old-fashioned. **b.** Run-down.
moth•er (mŭ*th*'ər) *n.* **1.** A female parent. **2.** An origin **:** source. **3.** A woman in a position of responsibility or authority. *—adj.* **1.** Of, pertaining to, or being a mother. **2.** Native <his *mother* country> *—v.* **1.** To give birth to. **2.** To care for like a mother **:** nourish and protect. **—moth'er•hood'** *n.* **—moth'er•less** *adj.* **—moth'er•li•ness** *n.* **—moth'er•ly** *adj.*
moth•er-in-law (mŭ*th*'ər-ĭn-lô') *n., pl.* **moth•ers-in-law.** The mother of one's spouse.
moth•er•land (mŭ*th*'ər-lănd') *n.* **1.** The country of one's birth. **2.** The native country of one's forebears.
moth•er-of-pearl (mŭ*th*'ər-əv-pûrl') *n.* The pearly internal layer of a mollusk shell.
mo•tif (mō-tēf') *n.* A thematic element that recurs in a musical, artistic, or literary work.
mo•tile (mōt'l, mō'tīl') *adj.* Moving or capable of moving spontaneously. **—mo•til'i•ty** (mō-tĭl'ĭ-tē) *n.*
mo•tion (mō'shən) *n.* **1.** The act or process of moving. **2.** A meaningful movement of the body or a bodily part **:** gesture. **3.** A formal proposal that action be taken, as by a legislative body. *—v.* To signal or direct by making a motion. **—mo'tion•less** *adj.*
motion picture *n.* A series of filmed images projected on a screen so rapidly that the illusion of motion is created. **—mo'tion-pic'ture** *adj.*
motion sickness *n.* Sickness caused by motion and marked by nausea.
mo•ti•vate (mō'tə-vāt') *v.* **-vat•ed, -vat•ing.** To provide with a motive **:** actuate. **—mo'ti•va'tion** *n.*
mo•tive (mō'tĭv) *n.* **1.** Something, as a reason or desire, acting as a spur to action. **2.** (*also* mō-tēv'). A musical motif. *—adj.* **1.** Causing or capable of causing motion. **2.** Of, relating to, or being a motive.
mot•ley (mŏt'lē) *adj.* **1.** Made up of a variety of components **:** heterogeneous. **2.** Multicolored.
mo•tor (mō'tər) *n.* **1.** Something that generates or imparts motion. **2.** A device that converts electrical energy into mechanical energy. **3.** A device that produces mechanical power from fuel **:** engine. *—adj.* **1.** Imparting or producing motion. **2.** Driven by or equipped with a motor. **3.** Of, relating to, or designed for motor vehicles. **4.** Of or relating to muscular movements. *—v.* To travel in a motor vehicle. **—mo'tor•ist** *n.*
mo•tor•bike (mō'tər-bīk') *n.* A light motorcycle.
mo•tor•boat (mō'tər-bōt') *n.* A boat driven by an internal-combustion engine.
mo•tor•cade (mō'tər-kād') *n.* A procession consisting of motor vehicles.
mo•tor•car (mō'tər-kär') *n.* An automobile.
motor court *n.* A motel.
mo•tor•cy•cle (mō'tər-sī'kəl) *n.* A 2-wheeled vehicle driven by an internal-combustion engine. **—mo'tor•cy'cle** *v.* **—mo'tor•cy'clist** *n.*
motor home *n.* A motor vehicle built on a truck or bus chassis and equipped to serve as a self-contained home during travel.
mo•tor•ize (mō'tə-rīz') *v.* **-ized, -iz•ing. 1.** To equip with a motor. **2.** To supply with motor-driven vehicles. **—mo'tor•i•za'tion** *n.*
mo•tor•man (mō'tər-mən) *n.* A driver of a locomotive, streetcar, or subway train.
motor scooter *n.* A small 2-wheeled vehicle resembling a scooter but having a low-powered gasoline engine.
motor vehicle *n.* A self-propelled motor-powered vehicle that does not run on rails but travels on wheels.
†motte *also* **mott** (mŏt) *n. W U.S.* A small stand of trees on a prairie.
mot•tle (mŏt'l) *v.* **-tled, -tling.** To mark with spots or streaks of different colors.

mot•to (mŏt'ō) *n., pl.* **-toes** *or* **-tos. 1.** A sentence, phrase, or word inscribed on something, as a coat of arms, to express its purpose or character. **2.** A brief expression of a guiding principle.
moue (mo͞o) *n.* A grimace : pout.
mould (mōld) *n. & v. esp. Brit. var. of* MOLD.
moult (mōlt) *v. & n. esp. Brit. var. of* MOLT.
mound (mound) *n.* **1.** A pile of earth, gravel, sand, rocks, or debris. **2.** A natural elevation, as a hillock. **3.** The slightly elevated pitcher's area in the center of a baseball diamond.
mount[1] (mount) *v.* **1.** To ascend or rise. **2.** To get up on <*mount* a camel> **3.** To increase in degree, amount, extent, or intensity. **4.** To arrange in an appropriate setting, esp. for display or study. **5. a.** To fix in position <*mount* cannon> **b.** To launch and carry out <*mount* an attack> *—n.* **1.** An animal, esp. a horse, on which to ride. **2.** A support to which something is affixed, as for display, study, or use.
mount[2] (mount) *n.* A lofty hill : mountain.
moun•tain (moun'tən) *n.* A natural elevation of the earth's surface higher than a hill.
mountain ash *n.* Any of various deciduous trees of the genus *Sorbus,* bearing clusters of small white flowers and bright orange-red berries.
mountain bike *n.* A sturdy bicycle having wide tires and horizontal handlebars, used for off-road cycling. **—mountain biking** *n.*

mountain bike

moun•tain•eer (moun'tə-nîr') *n.* **1.** A native or inhabitant of a mountainous area. **2.** Someone who climbs mountains for sport. **—moun'tain•eer'** *v.*
mountain goat *n.* A goatlike mammal, *Oreamnus americanus,* of North America, with short, curved black horns and yellowish-white hair and beard.
mountain laurel *n.* An evergreen shrub, *Kalmia latifolia,* of E North America, with poisonous leaves and clusters of pink or white flowers.
mountain lion *n.* A large, powerful wild cat, *Felis concolor,* of mountainous regions of North and South America.
moun•tain•ous (moun'tə-nəs) *adj.* **1.** Of, relating to, or being a region with many mountains. **2.** Very large : huge.
moun•tain•side (moun'tən-sīd') *n.* The side of a mountain.
moun•tain•top (moun'tən-tŏp') *n.* The top of a mountain.
moun•te•bank (moun'tə-băngk') *n.* A charlatan : quack.
Mount•ie *also* **Mount•y** (moun'tē) *n., pl.* **-ies.** *Can.* A member of the Royal Canadian Mounted Police.
mount•ing (moun'tĭng) *n.* A supporting frame or structure.
mourn (môrn, mōrn) *v.* To express or feel sorrow (for) : grieve. **—mourn'er** *n.*
mourn•ful (môrn'fəl, mōrn'-) *adj.* Feeling, expressing, arousing, or suggesting grief. **—mourn'ful•ly** *adv.* **—mourn'ful•ness** *n.*
mourn•ing (môr'nĭng, mōr'-) *n.* **1.** A sign, as the wearing of black clothing, of grief over a person's death. **2.** The period during which a person's death is mourned.
mourning dove *n.* A North American wild dove, *Zenaidura macroura,* that has a sorrowful call.
mouse (mous) *n., pl.* **mice** (mīs). **1.** Any of numerous small rodents of the families Muridae and Cricetidae, usu. having a long, narrow, almost hairless tail. **2.** A hand-held, button-activated input device that controls the movement of a cursor on a computer screen.
mous•er (mou'zer) *n.* An animal, esp. a cat, that is skilled at catching mice.
mouse•trap (mous'trăp') *n.* A trap set to catch mice.
mousse (mo͞os) *n.* A chilled and molded dish, esp. a dessert, made with whipped egg whites or cream and gelatin.
mous•tache (mŭs'tăsh', mə-stăsh') *n. var. of* MUSTACHE.
mous•y *also* **mous•ey** (mou'sē, -zē) *adj.* **-i•er, -i•est. 1.** Lacking vividness, as of color. **2.** Timid and fearful. **—mous'i•ness** *n.*
mouth (mouth) *n., pl.* **mouths** (mouth*z*). **1.** The bodily opening through which an animal takes food in. **2.** Something that resembles the mouth, as the natural opening of a cave or the opening in a container. *—v.* (mouth). **1. a.** To speak : pronounce. **b.** To utter in a declamatory manner. **2.** To articulate or form soundlessly. **—mouth'ful'** *n.*
mouth organ *n.* A harmonica.
mouth•piece (mouth'pēs') *n.* **1.** A part, as of a musical instrument, that is put in the mouth or with which the mouth makes contact. **2.** *Informal.* A spokesman.
mouth-to-mouth (mouth'tə-mouth') *adj.* Of, pertaining to, or being a method of artificial resuscitation in which the rescuer's mouth is placed over the victim's to force air into the victim's lungs every few seconds.
mouth•wash (mouth'wŏsh', -wôsh') *n.* A usu. flavored antiseptic liquid preparation for cleansing the mouth.
mouth•wa•ter•ing *or* **mouth-wa•ter•ing** (mouth'wô'tər-ĭng) *adj.* Appealing to the sense of taste : appetizing.
move (mo͞ov) *v.* **moved, mov•ing. 1.** To go

or cause to go from one place or point to another. **2.** To transfer (a piece in a board game). **3.** To change one's residence or place of business. **4.** To change or cause to change posture or position. **5.** To stir the emotions of. **6.** To initiate or cause to initiate action. **7.** To be busy or active. **8.** To make a formal motion, request, or proposal. **9.** To evacuate the bowels. **—move in.** To occupy as a residence or place of business. *—n.* **1.** The act of moving. **2.** A player's turn to move a piece in a board game. **3.** An action calculated to achieve an end **:** maneuver. **—mov'a•ble, move'a•ble** *adj.* **—mov'a•bly** *adv.*

move•ment (mo͞ov'mənt) *n.* **1.** The act or process of moving. **2.** The activities of a group toward the achievement of a goal. **3.** A trend **:** tendency. **4.** Activity **:** action. **5. a.** An evacuation of the bowels. **b.** Waste matter evacuated from the bowels. **6.** *Mus.* A primary section or division of a musical composition. **7.** A mechanism, as the works of a watch, that produces or transmits motion.

mov•er (mo͞o'vər) *n.* One that moves, esp. a company or person hired to move belongings, as furnishings, from one residence or place of business to another.

mov•ie (mo͞o'vē) *n. Informal.* **1.** A motion picture. **2. movies. a.** A showing of a motion picture. **b.** The motion-picture industry. **—mov'ie•go'er** *n.*

mov•ie•mak•er (mo͞o've-mā'kər) *n.* One who makes movies as a profession.

moving picture *n.* A motion picture.

mow[1] (mō) *v.* **mowed, mowed** *or* **mown** (mōn), **mow•ing. 1.** To cut down (e.g., grain or grass) with a machine or a scythe. **2.** To cut (e.g., grain or grass) from <*mow* the lawn> **—mow'er** *n.*

mow[2] (mou) *n.* The part of a barn where hay or grain is stored.

†**mo•zo** (mō'zō) *n., pl.* **-zos.** *W U.S.* A man who helps with a pack train or acts as a porter.

moz•za•rel•la (mŏt'sə-rĕl'ə) *n.* A soft smooth white cheese with a mild flavor.

much (mŭch) *adj.* **more** (môr, mōr), **most** (mōst). Great in amount, quantity, degree, or extent <*much* time> *—n.* **1.** A great amount, quantity, degree, or extent. **2.** Something remarkable or important <didn't amount to *much*> *—adv.* **more, most. 1.** To a great degree or extent <*much* prettier> **2.** About **:** approximately <said *much* the same thing>

mu•ci•lage (myo͞o'sə-lĭj) *n.* A sticky adhesive substance. **—mu'ci•lag'i•nous** (-lăj'ə-nəs) *adj.*

muck (mŭk) *n.* **1. a.** Moist, sticky dirt **:** filth. **b.** Mud. **2.** Moist animal dung **:** manure. **3.** Dark, fertile soil containing decayed organic matter. **—muck'y** *adj.*

muck•rake (mŭk'rāk') *v.* To search out and expose real or ostensible corruption on the part of well-known persons. **—muck'-rak'er** *n.*

mu•co•sa (myo͞o-kō'zə) *n.* A mucous membrane.

mu•cous (myo͞o'kəs) *adj.* Of, pertaining to, or secreting mucus.

mucous membrane *n.* A membrane covered with mucus-secreting glands that lines bodily channels that communicate with the air.

mu•cus (myo͞o'kəs) *n.* The viscous liquid secreted as a protective coating by glands in the mucous membrane.

mud (mŭd) *n.* **1.** Sticky, soft wet earth. **2.** Slanderous remarks. **—mud'di•ly** *adv.* **—mud'di•ness** *n.* **—mud'dy** *adj. & v.*

mud•dle (mŭd'l) *v.* **-dled, -dling. 1.** To make turbid **:** muddy. **2.** To mix up **:** jumble. **3.** To confuse, esp. with alcohol. **4.** To make a mess of **:** bungle. **—mud'dler** *n.*

mud•dle•head•ed (mŭd'l-hĕd'ĭd) *adj.* **1.** Mentally confused. **2.** Inept **:** stupid. **—mud'-dle•head'ed•ness** *n.*

mud•guard (mŭd'gärd') *n.* A shield over a wheel of a vehicle.

mud•slide (mŭd'slīd') *n.* A flow of mud, esp. a slow-moving one.

mud•sling•er (mŭd'slĭng'ər) *n.* Someone who makes malicious charges, esp. against a political opponent. **—mud'sling'ing** *n.*

Muen•ster *or* **Mun•ster** (mŭn'stər, mo͞on'-) *n.* A mild, semisoft, creamy fermented cheese.

mu•ez•zin (myo͞o-ĕz'ĭn, mo͞o-) *n.* A Muslim crier who calls the faithful to prayer 5 times a day.

muff[1] (mŭf) *v.* To spoil or ruin through clumsiness or carelessness. **—muff** *n.*

muff[2] (mŭf) *n.* A tubular covering with open ends into which the hands are put for warmth.

muf•fin (mŭf'ĭn) *n.* A small, soft cup-shaped bread that is often served hot.

muf•fle (mŭf'əl) *v.* **-fled, -fling. 1.** To wrap up snugly in order to protect or conceal. **2.** To pad or wrap up in order to deaden the sound of. **3.** To suppress. ★ ***syns:*** DAMPEN, DEADEN, MUTE, STIFLE

muf•fler (mŭf'lər) *n.* **1.** A scarf worn around the neck for warmth. **2.** A device that deadens sound, esp. that of an internal-combustion engine.

muf•ti (mŭf'tē) *n.* Civilian clothing.

mug[1] (mŭg) *n.* A cylindrical drinking cup, often with a handle.

mug[2] (mŭg) *n.* **1.** A person's face. **2.** An official photograph of a suspect's face. *—v.* **mugged, mug•ging. 1.** To assault, usu. with the intention of robbing. **2.** To make faces. **—mug'ger** *n.*

mug•gy (mŭg'ē) *adj.* **-gi•er, -gi•est.** Warm, close, and humid. **—mug'gi•ly** *adv.* **—mug'-gi•ness** *n.*

mug shot *n. Informal.* A photograph of a person's face, esp. for police files.

mug•wump (mŭg'wŭmp') *n.* One who acts independently, esp. in politics.

Mu•ham•mad•an (mo͝o-hăm'ĭ-dən) *or* **Mo•ham•med•an** (mō-) *adj.* Of or relating to Muhammad or Islam. *— n.* A Muslim. **—Mu•ham'mad•an•ism** *n.*

muk•luk (mŭk′lŭk′) *n.* **1.** A soft Eskimo boot of sealskin or reindeer skin. **2.** A slipper that resembles a mukluk.

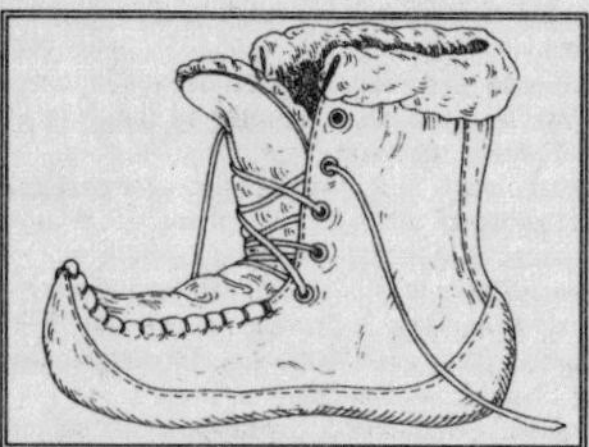

mukluk

mu•lat•to (mŏŏ-lăt′ō, -lä′tō, myŏŏ-) *n., pl.* **-tos** *or* **-toes. 1.** A person with one white and one black parent. **2.** One of mixed black and white ancestry.
mul•ber•ry (mŭl′bĕr′ē) *n.* Any of several trees of the genus *Morus,* bearing edible purplish-red berrylike fruit.
mulch (mŭlch) *n.* A protective covering, as of hay, placed on the earth around growing plants esp. to prevent moisture evaporation, protect roots from freezing, and retard the growth of weeds. **—mulch** *v.*
mulct (mŭlkt) *n.* A penalty, esp. a fine. —*v.* **1.** To penalize, esp. by fining. **2.** To defraud : swindle.
mule¹ (myōōl) *n.* **1.** A sterile hybrid animal that is the offspring of a female horse and a male donkey. **2.** *Informal.* An extremely stubborn person. **—mul′ish** *adj.* **—mul′ish•ly** *adv.* **—mul′ish•ness** *n.*
mule² (myōōl) *n.* An open shoe or slipper that leaves the heel bare.
mule deer *n.* A hoofed mammal, *Odocoileus hemionus,* of W North America, with long ears and 2-pronged antlers.
mule•skin•ner (myōōl′skĭn′ər) *n. Informal.* A muleteer.
mu•le•teer (myōō′lə-tîr′) *n.* One who drives mules.
mull¹ (mŭl) *v.* To heat and add sugar and spices to (e.g., wine).
mull² (mŭl) *v.* To think about : ponder.
mul•lah *also* **mul•la** (mŭl′ə, mŏŏl′ə) *n.* A Muslim religious teacher or leader, esp. one trained in law.
mul•lein (mŭl′ən) *n.* A tall plant of the genus *Verbascum,* esp. *V. thapsus,* with yellow flower clusters and downy leaves.
mul•let (mŭl′ĭt) *n., pl.* **mullet** *or* **-lets.** Any of various edible marine and freshwater fishes of the family Mugilidae.
mul•li•gan stew (mŭl′ĭ-gən) *n.* A stew of various meats and vegetables.
mul•li•ga•taw•ny (mŭl′ĭ-gə-tô′nē) *n.* A meat soup strongly flavored with curry.
mul•lion (mŭl′yən) *n.* A vertical strip that separates the panes of a window.
multi– *pref.* **1.** Many : much : multiple <*multi*colored> **2. a.** More than 1 <*multi*parous> **b.** More than 2 <*multi*lateral>
mul•ti•cul•tur•al (mŭl′tē-kŭl′chər-əl) *adj.* Of or including several cultures or ethnic groups.
mul•ti•dis•ci•pli•nar•y (mŭl′tĭ-dĭs′ə-plə-nĕr′ē) *adj.* Of, relating to, or utilizing a combination of academic disciplines.
mul•ti•far•i•ous (mŭl′tə-fâr′ē-əs) *adj.* Having much variety or diversity : diverse. **—mul′ti•far′i•ous•ly** *adv.*
mul•ti•flo•ra rose (mŭl′tə-flôr′ə, -flŏr′ə) *n.* A climbing or sprawling Asian shrub, *Rosa multiflora,* bearing small, fragrant flower clusters.
mul•ti•form (mŭl′tə-fôrm′) *adj.* Having many shapes, forms, or appearances.
mul•ti•lat•er•al (mŭl′tĭ-lăt′ər-əl) *adj.* **1.** Having many sides. **2.** Of, involving, or participated in by more than 2 governments or parties. **—mul′ti•lat′er•al•ly** *adv.*
mul•ti•lin•gual (mŭl′tə-lĭng′gwal) *adj.* Using or knowing several languages. **—mul′ti•lin′gual•ism** *n.*
mul•ti•me•di•a (mŭl′tē-mē′dē-ə, -tī-) *adj.* Including or involving the use of several media <a *multimedia* display> <a *multimedia* computer application> **—mul′ti•me′di•a** *n.*
mul•ti•na•tion•al (mŭl′tĭ-năsh′ən-əl, -năsh′nəl) *adj.* **1.** Of, relating to, or involving several countries. **2.** Having subsidiaries or op-

mul′ti•a′gen•cy *adj.*
mul′ti•branched′ *adj.*
mul′ti•cam′pus *adj.*
mul′ti•cell′ *adj.*
mul′ti•cel′lu•lar *adj.*
mul′ti•cen′ter *adj.*
mul′ti•cham′bered *adj.*
mul′ti•col′or *adj.*
mul′ti•col′ored *adj.*
mul′ti•cop′y *adj.*
mul′ti•cur′ren•cy *adj.*
mul′ti•de•nom′i•na′tion•al *adj.*
mul′ti•di•men′sion•al *adj.*
mul′ti•di•rec′tion•al *adj.*
mul′ti•dwell′ing *adj.*
mul′ti•el′e•ment *adj.*
mul′ti•eth′nic *adj.*
mul′ti•fac′et•ed *adj.*
mul′ti•fam′i•ly *adj.*
mul′ti•fo′cal *adj.*
mul′ti•fre′quen•cy *adj.*
mul′ti•func′tion•al *adj.*
mul′ti•hued′ *adj.*
mul′ti-in′dus•try *adj.*
mul′ti•lane′ *adj.*
mul′ti•lay′er *adj.*
mul′ti•lay′ered *adj.*
mul′ti•lev′el *adj.*
mul′ti•mem′ber *adj.*
mul′ti•mil′lion•aire′ *n.*
mul′ti•nu′cle•ar *adj.*
mul′ti•nu′cle•ate *adj.*
mul′ti•part′ *adj.*
mul′ti•par′ty *adj.*
mul′ti•pow′er *adj.*
mul′ti•pur′pose *adj.*
mul′ti•ra′cial *adj.*
mul′ti•sen′so•ry *adj.*
mul′ti•sid′ed *adj.*
mul′ti•speed′ *adj.*
mul′ti•state′ *adj.*
mul′ti•stor′ied *adj.*
mul′ti•stor′y *adj.*
mul′ti•syl•lab′ic *adj.*
mul′ti•track′ *adj.*
mul′ti•u′nit *adj.*
mul′ti•use′ *adj.*

erations in more than one country <a *multinational* corporation>
mul•tip•a•rous (mŭl-tĭp′ər-əs) *adj.* Giving birth to more than one offspring at a time.
mul•ti•ple (mŭl′tə-pəl) *adj.* Of, having, relating to, or consisting of more than one individual, element, or part **:** manifold. —*n. Math.* A number into which another number can be divided with no remainder.
mul•ti•ple-choice (mŭl′tə-pəl-chois′) *adj.* Offering several solutions from which the correct one is to be selected.
multiple sclerosis *n.* A degenerative disease of the central nervous system marked by hardening of tissue in the brain or spinal cord or both.
mul•ti•plex (mŭl′tə-plĕks′) *adj.* **1.** Manifold **:** multiple. **2.** Of, indicating, or being a communications system in which 2 or more messages can be transmitted simultaneously on the same circuit or radio channel. —**mul′ti•plex′** *v.*
mul•ti•pli•cand (mŭl′tə-plĭ-kănd′) *n.* A number to be multiplied by another.
mul•ti•pli•ca•tion (mŭl′tə-plĭ-kā′shən) *n.* **1.** The process of multiplying. **2.** The propagation of animals and plants. **3.** Repeated addition in which one number indicates how many times another is to be added to itself.
mul•ti•plic•i•ty (mŭl′tə-plĭs′ĭ-tē) *n., pl.* **-ties.** A large variety or number.
mul•ti•pli•er (mŭl′tə-plī′ər) *n.* A number by which another number is or is to be multiplied.
mul•ti•ply (mŭl′tə-plī′) *v.* **-plied, -ply•ing. 1.** To increase in number or amount, as by breeding. **2.** To perform the mathematical operation of multiplication (on).
mul•ti•sense (mŭl′tĭ-sĕns′) *adj.* Having several meanings.
mul•ti•stage (mŭl′tĭ-stāj′) *adj.* Consisting of or performed in successive stages <a *multistage* rocket>
mul•ti•tude (mŭl′tĭ-to͞od′, -tyo͞od′) *n.* A very large number. —**mul′ti•tu′di•nous** (-to͞od′n-əs, -tyo͞od′-) *adj.*
mul•ti•vi•ta•min (mŭl′tə-vī′tə-mĭn) *adj.* Containing several vitamins. —**mul′ti•vi′ta•min** *n.*
mum¹ (mŭm) *adj.* Not speaking **:** silent.
mum² (mŭm) *n. Informal.* A chrysanthemum.
mum•ble (mŭm′bəl) *v.* **-bled, -bling.** To utter or speak indistinctly, as by lowering the voice and partially closing the mouth. —**mum′ble** *n.* —**mum′bler** *n.*
mum•ble•ty-peg (mŭm′bəl-tē-pĕg′, mŭm′-blē-pĕg′) *also* **mum•ble-the-peg** (mŭm′-bəl-thə-pĕg′) *n.* A game in which the players throw a knife from different positions, the object being to stick the blade firmly in the ground.
mum•bo jum•bo (mŭm′bō jŭm′bō) *n.* **1.** An obscure or complicated ritual or incantation. **2.** Complicated and confusing activity or language.
mum•mer (mŭm′ər) *n.* **1.** Someone who acts in a pantomime. **2.** Someone wearing a mask or costume who participates in a celebration, esp. a festival. —**mum′mer•y** *n.*
mum•my (mŭm′ē) *n., pl.* **-mies.** The body of a human being or animal embalmed after death, as by the ancient Egyptians. —**mum′-mi•fy′** *v.*
mumps (mŭmps) *pl.n. (sing. or pl. in number).* An acute contagious viral disease characterized by swelling esp. of the salivary glands.
munch (mŭnch) *v.* To chew noisily.
mun•dane (mŭn-dān′, mŭn′dān′) *adj.* **1.** Of or pertaining to the world **:** worldly. **2.** Concerned with or characteristic of the ordinary. —**mun•dane′ly** *adv.*
mu•nic•i•pal (myo͞o-nĭs′ə-pəl) *adj.* **1.** Of, relating to, or typical of a municipality. **2.** Having local self-government. —**mu•nic′i•pal•ly** *adv.*
mu•nic•i•pal•i•ty (myo͞o-nĭs′ə-păl′ĭ-tē) *n., pl.* **-ties.** A political unit, as a city or town, that is incorporated and self-governing.
mu•nif•i•cent (myo͞o-nĭf′ĭ-sənt) *adj.* Generous in giving **:** lavish. —**mu•nif′i•cence** *n.* —**mu•nif′i•cent•ly** *adv.*
mu•ni•tions (myo͞o-nĭsh′ənz) *pl.n.* War materiel, esp. guns and ammunition.
Mun•ster (mŭn′stər, mo͝on′-) *n. var. of* MUENSTER.
mu•ral (myo͝or′əl) *n.* A painting applied directly to a wall surface. —**mu′ral•ist** *n.*
mur•der (mûr′dər) *n.* **1.** The crime of unlawfully killing a human being, esp. with malice aforethought. **2.** *Slang.* Something very difficult, dangerous, or uncomfortable. —*v.* **1.** To kill (a human being) unlawfully. **2.** To spoil or mar by ineptness **:** ruin. **3.** To put an end to **:** destroy. ★ ***syns:*** KILL, KNOCK OFF, LIQUIDATE, RUB OUT, SLAY, WASTE, WIPE OUT, ZAP —**mur′der•er** *n.*
mur•der•ous (mûr′dər-əs) *adj.* **1.** Intending or seeming to intend murder. **2.** Marked by or giving rise to murder. **3.** *Informal.* Very difficult, dangerous, or uncomfortable. —**mur′-der•ous•ly** *adv.*
murk (mûrk) *n.* Gloom **:** darkness. —**murk′-i•ly** *adv.* —**murk′i•ness** *n.* —**murk′y** *adj.*
mur•mur (mûr′mər) *n.* **1.** An indistinct, low, continuous sound. **2.** An indistinct complaint **:** mutter. **3.** An abnormal sound, usu. in the thoracic cavity, detectable by a stethoscope. —**mur′mur** *v.*
mur•rain (mûr′ĭn) *n.* A malignant and highly infectious disease of domestic plants or animals, as blight or anthrax.
mus•ca•tel (mŭs′kə-tĕl′) *n.* A rich, sweet wine.
mus•cle (mŭs′əl) *n.* **1. a.** Bodily tissue composed of fibers that contract and relax to cause movement or exert force. **b.** A contractile organ of muscle tissue. **2.** Muscular strength. **3.** Force. ★ ***syns:*** CLOUT, FORCE, POWER, WEIGHT —*v.* **-cled, -cling.** To make one's way by or as if by force.
mus•cle-bound (mŭs′əl-bound′) *adj.* Having some muscles that are overdeveloped and

lack the capacity to flex fully, usu. from too much exercise.

mus·cu·lar (mŭs′kyə-lər) *adj.* **1.** Of, relating to, or consisting of muscle. **2.** Having well-developed muscles : brawny. —**mus′cu·lar′i·ty** (-lăr′ĭ-tē) *n.*

muscular dystrophy *n.* A chronic noncontagious disease marked by gradual but irreversible muscular deterioration.

mus·cu·la·ture (mŭs′kyə-lə-cho͝or′, -chər) *n.* The system of muscles of the body or a bodily part.

muse[1] (myo͞oz) *v.* **mused, mus·ing.** To think about at length. —**mus′er** *n.*

muse[2] (myo͞oz) *n.* A source of inspiration.

mu·sette (myo͞o-zĕt′) *n.* **1.** A small French bagpipe. **2.** A small leather or canvas bag with a shoulder strap.

mu·se·um (myo͞o-zē′əm) *n.* An institution for the acquisition, preservation, and display of works of lasting artistic, historical, and scientific value.

mush (mŭsh) *n.* **1.** Meal, esp. cornmeal, boiled in water. **2.** Soft pulpy matter. **3.** *Informal.* Maudlin sentimentality. —**mush′i·ness** *n.* —**mush′y** *adj.*

mush·room (mŭsh′ro͞om′, -ro͝om′) *n.* A fleshy fungus of the class Basidiomycetes, characteristically having an umbrella-shaped cap borne on a stalk. —*v.* To multiply, grow, or expand rapidly.

mu·sic (myo͞o′zĭk) *n.* **1.** The art of organizing tones in combinations and sequences that constitute a cohesive, unified, continuous composition. **2.** Vocal or instrumental sounds having melody, rhythm, or harmony. **3. a.** A musical composition. **b.** A body of such compositions. **4.** An aesthetically pleasing or harmonious sound.

mu·si·cal (myo͞o′zĭ-kəl) *adj.* **1.** Of, relating to, or capable of producing music. **2.** Pleasing to the ear, esp. melodious. **3.** Having skill or an interest in music. —*n.* A musical comedy. —**mu′si·cal·ly** *adv.*

musical comedy *n.* A play or motion picture in which spoken dialogue alternates with songs and dances.

mu·si·cale (myo͞o′zĭ-kăl′) *n.* A social gathering at which a program of music is performed.

music box *n.* A box enclosing a mechanical device that produces music when activated.

mu·si·cian (myo͞o-zĭsh′ən) *n.* A performer or composer of music. —**mu·si′cian·ly** *adj.* —**mu·si′cian·ship′** *n.*

mu·si·col·o·gy (myo͞o′zĭ-kŏl′ə-jē) *n.* The historical, theoretical, and scientific study of music. —**mus′si·co·log′i·cal** (-kə-lŏj′ĭ-kəl) *adj.* —**mu′si·col′o·gist** *n.*

musk (mŭsk) *n.* A substance with a powerful odor that is secreted by an Asian deer, *Moschus moschiferus,* or produced synthetically and used in making perfume. —**musk′i·ness** *n.* —**musk′y** *adj.*

mus·keg (mŭs′kĕg′) *n.* A swamp or bog formed by accumulated sphagnum moss, leaves, and decayed matter resembling peat.

mus·kel·lunge (mŭs′kə-lŭnj′) *n., pl.* **muskellunge** *or* **-lung·es.** A large game fish, *Esox masquinongy,* of cooler fresh waters of North America.

mus·ket (mŭs′kĭt) *n.* A shoulder gun with a long barrel. —**mus′ket·eer′** *n.*

mus·ket·ry (mŭs′kĭ-trē) *n.* **1. a.** Muskets. **b.** The fire of muskets. **2.** Musketeers.

musk·mel·on (mŭsk′mĕl′ən) *n.* A variety of the melon *Cucumis melo,* as the cantaloupe, with a rough rind and usu. juicy edible flesh.

Mus·ko·ge·an (mŭs-kō′gē-ən) *n.* A family of American Indian languages that includes Choctaw, Chickasaw, Creek, and Seminole.

musk ox *n.* A large hoofed mammal, *Ovibos moschatus,* of N Canada and Greenland, with horns and a shaggy coat.

musk·rat (mŭsk′răt′) *n.* An aquatic rodent, *Ondatra zibethica,* of North America, with brown fur.

Mus·lim (mŭz′lĭm, mo͝os′-, mo͝oz′-) *or* **Mos·lem** (mŏz′ləm, mŏs′-) *n.* A believer in or adherent of Islam. —**Mus′lim** *adj.*

mus·lin (mŭz′lĭn) *n.* A plain-weave coarse or sheer cotton fabric.

†**muss** (mŭs) *v.* To make untidy or messy : disorder. —*n.* **1.** A state of untidiness : disorder. **2.** *Regional.* A squabble : row. —**muss′i·ly** *adv.* —**muss′i·ness** *n.* —**muss′y** *adj.*

mus·sel (mŭs′əl) *n.* **1.** A marine bivalve mollusk, esp. the edible *Mytilus edulis.* **2.** Any of several freshwater bivalve mollusks of the genera *Anodonta* and *Unio,* whose shells are a source of mother-of-pearl.

Mus·sul·man (mŭs′əl-mən) *n., pl.* **-men** *or* **-mans.** *Archaic.* A Muslim.

must[1] (mŭst) *v.* —Used to indicate necessity or obligation, probability, certainty or inevitability, or insistence. —*n.* **1.** An absolute requirement. **2.** Something that is indispensable.

must[2] (mŭst) *n.* Unfermented or fermenting fruit juice, usu. grape.

mus·tache *also* **mous·tache** (mŭs′tăsh′, mə-stăsh′) *n.* The hair that grows on the human upper lip.

mus·tang (mŭs′tăng′) *n.* A wild horse of the W North American plains, descended from Spanish horses.

mus·tard (mŭs′tərd) *n.* **1.** A plant of the genus *Brassica,* with 4-petaled yellow flowers and often pungent seeds. **2.** A condiment or medicinal preparation made from the powdered seeds of mustard.

mustard gas *n.* An oily volatile liquid used in warfare as a blistering agent.

mus·ter (mŭs′tər) *v.* **1.** To bring or come together : convene. **2.** To call or bring forth (e.g., courage). —*n.* **1.** A gathering, esp. of troops, as for review or roll call. **2.** The act of inspecting or examining critically.

must·n't (mŭs′ənt). Must not.

mus·ty (mŭs′tē) *adj.* **-ti·er, -ti·est.** Stale or moldy in taste or odor. —**mus′ti·ly** *adv.* —**mus′ti·ness** *n.*

mu·ta·ble (myo͞o′tə-bəl) *adj.* **1.** Capable of or

subject to change. 2. Apt to change. **—mu'ta·bil'i·ty, mu'ta·ble·ness** *n.*

mu·tant (myo͞ot'nt) *n.* An organism or individual that differs from the parental strain or strains as a result of mutation. **—mu'tant** *adj.*

mu·tate (myo͞o'tāt', myo͞o-tāt') *v.* **-tat·ed, -tat·ing.** To undergo or cause to undergo mutation. **—mu'ta'tive** *adj.*

mu·ta·tion (myo͞o-tā'shən) *n.* **1.** A change, as in form. **2.** *Biol.* **a.** A heritable alteration of the genes or chromosomes of an organism. **b.** A mutant.

mute (myo͞ot) *adj.* **mut·er, mut·est. 1.** Unable to speak **:** dumb. **2.** Not speaking or spoken **:** silent. *—n.* **1.** One who is incapable of speaking. **2.** One of various devices used for muffling, reducing, or softening the tone of a musical instrument. *—v.* **mut·ed, mut·ing.** To muffle, reduce, or soften the sound of. **—mute'ly** *adv.* **—mute'ness** *n.*

mu·ti·late (myo͞ot'l-āt') *v.* **-lat·ed, -lat·ing. 1.** To deprive of (an essential part, esp. a limb) **:** cripple or maim. **2.** To make imperfect by seriously damaging a part. **—mu'ti·la'tion** *n.* **—mu'ti·la'tive** *adj.* **—mu'ti·la'tor** *n.*

mu·ti·ny (myo͞ot'n-ē) *n., pl.* **-nies.** Open rebellion against lawful authority, esp. against superior officers. **—mu'ti·neer'** *n.* **—mu'ti·nous** *adj.* **—mu'ti·ny** *v.*

mutt (mŭt) *n. Slang.* A dog of mixed breed **:** mongrel.

mut·ter (mŭt'ər) *v.* **1.** To utter or speak indistinctly or in a low voice. **2.** To complain **:** grumble. **—mut'ter** *n.*

mut·ton (mŭt'n) *n.* The meat of a fully grown sheep.

mutton chops *pl.n.* Whiskers on the sides of the face that are shaped like chops of meat.

mu·tu·al (myo͞o'cho͞o-əl) *adj.* **1.** Having the same relationship each to the other <*mutual* enemies> **2.** Directed and received in equal amount <*mutual* admiration> **3.** Possessed in common <*mutual* avocations> **—mu'tu·al'i·ty** (-ăl'ĭ-tē) *n.*

mutual fund *n.* A company without fixed capitalization that sells its own shares and uses the pooled capital of its shareholders to invest in a variety of securities of other companies.

muu·muu (mo͞o'mo͞o') *n.* A dress of Hawaiian orig. that hangs loose from the shoulders.

muz·zle (mŭz'əl) *n.* **1. a.** The forward, projecting part of the head of certain animals **:** nose and jaws. **b.** A leather or wire device that fits over the muzzle to prevent biting or eating. **2.** The front end of the barrel of a gun. *—v.* **-zled, -zling. 1.** To put a muzzle on. **2.** To restrain from expressing **:** silence. **—muz'zler** *n.*

my (mī) *adj.* —Used attributively to indicate possession, agency, or reception of an action by the speaker <*my* hat><doing *my* chores><suffered *my* first defeat> *—interj.* —Used to express pleasure, surprise, or dismay.

my·al·gi·a (mī-ăl'jē-ə, -jə) *n.* Muscular pain, esp. when diffuse and nonspecific. **—my·al'gic** (-jĭk) *adj.*

my·ce·li·um (mī-sē'lē-əm) *n., pl.* **-li·a** (-lē-ə). A mass of branching threadlike filaments that form the main growing structure of a fungus. **—my·ce'li·al** *adj.*

my·col·o·gy (mī-kŏl'ə-jē) *n.* The scientific study of fungi. **—my'co·log'i·cal** (-kə-lŏj'ĭ-kəl) *adj.* **—my·col'o·gist** *n.*

my·co·tox·in (mī'kō-tŏk'sĭn) *n.* A toxin produced by a fungus.

my·e·li·tis (mī'ə-lī'tĭs) *n.* Inflammation of the bone marrow or the spinal column.

My·lar (mī'lär'). A trademark for a thin, strong polyester film.

my·na *or* **my·nah** (mī'nə) *n.* Any of various SE Asian birds of the family Sturnidae, related to the starlings, some of which are known for mimicry of human speech.

my·o·car·di·um (mī'ō-kär'dē-əm) *n., pl.* **di·a** (-dē-ə). The muscular tissue of the heart. **—my'o·car'di·al** *adj.*

my·o·pi·a (mī-ō'pē-ə) *n.* **1.** A visual defect in which distant objects appear fuzzy because their images are focused in front of rather than on the retina. **2.** Failure to think or plan ahead. **—my·op'ic** (mī-ŏp'ĭk, -ō'pĭk) *adj.* **—my·op'i·cal·ly** *adv.*

myr·i·ad (mîr'ē-əd) *adj.* Constituting an extremely large indefinite number **:** innumerable. **—myr'i·ad** *n.*

myr·i·a·me·ter (mîr'ē-ə-mē'tər) *n.* A metric unit of length equal to 10,000 meters.

myr·i·a·pod (mĭr'ē-ə-pŏd') *n.* An arthropod, as the centipede, having a segmented body and numerous legs.

myr·mi·don (mûr'mĭ-dŏn', -dən) *n.* A loyal, unquestioning follower.

myrrh (mûr) *n.* An aromatic gum resin yielded by several trees and shrubs of the genus *Commiphora,* of India, Arabia, and E Africa, used in perfumes and incense.

myr·tle (mûr'tl) *n.* **1.** An evergreen shrub of the genus *Myrtus,* esp. *M. communis,* with pink or white flowers and blue-black berries. **2.** PERIWINKLE[2].

my·self (mī-sĕlf') *pron.* **1.** The one identical with me. —Used: **a.** Reflexively <I dressed *myself.*> **b.** For emphasis <I *myself* agreed.> **2.** My normal or healthy condition or state <I have not been *myself* lately.>

mys·te·ri·ous (mĭ-stîr'ē-əs) *adj.* **1.** Of, relating to, or being a mystery <*mysterious* and enduring truths> **2.** Difficult or impossible to comprehend or explain <a *mysterious* phone call> ★ ***syns:*** ARCANE, CABALISTIC, MYSTIC, MYSTICAL, MYSTIFYING, UNACCOUNTABLE, UNEXPLAINABLE, UNFATHOMABLE **—mys·te'ri·ous·ly** *adv.* **—mys·te'ri·ous·ness** *n.*

mys·ter·y (mĭs'tə-rē) *n., pl.* **-ies. 1.** Something not fully understood or understandable. **2.** A mysterious quality or character. **3.** A fictional work dealing with a crime and its solution. **4.** A religious truth revealed to the elect.

mys•tic (mĭs'tĭk) *adj.* **1.** Of or relating to mysteries, mystics, or mysticism. **2.** Conveying or containing a sense of mystery : mysterious. —*n.* A person who practices or believes in mysticism.
mys•ti•cal (mĭs'tĭ-kəl) *adj.* **1.** Of, relating to, or stemming from direct communion with God or with ultimate reality. **2.** Spiritually symbolic. **3.** MYSTIC 1. —**mys'ti•cal•ly** *adv.*
mys•ti•cism (mĭs'tĭ-sĭz'əm) *n.* A spiritual discipline aiming at direct union or communion with God or with ultimate reality through trancelike contemplation or deep meditation.
mys•ti•fy (mĭs'tə-fī') *v.* **-fied, -fy•ing. 1.** To bewilder : perplex. **2.** To make mysterious. —**mys'ti•fi•ca'tion** *n.* —**mys'ti•fy'ing•ly** *adv.*
mys•tique (mĭ-stēk') *n.* **1.** A body of attitudes and beliefs associated with a group, person, thing, or idea. **2.** The special quality or skill required in an activity or occupation.
myth (mĭth) *n.* **1.** A traditional story that deals with supernatural beings, ancestors, or heroes that serve as primordial types in a primitive view of the world. **2.** A real or fictional story that appeals to the consciousness of a people by embodying its cultural ideals or by giving expression to deep, commonly felt emotions. **3.** A fictitious or imaginary person, idea, or thing. —**myth'i•cal, myth'ic** *adj.* —**myth'i•cal•ly** *adv.*
myth•mak•er (mĭth'mā'kər) *n.* A creator of myths or mythical situations.
my•thol•o•gy (mĭ-thŏl'ə-jē) *n., pl.* **-gies. 1.** A body of myths, esp. about the ancestors, deities, and heroes of a people. **2.** The systematic collection and study of myths. —**myth'o•log'i•cal** (mĭth'ə-lŏj'ĭ-kəl) *adj.* —**my•thol'o•gist** *n.*
myx•e•de•ma (mĭk'sĭ-dē'mə) *n.* A disease caused by decreased activity of the thyroid gland and marked by mental and physical deterioration.

Nn

n *or* **N** (ĕn) *n., pl.* **n's** or **N's. 1.** The 14th letter of the English alphabet. **2.** A speech sound represented by the letter *n.* **3.** Something with the shape of the letter N.
N *symbol for* NITROGEN.
Na *symbol for* SODIUM.
nab (năb) *v.* **nabbed, nab•bing.** *Slang.* **1.** To seize and arrest <*nabbed* the fugitive at the airport> **2.** To grab : snatch.
na•bob (nā'bŏb') *n.* A prominent, wealthy person.
na•celle (nə-sĕl') *n.* A separate streamlined enclosure mounted on an aircraft to house an engine, cargo, or the crew.
na•cho (nä'chō') *n.* A small, often triangular piece of tortilla topped with chili sauce or cheese and broiled.
na•cre (nā'kər) *n.* Mother-of-pearl. —**na'cre•ous** (-krē-əs) *adj.*
na•dir (nā'dər, -dîr') *n.* **1.** A point on the celestial sphere directly opposite the zenith. **2.** The lowest point.
nae (nā) *adv. Scot.* **1.** No. **2.** Not.
nag[1] (năg) *v.* **nagged, nag•ging. 1.** To bother by constant faultfinding, scolding, or complaining. **2.** To torment persistently, as with anxiety. **3.** To find fault, scold, or complain constantly. —*n.* One who nags. —**nag'ger** *n.* —**nag'ging•ly** *adv.*
nag[2] (năg) *n.* An old or worn-out horse.
Na•hum (nā'həm, nā'əm) *n.* —See table at BIBLE.
nai•ad (nā'əd, -ăd', nī'-) *n., pl.* **-a•des** (-ə-dēz') *or* **-ads.** *Gk. Myth.* One of the nymphs living in and presiding over brooks, fountains, and springs.
na•if *or* **na•ïf** (nä-ēf') *adj.* Naive.
nail (nāl) *n.* **1.** A thin, pointed piece of metal used as a fastener and designed to be hammered in. **2. a.** A fingernail or toenail. **b.** A talon or claw. —*v.* **1.** To fasten or attach with or as if with a nail. **2.** To shut or cover by fastening with nails. **3.** *Slang.* To stop and seize : catch <*nailed* the suspect> **4.** *Informal.* To strike : hit. —**nail down.** To establish decisively. —**nail'er** *n.*
nain•sook (nān'so͝ok') *n.* A soft, lightweight cotton fabric.
nai•ra (nī'rə) *n.* —See table at CURRENCY.
na•ive *or* **na•ïve** (nä-ēv') *adj.* **-iv•er, -iv•est. 1.** Not worldly or sophisticated : artless. **2.** Simple and credulous : ingenuous. —**na•ive'ly** *adv.* —**na•ive'ness** *n.*
na•ive•té *or* **na•ïve•té** (nä'ēv-tā') *n.* **1.** The quality or state of being naive. **2.** A naive action or statement.
na•ive•ty *or* **na•ïve•ty** (nä-ēv'tē, -ē'vĭ-tē) *n., pl.* **-ties.** Naiveté.
na•ked (nā'kĭd) *adj.* **1.** Without clothing on the body : nude. **2.** Without covering. **3.** Without disguise or embellishment. —**na'ked•ly** *adv.* —**na'ked•ness** *n.*
naked eye *n.* The eye unaided by an optical instrument, as a telescope.
nam•by-pam•by (năm'bē-păm'bē) *adj.* **1.** Insipid : sentimental. **2.** Indecisive : weak. —**nam'by-pam'by** *n.*
name (nām) *n.* **1.** A word or words by which an entity is called or designated. **2.** A usu. disparaging description or epithet. **3.** Appearance as opposed to reality <equality in *name* only> **4.** Reputation : renown. **5.** *Informal.* One who is famous. ★ ***syns:*** APPELLATION, COGNOMEN, DENOMINATION, DESIGNA-

TION, HANDLE, MONIKER, TAG —*v.* **named, nam•ing. 1.** To give a name to. **2.** To specify, identify, or cite by name. **3.** To nominate or appoint to an office or honor. **4.** To specify : fix. —**nam'a•ble, name'a•ble** *adj.*

name day *n.* The feast day of the saint after whom one is named.

name-drop (nām'drŏp') *v.* To mention casually the names of illustrious or famous people as a means of self-promotion. —**name'-drop'per** *n.* —**name'-drop'ping** *n.*

name•less (nām'lĭs) *adj.* **1.** Having no name. **2.** Anonymous<a *nameless* contributor> **3.** Inexpressible : indescribable <*nameless* horror> —**name'less•ness** *n.*

name•ly (nām'lē) *adv.* Specifically.

name•plate (nām'plāt') *n.* A plate or plaque, as on a door, inscribed with a name.

name•sake (nām'sāk') *n.* One having the same name as another, esp. one named after another.

nan•ny (năn'ē) *n., pl.* **-nies.** A children's nurse.

nanny goat *n.* A female goat.

nan•o•sec•ond (năn'ə-sĕk'ənd) *n.* One billionth (10^{-9}) sec.

nap[1] (năp) *n.* A short sleep, often during the day. —*v.* **napped, nap•ping. 1.** To sleep for a short period. **2.** To be unaware of or unprepared <caught our competitors *napping*>

nap[2] (năp) *n.* A soft or fuzzy surface on fabric or leather. —**nap'less** *adj.* —**napped** *adj.*

na•palm (nā'päm') *n.* **1.** An aluminum soap that forms an incendiary jelly when mixed with gasoline. **2.** A napalm jelly used in flame throwers and bombs.

nape (nāp) *n.* The back of the neck.

na•per•y (nā'pə-rē) *n.* Household linen, esp. table linen.

naph•tha (năf'thə, năp'-) *n.* A colorless flammable liquid derived from petroleum and used chiefly as a solvent.

naph•tha•lene (năf'thə-lēn', năp'-) *n.* A crystalline compound derived from coal tar and used in dyes, moth repellents, explosives, and solvents.

nap•kin (năp'kĭn) *n.* **1.** A piece of cloth or soft paper, used at meals to protect clothing or wipe the lips and fingers. **2.** A small cloth or towel. **3.** A sanitary napkin.

na•po•le•on (nə-pō'lē-ən, -pōl'yən) *n.* A pastry of flaky layers filled with custard cream.

narc *or* **nark** (närk) *n. Slang.* A police officer or government agent who deals with narcotics violations.

nar•cis•sism (när'sĭ-sĭz'əm) *n.* Excessive self-admiration or self-love. —**nar'cis•sist** *n.* —**nar'cis•sis'tic** *adj.*

nar•cis•sus (när-sĭs'əs) *n., pl.* **-es** *or* **-cis•si** (-sĭs'ī', -sĭs'ē). A widely grown plant of the genus *Narcissus,* with narrow grasslike leaves and white or yellow flowers having a cup- or trumpet-shaped crown.

nar•co•lep•sy (när'kə-lĕp'sē) *n.* A disorder marked by sudden and uncontrollable, often brief, attacks of deep sleep. —**nar'co•lep'tic** (-lĕp'tĭk) *adj. & n.*

nar•co•sis (när-kō'sĭs) *n., pl.* **-ses** (-sēz'). Deep, drug-induced unconsciousness.

nar•cot•ic (när-kŏt'ĭk) *n.* A habit-forming drug that dulls the senses, relieves pain, and induces sleep. —**nar•cot'ic** *adj.* —**nar•cot'i•cal•ly** *adv.*

nar•co•tism (när'kə-tĭz'əm) *n.* **1.** Addiction to narcotics. **2.** Narcosis.

nar•co•tize (när'kə-tīz') *v.* **-tized, -tiz•ing. 1.** To subject or treat with a narcotic. **2.** To put to sleep : soothe.

nar•is (nâr'ĭs) *n., pl.* **-es** (-ēz). A nostril.

nar•rate (năr'āt', nă-rāt') *v.* **-rat•ed, -rat•ing. 1.** To give a description or account : relate. **2.** To supply a running commentary for a performance, as of a motion picture. —**nar•ra'tion** *n.* —**nar'ra'tor** *n.*

nar•ra•tive (năr'ə-tĭv) *n.* **1.** A narrated account : story. **2.** The act or an example of narrating. —**nar'ra•tive** *adj.*

†**nar•row** (năr'ō) *adj.* **-er, -est. 1.** Small or slender in width. **2.** Limited in area or scope : confined. **3.** Rigid : inflexible. **4.** Barely enough <won by a *narrow* margin> **5.** *Regional.* Miserly : stingy. —*v.* To make or become narrow : contract. —*n.* **narrows.** A narrow body of water between 2 larger ones. —**nar'row•ly** *adv.* —**nar'row•ness** *n.*

nar•row-mind•ed (năr'ō-mīn'dĭd) *adj.* Lacking tolerance or sympathy : petty. —**nar'row-mind'ed•ly** *adv.* —**nar'row-mind'ed•ness** *n.*

nar•whal (när'wəl) *n.* An Arctic aquatic mammal, *Monodon monoceros,* having a long, spirally twisted ivory tusk in the male.

narwhal

†**nar•y** (nâr'ē) *adj. Regional.* Not one : no.

na•sal (nā'zəl) *adj.* **1.** Of or pertaining to the nose. **2.** Produced while exhaling air through the nose <a *nasal* sound> —**na•sal'i•ty** *n.* —**na'sal•ly** *adv.*

na•sal•ize (nā'zə-līz') *v.* **-ized, -iz•ing.** To make nasal or produce nasal sounds. —**na'sal•i•za'tion** *n.*

nas•cent (năs'ənt, nā'sənt) *adj.* Coming into existence : emergent. —**nas'cence** *n.*

na•stur•tium (nə-stûr'shəm, nă-) *n.* A plant of the genus *Tropaeolum,* with 5-petaled, usu. orange, yellow, or red flowers.

nas•ty (năs'tē) *adj.* **-ti•er, -ti•est. 1.** Disgustingly dirty : filthy. **2.** Morally offensive : obscene. **3.** Malicious : mean. **4.** Unpleasant. **5.** Dangerous or harmful. **—nas'ti•ly** *adv.* **—nas'ti•ness** *n.*

na•tal (nāt'l) *adj.* Of, pertaining to, or accompanying birth <*natal* trauma>

na•tal•i•ty (nā-tăl'ĭ-tē, nə-) *n., pl.* **-ties.** Birthrate.

na•tion (nā'shən) *n.* **1.** A group of people organized under one government. **2.** A tribe or federation, esp. of North American Indians. ★ ***syns:*** COUNTRY, LAND, STATE

na•tion•al (năsh'ə-nəl, năsh'nəl) *adj.* **1.** Of or belonging to a nation. **2.** Typical of the people of a nation. *—n.* A citizen of a nation. **—na'tion•al•ly** *adv.*

National Guard *n.* The militia reserve unit of a U.S. state, maintained by the state and federal governments and subject to active duty call by either.

na•tion•al•ism (năsh'ə-nə-lĭz'əm, năsh'nə-) *n.* **1.** Concern for or attachment to a particular nation's interests or culture. **2.** Advocacy of national independence. **—na'tion•al•ist** *n.* **—na'tion•al•is'tic** *adj.* **—na'tion•al•is'ti•cal•ly** *adv.*

na•tion•al•i•ty (năsh'ə-năl'ĭ-tē) *n., pl.* **-ties.** **1.** The condition of belonging to a particular nation by birth, origin, or naturalization. **2.** A people with common origins or traditions, often forming a nation.

na•tion•al•ize (năsh'ə-nə-līz', năsh'nə-) *v.* **-ized, -iz•ing.** **1.** To change from private to governmental control. **2.** To make national. **—na'tion•al•i•za'tion** *n.*

national monument *n.* A landmark maintained by a national government for public enjoyment or study.

national park *n.* A tract of land maintained by a national government for public recreation and cultural use.

national seashore *n.* A seacoast area maintained by a national government.

na•tion•wide (nā'shən-wīd') *adj.* Throughout a nation.

na•tive (nā'tĭv) *adj.* **1.** Belonging to one by nature : innate <*native* ability> **2.** Being such by birth or origin. **3.** Belonging to one by birth <my *native* country> **4.** Growing, living, or produced in a particular place : indigenous. *—n.* **1.** One born in or associated with a place by birth. **2. a.** An original inhabitant. **b.** A long-time resident. **3.** Something, as a plant or animal, that originated in a particular place. **—na'tive•ly** *adv.*

Native American *n.* An American Indian.

na•tiv•i•ty (nə-tĭv'ĭ-tē, nā-) *n., pl.* **-ties.** **1.** Birth, esp. the place, conditions, or circumstances of being born. **2. Nativity. a.** The birth of Jesus. **b.** Christmas.

nat•ty (năt'ē) *adj.* **-ti•er, -ti•est.** *Informal.* Neat and trim : dapper. **—nat'ti•ly** *adv.* **—nat'ti•ness** *n.*

nat•u•ral (năch'ər-əl, năch'rəl) *adj.* **1.** Existing in or produced by nature. **2.** Of or pertaining to nature. **3.** Following the usual or expected course of nature <death from *natural* causes> **4. a.** Not acquired : innate. **b.** Having a particular character by nature <a *natural* athlete> **5.** Free from pretension or artificiality. **6.** Expected and accepted. **7.** *Mus.* Not sharped or flatted. *—n.* **1.** *Informal.* One naturally suited or qualified. **2.** *Mus.* The sign (♮) placed before a note to nullify a preceding sharp or flat. **—nat'u•ral•ness** *n.*

natural childbirth *n.* Childbirth in which medical intervention, such as anesthesia or surgical aid, is minimized in favor of such techniques as controlled breathing and body position.

natural gas *n.* A mixture of gaseous hydrocarbons, chiefly methane, found with petroleum deposits and used as a fuel and in manufacturing organic compounds.

natural history *n.* The study of living things and natural objects and their origins and relationships.

nat•u•ral•ism (năch'ər-ə-lĭz'əm, năch'rə-) *n.* **1.** Realistic representation, esp. in art and literature. **2.** The philosophical doctrine that all phenomena can be explained by natural causes and laws. **—nat'u•ral•is'tic** *adj.* **—nat'u•ral•is'ti•cal•ly** *adv.*

nat•u•ral•ist (năch'ər-ə-lĭst, năch'rə-) *n.* **1.** One who studies natural history. **2.** One who advocates naturalism.

nat•u•ral•ize (năch'ər-ə-līz', năch'rə-) *v.* **-ized, -iz•ing.** **1.** To confer full citizenship upon (one of foreign birth). **2.** To adopt into widespread use. **3.** To adapt or become adapted to life in a new environment. **—nat'u•ral•i•za'tion** *n.*

nat•u•ral•ly (năch'ər-ə-lē, năch'rə-) *adv.* **1.** In a natural way. **2.** By nature : innately. **3.** Without a doubt : positively.

natural number *n.* One of the set of positive whole numbers : positive integer.

natural resource *n.* A necessary or beneficial material source, as of timber or a mineral deposit, occurring in nature.

natural science *n.* A science, as biology, chemistry, or physics, based primarily on quantitative phenomena and hypotheses of the physical world.

natural selection *n.* The principle that in a given environment individuals having characteristics that aid survival will produce more offspring and the proportion of individuals having such characteristics will increase with each succeeding generation.

na•ture (nā'chər) *n.* **1.** The physical world and its phenomena. **2.** The processes and forces producing and controlling the physical world. **3.** The world of living things <the serenity of *nature*> **4.** A primitive state of existence. **5.** Kind : type <an object of that *nature*> **6.** Intrinsic characteristics and qualities <the *nature* of the dilemma> **7.** One's basic character or disposition : temperament <had a kind *nature*> **—na'tured** *adj.*

na•tur•op•a•thy (nā'chə-rŏp'ə-thē) *n., pl.* **-thies.** A system of therapy that relies on natural remedies, such as sunlight, diet, and massage, to treat illness. **—na'tur•o•path'**

(nā'chər-ə-păth', nə-cho͝or'-) *n.* **—na•tur'o•path'ic** *adj.*

naught *also* **nought** (nôt) *n.* **1.** Nothing <all for *naught*> **2.** The figure 0 **:** zero.

naugh•ty (nô'tē) *adj.* **-ti•er, -ti•est. 1.** Unruly **:** disobedient <a *naughty* schoolboy> **2.** Indecent **:** improper. **—naugh'ti•ly** *adv.* **—naugh'ti•ness** *n.*

nau•se•a (nô'zē-ə, -zhə, -sē-ə, -shə) *n.* **1.** A stomach disturbance marked by a desire to vomit. **2.** Strong disgust **:** repugnance.

nau•se•ate (nô'zē-āt', -zhē-, -sē-, -shē-) *v.* **-at•ed, -at•ing.** To feel or cause to feel nausea. **—nau'se•at'ing•ly** *adv.*

nau•seous (nô'shəs, -zē-əs) *adj.* **1.** Causing nausea. **2.** Affected with nausea <felt *nauseous* all day> **—nau'seous•ly** *adv.*

nau•ti•cal (nô'tĭ-kəl) *adj.* Of, pertaining to, or typical of ships, shipping, sailors, or navigation. **—nau'ti•cal•ly** *adv.*

nautical mile *n.* —See table at MEASUREMENT.

nau•ti•lus (nôt'l-əs) *n., pl.* **-es** *or* **-li** (-lī'). A tropical marine mollusk of the genus *Nautilus,* having a spiral shell divided into air-filled chambers.

Nav•a•jo *also* **Nav•a•ho** (năv'ə-hō', nä'və-) *n., pl.* **-jo** *or* **-jos** *also* **-ho** *or* **-hos. 1.** A member of an American Indian people of Arizona, New Mexico, and SE Utah. **2.** Their Athabaskan language. **—Nav'a•jo'** *adj.*

na•val (nā'vəl) *adj.* Of, relating to, or having a navy.

naval stores *pl.n.* Products, as turpentine or pitch, orig. used to caulk the seams of wooden ships.

nave (nāv) *n.* The central part of a church from the main entrance to the chancel.

na•vel (nā'vəl) *n.* A small mark on the abdomen where the umbilical cord was attached to the fetus.

navel orange *n.* A sweet, usu. seedless orange with a navellike mark at one end.

nav•i•ga•ble (năv'ĭ-gə-bəl) *adj.* **1.** Sufficiently wide or deep to allow passage of ships. **2.** Able to be steered. **—nav'i•ga•bil'i•ty, nav'i•ga•ble•ness** *n.*

nav•i•gate (năv'ĭ-gāt') *v.* **-gat•ed, -gat•ing. 1.** To plan and direct the course of a ship or aircraft. **2.** To travel over or through water in a ship **:** sail. **3.** *Informal.* **a.** To make one's way. **b.** To walk. **—nav'i•ga'tion** *n.* **—nav'i•ga'tion•al** *adj.* **—nav'i•ga'tor** *n.*

na•vy (nā'vē) *n., pl.* **-vies. 1.** A nation's fleet, esp. of warships. **2.** *often* **Navy.** A national organization for naval defense.

navy bean *n.* A variety of the kidney bean, grown for its nutritious white seeds.

navy blue *n.* A dark blue.

nay (nā) *adv.* **1.** No. **2.** And moreover <was good-looking, *nay,* beautiful> *—n.* **1.** A denial or refusal. **2.** A negative vote.

nay•say•er (nā'sā'ər) *n.* **1.** One who is assertively negative in attitude. **2.** One who critically disagrees.

Na•zi (nät'sē, năt'-) *n., pl.* **-zis.** A member of the fascist party that held power (1933–45) in Germany under Adolf Hitler. **—Na'zi** *adj.* **—Na'zism, Na'zi•ism** *n.*

Nb *symbol for* NIOBIUM.

Nd *symbol for* NEODYMIUM.

Ne *symbol for* NEON.

Ne•an•der•thal (nē-ăn'dər-thôl', -tôl') *adj.* **1.** Of or relating to an extinct Stone Age species or race of humans. **2.** Rude or primitive. **—Ne•an'der•thal'** *n.*

neap tide (nēp) *n.* A tide of lowest range, occurring twice a month.

near (nîr) *adv.* **1.** To, at, or within a short distance or time <a house *near* the beach> **2.** Nearly **:** almost <*near* played out> **3.** In or with a close relationship. *—adj.* **1.** Close in distance, time, or degree <the *near* future> **2.** Closely related by kinship or association **:** intimate. **3.** Accomplished or missed by a narrow margin <a *near* bull's-eye> **4.** Short and direct. **5. a.** Closer of 2 or more. **b.** On the left side of a vehicle or draft team. ★ ***syns:*** CLOSE, IMMEDIATE, NEARBY, NIGH *—prep.* Close to <a motel *near* town> *—v.* To draw near or nearer (to). **—near'ness** *n.*

near beer *n.* A malt liquor not containing enough alcohol to be considered an alcoholic beverage.

near•by (nîr'bī') *adj. & adv.* Close at hand **:** adjacent.

near•ly (nîr'lē) *adv.* **1.** Almost but not quite. **2.** Closely or intimately.

near•sight•ed (nîr'sī'tĭd) *adj.* Afflicted with myopia **:** shortsighted. **—near'sight'ed•ly** *adv.* **—near'sight'ed•ness** *n.*

neat (nēt) *adj.* **1.** Clean and tidy. **2.** Orderly and precise **:** systematic. **3.** Skillfully or cleverly done **:** adroit. **4.** Undiluted <*neat* vodka> **5.** NET[2] 1. **6.** *Slang.* Fine **:** wonderful. ★ ***syns:*** ORDERLY, SHIPSHAPE, SPICK-AND-SPAN, TIDY, TRIM **—neat'ly** *adv.* **—neat'ness** *n.*

▲ ***word history:*** The adjective *neat* is derived from Old French *net,* which had several meanings. A basic sense of the French word was "free from dirt; clean." Liquor that contained no impurities was called *neat,* a sense that survives in the meaning "undiluted." An amount of money that was not liable to any reduction was also considered *neat.* A variant form of the Old French *net* had the same spelling and meanings but a different pronunciation. It survives in the English word *net,* meaning "remaining after all deductions." A *neat* profit and a *net* profit are in meaning and origin exactly the same.

neath *or* **'neath** (nēth) *prep.* Beneath.

neat's-foot oil (nēts'fo͝ot') *n.* A light yellow oil made from the feet and leg bones of cattle and used primarily to dress leather.

neb (nĕb) *n.* **1. a.** A bird's beak. **b.** A nose or snout. **2.** A sharp point.

neb•u•la (nĕb'yə-lə) *n., pl.* **-lae** (-lē') *or* **-las.** A large cloudlike mass of interstellar gas or dust, visible as a bright or dark patch in the sky depending on the way the mass reflects or absorbs light. **—neb'u•lar** *adj.*

neb•u•lize (nĕb'yə-līz') *v.* **-lized, -liz•ing.** To

change (a liquid) to a fine spray or mist. **—neb'u·li·za'tion** *n.* **—neb'u·liz'er** *n.*

neb·u·lous (nĕb'yə-ləs) *adj.* **1.** Misty, cloudy, or hazy. **2.** Indefinite in form or limits. **3.** Of or pertaining to a nebula. **—neb'u·los'i·ty** (-lŏs'ĭ-tē) *n.* **—neb'u·lous·ly** *adv.* **—neb'u·lous·ness** *n.*

nec·es·sar·y (nĕs'ĭ-sĕr'ē) *adj.* **1.** Absolutely required : indispensable. **2.** Needed to bring about a certain effect or result. **3. a.** Unavoidably determined by prior circumstances or conditions. **b.** Logically inevitable. ★ ***syns:*** ESSENTIAL, INDISPENSABLE, VITAL *—n., pl.* **-ies.** NECESSITY 1b. **—nec'es·sar'i·ly** *adv.*

ne·ces·si·tate (nə-sĕs'ĭ-tāt') *v.* **-tat·ed, -tat·ing. 1.** To make necessary. **2.** To compel or require. **—ne·ces'si·ta'tion** *n.*

ne·ces·si·ty (nə-sĕs'ĭ-tē) *n., pl.* **-ties. 1. a.** The quality or state of being necessary. **b.** Something necessary : requirement. **2.** Something inevitable. **3.** Neediness.

neck (nĕk) *n.* **1.** The bodily part linking the head and the trunk. **2.** The part of a garment that fits the neck. **3.** A somewhat narrow projection or part, as of land, a bottle, or a stringed musical instrument. **4.** A narrow margin <lost by a *neck*> *—v. Slang.* To kiss and caress. **—necked** *adj.*

neck·er·chief (nĕk'ər-chĭf) *n.* A scarf worn about the neck.

neck·lace (nĕk'lĭs) *n.* A neck ornament.

neck·line (nĕk'līn') *n.* The edge of a garment at or near the neck.

neck·tie (nĕk'tī') *n.* A narrow strip of material designed to be worn around the neck and tied in front.

ne·crol·o·gy (nə-krŏl'ə-jē, nĕ-) *n., pl.* **-gies. 1.** A list of usu. recently deceased people. **2.** An obituary. **—nec'ro·log'ic** (nĕk'rə-lŏj'ĭk), **nec'ro·log'i·cal** *adj.*

nec·ro·man·cy (nĕk'rə-măn'sē) *n.* **1.** Communication with the dead in order to foretell the future. **2.** Black magic : sorcery. **—nec'ro·man'cer** *n.* **—nec'ro·man'tic** *adj.*

ne·crop·o·lis (nə-krŏp'ə-lĭs, nĕ-) *n., pl.* **-lis·es** *or* **-leis** (-lās'). A cemetery, esp. a large elaborate one in an ancient city.

ne·cro·sis (nə-krō'sĭs, nĕ-) *n., pl.* **-ses** (-sēz'). Pathologic death of living plant or animal tissue. **—ne·crot'ic** (-krŏt'ĭk) *adj.*

nec·tar (nĕk'tər) *n.* **1.** The drink of the Greek gods. **2.** A good-tasting drink. **3.** A sweet liquid in various flowers gathered by bees for honey. **—nec'tar·ous** *adj.*

nec·tar·ine (nĕk'tə-rēn') *n.* A type of peach with a smooth glossy skin.

née *also* **nee** (nā) *adj.* Born. —Used to indicate the maiden name of a married woman.

need (nēd) *n.* **1.** A lack of something necessary, useful, or desirable. **2.** Obligation or requirement. **3.** Something necessary, useful, or desirable : requisite. **4.** Poverty or misfortune. ★ ***syns:*** EXIGENCY, NECESSITY *—v.* **1.** —Used as an auxiliary to express obligation or requirement <You *need* not go until tomorrow.> **2.** To require or desire urgently. **3.** To be in need or want.

need·ful (nēd'fəl) *adj.* Required : essential. **—need'ful·ness** *n.*

nee·dle (nēd'l) *n.* **1. a.** A thin, sharp-pointed steel sewing implement, with an eye at one end through which thread is passed and held. **b.** A similarly shaped implement, as one used in knitting. **2.** A thin pointed stylus that transmits vibrations from the grooves of a phonograph record. **3.** A thin pointer or indicator, as on a compass or gauge. **4.** A hypodermic needle. **5.** A stiff needle-shaped leaf, as of a fir tree. **6.** A thin, sharp projection, as a spine of a sea urchin or a crystal. *—v.* **-dled, -dling.** *Informal.* **1.** To provoke or prod. **2.** To tease.

nee·dle·point (nēd'l-point') *n.* Decorative stitching on canvas, usu. covering the entire surface of the material.

need·less (nēd'lĭs) *adj.* Unnecessary. **—need'less·ly** *adv.* **—need'less·ness** *n.*

nee·dle·work (nēd'l-wûrk') *n.* Work, as sewing or embroidery, done with a needle. **—nee'dle·work'er** *n.*

need·n't (nēd'nt). Need not.

needs (nēdz) *adv.* Of necessity <I must *needs* stay.>

need·y (nē'dē) *adj.* **-i·er, -i·est.** Being in want : poor. **—need'i·ness** *n.*

ne'er (nâr) *adv.* Never.

ne'er-do-well (nâr'do͞o-wĕl') *n.* An idle, unreliable person. **—ne'er'-do-well'** *adj.*

ne·far·i·ous (nə-fâr'ē-əs) *adj.* Wicked : despicable. **—ne·far'i·ous·ly** *adv.*

ne·gate (nə-gāt') *v.* **-gat·ed, -gat·ing. 1.** To nullify or make ineffective. **2.** To rule out : deny.

ne·ga·tion (nə-gā'shən) *n.* **1.** The act or process of negating. **2.** A denial, contradiction, or negative statement.

neg·a·tive (nĕg'ə-tĭv) *adj.* **1.** Indicating refusal, denial, contradiction, or disapproval. **2.** Not constructive or helpful. **3.** Not confident : unsure of oneself. **4.** *Math.* **a.** Less than zero. **b.** Of the sign (–) indicating a negative number or one that is to be subtracted. **5.** Of or having an electric charge that tends to repel electrons. **6.** Having light and dark areas opposite to those of the original photographic subject. *—n.* **1.** A negative statement, idea, or action. **2.** A word or part of a word, as *no* or *non-*, that indicates negation. **3.** The side in a debate that opposes or contradicts the question being debated. **4. a.** A negative photographic image. **b.** Photographic material, as a film or plate, having such an image. **5.** *Math.* A negative number. *—v.* **-tived, -tiv·ing. 1.** To refuse to accept or approve. **2.** To contradict or deny. **—neg'a·tive·ly** *adv.* **—neg'a·tive·ness, neg'a·tiv'i·ty** *n.*

neg·a·tiv·ism (nĕg'ə-tĭ-vĭz'əm) *n.* Habitual skepticism or resistance to the ideas, orders, or suggestions of others. **—neg'a·tiv·ist** *n.* **—neg'a·tiv·is'tic** *adj.*

ne·glect (nĭ-glĕkt') *v.* **1.** To pay no attention to : ignore. **2.** To fail to give proper care or attention to. **3.** To fail to do or accomplish, as through carelessness. *—n.* **1.** An act or instance of neglecting. **2.** The state of being neglected. **3.** Habitual lack of care. **—ne•glect′er, ne•glec′tor** *n.*

ne•glect•ful (nĭ-glĕkt′fəl) *adj.* Careless or unheeding. **—ne•glect′ful•ly** *adv.* **—ne•glect′ful•ness** *n.*

neg•li•gee (nĕg′lĭ-zhā′, nĕg′lĭ-zhā′) *n.* A woman's loose dressing gown, often of fine sheer fabric.

neg•li•gent (nĕg′lĭ-jənt) *adj.* **1.** Marked by or inclined to neglect, esp. habitually. **2.** Extremely careless. **3.** *Law.* Failing to take reasonable care, caution, or responsibility. **—neg′li•gence** *n.* **—neg′li•gent•ly** *adv.*

neg•li•gi•ble (nĕg′lĭ-jə-bəl) *adj.* Unworthy of consideration **:** insignificant.

ne•go•tia•ble (nĭ-gō′shə-bəl, -shē-ə-) *adj.* **1.** Able to be negotiated. **2.** Able to be transferred legally from one to another. **—ne•go′tia•bil′i•ty** *n.* **—ne•go′tia•bly** *adv.*

ne•go•ti•ate (nĭ-gō′shē-āt′) *v.* **-at•ed, -at•ing. 1.** To meet and discuss with another in order to reach an agreement. **2.** To settle by meeting and discussing <*negotiate* a peace treaty> **3.** To transfer title to or ownership of (e.g., notes) to another in exchange for equivalent value. **4.** To accomplish or cope with successfully. **—ne•go′ti•a′tion** *n.* **—ne•go′ti•a′tor** *n.*

Ne•gro (nē′grō) *n., pl.* **-groes.** A black person, esp. a person of African origin or descent. **—Ne′gro** *adj.*

Ne•groid (nē′groid′) *adj.* Of or being a proposed human racial classification distinguished by brown to black pigmentation and often tightly curled hair and including peoples indigenous to Africa south of the Sahara. **—Ne′groid** *n.*

Ne•he•mi•ah (nē′hə-mī′ə, nē′ə-) *n.* —See table at BIBLE.

neigh (nā) *n.* The long, high-pitched sound characteristic of a horse. **—neigh** *v.*

neigh•bor (nā′bər) *n.* **1.** One who lives near or is adjacent to another. **2.** A fellow human being. —*v.* **1.** To live or be located close by. **2.** To border on.

neigh•bor•hood (nā′bər-hŏŏd′) *n.* **1.** An area or section having distinguishing characteristics. **2.** The people living in a specific area or section. **3.** Approximate range or amount **:** vicinity.

neigh•bor•ly (nā′bər-lē) *adj.* Of or like a good neighbor **:** friendly. **—neigh′bor•li•ness** *n.*

neigh•bour (nā′bər) *n. esp. Brit. var. of* NEIGHBOR.

nei•ther (nē′*th*ər, nī′-) *adj.* Not one nor the other <*Neither* radio works.> —*pron.* Not the one nor the other <*Neither* of them works.> —*conj.* **1.** —Used with the correlative conjunction *nor* <*Neither* your house nor mine is big enough for the party.> **2.** Also not **:** nor <If you won't go, *neither* will I.>

nel•son (nĕl′sən) *n.* A wrestling hold in which pressure is applied with the palm of the hand against the opponent's neck.

nem•a•tode (nĕm′ə-tōd′) *n.* An often parasitic threadlike worm of the phylum Nematoda, as the hookworm.

nem•e•sis (nĕm′ĭ-sĭs) *n., pl.* **-ses** (-sēz′). **1.** One that brings about retribution or vengeance. **2.** Just punishment for wrongdoing. **3.** A seemingly unbeatable rival.

ne•o•clas•si•cism (nē′ō-klăs′ĭ-sĭz′əm) *n.* A revival or adaptation of classical forms, esp. in the arts. **—ne′o•clas′sic, ne′o•clas′si•cal** *adj.*

ne•o•dym•i•um (nē′ō-dĭm′ē-əm) *n. Symbol* **Nd** A bright silvery rare-earth element.

ne•o•fas•cism (nē′ō-făsh′ĭz′əm) *n.* A fringe movement inspired by the beliefs and methods of fascism or Nazism. **—ne′o•fas′cist** *adj. & n.*

ne•ol•o•gism (nē-ŏl′ə-jĭz′əm) *n.* A new word, phrase, or expression or a new meaning for an existing word. **—ne•ol′o•gis′tic, ne•ol′o•gis′ti•cal** *adj.*

ne•on (nē′ŏn′) *n. Symbol* **Ne** An inert gaseous element often used in display lights.

ne•o•nate (nē′ə-nāt′) *n.* A newborn child. **—ne′o•na′tal** *adj.*

ne•o•na•tol•o•gy (nē′ō-nā-tôl′ə-jē) *n.* The medical study of the first 60 days of an infant's life. **—ne′o•na•tol′o•gist** *n.*

ne•o-Na•zi (nē′ō-nät′sē, -năt′-) *n.* A member of a fringe group inspired by Adolf Hitler's Nazis. **—ne′o-Na′zism** *n.*

ne•o•phyte (nē′ə-fīt′) *n.* **1.** A new convert. **2.** A novice or beginner.

ne•o•plasm (nē′ə-plăz′əm) *n.* A tumor. **—ne′o•plas′tic** *adj.*

ne•o•prene (nē′ə-prēn′) *n.* A durable synthetic rubber resistant esp. to oil.

ne•pen•the (nĭ-pĕn′thē) *n.* Something that eases pain or grief.

neph•ew (nĕf′yo͞o) *n.* The son of one's brother or sister or of one's spouse's brother or sister.

ne•phrit•ic (nə-frĭt′ĭk) *adj.* **1.** Of or relating to the kidneys. **2.** Of, relating to, or afflicted with nephritis.

ne•phri•tis (nə-frī′tĭs) *n.* Inflammation of the kidneys.

nep•o•tism (nĕp′ə-tĭz′əm) *n.* Favoritism shown by those in high office to relatives or friends. **—nep′o•tist** *n.*

Nep•tune (nĕp′to͞on′, -tyo͞on′) *n.* The 8th planet from the sun. **—Nep•tu′ni•an** *adj.*

nep•tu•ni•um (nĕp-to͞o′nē-əm, -tyo͞o′-) *n. Symbol* **Np** A silvery, metallic, naturally radioactive element.

nerd (nûrd) *n. Slang.* An unpopular or socially inept person, esp. one regarded as excessively studious. **—nerd′y** *adj.*

nerve (nûrv) *n.* **1.** Any of the bundles of fibers extending from the central nervous system to the various organs and parts of the body and capable of relaying sensory stimuli and motor impulses throughout the body. **2. a.** Calm endurance **:** patience. **b.** Stamina **:** fortitude. **c.** Strong will **:** courage. **d.** *Informal.* Impudent boldness **:** audacity. **3. nerves.** Agitation brought about by fright, anxiety, or stress. —*v.* **nerved, nerv•ing.** To give strength or courage to.

nerve center *n.* A focal point of influence or control.

nerve•less (nûrv'lĭs) *adj.* **1.** Having little or no strength or energy. **2.** Displaying poise : calm. —**nerve'less•ly** *adv.* —**nerve'less•ness** *n.*

nerve-rack•ing *also* **nerve-wrack•ing** (nûrv'răk'ĭng) *adj.* Extremely irritating or distressing.

nerv•ous (nûr'vəs) *adj.* **1.** Of, affecting, or relating to the nerves or nervous system. **2.** Excitable : jumpy. **3.** Worried : apprehensive. —**nerv'ous•ly** *adv.* —**nerv'ous•ness** *n.*

nervous breakdown *n.* A severe or incapacitating emotional or psychic disorder.

nervous system *n.* A bodily mechanism in all multicellular animals except sponges that coordinates internal functions and responses to stimuli.

nerv•y (nûr'vē) *adj.* **-i•er, -i•est. 1.** Rudely bold or confident. **2.** Showing or requiring fortitude, energy, or stamina. **3.** Nervous.

–ness *suff.* State : condition : quality : degree <dark*ness*>

nest (nĕst) *n.* **1. a.** A shelter or receptacle constructed by a bird to hold its eggs and young. **b.** A similar receptacle that shelters an insect, fish, or animal. **2.** A warm, cozy place. **3.** A group of objects of graduated size that can be stacked together. —*v.* **1.** To construct or live in a nest. **2.** To fit snugly together or inside one another.

nest egg *n.* A sum of money saved for future use.

†nest•er (nĕs'tər) *n. W U.S.* A squatter, homesteader, or farmer who settles in cattle-grazing territory.

nes•tle (nĕs'əl) *v.* **-tled, -tling. 1. a.** To settle snugly and comfortably. **b.** To lie in a sheltered location. **2.** To snuggle contentedly. —**nes'tler** *n.*

nest•ling (nĕst'lĭng) *n.* A young bird not yet able to leave the nest.

net[1] (nĕt) *n.* **1.** Openwork fabric made of threads, cords, or ropes woven or knotted together. **2.** Something made of net, esp.: **a.** A device for capturing animals, as fish or butterflies. **b.** A mesh that acts as a barrier <a mosquito *net*> **c.** A mesh for holding the hair in place. **3.** A barrier strung between 2 posts in the center of a tennis, badminton, or volleyball court. **4.** Something that ensnares. —*v.* **net•ted, net•ting.** To catch in, protect, cover, or surround with or as if with a net.

net[2] (nĕt) *adj.* **1.** Remaining after all additions, subtractions, or adjustments have been made <*net* profits><*net* volume> **2.** Ultimate : final. —*n.* A net amount, as of profit or weight. —*v.* **net•ted, net•ting.** To bring in or yield as profit.

neth•er (nĕ*th*'ər) *adj.* Located beneath or below : lower : under <the *nether* regions>

net•su•ke (nĕt'sə-kē) *n.* A small Japanese toggle, usu. decorated with inlays or carving, used esp. to fasten a purse to a kimono sash.

netsuke

net•tle (nĕt'l) *n.* A plant of the genus *Urtica,* having toothed leaves covered with hairs that secrete a stinging fluid. —*v.* **-tled, -tling.** To vex : irritate.

net•work (nĕt'wûrk') *n.* **1.** An openwork fabric or structure in which cords, threads, wires, etc. are interwoven at regular intervals. **2.** Something resembling a net <a *network* of spies> **3.** A group of interconnected broadcasting stations that usu. share a large proportion of their programming. **4.** *Computer Sci.* A system of computers linked together to share information.

Neuf•châ•tel (no͞o'shə-tĕl', nœ'shä-) *n.* A soft cheese made from milk or cream.

neu•ral (no͝or'əl, nyo͝or'-) *adj.* Of or relating to a nerve or the nervous system.

neu•ral•gia (no͞o-răl'jə, nyo͞o-) *n.* Paroxysmal pain along a nerve. —**neu•ral'gic** *adj.*

neu•ras•the•ni•a (no͝or'əs-thē'nē-ə, nyo͝or'-) *n.* A neurotic condition characterized by fatigue, loss of memory, and feelings of anxiety and inadequacy. —**neu'ras•then'ic** (-thĕn'ĭk) *adj. & n.* —**neu'ras•then'i•cal•ly** *adv.*

neu•ri•tis (no͞o-rī'tĭs, nyo͞o-) *n.* Inflammation of a nerve, causing pain, loss of reflexes, and muscular atrophy. —**neu•rit'ic** (-rĭt'ĭk) *adj.*

neu•rol•o•gy (no͞o-rŏl'ə-jē, nyo͞o-) *n.* The scientifical and medical study of the nervous system and its disorders. —**neu'ro•log'i•cal** *adj.* —**neu•rol'o•gist** *n.*

neu•ron (no͝or'ŏn', nyo͝or'-) *also* **neu•rone** (-ōn') *n.* Any of the cells of nerve tissue consisting of a main portion containing the nucleus and cytoplasmic extensions, the cell body, the dendrites, and axons. —**neu•ron'ic** (-rŏn'ĭk) *adj.*

neu•ro•pa•thol•o•gy (no͝or'ō-pə-thŏl'ə-jē, nyo͝or'-) *n.* Study of diseases of the nervous system. —**neu'ro•path'o•log'ic** (-păth'ə-lŏj'ĭk), **neu'ro•path'o•log'i•cal** *adj.* —**neu'ro•pa•thol'o•gist** *n.*

neu•rop•a•thy (no͞o-rŏp'ə-thē, nyo͞o-) *n.* Disease of the nervous system.

neu•ro•sis (no͞o-rō'sĭs, nyo͞o-) *n., pl.* **-ses** (-sēz'). Any of various functional disorders of the mind or emotions with no obvious physical cause. —**neu•rot•ic** *adj. & n.* —**neu•rot'i•cal•ly** *adv.*

neu•ter (no͞o′tər, nyo͞o′-) *adj.* **1.** Neither masculine nor feminine in grammatical gender. **2.** *Biol.* Having no sexual organs. —*n.* **1. a.** The neuter grammatical gender. **b.** A neuter word. **2. a.** A castrated animal. **b.** An animal or plant with undeveloped sex glands or organs, esp. an undeveloped female insect, such as a worker in a colony of ants. —**neu′ter** *v.*

neu•tral (no͞o′trəl, nyo͞o′-) *adj.* **1.** Not supporting or favoring either side in a war, quarrel, or contest. **2.** Belonging to neither side nor party. **3.** *Chem.* Neither acid nor alkaline. **4.** *Physics.* Having a net electric charge of zero. **5.** Of or indicating a color, as gray, black, or white, with no hue : achromatic. —*n.* **1.** One that is neutral. **2.** A neutral color. **3.** A position in which a set of gears is disengaged with no power transmitted. —**neu•tral′i•ty** *n.* —**neu′tral•ly** *adv.*

neu•tral•ism (no͞o′trə-lĭz′əm, nyo͞o′-) *n.* The condition or policy of being neutral, esp. nonparticipation in a war. —**neu′tral•ist** *n.* —**neu′tral•is′tic** *adj.*

neu•tral•ize (no͞o′trə-līz′, nyo͞o′-) *v.* **-ized, -iz•ing. 1.** To make neutral. **2.** To counteract. —**neu′tral•i•za′tion** *n.* —**neu′tral•iz′er** *n.*

neutral spirits *n. (sing. or pl. in number).* Ethyl alcohol distilled at or above 190 proof, frequently used in alcoholic beverage blends.

neu•tri•no (no͞o-trē′nō, nyo͞o-) *n., pl.* **-nos.** A massless, electrically neutral, stable subatomic particle that travels at the speed of light.

neu•tron (no͞o′trŏn′, nyo͞o′-) *n.* An electrically neutral subatomic particle having approx. the mass of a proton. It is stable when bound in an atomic nucleus, contributing to the mass of the nucleus without affecting atomic number or electric charge.

neutron bomb *n.* A nuclear bomb that would produce many neutrons but little blast and thus destroy life but spare property.

nev•er (nĕv′ər) *adv.* **1.** Not ever. **2.** Not at all <*Never* mind.><*Never* fear.>

nev•er•more (nĕv′ər-môr′, -mōr′) *adv.* Never again.

nev•er-nev•er land (nĕv′ər-nĕv′ər) *n.* An illusory, idyllic, or ideal place.

nev•er•the•less (nĕv′ər-*th*ə-lĕs′) *adv.* Nonetheless.

ne•vus (nē′vəs) *n., pl.* **-vi** (-vī′). A congenital usu. pigmented growth or mark on the skin, as a mole : birthmark.

new (no͞o, nyo͞o) *adj.* **1. a.** Not old : recent <a *new* book> **b.** Never used before. **2.** Just discovered or learned <*new* evidence> **3.** Unfamiliar. **4.** Unaccustomed. **5.** Starting over again in a a cycle <the *new* moon> **6.** Changed for the better : rejuvenated. **7.** Coming after or taking the place of a previous one <a *new* model> **8.** Modern : current <*new* dances> —*adv.* Freshly : recently <*new*-mown hay> —**new′ness** *n.*

new•born (no͞o′bôrn′, nyo͞o′-) *adj.* **1.** Born very recently. **2.** Reborn. —*n.* A neonate.

new•com•er (no͞o′kŭm′ər, nyo͞o′-) *n.* One who has recently arrived.

New Deal *n.* The policies and programs for economic recovery, relief, and social security that President Franklin D. Roosevelt introduced during the 1930′s. —**New Dealer** *n.*

New Democratic Party *n. Can.* One of the 3 major political parties.

new•el (no͞o′əl, nyo͞o′-) *n.* **1.** The vertical support at the center of a circular staircase. **2.** A post that supports a handrail at the bottom or top of a staircase.

new•fan•gled (no͞o′făng′gəld, nyo͞o′-) *adj.* New : novel.

new•found (no͞o′found, nyo͞o-′) *adj.* Recently discovered <*newfound* wealth>

new•ly (no͞o′lē, nyo͞o′-) *adv.* **1.** Lately : recently <a *newly* baked pie> **2.** Once more : anew <a *newly* decorated room> **3.** In a new or different way : freshly <an old song *newly* arranged>

new•ly-wed *also* **new•ly•wed** (no͞o′lē-wĕd′, nyo͞o′-) *n.* One recently married.

new moon *n.* **1.** The phase of the moon that occurs when it is between the earth and the sun, visible as a thin crescent at sunset. **2.** The crescent moon.

news (no͞oz, nyo͞oz) *pl.n. (sing. in number).* **1.** Recent events and happenings, esp. notable or unusual ones. **2. a.** Information about notable recent events, esp. as reported by the media. **b.** A presentation of such information.

news•cast (no͞oz′kăst′, nyo͞oz′-) *n.* A radio or television broadcast of the news. —**news′cast′er** *n.*

news•let•ter (no͞oz′lĕt′ər, nyo͞oz′-) *n.* A printed report, usu. issued at regular intervals, giving news about or information of interest to a particular group.

news•pa•per (no͞oz′pā′pər, nyo͞oz′-) *n.* A usu. daily or weekly publication containing recent news, useful information, editorials, feature articles, and advertisements.

news•print (no͞oz′prĭnt′, nyo͞oz′-) *n.* Inexpensive paper made from wood pulp, used chiefly for newspapers.

news•reel (no͞oz′rēl′, nyo͞oz′-) *n.* A short film giving a visual report of recent events.

news•room (no͞oz′ro͞om′, -ro͝om′, nyo͞oz′-) A room, as in a newspaper office or a radio or television station, where news is prepared for release.

news•stand (no͞oz′stănd′, nyo͞oz′-) *n.* A booth, shop, or stand where newspapers, magazines, etc. are sold.

news•wor•thy (no͞oz′wûr′*th*ē, nyo͞oz′-) *adj.* Worthy of being reported : interesting or significant. —**news′wor′thi•ness** *n.*

news•y (no͞o′zē, nyo͞o′-) *adj.* **-i•er, -i•est.** *Informal.* Informative.

newt (no͞ot, nyo͞ot) *n.* A small semiaquatic salamander of the genus *Triturus.*

New Testament *n.* The Gospels, Acts, Epistles, and the Book of Revelation. —See table at BIBLE.

new•ton (no͞ot′n, nyo͞ot′n) *n. Physics.* The unit of force in the meter-kilogram-second system needed to accelerate a mass of 1 kilogram 1 meter per second per second.

New World *n.* The W Hemisphere.

New Year's Day *n.* Jan. 1, the first day of the year in the Gregorian calendar.

New Year's Eve *n.* The eve of New Year's Day, celebrated with merrymaking.

next (nĕkst) *adj.* **1.** Coming immediately after in time, order, or sequence. **2.** Nearest in position or space. —*adv.* **1.** Following in order immediately after the present or previous thing or action. **2.** On the first occasion after the present or previous one. —*prep.* Adjacent to : nearest.

nex•us (nĕk'səs) *n., pl.* **-us** *or* **-us•es.** A bond or link.

Nez Perce (nĕz' pûrs', nĕs') *n., pl.* **Nez Perce** *or* **-ces** (pûr'sĭz). **1.** A member of an American Indian people of W Idaho and NE Washington. **2.** Their language.

ngul•trum (ĕn-gŭl'trəm, ĕng-) *n.* —See table at CURRENCY.

ngwee (ĕn-gwē') *n., pl.* **ngwee.** —See table at CURRENCY.

Ni *symbol for* NICKEL.

ni•a•cin (nī'ə-sĭn) *n.* Nicotinic acid.

nib (nĭb) *n.* **1. a.** A sharp point or tip. **b.** The point of a pen. **2.** A bird's beak.

nib•ble (nĭb'əl) *v.* **-bled, -bling. 1.** To bite (at) with small, gentle bites. **2.** To eat (food) with small, quick bites. **—nib'ble** *n.* **—nib'bler** *n.*

nice (nīs) *adj.* **nic•er, nic•est. 1.** Enjoyable : pleasant. **2.** Appealing or attractive. **3.** Courteous and polite. **4.** Excessively fussy : fastidious. **5.** Showing discernment and subtlety. **6.** Skillful : deft <a *nice* shot> **—nice'ly** *adv.* **—nice'ness** *n.*

▲ ***word history:*** Since its adoption in the 13th cent. the word *nice* has developed from a term of abuse to a term of praise, a process called *melioration. Nice* is derived from Latin *nescius,* "ignorant," and was used in Middle English to mean "foolish; without sense." By the 15th cent. *nice* had acquired the sense "elegant" in conduct and dress, but not in a complimentary sense: *nice* meant "overrefined, overdelicate." This sense survives in the meanings "fastidious" and "precise, subtle." To the extent that delicacy, refinement, and precision have favorable connotations, *nice* developed corresponding senses.

ni•ce•ty (nī'sĭ-tē) *n., pl.* **-ties. 1.** Accuracy : exactness. **2.** A small or subtle detail or distinction. **3.** A dainty or elegant feature.

niche (nĭch, nēsh) *n.* **1.** An alcove or recess in a wall, as for displaying a statue. **2.** Something, as a position or activity, for which one is particularly suited.

nick (nĭk) *n.* A small shallow cut or chip on a surface. —*v.* To make a small shallow cut or chip in. **—in the nick of time.** At the very last moment.

nick•el (nĭk'əl) *n.* **1.** *Symbol* **Ni** A hard, silvery, ductile metallic element often used in alloys. **2.** A U.S. coin worth 5 cents, made of a nickel and copper alloy.

nick•el•o•de•on (nĭk'ə-lō'dē-ən) *n.* **1.** An early movie theater charging 5 cents admission. **2.** A player piano. **3.** A juke box.

nickel silver *n.* A hard, silvery alloy of copper, zinc, and nickel.

nick•name (nĭk'nām') *n.* **1.** A usu. descriptive name added to or replacing the actual name of a person, place, or thing. **2.** A shortened version or familiar form of a proper name. **—nick'name'** *v.*

▲ ***word history:*** A *nickname* is literally an additional name. The Middle English form of the word *nickname* was *ekename,* from *eke,* "addition" (related to the verb *eke*), and *name,* "name." *Ekename* acquired an initial *n* from the indefinite article *an,* which frequently preceded it: *an ekename* came to be spelled and pronounced as if it was *a nekename.* In modern times the first syllable *neke-* was respelled *nick-,* and *nickname* has been the usual form ever since.

nic•o•tine (nĭk'ə-tēn') *n.* A poisonous alkaloid found in tobacco and used in medicine and insecticides.

nic•o•tin•ic acid (nĭk'ə-tĭn'ĭk) *n.* A compound of carbon, hydrogen, and nitrogen that is a member of the vitamin B complex and is essential to living cells.

niece (nēs) *n.* A daughter of one's brother or sister or of one's spouse's brother or sister.

nif•ty (nĭf'tē) *adj.* **-ti•er, -ti•est.** *Slang.* First-rate : excellent.

nig•gard (nĭg'ərd) *n.* A miserly person : cheapskate. **—nig'gard•li•ness** *n.* **—nig•gard•ly** *adj. & adv.*

nig•gling (nĭg'lĭng) *adj.* **1.** Fastidious : finicky. **2.** Nagging or petty. **3.** Showing or demanding great care or attention to details. **—nig'gling•ly** *adv.*

†**nigh** (nī) *adv.* **1.** Near in space, time, or relationship. **2.** Nearly : almost. —*adj.* **1.** Being near in space, time, or relationship : close. **2.** *Regional.* Direct : short. —*prep.* Not far from : near.

night (nīt) *n.* **1.** The time between dusk and dawn, esp. the hours of darkness. **2.** Nightfall. **3.** Darkness. **4.** A time of gloom, obscurity, ignorance, or sadness.

night blindness *n.* Lessened ability to see in dim light. **—night'blind'** *adj.*

night•cap (nīt'kăp') *n.* **1.** A cloth covering for the head worn esp. in bed. **2.** *Informal.* A usu. alcoholic drink taken at the end of an evening's entertainment or just before bedtime.

night•clothes (nīt'klōz', -klō*th*z') *pl.n.* Clothing worn in bed.

night•club (nīt'klŭb') *n.* An establishment offering food, drink, and entertainment at night.

night crawler *n.* A large earthworm that comes out of the ground at night.

night•dress (nīt'drĕs') *n.* A nightgown.

night•fall (nīt'fôl') *n.* The approach of darkness : dusk.

night•gown (nīt'goun') *n.* A usu. loose garment worn in bed.

night·hawk (nīt′hôk′) *n.* **1.** A nocturnal bird of the genus *Chordeiles,* having tan to black streaked feathers. **2.** A night owl.
night·ie *or* **night·y** (nī′tē) *n., pl.* **-ies.** *Informal.* A nightgown.
night·in·gale (nīt′n-gāl′, nī′tĭng-) *n.* A European songbird, *Luscinia megarhynchos,* having brownish plumage and noted for its nocturnal song.
night·life (nīt′līf′) *n.* Entertainment or social activities available at night.
night·ly (nīt′lē) *adj.* **1.** Of or taking place during the night : nocturnal. **2.** Occurring or done every night. —**night′ly** *adv.*
night·mare (nīt′mâr′) *n.* **1.** A dream causing fear, horror, or distress. **2.** A highly distressing or frightening experience. —**night′mar′ish** *adj.* —**night′mar′ish·ly** *adv.* —**night′mar′ish·ness** *n.*

▲ ***word history:*** In Old and Middle English *mare* was a word denoting an evil spirit. Although the spirit was imagined to be female, the word *mare* is unrelated to the modern word *mare* meaning "female horse." *Nightmare* is a compound of *night* and the old word *mare;* it denoted an evil spirit thought to afflict sleeping persons by sitting on them and causing a feeling of suffocation. *Nightmare* was also used to denote both the feeling itself and the dream that produced it.

night owl *n.* One who stays up late.
night school *n.* A school offering classes in the evening.
night·shade (nīt′shād′) *n.* Any of several plants of the genus *Solanum,* many of them yielding a poisonous juice.
night·shirt (nīt′shûrt′) *n.* A long, loose shirt worn in bed.
night·stick (nīt′stĭk′) *n.* A heavy club carried by a police officer.
night·time (nīt′tīm′) *n.* The period between dusk and dawn.
ni·hil·ism (nī′ə-lĭz′əm, nī′hə-, nē′-) *n.* The philosophical doctrine that all values and beliefs are unknowable and worthless and that therefore existence is meaningless. —**ni′hil·ist** *n.* —**ni′hil·is′tic** *adj.*
nil (nĭl) *n.* Not anything : zero.
nim·ble (nĭm′bəl) *adj.* **-bler, -blest. 1.** Moving or acting with agility : deft. **2.** Clever in thinking, apprehending, or responding : quick-witted. —**nim′ble·ness** *n.* —**nim′bly** *adv.*
nim·bus (nĭm′bəs) *n., pl.* **-bi** (bī′) *or* **-es. 1.** A halo or bright light depicted about the head, as in a painting. **2.** An atmosphere or aura, as of mystery. **3.** A gray rain cloud covering the sky.
nin·com·poop (nĭn′kəm-po͞op′, nĭng′-) *n.* A stupid or silly person.
nine (nīn) *n.* **1.** The cardinal number equal to 8 + 1. **2.** The 9th in a set or sequence. **3.** Something having 9 parts, units, or members, as a baseball team. —**nine** *adj. & pron.* —**ninth** *n. & adj. & adv.*
nine·teen (nīn′tēn′) *n.* **1.** The cardinal number equal to 18 + 1. **2.** The 19th in a set or sequence. —**nine′teen′** *adj. & pron.* —**nine′teenth** *n. & adj. & adv.*
nine·ty (nīn′tē) *n., pl.* **-ties.** The cardinal number equal to 9 × 10. —**nine′ty** *adj. & pron.* —**nine′ti·eth** *n. & adj. & adv.*
nin·ja (nĭn′jə) *n., pl.* **-ja** *or* **-jas.** A 14th-cent. Japanese mercenary trained in the martial arts.
nin·ny (nĭn′ē) *n., pl.* **-nies.** A fool : dolt.
ni·o·bi·um (nī-ō′bē-əm) *n. Symbol* **Nb** A soft, silvery, ductile metallic element.
nip[1] (nĭp) *v.* **nipped, nip·ping. 1.** To grab and bite or pinch. **2.** To sever or remove by or as by nipping. **3.** To sting or chill, as with cold. **4.** To halt or retard the further growth or development of. **5.** *Slang.* **a.** To seize hastily. **b.** To steal. —*n.* **1.** A small, sharp bite or pinch. **2.** A small portion. **3.** Intensely sharp cold. **4.** A sharp, biting flavor : tang. —**nip and tuck.** Very close. —**nip′per** *n.* —**nip′ping·ly** *adv.*
nip[2] (nĭp) *n.* A small portion of an alcoholic beverage. —*v.* **nipped, nip·ping.** To drink (liquor) in small portions.
nip·per (nĭp′ər) *n.* **1. nippers.** A pincerlike tool used for grasping or nipping. **2.** A pincerlike part, as the large claw of a crab. **3.** A small boy.
nip·ple (nĭp′əl) *n.* **1.** A small conical projection on the surface of a mammary gland through which the milk passes. **2.** Something like a nipple, esp. the pierced rubber cap on a baby's bottle.
nip·py (nĭp′ē) *adj.* **-pi·er, -pi·est. 1.** Sharp or biting : tangy. **2.** Bitterly cold.
nir·va·na (nîr-vä′nə, nûr-) *n.* **1.** Often **Nirvana.** The state of perfect bliss in Buddhism in which the self is freed from suffering and desire and is united with the creator of the universe. **2.** A time or condition of great peace and joy.
nit (nĭt) *n.* The egg or offspring of a parasitic insect, esp. a louse. —**nit′ty** *adj.*
ni·ter (nī′tər) *n.* A colorless, white, or gray mineral of potassium nitrate, used to make gunpowder.
nit-pick (nĭt′pĭk′) *v. Informal.* To be concerned with or critical of trivial details.
ni·trate (nī′trāt′) *n.* **1.** A salt or ester of nitric acid. **2.** Fertilizer containing a salt of nitric acid. —*v.* **-trat·ed, -trat·ing.** To treat or combine with nitrate or nitric acid. —**ni·tra′tion** *n.*
ni·tre (nī′tər) *n. esp. Brit. var. of* NITER.
ni·tric (nī′trĭk) *adj.* Of, derived from, or containing nitrogen.
nitric acid *n.* A transparent, colorless, corrosive liquid used esp. to manufacture fertilizers and explosives.
ni·tri·fy (nī′trə-fī′) *vt.* **-fied, -fy·ing, -fies. 1.** To oxidize into nitric acid, nitrous acid, or any nitrate or nitrite, as by the action of soil bacteria. **2.** To treat or combine with nitrogen or nitrogen-containing compounds. —**ni′tri·fi·ca′tion** *n.* —**ni′tri·fi′er** *n.*
ni·trite (nī′trīt′) *n.* A salt or ester of nitrous acid.
ni·tro·cel·lu·lose (nī′trō-sĕl′yə-lōs′) *n.* A

pulpy substance formed by nitrating cellulose, used in plastics and explosives.

ni•tro•gen (nī'trə-jən) *n. Symbol* **N** A nonmetallic element occurring as a colorless, odorless, almost inert gas. **—ni•trog'e•nous** (nī-trŏj'ə-nəs) *adj.* **—ni'trous** *adj.*

ni•tro•glyc•er•in *also* **ni•tro•glyc•er•ine** (nī'trō-glĭs'ər-ĭn) *n.* A viscid, light yellow, highly volatile liquid used to make explosives and as a vasodilator.

nitrous acid *n.* An unstable inorganic acid existing only in solution.

nitrous oxide *n.* A colorless, sweet-smelling gas used as an anesthetic.

nit•ty-grit•ty (nĭt'ē-grĭt'ē, nĭt'ē-grĭt'ē) *n. Slang.* The fundamental facts.

nit•wit (nĭt'wĭt') *n. Informal.* A fool.

nix (nĭks) *Slang.* —*n.* Nothing. —*adv.* No. —*v.* To reject **:** deny.

no[1] (nō) *adv.* **1.** Not so. —Used to express denial, rejection, or disagreement. **2.** Not at all. —Used with a comparative form <*no* worse><*no* less> **3.** Not <like it or *no*> —*n., pl.* **noes.** A denial or rejection.

no[2] (nō) *adj.* **1.** Not one **:** not any. **2.** Not close to being **:** not at all.

No *symbol for* NOBELIUM.

no•bel•i•um (nō-bĕl'ē-əm, -bē'lē-) *n. Symbol* **No** A radioactive element produced synthetically in minute quantities.

Nobel Prize *n.* Any of the awards made annually by the Nobel Foundation for distinguished achievement in physics, chemistry, medicine or physiology, literature, economics, and the promotion of peace. **—No•bel'ist** *n.*

no•bil•i•ty (nō-bĭl'ĭ-tē) *n., pl.* **-ties. 1.** A social class set apart by high birth or rank. **2.** Noble status or rank. **3.** The quality or state of being noble.

no•ble (nō'bəl) *adj.* **-bler, -blest. 1.** Of or pertaining to the nobility. **2.** Morally good **:** virtuous. **3. a.** Superior in nature or character **:** exalted. **b.** Grand and stately <a *noble* vista> —*n.* A person of noble birth or rank. **—no'ble•ness** *n.* **—no'bly** *adv.*

no•ble•man (nō'bəl-mən) *n.* A man of noble birth or rank.

no•blesse o•blige (nō-blĕs' ō-blēzh') *n.* Honorable and charitable behavior regarded as the responsibility of persons of noble birth or rank.

no•ble•wom•an (nō'bəl-wo͝om'ən) *n.* A woman of noble birth or rank.

no•bod•y (nō'bŏd'ē, -bə-dē) *pron.* No person **:** not anyone. —*n., pl.* **-ies.** One of no significance or influence.

noc•tur•nal (nŏk-tûr'nəl) *adj.* **1.** Of, pertaining to, or happening during the night. **2.** Active at night. **—noc•tur'nal•ly** *adv.*

noc•turne (nŏk'tûrn') *n.* **1.** A painting of a night scene. **2.** A dreamy, romantic musical composition.

nod (nŏd) *v.* **nod•ded, nod•ding. 1.** To lower and raise the head rapidly, as in agreement. **2.** To convey or express by lowering and raising the head. **3.** To let the head droop forward, as in drowsiness. **4.** To be careless, as in a moment of abstraction. **5.** To droop, sway, or bend downward <flowers *nodding* in the wind> **—nod** *n.*

node (nōd) *n.* **1.** A swelling or bulge. **2.** *Bot.* The point on a stem where a leaf, bud, etc., is attached. **3.** *Physics.* A point or region of a vibrating or oscillating system where the amplitude of the vibration or oscillation is minimal. **—nod'al** *adj.*

node
Two examples of nodes:
(left) buckwheat and (right) rye grass

nod•ule (nŏj'o͞ol) *n.* **1.** A small node, as of body tissue. **2.** A small knoblike lump or outgrowth. **—nod'u•lar** *adj.*

No•ël *or* **No•el** (nō-ĕl') *n.* **1.** Christmas. **2. noël** *or* **noel.** A Christmas carol.

no-fault (nō'fôlt') *adj.* **1.** Of or designating an automobile insurance plan that compensates accident victims without establishing responsibility or blame. **2.** Of or designating a divorce that is granted without establishing blame.

nog•gin (nŏg'ĭn) *n.* **1.** A small cup or mug. **2.** An amount of liquid equal to ¼ pt. **3.** *Slang.* The head.

no-go (nŏ'gŏ') *adj. Slang.* Not in a suitable condition for functioning properly.

no-good (no'go͝od') *adj.* **1.** Having no worth, merit, or use. **2.** Despicable **:** vile. **—no'-good'** *n.*

no-hit (nō'hĭt') *adj. Baseball.* Of or being a game in which a pitcher allows the opposing team no hits or runs. **—no-hit'ter** *n.*

noise (noiz) *n.* **1.** Sound or a sound that is loud, disagreeable, or unwanted. **2.** Sound or a sound of any sort. **3.** A loud, confused clamor or commotion. **4.** *Physics.* A usu. random, persistent disturbance of a signal. **5.** *Computer Sci.* Meaningless data generated along with desired data. —*v.* **noised, nois•ing.** To spread the report or rumor of. **—noise'less** *adj.* **—noise'less•ly** *adv.*

noise•mak•er (noiz'mā'kər) *n.* One that makes noise, esp. a device for making noise at a celebration.

noi•some (noi'səm) *adj.* **1.** Disgusting **:** foul. **2.** Harmful or injurious. **—noi'some•ly** *adv.* **—noi'some•ness** *n.*

▲ ***word history:*** Neither in meaning

nor in origin does *noisome* have any connection with the word *noise;* the similarities are purely coincidental. *Noisome* is a compound formed in Middle English from *noy,* an obsolete word meaning "harm" or "annoyance," and the suffix *-some,* which is still current in Modern English where it is used to form adjectives with the gen. sense of "characterized by some quality."

nois•y (noi'zē) *adj.* **-i•er, -i•est. 1.** Producing noise. **2.** Marked by or full of noise. **—nois'i•ly** *adv.* **—nois'i•ness** *n.*

nol•le pros•e•qui (nŏl'ē prŏs'ĭ-kwī') *n. Law.* A declaration that the plaintiff in a civil case or the prosecutor in a criminal case will drop prosecution of all or part of a suit or indictment.

no•lo con•ten•de•re (nō'lō kən-tĕn'də-rē) *n. Law.* A plea in a criminal prosecution that subjects the defendant to conviction and punishment but allows denial of allegations in other proceedings.

no•mad (nō'măd') *n.* **1.** A member of a group of people who move about from place to place seeking food, water, and grazing land. **2.** A wanderer.

no•mad•ic (nō-măd'ĭk) *adj.* Wandering from place to place. ★ ***syns:*** ITINERANT, PERIPATETIC, ROAMING, ROVING, VAGABOND, VAGRANT **—no•mad'i•cal•ly** *adv.*

no man's land *n.* **1.** An unowned or unclaimed piece of property. **2.** Disputed land, esp. the territory between two entrenched armies. **3.** An ambiguous area or circumstance.

nom de guerre (nŏm' də gâr') *n.* A pseudonym.

nom de plume (nŏm' də plo͞om') *n.* A pen name.

no•men•cla•ture (nō'mən-klā'chər, nō-mĕn'klə-) *n.* An ordered set of names used in a particular art or science.

nom•i•nal (nŏm'ə-nəl) *adj.* **1.** Of, relating to, or like a name or names. **2.** In name but not in fact. **3.** Small **:** trifling. **4.** Of or pertaining to a noun. **—nom'i•nal•ly** *adv.*

nom•i•nate (nŏm'ə-nāt') *v.* **-nat•ed, -nat•ing. 1.** To present or select as a candidate, as for elective office. **2.** To designate or appoint to a position, honor, etc. **—nom'i•na'tion** *n.* **—nom'i•na'tor** *n.*

nom•i•na•tive (nŏm'ə-nə-tĭv) *adj.* Of or belonging to a grammatical case that usu. designates the subject of a verb. *—n.* The nominative case.

nom•i•nee (nŏm'ə-nē') *n.* One who has been nominated for an office, position, etc.

non– *pref.* Not <*non*combatant>

non•age (nŏn'ĭj, nō'nĭj) *n.* **1.** Legal minority. **2.** A time of youth or immaturity.

non•a•ge•nar•i•an (nŏn'ə-jə-nâr'ē-ən, nō'nə-) *n.* A person between 90 and 100 years old. **—non'a•ge•nar'i•an** *adj.*

non•a•ligned (nŏn'ə-līnd') *adj.* Not in alliance with any power bloc **:** neutral. **—non'a•lign'ment** *n.*

nonce (nŏns) *n.* The present time or occasion <Let's ignore that for the *nonce.*>

nonce word *n.* A word invented, occurring, or used only for a particular occasion.

non•cha•lant (nŏn'shə-länt') *adj.* Casually unconcerned. **—non'cha•lance'** *n.* **—non'cha•lant'ly** *adv.*

non•com (nŏn'kŏm') *n. Informal.* A noncommissioned officer.

non•com•bat•ant (nŏn'kəm-băt'nt, nŏn-kŏm'bə-tənt) *n.* **1.** A person serving in the armed forces whose duties do not include combat. **2.** A civilian in wartime, esp. one in a war zone.

non•com•mis•sioned officer (nŏn'kə-mĭsh'ənd) *n.* An enlisted member of the armed forces, as a sergeant, having a rank that confers leadership over others.

non•com•mit•tal (nŏn'kə-mĭt'l) *adj.* Not showing what one thinks or prefers.

non com•pos men•tis (nŏn kŏm'pəs mĕn'tĭs) *adj. Law.* Not of sound mind and hence not legally responsible.

non•con•duc•tor (nŏn'kən-dŭk'tər) *n.* Something that conducts little or no electricity, heat, sound, etc.

non•con•form•ist (nŏn'kən-fôr'mĭst) *n.* One who does not feel compelled to follow or accept traditional beliefs, customs, or practices. **—non'con•form'i•ty** *n.*

non•cred•it (nŏn-krĕd'ĭt) *adj.* Of or being an academic course that does not offer credit toward a degree.

non•dair•y (nŏn-dâr'ē) *adj.* Not made with dairy products.

non•de•script (nŏn'dĭ-skrĭpt') *adj.* Difficult to describe **:** undistinctive. **—non'de•script'** *n.*

non•dis•crim•i•na•tion (nŏn'dĭ-skrĭm'ə-nā'shən) *n.* The policy or practice of refraining from discrimination. **—non'dis•crim'i•na•to'ry** *adj.*

none (nŭn) *pron.* **1.** Not one. **2.** Not any. **3.** No part <*none* of our concern> *—adv.* Not at all <The professor was *none* too pleased with my answer.>

non•en•ti•ty (nŏn-ĕn'tĭ-tē) *n., pl.* **-ties. 1.** Something that does not exist in fact. **2.** One of little or no significance.

none•such (nŭn'sŭch') *n.* One having no equal. **—none'such'** *adj.*

none•the•less (nŭn'*th*ə-lĕs') *adv.* However **:** nevertheless.

non•e•vent (nŏn'ĭ-vĕnt') *n. Slang.* An event that does not take place or fails to meet one's expectations.

non•ex•ist•ent (nŏn'ĭg-zĭs'tənt) *adj.* Not existing **:** absent or lacking.

non•fat (nŏn'făt') *adj.* Lacking fat solids or having fat solids removed.

non•fea•sance (nŏn-fē'zəns) *n. Law.* Failure to perform an official duty or legal requirement.

non•fic•tion (nŏn-fĭk'shən) *n.* Writing based on fact rather than fiction.

non•flam•ma•ble (nŏm-flăm'ə-bəl) *adj.* Not flammable, esp. not readily ignited.

non·he·ro (nŏn-hîr′ō) *n.* An antihero.
no·nil·lion (nō-nĭl′yən) *n.* **1.** The cardinal number equal to 10^{30}. **2.** *esp. Brit.* The cardinal number equal to 10^{54}. **—no·nil′lion** *adj.* **—no·nil′lionth** *n.* & *adj.* & *adv.*
non·in·ter·ven·tion (nŏn′ĭn-tər-vĕn′shən) *n.* Failure to intervene, esp. an official policy of refusing to interfere in another nation's affairs. **—non′in·ter·ven′tion·ist** *n.*
non·met·al (nŏn-mĕt′l) *n.* A chemical element, as nitrogen or oxygen, lacking the characteristic properties of a metal. **—non′me·tal′lic** (nŏn′mə-tăl′ĭk) *adj.*
no-no (nō′nō′) *n. Informal.* Something unacceptable or not permissible.
non·ob·jec·tive (nŏn′əb-jĕk′tĭv) *adj.* Designating a style of graphic art in which objects are not depicted realistically.
no-non·sense (nō-nŏn′sĕns′, -səns) *adj.* Practical : serious.
non·pa·reil (nŏn′pə-rĕl′) *adj.* Without equal : matchless. *—n.* **1.** One having no equal. **2.** A small, usu. flat piece of chocolate covered with white sugar pellets.
non·par·ti·san (nŏn-pär′tĭ-zən) *adj.* Not influenced by or associated with one political party.
non·per·son (nŏn-pûr′sən) *n.* **1.** One whose existence is expunged from public attention, esp. for reasons of ideological deviation. **2.** One who has no legal or social standing.
non·plus (nŏn-plŭs′) *v.* **-plused, -plus·ing** *also* **-plussed, -plus·sing.** To confuse or perplex.
non·prof·it (nŏn-prŏf′ĭt) *adj.* Not intended to yield a profit.
non·pro·lif·er·a·tion (nŏn′prə-lĭf′ə-rā′shən) *adj.* Relating to or advocating the end of proliferation of nuclear weapons.
non·rep·re·sen·ta·tion·al (nŏn-rĕp′rĭ-zən-tā′shə-nəl) *adj.* Nonobjective.
non·res·i·dent (nŏn-rĕz′ĭ-dənt) *adj.* Not residing in a particlar place <a *nonresident* student> **—non·res′i·dent** *n.*
non·re·sis·tance (nŏn′rĭ-zĭs′təns) *n.* Complete obedience to authority even if arbitrary or unjust. **—non′re·sis′tant** *adj.*
non·re·stric·tive (nŏn′rĭ-strĭk′tĭv) *adj.* Indicating a word, clause, or phrase that is descriptive but not required by the meaning of the element it modifies.
non·rig·id (nŏn-rĭj′ĭd) *adj.* **1.** Not stiff or rigid. **2.** Designating a lighter-than-air aircraft that holds its shape by gas pressure.
non·sched·uled (nŏn-skĕj′o͞old) *adj.* Operating without a regular schedule of passenger or cargo flights.
non·sec·tar·i·an (nŏn′sĕk-târ′ē-ən) *adj.* Not restricted to a specific religion.
non·sense (nŏn′sĕns′, -səns) *n.* **1.** Foolish or senseless behavior or language. **2.** Something that is unimportant or of little use. **—non·sen′si·cal** *adj.*
non se·qui·tur (nŏn sĕk′wĭ-tər, -to͝or′) *n.* A statement that does not follow as the logical result of what came before it.
non·self (nŏn-sĕlf′) *n.* That which the immune system identifies as foreign to the body.
non·sex·ist (nŏn-sĕk′sĭst) *adj.* Not discriminating against individuals, esp. women, on the basis of gender.
non·skid (nŏn′skĭd′) *adj.* Designed to inhibit or prevent skidding.
non·stan·dard (nŏn-stăn′dərd) *adj.* Designating a word or usage that is usu. avoided by educated speakers and writers.
non·stick (nŏn′stĭk′) *adj.* Facilitating removal of adhered particles, as of food.
non·stop (nŏn′stŏp′) *adj.* **1.** Making no stops. **2.** Unceasing. **—non′stop′** *adv.*
non·sup·port (nŏn′sə-pôrt′, -pōrt′) *n. Law.* Failure to provide for the maintenance of one's dependents.
non·un·ion (nŏn-yo͞on′yən) *adj.* **1.** Not made by or belonging to a labor union. **2.** Not acknowledging a labor union.
non·ver·bal (nŏn-vûr′bəl) *adj.* **1.** Being other than verbal <*nonverbal* expression> **2.** Involving little use of language <a *nonverbal* aptitude test>
non·vi·o·lence (nŏn-vī′ə-ləns) *n.* The principle, policy, or practice of using only peaceful means to gain esp. political objectives. **—non·vi′o·lent** *adj.*
noo·dle[1] (no͞od′l) *n. Slang.* The head.
noo·dle[2] (no͞od′l) *n.* A narrow, flat strip of dried dough, usu. made with eggs.
nook (no͝ok) *n.* **1.** A corner, alcove, or recess, esp. as part of a larger room. **2.** A cozy or secluded place.
noon (no͞on) *n.* The middle of the day : 12 o'clock in the daytime. **—noon** *adj.*
noon·day (no͞on′dā′) *n.* Noon.
no one *pron.* No person : nobody.
noon·time (no͞on′tīm′) *n.* Noon.
noose (no͞os) *n.* A loop of rope secured by a slipknot so that it decreases in size as the rope is pulled.
no-par (nō′pär′) *adj.* Having no face value, as a stock.
nope (nōp) *adv. Slang.* No.
nor (nôr; nər *when unstressed*) *conj.* And not : or not : not either <We have neither time *nor* money for the project.>
Nor·dic (nôr′dĭk) *adj.* **1.** Scandinavian. **2.** Of a human physical type exemplified by the light-skinned, blond-haired peoples of Scandinavia. **—Nor′dic** *n.*
norm (nôrm) *n.* A model or pattern considered typical for a particular group.
nor·mal (nôr′məl) *adj.* **1.** Usual or ordinary : typical. **2. a.** Characterized by average growth or intelligence. **b.** Healthy in mind and body. *—n.* **1.** One that is normal : standard. **2.** The expected or usual condition or amount. **—nor·mal′i·ty, nor′mal·cy** *n.* **—nor′mal·ly** *adv.*
nor·mal·ize (nôr′mə-līz′) *v.* **-ized, -iz·ing.** To make or return to normal. **—nor′mal·i·za′tion** *n.* **—nor′mal·iz′er** *n.*
normal school *n.* A school for training esp. elementary-level teachers.
Nor·man (nôr′mən) *n.* **1.** A member of a

Scandinavian people who conquered Normandy in the 10th cent. **2.** A member of a people of Norman and French blood who invaded England in 1066. **3.** A native or resident of Normandy. —**Nor'man** *adj.*

nor·ma·tive (nôr'mə-tĭv) *adj.* Pertaining to or imposing a norm or standard. —**nor'ma·tive·ly** *adv.* —**nor'ma·tive·ness** *n.*

Norse (nôrs) *n., pl.* **Norse. 1.** The people of Scandinavia. **2.** The people of W Scandinavia, esp. the Norwegians. —**Norse** *adj.*

Norse·man (nôrs'mən) *n.* A member of an ancient Scandinavian people.

north (nôrth) *n.* **1. a.** The direction 90° counterclockwise from east. **b.** The point on the compass located at 0°. **2.** An area or region to the north of a given point. **3. North.** The N part of the U.S., esp. the states that fought for the Union during the Civil War. —*adj.* To, toward, of, from, facing, or in the north. —*adv.* In, from, or toward the north. —**north'er·ly** *adj. & adv.* —**north'ern** *adj.* —**north'ern·er** *n.* —**north'ern·most'** *adj.* —**north'ward** *adj. & adv.* —**north'wards** *adv.*

north·east (nôrth-ēst') *n.* **1.** The direction 45° counterclockwise from east and 45° clockwise from north. **2.** An area or region to the northeast of a given point. **3. Northeast.** Area of the NE U.S. including New England, N.Y., and sometimes Pa. and N.J. —**north·east'** *adj. & adv.* —**north·east'er·ly** *adj. & adv.* —**north·east'ern** *adj.* —**north·east'ward** *adj. & adv.* —**north·east'wards** *adv.*

North Pole *n.* The northernmost point of the earth.

North Star *n.* Polaris.

north·west (nôrth-wĕst') *n.* **1.** The direction 45° counterclockwise from north and 45° clockwise from west. **2.** An area or region to the northwest of a given point. —**north·west** *adj. & adv.* —**north·west'er·ly** *adj. & adv.* —**north·west'ern** *adj.* —**north·west'ward** *adj. & adv.* —**north·west'wards** *adv.*

nose (nōz) *n.* **1.** The section of the face or forward part of the head containing the nostrils and olfactory organs and forming the opening of the respiratory tract. **2.** The sense of smell. **3.** A capacity for discovering or detecting by or as if by smell. **4.** The forward end of a pointed structure, as an airplane, rocket, submarine, etc. —*v.* **nosed, nos·ing. 1.** To discover by or as if by smell. **2.** To touch or examine with the nose **:** nuzzle. **3.** To move forward or cause to move forward cautiously. **4.** *Informal.* To pry curiously **:** snoop.

nose·bleed (nōz'blēd') *n.* A nasal hemorrhage.

nose cone *n.* The protective forwardmost section of a rocket or missile.

nose dive *n.* **1.** A sudden, steep plunge made by an aircraft. **2.** A swift drop or fall. —**nose'-dive'** *v.*

nose·gay (nōz'gā') *n.* A small bouquet of flowers.

nos·ey (nō'zē) *adj. var. of* NOSY.

nosh (nŏsh) *n.* A snack. —**nosh** *v.*

no-show (nō'shō') *n. Slang.* A traveler who reserves space, as on an airplane, but neither claims nor cancels the reservation.

nos·tal·gia (nŏ-stăl'jə, nə-) *n.* A bittersweet yearning for things of the past. —**nos·tal'gic** *adj.*

nos·tril (nŏs'trəl) *n.* Either of the outer openings of the nose.

nos·trum (nŏs'trəm) *n.* **1.** A medicine with doubtful, usu. secret ingredients. **2.** A panacea for problems or evils.

nos·y *also* **nos·ey** (nō'zē) *adj.* **-i·er, -i·est.** *Informal.* Inquisitive **:** snoopy.

not (nŏt) *adv.* To no degree **:** in no manner or way. —Used to express negation, refusal, or denial.

†**no·ta·ble** (nō'tə-bəl) *adj.* **1. a.** Deserving notice **:** remarkable. **b.** Prominent **:** distinguished. **2.** (*also* nŏt'ə-bəl). *Archaic & Regional.* Diligent and efficient, esp. in household duties. —*n.* A well-known or distinguished person. —**no'ta·bil'i·ty** *n.* —**no'ta·bly** *adv.*

no·ta·rize (nō'tə-rīz') *v.* **-rized, -riz·ing.** To attest to and certify as a notary public. —**no'ta·ri·za'tion** *n.*

no·ta·ry (nō'tə-rē) *n., pl.* **-ries.** A notary public. —**no·tar'i·al** (nō-târ'ē-əl) *adj.*

notary public *n., pl.* **notaries public.** One legally authorized to witness signatures, certify documents, etc.

no·ta·tion (nō-tā'shən) *n.* **1. a.** A system of figures or symbols used in a specialized field to represent numbers, quantities, tones, or values. **b.** The use of such a system. **2.** A brief record **:** annotation.

notch (nŏch) *n.* **1.** A V-shaped cut. **2.** A steep-sided gap between mountains. **3.** *Informal.* A step or degree <a *notch* better> —*v.* **1.** To cut a notch in. **2.** To keep track of by or as if by making notches.

note (nōt) *n.* **1.** A brief record written down to aid the memory. **2.** A short, informal message or letter. **3.** A formal official or diplomatic communication. **4.** A comment or explanation, as on a passage in a text. **5. a.** A piece of paper money. **b.** A promissory note. **6.** *Mus.* **a.** A tone of designated pitch. **b.** The symbol for such a tone. **7.** A characteristic call or cry, as of a bird. **8.** A sign or hint of a certain quality <ended the petition on a *note* of despair> **9.** Consequence **:** distinction. **10.** Observation **:** heed. —*v.* **not·ed, not·ing. 1.** To perceive **:** notice. **2.** To write down. **3.** To make mention of **:** point out.

note·book (nōt'bo͝ok') *n.* A book with blank pages for writing in.

not·ed (nō'tĭd) *adj.* Famous **:** eminent.

note·wor·thy (nōt'wûr'*th*ē) *adj.* Significant **:** notable. —**note'wor'thi·ness** *n.*

noth·ing (nŭth'ĭng) *n.* **1.** Not anything <knows *nothing* about golf> **2.** No portion or part <*Nothing* is left of the cake.> **3.** One of no consequence or interest <The outcome is *nothing* to me.> **4.** Absence of anything perceptible <The music died away into *nothing.*> —*n.* **1.** One having no existence. **2.** One having no quantitative value : zero. **3. a.** Something trivial : trifle. **b.** An inconsequential person : nonentity. —*adv.* In no way or degree.

noth·ing·ness (nŭth′ĭng-nĭs) *n.* **1.** The quality or state of being nothing. **2.** Unoccupied space : emptiness. **3.** Lack of consequence : insignificance.

no·tice (nō′tĭs) *n.* **1.** Perception : observation. **2.** Consideration or polite respect. **3.** A published announcement. **4.** An announcement of purpose, esp. of one's intention to leave a job. **5.** A review, as of a play or book. —*v.* **-ticed, -tic·ing. 1.** To become aware of : perceive. **2.** To mention.

no·tice·a·ble (nō′tĭ-sə-bəl) *adj.* **1.** Easily attracting notice. **2.** Worthy of attention : significant. ★ ***syns:*** ARRESTING, CONSPICUOUS, MARKED, OBSERVABLE, OUTSTANDING, POINTED, PROMINENT, REMARKABLE, SALIENT, SIGNAL, STRIKING —**no′tice·a·bly** *adv.*

no·ti·fy (nō′tə-fī′) *v.* **-fied, -fy·ing.** To announce to : give notice to. —**no′ti·fi·ca′tion** *n.* —**no′ti·fi′er** *n.*

no·tion (nō′shən) *n.* **1.** An opinion or belief. **2.** A mental representation : idea. **3.** A whim or fancy <took a *notion* to go fishing> **4. notions.** Small useful articles, as buttons, needles, thread, etc. —**no′tion·al** *adj.*

no·to·ri·ous (nō-tôr′ē-əs, -tōr′-) *adj.* Having a usu. bad reputation : infamous. —**no′to·ri′e·ty** (-tə-rī′ĭ-tē) *n.*

no-trump (nō′trŭmp′) *n.* A declaration to play a hand without a trump suit in card games such as bridge. —**no′-trump′** *adj.*

not·with·stand·ing (nŏt′wĭth-stăn′dĭng, -wĭth-) *prep.* In spite of. —*adv.* All the same : nevertheless. —*conj.* Although.

nou·gat (no͞o′gət) *n.* A confection made of a sugar or honey paste mixed with nuts.

nought (nôt) *n. var. of* NAUGHT.

noun (noun) *n.* A word that names a person, place, or thing.

nour·ish (nûr′ĭsh, nŭr′-) *v.* **1.** To provide with the food or other substances needed for life : feed. **2.** To promote the growth or development of. **3.** To keep alive : sustain. —**nour′ish·ing** *adj.* —**nour′ish·ment** *n.*

nou·veau riche (no͞o′vō rēsh′) *n., pl.* **nou·veaux riches** (no͞o′vō rēsh′). A newly rich person.

nou·velle cuisine (no͞o-vĕl) *n.* Cooking that emphasizes the natural flavors of foods and the use of light sauces.

no·va (nō′və) *n., pl.* **-vae** (-vē) *or* **-vas.** A variable star that suddenly becomes very bright and then gradually dims over a period of time.

nov·el[1] (nŏv′əl) *n.* A book-length work of fiction. —**nov′el·ist** *n.* —**nov′el·is′tic** *adj.*

nov·el[2] (nŏv′əl) *adj.* Notably new, different, or unusual. —**nov′el·ly** *adv.*

nov·el·ette (nŏv′ə-lĕt′) *n.* A brief novel.

nov·el·ize (nŏv′ə-līz′) *v.* **-ized, -iz·ing.** To convert into a novelistic format. —**nov′el·i·za′tion** *n.*

no·vel·la (nō-vĕl′ə) *n., pl.* **-las** *or* **-vel·le** (-vĕl′ē). A novelette.

nov·el·ty (nŏv′əl-tē) *n., pl.* **-ties. 1.** The quality of being novel : newness. **2.** Something new or unusual. **3. novelties.** Small inexpensively produced items, as souvenirs or toys.

No·vem·ber (nō-vĕm′bər) *n.* The 11th month of the year, having 30 days.

no·ve·na (nō-vē′nə) *n., pl.* **-nas** *or* **-nae** (-nē). *Rom. Cath. Ch.* A devotion made on 9 consecutive days.

nov·ice (nŏv′ĭs) *n.* **1.** One new to a field or activity : beginner. **2.** One who has joined a religious order but has not yet taken the final vows.

no·vi·ti·ate (nō-vĭsh′ē-ĭt, -āt′) *n.* **1.** The period of training served by a religious novice. **2.** A place where novices train and live. **3.** NOVICE 2.

No·vo·cain (no′və-kān′). A trademark for the anesthetic procaine hydrochloride.

now (nou) *adv.* **1.** At the present time. **2.** At once : immediately. **3.** In the immediate past : recently. **4.** In the immediate future : soon. **5.** At this stage in the sequence of events : then. **6.** In these circumstances. **7.** —Used esp. to express reproof, issue a command, or make a request <*Now* hear this.> —*conj.* Seeing that : since. —*n.* The present. —*adj.* **1.** *Informal.* Of or pertaining to the present time. **2.** *Slang.* Trendy <the *now* look in sportswear>

now·a·days (nou′ə-dāz′) *adv.* In the present time.

no·way (nō′wā′) *also* **no·ways** (-wāz′) *adv.* Nowise.

no·where (nō′hwâr′, -wâr′) *adv.* Not anywhere. —*n.* A faraway or unknown place.

no-win (nō′wĭn′) *adj.* Incapable of affording victory or success.

no·wise (nō′wīz′) *adv.* In no way.

nox·ious (nŏk′shəs) *adj.* Harmful to health or morals.

noz·zle (nŏz′əl) *n.* A projecting spout, as at the end of a hose, through which something is discharged.

Np *symbol for* NEPTUNIUM.

nth (ĕnth) *adj.* **1.** Pertaining to an unspecified or indefinitely large whole number. **2.** Greatest : highest <to the *nth* degree>

nu·ance (no͞o-äns′, nyo͞o-, no͞o′äns′, nyo͞o′-) *n.* **1.** A slight or subtle gradation or variation. **2.** A subtle aspect or quality.

nub (nŭb) *n.* **1.** A protuberance or knob. **2.** Gist : core. —**nub′by** *adj.*

nub·bin (nŭb′ĭn) *n.* **1.** A small, imperfectly developed ear of corn. **2.** A similar small chunk or piece.

nu·bile (no͞o′bəl, -bīl′, nyo͞o′-) *adj.* Of marriageable age or condition.

nu·cle·ar (no͞o′klē-ər, nyo͞o′-) *adj.* **1.** Of, pertaining to, or forming a nucleus or nuclei. **2.** Using or derived from nuclear energy. **3.** Having or using nuclear weapons.

nuclear energy *n.* Energy released by a nuclear reaction.

nuclear family *n.* A family unit consisting of a mother and father and their children.

nuclear magnetic resonance *n.* The absorption of electromagnetic radiation of a specific frequency by an atomic nucleus placed in a strong magnetic field.

nuclear reaction *n.* A reaction that changes the structure, composition, or energy of an atomic nucleus.

nuclear reactor *n.* A device in which a nuclear chain reaction is initiated and controlled, thus producing heat used esp. to generate electricity.

nu•cle•ic acid (no͞o-klē′ĭk, nyo͞o-) *n.* A complex chemical compound essential to the functioning of all living cells.

nu•cle•on (no͞o′klē-ŏn′, nyo͞o′-) *n.* A proton or neutron, esp. as a component of an atomic nucleus. **—nu′cle•on′ic** *adj.*

nu•cle•on•ics (no͞o′klē-ŏn′ĭks, nyo͞o′-) *n.* *(sing. in number).* The study of the behavior of nucleons or atomic nuclei.

nu•cle•o•side (no͞o′klē-ə-sīd′, nyo͞o′-) *n.* A compound of a sugar and a purine or pyrimidine base.

nu•cle•o•tide (no͞o′klē-ə-tīd′, nyo͞o′-) *n.* Any of various organic compounds composed of a nucleoside combined with phosphoric acid.

nu•cle•us (no͞o′klē-əs, nyo͞o′-) *n., pl.* **-cle•i** (-klē-ī′) *or* **-es. 1.** A central or crucial element around which other elements are grouped. **2.** A basis for future growth or development. **3.** *Biol.* A complex, usu. spherical body within a living cell that controls the metabolism, growth, reproduction, and heredity of the cell. **4.** *Physics.* The positively charged core of an atom, made up of protons and neutrons and containing most of the mass of the atom. **—nu′cle•ate** (-ĭt) *adj.*

nu•clide (no͞o′klīd′, nyo͞o′-) *n. Physics.* An atomic nucleus characterized by its atomic number, atomic mass, and energy state. **—nu•clid′ic** (-klĭd′ĭk) *adj.*

nude (no͞od, nyo͞od) *adj.* Unclothed : naked. *—n.* **1.** The unclothed human figure or a representation of it. **2.** The state of being nude. **—nude′ness, nu′di•ty** *n.*

nudge (nuj) *v.* **nudged, nudg•ing.** To push or poke gently. **—nudge** *n.*

nud•ism (no͞o′dĭz′əm, nyo͞o′-) *n.* The practice of going nude, esp. for reasons of health. **—nud′ist** *n.*

nue•vo sol (no͞o-ā′vō sōl, nwĕ′vô) *n., pl.* **nuevo so•les** (sō′lās). —See table at CURRENCY.

nu•ga•to•ry (no͞o′gə-tôr′ē, -tōr′ē, nyo͞o′-) *adj.* **1.** Unimportant : trifling. **2.** Lacking force : invalid.

nug•get (nŭg′ĭt) *n.* A lump, as of gold.

nui•sance (no͞o′səns, nyo͞o′-) *n.* A source of inconvenience or vexation.

nuke (no͞ok, nyo͞ok) *Slang. —n.* **1.** A nuclear weapon. **2.** A nuclear-powered electric generating plant. *—v.* **nuked, nuk•ing.** To attack with nuclear weapons.

null (nŭl) *adj.* **1.** Devoid of legal or binding force : invalid. **2.** Having no consequence or value : insignificant. **3.** Amounting to nothing. *—n.* Nothing : zero. **—nul′li•ty** *n.*

null and void *adj.* NULL 1.

nul•li•fy (nŭl′ə-fī′) *v.* **-fied, -fy•ing. 1.** To deprive of legal force : annul. **2.** To counteract or negate. **—nul′li•fi•ca′tion** *n.*

numb (nŭm) *adj.* **1.** Lacking the power to feel or move normally. **2.** Stunned or paralyzed, as from shock or strong emotion. **—numb** *v.* **—numb′ness** *n.*

num•ber (nŭm′bər) *n.* **1.** Any of the set of positive integers. **2. numbers.** Arithmetic. **3.** A numeral or series of numerals for reference or identification. **4. a.** A total : sum. **b.** An indeterminate sum. **5.** Quantity of units or individuals. **6.** A multitude. **7.** An item in a group or series. **8.** *Gram.* The indication of the singularity or plurality of a linguistic form. **9. Numbers** *(sing. in number).* —See table at BIBLE. **10. numbers.** The numbers game. *—v.* **1.** To total in number or amount : add up to. **2.** To count or name one by one. **3.** To include in or belong to a group or category. **4.** To assign a number to. **5.** To restrict in number.

num•ber•less (nŭm′bər-lĭs) *adj.* Too many to be counted.

numbers game *n.* A lottery in which bets are made on an unpredictable number, as a daily stock-exchange figure.

nu•mer•a•ble (no͞o′mər-ə-bəl, nyo͞o′-) *adj.* Countable.

nu•mer•al (no͞o′mər-əl, nyo͞o′-) *n.* A symbol or mark representing a number.

nu•mer•ate (no͞o′mə-rāt′, nyo͞o′-) *v.* **-at•ed, -at•ing.** To enumerate : count. **—nu′mer•a′tion** *n.*

nu•mer•a•tor (no͞o′mə-rā′tər, nyo͞o′-) *n.* The expression above the line in a common fraction.

nu•mer•i•cal (no͞o-mĕr′ĭ-kəl, nyo͞o-) *also* **nu•mer•ic** (-ĭk) *adj.* Of, pertaining to, denoting, or expressed as a number or numbers. **—nu•mer′i•cal•ly** *adv.*

nu•mer•ol•o•gy (no͞o′mə-rŏl′ə-jē, nyo͞o′-) *n.* The occult study of numbers and their supposed influence on human beings. **—nu′mer•ol′o•gist** *n.*

nu•mer•ous (no͞o′mər-əs, nyo͞o′-) *adj.* Made up of many individuals or things. **—nu′mer•ous•ly** *adv.*

nu•mis•mat•ics (no͞o′mĭz-măt′ĭks, -mĭs-, nyo͞o′-) *n. (sing. in number).* The study or collection of coins, currency, and often medals. **—nu•mis′ma•tist** *n.*

num•skull *also* **numb•skull** (nŭm′skŭl′) *n.* A stupid person : dolt.

nun (nŭn) *n.* A woman member of a religious order.

nun•ci•o (nŭn′sē-ō′, no͝on′-) *n., pl.* **-os.** A high-ranking representative of the pope.

nup•tial (nŭp′shəl, -chəl) *adj.* Of or pertaining to marriage or the wedding ceremony. *—n. often* **nuptials.** A wedding.

nurse (nûrs) *n.* **1.** One specially trained to care for sick or disabled persons. **2.** One hired to care for a child. *—v.* **nursed, nurs•ing. 1.** To feed at the breast : suckle. **2.** To act as a nurse (for). **3.** To try to cure or treat <*nurse* a bad cold> **4.** To keep alive or healthy by constant attention or care **:** foster. **5.** To keep in the mind **:** harbor. **6.** To treat carefully **:** favor <*nursed* a sore foot> **7.** To consume slowly.

nurse•maid (nûrs′măd′) *n.* NURSE 2.

nurs•er•y (nûr′sə-rē, nûrs′rē) *n., pl.* **-ies. 1.** A room or area reserved for babies or children. **2. a.** A nursery school. **b.** A place where children are cared for temporarily. **3.** A place where plants are raised for sale, experimentation, etc.

nursery rhyme *n.* A short poem for children.

nursery school *n.* A school for children who are not old enough for kindergarten.

nurse's aide *n.* One who assists trained nurses, as by giving general patient care.

nursing home *n.* A private hospital for the care of the aged or chronically ill.

nurs•ling (nûrs′lĭng) *n.* **1.** An infant or young animal that is being suckled. **2.** One that is carefully tended.

nur•ture (nûr′chər) *n.* **1.** Sustenance **:** food. **2.** Upbringing **:** training. —*v.* **-tured, -tur•ing. 1.** To feed **:** nourish. **2.** To train or educate. **3.** To help grow or develop **:** cultivate. **—nur′tur•er** *n.*

nut (nŭt) *n.* **1. a.** A hard-shelled fruit or seed with an inner kernel. **b.** The often edible kernel of such fruits or seeds. **2.** *Slang.* **a.** An eccentric person. **b.** A fan or enthusiast. **3.** A ridge of wood at the end of the fingerboard or neck of stringed instruments over which the strings pass. **4.** A small block of metal or wood with a central, threaded hole designed to fit around and secure a bolt or screw.

nut•crack•er (nŭt′krăk′ər) *n.* A hinged implement for cracking nuts.

nut•hatch (nŭt′hăch′) *n.* A small bird of the family Sittidae, with a long, sharp bill.

nut•meat (nŭt′mēt′) *n.* The edible kernel of a nut.

nut•meg (nŭt′mĕg′) *n.* The hard, aromatic seed of a tropical evergreen tree, *Myristica fragrans,* used as a spice.

nu•tri•a (nōō′trē-ə, nyōō′-) *n.* The coypu or its thick, light-brown fur.

nu•tri•ent (nōō′trē-ənt, nyōō′-) *n.* Something that nourishes. **—nu′tri•ent** *adj.*

nu•tri•ment (nōō′trə-mənt, nyōō′-) *n.* Nourishment **:** food.

nu•tri•tion (nōō-trĭsh′ən, nyōō-) *n.* The process of nourishing or being nourished, esp. the process by which a living thing ingests and uses food. **—nu•tri′tion•al** *adj.* **—nu•tri′tion•al•ly** *adv.* **—nu•tri′tion•ist** *n.* **—nu′-tri•tive** (-trĭ-tĭv) *adj.*

nu•tri•tious (nōō-trĭsh′əs, nyōō-) *adj.* Giving nourishment. ★ ***syns:*** NOURISHING, NUTRIENT, NUTRITIVE **—nu•tri′tious•ly** *adv.* **—nu•tri′tious•ness** *n.*

nuts (nŭts) *Slang.* —*adj.* **1.** Crazy. **2.** Enthusiastic. —*interj.* —Used to express refusal, disappointment, or contempt.

nut•shell (nŭt′shĕl′) *n.* The shell enclosing the meat of a nut. **—in a nutshell.** In a few words **:** concisely.

nut•ty (nŭt′ē) *adj.* **-ti•er, -ti•est. 1.** Containing nuts or having a nutlike flavor. **2.** *Informal.* Eccentric **:** crazy. **—nut′ti•ly** *adv.* **—nut′ti•ness** *n.*

nux vom•i•ca (nŭks vŏm′ĭ-kə) *n.* A tree native to SE Asia, *Strychnos nux-vomica,* bearing poisonous seeds that are the source of strychnine.

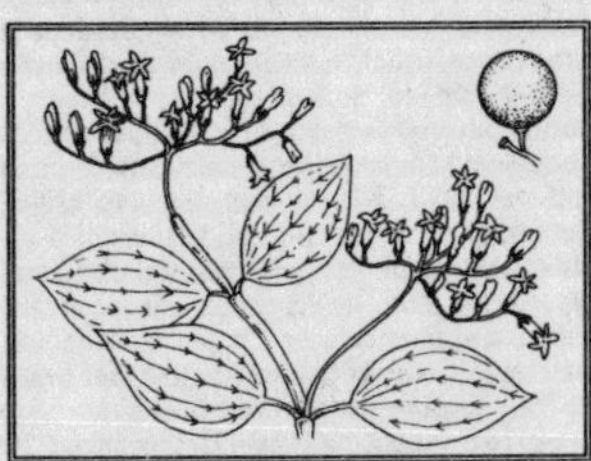

nux vomica

nuz•zle (nŭz′əl) *v.* **-zled, -zling. 1.** To rub or push against gently with or as if with the nose or snout. **2.** To cuddle together.

ny•lon (nī′lŏn′) *n.* **1.** A strong, resilient synthetic material. **2.** Fabric or yarn made from nylon. **3. nylons.** Stockings made of nylon.

nymph (nĭmf) *n.* **1.** *Gk. & Rom. Myth.* A female spirit inhabiting woodlands and waters. **2.** Any of various immature insects that undergo incomplete metamorphosis.

Oo

o *or* **O** (ō) *n., pl.* **o's** *or* **O's. 1.** The 15th letter of the English alphabet. **2.** A speech sound represented by the letter *o.* **3.** Something with the shape of the letter O. **4.** A zero. **5. O.** A human blood type of the ABO group.

O[1] (ō) *interj.* **1.** —Used before a name in formal address <Have mercy, *O* Lord.> **2.** —Used as an expression of surprise or strong emotion <*O* heavens>

O[2] *symbol for* OXYGEN.

oaf (ōf) *n.* A clumsy or stupid person. **—oaf′ish** *adj.* **—oaf′ish•ly** *adv.*

oak (ōk) *n.* A tree or shrub of the genus *Quercus,* bearing acorns as fruit and having hard, durable wood. **—oak′en** *adj.*

oak leaf cluster *n.* A U.S. military decoration of silver or bronze oak leaves and acorns added to various medals to denote an additional decoration.

oa•kum (ō′kəm) *n.* Loose hemp or jute fiber, occas. treated with pitch or tar, used mainly to caulk seams in wooden ships.

oar (ôr, ōr) *n.* **1.** A long, thin, usu. wooden pole with a blade at one end, used to row or occas. to steer a boat. **2.** An oarsman.

oar•lock (ôr′lŏk′, ōr′-) *n.* An often U-shaped device used as a fulcrum to hold an oar in place while rowing.

oars•man (ôrz′mən, ōrz′-) *n.* A rower, esp. in a racing crew.

o•a•sis (ō-ā′sĭs) *n., pl.* **-ses** (-sēz′). A fertile desert area, esp. one with water.

oat (ōt) *n.* **1.** A widely cultivated cereal grass, *Avena sativa.* **2.** *often* **oats** *(sing. or pl. in number).* The seeds of the oat, used as food or fodder. **—oat′en** *adj.*

oath (ōth) *n., pl.* **oaths** (ōthz, ōths). **1.** A solemn promise or declaration, often calling upon God as witness. **2.** A blasphemous use of a sacred name. **3.** A swearword.

oat•meal (ōt′mēl′) *n.* **1.** Meal of rolled or ground oats. **2.** A porridge made from rolled or ground oats.

O•ba•di•ah (ō′bə-dī′ə) *n.* —See table at BIBLE.

ob•bli•ga•to (ŏb′lĭ-gä′tō) *Mus. adv.* Not to be left out. —Used as a direction. **—ob′bli•ga′to** *adj. & n.*

ob•du•rate (ŏb′dŏŏ-rĭt, -dyŏŏ-) *adj.* **1.** Hard-hearted. **2.** Not yielding to persuasion : obstinate. **—ob′du•ra•cy** *n.*

o•be•di•ent (ō-bē′dē-ənt) *adj.* Obeying or willing to obey, as a command. ★ ***syns:*** AMENABLE, BIDDABLE, COMPLIANT, COMPLYING, CONFORMABLE, SUBMISSIVE, TRACTABLE **—o•be′di•ence** *n.*

o•bei•sance (ō-bā′səns, ō-bē′-) *n.* **1.** A gesture or body movement, as a bow, expressing deference. **2.** Deference : homage. **—o•bei′sant** *adj.*

ob•e•lisk (ŏb′ə-lĭsk′) *n.* **1.** A 4-sided usu. stone shaft tapering to a pyramidal point. **2.** DAGGER 2.

o•bese (ō-bēs′) *adj.* Extremely fat : grossly overweight. **—o•be′si•ty** *n.*

o•bey (ō-bā′) *v.* **1.** To carry out the instructions of. **2.** To comply with (a command).

ob•fus•cate (ŏb′fə-skāt′, ŏb-fŭs′kāt′) *v.* **-cat•ed, -cat•ing.** **1.** To make dark or obscure : cloud. **2.** To confuse. **—ob′fus•ca′tion** *n.* **—ob•fus′ca•to′ry** *adj.*

ob-gyn (ō′bē-jē′wī-ĕn′) *n. Informal.* **1.** The practice or field of obstetrics and gynecology. **2.** A specialist in this field.

o•bi (ō′bē) *n.* A wide sash worn with a kimono by Japanese women as part of the traditional dress.

O•bie (ō′bē) *n.* An annual award for achievement in off-Broadway theater.

o•bit (ō′bĭt, ō-bĭt′) *n.* An obituary.

o•bi•ter dic•tum (ō′bĭ-tər dĭk′təm) *n., pl.* **obiter dic•ta** (-tə). Something said in passing : incidental observation.

o•bit•u•ar•y (ō-bĭch′ōō-ĕr′ē) *n., pl.* **-ies.** A published death notice, usu. with a short biography of the deceased.

ob•ject¹ (əb-jĕkt′) *v.* **1.** To hold or present an opposing view : dissent. **2.** To feel or express disapproval. **—ob•jec′tion** *n.* **—ob•jec′tor** *n.*

ob•ject² (ŏb′jĭkt, -jĕkt′) *n.* **1.** Something perceptible, esp. to the sense of touch or vision. **2.** *Philos.* Something intelligible by the mind. **3.** A focus of attention or effort. **4.** The purpose of a specific action. **5. a.** A noun that receives or is affected by the action of a verb. **b.** A noun following and governed by a preposition.

ob•jec•ti•fy (əb-jĕk′tə-fī′) *v.* **-fied, -fy•ing.** To make objective.

ob•jec•tion•a•ble (əb-jĕk′shə-nə-bəl) *adj.* Offensive : disagreeable. **—ob•jec′tion•a•bil′i•ty** *n.* **—ob•jec′tion•a•bly** *adv.*

ob•jec•tive (əb-jĕk′tĭv) *adj.* **1.** Of or pertaining to a material object rather than a mental concept. **2.** Having actual existence. **3.** Not influenced by emotion or personal opinion. **4.** Designating the case of a noun or pronoun that serves as the object of a verb. *—n.* **1.** Something worked toward or aspired to : goal. **2. a.** The objective case. **b.** A word in the objective case. **3.** The lens in a microscope or telescope that is closest to the object. **—ob′jec•tiv′i•ty** *n.*

ob•jet d'art (ôb′zhĕ där′) *n., pl.* **ob•jets d'art** (ôb′zhĕ där′). A small object of artistic value.

ob•jur•gate (ŏb′jər-gāt′, ŏb-jûr′gāt′) *v.* **-gat•ed, -gat•ing.** To reprove sharply : berate. **—ob′jur•ga′tion** *n.*

ob•late (ŏb′lāt′, ŏb-lāt′) *adj.* Flattened at the poles, as the earth. **—ob′late′ly** *adv.*

ob•la•tion (ə-blā′shən, ŏ-blā′-) *n.* The act or ceremony of offering something in religious worship. **—ob•la′tion•al** *adj.*

ob•li•ga•tion (ŏb′lĭ-gā′shən) *n.* **1.** The act of binding oneself by a moral, social, or legal tie. **2.** A binding responsibility, as a contract or promise. **3.** The binding power of a law, contract, promise, or sense of duty. **4.** Indebtedness to another for a favor. **—ob′li•gate′** *v.*

o•blig•a•to•ry (ə-blĭg′ə-tôr′ē, -tōr′ē, ŏb′lĭ-gə-) *adj.* **1.** Morally or legally binding. **2.** Compulsory. **—o•blig′a•to′ri•ly** *adv.*

o•blige (ə-blīj′) *v.* **o•bliged, o•blig•ing.** **1.** To constrain. **2.** To make indebted or grateful. **3.** To perform a service or favor (for). **—o•blig′er** *n.* **—o•blig′ing•ly** *adv.*

o•blique (ō-blēk′, ə-blēk′) *adj.* **1. a.** Slanting or sloping : inclined. **b.** Designating geometric lines or planes that are neither parallel nor perpendicular. **2.** Devious or evasive. **—o•blique′ness, o•bliq′ui•ty** (ō-blĭk′wĭ-tē, ə-blĭk′-) *n.*

o•blit•er•ate (ə-blĭt′ə-rāt′) *v.* **-at•ed, -at•ing.** **1.** To eliminate completely. **2.** To make indecipherable : wipe out. **—o•blit′er•a′tion** *n.* **—o•blit′er•a′tive** (-ə-rā′tĭv, -ər-ə-tĭv) *adj.* **—o•blit′er•a′tor** *n.*

o•bliv•i•on (ə-blĭv′ē-ən) *n.* **1.** The state of being utterly forgotten. **2.** An act or instance of forgetting.

o•bliv•i•ous (ə-blĭv′ē-əs) *adj.* **1.** Not mindful : forgetful. **2.** Unaware.

ob•long (ŏb′lông′, -lŏng′) *adj.* **1.** Having a dimension, esp. 1 of 2 perpendicular dimensions, as width or length, greater than the other : rectangular. **2.** *Bot.* Having an elongated form. **—ob′long′** *n.*

ob•lo•quy (ŏb′lə-kwē) *n., pl.* **-quies. 1.** Abusive and defamatory language : calumny. **2.** Damage to one's reputation.

ob•nox•ious (ŏb-nŏk′shəs, əb-) *adj.* Highly disagreeable : repugnant.

o•boe (ō′bō) *n.* A tube-shaped woodwind instrument with keys and holes and a double-reed mouthpiece. **—o′bo•ist** *n.*

ob•scene (ŏb-sēn′, əb-) *adj.* **1.** Offensive to decency. **2.** Designed to incite lustful feelings. **3.** Repulsive : loathsome. ★ ***syns:*** COARSE, CRUDE, DIRTY, FILTHY, FOUL, GROSS, INDECENT, LEWD, NASTY, PROFANE, RANK, RAUNCHY, RAW, SCATOLOGICAL, SMUTTY **—ob•scen′i•ty** (-sĕn′ĭ-tē) *n.*

ob•scure (ŏb-skyŏŏr′, əb-) *adj.* **-scur•er, -scur•est. 1.** Deficient in light : dark. **2.** Indistinct : faint. **3.** Remote. **4.** Of humble station <an *obscure* civil servant> **5.** Not easily understood. —*v.* **-scured, -scur•ing. 1.** To make dim or indistinct. **2.** To conceal by or as if by covering. **—ob•scure′ly** *adv.* **—ob•scu′ri•ty** *n.*

ob•se•qui•ous (ŏb-sē′kwē-əs, əb-) *adj.* Fawning : servile. **—ob•se′qui•ous•ly** *adv.*

ob•se•quy (ŏb′sĭ-kwē) *n., pl.* **-quies.** *often* **obsequies.** A burial or funeral rite.

ob•ser•vance (əb-zûr′vəns) *n.* **1.** The act or practice of complying with something prescribed, as a law or rule. **2.** The act or custom of celebrating a ritual occasion, as a holiday. **3.** Observation.

ob•ser•va•tion (ŏb′zər-vā′shən) *n.* **1. a.** The act of observing. **b.** The condition of being observed. **2.** The act of noting and recording something as a phenomenon. **3.** A remark : comment. **—ob′ser•va′tion•al** *adj.* **—ob′ser•va′tion•al•ly** *adv.*

ob•ser•va•to•ry (əb-zûr′və-tôr′ē, -tōr′ē) *n., pl.* **-ries.** A building designed for making observations esp. of astronomical or meteorological phenomena.

ob•serve (əb-zûrv′) *v.* **-served, -serv•ing. 1.** To notice : perceive. **2.** To pay special attention to. **3.** To make a scientific observation of. **4.** To say casually : remark. **5.** To adhere to. **6.** To celebrate (e.g., a holiday). **—ob•serv′a•ble** *adj.* **—ob•serv′a•bly** *adv.* **—ob•ser′vant** *adj.* **—ob•serv′er** *n.*

ob•ses•sion (əb-sĕsh′ən, ŏb-) *n.* **1.** A persistent preoccupation with an idea or emotion. **2.** An idea or emotion causing a compulsive preoccupation. **—ob•sess′** *v.* **—ob•ses′sion•al** *adj.* **—ob•ses′sive** *adj.*

ob•sid•i•an (ŏb-sĭd′ē-ən) *n.* A shiny, usu. black or banded glass of volcanic origin.

ob•so•lesce (ŏb′sə-lĕs′) *v.* **-lesced, -lesc•ing.** To become obsolescent.

ob•so•les•cent (ŏb′sə-lĕs′ənt) *adj.* In the process of becoming obsolete. **—ob′so•les′cence** *n.* **—ob′so•les′cent•ly** *adv.*

ob•so•lete (ŏb′sə-lēt′, ŏb′sə-lēt′) *adj.* **1.** No longer in use. **2.** Outmoded in design.

ob•sta•cle (ŏb′stə-kəl) *n.* One that opposes or stands in the way of.

ob•ste•tri•cian (ŏb′stĭ-trĭsh′ən) *n.* A physician who specializes in obstetrics.

ob•stet•rics (ŏb-stĕt′rĭks, əb-) *n. (sing. or pl. in number).* The branch of medicine concerned with the care of women during and after pregnancy and childbirth. **—ob•stet′ric, ob•stet′ri•cal** *adj.*

ob•sti•nate (ŏb′stə-nĭt) *adj.* **1.** Stubbornly adhering to an opinion or course of action. **2.** Difficult to manage, control, or subdue. ★ ***syns:*** BULLHEADED, DOGGED, HARDHEADED, HEADSTRONG, INTRACTABLE, INTRANSIGENT, PERTINACIOUS, PERVERSE, PIGHEADED, REFRACTORY, STIFF-NECKED, STUBBORN, TOUGH, WILLFUL **—ob′sti•na•cy** (-nə-sē) *n.* **—ob′sti•nate•ly** *adv.*

ob•strep•er•ous (əb-strĕp′ər-əs, ŏb-) *adj.* Noisy and unruly, esp. in defiance. **—ob•strep′er•ous•ness** *n.*

ob•struct (əb-strŭkt′, ŏb-) *v.* **1.** To stop up (a passage) with obstacles. **2.** To hinder : impede. **3.** To cut off from view. **—ob•struct′er, ob•struc′tor** *n.* **—ob•struc′tion** *n.* **—ob•struc′tive** *adj.*

ob•struc•tion•ist (əb-strŭk′shə-nĭst, ŏb-) *n.* One who systematically blocks or delays a process. **—ob•struc′tion•ism** *n.*

ob•tain (əb-tān′, ŏb-) *v.* **1.** To gain possession of : acquire. **2.** To be widely accepted. **—ob•tain′a•ble** *adj.* **—ob•tain′er** *n.*

ob•trude (əb-trōōd′, ŏb-) *v.* **-trud•ed, -trud•ing.** To thrust (oneself or one's ideas) on without invitation. **—ob•trud′er** *n.* **—ob•tru′sion** (-trōō′zhən) *n.* **—ob•tru′sive** (-sĭv) *adj.*

ob•tuse (ŏb-tōōs′, -tyōōs′, əb-) *adj.* **1.** Not sharp : blunt. **2.** Slow in comprehension.

obtuse angle *n.* An angle less than 180° and greater than 90°.

ob•verse (ŏb-vûrs′, əb-, ŏb′vûrs′) *adj.* **1.** Turned toward the observer. **2.** Forming a counterpart. —*n.* (ŏb′vûrs′, ŏb-vûrs′, əb-). **1.** The side of a coin bearing the main stamp or design. **2.** A counterpart.

ob•vi•ate (ŏb′vē-āt′) *v.* **-at•ed, -at•ing.** To anticipate and prevent. **—ob′vi•a′tion** *n.* **—ob′vi•a′tor** *n.*

ob•vi•ous (ŏb′vē-əs) *adj.* Easily seen or discovered. **—ob′vi•ous•ly** *adv.*

oc•a•ri•na (ŏk′ə-rē′nə) *n.* A small simple wind

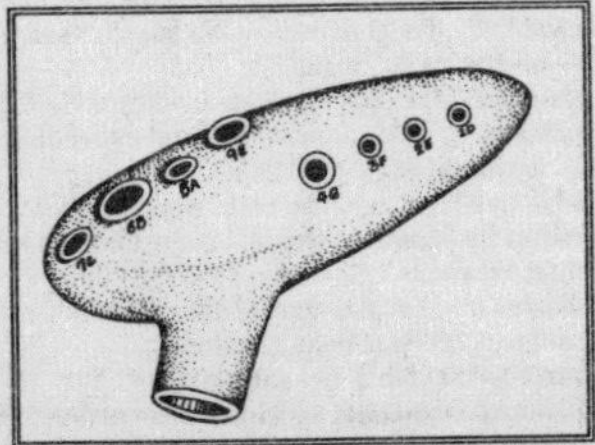

ocarina

instrument with a mouthpiece and finger holes.

oc•ca•sion (ə-kā'zhən) *n.* **1.** An event, esp. a notable event. **2.** The time at which something occurs. **3.** A favorable moment : opportunity. **4.** Something that brings on an event. **5.** A need created by particular circumstances. —*v.* To cause. —**on occasion** From time to time.

oc•ca•sion•al (ə-kā'zhə-nəl) *adj.* **1.** Happening from time to time : intermittent. **2.** Designed for or occurring on a special occasion. —**oc•ca'sion•al•ly** *adv.*

oc•ci•dent (ŏk'sə-dənt, -dĕnt') *n.* **1.** The west. **2. Occident.** Europe and the W Hemisphere. —**oc'ci•den'tal** *adj. & n.*

oc•clude (ə-klōōd') *v.* **-clud•ed, -clud•ing. 1.** To cause to become closed : obstruct. **2.** *Chem.* To adsorb or absorb. **3.** *Meteorol.* To force (air) upward from the earth's surface. **4.** To close so that the cusps of the teeth come together. —**oc•clu'sion** *n.*

occluded front *n.* The air front established when a warm front is occluded by a cold front.

oc•cult (ə-kŭlt', ŏ-kŭlt', ŏk'ŭlt') *adj.* **1.** Of or pertaining to supernatural phenomena or influences. **2.** Beyond the range of human comprehension. **3.** Available only to the initiate. —*n.* Occult practices or lore. —**oc•cult'ism** *n.* —**oc•cult'ist** *n.*

oc•cu•pan•cy (ŏk'yə-pən-sē) *n., pl.* **-cies. 1. a.** The act of taking or holding possession. **b.** The condition of being occupied. **2.** The period during which land or premises are occupied. —**oc'cu•pant** *n.*

oc•cu•pa•tion (ŏk'yə-pā'shən) *n.* **1.** An activity serving as one's regular employment. **2.** The process of occupying or state of being occupied. **3.** The taking possession of a territory by a foreign military force. —**oc'cu•pa'tion•al** *adj.*

occupational therapy *n.* Creative activity prescribed as a form of therapy. —**occupational therapist** *n.*

oc•cu•py (ŏk'yə-pī') *v.* **-pied, -py•ing. 1.** To take possession of and retain control over by force. **2.** To fill up (space or time). **3.** To live in. **4.** To hold (e.g., an office). **5.** To keep busy. —**oc'cu•pi'er** *n.*

oc•cur (ə-kûr') *v.* **-curred, -cur•ring. 1.** To come about. **2.** To be found : appear. **3.** To come to mind. —**oc•cur'rence** *n.* —**oc•cur'rent** *adj.*

o•cean (ō'shən) *n.* **1. a.** The whole body of salt water that covers nearly ¾ of the earth's surface. **b.** *often* **Ocean.** Any of the principal divisions of the ocean <the Pacific *Ocean*> **2.** A large quantity <*oceans* of food> —**o'ce•an'ic** *adj.*

o•cean•ar•i•um (ō'shə-nâr'ē-əm) *n., pl.* **-i•ums** *or* **-i•a** (-ē-ə). A large aquarium for the exhibition or study of marine life.

o•cean•og•ra•phy (ō'shə-nŏg'rə-fē) *n.* Study and exploration of the ocean and its phenomena. —**o'cean•og'ra•pher** *n.* —**o'cean•o•graph'ic** (-nə-grăf'ĭk), **o'cean•o•graph'i•cal** *adj.*

o•cean•ol•o•gy (ō'shə-nŏl'ə-jē) *n.* Oceanography. —**o'cean•o•log'ic, o'cean•o•log'i•cal** *adj.* —**o'cean•o•log'i•cal•ly** *adv.* —**o'cean•ol'o•gist** *n.*

o•cel•lus (ō-sĕl'əs) *n., pl.* **o•cel•li** (ō-sĕl'ī') The simple eye of many invertebrates. —**o•cel'lar** *adj.*

oc•e•lot (ŏs'ə-lŏt', ō'sə-) *n.* A wild cat, *Felis pardalis,* of SW U.S. and Central and South America, with a tawny spotted coat.

o•cher *or* **o•chre** (ō'kər) *n.* **1.** An earthy iron ore, occurring in brown, yellow, and red and used as a pigment. **2.** A yellowish orange. —**o'cher•ous, o'cher•y** *adj.*

o'clock (ə-klŏk') *adv.* According to the clock <five *o'clock*>

oc•ta•gon (ŏk'tə-gŏn') *n.* A polygon with 8 sides and angles. —**oc•tag'o•nal** (ŏk-tăg'ə-nəl) *adj.* —**oc•tag'o•nal•ly** *adv.*

oc•ta•he•dron (ŏk'tə-hē'drən) *n., pl.* **-drons** *or* **-dra** (-drə). A polyhedron with 8 plane surfaces.

oc•tal (ŏk'təl) *adj.* Of or being a number expressed in a numbering system of base 8.

oc•tane (ŏk'tān') *n.* **1.** Any of several hydrocarbon compounds occurring in petroleum. **2.** Octane number.

octane number *n.* A number measuring the antiknock rating of gasoline, based on the percentage of a particular form of octane contained in a sample of gasoline.

octane rating *n.* Octane number.

oc•tant (ŏk'tənt) *n.* 1/8 of a circle or of the circumference of a circle.

oc•tave (ŏk'tĭv, -tāv') *n.* **1.** *Mus.* **a.** The interval of 8 diatonic degrees between 2 tones. **b.** A tone 8 diatonic degrees above or below another tone. **2.** A group of 8.

oc•ta•vo (ŏk-tā'vō, -tä'-) *n., pl.* **-vos. 1.** A page size (approx. 6 × 9 in.), orig. obtained by folding a printer's sheet into 8 leaves. **2.** A book made up of octavo pages.

oc•tet (ŏk-tĕt') *n.* **1. a.** A musical composition for 8 voices or instruments. **b.** An ensemble of 8 musicians. **2.** A group of 8. **3.** The first 8 lines of a sonnet.

oc•til•lion (ŏk-tĭl'yən) *n.* **1.** The cardinal number equal to 10^{27}. **2.** *esp. Brit.* The cardinal number equal to 10^{48}.

Oc•to•ber (ŏk-tō'bər) *n.* The 10th month of the year, having 31 days.

▲ ***word history:*** The Roman year orig. began in March, and October was consequently the 8th month, as its name suggests: *October* is derived from Latin *octo,* "eight." The names of other months are also derived from the Latin names of numbers. *September,* the 7th month, is from *septem,* "seven"; *November,* the 9th month, is from *novem,* "nine"; *December,* the 10th month, is from *decem,* "ten." The months now known as July and August were orig. named *Quintilis,* "5th month," and *Sextilis,* "6th month."

oc•to•ge•nar•i•an (ŏk'tə-jə-nâr'ē-ən) *n.* A person between 80 and 90 years of age.

oc·to·pus (ŏk′tə-pəs) *n., pl.* **-es** *or* **-pi** (-pī′). A carnivorous nocturnal marine mollusk of the genus *Octopus* or related genera, with a saclike body and 8 tentacles bearing double rows of suckers.

octopus

oc·to·roon (ŏk′tə-ro͞on′) *n.* A person whose ancestry is 1/8 black.
oc·tu·ple (ŏk′tə-pəl, -to͞o′pəl, ŏk-tyo͞o′-) *adj.* **1.** Having 8 parts. **2.** Multiplied by 8. —*v.* **-pled, -pling.** To multiply or be multiplied by 8. —**oc′tu·ple** *n.*
oc·u·lar (ŏk′yə-lər) *adj.* **1.** Of or relating to the eye. **2.** Seen by the eye. —*n.* The eyepiece of an optical instrument.
oc·u·list (ŏk′yə-lĭst) *n.* **1.** An ophthalmologist. **2.** An optometrist.
OD (ō′dē′) *Slang.* —*n.* **1.** An overdose of a narcotic. **2.** One who has taken an overdose. —*v.* **OD′d, OD′ing.** To overdose.
odd (ŏd) *adj.* **1.** Deviating from the customary : unusual. **2. a.** In excess of the indicated number <20-*odd* students> **b.** Being a remainder <a few *odd* tickets still unsold> **3.** Being one of an incomplete set or pair. **4.** *Math.* Designating a number not divisible by 2. —**odd′ly** *adv.*
odd·ball (ŏd′bôl′) *n. Informal.* An eccentric person.
Odd Fellow *n.* A member of the Independent Order of Odd Fellows, a fraternal and benevolent secret society.
odd·i·ty (ŏd′ĭ-tē) *n., pl.* **-ties. 1.** One that is odd. **2.** The state or quality of being odd.
odd job *n.* A usu. temporary unskilled or menial job.
odd·ment (ŏd′mənt) *n.* Something left over : remnant.
odds (ŏdz) *pl.n.* **1.** An advantage assigned to a weaker side in a contest to equalize the chances of winning. **2.** A ratio expressing the probability of an outcome. **3.** The likelihood of something happening. —**at odds.** In conflict.
odds and ends *pl.n.* Miscellaneous items or remnants.
ode (ōd) *n.* A lyric poem usu. in praise of an object or person.
o·de·um (ō-dē′əm, ō′dē-) *n., pl.* **o·de·a** (ō-dē′-ə, ō′dē-ə) **1.** A small ancient Greek or Roman building used for public performances of poetry and music. **2.** A contemporary theater or music hall.
o·di·ous (ō′dē-əs) *adj.* Arousing hatred or repugnance : abhorrent. —**o′di·ous·ly** *adv.*
o·di·um (ō′dē-əm) *n.* **1.** The quality or state of being odious. **2.** Disgrace resulting from contemptible behavior.
o·dom·e·ter (ō-dŏm′ĭ-tər) *n.* An instrument for measuring distance traveled, as by a vehicle.
o·dor (ō′dər) *n.* **1.** The quality of something that stimulates the sense of smell. **2.** Repute : esteem. —**o′dor·if′er·ous** *adj.* —**o′dor·less** *adj.* —**o′dor·ous** *adj.*
o·dour (ŏ′dər) *n. esp. Brit. var. of* ODOR.
od·ys·sey (ŏd′ĭ-sē) *n.* An extended, adventurous wandering.
Oed·i·pus complex (ĕd′ə-pəs, ē′də-) *n. Psychoanal.* Unconscious sexual feelings in a child, esp. a boy, toward the parent of the opposite sex. —**Oed′i·pal** *adj.*
o′er (ôr, ōr) *prep. & adv.* Over.
oeu·vre (œ′vrə) *n., pl.* **oeu·vres** (œvrə) **1.** A work of art. **2.** The whole body of an artist's work.
of (ŭv, ŏv; əv *when unstressed*) *prep.* **1.** From. **2.** Caused by <his death *of* cancer> **3.** At a distance from. **4.** So as to be separated from <robbed *of* one's self-respect> **5.** From the total comprising <most *of* the cases> **6.** Made from. **7.** Associated with <a member *of* your religion> **8.** Belonging or connected to <the rungs *of* a ladder> **9.** Possessing <a person *of* courage> **10.** Containing <a basket *of* peaches> **11.** Specified as <a width *of* 20 feet> **12.** Directed toward <a love *of* dogs> **13.** Produced by. **14.** Marked or identified by <a year *of* discord> **15.** With reference to <speak *of* it tomorrow> **16.** Set aside for <needed a day *of* rest> **17.** Before : until <10 minutes *of* 12> **18.** During or on a specified time.
off (ôf, ŏf) *adv.* **1.** From a place or position <drive *off*> **2.** Distant in space or time. **3.** So as to be no longer on or connected. **4.** So as to be smaller or fewer. **5.** So as to be away from work or duty. —*adj.* **1.** Distant or removed <the *off* side of the pasture> **2.** Not on or connected. **3.** Not operating or operational. **4.** Canceled. **5.** Less or smaller. **6.** Below standard. **7.** In a specified condition <well *off*> **8.** Incorrect. **9.** Away from work or duty. —*prep.* **1.** So as to be removed from <The bird hopped *off* the branch.> **2.** Away from. **3.** By consuming or with the means provided by. **4.** Extending from <an artery *off* the heart> **5.** Not up to the usual standard of. **6.** So as to abstain from <went *off* drugs>
of·fal (ô′fəl, ŏf′əl) *n.* **1.** Waste parts, esp. the entrails and trimmings of a butchered animal. **2.** Refuse : filth.
off·beat (ôf′bēt′, ŏf′-) *n. Mus.* An unaccented beat. —*adj.* (ôf′bēt′, ŏf′-). *Slang.* Unconventional : eccentric.
off-Broad·way (ôf′brôd′wā′, ŏf′-) *adj.* Designating or relating to productions in theaters outside the Broadway entertainment district of New York City.

off-col•or (ôf'kŭl'ər, ŏf'-) *adj.* **1.** Varying from the standard or desired color. **2.** In poor taste : indecent.

of•fence (ə-fĕns') *n. esp. Brit. var. of* OFFENSE.

of•fend (ə-fĕnd') *v.* **1.** To arouse resentment, anger, or vexation in. **2.** To be displeasing (to). **3.** To commit a sin.

of•fense (ə-fĕns') *n.* **1.** The act of offending or the state of being offended. **2. a.** A breach of a social or moral code. **b.** A crime. **3.** (ŏf'-ĕns'). The act of attacking. **4.** (ŏf'ĕns'). The side that is attacking in a game or contest. **—of•fen'sive** *adj.* **—of•fen'sive•ly** *adv.* **—of•fen'sive•ness** *n.*

of•fer (ô'fər, ŏf'ər) *v.* **1.** To present for acceptance : tender. **2.** To place on sale. **3.** To propose as payment. **4.** To present as an act of worship. **5.** To provide : furnish. **6.** To present to an audience or to the public. ★ ***syns:*** EXTEND, PRESENT, PROFFER, TENDER, VOLUNTEER. **—of'fer** *n.* **—of'fer•er, of'fer•or** *n.* **—of'fer•ing** *n.*

of•fer•to•ry (ô'fər-tôr'ē, -tōr'ē, ŏf'ər-) *n., pl.* **-ries.** The presentation of offerings at a religious service.

off•hand (ôf'hănd', ŏf'-) *adv. & adj.* Without preparation : extemporaneously. **—off'hand'-ed•ly** *adv.*

off-hour (ôf'our', ŏf'-) *n.* A period of slack activity.

of•fice (ô'fĭs, ŏf'ĭs) *n.* **1. a.** A place in which business or professional activities are conducted. **b.** The personnel working in an office. **2.** A function or duty assigned to someone. **3.** A position of authority, as in a government or institution. **4.** A subdivision of a government. **5.** A public position <was elected to *office*> **6.** *often* **offices.** A favor. **7.** An ecclesiastical ceremony or service, esp. a rite for the dead.

of•fice•hold•er (ô'fĭs-hōl'dər, ŏf'ĭs-) *n.* A person holding a public office.

of•fi•cer (ô'fĭ-sər, ŏf'ĭ-) *n.* **1.** A person holding an office of authority, as in a government or corporation. **2.** A person holding a commission in the armed services. **3.** A licensed master, mate, chief engineer, or assistant engineer in the merchant marine. **4.** A member of a police force.

of•fi•cial (ə-fĭsh'əl) *adj.* **1.** Authorized by a proper authority. **2.** Suitable to a position of authority : formal. *—n.* **1.** One who holds an office or position. **2.** A sports referee or umpire. **—of•fi'cial•dom** *n.*

of•fi•ci•ant (ə-fĭsh'ē-ənt) *n.* One who officiates at a religious service.

of•fi•ci•ate (ə-fĭsh'ē-āt') *v.* **-at•ed, -at•ing. 1.** To carry out the functions and duties of an office or position. **2.** To preside at a religious service. **3.** To serve as a sports referee or umpire. **—of•fi'ci•a'tor** *n.*

of•fi•cious (ə-fĭsh'əs) *adj.* Excessively inclined to offer one's advice or services to others. **—of•fi'cious•ness** *n.*

off•ing (ô'fĭng, ŏf'ĭng) *n.* The near future <new developments in the *offing*>

off-key (ôf'-kē', ŏf'-) *adj.* **1.** *Mus.* Not in tune : flat or sharp. **2.** At odds with what is considered normal. **—off'-key'** *adv.*

off-limits (ôf-lĭm'ĭts, ŏf-) *adj.* Prohibited to a specific group.

off-line (ôf'līn', ŏf'-) *adj. Computer Sci.* Not controlled by a central computer.

off-off-Broad•way (ôf'ôf-brôd'wā', ŏf'ŏf-) *n.* A theatrical movement in New York City emphasizing experimental techniques and productions.

off-put•ting (ôf'po͝ot'ĭng, ŏf'-) *adj.* Disconcerting.

off-sea•son (ôf'-sē'zən, ŏf'-) *n.* A period marked by a slackening of activity.

off•set (ôf'sĕt', ŏf'-) *n.* **1.** Something that balances, compensates, or counteracts. **2.** A ledge or recess in a wall. **3.** A bend in a bar or pipe, enabling it to pass around an obstruction. **4.** Offset printing. *—v.* (ôf-sĕt', ŏf-) **1.** To counteract or compensate for. **2.** To print by offset. **3.** To form an offset in (a wall, pipe, or bar). **—off'set'** *adj.*

offset printing *n.* Printing by indirect image transfer.

off•shoot (ôf'sho͞ot', ŏf'-) *n.* One that branches out or develops from a source.

off•shore (ôf'shôr', -shōr', ŏf'-) *adj.* **1.** Moving or directed away from the shore. **2.** Located at a distance from the shore. **—off'-shore'** *adv.*

off•side *also* **off side** (ôf'sīd', ŏf'-) *adj.* Illegally forward or in advance of the ball or puck, as in football or hockey.

off•spring (ôf'sprĭng', ŏf'-) *n., pl.* **offspring. 1.** Progeny. **2.** A product : result.

off-stage (ôf'stāj', ŏf'-) *adj. & adv.* Away from or off the stage of a theater.

off-the-cuff (ôf'*th*ə-kŭf', ŏf'-) *adv. & adj.* Without preparation : impromptu.

off-the-rack (ôf'*th*ə-răk', ŏf'-) *adj.* Ready-made.

off-the-rec•ord (ôf'*th*ə-rĕk'ərd, ŏf'-) *adj. & adv.* Not for publication.

off-the-shelf (ôf'*th*ə-shĕlf', ŏf'-) *adj.* Available as an item carried in stock.

off-the-wall (ôf'*th*ə-wôl', ŏf'-) *adj. Informal.* Unconventional or bizarre.

off-track betting (ôf'trăk', ŏf'-) *n.* A system of gambling in which bets are placed away from a racetrack.

off-white (ôf'hwīt', -wīt', ŏf'-) *n.* A yellowish or grayish white.

off year *n.* **1.** A year in which a major election does not take place. **2.** A year of decreased production or activity.

oft (ôft, ŏft) *adv.* Often.

of•ten (ô'fən, ŏf'ən, ôf'tən, ŏf'-) *adv.* Many times : frequently.

of•ten•times (ô'fən-tīmz', ŏf'ən-, ôf'tən-, ŏf'-) *adv.* Repeatedly : frequently.

o•gee (ō'jē') *n.* **1.** A molding with an S-shaped profile. **2.** An arch formed by 2 S-shaped curves meeting at a point.

o•gle (ō'gəl, ô'-gəl) *v.* **o•gled, o•gling.** To stare (at), esp. amorously or impertinently.

o•gre (ō'gər) *n.* **1.** A monster or giant of folklore and legend that eats human beings. **2.** A cruel or dreaded person. **—o'gre·ish** (ō'gər-ĭsh, ō'grĭsh) *adj.* **—o'gress** *n.*

oh (ō) *interj.* **1.** —Used to express strong emotion, as fear, surprise, anger, or pain. **2.** —Used in direct address <*Oh,* sir! You forgot your coat.> **3.** —Used to indicate understanding of a statement.

ohm (ōm) *n.* A unit of electrical resistance equal to the resistance of a conductor through which a current of 1 amp flows when a potential difference of 1 volt is applied.

ohm·me·ter (ōm'mē'tər) *n.* An instrument for measuring the resistance of a conductor directly in ohms.

o·ho (ō-hō') *interj.* —Used esp. to express surprise or mock astonishment.

—oid *suff.* Like or representing <anthropo*oid*>

oil (oil) *n.* **1.** Any of several mineral and synthetic substances and animal and vegetable fats that are usu. thick, slippery, capable of being burned, liquid or easily melted, and insoluble in water. **2.** Petroleum. **3.** A substance having an oily consistency. **4.** An oil color. **5.** An oil painting. *—v.* To lubricate, coat, or polish with oil.

oil·cloth (oil'klôth', -klŏth') *n.* A cloth made waterproof by being treated with oil, clay, or paint.

oil color *n.* A paint consisting of pigment ground in oil.

oil field *n.* An area containing reserves of recoverable petroleum, esp. one that has been developed for production.

oil paint *n.* A paint in which the vehicle is a drying oil.

oil painting *n.* **1.** A painting in oil colors. **2.** The art of painting with oil colors.

oil·pa·per (oil'pā'pər) *n.* Paper treated with oil to make it transparent and water-repellent.

oil shale *n.* A dark-brown or black shale containing hydrocarbons from which petroleum can be produced by distillation.

oil·skin (oil'skĭn') *n.* **1.** Cloth treated with oil to make it waterproof. **2.** A protective garment made of oilskin.

oil slick *n.* A layer of oil on water.

oil·y (oi'lē) *adj.* **-i·er, -i·est. 1.** Of or like oil. **2.** Greasy. **3.** Excessively suave. **—oil'i·ly** *adv.* **—oil'i·ness** *n.*

oink (oingk) *n.* The characteristic grunting sound of a pig. **—oink** *v.*

oint·ment (oint'mənt) *n.* A viscous substance used on the skin as an emollient, cosmetic, or medicament.

O·jib·wa (ō-jĭb'wā', -wə) *also* **O·jib·way** (-wā') *n., pl.* **-wa** *or* **-was** *also* **-way** *or* **-ways. 1.** A member of an American Indian people inhabiting a region around Lake Superior. **2.** Their Algonquian language.

O.K. *or* **OK** *or* **o·kay** (ō'kā', ō-kā') *n., pl.* **O.K.'s** *or* **OK's** *or* **o·kays.** Approval **:** assent. *—v.* **O.K.'d, O.K.'ing** *or* **OK'd , OK'ing** *or* **o·kayed, o·kay·ing.** To approve of or consent to **:** authorize. *—interj.* —Used to express assent or approval. *—adj.* Acceptable. *—adv.* Acceptably.

o·ka·pi (ō-kä'pē) *n., pl.* **okapi** *or* **-pis.** A ruminant mammal, *Okapia johnstoni,* of C Africa, resembling a small giraffe.

O·kie (ō'kē) *n. Slang.* A migrant farm worker, esp. one from Okla. in the 1930's.

o·kra (ō'krə) *n.* A tall tropical and semitropical plant, *Hibiscus esculentus,* cultivated for its edible green pods.

old (ōld) *adj.* **1.** Having existed or lived for a relatively long time. **2.** Made in former times. **3.** Having or exhibiting the characteristics of age. **4.** Having existed for a specified time. **5.** Belonging to or being of an earlier time <my *old* high school> **6.** Known through long acquaintance <an *old* familiar face> **7.** —Used as an intensive <any *old* day> *—n.* Former times.

old country *n.* The native country of an immigrant.

old·en (ōl'dən) *adj.* Old **:** ancient.

Old English *n.* English from the middle of the 5th to the beginning of the 12th cent.

old fashioned *n.* A cocktail made of whiskey, fruit, sugar, and bitters.

old-fash·ioned (ōld'făsh'ənd) *adj.* Of a method or style once in vogue **:** outdated.

Old French *n.* French from the 9th to the early 16th cent.

Old Glory *n.* The U.S. flag.

old guard *n. often* **Old Guard.** A conservative, often reactionary element of a particular society, class, or political group.

old hand *n.* One who has long experience.

old hat *adj. Informal.* Old-fashioned.

old·ie (ōl'dē) *n.* Something old or outdated, esp. a song popular in an earlier time.

old lady *n. Slang.* **1.** One's mother. **2. a.** One's wife. **b.** One's girlfriend.

old-line (ōld'līn') *adj.* **1.** Having conservative or reactionary ideas. **2.** Traditional.

old maid *n.* **1.** *Informal.* A woman, esp. an older woman, who has not married. **2.** *Informal.* A prim and fussy person. **—old'maid'ish** *adj.*

old man *n. Slang.* **1.** One's father. **2. a.** One's husband. **b.** One's boyfriend.

old master *n.* **1.** An eminent European artist of the period from around 1500 to the early 1700's. **2.** A work by an old master.

Old Nick *n.* DEVIL 1.

old school *n.* A group that espouses traditional values or practices.

old·ster (ōld'stər) *n. Informal.* An old person.

Old Testament *n.* The 1st of the principal divisions of the Christian Bible. —See table at BIBLE.

old-tim·er (ōld'tī'mər) *n. Informal.* **1. a.** An oldster. **b.** An old hand. **2.** A very old or antiquated thing.

old wives' tale *n.* A piece of superstitious folklore.

old-world (ōld'wûrld') *adj.* Antique and picturesque.

Old World *n.* The E Hemisphere, Asia, Africa, and esp. Europe.

o·lé (ō-lā') *interj.* —Used to express excited approval. **—o·lé'** *n.*

o•le•ag•i•nous (ō′lē-ăj′ə-nəs) *adj.* **1.** Of or relating to oil. **2.** Unctuous **:** oily.

o•le•an•der (ō′lē-ăn′dər, ō′lē-ăn′-) *n.* A poisonous evergreen shrub of the genus *Nerium,* found in warm climates, bearing white, purple, or reddish flower clusters.

o•le•o (ō′lē-ō′) *n., pl.* **-os.** Margarine.

o•le•o•mar•ga•rine (ō′lē-ō-mär′jər-ĭn, -jə-rēn′) *n.* Margarine.

ol•fac•tion (ŏl-făk′shən, ōl-) *n.* **1.** The sense of smell. **2.** An act of smelling.

ol•fac•to•ry (ŏl-făk′tə-rē, -trē, ōl-) *adj.* Of or pertaining to the sense of smell.

ol•i•gar•chy (ŏl′ĭ-gär′kē) *n., pl.* **-chies. 1. a.** Government by a few, esp. by a small group or class. **b.** The persons and families making up such a group. **2.** A state governed by oligarchy. **—ol′i•garch′** *n.* **—ol′i•gar′chic, ol′i•gar′chi•cal** *adj.*

ol•i•gop•o•ly (ŏl′ĭ-gŏp′ə-lē, ō′lĭ-) *n., pl.* **-lies** A market condition in which there are so few sellers that the actions of any one of them can affect price and have a measurable impact on competitors. **—ol′i•gop′o•lis′tic** (-lĭs′tĭk) *adj.*

o•li•o (ō′lē-ō′) *n., pl.* **-os.** A miscellany.

ol•ive (ŏl′ĭv) *n.* **1.** An Old World semitropical evergreen tree, *Olea europaea,* with leathery leaves, yellow flowers, and small oval fruit used as food and a source of oil. **2.** A yellowish green. **—ol′ive** *adj.*

olive branch *n.* **1.** A branch of the olive tree regarded as a symbol of peace. **2.** A peace offering.

olive drab *n.* **1.** A dull brownish or grayish green. **2.** Cloth of an olive-drab color, often used for military uniforms.

olive oil *n.* Oil pressed from olives, used in cooking and as an ingredient of soaps.

ol•i•vine (ŏl′ə-vēn′) *n.* A usu. greenish mineral silicate of iron and magnesium.

O•lym•pi•an (ō-lĭm′pē-ən) *adj.* **1.** *Gk. Myth.* Of or relating to the gods and goddesses of Mount Olympus. **2.** Surpassing all others in scope. **3.** Of or relating to the Olympic games. **—O•lym′pi•an** *n.*

O•lym•pic games (ō-lĭm′pĭk) *pl. n.* **1.** An ancient Greek festival of athletic games and contests of dance and choral poetry, celebrated every 4 years to honor Zeus. **2.** An international athletic competition held every 4 years.

om•buds•man (ŏm′bŭdz′mən, -bo͝odz′-) *n.* **1.** A government official charged with investigating citizens' complaints against the government. **2.** One who investigates complaints, as from consumers, and helps to achieve settlements.

om•e•let *also* **om•e•lette** (ŏm′ə-lĭt, ŏm′lĭt) *n.* A dish made of eggs beaten with milk and cooked until set.

o•men (ō′mən) *n.* A phenomenon regarded as a portent of future good or evil. ★ *syns:* AUGURY, FORETOKEN, PORTENT, PRESAGE, PROGNOSTIC, PROGNOSTICATION

om•i•nous (ŏm′ə-nəs) *adj.* **1.** Of or being an omen, esp. an evil one. **2.** Threatening **:** menacing. **—om′i•nous•ly** *adv.*

o•mit (ō-mĭt′) *v.* **o•mit•ted, o•mit•ting. 1.** To leave out. **2.** To neglect **:** overlook. **—o•mis′sion** (-mĭsh′ən) *n.*

om•ni•bus (ŏm′nĭ-bŭs′) *n.* A bus. *—adj.* Including or providing for many items at once <an *omnibus* legislative bill>

om•ni•di•rec•tion•al (ŏm′nĭ-dĭ-rĕk′shə-nəl, -dī-) *adj.* Capable of receiving or transmitting signals in all directions.

om•ni•far•i•ous (ŏm′nĭ-fâr′ē-əs) *adj.* Of all kinds. **—om′ni•far′i•ous•ness** *n.*

om•nip•o•tent (ŏm-nĭp′ə-tənt) *adj.* Having absolute power or authority. *—n.* **Omnipotent.** God. **—om•nip′o•tence** *n.*

om•ni•pres•ence (ŏm′nĭ-prĕz′əns) *n.* The fact of being present everywhere. **—om′ni•pres′ent** *adj.*

om•nis•cient (ŏm-nĭsh′ənt) *adj.* Knowing everything. *—n.* **Omniscient.** God. **—om•nis′cience** *n.*

om•ni•vore (ŏm′nə-vôr′, -vōr′) *n.* An omnivorous animal.

om•niv•o•rous (ŏm-nĭv′ər-əs) *adj.* **1.** *Zool.* Eating both vegetable and animal substances. **2.** Eagerly absorbing everything available. **—om•niv′o•rous•ly** *adv.*

on (ŏn, ôn) *prep.* **1.** —Used to indicate: **a.** Position upon and in contact with. **b.** Location at or along. **c.** Proximity. **d.** Attachment to or suspension from. **2.** —Used to indicate movement or direction toward, against, or onto <jump *on* the platform><a march *on* Washington> **3.** —Used to indicate: **a.** Occurrence at a given time <*on* May 1st> **b.** The particular occasion or circumstance <*On* leaving the house, I heard the phone.> **4.** —Used to indicate: **a.** The object affected by perceptible action. **b.** The agent or agency of a specified action. **5.** —Used to indicate a source or basis <making money *on* the horses> **6.** —Used to indicate: **a.** The state or process of <*on* leave><*on* fire> **b.** The purpose of. **c.** A means of conveyance <ride *on* a subway> **d.** Availability by means of <a doctor *on* call> **e.** Association with. **f.** Addition or repetition <opened store *on* store> **7.** Concerning **:** about. **8.** In the possession of <not a cent *on* me> **9.** At the expense of <Dinner's *on* me.> *—adv.* **1.** In a position of covering or being in contact with something. **2.** In the direction of. **3.** Forward <moved *on* to a new job> **4.** In a continuous course. **5.** In or into operation or performance.

on•board (ŏn-bôrd′, -bōrd′, ôn-) *adj.* Carried aboard a vehicle.

once (wŭns) *adv.* **1.** One time only <*once* a year> **2.** At one time in the past. **3.** At any time **:** ever <Time, *once* gone, will never return.> **4.** By one degree of relationship <my first cousin, *once* removed> *—n.* One time. *—conj.* As soon as. *—adj.* Former <the *once* heavyweight champion>

once-o•ver (wŭns′ō′vər) *n. Informal.* A brief but comprehensive inspection.

on•co•gene (ŏn′kə-jēn, ŏng′-) *n.* A gene that causes the transformation of normal cells into cancerous tumor cells, esp. a viral gene.

—on′co·gen′ic (-jĕn′ĭk) *adj.* **—on′co·ge·nic′·i·ty** (-jə-nĭs′ĭ-tē) *n.*

on·co·gen·e·sis (ŏn′kō-jĕn′ĭ-sĭs, ŏng′-) *n.* The formation and development of tumors.

on·com·ing (ŏn′kŭm′ĭng, ôn′-) *adj.* Coming nearer.

one (wŭn) *adj.* **1.** Being a single unit or entity <*one* mile> **2.** Characterized by unity. **3.** Occurring or existing as something indefinite <We will meet again *one* day.> **4.** Single in kind. *—n.* **1.** A single individual **:** unit. **2.** The cardinal number represented by the symbol 1, designating the first such unit in a series. *—pron.* An indefinitely specified thing or person.

one-di·men·sion·al (wŭn′dĭ-mĕn′shə-nəl) *adj.* Lacking depth **:** superficial.

one-horse (wŭn′hôrs′) *adj.* Small and uninteresting <a *one-horse* town>

one·ness (wŭn′nĭs) *n.* **1.** Singleness. **2.** Sameness of character <the insipid *oneness* of institution food> **3.** Agreement **:** unity <*oneness* of mind>

one-night stand (wŭn′nīt′) *n.* A musical or dramatic performance given on one night only in a place.

on·er·ous (ŏn′ər-əs, ō′nər-) *adj.* Burdensome **:** oppressive. **—on′er·ous·ly** *adv.*

one·self (wŭn-sĕlf′) *also* **one's self** (wŭn sĕlf′, wŭnz sĕlf′) *pron.* **1.** One's own self <have confidence in *oneself*> **2.** One's normal or healthy condition.

one-shot (wŭn′shŏt′) *adj.* **1.** Effective after a single attempt. **2.** Being the only one <a *one-shot* opportunity>

one-sid·ed (wŭn′sī′dĭd) *adj.* **1.** Favoring one group **:** biased <a *one-sided* opinion> **2.** Unequal. **—one′-sid′ed·ness** *n.*

one-step (wŭn′stĕp′) *n.* A ballroom dance consisting of a series of rapid steps in 2/4 time. **—one′-step′** *v.*

one·time (wŭn′tīm′) *adj.* Former <a *onetime* diving champion>

one-time (wŭn′tīm′) *adj.* On only one occasion <a *one-time* medalist in 1980>

one-to-one (wŭn′tə-wŭn′) *adj.* **1.** Pairing each member of a class uniquely with a member of another class. **2.** Marked by proportional amounts on both sides.

one-track (wŭn′trăk′) *adj.* Intent on a single goal <a *one-track* mind>

one-up·man·ship (wŭn-ŭp′măn-shĭp′) *n.* *Informal.* The art of outdoing or showing up a rival.

one-way (wŭn′wā′) *adj.* **1.** Moving or allowing movement in only one direction. **2.** Relating to travel in only one direction.

on·go·ing (ŏn′gō′ĭng, ôn′-) *adj.* Currently taking place or developing.

on·ion (ŭn′yən) *n.* A plant, *Allium cepa,* cultivated worldwide for its rounded bulb having a pungent odor and taste.

▲ ***word history:*** The Latin source of the English word *onion* is *unio,* which is derived from Latin *unus,* "one." *Unio* had several meanings in Latin, among them "unity" and "union." *Unio* was also used to designate a kind of large pearl, and in rustic speech it designated a kind of onion. The exact reason for calling an onion *unio* is unknown. *Unio* was chosen perhaps because of the onion's single bulb, in contrast to the multisegmented garlic and shallot, both related to the onion. *Unio* could also have been chosen because of some pearllike quality of the bulb, such as roundness.

on·ion·skin (ŭn′yən-skĭn′) *n.* A tough, thin, translucent paper.

on-line (ŏn′līn′, ôn′-) *adj.* **1.** *Computer Sci.* **a.** Controlled by a central computer. **b.** Connected to a computer network. **c.** Accessible by a computer. **2.** Being in progress.

on·look·er (ŏn′lo͝ok′ər, ôn′-) *n.* One who looks on **:** spectator. **—on′look′ing** *adj.*

on·ly (ōn′lē) *adj.* Alone in kind **:** sole. *—adv.* **1.** Without anything or anyone else. **2. a.** At the very least. **b.** Merely. **3.** Solely **:** exclusively. *—conj.* But **:** except.

on·o·mat·o·poe·ia (ŏn′ə-măt′ə-pē′ə) *n.* The use or formation of words, as *hiss* or *cuckoo,* that have a sound imitating what they denote. **—on′o·mat′o·poe′ic** (-pē′ĭk), **on′o·mat′o·po·et′ic** (-pō-ĕt′ĭk) *adj.*

on·rush (ŏn′rŭsh′, ôn′-) *n.* **1.** A forward surge or flow. **2.** An assault.

on·set (ŏn′sĕt′, ôn′-) *n.* **1.** An assault. **2.** A beginning **:** outset.

on·shore (ŏn′shôr′, -shōr′, ôn′-) *adj.* **1.** Moving or directed toward the shore <an *onshore* breeze> **2.** Based or operating on or along the shore. **3.** Domestic <*onshore* industry> **—on′shore′** *adv.*

on·slaught (ŏn′slôt′, ôn′-) *n.* An attack.

on-stage (ŏn-stāj′, ôn-) *adj. & adv.* Toward or on the stage of a theater.

on·to (ŏn′to͞o′, ôn′-, ŏn′tə, ôn′-) *prep.* **1.** To a position on **:** upon. **2.** *Informal.* Aware of.

o·nus (ō′nəs) *n.* **1.** A burden, esp. an oppressive responsibility. **2.** Blame.

on·ward (ŏn′wərd, ôn′-) *adj.* Moving forward in space or time. *—adv. also* **on·wards** (-wərdz). In an onward direction.

on·yx (ŏn′ĭks) *n.* Chalcedony that occurs in colored bands and is used as a gemstone. *—adj.* Dark **:** black.

oo·dles (o͞od′lz) *pl.n.* *Informal.* A large amount **:** lots.

oomph (o͞omf) *n.* *Slang.* **1.** Boundless energy or enthusiasm. **2.** Sex appeal.

ooze[1] (o͞oz) *v.* **oozed, ooz·ing. 1.** To seep or flow out slowly. **2.** To vanish or ebb slowly **:** drain. ★ ***syns:*** BLEED, EXUDE, LEACH, PERCOLATE, SEEP, WEEP **—ooze** *n.* **—ooz′i·ness** *n.* **—ooz′y** *adj.*

ooze[2] (o͞oz) *n.* **1.** Soft, thin mud. **2.** Mudlike sediment covering the floor of lakes and oceans. **—ooz′i·ness** *n.* **—ooz′y** *adj.*

o·pah (ō′pə) *n.* A large brightly colored marine fish, *Lambris regius.*

o·pal (ō′pəl) *n.* A translucent, variously colored mineral composed of a form of silicon, often used as a gem. **—o′pal·ine′** (ō′pə-līn′, -lēn′) *adj.*

o·pal·es·cence (ō′pə-lĕs′əns) *n.* The quality

or state of exhibiting a milky iridescence like that of an opal. **—o'pal•esce'** *v.* **—o'pal•es'cent** *adj.*

o•paque (ō-pāk') *adj.* **1. a.** Impervious to the passage of light. **b.** Not reflecting light **:** lusterless. **2.** Unperceptive **:** obtuse. **—o•pac'i•ty** (-păs'ĭ-tē), **o•paque'ness** *n.*

op art *n.* Optical art.

op-ed page (ŏp-ĕd') *n.* A newspaper section, usu. located opposite the editorial page, featuring articles and columns presenting personal viewpoints.

o•pen (ō'pən) *adj.* **1.** Affording unobstructed entrance and exit. **2.** Not covered or concealed. **3.** Not sealed, fastened, or locked. **4.** Having spaces, gaps, or intervals <an *open* weave> **5.** Accessible to all. **6.** Vulnerable **:** susceptible. **7.** Available. **8.** Ready to transact business. **9.** Unoccupied. **10. a.** Candid <an *open* manner> **b.** Free from prejudice <an *open* mind> ★ ***syns:*** EXPOSED, UNCOVERED, UNPROTECTED —*v.* **1.** To release or become released from a closed position. **2.** To free from obstructions. **3.** To unfold. **4.** To remove the wrapping or cover from. **5.** To begin. **6.** To permit the use of. **7.** To make or become understanding or receptive. **8.** To reveal the secrets of. **9.** To come into view. **—open up. 1.** To begin firing a firearm. **2.** *Informal.* To speak or act freely. —*n.* **1.** The outdoors <camped in the *open*> **2.** An unconcealed state <bring a problem out into the *open*> **3.** A contest for both professionals and amateurs. **—o'pen•er** *n.* **—o'pen•ly** *adv.* **—o'pen•ness** *n.*

o•pen-air (ō'pən-âr') *adj.* Outdoor.

o•pen-and-shut (ō'pən-ən-shŭt') *adj.* Easily decided <an *open-and-shut* case>

open classroom *n.* A system of elementary education emphasizing informal individualized methods of teaching.

open door *n.* **1.** An unrestricted opportunity. **2.** Admission or access to all on equal terms. **—o'pen-door'** *adj.*

o•pen-end•ed (ō'pən-ĕn'dĭd) *adj.* **1.** Not restricted by definite limits or structure. **2.** Open to change. **3.** Inconclusive.

open enrollment *n.* A policy permitting admission of students without regard to academic qualifications.

o•pen•hand•ed (ō'pən-hăn'dĭd) *adj.* Generous. **—o'pen•hand'ed•ly** *adv.*

o•pen-heart (ō'pən-härt') *adj.* Of, relating to, or designating surgery in which the heart is open while its normal functions are performed by external apparatus.

o•pen-hearth (ō'pən-härth') *adj.* Designating a process of steel production in a furnace with a heat-reflecting roof.

open house *n.* An event to which all are welcome.

o•pen•ing (ō'pə-nĭng) *n.* **1.** An open space **:** aperture. **2.** An initial stage or period. **3.** A first performance, as of a play. **4.** A series of beginning moves in certain games, esp. chess. **5.** An opportunity. **6.** An unfilled job **:** vacancy. **7.** The act of becoming open or making open.

open letter *n.* A letter addressed to an individual but intended for general publication or distribution.

open loop *n. Computer Sci.* A control system that cannot correct or alter itself.

o•pen-mind•ed (ō'pən-mīn'dĭd) *adj.* Receptive to new ideas.

open shop *n.* A company employing both union and nonunion workers.

o•pen•work (ō'pən-wûrk') *n.* Ornamental work, as in cloth or metal, containing openings that form a pattern.

op•er•a[1] (ŏp'ər-ə, ŏp'rə) *n.* A theatrical work consisting of a dramatic performance set to music. **—op'er•at'ic** *adj.*

o•pe•ra[2] (ō'pər-ə, ŏp'ər-ə) *n. var. pl. of* OPUS.

op•er•a•ble (ŏp'ər-ə-bəl, ŏp'rə-) *adj.* **1.** Able to be used or operated. **2.** Able to be treated surgically.

opera glasses *pl.n.* Small binoculars for use esp. at theatrical performances.

opera house *n.* A theater designed primarily for operas.

op•er•and (ŏp'ər-ənd) *n. Math.* A quantity on which an operation is performed.

op•er•ate (ŏp'ə-rāt') *v.* **-at•ed, -at•ing. 1.** To run or function effectively. **2.** To have an effect or influence. **3.** To perform surgery. **4.** To direct or control the functioning of. ★ ***syns:*** HANDLE, RUN, USE, WORK

operating system *n. Computer Sci.* Software designed to complement or support the hardware of a system.

op•er•a•tion (ŏp'ə-rā'shən) *n.* **1.** An act, process, or method of operating. **2.** The condition of being operative. **3.** *Med.* A surgical procedure for remedying an injury or dysfunction in a living body. **4.** *Math.* A procedure performed in a specified sequence and in accordance with specific rules. **5.** *Computer Sci.* An action resulting from a single computer instruction. **6.** A military action or campaign. **—op'er•a'tion•al** *adj.* **—op'er•a'tion•al•ly** *adv.*

op•er•a•tive (ŏp'ər-ə-tĭv, ŏp'rə-, -ə-rā'tĭv) *adj.* **1.** Exerting force or influence. **2.** Efficient. **3.** In effect <*operative* rules> **4.** Of or relating to a surgical operation. —*n.* **1.** A skilled worker, esp. in industry. **2. a.** A secret agent. **b.** A detective.

op•er•a•tor (ŏp'ə-rā'tər) *n.* **1.** One that operates a machine. **2.** The manager or owner of a business. **3.** A symbol, as a multiplication sign, that denotes a mathematical operation. **4.** *Informal.* A shrewd and occas. unscrupulous person.

op•er•et•ta (ŏp'ə-rĕt'ə) *n.* A theatrical production similar to an opera but lighter in subject and style.

oph•thal•mic (ŏf-thăl'mĭk, ŏp-) *adj.* Of or pertaining to the eye.

oph•thal•mol•o•gy (ŏf'thăl-mŏl'ə-jē, ŏp'-, -thəl-) *n.* The medical field encompassing the functions, anatomy, pathology, and treatment of the eye. **—oph'thal•mol'o•gist** *n.*

oph•thal•mo•scope (ŏf-thăl'mə-skōp', ŏp-) *n.* An instrument consisting of a mirror with a central hole through which the eye is examined.

o·pi·ate (ō'pē-ĭt, -āt') *n.* **1.** A sedative drug containing opium or an opium derivative. **2.** Any drug. **3.** Something that numbs the senses or the mind.

o·pin·ion (ə-pĭn'yən) *n.* **1.** A belief held with confidence but not substantiated by positive knowledge. **2.** A conclusion based on special knowledge. **3.** A judgment of the value of a person or thing.

o·pin·ion·at·ed (ə-pĭn'yə-nā'tĭd) *adj.* Holding stubbornly and often unreasonably to one's personal opinions.

o·pi·um (ō'pē-əm) *n.* A bitter, yellowish-brown, highly addictive drug prepared from the pods of an Old World poppy and from which alkaloid drugs, as heroin, codeine, and morphine, are derived.

o·pos·sum (ə-pŏs'əm) *n., pl.* **-sum** *or* **-sums.** A nocturnal, arboreal marsupial of the family Didelphidae, esp. *Didelphis marsupialis,* of the W Hemisphere.

op·po·nent (ə-pō'nənt) *n.* One that opposes another or others. ★ ***syns:*** ADVERSARY, ANTAGONIST, OPPOSITION

op·por·tune (ŏp'ər-to͞on', -tyo͞on') *adj.* **1.** Favorable to a particular purpose. **2.** Occurring at an appropriate time.

op·por·tun·ist (ŏp'ər-to͞o'nĭst, -tyo͞o'-) *n.* One who takes advantage of circumstances for self-serving purposes. **—op'por·tun'ism** *n.* **—op'por·tun·is'tic** *adj.*

op·por·tu·ni·ty (ŏp'ər-to͞o'nĭ-tē, -tyo͞o'-) *n., pl.* **-ties. 1.** A favorable combination of circumstances. **2.** A chance for advancement <a job *opportunity*> ★ ***syns:*** BREAK, CHANCE, OCCASION, OPENING.

op·pose (ə-pōz') *v.* **-posed, -pos·ing. 1.** To be in conflict or contention with. **2.** To be in disagreement with. **3.** To place in contrasting position to. **—op·pos'a·ble** *adj.* **—op'po·si'tion** (ŏp'ə-zĭsh'ən) *n.*

op·po·site (ŏp'ə-zĭt, -sĭt) *adj.* **1.** Located or placed directly across from. **2.** Moving or tending away from each other. **3.** Sharply contrasting. *—n.* One that is opposite to another. *—adv.* In an opposite position. *—prep.* **1.** Across from or facing. **2.** In a complementary dramatic role.

op·press (ə-prĕs') *v.* **1.** To persecute or subjugate by force. **2.** To weigh heavily upon. **—op·pres'sion** *n.* **—op·pres'sive** *adj.* **—op·pres'sor** *n.*

op·pro·bri·ous (ə-prō'brē-əs) *adj.* **1.** Expressing contemptuous reproach. **2.** Disgraceful **:** ignoble.

op·pro·bri·um (ə-prō'brē-əm) *n.* **1.** Disgrace or humiliation resulting from shameful conduct. **2.** Scornful contempt or reproach. **3.** A cause of disgrace.

opt (ŏpt) *v.* To make a choice.

op·tic (ŏp'tĭk) *adj.* Of or pertaining to the eye or to vision.

op·ti·cal (ŏp'tĭ-kəl) *adj.* **1.** Of or pertaining to sight. **2.** Designed to assist vision <*optical* equipment> **3.** Of or pertaining to optics. **—op'ti·cal·ly** *adv.*

optical art *n.* Abstract art employing geometric designs or patterns.

optical disk *n. Computer Sci.* A plastic-coated disk that stores digital data as tiny pits etched into the surface and is read with a laser scanning the surface.

optical illusion *n.* A deceptive visual image.

op·ti·cian (ŏp-tĭsh'ən) *n.* One who makes or sells optical instruments and articles, as lenses and eyeglasses.

optic nerve *n.* Either of 2 sensory nerves connecting the retina with the brain.

op·tics (ŏp'tĭks) *n. (sing. in number). Physics.* Study of light and vision, chiefly of the generation, propagation, and detection of electromagnetic radiation with wavelengths greater than x-rays and shorter than microwaves.

op·ti·mal (ŏp'tə-məl) *adj.* Most favorable or desirable. **—op'ti·mal·ly** *adv.*

op·ti·mism (ŏp'tə-mĭz'əm) *n.* **1.** A disposition to expect the best possible outcome or to emphasize the most positive aspects of a situation. **2.** *Philos.* The doctrine that this world is the best of all possible worlds. **—op'ti·mist** *n.* **—op'ti·mis'tic** *adj.*

op·ti·mize (ŏp'tə-mīz') *v.* **-mized, -miz·ing. 1.** To improve to the greatest extent possible. **2.** To use most effectively.

op·ti·mum (ŏp'tə-məm) *n., pl.* **-ma** (-mə) *or* **-mums.** The best or most advantageous condition, degree, or amount. *—adj.* Most advantageous **:** best.

op·tion (ŏp'shən) *n.* **1.** The act of choosing **:** choice. **2.** A right to buy or sell something at a specified price within a specified time. **3.** Something chosen or available as a choice. **—op'tion·al** *adj.*

op·tom·e·try (ŏp-tŏm'ĭ-trē) *n.* The profession of examining the eyes and treating certain defects by means of corrective lenses. **—op·to·met'ric** (ŏp'tə-mĕt'rĭk) *adj.* **—op·tom'e·trist** *n.*

op·u·lent (ŏp'yə-lənt) *adj.* **1.** Having great wealth. **2.** Extravagant. **—op'u·lence** *n.*

o·pus (ō'pəs) *n., pl.* **o·per·a** (ō'pər-ə, ŏp'ər-ə) *or* **-es.** A creative work, esp. a musical composition.

or (ôr; *unstressed* ər) *conj.* —Used to indicate: **1. a.** An alternative, usu. only before the last in a series. **b.** The 2nd of 2 alternatives <I didn't know whether to laugh *or* cry.> **2.** An equivalent expression <claustrophobia, *or* fear of enclosed places> **3.** Indefiniteness <3 *or* 4>

—or[1] *suff.* One that performs an action <percolator>

—or[2] *suff.* Condition or activity <behavior>

or·a·cle (ôr'ə-kəl, ŏr'-) *n.* **1. a.** A shrine consecrated to a prophetic deity. **b.** One who serves a deity, esp. as a medium for prophecies, at such a shrine. **c.** A divine prophecy, often in the form of an enigmatic statement. **2.** One who gives wise advice. **—o·rac'u·lar** (ô-răk'yə-lər, ō-) *adj.*

o•ral (ôr′əl, ōr′-) *adj.* **1.** Spoken as opposed to written. **2.** Of or relating to the mouth <*oral* surgery> **3.** Used in or administered through the mouth.

oral contraceptive *n.* A pill containing hormones, taken usu. on a monthly schedule to prevent ovulation.

oral history *n.* **1.** Historical information obtained directly, as in interviews, from persons with firsthand knowledge. **2.** A written account based on oral history.

or•ange (ôr′ĭnj, ŏr′-) *n.* **1.** A semitropical evergreen tree of the genus *Citrus,* with white flowers and round, yellowish-red edible fruit having a sectioned interior and sweet, acid juice. **2.** A yellowish red.

or•ange•ade (ôr′ĭn-jād′, ŏr′-) *n.* A drink made of orange juice, sugar, and plain or carbonated water.

orange pekoe *n.* A grade of black tea.

or•ange•ry (ôr′ĭnj-rē, ŏr′-) *n., pl.* **-ries.** An enclosed place, as a greenhouse, where orange trees are cultivated.

o•rang•u•tan (ō-răng′ə-tăn′, ə-răng′-) *n.* An arboreal anthropoid ape, *Pongo pygmaeus,* of Borneo and Sumatra, with a shaggy coat, very long arms, and no tail.

o•rate (ô-rāt′, ō-rāt′, ôr′āt′, ōr′-) *v.* **o•rat•ed, o•rat•ing.** To speak in a pompous, declamatory manner.

o•ra•tion (ô-rā′shən, ō-rā′-) *n.* A formal speech, esp. one given on a special occasion.

or•a•tor (ôr′ə-tər, ŏr′-) *n.* **1.** A person who delivers an oration. **2.** A person skilled in the art of public speaking.

or•a•to•ri•o (ôr′ə-tôr′ē-ō′, -tōr′-, ŏr′-) *n., pl.* **-os.** A musical composition for voices and instruments, narrating a usu. sacred story without costumes or dramatic action.

or•a•to•ry[1] (ôr′ə-tôr′ē, -tōr′ē, ŏr′-) *n.* **1.** The art of speaking effectively in public. **2.** Rhetorical skill or style. **—or′a•tor′i•cal** *adj.*

or•a•to•ry[2] (ôr′ə-tôr′ē, -tōr′ē, ŏr′-) *n., pl.* **-ries.** A place for prayer, esp. a small private chapel.

orb (ôrb) *n.* **1.** A sphere. **2.** A celestial body. **3.** A jeweled sphere surmounted by a cross, as a symbol of royal power. **—or•bic′u•lar** (-bĭk′yə-lər) *adj.*

or•bit (ôr′bĭt) *n.* **1.** The path of a celestial body or artificial satellite as it revolves around another body. **2.** The path of a body in a field of force, esp. a path that surrounds another body. **3. a.** A range of activity or experience <one's social *orbit*> **b.** A range of control or influence. *—v.* **1.** To put into an orbit. **2.** To move or revolve in orbit. **—or′bit•al** *adj.*

or•ca (ôr′kə) *n.* The killer whale.

or•chard (ôr′chərd) *n.* **1.** Land used for the growing of fruit trees. **2.** The trees cultivated in an orchard.

or•ches•tra (ôr′kĭ-strə, -kĕs′trə) *n.* **1.** A large group of musicians performing together on various instruments. **2.** The area immediately in front of a stage where the musicians sit. **3. a.** The section of seats in a theater nearest the stage. **b.** The entire main floor of a theater. **—or•ches′tral** (-kĕs′trəl) *adj.* **—or•ches′tral•ly** *adv.*

or•ches•trate (ôr′kĭ-strāt′) *v.* **-trat•ed, -trat•ing. 1.** To arrange or compose (music) for performence by an orchestra. **2.** To organize or manage so as to achieve a desired effect. **—or′ches•tra′tion** *n.* **—or′ches•tra′tor, or′ches•trat′er** *n.*

or•chid (ôr′kĭd) *n.* **1.** A plant of the family Orchidaceae, found worldwide but chiefly in the tropics, with irregularly shaped flowers cultivated esp. for personal adornment. **2.** A light reddish purple.

or•dain (ôr-dān′) *v.* **1.** To install as a priest, minister, or rabbi. **2.** To order by virtue of established authority. **3.** To prearrange unalterably. **—or•dain′ment** *n.*

or•deal (ôr-dēl′, ôr′dēl′) *n.* A painful or difficult experience.

or•der (ôr′dər) *n.* **1.** A condition of coherent or logical arrangement among the individual elements of a group. **2.** The standard or prescribed state or condition of a thing. **3.** The established organization of a society. **4.** A sequential arrangement in time or space. **5.** The established sequence or procedure. **6.** An authoritative direction **:** command. **7.** A commission or instruction to buy or sell something. **8.** A meal or portion of food requested by a customer at a restaurant. **9. a.** A grade or rank of the Christian ministry. **b. orders.** The office of an ordained priest or minister. **10.** A group of people living under a religious rule. **11.** An organization of people bound by some common bond or social aim. **12.** A group of persons upon whom a sovereign or government has formally conferred honor <the *Order* of the British Empire> **13.** Degree of importance **:** rank. **14.** One of a number of styles of classical architecture. **15.** *Biol.* A taxonomic category of animals and plants, above a family and below a class. *—v.* **1.** To give a command (to). **2.** To give a command for. **3.** To request to be supplied with. **4.** To put into a systematic arrangement. **—on the order of. 1.** Similar to. **2.** Approximately. **—to order.** According to the buyer's specifications.

or•der•ly (ôr′dər-lē) *adj.* **1.** Having a systematic arrangement **:** neat. **2.** Well-behaved **:** peaceful. *—n., pl.* **-lies. 1.** One who performs unskilled work in a hospital. **2.** A soldier assigned to be a messenger or attendant to a superior officer. **—or′der•li•ness** *n.* **—or′der•ly** *adv.*

or•di•nal (ôr′dn-əl) *adj.* Designating a specified position in a numbered series. *—n.* An ordinal number.

ordinal number *n.* A number indicating position in a series, as first (1st) or second (2nd).

or•di•nance (ôr′dn-əns) *n.* **1.** An authoritative order or command. **2.** A municipal regulation or statute.

or•di•nar•i•ly (ôr′dn-âr′ə-lē, ôr′dn-ĕr′-) *adv.* As a general rule.

or•di•nar•y (ôr′dn-ĕr′ē) *adj.* **1.** Usual **:** normal. **2.** Of no exceptional quality **:** average.

★ *syns:* AVERAGE, COMMON, COMMONPLACE, PLAIN, RUN-OF-THE-MILL, UNEXCEPTIONAL —**or'di·nar'i·ness** *n.*

or·di·nate (ôr'dn-ĭt, -āt') *n. Math.* The coordinate representing the distance from a specified point to the *x*–axis, measured parallel to the *y*–axis.

or·di·na·tion (ôr'dn-ā'shən) *n.* The act of ordaining or the ceremony of being ordained.

ord·nance (ôrd'nəns) *n.* **1.** Military weapons, ammunition, and equipment. **2.** Heavy guns : artillery.

or·do (ôr'dō) *n., pl.* **-di·nes** (-də-nēz') *or* **-dos.** *Rom. Cath. Ch.* A calendar with directions for each day's Mass and office.

or·dure (ôr'jər) *n.* Excrement : dung.

ore (ôr, ōr) *n.* A mineral or rock from which a valuable substance, esp. a metal, can be extracted.

ö·re (œ'rə) *n., pl.* **ö·re.** —See table at CURRENCY.

o·re·ad (ôr'ē-ăd', ōr'-) *n. Gk. Myth.* A mountain nymph.

o·reg·a·no (ə-rĕg'ə-nō', ô-rĕg'-) *n.* An aromatic plant, *Origanum vulgare,* with pinkish flower spikes and leaves used as seasoning.

or·gan (ôr'gən) *n.* **1.** A musical instrument consisting of pipes of varying sizes that sound tones when supplied with air, and a keyboard and pedals that direct the flow of air from the bellows to the pipes. **2.** An instrument, as an electronic organ, that imitates the sound of the organ. **3.** *Biol.* A differentiated part of an organism, adapted for a specific function. **4.** A group or body that is part of a larger organization. **5.** An instrument of communication, esp. a periodical issued by an organization.

or·gan·dy *also* **or·gan·die** (ôr'gən-dē) *n., pl.* **-dies.** A stiff, transparent fabric of silk or cotton.

or·gan·elle (ôr'gə-nĕl') *n.* A differentiated structure within a cell, such as a vacuole, that performs a specific function.

or·gan·ic (ôr-găn'ĭk) *adj.* **1.** Of, pertaining to, or affecting an organ of the body. **2.** Of, pertaining to, or derived from living organisms. **3.** Grown with fertilizers that consist only of plant or natural matter, with no chemical additives. **4.** Like an organism in development or organization. **5.** Constituting a basic part : integral. **6.** *Chem.* Of or designating carbon compounds. —**or·gan'i·cal·ly** *adv.*

organic chemistry *n.* The chemistry of carbon compounds.

or·gan·ism (ôr'gə-nĭz'əm) *n.* **1.** A plant or animal. **2.** A system regarded as analogous to a living body <the social *organism*>

or·gan·ist (ôr'gə-nĭst) *n.* One who plays the organ.

or·gan·i·za·tion (ôr'gə-nĭ-zā'shən) *n.* **1.** An act of organizing or the process of being organized. **2.** The state or manner of being organized. **3.** Something organized or made into an ordered whole. **4.** A number of persons or groups united for a particular purpose. —**or'gan·i·za'tion·al** *adj.*

or·gan·ize (ôr'gə-nīz') *v.* **-ized, -iz·ing. 1.** To arrange or assemble into an orderly structured whole. **2.** To give a coherent form to. **3.** To arrange by coordinating and planning. **4.** To form or persuade to form a labor union. —**or'gan·iz'er** *n.*

or·gan·za (ôr-găn'zə) *n.* A sheer, stiff, silk or synthetic fabric.

or·gasm (ôr'găz'əm) *n.* The highest point of sexual excitement : climax. —**or·gas'mic, or·gas'tic** (-găs'tĭk) *adj.*

or·gy (ôr'jē) *n., pl.* **-gies. 1.** A revel involving unrestrained indulgence, esp. sexual activity. **2.** Excessive indulgence in a specific activity. —**or'gi·as'tic** (-ăs'tĭk) *adj.*

o·ri·el (ôr'ē-əl, ōr'-) *n.* A projecting bay window supported from below with a corbel or by brackets.

o·ri·ent (ôr'ē-ənt, -ĕnt', ōr'-) *n.* **1.** The east. **2. Orient.** The countries of Asia, esp. of E Asia. —*v.* (ôr'ē-ĕnt', ōr'-). **1.** To place or locate in a specified relation to the points of the compass. **2.** To determine the bearings of. **3.** To make or become familiar or acquainted with a situation. —**o'ri·en·ta'tion** *n.*

o·ri·en·tal (ôr'ē-ĕn'tl, ōr'-) *adj.* **1.** Eastern. **2.** *often* **Oriental.** Of or relating to the Orient. —*n. often* **Oriental.** A native or inhabitant of the Orient.

Oriental rug *n.* A rug made by hand in the Orient.

or·i·en·tate (ôr'ē-ĕn-tāt', -ən-, ōr'-) *v.* **-tat·ed, -tat·ing.** To orient.

or·i·fice (ôr'ə-fĭs, ŏr'-) *n.* An opening.

or·i·flamme (ôr'ə-flăm', ŏr'-) *n.* An inspiring symbol or standard.

o·ri·ga·mi (ôr'ĭ-gä'mē) *n.* The Japanese art of folding paper into decorative shapes.

or·i·gin (ôr'ə-jĭn, ŏr'-) *n.* **1.** The cause or source of something. **2.** Ancestry : derivation. **3.** A coming into being. **4.** *Math.* The point of intersection of coordinate axes. ★ *syns:* DERIVATION, FOUNTAIN, PROVENANCE, PROVENIENCE, ROOT, SOURCE, SPRING, WELL

o·rig·i·nal (ə-rĭj'ə-nəl) *adj.* **1.** Preceeding all others in time. **2.** New and unusual. **3.** Inventive. —*n.* **1.** A first form from which varieties arise or imitations are made. **2.** An authentic work of art as opposed to an imitation or reproduction. —**o·rig'i·nal'i·ty** (-năl'ĭ-tē) *n.*

o·rig·i·nate (ə-rĭj'ə-nāt') *v.* **-nat·ed, -nat·ing.** To bring or come into being. —**o·rig'i·na'tion** *n.* —**o·rig'i·na'tor** *n.*

o·ri·ole (ôr'ē-ōl', ōr'-) *n.* Any of various songbirds of the families Oriolidae and Icteridae, having bright yellow and black plumage in the males.

or·i·son (ôr'ĭ-sən, -zən, ŏr'-) *n.* A prayer.

Or·lon (ôr'lŏn'). A trademark for a synthetic acrylic fiber.

or·mo·lu (ôr'mə-lo͞o') *n.* An alloy resembling gold and used for decoration.

or·na·ment (ôr'nə-mənt) *n.* Something that decorates : embellishment. —*v.* (ôr'nə-mĕnt'). To furnish with ornaments. —**or'na·**

men′tal *adj.* —**or′na•men′tal•ly** *adv.* —**or′-na•men•ta′tion** *n.*
or•nate (ôr-nāt′) *adj.* Elaborately or heavily ornamented. —**or•nate′ly** *adv.*
or•ner•y (ôr′nə-rē) *adj.* **-i•er, -i•est.** Stubborn and ill-tempered.
or•ni•thol•o•gy (ôr′nə-thŏl′ə-jē) *n.* The scientific study of birds. —**or′ni•tho•log′i•cal** (-thə-lŏj′ĭ-kəl), **or′ni•tho•log′ic** *adj.* —**or′ni•thol′o•gist** *n.*
or•ni•thop•ter (ôr′nə-thŏp′tər) *n.* A machine shaped like an aircraft that is held aloft and propelled by wing movements.
o•ro•tund (ôr′ə-tŭnd′, ŏr′-, ōr′-) *adj.* **1.** Having a full sound **:** sonorous. **2.** Pompous.
or•phan (ôr′fən) *n.* A child whose parents are dead. —**or′phan** *v.*
or•phan•age (ôr′fə-nĭj) *n.* An institution for the care of children without parents.
or•ris (ôr′ĭs, ŏr′-) *n.* Any of several species of iris, esp. *Iris florentina,* with a fragrant root used in cosmetics and perfumes.
ort (ôrt) *n.* **1.** A scrap of food remaining after a meal. **2.** A bit.
or•tho•don•tia (ôr′thə-dŏn′shə) *also* **or•tho•don•tics** (-tĭks) *n.* The dental specialty and practice of correcting irregularities of the teeth. —**or′tho•don′tic** *adj.* —**or′tho•don′-tist** *n.*
or•tho•dox (ôr′thə-dŏks′) *adj.* **1.** Adhering to established or traditional beliefs, esp. in religion. **2.** Conforming to accepted standards. **3. Orthodox. a.** Of or designating any of the Christian churches of the Eastern Orthodox Church. **b.** Of or designating Orthodox Judaism. —**or′tho•dox′y** *n.*
Orthodox Judaism *n.* The branch of Judaism that is governed by adherence to the Torah as interpreted in the Talmud.
or•thog•o•nal (ôr-thŏg′ə-nəl) *adj. Math.* Pertaining to or composed of right angles.
or•thog•ra•phy (ôr-thŏg′rə-fē) *n., pl.* **-phies. 1.** Correct spelling. **2.** The area of language study dealing with systems of spelling. —**or′-tho•graph′ic** (-thə-grăf′ĭk) *adj.* —**or•thog′-raph•er** *n.*
or•tho•pe•dics *also* **or•tho•pae•dics** (ôr′-thə-pē′dĭks) *n. (sing. in number).* The branch of medicine that deals with injuries or disorders of the skeletal system. —**or′tho•pe′dic** *adj.* —**or′tho•pe′di•cal•ly** *adv.* —**or′tho•pe′-dist** *n.*
or•thot•ics (ôr-thŏt′ĭks) *n. (sing. in number).* The science that deals with the use of specialized mechanical devices to support or supplement impaired joints or limbs. —**or•thot′ic** *adj. & n.* —**or•thot′ist** (ôr-thŏt′ĭst, ôr′thə-tĭst) *n.*
or•to•lan (ôr′tə-lən) *n.* A small European bird, *Emberiza hortulana,* often eaten as a delicacy.
–ory *suff.* **1.** Of, involving, or tending toward <compensat*ory*> **2.** A place of or for <reformat*ory*>
Os *symbol for* OSMIUM.
Os•car (ŏs′kər). A trademark for any of the golden statuettes awarded each year by the Academy of Motion Picture Arts and Sciences for achievement in films.
os•cil•late (ŏs′ə-lāt′) *v.* **-lat•ed, -lat•ing. 1.** To swing back and forth with a regular motion. **2.** To waver between 2 or more choices. **3.** *Physics.* To vary between alternate extremes, usu. with a definable period. —**os′-cil•la′tion** *n.* —**os′cil•la′tor** *n.* —**os′cil•la•to′ry** (-lə-tôr′ē, -tōr′ē) *adj.*
os•cil•lo•scope (ŏ-sĭl′ə-skōp′, ə-sĭl′-) *n.* An instrument producing an instantaneous visual display on a fluorescent screen corresponding to oscillations of voltage and current. —**os•cil′lo•scop′ic** *adj.*
os•cu•late (ŏs′kyə-lāt′) *v.* **-lat•ed, -lat•ing.** To kiss. —**os′cu•la′tion** *n.*
–ose *suff.* Having **:** similar to <grandi*ose*>
o•sier (ō′zhər) *n.* A willow having long, wand-like branches used in basketry, esp. *Salix viminalis* or *S. purpurea.*
os•mi•um (ŏz′mē-əm) *n. Symbol* **Os** A hard, bluish-white metallic element, used for pen points and phonograph needles.
os•mo•sis (ŏz-mō′sĭs, ŏs-) *n.* **1.** The diffusion of fluid through a semipermeable membrane, as the wall of a living cell. **2.** A gradual, often unconscious process of assimilation <learned German by *osmosis*> —**os•mot′ic** (ŏz-mŏt′ĭk, ŏs-) *adj.*
os•prey (ŏs′prē, -prā′) *n., pl.* **-preys.** A large fish-eating hawk, *Pandion haliaetus,* having black and white plumage.
os•si•fy (ŏs′ə-fī′) *v.* **-fied, -fy•ing. 1.** To convert (e.g., cartilage) into bone. **2.** To set or become set into a rigidly conventional pattern. —**os′si•fi•ca′tion** *n.*
os•so bu•co (ō′sō bōō′kō) *n.* An Italian dish of veal shanks braised in white wine.
os•te•i•tis (ŏs′tē-ī′tĭs) *n.* Inflammation of bone or bony tissue.
os•ten•si•ble (ŏ-stĕn′sə-bəl, ə-stĕn′-) *adj.* Representing or appearing as such **:** professed. —**os•ten′si•bly** *adv.*
os•ten•ta•tion (ŏs′tĕn-tā′shən, -tən-) *n.* Lavish or pretentious display. —**os′ten•ta′tious** *adj.* —**os′ten•ta′tious•ly** *adv.*
os•te•o•ar•thri•tis (ŏs′tē-ō-är-thrī′tĭs) *n.* A degenerative disease of the joints.
os•te•op•a•thy (ŏs′tē-ŏp′ə-thē) *n.* A system that emphasizes manipulation esp. of the bones for treating disease. —**os′te•o•path′** (ŏs′tē-ə-păth′) *n.* —**os′te•o•path′ic** *adj.*
os•te•o•po•ro•sis (ŏs′tē-ō-pə-rō′sĭs) *n.* A disease in which the bones become extremely porous, occurring esp. in women following menopause. —**os′te•o•po•rot′ic** (-rŏt′ĭk) *adj.*
os•tra•cize (ŏs′trə-sīz′) *v.* **-cized, -ciz•ing.** To exclude from a group **:** shun. —**os′tra•cism** *n.*
os•trich (ŏs′trĭch, ô′strĭch) *n.* A large, swift, flightless bird of the genus *Struthio,* with a long bare neck and powerful legs.
oth•er (ŭth′ər) *adj.* **1. a.** Being or designating the remaining one of two or more <the *other* arm> **b.** Being or designating the remaining ones of several <*other* toys in the box> **2.** Different from that or those specified. **3.** Ad-

ditional : extra <He has no *other* suit.> **4.** Alternate <every *other* year> **5.** Of a past or future time. **6.** Of the recent past <just the *other* day> —*n.* **1. a.** The remaining one of two or more. **b. others.** The remaining ones of several. **2. a.** A different person or thing. **b.** An additional person or thing. —*pron.* A different or additional person or thing. —*adv.* In another way.

oth•er•wise (ŭth'ər-wīz') *adv.* **1.** Differently <believed *otherwise*> **2.** Under different circumstances <*Otherwise* I would have called.> **3.** In other respects. —*adj.* Different.

oth•er•world•ly (ŭth'ər-wûrld'lē) *adj.* **1.** Supernatural. **2.** Concerned with spiritual, intellectual, or imaginative matters. **—oth'er•world'li•ness** *n.*

o•ti•ose (ō'shē-ōs', ō'tē-) *adj.* **1.** Idle : lazy. **2.** Futile : ineffective.

o•ti•tis (ō-tī'tĭs) *n.* Inflammation of the ear.

o•to•lar•yn•gol•o•gy (ō'tō-lăr'ĭng-gŏl'ə-jē) *n.* A branch of medicine dealing with the ear, nose, and throat.

ot•ta•va (ŏ-tä'və) *adv. Mus.* At an octave lower or higher than written. —Used as a direction. **—ot•ta'va** *adj.*

ot•ter (ŏt'ər) *n., pl.* **-ter** *or* **-ters.** Any of several aquatic, carnivorous mammals of the genus *Lutra* and related genera, having webbed feet and thick fur.

ot•to•man (ŏt'ə-mən) *n.* **1.** An upholstered sofa without a back or arms. **2.** An upholstered or stuffed footstool.

Ot•to•man (ŏt'ə-mən) *n., pl.* **-mans.** A Turk, esp. of the Ottoman Empire. —*adj.* **1.** Of the Ottoman Empire. **2.** Turkish.

ou•bli•ette (ōō'blē-ĕt') *n.* A dungeon with a trap door in the ceiling as its only means of access.

ouch (ouch) *interj.* —Used to express sudden pain or distress.

ought (ôt) *v.* —Used to indicate: **1.** Duty or obligation <You *ought* to try harder.> **2.** Prudence or advisability <They *ought* to have health insurance> **3.** Desirability <You *ought* to have been there; it was interesting.> **4.** Likelihood or probability <I *ought* to finish soon.>

ou•gui•ya (ōō-gē'yə) *n.* —See table at CURRENCY.

ounce (ouns) *n.* **1.** —See table at MEASUREMENT. **2.** A tiny bit.

our (our) *adj.* Of or pertaining to us, esp. as possessors, agents, or objects of an action <*our* house><*our* being delayed>

ours (ourz) *pron.* That or those belonging to us <That boat is *ours.*> <*Ours* were the only suggestions adopted.>

our•selves (our-sĕlvz', är-) *pl. pron.* **1.** Those identical with us. —Used: **a.** Reflexively as the object of a verb or preposition <We hurt *ourselves.*> **b.** For emphasis <We *ourselves* were not involved.> **2.** Our normal state <We have not been *ourselves* since you left.>

—ous *suff.* Full of : having <joy*ous*> <fam*ous*> <glori*ous*>

oust (oust) *v.* To force out : eject.

oust•er (ou'stər) *n.* **1.** One that ousts. **2.** *Law.* Illegal or wrongful dispossession.

out (out) *adv.* **1.** In a direction away from the inside or center. **2.** Away from a home or business. **3.** Outdoors <put the dog *out*> **4. a.** To depletion, exhaustion, or extinction. **5.** To an end or conclusion <serve my time *out*> **6.** Into being, availability, circulation, or view <The new cars are *out.*> **7.** Into an unfashionable status <Wide ties have gone *out.*> **8.** *Baseball.* So as to be retired. —*adj.* **1.** Exterior : external. **2.** Not functioning, operating, or flowing. **3.** *Informal.* Not having an amount previously possessed <I am *out* $50.> **4.** Not to be considered. —*prep.* Forth from <fell *out* the window> —*n.* **1.** One that is out, esp. out of power. **2.** A means of evasion or escape. **3.** *Baseball.* A play in which a player is retired. —*v.* To be disclosed <Scandal will *out.*>

out– *pref.* In a way that surpasses, exceeds, or goes beyond <*out*do>.

out•age (ou'tĭj) *n.* A temporary suspension of operation, esp. of electric power.

out-and-out (out'n-out') *adj.* Utter.

out•back (out'băk') *n.* The remote, wild part of a country, as of Australia.

out•board (out'bôrd', -bōrd') *adj.* **1.** *Naut.* Located outside a vessel's hull. **2.** Located toward the end of the wing of an aircraft. **—out'board'** *adv.*

out•act' *v.*
out•ar'gue *v.*
out•bar'gain *v.*
out•bid' *v.*
out•bluff' *v.*
out•blus'ter *v.*
out•boast' *v.*
out•box' *v.*
out•brag' *v.*
out•bra'zen *v.*
out•build' *v.*
out•bul'ly *v.*
out•charm' *v.*
out•class' *v.*
out•climb' *v.*
out•cook' *v.*
out•dance' *v.*
out•daz'zle *v.*
out'de•bate' *v.*
out'de•liv'er *v.*
out'de•sign' *v.*
out•dis'tance *v.*
out•dress' *v.*
out•drink' *v.*
out•drive' *v.*
out•earn' *v.*
out•fight' *v.*
out•fish' *v.*
out•flat'ter *v.*
out•fly' *v.*
out•gain' *v.*
out•gam'ble *v.*
out•guess' *v.*
out•hit' *v.*
out•hunt' *v.*
out•hus'tle *v.*
out•jump' *v.*
out•kick' *v.*
out•last' *v.*
out•leap' *v.*
out•learn' *v.*
out•live' *v.*
out'ma•neu'ver *v.*
out'ma•nip'u•late' *v.*
out•march' *v.*

outboard motor *n.* A detachable engine mounted on the stern of a boat.

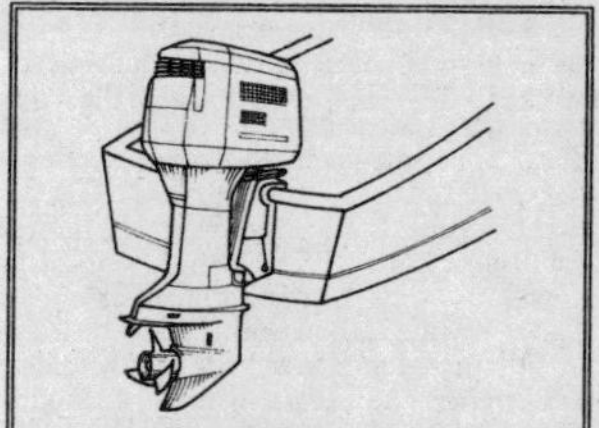

outboard motor

out•bound (out'bound') *adj.* Outward bound : going away.
out•break (out'brāk') *n.* A sudden occurrence : outburst.
out•build•ing (out'bĭl'dĭng) *n.* A building, as a shed or barn, that is separate from the main building.
out•burst (out'bûrst') *n.* A sudden eruption, as of emotion or activity.
out•cast (out'kăst') *n.* One who has been excluded from a group or society.
out•come (out'kŭm') *n.* A consequence.
out•crop (out'krŏp') *n.* A stratum or formation, as of bedrock, protruding through the soil level. **—out'crop'** *v.*
out•cry (out'krī') *n.* **1.** A loud clamor. **2.** A vociferous objection.
out•dat•ed (out-dā'tĭd) *adj.* Old fashioned : antiquated.
out•do (out-dōō') *v.* To exceed in achievement or performance.
out•door (out'dôr', -dōr') *also* **out-of-door** (out'əv-dôr', -dōr') *adj.* Done in, located in, or suitable for the open air.
out•doors (out-dôrz', -dōrz') *also* **out-of-doors** (out'əv-dôrz', -dōrz'). *—adv.* In or into the open air. *—n.* The open air.
out•er (ou'tər) *adj.* **1.** Located on the outside. **2.** Farther from the middle or center.
outer ear *n.* The external part of the ear.
out•er•most (ou'tər-mōst') *adj.* Most distant from the inside or center.
outer space *n.* A region of space beyond the limits of a celestial body or system.
out•face (out-fās') *v.* **-faced, -fac•ing. 1.** To overcome with a bold look : stare down. **2.** To resist : defy.
out•fall (out'fôl') *n.* The place where a sewer, drain, or stream discharges.
out•field (out'fēld') *n. Baseball.* The playing area extending outward from the infield. **—out'field'er** *n.*
out•fit (out'fĭt') *n.* **1.** A set of tools, clothes, or equipment for a specialized purpose. **2.** *Informal.* An association of persons, esp. a military unit or business organization. *—v.* To provide with specialized equipment or clothing.
out•flank (out-flăngk') *v.* To maneuver around and behind the flank of.
out•fox (out-fŏks') *v.* To outsmart.
out•go (out'gō') *n., pl.* **-goes.** Something that goes out, esp. money.
out•go•ing (out'gō'ĭng) *adj.* **1. a.** Departing : outbound. **b.** Relinquishing an office. **2.** Sociable : friendly.
out•grow (out-grō') *v.* **1.** To grow too large for. **2.** To lose in the process of maturing. **3.** To surpass in growth.
out•growth (out'grōth') *n.* **1.** Something that grows out of something else. **2.** A consequence : result.
out•house (out'hous') *n.* **1.** An outbuilding. **2.** An outdoor toilet.
out•ing (ou'tĭng) *n.* **1.** A pleasure trip. **2.** A walk outdoors.
out•land•ish (out-lăn'dĭsh) *adj.* Extremely unconventional : bizarre.
out•law (out'lô') *n.* **1.** A habitual criminal. **2.** One who is excluded from normal legal protection and rights. *—v.* **1.** To declare illegal. **2.** To deprive of legal protection. **—out'law'ry** *n.*
out•lay (out'lā') *n.* **1.** The spending of money. **2.** An amount spent : expenditure.
out•let (out'lĕt', -lĭt) *n.* **1.** An exit : vent. **2.** A means of release, as for emotion. **3.** A market for services or goods. **4.** *Elect.* A receptacle, esp. one mounted in a wall, that has a socket for a plug and is connected to a power supply.
out•line (out'līn') *n.* **1. a.** A line marking the outer edges of a figure or object. **b.** Shape. **2.** Drawing in which objects are delineated in contours without shading. **3.** A general account or description of a subject. ★ ***syns:***

out•mus'cle *v.*
out•num'ber *v.*
out•or'gan•ize' *v.*
out•pass' *v.*
out'per•form' *v.*
out•pitch' *v.*
out•play' *v.*
out•pol'i•tick *v.*
out•poll' *v.*
out•preach' *v.*
out•price' *v.*
out'pro•duce' *v.*
out•punch' *v.*
out•rank' *v.*
out•rate' *v.*
out•ri'val *v.*
out•roar' *v.*
out•row' *v.*
out•run' *v.*
out•sail' *v.*
out•scheme' *v.*
out•score' *v.*
out•scream' *v.*
out•sell' *v.*
out•shout' *v.*
out•shriek' *v.*
out•sing' *v.*
out•sit' *v.*
out•skate' *v.*
out•spend' *v.*
out•state' *v.*
out•stay' *v.*
out•stride' *v.*
out•strive' *v.*
out•swear' *v.*
out•swim' *v.*
out•swin'dle *v.*
out•talk' *v.*
out•throw' *v.*
out•trade' *v.*
out•vote' *v.*
out•wait' *v.*
out•walk' *v.*
out•wres'tle *v.*
out•write' *v.*

CONTOUR, DELINEATION, PROFILE, SILHOUETTE —*v.* **1.** To draw an outline of. **2.** To make a summary of.
out·look (out'lo͝ok') *n.* **1.** A place that offers a view of something. **2.** A point of view : attitude. **3.** Prospect.
out·ly·ing (out'lī'ĭng) *adj.* Comparatively distant from a center.
out·mod·ed (out-mō'dĭd) *adj.* **1.** No longer fashionable. **2.** Obsolete.
out of *prep.* **1. a.** From within to the outside of <went *out of* the country> **b.** From a given condition <came *out of* the coma> **c.** From a cause or source <made *out of* plastic> **2. a.** In a position beyond the range, sphere, or boundaries of. **b.** In a state different from the usual <*out of* practice> **3.** Because of <did it *out of* jealousy> **4.** From among.
out-of-bounds (out'əv-boundz') *adv. & adj.* Beyond the established limits.
out-of-date (out'əv-dāt') *adj.* Old-fashioned.
out-of-door (out'əv-dôr', -dōr') *adj. var. of* OUTDOOR.
out-of-doors (out'əv-dôrz', -dōrz') *adv. & n. var. of* OUTDOORS.
out-of-pock·et (out'-əv-pŏk'ĭt) *adj.* Designating expenses entailing the outlay of ready cash.
out-of-the-way (out'əv-*th*ə-wā') *adj.* **1.** Remote : secluded. **2.** Out of the ordinary.
out-of-town·er (out'əv-tou'nər) *n.* A person visiting from another city or town.
out·pa·tient (out'pā'shənt) *n.* A person who receives treatment at a hospital or clinic without being admitted as a patient.
out·port (out'pôrt', -pōrt') *n. Can.* A remote coastal village, esp. in Newf.
out·post (out'pōst') *n.* **1. a.** A detachment of troops stationed away from a main unit. **b.** The station occupied by an outpost. **2.** An outlying settlement.
out·pour·ing (out'pôr'ĭng, -pōr'-) *n.* Something that pours out or is poured out.
out·put (out'po͝ot') *n.* **1.** An amount produced during a given time. **2. a.** The power, energy, or work produced by a system. **b.** *Computer Sci.* The data produced from a specific input. **—out'put'** *v.*
out·rage (out'rāj') *n.* **1.** An extremely violent or vicious act. **2.** A gross offense to morality or decency. **3.** Resentful anger. —*v.* **-raged, -rag·ing. 1.** To commit an outrage upon. **2.** To produce anger in.
out·ra·geous (out-rā'jəs) *adj.* Exceeding the bounds of what is right and proper. ★ ***syns:*** ATROCIOUS, FLAGRANT, HEINOUS, MONSTROUS, SCANDALOUS, SHOCKING
ou·tré (o͞o-trā') *adj.* Highly unconventional : eccentric.
out·reach (out-rēch') *v.* To reach or go beyond. —*n.* An organized effort to extend services beyond usual limits.
out·rig·ger (out'rĭg'ər) *n.* **1.** A narrow float attached to a seagoing canoe by projecting spars for a stabilizing support. **2.** A vessel fitted with an outrigger.
out·right (out'rīt', -rīt') *adv.* **1.** Without reservation. **2.** Utterly. **3.** Straightway. —*adj.* (out'rīt'). **1.** Unqualified. **2.** Complete : thoroughgoing.
out·run (out-rŭn') *v.* **1.** To run faster than. **2.** To go beyond : exceed.
out·set (out'sĕt') *n.* Start : beginning.
out·shine (out-shīn') *v.* **1.** To shine brighter than. **2.** To surpass in beauty or excellence.
out·side (out-sīd', out'sīd') *n.* **1.** The part that faces out. **2.** The space beyond a limit. **3.** An utmost limit <I'll be gone 2 hours at the *outside.*> —*adj.* **1.** Originating or existing at a place beyond certain limits. **2.** Of, restricted to, or situated on the outside of a boundary. **3.** Extreme <an *outside* limit> **4.** Slight : slim <an *outside* chance> —*adv.* On or into the outside. —*prep.* **1.** On or to the outer side of. **2.** Beyond the limits of. **3.** Except for.
outside of *prep.* Outside.
out·sid·er (out-sī'dər) *n.* One who is not part of a particular group.
out·size (out'sīz') *n.* A very large size. **—out'size', out'sized'** *adj.*
out·skirts (out'skûrts') *pl.n.* The parts on the edge of a central area.
out·smart (out-smärt') *v.* To gain the advantage over by cunning or cleverness.
out·spo·ken (out-spō'kən) *adj.* **1.** Said without reserve : candid. **2.** Frank in speech. **—out·spo'ken·ly** *adv.*
out·stand·ing (out-stăn'dĭng, out'stan'-) *adj.* **1.** Projecting outward or upward. **2.** Conspicuous : prominent. **3.** Distinguished. **4.** Not resolved or settled.
out·stretch (out-strĕch') *v.* To extend.
out·strip (out-strĭp') *v.* **1.** To leave behind : outdistance. **2.** To surpass.
out·take (out'tāk') A take or scene of a motion picture that is not included in the final version.
out·ward (out'wərd) *adj.* **1.** Of or moving toward the exterior or outside. **2.** Purely external : superficial. —*adv.* Toward the outside. **—out'wards** *adv.*
out·weigh (out-wā') *v.* To exceed in weight or importance.
out·wit (out-wĭt') *v.* **-wit·ted, -wit·ting.** To outsmart.
ou·zo (o͞o'zō) *n., pl.* **-zos.** A colorless Greek liqueur flavored with aniseed.
o·va (ō'və) *n. pl. of* OVUM.
o·val (ō'vəl) *adj.* **1.** Shaped like an egg. **2.** Shaped like an ellipse. **—o'val** *n.*
o·va·ry (ō'və-rē) *n., pl.* **-ries. 1.** The female reproductive gland, typically occurring in pairs, in which ova are produced. **2.** *Bot.* The part of a pistil that contains ovules. **—o·var'i·an** (ō-vâr'ē-ən) *adj.*
o·vate (ō'vāt') *adj.* Oval.
o·va·tion (ō-vā'shən) *n.* Enthusiastic, prolonged applause.
ov·en (ŭv'ən) *n.* An enclosed compartment supplied with heat and used for baking or heating food.
ov·en·bird (ŭv'ən-bûrd') *n.* A North American warbler, *Seiurus aurocapillus,* that builds a dome-shaped nest on the ground.

o•ver (ō′vər) *prep.* **1.** Above <a sign *over* the window> **2.** Above and across <a jump *over* the brook> **3.** On the other side of. **4.** Upon. **5.** Throughout **:** during. **6.** More than in degree, quantity, or extent. **7.** Concerning <an argument *over* technique> *—adv.* **1.** Above the top or surface. **2. a.** Across to the other side. **b.** Across the edge <The milk spilled *over.*> **3. a.** Across a distance in a specific direction. **b.** To another specified place or position <moved the chair *over*> **4.** To a different opinion <won us *over*> **5.** To a different person, state, or title <sign *over* property> **6.** So as to be totally enclosed or covered <The pond froze *over* last night> **7.** Completely **:** thoroughly. **8. a.** From an upright position <The tree fell *over.*> **b.** From an upward to a reversed position <turn a magazine *over*> **9. a.** Again. **b.** In repetition <100 times *over*> **10.** In excess <$5 left *over*> **11.** —Used in 2-way radio transmission to indicate the end of a message. *—adj.* **1.** Upper **:** higher. **2.** External **:** outer. **3.** In excess.

over– *pref.* Excessive **:** excessively <*over*expose>

o•ver•act (ō′vər-ăkt′) *v.* To act with unnecessary exaggeration.

o•ver•age[1] (ō′vər-ĭj) *n.* A surplus.

o•ver•age[2] (ō′vər-āj′) *adj.* Over the required or proper age.

o•ver•all *also* **o•ver-all** (ō′vər-ôl′, ō′vər-ôl′) *adj.* **1.** From one end to the other. **2.** Including everything **:** comprehensive. *—adv.* In general.

o•ver•alls (ō′vər-ôlz′) *pl.n.* Loose-fitting trousers having a bib front and straps over the shoulders.

o•ver•arm (ō′vər-ärm′) *adj.* Done, thrown, or struck with the arm raised above the shoulder.

o•ver•awe (ō′vər-ô′) *v.* To overcome by inspiring awe.

o•ver•bal•ance (ō′vər-băl′əns) *v.* **1.** To outweigh. **2.** To throw off balance.

o•ver•bear (ō′vər-bâr′) *v.* **1.** To crush or bear down on with physical force. **2.** To prevail over **:** dominate.

o•ver•bear•ing (ō′vər-bâr′ĭng) *adj.* **1.** Overwhelming in power or authority **:** predominant. **2.** Arrogant.

o•ver•blown (ō′vər-blōn′) *adj.* **1.** Extremely fat. **2.** Inflated **:** exaggerated.

o•ver•board (ō′vər-bôrd′, -bōrd′) *adv.* Over the side of a ship into the water. **—go overboard.** To exhibit excessive enthusiasm, infatuation, etc.

o•ver•cap•i•tal•ize (ō′vər-kăp′ĭ-tl-īz′) *v.* **1.** To provide (e.g., a business) with excessive capital. **2.** To overestimate the value of (property). **—o′ver•cap′i•tal•i•za′tion** *n.*

o•ver•cast (ō′vər-kăst′, ō′vər-kăst′) *adj.* **1.** Clouded over **:** obscured. **2.** Gloomy.

o•ver•charge (ō′vər-chärj′) *v.* **1.** To charge an excessive price. **2.** To fill too full **:** overload. **—o′ver•charge′** *n.*

o•ver•cloud (ō′vər-kloud′) *v.* **1.** To make dark or gloomy. **2.** To become cloudy.

o•ver•coat (ō′vər-kōt′) *n.* A warm, heavy outer coat.

o•ver•come (ō′vər-kŭm′) *v.* **1.** To conquer **:** defeat. **2.** To prevail over **:** surmount. **3.** To affect deeply, as with fear or emotion.

o•ver•do (ō′vər-dōō′) *v.* To do, use, or stress to excess.

o•ver•dose (ō′vər-dōs′) *n.* An excessive dose, esp. of a narcotic. **—o′ver•dose′** *v.*

o•ver•draft (ō′vər-drăft′) *n.* The amount by which a bank account is overdrawn.

o•ver•draw (ō′vər-drô′) *v.* To draw against (a bank account) in excess of credit.

o•ver•dress (ō′vər-drĕs′) *v.* To dress too elaborately or formally.

o•ver•drive (ō′vər-drīv′) *n.* A gear of an automotive engine that transmits to the drive shaft a speed greater than the engine speed.

o•ver•due (ō′vər-dōō′, -dyōō′) *adj.* **1.** Being unpaid after becoming due. **2.** Expected but not yet come.

o′ver•anx′ious *adj.*
o′ver•at•tached′ *adj.*
o′ver•care′ful *adj.*
o′ver•chill′ *v.*
o′ver•cook′ *v.*
o′ver•cool′ *v.*
o′ver•cour′te•ous *adj.*
o′ver•crit′i•cal *adj.*
o′ver•crowd′ *v.*
o′ver•dar′ing *adj.*
o′ver•dec′o•rate′ *v.*
o′ver•de•mand′ *v.*
o′ver•de•vot′ed *adj.*
o′ver•de•vo′tion *n.*
o′ver•dil′i•gence *n.*
o′ver•dil′i•gent *n.*
o′ver•dis′ci•pline *v.*
o′ver•dra•mat′ic *adj.*
o′ver•drink′ *v.*
o′ver•ea′ger *adj.*
o′ver•ear′nest *adj.*
o′ver•ear′nest•ly *adv.*
o′ver•ed′u•cate′ *v.*
o′ver•e•lab′o•rate *adj.*
o′ver•el′e•gant *adj.*
o′ver•em•bel′lish *v.*
o′ver•e•mo′tion•al *adj.*
o′ver•em•phat′ic *adj.*
o′ver•en•thu′si•as′tic *adj.*
o′ver•ex•cit′a•ble *adj.*
o′ver•ex•cite′ *v.*
o′ver•ex•cite′ment *n.*
o′ver•ex•pand′ *v.*
o′ver•ex•pan′sion *n.*
o′ver•ex•pect′tant *adj.*
o′ver•ex•u′ber•ant *adj.*
o′ver•faith′ful *adj.*
o′ver•fa•mil′iar *adj.*
o′ver•fan′ci•ful *adj.*
o′ver•fas•tid′i•ous *adj.*
o′ver•fat′ten *v.*
o′ver•fed′ *adj.*
o′ver•feed′ *v.*
o′ver•fem′i•nine *adj.*
o′ver•fill′ *v.*
o′ver•fond′ness *n.*
o′ver•fre′quent *adj.*
o′ver•full′ *adj.*
o′ver•full′ness *n.*
o′ver•fur′nish *v.*
o′ver•gen′er•al•ize′ *v.*
o′ver•gen′er•ous *adj.*
o′ver•gra′cious *adj.*
o′ver•grate′ful *adj.*
o′ver•harsh′ *adj.*
o′ver•hast′y *adj.*
o′ver•heat′ *v.*
o′ver•help′ful *adj.*
o′ver•hon′est *adj.*
o′ver•i•de′al•ism′ *n.*
o′ver•im•ag′i•na′tive *adj.*
o′ver•in•clined′ *adj.*
o′ver•in•flate′ *v.*
o′ver•in•fla′tion *n.*
o′ver•in′flu•en′tial *adj.*
o′ver•in•sist′ence *n.*
o′ver•in•sist′ent *adj.*
o′ver•in•sure′ *v.*
o′ver•in′tel•lec′tu•al *adj.*

o•ver•es•ti•mate (ō′vər-ĕs′tə-māt′) *v.* **1.** To set too high an estimate on. **2.** To esteem too highly. —**o′ver•es′ti•mate** (-mĭt) *n.* —**o′ver•es′ti•ma′tion** *n.*

o•ver•ex•pose (ō′vər-ĭk-spōz′) *v.* To expose (a photographic film) too long or with too much light. —**o′ver•ex•po′sure** *n.*

o•ver•flow (ō′vər-flō′) *v.* **1.** To flow or run over the brim, top, or banks (of). **2.** To spread or pour over. —*n.* (ō′vər-flō′). **1.** A flood. **2.** An excess. **3.** An outlet for surplus liquid.

o•ver•grow (ō′vər-grō′) *v.* **1.** To choke or spread over with growth. **2.** To grow beyond usual size. —**o′ver•growth′** *n.*

o•ver•hand (ō′vər-hănd′) *also* **o•ver•hand•ed** (ō′vər-hăn′dĭd) *adj.* Thrown or struck with the hand raised above the shoulder. —**o′ver•hand′** *adv. & n.*

o•ver•hang (ō′vər-hăng′) *v.* **1.** To extend or project beyond. **2.** To loom over : menace. —**o′ver•hang′** *n.*

o•ver•haul (ō′vər-hôl′, ō′vər-hôl′) *v.* To examine thoroughly and make needed repairs. —**o′ver•haul′** *n.*

o•ver•head (ō′vər-hĕd′) *n.* The regular operating expenses of a business, including the costs of rent, utilities, upkeep, and taxes. —*adj.* (ō′vər-hĕd′). **1.** Located above the level of the head. **2.** Of or pertaining to overhead expenses. —**o′ver•head′** *adv.*

o•ver•hear (ō′vər-hîr′) *v.* To hear without the speaker's knowledge.

o•ver•joyed (ō′vər-joid′) *adj.* Filled with joy : elated.

o•ver•kill (ō′vər-kĭl′) *n.* **1.** Nuclear destructive capacity beyond what is needed to destroy a target. **2.** An action in excess of what is needed.

o•ver•land (ō′vər-lănd′, -lənd) *adj.* Over or by way of land. —**o′ver•land′** *adv.*

o•ver•lap (ō′vər-lăp′) *v.* **1.** To extend over and cover part of. **2.** To coincide partly with. —**o′ver•lap′** *n.*

o•ver•lay (ō′vər-lā′) *v.* **1.** To spread or lay on or over. **2.** To cover the surface of with a decorative layer <*overlay* silver with gold> —**o′ver•lay′** *n.*

o•ver•look (ō′vər-lo͝ok′) *v.* **1.** To look at from a higher position. **2.** To afford a view over. **3.** To fail to see : miss. **4.** To ignore deliberately : excuse. **5.** To watch over : supervise. —**o′ver•look′** *n.*

o•ver•lord (ō′vər-lôrd′) *n.* A lord with power or authority over other lords.

o•ver•ly (ō′vər-lē) *adv.* To an extreme or excessive degree.

o•ver•much (ō′vər-mŭch′) *adj.* In excess.

o•ver•night (ō′vər-nīt′) *adj.* **1.** Lasting for or remaining during a night. **2.** Immediate : sudden. —**o′ver•night′** *adv.*

o•ver•pass (ō′vər-păs′) *n.* An elevated road or bridge that crosses above a thoroughfare.

o•ver•play (ō′vər-plā′) *v.* **1.** To exaggerate. **2.** To rely too much on the strength of (one's position).

o•ver•pow•er (ō′vər-pou′ər) *v.* **1.** To overcome by superior force. **2.** To overwhelm.

o•ver•reach (ō′vər-rēch′) *v.* To miss or lose by attempting too much.

o•ver•ride (ō′vər-rīd′) *v.* **1.** To ride across. **2.** To take precedence over. **3.** To declare null and void.

o•ver•rule (ō′vər-ro͞ol′) *v.* **1.** To set aside by virtue of higher authority. **2.** To dominate by strong influence.

o•ver•run (ō′vər-rŭn′) *v.* **1.** To defeat and seize the positions of. **2.** To spread or swarm over destructively : infest. **3.** To extend or run beyond. **4.** To overflow. —**o′ver•run′** *n.*

o•ver•seas (ō′vər-sēz′, ō′vər-sēz′) *adv.* Across the sea : abroad. —**o′ver•seas′** *adj.*

o•ver•see (ō′vər-sē′) *v.* **1.** To direct : supervise. **2.** To inspect. —**o′ver•se′er** *n.*

o•ver•sexed (ō′vər-sĕkst′) *adj.* Having an immoderate sexual drive.

---

o′ver•in•tense′ *adj.*
o′ver•in′ter•est *n.*
o′ver•in•vest′ *v.*
o′ver•jeal′ous *adj.*
o′ver•keen′ *adj.*
o′ver•kind′ *adj.*
o′ver•large′ *adj.*
o′ver•lav′ish *adj.*
o′ver•lax′ *adj.*
o′ver•lib′er•al *adj.*
o′ver•live′ly *adj.*
o′ver•loud′ *adj.*
o′ver•loy′al *adj.*
o′ver•mag′ni•fy′ *v.*
o′ver•ma•ture′ *adj.*
o′ver•meek′ *adj.*
o′ver•mer′ci•ful *adj.*
o′ver•mix′ *v.*
o′ver•mod′est *adj.*
o′ver•moist′ *adj.*
o′ver•mois′ten *v.*
o′ver•mort′gage *v.*
o′ver•neat′ *adj.*
o′ver•neg•lect′ *v.*
o′ver•nerv′ous *adj.*
o′ver•nour′ish *v.*
o′ver•o•bese′ *adj.*
o′ver•ob•se′qui•ous *adj.*
o′ver•of•fi′cious *adj.*
o′ver•op′ti•mis′tic *adj.*
o′ver•or•nate′ *adj.*
o′ver•par•tic′u•lar *adj.*
o′ver•pas′sion•ate *adj.*
o′ver•pa′tri•ot′ic *adj.*
o′ver•pay′ *v.*
o′ver•pes′si•mis′tic *adj.*
o′ver•plain′ *adj.*
o′ver•pol′ish *v.*
o′ver•pop′u•lar *adj.*
o′ver•pop′u•lous *adj.*
o′ver•pre•cise′ *adj.*
o′ver•press′ *v.*
o′ver•pro•lif′ic *adj.*
o′ver•prom′i•nent *adj.*
o′ver•prompt′ *adj.*
o′ver•proud′ *adj.*
o′ver•pro•vide′ *v.*
o′ver•pro•voke′ *v.*
o′ver•pun′ish *v.*
o′ver•pun′ish•ment *n.*
o′ver•quan′ti•ty *n.*
o′ver•quick′ *adj.*
o′ver•qui′et *adj.*
o′ver•ra′tion•al *adj.*
o′ver•read′y *adj.*
o′ver•re′al•is′tic *adj.*
o′ver•re•flec′tive *adj.*
o′ver•re•li′ant *adj.*
o′ver•re•lig′ious *adj.*
o′ver•re•served′ *adj.*
o′ver•re•strain′ *v.*
o′ver•rich′ *adj.*
o′ver•right′eous *adj.*
o′ver•rig′id *adj.*
o′ver•rig′or•ous *adj.*
o′ver•rough′ *adj.*
o′ver•rude′ *adj.*
o′ver•sad′ *adj.*
o′ver•salt′ *v.*
o′ver•salt′y *adj.*
o′ver•sat′u•rate′ *v.*
o′ver•sat′u•ra′tion *n.*

o•ver•shad•ow (ō'vər-shăd'ō) *v.* **1.** To cast a shadow over. **2.** To make insignificant by comparison.
o•ver•shoe (ō'vər-sho͞o') *n.* A galosh or rubber worn over shoes as protection from water or snow.
o•ver•shoot (ō'vər-sho͞ot') *v.* **1.** To pass swiftly over or beyond. **2.** To miss by or as if by shooting something too far.
o•ver•sight (ō'vər-sīt') *n.* **1.** An inadvertent error or omission. **2.** Supervision.
o•ver•size (ō'vər-sīz') *also* **o•ver•sized** (ō'vər-sīzd') *adj.* Larger in size than usual.
o•ver•sleep (ō'vər-slēp') *v.* To sleep beyond the time for waking up.
o•ver•state (ō'vər-stāt') *v.* To state in exaggerated terms. **—o'ver•state'ment** *n.*
o•ver•stay (ō'vər-stā') *v.* To stay beyond the set limits or expected duration of.
o•ver•step (ō'vər-stĕp') *v.* To go beyond (a limit).
o•ver•stock (ō'vər-stŏk') *v.* To stock too much of. **—o'ver•stock'** *n.*
o•ver•stuff (ō'vər-stŭf') *v.* **1.** To stuff too much into. **2.** To cover entirely with thickly cushioned upholstery.
o•ver•sub•scribe (ō'vər-səb-skrīb') *v.* To subscribe to (e.g., a performance series) in excess of the supply available.
o•vert (ō-vûrt', ō'vûrt') *adj.* Not hidden or concealed **:** clearly evident.
o•ver•take (ō'vər-tāk') *v.* **1.** To catch up with. **2.** To pass after catching up with.
o•ver-the-count•er (ō'vər-*th*ə-koun'tər) *adj.* **1.** Not available on an officially recognized stock exchange. **2.** Available for sale without a prescription.
o•ver•throw (ō'vər-thrō') *v.* **1.** To overturn. **2.** To bring about the destruction or downfall of, esp. by force. **3.** To throw something over or beyond (a target). ★ ***syns:*** OVERTURN, SUBVERT, TOPPLE, TUMBLE **—o'ver•throw'** *n.*
o•ver•time (ō'vər-tīm') *n.* **1. a.** Working hours in excess of a normal working week. **b.** Payment for additional work beyond the normal working week. **2.** A period of playing time added after the set time for a sports contest. **—o'ver•time'** *adv.*
o•ver•tone (ō'vər-tōn') *n.* **1.** A harmonic. **2.** An implication **:** hint.
o•ver•ture (ō'vər-cho͝or', -chər) *n.* **1.** *Mus.* An instrumental introduction to a dramatic musical work, as an opera. **2.** An opening proposal or offer.
o•ver•turn (ō'vər-tûrn') *v.* **1.** To cause to turn over **:** upset. **2.** To defeat.
o•ver•view (ō'vər-vyo͞o') *n.* A brief comprehensive survey **:** summary.
o•ver•ween•ing (ō'vər-wē'nĭng) *adj.* **1.** Presumptuously arrogant. **2.** Immoderate.
o•ver•weight (ō'vər-wāt') *adj.* Above the normal or allowed weight.
o•ver•whelm (ō'vər-hwĕlm', -wĕlm') *v.* **1.** To flood over **:** engulf. **2.** To overcome utterly, as by physical or emotional force. **3.** To turn over **:** upset.
o•ver•work (ō'vər-wûrk') *v.* **1.** To work too hard. **2.** To use to excess <*overwork* an analogy>
o•ver•wrought (ō'vər-rôt') *adj.* **1.** Extremely nervous. **2.** Excessively ornate.
o•vi•duct (ō'vĭ-dŭkt') *n.* A tube through which the ova pass from an ovary to the uterus.
o•vip•a•rous (ō-vĭp'ər-əs) *adj.* Producing eggs that hatch outside the body.
o•void (ō'void') *also* **o•voi•dal** (ō-void'l) *adj.* Egg-shaped. **—o'void'** *n.*
o•vo•vi•vip•a•rous (ō'vō-vī-vĭp'ər-əs) *adj.* Producing eggs that hatch within the female's body.
o•vu•late (ō'vyə-lāt', ŏv'yə-) *v.* To produce and discharge ova. **—o'vu•la'tion** *n.*
o•vule (ō'vyo͞ol, ŏv'yo͞ol) *n.* *Bot.* A minute structure from which a plant develops after fertilization. **—o'vu•lar** *adj.*

o'ver•scent'ed *adj.*
o'ver•scru'pu•lous *adj.*
o'ver•sea'son *v.*
o'ver•sea'soned *adj.*
o'ver•se•cure' *adj.*
o'ver•sen'ti•men'tal *adj.*
o'ver•se're•ous *adj.*
o'ver•se•vere' *adj.*
o'ver•sharp' *adj.*
o'ver•shrink' *v.*
o'ver•skep'ti•cal *adj.*
o'ver•slow' *adj.*
o'ver•small' *adj.*
o'ver•smooth' *adj.*
o'ver•soak' *v.*
o'ver•soft' *adj.*
o'ver•sol'emn *adj.*
o'ver•so•lic'i•tous *adj.*
o'ver•so•phis'ti•cat'ed *adj.*
o'ver•so•phis'ti•ca'tion *n.*
o'ver•spar'ing *adj.*
o'ver•spe'cial•i•za'tion *n.*
o'ver•spe'cial•ize' *v.*
o'ver•spec'u•late' *v.*
o'ver•spec'u•la'tion *n.*
o'ver•spec'u•la'tive *adj.*
o'ver•stim'u•late' *v.*
o'ver•stim'u•la'tion *n.*
o'ver•strain' *v.*
o'ver•stress' *v.*
o'ver•stretch' *v.*
o'ver•striv'ing *adj.* & *n.*
o'ver•sub'tle *adj.*
o'ver•sub'tle•ty *n.*
o'ver•suf•fi'cient *adj.*
o'ver•su'per•sti'tious *adj.*
o'ver•sure' *adj.*
o'ver•sus•pi'cious *adj.*
o'ver•sus•pi'cious•ly *adv.*
o'ver•sweet' *adj.*
o'ver•sys'tem•at'ic *adj.*
o'ver•talk'a•tive *adj.*
o'ver•teach' *v.*
o'ver•tech'ni•cal *adj.*
o'ver•te•na'cious *adj.*
o'ver•ten'der *adj.*
o'ver•tense' *adj.*
o'ver•ten'sion *n.*
o'ver•thick' *adj.*
o'ver•thin' *adj.*
o'ver•thought'ful *adj.*
o'ver•thrift'y *adj.*
o'ver•tight' *adj.*
o'ver•tire' *v.*
o'ver•truth'ful *adj.*
o'ver•val'u•a•ble *adj.*
o'ver•ve'he•ment *adj.*
o'ver•ven'ti•late' *v.*
o'ver•ven'tur•ous *adj.*
o'ver•vig'or•ous *adj.*
o'ver•vi'o•lent *adj.*
o'ver•warm' *v.*
o'ver•weak' *adj.*
o'ver•wet' *adj.*
o'ver•will'ing *adj.*
o'ver•wise' *adj.*
o'ver•wor'ry *v.*
o'ver•young' *adj.*
o'ver•youth'ful *adj.*
o'ver•zeal'ous *adj.*
o'ver•zeal'ous•ly *n.*
o'ver•zeal'ous•ness *n.*

o•vum (ō′vəm) *n., pl.* **o•va** (ō′və). A female reproductive cell.
owe (ō) *v.* **owed, ow•ing. 1.** To be indebted to the amount of. **2.** To have a moral obligation to offer. **3.** To be in debt to. **4.** To be indebted or obliged for.
owing to *prep.* Because of.
owl (oul) *n.* Any of various often nocturnal birds of prey of the order Strigiformes, having a large head with a short, hooked beak. **—owl′ish** *adj.*
own (ōn) *adj.* Of or belonging to oneself or itself. *—pron. (sing. or pl. in number).* The one or ones belonging to oneself. *—v.* **1.** To have or possess. **2.** To confess **:** acknowledge. **—own up.** To confess fully. **—own′er** *n.* **—own′er•ship** *n.*
ox (ŏks) *n., pl.* **ox•en** (ŏk′sən). **1.** An adult castrated bull of the genus *Bos,* used as a draft animal. **2.** A bovine mammal.
ox•blood red (ŏks′blŭd′) *n.* A dark brownish red.
ox•bow (ŏks′bō′) *n.* **1.** A U-shaped wooden piece that fits around the neck of an ox and attaches to the yoke. **2. a.** A U-shaped bend in a river. **b.** The land enclosed by an oxbow.
ox•ford (ŏks′fərd) *n.* A sturdy low-cut shoe that is laced and tied over the instep.
ox•i•dant (ŏk′sĭ-dənt) *n.* An oxidizing agent.
ox•i•da•tion (ŏk′sĭ-dā′shən) *n.* **1.** Combination of a substance with oxygen. **2.** A reaction in which an element's valance is increased as a result of losing electrons. **—ox′i•da′tive** *adj.* **—ox′i•da′tive•ly** *adv.*
ox•ide (ŏk′sīd′) *n.* A compound of a radical or element with oxygen. **—ox•id′ic** (ŏk-sĭd′ĭk) *adj.*
ox•i•dize (ŏk′sĭ-dīz′) *v.* **-dized, -diz•ing.** *Chem.* **1.** To combine with oxygen. **2.** To coat with oxide. **—ox′i•diz′er** *n.*
ox•tail (ŏks′tāl′) *n.* The tail of an ox, esp. when used for food.
ox•y•a•cet•y•lene (ŏk′sē-ə-sĕt′l-ĭn, -ēn′) *adj.* Of or containing a mixture of oxygen and acetylene.
ox•y•gen (ŏk′sĭ-jən) *n. Symbol* **O** A colorless, tasteless, odorless, gaseous element that is essential to life and required for combustion. **—ox′y•gen′ic** *adj.*

▲ ***word history:*** The word *oxygen* was coined in French by the chemist Antoine Lavoisier in the 18th cent. soon after the element was isolated. The French word *oxygéne* was intended to mean "acid-producing," from Greek *oxus,* "sharp," used in the sense "acid," and the Greek suffix *-genēs,* "born," misinterpreted as "producing." Oxygen was considered at the time to be an essential component of an acid. Although this is not the case, the name *oxygen* has persisted for the element.

ox•y•gen•ate (ŏk′sĭ-jə-nāt′) *v.* **-at•ed, -at•ing.** To combine, treat, or mix with oxygen. **—ox′y•gen•a′tion** *n.*
oxygen tent *n.* A canopy placed usu. over the head and shoulders of a patient to provide oxygen at a higher level than normal.
oys•ter (oi′stər) *n.* An edible marine mollusk of the genus *Ostrea,* with a rough, irregularly shaped, double-hinged shell.
o•zone (ō′zōn′) *n.* **1.** A poisonous, blue, unstable gaseous form of oxygen, formed naturally from diatomic oxygen by electric discharge or exposure to ultraviolet radiation, used to purify water and as a bleach. **2.** *Informal.* Pure, clean air.
ozone layer *n.* A region of the upper atmosphere containing a relatively high concentration of ozone that absorbs solar ultraviolet radiation.
o•zo•no•sphere (ō-zō′nə-sfîr′) *n.* OZONE LAYER.

Pp

p *or* **P** (pē) *n., pl.* **p's** *or* **P's. 1.** The 16th letter of the English alphabet. **2.** A speech sound represented by the letter *p.*
P *symbol for* PHOSPHORUS.
Pa *symbol for* PROTACTINIUM.
pa′an•ga (päng′gə) *n.* —See table at CURRENCY.
pab•u•lum (păb′yə-ləm) *n.* An easily digested and usu. soft food.
PAC (păk) *n., pl.* **PAC's** *or* **PACs.** A political action committee.
pace (pās) *n.* **1. a.** A step made in walking **:** stride. **b.** The length of a pace. **2.** Rate of progress or movement. **3.** A gait of a horse in which the feet on one side move together. *—v.* **paced, pac•ing. 1.** To cover or walk at a pace, esp. a slow pace. **2.** To measure by paces. **3.** To regulate or set the pace of. **—pac′er** *n.*
pace•mak•er (pās′mā′kər) *n.* **1.** One that sets the pace, as in a race. **2. a.** Specialized muscle fibers of the heart that regulate the heartbeat. **b.** A surgically implanted electronic device used to stabilize or stimulate the heartbeat.
pach•y•derm (păk′ĭ-dûrm′) *n.* A large, hoofed thick-skinned mammal, as the rhinoceros or elephant.
pach•y•san•dra (păk′ĭ-săn′drə) *n.* Any of several plants of the genus *Pachysandra,* with evergreen leaves, grown as a ground cover.
pa•cif•ic (pə-sĭf′ĭk) *adj.* **1.** Tending to reduce conflict. **2.** Peaceful **:** serene.
pac•i•fi•er (păs′ə-fī′ər) *n.* **1.** One that paci-

fies. **2.** A device, as an artificial nipple, for a baby to suck or chew on.

pac•i•fism (păs'ə-fĭz'əm) *n.* Opposition to war or violence as a way to resolve disputes. **—pac'i•fist** *n.* **—pac'i•fis'tic** *adj.*

pac•i•fy (păs'ə-fī') *v.* **-fied, -fy•ing. 1.** To alleviate the anger or distress of **:** calm. **2.** To end war, fighting, or violence in. **—pac'i•fi•ca'tion** *n.*

pack (păk) *n.* **1. a.** A group of items wrapped or tied up **:** bundle. **b.** A container in which a bundle can be carried, esp. on the back. **2.** A complete set of related items, esp. playing cards. **3.** A large amount or number **:** heap. **4.** A group of animals or people. **5.** Absorbent material, as gauze, applied to a bodily part. —*v.* **1.** To roll, fold, or combine into a bundle. **2. a.** To put into a container, as for preservation. **b.** To place belongings in boxes or luggage for storing or transporting. **3.** To crowd or be crowded together **:** cram. **4.** To press or become pressed together **:** compact. **5.** *Informal.* To carry <*pack* a revolver> **6.** To send without ceremony <*packed* the children off to their aunt's> **7.** To organize the composition of in order to achieve a favorable or hoped-for result <*pack* a jury>

pack•age (păk'ĭj) *n.* **1.** A parcel **:** bundle. **2.** Something, as an offer, consisting of several items each of which must be accepted <a vacation *package*> —*v.* **-aged, -ag•ing.** To insert in or make into a package.

package store *n.* A store that sells alcoholic beverages in sealed bottles for consumption away from the premises.

pack animal *n.* An animal, as a mule, used to carry loads.

pack•er (păk'ər) *n.* One who packs, esp. one who processes and packs food products, as meats, for transportation and sale.

pack•et (păk'ĭt) *n.* **1.** A small bundle or package. **2.** A regularly scheduled passenger boat that carries cargo and mail.

pack•ing (păk'ĭng) *n.* Material in which something is packed, esp. to prevent seepage or breakage.

packing house *n.* A firm that processes and packs food products, esp. meat.

†**pack rat** *n.* **1.** A small North American rodent of the genus *Neotoma* that collects in its nest a wide variety of objects. **2.** *W U.S. Slang.* A petty thief. **3.** *Slang.* A collector or hoarder of miscellaneous objects.

pack•sad•dle (păk'săd'l) *n.* A saddle for a pack animal on which loads can be secured.

pact (păkt) *n.* An agreement, as between nations **:** treaty.

pad[1] (păd) *n.* **1.** Something soft that serves to line, stuff, or cushion. **2.** A drawing or writing tablet. **3.** The broad floating leaf of a water plant. **4.** The cushionlike underpart of the toes and feet of some animals. **5.** *Slang.* A person's living quarters. —*v.* **pad•ded, pad•ding. 1.** To line or stuff with soft material. **2.** To lengthen with extraneous or fraudulent material.

pad[2] (păd) *v.* **pad•ded, pad•ding.** To go on foot, esp. softly and nearly inaudibly.

pad•dle[1] (păd'l) *n.* **1.** A usu. wooden flat-bladed implement used to propel and steer a small boat, as a canoe. **2.** Something resembling a paddle, as: **a.** An implement used for mixing, stirring, or turning. **b.** A small wooden racket used in table tennis. **3.** A board on the circumference of a paddle wheel. —*v.* **-dled, -dling. 1.** To propel through water with or as if with a paddle. **2.** To mix, stir, or beat with a paddle.

pad•dle[2] (păd'l) *v.* **-dled, -dling. 1.** To dabble about in shallow water. **2.** To waddle **:** toddle.

paddle wheel *n.* A wheel with boards or paddles around its circumference, used to propel a ship.

pad•dock (păd'ək) *n.* A usu. enclosed area in which horses are kept, as for being saddled and displayed before a race.

pad•dy (păd'ē) *n., pl.* **-dies.** An irrigated, marshy, or flooded field in which rice is cultivated.

paddy wagon *n.* A police van for conveying suspects.

pad•lock (păd'lŏk') *n.* A detachable lock with a U-shaped piece that can be inserted through the staple of a hasp and then fastened. **—pad'lock'** *v.*

pa•dre (pä'drā, -drē) *n. Informal.* **1.** A priest. **2.** A military chaplain.

pae•an (pē'ən) *n.* A song of thanksgiving, praise, or exultation.

pa•gan (pā'gən) *n.* One who is not a Christian, Muslim, or Jew **:** heathen. **—pa'gan** *adj.*

page[1] (pāj) *n.* Someone hired to run errands or deliver messages, as in a hotel. —*v.* **paged, pag•ing.** To summon or call (a person) by name.

page[2] (pāj) *n.* **1.** A leaf, as of a book. **2.** One side of a page. —*v.* **paged, pag•ing. 1.** To paginate. **2.** To turn pages.

pag•eant (păj'ənt) *n.* An elaborate public spectacle, procession, or celebration. **—pag'eant•ry** *n.*

pag•i•nate (păj'ə-nāt') *v.* **-nat•ed, -nat•ing.** To number the pages of.

pa•go•da (pə-gō'də) *n.* A many-storied Buddhist tower, esp. one built as a shrine or memorial.

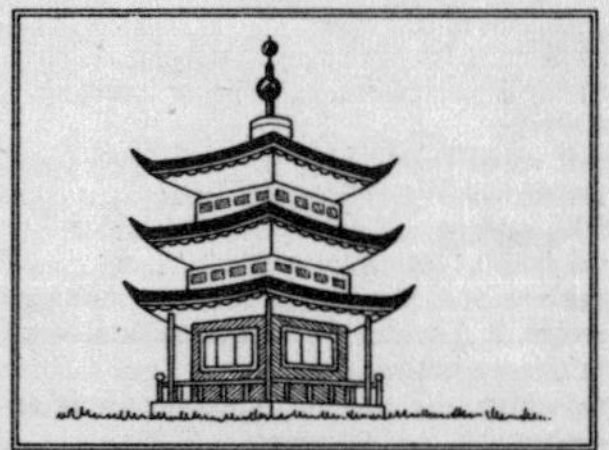

pagoda

paid (pād) *v. p.t. & p.p. of* PAY.
pail (pāl) *n.* A usu. cylindrical container with a handle : bucket.
pain (pān) *n.* **1.** Physical or mental suffering or distress, esp. an unpleasant sensation arising from injury or disease. **2. pains.** Effort : trouble. **3.** *Informal.* A nuisance : pest. **4.** Penalty <under *pain* of imprisonment> —*v.* To experience or cause pain. —**pain'ful** *adj.* —**pain'less** *adj.*
pain·kill·er (pān'kĭl'ər) *n.* Something, esp. a drug, that alleviates pain. —**pain'kill'ing** *adj.*
pains·tak·ing (pānz'tā'kĭng) *adj.* Diligent and attentive to detail : meticulously careful. —**pains'tak'ing·ly** *adv.*
paint (pānt) *n.* **1. a.** A mixture of a pigment and a liquid that is spread on a surface to form a decorative or protective coating. **b.** The pigment that is used in making paint. **c.** The film that is formed by the application of paint to a surface. **2.** Make-up. —*v.* **1.** To represent in a painting. **2.** To describe vividly in or as if in words. **3.** To decorate or coat with paint. **4.** To use cosmetics (on). **5.** To practice the art of painting pictures. **6.** To cover the surface of with a liquid medicine : swab.
paint·brush (pānt'brŭsh') *n.* A brush with which to apply paint.
paint·er[1] (pān'tər) *n.* One who paints.
pain·ter[2] (pān'tər) *n.* *Naut.* A rope used for tying up or towing a boat.
†pain·ter[3] (pān'tər) *n.* *Regional.* A mountain lion or lynx.
paint·ing (pān'tĭng) *n.* **1.** The art, process, or occupation of coating surfaces with paint. **2.** Something, as a picture, produced by the art of painting.
pair (pâr) *n., pl.* **pairs** *or* **pair. 1.** Two things that are similar in function or form. **2.** Something composed of 2 corresponding pieces or parts <a *pair* of scissors> **3.** Two persons or animals <an engaged *pair*><a *pair* of oxen> —*v.* **1.** To arrange in pairs. **2.** To form a pair.
pai·sa (pī-sä') *n., pl.* **-sa** (-sä') *or* **-sas.** —See table at CURRENCY.
pais·ley (pāz'lē) *adj.* Made of a soft wool fabric with colorful abstract swirled or curved shapes.
Pai·ute (pī'yo͞ot') *n., pl.* **-ute** *or* **-utes. 1.** A member of either of two distinct American Indian peoples, the Northern Paiute and the Southern Paiute, of the Great Basin. **2.** Their Shoshonean language.
pa·ja·mas (pə-jä'məz, -jăm'əz) *pl.n.* A loose-fitting 2-piece garment worn for lounging or sleeping.
pak choi (bäk' choi') *n.* A Chinese plant, *Brassica chinensis*, that is similar to the common cabbage and is used as a vegetable.
pal (păl) *n.* *Informal.* A good friend : chum.
pal·ace (păl'ĭs) *n.* **1.** The residence of a sovereign. **2.** A splendid house : mansion. —**pa·la'tial** (pə-lā'shəl) *adj.*
pal·a·din (păl'ə-dĭn) *n.* A heroic or knightly champion.
pal·an·quin (păl'ən-kēn') *n.* A covered litter for one person that is carried on poles on the shoulders of men.
pal·at·a·ble (păl'ə-tə-bəl) *adj.* Acceptable or agreeable to the taste.
pal·ate (păl'ĭt) *n.* **1.** The roof of the vertebrate mouth, consisting of a hard, bony forward part and a fleshy posterior part. **2.** The sense of taste. —**pal'a·tal** (-ə-təl) *adj.*
pa·lat·i·nate (pə-lăt'n-āt', -ĭt) *n.* The territory of a palatine.
pal·a·tine (păl'ə-tīn') *n.* **1.** An administrative official of the late Roman or Byzantine empire. **2.** A feudal lord having sovereign powers within his own domain. —*adj.* **1.** Of or pertaining to a palace. **2.** Of, relating to, or designating a palatine or palatinate.
pa·lav·er (pə-lăv'ər, -lä'vər) *n.* A long talk : parley. —**pa·lav'er** *v.*
pale[1] (pāl) *n.* **1.** A pointed stick, esp. a stake of a fence : picket. **2.** An area enclosed by a fence or boundary. —*v.* **paled, pal·ing.** To enclose with pales.
pale[2] (pāl) *adj.* **pal·er, pal·est. 1.** Lighter than usual or normal in complexion : pallid <*pale* cheeks> **2.** Of low color intensity : light <*pale* green> **3.** Of a low intensity of light : dim <a *pale sun*> —*v.* **paled, pal·ing.** To become or cause to become pale. —**pale'ness** *n.*
pa·le·og·ra·phy (pā'lē-ŏg'rə-fē) *n.* The study of ancient inscriptions and written documents. —**pa'le·og'ra·pher** *n.*
pa·le·on·tol·o·gy (pā'lē-ŏn-tŏl'ə-jē, -ən-) *n.* The study of forms of life existing in prehistoric or geologic times. —**pa'le·on·tol'o·gist** *n.*
pal·ette (păl'ĭt) *n.* **1.** An often oval board, usu. with a hole for the thumb, on which an artist mixes colors. **2.** The range of colors used by an artist.
pal·frey (pôl'frē) *n., pl.* **-freys.** *Archaic.* A saddle horse, esp. one for a woman to ride.
pal·imp·sest (păl'ĭmp-sĕst') *n.* Material, as vellum, that is used after having been written upon before and often shows traces of imperfectly erased writing.
pal·in·drome (păl'ĭn-drōm') *n.* A word, phrase, or sentence, as *Madam I'm Adam*, that reads the same backward or forward.
pal·ing (pā'lĭng) *n.* **1.** A pale, as that used for a fence : picket. **2.** Wood used in making pales. **3.** A fence made of pales.
pal·i·sade (păl'ĭ-sād') *n.* **1.** A fence of pales, esp. one forming a defense barrier or fortification. **2.** A line of steep cliffs, often along a river.
pall[1] (pôl) *n.* **1.** A heavy cloth covering, as of velvet, for a bier or coffin. **2.** A coffin. **3.** A gloomy atmosphere or effect.
pall[2] (pôl) *v.* **1.** To be or become dull, boring, or tiresome. **2.** To satiate : jade.
pal·la·di·um (pə-lā'dē-əm) *n.* *Symbol* **Pd** A soft, white metallic element used in many alloys.
pall·bear·er (pôl'bâr'ər) *n.* Someone who carries or attends the coffin at a funeral.
pal·let[1] (păl'ĭt) *n.* A portable platform on which materials, as cargo or freight, can be stored or moved.

pal•let² (păl'ĭt) *n.* A narrow, hard, often straw-filled bed or mattress.
pal•li•ate (păl'ē-āt') *v.* **-at•ed, -at•ing. 1.** To try to hide the seriousness of with apologies and excuses. **2.** To ease the pain or force of without curing. **—pal'li•a'tion** *n.* **—pal'li•a'-tive** *adj. & n.*
pal•lid (păl'ĭd) *adj.* **1.** Lacking in color : wan. **2.** Lacking in intensity : dull.
pal•lor (păl'ər) *n.* Extreme or abnormal paleness <a deathly *pallor*>
palm¹ (päm) *n.* The inner part of the hand between the wrist and the fingers. —*v.* To hide, pick up, or hold in the palm. **—palm off.** To dispose of or pass off by deception or fraud.
palm² (päm) *n.* **1.** Any of various chiefly tropical trees or shrubs of the family Palmaceae, usu. having an unbranched trunk with a crown of large featherlike or fanlike leaves. **2. a.** An emblem of victory. **b.** Victory : triumph.
pal•mate (păl'māt', päl'-, pä'māt') *also* **pal•mat•ed** (-mā'tĭd) *adj.* Resembling a hand with the fingers extended, as coral or antlers.
pal•met•to (păl-mĕt'ō) *n., pl.* **-tos** *or* **-toes.** A small, mostly tropical palm, esp. *Sabal palmetto,* with fan-shaped leaves.
palm•ist•ry (pä'mĭ-strē) *n.* The art or practice of predicting someone's future from the marks and patterns on the palms of his or her hands. **—palm'ist** *n.*
Palm Sunday *n.* The Sunday before Easter, celebrated in commemoration of Jesus's entry into Jerusalem.
palm•y (pä'mē) *adj.* **-i•er, -i•est. 1.** Of, relating to, or full of palm trees. **2.** Characterized by success or prosperity : flourishing.
pal•o•mi•no (păl'ə-mē'nō) *n., pl.* **-nos.** A golden or light-tan horse with a lighter tail and mane.
pal•pa•ble (păl'pə-bəl) *adj.* **1.** Capable of being felt or touched : tangible. **2.** Easily perceived : plain. **—pal'pa•bly** *adv.*
pal•pate (păl'pāt') *v.* **-pat•ed, -pat•ing.** To examine or explore by touch, esp. as an aid in medical diagnosis. **—pal•pa'tion** *n.*
pal•pi•tate (păl'pĭ-tāt') *v.* **-tat•ed, -tat•ing. 1.** To quiver : flutter. **2.** To beat more quickly than normal : throb. **—pal'pi•tat'ing•ly** *adv.* **—pal'pi•ta'tion** *n.*
pal•sy (pôl'zē) *n., pl.* **-sies. 1.** Paralysis. **2.** A condition characterized by tremor of the body or a bodily part. **—pal'sied** *adj.*
pal•ter (pôl'tər) *v.* **1.** To talk or act deceitfully or insincerely : equivocate. **2.** To quibble, esp. in doing business : haggle.
pal•try (pôl'trē) *adj.* **-tri•er, -tri•est. 1.** Trifling : trivial. **2.** Trashy : shabby. **3.** Contemptible : mean.
pam•pa (păm'pə) *n., pl.* **-pas** (-pəz, -pəs). In South America, a treeless grassland area.
pam•per (păm'pər) *v.* To treat with extreme indulgence : coddle.
pam•phlet (păm'flĭt) *n.* An often short publication with no binding and a paper cover. **—pam'phlet•eer'** *n.*
pan (păn) *n.* **1.** A wide, shallow, open vessel for household use. **2.** Something that resembles a pan. —*v.* **panned, pan•ning. 1.** To wash (gravel or earth) in a pan in search of precious metal, esp. gold. **2.** *Informal.* To criticize unfavorably and harshly. **—pan out.** *Informal.* To be successful.
pan•a•ce•a (păn'ə-sē'ə) *n.* A remedy for all ills, diseases, or difficulties : cure-all.
pa•nache (pə-năsh', -näsh') *n.* **1.** An ornamental cluster, as of feathers, esp. on a helmet. **2.** Vividness or dash in manner or action : verve.
Panama hat *n.* A hat braided by hand from the leaves of a plant of South and Central America.
Pan-A•mer•i•can (păn'ə-mĕr'ĭ-kən) *adj.* Of or relating to North, South, and Central America as a group.
pan•a•tel•a (păn'ə-tĕl'ə) *n.* A long, slender cigar.
pan•cake (păn'kāk') *n.* A flat, often thin cake made of batter fried on both sides.
pan•chro•mat•ic (păn'krō-măt'ĭk) *adj.* Sensitive to all colors <*panchromatic* film>
pan•cre•as (păng'krē-əs, păn'-) *n. Anat.* A long, irregularly shaped gland lying behind the stomach that secretes digestive enzymes and produces insulin. **—pan'cre•at'ic** (-ăt'-ĭk) *adj.*
pan•da (păn'də) *n.* **1.** A bearlike black and white animal, *Ailuropoda melanoleuca,* of mountainous regions of China and Tibet. **2.** A raccoonlike animal, *Ailurus fulgens,* with reddish fur and a ringed tail.
pan•dem•ic (păn-dĕm'ĭk) *adj.* Occurring or prevalent over a wide geographic area, as a disease : widespread. **—pan•dem'ic** *n.*
pan•de•mo•ni•um (păn'də-mō'nē-əm) *n.* Wild confusion or uproar : tumult.
pan•der (păn'dər) *n.* **1.** A go-between in sexual intrigues. **2.** A pimp. **3.** Someone who profits from exploiting the needs and weaknesses of others. —*v.* To act as a pander (for).
pan•dow•dy (păn-dou'dē) *n., pl.* **-dies.** Sliced fruit, esp. apples, sugared and spiced and baked with a thick top crust.
pane (pān) *n.* A single plate of glass, as in a section of a window or door.
pan•e•gy•ric (păn'ə-jĭr'ĭk, -jī'rĭk) *n.* **1.** A formal speech or written composition of commendation or praise. **2.** Elaborate praise. **—pan'e•gy'ri•cal** *adj.* **—pan'e•gy'rist** *n.*
pan•el (păn'əl) *n.* **1.** A flat, often rectangular piece, esp. of wood, that forms part of a surface or overlays it. **2.** A board on which controls or instruments are mounted. **3. a.** A list of persons selected for jury duty. **b.** A group of people who participate in a discussion or a game show, as on television. —*v.* **-eled, -el•ing** *or* **-elled, -el•ling. 1.** To furnish or decorate with panels. **2.** To impanel (a jury).
pan•el•ing (păn'ə-lĭng) *n.* **1.** A set of ornamental panels. **2.** A paneled wall.
pan•el•ist (păn'ə-lĭst) *n.* A member of a panel.
panel truck *n.* A small truck, as one used to make deliveries, with an enclosed body.

pang (păng) *n.* A sudden, brief, sharp spasm, as of pain.
pan•han•dle[1] (păn′hăn′dl) *v.* **-dled, -dling.** *Informal.* To ask for money or food, esp. on the street. —**pan′han′dler** *n.*
pan•han•dle[2] (păn′hăn′dl) *n.* A narrow strip, as of territory, that projects from a broader area.
pan•ic (păn′ĭk) *n.* A sudden, overpowering fear. —*v.* **-icked, -ick•ing.** To experience or cause to experience panic. —**pan′ick•y** *adj.*
pan•i•cle (păn′ĭ-kəl) *n. Bot.* An irregularly branched flower cluster. —**pan′i•cled** *adj.*
pan•jan•drum (păn-jăn′drəm) *n.* A personage of power and importance.
pan•nier (păn′yər, păn′ē-ər) *n.* A large basket, as one of a pair carried on either side of a pack animal or over a person's shoulders.
pan•o•ply (păn′ə-plē) *n., pl.* **-plies. 1.** A complete array of a warrior's armor and weapons. **2.** A protective covering. **3.** An impressive display **:** pomp.
pan•o•ram•a (păn′ə-răm′ə, -rä′mə) *n.* **1.** An unlimited view of what is visible in all directions. **2.** A picture or view that unrolls before a spectator. —**pan′o•ram′ic** *adj.*
pan•sy (păn′zē) *n., pl.* **-sies.** A garden plant, *Viola tricolor hortensis,* bearing flowers with rounded, velvety, variously colored petals.
pant (pănt) *v.* **1.** To breathe with difficulty and often in short gasps. **2.** To utter breathlessly or hurriedly. **3.** To feel a longing **:** yearn. —*n.* A short, labored breath.
pan•ta•loons (păn′tl-o͞onz′) *pl.n.* Trousers, esp. loose, baggy ones.
pan•the•ism (păn′thē-ĭz′əm) *n.* A doctrine identifying the Deity with the universe. —**pan′the•ist** *n.* —**pan′the•is′tic** *adj.*
pan•the•on (păn′thē-ŏn′, -ən) *n.* **1. a.** A temple that is dedicated to the gods. **b.** The gods of a people. **2.** A public building commemorating, honoring, and often serving as a place of burial for the great personages of a nation.
pan•ther (păn′thər) *n.* **1.** The leopard, *Panthera pardus,* esp. in its black, unspotted form. **2.** The mountain lion.
pant•ies (păn′tēz) *pl.n.* Underpants, esp. short ones, for women or children.
pan•to•mime (păn′tə-mīm′) *n.* **1.** Expressive communication solely by means of facial and bodily movements. **2.** A play in which pantomime is used instead of dialogue. —*v.* **-mimed, -mim•ing.** To express oneself in or represent by pantomime. —**pan′to•mim′ic** (-mĭm′ĭk) *adj.* —**pan′to•mim′ist** (-mī′mĭst, -mĭm′ĭst) *n.*
pan•try (păn′trē) *n., pl.* **-tries.** A closet or room in which food and dishes are stored.
pants (pănts) *pl.n.* **1.** Trousers. **2.** Underpants.
pant•suit *also* **pants suit** (pănt′so͞ot′) *n.* A woman's suit with trousers instead of a skirt.
pant•y•hose (păn′tē-hōz′) *pl.n.* A woman's one-piece undergarment that consists of stockings and underpants.
pant•y•waist (păn′tē-wāst′) *n.* A sissy.
†**pap**[1] (păp) *n.* **1.** *Regional.* A teat or nipple. **2.** Something resembling a nipple.
pap[2] (păp) *n.* **1.** Soft, easily digested food for invalids or infants. **2.** Something lacking real value or substance.
pa•pa (pä′pə, pə-pä′) *n.* Father.
pa•pa•cy (pā′pə-sē) *n., pl.* **-cies. 1.** The jurisdiction and office of a pope. **2.** The term of office of a pope. **3. Papacy.** *Rom. Cath. Ch.* The system of church government of which the pope is the head.
pa•pa•in (pə-pā′ĭn, -pī-) *n.* A protein-digesting enzyme obtained from the unripe fruit of the papaya and used as a meat tenderizer.
pa•pal (pā′pəl) *adj.* Of or relating to the pope or the papacy.
pa•paw *also* **paw•paw** (pô′pô′) *n.* A North American tree, *Asimina triloba,* bearing fleshy, edible fruit.
pa•pa•ya (pə-pī′ə) *n.* A tropical American tree, *Carica papaya,* bearing large, yellow, edible fruit.
pa•per (pā′pər) *n.* **1. a.** A material made of pulp obtained chiefly from wood and rags and used for printing or writing on, wrapping something in, and covering walls. **b.** A single sheet of paper. **2. a.** A document. **b. papers.** Documents that establish the bearer's identity. **3.** A newspaper. **4.** A written composition, as an essay or report. **5.** Wallpaper. —*v.* To cover with wallpaper. —**pa′per•y** *adj.*
pa•per•back (pā′pər-băk′) *n.* A book that has a flexible paper binding. —**pa′per•backed′** *adj.*
pa•per•board (pā′pər-bôrd′, -bōrd′) *n.* Cardboard.
pa•per•hang•er (pā′pər-hăng′ər) *n.* Someone who applies wallpaper. —**pa′per•hang′ing** *n.*
pa•per•weight (pā′pər-wāt′) *n.* A heavy object used to hold down loose papers.
pa•pier-mâ•ché (pā′pər-mə-shā′, păp′yā-) *n.* A material of waste paper mixed with paste or glue that can be shaped when wet.
pa•pil•la (pə-pĭl′ə) *n., pl.* **-pil•lae** (-pĭl′ē). A small projection from a bodily surface. —**pap′il•lar′y** (păp′ə-lĕr′ē, pə-pĭl′ə-rē) *adj.*
pap•il•lote (pä′pē-yōt′, păp′ē-) *n.* **1.** A frilled paper cover for decorating the bone end of a cooked chop or cutlet. **2.** Oiled parchment in which foods such as meat and fish are baked.
pa•poose (pă-po͞os′, pə-) *n.* An American Indian infant or very young child.
pa•pri•ka (pă-prē′kə, pə-, păp′rĭ-kə) *n.* A mild seasoning made from the ground pods of certain sweet red peppers.
Pap smear (păp) *n.* A Pap test.
Pap test *n.* A test in which a smear of a bodily secretion, esp. from the uterine cervix, is examined for the early detection of cancer.
pap•ule (păp′yo͞ol) *n.* A small inflammatory congested spot on the skin **:** pimple. —**pap′u•lar** (-yə-lər) *adj.*
pa•py•rus (pə-pī′rəs) *n., pl.* **-rus•es** *or* **-ri** (-rī′). **1.** A tall aquatic sedge, *Cyperus papyrus,* of N Africa. **2.** Paper made from papyrus, used in ancient times as a writing material.

par (pär) *n.* **1.** A normal standard or accepted average. **2.** A common and equal status or level : equality. **3.** The standard number of golf strokes needed by an expert to complete a hole. **4.** Face value, as of a security.

pa•ra (pä-rä', pä'rä) *n.* —See table at CURRENCY.

par•a•ble (păr'ə-bəl) *n.* A story that illustrates a moral lesson.

pa•rab•o•la (pə-răb'ə-lə) *n.* A plane curve formed by the locus of points equidistant from a fixed line and a fixed point not on the line. **—par'a•bol'ic** (păr'ə-bŏl'ĭk) *adj.*

par•a•chute (păr'ə-sho͞ot') *n.* A folding umbrella-shaped apparatus used to retard free fall from an aircraft or the motion of a vehicle. **—par'a•chute'** *v.* **—par'a•chut'ist** *n.*

pa•rade (pə-răd') *n.* **1.** A public procession, esp. a ceremonial one : march. **2.** A formal review of a body of troops. **3.** A long line : succession. **4.** An ostentatious display <a *parade* of elegant clothes> —*v.* **-rad•ed, -rad•ing.** **1.** To take part in or as if in a parade. **2.** To exhibit ostentatiously : show off. **3.** To take a leisurely walk : promenade. **—pa•rad'er** *n.*

par•a•digm (păr'ə-dīm', -dĭm') *n.* **1.** A listing of all the inflections of a noun or verb taken as a model for determining the forms of other words like it. **2.** A pattern : model. **—par'a•dig•mat'ic** (-dĭg-măt'ĭk) *adj.*

par•a•dise (păr'ə-dīs', -dīz') *n.* **1.** *often* **Paradise.** HEAVEN 2. **2.** A place or state of ideal beauty, loveliness, or rapture. **—par'a•dis'i•ac'** (-dĭz'ē-ăk'), **par'a•di•si'a•cal** (-dĭ-sī'ə-kəl, -zī'-) *adj.*

par•a•dox (păr'ə-dŏks') *n.* A statement that seems to conflict with common sense or to contradict itself but that may nevertheless be true. **—par'a•dox'i•cal** *adj.* **—par'a•dox'i•cal•ly** *adv.*

par•af•fin (păr'ə-fĭn) *n.* **1.** A waxy white or colorless substance that is used to make candles, lubricants, and sealing materials. **2.** *esp. Brit.* Kerosene. **—par'af•fin** *v.*

par•a•gon (păr'ə-gŏn', -gən) *n.* A pattern or model of perfection or excellence.

par•a•graph (păr'ə-grăf') *n.* **1.** A division of a composition that deals with a single aspect or idea and consists of one or more sentences. **2.** A mark (¶) used to indicate the beginning of a paragraph. —*v.* To arrange in or divide into paragraphs.

par•a•keet (păr'ə-kēt') *n.* Any of various small parrots usu. with long, tapering tails.

par•a•le•gal (păr'ə-lē'gəl) *adj.* Of, relating to, or being a person who is trained to assist a lawyer but is not licensed to practice law. **—par'a•le'gal** *n.*

par•al•lax (păr'ə-lăks') *n.* An apparent change in the position of an object caused by a change in observational position.

par•al•lel (păr'ə-lĕl', -ləl) *adj.* **1.** Moving or situated in the same direction but always separated by the same distance. **2.** Similar in comparable or corresponding parts : like. ★ *syns:* COEXTENSIVE, COLLATERAL, CONCURRENT —*n.* **1.** A parallel curve, line, or surface. **2. a.** Something that is analogous or similar to something else. **b.** A comparison that indicates analogy or similarity. **3.** One of the imaginary lines that encircles the earth parallel to the equator and represents a specified latitude. —*v.* **-leled, -lel•ing** *or* **-lelled, -lel•ling.** **1.** To extend or be parallel to. **2.** To be analogous or similar to. **—par'al•lel•ism** *n.*

par•al•lel•o•gram (păr'ə-lĕl'ə-grăm') *n.* A 4-sided plane figure with opposite sides equal and parallel.

pa•ral•y•sis (pə-răl'ĭ-sĭs) *n., pl.* **-ses** (-sēz'). Partial or complete loss of the ability to move or feel sensation. **—par'a•lyt'ic** (păr'ə-lĭt'ĭk) *adj. & n.*

par•a•lyze (păr'ə-līz') *v.* **-lyzed, -lyz•ing.** **1.** To affect with paralysis. **2.** To cause to be powerless or inoperative.

par•a•me•ci•um (păr'ə-mē'shē-əm, -sē-) *n., pl.* **-ci•a** (-shē-ə, -sē-ə) *or* **-ums.** Any of various usu. oval-shaped protozoans of the genus *Paramecium* that move by means of cilia.

par•a•med•ic (păr'ə-mĕd'ĭk) *n.* Someone trained to provide emergency medical treatment or to assist physicians. **—par'a•med'i•cal** *adj.*

pa•ram•e•ter (pə-răm'ĭ-tər) *n.* **1.** A constant in a mathematical expression whose values determine the specific form or characteristics of the expression. **2.** *Informal.* A typical element. **—par'a•met'ric** (păr'ə-mĕt'rĭk), **par'a•met'ri•cal** *adj.*

par•a•mil•i•tary (păr'ə-mĭl'ĭ-tĕr-ē) *adj.* Organized on a military pattern and esp. as an auxiliary military force.

par•a•mount (păr'ə-mount') *adj.* Of highest rank, power, or importance.

par•a•mour (păr'ə-mo͝or') *n.* A lover, esp. in an adulterous relationship.

par•a•noi•a (păr'ə-noi'ə) *n.* A psychosis marked by delusions of persecution or of grandeur. **—par'a•noid'** (-noid') *adj. & n.*

par•a•pet (păr'ə-pĭt, -pĕt') *n.* **1.** A low railing or wall, as along the edge of a balcony. **2.** An embankment or rampart to protect soldiers, as in a fort.

par•a•pher•na•lia (păr'ə-fər-nāl'yə, -fə-) *n.* *(sing. or pl. in number).* **1.** Personal belongings. **2.** The apparatus used in an activity : equipment.

par•a•phrase (păr'ə-frāz') *v.* **-phrased, -phras•ing** To restate the meaning of (e.g., a passage or text) in different words. ★ *syns:* REPHRASE, RESTATE, REWORD, TRANSLATE **—par'a•phrase'** *n.*

par•a•ple•gia (păr'ə-plē'jə, -jē-ə) *n.* Paralysis of the lower half of the body, including both legs. **—par'a•ple'gic** (-jĭk) *adj. & n.*

par•a•pro•fes•sion•al (păr'ə-prə-fĕsh'ə-nəl) *n.* Someone, as a teacher's aide, who is trained to assist a professional person.

par•a•psy•chol•o•gy (păr'ə-sī-kŏl'ə-jē) *n.* The study of phenomena, as telepathy and clairvoyance, that are inexplicable by known natural laws. **—par'a•psy'cho•log'i•cal** *adj.* **—par'a•psy•chol'o•gist** *n.*

par•a•quat (păr′ə-kwŏt′) *n.* A toxic yellow compound used as a herbicide.

par•a•site (păr′ə-sīt′) *n.* **1.** *Biol.* An organism, as a plant, that grows, feeds, and is sheltered on or in a different organism and contributes nothing to its host. **2.** Someone who depends on others, as for support, without providing adequate return. **—par′a•sit′ic** (-sĭt′ĭk) *adj.* **—par′a•sit•ism** (-sĭ-tĭz′əm, -sī-) *n.* **—par′a•sit•ize′** (-sĭ-tīz′) *v.*

par•a•si•tol•o•gy (păr′ə-sĭ-tŏl′ə-jē, -sī-) *n.* The scientific study of parasites, esp. animal parasites. **—par′a•si•tol′o•gist** *n.*

par•a•sol (păr′ə-sôl′, -sŏl′) *n.* A light umbrella used as a sunshade.

par•a•sym•pa•thet•ic nervous system (păr′ə-sĭm′pə- thĕt′ĭk) *n.* The part of the autonomic nervous system tending to dilate blood vessels, stimulate digestive secretions, and slow the heart.

par•a•thi•on (păr′ə-thī′ŏn′) *n.* A highly poisonous yellowish liquid used as an agricultural insecticide.

par•a•thy•roid gland (păr′ə-thī′roid′) *n.* Any of 4 small kidney-shaped glands that are adjacent to the thyroid gland and secrete a hormone necessary for calcium and phosphorus metabolism.

par•a•troops (păr′ə-tro͞ops′) *pl.n.* Troops that are equipped and trained to parachute from an aircraft. **—par′a•troop′er** *n.*

par•a•ty•phoid (păr′ə-tī′foid′) *n.* An acute food poisoning that resembles typhoid fever but is less severe.

par•boil (pär′boil′) *v.* To boil for a brief time.

par•cel (pär′səl) *n.* **1.** A wrapped package : bundle. **2.** A plot or portion of land. **3.** A group, as of things : collection. —*v.* **-celed, -cel•ing** *or* **-celled, -cel•ling. 1.** To divide into parts and give out. **2.** To make up into a parcel : package.

parcel post *n.* The section of the postal service that handles parcels.

parch (pärch) *v.* **1.** To make or become very dry, esp. with or from intense heat. **2.** To roast or toast (e.g., corn) with dry heat.

parch•ment (pärch′mənt) *n.* **1.** Sheepskin or goatskin prepared as a material for writing or drawing on. **2.** Something written or drawn on parchment.

par•don (pär′dn) *v.* **1.** To release from disfavor or punishment. **2.** To permit (an offense) to pass without punishment. **3.** To excuse : forgive. —*n.* **1.** *Law.* Exemption of a convicted person from the penalties of a crime or offense. **2.** Forgiveness, as for a fault or rudeness. **—par′don•a•ble** *adj.*

pare (pâr) *v.* **pared, par•ing. 1.** To remove an outer surface of : peel. **2.** To reduce by or as if by paring <*pared* his allowance>

par•e•go•ric (păr′ĭ-gôr′ĭk, -gŏr′-) *n.* A camphorated tincture of opium.

par•ent (pâr′ənt, păr′-) *n.* **1.** A mother or father. **2.** An ancestor : forefather. **3.** An origin : source. —*v.* To act or serve as a parent. **—par′ent•age** (-ən-tĭj) *n.* **—pa•ren′tal** (pə-rĕn′tl) *adj.* **—par′ent•hood′** *n.*

pa•ren•the•sis (pə-rĕn′thĭ-sĭs) *n., pl.* **-ses** (-sēz′). **1.** One of a pair of curved lines, ( ), used in writing and printing to enclose qualifying or explanatory remarks. **2.** A word, phrase, or sentence inserted into a passage by way of qualification or amplification. **—par′en•thet′i•cal** (păr′ən-thĕt′ĭ-kəl), **par′en•thet′ic** (-thĕt′ĭk) *adj.* **—par′en•thet′i•cal•ly** *adv.*

par•ent•ing (pâr′ən-tĭng, păr′-) *n.* The rearing of children by their parents.

pa•re•sis (pə-rē′sĭs, păr′ĭ-) *n.* A partial or slight paralysis.

par ex•cel•lence (pär′ ĕk-sə-läNS′) *adj.* Preeminent.

par•fait (pär-fā′) *n.* **1.** A sweet dessert of cream, eggs, and flavoring frozen together and served in a tall glass. **2.** A dessert consisting of variously flavored layers of ice cream or ices.

par•he•li•on (pär-hē′lē-ən, -hēl′yən) *n., pl.* **-he•li•a** (-hē′lē-ə, -hēl′yə). A bright spot appearing on either side of the sun, often on a luminous ring or halo.

pa•ri•ah (pə-rī′ə) *n.* An outcast.

pa•ri•e•tal (pə-rī′ĭ-tl) *adj.* **1.** Of, relating to, or forming the wall of a hollow anatomical structure. **2.** Of or relating to life or the regulation of life within a college.

par•i•mu•tu•el (păr′ĭ-myo͞o′cho͞o-əl) *n.* A betting system in which the winners divide the total amount bet, after the deduction of management expenses, in proportion to the sums they have wagered.

par•ing (pâr′ĭng) *n.* Something that has been pared off <carrot *parings*>

par•i pas•su (păr′ē păs′o͞o) *adv.* With equal pace, speed, or progress.

Paris green *n.* A poisonous emerald-green powder used as a pigment, wood preservative, and insecticide.

par•ish (păr′ĭsh) *n.* **1. a.** An administrative division of a diocese consisting of an area with its own church. **b.** The members of a parish. **2.** A civil district in the state of Louisiana that corresponds to a county.

pa•rish•ion•er (pə-rĭsh′ə-nər) *n.* A member of a parish.

par•i•ty (păr′ĭ-tē) *n., pl.* **-ties. 1.** Equality, as in value, position, or amount. **2.** The equivalent in value between 2 different kinds of currency.

park (pärk) *n.* **1.** A tract of land reserved for public use, as for recreation. **2.** An enclosed playing field : stadium <a baseball *park*> **3.** A place where vehicles, as cars, are stored or left. —*v.* To put or leave (a vehicle) standing for a time in a particular location.

par•ka (pär′kə) *n.* A warm hooded fur or cloth jacket.

parking meter *n.* A coin-operated device that registers the amount of time purchased for the parking of a motor vehicle.

Par•kin•son's disease (pär′kĭn-sənz) *n.* A progressive nervous disease that is marked by muscular tremor, partial facial paralysis, weakness, and impaired muscular control.

Parkinson's Law *n.* Any of several satirical observations propounded as economic laws, as "work expands to fill the time available for its completion."

park•way (pärk'wā') *n.* A wide landscaped highway.

par•lance (pär'ləns) *n.* A particular style of speaking : idiom <scientific *parlance*>

par•lay (pär'lā') *n.* A series of bets in which the winnings of the 1st and original stake are risked on subsequent wagers. —**par'lay'** *v.*

par•ley (pär'lē) *n., pl.* **-leys.** A discussion, esp. to resolve differences between opponents : conference. —**par'ley** *v.*

par•lia•ment (pär'lə-mənt) *n.* **1. Parliament.** The legislature of various countries, esp. the United Kingdom and Canada. **2.** An assembly that represents the members of a group. —**par'lia•men'ta•ry** (-mĕn'tə-rē, -mĕn'trē) *adj.*

par•lia•men•tar•i•an (pär'lə-mĕn-târ'ē-ən) *n.* One who is an expert in parliamentary rules, procedure, or debate.

par•lor (pär'lər) *n.* **1.** A room for entertaining visitors or for conversing. **2.** A business establishment <an ice-cream *parlor*>

par•lour (pär'lər) *n. esp. Brit. var. of* PARLOR.

par•lous (pär'ləs) *adj.* Full of peril : dangerous. —**par'lous•ly** *adv.*

Par•me•san (pär'mĭ-zän', -zăn', -zən) *n.* A hard, dry, sharp cheese often served grated.

par•mi•gia•na (pär'mĭ-jä'nə) *adj.* Covered or cooked with Parmesan cheese <chicken *parmigiana*>

pa•ro•chi•al (pə-rō'kē-əl) *adj.* **1.** Of, relating to, or supported by a church parish. **2.** Limited in range or understanding : provincial. —**pa•ro'chi•al•ly** *adv.*

parochial school *n.* A school that is run and supported by a religious group.

par•o•dy (păr'ə-dē) *n., pl.* **-dies. 1.** A musical or literary work that imitates another work, exaggerating the characteristics of the original to make it seem ridiculous. **2.** A travesty <a *parody* of justice> —**par'o•dist** *n.* —**par'o•dy** *v.*

pa•role (pə-rōl') *n.* **1.** The conditional release of a prisoner before the expiration of his or her term. **2.** Word of honor : pledge. —**pa•role'** *v.* —**pa•rol'ee'** *n.*

par•ox•ysm (păr'ək-sĭz'əm) *n.* A sudden attack or outburst, as of emotion : spasm. —**par'ox•ys'mal** *adj.*

par•quet (pär-kā') *n.* **1. a.** The forward part of the main floor of a theater. **b.** The main floor of a theater : orchestra. **2.** A parquetry floor.

par•quet•ry (pär'kĭ-trē) *n., pl.* **-ries.** Woodwork of inlaid pieces fitted together in a pattern.

par•ri•cide (păr'ĭ-sīd') *n.* **1.** Someone who murders his or her mother or father or a near relative. **2.** The act committed by a parricide. —**par'ri•cid'al** *adj.*

par•rot (păr'ət) *n.* Any of various tropical and semitropical birds of the order Psittaciformes, having short, hooked bills and brightly colored plumage. —*v.* To imitate or repeat mindlessly.

parrot fever *n.* Psittacosis.

par•ry (păr'ē) *v.* **-ried, -ry•ing. 1.** To turn aside (e.g., a weapon) : deflect. **2.** To avoid skillfully or adroitly : evade. —**par'ry** *n.*

parse (pärs) *v.* **parsed, pars•ing.** To identify the part of speech, form, and function of a word or group of words.

par•sec (pär'sĕk') *n.* A unit of astronomical length equal to 3.258 light-years.

par•si•mo•ny (pär'sə-mō'nē) *n.* Extreme reluctance to spend money or use resources : excessive frugality. —**par'si•mo'ni•ous** *adj.* —**par'si•mo'ni•ous•ly** *adv.*

pars•ley (pär'slē) *n.* A cultivated herb, *Petroselinum crispum,* with divided curly leaves used as a garnish and seasoning.

pars•nip (pär'snĭp') *n.* A plant, *Pastinaca sativa,* cultivated for its long rather strong-tasting edible root.

par•son (pär'sən) *n.* A clergyman, esp. a Protestant clergyman.

par•son•age (pär'sə-nĭj) *n.* The residence provided by a church for its parson.

part (pärt) *n.* **1.** A division, portion, or segment of a whole. **2.** A component of a machine. **3.** The role of an actor, as in a play. **4.** A task or function that must be performed in a common effort : duty. **5. a.** An individual melodic line for a particular instrument or voice. **b.** The score for such a line. **6.** A side in a controversy or dispute. **7.** *often* **parts.** A land, region, or territory. **8.** The line that forms when the hair divides, as from brushing or combing. —*v.* **1.** To divide, split, or break into parts : separate. **2.** To keep or put apart. **3.** To divide (the hair) into a part. **4.** To go away from someone. **5.** To leave : depart. **6.** To give up control or possession <wouldn't *part* with his car> —*adv.* In part : partially.

par•take (pär-tāk') *v.* **-took** (-to͝ok'), **-tak•en** (-tā'kən), **-tak•ing. 1.** To have or take a share (of) : participate (in). **2.** To take a helping, as of food. —**par•tak'er** *n.*

par•terre (pär-târ') *n.* **1.** A garden, esp. a flower garden, in which the beds and paths form a pattern. **2.** The section of a theater parquet situated under a rear balcony.

par•the•no•gen•e•sis (pär'thə-nō-jĕn'ĭ-sĭs) *n.* Reproduction without the conjunction of gametes of opposite sexes. —**par'the•no•ge•net'ic** (-jə-nĕt'ĭk) *adj.*

par•tial (pär'shəl) *adj.* **1.** Not total or complete : incomplete. **2.** According preference or favor to one side or person over another : biased. **3.** Especially fond <*partial* to classical music> —**par'ti•al'i•ty** (-shē-ăl'ĭ-tē, -shăl'ĭ-) *n.* —**par'tial•ly** *adv.*

par•tic•i•pate (pär-tĭs'ə-pāt') *v.* **-pat•ed, -pat•ing. 1.** To join with others in something : take part. **2.** To have a share in something. —**par•tic'i•pant** *n.* —**par•tic'i•pa'tion** *n.* —**par•tic'i•pa'tor** *n.* —**par•tic'i•pa•to'ry** *adj.*

par•ti•ci•ple (pär'tĭ-sĭp'əl) *n.* A word that both functions as an adjective and is used with an auxiliary verb to indicate certain tenses. **—par'ti·cip'i·al** *adj.*

par·ti·cle (pär'tĭ-kəl) *n.* **1.** A very small speck of solid matter. **2.** A subatomic particle. **3.** Any of a class of words, as many prepositions and conjunctions, that convey little meaning but help connect, specify, or limit the meanings of other words.

par·ti·col·ored (pär'tē-kŭl'ərd) *adj.* Marked by different tints or colors.

par·tic·u·lar (pər-tĭk'yə-lər) *adj.* **1.** Of, relating to, or associated with a specific person, thing, group, or category. **2.** Separate and distinct : individual. **3.** Special : exceptional. **4. a.** Mindful of details : meticulous. **b.** Difficult to please : fussy. —*n.* An individual fact, item, or detail. **—par·tic'u·lar'i·ty** *n.* **—par·tic'u·lar·ly** *adv.*

par·tic·u·lar·ize (pər-tĭk'yə-lə-rīz') *v.* **-ized, -iz·ing. 1.** To enumerate, describe, or state in detail : specify. **2.** To give details.

par·tic·u·late (pər-tĭk'yə-lĭt, -lāt') *adj.* Of or made up of separate particles. **—par·tic'u·late** *n.*

part·ing (pär'tĭng) *n.* **1.** A division : separation. **2.** The act of taking leave. —*adj.* Given, done, or said on departing <a *parting* embrace>

par·ti·san (pär'tĭ-zən) *n.* **1.** A supporter of another, as a party or cause. **2.** A guerrilla. **—par'ti·san** *adj.* **—par'ti·san·ship'** *n.*

par·ti·ta (pär-tē'tə) *n. Mus.* A set of related instrumental pieces, as a suite.

par·tite (pär'tīt') *adj.* Divided into parts.

par·ti·tion (pär-tĭsh'ən) *n.* **1.** The division of something into parts. **2.** Something that separates, esp. an interior structure dividing a larger area. —*v.* **1.** To divide into parts. **2.** To separate by a partition.

part·ly (pärt'lē) *adv.* To some degree or extent : in part.

part·ner (pärt'nər) *n.* **1.** One who is associated with another in a shared activity, esp.: **a.** One of 2 or more persons who jointly own a business. **b.** A husband or wife : spouse. **c.** Either of a pair of persons dancing together. **d.** One of a pair or a team in a game or sport. **2.** An ally. ★ ***syns:*** ALLY, ASSOCIATE, COLLEAGUE, CONFEDERATE **—part'ner·ship'** *n.*

part of speech *n.* One of the traditional grammatical classes, as noun or verb, into which words are placed according to their syntactic function.

par·took (pär-to͝ok') *v. p.t. of* PARTAKE.

par·tridge (pär'trĭj) *n., pl.* **-tridg·es** *or* **partridge.** Any of several plump-bodied game birds, esp. of the genera *Perdix* and *Alectoris.*

part song *n.* A song with 2 or more voice parts.

part-time (pärt'tīm') *adj.* During or for fewer than customary hours <*part-time* employment> **—part'-time'** *adv.*

par·tu·ri·tion (pär'cho͞o-rĭsh'ən, -chə-) *n.* Childbirth.

part·way (pärt'wā') *adv.* In part : partly.

par·ty (pär'tē) *n., pl.* **-ties. 1.** A social gathering, as for entertainment or pleasure. **2.** A group of people participating in a common activity or task <a work *party*> **3.** A group of persons organized to advance its political principles and support its candidates for office. **4.** A group or person involved in a proceeding or affair.

party line *n.* **1.** A telephone circuit shared by 2 or more subscribers within an exchange. **2.** The official policies or principles of a political party.

par·ve·nu (pär'və-no͞o', -nyo͞o') *n.* Someone who has suddenly or recently become wealthy or powerful but lacks the background or culture customarily associated with his new status.

pas (pä) *n., pl.* **pas** (pä, päz). A ballet step or series of steps.

Pascal *or* **PASCAL** *n. Computer Sci.* A high-level programming language that processes both numerical and textual data.

pas de deux (pä' də dœ') *n., pl.* **pas de deux.** A ballet figure or dance for 2 persons.

pa·sha (pä'shə, păsh'ə) *n.* Used formerly as a title for military and civil officers, esp. in Turkey and N Africa.

pass (păs) *v.* **1.** To move : proceed. **2.** To move or cause to move over, past, or beyond. **3.** To transfer or be transferred : circulate. **4.** To elapse or let elapse. **5.** To come to an end. **6.** To happen : occur. **7.** To go or be allowed to go without challenge <let the incident *pass*> **8.** To undergo or cause to undergo a trial, test, or course of study with success. **9.** To be accepted or viewed. **10.** To enact or be enacted, as by a legislature. **11.** To pronounce a legal judgment. **12.** To transfer (the puck or ball) to a teammate. **13.** To decline to play or bid, esp. in a card game. **14.** To go through (e.g., an obstacle). **15.** To discharge (bodily wastes). **—pass out.** To lose consciousness. **—pass up.** *Informal.* To turn down : decline. —*n.* **1.** The act of passing. **2.** A narrow passage in a mountain range : gap. **3. a.** A written permit or authorization to come or go freely or without charge. **b.** A written leave of absence from duty, esp. military duty. **4.** The act of transferring the puck or ball to a teammate. **5.** An effort : attempt. **6.** A situation : predicament. **7.** A sexual overture or gesture.

pass·a·ble (păs'ə-bəl) *adj.* **1.** Capable of being passed or traversed. **2.** Acceptable but not outstanding. **—pass'a·bly** *adv.*

pas·sage (păs'ĭj) *n.* **1.** The act of passing. **2.** A journey, esp. by air or water. **3.** The permission or right to travel, as on a ship. **4.** Something, as a channel or path, through, over, or along which something may pass. **5.** Enactment, as of a legislative measure. **6.** A selection or portion, as of a musical composition.

pas·sage·way (păs'ĭj-wā') *n.* A way that permits passage, as a corridor.

pass·book (păs'bo͝ok') *n.* A bankbook.

pas·sé (pă-sā') *adj.* **1.** No longer current : out-of-date. **2.** No longer young.

pas·sel (păs'əl) *n. Informal.* A large number or quantity.

pas·sen·ger (păs'ən-jər) *n.* Someone traveling in a vehicle or conveyance, as a car or train.
passe-par·tout (păs'-pär-to͞o') *n.* Something, such as a master key, that enables one to go or pass everywhere.
pass·er·by (păs'ər-bī', păs'ər-bī') *n., pl.* **pass·ers·by.** Someone who passes by.
pas·ser·ine (păs'ə-rīn') *adj.* Of or relating to birds of the order Passeriformes, which consists primarily of perching birds and songbirds.
pas·sim (păs'ĭm) *adv.* Here and there : in places throughout.
pass·ing (păs'ĭng) *adj.* **1.** Lasting only a brief time : transitory. **2.** Casual : superficial. —*n.* **1.** The act of one that passes. **2.** A place or means by which one can pass. **3.** Death.
pas·sion (păsh'ən) *n.* **1.** Powerful feeling. **2. a.** Love. **b.** Sexual desire : lust. **c.** The object of such love or desire. **3. a.** Great enthusiasm. **b.** The object of such enthusiasm. **4.** Anger : rage **5. Passion.** Christ's sufferings following the Last Supper to the time of his death. ★ ***syns:*** ARDOR, ENTHUSIASM, FERVOR, FIRE, ZEAL —**pas'sion·ate** *adj.* —**pas'sion·ate·ly** *adv.* —**pas'sion·less** *adj.*
pas·sion·flow·er (păsh'ən-flou'ər) *n.* A chiefly tropical American vine of the genus *Passiflora,* usu. bearing large, variously colored flowers.
pas·sive (păs'ĭv) *adj.* **1.** Not active but acted upon. **2.** Unresisting : submissive. **3.** Indicating that the grammatical subject of a verb is the recipient or object of the action expressed by the verb. —*n.* **1.** The passive voice of a verb. **2.** A verb form in the passive voice. —**pas'sive·ly** *adv.* —**pas·siv'i·ty** (pă-sĭv'ĭ-tē), **pas'sive·ness** *n.*
pass·key (păs'kē') *n.* **1.** A master key. **2.** A skeleton key.
Pass·o·ver (păs'ō'vər) *n.* A Jewish holiday that is celebrated in the spring and commemorates the exodus from Egypt.
pass·port (păs'pôrt', -pōrt') *n.* An official document issued by a nation that certifies the identity and citizenship of the holder and grants him or her its protection during travel abroad.
pass·word (păs'wûrd') *n.* **1.** A secret word or phrase that one uses to gain admittance or access to information. **2.** A sequence of characters required to gain access to a computer system.
past (păst) *adj.* **1.** Having happened or existed in a time before the present : bygone. **2. a.** Before the present time : ago <12 months *past*> **b.** Just elapsed or gone by <the *past* week> **3.** Of, relating to, or being a verb tense or form used to express time that has gone by. —*n.* **1.** The time before the present. **2. a.** A person's background or history. **b.** A questionable or secret personal past life. **3. a.** The past tense. **b.** A verb form in the past tense. —*adv.* So as to go beyond <The plane flew *past.*> —*prep.* Beyond, as in position or time.
pas·ta (pä'stə) *n.* **1.** A paste, as macaroni, or dough, as ravioli, made of flour and water. **2.** A cooked dish of pasta.
paste (pāst) *n.* **1.** A viscous substance, as a mixture of flour and water, used to stick things together. **2.** Dough, as that used for making pastry. **3.** A food made smooth or creamy by grinding or pounding <tomato *paste*> **4.** A brilliant glass used in artificial gems. —*v.* **past·ed, past·ing. 1.** To cause to stick together by applying paste. **2.** *Slang.* To hit : punch.
paste·board (pāst'bôrd', -bōrd') *n.* A firm board that is made of sheets of paper pasted together.
pas·tel (pă-stĕl') *n.* **1. a.** A paste made of ground pigment. **b.** A crayon made of pastel. **2.** A picture or drawing in pastel. **3.** A light or pale tint.
pas·tern (păs'tərn) *n.* The portion of a horse's foot between the joint at the hoof and the fetlock.
pas·teur·i·za·tion (păs'chə-rĭ-zā'shən) *n.* A process in which a liquid, as milk, is heated to the temperature at which most disease-producing microorganisms are destroyed. —**pas'teur·ize'** (-rīz') *v.*
pas·tiche (pă-stēsh', pä-) *n.* **1.** A work, as a musical composition, that is made up of selections from various different works. **2.** A hodgepodge : potpourri.
pas·tille (pă-stēl') *also* **pas·til** (păs'tĭl) *n.* A medicated or aromatic lozenge.
pas·time (păs'tīm') *n.* Something that occupies the time pleasantly : diversion.
pas·tor (păs'tər) *n.* A Christian minister or priest, esp. one who leads a congregation. —**pas'tor·ate** *n.*
pas·tor·al (păs'tər-əl) *adj.* **1.** Of or relating to shepherds or to life in the country. **2.** Of or relating to a pastor or his duties.
pas·to·rale (păs'tə-räl', -răl') *n.* A vocal or instrumental composition with a theme that suggests idyllic rural life.
†**pas·to·ri·um** (pă-stôr'ē-əm, -stōr'-) *n.* *S U.S.* The residence of a pastor : parsonage.
past participle *n.* A participle that expresses action that is completed. —Used to form the passive voice and the perfect tenses.
pas·tra·mi (pə-strä'mē) *n.* Highly seasoned smoked beef, usu. prepared from breast or shoulder cuts.
pas·try (pā'strē) *n., pl.* **-tries. 1.** A paste of water, flour, and shortening used for baked crusts, as of pies and tarts. **2.** Baked and esp. sweet goods made with pastry.
pas·tur·age (păs'chər-ĭj) *n.* Pasture.
pas·ture (păs'chər) *n.* **1.** Plants, as grass, on which grazing livestock feed. **2.** A tract of land on which livestock graze. —*v.* **-tured, -tur·ing. 1.** To herd (animals) into a pasture for grazing. **2.** To graze.
past·y¹ (pā'stē) *adj.* **-i·er, -i·est.** Resembling paste, esp. in being pale and unhealthy-looking.
pas·ty² (păs'tē) *n., pl.* **-ties.** A pie with a filling of seasoned meat or fish.
▲ ***word history:*** The noun *pasty²*, "meat

pie," was borrowed from Old French *pastee* in the 13th cent. *Pastee* is derived from Old French *paste,* literally "paste," which orig. referred to an edible dough of flour and liquid. Old French *pastee* is descended from the same word as Italian *pasta.* The modern French form of *pastee* is *pâté,* which was borrowed into English in the 18th cent. as a synonym for *pasty*[2]. *Pâté* in English now denotes the meat alone, without its pastry crust. *Patty* is an anglicized variant of *pâté.*

pat (păt) *v.* **pat·ted, pat·ting. 1. a.** To tap lightly with the open hand or something flat. **b.** To tap softly, esp. with the flat of the hand, as a gesture of affection. **2.** To smooth, flatten, or shape by tapping. —*n.* **1.** A light or gentle tap, esp. with a flat implement or the open hand. **2.** The sound made by a pat. **3.** A small, flat, usu. rectangular mass, as of butter. —*adj.* **1.** Precisely suited to the purpose or occasion. **2.** Learned or memorized exactly. **3.** Glib : facile <a *pat* answer> **4.** Not moving : unyielding. —*adv.* In a pat manner. —**pat'ly** *adv.* —**pat'ness** *n.*

pa·ta·ca (pə-tä'kə) *n.* —See table at CURRENCY.

patch (păch) *n.* **1.** A piece of fabric used to cover or reinforce a worn or weakened area in a garment. **2.** A piece of cloth affixed to a garment as an insignia, as of military rank. **3.** A protective pad, dressing, or bandage worn over an injured or missing eye. **4.** A small area that differs from what surrounds it <a *patch* of snow> —*v.* **1.** To cover or reinforce with a patch. **2.** To put together or repair, esp. hastily.

patch test *n.* A test for allergic reaction in which a suspected allergen is applied to the skin with a small surgical pad.

patch·work (păch'wûrk') *n.* **1.** Something that consists of pieces of various colors, shapes, materials, or sizes. **2.** A miscellany : jumble.

patch·y (păch'ē) *adj.* **-i·er, -i·est. 1.** Consisting of or marked by patches : spotty. **2.** Uneven in quality or performance.

pate (pāt) *n.* The top of the head.

pâ·té (pä-tā', pă-) *n.* **1.** A paste of seasoned and spiced meat. **2.** A small pastry filled with fish or meat.

pa·tel·la (pə-tĕl'ə) *n., pl.* **-tel·lae** (-tĕl'ē). A flat, triangular bone that forms the front of the knee joint : kneecap.

pat·en (păt'n) *n.* **1.** A plate, esp. one for the Eucharistic bread. **2.** A thin metal disk.

pat·ent (păt'nt) *n.* **1.** A governmental grant assuring an inventor the sole right to his invention for a period of time. **2.** Something that is patented. —*adj.* **1.** (*also* pāt'nt). Obvious : evident. **2.** Protected by a patent. —*v.* **1.** To obtain a patent for. **2.** To grant a patent to. —**pat'ent·ee'** *n.*

patent leather *n.* Leather finished to a smooth, shiny surface.

pa·ter·fa·mil·i·as (pā'tər-fə-mĭl'ē-əs, pä'-) *n., pl.* **pa·tres·fa·mil·i·as** (pā'trēz-). **1.** The male head of a household. **2.** The father of a family.

pa·ter·nal (pə-tûr'nəl) *adj.* **1.** Of, relating to, or typical of a father : fatherly. **2.** Inherited or received from a father. **3.** Of or relating to a father's side of a family. —**pa·ter'nal·ly** *adv.*

pa·ter·nal·ism (pə-tûr'nə-lĭz'əm) *n.* A practice or policy by which an authority treats or governs those under its jurisdiction in a paternal manner, esp. by filling their needs and regulating their behavior. —**pa·ter'nal·is'tic** *adj.*

pa·ter·ni·ty (pə-tûr'nĭ-tē) *n.* **1.** The state or fact of being a father : fatherhood. **2.** Paternal descent.

path (păth, päth) *n., pl.* **paths** (păthz, päthz, păths, päths). **1.** A way or track made by footsteps. **2.** A course : route. —**path'less** *adj.*

pa·thet·ic (pə-thĕt'ĭk) *adj.* Arousing sympathy, pity, or tenderness. —**pa·thet'i·cal·ly** *adv.*

path·find·er (păth'fīn'dər, päth'-) *n.* One who probes unexplored regions to discover a way : trailblazer.

path·o·gen (păth'ə-jən) *n.* An agent, esp. a microorganism such as a bacterium, that causes disease. —**path'o·gen'ic** (-jĕn'ĭk) *adj.* —**path'o·ge·nic'i·ty** (-jə-nĭs'ĭ-tē) *n.*

path·o·gen·e·sis (păth'ə-jĕn'ĭ-sĭs) *n.* The development of a diseased or morbid condition.

pa·thol·o·gy (pə-thŏl'ə-jē, pă-) *n., pl.* **-gies. 1.** The scientific and medical study of the nature of disease. **2.** The functional or anatomic manifestations of disease. —**path'o·log'i·cal** (păth'ə-lŏj'ĭ-kəl) *adj.* —**pa·thol'o·gist** *n.*

pa·thos (pā'thŏs') *n.* A quality or element that arouses pity, sympathy, or sorrow.

path·way (păth'wā', päth'-) *n.* A path.

pa·tience (pā'shəns) *n.* **1.** The fact, quality, or habit of being patient. **2.** *esp. Brit.* The game of solitaire.

pa·tient (pā'shənt) *adj.* **1.** Enduring affliction or pain without anger or complaint. **2.** Understanding : tolerant. **3.** Persevering : steadfast. —*n.* Someone receiving medical treatment. —**pa'tient·ly** *adv.*

pat·i·na (păt'n-ə, pə-tē'nə) *n.* A thin film of corrosion, usu. green, that forms on copper and bronze as a result of oxidation.

pat·i·o (păt'ē-ō') *n., pl.* **-os. 1.** An inner courtyard without a roof. **2.** A recreation area, usu. paved, near a residence.

pat·ois (păt'wä') *n., pl.* **-ois** (-wäz'). **1.** A regional dialect. **2.** Substandard or illiterate speech. **3.** Jargon.

pa·tri·arch (pā'trē-ärk') *n.* **1.** A man who is venerated as leader, father, or founder, as of a tribe or family. **2.** An ecclesiastical head, esp. in Eastern churches. **3.** A very old and revered man. —**pa'tri·ar'chal** *adj.* —**pa'tri·ar'chate** (-kĭt, -kāt') *n.* —**pa'tri·ar'chy** *n.*

pa·tri·cian (pə-trĭsh'ən) *n.* A member of the aristocracy. —**pa·tri'cian** *adj.*

pat·ri·cide (păt'rĭ-sīd') *n.* **1.** The act of murdering one's own father. **2.** One who has committed patricide. —**pat'ri·cid'al** (-sīd'l) *adj.*

pat·ri·lin·e·al (păt'rə-lĭn'ē-əl) *adj.* Relating to, based on, or tracing ancestral descent through the paternal line.

pat•ri•mo•ny (păt′rə-mō′nē) *n., pl.* **-nies.** Something, as property, inherited from one's father. —**pat′ri•mo′ni•al** *adj.*

pa•tri•ot (pā′trē-ət, -ŏt′) *n.* Someone who loves and defends his or her country. —**pa′-tri•ot′ic** (-ŏt′ĭk) *adj.* —**pa′tri•ot′i•cal•ly** *adv.* —**pa′tri•ot•ism** *n.*

pa•trol (pə-trōl′) *n.* **1. a.** The action of making a circuit about an area or beat for the purpose of observing or maintaining security. **b.** A person or group carrying out such an action. **2.** A detachment sent out to reconnoiter. —*v.* **-trolled, -trol•ling.** To engage in a patrol (of).

pa•trol•man (pə-trōl′mən) *n.* A policeman who patrols or polices an assigned area.

patrol wagon *n.* An enclosed police truck for conveying prisoners.

pa•trol•wom•an (pə-trōl′wŏŏm′ən) *n.* A policewoman who patrols or polices an assigned area.

pa•tron (pā′trən) *n.* **1.** Someone who acts as a special guardian or protector. **2.** Someone who supports or champions an artistically or socially worthwhile cause : sponsor <a *patron* of music> **3.** A regular customer.

pa•tron•age (pā′trə-nĭj, păt′rə-) *n.* **1.** The encouragement or support of a patron. **2. a.** The trade given by customers. **b.** Clientele : customers. **3.** The power to appoint people to governmental or political positions.

pa•tron•ess (pā′trə-nĭs) *n.* A woman who supports, protects, or champions someone or something.

pa•tron•ize (pā′trə-nīz′, păt′rə-) *v.* **-ized, -iz•ing. 1. a.** To be a patron to. **b.** To be a regular customer of. **2.** To act in an offensively condescending way toward. —**pa′tron•iz′ing•ly** *adv.*

pat•ro•nym•ic (păt′rə-nĭm′ĭk) *n.* A name that has been derived from that of a paternal ancestor, esp. by the addition of an affix. —**pat′ro•nym′ic** *adj.*

pa•troon (pə-trōōn′) *n.* A landholder in N.Y. and N.J. with certain feudal powers, esp. under Dutch colonial rule.

pat•sy (păt′sē) *n., pl.* **-sies.** *Slang.* A person who is victimized or cheated.

pat•ter[1] (păt′ər) *v.* To tap or pat quickly, lightly, and repeatedly. —**pat′ter** *n.*

pat•ter[2] (păt′ər) *v.* To speak glibly, rapidly, or mechanically. —*n.* **1.** The jargon of a specific group : lingo. **2.** Glib, rapid speech, as of a salesman.

▲ ***word history:*** The word *patter*[2] is derived from *pater,* a shortened form of *paternoster,* the Latin name for the Lord's Prayer. In medieval times Christian prayers were learned and recited in Latin; they were also often recited rapidly with no regard for the sense of the words. From this practice the name of the prayer became a general word for meaningless chatter. The verb *patter*[2] is derived from the noun.

pat•tern (păt′ərn) *n.* **1.** A decorative or artistic design. **2.** A model for use in making things. **3.** A combination of elements or characteristics : configuration. **4.** A model worthy of imitation. **5.** A specimen : sample. —*v.* To make, shape, form, or design according to a pattern.

pat•ty (păt′ē) *n., pl.* **-ties. 1.** A small flattened cake, as of chopped meat or minced food. **2.** A small pie.

patty shell *n.* A shell of puff pastry made to hold a filling of creamed meat, seafood, or vegetables.

pau•ci•ty (pô′sĭ-tē) *n.* Smallness of quantity or number : dearth.

paunch (pônch) *n.* A belly, esp. a potbelly. —**paunch′y** *adj.*

pau•per (pô′pər) *n.* A very poor person, esp. one who depends on charity. —**pau′per•ism** *n.* —**pau′per•ize′** *v.*

pause (pôz) *v.* **paused, paus•ing.** To stop, linger, or hesitate for a time. ★ ***syns:*** BIDE, LINGER, TARRY, WAIT —*n.* **1.** A temporary stop. **2. a.** A hesitation. **b.** A reason for hesitating. **3.** A sign indicating that a musical note or rest is to be held.

pa•vane *also* **pa•van** (pə-vän′, -văn′) *n.* **1.** A slow, stately court dance of the 16th cent. **2.** Music for a pavane.

pave (pāv) *v.* **paved, pav•ing.** To cover (e.g., a street) with a hard, smooth surface, as of concrete, for travel.

pave•ment (pāv′mənt) *n.* **1.** A surface that has been paved. **2.** The material used to make pavement.

pa•vil•ion (pə-vĭl′yən) *n.* **1.** A large, often ornate tent. **2.** A light, often ornamental roofed structure, as in a park, used for shelter or amusement.

pav•ing (pā′vĭng) *n.* Pavement.

paw (pô) *n.* The foot of an animal, as a cat, that has claws. —*v.* **1. a.** To strike or touch with a paw. **b.** To scrape or strike with a hoof. **2.** To handle rudely or clumsily. **3.** To make grabbing motions with the hands.

pawl (pôl) *n.* A hinged or pivoted device that fits into a notch of another machine part to drive it forward or prevent backward motion.

pawn[1] (pôn) *n.* **1.** Something given to another as security for a loan. **2.** The state of being held as a pledge. **3.** A hostage. —*v.* To deposit or give as security for a loan.

pawn[2] (pôn) *n.* **1.** A chessman of the lowest value. **2.** One used to advance another's purposes.

pawn•bro•ker (pôn′brō′kər) *n.* Someone who lends money on pledged property.

Paw•nee (pô-nē′) *n., pl.* **-nee** *or* **-nees. 1.** A member of an American Indian people formerly of KS and NE, now of OK. **2.** Their Caddoan language.

pawn•shop (pôn′shŏp′) *n.* The place where a pawnbroker conducts business.

paw•paw (pô′pô′) *n. var. of* PAPAW.

pay (pā) *v.* **paid** (pād), **pay•ing. 1.** To give to in return for goods purchased or services rendered. **2.** To give the amount required to discharge (a debt or obligation) : settle <*paid* his taxes> **3.** To requite. **4.** To yield as profit : return. **5.** To be worthwhile (to) <It *pays* to

study.> **6.** To suffer the consequences of <*paid* the price for lying> **7.** To bestow or give <*paying* close attention> —*adj.* **1.** Functioning only after payment for use has been made <a *pay* phone> **2.** Yielding or containing something valuable, as gold. —*n.* **1.** The fact of being paid, esp. by an employer **:** employ. **2.** Something paid, as wages. —**pay'a•ble** *adj.* —**pay•ee'** *n.* —**pay'er** *n.*

pay•check (pā'chĕk') *n.* **1.** A check issued to an employee in payment of wages or salary. **2.** Salary.

pay•load (pā'lōd') *n.* The revenue-producing load, as of cargo, that a vehicle can carry.

pay•mas•ter (pā'măs'tər) *n.* Someone in charge of a payroll.

pay•ment (pā'mənt) *n.* **1.** The act of paying. **2.** Something paid, as an amount.

pay•off (pā'ôf', -ŏf') *n.* **1.** Payment, as of a salary or bribe. **2.** *Informal.* The distribution of profits from an undertaking. **3.** *Informal.* The climax of a sequence of events or a narrative.

pay•o•la (pā-ō'lə) *n. Slang.* **1.** Bribery. **2.** A bribe.

pay•roll (pā'rōl') *n.* **1.** A list of employees who are entitled to receive wages. **2.** The amount of money to be paid to those on a payroll.

Pb *symbol for* LEAD.

PCB (pē'sē-bē') *n.* An industrial compound and environmental pollutant.

Pd *symbol for* PALLADIUM.

pea (pē) *n.* **1.** A vine, *Pisum sativum,* bearing round edible seeds in green pods. **2.** Any of several plants that are related to or resemble the pea.

peace (pēs) *n.* **1. a.** The absence of hostilities, as war. **b.** A treaty or agreement ending hostilities. **2.** A state of harmony, as between persons **:** concord. **3.** A state of security under the law <a disturbance of the *peace*> **4.** Freedom from disquieting feelings and thoughts **:** serenity. —**peace'a•ble** *adj.* —**peace'a•bly** *adv.* —**peace'ful** *adj.* —**peace'ful•ly** *adv.*

peace•keep•ing (pēs'kē'pĭng) *n.* The maintenance of peace, esp. the supervision and enforcement of a truce between hostile nations.

peace•mak•er (pēs'mā'kər) *n.* Someone who makes or tries to make peace.

peace•time (pēs'tīm') *n.* A time without war.

peach (pēch) *n.* A widely cultivated small tree, *Prunus persica,* bearing pink flowers and sweet, juicy edible fruit.

pea•cock (pē'kŏk') *n.* The male peafowl, having a crested head, brilliant blue or green plumage, and long iridescent tail feathers that can be spread like a fan.

pea•fowl (pē'foul') *n.* Either of 2 large Asiatic pheasants, *Pavo cristatus* or *P. muticus.*

pea•hen (pē'hĕn') *n.* The female peafowl.

pea jacket *n.* A short, warm, double-breasted jacket of heavy wool, worn esp. by sailors.

peak (pēk) *n.* **1.** An upward-projecting tapering point. **2. a.** The summit of a mountain or hill. **b.** A mountain. **3.** The visor of a hat or cap. **4.** The point of greatest intensity or development. —*v.* To bring to or achieve a maximum.

peak•ed (pē'kĭd) *adj.* Looking sickly and pale.

peal (pēl) *n.* **1.** The ringing of bells. **2.** A set of bells tuned to each other. **3.** A loud sound or series of sounds <*peals* of laughter> —*v.* To sound in peals **:** ring.

pea•nut (pē'nŭt', -nət) *n.* **1.** A pealike vine, *Arachis hypogaea,* bearing pods that ripen underground. **2.** The edible nutlike seed of the peanut.

pear (pâr) *n.* **1.** A widely cultivated tree, *Pyrus communis,* bearing white flowers and edible fruit. **2.** The fruit of the pear, spherical at the base and narrow at the stem.

pearl (pûrl) *n.* **1.** A smooth, lustrous, variously colored rounded deposit formed esp. around a grain of sand in the shells of certain mollusks and esteemed as a gem. **2.** Mother-of-pearl. **3.** One that is rare, precious, or fine. **4.** Something resembling a pearl. **5.** A yellowish white. —**pearl'y** *adj.*

peas•ant (pĕz'ənt) *n.* **1.** A member of the class comprising agricultural laborers and small farmers. **2.** An uneducated or ill-bred person. —**peas'ant•ry** *n.*

pea•shoot•er (pē'shōō'tər) *n.* A toy consisting of a small tube through which pellets, esp. dried peas, are blown.

peat (pēt) *n.* Partially carbonized vegetable matter, usu. mosses, obtained in wet ground, as bogs, and used as fertilizer and fuel. —**peat'y** *adj.*

peat moss *n.* **1.** A moss of the genus *Sphagnum,* growing in wet places. **2.** The partly carbonized remains of peat moss, used as a mulch and plant food.

peb•ble (pĕb'əl) *n.* A small, usu. round stone worn smooth by erosion. —*v.* **-bled, -bling.** To produce a rough, crinkled surface on (e.g., leather). —**peb'bly** *adj.*

pe•can (pĭ-kän', -kăn') *n.* A tree, *Carya illinoensis,* of the S U.S. bearing edible nuts.

pec•ca•dil•lo (pĕk'ə-dĭl'ō) *n., pl.* **-loes** *or* **-los.** A minor fault or offense.

pec•ca•ry (pĕk'ə-rē) *n., pl.* **-ries.** Either of 2 piglike tropical American mammals, *Tayassu tajacu* or *T. pecari,* with long, dark, dense bristles.

peck[1] (pĕk) *v.* **1.** To strike, tap, or pierce with or as if with the beak. **2.** To pick up with or as if with the beak. **3.** To kiss quickly and usu. without enthusiasm. —*n.* **1.** A mark or stroke made by pecking. **2.** A quick, usu. unenthusiastic kiss.

peck[2] (pĕk) *n.* —See table at MEASUREMENT.

pecking order *n.* **1.** A hierarchic social pattern within poultry flocks in which each member submits to pecking by higher-ranking members and can peck the lower-ranking members without being pecked in return. **2.** A social hierarchy in a human group based on status, authority, etc.

pec•tin (pĕk'tĭn) *n.* Any of various colloidal substances found in ripe fruits and used in making jelly. —**pec'tic** *adj.*

pec·to·ral (pĕk′tər-əl) *adj.* Of or relating to the chest or breast.

pec·u·late (pĕk′yə-lāt′) *v.* **-lat·ed, -lat·ing.** To embezzle. **—pec′u·la′tion** *n.*

pe·cu·liar (pĭ-kyo͞ol′yər) *adj.* **1.** Odd : queer. **2.** Distinctive : typical. **3.** Belonging exclusively to one group or person. **—pe·cu′li·ar′i·ty** (-kyo͞o′-lē-ăr′ĭ-tē, -kyo͞ol-yăr′-) *n.* **—pe·cu′liar·ly** *adv.*

pe·cu·ni·ar·y (pĭ-kyo͞o′nē-ĕr′ē) *adj.* Of, consisting of, or pertaining to money.

ped·a·gogue *also* **ped·a·gog** (pĕd′ə-gŏg′) *n.* A teacher, esp. a schoolteacher.

ped·a·go·gy (pĕd′ə-gō′jē, -gŏj′ē) *n.* The art, profession, or science of teaching. **—ped′a·gog′ic** (-gŏj′ĭk, -gō′jĭk), **ped′a·gog′i·cal** *adj.*

ped·al (pĕd′l) *n.* A lever, as on a musical instrument, that is operated by the foot. *—adj.* Of or pertaining to the foot. *—v.* **-aled, -al·ing** *or* **-alled, -al·ling. 1.** To operate or use a pedal. **2.** To ride a bicycle.

ped·ant (pĕd′nt) *n.* **1.** Someone, esp. an unimaginative teacher, who emphasizes trivial details of learning. **2.** Someone who makes a great show of learning or scholarship. **—ped′ant·ry** *n.*

pe·dan·tic (pĭ-dăn′tĭk) *adj.* Marked by a narrow, often ostentatious concern for book learning and formal rules. ★ ***syns:*** ACADEMIC, BOOKISH, DONNISH, FORMALISTIC, SCHOLASTIC **—pe·dan′ti·cal·ly** *adv.*

ped·dle (pĕd′l) *v.* **-dled, -dling.** To offer (goods) for sale while traveling about. **—ped′dler, ped′dlar** *n.*

ped·er·ast (pĕd′ə-răst′) *n.* A man who has sexual relations with a boy. **—ped′er·as′ty** *n.*

ped·es·tal (pĕd′ĭ-stəl) *n.* A base or support for an upright structure or part, as a column or statue.

pe·des·tri·an (pĭ-dĕs′trē-ən) *n.* A person who travels on foot. *—adj.* **1.** Traveling on foot. **2.** Commonplace : routine.

pe·di·at·rics (pē′dē-ăt′rĭks) *n. (sing. in number).* The branch of medicine dealing with the diseases and care of infants and children. **—pe′di·at′ric** *adj.* **—pe′di·a·tri′cian** (-ə-trĭsh′ən) *n.*

ped·i·cab (pĕd′ĭ-kăb′) *n.* A small 3-wheeled hooded passenger vehicle that is pedaled.

ped·i·cure (pĕd′ĭ-kyo͝or′) *n.* **1.** Care, esp. cosmetic care, of the toenails and feet. **2.** A single treatment of the toenails and feet. **—ped′i·cur′ist** *n.*

ped·i·gree (pĕd′ĭ-grē′) *n.* **1.** A line of ancestors : ancestry. **2.** A record of a line of ancestors, as of a purebred animal.

ped·i·ment (pĕd′ə-mənt) *n.* A gablelike triangular decorative or architectural element, as over the door of a building.

pe·dom·e·ter (pĭ-dŏm′ĭ-tər) *n.* An instrument that measures and registers the approx. distance one travels on foot.

pe·dun·cle (pĭ-dŭng′kəl, pē′dŭng′-) *n.* A stalklike supporting structure in some animals and plants.

peek (pēk) *v.* **1.** To look briefly : glance. **2.** To peer or look furtively, as from a hiding place. **—peek** *n.*

peel (pēl) *n.* A rind or skin, esp. of a fruit. *—v.* **1.** To strip the rind, skin, or bark from. **2.** To pull off (an outer covering). **3.** To shed the rind, skin, or bark. **4.** To come off in thin strips or layers. **—peel′er** *n.*

peen (pēn) *n.* The often wedge- or ball-shaped end of a hammerhead opposite the striking surface.

peep[1] (pēp) *v.* To utter a weak, high-pitched sound, as that of a baby bird. *—n.* A weak, high-pitched sound. **—peep′er** *n.*

peep[2] (pēp) *v.* **1.** To look furtively, as through a crack. **2.** To begin to be visible. *—n.* **1.** A quick or furtive look. **2.** The first appearance or glimpse. **—peep′er** *n.*

peep·hole (pēp′hōl′) *n.* A hole through which to peep.

peeping Tom *n.* A person who gets pleasure, esp. of a sexual nature, from secretly watching others.

peer[1] (pîr) *v.* **1.** To look searchingly or intently. **2.** To come partially into sight.

peer[2] (pîr) *n.* **1.** One of equal status with another. **2.** A nobleman. **—peer′age** *n.* **—peer′ess** *n.*

peer·less (pîr′lĭs) *adj.* Without equal : matchless. **—peer′less·ly** *adv.*

peeve (pēv) *v.* **peeved, peev·ing.** To cause to feel resentment : vex. *—n.* **1.** A grievance : vexation. **2.** A resentful mood or feeling.

pee·vish (pē′vĭsh) *adj.* Irritable in mood or disposition : petulant. **—pee′vish·ly** *adv.* **—pee′vish·ness** *n.*

pee·wee (pē′wē) *n.* One that is unusually small.

peg (pĕg) *n.* **1.** A small, pointed cylindrical piece, as of wood, used to fasten or pin things down or to fit a hole. **2.** A projecting piece similar to a peg used to mark a boundary or to act as a support. **3.** A degree : step. **4.** A throw, as of a ball. **5.** Something used as a reason, pretext, or occasion. *—v.* **pegged, peg·ging. 1.** To insert a peg into. **2.** To mark with pegs. **3.** To fix (e.g., a price) at a set level. **4.** *Informal.* To categorize. **5.** To throw. **6.** To work with diligence <*pegging* away at the job>

peg·ma·tite (pĕg′mə-tīt′) *n.* A coarse-grained granite.

pei·gnoir (pān-wär′, pĕn-) *n.* A woman's dressing gown : negligee.

pe·jo·ra·tive (pĭ-jôr′ə-tĭv, -jŏr′-, pĕj′ə-rā′tĭv) *adj.* Tending to make or become worse : derogatory.

Pe·king·ese *also* **Pe·kin·ese** (pē′kĭ-nēz′, -nēs′) *n.* A small, short-legged, flat-nosed, long-haired dog orig. bred in China.

pe·koe (pē′kō) *n.* A black tea made from small leaves.

pe·lag·ic (pə-lăj′ĭk) *adj.* Of or relating to the open ocean.

pelf (pĕlf) *n.* Wealth : money.

pel·i·can (pĕl′ĭ-kən) *n.* A large tropical or semitropical web-footed bird of the genus *Pelecanus*, with a large pouch under the lower bill in which it catches and holds fish.

pel·lag·ra (pə-lăg′rə, -lā′grə) *n.* A chronic disease caused by a lack of niacin and characterized by skin eruptions and digestive and nervous disorders. —**pel·lag'rous** *adj.*

pel·let (pĕl'ĭt) *n.* **1.** A small mass or ball, as of medicine. **2. a.** A bullet. **b.** A piece of small shot.

pell-mell *also* **pell·mell** (pĕl'mĕl') *adv.* **1.** In jumbled confusion. **2.** In disordered haste : headlong.

pel·lu·cid (pə-lo͞o'sĭd) *adj.* Very clear : transparent. —**pel·lu'cid·ly** *adv.*

pelt[1] (pĕlt) *n.* The skin of an animal, esp. with the fur on it.

pelt[2] (pĕlt) *v.* To strike with a series of missiles or blows.

pel·vis (pĕl'vĭs) *n., pl.* **-vis·es** *or* **-ves** (-vēz'). A basin-shaped structure of the vertebrate skeleton that rests on the lower limbs and supports the spinal column. —**pel'vic** *adj.*

pem·mi·can *also* **pem·i·can** (pĕm'ĭ-kən) *n.* Dried meat that is pounded into paste and mixed with fat.

pen[1] (pĕn) *n.* An instrument, often with a metal point and a supply of ink, used for writing. —*v.* **penned, pen·ning.** To write, esp. with a pen.

pen[2] (pĕn) *n.* A usu. small enclosure, esp. for animals. —*v.* **penned, pen·ning.** To confine in a pen : enclose.

pen[3] (pĕn) *n. Slang.* A penitentiary.

pe·nal (pē'nəl) *adj.* Of or relating to punishment, as for infractions of the law.

pe·nal·ize (pē'nə-līz', pĕn'ə-) *v.* **-ized, -iz·ing.** To impose a penalty on.

pen·al·ty (pĕn'əl-tē) *n., pl.* **-ties. 1.** A punishment for an offense or crime. **2.** Something that is forfeited when a person fails to meet the terms of an agreement. **3.** A handicap, loss, or disadvantage that results from an action.

pen·ance (pĕn'əns) *n.* **1.** A voluntary act of devotion or self-mortification to show sorrow for a sin or misdeed. **2.** *Eccles.* A sacrament that consists of contrition, confession, acceptance of punishment imposed by the confessor, and absolution.

Pe·na·tes (pĭ-nā'tēz') *pl.n.* The ancient Roman gods of the household.

pence (pĕns) *n. esp. Brit. var. pl. of* PENNY.

pen·chant (pĕn'chənt) *n.* A strong and continuous leaning : liking.

pen·cil (pĕn'səl) *n.* **1.** A writing or drawing implement that consists of or contains a thin stick of a marking substance, esp. graphite. **2.** Something resembling a pencil <an eyebrow *pencil*> —*v.* **-ciled, -cil·ing** *or* **-cilled, -cil·ling.** To write, mark, or draw with a pencil.

pen·dant *also* **pen·dent** (pĕn'dənt) *n.* A suspended ornament, as one hanging on a necklace. —*adj. var. of* PENDENT.

pen·dent *also* **pen·dant** (pĕn'dənt) *adj.* Hanging down. —*n. var. of* PENDANT

pend·ing (pĕn'dĭng) *adj.* **1.** Not yet settled or decided. 2. Impending. —*prep.* **1.** During. **2.** While awaiting : until.

pen·du·lous (pĕn'jə-ləs, pĕnd'yə-) *adj.* Hanging downward loosely : drooping.

pen·du·lum (pĕn'jə-ləm, pĕnd'yə-) *n.* An object hung from a fixed support so that it can swing freely back and forth.

pe·ne·plain *also* **pe·ne·plane** (pē'nə-plān') *n.* A large, nearly flat eroded land surface.

pen·e·trate (pĕn'ĭ-trāt') *v.* **-trat·ed, -trat·ing. 1.** To force a way into : pierce. **2.** To permeate. 3. To grasp the meaning or significance of : understand. **4.** To move profoundly. ★ *syns:* PERFORATE, PIERCE, PUNCTURE —**pen'e·tra·ble** (-trə-bəl) *adj.* —**pen'e·tra'tion** *n.*

pen·e·trat·ing (pĕn'i-trā'tĭng) *adj.* **1.** Having the ability to enter, pierce, or permeate <a *penetrating* scream> <*penetrating* cold> 2. Quick to perceive : discerning <a *penetrating* mind>

pen·guin (pĕng'gwĭn) *n.* Any of various flightless marine birds of the family Spheniscidae, of the S Hemisphere, with webbed feet and flipperlike wings.

pen·i·cil·lin (pĕn'ĭ-sĭl'ĭn) *n.* An antibiotic compound derived from a mold and used to prevent or treat various diseases and infections.

pen·in·su·la (pə-nĭn'sə-lə, -nĭns'yə-) *n.* A long, narrow piece of land that projects into water from a larger land mass. —**pen·in'su·lar** *adj.*

pe·nis (pē'nĭs) *n., pl.* **-nis·es** *or* **-nes** (-nēz'). The male organ of copulation in higher vertebrates and usu. of urination in mammals.

pen·i·tent (pĕn'ĭ-tənt) *adj.* Feeling a sense of sorrow and remorse for sins or misdeeds : repentant. —*n.* Someone who is penitent. —**pen'i·tence** *n.* —**pen'i·ten'tial** (-tĕn'shəl) *adj.*

pen·i·ten·tia·ry (pĕn'ĭ-tĕn'shə-rē) *n., pl.* **-ries.** A federal or state prison for those convicted of serious crimes. —*adj.* Resulting in or punishable by imprisonment in a penitentiary.

pen·knife (pĕn'nīf') *n.* A small pocketknife.

pen·light (pĕn'līt') *n.* A flashlight of approx. the size and shape of a fountain pen.

pen·man (pĕn'mən) *n.* **1.** A scribe. **2.** Someone with skill in penmanship. **3.** An author.

pen·man·ship (pĕn'mən-shĭp') *n.* The art, style, skill, or manner of handwriting.

pen name *also* **pen·name** (pĕn'nām') *n.* A pseudonym assumed by an author.

pen·nant (pĕn'ənt) *n.* **1.** A long, tapering nautical flag used for signaling or identification. **2.** A flag that resembles a pennant. **3.** A flag that symbolizes a championship.

pen·ni (pĕn'ē) *n., pl.* **pen·nis** *or* **pen·ni·a** (-ē-ə). —See table at CURRENCY.

pen·ni·less (pĕn'ĭ-lĭs) *adj.* Completely without money.

pen·non (pĕn'ən) *n.* **1.** A banner, esp. a long, narrow flag borne on a lance. **2.** A bird's wing : pinion.

pen·ny (pĕn'ē) *n., pl.* **pen·nies** *or* **pence** (pĕns). **1.** —See table at CURRENCY. **2.** A U.S. or Canadian coin worth 1 cent.

penny pincher *n. Informal.* A stingy person : miser. —**pen'ny-pinch'** *v.*

pen·ny·roy·al (pĕn′ē-roi′əl) *n.* A mint, *Mentha pulegium,* with aromatic hairy leaves and small bluish flowers.
pen·ny·weight (pĕn′ē-wāt′) *n.* A unit of troy weight equal to 24 grains, 1/20 of a troy oz., or approx. 1.555 g.
pen·ny-wise (pĕn′ē-wīz′) *adj.* Wise only in dealing with small matters.
Pe·nob·scot (pə-nŏb′skət, -skŏt′) *n., pl.* **-scot** *or* **-scots. 1.** A member of an American Indian people of central ME. **2.** Their Algonquian language.
pe·nol·o·gy (pē-nŏl′ə-jē) *n.* The theory and practice of criminal rehabilitation and prison management. **—pe·nol′o·gist** *n.*
pen·sion (pĕn′shən) *n.* An amount of money paid regularly, esp. to a person who has retired. —*v.* To pay or grant a pension to. **—pen′sion·er** *n.*
pen·sive (pĕn′sĭv) *adj.* Deeply thoughtful, often in a melancholy or musing way **:** reflective. **—pen′sive·ly** *adv.* **—pen′sive·ness** *n.*
pent (pĕnt) *adj.* Closed or shut up.
pen·ta·gon (pĕn′tə-gŏn′) *n.* A polygon having 5 sides and 5 interior angles. **—pen·tag′o·nal** (-tăg′ə-nəl) *adj.*
pen·tam·e·ter (pĕn-tăm′ĭ-tər) *n.* A line of verse that consists of 5 metrical feet.
pen·tath·lon (pĕn-tăth′lən, -lŏn′) *n.* An athletic contest consisting of 5 events for each participant.
Pen·te·cost (pĕn′tĭ-kôst′, -kŏst′) *n.* A Christian festival celebrated the 7th Sunday after Easter to commemorate the descent of the Holy Spirit upon the disciples. **—Pen′te·cos′tal** *adj.*
pent·house (pĕnt′hous′) *n.* A dwelling, esp. an apartment, built on the roof of a building.
pent-up (pĕnt′ŭp′) *adj.* Not given expression **:** repressed <*pent-up* grief>
pe·nul·ti·mate (pĭ-nŭl′tə-mĭt) *adj.* Next to last. **—pe·nul′ti·mate** *n.*
pe·num·bra (pĭ-nŭm′brə) *n., pl.* **-brae** (-brē) *or* **-bras.** A partial shadow, as in an eclipse, between regions of complete shadow and complete illumination.
pe·nu·ri·ous (pĭ-no͝or′ē-əs, -nyo͝or′-) *adj.* **1.** Stingy **:** miserly. **2.** Characterized by penury **:** extremely poor.
pen·u·ry (pĕn′yə-rē) *n.* Extreme poverty.
pe·on (pē′ŏn′) *n.* **1.** An unskilled agricultural laborer of Latin America. **2.** A person held in servitude to a creditor until an indebtedness is satisfied. **—pe′on·age** *n.*
pe·o·ny (pē′ə-nē) *n., pl.* **-nies.** A plant of the genus *Paeonia,* cultivated for its large, fragrant pink, red, or white flowers.
peo·ple (pē′pəl) *n., pl.* **people. 1.** Human beings <*People* laughed at him.> **2. a.** The body of persons living under one government in the same country **:** nationality <the French *people*> **b.** Enfranchised citizens **:** electorate. **3.** *pl.* **peoples.** A group of persons, often related, who share a common culture, language, or inherited condition of life. **4.** The mass of ordinary persons **:** populace <the *people* asserting their rights> **5.** Persons who constitute a group united by a common interest <scientific *people*> —*v.* **-pled, -pling.** To fill or furnish with people **:** populate.
pep (pĕp) *Informal.* —*n.* Energy **:** vigor. —*v.* **pepped, pep·ping.** To imbue with pep **:** invigorate. **—pep′py** *adj.*
pep·per (pĕp′ər) *n.* **1. a.** A tropical Asian vine, *Piper nigrum,* bearing small berrylike fruit. **b.** The dried fruit of the pepper used to make a pungent condiment. **2.** A bushy plant, *Capsicum frutescens* or *C. annuum,* related to the pepper and cultivated for its mild or pungent fruit, used as a vegetable or condiment. —*v.* **1.** To season or sprinkle with pepper. **2.** To sprinkle liberally <dark hair *peppered* with silver> **3.** To pelt with or as if with small missiles.
pep·per·corn (pĕp′ər-kôrn′) *n.* A dried berry of the pepper vine, *Piper nigrum.*
pep·per·mint (pĕp′ər-mĭnt′) *n.* **1.** A plant, *Mentha piperita,* having downy leaves that yield a pungent aromatic oil. **2.** A candy flavored with peppermint oil.
pep·per·y (pĕp′ə-rē) *adj.* **1.** Of, resembling, or containing pepper **:** hot and pungent. **2.** Hot-tempered. **3.** Fiery **:** scathing <a *peppery* temper>
pep·sin (pĕp′sĭn) *n.* **1.** An enzyme produced in the stomach that acts as a catalyst in the digestion of proteins. **2.** A digestive aid that contains pepsin.
pep·tic (pĕp′tĭk) *adj.* **1.** Pertaining to or aiding digestion. **2.** Caused by or pertaining to the action of digestive secretions.
pep·tide (pĕp′tīd′) *n.* Any of various natural or synthetic compounds consisting of two or more amino acids linked end to end.
per (pûr) *prep.* **1.** By the agency of. **2.** For, to, or by each. **3.** According to.
per·ad·ven·ture (pûr′əd-vĕn′chər) *adv. Archaic.* Perhaps **:** perchance. —*n.* Chance or uncertainty **:** doubt.
per·am·bu·late (pə-răm′byə-lāt′) *v.* **-lat·ed, -lat·ing.** To walk around **:** stroll. **—per·am′bu·la′tion** *n.*
per·am·bu·la·tor (pə-răm′byə-lā′tər) *n. esp. Brit.* A baby carriage.
per an·num (pər ăn′əm) *adv.* By, for, or in each year **:** annually.
per·cale (pər-kāl′) *n.* A fine, closely woven cotton fabric.
per cap·i·ta (pər kăp′ĭ-tə) *adv. & adj.* Of, by, or for each individual.
per·ceive (pər-sēv′) *v.* **-ceived, -ceiv·ing. 1.** To become aware of directly by the senses, esp. to see or hear. **2.** To achieve understanding or awareness of. **—per·ceiv′a·ble** *adj.* **—per·ceiv′a·bly** *adv.*
per·cent *also* **per cent** (pər-sĕnt′) —*adv.* Out of each hundred **:** per hundred. —*n.* **1.** One part in a hundred. **2.** A percentage.
per·cent·age (pər-sĕn′tĭj) *n.* **1.** A fraction or ratio with 100 as its denominator. **2.** A share or proportion in relation to a whole **:** part. **3.** Probability **:** odds. **4.** *Informal.* Profit **:** advantage.
per·cen·tile (pər-sĕn′tīl′) *n.* A number that

divides the range of a set of data so that a given percentage lies below it.

per·cept (pûr′sĕpt′) *n.* A mental impression of something perceived by the senses together with comprehension of what it is.

per·cep·ti·ble (pər-sĕp′tə-bəl) *adj.* Capable of being perceived. —**per·cep′ti·bil′i·ty** *n.* —**per·cep′ti·bly** *adv.*

per·cep·tion (pər-sĕp′shən) *n.* **1.** The act, process, or result of perceiving. **2.** The ability to perceive : understanding or insight.

per·cep·tive (pər-sĕp′tĭv) *adj.* **1.** Of or relating to perception. **2.a.** Having perception. **b.** Marked by perception : discerning. —**per·cep′tive·ly** *adv.*

per·cep·tu·al (pər-sĕp′cho͞o-əl) *adj.* Of, relating to, involving, or based on perception. —**per·cep′tu·al·ly** *adv.*

perch[1] (pûrch) *n.* **1.** Something, as a rod, that serves as a roost for a bird. **2.** A place where one can sit or rest : seat. —*v.* To alight or rest on or as if on a perch.

perch[2] (pûrch) *n., pl.* **perch** *or* **perch·es. 1.** Either of 2 freshwater food fishes, *Perca flavescens* or *P. fluviatilis.* **2.** Any of various fishes related or similar to the perch.

per·chance (pər-chăns′) *adv.* Maybe : perhaps.

per·cip·i·ent (pər-sĭp′ē-ənt) *adj.* Capable of perceiving, esp. perceiving readily and keenly. —**per·cip′i·ence** *n.*

per·co·late (pûr′kə-lāt′) *v.* **-lat·ed, -lat·ing. 1.** To filter or trickle through a porous substance. **2.** To force boiling water through (ground coffee) in order to draw out the essence. —**per′co·la′tion** *n.* —**per′co·la′tor** *n.*

per con·tra (pər kŏn′trə) *adv.* **1.** To the contrary. **2.** By way of contrast.

per·cus·sion (pər-kŭsh′ən) *n.* **1. a.** The hitting together of 2 bodies, esp. when noise is created. **b.** A vibration or impact caused by percussion. **2.** Detonation of a cap in a firearm. **3. a.** A musical instrument sounded by striking, as a drum. **b.** Percussion instruments as a group. —**per·cus′sion·ist** *n.*

percussion cap *n.* A thin metal cap containing gunpowder or another detonator that explodes on being struck.

per di·em (pər dē′əm) *adv.* For or by the day. —*n.* A daily fee or allowance.

per·di·tion (pər-dĭsh′ən) *n.* **1.** Everlasting damnation. **2.** Hell.

per·du·ra·ble (pər-do͝or′ə-bəl, -dyo͝or′-) *adj.* Extremely durable. —**per·du′ra·bil′i·ty** *n.* —**per·du′ra·bly** *adv.*

per·e·gri·nate (pĕr′ə-grə-nāt′) *v.* **-nat·ed, -nat·ing.** To travel around from place to place. —**per′e·gri·na′tion** *n.*

per·e·grine falcon (pĕr′ĭ-grĭn, -grēn′) *n.* A widely distributed bird of prey, *Falco peregrinus,* much used in falconry.

per·emp·to·ry (pə-rĕmp′tə-rē) *adj.* **1.** Terminating all debate or action <a *peremptory* decree> **2.** Admitting no refusal or contradiction : imperative. **3.** Expressing or of the nature of a command. **4.** Self-assured, sometimes excessively so : self-confident. —**per·emp′to·ri·ly** *adv.*

per·en·ni·al (pə-rĕn′ē-əl) *adj.* **1.** Lasting from year to year. **2.** Lasting indefinitely : perpetual. **3.** Recurring again and again. —*n.* A plant that lives for several or many years. —**per·en′ni·al·ly** *adv.*

per·fect (pûr′fĭkt) *adj.* **1.** Lacking in no essential : complete. **2.** Being without defect or fault : flawless. **3.** Exact : accurate. **4.** Absolute : utter <a *perfect* fool> **5.** Of, relating to, or constituting a verb form that expresses action completed before a fixed point of reference in time. ★ ***syns:*** CONSUMMATE, FAULTLESS, FLAWLESS, IMPECCABLE —*n.* **1.** The perfect tense. **2.** A verb or verb form in the perfect tense. —*v.* (pər-fĕkt′). To make perfect. —**per′fect·ly** *adv.* —**per′fect·ness** *n.*

per·fect·i·ble (pər-fĕk′tə-bəl) *adj.* Capable of making progress toward or achieving perfection. —**per·fect′i·bil′i·ty** *n.*

per·fec·tion (pər-fĕk′shən) *n.* **1.** The state or quality of being perfect. **2.** The process or act of perfecting. **3.** A perfect example of excellence.

per·fec·tion·ism (pər-fĕk′shə-nĭz′əm) *n.* A tendency to be dissatisfied with anything less than perfection. —**per·fec′tion·ist** *n.*

per·fec·to (pər-fĕk′tō) *n., pl.* **-tos.** A cigar that is thick in the center and tapers at each end.

per·fi·dy (pûr′fĭ-dē) *n.* Breach of loyalty or faith : treachery. —**per·fid′i·ous** (pər-fĭd′ē-əs) *adj.* —**per·fid′i·ous·ly** *adv.*

per·fo·rate (pûr′fə-rāt′) *v.* **-rat·ed, -rat·ing. 1.** To bore or punch a hole in : pierce. **2.** To make rows of holes in for easy separation. —**per′fo·ra′tion** *n.*

per·force (pər-fôrs′, -fōrs′) *adv.* By force of necessity.

per·form (pər-fôrm′) *v.* **1.** To begin and carry out : accomplish. **2.** To fulfill. **3.** To function in a certain way : act. **4.** To give a performance (of). —**per·form′er** *n.*

per·form·ance (pər-fôr′məns) *n.* **1.** The act, process, or manner of performing. **2.** A presentation, as of a musical work, before the public. **3.** An accomplishment : deed.

per·fume (pûr′fyo͞om′, pər-fyo͞om′) *n.* **1.** A fragrant substance, esp. a liquid, as one distilled from flowers. **2.** A usu. pleasing scent : odor. —*v.* (pər-fyo͞om′) **-fumed, -fum·ing.** To fill with or as if with perfume : scent.

per·fum·er·y (pər-fyo͞o′mə-rē) *n., pl.* **-ies. 1.** Perfumes in general. **2.** An establishment at which perfumes are made or sold.

per·func·to·ry (pər-fŭngk′tə-rē) *adj.* Done merely as a matter of routine and with little care or interest. —**per·func′to·ri·ly** *adv.* —**per·func′to·ri·ness** *n.*

per·go·la (pûr′gə-lə) *n.* A structure, as an arbor, with a roof of trelliswork.

per·haps (pər-hăps′) *adv.* Maybe but not surely : possibly.

per·i·car·di·um (pĕr′ĭ-kär′dē-əm) *n., pl.* **-di·a** (-dē-ə). The membranous sac that encloses the heart. —**per′i·car′di·al** *adj.*

per•i•gee (pĕr′ə-jē′) *n.* The point in the orbit of a satellite of the earth at which it is closest to the earth.

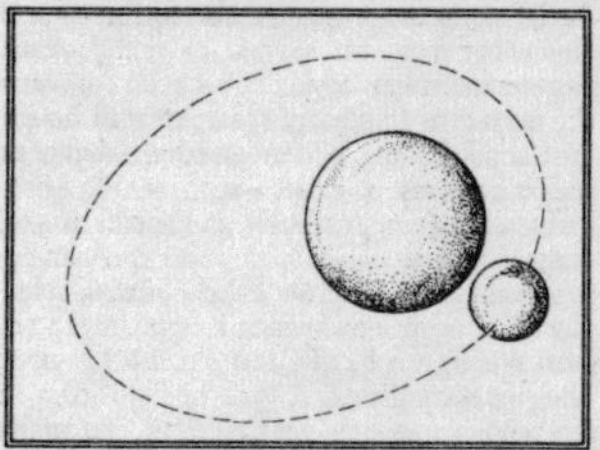

perigee

per•i•he•lion (pĕr′ə-hēl′yən) *n., pl.* **-lia** (-yə). The point in the orbit of a celestial body, as a planet, at which it is closest to the sun.
per•il (pĕr′əl) *n.* **1.** Danger. **2.** Something that is a source of danger. **—per′il•ous** *adj.* **—per′il•ous•ly** *adv.*
pe•rim•e•ter (pə-rĭm′ĭ-tər) *n.* The outer limits or boundary of an area.
per•i•ne•um (pĕr′ə-nē′əm) *n., pl.* **-ne•a** (-nē′ə). The portion of the body extending from the anus to the genitals.
pe•ri•od (pîr′ē-əd) *n.* **1. a.** An interval of time. **b.** An interval of time regarded as a phase in development **:** stage. **2.** An arbitrary temporal unit, as of an academic day. **3.** An occurrence or instance of menstruation. **4.** A point in time at which something ends **:** completion. **5. a.** The full stop at the end of a sentence. **b.** A punctuation mark (.) used to indicate the end of a sentence or an abbreviation. *—adj.* Of, pertaining to, or representing a particular historical period <a *period* stage setting>
pe•ri•od•ic (pîr′ē-ŏd′ĭk) *adj.* **1.** Having or marked by repeated cycles. **2.** Occurring or appearing at regular intervals. **3.** Happening now and then. **—pe′ri•od′i•cal•ly** *adv.* **—pe′ri•o•dic′i•ty** (-ə-dĭs′ĭ-tē) *n.*
pe•ri•od•i•cal (pîr′ē-ŏd′ĭ-kəl) *adj.* **1.** Periodic. **2. a.** Published at fixed intervals, usu. of more than one day. **b.** Of or pertaining to a publication issued at such intervals. *—n.* A periodical publication.
per•i•o•don•tal (pĕr′ē-ō-dŏn′tl) *adj.* Of or constituting tissue and structures that surround and support the teeth. **—per′i•o•don′tal•ly** *adv.* **—per′i•o•don′tist** *n.*
per•i•pa•tet•ic (pĕr′ə-pə-tĕt′ĭk) *adj.* Of, relating to, or carried on while walking or moving around.
pe•riph•er•y (pə-rĭf′ə-rē) *n., pl.* **-ies. 1.** The outermost part within a boundary. **2.** A region just beyond a boundary. **3.** An outer boundary. **—pe•riph′er•al** *adj.*
pe•riph•ra•sis (pə-rĭf′rə-sĭs) *n., pl.* **-ses** (-sēz′). **1.** The use of circumlocution. **2.** A roundabout expression.
per•i•scope (pĕr′ĭ-skōp′) *n.* An optical instrument that permits observation of objects from a position not in a direct line of sight. **—per′i•scop′ic** (-skŏp′ĭk) *adj.*
per•ish (pĕr′ĭsh) *v.* To become ruined, spoiled, or destroyed **:** die.
per•ish•a•ble (pĕr′ĭ-shə-bəl) *adj.* Apt to spoil or decay easily. *—n.* Something, esp. food, that is perishable.
per•i•stal•sis (pĕr′ĭ-stôl′sĭs, -stăl′-) *n.* Wavelike muscular contractions of the alimentary canal that propel material contained in it onward. **—per′i•stal′tic** (-stôl′tĭk, -stăl′-) *adj.*
per•i•style (pĕr′ĭ-stīl′) *n.* A tier of columns enclosing a court or surrounding a building.
per•i•to•ne•um (pĕr′ĭ-tə-nē′əm) *n., pl.* **-ne•a** (-nē′ə). The membrane that lines the walls of the abdominal cavity and encloses the viscera. **—per′i•to•ne′al** *adj.*
per•i•to•ni•tis (pĕr′ĭ-tə-nī′tĭs) *n.* Inflammation of the peritoneum.
per•i•wig (pĕr′ĭ-wĭg′) *n.* A wig.
▲ ***word history:*** For more than a cent. (approx. 1660–1780) decorative heads of false hair were almost universally worn by fashionable men and women in Europe. In English such headdresses were called *perukes* or *periwigs.* Both words are derived from Italian *perruca,* which orig. meant "bushy head of hair" and later "wig." *Perruca* was borrowed into French as *perruque,* which developed into two forms in English: *peruke* and *periwig,* which are synonymous. *Periwig* was shortened to *wig,* which is the form now in common use.
per•i•win•kle[1] (pĕr′ĭ-wĭng′kəl) *n.* Any of several small edible marine snails, esp. of the genus *Littorina,* with thick cone-shaped shells.
per•i•win•kle[2] (pĕr′ĭ-wĭng′kəl) *n.* A trailing evergreen plant of the genus *Vinca,* esp. *V. minor,* bearing blue flowers.
per•jure (pûr′jər) *v.* **-jured, -jur•ing.** To give false or misleading testimony while under oath. **—per′ju•ry** *n.*
perk[1] (pûrk) *v.* To raise (e.g., the head) pertly. **—perk up. 1.** To regain or cause to regain liveliness or spirit. **2.** To make spruce or trim in appearance **:** smarten. **—perk′i•ness** *n.* **—perk′y** *adj.*
perk[2] (pûrk) *n. Informal.* A perquisite.
perk[3] (pûrk) *v. Informal.* To percolate.
per•lite (pûr′līt′) *n.* A natural volcanic glass that in a heat-expanded form is used in plaster and concrete and in thermal and acoustic insulation.
perm (pûrm) *n. Informal.* A permanent.
per•ma•frost (pûr′mə-frôst′, -frŏst′) *n.* Permanently frozen subsoil occurring in perennially frigid areas.
per•ma•nent (pûr′mə-nənt) *adj.* Lasting indefinitely **:** enduring. *—n.* A long-lasting hair wave that is produced by the application of chemicals. **—per′ma•nence, per′ma•nen•cy** *n.* **—per′ma•nent•ly** *adv.*
permanent magnet *n.* A material that re-

tains induced magnetic properties after it is removed from a magnetic field.

permanent press *n.* A chemical process in which fabrics are permanently shaped and treated for wrinkle resistance.

permanent wave *n.* A permanent.

per•me•a•ble (pûr′mē-ə-bəl) *adj.* Capable of being permeated : penetrable. **—per′me•a•bil′i•ty** *n.* **—per′me•a•bly** *adv.*

per•me•ate (pûr′mē-āt′) *v.* **-at•ed, -at•ing. 1.** To flow or spread through : pervade. **2.** To pass through the openings or pores of. **—per′me•a′tion** *n.*

per•mis•si•ble (pər-mĭs′ə-bəl) *adj.* Admissible : allowable.

per•mis•sion (pər-mĭsh′ən) *n.* Consent, esp. official or formal consent.

per•mis•sive (pər-mĭs′ĭv) *adj.* **1.** Giving permission. **2.** Lenient, often excessively so : indulgent. **—per•mis′sive•ly** *adv.* **—per•mis′sive•ness** *n.*

per•mit (pər-mĭt′) *v.* **-mit•ted, -mit•ting. 1.** To give consent to or for : allow. **2.** To give an opportunity (to). *—n.* (pûr′mĭt′, pər-mĭt′). A document giving permission : license. **—per•mit′ter** *n.*

per•mu•ta•tion (pûr′myŏŏ-tā′shən) *n.* **1.** A complete change : transformation. **2.** *Math.* Any of the ordered subsets that can be formed from the elements of a set. **—per′mu•ta′tion•al** *adj.*

per•ni•cious (pər-nĭsh′əs) *adj.* Very harmful or destructive. **—per•ni′cious•ly** *adv.* **—per•ni′cious•ness** *n.*

per•o•ra•tion (pĕr′ə-rā′shən) *n.* The usu. formal concluding part of a speech.

per•ox•ide (pə-rŏk′sīd′) *n.* **1.** Hydrogen peroxide. **2.** An oxygen-containing compound that yields hydrogen peroxide when treated with an acid. *—v.* **-id•ed, -id•ing. 1.** To treat with peroxide. **2.** To bleach (hair) with hydrogen peroxide.

per•pen•dic•u•lar (pûr′pən-dĭk′yə-lər) *adj.* **1.** Forming or intersecting at right angles. **2.** Being at right angles to the plane of the horizon : vertical. **—per′pen•dic′u•lar** *n.* **—per′pen•dic′u•lar′i•ty** (-lăr′ĭ-tē) *n.* **—per′pen•dic′u•lar•ly** *adv.*

per•pe•trate (pûr′pĭ-trāt′) *v.* **-trat•ed, -trat•ing.** To be culpable of : commit. **—per′pe•tra′tion** *n.* **—per′pe•tra′tor** *n.*

per•pet•u•al (pər-pĕch′ōō-əl) *adj.* **1.** Lasting forever : unceasing. **2.** Continuing without or almost without interruption : constant. **—per•pet′u•al•ly** *adv.*

per•pet•u•ate (pər-pĕch′ōō-āt′) *v.* **-at•ed, -at•ing.** To cause to be perpetual : keep from dying out. **—per•pet′u•a′tion** *n.*

per•pe•tu•i•ty (pûr′pĭ-tōō′ĭ-tē, -tyōō′-) *n., pl.* **-ties. 1.** The state or quality of being perpetual. **2.** Everlasting time : eternity.

per•plex (pər-plĕks′) *v.* To confuse : bewilder. **—per•plex′ed•ly** (-plĕk′sĭd-lē) *adv.* **—per•plex′i•ty** (-plĕk′sĭ-tē) *n.*

per•qui•site (pûr′kwĭ-zĭt) *n.* Something, as a payment or privilege, received in addition to a regular wage or salary.

per se (pər sā′) *adv.* Of, in, or by itself.

per•se•cute (pûr′sĭ-kyōōt′) *v.* **-cut•ed, -cut•ing.** To harass in a way that causes suffering, esp. because of principles or religious belief : oppress. **—per′se•cu′tion** *n.* **—per′se•cu′tor** *n.*

per•se•vere (pûr′sə-vîr′) *v.* **-vered, -ver•ing.** To persist in an idea, purpose, or task despite obstacles. **—per′se•ver′ance** *n.* **—per′se•ver′ing•ly** *adv.*

Persian cat *n.* A stocky domestic cat with long silky fur.

Persian lamb *n.* The tightly curled, glossy fur of a young karakul lamb.

per•si•flage (pûr′sə-fläzh′) *n.* Light, frivolous, or jesting talk.

per•sim•mon (pər-sĭm′ən) *n.* A tree of the genus *Diospyros,* with hard wood and edible orange-red fruit.

per•sist (pər-sĭst′) *v.* **1.** To continue firmly and steadfastly despite obstacles. **2.** To continue in existence : endure. **—per•sist′ence, per•sist′en•cy** *n.* **—per•sist′ent** *adj.* **—per•sist′ent•ly** *adv.*

per•snick•e•ty (pər-snĭk′ĭ-tē) *adj.* Very fastidious : meticulous.

per•son (pûr′sən) *n.* **1.** A human being. **2.** The physical body of a human being. **3.** The personality of a human being : self. **4.** Reference, as indicated by any of 3 groups of pronouns, to the speaker, the individual addressed, and the individual spoken of.

per•so•na (pər-sō′nə) *n., pl.* **-nae** (-nē). A character in a literary or dramatic work.

per•son•a•ble (pûr′sə-nə-bəl) *adj.* Pleasing in personality : appealing.

per•son•age (pûr′sə-nĭj) *n.* A person of distinction or rank.

per•son•al (pûr′sə-nəl) *adj.* **1.** Of or pertaining to a person : private. **2.** Made or done in person <a *personal* appeal> **3.** Of or relating to the body or physical being <*personal* cleanliness> **4.** Pertaining to an individual, esp. in an objectionable way <disapproves of *personal* remarks> **5.** *Law.* Of or pertaining to movable property <*personal* belongings> **6.** Indicating grammatical person. *—n.* A usu. short item or notice in a newspaper that concerns a person or group or personal affairs. **—per′son•al•ly** *adv.*

personal computer *n.* A microcomputer for use by an individual.

per•son•al•i•ty (pûr′sə-năl′ĭ-tē) *n., pl.* **-ties. 1.** The distinctive qualities and traits of an individual. **2. a.** Social and personal traits that make a person appealing. **b.** A person having such traits. **3.** *Informal.* A famous person : celebrity. **4.** An objectionably personal remark <refused to engage in *personalities*>

per•son•al•ize (pûr′sə-nə-līz′) *v.* **-ized, -iz•ing.** To make personal, esp. by marking with one's name or initials.

per•son•al•ty (pûr′sə-nəl-tē) *n., pl.* **-ties.** *Law.* Personal property.

per•so•na non gra•ta (pər-sō′nə nŏn grä′tə, grăt′ə) *n.* One who is unwelcome or unacceptable, esp. to a foreign government.

per•son•i•fy (pər-sŏn'ə-fī') *v.* **-fied, -fy•ing. 1.** To represent or think of (e.g., an inanimate object) as having human qualities or form. **2.** To be the embodiment of. **—per•son'i•fi•ca'tion** *n.*

per•son•nel (pûr'sə-nĕl') *n.* The body of persons active in or employed by an organization, business, or service.

per•spec•tive (pər-spĕk'tĭv) *n.* **1.** A drawing or painting technique in which objects represented seem to have distance and depth. **2.** A mental view of the relationship of aspects of a subject to each other and to a whole. **3.** An idea of the relative importance of things.

per•spi•cac•i•ty (pûr'spĭ-kăs'ĭ-tē) *n.* Acuteness of understanding or mental perception. **—per'spi•ca'cious** (-kā'shəs) *adj.* **—per'spi•ca'cious•ly** *adv.*

per•spic•u•ous (pər-spĭk'yo͞o-əs) *adj.* Capable of being easily understood **:** plain and clear. **—per'spi•cu'i•ty** (pûr'spĭ-kyo͞o'ĭ-tē) *n.* **—per•spic'u•ous•ly** *adv.*

per•spi•ra•tion (pûr'spə-rā'shən) *n.* **1.** The salty moisture secreted by the sweat glands **:** sweat. **2.** The act of perspiring.

per•spire (pər-spīr') *v.* **-spired, -spir•ing.** To excrete perspiration.

per•suade (pər-swād') *v.* **-suad•ed, -suad•ing.** To cause to do or believe by means of reasoning, argument, or entreaty. **—per•suad'er** *n.* **—per•sua'sive** *adj.* **—per•sua'sive•ness** *n.*

per•sua•sion (pər-swā'zhən) *n.* **1.** The act or process of persuading or state of being persuaded. **2.** Belief, esp. religious belief.

pert (pûrt) *adj.* **1.** Impudently forward **:** saucy. **2.** High-spirited **:** lively. **3.** Trim and stylish **:** jaunty. **—pert'ly** *adv.*

per•tain (pər-tān') *v.* **1.** To refer **:** relate. **2.** To belong as a feature, adjunct, part, or accessory.

per•ti•na•cious (pûr'tn-ā'shəs) *adj.* **1.** Adhering firmly to a belief, purpose, or opinion. **2.** Stubbornly persistent **:** tenacious. **—per'ti•na'cious•ly** *adv.* **—per'ti•nac'i•ty** (-ăs'ĭ-tē) *n.*

per•ti•nent (pûr'tn-ənt) *adj.* Relating to the matter being discussed or considered **:** relevant <a *pertinent* comment> **—per'ti•nence, per'ti•nen•cy** *n.*

per•turb (pər-tûrb') *v.* To make anxious or uneasy **:** disquiet greatly. **—per'tur•ba'tion** (pûr'tər-bā'shən) *n.*

pe•ruke (pə-ro͞ok') *n.* A wig.

pe•ruse (pə-ro͞oz') *v.* **-rused, -rus•ing.** To read, esp. with great attention. **—pe•rus'al** *n.* **—pe•rus'er** *n.*

per•vade (pər-vād') *v.* **-vad•ed, -vad•ing.** To spread or be present in all parts of **:** permeate. **—per•va'sive** (-vā'sĭv, -zĭv) *adj.* **—per•va'sive•ly** *adv.*

per•verse (pər-vûrs') *adj.* **1.** Contrary to what is good or right **:** corrupt. **2.** Obstinately continuing in a fault or error. **—per•verse'ly** *adv.* **—per•verse'ness** *n.* **—per•ver'si•ty** (-vûr'sĭ-tē) *n.*

per•ver•sion (pər-vûr'zhən) *n.* **1.** The act of perverting or state of being perverted. **2.** A deviant form of sexual behavior.

per•vert (pər-vûrt') *v.* **1.** To lead away from the proper, right, or accepted course **:** corrupt. **2.** To use wrongly or improperly **:** misuse. *—n.* (pûr'vûrt'). A person who practices sexual perversion.

pe•se•ta (pə-sā'tə) *n.* —See table at CURRENCY.

pe•se•wa (pə-sə'wä) *n., pl* **-wa** *or* **-was.** —See table at CURRENCY.

pes•ky (pĕs'kē) *adj.* **-ki•er, -ki•est.** Causing irritation or vexation **:** annoying. **—pes'ki•ly** *adv.* **—pes'ki•ness** *n.*

pe•so (pā'sō) *n., pl.* **-sos.** —See table at CURRENCY.

pes•si•mism (pĕs'ə-mĭz'əm) *n.* A tendency to take the least hopeful view, as of a situation, or to anticipate the worst. **—pes'si•mist** *n.* **—pes'si•mis'tic** *adj.* **—pes'si•mis'ti•cal•ly** *adv.*

pest (pĕst) *n.* **1.** One that is annoying **:** nuisance. **2.** A plant or animal that is harmful or injurious to man.

pes•ter (pĕs'tər) *v.* To beset with petty and repeated annoyances **:** bother.

pes•ti•cide (pĕs'tĭ-sīd') *n.* A chemical substance used to kill pests, as rodents and insects. **—pes'ti•cid'al** (-sīd'l) *adj.*

pes•tif•er•ous (pĕ-stĭf'ər-əs) *adj.* **1.** Breeding, spreading, or contaminated with an infectious or epidemic disease. **2.** *Informal.* Annoying **:** irritating.

pes•ti•lence (pĕs'tə-ləns) *n.* A virulent, usu. fatal epidemic disease, esp. bubonic plague.

pes•ti•lent (pĕs'tə-lənt) *also* **pes•ti•len•tial** (pĕs'tə-lĕn'shəl) *adj.* **1.** Tending to destroy life **:** deadly. **2.** Likely to cause pestilence. **3.** Harmful, as to society **:** pernicious. **4.** Bothersome **:** troublesome.

pes•tle (pĕs'əl, pĕs'təl) *n.* A hand tool for crushing substances in a mortar.

pestle

pes•to (pĕs'tō) *n.* A sauce made of usu. fresh basil, garlic, pine nuts, olive oil, and grated cheese.

pet¹ (pĕt) *n.* **1.** An animal kept for enjoyment or as a companion. **2.** Someone or something of which one is esp. fond **:** favorite. *—adj.* **1.** Treated or kept as a pet <a *pet* cat> **2.** Particularly liked or indulged. *—v.* **pet•ted, pet•**

ting. 1. To stroke or pet gently : caress. **2.** To engage in amorous caressing and fondling.
pet² (pět) *n.* A fit of bad temper or irritation : pique.
pet·al (pĕt'l) *n.* One of the leaflike segments of a flower corolla.
pe·tard (pə-tärd') *n.* A bomb once used to break down a gate or blow apart a wall.
pet·cock (pĕt'kŏk') *n.* A small valve or faucet for draining pipes.
pe·ter (pē'tər) *v.* To lessen gradually and come to an end : run out <The water in the well *petered* out.>
Peter *n.* —See table at BIBLE.
pet·i·ole (pĕt'ē-ōl') *n. Bot.* A stalk attaching a leaf to a stem.
pe·tite (pə-tēt') *adj.* Small and slender.
pet·it four (pĕt'ē fôr', fōr', fo͝or', pə-tē') *n., pl.* **pet·its fours** *or* **pet·it fours** (pĕt'ē fôrz', fōrz', fo͝orz', pə-tē'). A small, decoratively frosted cake.
pe·ti·tion (pə-tĭsh'ən) *n.* **1.** A solemn request : entreaty. **2.** A formal written petition addressed to a superior. —*v.* To make a petition (to). —**pe·ti'tion·er** *n.*
pet·it point (pĕt'ē point') *n.* Needlepoint made with a small stitch.
pet·nap (pĕt'năp') *v.* **-napped, -nap·ping** *or* **-naped, -nap·ing.** To steal (a pet), usu. for profit. —**pet'nap'per** *n.*
pet·rel (pĕt'rəl) *n.* A small sea bird of the order Procellariiformes.
pet·ri·fy (pĕt'rə-fī') *v.* **-fied, -fy·ing. 1.** To change (e.g., wood) into a stony mass. **2.** To immobilize, as with terror. —**pet'ri·fac'tion** (pĕt'rə-făk'shən), **pet'ri·fi·ca'tion** (-fĭ-kā'shən) *n.*
pet·ro·chem·i·cal (pĕt'rō-kĕm'ĭ-kəl) *n.* A chemical obtained from natural gas or petroleum. —**pet'ro·chem'i·cal** *adj.* —**pet'ro·chem'is·try** *n.*
pet·ro·dol·lars (pĕt'rō-dŏl'ərz) *pl.n.* Currency derived by oil-exporting countries from the sale of petroleum abroad.
pet·ro·glyph (pĕt'rə-glĭf') *n.* A carving or line drawing on rock, esp. one made by prehistoric people. —**pet'ro·glyph'ic** *adj.*
pe·trog·ra·phy (pə-trŏg'rə-fē) *n.* The scientific classification of rocks. —**pe·trog'ra·pher** *n.* —**pet'ro·graph'ic** (pĕt'rəgrăf'ĭk), **pet'ro·graph'i·cal** *adj.*
pet·rol (pĕt'rəl) *n. esp. Brit.* Gasoline.
pet·ro·la·tum (pĕt'rə-lā'təm) *n.* A usu. colorless semisolid derived from petroleum and used esp. in medicinal ointments.
pe·tro·le·um (pə-trō'lē-əm) *n.* A thick, dark, flammable liquid that occurs naturally below the surface of the earth and is processed into such products as natural gas, gasoline, kerosene, and fuel oils.
petroleum jelly *n.* Petrolatum.
pe·trol·o·gy (pə-trŏl'ə-jē) *n.* The scientific study of the origin, composition, and structure of rocks. —**pet'ro·log'ic** (pĕt'rə-lŏj'ĭk), **pet'ro·log'i·cal** *adj.* —**pet'ro·log'i·cal·ly** *adv.* —**pe·trol'o·gist** *n.*
pet·ti·coat (pĕt'ē-kōt') *n.* A woman's skirt that is worn as an undergarment. —*adj.* Female : feminine.
pet·ti·fog·ger (pĕt'ē-fô'gər, -fŏg'ər) *n.* **1.** A petty, unscrupulous lawyer : shyster. **2.** Someone who quibbles over unimportant details. —**pet'ti·fog'** *v.*
pet·tish (pĕt'ĭsh) *adj.* Petulant : peevish. —**pet'tish·ly** *adv.*
pet·ty (pĕt'ē) *adj.* **-ti·er, -ti·est. 1.** Insignificant : trivial <a *petty* annoyance> **2.** Contemptibly narrow-minded or mean. **3.** Subordinate in rank. —**pet'ti·ly** *adv.* —**pet'ti·ness** *n.*
petty cash *n.* A small cash fund for incidental expenses, as in an office.
petty officer *n.* A noncommissioned officer in the U.S. Navy or Coast Guard.
pet·u·lant (pĕch'ə-lənt) *adj.* Characterized by fitful ill humor : irritable. —**pet'u·lance** *n.* —**pet'u·lant·ly** *adv.*
pe·tu·nia (pə-to͞on'yə, -tyo͞on'-) *n.* A widely grown plant of the genus *Petunia,* with funnel-shaped flowers.
pew (pyo͞o) *n.* One of the rows of benches for the congregation in a church.
pe·wee (pē'wē) *n.* Any of various small, brownish North American birds of the genus *Contopus.*
pew·ter (pyo͞o'tər) *n.* Any of numerous silver-gray alloys of tin with copper, antimony, and lead used esp. for tableware and kitchen utensils.
pe·yo·te (pā-ō'tē) *n.* **1.** MESCAL 1. **2.** A hallucinatory drug obtained from mescal.
pfen·nig (fĕn'ĭg) *n., pl.* **-nigs** *or* **pfen·ni·ge** (fĕn'ĭ-gə). —See table at CURRENCY.
pH (pē-āch') *n. Chem.* A numerical measure of the acidity or alkalinity of a chemical solution.
pha·e·ton (fā'ĭ-tn) *n.* **1.** A light, open 4-wheeled horse-drawn carriage. **2.** A large open autombile for 5 or more passengers.
phage (fāj) *n.* A bacteriophage.
phag·o·cyte (făg'ə-sīt') *n.* A cell, such as a white blood cell, that engulfs and absorbs foreign bodies in the bloodstream and tissues. —**phag'o·cyt'ic** (-sĭt'ĭk) *adj.*
pha·lanx (fā'lăngks') *n., pl.* **-lanx·es** *or* **pha·lan·ges** (fə-lăn'jēz', fā-). **1.** A close-knit or compact formation of persons, as troops. **2.** *pl.* **phalanges.** One of the bones of a finger or toe.
phal·a·rope (făl'ə-rōp') *n.* A small wading bird of the family Phalaropodidae, having lobed toes.
phal·lus (făl'əs) *n., pl.* **phal·li** (făl'ī') *or* **-lus·es. 1.** The penis. **2.** A representation of the penis. —**phal'lic** *adj.*
phan·tasm (făn'tăz'əm) *n.* **1.** A creation of the imagination : fantasy. **2.** A phantom. —**phan·tas'mal, phan·tas'mic** *adj.*
phan·tas·ma·go·ri·a (făn-tăz'mə-gôr'ē-ə,-gōr'-) *n.* A rapidly shifting sequence of haphazard imagery, as in a dream. —**phan·tas'-ma·go'ric** *adj.*
phan·tom (făn'təm) *n.* **1.** Something, as a ghost, that is sensed but that has no physical

reality : apparition. **2.** An image in the mind. **—phan'tom** *adj.*

Phar•aoh *also* **phar•aoh** (fâr'ō) *n.* A king of ancient Egypt.

phar•i•see (făr'ĭ-sē) *n.* **1. Pharisee.** A member of an ancient Jewish group that interpreted and observed the Mosaic law strictly. **2.** A hypocritical or sanctimonious person. **—phar'i•sa'i•cal** (-sā'ĭ-kəl) *adj.*

phar•ma•ceu•ti•cal (fär'mə-sōō'tĭ-kəl) *or* **phar•ma•ceu•tic** (-tĭk) *adj.* Of or pertaining to pharmacy or pharmacists. **—phar'ma•ceu'ti•cal•ly** *adv.*

phar•ma•cist (fär'mə-sĭst) *n.* Someone trained to practice pharmacy : druggist.

phar•ma•col•o•gy (fär'mə-kŏl'ə-jē) *n.* The scientific study of the composition, uses, and effects of drugs. **—phar'ma•co•log'ic** (-kə-lŏj'ĭk), **phar'ma•co•log'i•cal** *adj.* **—phar'ma•col'o•gist** *n.*

phar•ma•co•poe•ia (fär'mə-kə-pē'ə) *n.* **1.** A book containing a list of medicinal drugs with recommended procedures for their preparation and use. **2.** A stock or collection of drugs.

phar•ma•cy (fär'mə-sē) *n., pl.* **-cies. 1.** The techniques or practice of preparing and dispensing drugs. **2.** A drugstore.

pha•ros (fâr'ŏs') *n.* A lighthouse.

phar•ynx (făr'ĭngks) *n., pl.* **pha•ryn•ges** (fə-rĭn'jēz') *or* **-ynx•es.** The cavity connecting the nasal passages and mouth with the esophagus. **—pha•ryn'ge•al** (fə-rĭn'jē-əl, făr'ĭn-jē'əl) *adj.*

phase (fāz) *n.* **1.** A distinct stage of development. **2.** An aspect, as of a situation : part. **3.** One of the cyclic forms in which the moon or a planet appears. *—v.* **phased, phas•ing.** To carry out or plan systematically in phases. **—phase in** (*or* **out**). To introduce (or eliminate) in stages.

phase-in (fāz'ĭn') *n.* A systematic and gradual introduction.

phase•out (fāz'out') *n.* Systematic and gradual discontinuation.

pheas•ant (fĕz'ənt) *n.* Any of various long-tailed game birds of the family Phasianidae, with colorful plumage.

phen•cy•cli•dine (fĕn-sī'klĭ-dēn', -dĭn, -sĭk'-lĭ-) *n.* A drug used in veterinary medicine, also used illegally as a hallucinogen.

phe•no•bar•bi•tal (fē'nō-bär'bĭ-tôl') *n.* A white crystalline compound used as a sedative and hypnotic.

phe•nol (fē'nôl', -nōl') *n.* A caustic, poisonous crystalline compound obtained from benzene and used as a disinfectant and in making plastics and drugs.

phe•nom•e•non (fĭ-nŏm'ə-nŏn') *n., pl.* **-na** (nə) *or* **-nons. 1. a.** A fact or occurrence that can be perceived or observed. **b.** A rare fact or occurrence. **2.** An extremely outstanding or unusual person or thing : marvel. **—phe•nom'e•nal** *adj.* **—phe•nom'e•nal•ly** *adv.*

pher•o•mone (fĕr'ə-mōn') *n.* A chemical substance secreted by an animal that influences specific patterns of behavior in other members of the same species.

phi•al (fī'əl) *n.* A vial.

phi•lan•der (fĭ-lăn'dər) *v.* To make love casually or frivolously : dally.

phi•lan•thro•py (fĭ-lăn'thrə-pē) *n., pl.* **-pies. 1.** The effort to advance human well-being, as through charitable gifts or endowments. **2.** Benevolence toward mankind. **3.** A charitable institution. **—phil'an•throp'ic** (fĭl'ən-thrŏp'-ĭk), **phil'an•throp'i•cal** *adj.* **—phi•lan'thro•pist** *n.*

phi•lat•e•ly (fĭ-lăt'l-ē) *n.* The collection and study of postage stamps and postmarked materials. **—phil'a•tel'ic** (fĭl'ə-tĕl'ĭk) *adj.* **—phi•lat'e•list** *n.*

Phi•le•mon (fĭ-lē'mən, fī-) *n.* —See table at BIBLE.

phil•har•mon•ic (fĭl'här-mŏn'ĭk, fĭl'ər-) *adj.* Of or pertaining to a symphony orchestra. **—phil'har•mon'ic** *n.*

Phi•lip•pi•ans (fĭ-lĭp'ē-ənz) *pl.n. (sing. in number).* —See table at BIBLE.

phi•lip•pic (fĭ-lĭp'ĭk) *n.* An acrimonious verbal attack : tirade.

Phil•is•tine (fĭl'ĭ-stēn', fĭ-lĭs'tĭn, -tēn') *n.* **1.** A member of an ancient Palestinian people. **2. philistine.** A smug, materialistic person, esp. one who is indifferent to artistic, cultural, or intellectual values.

phil•o•den•dron (fĭl'ə-dĕn'drən) *n., pl.* **-drons** *or* **-dra** (-drə). Any of various climbing tropical American plants of the genus *Philodendron,* often grown as house plants.

▲ ***word history:*** The name *philodendron* literally means "fond of trees." It was given to a genus of tropical climbing plants because in their native habitat they twine around trees.

phi•lol•o•gy (fĭ-lŏl'ə-jē) *n.* **1.** The study of the chronological development of languages. **2.** The study of literature and of language as it is used in literature. **—phil'o•log'i•cal** (fĭl'ə-lŏj'ĭ-kəl) *adj.* **—phi•lol'o•gist** *n.*

phi•los•o•pher (fĭ-lŏs'ə-fər) *n.* **1.** An expert in or student of philosophy. **2.** Someone who thinks deeply : scholar. **3.** A calm, rational, self-assured person.

philosophers' stone *n.* An imaginary substance believed to have the power of transmuting base metal into gold.

phi•los•o•phize (fĭ-lŏs'ə-fīz') *v.* **-phized, -phiz•ing.** To speculate or reason like a philosopher.

phi•los•o•phy (fĭ-lŏs'ə-fē) *n., pl.* **-phies. 1. a.** A logical and critical study of the source and nature of human knowledge. **b.** A formal system of ideas based on such study. **2.** The sciences and liberal arts with the exception of law, medicine, and theology <a doctor of *philosophy*> **3.** A basic theory about a particular subject or sphere of activity <the *philosophy* of science> **4.** The set of values, ideas, and opinions of an individual or group. **—phil'o•soph'i•cal** (fĭl'-ə-sŏf'ĭ-kəl), **phil'o•soph'ic** *adj.* **—phil'o•soph'i•cal•ly** *adv.*

phil•ter *also* **phil•tre** (fĭl'tər) *n.* **1.** A love potion. **2.** A magic potion or charm.

phle•bi•tis (flĭ-bī'tĭs) *n.* Inflammation of a vein.
phlegm (flĕm) *n.* Thick mucus secreted esp. in the respiratory tract.
phleg•mat•ic (flĕg-măt'ĭk) *adj.* Having or suggesting a stolid, sluggish temperament : unemotional. —**phleg•mat'i•cal•ly** *adv.*
phlo•em (flō'ĕm') *n.* Vascular plant tissue through which food is conducted from the leaves to plant parts.
phlox (flŏks) *n., pl.* **phlox** *or* **phlox•es.** A plant of the genus *Phlox,* with terminal clusters of white, red, or purple flowers.
pho•bi•a (fō'bē-ə) *n.* A persistent illogical fear. —**pho'bic** *adj.*
phoe•be (fē'bē) *n.* A small, dull-colored North American bird of the genus *Sayornis.*
phoe•nix (fē'nĭks) *n.* A bird of legend said to consume itself by fire after centuries and rise renewed from its ashes.
phone (fōn) *Informal* —*n.* A telephone. —*v.* **phoned, phon•ing.** To call or transmit by telephone.
pho•neme (fō'nēm') *n.* One of the smallest speech units, as the *m* of *mat* and the *b* of *bat,* that distinguish one word or utterance from another. —**pho•ne'mic** (fə-nē'mĭk, fō-) *adj.* —**pho•ne'mics** *n.*
pho•net•ics (fə-nĕt'ĭks) *n. (sing. in number).* The study of the sounds of spoken language. —**pho•net'ic** *adj.* —**pho'ne•ti'cian** (fō'nĭ-tĭsh'ən) *n*
phon•ics (fŏn'ĭks) *n. (sing. in number).* A method of teaching beginning readers through the use of elementary phonetics.
pho•no•graph (fō'nə-grăf') *n.* An instrument that uses a vibrating needle to reproduce sound from a groove cut into a disc. —**pho'no•graph'ic** *adj.*
pho•nol•o•gy (fə-nŏl'ə-jē, fō-) *n.* The scientific study of the speech sounds of a language, including phonemics and phonetics and often sound changes over time. —**pho'no•log'ic** (fō'nə-lŏj'ĭk), **pho'no•log'i•cal** *adj.* —**pho•nol'o•gist** *n.*
pho•ny *also* **pho•ney** (fō'nē) *adj.* **-ni•er, -ni•est.** *Informal.* Not real or genuine : fake. —**pho'ny** *n.*
phos•phate (fŏs'făt') *n.* **1.** *Chem.* A salt or ester of phosphoric acid containing chiefly phosphorus and oxygen. **2.** A fertilizer containing compounds of phosphorus. —**phos•phat'ic** (fŏs-făt'ĭk) *adj.*
phos•phor (fŏs'fər, -fôr') *n.* A substance capable of emitting light when stimulated by incident radiation.
phos•pho•res•cence (fŏs'fə-rĕs'əns) *n.* **1.** The process or phenomenon of the persistent emission of light by a body after exposure to and removal of radiation. **2.** Organically generated emission of light : bioluminescence. —**phos'pho•resce'** *v.* —**phos'pho•res'cent** *adj.*
phos•phor•ic acid (fŏs-fôr'ĭk, -fŏr'-) *n.* A clear, colorless acid that is used in soaps, fertilizers, and detergents.
phos•pho•rus (fŏs'fər-əs) *n. Symbol* **P** A poisonous nonmetallic element used in safety matches, fertilizers, glass, and steel. —**phos•phor'ic** *adj.* —**phos'pho•rous** *adj.*
pho•to (fō'tō) *n., pl.* **-tos.** *Informal.* A photograph. —**pho'to** *v.*
pho•to•cell (fō'tō-sĕl') *n.* A photoelectric cell.
pho•to•chem•is•try (fō'tō-kĕm'ĭ-strē) *n.* The study of the effects of light on chemical reactions. —**pho'to•chem'i•cal** *adj.*
pho•to•com•po•si•tion (fō'tō-kŏm'pə-zĭsh'ən) *n.* A process by which printed matter is composed for reproduction by photographing type characters on film. —**pho'to•com•pose'** *v.*
pho•to•cop•y (fō'tō-kŏp'ē) *v.* To reproduce (printed matter) by a photographic process such as xerography. —**pho'to•cop'i•er** *n.* —**pho'to•cop'y** *n.*
pho•to•e•lec•tric (fō'tō-ĭ-lĕk'trĭk) *also* **pho•to•e•lec•tri•cal** (-trĭ-kəl) *adj.* Of or relating to electrical effects that result from or depend on the presence of light.
photoelectric cell *n.* An electronic device having an electrical output that varies in response to light.

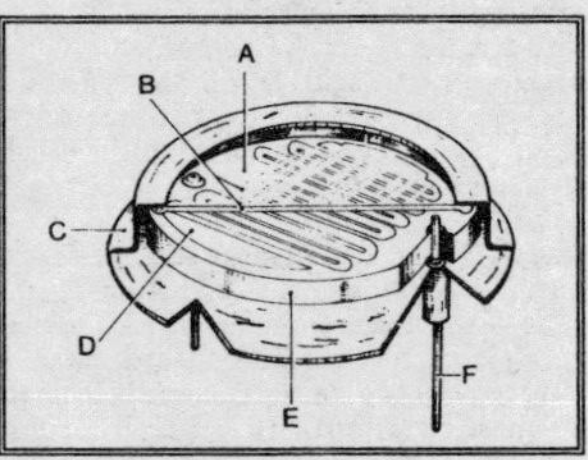

photoelectric cell
A. electrode, B. glass window, C. metal case, D. photoconductive material, E. ceramic substrate, F. base pin

pho•to•e•lec•tron (fō'tō-ĭ-lĕk'trŏn') *n.* An electron that is released in photoemission.
pho•to•e•mis•sion (fō'tō-ĭ-mĭsh'ən) *n.* The emission of photoelectrons from a metallic surface exposed to light or similar radiation.
pho•to•en•grav•ing (fō'tō-ĕn-grā'vĭng) *n.* **1.** The process of reproducing a drawing or photograph by transferring the image onto a metal plate in etched relief for printing. **2.** A reproduction made by photoengraving. —**pho'to•en•grave'** *v.*
photo finish *n.* A race finish so close that the winner can only be determined from a photograph of the finish.
pho•to•flash (fō'tō-flăsh') *n.* A flash bulb.
pho•to•gen•ic (fō'tə-jĕn'ĭk) *adj.* Suitable and esp. attractive as a subject for photography. —**pho'to•gen'i•cal•ly** *adv.*
pho•to•graph (fō'tə-grăf') *n.* An image, esp. a positive print, recorded by a camera and re-

produced on a photosensitive surface. —**pho'to·graph'** *v.*

pho·to·graph·ic (fō'tə-grăf'ĭk) *adj.* **1.** Of or used in photography or a photograph. **2.** Suggestive of a photograph, as in detail or accuracy. —**pho'to·graph'i·cal·ly** *adv.*

pho·tog·ra·phy (fə-tŏg'rə-fē) *n.* The process, art, technique, or profession of taking photographs. —**pho·tog'ra·pher** *n.*

pho·to·gra·vure (fō'tə-grə-vyŏŏr') *n.* The art or process of printing from an intaglio plate etched photographically.

pho·to·jour·nal·ism (fō'tō-jûr'nə-lĭz'əm) *n.* Journalism in which text is less important than pictorial matter, esp. photographs. —**pho'to·jour'nal·ist** *n.*

pho·tom·e·try (fō-tŏm'ĭ-trē) *n.* Measurement of the properties of light, esp. luminous intensity or flux. —**pho'to·met'ric** (fō'tə-mĕt'rĭk) *adj.* —**pho·tom'e·ter** *n.*

pho·ton (fō'tŏn') *n.* A quantum of electromagnetic energy. —**pho·ton'ic** *adj.*

pho·to-off·set (fō'tō-ôf'sĕt', -ŏf'-) *n.* Offset printing.

pho·to·re·cep·tor (fō'tō-rĭ-sĕp'tər) *n.* A nerve ending, cell, or group of cells specialized to sense or receive light.

pho·to·sen·si·tive (fō'tō-sĕn'sĭ-tĭv) *adj.* Sensitive to change as a result of exposure to light. —**pho'to·sen'si·tiv'i·ty** *n.*

pho·to·sphere (fō'tə-sfîr') *n.* The layer of a star, esp. the sun, that emits directly observable radiation, as light. —**pho'to·spher'ic** (-sfîr'ĭk, -sfĕr'-) *adj.*

Pho·to·stat (fō'tə-stăt'). A trademark for a device that makes photographic copies of graphic material.

pho·to·syn·the·sis (fō'tō-sĭn'thĭ-sĭs) *n.* The chemical process by which chlorophyll-containing plants use light to convert carbon dioxide and water into carbohydrates, releasing oxygen as a by-product. —**pho'to·syn'the·size'** (-sīz') *v.* —**pho'to·syn·thet'ic** (-thĕt'ĭk) *adj.*

pho·to·type·set·ting (fō'tō-tīp'sĕt'ĭng) *n.* Photocomposition.

pho·to·vol·ta·ic (fō'tō-vŏl-tā'ĭk, -vōl-) *adj.* Capable of producing a voltage when exposed to radiant energy, esp. light.

photovoltaic cell *n.* A solar cell.

phrase (frāz) *n.* **1.** A brief or concise expression. **2.** A sequence of 2 or more words that form a meaningful syntactic unit less completely predicated than a sentence. **3.** A portion of a musical composition that usu. consists of 4 to 8 measures. —*v.* **phrased, phras·ing. 1.** To write or express in words. **2.** To play music in a way that reveals its melodic phrases. —**phras'al** *adj.* —**phras'al·ly** *adv.*

phra·se·ol·o·gy (frā'zē-ŏl'ə-jē) *n., pl.* **-gies.** A style or manner of using words and phrases.

phren·ic (frĕn'ĭk, frē'nĭk) *adj. Anat.* Of or pertaining to the diaphragm.

phre·nol·o·gy (frĭ-nŏl'ə-jē) *n.* The study of the conformation of the human skull as a means of determining character and intelligence. —**phre·nol'o·gist** *n.*

phy·lac·ter·y (fĭ-lăk'tə-rē) *n., pl.* **-ies.** Either of 2 small leather boxes containing parchment strips inscribed with scriptural quotations that are worn on the forehead and the left arm esp. by orthodox Jewish men during weekday morning worship.

phy·log·e·ny (fī-lŏj'ə-nē) *n., pl.* **-nies.** The evolutionary development of a species of animal or plant.

phy·lum (fī'ləm) *n., pl.* **-la** (-lə). A broad category of the animal or plant kingdom into which organisms are divided.

phys·ic (fĭz'ĭk) *n.* A medicine, esp. a cathartic. —*v.* **-icked, -ick·ing.** To administer a physic to **:** purge.

phys·i·cal (fĭz'ĭ-kəl) *adj.* **1.** Of or relating to the body rather than the emotions or mind. **2.** Material rather than imaginary. **3. a.** Of, pertaining to, or produced by nonliving matter and energy. **b.** Of or pertaining to physics. ★ ***syns:*** ANIMAL, CARNAL, FLESHLY, SENSUAL —*n.* A medical examination to determine a person's physical condition. —**phys'i·cal·ly** *adv.*

physical education *n.* Instruction in the development, care, and exercise of the human body, including calisthenics, sports, and hygiene.

physical science *n.* A science, as chemistry, physics, or geology, that deals primarily with the properties of energy and nonliving matter.

physical therapy *n.* The treatment of disease or injury by means such as exercise, heat, baths, and massage. —**physical therapist** *n.*

phy·si·cian (fĭ-zĭsh'ən) *n.* A licensed medical doctor.

phys·i·cist (fĭz'ĭ-sĭst) *n.* A scientist specializing in physics.

phys·ics (fĭz'ĭks) *n. (sing. in number).* **1.** The science of matter and energy and of the interactions between them. **2.** Physical interactions, properties, laws, or processes.

phys·i·og·no·my (fĭz'ē-ŏg'nə-mē, -ŏn'ə-) *n., pl.* **-mies.** Facial expression and features, esp. as an indication of character.

phys·i·og·ra·phy (fĭz'ē-ŏg'rə-fē) *n.* The study of the structure and phenomena of the earth's surface. —**phys'i·og'ra·pher** *n.* —**phys'i·o·graph'ic** (-ə-grăf'ĭk) *adj.*

phys·i·ol·o·gy (fĭz'ē-ŏl'ə-jē) *n.* **1.** The scientific study of essential and typical life processes, activities, and functions. **2.** The vital processes and functions of an organism. —**phys'i·o·log'i·cal** (-ə-lŏj'ĭ-kəl), **phys'i·o·log'ic** *adj.* —**phys'i·o·log'i·cal·ly** *adv.* —**phys'i·ol'o·gist** *n.*

phys·i·o·ther·a·py (fĭz'ē-ō-thĕr'ə-pē) *n.* Physical therapy. —**phys'i·o·ther'a·peu'tic** *adj.* —**phys'i·o·ther'a·pist** *n.*

phy·sique (fĭ-zēk') *n.* The human body with respect to its muscular development, proportions, and appearance **:** build.

phy·to·plank·ton (fī'tō-plăngk'tən) *n.* Minute, free-floating aquatic plants.

pi[1] (pī) *n., pl.* **pis.** A transcendental number

that represents the ratio of the circumference of a circle to its diameter.

pi[2] *also* **pie** (pī) *n., pl.* **pis** *also* **pies.** Jumbled type.

pi•a•nis•si•mo (pē′ə-nĭs′ə-mō′) *adv. Mus.* Very softly. —Used as a direction. —**pi′a•nis′si•mo′** *adj. & n.*

pi•an•ist (pē-ăn′ĭst, pē′ə-nĭst) *n.* Someone who plays the piano.

pi•an•o[1] (pē-ăn′ō, -ä′nō) *n., pl.* **-os.** A musical instrument with a manual keyboard and felt-covered hammers that strike wire strings.

pi•a•no[2] (pē-ä′nō) *adv. Mus.* Softly. —Used as a direction. —**pi•a′no** *adj. & n.*

pi•an•o•for•te (pē-ăn′ō-fôr′tā, -tē, -fôrt′, -ä′-nō-) *n.* A piano.

pi•as•ter *also* **pi•as•tre** (pē-ăs′tər, -ä′stər) *n.* —See table at CURRENCY.

pi•az•za (pē-ăz′ə, -ä′zə) *n.* **1.** A public square, esp. in an Italian town. **2.** A porch.

pi•broch (pē′brŏKH′) *n.* A series of variations on a traditional dirge or martial theme for the bagpipe.

pic (pĭk) *n., pl.* **pics** *or* **pix.** *Slang.* **1.** A photograph. **2.** A movie.

pi•ca (pī′kə) *n.* **1.** A printer's type size equal to 12 points or approx. 1/6 in. **2.** A type size for typewriters, providing 10 characters to the inch.

pic•a•dor (pĭk′ə-dôr′) *n., pl.* **-dors** *or* **-do•res** (-dôr′ēz). A horseman in bullfighting who weakens the bull by lancing its neck muscles.

pic•a•resque (pĭk′ə-rĕsk′, pē′kə-) *adj.* Of, pertaining to, or involving rogues.

pic•a•yune (pĭk′ē-yo͞on′) *adj.* **1.** Of little importance or value **:** paltry. **2.** Mean in spirit **:** petty.

pic•ca•lil•li (pĭk′ə-lĭl′ē) *n.* A spicy relish of chopped and pickled vegetables.

pic•co•lo (pĭk′ə-lō′) *n., pl.* **-los.** A small flute with a hard, brilliant sound that is pitched an octave above an ordinary flute.

pick[1] (pĭk) *v.* **1.** To choose from a group **:** select. **2.** To gather by or as if by plucking <*pick* cotton> **3. a.** To remove an outer covering from. **b.** To remove, as by tearing off, bit by bit. **4.** To pull at with the fingers. **5.** To break up, detach, or pierce with a pointed or sharp instrument. **6.** To steal the contents of <*picks* pockets> **7.** To open without using a key <*pick* a lock> **8.** To pull gently or dig at. **9.** To cause deliberately **:** provoke <*pick* a fight> —**pick on.** To tease or harass. —**pick out.** To play the notes of singly or uncertainly <*picked out* the melody on the organ> —**pick up. 1.** To take on (e.g., freight or passengers). **2.** To become better **:** improve. **3.** To set in order **:** tidy. **4.** To learn, esp. without great effort. **5.** To arrest. —*n.* **1.** The act or right of choosing **:** selection. **2.** The choicest or best part. —**pick′er** *n.*

pick[2] (pĭk) *n.* **1.** A tool consisting of a curved bar sharpened at both ends and fitted to a long handle that is used for breaking up hard surfaces. **2.** A small flat piece, as of bone, used to pluck the strings of a musical instrument **:** plectrum.

pick•a•back (pĭk′ə-băk′) *adv. & n. var. of* PIGGYBACK.

pick•ax *or* **pick•axe** (pĭk′ăks′) *n.* A pick with one end of the blade pointed, the other end having a chisellike edge.

pick•er•el (pĭk′ər-əl, pĭk′rəl) *n., pl.* **-el** *or* **-els.** Any of various North American freshwater food and game fishes of the genus *Esox* that are related to but gen. smaller than the pike.

pick•er•el•weed (pĭk′ər-əl-wēd′, pĭk′rəl-) *n.* A North American plant, *Pontederia cordata,* found in freshwater shallows and having heart-shaped leaves and violet-blue flower spikes.

pick•et (pĭk′ĭt) *n.* **1.** A pointed stake, as one driven into the ground to support a fence. **2. a.** A detachment of soldiers on guard duty. **b.** A soldier on guard duty **:** sentinel. **3.** A person stationed outside a place of employment, esp. during a strike, to discourage entry by nonstriking workers or customers. —*v.* **1.** To secure, enclose, tether, mark out, or fortify with pickets. **2.** To guard with or post as a picket. **3.** To station pickets at <*picketing* a restaurant> **4.** To act as a picket.

picket line *n.* A line of people picketing a place of employment.

pick•ings (pĭk′ĭngz) *pl.n.* **1.** Scraps, esp. of edible food **:** leftovers. **2. a.** Result or gain from effort exerted <slim *pickings*> **b.** A share of spoils.

pick•le (pĭk′əl) *n.* **1.** A solution of brine or vinegar for flavoring and preserving food. **2.** A food, as a cucumber, preserved in a pickle. **3.** *Informal.* A difficult or troublesome situation **:** predicament. —*v.* **-led, -ling.** To flavor or preserve in a pickle.

pick•lock (pĭk′lŏk′) **1.** One who picks locks, esp. a thief. **2.** An instrument for picking a lock.

pick-me-up (pĭk′mē-ŭp′) *n. Informal.* Something, esp. an alcoholic drink, that invigorates or stimulates.

pick•pock•et (pĭk′pŏk′ĭt) *n.* Someone who steals from pockets.

pick•up (pĭk′ŭp′) *n.* **1.** The act or process of picking up. **2.** Acceleration. **3.** Renewed activity **:** improvement. **4.** *Electron.* **a.** A device for converting the oscillations of a phonograph needle into electrical impulses. **b.** The tone arm of a record player. **5. a.** The conversion of light or sound waves into electrical impulses. **b.** A device used for such conversion. **6.** A casual temporary acquaintance. **7.** A small, light truck with low sides and an open body.

pick•y (pĭk′ē) *adj.* **-i•er, -i•est.** *Informal.* Excessively meticulous **:** fussy.

pic•nic (pĭk′nĭk) *n.* An excursion in which members of a group eat a meal outdoors. —*v.* **-nicked, -nick•ing.** To go on a picnic. —**pic′-nick•er** *n.*

▲ ***word history:*** The word *picnic* is most probably derived from French *pique-nique,* whose origin is not known with absolute certainty. The word seems to have originated in the 18th cent., when it referred to a meal for which each guest contributed a dish to be served. At some point it became common to hold such parties outdoors, and by the 19th cent. *picnic* referred to any open-air meal.

pi•cot (pē′kō′) *n.* One of a series of small loops that form an ornamental edging, as on ribbon.

pic•to•graph (pĭk′tə-grăf′) *n.* **1.** A hieroglyph. **2.** A pictorial representation of numerical data or relationships. **—pic′to•graph′ic** *adj.*

pic•to•ri•al (pĭk-tôr′ē-əl, -tōr′-) *adj.* Of, pertaining to, or composed of pictures. **—pic•to′ri•al•ly** *adv.*

pic•ture (pĭk′chər) *n.* **1.** A representation that is drawn, painted, or photographed. **2.** A vivid, realistic verbal description. **3.** One that closely resembles another : image. **4.** An embodiment, as of a state of mind <the *picture* of health> **5.** A set of circumstances : situation. **6.** A motion picture. —*v.* **-tured, -tur•ing. 1.** To make a picture of. **2.** To visualize mentally. **3.** To describe vividly in words.

pic•tur•esque (pĭk′chə-rĕsk′) *adj.* **1.** Suggesting or resembling a picture <a *picturesque* colonial village> **2.** Quaintly attractive : charming. **3.** Strikingly expressive : vivid. **—pic′tur•esque′ly** *adv.* **—pic′tur•esque′ness** *n.*

picture window *n.* A large, usu. single-paned window that frames a broad view of the outside.

pid•dling (pĭd′lĭng) *adj.* Trivial : trifling.

pidg•in (pĭj′ĭn) *n.* A simplified medium of speech used for communication between groups who speak different languages.

pie[1] (pī) *n.* A baked pastry crust with a filling, as of fruit or meat.

pie[2] (pī) *n. var. of* PI[2].

pie•bald (pī′bôld′) *adj.* Patched or spotted <a *piebald* horse>

piece (pēs) *n.* **1.** A part, unit, or element of a whole : portion or fragment. **2.** One of a set or group <a *piece* of furniture> **3.** A musical, artistic, or literary work. **4.** An example : specimen. **5.** A coin. **6.** A firearm. —*v.* **pieced, piec•ing. 1.** To complete or mend by adding pieces. **2.** To unite into a whole : join.

pièce de ré•sis•tance (pē-ĕs′ də rā′zē-stäɴs′) *n.* **1.** The main dish of a meal. **2.** An outstanding example.

piece•meal (pēs′mēl′) *adv.* Bit by bit : gradually. **—piece′meal′** *adj.*

piece•work (pēs′wûrk′) *n.* Work that is paid for by the piece. **—piece′work′er** *n.*

pie chart *n.* A circular graph divided into sectors proportional to the relative size of the quantities represented.

pied (pīd) *adj.* Of more than one color in patches : piebald.

pied-à-terre (pyā′-dä-târ′) *n., pl.* **pieds-à-terre** (pyā-dä-târ′). A 2nd or temporary lodging.

pied•mont (pēd′mŏnt′) *n.* An area of land at the foot of a mountain or mountain range.

pie•plant (pī′plănt′) *n.* Rhubarb.

pier (pîr) *n.* **1.** A structure that extends into the water and is used to protect, secure, and provide access to vessels. **2.** A structure that supports the spans of a bridge. **3.** A vertical supporting structure.

pierce (pîrs) *v.* **pierced, pierc•ing. 1.** To puncture or pass into or through with or as if with a sharp instrument : stab. **2.** To make a hole in. **3.** To make a way through : penetrate. **—pierc′ing•ly** *adv.*

pi•e•ty (pī′ĭ-tē) *n., pl.* **-ties. 1.** Devotion to God : devoutness. **2.** Faithfulness and reverence to parents and family. **3.** A pious thought or act.

pi•e•zo•e•lec•tric•i•ty (pē-ā′zō-ĭ-lĕk-trĭs′ĭ-tē) *n.* The generation of electricity in dielectric crystals subjected to mechanical stress. **—pi•e′zo•e•lec′tric, pi•e′zo•e•lec′tri•cal** *adj.*

pif•fle (pĭf′əl) *n.* Foolish or trivial talk.

pig (pĭg) *n.* **1.** Any of several hoofed mammals with short legs, cloven hoofs, bristly hair, and a cartilaginous snout used for rooting, esp. the domesticated hog, *Sus scrofa,* when young. **2.** A person resembling a pig, as in being greedy or gross. **3.** A block of metal, usu. lead or iron, poured from a smelting furnace into a mold.

pi•geon (pĭj′ən) *n.* Any of several doves of the family Columbidae, with a prominent chest and short legs.

pi•geon•hole (pĭj′ən-hōl′) *n.* A small compartment, as in a desk, for holding letters and papers. —*v.* **1.** To place in a pigeonhole : file. **2.** To categorize : classify. **3.** To put aside indefinitely.

pi•geon-toed (pĭj′ən-tōd′) *adj.* Having toes that turn inward.

pig•gish (pĭg′ĭsh) *adj.* **1.** Like a pig : greedy or dirty. **2.** Pigheaded.

pig•gy (pĭg′ē) *Informal.* —*n., pl.* **-gies.** A little pig. —*adj.* Piggish.

pig•gy•back (pĭg′ē-băk′) *also* **pick•a•back** (pĭk′ə-) *adv.* **1.** On the shoulders and back. **2.** In, on, or by means of truck trailers carried on railroad flatcars. **—pig′gy•back′** *adj.*

pig•head•ed (pĭg′hĕd′ĭd) *adj.* Stubborn.

pig iron *n.* Crude iron as it is drawn from the blast furnace.

pig•let (pĭg′lĭt) *n.* A small young pig.

pig•ment (pĭg′mənt) *n.* **1.** A substance or material used as coloring. **2.** *Biol.* A substance, as hemoglobin or chlorophyll, that imparts a characteristic color to animal or plant tissue.

pig•men•ta•tion (pĭg′mən-tā′shən) *n. Biol.* **1.** Coloration of tissues by pigment. **2.** Deposition of pigment by cells.

pig•my (pĭg′mē) *n. & adj. var. of* PYGMY.

pig•nut (pĭg′nŭt′) *n.* A hickory tree, *Carya glabra* or *C. ovalis,* of the E U.S., bearing edible nuts.

pig•pen (pĭg′pĕn′) *n.* **1.** A pen in which pigs are kept. **2.** A very dirty place.

pig•skin (pĭg′skĭn′) *n.* **1. a.** The skin of a pig. **b.** Leather made from pigskin. **2.** *Informal.* **a.** A football. **b.** A saddle.

pig•sty (pĭg′stī′) *n.* A pigpen.

pig•tail (pĭg′tāl′) *n.* A plait of tightly braided hair.

pike[1] (pīk) *n.* A long spear with a sharp-pointed steel head once used by infantry.
pike[2] (pīk) *n., pl.* **pike** *or* **pikes. 1.** A large freshwater food and game fish, *Esox lucius,* having a long snout and a narrow body. **2.** A similar or related fish.
pike[3] (pīk) *n.* A turnpike.
pike[4] (pīk) *n.* A sharp point or spike, as the tip of spear.
pi·ker (pī'kər) *n. Slang.* A petty, stingy person.
pi·laf *or* **pi·laff** (pĭ-läf', pē'läf') *n.* A dish made of rice in a seasoned broth with shellfish, meat, or vegetables.
pi·las·ter (pī'lăs'tər, pĭ-lăs'-) *n.* A vertical column, often ornamental, that projects slightly from a wall.
pil·chard (pĭl'chərd) *n.* Any of various sardinelike fishes related to the herrings, esp. *Sardina pilchardus,* a commercially important edible species.
pile[1] (pīl) *n.* **1.** A mass of things in a heap. **2.** A large quantity or number. **3.** A funeral pyre. **4.** A very big building. **5.** A nuclear reactor. —*v.* **piled, pil·ing. 1.** To put into or form a pile **:** stack. **2.** To accumulate into a pile. **3.** To move forward in a group or mass <*pile* into a bus>
pile[2] (pīl) *n.* A heavy post or column, as of steel, driven into the ground as a foundation or support for a structure.
pile[3] (pīl) *n.* **1.** The surface of certain fabrics, as velvet and carpeting, consisting of cut or uncut loops of yarn. **2.** Soft, fine fur, hair, or wool. **—piled** *adj.*
piles (pīlz) *pl.n.* Hemorrhoids.
pil·fer (pĭl'fər) *v.* To steal articles of little value **:** filch. **—pil'fer·age** *n.*
pil·grim (pĭl'grĭm) *n.* **1.** A person who goes on a pilgrimage. **2.** Someone who travels in foreign countries. **3. Pilgrim.** One of a group of English Puritans who founded the colony of Plymouth in New England in 1620.
pil·grim·age (pĭl'grə-mĭj) *n.* **1.** A journey to a shrine or sacred place. **2.** An extended journey with a purpose.
pill (pĭl) *n.* **1.** A small tablet of medicine to be taken orally. **2. the pill.** *Informal.* An oral contraceptive. **3.** Something that is unpleasant but must be accepted. **4.** *Slang.* A disagreeable or boring person.
pil·lage (pĭl'ĭj) *v.* **-laged, -lag·ing.** To take loot **:** plunder. **—pil'lag·er** *n.*
pil·lar (pĭl'ər) *n.* A freestanding vertical shaft or column that serves as a support or stands alone as a monument.
pill·box (pĭl'bŏks') *n.* **1.** A small box for holding pills. **2.** An emplacement of reinforced concrete, esp. for a machine gun.
pil·lion (pĭl'yən) *n.* A cushion for a passenger behind the saddle on a motorcycle or horse.
pil·lo·ry (pĭl'ə-rē) *n., pl.* **-ries.** A wooden frame with holes in which the head and hands were locked as public punishment. —*v.* **-ried, -ry·ing. 1.** To put in a pillory. **2.** To expose to public abuse or ridicule.
pil·low (pĭl'ō) *n.* A cloth case filled with soft material, as down, and used to cushion a person's head during sleep. —*v.* **1.** To rest on or as if on a pillow. **2.** To serve as a pillow for. **—pil'low·y** *adj.*
pil·low·case (pĭl'ō-kās') *n.* A removable open-ended covering for a pillow.
pi·lot (pī'lət) *n.* **1.** Someone who operates or is licensed to operate an aircraft or spacecraft. **2.** Someone licensed to steer ships into and out of port. **3.** A helmsman. **4.** A leader or guide. **5.** A television program produced as a prototype of a proposed series. —*v.* **1.** To serve as the pilot of. **2.** To control the course of **:** conduct. —*adj.* Serving as a guide or model for future development or experiment <a *pilot* study>
pi·lot·age (pī'lə-tĭj) *n.* The technique or business of piloting.
pi·lot·house (pī'lət-hous') *n.* An enclosed area on the bridge or deck of a ship from which it is steered.
pilot light *n.* A small permanent flame used to ignite a gas burner or oven.
pi·men·to (pĭ-mĕn'tō) *also* **pi·mien·to** (pĭ-mĕn'tō, -myĕn'-) *n., pl.* **-tos.** A mild-flavored garden pepper, *Capsicum annuum,* with red fruit.
pimp (pĭmp) *n.* One who procures customers for a prostitute. **—pimp** *v.*
pim·per·nel (pĭm'pər-nĕl', -nəl) *n.* A low-growing plant, *Anagallis arvensis,* whose flowers close in wet weather.
pim·ple (pĭm'pəl) *n.* A small swelling on the skin that sometimes contains pus. **—pim'-ply** *adj.*
pin (pĭn) *n.* **1.** A small, straight, rigid piece of wire with a sharp point and a blunt head, used esp. for fastening. **2.** Something, as a hairpin, that resembles a pin in shape or use. **3.** An ornament fastened to clothing with a clasp **:** brooch or badge. **4.** A cylindrical piece of metal or wood used for supporting or fastening. **5.** One of the wooden clubs serving as the target in bowling. **6.** The staff bearing the pennant that marks a hole on a golf course. **7. pins.** *Informal.* The legs. —*v.* **pinned, pin·ning. 1.** To secure or fasten with or as if with a pin. **2.** To make contingent <*pinned* our future on his success> **3.** To hold fast **:** immobilize. **4.** To establish clearly **:** define <couldn't *pin* down the source of the trouble> **5.** To assign culpability for <tried to *pin* the theft on the stranger>
pin·a·fore (pĭn'ə-fôr', -fōr') *n.* A sleeveless apronlike garment.
pin·ball (pĭn'bôl') *n.* A game played on a device in which the player manipulates a ball over a slanted surface having obstacles and targets.
pince-nez (păNs-nā', păns-) *n., pl.* **pince-nez** (-nāz', -nā'). Eyeglasses clipped with a spring to the bridge of the nose.
pin·cer (pĭn'sər) *n.* **1. pincers.** A grasping implement with 2 jaws and 2 handles pivoted together to work in opposition. **2.** A

jointed, prehensile claw of certain arthropods, as a crab or lobster.

pinch (pĭnch) *v.* **1.** To squeeze between the thumb and forefinger or the jaws of an implement. **2.** To squeeze or compress so as to cause discomfort or pain. **3.** To shrivel : wither. **4.** To be thrifty or miserly. **5.** *Slang.* To steal. **6.** *Slang.* To arrest. —*n.* **1.** The act of pinching. **2.** An amount that can be held between the thumb and forefinger <a *pinch* of salt> **3.** A critical time : emergency. **4.** Strain : stress <felt the *pinch* of poverty> **5.** *Slang.* An arrest.

pinch-hit (pĭnch'hĭt') *v.* **1.** *Baseball.* To bat in place of another player, esp. when a hit is badly needed. **2.** *Informal.* To act as a substitute for another. —**pinch hitter** *n.*

pin curl *n.* A coiled strand of usu. damp hair secured with a bobby pin or clip and combed into a wave or curl when dry.

pin•cush•ion (pĭn'ko͝osh'ən) *n.* A firm cushion in which pins and needles are stuck when not in use.

pine[1] (pīn) *n.* **1.** An evergreen tree of the genus *Pinus,* bearing cones and clusters of needle-shaped leaves. **2.** The wood of a pine tree. —**pin'y, pine'y** *adj.*

pine[2] (pīn) *v.* **pined, pin•ing. 1.** To long for something : yearn. **2.** To lose health or vitality from longing or grief.

pin•e•al body (pĭn'ē-əl, pī'nē-) *n.* A small rudimentary glandular body of uncertain function located in the brain.

pine•ap•ple (pīn'ăp'əl) *n.* A tropical American plant, *Ananas comosus,* bearing a large, fleshy, edible fruit.

pin•feath•er (pĭn'fĕ*th*'ər) *n.* A growing feather still enclosed in its horny sheath, esp. one just emerging through the skin.

ping (pĭng) *n.* A high-pitched sound, as of a bullet striking metal. —**ping** *v.*

Ping-Pong (pĭng'pông', -pŏng'). A trademark for table tennis.

pin•head (pĭn'hĕd') *n.* **1.** The head of a pin. **2.** A stupid person : fool.

pin•hole (pĭn'hōl') *n.* A very small hole made by or as if by a pin.

pin•ion[1] (pĭn'yən) *n.* The wing of a bird. —*v.* **1.** To immobilize or restrain (a person) by binding the arms. **2.** To fix in place : hold fast.

pin•ion[2] (pĭn'yən) *n.* A small cogwheel designed to mesh with a larger cogwheel or a rack.

pink[1] (pĭngk) *n.* **1.** Any of various plants of the genus *Dianthus,* related to the carnation and often cultivated for their fragrant flowers. **2.** A light or pale red. **3.** The highest degree possible <the *pink* of health> —*adj.* **1.** Of the color pink. **2.** Sympathetic with or holding Communist opinions.

pink[2] (pĭngk) *v.* **1.** To stab or pierce lightly with a pointed instrument. **2.** To ornament with a pattern of perforations. **3.** To cut a notched or zigzag edge on, as to prevent raveling.

pink•eye *also* **pink eye** (pĭngk'ī') *n.* Acute contagious conjunctivitis.

pink•ie *also* **pink•y** (pĭng'kē) *n., pl.* **-ies.** The 5th or smallest finger.

pink slip *n. Informal.* A notice of termination of employment.

†**Pink•ster** *also* **Pinx•ter** (pĭngk'stər) *n. Regional.* Whitsunday.

pin money *n.* Money for incidental expenditures.

pin•nace (pĭn'əs) *n.* **1.** A small sailing boat once used as a tender. **2.** A small ship or ship's boat.

pin•na•cle (pĭn'ə-kəl) *n.* **1.** A small spirelike turret, as on a roof. **2.** A tall, pointed formation, as a mountain peak. **3.** The highest point : summit.

pinnacle

pin•nate (pĭn'āt') *adj.* Having like parts, as leaflets, arranged along each side of a common axis.

pi•noch•le *also* **pi•noc•le** (pē'nŭk'əl, -nŏk'-) *n.* A card game played with a special deck of 48 cards.

pi•ñon *also* **pin•yon** (pĭn'yən, -yōn') *n.* Any of several pine trees bearing edible, nutlike seeds, esp. *Pinus cembroides edulis,* of W North America.

pin•point (pĭn'point') *n.* **1.** The point of a pin. **2.** A very small spot or thing : particle. —*v.* To identify and locate precisely.

pin•prick (pĭn'prĭk') *n.* **1.** A very small puncture made by or as if by a pin. **2.** A small annoyance.

pin•stripe (pĭn'strīp') *n.* A fabric with thin, narrow stripes.

pint (pīnt) *n.* —See table at MEASUREMENT.

pin•to (pĭn'tō) *n., pl.* **-tos** *or* **-toes.** A horse with irregular spots or patches.

pint•size (pīnt'sīz') *also* **pint•sized** (-sīzd') *adj. Informal.* Very small.

pin•up (pĭn'ŭp') *n.* **1.** A picture, esp. of an attractive girl, to be pinned up on a wall. **2.** Someone, esp. a girl, considered suitable as the subject of a pinup. —**pin'up'** *adj.*

pin•wheel (pĭn'hwēl', -wēl') *n.* **1.** A toy consisting of a stick to which revolving vanes of paper or plastic are fastened. **2.** A firework in the form of a revolving wheel of colored flames.

pin•worm (pĭn'wûrm') *n.* A small nematode worm, *Enterobius vermicularis,* that infests the human intestines and rectum.

Pinx•ter (pĭngk'stər) *n. var. of* PINKSTER.
Pin•yin *or* **pin•yin** (pĭn'yĭn', -yĭn') *n.* A system for transliterating Chinese ideograms into the Roman alphabet.
pin•yon (pĭn'yən, -yōn') *n. var. of* PIÑON.
pi•o•neer (pī'ə-nîr') *n.* **1.** An early settler of an unknown or unclaimed territory. **2.** Someone who starts or leads others in the development of something new **:** innovator. **—pi'o•neer'** *v.*

▲ ***word history:*** The word *pioneer* is derived from French *pion,* "foot soldier." *Pioneer* orig. denoted a soldier whose task was to prepare the way for the main body of troops marching to a new area. From this use the word was applied to anyone who ventures into an unknown region.

pi•ous (pī'əs) *adj.* **1. a.** Reverently and earnestly religious **:** devout. **b.** Falsely and ostentatiously devout. **2.** Characterized by solemn hypocrisy. **3.** Of or pertaining to devotion **:** sacred. **4.** Having or showing a sense of duty **:** high-minded. **—pi'ous•ly** *adv.* **—pi'ous•ness** *n.*
pip[1] (pĭp) *n.* A small fruit seed, as of an orange.
pip[2] (pĭp) *n.* A dot that indicates numerical value, as on dice or dominoes.
pip[3] (pĭp) *n.* **1.** A disease of birds. **2.** An imaginary or minor human ailment.
pipe (pīp) *n.* **1.** A long hollow cylinder through which a fluid or gas can flow **:** tube. **2.** A tube with a small bowl at one end and a mouthpiece at the other that is used for smoking tobacco. **3. a.** A musical instrument, as a small flute, that consists of a tube. **b.** A bagpipe. *—v.* **piped, pip•ing. 1.** To convey in or as if in pipes. **2.** To play (music) on a pipe. **3.** To speak in a shrill voice. **—pipe down.** *Slang.* To stop talking **:** be quiet. **—pipe up.** *Slang.* To begin talking **:** speak up. **—pip'er** *n.*
pipe dream *n.* An unattainable or fantastic idea or hope.
pipe fitter *n.* One who installs and repairs piping systems.
pipe•line (pīp'līn') *n.* **1.** A channel of pipe for conveying fluids, esp. water or petroleum, over great distances. **2.** A direct channel through which information is transmitted. **—pipe'line'** *v.*
pipe organ *n.* ORGAN 1.
pi•pette *also* **pi•pet** (pī-pĕt') *n.* An open-ended and often graduated tube used for transferring small volumes of liquid.
pip•ing (pī'pĭng) *n.* **1.** A system of pipes. **2.** A narrow band or fold of material used to trim seams or edges.
pip•it (pĭp'ĭt) *n.* A widely distributed songbird of the genus *Anthus.*
pip•kin (pĭp'kĭn) *n.* A small earthenware or metal cooking pot.
pip•pin (pĭp'ĭn) *n.* **1.** Any of several varieties of apple. **2.** *Slang.* One that is greatly admired.
pip-squeak (pĭp'skwēk') *n.* A small or unimportant person.
pi•quant (pē'kənt, -känt', pē-känt') *adj.* **1.** Pleasantly pungent in taste or odor **:** spicy. **2.** Appealingly stimulating or provocative. **—pi'quan•cy** *n.* **—pi'quant•ly** *adv.*
pique (pēk) *n.* A feeling or fit of resentment stemming from wounded vanity or pride. *—v.* **piqued, piqu•ing. 1.** To cause to feel pique. **2.** To arouse <silence that *piqued* our curiosity>
pi•qué (pĭ-kā') *n.* A firm clothing fabric with ribs in various patterns.
pi•ra•nha *also* **pi•ra•ña** (pĭ-rän'yə, -răn'-) *n.* Any of several sharp-toothed tropical American freshwater fishes of the genus *Serrasalmus* that often attack animals.

piranha

pi•rate (pī'rĭt) *n.* **1.** Someone who commits robbery on the high seas. **2.** Someone who uses or reproduces the work of another illicitly or without authorization. **—pi'ra•cy** *n.* **—pi'rate** *v.* **—pi•rat'ic** (pī-răt'ĭk), **pi•rat'i•cal** *adj.* **—pi•rat'i•cal•ly** *adv.*
pi•rogue (pĭ-rōg') *n.* A canoe made from a hollowed tree trunk.
pir•ou•ette (pîr'o͞o-ĕt') *n.* A full turn of the body on the ball of the foot or the tip of the toe. **—pir'ou•ette'** *v.*
pis•ca•to•ri•al (pĭs'kə-tôr'ē-əl, -tōr'-) *adj.* Of or pertaining to fishing.
Pi•sces (pī'sēz') *n.* **1.** A constellation in the N Hemisphere. **2. a.** The 12th sign of the zodiac. **b.** One born under this sign.
pis•mire (pĭs'mīr', pĭz'-) *n.* An ant.
pis•ta•chi•o (pĭ-stăsh'ē-ō', -stä'shē-ō') *n., pl.* **-os.** A tree, *Pistacia vera,* bearing hard-shelled, edible nuts with a green kernel.
pis•til (pĭs'təl) *n.* The seed-bearing female reproductive organ of a flower.
pis•tol (pĭs'təl) *n.* A small firearm that can be held and fired with one hand.
pis•tol-whip (pĭs'təl-hwĭp', -wĭp') *v.* To beat with the barrel of a pistol.
pis•ton (pĭs'tən) *n.* A solid cylinder that fits into a larger cylinder and moves back and forth under fluid pressure, as in an engine, or displaces or compresses fluids, as in a pump.
pit[1] (pĭt) *n.* **1.** A natural or manmade hole in the ground. **2.** Hell. **3.** An enclosed space, as that used for cockfighting. **4. a.** A natural depression in the surface of a body, organ, or part. **b.** An indentation in the skin caused by injury or disease. **5.** The section directly in

front of a theater stage for the orchestra. **6.** The section of a commodities exchange where trading is carried on. **7.** An area for repair and refueling at an auto racecourse. **8. pits.** *Slang.* The worst <a situation that's the *pits*> —*v.* **pit•ted, pit•ting. 1. a.** To make pits in. **b.** To become marked with pits. **2.** To set into contest or competition.

pit[2] (pĭt) *n.* The single, central kernel of certain fruits, as a cherry or peach. —*v.* **pit•ted, pit•ting.** To extract the pit from.

pi•ta (pē'tə) *n.* Round, flat bread that is hollow inside and forms a pocket when cut.

pit•a•pat (pĭt'ə-păt') *n.* A rapid series of taps, steps, or beats.

pitch[1] (pĭch) *n.* **1.** A thick, dark, sticky substance derived esp. from the distillation residue of coal tar or petroleum. **2.** A resin derived from the sap of a conifer.

pitch[2] (pĭch) *v.* **1.** To throw, often toward a target **:** toss. **2.** *Baseball.* To throw (the ball) from the mound to the batter. **3.** To set up and fix in position <*pitched* the tent> **4.** To fix at a certain level <*pitched* her hopes too high> **5.** To fall forward **:** plunge. **6.** *Naut.* To dip bow and stern alternately. **7.** To slope downward. **—pitch in. 1.** To set to work vigorously. **2.** To cooperate with others in working toward a common goal. —*n.* **1.** An act or instance of pitching. **2.** A degree of slant. **3.** A level or degree of a state or quality <enthusiasm at a feverish *pitch*> **4.** Lowness or highness of a sound, esp. a musical sound. **5. a.** The throw of a baseball by a pitcher to a batter. **b.** The ball so thrown. **6.** *Slang.* A line of talk intended to persuade.

pitch-black (pĭch'blăk') *adj.* Extremely dark or black.

pitch•blende (pĭch'blĕnd') *n.* A brownish-black mineral that is the essential ore of uranium.

pitch-dark (pĭch'därk') *adj.* Extremely dark <a *pitch-dark* night>

pitch•er[1] (pĭch'ər) *n.* *Baseball.* The player who pitches the ball to the batter.

pitch•er[2] (pĭch'ər) *n.* A container, usu. with a handle and a lip or spout, for holding and pouring liquids.

pitcher plant *n.* An insectivorous plant of the genera *Sarracenia, Nepenthes,* or *Darlingtonia,* with pitcher-shaped leaves that trap insects.

pitch•fork (pĭch'fôrk') *n.* A large fork with widely spaced prongs used esp. for pitching hay.

pitch•man (pĭch'mən) *n.* A vender or peddler of small wares, esp. one with a colorful or high-powered sales talk.

pitch pipe *n.* A small pipe sounded to establish the pitch for singing a piece of music or tuning an instrument.

pit•e•ous (pĭt'ē-əs) *adj.* Arousing pity **:** sad. **—pit'e•ous•ly** *adv.*

pit•fall (pĭt'fôl') *n.* **1.** A trap, esp. a concealed pit in the ground used for snaring animals. **2.** An unexpected difficulty or hidden danger.

pith (pĭth) *n.* **1.** *Bot.* The soft, spongelike tissue in the center of the stems and branches of many vascular plants. **2.** The central or essential part **:** essence.

pith•y (pĭth'ē) *adj.* **-i•er, -i•est. 1.** Of or like pith. **2.** Terse, cogent, and meaningful. **—pith'i•ly** *adv.* **—pith'i•ness** *n.*

pit•i•a•ble (pĭt'ē-ə-bəl) *adj.* Pitiful.

pit•i•ful (pĭt'ĭ-fəl) *adj.* **1.** Deserving or arousing pity <a *pitiful* orphan> **2.** Meriting contempt **:** contemptible <a *pitiful* salary> **—pit'i•ful•ly** *adv.*

pit•i•less (pĭt'ĭ-lĭs) *adj.* Without pity **:** merciless. **—pit'i•less•ly** *adv.* **—pit'i•less•ness** *n.*

pi•ton (pē'tŏn') *n.* A metal spike, often with an eye through which a rope can be passed, that can be driven into ice or rock as a support, as in mountain climbing.

pit•tance (pĭt'ns) *n.* A small portion or amount, as of money.

pit•ter-pat•ter (pĭt'ər-păt'ər) *n.* A rapid series of light sounds or taps. **—pit'ter-pat'ter** *v.*

pi•tu•i•tar•y (pĭ-to͞o'ĭ-tĕr'ē, -tyo͞o'-) *n., pl.* **-ies.** A small, oval endocrine gland situated at the base of the vertebrate brain. **—pi•tu'i•tar'y** *adj.*

pit viper *n.* A venomous snake of the family Crotalidae, as a rattlesnake or copperhead, with a small pit on each side of the head.

pit•y (pĭt'ē) *n., pl.* **-ies. 1.** A feeling of sorrow for another's misfortune **:** compassion. **2.** A regrettable fact or situation. ★ ***syns:*** COMMISERATION, COMPASSION, SYMPATHY —*v.* **-ied, -y•ing.** To feel pity for.

piv•ot (pĭv'ət) *n.* **1.** A shaft or rod on which something turns. **2.** One on which the direction, development, or effect of something else depends. —*v.* To swing or turn on or as if on a pivot. **—piv'ot•al** *adj.*

pix[1] (pĭks) *n. var. of* PYX.

pix[2] (pĭks) *n. var. pl. of* PIC.

pix•el (pĭk'səl, -sĕl') *n.* The smallest image-forming unit of a computer video display.

pix•y *also* **pix•ie** (pĭk'sē) *n., pl.* **-ies.** An elfin or mischievous creature.

piz•za (pēt'sə) *n.* An open pie consisting of a crust covered usu. with a spiced mixture, as of tomatoes and cheese, and baked.

piz•zazz *also* **pi•zazz** (pĭ-zăz') *n.* *Slang.* Zest **:** flair.

piz•ze•ri•a (pēt'sə-rē'ə) *n.* A place where pizzas are baked and sold.

piz•zi•ca•to (pĭt'sĭ-kä'tō) *adv.* *Mus.* By plucking rather than bowing. —Used as a direction. **—piz'zi•ca'to** *adj.*

pj's (pē'jāz') *pl.n.* *Informal.* Pajamas.

plac•ard (plăk'ärd', -ərd) *n.* A notice, esp. a poster for display in a public place. —*v.* **1.** To announce in or as if in a placard. **2.** To post placards on, in, or throughout.

pla•cate (plā'kāt', plăk'āt') *v.* **-cat•ed, -cat•ing.** To mollify, esp. by yielding concessions **:** appease. **—plac'a•ble** *adj.*

place (plās) *n.* **1.** An area **:** region. **2.** An area, as a building, set aside for a particular use or purpose. **3.** A particular location, as a population center. **4.** A public square in a city or town. **5.** A position of employment : job. **6.** The position occupied by a substitute : stead. **7.** A relative position in a sequence or series : standing. **8. a.** A residence. **b.** A seat <took her *place* at the table> —*v.* **placed, plac·ing. 1.** To put in a particular place or order : set. **2.** To recognize : identify <couldn't *place* his face> **3.** To rank in a sequence or order. **4.** To make : give <*place* an order> **5.** To finish in 2nd place or among the first 3 finishers in a competition, as a race.

pla·ce·bo (plə-sē'bō) *n., pl.* **-bos** *or* **-boes. 1.** A substance having no medication that is administered for its psychological effect on a patient. **2.** An inert substance used as a control in an experiment.

place kick *n. Football.* The kicking, as for a field goal, of a ball that is held or placed in a fixed position on the ground. —**place'-kick'** *v.*

place mat *n.* A mat for a single setting at a meal.

place·ment (plās'mənt) *n.* **1.** The act or an instance of placing. **2.** The business or function of finding positions, as employment, for applicants.

pla·cen·ta (plə-sĕn'tə) *n., pl.* **-tas** *or* **-tae** (-tē). The vascular, membranous structure that supplies a mammalian fetus with nourishment before its birth and to which the fetus is attached by the umbilical cord. —**pla·cen'tal** (-sĕn'tl) *adj.*

plac·er (plăs'ər) *n.* A deposit left by a glacier or river that contains particles of valuable minerals.

plac·id (plăs'ĭd) *adj.* Marked by calm, quiet, or composure : serene. —**pla·cid'i·ty** (plə-sĭd'ĭ-tē) *n.* —**plac'id·ly** *adv.*

plack·et (plăk'ĭt) *n.* A slit in a dress, blouse, or skirt.

pla·gia·rize (plā'jə-rīz') *v.* **-rized, -riz·ing.** To take and use as one's own the ideas or writings of another. —**pla'gia·rism** *n.* —**pla'gia·rist** *n.*

plague (plāg) *n.* **1.** An affliction : calamity. **2.** A cause of irritation : nuisance. **3.** An infectious and often fatal epidemic disease, esp. bubonic plague. —*v.* **plagued, plagu·ing. 1.** To afflict with or as if with calamity or disease. **2.** To harass : pester.

plaice (plās) *n., pl.* **plaice** *or* **plaic·es. 1.** An edible marine flatfish, *Pleuronectes platessa,* of W European waters. **2.** A related flatfish, *Hippoglossoides platessoides,* of North American Atlantic waters.

plaid (plăd) *n.* **1.** A rectangular piece of wool of a tartan pattern worn esp. over one shoulder by Scottish Highlanders. **2.** A fabric, esp. of wool, with a tartan pattern. **3.** A tartan pattern. —**plaid** *adj.*

plain (plān) *adj.* **1.** Free from obstructions : open <in *plain* sight> **2.** Easy to understand : clear. **3.** Not complicated : simple <*plain* food> **4.** Straightforward : candid <*plain* talk> **5.** Common : ordinary <just *plain* folks> **6.** Having little ornamentation : undecorated. **7.** Not beautiful : homely. —*n.* An extensive region of level, treeless land. —*adv.* In a plain manner. —**plain'ly** *adv.* —**plain'ness** *n.*

plain·clothes man (plān'klōz') *also* **plain·clothes·man** (plān'klōz'mən) *n.* A police officer who wears civilian clothes while on duty.

Plains Indian (plānz) *n.* A member of any of the American Indian peoples inhabiting the Great Plains of North America.

plain·spo·ken (plān'spō'kən) *adj.* Candid : straightforward.

plaint (plānt) *n.* **1.** A complaint. **2.** An utterance of sorrow or grief : lamentation.

plain·tiff (plān'tĭf) *n.* The party that files a complaint in a lawsuit.

plain·tive (plān'tĭv) *adj.* Expressive of sorrow or melancholy : woeful. —**plain'tive·ly** *adv.* —**plain'tive·ness** *n.*

plait (plāt, plăt) *n.* **1.** A braid, esp. of hair. **2.** A pleat. —**plait** *v.*

plan (plăn) *n.* **1.** A method or scheme for achieving or doing something. **2.** An aim : goal. **3.** A diagram or drawing prepared to scale. —*v.* **planned, plan·ning. 1.** To draw up a plan of : design <*planned* a new shopping mall> **2.** To have in mind : intend. **3.** To formulate a way to achieve or do. —**plan'ner** *n.*

pla·nar (plā'nər, -när') *adj.* **1.** Of or in a geometric plane. **2.** Flat <a *planar* surface> —**pla·nar'i·ty** (plā-năr'ĭ-tē) *n.*

plane[1] (plān) *n.* **1.** A surface containing all the straight lines required to connect any 2 points on it. **2.** A level or flat surface. **3.** A level of development or existence. **4.** An airplane. **5.** A supporting surface of an airplane.

plane[2] (plān) *n.* A tool for leveling or smoothing a wood surface. —*v.* **planed, plan·ing.** To level or smooth with or as if with a plane. —**plan'er** *n.*

plan·et (plăn'ĭt) *n.* A nonluminous celestial body illuminated by light from a star around which it revolves. —**plan'e·tar'y** (-ĭ-tĕr'ē) *adj.*

plan·e·tar·i·um (plăn'ĭ-târ'ē-əm) *n., pl.* **-ums** *or* **-i·a** (-ē-ə). **1.** A device to project images of celestial bodies in their courses, as onto the inner surface of a dome. **2.** A room or building containing a planetarium.

plane tree *n.* A tree of the genus *Platanus,* with ball-shaped clusters of fruit and outer bark that usu. flakes off in patches.

plan·gent (plăn'jənt) *adj.* **1.** Deep and reverberating in sound. **2.** Plaintive. —**plan'gen·cy** *n.* —**plan'gent·ly** *adv.*

plank (plăngk) *n.* **1.** A long, thick board. **2.** An item in a political platform. —*v.* **1.** To cover with planks. **2.** To cook and serve (meat or fish) on a board. **3.** To set or put down with force.

plank·ing (plăng'kĭng) *n.* **1.** Planks as a whole. **2.** Something made of planks.

plank·ton (plăngk'tən) *n.* Microscopic plant and animal organisms that float or drift in great numbers in bodies of water. —**plank·ton'ic** (-tŏn'ĭk) *adj.*

pla•no•con•cave (plā'nō-kŏn-kāv', -kŏn'-kāv') *adj.* Flat or plane on one side and concave on the other.

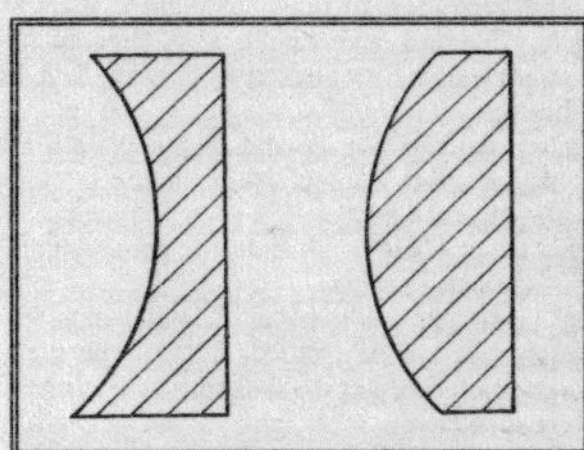
(Left) **planoconcave** *and* (right) **planoconvex**

pla•no•con•vex (plā'nō-kŏn-vĕks', -kŏn'-vĕks') *adj.* Flat or plane on one side and convex on the other.

plant (plănt) *n.* **1.** An organism typically having cellulose cell walls, manufacturing its own food by photosynthesis, and being incapable of locomotion. **2.** A soft-stemmed, herbaceous plant as distinguished from a tree or shrub. **3.** An establishment for industry or manufacturing **:** factory. **4.** The physical structures, equipment, and fixtures of an institution. —*v.* **1.** To place (e.g., seeds) in the ground for growing. **2.** To set firmly or forcibly in position. **3.** To start **:** establish. **4.** To instill <*plant* an idea> **5.** To place with intent to spy or deceive.

plan•tain[1] (plăn'tən) *n.* A weedy plant of the genus *Plantago,* esp. *P. major,* with a spike of small greenish flowers.

plan•tain[2] (plăn'tən) *n.* A large tropical plant, *Musa paradisiaca,* resembling the banana and bearing similar fruit.

plan•tar (plăn'tər, -tär') *adj.* Of, relating to, or located on the sole of the foot.

plan•ta•tion (plăn-tā'shən) *n.* **1.** A sizable group of trees or plants under cultivation. **2.** A large landed estate devoted to crop production, usu. by resident workers.

plant•er (plăn'tər) *n.* **1.** One that plants, esp. a sowing tool or machine. **2.** One who owns or manages a plantation. **3.** An ornamental container for a plant.

plaque (plăk) *n.* **1.** A flat piece often made of metal, ornamented or engraved for mounting, as on a building or memorial. **2.** An ornamental pin **:** brooch. **3.** A deposit that builds up on a tooth or the inner lining of a blood vessel.

plash (plăsh) *n.* **1.** A light splash. **2.** The sound of a plash. —**plash** *v.*

plas•ma (plăz'mə) *n.* **1.** The clear, liquid part of blood, lymph, or intramuscular fluid. **2.** The watery part of milk **:** whey. **3.** *Physics.* An electrically neutral, usu. hot gas composed of ions, electrons, and neutral particles. —**plas•mat'ic, plas'mic** *adj.*

plas•ter (plăs'tər) *n.* **1.** A paste that hardens while drying, used for covering walls and ceilings. **2.** Plaster of Paris. **3.** An often medicated pastelike mixture spread on a piece of material and applied to a part of the body. —*v.* To coat or cover with or as if with plaster. —**plas'ter•y** *adj.*

plas•ter•board (plăs'tər-bôrd', -bōrd') *n.* A wallboard made up of layers of fiberboard or paper over a plaster core.

plaster of Paris *n.* A quick-setting paste of white gypsum powder and water, used esp. for casts and statuary molds.

plas•tic (plăs'tĭk) *adj.* **1.** Capable of being shaped or molded **:** malleable. **2.** Of, marked by, or using expressive shaping or modeling <the *plastic* arts> **3.** Marked by artificiality **:** synthetic <the *plastic* world of advertising> —*n.* A synthetically produced material that can be molded and hardened into objects or formed into films or textile fibers. —**plas•tic'i•ty** (plă-stĭs'ĭ-tē) *n.* —**plas'ti•cize'** *v.*

plastic explosive *n.* A versatile explosive substance in the form of a moldable doughlike solid.

plastic surgery *n.* Surgery concerned with repairing, restoring, or remodeling bodily parts chiefly by bone or tissue transfer. —**plastic surgeon** *n.*

plas•tique (plă-stēk') *n.* A plastic explosive.

plate (plāt) *n.* **1.** A flat, thin piece of material, as metal. **2. a.** Forged, rolled, or cast metal in sheet form. **b.** A flat piece of engraved metal. **3. a.** A prepared surface, as of metal or plastic, from which printing is done. **b.** A print from such a surface. **c.** Something printed from an engraving. **4.** A sheet of glass or metal sensitized to light and used in photography. **5.** A part made of metal or plastic that is fitted to the gums to hold false teeth in place. **6.** *Baseball.* Home plate. **7.** A shallow, usu. circular dish. **8.** Food and service for one person. **9.** Household articles, as forks and knives, made of or plated with gold or silver. —*v.* **plat•ed, plat•ing. 1.** To cover with a thin layer of metal, esp. gold or silver. **2.** To make a printing surface from or for.

pla•teau (plă-tō') *n., pl.* **-teaus** *or* **-teaux** (-tōz'). **1.** A level expanse of elevated land. **2. a.** A stage of development. **b.** A stable period or state.

plate glass *n.* Rolled and polished glass in thick, strong sheets.

plat•en (plăt'n) *n.* **1.** A flat metal plate that holds the paper against the type in a printing press. **2.** The roller in a typewriter against which the keys hit.

plat•form (plăt'fôrm') *n.* **1.** An elevated horizontal surface, as for speakers or at a railroad station. **2.** A formal statement of principles or policy, as of a political party.

plat•ing (plā'tĭng) *n.* A thin layer, coating, or covering of metal or of metal plates.

plat•i•num (plăt'n-əm) *n.* *Symbol* **Pt** A silver-white, corrosive-resistant metallic element used esp. in jewelry.

plat•i•tude (plăt'ĭ-to͞od', -tyo͞od') *n.* A trite

and shallow idea or remark. **—plat'i•tu'di•nize'** *v.* **—plat'i•tu'di•nous** *adj.*
pla•ton•ic (plə-tŏn'ĭk, plā-) *adj.* Transcending sexual desire : purely intellectual or spiritual. **—pla•ton'i•cal•ly** *adv.*
pla•toon (plə-to͞on') *n.* **1.** A military unit usu. consisting of 2 or more squads. **2.** A group of players, esp. in football, acting as an offensive or defensive body.
plat•ter (plăt'ər) *n.* **1.** A large, shallow plate for serving food. **2.** *Slang.* A phonograph record.
plat•y•pus (plăt'ə-pəs) *n., pl.* **-es.** A semiaquatic, web-footed, egg-laying Australian mammal, *Ornithorhynchus anatinus*, with a snout resembling a duck's bill.
plau•dit (plô'dĭt) *n.* An act or expression of approval or praise.
plau•si•ble (plô'zə-bəl) *adj.* Appearing true, believable, or reasonable. **—plau'si•bil'i•ty** *n.* **—plau'si•bly** *adv.*
play (plā) *v.* **1.** To amuse oneself, as in recreation. **2.** To participate in (a game or sport). **3.** To do in jest <*play* a joke> **4.** To act frivolously or idly : trifle. **5.** To behave in a given way. **6.** To perform (a dramatic role). **7. a.** To perform on (an instrument). **b.** To perform (a piece). **8.** To be presented. **9.** To move lightly, rapidly, or sporadically. **10.** To make a pretense of being <*play* dead> **11.** To strive against in a game. **12. a.** To fill (a position) in a game. **b.** To use (e.g., a player or card) in a game. **13.** To perform (a role or part) in a process. **14. a.** To gamble. **b.** To make wagers on. **15.** To cause (e.g., a record or phonograph) to emit sounds. —*n.* **1. a.** A literary composition for the stage. **b.** The performance of a play. **2.** Recreational activity for pleasure, esp. the impulsive activity of children. **3.** Fun : jest. **4.** The act or manner of engaging in a game or sport. **5.** A way of operating. **6.** A maneuver in a game. **7.** Scope or freedom for action or use. **8.** Free motion, as of machinery. **—play ball.** To cooperate. **—play down.** To minimize the importance of. **—play up.** To give emphasis to. **—play'a•ble** *adj.* **—play'er** *n.*
pla•ya (plī'ə) *n.* A level area at the bottom of a desert basin that is at times covered with water.
play-act (plā'ăkt') *v.* **1.** To perform in a theatrical production. **2.** To make believe : pretend. **3.** To behave in an affected or insincere way. **—play'-act'ing** *n.*
play•back (plā'băk') *n.* The act or process of replaying a recording.
play•bill (plā'bĭl') *n.* An advertising poster for a play.
play•boy (plā'boi') *n.* A man devoted to the pursuit of pleasure.
player piano *n.* A mechanically operated piano using a punched paper roll to activate the keys.
play•ful (plā'fəl) *adj.* **1.** Full of high spirits : lively. **2.** Full of humor : jocular. **—play'ful•ly** *adv.* **—play'ful•ness** *n.*
play•girl (plā'gûrl') *n.* A woman devoted to the pursuit of pleasure.
play•go•er (plā'gō'ər) *n.* One who frequently goes to see plays.
play•ground (plā'ground') *n.* An area set aside for outdoor play and recreation, esp. for children.
play•house (plā'hous'). **1.** A theater. **2.** A small house for children to play in. **3.** A doll house.
playing card *n.* A card of a specified rank and suit that belongs to a deck and is used in playing card games.
playing field *n.* A field for games such as cricket and soccer.
play•mate (plā'māt') *n.* A friend in play.
play-off (plā'ôf', -ŏf') *n.* A sports contest or series of contests to determine a winner or championship.
play•pen (plā'pĕn') *n.* A portable enclosure in which a baby or small child can be left to play.
play•thing (plā'thĭng') *n.* A toy.
play•wright (plā'rīt') *n.* One who writes plays : dramatist.
pla•za (plä'zə, plăz'ə) *n.* **1.** An open area, esp. a public square, in a town or city. **2.** A shopping center or mall.
plea (plē) *n.* **1.** An appeal or urgent request. **2.** An explanation by way of defense or excuse : pretext. **3.** *Law.* A defendant's answer to a charge or indictment.
plea-bar•gain (plē'bär'gən) *v.* To make a pretrial agreement to plead guilty to a lesser charge if a more serious one is dropped. **—plea'-bar'gain•ing** *n.*
plead (plēd) *v.* **plead•ed** *or* **pled** (plĕd), **plead•ing.** **1.** To appeal fervently : entreat. **2.** To make an argument for or against something, as in a court. **3.** To give as an excuse <*plead* fatigue> **4.** *Law.* To put forward a formal plea of <*plead* not guilty> **5.** To present or argue (a case) before a court. **—plead'a•ble** *adj.*
pleas•ant (plĕz'ənt) *adj.* **1.** Affording pleasure : very agreeable. **2.** Pleasing in manner or appearance : amiable. **—pleas'ant•ly** *adv.* **—pleas'ant•ness** *n.*
pleas•ant•ry (plĕz'ən-trē) *n., pl.* **-ries.** **1.** An entertaining or humorous act or remark. **2.** An amiable social remark.
please (plēz) *v.* **pleased, pleas•ing.** **1.** To make happy or satisfied. **2.** To be the wish or will of <May it *please* the tribunal.> **3.** To be willing or disposed to <*Please* sit down.> **4.** To wish or prefer <We do as we *please.*> **—pleas'er** *n.*
pleas•ur•a•ble (plĕzh'ər-ə-bəl) *adj.* Giving pleasure : agreeable or gratifying. **—pleas'ur•a•bly** *adv.*
pleas•ure (plĕzh'ər) *n.* **1.** A feeling of enjoyment or satisfaction. **2.** Something that gives enjoyment. **3.** One's choice, wish, or preference.
pleat (plēt) *n.* A fold in fabric made by doubling the cloth back and stitching it down. **—pleat** *v.*
plebe (plēb) *n.* A 1st-year student at a military academy.

ple•be•ian (plĭ-bē'ən) *adj.* Vulgar : crude. —*n.* **1.** One of the common people. **2.** One who is considered vulgar or coarse.
pleb•i•scite (plĕb'ĭ-sīt') *n.* A direct vote by an electorate on an important issue or proposal.
plebs (plĕbz) *n., pl.* **ple•bes** (plē'bēz'). **1.** The commoners of ancient Rome. **2.** The common people : the masses.
plec•trum (plĕk'trəm) *n., pl.* **-trums** *or* **-tra** (-trə). A small, thin piece, as of metal or plastic, used to pluck the strings of an instrument, as a guitar.
pled (plĕd) *v. var. p.t. & p.p. of* PLEAD.
pledge (plĕj) *n.* **1.** A solemn vow or promise. **2.** Something given or held as security for the fulfillment of a debt or an obligation. **3.** One who has promised to join a fraternity. —*v.* **pledged, pledg•ing. 1.** To vow or promise solemnly. **2.** To put under obligation or commitment by or as if by a pledge. **3.** To give as security.
ple•na•ry (plē'nə-rē, plĕn'ə-) *adj.* **1.** Complete : full. **2.** Including all members qualified to attend. —**ple'na•ri•ly** *adv.*
plen•i•po•ten•ti•ar•y (plĕn'ə-pə-tĕn'shē-ĕr'ē, -shə-rē) *n., pl.* **-ies.** A diplomat given full authority to act for a government. —**plen'i•po•ten'ti•ar'y** *adj.*
plen•i•tude (plĕn'ĭ-to͞od', -tyo͞od') *n.* The quality or state of being full or abundant.
plen•te•ous (plĕn'tē-əs) *adj.* Plentiful. —**plen'te•ous•ness** *n.*
plen•ti•ful (plĕn'tĭ-fəl) *adj.* **1.** Existing in great abundance. **2.** Having or producing an abundance. —**plen'ti•ful•ly** *adv.* —**plen'ti•ful•ness** *n.*
plen•ty (plĕn'tē) *n.* **1.** An ample amount or supply. **2.** Abundance or prosperity.
ple•num (plē'nəm, plĕn'əm) *n., pl.* **ple•nums** *or* **ple•na** (plē'nə, plĕn'ə). **1.** An enclosure in which the air is at a pressure greater than that outside the enclosure. **2.** An assembly attended by all members.
pleth•o•ra (plĕth'ər-ə) *n.* An excess.
pleu•ra (plo͝or'ə) *n., pl.* **pleu•rae** (plo͝or'ē). Either of 2 membranous sacs lining the thoracic cavity and enveloping the lungs. —**pleu'ral** *adj.*
pleu•ri•sy (plo͝or'ĭ-sē) *n.* Inflammation of the pleura. —**pleu•rit'ic** (-rĭt'ĭk) *adj.*
Plex•i•glas (plĕk'sĭ-glăs'). A trademark for a strong, transparent thermoplastic.
plex•us (plĕk'səs) *n., pl.* **-us** *or* **-us•es.** An intertwining network, as of nerves or blood vessels.
pli•a•ble (plī'ə-bəl) *adj.* **1.** Flexible : pliant. **2.** Easily influenced by others. —**pli'a•bil'i•ty, pli'a•ble•ness** *n.* —**pli'a•bly** *adv.*
pli•ant (plī'ənt) *adj.* **1.** Flexible : pliable. **2.** Readily adaptable to change. —**pli'an•cy** *n.* —**pli'ant•ly** *adv.*
pli•ers (plī'ərz) *pl.n.* (*sing. or pl. in number*). A pincerslike tool for bending, cutting, or holding.
plight[1] (plīt) *n.* A condition or situation, esp. a distressing one.
plight[2] (plīt) *v.* To bind or promise by a pledge, esp. to promise to marry.
plink (plĭngk) *v.* To make or cause to make a metallic clinking sound.
plinth (plĭnth) *n.* A block or slab at the base of a column.
plod (plŏd) *v.* **plod•ded, plod•ding. 1.** To walk or proceed in or as if in a slow, heavy-footed way. **2.** To work doggedly or laboriously. —**plod'der** *n.* —**plod'ding•ly** *adv.*
plop (plŏp) *v.* **plopped, plop•ping. 1.** To fall or move with a sound resembling that of an object dropping into water. **2.** To drop or allow to drop heavily.
plot (plŏt) *n.* **1.** A small piece of ground <a garden *plot*> **2.** The series of actions or events of a literary work, as a novel. **3.** A secret, esp. illicit plan. ★ ***syns:*** COLLUSION, CONSPIRACY, INTRIGUE, MACHINATION, SCHEME —*v.* **plot•ted, plot•ting. 1.** To mark, note, or represent, as on a chart or map. **2.** To plan or scheme secretly : intrigue. —**plot'ter** *n.*
plough (plou) *n. & v. esp. Brit. var. of* PLOW.
plov•er (plŭv'ər, plō'vər) *n., pl.* **-ers** *or* **-er.** Any of various widely distributed wading birds of the family Charadriidae, with rounded bodies, short bills, and short tails.

plover

plow (plou) *n.* **1.** An implement used for breaking up, turning over, and cutting soil. **2.** An implement functioning like a plow, esp. a snowplow. —*v.* **1.** To break up, turn over, and cut (soil) with a plow. **2.** To remove snow (from) with a snowplow. **3.** To move or advance forcefully or laboriously. —**plow back.** To put (earned profits) back into one's business. —**plow'a•ble** *adj.* —**plow'er** *n.*
plow•share (plou'shâr') *n.* The cutting part of a plow.
ploy (ploi) *n.* A maneuver or scheme to outwit an opponent.
pluck (plŭk) *v.* **1.** To remove by pulling off or out : pick. **2.** To pull (e.g., hair or feathers) from. **3.** To pull at and release (the strings of an instrument) —*n.* **1.** The act of plucking. **2.** Courage and fortitude : spirit. —**pluck'er** *n.*
pluck•y (plŭk'ē) *adj.* **-i•er, -i•est.** Marked by spirit and courage. —**pluck'i•ly** *adv.* —**pluck'i•ness** *n.*
plug (plŭg) *n.* **1.** A device used to close an

opening. **2. a.** A fitting, usu. with metal prongs, attached to a cord and used in a socket to make an electrical connection. **b.** A spark plug. **3.** A fireplug. **4.** A cake of chewing tobacco. **5.** *Slang.* An inferior or worn-out horse. **6.** *Informal.* An instance of favorable publicity or free advertising. —*v.* **plugged, plug•ging. 1.** To stop up tightly with or as if with a plug. **2.** To connect or disconnect by means of a plug. **3.** *Slang.* To shoot with a bullet. **4.** *Informal.* To publicize or advertise favorably or insistently. **5.** *Informal.* To work persistently. —**plug'ger** *n.*

plum (plŭm) *n.* **1.** A shrub or small tree of the genus *Prunus,* bearing smooth-skinned, fleshy, edible fruit with a single hard-shelled pit. **2.** Something considered very desirable, as a prestigious job.

plum•age (plo͞o'mĭj) *n.* **1.** The feathers of a bird. **2.** Finery.

plumb (plŭm) *n.* A weight on the end of a line used to measure depth or test vertical alignment. —*adj.* **1.** Precisely vertical. **2.** *Informal.* Thorough **:** downright. —*adv.* **1.** Straight up and down. **2.** Thoroughly **:** completely. —*v.* To test the alignment or depth of with or as if with a plumb.

plumb•er (plŭm'ər) *n.* One who fits and repairs plumbing pipes and equipment.

plumb•ing (plŭm'ĭng) *n.* **1.** The equipment, as pipes and fixtures, of a water, gas, or sewage system. **2.** The activities or business of a plumber.

plume (plo͞om) *n.* A feather, esp. a large and showy one used for decoration. —*v.* **plumed, plum•ing. 1.** To adorn with or as if with feathers. **2.** To permit (oneself) to feel or show pride or satisfaction. —**plumed** *adj.* —**plum'y** *adj.*

plum•met (plŭm'ĭt) *v.* To fall or plunge straight downward.

plump¹ (plŭmp) *adj.* Having a full, rounded shape. —*v.* To make or become rounded and full. —**plump'ish** *adj.* —**plump'ly** *adv.* —**plump'ness** *n.*

plump² (plŭmp) *v.* **1.** To throw or drop down heavily or suddenly. **2.** To support someone or something strongly. —*n.* **1.** A heavy or sudden fall. **2.** The sound of a plump. —*adv.* **1.** Heavily or abruptly. **2.** Straight down or straight ahead. **3.** Without reservations **:** wholeheartedly.

plun•der (plŭn'dər) *v.* To deprive of goods or property forcibly and unlawfully **:** pillage. —*n.* Seized or stolen property or goods. —**plun'der•er** *n.*

plunge (plŭnj) *v.* **plunged, plung•ing. 1. a.** To cast oneself into or as if into water. **b.** To immerse or submerse. **2.** To enter or cause to enter abruptly into a specified state or activity. **3.** To fall or descend steeply or sharply **4.** To move swiftly or forcefully downward or forward. **5.** To gamble rashly. —**plunge** *n.*

plung•er (plŭn'jər) *n.* **1.** A machine part, as a piston, that works with a repeated plunging movement. **2.** A rubber suction cup on a handle that is used to clean out clogged drains and pipes.

plunk (plŭngk) *v. Informal.* **1.** To put down or drop heavily or suddenly. **2.** To make or cause to make a hollow, twanging sound. —**plunk** *n.* —**plunk'er** *n.*

plu•per•fect (plo͞o-pûr'fĭkt) *adj.* Of, relating to, or constituting a verb that designates an action or state completed before a specified or implied time in the past. —**plu•per'fect** *n.*

plu•ral (plo͝or'əl) *adj.* Of, relating to, or constituting a word form that designates more than one. —**plu'ral** *n.*

plu•ral•ism (plo͝or'ə-lĭz'əm) *n.* A condition of society in which numerous distinct ethnic, religious, or cultural groups coexist within one nation. —**plu'ral•ist** *n.* —**plu'-ral•is'tic** *adj.*

plu•ral•i•ty (plo͞o-răl'ĭ-tē) *n., pl.* **-ties. 1.** The condition of being plural. **2.** The number of votes cast for a winning candidate if this number is less than a majority but more than that cast for any other candidate. **3.** The excess of votes cast for a winner over the closest opposing candidate.

plu•ral•ize (plo͝or'ə-līz') *v.* **ized, -iz•ing.** To make plural. —**plu'ral•i•za'tion** *n.*

plus (plŭs) *prep.* **1.** Increased by <2 *plus* 2 equals 4> **2.** Along with **:** in addition to <has brains *plus* looks> —*adj.* **1.** Of or relating to addition. **2.** Greater than zero, as on a scale **:** positive. **3.** Added or extra. **4.** Slightly better than <a grade of C *plus*> —*n.* **1. a.** A symbol (+) designating addition. **b.** A positive number. **2.** Something added. **3.** A favorable factor **:** advantage.

plush (plŭsh) *n.* A velvetlike fabric with a soft, thick pile. —*adj.* Luxurious **:** elegant. —**plush'i•ly** *adv.* —**plush'i•ness** *n.* —**plush'ly** *adv.* —**plush'y** *adj.*

Plu•to (plo͞o'tō) *n.* The 9th and outermost planet from the sun.

plu•toc•ra•cy (plo͞o-tŏk'rə-sē) *n., pl.* **-cies. 1.** Governmental control by the wealthy. **2.** A governing group of wealthy people. —**plu'to•crat'** (-tə-krăt') *n.* —**plu'to•crat'ic** *adj.*

plu•ton (plo͞o'tŏn') *n.* Igneous rock formed beneath the surface of the earth. —**plu•ton'-ic** *adj.*

plu•to•ni•um (plo͞o-tō'nē-əm) *n. Symbol* **Pu** A radioactive, silvery metallic element used esp. in nuclear weapons.

plu•vi•al (plo͞o'vē-əl) *adj.* **1.** Of or relating to rain. **2.** Marked by abundant rain.

ply¹ (plī) *v.* **plied, ply•ing. 1.** To mold or twist together. **2.** To fold or double over (e.g., cloth). —*n., pl.* **plies. 1.** A layer or thickness, as of folded cloth or plywood. **2.** One of the twisted strands constituting yarn, rope, or thread.

ply² (plī) *v.* **plied, ply•ing. 1.** To use or wield (a tool). **2.** To perform (e.g., a trade) regularly. **3.** To traverse (a route or course) regularly. **4.** To keep supplying or presenting <*plied* us with tidbits>

Plym•outh Rock (plĭm'əth) *n.* An American breed of medium-sized domestic fowl raised for both meat and eggs.

Plymouth Rock

ply•wood (plī'wŏŏd') *n.* A construction material made of thin layers of wood glued and pressed together.

Pm *symbol for* PROMETHIUM.

pneu•mat•ic (nōō-măt'ĭk, nyōō-) *adj.* **1.** Of or relating to air or another gas. **2.** Filled with or operated by compressed air <a *pneumatic* tire><a *pneumatic* drill> **—pneu•mat'i•cal•ly** *adv.*

pneu•mo•co•ni•o•sis (nōō'mō-kō'nē-ō'sĭs, nyōō'-) *n.* A lung disease caused by prolonged inhalation of metallic or mineral dusts.

pneu•mo•nia (nōō-mōn'yə, nyōō-) *n.* An acute or chronic inflammatory disease of the lungs caused by viruses, bacteria, chemicals, or irritation. **—pneu•mon'ic** (-mŏn'ĭk) *adj.*

Po *symbol for* POLONIUM.

poach¹ (pōch) *v.* To cook in liquid below or just at the boiling point. **—poach'er** *n.*

poach² (pōch) *v.* To hunt or fish unlawfully, esp. by trespassing on private property. **—poach'er** *n.*

pock (pŏk) *n.* **1.** A pus-filled swelling of the skin caused by an eruptive disease, as smallpox. **2.** A pockmark.

pock•et (pŏk'ĭt) *n.* **1.** A pouch with an open top or side stitched into or onto a garment and used esp. for carrying small items. **2.** Something resembling a pocket in appearance or function. **3.** Monetary supply <out of *pocket*> **4.** A small area or group set apart from others. *—adj.* **1.** Of a size that fits in a pocket. **2.** Very small **:** miniature. *—v.* **1.** To deposit in or as if in a pocket. **2.** To take (e.g., money) illicitly. **—pock'et•ful'** *n.*

pock•et•book (pŏk'ĭt-bŏŏk') *n.* **1.** A wallet. **2.** A handbag. **3.** Supply of money.

pocket bread *n.* Pita.

pock•et•knife (pŏk'ĭt-nīf') *n.* A small knife with a folding blade.

pocket veto *n.* An indirect veto of a legislative bill by an executive through retention of the unsigned bill until the legislature has adjourned.

pock•mark (pŏk'märk') *n.* A scar left on the skin by an eruptive disease, as smallpox. **—pock'marked'** *adj.*

po•co (pō'kō) *adv. Mus.* A little. —Used as a direction.

†po•co•sin (pə-kō'sĭn) *n. SE U.S.* A swamp in an upland coastal region.

pod¹ (pŏd) *n.* **1.** *Bot.* A seed casing, as of a pea or bean, that splits open to release the enclosed seeds. **2.** An external housing, as for a jet engine or fuel, on an aircraft. **3.** A detachable compartment in a spacecraft for personnel or instruments.

pod² (pŏd) *n.* A school of marine mammals, such as seals or whales.

po•di•a•try (pə-dī'ə-trē) *n.* The professional study, care, and treatment of the feet. **—po•di'a•trist** *n.*

po•di•um (pō'dē-əm) *n., pl.* **-di•a** (-dē-ə) *or* **-ums. 1.** A raised platform for an orchestra conductor. **2.** A reading stand for a lecturer or public speaker.

po•em (pō'əm) *n.* A composition, usu. in verse, marked by language chosen esp. for its sound, beauty, and evocative power.

po•e•sy (pō'ĭ-zē, -sē) *n.* Poetry.

po•et (pō'ĭt) *n.* **1.** A writer of poetry. **2.** One having the power of lyrical expression.

po•et•as•ter (pō'ĭ-tăs'tər) *n.* A writer of inferior poems.

po•et•ess (pō'ĭ-tĭs) *n.* A woman who writes poems.

po•et•ic (pō-ĕt'ĭk) *or* **po•et•i•cal** (-ĭ-kəl) *adj.* **1.** Of or characteristic of poetry or poets. **2.** Written in verse. **3.** Highly fanciful or idealized. **—po•et'i•cal•ly** *adv.*

poetic justice *n.* An often ironically appropriate outcome in which wrongdoing is punished and virtue rewarded.

poetic license *n.* Artistic deviation from conventional form or fact to achieve a certain effect.

poet laureate *n., pl.* **poets laureate** *or* **poet laureates.** A poet appointed by the British monarch as chief poet of the kingdom for life.

po•et•ry (pō'ĭ-trē) *n.* **1.** The art or works of a poet. **2.** Writing in metrical verse.

po•grom (pə-grŭm', -grŏm', pō'grəm) *n.* An organized persecution or massacre, esp. of Jews.

poi (poi, pō'ē) *n.* A pastelike, often fermented Hawaiian food made from cooked taro root.

poign•ant (poin'yənt) *adj.* **1.** Emotionally painful or distressing. **2.** Deeply affecting **:** touching. **—poign'ance, poign'an•cy** *n.* **—poign'ant•ly** *adv.*

poin•ci•an•a (poin'sē-ăn'ə, -ä'nə) *n.* An ornamental tropical tree of the genus *Poinciana,* with large red or orange flowers.

poin•set•ti•a (poin-sĕt'ē-ə, -sĕt'ə) *n.* A tropical American shrub, *Euphorbia pulcherrima,* bearing usu. scarlet bracts around small yellow or greenish flowers.

point (point) *n.* **1.** A sharp or tapered end **:** tip. **2.** A tapering piece of land extending into water. **3.** A geometric object having no dimensions and no property other than location. **4.** A certain place or location. **5.** A given degree, stage, or condition. **6.** A definite moment in time. **7.** An important or essential factor, part, or idea. **8.** A purpose, objective, or reason. **9.** A separate item, element, or detail. **10.** A distinguishing quality or feature. **11.** A single unit, as in counting, measuring, or evaluating. **12. a.** A punctuation mark indicating a full stop. **b.** A decimal point. **13.** One of the 32 direction marks on a compass. —*v.* **1.** To aim : direct. **2.** To call attention to. **3.** To indicate the direction or position of, esp. by using the finger. **4.** To emphasize : stress. **5.** To be turned or directed. **—beside the point.** Not pertinent. **—to the point.** Pertinent.

point•blank (point′blăngk′) *adj.* **1.** Aimed straight at or being close to a mark or target. **2.** Forthright. —*adv.* **1.** With a direct aim. **2.** Without hesitating.

point•ed (poin′tĭd) *adj.* **1.** Having a sharp or tapered end. **2.** To the point : incisive. **3.** Clearly aimed at a particular person or group. **4.** Clearly evident : marked. **—point′ed•ly** *adv.* **—point′ed•ness** *n.*

point•er (poin′tər) *n.* **1.** A marker or device that indicates a number, as on a watch. **2.** A long, slender rod for pointing to a chart or blackboard. **3.** A hunting dog with a short-haired smooth coat. **4.** A helpful hint. **5.** *Computer Sci.* A word that directs the user to a core storage location.

poin•til•lism (point′tl-ĭz′əm, pwăn′-) *n.* A theory or technique of applying small strokes or dots of paint to a canvas so that they blend together when viewed from a distance. **—poin′til•list** *n. & adj.*

point•less (point′lĭs) *adj.* Devoid of meaning or purpose. **—point′less•ly** *adv.*

point of no return *n.* A crucial point, as in an action, beyond which return or reversal is no longer possible.

point of view *n.* **1.** A position from which things are considered. **2.** One's way of viewing things.

poise (poiz) *v.* **poised, pois•ing.** To bring into or be maintained in equilibrium : balance. —*n.* **1.** Balance : equilibrium. **2. a.** Composure. **b.** Bearing : carriage.

poi•son (poi′zən) *n.* A substance that causes injury, illness, or death, esp. by chemical means. —*v.* **1.** To kill or injure with poison. **2.** To put poison on or into. **3.** To have a destructive influence on : corrupt. **—poi′son•er** *n.* **—poi′son•ous** *adj.*

poison ivy *n.* A North American shrub or vine, *Rhus radicans,* bearing greenish flowers, whitish berries, and shiny trifoliate leaflets that cause a skin rash on contact.

poison oak *n.* A North American shrub, *Rhus toxicodendron* or *R. diversiloba,* related to poison ivy and causing a similar skin rash.

poison sumac *n.* A swamp shrub, *Rhus vernix,* of the SE U.S., with greenish-white berries and compound leaves that cause a skin rash similar to that caused by the related poison ivy.

poke (pōk) *v.* **poked, pok•ing.** **1.** To push or prod, as with an implement or finger. **2.** To make by or as if by poking. **3.** To thrust forward : stick out. **4.** To snoop or intrude. **5.** To rummage in a leisurely way. **6.** To proceed slowly. —*n.* A quick push, thrust, or jab.

pok•er[1] (pō′kər) *n.* A metal stick or bar for stirring a fire.

pok•er[2] (pō′kər) *n.* A card game played by 2 or more players who bet on the value of their hands in order to win a pool.

poker face *n.* An expressionless face, as that of an expert poker player. **—pok′er•faced′** *adj.*

poke•weed (pōk′wēd′) *n.* A North American plant, *Phytolacca americana,* with blackish-red berries, small white flowers, and a poisonous root.

pok•y *also* **poke•y** (pō′kē) *adj.* **-i•er, -i•est.** *Informal.* **1.** Irritatingly slow. **2.** Lacking adequate space.

pol (pôl) *n. Informal.* A politician.

po•lar (pō′lər) *adj.* **1.** Of or measured in relation to a pole, as of a magnet or sphere. **2.** Of or situated near the North or South Pole. **3.** Completely opposite.

polar bear *n.* A large white-furred bear, *Thalarctos maritimus,* of Arctic regions.

Po•lar•is (pō-lăr′ĭs, -lâr′-) *n.* A bright star near the N celestial pole, at the tip of Ursa Minor.

po•lar•i•ty (pō-lăr′ĭ-tē, -lâr′-) *n., pl.* **-ties.** **1.** Basic division or separation into opposing or contrary types, esp. of a physical property <magnetic *polarity*> **2.** The demonstration of 2 contrary tendencies. **3.** A designated polar extreme.

po•lar•ize (pō′lə-rīz′) *v.* **-ized, -iz•ing.** **1.** To cause polarity in. **2.** To set at opposite extremes. **3.** To acquire polarity : become polarized. **4.** To cause (light or radiation waves) to oscillate in a definite way. **—po′lar•i•za′tion** *n.*

pole[1] (pōl) *n.* **1.** Either extremity of an axis through a sphere, as the earth. **2.** Either of the earth's geographic poles. **3.** Either of 2 regions in a magnet at which the magnetism is concentrated. **4.** Either of a pair of oppositely charged electric terminals. **5.** Either of 2 forces in opposition.

pole[2] (pōl) *n.* **1.** A long, slender rod. **2.** An upright post. —*v.* **poled, pol•ing.** **1.** To push or move along (e.g., a boat) with a pole. **2.** To use poles in skiing.

pole•ax *or* **pole•axe** (pōl′ăks′) *n.* A medieval battle-ax consisting of an ax and hammer combination on a long pole.

pole•cat (pōl′kăt′) *n.* **1.** A carnivorous Old World mammal, *Mustela putorius,* with dark fur. **2.** A skunk.

po•lem•ic (pə-lĕm′ĭk) *n.* **1.** A verbal attack, esp. on opposing doctrines or opinions : controversy. **2. polemics** *(sing. or pl. in number).* The art or practice of controversy or debate. **—po•lem′ic, po•lem′i•cal** *adj.* **—po•lem′i•cist** *n.*

pole•star (pōl′stär′) *n.* **1.** The North Star. **2.** A guiding or determining principle.

pole vault *n.* An athletic contest in which each participant uses a long pole to vault over a high crossbar. —**pole′-vault′** *v.* —**pole′-vault′er** *n.*

po•lice (pə-lēs′) *n., pl.* **-lice. 1. a.** A division of government organized for maintenance of law and order and the prevention and investigation of crime. **b.** *(pl. in number).* The members of such a governmental division. **2.** An organized group functioning like a police force. **3.** Soldiers detailed to perform a specified task, as cleaning. —*v.* **-liced, -lic•ing. 1.** To guard or patrol, esp. to maintain order or enforce the law. **2.** To make (e.g., a military area) neat or clean.

po•lice•man (pə-lēs′mən) *n.* A member of a police force.

police state *n.* A repressive totalitarian political state utilizing a secret police force.

po•lice•wom•an (pə-lēs′wo͝om′ən) *n.* A woman who is a member of a police force.

pol•i•cy[1] (pŏl′ĭ-sē) *n., pl.* **-cies. 1.** A principle or course of action chosen to guide decision making. **2.** Prudent management.

pol•i•cy[2] (pŏl′ĭ-sē) *n., pl.* **-cies.** A written insurance contract.

pol•i•cy•hold•er (pŏl′ĭ-sē-hōl′dər) *n.* A holder of an insurance policy.

po•li•o (pō′lē-ō′) *n.* Poliomyelitis.

po•li•o•my•e•li•tis (pō′lē-ō-mī′ə-lī′tĭs) *n.* A contagious viral disease, esp. of children, that attacks the central nervous system and can result in paralysis.

pol•ish (pŏl′ĭsh) *v.* **1.** To make or become smooth and shiny, as by rubbing or chemical action. **2.** To develop or refine to a high degree. —*n.* **1.** A smooth, shiny surface : sheen. **2.** A substance used for polishing. **3.** Refinement of style or manners. —**polish off.** *Informal.* To finish or get rid of quickly. —**pol′ish•er** *n.*

pol•it•bu•ro (pŏl′ĭt-byo͝or′ō, pə-lĭt′-) *n.* A Communist Party executive committee that determines policy.

po•lite (pə-līt′) *adj.* **-lit•er, -lit•est. 1.** Marked by good manners and tactful behavior : courteous. **2.** Refined : urbane. —**po•lite′ly** *adv.* —**po•lite′ness** *n.*

pol•i•tesse (pŏl′ĭ-tĕs′, pô′lĭ-) *n.* Formal courtesy : decorum.

pol•i•tic (pŏl′ĭ-tĭk) *adj.* **1.** Wisely discerning, as in matters of policy. **2.** Shrewdly expedient. —**pol′i•tic•ly** *adv.*

po•lit•i•cal (pə-lĭt′ĭ-kəl) *adj.* **1.** Of or concerning the structure or affairs of government. **2.** Of or concerning politics, political parties, or politicians. —**po•lit′i•cal•ly** *adv.* —**po•lit′i•cize′** (-sīz′) *v.*

political action committee *n.* A committee formed by special-interest groups to raise money and make contributions to the campaigns of selected political candidates.

political science *n.* The study of government and political institutions. —**political scientist** *n.*

pol•i•ti•cian (pŏl′ĭ-tĭsh′ən) *n.* A person active in government or politics, esp. one holding a political office.

pol•i•tick (pŏl′ĭ-tĭk′) *v.* To engage in political discussion or campaigning.

po•lit•i•co (pə-lĭt′ĭ-kō′) *n., pl.* **-cos.** A politician.

pol•i•tics (pŏl′ĭ-tĭks′) *n.* **1.** *(sing. in number).* The art or science of government. **2.** *(sing. in number).* The policies, activities, and methods of a government or political party. **3.** *(pl. in number).* Factional intrigue or competition, as in a company. **4.** *(pl. in number).* One's general political standpoint.

pol•i•ty (pŏl′ĭ-tē) *n., pl.* **-ties. 1.** A political unit, as a nation or state. **2.** The form of government of a polity.

pol•ka (pōl′kə, pō′kə) *n.* **1.** A spirited dance of C European orig. **2.** Music for the polka. —**pol′ka** *v.*

poll (pōl) *n.* **1. a.** The casting and recording of votes in an election. **b.** The total votes cast or recorded. **c.** *often* **polls.** The place where votes are cast and counted. **2.** A public survey on a given issue. **3.** The head. —*v.* **1. a.** To receive (votes) in an election. **b.** To record the votes of. **2.** To question in a public survey. **3.** To clip a part of (an animal or plant). —**poll′er** *n.*

pol•len (pŏl′ən) *n.* Dustlike, usu. yellow grains containing the male reproductive cells of flowering plants.

pol•li•nate (pŏl′ə-nāt′) *v.* **-nat•ed, -nat•ing.** To fertilize by carrying pollen to the female part of (a plant). —**pol′li•na′tion** *n.* —**pol′li•na′tor** *n.*

pol•li•no•sis (pŏl′ə-nō′sĭs) *n.* Hay fever.

pol•li•wog *also* **pol•ly•wog** (pŏl′ē-wŏg′, -wôg′) *n.* A tadpole.

pol•lock *also* **pol•lack** (pŏl′ək) *n., pl.* **-lock** *or* **-locks** *also* **-lack** *or* **-lacks.** A marine food fish, *Pollachius virens,* of N Atlantic waters.

poll•ster (pōl′stər) *n.* One who takes or analyzes the results of public-opinion polls.

poll tax *n.* A fixed tax levied on persons, esp. as a requirement for voting.

pol•lute (pə-lo͞ot′) *v.* **-lut•ed, -lut•ing. 1.** To make unfit for or harmful to living things, esp. by the addition of waste substances. **2.** To render impure : corrupt. —**pol•lut′ant** *n.* —**pol•lut′er** *n.* —**pol•lu′tion** *n.*

po•lo (pō′lō) *n.* A game in which players on horseback try to drive a wooden ball through the opposing team's goal with long-handled mallets. —**po′lo•ist** *n.*

pol•o•naise (pŏl′ə-nāz′, pō′lə-) *n.* **1.** A Polish dance in which couples formally promenade in 3/4 time. **2.** Music for or in the style of the polonaise.

po•lo•ni•um (pə-lō′nē-əm) *n. Symbol* **Po** A naturally radioactive metallic element produced by the disintegration of radium.

pol•ter•geist (pōl′tər-gīst′) *n.* A mischievous ghost, esp. one that makes mysterious noises.

pol•troon (pŏl-tro͞on′) *n. Archaic.* An utter coward. —**pol•troon′er•y** *n.*

pol•y•an•dry (pŏl′ē-ăn′drē) *n.* The practice of having more than one husband at a time. —**pol′y•an′drous** *adj.*

pol•y•clin•ic (pŏl′ĭ-klĭn′ĭk) *n.* A clinic or hospital for a wide variety of illnesses.
pol•y•es•ter (pŏl′ē-ĕs′tər) *n.* A lightweight, strong, water-resistant synthetic resin used esp. in plastics and fibers.
pol•y•eth•yl•ene (pŏl′ē-ĕth′ə-lēn′) *n.* A lightweight, water-resistant thermoplastic resin used esp. in film or sheets for packaging and molded products.
po•lyg•a•my (pə-lĭg′ə-mē) *n.* The practice of having more than one husband or wife at a time. **—po•lyg′a•mist** *n.* **—po•lyg′a•mous** *adj.*
pol•y•glot (pŏl′ĭ-glŏt′) *adj.* **1.** Speaking, reading, or writing several languages. **2.** Written in or composed of several languages. **—pol′-y•glot′** *n.*
pol•y•gon (pŏl′ĭ-gŏn′) *n.* A flat, closed geometric figure bounded by 3 or more straight lines. **—po•lyg′o•nal** (pə-lĭg′ə-nəl) *adj.*
pol•y•graph (pŏl′ĭ-grăf′) *n.* An instrument that records fluctuations in physiological processes, as heartbeat and blood pressure, used esp. as a lie detector. **—pol′y•graph′ic** *adj.*
po•lyg•y•ny (pə-lĭj′ə-nē) *n.* The practice of having more than one wife at a time. **—po•lyg′y•nous** *adj.*
pol•y•he•dron (pŏl′ĭ-hē′drən) *n., pl.* **-drons** *or* **-dra** (-drə). A solid geometric figure bounded by polygons. **—pol′y•he′dral** *adj.*

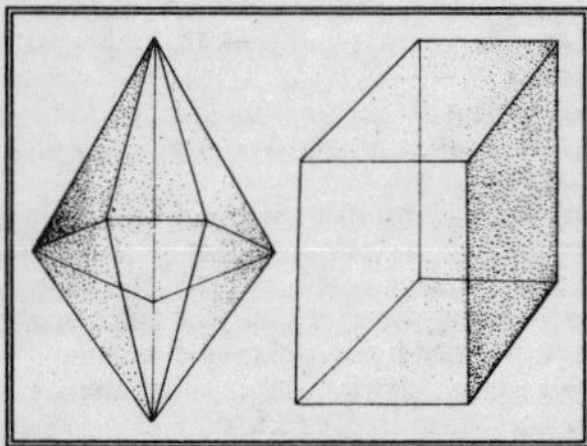

polyhedron
Two types of polyhedrons

pol•y•math (pŏl′ĭ-măth′) *n.* A person of extensive learning.
pol•y•mer (pŏl′ə-mər) *n.* A natural or synthetic compound consisting of similar molecules linked together. **—pol′y•mer′ic** (-mĕr′-ĭk) *adj.*
po•lym•er•ize (pŏl′ə-mə-rīz′, pə-lĭm′ə-) *v.* **-ized, -iz•ing.** To make or combine into a polymer. **—po•lym′er•i•za′tion** *n.*
pol•y•no•mi•al (pŏl′ĭ-nō′mē-əl) *adj.* Of or composed of more than 2 terms. *—n.* **1.** An algebraic function of 2 or more summed terms. **2.** A mathematical expression of 2 or more terms.
pol•yp (pŏl′ĭp) *n.* **1.** A coelenterate, as a hydra or coral, with a hollow, tubular body and a mouth opening usu. with tentacles. **2.** An abnormally projecting growth of mucous membrane. **—pol′yp•oid′** *adj.*
pol•y•pep•tide (pŏl′ē-pĕp′tīd′) *n.* A peptide containing many molecules of amino acids.
po•lyph•o•ny (pə-lĭf′ə-nē) *n.* Music consisting of several independent but harmonizing melodic parts. **—pol′y•phon′ic** (pŏl′ĭ-fŏn′ĭk) *adj.*
pol•y•sty•rene (pŏl′ĭ-stī′rēn′) *n.* A clear, hard, rigid thermoplastic polymer used esp. as insulation and in molded products.
pol•y•syl•la•ble (pŏl′ĭ-sĭl′ə-bəl) *n.* A word having at least 3 syllables. **—pol′y•syl•lab′ic** (-sĭ-lăb′ĭk) *adj.*
pol•y•tech•nic (pŏl′ĭ-tĕk′nĭk) *adj.* Of, dealing with, or instructing in technical or industrial arts or applied sciences.
pol•y•the•ism (pŏl′ĭ-thē-ĭz′əm) *n.* Belief in a number of gods. **—pol′y•the′ist** *n.* **—pol′y•the•is′tic** *adj.*
pol•y•un•sat•u•rat•ed (pŏl′ē-ŭn-săch′ə-rā′-tĭd) *adj.* Of or pertaining to an organic compound, as an oil or fat, that is rich in unsaturated bonds.
pol•y•u•re•thane (pŏl′ē-yŏŏr′ə-thān′) *n.* A thermoplastic or thermosetting resin used esp. in tough, resistant coatings and electrical insulation.
po•made (pə-mād′, -mäd′, pō-) *n.* A scented ointment for the hair. **—po•made′** *v.*
pome•gran•ate (pŏm′grăn′ĭt, pŭm′-) *n.* A semitropical Asian shrub or small tree, *Punica granatum,* cultivated for its fruit that has a tough reddish rind and many seeds.
pom•mel (pŭm′əl, pŏm′-) *n.* **1.** A knob on a sword handle. **2.** The raised knoblike front part of a saddle. *—v.* **-meled, -mel•ing** *or* **-melled, -mel•ling.** To beat severely : pummel.
pomp (pŏmp) *n.* **1.** Stately or splendid display. **2.** Pretentious or excessive display.
pom•pa•dour (pŏm′pə-dôr′, -dōr′) *n.* A puffy hairstyle in which the hair is swept straight up from the forehead.
pom•pa•no (pŏm′pə-nō′, pŭm′-) *n., pl.* **-no** *or* **-nos. 1.** A marine food fish of the genus *Trachinotus,* esp. *T. carolinus,* of tropical and temperate Atlantic waters. **2.** A small, edible butterfish, *Palometa simillima,* of American Pacific coastal waters.
pom•pom (pŏm′pŏm′) *also* **pom•pon** (-pŏn′) *n.* **1.** A small, decorative ball or tuft of material used esp. on caps. **2.** A small, buttonlike chrysanthemum or dahlia.
pom•pous (pŏm′pəs) *adj.* **1.** Suggesting ostentatious display. **2.** Marked by pretention or self-importance. **3.** Bombastic : grandiose. **—pom•pos′i•ty** (-pŏs′ĭ-tē) *n.*
pon•cho (pŏn′chō) *n., pl.* **-chos. 1.** A blanketlike loose outer garment having a hole in the middle for the head. **2.** A water-resistant garment resembling a poncho.
pond (pŏnd) *n.* A body of water smaller in size than a lake.
pon•der (pŏn′dər) *v.* **1.** To think about carefully : deliberate. **2.** To engage in contemplation. **—pon′der•er** *n.*
pon•der•o•sa pine (pŏn′də-rō′sə, -zə) *n.* A tall timber tree, *Pinus ponderosa,* of W North America, with dark-green needles.

pon·der·ous (pŏn′dər-əs) *adj.* **1. a.** Very heavy **:** massive. **b.** Clumsy **:** unwieldy. **2.** Lacking fluency of style. ★ ***syns:*** ELEPHANTINE, HEAVY-HANDED, LABORED —**pon′der·os′i·ty** (-də-rŏs′ĭ-tē), **pon′der·ous·ness** *n.* —**pon′der·ous·ly** *adv.*

pon·gee (pŏn-jē′, pŏn′jē′) *n.* A thin, soft, usu. tan silk fabric.

pon·iard (pŏn′yərd) *n.* A dagger.

pon·tiff (pŏn′tĭf) *n.* **1.** A bishop. **2.** A pope.

pon·tif·i·cal (pŏn-tĭf′ĭ-kəl) *adj.* Of or relating to a pontiff. —*n.* **pontificals.** The insignia and ceremonial vestments of a pontiff. —**pon·tif′i·cal·ly** *adv.*

pon·tif·i·cate (pŏn-tĭf′ĭ-kĭt, -kāt′) *n.* The state, office, or term of office of a pontiff. —*v.* (-kāt′) **-cat·ed, -cat·ing. 1.** To perform the duties and functions of a pontiff. **2.** To express oneself pompously or dogmatically. —**pon·tif′i·ca′tion** *n.* —**pon·tif′i·ca′tor** *n.*

pon·toon (pŏn-to͞on′) *n.* **1.** A flat-bottomed boat or supporting structure for a floating bridge. **2.** One of the floats supporting a seaplane.

po·ny (pō′nē) *n., pl.* **-nies. 1.** A horse that is small when full-grown. **2.** A translation used in preparing foreign-language lessons.

po·ny·tail (pō′nē-tāl′) *n.* A hair style in which the hair is gathered and fastened at the back of the head.

pooch (po͞och) *n. Slang.* A dog.

poo·dle (po͞od′l) *n.* A dog with a heavy, curly coat.

pooh-pooh (po͞o′po͞o′, po͞o-po͞o′) *v. Informal.* To regard with contempt **:** deride.

pool[1] (po͞ol) *n.* **1.** A body of water smaller than a pond. **2.** A puddle.

pool[2] (po͞ol) *n.* **1.** The total staked by all players in a gambling game. **2.** A mutually shared supply, as of resources. **3.** A business arrangement between competitors for common profit. **4.** Any of several billiards games played on a table with 6 pockets. —*v.* **1.** To combine in a shared fund for mutual use or advantage. **2.** To form or become a member of a pool.

poop[1] (po͞op) *n. Naut.* **1.** A raised structure in the stern of a ship. **2.** A poop deck.

poop[2] (po͞op) *v. Slang.* To exhaust or become exhausted.

poop[3] (po͞op) *n. Slang.* Inside information.

poop deck *n.* A small deck above the rear half of a ship's main deck.

poor (po͝or) *adj.* **1.** Lacking money and possessions. **2.** Lacking in quantity or quality **:** inadequate or inferior. **3.** Not productive <*poor* soil> **4.** Not favorable or satisfactory <a *poor* attitude> **5.** Deserving pity **:** unfortunate. ★ ***syns:*** BROKE, BUSTED, DESTITUTE, IMPOVERISHED, INDIGENT, NEEDY, PENNILESS, PENURIOUS, STRAPPED —**poor′ness** *n.*

poor boy *n.* HERO 4.

poor·house (po͝or′hous′) *n.* A publicly maintained home for destitute people.

†**poor·ly** (po͝or′lē) *adv.* In a poor manner. —*adj. Regional.* In poor health **:** ill.

poor-mouth (po͝or′mouth′, -mouth′) *v.* **1.** To claim poverty as an excuse or defense. **2.** To complain about lack of money.

pop[1] (pŏp) *v.* **popped, pop·ping. 1.** To make, cause to make, burst, or cause to burst with a sudden sharp, explosive sound. **2.** To go, come, or appear suddenly. **3.** To bulge from the sockets <eyes *popping* with delight> **4.** To thrust or put quickly or suddenly. **5.** To shoot (at). **6.** *Baseball.* To hit a pop fly. —*n.* **1.** A sudden sharp, explosive noise. **2.** A gunshot. **3.** A carbonated soft drink. —**pop′per** *n.*

pop[2] (pŏp) *n. Informal.* Father.

pop[3] (pŏp) *adj. Informal.* **1.** Of, pertaining to, or dealing with popular music. **2.** Of or pertaining to culture produced or influenced by the mass media. **3.** Of or pertaining to pop art.

pop art *n.* A style of art typically centering on commonplace objects that are sometimes physically incorporated into the work itself. —**pop artist** *n.*

pop·corn (pŏp′kôrn′) *n.* **1.** A variety of corn, *Zea mays everta,* with kernels that when heated pop to form small white puffs. **2.** The popped kernels of popcorn.

pope (pōp) *n. often* **Pope.** The head of the Roman Catholic Church.

pop fly *n. Baseball.* A short and high fly ball.

pop·gun (pŏp′gŭn′) *n.* A toy gun that shoots corks or pellets by air compression.

pop·in·jay (pŏp′ĭn-jā′) *n.* A conceited, often talkative person.

pop·lar (pŏp′lər) *n.* Any of several slender trees of the genus *Populus,* with triangular leaves and soft, light-colored wood.

pop·lin (pŏp′lĭn) *n.* A strong fabric with fine crosswise ridges.

pop·o·ver (pŏp′ō′vər) *n.* A light, hollow muffin that puffs up while baking.

pop·py (pŏp′ē) *n., pl.* **-pies.** A plant of the genus *Papaver,* with showy red, orange, or white flowers and milky white juice.

pop·py·cock (pŏp′ē-kŏk′) *n.* Nonsense.

Pop·si·cle (pŏp′sĭ-kəl, -sĭk′əl). A trademark for colored and flavored ice in the shape of a rectangle on 2 flat sticks.

pop·u·lace (pŏp′yə-ləs) *n.* **1.** The general public **:** masses. **2.** A population.

pop·u·lar (pŏp′yə-lər) *adj.* **1.** Widely liked. **2.** Of, relating to, or representing the general public. **3.** Widespread **:** prevalent. **4.** Generally affordable. **5.** Readily understandable. —**pop′u·lar′i·ty** (-lăr′ĭ-tē) *n.*

pop·u·lar·ize (pŏp′yə-lə-rīz′) *v.* **-ized, -iz·ing.** To make or become popular. —**pop′u·lar·i·za′tion** *n.* —**pop′u·lar·iz′er** *n.*

pop·u·late (pŏp′yə-lāt′) *v.* **-lat·ed, -lat·ing. 1.** To supply with a population. **2.** To live in **:** inhabit.

pop·u·la·tion (pŏp′yə-lā′shən) *n.* **1.** The people or total number of people in a given area. **2.** A group or set under statistical study. **3.** *Ecol.* All the plants or animals of the same kind found in a given area.

population explosion *n.* Great and rapid growth of a living population, esp. the unchecked increase in human population resulting from both increased infant survival and adult longevity.

pop•u•lism (pŏp′yə-lĭz′əm) *n.* Belief in or advocacy of the rights, interests, or wisdom of the common people. —**pop′u•list** *n.*

pop•u•lous (pŏp′yə-ləs) *adj.* **1.** Heavily populated. **2.** Filled up : crowded. —**pop′u•lous•ly** *adv.* —**pop′u•lous•ness** *n.*

por•ce•lain (pôr′sə-lĭn, pōr′-, pôrs′lĭn, pōrs′-) *n.* **1.** A hard, translucent ceramic made by firing and glazing a fine clay. **2.** An article made of porcelain.

porch (pôrch, pōrch) *n.* **1.** A roofed platform forming the entrance to a house. **2.** A verandah.

por•cine (pôr′sīn′) *adj.* Of, resembling, or typical of swine.

por•cu•pine (pôr′kyə-pīn′) *n.* Any of various rodents, including members of the Old World genus *Hystrix* and the New World genus *Erethizon*, that are covered with long, sharp quills.

pore[1] (pôr, pōr) *v.* **pored, por•ing. 1.** To read or examine with great care and attention <*pored* over the contract> **2.** To ponder : meditate.

pore[2] (pôr, pōr) *n.* A minute opening, as in the skin or a plant leaf, for the passage of fluid.

pork (pôrk, pōrk) *n.* The flesh of swine prepared for use as food.

pork barrel *n. Slang.* A government project or appropriation affording benefits to a specific politician's district.

pork•er (pôr′kər, pōr′-) *n.* A usu. young pig fattened for use as food.

por•no (pôr′nō) *also* **porn** (pôrn) *n. Slang.* Pornography.

por•nog•ra•phy (pôr-nŏg′rə-fē) *n.* Pictures, writing, or films designed to arouse sexual excitement. —**por•nog′ra•pher** *n.* —**por′no•graph′ic** (-nə-grăf′ĭk) *adj.*

po•rous (pôr′əs, pōr′-) *adj.* **1.** Containing pores. **2.** Capable of being permeated by gas or fluid. —**po•ros′i•ty** (pə-rŏs′ĭ-tē) *n.*

por•phy•ry (pôr′fə-rē) *n., pl.* **-ries.** A fine-grained igneous rock with large feldspar or quartz crystals.

por•poise (pôr′pəs) *n.* **1.** A gregarious aquatic mammal of the genus *Phocaena*, usu. with a blunt snout and a triangular dorsal fin. **2.** An aquatic mammal, as the dolphin, that is related to the porpoise.

por•ridge (pôr′ĭj, pŏr′-) *n.* Meal of grains or legumes boiled in water or milk.

por•rin•ger (pôr′ĭn-jər, pŏr′-) *n.* A shallow, one-handled cup or bowl.

port[1] (pôrt, pōrt) *n.* **1.** A town or city with a harbor. **2.** A harbor. **3.** A port of entry.

port[2] (pôrt, pōrt) *n.* The left side of a ship or aircraft facing toward the front. —*adj.* Of or on the port side. —*v.* To turn or shift the helm to the port side.

port[3] (pôrt, pōrt) *n.* **1.** A porthole. **2.** A vent or opening, as in an engine, for steam or fluid.

port[4] (pôrt, pōrt) *n.* A sweet fortified dark-red wine.

port•a•ble (pôr′tə-bəl, pōr′-) *adj.* Capable of being carried or moved. —**port′a•bil′i•ty** *n.* —**port′a•ble** *n.*

port•age (pôr′tĭj, pōr′-, pôr-täzh′) *n.* **1.** The carrying of boats and goods overland between one waterway and another. **2.** A route for portage. —*v.* **-aged, -ag•ing.** To carry over or make a portage.

por•tal (pôr′tl, pōr′-) *n.* A doorway or entrance, esp. one that is large and impressive.

port•cul•lis (pôrt-kŭl′ĭs, pōrt-) *n.* A grating that can be let down to prevent entrance to a fortified place.

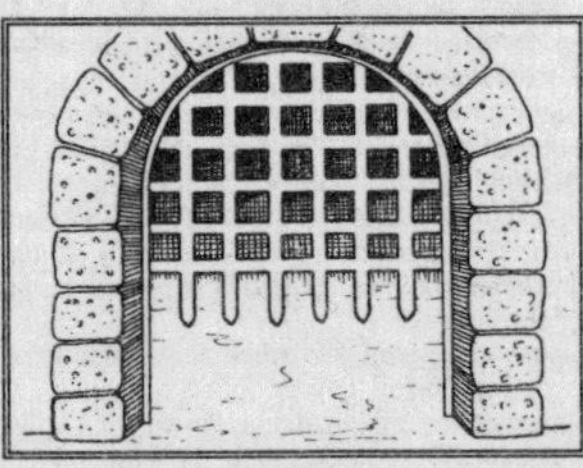

portcullis

porte-co•chère *or* **porte-co•chere** (pôrt′-kō-shâr′, pōrt′-) *n.* A roofed extension of a building over a driveway that shelters passengers getting into and out of vehicles.

por•tend (pôr-tĕnd′, pōr-) *v.* **1.** To give an indication or warning of in advance. **2.** To serve as an indication of.

por•tent (pôr′tĕnt′, pōr′-) *n.* **1.** An augury of a future event. **2.** Ominous significance. **3.** A cause of wonder or amazement.

por•ten•tous (pôr-tĕn′təs, pōr-) *adj.* **1.** Ominous : foreboding. **2.** Extraordinary : amazing. **3.** Marked by pompousness. —**por•ten′tous•ly** *adv.*

por•ter[1] (pôr′tər, pōr′-) *n.* **1.** One hired to carry travelers' baggage. **2.** An attendant in a railway sleeping or parlor car. **3.** One hired to do routine cleaning, as in a public building. —**por′ter•age** *n.*

por•ter[2] (pôr′tər, pōr′-) *n. esp. Brit.* A doorman or doorkeeper.

por•ter[3] (pôr′tər, pōr′-) *n.* A heavy dark beer.

por•ter•house (pôr′tər-hous′, pōr′-) *n.* A choice cut of beef containing a T-bone and a large piece of tenderloin.

port•fo•li•o (pôrt-fō′lē-ō′, pōrt-) *n., pl.* **-os. 1.** A flat carrying case for documents or drawings. **2.** The position and duties of a cabinet member or minister of state. **3.** The securities of an investor.

port•hole (pôrt′hōl′, pōrt′-) *n.* A small round opening in the side of a ship or an aircraft.

por•ti•co (pôr′tĭ-kō′, pōr′-) *n., pl.* **-coes** *or* **-cos.** A walkway or porch with a roof supported by a row of columns.

por•tière *or* **por•tiere** (pôrt-yâr′, pōrt-) *n.* A drapery hanging across a doorway.

por•tion (pôr′shən, pōr′-) *n.* **1.** A section or part of a whole. **2.** One's allotted part or share. **3.** A dowry. **4.** One's destiny **:** lot. —*v.* **1.** To divide and give out in portions. **2.** To give to as a portion. —**por′tion•a•ble** *adj.* —**por′tion•less** *adj.*

Portland cement *n.* A hydraulic cement made by roasting and grinding a clay-and-limestone mixture.

port•ly (pôrt′lē, pōrt′-) *adj.* **-li•er, -li•est.** Rather corpulent **:** stout. —**port′li•ness** *n.*

port•man•teau (pôrt-măn′tō′, pōrt-, pôrt′-măn-tō′, pōrt′-) *n., pl.* **-teaus** *or* **-teaux** (-tōz). A large piece of luggage.

portmanteau word *n.* A word, as *smog,* formed by merging the sounds and meanings of different words.

port of call *n.* A port where ships dock en route for cargo, overhaul, or supplies.

port of entry *n.* An official place of entrance or exit for foreign goods or travelers.

por•trait (pôr′trĭt, -trāt′, pōr′-) *n.* An artistic or photographic image of a person, esp. one showing the face.

por•trait•ist (pôr′trə-tĭst, pōr′-) *n.* A maker of portraits, esp. a painter.

por•trai•ture (pôr′trĭ-chŏŏr′, -chər, pōr′-) *n.* The art or practice of creating portraits.

por•tray (pôr-trā′, pōr-) *v.* **1.** To show by means of a picture. **2.** To describe verbally. **3.** To enact on the stage or screen. —**por•tray′al** *n.*

Port Sa•lut (pôr′ să-lōō′) *also* **Port du Sa•lut** (pôr′ dü să-lōō′) *n.* A semihard fermented cheese orig. made in France.

Por•tu•guese man-of-war (pôr′chə-gēz′, -gēs′) *n.* A chiefly tropical marine invertebrate organism of the genus *Physalia,* with a bluish bladderlike float and long stinging tentacles.

por•tu•lac•a (pôr′chə-lăk′ə, pōr′-) *n.* A plant of the genus *Portulaca,* esp. *P. grandiflora,* bearing fleshy stems and leaves and grown for its colorful flowers.

pose (pōz) *v.* **posed, pos•ing. 1.** To assume or place in a certain position, as for a portrait. **2.** To assume a certain manner or attitude, esp. for effect and often to deceive <*posed* as a naval officer> **3.** To put forth (e.g., a question). —*n.* **1.** A usu. sustained bodily posture, esp. one assumed in modeling. **2.** An affectation or pretense.

pos•er[1] (pō′zər) *n.* A person who poses.

pos•er[2] (pŏ′zər) *n.* A perplexing question.

po•seur (pō-zûr′) *n.* One who assumes a pose or attitude, esp. for effect.

posh (pŏsh) *adj.* Fashionable and smart.

pos•it (pŏz′ĭt) *v.* To take for granted without proof **:** postulate.

po•si•tion (pə-zĭsh′ən) *n.* **1.** The place or location occupied by something. **2.** The right or proper place. **3. a.** A way of being placed or arranged. **b.** A bodily posture <a sitting *position*> **4.** Relative place or situation <not in a *position* to argue> **5.** A viewpoint **:** attitude. **6.** A post of employment **:** job. **7.** Social status or official rank. —*v.* To place in proper position. —**po•si′tion•al** *adj.* —**po•si′tion•er** *n.*

pos•i•tive (pŏz′ĭ-tĭv) *adj.* **1. a.** Indicating affirmation, approval, or acceptance. **b.** Constructive **:** helpful. **2.** Expressed unequivocally <a *positive* denial> **3.** Incapable of being doubted or disproved. **4.** Absolutely certain **:** very confident. **5.** Existing in reality. **6.** *Math.* **a.** Greater than zero. **b.** Of the sign (+) indicating a positive number or one that is to be added. **7.** Of or having an electric charge that tends to attract electrons. **8.** Having the areas of light and dark in their natural relationship <a *positive* photographic print> **9.** Of or indicating the simple uncompared grammatical degree of an adjective or adverb. —*n.* **1.** A positive photographic image. **2.** A positive word form or the positive degree of an adjective or adverb. **3.** A positive number. **4.** A positive electric charge. —**pos′i•tive•ly** *adv.* —**pos′i•tive•ness** *n.*

pos•i•tron (pŏz′ĭ-trŏn′) *n.* The antiparticle of the electron.

pos•se (pŏs′ē) *n.* A group deputized by a sheriff, as for pursuing a lawbreaker.

pos•sess (pə-zĕs′) *v.* **1.** To have or own (e.g., property). **2.** To have as a quality, trait, or skill. **3.** To dominate **:** control. —**pos•ses′sor** *n.*

pos•sessed (pə-zĕst′) *adj.* Controlled by or as if by a supernatural force.

pos•ses•sion (pə-zĕsh′ən) *n.* **1. a.** The act or fact of possessing. **b.** The state of being possessed. **2.** Something owned **:** property. **3.** Control, as of one's emotions or actions. **4.** The state of being dominated, as by an evil spirit. **5.** A territory ruled by a foreign power.

pos•ses•sive (pə-zĕs′ĭv) *adj.* **1.** Displaying a desire to possess, esp. to control. **2.** Of or being a noun or pronoun case that indicates ownership. —*n.* **1.** The possessive case. **2.** A word or form in the possessive case. —**pos•ses′sive•ness** *n.*

pos•si•ble (pŏs′ə-bəl) *adj.* **1.** Capable of existing or being true. **2.** Capable of happening or being accomplished. **3.** Potential <*possible* hazards> **4.** Capable of being used for a certain purpose. —**pos′si•bil′i•ty** *n.* —**pos′si•bly** *adv.*

pos•sum (pŏs′əm) *n.* An opossum.

post[1] (pōst) *n.* **1.** An upright, usu. wooden or metal support. **2.** A stake set up as a marker or guide. **3.** The starting gate at a racecourse. —*v.* **1.** To put up (e.g., a notice) in a public place. **2.** To announce by or as if by a public notice <*post* test results> **3.** To protect (property) against trespassers by putting up signs. **4.** To enter (a name) on a public list.

post[2] (pōst) *n.* **1.** A base or garrison for military personnel. **2.** A soldier's or sentry's assigned station. **3.** A person's assigned position or duty. **4.** Employment, esp. in public office. **5.** A trading station. —*v.* **1.** To position or station in a particular place. **2.** To put forward (e.g., a bail bond).

post[3] (pōst) *n. esp. Brit.* **1. a.** A governmental

system for the transportation and delivery of mail. **b.** A mail delivery. **2.** A post office. —*v.* **1.** To make haste in riding or traveling. **2.** *esp. Brit.* To mail <*posted* the note> **3.** To make aware. **4.** To make entries in (an account book).

post– *pref.* **1.** Subsequent to **:** after <*post*script> **2.** Posterior to **:** behind <*post*nasal>

post•age (pō'stĭj) *n.* The fee for mailing something.

postage meter *n.* A machine used to print the amount of postage required on pieces of mail.

post•al (pō'stəl) *adj.* Of or relating to the post office or mail system.

postal card *n.* A postcard.

post•box *also* **post box** (pōst'bŏks') *n.* A mailbox.

post•card *also* **post card** (pōst'kärd') *n.* A card for a short message that can be mailed without an envelope.

post•date (pōst-dāt') *v.* **1.** To mark with a later date than the actual one <*postdate* a check> **2.** To come after in time.

post•doc•tor•al (pōst-dŏk'tər-əl) *adj.* Of or engaged in academic study beyond a doctor's degree <*postdoctoral* candidates>

post•er (pō'stər) *n.* A publicly posted, often decorative placard or advertisement.

pos•te•ri•or (pŏ-stîr'ē-ər, pō-) *adj.* **1.** Located behind or toward the back. **2.** Subsequent in time. —*n.* The human buttocks.

pos•ter•i•ty (pŏ-stĕr'ĭ-tē) *n.* **1.** Generations or time to come. **2.** The body of descendants from an ancestor.

pos•tern (pō'stərn, pŏs'tərn) *n.* A back gate or side entrance.

Post Exchange. A service mark for a general store on a military post for authorized personnel and their families.

post•grad•u•ate (pōst-grăj'o͞o-ĭt, -āt') *adj.* Of or engaged in academic study beyond a bachelor's degree. —**post•grad'u•ate** *n.*

post•haste (pōst'hāst') *adv.* As speedily as possible.

post•hu•mous (pŏs'chə-məs) *adj.* **1.** Given or taking place after one's death. **2.** Published after the death of the author. **3.** Born after the father has died. —**post'hu•mous•ly** *adv.*

post•hyp•not•ic (pōst'hĭp-nŏt'ĭk) *adj.* Of, relating to, or intended for the period following hypnosis.

pos•til•ion *also* **pos•til•lion** (pō-stĭl'yən, pə-) *n.* A rider on the left-hand lead horse of a team drawing a carriage.

post•lude (pōst'lo͞od') *n.* An organ solo at the conclusion of a church service.

post•man (pōst'mən) *n.* A mailman.

post•mark (pōst'märk') *n.* An official postal mark that cancels the stamp on a piece of mail. —**post'mark'** *v.*

post•mas•ter (pōst'măs'tər) *n.* One who officially manages a post office.

postmaster general *n., pl.* **postmasters general.** The chief official of a national postal system.

post me•rid•i•em (pōst' mə-rĭd'ē-əm) *adj.* After noon.

post•mis•tress (pōst'mĭs'trĭs) *n.* A woman in charge of a post office.

post•mor•tem (pōst-môr'təm) *adj.* **1.** Taking place or done after death. **2.** Of or relating to a postmortem. —*n.* **1.** A postmortem examination of a dead body, esp. to determine the cause of death **:** autopsy. **2.** *Informal.* An evaluation or review of a recent event.

post•na•sal (pōst-nā'zəl) *adj.* Of, in, or from the posterior part of the nasal cavity <a *postnasal* drip>

post•na•tal (pōst-năt'l) *adj.* Following birth.

post•ac'ci•dent *adj.*
post'ad•o•les'cent *adj.* & *n.*
post'am•pu•ta'tion *adj.*
post'ar•rest' *adj.*
post'a•tom'ic *adj.*
post•au'dit *n.*
post•bach'e•lor *adj.*
post'bap•tis'mal *adj.*
post-Bib'li•cal *adj.*
post'chlo•ri•na'tion *adj.*
post-Chris'tian *adj.*
post'civ•i•li•za'tion *adj.*
post•co'i•tal *adj.*
post•col'lege *adj.*
post'col•le'giate *adj.*
post'co•lo'ni•al *adj.*
post'-Co•lum'bi•an *adj.*
post'con•cep'tion *adj.*
post•con'quest *adj.*
post'con•so•nan'tal *adj.*
post'con•va•les'cent *adj.*
post'con•ven'tion *adj.*
post•cor'o•nar'y *adj.*
post•coup' *adj.*
post•cri'sis *adj.*
post•dead'line' *adj.*
post'de•bate' *adj.*
post'de•liv'er•y *adj.*
post'de•pres'sion *adj.*
post'de•val'u•a'tion *adj.*
post'ed•u•ca'tion•al *adj.*
post'e•lec'tion *adj.*
post'em•bry•on'ic *adj.*
post'e•mer'gen•cy *adj.*
post•ex'er•cise' *adj.*
post'ex•plo'sion *adj.*
post'ex•po'sure *adj.*
post'flight' *adj.*
post-Freud'i•an *adj.*
post'game' *adj.*
post•gla'cial *adj.*
post'grad•u•a'tion *adj.*
post'hi•ber•na'tion *adj.*
post•hos'pi•tal *adj.*
post•im'pact' *adj.*
post'im•pe'ri•al *adj.*
post'in•au'gu•ral *adj.*
post'in•de•pend'ence *adj.*
post'in•dus'tri•al *adj.*
post'in•fec'tion *adj.*
post'in•oc'u•la'tion *adj.*
post'ir•ra'di•a'tion *adj.*
post•lar'val *adj.*
post'launch' *adj.*
post'lib•er•a'tion *adj.*
post•mar'i•tal *adj.*
post'mas•tec'to•my *adj.*
post'me•di•e'val *adj.*
post'men•o•paus'al *adj.*
post•men'stru•al *adj.*
post'ne•o•na'tal *adj.*
post'pol•li•na'tion *adj.*
post•pri'mar'y *adj.*
post•pris'on *adj.*
post•pu'ber•ty *adj.*
post'pu•bes'cent *adj.*
post're•ces'sion *adj.*
post'-Ref•or•ma'tion *adj.*
post-Ren'ais•sance' *adj.*
post're•tire'ment *adj.*
post'rev•o•lu'tion•ar'y *adj.*
post•sea'son *adj.*
post•sur'gi•cal *adj.*
post•treat'ment *adj.*
post•tri'al *adj.*
post'vac•ci•na'tion *adj.*
post'-Vic•to'ri•an *adj.*
post'war' *adj.*

post office *n.* **1.** A governmental department in charge of the conveyance and delivery of the mails. **2.** A local office where mail is handled.

post·op·er·a·tive (pōst-ŏp′ər-ə-tĭv, -ŏp′rə-, -ŏp′ə-rā′-) *adj.* Following surgery.

post·paid (pōst′pād′) *adj.* Having the postage already paid.

post·par·tum (pōst-pär′təm) *adj.* Subsequent to childbirth.

post·pone (pōst-pōn′, pōs-pōn′) *v.* **-poned, -pon·ing.** To put off to a later time. **—post·pon′a·ble** *adj.* **—post·pone′ment** *n.* **—post·pon′er** *n.*

post·script (pōst′skrĭpt′, pōs′skrĭpt′) *n.* A usu. short message added after a letter has been completed.

post time *n.* The time just before the official start of a race after which no further betting is allowed.

pos·tu·lant (pŏs′chə-lənt) *n.* A candidate for membership in a religious order.

pos·tu·late (pŏs′chə-lāt′) *v.* **-lat·ed, -lat·ing.** To assume to be true. —*n.* (-lĭt, -lāt′). A self-evident or gen. accepted theory or statement **:** axiom. **—pos′tu·la′tion** *n.*

pos·ture (pŏs′chər) *n.* **1.** A way of carrying or positioning the body. **2.** Mode or status <a country's revolutionary *posture*> **3.** An attitude or tendency. —*v.* **-tured, -tur·ing.** To assume a pose, esp. for effect. **—pos′tur·er** *n.*

po·sy (pō′zē) *n., pl.* **-sies. 1. a.** A flower. **b.** A bouquet. **2.** *Archaic.* A short, usu. sentimental poem or motto.

pot (pŏt) *n.* **1.** A rounded, somewhat deep container used esp. in cooking and for holding plants. **2.** All the money staked in one hand of a card game. **3.** *Informal.* A pool of funds shared by all members of a group. **4.** *Slang.* Marijuana. **5.** *Computer Sci.* A section of computer storage for accumulated data. —*v.* **pot·ted, pot·ting. 1.** To put or plant in a pot. **2.** To cook or preserve in a pot. **3.** To shoot (game), esp. for food. **—pot′ful′** *n.*

po·ta·ble (pō′tə-bəl) *adj.* Fit to drink.

pot·ash (pŏt′ăsh′) *n.* Any of several chemical compounds that contain potassium, esp. a strongly alkaline material obtained from wood ashes and used esp. in fertilizers.

po·tas·si·um (pə-tăs′ē-əm) *n.* *Symbol* **K** A soft, silver-white, highly reactive metallic element used esp. in fertilizers.

potassium bromide *n.* A white crystalline salt used as a sedative and in developing photographs.

potassium carbonate *n.* A white salt used esp. in glass, pigments, and soaps.

potassium hydroxide *n.* A corrosive solid used as a bleach and in detergents.

potassium nitrate *n.* A soluble white crystalline salt used esp. to preserve meat and to make explosives and fertilizers.

po·ta·tion (pō-tā′shən) *n.* A drink, esp. an alcoholic beverage.

po·ta·to (pə-tā′tō) *n., pl.* **-toes.** A plant, *Solanum tuberosum,* widely grown for its starchy, edible tubers.

potato chip *n.* A very thin slice of potato deep-fried until crisp.

pot·bel·ly (pŏt′bĕl′ē) *n.* A sagging or protruding abdomen. **—pot′bel′lied** *adj.*

pot·boil·er (pŏt′boi′lər) *n.* A usu. inferior literary or artistic work produced solely to make a profit.

pot cheese *n.* Cottage cheese.

po·tent (pōt′nt) *adj.* **1.** Strong and powerful. **2.** Highly effective or influential. **3.** Strongly affecting the body or mind, as a drug or poison. **4.** Capable of having sexual intercourse. —Used of a male. **—po′ten·cy** *n.* **—po′tent·ly** *adv.*

po·ten·tate (pōt′n-tāt′) *n.* A powerful ruler **:** monarch.

po·ten·tial (pə-tĕn′shəl) *adj.* **1.** Not yet actual or real **:** latent <a *potential* problem> **2.** Capable of being developed <a *potential* source of energy> —*n.* **1.** Capacity for realization or development. **2.** The potential energy of a unit electric charge depending on its position in an electric circuit or field. **—po·ten′ti·al′i·ty** (-shē-ăl′ĭ-tē) *n.* **—po·ten′tial·ly** *adv.*

po·ten·ti·ate (pə-tĕn′chē-āt′) *v.* **-at·ed, -at·ing.** To increase the potency of (a drug) by administering a second drug at the same time.

pot·head (pŏt′hĕd′) *n.* *Slang.* A habitual smoker of marijuana.

poth·er (pŏ*th*′ər) *n.* A commotion or fuss.

pot·herb (pŏt′ûrb′, -hûrb′) *n.* A plant whose leaves, stems, or flowers are cooked and eaten or used as seasoning.

†pot·hole (pŏt′hōl′) *n.* **1.** A dent or hole, esp. in a road. **2.** *W U.S.* A place filled with mud or quicksand that is a hazard to cattle.

pot·hook (pŏt′ho͝ok′) *n.* An iron hook for hanging a pot over an open fire.

po·tion (pō′shən) *n.* A drink or dose, esp. of medicine or poison.

pot·luck (pŏt′lŭk′) *n.* **1.** The food on hand, esp. when offered to a guest at mealtime. **2.** Whatever happens to be available at a particular time.

pot·pie (pŏt′pī′) *n.* Meat or poultry stew covered with a pastry crust and baked in a deep dish.

pot·pour·ri (pō′po͝o-rē′) *n.* **1.** A miscellaneous combination or collection. **2.** A mixture of sweet-smelling dried flower petals and spices.

pot roast *n.* A cut of beef braised in a covered pot.

pot·sherd (pŏt′shûrd′) *n.* A pottery fragment found esp. at a dig.

pot shot *n.* **1.** A shot fired casually or at an easy target. **2.** A critical remark aimed at a vulnerable target.

pot·tage (pŏt′ĭj) *n.* A thick soup or stew.

pot·ter¹ (pŏt′ər) *n.* A maker of pottery.

pot·ter² (pŏt′ər) *v.* To putter.

pot·ter·y (pŏt′ə-rē) *n., pl.* **-ies. 1.** Molded and fired clay objects, as pots, bowls, and vases. **2.** The art or work of a potter. **3.** The workshop of a potter.

pouch (pouch) *n.* **1.** A small bag, esp. for carrying tobacco. **2.** A flexible bag, esp. for holding or transporting mail or diplomatic dispatches. **3.** *Zool.* A saclike anatomical structure, as one in which marsupials carry their young. —*v.* To assume the form of a pouch or pouchlike cavity. —**pouch'y** *adj.*

poul•ter•er (pōl'tər-ər) *n.* A dealer in poultry or poultry products.

poul•tice (pōl'tĭs) *n.* A soft, usu. warmed and medicated mass applied on cloth to a sore or inflamed body part. —**poul'tice** *v.*

poul•try (pōl'trē) *n.* Domestic fowl raised for meat or eggs.

pounce (pouns) *v.* **pounced, pounc•ing.** To seize by or as if by swooping or springing abruptly. —**pounce** *n.* —**pounc'er** *n.*

pound[1] (pound) *n., pl.* **pounds** *or* **pound. 1.** —See table at MEASUREMENT. **2.** —See table at CURRENCY.

▲ ***word history:*** The word *pound*[1], "a unit of currency," is a specialized use of the word *pound* meaning "a unit of weight." The word *pound*[1] is derived from Latin *pondo,* "a measure of weight." The orig. Latin word for "a pound weight" was *libra. Pondo,* which is actually the ablative case of *pondus,* "a weight," developed into a separate noun from the phrase *libra pondo,* "a pound by weight." *Pondo* descended into Old English as *pund,* which had the same meanings as modern *pound*[1]. The monetary unit was orig. the value of a pound weight of silver. The symbol £ still used for the British pound is a stylized *L* that stands for the Latin word *libra.*

pound[2] (pound) *v.* **1.** To strike forcefully or repeatedly. **2.** To pulverize or crush by beating. **3.** To instill by repetition. **4.** To move along or over heavily and loudly. **5.** To beat or throb rapidly and violently.

pound[3] (pound) *n.* A public enclosure for stray dogs and cats.

pound•age (poun'dĭj) *n.* Weight reckoned in pounds.

pound cake *n.* A cake rich in butter, sugar, and eggs.

pound-fool•ish (pound'fo͞o'lĭsh) *adj.* Not prudent in dealing with large amounts of money or weighty matters.

pour (pôr, pōr) *v.* **1.** To flow or cause to flow profusely or in a continuous stream. **2.** To supply abundantly. **3.** To rain hard.

pout (pout) *v.* **1.** To express disapproval or resentment by protruding the lips. **2.** To look sulky or sullen. —**pout** *n.*

pov•er•ty (pŏv'ər-tē) *n.* **1.** A chronic pressing need for money and material goods. **2.** Dearth. **3.** Inferior quality, as of soil.

pov•er•ty-strick•en (pŏv'ər-tē-strĭk'ən) *adj.* Completely impoverished.

POW (pē'ō'dŭb'əl-yo͞o) *n.* A prisoner of war.

pow•der (pou'dər) *n.* **1.** A dry substance composed of very fine particles. **2.** A medicine, cosmetic, or cleaning agent in the form of powder. **3.** An explosive mixture, as gunpowder. **4.** Light, dry snow. —*v.* **1.** To reduce to powder, as by pulverizing. **2.** To cover or dust with or as if with powder. —**pow'der•y** *adj.*

pow•der-puff (pou'dər-pŭf') *adj.* Of or being a usu. competitive activity for women. —*n.* **powder puff.** PUFF 3.

powder room *n.* A restroom for women.

†**pow•er** (pou'ər) *n.* **1.** The capacity or ability to do or accomplish something. **2.** *often* **powers.** A particular ability, capability, or skill. **3. a.** Strength, force, or might. **b.** Forceful impact : effectiveness. **4.** The authority or ability to control others. **5.** One having great authority or influence <a world *power*> **6.** Physical force or energy. **7.** The measured rate of time at which work is done or energy is transferred. **8.** Electrical energy : electricity. **9.** *Math.* The number of times a number or expression is to be multiplied by itself, as indicated by an exponent. **10.** The degree of magnification of an optical lens. **11.** *Regional.* A large number or amount. ★ ***syns:*** AUTHORITY, CLOUT, CONTROL —*v.* To supply (e.g., a motor or machine) with power. —**pow'er•less** *adj.*

power broker *n.* One, esp. a politician, who exerts strong influence by virtue of the individuals and votes he or she controls.

†**pow•er•ful** (pou'ər-fəl) *adj.* **1.** Having power, authority, or influence. **2.** *Regional.* Great <a *powerful* lot of harm> —*adv. Regional.* Very <It was *powerful* humid yesterday.> —**pow'er•ful•ly** *adv.*

pow•er•house (pou'ər-hous') *n.* **1.** A place where electrical power is generated. **2.** A forceful, energetic person.

power of attorney *n.* A legal document conferring authority to act as attorney or agent for another.

power plant *n.* **1.** The equipment making up the power source of a self-propelled unit, as a spacecraft. **2.** POWERHOUSE 1.

pow•wow (pou'wou') *n.* **1.** A North American Indian prayer ceremony, esp. before hunting or battle. **2.** *Informal.* A meeting or conference for discussion.

pox (pŏks) *n.* An eruptive disease, as smallpox, marked by pustules.

Pr *symbol for* PRASEODYMIUM.

prac•ti•ca•ble (prăk'tĭ-kə-bəl) *adj.* **1.** Capable of being done or put into effect. **2.** Capable of being used. —**prac'ti•ca•bil'i•ty** *n.* —**prac'ti•ca•bly** *adv.*

prac•ti•cal (prăk'tĭ-kəl) *adj.* **1.** Serving a purpose : useful. **2.** Resulting from or involving experience, practice, or use rather than theory or speculation. **3. a.** Inclined to action : unspeculative. **b.** Down-to-earth : sensible. **4.** Being so in effect : virtual. ★ ***syns:*** FUNCTIONAL, HANDY, SERVICEABLE, USEFUL, UTILITARIAN —**prac'ti•cal'i•ty** (-kăl'ĭ-tē) *n.* —**prac'ti•cal•ly** *adv.*

practical joke *n.* A prank played on someone to cause embarrassment. —**practical joker** *n.*

practical nurse *n.* A nurse who is usu. licensed by a state to provide routine patient care.

prac•tice (prăk'tĭs) *n.* **1.** A habit, custom, or method of doing something. **2. a.** Repetition to acquire or perfect a skill. **b.** Skill gained or maintained through repeated exercise. **3.** Actual performance or use <put knowledge into *practice*> **4.** The exercise of a profession. **5.** The business of a professional, as a doctor or lawyer. ★ ***syns:*** DRILL, EXERCISE, REHEARSAL, STUDY, TRAINING —*v.* **-ticed, -tic·ing. 1.** To make a habit or custom of <*practice* courteous driving> **2.** To do repeatedly in order to acquire proficiency. **3.** To pursue as a profession <*practice* medicine> **4.** To put into effect : apply.

prac·tise (prăk'tĭs) *n. & v. esp. Brit. var. of* PRACTICE.

prac·ti·tio·ner (prăk-tĭsh'ə-nər) *n.* One who practices a profession.

prae·tor (prē'tər) *n.* A magistrate of ancient Rome, ranking below a consul. —**prae·to'ri·an** (-tôr'ē-ən, -tōr'-) *adj.*

prag·mat·ic (prăg-măt'ĭk) *also* **prag·mat·i·cal** (-ĭ-kəl) *adj.* **1.** Concerned with practice rather than theory : practical. **2.** Of or pertaining to the theory or methods of pragmatism. —**prag·mat'i·cal·ly** *adv.*

prag·ma·tism (prăg'mə-tĭz'əm) *n.* **1.** The theory that actions and beliefs must be judged by their practical results. **2.** The use of practical means to solve problems. —**prag'ma·tist** *n.*

prai·rie (prâr'ē) *n.* A wide area of level or rolling grassland, as in the C U.S.

prairie dog *n.* A burrowing rodent of the genus *Cynomys,* of WC North America, with yellowish fur and a barklike call.

prairie schooner *n.* A large canvas-covered wagon used by pioneers in traveling across the North American prairies.

praise (prāz) *v.* **praised, prais·ing. 1.** To express approval of or admiration for. **2.** To extol or glorify (e.g., a deity or hero). ★ ***syns:*** ACCLAIM, APPLAUD, COMMEND, LAUD —**praise** *n.* —**praise'wor'thy** *adj.*

pra·line (prä'lēn', prā'-) *n.* A candy of boiled brown sugar or maple sugar in which nut kernels are embedded.

pram (prăm) *n. esp. Brit.* A baby carriage.

prance (prăns) *v.* **pranced, pranc·ing. 1.** To spring forward on the hind legs <*prancing* horses> **2. a.** To caper about. **b.** To swagger or strut. —**pranc'er** *n.* —**pranc'ing·ly** *adv.*

prank (prăngk) *n.* A playful or mischievous act or trick. ★ ***syns:*** ANTIC, CAPER, JOKE, LARK, MONKEYSHINE, SHENANIGAN, TOMFOOLERY, TRICK —**prank'ster** *n.*

pra·se·o·dym·i·um (prā'zē-ō-dĭm'ē-əm, -sē-) *n. Symbol* **Pr** A soft silvery rare-earth element used esp. in metallic alloys.

prate (prāt) *v.* **prat·ed, prat·ing.** To chatter idly and volubly.

prat·fall (prăt'fôl') *n.* A fall in which one lands on the buttocks.

pra·tique (pră-tēk') *n. Naut.* Clearance granted to a ship to proceed into a port after compliance with regulations.

prat·tle (prăt'l) *v.* **-tled, -tling. 1.** To prate. **2.** To babble childishly. —*n.* Foolish or childish talk.

prawn (prôn) *n.* An edible crustacean of the genus *Palaemonetes,* closely related to the shrimps.

pray (prā) *v.* **1.** To address God or a deity, esp. with devout petition. **2.** To request something fervently. **3.** To implore.

prayer (prâr) *n.* **1.** An expression, esp. of devout petition, addressed to God or a deity. **2.** A formal set of words used in praying. **3.** *often* **prayers.** A religious service esp. for the saying of prayers. **4.** An earnest entreaty. **5.** A minimal chance or hope.

prayer·ful (prâr'fəl) *adj.* **1.** Deeply religious : devout. **2.** Deeply sincere : earnest. —**prayer'ful·ly** *adv.*

praying mantis *n.* A predatory insect, *Mantis religiosa,* that holds its front legs folded as if in prayer.

pre– *pref.* **1. a.** Prior to : earlier <*pre*natal> **b.** Preparatory : preliminary <*pre*flight> **c.** In advance <*pre*heat> **2.** In front of <*pre*fix>

preach (prēch) *v.* **1.** To urge or advocate earnestly. **2.** To deliver (a sermon) formally. **3.**

pre'ad·mis'sion *n.*
pre'a·dult' *adj.*
pre'an·es·thet'ic *adj. & n.*
pre'ap·prove' *v.*
pre'ar·range' *v.*
pre'ar·range'ment *n.*
pre'as·sign' *v.*
pre·au'dit *n.*
pre-Bib'li·cal *adj.*
pre·bri'dal *adj.*
pre-Byz'an·tine' *adj.*
pre·chill' *v.*
pre-Chris'tian *adj.*
pre'civ·i·li·za'tion *n.*
pre·code' *v.*
pre·co'i·tal *adj.*
pre'col·lect' *v.*
pre'col·lec'tion *n.*
pre·col'lege *adj.*
pre'co·lo'ni·al *adj.*
pre'com·bus'tion *n.*
pre·com'pen·sate' *v.*
pre'com·pute' *v.*
pre'con·struct' *v.*
pre'con·vic'tion *n.*
pre·cook' *v.*
pre·cool' *v.*
pre·coun'sel *v.*
pre·crash' *adj.*
pre·crease' *v.*
pre·cut' *adj. & v.*
pre·dawn' *adj.*
pre'de·liv'er·y *adj.*
pre'de·par'ture *adj.*
pre·des'ig·nate' *v.*
pre'des·ig·na'tion *n.*
pre'de·val'u·a'tion *adj. & n.*
pre'de·vel'op·ment *n.*
pre'di·ag·no'sis *n.*
pre·din'ner *adj.*
pre'dis·close' *v.*
pre'dis·cov'er·y *n.*
pre·dusk' *adj.*
pre'dy·nas'tic *adj.*
pre-ed'it *v.*
pre'-e·lec'tion *adj. & n.*
pre'-en·dorse' *v.*
pre'-en·roll'ment *adj. & n.*
pre'-es·tab'lish *v.*
pre·fer'til·ize' *v.*
pre'fight' *adj.*
pre·file' *v.*
pre·for'mat' *v.*
pre·for'mu·late' *v.*
pre·freeze' *v.*
pre·game' *adj.*
pre'-His·pan'ic *adj.*
pre'im·pres'sion *n.*
pre'in·au'gu·ral *adj.*
pre'in·duc'tion *adj. & n.*
pre'in·dus'tri·al *adj.*
pre'in·va'sion *adj.*
pre·kin'der·gar'ten *adj. & n.*

To offer moral advice, esp. at length and tediously. —**preach'er** *n.* —**preach'ment** *n.* —**preach'y** *adj.*
pre·ad·o·les·cence (prē'ăd'l-ĕs'əns) *n.* The period between childhood and adolescence. —**pre'ad'o·les'cent** *n.* & *adj.*
pre·am·ble (prē'ăm'bəl) *n.* An introduction, esp. to a formal document.
pre·am·pli·fi·er (prē-ăm'plə-fī'ər) *n.* An electronic amplifier designed to augment very weak signals, as from a phonograph pickup, before they are further amplified.
preb·end (prĕb'ənd) *n.* **1.** An endowment of a cathedral or collegiate church from which a prebendary's stipend is drawn. **2.** The stipend drawn from a prebend.
preb·en·dar·y (prĕb'ən-dĕr'ē) *n., pl.* **-ies.** A member of the clergy granted a prebend for serving in a church.
pre·can·cer·ous (prē-kăn'sər-əs) *adj.* Tending or likely to become cancerous.
pre·car·i·ous (prĭ-kâr'ē-əs) *adj.* **1.** Perilously unstable. **2.** Dependent on chance : uncertain. —**pre·car'i·ous·ly** *adv.* —**pre·car'i·ous·ness** *n.*
pre·cau·tion (prĭ-kô'shən) *n.* A measure taken in advance to safeguard against harm. —**pre·cau'tion·ar'y** (-shə-nĕr'ē) *adj.*
pre·cede (prĭ-sēd') *v.* **-ced·ed, -ced·ing.** To come or be before in time, order, position, or rank. —**prec'e·dence** (prĕs'ĭ-dns, prĭ-sēd'-ns) *n.*
prec·e·dent (prĕs'ĭ-dnt) *n.* An instance, case, or decision that may serve as an example or justification for a later similar one. —*adj.* **pre·ce·dent** (prĭ-sēd'nt, prĕs'ĭ-dnt). Coming before : prior.
pre·cen·tor (prĭ-sĕn'tər) *n.* One who leads a church choir or congregation in singing.
pre·cept (prē'sĕpt') *n.* A general rule of conduct or procedure.
pre·cep·tor (prĭ-sĕp'tər, prē'sĕp'-) *n.* A teacher or tutor.
pre·cinct (prē'sĭngkt') *n.* **1.** An administrative district of a city or town <a police *precinct*> **2.** *often* **precincts.** An area or enclosure with definite boundaries. **3. precincts.** Surrounding areas : environs.
pre·ci·os·i·ty (prĕsh'ē-ŏs'ĭ-tē, prĕs'ē-) *n., pl.* **-ties.** Extreme fastidiousness.
pre·cious (prĕsh'əs) *adj.* **1.** Highly valuable : costly. **2.** Highly esteemed. **3.** Cherished : beloved. **4.** Affectedly refined.
prec·i·pice (prĕs'ə-pĭs) *n.* A very steep crag or cliff.
pre·cip·i·tant (prĭ-sĭp'ĭ-tənt) *adj.* Precipitate. —**pre·cip'i·tance** (-təns), **pre·cip'i·tan·cy** (-tən-sē) *n.*
pre·cip·i·tate (prĭ-sĭp'ĭ-tāt') *v.* **-tat·ed, -tat·ing. 1.** To cast down from a high place. **2.** To bring on, esp. abruptly or unexpectedly. **3.** To condense and fall as rain, hail, or snow. **4.** *Chem.* To separate (a solid substance) out of a solution. —*adj.* (-tĭt, -tāt'). **1.** Rushing headlong and heedlessly. **2.** Acting impulsively or rashly. **3.** Abrupt or unexpected. —*n.* (-tāt', -tĭt). *Chem.* A solid separated out from a solution. —**pre·cip'i·tate·ly** *adv.* —**pre·cip'i·tate·ness** *n.* —**pre·cip'i·ta'tor** *n.*
pre·cip·i·ta·tion (prĭ-sĭp'ĭ-tā'shən) *n.* **1.** Impetuous haste. **2. a.** Condensed water vapor that falls as rain, hail, or snow. **b.** The quantity of this water vapor. **3.** *Chem.* The production of a precipitate in a chemical reaction.
pre·cip·i·tous (prĭ-sĭp'ĭ-təs) *adj.* **1. a.** Like a precipice in being very steep. **b.** Having or marked by precipices. **2.** Precipitate. —**pre·cip'i·tous·ly** *adv.* —**pre·cip'i·tous·ness** *n.*
pré·cis (prā-sē') *n., pl.* **-cis** (-sēz'). A concise summary : abstract. —**pré·cis'** *v.*
pre·cise (prĭ-sīs') *adj.* **1.** Accurately stated or described : definite. **2.** Highly exact : correct. **3.** Distinct from others : particular <on this *precise* spot> **4.** Strictly observant of established forms and procedures. ★ ***syns:*** EXACT,

pre·knowl'edge *n.*
pre·la'bel *v.*
pre·launch' *adj.*
pre·law' *adj.*
pre·lit'er·a·cy *adj.* & *n.*
pre·mar'riage *adj.*
pre·meas'ure *v.*
pre·med'i·cate' *v.*
pre'me·di·e'val *adj.*
pre'men·o·paus'al *adj.*
pre·men'stru·al *adj.*
pre·merg'er *adj.*
pre·mix' *n.* & *v.*
pre·mix'ture *n.*
pre·mod'ern *adj.*
pre'mod·i·fi·ca'tion *n.*
pre·mod'i·fy' *v.*
pre·mois'ten *v.*
pre·mold' *v.*
pre'no·ti·fi·ca'tion *n.*
pre·no'ti·fy' *v.*
pre·num'ber *v.*
pre·nup'tial *adj.*
pre·o'pen·ing *adj.*
pre·or'der *v.*
pre·paste' *v.*
pre·plan' *v.*
pre·pri'mar'y *adj.*
pre·proc'ess *v.*
pre'pro·duc'tion *adj.* & *n.*
pre·pro'gram' *v.*
pre'pub·li·ca'tion *adj.* & *n.*
pre·pu'pal *adj.*
pre·pur'chase *v.*
pre·qual'i·fy' *v.*
pre're·ces'sion *adj.*
pre'-Ref·or·ma'tion *adj.*
pre're·lease' *adj.* & *n.*
pre-Ren'ais·sance' *adj.*
pre're·quire'ment *n.*
pre're·tire'ment *adj.* & *n.*
pre'-Rev·o·lu'tion *adj.*
pre'rev·o·lu'tion·ar'y *adj.*
pre'sale' *n.*
pre·sched'ule *v.*
pre·screen' *v.*
pre·sea'son *adj.* & *n.*
pre·show' *adj.*
pre·slice' *v.*
pre·sort' *v.*
pre·spec'i·fy' *v.*
pre·split' *adj.*
pre·stamp' *v.*
pre·ster'il·ize' *v.*
pre·sum'mit *adj.*
pre·sur'ger·y *adj.*
pre·sur'gi·cal *adj.*
pre·sweet'en *v.*
pre·tape' *v.*
pre'tax' *adj.*
pre·tel'e·vi'sion *adj.*
pre·tour'na·ment *adj.*
pre·train' *v.*
pre·train'ing *n.*
pre·treat' *v.*
pre·treat'ment *n.*
pre·tri'al *adj.* & *n.*
pre·trim' *v.*
pre'-Vic·to'ri·an *adj.*
pre'war' *adj.*
pre·wash' *v.*
pre·wrap' *v.*

IDENTICAL, VERY —**pre•cise'ly** *adv.* —**pre•cise'ness** *n.*

pre•ci•sion (prĭ-sĭzh'ən) *n.* The state, property, or quality of being precise.

pre•clude (prĭ-klo͞od') *v.* **-clud•ed, -clud•ing.** To make impossible : prevent.

pre•co•cious (prĭ-kō'shəs) *adj.* Marked by the early development of skills and abilities. —**pre•co'cious•ly** *adv.* —**pre•coc'i•ty** (-kŏs'ĭ-tē) *n.*

pre•cog•ni•tion (prē'kŏg-nĭsh'ən) *n.* Clairvoyant knowledge of something prior to its happening. —**pre•cog'ni•tive** *adj.*

pre-Co•lum•bi•an (prē'kə-lŭm'bē-ən) *adj.* Of, pertaining to, or originating in the Americas before the voyages of Columbus <*pre-Columbian* art>

pre•con•ceive (prē'kən-sēv') *v.* To form an opinion or conception of before knowing all the facts. —**pre'con•cep'tion** (-sĕp'shən) *n.*

pre•con•di•tion (prē'kən-dĭsh'ən) *n.* A prerequisite. —*v.* To put into a certain condition or mental attitude beforehand.

pre•cur•sor (prĭ-kûr'sər, prē'kûr'-) *n.* **1.** An indicator of one to come : forerunner. **2.** A predecessor.

pre•da•cious *or* **pre•da•ceous** (prĭ-dā'shəs) *adj.* Preying on other animals.

pre•date (prē-dāt') *v.* **1.** To come before in time : antedate. **2.** To mark with a date earlier than the actual one.

pre•da•tion (prĭ-dā'shən) *n.* **1.** The act of plundering or marauding. **2.** The capturing of prey as a means of maintaining life.

pred•a•to•ry (prĕd'ə-tôr'ē, -tōr'ē) *adj.* **1.** Of, relating to, or marked by plunder. **2.** Selfishly exploiting others. **3.** Predacious. —**pred'a•tor** *n.*

pre•de•cease (prē'dĭ-sēs') *v.* To die before (another).

pred•e•ces•sor (prĕd'ĭ-sĕs'ər, prē'dĭ-) *n.* **1.** One that comes before another, esp. in an office or function. **2.** An ancestor.

pre•des•ti•na•tion (prē-dĕs'tə-nā'shən) *n.* *Theol.* **1.** The act by which God is held to have unalterably predestined all events. **2.** The doctrine that the destiny of each soul has been foreordained by God.

pre•des•tine (prē-dĕs'tĭn) *v.* To destine in advance : foreordain.

pre•de•ter•mine (prē'dĭ-tûr'mĭn) *v.* To determine in advance. —**pre'de•ter'mi•na'tion** *n.* —**pre'de•ter'min•er** *n.*

pred•i•ca•ble (prĕd'ĭ-kə-bəl) *adj.* Capable of being asserted or predicated.

pre•dic•a•ment (prĭ-dĭk'ə-mənt) *n.* A difficult or distressing situation.

pred•i•cate (prĕd'ĭ-kāt') *v.* **-cat•ed, -cat•ing. 1.** To find a basis for : establish. **2.** To assert to be a quality or characteristic <*predicate* humanity's resilient spirit> —*n.* (-kĭt). The part of a sentence or clause that makes a statement about the subject. —**pred'i•ca'tion** *n.* —**pred'i•ca'tive** *adj.*

pre•dict (prĭ-dĭkt') *v.* To state in advance. ★ *syns:* FORECAST, FORETELL, PORTEND, PROGNOSTICATE —**pre•dict'a•bil'i•ty** *n.* —**pre•dict'a•ble** *adj.* —**pre•dict'a•bly** *adv.* —**pre•dic'tion** *n.* —**pre•dic'tor** *n.*

pre•di•gest (prē'dĭ-jĕst', -dī-) *v.* To subject to partial digestion, as by enzymatic action. —**pre'di•ges'tion** *n.*

pre•di•lec•tion (prĕd'l-ĕk'shən, prēd'l-) *n.* A natural or habitual preference.

pre•dis•pose (prē'dĭ-spōz') *v.* **1.** To incline or influence beforehand. **2.** To make susceptible. —**pre•dis'po•si'tion** *n.*

pre•dom•i•nant (prĭ-dŏm'ə-nənt) *adj.* **1.** Superior in power or importance : dominant. **2.** Most commonly occurring or existing : prevalent. —**pre•dom'i•nance** *n.* —**pre•dom'i•nant•ly** *adv.*

pre•dom•i•nate (prĭ-dŏm'ə-nāt') *v.* **1.** To be of greater strength, number, importance, or prominence. **2.** To have authority or controlling influence : dominate. —**pre•dom'i•nate•ly** *adv.*

pree•mie (prē'mē) *n.* *Informal.* A baby born prematurely.

pre•em•i•nent *or* **pre•em•i•nent** (prē-ĕm'ə-nənt) *adj.* Excelling all others : outstanding. —**pre•em'i•nence** *n.*

pre•empt *or* **pre•empt** (prē-ĕmpt') *v.* **1.** To gain buying rights to (public land) by settling before others. **2.** To take for oneself before others. **3.** To take the place of (a scheduled program). —**pre•emp'tion** *n.* —**pre•emp'tive** *adj.*

preen (prēn) *v.* **1.** To groom (feathers) with the beak. **2.** To primp. **3.** To take self-satisfied pride in (oneself).

pre•ex•ist *or* **pre•ex•ist** (prē'ĭg-zĭst') *v.* To exist before something else. —**pre'-ex•ist'ence** *n.* —**pre'-ex•ist'ent** *adj.*

pre•fab (prē'făb') *n.* A prefabricated building or structural part.

pre•fab•ri•cate (prē-făb'rĭ-kāt') *v.* To manufacture in standard sections for easy shipping and assembly. —**pre•fab'ri•ca'tion** *n.* —**pre•fab'ri•ca'tor** *n.*

pref•ace (prĕf'ĭs) *n.* An introductory statement or remark : foreword. —*v.* **-aced, -ac•ing.** To introduce or provide with a preface. —**pref'a•to'ry** (-ə-tôr'ē, -tōr'ē) *adj.*

pre•fect (prē'fĕkt') *n.* **1.** A high administrative official or magistrate. **2.** A student monitor, esp. in a private school. —**pre'fec'ture** (-fĕk'chər) *n.*

pre•fer (prĭ-fûr') *v.* **-ferred, -fer•ring. 1.** To select as being more desirable : favor. **2.** To present (e.g., a charge against another) before a legal authority. —**pref'er•a•ble** (prĕf'ər-ə-bəl) *adj.* —**pref'er•a•bly** *adv.*

pref•er•ence (prĕf'ər-əns) *n.* **1.** Choice : option. **2.** Partiality for something over another. **3.** One that is favored or chosen. —**pref'er•en'tial** (-ə-rĕn'shəl) *adj.*

pre•fer•ment (prĭ-fûr'mənt) *n.* Selection for promotion or favored treatment.

pre•fig•ure (prē-fĭg'yər) *v.* **1.** To indicate in advance : foreshadow. **2.** To imagine ahead of time. —**pre•fig'ure•ment** *n.*

pre•fix (prē'fĭks', prē-fĭks') *v.* To put (e.g., a title) before. —*n.* (prē'fĭks'). An affix that occurs at the beginning of a word.

pre•flight (prē′flīt′) *adj.* Readying for or taking place before aircraft flight.

preg•na•ble (prĕg′nə-bəl) *adj.* Unprotected against attack or capture, as a fort. **—preg′na•bil′i•ty** *n.*

preg•nant (prĕg′nənt) *adj.* **1.** Carrying an unborn fetus or offspring. **2.** Significant : meaningful. **—preg′nan•cy** *n.*

pre•heat (prē-hēt′) *v.* To heat (e.g., an oven) in advance.

pre•hen•sile (prĭ-hĕn′sĭl, -sīl′) *adj.* Adapted for seizing or holding, esp. by wrapping around.

prehensile
Two examples of prehensile tails: (left) *opossum and* (right) *spider monkey*

pre•his•tor•ic (prē′hĭ-stôr′ĭk, -stŏr′-) *also* **pre•his•tor•i•cal** (-ĭ-kəl) *adj.* Of, relating to, or belonging to the period prior to recorded history. **—pre′his•tor′i•cal•ly** *adv.*

pre•ig•ni•tion (prē′ĭg-nĭsh′ən) *n.* Ignition of fuel in an internal-combustion engine before the spark passes through the fuel.

pre•judge (prē-jŭj′) *v.* To judge before knowing all the facts. **—pre•judg′er** *n.* **—pre•judg′ment, pre•judge′ment** *n.*

prej•u•dice (prĕj′ə-dĭs) *n.* **1.** A bias for or against something formed without sufficient basis. **2.** Irrational intolerance of or hostility toward members of a certain race, religion, or group. **3.** Detriment, esp. to one's legal rights. *—v.* **-diced, -dic•ing. 1.** To fill with prejudice : bias. **2.** To be detrimental to. **—prej′u•di′cial** (-dĭsh′əl) *adj.*

prel•ate (prĕl′ĭt) *n.* A high-ranking member of the clergy, as a bishop or cardinal. **—prel′a•cy** (-ə-sē) *n.*

pre•lim•i•nar•y (prĭ-lĭm′ə-nĕr′ē) *adj.* Preceding or preparing for the main event or business. *—n., pl.* **-ies.** Something, as a remark, that is preliminary. **—pre•lim′i•nar′i•ly** (-nâr′ə-lē) *adv.*

pre•lit•er•ate (prē-lĭt′ər-ĭt) *adj.* Of or relating to a culture lacking a written language. **—pre•lit′er•ate** *n.*

prel•ude (prĕl′yo͞od′, prā′lo͞od′) *n.* **1.** An introductory or preliminary action, performance, or event. **2.** *Mus.* **a.** A piece or movement preceding the main theme. **b.** A short composition in free style. **c.** An organ solo played before a church service.

pre•mar•i•tal (prē-măr′ĭ-tl) *adj.* Existing or happening before marriage.

pre•ma•ture (prē′mə-to͝or′, -tyo͝or′, -cho͝or′) *adj.* Appearing, done, occurring, or born before the usual or correct time : early. **—pre′ma•ture′ly** *adv.*

pre•med (prē′mĕd′) *adj. Informal.* Premedical. *—n.* **1.** A premedical student. **2.** Premedical studies.

pre•med•i•cal (prē-mĕd′ĭ-kəl) *adj.* Preparing for or preceding the study of medicine.

pre•med•i•tate (prē-mĕd′ĭ-tāt′) *v.* To plan or plot beforehand. **—pre•med′i•tat′ed** *adj.* **—pre•med′i•ta′tion** *n.*

pre•mier (prē′mē-ər, prĭ-mîr′) *adj.* **1.** Foremost in importance or rank : chief. **2.** First or earliest in time. *—n.* (prĭ-mîr′). The chief executive or prime minister of a government. **—pre•mier′ship′** *n.*

pre•mière (prĭ-mîr′, prĭm-yâr′) *n.* An initial public presentation, as of a play or film. *—v.* **-mièred, -mièr•ing.** To present or receive an initial public presentation.

prem•ise (prĕm′ĭs) *n.* **1.** A postulate, assumption, or hypothesis serving as the basis of an argument. **2. premises.** Real estate and the structures on it. *—v.* **-ised, -is•ing.** To make or state as a premise.

pre•mi•um (prē′mē-əm) *n.* **1.** An award or prize. **2.** An additional sum paid esp. as an incentive : bonus. **3.** An additional amount charged above the nominal value. **4.** An exceptionally high value <put a *premium* on honesty> **5.** A payment, often in installments, for an insurance policy.

pre•mo•lar (prē-mō′lər) *n.* One of 8 paired bicuspids situated between the canines and molars. **—pre•mo′lar** *adj.*

pre•mo•ni•tion (prē′mə-nĭsh′ən, prĕm′ə-) *n.* **1.** An advance warning. **2.** A presentiment. **—pre•mon′i•to′ry** (-mŏn′ĭ-tôr′ē, -tōr′ē) *adj.*

pre•na•tal (prē-nāt′l) *adj.* Existing or happening before birth. **—pre•na′tal•ly** *adv.*

pre•oc•cu•py (prē-ŏk′yə-pī′) *v.* **1.** To absorb wholly the mind or attention of. **2.** To occupy beforehand or before another. **—pre•oc′cu•pa′tion** (-pā′shən) *n.* **—pre•oc′cu•pied′** *adj.*

pre•op•er•a•tive (prē-ŏp′ər-ə-tĭv, -ŏp′rə-, -ŏp′ə-rā′-) *adj.* Prior to surgery.

pre•or•bit•al (prē-ôr′bĭ-tl) *adj.* Occurring before establishment of an orbit.

pre•or•dain (prē′ôr-dān′) *v.* To decree or ordain in advance.

prep (prĕp) *Informal. —adj.* Preparatory. *—v.* **prepped, prep•ping. 1.** To study or train for something. **2.** To prepare for medical examination or surgery.

pre•pack•age (prē-păk′ĭj) *v.* To wrap or package (e.g., food) before selling.

prep•a•ra•tion (prĕp′ə-rā′shən) *n.* **1.** The act or process of preparing. **2.** The state of being prepared. **3.** *often* **preparations.** Preparatory measures. **4.** Something prepared, as a medicinal mixture.

pre•par•a•to•ry (prĭ-pâr′ə-tôr′ē, -tōr′ē, -păr′-) *adj.* Serving to prepare.

preparatory school *n.* A private school preparing students chiefly for college.

pre•pare (prĭ-pâr′) *v.* **-pared, -par•ing. 1.** To make or get ready for some purpose, task, or event. **2.** To produce by combining elements or ingredients. **3.** To provide in advance : equip. **4.** To put into writing.

pre•par•ed•ness (prĭ-pâr′ĭd-nĭs) *n.* A state of sufficient preparation, esp. for war.

pre•pay (prē-pā′) *v.* To pay or pay for ahead of time. **—pre•pay′ment** *n.*

pre•pon•der•ate (prĭ-pŏn′də-rāt′) *v.* **-at•ed, -at•ing.** To be superior in power, weight, number, or importance. **—pre•pon′der•ance** *n.* **—pre•pon′der•ant** *adj.* **—pre•pon′der•ant•ly** *adv.*

prep•o•si•tion (prĕp′ə-zĭsh′ən) *n.* A word, as *by,* that indicates the relation of a substantive to a verb, adjective, or another substantive. **—prep′o•si′tion•al** *adj.*

pre•pos•sess (prē′pə-zĕs′) *v.* **1.** To influence in advance : bias. **2.** To make a favorable impression on beforehand.

pre•pos•sess•ing (prē′pə-zĕs′ĭng) *adj.* Creating a favorable impression : pleasing.

pre•pos•ter•ous (prĭ-pŏs′tər-əs) *adj.* **1.** Beyond all reason : absurd. **2.** Ridiculous : silly. **—pre•pos′ter•ous•ly** *adv.* **—pre•pos′ter•ous•ness** *n.*

prep•pie *or* **prep•py** (prĕp′ē) *n., pl.* **-pies.** *Informal.* **1.** A student attending a preparatory school. **2.** A student or young adult who dresses and behaves traditionally and conservatively.

pre•pu•ber•ty (prē-pyōō′bər-tē) *n.* The period just before puberty.

pre•pu•bes•cence (prē′pyōō-bĕs′əns) *n.* Prepuberty. **—pre′pu•bes′cent** *adj.*

pre•puce (prē′pyōōs′) *n.* The foreskin.

pre•re•cord (prē′rĭ-kôrd′) *v.* To record (a radio or television program) ahead of time.

pre•req•ui•site (prē-rĕk′wĭ-zĭt) *adj.* Required as a preliminary condition. **—pre•req′ui•site** *n.*

pre•rog•a•tive (prĭ-rŏg′ə-tĭv) *n.* A special right or privilege, esp. of one holding a certain rank or status.

pres•age (prĕs′ĭj) *n.* **1.** An omen of a future event : portent. **2.** A premonition : foreboding. —*v.* **pre•sage** (prĭ-sāj′, prĕs′ĭj) **-saged, -sag•ing. 1.** To foreshadow : portend. **2.** To foretell : prophesy.

pres•by•o•pi•a (prĕz′bē-ō′pē-ə, prĕs′-) *n.* Inability of the eye, esp. with advancing age, to focus sharply on close objects. **—pres′by•op′ic** (-ŏp′ĭk, -ō′pĭk) *adj.*

pres•by•ter (prĕz′bĭ-tər, prĕs′-) *n.* **1.** An elder in the Presbyterian Church. **2.** A priest or minister.

pres•by•te•ri•an (prĕz′bĭ-tîr′ē-ən, prĕs′-) *adj.* **1.** Of or relating to legislative and judicial church government by presbyters. **2. Presbyterian.** Of or relating to a Presbyterian Church. —*n.* A member of a Presbyterian Church. **—pres′by•te′ri•an•ism** *n.*

Presbyterian Church *n.* Any of various Protestant churches governed by presbyters and traditionally Calvinist in doctrine.

pres•by•ter•y (prĕz′bĭ-tĕr′ē, prĕs′-) *n., pl.* **-ies. 1.** A governmental body in Presbyterian churches composed of the ministers and representative elders of a certain district. **2.** The part of a church set aside for the clergy officiating at a service.

pre•school (prē′skōōl′) *adj.* Of or intended for a child too young for kindergarten. **—pre′school′er** *n.*

pre•science (prē′shəns, prē′shē-əns, prĕsh′əns, prĕsh′ē-əns) *n.* Accurate foreknowledge or foresight of future events. **—pre′scient** *adj.* **—pre′sci•ent•ly** *adv.*

pre•scribe (prĭ-skrīb′) *v.* **-scribed, -scrib•ing. 1.** To impose as a rule or guide : direct. **2.** To order or recommend (e.g., a specific drug) in medical treatment. **—pre•scrip′tive** (-skrĭp′tĭv) *adj.*

pre•scrip•tion (prĭ-skrĭp′shən) *n.* **1.** The act or process of prescribing. **2. a.** A physician's written instruction for the preparation and use of a medicine. **b.** A medicine ordered by prescription. **c.** Specifications for corrective lenses.

pres•ence (prĕz′əns) *n.* **1.** The fact or state of being present. **2.** Immediate proximity in time or space. **3.** Someone or something that is present. **4. a.** Carriage or bearing, esp. stately bearing. **b.** Self-assured confidence : poise.

pres•ent[1] (prĕz′ənt) *n.* **1.** The current moment or period : now. **2. a.** The verb tense expressing action, condition, or state in the present. **b.** A verb form in the present tense. **3. presents.** *Law.* The document or instrument under examination. —*adj.* **1.** Currently existing or occurring. **2.** Being in view or at hand. **3.** Of, pertaining to, or being a verb tense or form that indicates the actual or hypothetical present.

pre•sent[2] (prĭ-zĕnt′) *v.* **1.** To introduce to another, esp. formally. **2.** To offer (e.g., a new play) to the public. **3.** To make a gift or award of or to. **4.** To put forth for consideration. **5.** To aim or salute with (a weapon). **6.** *Law.* To bring (a charge or indictment) before a court. —*n.* **pres•ent** (prĕz′ənt). A gift. **—pre•sent′a•ble** *adj.* **—pres′en•ta′tion** *n.*

pres•ent-day (prĕz′ənt-dā′) *adj.* Currently existing or occurring.

pre•sen•ti•ment (prĭ-zĕn′tə-mənt) *n.* An intuitive feeling that something will soon occur : premonition.

pres•ent•ly (prĕz′ənt-lē) *adv.* **1.** Shortly : soon. **2.** Currently : now.

present participle *n.* A participle that expresses present action, condition, or state and that is formed in English by adding *-ing* to the infinitive.

pres•er•va•tion•ist (prĕz′ər-vā′shə-nĭst) *n.* One who advocates preservation, esp. of natural areas or endangered species. **—pres′er•va′tion•ism** *n.*

pre•serve (prĭ-zûrv′) *v.* **-served, -serv•ing. 1.** To protect from harm. **2.** To maintain intact or unchanged. **3.** To prepare or treat in order to prevent spoilage or decay. —*n.* **1.** *often* **preserves.** Fruit preserved with sugar. **2.** An area for the safeguarding of wildlife or natural resources. —**pres'er•va'tion** (prĕz'ər-vā'shən) *n.* —**pre•serv'a•tive** *adj.* & *n.* —**pre•serv'er** *n.*

pre•set (prē'sĕt') *v.* To set (an automatic device) in advance.

pre•shrunk *also* **pre-shrunk** (prē'shrŭngk') *adj.* Processed during manufacture to minimize later shrinkage.

pre•side (prĭ-zīd') *v.* **-sid•ed, -sid•ing. 1.** To be in a position of control, esp. to serve as chairperson. **2.** To have or exercise authority.

pres•i•dent (prĕz'ĭ-dənt, -dĕnt') *n.* **1.** One selected to preside. **2.** *often* **President.** The chief of state of a republic, esp. the chief political executive of the U.S. **3.** The chief executive official of an organization, as a corporation. —**pres'i•den•cy** *n.* —**pres'i•den'tial** (-dĕn'shəl) *adj.*

Pres•i•dents' Day (prĕz'ĭ-dənts, -dĕnts) *n.* The 3rd Monday in Feb., a U.S. legal holiday commemorating the birthdays of George Washington and Abraham Lincoln.

pre•soak (prē-sōk') *v.* To soak before laundering.

press (prĕs) *v.* **1.** To exert steady force or pressure (against). **2.** To squeeze out the juice or contents of (e.g., grapes). **3. a.** To force into a desired shape or smoothness by steady pressure. **b.** To smooth by ironing. **4.** To urge insistently. **5.** To constrain : harass. **6.** To pursue with determination. **7.** To force one's way. **8.** To crowd together. **9.** To weigh heavily, as on the mind. —*n.* **1.** A machine or device for exerting pressure. **2.** A printing press. **3.** An establishment for printing. **4.** The art, process, or business of printing. **5. a.** Printed matter, esp. newspapers and periodicals. **b.** Persons, as reporters, employed in the news media. **c.** Comment and criticism by the news media. **6.** A crowd : throng. **7.** The act of applying pressure or the state of being pressed. **8.** Urgent claim or demand. **9.** The correctly creased state of a pressed garment or fabric. **10.** An upright storage closet. —**press'er** *n.*

press agent *n.* An agent hired to promote favorable publicity for a client.

press•ing (prĕs'ĭng) *adj.* Urgent : critical.

press•man (prĕs'mən, -măn') *n.* The operator of a printing press.

press•room (prĕs'ro͞om', -ro͝om') *n.* **1.** The location of the presses in a printing establishment. **2.** A room for reporters.

pres•sure (prĕsh'ər) *n.* **1.** The act of pressing or the state of being pressed. **2.** The application of steady force by one body in direct contact with another. **3.** The amount of force applied per unit of area of a surface. **4.** A compelling or constraining influence. **5.** Urgent requirements. **6.** A distressing or oppressive burden. —*v.* **-sured, -sur•ing.** To force, as by influencing or persuading.

pressure cooker *n.* **1.** An airtight metal pot that uses steam under pressure at high temperature to cook food quickly. **2.** A position of difficulty, stress, or anxiety.

pressure group *n.* A group that exerts pressure, esp. on legislators, in order to advance or safeguard its interests.

pressure suit *n.* An airtight suit worn in high-altitude aircraft or in spacecraft to protect against low-pressure conditions.

pres•sur•ize (prĕsh'ə-rīz') *v.* **-ized, -iz•ing.** To maintain (e.g., an aircraft cabin) at normal atmospheric pressure. —**pres'sur•i•za'tion** *n.*

pres•ti•dig•i•ta•tion (prĕs'tĭ-dĭj'ĭ-tā'shən) *n.* Sleight of hand. —**pres'ti•dig'i•ta'tor** *n.*

pres•tige (prĕ-stēzh', -stēj') *n.* A person's standing or repute in the opinion of others. —**pres•tig'ious** (-stĭj'əs, -stē'jəs) *adj.*

pres•to (prĕs'tō) *adv.* **1.** *Mus.* Very quickly. —Used as a direction. **2.** At once : immediately. —**pres'to** *adj.*

pre•sume (prĭ-zo͞om') *v.* **-sumed, -sum•ing. 1.** To assume to be true : take for granted. **2.** To act without authority or leave : dare. **3.** To take undue advantage of something <*presumed* on their hospitality> —**pre•sum'a•ble** *adj.* —**pre•sum'a•bly** *adv.* —**pre•sum'er** *n.*

pre•sump•tion (prĭ-zŭmp'shən) *n.* **1.** Audacious behavior or language : effrontery. **2. a.** An assumption or supposition based on reasonable evidence. **b.** Grounds for accepting or presuming. —**pre•sump'tive** *adj.* —**pre•sump'tive•ly** *adv.*

pre•sump•tu•ous (prĭ-zŭmp'cho͞o-əs) *adj.* Unduly or impertinently bold : forward. —**pre•sump'tu•ous•ness** *n.*

pre•sup•pose (prē'sə-pōz') *v.* **1.** To suppose beforehand : assume. **2.** To require as a necessary prior condition. —**pre•sup'po•si'tion** (-sŭp'ə-zĭsh'ən) *n.*

pre•teen (prē'tēn') *n.* A preadolescent child. —**pre'teen'** *adj.*

pre•tence (prē'tĕns', prĭ-tĕns') *n. esp. Brit. var. of* PRETENSE.

pre•tend (prĭ-tĕnd') *v.* **1.** To make believe : feign <*pretended* to be furious> **2.** To claim falsely : profess <didn't *pretend* to be an expert> **3.** To assert a claim, as to a throne. —**pre•tend'er** *n.*

pre•tense (prē'tĕns', prĭ-tĕns') *n.* **1.** A false and deceptive appearance or action. **2.** A false purpose : pretext. **3.** An outward show or attempt. **4.** An unsupported claim. **5.** Ostentatious display. **6.** Affectation.

pre•ten•tious (prĭ-tĕn'shəs) *adj.* **1.** Making claims, as to distinction or excellence. **2.** Extravagantly showy : ostentatious. —**pre•ten'sion** *n.* —**pre•ten'tious•ly** *adv.* —**pre•ten'tious•ness** *n.*

pret•er•it or **pret•er•ite** (prĕt'ər-ĭt) *adj.* Designating a verb tense used to express past or completed action or condition. —**pret'er•it** *n.*

pre•ter•nat•u•ral (prē'tər-năch'ər-əl, -năch'rəl) *adj.* **1.** Going beyond the ordinary course of nature. **2.** Having no natural explanation or cause. —**pre'ter•nat'u•ral•ly** *adv.* —**pre'ter•nat'u•ral•ness** *n.*

pre•text (prē′tĕkst′) *n.* A professed rather than a real reason.

pret•ti•fy (prĭt′ĭ-fī′) *v.* **-fied, -fy•ing.** To make pretty. **—pret′ti•fi•ca′tion** *n.*

†**pret•ty** (prĭt′ē) *adj.* **-ti•er, -ti•est. 1.** Pleasing or appealing, esp. in a delicate way. **2.** First-rate : fine. —Usu. used ironically <a *pretty* job of bungling> **3.** *Informal.* Sizable <a *pretty* sum> *—adv.* **1.** Somewhat : moderately <a *pretty* bad cut> **2.** *Regional.* In a pretty or pleasing way. *—v.* **-tied, -ty•ing.** *Informal.* To make pretty. **—pret′ti•ly** *adv.* **—pret′ti•ness** *n.*

pret•zel (prĕt′səl) *n.* A hard, salted cracker usu. shaped like a loose knot.

pre•vail (prĭ-vāl′) *v.* **1.** To win control : triumph. **2.** To be effective : succeed. **3.** To be common or frequent : predominate. **4.** To be in force or use : persist. **—prevail on** (*or* **upon).** To persuade successfully. **—pre•vail′er** *n.* **—pre•vail′ing•ly** *adv.*

prev•a•lent (prĕv′ə-lənt) *adj.* In widespread existence, occurrence, or use. **—prev′a•lence** *n.* **—prev′a•lent•ly** *adv.*

pre•var•i•cate (prĭ-văr′ĭ-kāt′) *v.* **-cat•ed, -cat•ing. 1.** To speak evasively : equivocate. **2.** To stray from the truth : lie. **—pre•var′i•ca′tion** *n.* **—pre•var′i•ca′tor** *n.*

pre•vent (prĭ-vĕnt′) *v.* **1.** To keep from taking place : ward off. **2.** To keep (someone) from acting. **—pre•vent′a•ble, pre•vent′i•ble** *adj.* **—pre•ven′tion** *n.*

pre•ven•tive (prĭ-vĕn′tĭv) *also* **pre•ven•ta•tive** (-tə-tĭv) *adj.* **1.** Protecting, as against failure : precautionary. **2.** Preventing disease. **—pre•ven′tive** *n.*

pre•view *also* **pre•vue** (prē′vyoo′) *—n.* **1.** An advance showing or viewing prior to public presentation. **2.** The presentation of excerpts from a forthcoming motion picture to advertise it. **3.** An advance indication. *—v.* **-viewed, -view•ing** *also* **-vued, -vu•ing.** To view or show beforehand.

pre•vi•ous (prē′vē-əs) *adj.* Existing or occurring earlier. **—pre′vi•ous•ly** *adv.*

previous to *prep.* Prior to : before.

pre•vi•sion (prĭ-vĭzh′ən) *n.* **1.** Foreknowledge : foresight. **2.** A prediction : forecast.

prey (prā) *n.* **1.** An animal hunted or seized for food. **2.** A victim. **3.** The act or habit of preying. *—v.* **1.** To seek or eat as prey. **2.** To take unfair advantage of : victimize. **3.** To have a detrimental effect <Guilt *preyed* on my mind.>

price (prīs) *n.* **1.** The sum of money expected or given for the sale of something. **2.** The cost at which something is obtained. **3.** The cost of bribing someone. *—v.* **priced, pric•ing. 1.** To set a price for. **2.** To ask or discover the price of.

price•less (prīs′lĭs) *adj.* Of incalcuable worth : invaluable.

price war *n.* A period of business competition in which competitors repeatedly undercut each other's prices.

pric•ey *also* **pric•y** (prī′sē) *adj.* **-i•er, -i•est.** *Informal.* Expensive.

prick (prĭk) *n.* **1. a.** An act or instance of piercing. **b.** The sensation of being pierced. **2.** A tiny mark or hole made by piercing. **3.** Something pointed or sharp, as a thorn. *—v.* **1.** To pierce lightly. **2.** To affect sharply with emotional pain. **3.** To outline by means of small perforations.

prick•le (prĭk′əl) *n.* **1.** A small, sharp spine or thorn, as on a plant. **2.** A slight tingling sensation. *—v.* **-led, -ling. 1.** To prick slightly, as with a thorn. **2.** To feel or cause tingling. **—prick′ly** *adj.*

prickly heat *n.* Inflammation of the sweat glands marked by an itching and tingling skin rash.

prickly pear *n.* A cactus of the genus *Opuntia,* with bristly flattened or cylindrical joints, usu. yellow flowers, and edible ovoid fruit.

pride (prīd) *n.* **1.** Proper respect for one's own dignity and worth. **2.** Pleasure or satisfaction over something done, achieved, or owned. **3.** A source of pride. **4.** Excessive self-esteem : conceit. *—v.* **prid•ed, prid•ing.** To take pride in (oneself). **—pride′ful** *adj.* **—pride′ful•ly** *adv.*

prie-dieu (prē-dyœ′) *n., pl.* **-dieus** *or* **-dieux** (-dyœz′). A low bench for kneeling in prayer, fitted with an elevated shelf for supporting a prayerbook or the elbows.

priest (prēst) *n.* **1.** A member of the clergy, esp. in the Roman Catholic, Eastern Orthodox, and Anglican churches, ranking below a bishop. **2.** A person having authority to perform religious rites. **—priest′hood′** *n.* **—priest′li•ness** *n.* **—priest′ly** *adj.*

priest•ess (prē′stĭs) *n.* A woman who presides over esp. pagan religious rites.

prig (prĭg) *n.* A smugly proper or prudish person. **—prig′gish** *adj.*

prim (prĭm) *adj.* **prim•mer, prim•mest.** Affectedly proper or precise : strait-laced. **—prim′ly** *adv.* **—prim′ness** *n.*

pri•ma•cy (prī′mə-sē) *n., pl.* **-cies. 1.** The state of ranking first. **2.** The rank, office, or duties of an ecclesiastical primate.

pri•ma don•na (prē′mə dŏn′ə, prĭm′ə) *n., pl.* **prima don•nas. 1.** The principal female soloist of an opera company. **2.** A self-centered or temperamental person.

pri•ma fa•cie (prī′mə fā′shē, fā′shə) *adj. & adv.* At first view : apparent <*prima facie* proof>

pri•mal (prī′məl) *adj.* **1.** First in time : primitive. **2.** First in importance : chief.

pri•mar•i•ly (prī-mĕr′ə-lē, -mâr′-) *adv.* **1.** In the first place. **2.** For the most part.

pri•ma•ry (prī′mĕr′ē, -mə-rē) *adj.* **1. a.** First in time or sequence : original. **b.** Serving to prepare. **2.** First in degree, quality, or importance : chief. **3.** Not derived from something else : firsthand <a *primary* source> **4.** Fundamental : basic <a *primary* need> ★ ***syns:*** CAPITAL, CARDINAL, CHIEF, DOMINANT, FIRST, FOREMOST, MAIN, PARAMOUNT, PREEMINENT, PREMIER, PRIME, PRINCIPAL, TOP *—n., pl.* **-ries. 1.** Something that is primary in time, sequence, or importance. **2.** A preliminary election in which party candidates are nominated for office by registered voters.

primary school *n.* **1.** A school that includes the first 3 or 4 grades and sometimes kindergarten. **2.** Elementary school.

pri•mate (prī'māt') *n.* **1.** (*also* -mĭt). The highest-ranking bishop of a province or country. **2.** One of the group of mammals that includes the lemurs, monkeys, apes, and human beings.

prime (prīm) *adj.* **1.** First in quality, importance, rank, or time <*prime* beef><his *prime* concern> **2.** Of or indicating a prime number. —*n.* **1.** The earliest phase of something, esp. dawn or spring. **2.** The most vigorous, flourishing, or successful stage or period. **3.** The best or most select part. **4.** A prime number. —*v.* **primed, prim•ing. 1.** To prepare (a gun or mine) for detonating. **2.** To put (e.g., a pump) in operation by filling with a liquid. **3.** To cover with a preliminary coat before painting. **4.** To teach or train beforehand.

prime meridian *n.* The meridian of 0° longitude at Greenwich, England, from which longitude E and W is measured.

prime minister *n.* **1.** The chief minister of a ruler or government. **2.** The head of the cabinet and often also the chief executive of a parliamentary democracy.

prime number *n.* A positive number that has no factor other than itself and 1.

prim•er[1] (prĭm'ər) *n.* **1.** An elementary textbook for teaching reading to children. **2.** A usu. small book covering the fundamentals of a topic.

prim•er[2] (prī'mər) *n.* **1.** One that primes. **2.** Material for priming a surface. **3.** A device for firing an explosive.

prime time *n.* The hours between 7 and 11 P.M., when the largest television audience is available. —**prime'-time'** *adj.*

pri•me•val (prī-mē'vəl) *adj.* Of or relating to the earliest ages **:** primordial.

prim•i•tive (prĭm'ĭ-tĭv) *adj.* **1.** Of or in an early stage of development. **2.** Crude or simple **:** unsophisticated <*primitive* technology> **3.** Of or pertaining to early human culture. **4.** Having skills acquired by oneself without formal training. —*n.* **1.** A member of a primitive society or culture. **2.** A self-taught artist. **3.** *Computer Sci.* A basic or fundamental unit of machine instruction or translation. —**prim'i•tive•ly** *adv.* —**prim'i•tive•ness** *n.*

prim•i•tiv•ism (prĭm'ĭ-tĭ-vĭz'əm) *n.* The style of art of primitive artists or cultures.

pri•mo•gen•i•tor (prī'mō-jĕn'ĭ-tər) *n.* An earliest ancestor.

pri•mo•gen•i•ture (prī'mō-jĕn'ĭ-cho͝or', -chər) *n.* **1.** The state of being the first-born child of a family. **2.** An exclusive right of the eldest child, esp. the eldest son, to inherit a family's estate.

pri•mor•di•al (prī-môr'dē-əl) *adj.* **1.** Existing first or in an original state **:** primeval. **2.** Fundamental **:** primary.

primp (prĭmp) *v.* To dress or arrange carefully **:** preen.

prim•rose (prĭm'rōz') *n.* A plant of the genus *Primula*, bearing tubular, variously colored 5-lobed flowers.

prince (prĭns) *n.* **1.** A male ruler of a principality. **2.** A male member of a royal family, esp. a son of the sovereign. **3.** An illustrious man, as in a group. —**prince'dom** *n.* —**prince'ly** *adj.*

prin•cess (prĭn'sĭs, -sĕs', prĭn-sĕs') *n.* **1.** A female ruler of a principality. **2.** A female member of a royal family, esp. a daughter of the sovereign. **3.** The wife of a prince.

prin•ci•pal (prĭn'sə-pəl) *adj.* Most important **:** chief. —*n.* **1.** The chief official of an elementary, junior high, or high school. **2.** A chief participant. **3.** A leading performer, as in a play. **4. a.** A financial holding as distinguished from its interest or revenue. **b.** A debt on which interest is calculated. **5.** *Law.* **a.** One who authorizes another to act as agent. **b.** One primarily responsible for an obligation. —**prin'ci•pal•ly** *adv.*

prin•ci•pal•i•ty (prĭn'sə-păl'ĭ-tē) *n., pl.* **-ties.** The territory, position, or jurisdiction of a prince.

principal parts *pl.n.* The series of inflected forms of a verb.

prin•ci•ple (prĭn'sə-pəl) *n.* **1.** A fundamental truth, law, or postulate. **2. a.** A rule or code of behavior. **b.** Moral or ethical standards in general **:** integrity. **3.** An underlying or established rule or policy. **4.** A scientific law underlying the working of natural phenomena or mechanical processes. **5.** A primary or original source.

prin•ci•pled (prĭn'sə-pəld) *adj.* Based on or acting from moral or ethical principles.

prink (prĭngk) *v.* To primp.

print (prĭnt) *n.* **1.** A mark made by pressing on a surface. **2.** Something marked or stamped with an impression. **3. a.** Inked impressions, as of lettering. **b.** Printed matter. **4.** A design or picture transferred from an engraved plate, wood block, or lithographic stone. **5.** The positive image of a photograph. **6. a.** Fabric stamped with a design. **b.** The design itself. —*v.* **1.** To stamp (e.g., a mark or design) on or in a surface. **2.** To mark or stamp (a surface) with a device, as a die. **3.** To produce by means of a printing press. **4.** To offer in printed form **:** publish. **5.** To write in block letters similar to commonly used printer's type. **6.** To make (a positive picture) on a photographically sensitive surface. —**print out.** To print automatically **:** produce a printout.

print•a•ble (prĭn'tə-bəl) *adj.* **1.** Capable of being printed or yielding a print. **2.** Suitable for publication.

printed circuit *n.* An electronic circuit made by applying a pattern of conductive metal to an insulating surface.

print•er (prĭn'tər) *n.* **1.** One that prints, esp. one whose occupation is printing. **2.** The part of a computer that produces printed matter.

print•ing (prĭn'tĭng) *n.* **1.** The art, operation, or business of producing printed matter. **2.**

Something printed. **3.** All the copies of a publication printed at one time.

printing press *n.* A machine that prints on a surface from inked type or plates.

print•out (prĭnt′out′) *n.* Printed material produced by a computer.

pri•or[1] (prī′ər) *adj.* **1.** Previous in time or order. **2.** Given or taking precedence, esp. in importance or value. **—pri•or′i•ty** (-ôr′ĭ-tē, -ŏr′-) *n.*

pri•or[2] (prī′ər) *n.* A monastic officer in charge of a priory.

pri•or•ess (prī′ər-ĭs) *n.* A nun in charge of a priory.

pri•or•i•tize (prī-ôr′ĭ-tīz′, -ŏr′-) *v.* **-tized, -tiz•ing.** To dispose of or handle in order of importance.

pri•or•y (prī′ə-rē) *n., pl.* **-ies.** A religious house governed by a prior or prioress.

prism (prĭz′əm) *n.* **1.** A geometric solid with equal and parallel polygons as ends and parallelograms as sides. **2.** A transparent prism with triangular ends and rectangular sides, used to refract light or disperse it into a spectrum. **3.** A decorative glass pendant, as on a chandelier. **—pris•mat′ic** (-măt′ĭk) *adj.*

pris•on (prĭz′ən) *n.* A place of confinement for accused or convicted persons.

pris•on•er (prĭz′ə-nər, prĭz′nər) *n.* **1.** A person held in confinement, esp. in a prison. **2.** A person not able or allowed to speak or act freely.

pris•sy (prĭs′ē) *adj.* **-si•er, -si•est.** Fussily prim and proper. **—pris′si•ly** *adv.* **—pris′si•ness** *n.*

pris•tine (prĭs′tēn′, prĭ-stēn′) *adj.* **1.** Of the earliest time or condition. **2.** Remaining in a pure, unspoiled state.

prith•ee (prĭth′ē, prĭth′ē) *interj. Archaic.* —Used to express a request or wish.

pri•va•cy (prī′və-sē) *n., pl.* **-cies. 1.** Seclusion or isolation from others. **2.** Secrecy.

pri•vate (prī′vĭt) *adj.* **1.** Secluded from others. **2. a.** Of or restricted to a single person : personal. **b.** Intimate : secret. **3.** Not for public use or participation. **4.** Owned or controlled by a person or group rather than the public or government. **5.** Not holding office <a *private* citizen> *—n.* An enlisted person of the lowest rank in the U.S. Army or Marine Corps. **—pri′vate•ly** *adv.*

▲ ***word history:*** The noun *private,* denoting a soldier of the lowest rank, developed from the adjective *private* in the sense "not holding an official or public position." Just as a private citizen is one who holds no public office, so a private soldier is one who has neither special responsibilities nor the rank that goes with them.

private detective *n.* A privately employed detective.

pri•va•teer (prī′və-tîr′) *n.* **1.** A privately owned vessel commissioned in wartime to seize enemy ships. **2.** The master or a crew member of a privateer. **—pri′va•teer′** *v.*

private eye *n.* A private detective.

private first class *n.* An enlisted person ranking above private and below corporal in the U.S. Army or Marine Corps.

pri•va•tion (prī-vā′shən) *n.* **1.** Lack of basic life necessities or comforts. **2.** An act or instance of deprivation.

pri•va•tize (prī′və-tīz′) *v.* **-tized, -tiz•ing.** To change (e.g., an industry) from governmental or public ownership or control to private enterprise. **—pri′va•ti•za′tion** *n.*

priv•et (prĭv′ĭt) *n.* A shrub, *Ligustrum vulgare* or *L. ovalifolium,* with small dark-green pointed leaves and white flower clusters, widely used for hedges.

priv•i•lege (prĭv′ə-lĭj) *n.* A special right or immunity granted to a person or group. **—priv′i•lege** *v.*

priv•i•leged (prĭv′ə-lĭjd) *adj.* **1.** Having or benefiting from a privilege. **2.** Legally exempted from disclosure <a *privileged* communication>

priv•y (prĭv′ē) *adj.* **1.** Made a party to secret information. **2.** Private or personal rather than official. *—n., pl.* **-ies.** A toilet, esp. an outhouse.

prize[1] (prīz) *n.* **1.** Something offered or awarded in a contest or lottery. **2.** Something worth pursuing or attaining. *—adj.* **1.** Offered or awarded as a prize. **2.** Given or deserving a prize. **3.** Outstanding : exceptional. *—v.* **prized, priz•ing.** To place a high value on : esteem.

prize[2] (prīz) *n.* Enemy property, esp. a vessel, captured in wartime.

†**prize**[3] (prīz) *v.* **prized, priz•ing.** To move or force with or as if with a lever : pry. *—n.* **1.** Leverage. **2.** *Regional.* Something used as a lever.

prize•fight (prīz′fīt′) *n.* A match between professional boxers. **—prize′fight′er** *n.* **—prize′fight′ing** *n.*

prize•win•ner (prīz′wĭn′ər) *n.* A winner of a prize. **—prize′win′ning** *adj.*

pro[1] (prō) *n., pl.* **pros. 1.** An argument in support of something. **2.** A person or side in favor of something. *—adv.* In favor. *—adj.* Favoring.

pro[2] (prō) *Informal. —n., pl.* **pros. 1.** A professional, esp. in sports. **2.** An expert in a given field. *—adj.* Professional <*pro* football>

pro-a•bor•tion (prō′ə-bôr′shən) *adj.* Favoring or supporting legalized abortion.

prob•a•bil•i•ty (prŏb′ə-bĭl′ĭ-tē) *n., pl.* **-ties. 1.** The state or quality of being probable. **2.** Something, as a situation, that is probable. **3.** *Math.* A number, esp. a ratio, expressing the likelihood of occurrence of a given event.

prob•a•ble (prŏb′ə-bəl) *adj.* **1.** Likely to be or become a reality. **2.** Plausible but not certain or proved. **—prob′a•bly** *adv.*

pro•bate (prō′bāt′) *n.* Legal determination of the validity of a will. *—v.* **-bat•ed, -bat•ing.** To prove the validity of (a will) by probate.

pro•ba•tion (prō-bā′shən) *n.* **1.** Determination during a trial period of a person's suitability, as for membership in a working or social group. **2.** The supervised release of a convicted offender on the promise of good conduct. **—pro•ba'tion•al, pro•ba'tion•ar'y** (-shə-nĕr'ē) *adj.*

pro•ba•tion•er (prō-bā'shə-nər) *n.* A person undergoing a period of probation.

pro•ba•tive (prō'bə-tĭv) *adj.* **1.** Serving to test or explore. **2.** Serving to prove.

probe (prōb) *n.* **1.** A device for investigating an unknown environment, as outer space. **2.** A slender instrument used esp. for examining a wound or bodily cavity. **3.** A careful examination or investigation with or as if with a probe. —*v.* **probed, prob•ing. 1.** To examine with a probe. **2.** To investigate painstakingly.

pro•bi•ty (prō'bĭ-tē) *n.* Moral uprightness **:** integrity.

prob•lem (prŏb'ləm) *n.* **1.** A difficult or perplexing question or issue. **2.** One that is troublesome or vexatious. **3.** A question proposed for consideration, discussion, or solution. **—prob'lem** *adj.*

prob•lem•at•ic (prŏb'lə-măt'ĭk) *or* **prob•lem•at•i•cal** (-ĭ-kəl) *adj.* **1.** Posing a problem or question. **2.** Open to doubt **:** dubious. **—prob'lem•at'i•cal•ly** *adv.*

pro bo•no (prō bō'nō) *adj.* Done for the public good without compensation.

pro•bos•cis (prō-bŏs'ĭs) *n., pl.* **-cis•es** *or* **-bos•ci•des** (-bŏs'ĭ-dēz'). **1.** A long, movable snout, as an elephant's trunk. **2.** A long, tubelike mouth part of certain insects.

pro•bus•ing (prō'bŭs'ĭng) *adj.* Favoring or supporting the busing of children to schools outside their neighborhoods as a means of achieving racial integration.

pro•caine hydrochloride (prō'kān') *n.* A white crystalline compound used as a local anesthetic.

pro•ce•dure (prə-sē'jər) *n.* **1.** A certain way of getting something done. **2.** An established series of steps. **3.** A prescribed or traditional set of forms to be followed. **—pro•ce'dur•al** *adj.*

pro•ceed (prō-sēd', prə-) *v.* **1.** To continue, esp. after stopping. **2.** To carry on an action or process. **3.** To go forward in an orderly way **:** advance. **4.** To issue **:** arise. **5.** To begin legal action.

pro•ceed•ing (prō-sē'dĭng, prə-) *n.* **1.** A course of action. **2.** Something transacted. **3. proceedings. a.** A succession of events **:** doings. **b.** A record of business conducted in an organization. **c.** Legal action.

pro•ceeds (prō'sēdz') *pl.n.* The profits from a business or fund-raising venture.

proc•ess (prŏs'ĕs', prō'sĕs') *n.* **1.** A series of steps or operations toward a desired result or product. **2.** A natural action or function marked by gradual change from one state to another. **3.** *Law.* **a.** A mandate to appear in court. **b.** The course of a judicial proceeding. **4.** A projecting part of an organ or organism. —*v.* **1.** To subject to a process. **2.** To prepare, treat, or convert esp. by a mechanical operation. **3.** *Computer Sci.* To perform operations on data.

pro•ces•sion (prə-sĕsh'ən) *n.* A group moving along esp. in an organized and ceremonial way **:** parade.

pro•ces•sion•al (prə-sĕsh'ə-nəl) *n.* **1.** Music to accompany a procession, esp. a hymn at the beginning of a church service. **2.** A formal procession.

proc•es•sor (prŏs'ĕs'ər) *n.* **1.** One that processes. **2. a.** A computer. **b.** A central processing unit of a computer. **c.** A program that translates another into a form acceptable to the computer being used.

pro-choice (prō'chois') *adj.* Supporting the legal right of women to choose whether or not to continue a pregnancy to term.

pro•claim (prō-klām', prə-) *v.* To declare officially and publicly. **—pro•claim'er** *n.* **—proc'la•ma'tion** (prŏk'lə-mā'shən) *n.*

pro•cliv•i•ty (prō-klĭv'ĭ-tē) *n., pl.* **-ties.** A natural inclination or tendency.

pro•con•sul (prō-kŏn'səl) *n.* **1.** The chief adminstrator of an ancient Roman province. **2.** A usu. powerful adminstrator in a modern colonial empire. **—pro•con'su•lar** *adj.* **—pro•con'su•late** *n.*

pro•cras•ti•nate (prə-krăs'tə-nāt', prō-) *v.* **-nat•ed, -nat•ing.** To put off until a later time **:** defer. **—pro•cras'ti•na'tion** *n.* **—pro•cras'ti•na'tor** *n.*

pro•cre•ate (prō'krē-āt') *v.* **-at•ed, -at•ing.** To beget or produce offspring. **—pro'cre•a'tion** *n.* **—pro'cre•a'tive** *adj.* **—pro'cre•a'tor** *n.*

pro•crus•te•an (prō-krŭs'tē-ən) *adj.* Coldly disregarding individual differences or special circumstances **:** ruthlessly inflexible.

proc•tor (prŏk'tər) *n.* One appointed to monitor college students, as at an examination. **—proc'tor** *v.* **—proc•to'ri•al** (-tôr'ē-əl, -tōr'-) *adj.*

proc•u•ra•tor (prŏk'yə-rā'tər) *n.* An administrator, esp. an official in charge of an ancient Roman province.

pro•cure (prō-kyo͝or', prə-) *v.* **-cured, -cur•ing. 1.** To get **:** acquire. **2.** To bring about **:** accomplish. **3.** To obtain (a prostitute or sexual partner) for another. **—pro•cur'er** *n.*

prod (prŏd) *v.* **prod•ded, prod•ding. 1.** To goad with a pointed object <*prod* cattle> **2.** To incite to action **:** urge. **—prod** *n.* **—prod'der** *n.*

prod•i•gal (prŏd'ĭ-gəl) *adj.* **1.** Extravagantly wasteful. **2.** Profuse **:** abundant. **—prod'i•gal** *n.* **—prod'i•gal'i•ty** (-găl'ĭ-tē) *n.* **—prod'i•gal•ly** *adv.*

pro•di•gious (prə-dĭj'əs) *adj.* **1.** Of very great size, force, or extent **:** immense. **2.** Extraordinary **:** wonderful. **—pro•di'gious•ly** *adv.* **—pro•di'gious•ness** *n.*

prod•i•gy (prŏd'ĭ-jē) *n., pl.* **-gies. 1.** An exceptionally talented child. **2.** Something marvelous **:** wonder.

pro•duce (prə-do͞os', -dyo͞os', prō-) *v.* **-duced, -duc•ing. 1.** To bring forth by a natural process **:** yield. **2.** To bring about **:** create. **3.** To make by a special process **:** manufacture. **4.** To cause to exist **:** give rise to. **5.** To present for inspection **:** show. **6.** To sponsor and present publicly. —*n.* (prŏd′o͞os, -yo͞os, prō′do͞os, -dyo͞os). Something produced, esp. agricultural products, as fruits and vegetables. —**pro•duc′er** *n.*

prod•uct (prŏd′əkt) *n.* **1.** Something produced by nature or by human or mechanical effort. **2.** *Math.* The number obtained by multiplying.

pro•duc•tion (prə-dŭk′shən, prō-) *n.* **1.** The act or process of producing. **2.** Something produced, as a play or film. —**pro•duc′tive** *adj.* —**pro•duc′tive•ly** *adv.* —**pro′duc•tiv′i•ty** (prō′dŭk-tĭv′ĭ-tē, prŏd′ək-), **pro•duc′tive•ness** *n.*

pro•em (prō′ĕm′) *n.* **1.** A preface. **2.** A prelude.

prof (prŏf) *n. Informal.* A professor.

pro•fane (prō-fān′, prə-) *adj.* **1.** Debasing what is sacred : blasphemous. **2.** Not religious in nature or use. **3.** Irreverent or vulgar <*profane* language> ★ ***syns:*** LAY, SECULAR, TEMPORAL, WORLDLY —*v.* **-faned, -fan•ing. 1.** To desecrate by treating contemptuously or irreverently : blaspheme. **2.** To put to an unworthy or degrading use : misuse. —**prof′a•na′tion** (prŏf′ə-nā′shən) *n.* —**pro•fan′a•to′ry** (-făn′ə-tôr′ē, -tōr′ē) *adj.* —**pro•fane′ly** *adv.* —**pro•fane′ness** *n.*

pro•fan•i•ty (prō-făn′ĭ-tē, prə-) *n., pl.* **-ties. 1.** The quality or state of being profane. **2. a.** Irreverent, abusive, or vulgar language. **b.** The use of profane language.

pro•fess (prə-fĕs′, prō-) *v.* **1.** To admit openly. **2.** To make a false show of. **3. a.** To claim skill or learning in. **b.** To practice (a profession or trade). **4.** To be an adherent of (a religion). —**pro•fess′ed•ly** (-fĕs′ĭd-lē) *adv.*

pro•fes•sion (prə-fĕsh′ən) *n.* **1.** An occupation usu. requiring advanced study and specialized training. **2.** The entire group of persons practicing a profession. **3.** An open declaration, esp. of religious faith.

pro•fes•sion•al (prə-fĕsh′ə-nəl) *adj.* **1.** Of, pertaining to, typical of, or practicing a profession. **2.** Engaged in a specified activity as a career. **3.** Engaging or engaged in for pay : not amateur <*professional* basketball> —*n.* One engaged in a profession. —**pro•fes′sion•al•ly** *adv.*

pro•fes•sion•al•ism (prə-fĕsh′ə-nə-lĭz′əm) *n.* **1.** Professional standing, techniques, attributes, or ethics. **2.** Participation in a profession, as organized athletics, for pay.

pro•fes•sion•al•ize (prə-fĕsh′ə-nə-līz′) *v.* **-ized, -iz•ing.** To make professional in character. —**pro•fes′sion•al•i•za′tion** *n.*

pro•fes•sor (prə-fĕs′ər) *n.* **1.** A faculty member of the highest rank in a college or university. **2.** A teacher, esp. at a college or university. —**pro′fes•so′ri•al** (prō′fĭ-sôr′ē-əl, -sōr′-, prŏf′ĭ-) *adj.*

prof•fer (prŏf′ər) *v.* To offer for acceptance. —**prof′fer** *n.*

pro•fi•cient (prə-fĭsh′ənt) *adj.* Highly competent in an art, skill, or field of knowledge : adept. —**pro•fi′cien•cy** *n.* —**pro•fi′cient•ly** *adv.*

pro•file (prō′fīl′) *n.* **1. a.** A view of something, esp. of a human head, from the side. **b.** A representation of a side view, esp. of a human head. **2.** The outline of something. **3.** A biographical sketch. —*v.* **-filed, -fil•ing. 1.** To depict in profile. **2.** To write a profile of.

prof•it (prŏf′ĭt) *n.* **1.** An advantage gained : benefit. **2.** Financial return after all business expenses have been met. —*v.* **1.** To gain financially. **2.** To gain an advantage : benefit. —**prof′it•less** *asj.*

prof•it•a•ble (prŏf′ĭ-tə-bəl) *adj.* Affording profit. ★ ***syns:*** ADVANTAGEOUS, FAT, LUCRATIVE, MONEYMAKING, REMUNERATIVE —**prof′it•a•bil′i•ty, prof′it•a•ble•ness** *n.* —**prof′it•a•bly** *adv.*

prof•i•teer (prŏf′ĭ-tîr′) *n.* One who profits unduly, esp. by selling goods in short supply. —**prof′i•teer′** *v.*

prof•li•gate (prŏf′lĭ-gĭt, -gāt′) *adj.* **1.** Heedlessly or extravagantly wasteful. **2.** Completely lacking in self-restraint : dissolute. —**prof′li•ga•cy** (-gə-sē) *n.* —**prof′li•gate** *n.* —**prof′li•gate•ly** *adv.*

pro for•ma (prō fôr′mə) *adj.* For the sake of form.

pro•found (prə-found′, prō-) *adj.* **1.** Of great depth : deep. **2.** Deeply felt or held. **3.** Penetrating : insightful. **4.** Complete : total <*profound* quiet> —**pro•found′ly** *adv.* —**pro•fun′di•ty** (-fŭn′dĭ-tē) *n.*

pro•fuse (prə-fyo͞os′, prō-) *adj.* Giving or given in great amount or quantity : abundant. —**pro•fuse′ly** *adv.* —**pro•fu′sion** (-fyo͞o′zhən), **pro•fuse′ness** *n.*

pro•gen•i•tor (prō-jĕn′ĭ-tər) *n.* **1.** An ancestor in a direct line. **2.** One that originates or sets a pattern for something.

prog•e•ny (prŏj′ə-nē) *n.* Offspring or descendants.

pro•ges•ter•one (prō-jĕs′tə-rōn′) *n.* A female hormone secreted by the ovary.

prog•na•thous (prŏg′nə-thəs) *adj.* Having jaws that jut beyond the upper face.

prog•no•sis (prŏg-nō′sĭs) *n., pl.* **-ses** (-sēz′). A prediction, esp. of the course and outcome of a disease.

prog•nos•tic (prŏg-nŏs′tĭk) *n.* **1.** A sign or omen of a future event. **2.** A prediction. —**prog•nos′tic** *adj.*

prog•nos•ti•cate (prŏg-nŏs′tĭ-kāt′) *v.* **-cat•ed, -cat•ing.** To predict from current indications. —**prog•nos′ti•ca′tion** *n.* —**prog•nos′ti•ca′tor** *n.*

pro•gram (prō′grăm′, -grəm) *n.* **1.** A list of the sequence of events or the subjects treated, as for a public presentation. **2.** A public presentation, performance, or entertainment. **3. a.** An organized plan of procedures : schedule. **b.** An organized effort to achieve a goal by stages. **4. a.** A set of logical steps for solving a problem. **b.** A coded set of instructions for a computer. **5.** Material for programmed instruction. —*v.* **-grammed, -gram•ming** *or* **-gramed, gram•ing. 1.** To include in a program : schedule. **2.** To provide (a computer) with a problem-solving program. —**pro•**

gram'ma·bil'i·ty *n.* —**pro'gram'ma·ble** *adj.* —**pro'gram·mat'ic** (prō'grə-măt'ĭk) *adj.* —**pro'gram'mer, pro'gram'er** *n.*

pro·gramme (prō'grăm', -grəm) *n.* & *v. esp. Brit. var. of* PROGRAM.

programmed instruction *n.* Instruction in which information is presented in discrete units, each requiring a correct response before the learner goes on to the next unit.

programming *or* **programing** *n.* The designing, scheduling, or planning of a program, esp. one for a computer.

prog·ress (prŏg'rĕs', -rĭs) *n.* **1.** Onward movement : advance. **2.** Gradual steady improvement. —*v.* **pro·gress** (prə-grĕs'). **1.** To move along : proceed. **2.** To advance toward a higher stage.

pro·gres·sion (prə-grĕsh'ən) *n.* **1.** Movement : progress. **2.** Advancement to a higher or different stage. **3.** A connected series : sequence.

pro·gres·sive (prə-grĕs'ĭv) *adj.* **1.** Moving forward : advancing. **2.** Continuing in steps or by stages or degrees. **3.** Advocating or working for political or social reform : liberal. **4.** Of or being a verb tense or form that expresses an action or condition in progress at the time indicated. —*n.* **1.** One that is progressive. **2.** A proponent of reform, as in politics and education. —**pro·gres'sive·ly** *adv.* —**pro·gres'sive·ness** *n.*

Progressive Conservative Party *n.* A Canadian political party.

pro·hib·it (prō-hĭb'ĭt, prə-) *v.* **1.** To forbid by law. **2.** To prevent : proscribe. —**pro·hib'i·to'ry** (-ĭ-tôr'ē, -tōr'ē) *adj.*

pro·hi·bi·tion (prō'ə-bĭsh'ən) *n.* **1.** The act of prohibiting or the state of being prohibited. **2.** A legal ban on the manufacture and sale of alcoholic beverages. —**pro'hi·bi'tion·ist** *n.*

pro·hib·i·tive (prō-hĭb'ĭ-tĭv, prə-) *adj.* **1.** Tending to prohibit. **2.** Tending to prevent purchase or use. —**pro·hib'i·tive·ly** *adv.*

proj·ect (prŏj'ĕkt', -ĭkt) *n.* **1.** A particular plan or intention. **2.** A planned or contemplated venture. —*v.* **pro·ject** (prə-jĕkt'). **1.** To protrude or cause to protrude. **2.** To throw forward or upward. **3.** To make (one's voice) clearly audible at a distance. **4.** To plan in the mind. **5.** To cause (light or an image) to fall upon a surface. —**pro·jec'tion** *n.*

pro·jec·tile (prə-jĕk'təl, -tīl') *n.* **1.** A projected missile, as a stone or bullet. **2.** A self-powered missile, as a rocket.

pro·jec·tion·ist (prə-jĕk'shə-nĭst) *n.* **1.** An operator of a motion-picture projector. **2.** One who makes maps.

pro·jec·tor (prə-jĕk'tər) *n.* A device for projecting images on a screen.

pro·lapse (prō-lăps') *Med. v.* **-lapsed, -laps·ing.** To fall or slip out of place, as a bodily organ. —**pro'lapse'** *n.*

pro·le·gom·e·non (prō'lĭ-gŏm'ə-nŏn', -nən) *n., pl.* **-na** (-nə). Introductory remarks. —**pro'le·gom'e·nous** *adj.*

pro·le·tar·i·an (prō'lĭ-târ'ē-ən) *adj.* Of, relating to, or characteristic of the proletariate. —**pro'le·tar'i·an** *n.*

pro·le·tar·i·at (prō'lĭ-târ'ē-ət) *n.* The working class, esp. industrial workers who earn their living by selling their labor.

pro-life (prō-līf') *adj.* Opposed to legalized abortion. —**pro-lif'er** *n.*

pro·lif·er·ate (prə-lĭf'ə-rāt') *v.* **-at·ed, -at·ing. 1.** To grow or produce by rapid multiplication of parts, as cells. **2.** To increase or spread rapidly. —**pro·lif'er·a'tion** *n.* —**pro·lif'er·a'tive** *adj.*

pro·lif·ic (prə-lĭf'ĭk) *adj.* **1.** Producing offspring or fruit in great numbers. **2.** Abundantly productive <a *prolific* novelist> —**pro·lif'i·cal·ly** *adv.*

pro·lix (prō-lĭks', prō'lĭks') *adj.* Long-winded : verbose. —**pro·lix'i·ty** (-lĭk'sĭ-tē) *n.* —**pro·lix'ly** *adv.*

pro·logue *also* **pro·log** (prō'lôg', -lŏg') *n.* An introduction, as to a play : preface.

pro·long (prə-lông', -lŏng') *v.* To lengthen in time, range, or extent. —**pro'lon·ga'tion** (prō'lông-gā'shən) *n.*

prom (prŏm) *n.* A formal dance usu. given by a class in high school or college.

prom·e·nade (prŏm'ə-nād', -näd') *n.* **1.** An unhurried walk : stroll. **2.** A public place for strolling. **3.** A formal march at the beginning of a ball. —**prom'e·nade'** *v.*

pro·me·thi·um (prə-mē'thē-əm) *n. Symbol* **Pm** A radioactive rare-earth metallic element.

prom·i·nence (prŏm'ə-nəns) *n.* **1.** The quality or state of being prominent : importance. **2.** Something that is prominent. **3.** A shining cloud of gas rising from the sun's surface.

prom·i·nent (prŏm'ə-nənt) *adj.* **1.** Jutting or bulging outward : projecting. **2.** Immediately noticeable : conspicuous. **3.** Widely known and esteemed.

pro·mis·cu·ous (prə-mĭs'kyo͞o-əs) *adj.* **1.** Made up of miscellaneous parts or kinds. **2.** Lacking discrimination or selectivity, esp. having a number of sexual partners. —**prom'is·cu'i·ty** (prŏm'ĭ-skyo͞o'ĭ-tē, prō'mĭ-), **pro·mis'cu·ous·ness** *n.* —**pro·mis'cu·ous·ly** *adv.*

prom·ise (prŏm'ĭs) *n.* **1.** An assurance that one will or will not do something specified : pledge. **2.** Something promised. **3.** A sign of what may be expected, esp. future development or success. ★ ***syns:*** COVENANT, GUARANTEE, PLEDGE, VOW —*v.* **-ised, -is·ing. 1.** To offer a promise (of). **2.** To give reason for expecting <Your future *promises* to be happy.> **3.** To portend <a sky that *promised* snow>

prom·is·ing (prŏm'ĭ-sĭng) *adj.* Giving hope of future excellence, benefit, or success. —**prom'is·ing·ly** *adv.*

prom·is·so·ry (prŏm'ĭ-sôr'ē, -sōr'ē) *adj.* Of, containing, or implying a promise.

promissory note *n.* A written promise to pay or repay a specified sum of money at a stated time or on demand.

pro·mo (prō'mō) *n., pl.* **-mos.** *Informal.* A promotional presentation.

prom·on·to·ry (prŏm'ən-tôr'ē, -tōr'ē) *n., pl.*

-ries. A high ridge of land or rock projecting into water, esp. into the sea.

pro•mote (prə-mōt′) *v.* **-mot•ed, -mot•ing. 1.** To raise to a higher position, rank, or class. **2.** To further the progress or growth of : advance. **3.** To advocate the adoption or use of. **4.** To try to sell or popularize by publicity. **—pro•mo′tion** *n.* **—pro•mo′tion•al** *adj.*

pro•mot•er (prə-mō′tər) *n.* **1.** An active advocate. **2.** A finance and publicity organizer, as of a sports event.

prompt (prŏmpt) *adj.* **1.** Acting or arriving on time : punctual. **2.** Done without delay : immediate. **3.** Ready to act quickly. —*v.* **1.** To incite to action. **2.** To encourage or inspire. **3.** To assist (e.g., a performer) by cueing. —*n.* **1.** A reminder : cue. **2.** *Computer Sci.* A symbol that appears on the screen indicating that the computer is ready to receive input. **—prompt′er** *n.* **—promp′ti•tude′** (prŏmp′tĭ-to͞od′, -tyo͞od′), **prompt′ness** *n.* **—prompt′ly** *adv.*

prom•ul•gate (prŏm′əl-gāt′, prō-mŭl′-) *v.* **-gat•ed, -gat•ing.** To make known or put into effect (e.g., a decree or law) by public declaration. **—prom′ul•ga′tion** *n.* **—prom′ul•ga′tor** *n.*

prone (prōn) *adj.* **1.** Lying flat or face downward. **2.** Having a tendency : inclined. **—prone′ly** *adv.* **—prone′ness** *n.*

prong (prông, prŏng) *n.* **1.** A sharply pointed end of a tool or utensil, as a fork. **2.** A slender pointed projection, as of a deer's antler.

prong•horn (prông′hôrn′, prŏng′-) *n.* A small antelopelike deer, *Antilocapra americana,* of W North American plains.

pro•noun (prō′noun′) *n.* One of a class of words used as substitutes for nouns and noun phrases.

pro•nounce (prə-nouns′) *v.* **-nounced, -nounc•ing. 1.** To produce or articulate (a word or speech sound). **2.** To declare officially, formally, or as an opinion. **—pro•nounce′a•ble** *adj.* **—pro•nun′ci•a′tion** (-nŭn′sē-ā′shən) *n.*

pro•nounced (prə-nounst′) *adj.* Strongly marked : unmistakable.

pro•nounce•ment (prə-nouns′mənt) *n.* **1.** A formal declaration. **2.** An authoritative statement.

pron•to (prŏn′tō) *adv. Informal.* Right away : immediately.

pro•nun•ci•a•men•to (prə-nŭn′sē-ə-mĕn′tō) *n., pl.* **-tos.** An edict.

proof (pro͞of) *n.* **1.** Evidence that establishes the truth or validity of something. **2.** Demonstration of the truth of a statement in mathematics or logic. **3.** The act of testing the truth or validity of something by experiment or trial. **4.** A trial impression, as of composed type or an engraved plate. **5.** The alcoholic strength of a liquor, expressed as twice the percentage of alcoholic content <120 *proof* whiskey> —*adj.* **1.** Able to withstand, repel, or resist : resistant. **2.** Of standard alcoholic strength or quality. —*v.* **1.** To proofread. **2.** To make resistant.

—proof *suff.* Safe from : resistant to <bullet*proof*>

proof•read (pro͞of′rēd′) *v.* To read and mark corrections in (printed, typed, or written material). **—proof′read′er** *n.*

prop[1] (prŏp) *n.* **1.** A support for keeping something upright. **2.** One depended on for support or aid. **—prop** *v.*

prop[2] (prŏp) *n.* A property on a stage or motion-picture set.

prop[3] (prŏp) *n. Informal.* A propeller.

prop•a•gan•da (prŏp′ə-găn′də) *n.* **1.** The systematic widespread promotion of a particular doctrine or idea. **2.** Material distributed to win people over to a particular doctrine. **—prop′a•gan′dist** *n.* **—prop′a•gan•dis′tic** *adj.* **—prop′a•gan′dize′** *v.*

prop•a•gate (prŏp′ə-gāt′) *v.* **-gat•ed, -gat•ing. 1.** To reproduce or cause to reproduce (offspring or new growth) : multiply. **2.** *Physics.* To spread or cause to spread through a medium <*propagate* light> **—prop′a•ga′tion** *n.*

pro•pane (prō′pān′) *n.* A gaseous hydrocarbon found in natural gas and petroleum and used as a fuel.

pro•pel (prə-pĕl′) *v.* **-pelled, -pel•ling. 1.** To thrust or drive forcefully onward. **2.** To impel to action : motivate.

pro•pel•lant *also* **pro•pel•lent** (prə-pĕl′ənt) *n.* Something, as an explosive charge or fuel, used to propel. **—pro•pel′lant** *adj.*

pro•pel•ler *also* **pro•pel•lor** (prə-pĕl′ər) *n.* A fanlike, usu. power-driven device for propelling aircraft or boats.

pro•pen•si•ty (prə-pĕn′sĭ-tē) *n., pl.* **-ties.** A natural inclination : bent.

prop•er (prŏp′ər) *adj.* **1.** Suitable : appropriate. **2.** Pertaining exclusively to a person or thing : peculiar. **3.** Correct by rule or convention. **4.** Strictly conforming to social convention. **5.** Strictly so called <the downtown *proper*> **—prop′er•ly** *adv.*

proper noun *n.* A noun that refers to a particular person, place, or thing.

prop•er•tied (prŏp′ər-tēd) *adj.* Owning property, as real estate, esp. as a chief source of income.

prop•er•ty (prŏp′ər-tē) *n., pl.* **-ties. 1.** Something owned, esp. real estate. **2.** A characteristic trait, quality, or attribute. **3.** The exclusive right to own something : ownership. **4.** A movable article other than costumes and scenery that is used in a play or movie. **—prop′er•ty•less** *adj.*

proph•e•cy (prŏf′ĭ-sē) *n., pl.* **-cies. 1.** A forewarning : prediction. **2.** The divinely inspired utterance of a prophet.

proph•e•sy (prŏf′ĭ-sī′) *v.* **-sied, -sy•ing. 1.** To reveal by or as if by divine inspiration. **2.** To foretell. **—proph′e•si′er** *n.*

proph•et (prŏf′ĭt) *n.* **1.** One whose revelations are divinely inspired. **2.** One who foretells the future.

proph•et•ess (prŏf′ĭ-tĭs) *n.* **1.** A woman who speaks by or as if by divine inspiration. **2.** The chief spokeswoman of a movement or cause.

pro•phet•ic (prə-fĕt′ĭk) *also* **pro•phet•i•cal** (-ĭ-kəl) *adj.* Of, pertaining to, or characteristic of a prophet or prophecy. —**pro•phet′i•cal•ly** *adv.*

pro•phy•lac•tic (prō′fə-lăk′tĭk, prŏf′ə-) *adj.* Serving to defend against or prevent something, esp. disease. —*n.* **1.** A prophylactic measure, drug, or device. **2.** A condom.

pro•phy•lax•is (prō′fə-lăk′sĭs, prŏf′ə-) *n., pl.* **-lax•es** (-lăk′sēz′). Protective treatment for or prevention of disease.

pro•pin•qui•ty (prə-pĭng′kwĭ-tē) *n.* **1.** Proximity in time or space. **2.** Kinship.

pro•pi•ti•ate (prō-pĭsh′ē-āt′) *v.* **-at•ed, -at•ing.** To win or win back the favor of : placate. —**pro•pi′ti•a′tion** *n.* —**pro•pi′ti•a•to′ry** (-ə-tôr′ē, -tōr′ē) *adj.*

pro•pi•tious (prə-pĭsh′əs) *adj.* Indicating a favorable condition or an auspicious outcome. —**pro•pi′tious•ly** *adv.*

prop-jet (prŏp′jĕt′) *n.* A turboprop.

pro•po•nent (prə-pō′nənt) *n.* A supporter of something : advocate.

pro•por•tion (prə-pôr′shən, -pōr′-) *n.* **1.** The relationship of a part to a whole or to another part as to magnitude, quantity, or degree : ratio. **2.** Harmonious relationship : symmetry or balance. **3.** *often* **proportions.** Dimensions. —*v.* **1.** To bring the size or dimensions of (different things) into proper relationship. **2.** To arrange with harmony and balance. —**pro•por′tion•al** *adj.* —**pro•por′tion•al•ly** *adv.* —**pro•por′tion•ate** *adj.* —**pro•por′tion•ate•ly** *adv.*

pro•pose (prə-pōz′) *v.* **-posed, -pos•ing. 1.** To present for consideration or action. **2.** To suggest (a person) for a position, office, or membership : nominate. **3.** To declare an intention : plan. **4.** To tender an offer, esp. of marriage. ★ ***syns:*** OFFER, POSE, PROPOUND, SUBMIT, SUGGEST —**pro•pos′al** *n.* —**pro•pos′er** *n.*

prop•o•si•tion (prŏp′ə-zĭsh′ən) *n.* **1. a.** Something, as a plan, proposed for consideration. **b.** A sexual overture. **2. a.** A statement to be discussed or analyzed. **b.** A statement in mathematics or logic. **3.** *Informal.* An often difficult situation <a sticky *proposition*> —*v. Informal.* To make a proposition to, esp. to make a sexual overture to. —**prop′o•si′tion•al** *adj.*

pro•pound (prə-pound′) *v.* To put forward for consideration or argument.

pro•pri•e•tar•y (prə-prī′ĭ-tĕr′ē) *adj.* **1.** Of, pertaining to, or characteristic of a proprietor. **2.** Owned, made, and sold by one holding a trademark or patent.

pro•pri•e•tor (prə-prī′ĭ-tər) *n.* An owner, as of a building or business. —**pro•pri′e•tor•ship′** *n.*

pro•pri•e•tress (prə-prī′ĭ-trĭs) *n.* A woman who is an owner, as of a business.

pro•pri•e•ty (prə-prī′ĭ-tē) *n., pl.* **-ties. 1.** The quality or state of being proper. **2.** Conformity to accepted standards of social conduct. **3. proprieties.** The rules and conventions of polite social behavior.

pro•pul•sion (prə-pŭl′shən) *n.* **1.** The act or process of propelling. **2.** A propelling force. —**pro•pul′sive** *adj.*

pro ra•ta (prō rā′tə, răt′ə, rä′tə) *adv.* In due proportion.

pro•rate (prō-rāt′, prō′rāt′) *v.* **-rat•ed, -rat•ing.** To divide, distribute, or assess on the basis of proportion. —**pro•ra′tion** *n.*

pro•rogue (prō-rōg′) *v.* **-rogued, -rogu•ing.** To adjourn or dissolve a session of (a legislature). —**pro′ro•ga′tion** *n.*

pro•sa•ic (prō-zā′ĭk) *adj.* **1.** Literal : matter-of-fact. **2.** Ordinary : commonplace. **3.** Lacking in imagination. —**pro•sa′i•cal•ly** *adv.* —**pro•sa′ic•ness** *n.*

pro•sce•ni•um (prō-sē′nē-əm) *n., pl.* **-ni•ums** *or* **-ni•a** (-nē-ə). The part of the stage that separates it from the audience.

pro•sciut•to (prō-shōō′tō) *n.* An aged, dry-cured, usu. thin-sliced Italian ham.

pro•scribe (prō-skrīb′) *v.* **-scribed, -scrib•ing. 1.** To make unlawful : prohibit. **2.** To banish : outlaw. —**pro•scrip′tion** (-skrĭp′shən) *n.* —**pro•scrip′tive** *adj.*

prose (prōz) *n.* Ordinary speech or writing as distinguished from verse or poetry.

pros•e•cute (prŏs′ĭ-kyōōt′) *v.* **-cut•ed, -cut•ing. 1.** To institute or subject to legal proceedings <*prosecute* an embezzler> **2.** To pursue to the end <*prosecute* a war> —**pros′e•cu′tion** *n.* —**pros′e•cu′tor** *n.* —**pros′e•cu•to′ri•al** (-tôr′ē-əl, -tōr′-) *adj.*

pros•e•lyte (prŏs′ə-līt′) *n.* A convert to a religion, doctrine, or party. —*v.* **-lyt•ed, -lyt•ing.** To proselytize.

pros•e•ly•tize (prŏs′ə-lə-tīz′) *v.* **-tized, -tiz•ing.** To convert (someone) from one religion, doctrine, or party to another. —**pros′e•ly•tiz′er** *n.*

pros•o•dy (prŏs′ə-dē) *n.* The study of the making of verses and esp. of metrical form. —**pro•sod′ic** (prə-sŏd′ĭk) *adj.*

pros•pect (prŏs′pĕkt′) *n.* **1.** Something anticipated : expectation. **2.** *often* **prospects.** Potential for success. **3. a.** A possible customer. **b.** A likely candidate. **4.** Direction of exposure, as to weather. **5. a.** A place affording an extensive view. **b.** The view itself. **c.** A scene. —*v.* To search about or explore, esp. for mineral deposits. —**pro•spec′tive** (prə-spĕk′tĭv) *adj.* —**pro•spec′tive•ly** *adv.* —**pros′pec′tor** *n.*

pro•spec•tus (prə-spĕk′təs) *n., pl.* **-tus•es.** A description of a proposed enterprise or venture distributed to prospective parties.

pros•per (prŏs′pər) *v.* To achieve success. ★ ***syns:*** BOOM, FLOURISH, THRIVE

pros•per•i•ty (prŏ-spĕr′ĭ-tē) *n.* Prosperous condition, esp. financially successful circumstances.

pros•per•ous (prŏs′pər-əs) *adj.* **1.** Successful : flourishing. **2.** Favorable : auspicious. ★ ***syns:*** COMFORTABLE, WELL-FIXED, WELL-HEELED, WELL-OFF, WELL-TO-DO

pros•tate (prŏs′tāt′) *n.* A gland at the base of the male urethra that secretes one of the major constituents of semen. —**pros•tat′ic** (prŏ-stăt′ĭk) *adj.*

pros•the•sis (prŏs-thē′sĭs) *n., pl.* **-ses** (-sēz′). An artificial replacement for a missing body part, such as a limb. **—pros•thet′ic** (-thĕt′ĭk) *adj.*

pros•ti•tute (prŏs′tĭ-to͞ot′, -tyo͞ot′) *n.* One hired as a sexual partner. *—v.* **-tut•ed, -tut•ing. 1.** To offer (oneself or another) as a paid sexual partner. **2.** To devote to an unworthy or debasing cause. **—pros′ti•tu′tion** *n.*

pros•trate (prŏs′trāt′) *adj.* **1.** Lying face down, as in submission or adoration. **2.** Lying flat, esp. on the ground <a *prostrate* tree trunk> **3.** In a state of helplessness **:** overcome <*prostrate* with grief> *—v.* **-trat•ed, -trat•ing. 1.** To put or throw down into a prostrate position. **2.** To lay low **:** overcome. **—pros•tra′tion** *n.*

pro•tac•tin•i•um (prō′tăk-tĭn′ē-əm) *n. Symbol* **Pa** A rare radioactive metallic element similar to uranium.

pro•tag•o•nist (prō-tăg′ə-nĭst) *n.* **1.** The leading character in a story or play. **2.** A champion of a cause.

pro•te•an (prō′tē-ən, prō-tē′-) *adj.* Easily taking on different shapes or forms.

▲ ***word history:*** The word *protean* comes from *Proteus,* the name of a Greek sea god who had the power to change his shape. Proteus had the gift of prophecy, but those who wanted to consult him had to bind him securely first. Proteus would then change into various shapes, as a wild boar, a tiger, a rush of water, and a raging fire. A questioner who could keep Proteus restrained until he returned to his orig. shape would receive an answer.

pro•tect (prə-tĕkt′) *v.* To guard from harm, attack, or injury **:** shield. **—pro•tec′tive** *adj.* **—pro•tec′tive•ly** *adv.*

pro•tec•tion (prə-tĕk′shən) *n.* **1.** The act of protecting or state of being protected. **2.** One that serves to protect. **3.** A system by which high duties are imposed on foreign competitors to protect domestic producers. **—pro•tec′tion•ism** *n.*

pro•tec•tor (prə-tĕk′tər) *n.* **1.** Someone or something that protects. **2.** One ruling a kingdom as regent. **—pro•tec′tor•ship′** *n.*

pro•tec•tor•ate (prə-tĕk′tər-ĭt) *n.* **1.** A guardian. **2. a.** Partial control by a superior power over a dependent political unit. **b.** A dependent political unit so controlled. **3.** The office or term of a protector.

pro•té•gé (prō′tə-zhā′) *n.* One whose well-being or career is furthered by an influential person. **—pro′té•gée′** *n.*

pro•tein (prō′tēn′, -tē-ĭn) *n.* Any of a very large group of complex organic compounds occurring in all living matter that are composed of amino acids and are essential for tissue growth and repair.

pro tem (prō tĕm′) *adv.* For the present.

pro tem•po•re (prō tĕm′pə-rē) *adv.* For the present **:** temporarily.

pro•test (prə-tĕst′, prō-) *v.* **1.** To object strongly (to), esp. formally or publicly. **2.** To declare earnestly **:** affirm. *—n.* (prō′tĕst′). **1.** The act of protesting, esp. disapproval or objection formally expressed. **2.** An individual or organized public demonstration of disapproval. **—prot′es•ta′tion** (prŏt′ĭ-stā′shən) *n.* **—pro•test′er** *n.*

Prot•es•tant (prŏt′ĭ-stənt) *n.* **1.** A member of one of the Christian churches arising from the Reformation. **2. protestant** (*also* prə-tĕs′-tənt). One who makes a protest or declaration. **—Prot′es•tant•ism** *n.*

Protestant Episcopal Church *n.* A U.S. church body orig. associated with the Church of England.

pro•to•col (prō′tə-kôl′, -kōl′, -kŏl′) *n.* **1.** A code of ceremony and etiquette followed by diplomats, heads of state, and the military. **2.** The orig. copy of a formal document, esp. of a treaty before ratification. **3.** A first draft or record, as of an agreement.

pro•ton (prō′tŏn′) *n.* A stable subatomic particle having a positive charge equal in magnitude to that of an electron.

pro•to•plasm (prō′tə-plăz′əm) *n.* The complex jellylike colloid that forms the living substance of plant and animal cells. **—pro′-to•plas′mic** (-plăz′mĭk) *adj.*

pro•to•type (prō′tə-tīp′) *n.* An original model after which other similar things are patterned. **—pro′to•typ′al** (-tī′pəl), **pro′to•typ′-ic** (-tĭp′ĭk), **pro′to•typ′i•cal** *adj.*

pro•to•zo•an (prō′tə-zō′ən) *n., pl.* **-zo•ans** *or* **-zo•a** (-zō′ə). Any of a very large group of one-celled, usu. microscopic organisms.

pro•tract (prō-trăkt′, prə-) *v.* To extend in time or space **:** prolong. **—pro•trac′tion** *n.* **—pro•trac′tive** *adj.*

pro•trac•tor (prō-trăk′tər) *n.* A semicircular graduated device for measuring and drawing angles.

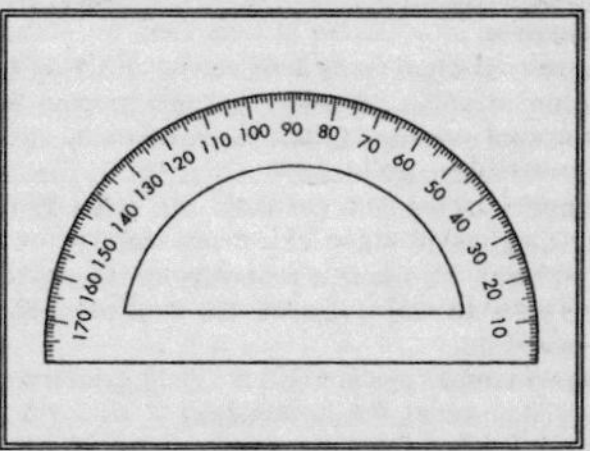

protractor

pro•trude (prō-tro͞od′) *v.* **-trud•ed, -trud•ing.** To thrust outward **:** project. **—pro•tru′-sion** *n.* **—pro•tru′sive** *adj.*

pro•tu•ber•ance (prō-to͞o′bər-əns, -tyo͞o′-) *n.* An object or part that bulges or swells outward. **—pro•tu′ber•ant** *adj.*

proud (proud) *adj.* **1.** Feeling greatly pleased or satisfied. **2.** Highly gratifying <my *proudest* possession> **3.** Having proper self-esteem. **4.** Worthy of honor and respect. **5.** Marked by dignity or majesty **:** stately. **6.** Having too much self-esteem : arrogant. 7. Spirited. —**proud'ly** *adv.*

prove (pro͞ov) *v.* **proved, proved** *or* **prov•en** (pro͞o'vən), **prov•ing. 1.** To show to be true or valid by evidence or argument. **2.** To demonstrate convincingly. **3.** To test the quality or worth of. **4.** To turn out to be. —**prov'a•ble** *adj.* —**prov'a•bly** *adv.* —**prov'er** *n.*

prov•e•nance (prŏv'ə-nəns) *n.* An origin or source.

prov•en•der (prŏv'ən-dər) *n.* **1.** Dry feed, as hay, for livestock. **2.** Food supplies.

pro•ve•nience (prə-vēn'yəns, -vē'nē-əns) *n.* Provenance.

prov•erb (prŏv'ûrb') *n.* **1.** A concise saying that illustrates a truth. **2. Proverbs** *(sing. in number).* —See table at BIBLE —**pro•ver'•bi•al** (prə-vûr'bē-əl) *adj.*

pro•vide (prə-vīd') *v.* **-vid•ed, -vid•ing. 1.** To supply or furnish (something needed or useful). **2.** To have or offer for use. **3.** To stipulate, as in a will. **4.** To take advance measures <*provide* against illness> **5.** To supply means of support <*provide* for one's dependents> —**pro•vid'er** *n.*

pro•vid•ed (prə-vī'dĭd) *conj.* On condition that.

prov•i•dence (prŏv'ĭ-dəns, -dĕns') *n.* **1.** The state or quality of being provident. **2. a.** Divine protection and guidance. **b. Providence.** God.

prov•i•dent (prŏv'ĭ-dənt, -dĕnt') *adj.* **1.** Showing prudent forethought. **2.** Economical : thrifty. —**prov'i•dent•ly** *adv.*

prov•i•den•tial (prŏv'ĭ-dĕn'shəl) *adj.* **1.** Of, pertaining to, or ordained by divine providence. **2.** Highly opportune : fortunate. —**prov'i•den'tial•ly** *adv.*

pro•vid•ing (prə-vī'dĭng) *conj.* With the proviso that : provided.

prov•ince (prŏv'ĭns) *n.* **1. a.** A political subdivision of a nation. **b.** *Can.* One of 10 such units in Canada. **2. provinces.** Outlying regions of a country away from the population centers or the capital. **3.** A domain, as of knowledge : sphere.

pro•vin•cial (prə-vĭn'shəl) *adj.* **1.** Of or relating to a province. **2.** Limited and narrow in perspective <a *provincial* point of view> —**pro•vin'cial•ism, pro•vin'ci•al'i•ty** (-shē-ăl'ĭ-tē) *n.*

provincial park *n. Can.* A park established by and under the jurisdiction of a province.

provincial parliament *n. Can.* The legislative assembly of a province.

provincial police *n. Can.* A police force maintained by a province.

proving ground *n.* A place for experimentation, as with new weapons or ideas.

pro•vi•sion (prə-vĭzh'ən) *n.* **1.** The act of providing. **2.** Something provided. **3.** *often* **provisions.** A supply of food and needed equipment. **4.** A measure taken in advance. **5.** A stipulation, as in a will. —*v.* To furnish with provisions.

pro•vi•sion•al (prə-vĭzh'ə-nəl) *adj.* Provided temporarily pending permanent arrangements. —**pro•vi'sion•al•ly** *adv.*

pro•vi•so (prə-vī'zō) *n., pl.* **-sos** *or* **-soes.** A clause with a condition or qualification : stipulation. —**pro•vi'so•ry** *adj.*

pro•voke (prə-vōk') *v.* **-voked, -vok•ing. 1.** To cause to be irritated or angry. **2.** To incite to action. **3.** To evoke. ★ ***syns:*** AROUSE, EXCITE, GOAD, IMPEL, INCITE, INFLAME, INSPIRE, INSTIGATE, KINDLE, MOTIVATE, MOVE, ROUSE, SPUR, STIMULATE —**prov'o•ca'tion** (prŏv-ə-kā'shən) *n.* —**pro•voc'a•tive** (prə-vŏk'ə-tĭv) *adj.*

pro•vo•lo•ne (prō'və-lō'nē) *n.* A smooth, hard, often smoked cheese orig. from Italy.

pro•vost (prō'vōst', prŏv'əst) *n.* A high-ranking administrative official, esp. of a university.

pro•vost marshal (prō'vō) *n.* The head of a military police unit.

prow (prou) *n.* **1.** The front of a ship : bow. **2.** A similar projecting part, as the forward end of a ski.

prow•ess (prou'ĭs) *n.* **1.** Outstanding bravery and skill, esp. in battle. **2.** Surpassing ability : excellence.

prowl (proul) *v.* To move about furtively or predatorily. —**prowl** *n.* —**prowl'er** *n.*

prowl car *n.* A squad car.

prox•i•mal (prŏk'sə-məl) *adj.* Proximate.

prox•i•mate (prŏk'sə-mĭt) *adj.* **1.** Very near : close. **2.** Immediate : direct.

prox•im•i•ty (prŏk-sĭm'ĭ-tē) *n.* The quality, state, or fact of being near : closeness.

prox•y (prŏk'sē) *n., pl.* **-ies. 1.** An authorized agent for another. **2.** Authority or written authorization to act for another.

Pro•zac (prō'zăk'). A trademark for an antidepressant drug.

prude (pro͞od) *n.* One excessively concerned with propriety or morality. —**prud'er•y** *n.* —**prud'ish** *adj.* —**prud'ish•ly** *adv.* —**prud'•ish•ness** *n.*

pru•dent (pro͞od'nt) *adj.* **1.** Handling practical matters judiciously. **2.** Managing carefully : provident. **3.** Behaving circumspectly : discreet. —**pru'dence** *n.* —**pru•den'tial** (pro͞o-dĕn'shəl) *adj.*

prune[1] (pro͞on) *n.* The partially dried fruit of the common plum.

prune[2] (pro͞on) *v.* **pruned, prun•ing. 1.** To cut or trim parts of (a plant or tree). **2.** To remove unnecessary or unwanted parts.

pru•ri•ent (pro͝or'ē-ənt) *adj.* Arousing or experiencing lustful feelings. —**pru'ri•ence** *n.* —**pru'ri•ent•ly** *adv.*

pry[1] (prī) *v.* **pried, pry•ing.** To look inquisitively or furtively : snoop.

pry[2] (prī) *v.* **pried, pry•ing. 1.** To raise, move, or open forcibly with or as if with a lever. **2.** To secure with effort or difficulty. —*n., pl.* **pries.** A tool for prying.

psalm (säm) *n.* **1.** A sacred song or poem. **2. Psalms.** *(sing. in number).* —See table at BIBLE. —**psalm'ist** *n.*

Psal•ter *also* **psal•ter** (sôl'tər) *n.* A book containing the Book of Psalms, esp. for use in church services.

p's and q's (pēz' ən kyo͞oz') *pl.n. Informal.* Proper conduct : manners.

pseu•do (so͞o'dō) *adj.* False : sham.

pseu•do•nym (so͞od'n-ĭm') *n.* An assumed name, esp. a pen name. **—pseu•don'y•mous** (so͞o-dŏn'ə-məs) *adj.*

psil•o•cy•bin (sĭl'ə-sī'bĭn, sī'lə-) *n.* A strongly hallucinogenic compound derived from the mushroom *Psilocybe mexicana.*

psit•ta•co•sis (sĭt'ə-kō'sĭs) *n.* A viral disease of parrots and related birds that is transmissible to humans.

pso•ri•a•sis (sə-rī'ə-sĭs) *n.* A chronic inflammatory skin disease marked by white scaly patches.

psych (sīk) *Informal.* *—n.* Psychology. *—v.* **1.** To prepare oneself mentally or emotionally. **2.** To intimidate by psychological means. **3.** To outguess or outwit.

psy•che (sī'kē) *n.* **1.** The soul or spirit. **2.** The mind.

psy•che•del•ic (sī'kĭ-dĕl'ĭk) *adj.* Of, producing, or marked by abnormal psychic effects, as hallucinations and perceptual distortions. **—psy'che•del'ic** *n.* **—psy'che•del'i•cal•ly** *adv.*

psy•chi•a•try (sĭ-kī'ə-trē, sī-) *n.* The branch of medicine dealing with the diagnosis and treatment of mental disorders. **—psy'chi•at'ric** (sī'kē-ăt'rĭk) *adj.* **—psy'chi•at'ri•cal•ly** *adv.* **—psy•chi'a•trist** *n.*

psy•chic (sī'kĭk) *also* **psy•chi•cal** (-kĭ-kəl) *adj.* **1.** Of or relating to the psyche. **2.** Of or caused by phenomena unexplainable by known natural laws. **3.** Responsive to supernatural or nonphysical phenomena. *—n.* **1.** One responsive to or influenced by psychic forces. **2.** One held to communicate with the spirit world.

psy•cho (sī'kō) *n. pl.* **-chos.** *Slang.* A psychopath. **—psy'cho** *adj.*

psy•cho•ac•tive (sī'kō-ăk'tĭv) *adj.* Chemically affecting the mind or behavior <a *psychoactive* drug>

psy•cho•a•nal•y•sis (sī'kō-ə-năl'ĭ-sĭs) *n.* A means of treating mental disorder through the analysis of usu. subconscious feelings and conflicts. **—psy'cho•an'a•lyst** (-ăn'ə-lĭst) *n.* **—psy'cho•an'a•lyt'ic** (-ăn'ə-lĭt'ĭk), **psy'cho•an'a•lyt'i•cal** *adj.* **—psy'cho•an'a•lyze'** (-līz') *v.*

psy•cho•bi•ol•o•gy (sī'kō-bī-ŏl'ə-jē) *n.* The study of the interactions between mental and biological processes. **—psy'cho•bi•ol'o•gist** *n.*

psy•cho•dra•ma (sī'kō-drä'mə, -drăm'ə) *n.* Psychotherapy in which individuals spontaneously act out roles assigned by the therapist.

psy•cho•gen•ic (sī'kō-jĕn'ĭk) *adj.* Arising in the mind or in emotional conflict.

psy•cho•lin•guis•tics (sī'kō-lĭng-gwĭs'tĭks) *n. (sing. in number).* The study of the interaction between psychological factors and linguistic behavior. **—psy'cho•lin'guist** *n.* **—psy'cho•lin•guis'tic** *adj.*

psy•chol•o•gy (sī-kŏl'ə-jē) *n., pl.* **-gies. 1.** The science of mind, emotions, and behavior. **2.** The emotional characteristics and behavior associated with an individual. **—psy'cho•log'i•cal** (-kə-lŏj'ĭ-kəl) *adj.* **—psy•chol'o•gist** *n.*

psy•cho•met•rics (sī'kə-mĕt'rĭks) *n. (sing. in number).* The branch of psychology that deals with testing and measuring psychological variables such as intelligence.

psy•chom•e•try (sī-kŏm'ĭ-trē) *n.* Psychometrics.

psy•cho•mo•tor (sī'kō-mō'tər) *adj.* Of or relating to movement or muscular activity associated with mental processes.

psy•cho•path (sī'kə-păth') *n.* A person with a mental disorder manifested esp. in aggressively antisocial behavior. **—psy'cho•path'ic** *adj.*

psy•cho•pa•thol•o•gy (sī'kō-pə-thŏl'ə-jē, -pă-) *n.* The study of the origin, growth, and symptoms of mental disorders. **—psy'cho•path'o•log'i•cal** (-păth'ə-lŏj'ĭ-kəl), **psy'cho•path'o•log'ic** *adj.* **—psy'cho•pa•thol'o•gist** *n.*

psy•cho•sis (sī-kō'sĭs) *n., pl.* **-ses** (-sēz'). A severe mental disorder marked by the degeneration of mental and social functioning and withdrawal from reality. **—psy•chot'ic** (-kŏt'ĭk) *adj. & n.*

psy•cho•so•mat•ic (sī'kō-sə-măt'ĭk) *adj.* Of, pertaining to, or caused by phenomena that are both physiological and psychological. **—psy'cho•so•mat'ic** *n.*

psy•cho•ther•a•py (sī'kō-thĕr'ə-pē) *n.* Treatment of emotional or mental disorders by psychological methods. **—psy'cho•ther'a•peu'tic** (-pyo͞o'tĭk) *adj.* **—psy'cho•ther'a•pist** *n.*

psy•cho•tro•pic (sī'kə-trō'pĭk, -trŏp'ĭk) *adj.* Having a mind-altering effect.

Pt *symbol for* PLATINUM.

ptar•mi•gan (tär'mĭ-gən) *n., pl.* **-gan** *or* **-gans.** A bird of the genus *Lagopus,* of N regions, with feathered feet.

PT boat (pē-tē') *n.* A fast, maneuverable boat used to torpedo enemy ships.

pto•maine *also* **pto•main** (tō'mān', tō-mān') *n.* Any of various sometimes poisonous nitrogenous products of protein putrefaction and decomposition.

ptomaine poisoning *n.* Food poisoning caused by bacteria or their toxins.

Pu *symbol for* PLUTONIUM.

pub (pŭb) *n.* A public tavern or bar.

pu•ber•ty (pyo͞o'bər-tē) *n.* The stage of human physical development in which sexual reproduction can first occur. **—pu'ber•tal, pu'ber•al** (-bər-əl) *adj.*

pu•bes•cent (pyo͞o-bĕs'ənt) *adj.* **1.** Covered with short soft hairs. **2.** Reaching or having arrived at puberty. **—pu•bes'cence** *n.*

pu•bic (pyo͞o'bĭk) *adj.* Of, relating to, or in the region of the pubis.

pu•bis (pyo͞o'bĭs) *n., pl.* **-bes** (-bēz'). The forward part of either of the hipbones, joining to form the front arch of the pelvis.

pub•lic (pŭb'lĭk) *adj.* **1.** Of, pertaining to, or affecting the community or the people as a whole <the *public* good> **2.** For the use of all <a *public* telephone> **3.** Participated in by the people or community <a *public* occasion> **4.** Serving or acting for the people or community <a *public* defender> **5.** Open to the knowledge of all. **6.** Widely known. ★ *syns:* DEMOCRATIC, GENERAL, POPULAR —*n.* **1.** The general populace. **2.** A body of people having a mutual interest. —**pub'lic·ly** *adv.*

pub·lic-ad·dress system (pŭb'lĭk-ə-drĕs') *n.* An electronic amplification system for projecting sound.

pub·li·can (pŭb'lĭ-kən) *n.* **1.** *esp. Brit.* The proprieter of a public house. **2.** A tax collector in the ancient Roman Empire.

pub·li·ca·tion (pŭb'lĭ-kā'shən) *n.* **1.** The act or process of publishing. **2.** Something published, as a magazine.

public domain *n.* **1.** Land under governmental ownership and control. **2.** The status of publications, products, and processes unprotected by copyright or patent.

public house *n. esp. Brit.* A licensed inn, tavern, or bar.

pub·li·cist (pŭb'lĭ-sĭst) *n.* One who publicizes, esp. a press agent.

pub·lic·i·ty (pŭ-blĭs'ĭ-tē) *n.* **1.** Information issued to attract public attention. **2.** Public attention or notoriety. **3.** The work of a publicist.

pub·li·cize (pŭb'lĭ-sīz') *v.* **-cized, -ciz·ing.** To bring to public attention.

public relations *pl.n. (sing. or pl. in number).* **1.** Methods and means by which a person or an organization seeks to promote a favorable relationship with the public. **2.** The degree of success in promoting good public relations.

public school *n.* **1.** A tax-supported U.S. school providing free education. **2.** A private secondary boarding school in Great Britain.

pub·lic-spir·i·ted (pŭb'lĭk-spĭr'ĭ-tĭd) *adj.* Dedicated to promoting the well-being of the general public.

public television *n.* Privately supported noncommercial television that provides educational and cultural programs for the public.

pub·lish (pŭb'lĭsh) *v.* **1.** To produce and present (printed and other material) for public distribution or sale. **2.** To publicize : announce. —**pub'lish·a·ble** *adj.* —**pub'lish·er** *n.* —**pub'lish·ment** *n.*

puck[1] (pŭk) *n.* A hard rubber disk used in ice hockey.

puck[2] (pŭk) *n.* A mischievous elf or sprite. —**puck'ish** *adj.*

puck·er (pŭk'ər) *v.* To draw up into wrinkles or folds. —*n.* A small wrinkle or fold.

pud·ding (po͝od'ĭng) *n.* A sweet custardlike or cakelike dessert.

pud·dle (pŭd'l) *n.* A small pool of liquid, esp. of muddy water.

pud·dling (pŭd'lĭng) *n.* The conversion of pig iron into pure iron by heat and agitation in an oxidizing atmosphere.

pu·den·dum (pyo͞o-dĕn'dəm) *n., pl.* **-da** (-də). A woman's external genital organs.

pudg·y (pŭj'ē) *adj.* **-i·er, -i·est.** Short and chubby. —**pudg'i·ness** *n.*

pueb·lo (pwĕb'lō) *n., pl.* **-los. 1.** A community of certain American Indian peoples of NM and AZ, typically consisting of multilevel adobe dwellings built around a central plaza. **2. Pueblo.** *pl.* **-blo** *or* **-blos.** A member of a people, such as the Hopi or Zuni, traditionally living in such communities.

pu·er·ile (pyo͞o'ər-əl, pyo͝or'əl) *adj.* Childishly silly : juvenile. —**pu'er·il'i·ty** (pyo͞o'ə-rĭl'ĭ-tē) *n.*

pu·er·per·al (pyo͞o-ûr'pər-əl) *adj.* Of or relating to childbirth.

puff (pŭf) *n.* **1. a.** A brief, usu. forceful discharge, as of smoke or air. **b.** A slight explosive sound made by a puff. **2.** A small swelling <*puffs* of clouds> **3.** A soft, light pad, esp. for applying powder. **4.** A light, flaky pastry. **5.** A highly complimentary review or recommendation. —*v.* **1.** To blow or come forth in puffs. **2.** To breathe heavily : pant. **3.** To give forth puffs, as of smoke. **4.** To swell or appear to swell. **5.** To inflate with pride or conceit. **6.** To praise or advertise extravagantly. —**puff'i·ly** *adv.* —**puff'i·ness** *n.* —**puff'y** *adj.*

puff·ball (pŭf'bôl') *n.* A rounded, often edible fungus of the genus *Lycoperdon* and related genera that when broken open releases spores in dustlike puffs.

puff·er (pŭf'ər) *n.* Any of various prickly, often poisonous, chiefly marine fishes capable of puffing up with water or air.

puff·er·y (pŭf'ə-rē) *n.* Favorable and often exaggeratedly flattering publicity.

puf·fin (pŭf'ĭn) *n.* Any of several sea birds of the genera *Fratercula* and *Lunda,* with black and white plumage and a flattened, brightly colored bill.

pug[1] (pŭg) *n.* **1.** A small dog, orig. bred in China, with a snub nose, a wrinkled face, and a curled tail. **2.** A short, upturned, somewhat flattened nose.

pug[2] (pŭg) *n. Slang.* A boxer.

pu·gi·lism (pyo͞o'jə-lĭz'əm) *n.* The sport of fighting with the fists : boxing. —**pu'gi·list** *n.* —**pu'gi·lis'tic** (-lĭs'tĭk) *adj.*

pug·na·cious (pŭg-nā'shəs) *adj.* Disposed to quarrel or fight : combative. —**pug·na'cious·ly** *adv.* —**pug·nac'i·ty** (-năs'ĭ-tē) *n.*

puis·sance (pwĭs'əns, pyo͞o'ĭ-səns) *n.* Power : might. —**puis'sant** *adj.*

puke (pyo͞ok) *v.* **puked, puk·ing.** *Slang.* To vomit.

puk·ka (pŭk'ə) *adj.* **1.** Authentic. **2.** First-rate.

pul (po͞ol) *n., pl.* **puls** *or* **pu·li** (po͞o'lē). —See table at CURRENCY.

pu·la (po͞o'lä) *n.* —See table at CURRENCY.

pul·chri·tude (pŭl'krĭ-to͞od', -tyo͞od') *n.* Physical beauty. —**pul'chri·tu'di·nous** (-to͞od'n-əs, -tyo͞od'-) *adj.*

pule (pyo͞ol) *v.* **puled, pul·ing.** To whine or whimper <a *puling* child>

Pu·lit·zer Prize (po͝ol'ĭt-sər, pyo͞o'lĭt-) *n.* Any of several awards conferred annually for accomplishment in various fields, as journalism, music, and literature.

pull (po͝ol) *v.* **1.** To apply force to so as to draw toward the force. **2.** To draw out or forth from a fixed position. **3.** To tug at. **4.** To break or tear apart. **5.** To stretch (e.g., taffy) repeatedly. **6.** To injure (a muscle or tendon) by straining. **7.** To move (e.g., a trailer) by automotive means. **8.** *Informal.* To carry out, esp. skillfully. **9.** To draw out (a knife or gun) in readiness for use. **10.** To produce (e.g., a printed proof) from type. **11.** *Informal.* To attract. **12.** To put on (clothing). **—pull off.** To accomplish despite difficulty. **—pull through.** To survive illness or trouble successfully. *—n.* **1.** The act or process of pulling. **2.** Force or effort used in pulling. **3.** A force that attracts or draws. **4.** A device used for pulling. **5.** *Slang.* Special advantage or influence. **—pull (oneself) together.** To regain one's composure.

pull·back (po͝ol'băk') *n.* An orderly withdrawal of military troops.

pul·let (po͝ol'ĭt) *n.* A young hen.

pul·ley (po͝ol'ē) *n., pl.* **-leys. 1.** A wheel with a grooved rim through which a rope or chain is run for hoisting or changing the direction of a pulling force. **2.** A wheel turned by or driving a belt.

pulley
Simple fixed pulley

Pull·man (po͝ol'mən) *n.* A railway sleeping car or parlor car.

pull·out (po͝ol'out') *n.* **1.** A military pullback. **2.** Something, as a magazine insert, to be pulled out.

pull·o·ver (po͝ol'ō'vər) *n.* A garment, esp. a sweater, put on by being pulled down over the head. **—pull'o'ver** *adj.*

pull-up (po͝ol'ŭp') *n.* The exercise of chinning.

pul·mo·nar·y (po͝ol'mə-nĕr'ē, pŭl'-) *adj.* Of, pertaining to, or affecting the lungs.

pulp (pŭlp) *n.* **1.** A soft, moist substance or mass. **2.** The soft juicy or fleshy part of a fruit or vegetable. **3.** Ground and moistened cellulose material used to make paper. **4.** The soft inner tissue of a tooth. **5.** A magazine printed on cheap paper and often containing lurid subject matter. **—pulp'i·ness** *n.* **—pulp'y** *adj.*

pul·pit (po͝ol'pĭt, pŭl'-) *n.* **1.** An elevated platform with a lectern used in preaching or conducting a church service. **2.** The ministry as a profession.

pulp·wood (pŭlp'wo͝od') *n.* Soft wood used in papermaking.

pul·sar (pŭl'sär') *n. Astron.* Any of several celestial objects emitting short intense bursts, as of radio waves or x-rays.

pul·sate (pŭl'sāt') *v.* **-sat·ed, -sat·ing.** To beat or vibrate rhythmically. **—pul·sa'tion** *n.* **—pul'sa'tor** *n.*

pulse (pŭls) *n.* **1.** The rhythmical expansion and contraction of the arteries generated by the regular beating of the heart. **2.** A quick temporary change in electrical or wave energy. *—v.* **pulsed, puls·ing.** To pulsate. **—pulse'less** *adj.*

pul·ver·ize (pŭl'və-rīz') *v.* **-ized, -iz·ing. 1.** To reduce or be reduced to tiny particles. **2.** To destroy completely : demolish. **—pul'ver·iz'a·ble** *adj.* **—pul'ver·i·za'tion** *n.* **—pul'ver·iz'er** *n.*

pu·ma (pyo͞o'mə) *n.* The mountain lion.

pum·ice (pŭm'ĭs) *n.* A light, porous volcanic rock used esp. as an abrasive.

pum·mel (pŭm'əl) *v.* **-meled, -mel·ing** *or* **-melled, -mel·ling.** To strike repeatedly : pound.

pump¹ (pŭmp) *n.* A device for moving a gas or liquid from one place or container to another. *—v.* **1.** To raise or move (liquid or gas) with a pump. **2.** To fill with air by means of a pump. **3.** To empty of water or air. **4.** To move up and down or back and forth. **5.** To force or propel with or as if with a pump. **6.** To question relentlessly.

pump² (pŭmp) *n.* A low shoe without laces or straps.

pum·per·nick·el (pŭm'pər-nĭk'əl) *n.* A coarse, dark, sour rye bread.

pump·kin (pŭmp'kĭn, pŭm'-, pŭng'-) *n.* A trailing vine, *Cucurbita pepo,* widely cultivated for its large pulpy round fruit with a thick, orange-yellow rind and many seeds.

pun (pŭn) *n.* A humorous play on a word that evokes more than one interpretation. **—pun** *v.*

punch¹ (pŭnch) *n.* **1.** A tool for piercing, perforating, cutting, or embossing. **2.** A tool for driving a pin, bolt, or nail in or out of a hole. *—v.* To use a punch on.

†punch² (pŭnch) *v.* **1.** To hit sharply with the fist. **2.** *W U.S.* To herd (cattle). *—n.* **1.** A blow with or as if with the fist. **2.** Vigor : energy. **—punch in** (*or* **out**). To check in (or out) formally at a job before (or after) a day's work.

punch³ (pŭnch) *n.* A beverage of fruit juices often with wine or liquor.

punch card *n.* A computer card punched with a pattern of holes or notches to represent data.

punch-drunk (pŭnch'drŭngk') *adj.* Dazed

or bewildered by or as if by too many blows to the head.

pun•cheon (pŭn′chən) *n.* A large cask for liquids.

punch line *n.* The phrase or sentence making the point of a joke.

punch•y (pŭn′chē) *adj.* **-i•er, -i•est. 1.** Marked by vigor or drive. **2.** Groggy or dazed from or as if from a blow.

punc•til•i•o (pŭngk-tĭl′ē-ō′) *n., pl.* **-os. 1.** A fine detail of formal conduct. **2.** Scrupulous observance of ceremony and etiquette.

punc•til•i•ous (pŭngk-tĭl′ē-əs) *adj.* Characterized by meticulous observance of the forms of conduct and etiquette. **—punc•til′i•ous•ly** *adv.*

punc•tu•al (pŭngk′chōō-əl) *adj.* Acting or being habitually on time : prompt. **—punc′tu•al′i•ty** (-ăl′ĭ-tē) *n.*

punc•tu•ate (pŭngk′chōō-āt′) *v.* **-at•ed, -at•ing. 1.** To provide (written material) with punctuation. **2.** To interrupt repeatedly. **3.** To give emphasis to.

punc•tu•a•tion (pŭngk′chōō-ā′shən) *n.* **1.** The use of standardized marks in written material to separate structural units and clarify meaning. **2.** The marks used in punctuating written material.

punc•ture (pŭngk′chər) *v.* **-tured, -tur•ing. 1.** To pierce with or as if with something sharp. **2.** To cause to collapse by or as if by puncturing. *—n.* **1.** An act or instance of puncturing. **2.** A small hole, as in a tire, made by puncturing.

pun•dit (pŭn′dĭt) *n.* One who is erudite or authoritative.

†pung (pŭng) *n. New England.* A low one-horse box sleigh.

pun•gent (pŭn′jənt) *adj.* **1.** Sharp or acrid to the taste or smell. **2.** Having a penetrating quality : biting or caustic. ★ ***syns:*** PIQUANT, SHARP, SPICY, ZESTY **—pun′gen•cy** (-jən-sē) *n.* **—pun′gent•ly** *adv.*

pun•ish (pŭn′ĭsh) *v.* **1.** To subject to a penalty for wrongdoing. **2.** To impose a penalty for. **3.** To treat roughly or injuriously. **—pun′ish•a•ble** *adj.*

pun•ish•ment (pŭn′ĭsh-mənt) *n.* **1.** A penalty for a crime or offense. **2.** Rough or injurious treatment.

pu•ni•tive (pyōō′nĭ-tĭv) *adj.* Imposing or aiming to impose punishment. **—pu′ni•tive•ly** *adv.* **—pu′ni•tive•ness** *n.*

punk[1] (pŭngk) *n.* **1.** Easily crumbled decayed wood used as kindling. **2.** A substance that smolders when lighted, used to ignite fireworks.

punk[2] (pŭngk) *Slang. n.* **1.** A young inexperienced or insignificant person. **2.** A young hoodlum or tough. **3.** Punk rock. *—adj.* **1.** Of inferior quality. **2.** In poor health. **3.** Of, relating to, or being a purposefully bizarre style of dress affected by punk rock groups.

†pun•kin (pŭng′kĭn) *n. Regional.* A pumpkin.

punk rock *n.* Hard rock music marked by themes of bitter hostility toward established society. **—punk rocker** *n.*

pun•ster (pŭn′stər) *n.* One giving to making puns.

punt[1] (pŭnt) *n.* A narrow flat-bottomed boat propelled by a long pole. *—v.* To propel (e.g., a punt) with a pole.

punt[2] (pŭnt) *n.* A play in which a football is dropped and kicked before it hits the ground. **—punt** *v.*

pu•ny (pyōō′nē) *adj.* **-ni•er, -ni•est.** Small or inferior in size, strength, or worth.

pup (pŭp) *n.* **1.** A puppy. **2.** The young of such animals as the seal and fox.

pu•pa (pyōō′pə) *n., pl.* **-pae** (-pē) *or* **-pas.** The inactive stage in the life cycle of many insects between the larval and adult forms. **—pu′pal** *adj.*

pu•pil[1] (pyōō′pəl) *n.* A young person being instructed by a teacher.

pu•pil[2] (pyōō′pəl) *n.* The dark opening in the center of the iris through which light enters the eye.

pup•pet (pŭp′ĭt) *n.* **1.** A figure of a person or animal manipulated by hand or by strings or wires. **2.** One whose actions are controlled by others. **—pup′pet•eer′** *n.* **—pup′pet•ry** *n.*

pup•py (pŭp′ē) *n., pl.* **-pies.** A young dog.

pup tent *n.* A waterproof shelter tent.

pur•blind (pûr′blīnd′) *adj.* **1.** Partially or nearly blind. **2.** Slow in understanding.

pur•chase (pûr′chĭs) *v.* **-chased, -chas•ing.** To acquire by paying money or its equivalent : buy. *—n.* **1.** Something purchased. **2.** The act or an instance of purchasing. **3.** A secure hold or position. **—pur′chas•a•ble** *adj.* **—pur′chas•er** *n.*

pur•dah (pûr′də) *n.* The Hindu practice of secluding women from public view.

pure (pyŏŏr) *adj.* **pur•er, pur•est. 1.** Having a homogeneous composition : unmixed. **2.** Free from impurities or contaminants : clean. **3.** Utter : sheer <*pure* foolishness> **4.** Free from faults : sinless. **5.** Chaste. **6.** Theoretical : abstract. **7.** Containing nothing inappropriate or unnecessary. **8.** Purebred. **—pure′ly** *adv.* **—pure′ness** *n.* **—pur′i•ty** *n.*

pure•bred (pyŏŏr′brĕd′) *adj.* Having many generations of ancestors of the same breed or kind. **—pure′bred′** *n.*

pu•rée (pyōō-rā′, pyŏŏr′ā′) *v.* **-réed, -rée•ing.** To press (cooked food) through a strainer. *—n.* Food or a dish, as soup, prepared by puréeing.

pur•ga•tion (pûr-gā′shən) *n.* An act or result of purging.

pur•ga•tive (pûr′gə-tĭv) *adj.* Tending to purge, esp. causing the bowels to empty. *—n.* A cathartic.

pur•ga•to•ry (pûr′gə-tôr′ē, -tōr′ē) *n., pl.* **-ries. 1.** *Rom. Cath. Ch.* An intermediate state in which the souls of those who have died in grace must atone for their sins before attaining heaven. **2.** A place or state of temporary punishment or suffering. **—pur′ga•to′ri•al** (-tôr′ē-əl, -tōr′-) *adj.*

purge (pûrj) *v.* **purged, purg•ing. 1.** To make clean or pure, esp. to free from sin or guilt. **2.** To rid of what is considered undesirable, esp. to rid of unwanted persons by harsh methods. **3.** To experience or cause emptying of the bowels. *—n.* **1.** The act, process, or result of purging, esp. the harsh elimination of unwanted persons. **2.** Something that purges, esp. a cathartic.

pu·ri·fy (pyŏŏr'ə-fī') *v.* **-fied, -fy·ing.** To make or become clean or pure. **—pu'ri·fi·ca'tion** *n.* **—pu'ri·fi'er** *n.*

Pu·rim (pŏŏr'ĭm) *n.* A Jewish holiday commemorating the deliverance of the Jews from massacre by the Persian official Haman.

pu·rine (pyŏŏr'ēn') *n.* **1.** A crystalline base used in organic synthesis and metabolism studies. **2.** A naturally occurring basic compound derived from or related to purine, as uric acid, adenine, and guanine.

pur·ism (pyŏŏr'ĭz'əm) *n.* Strict adherence to or demand for precision and correctness, esp. in language. **—pur'ist** *n.*

Pu·ri·tan (pyŏŏr'ĭ-tn) *n.* **1.** A member of a 16th- and 17th-cent. Protestant group of England and New England that opposed the elaborate ceremonies of the Church of England. **2. puritan.** An advocate of a very strict moral and religious code. **—pu'ri·tan'i·cal** (-tăn'ĭ-kəl) *adj.* **—pu'ri·tan'i·cal·ly** *adv.* **—pur'i·tan·ism** *n.*

purl[1] (pûrl) *v.* To flow in ripples or with a low murmuring sound. *—n.* The sound made by rippling water.

purl[2] (pûrl) *v.* To knit with a reversed stitch. *—n.* A reversed knitting stitch.

pur·lieu (pûrl'yōō, pûr'lōō) *n.* **1.** An outlying area, as of a city. **2. purlieus. a.** Outskirts **:** environs. **b.** Confines **:** borders.

pur·loin (pər-loin', pûr'loin') *v.* To steal.

pur·ple (pûr'pəl) *n.* **1.** A color with a hue between that of violet and red. **2.** Cloth or clothing of the color purple formerly worn as a symbol of royalty or high authority. *—adj.* **1.** Of the color purple. **2.** Showy and ornate <*purple* prose> **3.** Vulgar or profane <*purple* language> *—v.* **-pled, -pling.** To make or become purple. **—pur'plish** *adj.*

pur·port (pər-pôrt', -pōrt') *v.* To have or give the appearance of being or intending **:** profess. *—n.* (pûr'pôrt', -pōrt'). An apparent meaning or intention. **—pur·port'ed·ly** (-pôr'tĭd-lē, -pōr'-) *adv.*

pur·pose (pûr'pəs) *n.* **1.** An intended or desired result **:** goal. **2.** Determination **:** resolve. *—v.* **-posed, -pos·ing.** To intend to do **:** resolve. **—pur'pose·ful** *adj.* **—pur'pose·less** *adj.* **—pur'pose·ly** *adv.*

purr (pûr) *n.* A low, vibrating murmur characteristic of a contented cat. **—purr** *v.*

purse (pûrs) *n.* **1. a.** A small bag or pouch for money. **b.** A pocketbook or handbag. **2.** Financial resources **:** wealth. **3.** A sum of money tendered as a gift or prize. *—v.* **pursed, purs·ing.** To pucker or wrinkle.

purs·er (pûr'sər) *n.* A passenger ship's officer charged with keeping accounts.

purs·lane (pûr'slĭn, -slān') *n.* A trailing weed, *Portulaca oleracea,* with small yellow flowers, reddish stems, and fleshy leaves sometimes used in salads.

pur·su·ance (pər-sōō'əns) *n.* The act of putting something into effect.

pur·su·ant to (pər-sōō'ənt) *prep.* In accordance with **:** in carrying out.

pur·sue (pər-sōō') *v.* **-sued, -su·ing. 1.** To follow in order to catch **:** chase. **2.** To seek to achieve or accomplish. **3.** To proceed along (a course). **4.** To engage in or keep at (an activity). **—pur·su'er** *n.*

pur·suit (pər-sōōt') *n.* **1.** The act or an instance of pursuing. **2.** An activity regularly engaged in.

pu·ru·lent (pyŏŏr'ə-lənt, pyŏŏr'yə-) *adj.* Containing, discharging, or accompanied by pus. **—pu'ru·lence** *n.*

pur·vey (pər-vā') *v.* To supply or furnish (e.g., provisions), usu. as a service. **—pur·vey'ance** *n.* **—pur·vey'or** *n.*

pur·view (pûr'vyōō') *n.* **1.** Scope or extent of function, ability, or authority. **2.** Range of foresight, understanding, or experience.

pus (pŭs) *n.* A thick, yellowish-white fluid formed in infected tissue that contains bacteria, white blood cells, and tissue debris.

push (pŏŏsh) *v.* **1.** To press forcefully against in order to move. **2.** To move by exerting force **:** thrust. **3.** To press or urge forward vigorously. **4.** To pressure insistently. **5.** *Slang.* **a.** To publicize or sell, esp. aggressively. **b.** To sell illicitly <*push* drugs> *—n.* **1.** The act of pushing **:** thrust or shove. **2.** An energetic or insistent effort. **3.** A stimulus to action. **4.** *Informal.* Energy **:** drive. **—push around.** *Informal.* To attempt to intimidate.

push button *n.* A small button that when pressed activates something.

push·cart (pŏŏsh'kärt') *n.* A light cart pushed by hand.

push·er (pŏŏsh'ər) *n.* One that pushes, esp. one who sells narcotics illicitly.

push·o·ver (pŏŏsh'ō'vər) *n.* **1.** Something easily done. **2.** One easily defeated or deceived.

push-up (pŏŏsh'ŭp') *n.* An exercise performed with the face and hands to the floor that consists of pushing the body up and down with the arms.

push·y (pŏŏsh'ē) *adj.* **-i·er, -i·est.** *Informal.* Objectionably forward or aggressive. **—push'i·ly** *adv.* **—push'i·ness** *n.*

pu·sil·lan·i·mous (pyōō'sə-lăn'ə-məs) *adj.* Faint-hearted **:** cowardly. **—pu'sil·la·nim'i·ty** (-lə-nĭm'ĭ-tē) *n.* **—pu'sil·lan'i·mous·ly** *adv.*

puss[1] (pŏŏs) *n.* *Informal.* A cat.

puss[2] (pŏŏs) *n.* *Slang.* **1.** The mouth. **2.** The face.

puss·y[1] (pŏŏs'ē) *n., pl.* **-ies.** *Informal.* A cat.

pus·sy[2] (pŭs'ē) *adj.* **-si·er, -si·est.** Resembling or filled with pus.

pus·sy·cat (pŏŏs'ē-kăt') *n.* A cat.

puss·y·foot (pŏŏs'ē-fŏŏt') *v.* **1.** To move with stealth or wariness. **2.** *Slang.* To avoid taking a stand **:** equivocate.

pussy willow *n.* A North American shrub or small tree, *Salix discolor,* with silky catkins.

pus·tule (pŭs'chōōl', -tyōōl') *n.* A pus-filled blister. **—pus'tu·lar** *adj.*

put (pōŏt) *v.* **put, put•ting. 1.** To cause to be in a given position or location : place. **2.** To cause to be in a given state. **3.** To cause to undergo. **4.** To regard in a given way : attribute. **5.** To estimate : reckon. **6.** To impose or levy (e.g., a tax). **7.** To hurl for distance in the shot-put. **8.** To present for consideration or decision. **9.** To state : express <*putting* it bluntly> **10.** To translate. **11.** To arrange : adapt. **12.** To devote : apply <*put* effort into a project> **13.** To proceed on a particular course <*put* out to sea> **14.** To wager : bet. **—put down. 1.** To suppress : quell. **2.** *Slang.* To criticize, belittle, or humiliate. **—put in. 1.** To interpose : say. **2.** To spend time doing <*put in* 8 hours of typing> **3.** To enter (an offer, request, or application). **—put off. 1.** *Informal.* To repel. **2.** *Informal.* To evade. **3.** To postpone. **—put on. 1.** To don. **2.** To activate. **3.** To pretend to have. **4.** To mislead or tease. **5.** To add (e.g., weight). **—put out. 1.** To irritate or anger. **2.** To inconvenience. **3.** *Baseball.* To retire (a runner). **—put up. 1.** To build. **2.** To contribute. **3.** To offer for sale. **4.** To preserve (food). **5.** To accommodate. **6.** To endure. **—put up with.** To tolerate.

pu•ta•tive (pyōō'tə-tĭv) *adj.* Commonly regarded as such : supposed.

put-down (pōŏt'doun') *n. Slang.* A critical or belittling remark.

put-on (pōŏt'ŏn', -ôn') *adj.* Pretended : assumed. *—n. Slang.* **1.** The act of deliberately misleading someone. **2.** A hoax or joke : spoof.

put•out (pōŏt'out') *n. Baseball.* A play in which a batter or base runner is retired.

pu•tre•fy (pyōō'trə-fī') *v.* **-fied, -fy•ing.** To decay or cause to decay : rot. **—pu'tre•fac'tion** *n.* **—pu'tre•fac'tive** *adj.*

pu•tres•cent (pyōō-trĕs'ənt) *adj.* Becoming rotten : decaying. **—pu•tres'cence** *n.*

pu•trid (pyōō'trĭd) *adj.* **1.** Decomposed : rotten. **2.** Morally corrupt : vile. **—pu•trid'i•ty** *n.* **—pu'trid•ly** *adv.*

putsch (pōŏch) *n.* A sudden attempt to overthrow a government by a secret plot.

putt (pŭt) *n.* A light golf stroke made on the green to get the ball into the hole. **—putt** *v.*

put•tee (pŭ-tē', pŭt'ē) *n.* **1.** A strip of cloth wrapped around the lower leg. **2.** A leather gaiter.

putt•er[1] (pŭt'ər) *n.* **1.** A golf club used for putting. **2.** A golfer who is putting.

put•ter[2] (pŭt'ər) *v.* **1.** To busy oneself without getting much done. **2.** To tinker.

put•ty (pŭt'ē) *n., pl.* **-ties.** A doughlike cement of ground chalk and linseed oil, used esp. to fill cracks and secure panes of glass in sashes. **—put'ty** *v.*

puz•zle (pŭz'əl) *v.* **-zled, -zling. 1.** To confuse or perplex : bewilder. **2.** To be in a state of perplexity. **3.** To ponder laboriously <*puzzle* over an assignment> **4.** To use reasoning or ingenuity in solving. *—n.* **1.** Something that puzzles. **2.** A problem, game, or device that calls for inventive skill or reasoning. **—puz'zler** *n.*

PVC (pē'vē-sē') *n.* A common thermoplastic resin, used in a wide variety of manufactured products.

py•a (pē-ä') *n.* —See table at CURRENCY.

pyg•my *also* **pig•my** (pĭg'mē) *n., pl.* **-mies. 1.** One of very small size : dwarf. **2.** An insignificant individual. **3. Pygmy.** A member of any of several African and Asian peoples with a hereditary stature of from 4 to 5 ft. **—pyg'my** *adj.*

py•ja•mas (pə-jä'məz, -jăm'əz) *pl.n. esp. Brit. var. of* PAJAMAS.

py•lon (pī'lŏn') *n.* **1.** A monumental gateway, esp. to an Egyptian temple, consisting of a pair of truncated pyramids. **2.** A tower marking a prescribed turning point in an aircraft race. **3.** A steel tower supporting high-tension electric wires or cables.

py•or•rhe•a *or* **py•or•rhoe•a** (pī'ə-rē'ə) *n.* Inflammation of the tooth sockets.

pyr•a•mid (pĭr'ə-mĭd) *n.* **1.** A solid geometric figure having a polygon as its base and triangular faces that meet at a common point. **2.** A massive, monumental structure with a rectangular base and 4 triangular faces that meet at the top. *—v.* **1.** To heap up or build in or as if in pyramid form. **2.** To increase with rapidity and on a broadening base. **—py•ram'i•dal** (pĭ-răm'ĭ-dl) *adj.*

pyre (pīr) *n.* A pile of combustible material for burning a corpse as a funeral rite.

py•re•thrum (pī-rē'thrəm) *n.* **1.** An Old World plant of the genus *Chrysanthemum* and related genera, with showy flowers. **2.** An insecticide made from this plant.

Py•rex (pī'rĕks'). A trademark for any of several types of heat-resistant and chemical-resistant glassware.

py•rim•i•dine (pī-rĭm'ĭ-dēn', pĭ-) *n.* **1.** A liquid and crystalline basic organic compound. **2.** One of several basic compounds, as cytosine, that is similar to pyrimidine and is a component of RNA and DNA.

py•rite (pī'rīt') *n.* A yellowish-brown mineral sulfide containing iron and sulfur. **—py•rit'ic** (-rĭt'ĭk) *adj.*

py•ri•tes (pī-rī'tēz, pĭ-) *n., pl.* **-tes.** Any of a group of minerals composed chiefly of metallic sulfides, esp. of iron.

py•rol•y•sis (pī-rŏl'ĭ-sĭs) *n.* Chemical change effected by heat. **—py'ro•lyt'ic** (-rə-lĭt'ĭk) *adj.*

py•ro•ma•ni•a (pī'rō-mā'nē-ə, -mān'yə) *n.* An irresistible urge to set fires. **—py'ro•ma'ni•ac'** (-mā'nē-ăk') *n.*

py•ro•tech•nics (pī'rə-tĕk'nĭks) *n.* **1.** *(sing. in number).* A usu. large display of fireworks. **2.** *(sing. or pl. in number).* An impressively brilliant display, as of rhetoric or wit. **—py'ro•tech'nic, py'ro•tech'ni•cal** *adj.* **—py'ro•tech'ni•cal•ly** *adv.*

Pyr•rhic victory (pĭr'ĭk) *n.* A victory won at a staggering cost.

py•thon (pī'thŏn', -thən) *n.* Any of various nonvenomous Old World snakes of the family *Pythonidae* that suffocate their prey by coiling around it.

pyx *also* **pix** (pĭks) *n.* **1.** A container holding supplies of Eucharistic wafers. **2.** A container for taking the Eucharist to the sick.

Qq

q *or* **Q** (kyo͞o) *n., pl.* **q's** *or* **Q's. 1.** The 17th letter of the English alphabet. **2.** A speech sound represented by the letter *q*.

qin•dar•ka (kĭn-där′kə) *n.* —See table at CURRENCY.

q.t. (kyo͞o′tē′) *n. Slang.* Quiet <on the *q.t.*>

quack[1] (kwăk) *n.* The sound uttered by a duck. **—quack** *v.*

quack[2] (kwăk) *n.* **1.** A person who pretends to have medical expertise. **2.** A charlatan. **—quack** *v.* **—quack′er•y** *n.*

quad[1] (kwŏd) *n.* QUADRANGLE 2.

quad[2] (kwŏd) *n.* A quadruplet.

quad•ran•gle (kwŏd′răng′gəl) *n.* **1.** *Math.* A plane figure consisting of 4 points, no 3 of which lie on the same straight line, connected by straight lines. **2.** A rectangular area bordered by buildings.

quad•rant (kwŏd′rənt) *n.* **1.** *Geom.* **a.** A circular arc subtending a central angle of 90° : ¼ of a circle. **b.** The plane area bounded by 2 perpendicular radii and the arc they subtend. **2.** An instrument for determining altitudes.

quad•ra•phon•ic (kwŏd′rə-fŏn′ĭk) *adj.* Of or used in a stereophonic sound system having 2 additional channels.

quad•rat•ic (kwŏ-drăt′ĭk) *adj.* Of, relating to, or possessing mathematical quantities of the 2nd degree or less.

quad•ren•ni•al (kwŏ-drĕn′ē-əl) *adj.* **1.** Occurring once in 4 years. **2.** Lasting for 4 years. **—quad•ren′ni•al•ly** *adv.*

quad•ri•ceps (kwŏd′rĭ-sĕps′) *n.* The large four-part muscle at the front of the thigh.

quad•ri•lat•er•al (kwŏd′rə-lăt′ər-əl) *n.* A 4-sided polygon. **—quad′ri•lat′er•al** *adj.*

qua•drille (kwŏ-drĭl′, kwə-, kə-) *n.* **1.** A square dance of 5 figures performed by 4 couples. **2.** Music for the quadrille.

quad•ril•lion (kwŏ-drĭl′yən) *n.* **1.** The cardinal number equal to 10^{15}. **2.** *Brit.* The cardinal number equal to 10^{24}. **—quad•ril′lion** *adj. & pron.* **—quad•ril′lionth** *n. & adj. & adv.*

quad•ri•par•tite (kwŏd′rə-pär′tīt′) *adj.* **1.** Composed of or divided into 4 parts. **2.** Involving 4 participants.

quad•ri•ple•gi•a (kwŏd′rə-plē′jē-ə, -jə) *n.* Complete paralysis of the body from the neck down. **—quad′ri•ple′gic** *adj. & n.*

quad•ru•ped (kwŏd′rə-pĕd′) *n.* An animal having 4 feet.

quad•ru•ple (kwŏ-dro͞o′pəl, -drŭp′əl, kwŏd′-ro͞o-pəl) *adj.* **1.** Consisting of 4 parts. **2.** Multiplied by 4. **3.** *Mus.* Having 4 beats to the measure. **—quad•ru′ple** *n. & v.*

quad•ru•plet (kwŏ-drŭp′lĭt, -dro͞o′plĭt, kwŏd′rə-plĭt) *n.* **1.** One of 4 born at a single birth. **2.** A group or set of 4.

quad•ru•pli•cate (kwŏ-dro͞o′plĭ-kĭt) *adj.* **1.** QUADRUPLE 2. **2.** Reproduced or copied 4 times. —*n.* One of a set of 4 identical things. **—quad•ru′pli•cate′** (-kāt′) *v.* **—quad•ru′pli•ca′tion** *n.*

quaff (kwŏf, kwăf, kwôf) *v.* To drink heartily. —*n.* A hearty draft.

quag•mire (kwăg′mīr′, kwŏg′-) *n.* **1.** Land with a soft, yielding surface. **2.** A difficult or irksome situation.

qua•hog *also* **qua•haug** (kwô′hôg′, -hŏg′, kwō′-, kō′-) *n.* A hard-shelled edible clam of the Atlantic coast of North America.

quail[1] (kwāl) *n., pl.* **quail** *or* **quails. 1.** A small chickenlike game bird of the genus *Coturnix,* having a short tail. **2.** A bird, as the bobwhite, resembling the quail.

quail[2] (kwāl) *v.* To recoil in fear : cower.

quaint (kwānt) *adj.* **1.** Charmingly curious or old-fashioned. **2.** Unusual or unfamiliar : strange. **—quaint′ness** *n.*

quake (kwāk) *v.* **quaked, quak•ing. 1.** To tremble or shake. **2.** To shiver or tremble, as with fright. —*n.* **1.** A quaking. **2.** An earthquake. **—quak′y** *adj.*

Quak•er (kwā′kər) *n.* A member of the Society of Friends.

qual•i•fi•ca•tion (kwŏl′ə-fĭ-kā′shən) *n.* **1.** An act of qualifying or the state of being qualified. **2.** A quality, ability, or skill that makes one suitable for a given position or task. **3.** A restriction or modification.

qual•i•fied (kwŏl′ə-fīd′) *adj.* **1. a.** Competent. **b.** Having met the requirements for a specific position or task. **2.** Not total or wholehearted. ★ *syns:* LIMITED, MODIFIED, RESERVED, RESTRICTED

qual•i•fy (kwŏl′ə-fī′) *v.* **-fied, -fy•ing. 1.** To describe by specifying the characteristics of : characterize. **2.** To make competent or eligible for a task or position. **3.** To certify as competent or capable. **4.** To modify or restrict. **5.** To make less intense. **6.** To modify the meaning of (e.g., a noun). **—qual′i•fi′er** *n.*

qual•i•ta•tive (kwŏl′ĭ-tā′tĭv) *adj.* Of, relating to, or concerning quality.

qual•i•ty (kwŏl′ĭ-tē) *n., pl.* **-ties. 1.** Essential character : nature. **2. a.** An inherent or distinguishing attribute : property. **b.** A character trait. 3. Degree or grade of excellence. **4.** High social standing.

quality control *n.* Maintenance of proper standards in manufactured goods, esp. by regular inspection of the product.

qualm (kwŏm, kwôm) *n.* **1.** A sudden feeling of faintness or nausea. **2.** A sensation of doubt or uneasiness : misgiving. **3.** A conscience pang. ★ *syns:* COMPUNCTION, MISGIVING, RESERVATION, SCRUPLE

quan•da•ry (kwŏn′də-rē, -drē) *n., pl.* **-ries.** A perplexing situation or state.

quan•ti•fy (kwŏn′tə-fī′) *v.* **-fied, -fy•ing.** To determine or express the quantity of. **—quan′ti•fi′a•ble** *adj.*

quan•ti•ta•tive (kwŏn′tĭ-tā′tĭv) *adj.* Of, relating to, or expressed as a quantity, measure, or amount.

quan•ti•ty (kwŏn′tĭ-tē) *n., pl.* **-ties. 1.** A specified or undetermined number or amount.

2. A measurable whole. 3. A large number or amount <bought office supplies in *quantity*> ★ ***syns:*** AMOUNT, BODY, BULK, CORPUS, QUANTUM

quan•tum (kwŏn'təm) *n., pl.* **-ta** (-tə). **1.** A quantity or amount. **2.** *Physics.* An indivisible unit of energy, as a photon.

quantum theory *n. Physics.* A theory of dynamic systems in which variables are represented by abstract mathematical operators having properties that specify the behavior of the system.

quar•an•tine (kwôr'ən-tēn', kwŏr'-) *n.* **1. a.** A period of enforced isolation, as of a person, animal, ship, etc., to prevent the spread of a contagious disease. **b.** A place for such isolation. **2.** A state of enforced isolation or detention. **—quar'an•tine'** *v.*

quark (kwôrk) *n.* Any of a group of hypothetical subatomic particles having electric charges of magnitude ⅓ or ⅔ that of the electron, proposed as the fundamental units of matter.

quar•rel (kwôr'əl, kwŏr'-) *n.* **1.** An angry disagreement or dispute. **2.** A cause for complaint or dispute. *—v.* **-reled, -rel•ing** *or* **-relled, -rel•ling. 1.** To take part in a disagreement. **2.** To complain.

quar•ry¹ (kwôr'ē, kwŏr'ē) *n., pl.* **-ries. 1.** An animal hunted for food or sport. **2.** The object of a hunt or chase.

quar•ry² (kwôr'ē, kwŏr'ē) *n., pl.* **-ries.** An excavation or pit from which stone is cut or blasted. **—quar'ri•er** *n.* **—quar'ry** *v.*

quart (kwôrt) *n.* —See table at MEASUREMENT.

quar•ter (kwôr'tər) *n.* **1.** One of 4 equal parts. **2.** A coin valued at ¼ of the U.S. or Canadian dollar. **3.** ¼ of an hour. **4.** Any of the 4 divisions of the compass as defined by the cardinal points. **5. quarters. a.** A place of lodging or residence. **b.** Barracks. **6.** A section of a city. **7.** *often* **quarters.** An unspecified person or group <praise from all *quarters*> **8.** Mercy or clemency <give the enemy no *quarter*> *—v.* **1.** To cut or divide into 4 equal or equivalent parts. **2.** To dismember (a carcass) into 4 parts. **3.** To provide with shelter or lodgings. *—adj.* Being one of 4 equal or equivalent parts.

quar•ter•back (kwôr'tər-băk') *n. Football.* The offensive backfield player who directs the plays. **—quar'ter•back'** *v.*

quar•ter-deck (kwôr'tər-dĕk') *n.* The stern portion of the upper deck of a ship.

quarter horse *n.* A strong, muscular saddle horse orig. bred in the W U.S.

quar•ter•ly (kwôr'tər-lē) *adj.* Happening at 3-month intervals. *—n., pl.* **-lies.** A publication issued 4 times a year.

quar•ter•mas•ter (kwôr'tər-măs'tər) *n.* **1.** A military officer in charge of administering provisions and supplies. **2.** A petty officer in charge of the navigation of a ship.

quar•tet *also* **quar•tette** (kwôr-tĕt') *n.* **1.** A musical composition for instruments or voices. **2.** A set of 4 persons or things.

quar•tile (kwôr'tīl', -tĭl) *n. Statistics.* The portion of a frequency distribution containing one fourth of the total sample.

quar•to (kwôr'tō) *n., pl.* **-tos. 1.** A page size equal to ¼ whole sheet, orig. obtained by folding a sheet into quarters. **2.** A book made up of quarto pages.

quartz (kwôrts) *n.* A clear, hard, transparent mineral occurring abundantly as a component of granite and sandstone or as various pure crystals.

quartz•ite (kwôrt'sīt') *n.* A metamorphic rock formed by the recrystallization of quartz sandstone.

qua•sar (kwā'zär', -sär') *n.* A starlike object that emits radio waves and visible radiation and apparently has great speed and energy.

quash (kwŏsh, kwôsh) *v.* **1.** *Law.* To set aside or annul, esp. by judicial action. **2.** To crush or forcibly suppress.

qua•si (kwā'zī', -sī', kwä'zē, -sē) *adj.* Having a likeness to something : resembling <a *quasi* government>

qua•si-stel•lar object (kwā'zī-stĕl'ər, -sī-, kwä'zē-, -sē-). A quasar.

quat•rain (kwŏt'rān', kwŏ-trān') *n.* A stanza or poem consisting of 4 lines.

quat•re•foil (kăt'ər-foil', kăt'rə-) *n.* A stylized representation of a 4-petaled flower or a 4-lobed leaf.

quatrefoil

qua•ver (kwā'vər) *v.* **1.** To tremble, as from emotion or weakness. **2.** To speak in a tremulous voice. **—qua'ver** *n.*

quay (kē) *n.* A wharf.

quea•sy (kwē'zē) *adj.* **-si•er, -si•est.** Nauseated. **—quea'si•ness** *n.*

Qué•be•cois (kā'bĕ-kwä') *n.* A native of Quebec, esp. a French-speaking one.

queen (kwēn) *n.* **1.** The wife or widow of a king. **2.** A woman who is a monarch. **3.** A woman regarded as pre-eminent in a given field or domain. **4.** The chess piece with the most power. **5.** A playing card that has the figure of a queen on it. **6.** A fertile female in a colony of social insects, as bees, usu. the only one of its kind in the colony. **—queen'li•ness** *n.* **—queen'ly** *adj.*

queen mother *n.* The mother of a reigning monarch.

queen-size (kwēn'sīz') *adj.* **1.** Of, for, or being a bed approx. 60 in. by 80 in. <a *queen-size* mattress> **2.** Extra large.

queer (kwîr) *adj.* **1.** Different from the normal or expected **:** strange. **2.** Eccentric **:** odd. **3.** Suspicious. —*v. Slang.* **1.** To thwart or ruin. **2.** To put in a bad position.

quell (kwĕl) *v.* **1.** To suppress forcibly **:** put down. **2.** To pacify **:** quiet.

quench (kwĕnch) *v.* **1.** To put out (e.g., a fire) **:** extinguish. **2.** To squelch **:** dampen <couldn't *quench* our spirits> **3.** To satisfy **:** slake. **4.** To cool (metal) by immersing in liquid. **—quench'a•ble** *adj.*

que•nelle (kə-nĕl') *n.* A forcemeat dumpling poached in stock or water.

quer•u•lous (kwĕr'ə-ləs, kwĕr'yə-) *adj.* **1.** Constantly complaining or fretting **:** peevish. **2.** Uttering or expressing complaints or criticism. **—quer'u•lous•ness** *n.*

que•ry (kwîr'ē) *n., pl.* **-ries. 1.** A request for information **:** question. **2.** A doubt. **3.** A question mark. **—que'ry** *v.*

quest (kwĕst) *n.* **1.** A seeking or inquiring **:** search. **2.** An adventurous pursuit undertaken by a knight in medieval romance.

ques•tion (kwĕs'chən) *n.* **1.** An expression of inquiry requiring or inviting an answer. **2.** A point or subject open to debate. **3.** An unresolved matter **:** problem. **4.** A proposition brought up for consideration, as by an assembly. **5.** Uncertainty **:** doubt. **6.** Possibility **:** chance <no *question* of turning back now> —*v.* **1.** To put a question to. **2.** To interrogate, as a suspect or witness. **3.** To dispute.

ques•tion•a•ble (kwĕs'chə-nə-bəl) *adj.* **1.** Open to question or doubt **:** problematical. **2.** Of dubious morality or respectability. **—ques'tion•a•bly** *adv.*

question mark *n.* A punctuation symbol (?) placed at the end of a sentence to indicate a question.

ques•tion•naire (kwĕs'chə-nâr') *n.* A set of related questions, esp. one designed to gather statistical information from a sample population, as for a survey.

quet•zal (kĕt-säl') *n., pl.* **-zals** *or* **-za•les** (-sä'läs). **1.** A bird, *Pharomacrus mocino,* of Central America, having bronze-green and red plumage and long flowing tail feathers in the male. **2.** —See table at CURRENCY.

queue (kyo͞o) *n.* **1.** A line, as of people or vehicles, waiting a turn. **2.** *Computer Sci.* A sequence of stored data or programs awaiting processing. —*v.* **queued, queu•ing.** To form or wait in a line <*queued* up at the post office>

quib•ble (kwĭb'əl) *v.* **-bled, -bling.** To raise trivial objections, esp. over minor matters. **—quib'ble** *n.* **—quib'bler** *n.*

quiche (kēsh) *n.* Unsweetened custard baked in a pastry shell often with other ingredients, as vegetables or seafood.

▲ ***word history:*** A quiche may seem to be a quintessentially French dish, but the word *quiche* is actually a Gallicized German word. Quiche was orig. a specialty of Lorraine, a region in NE France bordering on Germany. The region was claimed by both countries at various times, and both French and German are spoken there. The word *quiche* is a borrowing of Alsatian German *küche,* a diminutive of *kuche,* "cake." The form *quiche* is a French spelling of the German word.

quick (kwĭk) *adj.* **1.** Moving or performing with speed and agility. **2.** Occurring or accomplished in a short time. **3.** Thinking, understanding, or responding rapidly and easily. **4.** Tending to react hastily or impulsively. —*n.* **1.** Raw or sensitive exposed flesh, as under the fingernails. **2.** The most sensitive aspect of one's emotions. **3.** The living <the *quick* and the dead> **—quick'ly** *adv.* **—quick'ness** *n.*

quick•en (kwĭk'ən) *v.* **1.** To make or become more rapid **:** accelerate. **2.** To vitalize. **3.** To stimulate **:** stir.

quick-freeze (kwĭk'frēz') *v.* To freeze (food) by a process sufficiently rapid to retain flavor and nutritional value.

quick•lime (kwĭk'līm') *n.* CALCIUM OXIDE.

quick•sand (kwĭk'sănd') *n.* A soft, shifting mass of loose sand mixed with water that yields easily to pressure and in which a heavy object tends to sink.

quick•sil•ver (kwĭk'sĭl'vər) *n.* The element mercury. —*adj.* Unpredictable.

▲ ***word history:*** The name *quicksilver* for the element mercury is a translation of Latin *argentum vivum,* literally "living silver." Mercury was so called because it is a silvery colored metal that is liquid at ordinary temperatures. In *quicksilver* the word *quick* preserves its original but now archaic sense "living, alive."

quick•step (kwĭk'stĕp') *n.* A march, esp. to accompany military quick time.

quick-tem•pered (kwĭk'tĕm'pərd) *adj.* Easily aroused to anger.

quick time *n.* A military marching pace of 120 steps per minute.

quick-wit•ted (kwĭk'wĭt'ĭd) *adj.* Quick to think and act **:** mentally alert.

quid[1] (kwĭd) *n.* A cut of something to be chewed, esp. a plug of tobacco.

quid[2] (kwĭd) *n., pl.* **quid** *or* **quids.** *esp. Brit.* A pound sterling.

quid pro quo (kwĭd' prō kwō') *n.* An equal exchange or substitution.

qui•es•cent (kwī-ĕs'ənt, kwē-) *adj.* Inactive **:** still. **—qui•es'cence** *n.*

qui•et (kwī'ĭt) *adj.* **1.** Making little or no sound **:** silent. **2.** Free of noise **:** hushed. **3.** Calm and unmoving **:** still. **4.** Free of agitation and turmoil. **5.** Restful **:** soothing. **6.** Marked by tranquillity. **7.** Not showy or obtrusive. —*n.* The state or quality of being quiet. —*v.* To make or become quiet. **—qui'et•ly** *adv.*

qui•e•tude (kwī'ĭ-to͞od', -tyo͞od') *n.* Quiet tranquillity.

qui•e•tus (kwī-ē'təs) *n.* **1.** Death. **2.** A final discharge, as of an obligation.

quill (kwĭl) *n.* **1.** The hollow stemlike principal shaft of a feather. **2.** A large wing or tail feather. **3.** A writing pen made from a long, stiff feather. **4.** One of the sharp hollow spines of a hedgehog or porcupine.

quilt (kwĭlt) *n.* A padded bed covering. **—quilt** *v.* **—quilt′ing** *n.*

quince (kwĭns) *n.* A tree, *Cydonia oblonga,* bearing white flowers and yellow applelike fruit, edible when cooked.

qui•nine (kwī′nīn′) *n.* A bitter, colorless, crystalline powder, obtained from cinchona and used as an antimalarial drug.

quinine water *n.* A carbonated beverage flavored with quinine.

quin•quen•ni•al (kwĭn-kwĕn′ē-əl, kwĭng-) *adj.* **1.** Occurring once every 5 years. **2.** Lasting for 5 years.

quin•sy (kwĭn′zē) *n.* Acute tonsillitis, often accompanied by fever and the formation of an abscess.

quint (kwĭnt) *n.* A quintuplet.

quin•tal (kwĭn′tl) *n.* A metric unit of mass equal to 100,000 grams.

quin•tes•sence (kwĭn-tĕs′əns) *n.* **1.** The pure, undiluted essence of something. **2.** The purest or most characteristic instance. **—quin′tes•sen′tial** (-tĭ-sĕn′shəl) *adj.*

quin•tet *also* **quin•tette** (kwĭn-tĕt′) *n.* **1.** A musical composition for 5 voices or instruments. **2.** An ensemble of 5 musicians. **3.** A group of 5.

quin•tile (kwĭn′tīl′, kwĭnt′l) *n. Statistics.* The portion of a frequency distribution containing one fifth of the total sample.

quin•til•lion (kwĭn-tĭl′yən) *n.* **1.** The cardinal number equal to 10^{18}. **2.** *esp. Brit.* The cardinal number equal to 10^{30}. **—quin•til′lion** *adj.* **—quin•til′lionth** *n. & adj. & adv.*

quin•tu•ple (kwĭn-to͞o′pəl, -tyo͞o′-, -tŭp′əl, kwĭn′tə-pəl) *adj.* **1.** Consisting of 5 parts. **2.** Multiplied by 5. **—quin•tu′ple** *n. & v.*

quin•tu•plet (kwĭn-tŭp′lĭt, -to͞o′plĭt, -tyo͞o′-plĭt, kwĭn′tə-plĭt) *n.* **1.** One of 5 born at a single birth. **2.** A group or set of 5.

quin•tu•pli•cate (kwĭn-to͞o′plĭ-kĭt, -tyo͞o′-). *adj.* **1.** QUINTUPLE 2. **2.** Reproduced or copied 5 times. —*n.* One of a set of 5 identical things. **—quin•tu′pli•cate′** (-kāt′) *v.*

quip (kwĭp) *n.* A witty, offhand remark. —*v.* **quipped, quip•ping.** To make a quip. **—quip′ster** *n.*

quire (kwīr) *n.* A uniform set of 24 or sometimes 25 sheets of paper : 1/20 ream.

quirk (kwûrk) *n.* **1.** A sudden sharp bend or crook. **2.** A peculiarity : idiosyncracy. **—quirk′i•ness** *n.* **—quirk′y** *adj.*

quirt (kwûrt) *n.* A riding whip with a lash of braided rawhide.

quis•ling (kwĭz′lĭng) *n.* A traitor, esp. one collaborating as the puppet of an occupying enemy force.

quit (kwĭt) *v.* **quit** *or* **quit•ted, quit•ting. 1.** To depart from : leave. **2.** To give up or withdraw from <*quit* school> **3.** To abandon or put aside. **4.** To cease to perform : stop. **—quit′ter** *n.*

quit•claim (kwĭt′klām′) *n.* The transfer of a title, right, or claim to another.

quite (kwīt) *adv.* **1.** To the fullest extent : completely. **2.** Actually : really. **3.** To a degree : rather <*quite* late>

quits (kwĭts) *adj.* Being on equal terms, as by payment or requital.

quit•tance (kwĭt′ns) *n.* **1.** Release from a debt, obligation, or penalty. **2.** Something given or done as recompense.

quiv•er[1] (kwĭv′ər) *v.* To shake or cause to shake with a rapid slight motion : tremble. **—quiv′er** *n.*

quiv•er[2] (kwĭv′ər) *n.* A portable case for arrows.

qui vive (kē vēv′) *n.* **1.** A challenge by a sentinel. **2.** Vigilance : alertness.

quix•ot•ic (kwĭk-sŏt′ĭk) *adj.* Idealistic in a romantic or impractical way. **—quix•ot′i•cal•ly** *adv.* **—quix′o•tism** *n.*

quiz (kwĭz) *v.* **1.** To question closely or repeatedly. **2.** To test the knowledge of by posing questions. —*n., pl.* **quiz•zes. 1.** A questioning or inquiry. **2.** A written or oral test. **—quiz′zer** *n.*

quiz•zi•cal (kwĭz′ĭ-kəl) *adj.* **1.** Showing puzzlement : perplexed. **2.** Teasing : mocking. **—quiz′zi•cal•ly** *adv.*

quoin (koin, kwoin) *n.* **1.** An exterior structural angle, as of a masonry wall. **2.** A stone forming a quoin : cornerstone.

quoin

quoit (kwoit, koit) *n.* **1. quoits** *(sing. in number).* A game in which iron or rope rings are pitched at a stake. **2.** A ring used in quoits.

quon•dam (kwŏn′dəm, -dăm′) *adj.* That once was : former.

quo•rum (kwôr′əm, kwōr′-) *n.* The minimum number of officers and members of a constituted body necessary for the valid transaction of business.

quo•ta (kwō′tə) *n.* **1. a.** A proportional share : allotment. **b.** A production assignment. **2.** The highest number or proportion, esp. of people, permitted admission, as to a nation, group, or institution.

quot•a•ble (kwō′tə-bəl) *adj.* Suitable for or worthy of quoting.

quo•ta•tion mark (kwō-tā′shən) *n.* Either of a pair of punctuation marks (“ ” *or* ‘ ’) used

esp. to designate the beginning and end of a quoted passage.
quote (kwōt) *v.* **quot•ed, quot•ing. 1.** To repeat or copy the words of (another), usu. acknowledging the source. **2.** To cite or refer to for authority or illustration. **3.** To state (a price) for securities, goods, or services. —*n. Informal.* **1.** Something quoted. **2.** A quotation mark. —**quo•ta'tion** *n.*
quoth (kwōth) *v. Archaic.* Uttered : said.
quo•tid•i•an (kwō-tĭd'ē-ən) *adj.* **1.** Recurring daily. **2.** Ordinary : everyday.
quo•tient (kwō'shənt) *n.* The quantity resulting from the division of one quantity by another.
QWER•TY (kwûr'tē) *adj.* Of or being the traditional configuration of typewriter or computer keyboard keys.

Rr

r *or* **R** (är) *n., pl.* **r's** *or* **R's. 1.** The 18th letter of the English alphabet. **2.** A speech sound represented by the letter *r.*
Ra *symbol for* RADIUM.
rab•bet (răb'ĭt) *n.* A groove along the edge of a board cut to fit another piece to form a joint. —*v.* **1.** To cut a rabbet in. **2.** To connect by a rabbet.
rab•bi (răb'ī') *n., pl.* **-bis. 1.** A person ordained for leadership of a Jewish congregation. **2.** A scholar qualified to interpret Jewish law. —**rab•bin'i•cal** (rə-bĭn'ĭ-kəl), **rab•bin'ic** *adj.*
rab•bin•ate (răb'ĭn-at') *n.* **1.** The office of a rabbi. **2.** Rabbis as a group.
rab•bit (răb'ĭt) *n., pl.* **-bits** *or* **-bit. 1.** A furry, long-eared, burrowing mammal of the family Leporidae. **2.** The fur of a rabbit.
rab•ble (răb'əl) *n.* A tumultuous crowd.
rab•ble-rous•er (răb'əl-rou'zər) *n.* A demagogue.
rab•id (răb'ĭd) *adj.* **1.** Afflicted with rabies. **2.** Extreme : fanatical. **3.** Raging : violent <*rabid* hostility> —**rab'id•ly** *adv.*
ra•bies (rā'bēz) *n.* An acute, infectious, often fatal viral disease of the central nervous system transmitted by the bite of an infected animal.
rac•coon (ră-kōōn') *n., pl.* **-coons** *or* **-coon. 1.** A North American mammal, *Procyon lotor,* with black, masklike facial markings and a bushy, black-ringed tail. **2.** The fur of a raccoon.
race[1] (rās) *n.* **1.** A division of the human population distinguished by physical characteristics transmitted by genes. **2.** A body of people united by a common history or nationality <the Spanish *race*> **3.** Humanity as a whole. **4.** A subspecies or breed, as of domestic animals. —**ra'cial** *adj.*
race[2] (rās) *n.* **1.** A competition of speed. **2.** A competition, as for an elective office. **3.** A rapid onward movement. **4. a.** A strong flow of water. **b.** The channel of a current of water. —*v.* **raced, rac•ing. 1.** To compete in a race (with). **2.** To move rapidly : rush. —**rac'er** *n.*
race•course (rās'kôrs') *n.* A racetrack.
race•horse (rās'hôrs') *n.* A horse bred and used for racing.
ra•ceme (rā-sēm', rə-) *n.* An inflorescence in which stalked flowers are arranged along a common stem.
race•track (rās'trăk') *n.* A course designed for racing.
rac•ism (rā'sĭz'əm) *n.* **1.** The belief that some races are inherently superior to others. **2.** Discrimination based on race. —**rac'ist** *n. & adj.*
rack (răk) *n.* **1.** A framework or stand for holding and usu. displaying something. **2.** A toothed metal bar designed to mesh with another toothed machine part. **3.** An instrument of torture for slowly stretching the victim's body. —*v.* **1.** To place in a rack. **2.** To torture on a rack. **3.** To torment <*racked* with pain> **4.** To strain with great effort <*racked* her brain trying to remember>
rack•et[1] *also* **rac•quet** (răk'ĭt) *n.* A light bat with a handle and netting stretched tightly across an open oval frame, used to strike a ball or shuttlecock.
rack•et[2] (răk'ĭt) *n.* **1.** An uproar or din. **2.** A fraudulent or dishonest business.
rack•et•eer (răk'ĭ-tîr') *n.* One engaged in an illegal business, esp. an extortionist.
rac•on•teur (răk'ŏn-tûr', -ən-) *n.* An accomplished and witty storyteller.
rac•quet•ball (răk'ĭt-bôl') *n.* A game played with a short racket and a rubber ball in a 4-walled court.
rac•y (rā'sē) *adj.* **-i•er, -i•est. 1.** Pungent : piquant. **2.** Slightly improper or indelicate. ★ *syns:* OFF-COLOR, RISQUHE, SPICY, SUGGESTIVE —**rac'i•ly** *adv.* —**rac'i•ness** *n.*
rad (răd) *n.* A unit of energy absorbed from ionizing radiation, equal to 0.01 joule per kg.
ra•dar (rā'där') *n.* A device for detecting the position, velocity, and size of distant objects by analysis of radio waves reflected from their surfaces.
ra•dar•scope (rā'där-skōp') *n.* The viewing screen of a radar receiver.
ra•di•al (rā'dē-əl) *adj.* **1.** Of or arranged like rays or radii. **2.** Having or marked by radiating parts. **3.** Directed along a radius.
radial tire *n.* A pneumatic tire strengthened by having the cords of its inner fabric laid at right angles to the center line of the tread.

ra•di•ant (rā'dē-ənt) *adj.* **1.** Emitting light or heat. **2.** Being or emitted as radiation. **3.** Filled with a strong, projecting quality <*radiant* with love> **4.** Glowing **:** brilliant. **—ra'di•ance, ra'di•an•cy** *n.*

ra•di•ate (rā'dē-āt') *v.* **-at•ed, -at•ing. 1.** To emit rays. **2.** To issue or be transmitted in rays. **3.** To spread out from a center. **4.** To manifest glowingly.

ra•di•a•tion (rā'dē-ā'shən) *n.* **1.** An act or process of radiating. **2.** *Physics.* **a.** Emission of energy in the form of electromagnetic waves or photons. **b.** Energy traveling in this form. **c.** A stream of particles.

radiation sickness *n.* An illness caused by overexposure to radiation, ranging in severity from nausea and diarrhea to hemorrhaging and death.

ra•di•a•tor (rā'dē-ā'tər) *n.* **1.** A framework of pipes that heats the surrounding air by means of a circulation of steam or hot water. **2.** A cooling device, as in an engine.

rad•i•cal (răd'ĭ-kəl) *adj.* **1.** Arising from or reaching a root or source **:** basic. **2.** Drastic **:** extreme. **3.** Favoring or effecting basic changes. —*n.* **1.** A supporter of basic changes, esp. political revolution. **2.** *Math.* **a.** The indicated root of a quantity. **b.** The sign ($\sqrt{}$) placed before a quantity indicating that its root is to be taken. **3.** *Chem.* An atom or group of atoms that has at least one unpaired electron. **—rad'i•cal•ness** *n.*

rad•i•cal•ism (răd'ĭ-kə-lĭz'əm) *n.* The beliefs or methods of political radicals.

ra•di•i (rā'dē-ī') *n. var. pl. of* RADIUS.

ra•di•o (rā'dē-ō') *n., pl.* **-os. 1.** The use of electromagnetic waves in the radio frequency range to transmit and receive electric signals without the use of wires. **2.** The equipment used to transmit or receive radio signals. **3.** The broadcast of programmed material to the public by radio. —*v.* **1.** To transmit (a message) by radio. **2.** To communicate (with) by radio.

ra•di•o•ac•tiv•i•ty (rā'dē-ō-ăk-tĭv'ĭ-tē) *n.* **1.** Spontaneous emission of radiation, as from unstable atomic nuclei. **2.** The radiation, such as alpha particles, emitted by a radioactive source. **—ra'di•o•ac'tive** *adj.*

radio astronomy *n.* Study of celestial phenomena by observation and analysis of their associated radio-frequency emissions.

radio beam *n.* A focused beam of radio signals used to guide ships or aircraft.

ra•di•o•car•bon (rā'dē-ō-kär'bən) *n.* Radioactive carbon, esp. carbon 14.

radio frequency *n.* An electromagnetic wave frequency used for radio and television transmission, in the range from about 10 kilohertz to about 300,000 megahertz.

ra•di•o•gram (rā'dē-ō-grăm') *n.* A message sent by wireless telegraphy.

ra•di•o•graph (rā'dē-ō-grăf') *n.* An image produced by radiation other than light, esp. by x-rays. **—ra'di•o•graph'** *v.* **—ra'di•o•graph'ic** *adj.* **—ra'di•o•graph'i•cal•ly** *adv.* **—ra'di•og'ra•phy** (-ŏg'rə-fē) *n.*

ra•di•o•i•so•tope (rā'dē-ō-ī'sə-tōp') *n.* A radioactive isotope of an element.

ra•di•o•lo•ca•tion (rā'dē-ō-lō-kā'shən) *n.* Detection of distant objects by radar.

ra•di•ol•o•gy (rā'dē-ŏl'ə-jē) *n.* The use of x-rays and other forms of radiation to diagnose and treat diseases. **—ra'di•o•log'i•cal** (-ə-lŏj'ĭ-kəl) *adj.* **—ra'di•ol'o•gist** *n.*

ra•di•om•e•ter (rā'dē-ŏm'ĭ-tər) *n.* A device for detecting and measuring radiation. **—ra'di•o•met'ric** (-ō-mĕt'rĭk) *adj.* **—ra'di•om'e•try** *n.*

ra•di•o•paque (rā'dē-ō-pāk') *adj.* Not allowing the passage of x-rays or other radiation. **—ra'di•o•pac'i•ty** (-ō-păs'ĭ-tē) *n.*

ra•di•o•sonde (rā'dē-ō-sŏnd') *n.* An instrument carried aloft usu. by balloon for transmitting meteorological data.

ra•di•o•te•leg•ra•phy (rā'dē-ō-tə-lĕg'rə-fē) *n.* Wireless telegraphy. **—ra'di•o•tel'e•graph'** (-tĕl'ĭ-grăf') *n.*

ra•di•o•tel•e•phone (rā'dē-ō-tĕl'ə-fōn') *n.* A telephone system for 2-way communication by means of radio. **—ra'di•o•te•leph'o•ny** (-tə-lĕf'ə-nē) *n.*

radio telescope *n.* A radio receiver for detecting and analyzying radio waves of extraterrestrial origin.

ra•di•o•ther•a•py (rā'dē-ō-thĕr'ə-pē) *n.* Treatment of disease by radiation.

radio wave *n.* A radio-frequency electromagnetic wave.

rad•ish (răd'ĭsh) *n.* A plant, *Raphanus sativus,* having a sharp-tasting edible root.

ra•di•um (rā'dē-əm) *n.* *Symbol* **Ra** A rare brilliant-white, highly radioactive metallic element used in radiotherapy.

ra•di•us (rā'dē-əs) *n., pl.* **-di•i** (-dē-ī') *or* **-us•es. 1. a.** A line segment between the center of a circle and any point on its circumference. **b.** A line segment between the center of a sphere and any point on its surface. **2.** A measure of circular area <every town within a *radius* of 50 miles> **3.** The shorter and thicker of the 2 bones of the forearm.

ra•don (rā'dŏn') *n.* *Symbol* **Rn** A colorless, radioactive, heavy gaseous element used in radiotherapy.

raf•fi•a (răf'ē-ə) *n.* A fiber from the leaves of an African palm tree, *Raphia ruffia,* used for mats and baskets.

raff•ish (răf'ĭsh) *adj.* **1.** Showy **:** flashy. **2.** Jaunty. **—raff'ish•ness** *n.*

raf•fle (răf'əl) *n.* A lottery in which a number of persons buy chances to win a prize. **—raf'fle** *v.*

raft[1] (răft) *n.* A low, floating structure of logs, planks, etc., used for water transport or as a platform. **—raft** *v.*

raft[2] (răft) *n.* *Informal.* A great number, amount, or collection.

raft•er (răf'tər) *n.* One of the sloping beams that support a pitched roof.

rag[1] (răg) *n.* A scrap of cloth.

rag[2] (răg) *v.* **ragged, rag•ging.** *Slang.* **1.** To taunt **:** tease. **2.** To scold.

rag[3] (răg) *n.* A piece of ragtime music.

ra•ga (rä'gə) *n.* A traditional form in Hindu music, usu. having a thematic set of tones and improvised variations.

rag•a•muf•fin (răg'ə-mŭf'ĭn) *n.* A dirty or untidily dressed child.

rage (rāj) *n.* **1. a.** Violent anger. **b.** A fit of anger. **2.** A craze : fad. —*v.* **raged, rag•ing. 1.** To be violently angry. **2.** To move or spread with violent force.

rag•ged (răg'ĭd) *adj.* **1.** Tattered. **2.** Dressed in tattered clothes. **3.** Having rough edges. **4.** Uneven <a *ragged* performance> —**rag'ged•ly** *adv.*

rag•lan (răg'lən) *n.* A loose garment with slanted shoulder seams and sleeves that extend in one piece to the neckline.

ra•gout (ră-gōō') *n.* A thick, spicy stew of meat and vegetables.

rag•time (răg'tīm') *n.* A jazz style marked by an elaborately syncopated melody and a steadily accented accompaniment.

rag•weed (răg'wēd') *n.* Any of several weeds of the genus *Ambrosia,* whose airborne pollen is a chief cause of hay fever.

raid (rād) *n.* **1.** A surprise attack, esp. by a small military force. **2.** A sudden and forcible entry. —*v.* To make a raid (on).

rail[1] (rāl) *n.* **1.** A horizontal bar supported at both ends or at intervals by posts, as in fences. **2.** A steel bar usu. used in pairs as a track for wheeled vehicles. **3.** A railroad. —*v.* To enclose or furnish with a rail.

rail[2] (rāl) *n.* A small brownish marsh bird of the family Rallidae.

rail[3] (rāl) *v.* To condemn or complain bitterly or abusively. —**rail'er** *n.*

rail•ing (rā'lĭng) *n.* A fence, balustrade, or barrier made of rails.

rail•ler•y (rā'lə-rē) *n., pl.* **-ies.** Good-natured teasing : banter.

rail•road (rāl'rōd') *n.* **1.** A road made of parallel steel rails on a bed of ties that provides a track for trains. **2.** A complete system of railroad track, along with stations, rolling stock, and other property. —*v.* **1.** To transport by railroad. **2.** *Informal.* **a.** To push through quickly so as to forestall discussion <*railroad* a bill through the legislature> **b.** To convict hastily or unfairly.

rail•way (rāl'wā') *n.* **1.** A railroad. **2.** A runway for wheeled vehicles.

rai•ment (rā'mənt) *n.* Clothing.

rain (rān) *n.* **1.** Water condensed from atmospheric vapor, falling to earth in drops. **2.** An abundant outpouring : shower. —*v.* **1.** To fall as or like rain. **2.** To send or pour down abundantly. —**rain out.** To force the postponement of because of rain. —**rain'i•ness** *n.* —**rain'y** *adj.*

rain•bow (rān'bō') *n.* An arc of spectral colors, esp. one appearing as a result of the refractive dispersion of sunlight in raindrops or mist.

rain check *n.* **1.** The stub of a ticket that entitles a holder to admission at a future date if the scheduled event is posponed because of bad weather. **2.** A postponement of the acceptance or fulfillment of an offer.

rain•coat (rān'kōt') *n.* A waterproof coat.

rain•fall (rān'fôl') *n.* **1.** A fall of rain. **2.** *Meteorol.* The quantity of water that falls over a specified area during a given time.

rain forest *n.* A dense usu. tropical evergreen forest having an annual rainfall of at least 100 in.

rain•mak•ing (rān'mā'kĭng) *n.* The action or ceremony of producing or trying to bring on rain. —**rain'mak'er** *n.*

rain•storm (rān'stôrm') *n.* A storm with heavy rain.

rain•wa•ter (rān'wô'tər, -wŏt'ər) *n.* Water that has fallen as rain.

raise (rāz) *v.* **raised, rais•ing. 1.** To cause to move upward : lift. **2.** To build : erect. **3.** To cause to appear <The sting *raised* a bump.> **4.** To increase the quantity, size, or worth of. **5.** To increase the strength, degree, or pitch of. **6.** To increase the rank or status of : promote. **7.** To grow or breed. **8.** To bring up : rear. **9.** To put forward for consideration. **10.** To stir up : arouse. **11.** To amass : collect <*raise* funds> **12.** To cause (dough) to rise. —*n.* An increase, as in amount or pay.

rai•sin (rā'zĭn) *n.* A dried usu. seedless grape.

rai•son d'ê•tre (rā'zôɴ dĕt'rə) *n.* Reason for existing.

ra•jah *or* **ra•ja** (rä'jə) *n.* A prince, chief, or ruler in India or the East Indies.

rake[1] (rāk) *n.* A garden tool with a long handle and teeth at the head. —*v.* **raked, rak•ing. 1.** To gather, loosen, or smooth with or as if with a rake. **2.** To gain in abundance <*raking* in the cash> **3.** To bring to light : uncover <*rake* up old scandals> **4.** To examine thoroughly <*rake* over the evidence> **5.** To aim heavy gunfire along the length of. —**rak'er** *n.*

rake[2] (rāk) *n.* A roué : libertine.

rake[3] (rāk) *n.* A slope, as of a ship's mast. —*v.* To slant or incline.

rake-off (rāk'ôf', -ŏf') *n. Slang.* A percentage of the profits.

rak•ish[1] (rā'kĭsh) *adj.* **1.** *Naut.* Trim and streamlined. **2.** Jaunty or showy. —**rak'ish•ly** *adv.* —**rak'ish•ness** *n.*

rak•ish[2] (rā'kĭsh) *adj.* Like a rake : dissolute. —**rak'ish•ly** *adv.* —**rak'ish•ness** *n.*

rale *also* **râle** (räl) *n.* An abnormal or pathological respiratory sound.

ral•ly (răl'ē) *v.* **-lied, -ly•ing. 1.** To gather or call together for a common purpose : assemble. **2.** To restore to order : reassemble. **3.** To rouse from decline or inactivity. **4.** To recover from a setback or disadvantage. —*n., pl.* **-lies. 1.** An assembly, esp. one intended to inspire enthusiasm. **2.** A sharp improvement or abrupt recovery.

ram (răm) *n.* **1.** A male sheep. **2.** A bar-shaped device used to drive, batter, or crush by impact. —*v.* **rammed, ram•ming. 1.** To strike against heavily : butt. **2.** To force into place. **3.** To stuff : cram.

Ram•a•dan (răm'ə-dän', răm'ə-dän') *n.* **1.**

The 9th month of the Muslim calendar. **2.** The fast held from sunrise to sunset during this period.

ram•ble (răm′bəl) *v.* **-bled, -bling. 1.** To walk aimlessly. **2.** To digress. **—ram′ble** *n.* **—ram′bling•ly** *adv.*

ram•bler (răm′blər) *n.* **1.** One that rambles. **2.** A climbing rose.

ram•bunc•tious (răm-bŭngk′shəs) *adj.* Unruly : boisterous.

ram•ie (răm′ē) *n.* A flexible fiber derived from the stems of an Asian plant, used in fabrics and cordage.

ram•i•fy (răm′ə-fī′) *v.* **-fied, -fy•ing. 1.** To branch out. **2.** To have branchlike consequences. **—ram′i•fi•ca′tion** *n.*

ramp (rămp) *n.* An inclined passage or roadway connecting different levels.

ram•page (răm′pāj′) *n.* A course of violent, destructive, or unrestrained action. —*v.* (răm-pāj′) **-paged, -pag•ing.** To move about wildly. **—ram•pa′geous** *adj.*

ram•pant (răm′pənt) *adj.* Growing or extending rapidly and without control : rife. **—ram′pan•cy** *n.* **—ram′pant•ly** *adv.*

ram•part (răm′pärt′, -pərt) *n.* A defensive embankment, often with a parapet.

ram•rod (răm′rŏd′) *n.* **1.** A metal rod for plunging the charge into a muzzle-loading firearm. **2.** A rod for cleaning the barrel of a firearm.

ram•shack•le (răm′shăk′əl) *adj.* Falling apart from poor construction or upkeep.

ran (răn) *v. p.t. of* RUN.

ranch (rănch) *n.* **1.** A large farm for raising livestock, as beef cattle, sheep, or horses. **2.** A large farm specializing in a kind of crop or animal <a mink *ranch*> —*v.* To work on or run a ranch.

†ran•che•ri•a (răn′chə-rē′ə) *n. SW U.S.* **1.** A Mexican herdsmen's hut. **2.** An Indian village.

†ran•che•ro (răn-châr′ō) *n., pl.* **-ros.** *SW U.S.* A rancher.

†ran•cho (răn′chō) *n., pl.* **-chos.** *SW U.S.* **1.** A hut or group of huts for housing ranch workers. **2.** A ranch.

ranch house *n.* A one-story house with a low-pitched roof.

ran•cid (răn′sĭd) *adj.* Having the rank odor or taste of spoiled fats or oils : putrid. **—ran•cid′i•ty, ran′cid•ness** *n.*

ran•cor (răng′kər) *n.* Bitter long-lasting resentment. **—ran′cor•ous** *adj.*

rand (rănd) *n.* —See table at CURRENCY.

ran•dom (răn′dəm) *adj.* **1.** Having no specific pattern or purpose : haphazard. **2.** Selected in such a way that each member of a set has an equal chance of being chosen.

ran•dom-ac•cess memory (răn′dəm-ăk′sĕs′) *n. Computer Sci.* A memory device in which information can be accessed in any order.

rang (răng) *v. p.t. of* RING[2].

range (rānj) *n.* **1.** An extent included or reached, esp. by perception, ability, or knowledge. **2.** An area of activity : sphere. **3.** An extent of variation <the daily temperature *range*> **4.** The maximum effective distance that can be traversed <within mortar *range*> **5.** A place for shooting at targets or testing weaponry. **6.** A tract of open land for grazing livestock. **7.** An act of roaming. **8.** A region in which a plant or animal is to be found. **9.** An extended series or chain, esp. of mountains. **10.** A large cooking stove with an oven and several burners. ★ ***syns:*** EXTENT, ORBIT, REACH, REALM, SCOPE, SPHERE —*v.* **ranged, rang•ing. 1.** To arrange in order, esp. in lines or rows. **2.** To classify. **3.** To roam or wander freely. **4.** To explore. **5.** To extend in a particular direction. **6.** To vary within specified limits.

rang•er (rān′jər) *n.* **1.** A rover. **2.** An armed, usu. mounted law officer. **3.** One who patrols and guards a forest or park.

rang•y (rān′jē) *adj.* **-i•er, -i•est.** Thin and long-limbed. **—rang′i•ness** *n.*

ra•ni *also* **ra•nee** (rä′nē) *n., pl.* **-nis** *also* **-nees.** The wife of a rajah.

rank[1] (răngk) *n.* **1.** Relative position in an ordered group. **2.** Position or status, as in society. **3.** Eminent position. **4.** An official grade <the *rank* of corporal> **5.** A row, line, or series. **6.** A line of soldiers or vehicles standing side by side in close order. **7. ranks.** Personnel, esp. enlisted military personnel. —*v.* **1.** To place in a row or rows. **2.** To classify. **3.** To hold a specified rank <*ranking* 2nd in the class> **4.** To take precedence over.

rank[2] (răngk) *adj.* **1.** Growing profusely or unmanageably <*rank* weeds> **2.** Strong and offensive in odor or taste. **3.** Indecent. **—rank′ly** *adv.* **—rank′ness** *n.*

rank and file *n.* **1.** The troops of an army. **2.** Ordinary members, as of a group or organization. **—rank′-and-file′** *adj.*

ran•kle (răng′kəl) *v.* **-kled, -kling. 1.** To be a source of persistent irritation or resentment. **2.** To become sore or inflamed.

ran•sack (răn′săk′) *v.* **1.** To search or rummage thoroughly. **2.** To pillage.

ran•som (răn′səm) *n.* **1.** The release of a detained person or property in return for payment. **2.** The price demanded or payment made. **—ran′som** *v.*

rant (rănt) *v.* To speak loudly, wildly, and at length : rave. **—rant′er** *n.*

rap[1] (răp) *v.* **rapped, rap•ping. 1.** To hit sharply : strike. **2.** To utter sharply. **3.** To criticize : blame. —*n.* **1.** A quick knock or blow. **2.** A reprimand. **3.** *Slang.* Blame or punishment.

rap[2] (răp) *n.* **1.** *Slang.* A talk or discussion. **2.** A form of popular music marked by spoken or chanted rhyming lyrics. — *v.* **rapped, rap•ping.** *Slang.* **1.** To converse freely and at length. **2.** To perform rap music.

ra•pa•cious (rə-pā′shəs) *adj.* **1.** Feeding on live prey. **2.** Ravenous : voracious. **3.** Plundering. **—ra•pa′cious•ly** *adv.* **—ra•pa′cious•ness, ra•pac′i•ty** (rə-păs′ĭ-tē) *n.*

rape[1] (rāp) *n.* **1.** The crime of forcing another person to submit to sexual intercourse. **2.** The act of seizing and carrying off **:** abduction. **3.** Abusive treatment **:** violation. **—rape** *v.* **—rap′ist** *n.*

rape[2] (rāp) *n.* A Eurasian plant, *Brassica napus,* cultivated as fodder and for its oil-rich seeds.

rap•id (răp′ĭd) *adj.* Very fast **:** swift. *—n. often* **rapids.** A fast-moving, steeply descending section of a river. **—ra•pid′i•ty** (rə-pĭd′ĭ-tē), **rap′id•ness** *n.*

rapid eye movement *n.* REM.

ra•pi•er (rā′pē-ər, rāp′yər) *n.* A long, slender, 2-edged sword.

rap•ine (răp′ĭn) *n.* Forcible seizure of another's property **:** plunder.

rap•pel (ră-pĕl′) *n.* The method of descending a sheer face, as of a cliff, by means of a double rope passed under the thigh and over the opposite shoulder. **—rap•pel′** *v.*

rappel

rap•port (ră-pôr′, -pōr′, rə-) *n.* A relationship, esp. a trustful or harmonious one.

rap•proche•ment (ră′prôsh-mäɴ′) *n.* A renewal of cordial relations, as between 2 governments.

rap•scal•lion (răp-skăl′yən) *n.* A rascal.

rapt (răpt) *adj.* **1.** Deeply delighted **:** enraptured. **2.** Deeply absorbed **:** engrossed.

rap•tor (răp′tər) *n.* A bird of prey. **—rap•to′ri•al** (-tôr′ē-əl, -tōr′-) *adj.*

rap•ture (răp′chər) *n.* A state or expression of ecstasy. **—rap′tur•ous** *adj.*

ra•ra a•vis (râr′ə ā′vĭs) *n.* One that is rare or unique.

rare[1] (râr) *adj.* **rar•er, rar•est. 1.** Occurring infrequently **:** uncommon. **2.** Highly valued owing to uncommonness **:** special. **3.** Thin in density **:** rarefied. **—rare′ly** *adv.* **—rare′ness** *n.* **—rar′i•ty** *n.*

rare[2] (râr) *adj.* **rar•er, rar•est.** Cooked only a short time <*rare* beef>

▲ ***word history:*** The adjective *rare[2]* meaning "lightly cooked" referred only to eggs until modern times. Its application to other foods, esp. meats, was considered an Americanism until recently, when it was adopted into British usage.

rare-earth element (râr′ûrth′) *n.* Any of the metallic elements with atomic numbers 57 through 71.

rar•e•fy (râr′ə-fī′, răr′-) *v.* **-fied, -fy•ing. 1.** To make or become thin, light, or less dense. **2.** To refine **:** purify. **—rar′e•fac′tion** *n.* **—rar′e•fac′tive** *adj.*

rar•ing (râr′ĭng) *adj. Informal.* Full of enthusiasm **:** eager <*raring* to go>

ras•cal (răs′kəl) *n.* **1.** A dishonest person **:** rogue. **2.** A playfully mischievous person. **—ras•cal′i•ty** *n.* **—ras′cal•ly** *adj.*

rash[1] (răsh) *adj.* Marked by ill-considered boldness or haste **:** impetuous.

rash[2] (răsh) *n.* **1.** A skin eruption. **2.** An outbreak of many occurrences <a *rash* of house fires>

rash•er (răsh′ər) *n.* **1.** A thin slice of fried or broiled bacon. **2.** A dish of rashers.

rasp (răsp) *n.* **1.** A coarse file having raised, pointed projections. **2.** A grating, abrasive sound or voice. *—v.* **1.** To scrape or file with or as if with a rasp. **2.** To utter in a grating voice. **3.** To grate upon (e.g., one's nerves). **—rasp′er** *n.* **—rasp′y** *adj.*

rasp•ber•ry (răz′bĕr′ē) *n.* **1.** A shrubby, usu. thorny plant of the genus *Rubus,* as *R. strigosus* of E North America, bearing edible, usu. reddish berries. **2.** *Slang.* A jeering or contemptuous sound made by exhaling so that the protruded tongue vibrates against the lips.

rat (răt) *n.* **1.** A long-tailed rodent similar to but larger than the mouse, esp. one of the genus *Rattus.* **2.** *Slang.* A despicable or treacherous person. *—v.* **rat•ted, rat•ting. 1.** To hunt or catch rats, esp. with dogs. **2.** *Slang.* To betray one's comrades.

ratch•et (răch′ĭt) *n.* A device consisting of a pawl that permits a wheel or bar to move in only one direction by engaging its sloping teeth. *—v.* To increase or decrease by increments.

rate[1] (rāt) *n.* **1.** A quantity measured with respect to another measured or fixed quantity <a *rate* of speed of 20 mph> **2.** A measure of a part to a whole **:** proportion <the mortality *rate*> **3.** A charge or payment calculated by means of a proportion or ratio. **4.** A level of quality. *—v.* **rat•ed, rat•ing. 1.** To calculate the value of **:** appraise. **2.** To assign or be assigned to a rank or class. **3.** *Informal.* To deserve **:** merit. **4.** *Informal.* To have status. **—at any rate. 1.** In any case. **2.** At least.

rate[2] (rāt) *v.* **rat•ed, rat•ing.** To berate.

rate of exchange *n.* The ratio at which a unit of currency may be exchanged for another.

rath•er (răth′ər, rä′thər) *adv.* **1.** Preferably. **2.** With more reason or justification. **3.** More accurately **:** exactly. **4.** Somewhat. **5.** On the contrary.

raths•kel•ler (răt′skĕl-ər, răth′-) *n.* A restaurant in the style of a German tavern.

rat•i•fy (răt′ə-fī′) *v.* **-fied, -fy•ing.** To approve formally and thereby validate <*ratify* a treaty> **—rat′i•fi•ca′tion** *n.*

rat•ing (rā′tĭng) *n.* **1.** A position assigned on a scale **:** standing. **2.** An evaluation of financial status <a credit *rating*>

ra•tio (rā′shō, -shē-ō′) *n., pl.* **-tios. 1.** The quotient of a pair of numbers, used as a means of comparing them. **2.** A relationship between the amounts or sizes of 2 things, expressed as a quotient : proportion.

ra·ti·oc·i·nate (răsh'ē-ŏs'ə-nāt') *v.* **-nat·ed, -nat·ing.** To think methodically : reason. **—ra'ti·oc'i·na'tion** *n.* **—ra'ti·oc'i·na'tive** *adj.* **—ra'ti·oc'i·na'tor** *n.*

ra·tion (răsh'ən, rā'shən) *n.* **1.** A fixed share or portion, esp. of allotted food. **2. rations.** Food allotted. —*v.* **1.** To provide with rations. **2.** To distribute : allot. **3.** To restrict to limited amounts.

ra·tio·nal (răsh'ə-nəl) *adj.* **1.** Having or exercising the power to reason. **2.** Of or consistent with reason. **3.** Of sound mind : sane. **4.** *Math.* Of or being a number expressible as an integer or a quotient of 2 integers. **—ra'tion·al'i·ty** *n.*

ra·tio·nale (răsh'ə-năl') *n.* **1.** A fundamental reason : rational basis. **2.** An exposition of guiding principles : justification.

ra·tio·nal·ism (răsh'ə-nə-lĭz'əm) *n.* The view that reason constitutes the only valid basis for action, belief, or faith. **—ra'tio·nal·ist** *n.* **—ra'tio·nal·is'tic** *adj.*

ra·tio·nal·ize (răsh'ə-nə-līz') *v.* **-ized, -iz·ing. 1.** To make rational. **2.** To cause to seem rational. **3.** To devise self-satisfying but incorrect explanations for (e.g., one's behavior). **—ra'tio·nal·i·za'tion** *n.*

rat·line *also* **rat·lin** (răt'lĭn) *n.* Any of the small ropes fastened horizontally to the shrouds of a ship.

rat·tan (ră-tăn', rə-) *n.* An Asian climbing palm of the genera *Calamus, Daemonorops,* or *Plectomia,* with strong, pliant stems used to make wickerwork.

rat·tle (răt'l) *v.* **-tled, -tling. 1.** To make or cause to make a quick succession of short, sharp sounds. **2.** To move with such sounds. **3.** To chatter. **4.** *Informal.* To unnerve : fluster. —*n.* **1.** A quick series of short, sharp sounds. **2.** A device, as a toy, that rattles when shaken. **3.** One or all of the dry, horny structures at the end of a rattlesnake's tail.

rat·tler (răt'lər) *n.* A rattlesnake.

rat·tle·snake (răt'l-snāk') *n.* A venomous New World snake of the genera *Crotalus* or *Sistrurus,* having a rattle at the end of the tail.

rat·tling (răt'lĭng) *Informal.* —*adj.* **1.** Animated : brisk. **2.** Very good. —*adv.* Especially <a *rattling* good party>

rat·ty (răt'ē) *adj.* **-ti·er, -ti·est. 1.** Characteristic of or overrun by rats. **2.** *Slang.* Dilapidated : shabby.

rau·cous (rô'kəs) *adj.* **1.** Loud and hoarse : strident. **2.** Boisterous : disorderly.

raun·chy (rôn'chē, rän'-) *adj.* **-chi·er, -chi·est.** *Slang.* **1.** Filthy : grubby. **2.** Obscene : vulgar <*raunchy* jokes> **—raun'chi·ly** *adv.* **—raun'chi·ness** *n.*

rav·age (răv'ĭj) *v.* **-aged, -ag·ing. 1.** To bring heavy destruction on : devastate. **2.** To sack : pillage. —*n.* **1.** The act of ravaging. **2.** Heavy damage. **—rav'ag·er** *n.*

rave (rāv) *v.* **raved, rav·ing. 1.** To speak irrationally or wildly. **2.** To rage : roar. **3.** To be wildly enthusiastic. —*n.* **1.** The act of raving. **2.** *Informal.* An extravagantly enthusiastic review or opinion.

rav·el (răv'əl) *v.* **-eled, -el·ing** *also* **elled, -el·ling. 1.** To separate the fibers or strands of (e.g., rope) : unravel. **2.** To complicate : confuse. —*n.* **1.** A raveled part. **2.** A loose thread. **3.** A tangle. **—rav'el·er** *n.*

rav·el·ing *also* **rav·el·ling** (răv'ə-lĭng) *n.* A thread separated from woven material.

ra·ven (rā'vən) *n.* A large bird, *Corvus corax,* with black plumage and a croaking cry. —*adj.* Black and glossy.

rav·en·ous (răv'ə-nəs) *adj.* **1.** Extremely hungry. **2.** Rapacious. **3.** Greedy. ★ ***syns:*** FAMISHED, HUNGRY, STARVING

ra·vine (rə-vēn') *n.* A steep, narrow cut in the earth's surface.

rav·i·o·li (răv'ē-ō'lē, rä'vē-) *pl.n.* Small casings of pasta filled with meat or cheese.

rav·ish (răv'ĭsh) *v.* **1.** To seize and carry off by force. **2.** To rape. **3.** To overwhelm with delight. **—rav'ish·ment** *n.*

rav·ish·ing (răv'ĭ-shĭng) *adj.* Alluring.

raw (rô) *adj.* **1.** Uncooked. **2. a.** Not refined or processed. **b.** Not coated or treated <*raw* wood> **3.** Inexperienced <*raw* recruits> **4.** Recently applied : fresh. **5.** Inflamed : sore. **6.** Damp and chilly. **7.** Unfair <a *raw* deal> **8.** Coarse : obscene. **—raw'ly** *adv.* **—raw'ness** *n.*

raw·boned (rô'bōnd') *adj.* Having a lean, gaunt, bony frame.

raw·hide (rô'hīd') *n.* **1.** The untanned hide of cattle. **2.** A whip or thong made of rawhide.

ray[1] (rā) *n.* **1.** A thin line or narrow beam of radiation, esp. visible light. **2.** A small amount : trace. **3. a.** A straight line extending from a point. **b.** A structure having this form, as a bony spine or a daisy petal.

ray[2] (rā) *n.* A marine fish of the order Rajiformes or Batoidei, having a horizontally flattened body and narrow tail.

ray·on (rā'ŏn') *n.* **1.** A synthetic textile fiber produced by forcing a cellulose solution through fine spinnerets. **2.** Fabric knit or woven from rayon.

raze (rāz) *v.* **razed, raz·ing.** To tear down : demolish.

ra·zor (rā'zər) *n.* An implement with a sharp-edged blade, used esp. for shaving.

razz (răz) *v.* *Slang.* To taunt with loud, scornful noises : heckle.

Rb *symbol for* RUBIDIUM.

re (rē, rā) *prep.* In reference to.

Re *symbol for* RHENIUM.

re– *pref.* **1.** Again : anew <*re*build> **2.** Backwards : back <*re*act>.

reach (rēch) *v.* **1.** To stretch out (a bodily part). **2.** To touch or try to grasp by stretching <couldn't *reach* the top shelf> **3.** To arrive at <*reach* a verdict> **4.** To succeed in communicating with. **5.** To extend (to). **6.** To amount to : aggregate. —*n.* **1.** The act or ability of stretching or thrusting out. **2.** The distance something can reach. **3.** An unbroken expanse. **4.** The range of one's understanding.

re•act (rē-ăkt') *v.* **1.** To act in response to a stimulus. **2.** To act in opposition. **3.** *Chem.* To undergo chemical change. —**re•ac'tant** *n.* —**re•ac'tive** *adj.*

re•ac•tance (rē-ăk'təns) *n.* Opposition to alternating electric current flow caused in a circuit by inductance and capacitance.

re•ac•tion (rē-ăk'shən) *n.* **1.** A response to a stimulus or the condition resulting from such a response. **2.** A contrary or opposing action. **3.** A political tendency to oppose progress or favor a return to former conditions. **4.** A chemical transformation or change. **5.** *Physics.* A nuclear reaction.

re•ac•tion•ar•y (rē-ăk'shə-nĕr'ē) *adj.* Opposing progress or favoring a return to former conditions. —**re•ac'tion•ar'y** *n.*

re•ac•tor (rē-ăk'tər) *n.* **1.** One that reacts. **2.** A nuclear reactor.

read (rēd) *v.* **read** (rĕd), **read•ing. 1.** To look through and take in the meaning of (written or printed words or symbols). **2.** To speak aloud the words of (written or printed material). **3.** To interpret the meaning of <*reading* the clues> **4.** To determine the thoughts or intent of <*read* someone's mind> **5.** To predict or foretell. **6.** To receive or comprehend (e.g. a radio message). **7.** To study <*read* philosophy> **8.** To learn by reading. **9.** To indicate or register <The speedometer *read* 60.> **10.** To have a certain wording or literary quality <How does the title *read*?> **11.** *Computer Sci.* To obtain (information) from a storage medium, such as a magnetic disk. —**read'a•bil'i•ty, read'a•ble•ness** *n.*

read•ing (rē'dĭng) *n.* **1.** Written or printed matter. **2.** A public recitation of written material. **3.** An interpretation. **4.** A specific form or variation of a text. **5.** Information indicated, as by a gauge.

read-on•ly memory (rēd'ōn'lē) *n.* A computer memory that allows access to stored data but prevents modification of the data.

read•out *also* **read-out** (rēd'out') *n. Computer Sci.* A presentation of data from storage or calculations.

read•y (rĕd'ē) *adj.* **-i•er, -i•est. 1.** Prepared or available for service or action. **2.** Mentally disposed **:** willing. **3.** Prompt in understanding or reacting <a *ready* wit> —*v.* **-ied, -y•ing.** To cause to be ready. —**read'i•ly** *adv.* —**read'i•ness** *n.*

read•y-made (rĕd'ē-mād') *adj.* Already made or prepared <*ready-made* pie crust>

re•a•gent (rē-ā'jənt) *n.* A substance used in a chemical reaction to detect, measure, or yield other substances.

re•al[1] (rē'əl, rēl) *adj.* **1.** Not imaginary or pretended **:** actual. **2.** Authentic or genuine <*real* gold> **3.** Essential **:** basic. **4.** Serious **:** substantial. **5.** *Law.* Of or constituting fixed or stationary property, as buildings or land. ★ ***syns:*** SUBSTANTIAL, SUBSTANTIVE, TANGIBLE —*adv. Informal.* Very.

re•al[2] (rā-äl') *n.* —See table at CURRENCY.

real estate *n.* Land owned as property, along with its natural resources and permanent buildings.

re•al•ism (rē'ə-lĭz'əm) *n.* **1.** Concern with factual truth and things as they really are **:** practicality. **2.** Artistic representation intended as an unidealized portrayal of objective reality. —**re'al•ist** *n.* —**re'al•is'tic** *adj.* —**re'al•is'ti•cal•ly** *adv.*

re•al•i•ty (rē-ăl'ĭ-tē) *n., pl.* **-ties. 1.** The quality or state of being actual or true. **2.** One that is real. **3.** The totality of all existing things.

re•al•ize (rē'ə-līz') *v.* **-ized, -iz•ing. 1.** To comprehend fully or correctly. **2.** To make real **:** fulfill <*realized* her potential> **3.** To obtain or achieve <*realize* a profit> —**re'al•iz'a•ble** *adj.* —**re'al•i•za'tion** *n.*

re•al•ly (rē'ə-lē, rē'lē) *adv.* **1.** In actual fact. **2.** Truly. **3.** Indeed.

realm (rĕlm) *n.* **1.** A kingdom. **2.** A field or sphere **:** domain.

---

re'ab•sorb' *v.*
re'ab•sorp'tion *n.*
re'ac•cept' *v.*
re'ac•com'mo•date' *v.*
re'ac•com'pa•ny *v.*
re'ac•cuse' *v.*
re'ac•quire' *v.*
re'a•dapt' *v.*
re'ad•dress' *v.*
re'ad•journ' *v.*
re'ad•journ'ment *n.*
re'ad•mis'sion *n.*
re'ad•mit' *v.*
re'ad•mit'tance *n.*
re'a•dopt' *v.*
re'ad•vance' *v.*
re•an'i•mate' *v.*
re•an'i•ma'tion *n.*
re'an•nex' *v.*
re'a•noint' *v.*
re'ap•pear' *v.*
re'ap•pear'ance *n.*
re'ap•ply' *v.*
re'ap•point' *v.*
re'ap•point'ment *n.*
re•ar'gue *v.*
re'as•cend' *v.*
re'as•cent' *n.*
re'as•sem'ble *v.*
re'as•sem'bly *n.*
re'as•sert' *v.*
re'as•ser'tion *n.*
re'as•sign' *v.*
re'as•sim'i•late' *v.*
re'as•so'ci•ate' *v.*
re'as•sume' *v.*
re'as•sump'tion *n.*
re'at•tach' *v.*
re'at•tack' *v.*
re'at•tain' *v.*
re'at•tempt' *v.*
re'a•vow' *v.*
re'a•wake' *v.*
re'a•wak'en *v.*
re•bill' *v.*
re•boil' *v.*
re•bur'y *v.*
re•car'ry *v.*
re•cel'e•brate' *v.*
re•chal'lenge *v.*
re•char'ter *v.*
re•check' *v.*
re•chris'ten *v.*
re•cir'cle *v.*
re•cir'cu•late' *v.*
re•clean' *v.*
re•clothe' *v.*
re•coin' *v.*
re•coin'age *n.*
re•col'o•nize' *v.*
re•col'or *v.*
re'com•bine' *v.*
re'com•mence' *v.*
re'com•mis'sion *n.*
re'com•mit' *v.*
re'com•mit'ment *n.*
re'con•dense' *v.*
re'con•duct' *v.*
re•con'quer *v.*
re•con'quest *n.*
re•con'se•crate' *v.*
re'con•sol'i•date' *v.*

real number *n.* A number that is rational or irrational and is not imaginary.
re•al•po•li•tik (rā-äl′pō′lĭ-tēk′) *n.* A diplomatic policy based on the aggressive pursuit of national interests without regard for ethical or philosophical considerations.
real time *n. Computer Sci.* The actual time in which a physical process under computer study or control occurs.
Re•al•tor (rē′əl-tər, -tôr′). A service mark for a real-estate agent affiliated with the National Association of Realtors.
re•al•ty (rē′əl-tē) *n., pl.* **-ties.** Real estate.
ream[1] (rēm) *n.* **1.** A quantity of paper, usu. 500 sheets. **2.** *often* **reams.** A great amount.
ream[2] (rēm) *v.* **1.** To enlarge or shape (e.g., a hole) with or as if with a reamer. **2.** To squeeze out (material) with a reamer.
ream•er (rē′mər) *n.* **1.** A tool for enlarging or shaping holes. **2.** A juicer with a conical, ridged center.
reap (rēp) *v.* **1.** To cut and gather (e.g., grain), as with a scythe or reaper. **2.** To harvest a crop from <*reap* a wheat field> **3.** To gain as a result of effort.
reap•er (rē′pər) *n.* One that reaps, esp. a machine for harvesting.
rear[1] (rîr) *n.* **1.** A hind part. **2.** A point or area farthest from the front. —*adj.* Of, at, or in the rear. —**rear′most′** *adj.*
rear[2] (rîr) *v.* **1.** To care for during early life. **2.** To lift upright : raise. **3.** To erect : build. **4.** To tend (plants or animals). **5.** To rise on the hind legs, as a horse.
rear admiral *n.* A naval officer ranking below a vice admiral and above a captain.
rear-end (rîr′ĕnd′) *v. Slang.* To run into (a motor vehicle) from behind. —**rear′-end′er** *n.*
rear•ward (rîr′wərd) *adj. & adv.* At or toward the rear. —**rear′wards** *adv.*
rea•son (rē′zən) *n.* **1.** The motive or basis for an action, decision, feeling, or belief. **2.** An underlying cause or fact that gives logical justification <no *reason* to delay> **3.** The ability or capacity for rational thought. **4.** Mental balance : sanity. —*v.* **1.** To use reason : think logically. **2.** To talk or discuss logically. **3.** To decide or determine by logical thinking. —**rea′son•ing** *n.*
rea•son•a•ble (rē′zə-nə-bəl) *adj.* **1.** Able to reason : rational. **2.** Consistent with reason : logical. **3.** Not extreme : moderate <*reasonable* rates> —**rea′son•a•bly** *adv.*
re•bate (rē′bāt′) *n.* A deduction from an amount charged or a return of part of a price paid. —*v.* (*also* rĭ-bāt′) **-bat•ed, -bat•ing.** To return (part of an amount) or deduct from (an amount due).
re•bel (rĭ-bĕl′) *v.* **-belled, -bel•ling. 1.** To refuse allegiance to and oppose by force an established authority. **2.** To defy or resist established convention. **3.** To feel strong unwillingness or revulsion. —*n.* **reb•el** (rĕb′əl). One who rebels or is rebellious.
re•bel•lion (rĭ-bĕl′yən) *n.* **1.** An uprising designed to change or overthrow an existing government or authority. **2.** Open defiance toward an authority or convention. ★ ***syns:*** INSURGENCE, INSURRECTION, MUTINY, REVOLT, UPRISING.
re•bel•lious (rĭ-bĕl′yəs) *adj.* **1.** Taking part in or favoring rebellion. **2.** Resisting direction or control : unruly.
re•birth (rē-bûrth′, rē′bûrth′) *n.* **1.** A reincarnation. **2.** A revival.
re•born (rē-bôrn′) *adj.* Emotionally or spiritually renewed.
re•bound (rē′bound′, rĭ-) *v.* **1.** To bounce or spring back after a collision. **2.** To recover, as from a decline. —*n.* (rē′bound′, rĭ-bound′). **1.** A bouncing or springing back : recoil. **2.** *Sports.* A rebounding basketball or hockey puck.
re•buff (rĭ-bŭf′) *n.* **1.** An abrupt or curt repulse or refusal. **2.** A check or setback. —*v.* **1.** To snub. **2.** To drive back.

re•con′sti•tute *v.*
re•con′sti•tu′tion *n.*
re′con•vene′ *v.*
re•cop′y *v.*
re•cross′ *v.*
re•crown′ *v.*
re•cul′ti•vate′ *v.*
re′ded•i•ca′tion *n.*
re′de•feat′ *v. & n.*
re′de•fine′ *v.*
re′de•mand′ *v.*
re•dem′on•strate′ *v.*
re′de•pos′it *v. & n.*
re′de•scend′ *v.*
re′de•scent′ *n.*
re′de•scribe′ *v.*
re′de•ter′mine *v.*
re′di•gest′ *v.*
re′dis•cov′er *v.*
re′dis•cov′er•y *n.*
re′dis•solve′ *v.*
re′dis•till′ *v.*
re′di•vide′ *v.*
re′di•vi′sion *n.*
re′do′ *v.*
re′draft′ *n.*
re•draw′ *v.*
re•drive′ *v.*
re•dry′ *v.*
re•dye′ *v.*
re-ed′it *v.*
re-el′e•vate′ *v.*
re′-em•bark′ *v.*
re′-em•bod′y *v.*
re′-em•brace′ *v.*
re′-e•merge′ *v.*
re′-e•mer′gence *n.*
re-em′i•grate′ *v.*
re′-en•cour′age *v.*
re′-en•cour′age•ment *n.*
re′-en•dow′ *v.*
re′-en•gage′ *v.*
re′-en•gage′ment *n.*
re′-en•grave′ *v.*
re′-en•list′ *v.*
re′-en•list′ment *n.*
re′-en•slave′ *v.*
re′-e•rect′ *v.*
re′-es•tab′lish *v.*
re′-es•tab′lish•ment *n.*
re′-e•val′u•ate′ *v.*
re′-e•val′u•a′tion *n.*
re′-ex•change′ *v.*
re′-ex•hib′it *v.*
re′-ex•pel′ *v.*
re′-ex•pe′ri•ence *v.*
re-ex•port′ *v.*
re•face′ *v.*
re•fash′ion *v.*
re•fas′ten *v.*
re•fire′ *v.*
re•fold′ *v.*
re•forge′ *v.*
re•for′mu•late′ *v.*
re′for•ti•fi•ca′tion *n.*
re•for′ti•fy′ *v.*
re•frame′ *v.*
re•freeze′ *v.*
re•fur′nish *v.*
re•gath′er *v.*
re•gild′ *v.*
re•glaze′ *v.*

re•buke (rĭ-byo͞ok′) *v.* **-buked, -buk•ing.** To reprove : reprimand. **—re•buke′** *n.*
re•bus (rē′bəs) *n.* A message containing pictures that represent words or syllables.
re•but (rĭ-bŭt′) *v.* **-but•ted, -but•ting.** To try to show to be false by presenting opposing arguments : argue against. **—re•but′tal** *n.* **—re•but′ter** *n.*
re•cal•ci•trant (rĭ-kăl′sĭ-trənt) *adj.* Stubbornly resistant to guidance : refractory. **—re•cal′ci•trance, re•cal′ci•tran•cy** *n.*
re•call (rĭ-kôl′) *v.* **1.** To ask or order to return. **2.** To recollect : remember. **3.** To cancel : revoke. **4.** To bring back : restore. *—n.* (*also* rē′kôl′). **1.** An act of recalling. **2.** The capacity to remember. **3.** An act of revoking : cancellation. **4.** The removal of an official from public office by popular vote. **5.** A request by the maker of a defective product for its return for repairs.
re•cant (rĭ-kănt′) *v.* To make a formal denial of (e.g. an earlier statement) : retract. **—re′can•ta′tion** *n.* **—re•cant′er** *n.*
re•cap[1] (rē-kăp′) *v.* To restore (a worn tire) by bonding new rubber onto the old casing. *—n.* (rē′kăp′). A recapped tire.
re•cap[2] (rē′kăp′) *v.* **-capped, -cap•ping.** To summarize. *—n.* A summary.
re•ca•pit•u•late (rē′kə-pĭch′ə-lāt′) *v.* **-lat•ed, -lat•ing.** To repeat in shorter form : summarize. **—re′ca•pit′u•la′tion** *n.* **—re•ca•pit′u•la′tive** *adj.*
re•cede (rĭ-sēd′) *v.* **-ced•ed, -ced•ing. 1.** To move away or back. **2.** To slope backward. **3.** To become or seem to become farther away. ★ ***syns:*** EBB, RETRACT, RETREAT
†re•ceipt (rĭ-sēt′) *n.* **1.** The act of receiving something or the fact of being received. **2. receipts.** The amount or quantity received <box office *receipts*> **3.** A written acknowledgment that something has been received. **4.** *Regional.* A recipe. *—v.* **1.** To indicate (a bill) as having been paid. **2.** To give or write a receipt for.
re•ceiv•a•ble (rĭ-sē′və-bəl) *adj.* **1.** Appropriate for being accepted. **2.** Waiting for payment : due <accounts *receivable*>
re•ceive (rĭ-sēv′) *v.* **-ceived, -ceiv•ing. 1.** To take (e.g., something given or sent) : get. **2.** To take into the mind. **3.** To meet with : encounter <*receive* kind treatment> **4.** To greet : welcome <*receive* a caller> **5.** To respond to <*received* the apology with dignity> **6.** *Electron.* To convert incoming electromagnetic waves into visible or audible signals. **7.** To accept as true or correct.
re•ceiv•er (rĭ-sē′vər) *n.* **1.** One that receives. **2.** *Law.* A person appointed to hold the property or funds of others during litigation. **3.** *Electron.* An apparatus, as a part of a radio, television, or telephone, that receives electrical signals and changes them into perceptible forms.

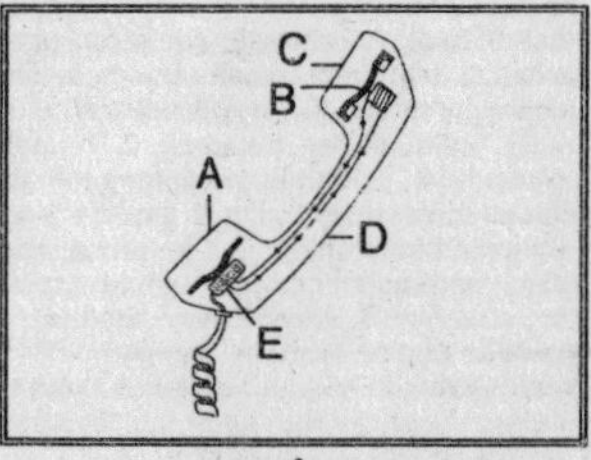

receiver
A. mouthpiece, B. electromagnet, C. receiver, D. handset, E. diaphragm

re•ceiv•er•ship (rĭ-sē′vər-shĭp′) *n. Law.* **1.** The office or tasks of a receiver. **2.** The state of being held by a receiver.
re•cent (rē′sənt) *adj.* **1.** Of, from, or happening at a time just before the present. **2.** Mod-

re•glue′ *v.*
re•grade′ *v.*
re•graft′ *v.*
re•grant′ *v.*
re•han′dle *v.*
re•heat′ *v.*
re•heel′ *v.*
re′hire′ *v.*
re′ig•nite′ *v.*
re′im•plant′ *v.*
re′im•port′ *v.*
re′im•pose′ *v.*
re′im•po•si′tion *n.*
re′im•preg′nate *v.*
re′im•press′ *v.*
re′im•print′ *v.*
re′im•pris′on *v.*
re′im•pris′on•ment *n.*
re′in•au′gu•rate′ *v.*
re′in•cite′ *v.*
re′in•cor′po•rate′ *v.*
re′in•cur′ *v.*
re′in•duce′ *v.*
re′in•fect′ *v.*
re′in•flame′ *v.*
re′in•form′ *v.*
re′in•fuse′ *v.*
re′in•hab′it *v.*
re′in•oc′u•late′ *v.*
re′in•oc′u•la′tion *n.*
re′in•scribe′ *v.*
re′in•sert′ *v.*
re′in•ser′tion *n.*
re′in•spect′ *v.*
re′in•spec′tion *n.*
re′in•spire′ *v.*
re′in•stall′ *v.*
re′in•stal•la′tion *n.*
re′in•struct′ *v.*
re′in•ter′ *v.*
re′in•ter′ro•gate′ *v.*
re′in•tro•duce′ *v.*
re′in•tro•duc′tion *n.*
re′in•vent′ *v.*
re′in•vest′ *v.*
re′in•ves′ti•gate′ *v.*
re′in•ves•ti•ga′tion *n.*
re′in•vest′ment *n.*
re′in•vite′ *v.*
re′in•volve′ *v.*
re•judge′ *v.*
re•kin′dle *v.*
re•la′bel *v.*
re•lace′ *v.*
re•launch′ *v.*
re•learn′ *v.*
re•light′ *v.*
re•load′ *n. & v.*
re•loan′ *n. & v.*
re′man•u•fac′ture *v.*
re•mar′ry *v.*
re•meas′ure *v.*
re•melt′ *v.*
re•merge′ *v.*
re•mi′grate *v.*
re′mi•gra′tion *n.*
re•mix′ *v.*
re′mod•i•fi•ca′tion *n.*
re•mod′i•fy′ *v.*
re•mold′ *v.*
re•name′ *v.*
re•nav′i•gate′ *v.*

ern : new. —**re'cent·ly** *adv.* —**re'cen·cy, re'-cent·ness** *n.*

re·cep·ta·cle (rĭ-sĕp'tə-kəl) *n.* **1.** A container. **2.** *Elect.* An electrical fitting connected to a power supply and designed to take a plug.

re·cep·tion (rĭ-sĕp'shən) *n.* **1.** An act or process of receiving something. **2.** A welcome or acceptance. **3.** A usu. large social gathering. **4.** *Electron.* **a.** The receiving of electromagnetic signals. **b.** The quality of received signals.

re·cep·tion·ist (rĭ-sĕp'shə-nĭst) *n.* An office employee who greets callers, gives information, and answers the telephone.

re·cep·tive (rĭ-sĕp'tĭv) *adj.* **1.** Able to receive. **2.** Ready to consider or listen <*receptive* to our plan> —**re'cep·tiv'i·ty, re·cep'tive·ness** *n.*

re·cep·tor (rĭ-sĕp'tər) *n.* **1.** A specialized nerve ending that senses or receives stimuli. **2.** A sense organ.

re·cess (rē'sĕs', rĭ-sĕs') *n.* **1. a.** A temporary halt in usual activities. **b.** The period of such a halt. **2.** *often* **recesses.** A remote, secret, or concealed place. **3.** An indentation, as in a wall. —*v.* **1.** To put in a recess. **2.** To make a recess in. **3.** To halt or pause for a recess.

re·ces·sion (rĭ-sĕsh'ən) *n.* **1.** The act of withdrawing or returning. **2.** The procession of clergy and choir members leaving a church after a service. **3.** An extended, moderate decline in general business activity.

re·ces·sion·al (rĭ-sĕsh'ə-nəl) *n.* A hymn sung during the exit of the clergy and choir after a church service.

re·ces·sive (rĭ-sĕs'ĭv) *adj.* **1.** Tending to recede. **2.** *Genetics.* Of or designating a gene that is not manifested in the organism when paired with a dominant gene for the same characteristic. —**re·ces'sive** *n.*

re·cher·ché (rə-shĕr'shā') *adj.* **1.** Uncommonly rare and exquisite : choice. **2.** Refined and elegant to an extreme.

re·cid·i·vism (rĭ-sĭd'ə-vĭz'əm) *n.* A tendency to slip back into a previous, esp. criminal, behavior pattern. —**re·cid'i·vist** *n.* —**re·cid'i·vis'tic** *adj.*

rec·i·pe (rĕs'ə-pē) *n.* **1.** A set of directions for preparing something, esp. food. **2.** A prescription or formula.

re·cip·i·ent (rĭ-sĭp'ē-ənt) *n.* One that receives.

re·cip·ro·cal (rĭ-sĭp'rə-kəl) *adj.* **1.** Given or felt by each to the other <*reciprocal* pledges><*reciprocal* esteem> **2.** Interchangeable. **3.** Complementary. —*n.* **1.** One that is reciprocal. **2.** *Math.* Either of a pair of numbers whose product is 1.

re·cip·ro·cate (rĭ-sĭp'rə-kāt') *v.* **-cat·ed, -cat·ing. 1.** To give and take mutually : interchange. **2.** To show or feel in response. **3.** To make a return for a gift or favor. —**re·cip'ro·ca'tion** *n.* —**re·cip'ro·ca'tive** *adj.* —**re·cip'ro·ca'tor** *n.*

reciprocating engine *n.* An engine in which the crankshaft is turned by pistons moving up and down in a cylinder.

rec·i·proc·i·ty (rĕs'ə-prŏs'ĭ-tē) *n.* **1.** A reciprocal relationship. **2.** An interchange of favors, esp. the exchange of trading rights between nations.

re·cit·al (rĭ-sīt'l) *n.* **1.** A public reading. **2.** A detailed account or narration. **3.** A music or dance performance, esp. by a soloist.

rec·i·ta·tion (rĕs'ĭ-tā'shən) *n.* **1.** An act of reciting. **2.** A spoken presentation of prepared lessons by a student.

re·cite (rĭ-sīt') *v.* **-cit·ed, -cit·ing. 1.** To say aloud (e.g., something memorized), esp. with an audience. **2.** To recount in detail. **3.** To enumerate : list. —**re·cit'er** *n.*

reck·less (rĕk'lĭs) *adj.* **1.** Careless. **2.** Heedless of consequences : rash.

reck·on (rĕk'ən) *v.* **1.** To calculate : compute. **2.** To consider : regard <*reckoned* him

re·no'ti·fy' *v.*
re'ob·tain' *v.*
re'oc·cu·pa'tion *n.*
re·oc'cu·py' *v.*
re'oc·cur' *v.*
re'oc·cur'rence *n.*
re'op·pose' *v.*
re'or·dain' *v.*
re'or·di·na'tion *n.*
re·o'ri·ent' *v.*
re·pac'i·fy' *v.*
re·pack' *v.*
re·paint' *v.* & *n.*
re·pa'per *v.*
re·pave' *v.*
re·pol'ish *v.*
re·pop'u·late' *v.*
re'pop·u·la'tion *n.*
re·pour' *v.*
re·proc'ess *v.*
re·pur'chase *v.*
re·pu'ri·fy' *v.*
re'pur·sue' *v.*
re·ra'di·ate' *v.*
re·read' *v.*
re're·cord' *v.*
re·route' *v.*
re·sad'dle *v.*
re·sail' *v.*
re·seal' *v.*
re·seat' *v.*
re·seed' *v.*
re·seg're·gate' *v.*
re·seize' *v.*
re·sell' *v.*
re·set'tle *v.*
re·set'tle·ment *n.*
re·sharp'en *v.*
re·ship' *v.*
re·ship'ment *n.*
re·sift' *v.*
re·sol'der *v.*
re·sole' *v.*
re'so·lid'i·fy' *v.*
re·sow' *v.*
re·spread' *v.*
re·stack' *v.*
re·strength'en *v.*
re·string' *v.*
re·stud'y *n.* & *v.*
re'sub·ject' *v.*
re'sub·jec'tion *n.*
re·sum'mon *v.*
re·sum'mons *n.*
re'sup·ply' *v.*
re·teach' *v.*
re·test' *v.*
re·tie' *v.*
re'trans·late' *v.*
re·trav'erse *v.*
re·type' *v.*
re·use' *v.*
re·u'til·ize' *v.*
re·ut'ter *v.*
re·val'ue *v.*
re·var'nish *v.*
re'ver·i·fi·ca'tion *n.*
re·ver'i·fy' *v.*
re·vin'di·cate *v.*
re·vin'di·ca'tion *n.*
re·voice' *v.*
re·warm' *v.*
re·wash' *v.*
re·weigh' *v.*
re·wire' *v.*

a fool> **3.** *Informal.* To think or assume <I *reckon* I'll be there.>

reck•on•ing (rĕk'ə-nĭng) *n.* **1.** An act of counting. **2.** An itemized bill. **3.** The determination of a geographic position, as of a ship, by calculation.

re•claim (rĭ-klām') *v.* **1.** To make fit for growing crops or living on <*reclaiming* marshes> **2.** To extract (useful substances) from wastes. **3.** To reform. **—rec'la•ma'tion** (rĕk'lə-mā'shən) *n.*

re•cline (rĭ-klīn') *v.* **-clined, -clin•ing.** To assume or cause to assume a prone or leaning position **:** lie or lay down.

re•cluse (rĭ-klo͞os', rĭ-klo͞os') *n.* One who retreats from the world to live in solitude. **—re•clu'sive** (-sĭv, -zĭv) *adj.*

rec•og•ni•tion (rĕk'əg-nĭsh'ən) *n.* **1.** An act of recognizing or the state of being recognized. **2.** An acknowledgment, esp. of the legitimacy of a government. **3.** Favorable notice.

re•cog•ni•zance (rĭ-kŏg'nĭ-zəns, -kŏn'ĭ-) *n. Law.* An obligation of record that commits a person to do something, as to make a court appearance. **—re•cog'ni•zant** *adj.*

rec•og•nize (rĕk'əg-nīz') *v.* **-nized, -niz•ing.** **1.** To know to be something perceived or experienced before <*recognize* a face> **2.** To acknowledge the validity or reality of <*recognized* the new government> **3.** To be aware or appreciative of. **—rec'og•niz'a•ble** *adj.* **—rec'og•niz'a•bly** *adv.*

re•coil (rĭ-koil') *v.* **1.** To spring or jerk back, as upon firing. **2.** To shrink back in fear or repulsion. **—re'coil'** (rē'koil', rĭkoil') *n.* **—re•coil'er** *n.*

rec•ol•lect (rĕk'ə-lĕkt') *v.* To recall to one's mind. **—rec'ol•lec'tion** *n.*

re•com•bi•nant DNA (rē-kŏm'bĭ-nənt) *n.* DNA from the genes of different species, divided and spliced together in a laboratory to produce new kinds of cells.

rec•om•mend (rĕk'ə-mĕnd') *v.* **1.** To represent to another as desirable or worthy **:** endorse. **2.** To make attractive <Her experience *recommends* her.> **3.** To advise <*recommend* a change of climate> **—rec'om•men•da'tion** *n.*

rec•om•pense (rĕk'əm-pĕns') *v.* **-pensed, -pens•ing.** To award compensation to or for. *—n.* **1.** Amends made, as for damage or loss. **2.** Payment for services.

rec•on•cile (rĕk'ən-sīl') *v.* **-ciled, -cil•ing.** **1.** To re-establish friendship between. **2.** To settle (e.g., a dispute). **3.** To bring (oneself) to acceptance. **4.** To make consistent or compatible <*reconcile* their opposing views> **—rec'on•cil'a•bil'i•ty** *n.* **—rec'on•cil'a•ble** *adj.* **—rec'on•cile'ment, rec'on•cil'i•a'tion** (-sĭl'ē-ā'shən) *n.* **—rec'on•cil'er** *n.* **—rec'on•cil'i•a•to'ry** (-sĭl'ē-ə-tôr'ē, -tōr'ē) *adj.*

rec•on•dite (rĕk'ən-dīt', rĭ-kŏn'dīt') *adj.* **1.** Not easily understood **:** abstruse. **2.** Concealed **:** hidden. **—rec'on•dite'ly** *adv.*

re•con•nais•sance (rĭ-kŏn'ə-səns, -zəns) *n.* An exploration of an area, esp. to obtain military information.

re•con•noi•ter (rē'kə-noi'tər, rĕk'ə-) *v.* **1.** To make a preliminary inspection (of). **2.** To make a reconnaissance.

re•con•sid•er (rē'kən-sĭd'ər) *v.* To consider again, esp. with intent to change an earlier decision. **—re'con•sid'er•a'tion** *n.*

re•con•struct (rē'kən-strŭkt') *v.* To construct again.

re•con•struc•tion (rē'kən-strŭk'shən) *n.* **1.** The act or result of reconstructing. **2. Reconstruction.** The period (1865–77) during which the Confederate states were administered by the federal government before being readmitted to the Union.

re•cord (rĭ-kôrd') *v.* **1.** To set down for preservation in writing or other permanent form. **2.** To register (sound or images) in permanent form for reproduction, esp. on a disk or tape. **3.** To register **:** indicate. *—n.* **rec•ord** (rĕk'ərd). **1.** An account, as of events, set down to preserve or transmit the truth. **2.** Information on a subject, collected and preserved. **3.** Known history of performance <your school *record*> **4.** The best performance known, as in a sports event. **5.** The highest or lowest statistical mark known. **6.** A disk designed to be played on a phonograph. **—off the record.** Not for publication.

re•cord•er (rĭ-kôr'dər) *n.* **1.** One that records <a video *recorder*> **2.** A usu. wooden flute with a mouthpiece like a whistle.

re•cord•ing (rĭ-kôr'dĭng) *n.* Something on which sound or visual images have been recorded.

re•count (rĭ-kount') *v.* To tell the facts or details of **:** describe.

re-count (rē-kount') *v.* To count again. *—n.* (rē'kount', rē-kount'). An additional count, as of votes cast.

re•coup (rĭ-ko͞op') *v.* **1.** To get an equivalent for <*recouped* his losses on the next bet> **2.** To reimburse.

re•course (rē'kôrs', -kōrs', rĭ-kôrs', -kōrs') *n.* **1.** A turning to for help or security. **2.** A source of aid or protection.

re•cov•er (rĭ-kŭv'ər) *v.* **1.** To get back **:** regain. **2.** To regain normal health, control, or balance. **3.** To win a favorable judgment in a lawsuit. ★ ***syns:*** RECOUP, REGAIN, RETRIEVE. **—re•cov'er•a•ble** *adj.* **—re•cov'er•y** *n.*

re-cov•er (rē-kŭv'ər) *v.* To cover anew.

rec•re•ant (rĕk'rē-ənt) *adj.* **1.** Unfaithful **:** disloyal. **2.** Cowardly. **—rec're•ance** *n.*

rec•re•ate (rĕk'rē-āt') *v.* **-at•ed, -at•ing.** To relax and divert (oneself).

re-cre•ate (rē'krē-āt') *v.* To create anew. **—re'-cre•a'tion** *n.*

rec•re•a•tion (rĕk'rē-ā'shən) *n.* Refreshment and relaxation of one's body or mind after work. **—rec're•a'tion•al** *adj.*

recreational vehicle *n.* A motor vehicle, as a camper or a mobile home, used for traveling and recreational activities.

re•crim•i•nate (rĭ-krĭm'ə-nāt') *v.* **-nat•ed, -nat•ing.** To counter one accusation with another. **—re•crim'i•na'tion** *n.*

re•cru•desce (rē'krōō-dĕs') *v.* **-desced, -desc•ing.** To break out again after a dormant period. **—re'cru•des'cence** *n.* **—re'cru•des'cent** *adj.*
re•cruit (rĭ-krōōt') *v.* **1.** To seek out and engage (someone) for work or service. **2.** To strengthen or raise (an armed force) by enlistment. **3.** To renew or restore <*recruited* her health> *—n.* A new member, esp. of a military force. **—re•cruit'er** *n.*
rec•ta (rĕk'tə) *n. var. pl. of* RECTUM.
rec•tan•gle (rĕk'tăng'gəl) *n.* A parallelogram with right angles. **—rec•tan'gu•lar** *adj.* **—rec•tan'gu•lar'i•ty** (-lăr'ĭ-tē) *n.*
rec•ti•fy (rĕk'tə-fī') *v.* **-fied, -fy•ing. 1.** To make right : correct. **2.** To refine : purify. **—rec'ti•fi'a•ble** *adj.* **—rec'ti•fi•ca'tion** *n.* **—rec'ti•fi'er** *n.*
rec•ti•lin•e•ar (rĕk'tə-lĭn'ē-ər) *adj.* Moving in, made up of, or marked by a straight line or lines.
rec•ti•tude (rĕk'tĭ-tōōd', -tyōōd') *n.* **1.** Moral integrity. **2.** Correctness.
rec•to (rĕk'tō) *n., pl.* **-tos.** A right-hand page of a book.
rec•tor (rĕk'tər) *n.* **1.** A member of the clergy in charge of a parish. **2.** *Rom. Cath. Ch.* A priest appointed to be head of a church, seminary, or university. **3.** The principal of certain schools or colleges.
rec•to•ry (rĕk'tə-rē) *n., pl.* **-ries.** A rector's residence.
rec•tum (rĕk'təm) *n., pl.* **-tums** *or* **-ta** (-tə). The lower portion of the alimentary canal between the colon and anus. **—rec'tal** *adj.*
re•cum•bent (rĭ-kŭm'bənt) *adj.* Lying down : reclining.
re•cu•per•ate (rĭ-kōō'pə-rāt', -kyōō'-) *v.* **-at•ed, -at•ing. 1.** To regain strength or health : recover. **2.** To recover from financial loss. **—re•cu'per•a'tion** *n.* **—re•cu'per•a'tive** (-pə-rā'tĭv, -pər-ə-tĭv) *adj.*
re•cur (rĭ-kûr') *v.* **-curred, -cur•ring.** To occur or come up again. **—re•cur'rence** *n.* **—re•cur'rent** *adj.*
re•curve (rē-kûrv') *v.* To curve backward or downward.
re•cy•cle (rē-sī'kəl) *v.* **-cled, -cling. 1.** To put through a cycle again. **2.** To recover useful materials from. **3.** To use again instead of discarding <*recycle* glass bottles> **4.** To recondition and adapt to a new use.
red (rĕd) *n.* **1. a.** Any of a group of colors whose hue is like that of blood. **b.** A pigment or dye with a red hue. **2.** *often* **Red.** A Communist. *—adj.* **red•der, red•dest. 1.** With a color like blood. **2.** Ruddy or flushed, esp. in the face <turned *red* with shame> **3.** *often* **Red.** Communist. **—in the red.** In debt.
red blood cell *n.* An erythrocyte.
red-blood•ed (rĕd'blŭd'ĭd) *adj.* Strong and virile. **—red'-blood'ed•ness** *n.*
red•breast (rĕd'brĕst') *n.* A robin or other bird with a red breast.
red•coat (rĕd'kōt') *n.* A British soldier esp. during the American Revolution.
†redd (rĕd) *v.* **redd•ed** *or* **redd, redd•ing.** *Regional.* To put in order : tidy <*redded* up the front room>
red•den (rĕd'n) *v.* To make or become red or reddish.
red•dish (rĕd'ĭsh) *adj.* Somewhat red.
†rede (rēd) *v.* **red•ed, red•ing.** *Regional.* To advise : counsel. **—rede** *n.*
re•deem (rĭ-dēm') *v.* **1.** To regain possession of by paying a specified sum. **2.** To pay off. **3.** To turn in (e.g., coupons) and receive something in exchange. **4.** To rescue or ransom. **5.** To save from sin. **6.** To make up for. **7.** To fulfill **—re•deem'a•ble** *adj.* **—re•deem'er** *n.*
re•demp•tion (rĭ-dĕmp'shən) *n.* An act of redeeming or the state of being redeemed. **—re•demp'tion•al, re•demp'tive, re•demp'to•ry** *adj.*
red-hand•ed (rĕd'hăn'dĭd) *adv. & adj.* In the act of doing something wrong.
red•head (rĕd'hĕd') *n.* A person with red hair. **—red'head'ed** *adj.*
red herring *n.* Something designed to divert attention from the matter at hand.
red-hot (rĕd'hŏt') *adj.* **1.** Glowing hot. **2.** Very recent <*red-hot* information>
re•dis•trict (rē-dĭs'trĭkt) *v.* To divide again into esp. election districts.
red-let•ter (rĕd'lĕt'ər) *adj.* Memorably happy <a *red-letter* occasion>
red•line (rĕd'līn') *v.* To discriminate against (an area or neighborhood) by refusing to grant fair loans, mortgages, or insurance policies.
red meat *n.* Meat, esp. beef, that is red before being cooked.
red•o•lent (rĕd'l-ənt) *adj.* **1.** Having a pleasant scent : aromatic. **2.** Suggestive : reminiscent. **—red'o•lence** *n.*
re•doubt (rĭ-dout') *n.* A small defensive fortification.
re•doubt•a•ble (rĭ-dou'tə-bəl) *adj.* **1.** Arousing awe or fear : formidable. **2.** Worthy of respect. **—re•doubt'a•bly** *adv.*
re•dound (rĭ-dound') *v.* **1.** To have an effect <achievements that *redound* to one's credit> **2.** To contribute : accrue.
red pepper *n.* **1.** The red podlike fruit of certain pepper plants. **2.** Cayenne pepper.
re•dress (rĭ-drĕs') *v.* **1.** To rectify : remedy. **2.** To make amends for or to. *—n.* (rē'drĕs', rĭ-drĕs'). **1.** Satisfaction for wrong done : amends. **2.** Correction.
Red River cart *n. Can.* A 2-wheeled horse-drawn cart formerly used in the Canadian West.
red snapper *n.* A marine food fish of the genus *Lutjanus,* with a reddish body.
red tape *n.* Official forms and bureaucratic procedures.
red tide *n.* Ocean waters discolored by floating masses of reddish, one-celled plantlike animals in numbers great enough to poison fish.
re•duce (rĭ-dōōs', -dyōōs') *v.* **-duced, -duc•ing. 1.** To lessen in extent, number, amount, degree, or price : diminish. **2.** To conquer : subject. **3.** To put in order. **4.** To separate into components : analyze. **5.** To bring to a sim-

pler or lower condition <*reduced* the farmers to poverty> **6.** To lose weight, esp. by dieting. **—re•duc'er** *n.* **—re•duc'i•bil'i•ty** *n.* **—re•duc'i•ble** *adj.* **—re•duc'i•bly** *adv.* **—re•duc'tion** (-dŭk'shən) *n.* **—re•duc'tive** *adj.*

re•dun•dant (rĭ-dŭn'dənt) *adj.* **1.** Exceeding what is required or natural. **2.** Unnecessarily repetitive. **—re•dun'dan•cy** *n.*

red-winged blackbird (rĕd'wĭngd') *n.* A North American blackbird, *Agelaius phoeniceus,* the male of which has scarlet patches on the wings.

red•wood (rĕd'wŏŏd') *n.* A very tall evergreen tree, *Sequoia sempervirens,* of coastal and N Calif., with soft, reddish wood.

reed (rēd) *n.* **1.** Any of several tall swamp or marsh grasses with jointed, hollow stalks. **2.** A primitive wind instrument made of a hollow reed stalk. **3.** *Mus.* **a.** A flexible strip of cane or metal set into the mouthpiece of certain instruments to create tone by vibrating. **b.** An instrument, as a clarinet, equipped with a reed. **—reed'i•ness** *n.* **—reed'y** *adj.*

reef[1] (rēf) *n.* A ridge of sand, coral, etc., that rises to or close to the water surface.

reef[2] (rēf) *n.* A part of a sail tucked in or rolled and tied down to reduce the amount of sail exposed to the wind. **—reef** *v.*

reef•er (rē'fər) *n. Slang.* Marijuana, esp. a marijuana cigarette.

reek (rēk) *v.* **1.** To smoke or steam **:** fume. **2.** To give off a stench. **3.** To be strongly and offensively suggestive <an arrangement *reeking* of corruption> **—***n.* **1.** A stench. **2.** Vapor **:** steam.

reel[1] (rēl) *n.* **1.** A device, as a cylinder or spool, that spins on an axis and is used for letting out and winding up rope, tape, or fishing line. **2.** The amount of material wound on a reel. **3.** A fast, lively folk dance. **—***v.* **1.** To wind on a reel. **2.** To bring in with a fishing rod and reel.

reel[2] (rēl) *v.* **1.** To fall back or be thrown off balance. **2.** To stagger or lurch. **3.** To feel dizzy or confused.

re-en•ter *or* **re•en•ter** (rē-ĕn'tər) *v.* To come in or enter again. **—re-en'trance** *n.*

re-en•try *or* **re•en•try** (rē-ĕn'trē) *n., pl.* **-tries.** *Aerospace.* Return of a missile or spacecraft to the earth's atmosphere after a space flight.

re•fec•to•ry (rĭ-fĕk'tə-rē) *n., pl.* **-ries.** A dining room, esp. in a monastery or college.

re•fer (rĭ-fûr') *v.* **-ferred, -fer•ring. 1.** To direct to a source of information or help. **2.** To attribute **:** assign. **3.** To submit to an authority. **4.** To direct the attention of. **5.** To make reference **:** allude. **6.** To turn to, as for information. **—ref'er•a•ble** (rĕf'ər-ə-bəl, rĭ-fûr'-) *adj.* **—re•fer'ral** *n.*

ref•e•ree (rĕf'ə-rē') *n.* **1.** One to whom matters are referred for settlement **:** arbitrator. **2.** *Sports.* An official who supervises play **:** umpire. **—ref'e•ree'** *v.*

ref•er•ence (rĕf'ər-əns, rĕf'rəns) *n.* **1.** An act of referring. **2.** Relation **:** regard <in *reference* to> **3.** An allusion to an event or situation. **4.** A note in a publication guiding the reader to another passage or source. **5.** The consultation of sources of information. **6. a.** One who is in a position to recommend or vouch for another, as for a position. **b.** A statement about someone's character or qualifications. **—ref'er•en'tial** (-ə-rĕn'shəl) *adj.*

ref•er•en•dum (rĕf'ə-rĕn'dəm) *n., pl.* **-dums** *or* **-da** (-də). **1.** The submission of a proposed law or other issue to a popular vote. **2.** The vote itself.

re•fill (rē-fĭl') *v.* To fill again. **—***n.* (rē'fĭl'). **1.** A product packaged to replace the contents of a container. **2.** An additional filling. **—re•fill'a•ble** *adj.*

re•fine (rĭ-fīn') *v.* **-fined, -fin•ing. 1.** To remove unwanted material from **:** purify. **2.** To free from coarseness. **3.** To make more precise or subtle. **4.** To improve **:** perfect.

re•fined (rĭ-fīnd') *adj.* **1.** Marked by good, well-informed taste and manners **:** cultivated. **2.** Purified. **3.** Precise or exact.

re•fine•ment (rĭ-fīn'mənt) *n.* **1.** An act or result of refining or the state of being refined. **2.** An improvement or elaboration. **3.** Fineness of thought, manners, or expression. **4.** A subtle or precise phrasing.

re•fin•er•y (rĭ-fī'nə-rē) *n., pl.* **-ies.** An industrial plant where crude substances, esp. petroleum, are purified.

re•fin•ish (rē-fĭn'ĭsh) *v.* To apply a new finish to (furniture). **—re•fin'ish•er** *n.*

re•flect (rĭ-flĕkt') *v.* **1.** To throw or bend back (e.g., light) from a surface. **2.** To mirror or be mirrored. **3.** To manifest **:** reveal. **4.** To think seriously **:** meditate. **—re•flec'tion** *n.* **—re•flec'tive** *adj.*

re•flec•tor (rĭ-flĕk'tər) *n.* One that reflects, esp. a surface that reflects light.

re•flex (rē'flĕks') *adj.* **1.** Turned, directed, or bent backward. **2.** Involuntary <A sneeze is a *reflex* response.> **—***n.* **1.** A reflection. **2.** *Physiol.* Involuntary response to a stimulus. **3.** *Psychol.* An unlearned or instinctive response.

re•flex•ive (rĭ-flĕk'sĭv) *adj. Gram.* **1.** Designating a verb with an identical subject and direct object. **2.** Designating a pronoun used as direct object of a reflexive verb. **—re•flex'ive** *n.* **—re•flex'ive•ly** *adv.*

re•for•est (rē-fôr'ĭst, -fŏr'-) *v.* To replant (an area) with forest trees. **—re•for'es•ta'tion** *n.*

re•form (rĭ-fôrm') *v.* **1.** To improve by removing defects or correcting errors. **2.** To remove abuse or malpractice in. **3.** To give up or cause to give up evil ways. **—***n.* **1.** An act of reforming. **2.** A change for the better. **3.** Moral improvement. **4.** Social or political change that seeks to remove corruption or malpractice.

re-form (rē'fôrm') *v.* To form again.

ref•or•ma•tion (rĕf'ər-mā'shən) *n.* **1.** An act of reforming or the state of being reformed. **2. Reformation.** The 16th-cent. movement leading to separation of the Protestant churches from the Roman Catholic Church. **—ref'or•ma'tion•al** *adj.*

re•for•ma•to•ry (rĭ-fôr′mə-tôr′ē, -tōr′ē) *n., pl.* **-ries.** A penal institution for reforming young offenders.

re•frac•tion (rĭ-frăk′shən) *n.* The bending of a wave path, as of light or sound, at the boundary between 2 different mediums. **—re•fract′** *v.* **—re•frac′tive** *adj.* **—re•frac′tive•ly** *adv.* **—re•frac′tive•ness, re′frac•tiv′i•ty** (rē′frăk-tĭv′ĭ-tē) *n.*

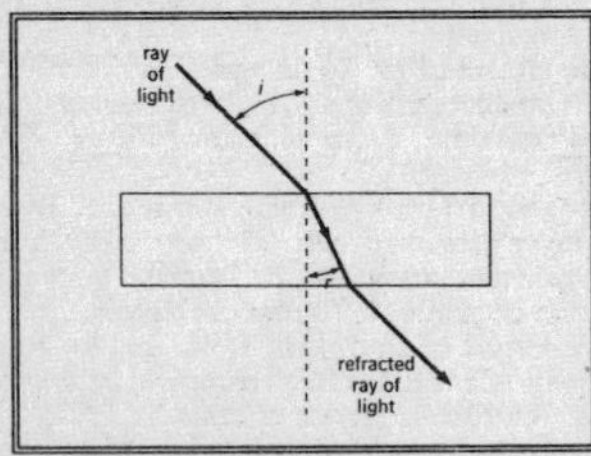

refraction
i, angle of incidence, r, angle of refraction

re•frac•to•ry (rĭ-frăk′tə-rē) *adj.* **1.** Obstinate **:** unmanageable. **2.** Difficult to melt or work. **3.** Not responsive to treatment. —*n., pl.* **-ries.** One that is refractory, esp. a heat-resistant material. **—re•frac′to•ri•ly** *adv.* **—re•frac′to•ri•ness** *n.*

re•frain[1] (rĭ-frān′) *v.* To hold oneself back <*refrain* from speaking> ★ ***syns:*** ABSTAIN, FORBEAR, KEEP, WITHHOLD

re•frain[2] (rĭ-frān′) *n.* A verse or phrase recurring throughout a song or poem.

re•fresh (rĭ-frĕsh′) *v.* **1.** To revive or become revived, as with rest or food. **2.** To make cool or clean **:** freshen. **3.** To renew by stimulation <*refreshed* her memory>

re•fresh•ment (rĭ-frĕsh′mənt) *n.* **1.** An act of refreshing or the state of being refreshed. **2.** Something that refreshes. **3. refreshments.** An assortment of light foods.

re•frig•er•ant (rĭ-frĭj′ər-ənt) *n.* A substance, as ammonia, water, or carbon dioxide, used for producing refrigeration.

re•frig•er•ate (rĭ-frĭj′ə-rāt′) *v.* **-at•ed, -at•ing. 1.** To chill (a substance) in a refrigerator. **2.** To preserve (food) by chilling. **—re•frig′er•a′tion** *n.*

re•frig•er•a•tor (rĭ-frĭj′ə-rā′tər) *n.* An insulated cabinet or room used for storing food at a low temperature.

ref•uge (rĕf′yo͞oj) *n.* **1.** The state of being protected, as from danger. **2.** A place providing protection **:** haven. ★ ***syns:*** ASYLUM, SANCTUARY, SHELTER

ref•u•gee (rĕf′yo͝o-jē′) *n.* One who flees for refuge, esp. from war or oppression.

re•ful•gent (rĭ-fo͝ol′jənt, -fŭl′-) *adj.* Shining radiantly. **—re•ful′gence** *n.*

re•fund (rĭ-fŭnd′, rē′fŭnd′) *v.* To give or pay back. —*n.* (rē′fŭnd′). **1.** A repayment of funds. **2.** The sum repaid.

re•fur•bish (rē-fûr′bĭsh) *v.* To make clean, bright, or new-looking again.

re•fuse[1] (rĭ-fyo͞oz′) *v.* **-fused, -fus•ing.** To decline to do, accept, give, or allow. **—re•fus′al** *n.*

ref•use[2] (rĕf′yo͞os) *n.* Something rejected or discarded as worthless **:** trash.

re•fute (rĭ-fyo͞ot′) *v.* **-fut•ed, -fut•ing.** To prove to be false or mistaken **:** disprove. **—re•fut′a•ble** *adj.* **—re•fut′a•bly** *adv.* **—ref•u•ta•tion** (rĕf′yo͝o-tā′shən) *n.*

re•gain (rē-gān′) *v.* **1.** To get back **:** recover. **2.** To reach again.

re•gal (rē′gəl) *adj.* Of or appropriate for a monarch **:** royal. **—re′gal•ly** *adv.*

re•gale (rĭ-gāl′) *v.* **-galed, -gal•ing. 1.** To give pleasure to. **2.** To entertain lavishly.

re•ga•lia (rĭ-gāl′yə) *n. (sing. or pl. in number).* **1.** Objects that symbolize royalty, as a crown and scepter. **2.** The distinguishing symbols of a rank, office, or group. **3.** Splendid attire **:** finery.

re•gard (rĭ-gärd′) *v.* **1.** To look at closely **:** watch. **2.** To look upon **:** consider <*regarded* his teacher as a friend> **3.** To have great esteem for. **4.** To relate to **:** concern. —*n.* **1.** A look **:** gaze. **2.** Careful attention **:** heed. **3.** Respect, affection, or esteem. **4. regards.** Good wishes **:** greetings. **5.** Reference **:** relation. **6.** A specific point or respect <right in that *regard,* but wrong in others> **—re•gard′ful** *adj.*

re•gard•ing (rĭ-gär′dĭng) *prep.* In reference to.

re•gard•less (rĭ-gärd′lĭs) *adj.* Heedless. —*adv.* In spite of everything **:** anyway.

re•gat•ta (rĭ-gä′tə, -găt′ə) *n.* A gathering of boats for racing.

re•gen•cy (rē′jən-sē) *n., pl.* **-cies. 1.** The office or government of a regent. **2.** The period during which a regent governs. **3.** A regent or group of regents.

re•gen•er•ate (rĭ-jĕn′ə-rāt′) *v.* **-at•ed, -at•ing. 1.** To reform morally or spiritually. **2.** To build, make, or start anew. **3.** *Biol.* To replace (e.g., a lost organ) by formation of new tissue. —*adj.* (-ər-ĭt). **1.** Morally or spiritually reformed. **2.** Restored **:** renewed. **—re•gen′er•a′tion** *n.* **—re•gen′er•a′tive** *adj.* **—re•gen′er•a′tor** *n.*

re•gent (rē′jənt) *n.* **1.** One who rules during the minority or disability of a monarch. **2.** One who serves on a governing board of an institution.

reg•gae (rĕg′ā) *n.* Popular music of Jamaican orig. having a strongly accentuated offbeat.

reg•i•cide (rĕj′ĭ-sīd′) *n.* **1.** The murder of a king. **2.** One who murders a king.

re•gime *also* **ré•gime** (rā-zhēm′, rĭ-) *n.* **1.** The government in power **:** administration. **2.** A system of management. **3.** A regimen.

reg•i•men (rĕj′ə-mən, -mĕn′) *n.* **1.** Rule **:** administration. **2.** A system, as of therapy or diet.

reg•i•ment (rĕj′ə-mənt) *n.* A military unit of ground or airborne troops composed of at least 2 battalions. —*v.* (-mĕnt′). **1.** To put into systematic order. **2.** To impose strict uniformity and discipline upon. **—reg′i•men′-**

tal *adj.* **—reg′i•men′tal•ly** *adv.* **—reg′i•men•ta′tion** *n.*

re•gion (rē′jən) *n.* **1.** A large, usu. continuous portion of a surface or space : area. **2.** An area of the body.

re•gion•al *adj.* **1.** Of, pertaining to, or typical of a geographic region. **2.** Of or limited to a particular region or district : localized.

reg•is•ter (rĕj′ĭ-stər) *n.* **1. a.** An official record of names, items, or statistics. **b.** A book for these entries. **2.** A device that automatically registers an amount or number <a cash *register*> **3.** An adjustable grill through which heated or cooled air is released. **4.** *Mus.* The range of a voice or instrument. *—v.* **1.** To enter in a register. **2.** To enroll formally. **3.** To indicate, as on a scale. **4.** To show (emotion). **5.** To cause (mail) to be handled with special care by payment of a fee. **6.** To place one's name on an official list of eligible voters. **—reg′is•tra•ble** *adj.* **—reg′is•trant** *n.*

registered nurse *n.* A nurse who has passed a test given by a state.

reg•is•trar (rĕj′ĭ-strär′, rĕj′ĭ-strär′) *n.* An officer, as of a college, who keeps records.

reg•is•tra•tion (rĕj′ĭ-strā′shən) *n.* **1.** The act of registering. **2.** The number registered : enrollment. **3.** A document certifying that one has registered.

reg•is•try (rĕj′ĭ-strē) *n., pl.* **-tries. 1.** Registration. **2.** A place or book for official records. **3.** A ship's registered nationality.

re•gress (rĭ-grĕs′) *v.* To go back to a former and usu. worse condition. *—n.* (rē′grĕs′). An act or way of going back : return. **—re•gres′sion** *n.* **—re•gres′sive** *adj.*

re•gret (rĭ-grĕt′) *v.* **-gret•ted, -gret•ting. 1.** To feel sorry or distressed about. **2.** To mourn. *—n.* **1.** A sense of loss for someone or something gone. **2.** Distress over having done the wrong thing. **3.** An expression of disappointment or sorrow. **4. regrets.** A polite declining of an invitation. **—re•gret′ful** *adj.* **—re•gret′ta•ble** *adj.* **—re•gret′ta•bly** *adv.*

reg•u•lar (rĕg′yə-lər) *adj.* **1.** Customary or normal : usual. **2.** Orderly, methodical, or symmetric. **3.** Conforming to a set procedure. **4.** Occurring at fixed intervals : periodic. **5.** Not varying : constant. **6.** Formally correct : proper. **7.** Thorough : out-and-out. **8.** Conforming to a standard mode of grammatical inflection. **9.** *Geom.* Having equal sides and angles. **10.** Of or constituting a nation's permanent army. *—n.* **1.** A loyal, dependable person. **2.** A soldier belonging to a regular army. **—reg′u•lar′i•ty** *n.*

regular army *n.* A nation's permanent standing army.

reg•u•lar•ize (rĕg′yə-lə-rīz′) *v.* **-ized, -iz•ing.** To make regular or cause to conform. **—reg′u•lar•i•za′tion** *n.*

reg•u•late (rĕg′yə-lāt′) *v.* **-lat•ed, -lat•ing. 1.** To direct or control in agreement with rules or laws. **2.** To adjust the amount, rate, or flow of <*regulate* traffic> **3.** To adjust for proper functioning. **—reg′u•la′tive** *adj.* **—reg′u•la′tor** *n.* **—reg′u•la•to′ry** *adj.*

reg•u•la•tion (rĕg′yə-lā′shən) *n.* **1.** An act of regulating. **2.** A principle, rule, or law for controlling behavior. **3.** A governmental order with the force of law.

re•gur•gi•tate (rē-gûr′jĭ-tāt′) *v.* **-tat•ed, -tat•ing.** To cast up (partly digested food) : vomit. **—re•gur′gi•ta′tion** *n.*

re•ha•bil•i•tate (rē′hĭ-bĭl′ĭ-tāt′) *v.* **-tat•ed, -tat•ing.** To restore to customary activity by education and therapy. **—re′ha•bil′i•ta′tion** *n.* **—re′ha•bil′i•ta′tive** *adj.*

re•hash (rē-hăsh′) *v.* To go over or present (old material) again. **—re′hash′** *n.*

re•hears•al (rĭ-hûr′səl) *n.* **1.** The act or process of practicing for a performance. **2.** An oral repetition or recital.

re•hearse (rĭ-hûrs′) *v.* **-hearsed, -hears•ing. 1.** To practice (e.g., a play or song) in preparation for a performance. **2.** To perfect by repetition. **3.** To recite or retell.

reign (rān) *n.* **1. a.** The exercise of power by a sovereign. **b.** The term during which a sovereign rules. **2.** Widespread influence : dominance <a *reign* of terror> *—v.* **1.** To exercise sovereign power. **2.** To have widespread influence : prevail.

re•im•burse (rē′ĭm-bûrs′) *v.* **-bursed, -burs•ing.** To pay back.

rein (rān) *n.* **1.** *often* **reins.** A long, narrow leather strap fastened to a bridle bit and used to control a horse or other animal. **2.** A means of restraint or guidance. *—v.* **1.** To hold back. **2.** To control or guide.

rein•deer (rān′dîr′) *n.* A large deer, *Rangifer tarandus,* of Arctic regions, having branched antlers.

re•in•force (rē′ĭn-fôrs′, -fōrs′) *v.* **-forced, -forc•ing. 1.** To give more strength or support to : strengthen. **2.** To strengthen militarily with troops or equipment. **3.** To encourage to behave in a desired way, as by giving a reward. **—re′in•forc′er** *n.*

re•in•state (rē′ĭn-stāt′) *v.* **-stat•ed, -stat•ing. 1.** To restore to a former condition or place. **2.** To bring back into use or existence. **—re′in•state′ment** *n.*

re•it•er•ate (rē-ĭt′ə-rāt′) *v.* To state again : repeat. **—re•it′er•a′tion** *n.* **—re•it′er•a′tive** *adj.*

re•ject (rĭ-jĕkt′) *v.* **1.** To refuse to accept or use : repudiate. **2.** To refuse to grant : deny <*rejected* his appeal> **3.** To throw away : discard. *—n.* (rē′jĕkt′). One rejected. **—re•jec′tion** *n.*

re•joice (rĭ-jois′) *v.* **-joiced, -joic•ing.** To be joyful. **—re•joic′er** *n.*

re•join (rĭ-join′) *v.* To answer : respond.

re-join (rĭ-join′) *v.* To join or come together again.

re•join•der (rĭ-join′dər) *n.* An answer, esp. to a reply.

re•ju•ve•nate (rĭ-jo͞o′və-nāt′) *v.* **-nat•ed, -nat•ing.** To restore to youthful vigor or appearance. **—re•ju′ve•na′tion** *n.* **—re•ju′ve•na′tor** *n.*

re•lapse (rĭ-lăps′) *v.* **-lapsed, -laps•ing.** To revert to an earlier condition, esp. after partial recovery from illness. *—n.* (rē′lăps′, rĭ-lăps′). The act of relapsing.

re•late (rĭ-lāt′) *v.* **-lat•ed, -lat•ing. 1.** To narrate : tell. **2.** To have relation or reference. **3.** *Informal.* To interact with other persons in a satisfying way <can't *relate* to strangers> **4.** To respond favorably.
re•lat•ed (rĭ-lā′tĭd) *adj.* **1.** Connected : associated. **2.** Connected by kinship, marriage, or common origin.
re•la•tion (rĭ-lā′shən) *n.* **1.** A natural or logical association between 2 or more things : connection. **2.** The connection of persons by blood or marriage : kinship. **3.** A relative. **4. relations. a.** Dealings or associations among persons or groups <diplomatic *relations*> **b.** Sexual intercourse. **5.** Reference : regard. **6.** An account or narration.
rel•a•tive (rĕl′ə-tĭv) *adj.* **1.** Connected : related. **2.** Considered with respect to others <his *relative* standing in the class> **3.** Referring to or modifying an antecedent <a *relative* pronoun> —*n.* **1.** One related to another by kinship. **2.** One that is relative. **3.** A relative grammatical term.
relative humidity *n.* A measure of the amount of water vapor in the air, expressed as a percentage of the maximum that the air could hold at the current temperature.
rel•a•tiv•i•ty (rĕl′ə-tĭv′ĭ-tē) *n.* **1.** The quality or state of being relative. **2.** *Physics.* **a.** Special relativity. **b.** General relativity.
re•lax (rĭ-lăks′) *v.* **1.** To make or become lax or less tight : loosen. **2.** To make or become less strict or severe. **3.** To relieve from effort : unburden. **4.** To cease working or straining : rest. **5.** To become less tense, formal, or reserved. **—re′lax•a′tion** *n.* **—relax′ed•ly** *adv.*
re•lax•ant (rĭ-lăk′sənt) *n.* Something, as a drug, that relaxes the muscles.
re•lay (rē′lā′, rĭ-lā′) *n.* **1.** A team or crew that relieves others at work <a *relay* of stagecoach horses> **2.** The act of passing something along. **3.** A relay race. **4.** *Elect.* A device that activates switches or other devices in an electric circuit in response to a small current or voltage charge. —*v.* **1.** To pass or send along by stages <*relay* a letter> **2.** To provide with fresh relays.
re-lay (rē-lā′) *v.* To lay again.
relay race *n.* A race between teams in which each member of each team runs a portion of the race and then is relieved by a teammate.
re•lease (rĭ-lēs′) *v.* **-leased, -leas•ing. 1.** To set free from confinement or restraint : liberate. **2.** To relieve from obligation or debt. **3.** To let go of : free. **4.** To permit sale, publication, performance, or circulation of. **5.** To give up (e.g., a claim). —*n.* **1.** The act of releasing. **2.** An authoritative discharge. **3.** A catch for locking and releasing, as on a machine. **4.** Something issued or made public <a news *release*> **—re•leas′a•ble** *adj.*
rel•e•gate (rĕl′ĭ-gāt′) *v.* **-gat•ed, -gat•ing. 1.** To consign to a lower position. **2.** To assign to a given class or category. **3.** To refer (e.g., a task) for performance or decision. **4.** To banish. **—rel′e•ga′tion** *n.*
re•lent (rĭ-lĕnt′) *v.* **1.** To become softened in attitude, temper, or resolve : give in. **2.** To slacken : abate.
re•lent•less (rĭ-lĕnt′lĭs) *adj.* **1.** Unyieldingly stern or harsh. **2.** Persistent.
rel•e•vant (rĕl′ə-vənt) *adj.* Related to the matter at hand. ★ ***syns:*** APROPOS, GERMANE, MATERIAL, PERTINENT **—rel′e•vance, rel′e•van•cy** *n.*
re•li•a•ble (rĭ-lī′ə-bəl) *adj.* Capable of being relied upon : dependable. **—re•li′a•bil′i•ty, re•li′a•ble•ness** *n.* **—re•li′a•bly** *adv.*
re•li•ance (rĭ-lī′əns) *n.* **1.** The act or condition of relying : dependence. **2.** Confidence : trust. **3.** One that is relied on. **—re•li′ant** *adj.* **—re•li′ant•ly** *adv.*
rel•ic (rĕl′ĭk) *n.* **1.** Something that has survived from a past culture or period. **2.** A keepsake : souvenir. **3.** An object of religious significance. **4. relics.** A corpse.
rel•ict (rĕl′ĭkt, rĭ-lĭkt′) *n.* **1.** *Ecol.* An organism or species of an earlier era surviving in a changed environment. **2.** A widow.
re•lief (rĭ-lēf′) *n.* **1.** A lessening of pain or discomfort : ease. **2.** Something that reduces pain or discomfort. **3.** Aid, as money or food, given to the needy, aged, or unfortunate. **4.** Release from a job, post, or duty. **5.** Figures or forms that project from a flat background, as in sculpture. **6.** Variations in elevation of a region.

relief
(Top) *Low relief and* (bottom) *high relief*

relief map *n.* A map showing variations in elevation of land, as with contour lines.
re•lieve (rĭ-lēv′) *v.* **-lieved, -liev•ing. 1.** To lessen the distress of : alleviate. **2.** To free from pain or trouble. **3.** To aid (one in need). **4.** To take away from. **5.** To release from a burden, duty, or task, esp. by acting as a replacement. **6.** To make less unpleasant or tiresome. **7.** To make clear or effective through contrast. **—re•liev′er** *n.*
re•lig•ion (rĭ-lĭj′ən) *n.* **1. a.** Belief in and reverence for a supernatural power accepted as the creator and governor of the universe. **b.** A personal or institutionalized system grounded in such belief. **2.** A belief, activity, or cause pursued with fervor and devotion. ★ ***syns:*** CREED, DENOMINATION, FAITH, PERSUASION, SECT
re•lig•ious (rĭ-lĭj′əs) *adj.* **1.** Of, pertaining to,

or teaching religion. **2.** Adhering to or showing religion. **3.** Faithful **:** conscientious. —*n., pl.* **religious.** One belonging to a religious order. —**re•lig′ious•ly** *adv.*

re•lin•quish (rĭ-lĭng′kwĭsh) *v.* **1.** To retire from. **2.** To give up doing, professing, or intending. **3.** To surrender. **4.** To release.

rel•i•quar•y (rĕl′ĭ-kwĕr′ē) *n., pl.* **-ies.** A receptacle for sacred relics.

rel•ish (rĕl′ĭsh) *n.* **1.** An appetite for something **:** liking. **2.** Pleasure **:** zest. **3.** A savory or spicy condiment served with food. **4.** The flavor of an appetizing food. —*v.* **1.** To enjoy. **2.** To give spice or flavor to.

re•live (rē-lĭv′) *v.* To experience again, esp. by using the imagination.

re•luc•tant (rĭ-lŭk′tənt) *adj.* **1.** Unwilling **:** averse <*reluctant* to go> **2.** Marked by unwillingness <a *reluctant* witness> —**re•luc′tance, re•luc′tan•cy** *n.*

re•ly (rĭ-lī′) *v.* **-lied, -ly•ing.** To trust confidently <*rely* on one's doctor for advice>

rem (rĕm) *n. Physics.* The amount of ionizing radiation needed to produce the same biological effect as 1 rad of high-penetration x-rays.

REM (rĕm) *n.* Rapid, periodic, jerky movement of the eyes during phases of the sleep cycle when dreaming occurs.

re•main (rĭ-mān′) *v.* **1.** To continue without change. **2.** To stay after the removal or loss of others. **3.** To be left as still to be dealt with <Repairs *remain* to be completed.> **4.** To persist or endure.

re•main•der (rĭ-mān′dər) *n.* **1.** Something left over **:** the rest. **2.** *Math.* **a.** In division, the difference between the dividend and the largest multiple of the divisor that is less than or equal to the dividend. **b.** The difference in subtraction. **3.** A book remaining with a publisher after sales have dropped, sold at a discount. —*v.* To sell (a book) as a remainder.

re•mains (rĭ-mānz′) *pl.n.* **1.** What is left after other parts have been removed or destroyed. **2.** A corpse.

re•mand (rĭ-mănd′) *v.* **1.** To send or order back. **2.** *Law.* To send back to prison or court for further action.

re•mark (rĭ-märk′) *n.* **1.** A casual or brief expression of opinion **:** comment. **2.** The act of noticing or mentioning. —*v.* **1.** To make a comment or observation. **2.** To take notice of **:** observe.

re•mark•a•ble (rĭ-mär′kə-bəl) *adj.* **1.** Worthy of being noticed or commented on. **2.** Extraordinary **:** uncommon. —**re•mark′a•ble•ness** *n.* —**re•mark′a•bly** *adv.*

re•me•di•al (rĭ-mē′dē-əl) *adj.* Meant to correct a deficiency <a *remedial* course in reading> —**re•me′di•al•ly** *adv.*

rem•e•dy (rĕm′ĭ-dē) *n., pl.* **-dies. 1.** Something, as medicine or therapy, that eases pain, treats disease, or corrects a disorder. **2.** Something that corrects a fault or error. —*v.* **-died, -dy•ing. 1.** To relieve or cure. **2.** To set right **:** rectify.

re•mem•ber (rĭ-mĕm′bər) *v.* **1.** To recall to the mind. **2.** To retain in the mind. **3.** To keep (someone) in one's thoughts or affections. **4.** To transmit greetings from.

re•mem•brance (rĭ-mĕm′brəns) *n.* **1.** An act of remembering or condition of being remembered. **2.** A memorial. **3.** The time spanned by one's memory. **4.** Something remembered **:** recollection. **5.** A memento **:** souvenir. **6.** A greeting.

Remembrance Day *n. Can.* Nov. 11, observed in memory of the victims of the World Wars.

re•mind (rĭ-mīnd′) *v.* To cause to remember. —**re•mind′er** *n.*

rem•i•nis•cence (rĕm′ə-nĭs′əns) *n.* **1.** The act or practice of recalling the past. **2.** A memory. **3.** *often* **reminiscences.** An account of bygone experiences. —**rem′i•nisce′** *v.* —**rem′i•nis′cent** *adj.*

re•miss (rĭ-mĭs′) *adj.* Lax in performing duties **:** negligent.

re•mis•si•ble (rĭ-mĭs′ə-bəl) *adj.* Capable of being remitted <*remissible* sins> —**re•mis′si•bil′i•ty** *n.* —**re•mis′si•bly** *adv.*

re•mis•sion (rĭ-mĭsh′ən) *n.* **1. a.** An act of remitting. **b.** The state or period of being remitted. **2.** A lessening of intensity, as of the symptoms of a disease.

re•mit (rĭ-mĭt′) *v.* **-mit•ted, -mit•ting. 1.** To send (money). **2. a.** To refrain from exacting (e.g., a punishment). **b.** To forgive <*remit* a sin> **3.** To relax **:** slacken. **4.** To abate **:** let up. —**re•mit′ta•ble** *adj.* —**re•mit′tal** *n.* —**re•mit′ter** *n.*

re•mit•tance (rĭ-mĭt′ns) *n.* Money or credit remitted.

rem•nant (rĕm′nənt) *n.* **1.** Something left over. **2.** A surviving trace **:** vestige.

re•mod•el (rē-mŏd′l) *v.* To remake with a new structure **:** reconstruct.

re•mon•strate (rĭ-mŏn′strāt′, rĕm′ən-) *v.* **-strat•ed, -strat•ing.** To say or speak in protest or reproof. —**re•mon′stra′tion, re•mon′strance** (-strəns) *n.* —**re•mon′stra•tive** (-strə-tĭv) *adj.*

rem•o•ra (rĕm′ər-ə) *n.* A marine fish of the family Echeneidae, with a sucking disk on its head with which it fastens itself to larger sea animals and ship hulls.

remora

re•morse (rĭ-môrs′) *n.* Deep moral anguish and regret for past misdeeds. —**re•morse′ful** *adj.* —**re•morse′less** *adj.*

re•mote (rĭ-mōt′) *adj.* **-mot•er, -mot•est. 1.** Situated far away. **2.** Distant in time. **3.** Barely perceptible **:** slight <a *remote* chance> **4.** Distant in relation <a *remote* cousin> **5.** Distant in manner **:** aloof.

remote control *n.* The control of an activity or machine from a distance, as by radioed instructions or coded signals.

re•move (rĭ-mo͞ov′) *v.* **-moved, -mov•ing. 1.** To move from a position occupied <*removed* the dishes> **2.** To take from one's person **:** doff. **3.** To take away **:** eliminate. **4.** To dismiss from office. **5.** To change one's residence or place of business **:** move. —*n.* **1.** An act of removing. **2.** Distance or degree of separation <at a safe *remove* from the blast> **—re•mov′a•ble** *adj.* **—re•mov′a•bly** *adv.* **—re•mov′al** *n.*

re•mu•ner•ate (rĭ-myo͞o′nə-rāt′) *v.* **-at•ed, -at•ing.** To pay (someone) for goods, services, etc. **—re•mu′ner•a′tion** *n.* **—re•mu′ner•a′tive** *n.* **—re•mu′ner•a′tor** *n.*

ren•ais•sance (rĕn′ĭ-säns′, -zäns′, rĭ-nā′səns) *n.* **1.** A revival **:** rebirth. **2. Renaissance.** The revival of classical art, literature, and learning in Europe during the 14th–16th cent. **3.** *often* **Renaissance.** A period of revived intellectual or artistic activity.

re•nal (rē′nəl) *adj.* Of or relating to the kidneys.

re•nas•cent (rĭ-năs′ənt, -nā′sənt) *adj.* Showing fresh growth or vigor. **—re•nas′cence** *n.*

rend (rĕnd) *v.* **rent** (rĕnt) *or* **rend•ed, rend•ing. 1.** To tear apart violently **:** split. **2.** To remove forcibly. **3.** To disturb as if by tearing <A scream *rent* the stillness.> **4.** To distress painfully. **—rend′er** *n.*

ren•der (rĕn′dər) *v.* **1.** To submit <*render* an account> **2.** To give or make available. **3.** To give (what is due). **4.** To surrender **:** yield. **5.** To represent verbally or artistically **:** depict. **6.** To translate. **7.** To cause to become **:** make. **8.** To melt down (e.g., fat) by heating. **—ren′der•er** *n.*

ren•dez•vous (rän′dā-vo͞o′, -də-) *n., pl.* **-vous** (-vo͞oz′). **1.** A meeting place or meeting arranged in advance. **2.** A popular gathering place. —*v.* To meet or bring together at a prearranged time and place.

ren•di•tion (rĕn-dĭsh′ən) *n.* **1.** An act of rendering. **2.** A performance of a musical or dramatic work. **3.** A translation.

ren•e•gade (rĕn′ĭ-gād′) *n.* **1.** One who rejects one's religion, cause, or allegiance for another. **2.** An outlaw. **—ren′e•gade′** *adj.*

re•nege (rĭ-nĭg′, -nĕg′) *v.* **-neged, -neg•ing. 1.** To fail to perform a promise or commitment. **2.** To fail to follow suit in a card game when able and obliged to do so. **—re•neg′er** *n.*

re•new (rĭ-no͞o′, -nyo͞o′) *v.* **1.** To make new or as if new again **:** restore. **2.** To take up once more **:** resume. **3.** To arrange for the extension of. **—re•new′al** *n.*

ren•net (rĕn′ĭt) *n.* An extract from a calf's stomach lining used for curdling milk to make cheeses.

ren•nin (rĕn′ĭn) *n.* A milk-coagulating enzyme derived from rennet.

re•nounce (rĭ-nouns′) *v.* **-nounced, -nounc•ing. 1.** To give up, esp. with a formal announcement. **2.** To reject **:** disown.

ren•o•vate (rĕn′ə-vāt′) *v.* **-vat•ed, -vat•ing.** To restore to good condition. **—ren′o•va′tion** *n.* **—ren′o•va′tor** *n.*

re•nown (rĭ-noun′) *n.* The quality of being widely known and honored **:** fame. **—re•nowned′** *adj.*

rent[1] (rĕnt) *n.* Periodic payment made by someone in return for the right to occupy or use another's property. —*v.* **1.** To obtain occupancy or use of (another's property) in return for periodic payments. **2.** To grant occupancy or use of (one's own property) in return for rent. **—rent′er** *n.*

rent[2] (rĕnt) *v. var. p.t. & p.p. of* REND. —*n.* **1.** An opening made by rending. **2.** A breach of relations between persons.

rent•al (rĕn′tl) *n.* **1.** An amount paid out or received as rent. **2.** Property rented or available for renting. **3.** An act of renting.

re•nun•ci•a•tion (rĭ-nŭn′sē-ā′shən) *n.* **1.** The act of renouncing. **2.** A declaration renouncing something. **—re•nun′ci•a′tive, re•nun′ci•a•to′ry** (-ə-tôr′ē, -tōr′ē) *adj.*

rep[1] (rĕp) *n.* A ribbed fabric.

rep[2] (rĕp) *n. Informal.* A representative.

re•pair[1] (rĭ-pâr′) *v.* **1.** To bring back to good or usable condition **:** fix. **2.** To make right **:** remedy. **3.** To refresh **:** renew. —*n.* **1.** The act or work of repairing. **2.** Operating condition after use or repairing <a car in good *repair*> **3.** An instance in which repairing is done. **—re•pair′a•ble** *adj.*

re•pair[2] (rĭ-pâr′) *v.* To go <*repair* to the drawing room>

re•pair•man (rĭ-pâr′măn′, -mən) *n.* One whose job is making repairs.

rep•a•ra•ble (rĕp′ər-ə-bəl) *adj.* Able to be repaired.

rep•a•ra•tion (rĕp′ə-rā′shən) *n.* **1.** An act or the process of repairing or making amends. **2.** Something done or paid as amends **:** compensation. **3. reparations.** Compensation required from a defeated nation for damage inflicted during a war. **—re•par′a•tive, re•par′a•to′ry** *adj.*

rep•ar•tee (rĕp′ər-tē′, -tā′, -är-) *n.* **1.** A quick, witty reply. **2.** Witty, combative conversation.

re•past (rĭ-păst′) *n.* **1.** A meal. **2.** The food eaten or offered at a meal.

re•pa•tri•ate (rē-pā′trē-āt′) *v.* **-at•ed, -at•ing.** To send back to the country of birth or citizenship. **—re•pa′tri•ate** (-ĭt, -āt′) *n.* **—re•pa′tri•a′tion** *n.*

re•pay (rĭ-pā′) *v.* **1.** To pay back (money). **2.** To give in return **:** requite <*repay* rudeness with rudeness> **—re•pay′ment** *n.*

re•peal (rĭ-pēl′) *v.* To revoke or rescind, esp. by a formal act. **—re•peal′** *n.*

re•peat (rĭ-pēt′) *v.* **1.** To say or do (something) again. **2.** To say in imitation of another. **3.** To manifest or express in the same way. **4.** To recite from memory. —*n.* **1.** The act of repeating. **2.** Something repeated. —**re•peat'a•ble** *adj.*

re•peat•ed (rĭ-pē'tĭd) *adj.* Said, done, or happening over and over. —**re•peat'ed•ly** *adv.*

re•pel (rĭ-pĕl') *v.* **-pelled, -pel•ling. 1.** To drive back : keep away <*repel* mosquitoes> **2.** To reject : spurn. **3.** To cause distaste or aversion in. **4.** To be unable to absorb or mix with. **5.** To push away or back by a force <Electric charges of like signs *repel* one another.> ★ ***syns:*** DISGUST, NAUSEATE, REPULSE, REVOLT, SICKEN

re•pel•lent (rĭ-pĕl'ənt) *adj.* **1.** Acting or tending to repel. **2.** Arousing strong distaste. **3.** Resistant to a particular substance <a water-*repellent* coat> —*n.* **1.** A substance for repelling insects. **2.** A substance or treatment that makes a surface resistant to something. —**re•pel'lence, re•pel'len•cy** *n.*

re•pent (rĭ-pĕnt') *v.* **1.** To feel regret or remorse (for). **2.** To resolve to reform oneself morally. —**re•pen'tance** *n.* —**re•pen'tant** *adj.* —**re•pen'tant•ly** *adv.*

re•per•cus•sion (rē'pər-kŭsh'ən, rĕp'ər-) *n.* **1.** An indirect or unforeseen effect of an event or action. **2.** A rebound or recoil. **3.** A reflection, esp. of sound : echo. —**re'per•cus'sive** *adj.*

rep•er•toire (rĕp'ər-twär') *n.* **1.** All of the songs, plays, etc., that a player or company is prepared to perform. **2.** The skills or accomplishments of a person or group.

rep•er•to•ry (rĕp'ər-tôr'ē, -tōr'ē) *n., pl.* **-ries. 1.** A repertoire. **2.** A theater in which a resident company performs a number of different plays during a season. **3.** A repository. —**rep'er•to'ri•al** *adj.*

rep•e•ti•tion (rĕp'ĭ-tĭsh'ən) *n.* **1.** An act, process, or instance of repeating or the condition of being repeated. **2.** Something repeated. —**rep'e•ti'tious, re•pet'i•tive** (rĭ-pĕt'ĭ-tĭv) *adj.*

re•pine (rĭ-pīn') *v.* **1.** To be discontented : fret. **2.** To yearn.

re•place (rĭ-plās') *v.* **1.** To put back in a previous place. **2.** To fill or take the place of. —**re•place'a•ble** *adj.* —**re•place'ment** *n.* —**re•plac'er** *n.*

re•play (rē-plā') *v.* To play (e.g., a video tape) again. —**re'play'** *n.*

re•plen•ish (rĭ-plĕn'ĭsh) *v.* To add a new supply to. —**re•plen'ish•ment** *n.*

re•plete (rĭ-plēt') *adj.* **1.** Abounding <a table *replete* with delicacies> **2.** Satiated. —**re•ple'tion, re•plete'ness** *n.*

rep•li•ca (rĕp'lĭ-kə) *n.* A copy or close reproduction, esp. of an art work.

rep•li•cate (rĕp'lĭ-kāt') *v.* **-cat•ed, -cat•ing.** To duplicate. —**rep'li•ca'tion** *n.*

re•ply (rĭ-plī') *v.* **-plied, -ply•ing.** To give an answer in writing or speech : respond. —*n., pl.* **-plies.** An answer : response. —**re•pli'er** *n.*

re•port (rĭ-pôrt', -pōrt') *n.* **1.** A usu. detailed and formal account. **2.** Common talk : rumor. **3.** Reputation : repute. **4.** An explosive noise : bang. —*v.* **1.** To present an account (of), often formally. **2.** To tell about : relate. **3.** To make known to the proper authorities. **4.** To write or supply an account (of) for publication or broadcast. **5.** To complain about <*reported* the suspicious character to the police> **6.** To present oneself <*report* for work on time>

re•port•age (rĕp'ər-täzh', rĭ-pôr'tĭj, -pōr'-) *n.* **1.** The reporting of news. **2.** Something reported.

report card *n.* A report of a student's progress sent to a parent or guardian.

re•port•ed•ly (rĭ-pôr'tĭd-lē, -pōr'-) *adv.* According to reports.

re•port•er (rĭ-pôr'tər, -pōr'-) *n.* **1.** One who reports. **2.** A writer or broadcaster of news. —**rep'or•to'ri•al** *adj.*

re•pose[1] (rĭ-pōz') *n.* **1.** An act of resting or the state of being at rest. **2.** Tranquillity. **3.** Poise : composure. —*v.* **-posed, -pos•ing. 1.** To lie or lay at rest. **2.** To lie supported by something. —**re•pose'ful** *adj.*

re•pose[2] (rĭ-pōz') *v.* **-posed, -pos•ing.** To place (e.g., trust) <They *reposed* their hopes in their children.>

re•pos•i•to•ry (rĭ-pŏz'ĭ-tôr'ē, -tōr'ē) *n., pl.* **-ries.** A place where things are stored, as for safekeeping.

re•pos•sess (rē'pə-zĕs') *v.* To regain or reclaim ownership of, esp. for failure to make payments. —**re'pos•ses'sion** *n.*

rep•re•hend (rĕp'rĭ-hĕnd') *v.* To express disapproval of. —**rep're•hen'sion** *n.*

rep•re•hen•si•ble (rĕp'rĭ-hĕn'sə-bəl) *adj.* Deserving of censure : blameworthy. —**rep're•hen'si•bly** *adv.*

rep•re•sent (rĕp'rĭ-zĕnt') *v.* **1.** To stand for : symbolize. **2.** To portray : depict. **3.** To be an example of. **4.** To act or speak on behalf of. **5.** To describe as having certain characteristics. ★ ***syns:*** EMBODY, EPITOMIZE, EXEMPLIFY, PERSONIFY, SYMBOLIZE, TYPIFY —**rep're•sent'a•bil'i•ty** *n.* —**rep're•sent'a•ble** *adj.*

rep•re•sen•ta•tion (rĕp'rĭ-zĕn-tā'shən, -zən-) *n.* **1.** An act of representing or the state of being represented. **2.** Something that represents. **3.** A statement, as of facts or accusations.

rep•re•sen•ta•tive (rĕp'rĭ-zĕn'tə-tĭv) *n.* **1.** One that exemplifies others of the same class. **2.** A delegate, agent, or spokesperson. **3. a.** A member of a legislative body chosen by popular vote. **b.** A member of the U.S. House of Representatives or of the lower house of a state legislature. —*adj.* **1.** Of or relating to government by representation. **2.** Authorized to act as an agent or delegate. **3.** Typical of others of the same class.

re•press (rĭ-prĕs') *v.* **1.** To hold back : restrain. **2.** To suppress : put down <*repress* an uprising> **3.** To exclude from the conscious mind. —**re•press'i•ble** *adj.* —**re•pres'sion** *n.* —**re•pres'sive** *adj.*

re•pres•sor (rĭ-prĕs'ər) *n.* **1.** One that represses. **2.** *Biol.* A chemical compound that prevents the synthesis of a protein by interfering with the actions of DNA.

re•prieve (rĭ-prēv′) *v.* **-prieved, -priev•ing. 1.** To delay the punishment of. **2.** To give temporary relief to. **—re•priev′a•ble** *adj.* **—re•prieve′** *n.*

rep•ri•mand (rĕp′rĭ-mănd′) *v.* To rebuke, esp. formally **:** censure. **—rep′ri•mand′** *n.*

re•print (rē′prĭnt′) *n.* **1.** A new or additional printing, as of a book, exactly like the original. **2.** A separately printed excerpt. **—re•print′** *v.* **—re•print′er** *n.*

re•pri•sal (rĭ-prī′zəl) *n.* An attack or other action intended to inflict injury in return for an injury suffered **:** retaliation.

re•prise (rĭ-prēz′) *n. Mus.* A repetition of a theme or phrase.

re•proach (rĭ-prōch′) *v.* To rebuke **:** blame. *—n.* **1.** Rebuke **:** blame. **2.** Shame **:** disgrace. **—re•proach′a•ble** *adj.*

rep•ro•bate (rĕp′rə-bāt′) *n.* A morally unprincipled person. *—adj.* Morally unprincipled **:** profligate. **—rep′ro•ba′tion** *n.*

re•pro•duce (rē′prə-do͞os′, -dyo͞os′) *v.* **-duced, -duc•ing. 1.** To produce an image or copy of. **2.** *Biol.* To generate offspring. **3.** To produce again **:** re-create. **4.** To undergo copying. **—re′pro•duc′er** *n.* **—re′pro•duc′i•ble** *adj.* **—re′pro•duc′tion** (-dŭk′shən) *n.* **—re′pro•duc′tive** *adj.*

re•proof (rĭ-pro͞of′) *n.* An act or expression of reproving **:** rebuke.

re•prove (rĭ-pro͞ov′) *v.* **-proved, -prov•ing. 1.** To rebuke **:** scold. **2.** To find fault with. **—re•prov′ing•ly** *adv.*

rep•tile (rĕp′tĭl, -tīl′) *n.* A cold-blooded, usu. egg-laying vertebrate of the class Reptilia, as a snake or turtle, having an outer covering of scales or horny plates. **—rep•til′i•an** (-tĭl′ē-ən, -tĭl′yən) *adj. & n.*

re•pub•lic (rĭ-pŭb′lĭk) *n.* **1. a.** A political order whose head of state is not a monarch but usu. a president. **b.** A nation with such a political order. **2. a.** A political order in which the power is held by the elected representatives of its citizens. **b.** A nation with such a political order.

re•pub•li•can (rĭ-pŭb′lĭ-kən) *adj.* **1.** Of, pertaining to, or favoring a republic. **2. Republican.** Of or relating to the U.S. Republican Party. *—n.* **1.** One who favors a republican form of government. **2. Republican.** A member of the U.S. Republican Party. **—re•pub′li•can•ism** *n.*

Republican Party *n.* One of the 2 major U.S. political parties, organized in 1854.

re•pu•di•ate (rĭ-pyo͞o′dē-āt′) *v.* **-at•ed, -at•ing. 1.** To reject as invalid or untrue. **2.** To refuse to recognize or pay. **3.** To disown. ★ ***syns:*** DENY, DISAVOW, DISCLAIM, DISOWN **—re•pu′di•a′tion** *n.*

re•pug•nant (rĭ-pŭg′nənt) *adj.* **1.** Arousing extreme dislike **:** offensive. **2.** *Logic.* Inconsistent. **—re•pug′nance** *n.*

re•pulse (rĭ-pŭls′) *v.* **-pulsed, -puls•ing. 1.** To drive back **:** repel. **2.** To reject rudely or coldly <*repulsed* his advances> *—n.* **1.** An act of repulsing or the state of being repulsed. **2.** A rejection. **—re•pul′sion** *n.*

re•pul•sive (rĭ-pŭl′sĭv) *adj.* **1.** Arousing extreme aversion **:** loathsome. **2.** Tending to drive off. **—re•pul′sive•ly** *adv.*

rep•u•ta•ble (rĕp′yə-tə-bəl) *adj.* Possessing a good reputation. **—rep′u•ta•bly** *adv.*

rep•u•ta•tion (rĕp′yə-tā′shən) *n.* **1.** The general estimation of a person or thing held by the public. **2.** The condition of being highly regarded.

re•pute (rĭ-pyo͞ot′) *n.* **1.** Reputation. **2.** A good reputation. *—v.* **-put•ed, -put•ing.** To regard **:** suppose.

re•put•ed (rĭ-pyo͞o′tĭd) *adj.* Assumed to be such <a *reputed* gangster> ★ ***syns:*** ALLEGED, CONJECTURAL, PUTATIVE, SUPPOSED **—re•put′ed•ly** *adv.*

re•quest (rĭ-kwĕst′) *v.* **1.** To ask for. **2.** To ask (someone) to do something. *—n.* **1.** The act of asking. **2.** Something asked for. **3.** The fact or condition of being requested <available on *request*>

req•ui•em (rĕk′wē-əm, rē′kwē-) *n.* **1. Requiem.** *Rom. Cath. Ch.* **a.** A mass for a deceased person. **b.** A musical composition for such a mass. **2.** A composition or service commemorating the dead.

re•quire (rĭ-kwīr′) *v.* **-quired, -quir•ing. 1.** To need. **2.** To insist upon **:** demand. **3.** To oblige **:** compel. **—re•quire′ment** *n.*

req•ui•site (rĕk′wĭ-zĭt) *adj.* Needed **:** necessary. *—n.* A necessity.

req•ui•si•tion (rĕk′wĭ-zĭsh′ən) *n.* **1.** A formal written request or demand for something needed. **2.** The state of being needed. **—req′ui•si′tion** *v.*

re•quite (rĭ-kwīt′) *v.* **-quit•ed, -quit•ing. 1.** To make return for <*requite* another's love> **2.** To avenge. **—re•quit′al** *n.*

rer•e•dos (rĕr′ĭ-dŏs′, rîr′-, rîr′dŏs′) *n.* The back of an open hearth of a fireplace.

re•run (rē′rŭn′) *n.* **1.** A repetition. **2.** Another showing of a recorded motion-picture or television program. **—re•run′** *v.*

re•scind (rĭ-sĭnd′) *v.* To make void **:** annul. **—re•scind′a•ble** *adj.* **—re•scind′er** *n.* **—re•scis′sion** (-sĭzh′ən) *n.*

res•cue (rĕs′kyo͞o) *v.* **-cued, -cu•ing.** To free from confinement or danger **:** save. **—res′cue** *n.* **—res′cu•er** *n.*

re•search (rĭ-sûrch′, rē′sûrch′) *n.* **1.** Scientific or scholarly investigation. **2.** Close, careful study. **—re•search′** *v.*

re•sec•tion (rĭ-sĕk′shən) *n.* The excision of part of an organ or structure by surgery.

re•sem•blance (rĭ-zĕm′bləns) *n.* A similarity in nature, form, or appearance.

re•sem•ble (rĭ-zĕm′bəl) *v.* **-bled, -bling.** To have a similarity to **:** be like.

re•sent (rĭ-zĕnt′) *v.* To feel angry or indignant about **:** object to. **—re•sent′ful** *adj.* **—re•sent′ful•ly** *adv.* **—re•sent′ment** *n.*

res•er•va•tion (rĕz′ər-vā′shən) *n.* **1.** The act of reserving or the condition of being reserved. **2.** Something reserved. **3.** A limiting qualification or exception. **4.** Land set apart by a government for a special purpose, esp. an area for the use of an American or Canadian

Indian people. **5.** An arrangement by which accommodations are secured ahead of time.

re·serve (rĭ-zûrv′) *v.* **-served, -serv·ing. 1.** To save for future use or a special purpose. **2.** To set apart for a particular person or use. **3.** To keep for oneself : retain. **4.** To defeat : put off. —*n.* **1.** Something saved for future use or a special purpose. **2.** The condition of being reserved <food held in *reserve*> **3.** Reticence. **4.** A reservation of public land. **5.** *often* **reserves.** A fighting force kept inactive until needed.

re·served (rĭ-zûrvd′) *adj.* **1.** Kept back or set aside. **2.** Reticent. —**re·serv′ed·ly** *adv.* —**re·serv′ed·ness** *n.*

res·er·voir (rĕz′ər-vwär′, -vwôr′, -vôr′) *n.* **1.** A body of water collected and stored for future use. **2.** A chamber for storing a fluid. **3.** A large supply : reserve.

re·side (rĭ-zīd′) *v.* **-sid·ed, -sid·ing. 1.** To live in a place : dwell. **2.** To be present : inhere. —**re·sid′er** *n.*

res·i·dence (rĕz′ĭ-dəns) *n.* **1.** The place where one lives. **2.** The act or a period of living somewhere.

res·i·den·cy (rĕz′ĭ-dən-sē, -dĕn′-) *n., pl.* **-cies. 1.** Residence. **2.** The period during which a physician receives specialized clinical training.

res·i·dent (rĕz′ĭ-dənt, -dĕnt′) *n.* **1.** One whose home is in a particular location. **2.** A physician serving a period of residency.

res·i·den·tial (rĕz′ĭ-dĕn′shəl) *adj.* **1.** Of or having residence. **2.** Containing or appropriate for residences.

re·sid·u·al (rĭ-zĭj′o͞o-əl) *adj.* Of, relating to, or left over as a residue. —*n.* **1.** An amount remaining : residue. **2.** A payment made to a performer for each repeat showing of a recorded television show.

res·i·due (rĕz′ĭ-do͞o′, -dyo͞o′) *n.* The remainder of something after treatment or removal of a part.

re·sign (rĭ-zīn′) *v.* **1.** To submit (oneself) to something unavoidable <*resigned* himself to waiting for the next bus> **2.** To give up (a job or position) : quit. **3.** To relinquish (a right, privilege, or claim).

res·ig·na·tion (rĕz′ĭg-nā′shən) *n.* **1.** An act of resigning. **2.** A formal statement that one is quitting a job. **3.** Passive acceptance, as of the unavoidable.

re·signed (rĭ-zīnd′) *adj.* Acquiescent. —**re·sign′ed·ly** *adv.*

re·sil·ience (rĭ-zĭl′yəns) *also* **re·sil·ien·cy** (-yən-sē) *n.* **1.** Ability to recover rapidly, as from misfortune : buoyancy. **2.** The property of a material that enables it to regain its original shape after being bent, stretched, or compressed : elasticity. —**re·sil′ient** *adj.* —**re·sil′ient·ly** *adv.*

res·in (rĕz′ĭn) *n.* **1.** A viscid substance that oozes from certain trees and plants, used in varnishes, synthetic plastics, and for many other purposes. **2.** Any of various artificial substances that have similar properties. —**res′in·ous** *adj.*

res·in·ate (rĕz′ə-nāt′) *v.* **-at·ed, -at·ing.** To impregnate or flavor with resin.

re·sist (rĭ-zĭst′) *v.* **1.** To oppose actively : strive against. **2.** To withstand. —**re·sist′er** *n.* —**re·sist′i·ble** *adj.*

re·sis·tance (rĭ-zĭs′təns) *n.* **1.** The act of resisting or the capacity to resist. **2.** A force that tends to oppose or retard motion. **3.** *Elect.* Opposition to electric current characteristic of a medium, substance, or circuit element. **4.** An underground organization seeking to overthrow a usu. totalitarian government. —**re·sis′tant** *adj.*

re·sis·tor (rĭ-zĭs′tər) *n.* An electric element used for providing resistance in a circuit.

res·o·lute (rĕz′ə-lo͞ot′) *adj.* Marked by firm determination : unwavering.

res·o·lu·tion (rĕz′ə-lo͞o′shən) *n.* **1.** Firm determination. **2. a.** The act of resolving. **b.** Something resolved, esp. a decision or expression of opinion adopted by a deliberative body. **3.** A solving, as of a problem.

re·solve (rĭ-zŏlv′) *v.* **-solved, -solv·ing. 1.** To make or cause to make a firm decision. **2.** To state formally in a resolution. **3.** To separate into component parts. **4.** To find a solution to. **5.** To deal with successfully : settle. —**re·solve** *n.* —**re·solv′a·ble** *adj.*

re·solved (rĭ-zŏlvd′) *adj.* Determined.

res·o·nance (rĕz′ə-nəns) *n.* **1.** The quality or state of being resonant. **2.** *Physics.* Enhancement of the response of a system to a periodic driving force oscillating at the frequency at which the system tends to oscillate naturally. **3.** Intensification of sound by sympathetic vibration.

res·o·nant (rĕz′ə-nənt) *adj.* **1.** Continuing to sound : echoing. **2.** Of or showing resonance. **3.** Having a full, deep, rich sound. —**res′o·nant·ly** *adv.*

res·o·nate (rĕz′ə-nāt′) *v.* **-nat·ed, -nat·ing. 1.** To show or produce resonance. **2.** To resound. —**res′o·na′tion** *n.*

res·o·na·tor (rĕz′ə-nā′tər) *n.* A hollow chamber or cavity that permits internal resonance, as of sound waves.

re·sort (rĭ-zôrt′) *v.* **1.** To have recourse <*resorted* to rationing> **2.** To go commonly or often : repair. —*n.* **1.** A place visited for relaxation or recreation. **2.** Recourse. **3.** One turned to for help or relief.

re·sound (rĭ-zound′) *v.* **1.** To be filled with sound : reverberate. **2.** To make a long, loud sound. —**re·sound′ing·ly** *adv.*

re·source (rē′sôrs′, -sōrs′, -zôrs′, -zōrs′, rĭ-) *n.* **1.** A source of support or aid. **2.** An ability to handle a situation in an effective manner. **3.** **resources. a.** Means that can be used profitably. **b.** Capital : assets. **4.** A natural resource.

re·source·ful (rĭ-sôrs′fəl, -sōrs′-, -zôrs′-, -zōrs′-) *adj.* Clever and imaginative, esp. in dealing with difficult situations. —**re·source′ful·ly** *adv.* —**re·source′ful·ness** *n.*

re·spect (rĭ-spĕkt′) *v.* **1.** To feel or show deferential regard for : esteem. **2.** To avoid violation of or inteference with. **3.** To relate to : concern. —*n.* **1.** Deferential regard : esteem.

2. The state of being regarded with deference or esteem. 3. Willingness to show consideration or appreciation. 4. **respects.** Polite expressions of consideration or deference <paid our *respects*> 5. A specific aspect, feature, or detail. 6. Relation : reference. **—re•spect'er** *n.* **—re•spect'ful** *adj.* **—re•spect'ful•ly** *adv.*

re•spect•a•ble (rĭ-spĕk'tə-bəl) *adj.* **1.** Deserving respect or esteem : worthy. **2.** Conventional or proper in conduct or appearance. **3.** Reasonably good. **4.** Considerable <a *respectable* amount> **—re•spect'a•bil'i•ty** *n.* **—re•spect'a•bly** *adv.*

re•spect•ing (rĭ-spĕk'tĭng) *prep.* With reference to.

re•spec•tive (rĭ-spĕk'tĭv) *adj.* Separate : particular <took their *respective* seats>

re•spec•tive•ly (rĭ-spĕk'tĭv-lē) *adv.* Singly in the order given.

res•pi•ra•tion (rĕs'pə-rā'shən) *n.* **1.** The act of inhaling and exhaling. **2.** The metabolic process by which an organism assimilates oxygen and releases carbon dioxide and other products of oxidation. **—res'pi•ra•to'ry** (-pər-ə-tôr'ē, -tōr'ē) *adj.*

res•pi•ra•tor (rĕs'pə-rā'tər) *n.* **1.** A device used in administering artificial respiration. **2.** A filtering device worn over the mouth and nose to protect the respiratory tract.

re•spire (rĭ-spīr') *v.* **-spired, -spir•ing. 1.** To breathe. **2.** To undergo the metabolic process of respiration.

res•pite (rĕs'pĭt) *n.* **1.** A short period of rest or relief. **2.** A temporary suspension.

re•splen•dent (rĭ-splĕn'dənt) *adj.* Full of splendor. **—re•splen'dence** *n.*

re•spond (rĭ-spŏnd') *v.* **1.** To reply : answer. **2.** To act because or at the prompting of something : react. **3.** To react positively.

re•spon•dent (rĭ-spŏn'dənt) *n.* **1.** One who responds. **2.** *Law.* A defendant in a divorce or equity case.

re•sponse (rĭ-spŏns') *n.* **1.** An act of responding. **2.** A reply : answer. **3.** A reaction to a stimulus.

re•spon•si•bil•i•ty (rĭ-spŏn'sə-bĭl'ĭ-tē) *n., pl.* **-ties. 1.** The quality, state, or fact of being responsible. **2.** One that a person is responsible for.

re•spon•si•ble (rĭ-spŏn'sə-bəl) *adj.* **1.** Having to account for one's actions : answerable <a government *responsible* to the people> **2.** Having a duty or obligation <*responsible* for washing the dishes tonight> **3.** Being a source or cause. **4.** Dependable. **5.** Involving important duties or obligations. **—re•spon'si•bly** *adv.*

re•spon•sive (rĭ-spŏn'sĭv) *adj.* **1.** Answering : responding. **2.** Promptly reacting to appeals or suggestions.

rest[1] (rĕst) *n.* **1.** A state or period of inactivity, relaxation, or sleep. **2.** Absence of motion. **3.** *Mus.* **a.** An interval of silence equal in duration to a note of the same value. **b.** The symbol indicating such a pause and its duration. **4.** A supporting device. *—v.* **1.** To stop work or motion. **2.** To give rest to. **3.** To lie down. **4.** To be at peace or ease. **5.** To be still or inactive. **6.** To be or cause to be supported. **7.** To depend : rely. **8.** To be placed or imposed <It *rests* with you to carry on.> **—rest'ful** *adj.* **—rest'ful•ly** *adv.*

rest[1]
A. note, B. rest

rest[2] (rĕst) *n.* **1.** The part left over : remainder. **2.** Those remaining <The *rest* are coming later.>

res•tau•rant (rĕs'tər-ənt, -tə-ränt') *n.* A place for serving meals to the public.

res•tau•ra•teur (rĕs'tər-ə-tûr') *n.* One who owns or runs a restaurant.

rest home *n.* An establishment where old or sick people are housed and cared for.

res•ti•tu•tion (rĕs'tĭ-to͞o'shən, -tyo͞o'-) *n.* **1.** An act of returning something to its rightful owner. **2.** An act of compensating for loss, damage, or injury.

res•tive (rĕs'tĭv) *adj.* **1.** Impatient under restriction or delay : uneasy. **2.** Hard to control : balky. **—res'tive•ness** *n.*

rest•less (rĕst'lĭs) *adj.* **1.** Without rest or quiet <*restless* sleep> **2. a.** Unable or unwilling to rest or be still. **b.** Nervous : fidgety. **—rest'less•ly** *adv.*

res•to•ra•tion (rĕs'tə-rā'shən) *n.* **1.** The act or an instance of restoring or the state of being restored. **2.** Something that has been restored to a previous condition.

re•stor•a•tive (rĭ-stôr'ə-tĭv, -stōr'-) *adj.* **1.** Of or for restoration. **2.** Tending to restore health or strength. **—re•stor'a•tive** *n.*

re•store (rĭ-stôr', -stōr') *v.* **-stored, -stor•ing. 1.** To put back into existence or use. **2.** To bring back to a former or original condition. **3.** To give back : return. ★ ***syns:*** REINSTATE, RENEW, REVIVE **—re•stor'er** *n.*

re•strain (rĭ-strān') *v.* **1.** To hold back. **2.** To take away the freedom of. **3.** To limit or restrict. **—re•strain'a•ble** *adj.*

re•straint (rĭ-strānt') *n.* **1.** An act of restraining or the condition of being restrained. **2.** Loss of freedom. **3.** A limitation. **4.** Something that restrains. **5.** Moderation in action or expression.

re•strict (rĭ-strĭkt') *v.* To hold within limits : confine. **—re•stric'tion** *n.* **—re•stric'tive** *adj.* **—re•stric'tive•ly** *adv.*

rest room *n.* A public lavatory.

re•sult (rĭ-zŭlt′) *v.* **1.** To happen or exist as a consequence. **2.** To end in a particular way. —*n.* A consequence : outcome. —**re•sul′tant** *adj.* & *n.*

re•sume (rĭ-zo͞om′) *v.* **-sumed, -sum•ing. 1.** To begin or take up again after an interruption. **2.** To occupy or assume again. —**re•sump′tion** (-zŭmp′shən) *n.*

ré•su•mé (rĕz′o͞o-mā′, rĕz′o͞o-mā′) *n.* A summary, esp. of one's personal history and employment experience.

re•sur•gent (rĭ-sûr′jənt) *adj.* Rising or surging again. —**re•sur′gence** *n.*

res•ur•rec•tion (rĕz′ə-rĕk′shən) *n.* **1.** An act of returning or bringing from death to life. **2. Resurrection.** *Theol.* **a.** The rising again of Jesus after the Crucifixion. **b.** The rising again of the dead at the Last Judgment. **3.** A revival. —**res′ur•rect′** *v.*

re•sus•ci•tate (rĭ-sŭs′ĭ-tāt′) *v.* **-tat•ed, -tat•ing.** To return to consciousness or life : revive. —**re•sus′ci•ta′tion** *n.* —**re•sus′ci•ta′tor** *n.*

re•tail (rē′tāl′) *n.* The sale of goods in small quantities to the public. —*v.* **1.** To sell at retail. **2.** To tell and retell. —**re′tail′** *adj.* & *adv.* —**re′tail′er** *n.*

re•tain (rĭ-tān′) *v.* **1.** To keep in one's possession : hold. **2.** To keep or hold in a certain place, condition, or position. **3.** To hold in the memory : remember. **4.** To hire (e.g., an attorney) by paying an initial fee. —**re•tain′a•ble** *adj.* —**re•tain′ment** *n.*

re•tain•er (rĭ-tā′nər) *n.* **1.** One that retains. **2. a.** An attendant in a noble household, as in feudal times. **b.** A domestic servant. **c.** An employee. **3.** The fee paid to engage a professional adviser.

re•take (rē-tāk′) *v.* **1.** To take again. **2.** To photograph again. —*n.* (rē′tāk′). A rephotographed scene, as for a film.

re•tal•i•ate (rĭ-tăl′ē-āt′) *v.* **-at•ed, -at•ing.** To return like for like, esp. evil for evil. —**re•tal′i•a′tion** *n.* —**re•tal′i•a•to′ry** *adj.*

re•tard (rĭ-tärd′) *v.* To slow the progress of : delay. —**re•tar′dant** *adj.* & *n.*

re•tar•da•tion (rē′tär-dā′shən) *n.* **1.** The act of retarding or state of being retarded. **2.** A delay. **3.** Mental deficiency.

re•tard•ed (rĭ-tär′dĭd) *adj.* Abnormally slow in mental or emotional development.

retch (rĕch) *v.* To try to vomit.

re•ten•tion (rĭ-tĕn′shən) *n.* **1.** An act of retaining or the state of being retained. **2.** The ability to retain. —**re•ten′tive** *adj.*

ret•i•cent (rĕt′ĭ-sənt) *adj.* Reluctant to speak freely. —**ret′i•cence** *n.*

ret•i•na (rĕt′n-ə) *n., pl.* **-nas** *or* **-nae** (-n-ē′). A delicate light-sensitive membrane lining the inner eyeball and connected to the brain by the optic nerve. —**ret′i•nal** *adj.*

ret•i•nue (rĕt′n-o͞o′, -yo͞o′) *n.* A group of attendants accompanying a high-ranking person. ★ ***syns:*** CORTEGE, ENTOURAGE, FOLLOWING, SUITE, TRAIN

re•tire (rĭ-tīr′) *v.* **-tired, -tir•ing. 1.** To withdraw, as for rest or seclusion. **2.** To go to bed. **3.** To give up working or serving, usu. because of advancing age. **4.** To remove from active service. **5.** To withdraw troops : retreat. **6.** To remove from circulation. **7.** *Baseball.* To cause (an offensive player) to no longer continue at bat or on base. —**re•tired′** *adj.* —**re•tir′ee′** *n.* —**re•tire′ment** *n.*

re•tir•ing (rĭ-tīr′ĭng) *adj.* Unobtrusive and reserved. —**re•tir′ing•ly** *adv.*

re•tort[1] (rĭ-tôrt′) *v.* **1.** To reply to, esp. in a quick, sharp way. **2.** To retaliate. —*n.* A quick, sharp reply. ★ ***syns:*** COMEBACK, COUNTER, REPARTEE, RIPOSTE

re•tort[2] (rĭ-tôrt′, rē′tôrt′) *n.* A closed laboratory vessel used for distillation or decomposition by heat.

re•touch (rē-tŭch′) *v.* **1.** To try to improve by adding details or small corrections : touch up. **2.** *Photog.* To change, esp. by taking out defects.

re•trace (rē-trās′) *v.* **1.** To trace again. **2.** To go back over <*retraced* his steps>

re•tract (rĭ-trăkt′) *v.* **1.** To take back : disavow <*retracted* the accusation> **2.** To draw back or in. —**re•tract′a•ble, re•tract′i•ble** *adj.* —**re•trac′tion** *n.*

re•trac•tile (rĭ-trăk′tĭl, -tīl′) *adj.* Able to be drawn back or in <*retractile* claws>

re•tread (rē-trĕd′) *v.* To fit (a worn tire) with a new tread. —*n.* (rē′trĕd′). A retreaded tire.

re•treat (rĭ-trēt′) *n.* **1.** An act of going back or withdrawing, esp. from danger or an enemy attack. **2.** A quiet, private place : refuge. **3.** A time of seclusion, esp. for quiet thought, prayer, or study. **4. a.** The signal for a military withdrawal. **b.** A bugle call that signals the lowering of the flag. —*v.* To make a retreat : withdraw.

re•trench (rĭ-trĕnch′) *v.* **1.** To cut down. **2.** To cut back expenses or operations.

ret•ri•bu•tion (rĕt′rə-byo͞o′shən) *n.* A suitable return, esp. punishment, for what one has done. —**re•trib′u•tive** (rĭ-trĭb′yə-tĭv), **re•trib′u•to′ry** (-tôr′ē, -tōr′ē) *adj.*

re•trieve (rĭ-trēv′) *v.* **-trieved, -triev•ing. 1.** To bring or get back : regain. **2.** To find and bring back (e.g., game) : fetch. **3.** To put right : rectify. —**re•triev′a•ble** *adj.* —**re•triev′a•bly** *adv.* —**re•triev′al** *n.*

re•triev•er (rĭ-trē′vər) *n.* **1.** One that retrieves. **2.** A dog trained to retrieve game.

ret•ro (rĕt′rō) *adj.* **1.** Retroactive. **2.** Involving or reminiscent of things past. —*n., pl.* **-ros.** A fashion, decor, or design reminiscent of an earlier period.

ret•ro•ac•tive (rĕt′rō-ăk′tĭv) *adj.* Applying to a period prior to enactment.

ret•ro•en•gine (rĕt′rō-ĕn′jĭn) *n.* A spacecraft's rocket engine producing thrust in a direction opposite to that of the spacecraft's motion, used to decelerate.

ret•ro•fire (rĕt′rō-fīr′) *v.* **-fired, -fir•ing.** To ignite. —Used of a retroengine.

ret•ro•fit (rĕt′rō-fĭt′) *v.* To provide with parts or equipment unavailable at the time of original manufacture. —**ret′ro•fit′** *n.*

ret•ro•grade (rĕt′rə-grād′) *adj.* **1.** Moving or

directed backward. 2. Reverting to an earlier or inferior condition. —*v.* **1.** To move backward. **2.** To decline : degenerate.

ret•ro•gress (rĕt′rə-grĕs′, rĕt′rə-grĕs′) *v.* To go backward, esp. to an earlier or worse condition. **—ret′ro•gres′sion** *n.* **—ret′ro•gres′sive** *adj.*

ret•ro•rock•et (rĕt′rō-rŏk′ĭt) *n.* A retro-engine.

ret•ro•spect (rĕt′rə-spĕkt′) *n.* A consideration or review of past events. **—ret′ro•spec′tion** *n.* **—ret′ro•spec′tive** *adj. & n.*

ret•ro•vi•rus (rĕt′rō-vī′rəs, rĕt′rə-vī′-) *n.* A virus, such as the one causing AIDS, that contains RNA and an enzyme that can create DNA using RNA as a template.

re•turn (rĭ-tûrn′) *v.* **1.** To go or come back. **2.** To give or send back to a former possessor. **3.** To reciprocate. **4.** To reply. **5.** To produce (e.g., profit). **6.** To deliver or submit (e.g., a verdict). **7.** To re-elect. —*n.* **1.** The act of returning or fact of being returned. **2.** Something returned. **3.** A recurrence. **4.** A reply. **5.** A profit : yield. **6.** An official report or document to be submitted. **7.** *Sports.* A ball sent or carried back. —*adj.* **1.** Of or involving a return <a *return* ticket> **2.** Given or done in return. **—re•turn′a•ble** *adj.* **—re•turn′ee′** *n.* **—re•turn′er** *n.*

re•un•ion (rē-yōōn′yən) *n.* **1.** The act or an instance of reuniting. **2.** A gathering of the separated members of a group.

re•u•nite (rē′yōō-nīt′) *v.* To come or bring together again.

rev (rĕv) *Informal.* —*n.* A revolution of a motor. —*v.* **revved, rev•ving.** To increase the speed or pace of <*rev* up an engine><*revving* up factory production>

re•vamp (rē-vămp′) *v.* **1.** To patch up : restore. **2.** To revise.

re•vanch•ism (rĭ-vănch′ĭz′əm) *n.* A political policy of seeking to win back lost national territory. **—re•vanch′ist** *n.*

re•veal (rĭ-vēl′) *v.* **1.** To make known. **2.** To bring to view : show clearly.

rev•eil•le (rĕv′ə-lē) *n.* A signal, as on a bugle, given to awaken soldiers early in the morning.

rev•el (rĕv′əl) *v.* **-eled, -el•ling** *or* **-elled, -el•ling. 1.** To take great pleasure <*reveled* in his triumph> **2.** To make merry : celebrate. —*n. often* **revels.** Merrymaking. **—rev′el•er** *n.* **—rev′el•ry** *n.*

rev•e•la•tion (rĕv′ə-lā′shən) *n.* **1.** An act of revealing. **2.** Something revealed, esp. something dramatic. **3. Revelation.** —See table at BIBLE. **—rev′e•la•to′ry** *adj.*

re•venge (rĭ-vĕnj′) *v.* **-venged, -veng•ing.** To impose or inflict injury in return for (injury or insult) : avenge. —*n.* **1.** The act of revenging. **2.** A desire for revenge. **—re•venge′ful** *adj.* **—re•veng′er** *n.*

rev•e•nue (rĕv′ə-nōō′, -nyōō′) *n.* **1.** Government income from all sources. **2.** Yield from investments.

re•ver•ber•ate (rĭ-vûr′bə-rāt′) *v.* **-at•ed, -at•ing. 1.** To echo : resound. **2.** To rebound or recoil. **—re•ver′ber•a′tion** *n.*

re•vere (rĭ-vîr′) *v.* **-vered, -ver•ing.** To regard with great devotion or respect.

rev•er•ence (rĕv′ər-əns) *n.* **1.** A profound feeling of awe and respect. **2.** An expression of respect, as a bow. **3. Reverence.** —Used as a form of address for certain members of the Christian clergy. **—rev′er•ence** *v.* **—rev′er•ent** *adj.*

rev•er•end (rĕv′ər-ənd) *adj.* **1.** Worthy of reverence. **2. Reverend.** —A title of respect for certain Christian clerics. —*n. Informal.* A cleric.

rev•er•en•tial (rĕv′ə-rĕn′shəl) *adj.* Expressing reverence. **—rev′er•en′tial•ly** *adv.*

rev•er•ie (rĕv′ə-rē) *n.* **1.** Abstracted musing. **2.** A daydream.

re•ver•sal (rĭ-vûr′səl) *n.* **1.** An act of reversing or the condition of being reversed. **2.** A change for the worse.

re•verse (rĭ-vûrs′) *adj.* **1.** Turned backward in position, order, or direction. **2.** Causing backward movement. —*n.* **1.** The contrary of something. **2.** A back or rear part. **3.** A change in fortune from better to worse. **4.** A mechanism for reversing movement, as a gear in a motor vehicle. —*v.* **-versed, -vers•ing. 1.** To turn to the opposite position or direction. **2.** To turn inside out or upside down. **3.** To transpose. **4.** *Law.* To revoke or annul (a decision or decree). **5.** To put or drive in reverse. **—re•vers′er** *n.* **—re•vers′i•ble** *adj. & n.*

re•vert (rĭ-vûrt′) *v.* **1.** To return to an earlier state, practice, or belief. **2.** *Law.* To return to a previous owner or the previous owner's heirs. **—re•ver′sion** *n.* **—re•ver′sion•ar′y** *adj.*

re•view (rĭ-vyōō′) *v.* **1.** To study or examine again. **2.** To look back on. **3.** To write or give a critical report on (e.g., a new book). **4.** *Law.* To examine (a decision or action) again, as in a higher court. **5.** To subject to a formal inspection <*review* troops> —*n.* **1.** A re-examination : reconsideration. **2.** A summary of previous material or past events. **3.** The act of restudying. **4.** An inspection or examination with the intention of evaluating. **5. a.** A critical report or essay that evaluates a work or performance. **b.** A periodical devoted to such reports. **6.** *Law.* A re-examination of an action or decision. ★ ***syns:*** COMMENT, COMMENTARY, CRITICISM, CRITIQUE, NOTICE

re•vile (rĭ-vīl′) *v.* **-viled, -vil•ing.** To denounce with abusive language. **—re•vile′ment** *n.* **—re•vil′er** *n.*

re•vise (rĭ-vīz′) *v.* **-vised, -vis•ing. 1.** To look over (a text) in order to improve or correct. **2.** To change : modify. **—re•vis′er, re•vi′sor** *n.* **—re•vi′sion** (-vĭzh′ən) *n.*

re•vi•tal•ize (rē-vīt′l-īz′) *v.* To give new life to. **—re•vi′tal•i•za′tion** *n.*

re•viv•al (rĭ-vī′vəl) *n.* **1.** An act of reviving or the state of being revived. **2.** A new presentation, as of an old film. **3.** An evangelistic meeting or series of meetings to reawaken religious faith.

re•vive (rĭ-vīv′) *v.* **-vived, -viv•ing. 1.** To return to life or consciousness. **2.** To impart new health, vigor, or spirit to. **3.** To restore to use or notice. **—re·viv'er** *n.*

re·viv·i·fy (rē-vĭv'ə-fī') *v.* **-fied, -fy·ing.** REVIVE 2. **—re·viv'i·fi·ca'tion** *n.*

re·voke (rĭ-vōk') *v.* **-voked, -vok·ing.** To nullify by canceling or reversing : annul. **—rev'o·ca·ble** (rĕv'ə-kə-bəl) *adj.* **—rev'o·ca'tion** *n.* **—re·vok'er** *n.*

re·volt (rĭ-vōlt') *v.* **1.** To try to overthrow one's rulers : rebel. **2.** To rise in strenuous opposition <*revolt* against new taxes> **3.** To fill with disgust : repel. *—n.* An uprising : rebellion.

re·volt·ing (rĭ-vōl'tĭng) *adj.* Disgustingly offensive. **—re·volt'ing·ly** *adv.*

rev·o·lu·tion (rĕv'ə-lōō'shən) *n.* **1. a.** Orbital motion about a point <Saturn's yearly *revolution* around the sun> **b.** Rotational motion about an axis. **2.** An abrupt overthrow of a government or group of rulers. **3.** A sudden or radical change in a system or state of affairs <a *revolution* in medicine> **—rev'o·lu'tion·ist** *n.*

rev·o·lu·tion·ar·y (rĕv'ə-lōō'shə-nĕr'ē) *adj.* **1.** Of, relating to, or promoting revolution. **2.** Marked by or effecting radical change. **—rev'o·lu'tion·ar'y** *n.*

rev·o·lu·tion·ize (rĕv'ə-lōō'shə-nīz') *v.* **-ized, -iz·ing.** To bring about radical changes in.

re·volve (rĭ-vŏlv') *v.* **-volved, -volv·ing. 1.** To move around a central point : orbit. **2.** To rotate : spin. **3.** To recur periodically. **4.** To consider : ponder. **—re·volv'a·ble** *adj.*

re·volv·er (rĭ-vŏl'vər) *n.* A handgun having a revolving cylinder with several cartridge chambers.

re·vue (rĭ-vyōō') *n.* A usu. satirical musical show with skits, songs, and dances.

re·vul·sion (rĭ-vŭl'shən) *n.* **1.** Sudden, strong disgust or loathing. **2.** Withdrawal from or aversion to something.

re·ward (rĭ-wôrd') *n.* Something given or offered for a special service, as the return of something lost. *—v.* **1.** To give a reward to or for. **2.** To recompense.

re·ward·ing (rĭ-wôrd'ĭng) *adj.* Yielding benefits or a sense of satisfaction.

re·word (rē-wûrd') *v.* To express again in different words.

Rh *symbol for* RHODIUM.

rhap·so·dize (răp'sə-dīz') *v.* **-dized, -diz·ing.** To express oneself with extravagant enthusiasm.

rhap·so·dy (răp'sə-dē) *n., pl.* **-dies. 1.** Extravagantly enthusiastic expression of feeling. **2.** A work, esp. a musical composition, marked by an impassioned style. **—rhap·sod'ic** (-sŏd'ĭk) *adj.* **—rhap·sod'i·cal·ly** *adv.* **—rhap'so·dist** *n.*

rhe·a (rē'ə) *n.* A flightless, 3-toed South American bird of the genus *Rhea,* resembling the ostrich.

rhe·ni·um (rē'nē-əm) *n. Symbol* **Re** A rare, dense, silvery-white metallic element used in electrical contacts and high-temperature thermocouples.

rhe·o·stat (rē'ə-stăt') *n.* A variable electrical resistor used to regulate current. **—rhe'o·stat'ic** *adj.*

rhe·sus monkey (rē'səs) *n.* A brownish monkey, *Macaca mulatta,* of India, often used in scientific research.

rhet·o·ric (rĕt'ər-ĭk) *n.* **1.** The art of the effective and persuasive use of language. **2.** Public speaking designed to persuade. **3.** Showy, bombastic language. **—rhe·tor'i·cal** (rĭ-tôr'ĭ-kəl, -tŏr-) *adj.* **—rhet'o·ri'cian** (rĕt'ə-rĭsh'ən) *n.*

rhetorical question *n.* A question to which one does not expect an answer.

rheum (rōōm) *n.* A thin watery mucous discharge from the eyes or nose.

rheu·mat·ic (rōō-măt'ĭk) *adj.* Of, relating to, or affected with rheumatism. *—n.* One affected with rheumatism.

rheumatic fever *n.* A severe infectious disease chiefly of children, marked by fever and painful inflammation of the joints and often resulting in permanent heart damage.

rheu·ma·tism (rōō'mə-tĭz'əm) *n.* A painful and disabling disorder of the muscles, tendons, joints, bones, or nerves.

rheu·ma·toid arthritis (rōō'mə-toid') *n.* A chronic disease characterized by stiffness and inflammation of the joints.

Rh factor (är'āch') *n.* Any of several substances in red blood cells that can cause severe antigenic reactions when mixed with blood lacking the factor.

rhine·stone (rīn'stōn') *n.* An artificial gem made of paste or glass in imitation of a diamond.

rhi·ni·tis (rī-nī'tĭs) *n.* Inflammation of the nasal mucous membranes.

rhi·no (rī'nō) *n., pl.* **-nos.** *Informal.* A rhinoceros.

rhi·noc·er·os (rī-nŏs'ər-əs) *n.* A large, thick-skinned mammal of the family Rhinocerotidae, of Africa and Asia, having 1 or 2 upright horns on the snout.

rhi·nol·o·gy (rī-nŏl'ə-jē) *n.* The anatomy, physiology, and pathology of the nose.

rhi·no·plas·ty (rī'nō-plăs'tē, -nə-) *n.* Plastic surgery of the nose.

rhi·zome (rī'zōm') *n.* A fleshy plant stem that grows horizontally under or along the ground, sending out roots below and leaves or shoots above.

Rh-neg·a·tive (är'āch-nĕg'ə-tĭv) *adj.* Not having an Rh factor.

rho·di·um (rō'dē-əm) *n. Symbol* **Rh** A hard, durable, silvery-white metallic element used to form high-temperature alloys and corrosion-resistant coatings.

rho·do·den·dron (rō'də-dĕn'drən) *n.* Any of various evergreen shrubs of the genus *Rhododendron,* having variously colored flower clusters.

rhom·boid (rŏm'boid') *n.* A parallelogram having unequal adjacent sides. **—rhom·boi'dal** *adj.*

rhom·bus (rŏm'bəs) *n., pl.* **-es** *or* **-bi** (-bī'). An equilateral parallelogram. **—rhom'bic** *adj.*

Rh-pos·i·tive (är′āch-pŏs′ĭ-tĭv) *adj.* Having an Rh factor.
rhu·barb (ro͞o′bärb′) *n.* **1.** A garden plant, *Rheum rhaponticum,* having long, fleshy, edible leafstalks. **2.** *Slang.* A noisy quarrel.
rhyme *also* **rime** (rīm)—*n.* **1. a.** Correspondence in the terminal sounds of words or of lines of verse. **b.** Verse having such correspondence. **2.** A word that corresponds with another in terminal sound <"Forlorn" is a *rhyme* for "outworn."> —*v.* **rhymed, rhym·ing** *also* **rimed, rim·ing. 1.** To be a rhyme. **2.** To compose verse. **3.** To use as a rhyme. **—rhym′er** *n.*
rhythm (rĭth′əm) *n.* **1.** A movement or action marked by regular recurrence of elements <the steady *rhythm* of knitting> **2.** *Mus.* A recurrent pattern formed by notes of differing stress and duration. **3. a.** The rise and fall of the voice in speech or of the mind's voice in reading. **b.** Poetic meter. **—rhyth′mi·cal, rhyth′mic** *adj.*
rhythm and blues *n.* A kind of music that combines elements of blues and jazz, marked by a strong backbeat.
rhythm method *n.* A birth-control method in which intercourse is avoided during the period of ovulation.
ri·al (rē-ôl′, -äl′) *n.* —See table at CURRENCY.
rib (rĭb) *n.* **1.** One of a series of long, paired, curved bones that extend from the spine toward the sternum and protect the chest cavity in most vertebrates. **2.** A rod that gives shape or support <the *ribs* of an umbrella> **3.** A raised ridge in fabric. —*v.* **ribbed, rib·bing. 1.** To support, shape, or provide with a rib or ribs. **2.** To make with ridges. **3.** *Slang.* To poke fun at.
rib·ald (rĭb′əld) *adj.* Marked by or indulging in coarse humor. **—rib′ald·ry** *n.*
rib·bon (rĭb′ən) *n.* **1.** A narrow strip or band of decorative fabric. **2. ribbons.** Ragged strips. **3.** An inked strip of cloth or polyethylene used in a typewriter, adding machine, etc.
ri·bo·fla·vin (rī′bō-flā′vĭn) *n.* The chief growth-promoting factor of the vitamin B complex, found in leafy vegetables, milk, egg yolks, and meat.
ri·bo·nu·cle·ic acid (rī′bō-no͞o-klē′ĭk, -nyo͞o-) *n.* A compound having a complicated, single-strand structure, found in the nucleus, cytoplasm, and ribosomes of all living cells and functioning in the synthesis of proteins : RNA.
ri·bo·some (rī′bə-sōm′) *n.* A spherical, RNA-containing particle in cytoplasm, active in the synthesis of protein. **—ri′bo·so′mal** *adj.*
rice (rīs) *n.* A cereal grass, *Oryza sativa,* with starchy edible seeds widely grown in warm regions.
†rice·bird (rīs′bûrd′) *n. S. U.S.* The bobolink.
rich (rĭch) *adj.* **1.** Having great wealth. **2.** Having great value or abundance <a *rich* harvest> **3.** Magnificent : luxurious. **4.** Abounding <*rich* in mineral resources> **5.** Extremely productive. **6.** Containing much fat or sugar <a *rich* pastry> **7. a.** Full and mellow <a *rich* baritone voice> **b.** Warm and strong in color. ★ ***syns:*** AFFLUENT, MONEYED, WEALTHY, WELL-TO-DO
rich·es (rĭch′ĭz) *pl.n.* **1.** Abundant wealth. **2.** Valuable possessions.
Rich·ter scale (rĭk′tər) *n.* A logarithmic scale used to express the magnitude of earthquakes.
rick (rĭk) *n.* A stack, as of straw or hay.
rick·ets (rĭk′ĭts) *n. (sing. in number).* A disease of children resulting from a lack of vitamin D and in defective bone growth.
rick·et·y (rĭk′ĭ-tē) *adj.* **-i·er, -i·est. 1.** Apt to fall apart : shaky. **2.** Feeble, with age. **3.** Of or affected with rickets.
rick·sha *or* **rick·shaw** (rĭk′shô′) *n.* A small, 2-wheeled Asian carriage drawn usu. by 1 person.
ric·o·chet (rĭk′ə-shā′) *v.* **-cheted** (-shād′), **-chet·ing** (-shā′ĭng) *also* **-chet·ted** (-shĕt′ĭd), **-chet·ting** (-shĕt′ĭng). To rebound from a surface. **—ric′o·chet′** *n.*
ri·cot·ta (rĭ-kŏt′ə) *n.* A soft, white, Italian cheese resembling cottage cheese.
rid (rĭd) *v.* **rid** *or* **rid·ded, rid·ding.** To make free : relieve <*rid* the house of vermin> **—rid′dance** *n.*
rid·dle[1] (rĭd′l) *v.* **-dled, -dling. 1.** To pierce with many small holes : perforate. **2.** To spread throughout <a paper *riddled* with spelling mistakes>
rid·dle[2] (rĭd′l) *n.* A puzzling question or situation requiring thought to be solved.
ride (rīd) *v.* **rode** (rōd), **rid·den** (rĭd′n), **rid·ing. 1.** To be conveyed in a vehicle or on an animal. **2.** To travel over a surface <a car that *rides* well> **3.** To float or move on or as if on water. **4.** To sit on and drive <*ride* a bicycle> **5.** To be carried upon <*riding* the waves> **6.** To take part in (e.g., a race) by sitting on and controlling an animal or vehicle. **7.** To cause to leave, esp. on horseback <*rode* him out of town> **8.** *Informal.* To ridicule. —*n.* **1.** An act of riding. **2.** A path for riding. **3.** A device, as at an amusement park, that one rides for pleasure or excitement. **—ride out.** To survive : outlast.
rid·er (rī′dər) *n.* **1.** One that rides. **2.** An addition to a document, esp. a clause added to a legislative bill.
ridge (rĭj) *n.* **1.** A long, narrow upper section or crest. **2.** A long, narrow land elevation. **3.** A line formed where 2 sloping surfaces meet, as on a roof. **4.** A narrow raised strip, as on cloth. **—ridge** *v.*
ridge·pole (rĭj′pōl′) *n.* A horizontal beam at the ridge of a roof, to which the rafters are attached.
rid·i·cule (rĭd′ĭ-kyo͞ol′) *n.* Words or actions intended to make people laugh scornfully at a person or thing. —*v.* **-culed, -cul·ing.** To make fun of. ★ ***syns:*** DERIDE, GIBE, MOCK, TAUNT, TWIT
ri·dic·u·lous (rĭ-dĭk′yə-ləs) *adj.* Meriting or inspiring ridicule : ludicrous.
ri·el (rē-ĕl′) *n.* —See table at CURRENCY.

rife (rīf) *adj.* **rif•er, rif•est. 1.** Common in occurrence : prevalent. **2.** Abounding.
riff (rĭf) *n.* A rhythmic phrase constantly repeated esp. in jazz. **—riff** *v.*
riff•raff (rĭf'răf') *n.* **1.** Disreputable people. **2.** Trash : rubbish.
ri•fle[1] (rī'fəl) *n.* A firearm having a long barrel containing spiral grooves. —*v.* **-fled, -fling.** To cut spiral grooves within.
ri•fle[2] (rī'fəl) *v.* **-fled, -fling.** To search through disruptively, esp. with intent to steal : ransack. **—ri'fler** *n.*
ri•fle•ry (rī'fəl-rē) *n.* The skill and practice of shooting a rifle.
rift (rĭft) *n.* **1. a.** *Geol.* A fault. **b.** A narrow rock fissure. **2.** A breach in friendly relations. —*v.* To split open : break.
†rig (rĭg) *v.* **rigged, rig•ging. 1.** To fit out with harness or equipment. **2.** To equip (a ship) with shrouds, sails, and yards. **3.** *Informal.* To dress : clothe <*rigged* out in her finery> **4.** To make or construct hastily. **5.** To manipulate dishonestly <*rig* the election> —*n.* **1.** The arrangement of masts, sails, and spars on a sailing vessel. **2.** Special equipment or gear. **3. a.** A truck, tractor, or tractor-trailer. **b.** A carriage with its horses. **4.** *Informal.* An outfit. **5.** An apparatus for drilling oil wells. **6.** *W U.S.* A saddle.
rig•a•ma•role (rĭg'ə-mə-rōl') *n. var. of* RIGMAROLE.
rig•ging (rĭg'ĭng) *n.* **1.** The system of ropes, chains, and tackle for supporting and maneuvering the masts, sails, and yards of a sailing ship. **2.** Equipment for a particular task, as construction work.
right (rīt) *n.* **1.** The side or direction opposite the left. **2.** That which is ethical, good, just, or proper. **3.** A conservative political group or faction. **4.** Something due to one by force of law or nature. **5.** A just moral or legal claim <the *right* to vote> —*adj.* **1. a.** Of or located on the side opposite the left. **b.** Toward this side <made a *right* turn> **2.** Of or inclined to politically conservative views or policies. **3.** Conforming with law, justice, or morality. **4.** In accord with fact, truth, or reason : correct. **5.** Fitting : appropriate. **6.** Advantageous : desirable. **7.** Made to be placed outward or upward <the *right* side of a sweater> —*adv.* **1.** In a straight line : directly. **2.** Properly : well <doesn't fit *right*> **3.** Precisely : just. **4.** Immediately. **5.** On or toward the right side. **6.** Very <the *Right* Honorable Prime Minister> **7.**—Used as an intensive <kept *right* on singing> —*v.* **1.** To restore to an upright or proper position. **2.** To put in order : set right. **3.** To redress <*right* an injustice>

▲ ***word history:*** The political sense of *right,* meaning "conservative" or "reactionary," goes back to the French Revolution. In the French National Assembly of 1789 the nobles sat on the president's right and the commoners on the left. The nobility as a group tended to be politically more conservative than the commoners. In later assemblies and parliaments seating continued to be assigned on the basis of political views as established in the first assembly.

right angle *n.* An angle of 90°, formed by 2 perpendicular line segments.
right away *adv.* Without delay.
right•eous (rī'chəs) *adj.* Meeting the standards of what is right and just. **—right'eous•ness** *n.*
right field *n. Baseball.* The portion of the outfield to the right as seen from home plate. **—right fielder** *n.*
right•ful (rīt'fəl) *adj.* **1.** Proper or right : just. **2.** Having a just claim <the *rightful* owner> **—right'ful•ly** *adv.*
right-hand (rīt'hănd') *adj.* **1.** On or toward the right side. **2.** Of or done by the right hand. **3.** Helpful and reliable.
right-hand•ed (rīt'hăn'dĭd) *adj.* **1.** Using the right hand more often and skillfully than the left. **2.** Of, for, or done by the right hand. **3.** Clockwise. **—right'-hand'ed, right'-hand'-ed•ly** *adv.*
right•ist (rī'tĭst) *n.* A political conservative or reactionary. **—right'ism** *n.*
right•ly (rīt'lē) *adv.* **1.** In a proper way : correctly. **2.** With honesty : justly.
right off *adv.* Straightaway : immediately.
right of way *also* **right-of-way** (rīt'əv-wā') *n.* **1.** *Law.* **a.** The right to pass over someone else's land. **b.** The path or area on which such passage is made. **2.** The strip of land over which railroads, pipelines, etc., run. **3.** The customary or legal right of a person or vehicle to pass before another.
right-to-life (rīt'tə-līf') *adj.* Pro-life. **—right'-to-lif'er** *n.*
right whale *n.* Any of several whales with a large head, whalebone plates in the mouth, and no dorsal fin.
rig•id (rĭj'ĭd) *adj.* **1.** Not bending : stiff. **2.** Not moving : stationary. **3.** Stern : severe. **—ri•gid'i•ty, rig'id•ness** *n.*
rig•ma•role (rĭg'mə-rōl') *also* **rig•a•ma•role** (-ə-mə-rōl') *n.* **1.** Incoherent speech. **2.** A needlessly complicated procedure.
rig•or (rĭg'ər) *n.* **1.** Strictness : severity. **2.** A trying circumstance : hardship. **3.** Precision. **4.** A shivering, as from a chill. **—rig'or•ous** *adj.* **—rig'or•ous•ly** *adv.*
rig•or mor•tis (rĭg'ər môr'tĭs) *n.* A temporary muscular stiffening after death.
rile (rīl) *v.* **riled, ril•ing.** To irritate : vex.
rill (rĭl) *n.* A small brook.
rim (rĭm) *n.* **1.** The outer edge of something. **2.** The outside of a wheel around which a tire fits. —*v.* **rimmed, rim•ming.** To provide with a rim.
rime[1] (rīm) *n.* A granular ice coating on plants, rocks, etc. **—rim'y** *adj.*
rime[2] (rīm) *n. & v. var. of* RHYME.
rind (rīnd) *n.* A tough outer covering, as the skin of a melon.
ring[1] (rĭng) *n.* **1.** A circular object or form with an empty circular center. **2.** A small circular band worn as an ornament on a finger. **3.** An enclosed area for staging exhibitions or contests. **4.** The sport of boxing. **5.** A group of

people acting together, esp. illegally. —*v.* **1.** To surround with a ring : encircle. **2.** To form into a ring.

ring² (rĭng) *v.* **rang** (răng), **rung** (rŭng), **ring•ing.** **1.** To make or cause to make a clear, resonant sound. **2.** To sound a bell as a summons or signal. **3.** To seem to a listener or observer : sound <a tale that *rings* true> **4.** To resound. **5.** To hear a persistent humming <Our ears *rang* from the explosion.> **6.** To telephone. —**ring up. 1.** To record, as on a cash register. **2.** To telephone. —*n.* **1.** The sound made by or as if by a bell. **2.** A loud, usu. continued or repeated sound. **3.** A telephone call. **4.** A particular sound or quality <a plan with a suspicious *ring*>

ring•er (rĭng′ər) *n.* **1.** One that rings a bell. **2.** *Slang.* A contestant entered fraudulently in a competition. **3.** *Slang.* One that strikingly resembles another.

ring•git (rĭng′gĭt′) *n.* —See table at CURRENCY.

ring•lead•er (rĭng′lē′dər) *n.* A leader, esp. in unlawful or underhand activities.

ring•let (rĭng′lĭt) *n.* A curled lock of hair.

ring•mas•ter (rĭng′măs′tər) *n.* A person who supervises and usu. introduces the acts in a circus ring.

ring•side (rĭng′sīd′) *n.* A place providing a close view, as of a prizefight.

ring•worm (rĭng′wûrm′) *n.* A contagious skin disease caused by a fungus and marked by ring-shaped itching patches.

rink (rĭngk) *n.* **1.** An area covered with smooth ice for skating. **2.** A smooth floor used for roller-skating.

rinse (rĭns) *v.* **rinsed, rins•ing. 1.** To wash lightly in water. **2.** To remove (e.g., soap) with water. —*n.* **1.** An act of rinsing. **2.** The liquid used for rinsing. **3.** A cosmetic solution used in tinting or conditioning the hair. —**rins′er** *n.*

ri•ot (rī′ət) *n.* **1.** A violent public disturbance. **2.** An uncontrolled outbreak, as of laughter. **3.** A profuse display. **4.** *Slang.* One that is irresistibly funny. —*v.* **1.** To take part in a riot. **2.** To engage in unrestrained revelry. —**ri′ot•ous** *adj.*

rip (rĭp) *v.* **ripped, rip•ping. 1.** To tear or become torn apart forcefully. **2.** To saw or split (wood) along the grain. **3.** To remove by pulling or tearing roughly. **4.** To move rapidly. **5.** To criticize harshly : excoriate. —*n.* A torn place : tear. —**rip off.** *Slang.* **1.** To steal (from). **2.** To swindle : defraud. —**rip′per** *n.*

ri•par•i•an (rĭ-pâr′ē-ən) *adj.* Of or on the bank of a natural course of water.

rip•cord (rĭp′kôrd′) *n.* A cord pulled to open a parachute.

ripe (rīp) *adj.* **rip•er, rip•est. 1.** Fully developed : mature. **2.** Fully prepared or aged for use. **3.** Suitable : opportune <The time was *ripe* for action.> —**ripe′ness** *n.*

rip•en (rī′pən) *v.* To make or become ripe.

rip-off (rĭp′ôf′, -ŏf′) *n. Slang.* **1.** A theft. **2.** A deception : swindle.

ri•poste (rĭ-pōst′) *n.* **1.** A quick thrust delivered after parrying a lunge in fencing. **2.** A quick, clever reply : retort. —**ri•poste′** *v.*

rip•ple (rĭp′əl) *v.* **-pled, -pling. 1.** To form or cause to form little waves on the surface. **2.** To waver gently in tone or volume. —**rip′ple** *n.*

rip•saw (rĭp′sô′) *n.* A saw for cutting wood along the grain.

rip tide *n.* A strong surface current flowing away from shore.

rise (rīz) *v.* **rose** (rōz), **ris•en** (rĭz′ən), **ris•ing. 1.** To go from a lower to a higher position. **2.** To assume a standing position after sitting, lying, or kneeling. **3.** To get out of bed. **4.** To increase in height, volume, or size. **5.** To increase in amount, number, or value. **6.** To increase in intensity or speed <The wind started to *rise.*> **7.** To advance in rank or condition. **8.** To slope upward. **9.** To appear above the horizon. **10.** To come into existence. **11.** To return to life. **12.** To be erected. **13.** To rebel. ★ ***syns:*** ASCEND, CLIMB, MOUNT, SOAR —*n.* **1.** An act of going up : ascent. **2.** A slope upward. **3.** The appearance of a celestial body above the horizon. **4.** An increase, as in height, amount, or intensity. **5.** An elevation in rank or condition. **6.** An origin : source **7.** *Informal.* An angry reaction.

ris•er (rī′zər) *n.* **1.** One who rises <an early *riser*> **2.** The vertical part of a step.

ris•i•bil•i•ty (rĭz′ə-bĭl′ĭ-tē) *n., pl.* **-ties. 1.** The capacity or tendency to laugh. **2.** *often* **risibilities.** One's sense of the comic. **3.** Laughter. —**ris′i•ble** *adj.* —**ris′i•bly** *adv.*

risk (rĭsk) *n.* The possibility of suffering harm or loss : danger. —*v.* **1.** To expose to the possibility of loss or damage. **2.** To incur the risk of. —**risk′y** *adj.*

ris•qué (rĭ-skā′) *adj.* Verging on impropriety or indelicacy : racy.

ris•sole (rĭ′sŏl, rē-sôl′) *n.* A small pastry-enclosed croquette usu. fried in deep fat.

rite (rīt) *n.* **1.** A formal, often religious procedure : ceremony. **2.** The prescribed form for a religious ceremony.

rit•u•al (rĭch′o͞o-əl) *n.* **1.** The form for conducting a ceremony. **2.** A ceremony or body of ceremonies. **3.** A procedure repeated customarily or automatically. —**rit′u•al** *adj.* —**rit′u•al•ism** *n.* —**rit′u•al•is′tic** *adj.* —**rit′u•al•is′ti•cal•ly** *adv.*

ritz•y (rĭt′sē) *adj.* **-i•er, -i•est.** *Slang.* Elegant : swank.

▲ ***word history:*** The word *ritzy* comes from the name of various celebrated hotels called *Ritz,* such as the *Hôtel Ritz* in Paris and the *Ritz Hotel* in London, which have a reputation for opulent elegance. They were founded by César Ritz, a Swiss hotelier who lived from 1850 to 1918.

ri•val (rī′vəl) *n.* **1.** One competing with another. **2.** One that equals or almost equals another. —*v.* **-valed, -val•ing** *also* **-valled, -val•ling. 1.** To try to equal or surpass. **2.** To be the equal of : match. —**ri′val** *adj.* —**ri′val•ry** *n.*

rive (rīv) *v.* **rived, rived** *or* **riv•en** (rĭv′ən),

riv•ing. 1. To tear or be torn apart : rend. **2.** To break into pieces : shatter.
riv•er (rĭv'ər) *n.* A relatively large natural stream of water.
riv•er•bank (rĭv'ər-băngk') *n.* The bank of a river.
riv•er•bed (rĭv'ər-bĕd') *n.* The area between the banks of a river covered or once covered by water.
riv•er•boat (rĭv'ər-bōt') *n.* A boat suitable for use on a river.
riv•er•side (rĭv'ər-sīd') *n.* The bank or side of a river.
riv•et (rĭv'ĭt) *n.* A metal bolt or pin used to join 2 or more objects by inserting it through a hole in each piece and then hammering the narrow end flat to form another head. —*v.* **1.** To fasten with or as if with a rivet. **2.** To engross (e.g., the attention).
riv•u•let (rĭv'yə-lĭt) *n.* A small stream.
ri•yal (rē-ôl', -äl') *n.* —See table at CURRENCY.
ri•yal-o•man•i (rē-ôl'ō-mä'nē, rē-äl'-) *n.* —See table at CURRENCY.
Rn *symbol for* RADON.
RNA (är'ĕn-ā') *n.* Ribonucleic acid.
roach[1] (rōch) *n.* A N European freshwater fish, *Rutilus rutilus.*
roach[2] (rōch) *n.* **1.** The cockroach. **2.** *Slang.* The butt of a marijuana cigarette.
road (rōd) *n.* **1.** An open, gen. public way for moving vehicles, persons, and animals. **2.** A course or path. **3. roads.** An anchorage for ships.
road•bed (rōd'bĕd') *n.* **1.** The foundation on which railroad ties, rails, and ballast are laid. **2.** The foundation of a road.
road•block (rōd'blŏk') *n.* **1.** An obstruction set up on a road to prevent or monitor passage. **2.** An obstacle : hindrance.
road•run•ner (rōd'rŭn'ər) *n.* A swift-running crested bird, *Geococcyx californianus,* of SW North America.
road•stead (rōd'stĕd') *n Naut.* A sheltered offshore anchorage area for ships.
road•ster (rōd'stər) *n.* An open car with a single wide seat.
road•way (rōd'wā') *n.* A road, esp. the part used by vehicles.
road•work (rōd'wûrk') *n.* **1.** Road construction or repairs. **2.** Physical training consisting of long outdoor runs.
roam (rōm) *v.* To move or travel aimlessly (through) : wander. **—roam'er** *n.*
roan (rōn) *adj.* Having a dark coat thickly sprinkled with white or gray <a *roan* colt> —*n.* A roan animal.
roar (rôr) *v.* **1.** To utter a long, deep, loud sound, esp. in rage or excitement. **2.** To utter with a long, deep, loud sound. **3.** To laugh loudly. **—roar** *n.* **—roar'er** *n.*
roast (rōst) *v.* **1.** To cook with dry heat. **2.** To expose to great heat. **3.** *Metallurgy.* To heat (ore) in order to purify, dehydrate, or oxidize. **4.** *Informal.* To criticize harshly. —*n.* **1.** A cut of meat suitable for roasting. **2.** An outing at which food is roasted.
rob (rŏb) *v.* **robbed, rob•bing. 1.** To take property unlawfully (from) : steal. **2.** To deprive unjustly <*robbed* me of my peace of mind> ★ ***syns:*** HEIST, HIT, HOLD UP, KNOCK OFF, RIP OFF, STICK UP. **—rob'ber** *n.* **—rob'ber•y** *n.*
robe (rōb) *n.* **1.** A long, flowing outer garment, esp. one worn on ceremonial occasions. **2.** A dressing gown or bathrobe. **3.** A blanket for the lap and legs. —*v.* **robed, rob•ing.** To dress in or don a robe.
rob•in (rŏb'ĭn) *n.* **1.** A North American songbird, *Turdus migratorius,* with a red breast and dark plumage. **2.** A small Old World bird, *Erithacus rubecula,* having an orange breast and a brown back.
ro•bot (rō'bət, -bŏt') *n.* **1.** A machine that looks like a human being and has the capacity to perform human tasks. **2.** A person who works mechanically. **3.** An automatic or remote-controlled device. **—ro•bot'ic** *adj.*
▲ ***word history:*** The word *robot* was invented by the Czech author Karel Čapek in his play *R.U.R.,* which stands for "Rossum's Universal Robots." The play was written in 1920 and was translated into English a few years later. The word *robot* quickly gained currency in English. Čapek derived the word from Czech *robota,* "forced labor, drudgery."
ro•bot•ics (rō-bŏt'ĭks) *n. (sing. in number).* The science and technology of robotic design.
ro•bust (rō-bŭst', rō'bŭst) *adj.* **1.** Full of health and strength : vigorous. **2.** Rich and full. **—ro• bust'ly** *adv.* **—ro•bust'ness** *n.*
roc (rŏk) An enormous, powerful, legendary bird of prey.
rock[1] (rŏk) *n.* **1. a.** A hard, naturally formed material of mineral origin. **b.** A piece of such material : stone. **2.** *Geol.* A mineral mass constituting a significant part of the earth's crust. **3.** One who is firm or dependable. **4. rocks.** *Slang.* Money. **—on the rocks. 1.** In or close to ruin. **2.** Served over ice cubes.
rock[2] (rŏk) *v.* **1.** To move back and forth, esp. rhythmically. **2.** To shake or sway violently, as from a blow. —*n.* **1.** A rocking motion. **2.** Rock 'n' roll.
rock-and-roll (rŏk'ən-rōl') *n. var. of* ROCK 'N' ROLL.
rock-bound (rŏk'bound') *adj.* Covered or bordered with rocks.
rock•er (rŏk'ər) *n.* **1.** One that rocks. **2.** A rocking chair. **3.** A curved support on which something, as a rocking chair, rocks.
rock•et (rŏk'ĭt) *n.* **1. a.** A device propelled through the air by a thrust developed by ejection of matter, esp. by the high-speed ejection of gaseous combustion products of solid or liquid fuels. **b.** An engine that produces a thrust in this way. **2.** A rocket-propelled explosive weapon. —*v.* To move rapidly and directly.
rock•et•ry (rŏk'ĭ-trē) *n.* The science and technology of designing, building, and flying rockets.

rock·ing chair (rŏk'ĭng) *n.* A chair mounted on rockers.
rocking horse *n.* A toy horse mounted on rockers.
rock 'n' roll *also* **rock-and-roll** (rŏk'ən-rōl') *n.* Popular music combining elements of blues and country music, marked by a heavily accented beat.
rock-ribbed (rŏk'rĭbd') *adj.* **1.** Rocky. **2.** Unyielding **:** stern.
rock salt *n.* Common salt in large chunks.
rock·y[1] (rŏk'ē) *adj.* **-i·er, -i·est. 1.** Made of, covered with, or full of rocks. **2.** Like rock, as in hardness. **—rock'i·ness** *n.*
rock·y[2] (rŏk'ē) *adj.* **-i·er, -i·est. 1.** Inclined or prone to sway unsteadily **:** shaky. **2.** Weak or dizzy. **—rock'i·ness** *n.*
ro·co·co (rə-kō'kō, rō'kə-kō') *adj.* **1.** Of or designating an artistic style marked by florid, ornate asymmetric ornamentation. **2.** Excessively elaborate. **—ro·co'co** *n.*
rod (rŏd) *n.* **1.** A thin, straight stick or bar. **2. a.** A stick used for whipping. **b.** Punishment. **3.** A fishing rod. **4.** A staff symbolizing rank or office. **5.** A measuring stick. **6.** —See table at MEASUREMENT.
rode (rōd) *v. p.t.* of RIDE.
ro·dent (rōd'nt) *n.* A mammal of the order Rodentia, as a mouse, rat, or beaver, having large incisors adapted for gnawing.
ro·de·o (rō'dē-ō', rō-dā'ō) *n., pl.* **-os. 1.** A cattle roundup. **2.** A public show featuring cowboy skills and competitions.
roe[1] (rō) *n.* The egg-laden ovary of a fish.
roe[2] (rō) *n.* The roe deer.
roe deer *n.* A small, delicately formed Eurasian deer, *Capreolus capreolus.*
roent·gen (rĕnt'gən, rŭnt'-) *n.* A unit of exposure to ionizing radiation, such as x-rays or gamma rays.
rog·er (rŏj'ər) *interj.* —Used in radio communications to indicate that a message has been received.
rogue (rōg) *n.* **1.** An unprincipled person **:** scoundrel. **2.** A playfully mischievous person **:** scamp. **—rog'uer·y** *n.* **—rog'uish** *adj.* **—rog'uish·ly** *adv.*
roil (roil) *v.* **1.** To make (a liquid) cloudy by stirring up sediment. **2.** To disturb **:** vex.
role *also* **rôle** (rōl) *n.* **1.** A part played by an actor. **2.** A function or position.
roll (rōl) *v.* **1.** To move on a surface by turning over and over. **2.** To move on wheels or rollers. **3.** To move with steady or increasing momentum. **4.** To go by **:** pass <The months *rolled* on.> **5.** To recur periodically. **6.** To sway or cause to sway from side to side, as a ship. **7.** To make a deep, prolonged sound, as thunder. **8.** To rotate <*rolled* his eyes in impatience> **9.** To pronounce with a trill <*roll* one's r's> **10.** To wrap (something) round and round upon itself or a center. **11.** To enfold in a covering. **12.** To spread or flatten with a roller <*roll* dough> **13.** To throw (dice). **—roll back.** To reduce to a previous level. —*n.* **1.** An act of rolling. **2.** Something rolled up in a cylinder. **3.** A list of names of members. **4. a.** A small rounded portion of bread. **b.** A food shaped like a tube with a filling <an egg *roll*> **5.** A swaying or rocking motion. **6.** A deep prolonged sound **:** rumble. **7.** A quick succession of short sounds <a drum *roll*>
roll·back (rōl'băk') *n.* A reduction, as of prices or wages, to a previous level.
roll call *n.* A reading aloud of a list of names of people to find out who is present.
roll·er (rō'lər) *n.* **1.** A small spokeless wheel, as on a roller skate. **2.** A rod around which something is wound. **3.** A heavy cylinder for leveling or crushing operations. **4.** A cylinder used for applying a liquid, as paint, to a surface. **5.** A heavy wave that breaks on the shore.
roller bearing *n.* A bearing using rollers to reduce friction between machine parts.
roller coaster *n.* A coiled elevated railway with small open cars operated as an amusement-park ride.
roller skate *n.* A skate with 4 wheels for skating on surfaces other than ice. **—roll'er-skate'** *v.* **—roller skater** *n.*
rol·lick (rŏl'ĭk) *v.* To frolic **:** romp. **—rol'lick** *n.* **—rol'lick·ing** *adj.*
rolling pin *n.* A smooth usu. wood cylinder for rolling dough.
ro·ly-po·ly (rō'lē-pō'lē) *adj.* Short and plump **:** pudgy.
ro·maine (rō-mān') *n.* A variety of lettuce, *Lactuca sativa longifolia,* having dark green leaves in a long, narrow head.
Ro·man (rō'mən) *adj.* **1.** Of or relating to Rome and its people, esp. ancient Rome. **2.** Latin. **3.** Of or relating to the Roman Catholic Church. **4. roman.** Of, set, or printed in the most common type style, characterized by upright letters. —*n.* **1.** A native or resident of Rome, esp. ancient Rome. **2.** Latin. **3. roman.** Roman type. **4. Romans.** —See table at BIBLE.
Roman candle *n.* A firework made of a tube from which balls of fire shoot out.
Roman Catholic Church *n.* The Christian church having the Bishop of Rome as its head. **—Roman Catholic** *adj. & n.* **—Roman Catholicism** *n.*
ro·mance (rō-măns', rō'măns') *n.* **1. a.** A medieval narrative of the adventures of chivalric heroes. **b.** A long, fictitious tale of adventure, heroism, or mystery. **c.** A quality or spirit suggestive of such tales. **2.** A story or film about a love affair. **3. a.** A love affair. **b.** Romantic involvement **:** love. —*adj.* **Romance.** Of, relating to, or designating the languages that developed from Latin, including French, Italian, Portuguese, Romanian, and Spanish. —*v.* (rō-măns') **-manced, -manc·ing. 1.** To invent fanciful stories. **2.** To carry on a courtship or love affair with **:** woo. **—ro·manc'er** *n.*
Ro·man·esque (rō'mə-nĕsk') *adj.* Of, relating to, or designating a style of architecture that prevailed in Europe from the 9th–12th cent. **—Ro'man·esque'** *n.*

Roman numeral *n.* A numeral formed with the characters I, V, X, L, C, D, or M based on the system used by the ancient Romans.

Ro•ma•no (rə-mä'nō, rō-) *n.* A dry, sharp-flavored, hard Italian cheese.

ro•man•tic (rō-măn'tĭk) *adj.* **1.** Of or marked by romance. **2.** Given to thoughts or feelings of adventure, heroism, or love. **3.** Imaginative but impractical : quixotic. **4.** Of love or strong, idealized affection. **5.** Of or characteristic of romanticism in the arts. —*n.* A romantic person.

ro•man•ti•cism (rō-măn'tĭ-sĭz'əm) *n.* An intellectual and artistic movement emphasizing strong emotion, imagination, freer forms, and the opposition of the individual to society. **—ro•man'ti•cist** *n.*

ro•man•ti•cize (rō-măn'tĭ-sīz') *v.* **-cized, -ciz•ing. 1.** To give a quality of adventure, heroism, or mystery to. **2.** To think or talk in a romantic way.

romp (rŏmp) *v.* **1.** To play or frolic boisterously. **2.** *Slang.* To win easily. **—romp** *n.*

romp•er (rŏm'pər) *n.* **1.** One that romps. **2. rompers.** A playsuit with short bloomers worn by small children.

rood (ro͞od) *n.* **1.** A cross or crucifix. **2.** A measure of land area equal to ¼ acre.

roof (ro͞of, ro͝of) *n.* **1.** The outside covering of the top of a building. **2.** The top covering of something <the *roof* of a vehicle> **3.** A vaulted inner structure. —*v.* To furnish or cover with a roof. **—roof'er** *n.*

roof•ing (ro͞o'fĭng, ro͝of'ĭng) *n.* Materials used in building a roof.

rook[1] (ro͝ok) *n.* A crowlike Old World bird, *Corvus frugilegus.* —*v. Slang.* To swindle : cheat.

rook[2] (ro͝ok) *n.* A chess piece that may move in a straight line across any number of unoccupied squares in a rank or file.

rook•er•y (ro͝ok'ə-rē) *n., pl.* **-ies. 1.** A place where rooks nest. **2.** A breeding ground of certain other birds and animals.

rook•ie (ro͝ok'ē) *n. Slang.* **1.** An untrained recruit. **2.** A novice player in sports. **3.** An inexperienced person.

room (ro͞om, ro͝om) *n.* **1.** Space that can be or is occupied. **2. a.** A part of a building set off by walls or partitions. **b.** The people within such an area <The whole *room* fell silent.> **3. rooms.** Living quarters. **4.** Opportunity or leeway. —*v.* To occupy a room. **—room'ful'** *n.* **—room'i•ness** *n.* **—room'y** *adj.*

room•er (ro͞o'mər, ro͝om'ər) *n.* A lodger.

room•ette (ro͞o-mĕt', ro͝om-ĕt') *n.* A small room in a railroad sleeping car.

room•ing house (ro͞o'mĭng, ro͝om'ĭng) *n.* A house where lodgers can rent rooms.

room•mate (ro͝om'māt', ro͞om'-) *n.* A person with whom one shares a room or apartment.

roost (ro͞ost) *n.* **1.** A perch on which birds sleep or rest. **2.** A place with perches for fowl or other birds. —*v.* To rest or sleep on or as if on a roost.

roost•er (ro͞o'stər) *n.* An adult male of the domestic fowl : cock.

root[1] (ro͞ot, ro͝ot) *n.* **1. a.** The usu. underground part of a plant that serves as support and draws water and nutrients from the soil. **b.** A similar underground plant part, as a tuber. **2.** The embedded part of a tooth, hair, or other body structure. **3.** A base : foundation. **4.** A source : origin. **5.** The essential part : heart. **6. roots.** Ties to a place or community. **7.** *Ling.* A word or word element from which other words or inflections are formed. **8.** *Math.* A number that when multiplied by itself an indicated number of times forms a product equal to a specified number <2 is a 4th *root* of 16.> —*v.* **1.** To grow a root or roots. **2.** To become or cause to become firmly established. **3.** To remove by or as if by the roots. **—root'less** *adj.* **—root'like'** *adj.*

root[2] (ro͞ot, ro͝ot) *v.* **1.** To dig with or as if with the snout. **2.** To rummage.

root[3] (ro͞ot, ro͝ot) *v.* **1.** To give encouragement to a team or contestant by cheering. **2.** To lend support. **—root'er** *n.*

root beer *n.* A carbonated soft drink flavored with certain plant-root extracts.

root canal *n.* **1.** A narrow pulp-filled cavity in a root of a tooth. **2.** A treatment in which diseased tissue from the root canal is removed.

root•stock (ro͞ot'stŏk', ro͝ot'-) *n.* **1.** A rhizome. **2.** A root used as a stock for plant propagation.

rope (rōp) *n.* **1.** A heavy, strong cord of twisted fiber. **2.** A string of items joined in one line by twisting, braiding, or beading. **3. ropes.** *Informal.* Specialized procedures or techniques <learned the *ropes*> —*v.* **roped, rop•ing. 1.** To fasten with or as if with rope. **2.** To enclose with a rope <*roped* off the accident scene> **3.** To lasso. **4.** *Informal.* To deceive : trick.

Roque•fort (rōk'fərt). A trademark for a tangy French cheese made from ewes' milk.

ror•qual (rôr'kwəl) *n.* Any of a family of baleen whales with a grooved throat and a small, pointed dorsal fin.

rorqual

Ror•schach test (rôr'shäk', -shäKH) *n.* A psychological test in which a subject's interpretations of standard inkblot patterns are used to analyze personality and detect emotional disorders.

ro·sa·ry (rō′zə-rē) *n., pl.* **-ries.** *Rom. Cath. Ch.* **1.** A series of prayers. **2.** A string of beads for counting prayers.

rose[1] (rōz) *n.* **1.** A shrub or vine of the genus *Rosa,* having prickly stems and variously colored, usu. fragrant flowers. **2.** A deep pink. **3.** A rosette.

rose[2] (rōz) *v. p.t. of* RISE.

ro·sé (rō-zā′) *n.* A pink, light wine.

ro·se·ate (rō′zē-ĭt, -āt′) *adj.* **1.** Rose-colored. **2.** Highly optimistic : cheerful.

rose·bud (rōz′bŭd′) *n.* A bud of a rose.

rose·bush (rōz′bo͝osh′) *n.* A shrub bearing roses.

rose-col·ored (rōz′kŭl′ərd) *adj.* **1.** Of the color rose. **2.** Overoptimistic.

rose·mar·y (rōz′mâr′ē) *n., pl.* **-ies.** An aromatic evergreen shrub, *Rosmarinus officinalis,* with leaves used esp. in cooking.

ro·sette (rō-zĕt′) *n.* **1.** An ornament of ribbon or silk that is gathered to resemble a rose. **2.** A roselike form or marking.

rose water *n.* A fragrant liquid made from rose petals steeped in water, used in cosmetics and cookery.

rose·wood (rōz′wo͝od′) *n.* The hard, often fragrant wood of any of several tropical trees, used in making furniture.

Rosh Ha·sha·nah (rŏsh′ hə-shä′nə, rōsh′) *n.* The Jewish New Year, a religious holiday celebrated in late Sept. or early Oct.

ros·in (rŏz′ĭn) *n.* A translucent resin obtained from the sap of pine trees, used to increase sliding friction on violin bows and as an ingredient in varnish, solder, and other products. **—ros′in·y** *adj.*

ros·ter (rŏs′tər, rô′stər) *n.* A list of names, esp. of personnel available for duty.

ros·trum (rŏs′trəm, rô′strəm) *n., pl.* **-trums** *or* **-tra** (-trə). A raised platform for public speakers.

ros·y (rō′zē) *adj.* **-i·er, -i·est. 1.** Pink or red in color. **2.** Promising : bright. **—ros′i·ly** *adv.* **—ros′i·ness** *n.*

rot (rŏt) *v.* **rot·ted, rot·ting.** To decompose : decay. *—n.* **1. a.** The process of rotting or condition of being rotten. **b.** Rotten matter. **2.** A plant disease marked by the breakdown of tissue. **3.** *Informal.* Foolish talk or writing.

ro·ta·ry (rō′tə-rē) *adj.* Of or marked by rotation, esp. axial rotation. *—n., pl.* **-ries. 1.** Something that rotates around an axis. **2.** A traffic circle.

ro·tate (rō′tāt′) *v.* **-tat·ed, -tat·ing. 1.** To turn on an axis. **2.** To move among positions in a recurring order. **3.** To plant (crops) in a fixed order of succession. **—ro′tat′a·ble** *adj.* **—ro·ta′tion** *n.* **—ro′ta′tor** *n.* **—ro′ta·to′ry** *adj.*

rote (rōt) *n.* **1.** Memorization by repetition without full comprehension. **2.** Thoughtless, mechanical repetition.

ro·tis·ser·ie (rō-tĭs′ə-rē) *n.* A cooking device with a rotating spit for roasting food.

ro·to·gra·vure (rō′tə-grə-vyo͝or′) *n.* **1.** An intaglio printing process in which the impression is transferred from an etched copper cylinder in a rotary printing press. **2.** The material printed by rotogravure.

ro·tor (rō′tər) *n.* **1.** A rotating part of an electrical or mechanical device. **2.** The assembly of rotating horizontal blades that supports a helicopter.

rot·ten (rŏt′n) *adj.* **1.** Decayed : decomposed. **2.** Putrid : fetid. **3.** Morally corrupt. **4.** Very bad : wretched <*rotten* luck>

rott·wei·ler (rŏt′wī′lər, rôt′vī′-) *n.* A German breed of dog having a stocky body, short black fur, and tan face markings.

ro·tund (rō-tŭnd′) *adj.* Rounded : plump. **—ro·tun′di·ty** *n.*

ro·tun·da (rō-tŭn′də) *n.* A circular building or hall, esp. one with a dome.

rou·ble (ro͞o′bəl) *n. var. of* RUBLE.

rou·é (ro͞o-ā′) *n.* A lecherous man : rake.

rouge (ro͞ozh) *n.* **1.** A red or pink cosmetic for coloring the cheeks or lips. **2.** A reddish powder used to polish metal and gems.

rough (rŭf) *adj.* **1.** Having an irregular surface : not smooth **2.** In violent motion : turbulent. **3.** Not gentle : violent or harsh <*rough* handling> **4.** Rude : uncouth. **5.** Difficult : trying. **6.** Harsh : grating. **7.** In a natural state <*rough* gems> **8.** Done hastily or incompletely <a *rough* sketch> *—n.* **1.** Rugged, overgrown ground. **2.** A crude or unfinished condition. **3.** A crude person : boor. *—v.* **1.** To make rough. **2.** To manhandle. **3.** To make or do hastily or incompletely <*rough* out a plan> **—rough′ly** *adv.* **—rough′ness** *n.*

rough·age (rŭf′ĭj) *n.* The coarse, indigestible parts of certain foods, as bran, that stimulate peristalsis.

rough·en (rŭf′ən) *v.* To make or become rough.

rough·hew (rŭf′hyo͞o′) *v.* **1.** To hew (e.g., timber) roughly, without finishing. **2.** To make in rough form.

rough·house (rŭf′hous′) *n.* Rowdy, boisterous play. **—rough′house′** *v.*

rough·neck (rŭf′nĕk′) *n.* A rowdy or uncouth person.

rough·shod (rŭf′shŏd′) *adj.* Marked by brutal force.

rou·lette (ro͞o-lĕt′) *n.* **1.** A gambling game in which players bet on which slot of a rotating disk a small ball will come to rest. **2.** A tool with a rotating toothed disk for making rows of dots or slits.

round (round) *adj.* **1.** Ball-shaped : spherical. **2.** Curved. **3.** Circular. **4.** Whole : full. **5.** Expressed as a whole number. **6.** Not exact : approximate. **7.** Full in tone : sonorous. *—n.* **1.** Something round, as a circle, globe, or disk. **2.** The hind leg of beef between the shank and rump. **3.** A recurring course or succession. **4.** *often* **rounds.** A series of customary or prescribed acts or stops <a postman on his *rounds*> **5.** A single distribution among members of a group <a *round* of drinks> **6.** An outburst of cheering or applause. **7.** A single shot or cartridge. **8.** An interval of play or action in various games. **9.** *Mus.* A composition in which each voice enters at a different time with the same melody. —*v.* **1.** To make or become round. **2.** To make or become plump : fill out. **3.** To bring to an end : finish. **4.** To go around. **5.** To surround. **6.** To express as a round number. —**round up.** To bring together. —*adv.* Around. —*prep.* **1.** Around. **2.** Throughout <*round* the year> —**in the round. 1.** Free standing <sculpture *in the round*> **2.** With the stage in the center of the audience.

round•a•bout (round'ə-bout') *adj.* Not direct : circuitous.

roun•de•lay (roun'də-lā') *n.* A poem or song with a regularly recurring refrain.

round•house (round'hous') *n.* **1.** A circular building for storing, servicing, and switching locomotives. **2.** A punch delivered with a sweeping sidearm movement.

round robin *n.* **1.** A tournament in which each contestant plays every other contestant in turn. **2.** A letter circulated among the members of a group.

round-shoul•dered (round'shōl'dərd) *adj.* Having the shoulders and upper back bent forward : stooped.

round table *n.* A discussion or conference with several participants.

round-the-clock (round'*thə*-klŏk') *adj.* Throughout a 24-hour day : continuous.

round trip *n.* A trip to a place and back, usu. over the same route.

round•up (round'ŭp') *n.* **1.** The herding together of cattle, as for shipping. **2.** A gathering up, as of suspects by the police. **3.** A summary.

round•worm (round'wûrm') *n.* A nematode.

rouse (rouz) *v.* **roused, rous•ing. 1.** To awaken from sleep or unconsciousness : arouse. **2.** To stir up, as to action : excite.

roust•a•bout (rou'stə-bout') *n.* **1.** An unskilled worker, esp. on a wharf or in an oil field. **2.** A laborer in a circus.

rout[1] (rout) *n.* **1.** A disorderly retreat. **2.** An overwhelming defeat. —**rout** *v.*

rout[2] (rout) *v.* **1.** To drive from a resting or hiding place. **2.** To dig up or gouge out. **3.** To rummage. —**rout'er** *n.*

route (ro͞ot, rout) *n.* **1. a.** A way for traveling : course. **b.** A means of achieving a goal. **2.** A regular course of travel. **3.** A highway. —*v.* **rout•ed, rout•ing. 1.** To send by a certain route. **2.** To assign a route to.

rou•tine (ro͞o-tēn') *n.* **1.** A series of activities performed regularly. **2.** A regularly performed show or presentation. —*adj.* **1.** According to standard procedure. **2.** Ordinary.

roux (ro͞o) *n.* A mixture of flour and fat cooked together and used as a thickening.

rove (rōv) *v.* **roved, rov•ing.** To wander about, esp. over a wide area : roam. —**rov'er** *n.* —**rov'ing** *adj.*

row[1] (rō) *n.* **1.** A number of persons or objects positioned next to each other, usu. in a straight line. **2.** A continuous line of buildings on a street. **3.** Succession <3 years in a *row*>

row[2] (rō) *v.* **1.** To propel (a boat) with oars. **2.** To carry or travel in a rowboat. —*n.* A trip by rowboat. —**row'er** *n.*

row[3] (rou) *n.* A noisy quarrel. —**row** *v.*

row•boat (rō'bōt') *n.* A small boat propelled by oars.

row•dy (rou'dē) *adj.* **-di•er, -di•est.** Noisy and disorderly. —**row'di•ness, row'dy•ism** *n.* —**row'dy** *n.*

row•el (rou'əl) *n.* A small toothed wheel inserted into a spur. —**row'el** *v.*

roy•al (roi'əl) *adj.* **1.** Of or relating to a king or queen. **2.** Fit for royalty : grand.

roy•al•ist (roi'ə-lĭst) *n.* A supporter of government by monarchs. —**roy'al•ism** *n.*

roy•al•ty (roi'əl-tē) *n., pl.* **-ties. 1.** Monarchs and their families as a group. **2.** The authority or status of monarchs. **3.** Royal quality or bearing. **4. a.** A share of the proceeds from the sale or performance of a work paid to the author or composer. **b.** A payment to an inventor or proprietor for the right to use his invention or services.

Ru *symbol for* RUTHENIUM.

rub (rŭb) *v.* **rubbed, rub•bing. 1.** To subject (a surface) to pressure and friction. **2.** To cause to move firmly along a surface. **3.** To contact or cause to contact with friction. **4.** To irritate : chafe. —**rub down.** To massage. —**rub out. 1.** To obliterate. **2.** *Slang.* To kill. —*n.* **1.** An act of rubbing. **2.** A massage. **3.** A difficulty : catch.

rub•ber[1] (rŭb'ər) *n.* **1.** A solid, elastic substance, derived from the coagulated and processed sap of various tropical plants or made synthetically. **2.** Something made of rubber, esp.: **a.** A waterproof overshoe. **b.** An eraser. **c.** *Slang.* A condom. **3.** One that rubs. —**rub'ber•y** *adj.*

▲ ***word history:*** The noun *rubber*[1], denoting a substance made from the sap of the rubber tree, is derived from the verb *rub,* since one of the first uses of this substance was rubbing out pencil marks.

rub•ber[2] (rŭb'ər) *n.* **1.** A series of games, as in bridge, of which a majority must be won to end play. **2.** An odd-numbered game that breaks a tie.

rubber band *n.* An elastic loop of rubber used to hold objects together.

rubber cement *n.* An adhesive of nonvulcanized rubber.

rub•ber•ize (rŭb'ə-rīz') *v.* **-ized, -iz•ing.** To treat or coat with rubber.

rub•ber•neck (rŭb'ər-nĕk') *v.* To stare wonderingly or inquisitively : gawk.

rub•bing (rŭb'ĭng) *n.* A representation of a raised or incised surface obtained by putting paper over the surface and rubbing with a marking agent.

rub•bish (rŭb'ĭsh) *n.* **1.** Worthless material : trash. **2.** Foolish talk : nonsense.

rub•ble (rŭb'əl) *n.* **1.** Fragments of crumbled rock or masonry. **2.** Irregular pieces of rock used in masonry.

rub•down (rŭb'doun') *n.* A massage.

rube (rōōb) *n. Slang.* An unsophisticated country person : bumpkin.
ru•bel•la (rōō-bĕl'ə) *n.* German measles.
ru•bi•cund (rōō'bĭ-kənd) *adj.* Ruddy. **—ru'bi•cun'di•ty** (-kŭn'dĭ-tē) *n.*
ru•bid•i•um (rōō-bĭd'ē-əm) *n. Symbol* **Rb** A soft, silvery, highly reactive element used in photoelectric cells.
ru•ble *or* **rou•ble** (rōō'bəl) *n.* —See table at CURRENCY.
ru•bric (rōō'brĭk) *n.* **1.** A title, heading, or initial letter of a manuscript or book, esp. when printed in ornamental red lettering. **2.** The name of a class or category. **3.** A direction in a liturgical book.
ru•by (rōō'bē) *n., pl.* **-bies. 1.** A deep-red, translucent corundum, greatly valued as a precious stone. **2.** A deep red. **—ru'by** *adj.*
ruche (rōōsh) *n.* A ruffle or pleat of fine fabric, as lace, used for trimming.
ruck•sack (rŭk'săk', rŏŏk'-) *n.* A knapsack.
ruck•us (rŭk'əs) *n. Informal.* A noisy disturbance.
rud•der (rŭd'ər) *n.* A hinged structure attached vertically to the stern of a vessel or aircraft for steering.
rud•dy (rŭd'ē) *adj.* **-di•er, -di•est.** Reddish or rosy, esp. in complexion. **—rud'di•ness** *n.*
rude (rōōd) *adj.* **rud•er, rud•est. 1.** Primitive : uncivilized. **2.** Lowly : humble. **3.** Ill-mannered : discourteous. **4.** Crude : makeshift. **5.** Abrupt : jarring <a *rude* surprise> ★ ***syns:*** DISCOURTEOUS, ILL-MANNERED, IMPOLITE, UNMANNERLY **—rude'ness** *n.*
ru•di•ment (rōō'də-mənt) *n. often* **rudiments 1.** A fundamental principle, element, or skill. **2.** Something in an undeveloped form : beginning. **3.** *Biol.* Vestigial. **—ru'di•men'ta•ry** (-mĕn'tə-rē) *adj.*
rue[1] (rōō) *v.* **rued, ru•ing.** To feel regret or sorrow (for). **—rue'ful** *adj.* **—rue'ful•ly** *adv.* **—rue'ful•ness** *n.*
rue[2] (rōō) *n.* An aromatic Eurasian plant, *Ruta graveolens,* with leaves that yield a volatile oil once used medicinally.
ruff (rŭf) *n.* **1.** A stiff, frilled or pleated circular collar worn in the 16th–17th cent. **2.** A collarlike fringe of feathers or fur around the neck of a bird or animal.
ruf•fi•an (rŭf'ē-ən, rŭf'yən) *n.* **1.** A rowdy fellow : tough. **2.** A thug.
ruf•fle (rŭf'əl) *n.* **1.** A decorative band of frilled or pleated fabric. **2.** A ruff. **3.** An annoyance : vexation. **4.** A ripple. *—v.* **-fled, -fling. 1.** To gather (fabric) into a ruffle. **2.** To erect (feathers or fur). **3.** To make or become rough or irregular. **4.** To fluster : discompose.
ru•fi•yaa (rōō'fē-yä') *n.* —See table at CURRENCY.
ru•fous (rōō'fəs) *adj.* Reddish to reddish-orange.
rug (rŭg) *n.* **1.** A piece of heavy fabric for covering a floor. **2.** *esp. Brit.* A piece of warm fabric or fur for the lap or legs.
rug•by (rŭg'bē) *n.* A kind of football in which players may kick, dribble, or run with the ball.
rug•ged (rŭg'ĭd) *adj.* **1.** Having a rough, irregular surface. **2.** Having strong features and deep wrinkles or furrows. **3.** Stormy : turbulent. **4.** Difficult to do or endure. **5.** Robust : hardy. **—rug'ged•ness** *n.*
rug•ger (rŭg'ər) *n. esp. Brit.* Rugby.
ru•in (rōō'ĭn) *n.* **1.** Total destruction or collapse. **2.** Total loss or defeat. **3.** The cause of total destruction or loss. **4.** *often* **ruins.** The remains of something destroyed or collapsed. *—v.* **1.** To destroy utterly. **2.** To injure or harm irreparably. **3.** To reduce to poverty : bankrupt. **—ru'in•a'tion** *n.* **—ru'in•ous** *adj.*
rule (rōōl) *n.* **1.** The act or power of governing. **2.** An authoritative statement of what may or may not be done : regulation. **3.** A usual or prevailing way of acting. **4.** A statement of what is true in most or all cases. **5.** A standard procedure or method. **6.** A straightedge : ruler. *—v.* **ruled, rul•ing. 1.** To exercise authority (over) : govern. **2.** To dominate by strong influence <*ruled* by his passions> **3.** To determine judicially : decree. **4.** To mark with straight parallel lines. **—rule out.** To exclude.
rul•er (rōō'lər) *n.* **1.** One that rules, esp. a sovereign. **2.** A straight rigid strip, as of wood or metal, for measuring lengths or drawing straight lines.
rul•ing (rōō'lĭng) *adj.* **1.** Exercising authority : governing. **2.** Predominant. *—n.* An official decision <a judge's *ruling*>
rum (rŭm) *n.* An alcoholic liquor distilled from fermented sugar cane or molasses.
rum•ba (rŭm'bə, rōōm'-) *n.* A rhythmical dance originating in Cuba or an adaptation of it. **—rum'ba** *v.*
rum•ble (rŭm'bəl) *v.* **-bled, -bling. 1.** To make a long, deep, rolling sound. **2.** To move with a rumbling sound. *—n.* **1.** A long, deep, rolling sound. **2.** Widespread expression of unrest. **3.** *Slang.* A gang fight. **4.** A separate compartment or seat at the rear of a carriage or automobile.
ru•mi•nant (rōō'mə-nənt) *n.* Any of various hoofed, cud-chewing mammals of the suborder Ruminantia, as a cow, sheep, deer, or giraffe. *—adj.* **1.** Cud-chewing. **2.** Meditative : reflective.
ru•mi•nate (rōō'mə-nāt') *v.* **-nat•ed, -nat•ing. 1.** To chew cud. **2.** To think or ponder at length. **—ru'mi•na'tion** *n.* **—ru'mi•na'tive** *adj.* **—ru'mi•na'tor** *n.*
rum•mage (rŭm'ĭj) *v.* **-maged, -mag•ing. 1.** To search thoroughly by turning over or disarranging things. **2.** To discover by searching in this way. **—rum'mage** *n.*
rum•my (rŭm'ē) *n.* A card game, the object of which is to procure sets of 3 or more cards of the same suit or rank.
ru•mor (rōō'mər) *n.* **1.** Information of uncertain truthfulness, usu. spread by talk. **2.** Hearsay. *—v.* To spread or tell by rumor.
ru•mour (rōō'mər) *n. & v. esp. Brit. var. of* RUMOR.
rump (rŭmp) *n.* **1. a.** An animal's fleshy hindquarters. **b.** A cut of meat from this part. **2.**

The human buttocks. **3.** A small remaining part.

rum·ple (rŭm'pəl) *v.* **-pled, -pling.** To form into untidy folds or creases : wrinkle or muss up. **—rum'ple** *n.* **—rum'ply** *adj.*

rum·pus (rŭm'pəs) *n.* A noisy ruckus.

rumpus room *n.* A family recreation room, often in the basement.

run (rŭn) *v.* **ran** (răn), **run, run·ning. 1.** To move swiftly on foot with both feet leaving the ground during each stride. **2.** To depart rapidly : flee. **3.** To carry at a rapid pace <*ran* the ball 12 yards> **4.** To make a quick trip or visit, esp. on foot or on wheels. **5.** To move about at will. **6.** To swim in large numbers, as migrating fish do. **7.** To turn for help : resort. **8.** To go on a regular route <The ferry *runs* hourly.> **9.** To drive : chase <*ran* him out of town> **10.** To become in the course of time. **11.** To participate or cause to participate in a race. **12.** To compete or present for elective office. **13.** To finish a race or contest in a specified position <*ran* 3rd in the primary> **14.** *Naut.* To sail or steer. **15.** To flow and spread, as dyes do in fabric. **16.** To flow or cause to flow <*run* water over dishes> **17.** To discharge (a liquid). **18.** To move or pass quickly <*ran* his toes through the grass> **19.** To thrust. **20.** To pass through by force <*run* a blockade> **21.** To subject oneself to <*run* a risk> **22.** To extend : stretch. **23.** To spread or climb while growing. **24.** To remain in effect <The contract *runs* for 2 years.> **25.** To vary : range <reactions that *ran* from dismay to delight> **26.** To incline : tend. **27. a.** To put or be in operation <*run* an engine><a motor that *runs* well> **b.** *Computer Sci.* To process or execute (a program or instruction). **28.** To manage : direct. **29.** To publish : print. **30.** To tear or unravel along a line <The stocking *ran.*> **31.** To recur <The defect *runs* in the family.> **32.** To accumulate <*run* up a big bill> **—run across.** To find by chance. **—run along.** To leave. **—run down. 1.** To stop for lack of power. **2.** To collide with and knock down. **3.** To chase and capture. **4.** To trace to a source. **—run in.** *Slang.* To arrest. **—run off.** To duplicate : copy. **—run out.** To become used up or exhausted. **—run through.** To present, rehearse, or examine quickly. —*n.* **1.** A pace faster than a walk. **2. a.** An act or period of running. **b.** A distance covered by running. **3.** A quick trip or visit. **4.** *Baseball.* A score made by advancing around the bases and reaching home plate safely. **5.** A migration of fish. **6.** Unrestricted freedom or use. **7.** A track or slope, as for skiers. **8.** A regular or scheduled route. **9.** A continuous period of operation, as of a printing press. **10.** A movement or flow. **11.** A small fast-flowing brook. **12.** A pipe or channel through which something flows. **13.** A continuous length, extent, series, or sequence <a *run* of bricks><a *run* of cold winters> **14.** A vein or seam, as of ore. **15.** A direction or tendency <the *run* of the grain in leather> **16.** An enclosure for domestic animals <a chicken *run*> **17.** A length of torn or unraveled stitches in fabric. **18.** A series of unexpected, urgent demands, as by bank depositors. **19.** A sustained condition <a *run* of bad luck> **20.** The average or common kind <the broad *run* of humanity> **—on the run. 1.** Hurrying about busily. **2.** In hiding or retreat.

run·a·bout (rŭn'ə-bout') *n.* A small, light auto, carriage, or motorboat.

run-a·round (rŭn'ə-round') *n.* Treatment marked by evasions, delays, or misinformation.

run·a·way (rŭn'ə-wā') *n.* **1.** One that has run away. **2.** *Informal.* An easy victory. —*adj.* **1.** Escaping or having escaped confinement. **2.** Out of control. **3.** Easily won.

run-down (rŭn'doun') *n.* A point-by-point summary. —*adj.* **1.** Falling apart : dilapidated. **2.** Worn-out : exhausted.

rune (ro͞on) *n.* **1.** One of the letters of an alphabet used by ancient Scandinavians and other Germanic peoples. **2.** A magic charm. **—ru'nic** *adj.*

rung[1] (rŭng) *n.* **1.** A bar that forms a step of a ladder. **2.** A crosspiece between the legs of a chair. **3.** A spoke of a wheel.

rung[2] (rŭng) *v. p.p. of* RING[2].

run-in (rŭn'ĭn') *n.* A quarrel : argument.

run·ner (rŭn'ər) *n.* **1.** One who runs. **2.** A contestant in a race. **3.** One who performs errands or delivers messages. **4.** A smuggler. **5.** A part that slides, esp.: **a.** The blade of an ice skate. **b.** One of the parallel structures on which a sled or sleigh moves. **6.** A supporting structure or groove in which a drawer or door slides. **7.** A long narrow carpet. **8.** *Bot.* **a.** A slender creeping stem that puts forth roots at intervals along its length. **b.** A plant with such a stem.

run·ner-up (rŭn'ər-ŭp') *n.* A contestant that takes 2nd place.

run·ning (rŭn'ĭng) *n.* **1.** The sport or activity of one who runs. **2.** Competition <in the *running* for the award> —*adj.* Continuous. —*adv.* Consecutively.

running mate *n.* The candidate or nominee for the lesser of 2 closely associated political offices.

run·ny (rŭn'ē) *adj.* **-ni·er, -ni·est.** Inclined to flow or discharge fluid.

run-off (rŭn'ôf', -ŏf') *n.* **1.** Overflow from a container. **2.** An added competition for breaking a tie.

run-of-the-mill (rŭn'əv-*th*ə-mĭl') *adj.* Not exceptional : ordinary.

runt (rŭnt) *n.* **1.** A small animal, esp. the smallest in a litter. **2.** A very small person. **—runt'i·ness** *n.* **—runt'y** *adj.*

run-through (rŭn'thro͞o') *n.* A complete but fast review or performance, as of a play.

run·way (rŭn'wā') *n.* **1.** A path or channel over which something runs. **2.** A narrow platform extending from a stage into an auditorium. **3.** A strip of paved level ground for aircraft to take off and land.

ru·pee (ro͞o-pē', ro͞o'pē) *n.* —See table at CURRENCY.

ru•pi•ah (ro͞o-pē′ə) *n., pl.* **-ah** *or* **-ahs.** —See table at CURRENCY.

rup•ture (rŭp′chər) *n.* **1.** The act of bursting or breaking open. **2.** A break in friendly or normal relations. **3.** A hernia. **—rup′tur•a•ble** *adj.* **—rup′ture** *v.*

ru•ral (ro͝or′əl) *adj.* Of the country or country life. **—ru•rual′i•ty** *n.*

ruse (ro͞os, ro͞oz) *n.* An action meant to confuse or mislead : wily deception.

rush[1] (rŭsh) *v.* **1.** To move or cause to move swiftly. **2.** To attack : charge <*rushed* the fort> **3.** To perform hastily. ★ ***syns:*** DASH, HASTEN, HURRY, HUSTLE, RACE, RUN, SCURRY, SPEED —*n.* **1.** A swift forward motion. **2.** Impatient movement toward or from a place. **3.** General haste or busyness. **4.** A sudden attack. **5.** A rapid, often noisy flow. —*adj.* Requiring haste.

rush[2] (rŭsh) *n.* A marsh plant of the family Juncaceae, with pliant hollow or pithy stems used to make baskets and mats.

rusk (rŭsk) *n.* Sweet raised bread baked until browned and dried.

rus•set (rŭs′ĭt) *n.* **1.** A reddish brown. **2.** A type of apple with a rough reddish-brown skin. **—rus′set** *adj.*

rust (rŭst) *n.* **1.** Any of various scaly or powdery reddish-brown ferric oxides that form a coating on iron and iron-containing materials exposed to oxygen and moisture. **2.** A plant disease caused by various parasitic fungi that make reddish or brownish spots on leaves and stems. **3.** A reddish brown. —*v.* **1.** To form rust (on). **2.** To corrode. **3.** To deteriorate through neglect or inactivity. **—rust′y** *adj.*

rus•tic (rŭs′tĭk) *adj.* **1.** Of or characteristic of country life : rural. **2.** Not sophisticated. **3.** Made of rough tree branches <a *rustic* shelter> —*n.* **1.** A rural person. **2.** A crude or simple person. **—rus′ti•cal•ly** *adv.* **—rus•tic′i•ty** (-tĭs′ĭ-tē) *n.*

rus•ti•cate (rŭs′tĭ-kāt′) *v.* **-cat•ed, -cat•ing.** To go or send to live in the country. **—rus′ti•ca′tion** *n.* **—rus′ti•ca′tor** *n.*

rus•tle (rŭs′əl) *v.* **-tled, -tling. 1.** To move or cause to move with soft crackling or fluttering sounds. **2.** *Informal.* To make or get by acting hastily <*rustle* up some food> **3.** To steal (cattle). **—rus′tle** *n.* **—rus′tler** *n.* **—rus′tling•ly** *adv.*

rut[1] (rŭt) *n.* **1.** A sunken track made by the wheels of passing vehicles. **2.** A fixed, unvarying routine. **—rut′ted** *adj.*

rut[2] (rŭt) *n.* A cyclically recurring condition of sexual excitement and activity, esp. in male deer.

ru•ta•ba•ga (ro͞o′tə-bā′gə) *n.* A Eurasian plant, *Brassica napobrassica,* having a thick, bulbous root used as food and fodder.

Ruth (ro͞oth) *n.* —See table at BIBLE.

ru•the•ni•um (ro͞o-thē′nē-əm) *n. Symbol* **Ru** A hard, white, acid-resistant metallic element.

ruth•less (ro͞oth′lĭs) *adj.* Lacking compassion : merciless. **—ruth′less•ly** *adv.*

RV (är′vē′) *n.* A recreational vehicle.

Rx (är′ĕks′) *n.* **1.** A prescription for medicine or medical appliances. **2.** A cure, remedy, or solution for a problem or a disorder.

▲ ***word history:*** There is no *x* in *Rx.* The spelling is an attempt to represent in ordinary letters the symbol ℞, which is merely a capital *R* with a slash through the tail. ℞ is a symbol for *recipe,* which orig. meant "a medicinal prescription" and only later came to mean "a formula used in cooking." *Recipe* is the imperative form of Latin *recipere,* "to take, receive." In Medieval Latin *recipe* often occurred as the first word of medicinal prescriptions directing one to take a certain quantity of a preparation.

rye (rī) *n.* **1.** A widely cultivated cereal grass, *Secale cereale,* whose seeds are used to make flour and whiskey. **2.** Whiskey distilled from rye.

Ss

s *or* **S** (ĕs) *n., pl.* **s's** *or* **S's. 1.** The 19th letter of the English alphabet. **2.** A speech sound represented by the letter *s.* **3. S** A grade indicating that a student's work is satisfactory. **4.** Something with the shape of the letter S.

S *symbol for* SULFUR.

–s[1] *suff.* Used to form plural nouns <book*s*>

–s[2] *suff.* Used to form the 3rd person sing. present tense of regular and most irregular verbs <walk*s*> <hit*s*>

–s[3] *suff.* Used to form adverbs <caught unaware*s* in the storm>

–'s *suff.* Used to form the possessive case <state'*s*> <women'*s*>

Sab•bath (săb′əth) *n.* **1.** Saturday, the 7th day of the week, set apart as a day of worship by Jews and some Christians. **2.** Sunday, the 1st day of the week, set apart as a day of worship by most Christians.

sab•bat•i•cal year *also* **sabbatical** (sə-băt′ĭ-kəl) *n.* A leave from work, esp. a paid leave of absence granted, as to a professor, usu. every 7th year, for rest, study, etc.

sa•ber (sā′bər) *n.* **1.** A cavalry sword with a single-edged curved blade. **2.** A light double-edged sword used in fencing.

Sa•bin vaccine (sā′bĭn) *n.* A polio vaccine administered orally.

sa•ble (sā′bəl) *n.* **1.** A carnivorous mammal, *Martes zibellina,* of N Europe and Asia, having soft dark fur. **2. a.** The color black, esp. in

heraldry. **b. sables.** Black mourning garments. **—sa′ble** *adj.*
sab•o•tage (săb′ə-täzh′) *n.* **1.** Destruction of property or obstruction of normal operations, as by enemy agents in a war. **2.** Treacherous action to defeat or hinder an endeavor. **—sab′o•tage′** *v.*
sab•o•teur (săb′ə-tûr′) *n.* A person who commits sabotage.
sa•bre (sā′bər) *n. esp. Brit. var. of* SABER.
sac (săk) *n.* A baglike or pouchlike part of an animal or plant.
sac•cha•rin (săk′ər-ĭn) *n.* A very sweet white crystalline powder used as a substitute for sugar.
sac•cha•rine (săk′ər-ĭn) *adj.* **1.** Of or like sugar : sweet. **2.** Insincerely or sickeningly sweet <a *saccharine* smile>
sac•er•do•tal (săs′ər-dōt′l, săk′-) *adj.* Of or relating to priests or the priesthood.
sa•chem (sā′chəm) *n.* A chief of an American Indian, esp. Algonquian tribe or confederation.
sa•chet (să-shā′) *n.* A small bag or packet filled with a sweet-smelling substance and used to scent clothes and linens.
sack[1] (săk) *n.* **1. a.** A large bag of strong, coarse material. **b.** A smaller bag, esp. of paper. **2.** *also* **sacque.** A loose-fitting garment for women and children. **3.** *Slang.* Dismissal from a job or position <got the *sack* for being late> **4.** *Slang.* A bed, mattress, or sleeping bag. **—***v.* **1.** To put into a sack. **2.** *Slang.* To fire from a job.
sack[2] (săk) *v.* To plunder : loot.
sack[3] (săk) *n.* A dry white wine popular in England in the 16th and 17th cent.
sack•cloth (săk′klôth′, -klŏth′) *n.* **1.** Sacking. **2. a.** A rough cloth of camel's hair, goat's hair, hemp, cotton, or flax. **b.** A garment made of sackcloth and worn as a symbol of sorrow or repentance.
sack•ing (săk′ĭng) *n.* Material, as burlap, used for making sacks.
sa•cra (sā′krə, săk′rə) *n. pl. of* SACRUM.
sac•ra•ment (săk′rə-mənt) *n.* **1.** In Christian churches, the rites instituted by Jesus that confer sanctifying grace. **2.** *often* **Sacrament. a.** The Eucharist. **b.** The consecrated elements of the Eucharist. **—sac′ra•men′tal** *adj.*
sa•cred (sā′krĭd) *adj.* **1.** Dedicated to or reserved for the worship of a deity. **2.** Regarded with religious veneration. **3.** Dedicated to or set apart for a single use, purpose, or person. **4.** Worthy of respect : venerable. **5.** Of or relating to religion. **—sa′cred•ly** *adv.* **—sa′cred•ness** *n.*
sacred cow *n.* One that is immune to attack or criticism.
sac•ri•fice (săk′rə-fīs′) *n.* **1. a.** The act of offering something, as an animal's life, to a deity, as in propitiation. **b.** A victim offered in sacrifice. **2. a.** Forfeiture of something valuable for the sake of something else. **b.** Something given up in this way. **3.** A loss <forced to sell at a *sacrifice*> **4.** *Baseball.* **a.** A fly ball enabling a runner to score after it is caught by a fielder. **b.** A bunt allowing a runner to advance a base while the batter is retired. **—***v.* **-ficed, -fic•ing. 1.** To offer as a sacrifice. **2.** To give up (something valuable) for the sake of something else. **3.** To sell or give at a loss. **4.** *Baseball.* To make a sacrifice. **—sac′ri•fi′cial** (-fĭsh′əl) *adj.*
sac•ri•lege (săk′rə-lĭj) *n.* Desecration, profanation, or theft of something sacred. **—sac′ri•le′gious** (-lĭj′əs, -lē′jəs) *adj.*
sac•ris•tan (săk′rĭ-stən) *n.* **1.** A person in charge of a sacristy. **2.** A sexton.
sac•ris•ty (săk′rĭ-stē) *n., pl.* **-ties.** A room in a church where vestments and sacred articles are kept : vestry.
sac•ro•il•i•ac (săk′rō-ĭl′ē-ăk′) *adj.* Of, relating to, or affecting the sacrum and ilium. **—***n.* The sacroiliac region or cartilage.
sac•ro•sanct (săk′rō-săngkt′) *adj.* Sacred and inviolable. **—sac′ro•sanc′ti•ty** *n.*
sa•crum (sā′krəm, săk′rəm) *n., pl.* **sa•cra** (sā′krə, săk′rə) A triangular bone consisting of 5 fused vertebrae and forming the posterior section of the pelvis. **—sa′cral** (sā′krəl) *adj.*
sad (săd) *adj.* **sad•der, sad•dest. 1.** Marked by unhappiness or sorrow. **2.** Expressing sorrow or regret. **3.** Causing sorrow or gloom. **4.** Deplorable <a *sad* state of affairs> **—sad′ly** *adv.* **—sad′ness** *n.*
sad•den (săd′n) *v.* To make sad.
sad•dle (săd′l) *n.* **1.** A leather seat for a rider, as of an animal or a bicycle. **2.** A cut of meat including a portion of the backbone and both loins. **—***v.* **-dled, -dling. 1.** To put a saddle on. **2.** To load down : encumber <*saddled* with too much work>
sad•dle•bag (săd′l-băg′) *n.* One of a pair of pouches that hang across the back of a horse behind the saddle or over the rear wheel of a bicycle or motorcycle.
sad•dle•bow (săd′l-bō′) *n.* The arched upper front part of a saddle.
saddle horse *n.* A horse bred or trained for riding.
saddle soap *n.* A mild soap used for cleaning and softening leather.
Sad•du•cee (săj′ə-sē′, săd′yə-) *n.* A member of an ancient Jewish sect that retained the older interpretation of the written Mosaic law. **—Sad′du•ce′an** *adj.*
sa•dism (sā′dĭz′əm, săd′ĭz′-) *n.* **1.** Abnormal enjoyment of cruelty. **2.** Extreme cruelty. **—sa′dist** *n.* **—sa•dis′tic** (sə-dĭs′tĭk) *adj.* **—sa•dis′ti•cal•ly** *adv.*
sa•do•mas•o•chism (sā′dō-măs′ə-kĭz′əm, săd′ō-) *n. Psychol.* Derivation of pleasure, esp. sexual gratification, from simultaneous sadism and masochism. **—sa′do•mas′o•chist** *n.* **—sa′do•mas′o•chis′tic** *adj.*
sa•fa•ri (sə-fä′rē) *n., pl.* **-ris. 1.** An expedition for hunting or exploring, esp. in E Africa. **2.** *Informal.* A journey or trip.
safe (sāf) *adj.* **saf•er, saf•est. 1.** Secure from harm, danger, or evil. **2.** Free from injury or danger : unhurt. **3.** Not risky : sure <a *safe* bet> **4.** Giving protection <a *safe* place> **5.**

Baseball. Having reached a base without being put out. —*n.* A usu. metal container used to store and protect valuables. —**safe'ly** *adv.* —**safe'ness** *n.*

safe-con·duct (sāf'kŏn'dŭkt) *n.* A document permitting safe passage through enemy lands.

safe-de·pos·it box (sāf'dĭ-pŏz'ĭt) *n.* A fireproof metal box, usu. in a bank vault, for storing valuables.

safe·guard (sāf'gärd') *n.* Something, as a device or course of action, that serves as a protection or defense. —*v.* To furnish a safeguard for : protect.

safe·keep·ing (sāf'kē'pĭng) *n.* The act of keeping safe or state of being kept safe.

safe·ty (sāf'tē) *n., pl.* **-ties. 1.** The state of being safe. **2.** A device designed to prevent accidents. **3.** *Football.* **a.** A play in which a member of the offensive team downs the ball behind his own goal line. **b.** One of 2 defensive backs.

safety glass *n.* A shatterproof material consisting of 2 sheets of glass with an intermediate layer of clear plastic.

safety match *n.* A match that can be ignited only when struck on a specially prepared surface.

safety pin *n.* A pin shaped like a clasp, with a guard covering the point.

safety razor *n.* A razor whose blade is held betweeen guards.

safety valve *n.* A valve, as in a steam boiler, that opens automatically when pressure reaches a hazardous level.

saf·flow·er (săf'lou'ər) *n.* A plant, *Carthamus tinctorius,* native to Asia, with orange flowers yielding a dyestuff and seeds that are the source of an oil used in cooking, cosmetics, paints, and medicine.

saf·fron (săf'rən) *n.* **1.** A plant, *Crocus sativus,* having flowers with orange stigmas. **2.** The dried stigmas of the saffron, used to color foods and as a spice.

sag (săg) *v.* **sagged, sag·ging. 1.** To droop, sink, or settle from or as if from pressure or weight. **2.** To lose strength, firmness, or resilience. **3.** To decline in amount or value <profits that *sagged*> —**sag** *n.*

sa·ga (sä'gə) *n.* **1.** A 12th- and 13th-cent. narrative of historical and legendary events and exploits in Iceland. **2.** A modern narrative resembling a saga.

sa·ga·cious (sə-gā'shəs) *adj.* Marked by keen perception : wise. —**sa·ga'cious·ly** *adv.* —**sa·gac'i·ty** (-găs'ĭ-tē) *n.*

sage[1] (sāj) *n.* One renowned for judgment and wisdom. —*adj.* **sag·er, sag·est.** Wise : judicious. —**sage'ly** *adv.* —**sage'ness** *n.*

sage[2] (sāj) *n.* **1.** A plant or shrub of the genus *Salvia,* esp. *S. officinalis,* with aromatic grayish-green leaves used as seasoning. **2.** Sagebrush.

sage·brush (sāj'brŭsh') *n.* A shrub, *Artemisia tridentata,* of arid regions of W North America, with aromatic sagelike leaves.

Sag·it·tar·i·us (săj'ĭ-târ'ē-əs) *n.* **1.** A constellation in the S Hemisphere. **2. a.** The 9th sign of the zodiac. **b.** One born under this sign.

sag·it·tate (săj'ĭ-tāt') *adj. Bot.* Shaped like an arrowhead <a *sagittate* leaf>

sagittate
Sagittate leaves

sa·go (sā'gō) *n., pl.* **-gos.** A powdery starch obtained from the pith of a tropical Asian palm.

sa·gua·ro (sə-gwä'rō, sə-wä'-) *n., pl.* **-ros.** A large cactus, *Carnegiea gigantea,* of the SW U.S. and N Mexico, with upward-curving branches and edible red fruit.

said (sĕd) *v. p.t. & p.p. of* SAY.

sail (sāl) *n.* **1.** A piece of strong fabric that catches the wind and causes a ship to move. **2.** *pl.* **sail** *or* **sails.** A sailing vessel. **3.** A trip in a sailing vessel. **4.** Something that resembles a sail. —*v.* **1.** To travel by sailing ship. **2.** To travel over or across in a ship <*sail* the Atlantic> **3.** To begin a voyage across water. **4.** To operate a sailing vessel, esp. for sport. **5.** To move quickly, smoothly, or effortlessly.

sail·board (sāl'bôrd', -bōrd') *n.* A small light sailboat with a flat hull. —**sail'board'** *v.* —**sail'board'er** *n.*

sail·boat (sāl'bōt') *n.* A boat propelled partly or wholly by sail.

sail·cloth (sāl'klôth', -klŏth') *n.* A strong canvas used to make sails or tents.

sail·fish (sāl'fĭsh') *n.* A large marine fish of the genus *Istiophorus,* with the upper jaw prolonged into a spearlike bone and a large, saillike dorsal fin.

sail·ing (sā'lĭng) *n.* The act or sport of operating, racing, or riding in a sailboat.

sail·or (sā'lər) *n.* **1.** One who sails, esp. a member of a ship's crew. **2.** An enlisted man in a navy.

saint (sānt) *n.* **1. a.** One officially recognized, esp. by canonization, as being entitled to public veneration. **b.** One who has died and gone to heaven. **2.** A patient, unselfish, highly virtuous person. —**saint'ed** *adj.* —**saint'hood'** *n.* —**saint'li·ness** *n.* —**saint'ly** *adj.*

Saint Ber·nard (bər-närd') *n.* A large, strong dog, orig. bred in Switzerland, formerly used to rescue lost travelers.

sake[1] (sāk) *n.* **1.** Reason : motive <arguing for the *sake* of arguing> **2.** Benefit : good <for the *sake* of the community>

sa•ke² *also* **sa•ki** (sä'kē) *n.* A Japanese alcoholic beverage made from rice.
sa•laam (sə-läm') *n.* **1.** An obeisance, esp. a low bow performed while placing the right palm on the forehead. **2.** A respectful ceremonial greeting performed esp. in Islamic countries. —**sa•laam'** *v.*
sa•la•cious (sə-lā'shəs) *adj.* Lewd **:** lascivious. —**sa•la'cious•ly** *adv.*
sal•ad (săl'əd) *n.* A usu. cold dish, as of raw vegetables, fruit, or meat, served with dressing.
sal•a•man•der (săl'ə-măn'dər) *n.* A small, lizardlike amphibian of the order Caudata, with porous, scaleless skin.
sa•la•mi (sə-lä'mē) *n.* A heavily spiced sausage made esp. of pork and beef.
sal•a•ry (săl'ə-rē, săl'rē) *n., pl.* **-ries.** Fixed compensation paid on a regular basis for services. —**sal'a•ried** *adj.*
sale (sāl) *n.* **1.** The act of selling. **2.** An opportunity to sell **:** demand. **3.** A disposal of goods at reduced prices. **4.** An auction. —**sal'a•ble, sale'a•ble** *adj.*
sales•clerk (sālz'klûrk') *n.* A person who sells goods in a store.
sales•man (sālz'mən) *n.* A man who sells goods or services. —**sales'man•ship'** *n.*
sales•per•son (sālz'pûr'sən) *n.* A salesclerk.
sales tax *n.* A tax levied on sales.
sales•woman (sālz'wo͝om'ən) *n.* A woman who sells goods or services.
sal•i•cyl•ic acid (săl'ĭ-sĭl'ĭk) *n.* A white crystalline acid used esp. to make aspirin.
sa•li•ent (sā'lē-ənt, sāl'yənt) *adj.* **1.** Projecting beyond a line or surface. **2.** Conspicuous **:** prominent.
sa•line (sā'lēn', -līn') *adj.* Of, relating to, or containing salt **:** salty. —**sa•lin'i•ty** (sə-lĭn'ĭ-tē) *n.*
Sa•lish (sā'lĭsh) *also* **Sa•lish•an** (-lĭ-shən) *n.* **1.** A family of American Indian languages of the NW U.S. and British Columbia. **2.** The group of Salish-speaking peoples. —**Sa'lish•an** *adj.*
sa•li•va (sə-lī'və) *n.* The watery, tasteless liquid secretion discharged into the mouth that aids digestion. —**sal'i•var'y** (săl'ə-vĕr'ē) *adj.*
sal•i•vate (săl'ə-vāt') *v.* **-vat•ed, -vat•ing.** To secrete saliva. —**sal'i•va'tion** *n.*
Salk vaccine (sôlk) *n.* A vaccine against poliomyelitis administered by injection.
sal•low (săl'ō) *adj.* Of a sickly yellow color <a *sallow* complexion>
sal•ly (săl'ē) *n., pl.* **-lies. 1.** A sudden rush forward, esp. in order to launch an assault **:** sortie. **2.** A sudden burst of activity **:** outbreak. **3.** A witticism **:** quip. **4.** An excursion **:** jaunt. —**sal•ly** *v.*
salm•on (săm'ən, sä'mən) *n., pl.* **salmon** *or* **-ons. 1.** A large food and game fish of the genera *Salmo* and *Oncorhynchus,* of N waters, having delicate pinkish flesh. **2.** A moderate, light, or strong yellowish pink. —**salm'on** *adj.*
sal•mo•nel•la (săl'mə-nĕl'ə) *n., pl.* **-nel•lae** (-nĕl'ē) *or* **-las** *or* **-la.** Any of various rod-shaped bacteria of the genus *Salmonella,* many of which are pathogenic.
sa•lon (sə-lŏn', sä-lôN') *n.* **1.** A large drawing room or reception room. **2.** A periodic gathering of prominent persons, as artists or literary figures. **3.** A fashionable commercial establishment <a beauty *salon*>
sa•loon (sə-lo͞on') *n.* **1.** A place where alcoholic drinks are sold and drunk **:** tavern. **2.** A large room, as for receptions or public entertainment, esp. on a passenger ship. **3.** *esp. Brit.* A sedan automobile.
sal•sa (säl'sə) *n.* **1.** A spicy sauce made of tomatoes, onions, and chili peppers. **2.** *Mus.* A popular form of Latin-American dance music.
sal soda *n.* A hydrated sodium carbonate used as a general cleanser.
salt (sôlt) *n.* **1.** A white crystalline solid, mainly sodium chloride, used esp. as a preservative and seasoning. **2.** Any of a large class of chemical compounds formed when one or more hydrogen ions of an acid are replaced by metallic ions. **3.** *often* **salts.** Any of various salts of inorganic acids used as cathartics. **4.** *Informal.* A sailor. —*adj.* **1.** Of or containing salt **:** salty. **2.** Preserved in salt or brine. —*v.* To season, sprinkle, or preserve with salt. —**salt away.** To lay aside and save (e.g., money). —**salt'i•ness** *n.* —**salt'y** *adj.*

▲ ***word history:*** The word *salt* is a native English word; over the centuries it has formed many compounds, most of which have obvious meanings. *Salt* is related to Latin *sal,* "salt," which has many derivatives in English whose origins are not immediately apparent. The word *salary* is perhaps the most notable word derived from *sal.* The Latin source of *salary* is *salarium,* which orig. meant "money given to soldiers to buy salt" but later meant "a stipend, wages." Salt, of course, was put on food, both as a seasoning and as a preservative. *Salad* and *sauce* orig. denoted salted accompaniments to a meal. *Salami* and *sausage* denote preparations of meat preserved with salt.

salt•box (sôlt'bŏks') *n.* A frame house with two stories in front and one in the rear and a long sloped roof.
salt•cel•lar (sôlt'sĕl'ər) *n.* A small dish for holding salt at the table.
sal•tine (sôl-tēn') *n.* A thin, crisp cracker sprinkled with coarse salt.
salt lick *n.* A deposit of exposed salt that animals lick.
salt•pe•ter (sôlt'pē'tər) *n.* **1.** Potassium nitrate. **2.** Sodium nitrate. **3.** Niter.
salt•shak•er (sôlt'shā'kər) *n.* A container for salt with a perforated top.
salt•water (sôlt'wô'tər, -wŏt'ər) *adj.* Of, consisting of, or living in salt water.
sa•lu•bri•ous (sə-lo͞o'brē-əs) *adj.* Conducive or favorable to health or well-being.
sal•u•tar•y (săl'yə-tĕr'ē) *adj.* **1.** Effecting improvement **:** remedial. **2.** Promoting health **:** wholesome.
sal•u•ta•tion (săl'yə-tā'shən) *n.* An expression or gesture of greeting or good will.

sa•lu•ta•to•ri•an (sə-lo͞o'tə-tôr'ē-ən, -tōr'-) *n.* The student with the 2nd highest academic rank in a class who delivers the opening address at graduation.

sa•lute (sə-lo͞ot') *v.* **-lut•ed, -lut•ing. 1.** To greet with politeness, respect, or honor. **2.** To pay respect to (a superior officer), as by raising the right hand to the forehead or cap. **3.** To honor ceremoniously. —*n.* An act, ceremony, or gesture of saluting.

sal•vage (săl'vĭj) *n.* **1. a.** The rescue of a ship, its crew, or its cargo, as from fire or shipwreck. **b.** The ship, crew, or cargo so rescued. **c.** Compensation given to those who aid in such a rescue. **2. a.** The act of saving endangered property from total loss. **b.** The property so saved. —*v.* **-vaged, -vag•ing.** To save from total loss or destruction. —**sal'vage•a•ble** *adj.*

sal•va•tion (săl-vā'shən) *n.* **1. a.** The act of saving or state of being saved, as from danger or destruction. **b.** A means or agent of salvation. **2.** Deliverance from sin or death : redemption.

salve (săv, säv) *n.* **1.** An analgesic or medicinal ointment, as for burns. **2.** Something that soothes or heals : balm. —*v.* **salved, salv•ing.** To soothe with or as if with salve.

sal•ver (săl'vər) *n.* A tray for serving food or drinks.

sal•vo (săl'vō) *n., pl.* **-vos** *or* **-voes. 1.** The firing of a number of weapons at the same time. **2.** A sudden outburst, as of cheers.

sa•mar•i•um (sə-mâr'ē-əm, -măr'-) *n. Symbol* **Sm** A pale-gray or silvery metallic rare-earth element.

same (sām) *adj.* **1.** Being exactly alike : identical. **2.** Alike, as in kind : similar. **3.** Being the one previously mentioned. ★ *syns:* IDENTICAL, SELFSAME, VERY —*adv.* In the same way. —*pron.* The very same one or ones. —**same'ness** *n.*

sam•o•var (săm'ə-vär') *n.* A metal urn with a spigot, used esp. in Russia to boil water for tea.

sam•pan (săm'păn') *n.* A flat-bottomed Asian skiff.

sam•ple (săm'pəl) *n.* A portion, piece, or segment that is representative of a whole : example. —*v.* **-pled, -pling.** To take a sample of, as for study.

sam•pler (săm'plər) *n.* A piece of cloth embroidered with designs or mottoes in various stitches.

sam•u•rai (săm'ə-rī') *n., pl.* **-rai** *or* **-rais. 1.** The feudal military aristocracy of Japan. **2.** A professional warrior belonging to the samurai.

San (sän) *n., pl.* **San** *or* **Sans. 1.** A member of a nomadic hunting people of SW Africa. **2.** The language of the San.

san•a•to•ri•um (săn'ə-tôr'ē-əm, -tōr'-) *n., pl.* **-ums** *or* **-ri•a** (-ē-ə). An institution for the treatment of chronic diseases or supervision of convalescence.

sanc•ta (săngk'tə) *n. var. pl. of* SANCTUM.

sanc•ti•fy (săngk'tə-fī') *v.* **-fied, -fy•ing. 1.** To make holy or sacred. **2.** To free from sin : purify. —**sanc'ti•fi•ca'tion** *n.*

sanc•ti•mo•ni•ous (săngk'tə-mō'nē-əs) *adj.* Feigning piety or righteousness. —**sanc'ti•mo'ni•ous•ly** *adv.* —**sanc'ti•mo'ni•ous•ness** *n.*

sanc•tion (săngk'shən) *n.* **1.** Authoritative approval or permission. **2.** A measure, as moral pressure or a fine, imposed to ensure compliance or conformity. —*v.* To give approval to : authorize.

sanc•ti•ty (săngk'tĭ-tē) *n., pl.* **-ties. 1.** Saintliness : godliness. **2.** The quality of being sacred : sacredness.

sanc•tu•ar•y (săngk'cho͞o-ĕr'ē) *n., pl.* **-ies. 1.** A sacred place, as a church, temple, or mosque. **2.** A place giving refuge or asylum <a game *sanctuary*>

sanc•tum (săngk'təm) *n., pl.* **-tums** *or* **-ta** (-tə). A private place, as an office, where one is free from intrusion.

sand (sănd) *n.* Loose, fine grains of disintegrated rock. —*v.* **1.** To sprinkle or cover with sand. **2.** To smooth or polish with an abrasive, as sandpaper. —**sand'y** *adj.*

san•dal (săn'dəl) *n.* **1.** A shoe with a sole fastened to the foot by thongs or straps. **2.** A light slipper or low-cut shoe fastened to the foot by an ankle strap.

san•dal•wood (săn'dəl-wo͝od') *n.* An Asian tree of the genus *Santalum*, esp. *S. album*, with aromatic yellowish heartwood used in cabinetmaking and wood carving.

sand•bag (sănd'băg') *n.* A bag filled with sand, often used in protective walls or dikes. —**sand'bag'** *v.*

sand•bank (sănd'băngk') *n.* A large mass of sand, as on a hillside or in a river.

sand•bar (sănd'bär') *n.* An offshore shoal of sand built up by waves or currents.

sand•blast (sănd'blăst') *n.* A high-velocity blast of air or steam carrying sand to etch glass or clean stone or metal surfaces. —**sand'blast'** *v.*

sand•box (sănd'bŏks') *n.* A low box containing sand for children to play in.

sand•hog (sănd'hôg', -hŏg') *n.* One who works in a caisson, as in the construction of underwater tunnels.

sand dollar *n.* Any of various thin circular echinoderms of sandy ocean bottoms of the N Atlantic and Pacific.

sand dollar

sand•lot (sănd′lŏt′) *n.* A vacant lot used esp. by children for unorganized sports. —**sand′lot′** *adj.*
sand•man (sănd′măn′) *n.* A folklore character who makes children sleepy.
sand•pa•per (sănd′pā′pər) *n.* Paper with a coating of abrasive material on one side, used for smoothing or polishing.
sand•pip•er (sănd′pī′pər) *n.* A small wading bird of the family Scolopacidae, usu. having a long, straight bill.
sand•stone (sănd′stōn′) *n.* Sedimentary rock formed of grains of quartz cemented together esp. by lime or silica.
sand•storm (sănd′stôrm′) *n.* A windstorm that carries clouds of sand.
sand trap *n.* A hazard on a golf course having a depression filled with sand.
sand•wich (sănd′wĭch) *n.* **1.** Two or more slices of bread with a filling, as meat, between them. **2.** Something resembling a sandwich. —*v.* To insert between 2 other things, esp. tightly.
sane (sān) *adj.* **san•er, san•est. 1.** Of sound mind. **2.** Having or showing sound judgment : reasonable. —**sane′ly** *adv.* —**sane′ness, san′i•ty** (săn′ĭ-tē) *n.*
sang (săng) *v. p.t. of* SING.
sang-froid (säN-frwä′) *n.* Composure : equanimity.
san•gui•nar•y (săng′gwə-nĕr′ē) *adj.* **1.** Accompanied by bloodshed **2.** Bloody.
san•guine (săng′gwĭn) *adj.* **1. a.** Of the color of blood : red. **b.** Ruddy. **2.** Cheerfully confident : optimistic. —**san•guin′i•ty** *n.* —**san•guin′e•ous** *adj.*
san•i•tar•i•an (săn′ĭ-târ′ē-ən) *n.* A public-health or sanitation expert.
san•i•tar•i•um (săn′ĭ-târ′ē-əm) *n., pl.* **-ums** *or* **-i•a** (-ē-ə). A sanatorium.
san•i•tar•y (săn′ĭ-tĕr′ē) *adj.* **1.** Of or relating to health. **2.** Free from elements, as filth or bacteria, that endanger health.
sanitary napkin *n.* A disposable pad worn to absorb menstrual flow.
san•i•ta•tion (săn′ĭ-tā′shən) *n.* **1.** The application of measures designed to protect public health. **2.** Disposal of sewage.
san•i•tize (săn′ĭ-tīz′) *v.* **-tized, -tiz•ing. 1.** To make sanitary. **2.** To make more acceptable by removing potentially offensive elements from.
sank (săngk) *v. p.t. of* SINK.
sans (sănz) *prep.* Without.
San•skrit (săn′skrĭt′) *n.* An ancient Indo-European language that is the classical language of India. —**San′skrit′** *adj.*
Santa Claus (klôz) *n.* The personification of Christmas, usu. represented as a jolly, fat, white-bearded, red-suited old man.
sap[1] (săp) *n.* **1.** The liquid that circulates through plant tissues, carrying food substances. **2.** Vigor : energy. **3.** *Slang.* A gullible person : dupe.
sap[2] (săp) *v.* **sapped, sap•ping. 1.** To weaken gradually. **2.** To undermine.
sa•pi•ent (sā′pē-ənt) *adj.* Wise : sagacious. —**sa′pi•ence** *n.*
sap•ling (săp′lĭng) *n.* A young tree.
sa•pon•i•fy (sə-pŏn′ə-fī′) *v.* To convert (an oil or fat) into soap by treating with an alkali. —**sa•pon′i•fi•ca′tion** *n.*
sap•phire (săf′īr′) *n.* **1.** A clear, deep-blue form of corundum valued as a gem. **2.** The deep-blue color of a gem sapphire.
sap•py (săp′ē) *adj.* **-pi•er, -pi•est. 1.** Full of sap. **2.** *Slang.* Silly or foolish : fatuous.
sap•ro•phyte (săp′rə-fīt′) *n.* A plant, as a mushroom, that derives its nourishment from decaying organic matter. —**sap′ro•phyt′ic** (-fĭt′ĭk) *adj.*
sap•suck•er (săp′sŭk′ər) *n.* Either of 2 small North American woodpeckers, *Sphyrapicus varius* or *S. thyrsoides.*
sap•wood (săp′wŏŏd′) *n.* Newly formed outer wood that lies just inside the cambium of a tree or woody plant.
Sar•a•cen (săr′ə-sən) *n.* **1.** A member of a pre-Islamic nomadic people of the Syrian-Arabian deserts. **2.** An Arab. **3.** A Muslim, esp. at the time of the Crusades.
sa•ran (sə-răn′) *n.* A thermoplastic resin derived from vinyl compounds and used esp. in the manufacture of packaging films.
sar•casm (sär′kăz′əm) *n.* **1.** A taunting or contemptuously ironic remark. **2.** The use of sarcasm. —**sar•cas′tic** (-kăs′tĭk) *adj.* —**sar•cas′ti•cal•ly** *adv.*
sar•co•ma (sär-kō′mə) *n., pl.* **-ma•ta** (-mə-tə) *or* **-mas.** A usu. malignant tumor derived from connective tissue.
sar•coph•a•gus (sär-kŏf′ə-gəs) *n., pl.* **-gi** (-jī′) *or* **-gus•es.** A stone coffin.
sar•dine (sär-dēn′) *n.* A small or half-grown edible herring or related fish of the family Clupeidae, often canned in oil.
sar•don•ic (sär-dŏn′ĭk) *adj.* Mockingly cynical : sarcastic. —**sar•don′i•cal•ly** *adv.*
sar•gas•so (sär-găs′ō) *n., pl.* **-sos.** Gulfweed.
sarge (särj) *n. Informal.* Sergeant.
sa•ri (sä′rē) *n.* A lightweight, wrapped outer garment worn chiefly by women of India and Pakistan.
sa•rong (sə-rông′, -rŏng′) *n.* A length of brightly colored cloth wrapped about the waist, worn by men and women in Malaysia, Indonesia, and the Pacific islands.
sar•sa•pa•ril•la (săs′pə-rĭl′ə, särs′-) *n.* **1.** The dried roots of a tropical American plant of the genus *Smilax,* used as a flavoring. **2.** A soft drink flavored with sarsaparilla extract.
sar•to•ri•al (sär-tôr′ē-əl, -tōr′-) *adj.* Of or relating to a tailor, tailoring, or tailored clothing.
sash[1] (săsh) *n.* An ornamental band worn around the waist or over the shoulder.
sash[2] (săsh) *n.* **1.** A frame that holds the glass panes of a window or door. **2.** The sliding section of a window.
sa•shay (să-shā′) *v. Informal.* To move or walk in an ostentatious manner : strut.
sa•shi•mi (sä-shē′mē) *n.* A Japanese dish of raw fish sliced very thin.
Sas•quatch (săs′kwăch′) *n.* A large, hairy, humanlike creature purported to exist in the Pacific Northwest and W Canada.

sass (săs) *Informal.* —*n.* Impudent, disrespectful speech. —*v.* To talk impudently or disrespectfully to.
sas•sa•fras (săs'ə-frăs') *n.* **1.** A North American tree, *Sassafras albidum,* with irregularly shaped leaves and aromatic bark. **2.** The dried root bark of the sassafras, used as flavoring and as a source of a volatile oil.
sas•sy (săs'ē) *adj.* **-si•er, -si•est.** Given to back talk : impudent.
sat (săt) *v. p.t. & p.p. of* SIT.
SAT (ĕs'ā-tē'). A trademark for Scholastic Aptitude Test.
Sa•tan (sāt'n) *n.* The devil.
sa•tang (sə-tăng') *n., pl.* **satang.** —See table at CURRENCY.
sa•tan•ic (sə-tăn'ĭk) *or* **sa•tan•i•cal** (-ĭ-kəl) *adj.* **1.** Of, relating to, or suggestive of Satan. **2.** Extremely evil : fiendish.
satch•el (săch'əl) *n.* A small bag for books or clothing, often having a shoulder strap.
sate (sāt) *v.* **sat•ed, sat•ing. 1.** To satisfy fully. **2.** To indulge excessively. ★ ***syns:*** CLOY, GLUT, GORGE, SATIATE, SURFEIT.
sa•teen (să-tēn') *n.* A durable cotton fabric with a smooth, glossy, satinlike finish.
sat•el•lite (săt'l-īt') *n.* **1.** A relatively small celestial body orbiting a larger one. **2.** A man-made object designed to orbit a celestial body. **3.** A subservient follower.
sa•ti•ate (sā'shē-āt') *v.* **-at•ed, -at•ing.** To sate. —**sa'ti•a'tion** *n.*
sa•ti•e•ty (sə-tī'ĭ-tē) *n.* The state of being excessively full : surfeit.
sat•in (săt'n) *n.* A smooth fabric, as of silk, nylon, or rayon, with a glossy face and dull back. —**sat'in•y** *adj.*
sat•in•wood (săt'n-wo͝od') *n.* A tree, *Chloroxylon swietenia,* of S Asia, with hard, yellowish, close-grained wood.
sat•ire (săt'īr') *n.* **1.** Irony, derision, or caustic wit used to attack or expose folly, vice, or stupidity. **2.** A literary work in which satire is used to ridicule or attack human vice or folly. —**sa•tir'i•cal** (sə-tîr'ĭ-kəl), **sa•tir'ic** *adj.* —**sa•tir'i•cal•ly** *adv.* —**sat'i•rist** *n.* —**sat'i•rize'** *v.*
sat•is•fac•tion (săt'ĭs-făk'shən) *n.* **1. a.** The fulfillment or gratification of a need, desire, or appetite. **b.** Pleasure derived from such fulfillment. **2.** Compensation for injury or loss : reparation. **3.** A source of fulfillment or gratification.
sat•is•fac•to•ry (săt'ĭs-făk'tə-rē) *adj.* Affording satisfaction. —**sat'is•fac'to•ri•ly** *adv.* —**sat'is•fac'to•ri•ness** *n.*
sat•is•fy (săt'ĭs-fī') *v.* **-fied, -fy•ing. 1.** To fulfill or gratify. **2.** To free from question or doubt : convince. **3. a.** To discharge (e.g., an obligation). **b.** To discharge an obligation to (a creditor). **4.** To comply with the requirements of (a standard or rule). **5.** To make reparation for : redress. —**sat'is•fy'ing•ly** *adv.*
sa•trap (sā'trăp', săt'răp') *n.* A petty ruler or official.
sat•u•rate (săch'ə-rāt') *v.* **-rat•ed, -rat•ing. 1.** To imbue or impregnate thoroughly. **2.** To soak or load to capacity. —**sat'u•ra•ble** *adj.* —**sat'u•ra'tion** *n.*
saturated fat *n.* A usu. animal fat composed predominantly of fatty acids having only single bonds in the carbon chain.
Sat•ur•day (săt'ər-dē, -dā') *n.* The 7th day of the week.
Saturday night special *n. Informal.* A cheap, easily obtainable handgun.
Sat•urn (săt'ərn) *n.* The 6th planet from the sun.
sat•ur•nine (săt'ər-nīn') *adj.* Having a melancholy or surly disposition : sardonic.
sat•yr (săt'ər, sā'tər) *n.* **1.** *Gk. Myth.* A woodland god often having the pointed ears, legs, and short horns of a goat. **2.** A lecherous man.
sauce (sôs) *n.* **1.** A dressing or relish for food. **2.** Stewed, sweetened fruit. **3.** *Informal.* Impertinence. —*v.* **sauced, sauc•ing. 1.** To season or dress with sauce. **2.** To add flavor or piquancy to. **3.** *Informal.* To be impertinent to.
sauce•pan (sôs'păn') *n.* A deep cooking pan with a handle.
sau•cer (sô'sər) *n.* A small, shallow dish for holding a cup.
sauc•y (sô'sē) *adj.* **-i•er, -i•est. 1.** Impertinent. **2.** Pert <a *saucy* glance> —**sauc'i•ly** *adv.* —**sauc'i•ness** *n.*
sau•er•bra•ten (sour'brät'n) *n.* Pot-roasted beef marinated before cooking.
sau•er•kraut (sour'krout') *n.* Salted and fermented chopped or shredded cabbage.
Sauk (sôk) *n., pl.* **Sauk** *or* **Sauks. 1.** A member of an American Indian people formerly of the upper Midwest, now mainly in Oklahoma. **2.** Their Algonquian language.
sault (so͞o) *n. Can.* A waterfall or rapids.
sau•na (sou'nə, sô'-) *n.* **1.** A steam bath with steam produced by water poured over heated rocks. **2.** A room or enclosure for a sauna.
saun•ter (sôn'tər) *v.* To walk at a leisurely pace : stroll. —**saun'ter** *n.*
sau•sage (sô'sĭj) *n.* Chopped and usu. highly seasoned meat, as pork, stuffed into a casing and cooked and cured.
sau•té (sō-tā', sô-) *v.* **-téed, -té•ing.** To fry lightly and quickly in a shallow pan using a small amount of fat or oil.
sau•terne (sō-tûrn', sô-) *n.* A relatively sweet white wine.
sav•age (săv'ĭj) *adj.* **1.** Wild. **2.** Uncivilized : primitive. **3.** Ferocious. **4.** Cruel or merciless : brutal. ★ ***syns:*** FERAL, WILD —*n.* **1.** A member of a primitive society. **2.** A fierce, vicious, or crude person. —**sav'age•ly** *adv.* —**sav'age•ry** *n.*
sa•van•na *also* **sa•van•nah** (sə-văn'ə) *n.* A flat, largely treeless grassland.
sa•vant (sə-vänt') *n.* A scholar.
save[1] (sāv) *v.* **saved, sav•ing. 1.** To rescue from harm, danger, or loss. **2.** To keep in a safe state : safeguard. **3.** To prevent the waste or loss of : conserve. **4.** To keep for future use : store. **5.** To deliver from sin : redeem. **6.** *Computer Sci.* To copy (data) from main memory to a storage medium. —**sav'er** *n.*

save[2] (sāv) *prep.* Except : but. —*conj.* Were it not.
sav•ing (sā'vĭng) *n.* **1.** Preservation from harm, danger, or loss. **2.** Avoidance of overspending : economy. **3. savings.** An amount, as of money, saved.
sav•ior (sāv'yər) *n.* **1.** One who saves another from harm or danger. **2. Savior.** Jesus.
sav•iour (sāv'yər) *n. esp. Brit. var. of* SAVIOR.
sa•voir-faire (săv'wär-fâr') *n.* The ability to say and do the correct thing : tact.
sa•vor (sā'vər) *n.* **1.** The taste or smell of something. **2.** A particular quality or flavor. —*v.* **1.** To have a particular taste, smell, or quality. **2.** To taste with enjoyment : relish. —**sa'vor•y** *adj.*
sa•vour (sā'vər) *n. & v. esp. Brit. var. of* SAVOR.
sav•vy (săv'ē) *Slang.* —*v.* **-vied, -vy•ing.** To know : comprehend. —*n.* Practical understanding : common sense.
saw[1] (sô) *n.* A tool with a thin, sharp-toothed metal blade used to cut hard materials. —*v.* **sawed, sawed** *or* **sawn** (sôn), **saw•ing. 1.** To cut or divide with or as if with a saw. **2.** To produce or shape with or as if with a saw.
saw[2] (sô) *n.* A trite or banal saying.

▲ ***word history:*** The noun *saw[2]*, "a saying," is descended from the same Germanic ancestor as the noun *saga*, "a narrative," and both are related to the verb *say. Saw* is a native English word whose Old English form was *sagu. Saga* was borrowed from Icelandic in the 18th cent. as the name of the historical legends of the Scandinavian peoples. In Old Norse and Old Icelandic *saga* basically meant a story or legend transmitted orally; the narratives now called *sagas* were written down several centuries after the events they recount.

saw[3] (sô) *v. p.t. of* SEE[1].
saw•dust (sô'dŭst') *n.* Small particles, as of wood, produced by sawing.
sawed-off (sôd'ôf', -ŏf') *adj.* **1.** Shortened <a *sawed-off* shotgun> **2.** *Slang.* Short.
saw•horse (sô'hôrs') *n.* A rack used to support something being sawed.
saw•mill (sô'mĭl') *n.* A plant or factory where logs are sawed into boards.
sawn (sôn) *v. var. p.p. of* SAW[1].
sax (săks) *n. Informal.* A saxophone.
sax•i•frage (săk'sə-frĭj, -frāj') *n.* A low-growing plant of the genus *Saxifraga*, with leaves sometimes arranged in a rosette.
Sax•on (săk'sən) *n.* A member of a West Germanic tribe that invaded England in the 5th cent. —**Sax'on** *adj.*
sax•o•phone (săk'sə-fōn') *n.* A keyed wind instrument with a reed mouthpiece and a curved conical metal body. —**sax'o•phon'-ist** *n.*
say (sā) *v.* **said** (sĕd), **say•ing. 1.** To utter aloud : pronounce. **2.** To express in words. **3.** To state positively : declare. **4.** To recite. **5.** To report or maintain : allege. **6.** To show : indicate <My watch *says* 2 o'clock.> —*n.* **1.** An assertion. **2.** A turn or opportunity to speak. **3.** The right or power to make a decision : authority.
say•ing (sā'ĭng) *n.* A familiar expression or sentiment : adage.
say-so (sā'sō') *n., pl.* **-sos.** *Informal.* **1.** An authoritative assertion. **2.** The right to make a final decision.
Sb *symbol for* ANTIMONY.
Sc *symbol for* SCANDIUM.
scab (skăb) *n.* **1.** The crustlike exudate that covers a healing wound. **2.** Any of various plant diseases characterized by crustlike spots. **3. a.** One who works while others are on strike : strikebreaker. **b.** One who is hired to replace a striking worker. —*v.* **scabbed, scab•bing. 1.** To form a scab. **2.** *Informal.* To act or work as a scab. —**scab'by** *adj.*
scab•bard (skăb'ərd) *n.* A sheath or case for the blade of a sword, dagger, or bayonet.
sca•bies (skā'bēz') *n.* A contagious skin disease caused by a mite, *Sarcoptes scabiei*, that is marked by severe itching.
scab•rous (skăb'rəs, skā'brəs) *adj.* **1.** Rough to the touch : scaly or scabby. **2.** Difficult to handle : thorny. **3.** Salacious.
scads (skădz) *pl.n. Informal.* A large amount <*scads* of money>
scaf•fold (skăf'əld, -ōld') *n.* **1.** A raised platform used by workers while constructing, painting, or repairing a structure. **2.** A platform on which condemned prisoners are executed.
sca•lar (skā'lər, -lär') *n.* A quantity, such as length or temperature, that is completely specified by a number on an appropriate scale. —**sca'lar** *adj.*
scal•a•wag (skăl'ə-wăg') *n. Informal.* A reprobate : rascal.
scald (skôld) *v.* **1.** To injure or burn with or as if with hot liquid or steam. **2.** To heat (a liquid) to a temperature just below the boiling point. —*n.* A bodily injury caused by scalding.
scale[1] (skāl) *n.* **1. a.** A small platelike structure that forms the protective outer covering esp. of fishes and reptiles. **b.** A similar part, as one of the overlapping structures that form the covering on the wings of butterflies and moths. **2.** A thin flake or crust, as of paint, rust, or dandruff. **3.** A plant disease or infestation caused by scale insects. —*v.* **scaled, scal•ing. 1.** To remove the scales of. **2.** To fall or come off in scales : flake. —**scal'y** *adj.*
scale[2] (skāl) *n.* **1. a.** A series of marks at fixed distances, used for measuring. **b.** An instrument having a scale. **2.** The size of a representation in proportion to the size of what it represents. **3. a.** A graduated series <a wage *scale*> **b.** Relative extent <living on a grand *scale*> **4.** A standard by which something can be estimated. **5.** An ascending or descending series of musical tones proceeding in accordance with a specified scheme of intervals. —*v.* **scaled, scal•ing. 1.** To climb up or over : ascend. **2.** To arrange in a particular propor-

tion or scale. **3.** To adjust or regulate according to a standard.

scale[3] (skāl) *n.* **1.** A weighing instrument or machine. **2.** Either of the pans, trays, or dishes of a balance.

scale insect *n.* Any of various small, destructive sucking insects of the family Coccidae, the females of which secrete and are covered by waxy scales on plant tissue.

sca•lene (skā′lēn′, skā-lēn′) *adj.* Having 3 unequal sides <a *scalene* triangle>

scal•lion (skăl′yən) *n.* A young onion before the enlargement of the bulb.

scal•lop (skŏl′əp, skăl′-) *n.* **1. a.** A marine mollusk of the family Pectinidae, with a fan-shaped, fluted bivalve shell. **b.** The fleshy, edible muscle of a scallop. **2.** One of a series of curves shaped like semicircles that form a border. —*v.* **1.** To border (e.g., cloth) with scallops. **2.** To bake in a sauce, often with bread crumbs.

scalp (skălp) *n.* The skin that covers the top of the human head. —*v.* **1.** To tear or cut the scalp from. **2.** *Informal.* To buy and resell (e.g., tickets) at greatly inflated prices. —**scalp′er** *n.*

scal•pel (skăl′pəl) *n.* A small straight knife with a thin, sharp blade used in surgery and dissection.

scam (skăm) *n. Slang.* A fraudulent scheme : swindle.

scamp (skămp) *n.* **1.** A scheming person : rogue. **2.** A playful, mischievous person.

scam•per (skăm′pər) *v.* To run hurriedly or playfully. —**scam′per** *n.*

scan (skăn) *v.* **scanned, scan•ning. 1.** To examine (something) closely. **2.** To look over rapidly but thoroughly. **3.** To analyze (verse) so as to show rhythmical patterns. **4.** *Electron.* **a.** To move a beam of light or electrons over (a surface) to reproduce or transmit an image. **b.** To move a radar beam over in search of a target. **c.** To search (e.g., a magnetic tape) automatically for specific data. —**scan** *n.* —**scan′ner** *n.*

scan•dal (skăn′dl) *n.* **1.** Something that offends public morality : disgrace. **2.** Malicious talk : gossip. —**scan′dal•ous** *adj.* —**scan′dal•ous•ly** *adv.*

scan•dal•ize (skăn′dl-īz′) *v.* **-ized, -iz•ing.** To shock the propriety or moral sense of. —**scan′dal•i•za′tion** *n.*

scandal sheet *n.* A newspaper whose stories are predominantly scandalous.

scan•di•um (skăn′dē-əm) *n. Symbol* **Sc** A silvery, lightweight metallic element.

scant (skănt) *adj.* **1.** Barely enough in amount or quantity : inadequate. **2.** Being slightly less than a specific measure. —*v.* To provide an inadequate amount of : skimp. —**scant′ly** *adv.* —**scant′ness** *n.*

scant•ling (skănt′lĭng, -lĭn) *n.* A small beam or section of timber, as an upright in a structural frame.

scant•y (skăn′tē) *adj.* **-i•er, -i•est.** Barely adequate or sufficient : meager. —**scant′i•ly** *adv.* —**scant′i•ness** *n.*

scape•goat (skāp′gōt′) *n.* One that is made an object of blame for others. ★ ***syns:*** FALL GUY, GOAT, PATSY, WHIPPING BOY

scape•grace (skāp′grās′) *n.* An unscrupulous or incorrigible person : reprobate.

scap•u•la (skăp′yə-lə) *n., pl.* **-lae** (-lē′) *or* **-las.** Either of a pair of large, flat, triangular bones that form the back part of the shoulder. —**scap′u•lar** *adj.*

scar (skär) *n.* **1.** A mark that remains after an injury has healed. **2.** A mark or sign of damage. —*v.* **scarred, scar•ring.** To mark with or form a scar.

scar•ab (skăr′əb) *n.* **1.** A large, broad-bodied beetle. **2.** An ornamental representation of a scarab.

scarce (skârs) *adj.* **scarc•er, scarc•est. 1.** Not common : rare. **2.** Insufficient to meet a demand or requirement. —**scar′ci•ty** *n.*

scarce•ly (skârs′lē) *adv.* **1.** By a narrow margin : barely. **2.** Hardly <*scarcely* ever watched television> **3.** Certainly not <could *scarcely* object>

scare (skâr) *v.* **scared, scar•ing.** To startle : frighten. —*n.* A state of alarm or panic. —**scare up.** To find or gather with considerable effort. —**scar′y** *adj.*

scare•crow (skâr′krō′) *n.* A roughly fashioned figure of a person used to scare birds away from growing crops.

scarf[1] (skärf) *n., pl.* **scarfs** *or* **scarves** (skärvz). **1.** A piece of cloth worn over the head or around the neck or shoulders. **2.** A long strip of cloth, as for a dresser.

scarf[2] (skärf) *n., pl.* **scarfs.** A joint made by cutting the ends of two pieces correspondingly and strapping or bolting them together. —**scarf** *v.*

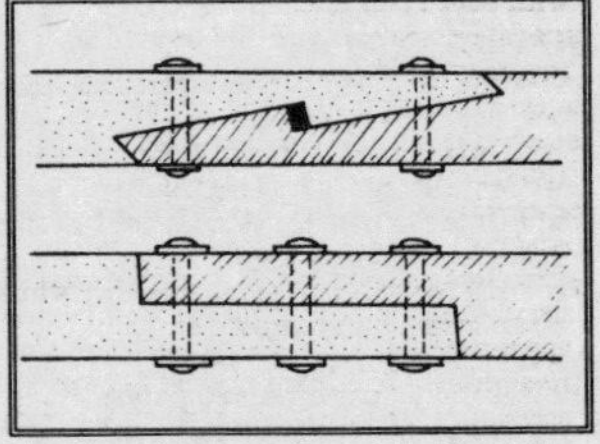

scarf[2]

scar•i•fy (skăr′ə-fī′) *v.* **-fied, -fy•ing. 1.** To make superficial cuts in : scratch. **2.** To criticize severely : flay.

scar•la•ti•na (skär′lə-tē′nə) *n.* Scarlet fever, esp. in a mild form.

scar•let (skär′lĭt) *n.* A strong or vivid red.

scarlet fever *n.* A severe contagious disease marked by a scarlet-colored rash and high fever.

scat (skăt) *v.* **scat•ted, scat•ting.** *Informal.* To leave hastily.

scath•ing (skā′thĭng) *adj.* Extremely harsh or bitterly severe.

sca•tol•o•gy (skə-tŏl′ə-jē, skă-) *n.* Interest in or preoccupation with obscenity. —**scat′o•log′i•cal** (skăt′l-ŏj′ĭ-kəl) *adj.*

scat•ter (skăt′ər) *v.* **1.** To break or cause to break up and go in many directions : disperse. **2.** To distribute irregularly : strew. ★ ***syns:*** DISPEL, DISPERSE, DISSIPATE

scat•ter•brain (skăt′ər-brān′) *n.* A disorganized, giddy person. —**scat′ter•brained′** *adj.*

scat•ter-gun (skăt′ər-gŭn′) *n.* A shotgun.

scatter rug *n.* A small rug that covers only part of a floor.

scav•enge (skăv′ənj) *v.* **-enged, -eng•ing.** To act as a scavenger.

scav•en•ger (skăv′ən-jər) *n.* **1.** An animal, as a vulture, that feeds on dead or decaying material. **2.** One who searches for something useful in discarded material.

sce•nar•i•o (sĭ-nâr′ē-ō′, -när′-) *n., pl.* **-os. 1.** A synopsis of a dramatic or literary plot. **2.** A screenplay.

scene (sēn) *n.* **1.** A view. **2.** The place where an action or event occurs : locale. **3. a.** One of the divisions of an act in a play. **b.** A short section of a motion picture. **4.** The scenery and properties for a dramatic presentation. **5.** A public display of passion or temper. **6.** *Slang.* **a.** A sphere of activity <the bar *scene*> **b.** A situation <a bad *scene*> —**sce′nic** *adj.*

scen•er•y (sē′nə-rē) *n.* **1.** A landscape. **2.** The structures or curtains on the stage of a theater that represent the play's setting.

scent (sĕnt) *n.* **1.** A smell : odor. **2.** A perfume. **3.** An odor left by the passing of an animal. **4.** The course or trail of an animal or fugitive that is being hunted or tracked. —*v.* **1.** To perceive by or as if by smelling. **2.** To fill with odor : perfume.

scep•ter (sĕp′tər) *n.* A rod or staff held by a sovereign as a sign of authority.

scep•tic (skĕp′tĭk) *n. var. of* SKEPTIC.

scep•ti•cism (skĕp′tĭ-sĭz′əm) *n. var. of* SKEPTICISM.

scep•tre (sĕp′tər) *n. & v. esp. Brit. var. of* SCEPTER.

sched•ule (skĕj′o͞ol) *n.* **1.** A written or printed list of items. **2.** A program of future events or appointments. **3.** A table of departure and arrival times. **4.** A plan allocating work and specifying deadlines for a project. —*v.* **-uled, -ul•ing. 1.** To place on a schedule. **2.** To set up a schedule for.

sche•ma (skē′mə) *n., pl.* **-ma•ta** (-mə-tə) *or* **-mas.** A diagrammatic presentation, as an outline.

sche•mat•ic (skē-măt′ĭk) *adj.* Of, relating to or in the form of a diagram or scheme. —**sche•mat′i•cal•ly** *adv.*

scheme (skēm) *n.* **1.** A plan for doing something. **2.** An orderly combination of related or successive parts : system. **3.** An underhand or secret plot : intrigue. —*v.* **schemed, schem•ing.** To plot underhandedly. —**schem′er** *n.*

scher•zo (skĕr′tsō) *n., pl.* **-zos** *or* **-zi** (-tsē). A lively musical movement.

Schick test (shĭk) *n.* A skin test for susceptibility to diphtheria.

schil•ling (shĭl′ĭng) *n.* —See table at CURRENCY.

schism (sĭz′əm, skĭz′-) *n.* **1.** A separation from or division within a religious body. **2.** Disunity. —**schis•mat′ic** (-măt′ĭk) *adj.*

schist (shĭst) *n.* A metamorphic rock made up of laminated layers of chiefly micaceous minerals. —**schis′tose′** (shĭs′tōs′), **schis′tous** (-təs) *adj.*

schis•to•so•mi•a•sis (shĭs′tō-sə-mī′ə-sĭs) *n.* A severe, gen. tropical disease caused by infestation with parasitic worms.

schiz•o•phre•ni•a (skĭt′sə-frē′nē-ə) *n.* A mental disorder marked by loss of awareness of reality, often with disturbances of behavior and the inability to reason. —**schiz′oid′** (skĭt′soid′) *adj. & n.* —**schiz′o•phren′ic** (-frĕn′ĭk) *adj. & n.*

schle•miel (shlə-mēl′) *n. Slang.* A bungler : dolt.

schlock (shlŏk) *n. Slang.* Cheap or inferior merchandise.

schmaltz *also* **schmalz** (shmälts) *n.* Excessively sentimental art or music. —**schmaltz′y** *adj.*

schnapps (shnäps, shnăps) *n.* A strong alcoholic liquor.

schnau•zer (shnou′zər, shnout′sər) *n.* A dog, orig. bred in Germany, having a wiry gray coat and a blunt muzzle.

schnoz•zle (shnŏz′əl) *also* **schnozz** (shnŏz) *n. Slang.* The human nose.

schol•ar (skŏl′ər) *n.* **1. a.** An erudite person. **b.** A person with much knowledge in a particular field. **2.** One who attends school : pupil. —**schol′ar•ly** *adv.*

schol•ar•ship (skŏl′ər-shĭp′) *n.* **1.** The methods and achievements of a scholar. **2.** Financial aid awarded to a student.

scho•las•tic (skə-lăs′tĭk) *adj.* Of or relating to schools. —**scho•las′ti•cal•ly** *adv.*

school[1] (sko͞ol) *n.* **1. a.** An institution for teaching and learning. **b.** The group of students attending a school. **2.** Attendance at or the process of being educated at a school. **3.** A group of persons of similar principles, beliefs, or opinions. —*v.* **1.** To instruct : educate. **2.** To discipline : train. —**school′boy′** *n.* —**school′girl′** *n.*

school[2] (sko͞ol) *n.* A large group of aquatic animals, esp. fish, swimming together.

school•book (sko͞ol′bo͝ok′) *n.* A textbook.

school•house (sko͞ol′hous′) *n.* A building used as a school.

school•marm (sko͞ol′märm′) *also* **school•ma′am** (-măm′) *n. Informal.* A woman who is a teacher, esp. a pedantic or old-fashioned one.

school•mas•ter (sko͞ol′măs′tər) *n.* A man who is a teacher or headmaster.

school•mate (sko͞ol′māt′) *n.* A school companion.

school•mis•tress (sko͞ol′mĭs′trĭs) *n.* A woman who is a teacher or headmistress.

school•room (sko͞ol′ro͞om′, -ro͝om′) *n.* A classroom in a school.

school•teach•er (sko͞ol′tē′chər) *n.* A person who teaches in a school.

school•work (sko͞ol′wûrk′) *n.* Lessons done at school or assigned as homework.

schoo•ner (sko͞o′nər) *n.* A fore-and-aft-rigged sailing vessel.

schuss (sho͝os) *v.* To make a fast straight run in skiing. —*n.* **1.** A straight downhill course for skiing. **2.** The act of schussing.

schwa (shwä) *n.* **1.** An unstressed vowel, as the *a* in *sofa* or *e* in *linen.* **2.** The symbol (ə) used to represent a schwa.

sci•at•i•ca (sī-ăt′ĭ-kə) *n.* **1.** Neuralgia of the nerve running down the back of the thigh. **2.** Chronic pain in the hip or thigh.

sci•ence (sī′əns) *n.* **1.** The study and theoretical explanation of natural phenomena. **2.** A systematic activity requiring study and method. **3.** Knowledge, esp. that acquired through experience. —**sci′en•tif′ic** (sī′ən-tĭf′ĭc) *adj.* —**sci′en•tif′i•cal•ly** *adv.* —**sci′en•tist** (sī′ən-tĭst) *n.*

science fiction *n.* Fiction in which imaginative scientific possibilities are used in the plot.

sci-fi (sī′fī′) *n. Informal.* Science fiction.

scim•i•tar (sĭm′ĭ-tər, -tär′) *n.* A short, curved, single-edged sword.

scin•til•la (sĭn-tĭl′ə) *n.* A tiny amount.

scin•til•late (sĭn′tə-lāt′) *v.* **-lat•ed, -lat•ing. 1.** To throw off sparks **:** flash. **2.** To be animated or brilliant. —**scin′til•la′tion** *n.*

sci•on (sī′ən) *n.* **1.** A descendant. **2.** A twig or shoot removed from one plant for grafting onto another.

scis•sors (sĭz′ərz) *pl.n. (sing. or pl. in number).* A cutting tool consisting of 2 blades joined and pivoted so that the cutting edges close against each other.

scissors kick *n.* A swimming kick in which the legs are opened and closed like scissors.

scle•ro•sis (sklə-rō′sĭs) *n., pl.* **-ses** (-sēz′). A thickening or hardening of a bodily part, as an artery. —**scle•rot′ic** (-rŏt′ĭk) *adj.*

scoff (skôf, skŏf) *v.* To show derision or mockery. —**scoff′er** *n.*

scoff•law (skŏf′lô′, skôf′-) *n.* One who habitually violates the law.

scold (skōld) *v.* To reprove severely **:** berate. —*n.* One who scolds.

sco•li•o•sis (skō′lē-ō′sĭs, skŏl′ē-) *n.* Abnormal lateral curvature of the spine.

sconce (skŏns) *n.* A decorative wall bracket for candles or electric lights.

scone (skōn, skŏn) *n.* A small biscuitlike pastry or quick bread baked on a griddle.

scoop (sko͞op) *n.* **1.** A shovellike utensil, usu. having a deep, curved bowl and a short handle. **2.** A ladle **:** dipper. **3.** The bucket of a power shovel or dredge. **4.** A scooping action or movement. **5.** *Slang.* An exclusive news story. —*v.* **1.** To lift out or up with or as if with a scoop. **2.** To hollow out by digging. **3.** *Slang.* To get the better of (a competitor) by getting a news scoop.

scoot (sko͞ot) *v.* To go quickly and suddenly. —**scoot** *n.*

scoot•er (sko͞o′tər) *n.* **1.** A child's vehicle consisting of a long footboard between 2 small end wheels, the forward wheel controlled by an upright steering bar. **2.** A motor scooter.

scope (skōp) *n.* **1.** The range of one's actions or thoughts. **2.** Space or opportunity to operate or function. **3.** The extent of an activity, situation, or subject.

–scope *suff.* An instrument for observing <micro*scope*>

scorch (skôrch) *v.* **1.** To burn slightly so as to change in color or flavor. **2.** To shrivel or parch with heat. —**scorch** *n.*

scorch•er (skôr′chər) *n.* **1.** One that scorches. **2.** *Informal.* A very hot day.

score (skôr, skōr) *n.* **1.** A notch or mark. **2.** A usu. numerical record of points made by competitors, as in a game. **3.** A result of a test or examination. **4. a.** An amount due **:** debt. **b.** A grievance that requires satisfaction **:** grudge. **5.** A group of 20 items. **6.** The written form of a musical arrangement or composition with all the orchestral or vocal parts indicated. **7.** *Informal.* **a.** The act or fact of gaining an advantage. **b.** The act of buying illicit drugs. **8.** A motive or reason. —*v.* **scored, scor•ing. 1. a.** To gain (a point or points) in or as if in a competitive event. **b.** To count or be worth as points. **2.** To achieve, win, or gain. **3.** To record the points in a competitive event. **4.** To mark with lines, notches, or cuts. **5.** To correct and assign a grade to. **6.** To arrange or compose a score for. **7.** To gain an advantage **:** succeed. —**score′less** *adj.* —**scor′er** *n.*

score•board (skôr′bôrd′, skōr′bōrd′) *n.* A large board for displaying the score of a game.

sco•ri•a (skôr′ē-ə, skōr′-) *n., pl.* **-ri•ae** (-ē-ē′) *Geol.* Rough particles of burnt, crustlike lava.

scorn (skôrn) *n.* **1.** Open contempt **:** disdain. **2.** An expression of scorn **:** derision. —*v.* To consider or treat with scorn **:** disdain. —**scorn′ful** *adj.*

Scor•pi•o (skôr′pē-ō′) *n.* **1.** A constellation in the S Hemisphere. **2. a.** The 8th sign of the zodiac. **b.** One born under this sign.

scor•pi•on (skôr′pē-ən) *n.* An arachnid of the order Scorpionida, having an erectile tail tipped with a poisonous sting.

Scor•pi•us (skôr′pē-əs) *n.* Scorpio 1.

Scot (skŏt) *n.* A native or inhabitant of Scotland.

scotch (skŏch) *v.* To put an end to **:** crush <*scotched* the rumor>

Scotch (skŏch) *n.* **1.** *(pl. in number).* The people of Scotland. **2.** Scots. **3.** A whiskey distilled in Scotland from malted barley. —**Scotch** *adj.* —**Scotch′man** *n.*

scot-free (skŏt′frē′) *adj.* Free from harm, punishment, obligation, or penalty.

Scots (skŏts) *adj.* Scottish. —*n.* The English dialect of Scotland.

Scots•man (skŏts′mən) *n.* A man who is a native or resident of Scotland.

Scots•wom•an (skŏts'wŏŏm'ən) *n.* A woman who is a native or resident of Scotland.
Scot•tish (skŏt'ĭsh) *adj.* Of, relating to, or characteristic of Scotland, its people, or its language. —*n.* **1.** Scots. **2.** *(pl. in number).* The people of Scotland.
scoun•drel (skoun'drəl) *n.* A wicked, dishonorable person : villain.
scour[1] (skour) *v.* **1.** To clean or polish by harsh rubbing, as with an abrasive agent. **2.** To remove by scrubbing.
scour[2] (skour) *v.* **1.** To range over or about (an area), esp. in a search. **2.** To move quickly : rush.
scourge (skûrj) *n.* **1.** A whip. **2.** A means of inflicting punishment or pain. **3.** A cause of affliction, as pestilence or war. —*v.* **scourged, scourg•ing. 1.** To flog. **2.** To chastise or punish severely.
scout[1] (skout) *v.* **1.** To observe or explore in order to obtain information. **2.** To search <*scout* around for bargains> —*n.* **1.** A person, aircraft, or ship sent out to obtain information. **2. a.** A member of the Boy Scouts. **b.** A member of the Girl Scouts. **3.** A person <a good *scout*>
scout[2] (skout) *v.* To reject contemptuously : scorn.
scout•mas•ter (skout'măs'tər) *n.* The adult leader in charge of a Boy Scout troop.
scow (skou) *n.* A large open barge used to transport freight, as gravel or garbage.
scowl (skoul) *v.* To lower or contract the brow, as in anger or displeasure. —**scowl** *n.* —**scowl'ing•ly** *adv.*
scrab•ble (skrăb'əl) *v.* **-bled, -bling. 1.** To scratch or grope about frantically. **2.** To struggle <*scrabbled* for a living> **3.** To ascend hastily : scramble. **4.** To scribble. —**scrab'ble** *n.* —**scrab'bler** *n.*
scrag•gly (skrăg'lē) *adj.* **-gli•er, -gli•est. 1.** Messy : unkempt. **2.** Irregular : uneven.
scram (skrăm) *v.* **scrammed, scram•ming.** *Slang.* To leave immediately.
scram•ble (skrăm'bəl) *v.* **-bled, -bling. 1.** To move rapidly, esp. on the hands and knees. **2.** To struggle or contend eagerly or urgently. **3.** To mix confusedly : jumble. **4.** To cook (eggs) by mixing and stirring while frying. **5.** *Electron.* To process (a signal) so that it cannot be used or understood without a special receiver. —**scram'ble** *n.* —**scram'bler** *n.*
scrap[1] (skrăp) *n.* **1.** A section or piece : fragment. **2.** Discarded waste material, esp. metal suitable for reprocessing. —*v.* **scrapped, scrap•ping. 1.** To separate into parts for salvage or disposal. **2.** To discard as worthless : junk.
scrap[2] (skrăp) *Slang.* —*v.* **scrapped, scrap•ping.** To fight, often with the fists. —*n.* A fight or scuffle : brawl. —**scrap'per** *n.* —**scrap'pi•ly** *adv.* —**scrap'pi•ness** *n.* —**scrap'py** *adj.*
scrap•book (skrăp'bŏŏk') *n.* A book with blank pages for mounting mementos.
scrape (skrāp) *v.* **scraped, scrap•ing. 1.** To rub (a surface) forcefully, as to clean, smooth, or shape. **2.** To remove by rubbing with a hard edge <*scrape* ice from a window> **3.** To bring or come into sliding, abrasive contact, often with a harsh grating sound. **4.** To injure the surface of by rubbing with something rough or sharp. **5.** To gather or produce with difficulty <*scrape* up new evidence> **6.** To practice small economies : skrimp. —*n.* **1.** The act or an instance of scraping. **2.** Something produced by scraping. **3.** *Slang.* **a.** An embarrassing or difficult situation. **b.** A fight : scuffle. —**scrap'er** *n.*
scratch (skrăch) *v.* **1.** To mark, injure, or scrape with or as if with the nails or claws. **2.** To rub to alleviate itching. **3.** To remove or cancel (e.g., a word) by or as if by drawing a line through. **4.** To make a rough, scraping sound. —*n.* **1.** A line or mark made by scratching. **2.** A harsh, scraping sound. —*adj.* **1.** Used for hasty notes or sketches <*scratch* paper> **2.** Done by chance. —**scratch'y** *adj.*
scratch•pad (skrăch'păd') *n.* A usu. high-speed internal register used for temporary storage in a computer memory.
scrawl (skrôl) *v.* To write quickly and often illegibly. —**scrawl** *n.* —**scrawl'y** *adj.*
scraw•ny (skrô'nē) *adj.* **-ni•er, -ni•est.** Thin and bony. —**scraw'ni•ness** *n.*
scream (skrēm) *v.* To utter a loud, piercing cry, as of pain. —*n.* **1.** A loud, piercing cry. **2.** *Slang.* One that is extremely funny.
scree (skrē) *n.* A mass of small stones or rock debris at the base of an incline or cliff.
screech (skrēch) *v.* **1.** To scream. **2.** To make a shrill, grating sound. —**screech** *n.*
screen (skrēn) *n.* **1.** An often movable frame used to protect, divide, conceal, or decorate <a mesh door *screen*> **2.** Something that serves to conceal <a smoke *screen*> **3.** A sieve used to separate fine particles from larger ones. **4. a.** A surface on which a picture is projected for viewing. **b.** The motion-picture industry. —*v.* **1.** To provide with a screen. **2.** To conceal, protect, guard, shield, or separate with or as if with a screen. **3.** To show or project (e.g., a motion picture) on a screen.
screen•ing (skrē'nĭng) *n.* **1.** Wire or plastic mesh used to make screens. **2.** A presentation, as of a motion picture.
screen•play (skrēn'plā') *n.* A motion-picture script.
screen test *n.* A short film sequence used to judge the talent or suitability of a person for a role in a motion picture. —**screen'-test'** *v.*
screw (skrōō) *n.* **1.** A metal piece resembling a nail with a helical or spiral groove and slotted head that can be turned by a screwdriver to fasten things together. **2.** A propeller, esp. for a ship or motorboat. —*v.* **1. a.** To fasten, attach, or tighten by or as if by means of a screw. **b.** To attach (e.g., a threaded cap) by twisting into place. **2.** To turn or twist out of shape : contort. **3.** To cheat. —**screw up.** *Slang.* To make a mess of (an undertaking).

screw•ball (skrōō'bôl') *n.* **1.** *Baseball.* A pitch that curves in the direction opposite that of a curve ball. **2.** *Slang.* An eccentric, whimsical, or irrational person.
screw•driv•er (skrōō'drī'vər) *n.* **1.** A tool for turning screws. **2.** A mixed drink of vodka and orange juice.
screw•y (skrōō'ē) *adj.* **-i•er, -i•est.** *Slang.* **1.** Insane : crazy. **2.** Absurdly odd, unusual, or inappropriate.
scrib•ble (skrĭb'əl) *v.* **-bled, -bling.** To write or draw in a hurried, careless manner. **—scrib'ble** *n.* **—scrib'bler** *n.*
scribe (skrīb) *n.* **1. a.** A professional copyist of manuscripts and documents. **b.** A public secretary or clerk. **2.** A writer, esp. a journalist.
scrim (skrĭm) *n.* A durable, loosely woven cotton or linen fabric.
scrim•mage (skrĭm'ĭj) *n. Football.* **1.** The play of the ball that follows the snap. **2.** A team's practice session. **—scrim'mage** *v.*
scrimp (skrĭmp) *v.* To economize severely. **—scrimp'y** *adj.*
scrim•shaw (skrĭm'shô') *n.* **1.** The art of carving or incising elaborate designs on whalebone or whale ivory. **2.** A decorative article made by scrimshaw.
scrip¹ (skrĭp) *n.* Paper money issued for temporary use.
scrip² (skrĭp) *n.* A certificate entitling the holder to a fractional share, as of stock.
script (skrĭpt) *n.* **1.** Handwriting, esp. a style with cursive characters. **2.** The text of a broadcast, play, or motion picture.
Scrip•ture (skrĭp'chər) *n.* **1. a.** A sacred writing or book. **b.** A passage from such a writing or book. **2.** *often* **Scriptures.** The Bible. **—Scrip'tur•al** *adj.*
scriv•en•er (skrĭv'ə-nər) *n.* A scribe.
scrod (skrŏd) *n.* A young haddock or cod.
scroll (skrōl) *n.* **1.** A roll, as of parchment, used esp. for writing. **2.** An ornament or ornamental design resembling a scroll. *—v. Computer Sci.* To display (text) with a continuous vertical or horizontal movement across the screen.
scroll saw *n.* A thin-bladed saw used to cut curved or irregular shapes.
scro•tum (skrō'təm) *n., pl.* **-ta** (-tə) *or* **-tums.** The external sac of skin that encloses the testes in most mammals. **—scro'tal** (skrōt'l) *adj.*
scrounge (skrounj) *v.* **scrounged, scroung•ing.** *Slang.* **1.** To forage or obtain by foraging. **2.** To cadge : mooch. **—scroung'er** *n.*
scrub¹ (skrŭb) *v.* **scrubbed, scrub•bing. 1.** To clean by rubbing, as with a brush. **2.** *Slang.* To cancel : drop <*scrubbed* the project> **—scrub** *n.*
scrub² (skrŭb) *n.* **1. a.** A stunted tree or shrub. **b.** A growth or tract of stunted vegetation. **2.** An undersized or underdeveloped domestic animal. **3.** One who is undersized or insignificant. **4.** A player not on a varsity or first team. **—scrub'by** *adj.*
scruff (skrŭf) *n.* The back of the neck.
scruf•fy (skrŭf'ē) *adj.* **-fi•er, -fi•est.** Shabby : unkempt.
scrump•tious (skrŭmp'shəs) *adj. Slang.* Delightful : first-rate.
scru•ple (skrōō'pəl) *n.* **1.** A dictate of conscience or ethical principle that tends to inhibit action. **2.** A tiny part or amount. **3.** A unit of apothecary weight equal to about 1.3 grams, or 20 grains.
scru•pu•lous (skrōō'pyə-ləs) *adj.* **1.** Having scruples : ethical. **2.** Painstaking : careful. **—scru'pu•lous•ly** *adv.*
scru•ti•nize (skrōōt'n-īz') *v.* **-nized, -niz•ing.** To inspect or observe carefully or critically. **—scru'ti•niz'er** *n.*
scru•ti•ny (skrōōt'n-ē) *n., pl.* **-nies. 1.** Close, careful inspection or study. **2.** Close observation : surveillance.
scu•ba (skōō'bə) *n.* An apparatus used by divers for breathing underwater.
scuba diver *n.* One who uses scuba gear in underwater swimming.
scud (skŭd) *v.* **scud•ded, scud•ding.** To move along quickly and easily. *—n.* Wind-driven clouds, snow, mist, or rain.
scuff (skŭf) *v.* **1.** To drag the feet while walking. **2.** To scrape or become scraped and roughened on the surface. *—n.* **1.** A mark or worn spot resulting from scuffing. **2.** A flat-soled, backless house slipper.
scuf•fle (skŭf'əl) *v.* **-fled, -fling. 1.** To fight or struggle in a confused manner at close quarters. **2. a.** To shuffle. **b.** To walk with shuffling steps. **—scuf'fle** *n.*
scull (skŭl) *n.* **1.** A long oar mounted on the stern of a boat and twisted from side to side. **2.** One of a pair of short oars used by a single oarsman. **3.** A light racing boat for 1, 2, or 4 oarsmen. *—v.* To propel (a boat) by using sculls.

scull

scul•ler•y (skŭl'ə-rē) *n., pl.* **-ies.** A room next to the kitchen where kitchen chores, as dishwashing, are done.
scul•lion (skŭl'yən) *n. Archaic.* A servant employed to do menial kitchen tasks.
sculpt (skŭlpt) *v.* To sculpture.
sculp•tor (skŭlp'tər) *n.* A person who produces sculptures.
sculp•tress (skŭlp'trĭs) *n.* A woman who produces sculptures.

sculp•ture (skŭlp′chər) *n.* **1.** The art of making 3-dimensional figures or designs, as by chiseling marble or casting metal. **2. a.** A work of art created by sculpture. **b.** Such works as a group. —*v.* **-tured, -tur•ing.** To fashion into, depict in, or decorate with sculpture. —**sculp′tur•al** *adj.*

scum (skŭm) *n.* **1.** A thin, filmy layer of material on the surface of a liquid. **2.** Worthless matter **:** refuse. **3.** Vile or despicable people **:** rabble.

scup•per (skŭp′ər) *n.* An opening in the side of a ship that allows water to run off.

scurf (skûrf) *n.* **1.** Scaly or flaky dry skin, as dandruff. **2.** A scaly crust covering a surface, esp. of a plant. —**scurf′y** *adj.*

scur•ri•lous (skûr′ə-ləs) *adj.* **1.** Tending to use vulgar or abusive language **:** foul-mouthed. **2.** Expressed in or containing vulgar or abusive language.

scur•ry (skûr′ē) *v.* **-ried, -ry•ing.** To scamper.

scur•vy (skûr′vē) *n.* A disease resulting from a deficiency of vitamin C and marked by spongy and bleeding gums, bleeding under the skin, and extreme weakness. —*adj.* **-vi•er, -vi•est.** Worthless **:** contemptible.

scut•tle[1] (skŭt′l) *n.* A small opening or hatch with a movable lid, esp. in the deck or hull of a ship. —*v.* **-tled, -tling. 1.** To cut a hole in (a ship's hull) in order to sink. **2.** *Informal.* To throw away **:** discard.

scut•tle[2] (skŭt′l) *n.* A metal pail used to carry coal.

scut•tle[3] (skŭt′l) *v.* **-tled, -tling.** To move with quick little steps **:** scurry.

scut•tle•butt (skŭt′l-bŭt′) *n. Slang.* Rumor or gossip.

scut•work (skŭt′wûrk′) *n. Informal.* Monotonous work or menial tasks.

scythe (sīth) *n.* A tool used for mowing or reaping, having a long, curved single-edged blade with a long, bent handle. —**scythe** *v.*

Se *symbol for* SELENIUM.

sea (sē) *n.* **1. a.** The body of salt water that covers most of the earth's surface. **b.** A relatively large body of salt water. **c.** A relatively large body of fresh water. **2.** The ocean's surface <a calm *sea*> **3.** Something that suggests the sea, as in vastness <a *sea* of humanity> —**at sea.** Confused **:** perplexed.

sea anemone *n.* A marine coelenterate of the class Anthozoa or Actinozoa, with a flexible, cylindrical body and petallike tentacles surrounding a central mouth.

sea•bed (sē′bĕd′) *n.* The bottom of a sea or ocean.

sea bird *n.* A bird, as an albatross, that frequents the open waters of the ocean.

sea•board (sē′bôrd′, -bōrd′) *n.* **1.** A seacoast. **2.** The land area near the sea.

sea•coast (sē′kōst′) *n.* Land bordering the sea.

sea•far•er (sē′fâr′ər) *n.* A sailor.

sea•far•ing (sē′fâr′ĭng) *n.* A sailor's calling. —**sea′far′ing** *adj.*

sea•food (sē′fo͞od′) *n.* Fish or shellfish, as flounder or lobster, eaten as food.

sea•go•ing (sē′gō′ĭng) *adj.* **1.** Made for ocean voyages or for use on the open sea. **2.** Seafaring.

sea gull *n.* A gull.

sea horse *n.* A small marine fish of the genus *Hippocampus*, swimming erect and having a horselike head.

seal[1] (sēl) *n.* **1. a.** A device with an engraved design used to stamp an impression on soft material, as wax. **b.** The impression made by such a device. **2.** Something, as a commercial hallmark, that serves to authenticate or verify. **3. a.** A fitting or closure that prevents a liquid or gas from entering or escaping. **b.** A material, as rubber, used to make such a fitting or closure. **4.** A small paper sticker used to decorate or fasten an envelope. —*v.* **1.** To affix a seal to, esp. as a mark of authenticity. **2.** To fasten with or as if with a seal. **3.** To fix irrevocably <Their fate was *sealed.*>

seal[2] (sēl) *n.* **1.** Any of various aquatic mammals of the families Phocidae and Otariidae, with a sleek, streamlined body and limbs modified into paddlelike flippers. **2.** The pelt or fur of a seal, esp. a fur seal. —*v.* To hunt seals. —**seal′er** *n.*

sea-lane (sē′lān′) *n.* An established or frequently used sea route.

seal•ant (sē′lənt) *n.* A sealing agent.

sea legs *pl.n. Informal.* The ability to walk without faltering on board ship.

sea level *n.* The level of the surface of the ocean, used as a standard in determining land elevation or sea depths.

sea lion *n.* An eared seal of the family Otariidae, esp. *Zalophus californianus,* of the N Pacific.

seal•skin (sēl′skĭn′) *n.* **1.** The pelt of a fur seal. **2.** A garment made of sealskin.

seam (sēm) *n.* **1.** The line formed by joining 2 pieces, esp. of material, at the edges, as by sewing. **2.** A crack or wrinkle. **3.** A thin stratum or layer, as of coal. —*v.* **1.** To join with or as if with a seam. **2.** To mark with a seamlike line, as a scar or wrinkle.

sea•man (sē′mən) *n.* **1.** A mariner or sailor. **2.** Any of the 3 lowest ranks in the U.S. Navy or Coast Guard.

sea•man•ship (sē′mən-shĭp′) *n.* The skill or art of handling a ship.

sea•mount (sē′mount′) *n.* An underwater mountain rising from the ocean floor and having a submerged summit.

seam•stress (sēm′strĭs) *n.* A woman who sews, esp. in order to make living.

seam•y (sē′mē) *adj.* **-i•er, -i•est.** Unpleasant **:** sordid <the *seamy* side of politics>

sé•ance (sā′äns′) *n.* **1.** A gathering of spiritualists to receive messages from spirits. **2.** A meeting or session.

sea•plane (sē′plān′) *n.* An aircraft capable of taking off from or landing on water.

sea•port (sē′pôrt′, -pōrt′) *n.* A port for seagoing ships.

sear (sîr) *v.* **1.** To make withered or dried up

: shrivel. **2.** To scorch, char, or burn the surface of.

search (sûrch) *v.* **1.** To look over carefully in order to find something. **2.** To examine carefully : probe. **3.** To seek <*searching* for an answer> **—search** *n.* **—search'er** *n.*

search•light (sûrch'līt') *n.* **1. a.** An apparatus for projecting a strong beam of light. **b.** The beam so projected. **2.** A flashlight.

search warrant *n.* A warrant legally authorizing a search.

sea•scape (sē'skāp') *n.* A view or depiction of the sea.

sea•shell (sē'shĕl') *n.* The calcareous shell of a marine mollusk.

sea•shore (sē'shôr', -shōr') *n.* Land bordering or near the sea.

sea•sick•ness (sē'sĭk'nĭs) *n.* Nausea caused by the pitching and rolling motions of a ship. **—sea'sick'** *adj.*

sea•side (sē'sīd') *n.* The seashore.

sea•son (sē'zən) *n.* **1.** One of the 4 divisions of the year, spring, summer, autumn, and winter. **2.** A period marked by particular activities, celebrations, or crops <the Christmas *season*> —*v.* **1.** To heighten the flavor of (food) by adding condiments. **2.** To add enjoyment or interest to. **3.** To bring to a suitable condition, as by aging. **4.** To make capable or fit through trial and experience. **—sea'son•al** *adj.*

sea•son•a•ble (sē'zə-nə-bəl) *adj.* **1.** Appropriate to the time or season. **2.** Occurring or performed at the proper time. **—sea'son•a•bly** *adv.*

sea•son•ing (sē'zə-nĭng) *n.* Something, as a spice, used to season : condiment.

season ticket *n.* A ticket that can be used during a specified period of time.

seat (sēt) *n.* **1.** Something, as a bench or chair, to sit on. **2.** A place where one may sit <found her *seat*> **3. a.** The buttocks. **b.** The part of a garment that covers the buttocks. **4.** A capital or center of activity or authority. **5.** Membership in a legislature or stock exchange. —*v.* **1. a.** To place on or in a seat. **b.** To cause or help to sit. **2.** To have or provide seats for.

seat belt *n.* An adjustable strap or harness that holds one securely in a seat, as in an automobile.

seat•ing (sē'tĭng) *n.* **1.** The act of providing with seats. **2.** The arrangement of seats, as in an auditorium.

sea urchin *n.* An echinoderm of the class Echinoidea, having a soft body enclosed in a thin, spiny shell.

sea wall *n.* A wall or embankment designed to prevent erosion of a shoreline.

sea•ward (sē'wərd) *adj.* & *adv.* At or toward the sea. **—sea'wards** *adv.*

sea•way (sē'wā') *n.* An inland waterway used by oceangoing ships.

sea•weed (sē'wēd') *n.* Any of numerous marine algae, as the kelp or rockweed.

sea•wor•thy (sē'wûr'*th*ē) *adj.* Fit for a voyage on the sea. —Used of a ship.

se•ba•ceous (sĭ-bā'shəs) *adj.* Of, relating to, or secreting fat or sebum.

se•cede (sĭ-sēd') *v.* **-ced•ed, -ced•ing.** To withdraw from an association or organization, esp. a political one. **—se•ces'sion** (-sĕsh'ən) *n.* **—se•ces'sion•ist** *n.*

se•clude (sĭ-klōōd') *v.* **-clud•ed, -clud•ing.** To remove, keep apart, or withdraw from others. **—se•clu'sion** (-klōō'zhən) *n.* **—se•clu'sive** (-sĭv) *adj.*

sec•ond[1] (sĕk'ənd) *n.* **1.** A unit of time equal to 1/60 of a minute. **2.** *Informal.* A very brief time : instant. **3.** *Math.* A unit of angular measure equal to 1/60 of a minute.

sec•ond[2] (sĕk'ənd) *adj.* **1.** Coming next after the first. **2.** Another <a *second* chance> **3.** Being inferior or subordinate <*second* to none> —*n.* **1.** The ordinal number matching the number 2 in a series. **2.** One that is second. **3.** An inferior or imperfect article, esp. of merchandise. **4.** The transmission gear in a motor vehicle that produces the next-to-slowest speed. —*v.* **1.** To give support to : assist. **2.** To endorse (e.g., a motion) as a means of bringing it to a vote. **—sec'ond, sec'ond•ly** *adv.*

sec•on•dar•y (sĕk'ən-dĕr'ē) *adj.* **1.** Of the 2nd rank : inferior. **2.** Not primary or original : derivative. **3.** Of or pertaining to a secondary school. **—sec'on•dar'i•ly** *adv.*

secondary school *n.* A school between elementary school and college.

sec•ond-class (sĕk'ənd-klăs') *adj.* **1.** Of secondary quality or status : inferior. **2.** Of or relating to travel accommodations ranking next below the first or highest class. **3.** Of or relating to a class of mail consisting mainly of newspapers and periodicals. **—sec'ond-class'** *adv.*

second cousin *n.* The child of one's parent's first cousin.

second generation *n.* *Computer Sci.* The period of computer technology that utilized solid-state circuitry and offline storage and highly developed software.

sec•ond-guess (sĕk'ənd-gĕs') *v.* **1.** To be critical of (e.g., a decision) after the event. **2.** To outguess.

sec•ond•hand (sĕk'ənd-hănd') *adj.* **1.** Not new : worn or used. **2.** Dealing in previously used merchandise. **3.** Obtained, derived, or borrowed from another. **—sec'ond•hand'** *adv.*

second lieutenant *n.* An officer in the U.S. Army, Air Force, or Marine Corps having the lowest commissioned grade.

second nature *n.* Deeply ingrained habits and characteristics.

second person *n.* The form of a pronoun or verb used in referring to the person addressed, as *you* and *may* in *you may go.*

sec•ond-rate (sĕk'ənd-rāt') *adj.* Inferior or mediocre in quality or value.

sec•ond-sto•ry man (sĕk'ənd-stôr'ē, -stōr'ē) *n.* A burglar who enters through an upstairs window.

sec•ond-string (sĕk'ənd-strĭng') *adj.* Being a substitute, as on a football team.

second wind *n.* Renewed strength or energy, as during a competition.

se•cre•cy (sē'krĭ-sē) *n.* **1.** The state or quality of being secret. **2.** The practice of keeping secrets.

se•cret (sē'krĭt) *adj.* **1.** Kept from general knowledge or view. **2.** Operating in a hidden or clandestine manner <*secret* police> **3.** Not frequented : secluded. **4.** Beyond common understanding : mysterious. ★ ***syns:*** CLANDESTINE, COVERT, HUSH-HUSH, UNDERCOVER —*n.* **1.** Something concealed from others. **2.** Something not readily understood : mystery. **3.** A method or formula for accomplishing something. —**se'cret•ly** *adv.*

sec•re•tar•i•at (sĕk'rĭ-târ'ē-ĭt) *n.* **1.** The department managed by a governmental secretary. **2.** The office or position of a governmental secretary.

sec•re•tar•y (sĕk'rĭ-tĕr'ē) *n., pl.* **-ies. 1.** A person hired to do clerical work, as handling correspondence, for a superior. **2.** An officer charged with keeping an organization's records, as minutes or correspondence. **3.** The head of a governmental department. **4.** A writing desk. —**sec're•tar'i•al** (-târ'ē-əl) *adj.*

se•crete[1] (sĭ-krēt') *v.* **-cret•ed, -cret•ing.** To produce and separate out (e.g., an oily substance) from cells or bodily fluids. —**se•cre'tion** *n.*

se•crete[2] (sĭ-krēt') *v.* **-cret•ed, -cret•ing.** To hide away : conceal.

se•cre•tive (sē'krə-tĭv, sĭ-krē'-) *adj.* Practicing or inclined to secrecy. —**se'cre•tive•ness** *n.*

Secret Service *n.* A branch of the U.S. Treasury Department charged with the suppression of counterfeiting and the protection of the President.

sect (sĕkt) *n.* **1.** A group of people, often part of a larger group, who are united by common interests or beliefs. **2.** A religious body, esp. one that has separated from a larger denomination.

sec•tar•i•an (sĕk-târ'ē-ən) *adj.* **1.** Of or relating to a sect. **2.** Narrow-minded : parochial. —*n.* **1.** A member of a sect. **2.** A narrow-minded or bigoted person. —**sec•tar'i•an•ism** *n.*

sec•tion (sĕk'shən) *n.* **1.** A part or piece of something : portion. **2.** A separate part, as of a newspaper. **3.** A view of the internal structure of a solid object as it would appear if cut straight through. **4.** A land unit of 640 acres or 1 sq. mi. —*v.* To divide into sections.

sec•tion•al (sĕk'shə-nəl) *adj.* **1.** Of, relating to, or like a section. **2.** Divided into or made up of sections. **3.** Not general : regional or local. —**sec'tion•al•ism** *n.*

sec•tor (sĕk'tər) *n.* **1.** *Math.* The part of a circle bounded by 2 radii and 1 of the intercepted arcs. **2.** A division of a defensive or offensive area for which one military unit is responsible. **3.** A distinct part <the agricultural *sector* of the economy>

sec•u•lar (sĕk'yə-lər) *adj.* **1.** Temporal rather than spiritual : worldly. **2.** Not religious or sacred. **3.** Not bound by monastic restrictions <*secular* clergy>

sec•u•lar•ism (sĕk'yə-lə-rĭz'əm) *n.* The belief that religious considerations should be excluded from civil affairs or public education. —**sec'u•lar•ist** *n.*

sec•u•lar•ize (sĕk'yə-lə-rīz') *v.* **-ized, -iz•ing. 1.** To change from ecclesiastical to lay or civil use or control. **2.** To make secular. —**sec'u•lar•i•za'tion** *n.*

se•cure (sĭ-kyo͝or') *adj.* **-cur•er, -cur•est. 1.** Free from harm, risk, or loss : safe. **2.** Free from anxiety or doubt : confident. **3.** Not likely to fail or give way : stable. **4.** Sure : certain. —*v.* **-cured, -cur•ing. 1.** To keep from harm, risk, or loss. **2.** To fasten firmly. **3.** To guarantee : ensure. **4.** To gain possession of : acquire. —**se•cure'ly** *adv.*

se•cu•ri•ty (sĭ-kyo͝or'ĭ-tē) *n., pl.* **-ties. 1.** Freedom from risk or danger : safety. **2.** Freedom from doubt, anxiety, or fear : confidence. **3.** Something given to assure the fulfillment of an obligation : pledge. **4. securities.** Written evidence of ownership or creditorship, esp. stocks or bonds. **5.** Measures designed to protect, as from theft, attack, or disclosure. **6.** *Computer Sci.* Prevention of the unauthorized use of a program or device.

se•dan (sĭ-dăn') *n.* **1.** A closed automobile having a front and rear seat. **2.** An enclosed chair carried on poles by 2 men.

se•date[1] (sĭ-dāt') *adj.* **-dat•er, -dat•est.** Serene and dignified : composed.

se•date[2] (sĭ-dāt') *v.* **-dat•ed, -dat•ing.** To administer a sedative to. —**se•da'tion** *n.*

sed•a•tive (sĕd'ə-tĭv) *adj.* Having a calming, soothing, or tranquilizing effect. —*n.* A sedative drug or agent.

sed•en•tar•y (sĕd'n-tĕr'ē) *adj.* Requiring or marked by much sitting.

sedge (sĕj) *n.* Any of various plants of the family Cyperaceae, resembling grasses but having solid stems.

sed•i•ment (sĕd'ə-mənt) *n.* **1.** Material that settles to the bottom of a liquid. **2.** Material, as stones, deposited by wind or water. —**sed'i•men'ta•ry** (-mĕn'tə-rē, -mĕnt'rē) *adj.* —**sed'i•men•ta'tion** *n.*

se•di•tion (sĭ-dĭsh'ən) *n.* Behavior or language that brings about rebellion against the established authority of the state. —**se•di'tious** *adj.*

se•duce (sĭ-do͞os', -dyo͞os') *v.* **-duced, -duc•ing. 1.** To draw away from duty or proper conduct : corrupt. **2.** To persuade or entice to have sexual intercourse. **3.** To beguile. —**se•duc'er** *n.* —**se•duc'tion** (-dŭk'shən) *n.* —**se•duc'tive** *adj.*

sed•u•lous (sĕj'ə-ləs) *adj.* Assiduous.

see[1] (sē) *v.* **saw** (sô), **seen** (sēn), **see•ing. 1.** To perceive by or have the power of sight. **2.** To comprehend. **3.** To have a mental picture of : visualize <*saw* the town as it once was> **4.** To know through firsthand experience : undergo. **5.** To take note of : heed. **6.** To encounter, esp. regularly. **7.** To visit, esp. for consultation <*seeing* a doctor> **8.** To attend

: view <*saw* a movie> **—see through. 1.** To understand the real character or nature of. **2.** To fulfill or finish (a task or obligation).

see² (sē) *n.* The authority, jurisdiction, or position of a bishop.

seed (sēd) *n., pl.* **seeds** *or* **seed. 1.** A fertilized and ripened plant ovule having an embryo capable of germinating to produce a new plant. **2.** A propagative part of a plant, as a bulb, tuber, or spore. **3.** A source : origin. **4.** Offspring : descendants. *—v.* **1.** To plant seeds in : sow. **2.** To remove the seeds from. **—go (*or* run) to seed. 1.** To progress to the seed-bearing stage. **2.** To deteriorate. **—seed′er** *n.*

seed•ling (sēd′lĭng) *n.* A young plant grown from a seed.

seed money *n.* Money required or given to start a new project.

seed•pod (sēd′pŏd′) *n.* A pod, as of a pea, that splits open when ripe.

seed•time (sēd′tīm′) *n.* A time for sowing seeds.

seed vessel *n. Bot.* A pericarp.

seed•y (sē′dē) *adj.* **-i•er, -i•est. 1.** Having numerous seeds. **2.** Run-down and shabby : unkempt. **3.** Squalid : disreputable.

see•ing (sē′ĭng) *conj.* Considering that.

seek (sēk) *v.* **sought** (sôt), **seek•ing. 1.** To make a search (for). **2.** To try to reach or obtain. **3.** To attempt : try. **—seek′er** *n.*

seem (sēm) *v.* **1.** To appear to be <*seemed* worried> **2.** To appear to oneself. **3.** To appear to exist or be true.

seem•ing (sē′mĭng) *adj.* Apparent : ostensible. **—seem′ing•ly** *adv.*

seem•ly (sēm′lē) *adj.* **-li•er, -li•est.** Proper : appropriate. **—seem′li•ness** *n.*

seen (sēn) *v. p.p. of* SEE¹.

seep (sēp) *v.* To pass slowly through small openings or pores : ooze. **—seep′age** *n.*

seer (sē′ər) *n.* A person supposedly able to visualize and thus predict the future.

seer•suck•er (sîr′sŭk′ər) *n.* A lightweight fabric, gen. of cotton or rayon, having a crinkled surface and usu. a striped pattern.

see•saw (sē′sô′) *n.* **1. a.** A game in which 2 children alternate in riding up and down on opposite ends of a long board balanced in the middle. **b.** The board used in seesaw. **2.** An up-and-down or back-and-forth movement. **—see′saw′** *v.*

seethe (sēth) *v.* **seethed, seeth•ing. 1.** To bubble, foam, boil, or churn. **2.** To be greatly agitated.

seg•ment (sĕg′mənt) *n.* **1.** Any of the parts into which something can be divided : section. **2.** *Math.* A section of a figure cut off by a line or plane. **—seg•ment′** (sĕg-mĕnt′) *v.* **—seg•ment′al** *adj.* **—seg′men•ta′tion** *n.*

seg•re•gate (sĕg′rĭ-gāt′) *v.* **-gat•ed, -gat•ing. 1.** To isolate from others. **2.** To impose racial segregation on.

seg•re•ga•tion (sĕg′rĭ-gā′shən) *n.* **1.** The act or process of segregating or the state of being segregated. **2.** The policy or practice of isolating or separating an ethnic group or race, as in schools, housing, and employment. **—seg′re•ga′tion•ist** *n.*

se•gue (sĕg′wā′, sā′gwā′) *v.* **-gued, -gu•ing.** To make a transition directly from one section or theme, as of music, to another.

seign•ior (sān-yôr′, sān′yôr′) *n.* A feudal lord. **—sei•gnio′ri•al** *adj.*

seine (sān) *n.* A large fishing net with weights at the lower edge and floats at the top. *—v.* To fish with a seine.

seis•mic (sīz′mĭk) *adj.* **1.** Of, relating to, or caused by an earthquake. **2.** Earthshaking. **—seis•mic′i•ty** (-mĭs′ĭ-tē) *n.*

seis•mo•gram (sīz′mə-grăm′) *n.* The record of an earth tremor made by a seismograph.

seis•mo•graph (sīz′mə-grăf′) *n.* An instrument for automatically detecting and measuring earthquakes and other ground vibrations. **—seis•mog′ra•pher** (sīz-mŏg′rə-fər) *n.* **—seis′mo•graph′ic** *adj.* **—seis•mog′ra•phy** *n.*

seis•mol•o•gy (sīz-mŏl′ə-jē) *n.* The science that deals with earthquakes and with the mechanical properties of the earth. **—seis′mo•log′ic** (-mə-lŏj′ĭk), **seis′mo•log′i•cal** *adj.* **—seis•mol′o•gist** *n.*

seize (sēz) *v.* **seized, seiz•ing. 1.** To take possession or hold of quickly and forcibly. **2.** To take prisoner : arrest. **3.** To take eagerly <*seized* the opportunity> **4.** To comprehend. **5.** To affect suddenly : overwhelm. **—sei′zure** (sē′zhər) *n.*

sel•dom (sĕl′dəm) *adv.* Rarely.

se•lect (sĭ-lĕkt′) *v.* To pick out or choose from a number of choices. *—adj.* **1.** Carefully picked or chosen. **2.** Choice <a *select* wine> **3.** Fastidious in selection : discriminating. **—se•lec′tive** *adj.* **—se•lec′tiv′i•ty** (-lĕk′tĭv′ĭ-tē) *n.*

se•lec•tee (sĭ-lĕk′tē′) *n.* One selected for military service.

se•lec•tion (sĭ-lĕk′shən) *n.* **1. a.** The act of selecting. **b.** One selected. **2.** A collection of carefully chosen persons or things. **3.** *Biol.* A process that favors or brings about the survival and perpetuation of one kind of organism rather than others.

selective service *n.* A system for drafting individuals for military service.

se•lect•man (sĭ-lĕkt′mən) *n.* One of a board of officers chosen annually in most New England towns to manage local affairs.

se•lect•wom•an (sĭ-lĕkt′wo͝om′ən) *n.* A woman who is a selectman.

sel•e•nite (sĕl′ə-nīt′) *n.* Gypsum in the form of clear colorless crystals.

se•le•ni•um (sĭ-lē′nē-əm) *n. Symbol* **Se** A nonmetallic element with chemical properties similar to sulfur.

sel•e•nog•ra•phy (sĕl′ə-nŏg′rə-fē) *n.* The study of the physical features of the moon.

sel•e•nol•o•gy (sĕl′ə-nŏl′ə-jē) *n.* The astronomical study of the moon.

self (sĕlf) *n., pl.* **selves** (sĕlvz). **1.** The essential being of one person as distinct from any other. **2.** A particular aspect of a person. **3.** Personal welfare, interest, or advantage : selfishness.

self– *pref.* **1.** Oneself : itself <*self*-control> **2.** Automatic : automatically <*self*-loading>

self-a•ban•doned (sĕlf'ə-băn'dənd) *adj.* Abandoned by oneself, esp. having yielded to one's impulses.

self-cen•tered (sĕlf'sĕn'tərd) *adj.* Concerned only with oneself : selfish. —**self'-cen'tered•ness** *n.*

self-com•posed (sĕlf'kəm-pōzd') *adj.* Having control over one's emotions.

self-con•scious (sĕlf'kŏn'shəs) *adj.* **1.** Uncomfortably aware of one's appearance or manner. **2.** Socially uncomfortable. **3.** Aware of one's individuality. —**self'-con'scious•ly** *adv.* —**self'-con'scious•ness** *n.*

self-con•tained (sĕlf'kən-tānd') *adj.* **1.** Complete within itself. **2.** Self-sufficient. **3.** Keeping to oneself : reserved.

self-de•fense (sĕlf'dĭ-fĕns') *n.* **1.** The act of defending oneself or what belongs to oneself. **2.** *Law.* The right to use whatever means reasonably necessary to protect oneself against violence or threatened violence.

self-de•struct (sĕlf'dĭ-strŭkt') *v.* To destroy oneself or itself.

self'-a•base'ment *n.*
self'-ac'cu•sa'tion *n.*
self'-act'ing *adj.*
self'-ad•dressed' *adj.*
self'-ad•just'ing *adj.*
self'-ad•min'is•tered *adj.*
self'-ad'mi•ra'tion *n.*
self'-ad•vance'ment *n.*
self'-ad'ver•tis'ing *adj.*
self'-ag•gran'dize•ment *n.*
self-aid' *n.*
self'-a•lign'ing *adj.*
self'-a•nal'y•sis *n.*
self'-ap•point'ed *adj.*
self'-ap•proved' *adj.*
self'-as•sert'ing *adj.*
self'-as•ser'tion *n.*
self'-as•ser'tive *adj.*
self'-as•sur'ance *n.*
self'-as•sured' *adj.*
self'-au'thor•ized' *adj.*
self'-a•ware'ness *n.*
self'-be•tray'al *n.*
self'-blame' *n.*
self'-charg'ing *adj.*
self'-clean'ing *adj.*
self'-clos'ing *adj.*
self'-com•mand' *n.*
self'-com•pla'cent *adj.*
self'-con•ceit' *n.*
self'-con•cerned' *adj.*
self'-con•demned' *adj.*
self'-con•duct'ed *adj.*
self'-con•fessed' *adj.*
self'-con'fi•dence *n.*
self'-con'fi•dent *adj.*
self'-con'flict *n.*
self'-con•grat'u•la'tion *n.*
self'-con•grat'u•la•tor'y *adj.*
self'-con'sti•tut'ed *adj.*
self'-con•sum'ing *adj.*
self'-con•tempt' *n.*
self'-con'tra•dic'tion *n.*
self'-con'tra•dic'to•ry *adj.*
self'-con•trol' *n.*
self'-cor•rect'ing *adj.*
self'-cor•rup'tion *n.*
self'-cre•at'ed *adj.*
self'-crit'i•cism *n.*
self'-cul'ti•va'tion *n.*
self'-cure' *n.*
self'-de•ceit' *n.*
self'-de•ceiv'ing *adj.*
self'-de•cep'tion *n.*
self'-de•feat'ing *adj.*
self'-de•frost'ing *adj.*
self'-deg'ra•da'tion *n.*
self'-de•lu'sion *n.*
self'-de•ni'al *n.*
self'-de•ny'ing *adj.*
self'-dep're•cat'ing *adj.*
self'-de•pre'ci•a'tion *n.*
self'-de•struc'tion *n.*
self'-de•struc'tive *adj.*
self'-de•ter'mi•na'tion *n.*
self'-di•rec'tion *n.*
self'-dis'ci•pline *n.*
self'-dis•cov'er•y *n.*
self'-dis•trust' *n.*
self'-doubt' *n.*
self'-driv'en *adj.*
self'-ed'u•cat'ed *adj.*
self'-em•ployed' *adj.*
self'-em•ploy'ment *n.*
self'-emp'ty•ing *adj.*
self'-es•teem' *n.*
self'-ev'i•dent *adj.*
self'-ex•am'i•na'tion *n.*
self'-ex•plain'ing *adj.*
self'-ex•plan'a•to'ry *adj.*
self'-ex•pres'sion *n.*
self'-feed'ing *adj.*
self'-fill'ing *adj.*
self'-for•get'ful *adj.*
self'-giv'ing *adj.*
self'-gov'ern•ing *adj.*
self'-gov'ern•ment *n.*
self'-guid'ance *n.*
self'-hard'en•ing *adj.*
self'-heal'ing *adj.*
self'-help' *n.*
self'-hyp•no'sis *n.*
self'-im'age *n.*
self'-im'mo•la'tion *n.*
self'-im•por'tance *n.*
self'-im•por'tant *adj.*
self'-im•posed' *adj.*
self'-im•prove'ment *n.*
self'-in•crim'i•na'tion *n.*
self'-in•duced' *adj.*
self'-in•dul'gence *n.*
self'-in•dul'gent *adj.*
self'-in•flict'ed *adj.*
self'-ink'ing *adj.*
self'-in•struct'ed *adj.*
self'-in•sur'ance *n.*
self'-in'ter•est *n.*
self'-light'ing *adj.*
self'-lim'it•ing *adj.*
self'-lock'ing *adj.*
self'-love' *n.*
self'-lu'bri•cat'ing *adj.*
self'-man'age•ment *n.*
self'-mas'ter•y *n.*
self'-mock'er•y *n.*
self'-mock'ing *adj.*
self'-mov'ing *adj.*
self'-oil'ing *adj.*
self'-op'er•at'ing *adj.*
self'-or•dained' *adj.*
self'-per•pet'u•at'ing *adj.*
self'-pit'y *n.*
self'-por'trait *n.*
self'-pos•sessed' *adj.*
self'-pos•ses'sion *n.*
self'-praise' *n.*
self'-pres'er•va'tion *n.*
self'-pro•claimed' *adj.*
self'-pro•pelled' *adj.*
self'-pro•pel'ling *adj.*
self'-pro•tec'tion *n.*
self'-re'al•i•za'tion *n.*
self'-re•cord'ing *adj.*
self'-re•gard' *n.*
self'-reg'is•ter•ing *adj.*
self'-reg'u•lat'ing *adj.*
self'-re•li'ance *n.*
self'-re•li'ant *adj.*
self'-re•proach' *n.*
self'-re•proof' *n.*
self'-re•spect' *n.*
self'-re•spect'ing *adj.*
self'-re•straint' *n.*
self'-re•veal'ing *adj.*
self'-rev'e•la'tion *n.*
self'-re•ward'ing *adj.*
self'-rule' *n.*
self'-sac'ri•fice' *n.*
self'-sac'ri•fic'ing *adj.*
self'-sat'is•fac'tion *n.*
self'-sat'is•fied' *adj.*
self'-seek'er *n.*
self'-seek'ing *adj.*
self'-serv'ice *n.*
self'-start'ing *adj.*
self'-stud'y *n.*
self'-styled' *adj.*
self'-suf•fi'cien•cy *n.*
self'-suf•fi'cient *adj.*
self'-sup•port'ing *adj.*
self'-sus•tain'ing *adj.*
self'-taught' *adj.*
self'-ther'a•py *n.*
self'-tor'ment *n.*
self'-trust' *n.*
self'-vin'di•ca'tion *n.*
self'-wind'ing *adj.*
self'-wor'ship *n.*

self-ef•fac•ing (sĕlf'ĭ-fā'sĭng) *adj.* Humble : modest. —**self'-ef•face'ment** *n.*
self-en•forc•ing (sĕlf'ĕn-fôr'sĭng, -fōr'-) *adj.* Having within itself the means or a guarantee of its enforcement <a *self-enforcing* order>
self-fer•til•i•za•tion (sĕlf'fûr'tl-ĭ-zā'shən) *n.* Fertilization by sperm from the same animal, as in some hermaphrodites, or by pollen from the same flower.
self-flag•el•la•tion (sĕlf'flăj'ə-lā'shən) *n.* Harsh criticism of oneself.
self-ful•fill•ing (sĕlf'fo͝ol-fĭl'ĭng) *adj.* **1.** Attaining one's own expectation or goals. **2.** Occurring largely as a result of having been predicted or expected <a *self-fulfilling* prophecy>
self•ish (sĕl'fĭsh) *adj.* Concerned only or primarily with oneself without regard for others. ★ *syns:* SELF-CENTERED, SELF-SEEKING —**self'ish•ness** *n.*
self•less (sĕlf'lĭs) *adj.* Without thought for oneself : unselfish. —**self'less•ly** *adv.* —**self'less•ness** *n.*
self-load•ing (sĕlf'lō'dĭng) *adj.* Semiautomatic, as a firearm.
self-made (sĕlf'mād') *adj.* Successful through one's own actions <a *self-made* millionaire>
self-pol•li•na•tion (sĕlf'pŏl'ə-nā'shən) *n.* The transfer of pollen from an anther to a stigma of the same flower.
self-right•eous (sĕlf'rī'chəs) *adj.* Piously or smugly convinced of one's own righteousness. —**self'-right'eous•ly** *adv.*
self•same (sĕlf'sām') *adj.* Exactly the same : identical. —**self'same'ness** *n.*
self-seal•ing (sĕlf'sē'lĭng) *adj.* Capable of sealing itself, as after a puncture.
self-serv•ing (sĕlf'sûr'vĭng) *adj.* Serving one's own interests, esp. without concern for the needs or interests of others.
self-start•er (sĕlf'stär'tər) *n.* **1.** A device for automatically starting an internal-combustion engine. **2.** An individual having initiative.
self-will (sĕlf'wĭl') *n.* Willfulness, esp. in satisfying one's own desires : stubbornness. —**self'-willed'** *adj.*
sell (sĕl) *v.* **sold** (sōld), **sell•ing. 1.** To exchange (e.g., goods or services) for money or its equivalent. **2. a.** To offer for sale. **b.** To be sold or on sale. **3.** To promote the sale, acceptance, or adoption of <tried to *sell* the idea to his parents> ★ *syns:* HANDLE, MARKET, MERCHANDISE, RETAIL, VEND —**sell out. 1.** To sell all of one's property. **2.** To betray. —**sell'er** *n.*
selt•zer (sĕlt'sər) *n.* **1.** Effervescent mineral water. **2.** Artificially carbonated water.
sel•vage *also* **sel•vedge** (sĕl'vĭj) *n.* The edge of a fabric woven so that it will not ravel.
selves (sĕlvz) *n. pl. of* SELF.
se•man•tic (sə-măn'tĭk) *adj.* Of or relating to meaning.
se•man•tics (sə-măn'tĭks) *n. (sing. in number).* **1.** The study of meaning in language, esp. with regard to historical changes. **2.** The study of the relationships between signs and symbols.
sem•a•phore (sĕm'ə-fôr', -fōr') *n.* **1.** A visual signaling apparatus with mechanically moving arms. **2.** A system for signaling with flags held in the hand. —**sem'a•phore'** *v.*
sem•blance (sĕm'bləns) *n.* **1.** A representation : likeness. **2.** An outward appearance or superficial show.
se•men (sē'mən) *n.* The thick, whitish secretion of the male reproductive organs.
se•mes•ter (sə-mĕs'tər) *n.* One of the 2 divisions of an academic year.
sem•i (sĕm'ī, sĕm'ē) *n., pl.* **sem•is.** *Informal.* **1.** A semitrailer. **2.** A semifinal.
semi– *pref.* **1.** Half of <*semi*circle> **2.** Partial : partially <*semi*professional> **3.** Occurring 2 times during <*semi*annual>
sem•i•an•nu•al (sĕm'ē-ăn'yo͞o-əl) *adj.* Occurring or issued twice a year.
sem•i•au•to•mat•ic (sĕm'ē-ô'tə-măt'ĭk) *adj.* Ejecting the shell and loading the succeeding

sem'i•ag'ri•cul'tur•al *adj.*
sem'i•an'i•mat'ed *adj.*
sem'i•ar'id *adj.*
sem'i•at•tached' *adj.*
sem'i•au•ton'o•mous *adj.*
sem'i•bar•bar'ic *adj.*
sem'i•bar'ren *adj.*
sem'i•bi'o•graph'ic *adj.*
sem'i•bleached' *adj.*
sem'i•civ'i•lized' *adj.*
sem'i•clas'si•cal *adj.*
sem'i•co•ag'u•lat'ed *adj.*
sem'i•col•laps'i•ble *adj.*
sem'i•con•cealed' *adj.*
sem'i•con'fi•dent *adj.*
sem'i•con•fine'ment *n.*
sem'i•con'scious *adj.*
sem'i•con•ser'va•tive *adj.*
sem'i•co•op'er•a•tive *adj.*
sem'i•cul'ti•vat'ed *adj.*
sem'i•cul'tured *adj.*
sem'i•dark'ness *adj.*
sem'i•deaf' *adj.*
sem'i•de•cay' *n.*
sem'i•de•cayed' *adj.*
sem'i•de•lir'i•ous *adj.*
sem'i•de•pend'ent *adj.*
sem'i•de•vel'oped *adj.*
sem'i•di•gest'ed *adj.*
sem'i•di•ur'nal *adj.*
sem'i•di•vine' *adj.*
sem'i•doc'u•men'ta•ry *adj. & n.*
sem'i•do•mes'ti•cat'ed *adj.*
sem'i•dor'mant *adj.*
sem'i•dry' *adj.*
sem'i•en•closed' *adj.*
sem'i•ex•pand'ed *adj.*
sem'i•ex•posed' *adj.*
sem'i•feu'dal•ism *n.*
sem'i•fic'tion•al *adj.*
sem'i•fixed' *adj.*
sem'i•flexed' *adj.*
sem'i•flu'id *adj.*
sem'i•for'mal *adj.*
sem'i•formed' *adj.*
sem'i•glaze' *n.*
sem'i•glazed' *adj.*
sem'i•gloss' *n.*
sem'i•god' *n.*
sem'i-Goth'ic *adj.*
sem'i•hard' *adj.*
sem'i•his•tor'i•cal *adj.*
sem'i•hos'tile *adj.*
sem'i•hu'mor•ous *adj.*
sem'i•hys•ter'i•cal *adj.*
sem'i-i'dle *adj.*
sem'i-in'de•pend'ent *adj.*
sem'i-in•tox'i•cat'ed *adj.*
sem'i-in'va•lid *adj. & n.*
sem'i-i•ron'ic *adj.*
sem'i•joc'u•lar *adj.*
sem'i•lib'er•al *adj.*

round of ammunition automatically but requiring a trigger squeeze for each shot. —Used of firearms.

sem•i•cir•cle (sĕm'ĭ-sûr'kəl) *n.* A half of a circle. —**sem'i•cir'cu•lar** (-kyə-lər) *adj.*

sem•i•co•lon (sĕm'ē-kō'lən) *n.* A mark of punctuation (;) that indicates a degree of separation greater than that of a comma but less that that of a period.

sem•i•con•duc•tor (sĕm'ē-kən-dŭk'tər) *n.* A solid crystalline substance, as selenium or silicon, that has electrical conductivity greater than an insulator but less than a conductor.

sem•i•fi•nal (sĕm'ē-fī'nəl) *adj.* Immediately preceding the final, as in a tournament. —*n.* A semifinal match or competition. —**sem'i•fi'nal•ist** *n.*

sem•i•month•ly (sĕm'ē-mŭnth'lē) *adj.* Happening or issued twice a month. —*n., pl.* **-lies.** A semimonthly event or publication. —**sem'•i•month'ly** *adv.*

sem•i•nal (sĕm'ə-nəl) *adj.* **1.** Of, pertaining to, or containing semen or seed. **2.** Of, relating to, or possessing the power to originate **:** creative <a *seminal* work of the impressionist style> —**sem'i•nal•ly** *adv.*

sem•i•nar (sĕm'ə-när') *n.* **1. a.** A course of study pursued by a group of advanced college or graduate students who do independent research under the guidance of a professor. **b.** A meeting of such a group. **2.** A meeting for an exchange of ideas.

sem•i•nar•y (sĕm'ə-nĕr'ē) *n., pl.* **-ies. 1. a.** A school where priests, ministers, or rabbis are educated and trained. **2.** A secondary school, esp. a private school for girls. —**sem'i•nar'•i•an** (-nâr'ē-ən) *n.*

Sem•i•nole (sĕm'ə-nōl') *n., pl.* **-nole** *or* **-noles. 1.** A member of an American Indian people of primarily Creek origin, now living in Oklahoma and S Florida. **2.** Their Muskogean language.

se•mi•ot•ics (sē'mē-ŏt'ĭks, sĕm'ē-, sē'mī-) *n. (takes sing. v.)* Semantics. —**se'mi•o•ti'cian** (-ə-tĭsh'ən) *n.*

sem•i•pal•mate (sĕm'ē-păl'māt', -päl'māt') *also* **sem•i•pal•mat•ed** (-mā'tĭd) *adj.* Having partial webbing between the toes, as some wading birds do.

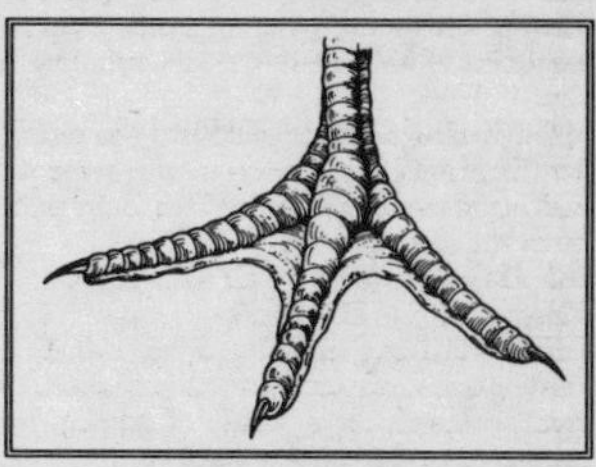

semipalmate
Semipalmate foot of a plover

sem•i•per•me•a•ble (sĕm'ē-pûr'mē-ə-bəl) *adj.* **1.** Somewhat permeable. **2.** Permeable to some molecules but not to all. —**sem'i•per'•me•a•bil'i•ty** *n.*

sem•i•pre•cious (sĕm'ē-prĕsh'əs) *adj.* Of smaller value than a precious stone.

sem•i•pri•vate (sĕm'ē-prī'vĭt) *adj.* Shared with usu. 1 to 3 other hospital patients <a *semiprivate* room>

sem•i•pro (sĕm'ē-prō') *adj. Informal.* Semiprofessional. —**sem'i•pro'** *n.*

sem•i•pro•fes•sion•al (sĕm'ē-prə-fĕsh'ə-nəl) *adj.* **1.** Participating in an activity for pay but not as a full-time occupation. **2.** Made up of or engaged in by semiprofessional players. —**sem'i•pro•fes'sion•al** *n.*

Sem•ite (sĕm'īt') *n.* **1.** A member of any of a group of linguistically-related Middle Eastern peoples, esp. Arabs and Jews. **2.** A Jew. —**Se•mit'ic** (sə-mĭt'ĭk) *adj.*

sem•i•tone (sĕm'ē-tōn') *n. Mus.* An interval of a half tone.

sem•i•trail•er (sĕm'ē-trā'lər) *n.* A trailer with a set or sets of wheels at the rear only, sup-

sem'i•liq'uid *adj.*
sem'i•lit'er•ate *adj.*
sem'i•lux'u•ry *n.*
sem'i•me•chan'i•cal *adj.*
sem'i•mil'i•tar'y *adj.*
sem'i•mo'bile *adj.*
sem'i•mod'er•ate *adj.*
sem'i•mod'ern *adj.*
sem'i•mute' *adj.*
sem'i•mys'ti•cal *adj.*
sem'i•myth'ic *adj.*
sem'i•neu•rot'ic *adj.*
sem'i•noc•tur'nal *adj.*
sem'i•pa•ral'y•sis *n.*
sem'i•pa'gan *adj.*
sem'i•pas'tor•al *adj.*
sem'i•per'ish•a•ble *adj.*
sem'i•per'ma•nent *adj.*
sem'i•pet'ri•fied' *adj.*
sem'i•plas'tic *adj.*
sem'i•po•lit'i•cal *adj.*
sem'i•pre•served' *adj.*
sem'i•prim'i•tive *adj.*
sem'i•prone' *adj.*
sem'i•pro•tect'ed *adj.*
sem'i•pub'lic *adj.*
sem'i•rad'i•cal *adj.*
sem'i•raw' *adj.*
sem'i•re•ac'tion•ar'y *adj.*
sem'i•re•lig'ious *adj.*
sem'i•res'o•lute' *adj.*
sem'i•re•spect'a•ble *adj.*
sem'i•re•tired' *adj.*
sem'i•re•tire'ment *n.*
sem'i•ro•man'tic *adj.*
sem'i•ru'ral *adj.*
sem'i•rus'tic *adj.*
sem'i•sa'cred *adj.*
sem'i•sa•tir'i•cal *adj.*
sem'i•sav'age *adj.*
sem'i•scho•las'tic *adj.*
sem'i•sci'en•tif'ic *adj.*
sem'i•se'cre•cy *n.*
sem'i•se'cret *adj.*
sem'i•se'ri•ous *adj.*
sem'i•shade' *n.*
sem'i•skilled' *adj.*
sem'i•soft' *adj.*
sem'i•sol'id *adj.*
sem'i•stiff' *adj.*
sem'i•sub•ur'ban *adj.*
sem'i•suc•cess'ful *adj.*
sem'i•sweet' *adj.*
sem'i•tai'lored *adj.*
sem'i•tech'ni•cal *adj.*
sem'i•tra•di'tion•al *adj.*
sem'i•trained' *adj.*
sem'i•trans•par'ent *adj.*
sem'i•truth'ful *adj.*
sem'i•vol'a•tile *adj.*
sem'i•vol'un•tar'y *adj.*
sem'i•wild' *adj.*
sem'i•year'ly *adj. & adv.*

ported in front by a truck tractor or towing vehicle.

sem·i·trop·i·cal (sĕm'ē-trŏp'ĭ-kəl) *adj.* Partly tropical.

sem·i·week·ly (sĕm'ē-wēk'lē) *adj.* Happening or issued twice a week. —*n., pl.* **-lies.** A semiweekly event or publication. —**sem'i·week'ly** *adv.*

sen (sĕn) *n., pl.* **sen.** —See table at CURRENCY.

sen·ate (sĕn'ĭt) *n.* The upper house in a bicameral legislature, as the U.S. Congress.

sen·a·tor (sĕn'ə-tər) *n.* A member of a senate. —**sen'a·to'ri·al** (-tôr'ē-əl, -tōr'-) *adj.* —**sen'a·to'ri·al·ly** *adv.*

send (sĕnd) *v.* **sent** (sĕnt), **send·ing. 1.** To cause to be conveyed or dispatched. **2.** To direct, allow, or enable to go. **3.** To give off (e.g., heat) **:** emit. **4.** To drive with force **:** propel. **5.** *Slang.* To transport with pleasure **:** delight. ★ ***syns:*** DISPATCH, FORWARD, ROUTE, SHIP, TRANSMIT —**send'er** *n.*

send·off (sĕnd'ôf', -ŏf') *n.* A demonstration of good wishes, as for the start of a new undertaking.

se·ne (sä'nä) *n., pl.* **sene.** —See table at CURRENCY.

se·nes·cent (sĭ-nĕs'ənt) *adj.* Growing old **:** aging. —**se·nes'cence** *n.*

se·nile (sē'nīl', sĕn'īl') *adj.* **1.** Of or proceeding from old age. **2.** Exhibiting the mental deterioration often associated with old age. —**se·nil'i·ty** (sə-nĭl'ĭ-tē) *n.*

sen·ior (sēn'yər) *adj.* **1.** Of or being the older of 2 **:** elder. **2.** Of higher rank or standing than another. **3.** Of or relating to the final year of high school or college. —*n.* **1.** A person who is older or of higher rank than another. **2.** A student in the final year of high school or college.

senior citizen *n.* An elderly, usu. retired person.

senior high school *n.* A school usu. including grades 10, 11, and 12.

sen·ior·i·ty (sēn-yôr'ĭ-tē, -yŏr'-) *n.* **1.** The state or fact of being senior. **2.** Priority over others by reason of service.

sen·i·ti (sĕn'ĭ-tē) *n., pl.* **seniti.** —See table at CURRENCY.

sen·na (sĕn'ə) *n.* A plant of the genus *Cassia,* with compound leaves that are dried and used medicinally as a cathartic.

se·ñor (sān-yôr') *n., pl.* **se·ñor·es** (sān-yôr'ās). The Spanish title of courtesy for a man, equivalent to English *Mr.* or *sir.*

se·ño·ra (sān-yôr'ə) *n., pl.* **se·ñor·as** (sān-yôr'əs). The Spanish title of courtesy for a married woman, equivalent to English *Mrs.* or *madam.*

se·ño·ri·ta (sān'yə-rē'tə) *n.* The Spanish title of courtesy for an unmarried woman or girl, equivalent to English *Miss.*

sen·sa·tion (sĕn-sā'shən) *n.* **1. a.** An awareness associated with the stimulation of a sense organ <the *sensation* of cold> **b.** The capacity to feel or perceive physically. **2.** A nonspecific feeling <a *sensation* of floating> **3. a.** A condition of strong interest and excitement. **b.** An event or object causing this condition. —**sen·sa'tion·al** *adj.*

sen·sa·tion·al·ism (sĕn-sā'shə-nə-lĭz'əm) *n.* The use of material or methods intended to shock, excite, or arouse curiosity.

sense (sĕns) *n.* **1. a.** One of the functions of sight, hearing, touch, smell, and taste. **b.** The faculty of perceiving by means of these functions. **2.** Ability to estimate, judge, appreciate, or understand <a *sense* of humor> **3.** A vague feeling or impression <a *sense* of doom> **4.** *often* **senses.** The ability to think or reason soundly <Come to your *senses.*> **5.** Significance **:** meaning. —*v.* **sensed, sens·ing. 1.** To perceive by or as if by the senses. **2.** To detect automatically <*sensed* victory>

sense·less (sĕns'lĭs) *adj.* **1.** Unconscious. **2.** Lacking sense **:** pointless. —**sense'less·ly** *adv.* —**sense'less·ness** *n.*

sen·si·bil·i·ty (sĕn'sə-bĭl'ĭ-tē) *n., pl.* **-ties. 1.** The capacity to perceive sensation. **2.** Refinement in feeling **:** sensitivity.

sen·si·ble (sĕn'sə-bəl) *adj.* **1.** Capable of perceiving or being perceived through or as if through the senses. **2.** Capable of **:** sensitive. **3.** Conscious **:** aware. **4.** Having or displaying good sense. —**sen'si·bly** *adv.*

sen·si·tive (sĕn'sĭ-tĭv) *adj.* **1.** Sensory. **2.** Responding readily to small changes of condition or environment. **3.** Readily affected, as by the emotions or circumstances of others. **4.** Easily offended, hurt, damaged, or irritated. —**sen'si·tive·ly** *adv.* —**sen'si·tiv'i·ty** (-tĭv'ĭ-tē), **sen'si·tive·ness** *n.*

sen·si·tize (sĕn'sĭ-tīz') *v.* **-tized, -tiz·ing.** To make or become sensitive. —**sen'si·ti·za'tion** *n.* —**sen'si·tiz'er** *n.*

sen·sor (sĕn'sər, -sôr') *n.* A device, as a photoelectric cell, that responds to a signal or stimulus.

sen·so·ry (sĕn'sə-rē) *adj.* Of or relating to the senses.

sen·su·al (sĕn'shōō-əl) *adj.* **1. a.** Of, relating to, or preoccupied with the gratification of the senses, esp. the sexual appetite. **b.** Suggesting sexuality **:** voluptuous. **2.** Not spiritual or intellectual **:** physical. —**sen'su·al·ist** *n.* —**sen'su·al'i·ty** (-ăl'ĭ-te) *n.* —**sen'su·al·ly** *adv.*

sen·su·ous (sĕn'shōō-əs) *adj.* **1.** Of or arising from the senses. **2.** Appealing to the senses. **3.** Voluptuous. —**sen'su·ous·ly** *adv.* —**sen'su·ous·ness** *n.*

sent (sĕnt) *v. p.t. & p.p. of* SEND.

sen·te (sĕn'tä) *n., pl.* **li·sen·te** (lē-sĕn'tä). —See table at CURRENCY.

sen·tence (sĕn'təns) *n.* **1.** A grammatical construction that contains a finite verb or verb phrase and usu. a subject and its predicate. **2. a.** A judicial decision, esp. one detailing punishment to be inflicted on a convicted person. **b.** The penalty imposed. —*v.* **-tenced, -tenc·ing.** To impose a sentence on (a convicted person). —**sen·ten'tial** (sĕn-tĕn'shəl) *adj.*

sen•ten•tious (sĕn-tĕn′shəs) *adj.* **1.** Given to or marked by the use of aphorisms. **2.** Abounding in or given to smug moralizing.

sen•tient (sĕn′shənt) *adj.* Capable of feeling or perceiving : conscious.

sen•ti•ment (sĕn′tə-mənt) *n.* **1.** A general cast of mind. **2.** An idea, opinion, or attitude based more on feeling than on reason. **3. a.** Susceptibility to emotion. **b.** Emotion, esp. romantic or nostalgic feeling. ★ ***syns:*** ATTITUDE, DISPOSITION, FEELING

sen•ti•men•tal (sĕn′tə-mĕn′tl) *adj.* **1.** Marked, swayed, or affected by sentiment. **2.** Arising from, expressive of, or appealing to the sentiments, esp. nostalgic or romantic feelings <*sentimental* pictures> **—sen′ti•men′tal•ism** *n.* **—sen′ti•men′tal•ist** *n.* **—sen′ti•men•tal′i•ty** (-tăl′ĭ-tē) *n.* **—sen′ti•men′tal•ly** *adv.*

sen•ti•men•tal•ize (sĕn′tə-mĕn′tl-īz′) *v.* **-ized, -iz•ing.** To be sentimental (about).

sen•ti•nel (sĕn′tə-nəl) *n.* One that guards or warns of approaching danger.

sen•try (sĕn′trē) *n., pl.* **-tries.** A guard, esp. a military guard : sentinel.

se•pal (sē′pəl) *n.* One of the usu. green segments forming the calyx of a flower.

sep•a•ra•ble (sĕp′ər-ə-bəl, sĕp′rə-) *adj.* Capable of being separated.

sep•a•rate (sĕp′ə-rāt′) *v.* **-rat•ed, -rat•ing. 1.** To put or keep apart : disjoin. **2.** To serve to keep apart, as a barrier does. **3.** To go different ways : part. **4.** To extract <*separate* cream from milk> ★ ***syns:*** DIVIDE, PART, PARTITION, SECTION, SEGMENT *—adj.* (sĕp′ər-ĭt, sĕp′rĭt). **1.** Set aside from others. **2.** Distinct from others. **3.** Particular : individual <*separate* directions> *—n.* (sĕp′ər-ĭt, sĕp′rĭt). A garment, as a skirt, designed to be worn in various combinations with other garments. **—sep′a•rate•ly** *adv.*

sep•a•ra•tion (sĕp′ə-rā′shən) *n.* **1.** The act or process of separating or the state of being separated. **2.** A place, line, or point of division. **3.** A space or interval that separates.

sep•a•ra•tist (sĕp′ər-ə-tĭst, sĕp′rə-, sĕp′ə-rā′-) *n.* A person who advocates separation, as from a political or religious affiliation. **—sep′a•ra•tism** *n.*

sep•a•ra•tor (sĕp′ə-rā′tər) *n.* One that separates, esp. an apparatus that separates cream from milk.

se•pi•a (sē′pē-ə) *n.* A grayish yellowish brown to dark brown.

sep•sis (sĕp′sĭs) *n.* The presence of disease-causing organisms or their toxins in the blood or body tissues.

Sep•tem•ber (sĕp-tĕm′bər) *n.* The 9th month of the year, having 30 days.

sep•tic (sĕp′tĭk) *adj.* **1.** Of, relating to, or having the nature of sepsis. **2.** Causing sepsis : putrefactive.

sep•ti•ce•mi•a (sĕp′tĭ-sē′mē-ə) *n.* A condition in which disease-causing microorganisms or their toxins are present in the bloodstream.

septic tank *n.* A tank in which sewage is decomposed by bacteria.

sep•tu•a•ge•nar•i•an (sĕp′to͞o-ə-jə-nâr′ē-ən, -tyo͞o-) *n.* One between the ages of 70 and 80. **—sep′tu•a•ge•nar′i•an** *adj.*

Sep•tu•a•gint (sĕp′cho͞o-ə-jĭnt′, sĕp′to͞o-) *n.* A 3rd cent. B.C. Greek translation of the Old Testament.

sep•tum (sĕp′təm) *n., pl.* **-ta** (-tə). A thin partition or membrane between two body cavities or soft masses of tissue.

sep•ul•cher (sĕp′əl-kər) *n.* A burial vault. *—v.* To put in a sepulcher : inter. **—se•pul′chral** (sə-pŭl′krəl) *adj.*

sep•ul•chre (sĕp′əl-kər) *n. & v. esp. Brit. var. of* SEPULCHER.

se•quel (sē′kwəl) *n.* **1.** Something that follows or comes after. **2.** A literary work forming the continuation of an earlier work. **3.** A result : outcome.

se•quence (sē′kwəns) *n.* **1.** The following of one thing after another. **2.** A number of things or events that follow each other. **3.** The order in which things or events occur or are arranged. **—se•quen′tial** (sĭ-kwĕn′shəl) *adj.* **—se•quen′tial•ly** *adv.*

se•quent (sē′kwənt) *adj.* **1.** Following : subsequent. **2.** Resultant : consequent.

se•ques•ter (sĭ-kwĕs′tər) *v.* **1.** To set apart : segregate. **2.** To withdraw : seclude. **—se′ques•tra′tion** (sē′kwĭ-strā′shən) *n.*

se•quin (sē′kwĭn) *n.* A small, usu. shiny decorative spangle.

se•quoi•a (sĭ-kwoi′ə) *n.* An extremely large evergreen tree of the genus *Sequoia,* which includes the redwood.

se•ra (sîr′ə) *n. var. pl. of* SERUM.

se•ra•glio (sĭ-răl′yō, -räl′-) *n., pl.* **-glios. 1.** A harem. **2.** The palace of a sultan.

se•ra•pe (sə-rä′pē) *n.* An often brightly colored woolen blanket worn as a cloak or poncho, esp. in certain parts of Mexico.

ser•aph (sĕr′əf) *n., pl.* **-aphs** *or* **-a•phim** (-ə-fĭm′). An angel of the highest order. **—se•raph′ic** (sə-răf′ĭk) *adj.*

sere (sîr) *adj.* Withered : dry.

ser•e•nade (sĕr′ə-nād′) *n.* Music performed to compliment or express love for someone. *—v.* **-nad•ed, -nad•ing.** To perform a serenade (to).

ser•en•dip•i•ty (sĕr′ən-dĭp′ĭ-tē) *n.* The faculty of discovering desirable or valuable things accidentally or unexpectedly. **—ser′en•dip′i•tous** *adj.*

se•rene (sə-rēn′) *adj.* **1.** Peaceful : calm. **2.** Perfectly clear <a *serene* moonlit sky> **—se•ren′i•ty** (sə-rĕn′ĭ-tē) *n.*

serf (sûrf) *n.* A medieval European peasant who was owned by a lord and bound to the land. **—serf′dom** *n.*

serge (sûrj) *n.* A twilled cloth of worsted or a blend of worsted and wool.

ser•geant (sär′jənt) *n.* **1.** A noncommissioned officer in the U.S. Army, Air Force, or Marine Corps ranking next above a corporal. **2.** A police officer ranking just below a captain or sometimes a lieutenant.

sergeant at arms *n., pl.* **sergeants at arms.** An officer charged with keeping order, as at the meeting of a legislature.

se•ri•al (sîr'ē-əl) *adj.* **1.** Consisting of or arranged in a series. **2.** Presented in installments <a *serial* television drama> —*n.* A serial story or play. —**se'ri•al•i•za'tion** *n.* —**se'ri•al•ize'** *v.* —**se'ri•al•ly** *adv.*

serial number *n.* One of a series of numbers used esp. for identification.

se•ries (sîr'ēz) *n., pl.* **series.** A number of things or events, esp. of the same kind, occurring in a row or following one after the other : succession.

se•ri•ous (sîr'ē-əs) *adj.* **1.** Grave : sober. **2.** Not jesting : earnest. **3.** Not trivial : weighty. **4.** Marked by or demanding thought, effort, or devotion. **5.** Giving cause for worry : dangerous. —**se'ri•ous•ly** *adv.* —**se'ri•ous•ness** *n.*

ser•mon (sûr'mən) *n.* **1.** A discourse delivered by a clergyman during a church service. **2.** An often long-winded lecture on duty or behavior. —**ser'mon•ize'** *v.* —**ser'mon•iz'er** *n.*

se•rol•o•gy (sĭ-rŏl'ə-jē) *n.* The medical science dealing with serums. —**se'ro•log'ic** (sîr'ə-lŏj'ĭk), **se'ro•log'i•cal** *adj.*

se•ro•neg•a•tive (sîr'ō-nĕg'ə-tĭv) *adj.* Showing a negative reaction to a test on blood serum for a disease.

se•ro•pos•i•tive (sîr'ō-pŏz'ĭ-tĭv) *adj.* Showing a positive reaction to a test on blood serum for a disease.

ser•pent (sûr'pənt) *n.* A snake.

ser•pen•tine (sûr'pən-tēn', -tīn') *adj.* **1.** Of or like a serpent in form or movement : sinuous. **2.** Subtly sly : cunning.

ser•rate (sĕr'āt') *also* **ser•rat•ed** (-ā'tĭd) *adj.* Having a notched sawlike edge.

ser•ried (sĕr'ēd) *adj.* Pressed or close together : crowded.

se•rum (sîr'əm) *n., pl.* **-rums** *or* **se•ra** (sîr'ə). **1.** The clear fluid obtained when whole blood is separated into its solid and liquid components. **2.** A liquid extracted from the tissues of an immunized animal and used esp. as an antitoxin.

ser•vant (sûr'vənt) *n.* **1.** One employed to perform household services. **2.** One that serves another.

serve (sûrv) *v.* **served, serv•ing. 1.** To be a servant (to). **2.** To prepare and offer <*serve* lunch> **3.** To supply service to : wait on <*serving* the public> **4.** To do a term of duty <*served* in the army > **5.** To put in : spend <*served* 6 years in the senate> **6.** To be of assistance to : benefit <*serving* the national interest> **7.** To meet the requirements of : satisfy <*serve* the purpose> **8.** To act in a specific capacity <*served* as chairman> **9.** To be used profitably by <a port that *serves* a wide region> **10.** To put a ball or shuttlecock into play, as in court games. —*n.* The act, right, or manner of serving a ball or shuttlecock. —**serv'er** *n.*

serv•ice (sûr'vĭs) *n.* **1.** The occupation of a servant. **2.** Employment, esp. for a government <public *service*> **3.** A government branch or department and its personnel <the civil *service*> **4. a.** One of the military forces of a nation. **b.** Duty in one of these forces. **5.** Work or duties performed for others <a housecleaning *service*> **6.** A facility offering repair or maintenance. **7.** A facility providing the public with a utility, as water or transportation. **8.** A religious ceremony or rite. **9.** Assistance : benefit. **10.** A set of utensils or dishes <a china *service*> **11.** The act, manner, or right of serving, as in tennis : serve. —*v.* **-iced, -ic•ing. 1.** To adjust, repair, or maintain. **2.** To provide or furnish a service to.

serv•ice•a•ble (sûr'vĭ-sə-bəl) *adj.* **1.** Ready or fit for service : useful. **2.** Capable of giving long service : durable.

serv•ice•man (sûr'vĭs-măn', -mən) *n.* **1.** A member of the military forces of a nation. **2.** A person whose work is the maintenance and repair of equipment.

service mark *n.* A symbol or mark used in the sale or advertising of services to distinguish them from the services of others.

service station *n.* A station where services, esp. repairs, can be obtained for motor vehicles.

serv•ice•wom•an (sûr'vĭs-wo͝om'ən) *n.* A woman member of the armed forces.

ser•vile (sûr'vəl, -vīl') *adj.* **1.** Slavishly submissive. **2.** Of or suitable to a servant or slave. ★ *syns:* OBSEQUIOUS, SLAVISH, SUBSERVIENT —**ser•vil'i•ty** (sər-vĭl'ĭ-tē) *n.*

serv•ing (sûr'vĭng) *n.* A helping.

ser•vi•tor (sûr'vĭ-tər, -tôr') *n.* A man servant : attendant.

ser•vi•tude (sûr'vĭ-to͞od', -tyo͞od') *n.* The state of being a slave or serf : bondage.

ser•vo (sûr'vō) *n., pl.* **-vos. 1.** A servomotor. **2.** A servomechanism.

ser•vo•mech•a•nism (sûr'vō-mĕk'ə-nĭz'əm) *n.* A feedback system composed of a sensory element, an amplifier, and a servomotor that automatically controls the functions of a mechanical device.

ser•vo•mo•tor (sûr'vō-mō'tər) *n.* A motor that controls the action of the mechanical device in a servomechanism.

ses•a•me (sĕs'ə-mē) *n.* A plant, *Sesamum indicum,* of tropical Asia, yielding small, flat seeds that are a source of oil.

ses•qui•cen•ten•ni•al (sĕs'kwĭ-sĕn-tĕn'ē-əl) *adj.* Occurring every 150 years. —*n.* A 150th anniversary.

ses•qui•pe•da•li•an (sĕs'kwĭ-pĭ-dā'lē-ən, -dāl'yən) *adj.* **1.** Containing many syllables : polysyllabic. **2.** Tending to use polysyllabic words.

ses•sion (sĕsh'ən) *n.* **1.** A meeting or series of meetings, as of a judicial or legislative body. **2.** A meeting devoted to a specific activity. **3.** A period during the day or year when a school holds classes.

ses•tet (sĕ-stĕt') *n.* A stanza making up the last 6 lines of a sonnet.

†**set¹** (sĕt) *v.* **set, set•ting. 1.** To put in a particular position : place. **2.** To cause to do or

be <*set* me thinking><*set* him free> **3. a.** To place in a firm or secure position **:** fix. **b.** To become firm, secure, or fixed. **4.** To prepare for proper functioning <*set* a trap> **5.** To adjust **:** regulate <*set* a timer> **6.** To arrange <*set* the table> **7. a.** To compose (music) to fit a text. **b.** To write (words) to fit a melodic line. **8.** To establish **:** settle <*set* the date> **9.** To place in a mounting or frame <*set* a jewel><*set* type> **10.** To cause to sit. **11.** To sit on eggs to hatch them. **12.** To make as an estimate of worth <*set* a high value on work> **13.** To sink below the horizon. **14.** To harden or congeal <cement *setting*> **15.** To have a particular course or direction. **16.** *Regional.* To sit. **—set back. 1.** To retard the progress of **:** hinder. **2.** *Informal.* To cost <That car *set* me *back* $8,000.> **—set forth. 1.** To present for consideration **:** propose. **2.** To express in words. **—set off. 1. a.** To cause to begin. **b.** To cause to explode. **2.** To call attention to by contrast **:** accentuate. **—set out. 1.** To undertake. **2.** To begin a journey. **—set up. 1.** To put together and erect. **2.** To establish **:** found. *—adj.* **1.** Fixed or determined by agreement or convention. **2.** Deliberate **:** intentional. **3.** Fixed and rigid. **4.** Unwilling to change <*set* in one's ways> **5.** Ready <*set* to go> *—n.* **1.** The act or process of setting. **2.** The way something is held or placed.

set[2] (sĕt) *n.* **1.** A group of persons or things of the same kind or sharing a common characteristic and usu. classed or associated together. **2.** An assemblage of parts that functions as a unit <a television *set*> **3.** A structure representing the place where the action of a play or motion picture takes place. **4.** *Math.* A collection of distinct elements <a *set* of integers> **5.** A group of games, as in tennis, that forms one unit or part of a match.

set•back (sĕt′băk′) *n.* An unanticipated delay or reverse in progress.

set•screw (sĕt′skrōō′) *n.* A screw used to hold 2 parts securely in position or to regulate the tension of a spring.

set•tee (sĕ-tē′) *n.* A small sofa with a back and arms.

set•ter (sĕt′ər) *n.* Any of several breeds of long-haired hunting dogs.

set•ting (sĕt′ĭng) *n.* **1.** The context and environment in which something occurs. **2.** The scenery for a dramatic performance. **3.** A mounting, as for a jewel.

set•tle (sĕt′l) *v.* **-tled, -tling. 1.** To put in order. **2.** To establish residence (in). **3.** To come or cause to come to rest <*settled* back in my chair> **4.** To restore tranquillity to **:** calm. **5.** To sink or cause to sink and condense. **6.** To end or resolve <*settle* a dispute> **7.** To fix through mutual accord. **8.** To make compensation or payment for (a claim or debt). **9.** To give by formal or legal process. **10.** To establish in a business or way of life. **11.** To become more composed **:** stabilize. **—set′tler** *n.*

set•tle•ment (sĕt′l-mənt) *n.* **1.** The act or process of settling. **2.** A small, relatively new community. **3.** Establishment, as of people in a new area. **4.** An adjustment or accord reached, as in financial matters. **5. a.** Transfer of property to provide for the future needs of a person. **b.** Property thus transferred. **6.** A welfare center offering community services to the needy.

set-to (sĕt′tōō′) *n., pl.* **-tos.** A brief but usu. angry conflict.

set•up (sĕt′ŭp′) *n.* **1.** *Informal.* The manner in which something is planned or arranged. **2.** *often* **setups.** *Informal.* Ice and nonalcoholic ingredients, as soda water, furnished to customers who add their own liquor. **3.** *Slang.* A competition or undertaking made easy to win or accomplish.

sev•en (sĕv′ən) *n.* **1.** The cardinal number equal to 6 + 1. **2.** The 7th in a set or sequence. **—sev′en** *adj. & pron.* **—sev′enth** *adj. & adv. & n.*

sev•en•teen (sĕv′ən-tēn′) *n.* **1.** The cardinal number equal to 16 + 1. **2.** The 17th in a set or sequence. **—sev′en•teen′** *adj. & pron.* **—sev′en•teenth′** *adj. & adv. & n.*

sev•en•teen-year locust (sĕv′ən-tēn′yîr′) *n.* A cicada, *Magicicada septendecim*, of the E U.S., having a nymphal stage in which it remains underground for 17 or sometimes 13 years.

seventh heaven *n.* A state of extreme happiness and satisfaction.

sev•en•ty (sĕv′ən-tē) *n., pl.* **-ties.** The cardinal number equal to 7 × 10. **—sev′en•ty** *adj. & pron.* **—sev′en•ti•eth** *adj. adv. & n.*

sev•er (sĕv′ər) *v.* To separate forcibly, as by cutting or breaking. **—sev′er•ance** *n.*

sev•er•al (sĕv′ər-əl, sĕv′rəl) *adj.* **1.** Being of a number greater than 2 or 3 but not many. **2.** Single **:** distinct. *—pron.* Several persons or things. **—sev′er•al•ly** *adv.*

sev•er•al•ty (sĕv′ər-əl-tē, sĕv′rəl-) *n., pl.* **-ties.** *Law.* **1.** A separate and individual right to possession or ownership. **2.** Property owned in severalty.

severance pay *n.* A sum of money, usu. based on length of employment, that an employee is eligible for on termination.

se•vere (sə-vîr′) *adj.* **-ver•er, -ver•est. 1.** Harshly unsparing **:** strict <*severe* terms> **2.** Corresponding strictly and inflexibly to established rule. **3.** Austere **:** somber. **4.** Extremely plain in style. **5.** Extremely intense <*severe* pain> **—se•vere′ly** *adv.* **—se•ver′i•ty** (-vĕr′ĭ-tē) *n.*

sew (sō) *v.* **sewed, sewn** (sōn) *or* **sewed, sew•ing. 1.** To make, close, repair, or attach with stitches made with a needle and thread. **2.** To work with a needle and thread <*sews* for a hobby>

sew•age (sōō′ĭj) *n.* Liquid and solid waste material that passes through sewers.

sew•er (sōō′ər) *n.* A channel or conduit to carry off waste material.

sew•er•age (sōō′ər-ĭj) *n.* **1.** A network of sewers. **2.** Sewage.

sew•ing (sō′ĭng) *n.* **1.** The act or occupation of one who sews. **2.** Something made or being made with needle and thread.

sewing machine *n.* A machine used for sewing.

sewn (sŏn) *v. var. p.p. of* SEW.

sex (sĕks) *n.* **1.** One of the 2 divisions, male and female, into which many living things are grouped. **2.** The physiological and functional differences that distinguish the male and female. **3.** Sexual intercourse. **—sex'less** *adj.*

sex•a•ge•nar•i•an (sĕk'sə-jə-nâr'ē-ən) *n.* One who is between the ages of 60 and 70. **—sex'-a•ge•nar'i•an** *adj.*

sex appeal *n.* Physical attractiveness that arouses sexual interest in another person.

sex chromosome *n.* One of a pair of chromosomes that in combination determine the sex of an individual in human beings, most animals, and some plants.

sex hormone *n.* An animal hormone, as estrogen or androgen, that affects the growth or function of the reproductive organs and the development of secondary sex characteristics.

sex•ism (sĕk'sĭz'əm) *n.* Prejudice or discrimination based on gender, esp. against women. **—sex'ist** *adj. & n.*

sex•tant (sĕk'stənt) *n.* An instrument used in navigation to measure the altitude between the plane of the horizon and a line extending to a celestial body.

sex•tet (sĕk-stĕt') *n.* **1. a.** A musical composition for 6 performers. **b.** A group of 6 musicians who perform a sextet. **2.** A group of 6 persons or things.

sex•ton (sĕk'stən) *n.* One who maintains church property.

sex•u•al (sĕk'shōō-əl) *adj.* Of, relating to, or involving sex, the sexes, or the sex organs. **—sex'u•al'i•ty** (-ăl'ĭ-tē) *n.* **—sex'u•al•ly** *adv.*

sexual intercourse *n.* Sexual union between human beings, gen. involving physical union of the sexual organs.

sex•y (sĕk'sē) *adj.* **-i•er, -i•est.** *Informal.* Arousing or intended to arouse sexual interest or desire : erotic. **—sex'i•ness** *n.*

shab•by (shăb'ē) *adj.* **-bi•er, -bi•est. 1.** Worn-out : ragged. **2.** Dressed in worn-out, frayed, or threadbare clothes. **3.** Contemptible : nasty. **—shab'bi•ly** *adv.* **—shab'bi•ness** *n.*

shack (shăk) *n.* A small, crude building.

shack•le (shăk'əl) *n.* **1.** A metal ring fastened or locked around the wrist or ankle of a prisoner. **2.** A device used to fasten or couple. **3.** Something that restrains or confines. —*v.* **-led, -ling.** To fasten, restrain, or confine with shackles.

shad (shăd) *n., pl.* **shad** *or* **shads.** A marine food fish of the genus *Alosa* that swims up rivers to spawn.

shade (shād) *n.* **1.** Comparative darkness caused by the interception of light rays. **2.** An area or space of shade. **3.** Shelter from the sun's rays. **4.** A device used to reduce or screen light. **5. shades.** *Slang.* Sunglasses. **6.** Relative obscurity. **7.** Degree of darkness of a color. **8.** A minor variation or difference. **9.** A small amount. **10.** A phantom : ghost. ★ *syns:* GRADATION, NUANCE —*v.* **shad•ed, shad•ing. 1.** To shield or screen from light or heat. **2.** To obscure : hide. **3.** To mark or draw indications of shade in <*shade* a drawing> **4.** To alter (e.g., meaning) by slight degrees.

shad•ing (shā'dĭng) *n.* **1.** Protection against light or heat. **2.** Marks, as lines, used to represent gradations of colors or darkness. **3.** A slight variation, gradation, or difference.

shad•ow (shăd'ō) *n.* **1.** Partial illumination in an area from which light is blocked by an opaque object. **2.** An image cast on a surface by an object blocking rays of light. **3. a.** Gloom : unhappiness. **b.** Something that causes gloom. **4.** A shaded area in a picture or photograph. **5.** A ghost : phantom. **6.** A slight indication, portion, or amount. —*v.* **1.** To throw a shadow on : shade. **2.** To represent vaguely or mysteriously. **3.** To follow secretly : trail. **—shad'ow•y** *adj.*

shad•ow•box (shăd'ō-bŏks') *v.* To box with an imaginary opponent, as for exercise. **—shad'ow•box'ing** *n.*

shad•y (shā'dē) *adj.* **-i•er, -i•est. 1.** Full of shade. **2.** Of questionable character. ★ *syns:* DOUBTFUL, DUBIOUS, FISHY, QUESTIONABLE, SUSPECT, SUSPICIOUS **—shad'i•ly** *adv.* **—shad'i•ness** *n.*

shaft (shăft) *n.* **1.** The long narrow body of an arrow or spear. **2.** An arrow or spear. **3.** One of 2 parallel poles by which an animal is harnessed to a vehicle. **4.** A ray or beam of light. **5.** The handle of an implement or tool. **6. a.** A cylindrical bar on which a rotating part turns. **b.** A similar bar that turns and transmits power. **7.** A long, narrow passage beneath the surface of the ground : tunnel. **8.** A vertical passage for an elevator. **9.** An air duct or conduit.

shag (shăg) *n.* **1.** A tangled or matted mass of hair, wool, or fiber. **2.** A coarse long nap, as on woolen cloth.

shag•bark (shăg'bärk') *n.* A North American hickory tree, *Carya ovata,* with shaggy bark.

shagbark
The shagbark hickory: detail of its bark, leaves, flowers, and fruit

shag•gy (shăg'ē) *adj.* **-gi•er, -gi•est. 1.** Having or consisting of long, rough hair, wool, or fibers. **2.** Rough and bushy or uneven <*shaggy* hair>

shah (shä) *n.* Used formerly as a title for the hereditary monarch of Iran.

shake (shāk) *v.* **shook** (shŏŏk), **shak•en** (shā'kən), **shak•ing. 1.** To move or cause to move up and down or back and forth with short, quick movements. **2.** To tremble or cause to tremble **:** quake. **3.** To throw off or displace by or as if by shaking <*shook* the snow from my coat> **4.** To bring or come to a particular condition by or as if by shaking. **5.** To agitate or disturb **:** disconcert <was *shaken* by the survivors' reports> **6.** To wave or brandish <*shake* one's fist> **7.** To clasp (hands) in greeting, farewell, or agreement. **8.** To make less firm **:** weaken <*shook* my confidence> *—n.* **1.** An act of shaking. **2. shakes.** *Informal.* Uncontrollable trembling. **3.** *Slang.* Deal **:** treatment <a fair *shake*> **—shake down.** *Informal.* **1.** To obtain money from by extortion. **2.** To make a complete search of. **3.** To subject to a shakedown test. **—shak'a•ble, shake'a•ble** *adj.*

shake•down (shāk'doun') *n.* **1.** *Informal.* Extortion of money. **2.** *Informal.* A complete search of a person or place. **3.** A test of performance, as of a new aircraft or ship.

shak•er (shā'kər) *n.* **1.** One that shakes <a salt *shaker*><a cocktail *shaker*> **2. Shaker.** A member of a Christian group originating in England in 1747.

shake•up (shāk'ŭp') *n.* A complete, often drastic reorganization.

shak•y (shā'kē) *adj.* **-i•er, -i•est. 1.** Tremulous **:** quaking. **2.** Rickety **:** unsound. **3.** Unreliable **:** precarious. **—shak'i•ly** *adv.* **—shak'i•ness** *n.*

shale (shāl) *n.* A rock consisting of claylike particles that split into layers easily.

shale oil *n.* A crude dark oil obtained from oil shale by heating and distillation.

shall (shăl) *v. p.t.* **should** (shŏŏd). —Used as an auxiliary to indicate simple futurity, determination or promise, inevitability, or command.

shal•lop (shăl'əp) *n.* An open boat having oars or sails or both.

shal•lot (shə-lŏt', shăl'ət) *n.* An onionlike plant, *Allium ascalonicum,* with a mild-flavored edible bulb.

shal•low (shăl'ō) *adj.* **1.** Not deep from bottom to top or surface. **2.** Lacking intellectual or emotional depth. *—n.* A shallow part or place in a body of water.

sham (shăm) *n.* **1.** Something or someone false that purports to be genuine **:** imitation. **2.** A decorative cover that simulates an article of household linen and is used in its place <a pillow *sham*> *—adj.* Not genuine **:** false. *—v.* **shammed, sham•ming.** To pretend to have or feel **:** feign. **—sham'mer** *n.*

sha•man (shä'mən, shā'-) *n.* A member of certain tribal societies who mediates between the visible and the spirit worlds for purposes of healing, divination, and control over natural events. **—sha'man•ism** *n.*

sham•ble (shăm'bəl) *v.* **-bled, -bling.** To walk awkwardly while shuffling the feet. **—sham'ble** *n.*

sham•bles (shăm'bəlz) *pl.n. (sing. in number).* A state or scene of complete disorder or destruction.

shame (shām) *n.* **1.** A painful feeling of guilt, embarrassment, or disgrace. **2.** The capacity to feel shame. **3.** A source of shame. **4.** Dishonor **:** disgrace. **5.** Something that is unfortunate or regrettable. *—v.* **shamed, sham•ing. 1.** To cause to feel shame. **2.** To bring disgrace upon. **—shame'ful** *adj.* **—shame'ful•ly** *adv.* **—shame'less** *adj.* **—shame'less•ly** *adv.*

shame•faced (shām'fāst') *adj.* **1.** Ashamed. **2.** Bashful. **—shame'fac'ed•ly** (-fā'sĭd-lē) *adv.*

sham•my (shăm'ē) *n.* Chamois leather.

sham•poo (shăm-pōō') *n., pl.* **-poos. 1.** A preparation, as of soap, used to wash the hair and scalp. **2.** A preparation used to clean rugs or upholstery. **3.** The act or process of washing or cleaning with shampoo. **—sham•poo'** *v.*

sham•rock (shăm'rŏk') *n.* A plant, as a clover, that has 3 leaflets and is regarded as the national emblem of Ireland.

shang•hai (shăng-hī') *v.* **1.** To force to board a ship and serve as a sailor. **2.** To compel to do something, esp. by force.

Shan•gri-la (shăng'grĭ-lä') *n.* An imaginary paradise on earth **:** utopia.

shank (shăngk) *n.* **1. a.** The portion of the human leg between the ankle and knee. **b.** A corresponding part in other vertebrates. **2.** A cut of meat, as lamb, from the leg. **3.** The part of an instrument or tool that connects the functioning part and the handle.

shan't (shănt, shänt). Shall not.

shan•tung (shăn-tŭng') *n.* A fabric, orig. of wild silk, with a nubby surface.

shan•ty (shăn'tē) *n., pl.* **-ties.** A roughly built or dilapidated cabin or shelter **:** shack.

shape (shāp) *n.* **1.** The outline or surface configuration of something **:** form. **2.** The contour of a person's body **:** figure. **3.** Condition, as for effective functioning <a swimmer in good *shape*> **4.** A form in which something may appear or exist. *—v.* **shaped, shap•ing. 1.** To take or cause to take form, esp. a particular form. **2.** To adjust to fit **:** adapt. **3.** To cause to take a particular course.

shape•less (shāp'lĭs) *adj.* **1.** Lacking definite shape. **2.** Lacking beauty or elegance of shape. **—shape'less•ly** *adv.* **—shape'less•ness** *n.*

shape•ly (shāp'lē) *adj.* **-li•er, -li•est.** Pleasing in shape. **—shape'li•ness** *n.*

shard (shärd) *n.* A piece broken off, esp. from a brittle substance **:** fragment.

share[1] (shâr) *n.* **1.** A portion belonging to an individual. **2.** One of the equal parts into which the capital stock of a corporation is divided. *—v.* **shared, shar•ing. 1.** To divide and parcel out in shares **:** apportion. **2.** To participate in, experience, or use in common. **—shar'er** *n.*

share[2] (shâr) *n.* A plowshare.

share·crop·per (shâr′krŏp′ər) *n.* A farmer who gives a share of the crop to the owner of the land he works.

share·hold·er (shâr′hōl′dər) *n.* A stockholder.

shark (shärk) *n.* **1.** Any of various often large and voracious marine fishes of the order Squaliformes, with a cartilaginous skeleton and small, toothlike scales. **2.** A ruthless, greedy person.

shark·skin (shärk′skĭn′) *n.* **1.** The skin of a shark or leather made from it. **2.** A material, as of rayon and acetate, with a smooth, shiny surface.

sharp (shärp) *adj.* **1.** Having a thin, keen edge or a fine point. **2.** Not rounded or smooth <a *sharp* chin> **3.** Not gradual : abrupt <a *sharp* drop> **4.** Distinct : clear <in *sharp* focus> **5.** Astute : shrewd <a *sharp* mind> **6.** Vigorous : energetic. **7.** Alert. **8.** Biting : harsh <*sharp* criticism> **9.** Sudden and shrill <a *sharp* blast of the horn> **10.** Intensely felt : severe <a *sharp* pain> **11.** *Mus.* **a.** Raised in pitch by a semitone. **b.** Above the correct pitch. **12.** *Informal.* Fashionable : stylish <a *sharp* suit> —*adv.* **1.** In a sharp manner. **2.** Precisely : exactly <came at 6 *sharp*> —*n.* **1.** *Mus.* **1.** A sign (♯) indicating that a note is a semitone higher than a given note. **2.** *Informal.* A shrewd cheater, esp. at gambling. —**sharp′ly** *adv.* —**sharp′ness** *n.*

sharp·en (shär′pən) *v.* To make or become sharp or sharper. —**sharp′en·er** *n.*

sharp·shoot·er (shärp′shōō′tər) *n.* An expert marksman.

shat·ter (shăt′ər) *v.* To smash or burst suddenly into pieces.

shat·ter·proof (shăt′ər-prōōf′) *adj.* Impervious or resistant to shattering.

shave (shāv) *v.* **shaved, shaved** *or* **shav·en** (shā′vən), **shav·ing. 1. a.** To remove (bodily hair, esp. the beard) from with a razor. **b.** To cut bodily hair, esp. the beard, close to the surface of the skin. **2. a.** To cut or scrape thin slices of or from. **b.** To cut or scrape into thin slices. **3.** To graze or come close to in passing. —*n.* The act or result of shaving.

shav·er (shra′vər) *n.* **1.** An electrically operated razor. **2.** *Informal.* A young boy.

shawl (shôl) *n.* A square or oblong piece of cloth worn as a covering for the head, neck, and shoulders.

Shaw·nee (shô-nē′) *n., pl.* **-nee** *or* **-nees. 1.** A member of an American Indian people formerly of the C Ohio Valley, now in Oklahoma. **2.** Their Algonquian language.

shay (shā) *n. Informal.* A chaise.

she (shē) *pron.* **1.** The female that is neither the speaker nor the hearer. <*She* left early.> **2.** Something, as a ship, traditionally regarded as feminine.

sheaf (shēf) *n., pl.* **sheaves** (shēvz). **1.** A bundle of stalks, esp. of grain. **2.** A collection of things held or bound together.

shear (shîr) *v.* **sheared, sheared** *or* **shorn** (shôrn, shōrn), **shear·ing. 1.** To remove (the fleece or hair) from by cutting with a sharp instrument : clip. **2.** To strip of by or as if by clipping. **3.** To cut with shears. —**shear′er** *n.*

shears (shîrz) *pl.n.* **1.** A cutting implement that resembles scissors but is gen. larger. **2.** An implement or machine that cuts with a scissorslike action.

sheath (shēth) *n., pl.* **sheaths** (shēthz, shēths). **1.** A case for a blade, as of a sword. **2.** A covering, part, or structure resembling a sheath. **3.** A close-fitting dress.

sheathe (shē*th*) *v.* **sheathed, sheath·ing. 1.** To insert into a sheath. **2.** To provide with a protective covering or structure.

sheath·ing (shē′*th*ĭng) *n.* **1.** A layer of material applied to the outer frame of a building to serve as a base for an exterior covering. **2.** An exterior protective covering on the underwater part of a ship's hull.

she·bang (shə-băng′) *n. Informal.* A situation, contrivance, or collection <mailed the whole *shebang*>

shed[1] (shĕd) *v.* **shed, shed·ding. 1.** To pour or cause to pour forth <*shed* tears><*shed* blood> **2.** To give off : emit <*shed* light> **3.** To throw off without penetration <Glass *sheds* water.> **4.** To cast off, esp. by a natural process <a snake *shedding* its skin>

shed[2] (shĕd) *n.* A small structure for storage or shelter.

she'd (shēd). **1.** She had. **2.** She would.

sheen (shēn) *n.* Luster : brightness.

sheep (shēp) *n., pl.* **sheep. 1.** A hoofed, thick-fleeced mammal of the genus *Ovis,* widely domesticated for wool and meat. **2.** A meek and submissive person.

sheep dog *also* **sheep·dog** (shēp′dôg′, -dŏg′) *n.* A dog that is trained to herd and guard sheep.

sheep·ish (shē′pĭsh) *adj.* **1.** Embarrassed and apologetic. **2.** Timid : shy. —**sheep′ish·ly** *adv.* —**sheep′ish·ness** *n.*

sheep·skin (shēp′skĭn′) *n.* **1. a.** The skin of a sheep either tanned with the fleece left on or in the form of leather. **b.** Parchment. **2.** A diploma.

sheer[1] (shîr) *v.* To swerve from a course.

sheer[2] (shîr) *adj.* **1.** Thin and fine : transparent. **2.** Absolute : utter <*sheer* stupidity> **3.** Almost perpendicular : very steep. —**sheer** *adv.* —**sheer′ness** *n.*

sheet[1] (shēt) *n.* **1.** A large piece of cloth, as cotton, used esp. as a bed covering. **2.** A piece of paper. **3.** A broad, continuous surface <a *sheet* of ice>

sheet[2] (shēt) *n.* **1.** A rope or chain that secures and regulates a sail. **2. sheets.** The spaces at either end of an open boat.

sheet·ing (shē′tĭng) *n.* **1.** Fabric, as plain cotton, made into sheets. **2.** Material, as plastic, manufactured in the form of a continuous sheet.

Sheet·rock (shēt′rŏk′). A trademark for plasterboard.

sheik (shēk, shāk) *n.* The leader of an Arab village, family, or tribe. —**sheik′dom** *n.*

shek•el (shĕk′əl) *n.* —See table at CURRENCY.

shelf (shĕlf) *n., pl.* **shelves** (shĕlvz). **1.** A flat, usu. narrow and rectangular structure fixed at right angles to a wall to hold or store things. **2.** Something, as a ledge of rock, that resembles a shelf.

shelf life *n.* The length of time during which a material can be stored without deteriorating.

shell (shĕl) *n.* **1. a.** The usu. hard outer covering of certain organisms, as a turtle. **b.** A similar outer covering of a fruit, egg, or nut. **2.** Something resembling a shell <a pastry *shell*> **3.** A long, narrow racing boat propelled by oarsmen. **4. a.** A case containing explosives and fired from a cannon. **b.** A case containing the charge, primer, and shot for smaller guns. —*v.* **1.** To remove from the shell : shuck. **2.** To fire shells at : bombard. —**shell out.** *Informal.* To pay. —**shell′er** *n.* —**shell′-like′** *adj.*

she'll (shēl). **1.** She will. **2.** She shall.

shel•lac (shə-lăk′) *n.* **1.** A purified lac formed into flakes and used esp. in varnishes. **2.** A thin varnish made by dissolving flake shellac in alcohol. —*v.* **-lacked, -lack•ing. 1.** To apply shellac (to). **2.** *Slang.* To defeat roundly.

shell bean *n.* A bean cultivated for its edible seeds rather than for its pods.

shell•fire (shĕl′fīr′) *n.* The shooting or firing of shells.

shell•fish (shĕl′fĭsh′) *n.* An aquatic animal, as a clam or lobster, with a shell or shell-like external covering.

shell shock *n.* A nervous disorder originating in trauma suffered under fire in modern warfare. —**shell′-shocked′** *adj.*

shel•ter (shĕl′tər) *n.* **1. a.** Something that provides protection or cover. **b.** A refuge. **2.** The state of being protected or covered. —*v.* To give protection or cover to.

shelve (shĕlv) *v.* **shelved, shelv•ing. 1.** To arrange or store on a shelf. **2.** To put aside or off. **3.** To slope : incline.

shelves (shĕlvz) *n. pl. of* SHELF.

shelv•ing (shĕl′vĭng) *n.* **1.** Shelves as a whole. **2.** Material for shelves.

she•nan•i•gan (shə-năn′ĭ-gən) *n. Informal.* **1.** A devious trick. **2.** *often* **shenanigans. a.** Playful activities : mischief. **b.** Shifty or questionable behavior.

shep•herd (shĕp′ərd) *n.* One who takes care of sheep. —*v.* To take care of as or in the manner of a shepherd. —**shep′herd•ess** *n.*

sher•bet (shûr′bĭt) *n.* A sweet, frozen dessert made of fruit juice, water or milk, and gelatin or egg whites.

sher•iff (shĕr′ĭf) *n.* A high law-enforcement official of a U.S. county.

sher•ry (shĕr′ē) *n., pl.* **-ries.** A fortified amber-colored wine.

Shet•land pony (shĕt′lənd) *n.* A small, compactly built pony.

shew (shō) *v. archaic var. of* SHOW.

shi•at•su (shē-ät′so͞o) *n.* Therapeutic massage with the thumbs and palms of those areas of the body used in acupuncture.

shib•bo•leth (shĭb′ə-ləth) *n.* **1.** A language usage that distinguishes the members of one group from another. **2.** A catchword : slogan.

shield (shēld) *n.* **1.** A piece of protective armor carried on the forearm. **2.** Something resembling a shield. **3.** Something that serves to conceal or protect. —*v.* To conceal or protect with or as if with a shield. —**shield′er** *n.*

shield law *n.* A law that protects journalists from being forced to reveal confidential sources of information.

shi•er (shī′ər) *adj. var. compar. of* SHY[1].

shi•est (shī′ĭst) *adj. var. superl. of* SHY[1].

shift (shĭft) *v.* **1.** To change or cause to change place, direction, or position. **2.** To exchange (one thing for another) : switch. **3.** To change gears in an automobile. **4.** To manage to take care of one's needs : get along. —*n.* **1.** A change from one place, direction, or position to another : transfer. **2. a.** A group of workers on duty at the same time. **b.** The working period of such a group. **3.** A gearshift. **4.** A woman's chemise, slip, or loose-fitting dress.

shift key *n.* A key on a typewriter or computer keyboard that changes letters from lower case to upper case.

shift•less (shĭft′lĭs) *adj.* Lacking efficiency, ambition, or purpose : inefficient or lazy. —**shift′less•ness** *n.*

shift•y (shĭf′tē) *adj.* **-i•er, -i•est. 1.** Crafty : tricky. **2.** Suggestive of trickiness : furtive. —**shift′i•ly** *adv.* —**shift′i•ness** *n.*

Shi•ite (shē′īt′) *n.* A member of the branch of Islam that regards the caliph Ali and his descendants as the legitimate successors to Muhammad. —**Shi′ism** *n.* —**Shi′ite′** *adj.*

shill (shĭl) *n. Slang.* Someone who works as a decoy, as in a gambling game, by posing as an innocent bystander or a customer.

shil•le•lagh (shə-lā′lē) *n.* A club : cudgel.

shil•ling (shĭl′ĭng) *n.* —See table at CURRENCY.

shil•ly-shal•ly (shĭl′ē-shăl′ē) *v.* **-lied, -ly•ing.** To be hesitant or indecisive : waver.

shim (shĭm) *n.* A thin wedge of material, as wood, used to fill space, as in leveling a chair on the floor.

shim•mer (shĭm′ər) *v.* To shine with a flickering or wavering light. —**shim′mer** *n.* —**shim′mer•y** *adj.*

†shim•my (shĭm′ē) *n., pl.* **-mies. 1.** A dance marked by rapid shaking of the body. **2.** An abnormal vibration or wobble, as in the steering mechanism of an automobile. **3.** *Regional.* A chemise. —**shim′my** *v.*

shin (shĭn) *n.* The front part of the leg below the knee and above the ankle. —*v.* **shinned, shin•ning.** To climb (e.g., a tree) by alternating gripping and pulling with the hands and legs.

shin•bone (shĭn′bōn′) *n.* The tibia.

shin•dig (shĭn′dĭg′) *n. Slang.* A usu. large and festive party.

shine (shīn) *v.* **shone** (shōn) *or* **shined, shin•ing. 1.** To emit or reflect light. **2.** To aim or direct the light of <*shining* the flashlight in the corner> **3.** To distinguish oneself : excel.

4. To make bright or glossy by polishing. —*n.* **1.** Radiance : brightness. **2.** A polish given to shoes. **3.** Fair weather.

shin•er (shī'nər) *n.* **1.** *Slang.* A black eye. **2.** Any of numerous small, silvery fishes of the family Cyprinidae.

shin•gle[1] (shĭng'gəl) *n.* **1.** A thin rectangular piece of material, as wood or asbestos, laid in overlapping rows to cover the roof or side of a house. **2.** *Informal.* A small signboard. —*v.* **-gled, -gling.** To apply shingles to. —**shin'gler** *n.*

shin•gle[2] (shĭng'gəl) *n.* **1.** Beach gravel consisting of coarse smooth pebbles. **2.** A beach covered with shingle.

shin•gles (shĭng'gəlz) *pl.n. (sing. or pl. in number).* A painful viral infection marked by skin eruptions along a nerve path.

shin•ny (shĭn'ē) *v.* **-nied, -ny•ing.** To climb by shinning.

Shin•to (shĭn'tō') *n.* A religion native to Japan, marked by the worship of nature spirits and ancestors. —**Shin'to•ism** *n.* —**Shin'to•ist** *n.*

shin•y (shī'nē) *adj.* **-i•er, -i•est.** Shining : bright. —**shin'i•ness** *n.*

ship (shĭp) *n.* **1.** A large vessel built for deep-water navigation. **2.** A ship's company. **3.** An airplane, airship, or spacecraft. —*v.* **shipped, ship•ping. 1.** To take or place on board a ship. **2.** To cause to be transported. **3.** To take (water) into a boat. **4.** To enlist for service on a ship.

–ship *suff.* **1.** Quality, state, or condition <scholar*ship*> **2.** Rank, status, or office <professor*ship*> **3.** Art, skill, or craft <penman*ship*>

ship•board (shĭp'bôrd', -bōrd') *n.* A ship.

ship•build•ing (shĭp'bĭl'dĭng) *n.* The business of building or designing ships. —**ship'build'er** *n.*

ship•mate (shĭp'māt') *n.* A fellow sailor.

ship•ment (shĭp'mənt) *n.* **1.** The act or process of shipping goods. **2.** The goods that are shipped.

ship•ping (shĭp'ĭng) *n.* **1.** The act or business of transporting goods. **2.** The body of ships that are in one port or belong to one country. —**ship'per** *n.*

ship•shape (shĭp'shāp') *adj.* In good order : tidy. —**ship'shape'** *adv.*

ship•worm (shĭp'wûrm') *n.* A wormlike marine mollusk of the genera *Teredo* and *Bankia* that bores into wood, often doing extensive damage.

ship•wreck (shĭp'rĕk') *n.* **1.** The remains of a wrecked ship. **2.** The destruction of a ship. **3.** Total destruction : ruin. —*v.* To suffer or cause to suffer shipwreck.

ship•wright (shĭp'rīt') *n.* A carpenter employed in ship construction or maintenance.

ship•yard (shĭp'yärd') *n.* A place where ships are built, repaired, and outfitted.

shire (shīr) *n.* A division of Great Britain, equivalent to a county.

shirk (shûrk) *v.* To avoid doing (work or duty). —**shirk'er** *n.*

shirr (shûr) *v.* **1.** To make shirring in (fabric). **2.** To bake (eggs) in buttered dishes.

shir•ring (shûr'ĭng) *n.* A decorative gathering of cloth into parallel rows.

shirt (shûrt) *n.* **1.** A garment for the upper body, usu. having a collar, sleeves, and a front opening. **2.** An undershirt.

shirt•ing (shûr'tĭng) *n.* Fabric for making shirts.

shirt•tail (shûrt'tāl') *n.* The part of a shirt that extends below the waist, esp. in the back.

shirt•waist (shûrt'wāst') *n.* A woman's dress or blouse styled to resemble a man's shirt.

shish ke•bab (shĭsh' kə-bŏb') *n.* Cubes of meat and vegetables, as onions, tomatoes, or green peppers, cooked on skewers.

shiv (shĭv) *n. Slang.* A knife or razor used esp. as a weapon.

shiv•er[1] (shĭv'ər) *v.* To shake from or as if from the cold : tremble. —**shiv'er** *n.* —**shiv'er•y** *adj.*

shiv•er[2] (shĭv'ər) *v.* To break or cause to break into fragments : shatter.

shoal[1] (shōl) *n.* **1.** A shallow place in a body of water. **2.** A sandbar or sandbank.

shoal[2] (shōl) *n.* A large group, esp. of fish.

shoat (shōt) *n.* A young pig.

shock[1] (shŏk) *n.* **1.** A violent impact or collision. **2.** A violent, unexpected disturbance of mental or emotional balance. **3.** An offense to the sense of decency or propriety : outrage. **4.** A physiological reaction to bodily trauma, usu. marked by loss of blood pressure and the lowering of vital signs. **5.** The effect caused by an electric current passing through the body. **6.** Apoplexy. **7.** A shock absorber. —*v.* **1.** To strike with great surprise, agitation, outrage, or disgust. **2.** To subject (an individual) to an electric shock.

shock[2] (shŏk) *n.* **1.** A number of sheaves of grain stacked upright in a field. **2.** A bushy mass <a *shock* of red hair>

shock absorber *n.* Any of various devices for absorbing mechanical shocks, esp. one used in automobiles.

shock•er (shŏk'ər) *n.* Something, as a sensational story or novel, that shocks.

shock•ing (shŏk'ĭng) *adj.* Highly disturbing or distasteful. —**shock'ing•ly** *adv.*

shock therapy *n.* The induction of convulsions by the use of electric current or drugs, as a treatment for mental illness.

shock troops *pl.n.* Military personnel specially trained to lead attacks.

shod•dy (shŏd'ē) *n., pl.* **-dies. 1. a.** Wool fibers obtained by shredding woolen rags or waste. **b.** Yarn or fabric made from shoddy. **2.** Inferior goods. —*adj.* **-di•er, -di•est. 1.** Consisting of or made of shoddy. **2.** Imitative in a cheap way : sham. **3.** Shabby. —**shod'di•ly** *adv.* —**shod'di•ness** *n.*

shoe (sho͞o) *n.* **1.** An outer covering for the human foot. **2.** A horseshoe. **3.** The outer casing of a rubber tire. **4.** The brake part that presses against the wheel or drum to slow or stop its motion. —*v.* **shod** (shŏd), **shoe•ing.** To provide or fit with shoes.

shoe•horn (sho͞o'hôrn') *n.* A curved tool, as of horn, used for putting on a shoe.
shoe•lace (sho͞o'lās') *n.* A cord used for lacing shoes.
shoe•mak•er (sho͞o'mā'kər) *n.* One who repairs or makes shoes.
shoe•string (sho͞o'strĭng') *n.* **1.** A shoelace. **2.** A very small amount of money.
sho•ji (shō'jē) *n.* A translucent screen used as a partition or door in a Japanese house.
shone (shōn) *v. var. p.t. & p.p. of* SHINE.
shoo-in (sho͞o'ĭn') *n. Informal.* An easy and sure winner.
shook (sho͝ok) *v. p.t. of* SHAKE.
shook-up (sho͝ok-ŭp') *adj. Slang.* Emotionally upset : disturbed.
shoot (sho͞ot) *v.* **shot** (shŏt), **shoot•ing. 1. a.** To hit, kill, or wound with a missile. **b.** To fire (a missile) from a weapon. **c.** To fire (a weapon). **2.** To send forth swiftly or forcibly <*shot* a rocket into space> **3.** To pass over, along, or through swiftly <*shoot* the rapids> **4.** To record on film : photograph. **5.** To stick or cause to stick out : extend. **6.** To move rapidly : dart. **7. a.** To begin to grow by or as if by germinating : sprout. **b.** To develop : mature. **8.** To propel (e.g., a ball) toward an objective. **—shoot up. 1.** *Informal.* To rise suddenly and rapidly. **2.** *Slang.* To inject (a narcotic) directly into a vein. *—n.* **1. a.** The young growth from a germinating seed : sprout. **b.** A plant part, as a leaf, that has just begun to grow or develop. **2.** A shooting party or match. **—shoot'er** *n.*
shooting iron *n. Informal.* A handgun, esp. a six-shooter.
shooting star *n.* METEOR 1.
shoot-out *also* **shoot•out** (sho͞ot'out') *n.* An armed confrontation in which opponents shoot firearms at one another.
shop (shŏp) *n.* **1.** A retail store. **2.** A place where goods are manufactured or repaired : factory. **3.** A workshop. *—v.* **shopped, shop•ping.** To visit stores to examine or buy merchandise. **—shop'per** *n.*
shop•keep•er (shŏp'kē'pər) *n.* An operator of a retail shop.
shop•lift•er (shŏp'lĭf'tər) *n.* Someone who steals merchandise on display in stores. **—shop'lift'** *v.* **—shop'lift'ing** *n.*
shop•talk (shŏp'tôk') *n.* Talk about or topics peculiar to a business or occupation.
shop•worn (shŏp'wôrn', -wōrn') *adj.* Tarnished, frayed, or faded from long display or too much handling in a store.
shore[1] (shôr, shōr) *n.* The land along the edge of a body of water, as an ocean.
shore[2] (shôr, shōr) *v.* **shored, shor•ing.** To support, as with an inclined timber : prop up.
shore bird *n.* A bird, as a sandpiper, that frequents coastal or inland shores.
shorn (shôrn, shōrn) *v. var. p.p. of* SHEAR.
short (shôrt) *adj.* **1.** Having little length or height. **2.** Of brief duration in time. **3.** Rudely abrupt : curt. **4.** Insufficient : inadequate. **5.** Not very great in distance. **6.** Containing a large amount of shortening : flaky. **7. a.** Not owning the stocks or commodities one is selling. **b.** Relating to or designating a sale of stocks or goods that the seller does not yet own but must produce to meet the terms of a contract. **8.** Being a speech sound or syllable of relatively brief duration. *—adv.* **1.** Suddenly and abruptly. **2.** At a point before a goal, limit, or target. **3.** Without owning what one is selling <sold *short*> *—n.* **1.** Something that is short. **2. shorts.** Trousers or underpants that extend to the knee or above. **3.** A short circuit. *—v.* To have or cause to have a short circuit. **—short'ness** *n.*
short•age (shôr'tĭj) *n.* A deficiency in the amount needed : insufficiency.
short•bread (shôrt'brĕd') *n.* A rich cookie made of flour, sugar, and butter.
short•cake (shôrt'kāk') *n.* A dessert consisting of a rich biscuit split, filled with fruit, and topped with cream.
short•change (shôrt'chānj') *v.* To give less change than is due, esp. intentionally.
short circuit *n. Elect.* A low-resistance connection, often accidentally established, between 2 points in a circuit. **—short'-cir'cuit** *v.*
short•com•ing (shôrt'kŭm'ĭng) *n.* A fault : failing.
short cut *n.* **1.** A shorter, more direct route than the one customarily taken. **2.** A faster method of doing something.
short•en (shôr'tn) *v.* To make or become short or shorter. **—short'en•er** *n.*
short•en•ing (shôr'tn-ĭng, shôrt'nĭng) *n.* A fat, as butter or lard, that makes cake or pastry light and flaky.
short•fall (shôrt'fôl') *n.* **1.** A failure to reach a need, level, or goal : shortage. **2.** The amount of a shortfall.
short•hand (shôrt'hănd') *n.* Any of several systems of rapid handwriting in which symbols and abbreviations represent words, phrases, and letters : stenography.
short-hand•ed (shôrt'hăn'dĭd) *adj.* Lacking the necessary number of workers.
short-horn (shôrt'hôrn') *n.* One of a breed of cattle orig. developed in England and having short curved horns.
short•list (shôrt'lĭst') *n.* A list of preferable items or candidates selected for final consideration. **—short'-list'** *v.*
short-lived (shôrt'lĭvd', -līvd') *adj.* Living or lasting for a brief time.
short•ly (shôrt'lē) *adv.* **1.** In a short time : soon. **2.** In a few words : succinctly.
short order *n.* Food quickly cooked and served, as at a diner.
short-range (shôrt'rānj') *adj.* **1.** Designed for short distances <a *short-range* missile> **2.** Relating to the near future.
short shrift *n.* **1.** A short respite granted a condemned person for confession before execution. **2.** Little sympathy or heed.
short•sight•ed (shôrt'sī'tĭd) *adj.* **1.** Nearsighted : myopic. **2.** Without foresight. **—short'sight'ed•ness** *n.*
short•stop (shôrt'stŏp') *n. Baseball.* **1.** The

position between 2nd and 3rd bases. **2.** The player who plays shortshop.

short story *n.* A short fictional prose narrative aiming at unity of characterization, theme, and effect.

short subject *n.* A brief film shown before a feature-length film.

short-tem•pered (shôrt'tĕm'pərd) *adj.* Easily moved to anger : irascible.

short-term (shôrt'tûrm') *adj.* **1.** Involving or occurring over a short time period. **2.** Of or relating to a financial transaction, as a loan, based on a time period usu. of less than one year.

short ton *n.* —See table at MEASUREMENT.

short wave *n.* A radio wave with a wavelength of 200 m or less. —**short'wave'** *adj.*

Sho•sho•ne *also* **Sho•sho•ni** (shō-shō'nē) *n., pl.* **-ne** or **-nes** *also* **-ni** *or* **-nis. 1.** A member of an American Indian people of W Wyoming, SE Idaho, and S Nevada. **2.** Their Uto-Aztecan language. —**Sho•sho'ne•an** *adj.*

shot[1] (shŏt) *n.* **1.** The discharge of a weapon, as a gun. **2.** *pl.* **shot. a.** A missile, as a bullet, that is fired from a weapon. **b.** A group of pellets to be fired from a shotgun. **3.** A throw, hit, stroke, or drive in any of several games. **4.** A marksman. **5.** Reach : range. **6.** A guess, try, or opportunity. **7.** The metal ball that is thrown for distance in the shot-put. **8. a.** A photograph. **b.** A single photographed scene or take in a motion picture. **9.** A hypodermic injection. **10.** A drink of liquor.

shot[2] (shŏt) *v. p.t. & p.p. of* SHOOT.

shot•gun (shŏt'gŭn') *n.* A gun with a smooth bore that fires a charge of small shot at close range.

shot-put (shŏt'po͝ot') *n.* An athletic event in which participants throw a heavy metal ball for distance. —**shot'-put'ter** *n.*

should (sho͝od) *v. p.t. of* **shall.** —Used to express duty, obligation, necessity, probability, expectation, or contingency.

shoul•der (shōl'dər) *n.* **1. a.** The part of the human body between the neck and upper arm. **b.** The joint connecting the arm with the trunk. **c.** The corresponding part of an animal's body. **2.** The edge along either side of a roadway. —*v.* **1.** To carry on or push with the shoulder. **2.** To take on : assume <*shoulder* blame>

shoulder belt *n.* An automobile safety belt that is worn diagonally across the body and over the shoulder.

shoulder blade *n.* The scapula.

should•n't (sho͝od'nt). Should not.

shout (shout) *n.* A loud cry : yell. —**shout** *v.* —**shout'er** *n.*

shove (shŭv) *v.* **shoved, shov•ing.** To push rudely or forcefully. —**shove** *n.*

shov•el (shŭv'əl) *n.* **1.** A tool with a long handle and a scoop for picking up material such as dirt and snow. **2.** The amount the scoop of a shovel can hold. —*v.* **-eled, -el•ing** *or* **-elled, -el•ling. 1.** To dig into, move, or remove with a shovel. **2.** To make or clear out with a shovel.

show (shō) *v.* **showed, shown** (shōn) *or* **showed, show•ing. 1.** To allow or cause to be seen : display <*show* surprise> **2.** To guide : conduct <*showed* me around town> **3.** To teach : instruct <*showed* her how to cook> **4.** To manifest : reveal <a coat that *showed* signs of wear> **5.** To bestow : confer <*showed* pity> **6.** To be visible <The moon *showed* in the treetops.> **7.** To establish : prove <*shows* that he cares> **8.** To finish 3rd or better in a race. ★ ***syns:*** DEMONSTRATE, DISPLAY, EVIDENCE, EVINCE, EXHIBIT, MANIFEST —**show off.** To behave or display ostentatiously or conspicuously. —**show up.** To put in an appearance : arrive —*n.* **1.** A demonstration : display. **2.** A false appearance : pretense. **3.** A spectacle. **4.** A public exhibition or theatrical presentation. **5.** *Informal.* An undertaking <tried to run the whole *show*> **6.** 3rd place or better in a race.

show•case (shō'kās') *n.* A case in which objects are displayed, as in a store. —*v.* **-cased, -cas•ing.** To display prominently and advantageously : feature.

show•down (shō'doun') *n.* An action, event, or circumstance that forces the settlement of a disputed issue.

show•er (shou'ər) *n.* **1.** A brief fall of rain, hail, snow, or sleet. **2.** An abundant flow : outflow <a *shower* of criticism> **3.** A party given in honor of someone to whom gifts are presented. **4.** A bath in which water is sprayed on the bather. —*v.* **1.** To spray : sprinkle. **2.** To bestow in abundance. **3.** To fall or pour down in a shower. **4.** To take a shower. —**show'er•y** *adj.*

show•ing (shō'ĭng) *n.* **1.** The act of displaying or presenting. **2.** Performance, as in a competition or test of skill.

show•man (shō'mən) *n.* **1.** A theatrical producer. **2.** Someone with a flair for visual or dramatic effectiveness. —**show'man•ship'** *n.*

show•off (shō'ôf', -ŏf') *n.* Someone who shows off : exhibitionist.

show place *also* **show•place** (shō'plās') *n.* A place that is shown, admired, or viewed for its beauty or historical interest.

show room *also* **show•room** (shō'ro͞om', -ro͝om') *n.* A room in which merchandise is displayed.

show•y (shō'ē) *adj.* **-i•er, -i•est.** Striking and conspicuous : flashy. —**show'i•ly** *adv.* —**show'i•ness** *n.*

shrank (shrăngk) *v. var. p.t. of* SHRINK

shrap•nel (shrăp'nəl) *n., pl.* **-nel. 1.** An artillery shell containing metal balls that explodes in the air. **2.** Fragments from a high-explosive shell.

shred (shrĕd) *n.* **1.** A long, narrow strip torn or cut off. **2.** A small amount : bit. —*v.* **shred•ded** *or* **shred, shred•ding.** To tear or cut into shreds.

shrew (shro͞o) *n.* **1.** Any of several very small mouselike mammals of the family Soricidae, with a narrow, pointed snout. **2.** A scold. —**shrew'ish** *adj.*

shrewd (shro͞od) *adj.* Clever and usu. practical. ★ ***syns:*** ASTUTE, CAGEY, SLICK —**shrewd'ly** *adv.* —**shrewd'ness** *n.*

shriek (shrēk) *n.* A loud, sharp, shrill cry : scream. —**shriek** *v.*

shrike (shrīk) *n.* Any of various carnivorous birds of the family Laniidae, having a hooked bill and often impaling their prey on sharp-pointed thorns.

shrill (shrĭl) *adj.* Thin and high-pitched : piercing. —*v.* To make a shrill sound. —**shrill'ness** *n.* —**shril'ly** *adv.*

shrimp (shrĭmp) *n., pl.* **shrimp** *or* **shrimps.** **1.** Any of various small, often edible marine crustaceans of the suborder Natantia. **2.** *Slang.* One that is small or unimportant.

shrine (shrīn) *n.* **1.** A receptacle for sacred relics. **2.** The tomb of a venerated person, esp. a saint. **3.** An object or site hallowed for its associations. —**shrine** *v.*

shrink (shrĭngk) *v.* **shrank** (shrăngk) *or* **shrunk** (shrŭngk), **shrunk** *or* **shrunk•en** (shrŭng'kən), **shrink•ing.** **1.** To become smaller, as from heat : contract. **2.** To lessen, as in amount : dwindle. **3.** To recoil : flinch. —*n. Slang.* A psychiatrist. —**shrink'a•ble** *adj.* —**shrink'er** *n.*

shrink•age (shrĭng'kĭj) *n.* **1.** The process of shrinking. **2.** A reduction in value : depreciation. **3.** The amount or extent to which something lessens or contracts.

shrinking violet *n. Informal.* A shy or retiring person.

shrink-wrap (shrĭngk'răp') *n.* A protective plastic film wound about articles of merchandise and then shrunk by heat to form a sealed package. —**shrink'-wrap'** *v.*

shrive (shrīv) *v.* **shrove** (shrōv) *or* **shrived, shriv•en** (shrĭv'ən) *or* **shrived, shriv•ing.** To hear the confession of and give absolution to.

shriv•el (shrĭv'əl) *v.* **-eled, -el•ing** *or* **-elled, -el•ling.** **1.** To shrink or cause to shrink and wrinkle. **2.** To lose or cause to lose vitality.

shroud (shroud) *n.* **1.** A cloth used to wrap a dead body. **2.** Something that screens, conceals, or protects. **3.** One of a set of ropes stretched from a vessels's masthead to the sides to support the mast. —*v.* To screen from view : conceal.

shrub (shrŭb) *n.* A low, woody plant that gen. has several stems. —**shrub'by** *adj.*

shrub•ber•y (shrŭb'ə-rē) *n., pl.* **-ies.** **1.** A group of shrubs. **2.** Shrubs in general.

shrug (shrŭg) *v.* **shrugged, shrug•ging.** To raise (the shoulders), esp. in doubt, indifference, or disdain. —**shrug off. 1.** To minimize. **2.** To rid oneself of. **3.** To wriggle out of (a garment). —**shrug** *n.*

shrunk (shrŭngk) *v. var. p.t. & p.p. of* SHRINK.

shrunk•en (shrŭng'kən) *v. var. p.p. of* SHRINK.

shtick (shtĭk) *n. Slang.* **1.** A characteristic talent, attribute, or trait. **2.** One's method of doing something. **3.** An entertainment routine.

shuck (shŭk) *n.* An outer covering : husk or shell. —*v.* **1.** To remove the shuck from. **2.** To cast off (e.g., clothing).

shud•der (shŭd'ər) *v.* To tremble convulsively, as from aversion or fear : shiver. —**shud'der** *n.*

shuf•fle (shŭf'əl) *v.* **-fled, -fling.** **1.** To move with a dragging or shambling gait. **2.** To move (something) from one place to another. **3.** To handle or mix together in a haphazard, disorderly fashion. **4.** To change the order of (e.g., playing cards) by mixing together. —**shuf'fle** *n.*

shuf•fle•board (shŭf'əl-bôrd', -bōrd') *n.* A game in which long-handled sticks are used to push disks along a smooth, level surface toward numbered squares.

shun (shŭn) *v.* **shunned, shun•ning.** To keep away from deliberately and esp. consistently : eschew. —**shun'ner** *n.*

shunt (shŭnt) *n.* **1.** The act or process of moving to an alternate course. **2.** A railroad switch. —*v.* **1.** To turn or cause to turn to one side. **2.** To shift or switch (a train or car) from one track to another.

shut (shŭt) *v.* **shut, shut•ting.** **1.** To move (e.g., a door) so as to cover an opening : close. **2.** To block entrance, passage, or access to. **3.** To lock up : confine. **4.** To halt, cease, or suspend operations (in) <*shut* down a factory> **5.** To close by bringing together the parts of <*shut* his book> —**shut out. 1.** To keep out. **2.** To prevent (an opposing player or team) from scoring in a game. —**shut up.** To be, cause to be, or become silent.

shut•down (shŭt'doun') *n.* A temporary stoppage of operations, as in a factory.

shut•eye (shŭt'ī') *n. Slang.* Sleep.

shut-in (shŭt'ĭn') *n.* Someone who has to stay indoors because of illness or disability.

shut•out (shŭt'out') *n.* A game in which one side does not score.

shut•ter (shŭt'ər) *n.* **1.** A usu. hinged movable cover for a window or door. **2.** A device on a camera that opens and shuts the lens opening to expose the film.

shut•ter•bug (shŭt'ər-bŭg') *n. Informal.* An amateur photographer.

shut•tle (shŭt'l) *n.* **1.** A device used in weaving that carries the woof threads between the warp threads. **2.** A vehicle, as a train or plane, that travels back and forth over an established, often short route. —*v.* **-tled, -tling.** To move back and forth like a shuttle.

shut•tle•cock (shŭt'l-kŏk') *n.* A light rounded object, as of cork, that has a crown of feathers and is used in badminton.

shy[1] (shī) *adj.* **shi•er** *or* **shy•er, shi•est** *or* **shy•est.** **1.** Readily frightened : timid. **2.** Bashfully reserved : diffident. **3.** Cautious : wary. **4.** *Informal.* Lacking : deficient. —*v.* **shied, shy•ing.** **1.** To move aside suddenly through fear. **2.** To draw back : recoil. —**shy'ly** *adv.* —**shy'ness** *n.*

shy[2] (shī) *v.* **shied, shy•ing.** To throw swiftly, esp. with a sideways motion : toss.

shy•lock (shī'lŏk') *n.* An unscrupulous moneylender : shark.

shy•ster (shī'stər) *n. Slang.* An unscrupulous or unethical politician or lawyer.

Si *symbol for* SILICON.
Siamese twin *n.* One of a set of twins born with their bodies joined.
sib•i•lant (sĭb'ə-lənt) *adj.* Producing, containing, or having a hissing sound. —*n.* A sibilant speech sound, as (s) or (z).
sib•ling (sĭb'lĭng) *n.* One of 2 or more offspring of the same parents.
sib•yl (sĭb'əl) *n.* A female prophet. —**sib'yl•line'** (-ə-līn', -lēn') *adj.*
sic[1] (sĭk, sēk) *adv.* So : thus. —Used in written material to indicate that a passage, phrase, or word is as it was in an original <wrote me that her mother was two [*sic*] busy to receive visitors>
sic[2] (sĭk) *v.* **sicced, sic•cing** *also* **sicked, sick•ing.** To urge to attack or harry.
sick (sĭk) *adj.* **1. a.** In poor health : ill. **b.** Nauseated. **2.** Of, pertaining to, or for sick persons <*sick* leave> **3.** Unwholesome : morbid. **4. a.** Revolted : disgusted. **b.** Experiencing an aversion from excess : weary <*sick* of working> **c.** Pining : longing. —**sick'ness** *n.*
sick•bay (sĭk'bā') *n.* The hospital and dispensary of a ship.
sick•bed (sĭk'bĕd') *n.* A bed in which a sick person lies.
sick•en (sĭk'ən) *v.* To make or become sick. —**sick'en•ing** *adj.*
sick•le (sĭk'əl) *n.* A semicircular blade attached to a handle used for cutting grain or tall grass.
sickle cell anemia *n.* A hereditary anemia marked by abnormal crescent-shaped red blood cells that are deficient in oxygen.
sick•ly (sĭk'lē) *adj.* **-li•er, -li•est. 1.** Prone to sickness : ailing. **2.** Of, caused by, or associated with sickness <a *sickly* look> **3.** Weak : feeble <a *sickly* smile>
sick•out (sĭk'out') *n.* An organized job action in which employees absent themselves from work on the pretext of illness.
side (sīd) *n.* **1.** A surface or border of an object, esp. the surface joining a bottom and a top. **2.** One of the 2 surfaces of a flat object, as a piece of paper. **3.** The part to the left or right of a vertical axis, as of the body. **4.** The space immediately beside someone or something. **5. a.** Something, as a set of opinions, considered as being opposite to another. **b.** One of the parties to a debate or dispute. **6.** An aspect or quality. —*adj.* **1.** Located to or on a side. **2.** To or from one side : oblique. **3.** Incidental <a *side* interest> **4.** Supplementary : additional <a *side* order of salad> —*v.* **sid•ed, sid•ing.** To support the opinion or position of a particular side. —**sid'ed** *adj.*
side•arm (sīd'ärm') *adj. Baseball.* Performed with a sideways motion of the arm. —**side'arm'** *adv.*
side arm *n.* A weapon, as a pistol, that can be carried at the side or waist.
side•board (sīd'bôrd', -bōrd') *n.* A piece of furniture that holds linens and tableware.
side•burns (sīd'bûrnz') *pl.n.* Whiskers down the sides of a man's face in front of the ears.
side•car (sīd'kär') *n.* A one-wheeled car for a passenger at the side of a motorcycle.
side effect *n.* A secondary and usu. untoward effect, esp. of a drug.
side•kick (sīd'kĭk') *n. Slang.* A close friend : pal.
side•light (sīd'līt') *n.* Incidental knowledge or information about a subject.
side•line (sīd'līn') *n.* **1.** A boundary line along either of the 2 sides of a playing court or field. **2.** A subsidiary activity, job, or line of merchandise.
side•long (sīd'lông', -lŏng') *adj.* Directed or tending to one side : oblique <a *sidelong* glance> —**side'long'** *adv.*
side•man (sīd'măn') *n.* A jazz musician.
si•de•re•al (sī-dîr'ē-əl) *adj.* Of, relating to, or measured by means of the stars.
side•sad•dle (sīd'săd'l) *n.* A saddle on which a woman may sit with both legs on the same side of the horse. —*adv.* On a sidesaddle.
side•show (sīd'shō') *n.* **1.** A small show offered in addition to a main attraction, as of a carnival. **2.** A subordinate incident.
side•split•ting (sīd'splĭt'ĭng) *adj.* Extremely funny : hilarious.
side•step (sīd'stĕp') *v.* **1.** To step out of the way of. **2.** To evade : avoid.
side stroke *n.* A swimming stroke performed on one side in which the arms are thrust forward alternately while the legs do a scissors kick.
side•swipe (sīd'swīp') *v.* To strike along the side in passing. —**side'swipe'** *n.*
side•track (sīd'trăk') *v.* **1.** To switch from a main railroad track to a siding. **2.** To deviate from a main issue, purpose, or course. —*n.* A railroad siding.
side•walk (sīd'wôk') *n.* A walk for pedestrians along the side of a street or road.
side wall *n.* One of the side surfaces of an automobile tire.
side•ways (sīd'wāz') *adv.* **1.** Toward, to, from, or at one side. **2.** With one side forward. —**side'ways'** *adj.*
side•wind•er (sīd'wīn'dər) *n.* A small rattlesnake, *Crotalus cerastes,* of the SW U.S. and Mexico, that moves by a distinctive lateral, looping bodily motion.
sid•ing (sī'dĭng) *n.* **1.** A short section of railroad track linked to a main track. **2.** Material used for covering the sides of a frame building.
si•dle (sīd'l) *v.* **-dled, -dling.** To move sideways, esp. furtively.
siege (sēj) *n.* **1.** The surrounding of a town or fortress by an army in order to capture it. **2.** A prolonged attack, as of illness.
si•er•ra (sē-ĕr'ə) *n.* A rugged mountain range whose tops have a serrate outline.
si•es•ta (sē-ĕs'tə) *n.* A rest or nap taken esp. after the midday meal.
sieve (sĭv) *n.* A wire mesh utensil used for straining, sifting, ricing, or puréeing. —**sieve** *v.*
sift (sĭft) *v.* **1.** To pass through or as if through a sieve. **2.** To separate by or as if by using a

sieve. **3.** To subject to careful examination. **—sift'er** *n.*

sigh (sī) *v.* **1.** To exhale a long, audible breath, as in sorrow, weariness, or relief. **2.** To experience grief or longing. **—sigh** *n.*

†**sight** (sīt) *n.* **1.** The act, process, or faculty of seeing. **2.** The range of a person's vision. **3.** Something seen : view. **4.** Something worth seeing. **5.** A device, as on a firearm, that guides the eye in aiming. **6.** *Regional.* A large number or quantity. —*v.* **1.** To catch sight of : see. **2.** To take aim.

sight•ed (sī'tĭd) *adj.* Capable of seeing.

sight•less (sīt'lĭs) *adj.* Unable to see : blind.

sight•ly (sīt'lē) *adj.* **-li•er, -li•est.** Pleasant to the sight.

sight-read (sīt'rēd') *v.* To read or perform (e.g., music) without preparation or prior study. **—sight'-read'er** *n.*

sight•see•ing (sīt'sē'ĭng) *n.* The act of traveling around to see places of interest. **—sight'se'er** *n.*

sign (sīn) *n.* **1.** Something suggesting the presence or existence of a fact, state, or quality : indication. **2.** A gesture that conveys an idea, wish, or command. **3.** A notice displayed publicly as an advertisement, to impart information, or to give guidance. **4.** A symbol. **5.** A portent : omen. **6.** A vestige or trace. **7.** One of the 12 divisions of the zodiac. ★ ***syns:*** EVIDENCE, INDICATION, INDICATOR, MANIFESTATION, MARK, SYMPTOM, TOKEN —*v.* **1.** To write one's signature on. **2.** To approve, guarantee, or ratify by affixing a signature or seal. **3.** To transfer or relinquish legally by signature. **4.** To make or mark with a sign : signal. **—sign off.** To stop transmission after identifying the broadcasting station. **—sign on.** To agree to or hire for work. **—sign out.** To record the departure of by signing. **—sign'er** *n.*

sig•nal (sĭg'nəl) *n.* **1.** A sign that serves to communicate a notice or warning. **2.** Something that indicates that action is to begin. **3. a.** *Electron.* An impulse or fluctuating electric quantity, as voltage or current, whose variations represent coded information. **b.** The sound, image, or message transmitted or received in electronic communications, as television. —*adj.* Out of the ordinary : outstanding. —*v.* **-naled, -nal•ing** *or* **-nalled, -nal•ling. 1.** To give a signal (to). **2.** To communicate or make known by signals. **—sig'nal•ly** *adv.*

sig•nal•ize (sĭg'nə-līz') *v.* **-ized, -iz•ing. 1.** To make noticeable. **2.** To point out in particular.

sig•na•to•ry (sĭg'nə-tôr'ē, -tōr'ē) *n., pl.* **-ries.** A signer of something, as a treaty.

sig•na•ture (sĭg'nə-cho͝or', -chər) *n.* **1.** A person's name as written by that person. **2.** Something, as a distinctive mark, that indicates identity. **3.** The symbol on a musical staff that indicates the key or meter.

sign•board (sīn'bôrd', -bōrd') *n.* A board that bears a sign.

sig•net (sĭg'nĭt) *n.* A seal, esp. one used to stamp official documents.

sig•nif•i•cance (sĭg-nĭf'ĭ-kəns) *n.* **1.** The state or quality of being significant : importance. **2.** The meaning of something : import. **3.** Implied meaning.

sig•nif•i•cant (sĭg-nĭf'ĭ-kənt) *adj.* **1.** Having or expressing meaning, often hidden meaning : meaningful. **2.** Important : weighty. **—sig•nif'i•cant•ly** *adv.*

sig•ni•fy (sĭg'nə-fī') *v.* **-fied, -fy•ing. 1.** To be a sign of : betoken. **2.** To make known by a sign : indicate. **3.** To have importance. **—sig'ni•fi•ca'tion** *n.*

sign language *n.* A communication system using hand gestures.

sign•post (sīn'pōst') *n.* A post that bears a sign.

Sikh (sēk) *n.* An adherent of a monotheistic religion of India combining elements of Hinduism and Islam. **—Sikh'ism** *n.*

si•lage (sī'lĭj) *n.* Fodder prepared for use by being stored and fermented in a silo.

si•lence (sī'ləns) *n.* **1.** The state, fact, or quality of being silent. **2.** The absence of sound : stillness. **3.** Failure or refusal to disclose : secrecy. —*v.* **-lenced, -lenc•ing. 1.** To cause to be silent : still. **2.** To suppress.

si•lenc•er (sī'lən-sər) *n.* A device for deadening the sound of a gunshot.

si•lent (sī'lənt) *adj.* **1.** Making no sound : quiet. **2. a.** Unwilling to speak : taciturn. **b.** Unable to speak : mute. **3.** Unexpressed : tacit. **4.** Unpronounced, as the *g* in *gnome.* ★ ***syns:*** HUSHED, NOISELESS, SOUNDLESS, STILL **—si'lent•ly** *adv.*

sil•hou•ette (sĭl'o͞o-ĕt') *n.* **1.** A representation of the outline of something, as a human profile, filled in with a solid color, esp. black. **2.** The outline of a body or object <the *silhouette* of a tree> —*v.* **-et•ted, -et•ting.** To represent or cause to be seen as a silhouette.

sil•i•ca (sĭl'ĭ-kə) *n.* A crystalline compound that occurs widely in mineral form, as quartz, sand, and flint.

sil•i•cate (sĭl'ĭ-kāt', -kĭt) *n.* Any of numerous compounds containing silicon, oxygen, and a metallic or organic radical.

si•li•ceous (sĭ-lĭsh'əs) *adj.* Of, pertaining to, containing, or resembling silica.

sil•i•con (sĭl'ĭ-kən, -kŏn') *n. Symbol* **Si** A nonmetallic element that occurs in both crystalline and amorphous forms and is used in glass, concrete, and silicones.

sil•i•cone (sĭl'ĭ-kōn') *n.* Any of a group of semi-inorganic polymers used in adhesives, lubricants, paints, and electrical insulation.

sil•i•co•sis (sĭl'ĭ-kō'sĭs) *n.* A disease of the lungs caused by inhalation of silica dust over a long time period.

silk (sĭlk) *n.* **1.** The fine, lustrous fiber produced by the larvae of certain insects, esp. the silkworm. **2.** Fabric or thread made from silk. **—silk'en** *adj.* **—silk'y** *adj.*

silk-cot•ton tree (sĭlk'kŏt'n) *n.* A tropical American tree, *Ceiba pentandra,* cultivated for its fruit containing the silklike fiber kapok.

silk screen *n.* A stencil method in which

ink is forced through a screen of fabric, esp. silk, onto a printing surface. **—silk′-screen′** *v.*

silk•worm (sĭlk′wûrm′) *n.* A caterpillar that produces a silk cocoon, esp. the larva of an Asian moth, *Bombyx mori,* that spins a cocoon of fine lustrous fiber.

sill (sĭl) *n.* A horizontal supporting member, as of wood, that forms the bottom part of a window or door frame.

sil•ly (sĭl′ē) *adj.* **-li•er, -li•est. 1.** Lacking or showing a lack of good sense : foolish or stupid. **2.** Lacking seriousness or substance : frivolous. **—sil′li•ness** *n.*

si•lo (sī′lō) *n., pl.* **-los. 1.** A pit or tall, cylindrical structure for the storage of fodder. **2.** An underground shelter for a missile.

silt (sĭlt) *n.* A sedimentary material consisting of fine mineral particles found esp. at the bottom of bodies of water. *—v.* To fill, cover, or obstruct with silt.

silt•stone (sĭlt′stōn′) *n.* Stone consisting mainly of hardened silt.

sil•ver (sĭl′vər) *n.* **1.** Symbol **Ag** A lustrous, white, ductile, malleable metallic element used in jewelry, tableware, and coinage. **2.** Coins made of silver. **3.** Household articles, esp. tableware, made of or plated with silver. **4.** A medium gray color. *—adj.* **1.** Of the color silver. **2.** Persuasive : eloquent. *—v.* To plate, cover, or decorate with or as if with silver.

silver bromide *n.* A crystalline compound used as the light-sensitive component on photographic plates and films.

sil•ver•fish (sĭl′vər-fĭsh′) *n.* A silvery, wingless insect, *Lepisma saccharina,* that causes damage to books and clothing.

silver iodide *n.* A pale-yellow powder used in photography and as an antiseptic.

silver nitrate *n.* A poisonous, colorless crystalline compound used in photography and as an external antiseptic.

sil•ver•smith (sĭl′vər-smĭth′) *n.* Someone who makes or repairs articles of silver.

sil•ver•ware (sĭl′vər-wâr′) *n.* Tableware, as forks, knives, and spoons, made of or plated with silver.

sim•i•an (sĭm′ē-ən) *adj.* Of, relating to, or resembling an ape or monkey. *—n.* An ape or monkey.

sim•i•lar (sĭm′ə-lər) *adj.* Having resemblance but not identical. **—sim′i•lar′i•ty** *n.* **—sim′i•lar•ly** *adv.*

sim•i•le (sĭm′ə-lē) *n.* A figure of speech in which 2 unlike things are compared, as in "hair like silk."

si•mil•i•tude (sĭ-mĭl′ĭ-to͞od′, -tyo͞od′) *n.* Resemblance : similarity.

sim•mer (sĭm′ər) *v.* **1.** To cook just below or at the boiling point. **2.** To be nearly at the point of erupting, as with emotion : seethe. **—sim′mer** *n.*

si•mon-pure (sī′mən-pyo͝or′) *adj.* **1.** Genuinely pure. **2.** Superficially or hypocritically virtuous.

sim•o•ny (sĭm′ə-nē, sī′mə-) *n.* Purchase or sale of ecclesiastical pardons or offices.

sim•pa•ti•co (sĭm-pä′tĭ-kō′, -păt′ĭ-) *adj.* **1.** Compatible : harmonious. **2.** Likable.

sim•per (sĭm′pər) *v.* To smile in an inane manner. **—sim′per** *n.*

sim•ple (sĭm′pəl) *adj.* **-pler, -plest. 1.** Having or composed of a single part or unit. **2.** Not difficult or complicated : easy. **3.** Without additions or qualifications : mere. **4.** Not showy or ornate : unadorned. **5.** Not affected : straightforward and unpretentious. **6.** Lacking or showing a lack of sense, intelligence, or education. **—sim′ple•ness** *n.* **—sim′ply** *adv.*

simple interest *n.* Interest paid only on the original principal, not on the interest accrued.

sim•ple-mind•ed (sĭm′pəl-mīn′dĭd) *adj.* **1.** Not sophisticated : artless. **2.** Stupid or foolish. **3.** Mentally defective.

simple sentence *n.* A sentence having only one clause, as *The dog growled.*

sim•ple•ton (sĭm′pəl-tən) *n.* A fool.

sim•plic•i•ty (sĭm-plĭs′ĭ-tē) *n.* **1.** Lack of showiness or ornateness : plainness. **2.** Lack of sophistication, affectation, or pretense : artlessness. **3.** Lack of complexity or difficulty. **4.** Foolishness.

sim•pli•fy (sĭm′plə-fī′) *v.* **-fied, -fy•ing.** To make simple or simpler. **—sim′pli•fi•ca′tion** *n.* **—sim′pli•fi′er** *n.*

sim•plis•tic (sĭm-plĭs′tĭk) *adj.* Spuriously simple because complexities or complications have been ignored. **—sim•plis′ti•cal•ly** *adv.*

sim•u•late (sĭm′yə-lāt′) *v.* **-lat•ed, -lat•ing. 1.** To have or duplicate the appearance, form, effect, or sound of. **2.** To pretend : feign. **—sim′u•la′tion** *n.* **—sim′u•la′tor** *n.*

si•mul•cast (sī′məl-kăst′, sĭm′əl-) *v.* To broadcast simultaneously by radio and television. **—si′mul•cast′** *n.*

si•mul•ta•ne•ous (sī′məl-tā′nē-əs, sĭm′əl-) *adj.* Occurring, existing, or carried out at the same time. **—si′mul•ta′ne•ous•ly** *adv.* **—si′mul•ta′ne•ous•ness** *n.*

sin (sĭn) *n.* **1.** The act of breaking a religious or moral law. **2.** An offense, error, or fault. *—v.* **sinned, sin•ning.** To commit a sin. **—sin′less** *adj.* **—sin′ner** *n.*

since (sĭns) *adv.* **1.** From then until now. **2.** Before now : ago. *—prep.* **1.** During the time after <haven't seen him *since* the party> **2.** Continuously after <has been at home *since* noon> *—conj.* **1.** As a result of the fact that : because. **2.** From the time at which.

sin•cere (sĭn-sîr′) *adj.* **-cer•er, -cer•est. 1.** Not deceitful or hypocritical : honest. **2.** Genuine : true. **—sin•cere′ly** *adv.* **—sin•cer′i•ty** (-sĕr′ĭ-tē) *n.*

si•ne•cure (sī′nĭ-kyo͝or′, sĭn′ĭ-) *n.* A position that pays a good salary but requires little or no work.

si•ne di•e (sī′nĭ dī′ē, sĭn′ā dē′ā′) *adv.* Without a future time or date being specified : indefinitely.

si•ne qua non (sĭn′ĭ kwä nōn′, nŏn′) *n.* An essential element.

sin•ew (sĭn′yo͞o) *n.* **1.** A tendon. **2.** Muscular power : strength. **—sin′ew•y** *adj.*

sin•ful (sĭn′fəl) *adj.* Characterized by or full of sin : wicked. —**sin′ful•ly** *adv.* —**sin′ful•ness** *n.*

sing (sĭng) *v.* **sang** (săng) *or* **sung** (sŭng), **sung, sing•ing. 1. a.** To use the voice to produce musical tones. **b.** To utter (e.g., a series of words) in musical tones. **2.** To produce musical sounds <canaries *singing*> **3.** To extol, esp. in verse or song. **4.** To produce a high-pitched, shrill sound <a teakettle *singing*> **5.** *Slang.* To give evidence or information. —**sing′er** *n.*

singe (sĭnj) *v.* **singed, singe•ing. 1.** To burn the surface of slightly : scorch. **2.** To remove the feathers, down, or bristles of with a flame.

sin•gle (sĭng′gəl) *adj.* **1.** Being one only : solitary. **2.** Consisting of only one form, feature, or part. **3.** Individual : separate. **4.** Designed or intended to accommodate one person or family. **5.** Unmarried. ★ ***syns:*** DISCRETE, INDIVIDUAL, SEPARATE, SINGULAR —*n.* **1.** A separate person or thing : individual. **2.** An accommodation for one person or family. **3.** An unmarried person. **4.** A dollar bill. **5.** A hit in baseball that enables the batter to reach 1st base. **6. singles.** A tennis match between 2 players, 1 on each side. —*v.* **-gled, -gling. 1.** To select or distinguish from among a group. **2.** To hit a single in baseball. —**sin′gle•ness** *n.* —**sin′gly** *adv.*

sin•gle-breast•ed (sĭng′gəl-brĕs′tĭd) *adj.* Closing in the center with very little overlap <a *single-breasted* coat>

single file *n.* A line of individuals one behind the other. —**single file** *adv.*

sin•gle-hand•ed (sĭng′gəl-hăn′dĭd) *adj.* Working or done without help from others : unassisted. —**sin′gle-hand′ed•ly** *adv.*

sin•gle-mind•ed (sĭng′gəl-mīn′dĭd) *adj.* Having a single overriding purpose.

sin•gle•ton (sĭng′gəl-tən) *n.* A playing card that is the only one of its suit in a player's hand.

sing•song (sĭng′sông′, -sŏng′) *n.* Monotonous regularity of rhythm or rhyme.

sin•gu•lar (sĭng′gyə-lər) *adj.* **1.** Of, pertaining to, or being a word form that denotes a single person, thing, or unit. **2.** Extraordinary : exceptional. **3.** Very odd : peculiar. —**sin′gu•lar** *n.* —**sin′gu•lar′i•ty** *n.* —**sin′gu•lar•ly** *adv.*

sin•is•ter (sĭn′ĭ-stər) *adj.* **1.** Suggesting evil : wicked. **2.** Threatening or presaging evil or trouble : ominous.

sink (sĭngk) *v.* **sank** (săngk) *or* **sunk** (sŭngk), **sunk** *or* **sunk•en** (sŭng′kən), **sink•ing. 1.** To submerge or cause to submerge beneath a surface. **2.** To descend slowly or bit by bit. **3.** To drive into the ground. **4.** To make (a shaft, hole, or well) in the earth by digging or drilling. **5.** To deteriorate in physical condition or strength. **6.** To become weaker, quieter, or less forceful. **7.** To slope downward : incline. **8.** To penetrate : seep. **9.** To invest. —*n.* **1.** A basin for water fixed to a wall or floor and connected with a drain. **2.** A cesspool. **3.** A sinkhole. —**sink′a•ble** *adj.*

sink•er (sĭng′kər) *n.* A weight used for sinking a fishing net or line.

sink•hole (sĭngk′hōl′) *n.* A natural depression in a land surface, esp. in a limestone region, that communicates with an underground passage, esp. a cavern.

sin•u•ous (sĭn′yo͞o-əs) *adj.* Having many bends or curves : winding. —**sin′u•os′i•ty** (-ŏs′ĭ-tē) *n.* —**sin′u•ous•ly** *adv.*

si•nus (sī′nəs) *n.* **1.** A bodily channel, esp. for the passage of blood. **2.** Any of several air-filled cavities in the cranial bones, esp. one communicating with the nostrils.

si•nus•i•tis (sī′nə-sī′tĭs) *n.* Inflammation of a sinus membrane.

Si•on (sī′ən) *n. var. of* ZION.

Siou•an (so͞o′ən) *n.* A large North American Indian language family spoken from Lake Michigan to the Rocky Mountains.

Sioux (so͞o) *n., pl.* **Sioux** (so͞o, so͞oz). **1.** A member of a group of American Indian peoples of the N Great Plains, now mainly in North and South Dakota. **2.** Any of their Siouan languages. —**Sioux** *adj.*

sip (sĭp) *v.* **sipped, sip•ping.** To drink in small quantities. —**sip** *n.*

si•phon *also* **sy•phon** (sī′fən) *n.* A bent tube through which liquid can be moved by means of atmospheric pressure up and over the lip of one container and down into another situated at a lower level. —*v.* To draw off through or as if through a siphon.

sir (sûr) *n.* **1.** —Used as a respectful form of address in place of a man's name. **2. Sir.** —Used as an honorific before the given or full name of a baronet or knight.

sire (sīr) *n.* **1. a.** A father. **b.** *Archaic.* A forefather. **2.** The male parent of an animal. **3.** *Archaic.* A form of address for a superior. —*v.* **sired, sir•ing.** To beget.

si•ren (sī′rən) *n.* **1.** A captivating or seductive woman. **2.** An often electrically operated whistle that makes a loud wailing sound as a signal or warning.

sir•loin (sûr′loin′) *n.* A cut of meat, esp. beef, from the upper loin.

si•roc•co (sĭ-rŏk′ō) *n., pl.* **-cos. 1.** A hot wind of S Europe, originating in the Sahara. **2.** A warm or hot southerly wind.

sir•up (sĭr′əp, sûr′-) *n. var. of* SYRUP.

si•sal (sī′zəl, -səl) *n.* A strong, sturdy cordage fiber obtained from the agave.

sis•sy (sĭs′ē) *n., pl.* **-sies. 1.** An effeminate man or boy. **2.** A cowardly or timorous person. —**sis′si•fy′** *v.*

sissy bar *n.* An inverted U-shaped bar rising from behind a motorcycle or bicycle seat to support the driver or a passenger.

sis•ter (sĭs′tər) *n.* **1.** A woman or girl having the same parents as another. **2.** A fellow member, as of a sorority. **3.** A nun. **4.** *esp. Brit.* A nurse. —**sis′ter•ly** *adj.*

sis•ter•hood (sĭs′tər-ho͝od′) *n.* **1.** The relationship or state of being a sister or sisters. **2.** The quality of being sisterly. **3.** A group, society, or community of sisters.

sis•ter-in-law (sĭs′tər-ĭn-lô′) *n., pl.* **sis•ters-**

in-law. 1. The sister of one's spouse. 2. The wife of one's brother.

sit (sĭt) *v.* **sat** (săt), **sit•ting. 1.** To assume a position with the body resting on the buttocks. **2.** To perch : roost. **3.** To cover eggs for hatching : brood. **4.** To keep one's seat on (a horse). **5.** To be located : lie. **6.** To pose for a photographer or artist. **7.** To be in session. **8.** To remain inactive, unused, or quiet. **9.** To baby-sit. **10. a.** To cause to sit : seat. **b.** To occupy a seat, as in a legislature. **—sit in. 1.** To be present or participate as a visitor. **2.** To take part in a sit-in. **—sit'ter** *n.*

si•tar (sĭ-tär') *n.* An Indian stringed instrument with a long, fretted neck and usu. 6 or 7 playing strings. **—si•tar'ist** *n.*

sit•com *also* **sit-com** (sĭt'kŏm') *n. Informal.* A situation comedy.

sit-down (sĭt'doun') *n.* A work stoppage in which employees remain in their place of work until their demands are met.

site (sīt) *n.* A location. *—v.* **sit•ed, sit•ing.** To locate : situate.

sit-in (sĭt'ĭn') *n.* A demonstration in which participants sit in seats or on the floor or ground in a public place as a means of protest.

sit•ting (sĭt'ĭng) *n.* **1.** The position or act of one that sits. **2.** A period during which one is seated. **3.** A session or term, as of a legislature.

sitting duck *n. Informal.* An easy target.

sit•u•ate (sĭch'o͞o-āt') *v.* **-at•ed, -at•ing.** To put in a certain position or place : locate.

sit•u•a•tion (sĭch'o͞o-ā'shən) *n.* **1.** A site : location. **2.** A set of circumstances : state. **3.** A position of employment.

situation comedy *n.* A humorous radio or television series consisting of episodes with the same characters.

sit-up (sĭt'ŭp') *n.* A form of exercise performed on the back in which the trunk is raised to a sitting position without the support of the arms and then returned to the orig. position.

six (sĭks) *n.* **1.** The cardinal number equal to 5 + 1. **2.** The 6th in a set or sequence. **3.** Something having 6 parts or units, esp. a motor vehicle with 6 cylinders. **—six** *adj. & pron.* **—sixth** *n. & adj. & adv.*

six-pack (sĭks'păk') *n.* **1.** A pack or container for 6 cans or bottles of a beverage sold together. **2.** The contents of a six-pack.

six-shoot•er (sĭks'sho͞o'tər) *n. Informal.* A revolver with 6 chambers.

six•teen (sĭk'stēn') *n.* **1.** The cardinal number equal to 15 + 1. **2.** The 16th in a set or sequence. **—six'teen'** *adj. & pron.* **—six'teenth'** *n., adj., & adv.*

six•ty (sĭk'stē) *n., pl.* **-ties.** The cardinal number equal to 6 × 10. **—six'ti•eth** *n. & adj. & adv.* **—six'ty** *adj. & pron.*

siz•a•ble *also* **size•a•ble** (sī'zə-bəl) *adj.* Fairly large. **—siz'a•bly** *adv.*

size[1] (sīz) *n.* **1.** Physical dimension, bulk, or extent : magnitude. **2.** One of a series of graduated dimensions by which manufactured articles are classified. *—v.* **sized, siz•ing.** To arrange or classify according to size. **—size up.** To form a judgment or opinion of.

size[2] (sīz) *n.* A gluey substance used to glaze or fill holes in paper, cloth, or wall surfaces. *—v.* **sized, siz•ing.** To glaze, fill, or coat with size.

siz•ing (sī'zĭng) *n.* SIZE[2].

siz•zle (sĭz'əl) *v.* **-zled, -zling. 1.** To make the hissing sound of frying fat. **2.** To seethe, as with indignation. **—siz'zle** *n.*

skate[1] (skāt) *n.* **1.** An ice skate. **2.** A roller skate. **—skate** *v.* **—skat'er** *n.*

skate[2] (skāt) *n.* Any of several marine fishes of the family Rajidae, with a flattened body and winglike fins.

skate[3] (skāt) *n.* A fellow <a good *skate*>

skate•board (skāt'bôrd', –bōrd') *n.* A short, narrow board to which roller-skate wheels are attached. **—skate'board'** *v.* **—skate'board'er** *n.*

ske•dad•dle (skĭ-dăd'l) *v.* **-dled, -dling.** *Informal.* To leave hastily : flee.

skeet (skēt) *n.* A form of trapshooting in which clay targets are thrown to simulate the flight of game birds.

skein (skān) *n.* A loose, long coil of thread or yarn.

skel•e•ton (skĕl'ĭ-tn) *n.* **1.** The internal vertebrate structure composed of bone and cartilage that protects and supports the soft organs and tissues. **2.** A structure that supports : framework. **3.** A brief plan : outline or sketch. **—skel'e•tal** *adj.*

skeleton key *n.* A key that can open more than one lock.

skep•tic *also* **scep•tic** (skĕp'tĭk) *n.* **1.** Someone who habitually doubts or questions. **2.** Someone inclined to philosophical or religious skepticism. **—skep'ti•cal** *adj.*

skep•ti•cism *also* **scep•ti•cism** (skĕp'tĭ-sĭz'əm) *n.* **1.** A doubting or questioning attitude. **2.** The philosophical doctrine that the attainment of absolute knowledge is impossible. **3.** Disbelief in religious principles or tenets.

sketch (skĕch) *n.* **1.** An undetailed drawing, esp. one made as a preliminary study. **2.** A rough outline, as of a book not yet completed. **3. a.** A brief or light literary composition. **b.** A short, often comical act in a revue or variety show. *—v.* To make a sketch (of). **—sketch'y** *adj.*

skew (skyo͞o) *v.* To place or turn at an angle : slant. *—n.* A slant.

skew•er (skyo͞o'ər) *n.* A long pin, as of metal, used to secure food and esp. meat while it cooks. **—skew'er** *v.*

ski (skē) *n., pl.* **skis.** One of a pair of long, flat runners for gliding over snow or water. *—v.* **skied, ski•ing.** To move or glide on skis. **—ski'er** *n.*

ski•bob (skē'bŏb') *n.* A vehicle for gliding downhill over snow, having a seat for the rider who wears small skis for balance.

skid (skĭd) *n.* **1.** The act or process of slipping or sliding sideways over a surface. **2. a.**

A plank or log forming a support or track on which something can be slid or rolled. **b.** PALLET[1]. **3.** A runner that forms part of the landing gear of an aircraft, as a helicopter. **4.** A wedge placed under a wheel to keep it from turning. —*v.* **skidded, skid•ding. 1.** To slip or slide sideways over a surface <a truck *skidding* on the icy road> **2.** To slide without revolving <a bicycle wheel *skidding* after the brakes were applied>

ski•doo (skĭ-do͞o′) *n. Can.* A motorized toboggan.

skid row *n. Slang.* A squalid district inhabited by derelicts.

skiff (skĭf) *n.* A boat with a flat bottom.

skil•ful (skĭl′fəl) *adj. esp. Brit. var. of* SKILLFUL.

ski lift *n.* A motor-driven conveyor for carrying skiers to the top of a mountain, trail, or slope.

skill (skĭl) *n.* **1.** Proficiency or ability **:** expertise. **2.** An art, trade, or technique, esp. one requiring use of the hands or body. —**skilled** *adj.*

skil•let (skĭl′ĭt) *n.* A frying pan.

skill•ful (skĭl′fəl) *adj.* **1.** Possessing, exercising, or showing skill. **2.** Requiring or done with skill. —**skill′ful•ly** *adv.* —**skill′ful•ness** *n.*

skim (skĭm) *v.* **skimmed, skim•ming. 1. a.** To remove floating matter or scum from (a liquid). **b.** To remove (floating matter) from <*skimmed* the foam from the boiling broth> **2.** To pass lightly and quickly over. **3.** To glance through or read quickly and superficially. —**skim′mer** *n.*

skim milk *n.* Milk from which the cream has been skimmed.

ski•mo•bile (skē′mō-bēl′, -mə-) *n.* A snowmobile.

skimp (skĭmp) *v.* **1.** To do without sufficient care or effort or with inferior material. **2.** To be sparing, esp. with money.

skimp•y (skĭm′pē) *adj.* **-i•er, -i•est.** Inadequate in fullness, size, or amount **:** scanty.

skin (skĭn) *n.* **1.** The tough, membranous tissue that forms the external covering of the animal body. **2.** An animal pelt, esp. when prepared for use, as in a garment. **3.** An outer covering or layer, as the rind of fruit. —*v.* **skinned, skin•ning. 1.** To remove the skin from. **2.** To injure the surface of by scraping. —**skin′less** *adj.*

skin diving *n.* Underwater swimming with a face mask, a snorkel or scuba equipment to permit breathing, and often flippers. —**skin′-dive′** *v.* —**skin diver** *n.*

skin flick *n.* A pornographic movie.

skin•flint (skĭn′flĭnt′) *n.* A miser.

skin graft *n.* A surgical graft of skin from one part of the body to another or from one individual to another.

†**skin•ner** (skĭn′ər) *n.* **1.** One who flays, dresses, or sells animal skins. **2.** *W U.S.* A mule driver.

skin•ny (skĭn′ē) *adj.* **-ni•er, -ni•est.** Very thin. —**skin′ni•ness** *n.*

skin•ny-dip (skĭn′ē-dĭp′) *v. Informal.* To swim in the nude. —**skin′ny-dip′ping** *n.*

skin•tight (skĭn′tīt′) *adj.* Fitted closely to the body.

skip (skĭp) *v.* **skipped, skip•ping. 1. a.** To move by hopping, jumping, or springing. **b.** To hop, jump, or spring lightly over. **2.** To pass from one point to another ignoring what intervenes. **3.** To pass over without considering, mentioning, or noticing **:** omit. **4.** *Informal.* To leave hastily and esp. furtively <*skip* town> —*n.* **1.** A skipping gait, movement, or step. **2.** An omission.

skip•per (skĭp′ər) *n.* The master of a ship, esp. a small one.

skir•mish (skûr′mĭsh) *n.* A minor encounter in war. —**skir′mish** *v.*

skirt (skûrt) *n.* **1.** The part of a garment, as a dress, that extends down from the waist. **2.** A garment that extends down from the waist. —*v.* **1.** To extend along the edge of **:** border. **2.** To pass around the edge or border of. **3.** To evade, esp. by circumlocution **:** avoid.

skit (skĭt) *n.* A short, often comic theatrical sketch.

ski touring *n.* Cross-country skiing engaged in for pleasure.

ski tow *n.* A ski lift.

skit•ter (skĭt′ər) *v.* To skip or glide rapidly or lightly along a surface.

skit•tish (skĭt′ĭsh) *adj.* **1.** Easily excited or frightened **:** nervous. **2.** Capricious or undependable.

skiv•vy (skĭv′ē) *n., pl.* **-vies.** *Slang. often* **skivvies.** Men's underwear consisting of an undershirt and shorts.

ski•wear (skē′wâr′) *n.* Clothing appropriate for skiing.

skulk (skŭlk) *v.* **1.** To lie in concealment **:** lurk. **2.** To move around stealthily. —**skulk′er** *n.*

skull (skŭl) *n.* The bony framework of the head that protects the brain.

skull•cap (skŭl′kăp′) *n.* A close-fitting cap without a brim.

skull•dug•ger•y *also* **skul•dug•ger•y** (skŭl-dŭg′ə-rē) *n.* Crafty or dishonest behavior **:** trickery.

skunk (skŭngk) *n.* **1.** Any of various New World mammals, esp. of the genus *Mephitis*, that have black and white fur and eject a foul-smelling secretion if startled. **2.** *Slang.* A despicable person. —*v. Slang.* To defeat overwhelmingly, esp. by preventing from scoring in a game.

skunk cabbage *n.* A North American swamp plant, *Symplocarpus foetidus*, bearing minute unpleasant-smelling flowers.

sky (skī) *n., pl.* **skies. 1.** The upper atmosphere. **2.** The celestial regions **:** heaven.

sky•cap (skī′kăp′) *n.* A porter employed at an airport.

sky•dive (skī′dīv′) *v.* To jump from an airplane and perform various maneuvers before opening the parachute. —**sky′div′er** *n.* —**sky′div′ing** *n.*

sky•jack (skī′jăk′) *v.* To hijack (an aircraft,

esp. one in flight). **—sky'jack'er** *n.* **—sky'-jack'ing** *n.*

sky·lark (skī'lärk') *n.* An Old World bird, *Alauda arvensis,* noted for singing while high in flight. —*v.* To frolic.

sky·light (skī'līt') *n.* A window in a ceiling or roof.

sky·line (skī'līn') *n.* **1.** The horizon. **2.** An outline seen against the sky.

sky marshal *n.* An armed federal law-enforcement officer assigned to prevent sky-jackings.

sky·rock·et (skī'rŏk'ĭt) *n.* A firework that shoots into the air and explodes brilliantly. —*v.* To rise suddenly and rapidly.

sky·scrap·er (skī'skrā'pər) *n.* An extremely tall building.

sky·ward (skī'wərd) *adv.& adj.* Toward the sky. **—sky'wards** *adv.*

sky·way (skī'wā') *n.* **1.** An airline route : air lane. **2.** An elevated highway.

sky·writ·ing (skī'rī'tĭng) *n.* Writing in the sky formed by the release of a visible vapor from an airplane. **—sky'writ'er** *n.*

slab (slăb) *n.* **1.** A broad, somewhat thick piece or slice. **2.** The outside piece cut from a log in squaring it for lumber.

slack (slăk) *adj.* **1.** Lacking in strength or liveliness : sluggish. **2.** Not active or busy. **3.** Not tense or taut : loose. **4.** Negligent : remiss. —*v.* **1.** To slacken. **2.** To slake (lime). —*n.* **1.** A part of something that is not drawn tight or that hangs loose. **2.** A period of reduced activity : lull. **3. slacks.** Long trousers for informal wear. **—slack'ly** *adv.* **—slack'-ness** *n.*

slack·en (slăk'ən) *v.* **1.** To make or become slower. **2.** To loosen.

slack·er (slăk'ər) *n.* Someone who shirks work or evades responsibility.

slag (slăg) *n.* The glassy refuse that remains after the smelting of metallic ore.

slain (slān) *v. p.p. of* SLAY.

slake (slāk) *v.* **slaked, slak·ing. 1.** To allay (e.g., thirst) : quench. **2.** To combine (lime) chemically with water or moist air.

sla·lom (slä'ləm) *n.* Downhill skiing, esp. in a race, along a zigzag course.

slam[1] (slăm) *v.* **slammed, slam·ming. 1.** To shut forcefully and noisily. **2.** To throw, drive, or strike with a loud, forceful impact. —*n.* A loud noise produced by a forceful impact : bang.

slam[2] (slăm) *n.* The winning of all or all but one of the tricks in a hand of bridge.

slam·mer (slăm'ər) *n. Slang.* A jail.

slan·der (slăn'dər) *n.* A false and malicious statement injurious to another's reputation. —*v.* To spread or utter slander about : defame. **—slan'der·ous** *adj.*

slang (slăng) *n.* A nonstandard vocabulary used esp. in casual speech and consisting of arbitrary and often ephemeral coinages and figures of speech. **—slang'i·ness** *n.* **—slang'-y** *adj.*

slant (slănt) *v.* **1.** To lie or cause to lie in an oblique direction : slope. **2.** To present or interpret so as to conform with a particular outlook. —*n.* **1.** A sloping plane, direction, line, or course. **2.** A particular or personal outlook. **—slant'ing·ly** *adv.* **—slant'wise'** *adv. & adj.*

slap (slăp) *n.* **1. a.** A sharp blow with the open hand. **b.** The sound of a slap. **2.** An injury to one's pride, esp. an insult. —*v.* **slapped, slap·ping. 1.** To give a slap to. **2.** To reprimand, insult, or criticize sharply.

slap·dash (slăp'dăsh') *adj.* Careless : slipshod. **—slap'dash'** *adv.*

slap·hap·py (slăp'hăp'ē) *adj. Slang.* Dazed, silly, or incoherent from or as if from blows to the head.

slap·stick (slăp'stĭk') *n.* A type of broad comedy marked by horseplay and farce.

slash (slăsh) *v.* **1.** To cut with forceful sweeping strokes. **2.** To make a slit in (a fabric or garment). **3.** To reduce greatly. —*n.* **1. a.** A forceful sweeping stroke, as with a sharp instrument. **b.** A cut made by slashing : gash. **2.** A virgule. **—slash'er** *n.*

slat (slăt) *n.* A flat, narrow thin strip, as of wood.

slate (slāt) *n.* **1. a.** A fine-grained rock that splits into thin layers with smooth surfaces. **b.** A writing surface or roofing tile made of slate. **2.** A list of political candidates running for office. —*v.* **slat·ed, slat·ing. 1.** To cover with slate. **2.** To schedule.

slath·er (slăth'ər) *v. Informal.* To spread thickly on or with.

slat·tern (slăt'ərn) *n.* An untidy woman. **—slat'tern·ly** *adj.*

slaugh·ter (slô'tər) *n.* **1.** The killing of livestock for food. **2.** The killing of a great number of people, esp. in battle : carnage. —*v.* **1.** To kill (livestock) for food : butcher. **2.** To kill savagely or in great numbers. **—slaugh'-ter·er** *n.*

slaugh·ter·house (slô'tər-hous') *n.* A place for butchering animals.

Slav (släv) *n.* A member of one of the Slavic-speaking peoples of E Europe.

slave (slāv) *n.* **1.** A person who is bound in servitude as the property of a person or household. **2.** A person completely controlled by a dominating influence <a *slave* to his work> —*v.* **slaved, slav·ing.** To work like a slave : labor.

slav·er[1] (slăv'ər, slā'vər) *v.* To slobber : drool. **—slav'er** *n.*

slav·er[2] (slā'vər) *n.* **1.** A ship engaged in slave traffic. **2.** A person who traffics in slaves.

slav·er·y (slā'və-rē, slāv'rē) *n.* **1.** Bondage to a master or household : servitude. **2.** The practice of owning slaves. **3.** Hard work : drudgery.

Slav·ic (slä'vĭk, slăv'ĭk) *adj.* Of or pertaining to the Slavs or their languages. —*n.* A branch of the Indo-European language family that includes Bulgarian, Czech, Polish, and Russian.

slav·ish (slā'vĭsh) *adj.* **1.** Resembling or befitting a slave : submissive. **2.** Showing no originality : imitative. **—slav'ish·ly** *adv.*

slaw (slô) *n.* Coleslaw.

slay (slā) *v.* **slew** (slo͞o), **slain** (slān), **slay·ing.** To kill, esp. by violent means. —**slay'er** *n.*

slea·zy (slē'zē) *adj.* **-zi·er, -zi·est. 1.** Lacking in substance : flimsy. **2.** Of poor quality : shoddy.

sled (slĕd) *n.* A vehicle mounted on runners used for coasting over snow or ice. —*v.* **sled·ded, sled·ding.** To convey or ride on a sled.

sledge[1] (slĕj) *n.* A vehicle on low runners for transporting loads over snow and ice.

sledge[2] (slĕj) *n.* A sledgehammer.

sledge·ham·mer (slĕdj'hăm'ər) *n.* A heavy, large hammer wielded with both hands.

sleek (slēk) *adj.* **1.** Lustrous and smooth : glossy. **2.** Neat and trim in appearance. —*v.* **1.** To make sleek. **2.** To cover up : conceal. —**sleek'ly** *adv.* —**sleek'ness** *n.*

sleep (slēp) *n.* **1.** A natural periodic state of rest marked by the suspension of consciousness. **2.** A state, as coma, that resembles sleep. —*v.* **slept** (slĕpt), **sleep·ing. 1.** To be in a state of sleep. **2.** To be in a state of quiet or inactivity. **3.** To spend in a period of sleep <*slept* away the afternoon> —**sleep'less** *adj.* —**sleep'less·ly** *adv.* —**sleep'less·ness** *n.*

sleep·er (slē'pər) *n.* **1.** One that sleeps. **2.** A sleeping car. **3.** *Informal.* Someone or something that achieves unexpected popularity, recognition, or success.

sleeping bag *n.* A warmly lined bag in which a person can sleep, esp. outdoors.

sleeping car *n.* A railroad car with sleeping accommodations.

sleeping sickness *n.* An often fatal endemic infectious disease of tropical Africa that is transmitted by the tsetse fly and marked by fever and lethargy.

sleep·walk·ing (slēp'wô'kĭng) *n.* Somnambulism. —**sleep'walk'er** *n.*

sleep·y (slē'pē) *adj.* **-i·er, -i·est. 1.** Ready to fall asleep : drowsy. **2.** Quiet, inactive, and often dull <a *sleepy* little town> —**sleep'i·ly** *adv.* —**sleep'i·ness** *n.*

sleet (slēt) *n.* **1.** Partially frozen rain. **2.** A thin coating of ice : glaze. —**sleet** *v.* —**sleet'y** *adj.*

sleeve (slēv) *n.* **1.** The part of a garment that covers the arm. **2.** An encasement into which something fits <a phonograph-record *sleeve*> —**sleeve'less** *adj.*

sleigh (slā) *n.* A light vehicle mounted on runners and used on ice or snow. —*v.* To ride in or drive a sleigh.

sleight (slīt) *n.* **1.** Deftness : dexterity. **2.** A sly trick : stratagem.

sleight of hand *n.* A trick so skillfully performed that its manner of execution cannot be observed.

slen·der (slĕn'dər) *adj.* **1.** Thin or slim. **2.** Inadequate in extent or amount : meager. —**slen'der·ly** *adv.* —**slen'der·ness** *n.*

slen·der·ize (slĕn'də-rīz') *v.* **-ized, -iz·ing.** To make or become slender.

slept (slĕpt) *v.* *p.t. & p.p. of* SLEEP.

sleuth (slo͞oth) *n.* *Informal.* A detective. —**sleuth** *v.*

slew[1] *also* **slue** (slo͞o) *n.* *Informal.* A large number or amount.

slew[2] (slo͞o) *v.* *p.t. of* SLAY.

slew[3] (slo͞o) *v. & n. var. of* SLUE[1].

slice (slīs) *n.* **1.** A thin, flat piece cut from something. **2.** A share : portion. **3.** An implement with a broad, flexible blade used esp. for serving food. **4.** A flight of a ball, as in golf, that curves off to the right if the player is right-handed or to the left if the player is left-handed. —*v.* **sliced, slic·ing. 1.** To cut into slices. **2.** To cut a slice from a larger piece. **3.** To hit (a ball) with a stroke causing a slice. —**slic'er** *n.*

slick (slĭk) *adj.* **1.** Smooth and slippery. **2.** Marked by deftness : adroit. **3.** Shrewd : clever. **4.** Superficially polished but without quality or depth. —*n.* **1.** A smooth area of water filmed with oil. **2.** *Informal.* A magazine with popular appeal that is printed on glossy paper. —*v.* To make smooth, glossy, or oily.

slick·er (slĭk'ər) *n.* **1.** A loose, glossy raincoat, often made of yellow oilcloth. **2.** *Informal.* A clever swindler.

slide (slīd) *v.* **slid** (slĭd), **slid·ing. 1.** To move or cause to move smoothly over a surface while keeping continuous contact. **2.** To lose one's balance and fall. **3.** To pass quietly : glide. ★ ***syns:*** COAST, DRIFT, GLIDE, SLIP —*n.* **1.** A sliding action or movement. **2.** A smooth surface on which something can slide. **3.** A part, as the bolt in certain locks, that operates by sliding. **4.** A photographic image on a transparent plate for projecting on a screen. **5.** A small glass plate on which specimens to be examined under a microscope can be mounted. **6.** A fall down a slope of a mass of ice, snow, earth, or rocks.

slid·er (slīd'ər) *n.* **1.** One that slides. **2.** A baseball pitch that curves slightly downward at the last moment.

slide rule *n.* A device for performing mathematical operations that consists of 2 logarithmically scaled rules mounted to slide along each other.

sliding scale *n.* A flexible scale in which prices or fees vary in accordance with another factor, as medical charges with a patient's income.

sli·er (slī'ər) *adj. var. compar. of* SLY.

sli·est (slī'ĭst) *adj. var. superl. of* SLY.

slight (slīt) *adj.* **1.** Small in amount or degree. **2.** Insignificant : unimportant. **3. a.** Slender and delicate. **b.** Frail. —*v.* **1.** To treat as insignificant. **2.** To ignore rudely : snub. **3.** To do or perform with negligence. —*n.* A deliberate act of disrespect or discourtesy. —**slight'ly** *adv.*

slim (slĭm) *adj.* **slim·mer, slim·mest. 1.** Slight : slender. **2.** Meager : scanty. —*v.* **slimmed, slim·ming.** To make or become slim. —**slim'ly** *adv.* —**slim'ness** *n.*

slime (slīm) *n.* **1.** Thick, sticky mud. **2.** A viscous, slippery substance, as that secreted by a slug. —**slim'y** *adj.*

sling (slĭng) *n.* **1.** A belt, rope, strap, or chain for securing something, as a load, that is to be

hoisted, lowered, secured, or carried. **2.** A weapon consisting of a looped strap from which a stone is thrown. —*v.* **slung** (slŭng), **sling•ing. 1.** To throw forcibly : fling. **2.** To place or carry in a sling. —**sling'er** *n.*
sling•shot (slĭng'shŏt') *n.* A Y-shaped stick with an elastic band used for throwing small stones.
slink (slĭngk) *v.* **slunk** (slŭngk), **slink•ing.** To move furtively or quietly.
slink•y (slĭng'kē) *adj.* **-i•er, -i•est. 1.** Furtive : stealthy. **2.** *Informal.* Sinuous.
slip¹ (slĭp) *v.* **slipped, slip•ping. 1.** To move or cause to move smoothly and quietly : glide. **2.** To lose one's balance or footing. **3.** To escape, esp. without being noticed. **4.** *Informal.* To decline in ability, strength, or performance. **5.** To pass unfinished or unnoticed. **6.** To make an error. —*n.* **1.** The act of slipping. **2.** An accident or mishap. **3.** An error : blunder. **4. a.** A docking place for a ship : pier. **b.** A space for a ship between 2 docks or wharves. **5.** A woman's undergarment serving as a lining for a dress. **6.** A pillowcase. —**slip'page** *n.*
slip² (slĭp) *n.* **1.** A twig or shoot cut from a plant for propagation. **2.** A strip, esp. of paper <a sales *slip*>
slip•cov•er (slĭp'kŭv'ər) *n.* A fitted, usu. cloth cover for a piece of furniture that can be slipped on and off.
slip•knot (slĭp'nŏt') *n.* A knot that slips along the rope or cord around which it is formed.
slipped disk *n.* A rupture of one of the cushioning disks between the spinal vertebrae that results in back pain.
slip•per (slĭp'ər) *n.* A light, low shoe that slips on and off easily.
slip•per•y (slĭp'ə-rē) *adj.* **-i•er, -i•est. 1.** Causing or tending to cause sliding, slipping, or falling. **2.** Untrustworthy : shifty. —**slip'per•i•ly** *adv.* —**slip'per•i•ness** *n.*
slip•shod (slĭp'shŏd') *adj.* Marked by carelessness : sloppy.
slip-stream (slĭp'strēm') *n.* The turbulent flow of air driven backward by the propeller of an aircraft.
slip-up (slĭp'ŭp') *n. Informal.* A mistake.
slit (slĭt) *n.* A straight, narrow tear or incision. —*v.* **slit•ted, slit•ting. 1.** To cut a slit in. **2.** To split.
slith•er (slĭth'ər) *v.* **1.** To slip and slide. **2.** To move in a sinuous manner, as a snake does : glide. —**slith'er•y** *adj.*
sliv•er (slĭv'ər) *n.* A thin, sharp-ended piece : splinter. —**sliv'er** *v.*
slob (slŏb) *n. Informal.* A coarse or slovenly person.
slob•ber (slŏb'ər) *v.* To let saliva dribble from the mouth. —**slob'ber** *n.*
slob ice *n. Can.* Chunks of disintegrating sea ice.
sloe (slō) *n.* The blue-black, plumlike fruit of a thorny Eurasian shrub, *Prunus spinosa.*
sloe-eyed (slō'īd') *adj.* Having slanted eyes.
sloe gin *n.* A liqueur with a gin base flavored with sloes.
slog (slŏg) *v.* **slogged, slog•ging. 1.** To walk slowly and heavily : plod. **2.** To work hard for long hours. **3.** To hit hard.
slo•gan (slō'gən) *n.* A phrase that expresses the nature or aims of an enterprise, cause, or group : motto.
sloop (slo͞op) *n.* A fore-and-aft-rigged sailing boat with one mast, a mainsail, and a jib.
slop (slŏp) *n.* **1.** Spilled or splashed liquid. **2.** Soft mud. **3.** Unappetizing, watery food or drink. **4.** *often* **slops.** Waste food used as animal feed : swill. —*v.* **slopped, slop•ping.** To spill or splash carelessly.
slope (slōp) *v.* **sloped, slop•ing.** To incline upward or downward : slant. —*n.* **1.** A stretch of ground forming an incline. **2. a.** An upward or downward incline : slant. **b.** The degree of such an incline.
slop•py (slŏp'ē) *adj.* **-pi•er, -pi•est. 1.** Wet : slushy or muddy. **2.** Messy : untidy.
sloppy joe (jō) *n.* Ground cooked meat in a usu. spicy sauce served on a bun.
slosh (slŏsh) *v.* To splash through a liquid, as water : flounder. —**slosh'y** *adj.*
slot (slŏt) *n.* **1.** A long, narrow groove or aperture. **2.** *Informal.* A position or place, as in a hierarchy : niche.
sloth (slōth, slôth, slŏth) *n.* **1.** Indolence : laziness. **2.** A slow-moving arboreal tropical American mammal of the family Bradypodidae. —**sloth'ful** *adj.*
slot machine *n.* A vending or gambling machine operated by insertion of a coin.
slouch (slouch) *n.* **1.** An awkward, relaxed, or drooping posture or gait. **2.** An inefficient or lazy person. —*v.* To sit, stand, or move with a slouch.
slough¹ (slo͞o, slou) *n.* **1.** A muddy hollow in the ground. **2.** A bog : swamp. **3.** A state of dejection.
slough² (slŭf) *n.* Something, esp. an outer layer or covering, that can be shed. —*v.* To cast off : shed.
slov•en (slŭv'ən) *n.* A habitually untidy or careless person. —**slov'en•ly** *adj.*
slow (slō) *adj.* **1.** Moving or proceeding at a low rate of speed. **2.** Taking or requiring more time than usual. **3.** Indicating a time earlier than the correct time. **4.** Naturally inactive : sluggish. **5.** Lacking in liveliness : boring. **6.** Not quick to comprehend : dull. ★ ***syns:*** DILATORY, POKY, TARDY —*adv.* In a slow manner. —*v.* **1.** To make or become slow or slower. **2.** To delay. —**slow'ly** *adv.* —**slow'ness** *n.*
slow burn *n.* A gradual build-up of anger.
slow•down (slō'doun') *n.* A slowing down, esp. in production.
slow motion *n.* A motion-picture technique in which the action as projected is slower than the original action.
sludge (slŭj) *n.* **1.** Mud, esp. that forming a deposit : ooze. **2.** Slushy matter, as that formed in the treatment of sewage. —**sludg'y** *adj.*
slue¹ *also* **slew** (slo͞o) *v.* **slued, slu•ing** *also* **slewed, slew•ing.** To turn to the side : twist. —**slue, slew** *n.*

slue[2] (slo͞o) *n. var. of* SLEW[1].

slug[1] (slŭg) *n.* **1.** A lump of metal, esp. a bullet. **2.** *Informal.* A small amount, esp. a jigger, of liquor. **3.** A metal disk used in place of a coin.

slug[2] (slŭg) *n.* A terrestrial gastropod mollusk, esp. of the genus *Limex,* that is related to the snails but has no shell.

slug[3] (slŭg) *v.* **slugged, slug·ging.** To strike heavily and hard, esp. with the fist. **—slug** *n.* **—slug′ger** *n.*

slug·gard (slŭg′ərd) *n.* An indolent person. **—slug′gard·ly** *adj.*

slug·gish (slŭg′ĭsh) *adj.* **1.** Slow in performance, response, or movement. **2.** Inactive : stagnant. **3.** Lazy : indolent. **—slug′gish·ly** *adv.* **—slug′gish·ness** *n.*

sluice (slo͞os) *n.* **1. a.** A manmade channel for water with a gate to control the flow. **b.** The gate in a sluice. **2.** A sluiceway. **3.** A sloping trough, as for floating logs. *—v.* **sluiced, sluic·ing. 1.** To flush with running water. **2.** To draw off by means of a sluice. **3.** To send (e.g., logs) through a sluice.

slum (slŭm) *n.* A squalid, heavily populated urban residential area marked by poverty and substandard housing. *—v.* **slummed, slum·ming.** To visit a slum, esp. out of curiosity.

slum·ber (slŭm′bər) *v.* **1. a.** To sleep. **b.** To doze. **2.** To be quiescent or dormant. *—n.* **1.** Sleep. **2.** A condition of quiescence or dormancy. **—slum′ber·er** *n.*

slum·ber·ous (slŭm′bər-əs) *also* **slum·brous** (-brəs) *adj.* **1.** Sleepy or sleeping. **2.** Tranquil : peaceful.

slump (slŭmp) *v.* **1.** To drop or sink suddenly. **2.** To slouch. **—slump** *n.*

slung (slŭng) *v. p.t. & p.p. of* SLING.

slunk (slŭngk) *v. p.t. & p.p. of* SLINK.

slur (slûr) *v.* **slurred, slur·ring. 1.** To pass over lightly or without due consideration. **2.** To pronounce indistinctly. **3.** *Mus.* To perform a succession of notes smoothly and without a break. *—n.* **1.** A derogatory remark : aspersion. **2.** *Mus.* A curved line connecting notes to indicate that they are to be slurred.

slurp (slûrp) *v.* To drink or eat noisily. **—slurp** *n.*

slush (slŭsh) *n.* **1.** Partially melted snow. **2.** Soft mud : mire. **—slush′y** *adj.*

slut (slŭt) *n.* **1.** A slatternly woman. **2.** A prostitute. **—slut′tish** *adj.*

sly (slī) *adj.* **sli·er, sli·est** *also* **sly·er, sly·est. 1.** Artfully clever : cunning. **2.** Stealthy : furtive. **3.** Playfully mischievous : roguish. ★ ***syns:*** FURTIVE, SECRETIVE, SURREPTITIOUS **—sly′ly** *adv.* **—sly′ness** *n.*

Sm *symbol for* SAMARIUM.

smack[1] (smăk) *v.* **1.** To press together and open (the lips) with a sharp noise. **2.** To slap or kiss with a sharp noise. *—n.* **1.** The sharp sound made by smacking the lips. **2.** A noisy slap or kiss. *—adv.* Directly and sharply <drove *smack* into a tree>

smack[2] (smăk) *n.* **1.** A distinctive flavor. **2.** A trace : suggestion. *—v.* **1.** To have a flavor. **2.** To have a trace : suggest.

smack[3] (smăk) *n.* A sailing boat used esp. in fishing.

smack[4] (smăk) *n. Slang.* Heroin.

smack·er (smăk′ər) *n.* **1.** A loud kiss. **2.** A resounding blow. **3.** *Slang.* A dollar.

small (smôl) *adj.* **1.** Little in size, extent, or quantity. **2.** Unimportant : trivial. **3.** Operating with limited resources or funds. **4.** Petty : mean. **5.** Humbled : humiliated. *—n.* A part that is smaller than the rest <the *small* of the back> **—small′ness** *n.*

small arms *pl.n.* Firearms that can be fired while held in the hand.

small calorie *n.* CALORIE 1.

small·pox (smôl′pŏks′) *n.* An acute, highly infectious viral disease marked by high fever and pustular eruptions.

small talk *n.* Casual conversation.

small·time (smôl′tīm′) *adj. Informal.* Of little standing : minor. **—small′tim′er** *n.*

smarm·y (smär′mē) *adj.* **-i·er, -i·est.** Marked by an insincere or exaggerated earnestness : unctuous.

smart (smärt) *adj.* **1. a.** Quick-witted : bright. **b.** Amusingly clever : witty. **2.** Fashionable : stylish. *—v.* **1.** To feel or cause to feel a sharp, stinging pain. **2.** To feel mental distress or pain. **—smart′ly** *adv.* **—smart′ness** *n.*

smart al·eck (ăl′ĭk) *n. Informal.* An obnoxiously arrogant or impudent person.

smart·en (smär′tn) *v.* To make or become smart or smarter.

smart·y (spär′tē) *n., pl.* **-ies.** A smart aleck.

smash (smăsh) *v.* **1.** To break or be broken into pieces. **2.** To throw or move forward violently so as to crush or shatter. **3.** To strike heavily : hit. **4.** To destroy completely : ruin. *—n.* **1.** The act or sound of smashing. **2.** Complete destruction : ruin. **3.** A collision : crash. **4.** A powerful overhand stroke, esp. in tennis. **5.** A resounding success : hit. *—adj. Informal.* Extraordinary : outstanding. **—smash′er** *n.*

smat·ter·ing (smăt′ər-ĭng) *n.* **1.** Slight or surface knowledge. **2.** A small, scattered amount or number.

smear (smîr) *v.* **1.** To cover, spread, or stain with a sticky, oily, or dirty substance. **2.** To soil : smudge. **3.** To injure the reputation of : slander. *—n.* A smudge or spot made by smearing. **—smear′y** *adj.*

smell (smĕl) *v.* **smelled** *or* **smelt** (smĕlt), **smell·ing. 1. a.** To perceive the odor of by means of the olfactory sense organs. **b.** To detect by or as if by use of these organs. **2.** To have or emit an odor. *—n.* **1. a.** The sense by which odors are perceived. **b.** The ability to perceive odors. **2.** The odor of something : scent. **3.** The act or an instance of smelling.

smelling salts *pl.n.* A preparation based on spirits of ammonia that is used esp. to relieve faintness.

smell·y (smĕl′ē) *adj.* **-i·er, -i·est.** Having a bad odor. ★ ***syns:*** FETID, FOUL, MALODOROUS, REEKING, STINKING.

smelt[1] (smĕlt) *v.* To melt or fuse (ores) in order to extract the metallic constituents.

smelt² (smĕlt) *n., pl.* **smelts** *or* **smelt.** Any of various small silvery food fishes of the family Osmeridae.

smelt·er (smĕl'tər) *n.* **1.** An establishment where ores are smelted. **2.** One that smelts.

smidg·en *also* **smidg·in** (smĭj'ən) *n Informal.* A minute quantity : bit.

smi·lax (smī'lăks') *n.* **1.** A plant of the genus *Smilax,* which includes various climbing vines. **2.** A glossy-leaved vine, *Asparagus asparagoides,* used in floral decoration.

smile (smīl) *n.* A facial expression in which the corners of the mouth curve upward to indicate pleasure, amusement, or derision. —*v.* **smiled, smil·ing. 1.** To have, exhibit, or form a smile. **2.** To show approval. **3.** To express with a smile. —**smil'ing·ly** *adv.*

smirch (smûrch) *v.* **1.** To soil, dirty, or stain. **2.** To disgrace. —**smirch** *n.*

smirk (smûrk) *v.* To smile in an obnoxiously conceited manner : simper. —**smirk** *n.* —**smirk'er** *n.*

smite (smīt) *v.* **smote** (smōt), **smit·ten** (smĭt'n) *or* **smote, smit·ing. 1.** To hit hard, esp. with the hand. **2.** To kill by smiting. **3.** To impress powerfully : affect.

smith (smĭth) *n.* A metalworker, esp. a blacksmith.

smith·er·eens (smĭ*th*'ə-rēnz') *pl.n. Informal.* Pieces : fragments.

smith·y (smĭth'ē, smĭ*th*'ē) *n., pl.* **-ies.** The shop of a smith, esp. a blacksmith.

smock (smŏk) *n.* A loose coatlike garment, often worn to protect the clothes while working. —*v.* To gather (fabric) in a decorative honeycomb pattern.

smog (smŏg, smôg) *n.* **1.** Fog mixed with smoke. **2.** Air pollution produced when sunlight causes hydrocarbons and nitrogen oxides from auto exhaust to combine. —**smog'gy** *adj.*

smoke (smōk) *n.* **1.** Vapor consisting of small particles of carbonaceous matter from the incomplete combustion of organic materials such as wood. **2.** A cloud of fine particles. **3.** A suspension of particles in a gaseous medium. —*v.* **smoked, smok·ing. 1.** To emit smoke. **2.** To inhale and exhale smoke from (e.g., a cigarette or cigar). **3.** To preserve (e.g., meat) by exposure to smoke. —**smoke'less** *adj.* —**smok'er** *n.* —**smok'y** *adj.*

smoke·house (smōk'hous') *n.* A structure in which meat or fish is smoked.

smoke screen *n.* **1.** A mass of smoke to conceal military operations. **2.** Something intended to conceal, mislead, or confuse.

smoke·stack (smōk'stăk') *n.* A large vertical pipe, as on a ship, through which smoke and combustion gases are emitted.

smol·der *also* **smoul·der** (smōl'dər) *v.* **1.** To burn with little smoke and without flame. **2.** To exist in a barely suppressed state. —**smol'der** *n.*

smooch (smo͞och) *n. Slang.* A kiss. —**smooch** *v.*

smooth (smo͞o*th*) *adj.* **1.** Not irregular or rough. **2.** Fine in texture or consistency. **3.** Free from jolts or jerks <a *smooth* ride> **4.** Without difficulties or obstructions. **5.** Agreeable and esp. ingratiating in manner. —*v.* **1.** To make or become smooth. **2.** To rid of difficulties or troubles. —**smooth'ly** *adv.* —**smooth'ness** *n.*

smor·gas·bord (smôr'gəs-bôrd', -bōrd') *n.* A buffet meal consisting of a variety of dishes.

smote (smōt) *v. p.t. & var. p.p. of* SMITE.

smoth·er (smŭ*th*'ər) *v.* **1.** To suffocate or be suffocated. **2.** To suppress or conceal. **3.** To cover thickly. —**smoth'er·y** *adj.*

smudge (smŭj) *v.* **smudged, smudg·ing.** To make dirty or blurred, esp. by rubbing : smear. —*n.* **1.** A smear or blotch. **2.** Dense smoke used to protect against frost or repel insects. —**smudg'y** *adj.*

smug (smŭg) *adj.* **smug·ger, smug·gest.** Self-righteous or self-satisfied : complacent. —**smug'ly** *adv.* —**smug'ness** *n.*

smug·gle (smŭg'əl) *v.* **-gled, -gling. 1.** To import or export illegally or without paying customs duties. **2.** To bring in or take out stealthily. —**smug'gler** *n.*

smut (smŭt) *n.* **1. a.** Something, as a particle of dirt, that smudges. **b.** A smudge. **2.** Obscene language or material. **3.** Any of several plant diseases caused by fungi and marked by the formation of black, powdery masses. **4.** Obscenity. —**smut'ty** *adj.*

Sn *symbol for* TIN.

snack (snăk) *n.* **1.** A hurried or light meal. **2.** Food eaten between meals. —**snack** *v.*

snaf·fle (snăf'əl) *n.* A jointed bit used on a horse's bridle.

snaffle

snag (snăg) *n.* **1.** A jagged or sharp protuberance. **2.** A part of a tree, esp. a stump, that protrudes from the surface of a body of water. **3.** An unforeseen obstacle or difficulty. —*v.* **snagged, snag·ging. 1.** To be caught on or as if on a snag. **2.** *Informal.* To catch quickly or unexpectedly : snatch.

snail (snāl) *n.* Any of numerous aquatic or terrestrial mollusks of the class Gastropoda, typically with a spiral, coiled shell, a broad retractile foot, and a distinct head.

snake (snāk) *n.* **1.** Any of various scaly, legless, occas. venomous reptiles of the suborder Serpentes, having a long, tapering body. **2.** An untrustworthy or insidious person. —*v.*

snaked, snak•ing. To move or drag with a snakelike motion. **—snak'i•ly** *adv.* **—snak'•y** *adj.*

snake•bite (snāk'bīt') *n.* **1.** The bite of a snake. **2.** Poisoning resulting from the bite of a venomous snake.

snap (snăp) *v.* **snapped, snap•ping. 1.** To make, cause to make, or break suddenly with a brisk, sharp cracking noise. **2.** To give way suddenly <His mind *snapped.*> **3.** To seize or snatch at something with or as if with the teeth. **4.** To speak abruptly, angrily, or sharply. **5.** To sparkle : flash <eyes *snapping* with anger> **6.** *Football.* To pass the ball to start a play. —*n.* **1.** The sound or act of snapping. **2.** A fastener or catch that opens and closes with a snap. **3.** A thin, crisp cookie. **4.** Vitality : energy. **5.** A short spell of cold weather. **6.** *Informal.* Something requiring little effort. **7.** *Football.* The passing of the ball that starts a play. **—snap'pish** *adj.* **—snap'py** *adj.*

snap bean *n.* A bean, as the string bean, grown for its crisp, edible pods.

snap•drag•on (snăp'drăg'ən) *n.* A plant, *Antirrhinum majus,* with 2-lipped, variously colored flower clusters.

snap•per (snăp'ər) *n., pl.* **-per** *or* **-pers.** Any of numerous marine food and game fishes of the family Lutjanidae.

snapping turtle *n.* Any of several New World freshwater turtles of the family Chelydridae, with powerful hooked jaws.

snap•shot (snăp'shŏt') *n.* A picture taken with a small hand-held camera.

snare[1] (snâr) *n.* **1.** A device, often consisting of a noose, for trapping small animals and birds. **2.** Something that entangles. **—snare** *v.* **—snar'er** *n.*

snare[2] (snâr) *n.* A string or wire stretched across the lower head of a drum.

snarl[1] (snärl) *v.* **1.** To growl angrily or ominously, esp. while baring the teeth. **2.** To speak in an angry or surly manner. **—snarl** *n.* **—snarl'ing•ly** *adv.*

snarl[2] (snärl) *n.* A tangle. —*v.* To become or cause to become tangled : knot.

snatch (snăch) *v.* **1.** To seize or try to seize something suddenly. **2.** To take suddenly and esp. illicitly : grab. —*n.* **1.** The act of snatching. **2.** A brief period. **3.** A fragment : bit <a *snatch* of an old story>

snaz•zy (snăz'ē) *adj.* **-zi•er, -zi•est.** Attractive in a flashy or showy way.

sneak (snēk) *v.* To move, take, or act in a quiet, stealthy way. ★ *syns:* CREEP, GLIDE, LURK, PROWL, SKULK, SLIDE, SLINK, SLIP, STEAL —*n.* **1.** A person who acts in a stealthy or underhanded way. **2.** An act or example of sneaking. **—sneak'i•ly** *adv.* **—sneak'i•ness** *n.* **—sneak'y** *adj.*

sneak•er (snē'kər) *n.* A usu. canvas sports shoe with a soft rubber sole.

sneer (snîr) *v.* To show contempt by curling the upper lip or by speaking in a derisive or scornful manner. **—sneer** *n.*

sneeze (snēz) *v.* **sneezed, sneez•ing.** To expel air forcibly through the nose and mouth by an involuntary convulsive action. **—sneeze** *n.*

snick•er (snĭk'ər) *n.* A partly stifled laugh. **—snick'er** *v.*

snide (snīd) *adj.* **snid•er, snid•est.** Sneakily derogatory. **—snide'ly** *adv.*

sniff (snĭf) *v.* **1.** To inhale audibly. **2.** To show contempt or disdain. **3.** To detect by or as if by sniffing. **—sniff** *n.*

snif•fle (snĭf'əl) *v.* **-fled, -fling.** To sniff frequently to prevent nasal discharge from running. —*n.* **1.** The act or sound of sniffling. **2. sniffles.** *Informal.* A head cold marked by sniffling. **—snif'fler** *n.*

snif•ter (snĭf'tər) *n.* A pear-shaped goblet used esp. for brandy.

snig•ger (snĭg'ər) *v.* To snicker. **—snig'ger** *n.* **—snig'ger•ing•ly** *adv.*

snip (snĭp) *v.* **snipped, snip•ping.** To cut or cut off with many quick strokes : clip. —*n.* **1.** A stroke made with shears or scissors. **2.** A small piece snipped off.

snipe (snīp) *n., pl.* **snipe** *or* **snipes.** A long-billed, brownish wading bird of the genus *Capella.* —*v.* **sniped, snip•ing. 1.** To shoot at individuals in the open from a hidden position. **2.** To make malicious attacks or remarks. **—snip'er** *n.*

snip•pet (snĭp'ĭt) *n.* A bit.

snip•py (snĭp'ē) *adj.* **-pi•er, -pi•est.** *Informal.* Impudent : impertinent.

snit (snĭt) *n. Slang.* Agitation : uproar.

snitch (snĭch) *v. Slang.* **1.** To steal : pilfer. **2.** To turn informer. **—snitch** *n.*

sniv•el (snĭv'əl) *v.* **-eled, -el•ing** *or* **-elled, -el•ling. 1.** To complain or speak tearfully : whine. **2.** To run at the nose. **—sniv'el** *n.* **—sniv'el•er** *n.*

snob (snŏb) *n.* Someone who considers himself socially superior and condescends to those he considers to be his inferiors. **—snob'ber•y** *n.* **—snob'bish** *adj.*

snob•bish (snŏb'ĭsh) *adj.* Characteristic of or resembling a snob. ★ *syns:* ELITIST, HIGH-HAT, SNOOTY, UPPITY. **—snob'bish•ly** *adv.* **—snob'bish•ness** *n.*

snood (sno͝od) *n.* A small netlike cap worn by women to hold the hair in place.

snoop (sno͞op) *Informal.* —*v.* To pry in a sly or intrusive manner. —*n.* One who snoops. **—snoop'y** *adj.*

snoot (sno͞ot) *n. Slang.* **1.** The snout. **2.** The nose. **3.** A snob.

snoot•y (sno͞o'tē) *adj.* **-i•er, -i•est.** *Informal.* Haughty : snobbish.

snooze (sno͞oz) *v.* **snoozed, snooz•ing.** *Informal.* To take a light nap : doze. **—snooze** *n.* **—snooz'er** *n.*

snore (snôr, snōr) *v.* **snored, snor•ing.** To breathe with a hoarse, harsh noise while sleeping. **—snore** *n.* **—snor'er** *n.*

snor•kel (snôr'kəl) *n.* A tube that projects above the surface of water, used by skin divers for breathing with the face submerged. **—snor'kel** *v.* **—snor'kel•er** *n.*

snort (snôrt) *n.* **1.** To force air noisily through

the nostrils. **2.** To express scorn, surprise, or anger by snorting. **3.** *Slang.* To inhale a drug. **—snort** *n.* **—snort'er** *n.*

snot (snŏt) *n. Slang.* **1.** Nasal mucus. **2.** A supercilious or contemptible person.

snout (snout) *n.* **1.** The long, projecting nose, jaws, or anterior facial part of an animal's muzzle. **2.** *Slang.* The human nose, esp. when excessively large.

snow (snō) *n.* **1.** Solid precipitation in the form of translucent ice crystals formed from water vapor in the upper atmosphere. **2.** A fall or shower of snow. —*v.* **1.** To fall to the earth as snow. **2.** To isolate or cover with or as if with snow. **3.** *Slang.* To overwhelm or deceive with insincere talk. **—snow'y** *adj.*

snow•ball (snō'bôl') *n.* A mass of snow formed into a ball. —*v.* To develop or accumulate at a rapidly increasing rate.

snow•bank (snō'băngk') *n.* A slope or rounded mass of snow.

snow•bound (snō'bound') *adj.* Confined or blockaded by snow.

snow•drift (snō'drĭft') *n.* Snow piled up by the wind.

snow•drop (snō'drŏp') *n.* Any of several bulbous plants of the genus *Galanthus,* with a nodding white flower that blooms in the early spring.

snow•fall (snō'fôl') *n.* **1.** A fall of snow. **2.** The amount of snow that falls in a particular storm or within a given time.

snow fence *n.* Temporary fencing of thin upright slats used to prevent snow from drifting onto roads and walks.

snow•mo•bile (snō'mō-bēl') *n.* A small automotive vehicle with skilike runners in front and tanklike treads used for driving in or traveling on snow.

snow pea *n.* A variety of the common pea having a soft thick edible pod.

snow•plow (snō'plou') *n.* A device or vehicle for removing snow.

snow•shoe (snō'sho͞o') *n.* A racketlike frame strung with leather strips that is attached to the shoe to prevent the foot from sinking into snow. **—snow'shoe'** *v.*

snow•storm (snō'stôrm') *n.* A storm with a heavy snowfall.

snow•suit (snō'so͞ot') *n.* A child's lined winter coveralls.

snow tire *n.* A tire with a deep tread that gives added traction on snow or ice.

snub (snŭb) *v.* **snubbed, snub•bing. 1.** To treat with contempt or scorn **:** slight. **2.** To check or stop the movement of by turning around a post. **—snub** *n.*

snub-nosed (snŭb'nōzd') *adj.* Having a short, stubby nose.

snuck (snŭk) *v. Informal. p.t. & p.p. of* SNEAK.

snuff[1] (snŭf) *v.* **1.** To draw in through the nostrils. **2.** To examine or sense by smell **:** sniff. —*n.* Finely pulverized tobacco that can be snuffed through the nostrils.

snuff[2] (snŭf) *v.* **1.** To cut off the charred portion of (a candle). **2.** To extinguish.

snuff•box (snŭf'bŏks') *n.* A small box for carrying snuff.

snuf•fle (snŭf'əl) *v.* **-fled, -fling. 1.** To breathe noisily, as through an obstructed nose. **2.** To sniffle. **—snuf'fle** *n.*

snug (snŭg) *adj.* **snug•ger, snug•gest. 1.** Pleasant and comfortable **:** cozy. **2.** Small but arranged well <a *snug* house> **3.** Close-fitting **:** tight <a *snug* winter jacket> **—snug, snug'ly** *adv.* **—snug'ness** *n.*

snug•gle (snŭg'əl) *v.* **-gled, -gling.** To lie or hold close **:** cuddle.

so (sō) *adv.* **1.** In the manner indicated or expressed **:** thus. **2. a.** To an extent indicated or expressed. **b.** To a great extent **:** very. **3.** As a result **:** consequently. **4.** Likewise **:** also. **5.** In truth **:** indeed <He did *so* lie.> —*conj.* With the result or consequence that <She didn't eat, *so* she lost weight.> —*pron.* **1.** The same <became a teacher and remained *so*> **2.** About that <needs a yard or *so* of silk for the blouse>

soak (sōk) *v.* **1.** To make or become thoroughly wet **:** saturate. **2.** To take in through or as if through pores **:** absorb. **3.** To be immersed in a liquid. **4.** *Slang.* To overcharge. —*n.* **1.** The act or process of soaking. **2.** *Slang.* A drunkard.

so-and-so (sŏ'ən-sŏ') *n., pl.* **-sos. 1.** One that is unnamed or unspecified. **2.** *Informal.* A nasty person **:** bastard.

soap (sōp) *n.* **1.** A cleansing agent made by the action of an alkali on natural oils and fats. **2.** *Slang.* A soap opera. —*v.* To treat, rub, or cover with soap. **—soap'y** *adj.*

soap•box (sōp'bŏks') *n.* An improvised platform on which a street orator stands.

soap opera *n.* A radio or television serial characterized by sentimentality and melodrama.

soap•stone (sōp'stōn') *n.* Steatite.

soar (sôr, sōr) *v.* **1.** To fly or glide high in the air. **2.** To rise suddenly above the normal level <*soaring* spirits><*soaring* prices>

sob (sŏb) *v.* **sobbed, sob•bing.** To weep with convulsive gasps. **—sob** *n.*

so•ber (sō'bər) *adj.* **1.** Abstemious in the use of liquor **:** temperate. **2.** Not intoxicated. **3.** Grave or serious **:** solemn. **4.** Marked by restraint **:** reasonable. —*v.* To make or become sober. **—so'ber•ly** *adv.* **—so•bri'e•ty, so'ber•ness** *n.*

so•bri•quet (sō'brĭ-kā', -kĕt') *n.* **1.** A nickname. **2.** An assumed name.

so-called (sō'kôld') *adj.* Commonly but often incorrectly named or designated.

soc•cer (sŏk'ər) *n.* A game played on a field by 2 teams who try to kick a round ball into the opposing team's goal.

▲ ***word history:*** Soccer, which is probably the most popular team sport everywhere except in the U.S., was invented in England. The word *soccer* is derived from *association.* The official name of the game is *Association Football,* that is, football as played under the rules of the Football Association of England, founded in 1863.

so•cia•ble (sō'shə-bəl) *adj.* **1.** Liking the company of others : friendly. **2.** Marked by friendly social relations. **—so'cia•bil'i•ty, so'cia•ble•ness** *n.* **—so'cia•bly** *adv.*
so•cial (sō'shəl) *adj.* **1.** Living in communities or groups. **2.** Of or relating to the life and interrelationships of human beings in society. **3.** Marked by friendly companionship with others. **4. a.** Of, pertaining to, or based on status in a specific society <wasn't his *social* equal> **b.** Of or pertaining to the upper classes. —*n.* An informal social gathering. **—so'cial•ly** *adv.*
social disease *n.* A venereal disease.
so•cial•ism (sō'shə-lĭz'əm) *n.* A social system or theory in which the producers possess political power and the means of producing and distributing goods. **—so'cial•ist** *n.* **—so'cial•is'tic** *adj.*
so•cial•ite (sō'shə-līt') *n.* A member of fashionable society.
so•cial•ize (sō'shə-līz') *v.* **-ized, -iz•ing. 1.** To place under government or group ownership or control. **2.** To adapt to the needs of society. **3.** To participate in social activities. **—so'cial•i•za'tion** *n.*
socialized medicine *n.* Provision of hospital and medical services at nominal cost by means of government regulation of health services and subsidies derived from taxation.
social science *n.* A science, as sociology or anthropology, that studies society and individual relationships in and to society.
social security *n.* A government program of monthly payments to the elderly, the disabled, and the unemployed, financed by taxation of employers and employees.
social work *n.* Activities and services designed to aid the poor and those with social problems. **—social worker** *n.*
so•ci•e•ty (sə-sī'ĭ-tē) *n., pl.* **-ties. 1. a.** The totality of social relationships among human beings. **b.** A group of human beings bound together by shared institutions and culture. **2. a.** The rich, privileged, and fashionable social class. **b.** The socially dominant members of a community. **3.** Companionship : company. **4.** An association of people with mutual aims or interests. **—so•ci'e•tal** *adj.*
Society of Friends *n.* A Christian denomination that rejects ritual, sacraments, a formal creed, a priesthood, and violence; Quakers.
so•ci•o•ec•o•nom•ic (sō'sē-ō-ĕk'ə-nŏm'ĭk, -ē'kə-, -shē-) *adj.* Of or involving both social and economic factors.
so•ci•ol•o•gy (sō'sē-ŏl'ə-jē, -shē-) *n.* The study of the organization, institutions, and development of human society. **—so'ci•o•log'ic** (-ə-lŏj'ĭk), **so'ci•o•log'i•cal** *adj.* **—so'ci•ol'o•gist** *n.*
so•ci•o•path (sŏ'sē-ə-păth', -shē-) *n.* A person manifesting antisocial behavior patterns or character traits. **—so'ci•o•path'ic** *adj.*
sock[1] (sŏk) *n., pl.* **socks** *or* **sox.** A stocking extending above the ankle and ending below the knee.
sock[2] (sŏk) *v. Slang.* To strike forcefully : punch. **—sock** *n.*
sock•et (sŏk'ĭt) *n.* An opening or cavity into which something fits.
socket wrench *n.* A wrench with a usu. interchangeable socket to fit over a nut or bolt.
sock•eye salmon (sŏk'ī') *n.* A salmon, *Oncorhynchus nerka,* of N Pacific coastal waters, that is a valuable food fish.
sod (sŏd) *n.* The surface of the soil held together by roots of grass : turf. —*v.* **sod•ded, sod•ding.** To cover with sod.
so•da (sō'də) *n.* **1. a.** Any of various forms of sodium carbonate. **b.** Chemically combined sodium. **2. a.** Soda water. **b.** A flavored carbonated soft drink. **c.** A drink made of carbonated water, flavoring, and often ice cream.
soda fountain *n.* A counter equipped for preparing and serving soft drinks, ice-cream dishes, and sandwiches.
so•dal•i•ty (sō-dăl'ĭ-tē) *n., pl.* **-ties. 1.** A society or association, esp. a devotional or charitable society in the Roman Catholic Church. **2.** Fellowship.
soda pop *n.* SODA 2b.
soda water *n.* A mixer or beverage of water charged with carbon dioxide.
sod•den (sŏd'n) *adj.* **1.** Thoroughly soaked : drenched. **2.** Soggy and heavy, as from improper cooking : doughy. **3.** Lacking in vitality or expressiveness : dull.
so•di•um (sō'dē-əm) *n.* Symbol **Na** A soft, light, extremely malleable silver-white metallic element.
sodium bicarbonate *n.* A white crystalline compound used esp. in making effervescent beverages and baking soda.
sodium carbonate *n.* **1.** A white powdery compound used in manufacturing ceramics, detergents, and soap. **2.** Any of various hydrated carbonates of sodium.
sodium chloride *n.* SALT 1.
sodium hydroxide *n.* An alkaline compound used in chemicals and soaps and in petroleum refining.
sodium nitrate *n.* A white crystalline compound used as a fertilizer and in solid rocket propellants and explosives.
sod•om•y (sŏd'ə-mē) *n.* **1.** Anal copulation of one male with another. **2.** Anal or oral copulation with a member of the opposite sex. **3.** Copulation with an animal.
so•ev•er (sō-ĕv'ər) *adv.* In any way : at all.
so•fa (sō'fə) *n.* An upholstered couch with a back and arms.
sofa bed *n.* A sofa whose seat unfolds to form a bed.
soft (sôft, sŏft) *adj.* **1.** Not hard or firm. **2.** Lacking stamina or robustness : flabby. **3.** Not rough, harsh, loud, or irritating. **4.** Mild : gentle. **5.** Easily swayed or affected emotionally. **6.** Lacking strength of character : weak. **7.** *Informal.* Mentally feeble. **8.** *Informal.* Not requiring much work or effort : easy <a *soft* job> **9.** Likely to fluctuate or devaluate. **10.** Containing relatively little dissolved min-

eral matter <*soft* water> **—soft, soft′ly** *adv.* **—soft′ness** *n.*

soft•ball (sôft′bôl′, sŏft′-) *n.* **1.** A game similar to baseball that is played on a smaller diamond with a larger, softer ball. **2.** The ball used in softball.

soft•bound (sôft′bound′, sŏft′-) *adj.* Not bound between hard covers.

soft coal *n.* Bituminous coal.

soft-core (sôft′kôr′, -kōr′, sŏft′-) *adj.* Being less explicit than hard-core material in depicting or describing sexual activity.

soft drink *n.* A nonalcoholic beverage.

soft•en (sô′fən, sŏf′ən) *v.* To make or become soft or softer. **—soft′en•er** *n.*

soft•heart•ed (sôft′här′tĭd, sŏft′-) *adj.* Easily moved to tenderness : sympathetic.

soft landing *n.* The landing of a space vehicle at a velocity low enough to prevent damaging or destructive impact.

soft palate *n.* The movable muscular fold suspended from the rear of the hard palate that closes off the nasal cavity from the oral cavity when swallowing.

soft-ped•al (sôft′pĕd′l, sŏft′-) *v. Informal.* To make less conspicuous : play down.

soft sell *n.* A method of selling or advertising that relies on subtle persuasion.

soft soap *n. Informal.* Sweet words : flattery. **—soft′-soap′** *v.*

soft•ware (sôft′wâr′, sŏft′-) *n. Computer Sci.* Data, as programs, routines, and symbolic languages, essential to the operation and maintenance of computers.

soft•wood (sôft′wo͝od′, sŏft′-) *n.* **1.** The wood of a coniferous tree. **2.** A tree yielding softwood. **—soft′wood′** *adj.*

soft•y (sôf′tē, sŏf′-) *n., pl.* **-ies.** *Informal.* Someone who finds it difficult to punish or be strict.

sog•gy (sŏg′ē, sô′gē) *adj.* **-gi•er, -gi•est.** Sodden with moisture : saturated. **—sog′gi•ly** *adv.* **—sog′gi•ness** *n.*

soi•gné *also* **soi•gnée** (swän-yā′) *adj.* **1.** Fashionable. **2.** Well-groomed : polished.

soil[1] (soil) *n.* **1.** The loose top layer of the earth's surface in which plant life can grow. **2.** Ground : earth. **3.** Land : country.

soil[2] (soil) *v.* **1.** To make or become dirty. **2.** To tarnish : disgrace. **3.** To corrupt morally : defile. *—n.* **1. a.** The state of being soiled. **b.** A stain. **2.** Excrement, esp. human excrement : waste.

soi•ree *or* **soi•rée** (swä-rā′) *n.* An evening reception or party.

so•journ (sō′jûrn′, sō-jûrn′) *v.* To stay in a place for a time. **—so′journ′** *n.* **—so′journ′er** *n.*

sol (sōl, sôl) *n., pl.* **so•les** (sō′lās). NUEVO SOL.

sol•ace (sŏl′əs) *n.* **1.** Comfort in sorrow, misfortune, or distress. **2.** A source of solace. **—sol′ace** *v.* **—sol′ac•er** *n.*

so•lar (sō′lər) *adj.* **1.** Of, relating to, or proceeding from the sun. **2.** Utilizing or operated by means of energy derived from the sun. **3.** Determined or measured with respect to the sun <the *solar* year>

solar battery *n.* A device that converts solar radiation into electrical energy.

solar cell *n.* A semiconductor device that converts solar radiation to electric energy.

solar flare *n.* A temporary outburst of solar gases from the sun's surface, a source of intense radiation.

so•lar•i•um (sō-lâr′ē-əm, -lăr′-) *n., pl.* **-i•a** (-ē-ə) *or* **-i•ums.** A glassed-in room or porch exposed to the sun.

solar plexus *n.* **1.** A network of nerves and nerve tissue situated behind the stomach. **2.** *Informal.* The pit of the stomach.

solar system *n.* The sun together with the celestial bodies that orbit it.

solar wind *n.* Plasma ejected at high speed from the sun's surface.

sold (sōld) *v. p.t. & p.p. of* SELL.

sol•der (sŏd′ər, sô′dər) *n.* Any of various alloys, esp. of tin and lead, used in the melted state to join or repair metal parts. *—v.* To join or repair with or as if with solder. **—sol′der•er** *n.*

▲ ***word history:*** The letter *l* in the word *solder* has a long history. The ancestor of *solder* is Latin *solidare,* "to make solid, to fasten together." The Latin word descended into Old French as *souder,* meaning "to join with melted metal"; loss of *l* in certain situations was a normal development in Old French. An *l* was reinserted in the Old French word by those who knew its derivation from Latin, and the variant *solder* existed alongside *souder.* These forms were both borrowed into English, as *solder* and *soder,* respectively, each being pronounced as it was spelled. The spelling *soder* eventually was displaced by *solder.* In British English both pronunciations still exist, but in American English the pronunciation without *l* has completely prevailed.

sol•dier (sōl′jər) *n.* **1.** Someone, esp. an enlisted person, who serves in an army. **2.** An active, loyal, and militant follower. *—v.* To serve as a soldier. **—sol′dier•ly** *adj.*

soldier of fortune *n.* One who engages in a military career in any army for money, pleasure, or adventure.

sol•dier•y (sōl′jə-rē) *n., pl.* **-ies. 1.** Soldiers as a group. **2.** A body of soldiers. **3.** The military profession.

sole[1] (sōl) *n.* **1.** The undersurface of the foot. **2.** The undersurface of a boot or shoe. *—v.* **soled, sol•ing.** To put a sole on (e.g., a shoe).

sole[2] (sōl) *adj.* Being the only one : single. **—sole′ly** *adv.*

sole[3] (sōl) *n., pl.* **sole** *or* **soles.** Any of various mainly marine flatfishes of the family Soleidae, valued as food.

sol•e•cism (sŏl′ĭ-sĭz′əm, sō′lĭ-) *n.* **1.** An error in grammar or word usage. **2.** A violation of etiquette. **—sol′e•cist** *n.*

sol•emn (sŏl′əm) *adj.* **1.** Deeply serious : grave. **2.** Performed with or marked by full religious ceremony. **3.** Formal in nature or character : ceremonious. **4.** Somber : gloomy. **—so•lem′ni•ty** (sə-lĕm′nĭ-tē), **sol′emn•ness** *n.* **—sol′emn•ly** *adv.*

sol•em•nize (sŏl'əm-nīz') *v.* **-nized, -niz•ing. 1.** To celebrate, honor, or observe with formal ceremonies. **2.** To perform (a marriage) with formal religious rites. **—sol'em•ni•za'tion** *n.*
so•le•noid (sō'lə-noid') *n.* A cylindrical coil of insulated wire in which an axial magnetic field is established by a flow of electric current.
so•lic•it (sə-lĭs'ĭt) *v.* **1.** To try to obtain. **2.** To beg : entreat. **3.** To tempt : entice. **—so•lic'i•ta'tion** *n.*
so•lic•i•tor (sə-lĭs'ĭ-tər) *n.* **1.** One that solicits. **2.** A lawyer, esp. the chief law officer of a city, town, or government department. **3.** *esp. Brit.* A lawyer who is not a barrister.
so•lic•i•tous (sə-lĭs'ĭ-təs) *adj.* **1.** Anxious and concerned : worried. **2.** Eager : desirous.
so•lic•i•tude (sə-lĭs'ĭ-to͞od', -tyo͞od') *n.* The state or quality of being solicitous.
sol•id (sŏl'ĭd) *adj.* **1.** Not liquid or gaseous. **2.** Not hollow. **3.** Being of the same character or substance throughout. **4.** Of, having, or involving 3 dimensions. **5.** Of a satisfactory and substantial character <*solid* pleasure> **6.** Written or printed without a space or hyphen. **7.** Upstanding and reliable : dependable. **8.** Sound : valid <a *solid* argument> **9.** Acting together : unanimous. **10.** Without gaps, crevices, or breaks : compact. *—n.* **1.** A solid body or substance. **2.** A geometric figure, as a cube, that has 3 dimensions. **—so•lid'i•fi•ca'tion** *n.* **—so•lid'i•fy'** *v.* **—so•lid'i•ty** (sə-lĭd'ĭ-tē), **sol'id•ness** *n.* **—sol'id•ly** *adv.*
sol•i•dar•i•ty (sŏl'ĭ-dăr'ĭ-tē) *n.* Unity arising from common purpose, sympathy, or interests : fellowship.
solid geometry *n.* The geometry of 3-dimensional figures and surfaces.
sol•id-state (sŏl'ĭd-stāt') *adj.* **1.** Of, relating to, or concerned with the physical properties of crystalline solids. **2.** Based on or composed principally or entirely of transistors or related semiconductor devices.
so•lil•o•quize (sə-lĭl'ə-kwīz') *v.* **-quized, -quiz•ing.** To deliver a soliloquy.
so•lil•o•quy (sə-lĭl'ə-kwē) *n., pl.* **-quies. 1.** A dramatic monologue in which a character's thoughts are revealed with no listener present. **2.** The act of speaking to oneself.
sol•i•taire (sŏl'ĭ-târ') *n.* **1.** A single gemstone, as a diamond, set by itself, esp. in a ring. **2.** A card game played by one person.
sol•i•tar•y (sŏl'ĭ-tĕr'ē) *adj.* **1.** Existing, being, or living alone. **2.** Happening, passed, or done alone. **3.** Secluded : remote. **4.** Only : sole. **—sol'i•tar'i•ness** *n.*
sol•i•tude (sŏl'ĭ-to͞od', -tyo͞od') *n.* **1.** The state of being alone : isolation. **2.** A secluded or lonely place.
so•lo (sō'lō) *n., pl.* **-los. 1.** *Mus.* A composition for a single voice or instrument with or without accompaniment. **2.** An action performed by one person. *—v.* To perform alone. **—so'lo** *adj. & adv.* **—so'lo•ist** *n.*
so•lon (sō'lən) *n.* **1.** A wise lawgiver. **2.** A lawmaker : legislator.
sol•stice (sŏl'stĭs, sōl'-) *n.* Either of 2 times of the year, approx. June 22 and Dec. 22, when the sun reaches the extreme point of its northward or southward motion in the sky. **—sol•sti'tial** (-stĭsh'əl) *adj.*
sol•u•ble (sŏl'yə-bəl) *adj.* **1.** Able to be dissolved. **2.** Able to be solved or explained. **—sol'u•bil'i•ty** *n.* **—sol'u•bly** *adv.*
sol•ute (sŏl'yo͞ot', sō'lo͞ot') *n.* A substance that has been dissolved.
so•lu•tion (sə-lo͞o'shən) *n.* **1. a.** A homogeneous mixture of 2 or more usu. liquid substances. **b.** Formation of such a mixture. **2. a.** The method or process of solving a problem. **b.** The answer to a problem.
solve (sŏlv) *v.* **solved, solv•ing.** To find a solution or answer to. **—solv'a•ble** *adj.*
sol•vent (sŏl'vənt) *adj.* **1.** Capable of meeting financial obligations. **2.** Having the capability to dissolve another substance. *—n.* A liquid that can dissolve another substance. **—sol'ven•cy** *n.*
so•mat•ic (sō-măt'ĭk, sə-) *adj.* Of or relating to the body : physical.
somatic cell *n.* Any cell of a plant or animal other than a germ cell.
som•ber (sŏm'bər) *adj.* **1.** Gloomy : dark. **2.** Melancholy : dejected.
som•bre (sŏm'bər) *adj. esp. Brit. var. of* SOMBER.
som•bre•ro (sŏm-brâr'ō) *n., pl.* **-ros.** A large, broad-brimmed felt or straw hat worn esp. in Mexico and the SW U.S.
some (sŭm) *adj.* **1.** Being an indefinite or unspecified number or quantity <*some* candy> **2.** Being unknown or unspecified by name <*Some* friend left a message.> **3.** A little or a few <*some* days past> *—pron.* An indefinite or unspecified number or quantity <*Some* of the roses wilted.> *—adv.* **1.** Approximately <*some* 10 books> **2.** *Informal.* Somewhat.
—some[1] *suff.* Marked by a specific quality, condition, or action <bother*some*>
—some[2] *suff.* A group of a specified number of members <two*some*>
some•bod•y (sŭm'bŏd'ē, -bŭd'ē, -bə-dē) *pron.* A person unspecified or unknown. *—n. Informal.* An important person.
some•day (sŭm'dā') *adv.* At an unspecified future time.
some•how (sŭm'hou') *adv.* In a way not specified or known.
some•one (sŭm'wŭn', -wən) *pron.* Somebody. *—n.* An important person.
some•place (sŭm'plās') *adv. & n.* Somewhere.
som•er•sault (sŭm'ər-sôlt') *n.* The act of rolling the body in a complete circle, with heels over head. **—som'er•sault'** *v.*
some•thing (sŭm'thĭng) *pron.* A thing undetermined or unspecified.
some•time (sŭm'tīm') *adv.* **1.** At an unstated or indefinite time. **2.** At an indefinite future time.
some•times (sŭm'tīmz') *adv.* Now and then : occasionally.

some•what (sŭm′hwŏt′, -wŏt′, -hwət, -wət′) *adv.* To some degree or extent.
some•where (sŭm′hwâr′, -wâr′) *adv.* At, in, or to an unspecified or unknown place.
som•nam•bu•lism (sŏm-năm′byə-lĭz′əm) *n.* The act of walking in one's sleep. **—som•nam′bu•list** *n.*
som•no•lent (sŏm′nə-lənt) *adj.* Sleepy : drowsy. **—som′no•lence** *n.*
son (sŭn) *n.* **1.** A male offspring. **2.** A male descendant. **3.** A male associated with a particular place, as a country or school.
so•nance (sō′nəns) *n.* Sound.
so•nar (sō′när′) *n.* A system or apparatus that uses reflected acoustic waves to detect and locate submerged objects.
so•na•ta (sə-nä′tä) *n. Mus.* An instrumental composition, as for the piano, in 3 or 4 movements contrasting in mood and tempo but related in key.
son•a•ti•na (sŏn′ə-tē′nə) *n.* A sonata with shorter movements than the typical sonata.
song (sông, sŏng) *n.* **1.** A usu. brief musical composition meant to be sung. **2.** The act or art of singing. **3.** Poetry. **—for a song.** For a small amount of money.
song•bird (sông′bûrd′, sŏng′-) *n.* A bird with a melodious call.
Song of Solomon *n.* —See table at BIBLE.
Song of Songs *n.* —See table at BIBLE.
song•ster (sông′stər, sŏng′-) *n.* A singer.
son•ic (sŏn′ĭk) *adj.* Of or pertaining to sound or the speed of sound.
sonic barrier *n.* The sudden sharp increase in aerodynamic drag experienced by aircraft approaching the speed of sound.
sonic boom *n.* A loud, explosive sound caused by an aircraft traveling at a supersonic speed.
son-in-law (sŭn′ĭn-lô′) *n., pl.* **sons-in-law.** The husband of one's daughter.
son•net (sŏn′ĭt) *n.* A fixed 14-line verse form, usu. in iambic pentameter, with a prescribed rhyme scheme.
son•o•gram (sŏn′ə-grăm′, sō′nə-) *n.* An image produced by ultrasonography.
so•no•rous (sə-nôr′əs, -nōr′-, sŏn′ər-) *adj.* **1.** Producing sound, esp. full, deep, or rich sound : resonant. **2.** Elevated : lofty. **—so•nor′i•ty** (sə-nôr′ĭ-tē, -nōr′-) *n.*
soon (so͞on) *adv.* **1.** In the near future. **2.** Early. **3.** Fast : quickly. **4.** Readily : willingly <I'd as *soon* stop right now.>
soot (so͝ot, so͞ot, sŭt) *n.* A fine black powder, mainly carbon, generated by the incomplete combustion of fuel, as wood or coal. **—soot′i•ness** *n.* **—soot′y** *adj.*
sooth (so͞oth) *n. Archaic.* Reality : truth.
soothe (so͞o*th*) *v.* **soothed, sooth•ing. 1.** To calm by showing concern : mollify. **2.** To ease the pain, discomfort, or distress of. **—sooth′er** *n.* **—sooth′ing•ly** *adv.*
sooth•say•er (so͞oth′sā′ər) *n.* One who predicts the future or foretells events.
sop (sŏp) *v.* **sopped, sop•ping. 1.** To soak, dip, or drench in a liquid : saturate. **2.** To take up by absorption. *—n.* Something given or conceded to placate : bribe.
soph•ism (sŏf′ĭz′əm) *n.* **1.** A plausible argument that is actually fallacious. **2.** Sophistry. **—soph′ist** *n.* **—so•phis′tic, so•phis′ti•cal** *adj.*
so•phis•ti•cate (sə-fĭs′tĭ-kĭt) *n.* A sophisticated person.
so•phis•ti•cat•ed (sə-fĭs′tĭ-kā′tĭd) *adj.* **1.** Experienced in the ways of the world : knowing. **2.** Complex : complicated <a *sophisticated* computer> **3.** Appealing to the tastes of a sophisticate <a *sophisticated* novel> ★ *syns:* COSMOPOLITAN, WORLDLY, WORLDLY-WISE **—so•phis′ti•ca′tion** *n.*
soph•ist•ry (sŏf′ĭ-strē) *n.* Plausible but fallacious argumentation or reasoning.
soph•o•more (sŏf′ə-môr′, -mōr′) *n.* A student in the 2nd year of college or high school.
soph•o•mor•ic (sŏf′ə-môr′ĭk, -mōr′-, -mŏr′-) *adj.* **1.** Of, pertaining to, or typical of a sophomore. **2.** Brash and overconfident but immature and ill-informed.
sop•o•rif•ic (sŏp′ə-rĭf′ĭk) *adj.* **1.** Inducing drowsiness or sleep. **2.** Drowsy : sleepy. **—sop′o•rif′ic** *n.*
so•pran•o (sə-prăn′ō, -prä′nō) *n., pl.* **-os. 1.** A singing voice of the highest range. **2. a.** A singer with a soprano. **b.** A part for a soprano.
sor•cer•y (sôr′sə-rē) *n.* The use of supernatural or magical powers : witchcraft. **—sor′cer•er** *n.* **—sor′cer•ess** *n.*
sor•did (sôr′dĭd) *adj.* **1.** Dirty : filthy. **2.** Squalid. **3.** Marked by moral degradation : base. **—sor′did•ly** *adv.* **—sor′did•ness** *n.*
sore (sôr, sōr) *adj.* **sor•er, sor•est. 1.** Causing or suffering pain or tenderness. **2.** Painful : sensitive. **3.** Causing sorrow, misery, or distress. **4.** Offended : angry. *—n.* **1.** An open skin lesion, wound, or ulcer. **2.** A source of distress or pain. **—sore′ly** *adv.* **—sore′ness** *n.*
sore•head (sôr′hĕd′, sōr′-) *n. Slang.* One easily offended or angered.
sore throat *n.* Inflammation of the tonsils, pharynx, or larynx.
sor•ghum (sôr′gəm) *n.* An Old World grass, *Sorghum vulgare,* grown as grain and forage and as a source of syrup.
so•ror•i•ty (sə-rôr′ĭ-tē, -rŏr′-) *n., pl.* **-ties.** A social club for women, esp. at a college.
sor•rel[1] (sôr′əl, sŏr′-) *n.* Any of several plants of the genus *Rumex,* with sour-tasting leaves.
sor•rel[2] (sôr′əl, sŏr′-) *n.* **1.** A reddish brown color. **2.** A horse of the color sorrel.
sor•row (sŏr′ō, sôr′ō) *n.* **1.** Mental suffering : anguish. **2.** A cause of sadness or grief. **3.** An expression of sadness or grief. **—sor′row•ful** *adj.* **—sor′row•ful•ly** *adv.*
sor•ry (sŏr′ē, sôr′ē) *adj.* **-ri•er, -ri•est. 1.** Feeling or showing sympathy, pity, or regret. **2.** Worthless : wretched. **3.** Sad : dismal. ★ *syns:* CONTRITE, PENITENT, REGRETFUL, REMORSEFUL, REPENTANT
sort (sôrt) *n.* **1.** A group or number of individuals having common attributes : class. **2.** Character : nature. **3.** Manner : way. *—v.* To arrange according to class, kind, or size : clas-

sify. **—out of sorts.** *Informal.* **1.** Somewhat sick. **2.** In a bad mood : grouchy.

sor·tie (sôr'tē, sôr-tē') *n.* **1.** An attack on enemy forces launched from a besieged place. **2.** A combat mission by a warplane. **—sor'tie** *v.*

SOS (ĕs'ō-ĕs') *n.* A call for rescue or help.

so-so (sō'sō') *adj.* Neither very good nor very bad : passable. **—so'-so'** *adv.*

sot (sŏt) *n.* A chronic drunkard.

sot·to vo·ce (sŏt'ō vō'chē) *adv.* In a quiet voice : softly.

sou·brette (so͞o-brĕt') *n.* A saucy, coquettish maid in a comedy or comic opera.

souf·flé (so͞o-flā') *n.* A light, fluffy dish made of egg yolks and stiffly beaten egg whites combined with other ingredients as a main dish or sweetened as a dessert.

sough (sŭf, sou) *v.* To make a soft sighing or rustling sound. **—sough** *n.*

sought (sôt) *v. p.t. & p.p. of* SEEK.

soul (sōl) *n.* **1.** The animating spiritual principle in a human being, often believed to survive death. **2.** A human being <not a *soul* at home> **3.** A central or active part. **4.** Embodiment : personification <the *soul* of honor> **5.** A person's spiritual, emotional, and moral nature. **6.** Intensity of emotion and expression, esp. in music. *—adj. Slang.* Of, relating to, or derived from American blacks and their culture.

soul·ful (sōl'fəl) *adj.* Filled with or expressing deep feeling. **—soul'ful·ly** *adv.*

sound[1] (sound) *n.* **1. a.** A vibratory disturbance in the pressure and density of a fluid, as air, capable of being detected by the organs of hearing. **b.** The sensation produced in the organs of hearing by such a disturbance. **2.** Noise <the *sound* of laughter> **3.** The distance within which something can be heard : earshot. **4.** A mental impression : implication. *—v.* **1.** To make or cause to make a sound. **2.** To seem to be <*sounds* sensible> **3.** To summon, order, or signal by a sound <*sound* a warning> **4.** To examine (e.g., a bodily organ) by causing it to emit sound. **—sound'less** *adj.*

sound[2] (sound) *adj.* **1.** Free from defect, damage, flaw, or disease. **2.** Solid. **3.** Strong : secure. **4.** Based on or showing valid reasoning or good judgment. **5.** Thorough <a *sound* defeat> **6.** Deep and undisturbed <*sound* sleep> **7.** Legally valid. ★ ***syns:*** FIRM, SECURE, SOLID, STABLE, STURDY, SURE **—sound'ly** *adv.* **—sound'ness** *n.*

sound[3] (sound) *n.* A long, relatively wide body of water larger than a channel or strait that often connects larger bodies of water.

sound[4] (sound) *v.* **1.** To measure the depth of (water), esp. by means of a weighted line. **2.** To attempt to learn the opinions or attitudes of : probe. **3.** To dive suddenly downward, as a whale does.

sound barrier *n.* The sonic barrier.

sounding board *n.* **1.** A thin board used in a musical instrument to increase resonance. **2.** A structure, as over a podium, designed to direct sound toward an audience. **3.** A person or group whose reactions, as to an idea, serve to help in an evaluation.

sound·proof (sound'pro͞of') *adj.* Permitting little or no sound to pass. **—sound'proof'** *v.* **—sound'proof'ing** *n.*

sound·track (sound'trăk') *n.* **1.** The strip on a motion-picture film that carries the sound recording. **2.** Music accompanying a motion picture.

soup (so͞op) *n.* A liquid food consisting of meat, fish, or vegetable stock, often with various solid ingredients added. **—soup up.** *Slang.* To increase the power or speed of.

soup·çon (so͞op-sôɴ') *n.* A tiny amount : trace.

soup·y (so͞o'pē) *adj.* **-i·er, -i·est. 1.** Having the appearance or consistency of soup. **2.** Foggy. **3.** *Informal.* Sentimental.

sour (sour) *adj.* **1.** Sharp, tart, or acid in taste. **2.** Rancid : spoiled <a *sour* smell> **3.** Disagreeable : unpleasant <a *sour* face> *—v.* To make or become sour. **—sour'ly** *adv.* **—sour'ness** *n.*

sour·ball (sour'bôl') *n.* A round piece of hard candy with a tart flavor.

source (sôrs, sōrs) *n.* **1.** A point of origin. **2.** The place of origin of a stream of water. **3.** One that supplies information.

sou·sa·phone (so͞o'zə-fōn', -sə-) *n.* A large brass wind instrument similar to the tuba, having a flaring bell.

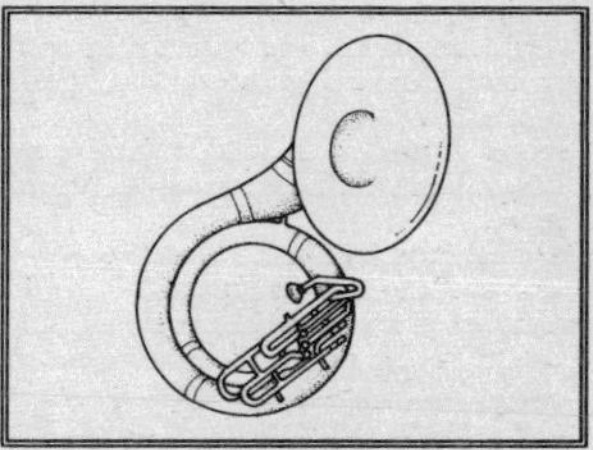

sousaphone

souse (sous) *v.* **soused, sous·ing. 1.** To immerse in a liquid. **2.** To drench. **3.** To steep in a brine : pickle. **4.** *Slang.* To make drunk. *—n.* **1.** The act or process of sousing. **2. a.** Something, as pork trimmings, steeped in pickle. **b.** Brine. **3.** *Slang.* A drunkard.

▲ ***word history:*** The orig. meaning of the verb *souse* was "to pickle" and of the noun, "pickled meat." Various liquids can be used to pickle or preserve food, but a common one is brine, which is very heavily salted water. The etymology of *souse* reflects this fact, for the word is ult. derived from the Germanic stem *sult-*, a variant of *salto-*, the direct ancestor of English *salt*. The Germanic stem, or a word derived from it, was borrowed into Old French as *sous*, and this form entered Middle English and became the modern word *souse*.

south (south) *n.* **1. a.** The direction 90° clockwise from east. **b.** The point on the compass 180° clockwise from north. **2.** An area or region to the south of a given point. **3. South.** The S part of the U.S., esp. the states that fought for the Confederacy during the Civil War. —*adj.* To, toward, of, from, facing, or in the south. —*adv.* In, from, or toward the south. —**south'er•ly** (sŭth'ər-lē) *adj. & adv.* —**south'ern** (sŭth'ərn) *adj.* —**south'ern•er** *n.* —**south'ern•most'** *adj.* —**south'ward** *adj. & adv.* —**south'wards** *adv.*

south•east (south-ēst', sou-ēst') *n.* **1.** The direction 45° clockwise from east and 45° counterclockwise from south. **2.** An area or region to the southeast of a given point. —**south•east'** *adj. & adv.* —**south•east'er•ly** *adj. & adv.* —**south•east'ern** *adj.* —**south•east'ward** *adj. & adv.* —**south•east'wards** *adv.*

south•paw (south'pô') *n.* A left-handed person, esp. a left-handed baseball pitcher. —**south'paw'** *adj.*

South Pole *n.* The southernmost point of the earth.

south•west (south-wĕst', sou-wĕst') *n.* **1.** The direction 45° clockwise from south and 45° counterclockwise from west. **2.** An area or region to the southwest of a given point. —**south•west'** *adj. & adv.* —**south•west'er•ly** *adj. & adv.* —**south•west'ern** *adj.* —**south•west'ward** *adj. & adv.* —**south•west'wards** *adv.*

sou•ve•nir (so͞o'və-nîr') *n.* Something kept as a token of remembrance : memento.

sov•er•eign (sŏv'ər-ən, sŏv'rən) *n.* **1.** The head of state in a monarchy. **2.** A British gold coin worth 1 pound. —*adj.* **1.** Supreme : paramount. **2.** Supreme in power or rank. **3.** Self-governing : independent. **4.** Of fine quality : excellent.

sov•er•eign•ty (sŏv'ər-ən-tē, sŏv'rən-) *n., pl.* **-ties. 1.** Supremacy of rule or authority. **2.** The rank, authority, or power of a sovereign. **3.** Political autonomy.

so•vi•et (sō'vē-ĕt', -ĭt, sŏv'ē-) *n.* **1.** A popularly elected legislative assembly in the former U.S.S.R. **2. Soviets.** The people and government of the former U.S.S.R.

sow¹ (sō) *v.* **sowed, sown** (sōn) *or* **sowed, sow•ing. 1.** To scatter (seed) for growing. **2.** To scatter with or as if with seed. **3.** To stir up : foment. —**sow'er** *n.*

sow² (sou) *n.* A fully grown female pig.

sox (sŏks) *n. var. pl. of* SOCK¹.

soy (soi) *n.* **1.** The soybean. **2.** A salty liquid condiment made by fermenting soybeans in brine.

soy•bean (soi'bēn') *n.* An Asian leguminous plant, *Glycine max,* cultivated for forage and for its nutritious, edible seeds.

†spa (spä) *n.* **1.** A mineral spring. **2.** A place, esp. a resort, having mineral springs. **3.** *Regional.* A soda fountain.

space (spās) *n.* **1. a.** A set of points or elements satisfying specified geometric conditions. **b.** The infinite 3-dimensional area within which all material bodies move and exist. **2.** The expanse in which the solar system, stars, and galaxies exist : universe. **3.** An empty area. **4.** A particular place, as a seat on a train. **5.** An interval or period of time. —*v.* **spaced, spac•ing.** To place, arrange, or organize with spaces between. —**spac'er** *n.*

space bar *n.* A bar of a typewriter or computer keyboard that introduces a blank space, as between words.

space•craft (spās'krăft') *n.* A vehicle designed for space travel.

spaced-out (spāst'out') *adj. Slang.* Stupefied from or as if from a drug : dopey.

space flight *n.* Flight beyond the atmosphere of the earth.

space heater *n.* A small, usu. portable device for heating an enclosed area.

space•man (spās'măn') *n.* A person who travels in outer space : astronaut.

space•port (spās'pôrt', -pōrt') *n.* An installation for testing and launching spacecraft.

space•ship (spās'shĭp') *n.* A spacecraft.

space shuttle *n.* A spacecraft serving as transportation between the earth and an orbiting space station.

space station *n.* A manned satellite designed for permanent orbit around the earth.

space suit *n.* A pressurized suit designed to permit the wearer relatively free movement in space.

space walk *n.* Activity or movement outside a spacecraft by an astronaut. —**space'-walk'** *v.* —**space walker** *n.*

spa•cious (spā'shəs) *adj.* Affording ample space : roomy. —**spa'cious•ly** *adv.* —**spa'cious•ness** *n.*

spade¹ (spād) *n.* A flat-bladed digging tool with a long handle. —*v.* **spad•ed, spad•ing.** To dig or cut with a spade.

spade² (spād) *n.* Any of a suit of playing cards marked with a black figure shaped like an inverted heart with a short stalk at the bottom.

▲ ***word history:*** The word *spade¹*, "digging tool," has no etymological relation to *spade²*, "suit of playing cards." *Spade¹* comes directly from Old English *spadu,* and *spade²* is from Italian *spada,* "sword." On Italian playing cards a broad-bladed sword was used as the symbol of a suit; this suit was called "spades" in English. Because the word *spade* was confused with the native English word, on English playing cards the symbol was reshaped to resemble a digging tool.

spade•work (spād'wûrk') *n.* The usu. hard and often uninteresting preliminary work in a project or activity.

spa•dix (spā'dĭks) *n., pl.* **-di•ces** (-dĭ-sēz'). A clublike stalk bearing tiny flowers, often enclosed in a sheathlike spathe.

spa•ghet•ti (spə-gĕt'ē) *n.* Pasta in the form of long, thin solid strings.

span¹ (spăn) *n.* **1.** The extent of space between 2 points or extremities, as of a bridge. **2.** The section between 2 intermediate supports of a bridge. **3.** Something, as a bridge, that spans. **4.** A unit of measure equal to approx. 9 in. **5.** A time period. —*v.* **spanned,**

span·ning. 1. To measure by or as if by the fully extended hand. **2.** To extend across.

span[2] (spăn) *n.* A pair of animals, as oxen, harnessed together.

span·dex (spăn'dĕks) *n.* A synthetic fabric used in making elastic clothing.

span·gle (spăng'gəl) *n.* A small disk of shiny material, as metal, used esp. on a dress for decoration. **—span'gle** *v.*

Span·iard (spăn'yərd) *n.* A native or inhabitant of Spain.

span·iel (spăn'yəl) *n.* Any of several dogs of usu. small size with drooping ears, short legs, and silky hair.

Span·ish (spăn'ĭsh) *adj.* Of or relating to Spain, its inhabitants, or their language or culture. *—n.* **1.** The Romance language of Spain and most of Central and South America. **2.** *(pl. in number).* The inhabitants of Spain.

Span·ish-A·mer·i·can (spăn'ĭsh-ə-mĕr'ĭ-kən) *adj.* **1.** Of or relating to the countries or people of Spanish America. **2.** Of or relating to people of Spanish descent residing in the U.S. **—Span'ish-A·mer'i·can** *n.*

Spanish fly *n.* **1.** A European blister beetle, *Lytta vesicatoria,* that secretes a substance capable of blistering the skin. **2.** A preparation made from the crushed, dried body of this beetle and once used medicinally and as an aphrodisiac.

Spanish moss *n.* A plant, *Tillandsia usneoides,* growing in long threadlike masses from trees.

spank (spăngk) *v.* To slap on the buttocks with an object or the open hand. **—spank** *n.* **—spank'er** *n.*

spank·ing (spăng'kĭng) *adj.* Fresh **:** brisk <a *spanking* breeze>

†span-new (spăn'no͞o', -nyo͞o') *adj. Regional.* Brand-new.

spar[1] (spär) *n.* A wooden or metal pole, as a mast or boom, that supports rigging.

spar[2] (spär) *v.* **sparred, spar·ring. 1.** To box without landing a heavy blow, esp. for practice. **2.** To dispute verbally.

spare (spâr) *v.* **spared, spar·ing. 1.** To refrain from destroying or harming **:** treat mercifully. **2.** To exempt from doing or experiencing something. **3.** To use with thrift or restraint. **4.** To do without **:** dispense with. *—adj.* **spar·er, spar·est. 1. a.** Kept in reserve <a *spare* bedroom> **b.** Beyond what is needed <*spare* cash> **2. a.** Not abundant. **b.** Thin or lean. *—n.* **1.** Something, esp. a tire, kept in reserve for future use. **2.** The act of knocking down all 10 pins with 2 successive rolls of a bowling ball. **—spare'ness** *n.*

spare·ribs (spâr'rĭbz') *pl.n.* A cut of pork ribs with most of the meat trimmed off.

spar·ing (spâr'ĭng) *adj.* Frugal **:** thrifty. **—spar'ing·ly** *adv.*

spark[1] (spärk) *n.* **1.** An incandescent particle, as one thrown off from burning wood or produced by friction. **2.** A flash of light **:** sparkle. **3.** A short luminous discharge of electricity. **4.** A factor or quality with the potential for development **:** seed. *—v.* **1.** To emit sparks. **2.** To stir up **:** rouse.

spark[2] (spärk) *n.* An elegant young man **:** dandy. *—v.* To woo **:** court.

spar·kle (spär'kəl) *v.* **-kled, -kling. 1.** To emit or shine with flashes of light **:** gleam. **2.** To flash with wit. **3.** To effervesce. *—n.* **1.** A gleaming particle **:** spark. **2.** Vivacity **:** animation. **—spar'kler** *n.*

sparkling water *n.* Water charged with carbon dioxide.

spark plug *n.* A device that ignites the fuel mixture in an engine by an electric spark.

spar·row (spăr'ō) *n.* A small singing bird of the family Fringillidae, with grayish or brownish plumage.

†spar·row·grass (spăr'ə-grăs', -grəs) *n. Regional.* Asparagus.

sparrow hawk *n.* A small, predatory North American falcon, *Falco sparverius,* or European hawk, *Accipter nisus.*

sparse (spärs) *adj.* **spars·er, spars·est.** Thinly distributed **:** meager. **—sparse'ly** *adv.* **—spar'si·ty** (spär'sĭ-tē) *n.*

spar·tan (spär'tn) *adj.* Marked by self-discipline, frugality, and often stoicism **:** austere. **—spar'tan** *n.*

spasm (spăz'əm) *n.* **1.** A sudden, involuntary muscular contraction. **2.** A sudden and temporary burst of activity, energy, or emotion. **—spas·mod'ic** (spăz-mŏd'ĭk) *adj.* **—spas·mod'i·cal·ly** *adv.*

spas·tic (spăs'tĭk) *adj.* Of, relating to, marked by, or affected by abnormal muscular spasms. **—spas'tic** *n.*

spat[1] (spăt) *v. var. p.t. & p.p. of* SPIT[1].

spat[2] (spăt) *n., pl.* **spat** *or* **spats.** A bivalve mollusk, as an oyster, in the larval stage.

spat[3] (spăt) *n.* A gaiter covering the ankle and the upper shoe.

spat[4] (spăt) *n.* A short, petty quarrel **:** tiff. **—spat** *v.*

spate (spāt) *n.* A sudden flood or outpouring **:** rush.

spathe (spā*th*) *n.* A leaflike part that encloses the base of the spadix of certain plants, as the calla.

spa·tial (spā'shəl) *adj.* Of or pertaining to space. **—spa'tial·ly** *adv.*

spat·ter (spăt'ər) *v.* **1.** To scatter, dash, or splash (a liquid) in drops. **2.** To throw off sprinkles or splashes.

spat·u·la (spăch'ə-lə) *n.* An implement with a flexible blade used esp. for spreading or mixing soft substances.

spav·in (spăv'ĭn) *n.* A bony deposit on the hock joint of a horse. **—spav'ined** *adj.*

spawn (spôn) *n.* **1.** The eggs of aquatic animals, as oysters, fishes, or frogs. **2.** Offspring, esp. produced in large numbers **:** brood. *—v.* **1.** To produce eggs. —Used of an aquatic animal. **2.** To produce offspring, esp. in large numbers. **3.** To generate.

spay (spā) *v.* To remove the ovaries of (a female animal).

speak (spēk) *v.* **spoke** (spōk), **spo·ken** (spō'kən), **speak·ing. 1.** To utter words **:** talk. **2.**

To express (e.g., one's thoughts) in words. **3.** To deliver a speech or lecture. **4.** To talk or be able to talk in (a language) <*speak* Russian>

speak•eas•y (spēk'ē'zē) *n., pl.* **-ies.** A place where alcoholic beverages are sold illegally.

speak•er (spē'kər) *n.* **1.** One who speaks. **2.** Someone who presides over a legislative assembly. **3.** A loudspeaker.

speak•er•phone (spē'kər-fōn') *n.* A telephone that contains both a loudspeaker and a microphone, allowing several persons to participate in a call at the same time.

spear (spîr) *n.* **1.** A weapon for throwing or thrusting that consists of a long shaft with a sharply pointed head. **2.** A shaft with a sharp point and barbs for catching fish. **3.** A spearlike stalk, as of asparagus. —*v.* To pierce, strike, or stab with or as if with a spear.

spear•head (spîr'hĕd') *n.* **1.** The military force that goes before others in an attack. **2.** A leading force in an action or endeavor. **—spear'head'** *v.*

spear•mint (spîr'mĭnt') *n.* A common mint, *Mentha spicata,* that yields an aromatic oil widely used as a flavoring.

spe•cial (spĕsh'əl) *adj.* **1.** Different from what is ordinary or usual **:** exceptional. **2.** Distinct from others **:** unique. **3.** Limited to or intended for a particular function, application, or occasion. **4.** Additional **:** extra. **5.** Regarded with particular favor. **—spe'cial** *n.* **—spe'cial•ly** *adv.*

special education *n.* Instruction designed for students whose learning needs cannot be met by a standard school curriculum.

Special Forces *pl.n.* A division of the U.S. Army composed of soldiers specially trained in guerrilla fighting.

spe•cial•ist (spĕsh'ə-lĭst) *n.* **1.** One, as a physician, who is devoted to a particular activity or branch of study. **2.** Any of several enlisted ranks in the U.S. Army.

spe•cial•ize (spĕsh'ə-līz') *v.* **-ized, -iz•ing. 1.** To focus one's efforts on a particular activity, study, or field. **2.** *Biol.* To adapt to a particular environment or function. **—spe'cial•i•za'tion** *n.*

special relativity *n.* The physical theory of space and time developed by Albert Einstein.

spe•cial•ty (spĕsh'əl-tē) *n., pl.* **-ties. 1.** A branch of study, occupation, or business in which one specializes. **2.** A product of special distinction <Pecan pie is the baker's *specialty.*> **3.** A special detail or feature.

spe•cie (spē'shē, -sē) *n.* Money in the form of coins.

spe•cies (spē'shēz, -sēz) *n., pl.* **-cies. 1. a.** A taxonomic classification category comprising organisms that are able to interbreed. **b.** An organism in this category. **2.** A kind **:** sort.

spe•cif•ic (spĭ-sĭf'ĭk) *adj.* **1.** Precisely specified **:** definite. **2.** Of, relating to, characterizing, or constituting a species. **3.** Special, unique, or distinctive, as a trait. **4.** Effective in the treatment and usu. the cure of a particular disease. —*n.* A specific remedy. **—spe•cif'i•cal•ly** *adv.* **—spec'i•fic'i•ty** (spĕs'ə-fĭs'ĭ-tē) *n.*

spec•i•fi•ca•tion (spĕs'ə-fĭ-kā'shən) *n.* **1.** Something that is specified **:** item. **2.** *often* **specifications.** A statement of particulars, esp. one describing materials, dimensions, and workmanship for the building, installation, or manufacture of something.

specific gravity *n.* **1.** The quotient of the measure of the mass of a solid or liquid divided by the measure of the mass of an equal volume of water at 4°C. **2.** The quotient of the measure of the mass of a gas divided by the measure of an equal volume of air or hydrogen under prescribed conditions of temperature and pressure.

spec•i•fy (spĕs'ə-fī') *v.* **-fied, -fy•ing.** To state, name, or mention explicitly, exactly, and unambiguously.

spec•i•men (spĕs'ə-mən) *n.* A part or element representative of an entire set or whole **:** sample.

spe•cious (spē'shəs) *adj.* Apparently attractive, true, or correct but not actually so **:** deceptive. **—spe'cious•ly** *adv.*

speck (spĕk) *n.* **1.** A small mark, flaw, or spot. **2.** A small particle **:** bit. —*v.* To mark with specks.

speck•le (spĕk'əl) *n.* A small speck. —*v.* **-led, -ling.** To cover or mark with or as if with speckles.

specs (spĕks) *pl.n. Informal.* **1.** Eyeglasses. **2.** SPECIFICATION 2.

spec•ta•cle (spĕk'tə-kəl) *n.* **1.** A public display, esp. on a large scale. **2.** Something exhibited to public view. **3. spectacles.** Eyeglasses. **—spec'ta•cled** *adj.*

spec•tac•u•lar (spĕk-tăk'yə-lər) *adj.* Of the nature of a spectacle **:** striking. —*n.* A lavish spectacle.

spec•ta•tor (spĕk'tā'tər) *n.* One who is present and watches **:** onlooker.

spec•ter (spĕk'tər) *n.* **1.** A ghost **:** apparition. **2.** A haunting or threatening vision <the *specter* of nuclear war>

spec•tral (spĕk'trəl) *adj.* **1.** Of, pertaining to, or resembling a specter. **2.** Of, relating to, or produced by a spectrum.

spec•tre (spĕk'tər) *n. esp. Brit. var. of* SPECTER.

spec•trom•e•ter (spĕk-trŏm'ĭ-tər) *n.* A spectroscope with scales for measuring the positions of spectral lines.

spec•tro•scope (spĕk'trə-skōp') *n.* An instrument used to resolve radiation into spectra and to make observations or recordings. **—spec'tro•scop'ic** (-skŏp'ĭk), **spec'tro•scop'i•cal** *adj.* **—spec'tro•scop'i•cal•ly** *adv.* **—spec•tros'co•pist** (spĕk-trŏs'kə-pĭst) *n.* **—spec•tros'co•py** *n.*

spec•trum (spĕk'trəm) *n., pl.* **-tra** (-trə) *or* **-trums. 1.** *Physics.* The distribution of a characteristic of a physical system or phenomenon, esp.: **a.** The distribution of energy emitted by a radiant source, as an incandescent body, arranged in order of wavelengths. **b.** A graphic or photographic representation of such a distribution. **2.** A broad range or sequence <a wide *spectrum* of feelings>

spec•u•late (spĕk′yə-lāt′) *v.* **-lat•ed, -lat•ing. 1.** To think deeply **:** reflect. **2.** To engage in a business venture offering the possibility of a large profit but entailing risk. **—spec′u•la′tion** *n.* **—spec′u•la′tive** *adj.* **—spec′u•la′tor** *n.*

speech (spēch) *n.* **1.** Manner or act of speaking. **2.** The faculty of speaking. **3.** Conversation. **4.** A public address. **5.** A language or dialect. ★ ***syns:*** DISCOURSE, TALK, UTTERANCE **—speech′less** *adj.*

speed (spēd) *n.* **1.** Rate of motion, action, activity, or performance. **2.** Rapidity **:** celerity. **3.** A gear in the transmission of a motor vehicle. **4.** *Slang.* An amphetamine drug. **5.** *Archaic.* Success **:** prosperity. —*v.* **sped** (spĕd) *or* **speed•ed, speed•ing. 1.** To move fast, esp. at a high or illegal rate of speed. **2.** To cause to go at an increased rate of speed **:** accelerate. **—speed′er** *n.* **—speed′i•ly** *adv.* **—speed′y** *adj.*

speed•boat (spēd′bōt′) *n.* A fast motorboat or launch.

speed•om•e•ter (spē-dŏm′ĭ-tər, spĭ-) *n.* **1.** An instrument that measures and indicates speed. **2.** An odometer.

speed•ster (spēd′stər) *n.* **1.** One that speeds. **2.** A fast car.

speed•up (spēd′ŭp′) *n.* Acceleration, esp. an acceleration in production without an increase in pay.

speed•way (spēd′wā′) *n.* **1.** A racecourse for motorcycles or automobiles. **2.** A road designed for high-speed traffic.

speed•well (spēd′wĕl′) *n.* A low-growing plant of the genus *Veronica,* with clusters of small, usu. blue flowers.

spe•le•ol•o•gy (spē′lē-ŏl′ə-jē) *n.* **1.** The study of the physical, geologic, and biological aspects of caves. **2.** Cave exploration. **—spe′le•ol′o•gist** *n.*

spell[1] (spĕl) *v.* **spelled** *or* **spelt** (spĕlt), **spell•ing. 1.** To name or write in order the letters of (a word). **2.** To signify **:** mean. **—spell out.** To state or explain explicitly.

spell[2] (spĕl) *n.* **1.** A formula supposed to have magic power **:** incantation. **2.** A state of bewitchment **:** trance. **3.** A compelling or dominating influence.

spell[3] (spĕl) *n.* **1.** An indefinite, often short period of time. **2.** *Informal.* A period of a particular kind of weather. **3.** One's turn at work **:** shift. **4.** A period of illness or distress **:** attack. —*v.* To relieve (another person) for a time by taking a turn.

spell•bind (spĕl′bīnd′) *v.* To hold by or as if by a spell **:** fascinate. **—spell′bind•er** *n.*

spell•bound (spĕl′bound′) *adj.* Bound by or as if by a spell **:** entranced.

spell•er (spĕl′ər) *n.* **1.** One who spells words. **2.** A textbook for teaching spelling.

spe•lun•ker (spĭ-lŭng′kər, spē′lŭng′kər) *n.* A person whose hobby is exploring caves. **—spe•lun′king** *n.*

spend (spĕnd) *v.* **spent** (spĕnt), **spend•ing. 1.** To use up or wear out **:** exhaust. **2.** To pay out (e.g., money) **:** expend. **3.** To pass (time). **4.** To waste **:** squander. **—spend′er** *n.*

spend•thrift (spĕnd′thrĭft′) *n.* One who squanders money.

spent (spĕnt) *adj.* Depleted of energy **:** exhausted.

sperm (spûrm) *n.* **1.** Spermatozoon. **2.** Semen. **—sper•mat′ic** (spər-măt′ĭk) *adj.*

sper•mat•o•zo•on (spər-măt′ə-zō′ŏn′, spûr′-mə-tə-, -ən) *n., pl.* **-zo•a** (-zō′ə). A male reproductive cell.

sper•mi•cide (spûr′mĭ-sīd′) *n.* A contraceptive agent that kills spermatozoa. **—sper′mi•cid′al** (-sīd′l) *adj.*

sperm whale *n.* A toothed whale, *Physeter catodon,* with a large head and a long, narrow lower jaw.

spew (spyo͞o) *v.* **1.** To vomit. **2.** To force or come out in a stream.

sphag•num (sfăg′nəm) *n.* A moss of the genus *Sphagnum,* growing in wet areas, as swamps, that decomposes to form peat.

sphere (sfîr) *n.* **1.** *Math.* A 3-dimensional geometric surface having all its points the same distance from a given point. **2.** A sphere-shaped figure or object **:** ball. **3.** A heavenly body, as a planet or star. **4.** An area, range, or extent of power, action, or influence **:** domain. **—spher′i•cal** (sfîr′ĭ-kəl, sfĕr′-) *adj.* **—spher′i•cal•ly** *adv.*

sphe•roid (sfîr′oid′, sfĕr′-) *n.* An ellipsoid generated by revolving an ellipse on or about one of its axes.

sphinc•ter (sfĭngk′tər) *n.* A ringlike muscle that closes a bodily passage or orifice.

sphinx (sfĭnks) *n., pl.* **sphinx•es** *or* **sphin•ges** (sfĭn′jēz′). **1.** An ancient Egyptian figure with the body of a lion and the head of a man, ram, or hawk. **2.** *Gk. Myth.* A monster having wings, a woman's head, and a lion's body, esp. one that destroyed all passers-by who could not answer the riddle it asked them. **3.** An enigmatic or mysterious person.

spice (spīs) *n.* **1.** A pungently aromatic vegetable substance, as cinnamon, pepper, or nutmeg, used to flavor or season food. **2.** Something that adds zest, flavor, and interest. **—spice** *v.* **—spic′y** *adj.*

spick-and-span *also* **spic-and-span** (spĭk′ən-spăn′) *adj.* **1.** Immaculately clean **:** spotless. **2.** Brand-new.

spic•ule (spĭk′yo͞ol) *n.* A small needlelike structure or part.

spi•der (spī′dər) *n.* **1.** Any of numerous 8-legged arachnids of the order Araneae that have a body divided into 2 parts and spin webs. **2.** A cast-iron frying pan with a long handle. **—spi′der•y** *adj.*

spiel (spēl, shpēl) *v. Slang.* To talk at length and usu. extravagantly. **—spiel** *n.*

spif•fy (spĭf′ē) *adj.* **-fi•er, -fi•est.** *Slang.* Stylish **:** smart.

spig•ot (spĭg′ət) *n.* A faucet.

spike[1] (spīk) *n.* **1.** A long, thick heavy nail. **2.** A sharp-pointed projection, as on the sole of a shoe to add traction. —*v.* **spiked, spik•**

ing. 1. To secure with spikes. **2.** To impale on, injure with, or pierce with a spike. **3.** To put an end to **:** suppress <*spike* a rebellion> **4.** *Slang.* To add alcoholic liquor to (a drink).

spike² (spīk) *n.* **1.** An ear of grain. **2.** *Bot.* A long stalkless or almost stalkless flower cluster.

spill (spĭl) *v.* **spilled** *or* **spilt** (spĭlt), **spill•ing. 1.** To cause or allow inadvertently to run out or flow. **2.** To shed (blood). **3.** To cause to fall, as from a horse. **4.** To run from or as if from a container **:** overflow. —*n.* **1.** An act of spilling. **2.** An amount spilled. **3.** Something spilled. **4.** A fall, as from a horse. **5.** A spillway. —**spill'age** *n.*

spill•way (spĭl'wā') *n.* A channel for the overflow of surplus water.

spin (spĭn) *v.* **spun** (spŭn), **spin•ning. 1. a.** To draw out (fibers) and twist into thread. **b.** To form (thread) by spinning. **2. a.** To form thread by extruding viscous filaments from the body. **b.** To construct from such filaments <*spinning* a cocoon> **3.** To tell slowly and esp. imaginatively <*spin* a story> **4.** To revolve or cause to revolve rapidly **:** twirl. **5.** To reel **:** whirl. **6.** To move quickly, as in a vehicle. —*n.* **1.** A rapid revolving motion. **2.** *Informal.* A short drive in a vehicle. **3.** *Slang.* Interpretation of someone's words or actions for political or personal advantage. —**spin'ner** *n.*

spin•ach (spĭn'ĭch) *n.* A widely cultivated plant, *Spinacia oleracea,* having dark-green edible leaves.

spi•nal (spī'nəl) *adj.* Of or near the spinal column or spinal cord. —**spi'nal•ly** *adv.*

spinal column *n.* The vertebrae enclosing the spinal cord and forming the supporting axis of the body.

spinal cord *n.* The part of the central nervous system extending from the brain along the back in the cavity of the spinal column.

spin•dle (spĭn'dl) *n.* **1.** A thin, rounded, tapering rod or pin holding a bobbin or spool on which thread is wound on a spinning wheel or machine. **2.** A slender rod that rotates or serves as an axis on which other parts rotate.

spin•dly (spĭn'dlē) *adj.* **-dli•er, -dli•est.** Elongated, thin, and usu. weak.

spin•drift (spĭn'drĭft') *n.* Sea spray blown by the wind.

spine (spīn) *n.* **1.** The spinal column. **2.** A sharp-pointed, projecting part on a plant or animal, as a quill. —**spin'y** *adj.*

spi•nel (spĭ-nĕl') *n.* A hard crystalline mineral valued as a gem.

spine•less (spīn'lĭs) *adj.* **1.** Lacking a spinal column. **2.** Lacking courage **:** cowardly.

spin•et (spĭn'ĭt) *n.* **1.** A small, compact upright piano. **2.** A harpsichord with a single keyboard.

spin•na•ker (spĭn'ə-kər) *n.* A large triangular sail set opposite the mainsail.

spin•ner•et (spĭn'ə-rĕt') *n.* A posterior structure in spiders and certain insect larvae that contains passages through which silky filaments are secreted.

spinning jenny *n.* An early machine with several spindles for spinning fibers.

spinning wheel *n.* A device for spinning yarn or thread that consists of a large foot- or hand-driven wheel and one spindle.

spin-off *also* **spin•off** (spĭn'ôf', -ŏf') *n.* A product, effect, or enterprise that is a byproduct of a larger or more complex one.

spin•ster (spĭn'stər) *n.* A woman who has remained single beyond the conventional age of marrying. —**spin'ster•hood'** *n.*

spiny lobster *n.* An edible marine crustacean of the family Palinuridae, having a spiny carapace and lacking the large pincers characteristic of the true lobster.

spi•ral (spī'rəl) *n.* **1.** The 2-dimensional locus of a point moving around a fixed center at an increasing or decreasing distance from the center. **2.** A helix. **3.** Something shaped like a spiral <*spirals* of smoke> **4.** A continuously expanding increase or decrease. —*adj.* **1.** Of or being a spiral. **2.** Helical. —*v.* **-raled, -ral•ing** *or* **-ralled, -ral•ling. 1.** To take or cause to take a spiral shape or course. **2.** To rise or fall with rapid acceleration. —**spi'ral•ly** *adv.*

spi•rant (spī'rənt) *n.* A consonant, as *f* or *s,* produced by forcing the breath through a constricted oral passage.

spire (spīr) *n.* **1.** The pointed tip of something that tapers upward. **2.** A formation or structure, as a steeple, that tapers upward to a point. —**spir'y** *adj.*

spi•re•a *also* **spi•rae•a** (spī-rē'ə) *n.* A plant or shrub of the genus *Spiraea,* with small white or pink flower clusters.

spir•it (spĭr'ĭt) *n.* **1.** A vital or animating force **:** soul. **2.** The part of a human being associated with the feelings and mind. **3.** Real meaning or sense **:** significance. **4.** A person. **5.** The prevailing tenor **:** tone <the *spirit* of the times> **6. Spirit.** The Holy Ghost. **7.** A ghost **:** specter. **8.** Mood **:** disposition. **9.** Animation and vigor. **10.** Strong loyalty <team *spirit*> **11.** *often* **spirits.** A distilled alcoholic liquor. ★ ***syns:*** BRIO, DASH, ÉLAN, ESPRIT, LIVELINESS, PEP —*v.* To carry away mysteriously or secretly. —**spir'it•less** *adj.*

spir•it•ed (spĭr'ĭ-tĭd) *adj.* **1.** Full of or marked by spirit. **2.** Courageous.

spir•i•tu•al (spĭr'ĭ-chōō-əl) *adj.* **1.** Of, relating to, or having the nature of spirit. **2.** Of or relating to religion or religious matters **:** ecclesiastical or sacred. —*n.* A religious song of African-American origin. —**spir'i•tu•al'i•ty** (-ăl'ĭ-tē) *n.* —**spir'i•tu•al•ize'** *v.* —**spir'i•tu•al•ly** *adv.*

spir•i•tu•al•ism (spĭr'ĭ-chōō-ə-lĭz'əm) *n.* The belief that the dead are able to communicate with the living, usu. through a medium. —**spir'i•tu•al•ist** *n.*

spir•i•tu•ous (spĭr'ĭ-chōō-əs) *adj.* Of or containing alcohol.

spi•ro•chete *also* **spi•ro•chaete** (spī'rə-kēt') *n.* Any of several twisted microorganisms of the order Spirochaetales, including those that cause syphilis.

spirt (spûrt) *n. & v. esp. Brit. var. of* SPURT.

spit[1] (spĭt) *n.* **1.** Saliva, esp. when ejected from the mouth. **2.** The act of spitting. —*v.* **spat** (spăt) *or* **spit, spit•ting. 1.** To eject (e.g., saliva) from the mouth. **2.** To send forth as if by spitting. **3.** To make a sputtering or hissing sound.

spit[2] (spĭt) *n.* **1.** A slender, pointed rod on which meat is skewered for roasting or broiling. **2.** A narrow point of land projecting into a body of water. —*v.* **spit•ted, spit•ting.** To skewer on or as if on a spit.

spit•ball (spĭt′bôl′) *n.* **1.** Paper chewed and shaped into a ball to be thrown as a projectile. **2.** *Baseball.* An illegal pitch in which the ball has been moistened on one side with saliva.

spite (spīt) *n.* Ill will with an urge to hurt, humiliate, or thwart : malice. —*v.* **spit•ed, spit•ing.** To treat with spite. **—in spite of.** Regardless of : notwithstanding. **—spite′ful** *adj.* **—spite′ful•ly** *adv.* **—spite′ful•ness** *n.*

spit•tle (spĭt′l) *n.* Saliva : spit.

spit•tle•bug (spĭt′l-bŭg′) *n.* An insect of the family Cercopidae, whose larvae form frothy masses of liquid on plant stems.

spit•toon (spĭ-to͞on′) *n.* A receptacle into which one may spit.

spitz (spĭts) *n.* A dog with a thick, usu. white coat and a tail curled over the back.

splash (splăsh) *v.* **1.** To dash (a liquid) about in flying masses. **2.** To dash a liquid on. **3.** To fall or move with the sound of splashing. **—splash** *n.* **—splash′y** *adj.*

splash•down (splăsh′doun′) *n.* The landing of a spacecraft or missile in the ocean.

splat[1] (splăt) *n.* A single slat, as of wood, in a chair back.

splat[2] (splăt) *n.* A slapping noise.

splat•ter (splăt′ər) *v.* To spatter. **—splat′ter** *n.*

splay (splā) *adj.* **1.** Turned or spread outward. **2.** Clumsy : awkward. —*v.* **1.** To spread apart or out. **2.** To slope or slant. **—splay** *n.*

splay•foot (splā′fo͝ot′) *n.* A deformed foot that is abnormally flat and turned out. **—splay′foot′ed** *adj.*

spleen (splēn) *n.* **1.** An organ located below the diaphragm in most vertebrates that functions to filter and store blood. **2.** Ill will : malice.

splen•did (splĕn′dĭd) *adj.* **1.** Brilliant with color or light : shining. **2.** Sumptuous : magnificent. **3.** Illustrious : grand. **4.** Excellent. **—splen′did•ly** *adv.*

splen•dif•er•ous (splĕn-dĭf′ər-əs) *adj.* Splendid.

splen•dor (splĕn′dər) *n.* **1.** Great luster or light : brilliance. **2.** Glory : magnificence.

splen•dour (splĕn′dər) *n. esp. Brit. var. of* SPLENDOR.

sple•net•ic (splĭ-nĕt′ĭk) *adj.* **1.** Splenic. **2.** Marked by ill will, malice, or irritability.

splen•ic (splĕn′ĭk) *adj.* Of, pertaining to, or near the spleen.

splice (splīs) *v.* **spliced, splic•ing. 1. a.** To join (e.g., 2 lengths of film) at the ends. **b.** To join (e.g., 2 ropes) by weaving together the strands. **2.** To join (e.g., 2 pieces of wood) by overlapping and binding together the ends. **—splice** *n.*

splint (splĭnt) *n.* **1.** Rigid material or a device used to immobilize an injured body part, as a fractured bone. **2.** A flexible wooden strip, as one used in basket making.

splin•ter (splĭn′tər) *n.* A thin, sharp piece of something, as wood or glass, split off lengthwise from a main body. —*v.* To split or cause to split into splinters.

split (splĭt) *v.* **split, split•ting. 1.** To divide, esp. cleanly, sharply, or suddenly, into lengthwise sections. **2.** To burst or break apart, esp. with force. **3.** To divide and share <*split* the bill> **4.** To separate into sections, layers, or parts. **5.** *Slang.* To leave, esp. suddenly. —*n.* **1.** The act or result of splitting. **2.** A breach : rupture.

split-lev•el (splĭt′lĕv′əl) *adj.* Built so that the floor levels of adjoining rooms are separated by approx. a half story.

split personality *n.* A psychological disorder in which a person exhibits 2 or more relatively distinct personalities.

split•ting (splĭt′ĭng) *adj.* Very acute : severe <a *splitting* headache>

splotch (splŏch) *n.* An irregularly shaped discolored area : blotch. **—splotch** *v.* **—splotch′y** *adj.*

splurge (splûrj) *n.* **1.** An extravagant expense or indulgence. **2.** An ostentatious display. **—splurge** *v.*

splut•ter (splŭt′ər) *v.* **1.** To make a short popping or spitting sound. **2.** To speak indistinctly and hastily. **—splut′ter** *n.*

spoil (spoil) *v.* **spoiled** *or* **spoilt** (spoilt), **spoil•ing. 1.** To impair in quality or value : damage. **2.** To destroy the perfection of : ruin. **3. a.** To harm the character of by overindulging. **b.** To pamper : coddle. **4.** *Archaic.* To rob : plunder. **5.** To become decayed : rot. **6.** To be very eager <*spoiling* for an argument> —*n.* **spoils. 1.** Loot seized by force : plunder. **2.** Political patronage at the disposal of a successful party or candidate. **—spoil′age** *n.* **—spoil′er** *n.*

spoil•sport (spoil′spôrt′) *n.* Someone whose behavior and reactions spoil the pleasure of others.

spoke[1] (spōk) *n.* **1.** One of the rods that connect the rim of a wheel to its hub. **2.** A rung of a ladder.

spoke[2] (spōk) *v. p.t. of* SPEAK.

spo•ken (spō′kən) *v. p.p. of* SPEAK.

spokes•man (spōks′mən) *n.* One who is authorized to speak on behalf of another or others.

spokes•per•son (spōks′pûr′sən) *n.* A spokesman or spokeswoman.

spokes•wom•an (spōks′wo͝om′ən) *n.* A woman authorized to speak on behalf of another or others.

spo•li•a•tion (spō′lē-ā′shən) *n.* The act of plundering, esp. in wartime.

sponge (spŭnj) *n.* **1.** Any of numerous primitive marine animals of the phylum Porifera, with a soft, porous skeleton. **2.** The absorbent skeleton of a sponge, used for such purposes as bathing, wiping, or cleaning. **3.** A substance or mass with spongelike properties. —*v.* **sponged, spong•ing. 1.** To bathe, wipe, or clean with a sponge. **2.** To fish for or gather sponges. **3.** *Slang.* To live by imposing on the generosity of another. **—spong'er** *n.* **—spong'y** *adj.*

sponge cake *n.* A light cake that contains no shortening.

sponge rubber *n.* A soft, porous rubber that resembles a sponge in texture.

spon•sor (spŏn'sər) *n.* **1.** Someone who takes the responsibility for another person or thing. **2.** A godparent. **3.** A business that finances a radio or television program in return for advertising time. **—spon'sor** *v.* **—spon'sor•ship'** *n.*

spon•ta•ne•ous (spŏn-tā'nē-əs) *adj.* **1.** Occurring, acting, or arising without apparent external cause. **2.** Produced or done naturally and voluntarily <*spontaneous* laughter> **—spon'ta•ne'i•ty** (-tə-nē'ĭ-tē, -nā'-) *n.* **—spon•ta'ne•ous•ly** *adv.*

spontaneous abortion *n.* MISCARRIAGE 2.

spontaneous combustion *n.* Ignition in a thermally isolated substance, as oily rags, caused by heat generated by slow internal oxidation.

spoof (spo͞of) *n.* **1.** Nonsense. **2.** A hoax. **3.** A good-natured satirical imitation : parody. **—spoof** *v.*

spook (spo͝ok) *Informal.* —*n.* A specter : ghost. —*v.* **1.** To haunt. **2.** To scare : frighten. **—spook'y** *adj.*

spool (spo͞ol) *n.* A cylinder on which thread, ribbon, wire, tape, or film is wound.

spoon (spo͞on) *n.* **1.** A cooking or eating utensil that consists of a small, shallow bowl on a handle. **2.** A shiny, curved metal fishing lure. —*v.* **1.** To scoop up and carry in or as if in a spoon. **2.** *Informal.* To kiss or caress. **—spoon'ful'** (-fo͝ol') *n.*

spoon•bill (spo͞on'bĭl') *n.* A wading bird of the subfamily Plataleidae, having a long, flat bill with a spoonlike tip.

spoon•er•ism (spo͞o'nə-rĭz'əm) *n.* An unintentional transposition of esp. initial sounds in 2 or more words, as *sew you to a sheet* for *show you to a seat.*

spoon-feed (spo͞on'fēd') *v.* **1.** To feed with a spoon. **2.** To provide information (to) in such completeness or detail that independent thought or action is precluded.

spoor (spo͝or) *n.* A trail or track of an animal, esp. a wild animal.

spo•rad•ic (spə-răd'ĭk) *adj.* Occurring at irregular intervals. **—spo•rad'i•cal•ly** *adv.*

spore (spôr, spōr) *n.* A usu. single-celled reproductive structure produced by nonflowering plants and certain lower animals.

sport (spôrt, spōrt) *n.* **1.** An amusing or interesting pastime : diversion. **2.** A physical activity, esp. one with a set form and body of rules. **3.** Jest : mockery <made *sport* of his discomfort> **4.** One who accepts an outcome, esp. an adverse one, with grace. **5.** *Informal.* One who leads a fast, extravagant life. **6.** A genetic mutation. —*v.* **1.** To have a good time : play. **2.** To show off : display. —*adj.* Of or appropriate for sport <*sport* fishing> **—sport'ive** *adj.* **—sport'y** *adj.*

sport•ing (spôr'tĭng, spōr'-) *adj.* **1.** Appropriate for or used in sports. **2.** Marked by sportsmanship. **3.** Of or relating to gambling. **4.** Offering a reasonable hope of success <a *sporting* chance>

sports car *n.* A low 1- or 2-passenger car designed for high-speed driving.

sports•cast (spôrts'kăst', spōrts'-) *n.* A television or radio broadcast of sports news or a sports event. **—sports'cast'er** *n.*

sports•man (spôrts'mən, spōrts'-) *n.* **1.** Someone who is active in sports. **2.** Someone who observes the rules of play and wins or loses with grace. **—sports'man•ship'** *n.*

sports•writ•er (spôrts'rī'tər) *n.* A writer about sports.

spot (spŏt) *n.* **1.** An area that differs sharply, as in color, from the area surrounding it. **2.** A location : position. **3.** *Informal.* A situation, esp. a dangerous or difficult one. —*v.* **spot•ted, spot•ting. 1.** To become or cause to become marked with spots. **2.** To notice : detect. —*adj.* **1.** Paid, made, or delivered immediately <*spot* cash> **2.** Done at random <a *spot* inspection> **—spot'less** *adj.* **—spot'less•ly** *adv.* **—spot'less•ness** *n.*

spot-check (spŏt'chĕk') *v.* To check or test at random. **—spot check** *n.*

spot•light (spŏt'līt') *n.* **1. a.** A beam of strong light used to illuminate a person, group, area, or object, as on a stage. **b.** A lamp that produces this light. **2.** Public attention. **—spot'light'** *v.*

spot•ter (spŏt'ər) *n.* One who watches for and reports something, as the approach of enemy aircraft.

spot•ty (spŏt'ē) *adj.* **-ti•er, -ti•est.** Inconsistent : uneven. **—spot'ti•ly** *adv.* **—spot'ti•ness** *n.*

spou•sal (spou'zəl, -səl) *n. often* **spousals.** Nuptials.

spouse (spous, spouz) *n.* One's wife or husband.

spout (spout) *v.* **1.** To issue forth or discharge copiously and forcibly. **2.** To utter or speak pompously. —*n.* **1.** A tube, hole, or pipe through which liquid spouts. **2.** A continuous stream of liquid.

sprain (sprān) *n.* **1.** A wrenching and laceration of the ligaments of a muscle or joint. **2.** The condition resulting from a sprain. —*v.* To cause a sprain in.

sprang (sprăng) *v. var. p.t. of* SPRING.

sprat (sprăt) *n.* **1.** A small marine food fish, *Clupea sprattus,* of NE Atlantic waters. **2.** A young herring.

sprawl (sprôl) *v.* **1.** To sit or lie with the arms and legs spread out awkwardly. **2.** To spread out or develop haphazardly. **—sprawl** *n.* **—sprawl'er** *n.*

spray[1] (sprā) *n.* **1.** Liquid moving in fine droplets or mist. **2. a.** A jet of vapor, as that discharged from a pressurized container. **b.** A device, as an atomizer, for discharging such a jet. *—v.* **1.** To disperse (a liquid) in the form of spray. **2.** To apply spray to (a surface). **—spray'er** *n.*

spray[2] (sprā) *n.* A branch or decorative arrangement of buds, flowers, or berries.

spray gun *n.* A device for applying a liquid in a spray.

spread (sprĕd) *v.* **spread, spread•ing. 1.** To open out fully or more fully. **2.** To push or force apart **:** stretch. **3.** To distribute over a surface **:** apply <*spread* paint on a wall> **4.** To distribute or be distributed widely over an area. **5.** To make or become widely known. **6.** To extend in time. **7.** To prepare (a table) for a meal. ★ ***syns:*** DIFFUSE, DISPERSE, RADIATE, SCATTER *—n.* **1.** The act or process of spreading. **2.** An open area **:** expanse. **3.** The extent to which something is or can be spread **:** range. **4.** A cloth cover for a table or bed. **5.** A food to be spread, as on bread. **6.** Printed matter extending across facing pages or adjacent columns. **7.** A difference, as between 2 totals **:** gap. **—spread'er** *n.*

spread•sheet (sprĕd'shēt') *n.* An accounting or bookkeeping program for a computer, displayed in multiple columns and rows.

spree (sprē) *n.* **1.** A drinking bout. **2.** Overindulgence in an activity <a shopping *spree*>

sprig (sprĭg) *n.* A small shoot of a plant **:** twig.

spright•ly (sprīt'lē) *adj.* **-li•er, -li•est.** Lively **:** vivacious. **—spright'li•ness** *n.*

spring (sprĭng) *v.* **sprang** (sprăng) *or* **sprung** (sprŭng), **sprung, spring•ing. 1.** To move forward or upward suddenly **:** jump. **2.** To break out, esp. suddenly **:** emerge. **3.** To move suddenly and with resilience. **4.** To come into existence **:** arise. **5.** To become warped, cracked, or bent, as wood. **6.** To release suddenly from a checked position <*spring* a trap> **7.** To produce unexpectedly and suddenly <*spring* a trick question> *—n.* **1.** An elastic device, esp. a coil of wire, that returns to its original shape when it is released after being compressed, extended, or twisted. **2.** Resilience **:** elasticity. **3.** The act of springing, esp. a jump or leap. **4.** A natural flow of water from the ground. **5.** An origin or source. **6.** The season between winter and summer. **—spring'y** *adj.*

spring•board (sprĭng'bôrd', -bōrd') *n.* **1.** A flexible board used in gymnastics and diving. **2.** *Informal.* A starting place.

spring•bok (sprĭng'bŏk') *n., pl.* **springbok** *or* **-boks.** A small white gazelle, *Antidorcas marsupialis,* of S Africa, capable of leaping high into the air.

†spring•er (sprĭng'ər) *n. U.S.* A cow about to calve.

spring fever *n.* Feelings of languor, restlessness, or yearning brought on by the coming of spring.

spring•time (sprĭng'tīm') *n.* SPRING 6.

sprin•kle (sprĭng'kəl) *v.* **-kled, -kling. 1.** To scatter about or release in small particles or drops. **2.** To rain or fall in small infrequent drops. ★ ***syns:*** BESPRINKLE, DUST, POWDER *—n.* **1.** An act of sprinkling. **2.** A light rainfall. **3.** A small amount. **—sprin'kler** *n.*

sprin•kling (sprĭng'klĭng) *n.* A small number or quantity **:** smattering.

sprint (sprĭnt) *n.* A short, fast run or race. *—v.* To run or race as fast as possible, usu. for a short distance. **—sprint'er** *n.*

sprite (sprīt) *n.* **1.** A small supernatural being **:** elf. **2.** A ghost.

sprock•et (sprŏk'ĭt) *n.* A toothlike part that projects from the rim of a sprocket wheel.

sprocket wheel *n.* A wheel rimmed with sprockets and used to engage the links of a chain in a pulley or drive a system.

sprout (sprout) *v.* **1.** To start growing and send out new growth. **2.** To develop or grow rapidly. *—n.* A young plant growth.

spruce[1] (sprōōs) *n.* **1.** A coniferous evergreen tree of the genus *Picea,* with needlelike foliage, drooping cones, and soft wood often used for paper pulp. **2.** Any of various trees similar or related to the spruce.

spruce[2] (sprōōs) *adj.* **spruc•er, spruc•est.** Tidy, neat, or trim. *—v.* **spruced, spruc•ing.** To make or become spruce.

sprung (sprŭng) *v. p.p. & var. p.t. of* SPRING.

spry (sprī) *adj.* **spri•er, spri•est** *or* **spry•er, spry•est.** Briskly active.

spud (spŭd) *n.* **1.** A sharp, spadelike digging tool. **2.** *Slang.* A potato.

spume (spyōōm) *n.* Foam or froth on a liquid.

spu•mo•ne *also* **spu•mo•ni** (spōō-mō'nē) *n.* An Italian frozen dessert of ice cream containing fruit, nuts, or candies.

spun (spŭn) *v. p.t. & p.p. of* SPIN.

spun glass *n.* **1.** Fiber glass. **2.** Fine blown glass with a delicate threading or filigree.

spunk (spŭngk) *n.* **1.** Tinder, as punk. **2.** *Informal.* Courage. **—spunk'y** *adj.*

spur (spûr) *n.* **1.** A device with a projecting point or sharp-toothed wheel behind, worn on a rider's boot and used to urge on a horse. **2.** An incentive. **3.** A spurlike attachment or projection, as the spinelike process on the leg of some birds. **4.** A side railroad track that connects with the main line. *—v.* **spurred, spur•ring. 1.** To urge (a horse) on with spurs. **2.** To move to action **:** prompt. **—spurred** *adj.*

spurge (spûrj) *n.* A chiefly tropical plant of the genus *Euphorbia,* having milky juice and small flowers.

spu•ri•ous (spyŏŏr'ē-əs) *adj.* Not authentic or genuine **:** false.

spurn (spûrn) *v.* To reject scornfully.

spurt (spûrt). *n.* **1.** A sudden, forcible gush. **2.** A sudden outbreak or short burst of effort or activity. *—v.* **1.** To squirt <oil *spurting* into the air> **2.** To show a sudden, brief increase in activity.

sput•nik (spŭt'nĭk, spōōt'-) *n.* An artificial earth satellite launched by the U.S.S.R.

sput•ter (spŭt'ər) *v.* **1. a.** To spit out small particles in short bursts. **b.** To make a coughing noise characteristic of sputtering. **2.** To speak excitedly or confusedly **:** stammer. **—sput'ter** *n.*

spu•tum (spyo͞o'təm) *n., pl.* **-ta** (-tə). Matter, as saliva or phlegm, that is expectorated.

spy (spī) *n., pl.* **spies. 1.** A secret agent employed, as by a government, to obtain intelligence. **2.** A person who furtively watches another or others. *—v.* **spied, spy•ing. 1.** To keep under surveillance with hostile intent. **2.** To see <*spied* a bluejay> **3.** To observe secretly <*spying* on the neighbors>

spy•glass (spī'glăs') *n.* **1.** A small telescope. **2. spyglasses.** Binoculars.

squab (skwŏb) *n.* A young, unfledged pigeon, esp. one used as food.

squab•ble (skwŏb'əl) *v.* **-bled, -bling.** To engage in a minor quarrel **:** bicker. **—squab'ble** *n.* **—squab'bler** *n.*

squad (skwŏd) *n.* **1.** A small organized group of soldiers. **2.** A small group engaged in a common enterprise.

squad car *n.* A police patrol car.

squad•ron (skwŏd'rən) *n.* Any of various military units, as of soldiers, planes, or ships.

squal•id (skwŏl'ĭd) *adj.* **1.** Wretched or unkempt in appearance. **2.** Morally repulsive **:** sordid.

squall[1] (skwôl) *n.* A harsh, loud yell or outcry. **—squall** *v.*

squall[2] (skwôl) *n.* A sudden, violent windstorm, often accompanied by rain or snow. **—squall'y** *adj.*

squal•or (skwŏl'ər) *n.* The quality or state of being squalid.

squan•der (skwŏn'dər) *v.* To spend extravagantly or wastefully **:** dissipate.

square (skwâr) *n.* **1.** A rectangle having 4 sides that are equal in length. **2.** Something having the shape of a square. **3.** A T-shaped or L-shaped instrument used for drawing or testing 90° angles. **4.** The product that results when a number is multiplied by itself. **5. a.** An open, often quadrilateral area at the intersection of 2 or more avenues or streets. **b.** A rectangular area bounded by streets **:** block. **6.** *Slang.* A rigidly conventional or unsophisticated person. *—adj.* **squar•er, squar•est. 1.** Having 4 equal sides and 4 90° angles. **2.** Forming a right angle <a board with *square* corners> **3.** Of, being, or expressed in units that measure area <*square* yards> **4.** Solid **:** substantial <a *square* meal> **5.** Fair **:** equitable <finally got a *square* deal> **6.** *Slang.* Stiffly conventional. **7.** Paid up **:** settled. *—v.* **squared, squar•ing. 1.** To cut a rectangular or square shape. **2.** To settle **:** adjust <*square* an account> **3.** To bring into harmony or conformity. **4.** To multiply (a quantity or number) by itself. **—square'ly** *adv.* **—square'ness** *n.*

square dance *n.* A dance in which couples in sets of 4 form squares. **—square'-dance'** *v.* **—square'-danc'er** *n.*

square-rigged (skwâr'rĭgd') *adj.* Having square sails set at right angles to the keel. **—square'-rig'ger** *n.*

square root *n.* A divisor of a quantity that when squared gives the quantity.

squash[1] (skwŏsh, skwôsh) *n.* A plant of the genus *Cucurbita,* grown in many varieties for its fleshy edible fruit.

squash[2] (skwŏsh, skwôsh) *v.* **1.** To beat, squeeze, or crush to a pulp. **2.** To put down **:** suppress <*squash* a revolt> *—n.* **1.** The act or sound of squashing. **2.** Something that has been squashed. **3.** A game played in a walled court by players who hit a hard rubber ball with a racket.

squash[2]

squat (skwŏt) *v.* **squat•ted, squat•ting. 1.** To sit on one's heels. **2.** To settle on land without having legal title. **3.** To settle on public land in order to obtain legal title. *—adj.* **squat•ter, squat•test.** Low and broad. *—n.* **1.** A squatting or crouching posture. **2.** The act of squatting or crouching. **—squat'ter** *n.*

squaw (skwô) *n.* A North American Indian woman, esp. a wife.

squawk (skwôk) *v.* **1.** To utter a harsh scream **:** screech. **2.** *Slang.* To make a noisy, angry protest. **—squawk** *n.*

squeak (skwēk) *v.* **1.** To make or utter a thin, shrill cry or sound. **2.** To pass or win by a narrow margin <*squeaked* through the test> **—squeak** *n.* **—squeak'y** *adj.*

squeal (skwēl) *v.* **1.** To make or utter a high, loud, drawn-out cry or sound. **2.** *Slang.* To betray a friend or a secret **:** snitch. **—squeal** *n.* **—squeal'er** *n.*

squea•mish (skwē'mĭsh) *adj.* **1.** Easily sickened or nauseated. **2.** Easily disgusted or offended **:** prudish. **3.** Excessively fastidious **:** oversensitive. **—squea'mish•ness** *n.*

squee•gee (skwē'jē') *n.* A tool having a rubber or leather blade set perpendicular to a handle, used to remove water from a flat surface, as a window. **—squee'gee'** *v.*

squeeze (skwēz) *v.* **squeezed, squeez•ing. 1.** To press hard on or together **:** compress. **2.** To extract by exerting pressure <*squeeze* juice from an orange> **3.** To extract dishonestly **:** extort. **4.** To make room or passage for by pressure **:** cram. *—n.* **1.** An act or instance of squeezing. **2.** An amount squeezed out. **3.** Financial pressure caused by short-

ages or narrowing economic margins. **—squeez'er** *n.*
squelch (skwĕlch) *v.* To suppress totally : squash. **—squelch** *n.*
squib (skwĭb) *n.* **1. a.** A firecracker. **b.** A firecracker that burns but does not explode. **2.** A short, often witty literary piece.
squid (skwĭd) *n., pl.* **squids** *or* **squid.** A marine cephalopod mollusk of the genera *Loligo, Rossia,* or related genera, having a usu. elongated body, 10 arms surrounding the mouth, and a vestigial internal shell.
squig•gle (skwĭg'əl) *n.* A short, wiggly mark or wavy line. **—squig'gle** *v.* **—squig'gly** *adj.*
squint (skwĭnt) *v.* **1.** To look with partly closed eyes. **2.** To close the eyes partly. **3.** To look to the side. **4.** To suffer from strabismus. **—squint** *n.*
squire (skwīr) *n.* **1.** A young nobleman attendant on and ranking just below a knight. **2.** An English country gentleman. **3.** A local dignitary, as a judge. **4.** A lady's escort. *—v.* **squired, squir•ing.** To accompany as a squire or escort.
squirm (skwûrm) *v.* **1.** To twist about in a writhing motion : wriggle. **2.** To experience or show distress. **—squirm** *n.*
squir•rel (skwûr'əl, skwŭr'-) *n.* A rodent of the genus *Sciurus* or related genera, usu. with gray or reddish-brown fur and a long, flexible, bushy tail.
squirt (skwûrt) *v.* To eject (liquid) quickly in a narrow stream. *—n.* **1.** A device for squirting. **2.** A quantity of liquid squirted. **3.** *Informal.* An impudent person.
squish (skwĭsh) *v.* **1.** To squash. **2.** To emit the sucking sound of soft mud being walked on. **—squish** *n.* **—squish'y** *adj.*
Sr *symbol for* STRONTIUM.
sRNA *n.* Transfer RNA.
stab (stăb) *v.* **stabbed, stab•bing. 1.** To wound or puncture with or as if with a pointed weapon. **2.** To thrust or lunge. *—n.* **1.** A thrust or lunge. **2.** A wound caused by stabbing. **3.** An attempt : try.
sta•bi•lize (stā'bə-līz') *v.* **-lized, -liz•ing. 1.** To make or become stable. **2.** To keep in a stable condition. **—sta'bi•li•za'tion** *n.* **—sta'bi•liz'er** *n.*
sta•ble[1] (stā'bəl) *adj.* **-bler, -blest. 1.** Resisting changes of condition or position. **2.** *Physics.* Having no known mode of decay. —Used of atomic particles. **3.** Unchanging and permanent : enduring. **4.** *Chem.* Not easily modified chemically. **5. a.** Dependable. **b.** Rational <a *stable* person> **—sta•bil'i•ty** (stə-bĭl'ĭ-tē) *n.*
sta•ble[2] (stā'bəl) *n.* **1.** A building for sheltering and feeding domestic animals, esp. horses and cattle. **2.** All of the racehorses belonging to one owner. *—v.* **-bled, -bling.** To keep or put in a stable.
stac•ca•to (stə-kä'tō) *adj.* **1.** *Mus.* Crisply separated. **2.** Composed of short, distinct parts or sounds. **—stac•ca'to** *n. & adv.*
stack (stăk) *n.* **1.** A large, usu. cone-shaped pile of straw or hay left outdoors for storage. **2.** An orderly mass or pile. **3.** A chimney or vertical exhaust pipe. **4. stacks.** The section of a library where most of the books are arranged on shelves. **5.** *Informal.* A large amount. *—v.* **1.** To pile up in a stack. **2.** To fix (e.g., a deck of playing cards) in order to cheat. **—stack up.** To bear comparison.
stack•up (stăk'ŭp') *n.* A number of airplanes awaiting landing instructions and circling at different altitudes.
sta•di•um (stā'dē-əm) *n.* A large, often open structure for holding athletic events.
staff (stăf) *n., pl.* **staffs** *or* **staves** (stāvz). **1.** A rod, pole, or stick, esp.: **a.** A walking stick : cane. **b.** A cudgel : club. **c.** A rod carried as a symbol of authority. **2.** *pl.* **staffs. a.** A group of assistants who aid an executive or director. **b.** A group of military or naval officers who do not participate in combat and who lack the authority to command. **3.** *Mus.* The set of horizontal lines on which notes are written. *—v.* **1.** To furnish with a staff. **2.** To serve on the staff of.
staff•er (stăf'ər) *n. Informal.* A staff member.
stag (stăg) *n.* **1.** The adult male of various deer, esp. the red deer. **2.** A man who attends a social function without a woman. *—adj.* Intended for men only <a *stag* party> *—adv.* Unaccompanied by a woman <went *stag* to the dance>
stage (stāj) *n.* **1.** A scaffold for workers. **2. a.** A raised platform on which dramatic performances are presented. **b.** The acting profession. **3.** The setting for an event. **4.** A resting or stopping place on a journey. **5.** A stagecoach. **6.** A level, degree, or period of time in the evolution of a process <a disease in its early *stages*> **7.** Any of a series of rocket propulsion units. *—v.* **staged, stag•ing. 1.** To produce or direct (a theatrical performance). **2.** To set up and put in motion <*staged* an attack>
stage•coach (stāj'kōch') *n.* A horse-drawn coach once used to transport mail, parcels, and passengers.
stage•craft (stāj'krăft') *n.* Skill in the use of theatrical techniques or devices.
stage•hand (stāj'hănd') *n.* One who works backstage in a theater.
stage-struck (stāj'strŭk') *adj.* Having a passionate desire to become an actor.
stag•ger (stăg'ər) *v.* **1.** To move unsteadily : totter. **2.** To cause to totter or sway. **3.** To lose strength or confidence. **4.** To overwhelm with a severe shock, defeat, or misfortune. **5. a.** To arrange on alternating sides of a median line. **b.** To schedule in overlapping time periods. *—n.* **1.** A staggering gait. **2. staggers** *(sing. in number).* A disease of the nervous system in animals, esp. a cerebrospinal disease of horses marked by loss of coordination.
stag•ger•ing (stăg'ər-ing) *adj.* Overwhelming <*staggering* medical bills> ★ ***syns:*** MIND-BLOWING, MIND-BOGGLING, OVERWHELMING, SPECTACULAR, STUNNING **—stag'ger•ing•ly** *adv.*

stag•nant (stăg′nənt) *adj.* **1.** Not flowing : still <*stagnant* water> **2.** Foul from standing still : stale <*stagnant* air> **3.** Not changing or growing : inactive <a *stagnant* period for sales>

stag•nate (stăg′nāt′) *v.* **-nat•ed, -nat•ing. 1.** To be or become stagnant. **2.** To fail to progress or develop : remain inactive. **—stag•na′tion** *n.*

staid (stād) *adj.* Sedate and reserved.

stain (stān) *v.* **1.** To discolor or become discolored : soil. **2.** To corrupt : taint. **3.** To color with dye. —*n.* **1.** A discolored spot. **2.** A blemish on one's moral character or reputation. **3.** A substance applied esp. to wood that penetrates the surface and imparts color. **—stain′less** *adj.*

stained glass *n.* Glass that is colored esp. for use in windows.

stainless steel *n.* Steel alloyed with chromium so as to inhibit corrosion, oxidation, or rusting.

stair (stâr) *n.* **1. stairs.** A flight of steps. **2.** One of a series of steps.

stair•case (stâr′kās′) *n.* A flight or series of flights of steps and a supporting structure connecting separate levels.

stair•way (stâr′wā′) *n.* A staircase.

stair•well (stâr′wĕl′) *n.* A vertical shaft containing a staircase.

stake (stāk) *n.* **1.** A sharpened piece, esp. of wood, for driving into the ground as a support or marker. **2. a.** A post to which an offender is bound for execution by burning. **b.** Execution by burning at the stake. **3. a.** Money or property risked in a bet or game of chance. **b.** The prize awarded the winner of a contest or race : purse. **4.** A share in an enterprise. —*v.* **staked, stak•ing. 1.** To indicate the boundaries of with or as if with stakes. **2.** To fasten or support with a stake. **3.** To tie to a stake. **4.** To gamble or risk : hazard. **5.** To provide working capital for. **—stake out. 1.** To assign (a police officer) to conduct surveillance of an area. **2.** To establish a stakeout on.

stake•out (stāk′out′) *n.* Police surveillance, as of a building or area.

sta•lac•tite (stə-lăk′tīt′) *n.* A cylindrical or conical deposit that projects downward from the roof of a cavern.

sta•lag•mite (stə-lăg′mīt′) *n.* A cylindrical or conical deposit that projects upward from the floor of a cavern.

stale (stāl) *adj.* **stal•er, stal•est. 1.** Having lost freshness, effervescence, or taste. **2.** Too old or overused to be effective. **3.** Impaired in efficacy or strength. ★ ***syns:*** FLAT, TIRED **—stale** *v.*

stale•mate (stāl′māt′) *n.* **1.** A position in chess in which only the king can move but only into check. **2.** A situation in which no further action can be taken : deadlock. **—stale′mate′** *v.*

stalk[1] (stôk) *n.* **1.** A stem or main axis of a plant. **2.** A slender or elongated support.

stalk[2] (stôk) *v.* **1.** To walk in a stiff, arrogant, or angry manner. **2.** To track (game) in a stealthy manner.

stall (stôl) *n.* **1.** An enclosure for a domestic animal in a barn or shed. **2.** An enclosure for selling or displaying merchandise, as at a fair : booth. **3. a.** An enclosed seat in a church chancel. **b.** A church pew. **4.** *esp. Brit.* A theater seat in the front part of the orchestra. **5.** A sudden loss in the power or effectiveness of an engine. —*v.* **1.** To put or lodge in a stall. **2.** To come or bring to a standstill inadvertently. **3.** To try to put off action through delaying tactics.

stal•lion (stăl′yən) *n.* A full-grown male horse that has not been castrated.

stal•wart (stôl′wərt) *adj.* **1.** Strong : robust. **2.** Steadfast : resolute.

sta•men (stā′mən) *n.* One of the pollen-producing reproductive organs of a flower, usu. consisting of an anther on a stalk.

stam•i•na (stăm′ə-nə) *n.* Endurance.

stam•i•nate (stăm′ə-nət, -nāt′) *adj. Bot.* **1.** Having stamens. **2.** Bearing stamens but no pistils.

stam•mer (stăm′ər) *v.* **1.** To make involuntary pauses or syllabic repetitions while speaking. **2.** To utter or say with a stammer. **—stam′mer** *n.* **—stam′mer•er** *n.*

stamp (stămp) *v.* **1.** To thrust (the foot) down heavily (on). **2.** To imprint or impress with a mark, design, or message. **3.** To put a gummed marker, as a postage stamp, on. **4.** To shape or cut out by forcing into or against a mold or die. —*n.* **1.** An act of stamping. **2. a.** An implement or device for stamping. **b.** An impression made by stamping. **3.** A mark or impression that indicates a fact, as approval or ownership. **4.** A postage stamp. **5.** A characteristic mark.

stam•pede (stăm-pēd′) *n.* **1.** A sudden, headlong rush, esp. of startled animals. **2.** *Can.* A rodeo with fair amusements, as the Calgary Stampede. —*v.* **-ped•ed, -ped•ing. 1.** To act or cause to act impulsively in or as if in a stampede. **2.** To cause to stampede.

stamping ground *n.* A customary or favorite environment.

stance (stăns) *n.* **1.** The position of a standing person or animal. **2.** An emotional or intellectual attitude.

stanch[1] *also* **staunch** (stônch, stŏnch) *v.* **1.** To stop or check the flow of. **2.** To check the flow of blood from (a wound).

stanch[2] (stônch, stŏnch) *adj. var. of* STAUNCH[1].

stan•chion (stăn′chən) *n.* A vertical pole, post, or support.

stand (stănd) *v.* **stood** (stŏŏd), **stand•ing. 1.** To take, be placed in, or maintain an upright or erect position. **2.** To assume or be in a specified position <*stand* straight> **3.** To remain valid, intact, or unchanged <The temperature *stands* at 32°.> **4.** To be situated or placed. **5.** To be in a specified position or degree : rank <*stood* at the head of the class> **6.** To remain stationary. **7.** To take up or maintain an attitude or conviction <*stand* fast> **8. a.** To resist **:** withstand <can *stand* high temperatures> **b.** To endure **:** bear <can't *stand* the suspense> **9.** To undergo <will *stand* trial> **10.** To set on end. —*n.* **1.** The act of standing. **2.** A stop on a performance tour. **3.** A small booth or stall for selling goods. **4.** A position one is prepared to defend <take a *stand*> **5. stands.** The seating area at a stadium or playing field. **6.** A witness stand. **7.** A rack or framework for holding something <a music *stand*> **8.** A growth of plants or trees. **—stand by. 1.** To be loyal to. **2.** To keep **:** fulfill. **3.** To be ready to act, esp. as a substitute. **—stand for.** To represent **:** symbolize. **—stand out.** To be prominent or outstanding. **—stand up. 1.** To prove valid, satisfactory, or durable. **2.** *Informal.* To fail to keep an appointment with <My date *stood* me *up.*>

stan•dard (stăn′dərd) *n.* **1.** A flag, as one serving as the emblem of a nation. **2.** Something accepted as a basis for comparison **:** criterion. **3.** A pedestal on which something is supported. **—stan′dard** *adj.*

stan•dard-bear•er (stăn′dərd-bâr′ər) *n.* **1.** One that bears the colors of a military unit. **2.** One in the forefront of a movement, cause, etc.

stan•dard•ize (stăn′dər-dīz′) *v.* **-ized, -iz•ing.** To cause to conform with a standard. **—stan′dard•i•za′tion** *n.*

standard of living *n.* A measure of the quality and quantity of goods and services enjoyed by a person, group, or nation.

standard time *n.* The time in any of the 24 zones into which the earth is divided longitudinally, usu. the mean solar time at the central meridian of each zone.

stand•by (stănd′bī′) *n., pl.* **-bys. 1.** One that is dependable. **2.** One kept in readiness to serve as a substitute.

stand•ee (stăn-dē′) *n.* One who stands.

stand-in (stănd′ĭn′) *n.* **1.** One who substitutes for an actor during camera and light adjustments. **2.** A substitute.

stand•ing (stăn′dĭng) *n.* **1 a.** Status with respect to achievement or reputation. **b.** High reputation **:** esteem. **2.** Length of time **:** duration. —*adj.* **1.** Remaining upright **:** erect. **2.** Made or performed from an upright position <*standing* jumps> **3.** Permanent and unchanging <a *standing* order> **4.** Not moving **:** stationary. **5.** Not flowing or circulating **:** stagnant.

stand-off (stănd′ôf′, -ŏf′) *n.* A tie, as in a competitive event **:** draw.

stand•off•ish (stănd-ô′fĭsh, -ŏf′ĭsh) *adj.* Not sociable **:** distant.

stand•out (stănd′out′) *n.* One that is extraordinary.

stand•point (stănd′point′) *n.* A point of view.

stand•still (stănd′stĭl′) *n.* A stop <production that came to a *standstill*>

stand•up *or* **stand-up** (stănd′ŭp′) *adj.* **1.** Erect **:** upright. **2.** Of, relating to, or being a performer who works alone and without props <a *standup* comedian>

stank (stăngk) *v. var. p.t. of* STINK.

stan•za (stăn′zə) *n.* One of the divisions of a poem, consisting of 2 or more lines. **—stan•za′ic** (-zā′ĭk) *adj.*

sta•pes (stā′pēz′) *n., pl.* **stapes** *or* **sta•pe•des** (stə-pē′dēz′). One of the 3 small bones of the inner ear.

staph•y•lo•coc•cus (stăf′ə-lō-kŏk′əs) *n., pl.* **-coc•ci** (-kŏk′sī′, -kŏk′ī′). Any of various spherical parasitic bacteria of the genus *Staphylococcus,* causing infections such as boils, septicemia, etc. **—staph′y•lo•coc′cal** (-kŏk′-əl), **staph′y•lo•coc′cic** (-kŏk′sĭk, -kŏk′ĭk) *adj.*

sta•ple[1] (stā′pəl) *n.* **1.** A major commodity grown or produced in a region. **2.** A major trade item in steady demand. **3.** A major element or feature. **4.** Raw material. **5.** Fiber, as of cotton or wool, graded with respect to length or fineness.

sta•ple[2] (stā′pəl) *n.* **1.** A U-shaped metal fastener with pointed ends designed to be driven into a surface to hold something, as a wire. **2.** A thin U-shaped piece of wire used as a fastening for materials such as paper or cloth. **—sta′ple** *v.* **—sta′pler** *n.*

star (stär) *n.* **1.** *Astron.* A self-luminous, self-containing mass of gas. **2.** Any of the celestial bodies that can be seen at night from the earth as usu. twinkling points of light. **3.** A symbol or graphic design that resembles a star. **4. a.** One who plays the leading role in a dramatic performance. **b.** An outstanding performer. **5.** An asterisk. **6. stars.** The constellations of the zodiac believed to influence personal destiny. **7. stars.** The future **:** destiny. —*v.* **starred, star•ring. 1.** To decorate with stars. **2.** To mark with an asterisk. **3.** To play or present in the leading role. **4.** To perform in an outstanding manner. **—star′dom** *n.* **—star′less** *adj.* **—star′ry** *adj.*

star•board (stär′bərd) *n.* The right side of a ship or aircraft facing forward. **—star′board** *adj. & adv.*

starch (stärch) *n.* **1.** Any of various nutrient carbohydrates that occur widely in plants, as potatoes or rice. **2.** A purified form of starch occurring chiefly as a white, tasteless powder used esp. for stiffening fabrics. —*v.* To stiffen (fabric) with starch. **—starch′i•ness** *n.* **—starch′y** *adj.*

stare (stâr) *v.* **stared, star•ing.** To look with an intent, direct gaze. **—stare** *n.* **—star′er** *n.*

star•fish (stär′fĭsh′) *n.* A marine echinoderm of the class Asteroidea, having 5 arms extending from a central disk.

stark (stärk) *adj.* **1.** Bare **:** blunt < the *stark* truth> **2.** Complete **:** total <*stark* poverty> **3.** Forbidding in appearance **:** barren <a *stark* wasteland> —*adv.* Completely <*stark* naked> **—stark′ly** *adv.* **—stark′ness** *n.*

star•let (stär′lĭt) *n.* A young motion-picture actress.

star•light (stär′līt′) *n.* The light produced by the stars.

star•ling (stär′lĭng) *n.* An Old World bird of

the family Sturnidae, with dark, often iridescent plumage, esp. *Sturnus vulgaris,* widely naturalized in the U.S.

star•lit (stär'lĭt') *adj.* Illuminated by the light of the stars.

star•ry-eyed (stär'ē-īd') *adj.* **1.** Naively enthusiastic. **2.** Marked by idealism.

Stars and Stripes *pl.n. (sing. or pl. in number).* The flag of the U.S.

Star-Span•gled Banner (stär'spăng'gəld) *n.* **1.** The flag of the U.S. **2.** The national anthem of the U.S.

star•struck *or* **star-struck** (stär'strŭk') *adj.* Fascinated by fame or famous people.

start (stärt) *v.* **1.** To begin to move, go, or act : commence. **2.** To move with a sudden involuntary motion : jerk. **3.** To put into operation, motion, or action. **4.** To introduce : originate. —*n.* **1.** A beginning. **2.** A sudden involuntarily bodily movement. **3.** A time or place at which to begin. **4.** A position of advantage over another : lead. —**start'er** *n.*

star•tle (stär'tl) *v.* **-tled, -tling. 1.** To cause to make a start, as of surprise. **2.** To fill with sudden surprise. ★ ***syns:*** JOLT, SHOCK —**star'tling•ly** *adv.*

starve (stärv) *v.* **starved, starv•ing. 1.** To suffer or die from hunger. **2.** To cause to starve. **3.** To suffer from deprivation. **4.** To compel or force by withholding. —**star•va'tion** *n.*

starve•ling (stärv'lĭng) *n.* One that is emaciated from or as if from starvation.

stash (stăsh) *v.* To put away or hide in a secret place. —*n.* **1.** A cache of money or valuables. **2.** Something hidden away.

sta•sis (stā'sĭs) *n., pl.* **-ses** (-sēz'). A state of balance, as among opposing forces.

state (stāt) *n.* **1.** A condition or mode of existence. **2.** An emotional or mental condition. **3.** A social position or rank. **4.** A form of government <a fascist *state*> **5.** A body politic, esp. one constituting a nation. **6.** One of the semiautonomous territorial subdivisions of a federal government, as the U.S. —*v.* **stat•ed, stat•ing. 1.** To express verbally. **2.** To establish : fix. —**state'hood'** *n.*

state•craft (stāt'krăft') *n.* The art of leading a country.

state house *n.* A building in which sessions of a state legislature are held.

state•less (stāt'lĭs) *adj.* Not having citizenship in a state or nation.

state•ly (stāt'lē) *adj.* **-li•er, -li•est. 1.** Marked by grace and dignity. **2.** Impressive : grand. —**state'li•ness** *n.*

state•ment (stāt'mənt) *n.* **1.** The act of stating or declaring. **2.** Something stated : declaration. **3.** An abstract of a financial account : bill. **4.** A monthly report sent to a debtor or bank depositor.

state of the art *n.* The highest level of development, as of a device, technique, or science, achieved at a particular time. —**state'-of-the-art'** *adj.*

state•room (stāt'ro͞om', -ro͝om') *n.* A private compartment on a train or ship.

state•side (stāt'sīd') *adj. & adv.* Of, to, or in the continental U.S.

states•man (stāts'mən) *n.* **1.** A leader in national or international affairs. **2.** One noted for disinterested public service. —**states'man•like', states'man•ly** *adj.* —**states'man•ship'** *n.*

states•wom•an (stāts'wo͝om'ən) *n.* **1.** A woman who is a leader in national or international affairs. **2.** A woman noted for disinterested public service.

state•wide (stāt'wīd') *adj. & adv.* Taking place throughout a state.

stat•ic (stăt'ĭk) *adj.* **1. a.** Not in motion : at rest. **b.** Marked by the absence of motion or progress. **2.** *Elect.* Of, relating to, or creating stationary electric charges. **3.** Of, relating to, or produced by random noise in a radio receiver. —*n.* **1.** Random noise in a radio receiver or visible specks on a television screen caused by atmospheric disturbances. **2.** *Slang.* **a.** Back talk. **b.** Obstruction. —**stat'i•cal•ly** *adv.*

sta•tion (stā'shən) *n.* **1.** The place or position where one stands or is directed to stand : post. **2.** The place from which a service is provided or operations are directed <a police *station*> **3.** A scheduled stopping place, as on a railroad or bus line : depot. **4.** Social standing : rank. **5.** A place having radio or television transmission equipment. —*v.* To post or place in a station. ★ ***syns:*** ASSIGN, POST, SET

sta•tion•ar•y (stā'shə-nĕr'ē) *adj.* **1. a.** Not moving. **b.** Not capable of being moved : fixed. **2.** Unchanging.

station break *n.* A pause in a broadcast program to allow for network or station identification.

sta•tion•er (stā'shə-nər) *n.* A person who sells stationery.

sta•tion•er•y (stā'shə-nĕr'ē) *n.* **1.** Writing paper and envelopes. **2.** Writing or typing materials.

station house *n.* **1.** A police station. **2.** A fire station.

station wagon *n.* An automobile having a fairly large interior, usu. a tailgate, and a row of folding or removable seats.

sta•tis•tic (stə-tĭs'tĭk) *n.* **1.** An item of numerical data. **2.** An estimate of a variable, as an average or mean, made on the basis of a sample taken from a larger set of data. —**sta•tis'ti•cal** (-tĭ-kəl) *adj.* —**sta•tis'ti•cal•ly** *adv.*

sta•tis•tics (stə-tĭs'tĭks) *n.* **1.** *(sing. in number).* The branch of mathematics that deals with the organization, analysis, collection, and interpretation of statistical data. **2.** *(pl. in number).* A collection or set of numerical data. —**stat'is•ti'cian** (stăt'ĭ-stĭsh'ən) *n.*

stat•u•ar•y (stăch'o͞o-ĕr'ē) *n., pl.* **-ies. 1.** Statues as a group. **2.** The art of making statues.

stat•ue (stăch'o͞o) *n.* A form or likeness sculpted, modeled, carved, or cast in material such as stone, clay, wood, or bronze.

stat•u•esque (stăch'o͞o-ĕsk') *adj.* Like a statue, esp. in size, grace, or dignity : stately.

stat•u•ette (stăch'o͞o-ĕt') *n.* A small statue.

stat·ure (stăch'ər) *n.* **1.** Natural height of a human or animal body when upright. **2.** A level of development or achievement.

sta·tus (stā'təs, stăt'əs) *n.* **1.** The state of a person or thing as defined by law, regulations, or customs. **2.** A relative or high position, esp. in a social system. **3.** A state of affairs : situation.

sta·tus quo (stā'təs kwō', stăt'əs) *n.* The current state of affairs.

stat·ute (stăch'o͞ot) *n.* **1.** A law enacted by the legislative assembly of a nation or state. **2.** A decree or edict.

statute of limitations *n. Law.* A statute setting a time limit on legal action in certain cases.

stat·u·to·ry (stăch'ə-tôr'ē, -tōr'ē) *adj.* **1.** Of or relating to a statute. **2.** Defined by or regulated by statute.

staunch[1] *also* **stanch** (stônch, stŏnch) *adj.* **1.** Firm and steadfast : loyal <a *staunch* ally> **2.** Solidly built or made. **—staunch'ly** *adv.*

staunch[2] (stônch, stŏnch) *v. var. of* STANCH[1].

stave (stāv) *n.* **1.** One of the narrow strips of wood forming part of the sides of a container, as a barrel. **2.** A heavy stick or pole : staff. **3.** A set of verses : stanza. —*v.* **staved** *or* **stove** (stōv), **stav·ing.** To break a hole in by or as if by puncturing staves. **—stave off.** To hold off : repel.

staves (stāvs) *n. var. pl. of* STAFF.

stay[1] (stā) *v.* **1.** To remain in one place or condition. **2.** To dwell : live. **3.** To pause : wait. **4.** To last : endure. **5.** To stop or halt : check. **6.** To delay (e.g., the carrying out of an order), as by legal action : suspend. **7.** To satisfy temporarily <*stayed* my hunger> **8.** To remain during or through <*stayed* the night> —*n.* **1.** A short visit or sojourn. **2.** A halt or pause. **3.** A postponement, as of an execution.

stay[2] (stā) *v.* To support or brace. —*n.* **1.** A part that props up or braces. **2.** A strip of rigid material, as bone or metal, used to stiffen a garment. **3. stays.** A corset.

stay[3] (stā) *n.* A rope or cable that serves as a brace or support for a mast or spar.

staying power *n.* Stamina : endurance.

stead (stĕd) *n.* **1.** The place or position of another. **2.** Advantage <intelligence that stood him in good *stead*>

stead·fast (stĕd'făst') *adj.* **1.** Not moving : fixed. **2.** Unyieldingly firm in purpose, faith, or attachment : loyal. **—stead'fast'ly** *adv.* **—stead'fast'ness** *n.*

stead·y (stĕd'ē) *adj.* **-i·er, -i·est. 1.** Firmly fixed or placed : stable. **2.** Not faltering : controlled. **3.** Not changing movement, direction, or quality <a *steady* rain> **4.** Not easily excited or upset : composed. **5.** Dependable : reliable. **6.** Regular <a *steady* customer> —*v.* **-ied, -y·ing.** To make or become steady : stabilize. **—stead'i·ly** *adv.* **—stead'i·ness** *n.* **—stead'y** *adv.*

stead·y-state theory (stĕd'ē-stāt') *n.* A cosmological theory that the expansion of the universe is compensated for by the continuous creation of matter.

steak (stāk) *n.* A piece of fish or meat, esp. beef, cut in a thick slice.

steal (stēl) *v.* **stole** (stōl), **sto·len** (stō'lən), **steal·ing. 1.** To take (the property of another) without permission or right. **2.** To take or enjoy secretly or furtively <*steal* a glimpse> **3.** To move or pass imperceptibly or secretly. **4.** *Baseball.* To gain (a base) without the ball being batted. —*n.* **1.** The act of stealing. **2.** *Slang.* A bargain.

stealth (stĕlth) *n.* Secret, surreptitious, or clandestine activity : furtiveness.

stealth·y (stĕl'thē) *adj.* **-i·er, -i·est.** Marked by or acting with stealth. **—stealth'i·ly** *adv.* **—stealth'i·ness** *n.*

steam (stēm) *n.* **1. a.** Water in the gaseous state, esp. when hot. **b.** The mist that forms when hot water vapor cools and condenses. **2.** A heating system in which steam generated in a boiler is piped to radiators. **3.** Energy : power. —*v.* **1.** To generate or emit steam. **2.** To turn into or escape as steam. **3.** To move by or as if by steam power. **4.** To expose to steam, as in cooking. **5.** *Informal.* To become angry : fume. **—steam'y** *adj.*

steam·boat (stēm'bōt') *n.* A steamship.

steam engine *n.* An engine in which the energy of hot steam is converted into mechanical power, esp. one in which the steam expands in a closed cylinder and drives a piston.

steam·er (stē'mər) *n.* **1.** A steamship. **2.** A container in which something is exposed to or treated with steam.

steam·fit·ter (stēm'fĭt'ər) *n.* One who installs and repairs heating, ventilating, refrigerating, or air-conditioning systems.

steam·roll·er (stēm'rō'lər) *n.* A vehicle equipped with a heavy roller for smoothing road surfaces. —*v.* **1.** To smooth or level with a steamroller. **2.** To overwhelm as if with a steamroller.

steam·ship (stēm'shĭp') *n.* A ship powered by steam.

steam shovel *n.* A steam-powered machine for excavating.

ste·a·tite (stē'ə-tīt') *n.* A solid form of talc used in ceramics and insulation.

steed (stēd) *n.* A spirited horse.

steel (stēl) *n.* **1.** Any of various hard, strong alloys of iron and carbon. **2.** A hard, unflinching quality. **3.** Something, as a sword, made of steel. —*v.* **1.** To plate, edge, or tip with steel. **2.** To make hard or strong : strengthen. **—steel'y** *adj.*

steel band *n.* A musical band composed chiefly of steel drums.

steel drum *n.* A metal percussion instrument fashioned from an oil barrel.

steel guitar *n.* A Hawaiian guitar.

steel-trap (stēl'trăp') *adj.* Very quick and keen : trenchant <a *steel-trap* mind>

steel wool *n.* Fine fibers of steel used esp. for cleaning or polishing.

steel·yard (stēl'yärd') *n.* A balance consisting of a scaled arm suspended off center, a hook at the shorter end on which to hang the object being weighed, and a counterbalance at the longer end that can be moved to find the weight.

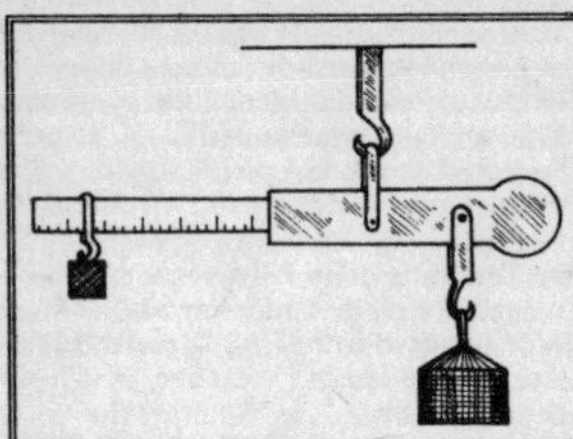

steelyard

steep¹ (stēp) *adj.* **1.** Sharply inclined : precipitous. **2.** Exorbitant. —**steep'ly** *adv.* —**steep'ness** *n.*
steep² (stēp) *v.* **1.** To soak or saturate in a liquid. **2.** To pervade : permeate <*steeped* in tradition>
steep•en (stē'pən) *v.* To make or become steeper.
stee•ple (stē'pəl) *n.* **1.** A tall tower, as one surmounting a church, often ending in a spire. **2.** A spire.
stee•ple•chase (stē'pəl-chās') *n.* A horse race across open land or over an obstacle course. —**stee'ple•chas'er** *n.*
stee•ple•jack (stē'pəl-jăk') *n.* A person who works on high structures, as steeples.
steer¹ (stîr) *v.* **1.** To direct the course of (e.g., a vehicle). **2.** To be guided or capable of being guided. **3.** To fix and travel on (a course). **4.** To direct : guide. —**steer'a•ble** *adj.* —**steers'man** *n.*
steer² (stîr) *n.* A young male of domestic cattle, esp. one castrated and raised for beef.
steer•age (stîr'ĭj) *n.* **1.** The act of steering. **2.** The section of a passenger ship affording the least expensive accommodations.
stein (stīn) *n.* A large mug, esp. for beer.
stel•lar (stĕl'ər) *adj.* **1.** Of, relating to, or consisting of stars. **2.** Of or befitting a star performer. **3.** Outstanding.
stem¹ (stĕm) *n.* **1. a.** The main ascending axis of a plant : stalk or trunk. **b.** A plant part supporting another part, as a flower. **2.** A part resembling a stem <the *stem* of a goblet> **3.** A line of genealogical descent. **4.** The part of a word to which affixes may be added, as to form inflections. —*v.* **stemmed, stem•ming. 1.** To derive from : originate. **2.** To make progress against.
stem² (stĕm) *v.* **stemmed, stem•ming. 1.** To plug up : stop. **2.** To check the flow or advance of : hold back.
stem•ware (stĕm'wâr') *n.* Glassware, as goblets, with stems.
stench (stĕnch) *n.* An offensive smell.
sten•cil (stĕn'səl) *n.* A sheet, as of plastic or cardboard, into which a design or lettering has been cut so that paint or ink applied to the sheet will reproduce the pattern on the surface beneath. —**sten'cil** *v.*
ste•nog•ra•phy (stə-nŏg'rə-fē) *n.* The skill or process of writing in shorthand. —**ste•nog'ra•pher** *n.* —**sten'o•graph'ic** (stĕn'ə-grăf'ĭk) *adj.*
sten•to•ri•an (stĕn-tôr'ē-ən, -tōr'-) *adj.* Very loud : booming.
step (stĕp) *n.* **1. a.** A single complete movement made by raising one foot and putting it down in another spot. **b.** Manner of walking : gait. **2. a.** A distance traversed in taking a step. **b.** A very short distance. **3.** A rest for the foot in ascending or descending. **4. a.** Any of a series of actions or measures taken to accomplish an end or goal. **b.** A stage in a process or degree in a scale. —*v.* **stepped, step•ping. 1. a.** To move by taking steps : walk. **b.** To step in a certain manner <*stepping* lively> **2.** To press the foot down or against. **3.** To measure by stepping. **4.** To make or arrange in or as if in a series of steps. —**step down. 1.** To resign, esp. from a high office. **2.** To reduce, esp. by degrees. —**step up.** To increase, esp. by degrees.
step•broth•er (stĕp'brŭth'ər) *n.* The son of one's stepparent by an earlier marriage.
step•child (stĕp'chīld') *n.* A stepson or stepdaughter.
step•daugh•ter (stĕp'dô'tər) *n.* The daughter of one's spouse by an earlier marriage.
step•fa•ther (stĕp'fä'*th*ər) *n.* One's mother's husband who is not one's natural father.
step•lad•der (stĕp'lăd'ər) *n.* A portable hinged ladder with steps.
step•moth•er (stĕp'mŭ*th*'ər) *n.* One's father's wife who is not one's natural mother.
step•par•ent (stĕp'pâr'ənt, -păr'-) *n.* A stepfather or stepmother.
steppe (stĕp) *n.* A vast arid, grassy plain found esp. in SE Europe and Siberia.
step•ping•stone (stĕp'ĭng-stōn') *n.* **1.** A stone on which to step, as in crossing a brook. **2.** A means of advancement.
step•sis•ter (stĕp'sĭs'tər) *n.* The daughter of one's stepparent by an earlier marriage.
step•son (stĕp'sŭn') *n.* The son of one's spouse by an earlier marriage.
step-up (stĕp'ŭp') *n.* An increase, as in size, amount, or activity.
–ster *suff.* **1.** One that is associated with, creates, or does <song*ster*> **2.** One that is <old*ster*>
stere (stîr) *n.* A unit of volume equal to one cubic meter.
ste•re•o (stĕr'ē-ō', stîr'-) *n., pl.* **-os. 1. a.** A stereophonic sound-reproduction system. **b.** Stereophonic sound. **2.** A stereoscopic system or photograph. —**ste're•o'** *adj.*
ster•e•o•phon•ic (stĕr'ē-ə-fŏn'ĭk, stîr'-) *adj.* Of, being, or used in a system of sound reproduction in which 2 separate channels are utilized in order to produce the effect of 3-dimensional sound distribution. —**ster'e•o•phon'i•cal•ly** *adv.*
ster•e•o•scope (stĕr'ē-ə-skōp', stîr'-) *n.* An

optical device through which 2 slightly different views of a scene are presented, one to each eye, giving a 3-dimensional illusion. —**ster′e•o•scop′ic** (-skŏp′ĭk) *adj.* —**ster′e•o•scop′i•cal•ly** *adv.*

ster•e•os•co•py (stĕr′ē-ŏs′kə-pē, stîr′-) *n.* The act of viewing objects in 3 dimensions.

ster•e•o•type (stĕr′ē-ə-tīp′, stîr′-) *n.* **1.** A conventional, formulaic, usu. highly simplified opinion, conception, or belief. **2.** A metal printing plate cast from a matrix made from a raised surface, as type. —*v.* **1.** To develop a stereotype about. **2.** To print from a stereotype. —**ster′e•o•typ′ic** (-tĭp′ĭk), **ster′e•o•typ′i•cal** *adj.*

ster•ile (stĕr′əl, -īl′) *adj.* **1.** Not capable of reproducing or producing : infertile or unproductive. **2.** Free from microorganisms, esp. those that cause disease. ★ ***syns:*** SANITARY, SANITIZED, STERILIZED —**ste•ril′i•ty** (stə-rĭl′ĭ-tē) *n.*

ster•il•ize (stĕr′ə-līz′) *v.* **-ized, -iz•ing.** To make sterile. —**ster′il•i•za′tion** *n.* —**ster′il•iz′er** *n.*

ster•ling (stûr′lĭng) *n.* **1.** British money. **2. a.** An alloy consisting of 92.5% silver with copper. **b.** Articles, as flatware, made of sterling. —*adj.* **1.** Of or expressed in British money. **2.** Made of sterling silver. **3.** First-rate.

stern[1] (stûrn) *adj.* **1.** Rigid : inflexible. **2.** Grim : forbidding. **3.** Harsh : austere. **4.** Firmly maintained. —**stern′ly** *adv.* —**stern′ness** *n.*

stern[2] (stûrn) *n.* The rear section of a ship or boat.

ster•num (stûr′nəm) *n., pl.* **-na** (-nə) *or* **-nums.** A long flat bone articulating with the cartilages of and forming the support of most of the ribs. —**stern′al** *adj.*

ster•oid (stîr′oid′, stĕr′-) *n.* Any of numerous naturally occurring, fat-soluble organic compounds, including many hormones.

steth•o•scope (stĕth′ə-skōp′) *n.* An instrument for listening to internal bodily sounds.

ste•ve•dore (stē′və-dôr′, -dōr′) *n.* A worker who loads or unloads ships.

stew (sto͞o, styo͞o) *v.* **1.** To cook by slowly boiling : simmer. **2.** *Informal.* To be anxious : worry. —*n.* **1.** A dish, esp. of meat and vegetables, cooked by stewing. **2.** *Informal.* A state of anxiety : worry.

stew•ard (sto͞o′ərd, styo͞o′-) *n.* **1.** One who manages another's financial affairs or property. **2.** A person responsible for the household affairs of a large institution, as an estate. **3.** A ship's officer responsible for provisions and dining arrangements. **4.** An attendant on a ship or aircraft. —**stew′ard•ship′** *n.*

stew•ard•ess (sto͞o′ər-dĭs, styo͞o′-) *n.* A woman flight attendant.

stick (stĭk) *n.* **1.** A slender, often long piece of wood, as a twig or branch. **2.** A cane or walking stick. **3.** Something that resembles a stick <a *stick* of dynamite> **4. sticks.** *Informal.* A rural area. **5.** *Informal.* A spiritless or dull person. —*v.* **stuck** (stŭk), **stick•ing. 1.** To pierce or prick with a sharply pointed object. **2. a.** To fasten by pushing in a pointed object. **b.** To impale. **3.** To attach with or as if with an adhesive, as glue. **4. a.** To be or cause to be fixed and unable to move. **b.** To become obstructed or jammed. **5. a.** To remain attached : adhere or cling. **b.** To remain firm, resolute, loyal, or faithful. **6.** To extend, project, or protrude. —**stick up.** To rob, esp. at gunpoint. —**stick up for.** To defend : support.

stick•er (stĭk′ər) *n.* **1.** One that sticks. **2.** An adhesive label. **3.** A thorn or barb.

stick-in-the-mud (stĭk′ĭn-*th*ə-mŭd′) *n. Informal.* One lacking initiative, imagination, or enthusiasm.

stick•le•back (stĭk′əl-băk′) *n.* A small freshwater or marine fish of the family Gasterosteidae, with erectile spines along the back.

stick•ler (stĭk′lər) *n.* One who insists on meticulous observance of detail.

stick shift *n.* A manually operated gearshift on an automobile.

stick•up (stĭk′ŭp′) *n. Slang.* A robbery, esp. at gunpoint.

stick•y (stĭk′ē) *adj.* **-i•er, -i•est. 1.** Having the property of sticking : adhesive. **2.** Very damp and warm : muggy. **3.** *Informal.* Unpleasant or difficult. ★ ***syns:*** HUMID, MUGGY, SOGGY

stiff (stĭf) *adj.* **1.** Not flexible or pliant. **2.** Not moving or functioning with ease. **3.** Stretched tight : taut. **4.** Rigidly formal. **5.** Not flowing easily : thick <a *stiff* batter> **6.** Strong : powerful <a *stiff* current> **7.** Difficult, laborious, or rigorous. **8.** Harsh : stern. **9.** Excessively high <a *stiff* price> ★ ***syns:*** STARCHY, STILTED, WOODEN —**stiff′ly** *adv.* —**stiff′ness** *n.*

stiff•en (stĭf′ən) *v.* To make or become stiff or stiffer. —**stiff′en•er** *n.*

stiff-necked (stĭf′nĕkt′) *adj.* Obstinate.

sti•fle[1] (stī′fəl) *v.* **-fled, -fling. 1.** To smother. **2.** To suffocate. **3.** To put out : extinguish. **4.** To cut off (e.g., the voice). **5.** To keep back : suppress <*stifle* a yawn>

sti•fle[2] (stī′fəl) *n.* A leg joint of certain quadrupeds, as the horse, analogous to the human knee.

stig•ma (stĭg′mə) *n., pl.* **stig•ma•ta** (stĭg-mä′tə, stĭg′mə-) *or* **-mas. 1.** A mark of infamy or disgrace. **2.** *pl.* **-mas.** *Bot.* The apex of the pistil of a flower, on which pollen is deposited at pollination. **3. stigmata.** Marks resembling the crucifixion wounds of Jesus. —**stig•mat′ic** (stĭg-măt′ĭk) *adj.*

stig•ma•tize (stĭg′mə-tīz′) *v.* **-tized, -tiz•ing. 1.** To brand as shameful or dishonorable. **2.** To mark with a stigma.

stile (stīl) *n.* A set of steps for crossing a wall or fence.

sti•let•to (stĭ-lĕt′ō) *n., pl.* **-tos** *or* **-toes.** A small dagger with a slender blade that tapers to a sharp point.

still[1] (stĭl) *adj.* **1.** Quiet : silent. **2.** Devoid of movement : stationary. **3.** Calm : peaceful. **4.** Of, relating to, or being a static photograph rather than a motion picture. —*n.* **1.** Quiet : silence. **2.** A still photograph, esp. one from a scene of a motion picture. —*adv.* **1.** Without motion <stood *still*> **2.** Up to or at the time indicated <*still* alive> **3.** Even or yet <*still* angrier> **4.** All the same : nevertheless. **—still** *v.* **—still'ness** *n.*

still² (stĭl) *n.* **1.** An apparatus for distilling liquids, esp. alcohols. **2.** A distillery.

still•birth (stĭl'bûrth') *n.* The birth of a dead fetus.

still•born (stĭl'bôrn') *adj.* Dead at birth.

still life *n., pl.* **still lifes.** A painting or photograph of inanimate objects, as flowers.

stilt (stĭlt) *n.* **1.** One of a pair of long, slender poles, each with a foot support, used for walking. **2.** A supporting pole for a structure that is raised above the level of the ground or water.

stilt•ed (stĭl'tĭd) *adj.* Stiffly formal.

Stil•ton (stĭl'tən) *n.* A rich, waxy cheese with a blue-green mold.

stim•u•lant (stĭm'yə-lənt) *n.* **1.** An agent that temporarily arouses or accelerates physiological or organic activity. **2.** A stimulus or incentive. **3.** An alcoholic beverage. **—stim'u•lant** *adj.*

stim•u•late (stĭm'yə-lāt') *v.* **-lat•ed, -lat•ing. 1.** To excite to activity or to heightened action. **2.** To act or serve as a stimulant or stimulus. **—stim'u•la'tion** *n.* **—stim'u•la'tive** *adj.*

stim•u•lus (stĭm'yə-ləs) *n., pl.* **-li** (-lī'). Something that stimulates. ★ ***syns:*** CATALYST, IMPETUS, IMPULSE, INCENTIVE, MOTIVATION, SPUR, STIMULANT

sting (stĭng) *v.* **stung** (stŭng), **sting•ing. 1.** To wound or prick painfully with or as if with a sharply pointed part or organ, as that of certain insects. **2.** To feel or cause to feel a sharp, smarting pain. **3.** To cause to suffer in the mind or feelings. ★ ***syns:*** BITE, BURN, SMART —*n.* **1.** An act of stinging. **2.** A wound or mark caused by or as if by stinging. **3.** A sharp, piercing organ or part, as of a bee, often ejecting a venomous secretion. **—sting'er** *n.*

sting•ray (stĭng'rā') *n.* A ray of the family Dasyatidae, having a whiplike tail with a venomous spine capable of inflicting severe injury.

stin•gy (stĭn'jē) *adj.* **-gi•er, -gi•est. 1.** Reluctant to give or spend. **2.** Skimpy : meager. ★ ***syns:*** CHEAP, CLOSE, MEAN, MISERLY, NIGGARDLY, PARSIMONIOUS, PENURIOUS, TIGHT, TIGHTFISTED **—stin'gi•ly** *adv.* **—stin'gi•ness** *n.*

stink (stĭngk) *v.* **stank** (stăngk) *or* **stunk** (stŭngk), **stunk, stink•ing. 1.** To give off a foul odor. **2. a.** To be highly offensive. **b.** To be in very bad repute. —*n.* A foul odor : stench **—stink'er** *n.*

stink•bug (stĭngk'bŭg') *n.* An insect of the family Pentatomidae, having a flattened body and emitting a foul odor.

stint (stĭnt) *v.* **1.** To restrict or limit. **2.** To be sparing or frugal. ★ ***syns:*** PINCH, SCRAPE, SCRIMP, SKIMP —*n.* **1.** An allotted amount of work. **2.** A restriction : limit. **3.** A period of time spent in an activity.

sti•pend (stī'pĕnd', -pənd) *n.* A regular fixed payment, as a salary or allowance.

stip•ple (stĭp'əl) *v.* **-pled, -pling. 1.** To draw, engrave, or paint in dots or short strokes. **2.** To apply (e.g., paint) in dots or short strokes. **—stip'ple** *n.*

stip•u•late (stĭp'yə-lāt') *v.* **-lat•ed, -lat•ing. 1.** To specify as a condition of an agreement. **2.** To make an agreement. ★ ***syns:*** DETAIL, PARTICULARIZE, SPECIFY **—stip'u•la'tion** *n.*

stir¹ (stûr) *v.* **stirred, stir•ring. 1.** To mix by passing an implement through in a repeated circular motion. **2.** To move or cause to move slightly. **3.** To incite, provoke, or agitate. **4.** To excite the emotions of. —*n.* **1.** The act of stirring. **2.** A commotion : fuss. **—stir'rer** *n.*

stir² (stûr) *n. Slang.* Prison.

stir-fry (stûr'frī') *v.* To fry (e.g., vegetables) quickly over high heat in a small amount of oil while stirring continuously.

stir•ring (stûr'ĭng) *adj.* **1.** Exciting : thrilling. **2.** Vigorous : lively.

stir•rup (stûr'əp, stĭr'-) *n.* A flat-based ring or loop hung from a horse's saddle to support the rider's foot.

stitch (stĭch) *n.* **1.** A single loop formed by a threaded needle, as in sewing. **2.** A single loop of yarn or thread around a knitting needle or crochet hook. **3.** A style of arranging the threads in sewing, knitting, or crocheting. **4.** A sudden sharp pain in the side. —*v.* **1.** To fasten or join with or as if with stitches. **2.** To make stitches : sew.

stoat (stōt) *n., pl.* **stoats** *or* **stoat.** *esp. Brit.* The ermine, esp. in its brown color phase.

stock (stŏk) *n.* **1.** The supply of goods kept on hand by a merchant or commercial establishment. **2.** *(sing. or pl. in number).* Animals kept or raised on a farm : livestock. **3. a.** A line of descent. **b.** The original from which a group of animals or plants is descended. **4.** The raw material used to make something. **5.** The broth from boiled meat or fish. **6.** A wooden supporting structure, block, or frame, as the part of a rifle to which the barrel is attached. **7.** The shares of a corporation. **8. stocks.** A pillory. **9.** A theatrical stock company. **10. a.** An assessment : estimate <took *stock* of the situation> **b.** Confidence or credence <put no *stock* in the rumor> —*v.* **1.** To provide with stock : supply. **2.** To gather and store a supply of something. —*adj.* **1.** Kept in stock. **2.** Standard <a *stock* response>

stock•ade (stŏ-kād') *n.* A barrier of upright posts set side by side in the ground for defense or imprisonment.

stock•bro•ker (stŏk'brō'kər) *n.* A broker who buys and sells securities.

stock car *n.* **1.** A car of a standard make specially equipped and modified for racing. **2.** A railroad car for carrying livestock.

stock company *n.* A group of actors and technicians attached to a single theater and performing in repertory.

stock exchange *n.* **1.** A place where securities, as stocks or bonds, are bought and sold. **2.** An association of stockbrokers.

stock•hold•er (stŏk′hōl′dər) *n.* A person who owns stock in a company.
stock•ing (stŏk′ĭng) *n.* A close-fitting, usu. knitted covering for the foot and leg.
stock market *n.* **1.** A stock exchange. **2.** The purchase and sale of stocks.
stock•pile (stŏk′pīl′) *n.* A supply stored for future use. **—stock′pile′** *v.*
stock-still (stŏk′stĭl′) *adj.* Motionless.
stock•y (stŏk′ē) *adj.* **-i•er, -i•est. 1.** Built solidly **:** sturdy. **2.** Plump **:** chubby.
stock•yard (stŏk′yärd′) *n.* A yard in which livestock is temporarily kept until slaughtered or shipped.
stodg•y (stŏj′ē) *adj.* **-i•er, -i•est. 1.** Dull and commonplace. **2.** Pompous **:** stuffy.
sto•ic (stō′ĭk) *also* **sto•i•cal** (-ĭ-kəl) *adj.* Apparently indifferent to or unaffected by pleasure or pain **:** impassive. **—sto′ic** *n.* **—sto′i•cal•ly** *adv.* **—sto′i•cism** *n.*
stoke (stōk) *v.* **stoked, stok•ing. 1.** To stir up and feed a fire. **2.** To feed fuel to and tend (a furnace). **—stok′er** *n.*
stole[1] (stōl) *n.* **1.** A long, narrow strip of linen or silk worn about the neck by priests and bishops. **2.** A long scarf of cloth or fur worn about a woman's shoulders.
stole[2] (stōl) *v. p.t. of* STEAL.
sto•len (stō′lən) *v. p.p. of* STEAL.
stol•id (stŏl′ĭd) *adj.* Feeling or exhibiting little emotion **:** apathetic. **—sto•lid′i•ty** (stə-lĭd′ĭ-tē) *n.* **—stol′id•ly** *adv.*
stom•ach (stŭm′ək) *n.* **1.** The enlarged saclike portion of the alimentary canal into which food passes from the esophagus. **2.** The abdomen. **3.** An appetite for food. **4.** A desire **:** inclination. —*v.* To tolerate.
stom•ach•ache (stŭm′ək-āk′) *n.* Abdominal pain.
sto•mach•ic (stə-măk′ĭk) *adj.* **1.** Of or relating to the stomach. **2.** Stimulating digestion in the stomach. **—sto•mach′ic** *n.*
stomp (stômp, stŏmp) *v.* To trample heavily (on) **:** stamp. —*n.* **1.** The act of stomping. **2.** A jazz dance marked by a rhythmical and heavy stamp.
stone (stōn) *n.* **1. a.** Hard or compacted mineral or earthy matter **:** rock. **b.** A small piece of this material. **2.** A gem. **3.** A seed, as of a cherry or plum, with a hard covering **:** pit. **4.** A hard mass of mineral matter that collects in a hollow bodily organ, as the kidney. **5.** *pl.* **stone.** A British unit of weight equal to 6.35 kgms or 14 lbs avoirdupois. —*v.* **stoned, ston•ing. 1.** To hurl or kill with stones. **2.** To remove the stones from. **—ston′y** *adj.*
Stone Age *n.* The earliest known period of human culture, marked by the use of stone implements and weapons.
stoned (stōnd) *adj. Slang.* **1.** Drunk. **2.** Being under the influence of a drug.
stone's throw *n.* A short distance.
stone•ware (stōn′wâr′) *n.* Heavy pottery.
stood (stŏŏd) *v. p.t. & p.p. of* STAND.
stooge (stōōj) *n.* **1.** The straight man to a comedian. **2.** Someone whose actions are controlled by another.
stool (stōōl) *n.* **1.** A backless and armless single seat. **2.** A low support on which to rest the feet. **3. a.** A toilet. **b.** Fecal matter.
stool pigeon *n. Slang.* **1.** A person functioning as a decoy. **2.** An informer, esp. for the police.
stoop[1] (stōōp) *v.* **1.** To bend forward from the waist. **2.** To lower oneself **:** condescend. —*n.* **1.** An act of stooping. **2.** A stooping posture.
stoop[2] (stōōp) *n.* A small platform or porch leading to the entrance of a house.
stop (stŏp) *v.* **stopped, stop•ping. 1.** To cease or cause to cease moving, acting, or operating. **2.** To close (an opening) by filling in, covering over, or plugging up. **3.** To obstruct or block. **4.** To desist from what one is doing <*stopped* reading> **5.** To halt for a brief visit or stay. ★ ***syns:*** CEASE, DESIST, DISCONTINUE, HALT, QUIT —*n.* **1. a.** An act of stopping. **b.** The state of being stopped **:** cessation. **2.** A point of completion **:** end. **3.** A stay or visit, as during a trip. **4.** A place stopped at. **5.** Something, as a plug, that obstructs or blocks. **6. a.** A tuned set of organ pipes producing tones similar in timbre. **b.** A knob, key, or pull that regulates such pipes. **—stop′page** *n.*
stop•cock (stŏp′kŏk′) *n.* A valve that regulates the flow of fluid through a pipe.
stop•gap (stŏp′găp′) *n.* An improvised substitute or temporary expedient.
stop•light (stŏp′līt′) *n.* **1.** A traffic signal. **2.** A light on the rear of a vehicle activated when the brakes are applied.
stop•o•ver (stŏp′ō′vər) *n.* **1.** A stop in the course of a journey. **2.** A place visited briefly during a journey.
stop•per (stŏp′ər) *n.* A device, as a cork or plug, for closing an opening.
stop•watch (stŏp′wŏch′) *n.* A watch with a hand that can be instantly started and stopped for exact measurement of time, as during a race.
stor•age (stôr′ĭj, stōr′-) *n.* **1. a.** The act of storing. **b.** The state of being stored. **c.** A space for storing goods. **2.** *Computer Sci.* The part of a computer that stores information for subsequent use or retrieval.
storage battery *n.* A group of rechargeable electric cells that function as a unit.
store (stôr, stōr) *n.* **1.** An establishment offering goods for sale. **2.** A supply set aside for future use. **3.** A storehouse. **4.** A great number or quantity **:** abundance. —*v.* **stored, stor•ing. 1.** To set aside or reserve for future use. **2.** To put away for safekeeping, as in a warehouse.
store•front (stôr′frŭnt′, stōr′-) *n.* **1.** The side of a store that faces a street. **2.** A room or suite of rooms on a storefront.
store•house (stôr′hous′, stōr′-) *n.* **1.** A building for the storage of goods **:** warehouse. **2.** An abundant source or supply.
store•keep•er (stôr′kē′pər, stōr′-) *n.* One who runs a retail store or shop.
store•room (stôr′rōōm′, -rŏŏm′, stōr′-) *n.* A room in which goods or supplies are stored.

sto•rey (stôr′ē, stôr′ē) *n. esp. Brit. var. of* STORY².
sto•ried (stôr′ēd, stōr′-) *adj.* Famous in story or history.
stork (stôrk) *n.* A large wading bird of the family Ciconiidae, with long legs and a long straight bill.
storm (stôrm) *n.* **1.** An atmospheric disturbance manifested in strong winds accompanied by rain, snow, hail, or sleet. **2.** A strong outburst or violent disturbance. **3.** A sudden, violent attack on a fortified place. —*v.* **1. a.** To blow forcefully. **b.** To rain, snow, hail, or sleet. **2.** To be very angry : rant and rave. **3.** To move tumultuously or angrily. **4.** To capture or try to capture by storm. —**storm′i•ness** *n.* —**storm′y** *adj.*
storm door *n.* An outer door added for protection against inclement weather.
storm window *n.* An outer window placed over an ordinary window to protect against inclement weather.
sto•ry¹ (stôr′ē, stōr′ē) *n., pl.* **-ries. 1.** A narration of an event or series of events. **2.** The plot of a narrative or dramatic work. **3.** A report, statement, or allegation of facts. **4.** A news article or broadcast. **5.** An anecdote. **6.** A lie.
sto•ry² (stôr′ē, stōr′ē) *n., pl.* **-ries.** One of the horizontal divisions of a building.
sto•ry•book (stôr′ē-bo͝ok′, stōr′-) *n.* A book containing a collection of stories, usu. for children.
sto•ry•tell•er (stôr′ē-tĕl′ər, stōr′-) *n.* **1.** One who tells or writes stories. **2.** *Informal.* A liar. —**sto′ry•tell′ing** *n.*
sto•tin•ka (stō-tĭng′kə) *n., pl.* **-ki** (-kē). See table at CURRENCY.
stoup (sto͞op) *n.* A font for holy water at the entrance of a church.
stout (stout) *adj.* **1.** Determined, bold, or brave. **2.** Physically strong : sturdy. **3.** Solid : substantial. **4.** Corpulent. **5.** Forceful : powerful. **6.** Staunch : firm. —*n.* A heavy, very dark beer or ale. —**stout′ly** *adv.*
stout•heart•ed (stout′här′tĭd) *adj.* Brave : courageous.
stove¹ (stōv) *n.* An apparatus that provides heat for warmth or cooking, using either fuel or electricity as a source of power.
stove² (stōv) *v. var. p.t. & p.p. of* STAVE.
stove•pipe (stōv′pīp′) *n.* A pipe, usu. of thin sheet iron, used to carry smoke or fumes from a stove to a chimney.
stow (stō) *v.* To put away, esp. in a neat, compact way. —**stow away. 1.** To store so as to be hidden. **2.** To be a stowaway.
stow•a•way (stō′ə-wā′) *n.* A person who hides aboard a vehicle, as a ship or aircraft, to avoid paying for passage.
stra•bis•mus (strə-bĭz′məs) *n.* An abnormality of the eyes in which one eye cannot focus with the other on an object.
strad•dle (străd′l) *v.* **-dled, -dling. 1.** To stand or sit astride (of). **2.** To appear to be in accord with both sides of an issue. —**strad′dle** *n.* —**strad′dler** *n.*
strafe (strāf) *v.* **strafed, straf•ing.** To attack (e.g., ground troops) with automatic weapon fire from low-flying aircraft.
strag•gle (străg′əl) *v.* **-gled, -gling. 1.** To fall behind. **2.** To proceed or spread out in a scattered or irregular group. —**strag′gler** *n.* —**strag′gly** *adj.*
straight (strāt) *adj.* **1.** Being without bends, curves, crooks, or angles. **2.** Not deviating from the proper or correct course <a *straight* thinker> **3.** Being in correct sequence or arrangement. **4.** Upright : honorable. **5.** Not diluted : pure <*straight* vodka> **6.** *Slang.* **a.** Conventional or conservative. **b.** Heterosexual. **c.** SQUARE 6. —*adv.* **1.** In a straight line : directly. **2.** In an erect posture : upright. **3.** Without detour or delay. **4.** Without circumlocution : candidly. —*n.* **1.** A straight line, part, piece, or position. **2.** A numerical sequence of 5 cards of various suits in a poker hand. —**straight′ly** *adv.* —**straight′ness** *n.*
straight angle *n.* An angle of 180°.
straight-a•way (străt′ə-wā′) *n.* A straight course, stretch, or track.
straight•edge (strāt′ĕj′) *n.* A rigid strip, as of wood, with a straight edge for testing or drawing straight lines.
straight•en (strāt′n) *v.* To make or become straight.
straight face *n.* A face betraying no emotion. —**straight′faced′** *adj.*
straight•for•ward (strāt-fôr′wərd) *adj.* **1.** Moving in a straight line : direct. **2.** Honest : candid.
straight-jack•et (strāt′jăk′ĭt) *n. var. of* STRAITJACKET.
straight man *n.* An entertainer serving as a foil for a comedian.
straight•way (strāt′wā′, -wā′) *adv.* At once : immediately.
strain¹ (strān) *v.* **1.** To draw or stretch tight. **2.** To exert to the limit. **3.** To injure by overuse or overexertion : wrench <*strain* a muscle> **4.** To force or stretch beyond the usual or proper limit. **5.** To pass or remove by passing through a strainer : filter. —*n.* **1.** Great tension or exertion, as of the emotions. **2.** An injury resulting from excessive effort or use. **3.** *Physics.* A deformation caused by stress.
strain² (strān) *n.* **1. a.** Ancestry : descent. **b.** A group or type having the same ancestry or line of descent. **2. a.** An inborn or inherited characteristic or tendency. **b.** A streak : trace. **3.** A musical tune.
strain•er (strā′nər) *n.* A device for separating liquids from solids.
strait (strāt) *n.* **1.** A narrow passage that connects 2 bodies of water. **2.** *often* **straits.** A situation of difficulty, perplexity, distress, or need. —*adj Archaic.* **1.** Narrow or constricted. **2.** Strict.
strait•en (strāt′n) *v.* **1.** To confine : limit. **2.** To cause to undergo hardship.
strait•jack•et *also* **straight•jack•et** (strāt′jăk′ĭt) *n.* **1.** A jacketlike garment of strong material used to bind the arms tightly

against the body as a means of restraining a violent or unmanageable patient or prisoner.
strait-laced (strāt-lāst′) *adj.* Strict in matters of behavior or morality.
strand¹ (strănd) *n.* Land bordering a body of water : shore. —*v.* **1.** To drive or be driven ashore. **2.** To put or leave in a helpless or difficult position.
strand² (strănd) *n.* **1.** Fibers or filaments twisted together to form a cable, rope, thread, or yarn. **2.** A single filament <a *strand* of hair> **3.** Something, as a string of pearls, that is plaited or twisted into a ropelike length.
strange (strānj) *adj.* **strang•er, strang•est. 1.** Previously unknown : new. **2. a.** Out of the ordinary : unusual. **b.** Peculiar : odd. **3.** Not of one's own kind, environment, or locality : exotic. **4.** Inexperienced : unacquainted. ★ ***syns:*** ECCENTRIC, ODD, PECULIAR, QUAINT, QUEER, UNUSUAL —**strange′ly** *adv.* —**strange′ness** *n.*
strang•er (strān′jər) *n.* **1.** One who is neither friend nor acquaintance. **2.** A foreigner. **3.** A newcomer.
stran•gle (străng′gəl) *v.* **-gled, -gling. 1. a.** To kill by choking : throttle. **b.** To smother. **2.** To repress, suppress, or stifle. —**stran′gler** *n.*
stran•gle•hold (străng′gəl-hōld′) *n.* **1.** An illegal wrestling hold that chokes an opponent. **2.** Something that restricts or suppresses freedom or progress.
stran•gu•late (străng′gyə-lāt′) *v.* **-lat•ed, -lat•ing.** *Pathol.* To compress, constrict, or obstruct so as to cut off circulation. —**stran′gu•la′tion** *n.*
strap (străp) *n.* A long, narrow strip of pliant material, as leather, used esp. for holding or fastening objects together. —*v.* **strapped, strap•ping. 1.** To bind or fasten with a strap. **2.** To flog with a strap. **3.** To sharpen (e.g., a razor).
strap•hang•er (străp′hang′ər) *n.* A passenger, as on a bus or subway, who grips a hanging strap for support.
strap•less (străp′lĭs) *adj.* Having no straps and esp. no shoulder straps.
strapped (străpt) *adj. Informal.* Having little or no money.
strap•ping (străp′ĭng) *adj.* Tall and strong.
stra•ta (strā′tə, străt′ə) *n. var. pl. of* STRATUM.
strat•a•gem (străt′ə-jəm) *n.* **1.** A military maneuver intended to surprise or deceive an enemy. **2.** A deception.
strat•e•gy (străt′ə-jē) *n., pl.* **-gies. 1.** The science or art of military command as applied to the general planning and conduct of full-scale combat operations. **2.** A plan of action, esp. for attaining a goal. —**stra•te′gic** (strə-tē′jĭk) *adj.* —**strat′e•gist** *n.*
strat•i•fy (străt′ə-fī′) *v.* **-fied, -fy•ing.** To form or lay down in layers or strata. —**strat′i•fi•ca′tion** *n.*
stra•tig•ra•phy (strə-tĭg′rə-fē) *n.* The study of rock strata. —**strat′i•graph′ic** (străt′ĭ-grăf′ĭk), **strat′i•graph′i•cal** *adj.*
strat•o•sphere (străt′ə-sfîr′) *n.* The part of the earth's atmosphere above the troposphere and below the mesophere. —**strat′o•spher′ic** *adj.*
stra•tum (strā′təm, străt′əm) *n., pl.* **-ta** (-tə) or **-tums. 1.** A horizontal layer, as one of a number of layers of rock of the same kind. **2.** A social level of persons with similar social, cultural, or economic status.
straw (strô) *n.* **1. a.** Stalks of grain, as wheat or oats, after threshing. **b.** A single stalk of threshed grain. **2.** A slender tube for sucking up a liquid. **3.** Something of little value or importance. —*adj.* **1.** Of the color of straw : yellowish. **2.** Made of straw. **3.** Of little value or force : unimportant.
straw•ber•ry (strô′bĕr′ē) *n.* **1.** Any of various low-growing plants of the genus *Fragaria,* with white flowers and red, fleshy fruit. **2.** The edible fruit of the strawberry.
straw boss *n. Informal.* A worker who acts as a boss or assistant foreman in addition to regular duties.
straw•flow•er (strô′flou′ər) *n.* An Australian plant, *Helichrysum bracteatum,* having flowers with variously colored bracts that retain their color when dried.
straw vote *n.* An unofficial poll or vote indicating the trend of political opinion.
stray (strā) *v.* **1.** To wander : roam. **2.** To deviate from a course : go astray. **3.** To digress. —*n.* A person or animal that has strayed and is lost. —*adj.* **1.** Strayed or having strayed : lost. **2.** Scattered <a few *stray* crumbs> —**stray′er** *n.*
streak (strēk) *n.* **1. a.** A mark, as a line, that differs in color or texture from its surroundings. **b.** A bolt of lightning. **2.** A character trait <a mean *streak*> **3.** *Informal.* A brief stretch : run <a *streak* of good luck> —*v.* **1.** To mark or become marked with streaks. **2.** To move rapidly : rush. —**streak′er** *n.* —**streak′y** *adj.*
stream (strēm) *n.* **1.** A body of water running over the earth's surface in a channel. **2.** A steady flow of a fluid. **3.** A continuous succession or flow. —*v.* **1.** To flow in or as if in a stream. **2.** To pour forth a stream of liquid. **3.** To move like a flowing stream. **4.** To wave or float outward <flags that *streamed* in the breeze>
stream•bed (strēm′bĕd′) *n.* The channel through which a natural stream of water runs or once ran.
stream•er (strē′mər) *n.* **1. a.** A long, narrow banner, flag, or pennant. **b.** A long, flowing strip of material. **2.** A newspaper headline running across a full page.
stream•lined (strēm′līnd′) *adj.* **1.** Designed or configured to offer minimum resistance to fluid flow. **2.** Improved in efficiency or look : simplified or modernized. —**stream′line′** *v.*
stream•lin•er (strēm′lī′nər) *n.* A streamlined passenger train.
street (strēt) *n.* **1.** A public thoroughfare in a city or town. **2.** The people living, working, or gathering in or along a street.

street•car (strēt′cär′) *n.* A car on rails that provides public transportation usu. along the streets.

street•walk•er (strēt′wô′kər) *n.* A prostitute who solicits in the street.

street•wise (strēt′wīz′) *adj.* Capable of surviving in the frequently violent environment of a large city.

strength (strĕngkth, strĕngth) *n.* **1.** The quality, state, or property of being strong : power. **2. a.** The power to resist force, stress, or wear. **b.** The power to resist attack. **3.** Concentration or potency, as of a drug. **4.** Intensity. **5.** Firmness : toughness. **6.** A source of power or force. **7.** Numerical force <a battalion at half *strength*>

strength•en (strĕngk′thən, strĕng′-) *v.* To make or become strong or stronger. **—strength′en•er** *n.*

stren•u•ous (strĕn′yo͞o-əs) *adj.* Requiring or marked by vigorous effort or exertion. **—stren′u•ous•ly** *adv.*

strep throat (strĕp) *n.* A throat infection caused by streptococci and marked by fever and inflammation of the tonsils.

strep•to•coc•cus (strĕp′tə-kŏk′əs) *n., pl.* **-coc•ci** (-kŏk′sī′, -kŏk′ī′). Any of various round to ovoid pathogenic bacteria of the genus *Streptococcus,* occurring in pairs or chains. **—strep′to•coc′cal** *adj.*

strep•to•my•cin (strĕp′tə-mī′sĭn) *n.* An antibiotic produced from mold cultures of bacteria of the genus *Streptomyces* and used esp. in the treatment of tuberculosis.

stress (strĕs) *n.* **1.** Importance or emphasis. **2.** Emphasis placed on a sound or syllable. **3.** A force that tends to strain or deform. **4.** Mental, emotional, or physical tension, strain, or distress. *—v.* **1.** To put emphasis on. **2.** To subject to strain or pressure. **3.** To accent. **—stress′ful** *adj.*

stretch (strĕch) *v.* **1. a.** To draw out to the full or a fuller length, breadth, or extent. **b.** To become or be capable of becoming stretched. **2.** To extend or cause to extend, as from one place to another. **3.** To put forth : hold out. **4.** To exert to the utmost : strain. **5.** To extend beyond proper or reasonable limits. **—6.** To prolong. *—n.* **1.** The act of stretching or state of being stretched. **2.** The degree to which something can be stretched. **3.** A continuous or unbroken expanse of space or time. **4.** A straight section of a racecourse, esp. the section just before the finish line. **—stretch′a•ble** *adj.* **—stretch′y** *adj.*

stretch•er (strĕch′ər) *n.* **1.** One that stretches. **2.** A litter, usu. of canvas stretched over a frame, for transporting the sick, wounded, or dead.

strew (stro͞o) *v.* **strewed, strewed** *or* **strewn** (stro͞on), **strew•ing. 1.** To scatter here and there. **2.** To cover by scattering. **3.** To be or become dispersed.

stri•a (strī′ə) *n., pl.* **stri•ae** (strī′ē′). **1.** A shallow groove or channel. **2.** A thin line or band, esp. one of a group that are parallel. **—stri′at′ed** *adj.* **—stri•a′tion** *n.*

strick•en (strĭk′ən) *v. var. p.p. of* STRIKE. *—adj.* **1.** Struck or injured, as by an arrow or bullet. **2.** Afflicted with strong emotion, illness, or trouble.

strict (strĭkt) *adj.* **1.** Exact : precise. **2.** Kept within specific and narrow limits. **3. a.** Imposing rigorous standards. **b.** Rigorously maintained or enforced : stringent. **—strict′ly** *adv.* **—strict′ness** *n.*

stric•ture (strĭk′chər) *n.* **1.** A restraint, limit, or restriction. **2.** An adverse criticism. **3.** *Pathol.* An abnormal constriction in a bodily duct or passage.

stride (strīd) *v.* **strode** (strōd), **strid•den** (strĭd′n), **strid•ing.** To walk vigorously with long steps. ★ ***syns:*** MARCH, STALK *—n.* **1. a.** A long step. **b.** The distance covered in a stride. **2.** *often* **strides.** A step forward : advance. **—strid′er** *n.*

stri•dent (strīd′nt) *adj.* Harsh, grating, and loud : shrill.

strife (strīf) *n.* **1.** Discord : conflict. **2.** A struggle : contention.

strike (strīk) *v.* **struck** (strŭk), **struck** *or* **strick•en** (strĭk′ən), **strik•ing. 1. a.** To hit with or as if with the hand. **b.** To inflict (a blow). **2. a.** To collide with. **b.** To cause to collide. **3.** To afflict suddenly, as with a disease or disorder. **4.** To indicate by a sound <a clock *striking* the hour> **5.** To produce by stamping, printing, or punching <*strike* a coin> **6.** To ignite (a match) by friction. **7.** To expunge or remove. **8.** To impress, esp. strongly or anew. **9.** To discover <*struck* oil> **10.** To affect deeply with (an emotion). **11.** To make or conclude <*struck* a deal> **12.** To assume (e.g., a pose). **13.** To stop working in protest against something or in support of demands made of an employer. **14.** To start out, esp. in a new direction. *—n.* **1.** An act or instance of striking. **2.** An attack, esp. a military air attack. **3.** A sudden achievement or valuable discovery, as of a precious mineral. **4. a.** *Baseball.* A pitched ball counted against the batter. **b.** The knocking down of all the pins in bowling with the first ball. **—strike out.** *Baseball.* To put or be put out with 3 strikes. **—strike up. 1.** To start or cause to start to sing or play. **2.** To initiate. **—strik′er** *n.*

strike•break•er (strīk′brā′kər) *n.* One who works or provides an employer with workers during a strike : scab. **—strike′break′ing** *n.*

strike•out (strīk′out′) *n. Baseball.* An act or instance of striking out.

strik•ing (strī′kĭng) *adj.* Extraordinarily impressive <a *striking* resemblance> **—strik′ing•ly** *adv.* **—strik′ing•ness** *n.*

string (strĭng) *n.* **1.** A cord, as of twisted fibers, for fastening, tying, or lacing. **2.** Something resembling a string. **3.** A set of objects with a cord running through them <a *string* of pearls> **4.** A series of related events, acts, or items arranged or falling in a line <a *string* of defeats> **5.** *Computer Sci.* A set of data arranged in ascending or descending sequence according to a key within the data. **6. a.** A cord stretched across the sounding board of a musical instrument that produces a tone when caused to vibrate. **b. strings.** Musical instruments with strings. 7. *often* **strings.** Hidden conditions or provisos. **8.** A cord or fiber in a plant. —*v.* **strung** (strŭng), **string•ing. 1.** To furnish, fasten, or tie with strings. **2.** To thread on a string. **3.** To make tense : tighten. **4.** To extend : stretch. **5.** To remove the strings from (vegetables). —**stringed** *adj.* —**string'y** *adj.*

string bean *n.* A bushy or climbing plant, *Phaseolus vulgaris,* cultivated for its narrow, green, edible pods.

strin•gent (strĭn'jənt) *adj.* **1.** Rigorously exacting : strict. **2.** Marked by scarcity, esp. of money. —**strin'gen•cy** *n.*

strip[1] (strĭp) *v.* **stripped, strip•ping. 1.** To remove the covering or clothing from. **2.** To divest, as of rank. **3.** To take or pull off : remove. **4.** To make bare, as by separating leaves from a stalk. **5.** To damage the threads or teeth of (e.g., a gear). **6.** To rob : despoil. **7.** To remove all one's clothes. —**strip'per** *n.*

strip[2] (strĭp) *n.* **1.** A long, slender piece, usu. of uniform width. **2.** An airstrip.

stripe (strīp) *n.* **1.** A long, narrow band distinguished, as by color, from its background. **2.** A strip of cloth worn on the sleeve of a uniform to show rank or length of service : chevron. **3.** Type : kind. —*v.* **striped, strip•ing.** To mark or provide with stripes.

striped bass *n.* A food and game fish, *Roccus saxatilis,* of North American coastal waters, with dark stripes along its sides.

strip•ling (strĭp'lĭng) *n.* A youth.

strip mine *n.* An open mine, esp. a coal mine, whose seams or outcrops run close to ground level and are exposed by the stripping of topsoil. —**strip-mine'** *v.*

strip•tease *also* **strip tease** (strĭp'tēz') *n.* An entertainment featuring a person who slowly removes clothing usu. to a musical accompaniment. —**strip'teas'er** *n.*

strive (strīv) *v.* **strove** (strōv) *or* **strived, striv•en** (strĭv'ən) *or* **strived, striv•ing. 1.** To exert strenuous efforts : labor. **2.** To struggle against : contend. —**striv'er** *n.*

strobe (strōb) *n.* **1.** A stroboscope. **2.** A strobe light.

strobe light *n.* A flash lamp that produces high-intensity short-duration light pulses by electric discharge in a gas.

stro•bo•scope (strō'bə-skōp') *n.* An instrument used to study moving objects by making them appear stationary, esp. with pulsed illumination or devices that intermittently interrupt observation. —**stro'bo•scop'ic** (-skŏp'ĭk) *adj.*

strode (strōd) *v. p.t. of* STRIDE.

stroke (strōk) *n.* **1.** An act of striking : blow. **2.** A sudden process, event, or action having a powerful effect <a *stroke* of luck> **3.** A single complete movement over or through water or air <a swimming *stroke*> **4.** A single movement or mark made by or as if by a pen or brush. **5.** A single complete movement of a machine part, as a piston. **6.** The striking or sound of striking of a clock, bell, or gong. **7.** Apoplexy. —*v.* **stroked, strok•ing.** To move the hand over gently : rub lightly.

stroll (strōl) *v.* To walk around in a leisurely way : amble. —**stroll** *n.*

stroll•er (strō'lər) *n.* **1.** One that strolls. **2.** A chairlike baby carriage.

strong (strông) *adj.* **1.** Physically powerful. **2.** Robust : healthy. **3.** Difficult to break : durable. **4.** Intense : violent <*strong* feelings> **5.** Persuasive or forceful. **6.** Drastic : extreme. **7.** Having a specified number of members or units <an orchestra 110 *strong*> —**strong'ly** *adv.*

strong-arm (strông'ärm') *adj. Informal.* Excessively forceful : coercive <*strong-arm* tactics> —**strong'-arm'** *v.*

strong•box (strông'bŏks') *n.* A stoutly made safe or box for storing valuables.

strong•hold (strông'hōld') *n.* A fortress.

strong•man (strông'măn') *n.* A political figure who exercises control by force.

strong-mind•ed (strông'mīn'dĭd) *adj.* Strong, determined, and independent in mind and will.

stron•ti•um (strŏn'chē-əm, -tē-) *n. Symbol* **Sr** A soft, readily oxidized metallic element used in various alloys.

strop (strŏp) *n.* A flexible strip, as of leather, used esp. to sharpen a razor. —*v.* **stropped, strop•ping.** To sharpen (a razor) on a strop.

stro•phe (strō'fē) *n.* A stanza of a poem.

strove (strōv) *v. var. p.t. of* STRIVE.

struck (strŭk) *v. p.t. & p.p. of* STRIKE. —*adj.* Shut down or affected by a labor strike.

struc•ture (strŭk'chər) *n.* **1.** Something made up of a number of parts assembled in a particular pattern. **2.** The way in which parts are combined or arranged to form a whole. **3.** Something constructed, as a building or bridge. —*v.* **-tured, -tur•ing.** To give structure to. —**struc'tur•al** *adj.*

stru•del (strōōd'l, shtrōōd'l) *n.* A pastry consisting of filling rolled up in a thin sheet of dough and baked.

strug•gle (strŭg'əl) *v.* **-gled, -gling. 1.** To exert strenuous efforts against resistance or opposition : strive. **2.** To progress with effort or difficulty. —*n.* **1.** Strenuous effort : striving. **2.** A battle : contest.

strum (strŭm) *v.* **strummed, strum•ming.** To play (a stringed instrument) by stroking the strings lightly with the fingers.

strum•pet (strŭm'pĭt) *n.* A prostitute.

strung (strŭng) *v. p.t. & p.p. of* STRING.

strung-out (strŭng'out') *adj. Slang.* Emotionally or physically debilitated from or as if from long-term drug use.

strut (strŭt) *v.* **strut•ted, strut•ting.** To walk in an affectedly self-important manner. —*n.* **1.** An affectedly self-important gait. **2.** A rod or bar for bracing against forces applied from the side.

strych•nine (strĭk'nīn', -nĭn, -nēn') *n.* A poisonous substance derived from certain plants and used to kill pests, as rodents, and as a stimulant.

stub (stŭb) *n.* **1.** A short end remaining after something has been used up or snapped off <a pencil *stub*> **2. a.** The part of a check or receipt kept as a record of payment made. **b.** The part of a ticket returned to the purchaser as proof of payment. —*v.* **stubbed, stub•bing.** To strike (e.g., one's toe) against something.

stub•ble (stŭb'əl) *n.* **1.** The short stalks, as of grain, that remain in the soil after a crop has been harvested. **2.** Something resembling stubble. —**stub'bly** *adj.*

stub•born (stŭb'ərn) *adj.* **1.** Unreasonably inflexible : obstinate and willful. **2.** Determined and persistent. **3.** Difficult to control or handle : resistant. —**stub'born•ly** *adv.* —**stub'born•ness** *n.*

stub•by (stŭb'ē) *adj.* **-bi•er, -bi•est.** Resembling a stub : short and thick.

stuc•co (stŭk'ō) *n., pl.* **-coes** *or* **-cos.** Plaster or cement used to coat exterior walls. —*v.* To cover or coat with stucco.

stuck (stŭk) *v. p.t. & p.p. of* STICK.

stuck-up (stŭk'ŭp') *adj. Informal.* Snobbish and supercilious : conceited.

stud[1] (stŭd) *n.* **1.** An upright post in the framework of a building to which sheets of lath, wallboard, or paneling are fastened. **2.** Something, as a knob or nail head, that projects from a surface. **3.** A small removable button used as an ornament or fastener, as on a shirt. —*v.* **stud•ded, stud•ding. 1.** To provide or decorate with studs. **2.** To strew : dot.

stud[2] (stŭd) *n.* A male animal, esp. a stallion, kept for breeding.

stud•book (stŭd'bo͝ok') *n.* A book in which the pedigrees of thoroughbred animals are recorded.

stud•ding (stŭd'ĭng) *n.* **1.** Studs, esp. for walls. **2.** Material used for studs.

stu•dent (sto͞od'nt, styo͞od'-) *n.* **1.** Someone who studies, esp. at a school or college. **2.** An attentive observer <a *student* of world affairs>

stud•ied (stŭd'ēd) *adj.* Carefully planned : contrived.

stu•di•o (sto͞o'dē-ō', styo͞o'-) *n., pl.* **-os. 1.** An artist's place of work. **2.** A place where an art is studied or taught. **3.** A place equipped for the production of motion pictures or television or radio programs.

studio couch *n.* A couch, usu. without a back, that can serve as a bed.

stu•di•ous (sto͞o'dē-əs, styo͞o'-) *adj.* **1.** Devoted to study. **2.** Earnestly diligent. —**stu'di•ous•ly** *adv.*

stud•y (stŭd'ē) *n., pl.* **-ies. 1.** The act or process of applying the mind to acquire knowledge. **2.** A close examination. **3.** A branch of knowledge. **4.** A room equipped and used esp. for writing and reading. —*v.* **-ied, -y•ing. 1.** To apply the mind to acquire knowledge or understanding of (a subject). **2.** To think about : ponder. **3.** To examine in detail : scrutinize.

stuff (stŭf) *n.* **1. a.** The material of which something consists or is made : essential substance. **b.** Raw material. **2.** Material of an unspecified nature or kind. **3.** Worthless objects. **4.** Words or ideas of little value. **5.** *esp. Brit.* Woven material, esp. woolens. **6.** Special capability. —*v.* **1. a.** To pack tightly : cram. **b.** To stop up : block. **2.** To fill (e.g., a turkey) with stuffing. **3.** To eat too much : gorge. —**stuff'er** *n.*

stuffed shirt *n. Informal.* A pompous, self-satisfied person.

stuff•ing (stŭf'ĭng) *n.* Material used to stuff, esp. a seasoned mixture used to fill meat, poultry, fish, or vegetables.

stuff•y (stŭf'ē) *adj.* **-i•er, -i•est. 1.** Lacking ventilation : close. **2.** Congested <a *stuffy* nose> **3.** *Informal.* Not very lively or interesting : stodgy.

stul•ti•fy (stŭl'tə-fī') *v.* **-fied, -fy•ing. 1.** To make ineffectual or useless : cripple. **2.** To cause to seem stupid or illogical. **3.** To make torpid or dull.

stum•ble (stŭm'bəl) *v.* **-bled, -bling. 1. a.** To trip and nearly fall. **b.** To move unsteadily : falter. **c.** To act or speak clumsily. **2.** To make an error, esp. a moral mistake : blunder. **3.** To come upon unexpectedly. —**stum'ble** *n.*

stum•ble•bum (stŭm'bəl-bŭm') *n. Slang.* **1.** A blundering or inept person. **2.** An inept or clumsy prizefighter.

stumbling block *n.* An impediment : obstacle.

stump (stŭmp) *n.* **1.** The part of a tree remaining in the ground after the top has fallen or been cut down. **2.** A part, as of a tooth, that is left after the main part has worn away or been cut off. **3.** An occasion or place for political speeches. —*v.* **1.** To clear stumps from (land). **2.** To travel around (an area) making political speeches. **3.** To walk stiffly and heavily. **4.** To puzzle : perplex. —**stump'er** *n.* —**stump'y** *adj.*

stun (stŭn) *v.* **stunned, stun•ning. 1.** To make senseless by or as if by a blow : daze. **2.** To stupefy, as with strong emotion : shock. —**stun** *n.*

stung (stŭng) *v. p.t. & p.p. of* STING.

stunk (stŭngk) *v. var. p.t. & p.p. of* STINK.

stun•ning (stŭn'ĭng) *adj.* Remarkably attractive. —**stun'ning•ly** *adv.*

stunt[1] (stŭnt) *v.* To hinder the growth or development of. —**stunt'ed** *adj.*

stunt[2] (stŭnt) *n.* **1.** A feat showing unusual skill, strength, or daring. **2.** Something unusual done esp. for publicity.

stu•pe•fy (sto͞o'pə-fī', styo͞o'-) *v.* **-fied, -fy•ing. 1.** To make physically groggy or dull. **2.** To astound : astonish. —**stu'pe•fac'tion** *n.* —**stu'pe•fi'er** *n.*

stu•pen•dous (sto͞o-pĕn'dəs, styo͞o-) *adj.* **1.** Causing amazement : astonishing. **2.** Of enormous size. —**stu•pen'dous•ly** *adv.*

stu•pid (sto͞o'pĭd, styo͞o'-) *adj.* **1.** Slow to understand : dull. **2.** Showing or resulting from lack of intelligence. ★ *syns:* DENSE, DUMB, OBTUSE, THICK —**stu•pid'i•ty** *n.* —**stu'pid•ly** *adv.*

stu•por (stōō′pər, styōō′-) *n.* **1.** A condition of reduced feeling or sense : numbness. **2.** A condition of apathy that is often caused by shock or stress : torpor. —**stu′por•ous** *adj.*
stur•dy (stûr′dē) *adj.* **-di•er, -di•est. 1.** Physically robust : strong. **2.** Mentally vigorous : resolute. —**stur′di•ly** *adv.* —**stur′di•ness** *n.*
stur•geon (stûr′jən) *n.* Any of various large freshwater and marine food fishes of the family Acipenseridae, valued as a source of caviar.
stut•ter (stŭt′ər) *v.* To speak with involuntary hesitation, prolongation, or repetition of sounds. —**stut′ter** *n.*
sty[1] (stī) *n., pl.* **sties. 1.** A pen or enclosure for pigs. **2.** An extremely messy or dirty place.
sty[2] (stī) *n., pl.* **sties.** Inflammation and swelling of a gland on the edge of an eyelid.
style (stīl) *n.* **1.** A way, method, or manner of saying, writing, or performing. **2.** Kind : sort. **3.** Individuality that is reflected in a person's actions and tastes. **4. a.** An elegant mode of life. **b.** Grace, elegance, or excellence in appearance or performance : distinction. **5. a.** The current fashion : vogue. **b.** A particular fashion. **6.** A scheme or custom adhered to in presenting printed material, including punctuation, spelling, capitalization, typography, and arrangement. **7.** A stylus. —*v.* **styled, styl•ing. 1.** To name : designate. **2.** To arrange, fashion, or design in a particular mode or style. —**sty•lis′tic** *adj.*
styl•ish (stī′lĭsh) *adj.* Conforming to the current style : fashionable. —**styl′ish•ly** *adv.* —**styl′ish•ness** *n.*
styl•ist (stī′lĭst) *n.* **1.** A specialist in style, esp. literary style. **2.** A designer of or consultant on style.
styl•ize (stī′līz′) *v.* **-ized, -iz•ing.** To conform to a style rather than representing according to nature.
sty•lus (stī′ləs) *n., pl.* **-lus•es** *or* **-li** (-lī′). **1.** A pointed instrument used for writing esp. on wax or for engraving. **2.** A phonograph needle.
sty•mie (stī′mē) *v.* **-mied, -mie•ing.** To frustrate : thwart.
styp•tic (stĭp′tĭk) *adj.* **1.** Astringent. **2.** Tending to arrest bleeding.
Sty•ro•foam (stī′rə-fōm′). A trademark for a light, resilient polystyrene plastic.
suave (swäv) *adj.* **suav•er, suav•est.** Smoothly but sometimes superficially gracious : urbane. —**suav′i•ty** *n.*
†**sub**[1] (sŭb) *n. Informal.* **1.** A submarine. **2.** *Regional.* HERO 4.
sub[2] (sŭb) *n. Informal.* A substitute. —**sub** *v.*
sub– *pref.* **1.** Below : under : beneath <*sub*soil> **2.** Subordinate : secondary <*sub*plot> **3.** Less than completely or normally : nearly : almost <*sub*human>
sub•al•tern (sə-bôl′tərn) *n.* **1.** A subordinate. **2.** *esp. Brit.* A military officer holding a rank below captain.
sub•a•tom•ic (sŭb′ə-tŏm′ĭk) *adj.* Of or pertaining to the constituents of the atom.
subatomic particle *n.* Any of various units of matter below the size of an atom.
sub•com•mit•tee (sŭb′kə-mĭt′ē) *n.* A subdivision of a committee.
sub•com•pact (sŭb-kŏm′păkt′) *n.* An automobile smaller in size than a compact.
sub•con•scious (sŭb-kŏn′shəs) *adj.* Existing or occurring below the threshold of consciousness. —**sub•con′scious** *n.* —**sub•con′scious•ly** *adv.* —**sub•con′scious•ness** *n.*
sub•con•ti•nent (sŭb′kŏn′tə-nənt) *n.* A very large land mass that is part of a continent.
sub•con•tract (sŭb-kŏn′trăkt′) *n.* A contract assigning some of the obligations of a contract to a 3rd party. —**sub′con•tract′** (-kən-trăkt′) *v.*
sub•cul•ture (sŭb′kŭl′chər) *n.* A cultural subgroup differentiated from a larger group by such factors as status, ethnic background, and religion.
sub•cu•ta•ne•ous (sŭb′kyōō-tā′nē-əs) *adj.* Located, used, or introduced beneath the skin <a *subcutaneous* injection>
sub•di•rec•to•ry (sŭb′dĭ-rĕk′tə-rē, -dī-) *n., pl.* **-ries.** *Computer Sci.* A subdivision within a larger directory that stores related files.
sub•di•vide (sŭb′dĭ-vīd′) *v.* **1.** To divide into smaller parts. **2.** To divide (land) into lots. —**sub′di•vi′sion** *n.*
sub•due (səb-dōō′, -dyōō′) *v.* **-dued, -du•ing. 1.** To subjugate : vanquish. **2.** To bring under control. **3.** To make less intense.
sub•group (sŭb′grōōp′) *n.* A subordinate group.
sub•head (sŭb′hĕd′) *n.* **1.** A heading of a subdivision of a printed work. **2.** A subordinate title or heading.
sub•ject (sŭb′jĭkt) *adj.* **1.** Under the authority, rule, or power of another. **2.** Disposed : prone <*subject* to infections> **3.** Liable <*subject* to misinterpretation> **4.** Dependent : contingent <permission *subject* to further discussion> —*n.* **1.** A person under the rule of another. **2.** The person or thing being dealt with or discussed : topic. **3.** An area or course of study. **4.** An individual as an object of study or experiment. **5.** A word, phrase, or clause about which something is predicated. —*v.* (səb-jĕkt′). **1.** To gain control over : subdue. **2.** To lay open : expose. **3.** To cause to undergo or experience. —**sub•jec′tion** (-jĕk′shən) *n.*
sub•jec•tive (səb-jĕk′tĭv) *adj.* **1.** Of or existing within an individual's mind rather than outside : personal. **2.** Of, pertaining to, or being a subject. —**sub•jec′tive•ly** *adv.* —**sub′jec•tiv′i•ty** *n.*
subject matter *n.* Matter being discussed, considered, or studied.
sub•join (sŭb-join′) *v.* To add on at the end : append.
sub ju•di•ce (sŭb jōō′dĭ-sē′, yōō′dĭ-kā′) *adv. Law.* Under judicial deliberation.
sub•ju•gate (sŭb′jə-gāt′) *v.* **-gat•ed, -gat•ing. 1.** To compel to submit : conquer. **2.** To enslave. —**sub′ju•ga′tion** *n.*

▲ ***word history:*** The word *subjugate* is borrowed from Latin *subjugare,* literally "to bring under the yoke." In accordance with an ancient Latin custom survivors of a defeated army were forced to pass under a symbolic yoke made of two upright spears, with a third used as a crossbar. The Romans regarded subjugation as the worst possible humiliation.

sub•junc•tive (sŭb-jŭngk′tĭv) *adj.* Of, pertaining to, or being a verb form or set of forms used to express uncertainty, desire, contingency, or unlikelihood. **—sub•junc′tive** *n.*

sub•let (sŭb-lĕt′) *v.* **1.** To rent (property held by lease) to another. **2.** To subcontract (work). **—sub′let′** *n.*

sub•li•mate (sŭb′lə-māt′) *v.* **-mat•ed, -mat•ing. 1.** *Chem.* To pass or cause to pass from a solid to a gas or from a gas to a solid without becoming a liquid. **2.** To modify the expression of (e.g., an impulse) so as to be socially acceptable. **—sub′li•ma′tion** *n.*

sub•lime (sə-blīm′) *adj.* **1.** Noble **:** lofty. **2.** Inspiring awe **:** awesome. *—v.* **-limed, -lim•ing.** *Chem.* To sublimate. **—su•blim′i•ty** (sə-blĭm′ĭ-tē) *n.*

sub•lim•i•nal (sŭb-lĭm′ə-nəl) *adj.* Not within the area of conscious perception or awareness. **—sub•lim′i•nal•ly** *adv.*

sub•lu•na•ry (sŭb′lo͞o′nə-rē) *adj.* Located beneath the moon.

sub•ma•chine gun (sŭb′mə-shēn′) *n.* An automatic or semiautomatic gun fired from the hip or shoulder.

sub•mar•gin•al (sŭb′mär′jə-nəl) *adj.* Being below a required minimum <*submarginal* living conditions>

sub•ma•rine (sŭb′mə-rēn′, sŭb′mə-rēn′) *adj.* Being or growing beneath the surface of the sea **:** undersea. *—n.* **1.** A ship that can operate both on the surface of the water and underwater. **2.** HERO 4.

sub•ma•rin•er (sub′mə-rē′nər, -măr′ə-) *n.* A crew member of a submarine.

sub•merge (səb-mûrj′) *v.* **-merged, -merg•ing. 1.** To place or plunge under the surface of a liquid, esp. water. **2.** To cover with water. **—sub•mer′gi•ble** *adj.* **—sub•mer′gence** *n.*

sub•merse (səb-mûrs′) *v.* **-mersed, -mers•ing.** To submerge. **—sub•mers′i•ble** *adj.* **—sub•mer′sion** *n.*

sub•mi•cro•scop•ic (sŭb′mī′-krə-skŏp′ĭk) *adj.* Too small to be seen with an optical microscope.

sub•min•i•a•ture (sŭb′mĭn′ē-ə-cho͝or′, -chər) *adj.* Extremely small.

sub•mit (səb-mĭt′) *v.* **-mit•ted, -mit•ting. 1.** To surrender to the authority, discretion, or will of another. **2.** To commit to the decision, consideration, or judgment of another. **3.** To offer as a suggestion or opinion. **4.** To acquiesce. **—sub•mis′sion** *n.* **—sub•mis′sive** *adj.* **—sub•mit′tal** *n.*

sub•nor•mal (sŭb-nôr′məl) *adj.* Being less than normal. **—sub′nor•mal′i•ty** *n.*

sub•or•bit•al (sŭb-ôr′bĭ-tl) *adj.* Of, being, or involving less than one orbit.

sub•or•di•nate (sə-bôr′dn-ĭt) *adj.* **1.** Of lower rank or class **:** inferior. **2.** Subject to the control or authority of another. **3.** Dependent on other elements in a sentence <a *subordinate* clause> *—n.* One that is subordinate. ★ *syns:* INFERIOR, JUNIOR, SUBALTERN, UNDERLING *—v.* (-nāt′) **-nat•ed, -nat•ing. 1.** To put in a lower rank or class. **2.** To make subservient. **—sub•or′di•na′tion** *n.* **—sub•or′di•na′tive** *adj.*

sub•orn (sə-bôrn′) *v.* To induce to commit an unlawful act, esp. perjury. **—sub′or•na′tion** *n.* **—sub•orn′er** *n.*

sub•plot (sŭb′plŏt′) *n.* A secondary plot in drama or fiction.

sub•poe•na (sə-pē′nə) *n.* A legal writ requiring the person named in it to appear in court. *—v.* To serve with a subpoena.

sub ro•sa (sŭb rō′zə) *adv.* In secret **:** covertly <negotiations held *sub rosa*>

sub•rou•tine (sŭb′ro͞o-tēn′) *n.* *Computer Sci.* A set of instructions that performs a specific task for a main routine.

sub•scribe (səb-scrīb′) *v.* **-scribed, -scrib•ing. 1.** To sign (one's name) to a document. **2.** To give testimony, attestation, or consent by signing one's name. **3. a.** To pledge to contribute. **b.** To contribute. **4.** To be in agreement <don't *subscribe* to your opinion> **5.** To contract to pay for and receive a periodical at regular intervals. **—sub•scrib′er** *n.*

sub•script (sŭb′skrĭpt′) *n.* A symbol or letter written next to and slightly below another character.

sub•scrip•tion (səb-skrĭp′shən) *n.* **1.** The act of signing one's name **:** signature. **2.** A purchase by signed order, as for issues of a periodical.

sub•se•quent (sŭb′sĭ-kwənt) *adj.* Following in order or time **:** succeeding. **—sub′se•quent•ly** *adv.* **—sub′se•quent•ness** *n.*

sub•ser•vi•ent (səb-sûr′vē-ənt) *adj.* **1.** Subordinate, as in condition or function. **2.** Servile **:** submissive **—sub•ser′vi•ence** *n.* **—sub•ser′vi•ent•ly** *adv.*

sub•set (sŭb′sĕt′) *n.* A mathematical set each of whose members is included within another set.

sub•side (səb-sīd′) *v.* **-sid•ed, -sid•ing. 1.** To move to a lower level **:** descend. **2.** To sink to the bottom of a liquid **:** settle. **3.** To become less agitated or intense **:** abate. **—sub•sid′ence** *n.*

sub•sid•i•ar•y (səb-sĭd′ē-ĕr′ē) *adj.* **1.** Providing support or assistance. **2.** Secondary, as in importance **:** subordinate. **3.** Of or pertaining to a subsidy. *—n., pl.* **-ies.** One that is subsidiary, esp. a company owned and controlled by another.

sub•si•dize (sŭb′sĭ-dīz′) *v.* **-dized, -diz•ing.** To provide or aid with a subsidy.

sub•si•dy (sŭb′sĭ-dē) *n., pl.* **-dies.** A financial grant, as that given by a government to a private undertaking or to another country.

sub•sist (səb-sĭst′) *v.* **1.** To exist or continue in existence. **2.** To have or receive what is necessary to maintain life.

sub•sis•tence (səb-sĭs′təns) *n.* **1.** The means necessary to maintain life. **2.** Existence. **—sub•sis′tent** *adj.*

sub•soil (sŭb′soil′) *n.* The layer of earth just beneath the surface soil.
sub•son•ic (sŭb′sŏn′ĭk) *adj.* **1.** Of or having less than audible frequency. **2.** Of, pertaining to, or being a speed less than that of sound in a designated medium.
sub•stance (sŭb′stəns) *n.* **1. a.** Matter that occupies space and has mass. **b.** Matter of a particular constitution or kind. **2. a.** Essential character **:** essence. **b.** The most basic or important quality or part **:** gist <the *substance* of the sermon> **3.** Actuality **:** reality <an idea without *substance*> **4.** Material belongings **:** property.
substance abuse *n.* Excessive use of addictive substances, esp. alcohol or narcotics.
sub•stan•dard (sŭb′stăn′dərd) *adj.* Being below a standard or norm.
sub•stan•tial (səb-stăn′shəl) *adj.* **1.** Having substance **:** material. **2.** Not imaginary **:** real. **3.** Solid and firm **:** strong. **4.** Providing sustenance **:** nourishing <a *substantial* breakfast> **5.** Considerable <a *substantial* snowfall> **6.** Moderately wealthy **:** well-to-do. **—sub•stan′tial•ly** *adv.*
sub•stan•ti•ate (səb-stăn′shē-āt′) *v.* **-at•ed, -at•ing.** To support with proof **:** verify. **—sub•stan′ti•a′tion** *n.*
sub•stan•tive (sŭb′stən-tĭv) *adj.* **1.** Substantial **:** real. **2.** Of, relating to, or being the essence of something **:** essential. —*n.* **1.** A noun. **2.** A group of words functioning as a noun. **—sub′stan•tive•ly** *adv.*
sub•sta•tion (sŭb′stā′shən) *n.* A subsidiary station, as of a post office.
sub•sti•tute (sŭb′stĭ-to͞ot′, -tyo͞ot′) *n.* One that takes the place of another. ★ ***syns:*** ALTERNATE, PINCH HITTER, REPLACEMENT, STAND-IN, SUB, SURROGATE —*v.* **-tut•ed, -tut•ing. 1.** To use or put in the place of another. **2.** To act as a substitute. **—sub′sti•tu′tion** *n.*
sub•strate (sŭb′strāt′) *n.* **1.** The material or substance on which an enzyme acts. **2.** A substratum.
sub•stra•tum (sŭb′strā′təm, -străt′əm) *n.* **1.** A layer that lies beneath. **2.** Subsoil.
sub•struc•ture (sŭb′strŭk′chər) *n.* An underlying support **:** foundation.
sub•sume (səb-so͞om′, -syo͞om′) *v.* **-sumed, -sum•ing.** To place in a larger or more comprehensive category.
sub•ten•ant (sŭb′-tĕn′ənt) *n.* One that rents property, as a house, from a tenant.
sub•tend (səb-tĕnd′) *v. Math.* To be opposite to and delimit <The hypotenuse *subtends* a right angle.>
sub•ter•fuge (sŭb′tər-fyo͞oj′) *n.* A trick or tactic used to escape, evade, or conceal.
sub•ter•ra•ne•an (sŭb′tə-rā′nē-ən) *adj.* **1.** Located, being, or operating underground. **2.** Hidden **:** secret <*subterranean* plots>
sub•text (sŭb′tĕkst′) *n.* The implicit meaning or theme of a literary text.
sub•ti•tle (sŭb′tīt′l) *n.* **1.** A subordinate and often explanatory title, as of a book. **2.** A printed translation of foreign-language dialogue projected at the bottom of a motion-picture screen.
sub•tle (sŭt′l) *adj.* **-tler, -tlest. 1.** Difficult to detect or analyze **:** barely perceptible. **2.** Marked by or having sharp discernment **:** keen. **3. a.** Expert **:** skillful. **b.** Sly **:** crafty. **—sub′tle•ty** *n.* **—sub′tly** *adv.*
sub•to•tal (sŭb′tōt′l) *n.* The total of part of a series of numbers. **—sub′to′tal** *v.*
sub•tract (səb-trăkt′) *v.* To take away (e.g., one number from another) by deducting. **—sub•trac′tion** *n.*
sub•tra•hend (sŭb′trə-hĕnd′) *n.* A quantity to be subtracted from another.
sub•trop•i•cal (sŭb-trŏp′ĭ-kəl) *adj.* Of, pertaining to, or being geographic areas adjacent to the tropics.
sub•urb (sŭb′ûrb′) *n.* **1.** A small, usu. residential community near a city. **2. suburbs.** A residential area in the vicinity of a city. **—sub•ur′ban** (sə-bûr′bən) *adj.*
sub•ur•ban•ite (sə-bûr′bə-nīt′) *n.* Someone who lives in a suburb.
sub•ur•bi•a (sə-bûr′bē-ə) *n.* **1.** Suburbs. **2.** Suburbanites as a cultural class.
sub•ven•tion (səb-vĕn′shən) *n.* A subsidy **:** endowment.
sub•vert (səb-vûrt′) *v.* **1.** To overthrow. **2.** To corrupt the character or morals of. **—sub•ver′sion** *n.* **—sub•ver′sive** *adj.*
sub•way (sŭb′wā′) *n.* **1.** An underground passage. **2.** An underground railroad, esp. one powered by electricity.
suc•ceed (sək-sēd′) *v.* **1. a.** To come next in order or time **:** follow. **b.** To replace another in an office or position. **2.** To accomplish or achieve something desired, intended, or attempted.
suc•cess (sək-sĕs′) *n.* **1.** The achievement of something desired, intended, or attempted. **2.** The gaining of fame or prosperity. **3.** One that succeeds. **—suc•cess′ful** *adj.* **—suc•cess′ful•ly** *adv.*
suc•ces•sion (sək-sĕsh′ən) *n.* **1.** The process or act of following in order. **2.** A group of persons or things that follow in order **:** sequence. **3.** The sequence, right, or act of succeeding to a title, throne, or estate.
suc•ces•sive (sək-sĕs′ĭv) *adj.* Following in uninterrupted order **:** consecutive. **—suc•ces′sive•ly** *adv.* **—suc•ces′sive•ness** *n.*
suc•ces•sor (sək-sĕs′ər) *n.* One that succeeds another, as to a throne.
suc•cinct (sək-sĭngkt′) *adj.* Marked by brevity **:** concise. **—suc•cinct′ly** *adv.* **—suc•cinct′ness** *n.*
suc•cor (sŭk′ər) *n.* Assistance **:** aid. **—suc′cor** *v.*
suc•co•tash (sŭk′ə-tăsh′) *n.* A mixture of cooked corn and lima or shell beans.
suc•cour (sŭk′ər) *n. esp. Brit. var. of* SUCCOR.
suc•cu•bus (sŭk′yə-bəs) *n., pl.* **-bus•es** *or* **-bi** (-bī′, -bē′). An evil spirit supposed to have sexual intercourse with a sleeping man.
suc•cu•lent (sŭk′yə-lənt) *adj.* **1.** Full of sap or juice **:** juicy. **2.** Having fleshy stems or

leaves that conserve moisture. —*n.* A succulent plant, as a cactus. —**suc'cu·lence** *n.* —**suc'cu·lent·ly** *adv.*

suc·cumb (sə-kŭm') *v.* **1.** To give in, as to something overpowering : yield. **2.** To die.

such (sŭch) *adj.* **1.** Of this or that kind. **2.** Of a quality that has been or is to be specified. —*adv.* To such a degree : so. —*pron.* **1.** Such a person or thing <a joke, if it can be be called *such*> **2.** The like <blouses, dresses, and *such*>

such·like (sŭch'līk') *adj.* Like : similar. —*pron.* A person or thing of a like kind.

suck (sŭk) *v.* **1. a.** To draw liquid in with the mouth. **b.** To draw liquid from by sucking <*suck* a lemon> **2.** To draw in by or as if by suction. —*n.* The act of sucking : suction.

suck·er (sŭk'ər) *n.* **1.** One that sucks. **2.** *Slang.* A person who is easily duped. **3.** A lollipop. **4.** A freshwater fish of the family Catostomidae, with thick lips adapted for feeding by suction. **5.** A part of an animal's body adapted for clinging by suction. **6.** A shoot growing from the base of a plant.

suck·le (sŭk'əl) *v.* **-led, -ling. 1.** To give or take milk from the breast or udder. **2.** To foster : rear.

suck·ling (sŭk'lĭng) *n.* A young mammal not yet weaned.

su·cre (so͞o'krā) *n.* —See table at CURRENCY.

su·crose (so͞o'krōs') *n.* A sugar obtained esp. from sugar cane and sugar beet.

suc·tion (sŭk'shən) *n.* **1.** The act or process of sucking. **2.** The act or process of drawing something, as ink, into a space, as the reservoir of a fountain pen, by producing a partial vacuum in the space.

sud·den (sŭd'n) *adj.* **1.** Coming or happening quickly or without warning <a *sudden* snowstorm> **2.** Abrupt : sharp <a *sudden* drop in the road> **3.** Marked by excessive haste : rash <a *sudden* departure> **4.** Rapid : fast. —**sud'den·ly** *adv.* —**sud'den·ness** *n.*

sudden death *n. Sports.* An extra period of play added to a tied game that ends when one team scores.

sudden infant death syndrome *n.* The unexpected death of an apparently healthy infant that usu. occurs during the first 4 months of life while sleeping.

suds (sŭdz) *pl.n.* **1.** Soapy water. **2.** Lather : foam. —**suds'y** *adj.*

sue (so͞o) *v.* **sued, su·ing. 1.** To satisfy a claim or redress a grievance by instituting legal proceedings. **2.** To make a request or appeal : entreat.

suede *also* **suède** (swād) *n.* **1.** Leather with a soft napped surface. **2.** Fabric with a surface resembling that of suede.

su·et (so͞o'ĭt) *n.* The hard fat around the kidneys of cattle and sheep from which tallow is obtained.

suf·fer (sŭf'ər) *v.* **1.** To endure or feel distress or pain. **2.** To sustain damage, injury, or loss. **3.** To be or seem to be at a disadvantage. **4.** To undergo : experience. **5.** To permit : allow. —**suf'fer·er** *n.*

suf·fer·ance (sŭf'ər-əns, sŭf'rəns) *n.* **1.** Endurance : forbearance. **2.** Approval or permission implied by failure to prohibit.

suf·fer·ing (sŭf'ər-ĭng, sŭf'rĭng) *n.* Mental or physical pain : misery.

suf·fice (sə-fīs') *v.* **-ficed, -fic·ing. 1.** To be adequate or sufficient. **2.** To answer a purpose or meet all requirements.

suf·fi·cient (sə-fĭsh'ənt) *adj.* As much as is needed or desired : enough. —**suf·fi'cien·cy** *n.* —**suf·fi'cient·ly** *adv.*

suf·fix (sŭf'ĭks') *n.* An affix appended to the end of a word.

suf·fo·cate (sŭf'ə-kāt') *v.* **-cat·ed, -cat·ing. 1.** To kill by depriving of oxygen. **2.** To die from a lack of oxygen. **3.** To stifle : suppress. —**suf'fo·ca'tion** *n.*

suf·fra·gan (sŭf'rə-gən) *n.* A bishop elected or appointed as an assistant to the bishop of a diocese. —**suf'fra·gan** *adj.* —**suf'fra·gan·ship'** *n.*

suf·frage (sŭf'rĭj) *n.* **1.** A vote. **2.** The right to vote : franchise.

suf·fra·gette (sŭf'rə-jĕt') *n.* A woman advocate of suffrage for women.

suf·fra·gist (sŭf'rə-jĭst) *n.* An advocate of the extension of suffrage, esp. to women.

suf·fuse (sə-fyo͞oz') *v.* **-fused, -fus·ing.** To spread through or over with or as if with liquid or light. —**suf·fu'sion** *n.*

sug·ar (sho͝og'ər) *n.* Any of a class of water-soluble crystalline carbohydrates with a characteristically sweet taste. —*v.* **1.** To coat, cover, or sprinkle with sugar. **2.** To make more palatable : sugar-coat.

sugar beet *n.* A beet, *Beta vulgaris,* with white roots from which sugar is obtained.

sugar cane *n.* A tall grass, *Saccharum officinarum,* that grows in warm regions and has thick stems that yield sugar.

sug·ar-coat (sho͝og'ər-kōt') *v.* To cause to seem more acceptable or appealing <*sugar-coated* the criticism with endearments>

sug·ar·less (sho͝og'ər-lĭs) *adj.* **1.** Containing no sugar. **2.** Sweetened with a substance other than sucrose.

sugar maple *n.* A maple tree, *Acer saccharum,* of E North America, with sap that is the source of maple sugar and syrup.

sug·ar·plum (sho͝og'ər-plŭm') *n.* A small candy in the shape of a ball.

sug·ar·y (sho͝og'ə-rē) *adj.* **-i·er, -i·est. 1.** Tasting of or containing sugar. **2.** Cloyingly or deceitfully sweet : saccharine.

sug·gest (səg-jĕst', sə-jĕst') *v.* **1.** To put forth (e.g., a plan or idea) for action or consideration : propose. **2.** To bring or call to mind by association : evoke. **3.** To make evident indirectly : imply. ★ ***syns:*** HINT, IMPLY, INSINUATE, INTIMATE

sug·gest·i·ble (səg-jĕs'tə-bəl, sə-jĕs'-) *adj.* Readily influenced by suggestion.

sug·ges·tion (səg-jĕs'chən, sə-jĕs'-) *n.* **1.** The act of suggesting. **2.** Something suggested. **3.** A slight trace : hint.

sug·ges·tive (səg-jĕs'tĭv, sə-jĕs'-) *adj.* **1.** Tending to suggest something, as ideas or thoughts. **2.** Tending to suggest something indecent or improper. **—sug·ges′tive·ly** *adv.* **—sug·ges′tive·ness** *n.*

su·i·cide (so͞o′ĭ-sīd′) *n.* **1.** The act of killing oneself intentionally. **2.** A person who commits suicide. **—su′i·cid′al** *adj.*

su·i·cid·ol·o·gy (so͞o′ĭ-sī-dŏl′ə-jē) *n.* The study of suicide, suicidal behavior, and suicide prevention. **—su′i·cid·ol′o·gist** *n.*

su·i gen·e·ris (so͞o′ī jĕn′ər-ĭs, so͞o′ē) *adj.* Being unique of its kind.

suit (so͞ot) *n.* **1.** A set of things to be used together <a *suit* of clothes> **2.** One of the 4 sets of playing cards constituting a deck. **3.** A court proceeding to recover a right or claim. **4.** The act of appealing or entreating, esp. courtship. —*v.* **1.** To meet the requirements or desires of **:** satisfy or please. **2.** To be appropriate or proper. **3.** To be becoming to.

suit·a·ble (so͞o′tə-bəl) *adj.* Appropriate for a particular purpose or occasion **:** proper. **—suit′a·bil′i·ty** *n.* **—suit′a·bly** *adv.*

suit·case (so͞ot′kās′) *n.* A flat and usu. rectangular piece of luggage.

suite (swēt) *n.* **1.** A staff of attendants, as for a monarch **:** retinue. **2.** A group of connected rooms used as a unit. **3.** (*also* so͞ot). A set of matched furniture. **4.** *Mus.* An instrumental composition consisting of several movements of varying characters or of material taken from a longer work.

suit·ing (so͞o′tĭng) *n.* Fabric from which suits of clothes are made.

suit·or (so͞o′tər) *n.* **1.** One who petitions or entreats. **2.** A man who courts a woman.

su·ki·ya·ki (so͞o′kē-yä′kē, skē-) *n.* A dish of Japanese orig. that consists of thinly sliced meat and vegetables cooked together, usu. with soy sauce.

sul·fa drug (sŭl′fə) *n.* Any of a group of synthetic organic compounds used to inhibit bacterial growth and activity.

sul·fa·nil·a·mide (sŭl′fə-nĭl′ə-mīd′) *n.* A white, odorless compound used to treat various bacterial infections.

sul·fate (sŭl′fāt′) *n.* A salt or ester of sulfuric acid.

sul·fide (sŭl′fīd′) *n.* A compound of sulfur and another element or radical.

sul·fur *also* **sul·phur** (sŭl′fər) *n. Symbol* S A pale-yellow nonmetallic element that occurs naturally in both free and combined forms and is used in gunpowder, rubber vulcanization, insecticides, pharmaceuticals, and industrial chemicals.

sulfur dioxide *n.* A colorless, very irritating gas that is used esp. in manufacturing sulfuric acid.

sul·fu·ric (sŭl-fyo͝or′ĭk) *adj.* Of, pertaining to, or containing sulfur.

sulfuric acid *n.* A very corrosive, dense, oily acid used esp. in the manufacture of a wide variety of chemicals.

sul·fur·ous (sŭl′fər-əs, sŭl-fyo͝or′əs) *adj.* **1.** Of, pertaining to, derived from, or containing sulfur. **2.** Emanating from or characteristic of burning sulfur <a *sulfurous* odor>

sulk (sŭlk) *v.* To be sullenly aloof or silent. —*n.* A sulky mood or display.

sulk·y[1] (sŭl′kē) *adj.* **-i·er, -i·est.** Given to sulking **:** moody. **—sulk′i·ly** *adv.* **—sulk′i·ness** *n.*

sulk·y[2] (sŭl′kē) *n., pl.* **-ies.** A light 2-wheeled 1-horse vehicle for 1 person.

sul·len (sŭl′ən) *adj.* **1.** Ill-humored and surly **:** morose. **2.** Gloomy or melancholy. **—sul′len·ly** *adv.* **—sul′len·ness** *n.*

sul·ly (sŭl′ē) *v.* **-lied, -ly·ing.** To soil or defile **:** taint.

sul·phur (sŭl′fər) *n. var. of* SULFUR.

sul·tan (sŭl′tən) *n.* A ruler of a Muslim country. **—sul′tan·ate′** (-tə-nāt′) *n.*

sul·tan·a (sŭl-tăn′ə, -tä′nə) *n.* **1.** The mother, wife, sister, or daughter of a sultan. **2. a.** A seedless, pale yellow grape. **b.** A raisin of the sultana.

sul·try (sŭl′trē) *adj.* **-tri·er, -tri·est. 1.** Hot and humid **:** muggy. **2.** Extremely hot **:** torrid. **3.** Voluptuous **:** sensual.

sum (sŭm) *n.* **1. a.** The result obtained by addition **:** total. **b.** An arithmetic problem. **2.** The whole quantity, amount, or number **:** aggregate. **3.** An amount of money. **4.** A summary. —*v.* **summed, sum·ming.** To find the sum of **:** add. **—sum up.** To recapitulate **:** summarize.

su·mac *also* **su·mach** (so͞o′măk′, sho͞o′-) *n.* A shrub or small trees of the genus *Rhus,* with compound leaves and clusters of small, usu. red berries.

sum·ma·rize (sŭm′ə-rīz′) *v.* **-rized, -riz·ing.** To state in a summary <*summarize* the report> **—sum′ma·ri·za′tion** *n.*

sum·ma·ry (sŭm′ə-rē) *n., pl.* **-ries.** A succinct statement of the principal points. —*adj.* **1.** Covering the principal points concisely **:** brief. **2.** Done quickly and without ceremony <*summary* dismissal> **—sum·mar′i·ly** (sə-mâr′ə-lē) *adv.*

sum·ma·tion (sə-mā′shən) *n.* A final statement that summarizes the principal points, esp. of the arguments in a trial.

sum·mer (sŭm′ər) *n.* The warmest season of the year, following spring and preceding autumn. —*v.* To pass the summer. **—sum′mer·y** *adj.*

sum·mer·house (sŭm′ər-hous′) *n.* A roofed structure that furnishes a shady refuge in a garden or park.

summer squash *n.* A squash that is eaten shortly after being picked rather than kept for storage.

sum·mer·time (sŭm′ər-tīm′) *n.* Summer.

sum·mit (sŭm′ĭt) *n.* The highest part, point, level, or degree.

sum·mon (sŭm′ən) *v.* **1.** To call together **:** convene. **2.** To send for **:** bid to come. **3.** To order to make an appearance in court. **4.** To call forth, esp. with effort **:** arouse <*summoned* up his nerve>

sum·mons (sŭm′ənz) *n., pl.* **-mons·es. 1.** A command or order to perform a particular duty or appear at a particular place. **2.** *Law.*

A notice summoning a defendant, witness, or juror to appear in court.

su•mo (sōō'mō) *n.* A stylized Japanese form of wrestling.

sump (sŭmp) *n.* **1.** A pit or hole that receives drainage. **2.** A cesspool.

sump•tu•ous (sŭmp'chōō-əs) *adj.* Very rich, expensive, luxurious, or splendid.

sun (sŭn) *n.* **1.** The star around which the earth and the other planets of the solar system orbit and whose heat and light sustain life on the earth. **2.** A star that is the center of a planetary system. **3.** The radiant energy, esp. visible light and heat, emitted by the sun : sunshine. —*v.* **sunned, sun•ning.** To bask in or expose to or as if to the rays of the sun. **—sun'less** *adj.*

sun•bathe (sŭn'bāth') *v.* To expose the body to sunlight. **—sun'bath'** (-băth', -bäth') *n.* **—sun'bath'er** *n.*

sun•belt *or* **Sun•belt** (sŭn'bĕlt') *n.* The S and SW states of the U.S.

sun block *n.* A preparation that prevents sunburn, usu. more protective than a sunscreen.

sun•bon•net (sŭn'bŏn'ĭt) *n.* A bonnet with a wide brim shading the face and neck from the sun.

sun•burn (sŭn'bûrn') *n.* An inflammation of the skin caused by overexposure to direct sunlight. —*v.* To affect or be affected with sunburn.

sun•burst (sŭn'bûrst') *n.* A design in the form of a central sunlike disk with radiating rays.

sun•dae (sŭn'dē, -dā') *n.* A portion of ice cream with a topping, as of syrup or nuts.

Sun•day (sŭn'dē, -dā') *n.* The first day of the week.

sun•der (sŭn'dər) *v.* To break apart.

sun•di•al (sŭn'dī'əl) *n.* An instrument that indicates the time of day from the shadow cast on a calibrated dial by a pointer.

sun•down (sŭn'doun') *n.* The time at which the sun sets.

sun•dries (sŭn'drēz) *pl.n.* Miscellaneous small items or articles.

sun•dry (sŭn'drē) *adj.* Miscellaneous.

sun•fish (sŭn'fĭsh') *n.* **1.** Any of various flat-bodied North American freshwater fishes of the family Centrarchidae. **2.** Any of several very large, round-bodied marine fishes of the family Molidae.

sun•flow•er (sŭn'flou'ər) *n.* A plant of the genus *Helianthus,* bearing large yellow-rayed dark-centered flowers with edible seeds rich in oil.

sung (sŭng) *v. p.p. & var. p.t. of* SING.

sun•glass•es (sŭn'glăs'ĭz) *pl.n.* Eyeglasses with tinted or polarized lenses to protect the eyes from the sun.

sunk (sŭngk) *v. p.p. & var. p.t. of* SINK.

sunk•en (sŭng'kən) *adj.* **1.** Fallen in : hollowed <*sunken* cheeks> **2.** Submerged <a *sunken* ship> **3.** Built or lying below a surrounding level <a *sunken* recreation room><a *sunken* pond>

sun lamp *n.* A lamp that emits a wide range of radiation and is used for cosmetic and therapeutic purposes.

sun•light (sŭn'līt') *n.* Sunshine.

sun•lit (sŭn'lĭt') *adj.* Illuminated by the light of the sun.

Sun•na *also* **Sun•nah** (sŏŏn'ə) *n.* The way of life prescribed as normative in Islam, based on the teachings and practices of Muhammad and on the Koran.

Sun•ni (sŏŏn'ē) *n., pl.* **-ni** *or* **-nis.** A member of the branch of Islam that accepts the first four caliphs as rightful successors of Muhammad. **—Sun'ni** *adj.* **—Sun'nite'** *n.*

sun•ny (sŭn'ē) *adj.* **-ni•er, -ni•est. 1.** Exposed to or full of sunshine. **2.** Bright and cheerful : merry.

sun•rise (sŭn'rīz') *n.* **1.** The first appearance of the sun above the horizon. **2.** The time of sunrise.

sun•roof (sŭn'rōōf', -rŏŏf') *n.* A car roof with a panel that can be slid back or lifted.

sun•screen (sŭn'skrēn') *n.* A preparation used to protect skin from the damaging rays of the sun.

sun•set (sŭn'sĕt') *n.* **1.** The disappearance of the sun below the horizon. **2.** The time of sunset.

sun•shade (sŭn'shād') *n.* Something, as a parasol or a billed cap, used as a shield against the sun's rays.

sun•shine (sŭn'shīn') *n.* **1.** The direct rays of the sun. **2.** A source of cheer or happiness. **—sun'shin'y** *adj.*

sun•spot (sŭn'spŏt') *n.* A dark spot that appears on the surface of the sun.

sun•stroke (sŭn'strōk') *n.* Heat stroke caused by exposure to the sun.

sun•tan (sŭn'tăn') *n.* A darkening of the skin from exposure to the sun. **—sun'tanned'** *adj.*

sun•up (sŭn'ŭp') *n.* Sunrise.

sup (sŭp) *v.* **supped, sup•ping.** To eat supper.

su•per[1] (sōō'pər) *n. Informal.* A superintendent, esp. of an apartment building.

su•per[2] (sōō'pər) *adj. Slang.* **1.** First-rate : excellent. **2.** Excessive in degree : extreme.

super– *pref.* **1.** Above : over : upon <*superimpose*> **2.** Superior in size, quality, number, or degree <*super*power> **3. a.** Exceeding a norm <*super*sonic> **b.** Excessive in degree or intensity <*super*subtle> **4.** More inclusive than a specified category <*super*order>

su•per•a•bun•dant (sōō'pər-ə-bŭn'dənt) *adj.* More than sufficient. **—su'per•a•bun'dance** *n.*

su•per•an•nu•at•ed (sōō'pər-ăn'yōō-ā'tĭd) *adj.* **1.** Retired from active duty because of age or infirmity. **2.** Obsolete.

su•perb (sōō-pûrb', sə-) *adj.* **1.** Of supreme quality : first-rate. **2.** Majestic : grand. **—su•perb'ly** *adv.*

su•per•car•go (sōō'pər-kär'gō) *n.* A merchant marine officer in charge of the cargo.

su•per•charg•er (sōō'pər-chär'jər) *n.* A device, as a compressor, for supplying air under

high pressure to an internal-combustion engine.
su•per•cil•i•ous (sōō'pər-sĭl'ē-əs) *adj.* Marked by or expressive of haughty scorn : disdainful. —**su'per•cil'i•ous•ly** *adv.*
su•per•class (sōō'pər-klăs') *n. Biol.* A taxonomic category ranking between a phylum and a class.
su•per•con•duc•tiv•i•ty (sōō'pər-kŏn'dŭk-tĭv'ĭ-tē) *n.* The complete loss of electrical resistance in certain metals and alloys at temperatures near absolute zero. —**su'per•con•duc'tive** (-kən-dŭk'tĭv) *adj.* —**su'per•con•duc'tor** *n.*
su•per•e•go (sōō'pər-ē'gō, -ĕg'ō) *n.* The part of the psyche that reflects the moral standards of the community and the conscience of authority.

su'per•a•chieve'ment *n.*
su'per•a•chiev'er *n.*
su'per•ac'id *adj.*
su'per•ac•tiv'i•ty *n.*
su'per•a•cute' *adj.*
su'per•a•dapt'a•ble *adj.*
su'per•aes•thet'ic *adj.*
su'per•af'flu•ence *n.*
su'per•a'gen•cy *n.*
su'per•al'ka•line *adj.*
su'per•am•bi'tious *adj.*
su'per•ar'du•ous *adj.*
su'per•ath•let'ic *adj.*
su'per•at•trac'tion *n.*
su'per•ben'e•fit *n.*
su'per•bomb' *n.*
su'per•brave' *adj.*
su'per•bright' *adj.*
su'per•bus'y *adj.*
su'per•can'did *adj.*
su'per•ca'pa•ble *adj.*
su'per•cau'tion *n.*
su'per•cer'e•mo'ni•ous *adj.*
su'per•chic' *adj.*
su'per•civ'i•lized' *adj.*
su'per•clean' *adj.*
su'per•co•los'sal *adj.*
su'per•com•plex' *adj.*
su'per•com•pres'sion *n.*
su'per•con'fi•dent *adj.*
su'per•con•glom'er•ate *n.*
su'per•con•ser'va•tive *adj.*
su'per•cool' *v.*
su'per•coun'try *n.*
su'per•crit'i•cal *adj.*
su'per•cul'ti•vat'ed *adj.*
su'per•cu'ri•ous *adj.*
su'per•cyn'i•cal *adj.*
su'per•del'i•cate *adj.*
su'per•de•luxe' *adj.*
su'per•de•mand' *n.*
su'per•de•vo'tion *n.*
su'per•dif'fi•cult' *adj.*
su'per•div'i•dend' *adj.*
su'per•ef•fec'tive *adj.*
su'per•ef•fi'cien•cy *n.*
su'per•ef•fi'cient *adj.*
su'per•e'go•ist *n.*
su'per•e•las'tic *adj.*
su'per•el'e•gance *n.*
su'per•el'o•quent *adj.*
su'per•em'i•nence *n.*
su'per•em'i•nent *adj.*
su'per•em'pha•sis *n.*
su'per•en•dur'ance *n.*
su'per•eth'i•cal *adj.*
su'per•ex•act'ing *adj.*
su'per•ex•cit'ed *adj.*
su'per•ex•pen'di•ture *n.*
su'per•ex•pres'sive *adj.*
su'per•fast' *adj.*
su'per•fem'i•nine *adj.*
su'per•fer'vent *adj.*
su'per•fine' *adj.*
su'per•flu'id *adj.* & *n.*
su'per•for'mal *adj.*
su'per•friend'ly *adj.*
su'per•fund' *n.*
su'per•gen'er•os'i•ty *n.*
su'per•glo'ri•ous *adj.*
su'per•gov'ern•ment *n.*
su'per•group' *n.*
su'per•growth' *n.*
su'per•heat' *v.*
su'per•he'ro *n.*
su'per•he•ro'ic *adj.*
su'per•her'o•ine *n.*
su'per•hit' *n.*
su'per•hype' *n.*
su'per•im•por'tant *adj.*
su'per•im•proved' *adj.*
su'per•in•cen'tive *n.*
su'per•in'di•vid'u•al•ist *n.*
su'per•in•dul'gence *n.*
su'per•in•dus'tri•ous *adj.*
su'per•in•gen'ious *adj.*
su'per•in•jus'tice *n.*
su'per•in•quis'i•tive *adj.*
su'per•in•sis'tent *adj.*
su'per•in'tel•lec'tu•al *adj.*
su'per•large' *adj.*
su'per•le'ni•ent *adj.*
su'per•li'ner *n.*
su'per•loy'al *adj.*
su'per•luck'y *adj.*
su'per•lux•u'ri•ous *adj.*
su'per•man' *n.*
su'per•mas'cu•line *adj.*
su'per•mil'i•tant *adj.*
su'per•mod'ern *adj.*
su'per•mod'est *adj.*
su'per•mun•dane' *adj.*
su'per•o•bese' *adj.*
su'per•ob'sti•nate *adj.*
su'per•of•fen'sive *adj.*
su'per•of•fi'cious *adj.*
su'per•op'ti•mis'tic *adj.*
su'per•or'di•nar'y *adj.*
su'per•or•gan'ic *adj.*
su'per•or'gan•ize' *v.*
su'per•pa'tient *adj.*
su'per•pa'tri•ot'ic *adj.*
su'per•phys'i•cal *adj.*
su'per•pi'ous *adj.*
su'per•po•lite' *adj.*
su'per•pow'er•ful *adj.*
su'per•pre•cise' *adj.*
su'per•pres'sure *n.*
su'per•prize' *n.*
su'per•pros'per•ous *adj.*
su'per•pure' *adj.*
su'per•race' *n.*
su'per•rad'i•cal *adj.* & *n.*
su'per•ra'tion•al *adj.*
su'per•re'al•ism *n.*
su'per•re'al•ist *adj.* & *n.*
su'per•re•fined' *adj.*
su'per•re•spect'a•ble *adj.*
su'per•rich' *adj.*
su'per•right'eous *adj.*
su'per•ro•man'tic *adj.*
su'per•safe' *adj.*
su'per•sar•cas'tic *adj.*
su'per•sat'is•fac'tion *n.*
su'per•scale' *n.*
su'per•schol'ar•ly *adj.*
su'per•school' *n.*
su'per•sci'en•tif'ic *adj.*
su'per•se'cre•cy *n.*
su'per•se'cret *adj.*
su'per•sell' *v.*
su'per•sen'si•tive *adj.*
su'per•sen'ti•men'tal *adj.*
su'per•se'ri•ous *adj.*
su'per•sim'pli•fy' *v.*
su'per•sleuth' *n.*
su'per•slick' *adj.*
su'per•smart' *adj.*
su'per•smooth' *adj.*
su'per•soft' *adj.*
su'per•sol'emn *adj.*
su'per•speed' *n.*
su'per•spy' *n.*
su'per•star' *n.*
su'per•state' *n.*
su'per•store' *n.*
su'per•stra'tum *n.*
su'per•strength' *n.*
su'per•stren'u•ous *adj.*
su'per•strict' *adj.*
su'per•strong' *adj.*
su'per•styl'ish *adj.*
su'per•sub'tle *adj.*
su'per•sweet' *adj.*
su'per•tank'er *n.*
su'per•ten'sion *n.*
su'per•thick' *adj.*
su'per•thin' *adj.*
su'per•thor'ough *adj.*
su'per•thrill'er *n.*
su'per•tight' *adj.*
su'per•ur'gent *adj.*
su'per•vig'i•lant *adj.*
su'per•vig'or•ous *adj.*
su'per•vi'tal *adj.*
su'per•weap'on *n.*
su'per•wide' *adj.*
su'per•wom'an *n.*
su'per•world'ly *adj.*
su'per•zeal'ous *adj.*

su•per•e•rog•a•to•ry (so͞o'pər-ə-rŏg'ə-tôr'ē, -tōr'ē) *adj.* Superfluous.

su•per•fi•cial (so͞o'pər-fĭsh'əl) *adj.* **1.** Of, pertaining to, affecting, or located on a surface. **2.** Concerned only with what is apparent. **3.** Lacking substance or depth. ★ *syns:* CURSORY, SHALLOW, SKETCHY —**su'per•fi'ci•al'i•ty** (-fĭsh'ē-ăl'ĭ-tē) *n.* —**su'per•fi'cial•ly** *adv.*

su•per•flu•ous (so͞o-pûr'flo͞o-əs) *adj.* Being beyond what is necessary, desirable, or sufficient : surplus. —**su'per•flu'i•ty** (so͞o'pər-flo͞o'ĭ-tē) *n.*

su•per•high•way (so͞o'pər-hī'wā') *n.* A broad highway, as an expressway, for high-speed traffic.

su•per•hu•man (so͞o'pər-hyo͞o'mən) *adj.* **1.** Being beyond or above the human : divine. **2.** Exceeding ordinary or normal human capability, power, or experience.

su•per•im•pose (so͞o'pər-ĭm-pōz') *v.* To place (one thing) on or over something else.

su•per•in•tend (so͞o'pər-ĭn-tĕnd') *v.* To supervise. —**su'per•in•ten'dence** *n.* —**su'per•in•ten'dent** *n.* & *adj.*

su•pe•ri•or (so͞o-pîr'ē-ər, sə-) *adj.* **1.** Of higher authority or rank. **2.** Of a higher kind or nature <*superior* knowledge> **3.** Of greater significance or value. **4.** Greater in amount or number. **5.** Haughty : arrogant. **6.** Seemingly indifferent, as to adversity or pain. **7.** Located higher up. —*n.* **1.** One who surpasses another in quality or is above another in rank. **2.** The head of a religious order or house. —**su•pe'ri•or'i•ty** (-pîr'ē-ôr'ĭ-tē, -ŏr'-) *n.*

su•per•la•tive (so͞o-pûr'lə-tĭv) *adj.* **1.** Of the highest degree of superiority : supreme. **2.** Of, pertaining to, or being the degree of comparison of an adjective or adverb that indicates the extreme or greatest extent or level. —*n.* **1.** One that is superlative. **2.** The very highest degree : peak. **3. a.** The superlative degree in a language. **b.** The superlative form of an adjective or adverb. —**su•per'la•tive•ly** *adv.*

su•per•mar•ket (so͞o'pər-mär'kĭt) *n.* A large self-service retail store at which food and household goods can be purchased.

su•per•nal (so͞o-pûr'nəl) *adj.* **1.** Heavenly : celestial. **2.** Of or coming from above.

su•per•nat•u•ral (so͞o'pər-năch'ər-əl) *adj.* **1.** Of or pertaining to an order of existence beyond the natural world. **2.** Of, pertaining to, or attributed to a divine agent. —**su'per•nat'u•ral•ly** *adv.*

su•per•no•va (so͞o'pər-nō'və) *n.* A rare and extremely bright nova.

su•per•nu•mer•ar•y (so͞o'pər-no͞o'mə-rĕr'ē, -nyo͞o'-) *adj.* Being in excess of the required, usual, or proper number : extra. —*n., pl.* **-ies. 1.** An extra thing or person. **2.** An actor who plays a nonspeaking part.

su•per•pow•er (so͞o'pər-pou'ər) *n.* An extremely influential and powerful nation.

su•per•sat•u•rate (so͞o'pər-săch'ə-rāt') *v.* To make (e.g., a chemical solution) more highly concentrated than is normally possible. —**su'per•sat'u•ra'tion** *n.*

su•per•scribe (so͞o'pər-skrīb') *v.* **-scribed, -scrib•ing.** To write on the upper part or outside. —**su'per•scrip'tion** *n.*

su•per•script (so͞o'pər-skrĭpt') *n.* A symbol or letter written next to and slightly above another character.

su•per•sede (so͞o'pər-sēd') *v.* **-sed•ed, -sed•ing. 1.** To take the place of : supplant. **2.** To set aside : displace.

su•per•son•ic (so͞o'pər-sŏn'ĭk) *adj.* Of, relating to, caused by, or moving at a speed greater than that of sound.

su•per•sti•tion (so͞o'pər-stĭsh'ən) *n.* **1.** A belief that is maintained despite evidence that it is unfounded or irrational. **2.** A belief, practice, or rite resulting from faith in chance, magic, or dogma. —**su'per•sti'tious** *adj.* —**su'per•sti'tious•ly** *adv.*

su•per•struc•ture (so͞o'pər-strŭk'chər) *n.* A structure built on top of something else.

su•per•vene (so͞o'pər-vēn') *v.* **-vened, -ven•ing.** To come or take place as something added, extraneous, or unexpected.

su•per•vise (so͞o'pər-vīz') *v.* **-vised, -vis•ing.** To direct and inspect the work, actions, or performance of : oversee. —**su'per•vi'sion** (-vĭzh'ən) *n.* —**su'per•vi'sor** *n.* —**su'per•vi'so•ry** (-vī'zə-rē) *adj.*

su•pine (so͞o-pīn', so͞o'pīn') *adj.* **1.** Lying on the back with the face upward. **2.** Not disposed to act : lethargic.

sup•per (sŭp'ər) *n.* The evening meal served when dinner is eaten at midday.

supper club *n.* A nightclub.

sup•plant (sə-plănt') *v.* To take the place of (another), esp. by underhand means or by force : supersede.

sup•ple (sŭp'əl) *adj.* **-pler, -plest. 1.** Readily bent without cracking or breaking : pliant. **2.** Marked by agility : limber. **3.** Yielding readily : compliant.

sup•ple•ment (sŭp'lə-mənt) *n.* **1.** Something that compensates for a deficiency or constitutes an addition. **2.** A part or section, as of a book, giving additional information or correcting errors. —*v.* (-mĕnt'). To be or provide a supplement to. —**sup'ple•men'ta•ry** (-mĕn'tə-rē, -mĕn'trē), **sup'ple•ment'al** (-mĕn'tl) *adj.*

sup•pli•ant (sŭp'lē-ənt) *n.* One who supplicates : pleader.

sup•pli•cant (sŭp'lĭ-kənt) *n.* A suppliant.

sup•pli•cate (sŭp'lĭ-kāt') *v.* **-cat•ed, -cat•ing. 1.** To ask for humbly and earnestly by or as if by praying. **2.** To make an earnest appeal. —**sup'pli•ca'tion** *n.*

sup•ply (sə-plī') *v.* **-plied, -ply•ing. 1.** To make available for use : furnish. **2.** To provide with what is lacking or needed. **3.** To fill sufficiently : satisfy <*supply* a lack> —*n., pl.* **-plies. 1.** The act of supplying. **2.** An amount or quantity, esp. of a commodity, that is available or needed. **3.** *often* **supplies.** A quantity, as of merchandise, held in reserve and dispensed when needed : provisions. **4.** The commodities available for meeting a demand or for purchase at a given price. —**sup•pli'er** *n.*

sup•port (sə-pôrt′, -pōrt′) *v.* **1.** To bear the weight of and maintain in position : hold up. **2.** To be able to bear : tolerate. **3.** To supply with the necessities of life, as food, shelter, and money : maintain. **4.** To corroborate : substantiate. **5.** To give aid or assistance to : back up. —*n.* **1.** The act of supporting or state of being supported. **2.** One that supports. —**sup•port′a•ble** *adj.* —**sup•port′er** *n.* —**sup•por′tive** *adj.*

sup•pose (sə-pōz′) *v.* **-posed, -pos•ing. 1.** To assume as true, esp. for the sake of argument. **2.** To consider likely or probable <I *suppose* you're right.> **3.** To expect <She's *supposed* to wait.>

sup•posed (sə-pōzd′, -pō′zĭd) *adj.* Accepted as being, often mistakenly. —**sup•pos′ed•ly** (-pō′zĭd-lē) *adv.*

sup•pos•ing (sə-pō′zĭng) *conj.* Assuming that.

sup•po•si•tion (sŭp′ə-zĭsh′ən) *n.* **1.** The act of supposing. **2.** Something supposed.

sup•pos•i•to•ry (sə-pŏz′ĭ-tôr′ē, -tōr′ē) *n., pl.* **-ries.** A solid medication designed for insertion into a bodily cavity, as the rectum, where it melts.

sup•press (sə-prĕs′) *v.* **1.** To put an end to, esp. by force : subdue <*suppress* a rebellion> **2.** To keep from being revealed, circulated, or published. **3.** To hold back : repress <*suppressed* her laughter> —**sup•pres′sion** *n.* —**sup•pres′sive** *adj.*

sup•pu•rate (sŭp′yə-rāt′) *v.* **-rat•ed, -rat•ing.** To discharge or form pus. —**sup′pu•ra′tion** *n.*

su•pra•na•tion•al (so͞o′prə-năsh′ə-nəl) *adj.* Extending beyond national boundaries or authority.

su•prem•a•cist (so͞o-prĕm′ə-sĭst) *n.* One who advocates the supremacy of a particular group.

su•prem•a•cy (so͞o-prĕm′ə-sē) *n., pl.* **-cies. 1.** The state or quality of being supreme. **2.** Supreme power, authority, or rank.

su•preme (sə-prēm′) *adj.* **1.** Of highest power, authority, or rank. **2.** Of greatest importance or finest quality. **3.** Final : ultimate <the *supreme* moment> —**su•preme′ly** *adv.* —**su•preme′ness** *n.*

Supreme Being *n.* God.

sur•cease (sûr′sēs′) *n.* Cessation, esp. a temporary end.

sur•charge (sûr′chärj′) *n.* **1.** An extra charge added to a cost or amount. **2.** Something overprinted on a postage stamp to give it a new value or denomination. **3.** An excessive burden : overload. —*v.* **1.** To charge an extra amount. **2.** To overcharge. **3.** To print a surcharge on (a stamp).

sur•cin•gle (sûr′sĭng′gəl) *n.* A girth that binds something, as a saddle or pack, to a horse's body.

sure (sho͝or) *adj.* **sur•er, sur•est. 1.** Impossible to doubt : certain. **2.** Firm and steady <a *sure* foothold> **3.** Feeling certainty : confident. **4.** Bound to happen : inevitable. **5.** Dependable : reliable. —*adv.* In a sure manner : surely. —**sure′ly** *adv.*

sure-fire (sho͝or′fīr′) *adj. Informal.* Certain to be successful.

sure-foot•ed (sho͝or′fo͝ot′ĭd) *adj.* Unlikely to stumble or fall.

sure•ty (sho͝or′ĭ-tē) *n., pl.* **-ties. 1.** The state of being sure : certainty. **2.** Something that secures, as against damage : guarantee. **3.** One who has agreed to be legally responsible for another person.

surf (sûrf) *n.* The waves of the sea as they break on the shoreline. —*v.* To engage in surfing. —**surf′er** *n.*

sur•face (sûr′fəs) *n.* **1.** The topmost or outside boundary of a body or object. **2.** Outward or superficial appearance. —*adj.* **1.** Of or situated on a surface. **2.** Superficial. —*v.* **-faced, -fac•ing. 1.** To provide with a surface. **2.** To rise or come to the surface.

surf•board (sûrf′bôrd′, -bōrd′) *n.* A long, narrow board used in surfing.

sur•feit (sûr′fĭt) *v.* To feed or supply to repletion : satiate. —*n.* **1. a.** Overindulgence, as in food or drink. **b.** Disgust caused by such overindulgence. **2.** An overabundant amount : excess.

surf•ing (sûr′fĭng) *n.* The sport of riding the surf into shore, esp. on a surfboard.

surge (sûrj) *v.* **surged, surg•ing. 1.** To move in or as if in billows or waves : swell. **2.** To increase suddenly to a high or excessive level. —*n.* **1.** A large wave of water : swell. **2.** A swelling like that of rolling waves <a *surge* of anger> **3.** A sudden increase <a *surge* of electric current>

sur•geon (sûr′jən) *n.* A physician who specializes in surgery.

sur•ger•y (sûr′jə-rē) *n., pl.* **-ies. 1.** The branch of medicine in which physical injury, deformity, and disease are treated by the cutting and removal or repair of bodily parts. **2.** A surgical operating room or laboratory. **3.** The work of a surgeon.

sur•gi•cal (sûr′jĭ-kəl) *adj.* **1.** Of, relating to, or characteristic of surgeons or surgery. **2.** Used in surgery. —**sur′gi•cal•ly** *adv.*

sur•ly (sûr′lē) *adj.* **-li•er, -li•est.** Bad-tempered and rude. —**sur′li•ness** *n.*

sur•mise (sər-mīz′) *v.* **-mised, -mis•ing.** To conjecture : guess. —**sur•mise′** *n.*

sur•mount (sər-mount′) *v.* **1.** To conquer : overcome. **2.** To ascend to or be at the top of. —**sur•mount′a•ble** *adj.*

sur•name (sûr′nām′) *n.* A person's last or family name.

sur•pass (sər-păs′) *v.* **1.** To be beyond the limits, capacity, or powers of. **2.** To be better, greater, or stronger than. ★ ***syns:*** EXCEED, EXCEL, OUTDO, OUTSHINE, OUTSTRIP, TRANSCEND —**sur•pass′ing•ly** *adv.*

sur•plice (sûr′plĭs) *n.* A loose-fitting white ecclestiastical vestment with full, flowing sleeves that is worn over a cassock.

sur•plus (sûr′pləs) *n.* An amount or quantity beyond what is used or needed : excess. —*adj.* Being a surplus.

sur•prise (sər-prīz′) *v.* **-prised, -pris•ing. 1.** To catch or take unawares. **2.** To attack without warning. **3.** To cause to feel astonishment : amaze. —*n.* **1.** A feeling of astonishment : amazement. **2.** Something that surprises. **3.** An attack made without warning. —**sur•pris′ing•ly** *adv.*

sur•re•al (sə-rē′əl) *adj.* Having the characteristics and qualities associated with surrealism : grotesque.

sur•re•al•ism (sə-rē′ə-lĭz′əm) *n.* A 20th-cent. literary and artistic movement in which fantastic imagery and incongruous juxtapositions are meant to express the workings of the subconscious. —**sur•re′al•ist** *n.* —**sur•re′al•is′tic** *adj.* —**sur•re′al•is′ti•cal•ly** *adv.*

sur•ren•der (sə-rĕn′dər) *v.* **1.** To give up control or possession of to another on demand or under compulsion. **2.** To give (oneself) over, as to an emotion : yield. —*n.* The act of surrendering.

sur•rep•ti•tious (sûr′əp-tĭsh′əs) *adj.* Made, done, or acting in secret : stealthy. —**sur′rep•ti′tious•ly** *adv.*

sur•rey (sûr′ē, sŭr′ē) *n., pl.* **-reys.** A horse-drawn 4-wheeled carriage with 2 seats.

sur•ro•gate (sûr′ə-gĭt, -gāt′, sŭr′-) *n.* **1.** A substitute. **2.** A judge in some U.S. states with jurisdiction over the probate of wills and settlement of estates.

sur•round (sə-round′) *v.* **1.** To extend around all edges of. **2.** To shut in on all sides so as to prevent escape : confine. ★ ***syns:*** CIRCLE, COMPASS, ENCIRCLE, ENCLOSE, GIRD, RING

sur•round•ings (sə-roun′dĭngz) *pl.n.* The conditions that surround one.

sur•tax (sûr′tăks′) *n.* A tax imposed in addition to a normal tax.

sur•veil•lance (sər-vā′ləns) *n.* Close observation, esp. of a person or group under suspicion.

sur•vey (sər-vā′, sûr′vā′) *v.* **1. a.** To look over and examine in detail. **b.** To study or view comprehensively. **2.** To determine the position, boundaries, area, and elevation of a part of the earth's surface by measuring angles and distances. —*n.* (sûr′vā′), *pl.* **-veys. 1.** A detailed examination : inspection. **2.** A comprehensive view <a *survey* of European history> **3. a.** The process of surveying land. **b.** A map or plan of surveyed land. —**sur•vey′or** *n.*

sur•vey•ing (sər-vā′ĭng) *n.* The act, profession, or science of making land surveys.

sur•vive (sər-vīv′) *v.* **-vived, -viv•ing. 1.** To continue to live or exist. **2.** To live longer than : outlive. —**sur•viv′al** *n.* —**sur•vi′vor** *n.*

sus•cep•ti•ble (sə-sĕp′tə-bəl) *adj.* **1.** Easily influenced, moved, or affected : sensitive. **2.** Prone to be subject <*susceptible* to infections> **3.** Capable of accepting or permitting <an argument not *susceptible* of proof> —**sus•cep′ti•bil′i•ty** *n.*

su•shi (so͞o′shē) *n.* A dish of Japanese origin that consists of thin slices of fresh raw fish or seaweed wrapped around a cake of cooked rice.

sus•pect (sə-spĕkt′) *v.* **1.** To believe without being sure : surmise. **2.** To be suspicious about : distrust. **3.** To consider to be guilty without proof. —*n.* (sŭs′pĕkt′). Someone who is suspected, esp. of a crime. —*adj.* (sŭs′pĕkt′). Open to or considered with suspicion.

sus•pend (sə-spĕnd′) *v.* **1.** To bar for a period from an office, privilege, or position. **2.** To cause to stop temporarily : interrupt. **3. a.** To put off for a time : postpone <*suspend* judgment> **b.** To make temporarily ineffective <*suspend* parking regulations> **4.** To hang, esp. so as to allow free movement except at the point of attachment. **5.** To keep from falling or sinking without apparent support <particles of cork *suspended* in wine>

sus•pend•er (sə-spĕn′dər) *n.* One of a pair of straps worn over the shoulders to support a skirt or trousers.

sus•pense (sə-spĕns′) *n.* **1.** Suspension. **2.** Apprehension resulting from uncertainty : anxiety. **3.** A feeling of pleasurable excitement as to a result. —**sus•pense′ful** *adj.*

sus•pen•sion (sə-spĕn′shən) *n.* **1.** The act of suspending or state of being suspended. **2.** A device by which something, as a mechanical part, is suspended. **3.** *Chem.* A noncolloidal dispersion of solid particles in a liquid.

suspension bridge *n.* A bridge whose roadway is hung from cables stretched between supporting towers.

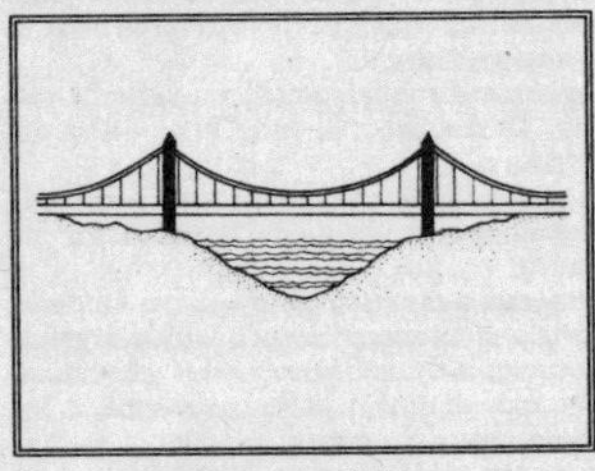

suspension bridge

sus•pi•cion (sə-spĭsh′ən) *n.* **1.** The act or an instance of suspecting something, esp. something wrong, without sufficient evidence or proof. **2.** A minute trace : hint.

sus•pi•cious (sə-spĭsh′əs) *adj.* **1.** Arousing or tending to arouse suspicion. **2.** Given to suspicion : distrustful. **3.** Expressing suspicion. —**sus•pi′cious•ly** *adv.*

sus•tain (sə-stān′) *v.* **1.** To hold up : support. **2.** To keep up : maintain <couldn't *sustain* their interest> **3.** To supply with nourishment. **4.** To support the spirits, courage, or resolution of. **5.** To withstand : endure <*sustain* a disappointment> **6.** To undergo : suffer <*sustained* an injury> **7.** To uphold as valid, true, or legal. **8.** To corroborate : confirm. ★ ***syns:*** BOLSTER, BUOY, PROP, SUPPORT, UPHOLD

sus•te•nance (sŭs′tə-nəns) *n.* **1.** The act of sustaining or state of being sustained. **2.** Something that nourishes : food. **3.** Something that sustains, strengthens, or supports. **4.** Means of maintaining life : livelihood.

su•ture (so͞o′chər) *n.* **1.** Material or a stitch used to join the edges of a wound or incision. **2.** A seamlike line of junction, as between 2 bones of the skull. **—su′ture** *v.*

su•ze•rain (so͞o′zər-ən, -zə-rān′) *n.* **1.** A feudal lord. **2.** A nation that controls the international affairs of another nation but permits it domestic sovereignty. **—su′ze•rain•ty** *n.*

svelte (sfĕlt) *adj.* **svelt•er, svelt•est.** Slender : willowy.

swab (swŏb) *n.* **1.** A small mass of absorbent material used esp. for cleaning or applying medicine. **2.** A mop, as that used to clean decks. **3.** *Slang.* A sailor. —*v.* **swabbed, swab•bing.** To clean, treat, or remove with a swab.

swad•dle (swŏd′l) *v.* **-dled, -dling. 1.** To wrap closely : envelop. **2.** To wrap (an infant) in strips of cloth.

swaddling clothes *pl.n.* **1.** Strips of cloth wrapped around a newborn infant to hold its legs and arms still. **2.** Restrictions imposed on the immature.

swag (swăg) *n. Slang.* Stolen money or property : booty.

swage (swāj) *n.* A tool used to shape metal. **—swage** *v.*

swag•ger (swăg′ər) *v.* **1.** To walk with an insolent or conceited air : strut. **2.** To brag : boast. **—swag′ger** *n.*

Swa•hi•li (swä-hē′lē) *n.* A Bantu language of E and C Africa that is widely used as a lingua franca.

swain (swān) *n.* **1.** A country youth, esp. a shepherd. **2.** A suitor.

swal•low[1] (swŏl′ō) *v.* **1.** To cause to pass into the stomach through the mouth. **2.** To consume as if by swallowing : engulf. **3.** To accept humbly : bear. **4.** *Slang.* To believe without questioning. **5.** To take back : retract <had to *swallow* his words> —*n.* **1.** The act of swallowing. **2.** The amount that can be swallowed at one time.

swal•low[2] (swŏl′ō) *n.* A bird of the family Hirundinidae, with long wings and a usu. forked tail.

swal•low•tail (swŏl′ō-tāl′) *n.* **1.** A deeply forked tail of or like that of a swallow. **2.** A butterfly of the family Papilionidae, with a taillike projection on each hind wing. **3.** A man's black coat worn for formal daytime occasions and having a long rounded and split tail.

swam (swăm) *v. p.t.* of SWIM.

swa•mi (swä′mē) *n.* A Hindu mystic or religious teacher.

swamp (swŏmp, swômp) *n.* A wet lowland region : marsh. —*v.* **1.** To cover with or drench in liquid. **2.** To deluge : overwhelm. **3.** To submerge by filling with water. **—swamp′i•ness** *n.* **—swamp′y** *adj.*

swamp fever *n.* Malaria.

swan (swŏn) *n.* A large aquatic bird, esp. of the genera *Cygnus* or *Olor,* with webbed feet, a long slender neck, and usu. white plumage.

swank (swăngk) *also* **swank•y** (swăng′kē) *adj.* **-i•er, -i•est. 1.** Fashionable and elegant. **2.** Ostentatious : showy. —*n.* **swank. 1.** Elegance. **2.** Ostentation : showiness.

swan's-down (swŏnz′doun′) *n.* **1.** The soft down of a swan. **2.** A soft woolen or cotton fabric with a thick nap.

swan song *n.* A farewell or final appearance, declaration, work, or act.

swap (swŏp) *v.* **swapped, swap•ping.** *Informal.* To trade one thing for another : exchange. **—swap** *n.*

sward (swôrd) *n.* Grass-covered ground.

swarm (swôrm) *n.* **1.** A large number of bees, together with a queen bee, moving together to start a new colony. **2.** A large number of persons or things, esp. when in motion : crowd. —*v.* **1.** To leave a beehive in a swarm. **2.** To gather in large numbers : throng. **3.** To be filled : teem <*swarming* with mosquitoes>

swart (swôrt) *adj.* Swarthy.

swar•thy (swôr′*th*ē) *adj.* **-thi•er, -thi•est.** Of dark color or complexion.

swash (swŏsh, swôsh) *v.* To move with a splashing sound. **—swash** *n.*

swash•buck•ler (swŏsh′bŭk′lər, swôsh′-) *n.* A flamboyant soldier, adventurer, or daredevil. **—swash′buck′ling** *adj.*

swas•ti•ka (swŏs′tĭ-kə) *n.* A symbol consisting of a Greek cross with the ends of the arms bent at right angles.

swat (swŏt) *v.* **swat•ted, swat•ting.** To hit with a sharp blow : slap. **—swat** *n.* **—swat′ter** *n.*

swatch (swŏch) *n.* A sample strip, as of fabric.

swath (swŏth, swôth) *n.* **1.** The width of a stroke of a scythe or mowing-machine blade. **2. a.** A path made in mowing. **b.** The cut grass or grain lying on a swath.

swathe (swŏ*th*, swô*th*) *v.* **swathed, swath•ing.** To wrap with or as if with bandages : bind.

sway (swā) *v.* **1.** To move or cause to move from side to side or back and forth. **2.** To bend to one side : veer. **3.** To vacillate. **4.** To exert control over or influence on. ★ ***syns:*** TEETER, TOTTER, WAVER, WEAVE, WOBBLE —*n.* **1.** The act of swinging from side to side or back and forth. **2.** Dominion : power. **3.** Influence.

sway•back (swā′băk′) *n.* An abnormal sagging of the spine. **—sway′backed′** *adj.*

swear (swâr) *v.* **swore** (swôr, swōr), **sworn** (swôrn, swōrn), **swear•ing. 1.** To declare solemnly under oath. **2.** To vow : promise. **3.** To use profanity : curse. **4.** To declare to be true while calling on God or something held sacred. **5.** To administer a legal oath to. **6.** To bind by or as if by means of an oath. **—swear in.** To administer an oath of office to. **—swear′er** *n.*

swear•word (swâr′wûrd′) *n.* An obscene or blasphemous word or phrase.

sweat (swĕt) *v.* **sweat•ed** *or* **sweat, sweat•ing. 1.** To excrete or cause to excrete salty liquid through the pores of the skin : perspire. **2.** To condense and accumulate drops of moisture on the surface. **3.** To work hard enough to sweat. **4.** *Informal.* To cause to work too hard **:** overwork. **5.** *Informal.* To be anxious **:** worry. —*n.* **1.** Salty liquid excreted by the sweat glands **:** perspiration. **2.** Moisture that condenses on a surface in the form of drops. **3.** *Informal.* A state of anxiety. **—sweat'y** *adj.*

sweat•er (swĕt'ər) *n.* A knitted or crocheted outer garment for the upper body.

sweat gland *n.* Any of the numerous small, tubular glands of the skin in most mammals that acts to secrete perspiration externally through pores.

sweat shirt *n.* A loose cotton jersey pullover.

sweat•shop (swĕt'shŏp') *n.* A shop or factory in which employees work long hours under bad conditions at low wages.

sweep (swēp) *v.* **swept** (swĕpt), **sweep•ing. 1.** To clean or remove with or as if with a brush. **2.** To touch lightly in passing over **:** brush. **3.** To move, remove, or convey by wind or rain. **4.** To surge or flow over with speed and sustained force <flood waters *sweeping* over the river bank> **5.** To move majestically or gracefully. **6.** To carry away, destroy, or remove by continuous action <*swept* the papers off the desk> —*n.* **1.** The act or motion of sweeping <the *sweep* of oars> **2.** Scope **:** range. **3.** An extent **:** reach <a *sweep* of ice> **4.** A surging or flowing force or movement. **5.** A contour **:** curve. **6.** A chimney sweep. **7.** The winning of all the stages or prizes in a contest. **—sweep'er** *n.*

sweep•back (swēp'băk') *n.* The backward slant of the leading edge of an airfoil.

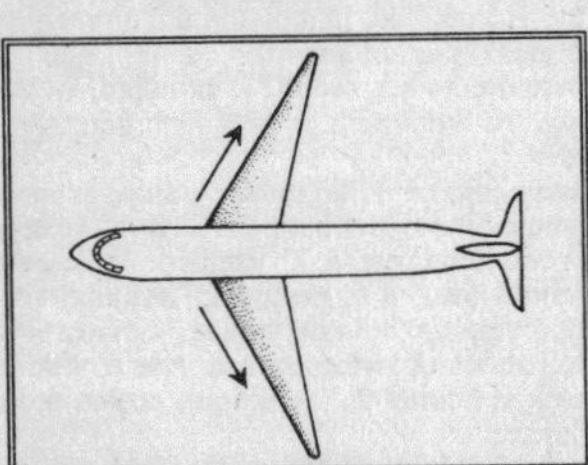

sweepback

sweep•ing (swē'pĭng) *adj.* **1.** Extending over a wide area. **2.** Curving. **3.** Thoroughgoing **:** extensive <*sweeping* changes> —*n.* **sweepings.** Things that are swept up **:** debris. **—sweep'ing•ly** *adv.*

sweep•stakes (swēp'stāks') *also* **sweep•stake** (-stāk') *n., pl.* **-stakes. 1.** A lottery in which the participants' contributions form a fund to be awarded as a prize to the winner or winners. **2.** An event or contest, as a horse race, whose result determines the winner of a sweepstakes.

sweet (swēt) *adj.* **1. a.** Having a sugary taste. **b.** Pleasing in taste. **2.** Pleasing to the senses or feelings <the *sweet* fragrance of lilacs> <a *sweet* satisfaction> **3.** Agreeable in disposition. **4.** Not salty or salted <*sweet* butter> **5.** Not spoiled, sour, or stale <*sweet* cream> —*n.* **1.** Something that is sweet. **2.** Candy. **3.** A dear or beloved person. **—sweet'ness** *n.*

sweet alyssum *n.* A widely cultivated plant, *Lobularia maritima,* bearing small, fragrant white or purplish flower clusters.

sweet•bread (swēt'brĕd') *n.* The thymus or pancreas of a young animal, as a calf, used for food.

sweet•bri•er *also* **sweet•bri•ar** (swēt'brī'ər) *n.* A European rose, *Rosa eglanteria,* with prickly stems, fragrant leaves, and pink flowers.

sweet corn *n.* An edible variety of corn, *Zea mays rugosa,* with kernels that are sweet when young.

sweet•en (swēt'n) *v.* To make or become sweet or sweeter. **—sweet'en•er** *n.*

sweet•en•ing (swēt'n-ĭng) *n.* Something used to sweeten.

sweet•heart (swēt'härt') *n.* One who is loved **:** dear.

sweet•meat (swēt'mēt') *n.* **1.** Candy. **2.** Crystallized or candied fruit.

sweet pea *n.* A climbing plant, *Lathyrus odoratus,* grown for its fragrant, variously colored flowers.

sweet pepper *n.* A pepper plant, *Capsicum frutescens grossum,* raised for its edible, bell-shaped, mild-flavored fruit.

sweet potato *n.* A tropical American vine, *Ipomoea batatas,* raised for its orange-colored edible root.

sweet-talk (swēt'tôk') *v.* To coax with flattery **:** cajole. **—sweet talk** *n.*

sweet tooth *n. Informal.* A fondness or desire for sweets, as pastry.

sweet Wil•liam (wĭl'yəm) *n.* A widely grown plant, *Dianthus barbatus,* with flat, dense varicolored flower clusters.

swell (swĕl) *v.* **swelled, swelled** *or* **swol•len** (swō'lən), **swell•ing. 1.** To increase in size, volume, force, number, or intensity. **2. a.** To expand excessively or abnormally, as from internal pressure. **b.** To bulge **:** protrude. **3.** To fill or be filled with an emotion <*swelled* with self-importance> —*n.* **1.** A long ocean wave that moves continuously without breaking. **2.** A gradual increase, as in size or volume. **3.** *Informal.* One who is fashionably dressed or prominent in fashionable society. —*adj.* **1.** *Informal.* Stylish. **2.** Fine **:** excellent.

swelled head *n.* An unduly high opinion of oneself **:** conceit.

swell•head (swĕl'hĕd') *n.* Someone with a swelled head. **—swell'head'ed** *adj.*

swell•ing (swĕl'ĭng) *n.* **1.** The state of being swollen. **2.** Something that is swollen.

swel•ter (swĕl'tər) *v.* To suffer from oppressive heat.

swept (swĕpt) *v. p.t. & p.p. of* SWEEP.

swerve (swûrv) *v.* **swerved, swerv•ing.** To turn aside abruptly from a straight or direct course : veer. **—swerve** *n.*
swift (swĭft) *adj.* **1.** Moving or capable of moving with great speed. **2.** Occurring, coming, or accomplished quickly. *—n.* Any of several dark-colored birds of the family Apodidae, with long, slender wings. **—swift'ly** *adv.* **—swift'ness** *n.*
swig (swĭg) *Informal. —n.* A long draft of a liquid : gulp. **—swig** *v.*
swill (swĭl) *n.* **1.** A mixture of edible garbage and liquid fed to animals. **2.** Refuse : garbage. *—v.* **1.** To drink greedily or to excess. **2.** To feed (animals) with swill.
swim (swĭm) *v.* **swam** (swăm), **swum** (swŭm), **swim•ming. 1.** To propel oneself through water by movements of the body or parts of the body. **2.** To move smoothly as though gliding. **3.** To be flooded or covered with or as if with a liquid. **4.** To feel dizzy : reel. **5.** To cross by swimming. *—n.* The act or a period of swimming. **—in the swim.** *Informal.* Participating or involved in the main current of affairs or activities. **—swim'mer** *n.*
swim•ming•ly (swĭm'ĭng-lē) *adv.* With ease and success.
swim•suit (swĭm'so͞ot') *n.* A garment worn for swimming.
swin•dle (swĭn'dl) *v.* **-dled, -dling.** To cheat out of money or property : defraud. **—swin'dle** *n.* **—swin'dler** *n.*
swine (swīn) *n., pl.* **swine. 1.** A hoofed mammal of the family Suidae, which includes pigs and hogs. **2.** A despicable person. **—swin'ish** *adj.*
swing (swĭng) *v.* **swung** (swŭng), **swing•ing. 1.** To move or cause to move freely back and forth suspended or as if suspended from above. **2.** To walk or move with a free swaying motion. **3.** To move in a broad arc. **4.** To turn or move in place on a pivot or hinge. **5.** *Slang.* To be executed by hanging. **6.** To manage successfully. **7.** To have a compelling rhythm. **8.** *Slang.* To be up-to-date and spirited. *—n.* **1.** The act of swinging. **2.** The distance through which something travels while swinging. **3.** A seat suspended from above on which to swing for amusement. **4.** Music based on jazz but usu. played by a larger band and marked by simpler harmonic and rhythmic patterns. **—swing'er** *n.*
swing shift *n. Informal.* A factory work shift between the day and night shifts that lasts from approx. 4 P.M. to midnight.
swipe (swīp) *n.* A heavy sweeping blow or stroke. *—v.* **swiped, swip•ing. 1.** To strike with or make a swipe. **2.** *Slang.* To filch : steal.
swirl (swûrl) *v.* To move with a rotating motion like that of a whirlpool : spin. **—swirl** *n.* **—swirl'y** *adj.*
swish (swĭsh) *v.* **1.** To make or move with a hissing sound. **2.** To make or move with a rustling sound. **—swish** *n.*
Swiss (swĭs) *n., pl.* **Swiss.** A native or inhabitant of Switzerland. **—Swiss** *adj.*
Swiss chard *n.* Chard.
Swiss cheese *n.* A hard pale-yellow or white cheese with large holes.
Swiss steak *n.* A round or shoulder steak that is pounded with flour and braised.
switch (swĭch) *n.* **1.** A thin flexible rod, stick, whip, or twig. **2.** A blow administered with a switch. **3.** A device for breaking or opening an electric circuit. **4.** A device for transferring a railroad locomotive or car from one track to another. **5.** A shift from one thing to another. **6.** A thick strand of hair used to supplement one's own hair in a coiffure. *—v.* **1.** To whip with or as if with a switch : lash. **2.** To swish back and forth : whisk. **3.** To change : exchange. **4.** To connect, disconnect, or transfer by operating a switch.
switch•back (swĭch'băk') *n.* A road, railroad, or trail that ascends a steep incline in a zigzag course.
switch•blade knife (swĭch'blād') *n.* A pocket knife with a blade operated by a spring.
switch•board (swĭch'bôrd', -bōrd') *n.* A panel on which switches for operating and controlling electric circuits are mounted.
switch hitter *n.* A baseball player who can bat with both the right and the left hand.
switch•man (swĭch'mən) *n.* Someone who operates a railroad switch.
swiv•el (swĭv'əl) *n.* A coupling device, as a link or pivot, that permits attached parts to rotate freely. *—v.* **-eled, -el•ing** *or* **-elled, -el•ling.** To rotate or turn on or as if on a swivel.
swiz•zle stick (swĭz'əl) *n.* A rod for stirring mixed drinks.
swol•len (swō'lən) *v. var. p.p. of* SWELL.
swoon (swo͞on) *v.* To faint. **—swoon** *n.*
swoop (swo͞op) *v.* To pounce swiftly and suddenly like a bird descending on its prey. **—swoop** *n.*
sword (sôrd) *n.* **1.** A weapon consisting of a long, pointed cutting or thrusting blade. **2.** A symbol of martial power or authority. **3.** The use of force, as in war.
sword•fish (sôrd'fĭsh') *n.* A very large marine game and food fish, *Xiphias gladius,* with the upper jaw projecting in a long, swordlike extension.
sword•play (sôrd'plā') *n.* The act, skill, or art of using a sword.
swords•man (sôrdz'mən) *n.* Someone skilled in the use of the sword. **—swords'man•ship'** *n.*
sword•tail (sôrd'tāl') *n.* A small, brightly colored freshwater fish, *Xiphophorus helleri,* of Central America.
swore (swôr, swōr) *v. p.t. of* SWEAR.
sworn (swôrn, swōrn) *v. p.p. of* SWEAR.
swum (swŭm) *v. p.p. of* SWIM.
swung (swŭng) *v. p.t. & p.p. of* SWING.
syb•a•rite (sĭb'ə-rīt') *n.* Someone who is devoted to pleasure and luxury. **—syb'a•rit'ic** (-rĭt'ĭk) *adj.*
syc•a•more (sĭk'ə-môr', -mōr') *n.* **1.** A North American deciduous tree, *Platanus occidentalis,* with lobed leaves and ball-like seed clusters. **2.** An Old World tree, *Acer pseudopla-*

tanus, that resembles and is related to the maples.

syc•o•phant (sĭk′ə-fənt, -făntʹ) *n.* An obsequious flatterer. —**syc′o•phan•cy** *n.* —**syc′o•phan′tic** (-fănʹtĭk) *adj.*

syl•la•bar•y (sĭlʹə-bĕr′ē) *n., pl.* **-ies.** A list of syllables, esp. a list or set of written characters, each representing a syllable.

syl•lab•i•cate (sə-lăbʹĭ-kāt′) *v.* **-cat•ed, -cat•ing.** To divide or form into syllables. —**syl•lab′i•ca′tion** *n.*

syl•lab•i•fy (sə-lăbʹə-fī′) *v.* **-fied, -fy•ing.** To syllabicate. —**syl•lab′i•fi•ca′tion** *n.*

syl•la•ble (sĭlʹə-bəl) *n.* **1.** A unit of spoken language that consists of a single uninterrupted sound and forms a whole word, as *cat,* or a division of a word, as *dif-* in *difficult.* **2.** One or more letters or phonetic symbols representing a syllable. —**syl•lab′ic** (sə-lăbʹĭk) *adj.*

syl•la•bus (sĭlʹə-bəs) *n., pl.* **-bus•es** *or* **-bi** (-bī′). A brief outline of the main points of a book, lecture, or course of study.

syl•lo•gism (sĭlʹə-jĭz′əm) *n.* A formal argument consisting of a major premise and a minor premise and a conclusion that is logically derived from the premises. —**syl′lo•gis′tic** *adj.*

sylph (sĭlf) *n.* **1.** An imaginary being believed to inhabit the air. **2.** A gracefully slim woman.

syl•van (sĭlʹvən) *adj.* **1.** Of, relating to, living in, or typical of forest regions. **2.** Abounding in trees : wooded.

sym•bi•o•sis (sĭm′bē-ōʹsĭs, -bī-) *n. Biol.* The living together in close association of 2 unlike organisms, esp. when mutually advantageous. —**sym′bi•ot′ic** (-ŏtʹĭk) *adj.*

sym•bol (sĭmʹbəl) *n.* **1.** Something that represents or stands for something else, as by resemblance or association. **2.** A written or printed character or sign representing an element, operation, quantity, quality, or relation, as in mathematics, chemistry, or music. —**sym•bol′ic** (-bŏlʹĭk), **sym•bol′i•cal** *adj.* —**sym•bol′i•cal•ly** *adv.*

sym•bol•ism (sĭmʹbə-lĭz′əm) *n.* The use of symbols to represent invisible, intangible, or abstract things.

sym•bol•ize (sĭmʹbə-līz′) *v.* **-ized, -iz•ing. 1.** To serve as or be a symbol of : stand for. **2.** To represent by a symbol. —**sym′bol•i•za′tion** *n.*

sym•me•try (sĭmʹĭ-trē) *n., pl.* **-tries. 1.** Correspondence in form, size, and arrangement of parts on opposite sides of a boundary, as a dividing line or around an axis. **2.** An arrangement characterized by balance and harmonious proportions. —**sym•met′ric** (sĭ-mĕtʹrĭk), **sym•met′ri•cal** *adj.* —**sym•met′ri•cal•ly** *adv.*

sym•pa•thet•ic (sĭm′pə-thĕtʹĭk) *adj.* **1.** Of, marked by, feeling, or resulting from sympathy. **2.** Favorably disposed : approving. —**sym′pa•thet′i•cal•ly** *adv.*

sympathetic nervous system *n.* The part of the autonomic nervous system that tends to depress secretion, decrease smooth-muscle tone and contractility, and cause vascular contraction.

sym•pa•thize (sĭmʹpə-thīz′) *v.* **-thized, -thiz•ing. 1.** To express or feel sympathy. **2.** To share another's feelings. —**sym′pa•thiz′er** *n.*

sym•pa•thy (sĭmʹpə-thē) *n., pl.* **-thies. 1. a.** A relationship between individuals in which whatever affects one affects the other in a similar way. **b.** Mutual affection or understanding. **2. a.** The capacity to share another's feelings. **b.** A feeling or expression of sorrow for another's distress or loss. **c.** Pity : compassion. **3.** Favor : accord.

sym•pho•ny (sĭmʹfə-nē) *n., pl.* **-nies. 1.** A large and elaborate sonata for orchestra. **2.** A large orchestra with string, wind, and percussion sections. **3.** Harmony, esp. of sound. —**sym•phon′ic** (-fŏnʹĭk) *adj.*

sym•po•si•um (sĭm-pōʹzē-əm) *n., pl.* **-si•ums** *or* **-si•a** (-zē-ə). **1.** A meeting at which a particular topic is discussed by several participants. **2.** A collection of written opinions on a particular topic.

symp•tom (sĭmpʹtəm) *n.* **1.** A change in bodily sensation, function, or appearance that indicates disorder, abnormality, or disease. **2.** A sign : indication. —**symp′to•mat′ic** (-tə-mătʹĭk) *adj.*

syn•a•gogue *also* **syn•a•gog** (sĭnʹə-gŏg′) *n.* **1.** A meeting place for Jewish worship and religious instruction. **2.** A Jewish congregation.

syn•apse (sĭnʹăps′) *n.* The point at which a nerve impulse is transmitted from an axon of one neuron to the dendrite of another.

sync *also* **synch** (sĭngk) *Informal.* —*n.* Synchronization. —*v.* To synchronize.

syn•chro•nize (sĭngʹkrə-nīz′, sĭnʹ-) *v.* **-nized, -niz•ing. 1.** To take place or cause to take place at the same moment. **2.** To operate or cause to operate in unison. **3.** To cause to agree precisely in rate or time. **4.** To represent or arrange to indicate coexistence or parallel occurrence. —**syn′chro•ni•za′tion** *n.* —**syn′chro•niz′er** *n.*

syn•chro•nous (sĭngʹkrə-nəs, sĭnʹ-) *adj.* **1.** Taking place or existing at the same time. **2.** Moving or operating together at the same rate. —**syn′chro•nous•ly** *adv.*

syn•co•pate (sĭngʹkə-pāt′, sĭnʹ-) *v.* **-pat•ed, -pat•ing.** To shift a regular musical accent to a beat that is normally weak. —**syn′co•pa′tion** *n.*

syn•co•pe (sĭngʹkə-pē, sĭnʹ-) *n.* **1.** The shortening of a word by dropping a sound, letter, or syllable from the middle, as in *bo's'n* for *boatswain.* **2.** *Pathol.* A brief loss of consciousness : swoon.

syn•di•cate (sĭnʹdĭ-kĭt) *n.* **1.** A group of people who form an association to undertake a project or carry out a business transaction. **2.** An agency that sells materials for simultaneous publication in a number of periodicals or newspapers. —*v.* (-kāt′) **-cat•ed, -cat•ing. 1.** To manage as or organize into a syndicate. **2.** To publish through a syndicate. —**syn′di•ca′tion** *n.*

syn•drome (sĭn′drōm′) *n.* A set of symptoms that together characterize a disease or disorder.

syn•er•gism (sĭn′ər-jĭz′əm) *also* **syn•er•gy** (-ər-jē) *n.* The combined action of 2 or more substances or agencies to achieve an effect greater than that of which each is individually capable. —**syn•er′gic** (sĭ-nûr′jĭk) *adj.* —**syn′er•gist** *n.* —**syn′er•gis′tic** *adj.* —**syn′er•gis′ti•cal•ly** *adv.*

syn•od (sĭn′əd) *n.* A council or assembly, esp. of churches or church officials. —**syn′od•al** (sĭn′ə-dl), **sy•nod′i•cal** (sĭ-nŏd′ĭ-kəl), **sy•nod′ic** (-ĭk) *adj.*

syn•o•nym (sĭn′ə-nĭm′) *n.* A word whose meaning is identical or almost identical to that of another word in the same language. —**syn•on′y•mous** (sĭ-nŏn′ə-məs) *adj.* —**syn•on′y•my** *n.*

syn•op•sis (sĭ-nŏp′sĭs) *n., pl.* **-ses** (-sēz′). A shortened statement or outline, as of a narrative **:** abstract.

syn•tax (sĭn′tăks′) *n.* The way in which words are put together to form sentences, clauses, and phrases. —**syn•tac′tic** (-tăk′tĭk), **syn•tac′ti•cal** *adj.*

syn•the•sis (sĭn′thĭ-sĭs) *n., pl.* **-ses** (-sēz′). The combination of elements, parts, or substances into a whole. —**syn′the•size′** *v.*

syn•the•siz•er (sĭn′thĭ-sī′zər) *n.* An electronic device that duplicates the sounds of musical instruments.

syn•thet•ic (sĭn-thĕt′ĭk) *adj.* **1.** Of, relating to, or involving synthesis. **2. a.** Not genuine. **b.** Manmade. —**syn•thet′ic** *n.* —**syn•thet′i•cal•ly** *adv.*

syph•i•lis (sĭf′ə-lĭs) *n.* A chronic infectious venereal disease caused by a spirochete. —**syph′i•lit′ic** (-lĭt′ĭk) *adj. & n.*

sy•phon (sī′fən) *n. & v. var. of* SIPHON.

sy•ringe (sə-rĭnj′, sîr′ĭnj) *n.* **1.** A medical instrument for injecting fluids into or drawing them from the body. **2.** A hypodermic syringe. —**syr•inge′** *v.*

syr•up *also* **sir•up** (sĭr′əp, sûr′-) *n.* A thick, sweet liquid, esp. that made by boiling sugar and water. —**syr′up•y** *adj.*

sys•tem (sĭs′təm) *n.* **1.** A group of elements that interact and function together as a whole. **2. a.** The human body as a functional unit. **b.** A group of bodily organs that together perform a vital function <the vascular *system*> **3.** A procedure **:** method. **4.** An orderly pattern or arrangement. —**sys′tem•at′ic** (-tə-măt′ĭk) *adj.* —**sys′tem•at′i•cal•ly** *adv.*

sys•tem•a•tize (sĭs′tə-mə-tīz′) *v.* **-tized, -tiz•ing.** To form into or reduce to a system. —**sys′tem•a•ti•za′tion** *n.*

sys•tem•ic (sĭ-stĕm′ĭk) *adj.* Of, pertaining to, or affecting the whole body.

sys•tem•ize (sĭs′tə-mīz′) *v.* **-ized, -iz•ing.** To systematize.

systems analysis *n.* The use of mathematical means to study an activity, determine its desired goal, and formulate the most efficient means of attaining it. —**systems analyst** *n.*

sys•to•le (sĭs′tə-lē) *n.* The rhythmic contraction of the heart by means of which blood is driven through the aorta and pulmonary artery. —**sys•tol′ic** (sĭ-stŏl′ĭk) *adj.*

Tt

t *or* **T** (tē) *n., pl.* **t's** *or* **T's. 1.** The 20th letter of the English alphabet. **2.** A speech sound represented by the letter *t*. **3.** Something with the shape of the letter T. —**to a T.** Perfectly <The job suits me *to a T.*>

Ta *symbol for* TANTALUM.

tab (tăb) *n.* **1.** A small projecting loop, tag, etc., to help in opening, handling, or identifying something. **2.** *Informal.* An amount paid or owed, as for a meal. —**keep tabs on.** To keep close watch on.

Ta•bas•co (tə-băs′kō). A trademark for a spicy sauce made from red peppers.

tab•by (tăb′ē) *n., pl.* **-bies. 1.** A domestic cat with darkish striped or mottled fur. **2.** A female cat.

tab•er•na•cle (tăb′ər-năk′əl) *n.* **1.** *often* **Tabernacle.** The portable sanctuary in which the ancient Jews carried the Ark of the Covenant through the desert. **2.** A container on an altar for the consecrated Eucharist. **3.** A temple.

ta•ble (tā′bəl) *n.* **1.** A flat-topped piece of furniture supported by legs. **2.** An orderly arrangement of data. **3.** A brief outline or listing. **4.** A flat usu. inscribed tablet. —*v.* **-bled, -bling. 1.** To place on a table. **2.** To list or record in a table. **3.** To postpone, as legislation.

tab•leau (tăb′lō′, tă-blō′) *n., pl.* **-leaux** (-lōz′, -blōz′) *or* **-leaus. 1.** A vivid depiction. **2.** A stage scene in which costumed actors neither speak nor move.

ta•ble•cloth (tā′bəl-klôth′, -klŏth′) *n.* A cloth to cover a table, esp. during a meal.

ta•ble d'hôte (tā′bəl dōt′) *n., pl.* **ta•bles d'hôte** (tā′bəl dōt′). A full-course restaurant meal offered at a fixed price.

ta•ble•land (tā′bəl-lănd′) *n.* A flat elevated region **:** plateau.

ta•ble•spoon (tā′bəl-spo͞on′) *n.* **1.** A large serving spoon. **2.** A household cooking measure equal to 3 teaspoons or ½ fl oz (15 ml). —**ta′ble•spoon′ful′** *n.*

tab•let (tăb′lĭt) *n.* **1.** A flat piece of stone, ivory, etc., fit for or bearing an inscription. **2.** A pad consisting of sheets of writing paper

glued at one edge. **3.** Oral medication in the form of a small flat pellet.
table tennis *n.* A game resembling tennis that is played on a table with light wooden paddles and a small plastic ball.
ta•ble•ware (tā'bəl-wâr') *n.* The dishes, glassware, and silverware used in setting a dining table.
tab•loid (tăb'loid') *n.* A small-format illustrated newspaper with short, often sensational news items.
ta•boo *also* **ta•bu** (tə-bōō', tă-) —*n., pl.* **-boos** *also* **-bus. 1.** A prohibition against doing, using, or mentioning something because of its sacred and inviolable nature. **2.** A cultural prohibition against some word or act. —*adj.* **1.** Set apart as inviolable. **2.** Banned for social or moral reasons. —**ta•boo'** *v.*
tab•u•lar (tăb'yə-lər) *adj.* **1.** Arranged in a table or list. **2.** Calculated by means of a table. —**tab'u•lar•ly** *adv.*
tab•u•late (tăb'yə-lāt') *v.* **-lat•ed, -lat•ing.** To condense and list, as in a table. —**tab'u•la'tion** *n.* —**tab'u•la'tor** *n.*
ta•chom•e•ter (tə-kŏm'ĭ-tər) *n.* An instrument for determining speed, as of a rotating shaft. —**tach'o•met'ric** (tăk'ə-mĕt'rĭk) *adj.* —**ta•chom'e•try** *n.*
tach•y•car•di•a (tăk'ĭ-kär'dē-ə) *n.* Excessively rapid heartbeat.
tac•it (tăs'ĭt) *adj.* **1.** Expressed nonverbally : unspoken. **2.** Expressed indirectly : implied. —**tac'it•ly** *adv.* —**tac'it•ness** *n.*
tac•i•turn (tăs'ĭ-tûrn') *adj.* Uncommunicative. —**tac'i•tur'ni•ty** (-tûr'nĭ-tē) *n.*
tack[1] (tăk) *n.* **1.** A small flat-headed nail with a sharp point. **2. a.** The direction of a ship with respect to the trim of its sails. **b.** The act of changing from one direction to another. **3.** An approach or course of action. **4.** An alternating course. **5.** A loose, temporary sewing stitch. —*v.* **1.** To secure or attach with a tack. **2.** To append as an extra item. **3.** To change a ship's course. **4.** To sew with loose stitches. —**tack'er** *n.*
tack[2] (tăk) *n.* The harness for a horse, including the bridle and saddle.
tack•le (tăk'əl) *n.* **1.** Equipment or gear for an occupation or sport, esp. fishing. **2.** (*also* tā'kəl). A system of ropes and pulley blocks for hoisting and pulling weights esp. on a ship. **3.** *Football.* **a.** A lineman positioned between guard and end. **b.** The act of stopping an opposing player by seizing and bringing him down. —*v.* **-led, -ling. 1.** To take on : deal with (e.g., a problem). **2.** *Football.* To seize and bring down (an opposing player). —**tack'ler** *n.*
tack•y[1] (tăk'ē) *adj.* **-i•er, -i•est.** Somewhat sticky, as a newly painted surface. —**tack'i•ness** *n.*
tack•y[2] (tăk'ē) *adj.* **-i•er, -i•est.** *Informal.* **1.** Shabby. **2. a.** Not stylish <*tacky* clothes> **b.** Vulgar : tasteless <*tacky* jokes> —**tack'i•ly** *adv.* —**tack'i•ness** *n.*
ta•co (tä'kō) *n., pl.* **-cos.** A folded tortilla filled with ground meat, cheese, beans, etc.
tac•o•nite (tăk'ə-nīt') *n.* A fine-grained rock containing hematite and mined as a low-grade iron ore.
tact (tăkt) *n.* The ability to do or say the right thing at the right time : diplomacy. —**tact'ful** *adj.* —**tact'less** *adj.*
tac•tic (tăk'tĭk) *n.* **1.** An expedient for achieving an end. **2. tactics** *(sing. in number).* **a.** The science of using strategy to gain military objectives. **b.** Skillful maneuvering to achieve a goal. —**tac'ti•cal** *adj.* —**tac•ti'cian** *n.*
tac•tile (tăk'təl, -tīl') *adj.* **1.** Of, perceptible to, or issuing from the sense of touch. **2.** Used for feeling <a *tactile* organ> —**tac•til'i•ty** (-tĭl'ĭ-tē) *n.*
tad (tăd) *n. Informal.* **1.** A small boy. **2.** A small amount or degree.
tad•pole (tăd'pōl') *n.* A frog or toad larva, with a tail and external gills.
tae kwon do (tī' kwŏn' dō') *n.* A Korean art of self-defense.
taf•fe•ta (tăf'ĭ-tə) *n.* A crisp, glossy fabric esp. of silk, rayon, or nylon.
taf•fy (tăf'ē) *n., pl.* **-fies.** A chewy candy made of molasses or brown sugar.
tag[1] (tăg) *n.* **1.** A piece of paper, plastic, metal, etc., attached or hung in order to identify, classify, or label. **2.** A hard tip on a shoelace. **3.** A descriptive term or epithet. **4.** A cliché —*v.* **tagged, tag•ging. 1.** To use a tag for labeling or identifying. **2.** To follow along after. —**tag'ger** *n.*
tag[2] (tăg) *n.* **1.** A children's game in which a player runs after the others and attempts to touch one of them. **2.** *Baseball.* The act of making an out by touching a runner with the ball. —*v.* **tagged, tag•ging. 1.** To touch in or as if in a game of tag. **2.** *Baseball.* To touch (a runner) with the ball in order to make an out. —**tag'ger** *n.*
tai chi *or* **Tai Chi** (tī' chē', jē') *n.* A Chinese system of physical exercise designed esp. for self-defense and meditation.
tai•ga (tī'gə) *n.* The subarctic evergreen forest of N Eurasia just S of the tundra.
tail (tāl) *n.* **1. a.** The hindmost part or an extension beyond the main part of an animal's body. **b.** The hindmost, rear, or lower part of something. **2.** Something that looks, hangs, or trails like an animal's tail. **3. tails.** The reverse side of a coin <Heads I win, *tails* you win.> **4. tails.** Formal evening attire for men. **5.** One who follows or keeps close watch on another. —*v.* To follow <The detective *tailed* the suspect.>
tail•gate (tāl'gāt') *n.* A hinged section at the rear of a truck, wagon, etc. for loading and unloading. —*v.* **-gat•ed, -gat•ing.** To follow too closely behind (another vehicle).
tail•ings (tā'lĭngz) *pl.n.* Refuse or dross remaining after ore has been processed.
tail•light (tāl'līt') *n.* A warning light at the rear of a vehicle.
tai•lor (tā'lər) *n.* One who makes, mends, and alters clothing. —*v.* **1.** To fashion (a garment). **2.** To make or adapt for a specific purpose.

tai·lor-made (tā'lər-mād') *adj.* **1.** Made to order. **2.** Perfectly suited.
tail pipe *n.* The pipe through which exhaust gases from an engine are discharged.
tail·spin (tāl'spĭn') *n.* **1.** The nose-down spiraling descent of an aircraft. **2.** An abrupt decline. **3.** An emotional collapse.
tail wind *n.* A wind blowing in the same direction as that in which an aircraft, ship, etc. is traveling.
taint (tānt) *v.* **1.** To affect with something objectionable. **2.** To make rotten : spoil. **3.** To corrupt morally. —*n.* **1.** A moral blemish or defect. **2.** A corrupting influence.
ta·ka (tä'kə) *n.* —See table at CURRENCY.
take (tāk) *v.* **took** (to͝ok), **tak·en** (tā'kən), **tak·ing.** **1.** To get possession of. **2.** To grip and hold with the hands. **3.** To carry or cause to go with one to a different place. **4.** To convey or conduct to a different place. **5.** To remove from an occupied position. **6.** To please greatly : charm. **7.** To put into one's body, as air, food, medicine, etc. **8. a.** To assume for oneself. **b.** To commit oneself to : undertake. **9.** To govern grammatically <A transitive verb *takes* a direct object.> **10.** To select : choose. **11.** To use for conveying or traveling. **12.** To make use of : occupy. **13.** To require or need. **14.** To measure or observe in order to determine <*take* a reading> **15.** To record by writing. **16.** To make by a photographic process. **17.** To accept or receive, as money, counsel, etc. **18.** To undergo or endure (e.g., criticism). **19.** To follow or pursue (e.g., a lead). **20.** To engage in : do. **21.** To let in : admit <The cellar *took* water.> **22.** To react to in a given way <*took* us seriously> **23.** To deduct : subtract. **24.** To study <*take* chemistry> **25.** To be effective : work. **26.** To come to be <*took* ill> **27.** To swindle : cheat. —**take after.** To look or act like : resemble. —**take back.** To retract or deny (e.g., a statement). —**take in.** **1.** To look at : view. **2.** To include : contain. **3.** To fathom : understand. **4.** To deceive : swindle. —**take off.** **1.** To remove. **2.** To leave the ground, as an aircraft. **3.** *Informal.* To go away : depart. —**take on.** **1.** To hire. **2.** To compete against. —**take over.** To gain control or management (of). —*n.* **1. a.** The act or process of acquiring. **b.** The quantity acquired, esp. at one time. **2.** The total admission receipts to an event. **3.** The nonstop running of filming or recording equipment. —**tak'er** *n.*
take·off (tāk'ôf', -ŏf') *n.* **1.** The act or process of rising up in flight. **2.** *Informal.* An amusing imitation of someone.
take-out (tāk'out') *n.* Something, as food, that is consumed away from the premises. —**take'-out'** *adj.*
take·o·ver *also* **take-o·ver** (tāk'ō'vər) *n.* The act or process of taking control or management of or responsibility for.
tak·ing (tā'kĭng) *n.* **1.** The act or process of possessing. **2. takings.** Something received, esp. money.
ta·la (tä'lə) *n.* —See table at CURRENCY.
talc (tălk) *n.* A soft, fine-grained, soapy-textured mineral used esp. in making talcum powder.
tal·cum powder (tăl'kəm) *n.* A fine body powder made from purified talc.
tale (tāl) *n.* **1.** A recital of events <a *tale* of woe> **2.** A usu. fictitious narrative. **3.** A false or malicious story.
tal·ent (tăl'ənt) *n.* **1.** A mental or physical ability : aptitude. **2. a.** Superior natural ability : genius. **b.** A person or people with such ability. **3.** Any of various ancient coins or weights. —**tal'ent·ed** *adj.*
tal·is·man (tăl'ĭs-mən, -ĭz-) *n.* An object held to have magical or protective powers : charm. —**tal'is·man'ic** (-măn'ĭk) *adj.*
talk (tôk) *v.* **1.** To utter words. **2. a.** To communicate by speech. **b.** To discuss <*talk* politics> **3.** To use (a language) in communicating. **4.** To engage in gossip or idle chatter. **5.** To negotiate. **6.** To consult or confer <*talked* with the lawyer> **7.** To influence : persuade. —**talk back.** To make a rude reply. —**talk down.** To speak condescendingly. —**talk over.** To discuss esp. in depth. —*n.* **1.** The act of conversing. **2.** A way of speaking. **3.** An informal address. **4.** Hearsay : rumor. **5.** A subject or topic of conversation. **6.** A conference or negotiation. —**talk'er** *n.*
talk·a·tive (tô'kə-tĭv) *adj.* Tending to talk excessively. —**talk'a·tive·ness** *n.*
talk·ing-to (tô'kĭng-to͞o') *n., pl.* **-tos.** *Informal.* A reprimand : scolding.
tall (tôl) *adj.* **1.** Of greater than average height. **2.** Of a designated height. **3.** Imaginary : fanciful <a *tall* tale> **4.** Unusually big, long, or difficult. ★ *syns:* HIGH, LOFTY, TOWERING. —*adv.* Straight, as in pride <walk *tall*> —**tall'ness** *n.*
tal·low (tăl'ō) *n.* Hard fat rendered esp. from cattle or sheep and used in candles, soaps, and lubricants. —**tal'low·y** *adj.*
tal·ly (tăl'ē) *n., pl.* **-lies.** **1.** A stick that is notched in keeping count. **2.** A reckoning or score. —*v.* **-lied, -ly·ing.** **1.** To count, reckon, or score. **2.** To match.
tal·ly·ho (tăl'ē-hō') *interj.* —Used in fox hunting when the fox is sighted.
Tal·mud (täl'mo͝od', tăl'məd) *n.* The early authoritative religious writings that form the basis of Orthodox Judaism. —**Tal·mu'dic, Tal·mu'di·cal** *adj.*
tal·on (tăl'ən) *n.* The claw of a bird or animal that seizes other animals as prey.
ta·lus (tā'ləs) *n., pl.* **-li** (-lī). The bone that articulates with the tibia and fibula to form the ankle joint.
ta·ma·le (tə-mä'lē) *n.* Chopped meat, chili, and seasonings wrapped in cornhusks and steamed.
tam·a·rack (tăm'ə-răk') *n.* A North American larch tree, esp. *Larix laricina,* with short deciduous needles.
tam·a·rind (tăm'ə-rĭnd') *n.* A tropical tree, *Tamarindus indica,* with red-striped yellow flowers and pulpy acid fruit.
tam·a·risk (tăm'ə-rĭsk') *n.* A native Eurasian

shrub or small tree of the genus *Tamarix,* with pink flower clusters.

tam·ba·la (tăm-bä′lə) *n.* —See table at CURRENCY.

tam·bou·rine (tăm′bə-rēn′) *n.* A percussion instrument consisting of a small drumhead with jingling disks in the rim.

tame (tām) *adj.* **tam·er, tam·est. 1.** Brought from a wild to a manageable or domesticated state. **2. a.** Naturally gentle. **b.** Docile or submissive. **3.** Dull. **—tame** *v.* **—tame′ly** *adv.* **—tam′er** *n.*

tam-o′-shan·ter (tăm′ə-shăn′tər) *n.* A Scottish cap with a flat, circular top.

tamp (tămp) *v.* To pack down tightly by repeated light blows.

tam·per (tăm′pər) *v.* **1.** To handle something idly, ignorantly, or injuriously. **2.** To make clandestine or illicit arrangements <*tamper* with a contract> ★ ***syns:*** FOOL, MEDDLE, MESS, MONKEY, TINKER

tam·pon (tăm′pŏn′) *n.* An absorbent plug inserted into a wound or bodily cavity.

tan (tăn) *v.* **tanned, tan·ning. 1.** To make (hide) into leather, esp. by exposure to tannin. **2.** To make or become brown by exposure to sunlight. **3.** *Informal.* To spank hard. —*n.* **1.** A light yellowish brown. **2.** The brownish color of skin exposed to sunlight. **—tan** *adj.*

tan·a·ger (tăn′ə-jər) *n.* A New World bird of the family Thraupidae, often with brightly colored plumage in the male.

tan·bark (tăn′bärk′) *n.* The bark of certain trees, used as a source of tannin.

tan·dem (tăn′dəm) *n.* **1.** A bicycle for 2 or more persons. **2.** An arrangement of 2 or more persons, animals, or things placed 1 behind the other. **3.** A 2-wheeled carriage drawn by horses harnessed in tandem. **—tan′dem** *adj. & adv.*

tang (tăng) *n.* **1.** A distinctively pungent taste or smell. **2.** A projecting part that joins a tool to its handle. **—tang′y** *adj.*

tan·gent (tăn′jənt) *adj.* Touching at a single point or along a line but not intersecting. —*n.* **1.** A line, curve, or surface that is tangent with another. **2.** A sudden change of course : digression. **—tan′gen·cy** (-jən-sē) *n.* **—tan·gen′tial** *adj.*

tan·ger·ine (tăn′jə-rēn′) *n.* A widely cultivated citrus tree, *Citrus nobilis deliciosa,* bearing easily peeled deep-orange fruit.

tan·gi·ble (tăn′jə-bəl) *adj.* **1.** Discernible by touch. **2.** Existing in reality : concrete. —*n.* **1.** Something tangible. **2. tangibles.** Appraisable assets. **—tan′gi·bil′i·ty, tan′gi·ble·ness** *n.* **—tan′gi·bly** *adv.*

tan·gle (tăng′gəl) *v.* **-gled, -gling. 1.** To mix together in a confused mass : snarl. **2.** To be or become complicated or confused : entangle. **3.** *Informal.* To wrestle. —*n.* **1.** An intertwined mass. **2.** A confused or muddled condition. **—tang′ler** *n.*

tan·go (tăng′gō) *n., pl.* **-gos.** A Latin-American ballroom dance marked by long gliding steps. **—tan′go** *v.*

tan·gram (tăng′grəm) *n.* A Chinese puzzle made of a square cut into five triangles, a square, and a rhomboid, to be reassembled into different figures.

tangram

tank (tăngk) *n.* **1.** A large receptacle for fluids or gases. **2.** An enclosed, heavily armored and armed military vehicle that moves on caterpillar treads.

tan·kard (tăng′kərd) *n.* A large drinking cup with a handle and a hinged lid.

tank·er (tăng′kər) *n.* A ship, truck, or plane equipped with tanks for transporting large amounts of liquid, as oil.

tan·ner (tăn′ər) *n.* One who tans hides.

tan·ner·y (tăn′ə-rē) *n., pl.* **-ies.** A place where hides are tanned for leather.

tan·nic acid (tăn′ĭk) *n.* An astringent substance obtained from certain fruits and bark and used esp. in tanning.

tan·nin (tăn′ĭn) *n.* **1.** Tannic acid. **2.** A substance used in tanning hides.

tan·ta·lize (tăn′tl-īz′) *v.* **-lized, -liz·ing.** To tease or harass by showing but keeping out of reach something highly desirable. ★ ***syns:*** BAIT, TEASE, TORMENT **—tan′ta·li·za′tion** *n.* **—tan′ta·liz′er** *n.* **—tan′ta·liz′ing·ly** *adv.*

tan·ta·lum (tăn′til-əm) *n. Symbol* **Ta** A very hard corrosion-resistant ductile metallic element.

tan·ta·mount (tăn′tə-mount′) *adj.* Identical in effect or value.

tan·trum (tăn′trəm) *n.* An outburst of anger, rage, etc.

Tao·ism (tou′ĭz′əm, dou′-) *n.* A Chinese philosophy and system of religion based on the teachings of Lao-tse in the 6th cent. B.C. **—Tao′ist** *n.* **—Tao·is′tic** *adj.*

tap¹ (tăp) *v.* **tapped, tap·ping. 1.** To strike lightly or repeatedly. **2.** To repair or reinforce (shoe heels or toes) by putting on a tap. **3.** To choose, as for membership. —*n.* **1.** A slight, audible blow. **2.** A layer of material or a metal plate applied to the toe or heel of a shoe.

tap² (tăp) *n.* **1.** A valve and spout for regulating fluid flow : faucet or spigot. **2.** An alcoholic beverage drawn from a tap. **3.** A tool to cut threads in an internal screw. **4.** A point at which a connection is made in an electric circuit. **5.** *Med.* Removal of bodily fluid <a spinal *tap*> —*v.* **tapped, tap·ping. 1.** To provide with a spigot or tap. **2.** To make a hole in for drawing off liquid. **3.** To draw (liquid) from a container. **4.** To connect a local outlet with (a main gas or water pipe). **5. a.** To monitor by a wiretap. **b.** To make a connection in (an electric power line). **6.** To cut screw threads in (a collar or socket). **7.** To make use of : draw from.

tap dance *n.* A dance in which the clicking heels and toes of the dancer's shoes sound out the rhythm. **—tap'-dance'** *v.* **—tap dancer** *n.*

tape (tāp) *n.* **1.** A strong, narrow strip of woven fabric. **2.** A long, narrow, flexible strip, as of paper or metal. **3.** Magnetized recording tape. **4.** A string stretched across the finish line of a race. *—v.* **taped, tap•ing. 1.** To fasten, wrap, or support with tape. **2.** To measure with a measuring tape. **3.** To make a tape recording (of).

tape deck *n.* A tape recorder and player having no built-in amplifiers or speakers, used as a component in a high-fidelity sound system.

tape measure *n.* A device for linear measuring, consisting of a tape marked off in a scale.

ta•per (tā'pər) *n.* **1.** A slender candle or long, wax-coated wick. **2.** A gradual lessening in thickness or width. *—v.* **1.** To make or become gradually thinner toward one end. **2.** To slacken off.

tape recorder *n.* An instrument capable of recording and usu. playing back sound on magnetic tape. **—tape'-re•cord** *v.* **—tape re•cording** *n.*

tap•es•try (tăp'ĭ-strē) *n., pl.* **-tries.** A rich, heavy cloth woven with multicolored pictorial designs, used esp. as a wall hanging. **—tap'es•tried** *adj.*

tape•worm (tāp'wûrm') *n.* A long ribbonlike parasitical worm of the class Cestoda that lives in vertebrate intestines.

tap•i•o•ca (tăp'ē-ō'kə) *n.* A beadlike cassava starch used esp. for puddings.

ta•pir (tā'pər, tə-pîr') *n.* A tropical American or Asian mammal of the genus *Tapirus,* with a heavy body, short legs, and a long, fleshy snout.

tap•room (tăp'ro͞om', -ro͝om') *n.* A bar or barroom.

tap•root (tăp'ro͞ot', -ro͝ot') *n.* The usu. large main root of a plant, growing straight downward from the stem and sending out smaller side roots.

taps (tăps) *pl.n. (sing. in number).* A bugle call sounded at night to signal lights out or at funerals and memorial services.

tar¹ (tär) *n.* A thick, dark, oily substance distilled esp. from wood, coal, or peat. *—v.* **tarred, tar•ring.** To cover or treat with tar. **—tar'ry** *adj.*

tar² (tär) *n. Informal.* A sailor.

tar•an•tel•la (tăr'ən-tĕl'ə) *n.* A spirited, whirling dance of S Italy.

ta•ran•tu•la (tə-răn'chə-lə) *n., pl.* **-las** *or* **-lae** (-lē'). Any of various large, hairy, chiefly tropical spiders of the family Theraphosidae that can inflict a painful bite.

tar•dy (tär'dē) *adj.* **-di•er, -di•est. 1. a.** Later than expected. **b.** Tending to delay. **2.** Moving slowly : sluggish. **—tar'di•ly** *adv.* **—tar'di•ness** *n.*

tare¹ (târ) *n.* A weed growing esp. in grain fields.

tare² (târ) *n.* The weight of a container or wrapper, subtracted from the gross weight to obtain the net weight.

tar•get (tär'gĭt) *n.* **1. a.** A marked surface to shoot at. **b.** Something aimed or shot at. **2.** An object of attack or criticism. **3.** A desired goal. *—v.* To make into a target.

tar•iff (tăr'ĭf) *n.* **1. a.** A list or system of taxes governmentally imposed on imported or exported goods. **b.** A tax of this kind. **2.** A scale of rates or charges.

tar•mac (tär'măk') *n.* A bituminous road or surface, esp. an airport runway.

tar•nish (tär'nĭsh) *v.* **1.** To lose or cause to lose luster. **2.** To spoil or taint. **—tar'nish** *n.* **—tar'nish•a•ble** *adj.*

ta•ro (tär'ō, tăr'ō) *n., pl.* **-ros.** A tropical Asian plant, *Colocasia esculenta,* with broad leaves and a large, starchy, edible tuber.

tar•ot (tăr'ō) *n.* Any of a set of 22 fortune-telling cards depicting vices, virtues, and elemental forces.

tarp (tärp) *n. Informal.* A tarpaulin.

tar•pau•lin (tär-pô'lĭn, tär'pə-) *n.* A sheet of waterproof canvas.

tar•pon (tär'pən) *n., pl.* **-pon** *or* **-pons.** A large, silvery game fish, *Megalops atlantica,* of Atlantic coastal waters.

tarpon

tar•ra•gon (tăr'ə-gŏn', -gən) *n.* A native Eurasian aromatic herb, *Artemisia dracunculus,* with leaves used as seasoning.

tar•ry (tăr'ē) *v.* **-ried, -ry•ing. 1.** To delay or be late in coming or going : linger. **2.** To stay for a time : sojourn. **—tar'ri•er** *n.*

tar•sus (tär'səs) *n., pl.* **-si** (-sī'). The part of the vertebrate foot between the leg and the metatarsus : the ankle. **—tar'sal** *adj.*

tart¹ (tärt) *adj.* **1.** Pungent or pleasantly sour to the taste. **2.** Sharp in tone or meaning. **—tart'ly** *adv.* **—tart'ness** *n.*

tart² (tärt) *n.* **1.** A pastry shell or pie filled with fruit, custard, etc. **2.** A prostitute.

tar•tan (tär′tn) *n.* Any of numerous plaid fabric patterns of Scottish origin consisting of stripes of varying widths and colors crossing at right angles against a solid background. —**tar′tan** *adj.*

tar•tar (tär′tər) *n.* **1.** A reddish crustlike deposit from grapes formed esp. on the sides of wine casks. **2.** A hard deposit on the teeth, composed of food, secretions, and calcium salts. —**tar•tar′ic** *adj.*

Tar•tar (tär′tər) *n.* **1.** A member of any of the Mongolian peoples of C Asia who invaded W Asia and E Europe in the 13th cent. **2.** A fierce or violent person.

tar•tar sauce *also* **tar•tare sauce** (tär′tər) *n.* A mayonnaise sauce containing chopped onion and pickles.

task (tăsk) *n.* **1.** A piece of work usu. assigned to be done. **2.** A difficult undertaking. ★ ***syns:*** CHORE, DUTY, JOB, STINT —*v.* To overburden.

task force *n.* A temporary grouping to accomplish a goal.

task•mas•ter (tăsk′măs′tər) *n.* One who imposes heavy or burdensome work.

Tasmanian devil *n.* A burrowing carnivorous marsupial, *Sarcophilus harrisii,* with a long, almost hairless tail.

tas•sel (tăs′əl) *n.* **1.** An ornamental bunch of threads or cords fastened at one end and hung on curtains, clothing, etc. **2.** Something resembling a tassel, as the male flower cluster of a corn plant. —*v.* **-seled, -sel•ing** *or* **-selled, -sel•ling. 1.** To decorate with tassels. **2.** To put forth tassels.

taste (tāst) *v.* **tast•ed, tast•ing. 1.** To determine the flavor of by putting into the mouth. **2.** To ingest a small amount (of) esp. as a sample. **3.** To partake of **:** experience. **4.** To have a particular flavor. —*n.* **1.** The sense by which the qualities of sweet, sour, salty, and bitter are perceived in the mouth. **2.** A distinctive sensation produced by or as if by a substance taken into the mouth **:** flavor. **3.** A small amount tasted or eaten. **4.** A first or limited experience. **5.** A personal liking. **6. a.** Ability to discern what is aesthetically pleasing or appropriate. **b.** A sense of moral or social propriety. —**tast′a•ble** *adj.* —**taste′ful** *adj.* —**taste′less** *adj.* —**tast′er** *n.*

taste bud *n.* Any of the numerous cells on the tongue that are the end organs of the sense of taste.

tast•y (tā′stē) *adj.* **-i•er, -i•est.** Agreeable in flavor **:** savory. —**tast′i•ly** *adv.* —**tast′i•ness** *n.*

tat (tăt) *v.* **tat•ted, tat•ting.** To do or make by tatting. —**tat′ter** *n.*

tat•ter (tăt′ər) *n.* **1.** A torn and hanging shred. **2. tatters.** Ragged clothing. —*v.* To make or become torn or shredded.

tat•ter•de•ma•lion (tăt′ər-də-māl′yən, -măl′-) *n.* A ragged unkempt person, esp. a child. —**tat′ter•de•ma′lion** *adj.*

tat•ting (tăt′ĭng) *n.* **1.** A delicate lace made by looping and knotting thread on a small hand shuttle. **2.** The art of making tatting.

tat•tle (tăt′l) *v.* **-tled, -tling. 1.** To betray the secrets of another by gossiping. **2.** To chatter idly. —**tat′tler** *n.*

tat•tle•tale (tăt′l-tāl′) *n.* One who tattles on others **:** informer.

tat•too[1] (tă-to͞o′) *n.* **1.** A military drum or bugle call to quarters at night. **2.** A rhythmic drumming or tapping.

tat•too[2] (tă-to͞o′) *n.* A mark or design made on the skin by pricking and ingraining an indelible dye or by raising scars. —**tat•too′** *v.* —**tat•too′er** *n.*

taught (tôt) *v. p.t. & p.p. of* TEACH.

taunt (tônt) *v.* To jeer at **:** deride. —*n.* A scornful remark. —**taunt′ing•ly** *adv.*

taupe (tōp) *n.* A brownish gray or a yellowish brown. —**taupe** *adj.*

Tau•rus (tôr′əs) *n.* **1.** A constellation in the N Hemisphere. **2. a.** The 2nd sign of the zodiac. **b.** One born under this sign.

taut (tôt) *adj.* **1.** Pulled or drawn tight. **2.** Emotionally tense. **3.** Kept in tidy shape.

tau•tol•o•gy (tô-tŏl′ə-jē) *n., pl.* **-gies. 1. a.** Needless repetition esp. in speech or writing **:** redundancy. **b.** An instance of tautology. **2.** A statement that is always true because it includes all logical possibilities. —**tau′to•log′i•cal** (tô′tə-lŏj′ĭ-kəl) *adj.*

tav•ern (tăv′ərn) *n.* **1.** An establishment licensed to sell alcoholic beverages to be consumed on the premises. **2.** An inn where travelers may lodge.

taw•dry (tô′drē) *adj.* **-dri•er, -dri•est.** Cheap and garish **:** gaudy. —**taw′dri•ly** *adv.* —**taw′dri•ness** *n.*

▲ ***word history:*** The word *tawdry* is an alteration of the name *Saint Audrey,* an Anglo-Saxon princess who died of a throat ailment. A fair was held annually in her honor at which cloth neckbands, called *tawdry laces,* were sold. These must have been showy but inexpensive souvenirs, because the word *tawdry* became an adjective in its own right meaning "gaudy."

taw•ny (tô′nē) *n.* A light golden brown or brownish orange. —**taw′ny** *adj.*

tax (tăks) *n.* **1.** A payment imposed upon persons or groups for governmental support. **2.** A heavy demand **:** strain. —*v.* **1.** To place a tax on (income, property, or goods). **2.** To require a tax from. **3.** To make excessive demands upon. **4.** To make a charge against **:** accuse. —**tax′a•ble** *adj.* —**tax•a′tion** *n.* —**tax′er** *n.* —**tax′pay′er** *n.*

tax•i (tăk′sē) *n., pl.* **-is** *or* **-ies.** A taxicab. —*v.* **-ied, -i•ing. 1.** To transport or go by taxicab. **2.** To move slowly on the ground or water before taking off or after landing.

tax•i•cab (tăk′sē-kăb′) *n.* An automobile that transports passengers for a charge.

tax•i•der•my (tăk′sĭ-dûr′mē) *n.* The art of preparing, stuffing, and mounting animal skins. —**tax′i•derm′ist** *n.*

tax•on•o•my (tăk-sŏn′ə-mē) *n.* The science, laws, or principles of classifying living organisms in specially named categories based on shared characteristics and natural relationships. —**tax′o•nom′ic** (-sə-nŏm′ĭk), **tax′o•nom′i•cal** *adj.* —**tax′o•nom′i•cal•ly** *adv.* —**tax•on′o•mist** *n.*

tax shelter *n.* A financial strategy or provision that reduces current taxes.

Tb *symbol for* TERBIUM.

T-bone (tē′bōn′) *n.* A small, thick steak tenderloin containing a T-shaped bone.

Tc *symbol for* TECHNETIUM.

T cell *n.* A white blood cell that has various roles in the immune system, including recognition of foreign antigens and activation of other immune cells.

Te *symbol for* TELLURIUM.

tea (tē) *n.* **1. a.** An Asian shrub, *Thea sinensis* or *Camellia sinensis,* with fragrant white flowers and evergreen leaves. **b.** The dried leaves of this shrub, used to make a drink by steeping in boiling water. **c.** The drink so made. **2.** A drink resembling tea <herbal *tea*> **3.** A light meal or a social gathering at which tea is served.

teach (tēch) *v.* **taught** (tôt), **teach•ing. 1.** To communicate knowledge or skill (to). **2.** To provide instruction in. **3.** To give insight by example or experience. ★ ***syns:*** INSTRUCT, TRAIN, TUTOR —**teach′a•bil′i•ty, teach′a•ble•ness** *n.* —**teach′a•ble** *adj.* —**teach′a•bly** *adv.* —**teach′er** *n.*

teach•ing (tē′chĭng) *n.* **1.** The act, practice, or occupation of teachers. **2.** Something taught, esp. a precept or doctrine.

teak (tēk) *n.* A tall, evergreen Asian tree, *Tectona grandis,* with hard, durable, yellowish-brown wood used esp. in shipbuilding and furniture-making. —**teak** *adj.*

tea•ket•tle (tē′kĕt′l) *n.* A covered kettle with a handle and a spout, used esp. for boiling water for tea.

teal (tēl) *n.* Any of several small wild river ducks, esp. one of the genus *Anas,* with brightly marked plumage.

team (tēm) *n.* **1.** Two or more draft animals harnessed to a farm implement or a vehicle. **2.** Two or more players on the same side in a game. **3.** A group working together. —*v.* **1.** To join together (animals) in a team. **2.** To unite in a team. —**team′mate** *n.* —**team′work′** *n.*

team•ster (tēm′stər) *n.* **1.** One who drives a team of draft animals. **2.** One whose occupation is truck driving.

tea•pot (tē′pŏt′) *n.* A covered pot with a spout, for preparing and pouring tea.

tear[1] (târ) *v.* **tore** (tôr, tōr), **torn** (tôrn, tōrn), **tear•ing. 1.** To pull apart or become divided into pieces. **2.** To make (a hole) by or as if by ripping. **3.** To lacerate (the skin). **4.** To separate or remove by force. **5.** To divide or disrupt emotionally. **6.** To move with great haste. —**tear down.** To demolish : destroy. —*n.* A hole, rip, or flaw.

tear[2] (tîr) *n.* **1.** A drop of the clear salty fluid that moistens the eye and the inner eyelid. **2. tears.** The act of crying. —*v.* To become full of tears. —**tear′ful** *adj.* —**tear′ful•ness** *n.* —**tear′i•ly** *adv.* —**tear′i•ness** *n.* —**tear′y** *adj.*

tear gas (tîr) *n.* A chemical substance that causes severe eye and respiratory irritation when dispersed.

tear-jerk•er (tîr′jûr′kər) *n. Slang.* An extremely sad story, drama, or performance.

tease (tēz) *v.* **teased, teas•ing. 1.** To vex or annoy by taunting or making fun of. **2.** To try to get by coaxing or begging. **3.** To tantalize. **4.** To comb apart and lay straight the fibers of (wool). **5.** To raise the nap of (cloth) with a teasel. **6.** To give (the hair) a bouffant effect by combing. —**teas′er** *n.*

tea•sel *also* **tea•zel** *or* **tea•zle** (tē′zəl) *n.* **1.** An Old World plant of the genus *Dipsacus,* with thistlelike flowers surrounded by stiff bristles. **2.** The bristly flower head of *D. fullonum,* used to produce a napped surface on fabrics.

tea•spoon (tē′spo͞on′) *n.* **1.** A small spoon used esp. for stirring and for eating desserts. **2.** A household cooking measure equal to ⅓ tbsp (about 5 ml). —**tea′spoon′ful′** *n.*

teat (tēt, tĭt) *n.* A nipple.

tech•ne•ti•um (tĕk-nē′shē-əm) *n. Symbol* **Tc** A silvery-gray, radioactive, artificially produced metallic element.

tech•ni•cal (tĕk′nĭ-kəl) *adj.* **1.** Of, relating to, or derived from technique. **2.** Of a particular subject : specialized. **3.** Of or using scientific knowledge. **4.** In principle rather than practice. **5.** Of, relating to, or derived from technology. —**tech′ni•cal•ly** *adv.* —**tech′ni•cal•ness** *n.*

tech•ni•cal•i•ty (tĕk′nĭ-kăl′ĭ-tē) *n., pl.* **-ties. 1.** The quality or state of being technical. **2.** A point or detail having meaning only to a specialist.

tech•ni•cian (tĕk-nĭsh′ən) *n.* A person highly skilled in a certain field or process.

Tech•ni•col•or (tĕk′nĭ-kŭl′ər). A trademark for a motion-picture color process.

tech•nique (tĕk-nēk′) *n.* **1.** The systematic procedure by which a complex or scientific task is accomplished. **2.** *also* **tech•nic** (tĕk′nĭk). The degree of expertise shown in a procedure or performance.

tech•noc•ra•cy (tĕk-nŏk′rə-sē) *n., pl.* **-cies.** Government by technical experts, esp. scientists and engineers. —**tech′no•crat′** (-nə-krăt′) *n.* —**tech′no•crat′ic** *adj.*

tech•nol•o•gy (tĕk-nŏl′ə-jē) *n., pl.* **-gies. 1.** The application of scientific knowledge, esp. in industry or business. **2.** The methods and materials of applied science. —**tech′no•log′i•cal** (-nə-lŏj′ĭ-kəl) *adj.* —**tech•nol′o•gist** *n.*

tec•ton•ics (tĕk-tŏn′ĭks) *n. (sing. in number).* **1.** The art or science of construction. **2.** The geology of structural changes in the earth's crust. —**tec•ton′ic** *adj.*

ted•dy bear (tĕd′ē) *n.* A stuffed toy bear.

te•di•ous (tē′dē-əs) *adj.* Wearisome : boring. —**te′di•ous•ness** *n.*

te•di•um (tē′dē-əm) *n.* The quality or state of being tedious : boredom.

tee (tē) *n.* **1.** A small peg stuck in the ground for holding a golf ball for a first stroke. **2.** The raised area from which a golfer tees off. —*v.* **teed, tee•ing.** To place (a ball) on a golf tee.

—tee off. 1. To make one's first stroke toward a hole from the tee. **2.** *Slang.* To begin. **3.** *Slang.* To annoy or anger.
teem (tēm) *v.* To be full of : abound.
teen (tēn) *adj.* Teenage. —*n.* One between 13 and 19 : teenager.
teen•age *or* **teen-age** (tēn'āj') *also* **teen•aged** *or* **teen-aged** (-ājd') *adj.* Of, relating to, or descriptive of those aged 13 through 19. **—teen'ag'er** *n.*
teens (tēnz) *pl.n.* **1.** The numbers 13 through 19. **2.** The years of life between ages 13 and 19.
tee•ny (tē'nē) *adj.* **-ni•er, -ni•est.** *Informal.* Very small : tiny.
tee•pee (tē'pē) *n. var. of* TEPEE.
tee shirt (tē'shûrt') *n. var. of* T-SHIRT.
tee•ter (tē'tər) *v.* **1.** To walk or move unsteadily. **2.** To vacillate. **—tee'ter** *n.*
teeth (tēth) *n. pl. of* TOOTH.
teethe (tē*th*) *v.* **teethed, teeth•ing.** To grow or cut one's teeth.
tee•to•tal•er (tē-tōt'l-ər) *n.* One who abstains from alcoholic beverages. **—tee•to'tal•ism** *n.*
▲ ***word history:*** The word *teetotaler* is derived from the phrase *teetotal abstainer,* which was coined by temperance workers in the 1830's. The syllable *tee-* is simply a spelling of the pronunciation of the letter T, which is the reduplication of the initial letter of *total. Teetotal* was therefore a catchy way of saying "absolutely total."
Tef•lon (tĕf'lŏn'). A trademark for a durable plastic used as a nonstick coating.
tek•tite (tĕk'tīt') *n.* A usu. small and round, dark brown to green glassy rock that may be of meteoric origin.
tel•e•cast (tĕl'ĭ-kăst') *v.* **-cast** *or* **-cast•ed, -cast•ing.** To broadcast (a program) by television. **—tel'e•cast'** *n.*
tel•e•com•mu•ni•ca•tion (tĕl'ĭ-kə-myo͞o'nĭ-kā'shən) *n. often* **telecommunications** *(sing. in number).* The science and technology of sending messages by electrical or electronic means.
tel•e•com•mut•ing (tĕl'ĭ-kə-myo͞o'tĭng) *n.* The practice of working at home by using a modem and a computer terminal connected with one's business office. **—tel'e•com•mute'** *v.* **—tel'e•com•mut'er** *n.*
tel•e•con•fer•ence (tĕl'ĭ-kŏn'fər-əns, -frəns) *n.* A conference held among people in different locations with telecommunications equipment.
tel•e•gen•ic (tĕl'ə-jĕn'ĭk, -jē'nĭk) *adj.* Having a pleasing appearance on television.
tel•e•gram (tĕl'ĭ-grăm') *n.* A message or communication transmitted by telegraph.
tel•e•graph (tĕl'ĭ-grăf') *n.* **1.** A communications system in which a transmission is sent, either by wire or radio, to a receiving station. **2.** A message sent by telegraph : telegram. —*v.* To send or communicate by telegraph. **—te•leg'ra•pher** (tə-lĕg'rə-fər), **te•leg'ra•phist** *n.* **—tel'e•graph'ic** *adj.* **—tel'e•graph'i•cal•ly** *adv.* **—te•leg'ra•phy** *n.*
tel•e•ki•ne•sis (tĕl'ə-kĭ-nē'sĭs, -kī-) *n.* Movement of objects by scientifically inexplicable means. **—tel'e•ki•net'ic** (-nĕt'ĭk) *adj.* **—tel'e•ki•net'i•cal•ly** *adv.*
tel•e•mar•ket•ing (tĕl'ə-mär'kĭ-tĭng) *n.* Use of the telephone in marketing. **—tel'e•mar'ket•er** *n.*
te•lem•e•try (tə-lĕm'ĭ-trē) *n.* The science and technology of the transmission and measurement of data from a distant source, as a spacecraft. **—tel'e•me'ter** (tĕl'ə-mē'tər) *n.* **—tel'e•met'ric** (tĕl'ə-mĕt'rĭk), **tel'e•met'ri•cal** *adj.*
te•lep•a•thy (tə-lĕp'ə-thē) *n.* Communication between individuals by mental processes rather than ordinary sensory means. **—tel'e•path'ic** (tĕl'ə-păth'ĭk) *adj.* **—tel'e•path'i•cal•ly** *adv.* **—te•lep'a•thist** *n.*
tel•e•phone (tĕl'ə-fōn') *n.* An electronic device or system for sound reception or reproduction at a distance. —*v.* **-phoned, -phon•ing. 1.** To communicate (with) by telephone. **2.** To transmit by telephone. **—tel'e•phon'er** *n.*
te•leph•o•ny (tə-lĕf'ə-nē) *n.* The science and technology of electrical sound transmission between distant points. **—tel'e•phon'ic** (-fŏn'ĭk) *adj.*
tel•e•pho•to (tĕl'ə-fō'tō) *adj.* Of, relating to, or being a photographic lens or lens system for producing a large image of a distant object. **—tel'e•pho'to•graph'** *n. & v.* **—tel'e•pho'to•graph'ic** *adj.* **—tel'e•pho'tog'ra•phy** *n.*
tel•e•play (tĕl'ə-plā') *n.* A play written or adapted for television.
tel•e•scope (tĕl'ĭ-skōp') *n.* An arrangement of lenses or mirrors or both that collects light, allowing observation of remote objects, esp. stars and planets. —*v.* **-scoped, -scop•ing. 1.** To slide or cause to slide one within another, as the tubular parts of a hand telescope. **2.** To make shorter : condense. **—tel'e•scop'ic** (-skŏp'ĭk) *adj.* **—tel'e•scop'i•cal•ly** *adv.*
tel•e•thon (tĕl'ə-thŏn') *n.* A long telecast usu. for fund-raising.
Tel•e•type (tĕl'ĭ-tīp'). A trademark for a teletypewriter.
tel•e•type•writ•er (tĕl'ĭ-tīp'rī'tər) *n.* A telegraphlike typewriter that either transmits or receives electrically coded messages.
tel•e•van•gel•ist (tĕl'ĭ-văn'jə-lĭst) *n.* An evangelist who conducts religious telecasts. **—tel'e•van'gel•ism** *n.*
tel•e•vise (tĕl'ə-vīz') *v.* **-vised, -vis•ing.** To broadcast by television : telecast.
tel•e•vi•sion (tĕl'ə-vĭzh'ən) *n.* **1.** Transmission and reception of images and usu. sound by electronic means. **2.** A receiving device that reproduces transmitted images on a screen. **3.** The television industry.
tel•ex (tĕl'ĕks') *n.* **1.** A communications system consisting of teletypewriters connected to a telephonic network. **2.** A message sent or received by such a system. **—tel'ex'** *v.*
tell (tĕl) *v.* **told** (tōld), **tell•ing. 1.** To describe or relate : narrate. **2.** To express in words : say. **3.** To make known. **4.** To direct

: command. **5.** To perceive or discern by observation. **6.** To have a marked effect or impact <The strain on the team began to *tell.*> **—tell off.** *Informal.* To scold or criticize. **—tell'a•ble** *adj.*

tell•er (tĕl'ər) *n.* **1.** One who tells or narrates. **2.** A bank employee who handles money paid out and received.

tell•ing (tĕl'ĭng) *adj.* **1.** Effective : forceful. **2.** Meaningful. **—tell'ing•ly** *adv.*

tell•tale (tĕl'tāl') *n.* One that reveals information or secrets. **—tell'tale'** *adj.*

tel•lu•ri•um (tĕ-lŏŏr'ē-əm, tə-) *n. Symbol* **Te** A brittle, silvery-white, sulfurlike metallic element used esp. in alloys.

te•mer•i•ty (tə-mĕr'ĭ-tē) *n.* Audacity.

tem•per (tĕm'pər) *v.* **1.** To modify by the addition of something. **2.** To bring to the right degree of texture or firmness, esp. to harden or toughen (a metal), as by gradual heating and cooling. **3.** To tune (a keyboard instrument). *—n.* **1.** A usual state of mind or emotions. **2.** Mental or emotional composure. **3. a.** A tendency to become irritable or angry. **b.** A violent outburst of anger. **4.** The degree of hardness achieved by tempering. **—tem'per•a•ble** *adj.*

tem•per•a (tĕm'pər-ə) *n.* **1.** A type of paint made by mixing pigment with a water-soluble substance such as size or egg yolk. **2.** Painting done with tempera.

tem•per•a•ment (tĕm'pər-ə-mənt, -prə-mənt) *n.* **1.** A person's characteristic way of thinking, behaving, and reacting : disposition. **2.** Undue irritability or sensitivity. **—tem'per•a•men'tal** *adj.*

tem•per•ance (tĕm'pər-əns, -prəns) *n.* **1.** Moderation in one's appetites or emotions : self-restraint. **2.** Moderation in or total abstinence from drinking alcoholic beverages.

tem•per•ate (tĕm'pər-ĭt, -prĭt) *adj.* **1.** Practicing moderation and self-restraint. **2.** Not excessive or extreme. **3.** Of or having a mild or moderate climate.

tem•per•a•ture (tĕm'pər-ə-chŏŏr', -chər, tĕm'prə-) *n.* **1.** The relative hotness or coldness of a body or environment as measured on a standard scale. **2.** An abnormally high body temperature usu. as a result of illness.

tem•pered (tĕm'pərd) *adj.* Having a particular disposition <hot-*tempered*>

tem•pest (tĕm'pĭst) *n.* A violent storm often with rain, snow, hail, etc.

tem•pes•tu•ous (tĕm-pĕs'chŏŏ-əs) *adj.* Of or resembling a tempest : turbulent. **—tem•pes'tu•ous•ness** *n.*

tem•plate (tĕm'plĭt) *n.* A gauge or pattern, as a thin metal plate, used in making or copying something accurately.

tem•ple[1] (tĕm'pəl) *n.* **1.** A place or house of worship, esp. a synagogue. **2.** A place devoted to a special purpose.

tem•ple[2] (tĕm'pəl) *n.* The flattened area on either side of the forehead.

tem•po (tĕm'pō) *n., pl.* **-pos** *or* **-pi** (-pē). **1.** The speed at which a musical composition is to be played. **2.** A rate or rhythm of something : pace.

tem•po•ral[1] (tĕm'pər-əl, -prəl) *adj.* **1.** Of, pertaining to, or limited by time. **2.** Of or pertaining to worldly or secular matters.

tem•po•ral[2] (tĕm'pər-əl, -prəl) *adj.* Of or near the temples or sides of the head.

tem•po•rar•y (tĕm'pə-rĕr'ē) *adj.* Having a limited duration or use : impermanent. *—n., pl.* **-ies.** A temporary worker, as in an office. **—tem'po•rar'i•ly** *adv.*

tem•po•rize (tĕm'pə-rīz') *v.* **-rized, -riz•ing. 1.** To postpone acting or deciding in order to gain time. **2.** To adapt to circumstances. **—tem'po•ri•za'tion** *n.*

tempt (tĕmpt) *v.* **1.** To draw into a wrong or foolish course of action. **2.** To attract : invite. **3.** To risk provoking, as fate. **4.** To incline strongly <was *tempted* to quit> ★ ***syns:*** ALLURE, ENTICE, INVEIGLE, LURE, SEDUCE **—temp•ta'tion** *n.* **—tempt'er** *n.* **—tempt'ress** *n.*

tem•pu•ra (tĕm'pŏŏ-rə, tĕm-pŏŏr'ə) *n.* A Japanese dish of batter-dipped deep-fried vegetables and seafood.

ten (tĕn) *n.* **1.** The cardinal number equal to 9 + 1. **2.** The 10th in a set or sequence. **3.** A 10-dollar bill. **—ten** *adj. & pron.* **—tenth** *n. & adj. & adv.*

ten•a•ble (tĕn'ə-bəl) *adj.* Capable of being defended or sustained. **—ten'a•bil'i•ty, ten'a•ble•ness** *n.* **—ten'a•bly** *adv.*

te•na•cious (tə-nā'shəs) *adj.* **1.** Holding firmly, stubbornly, or persistently. **2.** Tending to cling or adhere. **3.** Retaining easily and well <a *tenacious* memory> **—te•na'cious•ly** *adv.* **—te•nac'i•ty** (-năs'ə-tē), **te•na'cious•ness** *n.*

ten•an•cy (tĕn'ən-sē) *n., pl.* **-cies. 1.** The possession or occupancy by lease or rent of another's land or building. **2.** The duration of a tenant's occupancy.

ten•ant (tĕn'ənt) *n.* **1.** One who pays rent to occupy another's property. **2.** An inhabitant : dweller.

Ten Commandments *n. Bible.* The 10 moral laws given to Moses by God.

tend[1] (tĕnd) *v.* **1.** To be directed, as a course of travel. **2. a.** To be apt or likely <Stress *tends* to cause illness.> **b.** To be inclined <*tends* toward stinginess>

tend[2] (tĕnd) *v.* **1.** To look after : take care of. **2.** To serve at : manage, as a bar.

ten•den•cy (tĕn'dən-sē) *n., pl.* **-cies. 1.** An inclination to think or behave in a particular way. **2.** A general drift or trend.

ten•den•tious (tĕn-dĕn'shəs) *adj.* Tending toward a certain point of view : biased.

ten•der[1] (tĕn'dər) *adj.* **1.** Easily damaged : fragile. **2.** Young : immature. **3. a.** Easily hurt <*tender* skin> **b.** Painful : sore <a *tender* tooth> **4.** Readily cut or chewed. **5.** Kind : gentle. **6.** Sympathetic. **—ten'der•ly** *adv.* **—ten'der•ness** *n.*

ten•der[2] (tĕn'dər) *n.* **1.** A formal bid or offer. **2.** Something offered, esp. money <legal *tender*> *—v.* To offer or present formally. **—ten'der•er** *n.*

tend•er[3] (tĕn'dər) *n.* **1.** One who tends something. 2. *Naut.* A small vessel that services larger vessels. **3.** A railroad car carrying fuel and water for the locomotive, to which it is attached.

ten•der•foot (tĕn′dər-fo͝ot′) *n., pl.* **-foots** *or* **-feet. 1.** One not used to rough outdoor life. 2. A novice.

ten•der•heart•ed (tĕn′dər-här′tĭd) *adj.* Compassionate. **—ten′der•heart′ed•ly** *adv.* **—ten′der•heart′ed•ness** *n.*

ten•der•ize (tĕn′də-rīz′) *v.* **-ized, -iz•ing.** To make (meat) tender, as by pounding or marinating. **—ten′der•iz′er** *n.*

ten•der•loin (tĕn′dər-loin′) *n.* **1.** A tender portion of a beef or pork loin. **2.** A city district notorious for vice and corruption.

ten•di•ni•tis *also* **ten•do•ni•tis** (tĕn′də-nī′tĭs) *n.* Inflammation of a tendon.

ten•don (tĕn′dən) *n.* A band of tough, fibrous tissue connecting a muscle and a bone. **—ten′di•nous** *adj.*

ten•dril (tĕn′drəl) *n.* **1.** A slender coiling stemlike part by which a climbing plant attaches itself to a support. **2.** Something, as a ringlet of hair, resembling a tendril.

ten•e•brous (tĕn′ə-brəs) *adj.* Dark and gloomy.

ten•e•ment (tĕn′ə-mənt) *n.* **1.** A building used as a dwelling. **2.** A low-rent apartment building that is minimally maintained.

ten•et (tĕn′ĭt) *n.* A basic principle, doctrine, or dogma.

ten-gal•lon hat (tĕn′găl′ən) *n.* A wide-brimmed felt hat with a tall crown.

ten•nis (tĕn′ĭs) *n.* A game played with rackets and a light ball by 2 or 4 players on a court divided by a net.

ten•on (tĕn′ən) *n.* A projecting piece, as on wood, designed to fit into a mortise.

ten•or (tĕn′ər) *n.* **1.** General meaning **:** purport. **2. a.** A male singing voice higher than a baritone. **b.** A singer with a tenor voice. **c.** A part written for a tenor.

ten•pin (tĕn′pĭn′) *n.* **1.** A bowling pin grouped in sets of 10 for playing tenpins. **2. tenpins** *(sing. in number).* The game of bowling with tenpins.

tense[1] (tĕns) *adj.* **tens•er, tens•est. 1.** Stretched tightly **:** taut. **2.** Experiencing emotional tension. 3. Distressingly suspenseful. *—v.* **tensed, tens•ing.** To make or become tense. **—ten′si•ty** *n.*

tense[2] (tĕns) *n.* Any of the inflected forms of a verb that designate the time of the action or state.

ten•sile (tĕn′səl, -sīl′) *adj.* **1.** Of, relating to, or involving tension. **2.** Capable of being stretched. **—ten•sil′i•ty** *n.*

ten•sion (tĕn′shən) *n.* **1.** The act or process of stretching or the state of being stretched. **2.** A force that tends to stretch something. **3. a.** Mental or emotional strain. **b.** A forced often hostile mutual relation. **4.** Voltage or electrical potential.

tent (tĕnt) *n.* A movable shelter consisting of material stretched over a supporting framework. *—v.* To shelter in a tent.

ten•ta•cle (tĕn′tə-kəl) *n.* A long flexible unjointed projection from the bodies of certain invertebrates, as an octopus. **—ten•tac′u•lar** (-tăk′yə-lər) *adj.*

ten•ta•tive (tĕn′tə-tĭv) *adj.* **1.** Experimental or provisional in nature **:** not definite. **2.** Hesitant **:** unsure. **—ten′ta•tive•ly** *adv.*

ten•ter•hook (tĕn′tər-ho͝ok′) *n.* A hooked nail used to fasten cloth on a framework for drying and stretching. **—on tenterhooks.** Anxious or suspenseful.

ten•u•ous (tĕn′yo͞o-əs) *adj.* **1.** Slender in form **:** fine. **2.** Rarefied, as high-altitude air. **3.** Lacking substance or significance. ★ ***syns:*** FEEBLE, FLIMSY, INSUBSTANTIAL, UNSUBSTANTIAL **—ten′u•ous•ness** *n.*

ten•ure (tĕn′yər, -yo͝or′) *n.* **1.** The act, state, right, or period of holding something, as land or an office. **2.** The conditions by which something is held. **3.** Permanence of position. **—ten′ured** *adj.*

te•pee (tē′pē) *n.* A portable dwelling of certain American Indian peoples, consisting of a conical framework of poles covered with skins or bark.

tep•id (tĕp′ĭd) *adj.* **1.** Lukewarm. **2.** Half-hearted. **—tep′id•ly** *adv.*

te•qui•la (tə-kē′lə) *n.* An alcoholic liquor made from a fleshy-leaved Central American agave plant, *Agave tequilana.*

ter•a•to•gen•ic (tĕr′ə-tə-jĕn′ĭk) *adj.* Causing fetal malformations.

ter•bi•um (tûr′bē-əm) *n. Symbol* **Tb** A soft, silvery-gray metallic rare-earth element used as a laser material.

ter•cen•ten•a•ry (tûr′sĕn-tĕn′ə-rē, tərsĕn′tə-nĕr′ē) *n., pl.* **-ries. 1.** A time span of 300 years. 2. A 300th anniversary or its celebration. **—ter′cen•ten′a•ry** *adj.*

ter•cen•ten•ni•al (tûr′sĕn-tĕn′ē-əl) *n. & adj.* Tercentenary.

ter•i•ya•ki (tĕr′ē-yä′kē) *n.* A Japanese dish of grilled or broiled slices of marinated meat or shellfish.

term (tûrm) *n.* **1. a.** A limited duration <a school *term*> **b.** A designated period for one to serve. **2. a.** A point of time initiating or terminating a period. **b.** A set date, as for paying money owed. **c.** The end of a normal pregnancy. **3. a.** A word or phrase having a precise meaning <a technical *term*> **b. terms.** Words or manner of expression <spoke in plain *terms*> **4. terms. a.** Conditions or provisions <the *terms* of a treaty> **b.** Mutual relations <on friendly *terms*> **5.** *Math.* **a.** Each of the numbers connected by plus or minus signs in an equation or series. **b.** Either number of a ratio. *—v.* To designate with a term **:** call.

ter•ma•gant (tûr′mə-gənt) *n.* A scolding, shrewish woman.

ter•mi•nal (tûr′mə-nəl) *adj.* **1.** Of, located at, or forming the boundary or end of something. **2.** In conclusion **:** final. **3.** Of or taking place in a term or every term. **4.** Resulting in death **:** fatal. *—n.* **1.** An ending or extreme point, limit, or part. **2.** An electrical connection point in a component. **3.** A station at the end of a railway, bus line, or airline. **4.** *Computer Sci.* A device through which data can enter or leave a computer system.

ter•mi•nate (tûr′mə-nāt′) *v.* **-nat•ed, -nat•ing. 1.** To come or bring to an end : conclude. **2.** To discontinue the employment of : fire. **—ter′mi•na•ble** *adj.* **—ter′mi•na′tion** *n.* **—ter′mi•na′tor** *n.*

ter•mi•nol•o•gy (tûr′mə-nŏl′ə-jē) *n., pl.* **-gies.** The technical vocabulary of a specific trade, science, or art.

ter•mi•nus (tûr′mə-nəs) *n., pl.* **-es** *or* **-ni** (-nī′). **1.** The final point : end. **2.** The terminal of a transportation line.

ter•mite (tûr′mīt′) *n.* Any of numerous highy destructive social insects of the order Isoptera that usu. feed on wood.

tern (tûrn) *n.* Any of various sea birds of the genus *Sterna* and related genera, with narrow wings and a forked tail.

terp•si•cho•re•an (tûrp′sĭ-kə-rē′ən, -kôr′ē-ən, -kōr′-) *adj.* Of or pertaining to dancing. —*n.* A dancer.

ter•race (tĕr′əs) *n.* **1.** An open porch or balcony. **2.** An open area adjoining a house : patio. **3.** A flat-topped mound of earth with vertical or sloping sides. **4.** A row of dwellings built on a raised or sloping site. —*v.* **-raced, -rac•ing.** To make into or supply with a terrace.

ter•ra cot•ta (tĕr′ə kŏt′ə) *n.* **1.** A hard ceramic pottery and building clay. **2.** A brownish orange. **—ter′ra-cot′ta** *adj.*

ter•rain (tə-rān′, tĕ-) *n.* A tract of land esp. with respect to its physical features.

ter•ra•pin (tĕr′ə-pĭn) *n.* An aquatic, often edible North American turtle of the genus *Malaclemys* and related genera.

ter•rar•i•um (tə-râr′ē-əm, -răr′-) *n., pl.* **-ums** *or* **-i•a** (-ē-ə). A usu. closed glass container for growing small plants or keeping small animals, as turtles or lizards.

ter•res•tri•al (tə-rĕs′trē-əl) *adj.* **1.** Of or pertaining to the earth or its inhabitants. **2.** Living or growing on land <*terrestrial* animals> —*n.* A terrestrial inhabitant. **—ter•res′tri•al•ly** *adv.*

ter•ri•ble (tĕr′ə-bəl) *adj.* **1.** Causing great fear or dread. **2.** Extreme : intense <*terrible* cold> **3.** Very difficult or distressing <a *terrible* dilemma> **4. a.** Unpleasant : disagreeable. **b.** Of inferior quality. **—ter′ri•ble•ness** *n.* **—ter′ri•bly** *adv.*

ter•ri•er (tĕr′ē-ər) *n.* An active small dog orig. bred to dig for burrowing game.

ter•rif•ic (tə-rĭf′ĭk) *adj.* **1.** Causing great fear : terrifying. **2.** *Informal.* Very good : excellent <a *terrific* idea> **3.** Causing awe or amazement. **4.** Very bad or intense <*terrific* pain> **—ter•rif′i•cal•ly** *adv.*

ter•ri•fy (tĕr′ə-fī′) *v.* **-fied, -fy•ing.** To fill with fear.

ter•ri•to•ry (tĕr′ĭ-tôr′ē, -tōr′ē) *n., pl.* **-ries. 1.** A usu. sizable geographic area : region. **2.** The land and waters under the jurisdiction of a state, nation, or sovereign. **3. Territory.** A part of a nation not accorded full status. **4.** The area to which one is assigned as an agent or representative. **5.** A field of interest or activity. **—ter′ri•to′ri•al** *adj.* **—ter′ri•to′ri•al•ly** *adv.*

ter•ror (tĕr′ər) *n.* **1.** Overwhelmingly intense fear. **2.** One that causes terror. **3.** Violence by a group to achieve a usu. political objective.

ter•ror•ism (tĕr′ə-rĭz′əm) *n.* The political use of violence or intimidation. **—ter′ror•ist** *n.* **—ter′ror•is′tic** *adj.*

ter•ror•ize (tĕr′ə-rīz′) *v.* **-ized, -iz•ing. 1.** To fill with great fear : terrify. **2.** To control and dominate by intimidation or violence. **—ter′ror•i•za′tion** *n.* **—ter′ror•iz′er** *n.*

ter•ry cloth (tĕr′ē) *n.* An absorbent pile fabric with uncut loops on both sides.

terse (tûrs) *adj.* **ters•er, ters•est.** Brief : concise. **—terse′ly** *adv.* **—terse′ness** *n.*

tes•sel•late (tĕs′ə-lāt′) *v.* **-lat•ed, -lat•ing.** To form into or ornament with a mosaic pattern. **—tes′sel•la′tion** *n.*

test (tĕst) *n.* **1.** A means of examining or evaluating something. **2.** Something devised and administered to determine one's skill, knowledge, intelligence, etc. **3.** A criterion in measuring or examining : standard. **—test** *v.* **—test′er** *n.*

tes•ta•ment (tĕs′tə-mənt) *n.* **1.** The legal disposition of one's personal property by a written will. **2. Testament.** Either of the 2 principal sections of the Bible, the Old Testament and the New Testament. **3.** A statement of belief. **4.** Convincing evidence. **—tes′ta•men′ta•ry** *adj.*

tes•tate (tĕs′tāt′) *adj.* Having made a valid will.

tes•ta•tor (tĕs′tā′tər) *n.* One who has made a valid will. **—tes•ta′trix** *n.*

tes•ti•cle (tĕs′tĭ-kəl) *n.* A testis. **—tes•tic′u•late** (tĕs-tĭk′yə-lĭt), **tes•tic′u•lar** (-lər) *adj.*

tes•ti•fy (tĕs′tə-fī′) *v.* **-fied, -fy•ing. 1.** To give evidence under oath. **2.** To serve as evidence or proof. **3.** To affirm publicly. **—tes′ti•fi′er** *n.*

tes•ti•mo•ni•al (tĕs′tə-mō′nē-əl, -mōn′yəl) *n.* **1.** A formal statement attesting to something. **2.** A written statement affirming another's good character or value. **3.** Something given as a formal tribute. **—tes′ti•mo′ni•al** *adj.*

tes•ti•mo•ny (tĕs′tə-mō′nē) *n., pl.* **-nies. 1. a.** A solemn declaration or affirmation made under oath. **b.** The total of such declarations in a specific legal case. **2.** Supporting evidence : proof. **3.** A public declaration of religious experience.

tes•tis (tĕs′tĭs) *n., pl.* **-tes** (-tēz′). The male sperm-producing gland, one of a pair in a pouchlike enclosure.

tes•tos•ter•one (tĕs-tŏs′tə-rōn′) *n.* A male sex hormone.

test tube *n.* A clear glass cylinder usu. closed at one end, used in laboratory experiments.

test-tube baby (tĕst′to͞ob′) *n.* A baby conceived outside the womb through fertilization of an egg removed from the mother.

tes•ty (tĕs′tē) *adj.* **-ti•er, -ti•est.** Showing or marked by ill humor : irritable. **—tes′ti•ly** *adv.* **—tes′ti•ness** *n.*
Tet (tĕt) *n.* The lunar New Year as celebrated in Southeast Asia.
tet•a•nus (tĕt′n-əs) *n.* An often fatal bacterial disease marked by muscular spasms and rigidity esp. of the jaw.
tête-à-tête (tāt′ə-tāt′) *n.* A private conversation between 2 persons. **—tête′à-tête′** *adj. & adv.*
teth•er (tĕth′ər) *n.* **1.** A rope or chain that allows an animal limited freedom to move about. **2.** The limit of one's resources or strength. *—v.* To restrict with or as if with a tether.
Te•ton (tē′tŏn′) *n., pl.* **-ton** *or* **-tons.** A member of the largest and westernmost of the Sioux peoples.
tet•ra•cy•cline (tĕt′rə-sī′klēn′) *n.* A yellow crystalline compound.
tet•ra•eth•yl lead (tĕt′rə-ĕth′əl) *n.* An oily poisonous lead compound used as an antiknock agent in gasoline.
tet•ra•he•dron (tĕt′rə-hē′drən) *n., pl.* **-drons** *or* **-dra** (-drə). A polyhedron with 4 triangular faces. **—tet′ra•he′dral** *adj.*

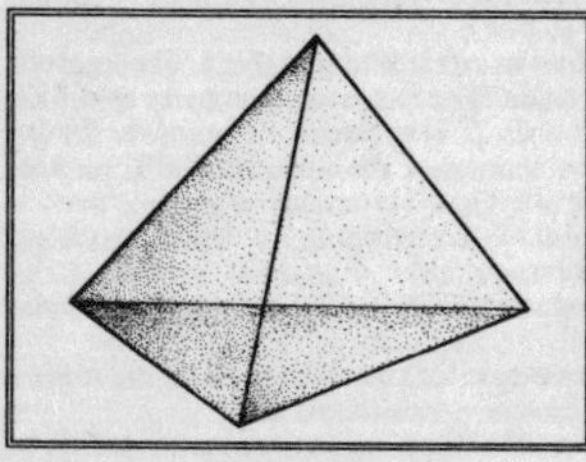

tetrahedron

te•tram•e•ter (tĕ-trăm′ĭ-tər) *n.* A line of verse with 4 metrical feet.
Teu•ton (to͞ot′n, tyo͞ot′n) *n.* **1.** A member of an ancient N European people. **2.** A German. **—Teu•ton′ic** *adj. & n.*
text (tĕkst) *n.* **1.** The wording or words of an author's work. **2.** The main body of a printed work. **3.** A Scriptural passage to be treated in a sermon. **4.** The theme of a discourse. **5.** A textbook. **—tex′tu•al** (tĕks′cho͞o-əl) *adj.* **—tex′tu•al•ly** *adv.*
text•book (tĕkst′bo͝ok′) *n.* A book used in studying a subject.
tex•tile (tĕk′stīl′, -stəl) *n.* **1.** Cloth esp. when knitted or woven. **2.** Fiber or yarn for making cloth. **—tex′tile** *adj.*
tex•ture (tĕks′chər) *n.* **1.** The surface look or feel of something. **2.** The basic make-up or structure of a substance. **3.** Distinctive or identifying character. **—tex′tur•al** *adj.* **—tex′tur•al•ly** *adv.*
—th¹ *suff. var. of* -ETH¹.
—th² *or* **—eth** *suff.* —Used to form ordinal numbers <hundred*th*>
Th *symbol for* THORIUM.
thal•a•mus (thăl′ə-məs) *n., pl.* **-mi** (-mī′). *Anat.* A large rounded mass of gray nerve tissue at the base of the brain that relays sensory stimuli to the brain cortex. **—tha•lam′-ic** (thə-lăm′ĭk) *adj.*

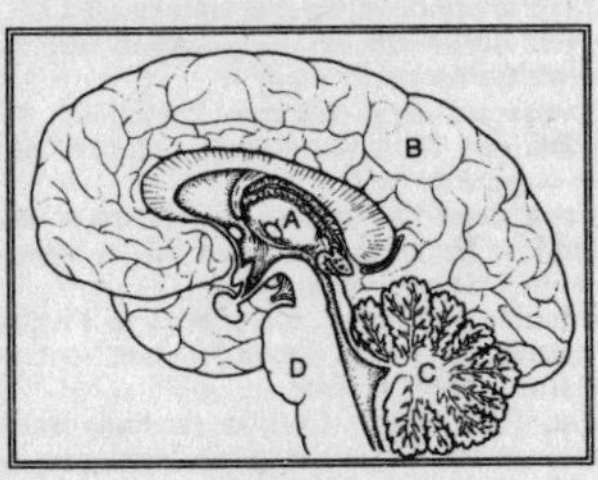

thalamus
A. thalamus, B. cerebrum, C. cerebellum, D. medulla oblongata

tha•lid•o•mide (thə-lĭd′ə-mīd′) *n.* A sedative found to cause severe fetal abnormalities when used by pregnant women.
thal•li•um (thăl′ē-əm) *n. Symbol* **Tl** A soft, malleable, highly toxic metallic element used esp. in rodent and ant poisons.
than (*th*ăn; *th*ən *when unstressed*) *conj.* **1.** —Used to indicate the second element or clause after a comparative adjective or adverb <You are much taller *than* I am.> **2.** —Used in statements of preference <would rather walk *than* ride> *—prep.* In comparison with.
thane (thān) *n.* A Scottish feudal lord.
thank (thăngk) *v.* **1.** To express one's thanks to. **2.** To hold responsible : credit.
thank•ful (thăngk′fəl) *adj.* Showing or feeling gratitude : grateful. **—thank′ful•ly** *adv.* **—thank′ful•ness** *n.*
thank•less (thăngk′lĭs) *adj.* **1.** Ungrateful. **2.** Unappreciated. **—thank′less•ly** *adv.* **—thank′less•ness** *n.*
thanks (thăngks) *pl.n.* An expression of appreciation. *—interj.* —Used to express gratefulness. **—thanks to.** Because of.
thanks•giv•ing (thăngks-gĭv′ĭng) *n.* An act of expressing gratitude, esp. to God.
Thanksgiving Day *n.* A U.S. holiday celebrated on the 4th Thursday of Nov.
that (*th*ăt; *th*ət *when unstressed) adj., pl.* **those** (*th*ōz). **1.** Being the one present or under discussion <*that* cat> **2.** Being less immediate than or contrasted with another <this room or *that* one> *—pron., pl.* **those. 1.** The one that is present or being discussed <*That* is our car.> **2.** Who, whom, or which <friends *that* are far away><jobs *that* are available> **3.** In, on, by, or with which <the day *that* you were sick> **4.** The one that is less immediate than or contrasted with another <This is mine, *that* is yours.> **5.** Something just mentioned <After *that,* we quit.>

—*adv.* To such an extent **:** so <Are you *that* tired?> —*conj.* **1.** —Used to introduce a dependent clause. **2.** —Used to introduce an expression of desire.

thatch (thăch) *n.* Plant material, as straw, reeds, or palm fronds, used for roofing. —*v.* To overlay with or as if with thatch.

thaw (thô) *v.* **1.** To change or cause to change from a frozen to a soft or liquid state. **2.** To grow warmer so that snow and ice melt. **3.** To become less formal or reserved **:** relax. **—thaw** *n.*

the (*th*ē *before a vowel; th*ə *before a consonant*) *def. art.* **1.** —Used as a determiner before nouns and noun phrases designating particular persons or things. **2.** —Used before a singular noun to make it general <*the* human brain> **3.** —Used before an adjective functioning as a noun <*the* strong and *the* weak> **4.** —Used like a preposition before a noun, meaning *per.* —*adv.* To that or what extent <*the* quicker *the* better>

the•a•ter *or* **the•a•tre** (thē′ə-tər) *n.* **1.** A building or outdoor structure for presenting dramatic performances or motion pictures. **2.** A usu. large room with tiers of seats, as for lectures. **3.** Dramatic works or production. **4.** A context for dramatic events. **5.** An area of military operations.

the•at•ri•cal (thē-ăt′rĭ-kəl) *adj.* **1.** Of or appropriate for the theater. **2.** Marked by exaggeration. **3.** Extravagant. —*n.* **theatricals.** Performance of theatrical works. **—the•at′ri•cal′i•ty, the•at′ri•cal•ness** *n.* **—the•at′ri•cal•ly** *adv.*

the•at•rics (thē-ăt′rĭks) *pl.n.* **1.** *(sing. in number).* Theatricals. **2.** Behavior contrived for effect.

the•be (thā′bā) *n., pl.* **thebe.** —See table at CURRENCY.

thee (*th*ē) *pron. archaic objective case of* THOU.

theft (thĕft) *n.* The act or an instance of stealing **:** larceny.

their (*th*âr; *th*ər *when unstressed) pron. possessive case of* THEY. —Used before a noun as a modifier.

theirs (*th*ârz) *pron.* That or those belonging to them.

the•ism (thē′ĭz′əm) *n.* Belief in a god or gods. **—the′ist** *n.* **—the•is′tic** *adj.*

them (*th*ĕm; *th*əm *when unstressed) pron. objective case of* THEY. —Used as the direct or indirect object of a verb or as the object of a preposition.

theme (thēm) *n.* **1.** A subject or topic. **2.** The subject of a work of art. **3.** A short composition written esp. by a student. **4.** The principal melody of a musical composition or movement. **—the•mat′ic** (thĭ-măt′ĭk) *adj.* **—the•mat′i•cal•ly** *adv.*

theme park *n.* An amusement park in which all the settings and attractions have a central theme.

them•selves (*th*ĕm-sĕlvz′, *th*əm-) *pron.* They or them. —Used: **1.** Reflexively as the direct or indirect object of a verb or as the object of a preposition <helped *themselves* to the pie><bought *themselves* a house> <billed it to *themselves*> **2.** For emphasis <They *themselves* couldn't be sure.>

then (*th*ĕn) *adv.* **1.** At that past time. **2.** After that **:** next. **3.** At a future time. **4.** In that case. **5.** Moreover. **6.** However. —*n.* That time or instance. —*adj.* Being or acting so at that time.

thence (*th*ĕns, thĕns) *adv.* **1.** From there on. **2.** From that fact, event, or origin. **3.** From then on.

thence•forth (*th*ĕns-fôrth′, thĕns-) *adv.* From that time on.

thence•for•ward (*th*ĕns-fôr′wərd, thĕns-) *also* **thence•for•wards** (-wərdz) *adv.* From then on.

the•oc•ra•cy (thē-ŏk′rə-sē) *n., pl.* **-cies. 1.** A government ruled by or subject to religious authority. **2.** A state governed by a theocracy. **—the′o•crat′** *n.* **—the′o•crat′ic** *adj.* **—the′o•crat′i•cal•ly** *adv.*

the•ol•o•gy (thē-ŏl′ə-jē) *n., pl.* **-gies. 1.** The study of the nature of God, of religious ideas, beliefs, and practices, and esp. of humankind's relation to God. **2.** An organized body of opinions about such a relationship. **—the′o•lo′gi•an** (thē′ə-lō′jən) *n.* **—the′o•log′i•cal** (-lŏg′ĭ-kəl) *adj.* **—the′o•log′i•cal•ly** *adv.*

the•o•rem (thē′ə-rəm) *n.* **1.** An idea proven or assumed to be true **:** proposition. **2.** *Math.* A statement whose truth can be proved on the basis of a given set of axioms.

the•o•rize (thē′ə-rīz′) *v.* **-rized, -riz•ing.** To conceptualize or analyze theories. **—the′o•re•ti′cian** *n.* **—the′o•ri•za′tion** *n.* **—the′o•riz′er, the′o•rist** *n.*

the•o•ry (thē′ə-rē) *n., pl.* **-ries. 1.** A general principle formulated to account for certain observable phenomena **:** hypothesis. **2.** A body of principles governing the study or practice of an art or discipline. **3.** Abstract reasoning. **4.** An assumption or guess. **—the′o•ret′i•cal** (-rĕt′ĭ-kəl) *adj.* **—the′o•ret′i•cal•ly** *adv.*

the•os•o•phy (thē-ŏs′ə-fē) *n., pl.* **-phies.** Religious theory based on mystical insight into the nature of God. **—the′o•soph′ic** (-ə-sŏf′ĭk), **the′o•soph′i•cal** *adj.* **—the′o•soph′i•cal•ly** *adv.* **—the•os′o•phist** *n.*

ther•a•peu•tic (thĕr′ə-pyo͞o′tĭk) *adj.* Having the power to heal or cure. **—ther′a•peu′ti•cal•ly** *adv.*

ther•a•peu•tics (thĕr′ə-pyo͞o′tĭks) *n. (sing. in number).* Medical treatment of disease **:** therapy. **—ther′a•peu′tist** *n.*

ther•a•py (thĕr′ə-pē) *n., pl.* **-pies.** A procedure designed to treat disease, illness, or disability. **—ther′a•pist** *n.*

there (*th*âr) *adv.* **1.** In or at that place <Let's sit *there.*> **2.** To, into, or toward that place <took the train *there*> **3.** In that matter <I agree with you *there.*> —*n.* That place or point <got out of *there* fast> —*pron.* —Used to introduce a sentence or clause.

there•a•bouts (*th*âr′ə-bouts′) *also* **there•a•bout** (-bout′) *adv.* **1.** Near that number or degree. **2.** Near that place or time.

there•af•ter (*th*âr-ăf′tər) *adv.* Afterward.
there•at (*th*âr-ăt′) *adv.* **1.** At that place. **2.** At that time. **3.** By reason of that.
there•by (*th*âr-bī′) *adv.* **1.** By means of that. **2.** With reference to that.
there•fore (*th*âr′fôr′, -fōr′) *adv.* For that reason : in consequence.
there•from (*th*âr-frŭm′, -frŏm′) *adv.* From this or that.
there•in (*th*âr-ĭn′) *adv.* **1.** In that place. **2.** In that circumstance or respect.
there•in•af•ter (*th*âr′ĭn-ăf′tər) *adv.* In a later part, as of a book or speech.
there•of (*th*âr-ŭv′, -ŏv′) *adv.* **1.** Of that or it. **2.** From that origin or cause.
there•on (*th*âr-ŏn′, -ôn′) *adv.* **1.** On or upon that. **2.** Directly following that.
there•to (*th*âr-to͞o′) *adv.* To that or it.
there•to•fore (*th*âr′tə-fôr′, -fōr′) *adv.* Before that.
there•un•to (*th*âr′ŭn-to͞o′) *adv.* Thereto.
there•up•on (*th*âr′ə-pŏn′, -pôn′) *adv.* **1.** On or upon that or it. **2.** Directly following that. **3.** For that reason : therefore.
there•with (*th*âr-wĭth′, -wĭ*th*′) *adv.* **1.** With that or it. **2.** Directly after that.
ther•mal (thûr′məl) *adj.* **1.** Of, making use of, producing, or caused by heat. **2.** Designed to retain body heat <*thermal* underwear> —**ther′mal•ly** *adv.*
ther•mo•dy•nam•ics (thûr′mō-dī-năm′ĭks) *n. (sing. in number).* Physics that deals with the relationships between heat and other forms of energy. —**ther′mo•dy•nam′ic** *adj.* —**ther′mo•dy•nam′i•cal•ly** *adv.*
ther•mom•e•ter (thər-mŏm′ĭ-tər) *n.* An instrument for measuring temperature, esp. a glass tube in which mercury rises and falls with temperature variations. —**ther′mo•met′ric, ther′mo•met′ri•cal** *adj.*
ther•mo•nu•cle•ar (thûr′mō-no͞o′klē-ər) *adj.* **1.** Of or derived from the fusion of atomic nuclei at high temperatures or the energy so produced. **2.** Of atomic weapons based on nuclear fusion.
ther•mo•plas•tic (thûr′mə-plăs′tĭk) *adj.* Soft and pliable when heated but hard when cooled. —**ther′mo•plas′tic** *n.*
Ther•mos bottle (thûr′məs). A trademark for a flask designed to maintain the desired temperature of the contents.
ther•mo•set•ting (thûr′mō-sĕt′ĭng) *adj.* Hardening permanently when heated.
ther•mo•stat (thûr′mə-stăt′) *n.* A device that automatically responds to temperature changes and activates switches controlling equipment such as furnaces, refrigerators, and air conditioners. —**ther′mo•stat′ic** *adj.* —**ther′mo•stat′i•cal•ly** *adv.*
the•sau•rus (thĭ-sôr′əs) *n., pl.* **-es** *or* **-sau•ri** (-sôr′ī′). **1.** A book of selected words or concepts, as a specialized vocabulary of a given field such as medicine or music. **2.** A book of synonyms.

▲ ***word history:*** A thesaurus is literally a treasury of words and information, for the word itself comes form Greek *thesauros,* "treasure." The Romans borrowed the Greek word, and Latin *thesaurus* developed into Old French *tresor,* which was borrowed into English as *treasure.* The Latin word *thesaurus* was used in titles of English books in early modern times, but it did not become a generic term for a particular kind of book until the 19th cent.

these (*th*ēz) *pron. pl. of* THIS.
the•sis (thē′sĭs) *n., pl.* **-ses** (-sēz′). **1.** A statement advanced for consideration and maintained by argument. **2.** A formal paper or treatise written, as by a degree candidate, after original academic research.
thes•pi•an *also* **Thes•pi•an** (thĕs′pē-ən) —*adj.* Of or relating to drama. —*n.* A stage performer.
Thes•sa•lo•ni•ans (thĕs′ə-lō′nē-ənz) *pl.n. (sing. in number).* —See table at BIBLE.
thews (tho͞oz, thyo͞oz) *pl.n.* **1.** Sinews or muscles. **2.** Muscular strength or power.
they (*th*ā) *pron.* **1.** The ones just mentioned. —Used as the plural of *he, she,* and *it.* **2.** People in general.
they'd (*th*ād). **1.** They had. **2.** They would.
they'll (*th*āl). They will.
they're (*th*âr). They are.
they've (*th*āv). They have.
thi•a•mine (thī′ə-mĭn, -mēn′) *also* **thi•a•min** (-mĭn) *n.* A B-complex vitamin essential for normal metabolic and nerve functioning.
thick (thĭk) *adj.* **1. a.** Having considerable depth or extent from one surface or side to the other <a *thick* board> **b.** Determined by measurement <10 in. *thick*> **2.** Heavily or stockily built. **3.** Packed densely or abundantly. **4.** Having a viscous consistency. **5.** Numerous : abounding. **6.** Uttered indistinctly. **7.** Noticeable <a *thick* accent> **8.** Lacking mental quickness. **9.** *Informal.* Friendly. **10.** *Informal.* Excessive. —*n.* **1.** The thickest part of something. **2.** The most active or crowded part. —**thick′ly** *adv.* —**thick′ness** *n.*
thick•en (thĭk′ən) *v.* **1.** To make or become thick. **2.** To make more complex. —**thick′en•er** *n.* —**thick′en•ing** *n.*
thick•et (thĭk′ĭt) *n.* A close-packed growth of shrubs, small trees, etc.
thick•set (thĭk′sĕt′) *adj.* Having a stout, stocky body.
thick-skinned (thĭk′skĭnd′) *adj.* **1.** Having a thick skin. **2.** Not easily offended.
thief (thēf) *n., pl.* **thieves** (thēvz). One that steals, esp. furtively.
thieve (thēv) *v.* **thieved, thiev•ing.** To engage in or take by theft. —**thiev′er•y** *n.*
thigh (thī) *n.* The part of the vertebrate leg between the hip and the knee.
thigh•bone (thī′bōn′) *n.* The femur, extending from the hip to the knee.
thim•ble (thĭm′bəl) *n.* A small, cuplike guard worn to protect the finger in needlework. —**thim′ble•ful′** *n.*
thin (thĭn) *adj.* **thin•ner, thin•nest. 1.** Having little depth or extent from one surface or

side to the other <a *thin* board> **2.** Fine in diameter <a *thin* wire> **3.** Slender in build. **4.** Not densely packed or abundant **:** sparse. **5. a.** Having a fluid consistency. **b.** Rarefied <*thin* air> **6.** Lacking force or substance. **—thin** *v.* **—thin'ly** *adv.* **—thin'ness** *n.*

thine (*th*īn) *pron. Archaic & Poetic.* That which belongs to thee. —Used as a possessive form of *thou.*

thing (thĭng) *n.* **1.** Something that has a separate existence **:** entity. **2.** A real or material object. **3.** An inanimate object as distinguished from an animate being. **4.** A living being. **5. things. a.** Personal belongings. **b.** General conditions. **6.** A garment <not a *thing* to wear> **7.** An act or deed. **8.** A conception, idea, or utterance. **9.** A matter to be treated **:** concern. **10.** An incident **:** happening. **11.** An item or detail. **12.** A mild phobia or fixation. **13.** *Slang.* Something one enjoys or does esp. well.

think (thĭngk) *v.* **thought** (thôt), **think•ing. 1.** To formulate (a thought) in the mind. **2.** To reflect on **:** ponder. **3.** To exercise the power of reason. **4.** To have a view (about) **:** believe. **5.** To recall **:** remember. **6.** To visualize. **7.** To weigh or consider. **8.** To dispose the mind in a given way <*think* big> **—think up.** To invent. **—think'a•ble** *adj.* **—think'er** *n.*

thin•ner (thĭn'ər) *n.* A liquid, as turpentine, mixed with paint to make it flow more easily.

thin-skinned (thĭn'skĭnd') *adj.* **1.** Having a thin skin or rind. **2.** Easily offended.

third (thûrd) *n.* **1.** The ordinal number that matches the number 3 in a series. **2.** One of 3 equal parts. **3.** The 3rd forward gear in the transmission of a motor vehicle. **—third** *adj. & adv.* **—third'ly** *adv.*

third degree *n.* Physical or mental torture to obtain information or a confession from a prisoner.

third-de•gree burn (thûrd'dĭ-grē') *n.* A severe burn marked by destruction of the epidermis and exposure of nerve endings.

third person *n.* The pronouns or verb forms used when making reference to a person or thing other than the speaker or writer or the one spoken to.

Third World *n.* Underdeveloped or developing countries, esp. those not allied with the Communist or non-Communist blocs.

thirst (thûrst) *n.* **1. a.** A dry feeling in the mouth related to a wish to drink. **b.** The wish to drink. **2.** A fervent wish or craving. *—v.* **1.** To experience thirst. **2.** To have a craving **:** yearn. **—thirst'i•ly** *adv.* **—thirst'i•ness** *n.* **—thirst'y** *adj.*

thir•teen (thûr'tēn') *n.* **1.** The cardinal number equal to 12 + 1. **2.** The 13th in a set or sequence. **—thir'teen'** *adj. & pron.* **—thir'teenth'** *n. & adj. & adv.*

thir•ty (thûr'tē) *n., pl.* **-ties.** The cardinal number equal to 3 × 10. **—thir'ti•eth** *n. & adj. & adv.* **—thir'ty** *adj. & pron.*

this (*th*ĭs) *pron., pl.* **these** (*th*ēz). **1.** The one that is present or being discussed <*This* is our car.> **2.** Something about to be said <Now hear *this.*> **3.** The one that is more immediate than or contrasted with another <*This* is mine, that is yours.> **4.** The present time **:** now. *—adj., pl.* **these. 1.** Being present or under discussion. **2.** Being more immediate than or contrasted with another. **3.** Being about to be said. *—adv.* To such an extent.

this•tle (thĭs'əl) *n.* Any of various plants, chiefly of the genera *Cirsium, Carduus,* or *Onopordum,* with usu. purplish flowers and prickly leaves.

this•tle•down (thĭs'əl-doun') *n.* The silky, fluffy material attached to the seeds of a thistle.

thith•er (thĭ*th*'ər, *th*ĭ*th*'-) *adv.* To that place **:** there. *—adj.* Being on the farther or more distant side.

thole pin (thōl) *n.* A peg set in pairs in the gunwale of a boat to hold oars in place.

thong (thông, thŏng) *n.* A narrow strip of material, as leather, used esp. for binding.

tho•rax (thôr'ăks', thōr'-) *n., pl.* **-es** *or* **tho•ra•ces** (thôr'ə-sēz', thōr'-). **1.** The section of the mammalian body between the neck and the abdomen **:** chest cavity. **2.** The middle section of the 3-part body of an insect. **—tho•rac'ic** (thə-răs'ĭk) *adj.*

tho•ri•um (thôr'ē-əm, thōr'-) *n. Symbol* **Th** A silvery-white radioactive metallic element used in magnesium alloys.

thorn (thôrn) *n.* **1. a.** A sharp, woody projection on a plant stem. **b.** A shrub, tree, or plant bearing such projections. **2.** One that causes irritation or annoyance. **—thorn'i•ness** *n.* **—thorn'y** *adj.*

thor•ough (thûr'ō, thŭr'ō) *adj.* **1.** Intensive **:** complete. **2.** Very careful or accurate. **3.** Absolute **:** unqualified. **—thor'ough•ly** *adv.* **—thor'ough•ness** *n.*

thor•ough•bred (thûr'ō-brĕd', thûr'ə-, thŭr'-) *adj.* Of pure breeding stock. *—n.* **1.** An animal bred of pure or pedigreed stock. **2. Thoroughbred.** Any of an English breed of racehorses.

thor•ough•fare (thûr'ō-fâr', thûr'ə-, thŭr'-) *n.* A public street, road, or highway.

thor•ough•go•ing (thûr'ō-gō'ĭng, thûr'ə-, thŭr'-) *adj.* **1.** Complete. **2.** Absolute.

those (*th*ōz) *adj. & pron. pl. of* THAT.

thou (*th*ou) *pron. Archaic.* The person spoken to **:** you.

though (*th*ō) *adv.* None the less **:** however. *—conj.* **1.** Regardless of the fact that **:** although. **2.** Supposing that **:** even if.

thought (thôt) *v. p.t. & p.p. of* THINK *—n.* **1.** The act, process, or power of thinking. **2.** A product of thinking **:** idea. **3.** A body of ideas, as of a given time or place in history. **4.** Attentive consideration. **5.** An opinion, viewpoint, or belief. **6.** A small amount or degree.

thought•ful (thôt'fəl) *adj.* **1.** Contemplative. **2.** Marked by careful thought. **3.** Considerate. **—thought'ful•ness** *n.*

thought•less (thôt'lĭs) *adj.* **1.** Careless. **2.** Reckless **:** rash. **3.** Inconsiderate. **—thought'less•ness** *n.*

thou•sand (thou'zənd) *n.* The cardinal number equal to 10 × 100 or 10^3. **—thou'sand** *adj. & pron.* **—thou'sandth** *n. & adj. & adv.*

thrall (thrôl) *n.* **1.** A slave or serf. **2.** Bondage : servitude. **—thrall'dom** (-dəm), **thral'dom** *n.*

thrash (thrăsh) *v.* **1.** To strike or beat with or as if with a whip. **2.** To move violently about. **3.** To defeat : vanquish. **4.** To discuss fully <*thrash* out the problem> **5.** To thresh (grain).

thrash•er (thrăsh'ər) *n.* A long-tailed New World songbird of the genus *Toxostoma,* often with a spotted breast.

thread (thrĕd) *n.* **1.** A fine, thin cord made of 2 or more fibrous strands twisted together. **2.** Something resembling a thread <a *thread* of smoke> **3.** A ridge that winds around a screw, nut, or bolt. **4.** A cohesive element. *—v.* **1.** To pass a thread through (e.g., a needle). **2.** To string on a thread. **3.** To make one's way cautiously. **—thread'y** *adj.*

thread•bare (thrĕd'bâr') *adj.* **1.** So worn that the threads show through : shabby. **2.** Hackneyed : trite.

threat (thrĕt) *n.* **1.** An expression of the intent to inflict harm. **2.** A possible source of danger : menace.

threat•en (thrĕt'n) *v.* **1.** To make a threat (against). **2.** To menace. **3.** To give warning signs of : portend. **—threat'en•er** *n.* **—threat'en•ing•ly** *adv.*

three (thrē) *n.* **1.** The cardinal number equal to 2 + 1. **2.** The 3rd in a set or sequence. **3.** Something having 3 parts, units, or members. **—three** *adj. & pron.*

three-D *or* **3-D** (thrē'dē') *adj.* Three-dimensional.

three-di•men•sion•al (thrē'dĭ-mĕn'shən-əl) *adj.* **1.** Of or having 3 dimensions. **2.** Producing visual images that give an illusion of depth and perspective.

three-fold (thrē'fōld') *adj.* **1.** Having or consisting of 3 parts. **2.** Three times as many or as much. **—three'fold'** *adv.*

three•score (thrē'skôr', -skōr') *adj.* Being 3 × 20 : 60. **—three'score'** *n.*

three•some (thrē'səm) *n.* Three persons or things together.

thren•o•dy (thrĕn'ə-dē) *n., pl.* **-dies.** A song of mourning. **—thren'o•dist** *n.*

thresh (thrĕsh) *v.* **1.** To separate the seeds from (cereal plants) by striking or beating. **2.** To beat severely : thrash.

thresh•old (thrĕsh'ōld', -hōld') *n.* **1.** A horizontal length of wood or stone serving as a doorsill. **2.** An entranceway. **3.** The place or point of beginning. **4.** The lowest level or intensity at which a stimulus is perceptible or can produce an effect.

threw (thro͞o) *v. p.t. of* THROW.

thrice (thrīs) *adv.* **1.** Three times. **2.** Threefold in manner or degree.

thrift (thrĭft) *n.* Prudent management of money and other resources. **—thrift'i•ly** *adv.* **—thrift'i•ness** *n.* **—thrift'y** *adj.*

thrill (thrĭl) *v.* **1.** To experience or cause to experience sudden intense excitement, joy, fear, etc. **2.** To quiver : vibrate. **—thrill** *n.* **—thrill'ing•ly** *adv.*

thrive (thrīv) *v.* **throve** (thrōv) *or* **thrived, thrived** *or* **thriven** (thrĭv'ən), **thriving. 1.** To be healthy or do well : flourish. **2.** To be successful : prosper.

throat (thrōt) *n.* **1.** The section of the digestive tract forming a passage between the back of the mouth and the esophagus. **2.** The front section of the neck.

throat•y (thrō'tē) *adj.* **-i•er, -i•est.** Sounded or apparently coming from deep in the throat : guttural or husky. **—throat'i•ly** *adv.* **—throat'i•ness** *n.*

throb (thrŏb) *v.* **throbbed, throb•bing. 1.** To beat quickly or forcefully : pound. **2.** To vibrate or sound slowly and rhythmically. **—throb** *n.* **—throb'bing•ly** *adv.*

throe (thrō) *n.* **1.** *often* **throes.** A severe pang or spasm of pain, as in childbirth. **2. throes.** A very painful or effortful struggle.

throm•bo•sis (thrŏm-bō'sĭs) *n., pl.* **-ses** (-sēz'). The development or presence of a thrombus.

throm•bus (thrŏm'bəs) *n., pl.* **-bi** (-bī'). A blood clot occluding a blood vessel or formed in a heart cavity.

throne (thrōn) *n.* **1.** The ceremonial chair of a monarch, bishop, etc. **2.** The rank or power of a monarch.

throng (thrŏng) *n.* A large crowd : multitude. *—v.* **1.** To crowd into or around : fill. **2.** To move in or as if in a crowd.

throt•tle (thrŏt'l) *n.* **1.** An engine valve that regulates the vaporized fuel or steam flow. **2.** A lever or pedal controlling the throttle. *—v.* **-tled, -tling. 1.** To control (an engine speed or fuel) with a throttle. **2.** To choke (a person). **3.** To prevent by force : suppress. **—throt'tler** *n.*

through (thro͞o) *prep.* **1.** In one side and out the opposite or another side of <came *through* the tunnel> **2.** In the midst of <flew *through* the clouds> **3.** By way of <got in *through* the cellar> **4.** By means of <found the job *through* an ad> **5.** Around <biked *through* Europe> **6.** For the duration of <slept *through* the movie> **7.** At or to the end of <We're *through* the worst part.> **8.** As a result of <failed *through* carelessness> *—adv.* **1.** In one end or side and out the other. **2.** From start to finish. **3.** Completely <chilled *through*> *—adj.* **1.** Extending from one end, side, or surface to another. **2.** Allowing unobstructed passage : direct. **3.** Finished. **4.** No longer effective or valued.

through•out (thro͞o-out') *prep.* Through the whole extent or duration of. *—adv.* **1.** Everywhere. **2.** From start to finish.

throve (thrōv) *v. var. p.t. of* THRIVE.

throw (thrō) *v.* **threw** (thro͞o), **thrown** (thrōn), **throw•ing. 1.** To cause to move through the air with a flinging motion of the arm. **2. a.** To hurl forcefully, as in anger. **b.** To cause to fall. **3.** To direct : cast <*threw* a glance my way> **4.** To put on or take off (clothing) hurriedly. **5.** *Informal.* To be the giver of (a party or social affair). **6.** *Informal.* To lose (a contest) by design. **7.** To move (a controlling lever or switch). **8.** To put abruptly into a given state <The threat *threw* us into turmoil.> **—throw up.** To vomit. *—n.* **1.** The act of throwing. **2.** The distance or height to which a projectile is or can be thrown. **3.** A light scarf, shawl, or coverlet.

throw•back (thrō'băk') *n.* A reversion to an ancestral type or earlier stage **:** atavism.

thru (thro͞o) *prep. & adv. & adj. Informal.* Through.

thrum (thrŭm) *v.* **thrummed, thrum•ming.** To play idly on (a stringed instrument). **—thrum** *n.*

thrush (thrŭsh) *n.* A songbird of the family Turdidae, usu. with brownish upper plumage and a spotted breast.

thrust (thrŭst) *v.* **thrust, thrust•ing. 1.** To push or shove with force. **2.** To stab, as with a dagger. **3.** To force (oneself or another) into a particular state or situation. **4.** To interject (e.g., comments). *—n.* **1.** A sudden forceful push or shove. **2. a.** A force or pressure that drives an object. **b.** The propelling force produced in a rocket or jet engine by the high-velocity rearward discharge of fuel gases. **3.** A stab with a pointed weapon. **4.** Stress or pressure of one part of a structure against another. **5.** General direction or tendency.

thru•way *also* **through•way** (thro͞o'wā') *n.* A multilane highway **:** expressway.

thud (thŭd) *n.* **1.** A dull thumping sound. **2.** A blow or fall causing a thud. **—thud** *v.*

thug (thŭg) *n.* A tough or violent ruffian, hoodlum, or gangster. **—thug'ger•y** *n.* **—thug'gish** *adj.*

thu•li•um (tho͞o'lē-əm) *n. Symbol* **Tm** A silvery rare-earth metallic element.

thumb (thŭm) *n.* **1.** The short first digit of the hand, capable of touching the other 4 fingers. **2.** The part of a mitten or glove that fits over the thumb. *—v.* **1.** To browse rapidly through (a publication). **2.** To dirty or impair by excess handling. **3.** *Informal.* To hitchhike by signaling with the thumb.

thumb•nail (thŭm'nāl') *n.* The nail of the thumb. *—adj.* Concise <a *thumbnail* sketch>

thumb•screw (thŭm'skro͞o') *n.* **1.** A screw that can be turned with the thumb and index finger. **2.** An instrument of torture that crushed the thumb.

thumb•tack (thŭm'tăk') *n.* A tack with a round, smooth head that can be pressed into place with the thumb.

thump (thŭmp) *n.* **1.** A blow with something blunt or weighty. **2.** The dull or muffled sound made by such a blow **:** thud. *—v.* **1.** To hit with something blunt or dull so as to make a thump. **2.** To throb **:** pound.

thun•der (thŭn'dər) *n.* **1.** The explosive or rumbling sound following a discharge of lightning. **2.** A loud rumbling noise similar to thunder. *—v.* **1.** To produce thunder or thunderlike sounds. **2.** To utter loudly. **—thun'der•ous** *adj.*

thun•der•bolt (thŭn'dər-bōlt') *n.* A discharge of lightning immediately followed by thunder.

thun•der•clap (thŭn'dər-klăp') *n.* A loud crash of thunder.

thun•der•cloud (thŭn'dər-kloud') *n.* A large, dark cloud carrying an electric charge and producing thunder and lightning.

thun•der•head (thŭn'dər-hĕd') *n.* The swollen upper part of a thundercloud.

thun•der•show•er (thŭn'dər-shou'ər) *n.* A brief, sometimes heavy rainstorm with thunder and lightning.

thun•der•storm (thŭn'dər-stôrm') *n.* A rainstorm with thunder and lightning.

thun•der•struck (thŭn'dər-strŭk') *adj.* Astounded **:** amazed.

Thurs•day (thûrz'dē, -dā') *n.* The 5th day of the week.

thus (*th*ŭs) *adv.* **1.** In this or that way. **2.** To such an extent or degree. **3.** Therefore.

thwack (thwăk) *v.* To strike hard with something flat **:** whack. **—thwack** *n.*

thwart (thwôrt) *v.* To keep from happening **:** frustrate. *—n.* A seat placed across a boat for an oarsman. *—adj.* Extending across something **:** transverse. *—adv. & prep. Archaic.* Across.

thy (*th*ī) *adj. Archaic.* Of thee or thyself. —Used as a possessive form of *thou.*

thyme (tīm) *n.* An aromatic plant of the genus *Thymus,* esp. *T. vulgaris,* of S Europe, with leaves used in cooking.

thy•mine (thī'mēn') *n.* A pyrimidine base that is an essential constituent of deoxyribonucleic acid.

thy•mus (thī'məs) *n.* **1.** A glandlike structure near the throat that is usu. vestigial in adults. **2.** A similar structure in other vertebrate animals, used esp. as a sweetbread. **—thy'mic** *adj.*

thy•roid (thī'roid') *adj.* Of or pertaining to the thyroid gland. *—n.* **1.** The thyroid gland. **2.** A medicine prepared from the thyroid gland of certain domestic animals.

thyroid gland *n.* A 2-lobed endocrine gland located at the base of the neck in humans and producing thyroxin.

thy•rox•in (thī-rŏk'sĭn) *also* **thy•rox•ine** (-sēn', -sĭn) *n.* An iodine-containing hormone produced by the thyroid gland to regulate growth and metabolism and made synthetically to treat thyroid disorders.

thy•self (*th*ī-sĕlf') *pron. Archaic.* Yourself.

Ti *symbol for* TITANIUM.

ti•ar•a (tē-ăr'ə, -âr'ə, -är'ə) *n.* **1.** An often bejeweled, crownlike ornamental headdress worn by women on formal occasions. **2.** The tall triple crown worn by the pope.

tib•i•a (tĭb'ē-ə) *n., pl.* **-i•ae** (-ē-ē') *or* **-as.** The larger inner bone of the vertebrate lower leg. **—tib'i•al** *adj.*

tic (tĭk) *n.* A recurring muscular spasm, usu. in the face or limbs.

tick¹ (tĭk) *n.* **1.** A light rhythmical tapping

sound, as made by a clock. **2.** A small check mark used on a list or to call attention to an item. **—tick** *v.*

tick[2] (tĭk) *n.* Any of numerous bloodsucking parasitic arachnids of the family Ixodidae or louselike insects of the family Hippoboscidae, many of which are carriers of disease.

tick[3] (tĭk) *n.* **1.** The sturdy fabric used to cover a mattress or pillow. **2.** Ticking.

tick•er (tĭk′ər) *n.* **1.** A telegraphic printing or display device that automatically receives and records news or stock-market quotations. **2.** *Slang.* The human heart.

ticker tape *n.* The strip of paper on which a telegraphic ticker prints.

tick•et (tĭk′ĭt) *n.* **1.** A paper slip or card entitling its holder to a specified service or privilege. **2.** A certifying document or license. **3.** An identifying or descriptive tag. **4.** A list of political candidates supported by a party or group. **5.** A legal summons for a violation. —*v.* **1.** To supply with a ticket. **2.** To label. **3.** To designate for a certain use. **4.** To serve with a legal summons.

tick•ing (tĭk′ĭng) *n.* A strong, sturdy, often striped fabric used to make casings for pillows and mattresses.

tick•le (tĭk′əl) *v.* **-led, -ling. 1.** To touch (a bodily part) lightly so as to cause twitching or laughter. **2.** To delight or amuse. **3.** To experience a tingling or twitching sensation. **—tick′le** *n.* **—tick′ler** *n.*

tick•lish (tĭk′lĭsh) *adj.* **1.** Sensitive to being tickled. **2.** Easily upset or offended. **3.** Requiring diplomacy or delicacy.

tick-tack-toe *also* **tic-tac-toe** (tĭk′-tăk-tō′) *n.* A game in which each of 2 players tries to make a line of 3 X's or 3 O's inside a 9-space box.

tidal wave *n.* **1.** An unusual rise of water along the seashore esp. as a result of strong winds. **2.** A very large ocean wave caused esp. by an earthquake. **3.** A widespread display, as of opinion or sentiment.

tid•bit (tĭd′bĭt′) *n.* A choice bit, esp. of food or gossip.

tide (tīd) *n.* **1. a.** The periodic rise and fall of the surface level of the oceans, caused by the gravitational pull of the moon and sun. **b.** A particular occurrence of a tide. **c.** The water that moves in a tide. **2.** A forceful trend. **3.** A time or season. **—tid′al** *adj.*

tide•land (tīd′lănd′) *n.* Coastal land that is under water during high tide.

tide•wa•ter (tīd′wô′tər, -wŏt′ər) *n.* **1.** Water that inundates the land when the tide is very high. **2.** River water and streams affected by tides. **3.** Low coastal land.

tid•ings (tī′dĭngz) *pl.n.* News.

ti•dy (tī′dē) *adj.* **-di•er, -di•est. 1.** Neat and clean **:** orderly. **2.** *Informal.* Substantial <a *tidy* sum of money> —*v.* **-died, -dy•ing.** To make (things) orderly. **—ti′di•ly** *adv.* **—ti′di•ness** *n.*

tie (tī) *v.* **tied, ty•ing. 1.** To bind or secure with a cord, rope, line, etc. **2.** To fasten by bringing together and knotting strings or laces. **3.** To form (a knot or bow). **4.** To make a knot or bow in. **5.** To link **:** unite. **6.** To match (an opponent or score) in a competition. ★ ***syns:*** BIND, KNOT, SECURE —*n.* **1.** A cord, string, rope, etc. by which something is tied. **2.** A necktie. **3.** Something that unites. **4.** An equality of scores, votes, etc. **5.** A beam, rod, etc., that gives structural support. **6.** A timber laid crosswise to support railway tracks.

tie-dye (tī′dī′) *n.* A method of dyeing fabric by tying parts of it to prevent absorption of the dye, creating a streaked or mottled pattern. **—tie′-dye′** *v.*

tier (tîr) *n.* A row or layer, esp. one of a series of rows arranged one above or behind another. **—tiered** *adj.*

tie-up (tī′ŭp′) *n.* **1.** A temporary suspension or delay. **2.** A connection.

tiff (tĭf) *n.* **1.** A fit of annoyance. **2.** A petty dispute. **—tiff** *v.*

ti•ger (tī′gər) *n.* A large carnivorous Asian cat, *Panthera tigris,* with a tawny black-striped coat. **—ti′gress** *n.*

ti•ger-eye (tī′gər-ī′) *also* **ti•ger's-eye** (tī′-gərz-) *n.* A yellow-brown gemstone.

tiger lily *n.* An Asian plant, *Lilium tigrinum,* with black-spotted orange flowers.

†tight (tīt) *adj.* **1.** So close in construction or texture that air, water, etc., cannot penetrate. **2.** Fixed firmly in place. **3.** Set closely together **:** compact. **4.** Stretched taut. **5.** Fitting uncomfortably close <*tight* boots> **6.** Constricted **:** compressed. **7.** Close-fisted **:** stingy. **8.** Difficult <was in a *tight* spot> **9.** Evenly matched <a *tight* race> **10.** *Slang.* Intoxicated. **11.** *Regional.* Neat and trim. —*adv.* **1.** In a firm way. **2.** In a deep or sound way. **—tight′ly** *adv.* **—tight′ness** *n.*

tight•en (tīt′n) *v.* To make or become tight. **—tight′en•er** *n.*

tight•fist•ed (tīt′fĭs′tĭd) *adj.* Stingy.

tight•lipped (tīt′lĭpt′) *adj.* Reticent.

tight•rope (tīt′rōp′) *n.* A tightly stretched rope or wire high above the ground on which acrobats perform.

tights (tīts) *pl.n.* A tight-fitting stretchable garment designed esp. for the lower half of the body.

tight•wad (tīt′wŏd′) *n.* *Slang.* A stingy person **:** miser.

til•de (tĭl′də) *n.* A diacritical mark (˜) used to indicate certain nasal sounds in Spanish and Portuguese, as in *piñon* or *São.*

tile (tīl) *n.* **1.** A thin slab of baked clay, plastic, concrete, etc., used to cover walls, floors, or roofs. **2.** A short earthenware pipe used in drains, chimneys, etc. **—tile** *v.*

till[1] (tĭl) *v.* To plow, harrow, and fertilize (land) before planting. **—till′a•ble** *adj.*

till[2] (tĭl) *prep.* Until. —*conj.* **1.** Until. **2.** Before or unless.

till[3] (tĭl) *n.* A small drawer for money, esp. in a store or bank.

till•age (tĭl′ĭj) *n.* **1.** The work of cultivating land. **2.** Cultivated land.

till•er[1] (tĭl′ər) *n.* A person or machine that tills land.
till•er[2] (tĭl′ər) *n.* A steering lever used to turn a boat's rudder from side to side.
tilt (tĭlt) *v.* **1.** To tip or cause to tip, as by raising one end. **2.** To engage in a joust. —*n.* **1.** A sloping surface or direction. **2.** A joust with lances. **3.** A spirited verbal contest —**at full tilt.** As fast as possible.
tim•ber (tĭm′bər) *n.* **1.** Growing trees or wooded land. **2. a.** Wood used for building : lumber. **b.** A finished piece of wood, esp. a structural beam. **c.** A curved support in a ship's frame. —**tim′bered** *adj.*
tim•ber•line (tĭm′bər-līn′) *n.* The height or limit beyond which trees do not grow in mountainous or artic regions.
tim•bre (tĭm′bər, tăm′-) *n.* The quality of a sound that makes it distinct from others of the same pitch and volume.
time (tīm) *n.* **1. a.** A continuous measurable quantity in which events occur in apparently irreversible order. **b.** An interval bounded by 2 points of this quantity : duration. **c.** A numerical measure of this interval, as in years, days, or minutes. **d.** A number representing a given point, as the present, as determined from a given point in the past. **e.** A system of numerical measure for this quantity <standard *time*> **2.** *often* **times.** A particular period in history : era. **3.** An opportune moment. **4.** A fixed or customary moment or period <dinner *time*> **5.** One of a series of instances <tried 3 *times*> **6.** An occasion associated with a certain experience <had a great *time*> **7.** *Informal.* A period in prison. **8.** Rate of speed. **9.** A musical meter. **10. a.** The regular period of work. **b.** The pay received. —*adj.* **1.** Of or pertaining to time. **2.** Set to operate at a certain moment. **3.** Of or pertaining to paying in installments. —*v.* **timed, tim•ing.** **1.** To arrange the time for (an event or occasion) : schedule. **2.** To adjust (a timepiece) to keep accurate time. **3.** To adjust or control so that movements or events occur in proper sequence. **4.** To set, maintain, or record the pace or duration of. —**on time. 1.** According to schedule : promptly. **2.** By making successive payments. —**tim′er** *n.*
time bomb *n.* **1.** A bomb that can be set to detonate at a particular time. **2.** Something that threatens eventual disaster.
time clock *n.* An instrument that records the times employees begin and finish work.
time-hon•ored (tīm′ŏn′ərd) *adj.* Respected because of age or long tradition.
time•keep•er (tīm′kē′pər) *n.* **1.** A timepiece. **2.** One who times a contest or contestants or records employee work hours.
time-lapse (tīm′lăps′) *adj.* Of or using a technique that photographs a slow process in such a way as to give an accelerated view of that process.
time•less (tīm′lĭs) *adj.* **1.** Having no limit or end : eternal. **2.** Unaffected by time : ageless. —**time′less•ness** *n.*
time•ly (tīm′lē) *adj.* **-li•er, -li•est.** Occurring or done at an opportune or appropriate time. —**time′li•ness** *n.*
time-out (tīm′out′) *n.* A brief period of rest or consultation during a game.
time•piece (tīm′pēs′) *n.* An instrument, as a clock or watch, that measures, records, or indicates time.
times (tīmz) *prep.* Multiplied by.
time-shar•ing (tīm′shâr′ĭng) *n.* **1.** Simultaneous sharing of a computer by many users at different sites. **2.** Joint ownership with individual use of vacation property.
time•ta•ble (tīm′tā′bəl) *n.* A schedule listing the time at which certain events, as arrivals and departures at a transportation station, are expected to take place.
time•worn (tīm′wôrn′, -wōrn′) *adj.* **1.** Impaired or affected by long wear or use. **2.** Hackneyed : trite.
tim•id (tĭm′ĭd) *adj.* **1.** Fearful. **2.** Lacking in self-confidence : shy. —**ti•mid′i•ty, tim′id•ness** *n.* —**tim′id•ly** *adv.*
tim•or•ous (tĭm′ər-əs) *adj.* Easily frightened : timid. —**tim′or•ous•ly** *adv.*
tim•o•thy (tĭm′ə-thē) *n.* A native Eurasian grass, *Phleum pratense,* with narrow, cylindrical flower spikes, grown for hay.
Tim•o•thy (tĭm′ə-thē) *n.* —See table at BIBLE.
tim•pa•ni *also* **tym•pa•ni** (tĭm′pə-nē) *pl.n.* A set of kettledrums in an orchestra. —**tim′pa•nist** *n.*
tin (tĭn) *n.* **1.** *Symbol* **Sn** A soft silvery malleable metallic element. **2.** A container or box made of or plated with tin. **3.** *esp. Brit.* A can in which food is preserved. —*v.* **tinned, tin•ning. 1.** To coat or plate with tin. **2.** *esp. Brit.* To preserve in tins.
tinc•ture (tĭngk′chər) *n.* **1.** A pigment for dyeing. **2.** A shade of a color : tint. **3.** A slight trace. **4.** An alcohol solution of a medicine that does not change readily into a vapor. —*v.* **-tured, -tur•ing.** To tint.
tin•der (tĭn′dər) *n.* Readily ignited material used for kindling.
tin•der•box (tĭn′dər-bŏks′) *n.* **1.** A metal box for holding tinder. **2.** A firetrap. **3.** A highly dangerous or explosive situation.
tine (tīn) *n.* A narrow pointed part, as of a fork or an antler.
tin•foil (tĭn′foil′) *n.* A thin pliable sheet of aluminum or a tin alloy.
tinge (tĭnj) *v.* **tinged** (tĭnjd), **tinge•ing** *or* **ting•ing. 1.** To impart a trace of color to : tint. **2.** To affect slightly, as by admixture. —*n.* A slight trace, as of color or flavor.
tin•gle (tĭng′gəl) *v.* **-gled, -gling.** To feel or cause a prickling, stinging sensation. —**tin′gle** *n.* —**tin′gler** *n.* —**tin′gly** *adj.*
tink•er (tĭng′kər) *n.* **1.** One who usu. travels from place to place mending household utensils. **2.** One unskillful at making repairs : bungler. —*v.* **1.** To do a tinker's work. **2.** To toy with machine parts experimentally in an effort to repair.
tin•kle (tĭng′kəl) *v.* **-kled, -kling.** To make or cause to make a series of metallic ringing

sounds <bells *tinkling*> **—tin'kle** *n.* **—tin'kly** *adj.*

tin·ny (tĭn'ē) *adj.* **-ni·er, -ni·est. 1.** Of, having, yielding, or suggestive of tin. **2.** Of or producing a thin metallic sound.

tin plate *n.* Thin sheet iron or steel coated with tin. **—tin'-plate'** *v.*

tin·sel (tĭn'səl) *n.* **1.** Very slender strips or threads of a glittering material, as metal foil, used for decoration. **2.** Something showy but worthless. **—tin'sel** *adj.*

tin·smith (tĭn'smĭth') *n.* A person who makes and repairs tin articles.

tint (tĭnt) *n.* **1.** A shade of a color, esp. a pale or faint variation : tinge. **2.** A slight coloration : hue. **3.** A barely detectable degree : trace. **4.** A dye for the hair. *—v.* To give a tint to or take on a tint.

tin·tin·nab·u·la·tion (tĭn'tĭ-năb'yə-lā'shən) *n.* The ringing of bells.

tin·type (tĭn'tīp') *n.* A positive photograph made directly on a treated iron plate.

tin·work (tĭn'wûrk') *n.* **1.** Work in tin. **2. tinworks** *(sing. or pl. in number).* A place where tin is smelted and rolled.

ti·ny (tī'nē) *adj.* **-ni·er, -ni·est.** Very small : minute.

—tion *suff.* Action : process <absorp*tion*>

tip¹ (tĭp) *n.* **1.** The end of something, esp. of something pointed or projecting. **2.** A piece or attachment designed to be fitted to the end of something. *—v.* **tipped, tip·ping. 1.** To provide with a tip. **2.** To cover, ornament, or remove the tip of.

tip² (tĭp) *v.* **tipped, tip·ping. 1.** To topple over : upset. **2.** To tilt. **—tip** *n.*

tip³ (tĭp) **tipped, tip·ping. 1.** To strike softly : tap. **2.** *Baseball.* To hit (the ball) with the side of the bat so that it glances off. *—n.* A light blow : tap.

tip⁴ (tĭp) *n.* **1.** A small sum of money given as an acknowledgment of services rendered : gratuity. **2. a.** Advance or inside information given as a guide to action. **b.** A helpful hint. *—v.* **tipped, tip·ping. 1.** To give a gratuity (to). **2.** To provide advance or inside information to. **—tip'per** *n.*

ti·pi (tē'pē) *n. var. of* TEPEE.

tip-off (tĭp'ôf', -ŏf') *n.* **1.** *Informal.* An item of advance or inside information. **2.** *Basketball.* The act or practice of beginning a game or overtime period with a jump ball.

tip·pet (tĭp'ĭt) *n.* **1.** A covering for the shoulders, as of fur, with long ends that hang in front. **2.** A long hanging part, as of a sleeve, hood, or cape.

tip·ple (tĭp'əl) *v.* **-pled, -pling.** To drink alcoholic beverages, esp. to excess. *—n.* Alcoholic liquor. **—tip'pler** *n.*

tip·ster (tĭp'stər) *n. Informal.* A person who sells inside information, as to those who gamble or bet.

tip·sy (tĭp'sē) *adj.* **-si·er, -si·est. 1.** Slightly inebriated. **2.** Likely to tip over. **—tip'si·ly** *adv.* **—tip'si·ness** *n.*

tip·toe (tĭp'tō') *v.* To walk stealthily on or as if on the tips of one's toes. *—n.* The tip of a toe. *—adj.* **1.** Standing or walking on or as if on the tips of one's toes. **2.** Stealthy : wary. *—adv.* On or as if on tiptoe.

tip·top (tĭp'tŏp') *n.* **1.** The highest point : apex. **2.** The highest degree of quality or excellence. **—tip'top'** *adj. & adv.*

ti·rade (tī'rād', tī-rād') *n.* A long angry or violent speech, usu. of a censorious or denunciatory nature. ★ ***syns:*** DIATRIBE, FULMINATION, HARANGUE, JEREMIAD, OBLOQUY, PHILIPPIC

tire¹ (tīr) *v.* **tired, tir·ing. 1.** To make or become weary : fatigue. **2.** To make or become uninterested or bored.

tire² (tīr) *n.* **1.** A covering for a wheel, usu. made of rubber reinforced with cords of nylon or fiber glass and filled with compressed air. **2.** A hoop, as of rubber or metal, fitted around a wheel.

tired (tīrd) *adj.* **1. a.** Marked by weariness : fatigued. **b.** Not enthusiastic : bored. **2.** Lacking originality : trite <a *tired* joke>

tire·less (tīr'lĭs) *adj.* Not tiring easily : indefatigable. **—tire'less·ly** *adv.*

tire·some (tīr'səm) *adj.* **1.** Causing fatigue : wearisome. **2.** Causing boredom : tedious. **3.** Causing annoyance : bothersome. **—tire'some·ness** *n.*

'tis (tĭz). It is.

tis·sue (tĭsh'o͞o) *n.* **1.** *Biol.* **a.** An aggregation of morphologically and funtionally similar cells. **b.** Cellular matter regarded as a collective entity. **2.** A soft, absorbent piece of paper used as a disposable handkerchief or towel. **3.** *also* **tissue paper.** Thin, nearly translucent paper used for packing, wrapping, or protecting delicate articles. **4.** A light, thin, sheer cloth. **5.** An interrelated number of things <a *tissue* of lies>

tit (tĭt) *n.* **1.** Any of various small European birds of the family Paridae, related to and resembling the American chickadees. **2.** A bird similar or related to the tit.

ti·tan (tīt'n) *n.* One that is great in size, importance, or achievement.

ti·tan·ic (tī-tăn'ĭk) *adj.* **1.** Having great stature or enormous strength : huge. **2.** Enormous in scope, power, or influence.

ti·ta·ni·um (tī-tā'nē-əm, tĭ-) *n. Symbol* **Ti** A strong, shiny white metal element that is highly resistant to corrosion.

tithe (tī*th*) *n.* **1.** A 10th part of one's income, contributed voluntarily for charity or due as a tax for the support esp. of the church. **2.** A 10th part. **—tithe'** *v.* **—tith'er** *n.*

tit·il·late (tĭt'ə-lāt') *v.* **-lat·ed, -lat·ing. 1.** To stimulate by touching or tickling lightly. **2.** To excite pleasingly. **—tit'il·lat'ing·ly** *adv.* **—tit'il·la'tion** *n.*

ti·tle (tīt'l) *n.* **1.** An identifying name given to something, as a book, play, film, etc. **2. a.** Written matter included in a film or television program to give credits. **b.** A subtitle in a film. **3.** *Law.* **a.** The aggregate evidence that gives rise to a legal right of possession or control. **b.** The document that constitutes this evidence, as a deed. **4.** Something that justifies a claim. **5.** A formal appellation attached to a person or family by virtue of office, rank, hereditary privilege, etc. **6.** A descriptive appellation : epithet. **7.** A championship in sports. —*v.* **-tled, -tling.** To provide with a title : confer a name on.

ti•tle•hold•er (tīt'l-hōl'dər) *n.* One that holds a title, esp. for a championship.

tit•mouse (tĭt'mous') *n.* **1.** Any of several small, grayish, crested North American birds of the genus *Parus.* **2.** TIT 1.

ti•tra•tion (tī-trā'shən) *n.* Determination of the concentration of a solute by measuring the amount of an added reagent needed to complete a reaction.

tit•ter (tĭt'ər) *v.* To utter a suppressed, nervous giggle. —**tit'ter** *n.*

tit•tle (tĭt'l) *n.* The smallest bit : jot.

tit•tle-tat•tle (tĭt'l-tăt'l) *n.* Petty gossip. —*v.* To engage in gossip.

tit•u•lar (tĭch'ōō-lər) *adj.* **1.** Of or having a title. **2.** In name only <the *titular* head of the department> —**tit'u•lar•ly** *adv.*

Ti•tus (tī'təs) *n.* —See table at BIBLE.

tiz•zy (tĭz'ē) *n., pl.* **-zies.** *Slang.* A nervous, excited state of confusion : snit.

Tl *symbol for* THALLIUM.

Tm *symbol for* THULIUM.

TNT (tē'ĕn-tē') *n.* Trinitrotoluene.

to (tōō; *unstressed* tə) *prep.* **1.** In a direction toward <went to *town*> <turned *to* us and spoke> **2. a.** Reaching as far as <rotten *to* the core> **b.** To the extent of <beaten *to* death> **c.** With the resultant condition of <torn *to* bits> **3.** Toward a specified state <his rise *to* power> **4.** In contact with <a face pressed *to* the glass> **5.** In front of <stood face *to* face> **6.** —Used to indicate possession <I have the belt *to* this coat.> **7.** Concerning <deaf *to* our pleas> **8.** In a given relationship with <at right angles *to* the line> **9.** As an accompaniment of <danced *to* the music> **10.** In respect of <the secret *to* my success> **11.** Composing <4 qts *to* a gal> **12.** In harmony with <not *to* my taste> **13.** In comparison with. **14. a.** Before <The time is 5 minutes *to* 10.> **b.** Until <worked from 8 *to* 4> **15. a.** For the purpose of <went out *to* dinner> **b.** In honor of. **16.** —Used before a verb to indicate the infinitive <I'd like *to* rest.> —Also used alone when the infinitive is understood <Rest if you want *to*.> **17. a.** —Used to indicate the relationship of a verb with its complement <refer *to* a thesaurus><refer me *to* a thesaurus> **b.** —Used with a reflexive pronoun to indicate exclusivity or separateness <had the train all *to* ourselves> —*adv.* **1.** In a direction toward <ran *to* and fro> **2.** Into a shut or closed position <pushed the gate *to*> **3.** Into a state of consciousness <The doctor brought the patient *to*.> **4.** Into a state of action <sat down to eat and fell *to*>

toad (tōd) *n.* Any of numerous tailless amphibians chiefly of the family Bufonidae, resembling the frogs but having rougher, drier skin.

toad•stool (tōd'stōōl') *n.* A poisonous or inedible fungus with an umbrella-shaped fruiting body.

toad•y (tō'dē) *n., pl.* **-ies.** One who obsequiously flatters or defers to others in order to gain favor : sycophant. —**toady** *v.*

toast[1] (tōst) *v.* **1.** To heat and brown (e.g., bread) by placing it in a toaster or close to a fire. **2.** To warm thoroughly, as before a fire. —*n.* Sliced bread that has been heated and browned. —**toast'y** *adj.*

toast[2] (tōst) *n.* **1.** The act of drinking to the health of or in honor of another. **2.** The one honored by a toast. **3.** One receiving much attention or acclaim <the *toast* of Hollywood> —*v.* To drink or propose a drink in honor of or the health of.

toast•er (tō'stər) *n.* A device for toasting bread, esp. by electrically heated coils.

toast•mas•ter (tōst'măs'tər) *n.* One who introduces speakers at a banquet. —**toast'mis'tress** *n.*

to•bac•co (tə-băk'ō) *n., pl.* **-cos** *or* **-coes. 1.** A tropical American plant of the genus *Nicotiana,* esp. *N. tabacum* widely cultivated for its leaves, which are dried and processed for smoking or chewing as snuff. **2.** Products made from tobacco.

to•bac•co•nist (tə-băk'ə-nĭst) *n.* A dealer in tobacco.

To•bit (tō'bĭt) *n.* —See table at BIBLE.

to•bog•gan (tə-bŏg'ən) *n.* A long, narrow sled without runners, made of thin boards curved upward at the front end. —*v.* **1.** To ride on a toboggan. **2.** To decline sharply <sales that *tobogganed*> —**to•bog'gan•er, to•bog'gan•ist** *n.*

toc•sin (tŏk'sĭn) *n.* **1.** An alarm sounded on a bell. **2.** A warning.

to•day *also* **to-day** (tə-dā'). —*adv.* **1.** On or during the present day. **2.** At or during the present time. —*n.* The present time, day, or period.

tod•dle (tŏd'l) *v.* **-dled, -dling.** To walk unsteadily with short steps. —**tod'dler** *n.*

tod•dy (tŏd'ē) *n., pl.* **-dies.** A drink of brandy or other liquor mixed with hot water, sugar, and spices.

to-do (tə-dōō') *n., pl.* **-dos** (-dōōz'). *Informal.* Commotion : fuss.

toe (tō) *n.* **1.** One of the extensions from the foot, esp. of a vertebrate animal. **2.** The part of a shoe, sock, or boot covering the toes. **3.** Something resembling a toe. —*v.* **toed, toe•ing.** To touch, kick, or reach with the toe. —**on (one's) toes.** Prepared to act : alert.

toe•a (toi'ə) *n., pl.* **toea.** —See table at CURRENCY.

toe•hold (tō'hōld') *n.* **1.** A small indentation on which the toe can find support in climbing. **2.** A slight advantage.

toe•nail (tō'nāl') *n.* The nail on a toe.

tof•fee (tŏf'ē, tô'fē) *n.* A hard, chewy candy made of brown sugar and butter.

to•fu (tō'fōō) *n.* Bean curd.

tog (tŏg, tôg) *Informal.* —*n.* **1.** A coat or cloak. **2. togs.** Clothes <jogging *togs*> —*v.* **togged,**

tog•ging. To clothe or dress <*togged* themselves out in high boots>

to•ga (tō'gə) *n.* A loosely draped outer garment worn in public by citizens in ancient Rome. **—to'gaed** *adj.*

to•geth•er (tə-gĕ*th*'ər) *adv.* **1.** In or into a single mass, group, or place <gathered *together* for dinner> **2.** Mutually or reciprocally <couldn't get along *together*> **3.** Regarded collectively **:** jointly. **4.** Simultaneously. **5.** In accord or harmony <stood *together* on the issue> **6.** *Informal.* In an effective, coherent condition <Get yourself *together* and stop complaining.> *—adj. Slang.* **1.** In tune with what is going on **:** hip <a *together* person> **—to•geth'er•ness** *n.*

tog•gle (tŏg'əl) *n.* An ornamental crosspiece or button, as of wood or bone, inserted into a loop as a fastening. *—v. Computer Sci.* To switch from one to the other of 2 possible states.

tog•gle switch (tŏg'əl) *n.* A switch in which a projecting lever with a spring is used to open or close an electric circuit.

toil[1] (toil) *v.* **1.** To work laboriously and continuously. **2.** To advance with difficulty. **—toil'some** *adj.*

toil[2] (toil) *n. often* **toils.** An entanglement <caught up in the *toils* of politics>

toi•let (toi'lĭt) *n.* **1. a.** An apparatus consisting of a porcelain bowl fitted with a hinged seat and a flushing device, used for the disposal of bodily wastes. **b.** A room or stall containing such an apparatus. **2.** TOILETTE 1. **3.** *Archaic.* A dressing table. **4.** Dress **:** attire.

toi•let•ry (toi'lĭ-trē) *n., pl.* **-ries.** An article or cosmetic for grooming oneself.

toi•lette (twä-lĕt') *n.* **1.** The act or process of dressing or grooming oneself. **2.** One's dress or style of dress.

toilet water *n.* A scented liquid weaker than perfume and stronger than cologne.

To•kay (tō-kā') *n.* A sweet, gold-colored dessert wine.

to•ken (tō'kən) *n.* **1.** An indication or representation of a fact, event, or emotion **:** sign. **2.** A symbol or evidence of authority, validity, or identity. **3.** A keepsake. **4.** A piece of stamped metal used as a substitute for money. *—adj.* **1.** Done as an indication or pledge <a *token* contribution> **2. a.** Perfunctory. **b.** Merely symbolic <a *token* minority on the school board>

told (tōld) *v. p.t. & p.p. of* TELL.

tol•er•a•ble (tŏl'ər-ə-bəl) *adj.* **1.** Able to be tolerated. **2.** Allowable **:** permissible. **3.** Fair **:** passable. **—tol'er•a•bil'i•ty, tol'er•a•ble•ness** *n.* **—tol'er•a•bly** *adv.*

tol•er•ance (tŏl'ər-əns) *n.* **1.** Recognition of and respect for the opinions, beliefs, or actions of others. **2. a.** The amount of variation from a standard that is allowed. **b.** The permissible deviation from a specified value of a structural dimension. **3.** Capacity to withstand pain or hardship. **4. a.** Physiological resistance to poison. **b.** Capacity to absorb a drug continuously or in large dosages without adverse effect. **—tol'er•ant** *adj.* **—tol'er•ant•ly** *adv.*

tol•er•ate (tŏl'ə-rāt') *v.* **-at•ed, -at•ing. 1.** To allow. **2.** To recognize and respect (the rights, opinions, or practices of others). **3.** To put up with. **4.** *Med.* To have tolerance for (a drug or poison). **—tol'er•a'tion** *n.*

toll[1] (tōl) *n.* **1.** A fixed fee or tax, esp. for passage across a bridge or along a road. **2.** A charge for a service, as a person-to-person telephone call. **3.** The extent or amount of loss or destruction caused by a disaster. ★ ***syns:*** CHARGE, EXACTION, FEE

toll[2] (tōl) *v.* **1.** To sound (a large bell) in slowly repeated single tones. **2.** To announce or call together by tolling. *—n.* **1.** An act of tolling. **2.** The sound of a bell that is tolled.

toll•booth (tōl'bo͞oth') *n.* A booth at a tollgate where a toll is collected.

toll•gate (tōl'gāt') *n.* A place, often equipped with a gate, at which vehicles must stop and pay a toll to secure passage.

toll•house (tōl'hous') *n.* A tollbooth.

tol•u•ene (tŏl'yo͞o-ēn') *n.* A colorless flammable liquid derived from coal tar or petroleum and used in high-octane fuels.

tom (tŏm) *n.* The male of various animals, esp. a male cat or turkey.

tom•a•hawk (tŏm'ə-hôk') *n.* A light ax once used as a tool or weapon by North American Indians. **—tom'a•hawk'** *v.*

to•ma•to (tə-mā'tō, -mä'-) *n., pl.* **-toes.** A plant, *Lycopersicon esculentum,* native to South America, widely cultivated for its edible, fleshy, usu. red fruit.

tomb (to͞om) *n.* **1.** A chamber or vault for burying the dead. **2.** A place of burial. **3.** A monument commemorating the dead.

tom•boy (tŏm'boi') *n.* A girl whose behavior is like that held to be characteristic of a boy. **—tom'boy'ish** *adj.*

tomb•stone (to͞om'stōn') *n.* A gravestone.

tom•cat (tŏm'kăt') *n.* A male cat.

tome (tōm) *n.* A large or scholarly book.

tom•fool (tŏm'fo͞ol') A stupid, foolish person **:** blockhead. *—adj.* Foolish **:** stupid. **—tom'fool'er•y** *n.*

tom•my•rot (tŏm'ē-rŏt') *n.* Nonsense.

to•mog•ra•phy (tō-mŏg'rə-fē) *n.* A method for making x-ray pictures of a plane section of an object.

to•mor•row (tə-môr'ō, -mŏr'ō) *n.* **1.** The day immediately following today. **2.** The near future. *—adv.* On or for the day immediately following today.

tom•tit (tŏm'tĭt') *n.* A small bird, as a tit.

tom-tom (tŏm'tŏm') *n.* **1.** Any of various drums having small heads that are beaten with the hands. **2.** A monotonous rhythmical drumbeat or similar sound.

ton (tŭn) *n.* **1.**—See table at MEASUREMENT. **2.** *Informal.* A large amount.

to•nal•i•ty (tō-năl'ə-tē) *n., pl.* **-ties.** *Mus.* The arrangement of the tones and chords of a composition in relation to a tonic.

tone (tōn) *n.* **1.** A sound that has a distinct pitch, duration, loudness, and quality. **2.** *Mus.*

The characteristic quality or timbre of a specific instrument or voice. **3.** A style or mode of expression. **4.** General quality, effect, or atmosphere. **5.** A color or shade of color. **6.** *Physiol.* **a.** The tension in muscles at rest. **b.** Normal firmness of body tissues. —*v.* **toned, ton•ing. 1.** To give a particular inflection or tone to. **2.** To soften or change the color of. **3.** To sound monotonously. **4.** To harmonize in color. **—to'nal** *adj.* **—to'nal•ly** *adv.*

tone arm *n.* The pivoted arm of a record player that holds the cartridge and stylus.

ton•er (tō'nər) *n.* One that tones, esp. a powdery ink used dry or suspended in a liquid to produce a photocopy.

tong (tông, tŏng) *n.* **1.** A Chinese association or political party. **2.** An association of Chinese in the U.S., believed to be involved in organized crime.

tongs (tôngz, tŏngz) *pl.n. (sing. or pl. in number).* An implement that consists of 2 arms joined at 1 end by a hinge or pivot, used for holding or grasping something.

tongue (tŭng) *n.* **1.** The fleshy, muscular organ attached in most vertebrates to the bottom of the mouth that is the main organ of taste, moves to facilitate chewing and swallowing, and, in humans, acts in speech. **2.** The tongue of an animal, as a lamb, used as food. **3.** A language or dialect. **4.** Style or quality of utterance <your sharp *tongue*> **5.** The flap of material under the laces or buckles of a shoe. **6.** Something resembling a tongue, as in shape <*tongues* of flames>

tongue-in-cheek (tŭng'ən-chēk') *adj.* Ironic or facetiously exaggerated.

tongue-lash•ing (tŭng'lăsh'ĭng) *n. Informal.* A harsh scolding.

tongue-tied (tŭng'tīd') *adj.* Speechless, as from shyness or astonishment.

tongue twister *n.* A word or expression hard to articulate rapidly, usu. due to a succession of similar consonantal sounds.

†ton•ic (tŏn'ĭk) *n.* **1.** An invigorating, refreshing, or restorative agent. **2.** *Mus.* The first note of a diatonic scale. **3. a.** Quinine water. **b.** *Regional.* A flavored carbonated beverage. —*adj.* **1.** Stimulating mental, physical, or emotional vigor. **2.** *Mus.* Of or based on the tonic.

to•night (tə-nīt'). *adv.* On or during the coming or present night. —*n.* This night or the night of this day.

ton•nage (tŭn'ĭj) *n.* **1.** The number of tons of water a ship will displace when afloat. **2.** The capacity of a merchant ship expressed in units of 100 cu ft. **3.** A duty or charge per ton on cargo. **4.** The total shipping of a port or country, computed in tons. **5.** Weight measured in tons.

tonne (tŭn) *n. Can.* A metric ton.

ton•sil (tŏn'səl) *n.* A mass of tissue similar to that found in lymph nodes, esp. either of 2 such masses located on both sides of the inner wall of the throat.

ton•sil•lec•to•my (tŏn'sə-lĕk'tə-mē) *n., pl.* **-mies.** The removal of a tonsil or tonsils by means of surgery.

ton•sil•li•tis (tŏn'sə-lī'tĭs) *n.* Inflammation of a tonsil or tonsils.

ton•so•ri•al (tŏn-sôr'ē-əl, -sōr'-) *adj.* Of or pertaining to a barber or to barbering.

ton•sure (tŏn'shər) *n.* **1.** The act of shaving the crown of the head, esp. prior to becoming a priest or a monk. **2.** The part of a head that has been shaved.

ton•y (tō'nē) *adj.* **-i•er, -i•est.** *Informal.* Expensive, luxurious, or exclusive.

To•ny (tō'nē) *n.* An annual award for outstanding theatrical achievement.

too (to͞o) *adv.* **1.** As well **:** also <I'm coming *too.*> **2.** More than sufficiently <You study *too* much.> **3.** Extremely <They're only *too* willing to help.>

took (to͝ok) *v. p.t. of* TAKE.

tool (to͞ol) *n.* **1.** An implement or machine used to do work or perform a task. **2.** Something regarded as necessary to the performance of one's occupational or professional tasks <Words are the *tools* of my trade.> **3.** One utilized to carry out the designs of another. —*v.* **1.** To work or shape with a tool or tools. **2.** To equip (e.g., a factory) for production by providing tools and machinery. **3.** *Informal.* To travel in a vehicle <*tooled* around town in my new car>

toot (to͞ot) *v.* To sound or cause to sound, esp. in short bursts <*tooted* the car horn> **—toot** *n.* **—toot'er** *n.*

tooth (to͞oth) *n., pl.* **teeth** (tēth). **1. a.** One of a set of hard bonelike structures rooted in sockets in the jaws of most vertebrates, typically composed of a core of soft pulp surrounded by a layer of hard dentine coated with cement or enamel. **b.** A similar structure in invertebrates. **2.** A small, notched, projecting part resembling a tooth, as on a comb, saw, or leaf. **3. teeth. a.** Something destructive in its concentrated force <the *teeth* of the storm> **b.** Effective means of enforcement <regulations with *teeth* to them> **4.** Taste or appetite. **—toothed** *adj.* **—tooth'less** *adj.*

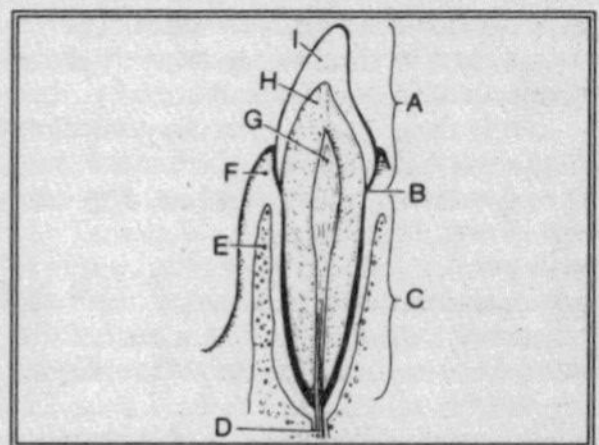

tooth
Cross section of a tooth showing: A. crown, B. neck, C. root, D. root canal, E. bone, F. gum, G. pulp, H. dentine, I. enamel

tooth•ache (to͞oth'āk') *n.* An aching pain in or near a tooth.

tooth•brush (to͝oth′brŭsh′) *n.* A small brush used to clean the teeth.
tooth•paste (to͝oth′pāst′) *n.* A paste for cleaning teeth.
tooth•pick (to͝oth′pĭk′) *n.* A small piece of wood or plastic for removing food particles from between the teeth.
tooth•pow•der (to͝oth′pou′dər) *n.* A powder for cleaning teeth.
tooth•some (to͝oth′səm) *adj.* **1.** Delicious <a *toothsome* morsel of cake> **2.** Attractive <a *toothsome* business offer>
tooth•y (to͞o′thē) *adj.* **-i•er, -i•est.** Having prominent teeth. **—tooth′i•ly** *adv.*
top[1] (tŏp) *n.* **1.** The highest part, point, surface, or end. **2.** The crown of the human head. **3.** The part of a plant, as of a rutabaga, above the ground. **4.** A part, as a lid or cap, that covers or forms the uppermost section of something <a box *top*> **5.** The highest degree, pitch, or point. **6.** The highest position or rank. **7.** The earliest part <the *top* of the 8th inning> —*v.* **topped, top•ping. 1.** To provide with, form, or function as a top. **2.** To reach the top of. **3.** To surpass **:** exceed.
top[2] (tŏp) *n.* A toy consisting of a symmetric rigid body spun on a pointed end about the axis of symmetry.
to•paz (tō′păz′) *n.* **1.** A colorless, blue, yellow, brown, or pink aluminum silicate mineral valued as a gemstone. **2.** A yellow gemstone, esp. a yellow sapphire or corundum. **3.** A light-yellow quartz.
top•coat (tŏp′kōt′) *n.* A light overcoat.
top-dress (tŏp′drĕs′) *v.* To cover (e.g., land) with loose material not worked in, esp. to cover with fertilizer.
top•er (tō′pər) *n.* A drunkard.
top•flight (tŏp′flīt′) *adj.* First-rate.
top hat *n.* A man's hat having a narrow brim and a tall crown shaped like a cylinder, and usu. made of silk.
top-heav•y (tŏp′hĕv′ē) *adj.* Likely to topple over because of too much weight or bulk at the top.
to•pi•ar•y (tō′pē-ĕr′ē) *n., pl.* **-ies. 1.** The art of trimming live shrubs or trees into decorative shapes. **2.** A plant so trimmed.
top•ic (tŏp′ĭk) *n.* **1.** A subject discussed in a speech, essay, thesis, etc. **:** theme. **2.** A subject of discussion or conversation. **3.** A subdivision of a theme, thesis, or outline.
top•i•cal (tŏp′ĭ-kəl) *adj.* **1.** Of or belonging to a particular location or place **:** local. **2.** Of current interest **:** contemporary <*topical* issues> **3.** *Med.* Of or applied to an isolated part of the body. **4.** Of or relating to a particular topic or topics. **—top′i•cal′i•ty** (-kăl′ə-tē) *n.* **—top′i•cal•ly** *adv.*
top•knot (tŏp′nŏt′) *n.* **1.** A crest or knot of hair or feathers on the crown of the head. **2.** An ornamental ribbon or bow worn as a headdress.
top•less (tŏp′lĭs) *adj.* **1.** Having no top <*topless* jars> **2.** So high as to appear to extend out of sight <*topless* towers>
top•most (tŏp′mōst′) *adj.* Being the highest **:** uppermost.
top•notch (tŏp′nŏch′) *adj. Informal.* First-rate <a *topnotch* writer>
to•pog•ra•phy (tə-pŏg′rə-fē) *n., pl.* **-phies. 1.** Detailed and precise description of a place or region. **2.** The technique of graphically representing the exact physical features of a place or region on a map. **3.** The physical features of a place or region. **4.** The surveying of the features of a region or place. **—to•pog′ra•pher** *n.* **—top′o•graph′ic** (tŏp′ə-grăf′ĭk), **top′o•graph′i•cal** *adj.* **—top′o•graph′i•cal•ly** *adv.*
top•ping (tŏp′ĭng) *n.* A frosting, garnish, or sauce for food.
top•ple (tŏp′əl) *v.* **-pled, -pling. 1.** To overturn. **2.** To overthrow. **3.** To fall.
top round *n.* A cut of meat taken from the inner section of a round of beef.
tops (tŏps) *adj. Slang.* First-rate.
top•sail (tŏp′səl, -sāl′) *n. Naut.* **1.** A square sail set above the lowest sail on the mast of a square-rigged ship. **2.** A triangular or square sail set above the gaff of a lower sail on a fore-and-aft-rigged ship.
top-se•cret (tŏp′sē′krĭt) *adj.* Designating documents or data of the highest level of security classification.
top•side (tŏp′sīd′) *n.* **1.** *often* **topsides.** The upper parts of a ship above the main deck. **2.** The highest position of authority. —*adv. & adj.* **1.** On or to the upper decks of a ship. **2.** In a position of authority.
top•soil (tŏp′soil′) *n.* The usu. fertile layer of soil at the surface of the ground.
top•sy-tur•vy (tŏp′sē-tûr′vē) *adv.* **1.** Upside-down. **2.** In complete disarray. —*adj.* In a confused or disordered state. —*n.* Confusion **:** disorder. **—top′sy-tur′vi•ly** *adv.* **—top′sy-tur′vi•ness** *n.*
toque (tōk) *n.* A small, close-fitting hat with no brim, worn by women.
to•rah *also* **To•rah** (tôr′ə, tōr′ə) *n.* **1.** The complete body of Jewish religious law and learning. **2.** The first 5 books of the Hebrew Scriptures. —See table at BIBLE. **3.** The scroll on which these scriptures are written, used in a synagogue during services.
torch (tôrch) *n.* **1.** A portable light consisting of flaming material wound about the end of a stick of wood. **2.** A portable device that burns a fuel, usu. a gas, often with a supply of oxygen, to produce a flame hot enough for welding, brazing, or cutting metal. **3.** Something that illuminates. **4.** *esp. Brit.* A flashlight. —*v. Slang.* To set fire to <*torched* the building>
torch song *n.* A sentimental popular song, esp. one lamenting a lost or unrequited love. **—torch singer** *n.*
tore (tôr, tōr) *v. p.t. of* TEAR[1].
tor•e•a•dor (tôr′ē-ə-dôr′) *n.* A bullfighter.
tor•ment (tôr′mĕnt′) *n.* **1.** Extreme physical pain or mental anguish. **2.** A source of harassment, annoyance, or pain. **3.** Torture inflicted on prisoners being interrogated. —*v.* (tôr-mĕnt′, tôr′mĕnt′). **1.** To cause to undergo great

pain or anguish. **2.** To upset or agitate greatly. **3.** To annoy, pester, or harass. **—tor•ment'ing•ly** *adv.* **—tor•men'tor** *n.*

torn (tôrn, tōrn) *v. p.p. of* TEAR[1].

tor•na•do (tôr-nā'dō) *n., pl.* **-does** *or* **-dos. 1.** A rotating column of air usu. accompanied by a funnel-shaped downward extension of a thundercloud and having a vortex several hundred yds in diameter whirling destructively at speeds of up to 300 mph. **2.** A violently destructive whirlwind.

tor•pe•do (tôr-pē'dō) *n., pl.* **-does.** A self-propelled underwater missile launched from a ship, submarine, or aircraft and designed to explode near a target or on contact with it. **—tor•pe'do** *v.*

▲ ***word history:*** The original sense of *torpedo* in English was "electric ray," a fish that produces an electric charge. The word was borrowed from Latin *torpedo,* which also denoted the same fish but which basically meant "numbness." *Torpedo* is related to *torpidus,* "numb," the Latin source of English *torpid.* The word *torpedo* was first applied to drifting underwater mines in the early 19th cent.; self-propelled torpedoes were a later invention.

torpedo boat *n.* A fast boat fitted with torpedo tubes.

tor•pid (tôr'pĭd) *adj.* **1.** Having been deprived of the power of motion or feeling : benumbed. **2.** Dormant : hibernating. **3.** Apathetic : spiritless. **—tor•pid'i•ty** *n.* **—tor'pid•ly** *adv.*

tor•por (tôr'pər) *n.* **1.** Mental or physical inactivity or insensibility : sluggishness. **2.** Apathy : dullness.

torque (tôrk) *n.* **1.** The capability or tendency of a force for producing torsion or rotation about an axis. **2.** A turning or twisting force.

tor•rent (tôr'ənt, tŏr'-) *n.* **1.** A swift, turbulent stream. **2.** A deluge. **3.** An overwhelming flow <*torrents* of criticism> **—tor•ren'tial** (tô-rĕn'shəl, tə-) *adj.*

tor•rid (tôr'ĭd, tŏr'-) *adj.* **1.** Dried by the heat of the sun : parched. **2.** Scorching : burning. **3.** Passionate : ardent <a *torrid* love affair> **—tor•rid'i•ty, tor'rid•ness** *n.* **—tor'rid•ly** *adv.*

Torrid Zone *n.* The region of the earth's surface between the tropics of Cancer and Capricorn.

tor•sion (tôr'shən) *n.* **1.** The act of twisting or turning or the state of being twisted or turned. **2.** Stress produced when one end of an object is twisted out of line with the other. **—tor'sion•al** *adj.*

tor•so (tôr'sō) *n., pl.* **-sos** *or* **-si** (-sē'). **1.** TRUNK 2. **2.** A statue of the trunk of the human body.

tort (tôrt) *n. Law.* A wrongful act, damage, or injury done willfully, negligently, or in circumstances involving strict liability for which a civil suit can be brought.

torte (tôrt, tôr'tə) *n., pl.* **tortes** *or* **tor•ten** (tôr'tn). A rich cake made with many eggs and little flour and usu. containing chopped nuts.

tor•tel•li•ni (tôr'tl-ē'nē) *n.* Small stuffed pasta dumplings.

tor•til•la (tôr-tē'yə) *n.* A thin, round, unleavened bread, usu. made from cornmeal or flour and served hot with toppings of ground meat or cheese.

tor•toise (tôr'təs) *n.* **1.** A terrestrial turtle, esp. one of the family Testudinidae, with thick, scaly limbs. **2.** One that moves or acts slowly.

tor•toise•shell *also* **tor•toise-shell** *or* **tortoise shell** (tôr'təs-shĕl') *n.* The mottled, horny, translucent brownish covering of the carapace of certain sea turtles, used to make combs, jewelry, etc.

tor•tu•ous (tôr'cho͞o-əs) *adj.* **1.** Marked by or having repeated turns or bends : twisting. **2.** Not straightforward : devious. **3.** Complex. **—tor'tu•ous•ly** *adv.* **—tor'tu•ous•ness** *n.*

tor•ture (tôr'chər) *n.* **1. a.** Infliction of severe physical pain as punishment or coercion. **b.** The state of being tortured. **2.** Mental anguish. **3.** Something causing pain or anguish. *—v.* **-tured, tur•ing. 1.** To subject (a person or animal) to torture. **2.** To afflict with great physical or mental pain. **3.** To twist or turn abnormally : distort. **—tor'tur•er** *n.* **—tor'tur•ous** *adj.*

To•ry (tôr'ē, tōr'ē) *n., pl.* **-ries. 1.** A member of a British political party, founded in 1689, known as the Conservative Party since about 1832. **2.** An American siding with the English side during the Amer. Revolution. **3.** A member of a Conservative Party, as in Canada. **—To'ry•ism** *n.*

toss (tôs, tŏs) *v.* **1.** To throw or be heaved about continuously <*tossed* by the waves> **2.** To throw lightly with or as if with the hand or hands <*toss* a ball> **3.** *Informal.* To discuss casually. **4.** To move or lift (the head) with a sudden motion. **5.** To throw to the ground. **6.** To flip a coin in order to make a decision. **7.** To mix (a salad) with a dressing. **8.** To move oneself about restlessly <*tossed* in my sleep> ★ ***syns:*** HEAVE, PITCH, ROCK, ROLL *—n.* **1.** The act of tossing or state of being tossed. **2.** A rapid movement or lift, as of the head.

toss•up (tôs'ŭp', tŏs'-) *n.* **1.** The flip of a coin to decide an issue. **2.** An even chance.

tot[1] (tŏt) *n.* **1.** A young child. **2.** A small amount, as of liquor <a *tot* of brandy>

tot[2] (tŏt) *v.* **tot•ted, tot•ting.** To total <*totted* up the bill>

to•tal (tōt'l) *n.* **1.** A number or quantity reached by addition : sum. **2.** A whole quantity : entirety. *—adj.* **1.** Being the whole : entire. **2.** Complete : absolute. *—v.* **-taled, -tal•ing** *or* **-talled, -tal•ling. 1.** To find the sum of. **2.** To equal a total of <The number of victims *totals* 200.> **3.** *Slang.* To demolish (a vehicle) completely. **—to'tal•ly** *adv.*

to•tal•i•tar•i•an (tō-tăl'ə-târ'ē-ən) *adj.* Having or exercising complete political control. **—to•tal'i•tar'i•an** *n.* **—to•tal'i•tar'i•an•ism** *n.*

to·tal·i·ty (tō-tăl′ə-tē) *n., pl.* **-ties. 1.** The state of being total. **2.** An aggregate sum.
to·tal·iz·er (tōt′l-ī′zər) *n.* **1.** A pari-mutuel machine. **2.** An adding machine.
tote (tōt) *v.* **tot·ed, tot·ing. 1.** To haul, esp. on the back or in the arms **:** lug. **2.** To have on one's person. —*n.* **1.** A load **:** burden. **2.** A tote bag. —**tot′er** *n.*
tote bag *n. Informal.* A large handbag or shopping bag.
to·tem (tō′təm) *n.* **1. a.** An animal, plant, or natural object serving as the emblem of a clan or family by virtue of an asserted ancestral relationship. **b.** A representation of this being. **2.** A venerated symbol.
totem pole *n.* **1.** A post carved and painted with totems and erected in front of a dwelling, as among certain American Indian peoples. **2.** *Slang.* A hierarchy.
tot·ter (tŏt′ər) *v.* **1. a.** To sway as if about to fall. **b.** To appear about to collapse <a *tottering* government> **2.** To move unsteadily. **3.** To waver **:** vacillate <*tottered* between capitulation and resistance> —**tot′ter** *n.* —**tot′ter·y** *adj.*
tou·can (to͞o′kăn′, -kän′) *n.* Any of various tropical American birds of the family Ramphastidae, having brightly colored plumage and a very large bill.
touch (tŭch) *v.* **1.** To cause or allow a bodily part, esp. the hand or fingers, to come into contact with so as to feel. **2. a.** To bring something into contact with <*touched* the metal plate with a wire> **b.** To bring (one thing) into contact with something else <*touch* a wire to the metal plate> **3.** To tap, press, or strike lightly. **4.** To lay hands on in violence <I never *touched* you> **5.** To eat or drink **:** taste <You didn't *touch* your dinner.> **6.** To disturb by handling. **7.** To reach <*touch* land> **8.** To measure up to **:** equal. **9.** To deal with as a subject. **10.** To be relevant to **:** concern. **11.** To have an effect on **:** move emotionally. —**touch down.** To land or make contact with a landing surface, as an aircraft or spacecraft. —**touch off. 1.** To cause to explode **:** fire. **2.** To initiate (e.g., a chain of events) **:** trigger. —**touch up.** To improve by making small changes or additions. —*n.* **1.** An act or instance of touching. **2.** The physiological sense by which external objects or forces are perceived through contact with the body. **3.** A sensation experienced in touching something with a characteristic texture. **4.** A light tap or shove. **5.** An improving change or addition. **6.** A mild attack <a *touch* of indigestion> **7.** A tiny amount **:** trace <a *touch* of garlic> **8. a.** A manner or technique of striking the keys of a keyboard instrument, as a piano or typewriter. **b.** The resistance to being struck by the fingers characteristic of a keyboard. **9.** A characteristic way or style of doing things. **10.** The state of being in contact or communication <Let's keep in *touch.*> —**touch′a·ble** *adj.*
touch·back (tŭch′băk′) *n. Football.* A play in which one recovers a ball propelled by an opposing player and touches it to the ground behind one's own goal line.
touch·down (tŭch′doun′) *n.* **1.** *Football.* A play worth 6 points, accomplished by being in possession of the ball when it is declared dead on or behind the opponent's goal line. **2.** The contact of an aircraft or spacecraft with the landing surface.
tou·ché (to͞o-shā′) *interj.* —Used to express concession to an opponent for a point well made, as in an argument.
touch football *n.* A variety of football played on an improvised field and without protective equipment, involving the substitution of touching for tackling.
touch·ing (tŭch′ĭng) *adj.* Causing a sympathetic reaction **:** moving.
touch·stone (tŭch′stōn′) *n.* **1.** A hard black stone once used to test the quality of gold or silver. **2.** A criterion.
touch-tone (tŭch′tōn′) *adj.* Of or being a telephone dialing system using push buttons that generate tones of differing pitch.
touch-type (tŭch′tīp′) *v.* To type without having to look at the keyboard.
touch·up (tŭch′ŭp′) *n.* The act or process of finishing or improving by small alterations and additions.
touch·y (tŭch′ē) *adj.* **-i·er, -i·est. 1.** Easily taking offense **:** oversensitive. **2.** Requiring tact or skill <a *touchy* situation> —**touch′i·ly** *adv.* —**touch′i·ness** *n.*
tough (tŭf) *adj.* **1.** So strong and resilient as to withstand great strain without tearing or breaking. **2.** Difficult to chew or cut <a *tough* steak> **3.** Physically hardy **:** rugged. **4.** Severe <a *tough* winter> **5.** Vicious **:** rough <a *tough* hoodlum> **6.** Demanding or troubling **:** difficult. **7.** Strong-minded **:** resolute. **8.** *Informal.* Unfortunate <a *tough* break> —*n.* A thug. —**tough′ly** *adv.* —**tough′ness** *n.*
tough·en (tŭf′ən) *v.* To make or become tough. —**tough′en·er** *n.*
tough-mind·ed (tŭf′mīn′dĭd) *adj.* Not sentimental or afraid. —**tough′-mind′ed·ly** *adv.* —**tough′-mind′ed·ness** *n.*
tou·pee (to͞o-pā′) *n.* A partial wig or hair piece worn to cover a bald spot.
tour (to͝or) *n.* **1.** A trip including visits to points of interest. **2.** A group organized for a tour. **3.** A journey to fulfill a schedule of engagements in several places <a concert *tour*> **4.** A shift, as in a factory. **5.** A period of service at a single place or job. —*v.* To go on tour or make a tour of.
tour de force (to͝or′ də fôrs′) *n.* A feat of strength or virtuosity.
tour·ism (to͝or′ĭz′əm) *n.* **1.** Traveling for pleasure. **2.** The business of providing tours and services for tourists.
tour·ist (to͝or′ĭst) *n.* A person who travels for pleasure.
tourist class *n.* Travel accommodations less luxurious than first class or cabin class.
tour·ma·line (to͝or′mə-lĭn, -lēn′) *n.* A complex crystalline silicate used in electronic in-

strumentation and valued as a gem in certain varieties.

tour•na•ment (to͝or′nə-mənt, tûr′-) *n.* **1.** A contest involving a number of competitors who vie against each other in a series of games or trials. **2.** A medieval sport in which 2 groups of mounted contestants fought with blunted lances or swords.

tour•ne•dos (to͝or′nə-dō′) *n., pl.* **tour•ne•dos** (-dō′, -dōz′). A fillet of beef cut from the tenderloin.

tour•ney (to͝or′nē, tûr′-) *n., pl.* **-neys.** A tournament.

tour•ni•quet (to͝or′nĭ-kĭt, -kā′, tûr′-) *n.* A device, as a cloth band tightened around a limb, used to temporarily stop the flow of blood through a large artery.

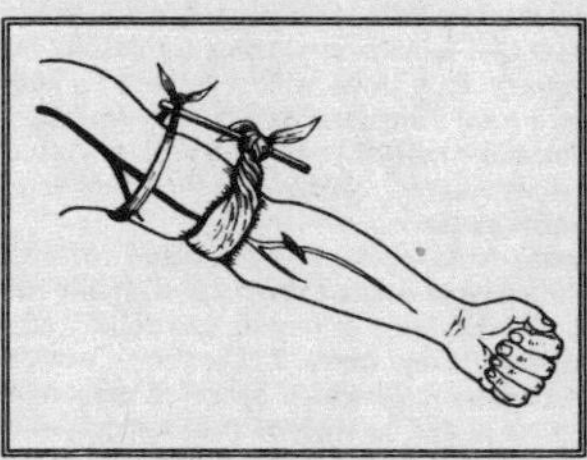

tourniquet

tou•sle (tou′zəl) *v.* **-sled, -sling.** To disarrange : muss.

tout (tout) *v. Informal.* **1.** To obtain or sell information on (e.g., a racehorse) for the guidance of bettors. **2.** To publicize or praise highly. —*n.* One who obtains information on racehorses and sells it to bettors. —**tout′er** *n.*

tow[1] (tō) *v.* To pull or draw along behind as by a rope or chain. —*n.* **1.** An act of towing or the state of being towed. **2.** Something, as a tugboat, that tows. **3.** A rope or cable used in towing <a ski *tow*> —**tow′age** *n.* —**tow′er** *n.*

tow[2] (tō) *n.* Coarse broken flax or hemp fiber prepared for spinning.

to•ward (tôrd, tōrd, tə-wôrd′) *also* **to•wards** (tôrdz, tōrdz, tə-wôrdz′) *prep.* **1.** In the direction of <driving *toward* them> **2.** In a position facing <had your back *toward* me> **3.** Somewhat before in time : approaching <It began to sleet *toward* morning.> **4.** With regard to <didn't like my attitude *toward* the work> **5.** In furtherance or partial fulfillment of <paid only $20 *toward* the bill> **6.** By way of achieving <efforts *toward* reconciliation>

tow-a•way zone (tō′ə-wā′) *n.* A no-parking zone from which cars may be legally towed.

tow•el (tou′əl) *n.* A piece of absorbent cloth or paper used for wiping or drying. —*v.* **-eled, -el•ing** *or* **-elled, -el•ling.** To wipe or rub dry with a towel.

tow•el•ette (tou′ə-lĕt′) *n.* A small, usu. moist piece of material used for cleansing, as of the hands or face.

tow•el•ing (tou′əl-ĭng) *n.* A fabric of cotton or linen used for making towels.

tow•er (tou′ər) *n.* **1. a.** A very tall building : skyscraper. **b.** An extremely tall part of a building. **2.** A tall framework or structure for observing, signaling, or pumping. —*v.* To rise to a noticeable height : loom.

tow•er•ing (tou′ər-ĭng) *adj.* **1.** Of impressive height. **2.** Outstanding : pre-eminent <*towering* scientific achievements> **3.** Fiercely intense <a *towering* rage>

tow•head (tō′hĕd′) *n.* **1.** A head of white-blond hair. **2.** One with a towhead. —**tow′head′ed** *adj.*

tow•hee (tō′hē, tō-hē′) *n.* A North American bird of the genera *Pipilo* or *Chlorura,* esp. *P. erythrophthalmus,* with black, white, and rust plumage in the male.

town (toun) *n.* **1.** An often incorporated population center larger than a village and smaller than a city. **2.** *Informal.* A city. **3.** The residents of a town. —**go to town.** *Slang.* To go all out. —**towns′man** *n.* —**towns′wom′an** *n.*

town clerk *n.* A public official who keeps the records of a town.

town hall *n.* The building that contains the offices of the public officials of a town and houses the town council and courts.

town house *n.* **1.** A city residence. **2.** One of a row of houses connected by common side walls.

town meeting *n.* A legislative assembly of townspeople.

town•ship (toun′shĭp′) *n.* **1.** A subdivision of a county in many U.S. states. **2.** A unit of land area used in surveying, equal to 36 sections or 36 sq mi.

towns•peo•ple (tounz′pē′pəl) *pl.n.* The residents of a town or city.

tow•path (tō′păth′, -päth′) *n.* A path beside a river or canal used by people or animals towing boats.

tow truck *n.* WRECKER 2a.

tox•e•mi•a (tŏk-sē′mē-ə) *n.* A condition in which the blood contains toxins, either produced by microorganisms that infect the body or by body cells through faulty metabolism or absorbed from an external source. —**tox•e′mic** *adj.*

tox•ic (tŏk′sĭk) *adj.* **1.** Of or relating to a toxin. **2.** Harmful, destructive, or deadly <*toxic* wastes><*toxic* fumes> —**tox′i•cal•ly** *adv.* —**tox•ic′i•ty** (-sĭs′ə-tē) *n.*

tox•i•col•o•gy (tŏk′sĭ-kŏl′ə-jē) *n.* The study of the nature, effects, and detection of poisons and the treatment of poisoning. —**tox′i•co•log′i•cal** (-kə-lŏj′ĭ-kəl) *adj.* —**tox′i•col′o•gist** *n.*

tox•i•co•sis (tŏk′sĭ-kō′sĭs) *n., pl.* **-ses** (-sēz′). A pathological condition resulting from poisoning.

tox•in (tŏk′sĭn) *n.* A poisonous substance, having a protein structure, that is secreted by certain organisms and is capable of causing toxicosis when introduced into the body tissues but is also capable of inducing production of an antitoxin.

toy (toi) *n.* **1.** An object designed or meant for a child to play with. **2.** Something insignificant : trifle. **3.** A small ornament : bauble. **4.** A diminutive thing, as a dog of a very small breed or one much smaller than is characteristic of its breed. —*v.* To entertain oneself idly : trifle.

trace[1] (trās) *n.* **1.** A visible sign or mark of a person, thing, or event that was once present, but is no longer. **2. a.** A very small amount <a *trace* of smoke> **b.** A constituent, as a chemical compound or element, present in less than standard quantities. ★ ***syns:*** RELIC, REMAINS, VESTIGE —*v.* **traced, trac•ing. 1.** To follow the track or trail of. **2.** To follow the successive stages in the development or progress of <*trace* the development of a culture> **3.** To locate or discover (e.g., a cause) by researching evidence. **4.** To sketch (a figure). **5.** To form (e.g., letters) with careful concentration. **6.** To copy by following lines seen through a sheet of transparent paper. **—trace′a•bil′i•ty** *n.* **—trace′a•ble** *adj.* **—trace′a•bly** *adv.* **—trac′er** *n.*

trace[2] (trās) *n.* Either of 2 side straps or chains that connect a harnessed draft animal to the vehicle it pulls.

tracer bullet *n.* A bullet that leaves a luminous or smoky trail.

trac•er•y (trā′sə-rē) *n., pl.* **-ies.** Ornamental work of interlaced, ramefied lines, as the lacy openwork in a Gothic window.

tra•che•a (trā′kē-ə) *n., pl.* **-che•ae** (-kē-ē′) *or* **-as.** A respiratory passage leading from the larynx to the bronchi.

tra•che•ot•o•my (trā′kē-ŏt′ə-mē) *n., pl.* **-mies.** Surgical incision into the trachea via the neck.

track (trăk) *n.* **1.** A mark, as a footprint, wheel rut, etc., or a trail of marks left behind by something <tire *tracks*> **2.** A path or course over which something moves or may move. **3.** A course of action : method. **4. a.** A road or course set up for running or racing. **b.** Athletic competition on such a course. **c.** Track and field. **5.** A rail or set of parallel rails on which a rail vehicle, as a train, runs. —*v.* **1.** To follow the footprints or trail of. **2.** To pursue successfully. **3.** To deposit (e.g., matter carried on the shoes). **—track′a•ble** *adj.* **—track′er** *n.*

track•age (trăk′ĭj) *n.* Railway tracks.

track and field *n.* Athletic events, as the long jump or the shot-put, performed on a running track and associated field.

track meet *n.* A track and field meet.

track•suit (trăk′so͞ot′) *n.* A loose-fitting jacket and pants worn while exercising.

tract[1] (trăkt) *n.* **1.** A stretch of land. **2.** *Anat.* **a.** A system of body organs and tissues that together perform a specialized function <the digestive *tract*> **b.** A bundle of nerve fibers with a common origin, termination, and function.

tract[2] (trăkt) *n.* A paper or pamphlet containing a declaration or appeal, esp. one distributed by a special interest group.

trac•ta•ble (trăk′tə-bəl) *adj.* **1.** Easily managed : obedient. **2.** Easily handled or worked. **—trac′ta•bil′i•ty, trac′ta•ble•ness** *n.* **—trac′ta•bly** *adv.*

tract house *n.* One of numerous houses of similar design constructed on a tract of land. **—tract housing** *n.*

trac•tile (trăk′təl, -tīl′) *adj.* Capable of being drawn out in length : ductile <*tractile* metals> **—trac•til′i•ty** (-tĭl′ĭ-tē) *n.*

trac•tion (trăk′shən) *n.* **1.** The act of pulling, as a load over a surface. **2.** The state of being pulled. **3.** The friction that prevents a wheel from slipping or skidding over the surface on which it runs. **4.** The ability of an apparatus, as a railroad engine, to pull loads. **—trac′tive** *adj.*

trac•tor (trăk′tər) *n.* **1.** A gasoline- or diesel-powered vehicle with large, heavily treaded tires that is used in farming for pulling machinery. **2.** A truck with a cab and no body, used for pulling large vehicles, as trailers.

trac•tor-trail•er (trăk′tər-trā′lər) *n.* A truck consisting of a tractor attached to a semitrailer or trailer.

trade (trād) *n.* **1.** An occupation requiring skilled labor : craft <the *trade* of a plumber> **2.** The business of buying and selling commodities : commerce. **3.** The people working in or associated with a specified industry or business. **4.** The customers of a specified industry or business. **5.** An instance of buying or selling : transaction. **6.** Exchange of one thing for another. —*v.* **trad•ed, trad•ing. 1. a.** To engage in buying, selling, or bartering. **b.** To make an exchange of one thing for another. **2.** To shop as regular customers. **—trade in.** To give (an old or used item) as partial payment on a new purchase. **—trade on.** To put to advantage : utilize <*traded on* looks and charm> **—trad′a•ble** *adj.* **—trad′er** *n.*

trade-in (trād′ĭn′) *n.* **1.** Merchandise accepted as partial payment for a new purchase. **2.** A transaction involving a trade-in.

trade•mark (trād′märk′) *n.* A device, as a symbol or name, that identifies a product, is officially registered, and is restricted by law to the exclusive use of the owner or manufacturer.

trade•off *also* **trade-off** (trād′ôf′, -ŏf′) *n.* Exchange of one thing in return for another, esp. a giving up of something valued or desirable for another thought to be more valuable or desirable.

trade school *n.* A secondary school providing instruction in skilled trades.

trades•man (trādz′mən) *n.* **1.** One engaged in the retail trade, esp. a shopkeeper : dealer. **2.** A skilled worker.

trade union *n.* A labor union, esp. one whose membership is limited to people in the same trade. **—trade unionism** *n.* **—trade unionist** *n.*

trade wind *n.* One of an extremely consistent system of winds occupying most of the tropics, blowing toward the equator, northeasterly in the N Hemisphere and southeasterly in the S Hemisphere.

trading post *n.* A store in a remote and thinly populated area established by traders to barter supplies for local products.

trading stamp *n.* A stamp given by a retailer to a buyer for a purchase of a specified amount and intended to be redeemed in quantity for merchandise.

tra•di•tion (trə-dĭsh'ən) *n.* **1.** Transmittal of elements of a culture from one generation to another, esp. by oral communication. **2.** A set of customs and usages transmitted from one generation to another and viewed as a coherent body of precedents influencing the present **:** heritage. **3.** A time-honored practice or set of such practices. **—tra•di'tion•al** *adj.* **—tra•di'tion•al•ist** *n.* **—tra•di'tion•al•ly** *adv.*

tra•duce (trə-dōōs', -dyōōs') *v.* **-duced, -duc•ing. 1.** To speak falsely of **:** misrepresent. **2.** To betray **:** violate. **—tra•duce'ment** *n.* **—tra•duc'er** *n.*

traf•fic (trăf'ĭk) *n.* **1. a.** Commercial exchange of goods **:** commerce <heavy *traffic* in steel> **b.** Illegal or improper commercial activity <drug *traffic*> **2. a.** The business of moving passengers and cargo through a transportation system. **b.** The amount of cargo or number of passengers conveyed in a transportation system. **3. a.** Passage of persons, vehicles, or messages through transportation routes. **b.** The number, as of vehicles, in transit <heavy *traffic* on the expressways> **4.** Dealings between groups or individuals. *—v.* **-ficked, -fick•ing. 1.** To carry on trade in. **2.** To travel over <roads that are heavily *trafficked*> **—traf'fick•er** *n.*

traffic light *n.* A signal that flashes a red, green, or yellow warning light to direct vehicular and pedestrian traffic to stop, go, or proceed with caution.

tra•ge•di•an (trə-jē'dē-ən) *n.* **1.** A writer of tragedies. **2.** A performer of tragic roles.

tra•ge•di•enne (trə-jē'dē-ĕn') *n.* An actress who performs tragic roles.

trag•e•dy (trăj'ə-dē) *n., pl.* **-dies. 1. a.** A dramatic or literary work that ends with great misfortune or ruin for the main character or characters. **b.** The literary genre of tragic dramatic works. **2.** A dramatic, unhappy, often disastrous event, esp. one of moral significance. **3.** A tragic element or aspect.

trag•ic (trăj'ĭk) *adj.* **1.** Relating to or having the nature of tragedy. **2.** Writing or performing in tragedy. **—trag'i•cal•ly** *adv.*

trail (trāl) *v.* **1. a.** To permit to drag or stream behind. **b.** To be dragged along behind. **2.** To follow the tracks or scent of, as in hunting <dogs *trailing* deer> **3.** To lag behind <*trailing* by 10 points in the first half> **4.** To extend, grow, or droop along or over a surface <grape vines *trailing* over an arbor> **5.** To become gradually weaker **:** dwindle <voices *trailing* off in the distance> *—n.* **1.** Something that hangs loose and long <*trails* of ribbons> **2.** Something that is drawn along or follows behind **:** train. **3. a.** A mark, trace, course, or path left by a moving body <white jet *trails*> **b.** Scent **:** track <the *trail* of a wolf> **c.** A beaten track or blazed path. **4.** The act of trailing.

trail bike *n.* A small motorcycle designed for cross-country, off-road riding.

trail•blaz•er (trāl'blā'zər) *n.* **1.** One that blazes a trail. **2.** A pioneer in a specific field of endeavor. **—trail'blaz'ing** *adj.*

trail•er (trā'lər) *n.* **1.** One that trails. **2.** A large transport vehicle designed to be hauled by a heavy-duty vehicle, as a truck or tractor. **3.** A furnished van pulled by a truck or car and used as a house or office.

trailer park *n.* An area in which parking space for house trailers is rented.

trailing arbutus *n.* A low-growing plant, *Epigaea repens,* of E North America, with evergreen leaves and fragrant pink or white flower clusters.

train (trān) *n.* **1.** A part of a long gown that trails behind the wearer. **2.** A staff of attendants **:** retinue. **3.** A long moving line, as of persons or vehicles. **4.** A string of railroad cars coupled together and pulled by a locomotive. **5.** An orderly series of related thoughts or events **:** sequence. *—v.* **1.** To instruct or condition to some manner of behavior or performance. **2.** To make proficient through special instruction and drill. **3.** To make or become fit for an athletic performance. **4.** To cause (e.g., a plant) to grow in or take on a desired shape or course. **5.** To direct **:** aim. **—train'a•ble** *adj.* **—train•ee'** *n.* **—train'er** *n.* **—train'ing** *n.*

train•man (trān'mən) *n.* A crew member on a railroad train, esp. the brakeman.

traipse (trāps) *v.* **traipsed, traips•ing.** To walk about aimlessly or intrusively.

trait (trāt) *n.* **1.** A distinguishing feature, as of one's character. **2.** A characteristic that is inherited.

trai•tor (trā'tər) *n.* **1.** One who betrays a cause or another's confidence. **2.** One who commits treason. **—trai'tor•ous** *adj.*

tra•jec•to•ry (trə-jĕk'tə-rē) *n., pl.* **-ries. 1.** The path of a moving object, as a projectile, esp. such a path in 3 dimensions. **2.** *Math.* A curve that cuts all of a given family of curves or surfaces at the same angle.

tram (trăm) *n.* **1.** *esp. Brit.* **a.** A streetcar. **b.** A cable car. **2.** A 4-wheeled, open wagon or iron car run on tracks in a coal mine.

tram•mel (trăm'əl) *n.* **1.** A shackle for teaching a horse to amble. **2.** *often* **trammels.** A restriction on free activity or movement. *—v.* **-meled, -mel•ing** *or* **melled, -mel•ling. 1.** To hinder, restrict, or confine. **2.** To ensnare **:** enmesh.

tramp (trămp) *v.* **1.** To walk with a heavy step **:** trudge. **2. a.** To go on foot **:** hike. **b.** To wander about aimlessly. **3.** To trample <*tramp* down snow> *—n.* **1. a.** A heavy footfall. **b.** The sound made by heavy footsteps. **2.** A trip made by walking **:** hike. **3.** One who travels about aimlessly on foot, doing odd jobs or begging for a living **:** vagrant. **4. a.** A prostitute. **b.** A promiscuous person. **5.** A cargo ship having no regular schedule but taking on freight wherever it may be found and unloading it wherever required. **—tramp'er** *n.*

tram•ple (trăm'pəl) *v.* **-pled, -pling. 1.** To tread heavily so as to bruise, crush, or destroy. **2.** To treat ruthlessly, as if tramping on. **—tram'ple** *n.* **—tram'pler** *n.*

tram•po•line (trăm'pə-lēn') *n.* A device for performing acrobatic feats, consisting of a sheet of taut canvas attached with springs to a metal frame. **—tram'po•lin'ist** *n.*

trance (trăns) *n.* **1.** A dreamlike mental condition, as produced by hypnosis or drugs. **2.** The condition of being so lost in thought as to be unaware of one's surroundings. **3.** A dazed state, as between sleeping and waking **:** stupor. ★ ***syns:*** ABSTRACTION, MUSE, REVERIE, STUDY

tran•quil (trăn'kwəl) *adj.* **1.** Free from disturbance **:** serene. **2.** Steady **:** even <a *tranquil* flame> **—tran•quil'li•ty, tran•quil'i•ty** *n.* **—tran'quil•ly** *adv.*

tran•quil•ize *also* **tran•quil•lize** (trăn'kwə-līz') *v.* **-ized, -iz•ing** *also* **-lized, -liz•ing.** To make or become tranquil. **—tran'quil•i•za'tion** *n.*

tran•quil•iz•er (trăn'kwə-līz'ər) *n.* A drug used to calm or pacify.

trans•act (trăn-săkt', -zăkt') *v.* To do, perform, carry out, manage, or conduct (e.g., business). **—trans•ac'tor** *n.*

trans•ac•tion (trăn-săk'shən, -zăk'shən) *n.* **1.** The act of transacting or the fact of being transacted. **2.** Something transacted. **3. transactions.** The proceedings, as of a convention. **—trans•ac'tion•al** *adj.*

trans•at•lan•tic (trăns'ət-lăn'tĭk, trănz'ət-) *adj.* **1.** Situated on the other side of the Atlantic. **2.** Traversing the Atlantic.

trans•ceiv•er (trăn-sē'vər, -zē'-) *n.* A module composed of a radio receiver and transmitter.

tran•scend (trăn-sĕnd') *v.* **1. a.** To pass beyond (a human limit). **b.** To exist above and independent of (material experience or the universe). **2.** To surpass.

tran•scen•dent (trăn-sĕn'dənt) *adj.* **1.** Surpassing all others **:** pre-eminent. **2.** Above and independent of the material universe. **—tran•scen'dence, tran•scen'den•cy** *n.* **—tran•scen'dent•ly** *adv.*

tran•scen•den•tal (trăn'sĕn-dĕnt'l) *adj.* **1.** Of or relating to transcendentalism. **2.** Rising above common thought or ideas **:** mystical. **—tran'scen•den'tal•ly** *adv.*

tran•scen•den•tal•ism (trăn'sən-dĕnt'l-ĭz'əm) *n.* The philosophical belief that knowledge of reality comes from intuition rather than from objective experience. **—tran'scen•den'tal•ist** *n.*

transcendental number *n.* An irrational number that cannot occur as a root or solution of any algebraic equation whose coefficients are all rational numbers.

trans•con•ti•nen•tal (trăns'kŏn'tə-nĕn'təl, trănz'-) *adj.* Traversing a continent.

tran•scribe (trăn-skrīb') *v.* **-scribed, -scrib•ing. 1. a.** To make a copy of by writing out fully, as from shorthand notes or via an electronic medium <*transcribe* a memorandum> **b.** To transfer (information) from one recording and storing system to another. **2.** To arrange or adapt (a musical composition) for a voice or instrument other than the original. **3.** To record, usu. on tape, for broadcasting at some later date **—tran•scrib'a•ble** *adj.* **—tran•scrib'er** *n.*

tran•script (trăn'skrĭpt') *n.* Transcribed matter, esp. a written, typewritten, or printed copy, as of an academic record.

tran•scrip•tion (trăn-skrĭp'shən) *n.* **1.** The act or process of transcribing. **2.** Something transcribed, esp.: **a.** An arrangement of a musical composition other than the original. **b.** A television or radio program that is recorded. **—tran•scrip'tion•al** *adj.* **—tran•scrip'tion•al•ly** *adv.*

trans•cul•tu•ra•tion (trăns'kŭl-chə-rā'shən) *n.* Cultural change brought about by the introduction of elements of a foreign culture.

trans•duc•er (trăns-dōō'sər, -dyōō'-, trănz-) *n.* A substance or device, as a photoelectric cell, that converts input energy of one form into output energy of another. **—trans•duce'** *v.*

tran•sept (trăn'sĕpt') *n.* Either of the 2 lateral arms of a church built in the shape of a cross.

trans•fer (trăns-fûr', trăns'fər) *v.* **-ferred, -fer•ring. 1.** To carry, remove, or shift from one person, position, or place to another. **2.** To convey or make over the possession or legal title of (e.g., property) to another. **3.** To shift (e.g., a design) from one surface to another. **4.** To change from one motor carrier to another. —*n.* (trăns'fər). **1.** *also* **trans•fer•al** (trăns-fûr'-əl). Conveyance or removal of a thing from one person or place to another. **2.** *also* **transferal.** One that has or has been transferred. **3.** A ticket that entitles a passenger to change from one motor carrier to another. **4.** *also* **transferal.** *Law.* Conveyance of title or property from one party to another. **—trans•fer'a•bil'i•ty** *n.* **—trans•fer'a•ble** *adj.* **—trans•fer'ence** *n.* **—trans•fer'er** *n.*

trans•fer•al *also* **trans•fer•ral** (trăns'fûr-əl) *n.* A transfer.

transfer RNA *n.* A ribonucleic acid that acts as a carrier in the transport of a specific amino acid to the site where a protein molecule is being synthesized.

trans•fig•ure (trăns-fĭg'yər) *v.* **-ured, -ur•ing. 1.** To transform the figure or outward appearance of. **2.** To glorify **:** exalt. **—trans•fig'u•ra'tion** *n.*

trans•fix (trăns-fĭks') *v.* **1.** To pierce with or as if with a pointed weapon. **2.** To make motionless, as with terror, amazement, or awe. **—trans•fix'ion** *adj.*

trans•form (trăns-fôrm') *v.* **1.** To alter markedly the appearance or form of. **2.** To change the nature, function, or condition of **:** convert <a steam engine *transforming* heat into

energy> —**trans•form'a•ble** *adj.* —**trans•form'a•bly** *adv.* —**trans'for•ma'tion** *n.* —**trans•form'er** *n.*

trans•fuse (trăns-fyōōz') *v.* **-fused, -fus•ing. 1.** To transfer (liquid) by pouring from one container into another. **2.** To permeate, imbue, or instill. **3.** *Med.* To inject a liquid, as plasma, into the bloodstream. —**trans•fus'er** *n.* —**trans•fu'sion** *n.*

trans•gress (trăns-grĕs', trănz-) *v.* **1.** To breach (a boundary or limit). **2.** To act in violation of (e.g., a law). —**trans•gress'i•ble** *adj.* —**trans•gres'sion** *n.* —**trans•gres'sive** *adj.* —**trans•gres'sor** *n.*

tran•sient (trăn'shənt, -zhənt, -zē-ənt) *adj.* **1.** Lasting only a short time **:** transitory. **2.** Passing through from one place to another <*transient* farm laborers> —**tran'sience, tran'sien•cy** *n.* —**tran'sient** *n.* —**tran'sient•ly** *adv.*

tran•sis•tor (trăn-zĭs'tər, trăn-sĭs'-) *n.* **1.** A 3-terminal semiconductor device for amplification, switching, and detection. **2.** A radio fitted with transistors. —**tran•sis'tor•i•za'tion** *n.* —**tran•sis'tor•ize'** *v.*

tran•sit (trăn'sĭt, -zĭt) *n.* **1. a.** Passage over, across, or through. **b.** Conveyance of goods or persons from place to place, esp. on a local system of public transport. **2.** An instrument used in surveying that measures horizontal and vertical angles.

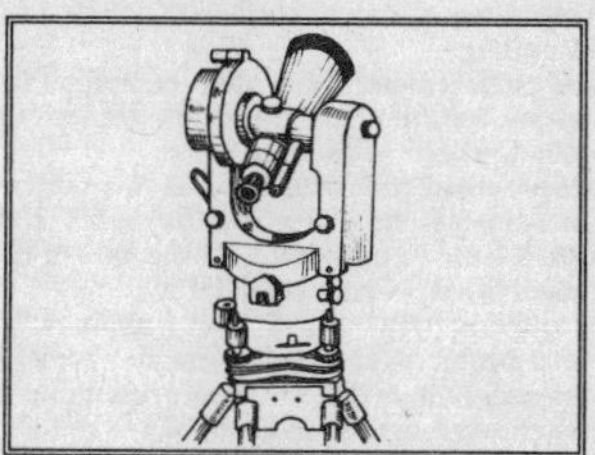

transit

tran•si•tion (trăn-zĭsh'ən, -sĭsh'ən) *n.* **1.** An act, process, or instance of changing from one state, form, activity, or place to another. **2.** Passage from one subject to another, as in discourse. —**tran•si'tion•al** *adj.* —**tran•si'tion•al•ly** *adv.*

tran•si•tive (trăn'sə-tĭv, trăn'zə-) *adj.* **1.** Expressing an action carried from the subject to the object and requiring a direct object to complete the meaning. —Used of a verb. **2.** Marked by or effecting transition. —*n.* A transitive verb. —**tran'si•tive•ly** *adv.* —**tran'si•tive•ness, tran'si•tiv'i•ty** *n.*

tran•si•to•ry (trăn'sə-tôr'ē, -tōr'ē, trăn'zə-) *adj.* Lasting only a short time. ★ ***syns:*** MOMENTARY, PASSING, SHORT-LIVED, TEMPORARY, TRANSIENT —**tran'si•to'ri•ly** *adv.* —**tran'si•to'ri•ness** *n.*

trans•late (trăns-lāt', trănz-, trăns'lāt', trănz'-) *v.* **-lat•ed, -lat•ing. 1.** To express in another language while retaining the original sense. **2.** To simplify or explain. **3.** To change from one form or style to another **:** convert <*translate* ideas into reality> —**trans•lat'a•bil'i•ty, trans•lat'a•ble•ness** *n.* —**trans•lat'a•ble** *adj.* —**trans•la'tion** *n.* —**trans•la'tor** *n.*

trans•lit•er•ate (trăns-lĭt'ə-rāt', trănz-) *v.* **-at•ed, -at•ing.** To write (words or letters) in the corresponding characters of another alphabet. —**trans•lit'er•a'tion** *n.*

trans•lu•cent (trăns-lōō'sənt, trănz-) *adj.* Admitting and diffusing light so that objects beyond cannot be clearly perceived. —**trans•lu'cence, trans•lu'cen•cy** *n.*

trans•mi•grate (trăns-mī'grāt', trănz-) *v.* To pass into another body after death. —Used of the soul. —**trans'mi•gra'tion** *n.* —**trans•mi'gra'tor** *n.* —**trans•mi'gra•to'ry** (-grə-tôr'ē, -tōr'ē) *adj.*

trans•mis•si•ble (trăns-mĭs'ə-bəl, trănz-) *adj.* Capable of undergoing transmission <*transmissible* viruses>

trans•mis•sion (trăns-mĭsh'ən, trănz-) *n.* **1.** The act of transmitting or state of being transmitted. **2.** Something, as a voice or message, that is transmitted. **3.** An automotive assembly of gears and associated parts by which power is transmitted from the engine to a driving axle. **4.** Passage of modulated carrier waves from a transmitter. —**trans•mis'sive** *adj.*

trans•mit (trăns-mĭt', trănz-) *v.* **-mit•ted, -mit•ting. 1.** To convey or dispatch from one person, thing, or place to another. **2.** To cause to spread a contagious disease <*transmit* an infection> **3.** To convey to others by heredity. **4.** *Electron.* To send (a signal) as by wire or radio. **5.** *Physics.* To cause (a disturbance) to propagate through a medium. —**trans•mis'si•ble, trans•mit'ta•ble** *adj.* —**trans•mit'tal** *n.*

trans•mit•ter (trăns-mĭt'ər, trănz-) *n.* One that transmits, as: **a.** A telegraphic sending instrument. **b.** The part of a telephone that converts sounds into electrical impulses. **c.** Electronic equipment that generates and amplifies a carrier wave and sends out the resulting signal.

trans•mog•ri•fy (trăns-mŏg'rə-fī', trănz-) *v.* **-fied, -fy•ing.** To change into a different, esp. fantastic or bizarre shape or form. —**trans•mog'ri•fi•ca'tion** *n.*

trans•mute (trăns-myōōt', trănz-) *v.* **-mut•ed, -mut•ing.** To change from one nature, form, substance, or state into another. —**trans•mut'a•bil'i•ty** *n.* —**trans•mut'a•ble** *adj.* —**trans•mut'a•bly** *adv.* —**trans'mu•ta'tion** *n.*

trans•na•tion•al (trăns-năsh'ə-nəl, trănz-) *adj.* **1.** Reaching beyond national boundaries. **2.** Of or involving several nations or nationalities.

trans•o•ce•an•ic (trăns'ō-shē-ăn'ĭk, trănz'-) *adj.* **1.** Situated on the other side of the ocean. **2.** Traversing the ocean.

tran•som (trăn'səm) *n.* **1. a.** A small, often

hinged window above another window or a door. **b.** The horizontal crosspiece to which such a window is hinged. **2.** A horizontal piece of wood or stone in a window that serves to divide it. —**tran'somed** *adj.*

tran·son·ic (trăn-sŏn'ĭk) *adj.* Of or relating to aerodynamic flow or flight conditions at speeds close to the speed of sound.

trans·pa·cif·ic (trăns'pə-sĭf'ĭk) *adj.* **1.** Situated on the other side of the Pacific. **2.** Traversing the Pacific.

trans·par·ent (trăns-pâr'ənt, -păr'ənt) *adj.* **1.** Capable of transmitting light so that objects and images beyond can be clearly perceived. **2.** Permeable to electromagnetic radiation of specified frequencies. **3.** So fine or delicate in texture that objects may be easily seen on the other side : diaphanous. **4. a.** Easily detected : obvious. **b.** Readily understandable. —**trans·par'en·cy** *n.* —**trans·par'ent·ly** *adv.*

tran·spire (trăn-spīr') *v.* **-spired, -spir·ing. 1.** To give off (vapor containing waste products) through animal or plant pores. **2.** To be revealed. **3.** To take place. —**tran'spi·ra'tion** *n.*

trans·plant (trăns-plănt', -plänt') *v.* **1.** To remove (a living plant) from the place where it is growing and plant it in another place. **2.** To relocate. **3.** *Med.* To transfer (an organ or tissue) from one body or bodily part to another. —**trans'plant'** *n.* —**trans·plant'a·ble** *adj.* —**trans'plan·ta'tion** *n.*

trans·po·lar (trăns-pō'lər) *adj.* Extending across or crossing over either of the geographic polar regions.

trans·port (trăns-pôrt', -pōrt') *v.* **1.** To convey from one place to another. **2.** To affect with strong emotion. **3.** To send across the sea to a penal colony. —*n.* (trăns'pôrt', -pōrt'). **1.** The act or process of transporting. **2.** The state of being carried away by emotion. **3.** A ship or aircraft for transporting troops or military equipment. **4.** A vehicle, as an airplane, for transporting mail, freight, or passengers. —**trans·port'a·bil'i·ty** *n.* —**trans·port'a·ble** *adj.* —**trans'por·ta'tion** *n.* —**trans·port'er** *n.*

trans·pose (trăns-pōz') *v.* **-posed, -pos·ing. 1.** To reverse the order or place of. **2.** To move into a different position or order. **3.** *Mus.* To write or perform (a composition) in a key other than the one in which it was written. —**trans·pos'a·ble** *adj.* —**trans·pos'er** *n.* —**trans'po·si'tion** *n.*

trans·sex·u·al (trăns-sĕk'sho͞o-əl) *n.* **1.** One predisposed to become a member of the opposite sex. **2.** One whose sex has been changed externally by surgery.

trans·ship (trăns-shĭp') *also* **tran·ship** (trăn-) *v.* To transfer (cargo) from one vessel or vehicle to another for reshipment. —**trans·ship'ment** *n.*

tran·sub·stan·ti·a·tion (trăn'səb-stăn'shē ā'shən) *n. Theol.* The doctrine that the brea and wine of the Eucharist are transform into the true presence of Christ, althou their appearance is the same.

trans·u·ran·ic (trăns'yo͞o-răn'ĭk, -rā' trănz'-) *adj.* Having an atomic number higher than 92.

trans·ver·sal (trăns-vûr'səl, trănz-) *adj.* Transverse. —*n.* A line intersecting a system of lines. —**trans·ver'sal·ly** *adv.*

trans·verse (trăns-vûrs', trănz-, trăns'vûrs', trănz'-) *adj.* Located or lying across. —*n.* (trăns'vûrs', trănz'). Something, as a part or beam, that is transverse. ★ ***syns:*** CROSSING, CROSSWISE, THWART, TRANSVERSAL, TRAVERSE —**trans·verse'ly** *adv.*

trans·ves·tism (trăns-vĕs'tĭz-əm) *n.* The practice of adopting the dress and often the manners or behavior of the other sex. —**trans·ves'tite** (-tīt) *n. & adj.*

trap (trăp) *n.* **1.** A device, as a net or a clamplike apparatus that springs shut suddenly, for catching and holding animals. **2.** A stratagem or device used to trick or surprise an unsuspecting victim. **3. a.** A receptacle, as a grease trap, for collecting waste materials. **b.** A device for sealing a passage, as a drainpipe, against the escape of gases. **4.** A device that hurls clay pigeons, balls, or disks into the air to be shot at. **5.** A land hazard, as a sand-filled depression, on a golf course. **6.** A light 2-wheeled carriage with springs. **7.** A trap door. **8. traps.** Percussion instruments. —*v.* **trapped, trap·ping. 1.** To catch in or as if in a trap. **2.** To trap furbearing animals. —**trap'per** *n.*

trap door *n.* A movable door in a floor, roof, or ceiling.

tra·peze (tră-pēz') *n.* A short horizontal bar suspended from 2 parallel ropes, used for acrobatic stunts or exercise.

trap·e·zoid (trăp'ə-zoid') *n.* **1.** A quadrilateral having one pair of parallel sides. **2.** A small bone in the wrist near the base of the index finger. —**trap'e·zoi'dal** *adj.*

trap·ping (trăp'ĭng) *n.* **1.** *often* **trappings.** An ornamental covering or harness for a horse. **2. trappings. a.** Articles of dress or adornment. **b.** Outward signs or indications.

trap·shoot·ing (trăp'sho͞o'tĭng) *n.* The sport of shooting at clay pigeons.

trash (trăsh) *n.* **1.** Worthless, discarded material : junk. **2.** Worthless literary or artistic matter. **3.** One considered ignorant or contemptible. —**trash'y** *adj.*

trau·ma (trou'mə, trô'-) *n., pl.* **-mas** *or* **-ma·ta** (-mə-tə). **1.** *Pathol.* A wound, esp. one caused by sudden physical injury. **2.** *Psychiat.* An emotional shock that creates substantial and lasting damage to the psychological development of the individual, gen. leading to neurosis. **3.** Something that severely jars the mind or emotions. ★ ***syns:*** BLOW, JOLT, SHOCK —**trau·mat'ic** *adj.* —**trau·mat'i·cal·ly** *adv.* —**trau'ma·tize'** *v.*

tra·vail (trə-vāl', trăv'āl') *n.* **1.** Strenuous physical or mental exertion. **2.** Tribulation : distress. **3.** The labor of childbirth. **4.** *Can.* A travois. —*v.* **1.** To labor strenuously : toil. **2.** To undergo the labor of childbirth.

trav·el (trăv'əl) *v.* **-eled, -el·ing** *or* **-elled, -el·ling. 1.** To move from one place to another :

journey. **2.** To journey from one place to another as a sales representative. **3.** To be transmitted, as sound. **4.** To associate <*travels* in a fast circle> **5.** To admit of being transported <Some perishable goods *travel* poorly.> —*n.* **1.** The act or process of traveling. **2.** *often* **travels. a.** A series of journeys. **b.** A written account of a series of journeys. —**trav'el·er** *n.*

▲ ***word history:*** The hardships of making a journey in earlier times is reflected in the etymological identity of the words *travel* and *travail.* Both are derived from Old French *travailler,* which orig. meant "to torment, trouble" and later came to mean "to be troubled, be in pain, work hard." *Travailler* was borrowed into English as *travail,* which at first had the same meanings as the Old French word but later came to mean "to toil, make a difficult journey," and simply "to journey." *Travel* was orig. a variant of *travail,* but it has now become a separate word used exclusively in the sense "to journey."

travel agency *n.* An agency that arranges for travel itineraries, tickets, and accommodations. —**travel agent** *n.*

travel bureau *n.* A travel agency.

traveler's check *n.* An internationally redeemable draft available in various denominations and valid only with the holder's own endorsement against his or her original signature.

trav·e·logue *also* **trav·e·log** (trăv'ə-lôg', -lŏg') *n.* A lecture illustrated by slides or a narrated film about travels.

tra·verse (trə-vûrs', trăv'ərs) *v.* **-versed, -vers·ing. 1.** To pass across, over, or through. **2.** To move forward and backward over. **3.** To extend across <a bridge *traversing* a gorge> **4.** To go counter to **:** thwart. —*n.* **1. a.** The act of traversing. **b.** A route or path across. **2.** Something lying across something else, as a transom. —*adj.* Transverse. —**trav'ers·a·ble** *adj.* —**tra·vers'al** *n.* —**tra·vers'er** *n.*

trav·es·ty (trăv'ĭ-stē) *n., pl.* **-ties.** A grotesque imitation with intent to ridicule. —*v.* **-tied, -ty·ing.** To make a travesty of.

tra·vois (trə-voi', trăv'oi') *n., pl.* **tra·vois** (trə-voiz', trăv'oiz') *or* **-es.** A frame slung between trailing poles and pulled by a dog or horse, formerly used by Plains Indians as a conveyance for goods and belongings.

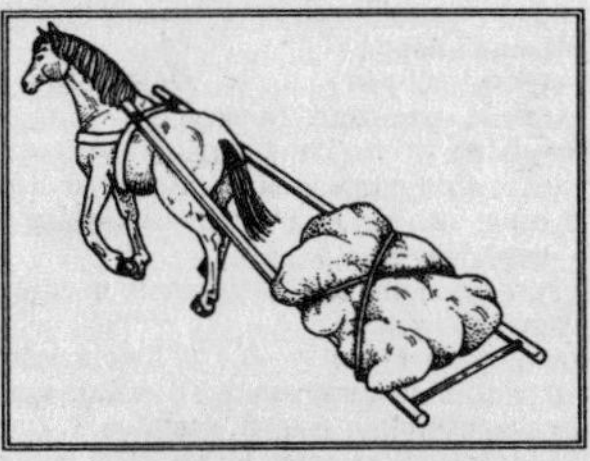

travois

trawl (trôl) *n.* A large tapered and flattened or conical fishing net towed along the sea floor. —**trawl** *v.*

tray (trā) *n.* A flat, shallow container having a raised edge, used for holding, carrying, or displaying something.

treach·er·ous (trĕch'ər-əs) *adj.* **1.** Disloyal **:** traitorous. **2. a.** Undependable. **b.** Dangerous. —**treach'er·ous·ly** *adv.* —**treach'er·ous·ness** *n.*

treach·er·y (trĕch'ə-rē) *n., pl.* **-ies. 1.** Deliberate betrayal of confidence or trust **:** perfidy. **2.** An act or instance of betraying confidence or trust.

trea·cle (trē'kəl) *n.* **1.** Cloying sentiment. **2.** *esp. Brit.* Molasses. —**trea'cly** *adj.*

tread (trĕd) *v.* **trod** (trŏd), **trod·den** (trŏd'n) *or* **trod, tread·ing. 1.** To walk over, on, or along. **2.** To stamp or trample. **3.** To execute (e.g., a step or measure) by walking or dancing. —*n.* **1.** The act, manner, sound, or an instance of treading. **2.** The horizontal section of a step in a staircase. **3.** The portion of a wheel that makes contact with the ground or rails. **4.** The grooved surface of a tire.

tread·le (trĕd'l) *n.* A foot pedal for activating a circular drive, as in a potter's wheel or sewing machine.

tread·mill (trĕd'mĭl') *n.* **1.** A mechanism activated by walking on the moving steps of a wheel or treading an endless sloping belt. **2.** A monotonous task.

trea·son (trē'zən) *n.* **1.** Violation of allegiance toward one's country or sovereign, esp. the betrayal of one's own country by waging war against it or by consciously and purposely acting to aid its enemies. **2.** A betrayal of trust or confidence. —**trea'son·a·ble** *adj.* —**trea'son·ous** *adj.*

treas·ure (trĕzh'ər) *n.* **1.** Accumulated or hidden wealth, as jewels or money. **2.** One regarded as esp. valuable. —*v.* **-ured, -ur·ing. 1.** To accumulate and save for future use. **2.** To value greatly **:** cherish.

treas·ur·er (trĕzh'ər-ər) *n.* A person having charge of funds or revenues, esp. a financial officer for a government, company, or society. —**treas'ur·er·ship'** *n.*

treas·ure-trove (trĕzh'ər-trōv') *n.* **1.** Unclaimed treasure found hidden. **2.** A valuable discovery **:** trove.

treas·ur·y (trĕzh'ə-rē) *n., pl.* **-ies. 1.** A place where treasure is kept. **2.** A place where private or public funds are kept and managed. **3.** Public funds or revenues. **4.** A collection of valuable things. **5. Treasury.** The governmental department in charge of the collection, management, and expenditure of public revenue.

treat (trēt) *v.* **1.** To have to do with or behave in a specified manner toward. **2.** To consider or regard in a given manner. **3.** To deal with in speech or writing. **4.** To represent or deal with in a specified style or manner. **5.** To provide food or entertainment for (another) at one's own expense <*treated* me to dinner> **6.** To subject to an action, process, or change

<*treat* sick patients><*treat* the garden with compost> —*n.* **1.** The act of treating. **2.** Something, as one's food or entertainment, paid for by another person. **3.** A special delight <A trip to Paris was a real *treat.*> —**treat'a•ble** *adj.* —**treat'er** *n.*

trea•tise (trē'tĭs) *n.* A formal written account treating a subject systematically.

treat•ment (trēt'mənt) *n.* **1.** The act or manner of treating **:** handling. **2.** Medical application of remedies so as to effect a cure **:** therapy.

trea•ty (trē'tē) *n., pl.* **-ties.** A formal agreement between 2 or more states or nations. ★ ***syns:*** ACCORD, AGREEMENT, CONCORD, CONVENTION, PACT

treb•le (trĕb'əl) *adj.* **1.** Triple **:** threefold. **2.** *Mus.* Of, having, or performing the highest part, voice, or range. **3.** Having a high pitch **:** shrill. —*n.* **1.** *Mus.* The highest part, voice, instrument, or range **:** soprano. **2.** A high, shrill voice or sound. —*v.* **-led, -ling.** To increase 3 times **:** triple. —**treb'le•ness** *n.* —**treb'ly** *adv.*

treble clef *n. Mus.* A symbol centered on the 2nd line from the bottom of a staff to indicate G above middle C.

treble clef

tree (trē) *n.* **1.** A usu. tall woody plant having comparatively great height and a single trunk. **2.** A plant, as a shrub, resembling a tree in form or size. **3.** Something similar to a tree, as a pole with pegs for hanging clothes. **4.** A diagram with a branching form, as one used to show family descent. —*v.* **treed, tree•ing. 1.** To force to climb a tree in evasion of pursuit. **2.** *Informal.* To force into a difficult position **:** corner. —**tree'less** *adj.* —**tree'like'** *adj.*

tree farm *n.* Forested land on which trees are grown commercially.

tree frog *n.* A small, arboreal frog of the genus *Hyla* and related genera, with long toes terminating in adhesive disks.

tree line *n.* **1.** The limit of N or S latitude beyond which trees cannot grow except as stunted forms. **2.** A timberline.

tree of heaven *n.* The ailanthus.

tre•foil (trē'foil', trĕf'oil') *n.* **1.** Any of various plants of the genera *Trifolium, Lotus,* and related genera, having compound leaves with 3 leaflets. **2.** A stylized representation of a trefoil leaf.

trek (trĕk) *v.* **trekked, trek•king.** To make a slow, arduous journey. —*n.* A journey or leg of a journey, esp. when slow and difficult. —**trek'ker** *n.*

trel•lis (trĕl'ĭs) *n.* A frame supporting open latticework, used for training vines and other climbing plants.

trem•ble (trĕm'bəl) *v.* **-bled, -bling. 1.** To shake involuntarily, as from fear, cold, or weakness. **2.** To feel or express fear or anxiety. —**trem'ble** *n.* —**trem'bler** *n.* —**trem'bly** *adj.*

tre•men•dous (trĭ-mĕn'dəs) *adj.* **1.** Fearful **:** terrible. **2. a.** Particularly large **:** enormous. **b.** *Informal.* Marvelous **:** wonderful. —**tre•men'dous•ly** *adv.*

trem•o•lo (trĕm'ə-lō') *n., pl.* **-los.** *Mus.* A vibrating effect made by quickly repeating one tone or by quickly alternating two tones.

trem•or (trĕm'ər) *n.* **1.** A slight vibrating or shaking movement, as of the earth. **2.** Involuntary trembling of the body.

trem•u•lous (trĕm'yə-ləs) *adj.* **1.** Vibrating **:** quivering **:** trembling. **2.** Timid **:** fearful. —**trem'u•lous•ly** *adv.*

trench (trĕnch) *n.* **1.** A furrow. **2. a.** A ditch. **b.** A ditch embanked with its own soil used for protection, esp. in warfare. —*v.* **1.** To cut or dig a trench. **2.** To fortify with a trench. **3.** To encroach <*trenched* on my land> —**trench'er** *n.*

trench•ant (trĕn'chənt) *adj.* **1.** Forcefully effective **:** vigorous. **2.** Very perceptive **:** incisive. —**trench'an•cy** *n.*

trench coat *n.* A loose-fitting, belted raincoat with numerous pockets and flaps.

trench•er (trĕn'chər) *n.* A wooden cutting or serving board.

trench•er•man (trĕn'chər-mən) *n.* A hearty eater.

trench foot *n.* A condition of the feet resembling frostbite caused by prolonged exposure to damp cold.

trench mouth *n.* Contagious gingivitis.

trend (trĕnd) *n.* **1.** A general inclination or tendency **:** drift. **2.** A direction of movement **:** course. —*v.* To have a specified direction or tendency. —**trend'set'ter** *n.*

trend•y (trĕn'dē) *adj.* **-i•er, -i•est.** *Informal.* Of or being in accord with the latest fashion or fad <*trendy* attire> —**trend'i•ly** *adv.* —**trend'i•ness** *n.*

tre•pan (trĭ-păn') *n.* A trephine. —*v.* **-panned, -pan•ning.** To trephine.

tre•phine (trĭ-fīn') *n.* A surgical instrument with sawlike edges, used for cutting out disks of bone, usu. from the skull. —**tre•phine** *v.* —**treph'i•na'tion** *n.*

trep•i•da•tion (trĕp'ə-dā'shən) *n.* Great alarm or dread.

tres•pass (trĕs'pəs, -păs') *n.* **1.** To commit a sin or offense **:** transgress. **2.** To infringe upon another's privacy, time, or attention. **3.** *Law.* To invade the property, rights, or person of another without consent. —*n.* **1.** A transgression. 2. *Law.* The act of trespassing. **—tres'pass•er** *n.*

tress (trĕs) *n.* **1.** A lock of hair. **2. tresses.** A woman's long hair.

tres•tle (trĕs'əl) *n.* **1.** A horizontal beam or bar held up by 2 pairs of legs and used as a support, as for a table. **2.** A framework composed of vertical, slanted supports and horizontal crosspieces holding up a bridge.

trey (trā) *n.* A card, die, or domino with 3 pips **:** three.

tri•a•ble (trī'ə-bəl) *adj.* **1.** Capable of being tried or tested. **2.** *Law.* Subject to judicial examination. **—tri'a•ble•ness** *n.*

tri•ad (trī'ăd', -əd) *n.* A group of 3 persons or things. **—tri•ad'ic** *adj.*

tri•age (trē-äzh', trē'äzh') *n.* A process for sorting injured people into groups based on their need for medical treatment.

tri•al (trī'əl, trīl) *n.* **1.** *Law.* Examination and hearing of evidence before a court to decide the issue of specified charges or claims. **2.** The act or process of trying and proving by use and experience **:** experiment. **3.** An effort or attempt. **4.** A source of vexation or distress that tests patience and endurance. *—adj.* **1.** *Law.* Of or relating to a trial. **2.** Made, done, performed, or used during a test or experiment.

tri•an•gle (trī'ăng'gəl) *n.* **1.** A plane geometric figure with 3 angles and 3 sides. **2.** Something shaped like a triangle. **3.** *Mus.* A percussion instrument composed of a piece of metal formed into a triangle. **—tri•an'gu•lar** *adj.* **—tri•an'gu•lar'i•ty** *n.*

tri•an•gu•late (trī-ăng'gyə-lāt') *v.* **-lat•ed, -lat•ing. 1.** To divide into triangles. **2.** To measure by trigonometry. **—tri•an'gu•late•ly** *adv.* **—tri•an'gu•la'tion** *n.*

tri•ath•lon (trī-ăth'lən, -lŏn') *n.* An athletic contest consisting of 3 successive events, usu. long-distance swimming, bicycling, and running. **—tri•ath'lete** *n.*

tribe (trīb) *n.* **1.** A system of social organization comprising several villages, districts, bands, lineages, or other groups that share a common ancestry, culture, language, and name. **2.** A group sharing a common occupation, interest, or habit. **—trib'al** *adj.* **—trib'al•ism** *n.* **—trib'al•ly** *adv.* **—tribes'man** *n.* **—tribes'wom'an** *n.*

trib•u•la•tion (trĭb'yə-lā'shən) *n.* **1.** Great trial, affliction, or distress. **2.** A cause of great distress.

tri•bu•nal (trī-byōō'nəl, trĭ-) *n.* **1.** A court of justice <a military *tribunal*> **2.** One empowered to determine or judge.

trib•une (trĭb'yōōn', trĭ-byōōn') *n.* **1.** An ancient Roman official chosen by the plebs to protect their rights against the patricians. **2.** A protector or champion of the people. **—trib'u•nar'y** *adj.*

trib•u•tar•y (trĭb'yə-tĕr'ē) *adj.* **1.** Flowing into another. **2.** Contributory. **3.** Of the nature of or paying tribute. *—n., pl.* **-ies. 1.** A river or stream flowing into a larger river or stream. **2.** One that pays tribute.

trib•ute (trĭb'yōōt) *n.* **1.** A gift or testimonial expressing gratitude or admiration. **2.** Money or valuables given by a ruler or nation to another in submission or as the price for protection.

trice (trīs) *n.* An extremely short period of time **:** instant.

tri•ceps (trī'sĕps') *n.* A large 3-headed muscle running along the back of the upper arm and functioning to extend the forearm.

tri•cer•a•tops (trī-sĕr'ə-tŏps') *n.* A 3-horned herbivorous dinosaur of the genus *Triceratops.*

tri•chi•na (trĭ-kī'nə) *n., pl.* **-nae** (-nē) *or* **-nas.** A parasitic nematode worm infesting the intestines of mammals.

trich•i•no•sis (trĭk'ə-nō'sĭs) *n.* A disease caused by trichinae-infested pork that has not been cooked enough and marked by fever, muscular swelling, and pain.

trick (trĭk) *n.* **1.** An indirect, often deceptive or fraudulent means of achieving an end. **2.** A mischievous act **:** prank. **3.** A stupid, disgraceful, or childish act. **4.** A mannerism. **5.** A special skill **:** knack. **6.** A feat of magic or legerdemain. **7.** A difficult, dexterous, or clever act designed to amuse or impress. **8.** The cards played in a single round in a card game. *—v.* **1.** To cheat or deceive. **2.** To adorn <*tricked* out in rhinestones> *—adj.* Weak, defective, or likely to fail <a *trick* elbow>

trick•er•y (trĭk'ə-rē) *n., pl.* **-ies.** Deception by stratagem.

trick•le (trĭk'əl) *v.* **-led, -ling. 1.** To fall or flow in drops or droplets or in a thin stream. **2.** To move or advance slowly or bit by bit. **—trick'le** *n.*

trick•ster (trĭk'stər) *n.* One that plays tricks **:** swindler.

trick•y (trĭk'ē) *adj.* **-i•er, -i•est. 1.** Given to or marked by trickery **:** wily. **2.** Requiring skill or caution <a *tricky* pastry recipe> **—trick'i•ly** *adv.* **—trick'i•ness** *n.*

tri•col•or (trī'kŭl'ər) *n.* **1.** A flag of 3 colors. **2.** The French flag. **—tri'col'ored** *adj.*

tri•corn *also* **tri•corne** (trī'kôrn') *n.* A hat whose brim is turned up on 3 sides.

tri•cor•nered (trī'kôr'nərd) *adj.* Having 3 corners.

tri•cy•cle (trī'sĭk'əl, -sĭ-kəl) *n.* A vehicle with 3 wheels, usu. pedal-propelled.

tri•dent (trīd'ənt) *n.* A long, 3-pronged fork, weapon, or spear.

tried (trīd) *adj.* Thoroughly tested and proved to be good or reliable.

tri•en•ni•al (trī-ĕn'ē-əl) *adj.* **1.** Occurring every 3rd year. **2.** Lasting 3 years. **—tri•en'ni•al** *n.* **—tri•en'ni•al•ly** *adv.*

tri•fle (trī'fəl) *n.* **1.** Something unimportant or of little value. **2.** A small amount **:** jot. **3.** Cake soaked in wine or brandy and topped with jam. *—v.* **-fled, -fling. 1.** To handle something as if it were of little importance or value. **2.** To toy with something <*trifle* with someone's affections> **3.** To waste (e.g., time). **—tri'fler** *n.*

tri•fling (trī'flĭng) *adj.* **1.** Of little importance : insignificant. **2.** Marked by frivolity. **—tri′fling·ly** *adv.*

tri·fo·cal (trī-fō′kəl) *adj.* Having 3 focal lengths. *—pl.n.* **trifocals.** Eyeglasses with trifocal lenses.

trig[1] (trĭg) *adj.* **1.** Neat and trim : tidy. **2.** Being in good condition. **—trig** *v.* **—trig′ly** *adv.* **—trig′ness** *n.*

trig[2] (trĭg) *n.* Trigonometry.

trig·ger (trĭg′ər) *n.* **1.** The small lever of a firearm that is pressed by the finger to discharge it. **2.** A similar device that releases or activates a mechanism. **3.** Stimulus. *—v.* To set off : activate.

trigonometric function *n.* A function of an angle expressed as a ratio of 2 of the sides of a right triangle that contains the angle.

trig·o·nom·e·try (trĭg′ə-nŏm′ə-trē) *n.* The study of the properties and applications of trigonometric functions. **—trig′o·no·met′ric —trig′o·no·met′ri·cal** *adj.* **—trig′o·no·met′ri·cal·ly** *adv.*

tri·lat·er·al (trī-lăt′ər-əl) *adj.* Having three sides. **—tri·lat′er·al·ly** *adv.*

tril·by (trĭl′bē) *n., pl.* **-bies.** *esp. Brit.* A soft felt hat with a deeply creased crown.

trill (trĭl) *n.* **1.** A tremulous sound : warble. **2.** *Mus.* Rapid alternating of 2 tones a whole or a half tone apart. **3. a.** A rapid vibration of one speech organ against another. **b.** A sound pronounced with a trill, as Spanish *rr.* *—v.* **1.** *Mus.* To sound, sing, or play with a trill. **2.** To articulate with a trill.

tril·lion (trĭl′yən) *n.* **1.** The cardinal number equal to 10^{12}. **2.** *esp. Brit.* The cardinal number equal to 10^{18}. **—tril′lion** *adj. & pron.* **—tril′lionth** *n. & adj. & adv.*

tril·o·gy (trĭl′ə-jē) *n., pl.* **-gies.** A series of 3 literary works that are related in subject matter or theme.

trim (trĭm) *v.* **trimmed, trim·ming. 1.** To neaten by clipping or pruning. **2.** To remove excess from by cutting <*trimmed* the budget> **3.** To decorate : ornament. **4.** *Informal.* To defeat soundly. **5.** *Naut.* **a.** To adjust (the sails and yards) for proper wind reception. **b.** To balance (a ship) by shifting the contents. **6.** To balance (an aircraft) in flight by regulating the control surfaces and tabs. *—n.* **1.** State of order, arrangement, or appearance : condition <in good *trim*> **2. a.** Exterior ornamentation, as moldings or framework. **b.** Ornamentation, as for clothing. **3.** Rejected or excised material. **4. a.** The readiness of a vessel for sailing. **b.** The balance or position of a ship or aircraft. *—adj.* **trim·mer, trim·mest. 1.** In good order. **2.** Having neat, pleasing forms or lines <a *trim* figure> <a *trim* sailboat> **—trim′ly** *adv.* **—trim′mer** *n.* **—trim′ness** *n.*

tri·mes·ter (trī-mĕs′tər) *n.* A stage or period of 3 months.

trim·ming (trĭm′ĭng) *n.* **1.** Material added as an ornament or decoration. **2. trimmings.** Accessories <turkey and *trimmings*> **3.** *Informal.* A sound defeat.

trin·i·ty (trĭn′ə-tē) *n., pl.* **-ties. 1.** A group of 3 members in union : triad. **2. Trinity.** The union of the Father, Son, and Holy Ghost in a single Godhead.

trin·ket (trĭng′kĭt) *n.* **1.** A small ornament. **2.** A trivial thing : trifle.

tri·ni·tro·tol·u·ene (trī-nī′trō-tŏl′yo͞o-ēn′) *n.* A yellow crystalline compound used chiefly as a high explosive : TNT.

tri·o (trē′ō) *n., pl.* **-os. 1.** A group or set of 3. **2.** *Mus.* **a.** A composition for 3 performers. **b.** The group performing a trio.

trip (trĭp) *n.* **1.** Travel from one place to another : journey. **2.** *Slang.* **a.** A hallucinatory experience induced by a psychedelic drug. **b.** An exciting experience. **3.** A stumble : fall. **4. a.** A device, as a pawl, for triggering a mechanism. **b.** The action of a trip. *—v.* **tripped, trip·ping. 1.** To stumble or cause to stumble : fall. **2.** To move nimbly with light, rapid steps : skip. **3.** To make a mistake. **4.** To release or be released, as a catch, switch, or trigger.

tri·par·tite (trī-pär′tīt′) *adj.* **1.** Made up of or divided into 3 parts. **2.** Pertaining to or carried out by 3 parties.

tripe (trīp) *n.* **1.** The stomach lining of ruminants, esp. oxen, used as food. **2.** *Informal.* Something worthless : rubbish.

tri·ple (trĭp′əl) *adj.* **1.** Having 3 parts. **2.** Multiplied by 3. *—n.* **1.** A number or amount 3 times greater than another. **2.** A group or set of 3. **3.** *Baseball.* A 3-base hit. *—v.* **-pled, -pling. 1.** To make or become 3 times as large in number or amount. **2.** *Baseball.* To hit a triple. **—tri′ply** *adv.*

trip·let (trĭp′lĭt) *n.* **1.** A group or set of 3 of a kind. **2.** One of 3 born at a single birth.

tri·plex (trĭp′lĕks′, trī′plĕks′) *adj.* Consisting of 3 parts <*triplex* windows> *—n.* Something triplex, as a building containing 3 apartments.

trip·li·cate (trĭp′lĭ-kĭt) *n.* A set of 3 identical things or copies <typed in *triplicate*> *—v.* (trĭp′lĭ-kāt′) **-cat·ed, -cat·ing.** To make 3 identical copies of. **—trip′li·cate·ly** *adv.* **—trip′li·ca′tion** *n.*

trip·ping·ly (trĭp′ĭng-lē) *adv.* Lightly and easily : fluently.

tri·pod (trī′pŏd′) *n.* A 3-legged object, as a cauldron, stool, or table.

trip·tych (trĭp′tĭk) *n.* A work of art composed of 3 hinged or folding panels.

tri·reme (trī′rēm′) *n.* An ancient Greek or Roman galley or warship, with 3 banks of oars on each side.

tri·sect (trī′sĕkt′, trī-sĕkt′) *v.* To divide into 3 equal parts. **—tri′sec′tion** *n.*

tris·mus (trĭz′məs) *n.* Lockjaw. **—tris′mic** *adj.*

trite (trīt) *adj.* **trit·er, trit·est.** Devoid of freshness or appeal due to overuse. ★ ***syns:*** BANAL, COMMONPLACE, HACKNEYED, PLATITUDINOUS, TIMEWORN

trit·i·um (trĭt′ē-əm, trĭsh′ē-) *n.* A rare radioactive hydrogen isotope with atomic mass 3, prepared artificially as a tracer and a constituent of hydrogen bombs.

tri•umph (trī'əmf) *v.* **1.** To be victorious : win. **2.** To be jubilant : exult. —*n.* **1.** An instance or the fact of being victorious : success. **2.** Jubilant exultation. —**tri•um'phal** *adj.* —**tri•um'phant** *adj.* —**tri•um'phant•ly** *adv.* —**tri'umph•er** *n.*

tri•um•vir (trī-ŭm'vər) *n., pl.* **-virs** or **-vi•ri** (-və-rī'). One of a group of 3 men who shared public administration or civil authority, as in ancient Rome. —**tri•um'vi•ral** *adj.* —**tri•um'vi•rate** *n.*

tri•va•lent (trī-vā'lənt) *adj.* Having valence 3. —**tri•va'lence, tri•va'len•cy** *n.*

triv•et (trĭv'ĭt) *n.* **1.** A 3-legged stand. **2.** A metal stand with short feet, used under a hot dish or platter on a table.

triv•i•a (trĭv'ē-ə) *pl.n.* Insignificant or superfluous matters. ★ ***syns:*** MINUTIAE, TRIFLES, TRIVIALITY

triv•i•al (trĭv'ē-əl) *adj.* **1.** Relatively insignificant : unimportant. **2.** Commonplace : ordinary. —**triv'i•al'i•ty** *n.* —**triv'i•al•ize'** *v.*

–trix *suff.* A woman associated with a specified thing <execu*trix*>

tRNA (tē'är-ĕn'ā') *n.* Transfer RNA.

tro•che (trō'kē) *n.* A small, usu. round medicinal lozenge.

tro•chee (trō'kē) *n.* A metrical foot in prosody consisting of a stressed syllable followed by an unstressed syllable. —**tro•cha'•ic** (-kā'ĭk) *adj. & n.*

trod (trŏd) *v. p.t. & var. p.p. of* TREAD.

trod•den (trŏd'n) *v. p.p. of* TREAD.

troi•ka (troi'kə) *n.* **1.** A small Russian carriage drawn by a team of 3 horses abreast. **2.** A group or association of 3.

Tro•jan (trō'jən) *n.* **1.** A native or resident of ancient Troy. **2.** A courageous, determined, or energetic person. —**Tro'jan** *adj.*

Trojan horse *n.* A subversive group or device placed within enemy ranks.

troll[1] (trōl) *v.* **1.** To fish for by running a baited line behind a slowly moving boat. **2.** To trail (a baited line) in fishing. **3.** To sing the parts of (e.g., a round). **4.** To sing lustily. —*n.* **1.** The act of trolling for fish. **2.** A lure used for trolling. **3.** A musical round. —**troll'•er** *n.*

troll[2] (trōl) *n.* A creature of Scandinavian folklore variously portrayed as a dwarf or a giant living in caves or under bridges.

trol•ley *also* **trol•ly** (trŏl'ē) *n., pl.* **-leys** *also* **-lies.** **1.** A streetcar. **2.** A wheeled cage or basket hung from and traveling on an overhead track. **3.** A device that gathers electric current, as from an overhead wire or a 3rd rail, and transmits it to the motor of an electric vehicle.

trolley bus *n.* A trackless bus that is powered by electricity from an overhead wire.

trolley car *n.* A streetcar.

trol•lop (trŏl'əp) *n.* **1.** A slattern. **2.** A sexually promiscuous woman.

trom•bone (trŏm-bōn', trəm-, trŏm'bōn') *n.* A brass musical instrument with a movable U-shaped slide for producing different pitches. —**trom•bon'ist** *n.*

tromp (trŏmp) *v. Informal.* **1.** To tramp. **2.** To trample underfoot. **3.** To trounce.

trompe l'oeil (trômp'loi') *n.* **1.** A style of painting that creates an illusion of photographic reality. **2.** A trompe l'oeil effect.

troop (tro͞op) *n.* **1.** A group or company of people or animals. **2. a.** A group of soldiers. **b. troops.** Military units : soldiers. —*v.* To advance or go as a throng.

troop carrier *n.* A transport aircraft for deploying troops.

troop•er (tro͞o'pər) *n.* **1. a.** A cavalry soldier. **b.** A cavalry horse. **2.** A mounted police officer. **3.** A state police officer.

troop•ship (tro͞op'shĭp') *n.* A ship for transporting troops.

trope (trōp) *n.* Figurative use of a word or expression : figure of speech.

tro•phy (trō'fē) *n., pl.* **-phies.** Something, as a prize or memento won or received as a symbol of achievement or victory.

trop•ic (trŏp'ĭk) *n.* **1.** Either of 2 parallels of latitude that constitute the boundaries of the Torrid Zone. **2. tropics.** The region of the earth's surface lying between these latitudes. —*adj.* Of or pertaining to the tropics : tropical.

trop•i•cal (trŏp'ĭ-kəl) *adj.* **1.** Of, occurring in, or typical of the tropics. **2.** Hot and humid : torrid. —**trop'i•cal•ly** *adv.*

tropic of Cancer *n.* The parallel of latitude 23° 27′ N of the equator and the N boundary of the Torrid Zone.

tropic of Capricorn *n.* The parallel of latitude 23° 27′ S of the equator and the S boundary of the Torrid Zone.

tro•pism (trō'pĭz'əm) *n.* Growth or movement of a plant or animal in response to an external stimulus.

tro•po•sphere (trō'pə-sfîr', trŏp'ə-) *n.* The lowest region of the atmosphere between the earth's surface and the lower stratosphere, marked by decreasing temperature with increasing altitude.

trot (trŏt) *n.* **1.** A gait of a 4-footed animal in which diagonal pairs of legs move forward together. **2.** A gait of a person, faster than a walk : jog. **3.** *Informal.* A literal translation of a text, used esp. by students : pony. —*v.* **trot•ted, trot•ting.** **1.** To go or advance at a trot. **2.** To hurry. —**trot'ter** *n.*

troth (trôth, trŏth, trōth) *n.* **1.** Good faith : fidelity. **2. a.** One's pledged fidelity. **b.** Betrothal. —**troth** *v.*

trou•ba•dour (tro͞o'bə-dôr', -dōr', -do͝or') *n.* **1.** One of a class of 12th- and 13th-cent. lyric poets in Provence, N Italy, and N Spain who composed songs in complex metrical form. **2.** A strolling minstrel.

trou•ble (trŭb'əl) *n.* **1.** Distress, affliction, danger, or need <in *trouble* with the authorities> **2.** A cause or source of distress, affliction, danger, or need. **3.** Pains : exertion <went to a lot of *trouble* to give us a good time> **4.** Pain, disease, or malfunction <heart *trouble*><car *trouble*> —*v.* **-bled, -bling.** **1.** To stir up : agitate. **2.** To afflict with discomfort or pain. **3.** To cause confusion or distress in : perturb. **4.** To inconvenience : bother. **5.** To take pains. **—troub'ler** *n.* **—troub'ling•ly** *adv.*

trou•ble•mak•er (trŭb'əl-mā'kər) *n.* One that makes trouble.

trou•ble-shoot•er (trŭb'əl-sho͞o'tər) *n.* One who pinpoints and gets rid of sources of trouble. **—trou'ble-shoot'** *v.*

trou•ble•some (trŭb'əl-səm) *adj.* **1.** Causing trouble or anxiety. **2.** Difficult to treat, manage, or cope with. ★ ***syns:*** MEAN, PESKY, TRYING, VEXATIOUS, WICKED **—trou'ble•some•ly** *adv.* **—trou'ble•some•ness** *n.*

trough (trôf, trŏf) *n.* **1.** A long, shallow receptacle, esp. one to hold food and water for animals. **2.** A gutter below the eaves of a roof. **3.** A long, narrow depression, as between waves. **4.** A low point in a business cycle or on a statistical graph. **5.** *Meteorol.* An elongated region of low atmospheric pressure, often associated with a front.

trounce (trouns) *v.* **trounced, trounc•ing. 1.** To beat : thrash. **2.** To defeat soundly : whip.

troupe (tro͞op) *n.* A company, esp. of theatrical performers. —*v.* **trouped, troup•ing.** To tour with a company of performers. **—troup'er** *n.*

trou•sers (trou'zərz) *pl.n.* An outer garment for covering the body from the waist to the ankles, with sections that fit each leg separately.

trous•seau (tro͞o'sō', tro͞o-sō') *n., pl.* **-seaux** (-sōz', -sōz') *or* **-seaus.** The wardrobe and household goods, esp. linens, assembled by a bride.

trout (trout) *n., pl.* **trout** *or* **trouts.** A freshwater anadromous food or game fish of the genera *Salvelinus* and *Salmo,* related to the salmon.

trove (trōv) *n.* **1.** Something valuable discovered or found : find. **2.** A collection of usu. valuable objects.

trow (trō) *v. Archaic.* To suppose : think.

trow•el (trou'əl) *n.* **1.** A flat-bladed hand tool for spreading, smoothing, or shaping such substances as cement, plaster, or mortar. **2.** A small scoop-shaped gardening tool. **—trow'el** *v.* **—trow'el•er** *n.*

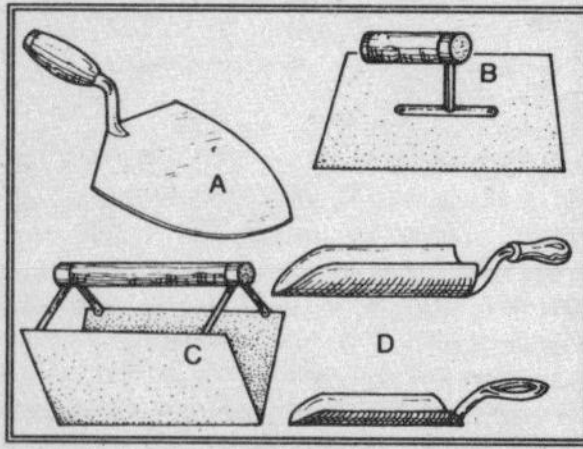

trowel
Four types of trowels: A. brick, B. plaster, C. corner, and D. garden

troy (troi) *adj.* Of, pertaining to, or expressed in troy weight.

troy weight *n.* A system of units of weight in which the pound consists of 12 oz, 240 pennyweights, or 5,760 grains.

tru•ant (tro͞o'ənt) *n.* One who avoids doing work or fulfilling a duty, esp. one who is absent from school without permission. **—tru'an•cy** *n.* **—tru'ant** *adj.*

truce (tro͞os) *n.* A temporary cessation of hostilities by mutual agreement : armistice.

truck[1] (trŭk) *n.* **1.** An automotive vehicle designed to carry heavy loads. **2.** A 2-wheeled barrow with a pair of handles at one end for moving heavy objects by hand. **3.** A swiveling frame with wheels at each end of a railroad car, locomotive, or streetcar, used to support and guide. —*v.* **1.** To drive a truck. **2.** To carry by truck. **—truck'er** *n.*

truck[2] (trŭk) *v.* **1.** To barter : exchange. **2.** To have dealings or commerce : traffic. —*n.* **1.** Garden produce, esp. vegetables, raised for the market. **2.** Barter : exchange. **3.** *Informal.* Dealings. **—truck'load'** *n.*

truck•age (trŭk'ĭj) *n.* **1.** Transport of goods by truck. **2.** The charge for truckage.

truck farm *n.* A farm raising vegetables for the market. **—truck farmer** *n.* **—truck farming** *n.*

truck•ing (trŭk'ing) *n.* TRUCKAGE 1.

truck•le (trŭk'əl) *v.* **-led, -ling.** To yield weakly to another's will : submit.

truc•u•lent (trŭk'yə-lənt) *adj.* **1.** Fierce : savagely cruel. **2.** Belligerent : pugnacious. **—truc'u•lence** *n.* **—truc'u•lent•ly** *adv.*

trudge (trŭj) *v.* **trudged, trudg•ing.** To walk heavily and laboriously : plod. —*n.* A long, wearying walk.

true (tro͞o) *adj.* **tru•er, tru•est. 1.** Consistent with reality or fact <a *true* statement> **2.** Real : genuine. **3.** Loyal : faithful. **4.** Legitimate : rightful <the *true* successor> **5.** Conforming exactly to an orig. pattern or standard. **6.** Rightfully so called. **7.** Determined with reference to the earth's axis, not the magnetic poles <*true* south> ★ ***syns:*** GENUINE, REAL, SINCERE —*adv.* **1.** Truthfully. **2.** Precisely : accurately. **3.** Without deviation from an ancestral type or stock <breed *true*> —*v.* **trued, tru•ing** *or* **true•ing.** To adjust so as to conform with a standard, esp. of accuracy. —*n.* **1.** Truth. **2.** Accurate adjustment or alignment. **—tru'ly** *adv.*

true-blue (tro͞o'blo͞o') *n.* A truly loyal person. **—true'-blue'** *adj.*

true•love (tro͞o'lŭv') *n.* One who is beloved : sweetheart.

truf•fle (trŭf'əl) *n.* **1.** Any of various edible underground fungi, esp. of the genus *Tuber,* esteemed as a delicacy. **2.** A chocolate confection shaped like a ball.

tru•ism (tro͞o'ĭz'əm) *n.* An obvious or self-evident truth.

trump (trŭmp) *n.* **1.** A suit any of whose cards outrank all other cards for the duration of a hand. **2.** A card of a trump. —*v.* To play a trump card. —**trump up.** To concoct, esp. fraudulently : fabricate.

trump•er•y (trŭm′pə-rē) *n.* **1.** Worthless items : junk. **2.** Nonsense.

trum•pet (trŭm′pĭt) *n.* **1.** A brass wind instrument consisting of a long metal tube with a flared bell at one end and a mouthpiece at the other. **2.** Something resembling a trumpet in shape or sound. **3.** A horn-shaped instrument for directing sound into the ear of a partially deaf person. —*v.* **1.** To play a trumpet. **2.** To proclaim loudly. —**trum′pet•er** *n.*

trun•cate (trŭng′kāt′) *v.* **-cat•ed, -cat•ing.** To shorten by or as if by cutting off. —**trun′ca′tion** *n.*

trun•cheon (trŭn′chən) *n.* A club carried by policemen.

trun•dle (trŭnd′l) *v.* **-dled, -dling.** To push or move on wheels : roll.

trundle bed *n.* A low bed, usu. on casters, that can be slid under another bed.

trunk (trŭngk) *n.* **1.** The principal woody stem of a tree. **2.** The body of a human being excluding the limbs and head. **3.** The main section or part of something. **4.** A box or case in which clothes or belongings can be packed, as for storage or travel. **5.** The covered luggage compartment of an automobile. **6.** The long, prehensile snout of an elephant : proboscis. **7. trunks.** Men's shorts worn esp. for athletics.

trunk line *n.* The main line of a communications or transportation system.

truss (trŭs) *n.* **1.** A device worn to keep a hernia in place. **2.** A framework, as of wood or metal, supporting a structure such as a bridge. —*v.* **1.** To tie securely : bind. **2.** To brace or support with a truss.

trust (trŭst) *n.* **1.** Firm reliance in the honesty, dependability, strength, or character of someone or something. **2.** One in which faith or confidence is placed. **3.** Care : custody. **4. a.** Something given into one's care for the benefit or interest of another : charge. **b.** The state and obligation resulting from this. **5.** Reliance on something in the future : hope. **6.** An interest in property that is held by one party for the benefit of another. **7.** A combination of corporations or firms formed esp. for the purpose of reducing competition. **8.** Confidence in a person's willingness and ability to pay : credit. —*v.* **1.** To have or place confidence in : rely. **2.** To be confident : hope. **3.** To assume or expect. **4.** To believe. **5.** To entrust. **6.** To allow to have, use, or care for without misgivings. **7.** To extend financial credit to.

trust company *n.* A commercial bank that manages trusts.

trus•tee (trŭs-tē′) *n.* **1.** A person or agent to whom the property of a beneficiary is legally entrusted. **2.** A member of a board that directs the policies and funds of an institution, as a hospital or college. —**trus•tee′ship′** *n.*

trust•ful (trŭst′fəl) *adj.* Full of trust and confidence. —**trust′ful•ly** *adv.*

trust territory *n.* A colony or territory placed under the administration of a country by commission of the United Nations.

trust•wor•thy (trŭst′wûr′*th*ē) *adj.* Worthy of trust : reliable. —**trust′wor′thi•ly** *adv.* —**trust′wor′thi•ness** *n.*

trust•y (trŭs′tē) *adj.* **-i•er, -i•est.** Reliable : trustworthy. —*n., pl.* **-ies.** A trusted person, esp. a convict held worthy of trust and granted special privileges.

truth (tro͞oth) *n., pl.* **truths** (tro͞o*th*z, tro͞oths). **1.** Accordance with knowledge, fact, or actuality. **2.** The real state of affairs : fact. **3.** Actuality : reality. **4.** A statement that is or is accepted as being true. **5.** The state of being truthful : honesty.

truth•ful (tro͞oth′fəl) *adj.* **1.** Telling or inclined to tell the truth : honest. **2.** Corresponding to fact or reality. —**truth′ful•ly** *adv.* —**truth′ful•ness** *n.*

try (trī) *v.* **tried, try•ing. 1.** To subject to trial or test, as to determine strength or effect. **2. a.** To hear or examine by judicial process. **b.** To ascertain the guilt or innocence of (an accused person) in a court of law. **3.** To subject to hardship, affliction, or strain : tax. **4.** To separate impurities from (fat) by melting : render. **5.** To make an effort to do something : attempt. —**try on.** To put on (e.g., a garment) to test appearance and fit. —*n., pl.* **tries.** An attempt.

try•ing (trī′ĭng) *adj.* Causing severe strain, annoyance, or distress. —**try′ing•ly** *adv.*

try•out (trī′out′) *n.* A test to determine the skills of applicants, as for a role in a play.

tryp•sin (trĭp′sĭn) *n.* One of the enzymes of the pancreatic juice, active in the digestive processes. —**tryp′tic** *adj.*

try square *n.* A ruled metal straightedge set at right angles to a wooden straight piece, used esp. by carpenters to measure and mark square work.

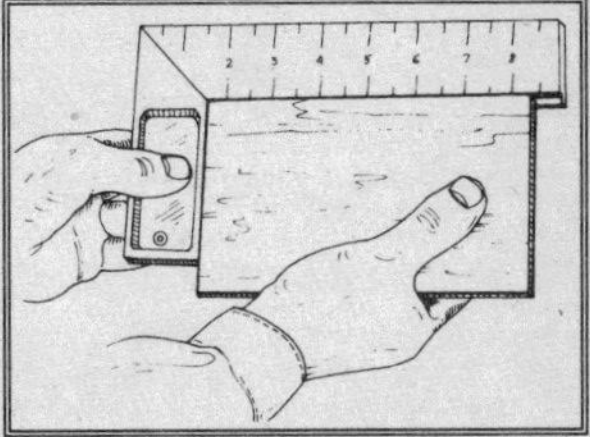

try square

tryst (trĭst) *n.* **1.** An agreement, esp. between lovers, to meet. **2.** A meeting or meeting place for a tryst.

tsar (zär) *n. var. of* CZAR.

tset•se fly (tsĕt′sē, tsē′sē) *n.* An African fly of the genus *Glossina* that often carries and transmits the microorganisms that cause sleeping sickness.

T-shirt *also* **tee shirt** (tē′shûrt′) *n.* A short-sleeved, collarless men's undershirt. **2.** An outer shirt that resembles a T-shirt.

T-square (tē'skwâr') *n.* A ruler with a crosspiece at one end for establishing and drawing parallel lines.

tsu•na•mi (tsŏŏ-nä'mē) *n.* A huge ocean wave caused by an underwater earthquake or volcanic eruption.

tub (tŭb) *n.* **1.** A low, round, flat-bottomed vessel, as one used for washing. **2. a.** A bathtub. **b.** A bath taken in a bathtub.

tu•ba (tōō'bə, tyōō'-) *n.* A large valved brass wind instrument with a bass pitch.

tu•bal (tōō'bəl, tyōō'-) *adj.* Of, relating to, or taking place in a tube, esp. the Fallopian tube <a *tubal* pregnancy>

tu•bal ligation (tōō'bəl, tyōō'-) *n.* A method of female sterilization in which the fallopian tubes are surgically tied.

tu•bate (tōō'bāt', tyōō'-) *ajd.* Forming or having a tube.

tub•by (tŭb'ē) *adj.* **-bi•er, -bi•est.** Short and fat **:** pudgy.

tube (tōōb, tyōōb) *n.* **1.** A hollow cylinder, esp. one that conveys fluids **:** channel. **2.** A small, flexible cylindrical container sealed at one end from which substances such as pigments and toothpaste can be squeezed. **3. a.** An electron tube. **b.** A vacuum tube. **4.** *esp. Brit.* A subway. **5.** An airtight rubber tube inside a tire that holds air under pressure. **6.** *Informal.* Television. **—tubed** *adj.* **—tube'less** *adj.*

tu•ber (tōō'bər, tyōō'-) *n.* A swollen, usu. underground stem, as that of the potato, bearing buds from which new plants arise.

tu•ber•cle (tōō'bər-kəl, tyōō'-) *n.* **1.** A small, knobby protuberance or excrescence, as on a plant or animal. **2.** *Pathol.* **a.** A tubercular lesion. **b.** A nodule or swelling.

tubercle bacillus *n.* A rod-shaped bacterium, *Mycobacterium tuberculosis,* the cause of tuberculosis.

tu•ber•cu•lar (tŏŏ-bûr'kyə-lər, tyŏŏ-) *adj.* **1.** TUBERCULATE 1. **2.** Of, relating to, or afflicted with tuberculosis.

tu•ber•cu•late (tŏŏ-bŭr'kyə-lĭt, tyŏŏ-) *adj.* **1.** Of, pertaining to, or covered with tubercles. **2.** TUBERCULAR 2.

tu•ber•cu•lin (tŏŏ-bûr'kyə-lĭn, tyŏŏ-) *n.* A substance derived from cultures of tubercle bacilli and used in diagnosing and treating tuberculosis.

tu•ber•cu•lo•sis (tŏŏ-bûr'kyə-lō'sĭs, tyŏŏ-) *n.* A communicable disease of humans and animals that is caused by a microorganism and marked by lesions, esp. of the lung. **—tu•ber'cu•lous** *adj.*

tube•rose (tōōb'rōz', tyōōb'-) *n.* A tuberous plant, *Polianthes tuberosa,* native to Mexico, grown for its fragrant flowers.

tu•ber•ous (tōō'bər-əs, tyōō'-) Of, bearing, or being a plant tuber.

tub•ing (tōō'bĭng, tyōō'-) *n.* **1. a.** A system of tubes. **b.** A length of tube. **2.** Fabric in the form of a tube.

tu•bule (tōō'byōōl, tyōō'-) *n.* An extremely small tube.

tu•bu•lar (tōō'byə-lər, tyōō'-) *adj.* Consisting of or having the form of a tube.

tuck (tŭk) *n.* A flattened fold in fabric that is stitched in place to decorate or adjust fit. **—*v.*** **1.** To make tucks in. **2.** To turn under the edge of (e.g., a blanket or shirt) in order to secure. **3.** To cover snugly by tucking in sheets and blankets. **4.** To put in a snug, safe, or concealed place.

tuck•er (tŭk'ər) *v. Informal.* To tire out **:** exhaust.

—tude *suff.* A condition, state, or quality <exact*itude*>

Tues•day (tōōz'dē, tyōōz'-, -dā') *n.* The 3rd day of the week.

tu•fa (tōō'fə, tyōō'-) *n.* Calcareous and siliceous rock deposited by springs, streams, or ground water. **—tu•fa'ceous** *adj.*

tuft (tŭft) *n.* **1.** A small cluster of flexible, elongated strands, as of hair, attached or growing close together. **2.** A clump, esp. of threads fastened at the base and cut off very short, used esp. as decoration. **—*v.*** To decorate or provide with tufts.

tug (tŭg) *v.* **tugged, tug•ging. 1.** To pull and strain vigorously (at). **2.** To move by pulling vigorously. **3.** To tow by tugboat. **—*n.*** **1. a.** A vigorous pull. **b.** A strong pulling force. **2.** A tugboat. **—tug'ger** *n.*

tug•boat (tŭg'bōt') *n.* A powerfully built small boat used for towing larger vessels.

tug of war *n.* **1.** A contest in which 2 teams tug against each other at opposite ends of a rope. **2.** A struggle for supremacy.

tu•grik (tōō'grĭk) *n.* —See table at CURRENCY.

tu•i•tion (tōō-ĭsh'ən, tyōō-) *n.* **1.** A payment or fee for instruction, as at a college. **2.** Teaching **:** instruction.

tu•la•re•mi•a (tōō'lə-rē'mē-ə, tyōō'-) *n.* An infectious bacterial disease transmitted to humans by infected rodents and marked by fever and swelling of the lymph nodes.

tu•lip (tōō'lĭp, tyōō'-) *n.* **1.** Any of various bulb-bearing plants of the genus *Tulipa,* widely grown for their variously colored flowers. **2.** A flower of a tulip.

tulip tree *n.* A tall deciduous tree, *Liriodendron tulipifera,* with large green and orange flowers and yellowish soft wood.

tulle (tōōl) *n.* A fine starched silk, rayon, or nylon net used esp. for veils, gowns, and ballet tutus.

tum•ble (tŭm'bəl) *v.* **-bled, -bling. 1.** To perform acrobatic feats, as rolls, somersaults, and twists. **2.** To roll end over end. **3.** To spill out in confusion, haste, and disorder. **4.** To fall or cause to fall headlong. **5.** To decline, esp. suddenly **:** collapse. **6.** *Slang.* To come suddenly to understand. **—*n.*** **1.** An act of tumbling **:** fall. **2.** A state of disorder or confusion.

tum•ble-down (tŭm'bəl-doun') *adj.* Ramshackle **:** dilapidated.

tum•bler (tŭm'blər) *n.* **1.** A gymnast or acrobat. **2.** A drinking glass with no handle or stem. **3.** The part in a lock that throws the bolt when a key is used.

tum·ble·weed (tŭm′bəl-wēd′) *n.* A plant, esp. of the genus *Amaranthus,* that breaks off from its roots when withered and is rolled about by the wind.

tum·brel *or* **tum·bril** (tŭm′brəl) *n.* **1.** A cart, esp. one that can be tilted to discharge a load. **2.** A crude cart that was used to carry condemned prisoners to a place of execution, as during the French Revolution.

tu·mid (tōō′mĭd, tyōō′-) *adj.* **1.** Distended : swollen. **2.** Overblown, esp. in language : bombastic. **—tu·mid′i·ty** *n.*

tum·my (tŭm′ē) *n., pl.* **-mies.** *Informal.* The abdomen : stomach.

tu·mor (tōō′mər, tyōō′-) *n.* A circumscribed noninflammatory growth arising from existing tissue but growing independently of the normal rate or structural development of such tissue and serving no physiological function. **—tu′mor·ous** *adj.*

tu·mult (tōō′məlt, tyōō′-) *n.* **1.** The turmoil of a crowd with its accompanying din and commotion. **2.** A turbulent uprising : riot. **3.** Agitation of the emotions or mind.

tu·mul·tu·ous (tōō-mŭl′chōō-əs, tyōō-) *adj.* **1.** Marked by or causing tumult. **2.** Confusedly or violently agitated.

tun (tŭn) *n.* A large cask.

tu·na (tōō′nə, tyōō′-) *n., pl.* **-na** *or* **-nas.** An often large marine food fish of the genus *Thunnus* and related genera, commercially important as a source of canned fish.

tun·dra (tŭn′drə) *n.* A treeless area of Arctic regions with a subsoil that is permanently frozen.

tune (tōōn, tyōōn) *n.* **1.** A melody, esp. a simple and easily remembered one. **2.** Correct musical pitch. **3.** Harmony or agreement <in *tune* with modern times> *—v.* **tuned, tun·ing. 1.** To adjust so as to be in correct musical pitch. **2.** To adjust (e.g., an engine) for most efficient performance. **3.** To adjust a radio or television receiver to receive a broadcast. **—tun′a·ble, tune′a·ble** *adj.* **—tun′a·bly** *adv.* **—tun′er** *n.*

tune·ful (tōōn′fəl, tyōōn′-) *adj.* **1.** Musical : melodious. **2.** Producing music. **—tune′ful·ly** *adv.* **—tune′ful·ness** *n.*

tune·less (tōōn′lĭs, tyōōn′-) *adj.* **1.** Not melodious. **2.** Producing no music. **—tune′less·ly** *adv.* **—tune′less·ness** *n.*

tune-up (tōōn′ŭp′, tyōōn′-) *n.* **1.** Adjustment of a motor or engine for maximum efficiency. **2.** An engine warm-up.

tung·sten (tŭng′stən) *n. Symbol* **W** A hard metallic element that is resistant to corrosion and high temperatures.

tu·nic (tōō′nĭk, tyōō′-) *n.* **1.** A loose-fitting garment extending to the knees, worn esp. by the ancient Greeks and Romans. **2.** A usu. hip-length jacket or blouse.

tuning fork *n.* A 2-pronged metal device that makes a sound of fixed pitch when struck that is used as a reference, as in tuning musical instruments.

tun·nel (tŭn′əl) *n.* A passageway under the ground or the water. *—v.* **-neled, -nel·ing** *or* **-nelled, -nel·ling.** To make a tunnel under or through.

tun·ny (tŭn′ē) *n., pl.* **-ny** *or* **-nies.** Tuna.

tur·ban (tûr′bən) *n.* **1.** A headdress that is worn esp. by Muslims and consists of a long scarf wound around the head. **2.** A woman's close-fitting hat like a turban.

tur·bid (tûr′bĭd) *adj.* **1.** Opaque with suspended sediment or foreign particles <a *turbid* lake> **2.** Heavy, dense, or dark, as with smoke. **3.** In turmoil : confused <*turbid* emotions> **—tur′bid·ly** *adv.* **—tur′bid·ness, tur′bid′i·ty** *n.*

tur·bine (tûr′bĭn, -bīn′) *n.* A machine in which the kinetic energy of a moving fluid is converted to mechanical power by the reaction of the fluid with a series of buckets, paddles, or blades fitted around the circumference of a wheel or cylinder.

tur·bo·fan (tûr′bō-făn′) *n.* **1.** A turbojet engine in which a fan supplements the total thrust by forcing air diverted from the main engine directly into the hot turbine exhaust. **2.** An aircraft with a turbofan.

tur·bo·jet (tûr′bō-jĕt′) *n.* **1.** A jet engine having a turbine-driven compressor and developing thrust from the exhaust of hot gases. **2.** An aircraft with a turbojet.

tur·bo·prop (tûr′bō-prŏp′) *n.* **1.** A turbojet engine used to drive an external propeller. **2.** An aircraft equipped with a turboprop.

tur·bot (tûr′bət) *n., pl.* **-bot** *or* **-bots.** A European flatfish, *Psetta maxima,* that is a highly regarded food fish.

tur·bu·lent (tûr′byə-lənt) *adj.* **1.** Marked by violent agitation : disturbed. **2.** Causing disturbance or unrest. **—tur′bu·lence** *n.* **—tur′bu·lent·ly** *adv.*

tu·reen (tōō-rēn′, tyōō-) *n.* A broad deep dish, often with a cover from which foods, as soups or stews, are served.

turf (tûrf) *n.* **1. a.** The surface layer of earth with its dense growth of grass and matted roots. **b.** A piece of turf. **2.** A piece of peat burned as fuel. **3. a.** A racetrack. **b.** The business or sport of horse racing. *—v.* To cover with turf.

tur·gid (tûr′jĭd) *adj.* **1.** Marked by swelling : distended. **2.** Excessively grand in language or style : pompously ornate. **—tur·gid′i·ty, tur′gid·ness** *n.*

Turk (tûrk) *n.* **1.** A native or inhabitant of Turkey. **2.** An Ottoman.

tur·key (tûr′kē) *n., pl.* **-keys. 1.** A large, widely domesticated North American bird, *Meleagris gallopavo,* with a bare head and neck with fleshy wattles. **2.** The flesh of a turkey used as food.

turkey buzzard *n.* A New World vulture, *Cathartes aura,* with dark plumage and a bare red head and neck.

Turk·ish bath (tûr′kĭsh) *n.* A steam bath that is followed by a shower and massage.

Turkish towel *n.* A cotton towel with a thick nap.

tur·mer·ic (tûr′mər-ĭk) *n.* **1.** An Indian plant, *Curcuma longa,* with yellow flowers and an aromatic rootstock. **2.** The powdered rootstock of the turmeric used as a spice and as a yellow dye.

tur•moil (tûr′moil) *n.* A state of great confusion or agitation.

turn (tûrn) *v.* **1. a.** To move or cause to move around a center or axis **:** revolve or rotate <*turned* the doorknob> **b.** To alter or control the functioning of by revolving or rotating. **2.** To shape on a lathe <*turn* a chair leg> **3.** To form or articulate with elegance or distinction <*turn* a phrase> **4. a.** To change or cause to change position so as to show another surface or side. **b.** To change or cause to change position by rotating **:** pivot. **5.** To injure by twisting **:** wrench <*turned* her ankle> **6.** To nauseate or become nauseated **:** upset. **7. a.** To set in a particular course or direction <*turning* his head to face the mirror> **b.** To change one's course or direction. **8.** To make a course around or about <*turn* the corner> **9.** To direct (e.g., the attention) toward or away from something <*turn* your thoughts to your work> **10.** To make or become antagonistic. **11.** To send or drive <*turning* the trespasser off his property> **12.** To transform or become transformed **:** change. **13.** To reach or exceed <has already *turned* 65> **14.** To have recourse **:** resort. **15.** To be contingent **:** hinge. **16.** To change or cause to change color. **17.** To spoil or cause to spoil **:** sour. **18.** To be, seem to be, or become dizzy **:** whirl. **—turn down.** To refuse to accept **:** reject. **—turn in.** 1. To give over to another **:** hand in. 2. *Informal.* To go to bed. **—turn off. 1.** To stop the flow or operation of. 2. *Slang.* To affect with dislike, revulsion, or displeasure. **—turn on. 1.** To start the flow or operation of. 2. *Slang.* **a.** To affect with pleasure or excitement. **b.** To use a drug in order to get high. **—turn out. 1.** To shut off (e.g., a light). **2.** To arrive and assemble. 3. To produce <*turning out* good work> **4.** To come or prove to be in the end **:** result. **—turn over. 1.** To think about **:** ponder. **2.** To transfer to another <*turned over* his paycheck to his mother> **—turn up. 1.** To cause to increase, as in volume. **2.** To find or be found. **3.** To appear **:** arrive. —*n.* **1.** The act of turning around a center or axis **:** revolution or rotation. **2.** A change of direction <a sharp *turn* to the right> **3.** A change, as in a trend or course of events <a *turn* for the worse> **4.** An opportunity to do something, esp. in a particular order <your *turn* to play> **5.** Natural inclination, style, or aptitude <a scientific *turn* of mind> **6.** A deed or action that affects another <a good *turn*> **7.** A short excursion or walk <took a *turn* around the park> **8.** A single twist, as of wire around a spool. **9.** A distinctive fashioning <a pretty *turn* of phrase> **10.** A momentary shock or scare. **—turn′er** *n.*

†turn•a•bout (tûrn′ə-bout′) *n.* **1.** A change and esp. a reversal in direction, opinion, allegiance, or policy. **2.** *Regional.* A dance or party to which girls invite boys.

turn•buck•le (tûrn′bŭk′əl) *n.* A metal coupling, used for tightening a rod or wire rope, having an oblong piece internally threaded at both ends into which a threaded rod is screwed.

turn•coat (tûrn′kōt′) *n.* One, esp. a traitor, who abandons a side or party to which he has given, owes, or professes allegiance.

turning point *n.* A point at which a decisive change takes place.

tur•nip (tûr′nĭp) *n.* A cultivated plant, *Brassica rapa*, with a large edible root.

turn•key (tûrn′kē′) *n.* The person in charge of the keys in a prison **:** jailer.

turn•off (tûrn′ôf′, -ŏf′) *n.* **1.** A place for turning off, esp. a highway exit. **2.** *Slang.* Something distasteful or disgusting.

turn•on (tûrn′ŏn′, -ôn′) *n. Slang.* Something that causes pleasurable excitement.

turn•out (tûrn′out′) *n.* **1.** The number of people present at a gathering **:** attendance. **2.** An outfit of clothing. **3.** A widened section in a highway where vehicles can pass.

turn•o•ver (tûrn′ō′vər) *n.* **1.** The act of turning over **:** upset. **2.** A reversal **:** change. **3.** A filled pastry with half the crust turned over the other half. **4.** The number of times a stock of goods is purchased, sold, and restocked during a given period. **5.** The volume of business transacted during a given period. **6. a.** The number or workers hired within a given period to replace those who have left. **b.** The ratio of this number to the number of workers employed.

turn•pike (tûrn′pīk′) *n.* A highway, esp. a superhighway with tollgates.

turn•stile (tûrn′stīl′) *n.* A device permitting the passage of one person at a time that consists of horizontal arms set into and revolving around a central post.

turn•ta•ble (tûrn′tā′bəl) *n.* A circular rotating platform, as that used for turning a phonograph record or locomotive.

tur•pen•tine (tûr′pən-tīn′) *n.* **1.** A sticky mixture of resin and oil obtained from certain pine trees. **2.** A thin, volatile oil distilled from a turpentine and used esp. as a paint thinner and solvent.

tur•pi•tude (tûr′pə-to͞od′, -tyo͞od′) *n.* Vileness **:** depravity.

tur•quoise (tûr′kwoiz′, -koiz′) *n.* **1.** A bluish-green mineral containing aluminum and copper and valued as a gem. **2.** A light bluish green. **—tur′quoise′** *adj.*

tur•ret (tûr′ĭt) *n.* **1.** A small, usu. ornamental tower on a building. **2.** A tower-shaped, usu. rotating armored structure, as on a warship or tank, on which guns are mounted. **3.** A rotating cylindrical block, as on a lathe, for holding various tools for successive use. **—tur′ret•ed** *adj.*

tur•tle¹ (tûrt′l) *n.* Any of various reptiles of the order Chelonia with the body encased in a carapace into which the head, legs, and tail can be retracted.

tur•tle[2] (tûrt'l) *n. Archaic.* A turtledove.

tur•tle•dove (tûrt'l-dŭv') *n.* A slender European dove, *Streptopelia turtur*, with a soft, purring coo.

tur•tle•neck (tûrt'l-nĕk') *n.* **1.** A high, turned-down collar fitting closely around the neck. **2.** A sweater with a turtleneck.

tusk (tŭsk) *n.* A pointed elongated tooth, as of an elephant or walrus, that projects outside the closed mouth.

tusk•er (tŭs'kər) *n.* An animal, as a wild boar, that has tusks.

tus•sle (tŭs'əl) *v.* **-sled, -sling.** To fight roughly **:** scuffle. **—tus'sle** *n.*

tus•sock (tŭs'ək) *n.* A thick tuft, esp. of grass **:** clump. **—tus'sock•y** *adj.*

tu•te•lage (to͞o'tə-lĭj, tyo͞o'-) *n.* **1.** The function or act of being a guardian **:** guardianship. **2.** Instruction, esp. that provided by a tutor. **3.** The state of being under a guardian or tutor.

tu•te•lar•y (to͞ot'l-ĕr'ē, tyo͞ot'-) *adj.* **1.** Being or serving as a guardian or protector <*tutelary* gods> **2.** Of or pertaining to a guardian or guardianship. **—tu'te•lar'y** *n.*

tu•tor (to͞o'tər, tyo͞o'-) *n.* A person who is responsible for instructing another, esp. one who gives individual or private instruction. —*v.* To act as a tutor (to). **—tu•to'ri•al** (-tôr'ē-əl, -tōr'-) *adj.* **—tu'tor•ship'** *n.*

tut•ti-frut•ti (to͞o'tē-fro͞o'tē) *n.* A confection, esp. ice cream, that contains various chopped candied fruits.

tu•tu (to͞o'to͞o) *n.* A very short projecting ballet skirt of gathered sheer fabric.

tux (tŭks) *n. Informal.* A tuxedo.

tux•e•do (tŭk-sē'dō) *n., pl.* **-dos. 1.** A man's semiformal, usu. black tailless jacket. **2.** A semiformal suit with a tuxedo jacket.

TV (tē-vē') *n.* Television.

twad•dle (twŏd'l) *n.* Trivial, foolish, or idle talk. **—twad'dle** *v.* **—twad'dler** *n.*

twain (twān) *n.* Two.

twang (twăng) *n.* **1.** A sharp, ringing sound like that made by the plucked string of a musical instrument. **2.** Nasal resonance or tone of voice. —*v.* **1.** To emit or cause to emit a twang. **2.** To speak in a nasal twang. **—twang'y** *adj.*

'twas (twŭz). It was.

tweak (twēk) *v.* To pinch sharply and twist. **—tweak** *n.*

tweed (twēd) *n.* **1.** A coarse woolen fabric usu. woven in a twill weave, often in several colors. **2. tweeds.** Clothing, esp. a suit, made of tweed.

tweed•y (twē'dē) *adj.* **-i•er, -i•est. 1.** Made of or resembling tweed. **2.** Wearing or fond of wearing tweeds.

tweet (twēt) *v.* To utter a weak chirping sound. **—tweet** *n.*

tweet•er (twē'tər) *n.* A loudspeaker that reproduces high-pitched sounds.

tweez•ers (twē'zərz) *pl.n.* A small, pincerlike device used for grasping or plucking small things.

Twelfth Night *n.* Jan. 5, the eve of Epiphany.

twelve (twĕlv) *n.* **1.** The cardinal number equal to 11 + 1. **2.** The 12th in a set or sequence. **—twelve** *adj. & pron.* **—twelfth** *n. & adj. & adv.*

twen•ty (twĕn'tē) *n.* The cardinal number equal to 2 × 10. **—twen'ti•eth** *n. & adj. & adv.* **—twen'ty** *adj. & pron.*

twerp *also* **twirp** (twûrp) *n.* A contemptible or unimportant person.

twice (twīs) *adv.* **1.** In 2 cases or on 2 occasions. **2.** In doubled degree or quantity <works *twice* as hard>

twid•dle (twĭd'l) *v.* **-dled, -dling. 1.** To turn around idly or lightly **:** twirl. **2.** To toy idly with something **:** trifle.

twig (twĭg) *n.* A small branch or slender shoot. **—twig'gy** *adj.*

twi•light (twī'līt') *n.* **1.** The soft, diffuse light cast by the sun when it is below the horizon, esp. following sunset. **2.** A period or state of decline.

twill (twĭl) *n.* **1.** A textile weave that produces parallel ribs on the surface of a fabric. **2.** A fabric with a twill. **—twilled** *adj.*

twin (twĭn) *n.* **1.** One of 2 born at a single birth. **2.** One of 2 similar or identical persons or things **:** counterpart. —*adj.* **1.** Being 1 or both of 2 offspring produced at the same birth <a *twin* sister><*twin* boys> **2.** Being 1 of 2 similar or identical persons or things <*twin* houses> **3.** Consisting of 2 similar or identical parts. —*v.* **twinned, twin•ning. 1.** To give birth to twins. **2.** To be paired or coupled.

twine (twīn) *v.* **twined, twin•ing. 1.** To twist together (e.g., threads) **:** intertwine. **2.** To form by twisting. **3.** To coil about **:** wind. **4.** To move in a winding manner. —*n.* A strong thread, string, or cord consisting of 2 or more strands twisted together.

twinge (twĭnj) *n.* **1.** A sudden, sharp pain. **2.** An emotional or mental pang. —*v.* **twinged, twing•ing.** To feel or cause to feel a sudden sharp pain.

twin•kle (twĭng'kəl) *v.* **-kled, -kling. 1.** To shine or cause to shine with a sparkling or intermittent light. **2.** To be bright, as with happiness **:** sparkle. **3.** To wink or blink. —*n.* **1.** An intermittent gleam of light. **2.** A sparkle, as of merriment, in the eye. **3.** A very brief interval **:** twinkling. **—twin'kler** *n.*

twin•kling (twĭng'klĭng) *n.* An instant.

twirl (twûrl) *v.* To rotate or cause to rotate briskly **:** whirl. **—twirl** *n.*

twirp (twûrp) *n. var. of* TWERP.

twist (twĭst) *v.* **1.** To wind (2 or more threads) together to make a single strand. **2.** To coil around something **:** twine. **3. a.** To give a spiral shape to. **b.** To form a spiral shape. **4.** To open or break off by turning. **5.** To wrench and injure <*twisted* his leg> **6.** To change the true form, shape, or meaning of **:** distort. **7.** To move in a winding course. **8.** To revolve or rotate. —*n.* **1.** Something formed by winding or twisting. **2. a.** The act of twisting. **b.** the state of being twisted. **3. a.** A spin or twirl. **b.** A spiral curve or turn. **4.** Torsional strain or stress. **5.** A wrench, as of a joint. **6.** An unexpected development. **7.** A distortion in form or meaning. **8.** A new or unexpected procedure, system, or approach.

twist•er (twĭs'tər) *n.* **1.** One that twists. **2.** A ball thrown or batted with a twist. **3.** *Informal.* **a.** A cyclone. **b.** A tornado.

twit (twĭt) *v.* **twit•ted, twit•ting.** To tease or taunt, esp. about a mistake or fault.

†twitch (twĭch) *v.* **1.** To move, cause to move, or pull with a jerk. **2.** To move spasmodically. —*n.* **1.** An involuntary muscular jerk. **2.** A sudden pull or tug. **3.** *W U.S.* A looped cord used to restrain a horse by tightening it around the upper lip.

twit•ter (twĭt'ər) *v.* **1.** To make a series of chirping sounds. **2.** To chatter, esp. nervously or excitedly. —*n.* **1.** A series of chirping sounds. **2.** Excitement or agitation : flutter. —**twit'ter•y** *adj.*

twixt *also* **'twixt** (twĭkst) *prep. & adv.* Betwixt : between.

two (to͞o) *n.* **1.** The cardinal number equal to 1 + 1. **2.** The 2nd in a set or sequence. **3.** Something with 2 parts, units, or members. —**two** *adj. & pron.*

two-bit (to͞o'bĭt') *adj. Slang.* Cheap or insignificant : trifling.

two bits *pl.n. Informal.* **1.** Twenty-five cents. **2.** A petty sum.

two-by-four (to͞o'bī-fôr', -fōr', to͞o'bə-) *n.* A length of lumber 2 in thick and 4 in wide, or that is slightly smaller after it is dressed.

two-di•men•sion•al (to͞o'dĭ-mĕn'shə-nəl, -dī-) *adj.* **1.** Having only 2 dimensions, esp. length and width. **2.** Lacking depth <a movie with *two-dimensional* characters>

two-faced (to͞o'fāst') *adj.* **1.** Having 2 faces. **2.** Double-dealing or hypocritcal : treacherous. —**two'-fac'ed•ly** *adv.*

two•fold (to͞o'fōld', -fōld') *adj.* **1.** Having 2 parts or units. **2.** Being twice as much or as many : double. —**two'fold'** *adv.*

two-ply (to͞o'plī') *adj.* Consisting of 2 layers, thicknesses, or strands.

two•some (to͞o'səm) *n.* **1.** Two persons or things : pair. **2.** A golf game for 2 players.

two-time (to͞o'tīm') *v. Slang.* To deceive or be unfaithful to. —**two'-tim'er** *n.*

two-way (to͞o'wā') *adj.* Affording movement or permitting communication in 2 directions.

—ty *suff.* Condition : quality <novel*ty*>

ty•coon (tī-ko͞on') *n. Informal.* A businessman of power and wealth : magnate.

tyke (tīk) *n.* **1.** A small child. **2.** A mongrel dog : cur.

tym•pa•ni (tĭm'pə-nē) *n. var. of* TIMPANI.

tym•pan•ic membrane (tĭm-păn'ĭk) *n.* The thin, semitransparent, oval membrane separating the middle and external ear.

tym•pa•num (tĭm'pə-nəm) *n., pl.* **-na** (-nə) *or* **-nums.** **1.** The middle ear. **2.** The tympanic membrane.

type (tīp) *n.* **1. a.** A group, kind, or class sharing common traits or characteristics : category. **b.** An individual having the characteristics of such a group, kind, or class : variety or sort <a tree of the deciduous *type*> **2.** An example : model. **3.** Small blocks, usu. of metal, with raised characters that leave a printed impression when inked and pressed upon paper. **4.** Printed or typewritten letters or characters : print. —*v.* **typed, typ•ing. 1.** To classify or identify according to type. **2.** To typewrite.

type•cast (tīp'kăst') *v.* **1.** To cast (an actor) repeatedly in the same kind of role. **2.** To cast (an actor) in a role requiring characteristics typical of the actor in real life.

type•face (tīp'fās') *n.* A design or style of printing type.

type•script (tīp'skrĭpt') *n.* Typewritten material, as the manuscript of a book.

type•set•ter (tīp'sĕt'ər) *n.* Someone who sets type : compositor. —**type'set'** *v. & adj.* —**type'set'ting** *n.*

type•write (tīp'rīt') *v.* To write with or use a typewriter.

type•writ•er (tīp'rī'tər) *n.* A machine for writing letters and characters by means of manually activated keys that strike the paper through an inked ribbon.

ty•phoid (tī'foid') *n.* An acute, highly infectious bacterial disease transmitted by contaminated water or food marked by high fever and intestinal hemorrhaging. —**ty'phoid'** *adj.*

ty•phoon (tī-fo͞on') *n.* A tropical hurricane in the W Pacific or the China Sea.

ty•phus (tī'fəs) *n.* A severe infectious disease caused by microorganisms of the genus *Rickettsia,* and marked by severe headache, high fever, delirium, and red rash.

typ•i•cal (tĭp'ĭ-kəl) *also* **typ•ic** (-ĭk) *adj.* **1.** Exhibiting the essential traits and characteristics of a kind, class, or group <a *typical* urban community> **2.** Of or relating to a representative specimen : characteristic. **3.** Conforming to or being a type. —**typ'i•cal•ly** *adv.* —**typ'i•cal•ness** *n.*

typ•i•fy (tĭp'ə-fī') *v.* **-fied, -fy•ing. 1.** To be a typical or characteristic example of. **2.** To represent by an image, model, or form. —**typ'i•fi•ca'tion** *n.*

typ•ist (tī'pĭst) *n.* An operator of a typewriter.

ty•po (tī'pō) *n., pl.* **-pos.** *Informal.* An error in setting type or in typewriting.

ty•pog•ra•phy (tī-pŏg'rə-fē) *n.* **1.** The act or art of printing with type. **2.** The arrangement and appearance of printed material. —**ty•pog'ra•pher** *n.* —**ty'po•graph'i•cal** (-pə-grăf'ĭ-kəl), **ty'po•graph'ic** *adj.*

ty•ran•ni•cal (tĭ-răn'ĭ-kəl, tī-) *also* **ty•ran•nic** (-răn'ĭk) *adj.* Of, relating to, or characteristic of a tyrant : despotic. —**ty•ran'ni•cal•ly** *adv.*

tyr•an•nize (tĭr'ə-nīz') *v.* **-nized, -niz•ing. 1.** To rule as a tyrant. **2.** To treat or act as a tyrant might. —**tyr'an•niz'er** *n.*

ty•ran•no•saur (tĭ-răn'ə-sôr', tī-) *n.* A carnivorous dinosaur of the genus *Tyrannosaurus,* with small forelimbs and a large head.

tyr•an•nous (tĭr'ə-nəs) *adj.* Tyrannical.
tyr•an•ny (tĭr'ə-nē) *n., pl.* **-nies. 1.** A government in which the ruler has absolute power. **2.** The unjust or cruel exercise of power. **3.** A tyrannical act. **4.** A state of severity **:** rigor.
ty•rant (tī'rənt) *n.* **1.** An absolute ruler, esp. an unjust, oppressive, or cruel one. **2.** Someone who exercises power, control, or authority unfairly or harshly.
tyre (tīr) *n. esp. Brit. var. of* TIRE[2].
ty•ro *also* **ti•ro** (tī'rō) *n., pl.* **-ros.** A beginner **:** novice.
tzar (zär) *n. var. of* CZAR.

Uu

u *or* **U** (yo͞o) *n., pl.* **u's** *or* **U's. 1.** The 21st letter of the English alphabet. **2.** A speech sound represented by the letter *u*. **3. U.** A grade indicating that a student's work is unsatisfactory. **4.** Something with the shape of the letter U.
U *symbol for* URANIUM.
u•biq•ui•tous (yo͞o-bĭk'wĭ-təs) *adj.* Being or seeming to be present everywhere. **—u•biq'ui•tous•ly** *adv.* **—u•biq'ui•ty** *n.*
U-boat (yo͞o'bōt') *n.* A German submarine.
ud•der (ŭd'ər) *n.* The large pouchlike mammary gland of a cow, ewe, or goat, having 2 or more teats.
UFO (yo͞o'ĕf-ō') *n., pl.* **UFOs** *or* **UFO's.** An unidentified flying object.
u•fol•o•gy (yo͞o-fŏl'ə-jē) *n.* Study of unidentified flying objects. **—u•fol'o•gist** *n.*
ugh (ŭg, ŭk) *interj.* —Used to express horror or disgust.
ug•ly (ŭg'lē) *adj.* **-li•er, -li•est. 1.** Unpleasant to look at. **2.** Offensive <*ugly* gossip> **3.** Deserving censure <an *ugly* crime> **4.** Menacing <an *ugly* sky> **5.** Having or showing a bad temper. ★ ***syns:*** HIDEOUS, UNSIGHTLY **—ug'li•ness** *n.*
uh (ŭ) *interj.* —Used to express hesitation or uncertainty.
uh-huh (ə-hŭ') *interj. Informal.* —Used to express the affirmative.
u•kase (yo͞o-kās', -kāz', yo͞o'kās', -kāz') *n.* An official decree **:** edict.
u•ku•le•le (yo͞o'kə-lā'lē, o͞o'kə-) *n.* A small 4-stringed Hawaiian guitar.
ul•cer (ŭl'sər) *n.* **1.** An often festering lesion in skin or mucous membrane resulting in destruction of the tissue. **2.** Something that corrupts. **—ul'cer•ous** *adj.*
ul•cer•ate (ŭl'sə-rāt') *v.* **-at•ed, -at•ing.** To make or become affected with or as if with an ulcer. **—ul'cer•a'tion** *n.* **—ul'cer•a'tive** (-sə-rā'tĭv, -sər-ə-tĭv) *adj.*
ul•na (ŭl'nə) *n., pl.* **-nae** (-nē') *or* **-nas.** The inner, larger bone of the forearm. **—ul'nar** *adj.*
ul•ster (ŭl'stər) *n.* A long loose overcoat.
ul•te•ri•or (ŭl-tîr'ē-ər) *adj.* **1.** Going beyond what is obvious or admitted **:** concealed. **2.** Lying beyond a particular area or region **:** farther.
ul•ti•mate (ŭl'tə-mĭt) *adj.* **1.** Final **:** conclusive <the *ultimate* defeat> **2.** Most extreme **:** greatest <the *ultimate* crime> **3.** Unable to be further divided or analyzed, as a subatomic particle. **4.** Fundamental **:** basic <*ultimate* truths> **5.** Most remote in time or space. *—n.* Something that is ultimate. **—ul'ti•mate•ly** *adv.*
ul•ti•ma•tum (ŭl'tə-mā'təm, -mä'-) *n., pl.* **-tums** *or* **-ta** (-tə). A final proposal, demand, or offer, as in negotiating.
ul•ti•mo (ŭl'tə-mō') *adv.* In or of the month just past.
ul•tra (ŭl'trə) *adj.* Exceeding the usual, average, etc. **:** extreme. *—n.* One with extreme views, esp. in politics.
ultra– *pref.* **1.** Beyond the range, scope, or limit of <*ultra*microscope> **2.** Beyond the usual degree **:** extreme <*ultra*liberal>
ul•tra•con•ser•va•tive (ŭl'trə-kən-sûr'və-tĭv) *adj.* Conservative to an extreme, esp. in political beliefs **:** reactionary. **—ul'tra•con•ser'va•tism** *n.* **—ul'tra•con•ser'va•tive** *n.*
ul•tra•high (ŭl'trə-hī') *adj.* Exceedingly high.
ultrahigh frequency *n.* A band of radio frequencies from 300 to 3,000 megahertz.
ul•tra•lib•er•al (ŭl'trə-lĭb'ər-əl, -lĭb'rəl) *adj.* Liberal to an extreme, esp. in political beliefs **:** radical. **—ul'tra•lib'er•al** *n.* **—ul'tra•lib'er•al•ism** *n.*
ul•tra•ma•rine (ŭl'trə-mə-rēn') *n.* **1.** A blue pigment made esp. from powdered lapis lazuli. **2.** A bright deep blue. *—adj.* **1.** Having a bright deep-blue color. **2.** Of or located beyond the sea.
ul•tra•mi•cro•scope (ŭl'trə-mī'krə-skōp') *n.* A microscope that uses high-intensity light for the study of very minute particles. **—ul'tra•mi•cros'co•py** (-krŏs'kə-pē) *n.*
ul•tra•mi•cro•scop•ic (ŭl'trə-mī'krə-skŏp'ĭk) *adj.* **1.** So small as to be invisible with an ordinary microscope. **2.** Of or pertaining to an ultramicroscope.
ul•tra•mod•ern (ŭl'trə-mŏd'ərn) *adj.* Extremely modern or advanced in ideas or style. **—ul'tra•mod'ern•is'tic** *adj.*
ul•tra•mon•tane (ŭl'trə-mŏn'tān', -mŏn-tān') *adj.* Of or relating to peoples or countries beyond the mountains, esp. the Alps. **—ul'tra•mon'tane'** *n.*
ul•tra•son•ic (ŭl'trə-sŏn'ĭk) *adj.* Relating to, consisting of, or using sound frequencies inaudible to humans, above approx. 20,000 hertz.

ul•tra•son•ics (ŭl′trə-sŏn′ĭks) *n. (sing. in number).* The scientific study and practical application of ultrasonic sound.
ul•tra•so•nog•ra•phy (ŭl′trə-sə-nŏg′rə-fē) *n.* Diagnostic use of ultrasonic waves to visualize internal body structures. **—ul′tra•son′o•graph′ic** (-sŏn′ə-grăf′ĭk, -sō′nə-) *adj.*
ul•tra•sound (ŭl′trə-sound′) *n.* Ultrasonic sound.
ul•tra•vi•o•let (ŭl′trə-vī′ə-lĭt) *adj.* Of, producing, or using radiation with wavelengths just shorter than those of visible light and just longer than those of x-rays. **—ul′tra•vi′o•let** *n.*
ul•u•late (ŭl′yə-lāt′) *v.* **-lat•ed, -lat•ing.** To wail or howl loudly. **—ul′u•la′tion** *n.*
um•bel (ŭm′bəl) *n. Bot.* A rounded or flat-topped flower cluster in which the individual flower stalks radiate from approx. the same point on the main stem, as in carrots and parsley. **—um′bel•late′** *adj.*
um•ber (ŭm′bər) *n.* **1.** A natural brown earth containing chiefly iron and manganese oxides and used as pigment. **2.** A dark reddish brown. **—um′ber** *adj.*
um•bil•i•cal (ŭm-bĭl′ĭ-kəl) *adj.* Of, relating to, or near the umbilical cord or navel. *—n.* An umbilical cord.
umbilical cord *n.* **1.** The cordlike structure by which the fetus is joined at the navel to the placenta and which nourishes the fetus and removes its wastes. **2.** A line attached to a spacecraft that supplies an astronaut working outside the vehicle with air and usu. a means of communication.
um•bil•i•cus (ŭm-bĭl′ĭ-kəs, ŭm′bə-lī′kəs) *n., pl.* **-ci** (-sī′). The navel.
um•bra (ŭm′brə) *n., pl.* **-brae** (-brē). **1.** A dark area, esp. the darkest part of a shadow. **2.** The shadow thrown by the moon on a part of the earth during a total solar eclipse.
um•brage (ŭm′brĭj) *n.* **1.** A feeling of resentment or offense <took *umbrage* at the slight> **2.** *Archaic.* Shadow, shade, or a source of shade.
um•brel•la (ŭm-brĕl′ə) *n.* **1.** A collapsible covering mounted on a handle that is used for protection from the rain or sun. **2.** Something that covers or protects. **3.** Something that encompasses many different elements or groups.
umbrella bird *n.* A tropical American bird, *Cephalopterus ornatus,* having a retractile crest and a long feathered wattle.

umbrella bird

u•mi•ak (ōō′mē-ăk′) *n.* An open Eskimo boat made of wood and covered with skins.
um•laut (ŏŏm′lout′) *n.* **1.** A vowel changed in sound by partial assimilation to a vowel in the next syllable. **2.** The diacritical mark (¨) placed esp. over a German vowel to indicate an umlaut.
um•pire (ŭm′pīr′) *n.* **1.** One who rules on plays, as in baseball. **2.** One empowered to settle a dispute. **—um′pire′** *v.*
ump•teen (ŭmp-tēn′, ŭm-) *adj. Informal.* Of an indefinitely large number. **—ump•teenth′** *adj.*
un–[1] *pref.* Not or opposite <*un*pleasant>
un–[2] *pref.* **1.** Reversal or cancellation of an action <*un*do> **2.** Release or removal from <*un*fetter>
un•a•ble (ŭn-ā′bəl) *adj.* **1.** Not able. **2.** Lacking mental capability.
un•ac•com•pa•nied (ŭn′ə-kŭm′pə-nēd) *adj.* **1.** Being without a companion **:** alone. **2.** *Mus.* Having no accompaniment **:** solo.
un•ac•count•a•ble (ŭn′ə-koun′tə-bəl) *adj.* **1.** Incapable of being explained. **2.** Not to be held responsible. **—un′ac•count′a•bil′i•ty** *n.* **—un′ac•count′a•bly** *adv.*
un•ac•count•ed (ŭn′ə-koun′tĭd) *adj.* Not explained or understood <The mistake was *unaccounted* for.>
un•ac•cus•tomed (ŭn′ə-kŭs′təmd) *adj.* **1.** Not customary or usual <*unaccustomed* boldness> **2.** Not habituated or used to <*unaccustomed* to hardship>
un•a•dul•ter•at•ed (ŭn′ə-dŭl′tə-rā′tĭd) *adj.* Free from extraneous elements **:** pure.
un•ad•vised (ŭn′əd-vīzd′) *adj.* **1.** Not informed or counseled. **2.** Not prudent **:** rash. **—un′ad•vis′ed•ly** *adv.*
un•af•fect•ed (ŭn′ə-fĕk′tĭd) *adj.* **1.** Not affected. **2.** Free from affectation. **—un′af•fect′•ed•ness** *n.*
un•al•loyed (ŭn′ə-loid′) *adj.* **1.** Not alloyed, as a metal **:** pure. **2.** Unqualified **:** absolute <an *unalloyed* success>
un-A•mer•i•can (ŭn′ə-mĕr′ĭ-kən) *adj.* Considered contrary to the institutions or principles of the U.S.
u•nan•i•mous (yōō-năn′ə-məs) *adj.* **1.** Being in complete agreement. **2.** Based on the assent or agreement of all. **—u′na•nim′i•ty** (yōō′nə-nĭm′ĭ-tē) *n.* **—u•nan′i•mous•ly** *adv.*
un•ap•proach•a•ble (ŭn′ə-prō′chə-bəl) *adj.* **1.** Not friendly. **2.** Not able to be reached. **3.** Without equal **:** unrivaled.
un•armed (ŭn-ärmd′) *adj.* Lacking means of defense, as weapons.
un•as•sail•a•ble (ŭn′ə-sā′lə-bəl) *adj.* **1.** Not open to doubt **:** undeniable. **2.** Not open to attack **:** impregnable. **—un′as•sail′a•bil′i•ty** *n.* **—un′as•sail′a•bly** *adv.*
un•as•sist•ed (ŭn′ə-sĭs′tĭd) *adj.* **1.** Not assisted. **2.** *Sports.* Designating a play handled without an assist.
un•as•sum•ing (ŭn′ə-sōō′mĭng) *adj.* Modest **:** reserved.

un•at•tached (ŭn′ə-tăcht′) *adj.* **1.** Not attached. **2.** Not married or engaged.

un•a•vail•ing (ŭn′ə-vā′lĭng) *adj.* Unsuccessful : futile. —**un′a•vail′ing•ly** *adv.*

un•a•void•a•ble (ŭn′ə-voi′də-bəl) *adj.* Certain to occur : inevitable. —**un′a•void′a•bil′i•ty** *n.* —**un′a•void′a•bly** *adv.*

un•a•ware (ŭn′ə-wâr′) *adj.* Not consciously aware. —*adv.* Unawares.

un•a•wares (ŭn′ə-wârz′) *adv.* **1.** Without warning : by surprise. **2.** Without forethought : unprepared.

un•bal•anced (ŭn-băl′ənst) *adj.* **1.** Not in proper balance. **2. a.** Mentally deranged. **b.** Not of sound judgment. **3.** Not adjusted so that credits are equal to debits.

un•bar (ŭn-bär′) *v.* To open.

un•bear•a•ble (ŭn-bâr′ə-bəl) *adj.* Not endurable : intolerable. —**un•bear′a•bly** *adv.*

un•beat•a•ble (ŭn-bē′tə-bəl) *adj.* Impossible to defeat or outdo.

un•beat•en (ŭn-bēt′n) *adj.* **1.** Never beaten. **2.** Not walked or trampled on. **3.** Not pounded or whipped.

un•be•com•ing (ŭn-bĭ-kŭm′ĭng) *adj.* **1.** Not pleasing : unattractive. **2.** Not proper : indecorous. —**un•be•com′ing•ly** *adv.*

un•be•known (ŭn′bĭ-nōn′) *or* **un•be•knownst** (-nōnst′) *adj.* Without one's knowledge : not known.

un•be•lief (ŭn′bĭ-lēf′) *n.* Lack of belief, esp. religious belief. —**un′be•liev′er** *n.* —**un′be•liev′ing** *adj.*

un•be•liev•a•ble (ŭn′bĭ-lē′və-bəl) *adj.* Not to be believed : incredible. —**un′be•liev′a•bly** *adv.*

un•bend (ŭn-bĕnd′) *v.* **1.** To make or become straight : straighten. **2.** To make or become relaxed : unwind.

un•bend•ing (ŭn-bĕn′dĭng) *adj.* Inflexible : unyielding.

un•bid•den (ŭn-bĭd′n) *also* **un•bid** (-bĭd′) *adj.* Not asked or invited.

un•bind (ŭn-bīnd′) *v.* **1.** To untie. **2.** To set free.

un•blink•ing (ŭn-blĭng′kĭng) *adj.* **1.** Not blinking. **2.** Showing little emotion. **3.** Willing to face reality.

un•blush•ing (ŭn-blŭsh′ĭng) *adj.* **1.** Lacking remorse : shameless. **2.** Not becoming red-faced. —**un•blush′ing•ly** *adv.*

un•bolt (ŭn-bōlt′) *v.* To remove the bolts from : unlock.

un•born (ŭn-bôrn′) *adj.* **1.** Not yet born. **2.** Not yet in existence.

un•bos•om (ŭn-bo͝oz′əm, -bo͞o′zəm) *v.* **1.** To reveal : divulge. **2.** To divulge the thoughts or feelings of (oneself).

un•bound•ed (ŭn-boun′dĭd) *adj.* Having no bounds or limits : unrestrained.

un•bowed (ŭn-boud′) *adj.* **1.** Not bowed or bent. **2.** Not subdued : unyielding.

un•bri•dled (ŭn-brīd′ld) *adj.* **1.** Not wearing a bridle. **2.** Unbounded : unrestrained.

un•bro•ken (ŭn-brō′kən) *adj.* **1.** Not broken : whole. **2.** Not breached or violated. **3.** Continuing without interruption. **4.** Not tamed or subdued.

un•bur•den (ŭn-bûr′dn) *v.* **1.** To free from a burden. **2.** To free (oneself) from fears or cares.

un•but•ton (ŭn-bŭt′n) *v.* **1.** To undo the buttons (of). **2.** To open by or as if by undoing buttons. **3.** To relax : unbend.

un•called-for (ŭn-kôld′fôr′) *adj.* **1.** Not requested. **2.** Unwarranted : gratuitous.

un•can•ny (ŭn-kăn′ē) *adj.* **-ni•er, -ni•est. 1.** Mysterious : strange. **2.** Seemingly supernatural or superhuman. —**un•can′ni•ly** *adv.* —**un•can′ni•ness** *n.*

un•ceas•ing (ŭn-sē′sĭng) *adj.* Never ceasing : incessant. —**un•ceas′ing•ly** *adv.*

un•cer•e•mo•ni•ous (ŭn-sĕr′ə-mō′nē-əs) *adj.* **1.** Marked by informality. **2.** Rudely abrupt. —**un•cer′e•mo′ni•ous•ly** *adv.* —**un•cer′e•mo′ni•ous•ness** *n.*

un•cer•tain (ŭn-sûr′tn) *adj.* **1.** Not sure : doubtful. **2.** Not capable of being known in advance. **3.** Not yet determined or settled. **4.** Likely to change : variable. —**un•cer′tain•ly** *adv.* —**un•cer′tain•ty** *n.*

un•char•i•ta•ble (ŭn-chăr′ĭ-tə-bəl) *adj.* Judging others too harshly. —**un•char′i•ta•ble•ness** *n.* —**un•char′i•ta•bly** *adv.*

un•chart•ed (ŭn-chär′tĭd) *adj.* **1.** Not charted on a map or plan : unexplored. **2.** Not known : unfamiliar.

un•chaste (ŭn-chāst′) *adj.* Not chaste : morally impure. —**un•chaste′ly** *adv.*

un•chris•tian (ŭn-krĭs′chən) *adj.* **1.** Not of the Christian religion. **2.** Contrary to the Christian spirit.

un•cial (ŭn′shəl, -shē-əl) *adj.* Of or relating to a script with rounded capital letters found esp. in Greek and Latin manuscripts of the 4th to the 8th cent. —**un′cial** *n.*

uncial

un•cir•cum•cised (ŭn-sûr′kəm-sīzd′) *adj.* **1.** Not circumcised. **2.** Heathen.

un•civ•il (ŭn-sĭv′əl) *adj.* **1.** Not civilized. **2.** Discourteous : rude.

un•civ•i•lized (ŭn-sĭv′ə-līzd′) *adj.* Not civilized : barbarous.

un•clad (ŭn-klăd′) *adj.* Naked.

un•clasp (ŭn-klăsp′) *v.* **1.** To loosen the clasp of. **2.** To release from a clasp or hold.

un•cle (ŭng′kəl) *n.* **1.** The brother of one's father or mother. **2.** The spouse of one's aunt. —*interj. Slang.* —Used to indicate capitulation, as in a fight.

un•clean (ŭn-klēn′) *adj.* **1.** Not clean : dirty or foul. **2.** Immoral : unchaste. **3.** Ceremonially or religiously unfit.

un•clean•ly (ŭn-klĕn′lē) *adj.* **-li•er, -li•est.** Habitually unclean in mind or body. **—un•clean′li•ness** *n.*

Uncle Sam (săm) *n.* A figure of a tall thin white-bearded man that symbolizes the U.S. or the U.S. government.

Uncle Tom (tŏm) *n.* A black man regarded as being unduly deferential or subservient to whites. **—Uncle Tom′ism** *n.*

un•cloak (ŭn-klōk′) *v.* **1.** To remove a cloak or covering from. **2.** To reveal.

un•close (ŭn-klōz′) *v.* **1.** To open. **2.** To disclose.

un•clothe (ŭn-klō*th*′) *v.* To undress or uncover.

un•com•fort•a•ble (ŭn-kŭm′fər-tə-bəl, -kŭmf′-tə-bəl) *adj.* **1.** Feeling mental or physical discomfort. **2.** Causing discomfort : troubling. **—un•com′fort•a•bly** *adv.*

un•com•mit•ted (ŭn′kə-mĭt′ĭd) *adj.* Not committed to or involved in a particular cause or course of action.

un•com•mon (ŭn-kŏm′ən) *adj.* **1.** Not commonly found. **2.** Surpassing the usual. ★ ***syns:*** EXCEPTIONAL, EXTRAORDINARY, RARE, REMARKABLE, SINGULAR, UNUSUAL **—un•com′mon•ly** *adv.*

un•com•mu•ni•ca•tive (ŭn′kə-myōō′nĭ-kā′tĭv, -kə-tĭv) *adj.* Not inclined or willing to talk : taciturn.

un•com•pro•mis•ing (ŭn-kŏm′prə-mī′zĭng) *adj.* Unwilling to compromise.

un•con•cern (ŭn′kən-sûrn′) *n.* **1.** Lack of interest : indifference. **2.** Freedom from anxiety or concern.

un•con•cerned (ŭn′kən-sûrnd′) *adj.* **1.** Indifferent. **2.** Free from anxiety or concern. **—un′con•cern′ed•ly** *adv.*

un•con•di•tion•al (ŭn′kən-dĭsh′ə-nəl) *adj.* Not subject to limitations or reservations. **—un′con•di′tion•al•ly** *adv.*

un•con•di•tioned (ŭn′kən-dĭsh′ənd) *adj.* **1.** Unconditional. **2.** *Psychol.* Not acquired by learning or conditioning <an *unconditioned* response>

un•con•quer•a•ble (ŭn-kŏng′kər-ə-bəl) *adj.* Incapable of being conquered or defeated : indomitable.

un•con•scion•a•ble (ŭn-kŏn′shə-nə-bəl) *adj.* **1.** Not guided or restrained by conscience : unscrupulous. **2.** Exceeding reasonable limits : excessive. **—un•con′scion•a•bly** *adv.*

un•con•scious (ŭn-kŏn′shəs) *adj.* **1.** Not available to or observable by the conscious mind <*unconscious* feelings> **2.** Temporarily lacking conscious awareness, as in sleep or a coma. **3.** Not consciously realized or controlled : involuntary. *—n.* The part of the mind inaccessible to conscious awareness or control. **—un•con′scious•ly** *adv.* **—un•con′scious•ness** *n.*

un•con•sti•tu•tion•al (ŭn′kŏn-stĭ-tōō′shə-nəl, -tyōō′-) *adj.* Incompatible with the constitution of a country or organized group. **—un′con•sti•tu′tion•al′i•ty** *n.* **—un′con•sti•tu′tion•al•ly** *adv.*

un•con•trol•la•ble (ŭn′kən-trō′lə-bəl) *adj.* Incapable of being controlled or restrained. **—un′con•trol′la•bly** *adv.*

un•con•ven•tion•al (ŭn′kən-vĕn′shə-nəl) *adj.* Not conforming to convention : unusual. **—un′con•ven′tion•al′i•ty** *n.* **—un′con•ven′tion•al•ly** *adv.*

un•cork (ŭn-kôrk′) *v.* **1.** To pull the cork from. **2.** To free from a sealed or confined condition.

un•cou•ple (ŭn-kŭp′əl) *v.* To disconnect (e.g., railroad cars). **—un•cou′pler** *n.*

un•couth (ŭn-kōōth′) *adj.* **1.** Speaking or acting crudely : unrefined. **2.** Awkward or clumsy : ungainly. **—un•couth′ly** *adv.* **—un•couth′ness** *n.*

un•cov•er (ŭn-kŭv′ər) *v.* **1.** To take the cover from. **2.** To lay bare : disclose. **3.** To remove the hat from in courtesy or respect.

un•cross (ŭn-krôs′, -krŏs′) *v.* To change the crossed position of (e.g., one's legs).

unc•tion (ŭngk′shən) *n.* **1.** The act of anointing, as in a consecration ceremony or ritual of healing. **2.** An ointment, salve, or oil used for anointing. **3.** Something soothing or restorative : balm. **4.** Exaggerated sincerity and desire to please.

unc•tu•ous (ŭngk′chōō-əs) *adj.* **1.** Full of oil or grease. **2.** Unduly ingratiating <an *unctuous* manner> **—unc′tu•ous•ly** *adv.* **—unc′tu•ous•ness** *n.*

un•cut (ŭn-kŭt′) *adj.* **1.** Not sliced, carved, etc. **2.** Not shortened or abridged. **3.** Not shaped or polished, as a gemstone. **4.** Not slit or trimmed, as book pages.

un•daunt•ed (ŭn-dôn′tĭd, -dän′-) *adj.* Not discouraged : resolute. **—un•daunt′a•ble** *adj.* **—un•daunt′ed•ly** *adv.*

un•de•ceive (ŭn′dĭ-sēv′) *v.* To free from illusion or misconception.

un•de•cid•ed (ŭn′dĭ-sī′dĭd) *adj.* **1.** Not yet determined : unsettled. **2.** Having arrived at no decision : irresolute.

un•de•mon•stra•tive (ŭn′dĭ-mŏn′strə-tĭv) *adj.* Not inclined to show one's feelings : reserved. **—un′de•mon′stra•tive•ly** *adv.* **—un′de•mon′stra•tive•ness** *n.*

un•de•ni•a•ble (ŭn′dĭ-nī′ə-bəl) *adj.* **1.** Not open to denial or doubt. **2.** Indisputably good or authentic. **—un′de•ni′a•bly** *adv.*

un•der (ŭn′dər) *prep.* **1. a.** Lower than : below <*under* the house> **b.** So as to be covered or concealed by <*under* my coat> **2.** Below the surface of <*under* the ice> **3.** Assuming the disguise of <*under* a pen name> **4.** Less, smaller, or lower than <paid *under* $50 for it> **5.** Less or lower than the requisite amount or degree of <*under* legal age> **6.** Lower in rank or status than. **7.** Subject to the authority or control of <worked *under* the governor> **8.** Acted on or affected by <*under* great stress> **9.** Bound or obligated by <*under* oath> **10.** Within the designation or grouping of <filed *under* expenses> **11.** Subject to : undergoing <*under* dispute>

12. On account of <*under* the circumstances> —*adv.* **1.** In or into a place lower than or covered by something. **2. a.** Into a state of submission, inferiority, or defeat. **b.** Into an unconscious state. **3.** So as to be covered or submerged. **4.** Lower than a given quantity or level. —*adj.* **1.** Located lower than or beneath something else <the *under* lip> **2.** Subordinate in rank or importance. **3.** Lower or less in amount, caliber, or degree.

under– *pref.* **1.** Location below or beneath <*under*water> **2.** Subordination in rank or importance <*under*graduate> **3.** Degree, rate, or quantity that is lower or less than normal <*under*privileged>

un•der•a•chieve (ŭn′dər-ə-chēv′) *v.* To fail to perform at an expected level of ability, esp. in school. **—un′der•a•chiev′er** *n.*

un•der•age (ŭn′dər-āj′) *adj.* Not having reached the customary or legal age.

un•der•arm (ŭn′dər-ärm′) *adj.* **1. a.** Located or placed under the arm. **b.** Used in the armpit <*underarm* deodorant> **2.** Underhand <an *underarm* pitch> —*adv.* With an underarm movement. —*n.* The hollow under the arm **:** armpit.

un•der•bel•ly (ŭn′dər-bĕl′ē) *n.* **1.** The underside of an animal's body. **2.** A vulnerable area or part.

un•der•bid (ŭn′dər-bĭd′) *v.* **1.** To bid lower than (a competitor). **2.** To bid too low, as in bridge. **—un′der•bid′** *n.* **—un′der•bid′der** *n.*

un•der•brush (ŭn′dər-brŭsh′) *n.* Small trees, shrubs, etc., growing thickly beneath taller trees.

un•der•car•riage (ŭn′dər-kăr′ĭj) *n.* **1.** A supporting framework or structure, as of a motor vehicle. **2.** The landing mechanism of an aircraft.

un•der•charge (ŭn′dər-chärj′) *v.* To charge (someone) an insufficient amount. **—un′der•charge′** *n.*

un•der•class•man (ŭn′dər-klăs′mən) *n.* A freshman or sophomore at a secondary school or college.

un•der•clothes (ŭn′dər-klōz′, -klō*thz*′) *pl.n.* Underwear.

un•der•cloth•ing (ŭn′der-klō′*th*ĭng) *n.* Underclothes.

un•der•coat (ŭn′dər-kōt′) *n.* **1.** A coat worn beneath another. **2.** A growth of short hair, fur, or feathers partly covered by a longer outer growth. **3. a.** *also* **un•der•coat•ing** (-kō′tĭng). A coat of paint or sealing material applied before a final coat or finish. **b.** A tarlike rust-preventive substance sprayed on the underside of a motor vehicle. —*v.* To apply an undercoat to.

un•der•cov•er (ŭn′dər-kŭv′ər) *adj.* Acting or carried on in secret.

un•der•cur•rent (ŭn′dər-kûr′ənt, -kŭr′-) *n.* **1.** A current, as of water or air, flowing beneath another current or surface. **2.** An underlying tendency or force.

un•der•cut (ŭn′dər-kŭt′) *v.* **1.** To cut into an underlying part. **2.** To undersell or work for less money than. **3.** To hamper or weaken the effectiveness of. **4. a.** To strike (a golf ball or baseball) downward and forward so as to impart backspin. **b.** To cut or slice (e.g., a tennis ball) with an underarm stroke. **—un′der•cut′** *n.*

un•der•de•vel•oped (ŭn′dər-dĭ-vĕl′əpt) *adj.* **1.** Not developed in a full or normal way. **2.** Delayed in economic and industrial development.

un•der•dog (ŭn′dər-dôg′, -dŏg′) *n.* **1.** A loser or expected loser in a contest or struggle. **2.** One in a disadvantageous position.

un•der•done (ŭn′dər-dŭn′) *adj.* Not sufficiently cooked.

un•der•dressed (ŭn′dər-drĕst′) *adj.* **1.** Dressed too informally. **2.** Not wearing enough warm or protective clothing.

un•der•em•ployed (ŭn′dər-ĕm-ploid′) *adj.* Employed at a low-paying job for which one is overqualified. **—un′der•em•ploy′ment** *n.*

un•der•es•ti•mate (ŭn′dər-ĕs′tə-māt′) *v.* To make too low an estimate of. **—un′der•es′ti•ma′tion** *n.*

un•der•ex•pose (ŭn′dər-ĭk-spōz′) *v.* To expose (film) to light for too short a time to produce normal image contrast. **—un′der•ex•po′sure** *n.*

un•der•foot (ŭn′dər-fo͝ot′) *adv.* **1.** Underneath the feet. **2.** In the way.

un•der•gar•ment (ŭn′dər-gär′mənt) *n.* A garment worn under others.

un•der•go (ŭn′dər-gō′) *v.* **1.** To be subjected to. **2.** To suffer through **:** endure.

un•der•grad•u•ate (ŭn′dər-grăj′o͞o-ĭt) *n.* A college or university student who is studying for a bachelor's degree.

un•der•ground (ŭn′dər-ground′) *adj.* **1.** Below the earth's surface. **2.** Acting or conducted in secret. **3.** Of or relating to an avant-garde movement or its films, publications, etc. —*n.* **1.** A secret political organization, esp. one seeking to overthrow a government. **2.** *esp. Brit.* An underground railway **:** subway. **3.** An avant-garde or nonestablishment movement or group. —*adv.* (ŭn′dər-ground′). **1.** Below the ground. **2.** In secret **:** clandestinely.

un•der•growth (ŭn′dər-grōth′) *n.* Low-growing underbrush esp. in a forest.

un•der•hand (ŭn′dər-hănd′) *adj.* **1.** Done secretly and deceitfully. **2.** Done with the hand kept below shoulder level <an *underhand* pitch> —*adv.* **1.** With an underhand action. **2.** In an underhand way.

un•der•hand•ed (ŭn′dər-hăn′dĭd) *adj. & adv.* Underhand. **—un′der•hand′ed•ly** *adv.* **—un′der•hand′ed•ness** *n.*

un•der•lie (ŭn′dər-lī′) *v.* **1.** To be situated under or below. **2.** To be the basis for.

un•der•line (ŭn′dər-līn′, ŭn′dər-līn′) *v.* **1.** To draw a line under. **2.** To place emphasis on. **—un′der•line′** *n.*

un•der•ling (ŭn′dər-lĭng) *n.* One in a subordinate position.

un•der•ly•ing (ŭn′dər-lī′ĭng) *adj.* **1.** Located under or below. **2.** Fundamental <*underlying* truths> **3.** Implicit <an *underlying* meaning>

un•der•mine (ŭn′dər-mīn′) *v.* **1.** To excavate a mine or tunnel underneath. **2.** To weaken or impair gradually.

un•der•most (ŭn′dər-mōst′) *adj.* & *adv.* Lowest in position, rank, or place.

un•der•neath (ŭn′dər-nēth′) *adv.* **1.** In a place below or beneath. **2.** On the underside or lower side. —*prep.* **1.** Below : beneath. **2.** Under the controlling authority of. —*n.* The underside.

un•der•nour•ished (ŭn′dər-nûr′ĭsht) *adj.* Lacking sufficient nourishment for proper health and growth. —**un′der•nour′ish•ment** *n.*

un•der•pants (ŭn′dər-pănts′) *pl.n.* Pants or shorts worn under outer clothing.

un•der•pass (ŭn′dər-păs′) *n.* A part of a road that passes underneath another road or a railroad.

un•der•pay (ŭn′dər-pā′) *v.* To pay less than is required or deserved.

un•der•pin•ning (ŭn′dər-pĭn′ĭng) *n.* **1.** Material or masonry used to support a structure. **2.** *often* **underpinnings. a.** A support or foundation. **b.** *Informal.* The legs. —**un′der•pin′** *v.*

un•der•play (ŭn′dər-plā′, ŭn′dər-plā′) *v.* **1.** To play down. **2.** To play (a role) in a restrained way.

un•der•priv•i•leged (ŭn′dər-prĭv′ə-lĭjd) *adj.* Socially or economically disadvantaged <*underprivileged* children>

un•der•pro•duc•tion (ŭn′dər-prə-dŭk′shən) *n.* Production of less than the usual quantity or below demand.

un•der•rate (ŭn′dər-rāt′) *v.* To rate too low : underestimate.

un•der•score (ŭn′dər-skôr′, -skōr′) *v.* **1.** To draw a line under. **2.** To emphasize. —**un′der•score′** *n.*

un•der•sea (ŭn′dər-sē′) *adj.* & *adv.* Under the surface of the sea. —**un′der•seas′** *adv.*

un•der•sec•re•tar•y (ŭn′dər-sĕk′rĭ-tĕr′ē) *n.* An official immediately subordinate, esp. to a cabinet member.

un•der•sell (ŭn′dər-sĕl′) *v.* To sell for less money than (a competitor).

un•der•shirt (ŭn′dər-shûrt′) *n.* A shirtlike undergarment.

un•der•shoot (ŭn′dər-sho͞ot′) *v.* **1.** To shoot or land short of (a target). **2.** To land short of (a runway) in piloting an aircraft.

un•der•shorts (ŭn′dər-shôrts′) *pl.n.* Short underpants.

un•der•shot (ŭn′dər-shŏt′) *adj.* **1.** Moved or turned by water passing underneath, as a water wheel. **2.** Projecting beyond an upper part <an *undershot* jaw>

un•der•side (ŭn′dər-sīd′) *n.* The side or surface that is on the bottom.

un•der•signed (ŭn′dər-sīnd′) *n., pl.* **undersigned.** One whose name is signed at the end of a document.

un•der•sized (ŭn′dər-sīzd′) *also* **un•der•size** (-sīz′) *adj.* Of a smaller size than is usual, expected, or normal.

un•der•skirt (ŭn′dər-skûrt′) *n.* A skirt, as a petticoat, worn under an outer skirt.

un•der•slung (ŭn′dər-slŭng′) *adj.* Suspended by springs attached below the axles. —Used of a vehicle chassis.

un•der•stand (ŭn′dər-stănd′) *v.* **1.** To perceive and comprehend the meaning and significance of. **2.** To be thoroughly familiar with or expert in. **3.** To grasp the intended meaning of what is expressed by. **4.** To be tolerantly or sympathetically disposed. **5.** To find out in a roundabout way. **6.** To draw as a conclusion. **7.** To accept as agreed upon. —**un′der•stand′a•ble** *adj.* —**un′der•stand′a•bly** *adv.*

un•der•stand•ing (ŭn′dər-stăn′dĭng) *n.* **1.** Ability to comprehend : perception. **2.** Capacity to think, learn, judge, etc. **3.** Individual judgment or interpretation. **4.** Accord of thought or feeling. **5.** A mutual agreement esp. to reconcile differences. —*adj.* Disposed to kindness, compassion, tolerance, etc.

un•der•state (ŭn′dər-stāt′) *v.* **1.** To state as less than is the actual situation. **2.** To state unemphatically esp. for dramatic effect. —**un′der•state′ment** *n.*

un•der•stat•ed (ŭn′dər-stā′tĭd) *adj.* Exhibiting restrained good taste <an *understated* décor> —**un′der•stat′ed•ly** *adv.*

un•der•stood (ŭn′dər-sto͝od′) *adj.* **1.** Agreed upon : settled. **2.** Implicit.

un•der•stud•y (ŭn′dər-stŭd′ē) *v.* **1.** To learn (another's role) so as to be able to substitute if necessary. **2.** To serve as an understudy to. —**un′der•stud′y** *n.*

un•der•take (ŭn′dər-tāk′) *v.* **1.** To set about doing, as a task. **2.** To obligate oneself : pledge. **3.** To guarantee.

un•der•tak•er (ŭn′dər-tā′kər) *n.* One who prepares the dead for burial and usu. serves as funeral director.

▲ ***word history:*** The subject of death has always inspired euphemism; the word *undertaker* is one example. Derived from the verb *undertake,* "to take upon oneself," *undertaker* orig. denoted one who undertakes any kind of task. Around 1700, during a period of general refinement of speech and manners, the word *undertaker* was applied specifically to those who undertake to prepare the dead for the grave.

un•der•tak•ing (ŭn′dər-tā′kĭng) *n.* **1.** Something undertaken. **2.** A promise or guarantee. **3.** The business or duties of an undertaker.

un•der-the-count•er (ŭn′dər-*th*ə-koun′tər) *adj.* Transacted or sold illicitly.

un•der•tone (ŭn′dər-tōn′) *n.* **1.** A low or quiet voice tone. **2.** A pale or subdued color, esp. one visible through another color. **3.** An underlying emotional quality <*undertones* of sadness>

un•der•tow (ŭn′dər-tō′) *n.* An underwater current running opposite to the surface current.

un•der•val•ue (ŭn′dər-văl′yo͞o) *v.* **1.** To place too little a value on. **2.** To hold in low regard or esteem.

un•der•wa•ter (ŭn′dər-wô′tər, -wŏt′ər) *adj.* Under the surface of water. —**un′der•wa′ter** *adv.*

un•der•wear (ŭn′dər-wâr′) *n.* Garments worn next to the skin : underclothes.
un•der•weight (ŭn′dər-wāt′) *adj.* Of less than the normal, usual, or requisite weight. **—un′der•weight′** *n.*
un•der•world (ŭn′dər-wûrld′) *n.* **1.** *Gk. & Rom. Myth.* The nether world, esp. the abode of the dead : Hades. **2.** The world of organized crime.
un•der•write (ŭn′dər-rīt′) *v.* **1.** To write at the end of, esp. to sign (a document). **2.** To agree to finance (an enterprise). **3.** To sign (an insurance policy) so as to assume liability in case of specified losses. **4.** To agree to purchase (stock in a new enterprise) usu. at a fixed date and price. **—un′der•writ′er** *n.*
un•de•sir•a•ble (ŭn′dĭ-zīr′ə-bəl) *adj.* Not desirable. **—un′de•sir′a•ble** *n.* **—un′de•sir′a•bly** *adv.*
un•dies (ŭn′dēz) *pl.n. Informal.* Underwear, esp. children's underpants.
un•do (ŭn-do͞o′) *v.* **1.** To reverse, erase, or annul. **2.** To unfasten or loosen. **3.** To open by unwrapping. **4. a.** To cause the downfall of. **b.** To upset : confuse.
un•do•ing (ŭn-do͞o′ĭng) *n.* **1.** Reversal or annulment. **2.** Loosening or untying. **3. a.** Ruin. **b.** A cause of ruin : downfall.
un•doubt•ed (ŭn-dou′tĭd) *adj.* Not doubted or questioned : accepted completely. **—un•doubt′ed•ly** *adv.*
un•dress (ŭn-drĕs′) *v.* To take off the clothing of. *—n.* **1.** Casual attire. **2.** The state of being naked.
un•due (ŭn-do͞o′, -dyo͞o′) *adj.* **1.** Exceeding a normal or reasonable limit : excessive. **2.** Improper or unlawful.
un•du•lant (ŭn′jə-lənt, ŭn′dyə-, ŭn′də-) *adj.* Undulating : wavelike.
un•du•late (ŭn′jə-lāt′, ŭn′dyə-, ŭn′də-) *v.* **1.** To rise and fall or move from side to side in a smooth wavelike motion. **2.** To have a wavy look or shape. **—un′du•la′tion** *n.*
un•du•ly (ŭn-do͞o′lē, -dyo͞o′-) *adv.* **1.** To an excessive degree. **2.** Improperly.
un•dy•ing (ŭn′dī′ĭng) *adj.* Being without end : everlasting.
un•earned (ŭn-ûrnd′) *adj.* **1.** Not merited <*unearned* praise> **2.** Not acquired by labor or service.
un•earth (ŭn-ûrth′) **1.** To dig up out of the earth. **2.** To disclose : uncover.
un•earth•ly (ŭn-ûrth′lē) *adj.* **-li•er, -li•est. 1.** Not of the natural world : supernatural. **2.** Frighteningly unexplainable : weird. **3.** Unreasonable : absurd <an *unearthly* hour for visitors>
un•eas•y (ŭn-ē′zē) *adj.* **1.** Causing or feeling discomfort or distress. **2.** Not easy : difficult. **3.** Awkward or embarrassed. **4.** Restless. **5.** Unstable : uncertain. **—un•eas′i•ly** *adv.* **—un•eas′i•ness** *n.*
un•em•ployed (ŭn′ĕm-ploid′) *adj.* **1.** Not employed : out of work. **2.** Not put to use : inactive. **—un′em•ploy′ment** *n.*
un•e•qual (ŭn-ē′kwəl) *adj.* **1.** Not the same, as in quantity, size, value, etc. **2.** Having unbalanced sides or parts : asymmetric. **3.** Not even or consistent : variable. **4.** Lacking sufficient ability : inadequate.
un•e•qualed (ŭn-ē′kwəld) *adj.* Having no equal or match : unrivaled.
un•e•quiv•o•cal (ŭn′ĭ-kwĭv′ə-kəl) *adj.* Not doubtful or uncertain : clear. **—un′e•quiv′o•cal•ly** *adv.*
un•err•ing (ŭn-ûr′ĭng, -ĕr′-) *adj.* Consistently accurate. **—un′err′ing•ly** *adv.*
un•es•sen•tial (ŭn′ĭ-sĕn′shəl) *adj.* Dispensable. *—n.* Something dispensable.
un•e•ven (ŭn-ē′vən) *adj.* **1.** Having a rough, irregular surface. **2.** Deviating from the straight or parallel. **3.** Varying in uniformity or consistency. **4.** Not balanced or equitable : unfair. **5.** Not divisible by 2 <an *uneven* number> **—un•e′ven•ly** *adv.* **—un•e′ven•ness** *n.*
un•e•vent•ful (ŭn′ĭ-vĕnt′fəl) *adj.* Lacking in significant events. **—un′e•vent′ful•ly** *adv.* **—un′e•vent′ful•ness** *n.*
un•ex•am•pled (ŭn′ĭg-zăm′pəld) *adj.* Without parallel : unequaled.
un•ex•cep•tion•a•ble (ŭn′ĭk-sĕp′shə-nə-bəl) *adj.* Beyond objection : irreproachable. **—un′ex•cep′tion•a•bly** *adv.*
un•ex•cep•tion•al (ŭn′ĭk-sĕp′shə-nəl) *adj.* **1.** Not varying from a norm : usual. **2.** Not subject to exceptions : absolute. **—un′ex•cep′tion•al•ly** *adv.*
un•ex•pect•ed (ŭn′ĭk-spĕk′tĭd) *adj.* Not anticipated beforehand. **—un′ex•pect′ed•ly** *adv.* **—un′ex•pect′ed•ness** *n.*
un•fail•ing (ŭn-fā′lĭng) *adj.* **1.** Not running out : inexhaustible. **2.** Constant : dependable. **3.** Incapable of error : infallible. **—un•fail′ing•ly** *adv.*
un•fair (ŭn-fâr′) *adj.* **1.** Marked by a lack of justice or honesty : biased. **2.** Not ethical, esp. in business affairs. ★ *syns:* INEQUITABLE, UNEQUAL, UNJUST **—un•fair′ly** *adv.* **—un•fair′ness** *n.*
un•faith•ful (ŭn-fāth′fəl) *adj.* **1.** Lacking in loyalty. **2.** Guilty of adultery. **3.** Not accurately reflecting the original. **—un•faith′ful•ly** *adv.* **—un•faith′ful•ness** *n.*
un•fa•mil•iar (ŭn′fə-mĭl′yər) *adj.* **1.** Not previously known : strange <an *unfamiliar* street> **2.** Not acquainted or conversant <*unfamiliar* with the topic> **—un′fa•mil•iar′i•ty** (-mĭl-yăr′ĭ-tē, -mĭl′ē-ăr′-) *n.*
un•fa•vor•a•ble (ŭn-fā′vər-ə-bəl, -fā′vrə-) *adj.* **1.** Not favorable or propitious. **2.** Negative : opposed. **—un•fa′vor•a•bly** *adv.*
un•feel•ing (ŭn-fē′lĭng) *adj.* **1.** Not sympathetic : hardhearted. **2.** Having no sensation : numb. **—un•feel′ing•ly** *adv.*
un•feigned (ŭn-fānd′) *adj.* Not pretended : authentic. **—un•feign′ed•ly** *adv.*
un•fet•ter (ŭn-fĕt′ər) *v.* To free from fetters or restraints, esp. to liberate.
un•fit (ŭn-fĭt′) *adj.* **1.** Not appropriate for a given purpose. **2.** Not qualified : incompetent. **3.** In poor mental or bodily health. *—v.* To disqualify. **—un•fit′ly** *adv.* **—un•fit′ness** *n.*
un•flap•pa•ble (ŭn-flăp′ə-bəl) *adj. Slang.*

Not easily upset : cool and collected. —**un·flap'pa·bil'i·ty** *n.* —**un·flap'pa·bly** *adv.*
un·fledged (ŭn-flĕjd') *adj.* **1.** Not yet having fully developed flight feathers. **2.** Lacking experience or maturity.
un·flinch·ing (ŭn-flĭn'chĭng) *adj.* Standing firm and unyielding : resolute. —**un·flinch'ing·ly** *adv.*
un·fold (ŭn-fōld') *v.* **1.** To open up the folds of and spread out. **2.** To become gradually visible. **3.** To make known or develop gradually. —**un·fold'ment** *n.*
un·fore·seen (ŭn'fər-sēn') *adj.* Not anticipated in advance : unexpected.
un·for·get·ta·ble (ŭn'fər-gĕt'ə-bəl) *adj.* Extremely memorable. —**un'for·get'ta·bly** *adv.*
un·for·mat·ted (ŭn-fôr'măt'ĭd) *adj.* *Computer Sci.* **1.** Designating input or output data not edited before display. **2.** Designating a disk that has not been electronically initialized to accept data.
un·formed (ŭn-fôrmd') *adj.* **1.** Having no definite form or structure : amorphous. **2.** Not yet fully developed : immature.
un·for·tu·nate (ŭn-fôr'chə-nĭt) *adj.* **1.** Having bad luck. **2.** Causing misfortune. **3.** Inappropriate <an *unfortunate* remark> ★ ***syns:*** AWKWARD, INAPPROPRIATE, INFELICITOUS, UNHAPPY —*n.* A victim of misfortune. —**un·for'tu·nate·ly** *adv.*
un·found·ed (ŭn-foun'dĭd) *adj.* Having no basis in fact : groundless.
un·fre·quent·ed (ŭn'frĭ-kwĕn'tĭd, ŭn-frē'kwən-) *adj.* Infrequently visited <an *unfrequented* spot>
un·friend·ly (ŭn-frĕnd'lē) *adj.* **1.** Not friendly : aloof or hostile. **2.** Not favorable. —**un·friend'li·ness** *n.*
un·frock (ŭn-frŏk') *v.* To deprive (a member of the clergy) of rightful privileges and functions.
un·furl (ŭn-fûrl') *v.* To unfold or unroll.
un·gain·ly (ŭn-gān'lē) *adj.* **-li·er, -li·est.** Lacking grace or ease of movement : awkward. —**un·gain'li·ness** *n.*
un·god·ly (ŭn-gŏd'lē) *adj.* **1.** Lacking reverence for God : impious. **2.** Marked by wickedness : sinful. **3.** *Informal.* Outrageous : absurd <got up at an *ungodly* hour> —**un·god'li·ness** *n.*
un·gov·ern·a·ble (ŭn-gŭv'ər-nə-bəl) *adj.* Uncontrollable : unruly.
un·gra·cious (ŭn-grā'shəs) *adj.* **1.** Discourteous : rude. **2.** Not pleasant : disagreeable. —**un·gra'cious·ly** *adv.* —**un·gra'cious·ness** *n.*
un·grate·ful (ŭn-grāt'fəl) *adj.* **1.** Not thankful. **2.** Unpleasant : distasteful. —**un·grate'ful·ly** *adv.* —**un·grate'ful·ness** *n.*
un·guard·ed (ŭn-gär'dĭd) *adj.* **1.** Without protection or defense. **2.** Indiscreet.
un·guent (ŭng'gwənt) *n.* A soothing or healing salve : ointment.
un·gu·late (ŭng'gyə-lĭt, -lāt') *adj.* Having hoofs. —*n.* An ungulate mammal.
un·hal·lowed (ŭn-hăl'ōd) *adj.* **1.** Not holy or consecrated. **2.** Impious : irreverent.
un·hand (ŭn-hănd') *v.* To let go of.
un·hap·py (ŭn-hăp'ē) *adj.* **1.** Sad : sorrowful. **2.** Causing misfortune : unlucky. **3.** Not suitable : inappropriate. **4.** Not pleased or satisfied. —**un·hap'pi·ly** *adv.* —**un·hap'pi·ness** *n.*
un·health·y (ŭn-hĕl'thē) *adj.* **1.** In poor health : sick. **2.** Being a sign or symptom of poor health. **3.** Not contributing to health : unwholesome. **4.** Morally harmful. —**un·health'i·ly** *adv.* —**un·health'i·ness** *n.*
un·heard (ŭn-hûrd') *adj.* **1.** Not heard. **2.** Not accorded a hearing : not listened to.
un·heard-of (ŭn-hûrd'ŭv', -ŏv') *adj.* Never before known or heard of, esp. unprecedented.
un·hinge (ŭn-hĭnj') *v.* **1. a.** To take from hinges. **b.** To take the hinges from. **2.** To make mentally unbalanced.
un·ho·ly (ŭn'hō'lē) *adj.* **1.** Not holy or sacred. **2.** Morally bad : wicked. **3.** *Informal.* Outrageous : terrible <an *unholy* mess> —**un·ho'li·ness** *n.*
un·hook (ŭn-ho͝ok') *v.* **1.** To release or remove from a hook. **2.** To loosen or unfasten the hooks of.
un·horse (ŭn-hôrs') *v.* **1.** To unseat from a horse. **2.** To force from an occupied position, esp. to overthrow.
u·ni·cam·er·al (yo͞o'nĭ-kăm'ər-əl) *adj.* Having one legislative chamber.
u·ni·cel·lu·lar (yo͞o'nĭ-sĕl'yə-lər) *adj.* Consisting of a single cell, as a protozoan.
u·ni·corn (yo͞o'nĭ-kôrn') *n.* A legendary animal resembling a horse, with a long spiraled horn in the center of its forehead.
unicorn plant *n.* A plant, *Proboscidea louisiana,* of the S U.S., having yellowish flowers mottled with purple and a beaked pod.
u·ni·cy·cle (yo͞o'nĭ-sī'kəl) *n.* A one-wheeled vehicle that is usu. pedaled.
un·i·den·ti·fied flying object (ŭn'ī-dĕn'tə-fīd') *n.* An apparently flying object that cannot be identified or explained.
u·ni·form (yo͞o'nə-fôrm') *adj.* **1.** Never changing or varying. **2.** Identical with another or others. —*n.* An outfit that distinguishes the wearer as belonging to a particular group. —**u'ni·for'mi·ty, u'ni·form'ness** *n.* —**u'ni·form'ly** *adv.*
u·ni·fy (yo͞o'nə-fī') *v.* **-fied, -fy·ing.** To consolidate : unite. —**u'ni·fi·ca'tion** *n.* —**u'ni·fi'er** *n.*
u·ni·lat·er·al (yo͞o'nĭ-lăt'ər-əl) *adj.* **1.** Of, relating to, involving, or affecting only one side. **2.** Obligating only one of two or more persons, parties, or nations <a *unilateral* treaty> —**u'ni·lat'er·al·ly** *adv.*
un·im·peach·a·ble (ŭn'ĭm-pē'chə-bəl) *adj.* Beyond dispute or reproach : unquestionable <*unimpeachable* integrity> —**un'im·peach'a·bly** *adv.*
un·in·hib·it·ed (ŭn'ĭn-hĭb'ĭ-tĭd) *adj.* Without inhibitions, esp. exuberantly unconstrained. —**un'in·hib'it·ed·ly** *adv.*
un·in·tel·li·gent (ŭn'ĭn-tĕl'ə-jənt) *adj.* Showing a lack of intelligence.
un·in·tel·li·gi·ble (ŭn'ĭn-tel'ə-jə-bəl) *adj.*

Difficult or impossible to comprehend <*unintelligible* speech> **—un'in·tel'li·gi·bly** *adv.*

un·in·ter·est·ed (ŭn-ĭn'trĭs-tĭd, -ĭn'tə-rĕs'-tĭd) *adj.* **1.** Having no concern with or share in something, esp. having no financial or property interest. **2.** Not interested. ★ ***syns:*** DETACHED, INCURIOUS, INDIFFERENT, REMOTE, UNCONCERNED

un·ion (yo͞on'yən) *n.* **1. a.** The act or an instance of uniting. **b.** The state of being united. **c.** An alliance or confederation of persons, parties, or political entities for mutual interest or advantage. **2. a.** A marital partnership. **b.** A sexual uniting. **3.** A labor union. **4.** A device for joining or coupling pipes, rods, etc. **5.** A design on a flag signifying the union of 2 or more political entities. **6. Union.** The U.S. esp. during the Civil War.

un·ion·ism (yo͞on'yə-nĭz'əm) *n.* **1.** The theory, principle, or policy of forming or being loyal to a union. **2.** The principles or system of a union, esp. a labor or trade union. **—un'ion·ist** *n.*

un·ion·ize (yo͞on'yə-nīz') *v.* **-ized, -iz·ing.** To form into or cause to become a member of a labor or trade union. **—un'ion·i·za'tion** *n.*

union jack *n.* **1.** A national flag composed entirely of a union. **2. Union Jack.** The national flag of the United Kingdom.

union shop *n.* An establishment whose employees are required to be or become union members.

u·nique (yo͞o-nēk') *adj.* **1.** Being the only one. **2.** Being without an equal. ★ ***syns:*** INCOMPARABLE, MATCHLESS, PEERLESS, UNEQUALED, UNPARALLELED, UNRIVALED **—u·nique'ly** *adv.*

u·ni·sex (yo͞o'nĭ-sĕks') *adj.* Appropriate for or common to both sexes <*unisex* clothes>

u·ni·sex·u·al (yo͞o'nĭ-sĕk'sho͞o-əl) *adj.* Of, pertaining to, or confined to one sex.

u·ni·son (yo͞o'nĭ-sən, -zən) *n.* **1.** *Mus.* **a.** Sameness of pitch. **b.** The combination of tones or parts sounding simultaneously at the same pitch or in octaves. **2.** Simultaneous utterance of the same words by 2 or more persons. **3.** Harmonious agreement.

u·nit (yo͞o'nĭt) *n.* **1.** One considered to constitute part of a whole. **2.** An exact quantity used as a standard of measurement. **3.** Something that performs a particular function, as in a machine or system. **4.** The number 1.

u·ni·tard (yo͞o'nĭ-tärd') *n.* A one-piece tight-fitting leotard and tights combination, sometimes with foot straps.

U·ni·tar·i·an (yo͞o'nĭ-târ'ē-ən) *n.* A member of a Christian denomination that emphasizes freedom and tolerance in religious belief. **—U'ni·tar'i·an·ism** *n.*

u·ni·tar·y (yo͞o'nĭ-tĕr'ē) *adj.* **1.** Of or relating to a unit or units. **2.** Having the nature of a unit : whole.

u·nite (yo͞o-nīt') *v.* **u·nit·ed, u·nit·ing.** **1.** To bring or put together so as to make a whole. **2.** To join together for a common purpose. **3.** To become consolidated.

United Nations *pl.n. (sing. or pl. in number).* An international organization comprising most of the countries of the world, formed in 1945 to promote peace, security, and economic development.

unit pricing *n.* The pricing of goods based on cost per standard unit, as the ounce or pound.

u·ni·ty (yo͞o'nĭ-tē) *n., pl* **-ties. 1.** The state of being united into a whole. **2.** Agreement : accord. **3.** Unification of parts into a whole. **4.** Arrangement of elements in an artistic or literary work so that each contributes to the main theme. **5.** Unchanging singleness of purpose or action. **6.** *Math.* The smallest whole numerical unit : l.

u·ni·va·lent (yo͞o'nĭ-vā'lənt) *adj.* **1.** Having valence 1. **2.** Having a single valence.

u·ni·valve (yo͞o'nĭ-vălv') *n.* A mollusk, as a snail, with a single shell.

u·ni·ver·sal (yo͞o'nə-vûr'səl) *adj.* **1.** Including, involving, or affecting the whole world : worldwide. **2.** Relating to, involving, or affecting all those belonging to a given class or group. **3.** Used by or common to all <a *universal* language> **4.** Of or relating to the universe : cosmic. **5.** Having or adjustable to a variety of sizes or uses. **—u'ni·ver·sal'i·ty** *n.* **—u'ni·ver'sal·ly** *adv.*

universal donor *n.* One having blood type O.

U·ni·ver·sal·ism (yo͞o'nə-vûr'sə-lĭz'əm) *n.* The theological doctrine of universal salvation. **—U'ni·ver'sal·ist** *n.*

universal joint *n.* A joint or coupling that permits machine parts not in the same line limited movement in any direction while transmitting rotary motion.

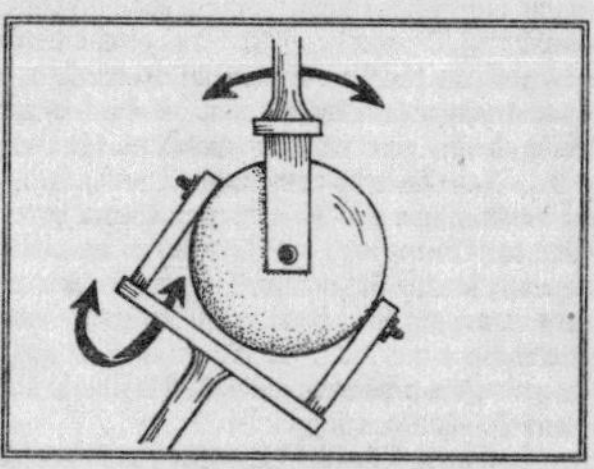

universal joint

Universal Product Code *n.* A series of vertical bars of varying widths printed on consumer product packages and used esp. for inventory control.

u·ni·verse (yo͞o'nə-vûrs') *n.* **1.** All existing space and matter regarded as a whole. **2. a.** The planet earth. **b.** All humankind.

u·ni·ver·si·ty (yo͞o'nə-vûr'sĭ-tē) *n., pl.* **-ties.** An institution of higher learning that offers degrees in undergraduate, graduate, and professional school divisions.

un•just (ŭn-jŭst') *adj.* Marked by a lack of justice or fairness. —**un•just'ly** *adv.*

un•kempt (ŭn-kĕmpt') *adj.* **1.** Not brushed or combed. **2.** Untidy : messy.

un•kind (ŭn-kīnd') *adj.* Lacking in concern, sympathy, or understanding. —**un•kind'li•ness** *n.* —**un•kind'ly** *adj. & adv.* —**un•kind'ness** *n.*

un•know•ing (ŭn-nō'ĭng) *adj.* Not informed or aware. —**un•know'ing•ly** *adv.*

un•known (ŭn-nōn') *adj.* **1.** Not familiar : strange. **2.** Not identified or determined <an *unknown* amount> —**un•known'** *n.*

un•law•ful (ŭn-lô'fəl) *adj.* **1.** Against the law. **2.** Immoral. **3.** Illegitimate. —**un•law'ful•ly** *adv.* —**un•law'ful•ness** *n.*

un•lead•ed (ŭn-lĕd'ĭd) *adj.* Containing no tetraethyl lead, as gasoline.

un•learn (ŭn-lûrn') *v.* To forget.

un•learn•ed (ŭn-lûr'nĭd) *adj.* **1.** Having little or no education. **2.** (ŭn-lûrnd'). Not learned or acquired through training or studying <an *unlearned* response>

un•leash (ŭn-lēsh') *v.* To loose from or as if from a leash.

un•less (ŭn-lĕs') *conj.* Except on the condition or under the circumstances that.

un•let•tered (ŭn-lĕt'ərd) *adj.* Not educated, esp. unable to read and write.

un•like (ŭn-līk') *adj.* **1.** Not alike : dissimilar. **2.** Not equal, as in quantity or strength. —*prep.* **1.** Different from <a flavor *unlike* any other> **2.** Not characteristic of <*unlike* them to be late> —**un•like'ness** *n.*

un•like•ly (ŭn-līk'lē) *adj.* **1.** Not likely or plausible. **2.** Likely to fail : not promising. ★ *syns:* DOUBTFUL, IMPROBABLE —**un•like'li•hood, un•like'li•ness** *n.*

un•lim•ber (ŭn'lĭm'bər) *v.* To prepare for action.

un•load (ŭn-lōd') *v.* **1. a.** To take the load or cargo from. **b.** To take (cargo) from. **2. a.** To unburden (one's mind) of something oppressive. **b.** To give vent to (troubles, problems, etc.). **3. a.** To take the charge from (a gun). **b.** To fire (a gun). **4.** To dispose of, esp. by selling in volume.

un•lock (ŭn-lŏk') *v.* **1.a.** To open (a lock) esp. by turning a key. **b.** To open (a door, trunk, etc.) by unlocking. **2.** To make accessible <*unlock* a closed mind> **3.** To find a solution to <*unlock* a puzzle>

un•looked-for (ŭn-lŏŏkt'fôr') *adj.* Not expected : unforeseen.

un•loose (ŭn-lōōs') *also* **un•loos•en** (-lōō'sən) *v.* **1.** To let loose, as by unfastening. **2.** To ease or release, as a firm grip.

un•luck•y (ŭn-lŭk'ē) *adj.* **1.** Having bad luck : unfortunate. **2.** Forecasting misfortune : inauspicious. **3.** Unsuitable or disappointing <an *unlucky* selection> —**un•luck'i•ly** *adv.* —**un•luck'i•ness** *n.*

un•make (ŭn-māk') *v.* **1.** To reverse or nullify : undo. **2.** To deprive of status, rank, or power : depose. **3.** To cause the ruin of.

un•man•ly (ŭn-măn'lē) *adj.* **1. a.** Not brave : cowardly. **b.** Dishonorable **2.** Effeminate.

un•manned (ŭn-mănd') *adj.* Lacking or designed to operate without a crew <an *unmanned* spacecraft>

un•man•nered (ŭn-măn'ərd) *adj.* **1.** Having bad manners : rude. **2.** Without pretense or pause : unaffected.

un•man•ner•ly (ŭn-măn'ər-lē) *adj.* Ill-mannered. —**un•man'ner•li•ness** *n.*

un•mask (ŭn-măsk') *v.* **1.** To take away a mask (from). **2.** To reveal the true nature of : expose.

un•mean•ing (ŭn-mē'nĭng) *adj.* Lacking meaning or sense.

un•men•tion•a•ble (ŭn-mĕn'shə-nə-bəl) *adj.* Unsuitable or improper as a subject of conversation. —*pl.n.* **unmentionables.** *Informal.* Underwear.

un•mer•ci•ful (ŭn-mûr'sĭ-fəl) *adj.* **1.** Without mercy : pitiless. **2.** Excessive : immoderate. —**un•mer'ci•ful•ly** *adv.* —**un•mer'ci•ful•ness** *n.*

un•mind•ful (ŭn-mīnd'fəl) *adj.* Inattentive : oblivious.

un•mis•tak•a•ble (ŭn'mĭ-stā'kə-bəl) *adj.* Clearly evident. —**un'mis•tak'a•bly** *adv.*

un•mit•i•gat•ed (ŭn-mĭt'ĭ-gā'tĭd) *adj.* **1.** Not lessened or relieved <*unmitigated* tension> **2.** Absolute : thoroughgoing <*unmitigated* impudence>

un•mor•al (ŭn-môr'əl, -mŏr'-) *adj.* Having no moral perception : amoral.

un•nat•u•ral (ŭn-năch'ər-əl, -năch'rəl) *adj.* **1.** Against natural law, esp. abnormal or unusual. **2.** Affected or artificial, as in behavior. **3.** Contrary to natural feelings : inhuman. —**un•nat'u•ral•ly** *adv.* —**un•nat'u•ral•ness** *n.*

un•nec•es•sar•y (ŭn-nĕs'ĭ-sĕr'ē) *adj.* Not necessary : uncalled-for. —**un•nec'es•sar'i•ly** *adv.*

un•nerve (ŭn-nûrv') *v.* To deprive of courage or composure.

un•num•bered (ŭn-nŭm'bərd) *adj.* **1.** Too numerous to be counted. **2.** Not identified by a number.

un•ob•tru•sive (ŭn'əb-trōō'sĭv, -zĭv) *adj.* Not noticeable. —**un'ob•tru'sive•ly** *adv.*

un•oc•cu•pied (ŭn-ŏk'yə-pīd') *adj.* **1.** Not occupied : empty. **2.** Doing little : idle.

un•or•gan•ized (ŭn-ôr'gə-nīzd') *adj.* **1.** Not ordered, coordinated, or systematized. **2.** Not organized into a union.

un•pack (ŭn-păk') *v.* **1.** To remove packed things (from). **2.** To take from a container, parcel, or packaging.

un•par•al•leled (ŭn-păr'ə-lĕld') *adj.* Without equal : matchless.

un•par•lia•men•ta•ry (ŭn'pär-lə-mĕn'tə-rē, -mĕn'trē) *adj.* Not according to parliamentary practice.

un•peo•ple (ŭn-pē'pəl) *v.* To reduce sharply the population of.

un•pleas•ant (ŭn-plĕz'ənt) *adj.* Not pleasant : offensive. —**un•pleas'ant•ly** *adv.* —**un•pleas'ant•ness** *n.*

un•plug (ŭn-plŭg') *v.* **1.** To withdraw a plug, stopper, or obstruction from. **2.** To disconnect (an electric appliance).

un·plumbed (ŭn-plŭmd′) *adj.* **1.** Not tested or measured with a plumb. **2.** Not explored or understood in depth.

un·pop·u·lar (ŭn-pŏp′yə-lər) *adj.* Not generally liked or approved of. **—un·pop′u·lar′i·ty** (-lăr′ĭ-tē) *n.*

un·prec·e·dent·ed (ŭn-prĕs′ĭ-dĕn′tĭd) *adj.* Not done or known before : novel.

un·pre·dict·a·ble (ŭn′prĭ-dĭk′tə-bəl) *adj.* Not capable of being known beforehand. **—un′pre·dict′a·bil′i·ty** *n.* **—un′pre·dict′a·bly** *adv.*

un·pre·pared (ŭn′prĭ-pârd′) *adj.* **1.** Not prepared or equipped. **2.** Not done or rehearsed in advance. **—un′pre·par′ed·ly** *adv.* **—un′pre·par′ed·ness** *n.*

un·pre·ten·tious (ŭn′prĭ-tĕn′shəs) *adj.* Not pretentious : modest.

un·prin·ci·pled (ŭn-prĭn′sə-pəld) *adj.* Unscrupulous.

un·print·a·ble (ŭn-prĭn′tə-bəl) *adj.* Improper or unfit for publication.

un·pro·fes·sion·al (ŭn′prə-fĕsh′ə-nəl) *adj.* **1.** Contrary to the standards or ethics of a profession. **2.** Lacking professional competence : amateurish.

un·prof·it·a·ble (ŭn-prŏf′ĭ-tə-bəl) *adj.* **1.** Producing no profit. **2.** Serving no purpose.

un·qual·i·fied (ŭn-kwŏl′ə-fīd′) *adj.* **1.** Lacking the requisite qualifications. **2.** Unreserved : absolute.

un·ques·tion·a·ble (ŭn-kwĕs′chə-nə-bəl) *adj.* Not open to doubt or dispute : certain. **—un·ques′tion·a·bly** *adv.*

un·qui·et (ŭn-kwī′ĭt) *adj.* **1.** Anxious : distressed. **2.** Violently disturbed : turbulent.

un·quote (ŭn′kwōt′) *n.* —Used by a speaker to indicate the end of a quotation.

un·rav·el (ŭn-răv′əl) *v.* **1. a.** To disentangle (threads). **b.** To undo the knitted or woven fabric of. **2.** To clarify : solve.

un·read (ŭn-rĕd′) *adj.* **1.** Not read or studied. **2.** Not educated : unlearned.

un·read·a·ble (ŭn-rē′də-bəl) *adj.* **1.** Not legible. **2. a.** Too dull to read. **b.** Too difficult to understand.

un·re·al (ŭn-rē′əl, -rēl′) *adj.* Not real or substantial : illusory. **—un′re·al′i·ty** *n.*

un·rea·son·a·ble (ŭn-rē′zə-nə-bəl) *adj.* **1.** Not governed by reason : irrational or absurd. **2.** Exceeding reasonable limits : immoderate. **—un·rea′son·a·ble·ness** *n.* **—un·rea′son·a·bly** *adv.*

un·re·gen·er·ate (ŭn′rĭ-jĕn′ər-ĭt) *adj.* **1.** Not morally or spiritually reformed or regenerated. **2.** Stubborn : obstinate.

un·re·lent·ing (ŭn′rĭ-lĕn′tĭng) *adj.* **1.** Relentless : unyielding. **2.** Not lessening in intensity or pace. **—un′re·lent′ing·ly** *adv.*

un·re·li·a·ble (ŭn′rĭ-lī′ə-bəl) *adj.* Not to be depended on or trusted. **—un′re·li′a·bil′i·ty** *n.* **—un′re·li′a·bly** *adv.*

un·re·mit·ting (ŭn′rĭ-mĭt′ĭng) *adj.* Never letting up : continuous. **—un′re·mit′ting·ly** *adv.*

un·re·served (ŭn′rĭ-zûrvd′) *adj.* **1.** Not set aside for a specific person or use. **2.** Wholehearted. **3.** Not reticent : frank and open. **—un′re·serv′ed·ly** *adv.*

un·rest (ŭn-rĕst′) *n.* A state of turmoil.

un·re·strained (ŭn′rĭ-strānd′) *adj.* **1.** Not checked or controlled. **2.** Not forced or affected : natural.

un·ripe (ŭn-rīp′) *adj.* Not ripe or mature.

un·ri·valed (ŭn-rī′vəld) *adj.* Unequaled.

un·roll (ŭn-rōl′) *v.* **1.** To unwind (something rolled). **2.** To reveal : disclose.

un·ruf·fled (ŭn-rŭf′əld) *adj.* Not agitated or upset : calm.

un·ru·ly (ŭn-rōō′lē) *adj.* **-li·er, -li·est.** Difficult to control or subdue.

un·sad·dle (ŭn-săd′l) *v.* **1.** To take the saddle off. **2.** To unhorse.

un·sat·u·rat·ed (ŭn-săch′ə-rā′tĭd) *adj.* **1.** Of or relating to a compound, esp. of carbon, containing atoms that share more than one valence bond <*unsaturated* fats> **2.** Capable of dissolving more of a solute at a given temperature.

un·sa·vor·y (ŭn-sā′və-rē) *adj.* **1.** Tasting unpleasant or insipid. **2.** Not to one's liking : disagreeable. **3.** Morally repellent. **—un·sa′vor·i·ly** *adv.* **—un·sa′vor·i·ness** *n.*

un·scathed (ŭn-skāthd′) *adj.* Not injured or harmed.

un·schooled (ŭn-skōōld′) *adj.* Not instructed or trained.

un·sci·en·tif·ic (ŭn-sī′ən-tĭf′ĭk) *adj.* Not conforming to the principles or methods of science. **—un·sci′en·tif′i·cal·ly** *adv.*

un·scram·ble (ŭn-skrăm′bəl) *v.* **1.** To straighten out : disentangle. **2.** To restore (a scrambled message) to intelligible form.

un·screw (ŭn-skrōō′) *v.* **1.** To loosen by or as if by turning. **2.** To take out the screws from.

un·scru·pu·lous (ŭn-skrōō′pyə-ləs) *adj.* Lacking scruples or principles : unprincipled. **—un·scru′pu·lous·ly** *adv.* **—un·scru′pu·lous·ness** *n.*

un·seal (ŭn-sēl′) *v.* To break open or remove the seal from.

un·sea·son·a·ble (ŭn-sē′zə-nə-bəl) *adj.* **1.** Not suitable for or typical of the season. **2.** Badly timed. **—un·sea′son·a·bly** *adv.*

un·seat (ŭn-sēt′) *v.* **1.** To remove from a seat or throw from a saddle. **2.** To force out of office : depose.

un·seem·ly (ŭn-sēm′lē) *adj.* Improper : unbecoming <*unseemly* behavior>

un·sel·fish (ŭn-sĕl′fĭsh) *adj.* Willing to give or share : generous. **—un·sel′fish·ly** *adv.* **—un·sel′fish·ness** *n.*

un·set·tle (ŭn-sĕt′l) *v.* **1.** To make unstable : disrupt. **2.** To make upset : disturb.

un·set·tled (ŭn-sĕt′əld) *adj.* **1.** Marked by disorder and unrest. **2.** Not decided : unresolved. **3.** Not paid, as an account. **4.** Not populated. **5.** Not fixed or established, as in situation or character.

un·shak·a·ble (ŭn-shā′kə-bəl) *adj.* Not wavering : steadfast.

un·sheathe (ŭn-shēth′) *v.* To take from or as if from a sheath.

un·sight·ly (ŭn-sīt′lē) *adj.* Not pleasant to look at : unattractive or repulsive. —**un·sight′li·ness** *n.*
un·skilled (ŭn-skĭld′) *adj.* **1.** Having no skills or training, esp. in a given kind of work. **2.** Requiring no special skill <*unskilled* labor> **3.** Showing no skill : crude.
un·skill·ful (ŭn-skĭl′fəl) *adj.* Lacking in skill or proficiency : inexpert. —**un·skill′ful·ly** *adv.* —**un·skill′ful·ness** *n.*
un·so·cia·ble (ŭn-sō′shə-bəl) *adj.* Not disposed to social activities. —**un·so′cia·bil′i·ty** *n.* —**un·so′cia·bly** *adv.*
un·so·phis·ti·cat·ed (ŭn′sə-fĭs′tĭ-kā′tĭd) *adj.* **1.** Inexperienced in the ways of the world : naive. **2.** Not complex : simple.
un·sound (ŭn-sound′) *adj.* **1.** Not solidly made or placed. **2.** Unhealthy in mind or body. **3.** Founded on fallacy : illogical. —**un·sound′ly** *adv.* —**un·sound′ness** *n.*
un·spar·ing (ŭn-spâr′ĭng) *adj.* **1.** Liberal : generous. **2.** Pitiless : severe. —**un·spar′ing·ly** *adv.* —**un·spar′ing·ness** *n.*
un·speak·a·ble (ŭn-spē′kə-bəl) *adj.* **1.** Incapable of being expressed or described. **2.** Indescribably bad. ★ ***syns:*** ABOMINABLE, FRIGHTFUL, REVOLTING, SHOCKING, SICKENING —**un·speak′a·bly** *adv.*
un·spo·ken (ŭn-spō′kən) *adj.* Not expressed in words.
un·spot·ted (ŭn-spŏt′ĭd) *adj.* **1.** Not marked or covered with spots. **2.** Free from moral blemish : unsullied.
un·sta·ble (ŭn-stā′bəl) *adj.* **1.** Not firmly or steadily fixed, made, etc. **2.** Tending to change or fluctuate. **3. a.** Of inconstant temperament : capricious. **b.** Mentally unbalanced or emotionally maladjusted. **4.** Decomposing readily <an *unstable* chemical compound> **5.** *Physics.* **a.** Decaying with relatively short lifetime, as a subatomic particle. **b.** Radioactive, as an atomic nucleus. —**un·sta′bly** *adv.*
un·stead·y (ŭn-stĕd′ē) *adj.* **1.** Not firm or secure : unstable. **2.** Inconstant : variable. **3.** Not consistent : erratic. —**un·stead′i·ly** *adv.* —**un·stead′i·ness** *n.*
un·stick (ŭn-stĭk′) *v.* To free from a stuck position.
un·stop (ŭn-stŏp′) *v.* **1.** To withdraw a stopper from. **2.** To remove a blockage from : open.
un·stressed (ŭn-strĕst′) *adj.* **1.** Not stressed or accented. —Used of a syllable. **2.** Not given emphasis.
un·struc·tured (ŭn-strŭk′chərd) *adj.* **1.** Lacking form or arrangement. **2.** Lacking formal regulation, discipline, etc.
un·strung (ŭn′strŭng′) *adj.* **1.** Having the strings loosened or disconnected. **2.** Feeling nervous tension : upset.
un·stud·ied (ŭn-stŭd′ēd) *adj.* **1.** Not forced or contrived : natural. **2.** Not gained by study.
un·sub·stan·tial (ŭn′səb-stăn′shəl) *adj.* **1.** Lacking substance or reality. **2.** Lacking firmness or strength : flimsy. **3.** Lacking a factual basis : not valid.
un·suit·a·ble (ŭn-so͞o′tə-bəl) *adj.* Not suitable. ★ ***syns:*** IMPROPER, INAPPROPRIATE, MALAPROPOS, UNBECOMING, UNFIT, UNSEEMLY —**un·suit′a·bil′i·ty, un·suit′a·ble·ness** *n.* —**un·suit′a·bly** *adv.*
un·sung (ŭn-sŭng′) *adj.* **1.** Not sung. **2.** Not praised or celebrated, as in poetry.
un·tan·gle (ŭn-tăng′gəl) *v.* **1.** To free from tangles. **2.** To clear up : settle.
un·taught (ŭn-tôt′) *adj.* **1.** Not educated : unlettered. **2.** Not acquired by study.
un·thank·ful (ŭn-thăngk′fəl) *adj.* **1.** Not thankful : ungrateful. **2.** Not appreciated : thankless <an *unthankful* job>
un·think·a·ble (ŭn-thĭng′kə-bəl) *adj.* Inconceivable : unimaginable.
un·think·ing (ŭn-thĭng′kĭng) *adj.* Marked by or resulting from lack of forethought. —**un·think′ing·ly** *adv.*
un·ti·dy (ŭn-tī′dē) *adj.* Not tidy : messy. —**un·ti′di·ly** *adv.* —**un·ti′di·ness** *n.*
un·tie (ŭn-tī′) *v.* **1.** To loosen or unfasten (something tied). **2.** To free from a bond or restraint. **3.** To straighten out : resolve.
un·til (ŭn-tĭl′) *prep.* **1.** Up to the time of <jogged *until* dark> **2.** Before a given time <can't go *until* summer> —*conj.* **1.** Up to the time that <swam *until* it was noon> **2.** Before <won't come *until* my car is fixed> **3.** To the point or extent that <I worked *until* I was exhausted.>
un·time·ly (ŭn-tīm′lē) *adj.* **1.** Inopportune. **2.** Premature. —**un·time′li·ness** *n.* —**un·time′ly** *adv.*
un·to (ŭn′to͞o) *prep.* To.
un·told (ŭn-tōld′) *adj.* **1.** Not related or revealed, as secrets. **2.** Incalculable.
un·touch·a·ble (ŭn-tŭch′ə-bəl) *adj.* **1.** Not permitted to be touched. **2.** Incapable of being reached or obtained. —*n. often* **Untouchable.** A member of the lowest Hindu social class, whose touch was considered unclean by Hindus of higher castes.
un·to·ward (ŭn-tôrd′, -tōrd′, ŭn′tə-wôrd′) *adj.* **1.** Not propitious : unfavorable. **2.** Unruly or obstinate.
un·true (ŭn-tro͞o′) *adj.* **1.** Contrary to the truth : false. **2.** Departing from a standard : inexact. **3.** Not faithful : disloyal.
un·truth (ŭn-tro͞oth′) *n.* **1.** Something untrue : falsehood. **2.** The state of being false. —**un·truth′ful** *adj.* —**un·truth′ful·ly** *adv.* —**un·truth′ful·ness** *n.*
un·tu·tored (ŭn-to͞o′tərd, -tyo͞o′-) *adj.* **1.** Not formally educated. **2.** Not learned : inborn. **3.** Unsophisticated : naive.
un·twist (ŭn-twĭst′) *v.* To loosen or separate the twisted strands or parts of.
un·used (ŭn-yo͞ozd′, -yo͞ost′) *adj.* **1.** Not put to use. **2.** Never before used. **3.** Unaccustomed <*unused* to rich food>
un·u·su·al (ŭn-yo͞o′zho͞o-əl) *adj.* Not usual : uncommon or extraordinary. —**un·u′su·al·ly** *adv.* —**un·u′su·al·ness** *n.*
un·ut·ter·a·ble (ŭn-ŭt′ər-ə-bəl) *adj.* **1.** Not capable of being expressed or described : inexpressible. **2.** Not pronounceable. —**un·ut′ter·a·bly** *adv.*
un·var·nished (ŭn-vär′nĭsht) *adj.* **1.** Not

coated with varnish. **2.** Not embellished or disguised **:** plain.

un•veil (ŭn-vāl′) *v.* **1.** To take a veil or other covering from. **2.** To uncover **:** reveal. **3.** To take off one's veil.

un•voiced (ŭn-voist′) *adj.* **1.** Not uttered or expressed **:** unsaid. **2.** Uttered without vibrating the vocal cords **:** voiceless.

un•war•rant•a•ble (ŭn-wôr′ən-tə-bəl, -wŏr′-) *adj.* Not justifiable or excusable. **—un•war′rant•a•bly** *adv.*

un•war•rant•ed (ŭn-wôr′ən-tĭd, -wŏr′-) *adj.* Incapable of being justified or substantiated **:** groundless.

un•war•y (ŭn-wâr′ē) *adj.* Not guarded or cautious **:** gullible. **—un•war′i•ly** *adv.* **—un•war′i•ness** *n.*

un•well (ŭn-wĕl′) *adj.* Not well **:** sick.

un•whole•some (ŭn-hōl′səm) *adj.* **1.** Not conducive to health **:** unhealthy. **2.** Morally harmful or corrupt. **—un•whole′some•ly** *adv.* **—un•whole′some•ness** *n.*

un•wield•y (ŭn-wēl′dē) *adj.* Hard to manage because of shape or size **:** clumsy.

un•will•ing (ŭn-wĭl′ĭng) *adj.* **1.** Not willing **:** loath. **2.** Marked by reluctance <an *unwilling* promise> **—un•will′ing•ly** *adv.* **—un•will′ing•ness** *n.*

un•wind (ŭn-wīnd′) *v.* **1.** To undo (something rolled or coiled). **2.** To become unrolled or untwisted. **3.** To become free of tension **:** relax.

un•wise (ŭn-wīz′) *adj.* Lacking wisdom or good judgment. **—un•wise′ly** *adv.*

un•wit•ting (ŭn-wĭt′ĭng) *adj.* **1.** Not intended **:** inadvertent. **2.** Unknowing **:** unaware. **—un•wit′ting•ly** *adv.*

un•wont•ed (ŭn-wôn′tĭd, -wōn′-, -wŭn′-) *adj.* Not customary or usual.

un•world•ly (ŭn-wûrld′lē) *adj.* **1.** Not of this world **:** spiritual rather than secular. **2.** Concerned with spiritual or religious matters. **3.** Unsophisticated **:** naive. **—un•world′li•ness** *n.*

un•wor•thy (ŭn-wûr′thē) *adj.* **1.** Not deserving <*unworthy* of praise> **2.** Not befitting **:** unbecoming <a deed *unworthy* of them> **3.** Base **:** despicable. **—un•wor′thi•ly** *adv.* **—un•wor′thi•ness** *n.*

un•writ•ten (ŭn-rĭt′n) *adj.* **1.** Not written down. **2.** Effective through custom or tradition <an *unwritten* rule>

un•yoke (ŭn-yōk′) *v.* **1.** To free from a yoke. **2.** To disjoin **:** disconnect.

up (ŭp) *adv.* **1.** From a lower level or position to a higher one. **2.** In, to, or toward a higher level or position. **3.** To or into an upright position. **4. a.** Above a surface, as of ground or water. **b.** Above the horizon <The moon came *up.*> **5.** So as to be considered <brought the subject *up* again> **6.** In or toward a place or position considered as higher, as on a map, chart, or scale. **7.** To or at a greater charge or fee. **8.** Into an improved, intensified, or advanced state. **9.** With or to a higher volume **:** louder. **10.** Into a highly active state <A storm came *up.*> **11.** So as to uproot <pulling *up* carrots> **12.** Into parts or pieces <cut *up* the meat> **13.** —Used as an intensive <tidied *up*> **14.** Completely **:** entirely <drank it all *up*> *—adj.* **1.** Moving or aimed upward <an *up* escalator> **2.** Being out of bed. **3.** Comparatively high <Prices are *up.*> **4.** *Informal.* Taking place **:** happening <Tell me what's *up.*> **5.** Under consideration. **6.** At an end <Time's *up* for today.> **7.** *Informal.* Highly informed <not *up* on politics> **8.** Being in advance of an opponent <*up* 2 holes in a golf match> **9.** *Baseball.* Being next at bat. **10.** Standing trial <*up* for homicide> *—prep.* **1.** To, toward, or at a higher point of or on <climbed *up* the hill> **2.** Toward or at a more distant point <lives *up* the block> **3.** Toward the source or origin of <*up* the Seine> *—n.* **1.** An upward slope. **2.** An upward movement or trend <a sudden *up* in prices> **3.** *Slang.* Excitement or euphoria. *—v.* **upped, up•ping. 1.** To cause to be greater <*upped* our chances of winning> **2.** To move or cause to move upward. **3.** *Informal.* To act abruptly <just *upped* and left home> **—on the up and up.** Open and aboveboard. **—up to. 1.** Involved in <What are you *up to*?> **2.** *Informal.* Ready or prepared for <not *up to* seeing people> **3.** The responsibility of <The choice is *up to* you.>

up-and-com•ing (ŭp′ən-kŭm′ĭng) *adj.* Having potential **:** promising.

U•pan•i•shad (o͞o-păn′ĭ-shăd′) *n.* One of a collection of philosophical discourses contributing to ancient Hindu theology.

up•beat (ŭp′bēt′) *n. Mus.* An unaccented and esp. the final beat of a measure. *—adj. Informal.* Happy **:** optimistic.

up•braid (ŭp-brād′) *v.* To reproach or criticize harshly. **—up•braid′er** *n.*

up•bring•ing (ŭp′brĭng′ĭng) *n.* The process of rearing and training a child.

up•com•ing (ŭp′kŭm′ĭng) *adj.* About to appear or take place.

up•coun•try (ŭp′kŭn′trē) *n.* The interior of a country. *—adj.* (ŭp′kŭn′trē). Of, relating to, located in, or coming from the upcountry. **—up•coun′try** *adv.*

up•date (ŭp-dāt′) *v.* **1.** To bring up to date <*update* a news story> **2.** To modernize. **—up′date′** *n.*

up•draft (ŭp′drăft′) *n.* A current of air flowing upward.

up•end (ŭp-ĕnd′) *v.* **1.** To set on end. **2.** To overturn or defeat.

up-front (ŭp′frŭnt′) *adj.* **1.** Straightforward **:** frank <an *up-front* discussion of grievances> **2.** Required in advance <*up-front* cash>

up•grade (ŭp′grād′) *v.* To increase the rank, grade, or standard of. *—n.* **1.** Something that upgrades. **2.** An upward slope.

up•heav•al (ŭp-hē′vəl) *n.* **1.** The process or an instance of being lifted forcefully upward. **2.** An abrupt and violent change or tumult <a political *upheaval*> **3.** *Geol.* An uplifting of the earth's crust.

up•hill (ŭp′hĭl′) *adj.* **1.** Going up an incline or hill. **2.** Prolonged and laborious **:** difficult.

—*n.* An upward slope. —*adv.* (ŭp′hĭl′). **1.** Upward on an incline. **2.** Against adversity.
up•hold (ŭp-hōld′) *v.* **1.** To raise or hold aloft. **2.** To keep from falling. **3.** To defend or affirm despite opposition <*upheld* our beliefs> —**up•hold′er** *n.*
up•hol•ster (ŭp-hōl′stər) *v.* To provide (furniture) with padding, cushions, a fabric covering, etc. —**up•hol′ster•er** *n.*
up•hol•ster•y (ŭp-hōl′stər-ē, -hōl′strē) *n., pl.* **-ies. 1.** An upholsterer's materials. **2.** The business or craft of upholstering.
up•keep (ŭp′kēp′) *n.* **1.** Maintenance in proper operation and repair. **2.** The cost of maintenance.
up•land (ŭp′lənd, -lănd′) *n.* The elevated areas of a country, region, or tract of land. —**up′land** *adj.* —**up′land•er** *n.*
up•lift (ŭp-lĭft′) *v.* **1.** To lift or raise up. **2.** To elate. **3.** To elevate socially, morally, or intellectually. —*n.* (ŭp′lĭft′). **1.** A lifting up, esp. a geologic upheaval. **2.** A movement supporting social, moral, or intellectual improvement.
up•load (ŭp′lōd′) *v.* To transfer (data or programs), usu. from a peripheral computer or device to a central computer.
up•most (ŭp′mōst′) *adj.* Uppermost.
up•on (ə-pŏn′, ə-pôn′) *prep.* On.
up•per (ŭp′ər) *adj.* **1.** Higher in location, position, or status. **2. Upper.** Being a later division of a specific archaeological or geologic period. —*n.* **1.** The part of footwear above the sole. **2.** *Slang.* A drug used as a stimulant.
upper case *n.* The case of printing type containing the capital letters. —**up′per-case′** *adj.*
upper class *n.* The highest socioeconomic class in a society. —**up′per-class′** *adj.*
up•per•class•man (ŭp′ər-klăs′mən) *n.* A junior or senior in a secondary school or college.
upper crust *n. Informal.* The pre-eminent social class or group.
up•per•cut (ŭp′ər-kŭt′) *n.* A short swinging blow aimed upward, as at an opponent's chin in boxing.
upper hand *n.* A controlling position **:** advantage.
up•per•most (ŭp′ər-mōst′) *adj.* Highest or foremost in position, place, rank, or influence. —**up′per•most′** *adv.*
up•pi•ty (ŭp′ĭ-tē) *adj. Informal.* Arrogant or snobbish.
up•raise (ŭp-rāz′) *v.* To uplift.
up•right (ŭp′rīt′) *adj.* **1.** In a vertical position or direction. **2.** Adhering to moral principles **:** honorable. —*n.* Something standing upright, as a building beam. —**up′right′** *adv.* —**up′right′ly** *adv.* —**up′right′ness** *n.*
upright piano *n.* A piano whose strings are mounted in a vertical direction.
up•ris•ing (ŭp′rī′zĭng) *n.* A revolt.
up•roar (ŭp′rôr′, -rōr′) *n.* A state of violent commotion **:** tumult. ★ *syns:* BROUHAHA, SENSATION, STIR, TO-DO
up•roar•i•ous (ŭp-rôr′ē-əs, -rōr′-) *adj.* **1.** Characterized by uproar. **2.** Boisterous <*uproarious* laughter> **3.** Hilarious <*uproarious* comedy> —**up•roar′i•ous•ly** *adv.* —**up•roar′i•ous•ness** *n.*
up•root (ŭp-ro͞ot′, -ro͝ot′) *v.* To unearth or detach completely by or as if by pulling up the roots. —**up•root′er** *n.*
up•scale (ŭp′skāl′) *adj.* Intended for or relating to high-income consumers. —**up•scale′** *v.*
up•set (ŭp-sĕt′) *v.* **-set, -set•ting. 1.** To overturn or cause to tip over. **2.** To throw into disorder or confusion **:** unsettle. **3.** To distress mentally, emotionally, or physically. **4.** To win a victory over, esp. unexpectedly. —*n.* (ŭp′sĕt′). **1.** An act of upsetting or the state of being upset. **2.** A disturbance of usual functioning, order, etc. **3.** A game or contest in which the favorite is unexpectedly defeated. —*adj.* (ŭp-sĕt′). **1.** Overturned **:** tipped over. **2.** Disordered **:** unsettled. **3.** Distressed **:** troubled. —**up•set′ter** *n.*
up•shot (ŭp′shŏt′) *n.* Outcome **:** result.
up•side-down *also* **upside down** (ŭp′sīd-doun′) *adv.* **1.** With the upper part or side on the bottom. **2.** In or into utter disorder or confusion. —**up′side-down′** *adj.*
up•stage (ŭp′stāj′) *adj. & adv.* At or toward the back part of a stage. —*v.* (ŭp-stāj′). **1.** To distract audience attention from (another actor), as by remaining upstage. **2.** *Informal.* To steal the show from or get the better of. **3.** *Informal.* To treat condescendingly.
up•stairs (ŭp′stârz′) *adv.* **1.** To or on an upper floor. **2.** To or at a higher level or position. —*adj.* (ŭp′stârz′). Of, pertaining to, or situated on the upper floors. —*n. (sing. in number).* The upper section of a house or other building.
up•stand•ing (ŭp-stăn′dĭng, ŭp′stăn′-) *adj.* **1.** Erect. **2.** Morally upright.
up•start (ŭp′stärt′) *n.* One made self-important by new wealth or power.
up•state (ŭp′stāt′) *adv.* At, toward, or to the part of a state located inland or esp. N of a large city. —**up′state′** *adj. & n.*
up•stream (ŭp′strēm′) *adv.* **1.** At, toward, or to the source of a stream. **2.** Against the current. —**up′stream′** *adj.*
up•stroke (ûp′strōk′) *n.* An upward stroke, as of a brush or pen.
up•surge (ŭp′sûrj′) *n.* An abrupt or rapid rise. —**up•surge′** *v.*
up•swept (ŭp′swĕpt′) *adj.* Swept upward <an *upswept* hairdo>
up•swing (ŭp′swĭng′) *n.* An upward swing or trend, esp. a noticeable increase.
up•take (ŭp′tāk′) *n.* **1.** A flue for the upward passage of smoke or air. **2.** *Informal.* Understanding **:** comprehension <slow on the *uptake*> **3.** An act or instance of absorbing esp. into living tissue.
up•tight *also* **up tight** (ŭp′tīt′) *adj. Slang.* **1.** Tense or nervous. **2.** Angry **:** outraged. **3.** Rigidly conventional.

up-to-date (ŭp′tə-dāt′) *adj.* **1.** Most recent **:** current <an *up-to-date* directory> **2.** In step with the times **:** modern. **—up′to-date′ness** *n.*

up•town (ŭp′toun′) *adv.* To, toward, or in the upper section of a city. *—n.* The section of a city located uptown. **—up′town′** *adj.*

up•turn (ŭp′tûrn′) *n.* An upward trend, as in business or prices. *—v.* (*also* ŭp-tûrn′). **1.** To dig up and turn over, as soil. **2.** To turn or direct upward.

up•ward (ŭp′wərd) *also* **up•wards** (-wərdz) *adv.* From a lower place, level, or position to or toward a higher one. *—adj.* **upward.** Directed toward a higher place or position. **—upwards (***or* **upward) of.** More than <interviewed *upwards of* 50 candidates> **—up′-ward•ly** *adv.*

up•well•ing (ŭp-wĕl′ĭng, ŭp′wĕl′-) *n.* The act of rising up from or as if from a lower source <an *upwelling* of emotion>

up•wind (ŭp′wĭnd′) *adv. & adj.* In or toward the direction from which the wind is blowing.

u•ra•cil (yŏŏr′ə-sĭl) *n.* A nitrogenous pyrimidine base that is a constituent of RNA.

u•rae•us (yŏŏ-rē′əs) *n.* A figure of the sacred serpent depicted on the headdress of ancient Egyptian rulers and deities as an emblem of sovereignty.

uraeus

u•ra•ni•um (yŏŏ-rā′nē-əm) *n. Symbol* **U** A heavy silvery-white radioactive metallic element used esp. in research and in nuclear fuels and weapons.

U•ra•nus (yŏŏr′ə-nəs, yŏŏ-rā′nəs) *n.* The 7th planet of the solar system in order of distance from the sun.

ur•ban (ûr′bən) *adj.* **1.** Of or constituting a city. **2.** Typical of the city or city life.

ur•bane (ûr-bān′) *adj.* Polished and elegant in manner or style **:** suave. **—ur′bane′ly** *adv.* **—ur•ban′i•ty** (-băn′ĭ-tē) *n.*

▲ ***word history:*** *Urban* and *urbane* are both derived from Latin *urbanus,* "belonging to a city," and they were once synonymous in meaning. *Urbane* was borrowed first, from Old French *urbain,* and it preserved the French pattern of stress. After *urban* was borrowed directly from Latin *urbanus, urbane* developed the more specialized sense of "refined, polite, elegant." These desirable qualities were considered to be characteristic of urban rather than country folk.

ur•ban•ite (ûr′bə-nīt′) *n.* One who lives in a city.

ur•ban•ize (ûr′bə-nīz′) *v.* **-ized, -iz•ing.** To impart an urban character to.

ur•chin (ûr′chĭn) *n.* A mischievous child.

u•re•a (yŏŏ-rē′ə) *n.* A white chemical compound found in body fluids and esp. the urine of mammals.

u•re•mi•a (yŏŏ-rē′mē-ə) *n.* A toxic condition resulting from abnormal accumulation of urea in the blood. **—u•re′mic** *adj.*

u•re•ter (yŏŏ-rē′tər, yŏŏr′ĭ-tər) *n.* Either of the ducts that carry urine from the kidneys to the bladder.

u•re•thra (yŏŏ-rē′thrə) *n., pl.* **-thras** *or* **-thrae** (-thrē). The canal through which urine is discharged and that in the male also serves as the seminal duct. **—u•re′thral** *adj.*

urge (ûrj) *v.* **urged, urg•ing. 1.** To push or drive forcefully onward **:** impel. **2.** To plead with esp. insistently. **3.** To recommend strongly and persistently. ★ ***syns:*** EXHORT, PRESS, PROD, PROMPT. *—n.* An impelling force, influence, or impulse.

ur•gent (ûr′jənt) *adj.* **1.** Demanding immediate attention. **2.** Urging persistently. **—ur′-gen•cy** *n.* **—ur′gent•ly** *adv.*

u•ric (yŏŏr′ĭk) *adj.* Of, pertaining to, or present in urine.

uric acid *n.* A white crystalline compound, the end product of purine metabolism in humans and other primates, birds, terrestrial reptiles, and most insects.

u•ri•nal (yŏŏr′ə-nəl) *n.* **1.** An upright wall fixture used by males for urinating. **2.** A receptacle for urine used esp. by bedridden persons.

u•ri•nal•y•sis (yŏŏr′ə-năl′ĭ-sĭs) *n.* Laboratory analysis of urine.

u•ri•nar•y (yŏŏr′ə-nĕr′ē) *adj.* **1.** Pertaining to, taking place in, or constituting organs for the production and excretion of urine. **2.** Of or pertaining to urine.

urinary bladder *n.* A muscular membranous sac in the forward part of the pelvic cavity for the temporary storage of urine before excretion.

u•ri•nate (yŏŏr′ə-nāt′) *v.* **-nat•ed, -nat•ing.** To empty the bladder of urine.

u•rine (yŏŏr′ĭn) *n.* A yellowish fluid secreted by the kidneys and containing dissolved bodily wastes.

urn (ûrn) *n.* **1.** A vaselike container used esp. to hold the ashes after cremation. **2.** A closed container with a spout, used for serving coffee or tea.

u•ro•gen•i•tal (yŏŏr′ō-jĕn′ĭ-tl) *adj.* Of or pertaining to both the urinary and genital organs or their functions.

u•rol•o•gy (yŏŏ-rŏl′ə-jē) *n.* The branch of medicine concerned with the urinary or urogenital tract. **—u•rol′o•gist** *n.*

Ur•sa Major (ûr′sə) *n.* A constellation in the N Hemisphere containing the Big Dipper.

Ursa Minor *n.* A ladle-shaped constellation with the star Polaris at the tip of the handle.

ur•sine (ûr′sīn′) *adj.* Of or characteristic of a bear.

ur•ti•car•i•a (ûr′tĭ-kâr′ē-ə) *n.* Hives.

us (ŭs) *pron. The objective case of* WE. —Used: **1.** As the direct object of a verb <The schedule exhausted *us.*> **2.** As the indirect object of a verb <They rented *us* the cottage.> **3.** As the object of a preposition <mailed a letter off to *us*>

us•a•ble *also* **use•a•ble** (yo͞o′zə-bəl) *adj.* **1.** Capable of being used. **2.** Fit for use. —**us′a•bil′i•ty** *n.* —**us′a•bly** *adv.*

us•age (yo͞o′sĭj, -zĭj) *n.* **1.** The act or way of using something. **2.** A customary or habitual way of doing something. **3.** The way in which language or its elements are used. **4.** A particular expression in speech or writing <a nonstandard *usage*>

use (yo͞oz) *v.* **used, us•ing. 1.** To put into action or service **:** employ for some purpose. **2.** To employ regularly <*uses* public transportation> **3.** To behave toward **:** treat. **4.** *Informal.* To exploit for one's advantage. **5.** To partake of as a habit <*uses* tobacco> **6.** —Used in the past tense with *to* to denote earlier practice, fact, or state <They *used* to be rich.> —**use up.** To consume or exhaust totally. —*n.* (yo͞os). **1.** The act of using something. **2.** The state or fact of being used. **3.** The way of using **:** usage. **4. a.** The permission, privilege, or benefit of using something. **b.** The ability to use something, as an arm, leg, etc. **5.** Necessity or reason to use <had no more *use* for the car> **6.** The quality of being useful for some purpose **:** usefulness. **7.** The purpose for which something is used **:** function. **8.** Accustomed practice. **9.** *Law.* **a.** The enjoyment of property, as by occupying or utilizing it. **b.** The profit or benefit of property held in trust. —**used to.** Accustomed or habituated to <can't get *used to* the noise> —**us′er** *n.*

used (yo͞ozd) *adj.* Previously owned **:** secondhand <new and *used* appliances>

use•ful (yo͞os′fəl) *adj.* Of particular use or advantage **:** serviceable. —**use′ful•ly** *adv.* —**use′ful•ness** *n.*

use•less (yo͞os′lĭs) *adj.* **1.** Having little purpose or worth. **2.** Of no avail **:** futile <It's *useless* to worry.> —**use′less•ly** *adv.* —**use′less•ness** *n.*

us•er-friend•ly (yo͞o′zər-frĕnd′lē) *adj.* Easy to use or learn. —**us′er-friend′li•ness** *n.*

ush•er (ŭsh′ər) *n.* **1.** One who conducts people to their seats, as in a theater or church. **2.** An official who goes before persons of rank in a procession. —*v.* **1.** To conduct **:** escort. **2.** To precede as an usher or forerunner. **3.** To begin or introduce <a party to *usher* in the new year>

u•su•al (yo͞o′zho͞o-əl) *adj.* **1.** Common **:** ordinary. **2.** Customary **:** regular. —**u′su•al•ly** *adv.* —**u′su•al•ness** *n.*

u•su•fruct (yo͞o′zə-frŭkt′, -sə-) *n. Law.* The right to utilize and enjoy the profits and advantages of something, as property, belonging to another.

u•su•rer (yo͞o′zhər-ər) *n.* One who lends money at an excessive interest rate.

u•su•ri•ous (yo͞o-zho͝or′ē-əs) *adj.* Relating to, practicing, or being usury. —**u•su′ri•ous•ly** *adv.* —**u•su′ri•ous•ness** *n.*

u•surp (yo͞o-sûrp′, -zûrp′) *v.* To seize and hold illegally and by force. —**u′sur•pa′tion** *n.* —**u•surp′er** *n.*

u•su•ry (yo͞o′zhə-rē) *n., pl.* **-ries. 1.** The act or practice of lending money at excessive interest rates. **2.** An exorbitant or illegal rate of interest.

Ute (yo͞ot) *n., pl.* **Ute** *or* **Utes. 1.** A member of an American Indian people of Utah, Colorado, and N New Mexico. **2.** Their Uto-Aztecan language.

u•ten•sil (yo͞o-tĕn′səl) *n.* **1.** An implement or container for household and esp. kitchen use. **2.** A useful implement or tool.

u•ter•us (yo͞o′tər-əs) *n.* A hollow, muscular organ of female mammals, in which young develop and usu. are nourished prior to birth. —**u′ter•ine** (-ĭn, -tə-rīn′) *adj.*

u•tile (yo͞o′tl, yo͞o′tīl′) *adj.* Useful.

u•til•i•tar•i•an (yo͞o-tĭl′ĭ-târ′ē-ən) *adj.* **1.** Of, relating to, or based on utility. **2.** Stressing useful rather than aesthetic qualities. **3.** Adhering to or supporting utilitarianism. —*n.* A supporter of utilitarianism.

u•til•i•tar•i•an•ism (yo͞o-tĭl′ĭ-târ′ē-ə-nĭz′-əm) *n.* The philosophical doctrine that action should be based on the usefulness of its effects and that only the useful is good or worthwhile.

u•til•i•ty (yo͞o-tĭl′ĭ-tē) *n., pl.* **-ties. 1.** The quality or state of being useful **:** usefulness. **2.** Something designed for practical use. **3.** A company that offers a governmentally regulated public service. **4.** A public service, as electricity, heat, or water, provided by a utility company.

u•til•ize (yo͞ot′l-īz′) *v.* **-ized, -iz•ing.** To put to use **:** make profitable use of. —**u′til•iz′a•ble** *adj.* —**u′til•i•za′tion** *n.*

ut•most (ŭt′mōst′) *adj.* **1.** Most distant **:** extreme. **2.** Of the greatest amount or degree. —**ut′most′** *n.*

U•to-Az•tec•an (yo͞o′tō-ăz′tĕk′ən) *n.* A language family of North and Central America that includes Ute, Hopi, and Shoshone.

u•to•pi•a (yo͞o-tō′pē-ə) *n.* **1.** *often* **Utopia.** A place in which there is sociopolitical perfection. **2.** An impractically idealistic goal or scheme, esp. for a perfect society. —**u•to′pi•an** *adj. & n.*

ut•ter¹ (ŭt′ər) *v.* **1.** To express verbally **:** speak. **2.** To produce as sound <*utter* a cry> **3.** To begin the circulation of (counterfeit money or a forgery). —**ut′ter•a•ble** *adj.* —**ut′ter•er** *n.*

ut•ter² (ŭt′ər) *adj.* Completely such, without qualification or exception. ★ ***syns:*** ALL-

OUT, ARRANT, COMPLETE, CONSUMMATE, FLAT, OUT-AND-OUT, OUTRIGHT, POSITIVE, PURE, SHEER, THOROUGH, TOTAL, UNMITIGATED, UNQUALIFIED

ut•ter•ance (ŭt′ər-əns) *n.* **1. a.** The act of uttering. **b.** The power or way of speaking. **2.** Something uttered.

ut•ter•ly (ŭt′ər-lē) *adv.* Completely.

ut•ter•most (ŭt′ər-mōst′) *adj.* Most distant or extreme : utmost. **—ut′ter•most** *n.*

U-turn (yo͞o′tûrn′) *n.* A turn in which the direction of travel is reversed <The driver made an illegal *U-turn.*>

u•vu•la (yo͞o′vyə-lə) *n.* The fleshy cone-shaped projection hanging above the back of the tongue. **—u′vu•lar** *adj.*

ux•o•ri•ous (ŭk-sôr′ē-əs, -sōr′-, ŭg-zôr′-, -zōr′-) *adj.* Unduly fond of or submissive to one's wife. **—ux•o′ri•ous•ly** *adv.* **—ux•o′ri•ous•ness** *n.*

Vv

v *or* **V** (vē) *n.,pl.* **v's** or **V's. 1.** The 22nd letter of the English alphabet. **2.** A speech sound represented by the letter *v.* **3.** Something with the shape of the letter V. **4.** The Roman numeral for 5.

V *symbol for* VANADIUM.

va•can•cy (vā′kən-sē) *n., pl.* **-cies. 1.** The state of being unoccupied or vacant. **2.** An empty space. **3.** An unfilled or unoccupied office, position, or accommodation.

va•cant (vā′kənt) *adj.* **1.** Holding nothing : empty. **2.** Without an occupant or incumbent. **3. a.** Lacking intelligence. **b.** Expressionless : blank. **4.** Not filled with activity.

va•cate (vā′kāt′) *v.* **-cat•ed, -cat•ing. 1.** To cease to occupy : make vacant. **2.** *Law.* To make void.

va•ca•tion (vā-kā′shən) *n.* A period of time for pleasure, rest, or relaxation, esp. one with pay granted to an employee. *—v.* To take or spend a vacation.

va•ca•tion•land (vā-kā′shən-lănd′) *n.* A place with special attractions and facilities for vacationers.

vac•ci•nate (văk′sə-nāt′) *v.* **-nat•ed, -nat•ing.** To inoculate with a vaccine so as to produce immunity to an infectious disease, as smallpox.

vac•ci•na•tion (văk′sə-nā′shən) *n.* **1.** Inoculation with a vaccine. **2.** A scar on the skin caused by vaccinating.

vac•cine (văk-sēn′) *n.* A liquid suspension of weakened or killed microorganisms, as of bacteria or viruses, injected into a person or animal as protection against disease.

vac•il•late (văs′ə-lāt′) *v.* **-lat•ed, -lat•ing. 1.** To sway from side to side : oscillate. **2.** To show indecision : waver. **—vac′il•la′tion** *n.* **—vac′il•la′tor** *n.*

va•cu•i•ty (vă-kyo͞o′ĭ-tē) *n., pl.* **-ties. 1.** Complete absence of matter : emptiness. **2.** An empty space. **3.** Total lack of ideas. **4.** Something, esp. a remark, that is vacuous.

vac•u•ole (văk′yo͞o-ōl′) *n.* A small cavity in cell protoplasm.

vac•u•ous (văk′yo͞o-əs) *adj.* **1.** Empty : blank. **2. a.** Lacking intelligence : stupid. **b.** Pointless : inane. **—vac′u•ous•ly** *adv.*

vac•u•um (văk′yo͞o-əm, -yo͞om) *n., pl.* **-ums** *or* **-u•a** (-yo͞o-ə). **1.** A space empty of matter. **2.** A state of emptiness : void. *—v.* To clean with a vacuum cleaner.

vacuum bottle *n.* A flask or bottle with a vacuum between its inner and outer walls, designed to maintain the desired temperature of the contents.

vacuum cleaner *n.* An electrical appliance that cleans surfaces by suction.

vac•u•um-packed (văk′yo͞o-əm-păkt′, -yo͞om-, -yəm-) *adj.* Packed in a container that has had most of the air removed before being sealed.

vacuum tube *n.* An electron tube having an internal vacuum high enough to permit electrons to move with low interaction with any remaining gas molecules.

va•de me•cum (vā′dē mē′kəm) *n., pl.* **vade me•cums.** Something useful, as a manual, that one carries about constantly.

vag•a•bond (văg′ə-bŏnd′) *n.* **1.** A homeless person who moves from place to place. **2.** A tramp. **—vag′a•bond′** *adj.*

va•gar•y (vā′gə-rē, və-gâr′ē) *n., pl.* **-ies.** A capricious or eccentric idea or action. **—va•gar′i•ous** *adj.*

va•gi•na (və-jī′nə) *n., pl.* **-nas** *or* **-nae** (-nē). *Anat.* The passage leading from the uterus to the vulva in female mammals. **—vag′i•nal** (văj′ə-nəl) *adj.*

vag•i•ni•tis (văj′ə-nī′tĭs) *n.* Inflammation of the vagina.

va•grant (vā′grənt) *n.* **1.** One who roams from place to place without a permanent home or job. **2.** One, as a drunkard, who lives on the streets and is considered a public nuisance. *—adj.* **1.** Roaming from place to place without a job. **2.** Moving in a random way. **—va′gran•cy** *n.*

vague (vāg) *adj.* **vagu•er, vagu•est. 1.** Not clearly outlined or expressed. **2.** Having an indefinite shape or form. **3.** Indistinctly perceived. ★ ***syns:*** CLOUDY, FOGGY, FUZZY, HAZY, INDEFINITE, INDISTINCT, MISTY, UNCLEAR **—vague′ly** *adv.*

vain (vān) *adj.* **1.** Not yielding the desired outcome : fruitless. **2.** Lacking substance or worth. **3.** Unduly proud of one's appearance or achievement. **—in vain. 1.** Fruitlessly. **2.**

Irreverently <took the Lord's name *in vain*> —**vain'ly** *adv.*
vain•glo•ry (vān'glôr'ē, -glōr'ē) *n., pl.* **-ries. 1.** Boastful and unwarranted pride. **2.** Vain, pretentious display.
val•ance (văl'əns) *n.* **1.** A short ornamental curtain hanging from an edge, as of a bed. **2.** A decorative frame or drapery across the top of a window.

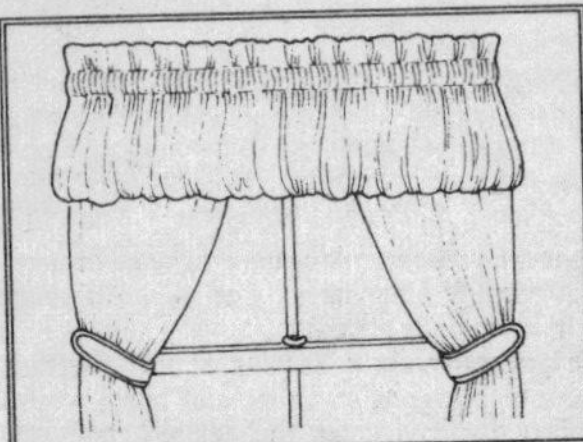

valance

vale (vāl) *n.* A valley.
val•e•dic•tion (văl'ĭ-dĭk'shən) *n.* An act or expression of leave-taking.
val•e•dic•to•ri•an (văl'ĭ-dĭk-tôr'ē-ən, -tōr'-) *n.* A student, usu. the one ranking highest in a graduating class, who delivers the valedictory at a commencement.
val•e•dic•to•ry (văl'ĭ-dĭk'tə-rē) *adj.* Of or constituting a farewell. —*n., pl.* **-ries.** A farewell speech, esp. one delivered by a valedictorian at a commencement exercise.
va•lence (vā'ləns) *also* **va•len•cy** (-lən-sē) *n., pl.* **-lenc•es** *also* **-len•cies** *n.* **1.** *Chem.* The capability of an atom or group of atoms to combine in particular proportions with other atoms or groups of atoms. **2.** A whole number used to represent this capability.
val•en•tine (văl'ən-tīn') *n.* **1.** A person chosen as one's sweetheart on Valentine's Day. **2.** A usu. sentimental greeting card sent to one's valentine.
Valentine's Day *or* **Valentines Day** *n.* Feb. 14, when valentines are traditionally exchanged.
val•et (văl'ĭt, vă-lā') *n.* **1.** A man's personal male attendant. **2.** A hotel employee who performs personal services for guests.
val•e•tu•di•nar•i•an (văl'ĭ-tōōd'n-âr'ē-ən, -tyōōd'-) *n.* A weak or sickly person, esp. one constantly concerned with health matters. —**val'e•tu'di•nar'i•an•ism** *n.*
val•iant (văl'yənt) *adj.* Having or exhibiting valor. —**val'iance** *n.*
val•id (văl'ĭd) *adj.* **1.** Founded on truth or fact. **2.** Having legal force. —**va•lid'i•ty** (və-lĭd'ĭ-tē), **val'id•ness** *n.*
val•i•date (văl'ĭ-dāt') *v.* **-dat•ed, -dat•ing. 1.** To declare or make legally valid. **2.** To verify : substantiate. —**val'i•da'tion** *n.*
va•lise (və-lēs') *n.* A small suitcase.
Val•i•um (văl'ē-əm). A trademark for the tranquilizer diazepam.
val•ley (văl'ē) *n., pl.* **-leys. 1.** An elongated lowland between mountain ranges or hills, often having a river running along the bottom. **2.** A channel formed by the joining of 2 roof slopes.
val•or (văl'ər) *n.* Bravery : courage. —**val'or•ous** *adj.*
val•our (văl'ər) *n. esp. Brit. var. of* VALOR.
val•u•a•ble (văl'yōō-ə-bəl, văl'yə-) *adj.* **1.** Of high monetary value. **2.** Of great importance or use. ★ *syns:* INVALUABLE, PRECIOUS, PRICELESS —*n. often* **valuables.** A personal possession of high monetary value.
val•u•ate (văl'yōō-āt') *v.* **-at•ed, -at•ing.** To set a value on. —**val'u•a'tor** *n.*
val•u•a•tion (văl'yōō-ā'shən) *n.* **1.** An act or the process of assessing price or value. **2.** Assessed value or price.
val•ue (văl'yōō) *n.* **1.** An amount regarded as a fair equivalent for something, esp. goods or services. **2.** Material worth. **3.** Worth in importance or usefulness to the possessor. **4.** A standard or principle regarded as desirable or worthwhile. **5.** Precise meaning, as of a term. **6.** *Math.* A calculated or assigned numerical quantity. **7.** *Mus.* The relative length of a rest or tone. —*v.* **-ued, -u•ing. 1.** To determine or estimate the worth or value of. **2.** To regard highly. **3.** To rate according to usefulness, importance, or worth. —**val'ue•less** *adj.*
val•ue-ad•ded tax (văl'yōō-ăd'ĭd) *n.* A tax on the estimated market value of a product added at each stage of its manufacture and ult. passed on to the consumer.
valve (vălv) *n.* **1.** *Anat.* A membranous structure in a hollow organ or passage, as a vein or artery, that slows or prevents the backward movement of a fluid. **2. a.** A mechanical device that regulates the flow of gases, liquids, or loose materials by blocking and uncovering openings. **b.** The movable part of such a device. **c.** A device in a brass wind instrument used to vary the length of the column of air and thus control the pitch. **3.** *Biol.* Either of the paired hinged shells of many mollusks. —**valved** *adj.* —**val'vu•lar** (văl'vyə-lər) *adj.*
va•moose (vă-mōōs', və-) *v.* **-moosed, -moos•ing.** *Slang.* To leave hurriedly.
vamp[1] (vămp) *n.* **1.** The part of a shoe or boot that covers the instep and sometimes extends over the toes. **2.** An improvised musical accompaniment. —*v.* **1.** To provide (a shoe or boot) with a new vamp. **2.** To patch up (something old). **3.** *Mus.* To improvise.
vamp[2] (vămp) *n. Informal.* A woman who exploits or seduces men. —**vamp** *v.*
vam•pire (văm'pīr') *n.* **1.** A reanimated corpse held to suck the blood of sleeping persons at night. **2.** One who preys on others. **3.** A tropical American bat erroneously thought to feed on the blood of living mammals. —**vam'pir•ism** *n.*
van[1] (văn) *n.* **1.** A large closed truck or wagon. **2.** *esp. Brit.* A closed railroad car for carrying freight or baggage.

van[2] (văn) *n.* The vanguard **:** forefront.
va·na·di·um (və-nā′dē-əm) *n. Symbol* **V** A white ductile metallic element.
Van Al·len belt (văn ăl′ən) *n.* Either of 2 zones surrounding the planet at various high altitudes in which highly energetic charged particles are trapped in the earth's magnetic field.
Van·dal (văn′dl) *n.* **1.** A member of a Germanic people that overran Gaul, Spain, and N Africa and sacked Rome in A.D. 455. **2. vandal.** One who maliciously destroys or defaces property. **—van′dal·ize′** *v.*
van·dal·ism (văn′dl-ĭz′əm) *n.* The malicious destruction or defacement of public or private property.
Van·dyke beard (văn-dīk′) *n.* A short, pointed beard.

Vandyke beard

vane (vān) *n.* **1.** A device that pivots on an elevated object, as a rooftop or spire, to indicate wind direction. **2.** One of a number of thin, rigid blades radially mounted along an axis that is used to turn or is turned by a fluid. **3.** One of the stabilizing fins attached to the tail of a missile.
van·guard (văn′gärd′) *n.* **1.** An army or fleet's foremost position. **2.** The leading position in a movement or trend.
va·nil·la (və-nĭl′ə) *n.* **1.** A tropical American orchid of the genus *Vanilla,* esp. *V. planifolia,* cultivated for its long, narrow, aromatic seedpods. **2.** A flavoring extract prepared from the seedpod of the vanilla.
van·ish (văn′ĭsh) *v.* **1.** To disappear, esp. quickly or in an unexplained way. **2.** To pass out of existence. **—van′ish·er** *n.*
van·i·ty (văn′ĭ-tē) *n., pl.* **-ties. 1.** Excessive pride **:** conceit. **2.** Lack of usefulness **:** worthlessness. **3.** Something vain or futile. **4.** A vanity case. **5.** A dressing table.
vanity case *n.* **1.** A woman's compact. **2.** A small case for toiletries or cosmetics.
vanity plate *n.* A usu. more expensive license plate for a motor vehicle having a combination of numbers or letters chosen by the vehicle's owner.
vanity press *n.* A publisher that publishes a book at the author's expense.
van·quish (văng′kwĭsh, văn′-) *v.* **1.** To defeat in battle. **2.** To overcome **:** suppress.
van·tage (văn′tĭj) *n.* **1.** Superiority in a conflict or competition. **2.** A strategic position providing superiority.
vap·id (văp′ĭd) *adj.* Lacking liveliness or interest. **—va·pid′i·ty** (vă-pĭd′ĭ-tē, və-), **vap′id·ness** *n.* **—vap′id·ly** *adv.*
va·por (vā′pər) *n.* **1.** A faintly visible suspension of fine particles of matter in the air, as mist or fog. **2.** The gaseous state of a substance that under normal circumstances is liquid or solid. **3. vapors.** *Archaic.* Hysteria. **—va′por·ish** *adj.*
va·por·ize (vā′pə-rīz′) *v.* **-ized, -iz·ing.** To convert or be converted into vapor. **—va′por·i·za′tion** *n.* **—va′por·iz′er** *n.*
va·por·ous (vā′pər-əs) *adj.* **1.** Relating to or like vapor. **2. a.** Producing vapors. **b.** Giving off or full of vapors. **3.** Insubstantial or vague. **—va′por·ous·ly** *adv.*
vapor trail *n.* A contrail.
va·pour (vā′pər) *n. & v. esp. Brit. var. of* VAPOR.
†va·que·ro (vä-kâr′ō) *n., pl.* **-ros.** *SW U.S.* A cowboy.
var·i·a (vâr′ē-ə, văr′-) *n.* A miscellany, esp. of literary works.
var·i·a·ble (vâr′ē-ə-bəl) *adj.* **1.** Tending or apt to vary. **2.** Fickle **:** inconstant. *—n.* **1.** Something that varies. **2.** *Math.* **a.** A quantity that may assume any of a set of values. **b.** A symbol representing such a quantity. **—var′i·a·bil′i·ty, var′i·a·ble·ness** *n.* **—var′i·a·bly** *adv.*
var·i·ance (vâr′ē-əns) *n.* **1. a.** Difference. **b.** A degree of variation. **2.** A difference of opinion. **3.** *Law.* A license to engage in an act contrary to a usual rule.
var·i·ant (vâr′ē-ənt) *adj.* **1.** Having or showing variation. **2.** Tending or apt to vary **:** variable. *—n.* Something that differs in form only slightly from something else <a spelling *variant*>
var·i·a·tion (vâr′ē-ā′shən) *n.* **1.** The process or result of varying. **2.** Extent or degree of varying. **3.** Something slightly different from another of the same type. **4.** *Mus.* An altered version of a given theme, with modifications in melody, key, or rhythm.
var·i·col·ored (vâr′ĭ-kŭl′ərd) *adj.* VARIEGATED 1.
var·i·cose (văr′ĭ-kōs′) *adj.* Abnormally swollen and knotted <*varicose* veins>
var·ied (vâr′ēd) *adj.* **1.** Characterized by variety. **2.** Altered **:** modified.
var·i·e·gat·ed (vâr′ē-ĭ-gā′tĭd, vâr′ĭ-gā′-, văr′-) *adj.* **1.** Having streaks or marks of different colors. **2.** Marked by variety.
va·ri·e·ty (və-rī′ĭ-tē) *n., pl.* **-ties. 1.** The state or quality of being varied or various. **2.** A number of varied things, esp. of a particular group. **3.** A group set off from other groups by specific characteristics. **4.** A living thing, esp. a plant, belonging to a subdivision of a species.
variety store *n.* A retail store that carries a variety of usu. inexpensive merchandise.
var·i·ous (vâr′ē-əs) *adj.* **1. a.** Of diverse kinds. **b.** Different. **2.** Several. **3.** Versatile. **4.** Indi-

vidual and separate. **—var'i•ous•ly** *adv.* **—var'i•ous•ness** *n.*

var•let (vär'lĭt) *n. Archaic.* **1.** A servant. **2.** A rascal **:** knave.

var•mint (vär'mĭnt) *n. Informal.* **1.** A dangerous or troublesome animal. **2.** A despised or obnoxious person.

var•nish (vär'nĭsh) *n.* **1.** An oil-based paint for coating a surface with a hard, transparent, shiny film. **2.** The smooth coating or gloss produced by applying varnish. **3.** A deceptively attractive outward appearance. **—var'nish** *v.*

var•si•ty (vär'sĭ-tē) *n., pl.* **-ties.** The best team representing a school or club.

var•y (vâr'ē) *v.* **-ied, -y•ing. 1.** To undergo or cause change **:** alter. **2.** To make different. **3.** To diverge **:** deviate.

vas (văs) *n., pl.* **va•sa** (vā'zə). *Anat.* A vessel or duct.

vas•cu•lar (văs'kyə-lər) *adj. Biol.* Of, having, or forming vessels for the circulation of fluids, as blood or sap.

vas def•er•ens (văs' dĕf'ər-ənz, -ə-rĕnz') *n.* The duct in male vertebrate animals through which sperm passes from a testis to the ejaculatory duct.

vase (vās, vāz, väz) *n.* An open container for holding cut flowers.

va•sec•to•my (vă-sĕk'tə-mē) *n., pl.* **-mies.** A method of sterilization involving the surgical excision of a part of the vas deferens.

Vas•e•line (văs'ə-lēn'). A trademark for a petrolatum.

vas•o•con•stric•tion (văs'ō-kən-strĭk'shən) *n.* Constriction of a blood vessel. **—vas'o•con•stric'tor** *n.*

vas•o•dil•a•ta•tion (văs'ō-dĭl'ə-tā'shən, -dī'lə-) *n.* Dilatation of a blood vessel. **—vas'o•di•la'tor** (-dī-lā'tər, -dĭ-) *n.*

vas•sal (văs'əl) *n.* **1.** One who was granted land from a feudal lord in return for homage and military service. **2.** One who is subordinate or subservient to another. **—vas'sal•age** *n.*

vast (văst) *adj.* Very great in size or extent. **—vast'ly** *adv.* **—vast'ness** *n.*

vat (văt) *n.* A large tub or cask for storing or holding liquids.

vat•ic (văt'ĭk) *adj.* Prophetic **:** oracular.

Vat•i•can (văt'ĭ-kən) *n.* **1.** The official papal residence. **2.** The papal government.

va•tu (vä'tōō) *n.* —See table at CURRENCY.

vaude•ville (vôd'vĭl', vōd'-, vô'də-) *n.* A stage show consisting of a number of short acts, as slapstick comedy, songs, and dances. **—vaude•vil'lian** *n.*

vault[1] (vôlt) *n.* **1. a.** An arched roof or ceiling. **b.** Something resembling a vault, as the sky. **2.** An underground room having arched walls and ceiling, as a storeroom. **3.** A room, as in a bank, for the safekeeping of valuables. **4.** A burial chamber. *—v.* To construct or supply with a vault.

vault[2] (vôlt) *v.* To leap or jump (over), esp. by holding a long pole or with the hands supported on the barrier. **—vault** *n.*

vaunt (vônt, vŏnt) *v.* To boast. **—vaunt** *n.* **—vaunt'ing•ly** *adv.*

VCR (vē'sē-är') *n., pl.* **VCR's.** An electronic device for recording and playing back video images and sound on a videocassette.

VDT (vē'dē-tē') *n., pl.* **VDT's.** *Computer Sci.* A device using the screen of a cathode-ray tube to display data and graphic images.

-'ve. Have <I'*ve* been invited.>

veal (vēl) *n.* The meat of a calf.

vec•tor (vĕk'tər) *n.* **1.** *Math.* A quantity that has magnitude and a direction. **2.** An organism that transmits disease-carrying germs. **—vec•to'ri•al** *adj.*

veep (vēp) *n. Slang.* A vice president.

veer (vîr) *v.* To shift from one course or direction to another. **—veer** *n.*

veg•an (vĕj'ən, -ăn') *n.* A strict vegetarian who uses no products derived from animals, as soap or leather. **—veg'an•ism** *n.*

veg•e•ta•ble (vĕj'tə-bəl, vĕj'ĭ-tə-) *n.* **1.** A plant, as the beet or spinach, raised for an edible part, as the root or leaves. **2.** One who leads a dull, passive, or merely physical existence. **—veg'e•ta•ble** *adj.*

veg•e•tar•i•an (vĕj'ĭ-târ'ē-ən) *n.* A person whose diet includes mainly plants and plant products and who eats no meat. *—adj.* **1.** Consuming only plants and plant products. **2.** Consisting only of plants and plant products. **—veg'e•tar'i•an•ism** *n.*

veg•e•tate (vĕj'ĭ-tāt') *v.* **-tat•ed, -tat•ing. 1.** To sprout or grow as a plant does. **2.** To lead a life characterized by little physical energy or mental effort.

veg•e•ta•tion (vĕj'ĭ-tā'shən) *n.* **1.** The act or process of vegetating. **2.** Plants or plant life in general.

veg•e•ta•tive (vĕj'ĭ-tā'tĭv) *adj.* **1.** Of, relating to, or typical of plants or plant growth. **2.** *Biol.* **a.** Of or capable of growth. **b.** Of or relating to growth or physical change rather than sexual processes.

ve•he•ment (vē'ə-mənt) *adj.* **1.** Marked by vigorous or forceful expression or intense emotion. **2.** Characterized by or full of vigor. **—ve'he•mence** *n.*

ve•hi•cle (vē'ĭ-kəl) *n.* **1.** A device, as a piece of mechanized equipment, for transporting goods, passengers, or equipment. **2.** A medium, as a painting or novel, through which something is expressed or accomplished. **3.** A substance, as oil, in which paint pigments are mixed for application. **—ve•hic'u•lar** (vē-hĭk'yə-lər) *adj.*

veil (vāl) *n.* **1.** A piece of usu. fine, transparent cloth worn by women over the head, shoulders, and often part of the face. **2. a.** The part of a nun's headdress that frames the face and falls over the shoulders. **b.** The life or vows of a nun <took the *veil*> **3.** Something that conceals or screens. *—v.* To cover or conceal with or as if with a veil.

vein (vān) *n.* **1.** *Anat.* A vessel that transports blood toward the heart. **2.** One of the narrow branching tubes forming the framework of an insect's wing or a leaf. **3.** *Geol.* A deposit of an ore in the earth. **4.** A wavy streak of color, as in marble. **5.** A pervading quality or character. **6.** A manner or mode. —*v.* To fill or mark with veins.

Vel•cro (vĕl'krō'). A trademark for a fastening tape used esp. for cloth products.

veldt (fĕlt, vĕlt) *n. So. Afr.* An open grazing area.

vel•lum (vĕl'əm) *n.* A fine parchment prepared from the skins of calf, lamb, or kid and used for writing on and for binding fine books.

ve•loc•i•ty (və-lŏs'ĭ-tē) *n., pl.* **-ties. 1.** Rapidity **:** speed. **2.** *Physics.* A vector quantity whose magnitude is a body's speed and whose direction is the body's direction of motion.

ve•loc•i•pede (və-lŏs'ə-pēd') *n.* **1.** An early bicycle propelled by pushing the feet along the ground. **2.** A tricycle.

velocipede

ve•lour *or* **ve•lours** (və-lo͝or') *n., pl.* **-lours** (-lo͝or'). A velvetlike fabric with a short thick nap.

ve•lum (vē'ləm) *n., pl.* **-la** (-lə). The soft back part of the palate. —**ve'lar** *adj.*

vel•vet (vĕl'vĭt) *n.* **1.** A fabric made usu. of silk or a synthetic fiber and having a smooth, dense pile. **2.** Something resembling velvet. **3.** The soft skin covering the growing antlers of a deer. —**vel'vet•y** *adj.*

vel•vet•een (vĕl'vĭ-tēn') *n.* A velvetlike cotton fabric.

ve•na ca•va (vē'nə kā'və) *n., pl.* **ve•nae ca•vae** (vē'nē kā'vē). Either of the 2 large veins that return blood to the right atrium of the heart in vertebrates that breathe air.

ve•nal (vē'nəl) *adj.* Open or susceptible to bribery. —**ve•nal'i•ty** (vē-năl'ĭ-tē) *n.*

vend (vĕnd) *v.* To sell.

vend•ee (vĕn-dē') *n.* A buyer.

vend•er *also* **ven•dor** (vĕn'dər) *n.* **1.** One that sells. **2.** A vending machine.

ven•det•ta (vĕn-dĕt'ə) *n.* A feud between families, esp. one involving revenge killings.

vending machine *n.* A coin-operated machine for dispensing merchandise.

ve•neer (və-nîr') *n.* **1.** A thin surface layer of a better material covering an inferior one. **2.** Superficial outward show. —*v.* To cover with a veneer.

ven•er•a•ble (vĕn'ər-ə-bəl) *adj.* **1.** Worthy of respect by reason of age, dignity, or position. **2.** Deserving respect for historic or religious associations. —**ven'er•a•bil'i•ty** *n.*

ven•er•ate (vĕn'ə-rāt') *v.* **-at•ed, -at•ing.** To regard with respect or deference. —**ven'er•a'tion** *n.*

venereal disease *n.* A contagious disease, as gonorrhea or syphilis, transmitted by sexual contact.

ve•ne•re•ol•o•gy (və-nîr'ē-ŏl'ə-jē) *n.* The study of venereal diseases. —**ve•ne're•ol'o•gist** *n.*

Ve•ne•tian blind (və-nē'shən) *n.* A blind with thin horizontal slats that can be set at a desired angle to control the amount of light that comes in between them.

venge•ance (vĕn'jəns) *n.* The act of causing harm to another in retribution for a wrong or injury.

venge•ful (vĕnj'fəl) *adj.* Desiring vengeance. —**venge'ful•ness** *n.*

ve•ni•al (vē'nē-əl, vēn'yəl) *adj.* Easily forgiven or excused.

ve•ni•re (və-nī'rē) *n.* A writ summoning persons to appear in court as jurors. —**ve•ni're•man** *n.*

ven•i•son (vĕn'ĭ-sən, -zən) *n.* The edible flesh of a deer.

ven•om (vĕn'əm) *n.* **1.** A poisonous secretion of an animal, as a snake or scorpion, usu. transmitted by a sting or bite. **2.** Malice **:** spite. —**ven'om•ous** *adj.*

ve•nous (vē'nəs) *adj.* **1.** Of or relating to veins. **2.** *Physiol.* Returning to the heart through a vein, esp. one of the larger veins.

vent[1] (vĕnt) *n.* **1.** A way of leaving a restricted space. **2.** An opening for the passage or escape of a liquid, gas, or vapor. —*v.* **1.** To give forceful expression to. **2.** To discharge through a vent. **3.** To provide with a vent.

vent[2] (vĕnt) *n.* A vertical slit in a garment, as a jacket or skirt.

ven•ti•late (vĕn'tl-āt') *v.* **-lat•ed, -lat•ing. 1.** To cause fresh air to circulate in. **2.** To provide with a vent. **3.** To expose to public examination or discussion. —**ven'ti•la'tion** *n.* —**ven'ti•la'tor** *n.*

ven•tral (vĕn'trəl) *adj.* **1.** Of, relating to, or near the belly. **2.** Of or relating to the lower surface of the body of an animal.

ven•tri•cle (vĕn'trĭ-kəl) *n.* A cavity in an anatomical organ, esp. either of the chambers of the heart that contract to pump blood into arteries. —**ven•tric'u•lar** (vĕn-trĭk'yə-lər) *adj.*

ven•tril•o•quism (vĕn-trĭl'ə-kwĭz'əm) *also* **ven•tril•o•quy** (-kwē) *n.* A means of producing vocal sounds so that they seem to come from a source other than the speaker, as from a mechanical or hand-operated dummy. —**ven•tril'o•quist** *n.*

ven•ture (vĕn'chər) *n.* **1.** A course of action involving risk or danger. **2.** Something at hazard in a venture. —*v.* **-tured, -tur•ing. 1.** To expose to risk or danger. **2.** To brave the dangers of. **3.** To dare to express <*ventured* an opinion> —**ven'tur•er** *n.* —**ven'ture•some, ven'tur•ous** *adj.*

ven•ue (vĕn′yōō) *n.* **1.** The locality where a crime or other cause of legal action occurs. **2.** The place where a gathering or public event, as a concert, is held.

Ve•nus (vē′nəs) *n.* The 2nd planet from the sun. —**Ve•nu′sian** (vĭ-nōō′zhən, -nyōō′-) *adj.*

Ve•nus′s-fly•trap (vē′nə-sĭz-flī′trăp′) *n.* A plant, *Dionaea muscipula,* of boggy areas of the SE U.S., with hinged, spined leaf blades that close to entrap insects.

ve•ra•cious (və-rā′shəs) *adj.* **1.** Truthful : honest. **2.** True : accurate. —**ve•ra′cious•ly** *adv.* —**ve•ra′cious•ness** *n.*

ve•rac•i•ty (və-răs′ĭ-tē) *n., pl.* **-ties. 1.** Devotion to the truth. **2.** Accuracy.

ve•ran•dah *or* **ve•ran•da** (və-răn′də) *n.* A usu. roofed and often partly enclosed porch or balcony extending along the outside of a building.

verb (vûrb) *n.* **1.** The part of speech that expresses action, existence, or occurrence in most languages. **2.** Any of the words within this part of speech, as *be, walk,* or *think.*

ver•bal (vûr′bəl) *adj.* **1.** Of or relating to words. **2.** Having to do with words rather than with the ideas they represent. **3.** Expressed in speech. **4.** Word for word : literal. **5.** Relating to or derived from a verb. —*n.* A noun, adjective, or other word derived from a verb and retaining some of the verb's characteristics. —**ver′bal•ly** *adv.*

ver•bal•ize (vûr′bə-līz′) *v.* **-ized, -iz•ing. 1.** To express in words. **2.** To convert into a verb. —**ver′bal•i•za′tion** *n.*

ver•ba•tim (vər-bā′tĭm) *adv. & adj.* Using precisely the same words : word for word.

ver•be•na (vər-bē′nə) *n.* A New World plant of the genus *Verbena,* with variously colored flower clusters.

ver•bi•age (vûr′bē-ĭj) *n.* **1.** More words than are needed : wordiness. **2.** The way in which one expresses oneself : wording.

ver•bose (vər-bōs′) *adj.* Using or having more words than required. —**ver•bos′i•ty** (-bŏs′ĭ-tē) *n.*

ver•bo•ten (vər-bōt′n) *adj.* Forbidden.

ver•dant (vûr′dənt) *adj.* **1.** Covered with growing plants. **2.** Green in color. —**ver′dan•cy** *n.* —**ver′dant•ly** *adv.*

ver•dict (vûr′dĭkt) *n.* **1.** The decision arrived at by a jury at the end of a trial. **2.** A judgment.

ver•di•gris (vûr′dĭ-grēs′, -grĭs) *n.* A green coating or crust of copper salts that forms on copper, brass, and bronze exposed to sea water or air for a long time.

ver•dure (vûr′jər) *n.* **1.** The green color of healthy growing plants. **2.** Vegetation.

verge[1] (vûrj) *n.* **1.** An edge or rim : brink. **2.** The point beyond which an action or condition is likely to start or happen. **3.** A staff or rod carried as a symbol of authority. —*v.* **verged, verg•ing.** To border on.

verge[2] (vûrj) *v.* **verged, verg•ing. 1.** To tend or incline. **2.** To be in transition.

ver•i•fy (vĕr′ə-fī′) *v.* **-fied, -fy•ing. 1.** To prove the truth of by presenting evidence or testimony. **2.** To test the accuracy of. —**ver′i•fi′a•ble** *adj.* —**ver′i•fi•ca′tion** *n.* —**ver′i•fi′er** *n.*

ver•i•ly (vĕr′ə-lē) *adv.* **1.** In fact : certainly. **2.** Assuredly : truly.

ver•i•si•mil•i•tude (vĕr′ĭ-sə-mĭl′ĭ-tōōd′, -tyōōd′) *n.* **1.** The quality or state of appearing to be true : likelihood. **2.** Something appearing to be real or true.

ver•i•ta•ble (vĕr′ĭ-tə-bəl) *adj.* True : unquestionable. —**ver′i•ta•bly** *adv.*

ver•i•ty (vĕr′ĭ-tē) *n., pl.* **-ties. 1.** The quality or state of being real or true. **2.** A statement or principle regarded as established and permanent truth.

ver•mi•cel•li (vûr′mə-chĕl′ē, -sĕl′ē) *n.* Pasta in long strings thinner than spaghetti.

ver•mi•cide (vûr′mĭ-sīd′) *n.* An agent for killing worms. —**ver′mi•cid′al** *adj.*

ver•mi•form (vûr′mə-fôrm′) *adj.* Wormlike in shape.

vermiform appendix *n.* A slender, closed tube attached to the large intestine.

ver•mi•fuge (vûr′mə-fyōōj′) *n.* An agent that destroys or expels intestinal worms.

ver•mil•ion *also* **ver•mil•lion** (vər-mĭl′yən) *n.* A bright red.

ver•min (vûr′mĭn) *n., pl.* **vermin.** An insect or animal that is destructive, annoying, or harmful to health, as a cockroach or rat. —**ver′min•ous** *adj.*

ver•mouth (vər-mōōth′) *n.* A sweet red or dry white wine flavored with herbs.

ver•nac•u•lar (vər-năk′yə-lər) *n.* **1.** The normal spoken language of a country or region. **2.** The idiom of a specific profession or trade. —**ver•nac′u•lar** *adj.*

ver•nal (vûr′nəl) *adj.* Of, relating to, or happening in the spring. —**ver′nal•ly** *adv.*

ver•ni•er (vûr′nē-ər) *n.* A small auxiliary scale attached parallel to a main scale to indicate fractional parts of the smallest divisions of the larger scale.

vernier caliper *n.* A measuring instrument with an L-shaped frame with a linear scale along its longer arm and a L-shaped sliding attachment with a vernier scale.

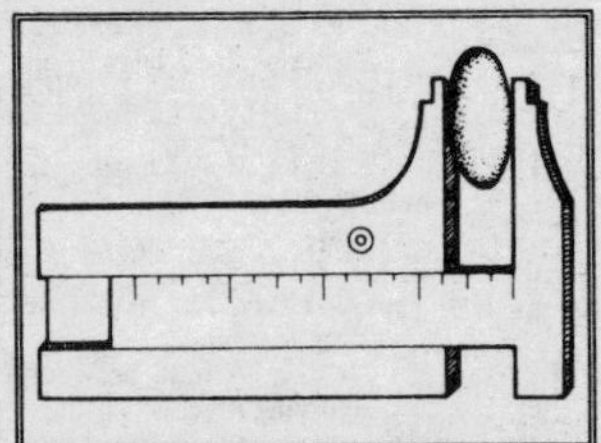

vernier caliper

ve•ron•i•ca (və-rŏn′ĭ-kə) *n.* Any of various plants of the genus *Veronica,* including the speedwell.

ver•sa•tile (vûr′sə-təl, -tīl′) *adj.* **1.** Capable of doing many things. 2. Having many functions or uses. —**ver′sa•til′i•ty** *n.*

verse[1] (vûrs) *n.* **1.** Writing that has meter or rhyme : poetry. **2. a.** A line of poetry. **b.** A stanza. **3.** A particular type of metrical composition, as blank verse. **4.** A subdivision of a chapter of the Bible.

verse[2] (vûrs) *v.* **versed, vers•ing.** To make familiar or skilled <*verse* oneself in economics>

ver•si•cle (vûr′sĭ-kəl) *n.* A short sentence chanted by a priest and followed by a congregational response.

ver•si•fy (vûr′sə-fī′) *v.* **-fied, -fy•ing. 1.** To put into verse form. **2.** To write verses. —**ver′si•fi•ca′tion** *n.* —**ver′si•fi′er** *n.*

ver•sion (vûr′zhən, -shən) *n.* **1.** A description or account told from a particular point of view. **2.** A translation of a written work, esp. the Bible. **3.** A particular form or variation. **4.** An adaptation of a work of literature or art into another medium.

ver•so (vûr′sō) *n., pl.* **-sos.** The left-hand page of a book.

ver•sus (vûr′səs) *prep.* **1.** Against <the Yankees *versus* the Orioles> **2.** In contrast with <compromise *versus* defeat>

ver•te•bra (vûr′tə-brə) *n., pl.* **-brae** (-brē) *or* **-bras.** Any of the bones or cartilaginous segments making up the spinal column. —**ver′te•bral** *adj.*

ver•te•brate (vûr′tə-brāt′, -brĭt) *adj.* **1.** Having a backbone. **2.** Of or typical of vertebrates. —*n.* A member of the subphylum Vertebrata that includes the fishes, amphibians, reptiles, birds, and mammals, all of which have a backbone.

ver•tex (vûr′tĕks′) *n., pl.* **-es** *or* **-ti•ces** (-tĭ-sēz′). **1.** The apex. **2. a.** The point at which the sides of an angle intersect. **b.** The point of a triangle opposite and farthest away from its base. **c.** A point on a polyhedron common to 3 or more sides.

ver•ti•cal (vûr′tĭ-kəl) *adj.* **1.** Being at right angles to the horizon. **2.** Directly overhead. ★ *syns:* PERPENDICULAR, PLUMB, UPRIGHT —*n.* **1.** A vertical line or plane. **2.** A vertical position. —**ver′ti•cal′i•ty** (-kăl′ĭ-tē), **ver′ti•cal•ness** *n.*

ver•tig•i•nous (vər-tĭj′ə-nəs) *adj.* **1.** Turning about an axis. **2.** Affected by or likely to cause vertigo. —**ver•tig′i•nous•ly** *adv.*

ver•ti•go (vûr′tĭ-gō′) *n., pl.* **-goes** *or* **-gos.** The sensation of dizziness.

ver•vain (vûr′vān′) *n.* A plant of the genus *Verbena,* with spikes of small blue or white flowers.

verve (vûrv) *n.* **1.** Energy and vigor, esp. in artistic performance or composition. **2.** Liveliness : vitality.

ver•y (vĕr′ē) *adv.* **1.** To a high degree : extremely. **2.** Absolutely : truly <the *very* best we can buy> **3.** Exactly <the *very* same person> —*adj.* **-i•er, -i•est. 1.** Complete : absolute. **2.** Identical <the *very* complaints of yesterday> **3.** —Used as an intensive to emphasize the importance of the thing mentioned <The *very* earth trembled.> **4.** Particularly suitable <the *very* thing for a cold> **5.** Mere <awed by the *very* mention of the name> **6.** Actual <caught in the *very* act>

very high frequency *n.* A band of radio frequencies ranging between 30 and 300 megahertz.

very low frequency *n.* A band of radio frequencies between 3 and 30 kilohertz.

ves•i•cant (vĕs′ĭ-kənt) *n.* A blistering agent, as mustard gas, used in chemical warfare. —**ves′i•cant** *adj.*

ves•i•cle (vĕs′ĭ-kəl) *n.* **1.** A small bladderlike cavity or cell. **2.** *Pathol.* A serum-filled blister. —**ve•sic′u•lar** (və-sĭk′yə-lər) *adj.*

ves•per (vĕs′pər) *n.* **1.** A bell for summoning people to vespers. **2. Vesper.** The evening star.

ves•pers *also* **Ves•pers** (vĕs′pərz) *pl.n.* A service of worship in the late afternoon or evening.

ves•sel (vĕs′əl) *n.* **1. a.** A hollow utensil used as a container, esp. for liquids. **b.** One regarded as an agent of some quality <a *vessel* of innocence> **2.** A craft, esp. one bigger than a rowboat, intended for navigation on water. **3.** *Anat.* A duct or other tube for circulating a bodily fluid.

vest (vĕst) *n.* **1.** A sleeveless and collarless garment, either open or fastening in front, worn over a shirt and often under a suit coat or jacket. **2.** *esp. Brit.* An undershirt. —*v.* **1.** To clothe or dress with or as if with ecclesiastical vestments. **2.** To place in the possession of. **3.** To place (e.g., authority) in the hands of.

ves•tal (vĕs′təl) *adj.* Chaste : virginal. —*n.* A woman who is a virgin.

vested interest *n.* **1.** A strong commitment to something, as an institution, from which one receives political or economic benefit. **2.** A group with a vested interest.

ves•ti•bule (vĕs′tə-byo͞ol′) *n.* **1.** A small entrance hall or passage. **2.** *Anat.* A cavity, chamber, or channel that serves as an approach or entrance to another cavity. —**ves•tib′u•lar** *adj.*

ves•tige (vĕs′tĭj) *n.* A visible sign of something that no longer exists.

ves•tig•i•al (vĕ-stĭj′ē-əl, -stĭj′əl) *adj.* **1.** Of, pertaining to, or being a vestige. **2.** *Biol.* Existing or persisting as a degenerate bodily structure. —**ves•tig′i•al•ly** *adv.*

vest•ment (vĕst′mənt) *n.* **1.** A garment, esp. a ceremonial or official robe. **2.** Any of the ritual robes worn by members of the clergy or assistants at religious services.

vest-pock•et (vĕst′pŏk′ĭt) *adj.* Relatively small : diminutive.

ves•try (vĕs′trē) *n., pl.* **-tries. 1.** A room in a church where the clergy don their vestments : sacristy. **2.** A church meeting room. **3.** A committee administering the affairs of an Episcopal parish.

ves•try•man (vĕs′trē-mən) *n.* A vestry member.

ves•ture (vĕs′chər) *n.* **1.** Clothing. **2.** Something that covers.

vet (vĕt) *n. Informal.* **1.** A veterinarian. **2.** A veteran.

vetch (vĕch) *n.* A climbing plant of the genus *Vicia,* bearing pinnate leaves and small, usu. purplish flowers.

vet•er•an (vĕt′ər-ən, vĕt′rən) *n.* **1.** One with a long record of service in a particular activity or capacity. **2.** One who has served in the armed forces.

Veterans Day *n.* Nov. 11, a U.S. holiday commemorating the armistice ending World War I in 1918 and honoring veterans of the armed services.

vet•er•i•nar•i•an (vĕt′ər-ə-nâr′ē-ən, vĕt′rə-) *n.* One trained and qualified to give medical treatment to animals.

vet•er•i•nar•y (vĕt′ər-ə-nĕr′ē, vĕt′rə-) *adj.* Of, pertaining to, or being the science of the diagnosis and treatment of animals. *—n., pl.* **-ies.** A veterinarian.

ve•to (vē′tō) *n., pl.* **-toes. 1. a.** The right or power of a branch of government or of a governmental office to reject a bill passed by a legislature and thus delay or prevent its enactment. **b.** The exercise of this right. **2.** An authoritative rejection of a proposed act. *—v.* **-toed, -to•ing. 1.** To prevent enactment of (a legislative bill) by exercising the power of veto. **2.** To forbid.

vex (vĕks) *v.* **1.** To annoy or bother. **2.** To baffle. **3.** To discuss at length.

vex•a•tion (vĕk-sā′shən) *n.* **1.** An act of vexing or the state of being vexed. **2.** A source of annoyance. **—vex•a′tious** *adj.* **—vex•a′tious•ly** *adv.*

vi•a (vī′ə, vē′ə) *prep.* By way of.

vi•a•ble (vī′ə-bəl) *adj.* **1.** Capable of living, as a newborn infant or a fetus arriving at a stage of development that will allow it to live. **2.** Capable of living or developing under favorable conditions. **3.** Capable of being successful or continuing to be effective. **—vi′a•bil′i•ty** *n.* **—vi′a•bly** *adv.*

vi•a•duct (vī′ə-dŭkt′) *n.* A bridge consisting of a series of arches for carrying a road or railroad over a wide valley or over other roads or railroads.

vi•al (vī′əl) *n.* A small container, used esp. for liquids.

vi•and (vī′ənd) *n.* **1.** An item of food. **2. viands.** Provisions.

vibes (vībz) *pl.n.* **1.** *Informal.* A vibraphone. **2.** *Slang.* VIBRATIONS *4.*

vi•brant (vī′brənt) *adj.* **1.** Displaying, marked by, or caused by vibration. **2.** Full of energy : vigorous. **—vi′brance, vi′bran•cy** *n.* **—vi′brant•ly** *adv.*

vi•bra•phone (vī′brə-fōn′) *n.* A percussion instrument resembling the marimba but with rotating disks and metal bars in the resonators to cause a vibrato. **—vi′bra•phon′ist** *n.*

vi•brate (vī′brāt′) *v.* **-brat•ed, -brat•ing. 1.** To move or cause to move back and forth rapidly. **2.** To produce a sound. **3.** To respond emotionally. **4.** To waver in making choices. **—vi′bra′tor** *n.* **—vi′bra•to′ry** (-brə-tôr′ē, -tōr′ē) *adj.*

vi•bra•tion (vī-brā′shən) *n.* **1.** The act of vibrating or state of being vibrated. **2.** *Physics.* Quick motion of a particle or of an elastic solid back and forth in a straight line on both sides of a center position. **3.** A single vibrating motion : quiver. **4. vibrations.** *Slang.* An emotional aura that can be instinctively sensed. **—vi•bra′tion•al** *adj.*

vi•bra•to (vĭ-brä′tō, vē-) *n., pl.* **-tos.** *Mus.* A tremulous or pulsating effect created in a vocal or instrumental tone by minute and rapid variations in pitch.

vi•bur•num (vī-bûr′nəm) *n.* A shrub or tree of the genus *Viburnum,* bearing small white flower clusters and black or red berries.

vic•ar (vĭk′ər) *n.* **1.** A parish priest in the Church of England. **2.** A cleric in the Episcopal Church in charge of a chapel. **3.** One who serves as a substitute for another. **—vi•car′i•al** (vī-kâr′ē-əl) *adj.*

vic•ar•age (vĭk′ər-ĭj) *n.* **1.** The residence of a vicar. **2.** A vicar's benefice.

vicar general *n., pl.* **vicars general.** *Rom. Cath. Ch.* A priest acting as an administrative deputy to a bishop.

vi•car•i•ous (vī-kâr′ē-əs, vĭ-) *adj.* **1.** Endured or undergone by one person acting for another. **2.** Acting in place of someone else. **3.** Felt or experienced as if one were participating in the feelings or experience of another. **—vi•car′i•ous•ly** *adv.* **—vi•car′i•ous•ness** *n.*

vice[1] (vīs) *n.* **1.** A degrading or immoral habit or practice. **2.** Wicked or evil conduct. **3.** Sexual immorality, esp. prostitution. **4.** A personal failing.

vice[2] (vīs) *n. var. of* VISE.

vice[3] (vīs) *n.* A person acting in the place of another <the *vice*-chairman> *—prep.* **vi•ce** (vī′sē). In place of.

vice admiral *n.* A U.S. naval officer ranking next beneath an admiral.

vice•ge•rent (vīs-jîr′ənt) *n.* One appointed by a head of state to act as an administrative deputy.

vi•cen•ni•al (vī-sĕn′ē-əl) *adj.* Occurring once every 20 years.

vice president *n.* **1.** An officer ranking next beneath a president and having authority to take his place in case of absence, illness, or death. **2.** A deputy of a president, esp. in a corporation, who is head of a department. **—vice-pres′i•den•cy** *n.*

vice•re•gal (vīs-rē′gəl) *adj.* Of or pertaining to a viceroy.

vice•roy (vīs′roi′) *n.* A governor of a country, colony, or province ruling as the representative of a sovereign. **—vice′roy′al•ty** *n.*

vice squad *n.* A police division whose task is to control gambling and prostitution.

vi•ce ver•sa (vī′sə vûr′sə, vīs vûr′-) *adv.* With the meaning or order reversed.

vi•chys•soise (vĭsh′ē-swäz′, vē′shē-) *n.* A creamy, thick potato soup made from chicken stock, flavored with leeks or onions, and usu. served cold.

vi•cin•i•ty (vĭ-sĭn'ĭ-tē) *n., pl.* **-ties. 1.** The state of being near in space or relationship. **2.** A surrounding area.
vi•cious (vĭsh'əs) *adj.* **1.** Addicted to vice or depravity : evil. **2.** Malicious : spiteful <*vicious* rumors> **3.** Marked by violence or ferocity <a *vicious* storm> **4.** Savagely aggressive : dangerous. **—vi'cious•ly** *adv.*
vi•cis•si•tude (vĭ-sĭs'ĭ-to͞od', -tyo͞od') *n.* **1.** *often* **vicissitudes.** A change or variation. **2.** The quality of being changeable.
vic•tim (vĭk'tĭm) *n.* **1.** One harmed or killed by another. **2.** A living creature slain and offered to a deity as a sacrifice. **3.** One harmed by an act, circumstance, or condition <*victims* of disaster>
vic•tim•ize (vĭk'tə-mīz') *v.* **-ized, -iz•ing. 1.** To subject to fraud. **2.** To make a victim of. **—vic'tim•i•za'tion** *n.*
vic•tor (vĭk'tər) *n.* One who vanquishes or defeats an adversary.
vic•to•ri•a (vĭk-tôr'ē-ə, -tōr'-) *n.* A light 4-wheeled horse-drawn carriage for 2 with a folding top and a raised seat in front for the driver.
Victoria Day *n. Can.* The first Monday preceding May 25, a national holiday commemorating Queen Victoria's birthday.
Vic•to•ri•an (vĭk-tôr'ē-ən, -tōr'-) *adj.* **1.** Of or relating to the period of Queen Victoria's reign. **2.** Relating to or displaying moral qualities or standards that are usu. associated with the time of Queen Victoria. —*n.* One belonging to or typical of the Victorian period.
vic•to•ri•ous (vĭk-tôr'ē-əs, -tōr'-) *adj.* **1.** Being the winner in a struggle or contest. **2.** Typical of or expressing victory. **—vic•to'ri•ous•ly** *adv.* **—vic•to'ri•ous•ness** *n.*
vic•to•ry (vĭk'tə-rē) *n., pl.* **-ries. 1.** Defeat of an enemy, as in wartime. **2.** Success in a struggle against an obstacle or opponent. ★ *syns:* CONQUEST, TRIUMPH, WIN
vict•ual (vĭt'l) *n.* **1.** Food suitable for consumption. **2. victuals.** Items of food : provisions. **—vict'ual** *v.*

▲ ***word history:*** *Victual* was borrowed from Old French *vitaille,* and until the 16th cent. the spelling of the word conformed to its pronunciation, which rhymes with *little.* During the Renaissance and the renewal of interest in classical languages and literature, scholars pedantically revised the spelling of English words to reflect their origins. *Victual* comes ult. from Late Latin *victualia,* "provisions." The pronunciation has never reflected this artificial respelling, and the form *vittle,* which adheres more closely to the actual sound of the word, is still sometimes seen.

vict•ual•er *also* **vict•ual•ler** (vĭt'l-ər) *n.* A supplier of provisions.
vi•cu•ña *or* **vi•cu•na** (vĭ-ko͞on'yə, -ko͞o'nə, -kyo͞o'nə, və-) *n.* **1.** A llamalike ruminant mammal, *Vicugna vicugna,* of the Andes, with a fine, silky fleece. **2.** Cloth made from this fleece.
vi•de (vī'dē, vē'dā'). See. —Used to direct a reader's attention <*Vide* page 31.>
vi•del•i•cet (vĭ-dĕl'ĭ-sĭt', vī-) *adv.* That is to say : namely. —Used to introduce examples or lists.
vid•e•o (vĭd'ē-ō') *adj.* **1.** Of or relating to television, esp. to televised pictures. **2.** Of or relating to videotape equipment or technology. —*n.* **1.** The visual part of a telecast. **2.** Television. **3.** A videotape or videocassette.
video camera *n.* A portable, hand-held camera that records on videocassettes for playback on a television set.
vid•e•o•cas•sette (vĭd'ē-ō-kə-sĕt', -kă-) *n.* A cassette containing videotape.
videocassette recorder *n.* A VCR.
vid•e•o•disc *also* **vid•e•o•disk** (vĭd'ē-ō-dĭsk') *n.* A disc recording of sounds and images, as of a film, that may be played on a television set.
video display terminal *n.* A VDT.
video game *n.* A computerized game in which the player or players control images on a display screen.
vid•e•og•ra•phy (vĭd'ē-ŏg'rə-fē) *n.* The art of making video shows or movies with a video camera. **—vid'e•og'ra•pher** *n.*
vid•e•o•phone (vĭd'ē-ō-fōn') *n.* A telephone equipped for both audio and video transmission.
vid•e•o•tape (vĭd'ē-ō-tāp') *n.* A magnetic tape used to record visual images and associated sound for subsequent playback or broadcasting. **—vid'e•o•tape'** *v.*
video terminal *n.* A computer input-output device utilizing a cathode-ray tube to display data on a screen.

video terminal

vie (vī) *v.* **vied, vy•ing.** To engage in a struggle or contest : contend. **—vi'er** *n.*
view (vyo͞o) *n.* **1.** The act of examining : inspection. **2.** A systematic survey. **3.** Opinion. **4.** The field of vision. **5.** A scene : vista. **6.** A picture of a scene. **7.** A way of seeing something, as from a particular position <an aerial *view* of the fortifications> **8.** An intention <wrote the book with a *view* to publication> —*v.* **1.** To see. **2. a.** To examine. **b.** To survey mentally : consider. **—view'er** *n.*
view finder *n.* FINDER 2.
view•point (vyo͞o'point') *n.* A point of view.
vi•ges•i•mal (vī-jĕs'ə-məl) *adj.* **1.** Twentieth. **2.** Based on or relating to 20.

vig·il (vĭj′əl) *n.* **1.** A watch kept at night. **2.** The day before a religious festival, observed by devotional preparation.

vig·i·lance (vĭj′ə-ləns) *n.* Alert watchfulness. —**vig′i·lant** *adj.*

vig·i·lan·te (vĭj′ə-lăn′tē) *n.* A member of a group of volunteers that without authority assumes police powers, as pursuing and punishing criminal suspects.

vi·gnette (vĭn-yĕt′, vēn-) *n.* **1.** A decorative design at the opening or end of a book or a chapter of a book. **2.** An unbordered portrait that shades off into the surrounding color at the edges. **3.** A short, descriptive literary sketch.

vig·or (vĭg′ər) *n.* **1.** Physical strength or energy. **2.** Intensity.

vig·or·ous (vĭg′ər-əs) *adj.* **1.** Healthy and energetic : robust. **2.** Lively : forceful. —**vig′or·ous·ly** *adv.* —**vig′or·ous·ness** *n.*

vig·our (vĭg′ər) *n. esp. Brit. var. of* VIGOR.

Vi·king (vī′kĭng) *n.* One of a seafaring Scandinavian people who raided settlements on the coasts of N and W Europe from the 8th to the 10th cent.

vile (vīl) *adj.* **vil·er, vil·est. 1.** Disgusting : loathsome. **2.** Objectionable : unpleasant. **3.** Miserable : wretched. **4.** Depraved : ignoble. —**vile′ly** *adv.* —**vile′ness** *n.*

vil·i·fy (vĭl′ə-fī′) *v.* **-fied, -fy·ing.** To defame : denigrate. —**vil′i·fi·ca′tion** *n.* —**vil′i·fi′er** *n.*

vil·la (vĭl′ə) *n.* **1.** An often large and luxurious house in the country. **2.** *esp. Brit.* A middle-class suburban house.

vil·lage (vĭl′ĭj) *n.* **1.** A small group of dwellings in a rural area. **2.** An incorporated community smaller than a town in some U.S. states. **3.** The inhabitants of a village. —**vil′lag·er** *n.*

vil·lain (vĭl′ən) *n.* **1.** A wicked or evil person. **2.** A fictional or dramatic character typically at odds with the hero. **3.** *var. of* VILLEIN. —**vil′lain·ous** *adj.*

vil·lain·y (vĭl′ə-nē) *n., pl.* **-ies. 1.** Villainous conduct. **2.** Baseness of character or mind. **3.** A treacherous or wicked act.

vil·lein *also* **vil·lain** (vĭl′ən) *n.* One of a class of feudal serfs holding the legal status of freemen in their dealings with everyone except their lord. —**vil′lein·age** *n.*

vil·lous (vĭl′əs) *also* **vil·lose** (-lōs′) *adj.* Covered with fine hairs or villi.

vil·lus (vĭl′əs) *n., pl.* **vil·li** (vĭl′ī′) **1.** *Anat.* A minute projection arising from a mucous membrane. **2.** *Bot.* A fine hairlike epidermal outgrowth.

vim (vĭm) *n.* Ebullient vitality.

vin·ai·grette (vĭn′ə-grĕt′) *n.* **1.** A small decorative bottle with a perforated top for holding an aromatic preparation such as smelling salts. **2.** A dressing of vinegar or lemon juice and oil flavored with herbs.

vin·ci·ble (vĭn′sə-bəl) *adj.* Capable of being vanquished or overcome.

vin·di·cate (vĭn′dĭ-kāt′) *v.* **-cat·ed, -cat·ing. 1.** To clear of blame or suspicion with corroboration or proof. **2.** To justify or support <*vindicate* one's faith> **3.** To justify or prove the value of, esp. in light of subsequent events. ★ ***syns:*** ABSOLVE, AQUIT, CLEAR, EXONERATE —**vin′di·ca′tion** *n.* —**vin′di·ca′tor** *n.*

vin·dic·tive (vĭn-dĭk′tĭv) *adj.* **1.** Having or showing a desire for revenge. **2.** Meant to cause harm or pain. ★ ***syns:*** REVENGEFUL, SPITEFUL, VENGEFUL —**vin·dic′tive·ly** *adv.* —**vin·dic′tive·ness** *n.*

vine (vīn) *n.* **1. a.** A plant with a flexible stem that grows along the ground or climbs or clings to a surface for support. **b.** The stem of such a plant. **2.** A grapevine.

vin·e·gar (vĭn′ĭ-gər) *n.* An impure dilute solution of acetic acid, obtained by fermentation and used in flavoring and preserving food. —**vin′e·gar·y** *adj.*

vin·e·gar·roon (vĭn′ĭ-gə-ro͞on′) *n.* A large nonvenomous scorpionlike arachnid, *Mastigoproctus giganteus,* that gives off a strong vinegary odor when disturbed.

vinegarroon

vine·yard (vĭn′yərd) *n.* Ground planted with cultivated grapevines.

vin·i·cul·ture (vĭn′ĭ-kŭl′chər, vī′nĭ-) *n.* Cultivation of grapes : viticulture.

vi·no (vē′nō) *n., pl.* **-nos.** Wine.

vin or·di·naire (văɴ′ ôr-dē-nâr′) *n., pl.* **vins or·di·naires** (văɴ′ ôr-dē-nâr′) Inexpensive table wine.

vin·tage (vĭn′tĭj) *n.* **1.** The grapes or wine produced from a particular vineyard or district in one season. **2.** Wine identified as to year and vineyard or district of origin. **3.** The harvesting of a grape crop. **4.** A year or time of origin <a uniform of 1914 *vintage*> —*adj.* **1.** Of or relating to a vintage. **2.** Characterized by excellence and lasting popularity. **3.** Representative of the best <stories that were *vintage* Saroyan>

vint·ner (vĭnt′nər) *n.* **1.** A wine merchant. **2.** A wine maker.

vi·nyl (vī′nəl) *n.* Any of various tough, flexible, shiny plastics used esp. for coverings and clothing.

vi·ol (vī′əl) *n.* Any of a family of stringed instruments, chiefly of the 16th and 17th cent., with a fretted fingerboard, usu. 6 strings, and a flat back.

vi•o•la (vē-ō'lə) *n.* A stringed instrument of the violin family, somewhat bigger than a violin and having a deeper tone.

vi•o•la•ble (vī'ə-lə-bəl) *adj.* Capable of being violated.

vi•o•late (vī'ə-lāt') *v.* **-lat•ed, -lat•ing. 1.** To break (e.g. a law). **2.** To injure the person or property of, esp. to rape. **3.** To desecrate. **—vi'o•la'tion** *n.* **—vi'o•la'tor** *n.*

vi•o•lence (vī'ə-ləns) *n.* **1.** Physical force employed so as to damage or injure. **2.** An instance of violent action. **3.** Intensity <the *violence* of the tornado> **4.** Damage or abuse, as to meaning or content <do *violence* to a song> **5.** Fervor : vehemence.

vi•o•lent (vī'ə-lənt) *adj.* **1.** Characterized or caused by great physical force. **2.** Having or showing great emotional force. **3.** Intense : severe. **4.** Caused by force rather than by natural causes <a *violent* death>

vi•o•let (vī'ə-lĭt) *n.* **1.** A low-growing plant of the genus *Viola,* bearing flowers that are purplish-blue or occas. white or yellow. **2.** A bluish purple.

vi•o•lin (vī'ə-lĭn') *n.* A stringed instrument played with a bow and having 4 strings and an unfretted fingerboard. **—vi'o•lin'ist** *n.*

vi•o•lon•cel•lo (vē'ə-lən-chĕl'ō) *n., pl.* **-los.** A cello. **—vi'o•lon•cel'list** *n.*

VIP (vē'ī-pē') *n., pl.* **VIPs.** *Informal.* A very important person.

vi•per (vī'pər) *n.* **1.** A venomous snake of the family Viperidae, esp. a common Eurasian species, *Vipera berus.* **2.** A venomous or presumably venomous snake. **3.** A treacherous person. **—vi'per•ous** *adj.*

vi•ra•go (vĭ-rä'gō) *n., pl.* **-goes** *or* **-gos.** A strident, domineering woman.

vi•ral (vī'rəl) *adj.* Of, pertaining to, or resulting from a virus.

vir•e•o (vîr'ē-ō') *n., pl.* **-os.** Any of various small New World birds of the genus *Vireo,* with greenish or grayish plumage.

vir•gin (vûr'jĭn) *n.* **1.** One who has never engaged in sexual intercourse. **2. Virgin.** The mother of Jesus. **3. Virgin.** VIRGO **2.** *—adj.* **1.** Typical of or suitable for a virgin. **2.** In a natural or unchanged state <*virgin* forests> **3.** Extracted from the first pressing <*virgin* olive oil> **—vir•gin'i•ty** *n.*

vir•gin•al[1] (vûr'jə-nəl) *adj.* **1.** Of or pertaining to a virgin. **2.** Untouched : fresh.

vir•gin•al[2] (vûr'jə-nəl) *n. often* **virginals.** A small rectangular harpsichord without legs, popular in the 16th and 17th cent.

Virginia creeper *n.* A North American climbing vine, *Parthenocissus quinquefolia,* bearing compound leaves and bluish-black berries.

Virginia reel *n.* An American country dance in which couples perform various steps together to the instructions of a caller.

Vir•go (vûr'gō, vîr'-) *n.* **1.** A constellation in the region of the celestial equator. **2. a.** The 6th sign of the zodiac. **b.** One born under this sign.

vir•gule (vûr'gyo͞ol) *n.* A diagonal mark (/) used esp. to denote alternatives, as in *and/or,* and to stand for the word *per,* as in *feet/second.*

vi•ri•cide (vī'rĭ-sīd') *n.* An agent that destroys viruses.

vir•i•des•cent (vîr'ĭ-dĕs'ənt) *adj.* Green or somewhat green. **—vir'i•des'cence** *n.*

vir•ile (vĭr'əl) *adj.* **1.** Typical of or appropriate to a man. **2.** Having or showing energy and vigor. **3.** Able to perform sexually as a male. **—vi•ril'i•ty** (vĭ-rĭl'ĭ-tē) *n.*

vi•rol•o•gy (vī-rŏl'ə-jē) *n.* The study of viruses and viral diseases. **—vi•rol'o•gist** *n.*

vir•tu (vər-to͞o', vĭr-) *n.* **1.** A knowledge or love of fine objects of art. **2.** Objects of art, esp. antiques.

vir•tu•al (vûr'cho͞o-əl) *adj.* Existing or resulting in effect though not in actual fact. **—vir'tu•al'i•ty** (-ăl'ĭ-tē) *n.*

virtual reality *n. Computer Sci.* A computer simulation of a real or imaginary system that enables a user to perform operations on the simulated system and shows the effects in real time.

vir•tue (vûr'cho͞o) *n.* **1. a.** Moral excellence. **b.** An example of moral excellence <the *virtue* of generosity> **2.** Chastity, esp. of a girl or woman. **3.** A particular beneficial quality : advantage. **4.** Effective power <believed in the *virtue* of meditation> **—by virtue of.** By reason of.

vir•tu•o•so (vûr'cho͞o-ō'sō) *n., pl.* **-sos** *or* **-si** (-sē). **1.** A musical performer of unusual excellence. **2.** One with outstanding talent in any field, esp. in the arts. **—vir'tu•os'i•ty** *n.*

vir•tu•ous (vûr'cho͞o-əs) *adj.* **1.** Displaying virtue : righteous. **2.** Chaste : pure.

vir•u•lent (vîr'yə-lənt, vîr'ə-) *adj.* **1.** Extremely poisonous or pathogenic. **2.** Bitterly hostile or malicious. **—vir'u•lence** *n.* **—vir'u•lent•ly** *adv.*

vi•rus (vī'rəs) *n.* **1.** Any of various submicroscopic pathogens consisting essentially of a particle of nucleic acid enclosed in protein and able to replicate only within a living cell. **2.** A corrupting influence. **3.** A computer virus.

vi•sa (vē'zə) *n.* An official authorization appended to a passport allowing entry into a specific country.

vis•age (vĭz'ĭj) *n.* The face or facial expression of a person.

vis-à-vis (vē'zə-vē') *n., pl.* **vis-à-vis** (-vēz', -vē'). One of 2 persons or things opposite or corresponding to the other. *—adv.* Face to face. *—prep.* **1.** Compared with. **2.** In relation to. **—vis'-à-vis'** *adj.*

vis•cer•a (vĭs'ər-ə) *pl.n.* The internal organs of the body, esp. those within the thorax and abdomen.

vis•cer•al (vĭs'ər-əl) *adj.* **1.** Relating to or located in the viscera. **2.** Profound : intense <*visceral* grief>

vis•cid (vĭs'ĭd) *adj.* **1.** Thick and sticky. **2.** Covered with a sticky coating. **—vis•cid'i•ty** (vĭ-sĭd'ĭ-tē) *n.* **—vis'cid•ly** *adv.*

vis•cose (vĭs'kōs') *n.* A thick, brown solution made from cellulose and used in manufacturing rayon and cellophane. —*adj.* Viscous.

vis•cos•i•ty (vĭ-skŏs'ĭ-tē) *n., pl.* **-ties.** The condition or property of being viscous.

vis•count (vī'kount') *n.* A peer ranking beneath an earl and above a baron. —**vis'count'cy** *n.* —**vis'count'ess** *n.*

vis•cous (vĭs'kəs) *adj.* **1.** Having relatively high resistance to flow. **2.** Having a heavy, gluey quality. —**vis'cous•ly** *adv.*

vise *also* **vice** (vīs) *n.* A clamping apparatus consisting of 2 jaws opened or closed by a screw or lever, used in carpentry or metalworking to hold a piece in position.

vise

vis•i•bil•i•ty (vĭz'ĭ-bĭl'ə-tē) *n., pl.* **-ties. 1.** The fact, state, or degree of being visible. **2.** The range of vision under given weather conditions.

vis•i•ble (vĭz'ə-bəl) *adj.* **1.** Capable of being seen. **2.** Apparent. —**vis'i•bly** *adv.*

vi•sion (vĭzh'ən) *n.* **1.** The faculty of sight. **2.** Unusual ability in foreseeing what is going to happen. **3.** A mental image created by the imagination. **4.** The mystical experience of seeing as if with the eyes the supernatural or a supernatural being. **5.** One of great beauty.

vi•sion•ar•y (vĭzh'ə-nĕr'ē) *adj.* **1.** Marked by foresight. **2.** Having the nature of fantasies or dreams. **3.** Existing only in the imagination : not practicable. —*n., pl.* **-ies. 1.** One who has visions. **2.** One given to impractical ideas.

vis•it (vĭz'ĭt) *v.* **1.** To go or come to see (a person). **2.** To go or come to see (a place), as on a tour. **3.** To stay with as a guest. **4.** To afflict. **5.** To inflict punishment for <*visit* the sins of the fathers upon the children> **6.** *Informal.* To chat. —**vis'it** *n.* —**vis'i•tor, vis'i•tant** *n.*

vis•i•ta•tion (vĭz'ĭ-tā'shən) *n.* **1.** A visit, esp. an official one. **2.** A parent's right to visit a child or have a child as a visitor, as specified in a divorce or separation order. **3.** A punishment or blessing regarded as being divinely ordained.

visiting nurse *n.* A registered nurse employed by a hospital or public health agency to promote community health.

vi•sor *also* **vi•zor** (vī'zər) *n.* **1.** A piece projecting from the front of a cap to shade the eyes or protect against wind or rain. **2.** A fixed or movable shield against glare over the windshield of a motor vehicle. **3.** The front piece of the helmet of a suit of armor, able to be raised or lowered.

vis•ta (vĭs'tə) *n.* **1.** A distant view, esp. through a passage or opening. **2.** A mental view of a series of events.

vi•su•al (vĭzh'ōō-əl) *adj.* **1.** Of or relating to the sense of sight. **2.** Visible. **3.** Done or controlled by using sight alone. **4.** Of or relating to communication of instruction by means of vision <*visual* aids>

vi•su•al•ize (vĭzh'ōō-ə-līz') *v.* **-ized, -iz•ing.** To form a mental image of. —**vi'su•al•i•za'tion** *n.* —**vi'su•al•iz'er** *n.*

vi•ta (vī'tə, vē'-) *n.* A résumé.

vi•tal (vīt'l) *adj.* **1.** Of or characteristic of life. **2.** Essential to life. **3.** Full of life : animated. **4.** Very important. —**vi'tal•ly** *adv.*

vi•tal•i•ty (vī-tăl'ĭ-tē) *n., pl.* **-ties. 1.** The characteristic that distinguishes the living from the nonliving. **2.** The capacity to grow or develop. **3.** Physical or intellectual vigor : energy.

vi•tal•ize (vīt'l-īz') *v.* **-ized, -iz•ing. 1.** To endow with life. **2.** To invigorate. —**vi'tal•i•za'tion** *n.* —**vi'tal•iz'er** *n.*

vital signs *pl.n. Med.* A person's pulse rate, temperature, and respiratory rate.

vital statistics *pl.n.* Statistics concerning births, deaths, marriages, and migrations.

vi•ta•min (vī'tə-mĭn) *n.* Any of various relatively complex organic substances that occur in small amounts in animal and plant tissue and are essential for the continuation of normal life functions.

▲ ***word history:*** *Vitamin* was borrowed from German *Vitamine,* which is a compound of Latin *vita,* "life," and the scientific suffix *–amine,* "amine, an organic compound of nitrogen." It was at first believed that vitamins were based on amino acids. Although this was later found to be untrue, the name *vitamin* was kept.

vitamin A *n.* A vitamin or mixture of vitamins found esp. in fish-liver oils that is necessary for normal cell growth and sight.

vitamin B *n.* **1.** Vitamin B complex. **2.** A member of the vitamin B complex, esp. vitamin B_1.

vitamin B_1 *n.* Thiamine.

vitamin B_2 *n.* Riboflavin.

vitamin B_{12} *n.* A complex cobalt-containing compound occurring in liver and essential for normal blood formation.

vitamin B complex *n.* A related group of vitamins orig. held to be a single substance and found mainly in yeast, eggs, liver, and certain vegetables.

vitamin C *n.* Ascorbic acid.

vitamin D *n.* Any of several related sterols made active by exposure to ultraviolent light or obtained from milk, fish, and eggs and necessary for normal bone growth.

vitamin E *n.* Any of several related oils found mainly in grains and vegetable oils and used esp. in treating sterility.

vitamin G *n.* Riboflavin.
vitamin H *n.* Biotin.
vitamin K *n.* Any of several artificial or natural substances essential for the normal clotting of blood.
vi·ti·ate (vĭsh'ē-āt') *v.* **-at·ed, -at·ing. 1.** To impair the quality or value of. **2.** To corrupt morally. **3.** To invalidate. **—vi'ti·a'tion** *n.* **—vi'ti·a'tor** *n.*
vit·i·cul·ture (vĭt'ĭ-kŭl'chər) *n.* Cultivation of grapes. **—vit'i·cul'tur·al** *adj.* **—vit'i·cul'tur·ist** *n.*
vit·re·ous (vĭt'rē-əs) *adj.* **1.** Relating to or similar to glass. **2.** Of or relating to the vitreous humor.
vitreous humor *n.* Clear gelatinous matter that fills the section of the eyeball between the retina and the lens.
vit·ri·fy (vĭt'rə-fī') *v.* **-fied, -fy·ing.** To make into glass or a similar substance, esp. by heat fusion. **—vit'ri·fi·ca'tion** *n.*
vit·ri·ol (vĭt'rē-ōl') *n.* **1.** *Chem.* **a.** Sulfuric acid. **b.** Any of various sulfates of metals. **2.** Bitter or sharp expression or feeling. **—vit'ri·ol'ic** *adj.*
vit·tles (vĭt'lz) *pl.n. nonstandard var. of* VICTUALS.
vi·tu·per·ate (vī-to͞o'pə-rāt', -tyo͞o'-, vĭ-) *v.* **-at·ed, -at·ing.** To berate. **—vi·tu'per·a'tion** *n.* **—vi·tu'per·a·tive** *adj.*
vi·va (vē'və) *interj.* —Used to express approval.
vi·va·ce (vē-vä'chā) *adv. & adj. Mus.* In a lively manner. —Used as a direction.
vi·va·cious (vĭ-vā'shəs, vī-) *adj.* Filled with animation : lively. **—vi·va'cious·ly** *adv.* **—vi·va'cious·ness, vi·vac'i·ty** (vĭ-văs'ĭ-tē, vī-) *n.*
vi·var·i·um (vī-vâr'ē-əm) *n., pl.* **-ums** *or* **-i·a** (-ē-ə) An enclosure for keeping living animals for research or observation.
vi·va vo·ce (vī'və vō'sē) *adv. & adj.* By word of mouth.
viv·id (vĭv'ĭd) *adj.* **1.** Bright : brilliant. **2.** Having intensely bright colors. **3. a.** Evoking lifelike images in the mind. **b.** Active <a *vivid* imagination> **—viv'id·ly** *adv.*
viv·i·fy (vĭv'ə-fī') *v.* **-fied, -fy·ing. 1.** To give or bring life to. **2.** To make livelier. **—viv'i·fi·ca'tion** *n.* **—viv'i·fi'er** *n.*
vi·vip·a·rous (vī-vĭp'ər-əs, vĭ-) *adj. Zool.* Giving birth to living offspring that develop inside the body of the mother rather than hatching from eggs. **—vi'vi·par'i·ty** (vī'və-păr'ĭ-tē, vĭv'ə-) *n.*
viv·i·sec·tion (vĭv'ĭ-sĕk'shən) *n.* Dissection of or operation on a living animal, esp. for scientific research. **—viv'i·sect'** *v.*
vix·en (vĭk'sən) *n.* **1.** A female fox. **2.** A shrewish woman. **—vix'en·ish** *adj.*
vi·zier *also* **vi·zir** (vĭ-zîr') *n.* A high officer in a Muslim government, esp. in the Ottoman Empire.
vi·zor (vī'zər) *n. var. of* VISOR.
V-neck (vē'nĕk') *n.* A V-shaped neckline.
vo·ca·ble (vō'kə-bəl) *n.* A word regarded only as a sequence of letters or sounds instead of as a unit of meaning.
vo·cab·u·lar·y (vō-kăb'yə-lĕr'ē) *n., pl.* **-ies. 1.** A list of words and often phrases, usu. in an alphabetical arrangement and translated or defined. **2.** All the words of a language. **3.** All the words used and understood by a particular person.
vo·cal (vō'kəl) *adj.* **1.** Of, relating to, or composed for the human voice. **2.** Uttered by the voice. **3.** Having a voice and able to emit sound or speech. **4.** Full of voices. **5.** Speaking freely and loudly : outspoken. *—n.* **1.** A vocal sound. **2.** A popular piece of music for a singer. **—vo'cal·ly** *adv.*
vocal cords *pl.n.* The lower of 2 pairs of bands or folds in the larynx that vibrate when drawn together and when air is passed up from the lungs, thereby producing vocal sounds.
vo·cal·ic (vō-kăl'ĭk) *adj.* Relating to or being the nature of a vowel or vowels.
vo·cal·ist (vō'kə-lĭst) *n.* A singer.
vo·cal·ize (vō'kə-līz') *v.* **-ized, -iz·ing. 1.** To give vocal expression to. **2.** To change (a consonant) into a vowel. **3.** To use the voice, esp. to sing. **—vo'cal·i·za'tion** *n.* **—vo'cal·iz'er** *n.*
vo·ca·tion (vō-kā'shən) *n.* **1.** A profession, esp. one to which an individual is particularly suited. **2.** A predisposition or urge to take up a particular type of work, esp. religious work. **—vo·ca'tion·al** *adj.*
vocational school *n.* A school that offers instruction in skilled trades such as mechanics or carpentry.
voc·a·tive (vŏk'ə-tĭv) *adj.* Relating to or being a grammatical case, as in Latin, used to designate the one being addressed. **—voc'a·tive** *n.*
vo·cif·er·ate (vō-sĭf'ə-rāt') *v.* **-at·ed, -at·ing.** To cry out or utter vehemently. **—vo·cif'er·a'tion** *n.*
vo·cif·er·ous (vō-sĭf'ər-əs) *adj.* Making an outcry. **—vo·cif'er·ous·ly** *adv.*
vod·ka (vŏd'kə) *n.* A colorless alcoholic liquor distilled from fermented wheat or rye mash, potatoes, or corn.
vogue (vōg) *n.* **1.** Prevailing fashion or style. **2.** Popularity. **—vogu'ish** *adj.*
voice (vois) *n.* **1. a.** The sound produced by the vocal organs of a vertebrate, esp. a human being. **b.** The ability to produce such sounds. **2.** A sound resembling vocal utterance. **3.** The specified quality or timbre of vocal sound <a *soft* voice> **4. a.** A medium or agency of expression <give *voice* to one's feelings> **b.** The opportunity to express an opinion or choice. **5.** *Gram.* A verb form showing the relation between the subject and the action expressed by the verb. **6. a.** Musical tone produced by vibrating vocal chords and resonated within the throat and head cavities. **b.** A singer <a choir of 300 *voices*> **c.** Any of the melodic parts in a vocal composition. *—v.* **voiced, voic·ing. 1.** To give voice to : utter. **2.** To pronounce with vibration of the vocal cords. **3.** *Mus.* To regulate the tone of (e.g., the pipes of an organ). **—voice'less** *adj.*
voice box *n.* The larynx.

voice mail *n.* An interactive computerized system for answering and routing telephone calls and recording messages.
voice-o•ver (vois′ō′vər) *n.* The voice of a film or television narrator who does not appear on camera.
voice•print (vois′prĭnt′) *n.* An electronically recorded graphic representation of a person's voice.
void (void) *adj.* **1.** Containing no matter : empty. **2.** Unoccupied, as a position or a building : vacant. **3.** Devoid : lacking. **4.** Useless : ineffective. **5.** Lacking legal force : null. —*n.* **1.** An empty space. **2.** A feeling or state of emptiness or loneliness. —*v.* **1.** To make void or of no effect. **2. a.** To empty. **b.** To evacuate (body wastes). **3.** To vacate. —**void′a•ble** *adj.* —**void′er** *n.*
voile (voil) *n.* A sheer fabric used esp. for making light clothing and curtains.
vol•a•tile (vŏl′ə-tl, -tīl′) *adj.* **1.** Evaporating readily at normal pressures and temperatures. **2.** Changeable, esp.: **a.** Fickle. **b.** Given to violence. **c.** Ephemeral. —**vol′a•til′i•ty** (-tĭl′ĭ-tē) *n.* —**vol′a•til•ize′** *v.*
vol-au-vent (vô′lō-väN′) *n.* A small pastry shell with a filling, as of meat or fish.
vol•can•ic (vŏl-kăn′ĭk) *adj.* **1.** Relating to or produced by a volcano. **2.** Violent.
vol•can•ism (vŏl′kə-nĭz′əm) *also* **vul•can•ism** (vŭl′-) *n.* Volcanic force.
vol•ca•no (vŏl-kā′nō) *n., pl.* **-noes** *or* **-nos. 1.** A vent in the earth's crust through which molten rock, ash, and gases are ejected. **2.** A mountain formed by the materials ejected from a volcano.
vole (vōl) *n.* Any of various short-tailed rodents of the genus *Microtus* and related genera, similar to rats or mice.
vo•li•tion (və-lĭsh′ən) *n.* **1.** An act of choosing, using one's own will. **2.** A conscious choice. **3.** The power of choosing.
vol•ley (vŏl′ē) *n., pl.* **-leys. 1. a.** Simultaneous discharge of a number of missiles. **b.** The missiles so discharged. **2.** A bursting forth of many things at the same time or in rapid succession <a *volley* of oaths> **3.** A shot, esp. in tennis, in which the ball is hit before touching the ground. —*v.* **1.** To discharge or be discharged in a volley. **2.** To hit (e.g., a tennis ball) before it touches the ground. —**vol′ley•er** *n.*
vol•ley•ball (vŏl′ē-bôl′) *n.* A court game in which one team tries to score by making the ball hit the ground on the opposing team's side of a high net.
volt (vōlt) *n.* A unit of electric potential and electromotive force, equal to the difference of electric potential between the 2 ends of a conductor that has a resistance of 1 ohm and through which a current of 1 ampere is flowing.
volt•age (vōl′tĭj) *n.* Electromotive force, usu. expressed in volts.
vol•ta•ic (vŏl-tā′ĭk, vōl-, vôl-) *adj.* Relating to or designating electricity produced by chemical action.
volte-face (vôlt′fäs′, vôl′tə-) *n.* A reversal : about-face.
volt•me•ter (vōlt′mē′tər) *n.* An instrument for measuring differences of electric potential in volts.
vol•u•ble (vŏl′yə-bəl) *adj.* Fluent in speech. —**vol′u•bil′i•ty, vol′u•ble•ness** *n.* —**vol′u•bly** *adv.*
vol•ume (vŏl′yo͞om, -yəm) *n.* **1.** A book. **2.** One book of a set. **3. a.** The size of a 3-dimensional object or region of space. **b.** The capacity of such a region or object. **4.** A quantity : amount. **5. a.** The loudness of a sound. **b.** A control, as on a radio, for regulating loudness.
vol•u•met•ric (vŏl′yə-mĕt′rĭk) *adj.* Of or relating to measurement of volume. —**vol′u•met′ri•cal•ly** *adv.*
vo•lu•mi•nous (və-lo͞o′mə-nəs) *adj.* **1.** Having great volume, size, or quantity. **2.** Filling or sufficient to fill many volumes. **3.** Consisting of many coils or folds.
vol•un•tar•y (vŏl′ən-tĕr′ē) *adj.* **1. a.** Arising from one's own free will. **b.** Acting on one's own initiative. **2.** Acting willingly and without reward. **3.** *Law.* Intentional <*voluntary* manslaughter> ★ ***syns:*** DELIBERATE, INTENTIONAL, WILLFUL —*n., pl.* **-ies.** Solo organ music played at a church service. —**vol′un•tar′i•ly** *adv.*
vol•un•teer (vŏl′ən-tîr′) *n.* One who serves or acts of his or her own free will. —*v.* **1.** To offer or give of one's own accord. **2.** To offer oneself as a volunteer.
vol•un•teer•ism (vŏl′ən-tîr′ĭz′əm) *n.* Use of or reliance on volunteers.
vo•lup•tu•ar•y (və-lŭp′cho͞o-ĕr′ē) *n., pl.* **-ies.** One whose life is devoted to sensual pleasures. —**vo•lup′tu•ar′y** *adj.*
vo•lup•tu•ous (və-lŭp′cho͞o-əs) *adj.* **1.** Characterized by or giving sensual gratification. **2.** Given over to sensual pleasures. —**vo•lup′tu•ous•ness** *n.*
vo•lute (və-lo͞ot′) *n.* A scroll-like decoration, as on a column.
vom•it (vŏm′ĭt) *v.* **1.** To eject the contents of the stomach through the mouth. **2.** To eject in a gush. —*n.* Matter ejected from the stomach by vomiting.
voo•doo (vo͞o′do͞o) *n.* **1.** A religious cult marked by a belief in sorcery, primitive deities, and fetishes. **2.** A spell or curse held to possess magic power. —**voo′doo•ism** *n.* —**voo′doo•is′tic** *adj.*
vo•ra•cious (vô-rā′shəs, və-) *adj.* **1.** Consuming or eager to consume large quantities of food. **2.** Avid : insatiable. —**vo•ra′cious•ly** *adv.* —**vo•rac′i•ty** (-răs′ĭ-te), **vo•ra′cious•ness** *n.*
vor•tex (vôr′tĕks′) *n., pl.* **-es** *or* **-ti•ces** (-tĭ-sēz′). A mass of fluid whirling about an axis : whirlpool.
vo•ta•ry (vō′tə-rē) *n., pl.* **-ries. 1.** A person bound by religious vows : monk or nun. **2.** A fervent devotee to a religion or ideal.
vote (vōt) *n.* **1. a.** A choice made, as for a candidate for office or in a referendum, in

or as if in an election. **b.** The way in which such a choice is indicated, as by a ballot. **2.** The number of votes cast in an election or to resolve an issue. **3.** A group of voters <the farm *vote*> **4.** The result of an election. **5.** The right to vote. —*v.* **vot•ed, vot•ing. 1.** To indicate one's preference by a vote. **2.** To bring into existence by a vote. **3.** To pronounce by general agreement. —**vote'less** *adj.* —**vot'er** *n.*

vo•tive (vō'tĭv) *adj.* Dedicated or performed in fulfillment of a vow.

vouch (vouch) *v.* **1.** To verify by supplying proof. **2.** To give a personal assurance. **3.** To corroborate.

vouch•er (vou'chər) *n.* **1.** One who vouches. **2.** A document giving proof of a business transaction.

vouch•safe (vouch-sāf', vouch'sāf') *v.* **-safed, -saf•ing.** To condescend to grant.

vow (vou) *n.* **1.** A solemn promise or pledge that commits one to act or behave in a particular way. **2.** A formal assertion. —*v.* **1.** To promise solemnly. **2.** To assert formally. **3.** To make a promise. —**take vows.** To enter a religious order.

vow•el (vou'əl) *n.* **1.** A speech sound produced by relatively free passage of breath through the larynx and mouth, usu. forming the central sound of a syllable. **2.** A letter that represents a vowel, as *a, e, i, o, u,* and sometimes *y.*

vox pop•u•li (vŏks' pŏp'yə-lī') *n.* Popular sentiment.

voy•age (voi'ĭj) *n.* A long journey, esp. on a ship. —**voy'age** *v.* —**voy'ag•er** *n.*

vo•ya•geur (voi'ə-zhûr', vwä'yä-) *n.* A woodsman or guide, esp. one who transports furs and supplies between isolated posts in the U.S. and Canadian NW.

vo•yeur (voi-yûr') *n.* One who habitually seeks sexual gratification from observing the sexual activities of others. —**vo•yeur'ism** *n.* —**vo'yeur•is'tic** *adj.* —**vo'yeur•is'ti•cal•ly** *adv.*

vul•can•ism (vŭl'kə-nĭz'əm) *n. var. of* VOLCANISM.

vul•ca•nite (vŭl'kə-nīt') *n.* A hard rubber made by vulcanization.

vul•can•ize (vŭl'kə-nīz') *v.* **-ized, -iz•ing.** To increase the strength and resilience of (e.g., rubber) by combination with additives, as sulfur, under heat and pressure. —**vul'can•i•za'tion** *n.* —**vul'can•iz'er** *n.*

vul•gar (vŭl'gər) *adj.* **1.** Of or associated with the great masses of people. **2.** Spoken by or expressed in language used by the common people. **3.** Deficient in taste or delicacy. **4.** Indecent. —**vul'gar•ly** *adv.*

vul•gar•i•an (vŭl-gâr'ē-ən) *n.* A vulgar person.

vul•gar•ism (vŭl'gə-rĭz'əm) *n.* **1.** An obscene word or expression. **2.** A word, phrase, or expression used chiefly by uncultivated persons.

vul•gar•i•ty (vŭl-găr'ĭ-tē) *n., pl.* **-ties. 1.** The quality or state of being vulgar. **2.** Something vulgar, as an act or expression.

vul•gar•ize (vŭl'gə-rīz') *v.* **-ized, -iz•ing. 1.** To make vulgar : debase. **2.** To popularize. —**vul'gar•i•za'tion** *n.*

Vul•gate (vŭl'gāt', -gĭt) *n.* The Latin translation of the Bible made at the end of the 4th cent., now used in a revised form by the Roman Catholic Church.

vul•ner•a•ble (vŭl'nər-ə-bəl) *adj.* **1.** Susceptible to physical injury. **2.** Susceptible to attack. **3. a.** Subject to criticism or censure. **b.** Liable to yield to temptation or persuasion. **4.** Being in a position to receive greater penalties or bonuses. —Used of a pair that has won one game of a rubber in bridge. —**vul'ner•a•bil'i•ty** *n.* —**vul'ner•a•bly** *adv.*

vul•pine (vŭl'pīn') *adj.* **1.** Of, relating to, or typical of a fox. **2.** Cunning.

vul•ture (vŭl'chər) *n.* **1.** Any of various large carrion-eating birds of the New World family Cathartidae or Old World family Accipitridae, with dark plumage and a naked head and neck. **2.** A greedy person.

vulture
California condor

vul•va (vŭl'və) *n., pl.* **-vae** (-vē'). The external parts of the female genitalia. —**vul'val, vul'var** *adj.*

Ww

w *or* **W** (dŭb′əl-yōō) *n., pl.* **w's** *or* **W's. 1.** The 23rd letter of the English alphabet. **2.** A speech sound represented by the letter *w.* **3.** Something with the shape of the letter W.

W *symbol for* TUNGSTEN.

WAC (wăk) *n.* A member of the U.S. Women's Army Corps.

wack•y *also* **whack•y** (wăk′ē) *adj.* **-i•er, -i•est.** *Slang.* Eccentric or silly.

wad (wŏd) *n.* **1.** A small soft mass of fibrous material used for padding, stuffing, or packing. **2.** Material, as tobacco or chewing gum, pressed into a ball, roll, or lump. **3.** A flexible plug for holding shot or a gunpowder charge in place in a cartridge. **4.** *Informal.* **a.** A thick roll of papers or paper money. **b.** A sizable amount, esp. of money. **—wad** *v.*

wad•ding (wŏd′ĭng) *n.* **1.** Wads as a whole. **2.** A sheet of cotton or wool used for packing, padding, or stuffing. **3.** Material for shotgun wads.

wad•dle (wŏd′l) *v.* **-dled, -dling.** To take short steps and tilt slightly from side to side. **—wad′dle** *n.* **—wad′dler** *n.*

wad•dy[1] (wŏd′ē) *n., pl.* **-dies.** *Austral.* A heavy straight stick or club thrown as a weapon by aborigines. **—wad′dy** *v.*

†**wad•dy**[2] *also* **wad•die** (wŏd′ē) *n., pl.* **-dies.** *W U.S.* **1.** A cowboy. **2.** A rustler.

wade (wād) *v.* **wad•ed, wad•ing. 1.** To walk in or through a medium, as water or mud, that hampers movement. **2.** To make one's way with difficulty. **3.** To begin vigorously or resolutely.

wad•er (wā′dər) *n.* **1.** One that wades. **2.** A wading bird. **3. waders.** Waterproof hip boots or trousers worn esp. by fishermen.

wa•di (wä′dē) *n., pl.* **-dis** *also* **-dies.** A dry gully or riverbed in N Africa or SW Asia that fills up only during the rainy season.

wading bird *n.* A long-legged bird, as a heron, that looks for food in shallow water.

WAF (wăf) *n.* A member of the Women in the Air Force.

wa•fer (wā′fər) *n.* **1.** A small flat crisp cookie, cracker, or candy. **2.** A very thin round piece of unleavened bread used in Communion. **3.** *Electron.* A thin semiconductor slice on which an integrated circuit can be formed.

waf•fle[1] (wŏf′əl) *n.* Pancake batter baked into a light crisp cake in a waffle iron.

waf•fle[2] (wŏf′əl) *v.* **-fled, -fling.** *Informal.* To use words evasively **:** equivocate.

waffle iron *n.* An electric appliance with 2 hinged metal plates marked with an indented pattern, as of squares, that are pressed into waffle batter as it cooks.

waft (wäft, wăft) *v.* To move or drift gently by or as if by the motion of air or water. *—n.* **1.** Something conveyed through the air <a *waft* of perfume> **2.** A gentle breeze.

wag[1] (wăg) *v.* **wagged, wag•ging. 1.** To move or cause to move quickly and repeatedly from side to side or up and down. **2.** To move (the tongue) in conversation or chatter. ★ *syns:* LASH, SWITCH, WAGGLE, WAVE **—wag** *n.* **—wag′ger** *n.*

wag[2] (wăg) *n.* A witty, playful person **:** joker. **—wag′gish** *adj.*

wage (wāj) *n.* **1.** Remuneration for labor or services. **2. wages** *(sing. or pl. in number).* A fitting return or just desert. *—v.* **waged, wag•ing.** To begin or conduct (a war or campaign.)

wa•ger (wā′jər) *n.* A bet **:** stake. *—v.* To make a bet. **—wa′ger•er** *n.*

wag•ger•y (wăg′ə-rē) *n., pl.* **-ies. 1.** Whimsical playfulness **:** drollery. **2.** A playful act or remark **:** jest.

wag•gle (wăg′əl) *v.* **-gled, -gling.** To move quickly from side to side or back and forth **:** wag. **—wag′gle** *n.* **—wag′gly** *adj.*

wag•on (wăg′ən) *n.* **1.** A 4-wheeled vehicle, esp. one drawn by horses and used for transporting loads or goods. **2. a.** A station wagon. **b.** A patrol wagon. **3.** A child's low 4-wheeled cart with a long handle.

wagon train *n.* A column of wagons traveling cross-country, as in pioneer days.

wag•tail (wăg′tāl′) *n.* A bird of the genus *Motacilla* or related genera, with a long, constantly wagging tail.

wa•hi•ne (wä-hē′nē, -nā′) *n.* **1.** A Polynesian woman. **2.** A woman surfer.

wa•hoo[1] (wä′hōō) *n., pl.* **-hoos.** A shrub or small tree, *Euonymus atropurpureus,* of E North America, with small purplish flowers and red fruit.

†**wa•hoo**[2] (wä′hoo′) *interj. esp. W U.S.* —Used to express exuberance.

waif (wāf) *n.* **1. a.** A lost, homeless, or abandoned child. **b.** A young animal that has strayed. **2.** Something found and unclaimed, as an object cast up by the sea.

wail (wāl) *v.* **1.** To make a loud, mournful cry. **2.** To make a long, loud, high-pitched sound <sirens *wailing*> **—wail** *n.* **—wail′ful** *adj.* **—wail′ing•ly** *adv.*

wain (wān) *n.* **1.** A large open wagon for farm use. **2. Wain.** The Big Dipper.

wain•scot (wān′skət, -skŏt′, -skōt′) *n.* **1.** A usu. wooden facing or paneling applied to the walls of a room. **2.** The lower part of an interior wall when finished in a different material. **—wain′scot** *v.*

wain•scot•ing *also* **wain•scot•ting** (wān′skə-tĭng, -skŏt′ĭng, -skō′tĭng) *n.* **1.** A wainscot. **2.** Material for a wainscot.

wain•wright (wān′rīt′) *n.* One who builds and repairs wagons.

waist (wāst) *n.* **1.** The somewhat narrowed part of the body between the rib cage and the pelvis. **2. a.** The part of a garment that fits around the waist. **b.** A garment, as a blouse or bodice, worn on the upper body. **c.** A child's undershirt, to which other clothing may be fastened. **3.** The middle section or part of something, esp. when narrower than the rest. **—waist′ed** *adj.*

waist•band (wāst′bănd′) *n.* A cloth band, as on a skirt, that circles the waist.

waist•coat (wĕs′kĭt, wāst′kōt′) *n. esp. Brit.* A vest for men.

waist•line (wāst′līn′) *n.* **1. a.** The narrowest part of the waist. **b.** The measurement of this part. **2.** The juncture of the skirt and bodice of a dress.

wait (wāt) *v.* **1.** To remain inactive until something anticipated occurs. **2.** To put off until later. **3. a.** To be in attendance, as a waiter, waitress, or salesperson. **b.** To serve at meals <*wait* on table> **4.** To be prepared or ready <a hot meal *waiting*> —*n.* Time spent in waiting. **—in wait.** In hiding, awaiting a chance to attack.

wait•er (wā′tər) *n.* **1.** A man who serves at meals, as in a restaurant. **2.** A tray or salver.

wait•ing game (wā′tĭng) *n.* A strategy in which advantage is sought through the use of delaying tactics.

waiting room *n.* A room for the use of persons waiting, as to see a doctor.

wait•ress (wā′trĭs) *n.* A woman who serves at meals, as in a restaurant.

waive (wāv) *v.* **waived, waiv•ing. 1.** To relinquish (a right or claim) voluntarily. **2.** To dispense with or postpone.

waiv•er (wā′vər) *n.* **1.** The deliberate waiving of a right, claim, or privilege. **2.** A formal document indicating a waiver.

wake¹ (wāk) *v.* **woke** (wōk), **waked** (wākt) *or* **woke** *or* **wo•ken** (wō′kən), **wak•ing. 1.** To bring or come from sleep **:** awaken. **2.** To keep a vigil, esp. over a deceased person. **3.** To be or stay awake. **4.** To rouse to awareness **:** alert. **5.** To stir up **:** stimulate. —*n.* A vigil, esp. over a corpse before the burial.

wake² (wāk) *n.* **1.** The visible turbulence left by a vessel moving through water. **2.** A track or course left behind.

wake•ful (wāk′fəl) *adj.* **1.** Not sleeping, whether involuntarily or by choice **:** sleepless. **2.** Vigilant. **—wake′ful•ness** *n.*

wak•en (wā′kən) *v.* **1.** To awaken from sleep. **2.** To stir up from a dormant state.

wale (wāl) *n.* **1. a.** A ridge in some fabrics, as corduroy. **b.** The weave or texture of such fabric <a wide *wale*> **2.** A skin welt made by a lash or blow. —*v.* **waled, wal•ing.** To mark (the skin) with wales.

walk (wôk) *v.* **1.** To move or cause to go on foot over a surface at a pace slower than a run. **2.** To go or pass over, on, or through by walking. **3.** To behave in a certain way. **4.** *Baseball.* To advance or cause to advance to first base after 4 balls have been pitched. —*n.* **1.** The act or an example of walking. **2.** A distance to be walked. **3.** A place on which to walk. **4.** A way of walking **:** gait. **5.** *Baseball.* The automatic advance of a batter to first base after receiving 4 balls. **6. a.** A way of acting or living. **b.** Status or occupation. **—walk′er** *n.*

walk•a•way (wôk′ə-wā′) *n.* A contest, competition, or victory won with ease.

walk•ie-talk•ie (wô′kē-tô′kē) *n.* A portable, battery-operated radio transmitter and receiver.

walk-in (wôk′ĭn′) *adj.* Big enough to walk into, as a closet or refrigerator. —*n.* **1.** An easy win. **2.** One who walks in.

walking papers *pl.n. Informal.* Notice of dismissal.

walking stick *n.* **1.** A cane used in walking. **2.** Any of various insects of the family Phasmidae that look like twigs or sticks.

walk-on (wôk′ŏn′, -ôn′) *n.* A small role in a play, usu. without speaking lines.

walk•out (wôk′out′) *n.* **1.** A labor strike. **2.** The act of leaving a meeting, organization, etc., as a sign of disapproval.

walk•o•ver (wôk′ō′vər) *n.* A walkaway.

walk•up *also* **walk-up** (wôk′ŭp′) *n.* A building of several stories with no elevator or an apartment or office in such a building. **—walk′up** *adj.*

wall (wôl) *n.* **1.** A vertical structure or partition that serves to enclose or separate. **2.** A continuous defensive rampart. **3.** Something that rises, separates, surrounds, or protects like a wall. —*v.* To provide or close up with or as if with a wall.

wal•la•by (wŏl′ə-bē) *n., pl.* **-bies.** An Australian marsupial of the genus *Wallabia* or related genera that resembles the kangaroo but is gen. smaller.

wal•la•roo (wŏl′ə-ro͞o′) *n., pl.* **-roos.** A kangaroo, *Macropus robustus* or *Osphranter robustus,* of hilly regions of Australia.

wall•board (wôl′bôrd′, -bōrd′) *n.* A structural material, as paper-coated gypsum plaster, used in large sheets to cover inside walls and ceilings.

wal•let (wŏl′ĭt) *n.* A small flat folding case for carrying paper money, cards, etc.

wall•eye (wôl′ī′) *n.* **1. a.** An eye abnormally directed out to the side of the face. **b.** An eye with an opaque or white cornea. **2.** A North American freshwater food and game fish, *Stizostedium vitreum,* with large, conspicuous eyes. **—wall′eyed′** *adj.*

wall•flow•er (wôl′flou′ər) *n.* **1. a.** A widely cultivated European plant *Cheiranthus cheiri,* with fragrant yellow, orange, or brownish flowers. **b.** A similar plant, *Erysimum asperum,* of the W U.S. **2.** *Informal.* One who only looks on at a dance or party esp. from shyness or unpopularity.

Wal•loon (wŏ-lo͞on′) *n.* One of a French-speaking people of Celtic descent inhabiting S and SE Belgium.

wal•lop (wŏl′əp) *v.* **1.** To thrash soundly. **2.** To hit with a hard blow. —*n.* **1.** A hard blow. **2.** An impact. **—wal′lop•er** *n.*

wal•lop•ing (wŏl′ə-pĭng) *adj. Informal.* **1.** Very large. **2.** Very impressive. —*n.* A sound thrashing or defeat.

wal•low (wŏl′ō) *v.* **1.** To roll around in or as if in muddy water or deep mud. **2.** To take luxurious pleasure **:** revel. **3.** To be or become plentifully supplied with something. —*n.* A place where animals wallow.

wall•pa•per (wôl′pā′pər) *n.* Heavy colored or

patterned paper used to cover interior walls. —**wall'pa'per** *v.*

wal•nut (wôl'nŭt', -nət) *n.* **1.** Any of several trees of the genus *Juglans*, with round, sticky fruit that encloses an edible nut. **2.** The hard, dark-brown wood of a walnut, used esp. for furniture.

wal•rus (wôl'rəs, wŏl'-) *n.* A large Arctic marine mammal, *Odobenus rosmarus*, related to the seals and sea lions and having tough, wrinkled skin and large tusks.

waltz (wôlts) *n.* **1.** A gliding dance in 3/4 time. **2.** Music to accompany the waltz. —*v.* **1.** To dance the waltz (with). **2.** To move or progress lightly or easily.

Wam•pa•no•ag (wăm'pə-nō'ăg) *n., pl.* **-ag** *or* **-ags. 1.** A member of an American Indian people of E Rhode Island and SE Massachusetts. **2.** Their Algonquian language.

wam•pum (wŏm'pəm, wôm'-) *n.* **1.** Small strung beads of polished shells, once used by North American Indians as currency or jewelry. **2.** *Informal.* Money.

wan (wŏn) *adj.* **wan•ner, wan•nest. 1.** Abnormally pale. **2.** Weak or faint <a *wan* smile> —**wan'ly** *adv.* —**wan'ness** *n.*

wand (wŏnd) *n.* **1.** A thin rod carried in a procession **:** scepter. **2.** A thin rod used by a magician, diviner, or sorcerer.

wan•der (wŏn'dər) *v.* **1.** To move or travel about aimlessly **:** roam. **2.** To go in a roundabout or leisurely way. **3.** To stray from a given place, group, or topic. **4.** To think or speak disjointedly. **5.** To go astray morally. —**wan'der•er** *n.* —**wan'der•ing•ly** *adv.*

wandering jew *n.* A trailing plant native to tropical America, *Tradescantia fluminensis* or *Zebrina pendula*, with usu. variegated foliage and popular as a house plant.

wan•der•lust (wŏn'dər-lŭst') *n.* A strong, persistent urge to travel.

wane (wān) *v.* **waned, wan•ing. 1.** To grow gradually less illuminated when passing from full to new <The old moon *wanes.*> **2.** To decrease gradually **:** decline. **3.** To near an end. —*n.* **1.** The period during which the moon wanes. **2.** A gradual decrease or deterioration.

wan•gle (wăng'gəl) *v.* **-gled, -gling. 1.** To do or get by connivance. **2.** To manipulate, esp. by deception or fraud. —**wan'gler** *n.*

Wan•kel engine (väng'kəl, wăng'-) *n.* An internal-combustion engine in which a triangular rotor replaces the pistons.

want (wŏnt, wônt) *v.* **1.** To desire greatly **:** wish. **2.** To be deficient in **:** lack <The novel *wants* cohesiveness.> **3.** To need **:** require. **4.** To be needy. **5.** To seek with intent to capture. —*n.* **1.** Lack of a usual or necessary amount. **2.** Urgent need **:** impoverishment. **3.** A need, desire, or requirement. **4.** A character fault or flaw.

want ad *n.* A classified advertisement.

want•ing (wŏn'tĭng, wôn'-) *adj.* **1.** Not present. **2.** Below standards or expectations. **3.** Deficient <*wanting* in tact> —*prep.* **1.** Without. **2.** Minus **:** less.

wan•ton (wŏn'tən) *adj.* **1. a.** Lascivious **:** lewd. **b.** Suggesting sexuality. **2.** Cruel and merciless **:** inhumane. **3.** Unduly extravagant. **4.** Lacking sound reason or cause **:** unjust. **5.** Excessively playful **:** frolicsome. —*n.* A wanton person. —**wan'ton•ly** *adv.*

wap•i•ti (wŏp'ĭ-tē) *n., pl.* **-ti** *or* **-tis.** A large North American deer, *Cervus canadensis*, having high branching antlers **:** elk.

war (wôr) *n.* **1.** Armed conflict between nations, states, or factions. **2.** A determined struggle esp. for a specific goal <a *war* against illiteracy> **3.** A state of antagonism or discord. **4.** Military techniques or procedures as a science. —*v.* **warred, war•ring. 1.** To engage in armed conflict. **2.** To struggle or contend.

war•ble (wôr'bəl) *v.* **-bled, -bling.** To sing a sequence of melodious trilling sounds. —**war•ble** *n.*

war•bler (wôr'blər) *n.* **1.** Any of various small, often yellowish New World birds of the family Parulidae. **2.** Any of various small brownish or grayish Old World birds of the subfamily Silviinae.

war bonnet *n.* A headdress with a trailing feathered extension worn ceremonially by some North American Indians.

war crime *n. often* **war crimes.** A crime, as genocide, committed during wartime. —**war criminal** *n.*

ward (wôrd) *n.* **1. a.** A division in a hospital <a maternity *ward*> **b.** A room in a hospital usu. for 2 or more patients. **c.** A division in a penal institution. **2.** A division of a city or town for administrative and representative purposes. **3.** A minor or incompetent person under the protection of a legal guardian or a court. **4. a.** The state of being in custody. **b.** The act of guarding or protecting. **5.** A defense. —*v.* To avert <*ward* off an attack>

-ward *or* **-wards** *suff.* Direction toward <earth*ward*><north*ward*>

war•den (wôr'dn) *n.* **1.** The administrative head of a prison. **2.** An official whose duty it is to enforce certains laws and governmental orders <a fire *warden*> **3.** A churchwarden.

ward•er (wôr'dər) *n.* One employed to stand guard or keep watch.

ward heel•er (hē'lər) *n. Slang.* A local worker for a powerful political machine.

ward•robe (wôr'drōb') *n.* **1.** A cabinet, closet, or room for clothes. **2.** All the clothing belonging to an individual.

ward•room (wôrd'ro͞om', -ro͝om') *n.* A room on a warship in which commissioned officers may dine and lounge.

ward•ship (wôrd'shĭp') *n.* **1.** The state of being a ward or under a guardian's care. **2.** The act or right of guardianship **:** custody.

ware (wâr) *n.* **1.** Manufactured or handmade articles of the same general kind <table*ware*> **2.** Articles made of fired clay **:** pottery or ceramics. **3. wares.** Articles for sale **:** merchandise.

ware•house (wâr'hous') *n.* A usu. large building for the storage of goods or merchandise. —**ware'house'** *v.*

war•fare (wôr′fâr′) *n.* **1.** Armed conflict between enemies. **2.** Struggle **:** discord.
war•head (wôr′hĕd′) *n.* The part of a projectile, as a bomb or guided missile, that houses the charge.
war-horse (wôr′hôrs′) *n.* **1.** A horse used in battle. **2.** *Informal.* A veteran esp. of military or political life.
war•like (wôr′līk′) *adj.* **1.** Inclined to fight or make war. **2.** Of or relating to war. **3.** Portending or indicating war.
war•lock (wôr′lŏk′) *n.* A male witch or wizard.
war•lord (wôr′lôrd′) *n.* A military commander exercising civil power in a given region, whether in nominal allegiance to the national government or in defiance of it.
warm (wôrm) *adj.* **1.** Neither cool nor very hot **:** moderately hot. **2. a.** Giving off a moderate amount of heat, as the sun. **b.** Helping to retain bodily heat <*warm* clothes> **3.** Feeling sensations of high bodily heat, as from vigorous exercise. **4.** Enthusiastic **:** ardent <*warm* praises> **5.** Marked by excitement or emotional tensions. **6.** Freshly made, as a trail or scent. **7.** Close to a goal, as in a game or search. **8.** *Informal.* Distressing or dangerous <made things *warm* for the suspect> **9.** Marked by warmth of color, tone, or feeling. —*v.* **1.** To make or become somewhat high in temperature. **2.** To make lively or spirited. **3.** To inspire with pleasant feelings. **4.** To become kindly disposed. **5.** To become gradually more ardent or animated, as in public speaking. —**warm up.** To make or become prepared for action, as by preliminary practicing or exercising. —**warm′er** *n.* —**warm′ish** *adj.* —**warm′ly** *adv.*
warm-blood•ed (wôrm′blŭd′ĭd) *adj.* Having a relatively constant warm body temperature unrelated to the temperature of the surroundings, as a bird or mammal. —**warm′-blood′ed•ness** *n.*
warm-heart•ed (wôrm′här′tĭd) *adj.* Marked by emotional warmth **:** kind and friendly. —**warm′heart′ed•ly** *adv.* —**warm′-heart′ed•ness** *n.*
war•mon•ger (wôr′mŭng′gər, -mŏng′-) *n.* One who favors or tries to stir up war. —**war′mon′ger•ing** *n.* & *adj.*
warmth (wôrmth) *n.* **1.** The quality or state of being warm. **2.** Kindness, friendliness, etc. **3.** Excitement or intensity.
warm-up (wôrm′ŭp′) *n.* An act, method, or time of warming up.
warn (wôrn) *v.* **1.** To alert to danger. **2.** To admonish or advise as to action or conduct. **3.** To direct to go or remain away. **4.** To notify or inform beforehand. ★ ***syns:*** ALERT, CAUTION, FOREWARN
warn•ing (wôr′nĭng) *n.* **1.** An intimation esp. of impending danger. **2. a.** A sign or notice of impending danger. **b.** The act of giving such a sign. —*adj.* Serving as a warning. —**warn′ing•ly** *adv.*
warp (wôrp) *v.* **1.** To distort or become bent out of shape, as wood. **2.** To deviate or cause to deviate from a proper course. **3.** *Naut.* To move (a vessel) by hauling on a line attached to a piling, anchor, or pier. —*n.* **1.** The state of being warped. **2.** A distortion or twist. **3.** The lengthwise threads in a woven fabric, crossed at right angles by the woof threads.
war•path (wôr′păth′, -päth′) *n.* **1.** A course that leads to warfare or battle. **2.** A hostile course or mood <on the *warpath*>
war•plane (wôr′plān′) *n.* An aircraft equipped for combat.
war•rant (wôr′ənt, wŏr′-) *n.* **1.** Authorization or justification. **2.** Something that assures, proves, or guarantees. **3.** A written authorization, esp. a legal writ authorizing a search, seizure, or arrest. **4.** A certificate of appointment to the rank of warrant officer. —*v.* **1.** To give proof of **:** bear witness to. **2.** To vouch for. **3. a.** To guarantee (a product) to be as represented. **b.** To guarantee (a buyer) insurance against damage or loss. **4.** To call for or merit. **5.** To grant authorization to. —**war′rant•a•ble** *adj.* —**war′ran•tee′** *n.* —**war′ran•tor** *n.*
warrant officer *n.* A military officer ranking below a commissioned officer and above a noncommissioned officer.
war•ran•ty (wôr′ən-tē, wŏr′-) *n., pl.* **-ties. 1.** Official authorization. **2.** Justification for a course of action. **3.** A legally binding written guarantee.
war•ren (wôr′ən, wŏr′-) *n.* **1.** A living and breeding area for rabbits. **2.** A crowded dwelling place or locality.
war•ri•or (wôr′ē-ər, wŏr′-) *n.* One who fights in a war, esp. a battle veteran.
war•ship (wôr′shĭp′) *n.* A ship equipped for combat.
wart (wôrt) *n.* **1.** A small, usu. hard outgrowth on the skin, esp. one produced by a virus. **2.** A wartlike protuberance, as on a plant. —**wart′y** *adj.*
wart hog *n.* A wild African tusked hog, *Phacochoerus aethiopicus,* with wartlike swellings on the face.

wart hog

war•y (wâr′ē) *adj.* **-i•er, -i•est. 1.** Alert to danger **:** watchful. **2.** Marked by caution **:** careful. —**war′i•ly** *adv.* —**war′i•ness** *n.*
was (wŏz, wŭz; wəz *when unstressed*) *v. 1st & 3rd person sing. p.t. of* BE.

†**wash** (wŏsh, wôsh) *v.* **1.** To cleanse usu. with water and soap or detergent. **2.** To make oneself clean. **3.** To cleanse of moral corruption. **4.** To make somewhat wet. **5.** To flow over or along. **6.** To carry or be carried away by water. **7.** To erode or destroy by water. **8.** To cover (e.g., a canvas) with a thin, watery layer of paint or other coloring. **9.** To pour or shake water through to separate out valuable material. **10.** *Informal.* To hold up under inspection <Your story just won't *wash.*> —*n.* **1.** An act, process, or instance of washing or undergoing washing. **2.** A quantity of soiled or laundered clothes, linens, etc. **3. a.** A liquid used in cleansing or coating something. **b.** A thin coating, as of water color or whitewash. **4.** A turbulent rush or surge of air or water. **5.** Liquid refuse **:** swill. **6.** Soil erosion by the action of moving water. **7.** *W U.S.* The dry bed of a stream.

wash•a•ble (wŏsh'ə-bəl, wô'shə-bəl) *adj.* Able to withstand washing without damage <a *washable* fabric>

wash-and-wear (wŏsh'ən-wâr', wôsh'-) *adj.* Requiring little or no ironing after being washed <a *wash-and-wear* shirt>

wash•ba•sin (wôsh'bā'sĭn) *n.* A basin for washing **:** washbowl.

wash•board (wŏsh'bôrd', -bōrd', wôsh'-) *n.* A corrugated board on which clothes can be scrubbed clean.

wash•bowl (wŏsh'bōl', wôsh'-) *n.* A water basin esp. for washing one's hands and face.

wash•cloth (wŏsh'klôth', -klŏth', wôsh'-) *n.* A small cloth for washing oneself.

washed-out (wŏsht'out', wôsht'-) *adj.* **1. a.** Faded. **b.** Pale. **2.** *Informal.* Tired out.

wash•er (wŏsh'ər, wô'shər) *n.* **1.** One that washes, esp. a machine for washing clothes or dishes. **2.** A small disk or plate used under a nut or at an axle bearing to relieve friction or prevent leakage.

wash•er•wom•an (wŏsh'ər-wo͝om'ən, wô'shər-) *n.* A woman who launders clothes for a living **:** laundress.

wash•ing (wŏsh'ĭng, wô'shĭng) *n.* **1.** A batch of articles washed or to be washed **:** laundry. **2.** The material remaining after an ore has been washed. **3.** A thin coating.

washing soda *n.* A hydrated carbonate of sodium, used as an all-purpose cleanser.

wash•out (wŏsh'out', wôsh'-) *n.* **1.** The removal or erosion of something by water. **2.** A total failure.

wash•room (wŏsh'ro͞om', -ro͝om', wôsh'-) *n.* A rest room or lavatory.

wash•stand (wŏsh'stănd', wôsh'-) *n.* **1.** A small table with a basin and a pitcher of water for washing. **2.** A stationary washbowl, esp. in a bathroom.

wash•tub (wŏsh'tŭb', wôsh'-) *n.* A tub for washing clothes.

wash•y (wŏsh'ē, wô'shē) *adj.* **-i•er, -i•est. 1.** Having a watery consistency **:** diluted. **2.** Lacking force, intensity, or definition.

was•n't (wŏz'ənt, wŭz'-). Was not.

wasp (wŏsp, wôsp) *n.* Any of numerous insects, chiefly of the superfamilies Vespoidea and Sphecoidea, having a slender body with a constricted abdomen, the female of which is capable of inflicting a painful sting.

Wasp *or* **WASP** (wŏsp, wôsp) *n.* A white American Protestant whose ancestors were Anglo-Saxon. —**Wasp'ish, Wasp'y** *adj.*

wasp•ish (wŏs'pĭsh, wô'spĭsh) *adj.* **1.** Of or typical of a wasp. **2.** Easily vexed **:** snappish. —**wasp'ish•ness** *n.*

wasp waist *n.* A very narrow waist. —**wasp'-waist'ed** *adj.*

was•sail (wŏs'əl, wŏ-sāl') *n.* **1. a.** An English toast given to someone's health in former times. **b.** The alcoholic beverage used in giving this toast. **2.** A festive occasion with much drinking. —*v.* To drink a wassail (to) **:** toast. —**was'sail•er** *n.*

Was•ser•mann test (wä'sər-mən) *n.* A blood test for syphilis.

wast•age (wā'stĭj) *n.* **1.** Loss by use, wear, decline, destruction, or wastefulness. **2.** Something wasted or lost by wear.

waste (wāst) *v.* **wast•ed, wast•ing. 1.** To use or expend carelessly or needlessly **:** squander. **2.** To grow or cause to grow gradually thinner or weaker, as from illness. **3. a.** To fail to use, as an opportunity. **b.** To be available without being put to use <Time is *wasting.*> **4.** To destroy completely **:** devastate. **5.** *Slang.* To murder. ★ ***syns:*** CONSUME, DEVOUR, EXPEND, SQUANDER —*n.* **1. a.** The act or an example of wasting. **b.** The condition of being wasted. **2.** Gradual loss through wastefulness. **3.** Worthless or useless material that is produced as a by-product or discarded as refuse. **4.** Unusable digestive residue eliminated from the body. **5.** A barren region. —**wast'er** *n.* —**waste'ful** *adj.*

waste•bas•ket (wāst'băs'kĭt) *n.* A container for wastepaper or trash.

waste•land (wāst'lănd') *n.* Uncultivated or uninhabited land, as a desert.

waste•pa•per (wāst'pā'pər) *n.* Discarded paper.

wast•rel (wā'strəl) *n.* **1.** One who wastes, esp. a spendthrift. **2.** A lazy person **:** idler.

watch (wŏch) *v.* **1.** To look at or observe attentively and usu. continuously. **2.** To wait expectantly <*watch* for a chance> **3.** To be on the alert. **4.** To keep guard or vigil. **5.** To keep informed about. **6.** To keep guard over **:** tend. ★ ***syns:*** EYE, OBSERVE, SCRUTINIZE —*n.* **1.** The act of staying awake esp. to guard or attend. **2.** A period of attentive observation. **3.** One or several serving to guard or protect <a night *watch*> **4.** The post or period of duty of one who keeps watch. **5.** A small, portable timepiece worn or carried on the person. **6.** *Naut.* **a.** A designated period of time for certain crew members to be on duty. **b.** The crew members on duty during a given watch. —**watch'er** *n.*

watch•dog (wŏch'dôg', -dŏg') *n.* **1.** A dog trained to guard esp. private property against intruders. **2.** One who serves as a guardian against waste, loss, or illegal practices.

watch•ful (wŏch'fəl) *adj.* Constantly on the alert, esp. for danger. —**watch'ful•ly** *adv.* —**watch'ful•ness** *n.*

watch•mak•er (wŏch'mā'kər) *n.* A maker or repairer of watches.

watch•man (wŏch'mən) *n.* One employed to keep watch : guard.

watch•tow•er (wŏch'tou'ər) *n.* A tower for a lookout or sentinel.

watch•word (wŏch'wûrd') *n.* **1.** A secret word or phrase spoken to a guard to gain entrance. **2.** A slogan.

wa•ter (wô'tər, wŏt'ər) *n.* **1.** A clear liquid compound of hydrogen and oxygen that is essential for most plant and animal life. **2.** A form of water, as rain, ice, or steam. **3. a.** A body of water, as an ocean, lake, or river. **b.** An area or quantity of water, esp. ocean water near or controlled by a country. **4.** A bodily fluid, as urine or tears. **5.** A solution containing and resembling water <soda *water*> **6.** A pattern or finish, as of a fabric, marked by a wavy luster. **7. a.** Clearness and luster of a precious gem. **b.** Degree of completeness. —Used esp. in the phrase *of the first water.* —*v.* **1.** To make wet by supplying with water. **2. a.** To give drinking water to. **b.** To get or take on water. **3.** To mix or dilute with or as if with water. **4.** To give a wavy finish or luster to the surface of (e.g., silk or metal). **5.** To produce or discharge a watery fluid.

water bed *n.* A bed consisting of a tough, heavy plastic bag filled with water.

wa•ter•borne (wô'tər-bôrn', -bōrn', wŏt'ər-) *adj.* Supported, transported, or transmitted by water.

water buffalo *n.* A large, often domesticated Asian or African buffalo, *Bubalus bubalis,* with spreading horns.

water chestnut *n.* A Chinese sedge, *Eleocharis tuberosa,* with an edible, succulent corm used esp. in Oriental cookery.

water closet *n.* A small room with a toilet and often a sink.

water color *also* **wa•ter•col•or** (wô'tər-kŭl'ər, wŏt'ər-) *n.* **1.** A paint in which water rather than oil is mixed with the coloring material. **2.** A picture done in water colors. **3.** The art or process of using water colors. —**water colorist** *n.*

wa•ter•course (wô'tər-kôrs', -kōrs', wŏt'ər-) *n.* **1.** A waterway. **2.** A channel through which water flows.

wa•ter•craft (wô'tər-krăft', wŏt'ər-) *n.* A boat or ship.

wa•ter•cress (wô'tər-krĕs', wŏt'ər-) *n.* A freshwater plant, *Nasturtium officinale,* with pungent edible leaves.

wa•ter•fall (wô'tər-fôl', wŏt'ər-) *n.* A natural stream of water descending from a steep height.

wa•ter•fowl (wô'tər-foul', wŏt'ər-) *n.* **1.** A swimming bird usu. found in freshwater areas. **2.** Swimming birds as a group.

wa•ter•front (wô'tər-frŭnt', wŏt'ər-) *n.* **1.** Land bordering a body of water, as a harbor or lake. **2.** The district of a town or city that borders the water, esp. a wharf district.

water gap *n.* A transverse gap in a mountain ridge through which a stream runs.

watering place *n.* A health resort with mineral springs for drinking, bathing, etc.

water lily *n.* An aquatic plant of the genus *Nymphaea,* with floating leaves and variously colored often fragrant flowers.

water line *n.* **1.** The line on a ship's hull to which the water surface rises. **2.** A line on a ship's hull indicating the depth to which the ship sinks when carrying cargo.

wa•ter-logged (wô'tər-lôgd', -lŏgd', wŏt'ər-) *adj.* So filled or saturated with water as to be heavy or unwieldy.

wa•ter•mark (wô'tər-märk', wŏt'ər-) *n.* **1.** A mark indicating the height to which water has risen, esp. the height of high and low tide. **2.** A very faintly visible design impressed on paper during manufacture. —*v.* To mark (paper) with a watermark.

wa•ter•mel•on (wô'tər-mĕl'ən, wŏt'ər-) *n.* A native African vine, *Citrullus vulgaris,* grown for its large, edible fruit, which has a hard green rind and sweet pink flesh.

water moccasin *n.* A venomous snake, *Agkistrodon piscivorus,* of lowlands and swampy areas of the S U.S.

water ouzel *n.* A small bird of the genus *Cinclus* that feeds along the bottom of swift-moving streams.

water polo *n.* A water sport with 2 teams of swimmers that try to push, throw, or carry a ball into the other's goal.

wa•ter•pow•er (wô'tər-pou'ər, wŏt'ər-) *n.* The energy of swift-moving water as used esp. for generating electricity.

wa•ter•proof (wô'tər-pro͞of', wŏt'ər-) *adj.* Capable of keeping water from penetrating. —*n.* **1.** A waterproof fabric or material. **2.** *esp. Brit.* A raincoat : slicker. —*v.* To treat in order to make waterproof.

wa•ter-re•pel•lent (wô'tər-rĭ-pĕl'ənt, wŏt'ər-) *adj.* Treated to resist water but not completely waterproof.

wa•ter-re•sis•tant (wô'tər-rĭ-zĭs'tənt, wŏt'ər-) *adj.* Water-repellent.

wa•ter•shed (wô'tər-shĕd', wŏt'ər-) *n.* **1.** A ridge between regions whose water drains into 2 different river systems. **2.** The region or area drained by a river system or other body of water. **3.** A critical point serving as a dividing line.

wa•ter•side (wô'tər-sīd', wŏt'ər-) *n.* Land alongside a body of water.

wa•ter-ski *also* **water ski** (wô'tər-skē', wŏt'ər-) *n.* One of a pair of short, broad skis worn while skimming over water behind a towing motorboat. —**wa'ter-ski'** *v.* —**wa'ter-ski'er** *n.*

wa•ter•spout (wô'tər-spout', wŏt'ər-) *n.* **1.** A hole or pipe from which water is discharged. **2.** A tornado or whirlwind over an ocean or lake that appears as a whirling funnel-shaped column of spray and mist.

water strider *n.* An insect of the family

Gerridae, with long, slender legs for supporting itself on the water surface.

water table *n.* The upper limit of a zone of underground rock that is entirely saturated with water.

wa·ter·tight (wô'tər-tīt', wŏt'ər-) *adj.* **1.** Tight enough to prevent water from getting in. **2.** Incapable of being misinterpreted, thwarted, etc. **:** flawless.

wa·ter·way (wô'tər-wā', wŏt'ər-) *n.* A navigable body of water.

water wheel *n.* A wheel propelled by falling or flowing water.

water wings *pl.n.* An inflatable device used to support one's body in water.

wa·ter·works (wô'tər-wûrks', wŏt'ər-) *pl.n.* *(sing. or pl. in number).* A system of reservoirs, pipes, and pumping stations, that supplies water to a city or town.

wa·ter·y (wô'tə-rē, wŏt'ə-) *adj.* **-i·er, -i·est. 1.** Filled with or containing water. **2.** Resembling or reminiscent of water. **3.** Weak or thin **:** diluted. **4.** Lacking force or effectiveness. **—wa'ter·i·ness** *n.*

watt (wŏt) *n.* A unit of electrical power equal to 1 joule per sec.

watt·age (wŏt'ĭj) *n.* Amount of electrical power expressed in watts.

wat·tle (wŏt'l) *n.* **1.** Sticks and twigs, branches, reeds, etc., woven into a construction material, as for walls or fences. **2.** A fleshy, often vividly colored flap of skin hanging from the head or neck of certain birds and lizards.

wave (wāv) *v.* **waved, wav·ing. 1.** To move or cause to move back and forth or up and down **:** flap or flutter. **2.** To signal or express by waving <*wave* good-bye> **3.** To arrange or fall in curves or curls, as hair. *—n.* **1.** An undulating ridge or swell on the surface of water. **2.** An undulation or succession of rippling movements in or on a surface <*waves* of tall grass> **3.** A curve or an arrangement of curves, as in the hair. **4.** An up-and-down or back-and-forth movement. **5. a.** A sweeping or surging movement <*waves* of protest> **b.** A peak of activity <a buying *wave*> **6.** A persistent condition of unusually hot or cold weather. **7.** *Physics.* A disturbance or oscillation that passes energy from point to point in a medium or in space <a sound *wave*> **—wave'like** *adj.*

Wave (wāv) *n.* A member of the women's reserve of the U.S. Navy.

wave·band (wāv'bănd') *n.* A range of radio frequencies.

wave·form (wāv'fôrm') *n.* Mathematical representation of a wave.

wave·length (wāv'lĕngth') *n.* The distance in a periodic wave between 2 points of corresponding phases.

wave·let (wāv'lĭt) *n.* A small wave.

wa·ver (wā'vər) *v.* **1.** To sway unsteadily back and forth. **2.** To be undecided or irresolute **:** vacillate. **3.** To weaken in force or purpose <My courage began to *waver.*> **4.** To have a trembling or quavering sound. **5.** To flicker or flutter, as candlelight. **—wa'ver** *n.* **—wa'ver·ing·ly** *adv.*

wav·y (wā'vē) *adj.* **-i·er, -i·est. 1.** Having or moving in waves. **2.** Characterized by wavelike or winding curves.

wax[1] (wăks) *n.* **1.** Any of various natural yellowish solid or soft, sticky substances, as beeswax, that when heated melt or soften easily. **2.** A waxy substance occurring naturally in the ears. **3.** A solid plastic or very thick liquid material, as paraffin. **4.** A commercial preparation containing wax and used esp. for shining surfaces. *—v.* To treat or shine with wax.

wax[2] (wăks) *v.* **1.** To grow gradually more illuminated when passing from new to full <The new moon *waxes.*> **2.** To increase gradually, as in quantity or strength. **3.** To become <The weather *waxed* cool.>

wax bean *n.* A variety of snap bean with long, pale-yellow pods.

wax·en (wăk'sən) *adj.* **1.** Made of or coated with wax. **2.** Pale-yellow or very smooth like wax <a *waxen* complexion>

wax myrtle *n.* A shrub, *Myrica cerifera,* of the SE U.S., bearing with evergreen leaves and small, waxy berrylike fruit.

wax paper *or* **waxed paper** *n.* Paper treated against moisture with wax.

wax·wing (wăks'wĭng') *n.* A crested bird of the genus *Bombycilla,* with brownish plumage and red-tipped wing feathers.

wax·work (wăks'wûrk') *n.* **1.** A usu. life-size figure made of wax. **2. waxworks.** *(sing. or pl. in number).* An exhibition of waxwork representing famous persons.

wax·y (wăk'sē) *adj.* **-i·er, -i·est. 1.** Like wax in texture or appearance. **2.** Consisting of or full of wax. **—wax'i·ness** *n.*

†way (wā) *n.* **1.** A manner or fashion. **2.** A means, method, or technique. **3.** An aspect or feature. **4.** A characteristic or tendency. **5.** A customary manner of living, acting, or doing. **6.** A passage leading from one place to another. **7.** Progress toward a goal. **8.** Sufficient room for passing <make *way*> **9.** An extent of linear space **:** distance. **10.** Direction of movement or location. **11.** Facility **:** talent. **12.** Freedom to do as one likes. **13.** A course of conduct or action <did it the hard *way*> **14.** A condition or state of affairs <That's the *way* it is.> **15.** *Informal.* A district or locality. **—out of the way. 1.** Remote. **2.** Improper. **—under way.** Actively progressing.

way·bill (wā'bĭl') *n.* A list of goods, charges, and shipping instructions accompanying a shipment.

way·far·er (wā'fâr'ər) *n.* One who travels, esp. on foot. **—way'far'ing** *adj.* **&** *n.*

way·lay (wā'lā') *v.* **1.** To attack from ambush. **2.** To accost or intercept in an attempt to speak with. **—way'lay'er** *n.*

way-out (wā'out') *adj. Slang.* Very unconventional **:** far-out.

ways and means *pl.n.* **1.** Ways of funding a specific project or accomplishing a specific goal. **2.** A committee in charge of ways and means.

way·side (wā'sīd') *n.* Land at the immediate edge of a road.

way station *n.* An intermediate stop on a travel route.

way·ward (wā'wərd) *adj.* **1.** Willful : intractable <a *wayward* child> **2.** Capricious : unpredictable <a *wayward* breeze>

we (wē) *pron.* **1.** —Used to refer to the person speaking or writing plus another or others. **2.** —Used instead of *I* in an official capacity by a monarch or by an editor or writer. **3.** People in general.

weak (wēk) *adj.* **1.** Having little strength or energy : feeble. **2.** Easily damaged or broken : fragile. **3.** Marked by, indicative of, or resulting from insufficient intellect, character, strength, or will power. **4.** Lacking the usual or required strength <*weak* broth> **5.** Lacking the ability to function normally <*weak* lungs> **6.** Having inadequate capability or skills <a *weak* administrator> **7.** Unconvincing <a *weak* alibi> **8.** Not forceful or intense <a *weak* little voice><*weak* sunlight> **9.** Of or being a verb whose past tense and past participle are formed by adding *-ed, -d, or -t.* **—weak'ly** *adv.*

weak·en (wē'kən) *v.* To make or become weak. **—weak'en·er** *n.*

weak·fish (wēk'fĭsh') *n.* A marine food and game fish of the genus *Cynoscion*, esp. *C. regalis* of N Atlantic waters.

weak-kneed (wēk'nēd') *adj.* Lacking in courage or determination.

weak·ling (wēk'lĭng) *n.* One of weak constitution or character.

weak·ly (wēk'lē) *adj.* **-li·er, -li·est.** Feeble : sickly.

weak·ness (wēk'nĭs) *n.* **1.** The state or sensation or an instance of being weak. **2.** A defect or shortcoming. **3. a.** A particular fondness. **b.** An object of special liking.

weal[1] (wēl) *n.* Well-being : welfare.

weal[2] (wēl) *n.* WELT 3.

wealth (wĕlth) *n.* **1.** Abundance of riches, resources, or valuable possessions. **2.** An abundant amount <a *wealth* of information> **3.** All goods, property, and resources having monetary value.

wealth·y (wĕl'thē) *adj.* **-i·er, -i·est. 1.** Having much wealth : affluent. **2.** Richly supplied : abundant.

wean (wēn) *v.* **1.** To train (a young child or mammal) to stop nursing and take other nourishment. **2.** To rid of a dependence on something undesirable.

weap·on (wĕp'ən) *n.* **1.** An instrument or device used for offense or defense. **2.** A means employed to contend with another.

weap·on·ry (wĕp'ən-rē) *n.* **1.** Design and manufacture of weapons. **2.** Weapons.

wear (wâr) *v.* **wore** (wôr, wōr), **worn** (wôrn, wōrn), **wear·ing. 1.** To have on or put on, as clothes or accessories. **2.** To bear regularly on one's person <*wears* a mustache> **3.** To affect or display <always *wearing* a grin> **4.** To maintain in a certain way <*wore* my hair in pigtails> **5.** To damage or expend by or as if by excessive use, friction, or exposure to weather. **6.** To make by continual use or exposure. **7.** To exhaust or become exhausted. **8.** To hold up under long or hard use : last. **9.** To pass gradually <The day *wore* on.><The anesthetic *wore off.*> **—wear down.** To weaken the resistance of by constant pressure. *—n.* **1. a.** The act of wearing. **b.** The state of being worn : use. **2.** Clothing, esp. of a specific type or for a specific use <children's *wear*> <beach *wear*> **3.** Gradual depreciation or decline resulting from use or age. **4.** Durability. **—wear'a·bil'i·ty** *n.* **—wear'a·ble** *adj.*

wear and tear *n.* Depreciation, damage, or loss resulting from ordinary use.

wea·ri·some (wîr'ē-səm) *adj.* Causing fatigue : tedious. **—wea'ri·some·ly** *adv.*

wea·ry (wîr'ē) *adj.* **-ri·er, -ri·est. 1.** Feeling fatigued. **2.** Indicative of fatigue. **3.** Exhausted of patience. *—v.* **-ried, -ry·ing.** To make or become fatigued. **—wea'ri·ly** *adv.* **—wea'ri·ness** *n.*

wea·sel (wē'zəl) *n.* **1.** A long-tailed carnivorous mammal of the genus *Mustela*, with a long, slender body and short legs. **2.** A sneaky, devious person. *—v.* To speak or act evasively.

weath·er (wĕth'ər) *n.* **1.** The state of the atmosphere in terms of temperature, humidity, wind velocity, and barometric pressure. **2.** Stormy or disagreeable atmospheric conditions. *—v.* **1.** To subject to or resist the action of weather. **2.** To change through exposure to the weather. **3.** To survive successfully.

weath·er-beat·en (wĕth'ər-bēt'n) *adj.* **1.** Impaired by exposure to the elements. **2.** Tanned and leathery from being exposed to the weather <*weather-beaten* skin>

weath·er·cock (wĕth'ər-kŏk') *n.* **1.** A weather vane often in the form of a cock. **2.** A fickle or changeable person.

weath·er·ize (wĕth'ə-rīz') *v.* To make repairs and improvements on as a protective measure against cold weather.

weath·er·man (wĕth'ər-măn') *n.* One who reports or forecasts the weather.

weath·er·proof (wĕth'ər-pro͞of') *adj.* Capable of being exposed to weather without impairment. *—v.* To make weatherproof.

weather stripping *n.* A narrow piece of material fitted around doors and windows to make a seal against cold weather. **—weath'er-strip'** *v.*

weather vane *n.* A vane that turns to indicate the direction the wind is blowing.

weave (wēv) *v.* **wove** (wōv) *or* **weaved, wo·ven** (wō'vən), **weav·ing. 1. a.** To make (cloth) by interlacing woof and warp threads on a loom. **b.** To interlace (threads or strands) into cloth. **2.** To make (e.g, a basket or rug) by intertwining the materials of. **3.** To bring together into a whole. **4.** To wind or twine into a material or work. **5.** To spin (a spider's web).

6. To make one's way by moving in and out. —*n.* A pattern or technique of weaving. **—weav'er** *n.*

web (wĕb) *n.* **1.** A fabric on or being taken from a loom. **2.** An interlacing of materials that forms a latticed or woven structure. **3.** A cobweb. **4.** Something intricately constructed, as an entanglement or snare. **5.** A complicated network <a *web* of electrical wires> **6.** A piece of skin or membrane, esp. one joining the toes of certain water birds. **7.** A thin metal sheet, plate, or strip in a structural element. —*v.* **webbed, web•bing. 1.** To cover, join, or provide with a web. **2.** To entangle in or as if in a web. **—webbed** *adj.*

web•bing (wĕb'ĭng) *n.* A strong closely woven fabric used esp. for seat belts, brake linings, or upholstery.

web-foot•ed (wĕb'fo͝ot'ĭd) *adj.* Having webbed feet.

wed (wĕd) *v.* **wed•ded, wed** *or* **wed•ded, wed•ding. 1.** To take as a spouse : marry. **2.** To unite (a couple) in marriage. **3.** To unite closely.

we'd (wēd). **1.** We had. **2.** We should. **3.** We would.

wed•ding (wĕd'ĭng) *n.* **1.** A matrimonial ceremony or celebration. **2.** A marriage anniversary or its celebration. **3.** A joining together in close association.

wedge (wĕj) *n.* **1.** A tapered triangular piece of wood or metal used for splitting, tightening, securing, or levering. **2.** Something wedge-shaped. **3.** Something, as an action, idea, or policy that causes division or disruption among people. —*v.* **wedged, wedg•ing. 1.** To force apart or divide with or as if with a wedge. **2.** To make fast with a wedge. **3.** To squeeze into a limited space.

wed•lock (wĕd'lŏk') *n.* The state of being married : marriage.

Wednes•day (wĕnz'dē, -dā') *n.* The 4th day of the week.

wee (wē) *adj.* **we•er, we•est. 1.** Very small. **2.** Very early <the *wee* hours>

weed[1] (wēd) *n.* A plant held to have no value, esp. one growing plentifully and detrimentally in a garden, lawn, etc. —*v.* **1.** To remove or rid of weeds. **2.** To get rid of as undesirable or unfit. **—weed'er** *n.* **—weed'i•ness** *n.* **—weed'y** *adj.*

weed[2] (wēd) *n.* **1.** A symbol of mourning, as a black arm band. **2. weeds.** Black clothes worn by a widow in mourning. **3.** *often* **weeds.** A garment.

week (wēk) *n.* **1.** A period of 7 days, esp. a period that begins on a Sunday and ends the following Saturday. **2.** The school or business hours of a calendar week.

week•day (wēk'dā') *n.* **1.** Any day of the week excluding Sunday. **2.** A day not included in the weekend.

week•end (wēk'ĕnd') *n.* The end of the school or business week, esp. the period from Friday evening through Sunday evening. —*v.* To pass the weekend.

week•ly (wēk'lē) *adv.* **1.** Once a week or every week. **2.** By the week : per week. —*adj.* **1.** Done, taking place, or issued every week. **2.** Made or figured by the week. —*n., pl.* **-lies.** A newspaper or magazine issued once a week.

ween (wēn) *v.* **weened, ween•ing.** *Archaic.* To think : imagine.

weep (wēp) *v.* **wept** (wĕpt), **weep•ing. 1.** To express emotion, as sorrow or joy, by shedding tears : cry. **2.** To ooze or exude (drops of a liquid). —*n. often* **weeps.** A fit of weeping. **—weep'er** *n.*

weep•ing (wē'pĭng) *adj.* **1.** Shedding tears : tearful. **2.** Having long, slender, drooping branches <a *weeping* willow> —*n.* The act of shedding tears.

weep•y (wē'pē) *adj.* **-i•er, -i•est.** Given to weeping : tearful.

wee•vil (wē'vəl) *n.* Any of various beetles, chiefly of the family Curculionidae, that usu. have a downward-curving snout and are damaging to plants and plant products. **—wee'vil•y, wee'vil•ly** *adj.*

weft (wĕft) *n.* **1.** The horizontal threads in weaving : woof. **2.** Fabric that is woven.

weigh (wā) *v.* **1.** To find out the weight of by or as if by using a scale or similar instrument. **2.** To balance carefully in the mind : ponder. **3.** *Naut.* To hoist up (an anchor) prior to sailing. **4.** To have or be of a particular weight. **5.** To have influence or importance : count <testimony *weighing* in our favor> **6.** To burden : oppress.

weight (wāt) *n.* **1.** Heaviness or mass of an object as determined by weighing. **2. a.** The gravitational force exerted on an object. **b.** A unit measure of this force, as an ounce or pound. **c.** A system of such units. **3.** An object used chiefly to exert a downward force, as a solid used for making scientific measurements. **4.** An object, as a paperweight, for holding something down. **5.** A heavy object, as a barbell, used in weightlifting. **6.** A burden <the *weight* of many tasks> **7.** The greatest portion <the *weight* of the evidence> **8.** Authoritative influence or importance. —*v.* **1.** To make heavy with or as if with a weight. **2.** To burden or oppress.

weight•less (wāt'lĭs) *adj.* **1.** Having very little weight. **2.** Experiencing little or no gravitational force, as an orbiting object.

weight•lift•ing (wāt'lĭf'tĭng) *n.* The lifting of barbells for exercise or in athletic events.

weight•y (wā'tē) *adj.* **-i•er, -i•est. 1. a.** Having great weight : heavy. **b.** Fat. **2.** Of great importance. **3.** Burdensome. **4.** Authoritative. **—weight'i•ly** *adv.* **—weight'i•ness** *n.*

Wei•mar•an•er (vī'mä-rä'nər, wī'-) *n.* A large dog with a smooth grayish coat.

weir (wîr) *n.* **1.** A dam built to direct or back up the flow of water. **2.** A fence or barrier, as of branches or net, placed in a stream to catch or retain fish.

weird (wîrd) *adj.* **1.** Having a mysterious or unearthly quality. **2.** Of an odd, bizarre, or inexplicable nature. ★ ***syns:*** EERIE, UNCANNY, UNEARTHLY

▲ ***word history:*** When Macbeth referred

to the witches on the heath as the "weird sisters" he was not being insulting, he was being etymological and innovative at the same time. The phrase *weird sisters* orig. referred to the Fates, the 3 women of classical myth who controlled the destiny of each individual person. The phrase was also extended to include women who prophesied or possessed other attributes of the Fates. *Weird* by itself was a noun that orig. meant "fate" or "destiny" pure and simple, and in medieval times the word was used to translate *Parca,* the Latin word for "Fate." This use of *weird* lost currency during the modern period, surviving primarily in the phrase "weird sisters," where it was interpreted as an adjective. The great prestige of Shakespeare preserved this use of *weird,* which was extended to its current meaning by 19th-cent. poets and writers.

weird•ie *also* **weird•y** (wîr'dē) *n. pl.* **-ies.** *Slang.* A weirdo.

weird•o (wîr'dō) *n., pl.* **-oes.** *Slang.* One that is strange or bizarre.

wel•come (wĕl'kəm) *v.* **-comed, -com•ing. 1.** To greet or extend hospitality cordially to. **2.** To accept willingly or gladly <*welcome* an opportunity> *—n.* A warm greeting or reception. *—adj.* **1.** Greeted or received warmly. **2.** Pleasing **:** gratifying. **3.** Willingly invited or allowed. **4.** —Used in the phrase "you're welcome" to acknowledge thanks. *—interj.* —Used as a cordial greeting.

weld (wĕld) *v.* **1.** To unite (metal parts) by applying heat and sometimes pressure. **2.** To bring closely together **:** unite. *—n.* A union or joint formed by welding.

wel•fare (wĕl'fâr') *n.* **1.** The state of being healthy, happy, or prosperous **:** general well-being. **2.** Organized efforts by a community or private agency to improve the circumstances of the poor. **3.** Governmental aid to the disadvantaged or disabled.

well[1] (wĕl) *n.* **1.** A deep excavation to obtain a natural deposit, as water, oil, or gas. **2.** A spring or fountain serving as a natural source of water. **3.** A valuable source of supply. **4.** A container or reservoir for a liquid. **5.** A vertical opening through floors, as for a staircase. **6.** An enclosure around the pumps in a ship's hold. *—v.* To rise to the surface and flow forth.

well[2] (wĕl) *adv.* **bet•ter** (bĕt'ər), **best** (bĕst). **1.** In a good or correct fashion **:** properly. **2.** With skill or proficiency **:** expertly. **3.** In a satisfactory or sufficient way <dined *well*> **4.** In an effective or successful way <communicates *well* with teen-agers> **5.** Comfortably or affluently <too poor to live *well*> **6.** Favorably **:** positively <spoke *well* of you> **7.** Thoroughly **:** completely <*well* insulated> **8.** Exactly **:** clearly <I recall it *well.*> **9.** To a considerable extent or degree <*well* over 50> **10.** With reason or justification <can't very *well* refuse>. **11.** In all probability <They may *well* be lying.> **12.** Prudently **:** advisably <You would do *well* to keep quiet.> **13.** Closely **:** familiarly <knew them *well*> **14.** Attentively <listen *well*> *—adj.* **1. a.** In good health. **b.** Recovered or healed. **2.** In a satisfactory or agreeable state <All is *well* with us.> **3. a.** Prudent <It would be *well* not to interfere.> **b.** Fortunate <It is *well* that they left early.>

we'll (wēl). **1.** We will. **2.** We shall.

well-ap•point•ed (wĕl'ə-poin'tĭd) *adj.* Having a full array of suitable furnishings or equipment.

well-bal•anced (wĕl'băl'ənst) *adj.* **1.** Balanced evenly in amount, extent, or degree. **2.** Mentally sound **:** sensible.

well-be•ing (wĕl'bē'ĭng) *n.* The state of being gen. healthy, happy, or prosperous.

well-born (wĕl'bôrn') *adj.* Of good ancestry or breeding stock.

well-bred (wĕl'brĕd') *adj.* Having or indicating good breeding **:** polite and refined.

well-dis•posed (wĕl'dĭ-spōzd') *adj.* Inclined to be kindly, friendly, or receptive.

well-done (wĕl'dŭn') *adj.* **1.** Done properly or proficiently. **2.** Cooked thoroughly.

well-fixed (wĕl'fĭkst') *adj. Informal.* In good financial circumstances **:** well-to-do.

well-found•ed (wĕl'foun'dĭd) *adj.* Based on reliable judgment or evidence.

well-groomed (wĕl'gro͞omd') *adj.* **1.** Neat, clean, and carefully dressed. **2.** Well cared for <a *well-groomed* lawn>

well-ground•ed (wĕl'groun'dĭd) *adj.* **1.** Knowledgeable about the basics of a subject. **2.** Well-founded.

well-heeled (wĕl'hēld') *adj. Slang.* Well-fixed **:** well-to-do.

well-knit (wĕl'nĭt') *adj.* Strongly knit, esp. strongly and firmly constructed <a *well-knit* physique> <a *well-knit* play>

well-known (wĕl'nōn') *adj.* **1.** Widely known. **2.** Fully known.

well-man•nered (wĕl'măn'ərd) *adj.* Having good manners **:** polite.

well-mean•ing (wĕl'mē'nĭng) *adj.* Meaning or meant to be helpful.

well•ness (wĕl'nĭs) *n.* The condition of good physical and mental health, esp. when maintained by proper diet and exercise.

well-nigh (wĕl'nī') *adv.* Very nearly.

well-off (wĕl'ôf', -ŏf') *adj.* Being in fortunate circumstances, esp. well-to-do.

well-read (wĕl'rĕd') *adj.* Well informed through extensive reading.

well-spo•ken (wĕl'spō'kən) *adj.* **1.** Spoken with aptness or propriety. **2.** Speaking skillfully and esp. courteously.

well•spring (wĕl'sprĭng') *n.* **1.** The source of a stream or spring. **2.** A source.

well-timed (wĕl'tīmd') *adj.* Happening or done at a timely moment **:** opportune.

well-to-do (wĕl'tə-do͞o') *adj.* Wealthy.

well-turned (wĕl'tûrnd') *adj.* **1.** Nicely shaped or formed. **2.** Skillfully or appropriately expressed.

well-wish•er (wĕl'wĭsh'ər) *n.* One who extends good wishes.

well-worn (wĕl'wôrn', -wōrn') *adj.* **1.** Im-

paired from much use. **2.** Hackneyed from much repetition.
welsh (wĕlsh, wĕlch) *v. Slang.* **1.** To cheat by not paying a debt or bet. **2.** To neglect to discharge an obligation. **—welsh'er** *n.*
Welsh (wĕlsh) *n.* **1.** *(pl. in number).* The people inhabiting Wales. **2.** The Celtic language of Wales. **—Welsh** *adj.* **—Welsh'man** *n.* **—Welsh'wom'an** *n.*
▲ ***word history:*** The Welsh are the descendants of the Celts who lived in Britain before the Roman and Germanic invasions. The Welsh called themselves the *Cymry,* but the invading Anglo-Saxons called them *Wealas,* which in Old English meant "foreigners." *Wealas* became *Wales* in Modern English; *Wælisc,* the adjective derived from *Wealas,* became modern *Welsh.*
Welsh cor·gi (kôr'gē) *n.* A short-legged dog orig. bred in Wales, with a long body and a foxlike head.
Welsh rabbit *also* **Welsh rarebit** *n.* A hot dish of melted cheese poured over toast or crackers.
welt (wĕlt) *n.* **1.** A strip of material, as leather, stitched into a shoe between the sole and the upper. **2.** A strip or cord sewn into a seam to reinforce or trim it. **3.** A ridge or slight swelling raised on the skin by a blow or lash or by an allergic reaction. —*v.* **1.** To provide with a welt. **2.** To beat or whip severely.
wel·ter (wĕl'tər) *v.* **1.** To wallow, roll, or toss about, as in mud or waves. **2.** To lie drenched in a liquid, esp. blood. **3.** To billow and swell, as the sea. —*n.* **1.** An agitated rolling and tossing **:** turbulence. **2. a.** Great confusion **:** turmoil. **b.** A disorderd mass or jumble.
wel·ter·weight (wĕl'tər-wāt') *n.* A boxer or wrestler weighing 136 to 147 lb.
wen (wĕn) *n.* A cyst containing oily secretions from the skin.
wench (wĕnch) *n. Archaic.* **1.** A young girl or woman. **2.** A woman servant. **3.** A prostitute.
wend (wĕnd) *v.* To go on (one's way).
went (wĕnt) *v. p.t. of* GO.
wept (wĕpt) *v. p.t. & p.p. of* WEEP.
were (wûr) *v.* **1.** *2nd person sing. p.t. of* BE. **2.** *1st, 2nd, & 3rd person pl. p.t. of* BE. **3.** *Past subjunctive of* BE.
we're (wîr). We are.
were·n't (wûrnt, wûr'ənt). Were not.
were·wolf (wîr'wo͝olf', wûr'-, wâr'-) *n.* A person thought capable of taking on the form of a wolf.
wes·kit (wĕs'kĭt) *n.* A waistcoat **:** vest.
west (wĕst) *n.* **1. a.** The general direction opposite to sunrise. **b.** The point on the mariner's compass 90° counterclockwise from north. **2.** *often* **West.** An area or region lying in a western direction from a certain point. **3. West.** Europe and the Western Hemisphere **:** the Occident. —*adj.* Of, at, toward, or coming from the west. —*adv.* To or toward the west. **—west'er·ly** *adv. & adj.* **—west'ward** *adv. & adj.* **—west'wards** *adv.*
west·ern (wĕs'tərn) *adj.* **1.** Lying toward the west. **2.** Coming from the west. **3.** *often* **Western. a.** Of, typical of, or found in regions designated as western. **b.** Of or typical of Europe and the Western Hemisphere. —*n. often* **Western.** A novel, film, or broadcast about frontier life in the American West. **—west'ern·er, West'ern·er** *n.*
West·ern·ize (wĕs'tər-nīz') *v.* **-ized, -iz·ing.** To convert to the ways or ideas of the West. **—West'ern·i·za'tion** *n.*
wet (wĕt) *adj.* **wet·ter, wet·test. 1.** Covered or saturated with a liquid, esp. water. **2.** Marked by rain **:** rainy. **3.** Not yet dry or hardened, as paint or plaster. **4.** Permitting or favoring the sale of alcoholic beverages <a *wet* town> —*n.* **1.** Something wet, esp. water. **2.** Moisture **:** wetness. **3.** Rainy or snowy weather. **4.** One supporting the sale of liquor. —*v.* **wet** *or* **wet·ted, wet·ting.** To make or become wet. **—wet'ly** *adv.* **—wet'ness** *n.*
wet blanket *n. Informal.* One that dampens the enjoyment of others.
weth·er (wĕth'ər) *n.* A male sheep castrated before maturity.
wet·land (wĕt'lănd') *n.* A wet, swampy lowland area.
wet nurse *n.* A woman who nurses and cares for another woman's child.
wet suit *n.* A tight-fitting permeable suit, as of rubber, worn esp. by skin divers.
we've (wēv). We have.
whack (hwăk, wăk) *v.* To strike with a sharp, resounding blow **:** slap. —*n.* **1.** A loud, hard blow or slap. **2.** The resounding noise made by a whack. **3.** *Informal.* An attempt **:** try. **—out of whack.** Not functioning properly.
whack·y (hwăk'ē, wăk'ē) *adj. var. of* WACKY.
whale[1] (hwāl, wāl) *n.* **1.** Any of various often very large marine mammals of the order Cetacea, having a gen. fishlike form, flippers, and a tail with horizontal flukes. **2.** *Informal.* An unusually impressive example <had a *whale* of a time> —*v.* **whaled, whal·ing.** To hunt whales.
whale[2] (hwāl, wāl) *v.* **whaled, whal·ing. 1.** To strike forcefully and repeatedly. **2.** To thrash about.
whale·boat (hwāl'bōt', wāl'-) *n.* A long rowboat with pointed ends, formerly used in whaling.
whale·bone (hwāl'bōn', wāl'-) *n.* **1.** The flexible, hornlike substance forming plates or strips in the upper jaw of certain large whales. **2.** A strip of whalebone used esp. to stiffen a corset.
whal·er (hwā'lər, wā'-) *n.* **1.** One engaged in whaling. **2.** A whaleboat.
whal·ing (hwā'lĭng, wāl-) *n.* The business or practice of hunting, killing, and processing whales.
wham (hwăm, wăm) *n.* **1.** A loud, hard blow. **2.** The sound of such a blow. —*v.* **whammed, wham·ming.** To hit or smash into loudly and forcefully.
wham·my (hwăm'ē, wăm'ē) *n., pl.* **-mies.** *Slang.* An evil spell **:** hex.
wharf (hwôrf, wôrf) *n., pl.* **wharves** (hwôrvz,

wôrvz) *or* **wharfs.** A dock or pier at which ships are loaded or unloaded.
wharf•age (hwôr′fĭj, wôr′-) *n.* **1.** Permission to use a wharf. **2.** A charge or fee for such permission and use.
what (hwŏt, hwŭt, wŏt, wŭt; hwət, wət *when unstressed*) *pron.* **1.** Which thing, event, kind, character, etc. <*What* do you want?> <*What's* this?><*What* is it to me?> **2. a.** That which <I saw *what* you did.> **b.** Whatever thing or anything that <Say *what* you want.> **3.** *Informal.* Something unspecified <Do you know *what*?> *—adj.* **1.** Which one or ones <*What* shirt will you wear?> **2.** As much or as many **:** whatever <solved *what* problems arose> **3.** How great, remarkable, etc. <*What* foolishness> *—adv.* **1.** In which way <*What* do you care?> **2.** Because of <busy *what* with job and school>
what•ev•er (hwŏt-ĕv′ər, hwŭt-, wŏt-, wŭt-) *pron.* **1.** Anything that <did *whatever* we could> **2.** No matter what <*Whatever* happens, be sure to call me.> **3.** *Informal.* Which thing or things **:** what <*Whatever* have they done?> *—adj.* Of any kind at all <no money *whatever*>
what•not (hwŏt′nŏt′, hwŭt′-, wŏt′-, wŭt′-) *n.* A set of open shelves for small objects.
what•so•ev•er (hwŏt′sō-ĕv′ər, hwŭt′-, wŏt′-, wŭt′-) *pron. & adj.* Whatever.
wheal (hwēl, wēl) *n.* A small acute swelling on the surface of the skin.
wheat (hwēt, wēt) *n.* **1.** A cereal grass of the genus *Triticum,* esp. *T. aestivum,* widely cultivated in many varieties for its commercially important grain. **2.** The grain of the wheat plant ground into flour. **—wheat′en** *adj.*
wheat germ *n.* The embryo of wheat kernels, rich in vitamins and used as a cereal or food supplement.
whee•dle (hwēd′l, wēd′l) *v.* **-dled, -dling.** To persuade or obtain by flattery or cajolery **:** coax. **—whee′dler** *n.* **—whee′dling•ly** *adv.*
wheel (hwēl, wēl) *n.* **1. a.** A disk or ring joined to a hub by spokes and designed to turn around a central axle or shaft. **b.** Something resembling a wheel in shape or function. **c.** Something having a wheel as its main part, esp. the steering device of a vehicle. **d.** *Informal.* A bicycle. **2. wheels.** Moving or energizing forces <the *wheels* of big business> **3.** A rotation around an axis. **4. wheels.** *Slang.* An automobile. **5.** *Slang.* One having great power or influence <a big *wheel* in politics> *—v.* **1.** To move or transport on or as if on wheels or in a vehicle. **2.** To turn or cause to turn around or as if around a central axis. **3.** To change direction esp. by pivoting. **4.** To reverse one's opinion or practice.
wheel•bar•row (hwēl′băr′ō, wēl′-) *n.* A usu. one-wheeled vehicle with handles, used to transport small loads.
wheel•base (hwēl′bās′, wēl′-) *n.* The distance in inches from front to rear axle in an automotive vehicle.
wheel•chair (hwēl′châr′, wēl′-) *n.* A chair mounted on wheels esp. for the use of persons unable to walk by themselves.
wheel•er (hwē′lər, wē′-) *n.* Something that has wheels <a 2-*wheeler*>
wheel•er-deal•er (hwē′lər-dē′lər, wē′-) *n.* *Informal.* One who wheels and deals, esp. a shrewd businessman or politician.
wheel house *n.* A pilothouse.
wheel•wright (hwēl′rīt′, wēl′-) *n.* A builder and repairer of wheels.
wheeze (hwēz, wēz) *v.* **wheezed, wheez•ing.** To make a hoarse whistling sound in breathing. *—n.* **1.** A wheezing sound. **2.** An old joke or cliché. **—wheez′er** *n.*
wheez•y (hwē′zē, wē′-) *adj.* **-i•er, -i•est. 1.** Tending to wheeze. **2.** Having or making a wheezing sound. **—wheez′i•ly** *adv.* **—wheez′i•ness** *n.*
whelk (hwĕlk, wĕlk) *n.* Any of various large, sometimes edible marine snails of the family Buccinidae, with turreted shells.
whelp (hwĕlp, wĕlp) *n.* **1.** The young of a mammal such as a dog or wolf. **2.** An insolent or base young fellow. *—v.* To give birth to (whelps).
when (hwĕn, wĕn) *adv.* **1.** At what time <*When* will the train arrive?> **2.** At which time <a year *when* we traveled> *—conj.* **1.** At the time that <Start *when* I give the signal.> **2.** Every time that **:** whenever <afraid *when* they're alone> **3.** While on the contrary **:** although <playing *when* we should be working> **4.** Considering that **:** if <How can you succeed *when* you won't try?> *—pron.* What or which time <By *when* will it be ready?> *—n.* The time or date of an event.
whence (hwĕns, wĕns) *adv.* **1.** From what place, cause, or origin <*Whence* came all this money?> **2.** From which <the country *whence* we came> *—conj.* By reason of which.
when•ev•er (hwĕn-ĕv′ər, wĕn-) *adv.* At whatever time **:** when. *—conj.* At whatever or every time that.
when•so•ev•er (hwĕn′sō-ĕv′ər, wĕn′-) *adv. & conj.* At whatever time **:** whenever.
where (hwâr, wâr) *adv.* **1.** At or in what place <*Where* are you?> **2.** To or toward what place or end <*Where* is this discussion leading?> **3.** From what place or origin <*Where* did you hear that story?> *—conj.* **1. a.** At or in what place <don't know *where* they are> **b.** At or in which place <the house *where* we stayed> **2.** In or to a place in which or to which <went *where* we could find work> **3.** Wherever <my dog goes *where* I go.> **4.** While on the contrary **:** whereas <had 3 cars, *where* we had none> **5.** In a situation in which <useless *where* common sense is needed> *—n.* **1.** The location or occasion. **2.** What place <*Where* are you from?>
where•a•bouts (hwâr′ə-bouts′, wâr′-) *adv.* In, at, or near what location <*Whereabouts* can we find them?> *—n. (sing. or pl. in number).* Approximate location <just discovered its *whereabouts*>
where•as (hwâr-ăz′, wâr-) *conj.* **1.** It being

the fact that : since. 2. While on the contrary : although.
where·at (hwâr-ăt′, wâr-) *conj.* 1. Toward or at which place. 2. Whereupon.
where·by (hwâr-bī′, wâr-) *conj.* By or through which.
where·fore (hwâr′fôr′, -fōr′, wâr′-) *adv.* For what reason : why. —*n.* A reason.
where·in (hwâr-ĭn′, wâr-) *adv.* In what way : how. —*conj.* In which thing, location, or circumstance.
where·of (hwâr-ŏv′, -ŭv′, wâr-) *conj.* 1. Of what. 2. Of which or whom.
where·on (hwâr-ŏn′, -ôn′, wâr-) *conj.* On which or what.
where·so·ev·er (hwâr′sō-ĕv′ər, wâr′-) *conj. Archaic.* Wherever.
where·to (hwâr-to͞o′, wâr-) *conj.* To which. —*adv.* To what place or end.
where·up·on (hwâr′ə-pŏn′, -pôn′, wâr′-) *conj.* 1. On or upon which. 2. Following and as a result of which.
wher·ev·er (hwâr-ĕv′ər, wâr-) *adv.* 1. In or to whatever place. 2. Where. —Used as an intensive <*Wherever* did you disappear?> —*conj.* In or to whatever place or circumstance.
where·with (hwâr′wĭth′, -wĭ*th*′, wâr′-) *conj.* With or by means of which.
where·with·al (hwâr′wĭ*th*-ôl′, -wĭth-, wâr′-) *n.* The necessary means or resources, esp. money.
wher·ry (hwĕr′ē, wĕr′ē) *n., pl.* **-ries.** A light, swift rowboat used esp. in racing.

wherry

whet (hwĕt, wĕt) *v.* **whet·ted, whet·ting.** 1. To sharpen or hone. 2. To stimulate <*whet* the appetite>
wheth·er (hwĕ*th*′ər, wĕ*th*′-) *conj.* 1. —Used in indirect questions to introduce an alternative <We need to know *whether* you'll come.> 2. —Used to introduce alternative possibilities <*Whether* we win or lose, we must play fair.> 3. Either <succeeded *whether* by ability or luck>
whet·stone (hwĕt′stōn′, wĕt′-) *n.* A stone for sharpening knives, scissors, etc.
whew (hwo͞o, hwyo͞o) *interj.* —Used to express amazement, relief, or fatigue.
whey (hwā, wā) *n.* The watery part of milk that separates from the curds.
which (hwĭch, wĭch) *pron.* 1. What one or ones <*Which* is yours?> 2. The one or ones that <I just want that *which* is mine.> 3. The one or ones previously named or implied <my car, *which* is old but dependable> 4. Whatever one or ones : whichever <Buy *which* looks best.> —*adj.* 1. What one or ones of. 2. Any one of. 3. Being the one or ones just mentioned.
which·ev·er (hwĭch-ĕv′ər, wĭch-) *pron.* Whatever one or ones which. —*adj.* Being anyone of which : no matter which.
which·so·ev·er (hwĭch′sō-ĕv′ər, wĭch′-) *pron. & adj.* Whichever.
whiff (hwĭf, wĭf) *n.* 1. A slight gust, as of air or smoke. 2. A slight passing smell. 3. An inhalation, as of smoke or scent. —*v.* 1. To carry or be conveyed in slight gusts : waft. 2. To sniff : smell.
whif·fle·tree (hwĭf′əl-trē, wĭf′-) *n.* The pivoted crossbar to which the traces of a harness are hitched.
Whig (hwĭg, wĭg) *n.* 1. A member of an 18th- and 19th-cent. English political party opposed to the Tories. 2. A colonist who advocated independence from England during the American Revolution.
while (hwīl, wīl) *n.* 1. A length of time <Let's walk a *while.*> 2. Time or effort used <well worth her *while*> —*conj.* 1. a. As long as <*While* you're up, please get me a drink.> b. During the time that <arrived *while* you were sleeping> 2. At the same time that : although <*While* comfortable, we're not rich.> —*v.* **whiled, whil·ing.** To cause to pass, esp. agreeably <*whiled* away the summer day>
whi·lom (hwī′ləm, wī′-) *adv. Archaic.* At a former time : formerly.
whilst (hwīlst, wīlst) *conj.* While.
whim (hwĭm, wĭm) *n.* A sudden, capricious, or arbitrary notion or impulse.
whim·per (hwĭm′pər, wĭm′-) *v.* To cry with weak whining sounds. —**whim′per** *n.* —**whim′per·er** *n.*
whim·si·cal (hwĭm′zĭ-kəl, wĭm′-) *adj.* 1. Full of whim, fancy, or caprice. 2. Erratic or unpredictable. —**whim′si·cal′i·ty** (-kăl′ĭ-tē) *n.* —**whim′si·cal·ly** *adv.*
whim·sy *also* **whim·sey** (hwĭm′zē, wĭm′-) *n., pl.* **-sies** *also* **-seys** 1. A whimsical idea or fancy. 2. Something quaint, fanciful, etc., esp. a fanciful style of humor.
whine (hwīn, wīn) *v.* **whined, whin·ing.** 1. To make a high-pitched, plaintive sound, as in pain or protest. 2. To complain in a childish, irritating way. 3. To make a continuous high-pitched sound, as an engine or machine. —**whine** *n.* —**whin′y** *adj.*
whin·ny (hwĭn′ē, wĭn′ē) *v.* **-nied, -ny·ing.** To neigh softly, as a horse. —**whin′ny** *n.*
whip (hwĭp, wĭp) *v.* **whipped, whip·ping.** 1. To strike repeatedly, as with a lash or rod. 2. To subject to punishment by or as if by whipping. 3. To drive or impel to action by or as if by whipping. 4. To beat into a froth or foam <*whip* egg whites> 5. To move, pull, or grab abruptly <*whipped* out a pen> 6. To bind

(e.g., a rope) with cord to strengthen or prevent fraying. **7.** To defeat soundly. **8.** To move swiftly or nimbly. **9.** To thrash about like a lash. **—whip up. 1.** To stir up **:** excite <*whipped up* the crowd> **2.** To put together quickly, as a meal. *—n.* **1.** A pliable rod or lash used in whipping. **2.** A blow, motion, or stroke with or as if with a whip. **3.** A legislative member selected to enforce party discipline and ensure attendance. **4.** A dessert made with whipped cream or stiffly beaten egg whites. **—whip'per** *n.*

whip•cord (hwĭp'kôrd', wĭp'-) *n.* **1.** A tough worsted fabric with a diagonally ribbed or corded surface. **2.** A strong thin twisted or braided cord esp. for making whiplashes. **3.** A tough cord of catgut.

whip•lash (hwĭp'lăsh', wĭp'-) *n.* **1.** The lash of a whip. **2.** Injury to the neck or spine caused by an abrupt forward or backward jerking motion of the head, as in an automobile collision.

whip•per•snap•per (hwĭp'ər-snăp'ər, wĭp'-) *n.* One who is small, unimportant, or impertinent.

whip•pet (hwĭp'ĭt, wĭp'-) *n.* A short-haired, swift-running dog of a breed developed in England, resembling but smaller than the greyhound.

whipping boy *n.* One bearing blame for others **:** scapegoat.

whip•poor•will (hwĭp'ər-wĭl', wĭp'-) *n.* A brownish nocturnal North American bird, *Caprimulgus vociferus.*

whip•saw (hwĭp'sô', wĭp'-) *n.* A long narrow crosscut saw operated by 2 persons. *—v.* **1.** To saw with a whipsaw. **2.** To defeat or best in 2 ways at once.

whir (hwûr, wûr) *v.* **whirred, whir•ring.** To move or revolve rapidly with a buzzing or humming sound. *—n.* **1.** A sustained buzzing or vibrating sound. **2.** An excited bustle of activity.

whirl (hwûrl, wûrl) *v.* **1.** To spin, rotate, or twirl briskly. **2.** To wheel or pivot, changing direction. **3.** To have a spinning or reeling sensation. **4.** To move or drive at a high speed. **5.** To move or drive in a circular course, esp. rapidly or forcefully. *—n.* **1.** A swift whirling or rotating motion. **2.** One that whirls or undergoes whirling. **3.** A rapid succession or round of events <the social *whirl*> **4.** A confused condition **:** tumult. **5.** *Informal.* A brief try **:** attempt <gave skiing a *whirl*> **—whirl'er** *n.*

whirl•i•gig (hwûr'lĭ-gĭg', wûr'-) *n.* **1.** A toy that whirls. **2.** A carousel. **3.** Something that constantly whirls or changes.

whirl•pool (hwûrl'po͞ol', wûrl'-) *n.* A rapid rotary current of water, as from the meeting of 2 tides.

whirl•wind (hwûrl'wĭnd', wûrl'-) *n.* **1.** A small, often violently whirling column of air. **2.** A confused bustle or rush. *—adj.* Very fast or rushed <a *whirlwind* tour>

whirl•y•bird (hwûr'lē-bûrd', wûr'-) *n. Slang.* A helicopter.

whisk (hwĭsk, wĭsk) *v.* **1.** To move or cause to move with brisk little sweeping or brushing motions. **2.** To whip (eggs or cream) esp. by hand. **3.** To move quickly and spryly. *—n.* **1.** A brisk little sweeping motion. **2.** A whiskbroom. **3.** A hand utensil used to whip foods.

whisk•broom (hwĭsk'bro͞om', -bro͝om', wĭsk'-) *n.* A small short-handled broom used esp. as a clothes brush.

whisk•er (hwĭs'kər, wĭs'-) *n.* **1. a. whiskers.** The hair growing on a man's cheeks and chin and above the upper lip. **b.** A single hair of this growth. **2.** A long hair or bristle near the mouth of certain animals. **—whisk'ered, whisk'er•y** *adj.*

whis•key (hwĭs'kē, wĭs'-) *n., pl.* **-keys.** A liquor distilled from corn, rye, or barley.

whis•ky (hwĭs'kē, wĭs'-) *n. Scot. var. of* WHISKEY.

whis•per (hwĭs'pər, wĭs'-) *v.* **1.** To speak or say in a very low, muted voice. **2.** To tell in private or in secret. **3.** To make a soft rustling or hissing sound. *—n.* **1.** An act or instance of whispering. **2.** Soft low speech produced by whispering. **3.** A low rustling sound. **4.** A whispered message, esp. of gossip or scandal.

whist (hwĭst, wĭst) *n.* A card game played with 52 cards by 4 players in 2 teams.

whis•tle (hwĭs'əl, wĭs'-) *v.* **-tled, -tling. 1.** To make a clear shrill sound by forcing air through the teeth or through puckered lips or by blowing on or through an instrument or device. **2.** To make a high-pitched sound, esp. by rapid movement through the air. **3.** To make or express by whistling <*whistled* their approval> **4.** To summon or signal by whistling. *—n.* **1.** An instrument or device that uses a jet of air or steam to make a whistling sound. **2.** A sound produced by a device or by whistling through the teeth or lips. **3.** A whistling sound made by an animal or a moving projectile. **—whis'tler** *n.*

whistle stop *n.* **1.** A small town at which a train stops only on signal. **2.** A brief appearance of a candidate for office, as on the observation platform of a train.

whit (hwĭt, wĭt) *n.* The smallest bit.

white (hwīt, wīt) *n.* **1.** A color of maximum lightness that is the opposite of black. **2.** The white or light-colored part of something, as an egg or the eyeball. **3. whites.** White clothes, esp. as a part of an outfit or uniform. **4.** *also* **White.** A member of a racial group having light skin coloration, esp. one of European origin. *—adj.* **whit•er, whit•est. 1.** Of or almost of the color white. **2.** Having a light color **:** pale. **3.** *also* **White.** Of or belonging to a racial group having light skin coloration, esp. one of European origin. **4.** Pale gray or silvery, as hair. **5.** Marked by snow <a *white* Christmas in Vermont> **6.** Ardent **:** impassioned. **7.** Morally unblemished **:** pure. **8.** Not written or printed on **:** blank. **9.** Ultraconservative in politics. **—white'ness** *n.*

white ant *n.* A termite.

white•bait (hwīt′bāt′, wīt′-) *n.* The edible young of herring or other small fish.
white blood cell *n.* A leukocyte.
white•cap (hwīt′kăp′, wīt′-) *n.* A wave capped with foam.
white-col•lar (hwīt′kŏl′ər, wīt′-) *adj.* Of or relating to workers whose occupations usu. do not involve manual labor.
white elephant *n.* **1.** A rare pale-colored Asian elephant sometimes venerated in parts of SE Asia. **2.** A possession of little practical value that requires much care and expense. **3.** Something no longer wanted by its owner but possibly of value to others.
white-faced (hwīt′fāst′, wīt′-) *adj.* **1.** Having a pallid complexion. **2.** Having a white patch extending from the muzzle to the forehead <*white-faced* cattle>
white feather *n.* A sign of cowardice.
white•fish (hwīt′fĭsh′, wīt′-) *n.* Any of various North American silvery freshwater food fishes of the genus *Coregonus.*
white flag *n.* A white flag or cloth raised to signal a truce or surrender.
white gold *n.* A pale alloy of gold and nickel that resembles platinum.
white•head (hwīt′hĕd′) *n.* A small whitish bump under the skin, caused by retained secretion of a sebaceous gland.
white heat *n.* **1.** An intensely hot temperature at which a substance glows with a bright white light. **2.** A state of intense emotion. **—white′-hot′** *adj.*
White House *n.* **1.** The executive branch of the U.S. government. **2.** The residence of the President of the U.S.
white lead *n.* A heavy white poisonous lead compound used in paint.
white lie *n.* A diplomatic untruth.
white matter *n.* Whitish nerve tissue, esp. of the brain and spinal cord, consisting chiefly of nerve fibers in fatty sheaths.
whit•en (hwīt′n, wīt′n) *v.* To make or become white. **—whit′en•er** *n.*
white noise *n.* Acoustical or electrical noise in which the intensity is the same at all frequencies within a given band.
white pine *n.* A timber tree of E North America that has needles in clusters of 5 and durable, easily worked wood.
white sauce *n.* A sauce made with butter, flour, and milk, cream, or stock.
white slave *n.* A woman forced into prostitution. **—white slavery** *n.*
white•wall (hwīt′wôl′, wīt′-) *n.* An automotive tire with a white band on the visible side wall.
white•wash (hwīt′wŏsh′, -wôsh′, wīt′-) *n.* **1.** A preparation of lime and water and often whiting, size, or glue for whitening exterior walls, fences, etc. **2.** A glossing over or covering up, as of faults or crime. —*v.* **1.** To whiten with or as if with whitewash. **2.** To try to excuse or ignore (e.g., a fault).
white water *n.* Turbulent or frothy water, as in rapids. **—white′-wa′ter** *adj.*
white whale *n.* A small whale chiefly of N waters, *Delphinapterus leucas,* that is white when full-grown.
whith•er (hwĭth′ər, wĭth′-) *adv.* **1.** To what place, end, or circumstance. **2.** To which designated place. **3.** Wherever.
whit•ing[1] (hwī′tĭng, wī′-) *n.* A pulverized chalk used esp. in paints and putty.
whit•ing[2] (hwī′tĭng, wī′-) *n.* A food fish, *Gadus merlangus,* of European Atlantic waters, related to the cod.
whit•ish (hwī′tĭsh, wī′-) *adj.* Somewhat white in color.
whit•low (hwĭt′lō, wĭt′-) *n.* A pus-filled infection near the nail of a finger or toe.
Whit•sun•day (hwĭt′sŭn′dē, -sən-dā′, wĭt′-) *n.* Pentecost.
whit•tle (hwĭt′l, wĭt′l) *v.* **-tled, -tling. 1. a.** To pare small bits or shavings from (wood) with a knife. **b.** To shape (an object) by whittling. **2.** To reduce or remove gradually as if by whittling. **—whit′tler** *n.*
whiz *also* **whizz** (hwĭz, wĭz). —*v.* **whizzed, whiz•zing. 1.** To make a whirring or hissing sound, as of a projectile speeding through air. **2.** To speed by. —*n., pl.* **whiz•zes. 1.** A whirring or hissing sound. **2.** *Slang.* One with notable expertise <a computer *whiz*>
who (hōō) *pron.* **1.** What or which individual or group <*Who* found it?><*Who* are they?> **2.** The individual or group that <The students *who* left got jobs.>
whoa (hwō, wō) *interj.* Used as a command to stop, as to a horse.
who'd (hōōd). **1.** Who would. **2.** Who had.
who•dun•it (hōō-dŭn′ĭt) *n. Informal.* A detective or mystery story.
who•ev•er (hōō-ĕv′ər) *pron.* Whatever person <*Whoever* took it will be caught.>
whole (hōl) *adj.* **1.** Having no part or element missing **:** complete. **2.** Not divided into units or sections <a *whole* acre> **3.** In good health or condition **:** sound. **4.** Being the entire quantity, duration, or extent <laughed the *whole* time> **5.** *Math.* Not in fractional units **:** integral. —*n.* **1.** Something lacking no part or element. **2.** A complete entity, unity, or system. **—on the whole. 1.** All things considered. **2.** In general. **—whole′ness** *n.*
whole•heart•ed (hōl′här′tĭd) *adj.* Wholly committed, enthusiastic, or sincere.
whole number *n.* An integer.
whole•sale (hōl′sāl′) *n.* The sale of goods in quantity esp. for resale by a retailer. —*adj.* **1.** Of, relating to, or involved in wholesaling. **2.** Sold in quantity, usu. at a lower price. **3.** Made or done indiscriminately. —*v.* **-saled, -sal•ing. 1.** To sell or be sold at wholesale. **2.** To engage in wholesale selling. **—whole′sale′** *adv.* **—whole′sal′er** *n.*
whole•some (hōl′səm) *adj.* **1.** Contributing or conducive to health or well-being <*wholesome* food> **2.** Having or indicating sound physical or mental health <a *wholesome* attitude> **—whole′some•ly** *adv.* **—whole′some•ness** *n.*
whole-wheat (hōl′hwēt′, -wēt′) *adj.* Made

from ground wheat kernels from which no part has been removed.
who'll (ho͞ol). **1.** Who will. **2.** Who shall.
whol•ly (hō'lē, hōl'lē) *adv.* **1.** Entirely : totally. **2.** Exclusively : solely.
whom (ho͞om) *pron. objective case of* WHO.
whom•ev•er (ho͞om-ĕv'ər) *pron. objective case of* WHOEVER.
whom•so•ev•er (ho͞om'sō-ĕv'ər) *pron. objective case of* WHOSOEVER.
whoop (hwo͞op, ho͞op, wo͞op) *n.* **1.** A loud shout or hooting cry, as of excitement or triumph. **2.** The convulsive gasp typical of whooping cough. —*v.* **1.** To shout loudly. **2.** To utter with a whoop. **3.** To gasp convulsively, as in whooping cough. **4.** To urge or cheer on with a whoop. —**whoop'er** *n.*
whooping cough *n.* An infectious disease that causes spasms of coughing often followed by deep, noisy inspiration.
whooping crane *n.* A large, long-legged, nearly extinct North American bird, *Grus americana,* with black and white plumage and a shrill, trumpeting cry.

whooping crane

whoops (hwo͝ops, wo͝ops, hwo͞ops, wo͞ops) *interj.* —Used to express mild surprise or apology.
whoosh (hwo͝osh, wo͝osh, hwo͞osh, wo͞osh) *v.* To make a gushing, rushing, or hissing sound. —**whoosh** *n.*
whop (hwŏp, wŏp) *v.* **whopped, whop•ping. 1.** To beat : thrash. **2.** To defeat completely. —*n.* A heavy blow or thump.
whop•per (hwŏp'ər, wŏp'-) *n.* **1.** Something unusually large or extraordinary. **2.** A flagrant lie.
whop•ping (hwŏp'ĭng, wŏp'-) *adj.* Exceptionally large.
whore (hôr, hōr) *n.* A prostitute. —**whor'ish** *adj.* —**whor'ish•ly** *adv.*
whorl (hwôrl, wôrl, hwûrl, wûrl) *n.* **1.** Something having a coiled, curved, or spiral form, as a ridge of a fingerprint. **2.** An arrangement esp. of leaves or petals radiating from a single axis. —**whorled** *adj.*
who's (ho͞oz). **1.** Who is. **2.** Who has.
whose (ho͞oz) *pron. (sing. or pl. in number).* That which belongs to whom. —*adj.* Of or relating to whom or which.
who•so•ev•er (ho͞o'sō-ĕv'ər) *pron.* Whoever.
why (hwī, wī) *adv.* For what purpose, reason, or cause <*Why* were they fired?> —*conj.* **1.** The reason, cause, or purpose for which <Do you know *why* they were fired?> **2.** For which <can guess the reason *why* it happened> —*n., pl.* **whys.** The reason or cause. —*interj.* —Used to express mild indignation or surprise.
wick (wĭk) *n.* A cord or strand of soft fibers, as in a candle or an oil lamp, that draws up fuel to be burned.
wick•ed (wĭk'ĭd) *adj.* **1.** Morally bad : sinful. **2.** Marked by playful mischief. **3.** Causing harm, trouble, or distress. **4.** Obnoxious, as a vile odor. —**wick'ed•ly** *adv.* —**wick'ed•ness** *n.*
wick•er (wĭk'ər) *n.* **1.** A small flexible shoot or rodlike twig, as of willow, used esp. in making baskets and furniture. **2.** Woven wicker : wickerwork.
wick•er•work (wĭk'ər-wûrk') *n.* Articles, as baskets and furniture, made of wicker.
wick•et (wĭk'ĭt) *n.* **1.** A set of 3 upright sticks topped by 2 crossbars that forms the target of the bowler in cricket. **2.** A small usu. wire arch through which a player tries to hit the ball in croquet. **3.** A small door or gate, esp. one built in or near a larger one. **4.** A small windowlike opening, usu. with a grating, as at a box office.
wick•i•up (wĭk'ē-ŭp') *n.* A temporary dwelling used by certain nomadic American Indians, consisting of a frame hut covered with matting, bark, or brushwood.
wide (wīd) *adj.* **wid•er, wid•est. 1.** Extending over a large area : broad <a *wide* river> **2.** Measured across <paper 8 inches *wide*> **3.** Extensive in range or scope <a *wide* variety> **4.** Completely open or extended, as eyes or wings. **5.** Far from a goal, target, or truth. —*adv.* **1.** Over an extensive area. **2.** To the full extent. **3.** Deviating from the target : afield. —**wide'ly** *adv.* —**wide'ness** *n.*
wide-a•wake (wīd'ə-wāk') *adj.* **1.** Fully awake. **2.** Observant : alert.
wide-eyed (wīd'īd') *adj.* **1.** Having the eyes fully open. **2.** Astonished. **3.** Naive.
wid•en (wīd'n) *v.* To make or become wide. —**wid'en•er** *n.*
wide•spread (wīd'sprĕd') *adj.* **1.** Fully opened or spread out. **2.** Prevalent.
wid•geon (wĭj'ən) *n., pl.* **widgeon** *or* **-geons.** A wild duck, esp. *Mareca americana* of North America, with brownish plumage and a light head patch.
wid•ow (wĭd'ō) *n.* A woman who has not remarried after her husband's death. —*v.* To make a widow of. —**wid'ow•hood'** *n.*
wid•ow•er (wĭd'ō-ər) *n.* A man who has not remarried after his wife's death. —**wid'ow•er•hood'** *n.*
width (wĭdth, wĭtth) *n.* **1.** The quality, state, or fact of being wide. **2.** The extent of something from side to side : breadth. **3.** Something, as a piece of fabric or lumber, that has a specified width.
wield (wēld) *v.* **1.** To handle (e.g., a weapon

or tool) esp. skillfully. **2.** To employ (power or influence) affectively.

wie•ner (wē'nər) *n.* A frankfurter.

wife (wīf) *n., pl.* **wives** (wīvz). A married woman. **—wife'hood'** *n.* **—wife'ly** *adj.*

wig (wĭg) *n.* A covering of artificial or human hair for the head.

wig•gle (wĭg'əl) *v.* **-gled, -gling. 1.** To move or cause to move with rapid irregular side-to-side motions : jiggle. **2.** To proceed with a sinous motion : wriggle. **—wig'gle** *n.* **—wig'gler** *n.* **—wig'gly** *adj.*

wig•wam (wĭg'wŏm') *n.* A dwelling used by certain American Indians, typically consisting of an arched or cone-shaped framework covered with bark or hides.

wild (wīld) *adj.* **1.** Existing in a natural state : not cultivated or domesticated. **2.** Lacking discipline : unruly. **3.** Filled with or indicating intense, uncontrolled emotion. **4.** Marked by turbulence : stormy. **5.** Uncivilized : barbarous. **6.** Extravagant or outlandish <*wild* notions> **7.** Going astray of the mark or target. **8.** Representing any card desired rather than the actual one held or played <deuces *wild*> *—adv.* Out of control. *—n. often* **wilds.** A region not settled or cultivated by humans. **—wild'ly** *adv.* **—wild'ness** *n.*

wild card *n.* **1.** *Games.* A card whose value may vary during a game as assigned by its holder. **2.** *Computer Sci.* A symbol that stands for one or more characters in a string.

wild•cat (wīld'kăt') *n.* **1.** A small to medium-size wild feline, as an ocelot, lynx, or bobcat. **2.** One who is quick-tempered or fierce. **3.** An oil well drilled in an area not known to be productive. *—adj.* **1.** Having no certainty of profit or success. **2.** Undertaken without official authorization, as a labor strike. *—v.* **-cat•ted, -cat•ting.** To prospect for (oil or minerals) in an area regarded as unproductive. **—wild'cat'ter** *n.*

wil•de•beest (wĭl'də-bēst', vĭl'-) *n.* The gnu.

wil•der•ness (wĭl'dər-nĭs) *n.* An unsettled and uncultivated region.

wild-eyed (wīld'īd') *adj.* **1.** Having a wild look in the eyes. **2.** Impractical or extreme.

wild•fire (wīld'fīr') *n.* A raging fire that spreads very quickly.

wild•fowl (wīld'foul') *n.* A game bird, as a wild duck or goose.

wild-goose chase (wīld'gōōs') *n.* Pursuit of something beyond reach or hope.

wild•life (wīld'līf') *n.* Wild plants and animals, esp. wild animals living in their natural environment.

wild oat *n.* **1.** A native Eurasian grass, *Avena fatua,* related to the cultivated oat. **2. wild oats.** The excesses of youth.

wild rice *n.* A tall water grass of N North America, *Zizania aquatica,* that bears edible brownish grain.

wile (wīl) *n.* **1.** A stratagem or trick intended to entrap or deceive. **2.** A disarming or seductive manner. **3.** Deceitful cunning : guile. *—v.* **wiled, wil•ing. 1.** To entice with wiles. **2.** To while <*wile* away the long summer days>

will¹ (wĭl) *n.* **1.** The mental power or capability of choosing or deciding. **2.** An example of making a deliberate choice or decision. **3.** Control exercised over oneself : self-discipline. **4.** Something desired or determined, esp. by one holding power or authority. **5.** Inclination, intention, or wish <held against my *will*> **6.** Determined purpose or desire <the *will* to succeed> **7.** Disposition or attitude toward others <good *will*> **8.** A legal document indicating the distribution of a person's possessions after his or her death. *—v.* **1.** To decide upon or bring about by an act of the will. **2.** To order or decide by or as if by decree. **3.** To bequeath in a legal will. **4.** To intend to do. **—at will.** Freely.

will² (wĭl) *v. p.t.* **would** (wŏŏd). —Used to indicate: **1.** Simple futurity <I *will* go tomorrow.> **2.** Likelihood or certainty <You *will* rue that decision.> **3.** Readiness to act : willingness <*Will* you lend me your car?> **4.** Intention or determination <I *will* come no matter what.> **5.** Required action or command <You *will* do the dishes.> **6.** Customary action <*would* shop for hours> **7.** *Informal.* Probability <That *will* be the lawyer.> **8.** To wish, want, or desire <Go where you *will.*>

will•ful *also* **wil•ful** (wĭl'fəl) *adj.* **1.** Said or done deliberately. **2.** Stubborn. **—will'ful•ly** *adv.* **—will'ful•ness** *n.*

wil•lies (wĭl'ēz) *pl.n. Slang.* Feelings of nervousness.

will•ing (wĭl'ĭng) *adj.* **1.** Done, accepted, or given readily and voluntarily. **2.** Favorably inclined : ready. **3.** Acting or responding promptly. **4.** Volitional. **—will'ing•ly** *adv.* **—will'ing•ness** *n.*

wil•li•waw (wĭl'ē-wô') *n.* A sudden violent rush of cold air blowing from a mountainous coast to the sea.

will-o'-the-wisp (wĭl'ə-*th*ə-wĭsp') *n.* **1.** A light that glows over marshy ground at night. **2.** A misleading or deceptive goal.

wil•low (wĭl'ō) *n.* **1.** A deciduous tree or shrub of the genus *Salix,* usu. with narrow leaves, flowers borne in catkins, slender, flexible twigs used in wickerwork, and strong, lightweight wood.

wil•low•y (wĭl'ō-ē) *adj.* **-i•er, -i•est. 1.** Flexible : pliant. **2.** Slender and graceful.

will power *n.* Power to carry out one's desires or decisions : strength of mind.

wil•ly-nil•ly (wĭl'ē-nĭl'ē) *adv. & adj.* Whether desired or not.

wilt (wĭlt) *v.* **1.** To become or cause to become limp or withered. **2.** To lose vigor or force. **3.** To deprive of energy or courage. ★ ***syns:*** DROOP, FLAG, SAG *—n.* Any of various plant diseases marked by wilting or collapse.

wil•y (wī'lē) *adj.* **-i•er, -i•est.** Tricky : sly. **—wi'li•ness** *n.*

wim•ble (wĭm'bəl) *n.* A hand tool for boring holes. **—wim'ble** *v.*

wim•ple (wĭm′pəl) *n.* A cloth wound around the head and under the chin so that only the face is exposed, worn by women in medieval times and by some orders of nuns.

wimple

win (wĭn) *v.* **won** (wŭn), **win•ning. 1.** To gain victory in or as if in a contest. **2.** To gain by means of effort : earn <*win* fame> **3.** To receive for performance, as in a contest of skill or luck <*win* a prize> **4. a.** To gain the favor or support of <*won* the public> **b.** To cause (someone) to accept oneself in marriage. —*n.* A victory, esp. in a sports event. **—win′ner** *n.*

wince (wĭns) *v.* **winced, winc•ing.** To draw back or away involuntarily, as in pain.

winch (wĭnch) *n.* **1.** An apparatus for pulling or lifting, consisting of a drum around which a rope or cable attached to the load is wound as the load is moved. **2.** The crank used to turn a device such as a grindstone. **—winch** *v.* **—winch′er** *n.*

wind[1] (wĭnd) *n.* **1.** A natural or artificially produced movement of air. **2.** A prevailing influence : tendency. **3.** Air bearing a scent, as of game. **4. winds. a.** Wind instruments, as in an orchestra or band. **b.** The players of wind instruments. **5.** Intestinal gas : flatulence. **6. a.** Ability to breathe normally : respiration. **b.** Breath <had the *wind* knocked out of me> **7.** Empty or boastful words. **8.** An intimation or hint <got *wind* of their intentions> —*v.* **1.** To make short of breath <*winded* from the race> **2.** To perceive a scent of <The hounds *winded* a fox.> **3.** To allow (e.g., a horse) to rest in order to regain breath. **—wind′less** *adj.*

wind[2] (wīnd) *v.* **wound** (wound), **wind•ing. 1.** To wrap or be wrapped around something. **2.** To encircle in a series of coils. **3.** To move or proceed in a twisting course. **4.** To introduce indirectly : insinuate. **5.** To tighten the spring of <*wind* a watch> **6.** To turn, as a handle : crank. **7.** To lift or haul, as with a windlass or winch. ★ ***syns:*** COIL, CURL, ENTWINE, SNAKE, SPIRAL, TWINE, TWIST, WEAVE **—wind up.** *Informal.* **1.** To end : finish. **2.** To experience a given outcome of a course of action <*wound up* a millionaire> **3.** To swing the arm before pitching a ball. —*n.* A turn or twist. **—wind′er** *n.*

wind[3] (wīnd, wĭnd) *v.* **wind•ed** (wīn′dĭd, wĭn′-) *or* **wound** (wound), **wind•ing.** To sound (e.g., a horn or trumpet) by blowing.

wind•age (wĭn′dĭj) *n.* The influence of the wind on the course of a projectile moving through the air.

wind•bag (wĭnd′băg′) *n. Slang.* A tiresomely or idly garrulous person.

wind-blown (wĭnd′blōn′) *adj.* **1.** Blown or scattered by the wind. **2.** Growing or shaped in a way determined by the prevailing winds. **3.** Seeming or looking as if blown by the wind.

wind•break (wĭnd′brāk′) *n.* Something, as a hedge or fence, serving to lessen the force of the wind.

Wind-break•er (wĭnd′brā′kər). A trademark for an outer jacket having close-fitting, often elastic cuffs and waistband.

wind•burn (wĭnd′bûrn′) *n.* Irritation of the skin caused by wind.

wind-chill factor (wĭnd′chĭl′) *n.* The temperature of windless air that would have the same effect on exposed skin as a specified combination of temperature and wind speed.

wind•fall (wĭnd′fôl′) *n.* **1.** Something, as a tree or fruit, blown down by the wind. **2.** A sudden unlooked-for stroke of good luck.

wind•flow•er (wĭnd′flou′ər) *n.* ANEMONE 1.

wind•ing (wīn′dĭng) *adj.* **1.** Having a turning or twisting course. **2.** Spiral : curving. —*n.* Wire wound into a coil.

wind instrument (wĭnd) *n.* A musical instrument sounded by a current of air, esp. the player's breath.

wind•jam•mer (wĭnd′jăm′ər) *n.* A sailing ship or one of its crew members.

wind•lass (wĭnd′ləs) *n.* Any of various hauling or lifting machines similar to a winch and turned by a crank.

wind•mill (wĭnd′mĭl′) *n.* A mill or machine powered by the wind turning a wheel of adjustable blades or vanes.

win•dow (wĭn′dō) *n.* **1.** An opening, usu. framed and spanned with glass, built into a wall for light and air. **2.** A framework around a window : sash. **3.** A windowpane. **4.** A windowlike opening. **5.** A temporary period of a specified nature <a *window* of opportunity>

win•dow-dress•ing *also* **window dressing** (wĭn′dō-drĕs′ĭng) *n.* **1.** Decorative display of retail goods in store windows. **2.** A display made esp. to improve appearances or create a false favorable impression. **—win′dow-dress′er** *n.*

win•dow•pane (wĭn′dō-pān′) *n.* A pane of glass in a window.

win•dow-shop (wĭn′dō-shŏp′) *v.* To look at goods in store windows without going inside to buy. **—win′dow-shop′per** *n.* **—win′dow-shop′ping** *n.*

win•dow•sill (wĭn′dō-sĭl′) *n.* The sill at the bottom of a window opening.

wind•pipe (wĭnd′pīp′) *n.* The trachea.

wind•row (wĭnd′rō′) *n.* **1.** A row, as of leaves or snow, heaped up by the wind. **2.** A long row of cut hay or grain left to dry in a field before being bundled.

wind•shield (wĭnd′shēld′) *n.* A framed transparent screen located in front of the occupants of an automotive vehicle.

wind•sock (wĭnd′sŏk′) *n.* A large, conical, open-ended sleeve attached to a stand by a pivot so that it points in the direction of the wind blowing through it.

wind•storm (wĭnd′stôrm′) *n.* A storm with violent winds and very little rain.

wind•surf•ing (wĭnd′sûrf′ĭng) *n.* The sport of sailing while standing on a sailboard. **—wind′surf′** *v.* **—wind′surf′er** *n.*

wind•swept (wĭnd′swĕpt′) *adj.* Exposed to or driven by the wind.

wind tunnel (wĭnd) *n.* An enclosed chamber through which air is blown to study its effect on an aircraft, airfoil, etc.

wind-up (wīnd′ŭp′) *n.* **1. a.** The act of concluding **:** finish. **b.** A concluding part. **2.** *Baseball.* A pitcher's movements before pitching the ball.

wind•ward (wĭnd′wərd) *adj.* Facing or moving into the wind. *—n.* The point or side from which the wind blows. **—wind′ward** *adv.*

wind•y (wĭn′dē) *adj.* **-i•er, -i•est. 1. a.** Marked by or having much wind. **b.** Stormy **:** gusty. **2.** Exposed to the prevailing wind, esp. unsheltered. **3.** Tending toward or marked by prolonged, empty, or boastful talk. **—wind′i•ly** *adv.* **—wind′i•ness** *n.*

wine (wīn) *n.* **1. a.** The fermented juice of grapes, usu. containing 10–15% alcohol by volume. **b.** The fermented juice of various fruits or plants <blackberry *wine*> <rice *wine*> **2.** The dark purplish color of red wine. *—v.* **wined, win•ing.** To provide or entertain with drink or wine.

wine cooler *n.* A bottled mixture of wine, fruit juice, and sometimes soda water.

wine•glass (wīn′glăs′) *n.* A usu. stemmed glass for wine.

wine•press (wīn′prĕs′) *n.* A vat in which juice is expressed from grapes.

win•er•y (wī′nə-rē) *n., pl.* **-ies.** A wine-making establishment.

wing (wĭng) *n.* **1.** One of a pair of movable appendages that enable a bird, bat, or insect to fly. **2.** A plant or animal projection or part that resembles a wing. **3.** *Informal.* The human arm. **4.** One of a pair of airfoils positioned on each side of an aircraft fuselage to provide lift. **5.** Something resembling a wing esp. in form or function. **6.** An extension of a main building. **7.** A faction, as of a political party. **8.** *often* **wings.** The concealed area on either side of a stage for exits and entrances. **9.** A military aircraft unit or its pilots. **10.** The left or right flank of an army unit or navy fleet. **11.** A forward position or player, esp. in hockey. *—v.* **1.** To move on or as if on wings. **2.** To provide with wings. **3.** To do, gain, or accomplish by flying. **4.** To wound superficially. **—under (one's) wing.** In one's care. **—wing it.** *Informal.* To improvise. **—wing′less** *adj.* **—wing′like′** *adj.*

wing•ding (wĭng′dĭng′) *n. Slang.* A lively or extravagant party.

winged *adj.* **1.** (wĭngd). Having wings or winglike projections or extensions. **2.** (wĭng′ĭd). **a.** Moving swiftly on or as if on wings. **b.** Elevated **:** sublime.

wing nut *n.* A nut with winglike projections for thumb and forefinger leverage in turning.

wing•span (wĭng′spăn′) *n.* Wingspread, esp. of an aircraft.

wing•spread (wĭng′sprĕd′) *n.* **1.** The distance between the tips of the fully spread wings, as of a bird or an insect. **2.** The distance between the tips of an aircraft's wings.

wink (wĭngk) *v.* **1.** To close and open one eye deliberately, as to convey a message or signal. **2.** To shine or twinkle intermittently. **3.** To blink rapidly. **—wink at.** To ignore intentionally <*winked at* fraudulent practices> *—n.* **1. a.** The act of winking. **b.** A very short time, as that required for a wink. **2.** A brief sleep **:** nap.

Win•ne•ba•go (wĭn′ə-bā′gō) *n., pl.* **-go** *or* **-gos** *or* **-goes. 1.** A member of an American Indian people of Wisconsin, now also in Nebraska. **2.** Their Siouan language.

win•ning (wĭn′ĭng) *adj.* **1.** Victorious in competition. **2.** Charming **:** captivating. *—n* **1.** Victory **:** triumph. **2.** *often* **winnings.** Something won, esp. money.

win•now (wĭn′ō) *v.* **1.** To remove by a stream of air <*winnow* chaff from grain> **2.** To examine closely and carefully **:** sift. **3.** To separate out (something good or bad) as if by winnowing. **—win′now•er** *n.*

win•o (wī′nō) *n., pl.* **-os.** *Slang.* One addicted to drinking wine, esp. cheap wine.

win•some (wĭn′səm) *adj.* Very pleasant or agreeable **:** charming. **—win′some•ly** *adv.* **—win′some•ness** *n.*

win•ter (wĭn′tər) *n.* The season between autumn and spring, usu. the coldest time of the year. *—adj.* **1.** Of, relating to, or taking place in the winter. **2.** Planted in the autumn for spring or summer harvest <*winter* wheat> *—v.* **1.** To spend the winter <*wintered* in Florida> **2.** To keep, feed, or care for (e.g., cattle) during the winter.

win•ter•green (wĭn′tər-grēn′) *n.* A low-growing plant, *Gaultheria procumbens,* of E North America, with spicy, edible red berries and aromatic evergreen leaves that yield an oil or flavoring.

win•ter•ize (wĭn′tə-rīz′) *v.* **-ized, -iz•ing.** To equip or make ready for winter weather <*winterize* a car>

win•ter•kill (wĭn′tər-kĭl′) *v.* To kill by or perish from exposure to winter cold.

winter squash *n.* Any of several thick-rinded varieties of squash, such as the acorn squash, that can be stored for long periods.

win•ter•time (wĭn′tər-tīm′) *n.* The season of winter.

win•try (wĭn′trē) *also* **win•ter•y** (-tə-rē) **1.** Of or typical of winter. **2.** Cheerless and unfriendly <a *wintry* greeting> **—win′tri•ness** *n.*

wipe (wīp) *v.* **wiped, wip•ing. 1.** To clean or

dry by rubbing. **2.** To rid of by or as if by rubbing <*wipe* away the dirt> **3.** To pass over a surface <*wipe* a dustcloth over a table> **—wipe out. 1.** To destroy completely. **2.** *Informal.* To kill. **—wipe** *n.* **—wip'er** *n.*

wire (wīr) *n.* **1.** A usu. pliable, slender metal rod or strand used mainly to conduct electricity or for structural support. **2.** Wires bundled or twisted together to form a cable. **3. a.** A telegraph or telephone wire or service. **b.** A telegram or cablegram. **4.** An active telephone connection <hold the *wire*> **5.** The finish line of a race. **6.** *often* **wires.** Hidden manipulative influences affecting a person or group <pulled *wires* to get the position> *—v.* **wired, wir·ing. 1.** To join or attach with or as if with wire. **2.** To install a system of electrical wires in. **3. a.** To convey (a message) by telegraph. **b.** To telegraph to.

wire-draw (wīr'drô') *v.* **1.** To draw (metal) into wire. **2.** To draw out to great length or refinement.

wire-haired (wīr'hârd') *adj.* Having a stiff, wiry coat of hair, as a dog.

wire·less (wīr'lĭs) *n.* **1.** A radio telegraph or telephone system operating by electromagnetic waves. **2.** *esp. Brit.* Radio or radio communications. *—adj.* Having no wires.

Wire·pho·to (wīr'fō'tō). A trademark for a photograph electrically transmitted over telephone wires.

wire service *n.* A news-gathering organization that distributes syndicated copy electronically to subscribers.

wire·tap (wīr'tăp') *n.* A hidden listening or recording device tapped into an electric circuit. *—v.* To install or monitor a wiretap. **—wire'tap'per** *n.*

wir·ing (wīr'ĭng) *n.* A system of electric wires, esp. for electricity in a building.

wir·y (wīr'ē) *adj.* **-i·er, -i·est. 1.** Resembling wire, as stiff or kinky hair. **2.** Lean but strong. **—wir'i·ness** *n.*

wis·dom (wĭz'dəm) *n.* **1.** Insightful understanding of what is true, right, or enduring. **2.** Native good judgment <had the *wisdom* to leave well enough alone> **3.** The amassed learning of philosophers, scientists, and scholars.

Wisdom of Solomon *n.* —See table at BIBLE.

wisdom tooth *n.* The last tooth on each side of both jaws in humans.

wise[1] (wīz) *adj.* **wis·er, wis·est. 1.** Having great learning. **2.** Having discernment **:** sagacious. **3.** Sensible **:** prudent. **4. a.** Having awareness or information **:** knowing. **b.** Cunning **:** shrewd. **5.** *Slang.* Offensively bold or impudent. **—wise'ly** *adv.*

wise[2] (wīz) *n.* Manner or fashion <in this *wise*>

–wise *suff.* **1.** In a given way, direction, or position <counterclock*wise*> **2.** *Informal.* Regarding <dollar*wise*>

wise·a·cre (wīz'ā'kər) *n. Informal.* One who pretends to be learned or clever.

wise·crack (wīz'krăk') *n. Slang.* A witty or facetious remark. **—wise'crack'** *v.*

wish (wĭsh) *n.* **1.** A desire or longing for something. **2.** An expression of a wish <Make a *wish.*> **3.** Something desired. *—v.* **1.** To desire or long for **:** want. **2.** To make or express a wish for <*wished* us a safe trip> **3.** To bid <*wish* someone good night> **4.** To request or command <I *wish* you to go at once.> **5.** To force or impose upon another. **—wish'er** *n.*

wish·bone (wĭsh'bōn') *n.* The forked bone anterior to the breastbone of the majority of birds.

wish·ful (wĭsh'fəl) *adj.* **1.** Expressing a wish **:** longing. **2.** In keeping with wishes rather than fact. **—wish'ful·ly** *adv.* **—wish'ful·ness** *n.*

wish·y-wash·y (wĭsh'ē-wŏsh'ē, -wô'shē) *adj.* **-i·er, -i·est.** *Informal.* **1.** Weak or watery. **2.** Weak-willed **:** indecisive.

wisp (wĭsp) *n.* **1.** A small bunch of hay or straw. **2. a.** A thin piece, strip, etc. <a *wisp* of hair> **b.** A faint streak <a *wisp* of smoke> **3.** One that is slender, frail, or evanescent. **—wisp'y** *adj.*

wis·te·ri·a (wĭ-stîr'ē-ə) *also* **wis·tar·i·a** (-stâr'-) *n.* A woody vine of the genus *Wisteria,* with long, drooping purplish or white flower clusters.

wist·ful (wĭst'fəl) *adj.* Filled with longing. **—wist'ful·ly** *adv.* **—wist'ful·ness** *n.*

wit (wĭt) *n.* **1. a.** The ability to use words cleverly and humorously. **b.** One having this ability. **c.** Inventive skill or imagination. **2.** *often* **wits. a.** Ability to reason and understand. **b.** Intact mental powers **:** sanity. **—at (one's) wits' end.** At the end of one's mental resources.

witch (wĭch) *n.* **1. a.** An evil woman with magical powers, esp. in folklore. **b.** A sorceress. **2.** An ugly old woman. **3.** *Informal.* An irresistibly fascinating woman or girl.

witch·craft (wĭch'krăft') *n.* The use of magical powers **:** sorcery.

witch doctor *n.* A shamanistic healer, sorceror, or prophet, esp. among certain African peoples.

witch·er·y (wĭch'ə-rē) *n., pl.* **-ies. 1.** The use of magic **:** witchcraft. **2.** Exceptional power to fascinate.

witch hazel *n.* **1.** A shrub of the genus *Hamamelis,* esp. *H. virginiana,* of E North America, with yellow flowers. **2.** A spicy-smelling alcoholic solution made from the bark and leaves of witch hazel that is used as a mild astringent.

witch-hunt (wĭch'hŭnt') *n.* An intensive searching out and harassment of those with unpopular viewpoints <a political *witch-hunt*> **—witch'-hunt'ing** *n.*

witch·ing (wĭch'ĭng) *adj.* **1.** Pertaining to or suitable for witchcraft. **2.** Enchanting.

with (wĭth, wĭth) *prep.* **1.** In the company of <a cat *with* her kittens> **2.** Alongside <walk *with* your partner> **3.** Having, bearing, or wearing <a child *with* freckles> **4.** In a way marked by <drive *with* care> **5.** In the opinion or judgment of <It's O.K. *with* them if I stay.> **6.** In support of <We're *with* you on this issue.> **7.** Containing : including <tea *with* lemon> **8.** By means of <cooks *with* gas> **9.** In spite of : despite <*With* all our efforts, we're still broke.> **10.** At the same time as <sailed *with* high tide> **11.** In regard to : concerning <happy *with* my job> **12.** Compared to <on a par *with* classmates> **13.** Having been granted <We'll only marry *with* your approval.> **14.** In opposition or resistance to <fought *with* my brothers> **15.** As a result of <wept *with* relief> **16.** So as to join : to or onto <connect this piece *with* that one.> **17.** So as to be separated from <had to part *with* my savings.> **18.** In the passage of <got worse *with* each hour> **19.** In relation to <linked cancer *with* smoking> **20.** In the care or keeping of <left the car *with* me>

with•al (wĭ*th*-ôl′, wĭth-) *adv.* **1.** Besides : as well. **2.** However : nevertheless. **3.** *Archaic.* With that : therewith.

with•draw (wĭ*th*-drô′, wĭth-) *v.* **1.** To take back or away. **2.** To call back or retract <*withdrew* the complaint> **3.** To draw back : retreat. **4.** To end one's involvement in or use of something.

with•draw•al (wĭ*th*-drô′əl, wĭth-) *n.* **1.** The act, process, or an instance of withdrawing. **2.** An emotional or psychological detachment. **3. a.** Discontinuation of the use of a habit-forming substance. **b.** The physical and emotional reactions that are manifested upon withdrawal.

with•drawn (wĭ*th*-drôn′, wĭth-) *adj.* **1.** Isolated : remote. **2.** Retiring : shy. **3.** Emotionally detached.

withe (wĭth, wĭ*th*, wī*th*) *n.* A strong, pliable twig used esp. as a rope or binding.

with•er (wĭ*th*′ər) *v.* **1.** To shrivel or wilt from or as if from moisture loss. **2.** To lose or cause to lose freshness, force, or vigor. **3.** To render speechless or powerless.

with•ers (wĭ*th*′ərz) *pl.n.* The part of a horse's back between the shoulder blades.

with•hold (wĭth-hōld′, wĭ*th*-) *v.* **1.** To keep or hold back <*withhold* applause> **2.** To refrain from giving <*withhold* permission> **—with•hold′er** *n.*

withholding tax *n.* A tax on income withheld by one's employer.

with•in (wĭ*th*-ĭn′, wĭth-) *adv.* **1.** In or into the inner part : inside. **2.** Indoors. **3.** In oneself : inwardly. *—prep.* **1.** In the inner part of : inside. **2.** Inside the limits or extent of in time, degree, or distance. **3.** Not exceeding the fixed limits of. **4.** In the area or domain of. *—n.* An inside place or area <change from *within*>

with-it (wĭ*th*′ĭt) *adj. Slang.* Highly aware esp. of the latest trends.

†with•out (wĭ*th*-out′, wĭth-) *adv.* **1.** On the outside. **2.** Not indoors. **3.** With something lacking <had to do *without*> *—prep.* **1.** With someone or something absent or lacking <went *without* me> <walks *without* help> **2.** On or to the outer side of. *—conj. Regional.* Unless.

with•stand (wĭth-stănd′, wĭ*th*-) *v.* To resist or endure successfully.

wit•less (wĭt′lĭs) *adj.* Lacking intelligence or understanding. **—wit′less•ly** *adv.*

wit•ness (wĭt′nĭs) *n.* **1.** One who has personally seen, heard, or experienced something. **2.** Something that serves as proof or evidence. **3. a.** One who is requested to testify in court. **b.** One who is present at and can attest to a transaction. **4.** Affirmation : testimony <bear *witness*> *—v.* **1.** To be a witness of : see. **2.** To give proof or evidence of. **3.** To be the setting of <The town has *witnessed* much change.> **4.** To serve as a legal witness of <*witness* a will>

witness stand *n.* The place in a courtroom from which a witness presents testimony.

wit•ti•cism (wĭt′ĭ-sĭz′əm) *n.* A cleverly worded remark or saying.

wit•ty (wĭt′ē) *adj.* **-ti•er, -ti•est.** Cleverly humorous : amusing. **—wit′ti•ly** *adv.* **—wit′ti•ness** *n.*

wives (wīvz) *n. pl. of* WIFE.

wiz•ard (wĭz′ərd) *n.* **1.** One thought to have magical powers : sorcerer or magician. **2.** *Informal.* One with skill or expertise : whiz. **—wiz′ard•ry** *n.*

▲ ***word history:*** *Wizard* is a compound word formed from the adjective *wise,* "learned, sensible," and the suffix *-ard.* The word orig. meant "a wise man, philosopher." The suffix *-ard,* however, almost always has a pejorative or disparaging sense, as in the words *coward, drunkard,* and *sluggard. Wizard* was therefore often used contemptuously to mean "a so-called wise man," and from this use it came to mean "sorcerer" and "male witch."

wiz•ened (wĭz′ənd) *adj.* Shriveled and withered : dried up.

woad (wōd) *n.* An Old World plant, *Isatis tinctoria,* with leaves yielding a blue dye.

wob•ble (wŏb′əl) *v.* **-bled, -bling. 1.** To move or cause to move with an unsteady rocking motion. **2.** To tremble or quaver <a voice *wobbling* with fear> **3.** To be indecisive : vacillate. **—wob′ble** *n.* **—wob′bli•ness** *n.* **—wob′bly** *adj.*

woe (wō) *n.* **1.** A state of deep sorrow : grief. **2.** Misfortune : adversity.

woe•be•gone (wō′bĭ-gôn′, -gŏn′) *adj.* Mournful or wretched, esp. in appearance.

woe•ful (wō′fəl) *adj.* **1.** Full of woe : sorrowful. **2.** Pertaining to or causing woe. **3.** Lamentable : deplorable. **—woe′ful•ly** *adv.*

wok (wŏk) *n.* A metal pan with a convex bottom used esp. for stir-frying.

woke (wōk) *v. var. p.t. of* WAKE[1].

wo•ken (wō′kən) *v. var. p.p. of* WAKE[1].

wold (wōld) *n.* An open rolling stretch of upland.

wolf (wo͝olf) *n., pl.* **wolves** (wo͝olvz). **1.** A carnivorous mammal, *Canis lupus,* of N regions, or *C. rufus* or *C. niger,* of SW North America, related to and resembling the dog. **2.** A fierce or predacious person. **3.** *Slang.* A man who ardently pursues women. —*v.* To eat quickly and greedily. —**wolf'ish** *adj.* —**wolf'ish·ly** *adv.*

wolf·hound (wŏolf'hound') *n.* A large dog orig. used in wolf hunting.

wolf·ram (wŏol'frəm) *n.* Tungsten.

wol·ver·ine (wŏol'və-rēn') *n.* A carnivorous mammal, *Gulo gulo* or *G. luscus,* of N regions, with dark fur and a bushy tail.

wom·an (wŏom'ən) *n., pl.* **wom·en** (wĭm'ĭn). **1.** An adult female human being. **2.** Women as a group **:** womankind. **3.** Characteristic feminine qualities. **4.** A woman servant or attendant. **5.** *Informal.* **a.** A wife. **b.** A female lover or sweetheart.

wom·an·hood (wŏom'ən-hŏod') *n.* **1.** The state of being an adult human female. **2.** Womanly qualities, feelings, etc. **3.** Women in general **:** womankind.

wom·an·ish (wŏom'ə-nĭsh) *adj.* **1.** Of or typical of a woman. **2.** Effeminate.

wom·an·kind (wŏom'ən-kīnd') *n.* Women as a group.

wom·an·ly (wŏom'ən-lē) *adj.* **-li·er, -li·est.** Having qualities regarded as characteristic of and esp. admirable in women. —**wom'an·li·ness** *n.*

womb (wōom) *n.* **1.** The mammalian organ of gestation **:** uterus. **2.** A place where something develops.

wom·bat (wŏm'băt') *n.* An Australian marsupial, *Phascolomis ursinus* or *Lasiorhinus latifrons,* resembling a small bear.

wom·en (wĭm'ĭn) *n. pl. of* WOMAN.

wom·en·folk (wĭm'ĭn-fōk') *pl.n.* **1.** Women as a group. **2.** The female members of a family or community.

won[1] (wŭn) *v. p.t. & p.p. of* WIN.

won[2] (wôn) *n., pl.* **won.** —See table at CURRENCY.

won·der (wŭn'dər) *n.* **1. a.** One that excites amazement or admiration **:** marvel. **b.** The feeling aroused by something extraordinary or marvelous. **c.** The quality of arousing wonder. **2.** A feeling of uncertainty. —*v.* **1.** To feel amazement or admiration. **2.** To feel curiosity or uncertainty. **3.** To feel inquisitive or uncertain about.

won·der·ful (wŭn'dər-fəl) *adj.* **1.** Astonishing or marvelous. **2.** Exceptionally fine **:** excellent. —**won'der·ful·ly** *adv.*

won·der·land (wŭn'dər-lănd') *n.* **1.** An imaginary realm filled wih marvels. **2.** A place that arouses awe or admiration.

won·der·ment (wŭn'dər-mənt) *n.* **1.** A state or feeling of amazement. **2.** A cause of wonder **:** marvel. **3.** A state of being puzzled, uncertain, or curious.

won·drous (wŭn'drəs) *adj.* Remarkable **:** wonderful. —*adv. Archaic.* Wonderfully **:** amazingly. —**won'drous·ly** *adv.*

wonk (wŏngk) *n. Slang.* A student who studies excessively.

wont (wônt, wōnt) *adj.* **1.** Accustomed or used <was *wont* to speed> **2.** Apt or likely <is *wont* to be grumpy> —*n.* Habitual practice **:** custom.

won't (wōnt). Will not.

wont·ed (wôn'tĭd, wōn'-) *adj.* Accustomed **:** habitual.

won ton (wŏn' tŏn') *n., pl.* **won tons.** A noodle-dough dumpling filled with spiced minced pork, usu. served in soup.

woo (wōo) *v.* **1.** To court with the hope of marrying. **2.** To attempt to obtain or achieve <*woo* fame and fortune> **3.** To entreat insistently. —**woo'er** *n.*

wood (wŏod) *n.* **1. a.** The solid fibrous substance composing the main part of trees and shrubs below the outer covering. **b.** This substance used esp. for building material and fuel. **2.** *often* **woods.** A thick growth of trees somewhat smaller than a forest. **3.** An object, as a golf club, made of wood. —*adj.* **1.** Made of wood **:** wooden. **2.** Relating to wood as fuel or lumber. **3.** Inhabiting or growing naturally in woods. —*v.* **1.** To cover with a stand of trees. **2.** To furnish with wood, esp. for burning.

wood alcohol *n.* A flammable poisonous liquid used esp. as antifreeze.

wood·bine (wŏod'bīn') *n.* Any of various climbing vines, as an Old World honeysuckle, *Lonicera periclymenum,* or the Virginia creeper.

wood·block (wŏod'blŏk') *n.* A woodcut.

wood·chuck (wŏod'chŭk') *n.* A common rodent, *Marmota monax,* of N and E North America, with a short-legged, heavy-set body and grizzled brownish fur.

wood·cock (wŏod'kŏk') *n.* A game bird, *Scolopax rusticola* or *Philohela minor,* with short legs and a long bill.

wood·craft (wŏod'krăft') *n.* **1.** Skill in making things from wood. **2.** Skill and experience in woods-related activities, as hunting, fishing, or camping.

wood·cut (wŏod'kŭt') *n.* **1.** A wooden block whose surface is engraved with a design for printing. **2.** A print made from a woodcut.

wood·cut·ter (wŏod'kŭt'ər) *n.* One who cuts wood or trees esp. as a livelihood.

wood·ed (wŏod'ĭd) *adj.* Covered with trees or woods.

wood·en (wŏod'n) *adj.* **1.** Made or consisting of wood. **2.** Lacking in spirit or liveliness. **3.** Clumsy. —**wood'en·ly** *adv.*

wood·land (wŏod'lənd, -lănd') *n.* Land with a cover of trees and shrubs.

wood·peck·er (wŏod'pĕk'ər) *n.* Any of various birds of the family Picidae, with strong claws and a chisellike bill for drilling through bark and wood.

wood·pile (wŏod'pīl') *n.* A pile of wood, esp. when stacked for use as firewood.

wood·ruff (wŏod'rəf, -rŭf') *n.* A plant of the genus *Asperula,* esp. the Eurasian variety *A. odorata,* with small white flowers and fragrant leaves used esp. in sachets.

wood·shed (wŏod'shĕd') *n.* A shed for the storage of firewood.

woods·man (wŏodz'mən) *n.* One who lives, works, or spends much time in the woods, esp. one who is skilled in woodcraft.

woods•y (wŏŏd′zē) *adj.* **-i•er, -i•est.** Relating to or suggestive of the woods.
wood•wind (wŏŏd′wĭnd′) *n.* Any of a group of wind instruments, including the clarinet, oboe, flute, and bassoon.
wood•work (wŏŏd′wûrk′) *n.* Objects made of or work done in wood, esp. wooden moldings or doors.
wood•y (wŏŏd′ē) *adj.* **-i•er, -i•est. 1.** Of or containing wood. **2.** Typical or suggestive of wood. **3.** Abounding in trees : wooded.
woof (wŏŏf, wōōf) *n.* **1.** The threads that run crosswise in a woven fabric, at right angles to the warp threads. **2.** The texture of a woven fabric or the fabric itself.
woof•er (wŏŏf′ər) *n.* A loudspeaker that reproduces low-frequency sounds.
wool (wŏŏl) *n.* **1.** The soft, thick, often curly hair of some mammals, esp. sheep. **2.** Yarn, textiles, or garments made of wool. **3.** Something having the look or feel of wool.
wool•en *also* **wool•len** (wŏŏl′ən). *—adj.* Of, relating to, or made of wool. *—n. often* **woolens.** Wool textiles or garments.
wool•gath•er•ing (wŏŏl′găth′ər-ĭng) *n.* Idle indulgence in daydreams. **—wool′gath′er•er** *n.*
†**wool•ly** *also* **wool•y** (wŏŏl′ē). *adj.* **-li•er, -li•est** *also* **-i•er, -i•est. 1. a.** Of, relating to, or covered with wool. **b.** Like wool. **2.** Lacking clarity, as of thought. **3.** Marked by absence of law and order, as in American frontier times. *—n., pl.* **-lies** *also* **-ies. 1.** A garment made of wool. **2.** *W U.S. & Austral.* A sheep. **—wool′li•ness** *n.*
woolly bear *n.* The hairy caterpillar of a tiger moth, esp. that of *Isia isabella.*
woops (wŏŏps, wōōps) *interj. var. of* WHOOPS.
woo•zy (wōō′zē, wŏŏz′ē) *adj.* **-zi•er, -zi•est. 1.** Dazed : confused. **2.** Dizzy or nauseated. **—woo′zi•ness** *n.*
Worces•ter•shire (wŏŏs′tər-shîr′, -shər). A trademark for a spicy soy and vinegar sauce.
word (wûrd) *n.* **1. a.** A meaningful speech sound or succession of speech sounds that can be represented by graphic symbols. **b.** A written or printed representation of a word. **2.** A remark or comment. **3. words.** An argument. **4.** An assurance. **5.** An order to do something. **6.** News <sent *word* of their discovery> **7.** A password or watchword. **8. words.** The lyrics of a musical composition. **9. Word.** The Bible or Gospel. *—v.* To express orally or in writing. **—word′less** *adj.* **—word′less•ly** *adv.*
word•age (wûr′dĭj) *n.* **1.** Words in general. **2.** The number of words used, as in a novel. **3.** Choice of words : wording.
word•book (wûrd′bŏŏk′) *n.* A dictionary or specialized vocabulary.
word•ing (wûr′dĭng) *n.* The way in which words and phrases are used.
word play *n.* A clever or witty use of words, esp. a pun.
word processing *n.* A system of producing typewritten documents, as business letters, by use of automated typewriters and electronic text-editing equipment. **—word processor** *n.*
word•y (wûr′dē) *adj.* **-i•er, -i•est.** Marked by too many words. ★ ***syns:*** DIFFUSE, LONG-WINDED, PROLIX, VERBOSE **—word′i•ly** *adv.* **—word′i•ness** *n.*
wore (wôr, wōr) *v. p.t. of* WEAR.
work (wûrk) *n.* **1.** Physical or mental effort directed toward a goal. **2.** A job : employment <out of *work*> **3.** The activity that serves as one's regular source of livelihood : occupation. **4.** Something done as part of a job : task or duty. **5.** Quality of workmanship <careless *work*> **6. a.** Something brought about by an effort <the *work* of a mastermind> **b.** An act or deed, as of charity. **c. works.** The total production of a creative artist. **d. works.** Engineering structures, as bridges, roads, and dams. **7.** Something being produced, studied, or subjected to a process. **8. works** *(sing. in number).* A site of industry, as a factory or plant <iron *works*> **9. works.** The operating parts of a mechanism, as a clock. **10. the works.** *Slang.* Everything <ordered pizza with *the works*> **11.** The transfer of energy when a force is applied to a body. ★ ***syns:*** BUSINESS, EMPLOYMENT, JOB, OCCUPATION *—v.* **1.** To engage in physical or mental exertion. **2.** To have a job. **3.** To function or cause to function, esp. effectively. **4.** To have an influence or effect <Guilt *worked* on my conscience.> **5.** To become through gradual or repeated stress, pressure, or movement <The masonry *worked* loose.> **6.** To make a passage or way steadily or forcibly. **7.** To move or contort, as from painful emotion. **8.** To be handled or processed, as metal. **9.** To bring about : achieve <*works* wonders with children> **10.** To cause to expend effort <*worked* the dancers hard> **11.** To form or shape. **12.** To solve (a math problem) by figuring and reasoning. **13.** To achieve (a particular state) in stages. **14.** To plan or arrange. **15.** To excite or provoke <*worked* myself into a rage> **—work out. 1.** To find a solution for. **2.** To prove effective or appropriate. **3.** To exercise esp. regularly and strenuously.
work•a•ble (wûr′kə-bəl) *adj.* **1.** Capable of being done : practicable. **2.** Capable of being shaped, molded, or dealt with. **—work′a•bil′i•ty, work′a•ble•ness** *n.*
work•a•day (wûr′kə-dā′) *adj.* **1.** Of, relating to, or suitable for working days : everyday. **2.** Commonplace : ordinary.
work•a•hol•ic (wûr′kə-hô′lĭk, -hŏl′ĭk) *n.* One who has a compulsive and unrelenting need to work.
work•bench (wûrk′bĕnch′) *n.* A sturdy table used esp. by machinists or carpenters.
work•book (wûrk′bŏŏk′) *n.* **1.** A student's booklet of problems and exercises that is designed to be written in. **2.** A manual of instructions. **3.** A record book for work accomplished.
work•day (wûrk′dā′) *n.* **1.** A day that is part of one's workweek. **2.** The section of the day during which one works at a job.

work·er (wûr'kər) *n.* **1.** One that works <a slow *worker*> **2.** One who works for wages, esp. a manual or industrial laborer. **3.** A sterile ant, bee, or termite that performs specialized work in the colony.

work·fare (wûrk'fâr') *n.* A form of welfare in which aid recipients are required to perform public-service work.

work force *n.* **1.** The staff employed in a specific work project. **2.** All workers potentially available, as to a nation.

work·horse (wûrk'hôrs') *n.* **1.** A horse used primarily for labor. **2.** One who works tirelessly, esp. at difficult tasks.

work·ing (wûr'kĭng) *adj.* **1.** Of, relating to, used for, or spent in work. **2.** Adequate or enough for use or work. **3.** Capable of being used to further activity or work.

work·load (wûrk'lōd') *n.* The quantity of work assigned or accomplished in a specified time period.

work·man (wûrk'mən) *n.* **1.** One who performs usu. manual labor for wages. **2.** A skilled craftsman.

work·man·like (wûrk'mən-līk') *adj.* Of or worthy of a skillful worker or craftsman.

work·man·ship (wûrk'mən-shĭp') *n.* **1.** The craftsmanship of a workman. **2.** The quality of a craftsman's work.

work·out (wûrk'out') *n.* **1.** A usu. strenuous period of exercise or practice. **2.** An arduous task.

work·place (wûrk'plās') *n.* **1.** A place where people are employed. **2.** The work setting in general.

work·room (wûrk'ro͞om', -ro͝om') *n.* A room used esp. for work done by hand.

work·shop (wûrk'shŏp') *n.* **1.** A place where manual or industrial work is done. **2. a.** A group of people who meet regularly for a seminar in a particular field. **b.** A usu. short educational program in which small groups deal with specific problems.

work·space (wûrk'spās') *n.* An area used or allocated for one's work, as in an office.

work·sta·tion (wûrk'stā'shən) *n.* An area, as in an office, equipped for one worker, often including a computer terminal.

work-stud·y (wûrk'stŭd'ē) *adj.* Of or being an academic program that enables students to gain work experience and make money while continuing their studies.

work·ta·ble (wûrk'tā'bəl) *n.* A table for a particular task or activity.

work·week (wûrk'wēk') *n.* The total number of hours, as 35 or 40, required to be worked in one week.

world (wûrld) *n.* **1.** The planet earth. **2.** All of creation **:** the universe. **3.** The earth and all that inhabit it. **4.** The human race. **5.** The public **:** society. **6.** A specific region of the earth. **7.** A sphere or domain <the insect *world*> **8.** A field or sphere of human interest or effort <the sports *world*> **9.** Individual existence, experience, etc. **10.** Secular life and its affairs. **11.** A great amount <a *world* of misfortune> **12.** A celestial body, esp. a planet <extraterrestrial *worlds*>

world·ly (wûrld'lē) *adj.* **-li·er, -li·est. 1.** Of or concerned with temporal rather than spiritual or religious matters. **2.** Worldly-wise. **—world'li·ness** *n.*

world·ly-wise (wûrld'lē-wīz') *adj.* Having a shrewd understanding of human affairs **:** sophisticated.

world·wide (wûrld'wīd') *adj.* Universal in scope or extent. **—world'wide'** *adv.*

worm (wûrm) *n.* **1.** Any of various invertebrates, as those of the phyla Annelida, Nematoda, or Platyhelminthes, that have a long, flexible rounded or flattened body. **2.** Any of various insect larvae, as caterpillars or grubs, that have a soft elongated body. **3.** Something like a worm in movement or appearance. **4.** A force that inwardly torments or corrupts. **5.** A contemptible person. **6. worms.** Infestation with intestinal worms or wormlike parasites. —*v.* **1.** To move with or as if with the wriggling motion of a worm. **2.** To obtain by devious means <*wormed* a loan out of me> **3.** To rid of intestinal worms. **—worm'y** *adj.*

worm-eat·en (wûrm'ēt'n) *adj.* **1.** Infested with or damaged by worms. **2.** Affected by decay **:** rotten. **3.** Out-of-date.

worm gear *n.* **1.** A gear consisting of a rotating threaded shaft and a worm wheel that mesh together. **2.** A worm wheel.

worm gear

worm wheel *n.* The toothed wheel that meshes with the rotating threaded shaft of a worm gear.

worm·wood (wûrm'wo͝od') *n.* **1.** An aromatic plant of the genus *Artemisia,* esp. the European variety *A. absinthium,* that yields a bitter extract used in making absinthe. **2.** Something harsh or embittering.

worn (wôrn, wōrn) *v. p.p. of* WEAR. —*adj.* **1.** Affected or damaged by wear or use. **2.** Completely exhausted. **3.** Trite through overuse.

worn-out (wôrn'out', wōrn'-) *adj.* **1.** Worn or used up completely <*worn-out* clothes> **2.** Extremely tired.

wor·ri·some (wûr'ē-səm, wŭr'-) *adj.* **1.** Causing worry. **2.** Inclined to worry.

wor·ry (wûr'ē, wŭr'ē) *v.* **-ried, -ry·ing. 1.** To feel or cause to feel anxious or distressed. **2. a.** To grasp and tug at repeatedly <a dog *wor-*

rying a bone> **b.** To press or handle absentmindedly <*worry* a sore tooth> **3.** To irritate : annoy. —*n., pl.* **-ries. 1.** Mental anxiety or distress. **2.** A cause or source of worry. —**wor'ri•er** *n.*

wor•ry•wart (wûr'ē-wôrt', wŭr'-) *n. Informal.* One who tends to worry a great deal.

worse (wûrs) *adj.* **1.** More inferior. **2.** In poorer health. **3.** More disagreeable or severe. —*adv.* To a worse extent. —*n.* Something worse <a turn for the *worse*>

wors•en (wûr'sən) *v.* To make or become worse.

wor•ship (wûr'shĭp) *n.* **1. a.** Reverence for a deity or sacred object. **b.** A set of religious forms by which this reverence is expressed. **2.** Intense devotion to or esteem for a person or thing. **3.** *often* **Worship.** *esp. Brit.* A title of respect for some officials, as magistrates or mayors. —*v.* **-shiped, -ship•ing** *or* **-shipped, -ship•ping. 1.** To venerate as a deity. **2.** To love, admire, or esteem devotedly. **3.** To attend a religious service. —**wor'ship•er** *n.*

wor•ship•ful (wûr'shĭp-fəl) *adj.* **1.** Reverent or adoring. **2.** *esp. Brit.* Honorable by virtue of position or rank. —Used in titles of respect.

worst (wûrst) *adj.* **1.** Most inferior : least good. **2.** Most disagreeable or severe. **3.** Least desirable or satisfactory, esp. furthest from an ideal or standard. —*n.* One that is worst. —*adv.* In the worst way or degree. —*v.* To surpass : defeat.

wor•sted (wo͝os'tĭd, wûr'stĭd) *n.* **1.** Smooth, firmly twisted yarn made from long strands of wool. **2.** A firm, smooth fabric made from worsted.

wort (wûrt, wôrt) *n.* An herbaceous plant. —Usu. used in combination.

worth (wûrth) *n.* **1.** The quality of something that gives value or usefulness. **2.** Personal value or merit. **3.** The monetary value of something. **4.** The amount that a certain sum of money will buy <a dollar's *worth* of candy> **5.** Wealth : affluence. —*prep.* **1.** Equal in value to. **2.** Having money or property amounting to. **3.** Deserving of <a job *worth* doing>

worth•less (wûrth'lĭs) *adj.* **1.** Without value or use. **2.** Contemptible : despicable.

worth•while (wûrth'hwīl', -wīl') *adj.* Deserving of the time, effort, or expense involved. —**worth'while'ness** *n.*

wor•thy (wûr'*th*ē) *adj.* **-thi•er, -thi•est. 1.** Useful or valuable. **2.** Deserving respect : admirable. **3.** Meriting : deserving <*worthy* of attention> —*n., pl.* **-thies.** One who is respected or esteemed. —**wor'thi•ly** *adv.* —**wor'thi•ness** *n.*

would (wo͝od) *v. p.t. of* WILL[2].

would-be (wo͝od'bē') *adj.* Wishing or pretending to be <a *would-be* novelist>

would•n't (wo͝od'nt). Would not.

wound[1] (wo͞ond) *n.* **1.** An injury, esp. one in which the skin is lacerated or pierced. **2.** An emotional injury. —*v.* To injure by means of a wound.

wound[2] (wound) *v. p.t. & p.p.* of WIND[2].

wound[3] (wound) *v. var. p.t. & p.p. of* WIND[3].

wove (wōv) *v. var. p.t. of* WEAVE.

wo•ven (wō'vən) *v. p.p. of* WEAVE.

wow (wou) *interj.* —Used to express surprise, amazement, excitement, etc. —*n. Informal.* An extraordinary success. —*v.* To affect strongly and usu. agreeably.

†**wrack** (răk) *n.* **1.** Total destruction. **2. a.** Wreckage, esp. of a ship cast ashore. **b.** *Regional.* Violent destruction of a vehicle or building. **3.** Seaweed forming a tangled mass. —*v.* **1.** To ruin : wreck. **2.** To have a violent effect on <*wracked* by sobs>

wraith (rāth) *n.* **1.** An apparition or ghost. **2.** One that is insubstantial or shadowy.

wran•gle (răng'gəl) *v.* **-gled, -gling. 1.** To dispute noisily or angrily : quarrel. **2.** To achieve by argument. **3.** To herd (livestock). —**wran'gle** *n.* —**wran'gler** *n.*

wrap (răp) *v.* **wrapped** *or* **wrapt, wrap•ping. 1.** To arrange or fold about in order to cover or protect something. **2.** To enclose, encase, or enfold. **3.** To package, esp. with paper. **4.** To wind, fold, or twine about something. **5.** To envelop esp. so as to conceal. **6.** To be or cause to be completely engrossed <*wrapped* in thought> —**wrap up. 1.** To finish : end. **2.** To give a brief summary of. ★ ***syns:*** CLOAK, CLOTHE, ENFOLD, ENSHROUD, ENVELOP, ENWRAP, SHROUD, VEIL —*n.* **1.** A coat, shawl, etc., worn for warmth. **2.** A wrapper.

wrap•a•round (răp'ə-round') *n.* A dress or skirt open to the hem and fitted to the body by wrapping around. —**wrap'a•round'** *adj.*

wrap•per (răp'ər) *n.* **1.** One that wraps. **2. a.** Material in which something is wrapped. **b.** The tobacco leaf wrapped around a cigar. **3.** A loose robe.

wrap•ping (răp'ĭng) *n.* The material used for wrapping something.

wrap-up (răp'ŭp') *n.* A brief summary.

wrasse (răs) *n.* Any of numerous chiefly tropical, often brightly colored marine fishes of the family Labridae.

wrath (răth, rāth) *n.* **1.** Violent anger : fury. **2. a.** A manifestation of wrath. **b.** Divine punishment for sin. —**wrath'ful** *adj.* —**wrath'ful•ly** *adv.*

wreak (rēk) *v.* **1.** To inflict (vengeance or punishment) upon another. **2.** To give expression to <*wreak* one's anger>

wreath (rēth) *n., pl.* **wreaths** (rē*th*z, rēths). **1.** A ringlike band or circular form, as of intertwined flowers or pine boughs. **2.** A wreathlike ring or form.

wreathe (rē*th*) *v.* **wreathed, wreath•ing. 1.** To twist into a wreath or wreathlike contour. **2.** To move in coils or spirals. **3.** To take on or cause to take on the circular shape of a wreath.

wreck (rĕk) *v.* **1.** To damage or ruin by accident <*wrecked* the car> **2.** To tear down or blow up : demolish. **3.** To bring to a state of ruin. —*n.* **1.** The action of wrecking or state of being wrecked. **2. a.** Damaged remains, as of a wrecked ship or vehicle. **b.** A shipwreck. **c.** Cargo or debris washed ashore after a shipwreck. 3. One in a disabled or ruined state.

wreck•age (rĕk'ĭj) *n.* **1.** The act of wrecking or state of being wrecked. 2. The debris or remains of something wrecked.

wreck•er (rĕk'ər) *n.* **1. a.** One that wrecks. **b.** One engaged commercially in wrecking or demolishing something. **2. a.** A vehicle or ship that recovers or removes wrecks. **b.** A salvager of wrecked cargo.

wren (rĕn) *n.* A small, brownish bird of the family Troglodytidae that usu. holds its tail pointing upward.

wrench (rĕnch) *n.* **1.** An abrupt, forcible twisting movement. **2.** An injury, as to a muscle or joint, produced esp. by twisting. **3.** A tool for gripping, turning, or twisting an object such as a nut or bolt. —*v.* **1. a.** To twist or turn esp. violently. **b.** To twist and sprain <*wrenched* my ankle> **2.** To pull forcibly : wrest. **3.** To give emotional pain or anguish to. **4.** To distort the orig. meaning of. **—wrench'ing•ly** *adv.*

wrest (rĕst) *v.* **1.** To get by or as if by pulling with violent wrenching movements. **2.** To gain by or as if by force or violence. —*n.* A forcible twist or wrench.

wres•tle (rĕs'əl) *v.* **-tled, -tling. 1.** To fight by grappling and attempting to throw or immobilize one's opponent. **2.** To struggle to deal with or overcome <*wrestling* with unemployment> 3. To strive against in a wrestling match. —*n.* An act or instance of wrestling. **—wres'tler** *n.*

wres•tling (rĕs'lĭng) *n.* A gymnastic exercise or competition between 2 contenders who attempt to throw or immobilize each other by struggling hand-to-hand.

wretch (rĕch) *n.* **1.** An extremely unfortunate or miserable person. **2.** A vile or contemptible person.

wretch•ed (rĕch'ĭd) *adj.* **1.** Extremely unhappy : miserable. **2.** Of a poor or mean character <a *wretched* hovel> **3.** Extremely distressing : grievous <a *wretched* illness> **4.** Despicable : vile. 5. Inferior in quality or competence. **—wretch'ed•ly** *adv.* **—wretch'ed•ness** *n.*

wrig•gle (rĭg'əl) *v.* **-gled, -gling. 1.** To turn or twist about sinuously. **2.** To go forward by turning and twisting, as a snake. **3.** To get into or out of by subtle or devious means. **—wrig'gle** *n.* **—wrig'gly** *adj.*

wrig•gler (rĭg'lər) *n.* **1.** One that wriggles. **2.** The larval or pupal stage of a mosquito.

wring (rĭng) *v.* **wrung** (rŭng), **wring•ing. 1.** To twist and squeeze by hand or machine, esp. to extract liquid. **2.** To obtain by or as if by forcible twisting or compressing <*wring* a confession out of a suspect> **3.** To twist or wrench forcibly <*wring* someone's neck> **4.** To twist or press together (one's hands) in distress. **5.** To affect with emotional pain or distress.

wring•er (rĭng'ər) *n.* One that wrings, esp. a device with rollers that press out water from wet clothes.

wrin•kle (rĭng'kəl) *n.* **1.** A small fold, ridge, or crease, as on fabric or the skin. **2.** *Informal.* An ingenious innovation. ★ ***syns:*** ANGLE, GIMMICK, KICKER, TWIST —*v.* **-kled, -kling.** To form or cause to form wrinkles. **—wrin'kly** *adj.*

wrist (rĭst) *n.* **1.** The joint at which the hand and forearm come together. **2.** The arrangement of bones composing the wrist.

wrist•band (rĭst'bănd') *n.* The part of a sleeve or wrist watch encircling the wrist.

wrist watch *n.* A small timepiece worn on a band that encircles the wrist.

writ (rĭt) *n.* **1.** A written court order commanding an individual to perform or refrain from a specified act. **2.** Something written, esp. a formal document.

write (rīt) *v.* **wrote** (rōt), **writ•ten** (rĭt'n), **writ•ing. 1.** To form (symbols, letters, or words) on a surface, as with a pen or pencil. **2.** To inscribe the symbol, letters, or words of <*write* one's signature> **3.** To create and put down on paper. **4.** To communicate by writing <*wrote* the news to my family> **5.** To send a communication to <*write* me all the news> **—write in.** To vote for (a candidate not listed) by entering the name on the ballot. **—write off. 1.** To cancel as a loss <*write off* a debt> **2.** To make less in value.

write-in (rīt'ĭn') *n.* **1.** A vote cast by writing in the name of a candidate. **2.** A candidate whose name is written in.

writ•er (rī'tər) *n.* One who writes, esp. as an occupation : author.

writer's cramp *n.* A painful muscular spasm of the fingers or hand caused by prolonged writing.

write-up (rīt'ŭp') *n.* A written, usu. favorable report or review, as in a newspaper.

writhe (rīth) *v.* **writhed, writh•ing. 1.** To twist or squirm, as in pain. **2.** To move with a twisting or contorted motion, as a snake. **3.** To suffer acutely.

writ•ing (rī'tĭng) *n.* **1.** Written mode <an order put in *writing*> 2. Handwriting. 3. A written work, esp. a literary composition. **4.** The art or occupation of a writer.

wrong (rông, rŏng) *adj.* **1.** Being in error : incorrect. **2. a.** Against moral standards or legal codes. **b.** Unethical or unjust. **3.** Not needed, wanted, or intended <dialed the *wrong* number> **4.** Unsuitable : inappropriate. **5.** Not conforming to a fixed usage, method, or procedure. **6.** Being the side or surface opposite to the right or more prominent side. —*adv.* **1.** In an erroneous way. **2.** In an immoral or unjust manner. —*n.* **1.** Something that is unjust, injurious, or immoral. **2.** The state of being mistaken or at fault. —*v.* **1.** To do wrong to : harm. **2.** To treat dishonorably or unfairly. ★ ***syns:*** AGGRIEVE, OPPRESS, OUTRAGE, PERSECUTE **—wrong'er** *n.* **—wrong'ly** *adv.*

wrong•do•er (rông'do͞o'ər, rŏng'-) *n.* One who does wrong, esp. moral or legal wrong. **—wrong'do'ing** *n.*

wrong•ful (rông′fəl, rŏng′-) *adj.* **1.** Unethical : unjust. **2.** Unlawful : illegal. —**wrong′ful•ly** *adv.* —**wrong′ful•ness** *n.*
wrong-head•ed (rông′hĕd′ĭd, rŏng′-) *adj.* Obstinately wrong in judgment or opinion.
wrote (rōt) *v. p.t. of* WRITE.
wroth (rôth, rŏth) *adj.* Angry : wrathful.
wrought (rôt) *adj.* **1.** Made or fashioned. **2.** Hammered into shape, as metal. **3.** Delicately or elaborately made. **4.** Emotionally agitated. —Used with *up.*
wrought iron *n.* Commercial iron that is tough and malleable.
wrung (rŭng) *v. p.t. & p.p. of* WRING.
wry (rī) *adj.* **wri•er, wri•est** *also* **wry•er, wry•est. 1.a.** Abnormally bent to one side : crooked. **b.** Contorted to express distaste or displeasure <made a *wry* mouth> **2.** Ironically humorous. —**wry′ly** *adv.*
wun•der•kind (vo͝on′dər-kĭnd′, wŭn′-) *n.* **1.** A child prodigy. **2.** A person who achieves great success or acclaim at an early age.
wurst (wûrst, wo͝orst) *n.* Sausage.
wye (wī) *n.* The letter *y.*
WYSIWYG (wĭz′ē-wĭg′) *adj. Computer Sci.* Of or being a word-processing system in which the screen displays text exactly as it will be printed.

Xx

x *or* **X** (ĕks) *n., pl.* **x's** *or* **X's. 1.** The 24th letter of the English alphabet. **2.** Roman numeral for 10. **3.** An unknown or unnamed quantity. —*v.* **x'd, x'ing.** To cancel or delete with a series of *x*'s.
x-ax•is (ĕks′ăk′sĭs) *n.* The horizontal axis of a graph or chart.
X-chro•mo•some (ĕks′krō′mə-sōm′) *n.* The sex chromosome that is associated with female characteristics and occurs paired in the female and single in the male sex-chromosome pair.
Xe *symbol for* XENON.
xe•bec (zē′bĕk′) *n.* A 3-masted sailing ship with both square and triangular sails used in the Mediterranean.

xebec

xen•o•lith (zĕn′ə-lĭth′, zē′nə-) *n.* A rock fragment foreign to the igneous mass in which it occurs.
xe•non (zē′nŏn′) *n. Symbol* **Xe** A colorless, odorless gaseous element found in extremely small quantities in the air.
xen•o•phobe (zĕn′ə-fōb′, zē′nə-) *n.* One who fears, mistrusts, and dislikes foreigners or what is strange or foreign. —**xen′o•pho′bi•a** *n.* —**xen′o•pho′bic** *adj.*
xe•rog•ra•phy (zĭ-rŏg′rə-fē) *n.* A process for copying graphic material in which a negative image formed by a resinous powder on a charged plate is electrically transferred and fixed to a sheet of paper by means of heat. —**xe′ro•graph′ic** (zîr′ə-grăf′ĭk) *adj.*
xe•ro•phyte (zîr′ə-fīt′) *n.* A plant adapted to growing in an environment providing limited moisture. —**xe′ro•phyt′ic** (-fĭt′ĭk) *adj.*
Xe•rox (zîr′ŏks′). A trademark for a photocopying process or machine using xerography.
Xho•sa (kō′sä, -zə) *n., pl.* **-sa** *or* **-sas. 1.** A member of a Bantu people of South Africa. **2.** Their Bantu language.
X•mas (krĭs′məs, ĕks′məs) *n.* Christmas.

▲ ***word history:*** The character X in *Xmas* does not represent the letter *X* in the Roman alphabet but rather the Greek letter *chi.* The Greek form of *chi* is χ. *Chi* is the first letter of the Greek form of *Christ,* transliterated as *Khristos* or *Christos.* The symbol χ or *X* has been used as an abbreviation for *Christ* since earliest Christian times.

x-ra•di•a•tion (ĕks′rā′dē-ā′shən) *n.* **1.** Exposure to or treatment with x-rays. **2.** Radiation composed of x-rays.
x-ray *also* **X-ray** (ĕks′rā′) *n.* **1. a.** A relatively high-energy photon with a very short wavelength. **b.** A stream of such photons, capable of penetrating solids and used in radiography, radiology, and research. **2.** A photograph taken with x-rays. —*v.* To treat with or photograph with x-rays.

▲ ***word history:*** Wilhelm Roentgen, the German scientist who discovered x-rays, gave them the name *x-strahlen,* translated into English as "x-rays." He used *x,* the symbol for an unknown quantity, because he did not completely understand the nature of this kind of radiation.

x-ray astronomy *n.* Astronomy that deals with the properties of celestial bodies as indicated by the x-rays they emit.
x-ray star *n.* A celestial object resembling a star but emitting a major portion of its radiation in the form of x-rays.

xy•lem (zī'ləm) *n.* A woody tissue of vascular plants that conducts water and serves as a support, as for a stem.

xy•lo•phone (zī'lə-fōn') *n.* A musical instrument consisting of a mounted series of wooden bars graduated in length and played by striking with 2 small wooden mallets. **—xy'lo•phon'ist** *n.*

Yy

y *or* **Y** (wī) *n., pl.* **y's** *or* **Y's. 1.** The 25th letter of the English alphabet. **2.** Something with the shape of the letter Y.

Y *symbol for* YTTRIUM.

—y[1] *or* **—ey** *suff.* **1.** Characterized by : consisting of <rain*y*> <clay*ey*>**2.** Like <summer*y*> **3.** Tending or inclined toward <sleep*y*>

—y[2] *suff.* **1.** Condition : state : quality <jealous*y*> **2. a.** Activity <cooker*y*> **b.** Instance of a specified action <inquir*y*> **3. a.** Place for an activity <tanner*y*> **b.** Result or product of an activity <laundr*y*> **4.** Collection : body : group <soldier*y*>

—y[3] *suff.* **1.** Small one <pupp*y*> **2.** Dear one <dadd*y*>

yacht (yät) *n.* A relatively small motor-driven or sailing vessel that usu. has graceful lines and is used esp. for pleasure cruises or racing. **—yacht** *v.*

yacht•ing (yä'tĭng) *n.* The activity or sport of cruising or racing in a yacht.

yachts•man (yäts'mən) *n.* One who owns or sails a yacht. **—yachts'man•ship'** *n.*

ya•hoo (yä'hōō, yā'-) *n., pl.* **-hoos.** A crude or boisterous person.

Yah•weh (yä'wā') *also* **Yah•veh** (-vā') *n.* The God of the ancient Hebrews.

yak[1] (yăk) *n.* A long-haired bovine mammal, *Bos grunniens,* of Tibet and the mountains of C Asia, often domesticated.

yak[2] *also* **yack** (yăk) *v.* **yakked, yak•king** *also* **yacked, yacking.** *Slang.* To chatter or talk persistently and at length. **—yak, yack** *n.*

y'all (yôl) *pron. var. of* YOU-ALL.

†yam (yăm) *n.* **1.** A vine of the genus *Dioscorea* with a starchy edible root that is much used in the tropics as food. **2.** *S U.S.* A sweet potato with reddish flesh.

yam•mer (yăm'ər) *v.* **1.** To complain persistently : whine. **2.** To talk rapidly and often loudly : chatter. **—yam'mer** *n.*

yank (yăngk) *v.* To pull or jerk with a quick forceful movement. **—yank** *n.*

Yank (yăngk) *n. Informal.* A Yankee.

Yan•kee (yăng'kē) *n.* **1.a.** A native or resident of New England. **b.** A native or resident of the N U.S. **2.** A native or resident of the U.S. **—Yan'kee** *adj.*

yap (yăp) *v.* **yapped, yap•ping. 1.** To bark : yelp. **2.** *Slang.* To talk shrilly and relentlessly : jabber. *—n.* **1.** A bark : yelp. **2.** *Slang.* **a.** Shrill, relentless talk : chatter. **b.** The mouth. **—yap'per** *n.*

yard[1] (yärd) *n.* **1.** —See table at MEASUREMENT. **2.** A long tapering spar that is attached at right angles to a mast to support and spread the head of a square sail.

yard[2] (yärd) *n.* **1.** A small area of ground adjacent to a building. **2.** An often enclosed area together with its buildings set aside for a specific activity or business. **3.** An area with a system of tracks where railroad trains are made up and cars are switched, serviced, or stored. **4.** An enclosed area for livestock.

yard•age (yär'dĭj) *n.* The amount, extent, or length of something measured in yards.

yard•arm (yärd'ärm') *n.* Either end of the yard supporting a square sail.

yard•man (yärd'mən) *n.* A man employed esp. in a railroad yard.

yard•stick (yärd'stĭk') *n.* **1.** A graduated measuring stick one yard long. **2.** A standard for making a judgment or comparison.

▲ ***word history:*** A yardstick is literally a "stick-stick," for the word *yard* is the descendant of Old English *gerd,* which meant simply "a stick." Since sticks make convenient measuring devices, a stick of a certain length of this unit varied over the centuries; the current length of a yard was fixed in the 14th cent., during the reign of Edward III. The compound *yardstick* is a relatively recent coinage in which the word *yard* is used in the sense "a unit of length."

yar•mul•ke (yär'məl-kə, yä'məl-) *n.* A skullcap worn by Jewish males.

yarn (yärn) *n.* **1.** A continuous strand consisting of twisted fibers, as of wool, used in knitting or weaving. **2.** *Informal.* A long, often elaborate tale of real or fictitious adventures.

yar•row (yăr'ō) *n.* A pungent-smelling plant, *Achillea millefolium,* with usu. white or yellow flower clusters.

yaw (yô) *v.* **1.** *Naut.* To veer erratically from an intended course. **2.** To move unsteadily : weave. **—yaw** *n.*

yawl (yôl) *n.* **1.** A 2-masted fore-and-aft-rigged sailboat with the shorter mast at the stern abaft the tiller. **2.** A ship's small boat.

yawn (yôn) *v.* **1.** To take a deep inward breath with the mouth open wide, as from fatigue or boredom. **2.** To be wide open : gape <a *yawning* chasm> **—yawn** *n.* **—yawn'er** *n.* **—yawn'ing•ly** *adv.*

yawp *also* **yaup** (yôp) *v.* **1.** To utter a harsh cry : yelp. **2.** *Slang.* To talk loudly and stupidly. **—yawp** *n.* **—yawp'er** *n.*

yaws (yôz) *pl.n.* An infectious epidemic tropical skin disease marked by multiple pimples or pustules.

y-ax·is (wī'ăk'sĭs) *n.* The vertical axis of a graph or chart.

Yb *symbol for* YTTERBIUM.

Y-chro·mo·some (wī'krō'mə-sōm') *n.* The sex chromosome that is associated with male characteristics and occurs with one X-chromosome in the male sex-chromosome pair.

ye[1] (*thē*, yē) *adj. Archaic.* The.

▲ ***word history:*** The word *ye*[1], which is sometimes used in pseudoarchaic phrases such as "ye olde curiosity shoppe," is actually a variant spelling of the definite article *the.* The variant arose from a confusion of the lower-case letter *Y* with the letter þ, called *thorn,* which was used in medieval times to represent the sounds now spelled with *th.* In early printed English books the common manuscript abbreviations *ye* for *the* and *yt* for *that* were retained. The form *ye* as a living word has now died out.

ye[2] (yē) *pron. Archaic.* YOU 1. —Used esp. in literary or religious contexts and in certain dialects of English.

yea (yā) *adv.* **1.** Yes. **2.** Truly : indeed. —*n.* An affirmative vote or voter.

yeah (yĕ'ə, yă'ə, yā'ə) *adv. Informal.* Yes.

year (yîr) *n.* **1.** A period of time in the Gregorian calendar beginning on Jan. 1 and ending on Dec. 31 and consisting of 365 or 366 days. **2.** The period required for the earth to complete a revolution around the sun, consisting of 365 days, 5 hr, 49 min, and 12 sec. **3.** A period of time that is usu. shorter than but does not correspond to the calendar year <the academic *year*> **4. years.** Age <young in *years*> **5. years.** A long time <died *years* ago>

year·book (yîr'bo͝ok') *n.* **1.** A book published every year, esp. as a summary or report of facts. **2.** A book published as a record of the members and activities of the graduating class of a school.

year·ling (yîr'lĭng) *n.* An animal that is one year old or has not yet completed its second year. —*adj.* Being one year old.

year·long (yîr'lông', -lŏng') *adj.* Continuing through a year.

year·ly (yîr'lē) *adv.* Once every year : annually. —*adj.* Occurring once every year : annual. **—year'ly** *n.*

yearn (yûrn) *v.* **1.** To feel a strong desire or craving : long <*yearn* for solitude> **2.** To feel sympathy, pity, or tenderness.

yearn·ing (yûr'nĭng) *n.* A strong or tender longing.

year-round (yîr'round') *adj.* Existing, operating, or used throughout the year.

yeast (yēst) *n.* **1.** Any of various unicellular fungi of the genus *Saccharomyces* and related genera, reproducing by budding and capable of fermenting carbohydrates. **2.** A froth produced by and containing yeast cells that is present in or added to sugary substances, as fruit juices, in the making of alcoholic beverages. **3.** A commercial preparation in powdered or compressed form that contains yeast cells and is used esp. as a leavening agent. **4.** A cause of ferment or activity.

yeast·y (yē'stē) *adj.* **-i·er, -i·est. 1.** Of, relating to, or similar to yeast. **2.** Marked by ferment or agitation : unsettled. **3.** Full of unrestrained enthusiasm : exuberant. **4.** Frothy : frivolous. **—yeast'i·ness** *n.*

yegg (yĕg) *n. Slang.* A safecracker.

yell (yĕl) *v.* To scream or cry out loudly, as in fright or surprise : shout. —*n.* **1.** A loud cry : shout. **2.** A rhythmic cheer used esp. to show support for an athletic team, as at a college football game.

yel·low (yĕl'ō) *n.* **1.** The color of dandelions or ripe lemons. **2.** Something of the color yellow, as the yolk of an egg. **3. yellows.** Any of several plant diseases caused by viruses and marked by yellow discoloration of the foliage. —*adj.* **1.** Of the color yellow. **2.** Having a somewhat yellow skin or complexion. **3.** *Slang.* Cowardly. **4.** Featuring scandalous or sensational news items to attract or hold readers. —*v.* To make or become yellow. **—yel'low·ish** *adj.*

yel·low-bel·lied (yĕl'ō-bĕl'ēd) *adj. Slang.* Cowardly.

yellow birch *n.* A North American tree, *Betula lutea,* with yellowish bark and hard light-colored wood used for furniture.

yellow fever *n.* An acute infectious viral disease of warm regions that is transmitted by a mosquito and marked by fever, jaundice, and often hemorrhaging.

yellow jack *n.* **1.** Yellow fever. **2.** A yellow flag hoisted on a quarantined ship to warn of disease.

yellow jacket *n.* Any of several small wasps of the family Vespidae with yellow and black markings.

yelp (yĕlp) *v.* To utter a sharp, short, shrill cry or bark. **—yelp** *n.*

yen[1] (yĕn) *v. Informal.* A longing : yearning. **—yen** *v.*

yen[2] (yĕn) *n., pl.* **yen.** —See table at CURRENCY.

yen·ta (yĕn'tə) *n. Slang.* A prying, gossipy woman : busybody.

yeo·man (yō'mən) *n.* **1.** An independent farmer, esp. a member of a former class of English freeholding farmers ranking below the gentry. **2.** An officer or attendant in a noble or royal household. **3.** A petty officer who performs clerical duties.

yeo·man·ry (yō'mən-rē) *n.* The class of yeomen, esp. independent farmers.

yes (yĕs) *adv.* —Used to express affirmation, agreement, or consent, to contradict a preceding negative statement, or to introduce a more precise or emphatic statement. —*n., pl.* **yes·es. 1.** An affirmative or consenting reply. **2.** An affirmative vote or voter.

ye·shi·va *or* **ye·shi·vah** (yə-shē'və) *n.* **1.** A school for the study of the Talmud. **2.** A Jewish day school that offers instruction in both religious and secular subjects.

yes man *n. Informal.* A toady.

yes·ter·day (yĕs′tər-dā′, -dē) *n.* **1.** The day before today. **2.** Time in the recent past. —*adv.* **1.** On the day before today. **2.** Just a short while ago.

yes·ter·year (yĕs′tər-yîr′) *n.* **1.** Last year. **2.** Time in the recent past.

yet (yĕt) *adv.* **1.** At this time : now <not time to eat *yet*> **2.** Up to now : thus far <hasn't arrived *yet*> **3.** As previously : still <is *yet* a young man> **4.** In addition : besides <made *yet* another mistake> **5.** Even <a *yet* more beautiful house> **6.** Nevertheless <poor *yet* happy> **7.** At a future time : eventually <may *yet* come to understand> —*conj.* Nevertheless : but.

yet·i (yĕt′ē) *n.* The abominable snowman.

yew (yo͞o) *n.* Any of several evergreen trees or shrubs of the genus *Taxus,* with poisonous flat, dark-green needles, often poisonous scarlet berries, and fine-grained wood used esp. in cabinetmaking.

Yid·dish (yĭd′ĭsh) *n.* A language derived from German and Hebrew and spoken by Jews, esp. in E Europe. —**Yid′dish** *adj.*

yield (yēld) *v.* **1.** To bring forth by a natural process : bear. **2.** To produce as gain or profit : return <bonds *yielding* 11%> **3.** To give up possession of : relinquish. **4.** To grant to another : concede <had to *yield* the right of way> **5.** To give way, as to force or persuasion : submit. **6.** To defer to the superiority of someone else. ★ ***syns:*** BOW, CAPITULATE, FOLD, SUBMIT, SUCCUMB, SURRENDER —*n.* An amount yielded or obtained.

yield·ing (yēl′dĭng) *adj.* **1.** Giving way readily to pressure : flexible. **2.** Docile.

yip (yĭp) *n.* A sharp, quick high-pitched bark. —**yip** *v.*

yipe (yīp) *also* **yipes** (yīps) *interj.* —Used to express surprise, fear, or dismay.

yo·del (yōd′l) *v.* **-deled, -del·ing** *or* **-delled, -del·ling. 1.** To sing so that the voice alternates between chest voice and falsetto. **2.** To sing, call, or shout by yodeling. —**yo′del** *n.* —**yo′del·er** *n.*

yo·ga (yō′gə) *n.* **1.** *often* **Yoga.** A system of Hindu philosophy teaching control of the body and mind as a means of achieving spiritual insight and tranquillity. **2.** A system of exercises for promoting control of the body and mind.

yo·gi (yō′gē) *n., pl.* **-gis.** Someone who practices yoga.

yo·gurt *also* **yo·ghurt** (yō′gərt) *n.* An acidulous custardlike food made of milk fermented by bacteria.

yoke (yōk) *n.* **1.** A wooden bar with 2 U-shaped pieces that fit around the necks of a pair of draft animals working together. **2.** *pl.* **yoke.** A pair of draft animals coupled with a yoke. **3.** A frame placed across a person's shoulders to carry 2 equal loads one at each end. **4.** A vise or clamp that holds 2 parts together or in position. **5.** A shaped or fitted piece of a garment, esp. at the shoulders. **6.** Something that ties or connects : bond. **7.** Slavery : bondage. —*v.* **yoked, yok·ing. 1.** To join with or as if with a yoke : harness. **2.** To harness a draft animal to. **3.** To join together : bind.

yo·kel (yō′kəl) *n.* An unsophisticated country person : bumpkin.

yolk (yōk) *n.* **1.** The rounded yellow inner mass of nutritive material in the egg of a bird or reptile. **2.** An oily substance found in unprocessed sheep's wool.

▲ ***word history:*** The word *yolk,* meaning "the yellow part of an egg," is descended from Old English *geoloca. Geoloca* is a noun derived from the adjective *geolu,* the ancestor of *yellow. Yolk* and *yellow* are related to many other words such as *glass, gloaming, gleam,* and *gold,* denoting something bright, shining, or yellow-colored.

Yom Kip·pur (yŏm kĭp′ər, yōm′ kĭ-po͝or′) *n.* A Jewish holiday in Sept. or Oct., observed with prayer and fasting for the atonement of sins or wrongdoing.

†**yon** (yŏn) *adj. & adv.* Yonder. —*pron. Regional.* That one or those yonder.

yon·der (yŏn′dər) *adj.* Being at a distance but within sight. —*adv.* In, to, or at that place : over there.

yore (yôr, yōr) *n.* Time long past.

you (yo͞o) *pron.* **1.** The person or persons addressed <I'll do what *you* say.><*You* are naughty children.> **2.** A person in general : one <*You* can't be too careful.>

†**you-all** (yo͞o-ôl′) *also* **y'all** (yôl) *pron. SE U.S.* You. —Used in addressing 2 or more persons or referring to 2 or more persons one of whom is addressed.

you'd (yo͞od). **1.** You had. **2.** You would.

you'll (yo͞ol). **1.** You will. **2.** You shall.

young (yŭng) *adj.* **1.** Being in the first or an early period of growth, life, or development. **2.** Having qualities associated with youth : youthful. **3.** Lacking experience. **4.** Recently begun or formed : new. —*n., pl.* **young. 1.** Young persons : youth. **2.** Offspring, esp. of animals. —**young′ish** *adj.* —**young′ness** *n.* —**young′ster** *n.*

young·ling (yŭng′lĭng) *n.* A young person, plant, or animal.

your (yo͝or, yôr, yōr) *adj.* Of or relating to you or yourself.

you're (yo͝or). You are.

yours (yo͝orz, yôrz, yōrz) *pron.* That or those belonging to you.

your·self (yo͝or-sĕlf′, yôr-, yōr-, yər-) *pron., pl.* **-selves** (-sĕlvz′). That one identical with you. —Used: **a.** Reflexively <Don't exert *yourself.*><Are you mumbling to *yourself!*> **b.** For emphasis <You should solve the problem *yourself.*>

youth (yo͞oth) *n., pl.* **youths** (yo͞oths, yo͞o*thz*). **1.** The quality or state of being young. **2.** The time of life between childhood and adulthood. **3. a.** A young person, esp. a young man. **b.** Young people. **4.** The quality or state of being youthful.

youth·ful (yo͞oth′fəl) *adj.* **1.** Being still young. **2.** Of, pertaining to, or characteristic of youth. **3.** Having the freshness and energy typical of the young : vigorous. —**youth′ful·ly** *adv.* —**youth′ful·ness** *n.*
you've (yo͞ov). You have.
yowl (youl) *v.* To utter a long, loud, mournful howl or wail. —**yowl** *n.*
yo-yo (yō′yō) *n., pl.* **-yos.** A grooved spool wound around its center with string that is made to spin down from and reel up to the hand by winding and unwinding the string.
yt·ter·bi·um (ĭ-tûr′bē-əm) *n. Symbol* **Yb** A soft bright silvery rare-earth element.
yt·tri·um (ĭt′rē-əm) *n. Symbol* **Y** A silvery metallic element.
yu·an (yo͞o′än′) *n., pl.* **-an** *or* **-ans.** —See table at CURRENCY.
yuc·ca (yŭk′ə) *n.* Any of various chiefly tropical New World plants of the genus *Yucca* with stiff, pointed leaves and a terminal cluster of white flowers.
yuck (yŭk) *interj. Slang.* Used to express rejection or strong disgust. —**yuck′y** *adj.*
Yule *or* **yule** (yo͞ol) *n.* Christmas.

▲ ***word history:*** The word *Yule, gēol* in Old English, was orig. the name of a pagan Germanic religious festival held in midwinter. After the English were converted to Christianity, the name *Yule* was used for the feast of Christmas. The use of native words for Christian terms was encouraged in the Anglo-Saxon church; another example is the use of the name *Easter* for the feast of Jesus's Resurrection.

Yule log *n.* A large log used for the foundation of the traditional Christmas Eve fire.
Yule·tide *or* **yule·tide** (yo͞ol′tīd′) *n.* The Christmas season.
yum·my (yŭm′ē) *adj.* **-mi·er, -mi·est.** *Slang.* Delicious : delectable.
yup·pie (yŭp′ē) *n. Informal.* A young, affluent, usu. city-dwelling professional.
yurt (yûrt) *n.* A circular domed tent used by nomadic tribes of Siberia.

yurt

Zz

z *or* **Z** (zē) *n., pl.* **z's** *or* **Z's. 1.** The 26th letter of the English alphabet. **2.** A speech sound represented by the letter *z.* **3.** Something with the shape of the letter Z.
zaf·tig *or* **zof·tig** (zäf′tĭk, -tĭg) *adj. Slang.* **1.** Full-bosomed. **2.** Comfortably and pleasingly plump.
zai·bat·su (zī′bät′so͞o) *n., pl.* **zaibatsu.** A powerful family-controlled commercial combine of Japan.
zaire (zīr, zä-îr′) *n.* —See table at CURRENCY.
za·ny (zā′nē) *n., pl.* **-nies. 1.** A buffoon : clown. **2.** A person given to silly or foolish behavior. —*adj.* **-ni·er, -ni·est. 1.** Of or typical of a zany : clownish. **2.** Outlandishly ludicrous : absurd. —**za′ni·ly** *adv.* —**za′ni·ness** *n.*
zap (zăp) *v.* **zapped, zap·ping.** *Slang.* **1.** To destroy or kill with or as if with a burst of gunfire or electric current. **2.** To expose to radiation. —**zap′per** *n.*
z-ax·is (zē′ăk′sĭs) *n., pl.* **z-ax·es** (-sēz). *Math.* One of 3 axes in a 3-dimensional coordinate system.
za·zen (zä′zĕn′) *n.* Meditation as practiced in Zen Buddhism.
zeal (zēl) *n.* Enthusiastic and intensive interest, as in a cause or ideal : ardor.
zeal·ot (zĕl′ət) *n.* A zealous person, esp. a fanatical adherent of a cause.
zeal·ous (zĕl′əs) *adj.* Filled with, marked by, or motivated by zeal. —**zeal′ous·ly** *adv.* —**zeal′ous·ness** *n.*
ze·bra (zē′brə) *n.* Any of several horselike African mammals of the genus *Equus,* having conspicuous black or brown stripes on a whitish body.
ze·bu (zē′byo͞o, -bo͞o) *n.* A domesticated bovine mammal, *Bos indicus,* of Asia and Africa, having a prominent hump on the shoulders and a large dewlap.

zebu

Zech·a·ri·ah (zĕk′ə-rī′ə) *n.* —See table at BIBLE.
zed (zĕd) *n. esp. Brit.* The letter *z.*
Zeit·geist (tsīt′gīst′) *n.* The moral and intellectual atmosphere characteristic of an epoch or age : spirit of the times.
Zen (zĕn) *n.* A Japanese form of Buddhism reaching enlightenment through meditation, contemplation, and intuition.
ze·nith (zē′nĭth) *n.* **1.** The point in the sky that is directly overhead. **2.** The highest point : apex : climax.
ze·o·lite (zē′ə-līt′) *n.* Any of a group of hydrous aluminum silicate minerals or their corresponding synthetic compounds, used esp. as molecular filters and ion-exchange agents.
Zeph·a·ni·ah (zĕf′ə-nī′ə) *n.* —See table at BIBLE.
zeph·yr (zĕf′ər) *n.* **1.** A gentle breeze. **2.** A light, soft fabric, yarn, or garment.
zep·pe·lin (zĕp′ə-lĭn) *n.* A rigid dirigible with a long, cylindrical frame supported by internal gas cells.
ze·ro (zîr′ō, zē′rō) *n., pl.* **-ros** *or* **-roes. 1.** The numerical symbol "0" : cipher. **2.** The cardinal number indicating the absence of quantity. **3. a.** The point, as on a thermometer, from which measurements or degrees are reckoned. **b.** The temperature indicated by the numeral 0 on a thermometer. **4.** One that is unimportant : nonentity. **5.** The lowest point. —*adj.* **1.** Of, pertaining to, or being a zero. **2. a.** Without measurable or determinable value. **b.** Lacking : absent. —*v.* **-roed, -ro·ing.** To point at, aim at, or close in on something.

▲ ***word history:*** The word *zero,* "the numeral 0," is not only synonymous with the word *cipher* but is descended from the same Arabic source. The Arabic word *ṣifr* meant "empty" as well as "zero." *Zero* comes from the Italian form of *ṣifr, zefiro,* but *cipher* came into English through Medieval Latin *cifra.* Although *zero* was borrowed as a synonym of *cipher,* the two words have diverged in meaning. *Cipher* has developed the sense of "a code," whereas *zero* is used primarily as the name of the numeral, esp. in scientific use.

ze·ro-base (zîr′ō-bās′, zē′rō-) *or* **ze·ro-based** (-bāst′) *adj.* Having each expenditure or item justified as to need or cost.
zero hour *n.* The scheduled time for an action or operation to start.
zero population growth *n.* A rate of population increase limited to the number needed to replace the existing population.
ze·ro-sum game (zîr′ō-sŭm′, zē′rō-) *n.* A situation in which a gain by one person or side must be matched by a loss by another person or side.
zest (zĕst) *n.* **1.** An invigorating or keen quality : piquancy. **2.** Spirited enjoyment : relish. **3.** The outermost part of an orange or lemon rind, used as flavoring. —**zest′ful** *adj.* —**zest′ful·ly** *adv.* —**zest′y** *adj.*
zig·zag (zĭg′zăg′) *n.* **1. a.** A series of sharp turns in alternating directions. **b.** One of such a series. **2.** Something, as a pattern, marked by zigzags. —*adj.* Shaped like or forming a zigzag. —*adv.* In a zigzag path, course, or pattern. —**zig′zag′** *v.*
zilch (zĭlch) *n. Slang.* Zero : nothing.
zil·lion (zĭl′yən) *n. Informal.* An extremely large but unspecified number.
zinc (zĭngk) *n. Symbol* **Zn** A shiny bluish-white metallic element used to make a wide variety of alloys and to galvanize metals, as iron. —*v.* **zinced, zinc·ing** *or* **zincked, zinck·ing.** To coat with zinc : galvanize.
zinc ointment *n.* A salve containing approx. 20% zinc oxide, used in the treatment of skin disorders.
zinc oxide *n.* A white or yellowish powdery compound that is used as a pigment and in ointments and cosmetics.
zin·fan·del (zĭn′fən-dĕl′) *n.* A dry red wine produced in California.
zing (zĭng) *n.* **1.** A high-pitched humming sound. **2.** Vigor : vivacity. —**zing** *v.*
zing·er (zĭng′ər) *n. Informal.* A witty, often caustic remark.
zin·ni·a (zĭn′ē-ə) *n.* An American plant, *Zinnia elegans,* cultivated for its showy, colorful flowers.
Zi·on (zī′ən) *n.* **1. a.** The Jewish people. **b.** The Jewish homeland as a symbol of Judaism. **2.** The city of God : heaven. **3.** Utopia.
Zi·on·ism (zī′ə-nĭz′əm) *n.* A movement orig. for establishing a Jewish national homeland and state in Palestine, now concerned with the support of Israel. —**Zi′on·ist** *n.* —**Zi′on·is′tic** *adj.*
zip (zĭp) *n.* **1.** A short sharp hissing sound. **2.** *Informal.* Vim : energy. **3.** *Slang.* Zero : nothing. —*v.* **zipped, zip·ping. 1.** To act or move with facility, energy, or speed. **2.** To fasten or unfasten with a zipper.
Zip Code *also* **zip code** *or* **ZIP Code.** A trademark for a system to expedite the delivery of mail by assigning a 5-digit number to each postal delivery area in the U.S.
zip·per (zĭp′ər) *n.* A fastener that consists of 2 strips of tape each with a row of metal or plastic teeth that are interlocked by means of a sliding tab.
zip·py (zĭp′ē) *adj.* **-pi·er, -pi·est.** Full of energy : brisk : lively.
zir·con (zûr′kŏn′) *n.* A brown to colorless mineral, the transparent form of which is polished to form a gem.
zir·co·ni·um (zər-kō′nē-əm) *n. Symbol* **Zr** A shiny strong ductile metallic element used esp. in ceramics and alloys.
zit (zĭt) *n. Slang.* A pimple.
zith·er (zĭth′ər, zĭ*th*′-) *n.* A musical instrument with 30 to 40 strings played with the fingertips or a plectrum.
zi·ti (zē′tē) *n., pl.* **ziti.** Medium-sized tubular pasta.
zlo·ty (zlô′tē) *n., pl.* **-ty** *or* **-tys.** —See table at CURRENCY.
Zn *symbol for* ZINC.
zo·di·ac (zō′dē-ăk′) *n.* **1. a.** A band of the ce-

lestial sphere that extends approx. 8° on both sides of the ecliptic and encompasses the apparent paths of the principal planets, the moon, and the sun. **b.** This band divided into 12 astrological signs, each bearing the name of a constellation. **2.** A figure or diagram representing the zodiac. **—zo·di'a·cal** (-dī'ə-kəl) *adj.*

zof·tig (zäf'tĭk, -tĭg) *adj. var. of* ZAFTIG.

zom·bie *also* **zom·bi** (zŏm'bē) *n., pl.* **-bies** *also* **-bis. 1.a.** A snake god of voodoo cults. **b.** A supernatural power that according to voodoo belief enters into and reanimates a corpse. **2.** A person who is thought to look or behave like a reanimated corpse.

zon·al (zō'nəl) *also* **zo·na·ry** (-nə-rē) *adj.* **1.** Of or pertaining to a zone. **2.** Divided into zones. **—zon'al·ly** *adv.*

zone (zōn) *n.* **1.** A region or area distinguished or set apart from adjacent or surrounding parts by some feature or characteristic. **2.** A section of an area established for a specific purpose <a residential *zone*> **3.** *Archaic.* A belt or girdle. —*v.* **zoned, zon·ing.** To divide, mark off, or designate into zones. **—zo·na'tion** *n.*

zonk (zôngk, zŏngk) *v. Slang.* **1.** To stupefy : stun. **2.** To intoxicate or render senseless with drugs or alcohol.

zoo (zo͞o) *n., pl.* **zoos. 1.** A public park or large enclosure where animals are kept for public display. **2.** Something characterized by rampant confusion or disorder.

zo·o·ge·og·ra·phy (zō'ə-jē-ŏg'rə-fē) *n.* Study of the geographic distribution of animals. **—zo'o·ge·og'ra·pher** *n.* **—zo'o·ge'o·graph'ic, zo'o·ge'o·graph'i·cal** *adj.*

zoological garden *n.* ZOO 1.

zo·ol·o·gy (zō-ŏl'ə-jē) *n.* The biological science that deals with animals, animal life, and the animal kingdom. **—zo'o·log'i·cal** (-ə-lŏg'ĭ-kəl) *adj.* **—zo·ol'o·gist** *n.*

zoom (zo͞om) *v.* **1.** To make or move with a continuous loud buzzing sound. **2.** To climb suddenly and sharply in an airplane. **3.** To move upward sharply <Expenses *zoomed.*> **4.** To move quickly toward or away from a photographic subject while keeping the subject in focus. **—zoom** *n.*

zoom lens *n.* A camera lens whose focal length can be rapidly changed to permit continuous change in the size of the image without loss of focus.

zo·o·mor·phism (zō'ə-môr'fĭz'əm) *n.* **1.** The attribution of the form, characteristics, or qualities of an animal to a deity. **2.** The use of animal forms in graphic representation. **—zo'o·mor'phic** *adj.*

zo·o·phyte (zō'ə-fīt') *n.* An invertebrate animal, such as a sea anemone or sponge, that remains attached to a surface and superficially resembles a plant. **—zo'o·phyt'ic** (-fĭt'ĭk) *adj.*

zo·o·plank·ton (zō'ə-plăngk'tən) *n.* Plankton that consists of usu. microscopic animals.

zo·o·spore (zō'ə-spôr', -spōr') *n.* A motile asexual spore.

zo·ri (zôr'ē, zōr'ē) *n., pl.* **zori.** A flat Japanese sandal held by means of a thong passing between the big toe and the second toe.

Zo·ro·as·tri·an·ism (zôr'ō-ăs'trē-ə-nĭz'əm) *n.* The religion founded by Zoroaster. **—Zo'ro·as'tri·an** *n. & adj.*

Zou·ave (zo͞o-äv') *n.* A member of a French infantry unit, formerly composed of Algerian recruits, noted for their colorful oriental uniforms and precision drilling.

zounds (zoundz) *interj.* —Used to express surprise, anger, or indignation.

zoy·si·a (zoi'sē-ə, -zē-ə) *n.* A creeping grass of the genus *Zoysia* used as a lawn grass.

Zr *symbol for* ZIRCONIUM.

zuc·chet·to (zo͞o-kĕt'ō, tso͞o-) *n., pl.* **-tos.** *Rom. Cath. Ch.* A small skullcap worn by ecclesiastics.

zuc·chi·ni (zo͞o-kē'nē) *n., pl.* **-ni.** A type of summer squash that is long and narrow in shape and has a dark-green rind.

Zu·lu (zo͞o'lo͞o) *n., pl.* **-lu** *or* **-lus. 1.** A member of a people of SE Africa. **2.** The Bantu language of the Zulu. **—Zu'lu** *adj.*

Zu·ni (zo͞o'nē) *also* **Zu·ñi** (-nyē, -nē) *n., pl.* **-ni** *or* **-nis** *also* **-ñi** *or* **-ñis. 1.** A member of a Pueblo people of W New Mexico. **2.** The language of the Zuni.

zwie·back (swē'băk', swī'-, zwē'-, zwī'-) *n.* A usu. sweetened egg bread baked and then sliced and toasted.

zy·de·co (zī'dĭ-kō') *n.* Popular music of S Louisiana featuring the guitar, the accordion, and a washboard.

zy·go·mat·ic bone (zī'gə-măt'ĭk) *n.* The cheekbone.

zy·go·sis (zī-gō'sĭs, zĭ-) *n., pl.* **-ses** (-sēz). The union of gametes to form a zygote.

zy·gote (zī'gōt') *n.* A cell formed by the union of 2 gametes. **—zy·got'ic** (-gŏt'ĭk) *adj.* **—zy·got'i·cal·ly** *adv.*

zy·mur·gy (zī'mûr-jē) *n.* Technological chemistry that deals with fermentation processes, as in brewing.

Abbreviations

a *also* **a.** are (measurement).

A 1. *also* **a.** *or* **A.** acre. **2.** ampere. **3.** area.

Å angstrom.

AA Alcoholics Anonymous.

A.A. Associate in Arts.

AB Alberta.

A.B. 1. *or* **a.b.** able-bodied seaman. **2.** *Lat.* Artium Baccalaureus (Bachelor of Arts).

ac 1. acre. **2.** *or* **AC** alternating current.

a.c. *or* **a/c** air conditioning.

A.C. *Lat.* ante Christum (before Christ).

a/c account; account current.

acct. account; accountant.

acpt. acceptance.

acv actual cash value.

A.D. *Lat.* anno Domini (in the year of the Lord). —Usu. used in small capitals <A.D.>

ad int. *Lat.* ad interim (in the meantime).

ad loc. *Lat.* ad locum (to *or* at the place).

ADP automatic data processing.

AEC Atomic Energy Commission.

AF *also* **A.F. 1.** air force. **2.** audio frequency.

AFB air force base.

AFDC Aid to Families with Dependent Children.

AFL-CIO American Federation of Labor and Congress of Industrial Organizations.

A.G. *also* **AG** attorney general.

AI artificial intelligence.

AK *or* **Alas.** Alaska.

a.k.a. also known as.

AL *or* **Ala.** Alabama.

Alta. Alberta.

am *or* **AM** amplitude modulation.

A.M. *also* **a.m.** *Lat.* ante meridiem (before noon). —Usu. used in small capitals <A.M.>

Amex American Stock Exchange.

anon. anonymous.

AP *or* **A.P.** Associated Press.

ap. apothecary.

A/P accounts payable.

APB all points bulletin.

APO *or* **A.P.O.** Army Post Office.

APR annual percentage rate.

AR 1. *also* **A/R** accounts receivable. **2.** Arkansas.

ARC American Red Cross.

Ariz. Arizona.

Ark. Arkansas.

a/s air speed.

ASAP as soon as possible.

ASE American Stock Exchange.

ASL American Sign Language.

assoc. associate; association.

ASSR *or* **A.S.S.R.** Autonomous Soviet Socialist Republic.

asst. assistant.

atm *Physics.* atmosphere.

atm. *or* **atmos.** atmosphere; atmospheric.

at. no. *also* **at no** atomic number.

at wt atomic weight.

a.u. *or* **A.u.** angstrom unit.

A.U. astronomical unit.

AV *or* **A.V. 1.** atrioventricular. **2.** audiovisual. **3.** *Bible.* Authorized Version.

av. 1. *or* **Av.** avenue. **2.** avoirdupois.

a.v. *or* **a/v** *Lat.* ad valorem (in proportion to the value).

av. *or* **avdp.** avoirdupois.

ave. *or* **Ave.** avenue.

AWAC airborne warning and control system.

AYH American Youth Hostels.

AZ Arizona.

b. born.

B.A. 1. *Lat.* Baccalaureus Artium (Bachelor of Arts). **2.** British Academy.

BAC blood alcohol concentration.

B and E breaking and entering.

bar. 1. barometer; barometric. **2.** barrel.

bb *also* **b.b.** ball bearing.

bbl *or* **bbl.** barrel.

B.C. 1 before Christ. —Usu. used in small capitals <B.C.> **2.** *or* **BC** British Columbia.

B.C.E. before the Common Era. —Often used in small capitals <B.C.E.>

BCG bacillus Calmette-Guérin (tuberculosis vaccine).

b/d 1. barrels per day. **2.** brought down.

bd. ft. board foot.

BE Board of Education.

B/E 1. bill of entry. **2.** bill of exchange.

Bé Baumé scale.

BeV *Physics.* billion electron volts.

bf board foot.

b.f. *or* **B/F** brought forward.

BH bill of health.

BHT butylated hydroxytoluene.

BIA Bureau of Indian Affairs.

B/L bill of lading.

bldg. building.

BLS Bureau of Labor Statistics.

blvd. boulevard.

BM basal metabolism.

b.m. 1. board measure. **2.** bowel movement.

BMR basal metabolic rate.

B.O.D. biochemical oxygen demand.

bor. borough.

boul. boulevard.

bp boiling point.

BP blood pressure.

bpi *Computer Sci.* bits per inch; bytes per inch.

bps *Computer Sci.* bits per second.

B/R bills receivable.

bro. brother.

bros. brothers.

B.S. Bachelor of Science.

BSA Boy Scouts of America.

bsh. bushel.

Btu British thermal unit.
bu. 1. bureau. 2. *or* **bu** bushel.
BW 1. biological warfare. 2. *also* **b/w** black and white.
BYO bring your own.

C 1. Celsius. 2. centigrade.
c. *or* **C.** 1. century. 2. chapter. 3. circa. 4. copyright.
ca 1. centare. 2. circa.
CA California.
C.A. *or* **c.a.** chartered accountant.
c/a current account.
CAA Civil Aeronautics Authority.
CAB Civil Aeronautics Board.
C.A.F. cost and freight.
CAI computer-aided instruction.
cal calorie (small).
Cal calorie (large).
Cal. *or* **Calif.** California.
Can. *also* **Canad.** Canada; Canadian.
C & W country and western.
cap. 1. capacity. 2. capital (city). 3. capital letter.
car. carat.
CARE Cooperative for American Relief to Everywhere.
CAT 1. clear-air turbulence. 2. computerized axial tomography.
CATV community antenna television.
CB *or* **C.B.** citizens band.
C.B.D. cash before delivery.
CBW chemical and biological warfare.
cc 1. carbon copy. 2. cubic centimeter.
cc. chapters.
CCC 1. Civilian Conservation Corps. 2. Commodity Credit Corporation.
CCTV closed circuit television.
CCU coronary care unit.
ccw. counterclockwise.
CD 1. *also* **C/D** certificate of deposit 2. *also* **C.D.** civil defense. 3. compact disk.
c.d. cash discount.
CDC Centers for Disease Control and Prevention.
CDT *or* **C.D.T.** Central Daylight Time.
C.E. 1. chemical engineer. 2. civil engineer. 3. Common Era.
cent. 1. *Lat.* centum (hundred). 2. century.
CEO *also* **C.E.O.** chief executive officer.
cert. certificate; certification; certified.
CF cystic fibrosis.
cf. *Lat.* confer (compare).
c.f. *or* **C.F.** cost and freight.
C/F carried forward.
CFA chartered financial analyst.
c.f.i. *or* **C.F.I.** cost, freight, and insurance.
cfm *or* **c.f.m.** cubic feet per minute.
cfs *or* **c.f.s.** cubic feet per second.
cg centigram.
c.g. 1. center of gravity. 2. *or* **C.G.** consul general.
C.G. coast guard.
cgs *or* **CGS** centimeter-gram-second (system of units).
ch chain (measurement).
Ch.E. chemical engineer.
chg. 1. change. 2. charge.
Ci curie.
CI cost and insurance.
CIA Central Intelligence Agency.
CID Criminal Investigation Department.
c.i.f. *or* **C.I.F.** cost, insurance, and freight.
C.J. chief justice.
cl centiliter.
CLU chartered life underwriter.
cm centimeter.
CMA certified medical assistant.
cN centinewton.
C/N credit note.
CNS central nervous system.
CO 1. Colorado. 2. *or* **c.o.** commanding officer. 3. *or* **C.O.** conscientious objector.
co. 1. company. 2. county.
c.o. 1. carried over. 2. cash order.
c/o *also* **c.o.** care of.
COD *or* **C.O.D.** 1. cash on delivery. 2. collect on delivery.
coef. coefficient.
C. of C. chamber of commerce.
C. of E. Church of England.
C. of S. chief of staff.
Col. 1. *or* **COL** colonel. 2. Colorado.
COLA cost-of-living adjustment.
Colo. Colorado.
Cong. 1. Congregational. 2. Congress; Congressional.
Conn. Connecticut.
const. 1. *or* **Const.** constable. 2. constant. 3. *or* **Const.** constitution. 4. construction.
cont. 1. containing. 2. contents. 3. continent. 4. continue; continued. 5. contract.
contd. continued.
coop. cooperative.
CORE Congress of Racial Equality.
corp. corporation.
cos cosine.
COS *or* **C.O.S.** cash on shipment.
cosec cosecant.
cot cotangent.
CP 1. chemically pure. 2. command post. 3. Communist Party.
cp. compare.
CPA certified public accountant.
cpd. compound.
cpi characters per inch.
CPI consumer price index.
cpm 1. copies per minute. 2. cycles per minute.
CPR cardiopulmonary resuscitation.
cps 1. *also* **CPS** characters per second. 2. cycles per second.
CPU central processing unit.
CR *Psychol.* conditioned reflex; conditioned response.
CRT cathode-ray tube.
CS 1. capital stock. 2. conditioned stimulus.
C.S.A. Confederate States of America.
csc cosecant.
CSF cerebrospinal fluid.
CST *or* **C.S.T.** Central Standard Time.
CT 1. *or* **C.T.** Central Time. 2. *or* **Ct.** Connecticut.

ct. 1. cent. 2. certificate. 3. court.
ctf. certificate.
ctg. *or* **ctge.** cartage.
ctn cotangent.
ctn. carton.
cu. *or* **cu** cubic.
CV cardiovascular.
cw. clockwise.
c.w.o. cash with order.
cwt. hundredweight.
CY calendar year.
CZ *or* **C.Z.** Canal Zone.

d. 1. date. 2. died.
DA 1. delayed action. 2. deposit account.
D.A. *also* **DA** district attorney.
dag decagram.
DASD direct access storage device.
dB decibel.
dbl. double.
dc *or* **DC** direct current.
DC *or* **D.C.** District of Columbia.
D.C. *Mus.* da capo.
DCM Distinguished Conduct Medal.
D.D. 1. demand draft. 2. dishonorable discharge. 3. *Lat.* Divinitatis Doctor (Doctor of Divinity).
DDD Direct Distance Dialing.
D.D.S. 1. Doctor of Dental Science. 2. Doctor of Dental Surgery.
DE *or* **Del.** Delaware.
decd. deceased.
deg *or* **deg.** degree.
Dem. Democrat; Democratic.
dept. 1. department. 2. deputy.
Des. desert.
dev. deviation.
DEW distant early warning.
DF direction finder.
DFC Distinguished Flying Cross.
dg decigram.
D.H. Doctor of Humanities.
dia. diameter.
diam. diameter.
DJ disc jockey.
DJIA Dow-Jones Industrial Average.
dkg dekagram.
dkl dekaliter.
dkm dekameter.
dks dekastere.
dl deciliter.
D/L demand loan.
DLO dead letter office.
dm decimeter.
D.M.D. *Lat.* Dentariae Medicinae Doctor (Doctor of Dental Medicine).
DMZ demilitarized zone.
do. ditto.
DOA *Med.* dead on arrival.
DOB date of birth.
DOC Department of Commerce.
DOD Department of Defense.
DOE Department of Energy.
DOS Department of State.
DOT Department of Transportation.
doz. dozen.
DP 1. data processing. 2. dew point. 3. *also* **D.P.** displaced person.
DPH 1. Department of Public Health. 2. *also* **D.P.H.** Doctor of Public Health.
D.Ph. *or* **D.Phil.** Doctor of Philosophy.
dpi dots per inch.
DPT diphtheria, pertussis, tetanus (vaccine).
DPW Department of Public Works.
dr dram.
DR dead reckoning.
Dr. 1. doctor. 2. drive (in street names).
dr ap apothecaries' dram.
dr avdp avoirdupois dram.
dr t troy dram.
d.s. *or* **D.S.** *Mus.* dal segno.
DSC Distinguished Service Cross.
DSM Distinguished Service Medal.
DSO Distinguished Service Order.
DST *or* **D.S.T.** daylight-saving time.
DT 1. *or* **D.T.** daylight time. 2. delirium tremens.
D.V. 1. *Lat.* Deo volente (God willing). 2. *Bible.* Douay Version.
D.V.M. Doctor of Veterinary Medicine.
DWI driving while intoxicated.
dz. dozen.

E *also* **E.** *or* **e** *or* **e.** east.
ea. each.
EbN east by north.
EbS east by south.
EC European Community (Common Market).
E.C. Established Church.
ECG electrocardiogram.
ECM European Common Market.
Ed.M. *Lat.* Educationis Magister (Master of Education).
EDP electronic data processing.
EDT *or* **E.D.T.** Eastern Daylight Time.
e.e. errors excepted.
E.E. electrical engineer.
EEC European Economic Community.
EEG electroencephalogram.
EEO equal employment opportunity.
EFL English as a foreign language.
EFTS electronic funds transfer system.
e.g. *Lat.* exempli gratia (for example).
EHF extremely high frequency.
EHV extra high voltage.
EKG electrocardiogram; electrocardiograph.
ELF extremely low frequency.
emf *or* **EMF** electromotive force.
EMT emergency medical technician.
emu electromagnetic unit.
enc. *or* **encl.** enclosed; enclosure.
ENE east-northeast.
e.o. *Lat.* ex officio (by virtue of office).
e.o.m. end of month.
EP 1. European plan. 2. extended play.
EPA Environmental Protection Agency.
ER emergency room.
ERA 1. *Baseball.* earned run average. 2. Equal Rights Amendment.
ESE east-southeast.
ESL English as a second language.

ESOP employee stock ownership plan.
ESP extrasensory perception.
Esq. Esquire (title).
EST *or* **E.S.T.** Eastern Standard Time.
est. 1. established. 2. *Law.* estate.
ET 1. *or* **E.T.** Eastern Time. 2. elapsed time.
ETA *or* **e.t.a.** estimated time of arrival.
et al. *Lat.* et alii (and others).
etc. *Lat.* et cetera (and so forth).
ETD *or* **e.t.d.** estimated time of departure.
EURATOM European Atomic Energy Community.
eV electron volt.
EVA extravehicular activity.
exp *Math.* exponential.

F Fahrenheit.
f/ relative aperture of a lens.
FAA Federal Aviation Administration.
Fahr. Fahrenheit.
FAO Food and Agriculture Organization.
Far. Faraday.
fath *or* **fath.** fathom.
FBI Federal Bureau of Investigation.
FCA Farm Credit Administration.
FCC Federal Communications Commission.
FD 1. fatal dose. 2. fire department. 3. focal distance.
FDA Food and Drug Administration.
FDIC Federal Deposit Insurance Corporation.
FEP front end processor.
ff *Mus.* fortissimo.
ff. 1. folios. 2. following.
FHA Federal Housing Administration.
FHLBB Federal Home Loan Bank Board.
FICA Federal Insurance Contributions Act.
FIFO first in, first out.
fl fluid.
FL Florida.
fl. 1. *Lat.* floruit (flourished). 2. fluid.
Fla. Florida.
fl dr fluid dram.
Flor. Florida.
fl oz fluid ounce.
FM *or* **fm** frequency modulation.
fm. fathom.
fn. footnote.
FNMA Federal National Mortgage Association.
f.o.b. *also* **F.O.B.** free on board.
fp 1. foot-pound. 2. freezing point.
fpm *or* **f.p.m.** feet per minute.
FPO fleet post office.
fps *or* **f.p.s.** 1. feet per second. 2. frames per second.
FRB Federal Reserve Board.
FRS 1. Federal Reserve System. 2. *or* **F.R.S.** Fellow of the Royal Society.
FSA Federal Security Agency.
FSLIC Federal Savings and Loan Insurance Corporation.
ft foot.
FTC Federal Trade Commission.
fth. fathom.
ft-lb foot-pound.
fur. furlong.
FX foreign exchange.
FY fiscal year.
FYI for your information.

g 1. acceleration of gravity. 2. gram.
ga. gauge.
GA *or* **Ga.** Georgia.
gal. gallon.
GAO General Accounting Office.
GAR Grand Army of the Republic.
GATT General Agreement on Tariffs and Trade.
GAW guaranteed annual wage.
G.B. Great Britain.
gcd *or* **g.c.d.** greatest common divisor.
gcf *or* **g.c.f.** greatest common factor.
GCM Good Conduct Medal.
GCT *or* **G.c.t.** Greenwich civil time.
GED general equivalency diploma.
GHQ general headquarters.
gi gill (liquid measure).
GI 1. gastrointestinal. 2. general issue. 3. *also* **G.I.** Government Issue.
GIGO garbage in, garbage out.
gm gram.
GMT *or* **G.m.t.** Greenwich mean time.
GMW gram-molecular weight.
GNP gross national product.
GO general order.
GOP *or* **G.O.P.** Grand Old Party.
G.P. *or* **GP** general practitioner.
GPA grade-point average.
GPO 1. general post office. 2. Government Printing Office.
GQ general quarters.
GRE Graduate Record Examination.
gro. gross.
gr. wt. gross weight.
GS 1. general staff. 2. ground speed.
GSA 1. General Services Administration. 2. Girl Scouts of America.
GST *or* **G.s.t.** Greenwich sidereal time.
gtd. guaranteed.

hab. corp. habeas corpus.
Hb hemoglobin.
hcf *or* **h.c.f.** highest common factor.
hdqrs. headquarters.
HE high explosive.
hf high frequency.
hgb. hemoglobin.
hgt. height.
HHFA Housing and Home Finance Agency.
HI Hawaii.
H.I. Hawaiian Islands.
HMS *or* **H.M.S.** Her *or* His Majesty's Ship.
Hon. Honorable (title).
HOPE Health Opportunity for People Everywhere.
hp horsepower.
HPF highest possible frequency.
HQ *or* **h.q.** headquarters.
hr hour.
H.R. House of Representatives.

H.R.E. Holy Roman Emperor; Holy Roman Empire.
H.R.H. Her *or* His Royal Highness.
hrs hours.
HS *or* **H.S.** high school.
HST *or* **H.S.T.** Hawaiian Standard Time.
ht height.
HT 1. halftime. 2. halftone. 3. *or* **H.T.** Hawaiian Time. 4. hydrotherapy.
Hts. Heights.
HUD Housing and Urban Development.
HV 1. high velocity. 2. high-voltage.
HW 1. high water. 2. hot water.
HWM high-water mark.
hwy. highway.
hy. henry.
hyp. 1. hypotenuse. 2. hypothesis.
Hz hertz.

IA *or* **Ia.** Iowa.
IAS indicated air speed.
ib. *or* **ibid.** *Lat.* ibidem (in the same place).
ICBM intercontinental ballistic missile.
ICC Interstate Commerce Commission.
ICU intensive care unit.
ID 1. *or* **Id.** Idaho. 2. *also* **I.D.** identification.
id. *Lat.* idem (the same).
IDP integrated data processing.
IE industrial engineer.
i.e. *Lat.* id est (that is).
IF *or* **i.f.** intermediate frequency.
Ig immunoglobulin.
IG *or* **I.G.** inspector general.
ihp *or* **i.hp.** indicated horsepower.
IL *or* **Ill.** Illinois.
ILS instrument landing system.
IMF International Monetary Fund.
in *or* **in.** inch.
IN *or* **Ind.** Indiana.
inc. *also* **Inc.** incorporated.
INS Immigration and Naturalization Service.
intl. international.
inv. invoice.
I/O input/output.
IPA 1. International Phonetic Alphabet. 2. isopropyl alcohol.
ips *or* **i.p.s.** inches per second.
IQ *or* **I.Q.** intelligence quotient.
IR 1. information retrieval. 2. infrared.
IRA 1. Individual Retirement Account. 2. *also* **I.R.A.** Irish Republican Army.
IRBM intermediate range ballistic missile.
IRS Internal Revenue Service.
is. *or* **Is.** *or* **isl.** island.
ISBN International Standard Book Number.
IST insulin shock therapy.
isth. isthmus.
IU international unit.
IUD intrauterine device.
IV intravenous; intravenously.

J 1. current density. 2. joule.
J.C.D. *Lat.* Juris Canonici Doctor (Doctor of Canon Law).
JCL *Computer Sci.* job control language.
JCS *or* **J.C.S.** Joint Chiefs of Staff.
jct. junction.
JD 1. Justice Department. 2. *also* **J.D.** juvenile delinquent.
J.D. *Lat.* Jurum Doctor (Doctor of Laws).
JP *or* **J.P.** justice of the peace.
jr. *or* **Jr.** junior.
J.S.D. *Lat.* Juris Scientiae Doctor (Doctor of Juristic Science).
JV junior varsity.

k *or* **K** karat.
K 1. kelvin (temperature unit). 2. Kelvin (temperature scale). 3. kilobyte.
Kans. Kansas.
KB kilobyte.
kc kilocycle.
kcal kilocalorie.
kcs *or* **kc/s** kilocycles per second.
Ken. Kentucky.
keV kiloelectron volt.
kg kilogram.
kHz kilohertz.
km kilometer.
kmph kilometers per hour.
kmps kilometers per second.
KP kitchen police.
KS Kansas.
kt. karat.
kW kilowatt.
kWh kilowatt-hour.
KY *or* **Ky.** Kentucky.

l *or* **L** liter.
L lambert.
LA *or* **La.** Louisiana.
Lab. Labrador.
lat. latitude.
LB Labrador.
lb. *Lat.* libra (pound).
lc *also* **l.c.** lower case.
LC Library of Congress.
L/C letter of credit.
lcd *or* **l.c.d.** lowest common denominator.
LCD liquid crystal display.
lcm *or* **l.c.m.** least common multiple.
LD 1. learning disability; learning-disabled. 2. *Med.* lethal dose.
lf low frequency.
l.h. *also* **LH** left hand.
LIFO last in, first out.
ll *or* **ll.** lines.
LL.B. *Lat.* Legum Baccalaureus (Bachelor of Laws).
LL.D. *Lat.* Legum Doctor (Doctor of Laws).
LL.M. *Lat.* Legum Magister (Master of Laws).
lm lumen.
LM lunar module.
ln Napierian logarithm; natural logarithm.
LNG liquefied natural gas.
loc. cit. *Lat.* loco citato (in the place cited).
long. longitude.
LPG liquefied petroleum gas.
LPN *or* **L.P.N.** licensed practical nurse.

LSAT Law School Admissions Test.
LSD least significant digit.
l.t. *or* **LT** local time.
ltd. *or* **Ltd.** limited.
LW low water.
LWM low-water mark.

m 1. *Physics.* mass. 2. meter (measure).
M. Monsieur.
mA milliampere.
MA *or* **Mass.** Massachusetts.
M.A. *Lat.* Magister Artium (Master of Arts).
Man. Manitoba.
MAP modified American plan.
MASH Mobile Army Surgical Hospital.
max. maximum.
MB 1. Manitoba. 2. megabyte.
M.B.A. Master of Business Administration.
mc millicurie.
Mc megacycle.
MC 1. Marine Corps. 2. Medical Corps.
M.C. *or* **m.c.** master of ceremonies.
mcf thousand cubic feet.
MD or **Md.** Maryland.
M.D. *Lat.* Medicinae Doctor (Doctor of Medicine).
Mdm. Madam.
M.D.S. Master of Dental Surgery.
mdse. merchandise.
ME *or* **Me.** Maine.
M.E. 1. mechanical engineer. 2. medical examiner.
M.Ed. Master of Education.
mf medium frequency.
mF millifarad.
m.f. *Mus.* mezzo-forte.
M.F.A. Master of Fine Arts.
mfd. manufactured.
mfg. manufacture; manufactured; manufacturing.
MFN most-favored nation.
mfr. manufacture; manufacturer.
mg milligram.
mH millihenry.
MH 1. Medal of Honor. 2. mental health.
MHW mean high water.
MHz megahertz.
MI 1. Michigan. 2. military intelligence.
mi. mile.
MIA missing in action.
Mich. Michigan.
min. *or* **min** minute.
Minn. Minnesota.
misc. miscellaneous.
Miss. Mississippi.
mks meter-kilogram-second (system of units).
ml milliliter.
Mlle. Mademoiselle.
Mlles. Mesdemoiselles.
M.L.S. Master of Library Science.
MLW mean low water.
mm millimeter.
MM. Messieurs.
Mme. Madame.
Mmes. Mesdames.
MN 1. magnetic north. 2. Minnesota.
MO *or* **Mo.** Missouri.
mo. month.
m.o. *or* **M.O.** 1. mail order. 2. modus operandi 3. *also* **MO** money order.
mol wt molecular weight.
Mont. Montana.
mos. months.
mp *or* **m.p.** 1. melting point. 2. *Mus.* mezzo-piano.
MP *or* **M.P.** military police.
M.P. Member of Parliament.
mpg *or* **m.p.g.** miles per gallon.
mph *or* **m.p.h.** miles per hour.
Mr. Mister.
MRI magnetic resonance imaging.
ms *or* **msec** millisecond.
MS 1. Mississippi. 2. multiple sclerosis.
ms. *or* **MS.** *or* **ms** manuscript.
M.S. *or* **M.Sc.** *Lat.* Magister Scientiae (Master of Science).
MSG monosodium glutamate.
Msgr. Monseigneur; Monsignor.
mss. *or* **MSS.** *or* **mss** manuscripts.
MST *or* **M.S.T.** Mountain Standard Time.
MT 1. Montana. 2. *or* **M.T.** Mountain Time.
m.t. *or* **M.T.** metric ton.
mV millivolt.
MVP most valuable player.
mW milliwatt.
MW megawatt.

N *also* **N.** *or* **n** *or* **n.** north.
N.A. 1. not applicable. 2. not available.
NAACP National Association for the Advancement of Colored People.
NASA National Aeronautics and Space Administration.
NASDAQ National Association of Securities Dealers Automated Quotations.
natl. national.
NATO North Atlantic Treaty Organization.
NB 1. narrow band. 2. *or* **N.B.** New Brunswick.
n.b. *or* **N.B.** *Lat.* nota bene (note well).
NbE north by east.
NBS National Bureau of Standards.
NbW north by west.
NC 1. no charge. 2. *or* **N.C.** North Carolina.
NCAA National Collegiate Athletic Association.
NCO *or* **N.C.O.** noncommissioned officer.
NCV no commercial value.
ND *or* **N.D.** *or* **N.Dak.** North Dakota.
n.d. *or* **N.D.** no date.
NE 1. *or* **Nebr.** Nebraska. 2. northeast.
NET National Educational Television.
NF *or* **Newf.** *or* **Nfld.** Newfoundland.
n/f no funds.
NG *also* **N.G.** 1. National Guard. 2. no good.
NH *or* **N.H.** New Hampshire.
NIH National Institutes of Health.
NJ *or* **N.J.** New Jersey.
NLRB National Labor Relations Board.
nm 1. nanometer. 2. *or* **n.m.** nautical mile.
NM *or* **N.M.** *or* **N.Mex.** New Mexico.

NMR nuclear magnetic resonance.
NNE north-northeast.
NNW north-northwest.
no. *or* **No. 1.** north; northern. **2.** number.
nos. *or* **Nos.** numbers.
N.P. 1. notary public. **2.** nurse practitioner.
n.p.t. normal pressure and temperature.
NRC 1. National Research Council. **2.** Nuclear Regulatory Commission.
ns *or* **nsec** nanosecond.
NS *or* **N.S.** Nova Scotia.
n/s not sufficient.
NSC National Security Council.
NSE National Stock Exchange.
n.s.f. *or* **N.S.F.** not sufficient funds.
n.t.p. normal temperature and pressure.
nt. wt. *or* **n.wt.** net weight.
NV *or* **Nev.** Nevada.
NW northwest.
N.W.T. Northwest Territories.
NY *or* **N.Y.** New York.
NYSE New York Stock Exchange.

OAS Organization of American States.
o/c overcharge.
OCAS Organization of Central American States.
OCD Office of Civil Defense.
OCR optical character recognition.
OCS Officer Candidate School.
OD overdose.
O.D. 1. Doctor of Optometry. **2.** officer of the day. **3.** *also* **o/d** overdraft. **4.** overdrawn.
OED *also* **O.E.D.** Oxford English Dictionary.
OEM original equipment manufacturer.
OEO Office of Economic Opportunity.
OH Ohio.
OK *or* **Okla.** Oklahoma.
OMB Office of Management and Budget.
ON *or* **Ont.** Ontario.
op. cit. *Lat.* opere citato (in the work cited).
OPEC Organization of Petroleum Exporting Countries.
OR *or* **Or.** *or* **Ore.** Oregon.
O.R. *or* **OR** operating room.
OSHA U.S. Occupational Safety and Health Administration.
o.t. *or* **O.T. 1.** occupational therapy. **2.** overtime.
OTB off-track betting.
OTC *also* **O.T.C.** over-the-counter.
oz *also* **oz.** ounce.
oz ap apothecaries' ounce.
oz av *or* **oz avdp** avoirdupois ounce.
oz t troy ounce.

p 1. momentum. **2.** *or* **p.** *Mus.* piano (direction).
PA 1. *or* **Pa.** Pennsylvania. **2.** public-address system.
p.a. *Lat.* per annum (by the year).
P.A. *or* **P/A** power of attorney.
P and L profit and loss.
pat. patent.
patd. patented.
PBS Public Broadcasting Service.
PBX *also* **P.B.X.** Private Branch Exchange.
PC 1. personal computer. **2.** politically correct.
p.c. *also* **p/c** *or* **P/C** petty cash.
p/c *or* **P/C** prices current.
PCP phencyclidine.
pct. percent.
p.d. *or* **P.D.** per diem.
P.D. 1. Police Department. **2.** postal district.
PDT *or* **P.D.T.** Pacific Daylight Time.
PE *or* **P.E.I.** Prince Edward Island.
P.E. 1. physical education. **2.** *Statistics.* probable error. **3.** professional engineer.
P/E price/earnings.
pen. *or* **Pen.** peninsula.
Penn. *or* **Penna.** Pennsylvania.
pfd. preferred.
PH 1. Public Health. **2.** Purple Heart.
PHA Public Housing Administration.
Ph.D. *Lat.* Philosophiae Doctor (Doctor of Philosophy).
PHS Public Health Service.
PIN personal identification number.
pkwy. parkway.
PLO Palestine Liberation Organization.
p.m. *also* **P.M.** post mortem.
P.M. 1. *also* **p.m.** post meridiem. —Usu. used in small capitals <P.M.> **2.** Prime Minister.
P.M.G. postmaster general.
PMS premenstrual syndrome.
p.n. *or* **P/N** promissory note.
PO *or* **P.O.** *also* **p.o.** post office.
POE *or* **P.O.E. 1.** port of embarkation. **2.** port of entry.
pop. 1. popular. **2.** population.
POW *or* **P.O.W.** prisoner of war.
pp *or* **pp.** *Mus.* pianissimo.
ppb parts per billion.
ppd. 1. postpaid. **2.** prepaid.
ppm parts per million.
P.P.S. *also* **p.p.s.** *Lat.* post postscriptum (additional postscript).
ppt 1. parts per thousand. **2.** parts per trillion.
P.Q. *or* **PQ** Province of Quebec.
PR *or* **P.R. 1.** public relations. **2.** Puerto Rico.
PRO *also* **P.R.O.** public relations officer.
P.S. 1. *also* **p.s.** postscript. **2.** public school.
PSAT Preliminary Scholastic Aptitude Test.
psf *or* **p.s.f.** pounds per square foot.
psi *or* **p.s.i.** pounds per square inch.
PST *or* **P.S.T.** Pacific Standard Time.
P.T. *also* **PT** Pacific Time.
PTA Parent Teacher Association.
PTO 1. Parent Teacher Organization. **2.** Patent and Trademark Office.
p.t.o. *or* **PTO** please turn over.
PWA Public Works Administration.

q. 1. quart. **2.** quintal. **3.** quire.
Q.E.D. *Lat.* quod erat demonstrandum (which was to be demonstrated).
qt *or* **qt.** quart.
Que. Quebec.
q.v. *Lat.* quod vide (which see).

r *or* **R** radius.
R.A. **1.** *or* **RADM** rear admiral. **2.** *or* **RA** Regular Army.
RAF *also* **R.A.F.** Royal Air Force.
RAM random-access memory.
R & B rhythm and blues.
R & D research and development.
R and R rest and recreation.
RBC *or* **rbc** red blood cell.
RC **1.** Red Cross. **2.** Roman Catholic.
RCAF Royal Canadian Air Force.
RCMP Royal Canadian Mounted Police.
rd rod (unit of length).
RD **1.** registered dietician. **2.** rural delivery.
rd. **1.** *or* **Rd.** road. **2.** round.
RDA recommended daily allowance.
RDF radio direction finder.
rep. *or* **Rep.** representative.
Rep. Republican.
reqd. required.
Res. **1.** Reservation. **2.** Reservoir.
Rev. Ver. *Bible.* Revised Version.
RF radio frequency.
RFD *also* **R.F.D.** rural free delivery.
r.h. *also* **RH** right hand.
rhp *or* **r.hp.** rated horsepower.
RI *or* **R.I.** Rhode Island.
R.I.P. *Lat.* requiescat in pace (may she *or* he rest in peace).
rms root mean square.
RN **1.** registered nurse. **2.** Royal Navy.
RNA ribonucleic acid.
ROM read-only memory.
ROTC Reserve Officers' Training Corps.
rpm *or* **r.p.m.** revolutions per minute.
rps *or* **r.p.s.** revolutions per second.
RR *also* **R.R.** **1.** railroad. **2.** rural route.
RSV *Bible.* Revised Standard Version.
R.S.V.P. *or* **r.s.v.p.** *French.* répondez s'il vous plaît (please reply).
rte. route.
RV **1.** recreational vehicle. **2.** *Aerospace.* re-entry vehicle. **3.** *Bible.* Revised Version.
rwy. *or* **ry.** railway.

S *also* **S.** *or* **s** *or* **s.** south.
SA Salvation Army.
SAC Strategic Air Command.
SALT Strategic Arms Limitations Talks.
SAM surface-to-air-missile.
SASE self-addressed stamped envelope.
Sask. Saskatchewan.
S.B. *Lat.* Scientiae Baccalaureus (Bachelor of Science).
SBA Small Business Administration.
SbE south by east.
SbW south by west.
SC *or* **S.C.** South Carolina.
s.c. *also* **sc** small capitals.
S.C. Supreme Court.
SD **1.** sight draft. **2.** *or* **S.D.** South Dakota. **3.** special delivery. **4.** standard deviation.
S.Dak. South Dakota.
SE southeast.
SEATO Southeast Asia Treaty Organization.
sec **1.** secant. **2.** second.
SEC Securities and Exchange Commission.
SEM scanning electron microscope.
sen. *or* **Sen.** **1.** senate; senator. **2.** senior.
seq. *Lat.* sequens (the following).
SF science fiction.
sg specific gravity.
shf *or* **SHF** superhigh frequency.
SI *French.* Système Internationale d'Unités (International System of Units).
SIDS sudden infant death syndrome.
S.J. Society of Jesus.
SJC supreme judicial court.
SK Saskatchewan.
SLIP symmetric list processor.
so. *or* **So.** south; southern.
SOP standard operating procedure.
SPCA Society for the Prevention of Cruelty to Animals.
SPCC Society for the Prevention of Cruelty to Children.
SPF sun protection factor.
sp gr specific gravity.
sq. **1.** squadron. **2.** square.
Sr. **1.** *or* **sr.** senior. **2.** señor. **3.** sister (religious).
SRO **1.** single-room occupancy. **2.** standing room only.
SSA Social Security Administration.
SSE south-southeast.
SSI Supplemental Security Income.
SSR *or* **S.S.R.** Soviet Socialist Republic.
SSS Selective Service System.
SST supersonic transport.
SSW south-southwest.
ST standard time.
st. *or* **St.** street.
St. saint.
s.t. short ton.
STD sexually transmitted disease.
Ste. *French.* sainte (feminine form of saint).
STOL short takeoff and landing.
STP standard temperature and pressure.
sw short wave.
SW southwest.
SWAT Special Weapons and Tactics Team.

t **1.** ton. **2.** troy (system of weights).
t. teaspoonful; teaspoon.
T. tablespoon; tablespoonful.
TA teaching assistant.
tan tangent.
TAS **1.** telephone answering system. **2.** true air speed.
TB **1.** terabyte. **2.** *also* **T.B.** tuberculosis.
tbs. *or* **tbsp.** tablespoon; tablespoonful.
TEFL teaching English as a foreign language.
Tenn. Tennessee.
terr. **1.** terrace. **2.** territorial; territory.
TESL teaching English as a second language.
TESOL teachers of English to speakers of other languages.
test. **1.** testator. **2.** testatrix. **3.** testimony.
Tex. Texas.
TGIF thank God it's Friday.
THz terahertz.

TKO technical knockout.
t.l. *or* **t/l** total loss.
TLC tender loving care.
TM trademark.
t.m. true mean.
TN Tennessee.
tn. ton.
tnpk. *or* **tpk.** turnpike.
TNT trinitrotoluene.
tsp. teaspoon; teaspoonful.
TVA Tennessee Valley Authority.
TX Texas.

u.c. *also* **UC** upper case.
UCMJ Uniform Code of Military Justice.
UCS universal character set.
uhf *or* **UHF** ultrahigh frequency.
U.K. United Kingdom.
ULF ultra low frequency.
ult. 1. ultimate; ultimately. 2. ultimo.
UN *or* **U.N.** United Nations.
UNESCO United Nations Educational, Scientific, and Cultural Organization.
UNICEF United Nations International Children's Emergency Fund.
UPC Universal Product Code.
UPI *or* **U.P.I.** United Press International.
US *or* **U.S.** United States.
USA *or* **U.S.A.** 1. United States Army. 2. United States of America.
USAF United States Air Force.
U.S.C. United States Code.
U.S.C.A. United States Code Annotated.
USCG *also* **U.S.C.G.** United States Coast Guard.
USDA United States Department of Agriculture.
USIA United States Information Agency.
U.S.M. United States Mail.
USMA *also* **U.S.M.A.** United States Military Academy.
USMC *also* **U.S.M.C.** United States Marine Corps.
USN *also* **U.S.N.** United States Navy.
USNA *also* **U.S.N.A.** United States Naval Academy.
USO *or* **U.S.O.** United Service Organizations.
U.S.P. United States Pharmacopoeia.
U.S.P.O. *also* **USPO** United States Post Office.
USPS United States Postal Service.
U.S.S. 1. United States Senate. 2. *also* **USS** United States Ship.
USSR *or* **U.S.S.R.** Union of Soviet Socialist Republics.
UT 1. Universal time. 2. *or* **Ut.** Utah.
UV ultraviolet.
UW underwriter.

V 1. *Elect.* volt. 2. volume.
v. versus.
VA *or* **Va.** Virginia.
V.A. *also* **VA** Veterans' Administration.
val. 1. valley. 2. valuation; value.
VAT value-added tax.
V.C. 1. vice chairman. 2. vice chancellor. 3. vice consul. 4. Victoria Cross.
VD *also* **V.D.** venereal disease.
VDT video display terminal.
V.F. 1. *also* **VF** video frequency. 2. *also* **VF** visual field.
VFD volunteer fire department.
VFR visual flight rules.
VGA Video Graphics Array.
vhf *or* **VHF** very high frequency.
VI *or* **V.I.** Virgin Islands.
VIN vehicle identification number.
VISTA Volunteers in Service to America.
viz. *Lat.* videlicet (namely).
vlf *or* **VLF** very low frequency.
V.M.D. *Lat.* Veterinariae Medicinae Doctor (Doctor of Veterinary Medicine).
VN visiting nurse.
VP *or* **V.P.** vice president.
vs. versus.
V.S. veterinary surgeon.
V/STOL vertical short takeoff and landing.
VT 1. variable time. 2. *or* **Vt.** Vermont.
VTOL vertical takeoff and landing.
VTR videotape recorder.
VU volume unit.
v.v. vice versa.

W 1. *Elect.* watt. 2. *also* **W.** *or* **w** *or* **w.** west.
WA *or* **Wash.** Washington.
Wash. Washington.
WATS Wide-Area Telecommunications Service.
WBC *or* **wbc** white blood cell.
WbN west by north.
WbS west by south.
w.c. 1. water closet. 2. without charge.
WD *or* **W.D.** War Department.
WH watt-hour.
WHO World Health Organization.
W-hr watt-hour.
whsle. wholesale.
WI *or* **Wis.** Wisconsin.
w.i. when issued (financial stock).
WIA wounded in action.
wk. 1. weak. 2. week. 3. work.
WNW west-northwest.
WO *or* **W.O.** warrant officer.
w/o without.
WPA Work Projects Administration.
wpm *or* **w.p.m.** words per minute.
WSW west-southwest.
wt. weight.
WV *or* **W.Va.** West Virginia.
WW I *or* **W.W.I** World War I.
WW II *or* **W.W.II** World War II.
WY *or* **Wyo.** Wyoming.

yd yard (measurement).
YOB year of birth.
yr. 1. year. 2. younger. 3. your.
YT *or* **Y.T.** Yukon Territory.
ZPG zero population growth.

Biographical Entries

A

Aar•on (âr′ən, ăr′-), **Henry Louis ("Hank").** b. 1934. Amer. baseball player.

Ach•e•son (ăch′ĭ-sən), **Dean Gooderham.** 1893–1971. Amer. public official.

Ad•ams (ăd′əmz), **Abigail Smith.** 1744–1818. Amer. letter writer & wife of John Adams.

Adams, Henry Brooks. 1838–1918. Amer. historian.

Adams, John. 1735–1826. 2nd U.S. President (1797–1801) & political philosopher.

Adams, John Quincy. 1767–1848. 6th U.S. President (1825–29) & legislator.

Adams, Samuel. 1722–1803. Amer. Revolutionary leader.

Ad•dams (ăd′əmz), **Jane.** 1860–1935. Amer. social reformer & pacifist (Nobel, 1931).

Ad•di•son (ăd′ĭ-sən), **Joseph.** 1672–1719. English essayist. —**Ad′di•so′ni•an** *adj.*

Ad•en•au•er (ăd′n-ou′ər, äd′-), **Konrad.** 1876–1967. West German statesman.

Ad•ler (ăd′lər, äd′-), **Alfred.** 1870–1937. Austrian psychiatrist. —**Ad•le′ri•an** *adj.*

Aes•chy•lus (ĕs′kə-ləs, ē′skə-). 525–456 B.C. Greek dramatist. —**Aes′chy•le′an** (-lē′ən) *adj.*

Ae•sop (ē′səp, -sŏp′). 6th cent. B.C. Greek fabulist. —**Ae•so′pi•an** (ē-sō′pē-ən), **Ae•sop′ic** (ē-sŏp′ĭk) *adj.*

Ag•as•siz (ăg′ə-sē), **(Jean) Louis (Rodolphe).** 1807–73. Swiss-born Amer. naturalist.

A•gee (ā′jē), **James.** 1909–55. Amer. author & critic.

Ag•new (ăg′no͞o′, -nyo͞o′), **Spiro Theodore.** b. 1918. U.S. Vice President (1969–73); resigned.

A•gui•nal•do (ä′gē-näl′dô), **Emilio.** 1869–1964. Philippine revolutionary leader.

A•i•sha (ä′ē-shə). 611–78. Chief wife of Muhammad.

Ak•bar (ăk′bär). *the Great.* 1542–1605. Mogul emperor (1556–1605).

A•khe•na•ton *or* **A•khe•na•ten** (ä′kə-nä′tn, äk′nä′-). Egyptian pharaoh (1375–58 B.C.) & religious reformer.

Al•ar•ic (ăl′ər-ĭk). 370–410. Visigoth king & conqueror of Rome (410).

Al•bert (ăl′bərt), Prince. 1819–61. Consort of Queen Victoria of England.

Al•ci•bi•a•des (ăl′sə-bī′ə-dēz′). 450?–404 B.C. Athenian politician & general.

Al•cott (ôl′kət, -kŏt, ŏl′-), **Amos Bronson.** 1799–1888. Amer. educator & philosopher.

Alcott, Louisa May. 1832–88. Amer. author & reformer.

Al•ex•an•der (ăl′ĭg-zăn′dər, -zän′-). Name of 8 popes, esp.: **a. III.** d. 1181. Reigned 1159–81. **b. VI.** 1431?–1503. Reigned 1491–1503.

Alexander. Name of 3 Russian czars: **a. I.** 1777–1825. Ruled 1801–25. **b. II.** 1818–81. Ruled 1855–81; emancipated serfs (1861). **c. III.** 1845–94. Ruled 1881–94.

Alexander III. *the Great.* 356–23 B.C. Macedonian king (336–23) & conqueror of Greece, Persia, & Egypt. —**Al′ex•an′dri•an** *adj.*

Al•fon•so (ăl-fŏn′sō, -zō). Name of 6 kings of Portugal, esp.: **a. I.** 1112–85. Ruled 1139–85. **b. V.** 1432–81. Ruled 1438–81.

Alfonso XIII. 1886–1941. Spanish king (1886–1931, ruled 1902–31); abdicated.

Al•fred (ăl′frĭd). *the Great.* 849–99. West Saxon king (871–99), scholar, & lawmaker.

Al•ger (ăl′jər), **Horatio.** 1832–99. Amer. author.

A•li (ä-lē′). 600?–61. Muslim caliph (656–61); assassinated.

Ali, Muhammad. b. 1942. Amer. prizefighter.

Al•len (ăl′ən), **Ethan.** 1738–89. Amer. Revolutionary soldier.

Al•sop (ôl′səp, ŏl′-), **Joseph W., Jr.** (1910–89) & **Stewart** (1914–74). Amer. journalists.

A•men•ho•tep (ä′mən-hō′tĕp, ăm′ən-). Name of 4 Egyptian pharaohs, esp.: **a. III.** Reigned 1411?–1375 B.C. **b. IV.** AKHENATON.

Am•père (ăm′pîr, äɴ-pĕr′), **André Marie.** 1775–1836. French physicist.

A•mund•sen (ä′mənd-sən, ä′mo͝on-), **Roald.** 1872–1928. Norwegian polar explorer.

An•der•sen (ăn′dər-sən), **Hans Christian.** 1805–75. Danish author.

An•der•son (ăn′dər-sən), **Marian.** 1902–93. Amer. contralto.

Anderson, Maxwell. 1888–1959. Amer. playwright.

Anderson, Sherwood. 1876–1941. Amer. author.

An•dre•a del Sar•to (än-drā′ä dĕl′ sär′tō). 1486–1531. Italian painter.

An•drew (ăn′dro͞o), Saint. One of the 12 Apostles.

An•gel•i•co (ăn-jĕl′ĭ-kō′), Fra. *Giovanni da Fiesole.* 1387–1455. Italian painter.

Ång•ström (ăng′strəm, ông′strœm), **Anders Jonas.** 1814–74. Swedish physicist & astronomer.

Anne (ăn). 1665–1714. Queen of Great Britain & Ireland (1702–14).

Anne of Cleves (klēvz). 1515–57. English queen as 4th wife of Henry VIII.

A•nou•ilh (ä-no͞o′ē), **Jean.** 1910–87. French dramatist.

An•tho•ny (ăn′thə-nē), **Susan Brownell.** 1820–1906. Amer. reformer.

An•to•ni•us (ăn-tō′nē-əs), **Marcus.** MARK ANTONY.

Ap•u•lei•us (ăp′yə-lē′əs), **Lucius.** 2nd cent. A.D. Roman philosopher & satirist.

A•qui•nas (ə-kwī'nəs), Saint **Thomas.** 1225?–74. Italian theologian & philosopher.

Ar•a•fat (âr'ə-făt', ä-rä-fät'), **Yasir.** b. 1929. Palestinian leader (Nobel, 1994).

Ar•chi•me•des (är'kə-mē'dēz). 287?–12 B.C. Greek mathematician, engineer, & physicist. —**Ar'chi•me'de•an** *adj.*

Ar•is•toph•a•nes (ăr'ĭ-stŏf'ə-nēz). 448?–380? B.C. Athenian dramatist.

Ar•is•tot•le (ăr'ĭ-stŏt'l). 384–22 B.C. Greek philosopher. —**Ar'is•to•te'li•an** (ăr'ĭ-stə-tē'lē-ən, -tēl'yən) *adj.* & *n.*

Arm•strong (ärm'strông'), **Louis ("Satchmo").** 1900–71. Amer. jazz musician.

Ar•nold (är'nəld), **Benedict.** 1741–1801. Amer. Revolutionary general & traitor.

Arnold, Matthew. 1822–88. English poet & critic.

Ar•thur (är'thər), **Chester Alan.** 1829–86. 21st U.S. President (1881–85).

As•i•mov (ăz'ĭ-mŏf), **Isaac.** 1920–92. Russian-born Amer. author.

As•quith (ăs'kwĭth), **Herbert Henry.** 1852–1928. British prime minister (1908–16).

As•tor (ăs'tər), **John Jacob.** 1763–1848. German-born Amer. fur trader & capitalist.

A•ta•hual•pa (ä'tə-wäl'pə). 1502?–33. Incan emperor (1525–33); executed.

At•a•türk (ăt'ə-tûrk', ä'tə-), **Kemal.** See KEMAL ATATÜRK.

At•ti•la (ăt'l-ə, ə-tĭl'ə). *Scourge of the Gods.* 406?–53. King of the Huns (433?–53).

Att•lee (ăt'lē), **Clement Richard.** 1883–1967. British prime minister (1945–51).

At•tucks (ăt'əks), **Crispus.** 1723?–70. Killed in the Boston Massacre.

Au•den (ôd'n), **Wystan Hugh.** 1907–73. English-born Amer. author.

Au•du•bon (ô'də-bŏn', -bən), **John James.** 1785–1851. Haitian-born Amer. ornithologist & artist.

Au•gus•tine (ô'gə-stēn', ô-gŭs'tĭn), **Saint.** 354–430. Church father & philosopher. —**Au'gus•tin'i•an** (ô'gə-stĭn'ē-ən) *adj.* & *n.*

Au•gus•tus (ô-gŭs'təs). *Octavian.* 63 B.C.–A.D. 14. First Roman emperor (27 B.C.–A.D. 14). —**Au•gus'tan** *adj.* & *n.*

Au•re•lian (ô-rēl'yən, ô-rē'lē-ən). 212?–75. Roman emperor (270–75).

Aus•ten (ô'stən), **Jane.** 1775–1817. English author.

Aus•tin (ô'stən, ŏs'tən), **Stephen Fuller.** 1793–1836. Amer. political leader.

A•vo•ga•dro (ä'və-gä'drō, ăv'ə-), **Amedeo.** 1776–1856. Italian physicist.

B

Bach (bäKH, bäk). Family of German composers & musicians, including **Johann Sebastian** (1685–1750).

Ba•con (bā'kən), **Francis.** 1561–1626. English philosopher, essayist, courtier, jurist, & statesman. —**Ba•co'ni•an** *adj.* & *n.*

Bacon, Roger. 1214?–94. English friar, scientist, & philosopher.

Ba•den-Pow•ell (bād'n-pō'əl), Sir **Robert Stephenson Smyth.** 1857–1941. English soldier & founder of the Boy Scouts.

Bae•de•ker (bā'dĭ-kər), **Karl.** 1801–59. German guidebook publisher.

Baf•fin (băf'ĭn), **William.** 1584–1622. English explorer.

Bal•an•chine (băl'ən-chēn', băl'ən-chēn'), **George.** 1904–83. Russian-born Amer. choreographer.

Bal•bo•a (băl-bō'ə), **Vasco Núñez de.** 1475–1517. Spanish explorer.

Bald•win (bôld'wĭn), **James Arthur.** 1924–87. Amer. author.

Baldwin, Stanley. 1867–1947. British prime minister (1923–24, 1924–29, 1935–37).

Bal•four (băl'fo͝or', -fôr', -fōr'), **Arthur James.** 1848–1930. British prime minister (1902–5) & diplomat.

Bal•zac (bôl'zăk', băl'-, bäl-zäk'), **Honoré de.** 1799–1850. French author.

Bar•ba•ros•sa (bär'bə-rŏs'ə, -rôs'-). Holy Roman Emperor FREDERICK I.

Bar•ber (bär'bər), **Samuel.** 1910–81. Amer. composer.

Bar•num (bär'nəm), **Phineas Taylor ("P.T.").** 1810–91. Amer. showman.

Bar•ry•more (băr'ĭ-môr', -mōr'). Family of Amer. actors, including **Lionel Blythe** (1878–1954) & **Ethel** (1879–1959).

Bar•thol•o•mew (bär-thŏl'ə-myo͞o'), Saint. One of the 12 Apostles.

Bar•tók (bär'tŏk', -tôk'), **Béla.** 1881–1945. Hungarian pianist & composer.

Bar•ton (bär'tn), **Clara.** 1821–1912. Amer. nurse & founder of the Amer. Red Cross.

Ba•ruch (bə-ro͞ok'), **Bernard Mannes.** 1870–1965. Amer. stock broker & public official.

Ba•sie (bā'sē), **William ("Count").** b. 1904. Amer. jazz composer & band leader.

Ba•tis•ta y Zal•dí•var (bə-tēs'tə ē zäl-dē'vär'), **Fulgencio.** 1901–73. Cuban military & political leader; deposed & exiled (1959).

Baude•laire (bōd-lâr', -lĕr'), **Charles Pierre.** 1821–67. French poet & critic.

Beau•voir (bō-vwär'), **Simone de.** 1908–86. French author.

Beck•et (bĕk'ĭt), Saint **Thomas à.** 1118?–70. English Roman Catholic martyr.

Beck•ett (bĕk'ĭt), **Samuel.** 1906–89. Irish author (Nobel, 1969).

Bede (bēd) *Venerable Bede.* c. 673–735. English theologian, historian, & scientist.

Bee•cher (bē'chər), **Henry Ward.** 1813–87. Amer. clergyman, editor, & abolitionist.

Bee•tho•ven (bā'tō'vən), **Ludwig van.** 1770–1827. German composer.

Be•gin (bā'gĭn, bə-gēn'), **Menachem.** 1913–92. Russian-born Israeli statesman (Nobel, 1978).

Bell (bĕl), **Alexander Graham.** 1847–1922. Scottish-born Amer. inventor.

Bel•li•ni (bə-lē'nē). Family of Venetian painters, including **Jacopo** (1400?–70?), **Gentile** (1429?–1507), & **Giovanni** (1430?–1516).

Bel•low (bĕl'ō), **Saul.** b. 1915. Canadian-born Amer. novelist (Nobel, 1976).

Ben•e•dict of Nur•si•a (bĕn'ĭ-dĭkt', nûr'-shē-ə, -shə), Saint. 480?–543. Italian founder of the Benedictine order. —**Ben'e•dic'tine** (-tĭn, -tēn') *adj.* & *n.*

Be•nét (bĭ-nā'), **William Rose** (1886–1950) & **Stephen Vincent** (1898–1943). Amer. authors.

Ben Gur•i•on (bĕn gŏŏr'ē-ən, gŏŏr-yôn'), **David.** 1886–1973. Polish-born Israeli statesman.

Ben•nett (bĕn'ĭt), **Richard Bedford.** 1870–1947. Canadian prime minister (1930–1935).

Ben•tham (bĕn'thəm), **Jeremy.** 1748–1832. English author, reformer, & philosopher. —**Ben'tham•ite'** *n.*

Ben•ton (bĕn'tən), **Thomas Hart.** 1889–1975. Amer. artist & writer.

Berg•man (bûrg'mən), **Ingmar.** b. 1918. Swedish film director.

Bergman, Ingrid. 1915–82. Swedish actress.

Berg•son (bĕrg'sən, bĕrg-sôɴ'), **Henri Louis.** 1859–1941. French philosopher & author (Nobel, 1927).

Ber•ing *also* **Beh•ring** (bâr'ĭng, bĕr'-, bā'-rĭng), **Vitus.** 1680–1741. Danish navigator.

Berke•ley (bärk'lē, bûrk'-), **George.** 1685–1753. English-born Irish philosopher.

Ber•lin (bûr-lĭn'), **Irving.** 1888–1989. Russian-born Amer. songwriter.

Ber•li•oz (bĕr'lē-ōz', -ōs'), **(Louis) Hector.** 1803–69. French composer.

Bern•hardt (bûrn'härt', bĕr-när'), **Sarah.** 1844–1923. French actress.

Ber•ni•ni (bər-nē'nē), **Giovanni Lorenzo.** 1598–1680. Italian artist & architect.

Ber•noul•li (bər-nōō'lē). Family of Swiss mathematicians & scientists, including **Jakob** *or* **Jacques** (1654–1705), **Johann** *or* **Jean** (1667–1748), & **Daniel** (1700–82).

Bern•stein (bûrn'stīn', -stēn'), **Leonard.** 1918–90. Amer. conductor & composer.

Be•thune (bə-thōōn', -thyōōn'), **Mary McLeod.** 1875–1955. Amer. educator.

Bier•stadt (bîr'stăt', -shtät'), **Albert.** 1830–1902. German-born Amer. painter.

Bing•ham (bĭng'əm), **George Caleb.** 1811–79. Amer. genre painter.

Bis•marck (bĭz'märk', bĭs'-), Prince **Otto Eduard Leopold von.** 1815–98. Creator & first chancellor of the German Empire (1871–90). —**Bis•marck'i•an** *adj.*

Bi•zet (bē-zā'), **(Alexandre César Léopold) Georges.** 1838–75. French composer.

Black Hawk (blăk' hôk'). 1767–1838. Sauk leader.

Black•well (blăk'wĕl, -wəl), **Elizabeth** (1821–1910) & **Emily** (1826–1910). English-born Amer. physicians.

Blake (blāk), **William.** 1757–1827. English mystic, poet, & artist.

Bloom•er (blōō'mər), **Amelia Jenks.** 1818–94. Amer. social reformer.

Boc•cac•cio (bō-kä'chē-ō', -chō', bə-, bōk-kät'chō), **Giovanni.** 1313–75. Italian poet.

Bo•gart (bō'gärt), **Humphrey DeForest.** 1899–1957. Amer. actor.

Bohr (bôr, bōr), **Niels Henrik David.** 1885–1962. Danish physicist (Nobel, 1922).

Bol•eyn (bŏŏl'ĭn, bŏŏ-lĭn'), **Anne.** 1507–36. English queen as 2nd wife of Henry VIII; beheaded.

Bo•lí•var (bō'lə-vär', bŏl'ə-, bō-lē'vär), **Simón.** 1783–1830. Venezuelan soldier & South American liberator.

Bo•na•parte (bō'nə-pärt'). Corsican family, including: **a. Joseph.** 1768–1844. King of Naples (1806–8) & Spain (1808–13). **b.** NAPOLEON I. **c. Lucien.** 1775–1840. Politician & diplomat. **d. Louis.** 1778–1846. King of Holland (1806–10); abdicated. **e. Jérôme.** 1784–1860. King of Westphalia (1807).

Boole (bōōl), **George.** 1815–64. English mathematician & logician.

Boone (bōōn), **Daniel.** 1734–1820. Amer. frontiersman.

Booth (bōōth). Family of English & Amer. actors, including **John Wilkes** (1838–65), assassin of Abraham Lincoln.

Booth. Family of English and Amer. reformers, including **William** (1829–1912), founder of the Salvation Army.

Bor•den (bôr'dn), **Sir Robert.** 1854–1937. Canadian prime minister (1911–20).

Bor•ges (bôr'hās), **Jorge Luis.** 1899–1986. Argentinian author.

Bor•gia (bôr'jə, -jä, -zhə). Influential Italian family, including: **a. Cesare.** 1475?–1507. Cardinal, diplomat, & soldier. **b. Lucrezia.** 1480–1519. Patron of learning & the arts. **c. Rodrigo.** ALEXANDER VI.

Bosch (bŏsh, bôsh, bŏs, bôs), **Hieronymous.** 1450?–1516. Dutch painter.

Bos•well (bŏz'wĕl', -wəl), **James.** 1740–95. Scottish diarist & biographer.

Bot•ti•cel•li (bŏt'ĭ-chĕl'ē), **Sandro.** 1444?–1510. Italian painter.

Bour•bon (bŏŏr'bən, bŏŏr-bôɴ'). French royal family ruling in France (1589–1793), Spain (1700–1868, 1874–1931), & Naples & the Two Sicilies (1735–1861).

Bourke-White (bûrk'hwīt', -wīt'), **Margaret.** 1906–71. Amer. photographer.

Boyle (boil), **Robert.** 1627–91. British physicist & chemist.

Brad•ford (brăd'fərd), **William.** 1590–1657. English Puritan colonist in America.

Brad•street (brăd'strēt'), **Anne Dudley.** 1612–72. English-born colonial poet.

Bra•dy (brā'dē), **Mathew B.** 1823–96. Amer. pioneer photographer.

Brahe (brä, brä'hē, brä'ə), **Tycho.** 1546–1601. Danish astronomer.

Brahms (brämz), **Johannes.** 1833–97. German composer. —**Brahms'i•an** *adj.*

Braille (brāl), **Louis.** 1809?–52. French musician, educator, & inventor of writing & printing systems for the blind.

Bran•deis (brăn'dīs', -dīz'), **Louis Dembitz.** 1856–1941. Amer. jurist.

Brandt (bränt, brănt), **Willy.** 1913–92. West German statesman (Nobel, 1971).

Brant (brănt), **Joseph.** 1742–1807. Mohawk leader.

Braque (bräk, brăk), **Georges.** 1882–1963. French painter.

Braun (brôn, broun), **Wernher Magnus Maximilian von.** 1912–77. German-born Amer. rocket engineer.

Brecht (brĕkt, brĕKHt), **Bertolt.** 1898–1956. German poet & playwright.

Breu•ghel (broi′gəl, bro͞o′-, brœ′-). *var. of* BRUEGHEL.

Brezh•nev (brĕzh′nĕf, -nyĕf), **Leonid Ilyich.** 1906–82. Soviet statesman.

Bron•të (brŏn′tē). Family of English authors, including **Charlotte** (1816–55), **Emily Jane** (1818–48), & **Anne** (1820–49).

Brook (bro͝ok), **Rupert.** 1887–1915. English poet.

Brooks (bro͝oks), **Gwendolyn Elizabeth.** b. 1917. Amer. author.

Brown (broun), **John.** 1800–59. Amer. abolitionist; executed.

Brown•ing (brou′nĭng), **Elizabeth Barrett** (1806–61) & **Robert** (1812–89). English poets.

Broz (brōz, brôz), **Josip.** Marshal TITO.

Bruce (bro͞os), **Robert the.** ROBERT I of Scotland.

Bruck•ner (bro͝ok′nər), **Anton.** 1824–96. Austrian composer.

Brue•ghel *also* **Brue•gel** *or* **Breu•ghel** (broi′gəl, bro͞o′-, brœ′-). Flemish family of painters, including **Pieter** *the Elder* (1525?–69), **Pieter** *the Younger* (1564?–1637), & **Jan** (1568–1625).

Bru•nel•le•schi (bro͞o′nə-lĕs′kē), **Filippo.** 1377?–1446. Italian architect.

Bru•tus (bro͞o′təs), **Marcus Junius.** 85?–42 B.C. Roman politician, general, & assassin of Julius Caesar.

Bry•an (brī′ən), **William Jennings.** 1860–1925. Amer. lawyer & political leader.

Bu•ber (bo͞o′bər), **Martin.** 1878–1965. Austrian-born Judaic scholar & philosopher.

Bu•chan•an (byo͞o-kăn′ən, bə-), **James.** 1791–1868. 15th U.S. President (1857–61).

Buck (bŭk), **Pearl Sydenstricker.** 1892–1973. Amer. author (Nobel, 1938).

Bud•dha (bo͞o′də, bo͝od′ə). 563?–483? B.C. Indian philosopher & founder of Buddhism. **—Bud′dhist** *adj. & n.*

Buf•fa•lo Bill (bŭf′ə-lō bĭl′). William Frederick CODY.

Bul•finch (bo͝ol′fĭnch′), **Charles.** 1763–1844. Amer. architect.

Bunche (bŭnch), **Ralph Johnson.** 1904–71. Amer. diplomat (Nobel, 1950).

Bun•yan (bŭn′yən), **John.** 1628–88. English preacher & author.

Bur•bank (bûr′băngk′), **Luther.** 1849–1926. Amer. horticulturist.

Bur•ger (bûr′gər), **Warren Earl.** 1907–95. Amer. jurist.

Burke (bûrk), **Edmund.** 1729–97. British politician, orator, & author.

Burns (bûrnz), **Robert.** 1759–96. Scottish poet.

Burr (bûr), **Aaron.** 1756–1836. U.S. Vice President (1801–5), soldier, & adventurer; killed Alexander Hamilton in a duel.

Bur•ton (bûr′tn), Sir **Richard Francis.** 1821–90. English explorer & Orientalist.

Bush (bo͝osh), **George Herbert Walker.** b. 1924. 41st U.S. President (1989–93).

Byrd (bûrd), **Richard Evelyn.** 1888–1957. Amer. naval officer & polar explorer.

By•ron (bī′rən), **George Gordon.** 1788–1824. English poet. **—By•ron′ic** *adj.*

C

Ca•be•za de Va•ca (kə-bā′zə də vä′kə), **Alvar Núñez.** 1490?–1577? Spanish explorer & colonial administrator.

Cab•ot (kăb′ət), **John.** 1450–98. Italian-born explorer.

Cabot, Sebastian. 1476?–1557. Italian-born explorer & cartographer.

Cad•il•lac (kăd′l-ăk′), Sieur **Antoine de la Mothe.** 1656?–1730. French explorer.

Cae•sar (sē′zər), **Gaius Julius.** 100–44 B.C. Roman general, statesman, & historian. **—Cae•sar′e•an, Cae•sar′i•an** *adj.*

Cal•der (kôl′der, kŏl′-), **Alexander.** 1898–1976. Amer. sculptor.

Cal•houn (kăl-ho͞on′), **John Caldwell.** 1782–1850. U.S. Vice President (1824–32) & political philosopher.

Ca•lig•u•la (kə-lĭg′yə-lə). A.D. 12–41. Roman emperor (37–41).

Cal•vin (kăl′vĭn), **John.** 1509–64. French-born Swiss Protestant theologian.

Ca•mo•ëns (kăm′ō-ənz, kə-mō′-) *also* **Ca•mões** (kə-moiNsh′), **Luiz Vaz de.** 1524–80. Portuguese author.

Ca•mus (kä-mo͞o′), **Albert.** 1913–60. French author (Nobel, 1957).

Ca•na•let•to (kăn′ə-lĕt′ō), **Antonio.** 1697–1768. Italian painter.

Ca•nute (kə-no͞ot′, -nyo͞ot′). 994?–1035. King of England (1016–35), Denmark (1018–35), & Norway (1028–35).

Car•a•cal•la (kăr′ə-kăl′ə). 188–217. Roman emperor (211–17); assassinated.

Ca•ra•vag•gio (kăr′ə-vä′jō, -väzh′ō), **Michelangelo Amerighi** *or* **Merisa da.** 1565?–1609? Italian painter.

Cár•de•nas (kär′də-näs′), **Lázaro.** 1895–1970. Mexican soldier & statesman.

Car•los (kär′ləs, -lôs), Don. 1788–1855. Spanish pretender to the throne. **—Carl′ist** (kär′lĭst) *adj. & n.*

Car•lyle (kär-līl′, kär′līl), **Thomas.** 1795–1881. Scottish historian.

Car•ne•gie (kär′nə-gē, kär-nā′gē, -nĕg′ē), **Andrew.** 1835–1919. Scottish-born Amer. industrialist & philanthropist.

Car•ne•gie (kär′nə-gē), **Dale.** 1888–1955. Amer. author & educator.

Car•o•lin•gi•an (kăr′ə-lĭn′jē-ən) *also* **Car•lo•vin•gi•an** (kär′lə-vĭn′-). Dynasty of rulers in France (751–987), Germany (752–911), & Italy (774–961).

Car•ran•za (kə-răn′zə, -rän′-), **Venustiano.** 1859–1920. Mexican revolutionary statesman.

Car•roll (kâr'əl), **Lewis.** Charles Lutwidge DODGSON.

Car•son (kär'sən), **Christopher ("Kit").** 1809–68. Amer. frontiersman & Indian agent.

Car•ter (kär'tər), **James Earl ("Jimmy"), Jr.** b. 1924. 39th U.S. President (1977–81).

Car•tier (kär-tyā', kär'tē-ā'), **Jacques.** 1491–1557. French explorer.

Ca•ru•so (kə-ro͞o'sō, -zō), **Enrico.** 1873–1921. Italian-born operatic tenor.

Car•ver (kär'vər), **George Washington.** 1864?–1943. Amer. botanist, agricultural chemist, & educator.

Cas•satt (kə-săt'), **Mary Stevenson.** 1845–1926. Amer. painter.

Cas•tle•reagh (kăs'əl-rā'), Viscount. 1769–1822. British statesman.

Cas•tro (kăs'trō, kä'strō), **Fidel.** b. 1927. Cuban revolutionary premier (since 1959).

Cath•er (kăth'ər), **Willa Sibert.** 1873–1947. Amer. author.

Cath•e•rine (kăth'ər-ĭn, kăth'rĭn). Name of two empresses of Russia: **a. I.** 1684?–1727. Ruled 1725–27. **b. II.** *the Great.* 1729–96. Ruled 1762–96.

Catherine de Mé•di•cis (də mĕd'ə-chē', mā-də-sēs'). 1519–89. Queen of France as wife of Henry II & regent (1560–63).

Catherine of Ar•a•gon (ăr'ə-gŏn'). 1485–1536. Queen of England as 1st wife of Henry VIII.

Cat•lin (kăt'lĭn), **George.** 1796–1872. Amer. artist.

Ca•to (kā'tō), **Marcus Porcius.** *the Elder.* 234–149 B.C. Roman statesman & general.

Cato, Marcus Porcius. *the Younger.* 95–46 B.C. Roman statesman & philosopher.

Ca•tul•lus (kə-tŭl'əs), **Gaius Valerius.** 84?–54? B.C. Roman poet.

Ca•vour (kə-vo͝or', kä-vo͞or'), Conte **Camillo Benso di.** 1810–61. Italian political leader.

Cax•ton (kăk'stən), **William.** 1422?–91. First English printer.

Cel•li•ni (chə-lē'nē), **Benvenuto.** 1500–71. Italian artist.

Cel•si•us (sĕl'sē-əs, -shəs), **Anders.** 1701–44. Swedish astronomer.

Cer•van•tes Sa•a•ve•dra (sər-văn'tēz sä'ə-vā'drə), **Miguel de.** 1547–1616. Spanish author.

Cé•zanne (sā-zăn'), **Paul.** 1839–1906. French artist.

Cha•gall (shə-gäl', -găl'), **Marc.** 1887–1985. Russian-born artist.

Cham•ber•lain (chām'bər-lĭn). Family of English statesmen, including **(Arthur) Neville** (1869–1940), prime minister (1937–40).

Cham•plain (shăm-plān', shäN-plăN'), **Samuel de.** 1567?–1635. French explorer.

Chap•lin (chăp'lĭn), Sir **Charles Spencer ("Charlie").** 1889–1977. British-born actor, director, & producer.

Char•le•magne (shär'lə-mān'). *Charles I, Charles the Great.* 742–814. King of the Franks (768–814) & emperor of the West (800–14).

Charles (chärlz). *Prince of Wales.* b. 1948. British heir apparent.

Charles. Name of 2 kings of England: **a. I.** 1600–49. Ruled 1625–49; beheaded. **b. II.** 1630–85. Ruled 1660–85.

Charles. Name of 10 kings of France, esp.: **a. IV.** *the Fair.* 1294–1328. Ruled 1322–28. **b. V.** *the Wise.* 1337–80. Ruled 1364–80. **c. VI.** *the Well Beloved.* 1368–1422. Ruled 1380–1422. **d. VII.** 1403–61. Ruled 1422–61. **e. IX.** 1550–74. Ruled 1560–74. **f. X.** 1757–1836. Ruled 1824–30.

Charles. Name of 7 Holy Roman Emperors, esp.: **a. I.** *the Great.* CHARLEMAGNE. **b. V.** 1500–58. Ruled 1519–56; king of Spain as **Charles I** (1516–56).

Châ•teau•bri•and (shă-tō'brē-äN', shăt-ō'-), Vicomte **François René de.** 1768–1848. French political leader, diplomat, & author.

Chau•cer (chô'sər), **Geoffrey.** 1340?–1400. English poet. **—Chau•cer'i•an** (chô-sîr'ē-ən) *adj. & n.*

Chá•vez (chä'vĕz), **Cesar Estrada.** 1927–93. Amer. labor organizer.

Che•khov *also* **Che•kov** (chĕk'ôf, -ŏf, -ŏv), **Anton Pavlovich.** 1860–1904. Russian author. **—Che•kho'vi•an** (chĕ-kō'vē-ən) *adj.*

Che•ops (kē'ŏps). Egyptian king (2590–2567 B.C.).

Ches•ter•ton (chĕs'tər-tən), **Gilbert Keith.** 1874–1936. English author.

Chiang Kai-shek (chăng' kī'shĕk', jē-äng'). 1887–1975. Chinese military & political leader; exiled in Taiwan (1949–75).

Chi•ri•co (kîr'ĭ-kō', kē'rĭ-), **Giorgio de.** 1888–1978. Italian painter.

Cho•pin (shō-păn', -păN'), **Frédéric François.** 1810–49. Polish-born French composer.

Chou En-lai (jō' ĕn'lī'). ZHOU ENLAI.

Chris•tophe (krē-stôf'), **Henri.** 1767–1820. Haitian king (1811–20).

Chur•chill (chûr'chĭl', chûrch'hĭl'), Sir **Winston Leonard Spencer.** 1874–1965. English prime minister (1940–45, 1951–55; Nobel, 1953).

Cic•e•ro (sĭs'ə-rō'), **Marcus Tullius.** 106–43 B.C. Roman statesman, orator, & philosopher. **—Cic'e•ro'ni•an** *adj.*

Cid (sĭd), **the.** *Rodrigo or Ruy Díaz de Bivar.* 1040?–99. Spanish soldier & national hero.

Cin•cin•na•tus (sĭn'sə-năt'əs, -nā'təs), **Lucius Quinctius.** 519?–439 B.C. Roman general.

Clark (klärk), **Charles Joseph ("Joe").** b. 1939. Canadian prime minister (1979–80).

Clark, George Rogers. 1752–1818. Amer. military leader & frontiersman.

Clark, William. 1770–1838. Amer. Western explorer, soldier, & public official.

Clau•di•us (klô'dē-əs). Name of 2 Roman emperors: **a. I.** 10 B.C.–A.D. 54. Ruled 41–54. **b. II.** 214–70. Ruled 268–70.

Clau•se•witz (klou'zə-vĭts), **Karl von.** 1780–1831. Prussian army officer & military theorist.

Clay (klā), **Cassius Marcellus.** Muhammad ALI.

Clay, Henry. 1777–1852. Amer. statesman.
Cle·men·ceau (klĕm'ən-sō', klĕ-mäɴ-sō'), **Georges.** 1841–1929. French statesman.
Clem·ens (klĕm'ənz), **Samuel Langhorne.** *Mark Twain.* 1835–1910. Amer. author.
Cle·o·pat·ra (klē'ə-păt'rə, -pā'trə, -pä'-). 69–30 B.C. Egyptian queen.
Cleve·land (klēv'lənd), **(Stephen) Grover.** 1837–1908. 22nd & 24th U.S. President (1885–89, 1893–97).
Clin·ton (klĭn'tən), **William Jefferson.** b. 1946. 42nd U.S. President (since 1993).
Coc·teau (kŏk-tō', kôk-), **Jean.** 1891?–1963. French author.
Co·dy (kō'dē), **William Frederick.** *Buffalo Bill.* 1846–1917. Amer. frontier scout & showman.
Co·han (kō'hăn'), **George Michael.** 1878–1942. Amer. singer, songwriter, & playwright.
Cole·ridge (kōl'rĭj, kō'lə-rĭj), **Samuel Taylor.** 1772–1834. English poet, critic, & theologian.
Co·lette (kŏl-ĕt', kô-let'), **(Sidonie Gabrielle Claudine).** 1873–1954. French novelist.
Col·lins (kŏl'ĭnz), **Michael.** 1890–1922. Irish Sinn Fein leader.
Colt (kōlt), **Samuel.** 1814–62. Amer. inventor & manufacturer.
Co·lum·bus (kə-lŭm'bəs), **Christopher.** 1451?–1506. Italian navigator in service of Spain; traditional discoverer of America (1492). —**Co·lum'bi·an** *adj.*
Con·dor·cet (kôn-dôr-sĕ'), Marquis de. 1743–94. French revolutionary, philosopher, & mathematician.
Con·fu·cius (kən-fyo͞o'shəs). 551–479 B.C. Chinese philosopher. —**Con·fu'cian** *adj.*
Con·greve (kŏn'grēv', kŏng'-), **William.** 1670–1729. English playwright.
Con·rad (kŏn'răd'), **Joseph.** 1857–1924. Polish-born English novelist.
Con·sta·ble (kŭn'stə-bəl, kŏn'), **John.** 1776–1837. English landscape painter.
Con·stan·tine (kŏn'stən-tēn', -tīn'), Name of 2 Roman emperors, esp. **I,** *the Great,* 280?–337, ruled 306–37.
Cook (ko͝ok), **James.** *Captain Cook.* 1728–79. English navigator & explorer.
Coo·lidge (ko͞o'lĭj), **(John) Calvin.** 1872–1933. 30th U.S. President (1923–29).
Coo·per (ko͞o'pər), **James Fenimore.** 1789–1851. Amer. novelist.
Co·per·ni·cus (kō-pûr'nə-kəs, kə-), **Nicolaus.** 1473–1543. Polish astronomer. —**Co·per'ni·can** *adj.*
Cop·land (kōp'lənd), **Aaron.** 1900–90. Amer. composer.
Cop·ley (kŏp'lē), **John Singleton.** 1738–1815. Amer. portrait painter.
Cor·neille (kôr-nā'), **Pierre.** 1606–84. French dramatist.
Corn·wal·lis (kôrn-wŏl'ĭs, -wô'lĭs), **Charles.** 1738–1805. English military & political leader.
Co·ro·na·do (kôr'ə-nä'dō, kŏr'-), **Francisco Vásquez de.** 1510–54. Spanish explorer.
Co·rot (kô-rō', kə-), **Jean Baptiste Camille.** 1796–1875. French painter.
Cor·reg·gio (kə-rĕj'ō, -ē-ō'), **Antonio Allegri da.** 1494–1534. Italian painter.
Cor·tés *also* **Cor·tez** (kôr-tĕz', kôr'tĕz'), **Hernando** *or* **Fernando.** 1485–1547. Spanish explorer & conquistador.
Cou·loumb (ko͞o'lŏm', -lōm', ko͞o-lŏm', -lôɴ'), **Charles Augustin de.** 1736–1806. French physicist.
Cour·bet (ko͞or-bā'), **Gustave.** 1819–77. French painter.
Cow·ard (kou'ərd), Sir **Noel Pierce.** 1899–1973. English actor, author, & composer.
Cra·nach (krä'näKH'), **Lucas.** 1472–1553. German artist.
Crane (krān), **(Harold) Hart.** 1899–1932. Amer. poet.
Crane, Stephen. 1871–1900. Amer. author.
Cran·mer (krăn'mər), **Thomas.** 1489–1556. English prelate & religious reformer.
Cra·zy Horse (krā'zē hôrs'). 1849?–77. Sioux leader.
Cro·ce (krō'chā), **Benedetto.** 1866–1952. Italian philosopher, historian, & critic.
Crock·ett (krŏk'ĭt), **David ("Davy").** 1786–1836. Amer. politician & frontiersman.
Croe·sus (krē'səs). d. 546 B.C. Lydian king (560–46).
Crom·well (krŏm'wĕl', -wəl, krŭm'-), **Oliver** (1599–1658) & **Richard** (1626–1712). English military, political, & religious leaders. —**Crom·well'i·an** *adj.*
Cul·len (kŭl'ən), **Countée.** 1903–46. Amer. poet.
Cum·mings (kŭm'ĭngz), **Edward Estlin.** *e. e. cummings.* 1894–1962. Amer. poet.
Cun·ha (ko͞o'nyə), **Tristão da.** 1460?–1540. Portuguese navigator & explorer.
Cu·rie (kyo͝or'ē, kyo͝o-rē', kü-), *also* **Cu·rie-Jo·liot** (-zhô-lyō'), **Irene.** See JOLIOT-CURIE.
Curie, Pierre (1859–1906) & **Marie** (b. Poland, 1867–1934). French chemists & physicists (shared Nobel, 1903).
Cus·ter (kŭs'tər), **George Armstrong.** 1839–76. Amer. general.
Cy·rus (sī'rəs). 600?–529 B.C. *the Great.* Persian king (550–529) & founder of Persian empire.

D

Da·guerre (də-gâr'), **Louis Jacques Mandé.** 1787?–1851. French artist & inventor.
Da·li (dä'lē), **Salvador.** 1904–89. Spanish artist.
Dan·te A·li·ghie·ri (dän'tā äl'ə-gyâ'rē, dăn'-tē). 1265–1321. Italian poet. —**Dan'te·an** *adj.* & *n.* —**Dan·tesque'** (dăn-tĕsk') *adj.*
Dan·ton (däɴ-tôɴ'), **Georges Jacques.** 1759–94. French revolutionary leader.
Da·ri·us (də-rī'əs). Name of 3 kings of Persia, esp. I. *the Great.* 558?–486? B.C. Ruled 521–486 B.C.
Dar·row (dăr'ō), **Clarence Seward.** 1857–1938. Amer. lawyer.

Dar•win (där'wĭn), **Charles Robert.** 1809–82. English naturalist. —**Dar•win'i•an** *adj.*
Dau•mier (dō-myā', dō'mē-ā'), **Honoré.** 1808–79. French artist.
Da•vid (dä-vēd'), **Jacques Louis.** 1748–1825. French painter.
Da•vis (dā'vĭs), **Jefferson.** 1808–89. Amer. soldier & Confederate statesman.
Davis, Miles Dewey, Jr. 1926–91. Amer. musician.
Davis, Ruth Elizabeth ("Bette"). 1908–89. Amer. actress.
Da•vy (dā'vē), Sir **Humphrey.** 1778–1829. English chemist.
Dawes (dôz), **Charles Gates.** 1865–1951. U.S. Vice President (1925–29; Nobel, 1925).
Day (dā), **Dorothy.** 1897–1980. Amer. journalist & reformer.
Debs (dĕbz), **Eugene Victor.** 1855–1926. Amer. labor organizer & socialist leader.
De•bus•sy (də-byo͞o'sē), **Claude Achille.** 1862–1918. French composer.
De•ca•tur (dĭ-kā'tər), **Stephen.** 1779–1820. Amer. naval officer.
Deere (dîr), **John.** 1804–86. Amer. manufacturer & inventor.
De•foe (dĭ-fō'), **Daniel.** 1660–1731. English author.
De•gas (də-gä'), **(Hilaire Germain) Edgar.** 1834–1917. French painter.
de Gaulle (də gōl', gôl'), **Charles André Joseph Marie.** 1890–1970. French general & statesman.
de Koo•ning (dĭ ko͞o'nĭng), **Willem.** b. 1904. Dutch-born Amer. painter.
De•la•croix (dĕl'ə-krwä'), **(Ferdinand Victor) Eugène.** 1798–1863. French painter.
de la Mare (də lə mâr'), **Walter John.** 1873–1956. English author.
De La Warr (dĕl'ə wâr'), Baron. *Thomas West.* 1577–1618. English-born Amer. colonial administrator.
De•libes (də-lēb'), **(Clément Philibert) Léo.** 1836–91. French composer.
De Mille (də mĭl'), **Agnes George.** 1905–93. Amer. choreographer.
De Mille, Cecil Blount. 1881–1959. Amer. movie producer.
De•moc•ri•tus (dĭ-mŏk'rĭ-təs). 460?–357 B.C. Greek philosopher.
De•mos•the•nes (dĭ-mŏs'thə-nēz'). 385?–322 B.C. Greek orator.
Deng Xiao•ping (dŭng' shou'pĭng'). b. 1904. Chinese Communist leader.
Des•cartes (dā-kärt'), **René.** 1596–1650. French mathematician & philosopher. —**Car•te'sian** (kär-tē'zhən) *adj.*
de So•to (dĭ sō'tō), **Hernando.** 1496?–1542. Spanish explorer.
De Va•le•ra (dĕv'ə-lĕr'ə, -lîr'ə), **Eamon.** 1882–1975. Amer.-born Irish statesman.
Dew•ey (do͞o'ē, dyo͞o'ē), **George.** 1837–1917. Amer. naval officer.
Dewey, John. 1859–1952. Amer. philosopher & educator.
Dewey, Melvil. 1851–1931. Amer. librarian.
Dia•ghi•lev (dē-äg'ə-lĕf'), **Sergei Pavlovich.** 1872–1929. Russian ballet producer.
Dí•az (dē'äs, -äz), **Porfirio.** 1830–1915. Mexican general & statesman.
Dick•ens (dĭk'ĭnz), **Charles John Huffam.** 1812–70. English author. —**Dick•en'si•an** (dĭ-kĕn'zē-ən) *adj.*
Dick•in•son (dĭk'ĭn-sən), **Emily Elizabeth.** 1830–86. Amer. poet.
Di•de•rot (dē'də-rō', dē-drō'), **Denis.** 1713–1784. French philosopher & Encyclopedist.
Die•fen•ba•ker (dē'fən-bā'kər), **John George.** 1895–1979. Canadian prime minister (1957–63).
Di•em (dē-ĕm', dyĕm), **Ngo Dinh.** 1901–63. Vietnamese political leader; assassinated.
Die•trich (dē'trĭk, -trĭKH), **Marlene.** 1901?–92. German-born Amer. actress.
Di•Mag•gio (də-mä'zhē-ō, -măj'ē-ō), **Joseph Paul.** b. 1914. Amer. baseball player.
Di•o•cle•tian (dī'ə-klē'shən). 245–313. Roman emperor (284–305).
Di•og•e•nes (dī-ŏj'ə-nēz'). 412?–323 B.C. Greek philosopher.
Dis•ney (dĭz'nē), **Walter Elias ("Walt").** 1901–66. Amer. cartoonist & film producer.
Dis•rae•li (dĭz-rā'lē), **Benjamin.** 1804–81. British prime minister (1868, 1874–80).
Dodg•son (dŏj'sən), **Charles Lutwidge.** *Lewis Carroll.* 1832–98. English mathematician & author.
Dom•i•nic (dŏm'ə-nĭk), Saint. 1170–1221. Spanish-born founder of Dominican order. —**Do•min'i•can** (də-mĭn'ĭ-kən) *adj. & n.*
Don•a•tel•lo (dŏn'ə-tĕl'ō). 1386?–1466. Italian sculptor.
Don•i•zet•ti (dŏn'ĭ-zĕt'ē), **Gaetano.** 1797–1848. Italian composer.
Donne (dŭn), **John.** 1572?–1631. English poet.
Dopp•ler (dŏp'lər), **Christian Johann.** 1803–53. Austrian physicist.
Dos Pas•sos (dōs păs'ōs), **John Roderigo.** 1896–1970. Amer. novelist.
Dos•to•ev•ski *or* **Dos•to•yev•sky** (dŏs'tə-yef'skē, -toi-, -yĕv'-), **Feodor Mikhailovich.** 1821–81. Russian author. —**Dos'to•ev'ski•an** *adj.*
Doug•lass (dŭg'ləs), **Frederick.** 1817?–95. Amer. abolitionist & journalist.
Doyle (doil), Sir **Arthur Conan.** 1859–1930. English author.
Dra•co (drā'kō). 7th cent. B.C. Athenian lawgiver. —**Dra•co'ni•an** *adj.*
Drake (drāk), Sir **Francis.** 1540?–96. English naval hero & explorer.
Drei•ser (drī'sər, -zər), **Theodore (Herman Albert).** 1871–1945. Amer. author & editor.
Drey•fus (drī'fəs, drā'-), **Alfred.** 1859–1935. French army officer.
Dry•den (drīd'n), **John.** 1631–1700. English author.
Du Bois (do͞o bois'), **William Edward Burghardt ("W.E.B.").** 1868–1963. Amer. sociologist, educator, & author.
Du•champ (do͞o-shäN'), **Marcel.** 1887–1968. French-born modernist painter.

Dul·les (dŭl'ĭs), **John Foster.** 1888–1959. Amer. diplomat & statesman.

Du·mas (do͞o-mä', dyo͞o-), **Alexandre** (*Dumas père*; 1802–70) & **Alexandre** (*Dumas fils*; 1824–95). French authors.

Dun·can (dŭng'kən), **Isadora.** 1878–1927. Amer. dancer.

Dü·rer (do͝or'ər, dyo͝or'-), **Albrecht.** 1471–1528. German artist.

Du·va·lier (do͞o'väl-yā'), **François** (*Papa Doc*; 1907–71) & **Jean-Claude** (*Baby Doc*; b. 1951). Haitian political leaders.

Dvořák (də-vôr'zhäk'), **Anton** *or* **Antonin.** 1841–1904. Czech composer.

Dy·er (dī'ər), **Mary.** d. 1660. English-born Amer. Quaker martyr.

E

Ea·kins (ā'kĭnz), **Thomas.** 1844–1916. Amer. artist & educator.

Ear·hart (âr'härt'), **Amelia.** 1897–1937? Amer. aviator; lost on flight over the Pacific.

East·man (ēst'mən), **George.** 1854–1932. Amer. inventor & philanthropist.

Ed·dy (ĕd'ē), **Mary (Morse) Baker.** 1821–1910. Amer. founder of Christian Science.

E·den (ēd'n), Sir **(Robert) Anthony.** 1897–1977. British prime minister (1955–57).

Ed·i·son (ĕd'ĭ-sən), **Thomas Alva.** 1847–1931. Amer. inventor.

Ed·ward (ĕd'wərd). *the Confessor.* 1002–66. West Saxon king (1042–66).

Edward. *Prince of Wales, the Black Prince.* 1330–76. English soldier.

Edward. Name of 8 English kings: **a. I.** 1239–1307. Ruled 1272–1307. **b. II.** 1284–1327. Ruled 1307–27; murdered. **c. III.** 1312–77. Ruled 1327–77. **d. IV.** 1442–83. Ruled 1461–83. **e. V.** 1470–83. Ruled 1483; murdered. **f. VI.** 1537–53. Ruled 1547–53. **g. VII.** 1841–1910. Ruled 1901–10. **h. VIII.** Later *Duke of Windsor.* 1894–1972. Ruled 1936; abdicated. **—Ed·ward'i·an** (ĕd-wôr'de-ən, -wär'-) *adj. & n.*

Ed·wards (ĕd'wərdz), **Jonathan.** 1703–58. Amer. theologian & philosopher.

Ein·stein (īn'stīn'), **Albert.** 1879–1955. German-born Amer. theoretical physicist (Nobel, 1921).

Ei·sen·how·er (ī'zən-hou'ər), **Dwight David.** 1890–1969. 34th U.S. President (1953–61) & World War II commander.

Ei·sen·stein (ī'zən-stīn'), **Sergei Mikhailovich.** 1898–1948. Soviet filmmaker.

El·ea·nor of Aq·ui·taine (ĕl'ə-nər, -nôr'; ăk'wĭ-tān'). 1122?–1204. Queen of France & England.

El·gar (ĕl'gär', -gər), Sir **Edward.** 1857–1934. English composer.

El Grec·o (ĕl grĕk'ō). See GRECO.

El·i·ot (ĕl'ē-ət), **George.** *Mary Ann Evans.* 1819–80. English novelist.

Eliot, Thomas Stearns ("T.S."). 1888–1965. Amer.-born English critic & author (Nobel, 1948).

E·liz·a·beth (ĭ-lĭz'ə-bəth). Name of 5 English queens, esp.: **a. I.** 1533–1603. Ruled 1558–1603. **b.** b. 1900. Wife of George VI. **c. II.** b. 1926. Ruled since 1952. **—E·liz'a·be'than** (-bē'thən) *adj. & n.*

El·ling·ton (ĕl'ĭng-tən), **Edward Kennedy ("Duke").** 1899–1974. Amer. jazz composer, pianist, & bandleader.

Em·er·son (ĕm'ər-sən), **Ralph Waldo.** 1803–82. Amer. author. **—Em'er·so'ni·an** (ĕm'ər-sō'nē-ən) *adj.*

En·gels (ĕng'əlz, -əls), **Friedrich.** 1820–95. German socialist theorist & author.

Ep·ic·te·tus (ĕp'ĭk-tē'təs). 1st–2nd cent. A.D. Greek philosopher.

Ep·i·cu·rus (ĕp'ĭ-kyo͝or'əs). 342–270 B.C. Greek philosopher. **—Ep'i·cu·re'an** *adj. & n.*

E·ras·mus (ĭ-răz'məs), **Desiderius.** 1466?–1536. Dutch scholar & theologian.

Er·ic·son *also* **Er·ics·son** (ĕr'ĭk-sən), **Leif.** fl. c. 1000. Norwegian navigator.

Eth·el·red II (ĕth'əl-rĕd'). *the Unready.* 968?–1016. English king (978–1016).

Eu·clid (yo͞o'klĭd). 3rd cent. B.C. Greek mathematician & physicist. **—Eu·clid'e·an, Eu·clid'i·an** *adj.*

Eu·gé·nie (yo͞o'jə-nē, yo͞o-jē'-). 1826–1920. French empress as wife of Napoleon III.

Eu·rip·i·des (yo͞o-rĭp'ĭ-dēz'). 480?–406 B.C. Greek dramatist. **—Eu·rip'i·de'an** *adj.*

Ev·ans (ĕv'ənz), **Mary Ann.** George ELIOT.

F

Fa·ber·gé (făb'ər-zhā'), **Peter Carl.** 1846–1920. Russian designer & jeweler.

Far·a·day (făr'ə-dā'), **Michael.** 1791–1867. English physicist & chemist.

Far·ra·gut (făr'ə-gət), **David Glasgow.** 1801–70. Amer. admiral.

Fat·i·ma (făt'ə-mə). 606–32. Daughter of Muhammad.

Faulk·ner (fôk'nər), **William.** 1897–1962. Amer. author (Nobel, 1949).

Fawkes (fôks), **Guy.** 1570–1606. English conspirator; executed.

Fel·li·ni (fə-lē'nē), **Federico.** 1920–93. Italian filmmaker.

Fer·ber (fûr'bər), **Edna.** 1887–1968. Amer. author.

Fer·di·nand (fûr'dn-ănd'). Name of 5 kings of Castile & León, esp. **V.** 1452–1516. Ruled 1474–1504 with Isabella; also ruled Aragon (1479–1516) as **Ferdinand II** & Naples (1504–16) as **Ferdinand III.**

Ferdinand. 1. Name of 3 Holy Roman Emperors. **2.** Name of 2 Bourbon kings of Spain.

Fer·mi (fĕr'mē), **Enrico.** 1901–54. Italian-born Amer. physicist (Nobel, 1938).

Fich·te (fĭk'tə, fĭKH'-), **Johann Gottlieb.** 1762–1814. German philosopher.

Field·ing (fēl'dĭng), **Henry.** 1707–54. English author.

Fields (fēldz), **W.C.** 1880–1946. Amer. entertainer.

Fill·more (fĭl'môr', -mōr'), **Millard.** 1800–

74. 13th U.S. President (1850–53).
Fitz·ger·ald (fĭts-jĕr′əld), **F(rancis) Scott (Key).** 1896–1940. Amer. author.
Fitz·Ger·ald (fĭts-jĕr′əld), **Edward.** 1809–83. English poet & translator.
Flau·bert (flō-bâr′), **Gustave.** 1821–80. French author.
Flem·ing (flĕm′ĭng), Sir **Alexander.** 1881–1955. British bacteriologist (Nobel, 1945).
Ford (fôrd, fōrd), **Gerald Rudolph.** b. 1913. 38th U.S. President (1974–77).
Ford, Henry (1863–1947) & **Henry, Jr.** (1917–87). Amer. auto manufacturers.
For·ster (fôr′stər), **Edward Morgan ("E.M.").** 1879–1970. English author.
Fos·ter (fô′stər, fŏs′tər), **Stephen Collins.** 1826–64. Amer. songwriter.
Fou·cault (fo͞o-kō′), **Jean Bernard Léon.** 1819–68. French physicist.
France (frăns, fräNs), **Anatole.** 1844–1924. French author (Nobel, 1921).
Fran·cis (frăn′sĭs). Name of 2 French kings, esp. **I,** 1494–1547, ruled 1515–47.
Francis. Name of 2 Holy Roman Emperors, esp. **II,** 1768–1835, ruled 1792–1806.
Francis of As·si·si (ə-sē′zē, -sē, ə-sĭs′ē), Saint. 1182?–1226. Italian monk & founder of the Franciscan order. **—Fran·cis′can** (frăn-sĭs′kən) *adj. & n.*
Francis Jo·seph I (jō′zəf, -səf). 1830–1916. Austrian emperor (1848–1916).
Franck (frängk, fräNk), **César Auguste.** 1822–90. French organist & composer.
Fran·co (frăng′kō, fräng′-), **Francisco.** 1892–1975. Spanish soldier & dictator (1939–75).
Frank (frăngk, frängk), **Anne.** 1929–45. Dutch Jewish diarist.
Frank·furt·er (frăngk′fər-tər), **Felix.** 1882–1965. Austrian-born Amer. jurist.
Frank·lin (frăngk′lĭn), **Benjamin.** 1706–90. Amer. statesman, diplomat, author, scientist, & printer.
Franz Jo·sef I (fränts jō′səf, yō′zəf). FRANCIS JOSEPH I.
Fred·er·ick (frĕd′rĭk, -ər-ĭk). Name of 3 Holy Roman Emperors, esp. **I.** *Frederick Barbarossa.* 1123?–90. Ruled 1152–90 (crowned 1155); also king of Germany (1152–90) & Italy (1155–90).
Frederick. Name of 3 Prussian kings, esp. **II.** *the Great.* 1712–86. Ruled 1740–86.
Fré·mont (frē′mŏnt′), **John Charles.** 1813–90. Amer. soldier, explorer, & politician.
Freud (froid), **Anna.** 1895–1982. Austrian-born British psychoanalyst.
Freud, Sigmund. 1856–1939. Austrian physician & pioneer psychoanalyst. **—Freud′i·an** *adj. & n.*
Fro·bish·er (frō′bĭsh-ər), Sir **Martin.** 1535?–94. English navigator.
Fron·te·nac (frŏn′tə-năk′, frôNt-näk′), Comte **Louis de Buade de.** 1622–98. French colonial administrator.
Frost (frôst, frŏst), **Robert Lee.** 1874–1963. Amer. poet.
Ful·ler (fo͝ol′ər), **(Richard) Buckminster.** 1895–1983. Amer. architect & inventor.
Fuller, (Sara) Margaret. 1810–50. Amer. author, critic, & reformer.
Ful·ton (fo͝ol′tn), **Robert.** 1765–1815. Amer. artist, engineer, & inventor.

G

Gads·den (gădz′dən), **James.** 1788–1858. Amer. diplomat & railroad promoter.
Gage (gāj), **Thomas.** 1721–87. British general & colonial administrator.
Gains·bor·ough (gānz′bûr′ō, -bər-ə), **Thomas.** 1727–88. English painter.
Ga·len (gā′lən). 130?–201? Greek anatomist, physician, & author.
Ga·li·le·o Ga·li·lei (găl′ə-lē′ō găl′ə-lā′ē′, -lā′ō). 1564–1642. Italian astronomer & physicist. **—Gal′i·le′an** *adj.*
Gal·lau·det (găl′ə-dĕt′), **Thomas Hopkins.** 1787–1851. Amer. educator.
Gals·wor·thy (gălz′wûr′*th*ē), **John.** 1867–1933. English author (Nobel, 1932).
Gal·va·ni (găl-vä′nē, gäl-), **Luigi** *or* **Aloisio.** 1737–98. Italian physicist & physician.
Ga·ma (găm′ə, gä′mə), **Vasco da.** 1469?–1524. Portuguese explorer & administrator.
Gan·dhi (găn′dē, găn′), **Indira Nehru.** 1917–84. Indian political leader; assassinated.
Gandhi, Mohandas Karamchand ("Mahatma"). 1869–1948. Indian nationalist & spiritual leader; assassinated.
Gar·bo (gär′bō), **Greta.** 1905–90. Swedish-born Amer. actress.
Gar·ci·a Lor·ca (gär-sē′ə lôr′kä), **Federico.** 1899–1936. Spanish author.
García Már·quez (mär′kəs), **Gabriel.** b. 1928. Colombian-born author (Nobel, 1982).
Gar·field (gär′fēld′), **James Abram.** 1831–81. 20th U.S. President (1881); assassinated.
Gar·i·bal·di (găr′ə-bôl′dē), **Giuseppe.** 1807–82. Italian general & nationalist leader.
Gar·land (gär′lənd), **Judy.** 1922–69. Amer. actress & singer.
Gar·ri·son (găr′ĭ-sən), **William Lloyd.** 1805–79. Amer. abolitionist.
Gar·vey (gär′vē), **Marcus (Moziah) Aurelius.** 1887–1940. Jamaican black nationalist active in America; deported.
Gau·guin (gō-găN′), **(Eugène Henri) Paul.** 1848–1903. French painter.
Gauss (gous), **Karl Friedrich.** 1777–1855. German mathematician & astronomer.
Ge·net (zhə-nā′), **Jean.** 1910–86. French author.
Gen·ghis Khan (jĕng′gĭs kän′, gĕng′-). 1162?–1227. Mongol conqueror.
George (jôrj). Name of 6 kings of Great Britain, esp. **III.** 1738–1820. Ruled 1760–1820. **—Geor′gian** (jôr′jən) *adj. & n.*
Ge·ron·i·mo (jə-rŏn′ə-mō′). 1829–1909. Apache leader.
Gersh·win (gûrsh′wĭn), **George.** 1898–1937. Amer. composer.
Gershwin, Ira. 1896–1983. Amer. lyricist.
Gia·co·met·ti (jä-kə-mĕt′ē), **Alberto.** 1901–66. Swiss sculptor & painter.

Gib•bon (gĭb′ən), **Edward.** 1737–94. English historian.
Gide (zhēd), **André.** 1869–1951. French author (Nobel, 1947).
Gil•bert (gĭl′bərt), Sir **William Schwenck.** 1836–1911. English playwright & lyricist.
Gins•berg (gĭnz′bərg), **Allen.** b. 1926. Amer. poet.
Giot•to (jô′tō, jŏt′ō). 1266?–1337. Florentine painter, architect, & sculptor.
Glad•stone (glăd′stōn′), **William Ewart.** 1809–98. British prime minister (four times between 1868 & 1894).
Goe•thals (gō′thəlz), **George Washington.** 1858–1928. Amer. army engineer.
Goe•the (gœ′tə), **Johann Wolfgang von.** 1749–1832. German poet & dramatist.
Gogh (gō, gôKH, KHôKH), **Vincent van.** See VAN GOGH.
Go•gol (gô′gəl, gō′gôl), **Nikolai Vasilievich.** 1809–52. Russian author.
Gold•man (gōld′mən), **Emma.** 1869–1940. Russian-born Amer. anarchist.
Gold•smith (gōld′smĭth′), **Oliver.** 1728–74. Irish author.
Gom•pers (gŏm′pərz), **Samuel.** 1850–1924. English-born Amer. labor leader.
Good•man (go͝od′mən), **Benjamin David ("Benny").** 1909–86. Amer. musician.
Gor•ba•chev (gôr′bə-chôf′, -chŏf′, gər-bə-chôf′), **Mikhail Sergeyevich.** b. 1931. Russian president (1989–91; Nobel, 1990).
Gor•ki *also* **Gor•ky** (gôr′kē), **Maksim** *also* **Maxim.** 1868–1936. Russian author.
Go•ya y Lu•ci•en•tes (goi′ə ē lo͞o-sē-ĕn′-tēs), **Francisco José de.** 1746–1828. Spanish painter.
Gra•ham (grā′əm), **Martha.** 1894–1991. Amer. dancer & choreographer.
Grant (grănt), **Ulysses Simpson.** 1822–85. 18th U.S. President (1869–77) & Civil War general.
Graves (grāvz), **Robert Ranke.** 1895–1985. English-born Amer. author & critic.
Gray (grā), **Asa.** 1810–88. Amer. botanist.
Gray, Thomas. 1716–71. English poet.
Gre•co (grĕk′ō), **El.** 1541?–1614? Greek-born Spanish artist, architect, & scholar.
Gree•ley (grē′lē), **Horace.** 1811–72. Amer. journalist & politician.
Greene (grēn), **Graham.** 1904–91. English novelist.
Greg•o•ry (grĕg′ə-rē). Name of 16 popes, esp.: **a. I.** Saint. *the Great.* 540?–604. Reigned 590–604. **b. VII.** Saint. 1020?–85. Reigned 1073–85. **c. XIII.** 1502–85. Reigned 1572–85.
Grey (grā), Lady **Jane.** 1537–54. English queen (1553); executed for treason.
Grey, Zane. 1875–1939. Amer. author.
Grieg (grēg, grĭg), **Edvard Hagerup.** 1843–1907. Norwegian composer.
Grif•fith (grĭf′ĭth), **David Lewelyn Wark ("D.W.").** 1875–1948. Amer. filmmaker.
Grim•ké (grĭm′kē), **Sarah Moore** (1792–1873) & **Angeline Emily** (1805–79). Amer. feminists & abolitionists.
Grimm (grĭm), **Jakob Ludwig Karl** (1785–1863) & **Wilhelm Karl** (1786–1859). German philologists & folklorists.
Gro•pi•us (grō′pē-əs), **Walter Adolph.** 1883–1969. German-born Amer. architect.
Gus•ta•vus (gŭs-tā′vəs, -tä′-). Name of 6 kings of Sweden, esp. **II.** 1594–1632. Ruled 1611–32.
Gu•ten•berg (go͞ot′n-bûrg′), **Johann** *or* **Johannes.** 1400?–68? German printer & inventor of movable type.
Guth•rie (gŭth′rē), **Woodrow Wilson ("Woody").** 1912–67. Amer. folk singer.

H

Habs•burg (hăps′bûrg′, häps′bo͝ork′). *var. of* HAPSBURG.
Ha•dri•an (hā′drē-ən). A.D. 76–138. Roman emperor (117–38).
Hai•le Se•las•sie (hī′lē sə-lăs′ē, -lä′sē). 1891–1975. Ethiopian emperor (1930–74); exiled (1936–41) & deposed.
Hak•luyt (hăk′lo͞ot′), **Richard.** 1552–1616. English geographer.
Hale (hāl), **Edward Everett.** 1822–1909. Amer. clergyman & author.
Hale, Nathan. 1755–76. Amer. Revolutionary; hanged by the British as a spy.
Hal•ley (hăl′ē, hā′lē), **Edmund.** 1656–1742. English astronomer.
Hals (hälz, häls), **Frans.** 1580–1666. Dutch painter.
Ha•mil•car Bar•ca (hə-mĭl′kär′ bär′kə, hăm′əl-). 270?–228 B.C. Carthaginian general.
Ham•il•ton (hăm′əl-tən), **Alexander.** 1755?–1804. Amer. statesman & political & economic theorist; killed by Aaron Burr in a duel. **—Ham′il•to′ni•an** *adj.*
Ham•mar•skjöld (hăm′ər-shəld, -sho͞old′, -shēld′, hä′mər-), **Dag Hjalmar Agné Carl.** 1905–61. Swedish statesman & UN official (Nobel, 1961).
Ham•mer•stein (hăm′ər-stīn′, -stēn′), **Oscar, II.** 1895–1960. Amer. lyricist.
Ham•mu•ra•bi (hăm′ə-rä′bē). c. 20th or 18th cent. B.C. Babylonian king & lawgiver.
Ham•sun (häm′sən), **Knut.** 1859–1952. Norwegian author (Nobel, 1920).
Han (hän). Name of 3 Chinese dynasties: **Western Han,** 206 B.C.–A.D. 24; **Eastern Han,** A.D. 25–220; & **Later Han,** 947–50.
Han•cock (hăn′kŏk′), **John.** 1737–93. Amer. politician & Revolutionary leader.
Han•del (hăn′dl), **George Frederick.** 1685–1759. German-born English composer.
Han•ni•bal (hăn′ə-bəl). 247?–183 B.C. Carthaginian general.
Han•o•ver (hăn′ō′vər). English ruling family (1714–1901).
Haps•burg *also* **Habs•burg** (hăps′bûrg′, häps′bo͝ork′). Royal German family ruling Austria (1276–1740) & Spain (1516–1700).
Har•ding (här′dĭng), **Warren Gamaliel.** 1865–1923. 29th U.S. President (1921–23); died in office.

Har•dy (här'dē), **Thomas.** 1840–1928. English author.
Har•old (hăr'əld). Name of 2 kings of England: **a. I.** d. 1040. Ruled 1035–40. **b. II.** 1022–66. Ruled 1066.
Har•ri•man (hăr'ə-mən), **(William) Averell.** 1891–1986. Amer. financier & diplomat.
Har•ris (hăr'ĭs), **Joel Chandler.** 1848–1908. Amer. author & journalist.
Har•ri•son (hăr'ĭ-sən), **Benjamin.** 1833–1901. 23rd U.S. President (1889–93).
Harrison, William Henry. 1773–1841. Ninth U.S. President (1841); died in office.
Hart (härt), **Moss.** 1904–61. Amer. playwright, librettist, & director.
Har•vey (här'vē), **William.** 1578–1657. English physician, anatomist, & physiologist.
Hat•shep•sut (hăt-shĕp'so͞ot'). d. c. 1481 B.C. Egyptian queen.
Haw•thorne (hô'thôrn', hŏth'ôrn'), **Nathaniel.** 1804–64. Amer. author.
Haydn (hīd'n), **(Franz) Joseph ("Papa").** 1732–1809. Austrian composer.
Hayes (hāz), **Helen.** 1900–93. Amer. actress.
Hayes, Rutherford Birchard. 1822–93. 19th U.S. President (1877–81).
Haz•litt (hăz'lĭt, hāz'-), **William.** 1778–1830. English essayist.
Hearst (hûrst), **William Randolph.** 1863–1951. Amer. newspaper publisher.
Heath (hēth), **Edward Richard George.** b. 1916. British prime minister (1969–74).
He•gel (hā'gəl), **Georg Wilhelm Friedrich.** 1770–1831. German philosopher. —**He•ge'li•an** (hā-gā'lē-ən) *adj. & n.*
Hei•deg•ger (hī'dĕg'ər, -dĭ-gər), **Martin.** 1889–1976. German philosopher.
Hei•ne (hī'nə), **Heinrich.** 1797–1856. German lyric poet & critic.
Hei•sen•berg (hī'zən-bûrg', -bĕrk'), **Werner.** 1901–76. German physicist (Nobel, 1932).
Hell•man (hĕl'mən), **Lillian.** 1905–84. Amer. playwright.
Hem•ing•way (hĕm'ĭng-wā'), **Ernest Miller.** 1899?–1961. Amer. author (Nobel, 1954).
Hen•ry (hĕn'rē). *the Navigator.* 1394–1460. Portuguese prince.
Henry. Name of 8 kings of England, esp.: **a. II.** 1133–1189. Ruled 1154–89. **b. IV.** 1367–1413. Ruled 1399–1413. **c. V.** 1387–1422. Ruled 1413–22. **d. VI.** 1421–71. Ruled 1422–61, 1470–71. **e. VII.** 1457–1509. Ruled 1485–1509. **f. VIII.** 1491–1547. Ruled 1509–47.
Henry. Name of 4 kings of France, esp.: **a. II.** 1519–59. Ruled 1547–59. **b. IV.** *Henry of Navarre.* 1553–1610. Ruled 1589–1610.
Henry, Patrick. 1736–99. Amer. Revolutionary leader & orator.
Her•a•cli•tus (hĕr'ə-klī'təs). 6th–5th cent. B.C. Greek philosopher.
Her•od (hĕr'əd). *the Great.* 73?–4 B.C. King of Judea (40–4).
Herod An•ti•pas (ăn'tĭ-păs', -pəs). Ruler of Judea & tetrarch in Galilee (4 B.C.–A.D. 40).
He•rod•o•tus (hĭ-rŏd'ə-təs). *the Father of History.* 5th cent. B.C. Greek historian.
Her•schel (hûr'shəl). Family of English astronomers, including Sir **William** (1738–1822), **Caroline Lucretia** (1750–1848), & Sir **John Frederick William** (1792–1871).
Her•zl (hĕrt'səl), **Theodor.** 1860–1904. Hungarian-born Austrian founder of Zionism.
He•si•od (hē'sē-əd, hĕs'ē-). 8th cent. B.C. Greek poet.
Hes•se (hĕs'ə), **Hermann.** 1877–1962. German-born Swiss author (Nobel, 1946).
Hick•ok (hĭk'ŏk'), **James Butler ("Wild Bill").** 1837–76. Amer. frontier scout & marshal.
Hil•la•ry (hĭl'ə-rē), Sir **Edmund Percival.** b. 1919. New Zealand mountaineer.
Hil•lel (hĭl'ĕl). fl. 30 B.C.–A.D. 9. Palestinian rabbi.
Hip•poc•ra•tes (hĭ-pŏk'rə-tēz'). *the Father of Medicine.* 460?–377? B.C. Greek physician. —**Hip'po•crat'ic** (hĭp'ə-krăt'ĭk) *adj.*
Hi•ro•hi•to (hîr'ō-hē'tō). 1901–89. Japanese emperor (1926–89).
Hitch•cock (hĭch'kŏk'), **Alfred Joseph.** 1899–1980. British filmmaker.
Hit•ler (hĭt'lər), **Adolf.** 1889–1945. Austrian-born German Nazi dictator.
Hobbes (hŏbz), **Thomas.** 1588–1679. English philosopher. —**Hobbes'i•an** *adj. & n.*
Ho Chi Minh (hō' chē' mĭn'). 1890–1969. Vietnamese Communist leader.
Ho•garth (hō'gärth'), **William.** 1697–1764. English artist.
Ho•hen•zol•lern (hō'ən-zŏl'ərn). German royal family, ruling Brandenburg (1415–1918), Prussia (1701–1918), & Germany (1871–1918).
Ho•ku•sai (hō'ko͝o-sī', hō'ko͝o-sī'). 1760–1849. Japanese artist.
Hol•bein (hōl'bīn, hôl'-), **Hans.** *the Elder.* 1465?–1524. German painter.
Holbein, Hans. *the Younger.* 1497?–1543. German-born artist in England.
Hol•i•day (hŏl'ĭ-dā'), **Eleanor ("Billie").** *Lady Day.* 1915–59. Amer. singer.
Holmes (hōmz, hōlmz), **Oliver Wendell, Jr.** 1841–1935. Amer. jurist.
Ho•mer (hō'mər). fl. 850? B.C. Greek epic poet. —**Ho•mer'ic** (hō-mĕr'ĭk) *adj.*
Homer, Winslow. 1836–1910. Amer. painter.
Hoo•ver (ho͞o'vər), **Herbert Clark.** 1874–1964. 31st U.S. President (1929–33).
Hoover, J(ohn) Edgar. 1895–1972. Amer. director of FBI (1924–72).
Hop•kins (hŏp'kĭnz), **Gerard Manley.** 1844–89. English priest, poet, & artist.
Hop•per (hŏp'ər), **Edward.** 1882–1967. Amer. painter.
Hor•ace (hôr'əs, hŏr'-). 65–8 B.C. Roman poet. —**Ho•ra'tian** (hə-rā'shən) *adj.*
Hou•di•ni (ho͞o-dē'nē), **Harry.** 1874–1926. Amer. magician.
Hous•ton (hyo͞o'stən), **Samuel.** 1793–1863. Amer. general & politician.
How•ard (hou'ərd), **Catherine.** 1520?–42. Queen of England as 5th wife of Henry VIII

(1540–42); executed for adultery.

Howe (hou), **Elias.** 1819–67. Amer. inventor & manufacturer.

Howe, Julia Ward. 1819–1910. Amer. author, feminist, & philanthropist.

Howe, Sir **William.** 1729–1814. English general in America.

How•ells (hou′əlz), **William Dean.** 1837–1920. Amer. author & editor.

Hua Guo•feng •feng (hwä′ gwō′fŭng′). b. 1920. Chinese Communist leader.

Hub•ble (hŭb′əl), **Edwin Powell.** 1889–1953. Amer. astronomer.

Hud•son (hŭd′sən), **Henry.** d. 1611. English navigator & Arctic explorer.

Huer•ta (wĕr′tə, o͞o-ĕr′-), **Victoriano.** 1854–1916. Mexican statesman.

Hughes (hyo͞oz), **(James) Langston.** 1902–67. Amer. author.

Hu•go (hyo͞o′gō, ü-gō′), **Victor Marie.** 1802–85. French author.

Hull (hŭl), **Cordell.** 1871–1955. Amer. statesman (Nobel, 1945).

Hum•boldt (hŭm′bōlt′, ho͝om′-), Baron **(Friedrich Heinrich) Alexander von.** 1769–1859. German naturalist & author.

Hume (hyo͞om), **David.** 1711–76. Scottish philosopher & historian.

Hum•phrey (hŭm′frē, hŭmp′-), **Hubert Horatio.** 1911–78. U.S. Vice President (1965–69) & legislator.

Hur•ston (hûr′stən), **Zora Neale.** 1901?–60. Amer. author.

Huss *or* **Hus** (hŭs, ho͝os), **John** *or* **Jan.** 1374–1415. Bohemian religious reformer.

Hutch•in•son (hŭch′ĭn-sən), **Anne.** 1591–1643. English-born Amer. colonist.

Hux•ley (hŭks′lē), **Aldous Leonard.** 1894–1963. English author.

Huxley, Sir **Julian Sorell.** 1887–1975. English biologist & author.

Huxley, Thomas Henry. 1825–95. English biologist.

I

Ib•sen (ĭb′sən, ĭp′-), **Henrik.** 1828–1906. Norwegian dramatist.

Ig•na•tius of Loy•o•la (ĭg-nā′shəs, loi-ō′lə), Saint. 1491–1556. Spanish ecclesiastic & founder of the Society of Jesus.

In•gres (ăɴ′grə), **Jean Auguste Dominique.** 1780–1867. French painter.

In•no•cent (ĭn′ə-sənt). Name of 13 popes, esp. **III.** 1161–1216. Reigned 1198–1216.

Io•nes•co (ē′ə-nĕs′kō, yə-), **Eugène.** 1912–94. Romanian-born French dramatist.

Ir•ving (ûr′vĭng), **Washington.** 1783–1859. Amer. writer.

Is•a•bel•la I (ĭz′ə-bĕl′ə). 1451–1504. Queen of Castile & Aragon.

Ish•er•wood (ĭsh′ər-wo͝od′), **Christopher.** 1904–86. British-born Amer. writer.

I•van III Va•sil•ie•vich (ē-vän′, ī′vən; və-sĭl′yə-vĭch′). *the Great.* 1440–1505. Grand Duke of Muscovy (1462–1505).

Ivan IV Vasilievich. *the Terrible.* 1530–1584. Grand Duke of Muscovy (1533–84) & czar of Russia (1547–84).

Ives (īvz), **Charles Edward.** 1874–1954. Amer. composer.

J

Jack•son (jăk′sən), **Andrew.** *Old Hickory.* 1767–1845. Soldier & 7th U.S. President (1829–37). **—Jack•son′i•an** *adj. & n.*

Jackson, Mahalia. 1911–72. Amer. singer.

Jackson, Thomas Jonathan ("Stonewall"). 1824–63. Amer. Confederate general.

James (jāmz), Saint. *the Greater.* d. A.D. 44. One of the 12 Apostles; martyred.

James, Saint. One of the 12 Apostles.

James. Name of 6 kings of Scotland & Great Britain, esp.: **a. I.** 1566–1625. Ruled 1603–25 in England & 1567–1625 in Scotland as **James VI. b. II.** 1633–1701. Ruled 1685–88.

James, Henry. 1843–1916. Amer. novelist & critic. **—James′i•an** *adj. & n.*

James, Jesse Woodson. 1847–82. Amer. outlaw.

James, William. 1842–1910. Amer. psychologist & philosopher. **—James′i•an** *adj. & n.*

Jay (jā), **John.** 1745–1829. Amer. diplomat & jurist.

Jeanne d'Arc (zhäɴ därk′). JOAN OF ARC.

Jef•fer•son (jĕf′ər-sən), **Thomas.** 1743–1826. 3rd U.S. President (1801–9). **—Jef′fer•so′ni•an** (-sō′nē-ən) *adj. & n.*

Jen•ghis Khan *also* **Jen•ghiz Khan** (jĕn′gĭz kän′, -gĭs, jĕng′-). GENGHIS KHAN.

Je•sus (jē′zŭs) *also* **Je•sus Christ** (krīst). 4? B.C.–A.D. 29? Founder of Christianity.

Joan of Arc (jōn; ärk). 1412–31. French military leader & heroine.

John (jŏn), Saint. *the Evangelist.* One of the 12 Apostles & author of the 4th Gospel.

John, Saint. *the Baptist.* 5 B.C.–A.D. 30. Baptizer of Jesus.

John. Name of 21 popes, esp. **XXIII,** 1881–1963, reigned 1958–63.

John of Lack•land (lăk′lənd). 1167?–1216. English king (1199–1216).

John Paul (jŏn pôl, pŏl). Name of 2 popes, esp. **II.** b. 1920. Reigned since 1978.

Johns (jŏnz), **Jasper.** b. 1930. Amer. artist.

John•son (jŏn′sən), **Andrew.** 1808–75. 17th U.S. President (1865–69).

Johnson, Lyndon Baines. 1908–73. 36th U.S. President (1963–69).

Johnson, Philip Cortelyou. b. 1906. Amer. architect.

Johnson, Samuel. *Dr. Johnson.* 1709–84. English author & lexicographer. **—John•so′ni•an** (jŏn-sō′nē-ən) *adj. & n.*

Jo•li•et *also* **Jol•li•et** (jō′lē-ĕt′, jō′lē-ĕt′, zhô-lyā′), **Louis.** 1645–1700. French-Canadian explorer of America.

Jo•li•ot-Cu•rie (zhô-lyō′ kyo͞o-rē′), **Irène** (1897–1956) & **Frédéric** (1900–58). French physicists (Nobel, 1935).

Jones (jōnz), **John Paul.** 1747–92. Scottish-born Amer. naval officer.
Jon•son (jŏn'sən), **Benjamin ("Ben").** 1573–1637. English actor & author.
Jop•lin (jŏp'lĭn), **Scott.** 1868–1917. Amer. pianist & composer.
Joseph, Chief. 1840?–1904. Nez Percé leader.
Joule (jo͞ol, joul), **James Prescott.** 1818–89. English physicist.
Joyce (jois), **James.** 1882–1941. Irish author. —**Joyc'e•an** (joi'sē-ən) *adj.*
Juá•rez (hwä'rĕz, -räs), **Benito Pablo.** 1806–72. Mexican statesman.
Ju•das Is•car•i•ot (jo͞o'dəs ĭs-kăr'ē-ət). One of the 12 Apostles and betrayer of Jesus.
Jude (jo͞od), Saint. One of the 12 Apostles.
Jul•ian (jo͞ol'yən). 331–63. Roman emperor (361–63).
Jung (yo͝ong), **Carl Gustav.** 1875–1961. Swiss psychologist & psychiatrist.
Jus•tin•i•an (jŭ-stĭn'ē-ən). Name of 2 Byzantine emperors, esp. **I,** *the Great,* 483–565, ruled 527–65.
Ju•ve•nal (jo͞o'və-nəl). A.D. 60?–140? Roman satirist.

K

Ká•dar (kä'där), **János.** 1912–89. Hungarian statesman.
Kaf•ka (käf'kə, kăf'-), **Franz.** 1883–1924. Austrian author. —**Kaf'ka•esque'** (-ĕsk') *adj.*
Kahn (kän), **Louis I.** 1901–74. Estonian-born Amer. architect.
Ka•me•ha•me•ha (kə-mā'ə-mā'ə). Name of 5 kings of Hawaii, esp. **I,** *the Great,* 1753?–1819, ruled 1795–1819.
Kan•din•ski (kăn-dĭn'skē), **Vasili.** 1866–1944. Russian artist.
Kant (kănt, känt), **Immanuel.** 1724–1804. German philosopher. —**Kant'i•an** *adj.*
Keats (kēts), **John.** 1795–1821. English poet. —**Keats'i•an** *adj.*
Kel•ler (kĕl'ər), **Helen Adams.** 1880–1968. Amer. author & lecturer.
Kel•vin (kĕl'vĭn), 1st Baron. 1824–1907. Irish-born British physicist.
Ke•mal At•a•türk (kə-mäl' ăt'ə-tûrk', ä'-tə-). 1881–1938. Turkish statesman.
Ken•ne•dy (kĕn'ĭ-dē). Family of Amer. public officials, esp.: **a. John Fitzgerald ("Jack").** 1917–63. 35th U.S. President (1961–63); assassinated. **b. Robert Francis ("Bobby").** 1925–68. Legislator & attorney general; assassinated.
Ken•yat•ta (kĕn-yä'tə), **Jomo.** 1893?–1978. Kenyan statesman.
Kep•ler (kĕp'lər), **Johannes.** 1571–1630. German astronomer & mathematician.
Ker•ou•ac (kĕr'o͞o-ăk'), **Jean-Louis ("Jack").** 1922–69. Amer. author.
Key (kē), **Francis Scott.** 1779–1843. Amer. lawyer & poet.
Keynes (kānz), **John Maynard.** 1883–1943. English economist. —**Keynes'i•an** *adj. & n.*
Kho•mei•ni (kō-mā'nē, KHō-, hō-), Ayatollah **Ruholla.** 1900–88. Iranian leader.
Khru•shchev (kro͝osh-chĕf', -chôf', -chôv', -chĕv'), **Nikita Sergeevich.** 1894–1971. Soviet statesman.
Khu•fu (ko͞o'fo͞o'). CHEOPS.
Kier•ke•gaard (kîr'kĭ-gärd', -gôr'), **Sören Aaby.** 1813–55. Danish philosopher.
King (kĭng), **Martin Luther, Jr.** 1929–68. Amer. clergyman & civil-rights leader (Nobel, 1964); assassinated.
King, William Lyon Mackenzie. 1874–1950. Canadian prime minister (1921–26, 1926–30, 1935–48).
Kip•ling (kĭp'lĭng), **(Joseph) Rudyard.** 1865–1936. English author (Nobel, 1907).
Kis•sin•ger (kĭs'ĭn-jər), **Henry Alfred.** b. 1923. German-born Amer. diplomat (Nobel, 1973).
Klee (klā), **Paul.** 1879–1940. Swiss artist.
Knox (nŏks), **John.** 1505?–72. Scottish religious reformer.
Kos•ci•us•ko (kŏs'ē-ŭs'kō, kôsh-cho͝osh'-kō), **Thaddeus.** 1746–1817. Polish general & soldier in Amer. Revolution.
Ko•sy•gin (kə-sē'gən), **Aleksei Nikolaevich.** 1904–80. Soviet premier (1964–80).
Ku•blai Khan (ko͞o'blī kän') *also* **Ku•bla Khan** (-blə). 1216–94. Mongol emperor.

L

La•fa•yette (lä'fē-ĕt', lăf'ē-), Marquis de. 1757–1834. French military, political, & revolutionary leader.
La Fon•taine (lə fŏn-tān', fôN-tĕn'), **Jean de.** 1621–95. French poet & fabulist.
La•marck (lə-märk'), Chevalier de. 1744–1829. French naturalist.
Lamb (lăm), **Charles.** *Elia.* 1775–1834. English critic & essayist.
Lan•cas•ter (lăng'kə-stər, lăn'-). English royal house (1399–1461).
Lange (lăng), **Dorothea.** 1895–1965. Amer. photographer.
Lao-tse *also* **Lao-tzu** *or* **Lao-tsze** (lou'dzŭ'). 604?–531? B.C. Chinese philosopher.
La Roche•fou•cauld (lä rôsh-fo͞o-kō', rōsh-), Duc **François de.** 1613–80. French author.
La Salle (lə săl'), Sieur de. *Robert Cavelier.* 1643–87. French explorer in America.
Las Ca•sas (läs kä'səs), **Bartolomé de.** 1474–1566. Spanish missionary & historian.
Lau•ri•er (lôr'ē-ā', lŏr'-), Sir **Wilfrid.** 1841–1919. Canadian prime minister (1896–1911).
La•voi•sier (lə-vwä'zē-ā', lä-vwä-zyā'), **Antoine Laurent.** 1743–94. French pioneer chemist; guillotined.
Law•rence (lôr'əns, lŏr'-), **David Herbert ("D.H.").** 1885–1930. English novelist.
Lawrence, Thomas Edward ("T.E."). *Lawrence of Arabia.* 1888–1935. Welsh-born British soldier, adventurer, & author.
Laz•a•rus (lăz'ər-əs), **Emma.** 1849–87. Amer. poet & philanthropist.
Lea•key (lē'kē), **Louis Seymour Bazett.**

1903–72. English anthropologist.

Lear (lîr), **Edward.** 1812–88. English artist & author of nonsense verse.

Le Cor·bu·sier (lə kôr-bo͞o-zyā'). *Charles Edouard Jenneret.* 1887–1965. Swiss-born architect.

Le Duc Tho (lä' dŭk' tō'). 1911–90. Vietnamese political leader; declined 1973 Nobel.

Lee (lē), **Ann.** *Mother Ann.* 1736–84. English religious leader in America.

Lee, Henry ("Lighthorse Harry"). 1756–1818. Amer. Revolutionary commander.

Lee, Robert Edward. 1807–70. Amer. Confederate general.

Leeu·wen·hoek *or* **Leu·wen·hoek** (lā'vən-ho͝ok'), **Anton van.** 1632–1723. Dutch microscopy pioneer & naturalist.

Leib·nitz *or* **Leib·niz** (līb'nĭts, līp'-), Baron **Gottfried Wilhelm von.** 1646–1716. German philosopher & mathematician.

L'En·fant (län-fänt', läN-fäN'), **Pierre Charles.** 1754–1825. French-born engineer.

Le·nin (lĕn'ĭn), **Vladimir Ilich.** 1870–1924. Russian revolutionary leader. **—Len'in·ist'** *adj. & n.*

Leo (lē'ō). Name of 13 popes, esp.: **a. I.** Saint. *the Great.* 390?–461. Reigned 440–61. **b. III.** Saint. 750?–816. Reigned 795–816. **c. X.** 1475–1521. Reigned 1513–21.

Le·o·nar·do da Vin·ci (lē'ə-när'dō də vĭn'-chē, lā'-). 1452–1519. Florentine artist, engineer, musician, & scientist.

Le·o·pold (lē'ə-pōld'). Name of 3 kings of Belgium, esp. **II.** 1835–1909. Ruled 1865–1909.

Leu·wen·hoek (lā'vən-ho͝ok'). *var. of* LEEUWENHOEK.

Lé·vesque (lə-vĕk'), **René.** b. 1922. Canadian political leader.

Lew·is (lo͞o'ĭs), **Clive Staples ("C.S.").** 1898–1963. English novelist.

Lewis, John Llewellyn. 1880–1969. Amer. labor leader.

Lewis, Meriwether. 1774–1809. Amer. soldier & Western explorer.

Lewis, (Harry) Sinclair. 1885–1951. Amer. novelist (Nobel, 1930).

Li Bo (lē' bō'). *var. of* LI PO.

Lich·ten·stein (lĭk'tən-stīn', -stēn'), **Roy.** b. 1923. Amer. painter.

Li·li·u·o·ka·la·ni (lə-lē'ə-ō-kə-lä'nē). *Lydia Kamekeha Paki.* 1838–1917. Hawaiian queen (1891–93); deposed.

Lin Biao (lĭn' bē-ou'). 1907–71. Chinese political leader.

Lin·coln (lĭng'kən), **Abraham.** 1809–65. 16th U.S. President (1861–65); assassinated.

Lind·bergh (lĭnd'bûrg', lĭn'-), **Anne Spencer Morrow.** b. 1906. Amer. aviator & author.

Lindbergh, Charles Augustus. 1902–74. Amer. pioneer aviator.

Lin·nae·us (lĭ-nē'əs, -nā'-), **Carolus.** 1707–78. Swedish botanist. **—Lin·nae'an** *adj.*

Li Po (lē' pō', bō') *or* **Li Bo** (bō'). d. 762? Chinese poet.

Lip·pi (lĭp'ē), Fra **Filippo** *or* **Lippo** (1406?–69) **& Filippo** *or* **Filippino** (1457?–1504). Florentine painters.

Lis·ter (lĭs'tər), **Joseph.** 1827–1912. English founder of antiseptic surgery.

Liszt (lĭst), **Franz.** 1811–86. Hungarian pianist & composer.

Liv·ing·stone (lĭv'ĭng-stən), **David.** 1813–73. Scottish missionary & African explorer.

Liv·y (lĭv'ē), 59 B.C.–A.D. 17. Roman historian.

Lloyd George (loid jôrj'), **David.** 1863–1945. British prime minister (1916–22).

Locke (lŏk), **John.** 1632–1704. English philosopher.

Lodge (lŏj), **Henry Cabot.** 1850–1924. Amer. politician & author.

Lodge, Henry Cabot, Jr. 1902–85. Amer. politician & diplomat.

Lon·don (lŭn'dən), **John Griffith ("Jack").** 1876–1916. Amer. author.

Long·fel·low (lông'fĕl'ō, lŏng'-), **Henry Wadsworth.** 1807–82. Amer. poet.

Lor·ca (lôr'kə), **Federico García.** See GARCÍA LORCA.

Lou·is (lo͞o'ē, lo͞o-ē'). Name of 18 kings of France, esp. **a. XIV.** *the Sun King.* 1638–1715. Ruled 1643–1715. **b. XV.** 1710–74. Ruled 1715–74. **c. XVI.** 1754–93. Ruled 1774–92; executed. **d. XVIII.** 1755–1824. Ruled 1814–24.

Lou·is (lo͞o'ĭs), **Joseph ("Joe").** 1914–81. Amer. prizefighter.

Louis Phi·lippe (lo͞o'ē fĭ-lēp'). *the Citizen King.* 1773–1850. French king (1830–48).

Low·ell (lō'əl), **Amy.** 1874–1925. Amer. poet.

Lowell, James Russell. 1819–91. Amer. editor, poet, & diplomat.

Lowell, Robert Traill Spence, Jr. 1917–77. Amer. poet.

Loy·o·la (loi-ō'lə), Saint **Ignatius.** See IGNATIUS OF LOYOLA.

Luce (lo͞os), **Clare Boothe.** 1903–87. Amer. editor, politician, diplomat, & playwright.

Luce, Henry Robinson. 1898–1967. Amer. editor & publisher.

Lu·cre·tius (lo͞o-krē'shəs, -shē-əs). 96?–55 B.C. Roman philosopher & poet.

Luke (lo͝ok), Saint. Companion of St. Paul & author of the 3rd Gospel.

Lu·ther (lo͞o'thər), **Martin.** 1483–1546. German monk & Protestant religious reformer. **—Lu'ther·an** *adj. & n.*

M

Mac·Ar·thur (mĭk-är'thər), **Douglas.** 1880–1964. Amer. general.

Ma·cau·lay (mə-kô'lē), **Thomas Babington.** 1800–59. English historian & statesman.

Mac·don·ald (mək-dŏn'əld), Sir **John Alexander.** 1815–91. Canadian prime minister (1867–73, 1878–91).

Mac·Don·ald (mək-dŏn'əld), **(James) Ramsay.** 1866–1937. British prime minister

(1924, 1929–35).
Mach (mäk, mäKH), **Ernst.** 1838–1916. Austrian physicist & philosopher.
Mach·i·a·vel·li (măk'ē-ə-vĕl'ē), **Niccolò.** 1469–1527. Italian statesman & political theorist. —**Mach'i·a·vel'li·an** *adj. & n.*
Mac·ken·zie (mə-kĕn'zē), Sir **Alexander.** 1764–1820. Scottish explorer.
Mackenzie, Alexander. 1822–92. Scottish-born Canadian prime minister (1873–78).
Mac·Leish (mə-klēsh'), **Archibald.** 1892–1982. Amer. poet & dramatist.
Mac·mil·lan (mək-mĭl'ən), Harold. 1894–1986. British prime minister (1957–63).
Ma·de·ro (mə-dîr'ō), **Francisco.** 1873–1913. Mexican revolutionary & statesman.
Mad·i·son (măd'ĭ-sən), **Dolley Payne Todd.** 1768–1849. Amer. hostess & wife of James Madison.
Madison, James. 1751–1836. 4th U.S. President (1809–17).
Mae·ter·linck (mā'tər-lĭngk', mĕt'ər-, mä'-), Count **Maurice.** 1862–1949. Belgian poet, dramatist, & naturalist (Nobel, 1911).
Ma·gel·lan (mə-jĕl'ən), **Ferdinand.** 1480?–1521. Portuguese navigator; killed while circumnavigating the globe.
Ma·gritte (mə-grēt'), **René.** 1898–1967. Belgian painter.
Mah·ler (mä'lər), **Gustav.** 1860–1911. Austrian composer & conductor.
Mai·mon·i·des (mī-mŏn'ĭ-dēz'), **Moses.** 1135–1204. Spanish-born Jewish philosopher.
Mal·colm X (măl'kəm ĕks'). 1925–65. Amer. civil-rights leader; assassinated.
Mal·lar·mé (măl'är-mā'), **Stéphane.** 1842–98. French poet.
Mal·o·ry (măl'ə-rē), Sir **Thomas.** fl. 1470. English author.
Mal·raux (măl-rō'), **André.** 1901–76. French author & politician.
Mal·thus (măl'thəs, môl'-), **Thomas Robert.** 1766–1834. English economist. —**Mal·thu'sian** (măl-tho͞o'zhən, môl-) *adj. & n.*
Man·de·la (măn-dĕl'ə), **Nelson Rolihlahla.** b. 1918. South African political leader & president (since 1994).
Ma·nes (mā'nēz). 216?–76? Persian prophet.
Ma·net (mə-nā'), **Edouard.** 1832–83. French painter.
Mann (măn), **Horace.** 1796–1859. Amer. educator.
Mann (măn, män), **Thomas.** 1875–1955. German-born Amer. author (Nobel, 1929).
Mao Ze·dong (mou' dzŭ'do͝ong') *also* **Mao Tse-tung** (tsə-to͝ong'). 1893–1976. Chinese Communist leader.
Ma·rat (mə-rä'), **Jean Paul.** 1743–93. Swiss-born French revolutionary; assassinated.
Mar·co·ni (mär-cō'nē), **Guglielmo.** 1874–1937. Italian inventor (Nobel, 1909).
Mar·co Po·lo (mär'kō pō'lō). See POLO.
Mar·cos (mär'kōs, -kəs), **Ferdinand Edralin.** 1917–89. Philippine president (1965–86).
Mar·cus Au·re·li·us An·to·ni·nus (mär'kəs ô-rē'lē-əs ăn'tə-nī'nəs). 121–80. Roman emperor & philosopher.
Mar·gar·et of An·jou (mär'gə-rət, -grət; ăn-jo͞o', äN-zho͞o'). 1430–82. Queen of Henry IV of England.
Ma·ri·a The·re·sa (mə-rē'ə tə-rā'sə, -zə). 1717–80. Queen of Hungary & Bohemia.
Marie An·toi·nette (ăn'twə-nĕt'). 1755–93. Queen of France (1774–93) as wife of Louis XVI; executed.
Mark (märk), Saint. Author of the 2nd Gospel.
Mark An·to·ny (ăn'tə-nē) *or* **Mark An·tho·ny** (ăn'thə-nē). 83?–30 B.C. Roman orator, politician, & soldier.
Mar·lowe (mär'lō), **Christopher.** 1564–93. English dramatist & poet.
Mar·quette (mär-kĕt'), Père **Jacques.** 1637–75. French missionary & explorer.
Mar·shall (mär'shəl), **George Catlett.** 1880–1959. Amer. soldier, diplomat, & statesman (Nobel, 1953).
Marshall, John. 1755–1835. Amer. jurist & statesman.
Marshall, Thurgood. 1908–93. Amer. jurist.
Mar·tí (mär-tē'), **José Julian.** 1853–95. Cuban revolutionary leader and poet.
Mar·tial (mär'shəl). 1st cent. A.D. Roman epigrammist.
Mar·vell (mär'vəl), **Andrew.** 1621–78. English poet & satirist.
Marx (märks), **Karl.** 1818–83. German political philosopher & economist. —**Marx'i·an** *adj. & n.* —**Marx'ist** *adj. & n.*
Mary. Name of 2 English queens: **a. I.** *also* **Mary Tu·dor** (to͞o'dər). *Bloody Mary.* 1516–58. Ruled 1553–58. **b. II.** 1662–94. Ruled jointly with William III (1689–94).
Mary Queen of Scots (skŏts) *also* **Mary Stu·art** (sto͞o'ərt). 1542–87. Queen of Scotland (1542–67); beheaded.
Mas·sa·soit (măs'ə-soit'). 1580?–1661. Wampanoag Indian leader.
Mas·ters (măs'tərz), **Edgar Lee.** 1869–1950. Amer. poet.
Math·er (măth'ər), **Increase** (1639–1723) & **Cotton** (1663–1728). Amer. clergymen & authors.
Ma·tisse (mə-tēs', mä-), **Henri.** 1869–1954. French artist.
Mat·thew (măth'yo͞o), Saint. Apostle & author of the first Gospel.
Maugham (môm), **William Somerset.** 1874–1965. English author.
Mau·pas·sant (mō-pə-säN', mō'pə-sänt'), **(Henri René Albert) Guy de.** 1850–93. French author.
Mau·riac (môr-yäk', môr'ē-äk'), **François.** 1885–1970. French author (Nobel, 1952).
Max·i·mil·ian (măk'sə-mĭl'yən). 1832–67. Austrian archduke & emperor of Mexico (1864–67); executed.
Maximilian. Name of 2 Holy Roman Emperors: **a. I.** 1459–1519. Ruled 1493–1519. **b. II.** 1527–76. Ruled 1564–76.
Max·well, (măks'wĕl', -wəl), **James Clerk.** 1831–79. Scottish physicist.
Maz·zi·ni (mät-sē'nē), **Giuseppe.** 1805–72.

Italian revolutionary patriot.

Mc•Clel•lan (mə-klĕl'ən), **George Brinton.** 1826–85. Amer. general & politician.

Mc•Cul•lers (mə-kŭl'ərz), **Carson Smith.** 1917–67. Amer. author.

Mc•Kin•ley (mə-kĭn'lē), **William.** 1843–1901. 25th U.S. President (1897–1901); assassinated.

Mc•Lu•han (mə-klo͞o'ən), **(Herbert) Marshall.** 1911–81. Canadian educator.

Mead (mēd), **Margaret.** 1901–78. Amer. anthropologist.

Med•i•ci (mĕd'ə-chē'). Italian Renaissance family, including: **a. Cosimo de.** 1389–1464. Banker, art patron, & statesman. **b. Giovanni de.** LEO X. **c. Lorenzo de.** *Lorenzo the Magnificent.* 1449–92. Art patron & statesman.

Meigh•en (mē'ən), **Arthur.** 1874–1960. Canadian prime minister (1920–21, 1926).

Me•ir (mī'ər, mä-ĕr'), **Golda.** 1898–1978. Russian-born Israeli prime minister (1969–74).

Mel•ville (mĕl'vĭl), **Herman.** 1819–91. Amer. author.

Men•ci•us (mĕn'shē-əs). 4th cent. B.C. Chinese philosopher.

Menck•en (mĕng'kən), **Henry Louis.** 1880–1956. Amer. editor & critic.

Men•del (mĕn'dl), **Gregor Johann.** 1822–84. Austrian botanist. —**Men•de'li•an** (mĕn-dē'lē-ən, -dēl'yən) *adj.*

Men•de•le•ev (mĕn'də-lā'əf), **Dmitri Ivanovich.** 1834–1907. Russian chemist.

Men•dels•sohn (mĕn'dl-sən), **(Jakob Ludwig) Felix.** 1809–47. German composer.

Mer•ca•tor (mər-kā'tər), **Gerhardus.** 1512–94. Flemish geographer.

Mer•e•dith (mĕr'ĭ-dĭth), **George.** 1828–1909. English author.

Met•ter•nich (mĕt'ər-nĭk, -nĭKH), Prince **Klemens Wenzel Nepomuk Lothar von.** 1773–1859. Austrian statesman.

Mi•chel•an•ge•lo Buo•nar•ro•ti (mī'kəl-ăn'jə-lō' bwôn'ə-rô'tē, mĭk'əl-, mē'kə-län'-). 1475–1564. Italian sculptor, painter, architect, & poet.

Mies Van Der Ro•he (mēz' văn dər rō'ə, rō', mēs'), **Ludwig.** 1886–1969. German-born Amer. architect.

Mill (mĭl), **John Stuart.** 1806–73. English philosopher & economist.

Mil•lay (mĭ-lā'), **Edna St. Vincent.** 1892–1950. Amer. poet.

Mil•ler (mĭl'ər), **Arthur.** b. 1915. Amer. dramatist.

Mil•let (mĭ-lā'), **Jean François.** 1814–75. French painter.

Mil•ton (mĭl'tən), **John.** 1608–74. English poet.

Ming (mĭng). Chinese dynasty (1368–1644).

Min•u•it (mĭn'yo͞o-wĭt), **Peter.** 1580–1638. Dutch colonial administrator.

Mis•tral (mĭ-sträl'), **Gabriela.** 1889–1957. Chilean educator & poet (Nobel, 1945).

Mit•ter•rand (mē'tə-räN', -ränd'), **François Maurice.** b. 1916. French president (1981–95).

Mo•di•glia•ni (mō-dē'lē-ä'nē, -lyä'nē), **Amedeo.** 1884–1920. Italian artist.

Mo•ham•med (mō-hăm'ĭd). See MUHAMMAD.

Mo•lière (mōl-yâr'), **Jean Baptiste Poquelin.** 1622–73. French actor & playwright.

Mo•lo•tov (mŏl'ə-tôf', -tôv', môl'-), **Vyacheslav Mikhailovich.** 1890–1986. Russian statesman.

Mon•dri•an (môn'drē-än'), **Piet.** 1872–1944. Dutch painter.

Mo•net (mō-nā'), **Claude.** 1840–1926. French painter.

Mon•roe (mən-rō'), **James.** 1758–1831. 5th U.S. President (1817–25).

Mon•taigne (mŏn-tān'), **Michel Eyquem de.** 1533–92. French essayist.

Mon•ta•le (mōn-tä'lā), **Eugenio.** 1896–1981. Italian poet (Nobel, 1975).

Mont•calm de Saint-Ve•ran (mŏnt-käm' də săN'vā-räN'), Marquis **Louis Joseph de.** 1712–59. French commander in Canada.

Mon•tes•quieu (mŏn'tə-skyo͞o'), Baron **de la Brede et de.** *Charles de Secondat.* 1689–1755. French philosopher & jurist.

Mon•tes•so•ri (mŏn'tĭ-sôr'ē, -sōr'ē), **Maria.** 1870–1952. Italian physician & educator.

Mon•te•zu•ma II (mŏn'tə-zo͞o'mə). 1480?–1520. Last Aztec emperor in Mexico.

Moore (mo͝or), **Henry.** 1898–1986. English sculptor.

Moore, Marianne Craig. 1887–1972. Amer. poet.

More (môr, mōr), Saint (Sir) **Thomas.** 1478–1535. English statesman & author; beheaded for treason.

Mor•gan (môr'gən), **John Pierpont** (1837–1913) & **John Pierpont, Jr.** (1867–1943). Amer. financiers.

Morse (môrs), **Samuel Finley Breese.** 1791–1872. Amer. painter & inventor.

Mott (mŏt), **Lucretia Coffin.** 1793–1880. Amer. social reformer.

Mo•zart (mōt'särt'), **Wolfgang Amadeus.** 1756–91. Austrian composer.

Mu•ga•be (mo͞o-gä'bē), **Robert Gabriel.** b. 1925. Zimbabwean statesman.

Mu•ham•mad (mo͞o-hăm'ĭd, -hä'mĭd) *also* **Mo•ham•med** (mō-, mo͞o-). 570?–632. Arab prophet & founder of Islam.

Muhammad, Elijah. 1897–1975. Amer. religious leader.

Muir (myo͝or), **John.** 1838–1914. Scottish-born Amer. naturalist.

Munch (mo͝ongk), **Edvard.** 1863–1944. Norwegian artist.

Mu•ñoz Ma•rin (mo͞o-nyōs' mä-rēn'), **Luis.** 1898–1980. Puerto Rican statesman.

Mur•row (mûr'ō), **Edward Roscoe.** 1908–65. Amer. broadcast journalist.

Mus•so•li•ni (mo͞o'sə-lē'nē, mo͝os'ə-), **Benito.** *Il Duce.* 1883–1945. Italian Fascist dictator (1922–45); assassinated.

Mus•sorg•sky (mə-zôrg'skē, mo͞o-sôrg'skĭ), **Modest Petrovich.** 1835–81. Russian composer.

N

Na•bo•kov (nə-bô'kəf, nä'bə-kôf'), **Vladimir.** 1899–1977. Russian-born Amer. author.
Na•pi•er (nā'pē-ər, nə-pîr'), **John.** 1550–1617. Scottish mathematician.
Na•po•le•on I (nə-pō'lē-ən, -pōl'yən). *Napoleon Bonaparte.* 1769–1821. French emperor (1804–14); exiled. —**Na•po'le•on'ic** *adj.*
Napoleon III. *Charles Louis Napoleon Bonaparte.* 1808–73. French emperor (1852–70).
Nas•ser (nä'sər, năs'ər), **Gamal Abdel.** 1918–70. Egyptian soldier & statesman.
Na•tion (nā'shən), **Carry** *or* **Carrie.** 1846–1911. Amer. temperance reformer.
Neb•u•chad•nez•zar II (nĕb'ə-kəd-nĕz'ər, nĕb'yə-). King of Babylonia (605–562 B.C.).
Nef•er•ti•ti (nĕf'ər-tē'tē). 14th cent. B.C. Egyptian queen as wife of Akhenaton.
Neh•ru (nā'ro͞o), Pandits **Motilal** (1861–1931) & **Jawaharlal** (1889–1964). Indian nationalist leaders & statesmen.
Nel•son (nĕl'sən), **Horatio.** *Viscount Nelson.* 1758–1805. English admiral.
Ne•ro (nîr'ō, nē'rō). A.D. 37–68. Roman emperor (54–68).
Ne•ru•da (nā-ro͞o'də), **Pablo.** 1904–73. Chilean poet & diplomat (Nobel, 1971).
New•man (no͞o'mən, nyo͞o'-), **John Henry.** 1801–90. English prelate & theologian.
New•ton (no͞ot'n, nyo͞ot'n), Sir **Isaac.** 1642–1727. English mathematician, scientist, & philosopher. —**New•to'ni•an** *adj.*
Nich•o•las (nĭk'ə-ləs). Name of 2 czars of Russia: **a. I.** 1796–1855. Ruled 1825–55. **b. II.** 1868–1918. Ruled 1894–1918; executed.
Nie•tzsche (nē'chə, -chē), **Friedrich Wilhelm.** 1844–1900. German philologist & philosopher. —**Nie'tzsche•an** *adj. & n.*
Night•in•gale (nīt'n-gāl', nī'tĭng-), **Florence.** 1820–1910. English nursing pioneer.
Ni•jin•sky (nĭ-zhĭn'skē), **Vaslav.** 1890–1950. Russian-born dancer & choreographer.
Nim•itz (nĭm'ĭts), **Chester Williams.** 1885–1966. Amer. admiral.
Nix•on (nĭk'sən), **Richard Milhous.** 1913–94. 37th U.S. President (1969–74); resigned.
Nkru•mah (ən-kro͞o'mə, əng-), **Kwame.** 1909–72. Ghanaian statesman.
No•bel (nō-bĕl'), **Alfred Bernhard.** 1833–96. Swedish chemist & philanthropist.
Nos•tra•da•mus (nŏs'trə-dā'məs, -dä'-, nōs'-). 1503–66. French physician & astrologer.
Nu•re•yev (no͞o-rā'yəf, no͝or'ĭ-yĕv, -ĕf, -ĕv), **Rudolf.** 1938–93. Russian-born ballet dancer & choreographer.

O

Oak•ley (ōk'lē), **Annie.** 1860–1926. Amer. markswoman.
O•bre•gón (ō-brā-gôn'), **Alvaro.** 1880–1928. Mexican soldier & statesman.
O'Ca•sey (ō-kā'sē), **Sean.** 1880–1964. Irish playwright.
O'Con•nor (ō-kŏn'ər), **Flannery.** 1925–64. Amer. author.
Oc•ta•vi•an (ŏk-tā'vē-ən). AUGUSTUS.
O•dets (ō-dĕts'), **Clifford.** 1906–63. Amer. playwright.
Of•fen•bach (ô'fən-bäk'), **Jacques.** 1819–80. French composer.
O•gle•thorpe (ō'gəl-thôrp'), **James Edward.** 1696–1785. English soldier & colonizer.
O. Hen•ry (ō hĕn'rē). William Sidney PORTER.
O'Hig•gins (ō-hĭg'ĭnz), **Bernardo.** 1778–1842. Chilean general & statesman.
O'Keeffe (ō-kēf'), **Georgia.** 1887–1986. Amer. painter.
O•liv•i•er (ō-lĭv'ē-ā'), Sir **Laurence Kerr.** 1907–89. English actor and director.
Olm•sted (ōm'stĕd', -stĭd, ŏm'-), **Frederick Law.** 1822–1903. Amer. landscape architect.
O•mar Khay•yám (ō'mär kī-yäm', -ăm'). 1050–1123. Persian poet & mathematician.
O•nas•sis (ō-năs'ĭs, -nä'sĭs), **Jacqueline Lee Bouvier Kennedy.** 1929–94. Amer. socialite & editor.
O•ña•te (ôn-yä'tā), **Juan de.** 1549–1624? Spanish explorer & conquistador.
O'Neill (ō-nēl'), **Eugene Gladstone.** 1888–1953. Amer. playwright (Nobel, 1936).
Op•pen•hei•mer (ŏp'ən-hī'mər), **J(ulius) Robert.** 1904–67. Amer. physicist.
O•roz•co (ō-rôs'kō), **José Clemente.** 1883–1949. Mexican fresco painter.
Or•te•ga y Gas•set (ôr-tā'gə ē gä-sĕt'), **José.** 1883–1955. Spanish philosopher.
Or•well (ôr'wĕl', -wəl), **George.** *Eric Blair.* 1903–50. English author.
Os•ce•o•la (ŏs'ē-ō'lə, ō'sē-). 1804?–38. Seminole leader.
O•tis (ō'tĭs), **James.** 1725–83. Amer. Revolutionary politician & publicist.
Ot•to (ŏt'ō) *also* **O•tho** (ō'thō, ō'tō). Name of 4 Holy Roman Emperors, esp. **I,** *the Great,* 912–73, ruled 962–73.
Ov•id (ŏv'ĭd). 43 B.C.–A.D. 18. Roman poet.
Ow•en (ō'ĭn), **Robert.** 1771–1858. Welsh-born British manufacturer & reformer.
Owen, Robert Dale. 1801–77. Scottish-born Amer. social reformer.
Ow•ens (ō'ĭnz), **Jesse.** 1913–80. Amer. athlete.

P

Pa•ga•ni•ni (păg'ə-nē'nē, pä'gä-), **Nicolo.** 1782–1840. Italian violinist & composer.
Pah•la•vi (pä'lə-vē), **Mohammed Reza.** 1919–80. Iranian shah (1941–79); deposed.
Paine (pān), **Thomas.** 1737–1809. English-born Amer. author & Revolutionary leader.
Pal•la•dio (pə-lä'dē-ō), **Andrea.** 1508–80. Italian architect. —**Pal•la'di•an** *adj.*
Palm•er•ston (pä'mər-stən, päl'-), 3rd Viscount. *Henry John Temple.* 1784–1865. British prime minister (1855–58, 1859–65).
Papp (păp), **Joseph.** 1921–91. Amer. stage producer & director.

Park (pärk), **Mungo.** 1771–1806. Scottish explorer in Africa.

Park Chung Hee (pärk′ chŭng′ hē′). 1917–79. South Korean statesman.

Park•man (pärk′mən), **Francis.** 1823–93. Amer. historian.

Parks (pärks), **Rosa.** b. 1913. Amer. civil-rights leader.

Par•nell (pär-nĕl′, pär′nəl), **Charles Stewart.** 1846–91. Irish nationalist leader.

Parr (pär), **Catherine.** 1512–48. Queen of England as 6th wife of Henry VIII.

Pas•cal (păs-kăl′, päs-käl′), **Blaise.** 1623–62. French philosopher & mathematician.

Pas•ter•nak (păs′tər-năk′), **Boris.** 1890–1960. Russian author (Nobel, 1958).

Pas•teur (păs-tûr′), **Louis.** 1822–95. French chemist. —**Pas•teur′i•an** *adj.*

Pat•rick (păt′rĭk), Saint. 389?–461? Patron saint of Ireland.

Pat•ton (păt′n), **George Smith, Jr.** 1885–1945. Amer. general.

Paul (pôl), Saint. A.D. 5?–67? Apostle to the Gentiles. —**Paul′ine** (-īn) *adj.*

Paul. Name of 6 popes, esp.: **a. III.** 1468–1549. Reigned 1534–49. **b. VI.** 1897–1978. Reigned 1963–78.

Pau•ling (pô′lĭng), **Linus Carl.** 1901–94. Amer. chemist (Nobel, 1954, 1962).

Pav•lov (păv′lôf′, -lôv′), **Ivar Petrovich.** 1849–1936. Russian physiologist (Nobel, 1904). —**Pav•lo′vi•an** *adj.*

Pav•lo•va (păv′lə-və, păv-lō′-, päv′lə-, päv-lō′-), **Anna.** 1885–1931. Russian ballerina.

Peale (pēl), **Norman Vincent.** 1898–1993. Amer. clergyman & author.

Pear•son (pîr′sən), **Lester Bowles.** 1897–1972. Canadian prime minister (1963–68; Nobel, 1957).

Pea•ry (pîr′ē), **Robert Edwin.** 1856–1920. Amer. naval officer & Arctic explorer.

Pe•dro (pā′drō, -dro͞o). Name of 2 Brazilian emperors: **a. I.** 1798–1834. Ruled 1822–31; abdicated. **b. II.** 1825–91. Ruled 1831–89 (crowned 1841); forced to abdicate.

Peel (pēl), Sir **Robert.** 1788–1850. British prime minister (1834–35, 1841–46).

Pei (pā), **Ieoh Ming ("I.M.").** b. 1917. Chinese-born Amer. architect.

Penn (pĕn), **William.** 1644–1718. English Quaker colonizer in America.

Pepys (pēps), **Samuel.** 1633–1701? English diarist. —**Pepys′i•an** *adj.*

Per•i•cles (pĕr′ĭ-klēz′). d. 429 B.C. Athenian statesman & general.

Pe•rón (pā-rôn′, pə-). Argentinean popular & political leaders, including **Juan Domingo** (1895–1974), **Maria Eva Duarte de** (*Evita;* 1919–52), & **Isabel** (*Isabelita;* b. 1931).

Per•rault (pə-rō′), **Charles.** 1628–1703. French author.

Per•ry (pĕr′ē), **Matthew Calbraith.** 1794–1858. Amer. naval officer.

Perry, Oliver Hazard. 1785–1819. Amer. naval officer.

Per•shing (pûr′shĭng, -zhĭng), **John Joseph ("Black Jack").** 1860–1948. Amer. general.

Pé•tain (pā-tăɴ′), **Henri Philippe.** 1856–1951. French soldier & politician.

Pe•ter (pē′tər), Saint. d. A.D. 67? One of the 12 Apostles; martyred.

Peter. Name of 3 czars of Russia, esp. **I,** *the Great,* 1672–1725, ruled 1682–1725.

Pe•trarch (pē′trärk′, pĕt′rärk′), **Francesco.** 1304–74. Italian poet. —**Pe•trarch′an** (pĭ-trär′kən) *adj.*

Phid•i•as (fĭd′ē-əs). 5th cent. B.C. Athenian sculptor.

Phil•ip (fĭl′ĭp), Saint. One of the 12 Apostles.

Philip. d. 1676. Amer. Indian chief.

Philip. Name of 6 kings of France, esp. **II** *or* **Philip Au•gus•tus** (ô-gŭs′təs). 1165–1223. Ruled 1180–1223.

Philip. Name of 5 kings of Macedon, esp. **II,** 382–336 B.C. Ruled 359–36.

Philip. Name of 5 kings of Spain, esp. **II.** 1527–98. Ruled 1556–98.

Pia•get (pyä-zhā′), **Jean.** 1896–1980. Swiss psychologist.

Pi•cas•so (pĭ-kä′sō, -kăs′ō), **Pablo.** 1881–1973. Spanish artist.

Pierce (pîrs), **Franklin.** 1804–69. 14th U.S. President (1853–57).

Pi•late (pī′lət), **Pontius.** Roman governor of Judea (A.D. 26?–36?).

Pin•dar (pĭn′dər). 522?–443 B.C. Greek poet. —**Pin•dar′ic** (pĭn-dăr′ĭk) *adj.*

Pin•ter (pĭn′tər), **Harold.** b. 1930. English playwright.

Pi•ran•del•lo (pîr′ən-dĕl′ō), **Luigi.** 1867–1936. Italian author (Nobel, 1934).

Pi•ra•ne•si (pîr′ə-nā′zē), **Giambattista.** 1720–78. Italian architect & artist.

Pis•sar•ro (pĭ-sär′ō), **Camille.** 1830–1903. French painter.

Pitt (pĭt), **William.** 1759–1806. British prime minister (1783–1801, 1804–06).

Pi•us (pī′əs). Name of 12 popes, esp.: **a. V.** 1504–72. Reigned 1566–72. **b. IX.** 1792–1878. Reigned 1846–78. **c. X.** 1835–1914. Reigned 1903–14. **d. XII.** 1876–1958. Reigned 1939–58.

Pi•zar•ro (pĭ-zär′ō), **Francisco.** 1470?–1541. Spanish explorer & conquistador.

Planck (plängk), **Max Karl Ernst Ludwig.** 1858–1947. German physicist (Nobel, 1918).

Plan•tag•e•net (plăn-tăj′ə-nĭt). English ruling dynasty (1154–1485).

Pla•to (plā′tō). 427?–347 B.C. Greek philosopher. —**Pla•ton′ic** (plə-tŏn′ĭk) *adj.*

Plin•y (plĭn′ē). *the Elder.* A.D. 23–79. Roman scholar and naturalist.

Pliny. *the Younger.* A.D. 62–113. Roman consul & author.

Plu•tarch (plo͞o′tärk′). A.D. 46?–120? Greek biographer & philosopher.

Po•ca•hon•tas (pō′kə-hŏn′təs). 1595?–1617. Amer. Indian princess.

Poe (pō), **Edgar Allan.** 1809–49. Amer. author.

Polk (pōk), **James Knox.** 1795–1849. 11th U.S. President (1845–49).

Pol•lock (pŏl′ək), **Jackson.** 1912–56. Amer. artist.

Po•lo (pō'lō), **Marco.** 1254?–1325? Venetian traveler.

Pom•pey (pŏm'pē). *the Great.* 106–48 B.C. Roman general & statesman.

Ponce de Le•ón (pŏns' də lē'ən, lē-ōn'), **Juan.** 1460–1521. Spanish explorer.

Pon•ti•ac (pŏn'tē-ăk'). 1720?–69. Amer. Indian leader.

Pope (pōp), **Alexander.** 1688–1744. English poet & satirist.

Por•ter (pôr'tər), **Cole Albert.** 1891?–1964. Amer. composer.

Porter, William Sidney. *O. Henry.* 1862–1910. Amer. author.

Pou•lenc (pōō-lăNk'), **Francis.** 1899–1963. French composer.

Pound (pound), **Ezra Loomis.** 1885–1972. Amer. poet & critic.

Pow•ell (pou'əl), **Adam Clayton, Jr.** 1908–72. Amer. clergyman & politician.

Powell, John Wesley. 1834–1902. Amer. geologist & explorer.

Pow•ha•tan (pou'ə-tăn', pou-hăt'n). 1550?–1618. Amer. Indian chief.

Pres•cott (prĕs'kət, -kŏt'), **William Hickling.** 1796–1859. Amer. historian.

Pres•ley (prĕs'lē, prĕz'-), **Elvis Aron.** 1935–77. Amer. entertainer.

Priest•ley (prēst'lē), **Joseph.** 1733–1804. English clergyman & chemist.

Pro•kof•iev (prə-kôf'yəf, -yĕf', -yĕv'), **Sergei Sergeevich.** 1891–1953. Russian composer.

Pro•tag•o•ras (prō-tăg'ər-əs). 5th cent. B.C. Greek philosopher. —**Pro•tag'o•re'an** *adj.*

Proust (prōōst), **Marcel.** 1871–1922. French author. —**Proust'i•an** *adj.*

Ptol•e•my (tŏl'ə-mē). 2nd cent. A.D. Greek astronomer & geographer. —**Ptol'e•ma'ic** (tŏl'ə-mā'ĭk) *adj.*

Ptolemy. Name of 14 kings of Egypt, esp. **I,** 367?–283 B.C., reigned 305–285 B.C.

Puc•ci•ni (pōō-chē'nē), **Giacomo.** 1858–1924. Italian composer.

Pu•las•ki (pōō-lăs'kē, pə-), **Casimir.** 1748?–79. Polish patriot & general in America.

Pu•lit•zer (pōōl'ĭt-sər, pyōō'lĭt-), **Joseph.** 1847–1911. Hungarian-born Amer. journalist & publisher.

Push•kin (pōōsh'kĭn, pōōsh'-), **Aleksander Sergeevich.** 1799–1837. Russian author.

Py•thag•o•ras (pĭ-thăg'ər-əs). d. 497 B.C. Greek philosopher & mathematician. —**Py•thag'o•re'an** (-ə-rē'ən) *adj.*

Q

Que•zon y Mo•li•na (kā'sôn' ē mə-lē'nə), **Manuel Luis.** 1878–1944. Philippine statesman.

Quin•cy (kwĭn'zē, -sē), **Josiah.** 1744–75. Amer. Revolutionary patriot.

Quin•til•ian (kwĭn-tĭl'yən, -ē-ən). A.D. 35?–95? Roman rhetorician.

Quis•ling (kwĭz'lĭng), **Vidkun Abraham Lauritz.** 1887–1945. Norwegian army officer & political leader; executed for treason.

R

Ra•be•lais (răb'ə-lā', răb'ə-lā'), **François.** 1494?–1553. French humanist.

Ra•bin (rä-bēn'), **Itzhak** *or* **Yitzhak.** b. 1922. Israeli military & political leader (Nobel, 1994).

Rach•ma•ni•noff (rŏk-măn'ə-nôf', -nôv', räk-mä'nə-), **Sergei Vasilievich.** 1873–1943. Russian-born composer & pianist.

Ra•cine (rə-sēn', rä-), **Jean Baptiste.** 1639–99. French playwright.

Ra•leigh *or* **Ra•legh** (rô'lē, rŏl'ē), Sir **Walter.** 1552?–1618. English navigator, courtier, writer, & colonizer; executed.

Ram•e•ses (răm'ĭ-sēz') *or* **Ram•ses** (răm'sēz'). Name of 12 kings of Egypt, esp. **II.** Ruled 1292–1225 B.C.

Ram•say (răm'zē), Sir **William.** 1852–1916. British chemist (Nobel, 1904).

Ran•dolph (răn'dŏlf'), **Edmund Jennings.** 1753–1813. Amer. Revolutionary leader.

Raph•a•el (răf'ē-əl, rā'fē-, rä'-). 1483–1520. Italian artist.

Ras•pu•tin (răs-pyōō'tĭn, -pōō'-), **Grigori Efimovich.** 1871?–1916. Russian monk influential in czarist court; assassinated.

Ra•vel (rə-vĕl', rä-), **Maurice Joseph.** 1875–1937. French composer.

Rea•gan (rā'gən), **Ronald Wilson.** b. 1911. Actor & 40th U.S. President (1981–89).

Reed (rēd), **Walter.** 1851–1902. Amer. physician & army surgeon.

Rem•brandt van Rijn (rĕm'brănt' vän rīn', -bränt'). 1606–69. Dutch painter.

Ren•oir (rĕn'wär', rən-wär'), **Pierre Auguste.** 1841–1919. French painter.

Re•vere (rĭ-vîr'), **Paul.** 1735–1818. Amer. silversmith & Revolutionary patriot.

Reyn•olds (rĕn'əldz), Sir **Joshua.** 1723–92. English portrait painter.

Rhee (rē), **Syngman.** 1875–1965. Korean political leader.

Rhodes (rōdz), **Cecil John.** 1853–1902. English financier & colonizer.

Rich•ard (rĭch'ərd). Name of 3 English kings: **a. I.** *the Lion-Hearted.* 1157–99. Ruled 1189–99. **b. II.** 1367–1400. Ruled 1377–99. **c. III.** 1452–85. Ruled 1483–85.

Ri•che•lieu (rĭsh'ə-lōō', -lyōō', rē-shə-lyœ'), Duc de. 1585–1642. French prelate & political leader.

Rick•o•ver (rĭk'ō'vər), **Hyman George.** 1900–86. Amer. admiral.

Ri•el (rē-ĕl'), **Louis.** 1844–85. French-Canadian rebel; executed.

Ril•ke (rĭl'kə), **Rainer Maria.** 1875–1926. German-Austrian poet.

Rim•baud (răm-bō', răN-), **Jean Nicholas Arthur.** 1854–91. French poet.

Rim•ski-Kor•sa•kov *or* **Rim•sky-Kor•sa•kov** (rĭm'skē-kôr'sə-kôf', -kôv'), **Nikolai Andreyevich.** 1844–1908. Russian composer.

Ri•ve•ra (rĭ-vĕr'ə), **Diego.** 1886–1957. Mexican artist.

Rob•ert I (rŏb'ərt), *Robert Bruce, the Bruce.* 1274–1329. Scottish king (1306–29).

Robes•pierre (rōbz′pîr, -pē-âr′), **Maximilien François Marie Isidore de.** 1758–94. French revolutionary; guillotined.

Rob•in•son (rŏb′ĭn-sən), **Edwin Arlington.** 1869–1935. Amer. poet.

Robinson, John Roosevelt ("Jackie"). 1919–72. Amer. baseball player.

Rock•e•fel•ler (rŏk′ə-fĕl′ər). Amer. family including: **a. John Davison.** 1839–1937. Industrialist & philanthropist. **b. John Davison, Jr.** 1874–1960. Philanthropist. **c. Nelson Aldrich.** 1908–79. U.S. Vice President (1974–77).

Rock•ne (rŏk′nē), **Knute Kenneth.** 1888–1931. Norwegian-born Amer. football coach.

Rock•well (rŏk′wĕl′), **Norman.** 1894–1978. Amer. illustrator.

Rod•gers (rŏj′ərs), **Richard.** 1902–79. Amer. composer.

Ro•din (rō-dăn′, -dăN′), **François Auguste René.** 1840–1917. French sculptor.

Roent•gen (rĕnt′gən, -jən, rŭnt′-), **Wilhem Konrad.** 1845–1923. German physicist (Nobel, 1901).

Rolfe (rŏlf), **John.** 1585–1622. English colonist in America.

Ro•ma•nov (rō-mä′nəf, rō′mə-nôf′, -nŏf′). Russian ruling dynasty (1613–1917).

Rom•mel (rŏm′əl), **Erwin.** 1891–1944. German general.

Roo•se•velt (rō′zə-vĕlt′, rōz′vĕlt′, ro͞o′zə-), **(Anna) Eleanor.** 1884–1962. Amer. diplomat, author, & wife of Franklin Delano Roosevelt.

Roosevelt, Franklin Delano ("FDR"). 1882–1945. 32nd U.S. President (1933–45).

Roosevelt, Theodore. 1858–1919. 26th U.S. President (1901–9; Nobel, 1906).

Ros•si•ni (rō-sē′nē, rə-), **Gioacchino Antonio.** 1792–1868. Italian composer.

Roth•schild (rŏth′chīld, rŏths′-). Family of German bankers, including **Meyer Amschel** (1743–1812), **Salomon** (1774–1855), & **Nathan Meyer** (1777–1836).

Rous•seau (ro͞o-sō′), **Henri.** *Le Douanier Rousseau.* 1844–1910. French painter.

Rousseau, Jean Jacques. 1712–78. French author & philosopher.

Ru•bens (ro͞o′bənz), **Peter Paul.** 1577–1640. Flemish painter. —**Ru′ben•esque′** *adj.*

Ru•dolf I (ro͞o′dŏlf′), 1218–91. Holy Roman Emperor (1273–91) & founder of Hapsburg dynasty.

Ru•dolph (ro͞o′dŏlf′), **Wilma Glodean.** 1940–94. Amer. athlete.

Rus•kin (rŭs′kĭn), **John.** 1819–1900. English author & critic.

Rus•sell (rŭs′əl), Lord **Bertrand Arthur William.** 1872–1970. English pacifist, mathematician, & philosopher (Nobel, 1950).

Ruth (ro͞oth), **George Herman ("Babe").** 1895–1948. Amer. baseball player.

Ruth•er•ford (rŭ*th*′ər-fərd), **Ernest.** 1871–1937. New Zealand-born British physicist (Nobel, 1908).

S

Sa•bin (sā′bĭn), **Albert Bruce.** 1906–93. Amer. microbiologist & physician.

Sac•a•ja•we•a (săk′ə-jə-wē′ə). 1788?–1812. Shoshone guide.

Sa•dat (sə-dăt′, -dät′), **Anwar el-.** 1918–81. Egyptian statesman (Nobel, 1978); assassinated.

Sade (säd, săd, sād), Comte **Donatien Alphonse François de.** *Marquis de Sade.* 1740–1814. French author.

Saint Lau•rent (săN lô-räN′), **Louis Stephen.** 1882–1973. Canadian prime minister (1948–57).

Sa•kha•rov (sä′kə-rôf′, -rôv′), **Andrei Dimitrievich.** 1921–89. Russian physicist & dissident (Nobel, 1975).

Sal•a•din (săl′ə-dĭn). 1138–93. Sultan of Egypt & Syria.

Salk (sôlk), **Jonas Edward.** 1914–95. Amer. microbiologist.

Sam•o•set (săm′ə-sĕt′). d. 1653? Amer. Indian leader.

Sand (sănd, säNd), **George.** *Amandine Aurore Lucie Dupin.* 1804–76. French author.

Sand•burg (sănd′bûrg′, săn′-), **Carl.** 1878–1967. Amer. poet & biographer.

Sang•er (săng′ər), **Margaret Higgins.** 1883–1966. Amer. nurse and social reformer.

San Mar•tín (săn mär-tēn′, sän), **José de.** 1778–1850. Argentine revolutionary leader in South America.

San•ta An•na *or* **San•ta An•a** (săn′tə ăn′ə, sän′tə ä′nə), **Antonio López de.** 1795?–1876. Mexican military & political leader.

San•ta•ya•na (săn′tē-ä′nə, -tə-yä′-, sän′-), **George.** 1863–1952. Spanish-born Amer. educator, philosopher, & poet.

Sap•pho (săf′ō). 7th cent. B.C. Greek poet.

Sar•gent (sär′jənt), **John Singer.** 1856–1925. Amer. painter.

Sar•gon II (sär′gŏn′). d. 705 B.C. Assyrian king (722–705).

Sa•roy•an (sə-roi′ən), **William.** 1908–81. Amer. author.

Sar•tre (sär′trə, särt), **Jean Paul.** 1905–80. French philosopher & author (Nobel, 1964).

Saus•sure (sō-so͝or′), **Ferdinand de.** 1857–1913. Swiss pioneer linguist.

Sa•vo•na•ro•la (săv′ə-nə-rō′lə, sə-vŏn′ə-), **Girolamo.** 1452–98. Italian reformer; executed.

Scar•lat•ti (skär-lä′tē), **Alessandro** (1659–1725) & **(Giuseppe) Domenico** (1685–1767). Italian composers & musicians.

Schil•ler (shĭl′ər), **Johann Christoph Friedrich von.** 1759–1805. German poet, playwright, & historian.

Schlie•mann (shlē′män′), **Heinrich.** 1822–90. German-born Amer. archaeologist.

Schön•berg (shœn′bûrg, shûrn′-, shœn′-bĕrk′), **Arnold.** 1874–1951. Austrian composer.

Scho•pen•hau•er (shō′pən-hou′ər), **Arthur.** 1788–1860. German philosopher.

Schu•bert (sho͞o′bərt, -bĕrt′), **Franz Peter.** 1797–1828. Austrian composer.

Schu•mann (sho͞o'män', -mən), **Robert.** 1810–56. German composer.

Schweit•zer (shwīt'sər, shvīt'-), **Albert.** 1875–1965. French philosopher, physician, & musician (Nobel, 1952).

Scip•io (sĭp'ē-ō', skĭp'-), **Publius Cornelius.** *the Elder.* 237?–183 B.C. Roman military leader.

Scipio, Publius Cornelius. *the Younger.* 185–129 B.C. Roman general & politician.

Scott (skŏt), **Dred.** 1795?–1858. Amer. slave.

Scott, Robert Falcon. 1868–1912. English Antarctic explorer.

Scott, Sir **Walter.** 1771–1832. Scottish author.

Se•at•tle (sē-ăt'l). 1786?–1866. Amer. Indian leader.

Se•fe•ri•a•des (sĕf'ĕr-yä'*th*ēs), **Giorgos Stylianou.** 1900–71. Greek poet (Nobel, 1963).

Sen•e•ca (sĕn'ĭ-kə), **Lucius Annaeus.** *the Younger.* 4 B.C.–A.D. 65. Roman Stoic philosopher, writer, & politician.

Se•quoy•a *or* **Se•quoy•ah** (sĭ-kwoi'ə). 1770?–1843. Cherokee leader.

Se•ton (sēt'n), Saint **Elizabeth Ann Bayley.** *Mother Seton.* 1774–1821. Amer. religious leader.

Seu•rat (sə-rä'), **Georges Pierre.** 1859–91. French painter.

Sew•ard (so͞o'ərd), **William Henry.** 1801–72. Amer. statesman.

Sex•ton (sĕks'tən), **Anne.** 1928–74. Amer. poet.

Sey•mour (sē'môr', -mōr'), **Jane.** 1509?–37. Queen of England as 3rd wife of Henry VIII.

Shake•speare (shāk'spîr), **William.** 1564–1616. English playwright & poet. **—Shake•spear'e•an, Shake•spear'i•an** *adj. & n.*

Shaw (shô), **George Bernard.** 1856–1950. Irish-born English playwright (Nobel, 1925).

Shel•ley (shĕl'ē), **Mary Godwin Wollstonecraft.** 1797–1851. English author.

Shelley, Percy Bysshe. 1792–1822. English poet.

Sher•i•dan (shĕr'ĭ-dən), **Richard Brinsley.** 1751–1816. English playwright & politician.

Sher•man (shûr'mən), **Roger.** 1721–93. Amer. Revolutionary patriot & politician.

Sherman, William Tecumseh. 1820–91. Amer. Union general.

Shos•ta•ko•vich (shŏs'tə-kō'vĭch, -kô'-,), **Dimitri.** 1906–75. Russian composer.

Si•be•li•us (sĭ-bā'lē-əs, -bāl'yəs), **Jean.** 1865–1957. Finnish composer.

Sid•ney (sĭd'nē), Sir **Philip.** 1554–86. English poet, soldier, & politician.

Si•ha•nouk (sē'ə-no͝ok'), Prince **Norodom.** b. 1922. Cambodian statesman.

Si•kor•sky (sĭ-kôr'skē), **Igor Ivan.** 1889–1972. Russian-born Amer. aviation pioneer.

Si•na•tra (sə-nä'trə), **Francis Albert ("Frank").** b. 1915. Amer. entertainer.

Sin•clair (sĭn-klâr', sĭng-), **Upton Beall.** 1878–1968. Amer. author & reformer.

Sing•er (sĭng'ər), **Isaac Bashevis.** 1904–91. Polish-born Amer. Yiddish author (Nobel, 1978).

Sit•ting Bull (sĭt'ĭng bo͝ol'). 1834?–90. Sioux leader.

Skin•ner (skĭn'ər), **Burrhus Frederick ("B.F.").** 1904–90. Amer. psychologist.

Smith (smĭth), **Adam.** 1723–90. Scottish political economist & philosopher.

Smith, Bessie. 1894?–1937. Amer. blues singer.

Smith, John. 1580?–1631. English adventurer, colonist, explorer, & author.

Smith, Joseph. 1805–44. Amer. Mormon religious leader.

Smith•son (smĭth'sən), **James.** 1765–1829. English chemist & philanthropist.

Smol•lett (smŏl'ĭt), **Tobias George.** 1721–71. English novelist.

Soc•ra•tes (sŏk'rə-tēz'). 470?–399 B.C. Greek philosopher. **—So•crat'ic** (sō-krăt'ĭk) *adj.*

So•lon (sō'lən, -lŏn'). 638?–559 B.C. Athenian statesman & poet.

Sol•zhe•ni•tsyn (sōl'zhə-nēt'sĭn), **Aleksandr Isayevich.** b. 1918. Russian author (Nobel, 1970).

Soph•o•cles (sŏf'ə-klēz'). 496?–406 B.C. Greek dramatist. **—Soph'o•cle'an** *adj.*

Sou•sa (so͞o'zə, -sə), **John Philip.** 1854–1932. Amer. bandmaster & composer.

Spen•cer (spĕn'sər), **Herbert.** 1820–1903. English philosopher. **—Spen•ce'ri•an** *adj.*

Spen•ser (spĕn'sər), **Edmund.** 1552?–99. English poet. **—Spen•se'ri•an** *adj.*

Spi•no•za (spĭ-nō'zə), **Baruch** *or* **Benedict.** 1632–77. Dutch philosopher & theologian.

Squan•to (skwŏn'tō). d. 1622. Amer. Indian friend of Pilgrims.

Staël (stäl), Madame **de.** *Anne Louise Germaine Neckar.* 1766–1817. French novelist, critic, & literary patron.

Sta•lin (stä'lĭn, stăl'ĭn), **Joseph.** 1879–1953. Soviet Communist leader. **—Sta'lin•ist** *adj. & n.*

Stan•dish (stăn'dĭsh'), **Miles** *or* **Myles.** 1584?–1656. English colonist in America.

Stan•ley (stăn'lē), Sir **Henry Morton.** 1841–1904. Welsh-born African explorer.

Stan•ton (stăn'tən), **Elizabeth Cady.** 1815–1902. Amer. feminist & reformer.

Stein (stīn), **Gertrude.** 1874–1946. Amer. author.

Stein•beck (stīn'bĕk'), **John Ernst.** 1902–68. Amer. novelist (Nobel, 1962).

Sten•dhal (stĕn-däl'). *Marie Henri Beyle.* 1783–1842. French novelist & biographer.

Sterne (stûrn), **Laurence.** 1713–68. English satiric novelist.

Steu•ben (sto͞o'bən, styo͞o'-), Baron **Friedrich Wilhelm von.** 1730–94. Prussian-born Amer. Revolutionary military leader.

Ste•ven•son (stē'vən-sən), **Robert Louis Balfour.** 1850–94. Scottish poet & novelist.

Stieg•litz (stēg'lĭts), **Alfred.** 1864–1946. Amer. pioneer photographer.

Stone (stōn), **Lucy.** 1818–93. Amer. feminist.

Stowe (stō), **Harriet Elizabeth Beecher.** 1811–96. Amer. novelist & reformer.

Stra•di•va•ri (străd'ə-vâr'ē, -vär'ē) *also* **Stra•**

di•var•i•us (-vâr'ē-əs), **Antonio.** 1644–1737. Italian violinmaker.

Strauss (strous, shtrous) Family of Austrian composers, including **Johann** (1804–49), **Johann,** *the Waltz King* (1825–99), & **Josef** (1827–70).

Strauss, Richard. 1864–1949. German composer.

Stra•vin•sky (strə-vĭn'skē), **Igor Fëdorovich.** 1882–1971. Russian-born composer.

Strind•berg (strĭnd'bûrg), **(Johan) August.** 1849–1912. Swedish playwright & novelist.

Stu•art (sto͞o'ərt, styo͞o'-). Ruling house of Scotland (1371–1625) & Great Britain (1603–49, 1660–1714).

Stuart, Gilbert Charles. 1755–1828. Amer. painter.

Stuart, James Ewell Brown ("Jeb"). 1833–64. Amer. Confederate general.

Stuy•ve•sant (stī'vĭ-sənt), **Peter** *or* **Petrus.** 1592?–1672. Dutch colonial administrator.

Su•har•to (sə-här'tō, so͞o-), **Raden.** b. 1921. Indonesian military & political leader.

Su•kar•no (so͞o-kär'nō). 1901–70. Indonesian statesman.

Su•lei•man I (so͞o'lā-män', -lə-). 1490?–1566. Turkish sultan (1520–66).

Sul•li•van (sŭl'ə-vən), Sir **Arthur Seymour.** 1842–1900. English composer of operettas.

Sullivan, Louis Henri *or* **Henry.** 1856–1924. Amer. architect.

Sun Yat-sen (so͝on' yät'sĕn'). 1866–1925. Chinese revolutionary leader & statesman.

Swe•den•borg (swēd'n-bôrg'), **Emanuel.** 1688–1772. Swedish scientist & theologian.

Swift (swĭft), **Jonathan.** 1667–1745. Irish-born English satirist.

Synge (sĭng), **John Millington.** 1871–1909. Irish dramatist.

T

Tac•i•tus (tăs'ĭ-təs), **Publius Cornelius.** A.D. 55?–118? Roman historian & orator.

Taft (tăft), **William Howard.** 1857–1930. 27th U.S. President (1909–13) & jurist.

Ta•gore (tə-gôr', -gōr'), Sir **Rabindranath.** 1861–1941. Indian poet (Nobel, 1913).

Tal•ley•rand-Pé•ri•gord (tăl'ē-rănd'pĕr'-ə-gôr'), **Charles Maurice de.** 1754–1838. French statesman & diplomat.

Tam•er•lane (tăm'ər-lān') *or* **Tam•bur•laine** (-bər-). 1336?–1405. Mongol conqueror.

Tar•king•ton (tär'kĭng'tən), **(Newton) Booth.** 1869–1946. Amer. author.

Tay•lor (tā'lər), **Zachary.** 1784–1850. 12th U.S. President (1849–50) & army officer.

Tchai•kov•sky (chī-kôf'skē, -kôv'-), **Peter Ilich.** 1840–93. Russian composer.

Te•cum•seh (tĭ-kŭm'sə, -sē, -kŭmp'-) 1768–1813. Shawnee chief.

Ten•ny•son (tĕn'ĭ-sən), **Alfred.** *Alfred, Lord Tennyson.* 1809–92. English poet.

Te•re•sa (tə-rē'sə, -zə, -rā'-). *var. of* THERESA.

Teresa, Mother. b. 1910. Albanian-born Indian nun (Nobel,1979).

Thack•er•ay (thăk'ə-rē, thăk'rē), **William Makepeace.** 1811–63. English novelist.

Thant (thänt, thănt), **U.** 1909–74. Burmese UN secretary-general.

Thatch•er (thăch'ər), **Margaret Hilda.** b. 1925. British prime minister (1979–90).

The•o•do•ra (thē'ə-dôr'ə, -dōr'-). 508?–48. Byzantine empress as wife of Justinian I.

The•o•do•sius I (thē'ə-dō'shəs, -shē-əs). *the Great.* 346?–95. Roman emperor (379–95).

The•re•sa *or* **Te•re•sa** (tə-rē'sə, -zə, -rā'-), Saint. 1515–82. Spanish nun & mystic.

Thes•pis (thĕs'pĭs). 6th cent. B.C. Greek poet.

Thom•as (tŏm'əs), Saint. One of the 12 Apostles.

Thomas, Dylan Marlais. 1914–53. Welsh poet.

Thomas à Kem•pis (ə kĕm'pĭs, ä). 1380–1471. German ecclesiastic & writer.

Tho•reau (thə-rō', thôr'ō), **Henry David.** 1817–62. Amer. essayist & poet.

Thorpe (thôrp), **James Francis.** 1888–1953. Amer. Indian athlete.

Thu•cyd•i•des (tho͞o-sĭd'ĭ-dēz'). 471–400 B.C. Greek historian.

Thur•ber (thûr'bər), **James Grover.** 1894–1961. Amer. author & artist.

Ti•be•ri•us (tī-bîr'ē-əs). 42 B.C.–A.D. 37. Roman emperor (A.D. 14–37).

Til•lich (tĭl'ĭk), **Paul Johannes.** 1886–1965. German-born theologian & philosopher.

Tin•to•ret•to (tĭn'tə-rĕt'ō), **Il.** 1518–94. Italian painter.

Ti•tian (tĭsh'ən). 1477–1576. Italian painter.

Ti•to (tē'tō), Marshal. *Josip Broz.* 1892–1980. Yugoslavian statesman.

Tocque•ville (tōk'vĭl), **Alexis Charles Henri Maurice Clérel de.** 1805–59. French statesman, traveler, & historian.

To•jo (tō'jō'), **Hideki** *or* **Eiki.** 1885–1948. Japanese army officer & dictator (1941–44); executed.

Tol•stoy *or* **Tol•stoi** (tōl'stoi, tŏl'-), Count **Lev** *or* **Leo Nikolaevich.** 1828–1910. Russian author & philosopher. **—Tol•stoy'an, Tol•stoi'an** *adj.*

Tos•ca•ni•ni (tŏs'kə-nē'nē), **Arturo.** 1867–1957. Italian conductor.

Tou•louse-Lau•trec (to͞o-lo͞oz'lō-trĕk', -lə-), **Henri de.** 1864–1901. French artist.

Tous•saint L'Ou•ver•ture (to͞o-săN' lo͞o-vĕr-tür'), **Pierre Dominique.** 1743–1803. Haitian revolutionary & statesman.

Tra•jan (trā'jən). A.D. 52?–117. Roman emperor (98–117).

Trol•lope (trŏl'əp), **Anthony.** 1815–82. English novelist.

Trot•sky *or* **Trot•ski** (trŏt'skē, trôt'-), **Leon.** 1879–1940. Russian revolutionary; assassinated. **—Trot'sky•ite'** *adj. & n.*

Tru•deau (tro͞o-dō', tro͞o'dō'), **Pierre Elliott.** b. 1919. Canadian prime minister (1968–79 & 1980–84).

Tru•ji•llo Mo•li•na (tro͞o-hē'ō mō-lē'nə, -yō), **Rafael Leónidas.** 1891–1961. Dominican military & political leader.

Tru•man (tro͞o'mən), **Harry S.** 1884–1972.

33rd U.S. President (1945–53).
Truth (tro͞oth), **Sojourner.** 1797–1883. Amer. abolitionist.
Tub•man (tŭb′mən), **Harriet.** 1820–1913. Amer. abolitionist.
Tu•dor (to͞o′dər, tyo͞o′-). English ruling family (1485–1603).
Tur•ge•nev (to͝or-gān′yəf, -gĕn′-), **Ivan Sergeevich.** 1818–83. Russian novelist.
Tur•ner (tûr′nər), **Joseph Mallord William.** 1775–1851. English painter.
Turner, Nat. 1800–31. Amer. slave leader.
Tut•ankh•a•men (to͞o′tăng-kä′mən, -tăng-). fl. c. 1358 B.C. Egyptian pharaoh.
Twain (twān), **Mark.** Samuel Langhorne CLEMENS.
Ty•ler (tī′lər), **John.** 1790–1862. 10th U.S. President (1841–45).

U

Uc•cel•lo (o͞o-chĕl′lō), **Paolo.** 1397–1475? Italian painter.
U•na•mu•no (o͞o′nə-mo͞o′nō), **Miguel de.** 1864–1936. Spanish philosopher.
Ur•ban (ûr′bən). Name of 8 popes, esp. **II,** 1042?–99, reigned 1088–99.
U•tril•lo (yo͞o-trĭl′ō, o͞o-trē-ō′), **Maurice.** 1883–1955. French painter.

V

Va•lé•ry (văl′ə-rē′, və-lā-rē′), **Paul Ambroise.** 1871–1945. French poet.
Van Al•len (văn ăl′ən), **James Alfred.** b. 1914. Amer. physicist.
Van Bur•en (văn byo͝or′ən), **Martin.** 1782–1862. 8th U.S. President (1837–41).
Van•der•bilt (văn′dər-bĭlt′), **Cornelius** (1794–1877), **William Henry** (1821–85), & **Cornelius** (1843–99). Amer. financiers.
Van•dyke *or* **Van Dyck** (văn-dīk′), Sir **Anthony.** 1599–1641. Flemish painter.
van Eyck (văn īk′), **Jan.** 1370?–1440? Flemish painter.
van Gogh (văn gō′, gôKH′, vän KHÔKH′), **Vincent.** 1853–90. Dutch painter.
Var•gas (vär′gəs), **Getulio Dornelles.** 1883–1954. Brazilian statesman.
Va•sa•ri (və-zär′ē, -sär′ē), **Giorgio.** 1511–74. Italian artist & architect.
Vaughan Wil•liams (vôn wĭl′yəmz), **Ralph.** 1872–1958. English composer.
Vega (vā′gə), **Lope de.** 1562–1635. Spanish author.
Ve•láz•quez *or* **Ve•lás•quez** (və-läs′kəs), **Diego Rodríguez de Silva y.** 1599–1660. Spanish painter.
Ver•di (vâr′dē), **Giuseppe.** 1813–1901. Italian composer.
Ver•gil (vûr′jəl). *var. of* VIRGIL.
Ver•meer (vər-mîr′, -mâr′), **Jan.** 1632–75. Dutch painter.
Verne (vûrn, vĕrn), **Jules.** 1828–1905. French novelist.
Ver•ra•za•no (vĕr′ə-zä′nō), **Giovanni da.** 1485?–1528? Italian explorer.
Ves•puc•ci (vĕs-po͞o′chē, -pyo͞o′-), **Amerigo.** 1454–1512. Italian navigator & explorer.
Vic•tor Em•man•u•el II (vĭk′tər ĭ-măn′yo͞o-əl). 1820–78. Italian king (1861–78).
Vic•to•ri•a (vĭk-tôr′ē-ə, -tōr′-). 1819–1901. British queen (1837–1901) & empress of India (1876–1901). —**Vic•to′ri•an** *adj. & n.*
Vil•la (vē′ə, vē′yə), **Francisco ("Pancho").** 1877?–1923. Mexican revolutionary leader; assassinated.
Vin•cent de Paul (vĭn′sənt də pôl), Saint. 1581–1660. French ecclesiastic.
Vir•gil *also* **Ver•gil** (vûr′jəl). 70–19 B.C. Roman poet.
Vi•val•di (vĭ-väl′dē, -vôl′-), **Antonio.** 1675?–1741. Italian composer.
Vol•ta (vōl′tə, vôl′-), Count **Alessandro.** 1745–1827. Italian physicist.
Vol•taire (vōl-târ′, vŏl-, vôl-tĕr′). *François Marie Arouet.* 1694–1778. French author.
Von Neu•mann (vŏn noi′män′), **John.** 1903–57. Hungarian-born Amer. mathematician.

W

Wag•ner (väg′nər), **(Wilhelm) Richard.** 1813–83. German composer.
Wald•heim (vält′hīm′), **Kurt.** b. 1918. Austrian diplomat & UN secretary-general.
Wa•le•sa (wä-lĕn′sə, vä-wĕn′sä), **Lech.** b. 1943? Polish labor leader (Nobel, 1983).
Wal•lace (wŏl′ĭs), **Alfred Russel.** 1823–1913. English naturalist.
Wal•pole (wôl′pōl′, wŏl′-), **Horace** *or* **Horatio.** 1717–97. English author.
Wal•ton (wôl′tən), **Izaak.** 1593–1683. English fisherman & author.
War•hol (wôr′hôl′, -hōl′), **Andy.** 1928?–87. Amer. artist.
War•ren (wôr′ən, wŏr′-), **Earl.** 1891–1974. Amer. jurist.
Wash•ing•ton (wŏsh′ĭng-tən, wôsh′-), **Booker T(aliaferro).** 1856–1915. Amer. educator & author.
Washington, George. 1732–99. First U.S. President (1789–97) & Revolutionary soldier.
Watt (wŏt), **James.** 1736–1819. Scottish-born engineer & inventor.
Web•ster (wĕb′stər), **Daniel.** 1782–1852. Amer. politician, diplomat, & orator.
Webster, Noah. 1758–1843. Amer. lexicographer.
Wedg•wood (wĕj′wo͝od′), **Josiah.** 1730–95. English potter.
Weill (wīl, vīl), **Kurt.** 1900–50. German-born composer.
Weiz•mann (vīts′mən′, wīts′-, wīz′-), **Chaim.** 1874–1952. Polish-born Israeli chemist & statesman.
Welles (wĕlz), **(George) Orson.** 1915–85. Amer. actor, producer, & director.
Wel•ling•ton (wĕl′ĭng-tən). 1st Duke of.

Arthur Wellesley, the Iron Duke. 1769–1852. Irish-born British general & statesman.

Wells (wĕlz), **Herbert George ("H.G.").** 1866–1946. English author.

Wes•ley (wĕs′lē, wĕz′-), **John.** 1703–91. British founder of Methodism. —**Wes′ley•an** *adj.*

Whar•ton (hwôr′tn, wôr′-), **Edith Newbold Jones.** 1862–1937. Amer. author.

Wheat•ley (hwēt′lē, wēt′-), **Phillis.** 1753?–84. African-born Amer. poet.

Whist•ler (hwĭs′lər, wĭs′-), **James Abbott McNeill.** 1834–1903. Amer. artist.

Whit•man (whĭt′mən, wĭt′-), **Walter ("Walt").** 1819–92. Amer. poet.

Whit•ney (whĭt′nē, wĭt′-), **Eli.** 1765–1825. Amer. inventor & manufacturer.

Whit•ti•er (hwĭt′ē-ər, wĭt′-), **John Greenleaf.** 1807–92. Amer. poet.

Wilde (wīld), **Oscar Fingal O'Flahertie Wills.** 1854–1900. Irish poet & playwright.

Wil•der (wīl′dər), **Thornton (Niven).** 1897–1975. Amer. author.

Wil•kins (wĭl′kĭnz), **Roy.** 1901–81. Amer. civil-rights leader.

Wil•lard (wĭl′ərd), **Emma Hart.** 1787–1870. Amer. poet & educator.

Wil•liam (wĭl′yəm). Name of 4 kings of England, esp.: **a. I.** 1027–87. Ruled 1066–87. **b. III.** 1650–1702. Ruled 1689–1702.

William. Name of 2 kings of Prussia: **a. I.** 1797–1888. Ruled 1861–88. **b. II.** 1859–1941. Ruled 1888–1918.

William I. *Prince of Orange.* 1533–84. Dutch stadholder (1579–84).

Wil•liams (wĭl′yəmz), **Roger.** 1603?–83. English clergyman & founder of Rhode Island.

Williams, Thomas Lanier ("Tennessee"). 1911–83. Amer. playwright.

Williams, William Carlos. 1883–1963. Amer. physician & poet.

Wil•son (wĭl′sən), **(James) Harold.** 1916–95. British prime minister (1964–70, 1974–79).

Wilson, (Thomas) Woodrow. 1856–1924. 28th U.S. President (1913–21). —**Wil•so′ni•an** (-sō′nē-ən) *adj.*

Wind•sor (wĭn′zər). British ruling dynasty (since 1917).

Windsor, Duke of. EDWARD VIII.

Windsor, Wallis Warfield. *Duchess of Windsor.* 1896–1986. Amer. socialite.

Win•throp (wĭn′thrəp), **John** (1588–1649), **John** (1606–76), & **John** (1638–1707). English colonial administrators in America.

Wolfe (wo͝olf), **James.** 1727–59. English general in Canada.

Wol•sey (wo͝ol′zē), **Thomas.** 1475?–1530. English prelate & statesman.

Wood (wo͝od), **Grant.** 1892–1942. Amer. artist.

Wood•hull (wo͝od′hŭl′), **Victoria Clafin** (1838–1927) & **Tennessee** (1846–1923). Amer. publishers & feminists.

Woolf (wo͝olf), **(Adeline) Virginia (Stephen).** 1882–1941. English author.

Words•worth (wûrdz′wûrth′), **William.** 1770–1850. English poet.

Wren (rĕn), Sir **Christopher.** 1632–1723. English architect.

Wright (rīt), **Frank Lloyd.** 1869–1959. Amer. architect.

Wright, Richard. 1908–60. Amer. novelist.

Wright, Wilbur (1867–1912) & **Orville** (1871–1948). Amer. aviation pioneers.

Wyc•liffe (wĭk′lĭf′), **John.** 1320?–84. English religious reformer.

Wy•eth (wī′ĭth), **Newell Convers** (1882–1945) & **Andrew** (b. 1917). Amer. painters.

X

Xa•vi•er (zā′vē-ər, zăv′ē-), Saint **Francis.** 1506–52. Spanish missionary in Asia.

Xen•o•phon (zĕn′ə-fən, -fŏn′). 430?–355? B.C. Greek soldier & historian.

Xer•xes (zûrk′sēz′). Name of 2 kings of Persia, esp. **I,** *the Great,* 519?–465 B.C., ruled 486–465.

Y

Yeats (yāts), **William Butler.** 1865–1939. Irish author (Nobel, 1923). —**Yeats′i•an** *adj.*

Yel•tsin (yĕlt′sĭn), **Boris Nikolayevich.** b. 1931. Russian politician.

York (yôrk). English ruling house (1461–85).

Young (yŭng), **Brigham.** 1801–77. Amer. Mormon leader.

Young, Denton True ("Cy"). 1867–1955. Amer. baseball player.

Z

Za•pa•ta (zə-pä′tə), **Emiliano.** 1877?–1919. Mexican revolutionary.

Zar•a•thu•stra (zăr′ə-tho͞o′strə). ZOROASTER.

Zeno (zē′nō). 342?–270? B.C. Greek Stoic philosopher.

Zhou En•lai (jō ĕn-lī′). 1898–1976. Chinese statesman.

Zo•la (zō′lə, zō-lä′), **Emile.** 1840–1902. French author.

Zo•ro•as•ter (zôr′ō-ăs′tər, zôr′-). 6th cent. B.C. Persian prophet. —**Zo′ro•as′tri•an** *adj.*

Zwing•li (zwĭng′lē, swĭng′-), **Ulrich.** 1484–1531. Swiss religious reformer.

Geographic Entries

A

Aa•chen (ä'kən, ä'KHən). City of W Germany. Pop. 242,453.

Ab•a•dan (ä'bə-dän', ăb'ə-dăn'). City of SW Iran. Pop. 296,081.

Ab•er•deen (ăb'ər-dēn', ăb'ər-dēn'). Burgh of NE Scotland on the North Sea. Pop. 212,542.

Ab•i•djan (ăb'ĭ-jän'). Cap. of Ivory Coast in the S part. Pop. 1,500,000.

Ab•i•lene (ăb'ə-lēn'). City of W central TX WSW of Fort Worth. Pop. 106,654.

A•bruz•zi (ä-bro͞ot'sē, ə-) *also* **Abruzzi e Mo•li•se** (ā mô'lə-zā'). Region of central Italy on the Adriatic.

A•bu Dha•bi (ä'bo͞o dä'bē). Sheikdom & cap. of United Arab Emirates on the Persian Gulf. Pop. 242,975.

Ab•ys•sin•i•a (ăb'ĭ-sĭn'ē-ə). ETHIOPIA. **—Ab'ys•sin'i•an** *adj. & n.*

A•ca•di•a (ə-kā'dē-ə). Region & former French colony of E Canada. **—A•ca'di•an** *adj. & n.*

Ac•a•pul•co (ä'kə-po͝ol'kō, ăk'ə-) *or* **Acapulco de Juá•rez** (də hwär'əs, wär'-). City of S Mexico on the Pacific. Pop. 301,902.

Ac•cra (ăk'rə, ə-krä'). Cap. of Ghana in the S part. Pop. 859,640.

A•con•ca•gua (ăk'ən-kä'gwə, äk'-). Mountain, 22,835 ft (6,964.7 m), in the Andes of W Argentina near the Chilean border.

A•da•na (ä'də-nə, ə-dä'nə). City of S Turkey. Pop. 574,515.

Ad•dis Ab•a•ba (ăd'ĭs ăb'ə-bə). Cap. of Ethiopia. Pop. 1,408,068.

Ad•e•laide (ăd'l-ād'). City of S Australia NW of Melbourne. Metro. area pop. 983,200.

Ad•e•laide (ăd'l-ād'). City of S Australia NW of Melbourne. Metro. area pop. 983,200.

A•den (äd'n, ād'n). City of Yemen on the NW shore of the **Gulf of Aden,** W arm of the Arabian Sea. Pop. 271,600.

Ad•i•ron•dack Mountains (ăd'ə-rŏn'dăk') *also* **Ad•i•ron•dacks** (-dăks'). Range of NE NY.

A•dri•at•ic Sea (ā'drē-ăt'ĭk). Arm of the Mediterranean between Italy & the Balkan Peninsula.

Ae•ge•an Sea (ĭ-jē'ən). Arm of the Mediterranean between Greece & Turkey.

Af•ghan•i•stan (ăf-găn'ĭ-stăn'). Country of S central Asia. Cap. Kabul. Pop. 13,051,358. **—Af'ghan'** *adj. & n.*

Af•ri•ca (ăf'rĭ-kə). Second-largest continent, S of Europe & between the Atlantic & Indian oceans. **—Af'ri•can** *adj. & n.*

A•ga•na (ə-gä'nyə). Cap. of Guam on the W coast. Pop. 896.

A•gra (ä'grə). City of N central India. Pop. 694,191.

Ah•ma•da•bad *or* **Ah•me•da•bad** (ä'mə-də-bäd'). City of NW India. Pop. 2,059,725.

Aix-en-Pro•vence (āk'säN-prō-väNs', ĕk'-). City of SE France N of Marseilles. Pop. 121,327.

Aix-la-Cha•pelle (āks'lä-shə-pĕl', ĕks'-). AACHEN.

A•jac•cio (ä-yä'chō). Cap. of Corsica. Pop. 54,089.

Ak•kad *also* **Ac•cad** (ăk'ăd', ä'käd'). Ancient region of N Babylonia.

Ak•ron (ăk'rən). City of NE OH. Pop. 223,019.

Al•a•bam•a (ăl'ə-băm'ə). State of the S U.S. Cap. Montgomery. Pop. 4,062,608. **—Al'a•ba'mi•an** (-bā'mē-ən), **Al'a•bam'an** *adj. & n.*

A•las•ka (ə-lăs'kə). State of the U.S. in NW North America. Cap. Juneau. Pop. 551,947. **—A•las'kan** *adj. & n.*

Al•ba•ni•a (ăl-bā'nē-ə, -bān'yə). Republic of SE Europe on the Adriatic. Cap. Tiranë. Pop. 2,841,300. **—Al•ba'ni•an** *adj. & n.*

Al•ba•ny (ôl'bə-nē). Cap. of NY in the E on the Hudson. Pop. 101,082.

Al•ber•ta (ăl-bûr'tə). Province of W Canada. Cap. Edmonton. Pop. 2,237,724.

Al•bu•quer•que (ăl'bə-kûr'kē). City of central NM. Pop. 384,736.

Al•ca•traz (ăl'kə-trăz'). Island in San Francisco Bay, W CA.

A•lep•po (ə-lĕp'ō) *or* **A•lep** (ə-lĕp'). City of NW Syria. Pop. 985,413.

A•leu•tian Islands (ə-lo͞o'shən) *also* **A•leu•tians** (-shənz). Island chain of SW AK.

Al•ex•an•dri•a (ăl'ĭg-zăn'drē-ə). City of N Egypt on the Mediterranean. Pop. 2,821,000.

Al•ge•ri•a (ăl-jîr'ē-ə). Republic of NW Africa on the Mediterranean. Cap. Algiers. Pop. 16,948,000. **—Al•ge'ri•an** *adj. & n.*

Al•giers (ăl-jîrz'). Cap. of Algeria in the N on the Mediterranean. Pop. 1,523,000.

Al•i•can•te (ăl'ĭ-kăn'tē, ä'lē-kän'tē). City of SE Spain. Pop. 253,722.

Al•la•ha•bad (ăl'ə-hə-băd', ä'lə-hə-bäd'). City of N central India. Pop. 616,051.

Al•le•ghe•ny Mountains (ăl'ĭ-gā'nē) *also* **Al•le•ghe•nies** (-nēz). W part of the Appalachian Mts. extending from N PA to SW VA.

Al•len•town (ăl'ən-toun'). City of E PA NNW of Philadelphia. Pop. 105,090.

Al•ma-A•ta (ăl'mə-ä'tə, ăl'mə-ə-tä'). Cap. of Kazakhstan. Pop. 1,068,000.

Al Ma•na•mah (ăl'mə-năm'ə). *var. of* MANAMAH.

Alps (ălps). Mountain system of S central Europe rising to 15,771 ft (4,810.2 m).

Al•sace (ăl-săs', -sās'). Region & former province of E France between the Rhine & the Vosges Mts. **—Al•sa'tian** (-sā'shən) *adj. & n.*

Al•tai *or* **Al•tay** (ăl'tī'). Mountain system of central Asia.

Am•a•ril•lo (ăm'ə-rĭl'ō, -rĭl'ə). City of N TX in the Panhandle. Pop. 157,615.

Am·a·zon (ăm′ə-zŏn′, -zən). Second-longest river in the world, flowing c. 3,900 mi (6,275 km) from N Peru across N Brazil to a wide delta on the Atlantic.

A·mer·i·ca (ə-mĕr′ĭ-kə). The Western Hemisphere lands, including North America, South America, & Central America. —**A·mer′i·can** *adj. & n.*

American Sa·mo·a (sə-mō′ə). Unincorporated U.S. territory in the South Pacific comprising the E half of the Samoa Is. chain. Cap. Pago Pago. Pop. 32,279.

Am·i·ens (ăm′ē-ənz, ä-myăN′). City of N France. Pop. 131,332.

Am·man (ə-män′, ə-măn′). Cap. of Jordan in the N central part. Pop. 777,500.

A·moy (ä-moi′). XIAMEN.

Am·ster·dam (ăm′stər-dăm′). Constitutional cap. of the Netherlands, in the W part. Pop. 676,439.

An·a·heim (ăn′ə-hīm′). City of S CA SE of Los Angeles. Pop. 266,406.

An·a·to·li·a (ăn′ə-tō′lē-ə, -tōl′yə). Asian Turkey, usu. synonymous with Asia Minor. —**An′a·to′li·an** *adj. & n.*

An·chor·age (ăng′kər-ĭj′). City of S AK SSW of Fairbanks. Pop. 226,338.

An·da·lu·ci·a (än′də-lo͞o-sē′ə). ANDALUSIA.

An·da·lu·sia (ăn′də-lo͞o′zhə, -zhē-ə). Region of S Spain on the Mediterranean & the Atlantic. —**An′da·lu′sian** (-zhən) *adj. & n.*

An·des (ăn′dēz). Mountain system of W South America rising at many points to more than 22,000 ft (6,710 m).

An·dor·ra (ăn-dôr′ə, -dŏrə). Country of SW Europe between France & Spain in the E Pyrenees. Cap. Andorra la Vella. Pop. 38,051. —**An·dor′ran** *adj. & n.*

An·go·la (ăng-gō′lə, ăn-). Country of SW Africa on the Atlantic. Cap. Luanda. Pop. 8,140,000. —**An·go′lan** *adj. & n.*

An·guil·la (ăng-gwĭl′ə, ăn-). Island of the British West Indies in the N Leewards.

An·jou (ăn′jo͞o′, äN-zho͞o′). Region & former province of W France in the Loire valley.

An·ka·ra (ăng′kər-ə, äng′-). Cap. of Turkey in the W central part. Pop. 1,877,755.

An·nap·o·lis (ə-năp′ə-lĭs). Cap. of MD SSE of Baltimore. Pop. 33,187.

Ann Ar·bor (ăn är′bər). City of SE MI W of Detroit. Pop. 109,592.

An·ta·na·na·ri·vo (ăn′tə-năn′ə-rē′vō). Cap. of Madagascar. Pop. 700,000.

Ant·arc·tic Ocean (ănt-ärk′tĭk, -är′tĭk). Waters surrounding Antarctica, the S extensions of the Atlantic, Pacific, & Indian oceans.

Ant·arc·ti·ca (ănt-ärk′tĭ-kə, -är′tĭ-). Continent chiefly within the Antarctic Circle & asymmetrically centered on the South Pole.

An·ti·gua and Bar·bu·da (ăn-tē′gwə, -gə; bär-bo͞o′də). Country in the N Leewards, comprising Antigua & the smaller islands of Barbuda & Redonda. Cap. St. John's. Pop. 72,000. —**An·ti′guan** *adj. & n.*

An·til·les (ăn-tĭl′ēz). The West Indies except for the Bahamas.

An·ti·och (ăn′tē-ŏk′). Ancient town of Phrygia in SW Turkey.

Ant·werp (ănt′wûrp′, ăn′twərp). Port city of N Belgium. Pop. 490,524.

Ap·en·nines (ăp′ə-nīnz′). Mountain system of central Italy rising to 9,560 ft (2,915.8 m).

A·pi·a (ə-pē′ə). Cap. of Western Samoa on N Upolo Is. Pop. 33,170.

Ap·pa·la·chi·a (ăp′ə-lā′chē-ə, -chə, -lăch′ē-ə, -lăch′ə). Region of E U.S. containing the Appalachian Mts.

Ap·pa·la·chi·an Mountains (ăp′ə-lā′chē-ən, -chən, -lăch′ē-ən, -lăch′ən) *also* **the Ap·pa·la·chi·ans** (-ənz, -chənz). Mountain system of E North America rising to 6,684 ft (2,038.6 m).

Aq·ui·taine (ăk′wĭ-tān′). Historical region of SW France.

A·ra·bi·a (ə-rā′bē-ə). Peninsula of SW Asia between the Red Sea & the Persian Gulf. —**A·ra′bi·an** *adj. & n.*

Arabian Sea. NW part of the Indian Ocean between Arabia & India.

Ar·a·gon (ăr′ə-gŏn′). Region & former kingdom of NE Spain. —**Ar′a·go·nese′** (ăr′ə-gə-nēz′, -nēs′) *adj. & n.*

Ar·al Sea (ăr′əl). Inland sea of central Asia between S Kazakhstan and NW Uzbekistan.

Ar·an (ăr′ən). Three islands of W Ireland at the entrance to Galway Bay.

Ar·ca·di·a (är-kā′dē-ə). Region of ancient Greece in the Peloponnesus.

Arc·tic Ocean (ärk′tĭk, är′tĭk). Waters surrounding the North Pole between North America and Eurasia.

Ar·gen·ti·na (är′jən-tē′nə). Republic of SE South America. Cap. Buenos Aires. Pop. 27,947,446. —**Ar′gen·tine′** (-tēn′, -tīn′) *adj. & n.* —**Ar′gen·tin′e·an** (-tĭn′ē-ən) *adj. & n.*

Ar·i·zo·na (ăr′ĭ-zō′nə). State of the SW U.S. on the Mexican border. Cap. Phoenix. Pop. 3,677,985. —**Ar′i·zo′ni·an** *adj. & n.*

Ar·kan·sas (är′kən-sô′). **1.** (*also* är-kăn′zəs). River of the S central U.S. rising in central CO & flowing c. 1,450 mi (2,335 km) to the Mississippi in SE AR. **2.** State of the S central U.S. Cap. Little Rock. Pop. 2,362,239. —**Ar·kan′san** (är-kăn′zən) *adj. & n.*

Ark·han·gelsk (är-kăn′gĕlsk, -KHän′-). City of NW Russia. Pop. 408,000.

Ar·ling·ton (är′lĭng-tən). **1.** City of N TX. Pop. 261,721. **2.** County & unincorporated city of N VA near Washington, D.C. Pop. 170,936.

Ar·me·ni·a (är-mē′nē-ə, -mēn′yə). **1.** Region & former kingdom of Asia Minor. **2.** Country of Asia Minor S of Georgia. Cap. Yerevan. Pop. 3,317,000. —**Ar·me′ni·an** *adj. & n.*

Ar·no (är′nō). River of central Italy flowing c. 150 mi (240 km) to the Ligurian Sea.

A·ru·ba (ə-ro͞o′bə). Island of the Netherlands Antilles N of the Venezuela coast.

A·shan·ti (ə-shăn′tē, -shän′-) *or* **A·san·te** (-săn′-). Region & former kingdom of central Ghana, W Africa.

Ash·kha·bad (ăsh′kə-băd′, -bäd′). City of S central Turkmenistan. Pop. 356,000.

A•sia (ā′zhə, ā′shə). The world's largest continent occupying the E part of Eurasia & adjacent islands & separated from Europe by the Ural Mts. —**A′sian** *adj. & n.*

Asia Mi•nor (mī′nər). Peninsula of W Asia between the Black Sea & the Mediterranean.

As•ma•ra (ăz-mä′rə). City of N Ethiopia near the Red Sea. Pop. 474,241.

As•syr•i•a (ə-sîr′ē-ə). Ancient empire of W Asia in the upper valley of the Tigris. —**As•syr′i•an** *adj. & n.*

As•tra•khan (ăs′trə-kăn′). City of SW Russia on the Volga delta. Pop. 493,000.

A•sun•ción (ə-sōōn′sē-ōn′). Cap. of Paraguay in the S part. Pop. 455,517.

Ath•ens (ăth′ənz). Cap. of Greece in the E central part. Pop. 885,737.

At•lan•ta (ăt-lăn′tə). Cap. of GA in the NW part. Pop. 394,017.

At•lan•tic Ocean (ăt-lăn′tĭk). Second-largest ocean, extending from North & South America on the W to Europe & Africa on the E.

At•las (ăt′ləs). Mountain system of NW Africa rising to 13,665 ft (4,167.8 m).

At•ti•ca (ăt′ĭ-kə). Ancient region of E central Greece around Athens. —**At′tic** (ăt′ĭk) *adj.*

Au•gus•ta (ô-gŭs′tə, ə-gŭs′). Cap. of ME in the SW part NNE of Portland. Pop. 21,325.

Auk•land (ôk′lənd). City of New Zealand on NW North Is. Metro. area pop. 860,000.

Aus•ter•litz (ô′stər-lĭts′, ous′tər-). Town of SE Czech Republic.

Aus•tin (ô′stən, ŏs′tən). Cap. of TX in the S central part. Pop. 465,622.

Aus•tral•a•sia (ô′strə-lā′zhə, -shə). **1.** Islands of Oceania in the S Pacific, including Australia, New Zealand, New Guinea, & associated islands. **2.** OCEANIA. —**Aus′tral•a′sian** *adj. & n.*

Aus•tra•lia (ô-strāl′yə). **1.** The world's smallest continent, SE of Asia between the Pacific & Indian oceans. **2.** *or* **Commonwealth of Australia.** Country comprising the continent of Australia, the island state of Tasmania, two external territories, & several dependencies. Cap. Canberra. Pop. 15,544,500. —**Aus•tra′lian** *adj. & n.*

Aus•tri•a (ô′strē-ə). Federal republic of central Europe. Cap. Vienna. Pop. 7,555,338. —**Aus′tri•an** *adj. & n.*

Aus•tro•ne•sia (ô′strō-nē′zhə, -shə). Islands of the Pacific, including Indonesia, Melanesia, Micronesia, & Polynesia. —**Aus′tro•ne′sian** *adj. & n.*

Au•vergne (ō-vĕrn′, ō-vûrn′). Region & former province of S central France.

A•zer•bai•jan (ăz′ər-bī-jän′, ä′zər-). **1.** Region of NW Iran. **2.** Country of Transcaucasia N of Iran. Cap. Baku. Pop. 6,614,000.

A•zores (ā′zôrz, ā′zōrz, ə-zôrz′, ə-zōrz′). Islands in the N Atlantic W of mainland Portugal. —**A•zor′e•an, A•zor′i•an** *adj. & n.*

A•zov (ăs′ôf′, -ŏf′, ā′zŏf), **Sea of.** N arm of the Black Sea between Ukraine and Russia.

B

Bab•y•lon (băb′ə-lən, -lŏn′). Cap. of ancient Babylonia on the Euphrates R.

Bab•y•lo•ni•a (băb′ə-lō′nē-ə, -lōn′yə). Ancient country of SW Asia in the Euphrates valley. —**Bab′y•lo′ni•an** *adj. & n.*

Bagh•dad *or* **Bag•dad** (băg′dăd′). Cap. of Iraq. Metro. area pop. 2,200,000.

Ba•gui•o (bä′gē-ō′). Summer cap. of the Philippines in NW Luzon. Pop. 119,019.

Ba•ha•ma Islands (bə-hä′mə, -hā′-) *also* **Ba•ha•mas** (-məz). Island country in the Atlantic SE of FL. Cap. Nassau. Pop. 218,000. —**Ba•ha′mi•an** (-hā′mē-ən, -hä′-) , **Ba•ha′man** (-hä′mən, -hā′-) *adj. & n.*

Bah•rain *or* **Bah•rein** (bä-rān′). Sheikdom & archipelago in the Persian Gulf between Qatar & Saudi Arabia. Cap. Al Manamah. Pop. 350,798. —**Bah•rain′i** *adj. & n.*

Bai•kal *or* **Bay•kal** (bī-kôl′, -kŏl′). Lake of S central Russia.

Bai•ri•ki (bī-rē′kē). Cap. of Kiribati on Tarawa in the W central Pacific. Pop. 1,956.

Ba•ja Cal•i•for•ni•a (bä′hä kăl′ə-fôr′nyə). LOWER CALIFORNIA.

Bal•e•ar•ic (băl′ē-ăr′ĭk). Archipelago in the W Mediterranean E of Spain.

Ba•li (bä′lē). Island of Indonesia E of Java. —**Ba′li•nese′** (bä′lĭ-nēz′, -nēs′) *adj. & n.*

Bal•kan (bôl′kən). **1.** Mountain range extending from E Serbia through central Bulgaria to the Black Sea. **2.** Peninsula of SE Europe bounded by the Black Sea, Sea of Marmara, & the Aegean, Mediterranean, Ionian, & Adriatic seas.

Bal•tic Sea (bôl′tĭk, bŏl′-). Arm of the Atlantic in N Europe.

Bal•ti•more (bôl′tə-môr′, -mōr′, bŏl′-). City of N MD. Pop. 736,014.

Ba•ma•ko (bä′mə-kō′). Cap. of Mali in the SW on the Niger R. Pop. 502,000.

Ban•dar Se•ri Be•ga•wan (bŭn′dər sĕr′ē bə-gä′wən). Cap. of Brunei. Pop. 63,868.

Ban•dung (bän′dŏŏng′). City of Indonesia in W Java. Pop. 1,462,637.

Ban•ga•lore (băng′gə-lôr′, -lōr′). City of S central India W of Madras. Pop. 2,476,355.

Bang•kok (băng′kŏk′, băng-kŏk′). Cap. of Thailand in the SW part. Pop. 5,174,682.

Bang•la•desh (bäng′glə-dĕsh′, -dāsh′, băng′-). Republic of S Asia between India & Burma. Cap. Dacca. Pop. 87,052,000.

Ban•gui (bäng-gē′, bäN-). Cap. of Central African Republic. Pop. 340,000.

Ban•jul (bän′jōōl′). Cap. of Gambia on an island in the Gambia R. Pop. 44,536.

Bar•ba•dos (bär-bā′dəs, -dōz′, -dŏs′, -dōs′). Island country of the E West Indies. Cap. Bridgetown. Pop. 248,983. —**Bar•ba′di•an** *adj. & n.*

Bar•ba•ry (bär′bə-rē, -brē). Region of N Africa on the **Barbary Coast** between the W border of Egypt & the Atlantic.

Bar•bu•da (bär-bōō′də). Island of Antigua and Barbuda, in the West Indies.

Bar•ce•lo•na (bär′sə-lō′nə). City of NE Spain on the Mediterranean. Pop. 1,770,296.

Ba•rents Sea (băr′ənts, bär′-). Arm of the Arctic Ocean N of Norway & NW Russia.

Ba•ri (bä′rē). City of SE Italy on the Adriatic. Pop. 370,781.

Bar•qui•si•me•to (bär′kə-sə-mā′tō). City of NW Venezuela. Pop. 504,000.

Bar•ran•quil•la (băr′ən-kē′ə, -yə). City of N Colombia. Pop. 891,545.

Ba•sel (bä′zəl) *or* **Basle** (bäl). City of N Switzerland on the Rhine. Pop. 176,200.

Basque Provinces (băsk). Region of N Spain on the Bay of Biscay.

Bas•ra (bäs′rə, bŭs′-). City of SE Iraq on the Shatt-al-Arab. Pop. 616,700.

Basse•terre (băs-târ′, bäs-). Cap. of St. Christopher-Nevis. Pop. 14,725.

Basse-Terre (băs-târ′, bäs-). **1.** Island of the French West Indies in the Leewards. **2.** Cap. of Guadeloupe on **Basse-Terre** Island. Pop. 13,656.

Bat•on Rouge (băt′n ro͞ozh′). City of SE central LA NW of New Orleans. Pop. 219,531.

Ba•var•i•a (bə-vâr′ē-ə). Region & former duchy of S Germany. **—Ba•var′i•an** *adj. & n.*

Bei•jing (bā′jĭng′). Cap. of China in the NE part. Pop. 5,860,000.

Bei•rut (bā-ro͞ot′). Cap. of Lebanon in the W on the Mediterranean. Pop. 509,000.

Bel•a•rus (bĕl′ə-ro͞os′). *var. of* BELORUSSIA.

Be•lém (bə-lĕm′). Port city of NE Brazil near the mouth of the Amazon. Pop. 933,287.

Bel•fast (bĕl′făst′, bĕl-făst′). Cap. of Northern Ireland. Pop. 318,600.

Bel•gium (bĕl′jəm). Constitutional kingdom of NW Europe on the North Sea. Cap. Brussels. Pop. 9,858,017. **—Bel′gian** *adj. & n.*

Bel•grade (bĕl′grād′, -gräd′, bĕl-grād′). Cap. of Serbia and of Yugoslavia in N central Serbia. Pop. 936,200.

Be•lize (bə-lēz′). Country of Central America on the Caribbean. Cap. Belmopan. Pop. 145,353.

Bel•mo•pan (bĕl′mō-păn′). Cap. of Belize in the N central part. Pop. 2,935.

Be•lo Ho•ri•zon•te (bā′lō hôr′ĭ-zŏn′tē, bĕl′-ō). City of E Brazil. Pop. 1,780,855.

Be•lo•rus•sia (bĕl′ō-rŭsh′ə) *also* **Bye•lo•rus•sia** (bē-ĕl′ō-) *or* **Belarus** (bĕl′ə-ro͞os′). Country of E Europe E of Poland. Cap. Minsk. Pop. 9,942,000. **—Be′lo•rus′sian** *adj. & n.*

Ben•gal (bĕn-gôl′, bĕng-). Region of E India & Bangladesh on the **Bay of Bengal,** arm of the Indian Ocean. **—Ben′ga•lese′** (bĕn′gə-lēz′, -lēs′, bĕng′-) *adj. & n.*

Ben•gha•zi (bĕn-gä′zē, bĕng-găz′ē). City of NE Libya on the Mediterranean. Pop. 367,600.

Be•nin (bə-nĭn′, -nēn′). Country of W Africa. Cap. Porto-Novo. Pop. 3,567,000.

Ber•gen (bûr′gən, bĕr′-). City of SW Norway on inlets of the North Sea. Pop. 207,232.

Be•ring Sea (bîr′ĭng, bĕr′-). Part of the Pacific between Siberia & AK, joined to the Arctic Ocean by the **Bering Strait.**

Berke•ley (bûrk′lē). City of W CA N of Oakland. Pop. 102,724.

Berk•shire (bûrk′shîr′, -shər). Range of hills in W MA.

Ber•lin (bûr-lĭn′). Cap. of Germany in the NE. Divided (1945–90) into **East Berlin & West Berlin.** Pop. 3,034,118.

Ber•mu•da (bər-myo͞o′də). British colony in the Atlantic SE of Cape Hatteras. Cap. Hamilton. Pop. 56,000. **—Ber•mu′di•an** *adj. & n.*

Bern *or* **Berne** (bûrn, bĕrn). Cap. of Switzerland in the NW on the Aare. Pop. 140,600.

Bes•sa•ra•bi•a (bĕs′ə-rā′bē-ə). Region of Moldavia and W Ukraine. **—Bes′sa•ra′bi•an** *adj. & n.*

Beth•le•hem (bĕth′lĭ-hĕm′, -lē-əm). Town of the West Bank S of Jerusalem. Pop. 25,000.

Bho•pal (bō-päl′). City of central India NW of Nagpur. Pop. 671,018.

Bhu•tan (bo͞o-tăn′, -tän′). Kingdom of central Asia in the E Himalayas. Cap. Thimbu. Pop. 1,232,000. **—Bhu′tan•ese′** (bo͞o′tn-ēz′, -ēs′) *adj. & n.*

Bi•a•fra (bē-ăf′rə, -ä′frə). Region of E Nigeria. **—Bi•a′fran** *adj. & n.*

Bia•ly•stok (bē-ä′lĭ-stôk′). City of NE Poland. Pop. 245,400.

Bi•ki•ni (bĭ-kē′nē). Atoll in the Marshall Is. of the W central Pacific.

Bil•ba•o (bĭl-bä′ō, -bou′). City of N Spain near the Bay of Biscay. Pop. 397,541.

Bil•lings (bĭl′ĭngz). City of S MT ESE of Helena. Pop. 81,151.

Bir•ming•ham (bûr′mĭng-hăm′). **1.** (*also* -əm). City of central England. Pop. 1,022,300. **2.** City of N central AL. Pop. 265,968.

Bis•cayne Bay (bĭs-kān′, bĭs′kān′). Inlet of the Atlantic in SE FL.

Bish•kek (bĭsh′kĕk, bēsh′-). The cap. of Kirghiz in the N central part. Pop. 604,000.

Bis•marck (bĭz′märk′). **1.** Archipelago in the SW Pacific NE of New Guinea. **2.** Cap. of ND in the S central part. Pop. 49,256.

Bis•sau (bĭ-sou′). Cap. of Guinea-Bissau on an estuary of the Atlantic. Pop. 109,486.

Black Forest. Mountain range of SW Germany between the Rhine & the Neckar.

Black Hills. Mountains of SW SD & NE WY.

Black Sea Inland sea, between Europe & Asia.

Blue Nile (nīl). River of NE Africa flowing c. 1,000 mi (1,610 km) from NW Ethiopia to Khartoum, Sudan, where it merges with the White Nile to form the Nile.

Blue Ridge. Mountain range extending from S PA to N GA, part of the Appalachians.

Boe•o•tia (bē-ō′shə, -shē-ə). Ancient region of Greece N of Attica & the Gulf of Corinth. **—Boe•o′tian** *adj. & n.*

Bo•go•tá (bō′gə-tä′). Cap. of Colombia in the central part. Pop. 3,967,988.

Bo•he•mi•a (bō-hē′mē-ə). Historical region & former kingdom of W Czech Republic. **—Bo•he′mi•an** *adj. & n.*

Boi•se (boi′sē, -zē). Cap. of ID in the SW part near the OR border. Pop. 102,160.

Bo•liv•i•a (bə-lĭv′ē-ə). Republic of W South America. Caps. Sucre & La Paz. Pop. 6,429,226. **—Bo•liv′i•an** *adj. & n.*

Bo•lo•gna (bə-lōn'yə). City of N central Italy. Pop. 455,853. —**Bo•lo'gnan, Bo'lo•gnese'** (bō'lə-nēz', -nēs', -lən-yēz', -yēs') *adj. & n.*
Bom•bay (bŏm-bā'). Port city of W central India. Metro. area pop. 8,243,405.
Bonn (bŏn, bôn). Former cap. of West Germany, on the Rhine. Pop. 291,291.
Bo•phu•tha•tswa•na (bō'po͞o-tät-swä'nə). Autonomous Black homeland within South Africa. Cap. Mmabatho. Pop. 1,347,000.
Bor•deaux (bôr-dō'). City of SW France on the Garonne R. Pop. 208,159.
Bor•ne•o (bôr'nē-ō'). Island of the W Pacific SW of the Philippines. —**Bor'ne•an** *adj. & n.*
Bos•ni•a (bŏz'nē-ə). The N section of Bosnia-Herzegovina. —**Bos'ni•an** *adj. & n.*
Bos•ni•a-Her•ze•go•vi•na (bŏz'nē-ə-hĕrt'-sə-gō-vē'nə, -hûrt'-) *also* **Bosnia and Herzegovina.** Region and republic of NW Balkan Peninsula W of Serbia. Cap. Sarajevo. Pop. 3,710,965.
Bos•po•rus (bŏs'pər-əs) *also* **Bos•pho•rus** (-fər-). Strait separating European & Asian Turkey & joining the Black Sea & the Sea of Marmara.
Bos•ton (bô'stən, bŏs'tən). Cap. of MA. Pop. 574,283. —**Bos•to'ni•an** (bô-stō'nē-ən, bŏs-tō'-) *adj. & n.*
Both•ni•a (bŏth'nē-ə), **Gulf of.** N arm of the Baltic Sea between Sweden & Finland.
Bot•swa•na (bŏt-swä'nə). Republic of S central Africa. Cap. Gaborone. Pop. 973,000.
Boul•der (bōl'dər). City of N central CO NW of Denver. Pop. 83,312.
Brah•ma•pu•tra (brä'mə-po͞o'trə). River of S Asia flowing c. 1,800 mi (2,895 km) from SW Tibet to the **Bay of Bengal.**
Bran•den•burg (brăn'dən-bûrg', brän'dən-bo͝org'). Former duchy of N central Germany.
Bra•si•lia (brə-zĭl'yə). Cap. of Brazil NW of Rio de Janeiro. Pop. 1,176,935.
Bra•ti•sla•va (brăt'ĭ-slä'və, brä'tĭ-). Cap. of Slovakia. Pop. 409,100.
Bra•zil (brə-zĭl'). Republic of E South America. Cap. Brasília. Pop. 119,002,706. —**Bra•zil'i•an** *adj. & n.*
Braz•os (brăz'əs). River of E NM & central TX flowing c. 950 mi (1,528 km) to the Gulf of Mexico.
Braz•za•ville (brăz'ə-vĭl', brä'zə-vēl'). Cap. of Congo on the Congo R. Pop. 595,102.
Bre•men (brĕm'ən, brā'mən). City of NW Germany. Pop. 530,520.
Bre•scia (brĕsh'ə, brā'shə). City of N Italy E of Milan. Pop. 206,460.
Brest (brĕst). **1.** City of NW France. Pop. 156,060. **2.** *also* **Brest Li•tovsk** (lĭ-tôfsk'). City of SW Belorussia. Pop. 222,000.
Bridge•port (brĭj'pôrt', -pōrt'). City of SW CT on Long Is. Sound. Pop. 141,686.
Bridge•town (brĭj'toun'). Cap. of Barbados, West Indies. Pop. 7,466.
Brigh•ton (brīt'n). Borough of SE England on the English Channel S of London. Pop. 150,200.
Bris•bane (brĭz'bən, -bān'). City of E Australia. Pop. 734,750.
Bris•tol (brĭs'təl). City of SW England on the **Bristol Channel**, an inlet of the Atlantic separating Wales from SW England. Pop. 400,300.
Brit•ain (brĭt'n). UNITED KINGDOM.
British Co•lum•bi•a (kə-lŭm'bē-ə). Province of W Canada. Cap. Victoria. Pop. 2,744,467.
British Honduras. BELIZE.
British Isles. Islands off the NW coast of Europe comprising Great Britain, Ireland, & adjacent smaller islands.
British Vir•gin Islands (vûr'jĭn). British colony in the E Caribbean E of the U.S. Virgin Is. Cap. Road Town on Tortola Is. Pop. 12,034.
Brit•ta•ny (brĭt'n-ē). Region & former province of NW France.
Br•no (bûr'nō). City of SE Czech Republic SE of Prague. Pop. 383,443.
Bronx *or* **the Bronx** (brŏngks). Borough of New York City. Pop. 1,203,789.
Brook•lyn (bro͝ok'lĭn). Borough of New York City. Pop. 2,300,664.
Browns•ville (brounz'vĭl). City of S Texas on the Rio Grande. Pop. 98,962.
Bruges (bro͞ozh). City of NW Belgium E of Ostend. Pop. 118,218.
Bru•nei (bro͞o'nī'). Sultanate of NW Borneo. Cap. Bandar Seri Begawan. Pop. 191,765.
Brus•sels (brŭs'lz). Cap. of Belgium in the N central part. Metro. area pop. 2,395,000.
Bu•cha•rest (bo͞o'kə-rĕst', byo͞o'-). Cap. of Romania in the SE part. Pop. 1,995,156.
Bu•da•pest (bo͞o'də-pĕst', -pĕsht', byo͞o'-). Cap. of Hungary. Pop. 2,071,484.
Bue•nos Ai•res (bwā'nəs âr'ēz, īr'ĭz, bō'-nəs). Cap. of Argentina. Pop. 2,922,829.
Buf•fa•lo (bŭf'ə-lō'). City of W NY at the E end of Lake Erie. Pop. 328,123.
Bu•jum•bu•ra (bo͞o'jəm-bo͝or'ə). Cap. of Burundi in the W part. Pop. 229,980.
Bu•la•wa•yo (bo͝ol'ə-wä'ō, -wī'ō). City of SW Zimbabwe. Pop. 413,814.
Bul•gar•i•a (bŭl-gâr'ē-ə, bo͝ol-). Republic of SE Europe on the Black Sea. Cap. Sofia. Pop. 8,960,679. —**Bul•gar'i•an** *adj. & n.*
Bur•gun•dy (bûr'gən-dē). Region & former province of E France. —**Bur•gun'di•an** (bər-gŭn'dē-ən) *adj. & n.*
Bur•ki•na Fa•so (bər-kē'nə fä'sō). Country of W Africa. Cap. Ouagadougou. Pop. 6,965,886.
Bur•ma (bûr'mə). Officially (since 1989) **Myan•mar** (myän-mär'). Republic of SE Asia on the Bay of Bengal & the Andaman Sea. Cap. Rangoon. Pop. 35,313,905. —**Bur•mese'** (bər-mēz', -mēs'), **Bur'man** (bûr'mən) *adj. & n.*
Bu•run•di (bo͞o-ro͞on'dē). Republic of E central Africa NW of Tanzania. Cap. Bujumbura. Pop. 4,523,513. —**Bu•run'di•an** *adj. & n.*
Byd•goszcz (bĭd'gôsh', -gôsch'). City of N central Poland. Pop. 361,400.
Bye•lo•rus•sia (bē-ĕl'ō-rŭsh'ə). *var. of* BELORUSSIA.

Byz·an·tine Empire (bĭz′ən-tēn′, -tīn′). E part of the later Roman Empire.

By·zan·ti·um (bĭ-zăn′shē-əm, -shəm, -tē-əm). Ancient city of Thrace on the site of present-day Istanbul, Turkey.

C

Cá·diz (kə-dĭz′, kā′dĭz, kä′-). City of SW Spain NW of Gibralter on an inlet of the Atlantic. Pop. 160, 839.

Cai·ro (kī′rō). Cap. of Egypt on the Nile in the NE part. Pop. 6,205,000. —**Cai·rene′** (-rēn′) *adj. & n.*

Ca·la·bri·a (kə-lā′brē-ə, -lä′-). Region of S Italy, forming the toe of the Italian boot.

Ca·lais (kă-lā′, kăl′ā). City of N France on the Strait of Dover. Pop. 76,527.

Cal·cut·ta (kăl-kŭt′ə). City of E India on the Ganges delta. Metro. area pop. 3,305,006.

Cal·ga·ry (kăl′gə-rē). City of S Alta., Canada, S of Edmonton. Pop. 592,743.

Ca·li (kä′lē). City of W Colombia SW of Bogotá. Pop. 1,347,810.

Cal·i·for·nia (kăl′ə-fôr′nyə). State of the W U.S. on the Pacific. Cap. Sacramento. Pop. 29,839,250. —**Cal′i·for′nian** *adj. & n.*

Ca·ma·güey (kăm′ə-gwā′). City of E central Cuba. Pop. 244,091.

Cam·bo·di·a (kăm-bō′dē-ə). Country of SE Asia. Cap. Phnom Penh. Pop. 5,756,141. —**Cam·bo′di·an** *adj. & n.*

Cam·bridge (kām′brĭj). **1.** Borough of E central England NNE of London. Pop. 100,200. **2.** City of E MA near Boston. Pop. 95,802.

Cam·den (kăm′dən). City of W NJ opposite Philadelphia, PA. Pop. 87,492.

Cam·e·roon (kăm′ə-ro͞on′) *also* **Came·roun** (kăm-ro͞on′). Country of W central Africa. Cap. Yaoundé. Pop. 9,542,400.

Ca·naan (kā′nən). Ancient region of Palestine or the part of it W of the Jordan R.

Can·a·da (kăn′ə-də). Country of N North America. Cap. Ottawa. Pop. 23,343,181. —**Ca·na′di·an** (kə-nā′dē-ə n) *adj. & n.*

Ca·nar·y Islands (kə-nâr′ē). Spanish islands off the NW coast of Africa.

Ca·nav·er·al (kə-năv′ər-əl, -năv′rəl). Cape of E central Atlantic coast of FL.

Can·ber·ra (kăn′bər-ə, -bĕr′ə). Cap. of Australia in the SE part. Pop. 243,450.

Cannes (kăn). Resort city of SE France on the Mediterranean. Pop. 72,529.

Can·ter·bur·y (kăn′tər-bĕr′ē, -brē, -tə-). City of SE England ESE of London. Pop. 36,000.

Can·ton (kăn′tŏn′, kăn′tŏn′). GUANGZHOU.

Cape Bret·on Island (kāp brĕt′n, brĭt′-n). Island forming the NE part of N.S., Canada.

Cape Town *or* **Cape·town** (kāp′toun′). Legislative cap. of South Africa on the Atlantic in the extreme SW part. Pop. 859,940.

Cape Verde (vûrd). Island republic in the N Atlantic W of Senegal. Cap. Praia. Pop. 296,093.

Cap·pa·do·cia (kăp′ə-dō′shə, -shē-ə). Ancient region of Asia Minor in present-day central Turkey.

Ca·pri (kə-prē′, kăp′rē, kä′prē). Island of S Italy on the S edge of the Bay of Naples.

Ca·ra·cas (kə-rä′kəs, -răk′əs). Cap. of Venezuela, in the N part. Pop. 3,041,000.

Car·diff (kär′dĭf). City of SE Wales on Bristol Channel. Pop. 281,300.

Car·ib·be·an (kăr′ə-bē′ən, kə-rĭb′ē-). Sea of the N Atlantic bounded by the coasts of Central & South America & the West Indies.

Car·o·line (kăr′ə-līn′, -lĭn). Islands of the W Pacific E of the Philippines, part of the U.S. Trust Territory of the Pacific Is.

Car·pa·thi·an (kär-pā′thē-ən). Mountain system of central Europe.

Car·son City (kär′sən). Cap. of NV in the W part near the Calif. border. Pop. 40,443.

Car·ta·ge·na (kär′tə-gā′nə, -jē′-, -hā′-). City of NW Colombia on the Caribbean. Pop. 495,028.

Car·thage (kär′thĭj). Ancient city & state on the N coast of Africa. —**Car′tha·gin′i·an** (kär′thə-jĭn′ē-ən) *adj. & n.*

Cas·a·blan·ca (kăs′ə-blăng′kə, käz′-). City of NW Morocco. Pop. 2,139,204.

Cas·cade (kăs-kād′). Mountain range of NW U.S. rising to 14,410 ft (4,395.1 m).

Cash·mere (kăsh′mîr′, kăsh-mîr′). KASHMIR.

Cas·pi·an Sea (kăs′pē-ən). Salt lake between SE Europe & W Asia.

Cas·tile (kăs-tēl′). Region & former kingdom of central & N Spain. —**Cas·til′ian** (kă-stĭl′yən, kə-) *adj. & n.*

Cas·tries (kăs′trēz′, -trēs′). Cap. of St. Lucia in the British West Indies. Pop. 50,798.

Cat·a·lo·nia (kăt′l-ōn′yə, -ō′nē-ə). Region of NE Spain. —**Cat′a·lo′nian** *adj. & n.*

Cats·kill (kăt′skĭl′) *also* **Cats·kills** (-skĭlz). Mountain range in SE NY.

Cau·ca·sus (kô′kə-səs) *also* **Cau·ca·sia** (kô-kā′zhə, -shə). Region between the Black & Caspian seas including Georgia, Azerbaijan, Armenia, and part of SW Russia.

Cay·enne (kī-ĕn′, kā-). Cap. of French Guiana on **Cayenne Is.** Pop. 38,093.

Cay·man (kā-măn′, kā′mən) *also* **Cay·mans** (kā-mănz′, kā′mənz). British-administered island group in the Caribbean NW of Jamaica. Cap. Georgetown. Pop. 16,677.

Ce·dar Rapids (sē′dər). City of E central IA. Pop. 108,751.

Cel·e·bes (sĕl′ə-bēz′, sə-lē′bēz′). **1.** Sea of the W Pacific between Sulawesi & S Philippines. **2.** SULAWESI.

Cen·tral Af·ri·can Republic (sĕn′trəl ăf′-rĭ-kən). Country of central Africa. Cap. Bangui. Pop. 2,395,000.

Central A·mer·i·ca (ə-mĕr′ĭ-kə). Region of S North America from S border of Mexico to N border of Colombia. —**Central A·mer′i·can** *adj. & n.*

Cey·lon (sĭ-lŏn′, sā-). SRI LANKA. —**Cey′lo·nese′** (-nēz′, -nēs′) *adj. & n.*

Chad (chăd). Country of N central Africa. Cap. Ndjamena. Pop. 4,405,000.

Chal•dae•a *also* **Chal•de•a** (kăl-dē'ə). Ancient region of S Mesopotamia. —**Chal•dae'an, Chal•de'an** *adj. & n.*
Cham•pagne (shăm-pān'). Region & former province of NE France.
Cham•plain (shăm-plān'). Lake of NE NY, NW VT, & S Que., Canada.
Chang•chun (chăng'chōōn'). City of NE China in Manchuria. Pop. 1,480,000.
Chang Jiang (chäng' jē-äng'). YANGTZE.
Chang•sha (chăng'shä'). City of S China WSW of Shanghai. Pop. 1,123,900.
Charles•ton (chärl'stən). **1.** City of SE SC NE of Savannah. Pop 80,414. **2.** Cap. of WV in the W central part. Pop. 57,287.
Char•lotte (shär'lət). City of S NC near the SC border. Pop. 395,934.
Charlotte A•ma•lie (ə-mäl'yə). Cap. of the U.S. Virgin Is. on St. Thomas. Pop. 11,842.
Char•lotte•town (shär'lət-toun'). Cap. of P.E.I., Canada, on the S coast. Pop. 15,282.
Chat•ta•noo•ga (chăt'ə-nōō'gə). City of SE TN SE of Nashville. Pop. 152,466.
Chem•nitz (kĕm'nĭts). City of E central Germany SE of Leipzig. Pop. 318,917.
Cheng•chow (jŭng'jō'). ZHENGZHOU.
Cheng•du *also* **Cheng•tu** (chŭng'dōō'). City of central China. Pop. 1,590,000.
Ches•a•peake (chĕs'ə-pēk'). **1. Bay.** Inlet of the Atlantic in VA & MD. **2.** Independent city of SE VA. Pop. 151,976.
Chey•enne (shī-ăn', -ĕn'). Cap. of WY in the SE part. Pop. 50,008.
Chi•ca•go (shĭ-kä'gō, -kô'-). City of NE IL on Lake Michigan. Pop. 2,783,726.
Chi•hua•hua (chə-wä'wä). City of N Mexico. Pop. 385,603.
Chil•e (chĭl'ē). Republic of SW South America. Cap. Santiago. Pop. 11,329,736. —**Chil'e•an** *adj. & n.*
Chi•na (chī'nə). **1. Sea.** W part of the Pacific extending along the E coast of Asia from S Japan to the Malay Peninsula. **2.** *also* **People's Republic of China.** Country of E Asia. Cap. Beijing. Pop. 1,008,175,288. **3.** *also* **Republic of China.** TAIWAN.
Chit•ta•gong (chĭt'ə-gông', -gŏng'). City of SE Bangladesh. Pop. 980,000.
Chong•qing (chông'chē-ĭng'). City of S central China on the Yangtze. Pop. 2,080,000.
Chu•la Vis•ta (chōō'lə vĭs'tə). City of S CA near San Diego. Pop. 135,163.
Chung•king (chŏŏng'kĭng', jŏŏng'gĭng'). CHONGQING.
Cin•cin•na•ti (sĭn'sə-năt'ē, -năt'ə). City of extreme SW OH on the Ohio R. Pop. 364,040.
Ci•u•dad Juá•rez (sē'ōō-dăd' wär'ĕz, -ĕs, -əs, hwär'-). City of N Mexico on the Rio Grande opposite El Paso, TX. Pop. 544,496.
Cleve•land (klēv'lənd). City of NE OH on Lake Erie. Pop. 505,616.
Clyde (klīd). River of SW Scotland flowing 106 mi (170.6 km) NW to the Atlantic.
Co•cha•bam•ba (kō'chə-bäm'bə). City of E central Bolivia NNW of Sucre. Pop. 317,251.
Cod (kŏd), **Cape.** Peninsula of SE MA.
Co•logne (kə-lōn'). City of W Germany on the Rhine. Pop. 1,013,771.
Co•lom•bi•a (kə-lŭm'bē-ə, -lôm'-). Country of NW South America. Cap. Bogotá. Pop. 26,525,670. —**Co•lom'bian** *adj. & n.*
Co•lom•bo (kə-lŭm'bō). Cap. of Sri Lanka on the W coast. Metro. area pop. 587,647.
Col•o•ra•do (kŏl'ə-răd'ō, -rä'dō). **1.** River of the SW U.S. flowing 1,450 mi (2,333 km) to the Gulf of California. **2.** State of the W central U.S. Cap. Denver. Pop. 3,307,912. —**Col'o•ra'dan** *adj. & n.*
Colorado Springs. City of central CO SSE of Denver. Pop. 281,140.
Co•lum•bi•a (kə-lŭm'bē-ə). **1.** River of SE B.C., Canada, & NW U.S. flowing 1,210 mi (1,945 km) to the Pacific. **2. District of.** DISTRICT OF COLUMBIA. **3.** Cap. of SC in the central part. Pop. 98,052.
Co•lum•bus (kə-lŭm'bəs). **1.** City of W GA. Pop. 179,278. **2.** Cap. of OH in the central part. Pop. 632,910.
Com•mon•wealth of Nations (kŏm'ən-wĕlth'). Association consisting of the United Kingdom, its dependencies, & many former British colonies.
Com•o•ros (kŏm'ə-rōz'). Island country off SE Africa between Mozambique & Madagascar. Cap. Moroni. Pop. 346,992.
Con•a•kry (kŏn'ə-krē). Cap. of Guinea, W Africa. Metro. area pop. 600,000.
Con•cep•ción (kən-sĕp'sē-ōn', -sĕp'shən). City of W central Chile. Pop. 267,891.
Con•cord (kŏng'kərd). **1.** Town of E MA WNW of Boston. Pop. 17,076. **2.** Cap. of NH in the S central part. Pop. 36,006.
Con•go (kŏng'gō). **1.** River of central Africa flowing c. 2,900 mi (4,666 km) to the Atlantic. **2.** Republic of W central Africa. Cap. Brazzaville. Pop. 1,912,429. **3.** ZAIRE. —**Con'go•lese'** (-lēz', -lēs') *adj. & n.*
Con•nect•i•cut (kə-nĕt'ĭ-kət). State of the NE U.S. Cap. Hartford. Pop. 3,295,669.
Con•stan•ţa (kən-stăn'sə). City of SE Romania, on the Black Sea. Pop. 315,662.
Con•stan•tine (kŏn'stən-tēn') City of NE Algeria E of Algiers. Pop. 344,454.
Con•stan•ti•no•ple (kŏn'stăn-tə-nō'pəl). ISTANBUL.
Co•pen•ha•gen (kō'pən-hā'gən, -hä'-). Cap. of Denmark in the E. Pop. 482,937.
Cor•al (kôr'əl, kŏr'). Sea of the SW Pacific NE of Australia & SE of New Guinea.
Cór•do•ba (kôr'də-bə, -və). **1.** City of N central Argentina. Pop. 993,055. **2.** City of S Spain. Pop. 291,370. —**Cor'do•van** *adj. & n.*
Cor•inth (kôr'ĭnth, kŏr'). **1.** Isthmus connecting the Peloponnesus to the rest of Greece, crossed by the **Corinth Canal** (4 mi/ 6.4 km). **2.** Region of ancient Greece including the Isthmus of Corinth & adjacent NE Peloponnesus. —**Co•rin'thi•an** (kə-rĭn'thē-ən) *adj. & n.*
Cork (kôrk). City of S Ireland. Pop. 136,344.
Corn•wall (kôrn'wôl'). Region of extreme SW England. Pop. 46,144.

Cor•o•man•del Coast (kôr'ə-măn'dl). Region of SE India.

Cor•pus Chris•ti (kôr'pəs krĭs'tē). City of S TX. Pop. 257,453.

Cor•si•ca (kôr'sĭ-kə). Island of France in the Mediterranean N of Sardinia. —**Cor'si•can** *adj.* & *n.*

Cos (kŏs, kôs). KOS.

Cos•ta Ri•ca (kŏs'tə rē'kə). Country of Central America. Cap. San José. Pop. 2,534,000. —**Cos'ta Ri'can** (rē'kən) *adj.* & *n.*

Côte d'A•zur (kōt'də-zo͝or'). Mediterranean coast of SE France.

Cov•en•try (kŭv'ĭn-trē). City of central England ESE of Birmingham. Pop. 318,600.

Crac•ow *also* **Kra•ków** (krä'kou, krăk'ou, krā'kou, -kō). City of S Poland on the Vistula. Pop. 740,300.

Crete (krēt). Island of SE Greece in the E Mediterranean. —**Cre'tan** *adj.* & *n.*

Cri•me•a (krī-mē'ə, krĭ-). Peninsula of S Ukraine on the Black Sea & Sea of Azov. —**Cri•me'an** *adj.*

Cro•a•tia (krō-ā'shə, -shē-ə). Republic of S Europe along the NE Adriatic coast. Cap. Zagreb. Pop. 4,396,397. —**Cro•a'tian** *adj.* & *n.*

Cu•ba (kyo͞o'bə). Island republic in the Caribbean S of FL Cap. Havana. Pop. 9,723,605. —**Cu'ban** *adj.* & *n.*

Cu•lia•cán (ko͞ol'yə-kän'). City of W Mexico. Pop. 304,826.

Cum•ber•land (kŭm'bər-lənd). **1.** River of S KY & N TN flowing c. 690 mi (1,110 km) W to the Ohio. **2. Plateau** *or* **Mountains.** SW section of the Appalachians extending along the VA-KY border & into central TN. **3. Gap.** Pass, 1,304 ft (397.7 m), through the Cumberland Mts. near the junction of KY, VA, & TN borders.

Cu•ra•çao (ko͝or'ə-sō', -sou', kyo͝or'-). Island of the Netherland Antilles in the S Caribbean off the NW coast of Venezuela.

Cyc•la•des (sĭk'lə-dēz'). Group of islands of SE Greece in the S Aegean.

Cy•prus (sī'prəs). Island republic in the E Mediterranean S of Turkey. Cap. Nicosia. Pop. 692,731. —**Cyp'ri•ot** (sĭp'rē-ət), **Cyp'ri•ote'** (-ōt', -ət), **Cyp'ri•an** (-rē-ən) *adj.* & *n.*

Czech•o•slo•va•ki•a (chĕk'ə-slə-vä'kē-ə, -ō-slō-). Former country of central Europe (1945–93). Cap. Prague. —**Czech'o•slo'vak, Czech'o•slo•va'ki•an** *adj.* & *n.*

Czech Republic (chĕk). Country of central Europe. Cap. Prague. Pop. 10,291,927.

D

Dac•ca (dăk'ə, dä'kə). Cap. of Bangladesh in the E central part. Pop. 1,850,000.

Da•ho•mey (də-hō'mē). BENIN.

Da•kar (də-kär', dăk'är'). Cap. of Senegal in the W part on Cape Verde. Pop. 1,341,000.

Dal•las (dăl'əs). City of NE TX E of Fort Worth. Pop. 1,006,877.

Da•mas•cus (də-măs'kəs). Cap. of Syria in the SW part. Pop. 1,259,000. —**Dam'a•scene'** (dăm'ə-sēn') *adj.* & *n.*

Da Nang *or* **Da•nang** (də năng', dä' näng'). City of central Vietnam on the South China Sea. Pop. 318,655.

Dan•ube (dăn'yo͞ob). River of S central Europe rising in SW Germany & flowing c. 1,750 mi (2,816 km) SE to the Black Sea.

Dan•zig (dăn'sĭg, dän'-). GDAŃSK.

Dar•da•nelles (där'dn-ĕlz'). Strait connecting the Aegean with the Sea of Marmara.

Dar es Sa•laam (där'ĕs sə-läm'). Cap. of Tanzania in the E part. Pop. 757,346.

Day•ton (dāt'n). City of SW OH NNE of Cincinnati. Pop. 182,044.

Dead Sea (dĕd). Salt lake between Israel & Jordan.

Death Valley (dĕth). Desert basin of E CA & W NV.

Del•a•ware (dĕl'ə-wâr'). **1.** River of NE U.S. rising in E NY & flowing c. 280 mi (451 km) S to the Atlantic between E DE & SW NJ. **2.** State of the NE U.S. on the Atlantic. Cap. Dover. Pop. 668,696.

Del•hi (dĕl'ē). City of N central India on the Jumna R. Pop. 4,884,234.

Del•phi (dĕl'fī'). Ancient town of central Greece near Mt. Parnassus.

Den•mark (dĕn'märk'). Country of N Europe on Jutland & adjacent islands. Cap. Copenhagen. Pop. 5,112,130. —**Dane** (dān) *n.* —**Dan'ish** (dā'nĭsh) *adj.* & *n.*

Den•ver (dĕn'vər). Cap. of CO in the N central part. Pop. 467,610.

Der•by (där'bē). City of S central England NNW of London. Pop. 216,500.

Des Moines (dĭ moin'). Cap. of IA in the S central part. Pop. 193,187.

De•troit (dĭ-troit'). City of SE MI. Pop. 1,027,974.

Dev•il's Island (dĕv'ĭlz). Island in the Caribbean off French Guiana.

Diamond Head. Promontory, 761 ft (232.1 m) high, on SE coast of Oahu, HI.

Dien Bien Phu (dyĕn' byĕn' fo͞o'). Town of NW Vietnam near the Laos border.

Di•jon (dē-zhôɴ'). City of E France SE of Paris. Pop. 140,942.

Dis•trict of Co•lum•bi•a (dĭs'trĭkt'; kə-lŭm'bē-ə). Federal district of E U.S. coextensive with the city of Washington.

Dja•kar•ta (jə-kär'tə). *var. of* JAKARTA.

Dji•bou•ti (jĭ-bo͞o'tē). **1.** Country of E Africa on the Gulf of Aden. Pop. 226,000. **2.** Cap. of Djibouti in the SE part. Pop. 120,000.

Dne•pro•pe•trovsk (nĕp'rō-pə-trôfsk'). City of E central Ukraine. Pop. 1,153,000.

Dnie•per (nē'pər). River rising in W central Russia & flowing c. 1,420 mi (2,285 km) to the Black Sea.

Dnies•ter (nē'stər). River, c. 850 mi (1,368 km), of W Ukraine and E Moldavia.

Do•dec•a•nese (dō-dĕk'ə-nēz', -nēs'). Islands of SE Greece between Turkey & Crete.

Do•ha (dō'hə). Cap. of Qatar, SE Arabia, on the Persian Gulf. Pop. 190,000.

Do•lo•mites (dō'lə-mīts', dŏl'ə-). Range of the E Alps in NE Italy.
Dom•i•ni•ca (dŏm'ə-nē'kə, də-mĭn'ĭ-kə). Island republic in the E Caribbean. Cap. Roseau. Pop. 77,000.
Do•min•i•can Republic (də-mĭn'ĭ-kən). Republic of the West Indies on the E part of Hispaniola Is. Cap. Santo Domingo. Pop. 5,674,977.
Don (dŏn). River of SW Russia flowing 1,222 mi (1,966.2 km) into the NE Sea of Azov.
Do•netsk (də-nĕtsk'). City of E Ukraine. Pop. 1,021,000.
Dort•mund (dôrt'mənd, -mo͝ont'). City of W central Germany. Pop. 630,609.
Dou•a•la *or* **Du•a•la** (do͞o-ä'lə). City of SW Cameroon. Pop. 841,000.
Dou•ro (dôr'o͞o, dōr'-). River, c. 475 mi (764 km), of N Spain & N Portugal.
Do•ver (dō'vər). **1.** Strait between SE England & N France. **2.** Borough of SE England opposite Calais, France. Pop. 33,700. **3.** Cap. of DE in the central part. Pop. 27,630.
Dres•den (drĕz'dən). City of E central Germany. Pop. 507,692.
Du•bai (do͞o-bī'). City & sheikdom of E United Arab Emirates. Pop. 265,702.
Dub•lin (dŭb'lĭn). **1.** Cap. of Ireland in the E central part on the Irish Sea. Pop. 525,882. **—Dub'lin•er** *n.*
Duis•burg (do͞os'bûrg', do͞oz'-). City of W central Germany. Pop. 522,829.
Du•luth (də-lo͞oth'). City of NE MN on Lake Superior opposite Superior, WI Pop. 85,493.
Dun•kirk (dŭn'kûrk') *also* **Dun•kerque** (dœN-kĕrk'). City of N France on the North Sea. Pop. 73,120.
Du•ran•go (do͞o-răng'gō). City of N central Mexico. Pop 257,915.
Dur•ban (dûr'bən). City of E South Africa on the Indian Ocean. Pop. 677,760.
Dur•ham (dûr'əm). City of N central NC E of Greensboro. Pop. 136,611.
Du•shan•be (do͞o-shăm'bə, -shäm'-). Cap. of Tadzhikistan in the W part. Pop. 522,000.
Düs•sel•dorf (do͞os'əl-dôrf'). City of W central Germany on the Rhine. Pop. 565,893.
Dutch East Indies. INDONESIA.
Dutch Guiana. SURINAM.

E

East Berlin. See BERLIN.
East China Sea. Arm of the Pacific between E China & Ryukyu Is.
East•er Island (ē'stər). Chilean island in the S Pacific.
East Germany. See GERMANY.
East Indies. 1. Historically, the subcontinent of INDIA. **2.** MALAY Archipelago.
Eb•ro (ā'brō). River, c. 575 mi (925 km), of NE Spain flowing to the Mediterranean.
Ec•ua•dor (ĕk'wə-dôr'). Republic of NW South America. Cap. Quito. Pop. 8,050,630. **—Ec'ua•dor'i•an** *adj. & n.*
Ed•in•burgh (ĕd'n-bûr'ə). Cap. of Scotland in the E on the Firth of Forth. Pop. 446,361.
Ed•mon•ton (ĕd'mən-tən). Capital of Alta., Canada, in the central part. Pop. 532,246.
E•gypt (ē'jĭpt). Republic of NE Africa & SW Asia. Cap. Cairo. Pop. 48,503,000. **—E•gyp'tian** *adj. & n.*
El•ba (ĕl'bə). Italian island in the Tyrrhenian Sea.
El•be (ĕl'bə, ĕlb). River of Czech Republic and Germany flowing c. 725 mi (1,165 km) to the North Sea.
E•liz•a•beth (ĭ-lĭz'ə-bəth). City of NE NJ near Newark. Pop. 110,002.
El Pas•o (ĕl păs'ō). City of extreme W TX on the Rio Grande. Pop. 515,342.
El Sal•va•dor (ĕl săl'və-dôr'). Republic of Central America. Cap. San Salvador. Pop. 4,949,000. **—El Sal'va•dor'i•an** *adj. & n.*
Eng•land (ĭng'glənd). Part of the United Kingdom, the S part of the island of Great Britain. Pop. 46,220,955. **—Eng'lish** (-glĭsh) *adj. & n.*
English Channel. Arm of the Atlantic Ocean separating France & Great Britain.
Eph•e•sus (ĕf'ĭ-səs). Ancient city of Greek Asia Minor in present-day W Turkey.
E•qua•to•ri•al Guin•ea (ē'kwə-tôr'ē-əl gĭn'ē, -tōr'-, ĕk'wə-). Republic of W central Africa. Cap. Malabo. Pop. 300,000.
E•rie (îr'ē). **1.** One of the Great Lakes, between S Ont. & W NY, NW PA, N OH, & SE MI. **2.** City of NW PA on Lake Erie. Pop. 108, 718.
Er•i•tre•a (ĕr'ĭ-trē'ə, -trā'ə). Region of N Ethiopia. **—Er'i•tre'an** *adj. & n.*
Es•fa•han (ĕs'fə-hän'). *var. of* ISFAHAN.
Es•sen (ĕs'ən). City of W central Germany on the Ruhr R. Pop. 625,705.
Es•to•ni•a (ĕ-stō'nē-ə) *also* **Es•tho•ni•a** (ĕ-stō'-, ĕs-thō'-). Country of NW Europe. Cap. Tallinn. Pop. 1,530,000. **—Es•to'ni•an** *adj. & n.*
E•thi•o•pi•a (ē'thē-ō'pē-ə). Country of NE Africa. Cap. Addis Ababa. Pop. 32,775,000. **—E'thi•o'pi•an** *adj. & n.*
Et•na (ĕt'nə). Active volcano, 11,122 ft (3,392.2 m), in E Sicily.
Eu•gene (yo͞o-jēn'). City of W OR S of Salem. Pop. 112,669.
Eu•phra•tes (yo͞o-frā'tēz). River of SW Asia flowing c. 1,700 mi (2,735 km) from Turkey to the Persian Gulf.
Eur•a•sia (yo͝o-rā'zhə). Land mass comprising the continents of Europe & Asia. **—Eur•a'sian** *adj. & n.*
Eu•rope (yo͝or'əp). 6th-largest continent, extending W from the Dardanelles, Black Sea, & Ural Mts. to the Atlantic. **—Eur'o•pe'an** (yo͝or'ə-pē'ən) *adj. & n.*
Ev•ans•ville (ĕv'ənz-vĭl'). City of SW IN on the Ohio R. Pop. 126,272.
Ev•er•est (ĕv'ər-ĭst, ĕv'rĭst). Mountain, 29,028 ft (8,853.5 m), of the central Himalayas; highest elevation in the world.
Ev•er•glades (ĕv'ər-glādz'). Subtropical swamp area of S FL.

F

Faer•oe *or* **Far•oe** (fâr′ō). Islands of Denmark between Iceland & the Shetlands.

Fair•banks (fâr′băngks′). City of central AK NNE of Anchorage. Pop. 30,843.

Falk•land (fôk′lənd, fôlk′-). Islands of the S Atlantic E of the Strait of Magellan; claimed by Great Britain and Argentina.

Far•go (fär′gō). City of E ND E of Bismark. Pop. 74,111.

Far•oe (fâr′ō). *var. of* FAEROE.

Fez (fĕz) *also* **Fès** (fĕs). City of N central Morocco NE of Casablanca. Pop. 448,823.

Fi•ji (fē′jē). Island country of the SW Pacific comprising c. 800 islands. Cap. Suva. Pop. 686,000. —**Fi′ji•an** *adj. & n.*

Fin•ger Lakes (fĭng′gər). Eleven elongated glacial lakes in W central NY.

Fin•land (fĭn′lənd). Republic of N Europe. Cap. Helsinki. Pop. 4,893,748. —**Finn** (fĭn) *n.* —**Fin′nish** (fĭn′ĭsh) *adj. & n.*

Flan•ders (flăn′dərz). Region of NW Europe including part of N France & W Belgium & SW Netherlands.—**Flem′ing** (flĕm′ĭng) *n.* —**Flem′ish** (-ĭsh) *adj. & n.*

Flor•ence (flôr′əns, flŏr′). City of central Italy on the Arno R. Pop. 453,293. —**Flor′en•tine′** (-ən-tēn′, -tīn′) *adj. & n.*

Flor•i•da (flôr′ĭ-də, flŏr′-). State of the SE U.S. Cap. Tallahassee. Pop. 13,003,362. —**Flo•rid′i•an** (flə-rĭd′ē-ən), **Flor′i•dan** *adj. & n.*

Foo•chow (fo͞o′jō′, -chou′). FUZHOU.

For•mo•sa (fôr-mō′sə). TAIWAN.

For•ta•le•za (fôr′tl-ā′zə). City of NE Brazil on the Atlantic. Pop. 1,307,611.

Fort-de-France (fôr-də-fräNs′). Cap. of Martinique, French West Indies. Pop. 99,844.

Forth (fôrth, fōrth), **Firth of.** An inlet of the North Sea extending c. 55 mi (90 km) into SE Scotland.

Fort-La•my (fôr′lə-mē′). NDJAMENA.

Fort Lau•der•dale (lô′dər-dāl′). City of SE FL N of Miami Beach. Pop. 149,377.

Fort Wayne (wān). City of NE IN NE of Indianapolis. Pop. 173, 072.

Fort Worth (wûrth). City of NE TX W of Dallas. Pop. 447,619.

France (frăns). Republic of W Europe. Cap. Paris. Pop. 54,334,871. —**French** (frĕnch) *adj. & n.*

Frank•fort (frăngk′fərt). Cap. of KY in the N central part. Pop. 25,698.

Frank•furt (frănk′fərt, frängk′fo͝ort′) *or* **Frankfurt am Main** (äm mīn′). City of W central Germany on the Main R. Pop. 599,634.

Franz Jo•sef Land (frănts′ jō′zəf, -səf). Archipelago in the Arctic Ocean.

Fred•er•ic•ton (frĕd′rĭk-tən, -ər-ĭk-). Cap. of N.B., Canada. Pop. 43,723.

Free•town (frē′toun′). Cap. of Sierra Leone in the W part. Pop. 300,000.

Fre•mont (frē′mŏnt′). City of W CA SE of Oakland. Pop. 173,339.

French Gui•a•na (gē-ăn′ə, -ä′nə, gī-ăn′ə). French overseas department of NE South America. Cap. Cayenne. Pop. 72,012.

French Pol•y•ne•sia (pŏl′ə-nē′zhə, -shə). French overseas territory in the S central Pacific including the Society, Marquesas, Tuamotu, Gambier, & Tubuai Is.

Fres•no (frĕz′nō). City of S central CA SE of San Jose. Pop. 354,202.

Fri•sian (frĭzh′ən, frē′zhən). Chain of islands in the North Sea off the coasts of the Netherlands, Germany, & Denmark.

Frun•ze (fro͞on′zə). BISHKEK.

Fu•chou (fo͞o′jō′, -chou′). FUZHOU.

Fu•ji (fo͞o′jē). **1.** *or* **Fu•ji•ya•ma** (fo͞o′jē-ä′mə, -yä′-) *or* **Fu•ji•no•ya•ma** (-nō-) *or* **Fu•ji-san** (-sän′). Highest peak (12,388 ft/3,778.3 m) in Japan, in central Honshu. **2.** City of central Honshu, Japan. Pop. 205,751.

Fu•ji•ya•ma (fo͞o′jē-ä′mə, -yä′-). Mt. FUJI.

Fu•ku•o•ka (fo͞o′kə-wō′kə). City of N Kyushu, Japan. Pop. 1,008,588.

Fu•shun (fo͞o′sho͝on′). City of NE China E of Shenyang. Pop. 1,240,000.

Fu•zhou (fo͞o′jō′). City of SE China on the Min delta. Pop. 754,500.

G

Ga•bon (gă-bōN′). Republic of W central Africa. Cap. Libreville. Pop. 1,312,000.

Ga•bo•rone (gä′bə-rōn′, -rō′nē). Cap. of Botswana. Pop 72,000.

Ga•lá•pa•gos (gə-lä′pə-gəs, -lăp′ə-). Island group of Ecuador in the E Pacific.

Ga•la•ţi (gä-läts′, -lät′sē) *or* **Ga•latz** (gä′läts′). City of E Romania on the lower Danube. Pop. 268,000.

Ga•la•tia (gə-lā′shə, -shē-ə). Ancient country of central Asia Minor near modern Ankara, Turkey. —**Ga•la′tian** *adj. & n.*

Ga•li•cia (gə-lĭsh′ə, -ē-ə). **1.** Historical region of SE Poland & W Ukraine. **2.** Region & ancient kingdom of NW Spain. —**Ga•li′cian** *adj. & n.*

Gal•i•lee (găl′ə-lē′). **1. Sea of.** Freshwater lake bordered by Israel, Syria, & Jordan. **2.** Region of N Israel. —**Gal′i•le′an** *adj. & n.*

Gal•ves•ton (găl′vĭ-stən). City of SE TX. Pop. 59,070.

Gal•way (gôl′wā′). Region of W central Ireland.

Gam•bi•a (găm′bē-ə). Republic of W Africa on the Atlantic. Cap. Banjul. Pop. 696,000. —**Gam′bi•an** *adj. & n.*

Gan•ges (găn′jēz′) *or* **Gan•ga** (gŭng′gə). River of N India & Bangladesh flowing c. 1,560 mi (2,510 km) from the Himalayas to the Bay of Bengal.

Gar•land (gär′lənd). City of NE TX near Dallas. Pop. 180,650.

Gar•y (găr′ē, gâr′ē). City of NW IN on Lake Michigan. Pop. 116,646.

Gas•co•ny (găs′kə-nē). Region & former province of SW France.

Gaul (gôl). Ancient name for W Europe, comprising approx. modern France & Belgium.

Ga•za (gä′zə, găz′ə, gă′zə). City of SW Asia in the **Gaza Strip,** a Mediterranean coastal area adjoining Israel and Egypt. Pop. 118,272.

Ga•zi•an•tep (gä'zē-än-tĕp'). City of S Asian Turkey. Pop. 379,290.

Gdańsk (gə-dänsk', -dănsk'). City of N Poland on the Baltic Sea. Pop. 467,200.

Gel•sen•kir•chen (gĕl'zən-kîr'kən). City of W central Germany. Pop. 287,956.

Ge•ne•va (jə-nē'və). **1. Lake of.** Lake on the Swiss-French border between the Alps & the Jura Mts. **2.** City of SW Switzerland. Metro. area pop. 159,500.

Gen•o•a (jĕn'ə-wə, -ō-ə). City of NW Italy on the Ligurian Sea. Pop. 760,300.

George•town (jôrj'toun'). **1.** Cap. of the Cayman Is. on Grand Cayman. Pop. 7,617. **2.** Cap. of Guyana on the Atlantic. Pop. 78,500.

Geor•gia (jôr'jə). **1.** Region & republic of Asia Minor S of Russia. **2.** State of the SE U.S. Cap. Atlanta. Pop. 6,508,419. **—Geor'gian** *adj. & n.*

Ger•ma•ny (jûr'mə-nē). Country of N central Europe divided from 1949 to 1990 into **West Germany** and **East Germany.** Cap. Berlin. Bonn is the seat of government. Pop. 77,750,743.

Get•tys•burg (gĕt'ēz-bûrg'). Town of S PA, site of Civil War battle (1863). Pop. 7,025.

Gha•na (gä'nə, găn'ə). Republic of W Africa on the Gulf of Guinea. Cap. Accra. Pop. 12,205,574. **—Gha'na•ian, Gha'ni•an** *adj. & n.*

Ghats (gôts). Two mountain ranges of S India: the **Eastern Ghats** along the Bay of Bengal coast, & the **Western Ghats** along the Arabian Sea coast.

Ghent (gĕnt). City of W Belgium, NW of Brussels. Pop. 236,540.

Gib•ral•tar (jə-brôl'tər). British colony on the **Rock of Gibraltar,** a peninsula on the S coast of Spain in the **Strait of Gibraltar,** connecting the Mediterranean & Atlantic between Spain & N Africa. Pop. 29,648.

Gi•la (hē'lə). River of SW NM & S AZ flowing 630 mi (1,013.7 km) to the Colorado.

Gil•e•ad (gĭl'ē-əd). Mountain region of Jordan E of the Jordan R.

Gi•za (gē'zə). City of N Egypt on the Nile near Cairo. Pop. 1,608,400.

Glas•gow (glăs'kō, -gō, glăz'-). City of SW Scotland. Pop. 757,456. **—Glas•we'gian** (-wē'jən) *adj. & n.*

Glen•dale (glĕn'dāl'). **1.** City of S central AZ near Phoenix. Pop. 148,134. **2.** City of S CA near Los Angeles. Pop. 180,038.

Go•bi (gō'bē). Desert of central Asia, chiefly in Mongolia.

Godt•håb (gôt'hôb', gŏt'-). Cap. of Greenland on the SW coast. Pop. 10,559.

God•win Aus•ten (gŏd'wĭn ô'stən, ŏs'tən). Mountain in the Karakoram Range of N Pakistan, rising to 28,250 ft (8,616.3 m).

Goi•â•ni•a (goi-ăn'ē-ə). City of S central Brazil SE of Brasília. Pop. 702,858.

Go•lan Heights (gō'län', -lən). Hill region of NE Israel & SW Syria.

Go•mel (gō'məl, gô'). City of E Belorussia SE of Minsk. Pop. 465,000.

Good Hope (gŏŏd' hōp'), **Cape of.** Promontory on SW coast of South Africa.

Gor•ky *or* **Gor•ki** *also* **Gor•kiy** (gôr'kē). City of W Russia on the Volga. Pop. 1,399,000.

Gö•te•borg (yœ'tə-bôr'ē) *or* **Goth•en•burg** (gŏth'ən-bûrg', gŏt'n-). Port city of SW Sweden on the Kattegat. Pop. 430,763.

Gram•pi•ans (grăm'pē-ənz), **the.** Mountain range of central Scotland.

Gra•na•da (grə-nä'də). City of S Spain SE of Córdoba. Pop. 256,191.

Grand Canyon. Gorge of the Colorado R. in NW AZ, 217 mi (349.2 km) long, 4–18 mi (6.4–29 km) wide, & c. 1 mi (1.6 km) deep.

Grand Rapids. City of W central MI WNW of Lansing. Pop. 189,126.

Grand Turk (tûrk). Chief island of the Turks & Caicos Is. SE of the Bahamas.

Graz (gräts). City of SE Austria on the Mur SSW of Vienna. Pop. 243,166.

Great Barrier Reef. Largest coral reef in the world, off the NE coast of Australia.

Great Basin. Desert region of the W U.S. comprising most of NV & parts of UT, CA, ID, WY, & OR.

Great Brit•ain (brĭt'n). **1.** Island off the W coast of Europe comprising England, Scotland, & Wales. **2.** UNITED KINGDOM.

Great•er An•til•les (grā'tər ăn-tĭl'ēz). Island group of the West Indies including Cuba, Jamaica, Hispaniola, & Puerto Rico.

Great Lakes. Group of five freshwater lakes of central North America between the U.S. & Canada, including Lakes Superior, Huron, Erie, Ontario, & Michigan.

Great Plains. High grassland region of central North America extending from the Canadian provinces of Alta., Sask., & Man. S into TX.

Great Salt Lake. Shallow body of salt water of NW UT between the Wasatch Mts. & **Great Salt Lake Desert.**

Great Slave. Lake of S N.W.T., Canada.

Great Smoky Mountains. Part of the Appalachian system on the NC-TN border.

Greece (grēs). Republic of SE Europe. Cap. Athens. Pop. 9,740,417. **—Gre'cian** (grē'shən) *adj.* **—Greek** (grēk) *adj. & n.*

Green•land (grēn'lənd, -lănd'). Island of Denmark, in the North Atlantic off NE Canada. Cap. Godthåb. Pop. 55,171.

Greens•bor•o (grēnz'bûr'ə). City of N central NC E of Winston-Salem. Pop. 183,521.

Green•wich (grĭn'ĭj, -ĭch, grĕn'-). Borough of Greater London, SE England, on the Thames. Pop. 211,013.

Gre•na•da (grə-nā'də). Island in the Windward Is. of the West Indies, part of the nation of **Grenada,** including the S Grenadines. Cap. St. George's. Pop. 110,100.

Gren•a•dines (grĕn'ə-dēnz'). Archipelago in the Windward Is. of the E Caribbean, divided between Grenada & the nation of St. Vincent & the Grenadines.

Groz•ny *or* **Groz•nyy** (grôz'nē, grŏz'-). City of SW Russia SW of Astrakhan. Pop. 393,000.

Gua•da•la•ja•ra (gwŏd'l-ə-här'ə). City of SW

Mexico WNW of Mexico City. Pop. 1,626,152.

Gua•dal•ca•nal (gwŏd'l-kə-năl'). Island of the W Pacific, largest of the Solomon Is.

Gua•de•loupe (gwŏd'l-o͞op', gwŏd'l-o͞op'). Overseas department of France in the Leeward Is. Cap. Basse-Terre. Pop. 328,400.

Guam (gwäm). Island of the W Pacific, largest of the Mariana Is.; an unincorporated territory of the U.S. Cap. Agana. Pop. 105,979. —**Gua•ma'ni•an** (gwä-mā'nē-ən) *adj. & n.*

Guang•zhou (gwäng'jō'). City of S China. Pop. 2,570,000.

Guan•tá•na•mo (gwän-tä'nə-mo'). City of SE Cuba N of **Guantánamo Bay,** an inlet of the Caribbean. Pop. 166,558.

Gua•te•ma•la (gwä'tə-mä'lə). **1.** Republic of N Central America. Cap. Guatemala. Pop. 6,054,227. **2.** *also* **Guatemala City.** Capital of Guatemala in the S central part. Pop. 754,243. —**Gua'te•ma'lan** *adj. & n.*

Gua•ya•quil (gwī'ə-kēl', -kĭl). Port city of W Ecuador. Pop. 1,204,532.

Guern•sey (gûrn'zē). English island of the SW central English Channel.

Gui•an•a (gē-ăn'ə, -ä'nə, gī-ăn'ə). Region of NE South America, including SE Venezuela, part of N Brazil, & French Guiana, Surinam, & Guyana. —**Gui•an'an, Gui'a•nese'** (-nēz', -nēs') *adj. & n.*

Guin•ea (gĭn'ē). Republic of W central Africa on the Atlantic. Cap. Conakry. Pop. 4,830,000. —**Guin'e•an** *adj. & n.*

Guin•ea-Bis•sau (gĭn'ē-bĭ-sou'). Country of W central Africa on the Atlantic. Cap. Bissau. Pop. 777,214.

Guy•a•na (gī-ăn'ə). Republic of NE South America on the Atlantic. Cap. Georgetown. Pop. 918,000. —**Guy'a•nese'** *adj. & n.*

H

Hague (hāg), **The.** De facto cap. of the Netherlands in the W part. Pop. 445,213.

Hai•fa (hī'fa). City of NW Israel on the Mediterranean. Pop. 224,700.

Hai•phong (hī'fông'). City of NE Vietnam. Metro. area pop. 330,755.

Hai•ti (hā'tē). Country of the West Indies on W part of the island of Hispaniola. Cap. Port-au-Prince. Pop. 5,053,791. —**Hai'tian** (hā'shən, -tē-ən) *adj. & n.*

Hal•i•fax (hăl'ə-făks'). Cap. of N.S. on the Atlantic. Pop. 114,594.

Hal•le (hä'lə). City of central Germany WNW of Leipzig. Pop. 236,139.

Ham•burg (hăm'bûrg', häm'bo͝org', -bo͝ork'). City of N Germany on the Elbe. Pop. 1,592,447.

Ham•il•ton (hăm'əl-tən). **1.** Cap. of Bermuda on Bermuda Is. Pop. 1,676. **2.** City of S Ont., Canada, at W end of Lake Ontario SW of Toronto. Pop. 306,434.

Hamp•ton (hămp'tən). Independent city of SE VA on **Hampton Roads,** outlet of the James & Elizabeth rivers into Chesapeake Bay. Pop. 133,793.

Hang•zhou (häng'jo') *also* **Hang•chow** (hăng'chou', häng'jō'). City of E China. Pop. 1,250,000.

Han•no•ver *or* **Han•o•ver** (hăn'ō'vər, -ə-vər). City of NW Germany. Pop. 514,010.

Ha•noi (hă-noi', hə-, hä-). Cap. of Vietnam in the N part. Metro. area pop. 819,913.

Han•o•ver (hăn'ō'vər, -ə-vər). **1.** Former kindgom & province of NW Germany. **2.** *var. of* HANNOVER.

Ha•ra•re (hə-rär'ā). Cap. of Zimbabwe in the NE part. Pop. 656,011.

Har•bin (här'bĭn'). City of NE China in Manchuria. Pop. 2,630,000.

Har•lem (här'ləm). Section of New York City in N Manhattan.

Har•ris•burg (hăr'ĭs-bûrg'). Cap. of PA in the SE part. Pop. 52,376.

Hart•ford (härt'fərd). Cap. of CT in the N central part. Pop. 139,739.

Has•tings (hā'stĭngz). Borough of SE England on the Strait of Dover near. Pop. 75,900.

Hat•ter•as (hăt'ər-əs, hăt'rəs). Long barrier island off the E coast of NC with **Cape Hatteras** projecting from the SE part.

Ha•va•na (hə-văn'ə). Cap. of Cuba. Pop. 1,961,674. —**Ha•va'nan** *adj. & n.*

Ha•wai•i (hə-wä'ē, -yē, -wī'ē, -yē). **1.** Largest & southernmost island of the state of HI. **2.** State & island group **(Hawaiian Is.)** of the W U.S. in the central Pacific. Cap. Honolulu. Pop. 1,115,274. —**Ha•wai'ian** *adj. & n.*

Heb•ri•des (hĕb'rĭ-dēz'). Islands of W Scotland in the Atlantic, divided into the **Inner Hebrides** & the **Outer Hebrides.** —**Heb'ri•de'an** *adj. & n.*

Hei•del•berg (hīd'l-bûrg', -bo͝org'). City of SW Germany. Pop. 133,693.

Hei•long•jiang (hā'lo͝ong'jē-äng'). Province of extreme NE China.

Hel•e•na (hĕl'ə-nə). Cap. of MT in the W central part. Pop. 24,569.

Hel•les•pont (hĕl'əs-pŏnt'). DARDANELLES.

Hel•sin•ki (hĕl'sĭng'kē, hĕl-sĭng'-). Cap. of Finland in the S. Pop. 489,263.

Her•cu•la•ne•um (hûr'kyə-lā'nē-əm). Ancient city of S central Italy near Naples.

Her•mo•sil•lo (ĕr'mə-sē'ō, -yō). City of NW Mexico W of Chihuahua. Pop. 297,175.

Her•ze•go•vi•na (hĕrt'sə-gō-vē'nə, hûrt'-). S region of Bosnia-Herzegovina. —**Her'ze•go•vi'ni•an** *adj. & n.*

Hi•a•le•ah (hī'ə-lē'ə). City of SE FL near Miami. Pop. 188,004.

Hi•ga•shi•o•sa•ka (hē-gä'shē-ō-sä'kə). City of W central Honshu, Japan. Pop. 522,798.

Him•a•la•yas (hĭm'ə-lā'əz, hĭ-mäl'yəz) *also* **Him•a•la•ya Mountains** (hĭm'ə-lā'ə, hĭ-mäl'yə). Mountain system of S central Asia extending through Kashmir, N India, S Tibet, Nepal, Sikkim, & Bhutan. —**Him'a•la'yan** *adj. & n.*

Hin•du Kush (hĭn'do͞o ko͞osh'). Mountain range of SW Asia extending W from N Pakistan to NE Afghanistan.

Hi•ro•shi•ma (hîr'ə-shē'mə, hĭ-rō'shə-mə). City of SW Honshu, Japan. Pop. 1,044,129.

His•pan•io•la (hĭs′pən-yō′lə). Island of the West Indies E of Cuba, divided between Haiti & the Dominican Republic.

Ho Chi Minh City (hō′ chē′ mĭn′, shē′). City of S Vietnam. Metro. area pop. 2,441,185.

Hok•kai•do (hŏ-kī′dō). Second-largest island of Japan N of Honshu.

Hol•land (hŏl′ənd). NETHERLANDS. **—Hol′land•er** *n.*

Hol•ly•wood (hŏl′ē-wo͝od′). **1.** Community of S CA, part of Los Angeles. **2.** City of SE FL on the Atlantic. Pop. 121,697.

Hol•stein (hōl′stīn′, -stēn′). Region & former duchy of N Germany.

Hon•du•ras (hŏn-do͝or′əs, -dyo͝or′-). Country of N Central America. Cap. Tegucigalpa. Pop. 4,092,000. **—Hon•du′ran** *adj. &n.*

Hong Kong *also* **Hong•kong** (hŏng′kŏng′, -kŏng′, hông′kông′, -kông′). British crown colony on SE coast of China including **Hong Kong Is.** & adjacent areas. Cap. Victoria. Pop. 5,021,066.

Ho•ni•a•ra (hō′nē-är′ə). Cap. of the Solomon Is. on Guadalcanal. Pop. 14,942.

Hon•o•lu•lu (hŏn′ə-lo͞o′lo͞o). Cap. of HI on SE coast of Oahu. Pop. 365,272.

Hon•shu (hŏn′sho͞o). Island of Japan in the central part.

Hood (ho͝od), **Mount.** Volcanic peak, 11,235 ft (3,426.7 m), in the Cascade Range of NW OR.

Hor•muz *also* **Hor•moz** (hôr′mŭz′, hôr-mo͞oz′). Strait linking the Persian Gulf with the Gulf of Oman.

Horn (hôrn), **Cape.** Headland of extreme S Chile in the Tierra del Fuego archipelago.

Hous•ton (yo͞o′stən, hyo͞o′-). City of SE TX NW of Galveston. Pop. 1,630,553.

Huang (hwäng). YELLOW R.

Hud•son (hŭd′sən). **1.** Bay of the Atlantic in E central Canada. **2.** River, c. 315 mi (505 km), of E NY flowing S to the Atlantic at New York City.

Hue (hwā, hyo͞o-ā′). City of central Vietnam near the South China Sea. Pop. 165, 865.

Hun•ga•ry (hŭng′gə-rē). Country of central Europe. Cap. Budapest. Pop. 10,657,000. **—Hun•gar′i•an** (-gâr′ē-ən) *adj. & n.*

Hunts•ville (hŭnts′vĭl′). City of N central AL. Pop. 159,789.

Hu•ron (hyo͝or′ən, -ŏn′). 2nd-largest of the Great Lakes, between SE Ont., Canada, & E MI.

Hwang (hwäng). YELLOW R.

Hy•der•a•bad (hī′dər-ə-băd′, -bäd′, hī′drə-). **1.** City of central India. Pop. 2,187,262. **2.** City of S Pakistan. Pop. 745,000.

I

I•be•ri•a (ī-bîr′ē-ə). **1.** IBERIAN PENINSULA. **2.** Ancient Spain. **—I•be′ri•an** *adj. & n.*

Iberian Peninsula. Peninsula of SW Europe occupied by Spain & Portugal.

Ice•land (īs′lənd). Island republic in the North Atlantic. Cap. Reykjavík. Pop. 240,443. **—Ice′land•er** *n.* **—Ice•land′ic** *adj.*

I•da•ho (ī′də-hō′). State of the NW U.S. Cap. Boise. Pop. 1,011,486. **—I′da•ho′an** *adj. & n.*

I•gua•çú *also* **I•guas•sú** (ē′gwə-so͞o′). River, c. 380 mi (611 m), of S Brazil.

Ijs•sel *or* **IJs•sel** (ī′səl). River, c. 70 mi (112.6 km), of E Netherlands.

Ijs•sel•meer *or* **IJs•sel•meer** (ī′səl-mâr′, -mär′). Lake of NW Netherlands.

Il•li•nois (ĭl′ə-noi′, -noiz′). **1.** River, 273 mi (439.3 km), of N & W IL. **2.** State of N central U.S. Cap. Springfield. Pop. 11,466,682. **—Il′li•nois′an** (-noi′ən, -zən) *adj. & n.*

Il•lyr•i•a (ĭ-lîr′ē-ə). Ancient region of the NW Balkan Peninsula. **—Il•lyr′i•an** *adj. & n.*

In•chon (ĭn′chŏn′). City of NW South Korea on the Yellow Sea. Pop. 1,387,000.

In•de•pen•dence (ĭn′dĭ-pĕn′dəns). City of W MO E of Kansas City. Pop. 112,301.

In•di•a (ĭn′dē-ə). **1.** Peninsula & subcontinent of S Asia. **2.** Country of S Asia. Cap. New Delhi. Pop. 685,184,692. **—In′di•an** *adj. & n.*

Indian Ocean. Ocean extending from S Asia to Antarctica & from E Africa to SE Australia.

In•di•an•a (ĭn′dē-ăn′ə). State of N central U.S. Cap. Indianapolis. Pop. 5,564,228. **—In′di•an′i•an** *adj. & n.*

In•di•an•ap•o•lis (ĭn′dē-ə-năp′ə-lĭs). Cap. of IN in the central part. Pop. 741,952.

In•dies (ĭn′dēz). **1.** EAST INDIES. **2.** WEST INDIES.

In•do•chi•na (ĭn′dō-chī′nə). Peninsula of SE Asia occupied by Vietnam, Laos, Cambodia, Thailand, Burma, & the Malay Peninsula. **—In′do•chi′nese′** (-nēz′, -nēs′) *adj. & n.*

In•do•ne•sia (ĭn′də-nē′zhə, -shə, -dō-). Country of SE Asia. Cap. Jakarta. Pop. 147,490,298. **—In′do•ne′sian** *adj. & n.*

In•dus (ĭn′dəs). River of S central Asia rising in SW Tibet & flowing c. 1,900 mi (3,057 km) NW to the Arabian Sea.

In•ner Heb•ri•des (ĭn′ər hĕb′rĭ-dēz′). See HEBRIDES.

Inner Mon•go•li•a (mŏn-gō′lē-ə, -gōl′yə, mŏng-). Autonomous region of NE China.

Inns•bruck (ĭnz′bro͝ok′, ĭns′-). City of SW Austria WSW of Salzburg. Pop. 117,287.

I•o•ni•a (ī-ō′nē-ə). Ancient region of W Asia Minor along the Aegean coast. **—I•o′ni•an** *adj. & n.*

Ionian Sea. Arm of the Mediterranean between W Greece & S Italy & Sicily.

I•o•wa (ī′ə-wə). State of N central U.S. Cap. Des Moines. Pop. 2,787,424. **—I′o•wan** *adj. & n.*

I•ran (ĭ-răn′, ĭ-rän′, ī-răn′). Country of SW Asia. Cap. Teheran. Pop. 40,777,000. **—I•ra′ni•an** (ĭ-rā′nē-ən) *adj. & n.*

I•raq *also* **I•rak** (ĭ-răk′, ĭ-räk′). Country of SW Asia. Cap. Baghdad. Pop. 15,584,987. **—I•ra′qi** (ĭ-rä′kē, ĭ-răk′ē) *adj. & n.*

Ire•land (īr′lənd). **1.** Island of the British Isles in the N Atlantic W of Great Britain. **2.** Republic occupying most of Ireland. Cap. Dublin. Pop. 3,443,405. 3. NORTHERN IRELAND. —**I'rish** (ī'rĭsh) *adj. & n.*

Irish Sea. Waters of the N Atlantic between Ireland & Great Britain.

Ir•kutsk (îr-ko͞otsk'). City of S central Russia near Lake Baikal. Pop. 597,000.

Ir•ra•wad•dy (îr'ə-wŏd'ē). Chief river of Burma, flowing c. 1,000 mi (1,609 km) S to the Andaman Sea.

Ir•vine (ûr'vīn'). City of S CA SE of Santa Ana. Pop. 110,330.

Ir•ving (ûr'vĭng). Town of NE TX near Dallas. Pop. 155,037.

Is•fa•han (ĭs'fə-hän') *or* **Es•fa•han** (ĕs'-). City of central Iran. Pop. 927,000.

Is•lam•a•bad (ĭs-lä'mə-bäd', ĭz-lăm'ə-băd'). Cap. of Pakistan in the NE part. Pop. 201,000.

Is•ra•el (ĭz'rē-əl). **1.** Ancient kingdom of N Palestine. **2.** Country of SW Asia on the E Mediterranean. Cap. Jerusalem. Pop. 4,141,400. —**Is•rae'li** (ĭz-rā'lē) *adj. & n.*

Is•tan•bul (ĭs'tăn-bo͝ol', -tän-, -təm-). Largest city of Turkey, in the NW part. Pop. 2,772,708.

It•a•ly (ĭt'ə-lē). **1.** Peninsula of S Europe projecting into the Mediterranean. **2.** Country of S Europe including the peninsula of Italy, Sardinia, & Sicily. Cap. Rome. Pop. 56,243,935. —**I•tal'ian** (ĭ-tăl'yən) *adj. & n.*

Ith•a•ca (ĭth'ə-kə). Island of W Greece in the Ionian Is. —**Ith'a•can** *adj. & n.*

I•vo•ry Coast (ī'və-rē, īv'rē). Country of W Africa. Cap. Abidjan. Pop. 7,920,000.

I•wo Ji•ma (ē'wō jē'mə). Largest of the Volcano Is. of Japan in the NW Pacific.

I•zhevsk (ē-zhĕfsk'). City of W central Russia ENE of Kazan. Pop. 611,000.

Iz•mir (ĭz-mîr'). City of W Turkey on the Aegean. Pop. 757,854.

J

Jack•son (jăk'sən). Cap. of MS in the W central part. Pop. 196,637.

Jack•son•ville (jăk'sən-vĭl'). City of NE FL. Pop. 672,971.

Jai•pur (jī'po͝or'). City of NW India SW of Delhi. Pop. 977,165.

Ja•kar•ta *or* **Dja•kar•ta** (jə-kär'tə). Cap. of Indonesia on Java. Pop. 6,503,449.

Ja•mai•ca (jə-mā'kə). Island republic in the Caribbean S of Cuba. Cap. Kingston. Pop. 2,190,357. —**Ja•mai'can** *adj. & n.*

James•town (jāmz'toun'). **1.** Cap. of St. Helena in the S Atlantic. Pop. 1,516. **2.** Former village of SE VA; first permanent English settlement (1607) in America.

Ja•pan (jə-păn'). **1. Sea of.** Part of the Pacific between Japan & the Asian mainland. **2.** Country of Asia on an archipelago off the NE coast. Cap. Tokyo. Pop. 121,047,196. —**Jap'a•nese'** (jăp'ə-nēz', -nēs') *adj. & n.*

Ja•va (jä'və, jăv'ə). **1.** Sea between Java & Borneo. **2.** Island of Indonesia SE of Sumatra.

Jef•fer•son City (jĕf'ər-sən). Cap. of MO in the central part on the Missouri R. Pop. 35,481.

Jer•i•cho (jĕr'ĭ-kō'). **1.** Ancient city of Palestine. **2.** Town in the West Bank near the site of ancient Jericho. Pop. 5,312.

Jer•sey (jûr'zē). Largest of the Channel Is. in the English Channel.

Jersey City. City of NE NJ on the Hudson opposite Lower Manhattan. Pop. 228,537.

Je•ru•sa•lem (jə-ro͞o'sə-ləm, -zə-). Cap. of Israel in the E central part. Pop. 446,500.

Jid•da (jĭd'ə) *also* **Jed•da** (jĕd'ə). City of W central Saudi Arabia. Pop. 1,300,000.

Ji•lin (jē'lĭn'). **1.** Province of NE China. **2.** City of NE China. Pop. 882,700.

Ji•nan (jē'nän'). City of E China on the Yellow R. S of Tianjin. Pop. 1,430,000.

Jodh•pur (jŏd'pər, -po͝or'). City of W India SW of Delhi. Pop. 506,345.

Jo•han•nes•burg (jō-hăn'ĭs-bûrg', -hä'nĭs-). City of NE South Africa. Pop. 703,980.

Jor•dan (jôr'dn). **1.** River of NE Israel & NW Jordan. **2.** Country of SW Asia in NW Arabia. Cap. Amman. Pop. 2,595,100. —**Jor•da'ni•an** (jôr-dā'nē-ən) *adj. & n.*

Juan de Fu•ca (hwän' də fo͞o'kə, fyo͞o'-, wän'). Strait, c. 100 mi (161 km) long, between NW WA & Vancouver Is., B.C., Canada.

Ju•de•a *also* **Ju•dae•a** (jo͞o-dē'ə, -dā'-). Ancient region of S Palestine. —**Ju•de'an** *adj. & n.*

Ju•neau (jo͞o'nō'). Cap. of AK in the SE part. Pop. 26,751.

Ju•ra (jo͝or'ə). Range extending along the French-Swiss border.

Jut•land (jŭt'lənd). Peninsula of N Europe comprising mainland Denmark & N Germany.

K

Ka•bul (kä'bo͝ol, kə-bo͞ol'). Cap. of Afghanistan in the E part. Pop. 913,164.

Ka•go•shi•ma (kä'gə-shē'mə). City of S Kyushu, Japan. Pop. 505,360.

Ka•li•nin (kə-lē'nĭn). City of W central Russia NW of Moscow. Pop. 438,000.

Ka•li•nin•grad (kə-lē'nĭn-grăd'). City of extreme W Russia. Pop. 385,000.

Kam•chat•ka (kăm-chăt'kə). Peninsula of E Russia between the Sea of Okhotsk & the Bering Sea.

Kam•pa•la (käm-pä'lə). Cap. of Uganda in the S part on Lake Victoria. Pop. 458,503.

Kam•pu•che•a (kăm'pə-chē'ə, -po͞o-). CAMBODIA.

Kan•da•har (kăn'də-här'). City of SE Afghanistan. Pop. 178,409.

Ka•no (kä'nō). City of N Nigeria NE of Lagos. Pop. 475,000.

Kan•pur (kän'po͝or'). City of N India on the Ganges SE of Delhi. Pop. 1,481,879.

Kan•sas (kăn'zəs). State of the central U.S. Cap. Topeka. Pop. 2,485,600. —**Kan'san** (-zən) *adj. & n.*

Kansas City. 1. City of NE KS adjacent to Kansas City, MO. Pop. 149,767. **2.** City of W MO on the Missouri R. Pop. 435,146.

Kao•hsiung (gou'shē-o͝ong', kou'-). City of SW Taiwan on Formosa Strait. Pop. 1,248,175.

Ka•ra•chi (kə-rä'chē). City of S Pakistan on the Arabian Sea. Pop. 4,776,000.

Ka•ra•gan•da (kăr'ə-gən-dä'). City of central Kazakhstan. Pop. 617,000.

Karls•ru•he (kärlz'ro͞o'ə). City of SW Germany on the Rhine. Pop. 269,638.

Kash•mir (kăsh'mîr', kăsh-mîr'). Region & former state of N India & NE Pakistan.

Kat•man•du (kăt'măn-do͞o', kät'-). Cap. of Nepal in the central part. Pop. 235,160.

Ka•to•wi•ce (kä'tə-vēt'sə). City of S Poland WNW of Kraków. Pop. 363,300.

Kau•ai (kou'ī'). Island of HI NW of Oahu.

Kau•nas (kou'nəs, -näs'). City of central Lithuania. Pop. 405,000.

Ka•wa•sa•ki (kä'wə-sä'kē). City of E central Honshu, Japan. Pop. 1,040,802.

Ka•zakh•stan (kə-zäk'stän', -zŭkh-stän'). Country S of Russia NE of the Caspian Sea. Cap. Alma-Alta. Pop. 15,842,000.

Ka•zan (kə-zăn', zän'). City of W central Russia on the Volga. Pop. 1,047,000.

Ken•ne•dy (kĕn'ĭ-dē), **Cape.** CAPE CANAVERAL.

Ken•tuck•y (kən-tŭk'ē). State of E central U.S. Cap. Frankfort. Pop. 3,698,969. **—Ken•tuck'i•an** *adj. & n.*

Ken•ya (kĕn'yə, kēn'). Country of E central Africa. Cap. Nairobi. Pop. 15,327,061. **—Ken'yan** *adj. & n.*

Key Lar•go (kē lär'gō). Island off S FL, largest of the Florida Keys.

Key West (wĕst). City of extreme S FL on **Key West Is.** Pop. 24,832.

Khar•kov (kär'kôf', -kôv', -kəf). City of NE Ukraine E of Kiev. Pop. 1,554,000.

Khar•toum *also* **Khar•tum** (kär-to͞om'). Cap. of Sudan. Pop. 476,218.

Khmer Republic (kmĕr). CAMBODIA.

Khy•ber (kī'bər). Pass through the mountains between W Afghanistan & N Pakistan.

Ki•ev (kē'ĕf, -ĕv, -əf). Cap. of Ukraine in the N central part. Pop. 2,448,000.

Ki•ga•li (kĭ-gä'lē). Cap. of Rwanda in the central part. Pop. 156,700.

Kil•i•man•ja•ro (kĭl'ə-mən-jär'ō). Highest mountain in Africa, 19,340 ft (5,898.7 m), in NE Tanzania near the Kenya border.

Kim•ber•ley (kĭm'bər-lē). City of central South Africa. Pop. 70,920.

King•ston (kĭng'stən). Cap. of Jamaica in the SE part. Pop. 586,930.

Kings•town (kĭngz'toun'). Cap. of St. Vincent & the Grenadines. Pop. 18,378.

Kin•sha•sa (kĭn-shä'sə). Cap. of Zaire in the W part on the Congo R. Pop. 2,653,558.

Kir•ghiz (kîr-gēz'). Country of W central Asia. Cap. Bishkek. Pop. 3,967,000.

Ki•ri•ba•ti (kîr'ə-băs'). Island republic of the W central Pacific. Cap. Bairiki. Pop. 56,213.

Ki•rov (kē'rôf', -rôv', -rəf). City of W central Russia ENE of Moscow. Pop. 411,000.

Ki•san•ga•ni (kē'sən-gä'nē). City of N Zaire on the Congo R. Pop. 229,596.

Ki•shi•nev (kĭsh'ə-nĕf', -nĕv'). Cap. of Moldavia in the S part. Pop. 624,000.

Ki•ta•kyu•shu (kē-tä'kyo͞o-sho͞o). City of N Kyushu, Japan, on the coast. Pop. 1,065,078.

Kit•ty Hawk (kĭt'ē hôk'). Village of NE NC.

Ki•twe (kē'twā'). City of N central Zambia near the Zaire border. Pop. 314,794.

Klon•dike (klŏn'dīk'). River, c. 90 mi (145 km), of E central Y.T., Canada.

Knos•sos (nŏs'əs). Ancient city of N Crete.

Knox•ville (nŏks'vĭl', -vəl). City of E TN NE of Chattanooga. Pop. 165,121.

Ko•be (kō'bē', -bā'). City of S Japan on Osaka Bay in S Honshu. Pop. 1,367,390.

Ko•di•ak (kō'dē-ăk'). Island of S AK.

Ko•ly•ma (kə-lē'mə). **1.** River of NE Russia flowing c. 1,335 mi (2,148 km) N to the East Siberian Sea. **2.** Range of NE Russia.

Ko•re•a (kə-rē'ə). Peninsula & former country of E Asia, divided politically since 1948 between **North Korea** (cap. Pyongyang; pop. 22,419,000) & **South Korea** (cap. Seoul; pop. 47,793,000). **—Ko•re'an** *adj. & n.*

Kos (kŏs, kôs). Island of SE Greece in the N Dodecanese.

Kos•ci•us•ko (kŏs'ē-ŭs'kō), **Mount.** Highest mountain (7,316 ft/2,231.4 m) in Australia, in the SE part.

Ko•so•vo (kô'sə-vō'). Region of SW Serbia.

Kow•loon (kou'lo͞on'). City of Hong Kong colony on the SE coast of China. Metro. area pop. 799,123.

Kra•ków (krä'kou, krăk'ou, krā'kou, -kō). *var. of* CRACOW.

Kras•no•dar (krăs'nə-där'). City of SW Russia in the N Caucasus. Pop. 609,000.

Kras•no•yarsk (krăs'nə-yärsk'). City of S central Russia. Pop. 872,000.

Kri•voi Rog *or* **Kri•voy Rog** (krĭv'oi rōg', rôk'). City of S central Ukraine. Pop. 684,000.

Kua•la Lum•pur (kwä'lə lo͞om'po͝or', lŭm'-, ko͞o-ä'lə). Cap. of Malaysia on the SW Malay Peninsula. Pop. 937,817.

Kui•by•shev *or* **Kuy•by•shev** (kwē'bə-shĕf', -shĕv', ko͞o'ē-bə-). City of W Russia on the Volga ESE of Moscow. Pop. 1,257,000.

Ku•ma•mo•to (ko͞o'mə-mō'tō). City W Kyushu, Japan. Pop. 525,662.

Kun•ming (ko͞on'mĭng'). City of S China SW of Chongqing. Pop. 1,418,640.

Kurd•i•stan (ko͝or'dĭ-stăn', kûr'-). Region of SE Turkey, NE Iraq, & NW Iran.

Ku•rile *or* **Ku•ril** (kyo͝or'ēl', kyo͞o-rēl'). Island chain of extreme E Russia in the Pacific between Kamchatka Peninsula & N Hokkaido, Japan.

Kursk (ko͝orsk). City of W Russia SSW of Moscow. Pop. 420,000.

Ku•wait (kə-wāt'). **1.** Country of the NE Arabian Peninsula. Pop. 1,355,827. Cap. Kuwait. **2.** Cap. of Kuwait in the E central part. Pop. 60,365. **—Ku•wait'i** *adj. & n.*

Kwang•chow (gwäng'jō'). GUANGZHOU.

Kwang•ju (gwäng'jo͞o'). City of SW South Korea S of Seoul. Pop. 607,011.

Kyo•to (kē-ō'tō). City of S Honshu, Japan, NE of Osaka. Pop. 1,473,065.

Kyu•shu (kē-ōō'shōō). Third-largest island of SW Japan.

L

Lab•ra•dor (lăb'rə-dôr'). **1.** Peninsula of NE Canada between Hudson Bay & the Atlantic, divided between Que. & Newf. **2.** Mainland territory of Newf., Canada. —**Lab'ra•dor'e•an, Lab'ra•dor'i•an** *adj. & n.*

La•gos (lā'gŏs'). Cap. of Nigeria in the SW on the Gulf of Guinea. Pop. 1,404,000.

La•hore (lə-hōr', -hôr'). City of NE Pakistan near the Indian border. Pop. 2,685,000.

La•na•i (lə-nī'). Island of central HI.

Lan•chow (län'jō'). LANZHOU.

Lan•sing (lăn'sĭng). Cap. of MI in the S central part NW of Detroit. Pop. 127,321.

Lan•zhou (län'jō'). City of central China on the Yellow R. Pop. 1,500,000.

La•os (lous, lā'ŏs', lā'ōs). Country of SE Asia. Cap. Vientiane. Pop. 3,721,000. —**La•o'tian** (lā-ō'shən) *adj. & n.*

La Paz (lə păz', päz', päs'). Administrative cap. of Bolivia in the W part. Pop. 992,592.

Lap•land (lăp'lănd', -lənd). Region of N Scandinavia & NW Russia. —**Lap'land•er** *n.*

La Pla•ta (lä plä'tä). City of E central Argentina SE of Buenos Aires. Pop. 454,884.

La•re•do (lə-rā'dō). City of S TX on the Rio Grande SSW of San Antonio. Pop. 122,899.

La•ri•sa (lăr'ĭ-sə) *or* **La•ris•sa** (lə-rĭs'ə). City of E Greece in Thessaly. Pop. 102,048.

Las Pal•mas (läs päl'məs). Chief city of the Canary Is. of Spain, on Grand Canary Is. Pop. 377,353.

Las Ve•gas (läs vā'gəs). City of SE NV. Pop. 258,295.

Latin America. Countries of the Western Hemisphere S of the U.S. —**Lat'in A•mer'i•can** *n.* —**Lat'in-A•mer'i•can** *adj.*

Lat•vi•a (lăt'vē-ə). Country of N Europe on the Baltic. Cap. Riga. Pop. 2,604,000. —**Lat'vi•an** *adj. & n.*

Lau•sanne (lō-zăn', -zăn'). City of W Switzerland. Pop. 126,200.

La•val (lə-văl'). City of S Que., Canada, on the Ottawa R. near Montreal. Pop. 268,335.

Leb•a•non (lĕb'ə-nən). Country of SW Asia on the Mediterranean N of Israel. Cap. Beirut. Pop. 2,637,000. —**Leb'a•nese'** *adj. & n.*

Leeds (lēdz). Borough of N central England NE of Manchester. Pop. 718,100.

Lee•ward (lē'wərd). Islands of the West Indies in the N Lesser Antilles.

Leg•horn (lĕg'hôrn'). City of NW Italy on the Ligurian Sea. Pop. 175,371.

Le Ha•vre (lə hä'vrə, häv). City of N France on the English Channel. Pop. 199,388.

Leices•ter (lĕs'tər). City of central England ENE of Birmingham. Pop. 283,000.

Lei•den *also* **Ley•den** (līd'n). City of SW Netherlands NE of The Hague. Pop. 104,261.

Leip•zig (līp'sĭg, -sĭk). City of E central Germany SSW of Berlin. Pop. 558,994.

Lem•nos (lĕm'nŏs, -nəs) *also* **Lim•nos** (lēm'nôs'). Island of NE Greece in the Aegean.

Le•na (lē'nə, lā'-). River of E Russia flowing c. 2,670 mi (4,296 m) to the Arctic Ocean.

Len•in•grad (lĕn'ĭn-grăd'). SAINT PETERSBURG.

Le•ón (lā-ōn'). **1.** Region & former kingdom of NW Spain. **2.** City of central Mexico ENE of Guadalajara. Pop. 593,002.

Les•bos (lĕz'bŏs', -bəs) *also* **Les•vos** (-vôs'). Island of E Greece in the Aegean.

Le•so•tho (lə-sō'tō). Kingdom of S Africa, an enclave within E central South Africa. Cap. Maseru. Pop. 1,213,960.

Les•ser An•til•les (lĕs'ər ăn-tĭl'ēz). Island group of the E & S West Indies.

Le•vant (lə-vănt'). Countries bordering on the E Mediterranean. —**Le'van•tine'** (lĕv'ən-tīn', -tēn', lə-văn'-) *adj. & n.*

Lex•ing•ton (lĕk'sĭng-tən). **1.** City of N central KY ESE of Louisville. Pop. 204,165. **2.** Town of E MA near Boston. Pop. 28,974.

Ley•den (līd'n). *var. of* LEIDEN.

Lha•sa (lä'sə, lăs'ə). City of SW China, traditional cap. of Tibet. Pop. 105,897.

Li•be•ri•a (lī-bîr'ē-ə). Country of W Africa on the Gulf of Guinea. Cap. Monrovia. Pop. 1,911,000. —**Li•be'ri•an** *adj. & n.*

Li•bre•ville (lē'brə-vĭl', -vēl'). Cap. of Gabon in the NW part. Pop. 235,700

Lib•y•a (lĭb'ē-ə). Country of N Africa. Cap. Tripoli. Pop. 3,096,000. —**Lib'y•an** *adj. & n.*

Liech•ten•stein (lĭk'tən-stīn', -shtīn'). Principality in central Europe between Austria & Switzerland. Cap. Vaduz. Pop. 27,076.

Li•ège (lē-āzh', -ĕzh'). City of E Belgium. Pop. 207,496.

Li•gu•ri•a (lĭ-gyŏŏr'ē-ə). Region of NW Italy. —**Li•gu'ri•an** *adj. & n.*

Li•long•we (lĭ-lông'wā). Cap. of Malawi in the S central part. Pop. 103,000.

Li•ma (lē'mə). Cap. of Peru in the W central part. Metro. area pop. 3,968,972.

Lim•po•po (lĭm-pō'pō). River of SE Africa flowing c. 1,100 m (1,770 km) to the Indian Ocean.

Lin•coln (lĭng'kən). Cap. of NE in the SE part SW of Omaha. Pop. 191,972.

Linz (lĭnts). City of N Austria on Danube. Pop. 199,910.

Li•petsk (lē'pĕtsk'). City of W central Russia SSE of Moscow. Pop. 447,000.

Lis•bon (lĭz'bən). Cap. of Portugal in the W part on the Tagus R. Pop. 807,167.

Lith•u•a•ni•a (lĭth'ōō-ā'nē-ə). Country of N Europe on the Baltic. Cap. Vilnius. Pop. 3,570,000. —**Lith'u•a'ni•an** *adj. & n.*

Little Rock (rŏk). Cap. of AR in the central part. Pop. 175,795.

Liv•er•pool (lĭv'ər-pōōl'). Borough of NW England on the Mersey R. Pop. 518,900.

Li•vo•ni•a (lĭ-vō'nē-ə, -vōn'yə). Region comprising S Latvia & N Estonia. —**Li•vo'ni•an** *adj. & n.*

Li•vor•no (lē-vôr'nō). LEGHORN.

Lju•blja•na (lē-ōō'blē-ä'nə). Cap. of Slovenia on the Sava R. Pop. 205,600.
Loire (lwär, lə-wär'). River of W France, flowing c. 630 mi (1,014 km) to the Bay of Biscay.
Lom•bar•dy (lŏm'bər-dē). Region of N Italy. —**Lom'bard** *adj. & n.*
Lo•mé (lō-mā'). Cap. of Togo in the S part on the Gulf of Guinea. Pop. 369,926.
Lo•mond (lō'mənd), **Loch.** Largest lake in Scotland in the E central part.
Lon•don (lŭn'dən). **1.** City of SE Ont., Canada. Pop. 283,668. **2.** Cap. of the United Kingdom on the Thames R. in SE England. Metro. area pop. 6,851,400.
Long Beach (lông, lŏng). City of S CA SE of Los Angeles. Pop. 429,433.
Long Island. 1. Sound. Arm of the N Atlantic between Long Is. & CT **2.** Island, c. 120 mi (193 km) long, of SE NY.
Lor•raine (lō-rān', lô-). Region & former province of NE France.
Los An•ge•les (ăn'jə-ləs, -lēz', ăng'gə-ləs). City of S CA on the Pacific. Pop. 3,485,398.
Lou•i•si•an•a (lōō-ē'zē-ăn'ə, lōō'zē-). State of S central U.S. Cap. Baton Rouge. Pop. 4,238,216.
Lou•is•ville (lōō'ē-vĭl', -ə-vəl). City of NW KY. Pop. 269,063.
Lourdes (lŏŏrd, lŏŏrdz). Town of SW France at the foot of the Pyrenees. Pop. 17,425.
Low Countries. Belgium, the Netherlands, & Luxembourg.
Lower Cal•i•for•nia (kăl'ə-fôr'nyə). Peninsula of NW Mexico.
Lu•an•da (lōō-ăn'də) *also* **Lo•an•da** (lō-). Cap. of Angola in the W part. Pop. 1,200,000.
Lub•bock (lŭb'ək). City of NW TX S of Amarillo. Pop. 186,206.
Lu•cerne (lōō-sûrn'). City of central Switzerland. Pop. 61,000.
Luck•now (lŭk'nou). City of N central India ESE of Delhi. Pop. 859,721.
Lu•sa•ka (lōō-sä'kə). Cap. of Zambia in the S central part. Pop. 535,830.
Lux•em•bourg *or* **Lux•em•burg** (lŭk'səm-bûrg'). **1.** Country & grand duchy of W Europe. Cap. Luxembourg. Pop. 364,606. **2.** *also* **Luxembourg City.** Cap. of Luxembourg in the S part. Pop. 78,924.
Lu•zon (lōō-zŏn'). Island of the NW Philippines, largest of the archipelago.
Lvov (lə-vôf', -vôv'). City of W central Ukraine near the Polish border. Pop. 742,000.
Lyc•i•a (lĭsh'ē-ə, lĭsh'ə). Ancient country of SW Asia Minor. —**Lyc'i•an** *adj. & n.*
Lyd•i•a (lĭd'ē-ə). Ancient country of W central Asia Minor. —**Lyd'i•an** *adj. & n.*
Ly•on *or* **Ly•ons** (lē-ōN', lyôN). City of E central France. Pop. 413,095.

M

Maas (mäs). MEUSE.
Ma•cao *also* **Ma•cau** (mə-kou'). Portuguese overseas province of SE China. Cap. Macao (pop. 226,880). Pop. 238,413.
Mac•e•do•ni•a (măs'ĭ-dō'nē-ə, -dōn'yə). **1.** *also* **Mac•e•don** (-dən, -dŏn'). Ancient kingdom N of Greece. **2.** Historical region of SE Europe including parts of Greece, Bulgaria, & modern Macedonia. **3.** Republic of S central Balkan Peninsula. Cap. Skopje. Pop. 1,623,598. —**Mac'e•do'ni•an** *adj. & n.*
Mac•ken•zie (mə-kĕn'zē). **1.** Range of the N Rocky Mts. in NW Canada. **2.** River of NW Canada, 1,120 mi (1,800 km).
Ma•con (mā'kən). City of central GA SE of Atlanta. Pop. 106,612.
Mad•a•gas•car (măd'ə-găs'kər). Island republic off the SE coast of Africa. Cap. Antananarivo. Pop. 9,230,000. —**Mad'a•gas'can** *adj. & n.*
Ma•dei•ra (mə-dîr'ə, -dĕr'ə). Portuguese archipelago in the N Atlantic W of Morocco. —**Ma•dei'ran** *adj. & n.*
Mad•i•son (măd'ĭ-sən). Cap. of WI in the S central part. Pop. 191,262.
Mad•ras (mə-drăs', -dräs'). City of SE India on the Bay of Bengal. Pop. 3,276,622.
Ma•drid (mə-drĭd'). Cap. of Spain on the central plateau. Pop. 3,200,234.
Ma•du•rai (mä'də-rī'). City of S India SW of Madras. Pop. 820,891.
Mag•de•burg (măg'də-bûrg', mäg'də-bŏŏrg'). City of central Germany SW of Berlin. Pop. 289,075.
Ma•gel•lan (mə-jĕl'ən), **Strait of.** Channel separating S South America & Tierra del Fuego.
Main (mīn, mān). River of E Germany flowing c. 310 mi (500 km) to the Rhine.
Maine (mān). **1.** (*also* mĕn). Region of NW France S of Normandy. **2.** State of the NE U.S. Cap. Augusta. Pop. 1,233,223.
Mainz (mīnts). City of W central Germany SW of Frankfurt. Pop. 187,447.
Ma•jor•ca (mə-jôr'kə, -yôr'-). Spanish island of the Balearics.—**Ma•jor'can** *adj. & n.*
Mal•a•bar (măl'ə-bär'). Region of SW India.
Mal•a•bo (mä-lä'bō, măl'ə-bō'). Cap. of Equatorial Guinea. Pop. 30,710.
Má•la•ga (măl'ə-gə). City of S Spain NE of Gibraltar. Pop. 537,619.
Mal•a•gas•y Republic (măl'ə-găs'ē). MADAGASCAR.
Ma•la•wi (mə-lä'wē). Country of SE Africa. Cap. Lilongwe. Pop. 6,123,000. —**Ma•la'wi•an** *adj. & n.*
Ma•lay (mə-lā', mā'lā). **1.** Archipelago in the Indian & Pacific oceans between Australia & SE Asia. **2.** *also* **Ma•la•ya** (mə-lā'ə, mā-). Peninsula of SE Asia.—**Ma•la'yan** *adj. & n.*
Ma•lay•sia (mə-lā'zhə, -shə). Country of SE Asia. Cap. Kuala Lumpur. Pop. 13,486,433. —**Ma•lay'sian** *adj. & n.*
Mal•dives (môl'dīvz, măl'-). Island country in the Indian Ocean. Cap. Male. Pop. 181,453. —**Mal•div'i•an, Mal•di'van** *adj. & n.*
Ma•le (mä'lē). Cap. of the Maldives. Pop. 46,334.
Ma•li (mä'lē). Country of W Africa. Cap Bamako. Pop. 6,982,000. —**Ma'li•an** *adj. & n.*
Mal•lor•ca (mə-yôr'kä, -lyôr'-). MAJORCA.

Mal·ta (môl'tə). Island country in the Mediterranean S of Sicily. Cap. Valletta. Pop. 331,997. —**Mal·tese'** (-tēz', -tēs') *adj. & n.*
Mal·vin·as (măl-vē'nəs). FALKLAND.
Man (măn), **Isle of.** British island in the Irish Sea. —**Manx** (măngks) *adj. & n.*
Ma·na·gua (mə-näg'wə). Cap. of Nicaragua. Pop. 398,514.
Ma·nam·ah (mə-năm'ə) *or* **Al Manamah** (ăl'). Cap. of Bahrain. Pop. 108,684.
Ma·naus (mə-nous'). City of NW Brazil on the Rio Negro. Pop. 611,763.
Man·ches·ter (măn'chĕs'tər, -chĭ-stər). Borough of NE England NE of Liverpool. Pop. 490,000.
Man·chu·ri·a (măn-cho͝or'ē-ə). Region of NE China. —**Man·chu'ri·an** *adj. & n.*
Man·da·lay (măn'də-lā'). City of central Burma on the Irrawaddy. Pop. 532,895.
Man·hat·tan (măn-hăt'n). Borough of New York City, SE NY, mainly on **Manhattan Is.** Pop. 1,487,536. —**Man·hat'tan·ite'** (-īt') *n.*
Ma·nil·a (mə-nĭl'ə). City of SW Luzon, Philippines. Pop. 1,630,485.
Man·i·to·ba (măn'ĭ-tō'bə). Province of S central Canada. Cap. Winnipeg. Pop. 1,026,241. —**Man'i·to'ban** *adj. & n.*
Mann·heim (măn'hīm, män'-). City of SW Germany on the Rhine. Pop. 295,178.
Ma·pu·to (mə-po͞o'tō). Cap. of Mozambique on the Indian Ocean. Pop. 755,300.
Ma·ra·cai·bo (măr'ə-kī'bō, mä'rə-). City of NW Venezuela on **Lake Maracaibo,** largest lake of South America. Pop. 929,000.
Mar del Pla·ta (mär' dĕl plä'tə). City of E central Argentina. Pop. 414,696.
Mar·i·an·a Islands (mâr'ē-ăn'ə) *also* **Mar·i·an·as** (-əz). U.S.-administered island group in the W Pacific E of the Philippines.
Maritime Provinces *also* **the Mar·i·times** (măr'ĭ-tīmz'). Canadian provinces of N.S., N.B., & P.E.I.
Mar·ma·ra (mär'mər-ə), **Sea of.** Sea of NW Turkey between the Black & Aegean seas.
Marne (märn). River, c. 325 mi (523 km), of NE France.
Mar·que·sas Islands (mär-kā'səz). Archipelago, part of French Polynesia.
Mar·ra·kesh *or* **Mar·ra·kech** (mə-rä'kĭsh, măr'ə-kĕsh'). City of W central Morocco near the Atlas Mts. Pop. 439,728.
Mar·seilles (mär-sā', -sālz') *also* **Mar·seille** (-sā'). City of SE France on the Mediterranean. Pop. 874,436.
Mar·shall (mär'shəl). Islands in the central Pacific, part of U.S. Trust Territory of the Pacific.
Mar·tha's Vine·yard (mär'thəz vĭn'yərd). Island of SE MA off Cape Cod.
Mar·ti·nique (mär'tĭ-nēk', -tn-ēk'). French island & overseas department in the West Indies. Cap. Fort-de-France. Pop. 328,566.
Mar·y·land (mĕr'ə-lənd). State of the E central U.S. Cap. Annapolis. Pop. 4,798,622. —**Mar'y·land·er** *n.*
Mas·er·u (măz'ə-ro͞o'). Cap. of Lesotho in the W part. Pop. 14,686.
Mash·had (mə-shăd'). MESHED.
Mas·sa·chu·setts (măs'ə-cho͞o'sĭts). State of the NE U.S. Cap. Boston. Pop. 6,029,051.
Ma·ta·mo·ros (măt'ə-môr'əs, mä'tä-). City of NE Mexico on the Rio Grande opposite Brownsville, TX. Pop. 188,745.
Mat·ter·horn (măt'ər-hôrn', mä'tər-). Mountain, c. 14,685 ft (4,480 m), in the Pennine Alps on the Italian-Swiss border.
Mau·i (mou'ē). Island of HI NW of Hawaii Is.
Mau·re·ta·ni·a (môr'ĭ-tā'nē-ə, -tān'yə, mär'-). Ancient country of N Africa. —**Mau're·ta'ni·an** *adj. & n.*
Mau·ri·ta·ni·a (môr'ĭ-tā'nē-ə, -tān'yə, mär'-). Islamic republic of NW Africa. Cap. Nouakchott. Pop. 1,727,000. —**Mau'ri·ta'ni·an** *adj. & n.*
Mau·ri·tius (mô-rĭsh'əs, -ē-əs). Island country in the SW Indian Ocean. Cap. Port Louis. Pop. 1,023,934. —**Mau·ri'tian** *adj. & n.*
Mba·bane (əm-bə-bän'). Cap. of Swaziland in the NW part. Pop. 33,000.
Mc·Kin·ley (mĭ-kĭn'lē), **Mount.** Peak, 20,320 ft (6,198 m), in S central AK.
Mec·ca (mĕk'ə). City of W Saudi Arabia. Pop. 550,000.
Me·dan (mā-dän'). City of NE Sumatra, Indonesia. Pop. 1,378,955.
Me·del·lín (mĕd'l-ēn'). City of NW central Colombia NW of Bogotá. Pop. 1,473,351.
Me·di·na (mĭ-dē'nə). City of NW Saudi Arabia N of Mecca. Pop. 290,000.
Med·i·ter·ra·ne·an (mĕd'ĭ-tə-rā'nē-ən). Sea surrounded by Europe, Asia, Asia Minor, the Near East, & Africa, connecting with the Atlantic through the Strait of Gibraltar.
Me·kong (mā'kông', -kŏng'). River of SE Asia flowing c. 2,600 mi (4,185 km) to the South China Sea.
Mel·a·ne·sia (mĕl'ə-nē'zhə, -shə). Island group in the SW Pacific NE of Australia. —**Mel'a·ne'sian** *adj. & n.*
Mel·bourne (mĕl'bərn). City of SE Australia. Metro. area pop. 2,722,817.
Mem·phis (mĕm'fĭs, mĕmp'-). City of SW TN. Pop. 610,337.
Me·sa (mā'sə). City of S central AZ near Phoenix. Pop. 288,091.
Me·shed (mə-shĕd'). City of NE Iran. Pop. 1,130,000.
Mes·o·po·ta·mi·a (mĕs'ə-pə-tā'mē-ə). Ancient country of SW Asia between the Tigris & Euphrates rivers. —**Mes'o·po·ta'mi·an** *adj. & n.*
Mes·si·na (mĭ-sē'nə). City of NE Sicily. Pop. 240,121.
Meuse (myo͞oz, mz). River flowing c. 560 mi (901 km) from NE France to the North Sea.
Mex·i·cal·i (mĕk'sĭ-kăl'ē) City of NW Mexico near the CA border. Pop. 341,559.
Mex·i·co (mĕk'sĭ-kō'). **1. Gulf of.** Arm of the Atlantic bordering on E Mexico, SE U.S., & Cuba. **2.** Republic of NW Central America. Cap. Mexico City. Pop. 67,395,826. —**Mex'i·can** *adj. & n.*
Mexico City. Cap. of Mexico at the S end of the central plateau. Pop. 8,831,079.

Mi•am•i (mī-ăm'ē). City of SE FL on Biscayne Bay S of West Palm Beach. Pop. 358,548.
Miami Beach. City of SE FL near Miami. Pop. 92,639.
Mich•i•gan (mĭsh'ĭ-gən). **1. Lake.** Third-largest of the Great Lakes, between WI & MI. **2.** State of the N U.S. Pop. 9,328,784. Cap. Lansing. —**Mich'i•gan'der** *adj. & n.*
Mi•cro•ne•si•a (mī'krō-nē'zhə, -shə). Islands of the W Pacific E of the Philippines —**Mi'cro•ne'sian** *adj. & n.*
Middle East (ēst). Area of SW Asia & NE Africa. —**Middle East'ern** (ē'stərn) *adj. & n.*
Middle West (wĕst). Region of the N central U.S. —**Middle West'ern** (wĕs'tərn) *adj. & n.* —**Middle West'ern•er** *n.*
Mid•east (mĭd-ēst'). MIDDLE EAST. —**Mid•east'ern** *adj.* —**Mid•east'ern•er** *n.*
Mid•west (mĭd-wĕst'). MIDDLE WEST. —**Mid•west'ern** *adj.* —**Mid•west'ern•er** *n.*
Mi•lan (mĭ-lăn', -län'). City of N Italy. Pop. 1,634,638. —**Mil'a•nese'** (mĭl'ə-nēz', -nēs') *adj. & n.*
Mil•wau•kee (mĭl-wô'kē). City of SE WI on Lake Michigan. Pop. 628,088.
Min•da•na•o (mĭn'də-nä'ō, -nou'). Island of S Philippines NE of Borneo.
Min•do•ro (mĭn-dôr'ō, -dōr'ō). Island of W central Philippines S of Luzon.
Min•ne•ap•o•lis (mĭn'ē-ăp'ə-lĭs). City of SE MN adjacent to St. Paul. Pop. 368,383.
Min•ne•so•ta (mĭn'ĭ-sō'tə). State of the N U.S. Cap. St. Paul. Pop. 4,387,029. —**Min'ne•so'tan** *adj. & n.*
Mi•nor•ca (mĭ-nôr'kə). Spanish island in the Balearics.—**Mi•nor'can** *adj. & n.*
Minsk (mĭnsk). Cap. of Belorussia, in the central part. Pop. 1,472,000.
Mis•sis•sip•pi (mĭs'ĭ-sĭp'ē). **1.** River of central U.S. flowing 2,350 mi (3,780 km) to the Gulf of Mexico. **2.** State of the S U.S. Cap. Jackson. Pop. 2,586,443. —**Mis'sis•sip'pi•an** *adj. & n.*
Mis•sou•ri (mĭ-zŏŏr'ē, -zŏŏr'ə). **1.** River of the U.S. rising in W MT & flowing c. 2,565 mi (4,127 km) to the Mississippi. **2.** State of central U.S. Cap. Jefferson City. Pop. 5,137,804. —**Mis•sou'ri•an** *adj. & n.*
Mo•bile (mō-bēl', mō'bēl'). City of SW AL. Pop. 196,278.
Mo•des•to (mō-dĕs'tō). City of central CA SE of Stockton. Pop. 164,730.
Mog•a•dish•u (mŏg'ə-dĭsh'ōō, -dē'shōō). Cap. of Somalia. Pop. 400,000.
Mo•ja•ve *also* **Mo•ha•ve** (mō-hä'vē). Desert, of S CA SE of the Sierra Nevada.
Mol•da•vi•a (mŏl-dā'vē-ə, -dāv'yə). **1.** Historical region of E Romania. **2.** *also* **Mol•do•va** (môl-dô'və). Country of E Europe. Cap. Kishinev. Pop. 4,111,000. —**Mol•da'vi•an** *adj. & n.*
Mo•lo•kai (mŏl'ə-kī', mō'lə-). Island of HI between Oahu and Maui.
Mo•luc•cas (mə-lŭk'əz). Islands of E Indonesia. —**Mo•luc'can** *adj. & n.*
Mom•ba•sa (mŏm-bă'sə). City of SE Kenya. Pop. 341,148.
Mon•a•co (mŏn'ə-kō', mə-nä'kō). Principality on the Mediterranean, an enclave in SE France. Cap. Monaco *or* Monaco-Ville. Pop. 27,063. —**Mon'a•can** *adj. & n.*
Mon•go•li•a (mŏn-gō'lē-ə, -gōl'yə, mŏng-). **1.** Region of E central Asia. **2.** Country of N central Asia between Russia & China. Cap. Ulan Bator. Pop. 1,866,300. —**Mon•go'li•an** *adj. & n.*
Mon•ro•vi•a (mən-rō'vē-ə). Cap. of Liberia in the NW part. Pop. 243,243.
Mon•tan•a (mŏn-tăn'ə). State of the NW U.S. Cap. Helena. Pop. 803,655. —**Mon•tan'an** *adj. & n.*
Mont Blanc (mônt blăngk, môN bläN'). Mountain, 15,771 ft (4,810 m), in the Alps on the French-Italian border.
Mon•te Car•lo (mŏn'tē kär'lō). Town of Monaco on the Riviera. Pop. 11,599.
Mon•te•ne•gro (mŏn'tə-nē'grō, -nĕg'rō). Region of the W Balkan Peninsula on the Adriatic, part of the republic of Yugoslavia. Cap. Titograd. Pop. 502,207.
Mon•ter•rey (mŏn'tə-rā'). City of NE Mexico. Pop. 1,090,099.
Mon•te•vi•de•o (mŏn'tə-vĭ-dā'ō, -vĭd'ē-ō'). Cap. of Uruguay. Pop. 1,237,227.
Mont•gom•er•y (mŏnt-gŭm'ə-rē, -gŭm'rē). Cap. of AL in the central part. Pop. 187,106.
Mont•pel•ier (mŏnt-pēl'yər). Cap. of VT in the central part. Pop. 8,247.
Mon•tre•al (mŏn'trē-ôl') *or* **Mont•ré•al** (môN'rā-äl'). City of S Que. Canada. Pop. 980,354. —**Mon'tre•al'er** *n.*
Mont•ser•rat (mŏnt'sə-răt'). Island, one of the Leewards, in the British West Indies.
Mo•ra•vi•a (mə-rā'vē-ə). Region of Czech Republic. —**Mo•ra'vi•an** *adj. & n.*
Mo•roc•co (mə-rŏk'ō). Kingdom of NW Africa. Cap. Rabat. Pop. 20,419,555. —**Mo•roc'can** *adj. & n.*
Mo•ro•ni (mə-rō'nē). Cap. of the Comoros on Great Comoro Is. Pop. 20,112.
Mos•cow (mŏs'kou, -kō). Cap. of Russia in the W central part. Pop. 8,408,000.
Mo•selle (mō-zĕl'). River of NE France & W Germany flowing 320 mi (515 km) to the Rhine.
Mo•sul (mō-sōōl', mō'səl). City of N Iraq on the Tigris. Pop. 570,296.
Moul•mein (mōōl-mān', mōl-). City of S Burma on the Gulf of Martaban. Pop. 219,991.
Mo•zam•bique (mō'zəm-bēk'). Country of SE Africa. Cap. Maputo. Pop. 12,130,000. —**Mo'zam•bi'can** *adj. & n.*
Muk•den (mŏŏk'dən, mŭk'-, mŏŏk-dĕn'). SHENYANG.
Mul•tan (mŏŏl-tän'). City of E central Pakistan SW of Lahore. Pop. 694,000.
Mu•nich (myōō'nĭk). City of SE Germany near the Bavarian Alps. Pop. 1,314,865.
Mün•ster (mŏŏn'stər, mŭn'-, mĭn'-). City of W central Germany. Pop 272,626.
Mur•cia (mûr'shə, -shē-ə). **1.** Region & former Moorish kingdom of SE Spain. **2.** City of SE Spain. Pop. 200,300.

Mur•mansk (mo͝or-mănsk′, -mänsk′). City of NW Russia on Barents Sea. Pop. 419,000.
Mus•cat (mŭs′kăt′, -kət). Cap. of Oman on the Gulf of Oman. Pop. 30,000.
Myan•mar (myän-mär′). BURMA.
My•ce•nae (mī-sē′nē). Ancient Greek city in the NE Peloponnesus.
My•sore (mī-sôr′, -sōr′). City of S India. Pop. 441,754.

N

Na•ga•sa•ki (nä′gə-sä′kē, năg′ə-săk′ē). City of W Kyushu, Japan. Pop. 449,382.
Na•go•ya (nə-goi′ə). City of central Honshu, Japan. Pop. 2,116,350.
Nai•ro•bi (nī-rō′bē). Cap. of Kenya in the S central part. Pop. 827,775.
Na•mib•i•a (nə-mĭb′ē-ə). A country of SW Africa on the Atlantic Ocean. Cap. Windhoek. Pop. 1,099,000. —**Na•mib′i•an** *adj. & n.*
Nan•chang (năn′chăng′). City of SE China on the Gan R. Pop. 1,088,800.
Nan•jing (năn′jĭng′) *also* **Nan•king** (năn′-kĭng′, năn′-). City of E central China on the Yangtze. Pop. 2,250,000.
Nantes (nănts, näNt). City of W France on the Loire. Pop. 240,539.
Nan•tuck•et (năn-tŭk′ĭt). Island of SE MA S of Cape Cod.
Na•ples (nā′pəlz). City of S central Italy. Pop. 1,210,503. —**Ne′a•pol′i•tan** (nē′ə-pŏl′ĭ-tən) *adj. & n.*
Nash•ville (năsh′vĭl′). Cap. of TN in the central part. Pop. 488,374.
Nas•sau (năs′ô′). Cap. of the Bahamas, a port on New Providence. Pop. 135,000.
Na•tal (nə-tăl′, -täl′). City of NE Brazil on the Atlantic N of Recife. Pop. 376,446.
Na•u•ru (nä-o͞o′ro͞o). Atoll & republic of the central Pacific. Cap. Yaren. Pop. 8,000.
Na•varre (nə-vär′). Former kingdom of SW Europe extending from N Spain into France.
Naz•a•reth (năz′ə-rəth). Town of N Israel SE of Haifa. Pop. 46,300.
Ndja•me•na (ən-jä′mə-nə). Cap. of Chad on the Shari R. Pop. 303,000.
Near East. Region that includes nations of the E Mediterranean, the Arabian Peninsula, & sometimes NE Africa.
Ne•bras•ka (nə-brăs′kə). State of the central U.S. in the Great Plains. Cap. Lincoln. Pop. 1,584,617. —**Ne•bras′kan** *adj. & n.*
Ne•gev (nĕg′ĕv′) *or* **Ne•geb** (-eb′). Desert region of S Israel.
Nei Mong•gol (nā′ mŏn′gōl′, mŏng′-). INNER MONGOLIA.
Ne•me•a (nē′mē-ə). Ancient city of Greece W of Corinth. —**Ne′me•an** *adj. & n.*
Ne•pal (nə-pôl′, -päl′, -păl′). Kingdom of central Asia in the Himalayas between India & Tibet. Cap. Katmandu. Pop. 15,022,839. —**Nep′al•ese′** *adj. & n.*
Ness (nĕs), **Loch.** Lake of N central Scotland.
Neth•er•lands (nĕth′ər-ləndz). Kingdom of NW Europe on the North Sea. Constitutional cap. Amsterdam; de facto cap. The Hague. Pop. 14,394,600.
Netherlands An•til•les (ăn-tĭl′ēz). Autonomous territory of the Netherlands in the West Indies. Cap. Willemstad. Pop. 192,056.
Ne•tza•hual•có•yotl (nāt-sä′wäl-kō′yōt′l). City of S central Mexico. Pop. 1,341,230.
Ne•vad•a (nə-văd′ə, -vä′də). State of the W U.S. Cap. Carson City. Pop. 1,206,152. —**Ne•vad′an** *aj. & n.*
New•ark (no͞o′ərk, nyo͞o′-). City of NE NJ. Pop. 275,221.
New Bruns•wick (brŭnz′wĭk). Province of E Canada. Cap. Fredericton. Pop. 696,405.
New Cal•e•do•ni•a (kăl′ĭ-dō′nē-ə, -dōn′yə). French overseas territory in the SW Pacific. Cap. Nouméa. Pop. 145,368.
New•cas•tle (no͞o′kăs′əl, nyo͞o′-). **1.** City of SE Australia. Pop. 389,237. **2.** *or* **New•cas•tle-up•on-Tyne** (-ə-pŏn-tīn′). Borough of NE England on the Tyne R. Pop. 285,300.
New Del•hi (dĕl′ē). Cap. of India in the N central part. Pop. 273,036.
New Eng•land (ĭng′glənd). Section of the NE U.S. including ME, VT, NH, MA, CT, & RI.
New•found•land (no͞o′fən-lənd, -lănd′, -fənd-, nyo͞o′-). Province of E Canada. Cap. St. John's. Pop. 561,996. —**New′found•land•er** *n.*
New Guin•ea (gĭn′ē). Island in the SW Pacific N of Australia; divided between Indonesia & Papua New Guinea. —**New Guin′e•an** *adj. & n.*
New Hamp•shire (hămp′shər, -shîr′, hăm′-). State of the NE U.S. Cap. Concord. Pop. 1,113,915. —**New Hamp′shir•ite′** *n.*
New Ha•ven (hā′vən). City of S CT on Long Is. Sound. Pop. 130,474.
New Heb•ri•des (hĕb′rĭ-dēz′). Island group of the S Pacific E of Australia, forming the republic of Vanuatu.
New Jer•sey (jûr′zē). State of the E central U.S. on the Atlantic. Cap. Trenton. Pop. 7,748,634. —**New Jer′sey•ite′** *n.*
New Mex•i•co (mĕk′sĭ-kō′). State of the SW U.S. Cap. Santa Fe. Pop. 1,521,779. —**New Mex′i•can** *adj. & n.*
New Or•leans (ôr′lē-ənz, ôr′lənz, ôr-lēnz′). City of SE LA. Pop. 496,938.
Newport News. Independent city of SE VA. Pop. 170,045.
New Prov•i•dence (prŏv′ĭ-dəns). Island of the Bahamas in the West Indies.
New York (yôrk). **1.** State of the NE U.S. Cap. Albany. Pop. 18,044,505. **2.** *or* **New York City.** City of SE NY. Pop. 7,322,564.
New Zea•land (zē′lənd). Island country in the S Pacific SE of Australia. Cap. Wellington. Pop. 3,265,300. —**New Zea′land•er** *n.*
Ni•ag•a•ra (nī-ăg′rə, -ər-ə). River, flowing 34 mi (54.7 km) from Lake Erie to Lake Ontario.
Niagara Falls. Falls in the Niagara R. divided into the American Falls & the Canadian Falls.

Nia·mey (nē-ä′mä, nyä-mä′). Cap. of Niger in the SW on the Niger R. Pop. 399,100.
Nic·a·ra·gua (nĭk′ə-rä′gwə). **1.** Largest lake of Central America in SW Nicaragua. **2.** Republic of Central America. Cap. Managua. Pop. 2,823,979. **—Ni′ca·ra′guan** *adj. & n.*
Nice (nēs). City of SE France on the Mediterranean. Pop. 337,085.
Nic·o·bar Islands (nĭk′ə-bär′). Indian islands in the Bay of Bengal NW of Sumatra.
Nic·o·si·a (nĭk′ə-sē′ə). Cap. of Cyprus in the N central part. Pop. 48,221.
Ni·ger (nī′jər). **1.** River of W Africa flowing c. 2,600 mi (4,185 km) into the Gulf of Guinea. **2.** Republic of W central Africa. Cap. Niamey. Pop. 5,772,000.
Ni·ge·ri·a (nī-jîr′ē-ə). Republic of W Africa on the Gulf of Guinea. Cap. Lagos. Pop. 89,117,500. **—Ni·ge′ri·an** *adj. & n.*
Nile (nīl). Longest river in the world, flowing c. 4,160 mi (6,695 km) through E Africa to the Mediterranean in NE Egypt.
Nin·e·veh (nĭn′ə-və). Ancient cap. of the Assyrian Empire on the Tigris.
Nip·pon (nĭ-pŏn′). JAPAN.
Nor·folk (nôr′fək, -fôk). Independent city of SE VA. Pop. 261,229.
Nor·man·dy (nôr′mən-dē). Region & former province of NW France on the English Channel. **—Nor′man** *adj. & n.*
North America. N continent of the Western Hemisphere extending N from the Colombia-Panama border through Central America, the U.S., Canada, & the Arctic Archipelago to the N tip of Greenland. **—North American** *adj. & n.*
North Car·o·li·na (kăr′ə-lī′nə). State of the SE U.S. on the Atlantic. Cap. Raleigh. Pop. 6,657,630. **—North Car·o·lin′i·an** (-lĭn′ē-ən) *adj. & n.*
North Da·ko·ta (də-kō′tə). State of N central U.S. Cap. Bismarck. Pop. 641,364. **—North Da·ko′tan** *adj. & n.*
Northern Ireland. Component of the United Kingdom in the NE part of the island of Ireland. Cap. Belfast. Pop. 1,488,077.
North Korea. See KOREA.
North Sea. Arm of the Atlantic NW of central Europe & E of Great Britain.
Northwest Territories. Region of NW Canada including the Arctic Archipelago, the islands in Hudson Bay, & the mainland N of the Canadian provinces.
Nor·way (nôr′wā′). Kingdom of N Europe in the W part of the Scandinavian peninsula. Cap. Oslo. Pop. 4,122,707. **—Nor·we′gian** (nôr-wē′jən) *adj. & n.*
Not·ting·ham (nŏt′ĭng-əm). Borough of central England N of Leicester. Pop. 277,500.
Nouak·chott (nōō-äk′shŏt′). Cap. of Mauritania in the W part. Pop. 150,000.
Nou·mé·a (nōō-mā′ə). Cap. of New Caledonia on the island of New Caledonia. Pop. 60,112.
No·va Sco·tia (nō′və skō′shə). Province of E Canada. Cap. Halifax. Pop. 847,442. **—No′va Sco′tian** *adj. & n.*
No·vo·si·birsk (nō′vō-sə-bîrsk′). City of S central Russia on the Ob R. Pop. 1,393,000.
Nu·bi·a (nōō′bē-ə, nyōō′-). Desert region & ancient kingdom in the Nile valley of S Egypt & N Sudan. **—Nu′bi·an** *adj. & n.*
Nubian Desert. Desert of NE Sudan extending E of the Nile to the Red Sea.
Nue·vo La·re·do (nŏŏ-ā′vō lə-rā′dō). City of NE Mexico across the border from Laredo, TX. Pop. 184,662.
Nu·ku·a·lo·fa (nōō′kə-wə-lô′fə). Cap. of Tonga in the SW Pacific. Pop. 21,745.
Nu·rem·berg (nŏŏr′əm-bûrg′, nyŏŏr′-). City of SE Germany. Pop. 468,392.
Ny·as·a (nī-ăs′ə, nē-). Lake of SE Africa between Tanzania, Mozambique, & Malawi.

O

O·a·hu (ə-wä′hōō). Chief island of Hawaii between Molokai & Kauai.
Oak·land (ōk′lənd). City of W CA opposite San Francisco. Pop. 372,242.
Ob (ŏb, ôb). River, c. 2,300 mi (3,700 km), of W and central Russia.
O·ce·an·i·a (ō′shē-ăn′ē-ə , -ä′nē-ə). Collective name of islands in the S, W, & central Pacific, usu. including Australia & New Zealand. **—O′ce·an′i·an** *adj. & n.*
O·cean·side (ō′shən-sīd′). City of S CA NNW of San Diego. Pop. 128,398.
O·der (ō′dər). River of central Europe flowing c. 562 mi (904.3 km) from NE Czech Republic to the Baltic Sea.
O·des·sa (ō-dĕs′ə). City of S central Ukraine. Pop. 1,126,000.
O·hi·o (ō-hī′ō). **1.** River formed in W PA & flowing 981 mi (1,578.4 km) to the Mississippi in S IL. **2.** State of the N U.S. Cap. Columbus. Pop. 10,887,325. **—O·hi′o·an** *adj. & n.*
Oise (wäz). River, 186 mi (299.3 km), of S Belgium & N France.
O·ka·ya·ma (ō′kə-yä′mə). City of W Honshu, Japan. Pop. 572,423.
O·kee·cho·bee (ō′kə-chō′bē). Lake of SE FL N of the Everglades.
O·ke·fe·no·kee (ō′kə-fə-nō′kē). Large swamp of SE GA & N FL.
O·khotsk (ō-kŏtsk′), **Sea of.** NW arm of the Pacific W of the Kamchatka Peninsula.
O·ki·na·wa (ō′kĭ-nä′wə, -nou′-). **1.** Island group in the W Pacific SW of Japan. **2.** Largest island of the group.
O·kla·ho·ma (ō′klə-hō′mə). State of the SW U.S. Cap. Oklahoma City. Pop. 3,157,604. **—O′kla·ho′man** *adj. & n.*
Oklahoma City. Cap. of OK in the central part of the state. Pop. 444,719.
O·lym·pi·a (ō-lĭm′pē-ə, ə-lĭm′-). Cap. of WA on the S end of Puget Sound. Pop. 33,840.
O·lym·pus (ō-lĭm′pəs, ə-lĭm′-). Mountain range of N Greece, rising to 9,570 ft (2,920 m) at **Mount Olympus.**
O·ma·ha (ō′mə-hô′, -hä′). City of E NE on the Missouri R. Pop. 335,795.

O•man (ō-män′, ō-măn′). Sultanate of SE Arabian Peninsula. Cap. Muscat. Pop. 891,000. —**O•man′i** *adj. & n.*

Om•dur•man (ŏm′do͝or-män′). City of central Sudan. Pop. 526,287

Omsk (ômsk, ŏmsk). City of S central Russia. Pop. 1,108,000.

On•tar•i•o (ŏn-târ′ē-ō′). **1.** Smallest of the Great Lakes, between SE Ont., Canada, & NW NY. **2.** Province of E central Canada. Cap. Toronto. Pop. 8,625,107.

O•por•to (ō-pôr′tō, -pōr′-). City of NW Portugal. Pop. 327,368.

O•ran (ō-rän′). City of NW Algeria on the Mediterranean. Pop. 409,788.

Or•ange (ôr′ĭnj, ŏr′-). River, c. 1,300 mi (2,090 km), of Lesotho, South Africa, & Namibia.

Or•e•gon (ôr′ĭ-gən, -gŏn′, ŏr′-). State of the NW U.S. in the Pacific Northwest. Cap. Salem. Pop. 2,853,733. —**Or′e•go′ni•an** (-gō′nē-ən) *adj. & n.*

O•rel (ô-rĕl′, ō-rĕl′, ôr-yôl′). City of W Russia on the Oka R. Pop. 328,000.

O•ri•no•co (ôr′ə-nō′kō, ōr′-). River of Venezuela flowing c. 1,500 mi (2,415 km) to the Atlantic.

Ork•ney Islands (ôrk′nē) *also* **Ork•neys** (-nēz). Archipelago of c. 70 islands off the NE coast of Scotland.

Or•lan•do (ôr-lăn′dō). City of central FL ENE of Tampa. Pop. 164,693.

Or•muz (ôr′mŭz′, ôr-mo͞oz′). HORMUZ.

O•sa•ka (ō-sä′kə). City of S Honshu, Japan. Pop. 2,636,260.

Os•lo (ŏz′lō, ŏs′-). Cap. of Norway in the SE part. Pop. 448,747.

Ot•ta•wa (ŏt′ə-wə, -wä′, -wô′). Cap. of Canada in SE Ont. Pop. 295,163.

Ot•to•man Empire (ŏt′ə-mən). Turkish empire (1299–1919) in SW Asia, NE Africa, & SE Europe.

Oua•ga•dou•gou (wä′gə-do͞o′go͞o). Capital of Burkina Faso. Pop. 172,661.

O•zark Plateau (ō′zärk′) *also* **the O•zarks** (ō′zärks′). Upland region of S central U.S. extending from NW AR to E OK.

P

Pa•cif•ic (pə-sĭf′ĭk). Largest & deepest ocean, extending from the W Americas to E Asia & Australia.

Pacific Islands, Trust Territory of the. U.S.-administered islands of the W Pacific N & NE of New Guinea, including the Carolines, the Marianas (except Guam), & the Marshalls.

Pacific Northwest. Region of the NW U.S. usu. including WA & OR & sometimes SW B.C., Canada.

Pad•u•a (păj′o͞o-ə, păd′yo͞o-ə). City of NE Italy W of Venice. Pop. 231,337.

Pa•go Pa•go *also* **Pa•go•pa•go** *or* **Pan•go Pan•go** (päng′ō päng′ō, päng′gō päng′gō). Cap. of American Samoa on the S coast of Tutuila Is. Pop. 3,075.

Pak•i•stan (păk′ĭ-stăn′, pä′kĭ-stän′). Country of S Asia. Cap. Islamabad. Pop. 83,782,000. —**Pak′i•stan′i** *adj. & n.*

Pa•lau (pə-lou′) *or* **Pe•lew** (pə-lo͞o′). Islands within the Caroline group in the W Pacific.

Pa•lem•bang (pä′ləm-bäng′). City of SE Sumatra, Indonesia. Pop. 787,187.

Pa•ler•mo (pə-lûr′mō, -lâr′-). City of NW Sicily, Italy. Pop. 698,481.

Pal•es•tine (păl′ĭ-stīn′). Region of SW Asia between the E Mediterranean shore & the Jordan R. —**Pal′es•tin′i•an** (-stĭn′ē-ən) *adj. & n.*

Pal•ma (päl′mä) *also* **Pal•ma de Ma•llor•ca** (də mə-yôr′kə, məl-). City of SW Majorca Is., Spain. Pop. 311,197.

Pa•mirs (pə-mîrz′) *also* **Pa•mir** (-mîr′). Mountain region of S central Asia.

Pam•plo•na (păm-plō′nə). City of NE Spain near the Pyrenees. Pop. 181,688.

Pan•a•ma (păn′ə-mä′, -mô′). **1. Isthmus of.** Isthmus connecting North & South America & separating the Pacific from the Caribbean Sea. **2.** Ship canal across the Isthmus of Panama connecting the Caribbean Sea with the Pacific. **3.** Country of SW Central America. Cap. Panama. Pop. 1,795,012. **4.** *also* **Panama City.** Cap. of Panama in the central part. Pop. 398,172. —**Pan′a•ma′ni•an** (-mā′nē-ən) *adj. & n.*

Pan•go Pan•go (päng′ō päng′ō, päng′gō päng′gō). *var. of* PAGO PAGO.

Pap•u•a New Guin•ea (păp′yo͞o-ə no͞o′ gĭn′ē, nyo͞o′). Country of the W Pacific comprising the E half of New Guinea, the Bismarck Archipelago, the N Solomons, & adjacent islands. Cap. Port Moresby. Pop. 3,010,727. —**Pap′u•an New Guin′e•an** *n.*

Par•a•guay (păr′ə-gwī′, -gwā′). **1.** River, c. 1,300 mi. (2,092 km), of W Brazil & Paraguay. **2.** Country of S central South America. Cap. Asunción. Pop. 3,026,165. —**Par′a•guay′an** *adj. & n.*

Par•a•mar•i•bo (păr′ə-măr′ə-bō′). Cap. of Surinam. Pop. 102,297.

Pa•ra•ná (păr′ə-nä′). River, c. 2,040 mi. (3,282 km), of S central Brazil & E Argentina.

Par•is (păr′ĭs). Cap. of France in the N central part on the Seine. Pop. 2,149,900. —**Pa•ri′sian** (pə-rē′zhən, -rĭzh′ən) *adj. & n.*

Par•ma (pär′mə). City of N Italy SE of Milan. Pop. 176,750.

Par•nas•sus (pär-năs′əs) *also* **Par•nas•sós** (-nä-sōs′). Mountain, c. 8,060 ft (2,460 m), of central Greece N of the Gulf of Corinth.

Par•thi•a (pär′thē-ə). Ancient country of SW Asia. —**Par′thi•an** *adj. & n.*

Pas•a•de•na (păs′ə-dē′nə). **1.** City of S CA near Los Angeles. Pop. 131,591. **2.** City of S TX near Houston. Pop. 119,363.

Pat•er•son (păt′ər-sən). City of NE NJ N of Newark. Pop. 140,891.

Pat•na (pŭt′nə). City of NE India on the Ganges. Pop. 776,371.

Pá•trai (pä′trā) *also* **Pa•tras** (pə-trăs′, păt′rəs). City of S Greece. Pop. 111,607.

Peace (pēs). River, c. 945 mi (1,521 km), of N B.C. & N Alta., Canada.

Pearl Harbor. Inlet of the Pacific on S coast of Oahu, HI, W of Honolulu.
Pe•cos (pā'kəs). River of E NM & W TX flowing c. 926 mi (1,490 km) SE into the Rio Grande.
Pei•ping (pā'pĭng'). BEIJING.
Pe•king (pē'kĭng'). BEIJING.
Pel•o•pon•ne•sus *also* **Pel•o•pon•ne•sos** (pĕl'ə-pə-nē'səs) *or* **Pel•o•pon•nese** (pĕl'ə-pə-nēz', -nēs'). Peninsula forming the S part of Greece.—**Pel'o•pon•ne'sian** *adj. & n.*
Pen•nine Alps (pĕn'īn'). Range of the Alps along the Swiss-Italian border.
Penn•syl•va•nia (pĕn'səl-vān'yə , -vā'nē-ə). State of the E U.S. Cap. Harrisburg. Pop. 11,924,710. —**Penn'syl•va'nian** *adj. & n.*
Pe•or•i•a (pē-ôr'ē-ə, -ōr'-). City of central IL N of Springfield. Pop. 113,504.
Perm (pĕrm). City of W central Russia on the Kama R. Pop. 1,056,000.
Per•sia (pûr'zhə, -shə). IRAN. —**Per'sian** *adj. & n.*
Persian Gulf. Arm of the Arabian Sea between Arabia & SW Iran.
Perth (pûrth). City of SW Australia near the Indian Ocean. Metro. area pop. 809,035.
Pe•ru (pə-ro͞o'). Country of W South America on the Pacific. Cap. Lima. Pop. 17,031,221. —**Pe•ru'vi•an** (-vē-ən) *adj. & n.*
Phil•a•del•phi•a (fĭl'ə-dĕl'fē-ə). City of SE PA. Pop. 1,585,577. —**Phil'a•del'phi•an** *adj. & n.*
Phi•lip•pi (fə-lĭp'ī'). Ancient town of N central Macedonia, Greece.
Phil•ip•pines (fĭl'ə-pēnz'). Island country in the W Pacific SE of China. Cap. Manila. Pop. 48,098,460. —**Phil'ip•pine** *adj.*
Phnom Penh (pə-nôm' pĕn', nŏm' pĕn'). Cap. of Cambodia. Pop. 400,000.
Phoe•ni•cia (fĭ-nĭsh'ə, -ē-ə, -nē'shə, -shē-ə). Ancient maritime country along the E coast of the Mediterranean. —**Phoe•ni'cian** *adj. & n.*
Phoe•nix (fē'nĭks). Cap. of AZ in the S central part. Pop. 983,403.
Pied•mont (pēd'mŏnt'). **1.** Region of NW Italy. **2.** Plateau region of the E U.S. —**Pied'-mon•tese'** *adj. & n.*
Pierre (pîr). Cap. of SD in the central part. Pop. 12,906.
Pikes Peak (pīks). Mountain, 14,110 ft (4,303.6 m), in the Front Range of central CO.
Pi•rae•us (pī-rē'əs). Port city of E central Greece. Pop. 196,389.
Pi•sa (pē'zə, -sä). City of N central Italy. Pop. 91,156. —**Pi'san** *adj. & n.*
Pitts•burgh (pĭts'bûrg'). City of SW PA.
Pla•ta (plä'tə), **Río de la.** RÍO DE LA PLATA.
Platte (plăt). River, c. 310 mi (499 km), of S NE.
Plym•outh (plĭm'əth). **1.** Borough of SW England. Pop. 250,300. **2.** Town of SE MA SE of Boston. Pop. 45,608.
Po (pō). River of N Italy flowing c. 405 mi (652 km) E to the Adriatic.
Po•land (pō'lənd). Country of central Europe on the Baltic. Cap. Warsaw. Pop. 37,063,000. —**Po'lish** (pō'lĭsh) *adj. & n.*
Pol•y•ne•sia (pŏl'ə-nē'zhə, -shə). Scattered islands of the central & S Pacific. —**Pol'y•ne'sian** *adj. & n.*
Pom•er•a•ni•a (pŏm'ə-rā'nē-ə, -rān'yə). Historical region of N central Europe along the Baltic. —**Pom'er•a'ni•an** *adj. & n.*
Po•mo•na (pə-mō'nə). City of S CA near Los Angeles. Pop. 131,723.
Pom•pe•ii (pŏm-pā', -pā'ē). Ancient city of S Italy near Naples. —**Pom•pe'ian, Pom•pei'-ian** *adj. & n.*
Pon•ce (pôn'sā). City of S Puerto Rico on the Caribbean. Pop. 161,739.
Poo•na (po͞o'nə). City of W central India SE of Bombay. Pop. 1,203,351.
Port-au-Prince (pôrt'ō-prĭns', pōrt'-). Cap. of Haiti in the SW part. Pop. 684,284.
Port E•liz•a•beth (ĭ-lĭz'ə-bəth). City of SE South Africa. Pop. 281,600.
Port•land (pôrt'lənd, pōrt'-). **1.** City of SW ME on the Atlantic. Pop. 64,348. **2.** City of NW OR on the lower Columbia R. Pop. 437,319.
Port Lou•is (lo͞o'ĭs, lo͞o'ē, lo͞o-ē'). Cap. of Mauritius in the NW part. Pop. 136,812.
Port Mores•by (môrz'bē, mōrz'-). Cap. of Papua New Guinea. Pop. 123,624.
Pôr•to A•le•gre (pōr'to͞o ə-lĕ'grə). City of SE Brazil. Pop. 1,125,477.
Port of Spain (spān). Cap. of Trinidad and Tobago on the NW coast of Trinidad. Pop. 65,906.
Por•to-No•vo (pôr'tō-nō'vō, pōr'-). Cap. of Benin in the SE part. Pop. 123,000.
Port Sa•id (sä-ēd', sīd). City of NE Egypt. Pop. 374,000.
Por•tu•gal (pôr'chĭ-gəl, pōr'-). Country of SW Europe. Cap. Lisbon. Pop. 9,933,000. —**Por'-tu•gese'** (-gēz', -gēs') *adj. & n.*
Po•to•mac (pə-tō'mək). River of E U.S. rising in NE WV & flowing c. 285 mi (459 km) along the VA-MD border to Chesapeake Bay.
Pots•dam (pŏts'dăm'). City of NE Germany. Pop. 135,922.
Poz•nań (pōz'năn', -năn'yə, -nän', -nän'yə, pôz'-). City of W central Poland on the Warta R. Pop. 579,100.
Prague (präg). Cap. of Czech Republic in the W part on the Vltava R. Pop. 1,189,828.
Prai•a (prī'ə). Cap. of Cape Verde Is. on the SE coast of São Tiago Is. Pop. 37,480.
Pre•to•ri•a (prĭ-tôr'ē-ə, -tōr'-). Administrative cap. of South Africa. Pop. 435,100.
Prince Ed•ward Island (ĕd'wərd). Island & province of SE Canada. Cap. Charlottetown. Pop. 122,506.
Pro•vence (prō-väNs'). Region of SE France, on the Mediterranean. —**Pro'ven•çal'** (prō'-vən-säl') *adj. & n.*
Prov•i•dence (prŏv'ĭ-dəns, -dĕns'). Cap. of RI in the NE part. Pop. 160,728.
Pro•vo (prō'vō). City of N central UT SSE of Salt Lake City. Pop. 86,835.
Prus•sia (prŭsh'ə). Region & former state of N central Europe. —**Prus'sian** *adj. & n.*

Pueb•la (pōō-ĕb′lə, pwĕb′-). City of E central Mexico ESE of Mexico City. Pop. 835,759.

Puer•to Ri•co (pwĕr′tə rē′kō, pôrt′ə, pōrt′ə). Island of the West Indies E of Hispaniola; a self-governing commonwealth of the U.S. Cap. San Juan. Pop. 3,522,037. **—Puerto Ri′can** *adj. & n.*

Pu•get Sound (pyōō′jĭt). Inlet of the Pacific in NW WA.

Pun•jab (pŭn-jäb′, -jăb′, pŭn′jäb′, -jăb′). Region of NW India & NW Pakistan. **—Pun•ja′bi** *adj. & n.*

Pu•san (pōō′sän′). City of extreme SE South Korea. Pop. 3,517,000.

Pyong•yang (pē-ông′yäng′). Cap. of North Korea in the SW part. Pop. 1,283,000.

Pyr•e•nees (pîr′ə-nēz′). Mountain range along the French-Spanish border, rising to 11,168 ft (3,406.2 m). **—Pyr′e•ne′an** *adj.*

Q

Qa•tar (kä′tər). Country of E Arabia. Cap. Doha. Pop. 220,000.

Qing•dao (chĭng′dou′). City of E China on the Yellow Sea. Pop. 1,250,000.

Qi•qi•har (chē′chē′här′). City of NE China in Manchuria NW of Harbin. Pop. 995,200.

Que•bec (kwĭ-bĕk′) *or* **Qué•bec** (kā-). **1.** Province of E Canada. Cap. Quebec. Pop. 6,438,403. **2.** Cap. of Que., Canada, in the S part on the St. Lawrence R. Pop. 166,474. **—Que•beck′er, Que•bec′er** *n.*

Queens (kwēnz). Borough of New York City, SE NY, on W Long Is. Pop. 1,951,598.

Que•zon City (kā′sôn′, -sōn′). City of central Luzon, Philippines. Pop. 1,165,865.

Qui•to (kē′tō). Cap. of Ecuador in the N central part. Pop. 890,355.

R

Ra•bat (rə-bät′). Cap. of Morocco in the N part on the Atlantic. Pop. 518,616.

Ra•leigh (rô′lē, rä′-). Cap. of NC in the E central part. Pop. 207,951.

Ran•goon (răn-gōōn′, răng-). Cap. of Burma in the S central part. Pop. 2,458,712.

Rai•nier (rə-nîr′, rā-), **Mount.** Volcanic peak, 14,408 ft (4,394.4 m), of the Cascade Range in W central WA.

Ra•wal•pin•di (rä′wəl-pĭn′dē, roul-). City of NE Pakistan NNW of Lahore. Pop. 452,000.

Re•ci•fe (rə-sē′fə). City of NE Brazil on the Atlantic. Pop. 1,203,899.

Red (rĕd). **1.** Sea between NE Africa & Arabia. **2.** River of S central U.S. flowing 1,018 mi (1,638 km) along the TX-OK border & through AR & LA into the Mississippi.

Re•gi•na (rĭ-jī′nə). Cap. of Sask., Canada, in the S part. Pop. 162,613.

Reims *or* **Rheims** (rēmz, răNs). City of NE France ENE of Paris. Pop. 194,656.

Re•no (rē′nō′). City of W NV near the CA border. Pop. 133,850.

Ré•un•ion (rē-yōōn′yən). Island of France in the W Indian Ocean SW of Mauritius.

Rey•kja•vík (rā′kyə-vēk′, -vĭk′). Cap. of Iceland in the SW part. Pop. 88,745.

Rhine (rīn). River of W Europe rising in E Switzerland & flowing c. 820 mi (1,319 km) to the North Sea.

Rhode Island (rōd). State of the NE U.S. on the Atlantic. Cap. Providence. Pop. 1,005,984. **—Rhode Is′land•er** *n.*

Rhodes (rōdz). **1.** Island of SE Greece in the Aegean off SW Turkey.

Rho•de•sia (rō-dē′zhə). ZIMBABWE. **—Rho•de′sian** *adj. & n.*

Rhone *or* **Rhône** (rōn). River, c. 505 mi (812 km), of SW Switzerland & SE France.

Rich•mond (rĭch′mənd). **1.** Cap. of VA in the E central part. Pop. 203,056. **2.** Borough of New York City coextensive with Staten Is.

Ri•ga (rē′gə). Cap. of Latvia. Pop. 883,000.

Ri•o de Ja•nei•ro (rē′ō dā zhə-nâr′ō, dē). City of SE Brazil on Guanabara Bay. Pop. 5,090,700.

Rio Grande (grănd′, grăn′dē). River, c. 1,885 mi (3,033 km), of SW U.S., forming much of the U.S.-Mexican border.

Riv•er•side (rĭv′ər-sīd′). City of S CA NE of Santa Ana. Pop. 226,505.

Riv•i•er•a (rĭv′ē-ĕr′ə). Coastal resort area of SE France & NW Italy along the Mediterranean.

Ri•yadh (rē-äd′, -yäd′). Cap. of Saudi Arabia in the central part. Pop. 1,250,000.

Road Town (rōd). Cap. of the British Virgin Is. on Tortola Is. Pop. 2,479.

Ro•a•noke (rō′ə-nōk′). Island of NE NC, off the Atlantic coast between Albemarle & Pamlico sounds. Pop. 96,397.

Roch•es•ter (rŏch′ĭ-stər, -ĕs′tər). City of W NY ENE of Buffalo. Pop. 231,636.

Rock•ford (rŏk′fərd). City of N IL WNW of Chicago. Pop. 139,436.

Rock•y Mountains (rŏk′ē) *also* **Rockies** (rŏk′ēz). Mountain system of North America extending from N Mexico to NW AK.

Ro•ma•gna (rō-män′yə). Historical region of N central Italy.

Ro•ma•ni•a (rō-mā′nē-ə, -mān′yə) *or* **Ru•ma•ni•a** *also* **Rou•ma•ni•a** (rōō-). Country of SE Europe. Cap. Bucharest. Pop. 22,533,074. **—Ro•ma′ni•an** *adj. & n.*

Rome (rōm). Cap. of Italy in the W central part. Pop. 2,830,569.

Ro•sa•ri•o (rō-zär′ē-ō′, -sär′-). City of E central Argentina. Pop. 938,120.

Ro•seau (rō-zō′). Cap. of Dominica on the SW coast. Pop. 9,348.

Ros•tock (rŏs′tŏk′, rôs′tôk′). City of NE Germany near the Baltic. Pop. 241,116.

Ros•tov (rə-stôf′, -stôv′) *also* **Ros•tov-on-Don** (-ŏn-dôn′, -dŏn′). City of SW Russia on the Don near the Sea of Azov. Pop. 986,000.

Rot•ter•dam (rŏt′ər-dăm′) City of SW Netherlands. Pop. 555,341.

Ruhr (rŏŏr). River of NW Germany flowing 145 mi (233.3 km) W to the Rhine.

Ru•ma•ni•a (ro͞o-mā'nē-ə, -mān'yə) *var. of* ROMANIA.

Rush•more (rŭsh'môr', -mōr'). Mountain, 6,200 ft (1,891 m), in the Black Hills of W SD.

Rus•sia (rŭsh'ə). **1.** Former empire of E Europe & N Asia superseded by the USSR in 1917. **2.** Country of E Europe & W Asia. Cap. Moscow. Pop. 143,093,000. **3.** UNION OF SOVIET SOCIALIST REPUBLICS. **—Rus'sian** *adj. & n.*

Ru•the•nia (ro͞o-thēn'yə, -thē'nē-ə). Region of W Ukraine S of the Carpathians. **—Ru•the'ni•an** *adj. & n.*

Rwan•da *also* **Ru•an•da** (ro͞o-än'də). Country of E central Africa S of Uganda. Cap. Kigali. Pop. 5,109,000. **—Rwan'dan** *adj. & n.*

Ryu•kyu (rē-o͞o'ko͞o', -kyo͞o', -yo͞o'-). Islands of SW Japan.

S

Saar (sär, zär). **1.** River, c. 150 mi (241 km), of NE France & W Germany. **2.** SAARLAND.

Saar•land (sär'lănd', zär'-). Region of SW Germany in the Saar valley.

Sac•ra•men•to (săk'rə-mĕn'tō) Cap. of CA in the N central part. Pop. 369,365.

Sa•har•a (sə-hâr'ə, -här'ə). Vast desert of N Africa extending from the Atlantic to the Nile & from the Atlas Mts. S to the Sudan.

Sai•gon (sī-gŏn'). HO CHI MINH CITY.

Saint Chris•to•pher (krĭs'tə-fər). Island of the British West Indies; part of St. Christopher-Nevis.

Saint Chris•to•pher-Ne•vis (krĭs'tə-fər-nē'vĭs, -nĕv'ĭs) *also* **Saint Kitts and Ne•vis** (kĭts; nē'vĭs, nĕv'ĭs). Island country in the Leeward Is. Cap. Basseterre. Pop. 44,404.

Saint Croix (kroi). Largest of the U.S. Virgin Is. in the West Indies.

Saint-De•nis (săN-də-nē'). Cap. of Réunion on the Indian Ocean. Pop. 84,400.

Saint George's (jôr'jəz) *or* **Saint George** (jôrj). Cap. of Grenada in the West Indies. Pop. 7,500.

Saint He•le•na (hə-lē'nə). Island in the S Atlantic W of Angola, a British colony. Cap. Jamestown. Pop. 5,147.

Saint John (jŏn). One of the U.S. Virgin Is. in the West Indies.

Saint John's (jŏnz). **1.** Cap. of Antigua in the British West Indies. Pop. 24,359. **2.** Cap. of Newf., Canada. Pop. 83,770.

Saint Kitts and Nev•is (kĭts; nē'vĭs, nĕv'ĭs). SAINT CHRISTOPHER-NEVIS.

Saint Law•rence (lôr'əns, lŏr'-). River of SE Canada flowing 744 mi (1,197.1 km) NE from Lake Ontario to the **Gulf of St. Lawrence**, an arm of the NW Atlantic.

Saint Lou•is (lo͞o'ĭs). Independent city of E MO. Pop. 396,685.

Saint Lu•cia (lo͞o'shə, lo͞o-sē'ə). Island nation of the West Indies in the Windward Is. S of Martinique. Cap. Castries. Pop. 134,006.

Saint Mar•tin (mär'tn). Island of the West Indies in the W Leeward Is.; divided between France & the Netherlands.

Saint Paul (pôl). Cap. of MN in the SE adjacent to Minneapolis. Pop. 272,235.

Saint Pe•ters•burg (pē'tərz-bûrg'). **1.** City of NW Russia. Pop. 4,329,000. **2.** City of W central FL. Pop. 238,629.

Saint Pi•erre *or* **Saint-Pi•erre** (sānt' pîr', pē-âr', săN pyĕr'). **1.** Island of the St. Pierre and Miquelon group in the N Atlantic S of Newf., Canada. **2.** Cap. of St. Pierre and Miquelon on St. Pierre Is. Pop. 5,371.

Saint Pierre and Mi•que•lon (mĭk'ə-lŏn', mē-klôN'). French island group in the N Atlantic S of Newf., Canada. Cap. St. Pierre. Pop. 6,041.

Saint Tho•mas (tŏm'əs). Island of the U.S. Virgin Is. in the West Indies.

Saint Vin•cent and the Gren•a•dines (vĭn'sənt; grĕn'ə-dēnz'). Island nation in the central Windward Is. of the West Indies, comprising St. Vincent Is. & the N Grenadines. Cap. Kingstown. Pop. 108,704.

Sai•pan (sī-păn', -pän', sī'păn). Island of the W Pacific in the S Marianas, part of the U.S. Trust Territory of the Pacific Islands. **—Sai'pa•nese'** (-nēz', -nēs') *adj. & n.*

Sa•kai (sä'kī'). City of S Honshu, Japan, on Osaka Bay. Pop. 818,368.

Sa•kha•lin (săk'ə-lēn', -lən, săk'ə-lēn'). Island of SE Russia in the Sea of Okhotsk.

Sa•lem (sā'ləm). **1.** City of SE India SW of Madras. Pop. 308,716. **2.** Cap. of OR in the NW part. Pop. 107,786. **3.** City of NE MA NE of Boston. Pop. 38,091.

Sa•ler•no (sə-lûr'nō, -lĕr'-). City of S Italy on the Tyrrhenian Sea. Pop. 157,243.

Sa•li•nas (sə-lē'nəs). City of W CA S of San Francisco. Pop. 108,777.

Sa•lo•ni•ka (sə-lŏn'ĭ-kə, săl'ə-nē'kə). City of NE Greece. Pop. 406,413.

Salt Lake City. Cap. of UT in the N part near Great Salt Lake. Pop. 159,936.

Sal•va•dor (săl'və-dôr'). **1.** EL SALVADOR. **2.** (*also* săl'və-dôr'). City of E Brazil on the Atlantic. Pop. 1,501,981.

Sal•ween (săl'wēn'). River, c. 1,750 mi (2,816 km), of S central China and E Burma.

Salz•burg (sôlz'bûrg', sälz'-, sălz'-). City of W central Austria. Pop. 139,426.

Sa•mar•i•a (sə-măr'ē-ə, -mâr'-). **1.** Region and city of ancient Palestine in present-day NW Jordan. **2.** Ancient N kingdom of Israel. **—Sa•mar'i•tan** (-ĭ-tən) *adj. & n.*

Sam•ar•kand (săm'ər-kănd'). City of S Uzbekistan SW of Tashkent. Pop. 371,000.

Sa•mo•a (sə-mō'ə). Island group of the S Pacific ENE of Fiji; divided between **American Samoa & Western Samoa. —Sa•mo'an** *adj. & n.*

San•a *or* **Sa•n'a** *also* **Sa•naa** (să-nä', săn'ä). Cap. of Yemen. Pop. 277,800.

San An•to•ni•o (săn ăn-tō'nē-ō'). **1.** River, c. 200 mi (322 km), of S TX. **2.** City of S central TX. Pop. 935,933.

San Di•e•go (dē-ā'gō). City of S CA on the Pacific. Pop. 1,110,549.

San Fran•cis•co (frən-sĭs'kō). City of W CA

on a peninsula between the Pacific & **San Francisco Bay.** Pop. 723,959. —**San Fran·cis'can** (-kən) *n.*

San Jo·se (ə-zā', ō-, hō-). City of W CA SE of San Francisco. Pop. 782,248.

San Jo·sé (ə-zā', ō-, hō-). Cap. of Costa Rica in the central part. Pop. 277,800.

San Juan (wän', hwän'). **1.** City of NW Argentina W of Córdoba. Pop. 310,000. **2.** Cap. of Puerto Rico in the NE part. Pop. 424,600.

San Lu·is Po·to·sí (lo͞o-ēs' pō'tə-sē'). City of central Mexico NE of León. Pop. 362,371.

San Ma·ri·no (mə-rē'nō). **1.** Republic within N central Italy in the Apennines near the Adriatic. Cap. San Marino. Pop. 21,537. **2.** Cap. of San Marino. Pop. 4,628.

San Sal·va·dor (săl'və-dôr'). Cap. of El Salvador in the W central part. Pop. 445,100.

San·ta An·a (săn'tə ăn'ə). City of S CA. Pop. 293,742.

Santa Cat·a·li·na (kăt'l-ē'nə). Island of S CA in the S Santa Barbara Is.

Santa Cruz (kro͞oz). **1.** Islands of the W Pacific in the SE Solomon Is. **2.** Island of S CA in the N Santa Barbara Is. **3.** City of central Bolivia NE of Sucre. Pop. 441,717.

Santa Fe (fā'). Cap. of NM in the N central part. Pop. 55,859.

Santa Ro·sa (rō'zə). **1.** Island of S CA in the NW Santa Barbara Is. **2.** City of W CA N of San Francisco. Pop. 113,313.

San·ti·a·go (săn'tē-ä'gō, sän'-). **1.** Cap. of Chile in the central part. Metro. area pop. 425,924. **2.** *also* **Santiago de los Ca·ba·lle·ros** (dā' lôs kä'bə-lĕr'ōz, -bəl-yĕr'-). City of N Dominican Republic. Pop. 278,638. **3.** *also* **Santiago de Com·pos·te·la** (də kŏm'pə-stĕl'ə). City of NW Spain. Pop. 62,300.

Santiago de Cu·ba (də kyo͞o'bə). City of SE Cuba on the Caribbean. Pop. 349,444.

San·to Do·min·go (săn'tō də-mĭng'gō). Cap. of the Dominican Republic in the S part on the Caribbean. Pop. 1,313,712.

San·tos (săn'təs). City of SE Brazil on an offshore island. Pop. 410,933.

São Pau·lo (souɴ pou'lo͞o, -lō). City of SE Brazil SW of Rio de Janeiro. Pop. 8,493,226.

São To·mé (tə-mā'). **1.** Island forming part of the republic of São Tomé and Principe. **2.** Cap. of São Tomé and Principe on the SE coast of São Tomé Is. Pop. 17,380.

São Tomé and Prin·ci·pe (prēɴ'sē-pə). Island republic on the equator off the coast of W Africa. Cap. São Tomé. Pop. 73,631.

Sap·po·ro (sə-pôr'ō, -pōr'-). City of SW Hokkaido, Japan. Pop. 1,542,979.

Sar·a·gos·sa (săr'ə-gŏs'ə). City of NE Spain, on the Ebro R. Pop. 601,235.

Sa·ra·je·vo (săr'ə-yĕ-vō', sâr'ə-yā'-). Cap. of Bosnia-Herzegovina. Pop. 374,500.

Sa·ra·tov (sə-rä'təf). City of SW Russia on the Volga R. Pop. 899,000.

Sa·ra·wak (sə-rä'wäk, -wăk'). Region & state of Malaysia on NW Borneo.

Sar·din·i·a (sär-dĭn'ē-ə, -dĭn'yə). Island of Italy in the Mediterranean S of Corsica. —**Sar·din'i·an** *adj. & n.*

Sas·katch·e·wan (sə-skăch'ə-wən, -wän', săs-kăch'-). Province of S central Canada. Cap. Regina. Pop. 968,313.

Sa·u·di A·ra·bi·a (sou'dē ə-rā'bē-ə, sä-o͞o'-dē). Kingdom comprising most of the Arabian peninsula. Cap. Riyadh. Pop. 9,320,000. —**Sa·u'di, Sa·u'di A·ra'bi·an** *adj. & n.*

Sa·van·nah (sə-văn'ə). City of E GA on the Atlantic coast. Pop. 137,560.

Sa·voy (sə-voi'). Region & former duchy of SE France. —**Sa·voy'ard** (sə-voi'ärd', săv'oi-yärd') *adj. & n.*

Sax·on·y (săk'sə-nē). Former region & duchy of NW Germany. —**Sax'on** *adj. & n.*

Scan·di·na·vi·a (skăn'də-nā'vē-ə, -nāv'-yə). **1.** Peninsula of N Europe occupied by Norway & Sweden. **2.** Norway, Sweden, & Denmark, & sometimes also Iceland, Finland, & the Faeroe Is. —**Scan'di·na'vi·an** *adj. & n.*

Schles·wig (shlĕs'wĭg, -wĭk, slĕs'-). Region & former duchy of N Germany & S Denmark in S Jutland.

Scot·land (skŏt'lənd). Constituent country of the United Kingdom of Great Britain & Northern Ireland, in N Great Britain. Cap. Edinburgh. Pop. 5,149,500. —**Scots** (skŏts) *adj.* —**Scot'tish** (skŏt'ĭsh) *adj. & n.*

Scotts·dale (skŏts'dāl'). City of S central AZ near Phoenix. Pop. 130,069.

Scyth·i·a (sĭth'ē-ə, sĭ*th*-). Ancient region of SE Europe & SW Asia between the Danube & the Aral Sea. —**Scyth'i·an** *adj. & n.*

Se·at·tle (sē-ăt'l). City of W central WA on Puget Sound. Pop. 516,259.

Seine (sān, sĕn). River of N France flowing c. 480 mi (772 km) into the English Channel.

Se·ma·rang (sə-mär'äng). City of N Java, Indonesia, on the Java Sea. Pop. 1,026,671.

Sen·dai (sĕn-dī'). City of NE Honshu, Japan, on the Pacific. Pop. 700,248.

Sen·e·gal (sĕn'ĭ-gôl'). Country of W Africa. Cap. Dakar. Pop. 6,038,000. —**Sen'e·ga·lese'** (-gô'lēz', -lēs', -gə-) *adj. & n.*

Seoul (sōl). Cap. of South Korea in the NW part. Pop. 9,646,000.

Ser·bi·a (sûr'bē-ə). Region of the central Balkan Peninsula, part of the republic of Yugoslavia. Cap. Belgrade. Pop. 11,596,572. —**Ser'·bi·an** *adj. & n.*

Se·vas·to·pol (sə-văs'tə-pōl') *also* **Se·bas·to·pol** (-băs'-). City of S Ukraine in the Crimea on the Black Sea. Pop. 341,000.

Se·ville (sə-vĭl'). City of SW Spain on the Guadalquivir R. Pop. 672,435.

Sey·chelles (sā-shĕl', -shĕlz'). Island nation in the W Indian Ocean N of Madagascar. Cap. Victoria. Pop. 64,718.

Shan·dong (shän'do͝ong') *also* **Shan·tung** (shăn'tŭng'). Province of E China.

Shang·hai (shăng-hī'). City of E China Metro. area pop. 12,170,000.

Shas·ta (shăs'tə), **Mount.** Volcanic peak, 14,162 ft (4,319.4 m), of the Cascade Range in N CA.

Shef·field (shĕf'ēld'). Borough of N central England E of Manchester. Pop. 547,600.

Shen·an·do·ah (shĕn'ən-dō'ə). River, c. 150 mi (241 km), of N VA & NE WV.
Shen·yang (shŭn'yăng'). City of NE China ENE of Beijing. Pop. 3,250,000.
Shet·land (shĕt'lənd) *also* **Shet·lands** (-ləndz). Islands of N Scotland in the Atlantic NE of the Orkney Is.
Shi·jia·zhuang (shîr'jē-ä'jə-wäng'). City of NE China SW of Beijing. Pop. 1,127,800.
Shi·ko·ku (shĭ-kō'kōō). Island of S Japan between SW Honshu & E Kyushu.
Shi·raz (shē-räz'). City of SW Iran SSE of Esfahan. Pop. 800,000.
Shreve·port (shrēv'pôrt', -pōrt'). City of NW LA near the TX border. Pop. 198,525.
Si·am (sī-ăm'). THAILAND. —**Si'a·mese'** (sī'ə-mēz', -mēs') *adj. & n.*
Si·an (shē'än'). XI'AN.
Si·be·ri·a (sī-bîr'ē-ə). Region of central & E Russia from the Urals to the Pacific. —**Si·be'ri·an** *adj. & n.*
Si·chuan (sēch'wän'). Province of S central China.
Si·ci·ly (sĭs'ə-lē). Island of S Italy in the Mediterranean. —**Si·cil'ian** (sĭ-sĭl'yən) *adj. & n.*
Si·en·a (sē-ĕn'ə). City of central Italy. Pop. 61,888. —**Si'e·nese'** (-nēz', -nēs') *adj. & n.*
Si·er·ra Le·one (sē-ĕr'ə lē-ōn'). Country of W Africa. Cap. Freetown. Pop. 3,381,000.
Sierra Ma·dre (mä'drā). Mountain system of Mexico extending from SW to NE.
Sierra Ne·va·da (nə-văd'ə, -vä'də). **1.** Range of S Spain along the Mediterranean coast. **2.** Range of E CA rising to 14,494 ft (4,420.7 m).
Sik·kim (sĭk'ĭm). State & former semi-independent protectorate of NE India.
Si·le·sia (sī-lē'zhə, -zhē-ə, -shə, -shē-ə, sə-). Region of central Europe in SW Poland & N Czech Republic. —**Si·le'sian** *adj. & n.*
Si·nai (sī'nī'). **1. Mount.** Mountain, c. 7,500 ft (2,288 m), of NE Egypt on S Sinai Peninsula. **2.** Peninsula of NE Egypt.
Sin·ga·pore (sĭng'gə-pôr', -pōr', sĭng'ə-). **1.** Island off the S end of Malay Peninsula. **2.** Country of SE Asia comprising Singapore Is. & adjacent smaller islands. Cap. Singapore. Pop. 2,259,100. **3.** Cap. of Singapore.—**Sin'ga·por'e·an** *adj. & n.*
Sjael·land (shĕl'än'). Largest island of Denmark in the E part.
Skop·lje (skôp'lā', -yä') or **Skop·je** (-yä'). Cap. of Macedonia. Pop. 406,400.
Skye (skī). Island of NW Scotland in the Inner Hebrides.
Sla·vo·ni·a (slə-vō'nē-ə, -vōn'yə). Historical region of N Croatia. —**Sla·vo'ni·an** *adj. & n.*
Slo·vak·i·a (slō-vä'kē-ə, -văk'ē-ə). Country of central Europe. Cap. Bratislava. Pop. 4,991,168. —**Slo·vak'i·an** *adj. & n.*
Slo·ve·ni·a (slō-vē'nē-ə, -vēn'yə). Region & republic of the NW Balkan Peninsula. Cap. Ljubljana. Pop. 1,697,068. —**Slo'vene', Slo·ve'ni·an** *adj. & n.*
Smo·lensk (smō-lĕnsk'). City of W Russia. Pop. 331,000.
Smyr·na (smûr'nə). IZMIR.
Snake (snāk). River of NW U.S. rising in NW WY & flowing 1,038 mi (1,670 km) into the Columbia.
So·ci·e·ty (sə-sī'ĭ-tē). Islands of French Polynesia in the S Pacific E of Samoa.
So·fi·a (sō'fē-ə, sō-fē'ə). Cap. of Bulgaria in the W central part. Pop. 1,102,100.
Sol·o·mon Islands (sŏl'ə-mən) *also* **Sol·o·mons** (-mənz). **1.** Islands of the W Pacific E of New Guinea, divided between Papua New Guinea & the independent Solomon Is. **2.** Nation comprising the Solomons. Cap. Honiara. Pop. 212,868.
So·ma·li·a (sō-mä'lē-ə, -mäl'yə). Country of extreme E Africa. Cap. Mogadishu. Pop. 3,645,000. —**So·ma'li·an** *adj. & n.*
So·ma·li·land (sō-mä'lē-lănd', sə-). Region of E Africa including Somalia, Djibouti, & parts of E Ethiopia.
Somme (sŏm, sŭm). River, c. 150 mi (241 km), of N France.
Song·hua (sōōng'hwä'). River of Manchuria, NE China, flowing c. 1,150 mi (1,850 km) to the Amur.
Soo·chow (sōō'jō', -chou'). SUZHOU.
South Africa. Republic of S Africa. Caps. Pretoria & Cape Town. Pop. 24,208,140. —**South African** *adj. & n.*
South America. Continent of the S Western Hemisphere SE of North America between the Atlantic & the Pacific. —**South American** *adj. & n.*
South Bend. City of N IN near the MI border. Pop. 105,511.
South Car·o·li·na (kăr'ə-lī'nə). State of the SE U.S. Cap. Columbia. Pop. 3,505,707. —**South Car'o·lin'i·an** (-lĭn'ē-ən) *adj. & n.*
South China Sea. Arm of the W Pacific bounded by SE China, Taiwan, the Philippines, Borneo, & Vietnam.
South Da·ko·ta (də-kō'tə). State of the N central U.S. Cap. Pierre. Pop. 699,999. —**South Da·ko'tan** *adj. & n.*
South Korea. See KOREA.
South Seas. 1. All seas S of the equator. **2.** The S Pacific.
So·vi·et Union (sō'vē-ĕt', -ĭt, sŏv'ē-). UNION OF SOVIET SOCIALIST REPUBLICS.
So·we·to (sə-wē'tō). City of NE South Africa near Johannesburg. Pop. 868,550.
Spain (spān). Country of SW Europe including most of the Iberian Peninsula & the Balearic & Canary Is. Cap. Madrid. Pop. 38,872,389. —**Span'iard** (spăn'yərd) *n.* —**Span'ish** (spăn'ĭsh) *adj. & n.*
Spar·ta (spär'tə). City-state of ancient Greece in the SE Peloponnesus. —**Spar'tan** *adj. & n.*
Spice Islands (spīs). MOLUCCAS.
Split (splĭt). City of SW Croatia on the Dalmatian coast of the Adriatic. Pop. 193,600.
Spo·kane (spō-kăn'). City of E WA near the ID border. Pop. 177,196.
Spor·a·des (spôr'ə-dēz', spŏr'-). All the islands of Greece in the Aegean excepting the Cyclades.
Spring·field (sprĭng'fēld'). **1.** Cap. of IL in the central part. Pop. 105,227. **2.** City of SW MA on the Connecticut R. Pop. 156,983. **3.**

City of SW MO SE of Kansas City. Pop. 140,494.
Sri Lan•ka (srē läng'kə). Island nation in the Indian Ocean off SE India. Cap. Colombo. Pop. 14,848,364. —**Sri Lan'kan** *adj. & n.*
Sta•lin•grad (stä'lĭn-grăd', stăl'ĭn-). VOLGOGRAD.
Stam•ford (stăm'fərd). City of SW CT on Long Is. Sound. Pop. 108,056.
Stat•en (stăt'n). Island in New York Bay, SE NY, SW of Manhattan.
Stock•holm (stŏk'hōlm', -hōm'). Cap. of Sweden in the E part. Pop. 653,455.
Stock•ton (stŏk'tən). City of central CA. Pop. 210,943.
Stoke-on-Trent (stōk'ŏn-trĕnt', -ôn-). Borough of W central England. Pop. 250,700.
Stras•bourg (sträs'bŏŏrg', sträz'-). City of NE France near the Rhine R. Pop. 248,712.
Strat•ford-up•on-Av•on (străt'fərd-ə-pŏn-ā'vən). Borough of central England SSE of Birmingham. Pop. 20,941.
Stutt•gart (shtŏŏt'gärt', stŭt'-). City of SW Germany on the Neckar R. Pop. 561,567.
Sü•chow (sōō'jō', -chou', shōō'-). XUZHOU.
Su•cre (sōō'krā). Constitutional cap. of Bolivia in the central part. Pop. 86,609.
Su•dan (sōō-dăn'). Country of NE Africa S of Egypt. Cap. Khartoum. Pop. 20,569,364. —**Su'da•nese'** *adj. & n.*
Su•de•ten•land (sōō-dāt'n-lănd', -länt'). Region of N Czech Republic along the Polish border.
Su•ez (sōō-ĕz', sōō'ĕz'). **1. Gulf of.** N arm of the Red Sea off NE Egypt W of the Sinai Peninsula. **2.** Isthmus of NE Egypt connecting Africa & Asia & traversed by the **Suez Canal** (107 mi/172 km) from the Mediterranean to the Gulf of Suez. **3.** City of NE Egypt at the head of the Gulf of Suez. Pop. 254,000.
Su•la•we•si (sōō'lə-wā'sē). Island of central Indonesia on the equator E of Borneo.
Su•ma•tra (sōō-mä'trə). Island of W Indonesia in the Indian Ocean W of Borneo & the Malay Peninsula. —**Su•ma'tran** *adj. & n.*
Su•mer (sōō'mər). Ancient country of Mesopotamia in present-day S Iraq. —**Su•me'ri•an** *adj. & n.*
Sun•da (sŭn'də, sōōn'-) *also* **Sun•das** (-dəz). Islands of the W Malay Archipelago, comprising the **Greater Sundas** (Sumatra, Borneo, Java, & Sulawesi) & the **Lesser Sundas** (from Bali E to Timor).
Su•pe•ri•or (sōō-pîr'ē-ər). Largest & westernmost of the Great Lakes between the U.S. & Ont., Canada.
Su•ra•ba•ya *or* **Su•ra•ba•ja** (sŏŏr'ə-bī'ə). City of NE Java, Indonesia. Pop. 2,027,913.
Su•ri•nam (sŏŏr'ə-năm') *also* **Su•ri•na•me** (sü'rē-nä'mə). Country of NE South America on the Atlantic. Cap. Paramaribo. Pop. 354,860. —**Su'ri•nam•ese'** *adj. & n.*
Sus•que•han•na (sŭs'kwə-hăn'ə). River of the NE U.S. rising in central NY & flowing 444 mi (715 km) S to Chesapeake Bay.
Su•va (sōō'və). Cap. of Fiji on the SE coast of Viti Levu. Pop. 74,000.
Su•zhou (sōō'jō'). City of E China WNW of Shanghai. Pop. 695,500.
Sverd•lovsk (sfĕrd-lôfsk'). City of W central Russia. Pop. 1,300,000.
Swa•bi•a (swā'bē-ə). Region of SW Germany. —**Swa'bi•an** *adj. & n.*
Swa•zi•land (swä'zē-lănd'). Country of SE Africa. Cap. Mbabane. Pop. 585,000.
Swe•den (swēd'n). Country of N Europe on the E Scandinavian peninsula. Cap. Stockholm. Pop. 8,342,621. —**Swede** *n.* —**Swed'ish** *adj. & n.*
Swit•zer•land (swĭt'sər-lənd). Republic of W central Europe. Cap. Bern. Pop. 6,455,900. —**Swiss** (swĭs) *adj. & n.*
Syd•ney (sĭd'nē). City of SE Australia on an inlet of the Tasman Sea. Metro. area pop. 3,358,550.
Syr•a•cuse (sîr'ə-kyōōs', -kyōōz'). City of central NY. Pop. 163,860.
Sy•ri•a (sîr'ē-ə). Country of SW Asia on the E Mediterranean coast. Cap. Damascus. Pop. 9,052,628. —**Syr'i•an** *adj. & n.*
Szcze•cin (shchĕt'sēn'). City of NW Poland. Pop. 390,800.
Sze•chwan (sĕch'wän'). SICHUAN.

T

Ta•briz (tə-brēz'). City of NW Iran in Azerbaijan E of Lake Urmia. Pop. 852,000.
Ta•co•ma (tə-kō'mə). City of W central WA. Pop. 176,664.
Ta•dzhik•i•stan (tä-jĭk'ĭ-stăn', -stän', -jēk'-). Country of W central Asia bordering on Afghanistan & China. Cap. Dushanbe. Pop. 4,499,000.
Tae•gu (tă-gōō', tī-). City of SE South Korea NNW of Pusan. Pop. 1,607,458.
Tae•jon (tă-jôn', -jŏn', tī-). City of SW South Korea SSE of Seoul. Pop. 651,642.
Ta•hi•ti (tə-hē'tē). Island of the South Pacific in the Windward group of the Society Is., French Polynesia. —**Ta•hi'tian** *adj. & n.*
Ta•hoe (tä'hō). Lake on the CA-NV border W of Carson City, NV.
Tai•pei *also* **Tai•peh** (tī'pā', -bā'). Cap. of Taiwan in the N part. Pop. 2,327,621.
Tai•wan (tī'wän'). Island off the SE coast of China, constituting the Republic of China. Cap. Taipei. Pop. 18,457,923. —**Tai'wan•ese'** *adj. & n.*
Tai•yu•an *also* **Tai•yü•an** (tī'yōō-än'). City of NE China SW of Beijing. Pop. 1,390,000.
Tal•la•has•see (tăl'ə-hăs'ē). Cap. of FL in the Panhandle. Pop. 124,773.
Tal•linn *also* **Tal•lin** (tăl'ĭn, tä'lĭn). Cap. of Estonia in the NW part. Pop. 464,000.
Tam•pa (tăm'pə). City of W central FL on the Gulf of Mexico. Pop. 280,015.
Ta•nan•a•rive (tə-năn'ə-rēv'). ANTANANARIVO.
Tan•gan•yi•ka (tăn'gən-yē'kə, tăng'-), **Lake.** Lake of E central Africa between Zaire & Tanzania.

Tan•gier (tăn-jîr′) *also* **Tan•giers** (-jîrz′). City of N Morocco. Pop. 266,346.
Tang•shan (dăng′shăn′, tăng′-). City of NE China ESE of Beijing. Pop. 921,100.
Tan•za•ni•a (tăn′zə-nē′ə). Country of E central Africa. Cap. Dar es Salaam. Pop. 17,557,000. —**Tan•za′ni•an** *adj. & n.*
Ta•ran•to (tär′ən-tō′, tə-rän′tō). City of SE Italy. Pop. 242,774.
Tash•kent (tăsh-kĕnt′, -kĕnd′). City of E Uzbekistan. Pop. 2,030,000.
Tas•man (tăz′mən). Sea of the S Pacific between Australia & New Zealand.
Tas•ma•ni•a (tăz-mā′nē-ə, -mān′yə). Island state of SE Australia. —**Tas•ma′ni•an** *adj. & n.*
Tbi•li•si (tə-bĭl′ĭ-sē). Cap. of Georgia in the SE part. Pop. 1,158,000.
Te•gu•ci•gal•pa (tə-gōō′sə-găl′pə). Cap. of Honduras in the S central part. Pop. 532,500.
Te•he•ran *or* **Teh•ran** (tā′ə-răn′, -rän′). Cap. of Iran. Pop. 5,734,199.
Tel A•viv-Jaf•fa (tĕl′ə-vēv′jăf′ə, -yăf′ə). City of Israel in the central part on the Mediterranean. Pop. 323,400.
Tem•pe (tĕm′pē′). City of S central AZ near Phoenix. Pop. 141,865.
Ten•nes•see (tĕn′ĭ-sē′, tĕn′ĭ-sē′). State of the SE U.S. Cap. Nashville. Pop. 4,896,641. —**Ten′nes•se′an** *adj. & n.*
Te•noch•ti•tlán (tā-nôch′tē-tlän′). Ancient Aztec cap. on the site of present-day Mexico City.
Te•ton (tē′tŏn′, tēt′n) *also* **Te•tons** (tē′tŏnz, tēt′nz). Range of the Rockies in NW WY & SE ID, rising to 13,747 ft (4,192.8 m).
Tex•as (tĕk′səs). State of the S central U.S. Cap. Austin. Pop. 17,059,805. —**Tex′an** *adj. & n.*
Thai•land (tī′lănd′, -lənd). Country of SE Asia between Burma & Cambodia. Cap. Bangkok. Pop. 49,515,074. —**Thai** *adj. & n.*
Thames (tĕmz). River of S England flowing c. 210 mi (338 km) E to the North Sea.
Thebes (thēbz). **1.** *also* **The•bae** (thē′bē). Ancient cap. of Upper Egypt on the Nile in present-day central Egypt. **2.** Ancient city in E central Greece NW of Athens.
Thes•sa•lo•ni•ki (thĕs′ə-lə-nē′kē) *or* **Thes•sa•lo•ni•ca** (-nī′kə, -lŏn′ĭ-kə). SALONIKA.
Thes•sa•ly (thĕs′ə-lē). Region of E central Greece.—**Thes•sa′lian, Thes′sa•lo′ni•an** *adj. & n.*
Thim•bu (thĭm′bōō′) *also* **Thim•phu** (-pōō′). Cap. of Bhutan. Pop. 8,982.
Tho•hoy•an•dou (tō-hoi′ăn-dōō′). Cap. of Venda, black enclave in NE South Africa.
Thou•sand Islands (thou′zənd). Group of more than 1,500 islands of N NY & SE Ont., Canada, in the St. Lawrence.
Thrace (thrās). Ancient country of the SE Balkan Peninsula. —**Thra′cian** *adj. & n.*
Tian•jin (tē-än′jĭn′) *also* **Tien•tsin** (tē-ĕn′sĭn′, -ĕnt′-). City of NE China. Pop. 5,380,000.
Tian Shan (tē-än′ shän′). Mountains of central Asia extending ENE through W Kirghiz, extreme SW Kazakhstan, & NW China.
Ti•ber (tī′bər). River of central Italy flowing c. 251 mi (404 km) S & SW through Rome to the Tyrrhenian Sea.
Ti•bet (tə-bĕt′). Region & former semi-independent theocratic state of SW China. —**Ti•bet′an** *adj. & n.*
Ti•er•ra del Fue•go (tē-ĕr′ə dĕl fōō-ā′gō, fyōō-). **1.** Archipelago off S South America. **2.** Main island of this archipelago divided between Chile & Argentina.
Ti•gris (tī′grĭs). River of SW Asia flowing c. 1,150 mi (1,850 km) SE through Iraq to the Euphrates R.
Ti•jua•na (tē′ə-wä′nə, tē-wä′-). City of NW Mexico on the U.S. border. Pop. 363,154.
Tim•buk•tu *also* **Tim•buc•too** (tĭm′bŭk-tōō′, tĭm-bŭk′tōō). City of central Mali near the Niger R. Pop. 19,166.
Ti•mi•şoa•ra (tē′mēsh-wär′ə). City of W Romania. Pop. 303,499.
Ti•mor (tē′môr, tē-môr′). Island of SE Indonesia, in the Lesser Sundas.
Ti•ra•në *also* **Ti•ra•na** (tə-rä′nə). Cap. of Albania in the central part. Pop. 206,100.
Ti•rol (tə-rōl′, tī′rōl′, tī-rōl′). *var. of* TYROL.
Ti•ti•ca•ca (tĭt′ĭ-kä′kə). Largest freshwater lake in South America, in the Andes on the Bolivia-Peru border.
Ti•to•grad (tē′tō-grăd′). Cap. of Montenegro in the SE part. Pop. 73,000.
To•ba•go (tə-bā′gō). Island of Trinidad and Tobago in the SE West Indies.
To•go (tō′gō). Country of W Africa on the Gulf of Guinea. Cap. Lomhe. Pop. 2,742,945.
To•ky•o (tō′kē-ō′). Cap. of Japan, in E central Honshu. Pop. 8,353,674.
To•le•do (tə-lē′dō). **1.** City of central Spain SSW of Madrid. Pop. 57,778. **2.** City of NW OH on Lake Erie. Pop. 332,943.
Ton•ga (tŏng′gə). Island nation of the SW Pacific E of Fiji. Cap. Nukualofa. Pop. 96,592.
To•pe•ka (tə-pē′kə). Cap. of KS in the NE part W of Kansas City. Pop. 119,883.
To•ron•to (tə-rŏn′tō). Cap. of Ont., Canada, in the S part on Lake Ontario. Pop. 599,217.
Tor•to•la (tôr-tō′lə). Island of the West Indies, largest of the British Virgin Is.
Tor•tu•ga (tôr-tōō′gə). Island in the West Indies off N Haiti.
Tou•louse (tōō-lōōz′). City of S France on the Garonne SE of Bordeaux. Pop. 347,995.
To•ya•ma (tō-yä′mə). City of W central Honshu, Japan. Pop. 314,111.
Trans•cau•ca•sia (trăns′kô-kā′zhə, -zhē-ə, trănz′-). Region of Georgia, Armenia & Azerbaijan between the Caucasus Mts. & Turkey & Iran. —**Trans′cau•ca′sian** *adj. & n.*
Trans•kei (trăns-kā′, -kī′). Independent black African homeland in SE South Africa on the Indian Ocean coast. Cap. Umtata. Pop. 2,400,000. —**Trans•kei′an** *adj. & n.*
Trans•vaal (trăns-väl′, trănz-). Region & province of NE South Africa.
Tran•syl•va•nia (trăn′sĭl-vān′yə, -vā′nē-ə). Region of W Romania. —**Tran′syl•va′ni•an** *adj. & n.*

Tren•ton (trĕn′tən). Cap. of NJ in the W central part on the Delaware R. Pop. 88,675.
Tri•este (trē-ĕst′, -ĕs′tē). City of extreme NE Italy. Pop. 251,380.
Trin•i•dad (trĭn′ĭ-dăd′). Island of Trinidad and Tobago in the Atlantic off NE Venezuela. **—Trin′i•dad′i•an** *adj. & n.*
Trinidad and To•ba•go (tə-bā′gō). Country of SE West Indies, consisting of the islands of Trinidad & Tobago. Cap. Port of Spain. Pop. 1,059,825.
Trip•o•li (trĭp′ə-lē). Cap. of Libya in the NW on the Mediterranean. Pop. 858,500.
Troy (troi). Ancient city of NW Asia Minor near the Dardanelles.
Truk (trŭk, tro͝ok). Islands of the U.S. Trust Territory of the Pacific Is. in the central Carolines.
Tsi•nan (jē′nän′). JINAN.
Tsing•tao (chĭng′dou′, sĭng′tou′, tsĭng′-). QINGDAO.
Tu•a•mo•tu (to͞o′ə-mō′to͞o). Archipelago of French Polynesia in the S Pacific E of Tahiti.
Tuc•son (to͞o′sŏn′). City of SE AZ SSE of Phoenix. Pop. 405,390.
Tu•cu•mán (to͞o′kə-män′). City of NW Argentina NNW of Córdoba. Pop. 366,392.
Tu•la (to͞o′lə). City of W Russia S of Moscow. Pop. 532,000.
Tul•sa (tŭl′sə). City of NE OK NE of Oklahoma City. Pop. 367,302.
Tu•nis (to͞o′nĭs, tyo͞o′-). Cap. of Tunisia in the N part. Pop. 550,404.
Tu•ni•sia (to͞o-nē′zhə, -shə, -nĭzh′ə, -nĭsh′ə, tyo͞o-). Country of N Africa on the Mediterranean. Cap. Tunis. Pop. 5,588,209. **—Tu•ni′sian** *adj. & n.*
Tu•rin (to͝or′ĭn, tyo͝or′-). City of NW Italy on the Po WSW of Milan. Pop. 1,103,520.
Tur•key (tûr′kē). Country of SW Asia & SE Europe between the Mediterranean & the Black Sea. Cap. Ankara. Pop. 44,736,957. **—Tur′kish** (tûr′kĭsh) *adj. & n.*
Turk•men•i•stan (tûrk′mĕn-ĭ-stăn′, -stän′). Country of W central Asia E of the Caspian Sea. Cap. Ashkhabad. Pop. 3,189,000.
Turks and Cai•cos (tûrks; kā′kəs, kī′kōs). Island groups of the British West Indies in the Atlantic SE of the Bahamas.
Tus•ca•ny (tŭs′kə-nē′). Region of NW Italy. **—Tus′can** *adj. & n.*
Tu•va•lu (to͞o-vä′lo͞o). Island nation of the W Pacific N of Fiji. Cap. Funafuti. Pop. 7,349.
Ty•rol *or* **Ti•rol** (tə-rōl′, tī′rōl′, tĭ-rōl′). Region of the E Alps in W Austria & N Italy. **—Tyr′o•lese′** *adj. & n.*

U

U•fa (o͞o-fä′). City of W Russia. Pop. 1,064,000.
U•gan•da (yo͞o-găn′də, -gän′-). Country of E central Africa. Cap. Kampala. Pop. 12,636,179. **—U•gan′dan** *adj. & n.*
U•kraine (yo͞o-krān′). Country of E Europe. Pop. 50,840,000. **—U•krai′ni•an** *adj. & n.*
U•lan Ba•tor (o͞o′län bä′tôr′). Cap. of Mongolia in the N central part. Pop. 488,200.
Ul•ya•novsk (o͞ol-yä′nəfsk). City of W Russia on the Volga. Pop. 544,000.
Um•bri•a (ŭm′brē-ə). Region of central Italy. **—Um′bri•an** *adj. & n.*
Um•ta•ta (o͝om-tä′tə). Cap. of the Transkei in the W central part. Pop. 30,000.
Union of Soviet Socialist Republics. Former country of E Europe & N Asia with coastlines on the Baltic & Black seas & the Arctic & Pacific oceans.
U•nit•ed Ar•ab E•mir•ates (yo͞o-nī′tĭd ăr′əb ĭ-mîr′ĭts, ĕm′ər-). Country of E Arabia, a federation of seven sheikdoms. Cap. Abu Dhabi. Pop. 980,000.
United Arab Republic. EGYPT.
United Kingdom *or* **United Kingdom of Great Britain and Northern Ireland.** Country of W Europe comprising England, Scotland, Wales, & Northern Ireland. Cap. London. Pop. 55,648,994.
United States *or* **United States of America.** Country of central & NW North America with coastlines on the Atlantic, Pacific, & Arctic oceans. Cap. Washington, D.C. Pop. 249,632,692.
Upper Vol•ta (vŏl′tə, vōl′-, vôl′-). BURKINA FASO.
Ur (ûr, o͝or). Ancient city of Sumer, S Mesopotamia.
U•ral (yo͝or′əl). **1.** River of W Russia flowing 1,574 mi (2,533 km) W & S to the Caspian Sea. **2.** *also* **U•rals** (-əlz). Range of W Russia forming the traditional boundary between Europe & Asia.
U•ru•guay (o͝or′ə-gwī′, -gwā′, yo͝or′-). **1.** River of SE South America flowing c. 1,000 mi (1,609 km) W & S on the Brazil-Argentina & Argentina-Uruguay borders to the Río de la Plata. **2.** Country of SE South America. Cap. Montevideo. Pop. 2,788,429. **—U•ru•guay′an** *adj. & n.*
U•tah (yo͞o′tô′, -tä′). State of the W U.S. Cap. Salt Lake City. Pop. 1,727,784. **—U′tah•an** *adj. & n.*
U•trecht (yo͞o′trĕkt′). City of central Netherlands SSE of Amsterdam. Pop. 230,414.

V

Va•duz (vä-do͞ots′). Cap. of Liechtenstein in the W part on the Rhine. Pop. 4,927.
Va•len•ci•a (və-lĕn′chē-ə, -chə, -sē-ə). **1.** Region & former kingdom of E Spain. **2.** City of E Spain. Pop. 785,273. **3.** City of N Venezuela. Pop. 523,000.
Val•let•ta *also* **Va•let•ta** (və-lĕt′ə). Cap. of Malta on the NE coast. Pop. 14,042.
Val•pa•rai•so (văl′pə-rā′zō, -rī′-) *also* **Val•pa•ra•i•so** (väl′pä-rä-ē′sō). City of W central Chile on the Pacific. Pop. 271,580.
Van•cou•ver (văn-ko͞o′vər). **1.** Island of SW Canada in the Pacific off the SW B.C. mainland. **2.** City of SW B.C., Canada, opposite Vancouver Is. Pop. 414,281.

Va•nu•a•tu (vä'nōō-ä'tōō). Island republic of the S Pacific E of Australia. Cap. Vila. Pop. 138,000.

Va•ra•na•si (və-rä'nə-sē). City of N central India on the Ganges. Pop. 708,647.

Var•na (vär'nə). City of E Bulgaria on the Black Sea. Pop. 297,000.

Vat•i•can City (văt'ĭ-kən). Independent papal state within Rome, Italy. Pop. 736.

Ven•da (vĕn'də). Independent black African homeland in NE South Africa. Cap. Thohoyandou. Pop. 450,000.

Ven•e•zue•la (vĕn'ə-zwā'lə, -zwē'-). Country of N South America on the Caribbean. Cap. Caracas. Pop. 14,515,885. —**Ven'e•zue'lan** *adj. & n.*

Ven•ice (vĕn'ĭs). City of NE Italy on islets within a lagoon. Pop. 332,775. —**Ve•ne'tian** (və-nē'shən) *adj. & n.*

Ven•tu•ra (vĕn-tŏŏr'ə, -tyŏŏr'ə). City of SW CA on the Pacific. Pop. 92,575.

Ve•ra•cruz (vĕr'ə-krōōz', -krōōs') *or* **Ve•ra•cruz Lla•ve** (yä'vā). City of E central Mexico on the Gulf of Mexico. Pop. 255,646.

Ver•dun (vər-dŭn'). City of NE France on the Meuse R. Pop. 21,170.

Ver•mont (vər-mŏnt'). State of the NE U.S. Cap. Montpelier. Pop. 564,964. —**Ver•mont'er** *n.*

Ve•ro•na (və-rō'nə). City of N Italy. Pop. 238,553.

Ver•sailles (vər-sī', vĕr-). City of N central France near Paris. Pop. 91,014.

Ve•su•vi•us (və-sōō'vē-əs). Active volcano, 4,190 ft (1,278 m), of SW Italy.

Vi•chy (vĭsh'ē, vē'shē). City & resort of central France. Pop. 30,522.

Vic•to•ri•a (vĭk-tôr'ē-ə, -tōr'-). **1. Lake.** *also* **Victoria Ny•an•za** (nē-ăn'zə, nī-). Lake, c. 26,830 sq mi (69,490 sq km), of E central Africa in Uganda, Kenya, & Tanzania. **2.** Cap. of B.C., Canada, on SE Vancouver Is. Pop. 64,379. **3.** Cap. of Hong Kong colony on the NW coast of Hong Kong Is. Pop. 1,183,621. **4.** Cap. of the Seychelles on the NE coast of Mahé Is. Pop. 25,012.

Vi•en•na (vē-ĕn'ə). Cap of Austria in the NE part on the Danube. Pop. 1,515,666. —**Vi'en•nese'** (vē'ə-nēz', -nēs') *adj. & n.*

Vien•tiane (vyĕn-tyän'). Cap. of Laos in the N central part on the Mekong R. Pop. 132,253.

Viet•nam (vē-ĕt'näm', -năm', vē'ĕt-, vyĕt'-). Country of SE Asia in E Indochina on the South China Sea. Cap. Hanoi. Pop. 64,412,000. —**Viet'na•mese'** (-nə-mēz', -mēs') *adj. & n.*

Vi•la (vē'lə). Cap. of Vanuatu on Efate Is. in the SW Pacific. Pop. 14,797.

Vil•ni•us (vĭl'nē-əs) *or* **Vil•na** (-nə). Cap. of Lithuania in the SE part. Pop. 582,000.

Vir•gin•ia (vər-jĭn'yə). State of the E U.S. on Chesapeake Bay & the Atlantic. Cap. Richmond. Pop. 6,216,568. —**Vir•gin'ian** *adj. & n.*

Virginia Beach. Independent city of SE VA on the Atlantic near Norfolk. Pop. 393,069.

Virgin Islands of the United States. SW part of the Virgin Is. constituting a U.S. territory. Cap. Charlotte Amalie. Pop. 96,569.

Vi•sa•yan (və-sī'ən) *also* **Vi•sa•yans** (-ənz). Islands of the central Philippines between Luzon & Mindanao.

Vis•tu•la (vĭs'chə-lə, vĭsh'-,vĭs'tə-). Longest river of Poland, 678 mi (1,091 km), rising in the S & flowing N to the Baltic.

Vi•tebsk (vē'tĕpsk', -tĕbsk', vĭ-tĕpsk', -tĕbsk'). City of NE Belorussia on the Western Dvina R. NE of Minsk. Pop. 350,000.

Vi•ti Le•vu (vē'tē lĕv'ōō). Largest of the Fiji Is. in the S Pacific.

Vlad•i•vos•tok (vlăd'ə-və-stŏk', -vŏs'tŏk'). City of extreme SE Russia on the Sea of Japan. Pop. 648,000.

Vol•ga (vŏl'gə, vôl'-, vōl'-). River of W Russia flowing c. 2,300 mi (3,700 km) E & S to the Caspian Sea.

Vol•go•grad (vŏl'gə-grăd', vôl'-, vōl'-). City of SW Russia on the Volga. Pop. 999,000.

Vol•ta (vŏl'tə, vōl'-, vôl'-). River formed in central Ghana flowing 290 mi (467 km) S to the Atlantic.

Vo•ro•nezh (və-rô'nĭsh). City of W Russia on the Don SW of Lipetsk. Pop. 887,000.

Vo•ro•shi•lov•grad (vôr'ə-shē'ləf-grăd'). City of W Ukraine. Pop. 497,000.

Vosges (vōzh). Mountains of NE France.

W

Wa•co (wā'kō). City of E central TX S of Dallas-Fort Worth. Pop. 103,590.

Wai•ki•ki (wī'kĭ-kē'). Beach & resort district of Honolulu, HI.

Wake (wāk). Island of the W Pacific between HI & Guam, belonging to the U.S.

Wales (wālz). Principality of SW Great Britain W of England; part of the United Kingdom. Pop. 2,749,640. —**Welsh** (wĕlsh) *adj. & n.*

Wal•lis and Fu•tu•na (wŏl'ĭs; fə-tōō'nə). Two island groups of the SW Pacific W of Samoa & NE of Fiji; a French overseas territory. Pop. 9,129.

War•ren (wôr'ən, wŏr'-). City of SE MI near Detroit. Pop. 144,864.

War•saw (wôr'sô'). Cap. of Poland in the E central part. Pop. 1,651,225.

Wash•ing•ton (wŏsh'ĭng-tən, wôsh'-). **1.** State of the NW U.S. on the Pacific. Cap. Olympia. Pop. 4,887,941. **2.** Cap. of the U.S., coextensive with the District of Columbia. Pop. 609,909. —**Wash'ing•to'ni•an** *adj. & n.*

Wat•er•bury (wô'tər-bĕr'ē, wŏt'ər-). City of W central CT. Pop. 108,961.

Wa•ter•loo (wô'tər-lōō', wŏt'ər-, wô'tər-lōō'). Town of central Belgium near Brussels.

Wel•land (wĕl'ənd). **1.** Ship canal of SE Ont., Canada, connecting Lake Ontario with Lake Erie & by-passing Niagara Falls. **2.** City of SE Ont., Canada, on the Welland Ship Canal. Pop. 454,448.

Wel·ling·ton (wĕl'ĭng-tən). Cap. of New Zealand in extreme S North Is. Pop. 321,004.
Wes·sex (wĕs'ĭks). Region & ancient Anglo-Saxon kingdom of S England.
West Bank Disputed territory of SW Asia between Israel & Jordan.
West Berlin. See BERLIN.
Western Sa·mo·a (sə-mō'ə). Island nation of the S Pacific comprising the W half of the Samoa Is. Cap. Apia. Pop. 163,000.
West Germany. See GERMANY.
West In·dies (ĭn'dēz). Islands between SE North America & N South America, separating the Caribbean Sea & the Atlantic & including the Greater Antilles, the Lesser Antilles, & the Bahamas.
West·pha·lia (wĕst-fāl'yə, -fā'lē-ə). Region of W central Germany E of the Rhine —**West·pha'lian** *adj. & n.*
West Vir·gin·ia (vər-jĭn'yə). State of the E central U.S. Cap. Charleston. Pop. 1,801,625. —**West Vir·gin'ian** *adj. & n.*
Whid·bey (hwĭd'bē, wĭd'-). Island of NW WA in Puget Sound.
White·horse (hwīt'hôrs', wīt'). Cap. of Y.T., Canada, in the S part. Pop. 14,814.
White Nile (nīl). Section of the Nile River in Sudan flowing to Khartoum, where it joins the Blue Nile to form the Nile.
Whit·ney (hwĭt'nē, wĭt'-). **Mount.** Second-highest peak in the U.S., 14,494 ft (4,420.7 m), in the Sierra Nevada of E central CA.
Wich·i·ta (wĭch'ĭ-tô'). City of S central KS SW of Kansas City. Pop. 304,011.
Wies·ba·den (vēs'bäd'n, vĭs'-). City of W central Germany. Pop. 254,209.
Wight (wīt), **Isle of.** Island in the England Channel off S central England.
Wil·lem·stad (vĭl'əm-stät'). Cap. of the Netherland Antilles on the S coast of Curaçao. Pop. 95,000.
Wind·hoek (vĭnt'ho͝ok'). Cap. of Namibia in the central part. Pop. 61,369.
Wind·sor (wĭn'zər). City of S Ont., Canada, on the Detroit R. opposite Detroit, MI. Pop. 246,110.
Wind·ward (wĭnd'wərd). Islands of the SE West Indies, the S group of the Lesser Antilles from Martinique S to Grenada.
Win·ni·peg (wĭn'ə-pĕg'). Cap. of Man., Canada, in the SE part. Pop. 584,842.
Win·ston-Sa·lem (wĭn'stən-sā'ləm). City of N central NC. Pop. 143,485.
Wis·con·sin (wĭs-kŏn'sĭn). State of the N central U.S. Cap. Madison. Pop. 4,906,745. —**Wis·con'sin·ite'** *n.*
Worces·ter (wo͝os'tər). City of central MA W of Boston. Pop. 169,759.
Wro·claw (vrôt'släf'). City of SW Poland on the Oder R. Pop. 640,557.
Wu·han (wo͞o'hän'). City of E central China on the Yangtze. Pop. 3,287,720.
Wup·per·tal (vo͝op'ər-täl'). City of W central Germany. Pop. 371,283.
Wy·o·ming (wī-ō'mĭng). State of the W U.S. Cap. Cheyenne. Pop. 455,975. —**Wy·o'ming·ite'** *n.*

X

Xia·men (shyä'mən). City of SE China. Pop. 350,000.
Xi'an (shē'än'). City of central China SW of Beijing. Pop. 2,185,040.
Xi·ang (shē'äng'). River, c. 715 mi (1,150 km), of SE China.
Xin·gu (shēng-go͞o'). River of central & N Brazil flowing 1,230 mi (1,979.1 km) to the Amazon.
Xin·jiang Uy·gur (shĭn'jē-äng' wē'gər). Autonomous region of extreme W China.
Xi·zang (shēd'zäng'). TIBET.
Xu·zhou (sho͞o'jō'). City of E China NNW of Nanjing. Pop. 776,770.

Y

Yal·ta (yôl'tə). City of SE Ukraine in S Crimea on the Black Sea. Pop. 86,000.
Ya·lu (yä'lo͞o). River, c. 500 mi (805 km), forming part of the North Korea-China border.
Yang·tze (yăng'sē, yăngkt'-). Longest river of China & of Asia, flowing c. 3,450 mi (5,550 km) from Tibet to the East China Sea.
Yaoun·dé *or* **Yaun·dé** (youn-dē'). Cap. of Cameroon in the central part. Pop. 313,706.
Ya·ro·slavl (yär'ə-slä'vəl). City of W central Russia. Pop. 626,000.
Yel·low (yĕl'ō). River, c. 3,000 mi (4,830 km), of N China.
Yel·low·knife (yĕl'ō-nīf'). Cap. of N.W.T., Canada. Pop. 9,483.
Yel·low·stone (yĕl'ō-stōn'). River, 671 mi (1,079.6 km) long, of NW WY & MT.
Yem·en (yĕm'ən, yā'mən). Country of SW Asia at the S tip of the Arabian Peninsula. Cap. Sana. Pop. 10,183,000.
Ye·re·van (yĕr'ə-vän'). Cap. of Armenia in the W central part. Pop. 1,133,000.
Yo·ko·ha·ma (yō'kə-hä'mə). City of SE Honshu, Japan. Pop. 2,773,674.
Yon·kers (yŏng'kərz). City of SE NY N of New York City. Pop. 188,082.
York·town (yôrk'toun'). Village in SE VA.
Yu·ca·tán (yo͞o'kə-tăn', -tän'). Peninsula, mostly in SE Mexico, separating the Caribbean from the Gulf of Mexico.
Yu·go·sla·vi·a (yo͞o'gō-slä'vē-ə). Republic (since 1992) of SE Europe comprising Serbia and Montenegro; originally consisted of six constituent republics, four of which declared independence in 1991. Cap. Belgrade. Pop. 12,098,779. —**Yu'go·sla'vi·an** *adj. & n.*
Yu·kon (yo͞o'kŏn'). **1.** River flowing c. 2,000 mi (3,220 km) from S Y.T., Canada, through AK to the Bering Sea. **2.** Territory of NW Canada. Cap. Whitehorse. Pop. 23,504.

Z

Za·greb (zä'grĕb'). Cap. of Croatia in the N part on the Sava R. Pop. 768,700.
Zaire (zī'îr, zä-îr'). Republic of W central Af-

rica. Cap. Kinshasa. Pop. 34,491,000.

Zam•be•zi (zăm-bē′zē). River, c. 1,700 mi (2,735 km), of central & S Africa.

Zam•bi•a (zăm′bē-ə). Republic of S central Africa. Cap. Lusaka. Pop. 8,073,000. —**Zam′bi•an** *adj. & n.*

Zan•zi•bar (zăn′zə-bär′). **1.** Region of E Africa, part of Tanzania. **2.** Island off the NE coast of Tanzania.

Za•po•ro•zhe (zä′pə-rô′zhə). City of S Ukraine on the Dnieper R. Pop. 852,000.

Za•ra•go•za (zăr′ə-gō′zä, sä′rä-gō′sä). SARAGOSSA.

Zhda•nov (zhdä′nəf). City of SE Ukraine on the Sea of Azov. Pop. 522,000.

Zheng•zhou (jŭng′jō′). City of E central China SSW of Beijing. Pop. 1,404,050.

Zi•bo (zē′bō′). City of E China E of Jinan. Pop. 2,197,668.

Zim•bab•we (zĭm-bäb′wē, -wā). Republic of S central Africa. Cap. Harare. Pop. 9,122,000. —**Zim•bab′we•an** *adj. & n.*

Zu•lu•land (zo͞o′lo͞o-lănd′). Historical region of NE South Africa.

Zu•rich (zo͝or′ĭk). City of NE Switzerland. Pop. 369,522.

OXFORD WORLD'S CLASSICS

PERCY BYSSHE SHELLEY

Percy Bysshe Shelley was born in Horsham, Sussex on 4 August 1792, the eldest child of Timothy Shelley, a landowning Whig MP and later Baronet. He was educated at Syon House Academy, Isleworth, and at 12 was sent to Eton. At 18 he went up to University College, Oxford. Five months later, together with his friend Thomas Jefferson Hogg, he was expelled from Oxford for publishing and refusing to answer questions about a pamphlet entitled *The Necessity of Atheism*. The resulting estrangement from his family was soon compounded by his elopement to Scotland in 1811 with Harriet Westbrook, daughter of the proprietor of a London coffee house. In 1814 Shelley and Harriet separated, and he eloped again, this time to the Continent, with Mary Godwin, daughter of Mary Wollstonecraft and William Godwin. Harriet committed suicide in November 1816 and Mary and Shelley married the next month. After a spell back in England they departed for Italy early in 1818, where he wrote many of his best-known works. From this self-imposed exile Shelley never returned. He drowned in the Bay of Spezia in 1822, while sailing with his friend Edward Williams, who also drowned. In the course of his brief and controversial life Shelley produced an astonishing range of poetry and prose, including numerous lyric poems, plays, longer poems, polemical pamphlets, translations, and works of criticism and political philosophy.

Zachary Leader, Professor of English Literature at the University of Surrey Roehampton, has published widely on nineteenth- and twentieth-century literature. Among his books are *Revision and Romantic Authorship* (1996), *Romantic Period Writings 1798–1832: An Anthology* (co-edited with Ian Haywood) (1999) and (as editor) *The Letters of Kingsley Amis* (2000).

Michael O'Neill, Professor of English at the University of Durham, has published widely on Romantic and twentieth-century poetry. Among his books are *The Human Mind's Imaginings: Conflict and Achievement in Shelley's Poetry* (1989), *Percy Bysshe Shelley: A Literary Life* (1989), and *Romanticism and the Self-Conscious Poem* (1997).

OXFORD WORLD'S CLASSICS

For over 100 years Oxford World's Classics have brought readers closer to the world's great literature. Now with over 700 titles—from the 4,000-year-old myths of Mesopotamia to the twentieth century's greatest novels—the series makes available lesser-known as well as celebrated writing.

The pocket-sized hardbacks of the early years contained introductions by Virginia Woolf, T. S. Eliot, Graham Greene, and other literary figures which enriched the experience of reading. Today the series is recognized for its fine scholarship and reliability in texts that span world literature, drama and poetry, religion, philosophy and politics. Each edition includes perceptive commentary and essential background information to meet the changing needs of readers.

OXFORD WORLD'S CLASSICS

Percy Bysshe Shelley

The Major Works

Edited with an Introduction and Notes by
ZACHARY LEADER *and* MICHAEL O'NEILL

OXFORD
UNIVERSITY PRESS

Great Clarendon Street, Oxford OX2 6DP

Oxford University Press is a department of the University of Oxford.
It furthers the University's objective of excellence in research, scholarship,
and education by publishing worldwide in

Oxford New York

Auckland Bangkok Buenos Aires Cape Town Chennai
Dar es Salaam Delhi Hong Kong Istanbul Karachi Kolkata
Kuala Lumpur Madrid Melbourne Mexico City Mumbai Nairobi
São Paulo Shanghai Taipei Tokyo Toronto

Oxford is a registered trade mark of Oxford University Press
in the UK and in certain other countries

Published in the United States
by Oxford University Press Inc., New York

First published as an Oxford World's Classics paperback 2003
Reissued 2009

British Library Cataloguing in Publication Data

Data available

Library of Congress Cataloging in Publication Data

Data available

ISBN 978-0-19-953897-3

7

Typeset in Ehrhardt
by RefineCatch Limited, Bungay, Suffolk
Printed in Great Britain by
Clays Ltd, St Ives plc

CONTENTS

ACKNOWLEDGEMENTS

WE are grateful to various libraries and bodies for permission to quote from manuscripts in their possession. The following poems are quoted by kind permission of the Carl and Lily Pforzheimer Foundation, Inc.: 'A Cat in distress', 'To the Emperors of Russia and Austria', 'Zeinab and Kathema', 'Sonnet: On Launching Some Bottles Filled with *Knowledge* into the Bristol Channel', and 'Sonnet: To a Balloon, Laden with *Knowledge*'. The same Foundation has permitted us to use the literal transcription of *A Philosophical View of Reform* in *Shelley and His Circle*, volume vi, as copy-text for our selection from that work. We are deeply conscious of our debt to the editors of the transcription, Donald H. Reiman and Doucet Devin Fischer, and wish to thank them warmly. We, of course, take full responsibility for how we edit that transcription. We are also grateful to the Keeper of Special Collections and Western Manuscripts of the Bodleian Library, University of Oxford, for permission to quote from manuscripts in its possession (fuller details are given in our notes to each poem; relevant shelfmarks can be found under '*BSM*' in 'Abbreviations' at the head of Notes below, pp. 702–3). We are also grateful to Lord Abinger for his permission given through the Bodleian Library to use material from the Gisborne notebook (Oxford, Bodleian Library, [Abinger] Dep. d.475). For permission to publish material from the Scrope Davies Notebook, we are grateful to Barclays Bank. Other libraries and bodies which have kindly given us permission to publish texts based on manuscripts in their possession include Aberdeen University Library; the Bibliotheca Bodmeriana, Cologny-Genève; the British Library; Edinburgh University Library; Eton College Library; the Houghton Library, Harvard University; the Huntington Library, San Marino; the John Rylands University Library of Manchester; the Library of Congress; the Pierpont Morgan Library, New York; and the Syndics of Cambridge University Library.

Zachary Leader would like to thank Frank Kermode and Neil Fraistat for early advice and encouragement. Michael O'Neill would like to thank the University of Durham for research leave to work on the edition and the Arts and Humanities Research Board for an additional term of leave under its Research Leave Scheme. Both editors would like to thank Judith Luna at OUP for her patience and good sense, and Elizabeth Stratford for her meticulous copy-editing.

Many other individuals have helped us greatly. In particular we would like to thank the following for their help of various kinds: B. C. Barker-Benfield, Robert Carver, Richard Cronin, David Fuller, Basak Ertur, Doucet Devin Fischer, Gareth Reeves, Donald H. Reiman, Nicholas Roe, and Timothy Webb. Nora Crook deserves special mention for her generous readiness to discuss and expertly advise about many editorial problems. Responsibility for errors is, of course, the editors'.

The fine work of many editors of Shelley, past and present, has been of great benefit and stimulus to us. Of particular value to us among modern editions have been those of Timothy Webb for Everyman, Kelvin Everest and fellow-editors for Longman, Donald H. Reiman and Neil Fraistat for Johns Hopkins University Press, and Donald H. Reiman and Sharon B. Powers for Norton. The second edition of the Norton Shelley was published as we were going to press, but we have been able to consult it briefly. We are also indebted to the work of the editors of the *Bodleian Shelley Manuscripts* series and the relevant volumes in the *Manuscripts of the Younger Romantics* series, both under the general editorship of Donald H. Reiman.

INTRODUCTION

I

In *A Defence of Poetry* (written in 1821) Shelley celebrates the diversity of interpretations evoked by 'high poetry' (p. 693).[1] He is certainly a poet and a man able to stimulate divided responses. The current high standing he enjoys is shown by the number of major critical studies and editions of his writing that have appeared in the last few decades.[2] Yet what held sway for many years were the correspondingly adverse judgements of T. S. Eliot, who regarded Shelley's 'ideas' as 'repellent', and F. R. Leavis, who asserted that 'feeling in Shelley's poetry is divorced from thought'.[3] Causes for divisions of opinion about Shelley are not hard to find. The incendiary violence of his political rhetoric, full of volcanic eruptions and apocalyptic conflagrations, serves non-violence. He both champions and deplores Romantic idealism, sometimes in the same poem. His language has about it a momentum that detractors find overstated and admirers applaud, as the poetry 'Sweeps through the dull dense world, compelling there | All new successions to the forms they wear' (*Adonais*, ll. 382–3).

Shelley's private life has also caused controversy. The feeling that his personal conduct proves the dangerous or liberating nature of his ideas may explain the persistence of biographical readings of his work (or refusals to read the work). To insist too literally on biographical analyses of Shelley, however, would be to ignore his own conviction that 'The poet and the man are two different natures' (*L* 2. 310).

[1] Dates given in this Introduction to Shelley's writings refer to the date of publication, unless, as here, stated otherwise.

[2] In *Norton*[2] the key moment for the revival of Shelley's critical fortunes is dated as circa 1960, or, more precisely, 1958–9, years that saw the publication of pioneering critical, editorial, and textual work by Harold Bloom, Lawrence John Zillman, Charles H. Taylor, Jr., and Earl R. Wasserman: see Donald H. Reiman and Neil Fraistat, 'Shelley's Reputation before 1960: A Sketch', pp. 539–49, especially pp. 547–8. (For explanation of abbreviated references, see pp. 702–3.)

[3] T. S. Eliot, *The Use of Poetry and the Use of Criticism* (London, 1933), quoted from *Selected Prose of T. S. Eliot*, ed. and intro. Frank Kermode (London, 1975), 81 (for a more respectful view of Shelley, see Eliot's comments in 'What Dante Means to Me', in *To Criticize the Critic* (London, 1965), 130–2, on *The Triumph of Life*, especially the meeting between the Poet and Rousseau, which influenced Eliot's account of the 'familiar compound ghost' in 'Little Gidding'); F. R. Leavis, 'Shelley', in *Revaluation* (1936; Harmondsworth, 1972), 208.

Arguably, this opposition simplifies; there are times when Shelley's poetry thrives on blurring the gap between 'poet' and 'man'. But even when Shelley does express private feelings, as in his responses to literary slights in poems such as 'To —— (Lines to a Critic)', he is quick to relate his feelings to an ethical issue with wider political implications (here, how best to respond to hostility). Born on 4 August 1792, a few weeks before the September Massacres in France and months before the execution of Louis XVI, Shelley spent much of his career as a poet pondering the apparent failure of the French Revolution, staging in *Prometheus Unbound* (1820) an imaginative reworking of history that results, in the literary work, in successful liberation—not only from tyranny but also from the desire for revenge. Spared the first-hand disenchantment of the previous generation of Romantic poets, Wordsworth, Coleridge, and Southey, he attacks their 'gloom' (and Byron's 'misanthropy') in the Preface to *Laon and Cythna* (1817) (p. 132). For him, all these poets served as object-lessons in how not to read history.

Personally and poetically, Shelley thrived on conflict and dissent. The 'Son of a man of fortune in Sussex', as he described his situation in a letter to Godwin (*L* 1. 227), he received the education of an aristocrat who was expected to follow his father (Sir Timothy Shelley, a landowning Whig MP) into public life. He attended Eton, where contemporaries recalled his dislike of the practice of 'fagging' (whereby younger boys acted as the servants of older boys) and the baiting to which he was subjected. He proved to be an able scholar, adept at writing Latin verse and keen on science. Yet the youthful rebel was opposed to the institutions of school, university, and church. In March 1811 he was expelled from University College, Oxford, with his friend Thomas Jefferson Hogg, after refusing to disavow authorship of a pamphlet entitled *The Necessity of Atheism* (minimally altered in a long note to *Queen Mab* (1813), included here).

Expulsion from Oxford was followed by elopement and marriage in the same year to Harriet Westbrook, daughter of John Westbrook, businessman and owner of a London coffee house. The marriage was disapproved of by Shelley's father, who effectively broke off relations with his son.[4] Harriet was Shelley's loyal companion during a period of would-be political activism, which took him to Dublin in 1812 to campaign on behalf of Catholic Emancipation and repeal of the Act of

[4] For discussion of John Westbrook and analysis of Sir Timothy Shelley's opposition to the marriage, see *SC* 2. 866–8.

Union. She is the dedicatee of *Queen Mab*, which presents the youthful poet in full revolutionary flow, attacking tyranny and religion, and rounding off his poem with fire-breathing but closely argued essays on topics such as the desirability of free love and the horrors of meat-eating. However, by 1814 the marriage was under strain, and in that year Shelley fell in love and eloped with Mary Godwin, daughter of Mary Wollstonecraft and William Godwin, the poet's intellectual mentor. In the 1790s Godwin had influenced Wordsworth and others with his dispassionate exaltation of reason in *Enquiry Concerning Political Justice* (1793). Two decades later, he had fallen so far into obscurity that the youthful Shelley was surprised to discover he was still living: 'I had enrolled your name in the list of the honorable dead', he informed a no doubt mildly startled Godwin in a letter of 3 January 1812 (*L* I. 220). Later, Shelley outstripped Godwinian rationalism as he immersed himself in the poetry of his and previous ages, and in the writings of thinkers such as Plato. But Godwin did much to foster the poet's trust in unfettered enquiry.[5]

Shelley's refusal to abide by social convention caused great pain to himself and to others, especially the abandoned Harriet. In 1816, after a period of growing distress, she drowned herself in the Serpentine; within a month Shelley and Mary married. Yet to Virginia Woolf, at least, in a discussion of Shelley 'as son and as husband', it is apparent that 'his experiments, disastrous as they were in many ways, have helped us to greater sincerity and happiness in our own conflicts'.[6] The marriage was followed by a period of relative peace and productivity in Marlow, near Shelley's friend Thomas Love Peacock. In March 1818, though, the Shelleys set sail for Italy. This departure was prompted by several factors: the poet's financial and health problems; the wish to return Allegra, Byron's daughter by Claire Clairmont (Mary Shelley's half-sister), to her father; and Shelley's fear that his and Mary's children might be taken from them after a legal decision in March 1817 not to grant him custody of his two children by Harriet.

In Italy, Shelley and Mary experienced much suffering, at the heart of which were the deaths of their children: Clara, a year old, died in 1818 and 3-year-old William in 1819, resulting in subsequent emotional difficulties in the marriage. Shelley's work was badly received, largely on account of his heterodox views, though a number of

[5] See Pamela Clemit, 'Shelley's Godwin, 1812–1817', *Durham University Journal*, NS 54 (1993), 189–201.

[6] 'Not One of Us', in *The Essays of Virginia Woolf*, vol. 4: *1925–1928*, ed. Andrew McNeillie (London, 1994), 470.

reviewers recognized his poetic gifts. But his ability to communicate a fluid, dynamic vision in different literary forms is abundantly evident in his writings in Italy (1818–22), where he produced some of the finest poetry of the Romantic period. These writings include *Prometheus Unbound* and *Hellas* (1822), two lyrical dramas that take Greek models as their point of departure; *The Cenci* (1819), a five-act tragedy in blank verse; *The Mask of Anarchy* (written in 1819), a blend of masque and ballad; *Peter Bell the Third* (also written in 1819), a parody or mock-epic; *Letter to Maria Gisborne* (written in 1820), an epistle in verse; *The Witch of Atlas* (also written in 1820), a comic miniature epic or epyllion written in *ottava rima*; *Epipsychidion* (1821), a rhapsodic love poem in couplets that artfully reworks Dante's *Vita Nuova*; several Odes (including 'Ode to the West Wind' and 'Ode to Liberty', both 1820); sonnets showing formal innovation (examples are 'Ye hasten to the grave!', written in 1820, and 'England in 1819', written in 1819); shorter poems in various metrical forms (notably the poems to Jane Williams, written in 1821–2); *Adonais*, a pastoral elegy in Spenserian stanzas; and *The Triumph of Life* (written in 1822), a dream-vision written in *terza rima*. Often Shelley calls to mind a literary form or work only to offer a critique of the assumptions with which it is associated. *Adonais* ends in affirmation, but the affirmation differs from that found in elegies such as Milton's *Lycidas*: in place of Milton's Christian Heaven, Shelley puts his ambivalent trust in a self-created 'abode where the Eternal are' (l. 495). Dante's *Divine Comedy* is explicitly invoked by *The Triumph of Life* (ll. 471–6), but the Romantic poet substitutes his own blend of questioning and imagining for the theological certainties that inform the Italian poet's masterpiece.

Shelley lived in an age of turbulence, complexity, and change. More and more people lived in cities, unrepresented in Parliament. The country was locked in a war with Napoleonic France that would only come to an end with the Battle of Waterloo in 1815. After that victory a period of further reaction followed at home, a time of repression sharply analysed and attacked by Shelley, most concentratedly in 'England in 1819'.

George III was mad, and the self-indulgent Prince Regent the butt of lampoons. The government under Lord Liverpool refused to grant parliamentary reform, Catholic Emancipation, or the right to protest peacefully. Abroad, the Bourbons were restored in France and Spain, and Europe was subjected to counter-revolutionary pressures orchestrated by Metternich, Chancellor of Austria. Shelley looked eagerly for signs of social change domestically and internationally, as is evident from 'Ode to Liberty', inspired by the Spanish Revolution of 1820. His political, religious, and ethical views were underpinned by a belief in justice, equality, freedom, and the desirability of reform. In the prose work, *An Address to the People on the Death of the Princess Charlotte* (written in 1817), he shows a capacity for ironic yet visionary polemic, coupling the death of Princess Charlotte (daughter of the Prince Regent) with the executions of three labourers associated with the Pentridge Rising, which Shelley, along with other liberals, believed was fomented by a government informer. At the end, the Princess for whom Shelley enjoins his readers to mourn is not Charlotte but Liberty, whose resurrection he imagines as a 'glorious Phantom' (p. 631). The use of 'Phantom', with its implication of something yet to materialize, is characteristic. Confronted by a culture in retreat from political optimism, Shelley offers in much of his writing an ardent, self-aware Utopianism.

Shelley's interest in different poetic forms is the artistic analogue of his social experimentation and of his concern with process, in consciousness, history, and the cosmos.[7] Commitment to process, the condition of becoming, shapes his poetic practice. 'Language', he writes in *Prometheus Unbound*, is 'a perpetual Orphic song, | Which rules with daedal harmony a throng | Of thoughts and forms, which else senseless and shapeless were' (4. 415–17). In Shelley, these 'forms' negotiate with the as yet unformed. His words, whether apparently simple or evidently complex, allow us to experience the emergence of new possibilities. Turneresque in their swirls of energy, their delight in vanishings and manifestations, his descriptions of nature are the correlative of his longing for change. Reflecting on his use of different forms, Shelley worried whether 'it be wise to affect variety in compositions, or whether the attempt to excel in many ways does not debar from excellence in one particular kind' (*L* 2. 219). Yet it is his great distinction to be at once a poet of figurative, metrical, and syntactical constructions that mirror the desire for transformation, and a poet of audacious radical critique. Such critique is most evident in *Queen Mab*, but it is re-encountered in many later and formally quite different poems, such as those occasioned by Shelley's revulsion from and reflections on the Peterloo Massacre of 1819 (see the notes for *The Mask of Anarchy*). In this volume, we include a good number of the

[7] For a study of 'process' in Shelley, see Jerrold E. Hogle, *Shelley's Process: Radical Transference and the Development of his Major Works* (New York, 1988) .

'popular songs' which he hoped to publish after Peterloo, but which were too outspoken to find their way into print during his lifetime. They reveal a fusion of tough political thought, sharp-edged phrasing, and grim wit.

Shelley's variety is no matter of indecisiveness or personal instability.[8] His different styles and strategies often serve a common purpose, and can frequently be explained, in the first instance, by reference to his intended audiences. This awareness of audience shows in his instruction that *Queen Mab* be printed as 'A small neat Quarto, on fine paper & so as to catch the aristocrats: They will not read it, but their sons and daughters may' (*L* 1. 361). Later, *Prometheus Unbound* was addressed to 'the more select classes of poetical readers' (Preface, p. 232), while its near-contemporary, *The Cenci*, was aimed at 'the multitude' (*L* 2. 174). Ironically, his efforts to target audiences were often thwarted while other poets—pre-eminently Byron, at once friend, rival, and Jungian shadow—enjoyed far greater popularity. If Shelley's ideas outraged conservative reviewers, his style proved too searching for popular consumption. It is easier, from this distance, to hear in his work a poetic voice able to fuse affirmation and doubt, directness and complexity. *The Mask of Anarchy*, for example, excoriates with rare satiric edge the Liverpool administration. It opens with a 'ghastly masquerade' (l. 27) in which, like the political cartoonists active in the Regency, the narrator describes meeting 'Murder on the way—| He had a mask like Castlereagh' (ll. 5–6). As the poem develops, though, its ballad stanzas accommodate more than invective; they dramatize the desirability but also the difficulty of imagining a transition from anarchic misrule to freedom. The owner of the voice which addresses the reader on this subject is hard to identify; the likely candidate, the 'Earth | Which gave the sons of England birth' (ll. 139–40), is only proposed in a prolonged 'As if' clause (see ll. 139 and 146).[9] Shelley puts the problem of speaking into the foreground to

[8] For the construction of a 'schizoid' Shelley, see the comments of one of his major poetic heirs, W. B. Yeats, in *A Vision* (1937; London, 1981): 'Shelley out of phase writes pamphlets, and dreams of converting the world', p. 143.

[9] Stephen C. Behrendt in *Shelley and His Audiences* (Lincoln, Nebr., 1989) comments on the 'equivocation' that Shelley creates by his use of 'As if' (quoted from Michael O'Neill (ed.), *Shelley*, Longman Critical Readers (London, 1993), 134). Susan J. Wolfson, in *Formal Charges: The Shaping of Poetry in British Romanticism* (Stanford, Calif., 1997), finds that the 'syntaxes of *As if* have a reflexive effect of restraining the political agency of the oratory to a dream', p. 198. For thought-provoking questioning of Shelley's radicalism in this poem and elsewhere, see Donald H. Reiman, 'Shelley as Agrarian Reactionary', in *Norton*[2] 589–99, esp. pp. 596–7.

bring out the fact that he is cut off, by physical exile and social class, from the group to whose defence he would leap, and to assert that poetry's voice must frequently associate itself with hope and imagination.

For many readers, Shelley is a poet who is 'tameless, and swift, and proud', words he applies in 'Ode to the West Wind' (l. 56) to himself as well as to the wind, symbol of inspiration and herald of revolution. Yet J. S. Mill's assertion that 'It is only when under the overruling influence of some one state of feeling . . . that he writes as a great poet' is only partly right.[10] If there is a presiding 'state of feeling' in the 'Ode to the West Wind', it is made up of several constituents and continually redefined. In the final section, Shelley uses his modified sonnet form (four tercets with concluding couplet) to hold together various impulses. The section's opening blend of plea and imperative—'Make me thy lyre, even as the forest is' (l. 57)—announces a recovery from the mood of the previous section, in which a time of crisis is dramatized. The desire to be 'even as the forest is' implicitly recognizes, however, that the poet cannot simplify himself into a natural object like the forest. But Shelley's way of bringing out this separation is to push to the limit the possibility of identification with the natural: 'What if my leaves are falling like its own!' (l. 58) he exclaims in a line that plays one more figurative variation on the leaves that have already brought to mind 'ghosts' (l. 3), 'Pestilence-stricken multitudes' (l. 5), 'Loose clouds' (l. 16) (and, by extension, 'tangled boughs of Heaven and Ocean' (l. 17)), and 'The sapless foliage of the ocean' (l. 40). With impassioned humour in the midst of his desire for the recovery of inspiration, Shelley sees himself as a deciduous tree whose leaves are falling.

But if he hopes that the wind 'Will take from both [poet and forest] a deep, autumnal tone, | Sweet though in sadness' (ll. 60–1), he concedes in those final words that he is investing the natural scene with emotion. Thus, the subsequent plea for unity—'Be thou me, impetuous one!' (l. 62)—has built into it an awareness that the plea cannot be successful. Long before the cry 'Bethou' is mocked by Wallace Stevens in *Notes towards a Supreme Fiction* as 'A sound like any other' that 'will end' ('It Must Change', 6), Shelley has glimpsed its necessary failure. By the poem's close it is the poet who asserts his responsibility for meaning, drawing attention to 'the incantation of this verse' (l. 65), a

[10] J. S. Mill, 'Two Kinds of Poetry' (1833), quoted from *Shelley: Shorter Poems and Lyrics, A Casebook*, ed. Patrick Swinden (London, 1976), 58.

moment that sharpens the immediacy of the imaginative experience.[11] This experience is also sharpened by the image of words as scattered 'Ashes and sparks' (l. 67), reminding us of poetry's indirect and multiple ways of working on an audience. The disseminated sparks will kindle, the poem hopes, where they fall. As at the end of 'Mont Blanc' (written in 1816), Shelley concludes with a question (altered from a statement in the draft). In the earlier poem, the question teased us into recognizing the dependence of sense-making on 'the human mind's imaginings' (l. 143). In the 'Ode', the question looks rhetorical, demanding the answer 'yes, Spring will not be far behind', but it shows—covertly yet honestly—how Shelley's desires are communicated through potentially unstable metaphors: in political or poetic terms, there is no guarantee that Winter will give way to Spring.[12]

And yet it is by opening his poem to the possibility of deconstruction that Shelley persuades his reader of the need to 'believe in an optimism in which we are our own gods' (*L* 2. 125). Often he strikes a balance between sustaining hope and conceding that hope's only warrant may be the need to hope. In *Julian and Maddalo* (finished in 1819), he stages a debate between optimistic and pessimistic viewpoints, and while the narrator Julian articulates a Shelleyan belief in 'the power of man over his own mind' (Preface, p. 212), the poem is resistant to interpretations that take sides. Maddalo, modelled on Byron, is also an *alter ego* of the poet himself. Julian's enthusiasm and Maddalo's tragic cynicism are each presented as responses to being human that have their own authenticity. At stake for Julian, before the encounter with the Maniac, is the belief that 'it is our will | That thus enchains us to permitted ill' (ll. 170–1). Belief in the will's power is central to Julian's—and Shelley's—hopes of human betterment. Shelley's hostility to Christian orthodoxy has much to do with dislike of the acquiescence in some supposed divine will that he saw it as encouraging; the attractiveness to him of Godwin's *Political Justice* derives, in large part, from that work's advocacy of tireless aspiration. With qualifications, a vision of improvement governs Shelley's sense of history. In *A Philosophical View of Reform* (written in 1819–20), he traces the contest between 'the spirit of truth and the spirit of imposture' (p. 639), and asserts confidence in the victory of the

[11] See James Chandler in *England in 1819* (Chicago, 1998) on the 'representation of mutual making' in these lines; quoted from *Norton*[2] 718.

[12] See Ronald Tetreault's account in *The Poetry of Life: Shelley and Literary Form* (Toronto, 1987) of how at the close of the 'Ode', 'Shelley willingly surrenders his authority as poet to the reader' (quoted from O'Neill (ed.), *Shelley*, 140) .

former. At the same time, he grapples with 'the difficult and unbending realities of actual life' (p. 664), in keeping with his self-delineation in a letter to Leigh Hunt as 'one of those whom nothing will fully satisfy, but who [is] ready to be partially satisfied by all that is practicable' (*L* 2. 153). In *Julian and Maddalo* and *The Cenci*, the 'difficult and unbending realities of actual life' make themselves felt in the clash between theory and experience. After Julian and Maddalo have overheard the Maniac's soliloquy, their 'argument was quite forgot' (l. 520): Maddalo modulates from his earlier despair at the human condition into a more sympathetic awareness that creativity and pain may be complementary (ll. 544–6); Julian wishes, ineffectually yet with authentic concern, that he might act as psychotherapist to the Maniac and 'find | An entrance to the caverns of his mind' (ll. 572–3) in order to 'reclaim him from his dark estate' (l. 574).

In *The Cenci*, Shelley depicts the 'dark estate' of the human condition by attending to the 'caverns of the mind', or, as he calls it in the Preface to the play, 'the human heart' (p. 316). While still a teenager, Shelley had published two Gothic novels, *Zastrozzi* and *St. Irvyne* (both 1810), novels that show a relish for sensationalist plots involving vengeance, hatred, and passionate feeling. In his finest works, this strain of Gothicism transmutes, as it does in the portrait of Beatrice Cenci's father, the sadistic Count, into an altogether more harrowing awareness of the potential for evil in human beings. The play constructs traps even while voicing a desire for freedom. Beatrice, incestuously raped by her father, responds to her violation by contriving his death. The consequence is a Romantic revenge tragedy that dramatizes with great skill knotty moral dilemmas and induces in the audience a 'restless and anatomizing casuistry' (Preface, p. 317): we want to excuse Beatrice's involvement in her father's assassination yet we 'feel', as Shelley has it, 'that she has done what needs justification'.

2

Controversy about Shelley's worth has always centred on the poet's style, described with malign brilliance by William Hazlitt as 'a passionate dream, a straining after impossibilities, a record of fond conjectures, a confused embodying of vague abstractions'.[13] This style is controversial because the demands it places on the reader are

[13] From Hazlitt's unsigned review of *PP*, in the *Edinburgh Review*, July 1824; quoted from Theodore Redpath, *The Young Romantics and Critical Opinion 1807–1824* (London, 1973), 388.

inseparable from the challenges to received ideas posed by its contents. Among these challenges is Shelley's atheism, itself by no means an uncomplicated stance in the poetry and prose.[14] Even in the hostile attack on the Christian God in *Queen Mab*, in the Note appended to the words 'There is No God!' one comes across the following: 'This negation must be understood solely to affect a creative Deity. The hypothesis of a pervading Spirit coeternal with the universe, remains unshaken' (p. 79). There is what can look like a God-shaped hole in Shelley's work, variously filled by terms such as 'Necessity', 'Power', the 'One', and 'the unknown God', terms that hover between the status of imaginative fictions and sceptical but insistent hypotheses.[15] Shelley wishes to nullify the authority of a Jehovah-like deity conceived in the image and likeness of a tyrannical earthly ruler, but he is conscious of supra-rational intimations which seem evidence of what in *A Defence of Poetry* he calls a 'divinity in man' (p. 698). His dislike of Christianity as an institution coexists with a growing admiration for the 'sublime human character of Jesus Christ', a character 'deformed', we are told in a note to *Hellas*, 'by an imputed identification with a Demon, who tempted, betrayed, and punished the innocent beings who were called into existence by his sole will' (p. 587). The rhetoric is meant to provoke, and one can hear in it the accents of the Shelley who irritated Benjamin Robert Haydon (painter and friend of Keats) by 'saying in the most feminine and gentle voice, "As to that detestable religion, the Christian . . ."'[16] But the admiration for Jesus is heartfelt, as is a quasi-religious spirit of humanist ardour, heard in the essay 'On Christianity' (written in late 1817), where Christ's teachings are interpreted in Shelleyan terms as identifying 'God' with 'all that constitutes human perfection' (*Murray*, p. 259). What is manifest in such redefinitions is not muddle but a readiness to test and explore.

In 'Hymn to Intellectual Beauty' (written in 1816) Shelley rejects as 'Frail spells' (l. 29) attempts to conjure a 'voice from some sublimer world' (l. 25). The words 'God, and ghosts, and Heaven' (version A, l. 27) merely prove the futility of any 'endeavour' (version A, l. 28) to map an other-worldly realm. But Intellectual Beauty is endowed

[14] See David Fuller, 'Shelley and Jesus', *Durham University Journal*, NS 54 (1993), 211–23, Robert M. Ryan, *The Romantic Reformation: Religious Politics in English Literature, 1789–1824* (Cambridge, 1997), and Martin Priestman, *Romantic Atheism: Poetry and Freethought 1780–1830* (Cambridge, 2000).

[15] See *Queen Mab*, 6. 197; 'Mont Blanc', l. 16; *Adonais*, l. 460; and *Hellas*, l. 211.

[16] Quoted from Edmund Blunden, *Shelley: A Life Story* (1946; repr. London, 1965), 143.

with the qualities of godhead and addressed with spiritual fervour as Shelley composes his own 'Frail spells'. That it is also less an abstract idea than an eroticized anima-like figure could be seen as having personal implications. A key to Shelley's development may well have been his premature expulsion from a largely female household, the older brother of four sisters, with one of whom, Elizabeth, he wrote his first collection of poems, *Victor and Cazire* (1810). In some of his mature poetry, such as *Epipsychidion*, it is possible to regard Shelley as seeking an imaginative and emotional harmony akin to that which he experienced as a child.[17] Clearly, love and desire contribute a revolutionary if troubling power to the poetry. And yet Shelley is a figure hard simply to include in or exclude from the ranks of Romantic feminism. Against his admiration for the writings of his mother-in-law, Mary Wollstonecraft, his recognition that human liberation must involve both men and women ('Can man be free if woman be a slave?', as a line in *Laon and Cythna* (1817; Canto 2, stanza 43) has it), one might point to an anti-Wollstonecraftian drive to turn women from human beings into idealized objects.

That said, Shelley is so restless and enquiring in his investigations of idealism that he can seem his own severest critic, as is at least hinted by the debate provoked by the central figure of *Alastor* (1816). Is the Poet blamed for his 'self-centred seclusion' (p. 92)? Or is he admired for a tenacity and force of quest that inspires the poem's Narrator to praise him as a 'surpassing Spirit' (l. 714)? What fascinates is the intensity with which Shelley traces the tension between awareness of subjective desire and the longing to leave behind '*self*, that burr that will cling to one' (*L* 2. 109). In 'On Love' (written in 1818), he speaks of love as 'the bond and the sanction which connects not only man with man, but with everything which exists' (p. 632). But he also stresses the unknowableness of others and the genesis of love in an imagining of our own best selves. If Shelley's poetry is often about narcissism, about the lure of falling in love with one's own ideals, it confronts the dangers of such falling in love. The boundaries the verse wishes to break down reassert themselves to productive poetic effect; so, at the close of *Epipsychidion* the poem swings between a sense that words cannot describe the union with another rapturously yearned after in the preceding lines and the admission that such a union is impossible. In the late poems to Jane Williams, poems that occupy

[17] See *Sperry* for the connection between the poetry and 'the grown man who sought to recreate a lost harmony through a network of extraordinarily idealized personal relationships', p. ix.

a difficult zone between friendship and love, there is once more a longing for union. Shelley describes Jane's song as 'revealing | A tone | Of some world far from ours | Where music and moonlight and feeling | Are one' ('To Jane ('The keen stars were twinkling'), ll. 20–4). The writing is balanced between a recognition that the desired world is 'far from ours' and the assertion that Jane is, indeed, 'revealing' such a world.

The boundaries between the self and the world, or the private and the public, are fluid in Shelley's work. Though his writing bears the impress of his 'individual mind' (*Peter Bell the Third*, l. 303), he gives poetry a prominent social role, and unsettles the authority of the stable ego. In the essay 'On Life' (written in 1819), he offers a sceptical interrogation of personal identity: 'the existence of distinct individual minds similar to that which is employed in now questioning its own nature, is likewise found to be a delusion' (p. 635). It is characteristic of Shelley's rapidity of thought that the passage sees individuality as 'a delusion' but admits the need to believe in a 'distinct individual mind' capable of questioning its own nature. Shelleyan doubt is never automatic or superficial; he castigates a reductive scepticism in his attack on Enlightenment 'reasoners' in *A Defence of Poetry* (Notes, p. 834). At the same time, he never loses sight of the dangers of a fixed sense of self—whether embodied in the heroic yet hate-blinded resistance of Prometheus to Jupiter, or in the Wordsworthian 'hero' of *Peter Bell the Third*, unable to 'Fancy another situation | From which to dart his contemplation | Than that wherein he stood' (ll. 300–2).

The ability to imagine a different viewpoint is, in fact, crucial to the dialogue between author and reader which Shelley's poetry encourages. An increasingly central impulse in his writing is the wish to work on the reader's imagination, so that the reader will use that imagination to 'Fancy another situation'. As Shelley explains in the Preface to *Prometheus Unbound*, he aims to avoid 'Didactic poetry', to offer, instead, 'beautiful idealisms of moral excellence' (p. 232). If in *Queen Mab* his favoured style is assertion, a capacity for which never deserts him, he develops a capacity to subsume specific ideas within a more ambitious attempt to render the reader's mind 'the receptacle of a thousand unapprehended combinations of thought' (*A Defence of Poetry*, p. 681). In *Laon and Cythna*, narrative events—the story of the education and careers of two revolutionaries—are experienced through the filter of consciousness; much of the work's most compelling writing takes us close to dream, vision, and nightmare, and employs interlacing figurative suggestions. *Prometheus Unbound* does not shy away from abstraction: the Fury's speech to Prometheus in Act 1 asserts that 'The good want power . . . | The powerful goodness want' (1. 626–7) in an incisive analysis of political malaise. Yet, in the act of imagining a millennial universe which replaces hierarchy, power, and authority with harmony, delight in otherness, and freedom, Shelley shapes a language which is symbolic and, in some respects, untranslatable. Echoes and anticipations cluster in the spirit-voiced world of the lyrical drama, until in the final Act we inhabit a genuinely Utopian poetry. Even here, Shelley does not untether his language from reality; he is still capable of plain statement—'Familiar acts are beautiful through love' (4. 403)—and he often depicts the redeemed world of his imaginings through negative epithets that bring to mind, by contrast, things as they were (or are), as when human beings are said to be 'Equal, unclassed, tribeless and nationless' (3. 4. 195).[18] Moreover, his visions of transformation, such as Ione's and Panthea's descriptions of the moon and earth in Act 4, draw on his age's scientific knowledge, gathered into a metaphorical imagination that is also fertilized by memories of passages in Milton and Dante. The lyrical drama is sharply aware of the realities which it seeks to alter. In terms of its plot, this awareness of realities other than will and desire shows in the fact that neither Prometheus' resistance nor Asia's quest for answers and trust in love will, by themselves, bring about change. Something else is needed, a favourable concatenation of events and circumstance, embodied in the form of Demogorgon, a figure needed for the wheel of history to turn.

The aspiring upward spiral, rather than the determinist, revolving cycle, is the trajectory that Shelley would prefer history to describe. But it is part of his honesty that he is able, at the end of *Hellas*, his intervention on the side of the Greeks in their War of Independence against the Turks, to admit the tragic potential that lurks inside the messianic lyric cry, 'The world's great age begins anew' (l. 1060): 'The world is weary of the past,' he concludes, 'O might it die or rest at last!' (ll. 1100–1). 'A shadow tracks thy flight of fire' (l. 3), from 'The Two Spirits—An Allegory', is a line that one can apply to many of Shelley's later poems. In *Adonais* he is on the brink of rejecting this world in favour of 'the white radiance of Eternity' (l. 463), even though life's 'dome of many-coloured glass' (l. 462) has counterbalancing attractions. The unresting drive to explore the match or

[18] See Timothy Webb, 'The Unascended Heaven: Negatives in *Prometheus Unbound*', in Kelvin Everest (ed.), *Shelley Revalued: Essays from the Gregynog Conference* (Leicester, 1983).

mismatch between imaginative desire and historical event pervades his last, unfinished poem, *The Triumph of Life*, in which Shelley confronts the realities of post-Napoleonic Europe. For all its political gloom, however, *The Triumph of Life* is no straightforward retraction of earlier aspirations. For one thing, as always in Shelley, the stylishness of the writing is an advertisement for hope; for another, the quest to understand impels the poem beyond despair, driving the Narrator, just before the fragment breaks off, to ask, 'what is Life?' (l. 544). It is a question that resonates because we can hear within it, after the narrative of Rousseau's encounter with the 'shape all light' (l. 352), a further Shelleyan question, 'what should life be?' Had Shelley returned alive from his last, fatal boat-trip across the Gulf of Spezia, he would have continued to pose both questions with skill, power, and integrity.

3

This selection, organized chronologically, includes all but one of Shelley's longer poems, from *Queen Mab* onwards, in their entirety. Only *Laon and Cythna* (later *The Revolt of Islam*) is excerpted, though we have found space for almost a third of its 4,818 lines, including the Dedication, all of Cantos 1 and 2, and substantial extracts from Cantos 6–10 and 12 (plus the poem's prose Preface). In addition to a wide range of Shelley's shorter poems, we have included a representative sampling of his prose: the Prefaces to the longer poems, the most important of the lengthy Notes to *Queen Mab* (which include versions of *The Necessity of Atheism* and 'A Vindication of Natural Diet'), *An Address to the People on the Death of the Princess Charlotte*, *A Defence of Poetry*, almost all of *A Philosophical View of Reform*, and the essays 'On Love' and 'On Life'. Limitations of space have prevented us from including samples of Shelley's correspondence or any of his translations. The most important of the translations are of Plato's *Symposium*, canto 28 of Dante's *Purgatorio*, *The Cyclops* by Euripides, and the late, finely wrought Englishings of scenes from Calderón and Goethe. Shelley's extraordinary breadth of reading—including immersion in the works of many Latin and Greek authors, as well as in the King James Bible—is everywhere apparent in his poetry; the translations underline the force of his wish to achieve in his writing that 'identification of ourselves with the beautiful which exists in thought, action or person, not our own' (*A Defence of Poetry*, p. 682).

CHRONOLOGY

1792 Born 4 Aug. at Field Place, Horsham, Sussex, the eldest child of Timothy Shelley, landowner, Whig MP, later Baronet (1806).

1802–4 Educated at Syon House Academy, Isleworth, near London.

1804–10 Educated at Eton.

1810 Publishes two Gothic novels, *Zastrozzi* (spring) and *St. Irvine* (Dec.); *Original Poetry by Victor and Cazire* (written with his sister, Elizabeth, published and withdrawn, Sept.); and *Posthumous Fragments of Margaret Nicholson* (published Nov.). At University College, Oxford (from Oct.).

1811 Publishes the pamphlet *The Necessity of Atheism* (Feb., written with fellow undergraduate Thomas Jefferson Hogg); expelled with Hogg (25 Mar.) for refusing to answer questions about its publication. Meets the 16-year-old Harriet Westbrook (Jan.), elopes with and marries her (in Edinburgh, 29 Aug.).

1812 Visits Dublin and publishes two pamphlets on Irish political reform and Catholic Emancipation, *Address to the Irish People* and *Proposals for an Association . . . of Philanthropists* (Feb.); prints *Declaration of Rights* (Mar.). Becomes a vegetarian (Mar.). From 9 April lives in Wales, then Lynmouth, Devon, where he is under government surveillance (for radical activities); writes *Letter to Lord Ellenborough*; his servant is imprisoned in Aug. for distributing *Declaration of Rights* and *The Devil's Walk* (written winter 1811–12). Continued political activity in Tremadoc, North Wales (from Sept.), where William Madocks is building an embankment and model village; writes *Queen Mab*. Meets William Godwin (Oct.) and Thomas Love Peacock (Nov.). Copies out poems in the 'Esdaile Notebook' (Nov.–Dec.).

1813 Leaves Tremadoc (26 Dec.), in mysterious and threatening circumstances; visits Dublin and Killarney (Mar.); returns to London (Apr.). *A Vindication of Natural Diet* privately published (Apr.–May, later included as a note to *Queen Mab*). *Queen Mab* privately and anonymously published in May. Ianthe Shelley born (23 June). Moves to Bracknell, Berkshire (July), near Peacock.

1814 Privately publishes and distributes *A Refutation of Deism* (late 1813–early 1814). After a growing estrangement with Harriet, he meets and elopes with Mary Godwin, daughter of William Godwin and Mary Wollstonecraft (27 July); tours continent with Mary and her half-sister Claire Clairmont (returning to England 13 Sept.). Charles Shelley born to Harriet (30 Nov.).

1815 Mary's first child born (22. Feb.); dies two weeks later. After death of his grandfather (5 Jan.), financial problems are partially alleviated in June by a settlement agreed with his father (including a yearly annual allowance of £1,000). Moves to Bishopsgate, Windsor Park (Aug.).

1816 William Shelley born to Mary (24 Jan.). Publishes *Alastor . . . and Other Poems* (Feb.; *Alastor* itself written in late 1815). Tours Switzerland with Mary and Claire (25 May–29 Aug.); meets Byron at Lake Geneva, where S. writes 'Hymn to Intellectual Beauty' and 'Mont Blanc', and Mary begins writing *Frankenstein*. Returns to England 8 Sept., probably leaving the so-called 'Scrope Davies Notebook' with Byron (a notebook not returned to Shelley and only rediscovered in 1976); settles in Marlow. Suicides of Mary's half-sister Fanny Imlay (9 Oct.) and Harriet (9 Nov.). Leigh Hunt introduces S. to Keats and Horace Smith (Dec.). Marries Mary Godwin (30 Dec.).

1817 Publishes *A Proposal for Putting Reform to the Vote* (Mar.). The Lord Chancellor (Lord Eldon) denies S. custody of his two children by Harriet (27 Mar.). Writes *Laon and Cythna* (Apr.–Sept.; published Dec., then immediately suppressed by publisher). Clara Shelley born to Mary (2 Sept.). Works on *Rosalind and Helen* (Sept.). Writes *An Address to the People on the Death of the Princess Charlotte* (11–12 Nov., a limited number probably printed in 1817 (none survives); published posthumously, *c.*1843). Anonymous publication of *History of a Six Weeks' Tour* by Mary and S. (winter), including 'Mont Blanc'. Writes 'Ozymandias' (Dec.; published in the *Examiner*, in Jan. 1818).

1818 Publishes *The Revolt of Islam* (revised version of *Laon and Cythna*) in Jan. Leaves for Italy (13 Mar.). Meets Maria and John Gisborne at Livorno (Leghorn) (May). Moves to Bagni di Lucca (11 June), where he finishes *Rosalind and Helen*, translates Plato's *Symposium*, writes 'On Love'. Meets Byron in Venice (Aug.). Stays at Este, near Venice (until 5 Nov.), where he begins work on *Julian and Maddalo*, 'Lines Written among the Euganean Hills', and *Prometheus Unbound*. The one-year-old Clara Shelley dies in Venice (24 Sept.). Visits Rome (20–7 Nov.), then Naples (11 Dec.), where he tours Vesuvius and the Bay of Baiae and writes 'Stanzas Written in Dejection . . . near Naples' (Dec.).

1819 Visits Pompeii and Paestum (24–5 Feb.), returning to Rome on 5 March. Writes Acts 2 and 3 of *Prometheus Unbound* (Mar.–Apr.), finishes *Julian and Maddalo* (sent to Hunt in Aug.). Publishes *Rosalind and Helen . . . with Other Poems* (spring). William Shelley dies (7 June, aged three-and-a-half). Returns to Livorno (Leghorn) (17 June), where completes *The Cenci* (8 Aug.) and has it printed in

Italy, writes *The Mask of Anarchy* (Sept.; published posthumously, 1832). Moves to Florence (2 Oct.), where he writes 'Ode to the West Wind' (late Oct.), *Peter Bell the Third* (Oct.–Nov.), 'On Life' (Nov.–Dec.), *A Philosophical View of Reform* (begun Nov.; unfinished, published posthumously, 1920), 'England in 1819' (Dec.), and Act 4 of *Prometheus Unbound* (finished in Dec.). Percy Florence Shelley born (12 Nov.). Birth of S.'s 'Neapolitan charge', 'Elena Adelaide Shelley' (27 Dec.), registered by S. as his and Mary's child (died 9 June 1820), though it is unlikely that S., Mary, or Claire Clairmont were the child's natural parents.

1820 Moves to Pisa (late Jan.), where writes 'The Sensitive Plant' and publishes *The Cenci* in England (both in spring). Moves to Livorno (15 June–4 Aug.) and writes *Letter to Maria Gisborne*, 'To a Skylark', 'Ode to Liberty'. Moves to the Baths of San Giuliano, near Pisa (Aug.–Oct.) and writes *The Witch of Atlas*, *Swellfoot the Tyrant* (published Dec., and immediately suppressed), and 'Ode to Naples'. Publishes *Prometheus Unbound . . ., with Other Poems* (Aug.). Returns to Pisa (31 Oct.), begins friendship with Emilia Viviani (Dec.) to whom *Epipsychidion* will be addressed.

1821 Edward and Jane Williams, friends of S.'s cousin Thomas Medwin, come to live in Pisa (13 Jan.). Pirated edition of *Queen Mab* published in London by William Clark (who is subsequently imprisoned for its publication). Writes *Epipsychidion* (Jan.–Feb. (though drawing on material written before S. met Viviani); published May), *A Defence of Poetry* (Feb.–Mar.; published posthumously, 1840 [1839]), *Adonais* (Apr.–June; published July), and *Hellas* (Oct.; published 1822). Byron moves to Pisa (1 Nov.).

1822 At work on *Charles the First* (Jan.). Edward Trelawny arrives in Pisa (14 Jan.). Writes poems to Jane Williams (Jan.–July), translates scenes from Goethe and Calderón (Jan.–Feb.). *Hellas* published (Feb.). Moves with family and Edward and Jane Williams to Casa Magni at San Terenzo near Lerici (30 Apr.), where he works on *The Triumph of Life* (May–July; unfinished, posthumously published 1824). On 1 July sails on new boat, the *Don Juan*, to Livorno with Edward Williams (to meet Leigh Hunt and family); on return voyage both men drown with Charles Vivian, a deckhand (8 July). Cremated on 15 Aug. on the beach between La Spezia and Leghorn (his ashes are interred in the Protestant Cemetery in Rome, 1823).

1824 Publication of *Posthumous Poems*, edited by Mary S.; withdrawn from publication because of objections of Sir Timothy.

1839 Publication of Mary S.'s editions of Shelley's poetry (the first in four volumes, the second in one volume) and prose (though the title-page is dated 1840).

NOTE ON THE TEXT

SHELLEY's texts are notoriously difficult to edit. There are two main reasons for this: at his death, he left many poems and prose works unpublished and, indeed, on occasions, unfinished; he did not see proofs for many poems that he did publish during his lifetime. For these reasons, manuscript material is of unusual importance for editors of his work. We have drawn on this manuscript material heavily in editing our texts. Along with the volumes in the *Shelley and His Circle* series, the two series published over the last two decades by Garland, the *Bodleian Shelley Manuscripts* (*BSM*) series and the relevant volumes in the *Manuscripts of the Younger Romantics* (*MYR*) series, both under the general editorship of Donald H. Reiman, have made this manuscript material more widely available. As well as photofacsimiles of the manuscripts, they nearly always include transcriptions and a wealth of detailed commentary. Because each text by Shelley presents its own problems, we have indicated in each note to the poems and prose works our copy-text, referring the reader to relevant facsimile volumes.

Our editorial policy is one of fidelity to copy-text, while retaining the freedom to emend, where appropriate, in the light of other relevant printed or manuscript authorities and our own editorial judgement. Spellings have usually been modernized; occasionally, we have kept the original spelling when modernization would involve the sacrifice of some possibility of word-play (e.g. 'wrapt') or sound value (e.g. 'sate'). Punctuation has been modernized (usually involving the elimination or insertion of commas) when not to do so presents a serious obstacle to understanding. In matters of capitalization we have followed the practice in our copy-text and other relevant printed or manuscript authorities.

The degree sign (°) indicates a note at the end of the book.

'A Cat in distress'

1

A Cat in distress
Nothing more or less
Good folks I must faithfully tell ye,
As I am a sinner
It wants for some dinner
To stuff out its own little belly.

2

You mightn't easily guess
All the modes of distress
Which torture the tenants of earth,
And the various evils
Which like many devils
Attend the poor dogs from their birth.

3

Some a living require
And others desire
An old fellow out of the way,
And which is the best
I leave to be guessed
For I cannot pretend to say.

4

One wants society
T'other variety
Others a tranquil life,
Some want food
Others as good
Only require a wife.

5

But this poor little Cat
Only wanted a rat
To stuff out its own little maw,
And 'twere as good
Had some people such food
To make them hold their jaw.

To the Emperors of Russia and Austria Who Eyed the Battle of Austerlitz from the Heights whilst Buonaparte Was Active in the Thickest of the Fight

Coward Chiefs! who while the fight
  Rages in the plain below
Hide the shame of your affright
  On yon distant mountain's brow,
Does one human feeling creep
Through your hearts' remorseless sleep?
On that silence cold and deep
  Does one impulse flow
Such as fires the Patriot's breast,
Such as breaks the Hero's rest?

No, cowards! ye are calm and still.
  Keen frosts that blight the human bud
Each opening petal blight and kill
  And bathe its tenderness in blood.
Ye hear the groans of those who die,
Ye hear the whistling death-shots fly.
And when the yells of Victory
  Float o'er the murdered good,
Ye smile secure.—On yonder plain
  The game, if lost, begins again.

Think ye the restless fiend who haunts
  The tumult of yon gory field,
Whom neither shame nor danger daunts,
  Who dares not fear, who cannot yield,
Will not with Equalizing blow
Exalt the high, abase the low,°
And in one mighty shock o'erthrow
  The slaves that sceptres wield,
Till from the ruin of the storm
  Ariseth Freedom's awful form?

Hushed below the battle's jar
    Night rests silent on the Heath,
Silent save when vultures soar
    Above the wounded warrior's death.
How sleep ye now, unfeeling Kings!
    Peace seldom folds her snowy wings
On poisoned memory's conscience-stings,
    Which lurk bad hearts beneath,
Nor downy beds procure repose
Where crime and terror mingle throes.

Yet may your terrors rest secure.
    Thou Northern chief, why startest thou?°
Pale Austria, calm those fears. Be sure°
    The tyrant needs such slaves as you.°
Think ye the world would bear his sway
Were dastards such as you away?
No! they would pluck his plumage gay
    Torn from a nation's woe,
And lay him in the oblivious gloom
Where Freedom now prepares your tomb.

Zeinab and Kathema

Upon the lonely beach Kathema lay;
    Against his folded arm his heart beat fast.
Through gathering tears the Sun's departing ray
    In coldness o'er his shuddering spirit passed
And all unfelt the breeze of evening came
That fanned with quivering wing his wan cheek's feeble flame.

'Oh!' cried the mourner, 'could this widowed soul
    But fly where yonder Sun now speeds to dawn.'°
He paused—a thousand thoughts began to roll;
    Like waves they swept in restless tumult on,
Like those fast waves that quick-succeeding beat
Without one lasting shape the beach beneath his feet.

And now the beamless, broad and yellow sphere
Half sinking lingered on the crimson sea.
A shape of darksome distance does appear
Within its semicircled radiancy.
All sense was gone to his betrothed one—
His eye fell on the form that dimmed the setting sun,—

He thought on his betrothed . . . for his youth
With her that was its charm to ripeness grew.
All that was dear in love, or fair in truth,
With her was shared as childhood's moments flew,
And mingled with sweet memories of her
Was life's unveiling morn with all its bliss and care,

A wild and lovely Superstition's spell—
Love for the friend that life and freedom gave,
Youth's growing hopes that watch themselves so well,
Passion so prompt to blight, so strong to save,
And childhood's host of memories combine
Her life and love around his being to entwine.

And to their wishes with its joy-mixed pain
Just as the veil of hope began to fall,
The Christian murderers over-ran the plain,
Ravaging, burning and polluting all.
Zeinab was reft to grace the robber's land;
Each drop of kindred blood stained the invaders' brand.

Yes! they had come their holy book to bring
Which God's own son's apostles had compiled,
That charity and peace and love might spring
Within a world by God's blind ire defiled,
But rapine, war and treachery rushed before
Their hosts, and murder dyed Kathema's bower in gore.

Therefore his soul was widowed, and alone
He stood in the world's wide and drear expanse.
No human ear could shudder at his groan,
No heart could thrill with his unspeaking glance,
One only hope yet lingering dared to burn,
Urging to high emprise and deeds that danger spurn.

The glow has failed on Ocean's western line,
Faded from every moveless cloud above.
The moon is up—she that was wont to shine
And bless thy childish nights of guileless love,
Unhappy one, ere Christian rapine tore
All ties, and stained thy hopes in a dear mother's gore.

The form that in the setting Sun was seen
Now in the moonlight slowly nears the shore,
The white sails gleaming o'er the billows green
That sparkle into foam its prow before.
A wanderer of the deep it seems to be
On high adventures bent, and feats of chivalry.

Then hope and wonder filled the mourner's mind.
He gazed till vision even began to fail,
When to the pulses of the evening wind
A little boat approaching gave its sail,
Rode o'er the slow raised surges near the strand,
Ran up the beach and gave some stranger men to land.

'If thou wilt bear me to far England's shore
Thine is this heap, the Christian's God.'
The chief with gloating rapture viewed the ore
And his pleased avarice gave the willing nod.
They reach the ship, the freshening breezes rise
And smooth and fast they speed beneath the moonlight skies.

What heart e'er felt more ardent longings now?
What eye than his e'er beamed with riper hope
As curbed impatience on his open brow
There painted fancy's unsuspected scope,
As all that's fair the foreign land appeared
By ever present love, wonder and hope endeared?

Meanwhile through calm and storm, through night and day,
Unvarying in her aim the vessel went
As if some inward spirit ruled her way
And her tense sails were conscious of intent,
Till Albion's cliffs gleamed o'er her plunging bow
And Albion's river floods bright sparkled round her prow.

Then on the land in joy Kathema leaped
And kissed the soil in which his hopes were sown;
These even now in thought his heart has reaped.
Elate of body and soul he journeyed on
And the strange things of a strange land passed by
Like motes and shadows pressed upon his charmèd eye.°

Yet Albion's changeful skies and chilling wind,
The change from Cashmire's vale might well denote.
There Heaven and Earth are ever bright and kind,
Here blights and storms and damp forever float,
Whilst hearts are more ungenial than the zone,
Gross, spiritless, alive to no pangs but their own.

There flowers and fruits are ever fair and ripe,
Autumn there mingles with the bloom of spring,
And forms unpinched by frost or hunger's gripe,
A natural veil o'er natural spirits fling.
Here, woe on all but wealth has set its foot,
Famine, disease and crime even wealth's proud gates pollute.

Unquiet death and premature decay,
Youth tottering on the crutches of old age,
And ere the noon of manhood's riper day
Pangs that no art of medicine can assuage,
Madness and passion ever mingling flames,
And souls that well become such miserable frames—

These are the bribes which Art to man has given
To yield his taintless nature to her sway.
So might dank night with meteors tempt fair Heaven
To blot the sunbeam and forswear the day
Till gleams of baleful light alone might show
The pestilential mists, the darkness and the woe.

Kathema little felt the sleet and wind,
He little heeded the wide altered scene.
The flame that lived within his eager mind
There kindled all the thoughts that once had been.
He stood alone in England's varied woe,
Safe, mid the flood of crime that round his steps did flow.

It was an evening when the bitterest breath
Of dark December swept the mists along
That the lone wanderer came to a wild heath.
Courage and hope had stayed his nature long,
Now cold and unappeasèd hunger spent
His strength; sensation failed in total languishment.

When he awaked to life cold horror crept
Even to his heart, for a damp deathy smell
Had slowly come around him while he slept.
He started . . . lo! the fitful moonbeams fell
Upon a dead and naked female form
That from a gibbet high swung to the sullen storm.°

And wildly in the wind its dark hair swung,
Low mingling with the clangour of the chain,
Whilst ravenous birds of prey that on it clung
In the dull ear of night poured their sad strain,
And ghastlily her shapeless visage shone
In the unsteady light, half mouldered through the bone.

Then madness seized Kathema, and his mind
A prophecy of horror filled. He scaled
The gibbet which swung slowly in the wind
High o'er the heath.—Scarcely his strength availed
To grasp the chain, when by the moonlight's gleam
His palsied gaze was fixed on Zeinab's altered frame.

Yes! in those orbs once bright with life and love
Now full-fed worms bask in unnatural light;
That neck on which his eyes were wont to rove
In rapture, changed by putrefaction's blight.
Now rusts the ponderous links that creak beneath
Its weight, and turns to life the frightful sport of death.°

Then in the moonlight played Kathema's smile
Calmly.—In peace his spirit seemed to be.
He paused even like a man at ease awhile,
Then spoke—'My love! I will be like to thee,
A mouldering carcase or a spirit blest,
With thee corruption's prey, or Heavens happy guest.'

He twined the chain around his neck, then leaped
    Forward, in haste to meet the life to come.
An iron-souled son of Europe might have wept
    To witness such a noble being's doom,
As on the death scene Heaven indignant frowned
And Night in horror drew her veil the dead around.

For they had torn his Zeinab from her home.
    Her innocent habits were all rudely shriven—°
And dragged to live in love's untimely tomb
    To prostitution, crime and woe was driven.
The human race seemed leagued against her weal,
And indignation cased her naked heart in steel.

Therefore against them she waged ruthless war
    With their own arms of bold and bloody crime,
Even like a mild and sweetly-beaming star
    Whose rays were wont to grace the matin prime°
Changed to a comet horrible and bright
Which wild careers awhile then sinks in dark-red night.

Thus, like its God, unjust and pitiless,
    Crimes first are made and then avenged by man,
For where's the tender heart, whose hope can bless
    Or man's, or God's, unprofitable plan,
A universe of horror and decay,
Gibbets, disease, and wars and hearts as hard as they?

Sonnet

On Launching Some Bottles Filled with Knowledge *into the Bristol Channel*

Vessels of Heavenly medicine! may the breeze
Auspicious waft your dark green forms to shore;
Safe may ye stern the wide surrounding roar°
Of the wild whirlwinds and the raging seas:
And oh! if Liberty e'er deigned to stoop

From yonder lowly throne her crownless brow,
Sure she will breathe around your emerald group
The fairest breezes of her west that blow.°
Yes! she will waft ye to some freeborn soul
Whose eyebeam, kindling as it meets your freight,
Her heaven-born flame on suffering Earth will light
Until its radiance gleams from pole to pole
And tyrant-hearts with powerless envy burst
To see their night of ignorance dispersed.

Sonnet

To a Balloon, Laden with Knowledge

Bright ball of flame that through the gloom of even
Silently takest thine etherial way
And with surpassing glory dimm'st each ray
Twinkling amid the dark blue Depths of Heaven,
Unlike the Fire thou bearest, soon shalt thou
Fade like a meteor in surrounding gloom,
Whilst that, unquenchable, is doomed to glow
A watch-light by the patriot's lonely tomb,
A ray of courage to the oppressed and poor,
A spark though gleaming on the hovel's hearth
Which through the tyrant's gilded domes shall roar,
A beacon in the darkness of the Earth,
A Sun which o'er the renovated scene
Shall dart like Truth where Falsehood yet has been.

QUEEN MAB;

A PHILOSOPHICAL POEM

WITH NOTES

ÉCRASEZ L'INFAME!

Correspondance de Voltaire.°

Avia Pieridum peragro loca, nullius ante
Trita solo; juvat integros accedere fonteis;
Atque haurire: juvatque novos decerpere flores.

*   *   *   *   *   *   *

Unde prius nulli velarint tempora musae.
Primum quod magnis doceo de rebus; et arctis
Religionum animos nodis exsolvere pergo.—Lucret. lib. iv°

Δος που στῶ, καὶ κοσμον κινησω.—Archimedes°

To Harriet *****°

Whose is the love that, gleaming through the world,
Wards off the poisonous arrow of its scorn?
   Whose is the warm and partial praise,
   Virtue's most sweet reward?

Beneath whose looks did my reviving soul
Riper in truth and virtuous daring grow?
   Whose eyes have I gazed fondly on,
   And loved mankind the more?

Harriet! on thine:—thou wert my purer mind;
Thou wert the inspiration of my song;
   Thine are these early wilding flowers,
   Though garlanded by me.

Then press unto thy breast this pledge of love,
And know, though time may change and years may roll,
   Each flowret gathered in my heart
   It consecrates to thine.

I

How wonderful is Death,
Death and his brother Sleep!
One, pale as yonder waning moon
With lips of lurid blue;
The other, rosy as the morn
When throned on ocean's wave
It blushes o'er the world:
Yet both so passing wonderful!

Hath then the gloomy Power
Whose reign is in the tainted sepulchres
Seized on her sinless soul?
Must then that peerless form
Which love and admiration cannot view
Without a beating heart, those azure veins
Which steal like streams along a field of snow,
That lovely outline, which is fair
As breathing marble, perish?
Must putrefaction's breath
Leave nothing of this heavenly sight
But loathsomeness and ruin?
Spare nothing but a gloomy theme,
On which the lightest heart might moralize?
Or is it only a sweet slumber
Stealing o'er sensation,
Which the breath of roseate morning
Chaseth into darkness?
Will Ianthe wake again,°
And give that faithful bosom joy
Whose sleepless spirit waits to catch
Light, life and rapture from her smile?

Yes! she will wake again,
Although her glowing limbs are motionless,
And silent those sweet lips,
Once breathing eloquence,
That might have soothed a tiger's rage,
Or thawed the cold heart of a conqueror.
Her dewy eyes are closed,

And on their lids, whose texture fine
Scarce hides the dark blue orbs beneath,
The baby Sleep is pillowèd:
Her golden tresses shade
The bosom's stainless pride,
Curling like tendrils of the parasite
Around a marble column.

Hark! whence that rushing sound?
'Tis like the wondrous strain
That round a lonely ruin swells,
Which, wandering on the echoing shore,
The enthusiast hears at evening:
'Tis softer than the west wind's sigh;
'Tis wilder than the unmeasured notes
Of that strange lyre whose strings°
The genii of the breezes sweep:°
Those lines of rainbow light
Are like the moonbeams when they fall
Through some cathedral window, but the tints
Are such as may not find
Comparison on earth.

Behold the chariot of the Fairy Queen!
Celestial coursers paw the unyielding air;
Their filmy pennons at her word they furl,°
And stop obedient to the reins of light:
These the Queen of spells drew in,
She spread a charm around the spot,
And leaning graceful from the etherial car,
Long did she gaze, and silently,
Upon the slumbering maid.

Oh! not the visioned poet in his dreams,
When silvery clouds float through the wildered brain,
When every sight of lovely, wild and grand
Astonishes, enraptures, elevates,
When fancy at a glance combines
The wondrous and the beautiful,—
So bright, so fair, so wild a shape
Hath ever yet beheld,

As that which reined the coursers of the air,
And poured the magic of her gaze
Upon the maiden's sleep.

The broad and yellow moon
Shone dimly through her form—
That form of faultless symmetry;
The pearly and pellucid car
Moved not the moonlight's line:
'Twas not an earthly pageant:
Those who had looked upon the sight,
Passing all human glory,
Saw not the yellow moon,
Saw not the mortal scene,
Heard not the night-wind's rush,
Heard not an earthly sound,
Saw but the fairy pageant,
Heard but the heavenly strains
That filled the lonely dwelling.

The Fairy's frame was slight, yon fibrous cloud,°
That catches but the palest tinge of even,
And which the straining eye can hardly seize
When melting into eastern twilight's shadow,
Were scarce so thin, so slight; but the fair star
That gems the glittering coronet of morn,°
Sheds not a light so mild, so powerful,
As that which, bursting from the Fairy's form,
Spread a purpureal halo round the scene,°
Yet with an undulating motion,
Swayed to her outline gracefully.

From her celestial car
The Fairy Queen descended,
And thrice she waved her wand
Circled with wreaths of amaranth:°
Her thin and misty form
Moved with the moving air,
And the clear silver tones,
As thus she spoke, were such
As are unheard by all but gifted ear.

Fairy

Stars! your balmiest influence shed!
Elements! your wrath suspend!
Sleep, Ocean, in the rocky bounds
That circle thy domain!
Let not a breath be seen to stir
Around yon grass-grown ruin's height,
Let even the restless gossamer
Sleep on the moveless air!
Soul of Ianthe! thou,
Judged alone worthy of the envied boon
That waits the good and the sincere; that waits
Those who have struggled, and with resolute will
Vanquished earth's pride and meanness, burst the chains,
The icy chains of custom, and have shone
The day-stars of their age;—Soul of Ianthe!
Awake! arise!

Sudden arose
Ianthe's Soul; it stood
All beautiful in naked purity,
The perfect semblance of its bodily frame,
Instinct with inexpressible beauty and grace.
Each stain of earthliness
Had passed away, it reassumed
Its native dignity, and stood
Immortal amid ruin.

Upon the couch the body lay
Wrapt in the depth of slumber:°
Its features were fixèd and meaningless,
Yet animal life was there,
And every organ yet performed
Its natural functions: 'twas a sight
Of wonder to behold the body and soul.
The self-same lineaments, the same
Marks of identity were there:
Yet, oh, how different! One aspires to Heaven,
Pants for its sempiternal heritage,°

And ever changing, ever rising still,
Wantons in endless being.
The other, for a time the unwilling sport
Of circumstance and passion, struggles on;
Fleets through its sad duration rapidly;
Then like an useless and worn-out machine,
Rots, perishes, and passes.

Fairy

Spirit! who hast dived so deep;
Spirit! who hast soared so high;
Thou the fearless, thou the mild,
Accept the boon thy worth hath earned,
Ascend the car with me.

Spirit

Do I dream? is this new feeling
But a visioned ghost of slumber?
If indeed I am a soul,
A free, a disembodied soul,
Speak again to me.

Fairy

I am the Fairy MAB: to me 'tis given
The wonders of the human world to keep:
The secrets of the immeasurable past,
In the unfailing consciences of men,
Those stern, unflattering chroniclers, I find:
The future, from the causes which arise
In each event, I gather: not the sting
Which retributive memory implants
In the hard bosom of the selfish man;
Nor that ecstatic and exulting throb
Which virtue's votary feels when he sums up
The thoughts and actions of a well-spent day,
Are unforeseen, unregistered by me:
And it is yet permitted me, to rend
The veil of mortal frailty, that the spirit
Clothed in its changeless purity, may know
How soonest to accomplish the great end
For which it hath its being, and may taste

That peace, which in the end all life will share.
This is the meed of virtue; happy Soul,
Ascend the car with me!

The chains of earth's immurement
Fell from Ianthe's spirit;
They shrank and brake like bandages of straw
Beneath a wakened giant's strength.
She knew her glorious change,
And felt in apprehension uncontrolled
New raptures opening round:
Each day-dream of her mortal life,
Each frenzied vision of the slumbers
That closed each well-spent day,
Seemed now to meet reality.

The Fairy and the Soul proceeded;
The silver clouds disparted;
And as the car of magic they ascended,
Again the speechless music swelled,
Again the coursers of the air
Unfurled their azure pennons, and the Queen
Shaking the beamy reins
Bade them pursue their way.

The magic car moved on.
The night was fair, and countless stars
Studded heaven's dark blue vault,—
Just o'er the eastern wave
Peeped the first faint smile of morn:—
The magic car moved on—
From the celestial hoofs
The atmosphere in flaming sparkles flew,
And where the burning wheels
Eddied above the mountain's loftiest peak,
Was traced a line of lightning.
Now it flew far above a rock,
The utmost verge of earth,
The rival of the Andes, whose dark brow
Lowered o'er the silver sea.

Far, far below the chariot's path,
Calm as a slumbering babe,
Tremendous Ocean lay.
The mirror of its stillness showed
The pale and waning stars,
The chariot's fiery track,
And the grey light of morn
Tinging those fleecy clouds
That canopied the dawn.
Seemed it, that the chariot's way
Lay through the midst of an immense concave,
Radiant with million constellations, tinged
With shades of infinite colour,
And semicircled with a belt°
Flashing incessant meteors.

The magic car moved on.
As they approached their goal
The coursers seemed to gather speed;
The sea no longer was distinguished; earth
Appeared a vast and shadowy sphere;
The sun's unclouded orb
Rolled through the black concave;°
Its rays of rapid light
Parted around the chariot's swifter course,
And fell, like ocean's feathery spray
Dashed from the boiling surge
Before a vessel's prow.

The magic car moved on.
Earth's distant orb appeared
The smallest light that twinkles in the heaven;
Whilst round the chariot's way
Innumerable systems rolled,°
And countless spheres diffused
An ever-varying glory.
It was a sight of wonder: some
Were hornèd like the crescent moon;
Some shed a mild and silver beam
Like Hesperus o'er the western sea;°
Some dashed athwart with trains of flame,°

Like worlds to death and ruin driven;
Some shone like suns, and as the chariot passed,
Eclipsed all other light.

Spirit of Nature! here!
In this interminable wilderness
Of worlds, at whose immensity
Even soaring fancy staggers,
Here is thy fitting temple.
Yet not the lightest leaf
That quivers to the passing breeze
Is less instinct with thee:
Yet not the meanest worm
That lurks in graves and fattens on the dead
Less shares thy eternal breath.
Spirit of Nature! thou!
Imperishable as this scene,
Here is thy fitting temple.

2

If solitude hath ever led thy steps
To the wild ocean's echoing shore,
And thou hast lingered there,
Until the sun's broad orb
Seemed resting on the burnished wave,
Thou must have marked the lines
Of purple gold, that motionless
Hung o'er the sinking sphere:
Thou must have marked the billowy clouds
Edged with intolerable radiancy
Towering like rocks of jet
Crowned with a diamond wreath.
And yet there is a moment,
When the sun's highest point
Peeps like a star o'er ocean's western edge,
When those far clouds of feathery gold,
Shaded with deepest purple, gleam
Like islands on a dark blue sea;

Then has thy fancy soared above the earth,
And furled its wearied wing
Within the Fairy's fane.°

Yet not the golden islands
Gleaming in yon flood of light,
Nor the feathery curtains
Stretching o'er the sun's bright couch,
Nor the burnished ocean waves
Paving that gorgeous dome,
So fair, so wonderful a sight
As Mab's etherial palace could afford.
Yet likest evening's vault, that faery Hall!
As Heaven, low resting on the wave, it spread
Its floors of flashing light,
Its vast and azure dome,
Its fertile golden islands
Floating on a silver sea;
Whilst suns their mingling beamings darted
Through clouds of circumambient darkness,
And pearly battlements around
Looked o'er the immense of Heaven.

The magic car no longer moved.
The Fairy and the Spirit
Entered the Hall of Spells:
Those golden clouds
That rolled in glittering billows
Beneath the azure canopy
With the etherial footsteps trembled not:
The light and crimson mists,
Floating to strains of thrilling melody
Through that unearthly dwelling,
Yielded to every movement of the will.
Upon their passive swell the Spirit leaned,
And, for the varied bliss that pressed around,°
Used not the glorious privilege
Of virtue and of wisdom.

'Spirit!' the Fairy said,
And pointed to the gorgeous dome,

'This is a wondrous sight
And mocks all human grandeur;
But, were it virtue's only meed, to dwell°
In a celestial palace, all resigned
To pleasurable impulses, immured
Within the prison of itself, the will
Of changeless nature would be unfulfilled.
Learn to make others happy. Spirit, come!
This is thine high reward:—the past shall rise;
Thou shalt behold the present; I will teach
The secrets of the future.'

The Fairy and the Spirit
Approached the overhanging battlement.—
Below lay stretched the universe!
There, far as the remotest line
That bounds imagination's flight,
Countless and unending orbs
In mazy motion intermingled,
Yet still fulfilled immutably
Eternal nature's law.
Above, below, around
The circling systems formed
A wilderness of harmony;
Each with undeviating aim,
In eloquent silence, through the depths of space
Pursued its wondrous way.

There was a little light
That twinkled in the misty distance:
None but a spirit's eye
Might ken that rolling orb;
None but a spirit's eye,
And in no other place
But that celestial dwelling, might behold
Each action of this earth's inhabitants.
But matter, space and time
In those aerial mansions cease to act;
And all-prevailing wisdom, when it reaps
The harvest of its excellence, o'erbounds

Those obstacles, of which an earthly soul
Fears to attempt the conquest.

The Fairy pointed to the earth.
The Spirit's intellectual eye
Its kindred beings recognized.
The thronging thousands, to a passing view,
Seemed like an anthill's citizens.
How wonderful! that even
The passions, prejudices, interests,
That sway the meanest being, the weak touch
That moves the finest nerve,
And in one human brain
Causes the faintest thought, becomes a link
In the great chain of nature.

'Behold', the Fairy cried,
'Palmyra's ruined palaces!—°
Behold! where grandeur frowned;
Behold! where pleasure smiled;
What now remains?—the memory
Of senselessness and shame—
What is immortal there?
Nothing—it stands to tell
A melancholy tale, to give
An awful warning: soon
Oblivion will steal silently
The remnant of its fame.
Monarchs and conquerors there
Proud o'er prostrate millions trod—
The earthquakes of the human race;
Like them, forgotten when the ruin
That marks their shock is past.

'Beside the eternal Nile,
The Pyramids have risen.
Nile shall pursue his changeless way:
Those pyramids shall fall;
Yea! not a stone shall stand to tell
The spot whereon they stood;

Their very site shall be forgotten,
As is their builder's name!

'Behold yon sterile spot;
Where now the wandering Arab's tent
Flaps in the desert-blast.
There once old Salem's haughty fane°
Reared high to heaven its thousand golden domes,
And in the blushing face of day
Exposed its shameful glory.
Oh! many a widow, many an orphan cursed
The building of that fane; and many a father,
Worn out with toil and slavery, implored
The poor man's God to sweep it from the earth,
And spare his children the detested task
Of piling stone on stone, and poisoning
The choicest days of life,
To soothe a dotard's vanity.°
There an inhuman and uncultured race
Howled hideous praises to their Demon-God;
They rushed to war, tore from the mother's womb
The unborn child,—old age and infancy
Promiscuous perished; their victorious arms°
Left not a soul to breathe. Oh! they were fiends:
But what was he who taught them that the God°
Of nature and benevolence had given
A special sanction to the trade of blood?
His name and theirs are fading, and the tales
Of this barbarian nation, which imposture
Recites till terror credits, are pursuing°
Itself into forgetfulness.

'Where Athens, Rome, and Sparta stood,
There is a moral desert now:
The mean and miserable huts,
The yet more wretched palaces,
Contrasted with those ancient fanes,
Now crumbling to oblivion;
The long and lonely colonnades,
Through which the ghost of Freedom stalks,
Seem like a well-known tune,

Which in some dear scene we have loved to hear,
        Remembered now in sadness.
        But, oh! how much more changed,
        How gloomier is the contrast
        Of human nature there!
Where Socrates expired, a tyrant's slave,°
A coward and a fool, spreads death around—
        Then, shuddering, meets his own.
Where Cicero and Antoninus lived,
    A cowled and hypocritical monk
        Prays, curses and deceives.°

        'Spirit! ten thousand years
        Have scarcely passed away,
Since, in the waste where now the savage drinks
His enemy's blood, and aping Europe's sons,
      Wakes the unholy song of war,
      Arose a stately city,°
Metropolis of the western continent:
    There, now, the mossy column-stone,
Indented by time's unrelaxing grasp,
        Which once appeared to brave
        All, save its country's ruin;
        There the wide forest scene,
Rude in the uncultivated loveliness
        Of gardens long run wild,
Seems, to the unwilling sojourner, whose steps
    Chance in that desert has delayed,
Thus to have stood since earth was what it is.
    Yet once it was the busiest haunt,
Whither, as to a common centre, flocked
    Strangers, and ships, and merchandise:
        Once peace and freedom blessed
        The cultivated plain:
        But wealth, that curse of man,
Blighted the bud of its prosperity:
Virtue and wisdom, truth and liberty,
Fled, to return not, until man shall know
    That they alone can give the bliss
        Worthy a soul that claims
    Its kindred with eternity.

'There's not one atom of yon earth
But once was living man;
Nor the minutest drop of rain,
That hangeth in its thinnest cloud,
But flowed in human veins:
And from the burning plains
Where Lybian monsters yell,
From the most gloomy glens
Of Greenland's sunless clime,
To where the golden fields
Of fertile England spread
Their harvest to the day,
Thou canst not find one spot
Whereon no city stood.

How strange is human pride!
I tell thee that those living things,
To whom the fragile blade of grass,
That springeth in the morn
And perisheth ere noon,
Is an unbounded world;
I tell thee that those viewless beings,
Whose mansion is the smallest particle
Of the impassive atmosphere,
Think, feel and live like man;
That their affections and antipathies,
Like his, produce the laws
Ruling their moral state;
And the minutest throb
That through their frame diffuses
The slightest, faintest motion,
Is fixed and indispensable
As the majestic laws
That rule yon rolling orbs.'

The Fairy paused. The Spirit,
In ecstacy of admiration, felt
All knowledge of the past revived; the events
Of old and wondrous times,
Which dim tradition interruptedly
Teaches the credulous vulgar, were unfolded
In just perspective to the view;

Yet dim from their infinitude.
The Spirit seemed to stand
High on an isolated pinnacle;
The flood of ages combating below,
The depth of the unbounded universe
Above, and all around
Nature's unchanging harmony.

3

'Fairy!' the Spirit said,
And on the Queen of spells
Fixed her etherial eyes,
'I thank thee. Thou hast given
A boon which I will not resign, and taught
A lesson not to be unlearned. I know
The past, and thence I will essay to glean
A warning for the future, so that man
May profit by his errors, and derive
Experience from his folly:
For, when the power of imparting joy
Is equal to the will, the human soul
Requires no other heaven.'

Mab

Turn thee, surpassing Spirit!
Much yet remains unscanned.
Thou knowest how great is man,
Thou knowest his imbecility:°
Yet learn thou what he is;
Yet learn the lofty destiny
Which restless time prepares
For every living soul.

Behold a gorgeous palace, that, amid
Yon populous city, rears its thousand towers
And seems itself a city. Gloomy troops
Of sentinels, in stern and silent ranks,
Encompass it around: the dweller there
Cannot be free and happy; hearest thou not
The curses of the fatherless, the groans
Of those who have no friend? He passes on:

The King, the wearer of a gilded chain
That binds his soul to abjectness, the fool
Whom courtiers nickname monarch, whilst a slave
Even to the basest appetites—that man
Heeds not the shriek of penury; he smiles
At the deep curses which the destitute
Mutter in secret, and a sullen joy
Pervades his bloodless heart when thousands groan
But for those morsels which his wantonness
Wastes in unjoyous revelry, to save
All that they love from famine: when he hears
The tale of horror, to some ready-made face
Of hypocritical assent he turns,
Smothering the glow of shame, that, spite of him,
Flushes his bloated check.
Now to the meal
Of silence, grandeur, and excess, he drags
His palled unwilling appetite. If gold,°
Gleaming around, and numerous viands culled
From every clime, could force the loathing sense
To overcome satiety,—if wealth
The spring it draws from poisons not,—or vice,
Unfeeling, stubborn vice, converteth not
Its food to deadliest venom; then that king
Is happy; and the peasant who fulfils
His unforced task, when he returns at even,
And by the blazing faggot meets again
Her welcome for whom all his toil is sped,
Tastes not a sweeter meal.
Behold him now
Stretched on the gorgeous couch; his fevered brain
Reels dizzily awhile: but ah! too soon
The slumber of intemperance subsides,
And conscience, that undying serpent, calls
Her venomous brood to their nocturnal task.
Listen! he speaks! oh! mark that frenzied eye—
Oh! mark that deadly visage.

King

No cessation!
Oh! must this last for ever! Awful death,

I wish, yet fear to clasp thee!—Not one moment
Of dreamless sleep! O dear and blessed peace!
Why dost thou shroud thy vestal purity
In penury and dungeons? wherefore lurkest
With danger, death, and solitude; yet shun'st
The palace I have built thee? Sacred peace!
Oh visit me but once, but pitying shed
One drop of balm upon my withered soul.

Fairy

Vain man! that palace is the virtuous heart,
And peace defileth not her snowy robes
In such a shed as thine. Hark! yet he mutters;
His slumbers are but varied agonies,
They prey like scorpions on the springs of life.
There needeth not the hell that bigots frame
To punish those who err: earth in itself
Contains at once the evil and the cure;
And all-sufficing nature can chastise
Those who transgress her law—she only knows
How justly to proportion to the fault
The punishment it merits.
                                        Is it strange
That this poor wretch should pride him in his woe?
Take pleasure in his abjectness, and hug
The scorpion that consumes him? Is it strange
That, placed on a conspicuous throne of thorns,
Grasping an iron sceptre, and immured
Within a splendid prison, whose stern bounds
Shut him from all that's good or dear on earth,
His soul asserts not its humanity?
That man's mild nature rises not in war
Against a king's employ? No—'tis not strange.
He, like the vulgar, thinks, feels, acts and lives
Just as his father did; the unconquered powers
Of precedent and custom interpose
Between a *king* and virtue. Stranger yet,
To those who know not nature, nor deduce
The future from the present, it may seem,
That not one slave, who suffers from the crimes
Of this unnatural being; not one wretch,

Whose children famish, and whose nuptial bed
Is earth's unpitying bosom, rears an arm
To dash him from his throne!
                                        Those gilded flies
That, basking in the sunshine of a court,
Fatten on its corruption!—what are they?
—The drones of the community; they feed
On the mechanic's labour: the starved hind°
For them compels the stubborn glebe to yield°
Its unshared harvests; and yon squalid form,
Leaner than fleshless misery, that wastes
A sunless life in the unwholesome mine,
Drags out in labour a protracted death,
To glut their grandeur; many faint with toil,
That few may know the cares and woe of sloth.

Whence, thinkest thou, kings and parasites arose?
Whence that unnatural line of drones, who heap
Toil and unvanquishable penury
On those who build their palaces, and bring
Their daily bread?—From vice, black loathsome vice;
From rapine, madness, treachery, and wrong;
From all that genders misery, and makes
Of earth this thorny wilderness; from lust,
Revenge, and murder. . . . And when reason's voice,
Loud as the voice of nature, shall have waked
The nations; and mankind perceive that vice
Is discord, war, and misery; that virtue
Is peace, and happiness and harmony;
When man's maturer nature shall disdain
The playthings of its childhood;—kingly glare
Will lose its power to dazzle; its authority
Will silently pass by; the gorgeous throne
Shall stand unnoticed in the regal hall,
Fast falling to decay; whilst falsehood's trade
Shall be as hateful and unprofitable
As that of truth is now.
                                  Where is the fame
Which the vain-glorious mighty of the earth
Seek to eternize? Oh! the faintest sound
From time's light footfall, the minutest wave

That swells the flood of ages, whelms in nothing
The unsubstantial bubble. Aye! today
Stern is the tyrant's mandate, red the gaze
That flashes desolation, strong the arm
That scatters multitudes. Tomorrow comes!
That mandate is a thunder-peal that died
In ages past; that gaze, a transient flash
On which the midnight closed, and on that arm
The worm has made his meal.
The virtuous man,
Who, great in his humility, as kings
Are little in their grandeur; he who leads
Invincibly a life of resolute good,
And stands amid the silent dungeon-depths
More free and fearless than the trembling judge,
Who, clothed in venal power, vainly strove
To bind the impassive spirit;—when he falls,°
His mild eye beams benevolence no more:
Withered the hand outstretched but to relieve;
Sunk reason's simple eloquence, that rolled
But to appal the guilty. Yes! the grave
Hath quenched that eye, and death's relentless frost
Withered that arm: but the unfading fame
Which virtue hangs upon its votary's tomb;
The deathless memory of that man, whom kings
Call to their mind and tremble; the remembrance
With which the happy spirit contemplates
Its well-spent pilgrimage on earth,
Shall never pass away.

Nature rejects the monarch, not the man;
The subject, not the citizen: for kings
And subjects, mutual foes, for ever play
A losing game into each other's hands,
Whose stakes are vice and misery. The man
Of virtuous soul commands not, nor obeys.
Power, like a desolating pestilence,
Pollutes whate'er it touches; and obedience,
Bane of all genius, virtue, freedom, truth,
Makes slaves of men, and, of the human frame,
A mechanized automaton.
When Nero,

High over flaming Rome, with savage joy
Lowered like a fiend, drank with enraptured ear°
The shrieks of agonizing death, beheld
The frightful desolation spread, and felt
A new created sense within his soul
Thrill to the sight, and vibrate to the sound;
Thinkest thou his grandeur had not overcome
The force of human kindness? and, when Rome,
With one stern blow, hurled not the tyrant down,
Crushed not the arm red with her dearest blood,
Had not submissive abjectness destroyed
Nature's suggestions?
Look on yonder earth:
The golden harvests spring; the unfailing sun
Sheds light and life; the fruits, the flowers, the trees,
Arise in due succession; all things speak
Peace, harmony, and love. The universe,
In nature's silent eloquence, declares
That all fulfil the works of love and joy,—
All but the outcast man. He fabricates
The sword which stabs his peace; he cherisheth
The snakes that gnaw his heart; he raiseth up
The tyrant, whose delight is in his woe,
Whose sport is in his agony. Yon sun,
Lights it the great alone? Yon silver beams,
Sleep they less sweetly on the cottage thatch,
Than on the dome of kings? Is mother earth
A step-dame to her numerous sons, who earn
Her unshared gifts with unremitting toil;
A mother only to those puling babes
Who, nursed in ease and luxury, make men
The playthings of their babyhood, and mar,
In self-important childishness, that peace
Which men alone appreciate?

Spirit of Nature! no.
The pure diffusion of thy essence throbs
Alike in every human heart.
Thou, aye, erectest there°
Thy throne of power unappealable:
Thou art the judge beneath whose nod

Man's brief and frail authority
    Is powerless as the wind
    That passeth idly by.
Thine the tribunal which surpasseth
  The show of human justice,
    As God surpasses man.

    Spirit of Nature! thou
Life of interminable multitudes;
  Soul of those mighty spheres
Whose changeless paths through Heaven's deep silence lie;
  Soul of that smallest being,
    The dwelling of whose life
  Is one faint April sungleam;—
    Man, like these passive things,
Thy will unconsciously fulfilleth:
  Like theirs, his age of endless peace,
  Which time is fast maturing,
    Will swiftly, surely come;
And the unbounded frame, which thou pervadest,
    Will be without a flaw
  Marring its perfect symmetry.

4

How beautiful this night! the balmiest sigh,
Which vernal zephyrs breathe in evening's ear,
Were discord to the speaking quietude
That wraps this moveless scene. Heaven's ebon vault,
Studded with stars unutterably bright,
Through which the moon's unclouded grandeur rolls,
Seems like a canopy which love had spread
To curtain her sleeping world. Yon gentle hills,
Robed in a garment of untrodden snow;
Yon darksome rocks, whence icicles depend,°
So stainless, that their white and glittering spires
Tinge not the moon's pure beam; yon castled steep,
Whose banner hangeth o'er the time-worn tower
So idly, that rapt fancy deemeth it
A metaphor of peace;—all form a scene

Where musing solitude might love to lift
Her soul above this sphere of earthliness;
Where silence undisturbed might watch alone,
So cold, so bright, so still.
The orb of day,
In southern climes, o'er ocean's waveless field
Sinks sweetly smiling; not the faintest breath
Steals o'er the unruffled deep; the clouds of eve
Reflect unmoved the lingering beam of day;
And vesper's image on the western main
Is beautifully still. Tomorrow comes:
Cloud upon cloud, in dark and deepening mass,
Roll o'er the blackened waters; the deep roar
Of distant thunder mutters awfully;
Tempest unfolds its pinion o'er the gloom
That shrouds the boiling surge; the pitiless fiend,
With all his winds and lightnings, tracks his prey;
The torn deep yawns,—the vessel finds a grave
Beneath its jagged gulf.
Ah! whence yon glare
That fires the arch of heaven?—that dark red smoke
Blotting the silver moon? The stars are quenched
In darkness, and the pure and spangling snow
Gleams faintly through the gloom that gathers round!
Hark to that roar, whose swift and deaf'ning peals
In countless echoes through the mountains ring,
Startling pale midnight on her starry throne!
Now swells the intermingling din; the jar
Frequent and frightful of the bursting bomb;
The falling beam, the shriek, the groan, the shout,
The ceaseless clangour, and the rush of men
Inebriate with rage:—loud, and more loud
The discord grows; till pale death shuts the scene,
And o'er the conqueror and the conquered draws
His cold and bloody shroud.—Of all the men
Whom day's departing beam saw blooming there,
In proud and vigorous health; of all the hearts
That beat with anxious life at sunset there;
How few survive, how few are beating now!
All is deep silence, like the fearful calm
That slumbers in the storm's portentous pause;

Save when the frantic wail of widowed love
Comes shuddering on the blast, or the faint moan
With which some soul bursts from the frame of clay
Wrapped round its struggling powers.
The grey morn
Dawns on the mournful scene; the sulphurous smoke
Before the icy wind slow rolls away,
And the bright beams of frosty morning dance
Along the spangling snow. There tracks of blood
Even to the forest's depth, and scattered arms,
And lifeless warriors, whose hard lineaments
Death's self could change not, mark the dreadful path
Of the outsallying victors: far behind,°
Black ashes note where their proud city stood.
Within yon forest is a gloomy glen—
Each tree which guards its darkness from the day,
Waves o'er a warrior's tomb.
I see thee shrink,
Surpassing Spirit!—wert thou human else?
I see a shade of doubt and horror fleet
Across thy stainless features: yet fear not;
This is no unconnected misery,
Nor stands uncaused, and irretrievable.
Man's evil nature, that apology
Which kings who rule, and cowards who crouch, set up
For their unnumbered crimes, sheds not the blood
Which desolates the discord-wasted land.
From kings, and priests, and statesmen, war arose,
Whose safety is man's deep unbettered woe,
Whose grandeur his debasement. Let the axe
Strike at the root, the poison-tree will fall;°
And where its venomed exhalations spread
Ruin, and death, and woe, where millions lay
Quenching the serpent's famine, and their bones
Bleaching unburied in the putrid blast,
A garden shall arise, in loveliness
Surpassing fabled Eden.
Hath Nature's soul,
That formed this world so beautiful, that spread
Earth's lap with plenty, and life's smallest chord
Strung to unchanging unison, that gave

The happy birds their dwelling in the grove,
That yielded to the wanderers of the deep
The lovely silence of the unfathomed main,
And filled the meanest worm that crawls in dust
With spirit, thought, and love; on Man alone,
Partial in causeless malice, wantonly
Heaped ruin, vice, and slavery; his soul
Blasted with withering curses; placed afar
The meteor-happiness, that shuns his grasp,
But serving on the frightful gulf to glare,°
Rent wide beneath his footsteps?
                                        Nature!—no!
Kings, priests, and statesmen, blast the human flower
Even in its tender bud; their influence darts
Like subtle poison through the bloodless veins
Of desolate society. The child,
Ere he can lisp his mother's sacred name,
Swells with the unnatural pride of crime, and lifts
His baby-sword even in a hero's mood.
This infant-arm becomes the bloodiest scourge
Of devastated earth; whilst specious names,
Learnt in soft childhood's unsuspecting hour,
Serve as the sophisms with which manhood dims
Bright reason's ray, and sanctifies the sword
Upraised to shed a brother's innocent blood.
Let priest-led slaves cease to proclaim that man
Inherits vice and misery, when force
And falsehood hang even o'er the cradled babe,
Stifling with rudest grasp all natural good.

Ah! to the stranger-soul, when first it peeps
From its new tenement, and looks abroad
For happiness and sympathy, how stern
And desolate a tract is this wide world!
How withered all the buds of natural good!
No shade, no shelter from the sweeping storms
Of pitiless power! On its wretched frame,
Poisoned, perchance, by the disease and woe
Heaped on the wretched parent whence it sprung
By morals, law, and custom, the pure winds
Of heaven, that renovate the insect tribes,

May breathe not. The untainting light of day.
May visit not its longings. It is bound
Ere it has life: yea, all the chains are forged
Long ere its being: all liberty and love
And peace is torn from its defencelessness;°
Cursed from its birth, even from its cradle doomed
To abjectness and bondage!

Throughout this varied and eternal world
Soul is the only element, the block
That for uncounted ages has remained.
The moveless pillar of a mountain's weight
Is active, living spirit. Every grain
Is sentient both in unity and part,
And the minutest atom comprehends
A world of loves and hatreds; these beget
Evil and good: hence truth and falsehood spring;
Hence will and thought and action, all the germs
Of pain or pleasure, sympathy or hate,
That variegate the eternal universe.
Soul is not more polluted than the beams
Of heaven's pure orb, ere round their rapid lines
The taint of earth-born atmospheres arise.°

Man is of soul and body, formed for deeds
Of high resolve, on fancy's boldest wing
To soar unwearied, fearlessly to turn
The keenest pangs to peacefulness, and taste
The joys which mingled sense and spirit yield.
Or he is formed for abjectness and woe,
To grovel on the dunghill of his fears,
To shrink at every sound, to quench the flame
Of natural love in sensualism, to know
That hour as blest when on his worthless days
The frozen hand of death shall set its seal,
Yet fear the cure, though hating the disease.
The one is man that shall hereafter be;
The other, man as vice has made him now.

War is the statesman's game, the priest's delight,
The lawyer's jest, the hired assassin's trade,

And, to those royal murderers, whose mean thrones
Are bought by crimes of treachery and gore,
The bread they eat, the staff on which they lean.
Guards, garbed in blood-red livery, surround
Their palaces, participate the crimes°
That force defends, and from a nation's rage
Secures the crown, which all the curses reach
That famine, frenzy, woe and penury breathe.
These are the hired bravos who defend
The tyrant's throne—the bullies of his fear:°
These are the sinks and channels of worst vice,
The refuse of society, the dregs
Of all that is most vile: their cold hearts blend
Deceit with sternness, ignorance with pride,
All that is mean and villainous, with rage
Which hopelessness of good, and self-contempt,
Alone might kindle; they are decked in wealth,
Honour and power, then are sent abroad
To do their work. The pestilence that stalks
In gloomy triumph through some eastern land
Is less destroying. They cajole with gold,
And promises of fame, the thoughtless youth
Already crushed with servitude: he knows
His wretchedness too late, and cherishes
Repentance for his ruin, when his doom
Is sealed in gold and blood!
Those too the tyrant serve, who, skilled to snare
The feet of justice in the toils of law,
Stand, ready to oppress the weaker still;
And, right or wrong, will vindicate for gold,
Sneering at public virtue, which beneath
Their pitiless tread lies torn and trampled, where
Honour sits smiling at the sale of truth.

Then grave and hoary-headed hypocrites,
Without a hope, a passion, or a love,
Who, through a life of luxury and lies,
Have crept by flattery to the seats of power,
Support the system whence their honours flow. . . .
They have three words:—well tyrants know their use,
Well pay them for the loan, with usury

Torn from a bleeding world!—God, Hell, and Heaven.
A vengeful, pitiless, and almighty fiend,
Whose mercy is a nick-name for the rage
Of tameless tigers hungering for blood.
Hell, a red gulf of everlasting fire,
Where poisonous and undying worms prolong
Eternal misery to those hapless slaves
Whose life has been a penance for its crimes.
And Heaven, a meed for those who dare belie
Their human nature, quake, believe, and cringe
Before the mockeries of earthly power.°

These tools the tyrant tempers to his work,
Wields in his wrath, and as he wills destroys,
Omnipotent in wickedness: the while
Youth springs, age moulders, manhood tamely does
His bidding, bribed by short-lived joys to lend
Force to the weakness of his trembling arm.

They rise, they fall; one generation comes
Yielding its harvest to destruction's scythe.
It fades, another blossoms: yet behold!
Red glows the tyrant's stamp-mark on its bloom,
Withering and cankering deep its passive prime.
He has invented lying words and modes,
Empty and vain as his own coreless heart;
Evasive meanings, nothings of much sound,
To lure the heedless victim to the toils
Spread round the valley of its paradise.

Look to thyself, priest, conqueror, or prince!
Whether thy trade is falsehood, and thy lusts
Deep wallow in the earnings of the poor,
With whom thy master was:—or thou delight'st°
In numbering o'er the myriads of thy slain,
All misery weighing nothing in the scale
Against thy short-lived fame; or thou dost load
With cowardice and crime the groaning land,
A pomp-fed king. Look to thy wretched self!
Aye, art thou not the veriest slave that e'er
Crawled on the loathing earth? Are not thy days

Days of unsatisfying listlessness?
Dost thou not cry, ere night's long rack is o'er,
'When will the morning come?' Is not thy youth
A vain and feverish dream of sensualism?
Thy manhood blighted with unripe disease?°
Are not thy views of unregretted death
Drear, comfortless, and horrible? Thy mind,
Is it not morbid as thy nerveless frame,
Incapable of judgement, hope, or love?
And dost thou wish the errors to survive
That bar thee from all sympathies of good,
After the miserable interest
Thou hold'st in their protraction? When the grave
Has swallowed up thy memory and thyself,
Dost thou desire the bane that poisons earth
To twine its roots around thy coffined clay,
Spring from thy bones, and blossom on thy tomb,
That of its fruit thy babes may eat and die?°

5

Thus do the generations of the earth
Go to the grave, and issue from the womb,°
Surviving still the imperishable change
That renovates the world; even as the leaves
Which the keen frost-wind of the waning year
Has scattered on the forest soil, and heaped°
For many seasons there, though long they choke,
Loading with loathsome rottenness the land,
All germs of promise. Yet when the tall trees
From which they fell, shorn of their lovely shapes,
Lie level with the earth to moulder there,
They fertilize the land they long deformed,
Till from the breathing lawn a forest springs
Of youth, integrity, and loveliness,
Like that which gave it life, to spring and die.
Thus suicidal selfishness, that blights
The fairest feelings of the opening heart,
Is destined to decay, whilst from the soil
Shall spring all virtue, all delight, all love,

And judgment cease to wage unnatural war
With passion's unsubduable array.

Twin-sister of religion, selfishness!
Rival in crime and falsehood, aping all
The wanton horrors of her bloody play;
Yet frozen, unimpassioned, spiritless,
Shunning the light, and owning not its name;
Compelled, by its deformity, to screen
With flimsy veil of justice and of right,
Its unattractive lineaments, that scare
All, save the brood of ignorance: at once
The cause and the effect of tyranny;
Unblushing, hardened, sensual, and vile;
Dead to all love but of its abjectness,
With heart impassive by more noble powers°
Than unshared pleasure, sordid gain, or fame;
Despising its own miserable being,
Which still it longs, yet fears to disenthrall.

Hence commerce springs, the venal interchange
Of all that human art or nature yield;
Which wealth should purchase not, but want demand,
And natural kindness hasten to supply
From the full fountain of its boundless love,
For ever stifled, drained, and tainted now.
Commerce! beneath whose poison-breathing shade
No solitary virtue dares to spring,
But poverty and wealth with equal hand
Scatter their withering curses, and unfold
The doors of premature and violent death,
To pining famine and full-fed disease,
To all that shares the lot of human life,
Which poisoned body and soul, scarce drags the chain,
That lengthens as it goes and clanks behind.

Commerce has set the mark of selfishness,
The signet of its all-enslaving power
Upon a shining ore, and called it gold:
Before whose image how the vulgar great,
The vainly rich, the miserable proud,

The mob of peasants, nobles, priests, and kings,°
And with blind feelings reverence the power
That grinds them to the dust of misery.
But in the temple of their hireling hearts
Gold is a living god, and rules in scorn
All earthly things but virtue.

Since tyrants, by the sale of human life,
Heap luxuries to their sensualism, and fame
To their wide-wasting and insatiate pride,
Success has sanctioned to a credulous world
The ruin, the disgrace, the woe of war.
His hosts of blind and unresisting dupes
The despot numbers; from his cabinet
These puppets of his schemes he moves at will,
Even as the slaves by force or famine driven,
Beneath a vulgar master, to perform
A task of cold and brutal drudgery;—
Hardened to hope, insensible to fear,
Scarce living pulleys of a dead machine.
Mere wheels of work and articles of trade,
That grace the proud and noisy pomp of wealth!

The harmony and happiness of man
Yields to the wealth of nations; that which lifts°
His nature to the heaven of its pride,
Is bartered for the poison of his soul;
The weight that drags to earth his towering hopes,
Blighting all prospect but of selfish gain,
Withering all passion but of slavish fear,
Extinguishing all free and generous love
Of enterprise and daring, even the pulse
That fancy kindles in the beating heart
To mingle with sensation, it destroys,—
Leaves nothing but the sordid lust of self,
The grovelling hope of interest and gold,
Unqualified, unmingled, unredeemed
Even by hypocrisy.
And statesmen boast
Of wealth! The wordy eloquence that lives°
After the ruin of their hearts, can gild

The bitter poison of a nation's woe,
Can turn the worship of the servile mob
To their corrupt and glaring idol fame,
From virtue, trampled by its iron tread,
Although its dazzling pedestal be raised
Amid the horrors of a limb-strewn field,
With desolated dwellings smoking round.
The man of ease, who, by his warm fire-side,
To deeds of charitable intercourse
And bare fulfilment of the common laws
Of decency and prejudice, confines
The struggling nature of his human heart,
Is duped by their cold sophistry; he sheds
A passing tear perchance upon the wreck
Of earthly peace, when near his dwelling's door
The frightful waves are driven,—when his son
Is murdered by the tyrant, or religion
Drives his wife raving mad. But the poor man,°
Whose life is misery, and fear, and care;
Whom the morn wakens but to fruitless toil;
Who ever hears his famished offspring's scream,
Whom their pale mother's uncomplaining gaze
For ever meets, and the proud rich man's eye
Flashing command, and the heart-breaking scene
Of thousands like himself;—he little heeds
The rhetoric of tyranny; his hate
Is quenchless as his wrongs; he laughs to scorn
The vain and bitter mockery of words,
Feeling the horror of the tyrant's deeds,
And unrestrained but by the arm of power,
That knows and dreads his enmity.

The iron rod of penury still compels
Her wretched slave to bow the knee to wealth,
And poison, with unprofitable toil,
A life too void of solace, to confirm
The very chains that bind him to his doom.
Nature, impartial in munificence,
Has gifted man with all-subduing will.
Matter, with all its transitory shapes,
Lies subjected and plastic at his feet,°

That, weak from bondage, tremble as they tread.
How many a rustic Milton has passed by,
Stifling the speechless longings of his heart,
In unremitting drudgery and care!
How many a vulgar Cato has compelled°
His energies, no longer tameless then,
To mould a pin, or fabricate a nail!
How many a Newton, to whose passive ken
Those mighty spheres that gem infinity
Were only specks of tinsel, fixed in heaven
To light the midnights of his native town!°

Yet every heart contains perfection's germ:
The wisest of the sages of the earth,
That ever from the stores of reason drew
Science and truth, and virtue's dreadless tone,
Were but a weak and inexperienced boy,
Proud, sensual, unimpassioned, unimbued
With pure desire and universal love,
Compared to that high being, of cloudless brain,
Untainted passion, elevated will,
Which death (who even would linger long in awe
Within his noble presence, and beneath
His changeless eyebeam) might alone subdue.
Him, every slave now dragging through the filth
Of some corrupted city his sad life,
Pining with famine, swol'n with luxury,
Blunting the keenness of his spiritual sense
With narrow schemings and unworthy cares,
Or madly rushing through all violent crime,
To move the deep stagnation of his soul,—
Might imitate and equal.
                                        But mean lust
Has bound its chains so tight around the earth,
That all within it but the virtuous man
Is venal: gold or fame will surely reach
The price prefixed by selfishness, to all
But him of resolute and unchanging will;
Whom, nor the plaudits of a servile crowd,
Nor the vile joys of tainting luxury,
Can bribe to yield his elevated soul

To tyranny or falsehood, though they wield
With blood-red hand the sceptre of the world.

All things are sold: the very light of heaven
Is venal; earth's unsparing gifts of love,
The smallest and most despicable things
That lurk in the abysses of the deep,
All objects of our life, even life itself,
And the poor pittance which the laws allow
Of liberty, the fellowship of man,
Those duties which his heart of human love
Should urge him to perform instinctively,
Are bought and sold as in a public mart
Of undisguising selfishness, that sets
On each its price, the stamp-mark of her reign.
Even love is sold; the solace of all woe°
Is turned to deadliest agony, old age
Shivers in selfish beauty's loathing arms,
And youth's corrupted impulses prepare
A life of horror from the blighting bane
Of commerce; whilst the pestilence that springs°
From unenjoying sensualism, has filled
All human life with hydra-headed woes.

Falsehood demands but gold to pay the pangs
Of outraged conscience; for the slavish priest
Sets no great value on his hireling faith:
A little passing pomp, some servile souls,
Whom cowardice itself might safely chain,
Or the spare mite of avarice could bribe
To deck the triumph of their languid zeal,
Can make him minister to tyranny.
More daring crime requires a loftier meed:
Without a shudder, the slave-soldier lends
His arm to murderous deeds, and steels his heart
When the dread eloquence of dying men,
Low mingling on the lonely field of fame,
Assails that nature, whose applause he sells
For the gross blessings of a patriot mob,
For the vile gratitude of heartless kings,
And for a cold world's good word,—viler still!

There is a nobler glory, which survives
Until our being fades, and, solacing
All human care, accompanies its change;
Deserts not virtue in the dungeon's gloom,
And, in the precincts of the palace, guides
Its footsteps through that labyrinth of crime;
Imbues his lineaments with dauntlessness,°
Even when, from power's avenging hand, he takes
Its sweetest, last and noblest title—death;
—The consciousness of good, which neither gold,
Nor sordid fame, nor hope of heavenly bliss,
Can purchase; but a life of resolute good,
Unalterable will, quenchless desire
Of universal happiness, the heart
That beats with it in unison, the brain,
Whose ever wakeful wisdom toils to change
Reason's rich stores for its eternal weal.

This commerce of sincerest virtue needs°
No mediative signs of selfishness,
No jealous intercourse of wretched gain,
No balancings of prudence, cold and long;
In just and equal measure all is weighed,
One scale contains the sum of human weal,
And one, the good man's heart.
How vainly seek
The selfish for that happiness denied
To aught but virtue! Blind and hardened, they,
Who hope for peace amid the storms of care,
Who covet power they know not how to use,
And sigh for pleasure they refuse to give,—
Madly they frustrate still their own designs;
And, where they hope that quiet to enjoy
Which virtue pictures, bitterness of soul,
Pining regrets, and vain repentances,
Disease, disgust, and lassitude, pervade
Their valueless and miserable lives.

But hoary-headed selfishness has felt
Its death-blow, and is tottering to the grave:
A brighter morn awaits the human day,

When every transfer of earth's natural gifts
Shall be a commerce of good words and works;
When poverty and wealth, the thirst of fame,
The fear of infamy, disease and woe,
War with its million horrors, and fierce hell
Shall live but in the memory of time,
Who, like a penitent libertine, shall start,
Look back, and shudder at his younger years.

6

All touch, all eye, all ear,
The Spirit felt the Fairy's burning speech.
O'er the thin texture of its frame,
The varying periods painted changing glows,°
As on a summer even,
When soul-enfolding music floats around,
The stainless mirror of the lake
Re-images the eastern gloom,
Mingling convulsively its purple hues
With sunset's burnished gold.

Then thus the Spirit spoke:
'It is a wild and miserable world!
Thorny, and full of care,
Which every fiend can make his prey at will.
O Fairy! in the lapse of years,
Is there no hope in store?
Will yon vast suns roll on
Interminably, still illuming
The night of so many wretched souls,
And see no hope for them?
Will not the universal Spirit e'er
Revivify this withered limb of Heaven?'

The Fairy calmly smiled
In comfort, and a kindling gleam of hope
Suffused the Spirit's lineaments.
'Oh! rest thee tranquil; chase those fearful doubts,
Which ne'er could rack an everlasting soul,

That sees the chains which bind it to its doom.
Yes! crime and misery are in yonder earth,
Falsehood, mistake, and lust;
But the eternal world
Contains at once the evil and the cure.
Some eminent in virtue shall start up,
Even in perversest time:
The truths of their pure lips, that never die,
Shall bind the scorpion falsehood with a wreath
Of ever-living flame,
Until the monster sting itself to death.°

'How sweet a scene will earth become!
Of purest spirits a pure dwelling-place,
Symphonious with the planetary spheres;°
When man, with changeless nature coalescing,
Will undertake regeneration's work,
When its ungenial poles no longer point
To the red and baleful sun
That faintly twinkles there.°

'Spirit! on yonder earth,
Falsehood now triumphs; deadly power
Has fixed its seal upon the lip of truth!
Madness and misery are there!
The happiest is most wretched! Yet confide,
Until pure health-drops, from the cup of joy,
Fall like a dew of balm upon the world.
Now, to the scene I show, in silence turn,
And read the blood-stained charter of all woe,
Which nature soon, with recreating hand,
Will blot in mercy from the book of earth.
How bold the flight of passion's wandering wing,
How swift the step of reason's firmer tread,
How calm and sweet the victories of life,
How terrorless the triumph of the grave!
How powerless were the mightiest monarch's arm,
Vain his loud threat, and impotent his frown!
How ludicrous the priest's dogmatic roar!
The weight of his exterminating curse,
How light! and his affected charity,

To suit the pressure of the changing times,
What palpable deceit!—but for thy aid,
Religion! but for thee, prolific fiend,
Who peoplest earth with demons, hell with men,
And heaven with slaves!

'Thou taintest all thou lookest upon!—the stars,°
Which on thy cradle beamed so brightly sweet,
Were gods to the distempered playfulness
Of thy untutored infancy: the trees,
The grass, the clouds, the mountains, and the sea,
All living things that walk, swim, creep, or fly,
Were gods: the sun had homage, and the moon
Her worshipper. Then thou becamest, a boy,
More daring in thy frenzies: every shape,
Monstrous or vast, or beautifully wild,
Which, from sensation's relics, fancy culls;
The spirits of the air, the shuddering ghost,
The genii of the elements, the powers
That give a shape to nature's varied works,
Had life and place in the corrupt belief
Of thy blind heart: yet still thy youthful hands
Were pure of human blood. Then manhood gave
Its strength and ardour to thy frenzied brain;
Thine eager gaze scanned the stupendous scene,
Whose wonders mocked the knowledge of thy pride:
Their everlasting and unchanging laws
Reproached thine ignorance. Awhile thou stoodst
Baffled and gloomy; then thou didst sum up
The elements of all that thou didst know;
The changing seasons, winter's leafless reign,
The budding of the heaven-breathing trees,
The eternal orbs that beautify the night,
The sun-rise, and the setting of the moon,
Earthquakes and wars, and poisons and disease,
And all their causes, to an abstract point
Converging, thou didst bend, and called it GOD!
The self-sufficing, the omnipotent,
The merciful, and the avenging God!
Who, prototype of human misrule, sits
High in heaven's realm, upon a golden throne,

Even like an earthly king; and whose dread work,
Hell, gapes forever for the unhappy slaves
Of fate, whom he created in his sport,
To triumph in their torments when they fell!
Earth heard the name; earth trembled, as the smoke°
Of his revenge ascended up to heaven,
Blotting the constellations; and the cries
Of millions, butchered in sweet confidence
And unsuspecting peace, even when the bonds
Of safety were confirmed by wordy oaths
Sworn in his dreadful name, rung through the land;
Whilst innocent babes writhed on thy stubborn spear.
And thou didst laugh to hear the mother's shriek
Of maniac gladness, as the sacred steel
Felt cold in her torn entrails!

'Religion! thou wert then in manhood's prime:
But age crept on: one God would not suffice
For senile puerility; thou framedst
A tale to suit thy dotage, and to glut
Thy misery-thirsting soul, that the mad fiend
Thy wickedness had pictured, might afford
A plea for sating the unnatural thirst
For murder, rapine, violence, and crime,
That still consumed thy being, even when
Thou heard'st the step of fate;—that flames might light
Thy funeral scene, and the shrill horrent shrieks°
Of parents dying on the pile that burned
To light their children to thy paths, the roar
Of the encircling flames, the exulting cries
Of thine apostles, loud commingling there,
        Might sate thine hungry ear
        Even on the bed of death!

'But now contempt is mocking thy grey hairs;
Thou art descending to the darksome grave,
Unhonoured and unpitied, but by those
Whose pride is passing by like thine, and sheds,
Like thine, a glare that fades before the sun
Of truth, and shines but in the dreadful night
That long has lowered above the ruined world.

'Throughout these infinite orbs of mingling light,
Of which yon earth is one, is wide diffused
A spirit of activity and life,
That knows no term, cessation, or decay;
That fades not when the lamp of earthly life,
Extinguished in the dampness of the grave,
Awhile there slumbers, more than when the babe
In the dim newness of its being feels
The impulses of sublunary things,°
And all is wonder to unpractised sense:
But, active, steadfast, and eternal, still
Guides the fierce whirlwind, in the tempest roars,
Cheers in the day, breathes in the balmy groves,
Strengthens in health, and poisons in disease;
And in the storm of change, that ceaselessly
Rolls round the eternal universe, and shakes
Its undecaying battlement, presides,
Apportioning with irresistible law
The place each spring of its machine shall fill;
So that, when waves on waves tumultuous heap
Confusion to the clouds, and fiercely driven
Heaven's lightnings scorch the uprooted ocean-fords,
Whilst, to the eye of shipwrecked mariner,
Lone sitting on the bare and shuddering rock,
All seems unlinked contingency and chance:
No atom of this turbulence fulfils
A vague and unnecessitated task,
Or acts but as it must and ought to act.°
Even the minutest molecule of light,
That in an April sunbeam's fleeting glow
Fulfils its destined, though invisible work,
The universal Spirit guides; nor less,
When merciless ambition, or mad zeal,
Has led two hosts of dupes to battle-field,
That, blind, they there may dig each other's graves,
And call the sad work glory, does it rule
All passions: not a thought, a will, an act,
No working of the tyrant's moody mind,
Nor one misgiving of the slaves who boast
Their servitude, to hide the shame they feel,
Nor the events enchaining every will,

That from the depths of unrecorded time
Have drawn all-influencing virtue, pass
Unrecognized, or unforeseen by thee,
Soul of the Universe! eternal spring
Of life and death, of happiness and woe,
Of all that chequers the phantasmal scene
That floats before our eyes in wavering light,
Which gleams but on the darkness of our prison,
        Whose chains and massy walls
        We feel, but cannot see.°

'Spirit of Nature! all-sufficing Power,
Necessity! thou mother of the world!°
Unlike the God of human error, thou
Requirest no prayers or praises; the caprice
Of man's weak will belongs no more to thee
Than do the changeful passions of his breast
To thy unvarying harmony: the slave,
Whose horrible lusts spread misery o'er the world.
And the good man, who lifts, with virtuous pride,
His being, in the sight of happiness,
That springs from his own works; the poison-tree,
Beneath whose shade all life is withered up,
And the fair oak, whose leafy dome affords
A temple where the vows of happy love
Are registered, are equal in thy sight:
No love, no hate thou cherishest; revenge
And favouritism, and worst desire of fame
Thou knowest not: all that the wide world contains
Are but thy passive instruments, and thou
Regard'st them all with an impartial eye,
Whose joy or pain thy nature cannot feel,
    Because thou hast not human sense,
    Because thou art not human mind.

    'Yes! when the sweeping storm of time
Has sung its death-dirge o'er the ruined fanes
And broken altars of the almighty fiend,
Whose name usurps thy honours, and the blood
Through centuries clotted there, has floated down
The tainted flood of ages, shalt thou live

Unchangeable! A shrine is raised to thee,
 Which, nor the tempest breath of time,
 Nor the interminable flood,
 Over earth's slight pageant rolling,
  Availeth to destroy,—
The sensitive extension of the world,°
 That wondrous and eternal fane,
Where pain and pleasure, good and evil join,
To do the will of strong necessity,
 And life, in multitudinous shapes,
Still pressing forward where no term can be,
 Like hungry and unresting flame
Curls round the eternal columns of its strength.'°

7

Spirit

I was an infant when my mother went
To see an atheist burned. She took me there:
The dark-robed priests were met around the pile;
The multitude was gazing silently;
And as the culprit passed with dauntless mien,
Tempered disdain in his unaltering eye,
Mixed with a quiet smile, shone calmly forth:
The thirsty fire crept round his manly limbs;
His resolute eyes were scorched to blindness soon;
His death-pang rent my heart! the insensate mob
Uttered a cry of triumph, and I wept.
'Weep not, child!' cried my mother, 'for that man
Has said, "There is no God."'

Fairy

  There is no God!°
Nature confirms the faith his death-groan sealed:
Let heaven and earth, let man's revolving race,
His ceaseless generations tell their tale;
Let every part depending on the chain
That links it to the whole, point to the hand
That grasps its term! let every seed that falls
In silent eloquence unfold its store

Of argument: infinity within,
Infinity without, belie creation;
The exterminable spirit it contains
Is nature's only God; but human pride
Is skilful to invent most serious names
To hide its ignorance.
The name of God
Has fenced about all crime with holiness,
Himself the creature of his worshippers,
Whose names and attributes and passions change,
Seeva, Buddh, Foh, Jehovah, God, or Lord,°
Even with the human dupes who build his shrines,
Still serving o'er the war-polluted world
For desolation's watch-word; whether hosts
Stain his death-blushing chariot wheels, as on
Triumphantly they roll, whilst Brahmins raise
A sacred hymn to mingle with the groans;°
Or countless partners of his power divide
His tyranny to weakness; or the smoke
Of burning towns, the cries of female helplessness,
Unarmed old age, and youth, and infancy,
Horribly massacred, ascend to heaven
In honour of his name; or, last and worst,
Earth groans beneath religion's iron age,°
And priests dare babble of a God of peace,
Even whilst their hands are red with guiltless blood,
Murdering the while, uprooting every germ
Of truth, exterminating, spoiling all,
Making the earth a slaughter-house!

O Spirit! through the sense
By which thy inner nature was apprised
Of outward shows, vague dreams have rolled,
And varied reminiscences have waked
Tablets that never fade;°
All things have been imprinted there,
The stars, the sea, the earth, the sky,
Even the unshapeliest lineaments
Of wild and fleeting visions
Have left a record there
To testify of earth.

These are my empire, for to me is given
The wonders of the human world to keep,
And fancy's thin creations to endow
With manner, being, and reality;
Therefore a wondrous phantom, from the dreams
Of human error's dense and purblind faith,°
I will evoke, to meet thy questioning.
Ahasuerus, rise!°

A strange and woe-worn wight°
Arose beside the battlement,
And stood unmoving there.
His inessential figure cast no shade
Upon the golden floor;
His port and mien bore mark of many years,
And chronicles of untold ancientness
Were legible within his beamless eye:
Yet his cheek bore the mark of youth;
Freshness and vigour knit his manly frame;
The wisdom of old age was mingled there
With youth's primaeval dauntlessness;
And inexpressible woe,
Chastened by fearless resignation, gave
An awful grace to his all-speaking brow.

Spirit

Is there a God?

Ahasuerus

Is there a God!—aye, an almighty God,
And vengeful as almighty! Once his voice
Was heard on earth: earth shuddered at the sound;
The fiery-visaged firmament expressed
Abhorrence, and the grave of nature yawned
To swallow all the dauntless and the good
That dared to hurl defiance at his throne,
Girt as it was with power. None but slaves
Survived,—cold-blooded slaves, who did the work
Of tyrannous omnipotence; whose souls
No honest indignation ever urged
To elevated daring, to one deed

Which gross and sensual self did not pollute.
These slaves built temples for the omnipotent fiend,
Gorgeous and vast: the costly altars smoked
With human blood, and hideous paeans rung
Through all the long-drawn aisles. A murderer heard°
His voice in Egypt, one whose gifts and arts
Had raised him to his eminence in power,
Accomplice of omnipotence in crime,
And confidant of the all-knowing one.
These were Jehovah's words:

'From an eternity of idleness
I, God, awoke; in seven days' toil made earth
From nothing; rested, and created man:
I placed him in a paradise, and there
Planted the tree of evil, so that he
Might eat and perish, and my soul procure
Wherewith to sate its malice, and to turn,
Even like a heartless conqueror of the earth,
All misery to my fame. The race of men
Chosen to my honour, with impunity
May sate the lusts I planted in their heart.
Here I command thee hence to lead them on,
Until, with hardened feet, their conquering troops
Wade on the promised soil through woman's blood,
And make my name be dreaded through the land.
Yet ever burning flame and ceaseless woe
Shall be the doom of their eternal souls,
With every soul on this ungrateful earth,
Virtuous or vicious, weak or strong,—even all
Shall perish, to fulfil the blind revenge
(Which you, to men, call justice) of their God.'

The murderer's brow
Quivered with horror.
'God omnipotent,
Is there no mercy? must our punishment
Be endless? will long ages roll away,
And see no term? Oh! wherefore hast thou made
In mockery and wrath this evil earth?
Mercy becomes the powerful—be but just:

O God! repent and save.'
'One way remains:
I will beget a son, and he shall bear
The sins of all the world; he shall arise°
In an unnoticed corner of the earth,
And there shall die upon a cross, and purge
The universal crime; so that the few
On whom my grace descends, those who are marked
As vessels to the honour of their God,
May credit this strange sacrifice, and save
Their souls alive: millions shall live and die,
Who ne'er shall call upon their Saviour's name,
But, unredeemed, go to the gaping grave.
Thousands shall deem it an old woman's tale,
Such as the nurses frighten babes withal:
These in a gulf of anguish and of flame
Shall curse their reprobation endlessly,
Yet tenfold pangs shall force them to avow,
Even on their beds of torment, where they howl,
My honour, and the justice of their doom.
What then avail their virtuous deeds, their thoughts
Of purity, with radiant genius bright,
Or lit with human reason's earthly ray?
Many are called, but few will I elect.
Do thou my bidding, Moses!'
Even the murderer's cheek
Was blanched with horror, and his quivering lips
Scarce faintly uttered—'O almighty one,
I tremble and obey!'

O Spirit! centuries have set their seal
On this heart of many wounds, and loaded brain,
Since the Incarnate came: humbly he came,
Veiling his horrible Godhead in the shape
Of man, scorned by the world, his name unheard,
Save by the rabble of his native town,
Even as a parish demagogue. He led
The crowd; he taught them justice, truth, and peace,
In semblance; but he lit within their souls
The quenchless flames of zeal, and blessed the sword
He brought on earth to satiate with the blood

Of truth and freedom his malignant soul.
At length his mortal frame was led to death.
I stood beside him: on the torturing cross
No pain assailed his unterrestrial sense;
And yet he groaned. Indignantly I summed
The massacres and miseries which his name
Had sanctioned in my country, and I cried,
'Go! go!' in mockery.
A smile of godlike malice reillumined
His fading lineaments.—'I go', he cried,
'But thou shalt wander o'er the unquiet earth
Eternally.'——The dampness of the grave
Bathed my imperishable front. I fell,
And long lay tranced upon the charmèd soil.
When I awoke hell burned within my brain,
Which staggered on its seat; for all around
The mouldering relics of my kindred lay,
Even as the Almighty's ire arrested them.
And in their various attitudes of death
My murdered children's mute and eyeless skulls
Glared ghastily upon me.°
But my soul,
From sight and sense of the polluting woe
Of tyranny, had long learned to prefer
Hell's freedom to the servitude of heaven.°
Therefore I rose, and dauntlessly began
My lonely and unending pilgrimage,
Resolved to wage unweariable war
With my almighty tyrant, and to hurl
Defiance at his impotence to harm
Beyond the curse I bore. The very hand
That barred my passage to the peaceful grave
Has crushed the earth to misery, and given
Its empire to the chosen of his slaves.
These have I seen, even from the earliest dawn
Of weak, unstable and precarious power,
Then preaching peace, as now they practise war;
So, when they turned but from the massacre°
Of unoffending infidels, to quench
Their thirst for ruin in the very blood
That flowed in their own veins, and pitiless zeal

Froze every human feeling, as the wife
Sheathed in her husband's heart the sacred steel,
Even whilst its hopes were dreaming of her love;
And friends to friends, brothers to brothers stood
Opposed in bloodiest battle-field, and war,
Scarce satiable by fate's last death-draught waged,
Drunk from the winepress of the Almighty's wrath;°
Whilst the red cross, in mockery of peace,
Pointed to victory! When the fray was done,
No remnant of the exterminated faith
Survived to tell its ruin, but the flesh,
With putrid smoke poisoning the atmosphere,
That rotted on the half-extinguished pile.

Yes! I have seen God's worshippers unsheathe
The sword of his revenge, when grace descended,
Confirming all unnatural impulses,
To sanctify their desolating deeds;
And frantic priests waved the ill-omened cross
O'er the unhappy earth: then shone the sun
On showers of gore from the upflashing steel
Of safe assassination, and all crime
Made stingless by the spirits of the Lord,
And blood-red rainbows canopied the land.

Spirit! no year of my eventful being
Has passed unstained by crime and misery,
Which flows from God's own faith. I've marked his slaves
With tongues whose lies are venomous, beguile
The insensate mob, and, whilst one hand was red
With murder, feign to stretch the other out
For brotherhood and peace; and that they now
Babble of love and mercy, whilst their deeds
Are marked with all the narrowness and crime
That freedom's young arm dare not yet chastise,
Reason may claim our gratitude, who now
Establishing the imperishable throne
Of truth, and stubborn virtue, maketh vain
The unprevailing malice of my foe,
Whose bootless rage heaps torments for the brave,
Adds impotent eternities to pain,

Whilst keenest disappointment racks his breast,
To see the smiles of peace around them play,
To frustrate or to sanctify their doom.

Thus have I stood,—through a wild waste of years
Struggling with whirlwinds of mad agony,
Yet peaceful, and serene, and self-enshrined,
Mocking my powerless tyrant's horrible curse
With stubborn and unalterable will,
Even as a giant oak, which heaven's fierce flame
Had scathèd in the wilderness, to stand
A monument of fadeless ruin there;
Yet peacefully and movelessly it braves
The midnight conflict of the wintry storm,
  As in the sunlight's calm it spreads
  Its worn and withered arms on high
To meet the quiet of a summer's noon.

    The Fairy waved her wand:
    Ahasuerus fled
Fast as the shapes of mingled shade and mist,
That lurk in the glens of a twilight grove,
    Flee from the morning beam:
  The matter of which dreams are made
  Not more endowed with actual life
  Than this phantasmal portraiture
  Of wandering human thought.

8

The present and the past thou hast beheld:
It was a desolate sight. Now, Spirit, learn
  The secrets of the future.—Time!
Unfold the brooding pinion of thy gloom,
Render thou up thy half-devoured babes,°
And from the cradles of eternity,
Where millions lie lulled to their portioned sleep
By the deep murmuring stream of passing things,
Tear thou that gloomy shroud.—Spirit, behold
    Thy glorious destiny!

Joy to the Spirit came.
Through the wide rent in Time's eternal veil,
Hope was seen beaming through the mists of fear:
Earth was no longer hell;
Love, freedom, health, had given
Their ripeness to the manhood of its prime,
And all its pulses beat
Symphonious to the planetary spheres:
Then dulcet music swelled
Concordant with the life-strings of the soul;
It throbbed in sweet and languid beatings there,
Catching new life from transitory death,—
Like the vague sighings of a wind at even,
That wakes the wavelets of the slumbering sea
And dies on the creation of its breath,
And sinks and rises, fails and swells by fits,
Was the pure stream of feeling
That sprung from these sweet notes,
And o'er the Spirit's human sympathies
With mild and gentle motion calmly flowed.

Joy to the Spirit came,—
Such joy as when a lover sees
The chosen of his soul in happiness,
And witnesses her peace
Whose woe to him were bitterer than death,
Sees her unfaded cheek
Glow mantling in first luxury of health,
Thrills with her lovely eyes,
Which like two stars amid the heaving main
Sparkle through liquid bliss.

Then in her triumph spoke the Fairy Queen:
'I will not call the ghost of ages gone
To unfold the frightful secrets of its lore;
The present now is past,
And those events that desolate the earth
Have faded from the memory of Time,
Who dares not give reality to that
Whose being I annul. To me is given
The wonders of the human world to keep,

Space, matter, time, and mind. Futurity
Exposes now its treasure; let the sight
Renew and strengthen all thy failing hope.
O human Spirit! spur thee to the goal
Where virtue fixes universal peace,
And midst the ebb and flow of human things,
Show somewhat stable, somewhat certain still,
A lighthouse o'er the wild of dreary waves.

'The habitable earth is full of bliss;
Those wastes of frozen billows that were hurled
By everlasting snowstorms round the poles,
Where matter dared not vegetate or live,
But ceaseless frost round the vast solitude
Bound its broad zone of stillness, are unloosed;
And fragrant zephyrs there from spicy isles
Ruffle the placid ocean-deep, that rolls
Its broad, bright surges to the sloping sand,
Whose roar is wakened into echoings sweet
To murmur through the heaven-breathing groves
And melodize with man's blest nature there.

'Those deserts of immeasurable sand,
Whose age-collected fervours scarce allowed
A bird to live, a blade of grass to spring,
Where the shrill chirp of the green lizard's love
Broke on the sultry silentness alone,
Now teem with countless rills and shady woods,
Corn-fields and pastures and white cottages;
And where the startled wilderness beheld
A savage conqueror stained in kindred blood,
A tigress sating with the flesh of lambs
The unnatural famine of her toothless cubs,
Whilst shouts and howlings through the desert rang,
Sloping and smooth the daisy-spangled lawn,
Offering sweet incense to the sunrise, smiles
To see a babe before his mother's door,
Sharing his morning's meal
With the green and golden basilisk°
That comes to lick his feet.

'Those trackless deeps, where many a weary sail
Has seen above the illimitable plain,
Morning on night, and night on morning rise,
Whilst still no land to greet the wanderer spread
Its shadowy mountains on the sun-bright sea,
Where the loud roarings of the tempest-waves
So long have mingled with the gusty wind
In melancholy loneliness, and swept
The desert of those ocean solitudes,
But vocal to the seabird's harrowing shriek,°
The bellowing monster, and the rushing storm,
Now to the sweet and many mingling sounds
Of kindliest human impulses respond.
Those lonely realms bright garden-isles begem,
With lightsome clouds and shining seas between,
And fertile valleys, resonant with bliss,
Whilst green woods overcanopy the wave,
Which like a toil-worn labourer leaps to shore,
To meet the kisses of the flowrets there.

'All things are recreated, and the flame
Of consentaneous love inspires all life:°
The fertile bosom of the earth gives suck
To myriads, who still grow beneath her care,
Rewarding her with their pure perfectness:
The balmy breathings of the wind inhale
Her virtues, and diffuse them all abroad:
Health floats amid the gentle atmosphere,
Glows in the fruits, and mantles on the stream:
No storms deform the beaming brow of heaven,
Nor scatter in the freshness of its pride
The foliage of the ever verdant trees;
But fruits are ever ripe, flowers ever fair,
And autumn proudly bears her matron grace,
Kindling a flush on the fair cheek of spring,
Whose virgin bloom beneath the ruddy fruit
Reflects its tint and blushes into love.

'The lion now forgets to thirst for blood:
There might you see him sporting in the sun
Beside the dreadless kid; his claws are sheathed,°

His teeth are harmless, custom's force has made°
His nature as the nature of a lamb.
Like passion's fruit, the nightshade's tempting bane
Poisons no more the pleasure it bestows:
All bitterness is past; the cup of joy
Unmingled mantles to the goblet's brim,
And courts the thirsty lips it fled before.

'But chief, ambiguous man, he that can know
More misery, and dream more joy than all;
Whose keen sensations thrill within his breast
To mingle with a loftier instinct there,
Lending their power to pleasure and to pain,
Yet raising, sharpening, and refining each;
Who stands amid the ever-varying world,
The burden or the glory of the earth;
He chief perceives the change, his being notes
The gradual renovation, and defines
Each movement of its progress on his mind.

'Man, where the gloom of the long polar night
Lowers o'er the snow-clad rocks and frozen soil,
Where scarce the hardiest herb that braves the frost
Basks in the moonlight's ineffectual glow,
Shrank with the plants, and darkened with the night;
His chilled and narrow energies, his heart,
Insensible to courage, truth, or love,
His stunted stature and imbecile frame,
Marked him for some abortion of the earth,
Fit compeer of the bears that roamed around,
Whose habits and enjoyments were his own:
His life a feverish dream of stagnant woe,
Whose meagre wants, but scantily fulfilled,
Apprised him ever of the joyless length
Which his short being's wretchedness had reached;
His death a pang which famine, cold and toil
Long on the mind, whilst yet the vital spark
Clung to the body stubbornly, had brought:
All was inflicted here that earth's revenge
Could wreak on the infringers of her law;
One curse alone was spared—the name of God.

'Nor where the tropics bound the realms of day
With a broad belt of mingling cloud and flame,
Where blue mists through the unmoving atmosphere
Scattered the seeds of pestilence, and fed
Unnatural vegetation, where the land
Teemed with all earthquake, tempest and disease,
Was man a nobler being; slavery
Had crushed him to his country's bloodstained dust;
Or he was bartered for the fame of power,
Which all internal impulses destroying,
Makes human will an article of trade;
Or he was changed with Christians for their gold,
And dragged to distant isles, where to the sound
Of the flesh-mangling scourge, he does the work
Of all-polluting luxury and wealth,
Which doubly visits on the tyrants' heads
The long-protracted fullness of their woe;
Or he was led to legal butchery,°
To turn to worms beneath that burning sun,
Where kings first leagued against the rights of men,
And priests first traded with the name of God.°

'Even where the milder zone afforded man
A seeming shelter, yet contagion there,
Blighting his being with unnumbered ills,
Spread like a quenchless fire; nor truth till late
Availed to arrest its progress, or create
That peace which first in bloodless victory waved
Her snowy standard o'er this favoured clime:
There man was long the train-bearer of slaves,
The mimic of surrounding misery,
The jackal of ambition's lion-rage,
The bloodhound of religion's hungry zeal.

'Here now the human being stands adorning
This loveliest earth with taintless body and mind;
Blessed from his birth with all bland impulses,
Which gently in his noble bosom wake
All kindly passions and all pure desires.
Him, still from hope to hope the bliss pursuing,
Which from the exhaustless lore of human weal

Draws on the virtuous mind, the thoughts that rise
In time-destroying infiniteness, gift
With self-enshrined eternity, that mocks°
The unprevailing hoariness of age,
And man, once fleeting o'er the transient scene
Swift as an unremembered vision, stands
Immortal upon earth: no longer now
He slays the lamb that looks him in the face,°
And horribly devours his mangled flesh,
Which still avenging nature's broken law,
Kindled all putrid humours in his frame,
All evil passions, and all vain belief,
Hatred, despair, and loathing in his mind,
The germs of misery, death, disease, and crime.
No longer now the wingèd habitants,
That in the woods their sweet lives sing away,
Flee from the form of man; but gather round,
And prune their sunny feathers on the hands°
Which little children stretch in friendly sport
Towards these dreadless partners of their play.
All things are void of terror: man has lost
His terrible prerogative, and stands
An equal amidst equals: happiness
And science dawn though late upon the earth;
Peace cheers the mind, health renovates the frame;
Disease and pleasures cease to mingle here,
Reason and passion cease to combat there;
Whilst each unfettered o'er the earth extend
Their all-subduing energies, and wield
The sceptre of a vast dominion there;
Whilst every shape and mode of matter lends
Its force to the omnipotence of mind,
Which from its dark mine drags the gem of truth
To decorate its paradise of peace.'

9

'O happy Earth! reality of Heaven!°
To which those restless souls that ceaselessly
Throng through the human universe, aspire;

Thou consummation of all mortal hope!
Thou glorious prize of blindly-working will!
Whose rays, diffused throughout all space and time,
Verge to one point and blend forever there:
Of purest spirits thou pure dwelling-place!
Where care and sorrow, impotence and crime,
Languor, disease, and ignorance dare not come:
O happy Earth, reality of Heaven!

'Genius has seen thee in her passionate dreams,
And dim forebodings of thy loveliness
Haunting the human heart, have there entwined
Those rooted hopes of some sweet place of bliss
Where friends and lovers meet to part no more.
Thou art the end of all desire and will,
The product of all action; and the souls
That by the paths of an aspiring change
Have reached thy haven of perpetual peace,
There rest from the eternity of toil
That framed the fabric of thy perfectness.

'Even Time, the conqueror, fled thee in his fear;
That hoary giant, who, in lonely pride,
So long had ruled the world, that nations fell
Beneath his silent footstep. Pyramids,
That for millenniums had withstood the tide
Of human things, his storm-breath drove in sand
Across that desert where their stones survived
The name of him whose pride had heaped them there.
Yon monarch, in his solitary pomp,
Was but the mushroom of a summer day,
That his light-wingèd footstep pressed to dust:
Time was the king of earth: all things gave way
Before him, but the fixed and virtuous will,
The sacred sympathies of soul and sense,
That mocked his fury and prepared his fall.°

'Yet slow and gradual dawned the morn of love;
Long lay the clouds of darkness o'er the scene,
Till from its native heaven they rolled away:
First, crime triumphant o'er all hope careered

Unblushing, undisguising, bold and strong;
Whilst falsehood, tricked in virtue's attributes,
Long sanctified all deeds of vice and woe,
Till done by her own venomous sting to death,
She left the moral world without a law,
No longer fettering passion's fearless wing,
Nor searing reason with the brand of God.°
Then steadily the happy ferment worked;
Reason was free; and wild though passion went
Through tangled glens and wood-embosomed meads,
Gathering a garland of the strangest flowers,
Yet like the bee returning to her queen,
She bound the sweetest on her sister's brow,
Who meek and sober kissed the sportive child,
No longer trembling at the broken rod.

'Mild was the slow necessity of death:
The tranquil Spirit failed beneath its grasp,
Without a groan, almost without a fear,
Calm as a voyager to some distant land,
And full of wonder, full of hope as he.
The deadly germs of languor and disease
Died in the human frame, and purity
Blest with all gifts her earthly worshippers.
How vigorous then the athletic form of age!
How clear its open and unwrinkled brow!
Where neither avarice, cunning, pride, or care,
Had stamped the seal of grey deformity
On all the mingling lineaments of time.
How lovely the intrepid front of youth!
Which meek-eyed courage decked with freshest grace;
Courage of soul, that dreaded not a name,
And elevated will, that journeyed on
Through life's phantasmal scene in fearlessness,
With virtue, love, and pleasure, hand in hand.

'Then, that sweet bondage which is freedom's self,°
And rivets with sensation's softest tie
The kindred sympathies of human souls,
Needed no fetters of tyrannic law:
Those delicate and timid impulses

In nature's primal modesty arose,
And with undoubting confidence disclosed
The growing longings of its dawning love,
Unchecked by dull and selfish chastity,
That virtue of the cheaply virtuous,
Who pride themselves in senselessness and frost.°
No longer prostitution's venomed bane
Poisoned the springs of happiness and life;
Woman and man, in confidence and love,
Equal and free and pure together trod
The mountain-paths of virtue, which no more
Were stained with blood from many a pilgrim's feet.

'Then, where, through distant ages, long in pride
The palace of the monarch-slave had mocked
Famine's faint groan, and penury's silent tear,
A heap of crumbling ruins stood, and threw
Year after year their stones upon the field,
Wakening a lonely echo; and the leaves
Of the old thorn, that on the topmost tower
Usurped the royal ensign's grandeur, shook
In the stern storm that swayed the topmost tower
And whispered strange tales in the whirlwind's ear.

'Low through the lone cathedral's roofless aisles
The melancholy winds a death-dirge sung:
It were a sight of awfulness to see
The works of faith and slavery, so vast,
So sumptuous, yet so perishing withal!
Even as the corpse that rests beneath its wall.
A thousand mourners deck the pomp of death
Today, the breathing marble glows above
To decorate its memory, and tongues
Are busy of its life: tomorrow, worms
In silence and in darkness seize their prey.

'Within the massy prison's mouldering courts,
Fearless and free the ruddy children played,
Weaving gay chaplets for their innocent brows
With the green ivy and the red wall-flower,
That mock the dungeon's unavailing gloom;

The ponderous chains, and gratings of strong iron,
There rusted amid heaps of broken stone
That mingled slowly with their native earth:
There the broad beam of day, which feebly once
Lighted the cheek of lean captivity
With a pale and sickly glare, then freely shone
On the pure smiles of infant playfulness:
No more the shuddering voice of hoarse despair
Pealed through the echoing vaults, but soothing notes
Of ivy-fingered winds and gladsome birds
And merriment were resonant around.

'These ruins soon left not a wreck behind:°
Their elements, wide scattered o'er the globe,
To happier shapes were moulded, and became
Ministrant to all blissful impulses:
Thus human things were perfected, and earth,
Even as a child beneath its mother's love,
Was strengthened in all excellence, and grew
Fairer and nobler with each passing year.

'Now Time his dusky pennons o'er the scene
Closes in steadfast darkness, and the past
Fades from our charmèd sight. My task is done:
Thy lore is learned. Earth's wonders are thine own,
With all the fear and all the hope they bring.
My spells are past: the present now recurs.
Ah me! a pathless wilderness remains
Yet unsubdued by man's reclaiming hand.

'Yet, human Spirit, bravely hold thy course,
Let virtue teach thee firmly to pursue
The gradual paths of an aspiring change:
For birth and life and death, and that strange state
Before the naked soul has found its home,
All tend to perfect happiness, and urge
The restless wheels of being on their way,
Whose flashing spokes, instinct with infinite life,
Bicker and burn to gain their destined goal:
For birth but wakes the spirit to the sense
Of outward shows, whose unexperienced shape

New modes of passion to its frame may lend;
Life is its state of action, and the store
Of all events is aggregated there
That variegate the eternal universe;
Death is a gate of dreariness and gloom,
That leads to azure isles and beaming skies
And happy regions of eternal hope.
Therefore, O Spirit! fearlessly bear on:
Though storms may break the primrose on its stalk,
Though frosts may blight the freshness of its bloom,
Yet spring's awakening breath will woo the earth,
To feed with kindliest dews its favourite flower,
That blooms in mossy banks and darksome glens,
Lighting the green wood with its sunny smile.

'Fear not then, Spirit, death's disrobing hand,
So welcome when the tyrant is awake,
So welcome when the bigot's hell-torch burns;
'Tis but the voyage of a darksome hour,
The transient gulf-dream of a startling sleep.
Death is no foe to virtue: earth has seen
Love's brightest roses on the scaffold bloom,
Mingling with freedom's fadeless laurels there,
And presaging the truth of visioned bliss.
Are there not hopes within thee, which this scene
Of linked and gradual being has confirmed?
Whose stingings bade thy heart look further still,
When to the moonlight walk by Henry led,
Sweetly and sadly thou didst talk of death?
And wilt thou rudely tear them from thy breast,
Listening supinely to a bigot's creed,
Or tamely crouching to the tyrant's rod,
Whose iron thongs are red with human gore?
Never: but bravely bearing on, thy will
Is destined an eternal war to wage
With tyranny and falsehood, and uproot
The germs of misery from the human heart.
Thine is the hand whose piety would soothe
The thorny pillow of unhappy crime,
Whose impotence an easy pardon gains,
Watching its wanderings as a friend's disease:

Thine is the brow whose mildness would defy
Its fiercest rage, and brave its sternest will,
When fenced by power and master of the world.
Thou art sincere and good; of resolute mind,
Free from heart-withering custom's cold control,
Of passion lofty, pure and unsubdued.
Earth's pride and meanness could not vanquish thee,
And therefore art thou worthy of the boon
Which thou hast now received: virtue shall keep
Thy footsteps in the path that thou hast trod,
And many days of beaming hope shall bless
Thy spotless life of sweet and sacred love.
Go, happy one, and give that bosom joy
  Whose sleepless spirit waits to catch
  Light, life and rapture from thy smile.'

  The fairy waves her wand of charm.
Speechless with bliss the Spirit mounts the car,
  That rolled beside the battlement,
Bending her beamy eyes in thankfulness.
  Again the enchanted steeds were yoked,
  Again the burning wheels inflame
The steep descent of heaven's untrodden way.
  Fast and far the chariot flew:
  The vast and fiery globes that rolled
  Around the Fairy's palace-gate
Lessened by slow degrees, and soon appeared
Such tiny twinklers as the planet orbs
That there attendant on the solar power
With borrowed light pursued their narrower way.

    Earth floated then below:
  The chariot paused a moment there;
    The Spirit then descended:
The restless coursers pawed the ungenial soil,
Snuffed the gross air, and then, their errand done,
Unfurled their pinions to the winds of heaven.

  The Body and the Soul united then,
A gentle start convulsed Ianthe's frame:
Her veiny eyelids quietly unclosed;

Moveless awhile the dark blue orbs remained:
She looked around in wonder and beheld
Henry, who kneeled in silence by her couch,
Watching her sleep with looks of speechless love,
  And the bright beaming stars
  That through the casement shone.

NOTES TO 'QUEEN MAB'°

I.242–3

The sun's unclouded orb
Rolled through the black concave.

Beyond our atmosphere the sun would appear a rayless orb of fire in the midst of a black concave. The equal diffusion of its light on earth is owing to the refraction of the rays by the atmosphere, and their reflection from other bodies. Light consists either of vibrations propagated through a subtle medium, or of numerous minute particles repelled in all directions from the luminous body. Its velocity greatly exceeds that of any substance with which we are acquainted: observations on the eclipses of Jupiter's satellites have demonstrated that light takes up no more than 8′ 7″ in passing from the sun to the earth, a distance of 95,000,000 miles.—Some idea may be gained of the immense distance of the fixed stars, when it is computed that many years would elapse before light could reach this earth from the nearest of them; yet in one year light travels 5,422,400,000,000 miles, which is a distance 5,707,600 times greater than that of the sun from the earth.°

I.252–3

Whilst round the chariot's way
Innumerable systems rolled.

The plurality of worlds,—the indefinite immensity of the universe is a most awful subject of contemplation. He who rightly feels its mystery and grandeur, is in no danger of seduction from the falsehoods of religious systems, or of deifying the principle of the universe. It is impossible to believe that the Spirit that pervades this infinite machine, begat a son upon the body of a Jewish woman; or is angered at the consequences of that necessity, which is a synonym of itself. All that miserable tale of the Devil, and Eve, and an Intercessor, with the childish mummeries of the God of the Jews, is irreconcilable with the knowledge of the stars. The works of his fingers have borne witness against him.

The nearest of the fixed stars is inconceivably distant from the earth, and they are probably proportionably distant from each other. By a calculation of the velocity of light, Syrius is supposed to be at least 54,224,000,000,000 miles from the earth.° That which appears only like a thin and silvery cloud streaking the heaven, is in effect composed of innumerable clusters of suns, each shining with its own light, and illuminating numbers of planets that revolve around them. Millions and millions of suns are ranged around us, all attended by innumerable worlds, yet calm, regular, and harmonious, all keeping the paths of immutable necessity.

4.178–9

These are the hired bravos who defend
The tyrant's throne.

[This Note consists of an extended quotation from the fifth essay in part 2 of Godwin's collection of essays, *The Enquirer* (1797), followed by a version of 'Falsehood and Vice: a Dialogue', 'a little poem . . . strongly expressive of my abhorrence of despotism and falsehood'. S. rescued 'Falsehood and Vice' from the 'oblivion' of the unpublished *Esdaile Notebook*, where it exists in a slightly different form. The following extract from the Note begins in the penultimate paragraph of the Godwin quotation.]

[. . .] A soldier is a man whose business it is to kill those who never offended him, and who are the innocent martyrs of other men's iniquities. Whatever may become of the abstract question of the justifiableness of war, it seems impossible that the soldier should not be a depraved and unnatural being.

To these more serious and momentous considerations it may be proper to add a recollection of the ridiculousness of the military character. Its first constituent is obedience: a soldier is, of all descriptions of men, the most completely a machine; yet his profession inevitably teaches him something of dogmatism, swaggering, and self-consequence: he is like the puppet of a showman, who, at the very time he is made to strut and swell and display the most farcical airs, we perfectly know cannot assume the most insignificant gesture, advance either to the right or the left, but as he is moved by his exhibitor.—*Godwin's Enquirer, Essay* v.

I will here subjoin a little poem,° so strongly expressive of my abhorrence of despotism and falsehood, that I fear lest it never again may be depictured so vividly. This opportunity is perhaps the only one that ever will occur of rescuing it from oblivion.

FALSEHOOD AND VICE

A DIALOGUE

Whilst monarchs laughed upon their thrones
To hear a famished nation's groans,
And hugged the wealth wrung from the woe
That makes its eyes and veins o'erflow,—
Those thrones, high built upon the heaps

Of bones where frenzied famine sleeps,
Where slavery wields her scourge of iron,
Red with mankind's unheeded gore,
And war's mad fiends the scene environ:
Mingling with shrieks a drunken roar,
There Vice and Falsehood took their stand,
High raised above the unhappy land.

Falsehood

Brother! arise from the dainty fare,
Which thousands have toiled and bled to bestow;
A finer feast for thy hungry ear
Is the news that I bring of human woe.

Vice

And, secret one, what hast thou done,
To compare, in thy tumid pride, with me?
I, whose career, through the blasted year,
Has been tracked by despair and agony.

Falsehood

What have I done!—I have torn the robe
From baby truth's unsheltered form,
And round the desolated globe
Borne safely the bewildering charm:
My tyrant-slaves to a dungeon-floor
Have bound the fearless innocent,
And streams of fertilizing gore
Flow from her bosom's hideous rent,
Which this unfailing dagger gave. . . .
I dread that blood!—no more—this day
Is ours, though her eternal ray
  Must shine upon our grave.
Yet know, proud Vice, had I not given
To thee the robe I stole from heaven,
Thy shape of ugliness and fear
Had never gained admission here.

Vice

And know, that had I disdained to toil,
But sate in my loathsome cave the while,
And ne'er to these hateful sons of heaven,
GOLD, MONARCHY, and MURDER, given;
Hadst thou with all thine art essayed
One of thy games then to have played,

With all thine overweening boast,
Falsehood! I tell thee thou hadst lost!—
Yet wherefore this dispute?—we tend,
Fraternal, to one common end;
In this cold grave beneath my feet
Will our hopes, our fears, and our labours meet.

Falsehood

I brought my daughter, RELIGION, on earth:
She smothered Reason's babes in their birth;
But dreaded their mother's eye severe,—
So the crocodile slunk off slily in fear,
And loosed her bloodhounds from the den. . . .
They started from dreams of slaughtered men,
And, by the light of her poison eye,
Did her work o'er the wide earth frightfully:
The dreadful stench of her torches' flare,
Fed with human fat, polluted the air:
The curses, the shrieks, the ceaseless cries
Of the many-mingling miseries,
As on she trod, ascended high
And trumpeted my victory!—
Brother, tell what thou hast done.

Vice

I have extinguished the noon-day sun,
In the carnage-smoke of battles won:
Famine, murder, hell and power
Were glutted in that glorious hour
Which searchless fate had stamped for me
With the seal of her security. . . .
For the bloated wretch on yonder throne
Commanded the bloody fray to rise.
Like me he joyed at the stifled moan
Wrung from a nation's miseries;
While the snakes, whose slime even him *defiled*,
In ecstacies of malice smiled:
They thought 'twas theirs,—but mine the deed!
Theirs is the toil, but mine the meed—
Ten thousand victims madly bleed.
They dream that tyrants goad them there
With poisonous war to taint the air:
These tyrants, on their beds of thorn,
Swell with the thoughts of murderous fame,
And with their gains to lift my name.

Restless they plan from night to morn:
I—I do all; without my aid
Thy daughter, that relentless maid,
Could never o'er a death-bed urge
The fury of her venomed scourge.

Falsehood

Brother, well:—the world is ours;
And whether thou or I have won,
The pestilence expectant lowers
On all beneath yon blasted sun.
Our joys, our toils, our honours meet
In the milk-white and wormy winding-sheet:
A short-lived hope, unceasing care,
Some heartless scraps of godly prayer,
A moody curse, and a frenzied sleep
Ere gapes the grave's unclosing deep,
A tyrant's dream, a coward's start,
The ice that clings to a priestly heart,
A judge's frown, a courtier's smile,
Make the great whole for which we toil;
And, brother, whether thou or I
Have done the work of misery,
It little boots: thy toil and pain,
Without my aid, were more than vain;
And but for thee I ne'er had sate
The guardian of heaven's palace gate.

5.1–2

Thus do the generations of the earth
Go to the grave and issue from the womb.

[S.'s Note quotes Ecclesiastes 1: 4–7.]

5.4–6

Even as the leaves
Which the keen frost-wind of the waning year
Has scattered on the forest soil.

[S.'s Note quotes *Iliad* 6. 146–9.]

5.58

The mob of peasants, nobles, priests, and kings.

[S.'s Note quotes Lucretius, *De Rerum Natura* 2. 1–14.]

5.93–4

And statesmen boast
Of wealth!

[S.'s Note deplores the unequal distribution of wealth and the role of labour in society.]

5.112–13

or religion
Drives his wife raving mad.

I am acquainted with a lady of considerable accomplishments, and the mother of a numerous family, whom the Christian religion has goaded to incurable insanity. A parallel case is, I believe, within the experience of every physician.

Nam jam saepe homines patriam, carosque parentes
Prodiderunt, vitare Acherusia templa petentes.

Lucretius.°

5.189

Even love is sold.

Not even the intercourse of the sexes is exempt from the despotism of positive institution. Law pretends even to govern the indisciplinable wanderings of passion, to put fetters on the clearest deductions of reason, and, by appeals to the will, to subdue the involuntary affections of our nature. Love is inevitably consequent upon the perception of loveliness. Love withers under constraint: its very essence is liberty: it is compatible neither with obedience, jealousy, nor fear: it is there most pure, perfect, and unlimited, where its votaries live in confidence, equality, and unreserve.

How long then ought the sexual connection to last? what law ought to specify the extent of the grievances which should limit its duration? A husband and wife ought to continue so long united as they love each other: any law which should bind them to cohabitation for one moment after the decay of their affection, would be a most intolerable tyranny, and the most unworthy of toleration. How odious an usurpation of the right of private judgment should that law be considered, which should make the ties of friendship indissoluble, in spite of the caprices, the inconstancy, the fallibility, and capacity for improvement of the human mind. And by so much would the fetters of love be heavier and more unendurable than those of friendship, as love is more vehement and capricious, more dependent on those delicate peculiarities of imagination, and less capable of reduction to the ostensible merits of the object.

The state of society in which we exist is a mixture of feudal savageness and imperfect civilization. The narrow and unenlightened morality of the

Christian religion is an aggravation of these evils. It is not even until lately that mankind have admitted that happiness is the sole end of the science of ethics, as of all other sciences; and that the fanatical idea of mortifying the flesh for the love of God has been discarded. I have heard, indeed, an ignorant collegian adduce, in favour of Christianity, its hostility to every worldly feeling!°

But if happiness be the object of morality, of all human unions and disunions; if the worthiness of every action is to be estimated by the quantity of pleasurable sensation it is calculated to produce, then the connection of the sexes is so long sacred as it contributes to the comfort of the parties, and is naturally dissolved when its evils are greater than its benefits. There is nothing immoral in this separation. Constancy has nothing virtuous in itself, independently of the pleasure it confers, and partakes of the temporizing spirit of vice in proportion as it endures tamely moral defects of magnitude in the object of its indiscreet choice. Love is free: to promise for ever to love the same woman, is not less absurd than to promise to believe the same creed: such a vow, in both cases, excludes us from all enquiry. The language of the votarist is this: The woman I now love may be infinitely inferior to many others; the creed I now profess may be a mass of errors and absurdities; but I exclude myself from all future information as to the amiability of the one and the truth of the other, resolving blindly, and in spite of conviction, to adhere to them. Is this the language of delicacy and reason? Is the love of such a frigid heart of more worth than its belief?

The present system of constraint does no more, in the majority of instances, than make hypocrites or open enemies. Persons of delicacy and virtue, unhappily united to one whom they find it impossible to love, spend the loveliest season of their life in unproductive efforts to appear otherwise than they are, for the sake of the feelings of their partner or the welfare of their mutual offspring: those of less generosity and refinement openly avow their disappointment, and linger out the remnant of that union, which only death can dissolve, in a state of incurable bickering and hostility. The early education of their children takes its colour from the squabbles of the parents; they are nursed in a systematic school of ill humour, violence, and falsehood. Had they been suffered to part at the moment when indifference rendered their union irksome, they would have been spared many years of misery: they would have connected themselves more suitably, and would have found that happiness in the society of more congenial partners which is for ever denied them by the despotism of marriage. They would have been separately useful and happy members of society, who, whilst united, were miserable, and rendered misanthropical by misery. The conviction that wedlock is indissoluble holds out the strongest of all temptations to the perverse: they indulge without restraint in acrimony, and all the little tyrannies of domestic life, when they know that their victim is without appeal. If this connection were put on a rational basis, each would be assured that habitual ill temper would terminate in separation, and would check this vicious and dangerous propensity.

Prostitution is the legitimate offspring of marriage and its accompanying errors. Women, for no other crime than having followed the dictates of a natural appetite, are driven with fury from the comforts and sympathies of society. It is less venial than murder; and the punishment which is inflicted on her who destroys her child to escape reproach, is lighter than the life of agony and disease to which the prostitute is irrecoverably doomed. Has a woman obeyed the impulse of unerring nature;—society declares war against her, pitiless and eternal war: she must be the tame slave, she must make no reprisals; theirs is the right of persecution, hers the duty of endurance. She lives a life of infamy: the loud and bitter laugh of scorn scares her from all return. She dies of long and lingering disease: yet *she* is in fault, *she* is the criminal, *she* the forward and untameable child,—and society, forsooth, the pure and virtuous matron, who casts her as an abortion from her undefiled bosom! Society avenges herself on the criminals of her own creation; she is employed in anathematizing the vice today, which yesterday she was the most zealous to teach. Thus is formed one tenth of the population of London: meanwhile the evil is twofold. Young men, excluded by the fanatical idea of chastity from the society of modest and accomplished women, associate with these vicious and miserable beings, destroying thereby all those exquisite and delicate sensibilities whose existence cold-hearted worldlings have denied; annihilating all genuine passion, and debasing that to a selfish feeling which is the excess of generosity and devotedness. Their body and mind alike crumble into a hideous wreck of humanity; idiocy and disease become perpetuated in their miserable offspring, and distant generations suffer for the bigoted morality of their forefathers. Chastity is a monkish and evangelical superstition, a greater foe to natural temperance even than unintellectual sensuality; it strikes at the root of all domestic happiness, and consigns more than half of the human race to misery, that some few may monopolize according to law. A system could not well have been devised more studiously hostile to human happiness than marriage.

I conceive that, from the abolition of marriage, the fit and natural arrangement of sexual connection would result. I by no means assert that the intercourse would be promiscuous: on the contrary; it appears, from the relation of parent to child, that this union is generally of long duration, and marked above all others with generosity and self-devotion. But this is a subject which it is perhaps premature to discuss. That which will result from the abolition of marriage, will be natural and right, because choice and change will be exempted from restraint.

In fact, religion and morality, as they now stand, compose a practical code of misery and servitude: the genius of human happiness must tear every leaf from the accursed book of God, ere man can read the inscription on his heart. How would morality, dressed up in stiff stays and finery, start from her own disgusting image, should she look in the mirror of nature!

6.45–6

To the red and baleful sun
That faintly twinkles there.

[S's Note discusses the precession of the equinox and the possibility of there one day being 'a perfect identity between the moral and physical improvement of the human species'.]

6.171–3

No atom of this turbulence fulfils
A vague and unnecessitated task,
Or acts but as it must and ought to act.

[S's Note quotes Holbach's *Système de la Nature* (1774 edn.), 1.56.]

6.198°

Necessity, thou mother of the world!

[S.'s lengthy Note discusses the relation of necessity to liberty, morality, and divinity, drawing on the writings of Hume, Holbach, and Godwin.]

7.13

There is no God!

This negation must be understood solely to affect a creative Deity. The hypothesis of a pervading Spirit coeternal with the universe, remains unshaken.

A close examination° of the validity of the proofs adduced to support any proposition, is the only secure way of attaining truth, on the advantages of which it is unnecessary to descant: our knowledge of the existence of a Deity is a subject of such importance, that it cannot be too minutely investigated; in consequence of this conviction we proceed briefly and impartially to examine the proofs which have been adduced. It is necessary first to consider the nature of belief.

When a proposition is offered to the mind, it perceives the agreement or disagreement of the ideas of which it is composed. A perception of their agreement is termed *belief*. Many obstacles frequently prevent this perception from being immediate; these the mind attempts to remove, in order that the perception may be distinct. The mind is active in the investigation, in order to perfect the state of perception [of the relation which the component ideas of the proposition bear to each], which is passive: the investigation being confused with the perception, has induced many falsely to imagine that the mind is active in belief,—that belief is an act of volition,—in consequence of which it may be regulated by the mind. Pursuing, continuing this mistake, they have attached a degree of criminality to disbelief; of which, in its nature, it is incapable: it is equally incapable of merit.

Belief, then, is a passion, the strength of which, like every other passion, is in precise proportion to the degrees of excitement.

The degrees of excitement are three.

The senses are the sources of all knowledge to the mind; consequently their evidence claims the strongest assent.

The decision of the mind, founded upon our own experience, derived from these sources, claims the next degree.

The experience of others, which addresses itself to the former one, occupies the lowest degree.

[(A graduated scale, on which should be marked the capabilities of propositions to approach to the test of the senses, would be a just barometer of the belief which ought to be attached to them.)]

Consequently no testimony can be admitted which is contrary to reason; reason is founded on the evidence of our senses.

Every proof may be referred to one of these three divisions: it is to be considered what arguments we receive from each of them, which should convince us of the existence of a Deity.

1st. The evidence of the senses. If the Deity should appear to us, if he should convince our senses of his existence, this revolution would necessarily command belief. Those to whom the Deity has thus appeared have the strongest possible conviction of his existence. [But the God of Theologians is incapable of local visibility.]

2d. Reason. It is urged that man knows that whatever is, must either have had a beginning, or have existed from all eternity: he also knows, that whatever is not eternal must have had a cause. When this reasoning is applied to the universe, it is necessary to prove that it was created: until that is clearly demonstrated, we may reasonably suppose that it has endured from all eternity. [We must prove design before we can infer a designer. The only idea which we can form of causation is derivable from the constant conjunction of objects, and the consequent inference of one from the other.] In a case where two propositions are diametrically opposite, the mind believes that which is least° incomprehensible;—it is easier to suppose that the universe has existed from all eternity, than to conceive a being [beyond its limits] capable of creating it: if the mind sinks beneath the weight of one, is it an alleviation to increase the intolerability of the burden?

The other argument, which is founded on a man's knowledge of his own existence, stands thus. A man knows not only that he now is, but that once he was not; consequently there must have been a cause. [But our idea of causation is alone derivable from the constant conjunction of objects and the consequent inference of one from the other; and, reasoning experimentally,°] we can only infer from effects, causes exactly adequate to those effects. But there certainly is a generative power which is effected by certain instruments: we cannot prove that it is inherent in these instruments; nor is the contrary hypothesis capable of demonstration: we admit that the generative power is incomprehensible; but to suppose that the same effect is produced by an eternal, omniscient, omnipotent being,° leaves the cause in the same obscurity, but renders it more incomprehensible.

3d. Testimony. It is required that testimony should not be contrary to reason. The testimony that the Deity convinces the senses of men of his existence can only be admitted by us, if our mind considers it less probable that these men should have been deceived, than that the Deity should have appeared to them. Our reason can never admit the testimony of men, who not only declare that they were eye-witnesses of miracles, but that the Deity was irrational; for he commanded that he should be believed, he proposed the highest rewards for faith, eternal punishments for disbelief. We can only command voluntary actions; belief is not an act of volition; the mind is even passive, or involuntarily active: from this it is evident that we have no sufficient testimony, or rather that testimony is insufficient to prove the being of a God. It has been before shown that it cannot be deduced from reason. They alone, then, who have been convinced by the evidence of the senses, can believe it.

Hence it is evident that, having no proofs from either of the three sources of conviction, the mind *cannot* believe the existence of a [creative] God: it is also evident, that, as belief is a passion of the mind, no degree of criminality is attachable to disbelief; and that they only are reprehensible who neglect to remove the false medium through which their mind views any subject of discussion. Every reflecting mind must acknowledge that there is no proof of the existence of a Deity.

God is an hypothesis, and, as such, stands in need of proof: the *onus probandi* rests on the theist. Sir Isaac Newton says: *Hypotheses non fingo, quicquid enim ex phaenomenis non deducitur, hypothesis vocanda est, et hypothesis vel metaphysica, vel physicae, vel qualitatum occultarum, seu mechanicae, in philosophiâ locum non habent.*° To all proofs of the existence of a creative God apply this valuable rule. We see a variety of bodies possessing a variety of powers: we merely know their effects; we are in a state of ignorance with respect to their essences and causes. These Newton calls the phenomena of things; but the pride of philosophy is unwilling to admit its ignorance of their causes. From the phenomena, which are the objects of our senses, we attempt to infer a cause, which we call God, and gratuitously endow it with all negative and contradictory qualities. From this hypothesis we invent this general name, to conceal our ignorance of causes and essences. The being called God by no means answers with the conditions prescribed by Newton; it bears every mark of a veil woven by philosophical conceit, to hide the ignorance of philosophers even from themselves. They borrow the threads of its texture from the anthropomorphism of the vulgar. Words have been used by sophists for the same purposes, from the occult qualities of the peripatetics to the *effluvium* of Boyle and the *crinities* or *nebulae* of Herschel.° God is represented as infinite, eternal, incomprehensible; he is contained under every praedicate in non° that the logic of ignorance could fabricate. Even his worshippers allow that it is impossible to form any idea of him: they exclaim with the French poet,

Pour dire ce qu'il est, il faut être lui-même.°

Lord Bacon says, that 'atheism leaves to man reason, philosophy, natural piety, laws, reputation, and every thing that can serve to conduct him to virtue; but superstition destroys all these, and erects itself into a tyranny over the understandings of men: hence atheism never disturbs the government, but renders man more clear-sighted, since he sees nothing beyond the boundaries of the present life.'

[. . .]

7.67

Ahasuerus, rise!

[S.'s Note is a loose prose transcription of a translation of C. F. D. Schubart's poem 'Der ewige Jude. Eine lyrische Rhapsodie' (1783), about the Wandering Jew, Ahasuerus.]

7.135–6

I will beget a Son, and he shall bear
The sins of all the world.

[S.'s lengthy Note discusses the defects, illogicalities and tyrannies of the Christian religion.]

8.203–7

Him, (still from hope to hope the bliss pursuing,
Which, from the exhaustless lore of human weal
Draws on the virtuous mind,) the thoughts that rise
In time-destroying infiniteness, gift
With self-enshrined eternity, &c.°

Time is our consciousness of the succession of ideas in our mind. Vivid sensation, of either pain or pleasure, makes the time seem long, as the common phrase is, because it renders us more acutely conscious of our ideas. If a mind be conscious of an hundred ideas during one minute, by the clock, and of two hundred during another, the latter of these spaces would actually occupy so much greater extent in the mind as two exceed one in quantity. If, therefore, the human mind, by any future improvement of its sensibility, should become conscious of an infinite number of ideas in a minute, that minute would be eternity. I do not hence infer that the actual space between the birth and death of a man will ever be prolonged; but that his sensibility is perfectible, and that the number of ideas which his mind is capable of receiving is indefinite. One man is stretched on the rack during twelve hours; another sleeps soundly in his bed: the difference of time perceived by these two persons is immense; one hardly will believe that half an hour has elapsed, the other could credit that centuries had flown during his agony. Thus, the life of a man of virtue and talent, who should die in his thirtieth year, is, with regard to his own feelings, longer than that of a miserable priest-ridden slave, who dreams out a century of dullness. The one has perpetually cultivated his mental faculties, has rendered himself master of his thoughts, can abstract and generalize amid the lethargy of everyday business;—the other can slumber over the brightest moments of his being, and is unable to remember the happiest hour of his life. Perhaps the perishing ephemeron enjoys a longer life than the tortoise.

Dark flood of time!
Roll as it listeth thee—I measure not
By months or moments thy ambiguous course.
Another may stand by me on the brink
And watch the bubble whirled beyond his ken
That pauses at my feet. The sense of love,
The thirst for action, and the impassioned thought
Prolong my being: if I wake no more,
My life more actual living will contain
Than some grey veteran's of the world's cold school,
Whose listless hours unprofitably roll,
By one enthusiast feeling unredeemed.°

8.211–12°

No longer now
He slays the lamb that looks him in the face.

I hold that the depravity of the physical and moral nature of man originated in his unnatural habits of life. The origin of man, like that of the universe of which he is a part, is enveloped in impenetrable mystery. His generations either had a beginning, or they had not. The weight of evidence in favour of each of these suppositions seems tolerably equal; and it is perfectly unimportant to the present argument which is assumed. The language spoken however by the mythology of nearly all religions seems to prove, that at some distant period man forsook the path of nature, and sacrificed the purity and happiness of his being to unnatural appetites. The date of this event seems to have also been that of some great change in the climates of the earth, with which it has an obvious correspondence. The allegory of Adam and Eve eating of the tree of evil, and entailing upon their posterity the wrath of God, and the loss of everlasting life, admits of no other explanation than the disease and crime that have flowed from unnatural diet. Milton° was so well aware of this, that he makes Raphael thus exhibit to Adam the consequence of his disobedience.

Immediately a place
Before his eyes appeared: sad, noisome, dark:
A lazar-house it seem'd; wherein were laid
Numbers of all diseased: all maladies

Of ghastly spasm, or racking torture, qualms
Of heart-sick agony, all feverous kinds,
Convulsions, epilepsies, fierce catarrhs,
Intestine stone and ulcer, cholic pangs,
Daemoniac frenzy, moping melancholy,
And moon-struck madness, pining atrophy,
Marasmus, and wide-wasting pestilence,
Dropsies, and asthma, and joint-racking rheums.

And how many thousands more might not be added to this frightful catalogue!

The story of Prometheus is one likewise which, although universally admitted to be allegorical, has never been satisfactorily explained. Prometheus stole fire from heaven, and was chained for this crime to mount Caucasus, where a vulture continually devoured his liver, that grew to meet its hunger. Hesiod says, that, before the time of Prometheus, mankind were exempt from suffering; that they enjoyed a vigorous youth, and that death, when at length it came, approached like sleep, and gently closed their eyes. Again, so general was this opinion, that Horace,° a poet of the Augustan age, writes—

Audax omnia perpeti,
Gens humana ruit per vetitum nefas;
Audax Iapeti genus
Ignem fraude mala gentibus intulit:
Post ignem aetheriâ domo
Subductum, macies et nova febrium
Terris incubuit cohors,
Semotique prius tarda necessitas
Lethi corripuit gradum.

How plain a language is spoken by all this. Prometheus (who represents the human race) effected some great change in the condition of his nature, and applied fire to culinary purposes; thus inventing an expedient for screening from his disgust the horrors of the shambles. From this moment his vitals were devoured by the vulture of disease. It consumed his being in every shape of its loathsome and infinite variety, inducing the soul-quelling sinkings of premature and violent death. All vice arose from the ruin of healthful innocence. Tyranny, superstition, commerce, and inequality, were then first known, when reason vainly attempted to guide the wanderings of exacerbated passion. [. . .]

Man, and the animals whom he has infected with his society, or depraved by his dominion, are alone diseased. The wild hog, the mouflon,° the bison, and the wolf, are perfectly exempt from malady, and invariably die either from external violence, or natural old age. But the domestic hog, the sheep, the cow, and the dog, are subject to an incredible variety of distempers; and, like the corrupters of their nature, have physicians who thrive upon their miseries.

The supereminence of man is like Satan's, a supereminence of pain; and the majority of his species, doomed to penury, disease and crime, have reason to curse the untoward event, that by enabling him to communicate his sensations, raised him above the level of his fellow animals. But the steps that have been taken are irrevocable. The whole of human science is comprised in one question:—How can the advantages of intellect and civilization be reconciled with the liberty and pure pleasures of natural life? How can we take the benefits, and reject the evils of the system, which is now interwoven with all the fibres of our being?—I believe that abstinence from animal food and spirituous liquors would in a great measure capacitate us for the solution of this important question.

It is true, that mental and bodily derangement is attributable in part to other deviations from rectitude and nature than those which concern diet. The mistakes cherished by society respecting the connection of the sexes, whence the misery and diseases of unsatisfied celibacy, unenjoying prostitution, and the premature arrival of puberty necessarily spring; the putrid atmosphere of crowded cities; the exhalations of chemical processes; the muffling of our bodies in superfluous apparel; the absurd treatment of infants:—all these, and innumerable other causes, contribute their mite to the mass of human evil.°

Comparative anatomy teaches us that man resembles frugivorous animals in everything, and carnivorous in nothing; he has neither claws wherewith to seize his prey, nor distinct and pointed teeth to tear the living fibre. A Mandarin of the first class, with nails two inches long, would probably find them alone inefficient to hold even a hare. After every subterfuge of gluttony, the bull must be degraded into the ox, and the ram into the wether, by an unnatural and inhuman operation, that the flaccid fibre may offer a fainter resistance to rebellious nature. It is only by softening and disguising dead flesh by culinary preparation, that it is rendered susceptible of mastication or digestion; and that the sight of its bloody juices and raw horror does not excite intolerable loathing and disgust. Let the advocate of animal food force himself to a decisive experiment on its fitness, and, as Plutarch recommends, tear a living lamb with his teeth, and plunging his head into its vitals, slake his thirst with the steaming blood; when fresh from the deed of horror, let him revert to the irresistible instincts of nature that would rise in judgment against it, and say, Nature formed me for such work as this. Then, and then only, would he be consistent. [. . .]

What is the cause of morbid action in the animal system? Not the air we breathe, for our fellow denizens of nature breathe the same uninjured; not the water we drink (if remote from the pollutions of man and his inventions°), for the animals drink it too; not the earth we tread upon; not the unobscured sight of glorious nature, in the wood, the field, or the expanse of sky and ocean; nothing that we are or do in common with the undiseased inhabitants of the forest. Something then wherein we differ from them: our habit of altering our food by fire, so that our appetite is no longer a just criterion for the fitness of its gratification. Except in children, there remain no traces of that instinct which determines, in all other animals, what aliment is natural or otherwise; and so perfectly obliterated are they in the reasoning adults of our species, that it has become necessary to urge considerations drawn from comparative anatomy to prove that we are naturally frugivorous.

Crime is madness. Madness is disease. Whenever the cause of disease shall be discovered, the root, from which all vice and misery have so long overshadowed the globe, will lie bare to the axe. All the exertions of man, from that moment, may be considered as tending to the clear profit of his species. No sane mind in a sane body resolves upon a real crime. It is a man of violent passions, blood-shot eyes, and swollen veins, that alone can grasp the knife of murder. The system of a simple diet promises no Utopian advantages. It is no mere reform of legislation, whilst the furious passions and evil propensities of the human heart, in which it had its origin, are still unassuaged. It strikes at the root of all evil, and is an experiment which may be tried with success, not alone by nations, but by small societies, families, and even individuals. In no cases has a return to vegetable diet produced the slightest injury; in most it has been attended with changes undeniably beneficial. Should ever a physician be born with the genius of Locke, I am persuaded that he might trace all bodily and mental derangements to our unnatural habits, as clearly as that philosopher has traced all knowledge to sensation. What prolific sources of disease are not those mineral and vegetable poisons that have been introduced for its extirpation! How many thousands have become murderers and robbers, bigots and domestic tyrants, dissolute and abandoned adventurers, from the use of fermented liquors; who, had they slaked their thirst only with pure water, would have lived but to diffuse the happiness of their own unperverted feelings. How many groundless opinions and absurd institutions have not received a general sanction from the sottishness and intemperance of individuals! Who will assert that, had the populace of Paris satisfied their hunger at the ever-furnished table of vegetable nature, they would have lent their brutal suffrage to the proscription-list of Robespierre? Could a set of men, whose passions were not perverted by unnatural stimuli, look with coolness on an auto da fè? Is it to be believed that a being of gentle feelings, rising from his meal of roots, would take delight in sports of blood? Was Nero a man of temperate life? could you read calm health in his cheek, flushed with ungovernable propensities of hatred for the human race? Did Muley Ismael's° pulse beat evenly, was his skin transparent, did his eyes beam with healthfulness, and its invariable concomitants, cheerfulness and benignity? Though history has decided none of these questions, a child could not hesitate to answer in the negative. Surely the bile-suffused cheek of Buonaparte, his wrinkled brow, and yellow eye, the ceaseless inquietude of his nervous system, speak no less plainly the character of his unresting ambition than his murders and his victories. It is impossible, had Buonaparte descended from a race of vegetable feeders, that he could have had either the inclination or the power to ascend the throne of the Bourbons. The desire of tyranny could scarcely be excited in the individual, the power to tyrannize would certainly not be delegated by a society neither frenzied by inebriation nor rendered impotent and irrational by disease. [. . .]

[. . .] The change which would be produced by simpler habits [of diet] on political economy is sufficiently remarkable. The monopolizing eater of animal flesh would no longer destroy his constitution by devouring an acre at a meal, and many loaves of bread would cease to contribute to gout, madness and apoplexy, in the shape of a pint of porter, or a dram of gin, when appeasing the long-protracted famine of the hard-working peasant's hungry babies. The quantity of nutritious vegetable matter, consumed in fattening the carcase of an ox, would afford ten times the sustenance, undepraving indeed, and incapable of generating disease, if gathered immediately from the bosom of the earth. The most fertile districts of the habitable globe are now actually cultivated by men for animals, at a delay and waste of aliment absolutely incapable of calculation. It is only the wealthy that can, to any great degree, even now, indulge the unnatural craving for dead flesh, and they pay for the greater licence of the privilege by subjection to supernumerary diseases. Again, the spirit of the nation that should take the lead in this great reform, would insensibly become agricultural; commerce, with all its vice, selfishness and corruption, would gradually decline; more natural habits would produce gentler manners, and the excessive complication of political relations would be so far simplified, that every individual might feel and understand why he loved his country, and took a personal interest in its welfare. How would England, for example, depend on the caprices of foreign rulers, if she contained within herself all the necessaries, and despised whatever they possessed of the luxuries of life? How could they starve her into compliance with their views? Of what consequence would it be that they refused to take her woollen manufactures, when large and fertile tracts of the island ceased to be allotted to the waste of pasturage? On a natural system of diet, we should require no spices from India; no wines from Portugal, Spain, France, or Madeira; none of those multitudinous articles of luxury, for which every corner of the globe is rifled, and which are the causes of so much individual rivalship, such calamitous and sanguinary national disputes. In the history of modern times, the avarice of commercial monopoly, no less than the ambition of weak and wicked chiefs, seems to have fomented the universal discord, to have added stubbornness to the mistakes of cabinets, and indocility to the infatuation of the people. Let it ever be remembered, that it is the direct influence of commerce to make the interval between the richest and the poorest man wider and more unconquerable. Let it be remembered, that it is a foe to every thing of real worth and excellence in the human character. The odious and disgusting aristocracy of wealth is built upon the ruins of all that is good in chivalry or republicanism; and luxury is the forerunner of a barbarism scarce capable of cure. Is it impossible to realize a state of society, where all the energies of man shall be directed to the production of his solid happiness? Certainly, if this advantage (the object of all political speculation) be in any degree attainable, it is attainable only by a community which holds out no factitious incentives to the avarice and ambition of the few, and which is internally organized for the liberty, security and comfort of the many. None must be entrusted with power (and money is the completest species of power) who do not stand pledged to use it exclusively for the general benefit. But the use of animal flesh and fermented liquors, directly militates with this equality of the rights of man. The peasant cannot gratify these fashionable cravings without leaving his family to starve. Without disease and war, those sweeping curtailers of population, pasturage would include a waste too great to be afforded. The labour requisite to support a family is far lighter° than is usually supposed. The peasantry work, not only for themselves, but for the aristocracy, the army, and the manufacturers. [. . .]

I address myself not only to the young enthusiast, the ardent devotee of truth and virtue, the pure and passionate moralist, yet unvitiated by the contagion of the world. He will embrace a pure system, from its abstract truth, its beauty, its simplicity, and its promise of wide-extended benefit; unless custom has turned poison into food, he will hate the brutal pleasures of the chase by instinct; it will be a contemplation full of horror and disappointment to his mind, that beings capable of the gentlest and most admirable sympathies, should take delight in the death-pangs and last convulsions of dying animals. The elderly man, whose youth has been poisoned by intemperance, or who has lived with apparent moderation, and is afflicted with a variety of painful maladies, would find his account in a beneficial change produced without the risk of poisonous medicines. The mother, to whom the perpetual restlessness of disease, and unaccountable deaths incident to her children, are the causes of incurable unhappiness, would on this diet experience the satisfaction of beholding their perpetual healths and natural playfulness.° The most valuable lives are daily destroyed by diseases, that it is dangerous to palliate and impossible to cure by medicine. How much longer will man continue to pimp for the gluttony of death, his most insidious, implacable, and eternal foe?

Stanzas.—April, 1814

Away! the moor is dark beneath the moon,
    Rapid clouds have drank the last pale beam of even:
Away! the gathering winds will call the darkness soon,
    And profoundest midnight shroud the serene lights of heaven.

Pause not! The time is past! Every voice cries, Away!
    Tempt not with one last tear thy friend's ungentle mood:
Thy lover's eye, so glazed and cold, dares not entreat thy stay:
    Duty and dereliction guide thee back to solitude.°

Away, away! to thy sad and silent home;
Pour bitter tears on its desolated hearth;
Watch the dim shades as like ghosts they go and come,
And complicate strange webs of melancholy mirth.

The leaves of wasted autumn woods shall float around thine head:
The blooms of dewy spring shall gleam beneath thy feet:
But thy soul or this world must fade in the frost that binds the dead,
Ere midnight's frown and morning's smile, ere thou and
peace may meet.

The cloud shadows of midnight possess their own repose,
For the weary winds are silent, or the moon is in the deep:
Some respite to its turbulence unresting ocean knows;
Whatever moves, or toils, or grieves, hath its appointed sleep.

Thou in the grave shalt rest—yet till the phantoms flee
Which that house and heath and garden made dear to
thee erewhile,
Thy remembrance, and repentance, and deep musings are not free
From the music of two voices and the light of one sweet smile.

'O! there are spirits of the air'

Δάκρυσι διοίδω πότμον ἄποτμον°

O! there are spirits of the air,
And genii of the evening breeze,
And gentle ghosts, with eyes as fair
As star-beams among twilight trees:—
Such lovely ministers to meet
Oft hast thou turned from men thy lonely feet.

With mountain winds, and babbling springs,
And moonlight seas, that are the voice
Of these inexplicable things
Thou didst hold commune, and rejoice
When they did answer thee; but they
Cast, like a worthless boon, thy love away.

And thou hast sought in starry eyes
Beams that were never meant for thine,
Another's wealth:—tame sacrifice
To a fond faith! still dost thou pine?
Still dost thou hope that greeting hands,
Voice, looks, or lips, may answer thy demands?

Ah! wherefore didst thou build thine hope
On the false earth's inconstancy?
Did thine own mind afford no scope
Of love, or moving thoughts to thee?
That natural scenes or human smiles
Could steal the power to wind thee in their wiles?

Yes, all the faithless smiles are fled
Whose falsehood left thee broken-hearted;
The glory of the moon is dead;
Night's ghosts and dreams have now departed;
Thine own soul still is true to thee,
But changed to a foul fiend through misery.

This fiend, whose ghastly presence ever
Beside thee like thy shadow hangs,
Dream not to chase;—the mad endeavour
Would scourge thee to severer pangs.
Be as thou art. Thy settled fate,
Dark as it is, all change would aggravate.

To Wordsworth

Poet of Nature, thou hast wept to know
That things depart which never may return:
Childhood and youth, friendship and love's first glow,
Have fled like sweet dreams, leaving thee to mourn.
These common woes I feel. One loss is mine
Which thou too feel'st, yet I alone deplore.
Thou wert as a lone star, whose light did shine
On some frail bark in winter's midnight roar:
Thou hast like to a rock-built refuge stood

Above the blind and battling multitude:
In honoured poverty thy voice did weave
Songs consecrate to truth and liberty,—
Deserting these, thou leavest me to grieve,
Thus having been, that thou shouldst cease to be.

ALASTOR;

OR,

THE SPIRIT OF SOLITUDE

PREFACE

The poem entitled 'ALASTOR,' may be considered as allegorical of one of the most interesting situations of the human mind. It represents a youth of uncorrupted feelings and adventurous genius led forth by an imagination inflamed and purified through familiarity with all that is excellent and majestic, to the contemplation of the universe. He drinks deep of the fountains of knowledge, and is still insatiate. The magnificence and beauty of the external world sinks profoundly into the frame of his conceptions, and affords to their modifications a variety not to be exhausted. So long as it is possible for his desires to point towards objects thus infinite and unmeasured, he is joyous, and tranquil, and self-possessed. But the period arrives when these objects cease to suffice. His mind is at length suddenly awakened and thirsts for intercourse with an intelligence similar to itself. He images to himself the Being whom he loves. Conversant with speculations of the sublimest and most perfect natures, the vision in which he embodies his own imaginations unites all of wonderful, or wise, or beautiful, which the poet, the philosopher, or the lover could depicture. The intellectual faculties, the imagination, the functions of sense, have their respective requisitions on the sympathy of corresponding powers in other human beings. The Poet is represented as uniting these requisitions, and attaching them to a single image. He seeks in vain for a prototype of his conception. Blasted by his disappointment, he descends to an untimely grave.

The picture is not barren of instruction to actual men. The Poet's self-centred seclusion was avenged by the furies of an irresistible passion pursuing him to speedy ruin. But that Power which strikes the luminaries of the world with sudden darkness and extinction, by awakening them to too exquisite a perception of its influences, dooms to a slow and poisonous decay those meaner spirits that dare to abjure its dominion. Their destiny is more abject and inglorious as their delinquency is more contemptible and pernicious. They who, deluded by no generous error, instigated by no sacred thirst of doubtful knowledge, duped by no illustrious superstition, loving nothing on this earth, and cherishing no hopes beyond, yet keep aloof from sympathies with their kind, rejoicing neither in human joy nor mourning with human grief; these, and such as they, have their apportioned curse. They languish, because none feel with them their common nature. They are morally dead. They are neither friends, nor lovers, nor fathers, nor citizens of the world, nor benefactors of their country. Among those who attempt to exist without human sympathy, the pure and tender-hearted perish through the intensity and passion of their search after its communities, when the vacancy of their spirit suddenly makes itself felt. All else,° selfish, blind, and torpid, are those unforeseeing multitudes who constitute, together with their own, the lasting misery and loneliness of the world. Those who love not their fellow-beings, live unfruitful lives, and prepare for their old age a miserable grave.

'The good die first,
And those whose hearts are dry as summer dust,
Burn to the socket!'°

Nondum amabam, et amare amabam, quaerebam quid amarem, amans amare!

Confess. St. August.

Earth, ocean, air, beloved brotherhood!
If our great Mother has imbued my soul
With aught of natural piety to feel°
Your love, and recompense the boon with mine;
If dewy morn, and odorous noon, and even,
With sunset and its gorgeous ministers,
And solemn midnight's tingling silentness;
If autumn's hollow sighs in the sere wood,
And winter robing with pure snow and crowns
Of starry ice the grey grass and bare boughs;
If spring's voluptuous pantings when she breathes
Her first sweet kisses, have been dear to me;
If no bright bird, insect, or gentle beast
I consciously have injured, but still loved
And cherished these my kindred; then forgive
This boast, beloved brethren, and withdraw

No portion of your wonted favour now!
  Mother of this unfathomable world!
Favour my solemn song, for I have loved
Thee ever, and thee only; I have watched
Thy shadow, and the darkness of thy steps,
And my heart ever gazes on the depth
Of thy deep mysteries. I have made my bed
In charnels and on coffins, where black death
Keeps record of the trophies won from thee,
Hoping to still these obstinate questionings°
Of thee and thine, by forcing some lone ghost
Thy messenger, to render up the tale
Of what we are. In lone and silent hours,
When night makes a weird sound of its own stillness,
Like an inspired and desperate alchemist
Staking his very life on some dark hope,
Have I mixed awful talk and asking looks
With my most innocent love, until strange tears
Uniting with those breathless kisses, made
Such magic as compels the charmèd night
To render up thy charge: . . . and, though ne'er yet
Thou hast unveiled thy inmost sanctuary,
Enough from incommunicable dream,
And twilight phantasms, and deep noonday thought,
Has shone within me, that serenely now
And moveless, as a long-forgotten lyre
Suspended in the solitary dome
Of some mysterious and deserted fane,
I wait thy breath, Great Parent, that my strain
May modulate with murmurs of the air,
And motions of the forests and the sea,
And voice of living beings, and woven hymns
Of night and day, and the deep heart of man.°
  There was a Poet whose untimely tomb
No human hands with pious reverence reared,
But the charmed eddies of autumnal winds
Built o'er his mouldering bones a pyramid
Of mouldering leaves in the waste wilderness:—
A lovely youth,—no mourning maiden decked
With weeping flowers, or votive cypress wreath,°
The lone couch of his everlasting sleep:—

Gentle, and brave, and generous,—no lorn bard
Breathed o'er his dark fate one melodious sigh:
He lived, he died, he sung, in solitude.
Strangers have wept to hear his passionate notes,
And virgins, as unknown he passed, have pined
And wasted for fond love of his wild eyes.
The fire of those soft orbs has ceased to burn,
And Silence, too enamoured of that voice,
Locks its mute music in her rugged cell.
    By solemn vision, and bright silver dream,
His infancy was nurtured. Every sight
And sound from the vast earth and ambient air,
Sent to his heart its choicest impulses.
The fountains of divine philosophy
Fled not his thirsting lips, and all of great,
Or good, or lovely, which the sacred past
In truth or fable consecrates, he felt
And knew. When early youth had passed, he left
His cold fireside and alienated home
To seek strange truths in undiscovered lands.
Many a wide waste and tangled wilderness
Has lured his fearless steps; and he has bought
With his sweet voice and eyes, from savage men,
His rest and food. Nature's most secret steps
He like her shadow has pursued, where'er
The red volcano overcanopies
Its fields of snow and pinnacles of ice
With burning smoke, or where bitumen lakes°
On black bare pointed islets ever beat
With sluggish surge, or where the secret caves
Rugged and dark, winding among the springs
Of fire and poison, inaccessible
To avarice or pride, their starry domes
Of diamond and of gold expand above
Numberless and immeasurable halls,
Frequent with crystal column, and clear shrines
Of pearl, and thrones radiant with chrysolite.°
Nor had that scene of ampler majesty
Than gems or gold, the varying roof of heaven
And the green earth lost in his heart its claims
To love and wonder; he would linger long

In lonesome vales, making the wild his home,
Until the doves and squirrels would partake
From his innocuous hand his bloodless food,
Lured by the gentle meaning of his looks,
And the wild antelope, that starts whene'er
The dry leaf rustles in the brake, suspend
Her timid steps to gaze upon a form
More graceful than her own.
                                        His wandering step
Obedient to high thoughts, has visited
The awful ruins of the days of old:
Athens, and Tyre, and Balbec, and the waste
Where stood Jerusalem, the fallen towers
Of Babylon, the eternal pyramids,
Memphis and Thebes, and whatsoe'er of strange
Sculptured on alabaster obelisk,
Or jasper tomb, or mutilated sphynx,
Dark Ethiopia in her desert hills
Conceals. Among the ruined temples there,
Stupendous columns, and wild images
Of more than man, where marble daemons watch°
The Zodiac's brazen mystery, and dead men
Hang their mute thoughts on the mute walls around,°
He lingered, poring on memorials
Of the world's youth, through the long burning day
Gazed on those speechless shapes, nor, when the moon
Filled the mysterious halls with floating shades
Suspended he that task, but ever gazed
And gazed, till meaning on his vacant mind
Flashed like strong inspiration, and he saw
The thrilling secrets of the birth of time.°
   Meanwhile an Arab maiden brought his food,
Her daily portion, from her father's tent,
And spread her matting for his couch, and stole
From duties and repose to tend his steps:—
Enamoured, yet not daring for deep awe
To speak her love:—and watched his nightly sleep,
Sleepless herself, to gaze upon his lips
Parted in slumber, whence the regular breath
Of innocent dreams arose: then, when red morn
Made paler the pale moon, to her cold home

Wildered, and wan, and panting, she returned.°
The Poet wandering on, through Arabie
And Persia, and the wild Carmanian waste,
And o'er the aerial mountains which pour down
Indus and Oxus from their icy caves,
In joy and exultation held his way;
Till in the vale of Cashmire, far within°
Its loneliest dell, where odorous plants entwine
Beneath the hollow rocks a natural bower,
Beside a sparkling rivulet he stretched
His languid limbs. A vision on his sleep
There came, a dream of hopes that never yet
Had flushed his cheek. He dreamed a veilèd maid
Sate near him, talking in low solemn tones.
Her voice was like the voice of his own soul
Heard in the calm of thought; its music long,
Like woven sounds of streams and breezes, held
His inmost sense suspended in its web
Of many-coloured woof and shifting hues.
Knowledge and truth and virtue were her theme,
And lofty hopes of divine liberty,
Thoughts the most dear to him, and poesy,
Herself a poet. Soon the solemn mood
Of her pure mind kindled through all her frame
A permeating fire: wild numbers then°
She raised, with voice stifled in tremulous sobs
Subdued by its own pathos: her fair hands
Were bare alone, sweeping from some strange harp
Strange symphony, and in their branching veins
The eloquent blood told an ineffable tale.
The beating of her heart was heard to fill
The pauses of her music, and her breath
Tumultuously accorded with those fits
Of intermitted song. Sudden she rose,
As if her heart impatiently endured
Its bursting burden: at the sound he turned,
And saw by the warm light of their own life
Her glowing limbs beneath the sinuous veil
Of woven wind, her outspread arms now bare,
Her dark locks floating in the breath of night,
Her beamy bending eyes, her parted lips

Outstretched, and pale, and quivering eagerly.
His strong heart sunk and sickened with excess
Of love. He reared his shuddering limbs and quelled
His gasping breath, and spread his arms to meet
Her panting bosom: . . . she drew back a while,
Then, yielding to the irresistible joy,
With frantic gesture and short breathless cry
Folded his frame in her dissolving arms.
Now blackness veiled his dizzy eyes, and night
Involved and swallowed up the vision; sleep,
Like a dark flood suspended in its course,
Rolled back its impulse on his vacant brain.
 Roused by the shock he started from his trance—
The cold white light of morning, the blue moon
Low in the west, the clear and garish hills,
The distinct valley and the vacant woods,
Spread round him where he stood. Whither have fled
The hues of heaven that canopied his bower
Of yesternight? The sounds that soothed his sleep,
The mystery and the majesty of Earth,
The joy, the exultation? His wan eyes
Gaze on the empty scene as vacantly
As ocean's moon looks on the moon in heaven.
The spirit of sweet human love has sent
A vision to the sleep of him who spurned
Her choicest gifts. He eagerly pursues
Beyond the realms of dream that fleeting shade;
He overleaps the bounds. Alas! alas!
Were limbs, and breath, and being intertwined
Thus treacherously? Lost, lost, forever lost,
In the wide pathless desert of dim sleep,
That beautiful shape! Does the dark gate of death
Conduct to thy mysterious paradise,
O Sleep? Does the bright arch of rainbow clouds,
And pendent mountains seen in the calm lake,
Lead only to a black and watery depth,
While death's blue vault, with loathliest vapours hung,
Where every shade which the foul grave exhales
Hides its dead eye from the detested day,
Conduct, O Sleep, to thy delightful realms?
This doubt with sudden tide flowed on his heart,

The insatiate hope which it awakened, stung
His brain even like despair.
While daylight held
The sky, the Poet kept mute conference
With his still soul. At night the passion came,
Like the fierce fiend of a distempered dream,
And shook him from his rest, and led him forth
Into the darkness.—As an eagle grasped
In folds of the green serpent, feels her breast
Burn with the poison, and precipitates°
Through night and day, tempest, and calm, and cloud,
Frantic with dizzying anguish, her blind flight
O'er the wide aery wilderness: thus driven°
By the bright shadow of that lovely dream,°
Beneath the cold glare of the desolate night,
Through tangled swamps and deep precipitous dells,
Startling with careless step the moon-light snake,
He fled. Red morning dawned upon his flight,
Shedding the mockery of its vital hues
Upon his cheek of death. He wandered on
Till vast Aornos seen from Petra's steep°
Hung o'er the low horizon like a cloud;
Through Balk, and where the desolated tombs°
Of Parthian kings scatter to every wind
Their wasting dust, wildly he wandered on,
Day after day, a weary waste of hours,
Bearing within his life the brooding care
That ever fed on its decaying flame.
And now his limbs were lean; his scattered hair
Sered by the autumn of strange suffering
Sung dirges in the wind; his listless hand
Hung like dead bone within its withered skin;
Life, and the lustre that consumed it, shone
As in a furnace burning secretly
From his dark eyes alone. The cottagers,
Who ministered with human charity
His human wants, beheld with wondering awe
Their fleeting visitant. The mountaineer,
Encountering on some dizzy precipice
That spectral form, deemed that the Spirit of wind
With lightning eyes, and eager breath, and feet

Disturbing not the drifted snow, had paused
In its career: the infant would conceal
His troubled visage in his mother's robe
In terror at the glare of those wild eyes,
To remember their strange light in many a dream
Of after-times; but youthful maidens, taught
By nature, would interpret half the woe
That wasted him, would call him with false names
Brother, and friend, would press his pallid hand
At parting, and watch, dim through tears, the path
Of his departure from their father's door.
At length upon the lone Chorasmian shore°
He paused, a wide and melancholy waste
Of putrid marshes. A strong impulse urged
His steps to the seashore. A swan was there,
Beside a sluggish stream among the reeds.
It rose as he approached, and with strong wings
Scaling the upward sky, bent its bright course
High over the immeasurable main.
His eyes pursued its flight.—'Thou hast a home,
Beautiful bird; thou voyagest to thine home,
Where thy sweet mate will twine her downy neck
With thine, and welcome thy return with eyes
Bright in the lustre of their own fond joy.
And what am I that I should linger here,
With voice far sweeter than thy dying notes,
Spirit more vast than thine, frame more attuned
To beauty, wasting these surpassing powers
In the deaf air, to the blind earth, and heaven
That echoes not my thoughts?' A gloomy smile
Of desperate hope wrinkled his quivering lips.
For sleep, he knew, kept most relentlessly
Its precious charge, and silent death exposed,
Faithless perhaps as sleep, a shadowy lure,
With doubtful smile mocking its own strange charms.
Startled by his own thoughts he looked around.
There was no fair fiend near him, not a sight
Or sound of awe but in his own deep mind.
A little shallop floating near the shore°
Caught the impatient wandering of his gaze.
It had been long abandoned, for its sides

Gaped wide with many a rift, and its frail joints
Swayed with the undulations of the tide.
A restless impulse urged him to embark
And meet lone Death on the drear ocean's waste;
For well he knew that mighty Shadow loves
The slimy caverns of the populous deep.
The day was fair and sunny, sea and sky
Drank its inspiring radiance, and the wind
Swept strongly from the shore, blackening the waves.
Following his eager soul, the wanderer
Leaped in the boat, he spread his cloak aloft
On the bare mast, and took his lonely seat,
And felt the boat speed o'er the tranquil sea
Like a torn cloud before the hurricane.
As one that in a silver vision floats
Obedient to the sweep of odorous winds
Upon resplendent clouds, so rapidly
Along the dark and ruffled waters fled
The straining boat.—A whirlwind swept it on,
With fierce gusts and precipitating force,
Through the white ridges of the chafèd sea.
The waves arose. Higher and higher still
Their fierce necks writhed beneath the tempest's scourge
Like serpents struggling in a vulture's grasp.
Calm and rejoicing in the fearful war
Of wave ruining on wave, and blast on blast°
Descending, and black flood on whirlpool driven
With dark obliterating course, he sate:
As if their genii were the ministers
Appointed to conduct him to the light
Of those beloved eyes, the Poet sate
Holding the steady helm. Evening came on,
The beams of sunset hung their rainbow hues
High mid the shifting domes of sheeted spray
That canopied his path o'er the waste deep;
Twilight, ascending slowly from the east,
Entwined in duskier wreaths her braided locks
O'er the fair front and radiant eyes of day;
Night followed, clad with stars. On every side
More horribly the multitudinous streams
Of ocean's mountainous waste to mutual war

Rushed in dark tumult thundering, as to mock
The calm and spangled sky. The little boat
Still fled before the storm; still fled, like foam
Down the steep cataract of a wintry river;
Now pausing on the edge of the riven wave;
Now leaving far behind the bursting mass
That fell, convulsing ocean. Safely fled—
As if that frail and wasted human form
Had been an elemental god.
At midnight
The moon arose: and lo! the etherial cliffs°
Of Caucasus, whose icy summits shone
Among the stars like sunlight, and around
Whose caverned base the whirlpools and the waves
Bursting and eddying irresistibly
Rage and resound for ever.—Who shall save?—
The boat fled on,—the boiling torrent drove,—
The crags closed round with black and jagged arms,
The shattered mountain overhung the sea,
And faster still, beyond all human speed,
Suspended on the sweep of the smooth wave,
The little boat was driven. A cavern there
Yawned, and amid its slant and winding depths
Engulfed the rushing sea. The boat fled on
With unrelaxing speed.—'Vision and Love!'
The Poet cried aloud, 'I have beheld
The path of thy departure. Sleep and death
Shall not divide us long!'
The boat pursued
The windings of the cavern. Daylight shone
At length upon that gloomy river's flow;
Now, where the fiercest war among the waves
Is calm, on the unfathomable stream
The boat moved slowly. Where the mountain, riven,
Exposed those black depths to the azure sky,
Ere yet the flood's enormous volume fell
Even to the base of Caucasus, with sound
That shook the everlasting rocks, the mass
Filled with one whirlpool all that ample chasm;
Stair above stair the eddying waters rose,
Circling immeasurably fast, and laved

With alternating dash the gnarlèd roots
Of mighty trees, that stretched their giant arms
In darkness over it. I' the midst was left,
Reflecting, yet distorting every cloud,
A pool of treacherous and tremendous calm.
Seized by the sway of the ascending stream,
With dizzy swiftness, round, and round, and round,
Ridge after ridge the straining boat arose,
Till on the verge of the extremest curve,
Where, through an opening of the rocky bank,
The waters overflow, and a smooth spot
Of glassy quiet mid those battling tides
Is left, the boat paused shuddering.—Shall it sink
Down the abyss? Shall the reverting stress
Of that resistless gulf embosom it?
Now shall it fall?—A wandering stream of wind,
Breathed from the west, has caught the expanded sail,
And, lo! with gentle motion, between banks
Of mossy slope, and on a placid stream,
Beneath a woven grove it sails, and, hark!
The ghastly torrent mingles its far roar
With the breeze murmuring in the musical woods.
Where the embowering trees recede, and leave
A little space of green expanse, the cove
Is closed by meeting banks, whose yellow flowers°
Forever gaze on their own drooping eyes,
Reflected in the crystal calm. The wave
Of the boat's motion marred their pensive task,
Which nought but vagrant bird, or wanton wind,
Or falling spear-grass, or their own decay
Had e'er disturbed before. The Poet longed
To deck with their bright hues his withered hair,
But on his heart its solitude returned,
And he forbore. Not the strong impulse hid
In those flushed cheeks, bent eyes, and shadowy frame,
Had yet performed its ministry: it hung
Upon his life, as lightning in a cloud
Gleams, hovering ere it vanish, ere the floods
Of night close over it.
The noonday sun
Now shone upon the forest, one vast mass

Of mingling shade, whose brown magnificence
A narrow vale embosoms. There, huge caves,
Scooped in the dark base of their aery rocks
Mocking its moans, respond and roar forever.°
The meeting boughs and implicated leaves°
Wove twilight o'er the Poet's path, as led
By love, or dream, or god, or mightier Death,
He sought in Nature's dearest haunt, some bank,
Her cradle, and his sepulchre. More dark
And dark the shades accumulate. The oak,
Expanding its immense and knotty arms,
Embraces the light beech. The pyramids
Of the tall cedar overarching, frame
Most solemn domes within, and far below,
Like clouds suspended in an emerald sky,
The ash and the acacia floating hang
Tremulous and pale. Like restless serpents, clothed
In rainbow and in fire, the parasites,
Starred with ten thousand blossoms, flow around
The grey trunks, and, as gamesome infants' eyes,
With gentle meanings, and most innocent wiles,
Fold their beams round the hearts of those that love,
These twine their tendrils with the wedded boughs
Uniting their close union; the woven leaves
Make net-work of the dark blue light of day,
And the night's noontide clearness, mutable
As shapes in the weird clouds. Soft mossy lawns
Beneath these canopies extend their swells,
Fragrant with perfumed herbs, and eyed with blooms
Minute yet beautiful. One darkest glen
Sends from its woods of musk-rose, twined with jasmine,
A soul-dissolving odour, to invite
To some more lovely mystery. Through the dell,
Silence and Twilight here, twin-sisters, keep
Their noonday watch, and sail among the shades,
Like vaporous shapes half seen; beyond, a well,
Dark, gleaming, and of most translucent wave,
Images all the woven boughs above,
And each depending leaf, and every speck
Of azure sky, darting between their chasms;
Nor aught else in the liquid mirror laves

Its portraiture, but some inconstant star
Between one foliaged lattice twinkling fair,
Or painted bird, sleeping beneath the moon,
Or gorgeous insect floating motionless,
Unconscious of the day, ere yet his wings
Have spread their glories to the gaze of noon.
  Hither the Poet came. His eyes beheld
Their own wan light through the reflected lines
Of his thin hair, distinct in the dark depth
Of that still fountain; as the human heart,
Gazing in dreams over the gloomy grave,
Sees its own treacherous likeness there. He heard
The motion of the leaves, the grass that sprung
Startled and glanced and trembled even to feel
An unaccustomed presence, and the sound
Of the sweet brook that from the secret springs
Of that dark fountain rose. A Spirit seemed
To stand beside him—clothed in no bright robes
Of shadowy silver or enshrining light,
Borrowed from aught the visible world affords
Of grace, or majesty, or mystery;—
But, undulating woods, and silent well,
And leaping rivulet, and evening gloom
Now deepening the dark shades, for speech assuming
Held commune with him, as if he and it
Were all that was,—only . . . when his regard
Was raised by intense pensiveness, . . . two eyes,
Two starry eyes, hung in the gloom of thought,°
And seemed with their serene and azure smiles
To beckon him.
                         Obedient to the light
That shone within his soul, he went, pursuing
The windings of the dell.—The rivulet
Wanton and wild, through many a green ravine
Beneath the forest flowed. Sometimes it fell
Among the moss with hollow harmony
Dark and profound. Now on the polished stones
It danced; like childhood laughing as it went:
Then, through the plain in tranquil wanderings crept,
Reflecting every herb and drooping bud
That overhung its quietness.—'O stream!

Whose source is inaccessibly profound,
Whither do thy mysterious waters tend?
Thou imagest my life. Thy darksome stillness,
Thy dazzling waves, thy loud and hollow gulfs,
Thy searchless fountain, and invisible course
Have each their type in me: and the wide sky,
And measureless ocean may declare as soon
What oozy cavern or what wandering cloud
Contains thy waters, as the universe
Tell where these living thoughts reside, when stretched
Upon thy flowers my bloodless limbs shall waste
I' the passing wind!'
                    Beside the grassy shore
Of the small stream he went; he did impress
On the green moss his tremulous step, that caught
Strong shuddering from his burning limbs. As one
Roused by some joyous madness from the couch
Of fever, he did move; yet, not like him,
Forgetful of the grave, where, when the flame
Of his frail exultation shall be spent,
He must descend. With rapid steps he went
Beneath the shade of trees, beside the flow
Of the wild babbling rivulet, and now
The forest's solemn canopies were changed
For the uniform and lightsome evening sky.°
Grey rocks did peep from the spare moss, and stemmed
The struggling brook: tall spires of windlestrae°
Threw their thin shadows down the rugged slope,
And nought but gnarlèd roots of ancient pines
Branchless and blasted, clenched with grasping roots
The unwilling soil. A gradual change was here,
Yet ghastly. For, as fast years flow away,
The smooth brow gathers, and the hair grows thin
And white, and where irradiate dewy eyes
Had shone, gleam stony orbs:—so from his steps
Bright flowers departed, and the beautiful shade
Of the green groves, with all their odorous winds
And musical motions. Calm, he still pursued
The stream, that with a larger volume now
Rolled through the labyrinthine dell; and there
Fretted a path through its descending curves

With its wintry speed. On every side now rose
Rocks, which, in unimaginable forms,
Lifted their black and barren pinnacles
In the light of evening, and its precipice°
Obscuring the ravine, disclosed above,
Mid toppling stones, black gulfs and yawning caves,
Whose windings gave ten thousand various tongues
To the loud stream. Lo! where the pass expands
Its stony jaws, the abrupt mountain breaks,
And seems, with its accumulated crags,
To overhang the world: for wide expand
Beneath the wan stars and descending moon
Islanded seas, blue mountains, mighty streams,
Dim tracts and vast, robed in the lustrous gloom
Of leaden-coloured even, and fiery hills
Mingling their flames with twilight, on the verge
Of the remote horizon. The near scene,
In naked and severe simplicity,
Made contrast with the universe. A pine,
Rock-rooted, stretched athwart the vacancy
Its swinging boughs, to each inconstant blast
Yielding one only response, at each pause
In most familiar cadence, with the howl
The thunder and the hiss of homeless streams
Mingling its solemn song, whilst the broad river,
Foaming and hurrying o'er its rugged path,
Fell into that immeasurable void
Scattering its waters to the passing winds.
  Yet the grey precipice and solemn pine
And torrent, were not all;—one silent nook
Was there. Even on the edge of that vast mountain,
Upheld by knotty roots and fallen rocks,
It overlooked in its serenity
The dark earth, and the bending vault of stars.
It was a tranquil spot, that seemed to smile
Even in the lap of horror. Ivy clasped
The fissured stones with its entwining arms,
And did embower with leaves forever green,
And berries dark, the smooth and even space
Of its inviolated floor, and here
The children of the autumnal whirlwind bore,

In wanton sport, those bright leaves, whose decay,
Red, yellow, or etherially pale,°
Rivals the pride of summer. 'Tis the haunt
Of every gentle wind, whose breath can teach
The wilds to love tranquillity. One step,
One human step alone, has ever broken
The stillness of its solitude:—one voice
Alone inspired its echoes,—even that voice
Which hither came, floating among the winds,
And led the loveliest among human forms
To make their wild haunts the depository
Of all the grace and beauty that endued
Its motions, render up its majesty,
Scatter its music on the unfeeling storm,
And to the damp leaves and blue cavern mould,
Nurses of rainbow flowers and branching moss,
Commit the colours of that varying cheek,
That snowy breast, those dark and drooping eyes.
The dim and hornèd moon hung low, and poured
A sea of lustre on the horizon's verge
That overflowed its mountains. Yellow mist
Filled the unbounded atmosphere, and drank
Wan moonlight even to fullness: not a star
Shone, not a sound was heard; the very winds,
Danger's grim playmates, on that precipice
Slept, clasped in his embrace.—O, storm of death!
Whose sightless speed divides this sullen night:
And thou, colossal Skeleton, that, still
Guiding its irresistible career
In thy devastating omnipotence,
Art king of this frail world, from the red field
Of slaughter, from the reeking hospital,
The patriot's sacred couch, the snowy bed
Of innocence, the scaffold and the throne,
A mighty voice invokes thee. Ruin calls
His brother Death. A rare and regal prey
He hath prepared, prowling around the world;
Glutted with which thou mayst repose, and men
Go to their graves like flowers or creeping worms,
Nor ever more offer at thy dark shrine
The unheeded tribute of a broken heart.

When on the threshold of the green recess
The wanderer's footsteps fell, he knew that death
Was on him. Yet a little, ere it fled,
Did he resign his high and holy soul
To images of the majestic past,
That paused within his passive being now,
Like winds that bear sweet music, when they breathe
Through some dim latticed chamber. He did place
His pale lean hand upon the rugged trunk
Of the old pine. Upon an ivied stone
Reclined his languid head, his limbs did rest,
Diffused and motionless, on the smooth brink
Of that obscurest chasm;—and thus he lay,
Surrendering to their final impulses
The hovering powers of life. Hope and despair,
The torturers, slept; no mortal pain or fear
Marred his repose, the influxes of sense,
And his own being unalloyed by pain,
Yet feebler and more feeble, calmly fed
The stream of thought, till he lay breathing there
At peace, and faintly smiling:—his last sight
Was the great moon, which o'er the western line
Of the wide world her mighty horn suspended,
With whose dun beams inwoven darkness seemed
To mingle. Now upon the jagged hills
It rests, and still as the divided frame
Of the vast meteor sunk, the Poet's blood,°
That ever beat in mystic sympathy
With nature's ebb and flow, grew feebler still:
And when two lessening points of light alone°
Gleamed through the darkness, the alternate gasp
Of his faint respiration scarce did stir
The stagnate night:—till the minutest ray
Was quenched, the pulse yet lingered in his heart.
It paused—it fluttered. But when heaven remained
Utterly black, the murky shades involved
An image, silent, cold, and motionless,
As their own voiceless earth and vacant air.
Even as a vapour fed with golden beams
That ministered on sunlight, ere the west
Eclipses it, was now that wondrous frame—

No sense, no motion, no divinity—
A fragile lute, on whose harmonious strings
The breath of heaven did wander—a bright stream
Once fed with many-voicèd waves—a dream
Of youth, which night and time have quenched forever,
Still, dark, and dry, and unremembered now.
  O, for Medea's wondrous alchemy,°
Which wheresoe'er it fell made the earth gleam
With bright flowers, and the wintry boughs exhale
From vernal blooms fresh fragrance! O, that God,
Profuse of poisons, would concede the chalice
Which but one living man has drained, who now,°
Vessel of deathless wrath, a slave that feels
No proud exemption in the blighting curse
He bears, over the world wanders forever,
Lone as incarnate death! O, that the dream
Of dark magician in his visioned cave,
Raking the cinders of a crucible
For life and power, even when his feeble hand
Shakes in its last decay, were the true law
Of this so lovely world! But thou art fled
Like some frail exhalation; which the dawn
Robes in its golden beams,—ah! thou hast fled!
The brave, the gentle, and the beautiful,
The child of grace and genius. Heartless things
Are done and said i' the world, and many worms
And beasts and men live on, and mighty Earth
From sea and mountain, city and wilderness,
In vesper low or joyous orison,
Lifts still its solemn voice:—but thou art fled—
Thou canst no longer know or love the shapes
Of this phantasmal scene, who have to thee
Been purest ministers, who are, alas!
Now thou art not. Upon those pallid lips
So sweet even in their silence, on those eyes
That image sleep in death, upon that form
Yet safe from the worm's outrage, let no tear
Be shed—not even in thought. Nor, when those hues
Are gone, and those divinest lineaments,
Worn by the senseless wind, shall live alone°
In the frail pauses of this simple strain,

Let not high verse, mourning the memory
Of that which is no more, or painting's woe
Or sculpture, speak in feeble imagery
Their own cold powers. Art and eloquence,
And all the shows o' the world are frail and vain
To weep a loss that turns their lights to shade.
It is a woe too 'deep for tears,' when all°
Is reft at once, when some surpassing Spirit,
Whose light adorned the world around it, leaves
Those who remain behind, not sobs or groans,
The passionate tumult of a clinging hope;
But pale despair and cold tranquillity,
Nature's vast frame, the web of human things,
Birth and the grave, that are not as they were.

Mutability

We are as clouds that veil the midnight moon;
How restlessly they speed, and gleam, and quiver,
Streaking the darkness radiantly!—yet soon
Night closes round, and they are lost for ever:

Or like forgotten lyres, whose dissonant strings°
Give various response to each varying blast,
To whose frail frame no second motion brings
One mood or modulation like the last.

We rest.—A dream has power to poison sleep;
We rise.—One wandering thought pollutes the day;
We feel, conceive or reason, laugh or weep;
Embrace fond woe, or cast our cares away:

It is the same!—For, be it joy or sorrow,
The path of its departure still is free:
Man's yesterday may ne'er be like his morrow;
Nought may endure but Mutability.

Verses Written on Receiving a Celandine in a Letter from England

I thought of thee, fair Celandine,
As of a flower aery blue°
Yet small—thy leaves methought were wet
With the light of morning dew.
In the same glen thy star did shine
As the primrose and the violet,
And the wild briar bent over thee
And the woodland brook danced under thee.

Lovely thou wert in thine own glen
Ere thou didst dwell in song or story,
Ere the moonlight of a Poet's mind

Had arrayed thee with the glory
Whose fountains are the hearts of men—
Many a thing of vital kind
Had fed and sheltered under thee,
Had nourished their thoughts near to thee.

Yes, gentle flower, in thy recess
None might a sweeter aspect wear;
Thy young bud drooped so gracefully,
Thou wert so very fair—
Among the fairest, ere the stress
Of exile, death and injury
Thus withering and deforming thee
Had made a mournful type of thee—

A type of that whence I and thou
Are thus familar, Celandine—
A deathless Poet whose young prime
Was as serene as thine;
But he is changed and withered now,°
Fallen on a cold and evil time;°
His heart is gone—his fame is dim,
And Infamy sits mocking him.

Celandine! Thou art pale and dead,
Changed from thy fresh and woodland state.
Oh! that thy bard were cold, but he
Has lived too long and late.
Would he were in an honoured grave;
But that, men say, now must not be
Since he for impious gold could sell
The love of those who loved him well.

That he, with all hope else of good
Should be thus transitory
I marvel not—but that his lays
Have spared not their own glory,
That blood, even the foul god of blood
With most inexpiable praise,
Freedom and truth left desolate,
He has been bought to celebrate!°

They were his hopes which he doth scorn;
 They were his foes the fight that won;
That sanction and that condemnation
 Are now forever gone.
They need them not! Truth may not mourn
That with a liar's inspiration
Her majesty he did disown
Ere he could overlive his own.

They need them not, for Liberty,
 Justice and philosophic truth
From his divine and simple song°
 Shall draw immortal youth,
When he and thou shall cease to be
Or be some other thing, so long
As men may breathe or flowers may blossom
O'er the wide Earth's maternal bosom.

The stem whence thou wert disunited
 Since thy poor self was banished hither,
Now by that priest of Nature's care
 Who sent thee forth to wither
His window with its blooms has lighted,
And I shall see thy brethren there,
And each, like thee, will aye betoken
Love sold, hope dead, and honour broken.

Hymn to Intellectual Beauty

(VERSION A)

I

The awful shadow of some unseen Power°
 Floats though unseen amongst us,—visiting
 This various world with as inconstant wing
As summer winds that creep from flower to flower.—
Like moonbeams that behind some piny mountain shower,°
  It visits with inconstant glance

Each human heart and countenance;
Like hues and harmonies of evening,—
Like clouds in starlight widely spread,—
Like memory of music fled,—
Like aught that for its grace may be
Dear, and yet dearer for its mystery.

2

Spirit of BEAUTY, that doth consecrate
With thine own hues all thou dost shine upon
Of human thought or form,—where art thou gone?
Why dost thou pass away and leave our state,
This dim vast vale of tears, vacant and desolate?°
Ask why the sunlight not forever
Weaves rainbows o'er yon mountain river,
Why aught should fail and fade that once is shown,
Why fear and dream and death and birth
Cast on the daylight of this earth
Such gloom,—why man has such a scope
For love and hate, despondency and hope?

3

No voice from some sublimer world hath ever
To sage or poet these responses given—
Therefore the name of God, and ghosts, and Heaven,
Remain the records of their vain endeavour,
Frail spells—whose uttered charm might not avail to sever,
From all we hear and all we see
Doubt, chance, and mutability.
Thy light alone—like mist o'er mountains driven,
Or music by the night wind sent
Through strings of some still instrument,
Or moonlight on a midnight stream,
Gives grace and truth to life's unquiet dream.

4

Love, Hope, and Self-esteem, like clouds depart°
And come, for some uncertain moments lent.
Man were immortal, and omnipotent,
Didst thou, unknown and awful as thou art,

Keep with thy glorious train firm state within his heart.
  Thou messenger of sympathies,
  That wax and wane in lovers' eyes—
Thou—that to human thought art nourishment,
  Like darkness to a dying flame!°
  Depart not as thy shadow came,
  Depart not—lest the grave should be,
Like life and fear, a dark reality.

5

While yet a boy I sought for ghosts, and sped
 Through many a listening chamber, cave and ruin,
 And starlight wood, with fearful steps pursuing
Hopes of high talk with the departed dead.°
I called on poisonous names with which our youth is fed,
  I was not heard—I saw them not—°
  When musing deeply on the lot
Of life, at that sweet time when winds are wooing
  All vital things that wake to bring
  News of buds and blossoming,—
  Sudden, thy shadow fell on me;
I shrieked, and clasped my hands in ecstasy!

6

I vowed that I would dedicate my powers
 To thee and thine—have I not kept the vow?
 With beating heart and streaming eyes, even now
I call the phantoms of a thousand hours
Each from his voiceless grave: they have in visioned bowers
  Of studious zeal or love's delight
  Outwatched with me the envious night—
They know that never joy illumed my brow
  Unlinked with hope that thou wouldst free
  This world from its dark slavery,
  That thou—O awful LOVELINESS,
Wouldst give whate'er these words cannot express.

7

The day becomes more solemn and serene
 When noon is past—there is a harmony

In autumn, and a lustre in its sky,
Which through the summer is not heard or seen,
As if it could not be, as if it had not been!
Thus let thy power, which like the truth
Of nature on my passive youth
Descended, to my onward life supply
Its calm—to one who worships thee,
And every form containing thee,
Whom, SPIRIT fair, thy spells did bind
To fear himself, and love all human kind.°

Hymn to Intellectual Beauty

(VERSION B)

I

The lovely shadow of some awful Power
Walks though unseen amongst us, visiting
This peopled world with as inconstant wing
As summer winds that creep from flower to flower,
Like moonbeams that behind some piny mountain shower
It visits with a wavering glance
Each human heart and countenance;—
Like hues and harmonies of evening—
Like clouds in starlight widely spread,
Like memory of music fled
Like aught that for its grace might be
Dear, and yet dearer for its mystery.

2

Shadow of Beauty!—that doth consecrate
With thine own hues all thou dost fall upon
Of human thought or form, where art thou gone?
Why dost thou pass away and leave our state
A dark deep vale of tears, vacant and desolate?
Ask why the sunlight not forever
Weaves rainbows o'er yon mountain river,

Ask why aught fades away that once is shown,
Ask wherefore dream and death and birth
Cast on the daylight of this earth
Such gloom,—why man has such a scope
For love and joy, despondency and hope.

3

No voice from some sublimer world hath ever
To wisest poets these responses given,
Therefore the name of God and Ghosts and Heaven
Remain yet records of their vain Endeavour—
Frail spells, whose uttered charm might not avail to sever
From what we feel and what we see
Doubt, Chance and mutability.
Thy shade alone like mists o'er mountains driven
Or music by the night-wind sent
Through strings of some mute instrument
Or moonlight on a forest stream
Gives truth and grace to life's tumultuous dream.

4

Love, hope and self-esteem like clouds depart—
And come, for some uncertain moments lent.—
Man were immortal and omnipotent
Didst thou, unknown and awful as thou art
Keep with this glorious train firm state within his heart.
Thou messenger of sympathies
That wax and wane in lovers' eyes,
Thou that to the poet's thought art nourishment
As darkness to a dying flame,
Depart not as thy shadow came!
Depart not!—lest the grave should be
Like life and fear a dark reality.

5

While yet a boy I sought for ghosts, and sped
Through many a lonely chamber, vault and ruin
And starlight wood, with fearful step pursuing

Hopes of strange converse with the storied dead.
I called on that false name with which our youth is fed:
He heard me not—I saw them not—
When musing deeply on the lot
Of Life, at that sweet time when winds are wooing
All vocal things that live to bring
News of buds and blossoming—
Sudden thy shadow fell on me,
I shrieked and clasped my hands in ecstasy.

6

I vowed that I would dedicate my powers
To thee and thine—have I not kept the vow?
With streaming eyes and panting heart even now
I call the spectres of a thousand hours
Each from his voiceless grave, who have in visioned bowers
Of studious zeal or lore's delight
Outwatched with me the waning night
To tell that never joy illumed my brow
Unlinked with hope that thou wouldst free
This world from its dark slavery,
That thou, O, awful Loveliness!
Would give whate'er these words cannot express.

7

The day becomes more solemn and serene
When noon is past—there is a harmony
In Autumn and a lustre in the sky
Which through the summer is not heard or seen
As if it could not be—as if it had not been—
Thus let thy shade—which like the truth
Of Nature on my passive youth
Descended, to my onward life supply
Its hues, to one that worships thee
And every form containing thee
Whom, fleeting power! thy spells did bind
To fear himself and love all human Kind.

Mont Blanc

Lines Written in the Vale of Chamouni

(VERSION A)

1

The everlasting universe of things
Flows through the mind, and rolls its rapid waves,[°]
Now dark—now glittering—now reflecting gloom—
Now lending splendour, where from secret springs
The source of human thought its tribute brings
Of waters,—with a sound but half its own,[°]
Such as a feeble brook will oft assume
In the wild woods, among the mountains lone,
Where waterfalls around it leap for ever,
Where woods and winds contend, and a vast river
Over its rocks ceaselessly bursts and raves.[°]

2

Thus thou, Ravine of Arve—dark, deep Ravine—[°]
Thou many-coloured, many-voicèd vale,
Over whose pines, and crags, and caverns sail
Fast cloud shadows and sunbeams: awful scene,
Where Power in likeness of the Arve comes down
From the ice gulfs that gird his secret throne,
Bursting through these dark mountains like the flame
Of lightning through the tempest;—thou dost lie,
Thy giant brood of pines around thee clinging,
Children of elder time, in whose devotion
The chainless winds still come and ever came
To drink their odours, and their mighty swinging
To hear—an old and solemn harmony;
Thine earthly rainbows stretched across the sweep
Of the ethereal waterfall, whose veil
Robes some unsculptured image; the strange sleep[°]
Which when the voices of the desert fail
Wraps all in its own deep eternity;—
Thy caverns echoing to the Arve's commotion,

A loud, lone sound no other sound can tame;
Thou art pervaded with that ceaseless motion,
Thou art the path of that unresting sound—
Dizzy Ravine! and when I gaze on thee
I seem as in a trance sublime and strange
To muse on my own separate fantasy,
My own, my human mind, which passively
Now renders and receives fast influencings,
Holding an unremitting interchange
With the clear universe of things around;
One legion of wild thoughts, whose wandering wings
Now float above thy darkness, and now rest
Where that or thou art no unbidden guest,°
In the still cave of the witch Poesy,
Seeking among the shadows that pass by,°
Ghosts of all things that are, some shade of thee,
Some phantom, some faint image; till the breast°
From which they fled recalls them, thou art there!

3

Some say that gleams of a remoter world
Visit the soul in sleep,—that death is slumber,
And that its shapes the busy thoughts outnumber
Of those who wake and live.—I look on high;
Has some unknown omnipotence unfurled°
The veil of life and death? or do I lie
In dream, and does the mightier world of sleep
Spread far around and inaccessibly
Its circles? For the very spirit fails,
Driven like a homeless cloud from steep to steep
That vanishes among the viewless gales!
Far, far above, piercing the infinite sky,
Mont Blanc appears,—still, snowy, and serene—
Its subject mountains their unearthly forms
Pile around it, ice and rock; broad vales between
Of frozen floods, unfathomable deeps,
Blue as the overhanging heaven, that spread
And wind among the accumulated steeps;
A desert peopled by the storms alone,

Save when the eagle brings some hunter's bone,
And the wolf tracks her there—how hideously°
Its shapes are heaped around! rude, bare, and high,
Ghastly, and scarred, and riven.—Is this the scene
Where the old Earthquake-daemon taught her young
Ruin? Were these their toys? or did a sea
Of fire envelop once this silent snow?°
None can reply—all seems eternal now.
The wilderness has a mysterious tongue
Which teaches awful doubt, or faith so mild,°
So solemn, so serene, that man may be
But for such faith with nature reconciled;°
Thou hast a voice, great Mountain, to repeal
Large codes of fraud and woe; not understood
By all, but which the wise, and great, and good
Interpret, or make felt, or deeply feel.

4

The fields, the lakes, the forests, and the streams,
Ocean, and all the living things that dwell
Within the daedal earth; lightning, and rain,°
Earthquake, and fiery flood, and hurricane,
The torpor of the year when feeble dreams
Visit the hidden buds, or dreamless sleep
Holds every future leaf and flower;—the bound
With which from that detested trance they leap;
The works and ways of man, their death and birth,
And that of him and all that his may be;
All things that move and breathe with toil and sound
Are born and die; revolve, subside and swell.
Power dwells apart in its tranquillity
Remote, serene, and inaccessible:°
And *this*, the naked countenance of earth,
On which I gaze, even these primeval mountains
Teach the adverting mind. The glaciers creep°
Like snakes that watch their prey, from their far fountains,
Slow rolling on; there, many a precipice,
Frost and the Sun in scorn of mortal power
Have piled: dome, pyramid, and pinnacle,

A city of death, distinct with many a tower°
And wall impregnable of beaming ice.
Yet not a city, but a flood of ruin
Is there, that from the boundaries of the sky
Rolls its perpetual stream; vast pines are strewing
Its destined path, or in the mangled soil
Branchless and shattered stand; the rocks, drawn down
From yon remotest waste, have overthrown
The limits of the dead and living world,
Never to be reclaimed. The dwelling-place
Of insects, beasts, and birds, becomes its spoil;
Their food and their retreat for ever gone,
So much of life and joy is lost. The race
Of man flies far in dread; his work and dwelling
Vanish, like smoke before the tempest's stream,
And their place is not known. Below, vast caves°
Shine in the rushing torrents' restless gleam,
Which from those secret chasms in tumult welling°
Meet in the vale, and one majestic River,°
The breath and blood of distant lands, for ever
Rolls its loud waters to the ocean waves,
Breathes its swift vapours to the circling air.

5

Mont Blanc yet gleams on high:—the power is there,
The still and solemn power of many sights,
And many sounds, and much of life and death.
In the calm darkness of the moonless nights,
In the lone glare of day, the snows descend
Upon that Mountain; none beholds them there,
Nor when the flakes burn in the sinking sun,
Or the star-beams dart through them:—Winds contend
Silently there, and heap the snow with breath°
Rapid and strong, but silently! Its home
The voiceless lightning in these solitudes
Keeps innocently, and like vapour broods
Over the snow. The secret strength of things
Which governs thought, and to the infinite dome
Of heaven is as a law, inhabits thee!

And what were thou, and earth, and stars, and sea,
If to the human mind's imaginings
Silence and solitude were vacancy?°

Mont Blanc

(VERSION B)

Scene—Pont Pellisier in the Vale of Servox

In day the eternal universe of things
Flows through the mind, and rolls its rapid waves
Now dark, now glittering; now reflecting gloom,
Now lending splendour, where, from secret caves
The source of human thought its tribute brings
Of waters, with a sound not all its own:
Such as a feeble brook will oft assume
In the wild woods among the mountains lone
Where waterfalls around it leap forever
Where winds and woods contend, and a vast river
Over its rocks ceaselessly bursts and raves.

Thus thou Ravine of Arve, dark deep ravine,
Thou many coloured, many voicèd vale!
Over whose rocks and pines and caverns sail
Fast cloud shadows and sunbeams—awful scene,
Where Power in likeness of the Arve comes down
From the ice gulfs that gird his secret throne
Bursting through these dark mountains like the flame
Of lightning through the tempest—thou dost lie
Thy giant brood of pines around thee clinging
Children of elder time, in whose devotion
The charmèd winds still come, and ever came
To drink their odours, and their mighty swinging
To hear, an old and solemn harmony;
Thine earthly rainbows stretched across the sweep
Of the aerial waterfall, whose veil
Robes some unsculptured image; even the sleep
The sudden pause that does inhabit thee
Which when the voices of the desert fail

And its hues wane, doth blend them all and steep
Their periods in its own eternity;
Thy caverns echoing to the Arve's commotion
A loud lone sound no other sound can tame:
Thou art pervaded with such ceaseless motion
Thou art the path of that unresting sound:
Ravine of Arve! and when I gaze on thee
I seem as in a vision deep and strange
To muse on my own various fantasy,
My own, my human mind . . . which passively
Now renders and receives fast influencings
Holding an unforeseeing interchange
With the clear universe of things around:
A legion of swift thoughts, whose wandering wings
Now float above thy darkness, and now rest
Near the still cave of the witch Poesy
Seeking among the shadows that pass by,
Ghosts of the things that are, some form like thee,
Some spectre, some faint image; till the breast
From which they fled recalls them—thou art there.

Some say that gleams of a remoter world
Visit the soul in sleep—that death is slumber
And that its shapes the busy thoughts outnumber
Of those who wake and live. I look on high—
Has some unknown omnipotence unfurled
The veil of life and death? or do I lie
In dream, and does the mightier world of sleep
Spread far around, and inaccessibly
Its circles?—for the very spirit fails
Driven like a homeless cloud from steep to steep
That vanishes among the viewless gales.—
Far, far above, piercing the infinite sky
Mont Blanc appears, still, snowy and serene,
Its subject mountains their unearthly forms
Pile round it—ice and rock—broad chasms between
Of frozen waves, unfathomable deeps
Blue as the overhanging Heaven, that spread
And wind among the accumulated steeps,
Vast deserts, peopled by the storms alone
Save when the eagle brings some hunter's bone

And the wolf watches her—how hideously
Its rocks are heaped around, rude, bare and high,
Ghastly and scarred and riven!—is this the scene
Where the old Earthquake demon taught her young
Ruin? were these their toys? or did a sea
Of fire envelop once this silent snow?
None can reply—all seems eternal now.
This wilderness has a mysterious tongue
Which teaches awful doubt, or faith so mild
So simple, so serene that man may be
In such a faith with Nature reconciled.
Ye have a doctrine, Mountains, to repeal
Large codes of fraud and woe—not understood
By all, but which the wise and great and good
Interpret, or make felt, or deeply feel.

The fields, the lakes, the forests and the streams,
Ocean, and all the living things that dwell
Within the daedal Earth, lightning and rain,
Earthquake, and lava flood, and hurricane—
The torpor of the year, when feeble dreams
Visit the hidden buds, or dreamless sleep
Holds every future leaf and flower—the bound
With which from that detested trance they leap;
The works and ways of man, their death and birth
And that of him, and all that his may be,
All things that move and breathe with toil and sound
Are born and die, revolve, subside and swell—
Power dwells apart in deep tranquillity,
Remote, sublime, and inaccessible,
And this, the naked countenance of Earth
On which I gaze—even these primeval mountains
Teach the adverting mind.—the Glaciers creep
Like snakes that watch their prey, from their far fountains
Slow rolling on:—there, many a precipice
Frost and the Sun in scorn of human power
Have piled—dome, pyramid and pinnacle
A city of death, distinct with many a tower
And wall impregnable of shining ice . . .
A city's phantom . . . but a flood of ruin
Is there, that from the boundaries of the sky

Rolls its eternal stream . . . vast pines are strewing
Its destined path, or in the mangled soil
Branchless and shattered stand—the rocks drawn down
From yon remotest waste have overthrown
The limits of the dead and living world
Never to be reclaimed—the dwelling place
Of insects, beasts and birds becomes its spoil,
Their food and their retreat forever gone
So much of life and joy is lost—the race
Of man flies far in dread. His work and dwelling
Vanish like smoke before the tempest's stream
And their place is not known—below, vast caves
Shine in the gushing torrents' restless gleam
Which from those secret chasms in tumult welling
Meet in the vale—and one majestic river
The breath and blood of distant lands, forever
Rolls its loud waters to the Ocean waves,
Breathes its swift vapours to the circling air.

Mont Blanc yet gleams on high—the Power is there,
The still and solemn Power of many sights
And many sounds, and much of life and death.
In the calm darkness of the moonless nights
Or the lone light of day the snows descend
Upon that mountain—none beholds them there—
Nor when the sunset wraps their flakes in fire
Or the starbeams dart through them—winds contend
Silently there, and heap the snows, with breath
Blasting and swift—but silently—its home
The voiceless lightning in these solitudes
Keeps innocently, and like vapour broods
Over the snow. The secret strength of things
Which governs thought, and to the infinite dome
Of Heaven is as a column, rests on thee,
And what were thou and Earth and Stars and Sea
If to the human mind's imaginings
Silence and solitude were Vacancy?

To Constantia

Thy voice, slow rising like a Spirit, lingers
O'ershadowing me with soft and lulling wings;
The blood and life within thy snowy fingers
Teach witchcraft to the instrumental strings.
    My brain is wild, my breath comes quick,
    The blood is listening in my frame,
    And thronging shadows fast and thick
    Fall on my overflowing eyes,
    My heart is quivering like a flame;
As morning dew, that in the sunbeam dies,
I am dissolved in these consuming ecstasies.

I have no life, Constantia, but in thee;
Whilst, like the world-surrounding air, thy song
Flows on, and fills all things with melody:
Now is thy voice a tempest, swift and strong,
    On which, as one in trance, upborne
    Secure o'er woods and waves I sweep
    Rejoicing, like a cloud of morn:
    Now 'tis the breath of summer's night
    Which, where the starry waters sleep
Round western isles with incense-blossoms bright,
Lingering, suspends my soul in its voluptuous flight.

A deep and breathless awe, like the swift change
Of dreams unseen, but felt in youthful slumbers,
Wild, sweet, yet incommunicably strange,
Thou breathest now, in fast ascending numbers:
    The cope of Heaven seems rent and cloven°
    By the enchantment of thy strain,
    And o'er my shoulders wings are woven
    To follow its sublime career,
    Beyond the mighty moons that wane
Upon the verge of Nature's utmost sphere,°
Till the world's shadowy walls are past, and disappear.

Cease, cease—for such wild lessons madmen learn:
Long thus to sink,—thus to be lost and die
Perhaps is death indeed—Constantia turn!

Yes! in thine eyes a power like light doth lie,
Even though the sounds, its voice that were,°
Between thy lips are laid to sleep—
Within thy breath and on thy hair
Like odour it is lingering yet—
And from thy touch like fire doth leap:
Even while I write my burning cheeks are wet—
Such things the heart can feel and learn, but not forget!

LAON AND CYTHNA;

OR,

THE REVOLUTION

OF

THE GOLDEN CITY

A Vision of the Nineteenth Century

IN THE STANZA OF SPENSER

Δοζ που στω, καὶ κοσμον κινησω.—Archimedes°

PREFACE

The Poem which I now present to the world, is an attempt from which I scarcely dare to expect success, and in which a writer of established fame might fail without disgrace. It is an experiment° on the temper of the public mind, as to how far a thirst for a happier condition of moral and political society survives, among the enlightened and refined,° the tempests which have shaken the age in which we live. I have sought to enlist the harmony of metrical language, the etherial combinations of the fancy, the rapid and subtle transitions of human passion, all those elements which essentially compose a Poem, in the cause of a liberal and comprehensive morality, and in the view of kindling within the bosoms of my readers, a virtuous enthusiasm for those doctrines of liberty and justice, that faith and hope in something good, which neither violence, nor misrepresentation, nor prejudice, can ever totally extinguish among mankind.

For this purpose I have chosen a story of human passion in its most universal character, diversified with moving and romantic adventures, and appealing, in contempt of all artificial opinions or institutions, to the common sympathies of every human breast. I have made no attempt to recommend the motives which I would substitute for those at present governing mankind by methodical and systematic argument.° I would only awaken the feelings, so that the reader should see the beauty of true virtue, and be incited to those enquiries which have led to my moral and political creed, and that of some of the sublimest intellects in the world. The Poem, therefore (with the exception of the first Canto, which is purely introductory), is narrative, not didactic. It is a succession of pictures illustrating the growth and progress of individual mind aspiring after excellence, and devoted to the love of mankind; its influence in refining and making pure the most daring and uncommon impulses of the imagination, the understanding, and the senses; its impatience at 'all the oppressions which are done under the sun';° its tendency to awaken public hope and to enlighten and improve mankind; the rapid effects of the application of that tendency; the awakening of an immense nation from their slavery and degradation to a true sense of moral dignity and freedom; the bloodless dethronement of their oppressors, and the unveiling of the religious frauds by which they had been deluded into submission; the tranquillity of successful patriotism, and the universal toleration and benevolence of true philanthropy; the treachery and barbarity of hired soldiers; vice not the object of punishment and hatred, but kindness and pity; the faithlessness of tyrants; the confederacy of the Rulers of the World, and the restoration of the expelled Dynasty by foreign arms;° the massacre and extermination of the Patriots, and the victory of established power; the consequences of legitimate despotism, civil war, famine, plague, superstition, and an utter extinction of the domestic affections; the judicial murder of the advocates of Liberty; the temporary triumph of oppression, that secure earnest of its final and inevitable fall; the transient nature of ignorance and error, and the eternity of genius and virtue. Such is the series of delineations of which the Poem consists. And if the lofty passions with which it has been my scope° to distinguish this story shall not excite in the reader a generous impulse, an ardent thirst for excellence, an interest profound and strong, such as belongs to no meaner desires—let not the failure be imputed to a natural unfitness for human sympathy in these sublime and animating themes. It is the business of the Poet to communicate to others the pleasure and the enthusiasm arising out of those images and feelings, in the vivid presence of which, within his own mind, consists at once his inspiration and his reward.

The panic which, like an epidemic transport, seized upon all classes of men during the excesses consequent upon the French Revolution, is gradually giving place to sanity. It has ceased to be believed, that whole generations of mankind ought to consign themselves to a hopeless inheritance of ignorance and misery, because a nation of men who had been dupes and slaves for centuries, were incapable of conducting themselves with the wisdom and tranquillity of freemen so soon as some of their fetters were partially loosened. That their conduct could not have been marked by any other characters than ferocity and thoughtlessness, is the historical fact from which liberty derives all its recommendations, and falsehood the worst features of its deformity. There is a reflux in the tide of human things which bears the shipwrecked hopes of men into a secure haven, after the storms are past. Methinks, those who now live have survived an age of despair.

The French Revolution may be considered as one of those manifestations of a general state of feeling among civilized mankind, produced by a defect of correspondence between the knowledge existing in society and the improvement, or gradual abolition, of political institutions. The year 1788 may be assumed as the epoch of one of the most important crises produced by this feeling. The sympathies connected with that event extended to every bosom. The most generous and amiable natures were those which participated the most extensively in these sympathies. But such a degree of unmingled good was expected, as it was impossible to realize. If the Revolution had been in every respect prosperous, then misrule and superstition would lose half their claims to our abhorrence, as fetters which the captive can unlock with the slightest motion of his fingers, and which do not eat with poisonous rust into the soul. The revulsion occasioned by the atrocities° of the demagogues and the re-establishment of successive tyrannies in France was terrible, and felt in the remotest corner of the civilized world. Could they listen to the plea of reason who had groaned under the calamities of a social state, according to the provisions of which, one man riots in luxury whilst another famishes for want of bread? Can he who the day before was a trampled slave, suddenly become liberal-minded, forbearing, and independent? This is the consequence of the habits of a state of society to be produced by resolute perseverance and indefatigable hope, and long-suffering and long-believing courage, and the systematic efforts of generations of men of intellect and virtue. Such is the lesson which experience teaches now. But on the first reverses of hope in the progress of French liberty, the sanguine eagerness for good overleapt the solution of these questions, and for a time extinguished itself in the unexpectedness of their result. Thus many of the most ardent and tender-hearted of the worshippers of public good, have been morally ruined by what a partial glimpse of the events they deplored appeared to show as the melancholy desolation of all their cherished hopes. Hence gloom and misanthropy have become the characteristics of the age in which we live, the solace of a disappointment that unconsciously finds relief only in the wilful exaggeration of its own despair. This influence has tainted the literature of the age with the hopelessness of the minds from which it flows. Metaphysics,° and enquiries into moral and political science, have become little else than vain attempts to revive exploded superstitions, or sophisms like those° of Mr Malthus, calculated to lull the oppressors of mankind into a security of everlasting triumph. Our works of fiction and poetry have been overshadowed by the same infectious gloom.° But mankind appear to me to be emerging from their trance. I am aware, methinks, of a slow, gradual, silent change. In that belief I have composed the following Poem.

I do not presume to enter into competition with our greatest contemporary Poets. Yet I am unwilling to tread in the footsteps of any who have preceded me. I have sought to avoid the imitation of any style of language or versification peculiar to the original minds of which it is the character, designing that even if what I have produced be worthless, it should still be properly my own. Nor have I permitted any system relating to mere words, to divert the attention of the reader from whatever interest I may have succeeded in creating, to my own ingenuity in contriving to disgust him according to the rules of criticism. I have simply clothed my thoughts in what appeared to me the most obvious and appropriate language. A person familiar with nature, and with the most celebrated productions of the human mind, can scarcely err in following the instinct, with respect to selection of language, produced by that familiarity.

There is an education peculiarly fitted for a Poet, without which, genius and sensibility can hardly fill the circle of their capacities. No education indeed can entitle to this appellation a dull and unobservant mind, or one, though neither dull nor unobservant, in which the channels of communication between thought and expression have been obstructed or closed. How far it is my fortune to belong to either of the latter classes, I cannot know. I aspire to be something better. The circumstances of my accidental education° have been favourable to this ambition. I have been familiar from boyhood with mountains and lakes, and the sea, and the solitude of forests: Danger which sports upon the brink of precipices, has been my playmate. I have trodden the glaciers of the Alps, and lived under the eye of Mont Blanc. I have been a wanderer among distant fields. I have sailed down mighty rivers, and seen the sun rise and set, and the stars come forth, whilst I have sailed night and day down a rapid stream among mountains. I have seen populous cities, and have watched the passions which rise and spread, and sink and change amongst assembled multitudes of men. I have seen the theatre of the more visible ravages of tyranny and war, cities and villages reduced to scattered groups of black and roofless houses, and the naked inhabitants sitting famished upon their desolated thresholds. I have conversed with living men of genius. The poetry of ancient Greece and Rome, and modern Italy, and our own country, has been to me like external nature, a passion and an enjoyment. Such are the sources from which the materials for the imagery of my Poem have been drawn. I have considered Poetry in its most comprehensive sense, and have read the Poets and the Historians and the Metaphysicians° whose writings have been accessible to me, and have looked upon the beautiful and majestic scenery of the earth as common sources of those elements which it is the province of the Poet to embody and combine. Yet the experience and the feelings to which I refer, do not in themselves constitute men Poets, but only prepares them to be the auditors of those who are. How far I shall be found to possess that more essential attribute of Poetry, the power of awakening in others sensations like those which animate my own bosom, is that which, to speak sincerely, I know not; and which with an acquiescent and contented spirit, I expect to be taught by the effect which I shall produce upon those whom I now address.

I have avoided, as I have said before, the imitation of any contemporary style. But there must be a resemblance which does not depend upon their own will, between all the writers of any particular age. They cannot escape from subjection to a common influence which arises out of an infinite combination of circumstances belonging to the times in which they live, though each is in a degree the author of the very influence by which his being is thus pervaded. Thus, the tragic Poets of the age of Pericles;° the Italian revivers of ancient learning; those mighty intellects of our own country that succeeded the Reformation, the translators of the Bible, Shakespeare, Spenser, the Dramatists of the reign of Elizabeth, and Lord Bacon;° the colder spirits of the interval that succeeded—all resemble each other and differ from every other in their several classes. In this view of things, Ford° can no more be called the imitator of Shakespeare, than Shakespeare the imitator of Ford. There were perhaps few other points of resemblance between these two men than that which the universal and inevitable influence of their age produced. And this is an influence which neither the meanest scribbler, nor the sublimest genius of any era can escape; and which I have not attempted to escape.

I have adopted the stanza of Spenser (a measure inexpressibly beautiful) not because I consider it a finer model of poetical harmony than the blank verse of Shakespeare and Milton, but because in the latter there is no shelter for mediocrity: you must either succeed or fail. This perhaps an aspiring spirit should desire. But I was enticed also, by the brilliancy and magnificence of sound which a mind that has been nourished upon musical thoughts can produce by a just and harmonious arrangement of the pauses of this measure. Yet there will be found some instances where I have completely failed in this attempt, and one, which I here request the reader to consider as an erratum, where there is left most inadvertently an alexandrine in the middle of a stanza.°

But in this, as in every other respect, I have written fearlessly. It is the misfortune of this age, that its Writers, too thoughtless of immortality, are exquisitely sensible to temporary praise or blame. They write with the fear of Reviews before their eyes. This system of criticism° sprang up in that torpid interval when Poetry was not. Poetry, and the art which professes to regulate and limit its powers, cannot subsist together. Longinus° could not have been the contemporary of Homer, nor Boileau of Horace. Yet this species of criticism never presumed to assert an understanding of its own: it has always, unlike true science, followed, not preceded the opinion of mankind, and would even now bribe with worthless adulation some of our greatest Poets to impose gratuitous fetters on their own imaginations, and become unconscious accomplices in the daily murder of all genius either not so aspiring or not so fortunate as their own. I have sought therefore to write, as I believe that Homer, Shakespeare, and Milton wrote, with an utter disregard of anonymous censure.° I am certain that calumny and misrepresentation, though it may move me to compassion, cannot disturb my peace. I shall understand the expressive silence of those sagacious enemies who dare not trust themselves to speak. I shall endeavour to extract from the midst of insult, and contempt, and maledictions, those admonitions which may tend to correct whatever imperfections such censurers may discover in this my first serious appeal to the Public.° If certain Critics were as clear-sighted as they are malignant, how great would be the benefit to be derived from their virulent writings! As it is, I fear I shall be malicious enough to be amused with their paltry tricks and lame invectives. Should the Public judge that my composition is worthless, I shall indeed bow before the tribunal from which Milton received his crown of immortality, and shall seek to gather, if I live, strength from that defeat, which may nerve me to some new enterprise of thought which may *not* be worthless. I cannot conceive that Lucretius,° when he meditated that poem whose doctrines are yet the basis of our metaphysical knowledge, and whose eloquence has been the wonder of mankind, wrote in awe of such censure as the hired sophists of the impure and superstitious noblemen of Rome might affix to what he should produce. It was at the period when Greece was led captive, and Asia made tributary to the Republic, fast verging itself to slavery and ruin, that a multitude of Syrian captives, bigoted to the worship of their obscene Ashtaroth,° and the unworthy successors of Socrates and Zeno,° found there a precarious subsistence by administering, under the name of freedmen, to the vices and vanities of the great. These wretched men were skilled to plead, with a superficial but plausible set of sophisms, in favour of that contempt for virtue which is the portion of slaves, and that faith in portents, the most fatal substitute for benevolence in the imaginations of men, which arising from the enslaved communities of the East, then first began to overwhelm the western nations in its stream. Were these the kind of men whose disapprobation the wise and lofty-minded Lucretius should have regarded with a salutary awe? The latest and perhaps the meanest of those who follow in his footsteps,° would disdain to hold life on such conditions.

The Poem now presented to the Public occupied little more than six months in the composition. That period has been devoted to the task with unremitting ardour and enthusiasm. I have exercised a watchful and earnest criticism on my work as it grew under my hands. I would willingly have sent it forth to the world with that perfection which long labour and revision is said to bestow. But I found that if I should gain something in exactness by this method, I might lose much of the newness and energy of imagery and language as it flowed fresh from my mind. And although the mere composition occupied no more than six months, the thoughts thus arranged were slowly gathered in as many years.°

I trust that the reader will carefully distinguish between those opinions which have a dramatic propriety in reference to the characters which they are designed to elucidate, and such as are properly my own. The erroneous and degrading idea which men have conceived of a Supreme Being, for instance, is spoken against, but not the Supreme Being itself. The belief which some superstitious persons whom I have brought upon the stage, express in the cruelty and malevolence of God,° is widely different from my own. In recommending also a great and important change in the spirit which animates the social institutions of mankind, I have avoided all flattery to those violent and malignant passions of our nature, which are ever on the watch to mingle with and to alloy the most beneficial innovations. There is no quarter given to Revenge, or Envy, or Prejudice. Love is celebrated everywhere as the sole law which should govern the moral world,

In the personal conduct of my Hero and Heroine, there is one circumstance which was intended to startle the reader from the trance of ordinary life. It was my object to break through the crust of those outworn opinions on which established institutions depend. I have appealed therefore to the most universal of all feelings, and have endeavoured to strengthen the moral sense, by forbidding it to waste its energies in seeking to avoid actions which are only crimes of convention. It is because there is so great a multitude of artificial vices, that there are so few real virtues. Those feelings alone which are benevolent or malevolent, are essentially good or bad. The circumstance of which I speak, was introduced, however, merely to accustom men to that charity and toleration which the exhibition of a practice widely differing from their own, has a tendency to promote.° Nothing indeed can be more mischievous, than many actions innocent in themselves, which might bring down upon individuals the bigoted contempt and rage of the multitude.°

DEDICATION

There is no danger to a man, that knows
What life and death is: there's not any law
Exceeds his knowledge: neither is it lawful
That he should stoop to any other law.

Chapman°

TO
MARY — —°

I

So now my summer-task is ended, Mary,
And I return to thee, mine own heart's home;
As to his Queen some victor Knight of Faery,°
Earning bright spoils for her enchanted dome;
Nor thou disdain, that ere my fame become
A star among the stars of mortal night,

If it indeed may cleave its natal gloom,
Its doubtful promise thus I would unite
With thy beloved name, thou Child of love and light.°

2

The toil which stole from thee so many an hour,
Is ended,—and the fruit is at thy feet!
No longer where the woods to frame a bower
With interlacèd branches mix and meet,
Or where with sound like many voices sweet,
Water-falls leap among wild islands green,
Which framed for my lone boat a lone retreat°
Of moss-grown trees and weeds, shall I be seen:
But beside thee, where still my heart has ever been.

3

Thoughts of great deeds were mine, dear Friend, when first
The clouds which wrap this world from youth did pass.
I do remember well the hour which burst
My spirit's sleep: a fresh May-dawn it was,
When I walked forth upon the glittering grass,
And wept, I knew not why; until there rose
From the near school-room, voices, that, alas!
Were but one echo from a world of woes—
The harsh and grating strife of tyrants and of foes.°

4

And then I clasped my hands and looked around—
—But none was near to mock my streaming eyes,
Which poured their warm drops on the sunny ground—
So without shame, I spake:—'I will be wise,
And just, and free, and mild, if in me lies
Such power, for I grow weary to behold
The selfish and the strong still tyrannize
Without reproach or check.' I then controlled
My tears, my heart grew calm, and I was meek and bold.

5

And from that hour did I with earnest thought
Heap knowledge from forbidden mines of lore,°

Yet nothing that my tyrants knew or taught
I cared to learn, but from that secret store
Wrought linkèd armour for my soul, before
It might walk forth to war among mankind;
Thus power and hope were strengthened more and more
Within me, till there came upon my mind
A sense of loneliness, a thirst with which I pined.

6

Alas, that love should be a blight and snare
To those who seek all sympathies in one!—°
Such once I sought in vain; then black despair,
The shadow of a starless night, was thrown
Over the world in which I moved alone:—
Yet never found I one not false to me,
Hard hearts, and cold, like weights of icy stone
Which crushed and withered mine, that could not be
Aught but a lifeless clog, until revived by thee.°

7

Thou Friend, whose presence on my wintry heart
Fell, like bright Spring upon some herbless plain;
How beautiful and calm and free thou wert
In thy young wisdom, when the mortal chain
Of Custom thou didst burst and rend in twain,°
And walked as free as light the clouds among,
Which many an envious slave then breathed in vain°
From his dim dungeon, and my spirit sprung
To meet thee from the woes which had begirt it long.

8

No more alone through the world's wilderness,
Although I trod the paths of high intent,
I journeyed now: no more companionless,
Where solitude is like despair, I went.—
There is the wisdom of a stern content
When Poverty can blight the just and good,°
When Infamy dares mock the innocent,°
And cherished friends turn with the multitude
To trample: this was ours, and we unshaken stood!

9

Now has descended a serener hour,
And with inconstant fortune, friends return;
Though suffering leaves the knowledge and the power
Which says:—Let scorn be not repaid with scorn.
And from thy side two gentle babes are born°
To fill our home with smiles, and thus are we
Most fortunate beneath life's beaming morn;
And these delights, and thou, have been to me
The parents of the Song I consecrate to thee.

10

Is it, that now my inexperienced fingers
But strike the prelude of a loftier strain?
Or, must the lyre on which my spirit lingers
Soon pause in silence, ne'er to sound again,
Though it might shake the Anarch Custom's reign,°
And charm the minds of men to Truth's own sway
Holier than was Amphion's? I would fain°
Reply in hope—but I am worn away,
And Death and Love are yet contending for their prey.°

11

And what art thou? I know, but dare not speak:
Time may interpret to his silent years.
Yet in the paleness of thy thoughtful cheek,
And in the light thine ample forehead wears,
And in thy sweetest smiles, and in thy tears,
And in thy gentle speech, a prophecy
Is whispered, to subdue my fondest fears:
And through thine eyes, even in thy soul I see
A lamp of vestal fire burning internally.°

12

They say that thou wert lovely from thy birth,
Of glorious parents, thou aspiring Child.
I wonder not—for One then left this earth°
Whose life was like a setting planet mild,
Which clothed thee in the radiance undefiled

Of its departing glory; still her fame
Shines on thee, through the tempests dark and wild
Which shake these latter days; and thou canst claim
The shelter, from thy Sire, of an immortal name.°

13

One voice came forth from many a mighty spirit,
Which was the echo of three thousand years;
And the tumultuous world stood mute to hear it,
As some lone man who in a desert hears
The music of his home:—unwonted fears
Fell on the pale oppressors of our race,
And Faith, and Custom, and low-thoughted cares,
Like thunder-stricken dragons, for a space
Left the torn human heart, their food and dwelling-place.

14

Truth's deathless voice pauses among mankind!
If there must be no response to my cry—
If men must rise and stamp with fury blind
On his pure name who loves them,—thou and I,
Sweet Friend! can look from our tranquillity
Like lamps into the world's tempestuous night,—
Two tranquil stars, while clouds are passing by
Which wrap them from the foundering seaman's sight,
That burn from year to year with unextinguished light.

ὅσαις δὲ βροτὸν ἔθνος ἀγλαΐαις ἁπτόμεσθα,
περαίνει πρὸς ἔσχατον
πλόον· ναυσὶ δ' οὔτε πεζὸς ἰὼν ἂν εὕροις
ἐς Ὑπερβορέων ἀγῶνα θαυματὰν ὁδόν.

Pind. *Pyth X*°

Canto First

I

When the last hope of trampled France had failed°
Like a brief dream of unremaining glory,
From visions of despair I rose, and scaled

The peak of an aerial promontory,
Whose caverned base with the vexed surge was hoary;
And saw the golden dawn break forth, and waken
Each cloud, and every wave:—but transitory
The calm: for sudden, the firm earth was shaken,
As if by the last wreck its frame were overtaken.°

2

So as I stood, one blast of muttering thunder
Burst in far peals along the waveless deep,
When, gathering fast, around, above and under,
Long trains of tremulous mist began to creep,
Until their complicating lines did steep°
The orient sun in shadow:—not a sound
Was heard; one horrible repose did keep°
The forests and the floods, and all around
Darkness more dread than night was poured upon the ground.

3

Hark! 'tis the rushing of a wind that sweeps
Earth and the ocean. See! the lightnings yawn°
Deluging Heaven with fire, and the lashed deeps
Glitter and boil beneath: it rages on,
One mighty stream, whirlwind and waves upthrown,
Lightning, and hail, and darkness eddying by.
There is a pause—the sea-birds, that were gone
Into their caves to shriek, come forth, to spy
What calm has fall'n on earth, what light is in the sky.

4

For, where the irresistible storm had cloven
That fearful darkness, the blue sky was seen
Fretted with many a fair cloud interwoven°
Most delicately, and the ocean green,
Beneath that opening spot of blue serene,
Quivered like burning emerald: calm was spread
On all below; but far on high, between
Earth and the upper air, the vast clouds fled,
Countless and swift as leaves on autumn's tempest shed.

5

For ever, as the war became more fierce
Between the whirlwinds and the rack on high,°
That spot grew more serene; blue light did pierce
The woof of those white clouds, which seemed to lie
Far, deep, and motionless; while through the sky
The pallid semicircle of the moon
Passed on, in slow and moving majesty;
Its upper horn arrayed in mists, which soon
But slowly fled, like dew beneath the beams of noon.

6

I could not choose but gaze; a fascination°
Dwelt in that moon, and sky, and clouds, which drew
My fancy thither, and in expectation
Of what I knew not, I remained:—the hue
Of the white moon, amid that heaven so blue,
Suddenly stained with shadow did appear;
A speck, a cloud, a shape, approaching grew,
Like a great ship in the sun's sinking sphere
Beheld afar at sea, and swift it came anear.

7

Even like a bark, which from a chasm of mountains,
Dark, vast, and overhanging, on a river
Which there collects the strength of all its fountains,
Comes forth, whilst with the speed its frame doth quiver,
Sails, oars, and stream, tending to one endeavour;
So, from that chasm of light a wingèd Form
On all the winds of heaven approaching ever
Floated, dilating as it came: the storm
Pursued it with fierce blasts, and lightnings swift and warm.

8

A course precipitous, of dizzy speed,
Suspending thought and breath; a monstrous sight!
For in the air do I behold indeed
An Eagle and a Serpent wreathed in fight:—°
And now relaxing its impetuous flight,
Before the aerial rock on which I stood,

The Eagle, hovering, wheeled to left and right,
And hung with lingering wings over the flood,
And startled with its yells the wide air's solitude.

9

A shaft of light upon its wings descended,
And every golden feather gleamed therein—
Feather and scale inextricably blended.
The Serpent's mailed and many-coloured skin
Shone through the plumes its coils were twined within
By many a swollen and knotted fold, and high
And far, the neck receding lithe and thin,
Sustained a crested head, which warily
Shifted and glanced before the Eagle's steadfast eye.°

10

Around, around, in ceaseless circles wheeling
With clang of wings and scream, the Eagle sailed°
Incessantly—sometimes on high concealing
Its lessening orbs, sometimes as if it failed,
Drooped through the air; and still it shrieked and wailed,
And casting back its eager head, with beak°
And talon unremittingly assailed
The wreathèd Serpent, who did ever seek
Upon his enemy's heart a mortal wound to wreak.

11

What life, what power, was kindled and arose
Within the sphere of that appalling fray!
For, from the encounter of those wondrous foes,
A vapour like the sea's suspended spray
Hung gathered: in the void air, far away,
Floated the shattered plumes; bright scales did leap,
Where'er the Eagle's talons made their way,
Like sparks into the darkness;—as they sweep,°
Blood stains the snowy foam of the tumultuous deep.

12

Swift chances in that combat—many a check,
And many a change, a dark and wild turmoil;

Sometimes the Snake around his enemy's neck
Locked in stiff rings his adamantine coil,
Until the Eagle, faint with pain and toil,
Remitted his strong flight, and near the sea
Languidly fluttered, hopeless so to foil
His adversary, who then reared on high
His red and burning crest, radiant with victory.

13

Then on the white edge of the bursting surge,
Where they had sunk together, would the Snake
Relax his suffocating grasp, and scourge
The wind with his wild writhings; for to break
That chain of torment, the vast bird would shake
The strength of his unconquerable wings
As in despair, and with his sinewy neck,
Dissolve in sudden shock those linkèd rings,
Then soar—as swift as smoke from a volcano springs.

14

Wile baffled wile, and strength encountered strength,
Thus long, but unprevailing:—the event°
Of that portentous fight appeared at length:°
Until the lamp of day was almost spent
It had endured, when lifeless, stark, and rent,°
Hung high that mighty Serpent, and at last
Fell to the sea, while o'er the continent,
With clang of wings and scream the Eagle passed,
Heavily borne away on the exhausted blast.

15

And with it fled the tempest, so that ocean
And earth and sky shone through the atmosphere—
Only, 'twas strange to see the red commotion
Of waves like mountains o'er the sinking sphere
Of sunset sweep, and their fierce roar to hear
Amid the calm: down the steep path I wound
To the seashore—the evening was most clear
And beautiful, and there the sea I found
Calm as a cradled child in dreamless slumber bound.

16

There was a Woman, beautiful as morning,
Sitting beneath the rocks, upon the sand
Of the waste sea—fair as one flower adorning
An icy wilderness—each delicate hand
Lay crossed upon her bosom, and the band
Of her dark hair had fall'n, and so she sate
Looking upon the waves; on the bare strand
Upon the sea-mark a small boat did wait,°
Fair as herself, like Love by Hope left desolate.

17

It seemed that this fair Shape had looked upon
That unimaginable fight, and now
That her sweet eyes were weary of the sun,
As brightly it illustrated her woe;
For in the tears which silently to flow
Paused not, its lustre hung: she watching aye
The foam-wreathes which the faint tide wove below
Upon the spangled sands, groaned heavily,
And after every groan looked up over the sea.

18

And when she saw the wounded Serpent make
His path between the waves, her lips grew pale,
Parted, and quivered; the tears ceased to break
From her immovable eyes; no voice of wail°
Escaped her; but she rose, and on the gale
Loosening her star-bright robe and shadowy hair
Poured forth her voice; the caverns of the vale
That opened to the ocean, caught it there,
And filled with silver sounds the overflowing air.

19

She spake in language whose strange melody
Might not belong to earth. I heard, alone,°
What made its music more melodious be,
The pity and the love of every tone;
But to the Snake those accents sweet were known
His native tongue and hers; nor did he beat

The hoar spray idly then, but winding on
Through the green shadows of the waves that meet
Near to the shore, did pause beside her snowy feet.

20

Then on the sands the Woman sate again,
And wept and clasped her hands, and all between,
Renewed the unintelligible strain
Of her melodious voice and eloquent mien;
And she unveiled her bosom, and the green
And glancing shadows of the sea did play
O'er its marmoreal depth:—one moment seen,°
For ere the next, the Serpent did obey
Her voice, and, coiled in rest in her embrace it lay.

21

Then she arose, and smiled on me with eyes
Serene yet sorrowing, like that planet fair,
While yet the day-light lingereth in the skies
Which cleaves with arrowy beams the dark-red air,
And said: 'To grieve is wise, but the despair
Was weak and vain which led thee here from sleep:
This shalt thou know, and more, if thou dost dare
With me and with this Serpent, o'er the deep,
A voyage divine and strange, companionship to keep.'

22

Her voice was like the wildest, saddest tone,
Yet sweet, of some loved voice heard long ago.
I wept. Shall this fair woman all alone,
Over the sea with that fierce Serpent go?
His head is on her heart, and who can know
How soon he may devour his feeble prey?—
Such were my thoughts, when the tide 'gan to flow;
And that strange boat, like the moon's shade, did sway
Amid reflected stars that in the waters lay.

23

A boat of rare device, which had no sail°
But its own curvèd prow of thin moonstone,

Wrought like a web of texture fine and frail,
To catch those gentlest winds which are not known
To breathe, but by the steady speed alone
With which it cleaves the sparkling sea; and now
We are embarked, the mountains hang and frown
Over the starry deep that gleams below,
A vast and dim expanse, as o'er the waves we go.°

24

And as we sailed, a strange and awful tale
That Woman told, like such mysterious dream
As makes the slumberer's cheek with wonder pale!
'Twas midnight, and around, a shoreless stream,
Wide ocean rolled, when that majestic theme
Shrined in her heart found utterance, and she bent
Her looks on mine; those eyes a kindling beam
Of love divine into my spirit sent,
And ere her lips could move, made the air eloquent.

25

'Speak not to me, but hear! much shalt thou learn,
Much must remain unthought, and more untold,
In the dark Future's ever-flowing urn:°
Know then, that from the depth of ages old,
Two Powers o'er mortal things dominion hold,
Ruling the world with a divided lot,
Immortal, all pervading, manifold,
Twin Genii, equal Gods—when life and thought°
Sprang forth, they burst the womb of inessential Nought.°

26

'The earliest dweller of the world alone,
Stood on the verge of chaos: Lo! afar
O'er the wide wild abyss two meteors shone,
Sprung from the depth of its tempestuous jar:°
A blood-red Comet and the Morning Star°
Mingling their beams in combat—as he stood,
All thoughts within his mind waged mutual war,
In dreadful sympathy—when to the flood°
That fair Star fell, he turned and shed his brother's blood.

27

'Thus evil triumphed, and the Spirit of evil,
One Power of many shapes which none may know,°
One Shape of many names; the Fiend did revel
In victory, reigning o'er a world of woe,
For the new race of man went to and fro,
Famished and homeless, loathed and loathing, wild,
And hating good—for his immortal foe,
He changed from starry shape, beauteous and mild,°
To a dire Snake, with man and beast unreconciled.

28

'The darkness lingering o'er the dawn of things,
Was Evil's breath and life: this made him strong
To soar aloft with overshadowing wings;
And the great Spirit of Good did creep among
The nations of mankind, and every tongue
Cursed, and blasphemed him as he passed; for none
Knew good from evil, though their names were hung
In mockery o'er the fane where many a groan,°
As King, and Lord, and God, the conquering Fiend did own.°

29

'The fiend, whose name was Legion; Death, Decay,
Earthquake and Blight, and Want, and Madness pale,
Wingèd and wan diseases, an array
Numerous as leaves that strew the autumnal gale;
Poison, a snake in flowers, beneath the veil
Of food and mirth, hiding his mortal head;
And, without whom all these might nought avail,
Fear, Hatred, Faith, and Tyranny, who spread
Those subtle nets which snare the living and the dead.

30

'His spirit is their power, and they his slaves
In air, and light, and thought, and language dwell;
And keep their state from palaces to graves,
In all resorts of men—invisible,
But when, in ebon mirror, Nightmare fell
To tyrant or impostor bids them rise,

Black-wingèd demon forms—whom, from the hell,
His reign and dwelling beneath nether skies,°
He loosens to their dark and blasting ministries.°

31

'In the world's youth his empire was as firm
As its foundations—soon the Spirit of Good,
Though in the likeness of a loathsome worm,
Sprang from the billows of the formless flood,
Which shrank and fled; and with that fiend of blood
Renewed the doubtful war—thrones then first shook,
And earth's immense and trampled multitude,
In hope on their own powers began to look,
And Fear, the demon pale, his sanguine shrine forsook.°

32

'Then Greece arose, and to its bards and sages,
In dream, the golden-pinioned Genii came,
Even where they slept amid the night of ages,
Steeping their hearts in the divinest flame,
Which thy breath kindled, Power of holiest name!
And oft in cycles since, when darkness gave
New weapons to thy foe, their sunlike fame
Upon the combat shone—a light to save,°
Like Paradise spread forth beyond the shadowy grave.

33

'Such is this conflict—when mankind doth strive
With its oppressors in a strife of blood,
Or when free thoughts, like lightnings are alive;
And in each bosom of the multitude
Justice and truth, with custom's hydra brood,°
Wage silent war;—when priests and kings dissemble
In smiles or frowns their fierce disquietude,
When round pure hearts, a host of hopes assemble,
The Snake and Eagle meet—the world's foundations tremble!

34

'Thou hast beheld that fight—when to thy home
Thou dost return, steep not its hearth in tears;

Though thou may'st hear that earth is now become
The tyrant's garbage, which to his compeers,°
The vile reward of their dishonoured years,
He will dividing give.—The victor Fiend
Omnipotent of yore, now quails, and fears
His triumph dearly won, which soon will lend
An impulse swift and sure to his approaching end.

35

'List, stranger list, mine is an human form,
Like that thou wearest—touch me—shrink not now!
My hand thou feel'st is not a ghost's, but warm
With human blood.—'Twas many years ago,
Since first my thirsting soul aspired to know
The secrets of this wondrous world, when deep
My heart was pierced with sympathy, for woe
Which could not be mine own—and thought did keep
In dream, unnatural watch beside an infant's sleep.°

36

'Woe could not be mine own, since far from men
I dwelt, a free and happy orphan child,
By the seashore, in a deep mountain glen;
And near the waves, and through the forests wild,
I roamed, to storm and darkness reconciled:
For I was calm while tempest shook the sky:
But when the breathless heavens in beauty smiled,
I wept, sweet tears, yet too tumultuously
For peace, and clasped my hands aloft in ecstacy.

37

'These were forebodings of my fate—before
A woman's heart beat in my virgin breast,
It had been nurtured in divinest lore:
A dying poet gave me books, and blest°
With wild but holy talk the sweet unrest
In which I watched him as he died away—
A youth with hoary hair—a fleeting guest
Of our lone mountains—and this lore did sway
My spirit like a storm, contending there alway.

38

'Thus the dark tale which history doth unfold,
I knew, but not, methinks, as others know,
For they weep not; and Wisdom had unrolled
The clouds which hide the gulf of mortal woe:
To few can she that warning vision show,
For I loved all things with intense devotion;
So that when Hope's deep source in fullest flow,°
Like earthquake did uplift the stagnant ocean
Of human thoughts—mine shook beneath the wide emotion.

39

'When first the living blood through all these veins
Kindled a thought in sense, great France sprang forth,
And seized, as if to break, the ponderous chains
Which bind in woe the nations of the earth.
I saw, and started from my cottage hearth;
And to the clouds and waves in tameless gladness,
Shrieked, till they caught immeasurable mirth—
And laughed in light and music: soon, sweet madness
Was poured upon my heart, a soft and thrilling sadness.

40

'Deep slumber fell on me:—my dreams were fire,
Soft and delightful thoughts did rest and hover
Like shadows o'er my brain; and strange desire,
The tempest of a passion, raging over
My tranquil soul, its depths with light did cover,
Which passed; and calm, and darkness, sweeter far
Came—then I loved; but not a human lover!
For when I rose from sleep, the Morning Star°
Shone through the woodbine wreaths which round my
casement were.

41

' 'Twas like an eye which seemed to smile on me.
I watched, till by the sun made pale, it sank
Under the billows of the heaving sea;
But from its beams deep love my spirit drank,

And to my brain the boundless world now shrank
Into one thought—one image—yes, for ever!
Even like the dayspring, poured on vapours dank,
The beams of that one Star did shoot and quiver
Through my benighted mind—and were extinguished never.

42

'The day passed thus: at night, methought in dream
A shape of speechless beauty did appear:°
It stood like light on a careering stream
Of golden clouds which shook the atmosphere;
A wingèd youth, his radiant brow did wear
The Morning Star: a wild dissolving bliss
Over my frame he breathed, approaching near,
And bent his eyes of kindling tenderness
Near mine, and on my lips impressed a lingering kiss,

43

'And said: "a Spirit loves thee, mortal maiden,
How wilt thou prove thy worth?" Then joy and sleep
Together fled, my soul was deeply laden,
And to the shore I went to muse and weep;
But as I moved, over my heart did creep
A joy less soft, but more profound and strong
Than my sweet dream; and it forbade to keep
The path of the seashore: that Spirit's tongue
Seemed whispering in my heart, and bore my steps along.

44

'How, to that vast and peopled city led,°
Which was a field of holy warfare then,
I walked among the dying and the dead,
And shared in fearless deeds with evil men,
Calm as an angel in the dragon's den—
How I braved death for liberty and truth,
And spurned at peace, and power, and fame; and when
Those hopes had lost the glory of their youth,
How sadly I returned—might move the hearer's ruth:°

45

'Warm tears throng fast! the tale may not be said—
Know then, that when this grief had been subdued,
I was not left, like others, cold and dead;°
The Spirit whom I loved, in solitude
Sustained his child: the tempest-shaken wood,
The waves, the fountains, and the hush of night—
These were his voice, and well I understood
His smile divine, when the calm sea was bright
With silent stars, and Heaven was breathless with delight.

46

'In lonely glens, amid the roar of rivers,
When the dim nights were moonless, have I known
Joys which no tongue can tell; my pale lip quivers
When thought revisits them:—know thou alone,
That after many wondrous years were flown,
I was awakened by a shriek of woe;
And over me a mystic robe was thrown,
By viewless hands, and a bright Star did glow
Before my steps—the Snake then met his mortal foe.'

47

'Thou fearest not then the Serpent on thy heart?'
'Fear it!' she said, with brief and passionate cry,
And spake no more: that silence made me start—
I looked, and we were sailing pleasantly,
Swift as a cloud between the sea and sky;
Beneath the rising moon seen far away,
Mountains of ice, like sapphire, piled on high
Hemming the horizon round, in silence lay
On the still waters—these we did approach alway.

48

And swift and swifter grew the vessel's motion,
So that a dizzy trance fell on my brain—
Wild music woke me: we had passed the ocean
Which girds the pole, Nature's remotest reign—
And we glode fast o'er a pellucid plain
Of waters, azure with the noontide day.

Etherial mountains shone around—a Fane
Stood in the midst, girt by green isles which lay
On the blue sunny deep, resplendent far away.°

49

It was a Temple, such as mortal hand
Has never built, nor ecstasy, nor dream,
Reared in the cities of enchanted land:
'Twas likest Heaven, ere yet day's purple stream
Ebbs o'er the western forest, while the gleam
Of the unrisen moon among the clouds
Is gathering—when with many a golden beam
The thronging constellations rush in crowds,
Paving with fire the sky and the marmoreal floods;

50

Like what may be conceived of this vast dome,°
When from the depths which thought can seldom pierce
Genius beholds it rise, his native home,
Girt by the deserts of the Universe.
Yet, nor in painting's light, or mightier verse,
Or sculpture's marble language can invest
That shape to mortal sense—such glooms immerse
That incommunicable sight, and rest
Upon the labouring brain and overburdened breast.

51

Winding among the lawny islands fair,
Whose blosmy forests starred the shadowy deep,°
The wingless boat paused where an ivory stair
Its fretwork in the crystal sea did steep,
Encircling that vast Fane's aerial heap:°
We disembarked, and through a portal wide
We passed—whose roof of moonstone carved, did keep
A glimmering o'er the forms on every side,
Sculptures like life and thought; immovable, deep-eyed.

52

We came to a vast hall, whose glorious roof
Was diamond, which had drunk the lightning's sheen

In darkness, and now poured it through the woof
Of spell-inwoven clouds hung there to screen
Its blinding splendour—through such veil was seen
That work of subtlest power, divine and rare;
Orb above orb, with starry shapes between,
And hornèd moons, and meteors strange and fair,
On night-black columns poised—one hollow hemisphere!

53

Ten thousand columns in that quivering light
Distinct—between whose shafts wound far away
The long and labyrinthine aisles—more bright
With their own radiance than the Heaven of Day;
And on the jasper walls around, there lay
Paintings, the poesy of mightiest thought,
Which did the Spirit's history display;
A tale of passionate change, divinely taught,
Which, in their wingèd dance, unconscious Genii wrought.

54

Beneath, there sate on many a sapphire throne,
The Great, who had departed from mankind,
A mighty Senate;—some whose white hair shone
Like mountain snow, mild, beautiful, and blind;°
Some, female forms, whose gestures beamed with mind;
And ardent youths, and children bright and fair;
And some had lyres whose strings were intertwined
With pale and clinging flames, which ever there
Waked faint yet thrilling sounds that pierced the crystal air.

55

One seat was vacant in the midst, a throne,
Reared on a pyramid like sculptured flame,
Distinct with circling steps which rested on
Their own deep fire—soon as the Woman came
Into that hall, she shrieked the Spirit's name
And fell; and vanished slowly from the sight.
Darkness arose from her dissolving frame,
Which gathering, filled that dome of woven light,
Blotting its spherèd stars with supernatural night.°

56

Then first, two glittering lights were seen to glide
In circles on the amethystine floor,
Small serpent eyes trailing from side to side,
Like meteors on a river's grassy shore,°
They round each other rolled, dilating more
And more—then rose, commingling into one,
One clear and mighty planet hanging o'er
A cloud of deepest shadow, which was thrown
Athwart the glowing steps and the crystalline throne.

57

The cloud which rested on that cone of flame
Was cloven; beneath the planet sate a Form,°
Fairer than tongue can speak or thought may frame,
The radiance of whose limbs rose-like and warm
Flowed forth, and did with softest light inform°
The shadowy dome, the sculptures, and the state
Of those assembled shapes—with clinging charm
Sinking upon their hearts and mine—He sate
Majestic, yet most mild—calm, yet compassionate.

58

Wonder and joy a passing faintness threw
Over my brow—a hand supported me,
Whose touch was magic strength: an eye of blue
Looked into mine, like moonlight, soothingly;
And a voice said—'Thou must a listener be
This day—two mighty Spirits now return,
Like birds of calm, from the world's raging sea,
They pour fresh light from Hope's immortal urn;
A tale of human power—despair not—list and learn!'

59

I looked, and lo! one stood forth eloquently,°
His eyes were dark and deep, and the clear brow
Which shadowed them was like the morning sky,
The cloudless Heaven of Spring, when in their flow
Through the bright air, the soft winds as they blow
Wake the green world—his gestures did obey

The oracular mind that made his features glow,
And where his curvèd lips half open lay,
Passion's divinest stream had made impetuous way.

60

Beneath the darkness of his outspread hair
He stood thus beautiful: but there was One°
Who sate beside him like his shadow there,
And held his hand—far lovelier—she was known
To be thus fair, by the few lines alone°
Which through her floating locks and gathered cloak
Glances of soul-dissolving glory, shone:—
None else beheld her eyes—in him they woke
Memories which found a tongue, as thus he silence broke.

Canto Second

1

The starlight smile of children, the sweet looks
Of women, the fair breast from which I fed,
The murmur of the unreposing brooks,
And the green light which, shifting overhead,
Some tangled bower of vines around me shed,
The shells on the sea-sand, and the wild flowers,
The lamp-light through the rafters cheerly spread,
And on the twining flax—in life's young hours
These sights and sounds did nurse my spirit's folded powers.

2

In Argolis, beside the echoing sea,°
Such impulses within my mortal frame
Arose, and they were dear to memory,
Like tokens of the dead:—but others came
Soon, in another shape: the wondrous fame
Of the past world, the vital words and deeds
Of minds whom neither time nor change can tame,
Traditions dark and old, whence evil creeds
Start forth, and whose dim shade a stream of poison feeds.

3

I heard, as all have heard, the various story
Of human life, and wept unwilling tears.
Feeble historians of its shame and glory,
False disputants on all its hopes and fears,
Victims who worshipped ruin,—chroniclers
Of daily scorn, and slaves who loathed their state
Yet flattering power had given its ministers
A throne of judgement in the grave:—'twas fate,°
That among such as these my youth should seek its mate.

4

The land in which I lived, by a fell bane°
Was withered up. Tyrants dwelt side by side,
And stabled in our homes,—until the chain
Stifled the captive's cry, and to abide
That blasting curse men had no shame—all vied
In evil, slave and despot; fear with lust,
Strange fellowship through mutual hate had tied,
Like two dark serpents tangled in the dust,
Which on the paths of men their mingling poison thrust.

5

Earth, our bright home, its mountains and its waters,
And the etherial shapes which are suspended
Over its green expanse, and those fair daughters,
The clouds, of Sun and Ocean, who have blended
The colours of the air since first extended
It cradled the young world, none wandered forth
To see or feel: a darkness had descended
On every heart: the light which shows its worth,°
Must among gentle thoughts and fearless take its birth.

6

This vital world, this home of happy spirits,
Was as a dungeon to my blasted kind,
All that despair from murdered hope inherits
They sought, and in their helpless misery blind,
A deeper prison and heavier chains did find,°
And stronger tyrants:—a dark gulf before,

The realm of a stern Ruler, yawned; behind,°
Terror and Time conflicting drove, and bore°
On their tempestuous flood the shrieking wretch from shore.

7

Out of that Ocean's wrecks had Guilt and Woe
Framed a dark dwelling for their homeless thought,°
And, starting at the ghosts which to and fro
Glide o'er its dim and gloomy strand, had brought
The worship thence which they each other taught.
Well might men loathe their life, well might they turn
Even to the ills again from which they sought
Such refuge after death!—well might they learn
To gaze on this fair world with hopeless unconcern!

8

For they all pined in bondage: body and soul,
Tyrant and slave, victim and torturer, bent
Before one Power, to which supreme control
Over their will by their own weakness lent,
Made all its many names omnipotent;
All symbols of things evil, all divine;
And hymns of blood or mockery, which rent
The air from all its fanes, did intertwine°
Imposture's impious toils round each discordant shrine.

9

I heard as all have heard, life's various story,
And in no careless heart transcribed the tale;
But, from the sneers of men who had grown hoary
In shame and scorn, from groans of crowds made pale
By famine, from a mother's desolate wail
O'er her polluted child, from innocent blood°
Poured on the earth, and brows anxious and pale
With the heart's warfare; did I gather food
To feed my many thoughts: a tameless multitude!

10

I wandered through the wrecks of days departed
Far by the desolated shore, when even°

O'er the still sea and jagged islets darted
The light of moonrise; in the northern Heaven,
Among the clouds near the horizon driven,
The mountains lay beneath one planet pale;
Around me, broken tombs and columns riven
Looked vast in twilight, and the sorrowing gale
Waked in those ruins grey its everlasting wail!

11

I knew not who had framed these wonders then,
Nor had I heard the story of their deeds;
But dwellings of a race of mightier men,
And monuments of less ungentle creeds
Tell their own tale to him who wisely heeds
The language which they speak; and now, to me
The moonlight making pale the blooming weeds,
The bright stars shining in the breathless sea,
Interpreted those scrolls of mortal mystery.

12

Such man has been, and such may yet become!
Aye, wiser, greater, gentler, even than they
Who on the fragments of yon shattered dome
Have stamped the sign of power—I felt the sway
Of the vast stream of ages bear away
My floating thoughts—my heart beat loud and fast—
Even as a storm let loose beneath the ray
Of the still moon, my spirit onward passed
Beneath truth's steady beams upon its tumult cast.

13

It shall be thus no more! too long, too long,
Sons of the glorious dead, have ye lain bound°
In darkness and in ruin.—Hope is strong,
Justice and Truth their wingèd child have found—°
Awake! arise! until the mighty sound
Of your career shall scatter in its gust
The thrones of the oppressor, and the ground
Hide the last altar's unregarded dust,
Whose Idol has so long betrayed your impious trust.°

14

It must be so—I will arise and waken
The multitude, and like a sulphurous hill,
Which on a sudden from its snows has shaken
The swoon of ages, it shall burst and fill
The world with cleansing fire: it must, it will—
It may not be restrained!—and who shall stand
Amid the rocking earthquake steadfast still,
But Laon? on high Freedom's desert land
A tower whose marble walls the leaguèd storms withstand!

15

One summer night, in commune with the hope
Thus deeply fed, amid those ruins grey
I watched, beneath the dark sky's starry cope;
And ever from that hour upon me lay
The burden of this hope, and night or day,
In vision or in dream, clove to my breast:
Among mankind, or when gone far away
To the lone shores and mountains, 'twas a guest
Which followed where I fled, and watched when I did rest.

16

These hopes found words through which my spirit sought
To weave a bondage of such sympathy,
As might create some response to the thought
Which ruled me now—and as the vapours lie
Bright in the outspread morning's radiancy,
So were these thoughts invested with the light
Of language: and all bosoms made reply
On which its lustre streamed, whene'er it might
Through darkness wide and deep those trancèd spirits smite.

17

Yes, many an eye with dizzy tears was dim,
And oft I thought to clasp my own heart's brother,
When I could feel the listener's senses swim,
And hear his breath its own swift gaspings smother
Even as my words evoked them—and another,
And yet another, I did fondly deem,

Felt that we all were sons of one great mother;
And the cold truth such sad reverse did seem,
As to awake in grief from some delightful dream.

18

Yes, oft beside the ruined labyrinth
Which skirts the hoary caves of the green deep,
Did Laon and his friend on one grey plinth,°
Round whose worn base the wild waves hiss and leap,
Resting at eve, a lofty converse keep:
And that this friend was false, may now be said
Calmly—that he like other men could weep
Tears which are lies, and could betray and spread
Snares for that guileless heart which for his own had bled.°

19

Then, had no great aim recompensed my sorrow,
I must have sought dark respite from its stress
In dreamless rest, in sleep that sees no morrow—
For to tread life's dismaying wilderness
Without one smile to cheer, one voice to bless,
Amid the snares and scoffs of humankind,
Is hard—but I betrayed it not, nor less
With love that scorned return, sought to unbind
The interwoven clouds which make its wisdom blind.°

20

With deathless minds which leave where they have passed
A path of light, my soul communion knew;
Till from that glorious intercourse, at last,
As from a mine of magic store, I drew
Words which were weapons;—round my heart there grew
The adamantine armour of their power,
And from my fancy wings of golden hue
Sprang forth—yet not alone from wisdom's tower,
A minister of truth, these plumes young Laon bore.

21

I had a little sister, whose fair eyes°
Were lodestars of delight, which drew me home°

When I might wander forth; nor did I prize
Aught human thing beneath Heaven's mighty dome
Beyond this child: so when sad hours were come,
And baffled hope like ice still clung to me,
Since kin were cold, and friends had now become
Heartless and false, I turned from all, to be,
Cythna, the only source of tears and smiles to thee.

22

What wert thou then? A child most infantine,
Yet wandering far beyond that innocent age
In all but its sweet looks and mien divine;
Even then, methought, with the world's tyrant rage
A patient warfare thy young heart did wage,
When those soft eyes of scarcely conscious thought,
Some tale, or thine own fancies would engage
To overflow with tears, or converse fraught
With passion, o'er their depths its fleeting light had wrought.

23

She moved upon this earth a shape of brightness,
A power, that from its objects scarcely drew
One impulse of her being—in her lightness
Most like some radiant cloud of morning dew,
Which wanders through the waste air's pathless blue,
To nourish some far desert: she did seem
Beside me, gathering beauty as she grew,
Like the bright shade of some immortal dream
Which walks, when tempest sleeps, the wave of life's dark stream.

24

As mine own shadow was this child to me,
A second self, far dearer and more fair;
Which clothed in undissolving radiancy,
All those steep paths which languor and despair
Of human things, had made so dark and bare,
But which I trod alone—nor, till bereft
Of friends, and overcome by lonely care,
Knew I what solace for that loss was left,
Though by a bitter wound my trusting heart was cleft.

25

Once she was dear, now she was all I had
To love in human life—this sister sweet,°
This child of twelve years old—so she was made°
My sole associate, and her willing feet
Wandered with mine where earth and ocean meet,
Beyond the aerial mountains whose vast cells°
The unreposing billows ever beat,
Through forests wide and old, and lawny dells,
Where boughs of incense droop over the emerald wells.

26

And warm and light I felt her clasping hand
When twined in mine: she followed where I went,
Through the lone paths of our immortal land.
It had no waste, but some memorial lent
Which strung me to my toil—some monument°
Vital with mind: then, Cythna by my side,
Until the bright and beaming day were spent,
Would rest, with looks entreating to abide,
Too earnest and too sweet ever to be denied.

27

And soon I could not have refused her—thus
Forever, day and night, we two were ne'er
Parted, but when brief sleep divided us:
And when the pauses of the lulling air°
Of noon beside the sea, had made a lair
For her soothed senses, in my arms she slept,
And I kept watch over her slumbers there,
While, as the shifting visions o'er her swept,
Amid her innocent rest by turns she smiled and wept.

28

And, in the murmur of her dreams was heard
Sometimes the name of Laon: suddenly
She would arise, and like the secret bird°
Whom sunset wakens, fill the shore and sky
With her sweet accents—a wild melody!
Hymns which my soul had woven to Freedom, strong

The source of passion whence they rose, to be;°
Triumphant strains, which, like a spirit's tongue,
To the enchanted waves that child of glory sung,

29

Her white arms lifted through the shadowy stream
Of her loose hair—oh, excellently great
Seemed to me then my purpose, the vast theme
Of those impassioned songs, when Cythna sate
Amid the calm which rapture doth create
After its tumult, her heart vibrating,
Her spirit o'er the ocean's floating state
From her deep eyes far wandering, on the wing
Of visions that were mine, beyond its utmost spring.

30

For, before Cythna loved it, had my song
Peopled with thoughts the boundless universe,
A mighty congregation, which were strong
Where'er they trod the darkness to disperse
The cloud of that unutterable curse
Which clings upon mankind:—all things became
Slaves to my holy and heroic verse,
Earth, sea and sky, the planets, life and fame
And fate, or whate'er else binds the world's wondrous frame.

31

And this beloved child thus felt the sway
Of my conceptions, gathering like a cloud
The very wind on which it rolls away:
Hers too were all my thoughts, ere yet endowed
With music and with light, their fountains flowed
In poesy; and her still and earnest face,
Pallid with feelings which intensely glowed
Within, was turned on mine with speechless grace,
Watching the hopes which there her heart had learned to trace.°

32

In me, communion with this purest being
Kindled intenser zeal, and made me wise

In knowledge, which in hers mine own mind seeing,
Left in the human world few mysteries:
How without fear of evil or disguise
Was Cythna!—what a spirit strong and mild,
Which death, or pain or peril could despise,
Yet melt in tenderness! what genius wild
Yet mighty, was enclosed within one simple child!

33

New lore was this—old age with its grey hair,
And wrinkled legends of unworthy things,
And icy sneers, is nought: it cannot dare
To burst the chains which life for ever flings
On the entangled soul's aspiring wings,
So is it cold and cruel, and is made
The careless slave of that dark power which brings
Evil, like blight on man, who still betrayed,
Laughs o'er the grave in which his living hopes are laid.

34

Nor are the strong and the severe to keep
The empire of the world: thus Cythna taught
Even in the visions of her eloquent sleep,
Unconscious of the power through which she wrought
The woof of such intelligible thought,
As from the tranquil strength which cradled lay
In her smile-peopled rest, my spirit sought
Why the deceiver and the slave has sway
O'er heralds so divine of truth's arising day.

35

Within that fairest form, the female mind
Untainted by the poison clouds which rest
On the dark world, a sacred home did find:
But else, from the wide earth's maternal breast,
Victorious Evil, which had dispossessed
All native power, had those fair children torn,
And made them slaves to soothe his vile unrest,
And minister to lust its joys forlorn,
Till they had learned to breathe the atmosphere of scorn.

36

This misery was but coldly felt, till she°
Became my only friend, who had indued
My purpose with a wider sympathy;
Thus, Cythna mourned with me the servitude
In which the half of humankind were mewed,°
Victims of lust and hate, the slaves of slaves;
She mourned that grace and power were thrown as food
To the hyena lust, who, among graves,
Over his loathed meal, laughing in agony, raves.

37

And I, still gazing on that glorious child,
Even as these thoughts flushed o'er her.—'Cythna sweet,°
Well with the world art thou unreconciled;
Never will peace and human nature meet
Till free and equal man and woman greet
Domestic peace; and ere this power can make
In human hearts its calm and holy seat,
This slavery must be broken'—as I spake,
From Cythna's eyes a light of exultation brake.

38

She replied earnestly:—'It shall be mine,
This task, mine, Laon!—thou hast much to gain;
Nor wilt thou at poor Cythna's pride repine,
If she should lead a happy female train
To meet thee over the rejoicing plain,
When myriads at thy call shall throng around
The Golden City'—Then the child did strain°
My arm upon her tremulous heart, and wound
Her own about my neck, till some reply she found.

39

I smiled, and spake not—'wherefore dost thou smile
At what I say? Laon, I am not weak,
And though my cheek might become pale the while,
With thee, if thou desirest, will I seek
Through their array of banded slaves to wreak
Ruin upon the tyrants. I had thought

It was more hard to turn my unpractised cheek
To scorn and shame, and this beloved spot
And thee, O dearest friend, to leave and murmur not.

40

'Whence came I what I am? thou, Laon, knowest
How a young child should thus undaunted be;
Methinks, it is a power which thou bestowest,
Through which I seek, by most resembling thee,
So to become most good, and great and free,
Yet far beyond this Ocean's utmost roar
In towers and huts are many like to me,
Who, could they see thine eyes, or feel such lore
As I have learnt from them, like me would fear no more.

41

'Think'st thou that I shall speak unskilfully,
And none will heed me? I remember now,
How once, a slave in tortures doomed to die,
Was saved, because in accents sweet and low
He sung a song his Judge loved long ago,
As he was led to death.—All shall relent
Who hear me—tears as mine have flowed, shall flow,
Hearts beat as mine now beats, with such intent
As renovates the world; a will omnipotent!

42

'Yes, I will tread Pride's golden palaces,
Through Penury's roofless huts and squalid cells
Will I descend, where'er in abjectness
Woman with some vile slave her tyrant dwells,
There with the music of thine own sweet spells
Will disenchant the captives, and will pour
For the despairing, from the crystal wells
Of thy deep spirit, reason's mighty lore,
And power shall then abound, and hope arise once more.

43

'Can man be free if woman be a slave?
Chain one who lives, and breathes this boundless air

To the corruption of a closèd grave!
Can they whose mates are beasts, condemned to bear
Scorn, heavier far than toil or anguish, dare
To trample their oppressors? in their home
Among their babes, thou knowest a curse would wear
The shape of woman—hoary crime would come°
Behind, and fraud rebuild religion's tottering dome.

44

'I am a child:—I would not yet depart.
When I go forth alone, bearing the lamp
Aloft which thou hast kindled in my heart,
Millions of slaves from many a dungeon damp
Shall leap in joy, as the benumbing cramp
Of ages leaves their limbs—no ill may harm
Thy Cythna ever—truth her radiant stamp
Has fixed, as an invulnerable charm
Upon her children's brow, dark falsehood to disarm.

45

'Wait yet awhile for the appointed day—
Thou wilt depart, and I with tears shall stand
Watching thy dim sail skirt the ocean grey;
Amid the dwellers of this lonely land
I shall remain alone—and thy command
Shall then dissolve the world's unquiet trance,
And, multitudinous as the desert sand
Borne on the storm, its millions shall advance,
Thronging round thee, the light of their deliverance.

46

'Then, like the forests of some pathless mountain,
Which from remotest glens two warring winds
Involve in fire, which not the loosened fountain
Of broadest floods might quench, shall all the kinds
Of evil, catch from our uniting minds
The spark which must consume them;—Cythna then
Will have cast off the impotence that binds
Her childhood now, and through the paths of men
Will pass, as the charmèd bird that haunts the serpent's den.

47

'We part!—O Laon, I must dare nor tremble°
To meet those looks no more!—Oh, heavy stroke,
Sweet brother of my soul! can I dissemble
The agony of this thought?'—As thus she spoke
The gathered sobs her quivering accents broke,
And in my arms she hid her beating breast.
I remained still for tears—sudden she woke
As one awakes from sleep, and wildly pressed
My bosom, her whole frame impetuously possessed.

48

'We part to meet again—but yon blue waste,
Yon desert wide and deep holds no recess,
Within whose happy silence, thus embraced
We might survive all ills in one caress:
Nor doth the grave—I fear 'tis passionless—
Nor yon cold vacant Heaven:—we meet again
Within the minds of men, whose lips shall bless
Our memory, and whose hopes its light retain
When these dissevered bones are trodden in the plain.'

49

I could not speak, though she had ceased, for now
The fountains of her feeling, swift and deep,
Seemed to suspend the tumult of their flow;
So we arose, and by the starlight steep
Went homeward—neither did we speak nor weep,
But pale, were calm with passion—thus subdued
Like evening shades that o'er the mountains creep,
We moved towards our home; where, in this mood,
Each from the other sought refuge in solitude.

From *Canto Sixth*

28

The autumnal winds, as if spellbound, had made
A natural couch of leaves in that recess°
Which seasons none disturbed, but in the shade

Of flowering parasites, did spring love to dress°
With their sweet blooms the wintry loneliness
Of those dead leaves, shedding their stars, whene'er
The wandering wind her nurslings might caress;
Whose intertwining fingers ever there,°
Made music wild and soft that filled the listening air.

29

We know not where we go, or what sweet dream
May pilot us through caverns strange and fair
Of far and pathless passion, while the stream
Of life, our bark doth on its whirlpools bear,
Spreading swift wings as sails to the dim air;
Nor should we seek to know, so the devotion
Of love and gentle thoughts be heard still there
Louder and louder from the utmost Ocean
Of universal life, attuning its commotion.

30

To the pure all things are pure! Oblivion wrapped°
Our spirits, and the fearful overthrow
Of public hope was from our being snapped,
Though linkèd years had bound it there; for now
A power, a thirst, a knowledge, which below
All thoughts, like light beyond the atmosphere,
Clothing its clouds with grace, doth ever flow,
Came on us, as we sate in silence there,
Beneath the golden stars of the clear azure air.

31

In silence which doth follow talk that causes
The baffled heart to speak with sighs and tears,
When wildering passion swalloweth up the pauses
Of inexpressive speech:—the youthful years
Which we together passed, their hopes and fears,
The common blood which ran within our frames,°
That likeness of the features which endears
The thoughts expressed by them, our very names,°
And all the wingèd hours which speechless memory claims,

32

Had found a voice:—and ere that voice did pass,
The night grew damp and dim, and through a rent
Of the ruin where we sate, from the morass,
A wandering Meteor by some wild wind sent,°
Hung high in the green dome, to which it lent
A faint and pallid lustre; while the song
Of blasts, in which its blue hair quivering bent,°
Strewed strangest sounds the moving leaves among;
A wondrous light, the sound as of a spirit's tongue.

33

The Meteor showed the leaves on which we sate,
And Cythna's glowing arms, and the thick ties°
Of her soft hair which bent with gathered weight
My neck near hers, her dark and deepening eyes,
Which, as twin phantoms of one star that lies
O'er a dim well, move, though the star reposes,
Swam in our mute and liquid ecstacies,
Her marble brow, and eager lips, like roses,
With their own fragrance pale, which spring but half uncloses.

34

The Meteor to its far morass returned:
The beating of our veins one interval
Made still; and then I felt the blood that burned°
Within her frame, mingle with mine, and fall
Around my heart like fire; and over all
A mist was spread, the sickness of a deep
And speechless swoon of joy, as might befall
Two disunited spirits when they leap
In union from this earth's obscure and fading sleep.

35

Was it one moment that confounded thus
All thought, all sense, all feeling, into one
Unutterable power, which shielded us
Even from our own cold looks, when we had gone
Into a wide and wild oblivion

Of tumult and of tenderness? or now
Had ages, such as make the moon and sun,
The seasons, and mankind their changes know,
Left fear and time unfelt by us alone below?°

36

I know not. What are kisses whose fire clasps
The failing heart in languishment, or limb
Twined within limb? or the quick dying gasps
Of the life meeting, when the faint eyes swim
Through tears of a wide mist boundless and dim,
In one caress? What is the strong control
Which leads the heart that dizzy steep to climb,
Where far over the world those vapours roll,
Which blend two restless frames in one reposing soul?

37

It is the shadow which doth float unseen,°
But not unfelt, o'er blind mortality,
Whose divine darkness fled not from that green
And lone recess, where lapped in peace did lie
Our linkèd frames; till, from the changing sky,
That night and still another day had fled;
And then I saw and felt. The moon was high,
And clouds, as of a coming storm, were spread
Under its orb,—loud winds were gathering overhead.

From *Canto Seventh*

30

'We live in our own world, and mine was made°
From glorious fantasies of hope departed:
Aye we are darkened with their floating shade,°
Or cast a lustre on them—time imparted
Such power to me, I became fearless-hearted,°
My eye and voice grew firm, calm was my mind,
And piercing, like the morn, now it has darted
Its lustre on all hidden things, behind
Yon dim and fading clouds which load the weary wind.

31

'My mind became the book through which I grew
Wise in all human wisdom, and its cave,
Which like a mine I rifled through and through,
To me the keeping of its secrets gave—
One mind, the type of all, the moveless wave°
Whose calm reflects all moving things that are,
Necessity, and love, and life, the grave,
And sympathy, fountains of hope and fear;
Justice, and truth, and time, and the world's natural sphere.

32

'And on the sand would I make signs to range
These woofs, as they were woven, of my thought;
Clear, elemental shapes, whose smallest change
A subtler language within language wrought:
The key of truths which once were dimly taught
In old Crotona;—and sweet melodies°
Of love, in that lorn solitude I caught
From mine own voice in dream, when thy dear eyes
Shone through my sleep, and did that utterance harmonize.

33

'Thy songs were winds whereon I fled at will,
As in a wingèd chariot, o'er the plain
Of crystal youth; and thou wert there to fill
My heart with joy, and there we sate again
On the grey margin of the glimmering main,
Happy as then but wiser far, for we
Smiled on the flowery grave in which were lain
Fear, Faith, and Slavery; and mankind was free,
Equal, and pure and wise, in wisdom's prophecy.

34

'For to my will my fancies were as slaves
To do their sweet and subtle ministries;
And oft from that bright fountain's shadowy waves
They would make human throngs gather and rise
To combat with my overflowing eyes,
And voice made deep with passion—thus I grew

Familiar with the shock and the surprise
And war of earthly minds, from which I drew
The power which has been mine to frame their thoughts anew.

35

'And thus my prison was the populous earth—
Where I saw—even as misery dreams of morn
Before the east has given its glory birth—
Religion's pomp made desolate by the scorn
Of Wisdom's faintest smile, and thrones uptorn,
And dwellings of mild people interspersed
With undivided fields of ripening corn,
And love made free,—a hope which we have nursed
Even with our blood and tears,—until its glory burst.

36

'All is not lost! there is some recompense
For hope whose fountain can be thus profound,
Even throned Evil's splendid impotence,°
Girt by its hell of power, the secret sound
Of hymns to truth and freedom—the dread bound
Of life and death passed fearlessly and well,
Dungeons wherein the high resolve is found,
Racks which degraded woman's greatness tell,
And what may else be good and irresistible.

37

'Such are the thoughts which, like the fires that flare
In storm-encompassed isles, we cherish yet
In this dark ruin—such were mine even there;°
As in its sleep some odorous violet,
While yet its leaves with nightly dews are wet,
Breathes in prophetic dreams of day's uprise,
Or, as ere Scythian frost in fear has met°
Spring's messengers descending from the skies,
The buds foreknow their life—this hope must ever rise.

38

'So years had passed, when sudden earthquake rent
The depth of ocean, and the cavern cracked

With sound, as if the world's wide continent
Had fallen in universal ruin wracked;
And through the cleft streamed in one cataract
The stifling waters:—when I woke, the flood
Whose banded waves that crystal cave had sacked
Was ebbing round me, and my bright abode
Before me yawned—a chasm desert, and bare, and broad.

39

'Above me was the sky, beneath the sea:
I stood upon a point of shattered stone,
And heard loose rocks rushing tumultuously
With splash and shock into the deep—anon
All ceased, and there was silence wide and lone.
I felt that I was free! the Ocean-spray
Quivered beneath my feet, the broad Heaven shone
Around, and in my hair the winds did play
Lingering as they pursued their unimpeded way.'

From *Canto Eighth*

4

'"What dream ye? Your own hands have built a home,°
Even for yourselves on a beloved shore:
For some, fond eyes are pining till they come,
How they will greet him when his toils are o'er,
And laughing babes rush from the well-known door!
Is this your care? ye toil for your own good—
Ye feel and think—has some immortal power
Such purposes? or in a human mood,
Dream ye that God thus builds for man in solitude?°

5

'"What then is God? ye mock yourselves, and give
A human heart to what ye cannot know:
As if the cause of life could think and live!
'Twere as if man's own works should feel, and show
The hopes, and fears, and thoughts from which they flow,
And he be like to them. Lo! Plague is free

To waste, Blight, Poison, Earthquake, Hail, and Snow,
Disease, and Want, and worse Necessity
Of hate and ill, and Pride, and Fear, and Tyranny.

6

'"What then is God? Some moon-struck sophist stood
Watching the shade from his own soul upthrown
Fill Heaven and darken Earth, and in such mood
The Form he saw and worshipped was his own,
His likeness in the world's vast mirror shown;
And 'twere an innocent dream, but that a faith
Nursed by fear's dew of poison, grows thereon,
And that men say, God has appointed Death°
On all who scorn his will, to wreak immortal wrath.

7

'"Men say they have seen God, and heard from God,
Or known from others who have known such things,
And that his will is all our law, a rod°
To scourge us into slaves—that Priests and Kings,
Custom, domestic sway, aye, all that brings
Man's freeborn soul beneath the oppressor's heel,
Are his strong ministers, and that the stings
Of death will make the wise his vengeance feel,
Though truth and virtue arm their hearts with tenfold steel.

8

'"And it is said, that God will punish wrong;°
Yes, add despair to crime, and pain to pain!
And his red hell's undying snakes among,°
Will bind the wretch on whom he fixed a stain,
Which, like a plague, a burden, and a bane,
Clung to him while he lived;—for, love and hate,
Virtue and vice, they say, are difference vain—
The will of strength is right—this human state
Tyrants, that they may rule, with lies thus desolate.

9

'"Alas, what strength? opinion is more frail
Than yon dim cloud now fading on the moon

Even while we gaze, though it awhile avail
To hide the orb of truth—and every throne
Of Earth or Heaven, though shadow, rests thereon,°
One shape of many names:—for this ye plough
The barren waves of ocean, hence each one
Is slave or tyrant; all betray and bow,
Command, or kill, or fear, or wreak, or suffer woe.

10

'"Its names are each a sign which maketh holy
All power—aye, the ghost, the dream, the shade
Of power,—lust, falsehood, hate, and pride, and folly;
The pattern whence all fraud and wrong is made,
A law to which mankind has been betrayed;
And human love is as the name well known
Of a dear mother, whom the murderer laid
In bloody grave, and into darkness thrown,
Gathered her wildered babes around him as his own.

11

'"O love! who to the hearts of wandering men
Art as the calm to Ocean's weary waves!
Justice, or truth, or joy! those only can
From slavery and religion's labyrinth caves
Guide us, as one clear star the seaman saves,—
To give to all an equal share of good,
To track the steps of freedom though through graves
She pass, to suffer all in patient mood,
To weep for crime, though stained with thy friend's dearest blood°

12

'"To feel the peace of self-contentment's lot,
To own all sympathies, and outrage none,
And in the inmost bowers of sense and thought,
Until life's sunny day is quite gone down,
To sit and smile with Joy, or, not alone,
To kiss salt tears from the worn cheek of Woe;
To live, as if to love and live were one,—
This is not faith or law, nor those who bow
To thrones on Heaven or Earth, such destiny may know.

13

'"But children near their parents tremble now,
Because they must obey—one rules another,
For it is said God rules both high and low,
And man is made the captive of his brother,°
And Hate is throned on high with Fear her mother,
Above the Highest—and those fountain-cells,
Whence love yet flowed when faith had choked all other,
Are darkened—Woman, as the bond-slave, dwells
Of man, a slave; and life is poisoned in its wells.

14

'"Man seeks for gold in mines, that he may weave
A lasting chain for his own slavery;—
In fear and restless care that he may live
He toils for others, who must ever be
The joyless thralls of like captivity;
He murders, for his chiefs delight in ruin;
He builds the altar, that its idol's fee
May be his very blood; he is pursuing
O, blind and willing wretch! his own obscure undoing.

15

'"Woman!—she is his slave, she has become
A thing I weep to speak—the child of scorn,
The outcast of a desolated home.
Falsehood, and fear, and toil, like waves have worn
Channels upon her cheek, which smiles adorn,
As calm decks the false Ocean:—well ye know
What Woman is, for none of Woman born,
Can choose but drain the bitter dregs of woe,
Which ever from the oppressed to the oppressors flow.°

16

'"This need not be; ye might arise, and will
That gold should lose its power, and thrones their glory;
That love, which none may bind, be free to fill
The world, like light; and evil faith, grown hoary
With crime, be quenched and die.—Yon promontory
Even now eclipses the descending moon!—

Dungeons and palaces are transitory—
High temples fade like vapour—Man alone
Remains, whose will has power when all beside is gone.

17

'"Let all be free and equal!—from your hearts
I feel an echo; through my inmost frame
Like sweetest sound, seeking its mate, it darts—
Whence come ye, friends? alas, I cannot name
All that I read of sorrow, toil, and shame,
On your worn faces; as in legends old
Which make immortal the disastrous fame
Of conquerors and impostors false and bold,
The discord of your hearts, I in your looks behold.

18

'"Whence come ye, friends? from pouring human blood
Forth on the earth? or bring ye steel and gold,
That Kings may dupe and slay the multitude?
Or from the famished poor, pale, weak, and cold,
Bear ye the earnings of their toil? unfold!
Speak! are your hands in slaughter's sanguine hue
Stained freshly? have your hearts in guile grown old?
Know yourselves thus! ye shall be pure as dew,
And I will be a friend and sister unto you.

19

'"Disguise it not—we have one human heart—°
All mortal thoughts confess a common home:
Blush not for what may to thyself impart
Stains of inevitable crime: the doom
Is this, which has, or may, or must become
Thine, and all humankind's. Ye are the spoil
Which Time thus marks for the devouring tomb,
Thou and thy thoughts and they, and all the toil°
Wherewith ye twine the rings of life's perpetual coil.

20

'"Disguise it not—ye blush for what ye hate,
And Enmity is sister unto Shame;

Look on your mind—it is the book of fate—
Ah! it is dark with many a blazoned name
Of misery—all are mirrors of the same;
But the dark fiend who with his iron pen
Dipped in scorn's fiery poison makes his fame
Enduring there, would o'er the heads of men
Pass harmless, if they scorned to make their hearts his den.

21

'"Yes, it is Hate, that shapeless fiendly thing
Of many names, all evil, some divine,
Whom self-contempt arms with a mortal sting;
Which, when the heart its snaky folds entwine
Is wasted quite, and when it doth repine
To gorge such bitter prey, on all beside
It turns with ninefold rage, as with its twine
When Amphisbaena some fair bird has tied,°
Soon o'er the putrid mass he threats on every side.

22

'"Reproach not thine own soul, but know thyself,
Nor hate another's crime, nor loathe thine own.
It is the dark idolatry of self,
Which, when our thoughts and actions once are gone,
Demands that man should weep, and bleed, and groan;
O vacant expiation! be at rest.—
The past is Death's, the future is thine own;
And love and joy can make the foulest breast
A paradise of flowers, where peace might build her nest."'

From *Canto Ninth*

21

'The blasts of autumn drive the wingèd seeds°
Over the earth,—next come the snows, and rain,
And frosts, and storms, which dreary winter leads
Out of his Scythian cave, a savage train;
Behold! Spring sweeps over the world again,
Shedding soft dews from her etherial wings;

Flowers on the mountains, fruits over the plain,
And music on the waves and woods she flings,
And love on all that lives, and calm on lifeless things.

22

'O Spring, of hope, and love, and youth, and gladness
Wind-wingèd emblem ! brightest, best and fairest!
Whence comest thou, when, with dark winter's sadness
The tears that fade in sunny smiles thou sharest?
Sister of joy, thou art the child who wearest
Thy mother's dying smile, tender and sweet;
Thy mother Autumn, for whose grave thou bearest
Fresh flowers, and beams like flowers, with gentle feet,
Disturbing not the leaves which are her winding-sheet.

23

'Virtue, and Hope, and Love, like light and Heaven,
Surround the world.—We are their chosen slaves.
Has not the whirlwind of our spirit driven
Truth's deathless germs to thought's remotest caves?°
Lo, Winter comes!—the grief of many graves,
The frost of death, the tempest of the sword,
The flood of tyranny, whose sanguine waves°
Stagnate like ice at Faith, the enchanter's word,
And bind all human hearts in its repose abhorred.

24

'The seeds are sleeping in the soil: meanwhile
The tyrant peoples dungeons with his prey,
Pale victims on the guarded scaffold smile
Because they cannot speak; and, day by day,
The moon of wasting Science wanes away
Among her stars, and in that darkness vast
The sons of earth to their foul idols pray,
And grey Priests triumph, and like blight or blast
A shade of selfish care o'er human looks is cast.

25

'This is the winter of the world;—and here
We die, even as the winds of Autumn fade,

Expiring in the frore and foggy air.—
Behold! Spring comes, though we must pass, who made
The promise of its birth,—even as the shade
Which from our death, as from a mountain, flings
The future, a broad sunrise; thus arrayed°
As with the plumes of overshadowing wings,
From its dark gulf of chains, Earth like an eagle springs.

26

'O dearest love! we shall be dead and cold
Before this morn may on the world arise;
Wouldst thou the glory of its dawn behold?
Alas! gaze not on me, but turn thine eyes
On thine own heart—it is a paradise°
Which everlasting spring has made its own,
And while drear Winter fills the naked skies,
Sweet streams of sunny thought, and flowers fresh blown,
Are there, and weave their sounds and odours into one.

27

'In their own hearts the earnest of the hope
Which made them great, the good will ever find;
And though some envious shade may interlope
Between the effect and it, One comes behind,
Who aye the future to the past will bind—
Necessity, whose sightless strength forever
Evil with evil, good with good must wind
In bands of union, which no power may sever:
They must bring forth their kind, and be divided never!°

28

'The good and mighty of departed ages
Are in their graves, the innocent and free,
Heroes, and Poets, and prevailing Sages,°
Who leave the vesture of their majesty
To adorn and clothe this naked world;—and we
Are like to them—such perish, but they leave
All hope, or love, or truth, or liberty,
Whose forms their mighty spirits could conceive
To be a rule and law to ages that survive.

29

'So be the turf heaped over our remains
Even in our happy youth, and that strange lot,
Whate'er it be, when in these mingling veins
The blood is still, be ours; let sense and thought
Pass from our being, or be numbered not
Among the things that are; let those who come
Behind, for whom our steadfast will has bought
A calm inheritance, a glorious doom,
Insult with careless tread our undivided tomb.

30

'Our many thoughts and deeds, our life and love,
Our happiness, and all that we have been,
Immortally must live, and burn and move,
When we shall be no more;—the world has seen
A type of peace; and as some most serene
And lovely spot to a poor maniac's eye,
After long years, some sweet and moving scene
Of youthful hope returning suddenly,
Quells his long madness—thus man shall remember thee.

31

'And Calumny meanwhile shall feed on us,
As worms devour the dead, and near the throne
And at the altar, most accepted thus
Shall sneers and curses be;—what we have done
None shall dare vouch, though it be truly known;
That record shall remain, when they must pass
Who built their pride on its oblivion;
And fame, in human hope which sculptured was,
Survive the perished scrolls of unenduring brass.

32

'The while we two, beloved, must depart,
And Sense and Reason, those enchanters fair,
Whose wand of power is hope, would bid the heart
That gazed beyond the wormy grave despair:
These eyes, these lips, this blood, seems darkly there
To fade in hideous ruin; no calm sleep
Peopling with golden dreams the stagnant air,

Seems our obscure and rotting eyes to steep
In joy;—but senseless death—a ruin dark and deep!

33

'These are blind fancies—reason cannot know
What sense can neither feel, nor thought conceive;
There is delusion in the world—and woe,
And fear, and pain—we know not whence we live,
Or why, or how, or what mute Power may give
Their being to each plant, and star, and beast,
Or even these thoughts:—Come near me! I do weave
A chain I cannot break—I am possessed
With thoughts too swift and strong for one lone human breast.

34

'Yes, yes—thy kiss is sweet, thy lips are warm—
O! willingly, beloved, would these eyes,
Might they no more drink being from thy form,
Even as to sleep whence we again arise,
Close their faint orbs in death: I fear nor prize
Aught that can now betide, unshared by thee—
Yes, Love when wisdom fails makes Cythna wise:
Darkness and death, if death be true, must be
Dearer than life and hope, if unenjoyed with thee.

35

'Alas, our thoughts flow on with stream, whose waters
Return not to their fountain—Earth and Heaven,
The Ocean and the Sun, the clouds their daughters,
Winter, and Spring, and Morn, and Noon, and Even,
All that we are or know, is darkly driven
Towards one gulf—Lo! what a change is come
Since I first spake—but time shall be forgiven,
Though it change all but thee!'—She ceased, night's gloom
Meanwhile had fallen on earth from the sky's sunless dome.

36

Though she had ceased, her countenance uplifted
To Heaven, still spake, with solemn glory bright;
Her dark deep eyes, her lips, whose motions gifted
The air they breathed with love, her locks undight;

'Fair star of life and love,' I cried, 'my soul's delight,
Why lookest thou on the crystalline skies?
O, that my spirit were yon Heaven of night,
Which gazes on thee with its thousand eyes!'°
She turned to me and smiled—that smile was Paradise!

From *Canto Tenth*

17

Day after day, when the year wanes, the frosts°
Strip its green crown of leaves, till all is bare;
So on those strange and congregated hosts
Came Famine, a swift shadow, and the air
Groaned with the burden of a new despair;
Famine, than whom Misrule no deadlier daughter
Feeds from her thousand breasts, though sleeping there
With lidless eyes, lie Faith, and Plague, and Slaughter,
A ghastly brood; conceived of Lethe's sullen water.°

18

There was no food, the corn was trampled down,
The flocks and herds had perished; on the shore
The dead and putrid fish were ever thrown;
The deeps were foodless, and the winds no more
Creaked with the weight of birds, but as before
Those wingèd things sprang forth, were void of shade;
The vines and orchards, Autumn's golden store,
Were burned;—so that the meanest food was weighed
With gold, and Avarice died before the god it made.

19

There was no corn—in the wide market-place
All loathliest things, even human flesh, was sold;
They weighed it in small scales—and many a face
Was fixed in eager horror then: his gold
The miser brought; the tender maid, grown bold
Through hunger, bared her scornèd charms in vain;
The mother brought her eldest born, controlled
By instinct blind as love, but turned again
And bade her infant suck, and died in silent pain.

20

Then fell blue Plague upon the race of man.°
'O, for the sheathèd steel, so late which gave
Oblivion to the dead, when the streets ran
With brothers' blood! O, that the earthquake's grave
Would gape, or Ocean lift its stifling wave!'
Vain cries—throughout the streets, thousands pursued
Each by his fiery torture howl and rave,
Or sit, in frenzy's unimagined mood,
Upon fresh heaps of dead; a ghastly multitude.

21

It was not hunger now, but thirst. Each well
Was choked with rotting corpses, and became
A cauldron of green mist made visible
At sunrise. Thither still the myriads came,
Seeking to quench the agony of the flame,
Which raged like poison through their bursting veins;
Naked they were from torture, without shame,
Spotted with nameless scars and lurid blains,°
Childhood, and youth, and age, writhing in savage pains.

22

It was not thirst but madness! many saw
Their own lean image everywhere, it went
A ghastlier self beside them, till the awe
Of that dread sight to self-destruction sent
Those shrieking victims; some, ere life was spent,
Sought, with a horrid sympathy, to shed
Contagion on the sound; and others rent
Their matted hair, and cried aloud, 'We tread
On fire! Almighty God his hell on earth has spread!'°

23

Sometimes the living by the dead were hid.
Near the great fountain in the public square,
Where corpses made a crumbling pyramid
Under the sun, was heard one stifled prayer
For life, in the hot silence of the air;
And strange 'twas, amid that hideous heap to see

Some shrouded in their long and golden hair,
As if not dead, but slumbering quietly
Like forms which sculptors carve, then love to agony.°

24

Famine had spared the palace of the king:—
He rioted in festival the while,
He and his guards and priests; but Plague did fling
One shadow upon all. Famine can smile°
On him who brings it food and pass, with guile
Of thankful falsehood, like a courtier grey,
The house-dog of the throne; but many a mile
Comes Plague, a wingèd wolf, who loathes alway
The garbage and the scum that strangers make her prey.°

25

So, near the throne, amid the gorgeous feast,
Sheathed in resplendent arms, or loosely dight°
To luxury, ere the mockery yet had ceased
That lingered on his lips, the warrior's might
Was loosened, and a new and ghastlier night
In dreams of frenzy lapped his eyes; he fell
Headlong, or with stiff eyeballs sate upright
Among the guests, or raving mad, did tell
Strange truths; a dying seer of dark oppression's hell.

26

The Princes and the Priests were pale with terror;
That monstrous faith wherewith they ruled mankind,
Fell, like a shaft loosed by the bowman's error,
On their own hearts: they sought and they could find
No refuge—'twas the blind who led the blind!
So, through the desolate streets to the high fane
Of their Almighty God, the armies wind°
In sad procession: each among the train
To his own Idol lifts his supplications vain.

27

'O God!' they cried, 'we know our secret pride
Has scorned thee, and thy worship, and thy name;

Secure in human power we have defied
Thy fearful might; we bend in fear and shame
Before thy presence; with the dust we claim
Kindred; be merciful, O King of Heaven!
Most justly have we suffered for thy fame
Made dim, but be at length our sins forgiven,
Ere to despair and death thy worshippers be driven.

28

'O God Almighty! thou alone hast power!°
Who can resist thy will? who can restrain
Thy wrath, when on the guilty thou dost shower
The shafts of thy revenge, a blistering rain?
Greatest and best, be merciful again!
Have we not stabbed thine enemies, and made
The Earth an altar, and the Heavens a fane,
Where thou wert worshipped with their blood, and laid
Those hearts in dust which would thy searchless works
have weighed?

29

'Well didst thou loosen on this impious City
Thine angels of revenge: recall them now;
Thy worshippers, abased, here kneel for pity,
And bind their souls by an immortal vow:
We swear by thee! and to our oath do thou
Give sanction, from thine hell of fiends and flame,
That we will kill with fire and torments slow,
The last of those who mocked thy holy name,
And scorned the sacred laws thy prophets did proclaim.'

30

Thus they with trembling limbs and pallid lips
Worshipped their own hearts' image, dim and vast,°
Scared by the shade wherewith they would eclipse
The light of other minds;—troubled they passed
From the great Temple;—fiercely still and fast
The arrows of the plague among them fell,
And they on one another gazed aghast,
And through the hosts contention wild befell,
As each of his own God the wondrous works did tell.°

31

And Oromaze, and Christ, and Mahomet,
Moses, and Buddh, Zerdusht, and Brahm, and Foh,°
A tumult of strange names, which never met
Before, as watchwords of a single woe,
Arose; each raging votary 'gan to throw
Aloft his armèd hands, and each did howl
'Our God alone is God!' and slaughter now
Would have gone forth, when from beneath a cowl
A voice came forth, which pierced like ice through every soul.

32

He was a Christian Priest from whom it came,°
A zealous man, who led the legioned west
With words which faith and pride had steeped in flame,
To quell the rebel Atheists; a dire guest
Even to his friends was he, for in his breast
Did hate and guile lie watchful, intertwined,
Twin serpents in one deep and winding nest;
He loathed all faith beside his own, and pined
To wreak his fear of God in vengeance on mankind.

33

But more he loathed and hated the clear light
Of wisdom and free thought, and more did fear,
Lest, kindled once, its beams might pierce the night,
Even where his Idol stood; for, far and near
Did many a heart in Europe leap to hear
That faith and tyranny were trampled down;
Many a pale victim, doomed for truth to share
The murderer's cell, or see, with helpless groan,
The priests his children drag for slaves to serve their own.

34

He dared not kill the infidels with fire
Or steel, in Europe: the slow agonies
Of legal torture mocked his keen desire:
So he made truce with those who did despise
His cradled Idol, and the sacrifice
Of God to God's own wrath,—that Islam's creed°
Might crush for him those deadlier enemies;

For fear of God did in his bosom breed
A jealous hate of man, an unreposing need.

35

'Peace! Peace!' he cried, 'when we are dead, the Day
Of Judgement comes, and all shall surely know
Whose God is God, each fearfully shall pay
The errors of his faith in endless woe!
But there is sent a mortal vengeance now
On earth, because an impious race had spurned
Him whom we all adore,—a subtle foe,
By whom for ye this dread reward was earned,
And thrones, which rest on faith in God, nigh overturned.°

36

'Think ye, because ye weep, and kneel, and pray,
That God will lull the pestilence? it rose
Even from beneath his throne, where, many a day
His mercy soothed it to a dark repose:
It walks upon the earth to judge his foes,
And what are thou and I, that he should deign
To curb his ghastly minister, or close
The gates of death, ere they receive the twain°
Who shook with mortal spells his undefended reign?

37

'Aye, there is famine in the gulf of hell,
Its giant worms of fire for ever yawn,—
Their lurid eyes are on us! those who fell
By the swift shafts of pestilence ere dawn,
Are in their jaws! they hunger for the spawn
Of Satan, their own brethren, who were sent
To make our souls their spoil. See! See! they fawn
Like dogs, and they will sleep with luxury spent,
When those detested hearts their iron fangs have rent!

38

'Our God may then lull Pestilence to sleep:—
Pile high the pyre of expiation now!
A forest's spoil of boughs, and on the heap
Pour venomous gums, which sullenly and slow,

When touched by flame, shall burn, and melt, and flow,
A stream of clinging fire,—and fix on high
A net of iron, and spread forth below
A couch of snakes, and scorpions, and the fry
Of centipedes and worms, earth's hellish progeny!

39

'Let Laon and Laone on that pyre,
Linked tight with burning brass, perish!—then pray
That, with this sacrifice, the withering ire
Of God may be appeased.' He ceased, and they°
A space stood silent, as far, far away
The echoes of his voice among them died;
And he knelt down upon the dust, alway
Muttering the curses of his speechless pride,°
Whilst shame, and fear, and awe, the armies did divide.

From *Canto Twelfth*

25

'When the consuming flames had wrapped ye round,°
The hope which I had cherished went away;
I fell in agony on the senseless ground,
And hid mine eyes in dust, and far astray
My mind was gone, when bright, like dawning day,
The Spectre of the Plague before me flew,
And breathed upon my lips, and seemed to say,
'They wait for thee, beloved;'—then I knew
The death-mark on my breast, and became calm anew.°

26

'It was the calm of love—for I was dying.
I saw the black and half-extinguished pyre
In its own grey and shrunken ashes lying;
The pitchy smoke of the departed fire
Still hung in many a hollow dome and spire
Above the towers like night; beneath whose shade
Awed by the ending of their own desire
The armies stood; a vacancy was made
In expectation's depth, and so they stood dismayed.

27

'The frightful silence of that altered mood,
The tortures of the dying clove alone,
Till one uprose among the multitude,
And said—"The flood of time is rolling on,
We stand upon its brink, whilst *they* are gone
To glide in peace down death's mysterious stream.
Have ye done well? they moulder flesh and bone,
Who might have made this life's envenomed dream
A sweeter draught than ye will ever taste, I deem.

28

'"These perish as the good and great of yore
Have perished, and their murderers will repent,
Yes, vain and barren tears shall flow before
Yon smoke has faded from the firmament
Even for this cause, that ye who must lament
The death of those that made this world so fair,
Cannot recall them now; but then is lent
To man the wisdom of a high despair,
When such can die, and he live on and linger here.

29

'"Ay, ye may fear not now the Pestilence,
From fabled hell as by a charm withdrawn;
All power and faith must pass, since calmly hence
In torment and in fire have Atheists gone;°
And ye must sadly turn away, and mourn
In secret, to his home each one returning,
And to long ages shall this hour be known;
And slowly shall its memory, ever burning,
Fill this dark night of things with an eternal morning.

30

'"For me the world is grown too void and cold,
Since hope pursues immortal destiny
With steps thus slow—therefore shall ye behold
How Atheists and Republicans can die—°
Tell to your children this!" then suddenly
He sheathed a dagger in his heart and fell;
My brain grew dark in death, and yet to me

There came a murmur from the crowd, to tell
Of deep and mighty change which suddenly befell.

31

'Then suddenly I stood, a wingèd Thought,
Before the immortal Senate, and the seat
Of that star-shining spirit, whence is wrought
The strength of its dominion, good and great,
The better Genius of this world's estate.
His realm around one mighty Fane is spread,
Elysian islands bright and fortunate,
Calm dwellings of the free and happy dead,
Where I am sent to lead!' these wingèd words she said,

32

And with the silence of her eloquent smile,
Bade us embark in her divine canoe;
Then at the helm we took our seat, the while
Above her head those plumes of dazzling hue
Into the winds' invisible stream she threw,
Sitting beside the prow: like gossamer,
On the swift breath of morn, the vessel flew
O'er the bright whirlpools of that fountain fair,
Whose shores receded fast, whilst we seemed lingering there;

33

Till down that mighty stream, dark, calm, and fleet,
Between a chasm of cedarn mountains riven,°
Chased by the thronging winds whose viewless feet,
As swift as twinkling beams, had, under Heaven,
From woods and waves wild sounds and odours driven,
The boat fled visibly—three nights and days,
Borne like a cloud through morn, and noon, and even,
We sailed along the winding watery ways
Of the vast stream, a long and labyrinthine maze.

34

A scene of joy and wonder to behold
That river's shapes and shadows changing ever,
Where the broad sunrise filled with deepening gold
Its whirlpools, where all hues did spread and quiver,
And where melodious falls did burst and shiver

Among rocks clad with flowers, the foam and spray
Sparkled like stars upon the sunny river,
Or when the moonlight poured a holier day,
One vast and glittering lake around green islands lay.

35

Morn, noon, and even, that boat of pearl outran
The streams which bore it, like the arrowy cloud
Of tempest, or the speedier thought of man,
Which flieth forth and cannot make abode,
Sometimes through forests, deep like night, we glode,
Between the walls of mighty mountains crowned
With Cyclopean piles, whose turrets proud,°
The homes of the departed, dimly frowned
O'er the bright waves which girt their dark foundations round.

36

Sometimes between the wide and flowering meadows,
Mile after mile we sailed, and 'twas delight
To see far off the sunbeams chase the shadows
Over the grass; sometimes beneath the night
Of wide and vaulted caves, whose roofs were bright
With starry gems, we fled, whilst from their deep
And dark-green chasms, shades beautiful and white,
Amid sweet sounds across our path would sweep,
Like swift and lovely dreams that walk the waves of sleep.

37

And ever as we sailed, our minds were full
Of love and wisdom, which would overflow
In converse wild, and sweet, and wonderful;
And in quick smiles whose light would come and go,
Like music o'er wide waves, and in the flow
Of sudden tears, and in the mute caress—
For a deep shade was cleft, and we did know,
That virtue, though obscured on Earth, not less
Survives all mortal change in lasting loveliness.

38

Three days and nights we sailed, as thought and feeling
Number delightful hours—for through the sky°

The spherèd lamps of day and night, revealing
New changes and new glories, rolled on high,
Sun, Moon, and moonlike lamps, the progeny
Of a diviner Heaven, serene and fair:
On the fourth day, wild as a wind-wrought sea
The stream became, and fast and faster bare
The spirit-wingèd boat, steadily speeding there.

39

Steady and swift, where the waves rolled like mountains
Within the vast ravine, whose rifts did pour
Tumultuous floods from their ten thousand fountains,
The thunder of whose earth-uplifting roar
Made the air sweep in whirlwinds from the shore,
Calm as a shade, the boat of that fair child
Securely fled, that rapid stress before,
Amid the topmost spray, and sunbows wild,°
Wreathed in the silver mist: in joy and pride we smiled.

40

The torrent of that wide and raging river
Is passed and our aerial speed suspended.
We look behind; a golden mist did quiver
When its wild surges with the lake were blended:
Our bark hung there, as on a line suspended°
Between two heavens, that windless waveless lake;
Which four great cataracts from four vales, attended
By mists, aye feed; from rocks and clouds they break,
And of that azure sea a silent refuge make.

41

Motionless resting on the lake awhile,
I saw its marge of snow-bright mountains rear
Their peaks aloft, I saw each radiant isle,
And in the midst, afar, even like a sphere°
Hung in one hollow sky, did there appear
The Temple of the Spirit; on the sound
Which issued thence, drawn nearer and more near,
Like the swift moon this glorious earth around,
The charmèd boat approached, and there its haven found.°

Ozymandias

I met a traveller from an antique land
Who said—'Two vast and trunkless legs of stone
Stand in the desert. Near them, on the sand,
Half sunk, a shattered visage lies, whose frown,
And wrinkled lip, and sneer of cold command,
Tell that its sculptor well those passions read
Which yet survive, stamped on these lifeless things,
The hand that mocked them and the heart that fed;°
And on the pedestal these words appear:
"My name is Ozymandias, King of Kings:
Look on my Works, ye Mighty, and despair!"
Nothing beside remains. Round the decay
Of that colossal Wreck, boundless and bare
The lone and level sands stretch far away.'

Lines Written among the Euganean Hills

October, 1818

Many a green isle needs must be
In the deep wide sea of misery,°
Or the mariner, worn and wan,
Never thus could voyage on
Day and night, and night and day,
Drifting on his dreary way,
With the solid darkness black
Closing round his vessel's track;
Whilst above the sunless sky,
Big with clouds, hangs heavily,
And behind the tempest fleet
Hurries on with lightning feet,
Riving sail, and cord, and plank,
Till the ship has almost drank
Death from the o'er-brimming deep;
And sinks down, down, like that sleep
When the dreamer seems to be
Weltering through eternity;

And the dim low line before
Of a dark and distant shore
Still recedes, as ever still
Longing with divided will,
But no power to seek or shun,
He is ever drifted on
O'er the unreposing wave
To the haven of the grave.
What, if there no friends will greet;
What, if there no heart will meet
His with love's impatient beat;
Wander wheresoe'er he may,
Can he dream before that day
To find refuge from distress
In friendship's smile, in love's caress?
Then 'twill wreak him little woe°
Whether such there be or no:
Senseless is the breast, and cold,
Which relenting love would fold;
Bloodless are the veins and chill
Which the pulse of pain did fill;
Every little living nerve
That from bitter words did swerve
Round the tortured lips and brow,
Are like sapless leaflets now
Frozen upon December's bough.
On the beach of a northern sea
Which tempests shake eternally,
As once the wretch there lay to sleep,
Lies a solitary heap,
One white skull and seven dry bones,
On the margin of the stones,
Where a few grey rushes stand,
Boundaries of the sea and land:
Nor is heard one voice of wail
But the sea-mews, as they sail°
O'er the billows of the gale;
Or the whirlwind up and down
Howling, like a slaughtered town,
When a king in glory rides
Through the pomp of fratricides:

Those unburied bones around
There is many a mournful sound;
There is no lament for him,
Like a sunless vapour dim
Who once clothed with life and thought
What now moves nor murmurs not.°

Aye, many flowering islands lie
In the waters of wide Agony:
To such a one this morn was led,
My bark by soft winds piloted:
'Mid the mountains Euganean
I stood listening to the paean,
With which the legioned rooks did hail
The sun's uprise majestical;
Gathering round with wings all hoar,
Through the dewy mist they soar
Like grey shades, till th' eastern heaven
Bursts, and then, as clouds of even,
Flecked with fire and azure lie
In the unfathomable sky,
So their plumes of purple grain,
Starred with drops of golden rain,
Gleam above the sunlight woods,
As in silent multitudes
On the morning's fitful gale
Through the broken mist they sail,
And the vapours cloven and gleaming
Follow down the dark steep streaming,
Till all is bright, and clear, and still,
Round the solitary hill.

Beneath is spread like a green sea
The waveless plain of Lombardy,
Bounded by the vaporous air,
Islanded by cities fair;
Underneath day's azure eyes
Ocean's nursling, Venice lies,
A peopled labyrinth of walls,
Amphitrite's destined halls,°
Which her hoary sire now paves

With his blue and beaming waves.
Lo! the sun upsprings behind,
Broad, red, radiant, half reclined
On the level quivering line
Of the waters crystalline;
And before that chasm of light,
As within a furnace bright,
Column, tower, and dome, and spire,
Shine like obelisks of fire,
Pointing with inconstant motion
From the altar of dark ocean
To the sapphire-tinted skies;
As the flames of sacrifice
From the marble shrines did rise,
As to pierce the dome of gold
Where Apollo spoke of old.°

Sun-girt City, thou hast been
Ocean's child, and then his queen;
Now is come a darker day,°
And thou soon must be his prey,
If the power that raised thee here
Hallow so thy watery bier.
A less drear ruin then than now,
With thy conquest-branded brow
Stooping to the slave of slaves°
From thy throne, among the waves
Wilt thou be, when the sea-mew
Flies, as once before it flew,
O'er thine isles depopulate,
And all is in its ancient state,
Save where many a palace gate
With green sea-flowers overgrown
Like a rock of ocean's own,
Topples o'er the abandoned sea
As the tides change sullenly.
The fisher on his watery way,
Wandering at the close of day,
Will spread his sail and seize his oar
Till he pass the gloomy shore,
Lest thy dead should, from their sleep

Bursting o'er the starlight deep,
Lead a rapid masque of death
O'er the waters of his path.

Those who alone thy towers behold
Quivering through aerial gold,
As I now behold them here,
Would imagine not they were
Sepulchres, where human forms,
Like pollution-nourished worms
To the corpse of greatness cling,
Murdered, and now mouldering:
But if Freedom should awake
In her omnipotence, and shake
From the Celtic Anarch's hold°
All the keys of dungeons cold,
Where a hundred cities lie
Chained like thee, ingloriously,
Thou and all thy sister band
Might adorn this sunny land,
Twining memories of old time
With new virtues more sublime;
If not, perish thou and they,
Clouds which stain truth's rising day
By her sun consumed away,
Earth can spare ye: while like flowers,
In the waste of years and hours,
From your dust new nations spring
With more kindly blossoming.

Perish—let there only be
Floating o'er thy hearthless sea,
As the garment of the sky
Clothes the world immortally,
One remembrance, more sublime
Than the tattered pall of time,
Which scarce hides thy visage wan;—
That a tempest-cleaving Swan°
Of the songs of Albion,
Driven from his ancestral streams
By the might of evil dreams,°

Found a nest in thee; and Ocean
Welcomed him with such emotion
That its joy grew his, and sprung
From his lips like music flung
O'er a mighty thunder-fit,
Chastening terror:—what though yet°
Poesy's unfailing River,
Which through Albion winds forever,
Lashing with melodious wave
Many a sacred Poet's grave,
Mourn its latest nursling fled?
What though thou with all thy dead
Scarce can for this fame repay
Aught thine own—oh, rather say,
Though thy sins and slaveries foul
Overcloud a sunlike soul?
As the ghost of Homer clings
Round Scamander's wasting springs;°
As divinest Shakespeare's might
Fills Avon and the world with light
Like Omniscient power, which he
Imaged 'mid mortality;
As the love from Petrarch's urn°
Yet amid yon hills doth burn,
A quenchless lamp by which the heart
Sees things unearthly; so thou art,
Mighty Spirit—so shall be
The City that did refuge thee.

Lo, the sun floats up the sky
Like thought-wingèd Liberty,
Till the universal light
Seems to level plain and height;
From the sea a mist has spread,
And the beams of morn lie dead
On the towers of Venice now,
Like its glory long ago.
By the skirts of that grey cloud
Many-domèd Padua proud
Stands, a peopled solitude,
'Mid the harvest-shining plain,

Where the peasant heaps his grain
In the garner of his foe,°
And the milk-white oxen slow
With the purple vintage strain,
Heaped upon the creaking wain,
That the brutal Celt may swill
Drunken sleep with savage will;
And the sickle to the sword
Lies unchanged, though many a lord,
Like a weed whose shade is poison,
Overgrows this region's foison,°
Sheaves of whom are ripe to come
To destruction's harvest home:
Men must reap the things they sow,
Force from force must ever flow,
Or worse; but 'tis a bitter woe
That love or reason cannot change
The despot's rage, the slave's revenge.

Padua, thou within whose walls
Those mute guests at festivals,
Son and Mother, Death and Sin,
Played at dice for Ezzelin,
Till Death cried, 'I win, I win!'
And Sin cursed to lose the wager,
But Death promised, to assuage her,
That he would petition for
Her to be made Vice-Emperor,
When the destined years were o'er,
Over all between the Po
And the eastern Alpine snow,
Under the mighty Austrian.°
Sin smiled so as Sin only can,
And since that time, aye, long before,
Both have ruled from shore to shore,
That incestuous pair, who follow
Tyrants as the sun the swallow,
As Repentance follows Crime,
And as changes follow Time.

In thine halls the lamp of learning,
Padua, now no more is burning;°

Like a meteor, whose wild way°
Is lost over the grave of day,
It gleams betrayed and to betray:
Once remotest nations came
To adore that sacred flame,
When it lit not many a hearth
On this cold and gloomy earth:
Now new fires from antique light
Spring beneath the wide world's might;
But their spark lies dead in thee,
Trampled out by tyranny.
As the Norway woodman quells,
In the depth of piny dells,
One light flame among the brakes,
While the boundless forest shakes,
And its mighty trunks are torn
By the fire thus lowly born:
The spark beneath his feet is dead,
He starts to see the flames it fed
Howling through the darkened sky
With a myriad tongues victoriously,
And sinks down in fear: so thou,°
O tyranny, beholdest now
Light around thee, and thou hearest
The loud flames ascend, and fearest:
Grovel on the earth: aye, hide
In the dust thy purple pride!

Noon descends around me now:
'Tis the noon of autumn's glow,
When a soft and purple mist
Like a vaporous amethyst,
Or an air-dissolvèd star
Mingling light and fragrance, far
From the curved horizon's bound
To the point of heaven's profound,
Fills the overflowing sky;
And the plains that silent lie
Underneath, the leaves unsodden
Where the infant frost has trodden
With his morning-wingèd feet,

Whose bright print is gleaming yet;
And the red and golden vines,
Piercing with their trellised lines
The rough, dark-skirted wilderness;
The dun and bladed grass no less,
Pointing from this hoary tower
In the windless air; the flower
Glimmering at my feet; the line
Of the olive-sandalled Apennine
In the south dimly islanded;
And the Alps, whose snows are spread
High between the clouds and sun;
And of living things each one;
And my spirit which so long
Darkened this swift stream of song,
Interpenetrated lie
By the glory of the sky:
Be it love, light, harmony,
Odour, or the soul of all
Which from heaven like dew doth fall,
Or the mind which feeds this verse
Peopling the lone universe.

Noon descends, and after noon
Autumn's evening meets me soon,
Leading the infantine moon,
And that one star, which to her°
Almost seems to minister
Half the crimson light she brings
From the sunset's radiant springs:
And the soft dreams of the morn
(Which like wingèd winds had borne
To that silent isle, which lies
'Mid remembered agonies,
The frail bark of this lone being)
Pass, to other sufferers fleeing,
And its ancient pilot, Pain,
Sits beside the helm again.

Other flowering isles must be
In the sea of life and agony:

Other spirits float and flee
O'er that gulf: even now, perhaps,
On some rock the wild wave wraps,
With folded wings they waiting sit
For my bark, to pilot it
To some calm and blooming cove,
Where for me, and those I love,
May a windless bower be built,
Far from passion, pain, and guilt,
In a dell 'mid lawny hills,
Which the wild sea-murmur fills,
And soft sunshine, and the sound
Of old forests echoing round,
And the light and smell divine
Of all flowers that breathe and shine:
We may live so happy there,
That the spirits of the air,
Envying us, may even entice
To our healing paradise
The polluting multitude;°
But their rage would be subdued
By that clime divine and calm,
And the winds whose wings rain balm
On the uplifted soul, and leaves
Under which the bright sea heaves;°
While each breathless interval
In their whisperings musical
The inspirèd soul supplies
With its own deep melodies,
And the love which heals all strife
Circling, like the breath of life,
All things in that sweet abode
With its own mild brotherhood:
They, not it, would change; and soon
Every sprite beneath the moon°
Would repent its envy vain,
And the earth grow young again.°

The Two Spirits—An Allegory

First Spirit

O Thou who plumed with strong desire°
Would float above the Earth—beware!
A shadow tracks thy flight of fire—°
        Night is coming.
Bright are the regions of the air
And when winds and beams [   ]°
It were delight to wander there—
        Night is coming!

Second Spirit

The deathless stars are bright above
If I should cross the shade of night.—°
Within my heart is the lamp of love
        And that is day—
And the moon will smile with gentle light
On my golden plumes where'er they move;
The meteors will linger around my flight
        And make night day.

First Spirit

But if the whirlwinds of darkness waken
Eclipse and Lightning and stormy rain—°
See, the bounds of the air are shaken,
        Night is coming.
And swift the clouds of the hurricane°
Yon declining sun have overtaken,
The clash of the hail sweeps o'er the plain—
        Night is coming.

Second Spirit

I see the glare and I hear the sound;
I'll sail on the flood of the tempest dark
With the calm within and light around
        Which makes night day;
And thou, when the gloom is deep and stark,
Look from thy dull earth slumberbound—
My moonlike flight thou then may'st mark
        On high, far away.

Some say there is a precipice
Where one vast pine hangs frozen to ruin
O'er piles of snow and chasms of ice
        Mid Alpine mountains;
And that the languid storm pursuing°
That wingèd shape forever flies
Round those hoar branches, aye renewing
        Its aery fountains.

Some say when the nights are dry and clear
And the death-dews sleep on the morass,
Sweet whispers are heard by the traveller
        Which make night day—
And a shape like his early love doth pass
Upborne by her wild and glittering hair,
And when he awakes on the fragrant grass
        He finds night day.

Stanzas Written in Dejection— December 1818, near Naples

The Sun is warm, the sky is clear,
The waves are dancing fast and bright,
Blue isles and snowy mountains wear
The purple noon's transparent might,
The breath of the moist earth is light
Around its unexpanded buds;
Like many a voice of one delight
The winds, the birds, the Ocean-floods;
The City's voice itself is soft, like Solitude's.

I see the Deep's untrampled floor°
With green and purple seaweeds strown,
I see the waves upon the shore°
Like light dissolved in star-showers, thrown;
I sit upon the sands alone;
The lightning of the noontide Ocean
Is flashing round me, and a tone

Arises from its measured motion,
How sweet! did any heart now share in my emotion.

Alas, I have nor hope nor health,
Nor peace within nor calm around,
Nor that content surpassing wealth
The sage in meditation found,°
And walked with inward glory crowned;
Nor fame nor power nor love nor leisure—
Others I see whom these surround,
Smiling they live and call life pleasure:
To me that cup has been dealt in another measure.°

Yet now despair itself is mild
Even as the winds and waters are;
I could lie down like a tired child
And weep away the life of care
Which I have borne and yet must bear,
Till Death like Sleep might steal on me,
And I might feel in the warm air
My cheek grow cold, and hear the sea
Breathe o'er my dying brain its last monotony.

Some might lament that I were cold,
As I, when this sweet day is gone,
Which my lost heart, too soon grown old,
Insults with this untimely moan—°
They might lament,—for I am one
Whom men love not, and yet regret;
Unlike this Day, which, when the Sun
Shall on its stainless glory set,
Will linger though enjoyed, like joy in Memory yet.

Sonnet ('Lift not the painted veil')

Lift not the painted veil which those who live°
Call Life; though unreal shapes be pictured there,
And it but mimic all we would believe
With colours idly spread,—behind, lurk Fear

And Hope, twin Destinies, who ever weave
Their shadows o'er the chasm, sightless and drear.°

I knew one who had lifted it . . . he sought,
For his lost heart was tender, things to love
But found them not, alas; nor was there aught
The world contains, the which he could approve.
Through the unheeding many he did move,
A splendour among shadows, a bright blot
Upon this gloomy world, a Spirit that strove°
For truth, and like the Preacher, found it not.°

JULIAN AND MADDALO

A CONVERSATION

The meadows with fresh streams, the bees with thyme,
The goats with the green leaves of budding spring,
Are saturated not—nor Love with tears.

Virgil's *Gallus*°

[PREFACE]

Count Maddalo is a Venetian nobleman of ancient family and of great fortune, who, without mixing much in the society of his countrymen, resides chiefly at his magnificent palace in that city. He is a person of the most consummate genius; and capable, if he would direct his energies to such an end, of becoming the redeemer of his degraded country. But it is his weakness to be proud: he derives, from a comparison of his own extraordinary mind with the dwarfish intellects that surround him, an intense apprehension of the nothingness of human life. His passions and his powers are incomparably greater than those of other men, and instead of the latter having been employed in curbing the former, they have mutually lent each other strength. His ambition preys upon itself, for want of objects which it can consider worthy of exertion. I say that Maddalo is proud, because I can find no other word to express the concentered° and impatient feelings which consume him; but it is on his own hopes and affections only that he seems to trample, for in social life no human being can be more gentle, patient, and unassuming than Maddalo. He is cheerful, frank, and witty. His more serious conversation is a sort of intoxication; men are held by it as by a spell. He has travelled much; and there is an inexpressible charm in his relation of his adventures in different countries.°

Julian is an Englishman of good family, passionately attached to those philosophical notions which assert the power of man over his own mind, and the immense improvements of which, by the extinction of certain moral superstitions, human society may be yet susceptible. Without concealing the evil in the world, he is for ever speculating how good may be made superior. He is a complete infidel, and a scoffer at all things reputed holy; and Maddalo takes a wicked pleasure in drawing out his taunts against religion. What Maddalo thinks on these matters is not exactly known. Julian, in spite of his heterodox opinions, is conjectured by his friends to possess some good qualities. How far this is possible, the pious reader will determine. Julian is rather serious.°

Of the Maniac° I can give no information. He seems by his own account to have been disappointed in love. He was evidently a very cultivated and amiable person when in his right senses. His story, told at length, might be like many other stories of the same kind: the unconnected exclamations of his agony will perhaps be found a sufficient comment for the text of every heart.

I rode one evening with Count Maddalo
Upon the bank of land which breaks the flow°
Of Adria towards Venice:—a bare strand°
Of hillocks, heaped from ever-shifting sand,
Matted with thistles and amphibious weeds,
Such as from earth's embrace the salt ooze breeds,
Is this;—an uninhabitable sea-side
Which the lone fisher, when his nets are dried,
Abandons; and no other object breaks
The waste, but one dwarf tree and some few stakes
Broken and unrepaired, and the tide makes
A narrow space of level sand thereon,
Where 'twas our wont to ride while day went down.
This ride was my delight.—I love all waste
And solitary places; where we taste
The pleasure of believing what we see
Is boundless, as we wish our souls to be:°
And such was this wide ocean, and this shore
More barren than its billows;—and yet more
Than all, with a remembered friend I love
To ride as then I rode;—for the winds drove
The living spray along the sunny air
Into our faces; the blue heavens were bare,°
Stripped to their depths by the awakening North,
And from the waves, sound like delight broke forth°
Harmonizing with solitude, and sent
Into our hearts aerial merriment.
So, as we rode, we talked; and the swift thought,
Winging itself with laughter, lingered not
But flew from brain to brain,—such glee was ours—
Charged with light memories of remembered hours,

None slow enough for sadness; till we came
Homeward, which always makes the spirit tame.
This day had been cheerful but cold, and now
The sun was sinking, and the wind also.
Our talk grew somewhat serious, as may be
Talk interrupted with such raillery
As mocks itself, because it cannot scorn
The thoughts it would extinguish:—'twas forlorn
Yet pleasing, such as once, so poets tell,
The devils held within the dales of Hell
Concerning God, freewill and destiny:
Of all that earth has been or yet may be,
All that vain men imagine or believe,
Or hope can paint or suffering may achieve,°
We descanted, and I (for ever still°
Is it not wise to make the best of ill?)
Argued against despondency, but pride
Made my companion take the darker side.
The sense that he was greater than his kind
Had struck, methinks, his eagle spirit blind
By gazing on its own exceeding light.
—Meanwhile the sun paused ere it should alight,
Over the horizon of the mountains;—Oh,
How beautiful is sunset, when the glow
Of Heaven descends upon a land like thee,
Thou Paradise of exiles, Italy!
Thy mountains, seas and vineyards and the towers
Of cities they encircle!—it was ours
To stand on thee, beholding it; and then
Just where we had dismounted, the Count's men
Were waiting for us with the gondola.—
As those who pause on some delightful way
Though bent on pleasant pilgrimage, we stood°
Looking upon the evening and the flood
Which lay between the city and the shore
Paved with the image of the sky . . . the hoar°
And aery Alps towards the North appeared
Through mist, an heaven-sustaining bulwark reared
Between the East and West; and half the sky
Was roofed with clouds of rich emblazonry
Dark purple at the zenith, which still grew

Down the steep West into a wondrous hue
Brighter than burning gold, even to the rent
Where the swift sun yet paused in his descent
Among the many-folded hills: they were
Those famous Euganean hills, which bear
As seen from Lido through the harbour piles
The likeness of a clump of peakèd isles—
And then—as if the Earth and Sea had been
Dissolved into one lake of fire, were seen
Those mountains towering as from waves of flame
Around the vaporous sun, from which there came
The inmost purple spirit of light, and made
Their very peaks transparent. 'Ere it fade,'
Said my companion, 'I will show you soon
A better station'—so, o'er the lagoon
We glided, and from that funereal bark
I leaned, and saw the city, and could mark
How from their many isles in evening's gleam
Its temples and its palaces did seem
Like fabrics of enchantment piled to Heaven.°
I was about to speak, when—'We are even
Now at the point I meant,' said Maddalo,
And bade the gondolieri cease to row.°
'Look, Julian, on the West, and listen well
If you hear not a deep and heavy bell.'
I looked, and saw between us and the sun
A building on an island; such a one
As age to age might add, for uses vile,
A windowless, deformed and dreary pile,
And on the top an open tower, where hung
A bell, which in the radiance swayed and swung.
We could just hear its hoarse and iron tongue.°
The broad sun sunk behind it, and it tolled
In strong and black relief.—'What we behold
Shall be the madhouse and its belfry tower,'°
Said Maddalo, 'and ever at this hour
Those who may cross the water hear that bell
Which calls the maniacs each one from his cell
To vespers.'—'As much skill as need to pray
In thanks or hope for their dark lot have they
To their stern maker,' I replied. 'O ho!

You talk as in years past,' said Maddalo.
''Tis strange men change not. You were ever still
Among Christ's flock a perilous infidel,
A wolf for the meek lambs—if you can't swim
Beware of Providence.' I looked on him,°
But the gay smile had faded in his eye.
'And such,'—he cried, 'is our mortality
And this must be the emblem and the sign
Of what should be eternal and divine!—
And like that black and dreary bell, the soul,
Hung in a heaven-illumined tower, must toll
Our thoughts and our desires to meet below
Round the rent heart and pray—as madmen do
For what? they know not, till the night of death
As sunset that strange vision, severeth
Our memory from itself, and us from all
We sought and yet were baffled!' I recall
The sense of what he said, although I mar
The force of his expressions. The broad star
Of day meanwhile had sunk behind the hill
And the black bell became invisible
And the red tower looked grey, and all between
The churches, ships and palaces were seen
Huddled in gloom;—into the purple sea
The orange hues of heaven sunk silently.
We hardly spoke, and soon the gondola
Conveyed me to my lodgings by the way.

The following morn was rainy, cold and dim.
Ere Maddalo arose, I called on him,
And whilst I waited with his child I played.°
A lovelier toy sweet Nature never made,
A serious, subtle, wild, yet gentle being,
Graceful without design and unforeseeing,
With eyes—oh speak not of her eyes!—which seem
Twin mirrors of Italian Heaven, yet gleam
With such deep meaning, as we never see
But in the human countenance: with me
She was a special favourite. I had nursed
Her fine and feeble limbs when she came first
To this bleak world; and she yet seemed to know

On second sight her ancient playfellow,
Less changed than she was by six months or so;
For after her first shyness was worn out
We sate there, rolling billiard balls about.
When the Count entered—salutations past—
'The words you spoke last night might well have cast
A darkness on my spirit—if man be
The passive thing you say, I should not see
Much harm in the religions and old saws°
(Though I may never own such leaden laws)
Which break a teachless nature to the yoke:°
Mine is another faith'—thus much I spoke,
And noting he replied not, added: 'See
This lovely child, blithe, innocent and free;
She spends a happy time with little care
While we to such sick thoughts subjected are
As came on you last night—it is our will
That thus enchains us to permitted ill—
We might be otherwise—we might be all
We dream of happy, high, majestical.
Where is the love, beauty and truth we seek
But in our mind? and if we were not weak
Should we be less in deed than in desire?'
'Aye, if we were not weak—and we aspire
How vainly to be strong!' said Maddalo;
'You talk Utopia.' 'It remains to know,'
I then rejoined, 'and those who try may find
How strong the chains are which our spirits bind—
Brittle perchance as straw . . . We are assured
Much may be conquered, much may be endured
Of what degrades and crushes us. We know
That we have power over ourselves to do
And suffer—what, we know not till we try;
But something nobler than to live and die—
So taught those kings of old philosophy
Who reigned, before Religion made men blind;°
And those who suffer with their suffering kind
Yet feel their faith, religion.' 'My dear friend,'°
Said Maddalo, 'my judgement will not bend
To your opinion, though I think you might
Make such a system refutation-tight

As far as words go. I knew one like you
Who to this city came some months ago
With whom I argued in this sort, and he
Is now gone mad,—and so he answered me.
Poor fellow! but if you would like to go
We'll visit him, and his wild talk will show
How vain are such aspiring theories.'
'I hope to prove the induction otherwise,
And that a want of that true theory, still
Which seeks a "soul of goodness" in things ill°
Or in himself or others has thus bowed
His being—there are some by nature proud,
Who patient in all else demand but this:
To love and be beloved with gentleness;
And being scorned, what wonder if they die
Some living death? this is not destiny
But man's own wilful ill.' As thus I spoke°
Servants announced the gondola, and we
Through the fast-falling rain and high-wrought sea
Sailed to the island where the madhouse stands.
We disembarked. The clap of tortured hands,
Fierce yells and howlings and lamentings keen,
And laughter where complaint had merrier been,
Moans, shrieks and curses and blaspheming prayers
Accosted us. We climbed the oozy stairs
Into an old courtyard. I heard on high,
Then, fragments of most touching melody
But looking up saw not the singer there—
Through the black bars in the tempestuous air
I saw, like weeds on a wrecked palace growing,
Long tangled locks flung wildly forth, and flowing,
Of those who on a sudden were beguiled
Into strange silence, and looked forth and smiled
Hearing sweet sounds.—Then I: 'Methinks there were
A cure of these with patience and kind care
If music can thus move . . . but what is he
Whom we seek here?' 'Of his sad history
I know but this,' said Maddalo: 'he came
To Venice a dejected man, and fame
Said he was wealthy, or he had been so:
Some thought the loss of fortune wrought him woe;

But he was ever talking in such sort
As you do—far more sadly—he seemed hurt,
Even as a man with his peculiar wrong,
To hear but of the oppression of the strong,
Or those absurd deceits (I think with you
In some respects, you know) which carry through
The excellent impostors of this earth
When they outface detection—he had worth,
Poor fellow! but a humourist in his way'—°
'Alas, what drove him mad?' 'I cannot say;
A lady came with him from France, and when
She left him and returned, he wandered then
About yon lonely isles of desert sand
Till he grew wild—he had no cash or land
Remaining,—the police had brought him here—
Some fancy took him and he would not bear
Removal; so I fitted up for him
Those rooms beside the sea, to please his whim
And sent him busts and books and urns for flowers
Which had adorned his life in happier hours,
And instruments of music—you may guess
A stranger could do little more or less
For one so gentle and unfortunate,
And those are his sweet strains which charm the weight
From madmen's chains, and made this Hell appear
A heaven of sacred silence, hushed to hear.'—
'Nay, this was kind of you—he had no claim
As the world says'—'None—but the very same
Which I on all mankind were I as he
Fallen to such deep reverse;—his melody°
Is interrupted now—we hear the din
Of madmen, shriek on shriek again begin;
Let us now visit him; after this strain
He ever communes with himself again,
And sees nor hears not any.' Having said
These words we called the keeper, and he led
To an apartment opening on the sea.—
There the poor wretch was sitting mournfully
Near a piano, his pale fingers twined
One with the other, and the ooze and wind
Rushed through an open casement, and did sway

His hair, and starred it with the brackish spray;
His head was leaning on a music book,
And he was muttering, and his lean limbs shook.
His lips were pressed against a folded leaf
In hue too beautiful for health, and grief
Smiled in their motions as they lay apart—°
As one who wrought from his own fervid heart
The eloquence of passion, soon he raised
His sad meek face and eyes lustrous and glazed
And spoke—sometimes as one who wrote and thought
His words might move some heart that heeded not
If sent to distant lands: and then as one
Reproaching deeds never to be undone
With wondering self-compassion; then his speech
Was lost in grief, and then his words came each
Unmodulated, cold, expressionless;
But that from one jarred accent you might guess
It was despair made them so uniform:
And all the while the loud and gusty storm
Hissed through the window, and we stood behind
Stealing his accents from the envious wind
Unseen. I yet remember what he said
Distinctly: such impression his words made.

'Month after month,' he cried, 'to bear this load
And as a jade urged by the whip and goad°
To drag life on, which like a heavy chain
Lengthens behind with many a link of pain!—
And not to speak my grief—O not to dare
To give a human voice to my despair
But live and move, and wretched thing! smile on
As if I never went aside to groan
And wear this mask of falsehood even to those
Who are most dear—not for my own repose—
Alas, no scorn or pain or hate could be
So heavy as that falsehood is to me—
But that I cannot bear more altered faces
Than needs must be, more changed and cold embraces,
More misery, disappointment and mistrust
To own me for their father . . . Would the dust
Were covered in upon my body now!

That the life ceased to toil within my brow!
And then these thoughts would at the least be fled;
Let us not fear such pain can vex the dead.

'What Power delights to torture us? I know
That to myself I do not wholly owe
What now I suffer, though in part I may.
Alas, none strewed sweet flowers upon the way
Where wandering heedlessly, I met pale Pain,
My shadow, which will leave me not again—
If I have erred, there was no joy in error,
But pain and insult and unrest and terror;
I have not as some do, bought penitence
With pleasure, and a dark yet sweet offence,
For then,—if love and tenderness and truth
Had overlived hope's momentary youth,
My creed should have redeemed me from repenting,
But loathèd scorn and outrage unrelenting
Met love excited by far other seeming
Until the end was gained . . . as one from dreaming
Of sweetest peace, I woke, and found my state
Such as it is.—
'O Thou, my spirit's mate°
Who, for thou art compassionate and wise,
Wouldst pity me from thy most gentle eyes
If this sad writing thou shouldst ever see—
My secret groans must be unheard by thee,
Thou wouldst weep tears bitter as blood to know
Thy lost friend's incommunicable woe.

'Ye few by whom my nature has been weighed
In friendship, let me not that name degrade
By placing on your hearts the secret load
Which crushes mine to dust. There is one road
To peace and that is truth, which follow ye!
Love sometimes leads astray to misery.
Yet think not though subdued—and I may well°
Say that I am subdued—that the full Hell
Within me would infect the untainted breast
Of sacred nature with its own unrest;
As some perverted beings think to find

In scorn or hate a medicine for the mind
Which scorn or hate have wounded—O how vain!
The dagger heals not but may rend again . . .
Believe that I am ever still the same
In creed as in resolve, and what may tame
My heart, must leave the understanding free
Or all would sink in this keen agony—
Nor dream that I will join the vulgar cry,
Or with my silence sanction tyranny,
Or seek a moment's shelter from my pain
In any madness which the world calls gain,
Ambition or revenge or thoughts as stern
As those which make me what I am, or turn
To avarice or misanthropy or lust . . .
Heap on me soon, O grave, thy welcome dust!
Till then the dungeon may demand its prey,
And poverty and shame may meet and say—
Halting beside me on the public way—
"That love-devoted youth is ours—let's sit
Beside him—he may live some six months yet."
Or the red scaffold, as our country bends,°
May ask some willing victim, or ye friends
May fall under some sorrow which this heart
Or hand may share or vanquish or avert;
I am prepared: in truth with no proud joy
To do or suffer aught, as when a boy
I did devote to justice and to love
My nature, worthless now! . . .
'I must remove
A veil from my pent mind. 'Tis torn aside!
O, pallid as death's dedicated bride,°
Thou mockery which art sitting by my side,
Am I not wan like thee? at the grave's call
I haste, invited to thy wedding-ball
To greet the ghastly paramour, for whom
Thou hast deserted me . . . and made the tomb
Thy bridal bed . . . But I beside your feet
Will lie and watch ye from my winding sheet—
Thus . . . wide awake, though dead . . . yet stay, O stay!
Go not so soon—I know not what I say—
Hear but my reasons . . . I am mad, I fear,

My fancy is o'erwrought . . . thou art not here . . .
Pale art thou, 'tis most true . . . but thou art gone,
Thy work is finished . . . I am left alone!—°

* * * * * * *

'Nay, was it I who wooed thee to this breast
Which, like a serpent, thou envenomest
As in repayment of the warmth it lent?
Didst thou not seek me for thine own content?
Did not thy love awaken mine? I thought
That thou wert she who said, "You kiss me not
Ever, I fear you cease to love me now"—
In truth I loved even to my overthrow°
Her, who would fain forget these words: but they
Cling to her mind, and cannot pass away.

* * * * * * *

'You say that I am proud—that when I speak
My lip is tortured with the wrongs which break
The spirit it expresses . . . Never one
Humbled himself before, as I have done!
Even the instinctive worm on which we tread
Turns, though it wound not—then with prostrate head
Sinks in the dust and writhes like me—and dies?
No: wears a living death of agonies!
As the slow shadows of the pointed grass
Mark the eternal periods, his pangs pass
Slow, ever-moving,—making moments be°
As mine seem—each an immortality!

* * * * * * *

'That you had never seen me—never heard
My voice, and more than all had ne'er endured
The deep pollution of my loathed embrace—
That your eyes ne'er had lied love in my face—
That, like some maniac monk, I had torn out
The nerves of manhood by their bleeding root
With mine own quivering fingers, so that ne'er
Our hearts had for a moment mingled there
To disunite in horror—these were not
With thee, like some suppressed and hideous thought
Which flits athwart our musings, but can find

No rest within a pure and gentle mind . . .
Thou sealedst them with many a bare broad word
And cearedst my memory o'er them—for I heard°
And can forget not . . . they were ministered
One after one, those curses. Mix them up
Like self-destroying poisons in one cup,
And they will make one blessing which thou ne'er
Didst imprecate for, on me,—death.

* * * * * *

'It were
A cruel punishment for one most cruel,
If such can love, to make that love the fuel
Of the mind's hell; hate, scorn, remorse, despair:
But *me*—whose heart a stranger's tear might wear
As water-drops the sandy fountain-stone,
Who loved and pitied all things, and could moan
For woes which others hear not, and could see
The absent with the glance of fantasy,
And with the poor and trampled sit and weep,
Following the captive to his dungeon deep;
Me—who am as a nerve o'er which do creep
The else unfelt oppressions of this earth°
And was to thee the flame upon thy hearth
When all beside was cold—that thou on me
Shouldst rain these plagues of blistering agony—
Such curses are from lips once eloquent
With love's too partial praise—let none relent
Who intend deeds too dreadful for a name
Henceforth, if an example for the same
They seek . . . for thou on me lookedst so, and so—
And didst speak thus . . . and thus . . . I live to show
How much men bear and die not!

* * * * * * *

'Thou wilt tell
With the grimace of hate how horrible
It was to meet my love when thine grew less;
Thou wilt admire how I could e'er address
Such features to love's work . . . this taunt, though true,
(For indeed nature nor in form nor hue
Bestowed on me her choicest workmanship)

Shall not be thy defence . . . for since thy lip
Met mine first, years long past, since thine eye kindled
With soft fire under mine, I have not dwindled
Nor changed in mind or body, or in aught
But as love changes what it loveth not
After long years and many trials.

'How vain
Are words! I thought never to speak again,
Not even in secret,—not to my own heart—
But from my lips the unwilling accents start
And from my pen the words flow as I write,°
Dazzling my eyes with scalding tears . . . my sight
Is dim to see that charactered in vain
On this unfeeling leaf which burns the brain
And eats into it . . . blotting all things fair
And wise and good which time had written there.

'Those who inflict must suffer, for they see
The work of their own hearts and this must be
Our chastisement or recompense—O child!
I would that thine were like to be more mild
For both our wretched sakes . . . for thine the most
Who feelest already all that thou hast lost
Without the power to wish it thine again;
And as slow years pass, a funereal train
Each with the ghost of some lost hope or friend
Following it like its shadow, wilt thou bend
No thought on my dead memory?

* * * * * *

'Alas, love,
Fear me not . . . against thee I would not move
A finger in despite. Do I not live
That thou mayst have less bitter cause to grieve?
I give thee tears for scorn and love for hate,
And that thy lot may be less desolate
Than his on whom thou tramplest, I refrain
From that sweet sleep which medicines all pain.°
Then, when thou speakest of me, never say
"He could forgive not." Here I cast away

All human passions, all revenge, all pride;
I think, speak, act no ill; I do but hide
Under these words like embers, every spark
Of that which has consumed me—quick and dark
The grave is yawning . . . as its roof shall cover
My limbs with dust and worms under and over
So let Oblivion hide this grief . . . the air
Closes upon my accents, as despair
Upon my heart—let death upon despair!'

He ceased, and overcome leant back awhile,
Then rising, with a melancholy smile
Went to a sofa, and lay down, and slept
A heavy sleep, and in his dreams he wept
And muttered some familiar name, and we
Wept without shame in his society.
I think I never was impressed so much;
The man who were not must have lacked a touch
Of human nature . . . then we lingered not,
Although our argument was quite forgot,
But calling the attendants, went to dine
At Maddalo's; yet neither cheer nor wine
Could give us spirits, for we talked of him
And nothing else, till daylight made stars dim;
And we agreed his was some dreadful ill
Wrought on him boldly, yet unspeakable,
By a dear friend; some deadly change in love
Of one vowed deeply which he dreamed not of;
For whose sake he, it seemed, had fixed a blot
Of falsehood on his mind which flourished not
But in the light of all-beholding truth;
And having stamped this canker on his youth
She had abandoned him . . . and how much more
Might be his woe, we guessed not—he had store
Of friends and fortune once, as we could guess
From his nice habits and his gentleness;
These were now lost . . . it were a grief indeed
If he had changed one unsustaining reed
For all that such a man might else adorn.
The colours of his mind seemed yet unworn;
For the wild language of his grief was high

Such as in measure were called poetry;
And I remember one remark which then
Maddalo made. He said: 'Most wretched men
Are cradled into poetry by wrong;
They learn in suffering what they teach in song.'

If I had been an unconnected man
I, from this moment, should have formed some plan
Never to leave sweet Venice,—for to me
It was delight to ride by the lone sea;
And then, the town is silent—one may write
Or read in gondolas by day or night,
Having the little brazen lamp alight,
Unseen, uninterrupted; books are there,
Pictures, and casts from all those statues fair
Which were twin-born with poetry, and all
We seek in towns, with little to recall
Regrets for the green country. I might sit
In Maddalo's great palace, and his wit
And subtle talk would cheer the winter night
And make me know myself, and the firelight
Would flash upon our faces, till the day
Might dawn and make me wonder at my stay:
But I had friends in London too: the chief
Attraction here, was that I sought relief
From the deep tenderness that maniac wrought
Within me—'twas perhaps an idle thought,
But I imagined that if day by day
I watched him, and but seldom went away,
And studied all the beatings of his heart
With zeal, as men study some stubborn art
For their own good, and could by patience find
An entrance to the caverns of his mind,
I might reclaim him from his dark estate:
In friendships I had been most fortunate—
Yet never saw I one whom I would call
More willingly my friend; and this was all
Accomplished not; such dreams of baseless good
Oft come and go in crowds and solitude
And leave no trace—but what I now designed
Made for long years impression on my mind.

The following morning urged by my affairs
I left bright Venice.

After many years
And many changes I returned; the name
Of Venice, and its aspect, was the same;
But Maddalo was travelling far away
Among the mountains of Armenia.
His dog was dead. His child had now become
A woman; such as it has been my doom
To meet with few, a wonder of this earth
Where there is little of transcendent worth,
Like one of Shakespeare's women: kindly she
And with a manner beyond courtesy
Received her father's friend; and when I asked
Of the lorn maniac, she her memory tasked
And told as she had heard the mournful tale:
'That the poor sufferer's health began to fail°
Two years from my departure, but that then
The Lady who had left him, came again.
Her mien had been imperious, but she now
Looked meek—perhaps remorse had brought her low.
Her coming made him better, and they stayed
Together at my father's—for I played
As I remember with the lady's shawl—
I might be six years old—but after all
She left him' . . . 'Why, her heart must have been tough:
How did it end?' 'And was not this enough?
They met—they parted'—'Child, is there no more?'
'Something within that interval which bore
The stamp of *why* they parted, *how* they met:
Yet if thine aged eyes disdain to wet
Those wrinkled cheeks with youth's remembered tears,
Ask me no more, but let the silent years
Be closed and ceared over their memory°
As yon mute marble where their corpses lie.'
I urged and questioned still, she told me how
All happened—but the cold world shall not know.

PROMETHEUS UNBOUND°

A LYRICAL DRAMA°

IN FOUR ACTS

Audisne haec, Amphiarae, sub terram abdite?°

PREFACE

The Greek tragic writers, in selecting as their subject any portion of their national history or mythology, employed in their treatment of it a certain arbitrary discretion. They by no means conceived themselves bound to adhere to the common interpretation or to imitate in story as in title their rivals and predecessors. Such a system would have amounted to a resignation of those claims to preference over their competitors which incited the composition. The Agamemnonian story was exhibited on the Athenian theatre with as many variations as dramas.

I have presumed to employ a similar licence. The *Prometheus Unbound* of Aeschylus supposed the reconciliation of Jupiter with his victim as the price of the disclosure of the danger threatened to his empire by the consummation of his marriage with Thetis. Thetis, according to this view of the subject, was given in marriage to Peleus, and Prometheus, by the permission of Jupiter, delivered from his captivity by Hercules.° Had I framed my story on this model, I should have done no more than have attempted to restore the lost drama of Aeschylus; an ambition which, if my preference to this mode of treating the subject had incited me to cherish, the recollection of the high comparison such an attempt would challenge might well abate. But, in truth, I was averse from a catastrophe so feeble as that of reconciling the Champion with the Oppressor of mankind. The moral interest of the fable, which is so powerfully sustained by the sufferings and endurance of Prometheus, would be annihilated if we could conceive of him as unsaying his high language and quailing before his successful and perfidious adversary. The only imaginary being resembling in any degree Prometheus is Satan; and Prometheus is, in my judgement, a more poetical character than Satan, because, in addition to courage, and majesty, and firm and patient opposition to omnipotent force, he is susceptible of being described as exempt from the taints of ambition, envy, revenge, and a desire for personal aggrandisement, which, in the Hero of *Paradise Lost*, interfere with the interest. The character of Satan engenders in the mind a pernicious casuistry which leads us to weigh his faults with his wrongs, and to excuse the former because the latter exceed all measure. In the minds of those who consider that magnificent fiction with a religious feeling it engenders something worse. But Prometheus is, as it were, the type of the highest perfection of moral and intellectual nature, impelled by the purest and the truest motives to the best and noblest ends.

This Poem was chiefly written upon the mountainous ruins of the Baths of Caracalla, among the flowery glades, and thickets of odoriferous blossoming trees, which are extended in ever widening labyrinths upon its immense platforms and dizzy arches suspended in the air. The bright blue sky of Rome, and the effect of the vigorous awakening of spring in that divinest climate, and the new life with which it drenches the spirits even to intoxication, were the inspiration of this drama.

The imagery which I have employed will be found, in many instances, to have been drawn from the operations of the human mind, or from those external actions by which they are expressed. This is unusual in modern poetry, although Dante and Shakespeare are full of instances of the same kind: Dante indeed more than any other poet, and with greater success. But the Greek poets, as writers to whom no resource of awakening the sympathy of their contemporaries was unknown, were in the habitual use of this power; and it is the study of their works (since a higher merit would probably be denied me) to which I am willing that my readers should impute this singularity.

One word is due° in candour to the degree in which the study of contemporary writings may have tinged my composition, for such has been a topic of censure with regard to poems far more popular, and indeed more deservedly popular, than mine. It is impossible that any one who inhabits the same age with such writers as those who stand in the foremost ranks of our own, can conscientiously assure himself that his language and tone of thought may not have been modified by the study of the productions of those extraordinary intellects. It is true that, not the spirit of their genius, but the forms in which it has manifested itself, are due less to the peculiarities of their own minds than to the peculiarity of the moral and intellectual condition of the minds among which they have been produced. Thus a number of writers possess the form, whilst they want the spirit of those whom, it is alleged, they imitate; because the former is the endowment of the age in which they live, and the latter must be the uncommunicated lightning of their own mind.

The peculiar style of intense and comprehensive imagery which distinguishes the modern literature of England, has not been, as a general power, the product of the imitation of any particular writer. The mass of capabilities remains at every period materially the same; the circumstances which awaken it to action perpetually change. If England were divided into forty republics, each equal in population and extent to Athens, there is no reason to suppose but that, under institutions not more perfect than those of Athens, each would produce philosophers and poets equal to those who (if we except Shakespeare) have never been surpassed. We owe the great writers of the golden age of our literature to that fervid awakening of the public mind which shook to dust the oldest and most oppressive form of the Christian religion. We owe Milton to the progress and development of the same spirit: the sacred Milton was, let it ever be remembered, a republican, and a bold inquirer into morals and religion. The great writers of our own age are, we have reason to suppose, the companions and forerunners of some unimagined change in our social condition or the opinions which cement it. The cloud of mind is discharging its collected lightning, and the equilibrium between institutions and opinions is now restoring, or is about to be restored.

As to imitation, poetry is a mimetic art. It creates, but it creates by combination and representation. Poetical abstractions are beautiful and new, not because the portions of which they are composed had no previous existence in the mind of man or in nature, but because the whole produced by their combination has some intelligible and beautiful analogy with those sources of emotion and thought, and with the contemporary condition of them: one great poet is a masterpiece of nature which another not only ought to study but must study. He might as wisely and as easily determine that his mind should no longer be the mirror of all that is lovely in the visible universe, as exclude from his contemplation the beautiful which exists in the writings of a great contemporary. The pretence of doing it would be a presumption in any but the greatest; the effect, even in him, would be strained, unnatural, and ineffectual. A poet is the combined product of such internal powers as modify the nature of others, and of such external influences as excite and sustain these powers; he is not one, but both. Every man's mind is, in this respect, modified by all the objects of nature and art; by every word and every suggestion which he ever admitted to act upon his consciousness; it is the mirror upon which all forms are reflected, and in which they compose one form. Poets, not otherwise than philosophers, painters, sculptors and musicians, are, in one sense, the creators, and, in another, the creations, of their age. From this subjection the loftiest do not escape. There is a similarity between Homer and Hesiod, between Aeschylus and Euripides, between Virgil and Horace, between Dante and Petrarch, between Shakespeare and Fletcher, between Dryden and Pope; each has a generic resemblance under which their specific distinctions are arranged. If this similarity be the result of imitation, I am willing to confess that I have imitated.

Let this opportunity be conceded to me of acknowledging that I have what a Scotch philosopher° characteristically terms, 'a passion for reforming the world':° what passion incited him to write and publish his book, he omits to explain. For my part I had rather be damned with Plato and Lord Bacon, than go to Heaven with Paley°and Malthus.° But it is a mistake to suppose that I dedicate my poetical compositions solely to the direct enforcement of reform, or that I consider them in any degree as containing a reasoned system on the theory of human life. Didactic poetry is my abhorrence; nothing can be equally well expressed in prose that is not tedious and supererogatory in verse. My purpose has hitherto been simply to familiarize the highly refined imagination of the more select classes of poetical readers with beautiful idealisms of moral excellence; aware that until the mind can love, and admire, and trust, and hope, and endure, reasoned principles of moral conduct are seeds cast upon the highway of life, which the unconscious passenger tramples into the dust, although they would bear the harvest of his happiness. Should I live to accomplish what I purpose, that is, produce a systematical history of what appear to me to be the genuine elements of human society, let not the advocates of injustice and superstition flatter themselves that I should take Aeschylus rather than Plato as my model.

The having spoken of myself with unaffected freedom will need little apology with the candid; and let the uncandid consider that they injure me less than their own hearts and minds by misrepresentation. Whatever talents a person may possess to amuse and instruct others, be they ever so inconsiderable, he is yet bound to exert them: if his attempt be ineffectual, let the punishment of an unaccomplished purpose have been sufficient; let none trouble themselves to heap the dust of oblivion upon his efforts; the pile they raise will betray his grave which might otherwise have been unknown.

DRAMATIS PERSONAE

PROMETHEUS.	ASIA. } Oceanides.
DEMOGORGON.	PANTHEA. } Oceanides.
JUPITER.	IONE. } Oceanides.
The EARTH.	The PHANTASM of JUPITER.
OCEAN.	The SPIRIT of the EARTH.
APOLLO.	The SPIRIT of the MOON.
MERCURY.	SPIRITS of the HOURS.
HERCULES.	SPIRITS. ECHOES. FAUNS.
	FURIES.

Act I°

SCENE.—*A ravine of icy rocks in the Indian Caucasus.* PROMETHEUS° *is discovered bound to the precipice.* PANTHEA *and* IONE *are seated at his feet. Time, night. During the Scene, morning slowly breaks.*

Prometheus. Monarch of Gods and Daemons, and all Spirits°
But One, who throng those bright and rolling worlds°
Which Thou and I alone of living things
Behold with sleepless eyes, regard this Earth
Made multitudinous with thy slaves, whom thou
Requitest for knee-worship, prayer, and praise,°
And toil, and hecatombs of broken hearts,°
With fear and self-contempt and barren hope;
Whilst me, who am thy foe, eyeless in hate,°
Hast thou made reign and triumph, to thy scorn,
O'er mine own misery and thy vain revenge.
Three thousand years of sleep-unsheltered hours,
And moments aye divided by keen pangs
Till they seemed years, torture and solitude,
Scorn and despair,—these are mine empire:
More glorious far than that which thou surveyest
From thine unenvied throne, O Mighty God!
Almighty, had I deigned to share the shame
Of thine ill tyranny, and hung not here
Nailed to this wall of eagle-baffling mountain,°
Black, wintry, dead, unmeasured; without herb,

Insect, or beast, or shape or sound of life.
Ah me! alas, pain, pain ever, forever!

No change, no pause, no hope! Yet I endure.
I ask the Earth, have not the mountains felt?
I ask yon Heaven, the all-beholding Sun,
Has it not seen? The Sea, in storm or calm,
Heaven's ever-changing Shadow, spread below,
Have its deaf waves not heard my agony?
Ah me! alas, pain, pain ever, forever!

The crawling glaciers pierce me with the spears
Of their moon-freezing crystals; the bright chains
Eat with their burning cold into my bones.
Heaven's wingèd hound, polluting from thy lips
His beak in poison not his own, tears up
My heart; and shapeless sights come wandering by,
The ghastly people of the realm of dream,
Mocking me; and the Earthquake-fiends are charged
To wrench the rivets from my quivering wounds
When the rocks split and close again behind;
While from their loud abysses howling throng
The genii of the storm, urging the rage
Of whirlwind, and afflict me with keen hail.
And yet to me welcome is day and night,
Whether one breaks the hoar frost of the morn,
Or starry, dim, and slow, the other climbs
The leaden-coloured east; for then they lead°
Their wingless, crawling Hours, one among whom
—As some dark Priest hales the reluctant victim—
Shall drag thee, cruel King, to kiss the blood
From these pale feet, which then might trample thee
If they disdained not such a prostrate slave.
Disdain? Ah no! I pity thee. What ruin
Will hunt thee undefended through wide Heaven!
How will thy soul, cloven to its depth with terror,
Gape like a hell within! I speak in grief,
Not exultation, for I hate no more,
As then, ere misery made me wise. The curse
Once breathed on thee I would recall. Ye Mountains,°
Whose many-voicèd Echoes, through the mist

Of cataracts, flung the thunder of that spell!
Ye icy Springs, stagnant with wrinkling frost,
Which vibrated to hear me, and then crept
Shuddering through India! Thou serenest Air,
Through which the Sun walks burning without beams!
And ye swift Whirlwinds, who on poisèd wings
Hung mute and moveless o'er yon hushed abyss,
As thunder, louder than your own, made rock
The orbèd world—if then my words had power,
Though I am changed so that aught evil wish
Is dead within; although no memory be
Of what is hate—let them not lose it now!
What was that curse? for ye all heard me speak.

First Voice (from the Mountains)

Thrice three hundred thousand years
  O'er the Earthquake's couch we stood:
Oft, as men convulsed with fears,
  We trembled in our multitude.

Second Voice (from the Springs)

Thunderbolts had parched our water,
  We had been stained with bitter blood,
And had run mute, 'mid shrieks of slaughter,
  Through a city and a solitude.

Third Voice (from the Air)

I had clothed, since Earth uprose,
  Its wastes in colours not their own,°
And oft had my serene repose
  Been cloven by many a rending groan.

Fourth Voice (from the Whirlwinds)

We had soared beneath these mountains
  Unresting ages; nor had thunder,
Nor yon volcano's flaming fountains,
  Nor any power above or under
  Ever made us mute with wonder.

First Voice

But never bowed our snowy crest
As at the voice of thine unrest.

Second Voice

Never such a sound before
To the Indian waves we bore.
A pilot asleep on the howling sea
Leaped up from the deck in agony,
And heard, and cried, 'Ah, woe is me!'
And died as mad as the wild waves be.

Third Voice

By such dread words from Earth to Heaven
My still realm was never riven:
When its wound was closed, there stood
Darkness o'er the day like blood.°

Fourth Voice

And we shrank back: for dreams of ruin
To frozen caves our flight pursuing
Made us keep silence—thus—and thus—
Though silence is as hell to us.

The Earth. The tongueless Caverns of the craggy hills
Cried, 'Misery!' then; the hollow Heaven replied,
'Misery!' and the Ocean's purple waves,
Climbing the land, howled to the lashing winds,
And the pale nations heard it, 'Misery!'

Prometheus. I hear a sound of voices: not the voice
Which I gave forth. Mother, thy sons and thou
Scorn him, without whose all-enduring will
Beneath the fierce omnipotence of Jove,
Both they and thou had vanished, like thin mist
Unrolled on the morning wind. Know ye not me,
The Titan? he who made his agony
The barrier to your else all-conquering foe?
O rock-embosomed lawns and snow-fed streams,
Now seen athwart frore vapours, deep below,°
Through whose o'ershadowing woods I wandered once
With Asia, drinking life from her loved eyes,
Why scorns the spirit which informs ye, now
To commune with me? me alone, who checked—
As one who checks a fiend-drawn charioteer—

The falsehood and the force of him who reigns
Supreme, and with the groans of pining slaves
Fills your dim glens and liquid wildernesses?
Why answer ye not, still? Brethren!

The Earth. They dare not.

Prometheus. Who dares? For I would hear that curse again.
Ha, what an awful whisper rises up!
'Tis scarce like sound: it tingles through the frame
As lightning tingles, hovering ere it strike.
Speak, Spirit! from thine inorganic voice°
I only know that thou art moving near
And love. How cursed I him?°

The Earth. How canst thou hear
Who knowest not the language of the dead?

Prometheus. Thou art a living spirit; speak as they.

The Earth. I dare not speak like life, lest Heaven's fell King
Should hear, and link me to some wheel of pain°
More torturing than the one whereon I roll.
Subtle thou art and good, and though the Gods
Hear not this voice, yet thou art more than God,
Being wise and kind: earnestly hearken now.

Prometheus. Obscurely through my brain, like shadows dim,
Sweep awful thoughts, rapid and thick. I feel
Faint, like one mingled in entwining love;
Yet 'tis not pleasure.

The Earth. No, thou canst not hear:
Thou art immortal, and this tongue is known
Only to those who die.

Prometheus. And what art thou,
O melancholy Voice?

The Earth. I am the Earth,
Thy mother; she within whose stony veins,
To the last fibre of the loftiest tree

Whose thin leaves trembled in the frozen air,
Joy ran, as blood within a living frame,
When thou didst from her bosom, like a cloud
Of glory, arise—a spirit of keen joy!
And at thy voice her pining sons uplifted
Their prostrate brows from the polluting dust,
And our almighty Tyrant with fierce dread
Grew pale, until his thunder chained thee here.
Then, see those million worlds which burn and roll
Around us: their inhabitants beheld
My spherèd light wane in wide Heaven; the sea
Was lifted by strange tempest, and new fire
From earthquake-rifted mountains of bright snow
Shook its portentous hair beneath Heaven's frown;
Lightning and Inundation vexed the plains;
Blue thistles bloomed in cities; foodless toads°
Within voluptuous chambers panting crawled;
When Plague had fallen on man and beast and worm,
And Famine; and black blight on herb and tree;
And in the corn, and vines, and meadow-grass,
Teemed ineradicable poisonous weeds
Draining their growth, for my wan breast was dry
With grief; and the thin air, my breath, was stained
With the contagion of a mother's hate°
Breathed on her child's destroyer; aye, I heard
Thy curse, the which, if thou rememberest not,
Yet my innumerable seas and streams,
Mountains, and caves, and winds, and yon wide air,
And the inarticulate people of the dead,
Preserve, a treasured spell. We meditate
In secret joy and hope those dreadful words
But dare not speak them.

Prometheus. Venerable Mother!
All else who live and suffer take from thee
Some comfort; flowers, and fruit, and happy sounds,
And love, though fleeting; these may not be mine.
But mine own words, I pray, deny me not.

The Earth. They shall be told. Ere Babylon was dust,
The Magus Zoroaster, my dead child,°

Met his own image walking in the garden.
That apparition, sole of men, he saw.
For know there are two worlds of life and death:
One that which thou beholdest; but the other
Is underneath the grave, where do inhabit
The shadows of all forms that think and live
Till death unite them and they part no more;
Dreams and the light imaginings of men,
And all that faith creates or love desires,
Terrible, strange, sublime and beauteous shapes.°
There thou art, and dost hang, a writhing shade,
'Mid whirlwind-shaken mountains; all the Gods
Are there, and all the Powers of nameless worlds,
Vast, sceptred Phantoms; heroes, men, and beasts;
And Demogorgon, a tremendous Gloom;°
And he, the Supreme Tyrant, on his throne
Of burning gold. Son, one of these shall utter
The curse which all remember. Call at will
Thine own ghost, or the ghost of Jupiter,
Hades or Typhon, or what mightier Gods
From all-prolific Evil since thy ruin
Have sprung, and trampled on my prostrate sons.
Ask, and they must reply: so the revenge
Of the Supreme may sweep through vacant shades,
As rainy wind through the abandoned gate
Of a fallen palace.

Prometheus. Mother, let not aught
Of that which may be evil, pass again
My lips, or those of aught resembling me.
Phantasm of Jupiter, arise, appear!°

Ione

My wings are folded o'er mine ears:
My wings are crossed over mine eyes:
Yet through their silver shade appears,
And through their lulling plumes arise,
A Shape, a throng of sounds:
May it be no ill to thee
O thou of many wounds!

Near whom, for our sweet sister's sake,
Ever thus we watch and wake.

Panthea°

The sound is of whirlwind underground,
  Earthquake, and fire, and mountains cloven;
The Shape is awful like the sound,
  Clothed in dark purple, star-inwoven.
A sceptre of pale gold,
  To stay steps proud, o'er the slow cloud,
His veinèd hand doth hold.
Cruel he looks, but calm and strong,
Like one who does, not suffers wrong.

Phantasm of Jupiter. Why have the secret powers of this strange world
Driven me, a frail and empty phantom, hither
On direst storms? What unaccustomed sounds
Are hovering on my lips, unlike the voice
With which our pallid race hold ghastly talk
In darkness? And, proud sufferer, who art thou?

Prometheus. Tremendous Image, as thou art must be
He whom thou shadowest forth. I am his foe,
The Titan. Speak the words which I would hear,
Although no thought inform thine empty voice.

The Earth. Listen! And though your echoes must be mute,
Grey mountains, and old woods, and haunted springs,
Prophetic caves, and isle-surrounded streams,
Rejoice to hear what yet ye cannot speak.

Phantasm. A spirit seizes me and speaks within:
It tears me as fire tears a thunder-cloud.

Panthea. See, how he lifts his mighty looks, the Heaven
Darkens above.

Ione. He speaks! O shelter me!

Prometheus. I see the curse on gestures proud and cold,
And looks of firm defiance, and calm hate,

And such despair as mocks itself with smiles,
Written as on a scroll . . . yet speak—O speak!

Phantasm

Fiend, I defy thee! with a calm, fixed mind,
All that thou canst inflict I bid thee do;
Foul Tyrant both of Gods and Humankind,
One only being shalt thou not subdue.
Rain then thy plagues upon me here,
Ghastly disease, and frenzying fear;
And let alternate frost and fire
Eat into me, and be thine ire
Lightning, and cutting hail, and legioned forms
Of furies, driving by upon the wounding storms.

Aye, do thy worst. Thou art omnipotent.
O'er all things but thyself I gave thee power,
And my own will. Be thy swift mischiefs sent
To blast mankind, from yon etherial tower.
Let thy malignant spirit move
Its darkness over those I love:
On me and mine I imprecate
The utmost torture of thy hate,
And thus devote to sleepless agony
This undeclining head while thou must reign on high.

But thou, who art the God and Lord: O thou
Who fillest with thy soul this world of woe,
To whom all things of Earth and Heaven do bow
In fear and worship: all-prevailing foe!
I curse thee! let a sufferer's curse
Clasp thee, his torturer, like remorse,
Till thine Infinity shall be
A robe of envenomed agony;
And thine Omnipotence a crown of pain
To cling like burning gold round thy dissolving brain.

Heap on thy soul, by virtue of this Curse,
Ill deeds; then be thou damned, beholding good;°
Both infinite as is the universe,
And thou, and thy self-torturing solitude.

An awful image of calm power
Though now thou sittest, let the hour
Come, when thou must appear to be
That which thou art internally,
And after many a false and fruitless crime
Scorn track thy lagging fall through boundless space and time.

Prometheus. Were these my words, O Parent?

The Earth. They were thine.

Prometheus. It doth repent me: words are quick and vain;
Grief for a while is blind, and so was mine.
I wish no living thing to suffer pain.

The Earth

Misery, oh misery to me,
That Jove at length should vanquish thee.
Wail, howl aloud, Land and Sea,
The Earth's rent heart shall answer ye.
Howl, Spirits of the living and the dead;
Your refuge, your defence lies fallen and vanquishèd.

First Echo

Lies fallen and vanquishèd?

Second Echo

Fallen and vanquishèd!

Ione

Fear not: 'tis but some passing spasm,
  The Titan is unvanquished still.
But see, where through the azure chasm
  Of yon forked and snowy hill,
Trampling the slant winds on high
  With golden-sandalled feet, that glow
Under plumes of purple dye,
Like rose-ensanguined ivory,
  A Shape comes now,
Stretching on high from his right hand
A serpent-cinctured wand.

Panthea. 'Tis Jove's world-wandering herald, Mercury.°

Ione

And who are those with hydra tresses
 And iron wings that climb the wind,
Whom the frowning God represses
 Like vapours steaming up behind,
Clanging loud, an endless crowd—

Panthea

These are Jove's tempest-walking hounds,°
Whom he gluts with groans and blood,
When charioted on sulphurous cloud
 He bursts Heaven's bounds.

Ione

Are they now led from the thin dead,
On new pangs to be fed?

Panthea. The Titan looks as ever, firm, not proud.

First Fury. Ha! I scent life!

Second Fury. Let me but look into his eyes!

Third Fury. The hope of torturing him smells like a heap
Of corpses to a death-bird after battle.

First Fury. Darest thou delay, O Herald? take cheer, Hounds
Of Hell: what if the Son of Maia soon
Should make us food and sport? Who can please long
The Omnipotent?

Mercury. Back to your towers of iron,
And gnash beside the streams of fire and wail°
Your foodless teeth! . . . Geryon, arise! and Gorgon,°
Chimaera, and thou Sphinx, subtlest of fiends,°
Who ministered to Thebes Heaven's poisoned wine,
Unnatural love, and more unnatural hate:°
These shall perform your task.

First Fury. Oh, mercy! mercy!
We die with our desire: drive us not back!

Mercury. Crouch then in silence.
Awful Sufferer,
To thee unwilling, most unwillingly
I come, by the great Father's will driven down,
To execute a doom of new revenge.
Alas! I pity thee, and hate myself
That I can do no more—aye from thy sight
Returning, for a season, Heaven seems Hell,
So thy worn form pursues me night and day,
Smiling reproach. Wise art thou, firm and good,
But vainly wouldst stand forth alone in strife
Against the Omnipotent; as yon clear lamps
That measure and divide the weary years
From which there is no refuge, long have taught,
And long must teach. Even now thy Torturer arms
With the strange might of unimagined pains
The powers who scheme slow agonies in Hell,
And my commission is to lead them here,
Or what more subtle, foul or savage fiends
People the abyss, and leave them to their task.
Be it not so . . . there is a secret known
To thee, and to none else of living things,
Which may transfer the sceptre of wide Heaven,
The fear of which perplexes the Supreme:
Clothe it in words, and bid it clasp his throne
In intercession; bend thy soul in prayer,
And like a suppliant in some gorgeous fane,
Let the will kneel within thy haughty heart;
For benefits and meek submission tame
The fiercest and the mightiest.

Prometheus. Evil minds
Change good to their own nature. I gave all
He has; and in return he chains me here
Years, ages, night and day: whether the Sun
Split my parched skin, or in the moony night
The crystal-wingèd snow cling round my hair:
Whilst my beloved race is trampled down

By his thought-executing ministers.°
Such is the tyrant's recompense—'tis just:
He who is evil can receive no good;
And for a world bestowed, or a friend lost,
He can feel hate, fear, shame; not gratitude:
He but requites me for his own misdeed.
Kindness to such is keen reproach, which breaks
With bitter stings the light sleep of Revenge.
Submission, thou dost know, I cannot try:
For what submission but that fatal word,
The death-seal of mankind's captivity,
Like the Sicilian's hair-suspended sword°
Which trembles o'er his crown, would he accept,
Or could I yield? Which yet I will not yield.
Let others flatter Crime, where it sits throned
In brief Omnipotence; secure are they:
For Justice, when triumphant, will weep down
Pity, not punishment, on her own wrongs,
Too much avenged by those who err. I wait,
Enduring thus, the retributive hour
Which since we spake is even nearer now.
But hark, the hell-hounds clamour: fear delay:
Behold! Heaven lowers under thy Father's frown.

Mercury. Oh, that we might be spared: I to inflict,
And thou to suffer! Once more answer me:
Thou knowest not the period of Jove's power?

Prometheus. I know but this, that it must come.

Mercury. Alas!
Thou canst not count thy years to come of pain?

Prometheus. They last while Jove must reign; nor more, nor less
Do I desire or fear.

Mercury. Yet pause, and plunge
Into Eternity, where recorded time,
Even all that we imagine, age on age,
Seems but a point, and the reluctant mind
Flags wearily in its unending flight,

Till it sink, dizzy, blind, lost, shelterless;
Perchance it has not numbered the slow years
Which thou must spend in torture, unreprieved.

Prometheus. Perchance no thought can count them, yet they pass.

Mercury. If thou might'st dwell among the Gods the while,
Lapped in voluptuous joy?

Prometheus. I would not quit
This bleak ravine, these unrepentant pains.

Mercury. Alas! I wonder at, yet pity thee.

Prometheus. Pity the self-despising slaves of Heaven,
Not me, within whose mind sits peace serene,
As light in the sun, throned: how vain is talk!
Call up the fiends.

Ione. O sister, look! White fire
Has cloven to the roots yon huge snow-loaded cedar;
How fearfully God's thunder howls behind!

Mercury. I must obey his words and thine: alas!
Most heavily remorse hangs at my heart!

Panthea. See where the child of Heaven with wingèd feet
Runs down the slanted sunlight of the dawn.

Ione. Dear sister, close thy plumes over thine eyes
Lest thou behold and die—they come, they come
Blackening the birth of day with countless wings,
And hollow underneath, like death.

First Fury. Prometheus!

Second Fury. Immortal Titan!

Third Fury. Champion of Heaven's slaves!

Prometheus. He whom some dreadful voice invokes is here,

Prometheus, the chained Titan. Horrible forms,
What and who are ye? Never yet there came
Phantasms so foul through monster-teeming Hell
From the all-miscreative brain of Jove;
Whilst I behold such execrable shapes,
Methinks I grow like what I contemplate,
And laugh and stare in loathsome sympathy.

First Fury. We are the ministers of pain, and fear,
And disappointment, and mistrust, and hate,
And clinging crime; and as lean dogs pursue
Through wood and lake some struck and sobbing fawn,
We track all things that weep, and bleed, and live,
When the great King betrays them to our will.

Prometheus. O many fearful natures in one name,
I know ye; and these lakes and echoes know
The darkness and the clangour of your wings.
But why more hideous than your loathèd selves
Gather ye up in legions from the deep?

Second Fury. We knew not that: Sisters, rejoice, rejoice!

Prometheus. Can aught exult in its deformity?

Second Fury. The beauty of delight makes lovers glad,
Gazing on one another: so are we.
As from the rose which the pale priestess kneels
To gather for her festal crown of flowers
The aerial crimson falls, flushing her cheek,
So from our victim's destined agony
The shade which is our form invests us round,
Else are we shapeless as our mother Night.

Prometheus. I laugh your power, and his who sent you here,
To lowest scorn. Pour forth the cup of pain.

First Fury. Thou thinkest we will rend thee bone from bone,
And nerve from nerve, working like fire within?

Prometheus. Pain is my element, as hate is thine;
Ye rend me now: I care not.

Second Fury. Dost imagine
We will but laugh into thy lidless eyes?

Prometheus. I weigh not what ye do, but what ye suffer,
Being evil. Cruel was the Power which called
You, or aught else so wretched, into light.

Third Fury. Thou think'st we will live through thee, one by one,
Like animal life, and though we can obscure not
The soul which burns within, that we will dwell
Beside it, like a vain loud multitude
Vexing the self-content of wisest men:
That we will be dread thought beneath thy brain,
And foul desire round thine astonished heart,
And blood within thy labyrinthine veins
Crawling like agony?

Prometheus. Why, ye are thus now:
Yet am I king over myself, and rule
The torturing and conflicting throngs within,
As Jove rules you when Hell grows mutinous.

Chorus of Furies

From the ends of the earth, from the ends of the earth,
Where the night has its grave and the morning its birth,
Come, come, come!
O ye who shake hills with the scream of your mirth
When cities sink howling in ruin; and ye
Who with wingless footsteps trample the sea,
And close upon Shipwreck and Famine's track
Sit chattering with joy on the foodless wreck;
Come, come, come!
Leave the bed, low, cold, and red,
Strewed beneath a nation dead;
Leave the hatred, as in ashes
Fire is left for future burning:
It will burst in bloodier flashes
When ye stir it, soon returning;
Leave the self-contempt implanted
In young spirits, sense-enchanted,
Misery's yet unkindled fuel;

Leave Hell's secrets half unchanted
To the maniac dreamer: cruel
More than ye can be with hate
Is he with fear.
Come, come, come!
We are steaming up from Hell's wide gate,
And we burden the blasts of the atmosphere,
But vainly we toil till ye come here.

Ione. Sister, I hear the thunder of new wings.

Panthea. These solid mountains quiver with the sound
Even as the tremulous air: their shadows make
The space within my plumes more black than night.

First Fury

Your call was as a wingèd car,
Driven on whirlwinds fast and far;
It rapt us from red gulfs of war.

Second Fury

From wide cities, famine-wasted;

Third Fury

Groans half heard, and blood untasted;

Fourth Fury

Kingly conclaves stern and cold,°
Where blood with gold is bought and sold;

Fifth Fury

From the furnace, white and hot,
In which—

A Fury

Speak not—whisper not:
I know all that ye would tell,
But to speak might break the spell
Which must bend the Invincible,
The stern of thought;
He yet defies the deepest power of Hell.

Fury

Tear the veil!

Another Fury

It is torn!

Chorus

The pale stars of the morn
Shine on a misery, dire to be borne,
Dost thou faint, mighty Titan? We laugh thee to scorn.
Dost thou boast the clear knowledge thou waken'dst for man?
Then was kindled within him a thirst which outran
Those perishing waters; a thirst of fierce fever,
Hope, love, doubt, desire—which consume him for ever.
One came forth of gentle worth,°
Smiling on the sanguine earth;
His words outlived him, like swift poison
Withering up truth, peace, and pity.
Look where round the wide horizon
Many a million-peopled city
Vomits smoke in the bright air.
Hark that outcry of despair!
'Tis his mild and gentle ghost
Wailing for the faith he kindled.
Look again, the flames almost
To a glow-worm's lamp have dwindled:
The survivors round the embers
Gather in dread.
Joy, joy, joy!
Past ages crowd on thee, but each one remembers,
And the future is dark, and the present is spread
Like a pillow of thorns for thy slumberless head.°

Semichorus I

Drops of bloody agony flow
From his white and quivering brow.
Grant a little respite now:
See, a disenchanted nation°
Springs like day from desolation;
To Truth its state is dedicate,

And Freedom leads it forth, her mate;
A legioned band of linkèd brothers,
Whom Love calls children—

Semichorus 2

'Tis another's—
See how kindred murder kin:
'Tis the vintage-time for death and sin:
Blood, like new wine, bubbles within;
Till Despair smothers
The struggling world, which slaves and tyrants win.°
[*All the* FURIES *vanish, except one.*

Ione. Hark, sister! what a low yet dreadful groan
Quite unsuppressed is tearing up the heart
Of the good Titan, as storms tear the deep,
And beasts hear the sea moan in inland caves.
Darest thou observe how the fiends torture him?

Panthea. Alas! I looked forth twice, but will no more.

Ione. What didst thou see?

Panthea. A woeful sight: a youth
With patient looks nailed to a crucifix.

Ione. What next?

Panthea. The heaven around, the earth below
Was peopled with thick shapes of human death,
All horrible, and wrought by human hands,
And some appeared the work of human hearts,
For men were slowly killed by frowns and smiles:
And other sights too foul to speak and live
Were wandering by. Let us not tempt worse fear
By looking forth: those groans are grief enough.

Fury. Behold, an emblem: those who do endure
Deep wrongs for man, and scorn, and chains, but heap
Thousandfold torment on themselves and him.

Prometheus. Remit the anguish of that lighted stare;
Close those wan lips; let that thorn-wounded brow
Stream not with blood; it mingles with thy tears!
Fix, fix those tortured orbs in peace and death,
So thy sick throes shake not that crucifix,
So those pale fingers play not with thy gore.
O horrible! Thy name I will not speak,
It hath become a curse. I see, I see
The wise, the mild, the lofty, and the just,
Whom thy slaves hate for being like to thee,
Some hunted by foul lies from their heart's home,
An early-chosen, late-lamented home,
As hooded ounces cling to the driven hind;°
Some linked to corpses in unwholesome cells;
Some—hear I not the multitude laugh loud?—
Impaled in lingering fire: and mighty realms
Float by my feet, like sea-uprooted isles,
Whose sons are kneaded down in common blood
By the red light of their own burning homes.

Fury. Blood thou canst see, and fire; and canst hear groans:
Worse things unheard, unseen, remain behind.

Prometheus. Worse?

Fury. In each human heart terror survives
The ravin it has gorged: the loftiest fear
All that they would disdain to think were true:
Hypocrisy and custom make their minds
The fanes of many a worship, now outworn.
They dare not devise good for man's estate,
And yet they know not that they do not dare.
The good want power, but to weep barren tears.
The powerful goodness want: worse need for them.
The wise want love; and those who love want wisdom;
And all best things are thus confused to ill.
Many are strong and rich, and would be just,
But live among their suffering fellow-men
As if none felt: they know not what they do.°

Prometheus. Thy words are like a cloud of wingèd snakes;
And yet I pity those they torture not.

Fury. Thou pitiest them? I speak no more! [*Vanishes.*

Prometheus. Ah woe!
Ah woe! Alas! pain, pain ever, forever!
I close my tearless eyes, but see more clear
Thy works within my woe-illumèd mind,
Thou subtle tyrant! Peace is in the grave.
The grave hides all things beautiful and good:
I am a God and cannot find it there:
Nor would I seek it: for, though dread revenge,
This is defeat, fierce King, not victory!
The sights with which thou torturest gird my soul
With new endurance, till the hour arrives
When they shall be no types of things which are.

Panthea. Alas! what sawest thou more?

Prometheus. There are two woes:
To speak and to behold; thou spare me one.
Names are there, Nature's sacred watch-words, they
Were borne aloft in bright emblazonry;
The nations thronged around, and cried aloud,
As with one voice, 'Truth, liberty, and love!'
Suddenly fierce confusion fell from Heaven
Among them: there was strife, deceit, and fear;
Tyrants rushed in, and did divide the spoil.
This was the shadow of the truth I saw.

The Earth. I felt thy torture, Son, with such mixed joy
As pain and virtue give. To cheer thy state,
I bid ascend those subtle and fair spirits,°
Whose homes are the dim caves of human thought,
And who inhabit, as birds wing the wind,
Its world-surrounding ether: they behold
Beyond that twilight realm, as in a glass,
The future: may they speak comfort to thee!

Panthea. Look, sister, where a troop of spirits gather,
Like flocks of clouds in spring's delightful weather,
Thronging in the blue air!

Ione. And see! more come,
Like fountain-vapours when the winds are dumb,
That climb up the ravine in scattered lines.
And hark! is it the music of the pines?
Is it the lake? Is it the waterfall?

Panthea. 'Tis something sadder, sweeter far than all.

Chorus of Spirits

From unremembered ages we
Gentle guides and guardians be
Of Heaven-oppressed mortality;
And we breathe, and sicken not,
The atmosphere of human thought:
Be it dim, and dank, and grey,
Like a storm-extinguished day,
Travelled o'er by dying gleams;
  Be it bright as all between
Cloudless skies and windless streams,
  Silent, liquid, and serene;
As the birds within the wind,
  As the fish within the wave,
As the thoughts of man's own mind
  Float through all above the grave,
We make there our liquid lair,
Voyaging cloudlike and unpent
Through the boundless element:
Thence we bear the prophecy
Which begins and ends in thee!

Ione. More yet come, one by one: the air around them
Looks radiant as the air around a star.

First Spirit

On a battle-trumpet's blast
I fled hither, fast, fast, fast,
'Mid the darkness upward cast.
From the dust of creeds outworn,
From the tyrant's banner torn,
Gathering round me, onward borne,

There was mingled many a cry—
'Freedom! Hope! Death! Victory!'
Till they faded through the sky;
And one sound above, around,
One sound beneath, around, above,
Was moving; 'twas the soul of love;
'Twas the hope, the prophecy,
Which begins and ends in thee.

Second Spirit

A rainbow's arch stood on the sea
Which rocked beneath, immovably;
And the triumphant storm did flee,
Like a conqueror, swift and proud,
Between, with many a captive cloud,
A shapeless, dark and rapid crowd,
Each by lightning riven in half:
I heard the thunder hoarsely laugh.
Mighty fleets were strewn like chaff
And spread beneath a hell of death
O'er the white waters. I alit
On a great ship lightning-split,
And speeded hither on the sigh
Of one who gave an enemy
His plank, then plunged aside to die.°

Third Spirit

I sate beside a sage's bed,
And the lamp was burning red
Near the book where he had fed,
When a Dream with plumes of flame
To his pillow hovering came,
And I knew it was the same
Which had kindled long ago
Pity, eloquence, and woe;
And the world awhile below
Wore the shade its lustre made.
It has borne me here as fleet
As Desire's lightning feet:
I must ride it back ere morrow,
Or the sage will wake in sorrow.

Fourth Spirit

On a poet's lips I slept
Dreaming like a love-adept
In the sound his breathing kept;
Nor seeks nor finds he mortal blisses,
But feeds on the aerial kisses
Of shapes that haunt thought's wildernesses.
He will watch from dawn to gloom
The lake-reflected sun illume
The yellow bees i' the ivy-bloom,
Nor heed nor see what things they be;
But from these create he can
Forms more real than living man,
Nurslings of immortality!
One of these awakened me,
And I sped to succour thee.

Ione. Behold'st thou not two shapes from the east and west
Come, as two doves to one beloved nest,
Twin nurslings of the all-sustaining air,
On swift still wings glide down the atmosphere?
And hark! their sweet, sad voices! 'tis despair
Mingled with love and then dissolved in sound.

Panthea. Canst thou speak, sister? all my words are drowned.

Ione. Their beauty gives me voice. See how they float
On their sustaining wings of skiey grain.
Orange and azure deepening into gold:
Their soft smiles light the air like a star's fire.

Chorus of Spirits

Hast thou beheld the form of Love?

Fifth Spirit

As over wide dominions
I sped, like some swift cloud that wings the wide air's wildernesses,
That planet-crested shape swept by on lightning-braided pinions,°
Scattering the liquid joy of life from his ambrosial tresses:
His footsteps paved the world with light; but as I passed 'twas fading,
And hollow Ruin yawned behind: great sages bound in madness,

And headless patriots, and pale youths who perished,
  unupbraiding,
Gleamed in the night I wandered o'er—till thou, O King
  of sadness,
Turned by thy smile the worst I saw to recollected gladness.

Sixth Spirit

Ah, sister! Desolation is a delicate thing:
It walks not on the earth, it floats not on the air,
But treads with lulling footstep, and fans with silent wing
The tender hopes which in their hearts the best and gentlest bear,
Who, soothed to false repose by the fanning plumes above
And the music-stirring motion of its soft and busy feet,
Dream visions of aerial joy, and call the monster Love,
And wake, and find the shadow Pain—as he whom now we greet.°

Chorus

Though Ruin now Love's shadow be,
Following him destroyingly
  On Death's white and wingèd steed,
Which the fleetest cannot flee,
  Trampling down both flower and weed,
Man and beast, and foul and fair,
Like a tempest through the air;
Thou shalt quell this horseman grim,
Woundless though in heart or limb.

Prometheus

Spirits! how know ye this shall be?

Chorus

  In the atmosphere we breathe,
As buds grow red when snow-storms flee
  From spring gathering up beneath,
Whose mild winds shake the elder brake,
And the wandering herdsmen know
That the white-thorn soon will blow:
Wisdom, Justice, Love, and Peace,
When they struggle to increase,
  Are to us as soft winds be

To shepherd boys, the prophecy
Which begins and ends in thee.

Ione. Where are the Spirits fled?

Panthea. Only a sense
Remains of them, like the omnipotence
Of music, when the inspired voice and lute
Languish, ere yet the responses are mute
Which through the deep and labyrinthine soul,
Like echoes through long caverns, wind and roll.

Prometheus. How fair these air-born shapes! and yet I feel
Most vain all hope but love; and thou art far,
Asia! who, when my being overflowed,
Wert like a golden chalice to bright wine
Which else had sunk into the thirsty dust.
All things are still: alas! how heavily
This quiet morning weighs upon my heart;
Though I should dream, I could even sleep with grief,
If slumber were denied not. I would fain
Be what it is my destiny to be,
The saviour and the strength of suffering man,
Or sink into the original gulf of things:
There is no agony, and no solace left;
Earth can console, Heaven can torment no more.

Panthea. Hast thou forgotten one who watches thee
The cold dark night, and never sleeps but when
The shadow of thy spirit falls on her?

Prometheus. I said all hope was vain but love: thou lovest.

Panthea. Deeply in truth; but the Eastern star looks white,°
And Asia waits in that far Indian vale
The scene of her sad exile; rugged once
And desolate and frozen, like this ravine;
But now invested with fair flowers and herbs,
And haunted by sweet airs and sounds, which flow
Among the woods and waters, from the ether
Of her transforming presence—which would fade
If it were mingled not with thine. Farewell!

Act 2

SCENE I.—*Morning. A lovely vale in the Indian Caucasus.* ASIA, *alone.*

Asia. From all the blasts of heaven thou hast descended:
Yes, like a spirit, like a thought, which makes
Unwonted tears throng to the horny eyes,
And beatings haunt the desolated heart,
Which should have learnt repose: thou hast descended
Cradled in tempests; thou dost wake, O Spring!
O child of many winds! As suddenly
Thou comest as the memory of a dream,
Which now is sad because it hath been sweet;
Like genius, or like joy which riseth up
As from the earth, clothing with golden clouds
The desert of our life . . .
This is the season, this the day, the hour;
At sunrise thou shouldst come, sweet sister mine,
Too long desired, too long delaying, come!
How like death-worms the wingless moments crawl!
The point of one white star is quivering still
Deep in the orange light of widening morn
Beyond the purple mountains; through a chasm
Of wind-divided mist the darker lake
Reflects it; now it wanes; it gleams again
As the waves fade, and as the burning threads
Of woven cloud unravel in pale air . . .
'Tis lost! and through yon peaks of cloud-like snow
The roseate sunlight quivers: hear I not
The Aeolian music of her sea-green plumes
Winnowing the crimson dawn?

PANTHEA *enters.*°

I feel, I see
Those eyes which burn through smiles that fade in tears,
Like stars half quenched in mists of silver dew.
Beloved and most beautiful, who wearest
The shadow of that soul by which I live,
How late thou art! the spherèd sun had climbed
The sea, my heart was sick with hope, before
The printless air felt thy belated plumes.

Panthea. Pardon, great Sister! but my wings were faint
With the delight of a remembered dream,
As are the noon-tide plumes of summer winds
Satiate with sweet flowers. I was wont to sleep
Peacefully, and awake refreshed and calm,
Before the sacred Titan's fall, and thy
Unhappy love, had made, through use and pity,
Both love and woe familiar to my heart
As they had grown to thine: erewhile I slept°
Under the glaucous caverns of old Ocean°
Within dim bowers of green and purple moss,
Our young Ione's soft and milky arms
Locked then, as now, behind my dark, moist hair,
While my shut eyes and cheek were pressed within
The folded depth of her life-breathing bosom:
But not as now, since I am made the wind
Which fails beneath the music that I bear
Of thy most wordless converse; since dissolved
Into the sense with which love talks, my rest
Was troubled and yet sweet; my waking hours
Too full of care and pain.

Asia. Lift up thine eyes,
And let me read thy dream.

Panthea. As I have said,
With our sea-sister at his feet I slept.
The mountain mists, condensing at our voice
Under the moon, had spread their snowy flakes,
From the keen ice shielding our linkèd sleep.
Then two dreams came. One, I remember not.
But in the other, his pale, wound-worn limbs
Fell from Prometheus, and the azure night
Grew radiant with the glory of that form
Which lives unchanged within, and his voice fell
Like music which makes giddy the dim brain,
Faint with intoxication of keen joy:
'Sister of her whose footsteps pave the world
With loveliness—more fair than aught but her,
Whose shadow thou art—lift thine eyes on me.'
I lifted them: the overpowering light

Of that immortal shape was shadowed o'er
By love; which, from his soft and flowing limbs,
And passion-parted lips, and keen, faint eyes,
Steamed forth like vaporous fire; an atmosphere
Which wrapped me in its all-dissolving power,
As the warm ether of the morning sun
Wraps ere it drinks some cloud of wandering dew.
I saw not, heard not, moved not, only felt
His presence flow and mingle through my blood
Till it became his life, and his grew mine,
And I was thus absorbed—until it passed,
And like the vapours when the sun sinks down,
Gathering again in drops upon the pines,
And tremulous as they, in the deep night
My being was condensed; and as the rays
Of thought were slowly gathered, I could hear
His voice, whose accents lingered ere they died
Like footsteps of far melody: thy name
Among the many sounds alone I heard
Of what might be articulate; though still
I listened through the night when sound was none.
Ione wakened then, and said to me:
'Canst thou divine what troubles me to-night?
I always knew what I desired before,
Nor ever found delight to wish in vain.
But now I cannot tell thee what I seek;
I know not; something sweet, since it is sweet
Even to desire; it is thy sport, false sister!
Thou hast discovered some enchantment old,
Whose spells have stolen my spirit as I slept
And mingled it with thine;—for when just now
We kissed, I felt within thy parted lips
The sweet air that sustained me, and the warmth
Of the life-blood, for loss of which I faint,
Quivered between our intertwining arms.'
I answered not, for the Eastern star grew pale,
But fled to thee.

Asia. Thou speakest, but thy words
Are as the air: I feel them not . . . Oh, lift
Thine eyes that I may read his written soul!

Panthea. I lift them, though they droop beneath the load
Of that they would express: what canst thou see
But thine own fairest shadow imaged there?

Asia. Thine eyes are like the deep, blue, boundless heaven
Contracted to two circles underneath
Their long, fine lashes: dark, far, measureless,
Orb within orb, and line through line inwoven.

Panthea. Why lookest thou as if a spirit passed?

Asia. There is a change; beyond their inmost depth
I see a shade, a shape: 'tis He, arrayed
In the soft light of his own smiles, which spread
Like radiance from the cloud-surrounded moon.
Prometheus, it is thine! depart not yet!
Say not those smiles that we shall meet again
Within that bright pavilion which their beams
Shall build o'er the waste world? The dream is told.
What shape is that between us? Its rude hair°
Roughens the wind that lifts it; its regard
Is wild and quick, yet 'tis a thing of air
For through its grey robe gleams the golden dew
Whose stars the noon has quenched not.

Dream

Follow! Follow!

Panthea. It is mine other dream.

Asia. It disappears.

Panthea. It passes now into my mind. Methought
As we sat here, the flower-infolding buds
Burst on yon lightning-blasted almond tree,°
When swift from the white Scythian wilderness°
A wind swept forth wrinkling the Earth with frost.
I looked, and all the blossoms were blown down;
But on each leaf was stamped, as the blue bells
Of Hyacinth tell Apollo's written grief,°
O, FOLLOW, FOLLOW!

Asia. As you speak, your words
Fill, pause by pause, my own forgotten sleep
With shapes. Methought among these lawns together
We wandered, underneath the young grey dawn,
And multitudes of dense, white, fleecy clouds
Were wandering in thick flocks along the mountains,
Shepherded by the slow, unwilling wind;
And the white dew on the new-bladed grass,
Just piercing the dark earth, hung silently;
And there was more which I remember not:
But on the shadows of the moving clouds
Athwart the purple mountain slope, was written
FOLLOW, O, FOLLOW! as they vanished by,
And on each herb, from which Heaven's dew had fallen,
The like was stamped, as with a withering fire.
A wind arose among the pines; it shook
The clinging music from their boughs, and then
Low, sweet, faint sounds, like the farewell of ghosts,
Were heard: O, FOLLOW, FOLLOW, FOLLOW ME!
And then I said: 'Panthea, look on me'.
But in the depth of those beloved eyes
Still I saw, FOLLOW, FOLLOW!

Echo

Follow, follow!

Panthea. The crags, this clear spring morning, mock our voices
As they were spirit-tongued.

Asia. It is some being
Around the crags. What fine clear sounds! O, list!

Echoes, unseen

Echoes we: listen!
We cannot stay:
As dew-stars glisten
Then fade away—
Child of Ocean!

Asia. Hark! Spirits speak! The liquid responses
Of their aerial tongues yet sound.

Panthea. I hear.

Echoes

O, follow, follow,
As our voice recedeth
Through the caverns hollow,
Where the forest spreadeth;

(*More distant*)

O, follow, follow;
Through the caverns hollow;
As the song floats thou pursue;
Where the wild bee never flew,
Through the noon-tide darkness deep,
By the odour-breathing sleep
Of faint nightflowers, and the waves
At the fountain-lighted caves,
While our music, wild and sweet,
Mocks thy gently falling feet,
Child of Ocean!

Asia. Shall we pursue the sound? It grows more faint
And distant.

Panthea. List! the strain floats nearer now.

Echoes

In the world unknown
Sleeps a voice unspoken;
By thy step alone
Can its rest be broken;
Child of Ocean!

Asia. How the notes sink upon the ebbing wind!

Echoes

O, follow, follow
Through the caverns hollow;
As the song floats thou pursue,
By the woodland noon-tide dew;
By the forests, lakes, and fountains,

Through the many-folded mountains;
To the rents, and gulfs, and chasms,
Where the Earth reposed from spasms,
On the day when He and thou
Parted, to commingle now;
Child of Ocean!

Asia. Come, sweet Panthea, link thy hand in mine,
And follow, ere the voices fade away.

SCENE 2.—*A forest, intermingled with rocks and caverns.* ASIA *and* PANTHEA *pass into it. Two young* FAUNS are sitting on a rock, listening.

Semichorus 1 of Spirits

The path through which that lovely twain
Have passed, by cedar, pine, and yew,°
And each dark tree that ever grew,
Is curtained out from Heaven's wide blue;
Nor sun, nor moon, nor wind, nor rain,
Can pierce its interwoven bowers;
Nor aught, save where some cloud of dew,
Drifted along the earth-creeping breeze
Between the trunks of the hoar trees,
Hangs each a pearl in the pale flowers°
Of the green laurel, blown anew;
And bends, and then fades silently,
One frail and fair anemone:
Or when some star of many a one
That climbs and wanders through steep night,
Has found the cleft through which alone
Beams fall from high those depths upon,
Ere it is borne away, away,
By the swift Heavens that cannot stay,
It scatters drops of golden light,
Like lines of rain that ne'er unite:
And the gloom divine is all around;
And underneath is the mossy ground.

Semichorus 2

There the voluptuous nightingales
Are awake through all the broad noonday.

When one with bliss or sadness fails,
And through the windless ivy-boughs,
Sick with sweet love, droops dying away
On its mate's music-panting bosom;
Another from the swinging blossom,
Watching to catch the languid close
Of the last strain, then lifts on high
The wings of the weak melody,
Till some new stream of feeling bear
The song, and all the woods are mute;
When there is heard through the dim air
The rush of wings, and rising there
Like many a lake-surrounded flute,
Sounds overflow the listener's brain
So sweet, that joy is almost pain.

Semichorus 1

There those enchanted eddies play
Of echoes, music-tongued, which draw,
By Demogorgon's mighty law,
With melting rapture, or sweet awe,
All spirits on that secret way,
As inland boats are driven to Ocean
Down streams made strong with mountain-thaw;
And first there comes a gentle sound
To those in talk or slumber bound,
And wakes the destined; soft emotion°
Attracts, impels them: those who saw
Say from the breathing earth behind°
There steams a plume-uplifting wind
Which drives them on their path, while they
Believe their own swift wings and feet
The sweet desires within obey:
And so they float upon their way,
Until, still sweet, but loud and strong,
The storm of sound is driven along,
Sucked up and hurrying: as they fleet
Behind, its gathering billows meet
And to the fatal mountain bear
Like clouds amid the yielding air.

First Faun. Canst thou imagine where those spirits live
Which make such delicate music in the woods?
We haunt within the least frequented caves
And closest coverts, and we know these wilds,
Yet never meet them, though we hear them oft:
Where may they hide themselves?

Second Faun. 'Tis hard to tell:
I have heard those more skilled in spirits say,
The bubbles, which the enchantment of the sun
Sucks from the pale faint water-flowers that pave
The oozy bottom of clear lakes and pools,
Are the pavilions where such dwell and float
Under the green and golden atmosphere
Which noontide kindles through the woven leaves;
And when these burst, and the thin fiery air,
The which they breathed within those lucent domes,
Ascends to flow like meteors through the night,
They ride on them, and rein their headlong speed,
And bow their burning crests, and glide in fire
Under the waters of the earth again.°

First Faun. If such live thus, have others other lives,
Under pink blossoms or within the bells
Of meadow flowers, or folded violets deep,
Or on their dying odours, when they die,
Or in the sunlight of the spherèd dew?

Second Faun. Aye, many more, which we may well divine.
But should we stay to speak, noontide would come,
And thwart Silenus find his goats undrawn,°
And grudge to sing those wise and lovely songs
Of fate, and chance, and God, and Chaos old,
And Love, and the chained Titan's woeful doom,
And how he shall be loosed, and make the earth
One brotherhood: delightful strains which cheer
Our solitary twilights, and which charm
To silence the unenvying nightingales.

SCENE 3.—*A pinnacle of rock among mountains.* ASIA *and* PANTHEA.

Panthea. Hither the sound has borne us—to the realm
Of Demogorgon, and the mighty portal,
Like a volcano's meteor-breathing chasm,°
Whence the oracular vapour is hurled up°
Which lonely men drink wandering in their youth,
And call truth, virtue, love, genius, or joy,
That maddening wine of life, whose dregs they drain
To deep intoxication, and uplift,
Like Maenads who cry loud, Evoe! Evoe!°
The voice which is contagion to the world.°

Asia. Fit throne for such a Power! Magnificent!
How glorious art thou, Earth! and if thou be
The shadow of some spirit lovelier still,
Though evil stain its work, and it should be
Like its creation, weak yet beautiful,
I could fall down and worship that and thee.
Even now my heart adoreth—Wonderful!
Look, sister, ere the vapour dim thy brain:
Beneath is a wide plain of billowy mist,
As a lake, paving in the morning sky,
With azure waves which burst in silver light,
Some Indian vale. Behold it, rolling on
Under the curdling winds, and islanding
The peak whereon we stand—midway, around,
Encinctured by the dark and blooming forests,
Dim twilight lawns and stream-illumèd caves,
And wind-enchanted shapes of wandering mist;
And far on high the keen sky-cleaving mountains
From icy spires of sunlike radiance fling
The dawn, as lifted Ocean's dazzling spray,
From some Atlantic islet scattered up,
Spangles the wind with lamp-like water-drops.
The vale is girdled with their walls, a howl
Of cataracts from their thaw-cloven ravines
Satiates the listening wind, continuous, vast,
Awful as silence. Hark! the rushing snow!
The sun-awakened avalanche! whose mass,
Thrice sifted by the storm, had gathered there

Flake after flake, in heaven-defying minds
As thought by thought is piled, till some great truth
Is loosened, and the nations echo round,
Shaken to their roots, as do the mountains now.°

Panthea. Look how the gusty sea of mist is breaking
In crimson foam, even at our feet! it rises
As Ocean at the enchantment of the moon
Round foodless men wrecked on some oozy isle.

Asia. The fragments of the cloud are scattered up;
The wind that lifts them disentwines my hair;
Its billows now sweep o'er mine eyes—my brain
Grows dizzy—seest those shapes within the mist?

Panthea. A countenance with beckoning smiles—there burns
An azure fire within its golden locks!
Another and another—hark! they speak!

Song of Spirits

To the deep, to the deep,
Down, down!
Through the shade of sleep,
Through the cloudy strife
Of Death and of Life;
Through the veil and the bar
Of things which seem and are,°
Even to the steps of the remotest throne,
Down, down!

While the sound whirls around,
Down, down!
As the fawn draws the hound,
As the lightning the vapour,
As a weak moth the taper;
Death, despair; love, sorrow;
Time both; today, tomorrow;
As steel obeys the Spirit of the stone,°
Down, down!

Through the grey, void abysm,
Down, down!

Where the air is no prism,
And the moon and stars are not,
And the cavern-crags wear not
The radiance of Heaven,
Nor the gloom to Earth given;
Where there is One pervading, One alone,
Down, down!

In the depth of the deep,
Down, down!
Like veiled lightning asleep,
Like the spark nursed in embers,
The last look Love remembers,
Like a diamond, which shines
On the dark wealth of mines,
A spell is treasured but for thee alone.
Down, down!

We have bound thee, we guide thee
Down, down!
With the bright form beside thee;
Resist not the weakness—
Such strength is in meekness
That the Eternal, the Immortal,°
Must unloose through life's portal
The snake-like Doom coiled underneath his throne°
By that alone.

SCENE 4.—*The Cave of* DEMOGORGON. ASIA *and* PANTHEA.

Panthea. What veilèd form sits on that ebon throne?

Asia. The veil has fallen!

Panthea. I see a mighty Darkness
Filling the seat of power; and rays of gloom
Dart round, as light from the meridian sun,
Ungazed upon and shapeless; neither limb,°
Nor form, nor outline; yet we feel it is
A living Spirit.

Demogorgon. Ask what thou wouldst know.

Asia. What canst thou tell?

Demogorgon. All things thou dar'st demand.

Asia. Who made the living world?

Demogorgon. God.

Asia. Who made all
That it contains—thought, passion, reason, will,
Imagination?

Demogorgon. God: Almighty God.

Asia. Who made that sense which, when the winds of spring
In rarest visitation, or the voice
Of one beloved heard in youth alone,
Fills the faint eyes with falling tears which dim
The radiant looks of unbewailing flowers,
And leaves this peopled earth a solitude
When it returns no more?

Demogorgon. Merciful God.

Asia. And who made terror, madness, crime, remorse,
Which from the links of the great chain of things
To every thought within the mind of man
Sway and drag heavily, and each one reels°
Under the load towards the pit of death;
Abandoned hope, and love that turns to hate;
And self-contempt, bitterer to drink than blood;
Pain, whose unheeded and familiar speech
Is howling, and keen shrieks, day after day;
And Hell, or the sharp fear of Hell?

Demogorgon. He reigns.

Asia Utter his name: a world pining in pain
Asks but his name: curses shall drag him down.

Demogorgon. He reigns.

Asia. I feel, I know it: who?

Demogorgon. He reigns.

Asia. Who reigns? There was the Heaven and Earth at first,°
And Light and Love; then Saturn, from whose throne
Time fell, an envious shadow; such the state
Of the earth's primal spirits beneath his sway,
As the calm joy of flowers and living leaves
Before the wind or sun has withered them
And semivital worms; but he refused
The birthrights of their being, knowledge, power,
The skill which wields the elements, the thought
Which pierces this dim universe like light,
Self-empire, and the majesty of love;
For thirst of which they fainted. Then Prometheus
Gave wisdom, which is strength, to Jupiter,
And with this law alone, 'Let man be free,'
Clothed him with the dominion of wide Heaven.
To know nor faith, nor love, nor law; to be
Omnipotent but friendless is to reign;
And Jove now reigned; for on the race of man
First famine, and then toil, and then disease,
Strife, wounds, and ghastly death unseen before,
Fell; and the unseasonable seasons drove,°
With alternating shafts of frost and fire,
Their shelterless, pale tribes to mountain caves:
And in their desert hearts fierce wants he sent,
And mad disquietudes, and shadows idle
Of unreal good, which levied mutual war,
So ruining the lair wherein they raged.
Prometheus saw, and waked the legioned hopes
Which sleep within folded Elysian flowers,
Nepenthe, Moly, Amaranth, fadeless blooms,°
That they might hide with thin and rainbow wings
The shape of Death; and Love he sent to bind
The disunited tendrils of that vine
Which bears the wine of life, the human heart;
And he tamed fire which, like some beast of prey
Most terrible, but lovely, played beneath
The frown of man; and tortured to his will

Iron and gold, the slaves and signs of power,
And gems and poisons, and all subtlest forms
Hidden beneath the mountains and the waves.
He gave man speech, and speech created thought,
Which is the measure of the universe;
And Science struck the thrones of earth and heaven,
Which shook, but fell not; and the harmonious mind
Poured itself forth in all-prophetic song;
And music lifted up the listening spirit
Until it walked, exempt from mortal care,
Godlike, o'er the clear billows of sweet sound;°
And human hands first mimicked and then mocked,°
With moulded limbs more lovely than its own,
The human form, till marble grew divine,
And mothers, gazing, drank the love men see
Reflected in their race, behold, and perish.°
He told the hidden power of herbs and springs,
And Disease drank and slept. Death grew like sleep.
He taught the implicated orbits woven°
Of the wide-wandering stars; and how the sun°
Changes his lair, and by what secret spell°
The pale moon is transformed, when her broad eye
Gazes not on the interlunar sea:°
He taught to rule, as life directs the limbs,
The tempest-wingèd chariots of the Ocean,
And the Celt knew the Indian. Cities then
Were built, and through their snow-like columns flowed
The warm winds, and the azure ether shone,
And the blue sea and shadowy hills were seen.
Such, the alleviations of his state,
Prometheus gave to man, for which he hangs
Withering in destined pain: but who rains down
Evil, the immedicable plague, which, while°
Man looks on his creation like a God
And sees that it is glorious, drives him on,°
The wreck of his own will, the scorn of earth,
The outcast, the abandoned, the alone?
Not Jove: while yet his frown shook heaven, aye, when
His adversary from adamantine chains°
Cursed him, he trembled like a slave. Declare
Who is his master? Is he too a slave?

Demogorgon. All spirits are enslaved which serve things evil.
Thou knowest if Jupiter be such or no.

Asia. Whom called'st thou God?

Demogorgon. I spoke but as ye speak,
For Jove is the supreme of living things.

Asia. Who is the master of the slave?

Demogorgon. If the abysm
Could vomit forth its secrets:—but a voice
Is wanting, the deep truth is imageless;
For what would it avail to bid thee gaze
On the revolving world? What to bid speak
Fate, Time, Occasion, Chance and Change? To these
All things are subject but eternal Love.

Asia. So much I asked before, and my heart gave
The response thou hast given; and of such truths
Each to itself must be the oracle.
One more demand; and do thou answer me
As my own soul would answer, did it know
That which I ask. Prometheus shall arise
Henceforth the sun of this rejoicing world:
When shall the destined hour arrive?

Demogorgon. Behold!

Asia. The rocks are cloven, and through the purple night
I see cars drawn by rainbow-wingèd steeds
Which trample the dim winds: in each there stands
A wild-eyed charioteer, urging their flight.
Some look behind, as fiends pursued them there,
And yet I see no shapes but the keen stars;
Others, with burning eyes, lean forth, and drink
With eager lips the wind of their own speed,
As if the thing they loved fled on before,
And now, even now, they clasped it. Their bright locks
Stream like a comet's flashing hair: they all
Sweep onward.

Demogorgon. These are the immortal Hours,
Of whom thou didst demand. One waits for thee.

Asia. A spirit with a dreadful countenance°
Checks its dark chariot by the craggy gulf.
Unlike thy brethren, ghastly charioteer,
What art thou? Whither wouldst thou bear me? Speak!

Spirit. I am the shadow of a destiny
More dread than is my aspect: ere yon planet
Has set, the Darkness which ascends with me
Shall wrap in lasting night Heaven's kingless throne.

Asia. What meanest thou?

Panthea. That terrible shadow floats
Up from its throne, as may the lurid smoke
Of earthquake-ruined cities o'er the sea.
Lo! it ascends the car; the coursers fly
Terrified: watch its path among the stars
Blackening the night!

Asia. Thus I am answered: strange!

Panthea. See, near the verge, another chariot stays;
An ivory shell inlaid with crimson fire,°
Which comes and goes within its sculptured rim
Of delicate strange tracery; the young spirit
That guides it has the dove-like eyes of hope;
How its soft smiles attract the soul! as light
Lures wingèd insects through the lampless air.

Spirit

My coursers are fed with the lightning,
  They drink of the whirlwind's stream,
And when the red morning is bright'ning
  They bathe in the fresh sunbeam;
  They have strength for their swiftness I deem:
Then ascend with me, daughter of Ocean.

I desire: and their speed makes night kindle;
  I fear: they outstrip the Typhoon;

Ere the cloud piled on Atlas can dwindle
We encircle the earth and the moon:
We shall rest from long labours at noon:
Then ascend with me, daughter of Ocean.

SCENE 5.—*The car pauses within a cloud on the top of a snowy mountain.* ASIA, PANTHEA, *and the* SPIRIT OF THE HOUR.

Spirit

On the brink of the night and the morning
My coursers are wont to respire;°
But the Earth has just whispered a warning
That their flight must be swifter than fire:
They shall drink the hot speed of desire!

Asia. Thou breathest on their nostrils, but my breath
Would give them swifter speed.

Spirit. Alas! it could not.°

Panthea. O Spirit! pause, and tell whence is the light
Which fills this cloud—the sun is yet unrisen.

Spirit. The sun will rise not until noon. Apollo
Is held in heaven by wonder; and the light
Which fills this vapour, as the aerial hue
Of fountain-gazing roses fills the water,
Flows from thy mighty sister.°

Panthea. Yes, I feel—

Asia. What is it with thee, sister? Thou art pale.

Panthea. How thou art changed! I dare not look on thee;
I feel, but see thee not. I scarce endure
The radiance of thy beauty. Some good change
Is working in the elements, which suffer
Thy presence thus unveiled. The Nereids tell°
That on the day when the clear hyaline°
Was cloven at thine uprise, and thou didst stand
Within a veinèd shell, which floated on
Over the calm floor of the crystal sea,

Among the Aegean isles, and by the shores
Which bear thy name, love, like the atmosphere
Of the sun's fire filling the living world,
Burst from thee, and illumined earth and heaven
And the deep ocean and the sunless caves,
And all that dwells within them; till grief cast°
Eclipse upon the soul from which it came:
Such art thou now; nor is it I alone,
Thy sister, thy companion, thine own chosen one,
But the whole world which seeks thy sympathy.
Hearest thou not sounds i' the air which speak the love
Of all articulate beings? Feelest thou not
The inanimate winds enamoured of thee? List! [*Music.*

Asia. Thy words are sweeter than aught else but his
Whose echoes they are: yet all love is sweet,
Given or returned. Common as light is love,
And its familiar voice wearies not ever.
Like the wide heaven, the all-sustaining air,
It makes the reptile equal to the God:
They who inspire it most are fortunate,
As I am now; but those who feel it most
Are happier still, after long sufferings,
As I shall soon become.

Panthea. List! Spirits speak.

Voice (in the air, singing)

Life of Life! thy lips enkindle
With their love the breath between them;
And thy smiles before they dwindle
Make the cold air fire; then screen them
In those looks, where whoso gazes
Faints, entangled in their mazes.

Child of Light! thy limbs are burning
Through the vest which seems to hide them,
As the radiant lines of morning
Through the clouds ere they divide them;
And this atmosphere divinest
Shrouds thee wheresoe'er thou shinest.

Fair are others; none beholds thee,
  But thy voice sounds low and tender
Like the fairest, for it folds thee
  From the sight, that liquid splendour,
And all feel, yet see thee never,
As I feel now, lost forever!

Lamp of Earth! where'er thou movest
  Its dim shapes are clad with brightness,
And the souls of whom thou lovest
  Walk upon the winds with lightness,
Till they fail, as I am failing,°
Dizzy, lost, yet unbewailing!

Asia

  My soul is an enchanted boat,
  Which, like a sleeping swan, doth float
Upon the silver waves of thy sweet singing;
  And thine doth like an angel sit
  Beside the helm conducting it,
Whilst all the winds with melody are ringing.
  It seems to float ever, forever,
  Upon that many-winding river,
  Between mountains, woods, abysses,
  A paradise of wildernesses!
Till, like one in slumber bound
Borne to the ocean, I float down, around,
Into a sea profound, of ever-spreading sound:

  Meanwhile thy spirit lifts its pinions
  In music's most serene dominions,
Catching the winds that fan that happy heaven;
  And we sail on, away, afar,
  Without a course, without a star,
But by the instinct of sweet music driven;
  Till through Elysian garden islets
  By thee, most beautiful of pilots,
  Where never mortal pinnace glided,
  The boat of my desire is guided:
Realms where the air we breathe is love,
Which in the winds and on the waves doth move,
Harmonizing this earth with what we feel above.

We have passed Age's icy caves,
And Manhood's dark and tossing waves,
And Youth's smooth ocean, smiling to betray:
Beyond the glassy gulfs we flee
Of shadow-peopled Infancy,
Through Death and Birth, to a diviner day;°
A paradise of vaulted bowers
Lit by downward-gazing flowers,
And watery paths that wind between
Wildernesses calm and green,
Peopled by shapes too bright to see,
And rest, having beheld; somewhat like thee;
Which walk upon the sea, and chant melodiously!°

Act 3

SCENE I.—*Heaven.* JUPITER *on his throne*; THETIS *and the other Deities assembled.*

Jupiter. Ye congregated Powers of Heaven, who share
The glory and the strength of him ye serve,
Rejoice! henceforth I am omnipotent.
All else has been subdued to me; alone
The soul of man, like unextinguished fire,
Yet burns towards Heaven with fierce reproach, and doubt,
And lamentation, and reluctant prayer,
Hurling up insurrection, which might make
Our antique empire insecure, though built
On eldest faith, and Hell's coeval, fear;
And though my curses through the pendulous air,°
Like snow on herbless peaks, fall flake by flake,°
And cling to it; though under my wrath's night
It climb the crags of life, step after step,
Which wound it, as ice wounds unsandalled feet,
It yet remains supreme o'er misery,
Aspiring, unrepressed, yet soon to fall:
Even now have I begotten a strange wonder,
That fatal child, the terror of the earth,°
Who waits but till the destined hour arrive,
Bearing from Demogorgon's vacant throne
The dreadful might of ever-living limbs
Which clothed that awful spirit unbeheld,
To redescend, and trample out the spark.

Pour forth Heaven's wine, Idaean Ganymede,°
And let it fill the daedal cups like fire,
And from the flower-inwoven soil divine
Ye all-triumphant harmonies arise,
As dew from earth under the twilight stars:
Drink! be the nectar circling through your veins
The soul of joy, ye ever-living Gods,
Till exultation burst in one wide voice
Like music from Elysian winds.

And thou

Ascend beside me, veilèd in the light
Of the desire which makes thee one with me,
Thetis, bright image of eternity!°
When thou didst cry, 'Insufferable might!
God! Spare me! I sustain not the quick flames,
The penetrating presence; all my being,°
Like him whom the Numidian seps did thaw
Into a dew with poison, is dissolved,°
Sinking through its foundations': even then
Two mighty spirits, mingling, made a third
Mightier than either, which, unbodied now,
Between us floats, felt, although unbeheld,
Waiting the incarnation, which ascends
(Hear ye the thunder of the fiery wheels
Griding the winds?) from Demogorgon's throne.°
Victory! victory! Feel'st thou not, O world,
The earthquake of his chariot thundering up
Olympus?

The Car of the HOUR *arrives.* DEMOGORGON *descends, and moves towards the throne of* JUPITER.

Awful shape, what art thou? Speak!

Demogorgon. Eternity. Demand no direr name.
Descend, and follow me down the abyss.
I am thy child, as thou wert Saturn's child;
Mightier than thee: and we must dwell together
Henceforth in darkness. Lift thy lightnings not.
The tyranny of Heaven none may retain,
Or reassume, or hold, succeeding thee:
Yet if thou wilt, as 'tis the destiny
Of trodden worms to writhe till they are dead,
Put forth thy might.

Jupiter. Detested prodigy!
Even thus beneath the deep Titanian prisons°
I trample thee! thou lingerest?
Mercy! mercy!
No pity, no release, no respite! Oh,
That thou wouldst make mine enemy my judge,

Even where he hangs, seared by my long revenge,
On Caucasus! He would not doom me thus.
Gentle, and just, and dreadless, is he not
The monarch of the world? What then art thou?
No refuge! no appeal!
Sink with me then,
We two will sink on the wide waves of ruin,
Even as a vulture and a snake outspent
Drop, twisted in inextricable fight,
Into a shoreless sea. Let Hell unlock
Its mounded oceans of tempestuous fire,
And whelm on them into the bottomless void
This desolated world, and thee, and me,
The conqueror and the conquered, and the wreck
Of that for which they combated.
Ai! Ai!°
The elements obey me not. I sink
Dizzily down, ever, forever, down.
And, like a cloud, mine enemy above
Darkens my fall with victory! Ai, Ai!

SCENE 2.—*The mouth of a great river in the island Atlantis.*° OCEAN° *is discovered reclining near the shore*; APOLLO° *stands beside him.*

Ocean. He fell, thou sayest, beneath his conqueror's frown?

Apollo. Aye, when the strife was ended which made dim
The orb I rule, and shook the solid stars.
The terrors of his eye illumined Heaven
With sanguine light, through the thick ragged skirts
Of the victorious Darkness, as he fell:
Like the last glare of day's red agony,
Which, from a rent among the fiery clouds,
Burns far along the tempest-wrinkled deep.

Ocean. He sunk to the abyss? To the dark void?

Apollo. An eagle so caught in some bursting cloud
On Caucasus, his thunder-baffled wings
Entangled in the whirlwind, and his eyes,
Which gazed on the undazzling sun, now blinded
By the white lightning, while the ponderous hail

Beats on his struggling form, which sinks at length
Prone, and the aerial ice clings over it.

Ocean. Henceforth the fields of Heaven-reflecting sea
Which are my realm, will heave, unstained with blood,°
Beneath the uplifting winds, like plains of corn
Swayed by the summer air; my streams will flow
Round many-peopled continents, and round
Fortunate isles; and from their glassy thrones
Blue Proteus and his humid nymphs shall mark
The shadow of fair ships, as mortals see
The floating bark of the light-laden moon
With that white star, its sightless pilot's crest,°
Borne down the rapid sunset's ebbing sea;
Tracking their path no more by blood and groans
And desolation, and the mingled voice
Of slavery and command; but by the light
Of wave-reflected flowers, and floating odours,
And music soft, and mild, free, gentle voices,
That sweetest music, such as spirits love.

Apollo. And I shall gaze not on the deeds which make
My mind obscure with sorrow, as eclipse
Darkens the sphere I guide; but list, I hear
The small, clear, silver lute of the young Spirit
That sits i' the morning star.

Ocean. Thou must away;
Thy steeds will pause at even, till when, farewell.
The loud deep calls me home even now to feed it
With azure calm out of the emerald urns
Which stand forever full beside my throne.
Behold the Nereids under the green sea,
Their wavering limbs borne on the wind-like streams,
Their white arms lifted o'er their streaming hair,
With garlands pied and starry sea-flower crowns,
Hastening to grace their mighty sister's joy.
[*A sound of waves is heard.*
It is the unpastured sea hungering for calm.°
Peace, monster; I come now. Farewell.

Apollo. Farewell.

SCENE 3.—*Caucasus.* PROMETHEUS, HERCULES, IONE, *the* EARTH, SPIRITS. ASIA, *and* PANTHEA, *borne in the Car with the* SPIRIT OF THE HOUR.

[HERCULES *unbinds* PROMETHEUS, *who descends.*

Hercules. Most glorious among spirits, thus doth strength
To wisdom, courage, and long-suffering love,
And thee, who art the form they animate,
Minister, like a slave.

Prometheus. Thy gentle words
Are sweeter even than freedom long desired
And long delayed.
Asia, thou light of life,
Shadow of beauty unbeheld; and ye,
Fair sister-nymphs, who made long years of pain
Sweet to remember, through your love and care;
Henceforth we will not part. There is a Cave°
All overgrown with trailing odorous plants,
Which curtain out the day with leaves and flowers,
And paved with veinèd emerald, and a fountain
Leaps in the midst with an awakening sound.
From its curved roof the mountain's frozen tears,
Like snow, or silver, or long diamond spires,
Hang downward, raining forth a doubtful light;
And there is heard the ever-moving air,
Whispering without from tree to tree, and birds,
And bees; and all around are mossy seats,
And the rough walls are clothed with long soft grass;
A simple dwelling, which shall be our own;
Where we will sit and talk of time and change,
As the world ebbs and flows, ourselves unchanged.°
What can hide man from mutability?
And if ye sigh, then I will smile; and thou,
Ione, shall chant fragments of sea-music,
Until I weep, when ye shall smile away
The tears she brought, which yet were sweet to shed.
We will entangle buds and flowers, and beams
Which twinkle on the fountain's brim, and make
Strange combinations out of common things,

Like human babes in their brief innocence;
And we will search, with looks and words of love,
For hidden thoughts, each lovelier than the last,
Our unexhausted spirits; and like lutes
Touched by the skill of the enamoured wind,
Weave harmonies divine, yet ever new,
From difference sweet where discord cannot be;
And hither come, sped on the charmèd winds
Which meet from all the points of heaven, as bees
From every flower aerial Enna feeds°
At their known island-homes in Himera,°
The echoes of the human world, which tell
Of the low voice of love, almost unheard,
And dove-eyed pity's murmured pain, and music,
Itself the echo of the heart, and all
That tempers or improves man's life, now free;
And lovely apparitions, dim at first,
Then radiant, as the mind, arising bright
From the embrace of beauty, whence the forms
Of which these are the phantoms, casts on them
The gathered rays which are reality,°
Shall visit us, the progeny immortal
Of Painting, Sculpture, and rapt Poesy,
And arts, though unimagined, yet to be.
The wandering voices and the shadows these
Of all that man becomes, the mediators
Of that best worship, love, by him and us
Given and returned; swift shapes and sounds, which grow
More fair and soft as man grows wise and kind,
And veil by veil, evil and error fall:
Such virtue has the cave and place around.
[*Turning to the* SPIRIT OF THE HOUR.
For thee, fair Spirit, one toil remains. Ione,
Give her that curvèd shell, which Proteus old°
Made Asia's nuptial boon, breathing within it
A voice to be accomplished, and which thou
Didst hide in grass under the hollow rock.

Ione. Thou most desired Hour, more loved and lovely
Than all thy sisters, this is the mystic shell;
See the pale azure fading into silver

Lining it with a soft yet glowing light:
Looks it not like lulled music sleeping there?

Spirit. It seems in truth the fairest shell of Ocean:
Its sound must be at once both sweet and strange.

Prometheus. Go, borne over the cities of mankind
On whirlwind-footed coursers: once again
Outspeed the sun around the orbèd world;
And as thy chariot cleaves the kindling air,
Thou breathe into the many-folded shell,
Loosening its mighty music; it shall be
As thunder mingled with clear echoes: then
Return; and thou shalt dwell beside our cave.
[*Kissing the ground*.
And thou, O Mother Earth!—

The Earth. I hear, I feel;
Thy lips are on me, and their touch runs down
Even to the adamantine central gloom
Along these marble nerves; 'tis life, 'tis joy,
And through my withered, old, and icy frame
The warmth of an immortal youth shoots down
Circling. Henceforth the many children fair
Folded in my sustaining arms; all plants,
And creeping forms, and insects rainbow-winged,
And birds, and beasts, and fish, and human shapes,
Which drew disease and pain from my wan bosom,
Draining the poison of despair; shall take
And interchange sweet nutriment; to me
Shall they become like sister-antelopes
By one fair dam, snow-white and swift as wind,
Nursed among lilies near a brimming stream.
The dew-mists of my sunless sleep shall float
Under the stars like balm: night-folded flowers
Shall suck unwithering hues in their repose:
And men and beasts in happy dreams shall gather
Strength for the coming day and all its joy:
And death shall be the last embrace of her
Who takes the life she gave, even as a mother,
Folding her child, says, 'Leave me not again.'

Asia. O mother! wherefore speak the name of death?
Cease they to love, and move, and breathe, and speak,
Who die?

The Earth. It would avail not to reply:
Thou art immortal, and this tongue is known
But to the uncommunicating dead.
Death is the veil which those who live call life:
They sleep, and it is lifted: and meanwhile
In mild variety the seasons mild
With rainbow-skirted showers, and odorous winds,
And long blue meteors cleansing the dull night,
And the life-kindling shafts of the keen sun's
All-piercing bow, and the dew-mingled rain
Of the calm moonbeams, a soft influence mild,
Shall clothe the forests and the fields, aye, even
The crag-built deserts of the barren deep,
With ever-living leaves, and fruit, and flowers.
And Thou! There is a Cavern where my spirit°
Was panted forth in anguish whilst thy pain
Made my heart mad, and those who did inhale it
Became mad too, and built a temple there,
And spoke, and were oracular, and lured
The erring nations round to mutual war,
And faithless faith, such as Jove kept with thee;
Which breath now rises, as among tall weeds
A violet's exhalation, and it fills
With a serener light and crimson air
Intense, yet soft, the rocks and woods around;
It feeds the quick growth of the serpent vine,
And the dark linkèd ivy tangling wild,°
And budding, blown, or odour-faded blooms
Which star the winds with points of coloured light,
As they rain through them, and bright, golden globes
Of fruit, suspended in their own green heaven;
And, through their veinèd leaves and amber stems,
The flowers whose purple and translucid bowls
Stand ever mantling with aerial dew,
The drink of spirits; and it circles round,
Like the soft waving wings of noonday dreams,
Inspiring calm and happy thoughts, like mine,

Now thou art thus restored. This Cave is thine.
Arise! Appear!

[*A* Spirit *rises in the likeness of a winged child.*

This is my torch-bearer,
Who let his lamp out in old time with gazing
On eyes from which he kindled it anew
With love, which is as fire, sweet daughter mine,
For such is that within thine own. Run, wayward,
And guide this company beyond the peak
Of Bacchic Nysa, Maenad-haunted mountain,°
And beyond Indus and its tribute rivers,°
Trampling the torrent streams and glassy lakes
With feet unwet, unwearied, undelaying;
And up the green ravine, across the vale,
Beside the windless and crystalline pool,
Where ever lies, on unerasing waves,
The image of a temple, built above,
Distinct with column, arch, and architrave,
And palm-like capital, and over-wrought,
And populous most with living imagery,
Praxitelean shapes, whose marble smiles°
Fill the hushed air with everlasting love.
It is deserted now, but once it bore
Thy name, Prometheus; there the emulous youths
Bore to thy honour through the divine gloom
The lamp which was thine emblem; even as those°
Who bear the untransmitted torch of hope
Into the grave, across the night of life,
As thou hast borne it most triumphantly
To this far goal of time. Depart, farewell.
Beside that temple is the destined Cave.

Scene 4.—*A forest. In the background a Cave.* Prometheus, Asia, Panthea, Ione, *and the* Spirit of the Earth.°

Ione. Sister, it is not earthly: how it glides
Under the leaves! how on its head there burns
A light, like a green star, whose emerald beams°
Are twined with its fair hair! how, as it moves,
The splendour drops in flakes upon the grass!
Knowest thou it?

Panthea. It is the delicate spirit
That guides the earth through heaven. From afar
The populous constellations call that light
The loveliest of the planets; and sometimes
It floats along the spray of the salt sea,
Or makes its chariot of a foggy cloud,
Or walks through fields or cities while men sleep,
Or o'er the mountain tops, or down the rivers,
Or through the green waste wilderness, as now,
Wondering at all it sees. Before Jove reigned
It loved our sister Asia, and it came
Each leisure hour to drink the liquid light
Out of her eyes, for which it said it thirsted
As one bit by a dipsas; and with her°
It made its childish confidence, and told her
All it had known or seen, for it saw much,
Yet idly reasoned what it saw; and called her,
For whence it sprung it knew not, nor do I,
'Mother, dear mother.'

Spirit of the Earth (*running to Asia*). Mother, dearest mother;
May I then talk with thee as I was wont?
May I then hide my eyes in thy soft arms,
After thy looks have made them tired of joy?
May I then play beside thee the long noons,
When work is none in the bright silent air?

Asia. I love thee, gentlest being, and henceforth
Can cherish thee unenvied: speak, I pray:
Thy simple talk once solaced, now delights.

Spirit of the Earth. Mother, I am grown wiser, though a child
Cannot be wise like thee, within this day;
And happier too; happier and wiser both.
Thou knowest that toads, and snakes, and loathly worms,
And venomous and malicious beasts, and boughs
That bore ill berries in the woods, were ever
An hindrance to my walks o'er the green world:
And that, among the haunts of humankind,
Hard-featured men, or with proud, angry looks,
Or cold, staid gait, or false and hollow smiles,

Or the dull sneer of self-loved ignorance,
Or other such foul masks, with which ill thoughts
Hide that fair being whom we spirits call man;
And women too, ugliest of all things evil,
(Though fair, even in a world where thou art fair,
When good and kind, free and sincere like thee),
When false or frowning made me sick at heart
To pass them, though they slept, and I unseen.
Well, my path lately lay through a great city;
Into the woody hills surrounding it:
A sentinel was sleeping at the gate:
When there was heard a sound, so loud, it shook
The towers amid the moonlight, yet more sweet
Than any voice but thine, sweetest of all,
A long, long sound, as it would never end;
And all the inhabitants leapt suddenly
Out of their rest, and gathered in the streets,
Looking in wonder up to Heaven, while yet
The music pealed along. I hid myself
Within a fountain in the public square,
Where I lay like the reflex of the moon
Seen in a wave under green leaves; and soon
Those ugly human shapes and visages
Of which I spoke as having wrought me pain,
Passed floating through the air, and fading still°
Into the winds that scattered them; and those
From whom they passed seemed mild and lovely forms
After some foul disguise had fallen, and all
Were somewhat changed, and after brief surprise
And greetings of delighted wonder, all
Went to their sleep again: and when the dawn
Came, wouldst thou think that toads, and snakes, and efts,
Could e'er be beautiful? yet so they were,
And that with little change of shape or hue:
All things had put their evil nature off:
I cannot tell my joy, when o'er a lake,
Upon a drooping bough with nightshade twined,
I saw two azure halcyons clinging downward°
And thinning one bright bunch of amber berries
With quick, long beaks, and in the deep there lay
Those lovely forms imaged as in a sky;

So with my thoughts full of these happy changes,
We meet again, the happiest change of all.

Asia. And never will we part, till thy chaste sister
Who guides the frozen and inconstant moon
Will look on thy more warm and equal light
Till her heart thaw like flakes of April snow
And love thee.

Spirit of the Earth. What; as Asia loves Prometheus?

Asia. Peace, wanton, thou art yet not old enough.
Think ye by gazing on each other's eyes
To multiply your lovely selves, and fill
With spherèd fires the interlunar air?

Spirit of the Earth. Nay, mother, while my sister trims her lamp
'Tis hard I should go darkling.

Asia. Listen! look!

[*The* SPIRIT OF THE HOUR *enters.*

Prometheus. We feel what thou hast heard and seen: yet speak.

Spirit of the Hour. Soon as the sound had ceased whose thunder filled
The abysses of the sky and the wide earth,
There was a change: the impalpable thin air
And the all-circling sunlight were transformed,
As if the sense of love, dissolved in them,
Had folded itself round the spherèd world.
My vision then grew clear, and I could see
Into the mysteries of the universe.
Dizzy as with delight I floated down,
Winnowing the lightsome air with languid plumes,
My coursers sought their birthplace in the sun,
Where they henceforth will live exempt from toil,
Pasturing flowers of vegetable fire;
And where my moonlike car will stand within
A temple, gazed upon by Phidian forms°
Of thee, and Asia, and the Earth, and me,

And you fair nymphs, looking the love we feel,
In memory of the tidings it has borne;
Beneath a dome fretted with graven flowers,
Poised on twelve columns of resplendent stone,
And open to the bright and liquid sky.
Yoked to it by an amphisbaenic snake°
The likeness of those wingèd steeds will mock°
The flight from which they find repose. Alas,°
Whither has wandered now my partial tongue
When all remains untold which ye would hear?
As I have said, I floated to the earth:
It was, as it is still, the pain of bliss
To move, to breathe, to be; I wandering went
Among the haunts and dwellings of mankind,
And first was disappointed not to see
Such mighty change as I had felt within
Expressed in outward things; but soon I looked,
And behold, thrones were kingless, and men walked
One with the other even as spirits do:
None fawned, none trampled; hate, disdain, or fear,
Self-love or self-contempt, on human brows
No more inscribed, as o'er the gate of hell,
'All hope abandon, ye who enter here';°
None frowned, none trembled, none with eager fear
Gazed on another's eye of cold command,
Until the subject of a tyrant's will
Became, worse fate, the abject of his own,
Which spurred him, like an outspent horse, to death.
None wrought his lips in truth-entangling lines
Which smiled the lie his tongue disdained to speak;
None, with firm sneer, trod out in his own heart
The sparks of love and hope, till there remained
Those bitter ashes, a soul self-consumed,
And the wretch crept a vampire among men,
Infecting all with his own hideous ill;
None talked that common, false, cold, hollow talk
Which makes the heart deny the *yes* it breathes,
Yet question that unmeant hypocrisy°
With such a self-mistrust as has no name.
And women, too, frank, beautiful, and kind
As the free heaven which rains fresh light and dew

On the wide earth, passed; gentle, radiant forms,
From custom's evil taint exempt and pure;
Speaking the wisdom once they could not think,
Looking emotions once they feared to feel,
And changed to all which once they dared not be,
Yet being now, made Earth like Heaven; nor pride,
Nor jealousy, nor envy, nor ill shame,
The bitterest of those drops of treasured gall,
Spoilt the sweet taste of the nepenthe, love.

Thrones, altars, judgement-seats, and prisons; wherein
And beside which, by wretched men were borne
Sceptres, tiaras, swords, and chains, and tomes
Of reasoned wrong, glozed on by ignorance,
Were like those monstrous and barbaric shapes,
The ghosts of a no more remembered fame,
Which, from their unworn obelisks, look forth
In triumph o'er the palaces and tombs
Of those who were their conquerors, mouldering round.
These imaged to the pride of kings and priests
A dark yet mighty faith, a power as wide
As is the world it wasted, and are now
But an astonishment; even so the tools
And emblems of its last captivity,
Amid the dwellings of the peopled earth,
Stand, not o'erthrown, but unregarded now.
And those foul shapes, abhorred by God and man,
Which under many a name and many a form
Strange, savage, ghastly, dark, and execrable,
Were Jupiter, the tyrant of the world;
And which the nations, panic-stricken, served
With blood, and hearts broken by long hope, and love
Dragged to his altars soiled and garlandless,
And slain amid men's unreclaiming tears,°
Flattering the thing they feared, which fear was hate,
Frown, mouldering fast, o'er their abandoned shrines:
The painted veil, by those who were, called life,
Which mimicked, as with colours idly spread,
All men believed and hoped, is torn aside;
The loathsome mask has fallen, the man remains
Sceptreless, free, uncircumscribed, but man:

Equal, unclassed, tribeless and nationless,
Exempt from awe, worship, degree: the king,
Over himself; just, gentle, wise: but man:
Passionless? no, yet free from guilt or pain,
Which were, for his will made or suffered them,
Nor yet exempt, though ruling them like slaves,
From chance, and death, and mutability,
The clogs of that which else might oversoar
The loftiest star of unascended Heaven,
Pinnacled dim in the intense inane.°

Act 4

SCENE. *A Part of the Forest near the Cave of* PROMETHEUS. PANTHEA *and* IONE *are sleeping: they awaken gradually during the first Song.*

Voice of Unseen Spirits

The pale stars are gone!
For the sun, their swift shepherd,
To their folds them compelling,
In the depths of the dawn,
Hastes, in meteor-eclipsing array, and they flee
Beyond his blue dwelling
As fawns flee the leopard.
But where are ye?

A Train of dark Forms and Shadows passes by confusedly, singing

Here, oh, here!
We bear the bier
Of the Father of many a cancelled year!
Spectres we
Of the dead Hours be,
We bear Time to his tomb in eternity.°

Strew, oh, strew
Hair, not yew!
Wet the dusty pall with tears, not dew!
Be the faded flowers
Of Death's bare bowers
Spread on the corpse of the King of Hours!

Haste, oh, haste!
As shades are chased,
Trembling, by day, from heaven's blue waste,
We melt away,
Like dissolving spray,
From the children of a diviner day,
With the lullaby

Of winds that die
On the bosom of their own harmony!

Ione

What dark forms were they?

Panthea

The past Hours weak and grey,
With the spoil which their toil
Raked together
From the conquest but One could foil.°

Ione

Have they passed?

Panthea

They have passed;
They outspeeded the blast,
While 'tis said, they are fled:

Ione

Whither, oh, whither?

Panthea

To the dark, to the past, to the dead.

Voice of Unseen Spirits

Bright clouds float in heaven,
Dew-stars gleam on earth,
Waves assemble on ocean,
They are gathered and driven
By the storm of delight, by the panic of glee!
They shake with emotion,
They dance in their mirth.
But where are ye?

The pine boughs are singing
Old songs with new gladness,
The billows and fountains
Fresh music are flinging,

Like the notes of a spirit, from land and from sea;
The storms mock the mountains
With the thunder of gladness.
But where are ye?

Ione. What charioteers are these?

Panthea. Where are their chariots?

Semichorus of Hours 1

The voice of the Spirits of Air and of Earth
Have drawn back the figured curtain of sleep°
Which covered our being and darkened our birth
In the deep.

A Voice

In the deep?

Semichorus 2

Oh, below the deep.

Semichorus 1

An hundred ages we had been kept
Cradled in visions of hate and care,
And each one who waked as his brother slept
Found the truth—

Semichorus 2

Worse than his visions were!

Semichorus 1

We have heard the lute of Hope in sleep;
We have known the voice of Love in dreams;
We have felt the wand of Power, and leap—

Semichorus 2

As the billows leap in the morning beams.

Chorus

Weave the dance on the floor of the breeze,
Pierce with song heaven's silent light,
Enchant the day that too swiftly flees,
To check its flight ere the cave of night.

Once the hungry Hours were hounds
Which chased the day like a bleeding deer,
And it limped and stumbled with many wounds
Through the nightly dells of the desert year.

But now, oh weave the mystic measure
Of music, and dance, and shapes of light,
Let the Hours, and the spirits of might and pleasure,
Like the clouds and sunbeams, unite.

A Voice.

Unite!

Panthea. See, where the Spirits of the human mind
Wrapped in sweet sounds, as in bright veils, approach.

Chorus of Spirits

We join the throng
Of the dance and the song,
By the whirlwind of gladness borne along;
As the flying-fish leap
From the Indian deep,
And mix with the sea-birds half asleep.

Chorus of Hours

Whence come ye, so wild and so fleet,
For sandals of lightning are on your feet,
And your wings are soft and swift as thought,
And your eyes are as love which is veilèd not?

Chorus of Spirits

We come from the mind
Of human kind,
Which was late so dusk, and obscene, and blind;
Now 'tis an ocean
Of clear emotion,
A heaven of serene and mighty motion.

From that deep abyss
Of wonder and bliss,

Whose caverns are crystal palaces;
    From those skiey towers
    Where Thought's crowned powers
Sit watching your dance, ye happy Hours!

    From the dim recesses
    Of woven caresses,
Where lovers catch ye by your loose tresses;
    From the azure isles,
    Where sweet Wisdom smiles,
Delaying your ships with her siren wiles.°

    From the temples high
    Of Man's ear and eye,
Roofed over Sculpture and Poesy;
    From the murmurings
    Of the unsealed springs
Where Science bedews his daedal wings.°

    Years after years,
    Through blood and tears,
And a thick hell of hatreds and hopes and fears,
    We waded and flew,
    And the islets were few
Where the bud-blighted flowers of happiness grew.

    Our feet now, every palm,
    Are sandalled with calm,
And the dew of our wings is a rain of balm;
    And, beyond our eyes,
    The human love lies
Which makes all it gazes on Paradise.

Chorus of Spirits and Hours

  Then weave the web of the mystic measure;
From the depths of the sky and the ends of the earth,
  Come, swift Spirits of might and of pleasure,
Fill the dance and the music of mirth,
  As the waves of a thousand streams rush by
  To an ocean of splendour and harmony!

Chorus of Spirits

Our spoil is won,
Our task is done,
We are free to dive, or soar, or run;
Beyond and around,
Or within the bound
Which clips the world with darkness round.°

We'll pass the eyes
Of the starry skies
Into the hoar deep to colonize:
Death, Chaos, and Night,
From the sound of our flight,
Shall flee, like mist from a tempest's might.

And Earth, Air, and Light,
And the Spirit of Might,
Which drives round the stars in their fiery flight;
And Love, Thought, and Breath,
The powers that quell Death,
Wherever we soar shall assemble beneath.

And our singing shall build
In the void's loose field
A world for the Spirit of Wisdom to wield;
We will take our plan
From the new world of man,
And our work shall be called the Promethean.

Chorus of Hours

Break the dance, and scatter the song;
Let some depart, and some remain.

Semichorus 1

We, beyond heaven, are driven along—

Semichorus 2

Us the enchantments of earth retain—

Semichorus 1

Ceaseless, and rapid, and fierce, and free,

With the Spirits which build a new earth and sea,
And a Heaven where yet Heaven could never be—

Semichorus 2

Solemn, and slow and serene, and bright
Leading the Day and outspeeding the Night,
With the powers of a world of perfect light—

Semichorus 1

We whirl, singing loud, round the gathering sphere,°
Till the trees, and the beasts, and the clouds appear
From its chaos made calm by love, not fear—

Semichorus 2

We encircle the oceans and mountains of earth,
And the happy forms of its death and birth
Change to the music of our sweet mirth.

Chorus of Hours and Spirits

Break the dance, and scatter the song,
   Let some depart, and some remain;
Wherever we fly we lead along
In leashes, like starbeams, soft yet strong,
   The clouds that are heavy with love's sweet rain.

Panthea. Ha! they are gone!

Ione. Yet feel you no delight
From the past sweetness?

Panthea. As the bare green hill,
When some soft cloud vanishes into rain,
Laughs with a thousand drops of sunny water
To the unpavilioned sky!

Ione. Even whilst we speak
New notes arise. What is that awful sound?

Panthea. 'Tis the deep music of the rolling world,
Kindling within the strings of the waved air
Aeolian modulations.

Ione. Listen too,
How every pause is filled with under-notes,
Clear, silver, icy, keen, awakening tones,
Which pierce the sense, and live within the soul,
As the sharp stars pierce winter's crystal air
And gaze upon themselves within the sea.

Panthea. But see where, through two openings in the forest
Which hanging branches overcanopy,
And where two runnels of a rivulet,
Between the close moss, violet-inwoven,
Have made their path of melody, like sisters
Who part with sighs that they may meet in smiles,
Turning their dear disunion to an isle
Of lovely grief, a wood of sweet sad thoughts;
Two visions of strange radiance float upon
The ocean-like enchantment of strong sound,
Which flows intenser, keener, deeper yet
Under the ground and through the windless air.

Ione. I see a chariot like that thinnest boat
In which the mother of the months is borne
By ebbing light into her western cave
When she upsprings from interlunar dreams,
O'er which is curved an orblike canopy
Of gentle darkness, and the hills and woods,
Distinctly seen through that dusk aery veil,
Regard like shapes in an enchanter's glass;°
Its wheels are solid clouds, azure and gold,
Such as the genii of the thunderstorm
Pile on the floor of the illumined sea
When the sun rushes under it; they roll
And move and grow as with an inward wind.
Within it sits a wingèd infant, white
Its countenance, like the whiteness of bright snow,
Its plumes are as feathers of sunny frost,
Its limbs gleam white, through the wind-flowing folds
Of its white robe, woof of ethereal pearl.
Its hair is white, the brightness of white light°
Scattered in strings; yet its two eyes are heavens
Of liquid darkness, which the Deity

Within seems pouring, as a storm is poured
From jagged clouds, out of their arrowy lashes,
Tempering the cold and radiant air around
With fire that is not brightness; in its hand°
It sways a quivering moonbeam, from whose point
A guiding power directs the chariot's prow
Over its wheelèd clouds, which, as they roll
Over the grass and flowers and waves, wake sounds
Sweet as a singing rain of silver dew.

Panthea. And from the other opening in the wood
Rushes, with loud and whirlwind harmony,°
A sphere, which is as many thousand spheres,
Solid as crystal, yet through all its mass
Flow, as through empty space, music and light:
Ten thousand orbs involving and involved,
Purple and azure, white and green and golden,
Sphere within sphere; and every space between
Peopled with unimaginable shapes,
Such as ghosts dream dwell in the lampless deep,
Yet each inter-transpicuous; and they whirl°
Over each other with a thousand motions,
Upon a thousand sightless axles spinning,
And with the force of self-destroying swiftness,
Intensely, slowly, solemnly roll on,
Kindling with mingled sounds, and many tones,
Intelligible words and music wild.
With mighty whirl the multitudinous Orb
Grinds the bright brook into an azure mist
Of elemental subtlety, like light;
And the wild odour of the forest flowers,
The music of the living grass and air,
The emerald light of leaf-entangled beams,
Round its intense yet self-conflicting speed,
Seem kneaded into one aerial mass
Which drowns the sense. Within the Orb itself,°
Pillowed upon its alabaster arms,
Like to a child o'erwearied with sweet toil,
On its own folded wings and wavy hair,
The Spirit of the Earth is laid asleep,
And you can see its little lips are moving,

Amid the changing light of their own smiles,
Like one who talks of what he loves in dream.

Ione. 'Tis only mocking the Orb's harmony.°

Panthea. And from a star upon its forehead, shoot,
Like swords of azure fire, or golden spears
With tyrant-quelling myrtle overtwined,°
Embleming Heaven and Earth united now,
Vast beams like spokes of some invisible wheel,
Which whirl as the Orb whirls, swifter than thought,
Filling the abyss with sunlike lightenings,
And perpendicular now, and now transverse,
Pierce the dark soil, and, as they pierce and pass,
Make bare the secrets of the earth's deep heart;
Infinite mine of adamant and gold,
Valueless stones, and unimagined gems,°
And caverns on crystalline columns poised
With vegetable silver overspread;
Wells of unfathomed fire, and water springs
Whence the great sea, even as a child, is fed,
Whose vapours clothe earth's monarch mountain-tops
With kingly, ermine snow. The beams flash on
And make appear the melancholy ruins
Of cancelled cycles; anchors, beaks of ships,
Planks turned to marble, quivers, helms, and spears,
And gorgon-headed targes, and the wheels
Of scythèd chariots, and the emblazonry
Of trophies, standards, and armorial beasts,
Round which death laughed, sepulchred emblems
Of dead destruction, ruin within ruin!
The wrecks beside of many a city vast,
Whose population which the earth grew over
Was mortal, but not human; see, they lie,
Their monstrous works and uncouth skeletons,
Their statues, homes, and fanes; prodigious shapes
Huddled in grey annihilation, split,
Jammed in the hard, black deep; and over these
The anatomies of unknown wingèd things,
And fishes which were isles of living scale,
And serpents, bony chains, twisted around
The iron crags, or within heaps of dust

To which the tortuous strength of their last pangs
Had crushed the iron crags; and over these
The jagged alligator, and the might
Of earth-convulsing behemoth, which once
Were monarch beasts, and on the slimy shores
And weed-overgrown continents of earth
Increased and multiplied like summer worms
On an abandoned corpse, till the blue globe
Wrapped deluge round it like a cloak, and they
Yelled, gasped, and were abolished; or some God
Whose throne was in a comet, passed, and cried,
'Be not!' And like my words they were no more.°

The Earth

The joy, the triumph, the delight, the madness!
The boundless, overflowing, bursting gladness!
The vaporous exultation, not to be confined!
  Ha! ha! the animation of delight
  Which wraps me, like an atmosphere of light,
And bears me as a cloud is borne by its own wind!

The Moon

    Brother mine, calm wanderer,
    Happy globe of land and air,
Some Spirit is darted like a beam from thee,
    Which penetrates my frozen frame,
    And passes with the warmth of flame,
With love, and odour, and deep melody
    Through me, through me!

The Earth

Ha! ha! the caverns of my hollow mountains,
My cloven fire-crags, sound-exulting fountains,
Laugh with a vast and inextinguishable laughter.
  The oceans, and the deserts, and the abysses,
  And the deep air's unmeasured wildernesses,
Answer from all their clouds and billows, echoing after.

  They cry aloud as I do: 'Sceptred Curse,
  Who all our green and azure universe
Threatenedst to muffle round with black destruction, sending

A solid cloud to rain hot thunder-stones,
And splinter and knead down my children's bones,
All I bring forth, to one void mass battering and blending;

'Until each crag-like tower, and storied column,
Palace, and obelisk, and temple solemn,
My imperial mountains crowned with cloud, and snow and fire;
My sea-like forests, every blade and blossom
Which finds a grave or cradle in my bosom,
Were stamped by thy strong hate into a lifeless mire:

'How art thou sunk, withdrawn, covered, drunk up
By thirsty nothing, as the brackish cup
Drained by a desert-troop, a little drop for all!
And from beneath, around, within, above,
Filling thy void annihilation, love
Bursts in like light on caves cloven by the thunder-ball.'

The Moon

The snow upon my lifeless mountains
Is loosened into living fountains,
My solid oceans flow, and sing, and shine:
A spirit from my heart bursts forth,
It clothes with unexpected birth
My cold bare bosom: Oh, it must be thine
On mine, on mine!

Gazing on thee I feel, I know
Green stalks burst forth, and bright flowers grow,
And living shapes upon my bosom move:
Music is in the sea and air,
Wingèd clouds soar here and there,
Dark with the rain new buds are dreaming of:
'Tis love, all love!

The Earth

It interpenetrates my granite mass,
Through tangled roots and trodden clay doth pass
Into the utmost leaves and delicatest flowers;
Upon the winds, among the clouds 'tis spread;
It wakes a life in the forgotten dead,
They breathe a spirit up from their obscurest bowers.

And like a storm, bursting its cloudy prison
With thunder, and with whirlwind, has arisen
Out of the lampless caves of unimagined being,
With earthquake shock and swiftness making shiver
Thought's stagnant chaos, unremoved for ever,
Till hate, and fear, and pain, light-vanquished shadows, fleeing,

Leave Man, who was a many-sided mirror
Which could distort to many a shape of error
This true fair world of things—a sea reflecting love;
Which over all his kind, as the sun's heaven
Gliding o'er ocean, smooth, serene, and even,
Darting from starry depths radiance and light, doth move.

Leave Man, even as a leprous child is left,
Who follows a sick beast to some warm cleft
Of rocks, through which the might of healing springs
is poured;
Then when it wanders home with rosy smile,
Unconscious, and its mother fears awhile
It is a spirit—then, weeps on her child restored.°

Man, oh, not men! a chain of linkèd thought,
Of love and might to be divided not,
Compelling the elements with adamantine stress;
As the sun rules, even with a tyrant's gaze,
The unquiet republic of the maze
Of planets, struggling fierce towards heaven's free wilderness.

Man, one harmonious soul of many a soul,
Whose nature is its own divine control,
Where all things flow to all, as rivers to the sea;
Familiar acts are beautiful through love;
Labour, and pain, and grief, in life's green grove
Sport like tame beasts—none knew how gentle they could be!

His will, with all mean passions, bad delights,
And selfish cares, its trembling satellites,
A spirit ill to guide, but mighty to obey,
Is as a tempest-wingèd ship, whose helm

Love rules, through waves which dare not overwhelm,
Forcing life's wildest shores to own its sovereign sway.

All things confess his strength. Through the cold mass
Of marble and of colour his dreams pass;
Bright threads whence mothers weave the robes their children wear;
Language is a perpetual Orphic song,°
Which rules with daedal harmony a throng
Of thoughts and forms, which else senseless and shapeless were.

The lightning is his slave; heaven's utmost deep
Gives up her stars, and like a flock of sheep
They pass before his eye, are numbered, and roll on!
The tempest is his steed, he strides the air;
And the abyss shouts from her depth laid bare,
'Heaven, hast thou secrets? Man unveils me; I have none.'

The Moon

The shadow of white death has passed
From my path in heaven at last,
A clinging shroud of solid frost and sleep;
And through my newly-woven bowers
Wander happy paramours,
Less mighty, but as mild as those who keep
Thy vales more deep.

The Earth

As the dissolving warmth of dawn may fold
A half-unfrozen dew-globe, green, and gold,
And crystalline, till it becomes a wingèd mist,
And wanders up the vault of the blue day,
Outlives the noon, and on the sun's last ray
Hangs o'er the sea, a fleece of fire and amethyst—

The Moon

Thou art folded, thou art lying
In the light which is undying
Of thine own joy, and heaven's smile divine;
All suns and constellations shower
On thee a light, a life, a power

Which doth array thy sphere; thou pourest thine
On mine, on mine!

The Earth

I spin beneath my pyramid of night°
Which points into the heavens, dreaming delight,
Murmuring victorious joy in my enchanted sleep;
As a youth lulled in love-dreams, faintly sighing,
Under the shadow of his beauty lying,
Which round his rest a watch of light and warmth doth keep.

The Moon

As in the soft and sweet eclipse
When soul meets soul on lovers' lips,
High hearts are calm, and brightest eyes are dull;
So when thy shadow falls on me,
Then am I mute and still, by thee
Covered; of thy love, Orb most beautiful,
Full, oh, too full!

Thou art speeding round the sun,
Brightest world of many a one,
Green and azure sphere, which shinest
With a light which is divinest
Among all the lamps of Heaven
To whom life and light is given;
I, thy crystal paramour,
Borne beside thee by a power
Like the polar Paradise,
Magnet-like, of lovers' eyes;
I, a most enamoured maiden,
Whose weak brain is overladen
With the pleasure of her love,
Maniac-like around thee move,
Gazing, an insatiate bride,
On thy form from every side,
Like a Maenad, round the cup
Which Agave lifted up°
In the weird Cadmaean forest.°
Brother, wheresoe'er thou soarest
I must hurry, whirl and follow

Through the heavens wide and hollow,
Sheltered by the warm embrace
Of thy soul from hungry space,
Drinking from thy sense and sight
Beauty, majesty, and might,
As a lover or chameleon
Grows like what it looks upon,
As a violet's gentle eye
Gazes on the azure sky
Until its hue grows like what it beholds,
As a grey and watery mist
Grows like solid amethyst
Athwart the western mountain it enfolds,
When the sunset sleeps
Upon its snow—

The Earth

And the weak day weeps°
That it should be so.
O gentle Moon, the voice of thy delight
Falls on me like thy clear and tender light
Soothing the seaman, borne the summer night
Through isles forever calm;
O gentle Moon, thy crystal accents pierce
The caverns of my pride's deep universe,
Charming the tiger Joy, whose tramplings fierce
Made wounds which need thy balm.

Panthea. I rise as from a bath of sparkling water,
A bath of azure light, among dark rocks,
Out of the stream of sound.

Ione. Ah me! sweet sister,
The stream of sound has ebbed away from us,
And you pretend to rise out of its wave,
Because your words fall like the clear soft dew
Shaken from a bathing wood-nymph's limbs and hair.

Panthea. Peace! peace! a mighty Power, which is as darkness,
Is rising out of Earth, and from the sky
Is showered like night, and from within the air
Bursts, like eclipse which had been gathered up

Into the pores of sunlight: the bright visions,
Wherein the singing spirits rode and shone,
Gleam like pale meteors through a watery night.

Ione. There is a sense of words upon mine ear.

Panthea. An universal sound like words. Oh, list!

Demogorgon

Thou Earth, calm empire of a happy soul,
Sphere of divinest shapes and harmonies,
Beautiful orb! gathering as thou dost roll
The love which paves thy path along the skies:°

The Earth

I hear: I am as a drop of dew that dies!

Demogorgon

Thou Moon, which gazest on the nightly Earth
With wonder, as it gazes upon thee,
Whilst each to men, and beasts, and the swift birth
Of birds, is beauty, love, calm, harmony:

The Moon

I hear: I am a leaf shaken by thee!

Demogorgon

Ye Kings of suns and stars, Daemons and Gods,
Etherial Dominations, who possess
Elysian, windless, fortunate abodes
Beyond Heaven's constellated wilderness:

A Voice from Above

Our great Republic hears: we are blest, and bless.

Demogorgon

Ye happy dead, whom beams of brightest verse
Are clouds to hide, not colours to portray,
Whether your nature is that universe
Which once ye saw and suffered—

A Voice from Beneath

Or as they
Whom we have left, we change and pass away.

Demogorgon

Ye elemental Genii, who have homes°
From man's high mind even to the central stone
Of sullen lead; from Heaven's star-fretted domes
To the dull weed some sea-worm battens on:

A Confused Voice

We hear: thy words waken Oblivion.

Demogorgon

Spirits, whose homes are flesh: ye beasts and birds,
Ye worms and fish; ye living leaves and buds;
Lightning and wind; and ye untameable herds,
Meteors and mists, which throng air's solitudes:

A Voice

Thy voice to us is wind among still woods.

Demogorgon

Man, who wert once a despot and a slave;
A dupe and a deceiver; a decay;
A traveller from the cradle to the grave
Through the dim night of this immortal day:

All

Speak: thy strong words may never pass away.

Demogorgon

This is the day, which down the void abysm
At the Earth-born's spell yawns for Heaven's despotism,°
And Conquest is dragged captive through the deep;°
Love, from its awful throne of patient power
In the wise heart, from the last giddy hour
Of dread endurance, from the slippery, steep,
And narrow verge of crag-like agony, springs
And folds over the world its healing wings.

Gentleness, Virtue, Wisdom, and Endurance,—
These are the seals of that most firm assurance
Which bars the pit over Destruction's strength;
And if, with infirm hand, Eternity,
Mother of many acts and hours, should free
The serpent that would clasp her with his length,
These are the spells by which to re-assume
An empire o'er the disentangled Doom.

To suffer woes which Hope thinks infinite;
To forgive wrongs darker than death or night;
To defy Power, which seems omnipotent;
To love, and bear; to hope, till Hope creates
From its own wreck the thing it contemplates;
Neither to change, nor falter, nor repent:°
This, like thy glory, Titan, is to be
Good, great and joyous, beautiful and free;
This is alone Life, Joy, Empire, and Victory.

THE CENCI

A TRAGEDY, IN FIVE ACTS

DEDICATION
TO
LEIGH HUNT ESQ.

My dear friend,

I inscribe with your name, from a distant country, and after an absence whose months have seemed years, this the latest of my literary efforts.

Those writings which I have hitherto published, have been little else than visions which impersonate my own apprehensions of the beautiful and the just. I can also perceive in them the literary defects incidental to youth and impatience; they are dreams of what ought to be, or may be. The drama which I now present to you is a sad reality.° I lay aside the presumptuous attitude of an instructor, and am content to paint, with such colours as my own heart furnishes, that which has been.

Had I known a person more highly endowed than yourself with all that it becomes a man to possess, I had solicited for this work the ornament of his name. One more gentle, honourable, innocent and brave; one of more exalted toleration for all who do and think evil, and yet himself more free from evil; one who knows better how to receive, and how to confer a benefit though he must ever confer far more than he can receive; one of simpler, and, in the highest sense of the word, of purer life and manners I never knew: and I had already been fortunate in friendships when your name was added to the list.

In that patient and irreconcilable enmity with domestic and political tyranny and imposture which the tenor of your life has illustrated, and which, had I health and talents should illustrate mine, let us, comforting each other in our task, live and die.

All happiness attend you!
Your affectionate friend,
PERCY B. SHELLEY.

Rome, May 29. 1819.

PREFACE°

A manuscript was communicated to me during my travels in Italy which was copied from the archives of the Cenci Palace at Rome, and contains a detailed account of the horrors which ended in the extinction of one of the noblest and richest families of that city during the Pontificate of Clement VIII,° in the year, 1599. The story is, that an old man having spent his life in debauchery and wickedness, conceived at length an implacable hatred towards his children; which showed itself towards one daughter under the form of an incestuous passion, aggravated by every circumstance of cruelty and violence. This daughter, after long and vain attempts to escape from what she considered a perpetual contamination both of body and mind, at length plotted with her mother-in-law and brother to murder their common tyrant. The young maiden who was urged to this tremendous deed by an impulse which overpowered its horror, was evidently a most gentle and amiable being, a creature formed to adorn and be admired, and thus violently thwarted from her nature by the necessity of circumstance and opinion. The deed was quickly discovered and in spite of the most earnest prayers made to the Pope by the highest persons in Rome the criminals were put to death. The old man had during his life repeatedly bought his pardon from the Pope for capital crimes of the most enormous and unspeakable kind, at the price of a hundred thousand crowns; the death therefore of his victims can scarcely be accounted for by the love of justice. The Pope, among other motives for severity, probably felt that whoever killed the Count Cenci deprived his treasury of a certain and copious source of revenue.° Such a story, if told so as to present to the reader all the feelings of those who once acted it, their hopes and fears, their confidences and misgivings, their various interests, passions and opinions acting upon and with each other, yet all conspiring to one tremendous end, would be as a light to make apparent some of the most dark and secret caverns of the human heart.

On my arrival at Rome I found that the story of the Cenci was a subject not to be mentioned in Italian society without awakening a deep and breathless interest; and that the feelings of the company never failed to incline to a romantic pity for the wrongs, and a passionate exculpation of the horrible deed to which they urged her, who has been mingled two centuries with the common dust. All ranks of people knew the outlines of this history, and participated in the overwhelming interest which it seems to have the magic of exciting in the human heart. I had a copy of Guido's picture of Beatrice which is preserved in the Colonna Palace, and my servant instantly recognized it as the portrait of *La Cenci*.°

This national and universal interest which the story produces and has produced for two centuries and among all ranks of people in a great City, where the imagination is kept for ever active and awake, first suggested to me the conception of its fitness for a dramatic purpose. In fact it is a tragedy which has already received from its capacity of awakening and sustaining the sympathy of men, approbation and success. Nothing remained as I imagined, but to clothe it to the apprehensions of my countrymen in such language and action as would bring it home to their hearts. The deepest and the sublimest tragic compositions, *King Lear* and the two plays in which the tale of Oedipus is told, were stories which already existed in tradition, as matters of popular belief and interest, before Shakespeare and Sophocles made them familiar to the sympathy of all succeeding generations of mankind.

This story of the Cenci is indeed eminently fearful and monstrous: anything like a dry exhibition of it on the stage would be insupportable. The person who would treat such a subject must increase the ideal, and diminish the actual horror of the events, so that the pleasure which arises from the poetry which exists in these tempestuous sufferings and crimes may mitigate the pain of the contemplation of the moral deformity from which they spring. There must also be nothing attempted to make the exhibition subservient to what is vulgarly termed a moral purpose. The highest moral purpose aimed at in the highest species of the drama, is the teaching the human heart, through its sympathies and antipathies, the knowledge of itself; in proportion to the possession of which knowledge, every human being is wise, just, sincere, tolerant and kind. If dogmas can do more, it is well: but a drama is no fit place for the enforcement of them. Undoubtedly, no person can be truly dishonoured by the act of another; and the fit return to make to the most enormous injuries is kindness and forbearance, and a resolution to convert the injurer from his dark passions by peace and love. Revenge, retaliation, atonement, are pernicious mistakes. If Beatrice had thought in this manner she would have been wiser and better; but she would never have been a tragic character: the few whom such an exhibition would have interested, could never have been sufficiently interested for a dramatic purpose, from the want of finding sympathy in their interest among the mass who surround them. It is in the restless and anatomizing casuistry° with which men seek the justification of Beatrice, yet feel that she has done what needs justification; it is in the superstitious horror with which they contemplate alike her wrongs and their revenge; that the dramatic character of what she did and suffered, consists.

I have endeavoured as nearly as possible to represent the characters as they probably were, and have sought to avoid the error of making them actuated by my own conceptions of right or wrong, false or true, thus under a thin veil converting names and actions of the sixteenth century into cold impersonations of my own mind. They are represented as Catholics, and as Catholics deeply tinged with religion. To a Protestant apprehension there will appear something unnatural in the earnest and perpetual sentiment of the relations between God and man which pervade the tragedy of the Cenci. It will especially be startled at the combination of an undoubting persuasion of the truth of the popular religion with a cool and determined perseverance in enormous guilt. But religion in Italy is not, as in Protestant countries, a cloak to be worn on particular days; or a passport which those who do not wish to be railed at carry with them to exhibit; or a gloomy passion for penetrating the impenetrable mysteries of our being, which terrifies its possessor at the darkness of the abyss to the brink of which it has conducted him. Religion coexists, as it were, in the mind of an Italian Catholic with a faith in that of which all men have the most certain knowledge. It is interwoven with the whole fabric of life. It is adoration, faith, submission, penitence, blind admiration; not a rule for moral conduct. It has no necessary connection with any one virtue. The most atrocious villain may be rigidly devout, and without any shock to established faith, confess himself to be so. Religion pervades intensely the whole frame of society, and is according to the temper of the mind which it inhabits, a passion, a persuasion, an excuse, a refuge; never a check. Cenci himself built a chapel in the court of his Palace, and dedicated it to St Thomas the Apostle, and established masses for the peace of his soul. Thus in the first scene of the fourth act Lucretia's design in exposing herself to the consequences of an expostulation with Cenci after having administered the opiate, was to induce him by a feigned tale to confess himself before death; this being esteemed by Catholics as essential to salvation; and she only relinquishes her purpose when she perceives that her perseverance would expose Beatrice to new outrages.

I have avoided with great care in writing this play the introduction of what is commonly called mere poetry, and I imagine there will scarcely be found a detached simile or a single isolated description, unless Beatrice's description of the chasm appointed for her father's murder should be judged to be of that nature.°

In a dramatic composition the imagery and the passion should interpenetrate one another, the former being reserved simply for the full development and illustration of the latter. Imagination is as the immortal God which should assume flesh for the redemption of mortal passion. It is thus that the most remote and the most familiar imagery may alike be fit for dramatic purposes when employed in the illustration of strong feeling, which raises what is low, and levels to the apprehension that which is lofty, casting over all the shadow of its own greatness. In other respects I have written more carelessly; that is without an over-fastidious and learned choice of words. In this respect I entirely agree with those modern critics° who assert that in order to move men to true sympathy we must use the familiar language of men. And that our great ancestors the ancient English poets are the writers a study of whom might incite us to do that for our own age which they have done for theirs. But it must be the real language of men° in general and not that of any particular class to whose society the writer happens to belong. So much for what I have attempted; I need not be assured that success is a very different matter; particularly for one whose attention has but newly been awakened to the study of dramatic literature.

I endeavoured whilst at Rome to observe such monuments of this story as might be accessible to a stranger. The portrait of Beatrice at the Colonna Palace is admirable as a work of art: it was taken by Guido during her confinement in prison. But it is most interesting as a just representation of one of the loveliest specimens of the workmanship of Nature. There is a fixed and pale composure upon the features: she seems sad and stricken down in spirit, yet the despair thus expressed is lightened by the patience of gentleness. Her head is bound with folds of white drapery from which the yellow strings of her golden hair escape, and fall about her neck. The moulding of her face is exquisitely delicate; the eyebrows are distinct and arched: the lips have that permanent meaning of imagination and sensibility which suffering has not repressed and which it seems as if death scarcely could extinguish. Her forehead is large and clear; her eyes which we are told were remarkable for their vivacity, are swollen with weeping and lustreless, but beautifully tender and serene. In the whole mien there is a simplicity and dignity which united with her exquisite loveliness and deep sorrow are inexpressibly pathetic. Beatrice Cenci appears to have been one of those rare persons in whom energy and gentleness dwell together without destroying one another: her nature was simple and profound. The crimes and miseries in which she was an actor and a sufferer are as the mask and the mantle in which circumstances clothed her for her impersonation on the scene of the world.

The Cenci Palace is of great extent; and though in part modernized, there yet remains a vast and gloomy pile of feudal architecture in the same state as during the dreadful scenes which are the subject of this tragedy. The Palace is situated in an obscure corner of Rome, near the quarter of the Jews, and from the upper windows you see the immense ruins of Mount Palatine half hidden under their profuse overgrowth of trees. There is a court in one part of the palace (perhaps that in which Cenci built the Chapel to St Thomas), supported by granite columns and adorned with antique friezes of fine workmanship and built up, according to the ancient Italian fashion, with balcony over balcony of open work. One of the gates of the palace formed of immense stones and leading through a passage, dark and lofty and opening into gloomy subterranean chambers, struck me particularly.

Of the Castle of Petrella, I could obtain no further information than that which is to be found in the manuscript.

DRAMATIS PERSONAE

COUNT FRANCESCO CENCI.
GIACOMO. } his sons.
BERNARDO. }
CARDINAL CAMILLO.
ORSINO, a prelate.
SAVELLA, the Pope's Legate.
OLIMPIO. } Assassins.
MARZIO. }
ANDREA, servant to Cenci.
Nobles, Judges, Guards, Servants.

LUCRETIA. Wife of Cenci, and Step-mother of his children.
BEATRICE, his daughter.

The Scene lies principally in Rome, but changes during the fourth Act to Petrella a castle among the Apulian Apennines.

Time. During the Pontificate of Clement VIII.

Act I

SCENE I.—*An apartment in the* CENCI *Palace.*
Enter COUNT CENCI, *and* CARDINAL CAMILLO.

Camillo. That matter of the murder is hushed up.°
If you consent to yield his Holiness
Your fief that lies beyond the Pincian gate.—°
It needed all my interest in the conclave
To bend him to this point: he said that you
Bought perilous impunity with your gold;
That crimes like yours if once or twice compounded
Enriched the Church, and respited from hell
An erring soul which might repent and live:—
But that the glory and the interest
Of the high throne he fills, little consist
With making it a daily mart of guilt
As manifold and hideous as the deeds
Which you scarce hide from men's revolted eyes.

Cenci. The third of my possessions—let it go!
Aye, I once heard the nephew of the Pope°
Had sent his architect to view the ground,
Meaning to build a villa on my vines
The next time I compounded with his uncle:
I little thought he should outwit me so!
Henceforth no witness—not the lamp—shall see
That which the vassal threatened to divulge
Whose throat is choked with dust for his reward.
The deed he saw could not have rated higher
Than his most worthless life:—it angers me!
Respited me from Hell!—So may the Devil
Respite their souls from Heaven. No doubt Pope Clement,
And his most charitable nephews, pray
That the apostle Peter and the saints
Will grant for their sake that I long enjoy
Strength, wealth, and pride, and lust, and length of days
Wherein to act the deeds which are the stewards
Of their revenue.—But much yet remains
To which they show no title.

Camillo. Oh, Count Cenci!
So much that thou mightst honourably live
And reconcile thyself with thine own heart
And with thy God, and with the offended world.
How hideously look deeds of lust and blood
Through those snow-white and venerable hairs!—
Your children should be sitting round you now,
But that you fear to read upon their looks
The shame and misery you have written there.
Where is your wife? Where is your gentle daughter?
Methinks her sweet looks, which make all things else
Beauteous and glad, might kill the fiend within you.
Why is she barred from all society
But her own strange and uncomplaining wrongs?
Talk with me, Count,—you know I mean you well.
I stood beside your dark and fiery youth
Watching its bold and bad career, as men
Watch meteors, but it vanished not—I marked
Your desperate and remorseless manhood; now
Do I behold you in dishonoured age
Charged with a thousand unrepented crimes.
Yet I have ever hoped you would amend,
And in that hope have saved your life three times.

Cenci. For which Aldobrandino owes you now°
My fief beyond the Pincian.—Cardinal,
One thing, I pray you, recollect henceforth,
And so we shall converse with less restraint.
A man you knew spoke of my wife and daughter—
He was accustomed to frequent my house;
So the next day *his* wife and daughter came
And asked if I had seen him; and I smiled:
I think they never saw him any more.

Camillo. Thou execrable man, beware!—

Cenci. Of thee?
Nay this is idle:—We should know each other.
As to my character for what men call crime,
Seeing I please my senses as I list,
And vindicate that right with force or guile,

It is a public matter, and I care not
If I discuss it with you. I may speak
Alike to you and my own conscious heart—
For you give out that you have half reformed me,
Therefore strong vanity will keep you silent
If fear should not; both will, I do not doubt.
All men delight in sensual luxury,
All men enjoy revenge; and most exult
Over the tortures they can never feel—
Flattering their secret peace with others' pain.
But I delight in nothing else. I love
The sight of agony, and the sense of joy,
When this shall be another's, and that mine.
And I have no remorse and little fear,
Which are, I think, the checks of other men.
This mood has grown upon me, until now
Any design my captious fancy makes
The picture of its wish, and it forms none
But such as men like you would start to know,
Is as my natural food and rest debarred
Until it be accomplished.

Camillo. Art thou not
Most miserable?

Cenci. Why, miserable?—
No.—I am what your theologians call
Hardened;—which they must be in impudence,
So to revile a man's peculiar taste.
True, I was happier than I am, while yet
Manhood remained to act the thing I thought;
While lust was sweeter than revenge; and now
Invention palls:—Aye, we must all grow old—
And but that there remains a deed to act
Whose horror might make sharp an appetite
Duller than mine—I'd do,—I know not what.
When I was young I thought of nothing else
But pleasure; and I fed on honey sweets:
Men, by St Thomas! cannot live like bees
And I grew tired:—yet, till I killed a foe,

And heard his groans, and heard his children's groans,
Knew I not what delight was else on earth,
Which now delights me little. I the rather
Look on such pangs as terror ill conceals,
The dry fixed eyeball; the pale quivering lip,
Which tell me that the spirit weeps within
Tears bitterer than the bloody sweat of Christ.°
I rarely kill the body which preserves,
Like a strong prison, the soul within my power,
Wherein I feed it with the breath of fear
For hourly pain.

Camillo. Hell's most abandoned fiend
Did never, in the drunkenness of guilt,
Speak to his heart as now you speak to me,
I thank my God that I believe you not.

Enter ANDREA.

Andrea. My Lord, a gentleman from Salamanca
Would speak with you.

Cenci. Bid him attend me in
The grand saloon.

[*Exit* ANDREA.

Camillo. Farewell; and I will pray
Almighty God that thy false, impious words
Tempt not his spirit to abandon thee.

[*Exit* CAMILLO.

Cenci. The third of my possessions! I must use
Close husbandry, or gold, the old man's sword,
Falls from my withered hand. But yesterday
There came an order from the Pope to make
Fourfold provision for my cursèd sons;
Whom I had sent from Rome to Salamanca,
Hoping some accident might cut them off;
And meaning if I could to starve them there.
I pray thee, God, send some quick death upon them!
Bernardo and my wife could not be worse
If dead and damned:—then, as to Beatrice—

[*looking around him suspiciously*

I think they cannot hear me at that door;
What if they should? And yet I need not speak
Though the heart triumphs with itself in words.
O, thou most silent air, that shalt not hear
What now I think! Thou, pavement, which I tread
Towards her chamber,—let your echoes talk
Of my imperious step scorning surprise,
But not of my intent!—Andrea!°

Enter ANDREA.

Andrea. My lord?

Cenci. Bid Beatrice attend me in her chamber
This evening:—no, at midnight and alone.

[*Exeunt.*

SCENE 2.—*A garden of the Cenci Palace.*

Enter BEATRICE *and* ORSINO, *as in conversation.*

Beatrice. Pervert not truth,
Orsino. You remember where we held
That conversation;—nay, we see the spot
Even from this cypress;—two long years are past
Since, on an April midnight, underneath
The moonlight ruins of mount Palatine,
I did confess to you my secret mind.

Orsino. You said you loved me then.

Beatrice. You are a Priest,
Speak to me not of love.

Orsino. I may obtain
The dispensation of the Pope to marry.
Because I am a Priest do you believe
Your image, as the hunter some struck deer,
Follows me not whether I wake or sleep?

Beatrice. As I have said, speak to me not of love;
Had you a dispensation, I have not;
Nor will I leave this home of misery
Whilst my poor Bernard, and that gentle lady
To whom I owe life, and these virtuous thoughts,

Must suffer what I still have strength to share.
Alas, Orsino! All the love that once
I felt for you, is turned to bitter pain.
Ours was a youthful contract, which you first
Broke, by assuming vows no Pope will loose.
And thus I love you still, but holily,
Even as a sister or a spirit might;
And so I swear a cold fidelity.
And it is well perhaps we shall not marry.
You have a sly, equivocating vein
That suits me not.—Ah, wretched that I am!
Where shall I turn? Even now you look on me
As you were not my friend, and as if you
Discovered that I thought so, with false smiles
Making my true suspicion seem your wrong.
Ah! no, forgive me; sorrow makes me seem
Sterner than else my nature might have been;
I have a weight of melancholy thoughts,
And they forbode,—but what can they forbode
Worse than I now endure?

Orsino. All will be well.
Is the petition yet prepared? You know
My zeal for all you wish, sweet Beatrice;
Doubt not but I will use my utmost skill
So that the Pope attend to your complaint.

Beatrice. Your zeal for all I wish;—Ah me, you are cold!
Your utmost skill . . . speak but one word . . . (*aside*) Alas!
Weak and deserted creature that I am,
Here I stand bickering with my only friend!
[*To* ORSINO.
This night my father gives a sumptuous feast,
Orsino; he has heard some happy news
From Salamanca, from my brothers there,
And with this outward show of love he mocks
His inward hate. 'Tis bold hypocrisy
For he would gladlier celebrate their deaths,
Which I have heard him pray for on his knees:
Great God! that such a father should be mine!
But there is mighty preparation made,

And all our kin, the Cenci, will be there,
And all the chief nobility of Rome.
And he has bidden me and my pale Mother
Attire ourselves in festival array.
Poor lady! She expects some happy change
In his dark spirit from this act; I none.
At supper I will give you the petition:
Till when—farewell.

Orsino. Farewell.

[*Exit* BEATRICE.

I know the Pope
Will ne'er absolve me from my priestly vow
But by absolving me from the revenue
Of many a wealthy see; and, Beatrice,
I think to win thee at an easier rate.
Nor shall he read her eloquent petition:
He might bestow her on some poor relation
Of his sixth cousin, as he did her sister,
And I should be debarred from all access.
Then as to what she suffers from her father,
In all this there is much exaggeration:—
Old men are testy and will have their way;
A man may stab his enemy, or his vassal,
And live a free life as to wine or women,
And with a peevish temper may return
To a dull home, and rate his wife and children;
Daughters and wives call this, foul tyranny.
I shall be well content if on my conscience
There rest no heavier sin than what they suffer
From the devices of my love—A net
From which she shall escape not. Yet I fear
Her subtle mind, her awe-inspiring gaze,
Whose beams anatomize me nerve by nerve°
And lay me bare, and make me blush to see
My hidden thoughts.—Ah, no! A friendless girl
Who clings to me, as to her only hope:—
I were a fool, not less than if a panther
Were panic-stricken by the Antelope's eye,
If she escape me.

[*Exit.*

SCENE 3.—*A magnificent Hall in the Cenci Palace. A Banquet.*
Enter CENCI, LUCRETIA, BEATRICE, ORSINO, CAMILLO, NOBLES.

Cenci. Welcome, my friends and Kinsmen; welcome ye,
Princes and Cardinals, pillars of the church,
Whose presence honours our festivity.
I have too long lived like an Anchorite,°
And in my absence from your merry meetings
An evil word is gone abroad of me;
But I do hope that you, my noble friends,
When you have shared the entertainment here,
And heard the pious cause for which 'tis given,
And we have pledged a health or two together,
Will think me flesh and blood as well as you;
Sinful indeed, for Adam made all so,
But tender-hearted, meek and pitiful.

First Guest. In truth, my Lord, you seem too light of heart,
Too sprightly and companionable a man,
To act the deeds that rumour pins on you.
[*To his companion*
I never saw such blithe and open cheer
In any eye!

Second Guest. Some most desired event,
In which we all demand a common joy,
Has brought us hither; let us hear it, Count.

Cenci. It is indeed a most desired event.
If when a parent from a parent's heart
Lifts from this earth to the great father of all
A prayer, both when he lays him down to sleep,
And when he rises up from dreaming it;
One supplication, one desire, one hope,
That he would grant a wish for his two sons
Even all that he demands in their regard—
And suddenly beyond his dearest hope,
It is accomplished, he should then rejoice,
And call his friends and kinsmen to a feast,
And task their love to grace his merriment,
Then honour me thus far—for I am he.

Beatrice (*to* LUCRETIA). Great God! How horrible! Some dreadful ill°
Must have befallen my brothers.

Lucretia. Fear not, Child,
He speaks too frankly.

Beatrice. Ah! My blood runs cold.
I fear that wicked laughter round his eye
Which wrinkles up the skin even to the hair.

Cenci. Here are the letters brought from Salamanca;
Beatrice, read them to your mother. God!
I thank thee! In one night didst thou perform,°
By ways inscrutable, the thing I sought.
My disobedient and rebellious sons
Are dead!—Why, dead!—What means this change of cheer?
You hear me not, I tell you they are dead;
And they will need no food or raiment more:
The tapers that did light them the dark way
Are their last cost. The Pope, I think, will not
Expect I should maintain them in their coffins.
Rejoice with me—my heart is wondrous glad.
[LUCRETIA *sinks, half fainting;* BEATRICE *supports her.*

Beatrice. It is not true!—Dear lady, pray look up.
Had it been true, there is a God in Heaven,
He would not live to boast of such a boon.
Unnatural man, thou knowest that it is false.

Cenci. Aye, as the word of God; whom here I call
To witness that I speak the sober truth;—
And whose most favouring Providence was shown
Even in the manner of their deaths. For Rocco
Was kneeling at the mass, with sixteen others,
When the Church fell and crushed him to a mummy,
The rest escaped unhurt. Cristofano°
Was stabbed in error by a jealous man,
Whilst she he loved was sleeping with his rival;
All in the self-same hour of the same night;
Which shows that Heaven has special care of me.

I beg those friends who love me, that they mark
The day a feast upon their calenders.
It was the twenty-seventh of December:°
Aye, read the letters if you doubt my oath.
[*The assembly appears confused; several of the guests rise.*

First Guest. Oh, horrible! I will depart.—

Second Guest. And I.—

Third Guest. No, stay!
I do believe it is some jest; though faith!
'Tis mocking us somewhat too solemnly.
I think his son has married the Infanta,°
Or found a mine of gold in El Dorado;°
'Tis but to season some such news; stay, stay!
I see 'tis only raillery by his smile.

Cenci (*filling a bowl of wine, and lifting it up*). Oh, thou bright wine whose purple splendour leaps
And bubbles gaily in this golden bowl
Under the lamplight, as my spirits do,
To hear the death of my accursèd sons!
Could I believe thou wert their mingled blood,
Then would I taste thee like a sacrament,°
And pledge with thee the mighty Devil in Hell,
Who, if a father's curses, as men say,
Climb with swift wings after their children's souls,
And drag them from the very throne of Heaven,
Now triumphs in my triumph!—But thou art
Superfluous; I have drunken deep of joy
And I will taste no other wine tonight.
Here, Andrea! Bear the bowl around.

A Guest (*rising*). Thou wretch!
Will none among this noble company
Check the abandoned villain?

Camillo. For God's sake
Let me dismiss the guests! You are insane,
Some ill will come of this.

Second Guest. Seize, silence him!

First Guest. I will!

Third Guest. And I!

Cenci (*addressing those who rise with a threatening gesture*). Who moves? Who speaks?

[*Turning to the Company.*

'Tis nothing,
Enjoy yourselves.—Beware! For my revenge
Is as the sealed commission of a king
That kills, and none dare name the murderer.

[*The Banquet is broken up; several of the Guests are departing.*

Beatrice. I do entreat you, go not, noble guests;
What, although tyranny and impious hate
Stand sheltered by a father's hoary hair?
What, if 'tis he who clothed us in these limbs
Who tortures them, and triumphs? What, if we,
The desolate and the dead, were his own flesh,
His children and his wife, whom he is bound
To love and shelter? Shall we therefore find
No refuge in this merciless wide world?
Oh, think what deep wrongs must have blotted out
First love, then reverence in a child's prone mind,°
Till it thus vanquish shame and fear! O, think°
I have borne much, and kissed the sacred hand
Which crushed us to the earth, and thought its stroke
Was perhaps some paternal chastisement!
Have excused much, doubted; and when no doubt
Remained, have sought by patience, love and tears
To soften him, and when this could not be
I have knelt down through the long sleepless nights
And lifted up to God, the father of all,
Passionate prayers: and when these were not heard
I have still borne,—until I meet you here,
Princes and kinsmen, at this hideous feast
Given at my brothers' deaths. Two yet remain,
His wife remains and I, whom if ye save not,
Ye may soon share such merriment again

As fathers make over their children's graves.
Oh! Prince Colonna, thou art our near kinsman,°
Cardinal, thou art the Pope's chamberlain,
Camillo, thou art chief justiciary,
Take us away!

Cenci. (*He has been conversing with* CAMILLO *during the first part of* BEATRICE*'s speech; he hears the conclusion, and now advances*.) I hope my good friends here
Will think of their own daughters—or perhaps
Of their own throats—before they lend an ear
To this wild girl.

Beatrice (*not noticing the words of Cenci*). Dare no one look on me?
None answer? Can one tyrant overbear
The sense of many best and wisest men?
Or is it that I sue not in some form
Of scrupulous law, that ye deny my suit?
Oh, God! That I were buried with my brothers!
And that the flowers of this departed spring
Were fading on my grave! And that my father
Were celebrating now one feast for all!

Camillo. A bitter wish for one so young and gentle;
Can we do nothing?—

Colonna. Nothing that I see.
Count Cenci were a dangerous enemy:
Yet I would second any one.

A Cardinal. And I.

Cenci. Retire to your chamber, insolent girl!

Beatrice. Retire thou, impious man! Aye, hide thyself
Where never eye can look upon thee more!
Wouldst thou have honour and obedience
Who art a torturer? Father, never dream,
Though thou mayst overbear this company,
But ill must come of ill.—Frown not on me!°

Haste, hide thyself, lest with avenging looks
My brothers' ghosts should hunt thee from thy seat!
Cover thy face from every living eye,
And start if thou but hear a human step:
Seek out some dark and silent corner, there,
Bow thy white head before offended God,
And we will kneel around, and fervently
Pray that he pity both ourselves and thee.

Cenci. My friends, I do lament this insane girl
Has spoilt the mirth of our festivity.
Good night, farewell; I will not make you longer
Spectators of our dull domestic quarrels.
Another time.—

[*Exeunt all but* CENCI *and* BEATRICE.

My brain is swimming round;
Give me a bowl of wine!
(*To* BEATRICE) Thou painted viper!
Beast that thou art! Fair and yet terrible!
I know a charm shall make thee meek and tame,
Now get thee from my sight!

[*Exit* BEATRICE.

Here, Andrea,
Fill up this goblet with Greek wine. I said
I would not drink this evening; but I must;
For, strange to say, I feel my spirits fail
With thinking what I have decreed to do.—

[*Drinking the wine.*

Be thou the resolution of quick youth
Within my veins, and manhood's purpose stern,
And age's firm, cold, subtle villainy;
As if thou wert indeed my children's blood
Which I did thirst to drink! The charm works well;
It must be done; it shall be done, I swear!°

[*Exit.*

END OF THE FIRST ACT.

Act 2

SCENE I.—*An apartment in the Cenci Palace.*
Enter LUCRETIA *and* BERNARDO.

Lucretia. Weep not, my gentle boy; he struck but me
Who have borne deeper wrongs. In truth, if he
Had killed me, he had done a kinder deed.
O, God Almighty, do thou look upon us,
We have no other friend but only thee!
Yet weep not; though I love you as my own
I am not your true mother.

Bernardo. Oh more, more,
Than ever mother was to any child,
That have you been to me! Had he not been
My father, do you think that I should weep?

Lucretia. Alas! Poor boy, what else couldst thou have done?
Enter BEATRICE.

Beatrice (*in a hurried voice*). Did he pass this way? Have you seen him, brother?
Ah! no, that is his step upon the stairs;
'Tis nearer now; his hand is on the door;
Mother, if I to thee have ever been
A duteous child, now save me! Thou, great God,
Whose image upon earth a father is,
Dost thou indeed abandon me! He comes;
The door is opening now; I see his face;
He frowns on others, but he smiles on me,
Even as he did after the feast last night.
Enter a Servant.
Almighty God, how merciful thou art!
'Tis but Orsino's servant.—Well, what news?

Servant. My master bids me say, the Holy Father
Has sent back your petition thus unopened.
[*Giving a paper*
And he demands at what hour 'twere secure
To visit you again?

Lucretia. At the Ave Mary.

[*Exit Servant.*

So, daughter, our last hope has failed; Ah me!
How pale you look; you tremble, and you stand
Wrapped in some fixed and fearful meditation,
As if one thought were over-strong for you.
Your eyes have a chill glare; O, dearest child!
Are you gone mad? If not, pray speak to me.

Beatrice. You see I am not mad; I speak to you.

Lucretia. You talked of something that your father did
After that dreadful feast? Could it be worse
Than when he smiled, and cried, 'My sons are dead!'
And every one looked in his neighbour's face
To see if others were as white as he?
At the first word he spoke I felt the blood
Rush to my heart, and fell into a trance;
And when it passed I sat all weak and wild;
Whilst you alone stood up, and with strong words
Checked his unnatural pride; and I could see
The devil was rebuked that lives in him.
Until this hour thus you have ever stood
Between us and your father's moody wrath°
Like a protecting presence: your firm mind
Has been our only refuge and defence:
What can have thus subdued it? What can now
Have given you that cold melancholy look,
Succeeding to your unaccustomed fear?

Beatrice. What is it that you say? I was just thinking
'Twere better not to struggle any more.
Men, like my father, have been dark and bloody,
Yet never—O! Before worse comes of it
'Twere wise to die: it ends in that at last.

Lucretia. Oh, talk not so, dear child! Tell me at once
What did your father do or say to you?
He stayed not after that accursèd feast
One moment in your chamber.—Speak to me.

Bernardo. Oh, sister, sister, prithee, speak to us!

Beatrice (*speaking very slowly with a forced calmness*). It was one word, Mother, one little word;
One look, one smile. (*wildly*)
Oh! He has trampled me
Under his feet, and made the blood stream down
My pallid cheeks. And he has given us all
Ditch water, and the fever-stricken flesh
Of buffaloes, and bade us eat or starve,
And we have eaten.—He has made me look
On my beloved Bernardo, when the rust
Of heavy chains has gangrened his sweet limbs,
And I have never yet despaired—but now!
What would I say? (*Recovering herself*)
Ah! no, 'tis nothing new.
The sufferings we all share have made me wild:
He only struck and cursed me as he passed;
He said, he looked, he did,—nothing at all
Beyond his wont, yet it disordered me.
Alas! I am forgetful of my duty,
I should preserve my senses for your sake.

Lucretia. Nay, Beatrice; have courage, my sweet girl.
If any one despairs it should be I.
Who loved him once, and now must live with him
Till God in pity call for him or me.
For you may, like your sister, find some husband,
And smile, years hence, with children round your knees;
Whilst I, then dead, and all this hideous coil°
Shall be remembered only as a dream.

Beatrice. Talk not to me, dear lady, of a husband.
Did you not nurse me when my mother died?
Did you not shield me and that dearest boy?
And had we any other friend but you
In infancy, with gentle words and looks,
To win our father not to murder us?
And shall I now desert you? May the ghost
Of my dead Mother plead against my soul

If I abandon her who filled the place
She left, with more, even, than a mother's love!

Bernardo. And I am of my sister's mind. Indeed
I would not leave you in this wretchedness,
Even though the Pope should make me free to live
In some blithe place, like others of my age,
With sports, and delicate food, and the fresh air.
Oh, never think that I will leave you, Mother!

Lucretia. My dear, dear children!

Enter CENCI, *suddenly*.

Cenci. What, Beatrice here!
Come hither! (*she shrinks back, and covers her face*)
Nay, hide not your face, 'tis fair;
Look up! Why, yesternight you dared to look
With disobedient insolence upon me,
Bending a stern and an inquiring brow
On what I meant; whilst I then sought to hide
That which I came to tell you—but in vain.

Beatrice (*wildly, staggering towards the door*). Oh, that the earth would gape! Hide me, oh God!°

Cenci. Then it was I whose inarticulate words
Fell from my lips, and who with tottering steps
Fled from your presence, as you now from mine.
Stay, I command you—from this day and hour
Never again, I think, with fearless eye,
And brow superior, and unaltered cheek,
And that lip made for tenderness or scorn,
Shalt thou strike dumb the meanest of mankind;
Me least of all. Now get thee to thy chamber!
Thou too, loathed image of thy cursèd mother,

[*to* BERNARDO

Thy milky, meek face makes me sick with hate!

[*Exeunt* BEATRICE *and* BERNARDO.

(*Aside*) So much has passed between us as must make
Me bold, her fearful.—'Tis an awful thing

To touch such mischief as I now conceive:
So men sit shivering on the dewy bank,
And try the chill stream with their feet; once in
How the delighted spirit pants for joy!

Lucretia (*advancing timidly towards him*). Oh, husband!
Pray forgive poor Beatrice,
She meant not any ill.

Cenci. Nor you perhaps?
Nor that young imp, whom you have taught by rote
Parricide with his alphabet? Nor Giacomo?
Nor those two most unnatural sons, who stirred
Enmity up against me with the Pope?
Whom in one night merciful God cut off:
Innocent lambs! They thought not any ill.
You were not here conspiring? You said nothing
Of how I might be dungeoned as a madman;
Or be condemned to death for some offence,
And you would be the witnesses?—This failing,
How just it were to hire assassins, or
Put sudden poison in my evening drink?
Or smother me when overcome by wine?
Seeing we had no other judge but God,
And he had sentenced me, and there were none
But you to be the executioners
Of his decree enregistered in heaven?
Oh, no! You said not this?

Lucretia. So help me God,
I never thought the things you charge me with!

Cenci. If you dare speak that wicked lie again
I'll kill you. What! It was not by your counsel
That Beatrice disturbed the feast last night?
You did not hope to stir some enemies
Against me, and escape, and laugh to scorn
What every nerve of you now trembles at?
You judged that men were bolder than they are;
Few dare to stand between their grave and me.

Lucretia. Look not so dreadfully! By my salvation
I knew not aught that Beatrice designed;
Nor do I think she designed any thing
Until she heard you talk of her dead brothers.

Cenci. Blaspheming liar! You are damned for this!
But I will take you where you may persuade
The stones you tread on to deliver you:
For men shall there be none but those who dare
All things—not question that which I command.
On Wednesday next I shall set out: you know
That savage rock, the Castle of Petrella,
'Tis safely walled, and moated round about:
Its dungeons underground, and its thick towers
Never told tales; though they have heard and seen
What might make dumb things speak.—Why do you linger?
Make speediest preparation for the journey!

[*Exit* LUCRETIA.

The all-beholding sun yet shines; I hear
A busy stir of men about the streets;
I see the bright sky through the window panes;
It is a garish, broad, and peering day;°
Loud, light, suspicious, full of eyes and ears,
And every little corner, nook and hole
Is penetrated with the insolent light.
Come, darkness! Yet, what is the day to me?°
And wherefore should I wish for night, who do
A deed which shall confound both night and day?
'Tis she shall grope through a bewildering mist
Of horror: if there be a sun in heaven°
She shall not dare to look upon its beams;
Nor feel its warmth. Let her then wish for night;
The act I think shall soon extinguish all
For me: I bear a darker deadlier gloom
Than the earth's shade, or interlunar air,
Or constellations quenched in murkiest cloud,
In which I walk secure and unbeheld
Towards my purpose.—Would that it were done!

[*Exit*.

SCENE 2.—*A chamber in the Vatican.*
Enter CAMILLO *and* GIACOMO, *in conversation.*

Camillo. There is an obsolete and doubtful law
By which you might obtain a bare provision
Of food and clothing—

Giacomo. Nothing more? Alas!
Bare must be the provision which strict law
Awards, and aged, sullen avarice pays.
Why did my father not apprentice me
To some mechanic trade? I should have then
Been trained in no highborn necessities
Which I could meet not by my daily toil.
The eldest son of a rich nobleman
Is heir to all his incapacities;
He has wide wants, and narrow powers. If you,
Cardinal Camillo, were reduced at once
From thrice-driven beds of down, and delicate food,°
An hundred servants, and six palaces,
To that which nature doth indeed require?—

Camillo. Nay, there is reason in your plea; 'twere hard.

Giacomo. 'Tis hard for a firm man to bear: but I
Have a dear wife, a lady of high birth,
Whose dowry in ill hour I lent my father
Without a bond or witness to the deed:
And children, who inherit her fine senses,
The fairest creatures in this breathing world;
And she and they reproach me not. Cardinal,
Do you not think the Pope would interpose
And stretch authority beyond the law?

Camillo. Though your peculiar case is hard, I know
The Pope will not divert the course of law.
After that impious feast the other night
I spoke with him, and urged him then to check
Your father's cruel hand; he frowned and said,
'Children are disobedient, and they sting
Their fathers' hearts to madness and despair,

Requiting years of care with contumely.
I pity the Count Cenci from my heart;
His outraged love perhaps awakened hate,
And thus he is exasperated to ill.
In the great war between the old and young
I, who have white hairs and a tottering body,
Will keep at least blameless neutrality.'

Enter ORSINO.

You, my good lord Orsino, heard those words.

Orsino. What words?

Giacomo. Alas, repeat them not again!
There then is no redress for me, at least
None but that which I may achieve myself,
Since I am driven to the brink.—But, say,
My innocent sister and my only brother
Are dying underneath my father's eye.
The memorable torturers of this land,
Galeaz Visconti, Borgia, Ezzelin,°
Never inflicted on their meanest slave
What these endure; shall they have no protection?

Camillo. Why, if they would petition to the Pope
I see not how he could refuse it—yet
He holds it of most dangerous example
In aught to weaken the paternal power,
Being, as 'twere, the shadow of his own.
I pray you now excuse me. I have business
That will not bear delay.

[*Exit* CAMILLO.

Giacomo. But you, Orsino,
Have the petition: wherefore not present it?

Orsino. I have presented it, and backed it with
My earnest prayers, and urgent interest;
It was returned unanswered. I doubt not
But that the strange and execrable deeds
Alleged in it—in truth they might well baffle
Any belief—have turned the Pope's displeasure
Upon the accusers from the criminal:
So I should guess from what Camillo said.

Giacomo. My friend, that palace-walking devil Gold
Has whispered silence to his Holiness:
And we are left, as scorpions ringed with fire,
What should we do but strike ourselves to death?°
For he who is our murderous persecutor
Is shielded by a father's holy name,
Or I would—(*stops abruptly*)

Orsino. What? Fear not to speak your thought.
Words are but holy as the deeds they cover:
A priest who has forsworn the God he serves;
A judge who makes Truth weep at his decree;
A friend who should weave counsel, as I now,
But as the mantle of some selfish guile;
A father who is all a tyrant seems,
Were the profaner for his sacred name.

Giacomo. Ask me not what I think; the unwilling brain
Feigns often what it would not; and we trust
Imagination with such fantasies
As the tongue dares not fashion into words,
Which have no words, their horror makes them dim
To the mind's eye.—My heart denies itself
To think what you demand.

Orsino. But a friend's bosom
Is as the inmost cave of our own mind
Where we sit shut from the wide gaze of day,
And from the all-communicating air.
You look what I suspected—

Giacomo. Spare me now!
I am as one lost in a midnight wood
Who dares not ask some harmless passenger
The path across the wilderness, lest he,
As my thoughts are, should be—a murderer.
I know you are my friend, and all I dare
Speak to my soul that will I trust with thee.
But now my heart is heavy and would take
Lone counsel from a night of sleepless care.
Pardon me, that I say farewell—farewell!

I would that to my own suspected self
I could address a word so full of peace.

Orsino. Farewell!—Be your thoughts better or more bold.
[*Exit* GIACOMO.

I had disposed the Cardinal Camillo
To feed his hope with cold encouragement:
It fortunately serves my close designs
That 'tis a trick of this same family
To analyse their own and other minds.
Such self-anatomy shall teach the will
Dangerous secrets: for it tempts our powers,
Knowing what must be thought, and may be done,
Into the depth of darkest purposes:
So Cenci fell into the pit; even I,
Since Beatrice unveiled me to myself,
And made me shrink from what I cannot shun,
Show a poor figure to my own esteem,
To which I grow half reconciled. I'll do
As little mischief as I can; that thought
Shall fee the accuser conscience.° (*After a pause*)
Now what harm
If Cenci should be murdered?—Yet, if murdered,
Wherefore by me? And what if I could take
The profit, yet omit the sin and peril
In such an action? Of all earthly things
I fear a man whose blows outspeed his words;
And such is Cenci: and while Cenci lives
His daughter's dowry were a secret grave
If a priest wins her.—Oh, fair Beatrice!
Would that I loved thee not, or loving thee
Could but despise danger and gold and all
That frowns between my wish and its effect,
Or smiles beyond it! There is no escape . . .
Her bright form kneels beside me at the altar,
And follows me to the resort of men,
And fills my slumber with tumultuous dreams,
So when I wake my blood seems liquid fire;
And if I strike my damp and dizzy head
My hot palm scorches it: her very name,
But spoken by a stranger, makes my heart

Sicken and pant; and thus unprofitably
I clasp the phantom of unfelt delights
Till weak imagination half possesses
The self-created shadow. Yet much longer
Will I not nurse this life of feverous hours:
From the unravelled hopes of Giacomo
I must work out my own dear purposes.
I see, as from a tower, the end of all:°
Her father dead; her brother bound to me
By a dark secret, surer than the grave;
Her mother scared and unexpostulating
From the dread manner of her wish achieved:
And she!—Once more take courage, my faint heart;
What dares a friendless maiden matched with thee?
I have such foresight as assures success:
Some unbeheld divinity doth ever,
When dread events are near, stir up men's minds
To black suggestions; and he prospers best,
Not who becomes the instrument of ill,
But who can flatter the dark spirit, that makes
Its empire and its prey of other hearts
Till it become his slave . . . as I will do. [*Exit.*

END OF THE SECOND ACT.

Act 3

SCENE I.—*An apartment in the Cenci Palace.*
LUCRETIA, *to her enter* BEATRICE.

Beatrice (*she enters staggering, and speaks wildly*). Reach me that handkerchief!—My brain is hurt;
My eyes are full of blood; just wipe them for me . . .
I see but indistinctly . . .

Lucretia. My sweet child,
You have no wound; 'tis only a cold dew
That starts from your dear brow . . . Alas! Alas!
What has befallen?

Beatrice. How comes this hair undone?
Its wandering strings must be what blind me so,
And yet I tied it fast.—O, horrible!
The pavement sinks under my feet! The walls
Spin round! I see a woman weeping there,
And standing calm and motionless, whilst I
Slide giddily as the world reels . . . My God!
The beautiful blue heaven is flecked with blood!°
The sunshine on the floor is black! The air
Is changed to vapours such as the dead breathe
In charnel pits! Pah! I am choked! There creeps
A changing, black, contaminating mist
About me . . . 'tis substantial, heavy, thick,
I cannot pluck it from me, for it glues
My fingers and my limbs to one another,
And eats into my sinews, and dissolves
My flesh to a pollution, poisoning
The subtle, pure, and inmost spirit of life!
My God! I never knew what the mad felt
Before; for I am mad beyond all doubt!

[*More wildly*

No, I am dead! These putrefying limbs
Shut round and sepulchre the panting soul
Which would burst forth into the wandering air!

[*A pause.*

What hideous thought was that I had even now?
'Tis gone; and yet its burden remains here
O'er these dull eyes . . . upon this weary heart!
O, world! O, life! O, day! O, misery!

Lucretia. What ails thee, my poor child? She answers not;
Her spirit apprehends the sense of pain,
But not its cause; suffering has dried away
The source from which it sprung . . .

Beatrice (*franticly*). Like Parricide.
Misery has killed its father: yet its father°
Never like mine . . . O, God! What thing am I?

Lucretia. My dearest child, what has your father done?

Beatrice (*doubtfully*). Who art thou, questioner? I have no father.
[*Aside*
She is the madhouse nurse who tends on me;
It is a piteous office.
[*To* LUCRETIA, *in a slow, subdued voice*
Do you know
I thought I was that wretched Beatrice
Men speak of, whom her father sometimes hales°
From hall to hall by the entangled hair;
At others, pens up naked in damp cells
Where scaly reptiles crawl, and starves her there,
Till she will eat strange flesh. This woeful story
So did I overact in my sick dreams,
That I imagined . . . no, it cannot be!
Horrible things have been in this wild world,
Prodigious mixtures, and confusions strange
Of good and ill; and worse have been conceived
Than ever there was found a heart to do.
But never fancy imaged such a deed
As . . . [*Pauses, suddenly recollecting herself*
Who art thou? Swear to me, ere I die
With fearful expectation, that indeed
Thou art not what thou seemest . . . Mother!

Lucretia. Oh!
My sweet child, know you . . .

Beatrice. Yet speak it not:
For then if this be truth, that other too
Must be a truth, a firm enduring truth,
Linked with each lasting circumstance of life,
Never to change, never to pass away.
Why so it is. This is the Cenci palace;
Thou art Lucretia; I am Beatrice.
I have talked some wild words, but will no more.
Mother, come near me: from this point of time,
I am . . . (*Her voice dies away faintly*)

Lucretia. Alas! What has befallen thee, child?
What has thy father done?

Beatrice. What have I done?
Am I not innocent? Is it my crime
That one with white hair, and imperious brow,
Who tortured me from my forgotten years,
As parents only dare, should call himself
My father, yet should be!—Oh, what am I?
What name, what place, what memory shall be mine?
What retrospects, outliving even despair?

Lucretia. He is a violent tyrant, surely, child:
We know that death alone can make us free;
His death or ours. But what can he have done
Of deadlier outrage or worse injury?
Thou art unlike thyself; thine eyes shoot forth
A wandering and strange spirit. Speak to me,
Unlock those pallid hands whose fingers twine
With one another.

Beatrice. 'Tis the restless life
Tortured within them. If I try to speak
I shall go mad. Aye, something must be done;
What, yet I know not . . . something which shall make°
The thing that I have suffered but a shadow
In the dread lightning which avenges it;

Brief, rapid, irreversible, destroying
The consequence of what it cannot cure.
Some such thing is to be endured or done:
When I know what, I shall be still and calm,
And never any thing will move me more
But now!—O blood, which art my father's blood,
Circling through these contaminated veins,
If thou, poured forth on the polluted earth,
Could wash away the crime, and punishment
By which I suffer . . . no, that cannot be!
Many might doubt there were a God above
Who sees and permits evil, and so die;
That faith no agony shall obscure in me.

Lucretia. It must indeed have been some bitter wrong;
Yet what, I dare not guess. Oh, my lost child,
Hide not in proud impenetrable grief
Thy sufferings from my fear.

Beatrice. I hide them not.
What are the words which you would have me speak?
I, who can feign no image in my mind
Of that which has transformed me. I, whose thought
Is like a ghost shrouded and folded up
In its own formless horror. Of all words,
That minister to mortal intercourse,
Which wouldst thou hear? For there is none to tell
My misery: if another ever knew
Aught like to it, she died as I will die,
And left it, as I must, without a name.
Death! Death! Our law and our religion call thee
A punishment and a reward . . . Oh, which
Have I deserved?

Lucretia. The peace of innocence;
Till in your season you be called to heaven.
Whate'er you may have suffered, you have done
No evil. Death must be the punishment
Of crime, or the reward of trampling down
The thorns which God has strewed upon the path
Which leads to immortality.

Beatrice. Aye, death . . .
The punishment of crime. I pray thee, God,
Let me not be bewildered while I judge.
If I must live day after day, and keep
These limbs, the unworthy temple of thy spirit,
As a foul den from which what thou abhorrest
May mock thee, unavenged . . . it shall not be!
Self-murder . . . no, that might be no escape,
For thy decree yawns like a Hell between
Our will and it:—O! In this mortal world°
There is no vindication and no law
Which can adjudge and execute the doom
Of that through which I suffer.

Enter ORSINO.

(*She approaches him solemnly*) Welcome, Friend!
I have to tell you that, since last we met,
I have endured a wrong so great and strange,
That neither life nor death can give me rest.
Ask me not what it is, for there are deeds
Which have no form, sufferings which have no tongue.

Orsino. And what is he who has thus injured you?

Beatrice. The man they call my father: a dread name.

Orsino. It cannot be . . .

Beatrice. What it can be, or not,
Forbear to think. It is, and it has been;
Advise me how it shall not be again.
I thought to die; but a religious awe
Restrains me, and the dread lest death itself
Might be no refuge from the consciousness
Of what is yet unexpiated. Oh, speak!

Orsino. Accuse him of the deed, and let the law
Avenge thee.

Beatrice. Oh, ice-hearted counsellor!
If I could find a word that might make known
The crime of my destroyer; and that done
My tongue should like a knife tear out the secret

Which cankers my heart's core; aye, lay all bare
So that my unpolluted fame should be
With vilest gossips a stale mouthèd story;
A mock, a bye-word, an astonishment:—
If this were done, which never shall be done,
Think of the offender's gold, his dreaded hate,
And the strange horror of the accuser's tale,
Baffling belief, and overpowering speech;
Scarce whispered, unimaginable, wrapped
In hideous hints . . . Oh, most assured redress!

Orsino. You will endure it then?

Beatrice. Endure?—Orsino,
It seems your counsel is small profit.
[*Turns from him, and speaks half to herself*
Aye,
All must be suddenly resolved and done.
What is this undistinguishable mist
Of thoughts, which rise, like shadow after shadow,
Darkening each other?

Orsino. Should the offender live?
Triumph in his misdeed? and make, by use,
His crime, whate'er it is, dreadful no doubt,
Thine element; until thou mayest become
Utterly lost; subdued even to the hue
Of that which thou permittest?

Beatrice (*to herself*). Mighty death!
Thou double-visaged shadow! Only judge!
Rightfullest arbiter!
[*She retires absorbed in thought*.

Lucretia. If the lightning
Of God has e'er descended to avenge . . .

Orsino. Blaspheme not! His high Providence commits
Its glory on this earth, and their own wrongs
Into the hands of men; if they neglect
To punish crime . . .

Lucretia. But if one, like this wretch,
Should mock, with gold, opinion, law and power?
If there be no appeal to that which makes
The guiltiest tremble? If because our wrongs,
For that they are unnatural, strange and monstrous,
Exceed all measure of belief? Oh, God!
If, for the very reasons which should make
Redress most swift and sure, our injurer triumphs?
And we, the victims, bear worse punishment
Than that appointed for their torturer?

Orsino. Think not
But that there is redress where there is wrong,
So we be bold enough to seize it.

Lucretia. How?
If there were any way to make all sure,
I know not . . . but I think it might be good
To . . .

Orsino. Why, his late outrage to Beatrice;
For it is such, as I but faintly guess,
As makes remorse dishonour, and leaves her
Only one duty, how she may avenge:
You, but one refuge from ills ill endured;
Me, but one counsel . . .

Lucretia. For we cannot hope
That aid, or retribution, or resource
Will arise thence, where every other one
Might find them with less need.

[BEATRICE *advances.*

Orsino. Then . . .

Beatrice. Peace, Orsino!
And, honoured Lady, while I speak, I pray,
That you put off, as garments overworn,
Forbearance and respect, remorse and fear,
And all the fit restraints of daily life,

Which have been borne from childhood, but which now
Would be a mockery to my holier plea.
As I have said, I have endured a wrong,
Which, though it be expressionless, is such
As asks atonement; both for what is past;
And lest I be reserved, day after day,
To load with crimes an overburdened soul,
And be . . . what ye can dream not. I have prayed
To God, and I have talked with my own heart,
And have unravelled my entangled will,
And have at length determined what is right.
Art thou my friend, Orsino? False or true?
Pledge thy salvation ere I speak.

Orsino. I swear
To dedicate my cunning, and my strength,
My silence, and whatever else is mine,
To thy commands.

Lucretia. You think we should devise
His death?

Beatrice. And execute what is devised,
And suddenly. We must be brief and bold.

Orsino. And yet most cautious.

Lucretia. For the jealous laws
Would punish us with death and infamy
For that which it became themselves to do.

Beatrice. Be cautious as ye may, but prompt. Orsino
What are the means?

Orsino. I know two dull, fierce outlaws,
Who think man's spirit as a worm's, and they
Would trample out, for any slight caprice,
The meanest or the noblest life. This mood
Is marketable here in Rome. They sell
What we now want.

Lucretia. Tomorrow before dawn,
Cenci will take us to that lonely rock,
Petrella, in the Apulian Apennines.
If he arrive there . . .

Beatrice. He must not arrive.

Orsino. Will it be dark before you reach the tower?

Lucretia. The sun will scarce be set.

Beatrice. But I remember.
Two miles on this side of the fort, the road
Crosses a deep ravine; 'tis rough and narrow,
And winds with short turns down the precipice;
And in its depth there is a mighty rock,
Which has, from unimaginable years,
Sustained itself with terror and with toil
Over a gulf, and with the agony
With which it clings seems slowly coming down;
Even as a wretched soul hour after hour,
Clings to the mass of life; yet clinging, leans;
And leaning, makes more dark the dread abyss
In which it fears to fall: beneath this crag,
Huge as despair, as if in weariness,
The melancholy mountain yawns . . . below,
You hear but see not an impetuous torrent
Raging among the caverns, and a bridge
Crosses the chasm; and high above there grow,
With intersecting trunks, from crag to crag,
Cedars, and yews, and pines; whose tangled hair
Is matted in one solid roof of shade
By the dark ivy's twine. At noonday here
'Tis twilight, and at sunset blackest night.°

Orsino. Before you reach that bridge make some excuse
For spurring on your mules, or loitering
Until . . .

Beatrice. What sound is that?

Lucr. Hark! No, it cannot be a servant's step;
It must be Cenci, unexpectedly
Returned . . . Make some excuse for being here.

Beatrice (*to* ORSINO, *as she goes out*). That step we hear approach must never pass
The bridge of which we spoke.

[*Exeunt* LUCRETIA *and* BEATRICE.

Orsino. What shall I do?
Cenci must find me here, and I must bear
The imperious inquisition of his looks
As to what brought me hither: let me mask
Mine own in some inane and vacant smile.

Enter GIACOMO, *in a hurried manner*.

How! Have you ventured hither? know you then
That Cenci is from home?

Giacomo. I sought him here;
And now must wait till he returns.

Orsino. Great God!
Weigh you the danger of this rashness?

Giacomo. Aye!
Does my destroyer know his danger? We
Are now no more, as once, parent and child,
But man to man; the oppressor to the oppressed;
The slanderer to the slandered; foe to foe:
He has cast Nature off, which was his shield,
And Nature casts him off, who is her shame;
And I spurn both. Is it a father's throat
Which I will shake, and say, I ask not gold;
I ask not happy years; nor memories
Of tranquil childhood; nor home-sheltered love;
Though all these hast thou torn from me, and more;
But only my fair fame; only one hoard
Of peace, which I thought hidden from thy hate,
Under the penury heaped on me by thee,
Or I will . . . God can understand and pardon,
Why should I speak with man?

Orsino. Be calm, dear friend.

Giacomo. Well, I will calmly tell you what he did.
This old Francesco Cenci, as you know,
Borrowed the dowry of my wife from me,
And then denied the loan; and left me so
In poverty, the which I sought to mend
By holding a poor office in the state.
It had been promised to me, and already
I bought new clothing for my ragged babes,
And my wife smiled; and my heart knew repose;
When Cenci's intercession, as I found,
Conferred this office on a wretch, whom thus
He paid for vilest service. I returned
With this ill news, and we sate sad together
Solacing our despondency with tears
Of such affection and unbroken faith
As temper life's worst bitterness; when he,
As he is wont, came to upbraid and curse,
Mocking our poverty, and telling us
Such was God's scourge for disobedient sons.
And then, that I might strike him dumb with shame,
I spoke of my wife's dowry; but he coined
A brief yet specious tale, how I had wasted
The sum in secret riot; and he saw
My wife was touched, and he went smiling forth.
And when I knew the impression he had made,
And felt my wife insult with silent scorn
My ardent truth, and look averse and cold,
I went forth too: but soon returned again;
Yet not so soon but that my wife had taught
My children her harsh thoughts, and they all cried,
'Give us clothes, father! Give us better food!
What you in one night squander were enough
For months!' I looked, and saw that home was hell.
And to that hell will I return no more
Until mine enemy has rendered up
Atonement, or, as he gave life to me
I will, reversing nature's law . . .

Orsino. Trust me,

The compensation which thou seekest here
Will be denied.

Giacomo. Then . . . Are you not my friend?
Did you not hint at the alternative,
Upon the brink of which you see I stand,
The other day when we conversed together?
My wrongs were then less. That word parricide,
Although I am resolved, haunts me like fear.

Orsino. It must be fear itself, for the bare word
Is hollow mockery. Mark, how wisest God
Draws to one point the threads of a just doom,
So sanctifying it: what you devise
Is, as it were, accomplishèd.

Giacomo. Is he dead?

Orsino. His grave is ready. Know that since we met
Cenci has done an outrage to his daughter.

Giacomo. What outrage?

Orsino. That she speaks not, but you may
Conceive such half conjectures as I do,
From her fixed paleness, and the lofty grief
Of her stern brow bent on the idle air,
And her severe unmodulated voice,
Drowning both tenderness and dread; and last
From this; that whilst her step-mother and I,
Bewildered in our horror, talked together
With obscure hints; both self-misunderstood
And darkly guessing, stumbling, in our talk,
Over the truth, and yet to its revenge,
She interrupted us, and with a look
Which told before she spoke it, he must die . . .

Giacomo. It is enough. My doubts are well appeased;
There is a higher reason for the act
Than mine; there is a holier judge than me,
A more unblamed avenger. Beatrice,

Who in the gentleness of thy sweet youth
Hast never trodden on a worm, or bruised
A living flower, but thou hast pitied it
With needless tears! Fair sister, thou in whom
Men wondered how such loveliness and wisdom
Did not destroy each other! Is there made
Ravage of thee? O, heart, I ask no more
Justification! Shall I wait, Orsino,
Till he return, and stab him at the door?

Orsino. Not so; some accident might interpose
To rescue him from what is now most sure;
And you are unprovided where to fly,
How to excuse or to conceal. Nay, listen:
All is contrived; success is so assured.
That . . .

Enter BEATRICE.

Beatrice. 'Tis my brother's voice! You know me not?

Giacomo. My sister, my lost sister!

Beatrice. Lost indeed!
I see Orsino has talked with you, and
That you conjecture things too horrible
To speak, yet far less than the truth. Now, stay not,
He might return: yet kiss me; I shall know
That then thou hast consented to his death.
Farewell, Farewell! Let piety to God,
Brotherly love, justice and clemency,
And all things that make tender hardest hearts
Make thine hard, brother. Answer not . . . farewell.
[*Exeunt severally*.

SCENE 2.—*A mean apartment in* GIACOMO'S *house*.
GIACOMO, *alone*.

Giacomo. 'Tis midnight, and Orsino comes not yet.
[*Thunder, and the sound of a storm*.
What! can the everlasting elements
Feel with a worm like man? If so the shaft

Of mercy-wingèd lightning would not fall
On stones and trees. My wife and children sleep:
They are now living in unmeaning dreams:
But I must wake, still doubting if that deed
Be just which was most necessary. O,
Thou unreplenished lamp! whose narrow fire
Is shaken by the wind, and on whose edge
Devouring darkness hovers! Thou small flame,
Which, as a dying pulse rises and falls,
Still flickerest up and down, how very soon,
Did I not feed thee, wouldst thou fail and be
As thou hadst never been! So wastes and sinks
Even now, perhaps, the life that kindled mine:
But that no power can fill with vital oil
That broken lamp of flesh. Ha! 'tis the blood°
Which fed these veins that ebbs till all is cold:
It is the form that moulded mine, which sinks
Into the white and yellow spasms of death:
It is the soul by which mine was arrayed
In God's immortal likeness which now stands
Naked before Heaven's judgement seat!

[*A bell strikes.*

One! Two!
The hours crawl on; and when my hairs are white
My son will then perhaps be waiting thus,
Tortured between just hate and vain remorse;
Chiding the tardy messenger of news
Like those which I expect. I almost wish
He be not dead, although my wrongs are great;
Yet . . . 'tis Orsino's step . . .

Enter ORSINO.

Speak!

Orsino. I am come
To say he has escaped.

Giacomo. Escaped!

Orsino. And safe.
Within Petrella. He passed by the spot
Appointed for the deed an hour too soon.

Giacomo. Are we the fools of such contingencies?
And do we waste in blind misgivings thus
The hours when we should act? Then wind and thunder,
Which seemed to howl his knell, is the loud laughter
With which Heaven mocks our weakness! I henceforth
Will ne'er repent of aught designed or done
But my repentance.

Orsino. See, the lamp is out.

Giacomo. If no remorse is ours when the dim air
Has drank this innocent flame, why should we quail
When Cenci's life, that light by which ill spirits
See the worst deeds they prompt, shall sink for ever?
No, I am hardened.

Orsino. Why, what need of this?
Who feared the pale intrusion of remorse
In a just deed? Although our first plan failed
Doubt not but he will soon be laid to rest.
But light the lamp; let us not talk i' the dark.

Giacomo (*lighting the lamp*). And yet once quenched I cannot thus relume°
My father's life: do you not think his ghost
Might plead that argument with God?

Orsino. Once gone
You cannot now recall your sister's peace;
Your own extinguished years of youth and hope;
Nor your wife's bitter words; nor all the taunts
Which, from the prosperous, weak misfortune takes;
Nor your dead mother; nor . . .

Giacomo. O, speak no more!
I am resolved, although this very hand
Must quench the life that animated it.

Orsino. There is no need of that. Listen: you know
Olimpio, the castellan of Petrella°
In old Colonna's time; him whom your father

Degraded from his post? And Marzio,
That desperate wretch, whom he deprived last year
Of a reward of blood, well earned and due?

Giacomo. I knew Olimpio; and they say he hated
Old Cenci so, that in his silent rage
His lips grew white only to see him pass.
Of Marzio I know nothing.

Orsino. Marzio's hate
Matches Olimpio's. I have sent these men,
But in your name, and as at your request,
To talk with Beatrice and Lucretia.

Giacomo. Only to talk?

Orsino. The moments which even now
Pass onward tomorrow's midnight hour
May memorize their flight with death: ere then
They must have talked, and may perhaps have done,
And made an end . . .

Giacomo. Listen! What sound is that?

Orsino. The housedog moans, and the beams crack: nought else.

Giacomo. It is my wife complaining in her sleep:
I doubt not she is saying bitter things
Of me; and all my children round her dreaming
That I deny them sustenance.

Orsino. Whilst he
Who truly took it from them, and who fills
Their hungry rest with bitterness, now sleeps
Lapped in bad pleasures, and triumphantly
Mocks thee in visions of successful hate
Too like the truth of day.

Giacomo. If e'er he wakes
Again, I will not trust to hireling hands . . .

Orsino. Why, that were well. I must be gone; good night!
When next we meet—may all be done—

Giacomo. And all
Forgotten—Oh, that I had never been!

[*Exeunt*.

END OF THE THIRD ACT.

Act 4

SCENE I.—*An apartment in the Castle of Petrella.*
Enter CENCI.

Cenci. She comes not; yet I left her even now
Vanquished and faint. She knows the penalty
Of her delay: yet what if threats are vain?
Am I now not within Petrella's moat?
Or fear I still the eyes and ears of Rome?
Might I not drag her by the golden hair?
Stamp on her? Keep her sleepless till her brain
Be overworn? Tame her with chains and famine?
Less would suffice. Yet so to leave undone
What I most seek! No, 'tis her stubborn will.°
Which by its own consent shall stoop as low
As that which drags it down.

Enter LUCRETIA.

Thou loathèd wretch!
Hide thee from my abhorrence; Fly, begone!
Yet stay! Bid Beatrice come hither.

Lucretia. Oh,
Husband! I pray for thine own wretched sake
Heed what thou dost. A man who walks like thee
Through crimes, and through the danger of his crimes,
Each hour may stumble o'er a sudden grave.
And thou art old; thy hairs are hoary grey;
As thou wouldst save thyself from death and hell,
Pity thy daughter; give her to some friend
In marriage: so that she may tempt thee not
To hatred, or worse thoughts, if worse there be.

Cenci. What! like her sister who has found a home
To mock my hate from with prosperity?
Strange ruin shall destroy both her and thee
And all that yet remain. My death may be
Rapid, her destiny outspeeds it. Go,
Bid her come hither, and before my mood
Be changed, lest I should drag her by the hair.

Lucretia. She sent me to thee, husband. At thy presence
She fell, as thou dost know, into a trance;
And in that trance she heard a voice which said,
'Cenci must die! Let him confess himself!
Even now the accusing Angel waits to hear
If God, to punish his enormous crimes,
Harden his dying heart!'

Cenci. Why—such things are . . .
No doubt divine revealings may be made.
'Tis plain I have been favoured from above,
For when I cursed my sons they died.—Aye . . . so . . .
As to the right or wrong, that's talk . . . repentance . . .
Repentance is an easy moment's work
And more depends on God than me. Well . . . well . . .
I must give up the greater point, which was
To poison and corrupt her soul.

[*A pause;* LUCRETIA *approaches anxiously, and then shrinks back as he speaks.*

One, two;
Aye . . . Rocco and Cristofano my curse
Strangled: and Giacomo, I think, will find
Life a worse Hell than that beyond the grave:
Beatrice shall, if there be skill in hate
Die in despair, blaspheming: to Bernardo,
He is so innocent, I will bequeath
The memory of these deeds, and make his youth
The sepulchre of hope, where evil thoughts
Shall grow like weeds on a neglected tomb.
When all is done, out in the wide Campagna,
I will pile up my silver and my gold;
My costly robes, paintings and tapestries;
My parchments and all records of my wealth,
And make a bonfire in my joy, and leave
Of my possessions nothing but my name;
Which shall be an inheritance to strip
Its wearer bare as infamy. That done,
My soul, which is a scourge, will I resign
Into the hands of him who wielded it;
Be it for its own punishment or theirs,
He will not ask it of me till the lash

Be broken in its last and deepest wound;
Until its hate be all inflicted. Yet,
Lest death outspeed my purpose, let me make
Short work and sure . . . [*Going*.

Lucretia (*stops him*). Oh, stay! It was a feint:
She had no vision, and she heard no voice.
I said it but to awe thee.

Cenci. That is well.
Vile palterer with the sacred truth of God,
Be thy soul choked with that blaspheming lie!
For Beatrice worse terrors are in store
To bend her to my will.

Lucretia. Oh! to what will?
What cruel sufferings more than she has known
Canst thou inflict?

Cenci. Andrea! Go call my daughter,
And if she comes not tell her that I come.
What sufferings? I will drag her, step by step,
Through infamies unheard of among men:
She shall stand shelterless in the broad noon
Of public scorn, for acts blazoned abroad,°
One among which shall be . . . What? Canst thou guess?
She shall become (for what she most abhors
Shall have a fascination to entrap
Her loathing will) to her own conscious self
All she appears to others; and when dead,°
As she shall die unshrived and unforgiven,
A rebel to her father and her God,
Her corpse shall be abandoned to the hounds;
Her name shall be the terror of the earth;
Her spirit shall approach the throne of God
Plague-spotted with my curses. I will make
Body and soul a monstrous lump of ruin.

Enter ANDREA.

Andrea. The lady Beatrice . . .

Cenci. Speak, pale slave! What
Said she?

Andrea. My Lord, 'twas what she looked; she said:
'Go tell my father that I see the gulf
Of Hell between us two, which he may pass,
I will not.'

[*Exit* ANDREA.

Cenci. Go thou quick, Lucretia,
Tell her to come; yet let her understand
Her coming is consent: and say, moreover,
That if she come not I will curse her.

[*Exit* LUCRETIA.

Ha!
With what but with a father's curse doth God
Panic-strike armèd victory, and make pale
Cities in their prosperity? The world's Father
Must grant a parent's prayer against his child
Be he who asks even what men call me.
Will not the deaths of her rebellious brothers
Awe her before I speak? For I on them
Did imprecate quick ruin, and it came.

Enter LUCRETIA.

Well; what? Speak, wretch!

Lucretia. She said, 'I cannot come;
Go tell my father that I see a torrent.
Of his own blood raging between us.'

Cenci (*kneeling*). God!
Hear me! If this most specious mass of flesh,°
Which thou hast made my daughter; this my blood,
This particle of my divided being;
Or rather, this my bane and my disease,
Whose sight infects and poisons me; this devil
Which sprung from me as from a hell, was meant
To aught good use; if her bright loveliness
Was kindled to illumine this dark world;
If nursed by thy selectest dew of love

Such virtues blossom in her as should make
The peace of life, I pray thee for my sake,
As thou the common God and Father art
Of her, and me, and all; reverse that doom!
Earth, in the name of God, let her food be
Poison, until she be encrusted round
With leprous stains! Heaven, rain upon her head
The blistering drops of the Maremma's dew,°
Till she be speckled like a toad; parch up
Those love-enkindled lips, warp those fine limbs
To loathèd lameness! All-beholding sun,
Strike in thine envy those life-darting eyes
With thine own blinding beams!

Lucretia. Peace! Peace!
For thine own sake unsay those dreadful words.
When high God grants he punishes such prayers.

Cenci (*leaping up, and throwing his right hand towards Heaven*). He does his will, I mine! This in addition,
That if she have a child . . .

Lucretia. Horrible thought!

Cenci. That if she ever have a child; and thou,°
Quick Nature! I adjure thee by thy God,
That thou be fruitful in her, and increase
And multiply, fulfilling his command,
And my deep imprecation! May it be
A hideous likeness of herself, that as
From a distorting mirror, she may see
Her image mixed with what she most abhors,
Smiling upon her from her nursing breast.
And that the child may from its infancy
Grow, day by day, more wicked and deformed,
Turning her mother's love to misery:
And that both she and it may live until
It shall repay her care and pain with hate,
Or what may else be more unnatural,
So he may hunt her through the clamorous scoffs
Of the loud world to a dishonoured grave.

Shall I revoke this curse? Go, bid her come,
Before my words are chronicled in heaven.°

[*Exit* LUCRETIA.

I do not feel as if I were a man,
But like a fiend appointed to chastise
The offences of some unremembered world.
My blood is running up and down my veins;
A fearful pleasure makes it prick and tingle:
I feel a giddy sickness of strange awe;
My heart is beating with an expectation
Of horrid joy.

Enter LUCRETIA.

What? Speak!

Lucretia. She bids thee curse;
And if thy curses, as they cannot do,
Could kill her soul . . .

Cenci. She would not come. 'Tis well,
I can do both: first take what I demand,
And then extort concession. To thy chamber!
Fly ere I spurn thee: and beware this night
That thou cross not my footsteps. It were safer
To come between the tiger and his prey.

[*Exit* LUCRETIA.

It must be late; mine eyes grow weary dim
With unaccustomed heaviness of sleep.
Conscience! Oh, thou most insolent of lies!
They say that sleep, that healing dew of heaven,
Steeps not in balm the foldings of the brain
Which thinks thee an impostor. I will go
First to belie thee with an hour of rest,
Which will be deep and calm, I feel: and then . . .
O, multitudinous Hell, the fiends will shake
Thine arches with the laughter of their joy!
There shall be lamentation heard in Heaven
As o'er an angel fallen; and upon Earth
All good shall droop and sicken, and ill things
Shall with a spirit of unnatural life
Stir and be quickened . . . even as I am now.°

[*Exit.*

SCENE 2.—*Before the Castle of Petrella.*
Enter BEATRICE *and* LUCRETIA *above on the ramparts.*

Beatrice. They come not yet.

Lucretia. 'Tis scarce midnight.

Beatrice. How slow
Behind the course of thought, even sick with speed.
Lags leaden-footed time!

Lucretia. The minutes pass . . .
If he should wake before the deed is done?

Beatrice. O, Mother! He must never wake again.
What thou hast said persuades me that our act
Will but dislodge a spirit of deep hell
Out of a human form.

Lucretia. 'Tis true he spoke
Of death and judgement with strange confidence
For one so wicked; as a man believing
In God, yet recking not of good or ill.°
And yet to die without confession! . . .

Beatrice. Oh!
Believe that heaven is merciful and just,
And will not add our dread necessity
To the amount of his offences.
Enter OLIMPIO *and* MARZIO, *below.*

Lucretia. See,
They come.

Beatrice. All mortal things must hasten thus
To their dark end. Let us go down.
[*Exeunt* LUCRETIA *and* BEATRICE *from above.*

Olimpio. How feel you to this work?

Marzio. As one who thinks

A thousand crowns excellent market price
For an old murderer's life. Your cheeks are pale.

Olimpio. It is the white reflexion of your own,
Which you call pale.

Marzio. Is that their natural hue?

Olimpio. Or 'tis my hate and the deferred desire
To wreak it, which extinguishes their blood.

Marzio. You are inclined then to this business?

Olimpio. Aye.
If one should bribe me with a thousand crowns
To kill a serpent which had stung my child,
I could not be more willing.

Enter BEATRICE *and* LUCRETIA, *below*.

Noble ladies!

Beatrice. Are ye resolved?

Olimpio. Is he asleep?

Marzio. Is all
Quiet?

Lucretia. I mixed an opiate with his drink:
He sleeps so soundly . . .

Beatrice. That his death will be
But as a change of sin-chastising dreams,
A dark continuance of the Hell within him,°
Which God extinguish! But ye are resolved?
Ye know it is a high and holy deed?

Olimpio. We are resolved.

Marzio. As to the how this act
Be warranted, it rests with you.

Beatrice. Well, follow!

Olimpio. Hush! Hark! What noise is that?

Marzio. Ha! some one comes!

Beatrice. Ye conscience-stricken cravens, rock to rest.
Your baby hearts. It is the iron gate,
Which ye left open, swinging to the wind,
That enters whistling as in scorn. Come, follow!
And be your steps like mine, light, quick and bold.

[*Exeunt.*

SCENE 3.—*An apartment in the Castle.*

Enter BEATRICE *and* LUCRETIA.

Lucretia. They are about it now.

Beatrice. Nay, it is done.

Lucretia. I have not heard him groan.

Beatrice. He will not groan.

Lucretia. What sound is that?

Beatrice. List! 'tis the tread of feet
About his bed.

Lucretia. My God!
If he be now a cold stiff corpse . . .

Beatrice. O, fear not
What may be done, but what is left undone:
The act seals all.

Enter OLIMPIO *and* MARZIO.

Is it accomplished?

Marzio. What?

Olimpio. Did you not call?

Beatrice. When?

Olimpio. Now.°

Beatrice. I ask if all is over?

Olimpio. We dare not kill an old and sleeping man;
His thin grey hair, his stern and reverent brow,
His veinèd hands crossed on his heaving breast,
And the calm innocent sleep in which he lay,
Quelled me. Indeed, indeed, I cannot do it.

Marzio. But I was bolder; for I chid Olimpio,
And bade him bear his wrongs to his own grave
And leave me the reward. And now my knife
Touched the loose wrinkled throat, when the old man
Stirred in his sleep, and said, 'God! hear, O, hear,
A father's curse! What, art thou not our father?'
And then he laughed. I knew it was the ghost

Of my dead father speaking through his lips,
And could not kill him.

Beatrice. Miserable slaves!
Where, if ye dare not kill a sleeping man,
Found ye the boldness to return to me
With such a deed undone? Base palterers!
Cowards and traitors! Why, the very conscience
Which ye would sell for gold and for revenge
Is an equivocation: it sleeps over°
A thousand daily acts disgracing men;
And when a deed where mercy insults heaven . . .
Why do I talk?

[*Snatching a dagger from one of them and raising it.*

Hadst thou a tongue to say,
'She murdered her own father,' I must do it!
But never dream ye shall outlive him long!

Olimpio. Stop, for God's sake!

Marzio. I will go back and kill him.

Olimpio. Give me the weapon, we must do thy will.

Beatrice. Take it! Depart! Return!

[*Exeunt* OLIMPIO *and* MARZIO.

How pale thou art!
We do but that which 'twere a deadly crime
To leave undone.

Lucretia. Would it were done!

Beatrice. Even whilst
That doubt is passing through your mind, the world
Is conscious of a change. Darkness and hell
Have swallowed up the vapour they sent forth
To blacken the sweet light of life. My breath°
Comes, methinks, lighter and the jellied blood°
Runs freely through my veins. Hark!

Enter OLIMPIO *and* MARZIO.

He is . . .

Olimpio. Dead!

Marzio. We strangled him that there might be no blood;
And then we threw his heavy corpse i' the garden
Under the balcony; 'twill seem it fell.

Beatrice (*giving them a bag of coin*). Here take this gold, and hasten to your homes.
And, Marzio, because thou wast only awed
By that which made me tremble, wear thou this!

[*Clothes him in a rich mantle*

It was the mantle which my grandfather
Wore in his high prosperity, and men
Envied his state: so may they envy thine.
Thou wert a weapon in the hand of God
To a just use. Live long and thrive! And, mark,
If thou hast crimes, repent: this deed is none.

[*A horn is sounded.*

Lucretia. Hark, 'tis the castle horn; my God! it sounds
Like the last trump.

Beatrice. Some tedious guest is coming.

Lucretia. The drawbridge is let down; there is a tramp
Of horses in the court; fly, hide yourselves!

[*Exeunt* OLIMPIO *and* MARZIO.

Beatrice. Let us retire to counterfeit deep rest;
I scarcely need to counterfeit it now:
The spirit which doth reign within these limbs
Seems strangely undisturbed. I could even sleep
Fearless and calm: all ill is surely past.

[*Exeunt.*

SCENE 4.—*Another apartment in the Castle.*
Enter on one side the Legate SAVELLA *introduced by a servant, and on the other* LUCRETIA *and* BERNARDO.

Savella. Lady, my duty to his Holiness
Be my excuse that thus unseasonably
I break upon your rest. I must speak with
Count Cenci; doth he sleep?

Lucretia (*in a hurried and confused manner*). I think he sleeps;
Yet wake him not, I pray, spare me awhile,
He is a wicked and a wrathful man;
Should he be roused out of his sleep tonight,
Which is, I know, a hell of angry dreams,
It were not well; indeed it were not well.
Wait till day break. . . . (*Aside*) O, I am deadly sick!

Savella. I grieve thus to distress you, but the Count
Must answer charges of the gravest import,
And suddenly; such my commission is.

Lucretia (*with increased agitation*). I dare not rouse him: I know none who dare . . .
'Twere perilous; . . . you might as safely waken
A serpent; or a corpse in which some fiend
Were laid to sleep.

Savella. Lady, my moments here
Are counted. I must rouse him from his sleep,
Since none else dare.

Lucretia (*aside*). O, terror! O, despair!
(*to* BERNARDO) Bernardo, conduct you the Lord Legate to
Your father's chamber.

[*Exeunt* SAVELLA *and* BERNARDO.
Enter BEATRICE.

Beatrice 'Tis a messenger
Come to arrest the culprit who now stands
Before the throne of unappealable God.°
Both Earth and Heaven, consenting arbiters,
Acquit our deed.

Lucretia. Oh, agony of fear!
Would that he yet might live! Even now I heard
The Legate's followers whisper as they passed
They had a warrant for his instant death.°
All was prepared by unforbidden means
Which we must pay so dearly, having done.
Even now they search the tower, and find the body;
Now they suspect the truth; now they consult
Before they come to tax us with the fact;
O, horrible, 'tis all discovered!

Beatrice. Mother,
What is done wisely, is done well. Be bold
As thou art just. 'Tis like a truant child
To fear that others know what thou hast done,
Even from thine own strong consciousness, and thus
Write on unsteady eyes and altered cheeks
All thou wouldst hide. Be faithful to thyself,
And fear no other witness but thy fear.
For if, as cannot be, some circumstance
Should rise in accusation, we can blind
Suspicion with such cheap astonishment,
Or overbear it with such guiltless pride,
As murderers cannot feign. The deed is done,
And what may follow now regards not me.
I am as universal as the light;
Free as the earth-surrounding air; as firm°
As the world's centre. Consequence, to me,

Is as the wind which strikes the solid rock
But shakes it not.

[*A cry within and tumult.*

Voices. Murder! Murder! Murder!

Enter BERNARDO *and* SAVELLA.

Savella (*to his followers*). Go, search the castle round; sound the alarm;
Look to the gates that none escape!

Beatrice. What now?

Bernardo. I know not what to say . . . my father's dead.

Beatrice. How; dead! he only sleeps; you mistake, brother.
His sleep is very calm, very like death;
'Tis wonderful how well a tyrant sleeps.
He is not dead?

Bernardo. Dead; murdered.

Lucretia (*with extreme agitation*). Oh, no, no,
He is not murdered though he may be dead;
I have alone the keys of those apartments.

Savella. Ha! Is it so?

Beatrice. My Lord, I pray excuse us;
We will retire; my mother is not well:
She seems quite overcome with this strange horror.

[*Exeunt* LUCRETIA *and* BEATRICE.

Savella. Can you suspect who may have murdered him?

Bernardo. I know not what to think.

Savella. Can you name any
Who had an interest in his death?

Bernardo. Alas!
I can name none who had not, and those most

Who most lament that such a deed is done;
My mother, and my sister, and myself.

Savella. 'Tis strange! There were clear marks of violence.
I found the old man's body in the moonlight
Hanging beneath the window of his chamber
Among the branches of a pine: he could not
Have fallen there, for all his limbs lay heaped
And effortless; 'tis true there was no blood . . . °
Favour me, Sir; it much imports your house
That all should be made clear; to tell the ladies
That I request their presence.

[*Exit* BERNARDO.

Enter Guards bringing in MARZIO.

Guard. We have one.

Officer. My Lord, we found this ruffian and another
Lurking among the rocks; there is no doubt
But that they are the murderers of Count Cenci:
Each had a bag of coin; this fellow wore
A gold-inwoven robe, which shining bright
Under the dark rocks to the glimmering moon
Betrayed them to our notice: the other fell
Desperately fighting.

Savella. What does he confess?

Officer. He keeps firm silence; but these lines found on him
May speak.

Savella. Their language is at least sincere.

[*Reads*.

'TO THE LADY BEATRICE.
That the atonement of what my nature
Sickens to conjecture may soon arrive,
I send thee, at thy brother's desire, those
Who will speak and do more than I dare
Write . . . Thy devoted servant,
ORSINO.'

Enter LUCRETIA, BEATRICE *and* BERNARDO.

Knowest thou this writing, Lady?

Beatrice. No.

Savella. Nor thou?

Lucretia. (*Her conduct throughout the scene is marked by extreme agitation.*) Where was it found? What is it? It should be
Orsino's hand! It speaks of that strange horror
Which never yet found utterance, but which made
Between that hapless child and her dead father
A gulf of obscure hatred.

Savella. Is it so?
Is it true, Lady, that thy father did
Such outrages as to awaken in thee
Unfilial hate?

Beatrice. Not hate, 'twas more than hate:
This is most true, yet wherefore question me?

Savella. There is a deed demanding question done;
Thou hast a secret which will answer not.

Beatrice. What sayest? My Lord, your words are bold and rash.

Savella. I do arrest all present in the name
Of the Pope's Holiness. You must to Rome.

Lucretia. O, not to Rome! Indeed we are not guilty.

Beatrice. Guilty! Who dares talk of guilt? My Lord,
I am more innocent of parricide
Than is a child born fatherless . . . Dear Mother,
Your gentleness and patience are no shield
For this keen-judging world, this two-edged lie,
Which seems, but is not. What! will human laws,
Rather will ye who are their ministers,
Bar all access to retribution first,

And then, when heaven doth interpose to do
What ye neglect, arming familiar things
To the redress of an unwonted crime,
Make ye the victims who demanded it
Culprits? 'Tis ye are culprits! That poor wretch
Who stands so pale, and trembling, and amazed,
If it be true he murdered Cenci, was
A sword in the right hand of justest God,
Wherefore should I have wielded it? Unless
The crimes which mortal tongue dare never name
God therefore scruples to avenge.

Savella. You own
That you desired his death?

Beatrice. It would have been
A crime no less than his, if for one moment
That fierce desire had faded in my heart.
'Tis true I did believe, and hope, and pray,
Aye, I even knew . . . for God is wise and just,
That some strange sudden death hung over him.
'Tis true that this did happen, and most true
There was no other rest for me on earth,
No other hope in Heaven . . . now what of this?

Savella. Strange thoughts beget strange deeds; and here are both:
I judge thee not.

Beatrice. And yet, if you arrest me,
You are the judge and executioner
Of that which is the life of life: the breath
Of accusation kills an innocent name,
And leaves for lame acquittal the poor life
Which is a mask without it. 'Tis most false
That I am guilty of foul parricide;
Although I must rejoice, for justest cause,
That other hands have sent my father's soul
To ask the mercy he denied to me.
Now leave us free: stain not a noble house
With vague surmises of rejected crime;
Add to our sufferings and your own neglect

No heavier sum: let them have been enough:
Leave us the wreck we have.

Savella. I dare not, Lady.
I pray that you prepare yourselves for Rome:
There the Pope's further pleasure will be known.

Lucretia. O, not to Rome! O, take us not to Rome!

Beatrice. Why not to Rome, dear mother? There as here
Our innocence is as an armèd heel
To trample accusation. God is there
As here, and with his shadow ever clothes
The innocent, the injured and the weak;
And such are we. Cheer up, dear Lady, lean
On me; collect your wandering thoughts. My Lord,
As soon as you have taken some refreshment,
And had all such examinations made
Upon the spot, as may be necessary
To the full understanding of this matter,
We shall be ready. Mother; will you come?

Lucretia. Ha! they will bind us to the rack, and wrest
Self-accusation from our agony!
Will Giacomo be there? Orsino? Marzio?
All present; all confronted; all demanding
Each from the other's countenance the thing
Which is in every heart! O, misery!
[*She faints, and is borne out.*

Savella. She faints: an ill appearance this.

Beatrice. My Lord,
She knows not yet the uses of the world.
She fears that power is as a beast which grasps
And loosens not: a snake whose look transmutes
All things to guilt which is its nutriment.
She cannot know how well the supine slaves
Of blind authority read the truth of things
When written on a brow of guilelessness:
She sees not yet triumphant Innocence

Stand at the judgement-seat of mortal man,
A judge and an accuser of the wrong
Which drags it there. Prepare yourself, My Lord;
Our suite will join yours in the court below.

[*Exeunt*.

END OF THE FOURTH ACT.

Act 5

SCENE I.—*An apartment in* ORSINO'S *Palace.*
Enter ORSINO *and* GIACOMO.

Giacomo. Do evil deeds thus quickly come to end?
O, that the vain remorse which must chastise
Crimes done, had but as loud a voice to warn
As its keen sting is mortal to avenge!
O, that the hour when present had cast off
The mantle of its mystery, and shown
The ghastly form with which it now returns
When its scared game is roused, cheering the hounds
Of conscience to their prey! Alas! Alas!
It was a wicked thought, a piteous deed,
To kill an old and hoary-headed father.

Orsino. It has turned out unluckily, in truth.

Giacomo. To violate the sacred doors of sleep;
To cheat kind nature of the placid death
Which she prepares for overwearied age;
To drag from Heaven an unrepentant soul
Which might have quenched in reconciling prayers
A life of burning crimes . . .

Orsino. You cannot say
I urged you to the deed.

Giacomo. O, had I never
Found in thy smooth and ready countenance
The mirror of my darkest thoughts; hadst thou
Never with hints and questions made me look
Upon the monster of my thought, until
It grew familiar to desire . . . °

Orsino. 'Tis thus
Men cast the blame of their unprosperous acts
Upon the abettors of their own resolve;
Or anything but their weak, guilty selves.

And yet, confess the truth, it is the peril
In which you stand that gives you this pale sickness
Of penitence; confess 'tis fear disguised
From its own shame that takes the mantle now
Of thin remorse. What if we yet were safe?

Giacomo. How can that be? Already Beatrice,
Lucretia and the murderer are in prison.
I doubt not officers are, whilst we speak,
Sent to arrest us.

Orsino. I have all prepared
For instant flight. We can escape even now,
So we take fleet occasion by the hair.

Giacomo. Rather expire in tortures, as I may.
What! will you cast by self-accusing flight
Assured conviction upon Beatrice?
She, who alone in this unnatural work,
Stands like God's angel ministered upon
By fiends; avenging such a nameless wrong
As turns black parricide to piety;
Whilst we for basest ends . . . I fear, Orsino,
While I consider all your words and looks,
Comparing them with your proposal now,
That you must be a villain. For what end
Could you engage in such a perilous crime,
Training me on with hints, and signs, and smiles,
Even to this gulf? Thou art no liar? No,
Thou art a lie! Traitor and murderer!
Coward and slave! But, no, defend thyself;

[*Drawing*.

Let the sword speak what the indignant tongue
Disdains to brand thee with.

Orsino. Put up your weapon.°
Is it the desperation of your fear
Makes you thus rash and sudden with a friend,
Now ruined for your sake? If honest anger
Have moved you, know, that what I just proposed
Was but to try you. As for me, I think,

Thankless affection led me to this point,
From which, if my firm temper could repent,
I cannot now recede. Even whilst we speak
The ministers of justice wait below:
They grant me these brief moments. Now if you
Have any word of melancholy comfort
To speak to your pale wife, 'twere best to pass
Out at the postern, and avoid them so.

Giacomo. O, generous friend! How canst thou pardon me?
Would that my life could purchase thine!

Orsino. That wish
Now comes a day too late. Haste; fare thee well!
Hear'st thou not steps along the corridor?

[*Exit* GIACOMO.

I'm sorry for it; but the guards are waiting
At his own gate, and such was my contrivance
That I might rid me both of him and them.
I thought to act a solemn comedy
Upon the painted scene of this new world,
And to attain my own peculiar ends
By some such plot of mingled good and ill
As others weave; but there arose a Power
Which grasped and snapped the threads of my device
And turned it to a net of ruin . . . Ha!

[*A shout is heard.*

Is that my name I hear proclaimed abroad?
But I will pass, wrapped in a vile disguise;
Rags on my back, and a false innocence
Upon my face, through the misdeeming crowd°
Which judges by what seems. 'Tis easy then
For a new name and for a country new,
And a new life, fashioned on old desires,
To change the honours of abandoned Rome.
And these must be the masks of that within,°
Which must remain unaltered . . . Oh, I fear
That what is past will never let me rest!
Why, when none else is conscious, but myself,
Of my misdeeds, should my own heart's contempt
Trouble me? Have I not the power to fly

My own reproaches? Shall I be the slave
Of . . . what? A word? which those of this false world°
Employ against each other, not themselves;
As men wear daggers not for self-offence.
But if I am mistaken, where shall I
Find the disguise to hide me from myself,
As now I skulk from every other eye?

[*Exit.*

SCENE 2.—*A Hall of Justice.*

CAMILLO, *Judges etc. are discovered seated*; MARZIO *is led in.*

First Judge. Accused, do you persist in your denial?
I ask you, are you innocent, or guilty?
I demand who were the participators
In your offence? Speak truth and the whole truth.

Marzio. My God! I did not kill him; I know nothing;
Olimpio sold the robe to me from which
You would infer my guilt.

Second Judge. Away with him!

First Judge. Dare you, with lips yet white from the rack's kiss
Speak false? Is it so soft a questioner,
That you would bandy lōver's talk with it
Till it wind out your life and soul? Away!

Marzio. Spare me! O, spare! I will confess.

First Judge. Then speak.

Marzio. I strangled him in his sleep.

First Judge. Who urged you to it?

Marzio. His own son Giacomo, and the young prelate
Orsino sent me to Petrella; there
The ladies Beatrice and Lucretia
Tempted me with a thousand crowns, and I
And my companion forthwith murdered him.
Now let me die.

First Judge. This sounds as bad as truth. Guards, there,
Lead forth the prisoners!

Enter LUCRETIA, BEATRICE *and* GIACOMO, *guarded*.

Look upon this man;
When did you see him last?

Beatrice. We never saw him.

Marzio. You know me too well, Lady Beatrice.

Beatrice. I know thee! How? where? when?

Marzio. You know 'twas I
Whom you did urge with menaces and bribes
To kill your father. When the thing was done
You clothed me in a robe of woven gold
And bade me thrive: how I have thriven, you see.
You my Lord Giacomo, Lady Lucretia,
You know that what I speak is true.

(BEATRICE *advances towards him; he covers his face, and shrinks back*.)

O, dart
The terrible resentment of those eyes
On the dead earth! Turn them away from me!
They wound: 'twas torture forced the truth. My Lords,
Having said this let me be led to death.

Beatrice. Poor wretch, I pity thee: yet stay awhile.

Camillo. Guards, lead him not away.

Beatrice. Cardinal Camillo,
You have a good repute for gentleness
And wisdom: can it be that you sit here
To countenance a wicked farce like this?
When some obscure and trembling slave is dragged
From sufferings which might shake the sternest heart
And bade to answer, not as he believes,
But as those may suspect or do desire
Whose questions thence suggest their own reply:
And that in peril of such hideous torments
As merciful God spares even the damned. Speak now

The thing you surely know, which is that you,
If your fine frame were stretched upon that wheel,
And you were told: 'Confess that you did poison
Your little nephew; that fair blue-eyed child
Who was the lodestar of your life': and though
All see, since his most swift and piteous death,
That day and night, and heaven and earth, and time,
And all the things hoped for or done therein
Are changed to you, through your exceeding grief,°
Yet you would say, 'I confess any thing,'
And beg from your tormentors, like that slave,
The refuge of dishonourable death.
I pray thee, Cardinal, that thou assert
My innocence.

Camillo (*much moved*). What shall we think, my lords?
Shame on these tears! I thought the heart was frozen
Which is their fountain. I would pledge my soul
That she is guiltless.

Judge. Yet she must be tortured.

Camillo. I would as soon have tortured mine own nephew
(If he now lived he would be just her age;
His hair, too, was her colour, and his eyes
Like hers in shape, but blue and not so deep)
As that most perfect image of God's love
That ever came sorrowing upon the earth.
She is as pure as speechless infancy!

Judge. Well, be her purity on your head, my Lord,
If you forbid the rack. His Holiness
Enjoined us to pursue this monstrous crime
By the severest forms of law; nay even
To stretch a point against the criminals.
The prisoners stand accused of parricide
Upon such evidence as justifies
Torture.

Beatrice. What evidence? This man's?

Judge. Even so.

Beatrice (*to* MARZIO). Come near. And who art thou thus chosen forth
Out of the multitude of living men
To kill the innocent?

Marzio. I am Marzio,
Thy father's vassal.

Beatrice. Fix thine eyes on mine;
Answer to what I ask.

[*Turning to the Judges*

I prithee mark
His countenance: unlike bold calumny
Which sometimes dares not speak the thing it looks,
He dares not look the thing he speaks, but bends
His gaze on the blind earth.

[*To* MARZIO

What! wilt thou say
That I did murder my own father?

Marzio. Oh!
Spare me! My brain swims round . . . I cannot speak . . .
It was that horrid torture forced the truth.
Take me away! Let her not look on me!
I am a guilty, miserable wretch;
I have said all I know; now, let me die!

Beatrice. My Lords, if by my nature I had been
So stern, as to have planned the crime alleged,
Which your suspicions dictate to this slave,
And the rack makes him utter, do you think
I should have left this two-edged instrument
Of my misdeed; this man, this bloody knife
With my own name engraven on the heft,
Lying unsheathed amid a world of foes,
For my own death? That with such horrible need
For deepest silence, I should have neglected
So trivial a precaution, as the making
His tomb the keeper of a secret written
On a thief's memory? What is his poor life?
What are a thousand lives? A parricide

Had trampled them like dust; and, see, he lives!
[*Turning to* MARZIO
And thou . . .

Marzio. Oh, spare me! Speak to me no more!
That stern yet piteous look, those solemn tones,
Wound worse than torture.
[*To the Judges*
I have told it all;
For pity's sake lead me away to death.

Camillo. Guards, lead him nearer the lady Beatrice,
He shrinks from her regard like autumn's leaf
From the keen breath of the serenest north.

Beatrice. Oh, thou who tremblest on the giddy verge
Of life and death, pause ere thou answerest me;
So mayest thou answer God with less dismay:
What evil have we done thee? I, alas!
Have lived but on this earth a few sad years
And so my lot was ordered, that a father
First turned the moments of awakening life
To drops, each poisoning youth's sweet hope; and then
Stabbed with one blow my everlasting soul;
And my untainted fame; and even that peace
Which sleeps within the core of the heart's heart;°
But the wound was not mortal; so my hate
Became the only worship I could lift
To our great father, who in pity and love,
Armed thee, as thou dost say, to cut him off;
And thus his wrong becomes my accusation;
And art thou the accuser? If thou hopest
Mercy in heaven, show justice upon earth:
Worse than a bloody hand is a hard heart.
If thou hast done murders, made thy life's path
Over the trampled laws of God and man,
Rush not before thy Judge, and say: 'My Maker,
I have done this and more; for there was one
Who was most pure and innocent on earth;
And because she endured what never any
Guilty or innocent endured before:

Because her wrongs could not be told, not thought;
Because thy hand at length did rescue her;
I with my words killed her and all her kin.'
Think, I adjure you, what it is to slay
The reverence living in the minds of men
Towards our ancient house, and stainless fame!
Think what it is to strangle infant pity,
Cradled in the belief of guileless looks,
Till it become a crime to suffer. Think
What 'tis to blot with infamy and blood
All that which shows like innocence, and is,
Hear me, great God! I swear, most innocent,
So that the world lose all discrimination
Between the sly, fierce, wild regard of guilt,
And that which now compels thee to reply
To what I ask: Am I, or am I not
A parricide?

Marzio. Thou art not!

Judge. What is this?

Marzio. I here declare those whom I did accuse
Are innocent. 'Tis I alone am guilty.

Judge. Drag him away to torments; let them be
Subtle and long drawn out, to tear the folds
Of the heart's inmost cell. Unbind him not
Till he confess.

Marzio. Torture me as ye will:
A keener pain has wrung a higher truth°
From my last breath. She is most innocent!
Bloodhounds, not men, glut yourselves well with me;
I will not give you that fine piece of nature
To rend and ruin.

[*Exit* MARZIO, *guarded*.

Camillo. What say ye now, my Lords?

Judge. Let tortures strain the truth till it be white°
As snow thrice sifted by the frozen wind.

Camillo. Yet stained with blood.

Judge (*to* BEATRICE). Know you this paper, Lady?

Beatrice. Entrap me not with questions. Who stands here
As my accuser? Ha! wilt thou be he,
Who art my judge? Accuser, witness, judge,
What, all in one? Here is Orsino's name;°
Where is Orsino? Let his eye meet mine.
What means this scrawl? Alas! Ye know not what,
And therefore on the chance that it may be
Some evil, will ye kill us?

Enter an OFFICER.

Officer. Marzio's dead.

Judge. What did he say?

Officer. Nothing. As soon as we
Had bound him on the wheel, he smiled on us,
As one who baffles a deep adversary;
And holding his breath, died.

Judge. There remains nothing
But to apply the question to those prisoners,
Who yet remain stubborn.

Camillo. I overrule
Further proceedings, and in the behalf
Of these most innocent and noble persons
Will use my interest with the Holy Father.

Judge. Let the Pope's pleasure then be done. Meanwhile
Conduct these culprits each to separate cells;
And be the engines ready: for this night
If the Pope's resolution be as grave,
Pious and just as once, I'll wring the truth
Out of those nerves and sinews, groan by groan.

[*Exeunt.*

SCENE 3.—*The cell of a prison.*

BEATRICE *is discovered asleep on a couch.*
Enter BERNARDO.

Bernardo. How gently slumber rests upon her face,
Like the last thoughts of some day sweetly spent
Closing in night and dreams, and so prolonged.
After such torments as she bore last night,
How light and soft her breathing comes. Ay, me!
Methinks that I shall never sleep again.
But I must shake the heavenly dew of rest
From this sweet folded flower, thus . . . wake! awake!
What, sister, canst thou sleep?

Beatrice (*awaking*). I was just dreaming
That we were all in Paradise. Thou knowest
This cell seems like a kind of Paradise
After our father's presence.

Bernardo. Dear, dear sister,
Would that thy dream were not a dream! O, God!
How shall I tell?

Beatrice. What wouldst thou tell, sweet brother?

Bernardo. Look not so calm and happy, or even whilst
I stand considering what I have to say
My heart will break.

Beatrice. See now, thou mak'st me weep:
How very friendless thou wouldst be, dear child,
If I were dead. Say what thou hast to say.

Bernardo. They have confessed; they could endure no more
The tortures . . .

Beatrice. Ha! What was there to confess?
They must have told some weak and wicked lie
To flatter their tormentors. Have they said
That they were guilty? O, white innocence,
That thou shouldst wear the mask of guilt to hide

Thine awful and serenest countenance
From those who know thee not!

Enter JUDGE *with* LUCRETIA *and* GIACOMO, *guarded*

Ignoble hearts!
For some brief spasms of pain, which are at least
As mortal as the limbs through which they pass,
Are centuries of high splendour laid in dust?
And that eternal honour which should live
Sunlike, above the reek of mortal fame,
Changed to a mockery and a byword? What!
Will you give up these bodies to be dragged
At horses' heels, so that our hair should sweep
The footsteps of the vain and senseless crowd,
Who, that they may make our calamity
Their worship and their spectacle, will leave
The churches and the theatres as void
As their own hearts? Shall the light multitude
Fling, at their choice, curses or faded pity,
Sad funeral flowers to deck a living corpse,
Upon us as we pass to pass away,
And leave . . . what memory of our having been?
Infamy, blood, terror, despair? O thou,
Who wert a mother to the parentless,
Kill not thy child! Let not her wrongs kill thee!
Brother, lie down with me upon the rack,
And let us each be silent as a corpse;
It soon will be as soft as any grave.
'Tis but the falsehood it can wring from fear
Makes the rack cruel.

Giacomo. They will tear the truth
Even from thee at last, those cruel pains:
For pity's sake say thou art guilty now.

Lucretia. O, speak the truth! Let us all quickly die;
And after death, God is our judge, not they;
He will have mercy on us.

Bernardo. If indeed
It can be true, say so, dear sister mine;

And then the Pope will surely pardon you,
And all be well.

Judge. Confess, or I will warp
Your limbs with such keen tortures . . .

Beatrice. Tortures! Turn
The rack henceforth into a spinning wheel!
Torture your dog, that he may tell when last
He lapped the blood his master shed . . . not me!
My pangs are of the mind, and of the heart,
And of the soul; aye, of the inmost soul,
Which weeps within tears as of burning gall
To see, in this ill world where none are true,
My kindred false to their deserted selves.
And with considering all the wretched life
Which I have lived, and its now wretched end,
And the small justice shown by Heaven and Earth
To me or mine; and what a tyrant thou art,
And what slaves these; and what a world we make,
The oppressor and the oppressed . . . such pangs compel
My answer. What is it thou wouldst with me?

Judge. Art thou not guilty of thy father's death?

Beatrice. Or wilt thou rather tax high-judging God
That he permitted such an act as that
Which I have suffered, and which he beheld;
Made it unutterable, and took from it
All refuge, all revenge, all consequence,
But that which thou hast called my father's death?
Which is or is not what men call a crime,
Which either I have done, or have not done;
Say what ye will. I shall deny no more.
If ye desire it thus, thus let it be,
And so an end of all. Now do your will;
No other pains shall force another word.°

Judge. She is convicted, but has not confessed.
Be it enough. Until their final sentence
Let none have converse with them. You, young Lord,
Linger not here!

Beatrice. O, tear him not away!

Judge. Guards, do your duty.

Bernardo (*embracing* BEATRICE). Oh! would ye divide
Body from soul?

Officer. That is the headsman's business.
[*Exeunt all but* LUCRETIA, BEATRICE, *and* GIACOMO.

Giacomo. Have I confessed? Is it all over now?
No hope! No refuge! O, weak, wicked tongue
Which hast destroyed me, would that thou hadst been
Cut out and thrown to dogs first! To have killed
My father first, and then betrayed my sister;
Aye, thee! the one thing innocent and pure
In this black guilty world, to that which I
So well deserve! My wife! my little ones!
Destitute, helpless and I . . . Father! God!
Canst thou forgive even the unforgiving,
When their full hearts break thus, thus! . . .
[*Covers his face and weeps*

Lucretia. O, my child!
To what a dreadful end are we all come!
Why did I yield? Why did I not sustain
Those torments? Oh, that I were all dissolved
Into these fast and unavailing tears,
Which flow and feel not!

Beatrice. What 'twas weak to do,
'Tis weaker to lament, once being done;
Take cheer! The God who knew my wrong, and made
Our speedy act the angel of his wrath,
Seems, and but seems to have abandoned us.
Let us not think that we shall die for this.
Brother, sit near me; give me your firm hand,
You had a manly heart. Bear up! Bear up!
O, dearest Lady, put your gentle head
Upon my lap, and try to sleep awhile:
Your eyes look pale, hollow and overworn,

With heaviness of watching and slow grief.
Come, I will sing you some low, sleepy tune,
Not cheerful, nor yet sad; some dull old thing,
Some outworn and unused monotony,
Such as our country gossips sing and spin,
Till they almost forget they live: lie down!°
So, that will do. Have I forgot the words?
Faith! They are sadder than I thought they were.

SONG

False friend, wilt thou smile or weep
When my life is laid asleep?
Little cares for a smile or a tear,
The clay-cold corpse upon the bier!
Farewell! Heigh ho!
What is this whispers low?
There is a snake in thy smile, my dear;
And bitter poison within thy tear.

Sweet sleep, were death like to thee,
Or if thou couldst mortal be,
I would close these eyes of pain;
When to wake? Never again.
O, World! Farewell!
Listen to the passing bell!
It says, thou and I must part,
With a light and a heavy heart.

[*The scene closes.*

SCENE 4.—*A Hall of the Prison.*
Enter CAMILLO *and* BERNARDO.

Camillo. The Pope is stern; not to be moved or bent.
He looked as calm and keen as is the engine
Which tortures and which kills, exempt itself
From aught that it inflicts; a marble form,
A rite, a law, a custom: not a man.
He frowned as if to frown had been the trick
Of his machinery, on the advocates
Presenting the defences, which he tore
And threw behind, muttering with hoarse, harsh voice:
'Which among ye defended their old father
Killed in his sleep?' Then to another: 'Thou

Dost this in virtue of thy place; 'tis well.'
He turned to me then, looking deprecation,°
And said these three words, coldly: 'They must die.'

Bernardo. And yet you left him not?

Camillo. I urged him still;
Pleading, as I could guess, the devilish wrong
Which prompted your unnatural parent's death.
And he replied. 'Paolo Santa Croce
Murdered his mother yester evening,
And he is fled. Parricide grows so rife
That soon, for some just cause no doubt, the young
Will strangle us all, dozing in our chairs.
Authority, and power, and hoary hair
Are grown crimes capital. You are my nephew,
You come to ask their pardon; stay a moment;
Here is their sentence; never see me more
Till, to the letter, it be all fulfilled.'

Bernardo. O, God, not so! I did believe indeed
That all you said was but sad preparation
For happy news. O, there are words and looks
To bend the sternest purpose! Once I knew them,
Now I forget them at my dearest need.
What think you if I seek him out, and bathe
His feet and robe with hot and bitter tears?
Importune him with prayers, vexing his brain
With my perpetual cries, until in rage
He strike me with his pastoral cross, and trample
Upon my prostrate head, so that my blood
May stain the senseless dust on which he treads,
And remorse waken mercy? I will do it!
O, wait till I return! [*Rushes out*.

Camillo. Alas! poor boy!
A wreck-devoted seaman thus might pray
To the deaf sea.

Enter LUCRETIA, BEATRICE *and* GIACOMO, *guarded*.

Beatrice. I hardly dare to fear
That thou bring'st other news than a just pardon.

Camillo. May God in heaven be less inexorable
To the Pope's prayers, than he has been to mine.
Here is the sentence and the warrant.

Beatrice (*wildly*). Oh,
My God! Can it be possible I have
To die so suddenly? So young to go°
Under the obscure, cold, rotting, wormy ground!
To be nailed down into a narrow place;
To see no more sweet sunshine; hear no more
Blithe voice of living thing; muse not again
Upon familiar thoughts, sad, yet thus lost—
How fearful! to be nothing! Or to be . . .
What? O, where am I? Let me not go mad!°
Sweet Heaven, forgive weak thoughts! If there should be
No God, no Heaven, no Earth in the void world;
The wide, grey, lampless, deep, unpeopled world!
If all things then should be . . . my father's spirit,
His eye, his voice, his touch surrounding me;
The atmosphere and breath of my dead life!
If sometimes, as a shape more like himself,
Even the form which tortured me on earth,
Masked in grey hairs and wrinkles, he should come
And wind me in his hellish arms, and fix
His eyes on mine, and drag me down, down, down!
For was he not alone omnipotent
On Earth, and ever present! Even though dead,
Does not his spirit live in all that breathe,
And work for me and mine still the same ruin,
Scorn, pain, despair? Who ever yet returned
To teach the laws of death's untrodden realm?°
Unjust perhaps as those which drive us now,
O, whither, whither?°

Lucretia. Trust in God's sweet love,
The tender promises of Christ: ere night
Think we shall be in Paradise.°

Beatrice. 'Tis past!
Whatever comes my heart shall sink no more.
And yet, I know not why, your words strike chill:

How tedious, false and cold seem all things. I°
Have met with much injustice in this world;
No difference has been made by God or man,
Or any power moulding my wretched lot,
'Twixt good or evil, as regarded me.
I am cut off from the only world I know,
From light, and life, and love, in youth's sweet prime.
You do well telling me to trust in God,
I hope I do trust in him. In whom else
Can any trust? And yet my heart is cold.

(*During the latter speeches* GIACOMO *has retired conversing with* CAMILLO, *who now goes out;* GIACOMO *advances.*)

Giacomo. Know you not, Mother . . . Sister, know you not?
Bernardo even now is gone to implore
The Pope to grant our pardon.

Lucretia. Child, perhaps
It will be granted. We may all then live
To make these woes a tale for distant years:
O, what a thought! It gushes to my heart
Like the warm blood.

Beatrice. Yet both will soon be cold.
O, trample out that thought! Worse than despair,
Worse than the bitterness of death, is hope:
It is the only ill which can find place
Upon the giddy, sharp and narrow hour°
Tottering beneath us. Plead with the swift frost
That it should spare the eldest flower of spring:
Plead with awakening Earthquake, o'er whose couch
Even now a city stands, strong, fair and free;
Now stench and blackness yawns, like death. O, plead
With famine, or wind-walking Pestilence,
Blind lightning, or the deaf sea, not with man!
Cruel, cold, formal man; righteous in words,
In deeds a Cain. No, Mother, we must die:
Since such is the reward of innocent lives;
Such the alleviation of worst wrongs.
And whilst our murderers live, and hard, cold men,
Smiling and slow, walk through a world of tears

To death as to life's sleep; 'twere just the grave
Were some strange joy for us. Come, obscure Death,
And wind me in thine all-embracing arms!
Like a fond mother hide me in thy bosom,
And rock me to the sleep from which none wake.
Live ye, who live, subject to one another
As we were once, who now . . .

BERNARDO *rushes in.*

Bernardo. Oh, horrible!
That tears, that looks, that hope poured forth in prayer,
Even till the heart is vacant and despairs,
Should all be vain! The ministers of death
Are waiting round the doors. I thought I saw
Blood on the face of one . . . what if 'twere fancy?
Soon the heart's blood of all I love on earth
Will sprinkle him, and he will wipe it off
As if 'twere only rain. O, life! O, world!
Cover me! let me be no more! To see
That perfect mirror of pure innocence
Wherein I gazed, and grew happy and good,
Shivered to dust! To see thee, Beatrice,
Who made all lovely thou didst look upon . . .
Thee, light of life . . . dead, dark! while I say, sister,
To hear I have no sister; and thou, Mother,
Whose love was a bond to all our loves . . . °
Dead! The sweet bond broken!

Enter CAMILLO *and Guards.*

They come! Let me
Kiss those warm lips before their crimson leaves
Are blighted . . . white . . . cold. Say farewell, before
Death chokes that gentle voice! O, let me hear
You speak!

Beatrice. Farewell, my tender brother. Think
Of our sad fate with gentleness, as now:
And let mild, pitying thoughts lighten for thee
Thy sorrow's load. Err not in harsh despair,
But tears and patience. One thing more, my child,
For thine own sake be constant to the love
Thou bearest us; and to the faith that I,

Though wrapped in a strange cloud of crime and shame,
Lived ever holy and unstained. And though
Ill tongues shall wound me, and our common name
Be as a mark stamped on thine innocent brow
For men to point at as they pass, do thou
Forbear, and never think a thought unkind
Of those, who perhaps love thee in their graves.
So mayest thou die as I do; fear and pain
Being subdued. Farewell! Farewell! Farewell!

Bernardo. I cannot say, farewell!

Camillo. O, Lady Beatrice!

Beatrice. Give yourself no unnecessary pain,
My dear Lord Cardinal. Here, Mother, tie
My girdle for me, and bind up this hair
In any simple knot; aye, that does well.
And yours I see is coming down. How often
Have we done this for one another; now
We shall not do it any more. My Lord,
We are quite ready. Well, 'tis very well.

THE END

THE MASK OF ANARCHY

WRITTEN ON THE OCCASION OF THE MASSACRE AT MANCHESTER

As I lay asleep in Italy°
There came a voice from over the Sea,
And with great power it forth led me
To walk in the visions of Poesy.

I met Murder on the way—
He had a mask like Castlereagh—°
Very smooth he looked, yet grim;
Seven bloodhounds followed him:°

All were fat; and well they might
Be in admirable plight,
For one by one, and two by two,
He tossed them human hearts to chew
Which from his wide cloak he drew.

Next came Fraud, and he had on,
Like Eldon, an erminèd gown;°
His big tears, for he wept well,
Turned to mill-stones as they fell.

And the little children, who
Round his feet played to and fro,
Thinking every tear a gem,
Had their brains knocked out by them.°

Clothed with the Bible, as with light,
And the shadows of the night,
Like Sidmouth, next, Hypocrisy°
On a crocodile rode by.°

And many more Destructions played
In this ghastly masquerade,
All disguised, even to the eyes,
Like Bishops, lawyers, peers or spies.

Last came Anarchy: he rode°
On a white horse, splashed with blood;
He was pale even to the lips,
Like Death in the Apocalypse.

And he wore a kingly crown,
And in his grasp a sceptre shone;
On his brow this mark I saw—
'I AM GOD, AND KING, AND LAW.'

With a pace stately and fast,
Over English land he passed,
Trampling to a mire of blood
The adoring multitude.

And a mighty troop around,
With their trampling shook the ground,
Waving each a bloody sword,
For the service of their Lord.

And with glorious triumph they
Rode through England proud and gay,
Drunk as with intoxication
Of the wine of desolation.

O'er fields and towns, from sea to sea,
Passed the Pageant swift and free,
Tearing up, and trampling down,
Till they came to London town:

And each dweller, panic-stricken,
Felt his heart with terror sicken
Hearing the tempestuous cry
Of the triumph of Anarchy.

For with pomp to meet him came
Clothed in arms like blood and flame,
The hired murderers, who did sing
'Thou art God, and Law, and King.

'We have waited, weak and lone
For thy coming, Mighty One!

Our purses are empty, our swords are cold,
Give us glory, and blood, and gold.'

Lawyers and priests, a motley crowd,
To the earth their pale brows bowed;
Like a bad prayer not overloud,
Whispering—'Thou art Law and God.'—

Then all cried with one accord
'Thou art King, and God, and Lord;
Anarchy, to thee we bow,
Be thy name made holy now!'

And Anarchy, the Skeleton,
Bowed and grinned to every one,
As well as if his education
Had cost ten millions to the nation.

For he knew the Palaces
Of our Kings were rightly his;
His the sceptre, crown, and globe,°
And the gold-inwoven robe.

So he sent his slaves before
To seize upon the Bank and Tower,°
And was proceeding with intent
To meet his pensioned Parliament°

When one fled past, a maniac maid,
And her name was Hope, she said:
But she looked more like Despair,
And she cried out in the air:

'My father Time is weak and grey
With waiting for a better day;
See how idiot-like he stands,
Fumbling with his palsied hands!

'He has had child after child
And the dust of death is piled
Over every one but me—
Misery, oh, Misery!'°

Then she lay down in the street,
Right before the horses' feet,
Expecting, with a patient eye,
Murder, Fraud and Anarchy,

When between her and her foes
A mist, a light, an image rose,
Small at first, and weak, and frail,
Like the vapour of a vale:

Till as clouds grow on the blast,
Like tower-crowned giants striding fast,
And glare with lightnings as they fly,
And speak in thunder to the sky,

It grew—a Shape arrayed in mail°
Brighter than the viper's scale,
And upborne on wings whose grain
Was as the light of sunny rain.

On its helm, seen far away,
A planet, like the Morning's, lay;°
And those plumes its light rained through
Like a shower of crimson dew.

With step as soft as wind it passed
O'er the heads of men—so fast
That they knew the presence there,
And looked—but all was empty air.

As flowers beneath May's footstep waken,
As stars from Night's loose hair are shaken,
As waves arise when loud winds call,
Thoughts sprung where'er that step did fall.

And the prostrate multitude
Looked—and ankle-deep in blood,
Hope, that maiden most serene,
Was walking with a quiet mien:

And Anarchy, the ghastly birth,
Lay dead earth upon the earth—
The Horse of Death tameless as wind
Fled, and with his hoofs did grind
To dust the murderers thronged behind.

A rushing light of clouds and splendour,
A sense awakening and yet tender
Was heard and felt—and at its close
These words of joy and fear arose

As if their own indignant Earth
Which gave the sons of England birth
Had felt their blood upon her brow,
And shuddering with a mother's throe

Had turnèd every drop of blood
By which her face had been bedewed
To an accent unwithstood—°
As if her heart cried out aloud:

'Men of England, heirs of Glory,
Heroes of unwritten story,
Nurslings of one mighty Mother,
Hopes of her, and one another,

'Rise like Lions after slumber
In unvanquishable number,
Shake your chains to Earth like dew
Which in sleep had fallen on you—
Ye are many—they are few.°

'What is Freedom?—ye can tell
That which slavery is, too well—
For its very name has grown
To an echo of your own.

''Tis to work and have such pay
As just keeps life from day to day
In your limbs, as in a cell
For the tyrants' use to dwell,

'So that ye for them are made
Loom, and plough, and sword, and spade,
With or without your own will bent
To their defence and nourishment.

''Tis to see your children weak
With their mothers pine and peak,°
When the winter winds are bleak—
They are dying whilst I speak.

''Tis to hunger for such diet
As the rich man in his riot
Casts to the fat dogs that lie
Surfeiting beneath his eye;

''Tis to let the Ghost of Gold°
Take from Toil a thousandfold
More than e'er its substance could
In the tyrannies of old.

'Paper coin—that forgery
Of the title deeds, which ye
Hold to something of the worth
Of the inheritance of Earth.

''Tis to be a slave in soul
And to hold no strong control
Over your own wills, but be
All that others make of ye.

'And at length when ye complain
With a murmur weak and vain
'Tis to see the Tyrant's crew
Ride over your wives and you—
Blood is on the grass like dew.

'Then it is to feel revenge
Fiercely thirsting to exchange
Blood for blood—and wrong for wrong—
Do not thus when ye are strong.

'Birds find rest, in narrow nest
When weary of their wingèd quest;
Beasts find fare, in woody lair
When storm and snow are in the air.°

'Asses, swine, have litter spread
And with fitting food are fed;
All things have a home but one—
Thou, oh, Englishman, hast none!°

'This is slavery—savage men
Or wild beasts within a den
Would endure not as ye do—
But such ills they never knew.

'What art thou, Freedom? O! could slaves
Answer from their living graves
This demand—tyrants would flee
Like a dream's dim imagery.

'Thou art not, as imposters say,
A shadow soon to pass away,
A superstition, and a name
Echoing from the cave of Fame.°

'For the labourer thou art bread,
And a comely table spread,
From his daily labour come
To a neat and happy home.

'Thou art clothes, and fire, and food
For the trampled multitude—
No—in countries that are free
Such starvation cannot be
As in England now we see.

'To the rich thou art a check,
When his foot is on the neck
Of his victim, thou dost make
That he treads upon a snake.°

'Thou art Justice—ne'er for gold
May thy righteous laws be sold
As laws are in England—thou
Shield'st alike both high and low.

'Thou art Wisdom—Freemen never
Dream that God will damn forever
All who think those things untrue
Of which Priests make such ado.

'Thou art Peace—never by thee
Would blood and treasure wasted be
As tyrants wasted them, when all
Leagued to quench thy flame in Gaul.°

'What if English toil and blood
Was poured forth, even as a flood?
It availed, Oh, Liberty!
To dim, but not extinguish thee.

'Thou art Love—the rich have kissed
Thy feet, and like him following Christ
Give their substance to the free
And through the rough world follow thee°

'Or turn their wealth to arms, and make
War for thy beloved sake
On wealth, and war, and fraud—whence they
Drew the power which is their prey.

'Science, Poetry and Thought
Are thy lamps; they make the lot
Of the dwellers in a cot
So serene, they curse it not.°

'Spirit, Patience, Gentleness,
All that can adorn and bless
Art thou—let deeds not words express
Thine exceeding loveliness.

'Let a great Assembly be
Of the fearless and the free

On some spot of English ground
Where the plains stretch wide around.

'Let the blue sky overhead,
The green earth on which ye tread,
All that must eternal be
Witness the solemnity.

'From the corners uttermost
Of the bounds of English coast,
From every hut, village and town
Where those who live and suffer moan
For others' misery or their own,

'From the workhouse and the prison
Where pale as corpses newly risen,
Women, children, young and old
Groan for pain, and weep for cold—

'From the haunts of daily life
Where is waged the daily strife
With common wants and common cares
Which sows the human heart with tares—°

'Lastly from the palaces
Where the murmur of distress
Echoes, like the distant sound
Of a wind alive around

'Those prison-halls of wealth and fashion
Where some few feel such compassion
For those who groan, and toil, and wail
As must make their brethren pale—

'Ye who suffer woes untold,
Or to feel, or to behold
Your lost country bought and sold
With a price of blood and gold—

'Let a vast Assembly be,
And with great solemnity

Declare with measured words that ye
Are, as God has made ye, free—

'Be your strong and simple words
Keen to wound as sharpened swords,
And wide as targes let them be°
With their shade to cover ye.

'Let the tyrants pour around
With a quick and startling sound,
Like the loosening of a sea
Troops of armed emblazonry.

'Let the charged artillery drive
Till the dead air seems alive
With the clash of clanging wheels,
And the tramp of horses' heels.

'Let the fixèd bayonet
Gleam with sharp desire to wet
Its bright point in English blood,
Looking keen as one for food.

'Let the horsemen's scimitars°
Wheel and flash, like sphereless stars°
Thirsting to eclipse their burning
In a sea of death and mourning.

'Stand ye calm and resolute,
Like a forest close and mute,
With folded arms and looks which are
Weapons of unvanquished war,

'And let Panic, who outspeeds
The career of armèd steeds,
Pass, a disregarded shade,
Through your phalanx undismayed.

'Let the laws of your own land,
Good or ill, between ye stand

Hand to hand and foot to foot,
Arbiters of the dispute,

'The old laws of England—they
Whose reverend heads with age are grey,
Children of a wiser day;
And whose solemn voice must be
Thine own echo—Liberty!

'On those who first should violate
Such sacred heralds in their state
Rest the blood that must ensue,
And it will not rest on you.

'And if then the tyrants dare
Let them ride among you there,
Slash, and stab, and maim, and hew—
What they like, that let them do.

'With folded arms and steady eyes,
And little fear, and less surprise,
Look upon them as they slay
Till their rage has died away.°

'Then they will return with shame
To the place from which they came,
And the blood thus shed will speak
In hot blushes on their cheek.

'Every woman in the land
Will point at them as they stand—
They will hardly dare to greet
Their acquaintance in the street.

'And the bold, true warriors
Who have hugged Danger in wars
Will turn to those who would be free,
Ashamed of such base company.

'And that slaughter to the Nation
Shall steam up like inspiration,

Eloquent, oracular;
A volcano heard afar.°

'And these words shall then become
Like oppression's thundered doom
Ringing through each heart and brain,
Heard again—again—again—

'"Rise like lions after slumber
In unvanquishable number—
Shake your chains to earth like dew
Which in sleep had fallen on you—
Ye are many—they are few"'.

Ode to the West Wind

1

O, wild West Wind, thou breath of Autumn's being,
Thou, from whose unseen presence the leaves dead
Are driven, like ghosts from an enchanter fleeing,°

Yellow, and black, and pale, and hectic red,
Pestilence-stricken multitudes: O, thou,°
Who chariotest to their dark wintry bed

The wingèd seeds, where they lie cold and low,
Each like a corpse within its grave, until
Thine azure sister of the Spring shall blow°

Her clarion o'er the dreaming earth, and fill
(Driving sweet buds like flocks to feed in air)
With living hues and odours plain and hill:

Wild Spirit, which art moving everywhere;
Destroyer and Preserver; hear, O, hear!°

2

Thou on whose stream, 'mid the steep sky's commotion,
Loose clouds like earth's decaying leaves are shed,°
Shook from the tangled boughs of Heaven and Ocean,°

Angels of rain and lightning: there are spread°
On the blue surface of thine airy surge,
Like the bright hair uplifted from the head

Of some fierce Maenad, even from the dim verge
Of the horizon to the zenith's height,
The locks of the approaching storm. Thou dirge°

Of the dying year, to which this closing night
Will be the dome of a vast sepulchre,
Vaulted with all thy congregated might

Of vapours, from whose solid atmosphere
Black rain, and fire, and hail will burst: O, hear!

3

Thou who didst waken from his summer dreams
The blue Mediterranean, where he lay,
Lulled by the coil of his crystalline streams,

Beside a pumice isle in Baiae's bay,°
And saw in sleep old palaces and towers
Quivering within the wave's intenser day,°

All overgrown with azure moss and flowers
So sweet, the sense faints picturing them! Thou
For whose path the Atlantic's level powers

Cleave themselves into chasms, while far below
The sea-blooms and the oozy woods which wear
The sapless foliage of the ocean, know

Thy voice, and suddenly grow grey with fear,
And tremble and despoil themselves: O, hear!

4

If I were a dead leaf thou mightest bear;
If I were a swift cloud to fly with thee;
A wave to pant beneath thy power, and share

The impulse of thy strength, only less free
Than thou, O, Uncontrollable! If even
I were as in my boyhood, and could be

The comrade of thy wanderings over Heaven,
As then, when to outstrip thy skiey speed
Scarce seemed a vision; I would ne'er have striven

As thus with thee in prayer in my sore need.°
Oh! lift me as a wave, a leaf, a cloud!
I fall upon the thorns of life! I bleed!°

A heavy weight of hours has chained and bowed
One too like thee: tameless, and swift, and proud.

5

Make me thy lyre, even as the forest is:
What if my leaves are falling like its own!
The tumult of thy mighty harmonies

Will take from both a deep, autumnal tone,
Sweet though in sadness. Be thou, Spirit fierce,
My spirit! Be thou me, impetuous one!

Drive my dead thoughts over the universe
Like withered leaves to quicken a new birth!°
And, by the incantation of this verse,

Scatter, as from an unextinguished hearth
Ashes and sparks, my words among mankind!
Be through my lips to unawakened earth

The trumpet of a prophecy! O, wind,
If Winter comes, can Spring be far behind?°

PETER BELL THE THIRD

BY MICHING MALLECHO, ESQ.°

Is it a party in a parlour—
Crammed just as they on earth were crammed,
Some sipping punch—some sipping tea;
But, as you by their faces see,
All silent and all——damned!

Peter Bell, by W. Wordsworth.°

Ophelia. What means this, my lord?
Hamlet. Marry, this is miching mallecho; it means mischief.

Shakespeare.°

DEDICATION
TO
THOMAS BROWN, ESQ., THE YOUNGER, H.F.°

Dear Tom—

Allow me to request you to introduce Mr Peter Bell to the respectable family of the Fudges; although he may fall short of those very considerable personages in the more active properties which characterize the Rat and the Apostate,° I suspect that even you their historian will be forced to confess that he surpasses them in the more peculiarly legitimate qualification of intolerable dullness.

You know Mr Examiner Hunt. That murderous and smiling villain at the mere sound of whose voice our susceptible friend the *Quarterly* fell into a paroxysm of eleutherophobia° and foamed so much acrid gall that it burned the carpet in Mr Murray's upper room,° and eating a hole in the floor fell like rain upon our poor friend's head, who was scampering from room to room like a bear with a swarm of bees on his nose:—it caused an incurable ulcer and our poor friend has worn a wig ever since. Well, this monkey° suckled with tiger's milk, this odious thief, liar, scoundrel, coxcomb and monster presented me to two of the Mr Bells.° Seeing me in his presence they of course uttered very few words and those with much caution. I scarcely need observe that they only kept company with him—at least I can certainly answer for one of them—in order to observe whether they could not borrow colours from any particulars of his private life for the denunciation they mean to make of him, as the member of an 'infamous and black conspiracy for diminishing the authority of that venerable canon, which forbids any man to mar his grandmother'; the effect of which in this on our moral and religious nation is likely to answer the purpose of the controversy. My intimacy with the younger Mr Bell naturally sprung from this introduction to his brothers. And in presenting him to you, I have the satisfaction of being able to assure you that he is considerably the dullest of the three.

There is this particular advantage in an acquaintance with any one of the Peter Bells; that if you know one Peter Bell, you know three Peter Bells; they are not one but three, not three but one. An awful mystery, after having caused torrents of blood, and having been hymned by groans enough to deafen the music of the spheres, is at length illustrated to the satisfaction of all parties in the theological world, by the nature of Mr Peter Bell.

Peter is a polyhedric Peter, or a Peter with many sides. He changes colours like a chameleon, and his coat like a snake. He is a Proteus° of a Peter. He was at first sublime, pathetic, impressive, profound; then dull; then prosy and dull; and now dull—'o so' dull! it is an ultra-legitimate° dullness.

You will perceive that it is not necessary to consider Hell and the Devil as supernatural machinery. The whole scene of my epic is in 'this world which is'—so Peter informed us before his conversion to *White Obi*°—

> the world of all of us, *and where*
> *We find our happiness, or not at all.*

Let me observe that I have spent six or seven days° in composing this sublime piece;—the orb of my moonlike genius has made the fourth part of its revolution round the dull earth which you inhabit, driving you mad whilst it has retained its calmness and its splendour, and I have been fitting this its last phase 'to occupy a permanent station in the literature of my country.'

Your works, indeed, dear Tom, sell better; but mine are far superior. The public is no judge; posterity sets all to rights.

Allow me to observe that so much has been written of Peter Bell, that the present history can be considered only, like the *Iliad*, as a continuation of that series of cyclic poems which have already been candidates for bestowing immortality upon, at the same time that they receive it from, his character and adventures. In this point of view, I have violated no rule of syntax in beginning my composition with a conjunction; the full stop which closes the poem continued by me being, like the full stops at the end of the *Iliad* and *Odyssey*, a full stop of a very qualified import.

Hoping that the immortality which you have given to the Fudges, you will receive from them; and in the firm expectation that when London shall be the habitation of bitterns,° when St Paul's and Westminster Abbey shall stand, shapeless and nameless ruins in the midst of an unpeopled marsh; when the piers of Waterloo bridge shall become the nuclei of islets of reeds and osiers and cast the jagged shadows of their broken arches on the solitary stream,—some transatlantic commentator will be weighing in the scales of some new and now unimagined system of criticism, the respective merits of the Bells and the Fudges, and of their historians,

I remain, Dear Tom,
Yours sincerely,
Miching Mallecho.

December 1, 1819.

P.S. Pray excuse the date of place;° so soon as the profits of this publication come in, I mean to hire lodgings in a more respectable street.

Prologue

Peter Bells, one, two and three,
O'er the wide world wandering be:—
First, the antenatal Peter,°
Wrapped in weeds of the same metre,
The so long predestined raiment
Clothed in which to walk his way meant
The second Peter, whose ambition
Is to link the proposition
As the mean of two extremes—
(This was learnt from Aldric's themes)°
Shielding from the guilt of schism
The orthodoxal syllogism:
The first Peter—he who was
Like the shadow in the glass
Of the second, yet unripe;
His substantial antitype.—°
Then came Peter Bell the Second,
Who henceforward must be reckoned

The body of a double soul—
And that portion of the whole
Without which the rest would seem
Ends of a disjointed dream.—
And the third is he who has
O'er the grave been forced to pass
To the other side, which is,—
Go and try else,—just like this.

Peter Bell the First was Peter
Smugger, milder, softer, neater,
Like the soul before it is
Born from *that* world into *this*.
The next Peter Bell was he
Predevote like you and me°
To good or evil as may come;
His was the severer doom.—
For he was an evil Cotter°
And a polygamic Potter.°
And the last is Peter Bell,
Damned since our first Parents fell,
Damned eternally to Hell—
Surely he deserves it well!

Part First

DEATH

And Peter Bell, when he had been
With fresh-imported Hell-fire warmed,
Grew serious—from his dress and mien
'Twas very plainly to be seen
Peter was quite reformed.

His eyes turned up, his mouth turned down;
His accent caught a nasal twang;
He oiled his hair; there might be heard°
The grace of God in every word
Which Peter said or sang.

But Peter now grew old, and had
An ill no doctor could unravel;

His torments almost drove him mad;—
Some said it was a fever bad—
  Some swore it was the gravel.°

His holy friends then came about
  And with long preaching and persuasion,
Convinced the patient, that without
The smallest shadow of a doubt
  He was predestined to damnation.

They said—'Thy name is Peter Bell;
  Thy skin is of a brimstone hue;
Alive or dead—aye, sick or well—
The one God made to rhyme with hell;
  The other, I think, rhymes with you.'°

Then Peter set up such a yell!—
  The nurse, who with some water gruel
Was climbing up the stairs, as well
As her old legs could climb them—fell,
  And broke them both—the fall was cruel.

The Parson from the casement leapt
  Into the lake of Windermere—°
And many an eel—though no adept
In God's right reason for it—kept
  Gnawing his kidneys half a year.

And all the rest rushed through the door,
  And tumbled over one another,
And broke their skulls.—Upon the floor
Meanwhile sate Peter Bell, and swore,
  And cursed his father and his mother;

And raved of God, and sin, and death,
  Blaspheming like an infidel;
And said, that with his clenchèd teeth
He'd seize the earth from underneath,
  And drag it with him down to Hell.

As he was speaking came a spasm,
  And wrenched his gnashing teeth asunder,

Like one who sees a strange phantasm
He lay,—there was a silent chasm
   Between his upper jaw and under.

And yellow death lay on his face;
   And a fixed smile that was not human
Told, as I understand the case,
That he was gone to the wrong place:—
   I heard all this from the old woman.

Then there came down from Langdale Pike
   A cloud with lightning, wind and hail;
It swept over the mountains like
An Ocean,—and I heard it strike
   The woods and crags of Grasmere vale.

And I saw the black storm come
   Nearer, minute after minute,
Its thunder made the cataracts dumb,
With hiss, and clash, and hollow hum
   It neared as if the Devil was in it.

The Devil *was* in it:—he had bought°
   Peter for half a crown; and when
The storm which bore him vanished, nought
That in the house that storm had caught
   Was ever seen again.

The gaping neighbours came next day—
   They found all vanished from the shore:
The Bible, whence he used to pray,
Half scorched under a hen-coop lay;
   Smashed glass—and nothing more!

Part Second

THE DEVIL

The Devil, I safely can aver,
   Has neither hoof, nor tail, nor sting;
Nor is he, as some sages swear,

A spirit, neither here nor there,
  In nothing—yet in everything.

He is—what we are; for sometimes°
  The Devil is a gentleman;
At others a bard bartering rhymes
For sack; a statesman spinning crimes,°
  A swindler, living as he can;

A thief, who cometh in the night,
  With whole boots and net pantaloons,
Like some one whom it were not right
To mention;—or the luckless wight
  From whom he steals nine silver spoons.

But in this case he did appear
  Like a slop-merchant from Wapping°
And with smug face, and eye severe
On every side did perk and peer°
  Till he saw Peter dead or napping.

He had on an upper Benjamin°
  (For he was of the driving schism)
In the which he wrapped his skin
From the storm he travelled in,
  For fear of rheumatism.

He called the ghost out of the corse;—
  It was exceedingly like Peter,—
Only its voice was hollow and hoarse—
It had a queerish look of course—
  Its dress too was a little neater.

The Devil knew not his name and lot;
  Peter knew not that he was Bell:
Each had an upper stream of thought,
Which made all seem as it was not;
  Fitting itself to all things well.°

Peter thought he had parents dear,
  Brothers, sisters, cousins, cronies,

In the fens of Lincolnshire;
He perhaps had found them there
   Had he gone and boldly shown his

Solemn phiz in his own village;°
   Where he thought, oft when a boy
He'd clomb the orchard walls to pillage°
The produce of his neighbour's tillage,
   With marvellous pride and joy.

And the Devil thought he had,
   Mid the misery and confusion
Of an unjust war, just made
A fortune by the gainful trade
Of giving soldiers rations bad—
   The world is full of strange delusion.

That he had a mansion planned
   In a square like Grosvenor square,°
That he was aping fashion, and
That he now came to Westmoreland
   To see what was romantic there.

And all this, though quite ideal,—
   Ready at a breath to vanish,—
Was a state not more unreal
Than the peace he could not feel,
   Or the care he could not banish.

After a little conversation
   The Devil told Peter, if he chose
He'd bring him to the world of fashion
By giving him a situation
   In his own service—and new clothes.

And Peter bowed, quite pleased and proud,
   And after waiting some few days
For a new livery—dirty yellow
Turned up with black—the wretched fellow
   Was bowled to Hell in the Devil's chaise.

Part Third

HELL

Hell is a city much like London—
  A populous and a smoky city;
There are all sorts of people undone,
And there is little or no fun done;
  Small justice shown, and still less pity.

There is a Castle, and a Canning,
  A Cobbett, and a Castlereagh;°
All sorts of caitiff corpses planning
All sorts of cozening for trepanning°
  Corpses less corrupt than they.

There is a * * *, who has lost°
  His wits, or sold them, none knows which;
He walks about a double ghost,
And though as thin as Fraud almost—
  Ever grows more grim and rich.

There is a Chancery Court, a King,°
  A manufacturing mob; a set
Of thieves who by themselves are sent
Similar thieves to represent;
  An Army;—and a public debt.

Which last is a scheme of Paper money,°
  And means—being interpreted—
'Bees, keep your wax—give us the honey
And we will plant while skies are sunny
  Flowers, which in winter serve instead.'

There is a great talk of Revolution—
  And a great chance of despotism—
German soldiers—camps—confusion—°
Tumults—lotteries—rage—delusion—
  Gin—suicide and methodism;°

Taxes too, on wine and bread,
 And meat, and beer, and tea, and cheese,
From which those patriots pure are fed
Who gorge before they reel to bed
 The tenfold essence of all these.

There are mincing women, mewing
 (Like cats, who *amant misere*)°
Of their own virtue, and pursuing
Their gentler sisters to that ruin,
 Without which—what were chastity?°

Lawyers—judges—old hobnobbers°
 Are there—Bailiffs—Chancellors—
Bishops—great and little robbers—
Rhymesters—pamphleteers—stock-jobbers—°
 Men of glory in the wars,—

Things whose trade is, over ladies
 To lean, and flirt, and stare, and simper,
Till all that is divine in woman
Grows cruel, courteous, smooth, inhuman,
 Crucified 'twixt a smile and whimper.

Thrusting, toiling, wailing, moiling,°
 Frowning, preaching—such a riot!
Each with never ceasing labour
Whilst he thinks he cheats his neighbour
 Cheating his own heart of quiet.

And all these meet at levees;—°
 Dinners convivial and political;—
Suppers of epic poets;—teas,
Where small talk dies in agonies;—
 Breakfasts professional and critical;—

Lunches and snacks so aldermanic
 That one would furnish forth ten dinners,
Where reigns a Cretan-tonguèd panic°
Lest news Russ, Dutch, or Alemannic°
 Should make some losers, and some winners

At conversazioni—balls—°
   Conventicles and drawing-rooms—°
Courts of law—committees—calls
Of a morning—clubs—book stalls—
   Churches—masquerades and tombs.

And this is Hell—and in this smother
   All are damnable and damned;
Each one damning, damns the other;
They are damned by one another,
   By none other are they damned.

'Tis a lie to say, 'God damns!'°
   Where was Heaven's Attorney General
When they first gave out such flams?°
Let there be an end of shams,
   They are mines of poisonous mineral.

Statesmen damn themselves to be
   Cursed; and lawyers damn their souls
To the auction of a fee;
Churchmen damn themselves to see
   God's sweet love in burning coals.

The rich are damned beyond all cure
   To taunt, and starve, and trample on
The weak and wretched: and the poor
Damn their broken hearts to endure
   Stripe on stripe, with groan on groan.°

Sometimes the poor are damned indeed
   To take,—not means for being blessed,—
But Cobbett's snuff, revenge; that weed°
From which the worms that it doth feed
   Squeeze less than they before possessed.

And some few, like we know who,°
   Damned—but God alone knows why—
To believe their minds are given
To make this ugly Hell a Heaven;
   In which faith they live and die.

Thus, as in a Town, plague-stricken,
  Each man be he sound or no
Must indifferently sicken;
As when day begins to thicken
  None knows a pigeon from a crow,—

So good and bad, sane and mad,
  The oppressor and the oppressed;
Those who weep to see what others
Smile to inflict upon their brothers;
  Lovers, haters, worst and best;

All are damned—they breathe an air,
  Thick, infected, joy-dispelling:
Each pursues what seems most fair,
Mining like moles, through mind, and there
Scoop palace-caverns vast, where Care
  In thronèd state is ever dwelling.

Part Fourth

SIN

Lo, Peter in Hell's Grosvenor square,
  A footman in the Devil's service!
And the misjudging world would swear
That every man in service there
  To virtue would prefer vice.

But Peter, though now damned, was not
  What Peter was before damnation.
Men oftentimes prepare a lot
Which ere it finds them, is not what
  Suits with their genuine station.

All things that Peter saw and felt
  Had a peculiar aspect to him;
And when they came within the belt
Of his own nature, seemed to melt
  Like cloud to cloud, into him.°

And so the outward world uniting
  To that within him, he became
Considerably uninviting
To those, who meditation slighting,
  Were moulded in a different frame.

And he scorned them, and they scorned him;
  And he scorned all they did; and they
Did all that men of their own trim°
Are wont to do to please their whim,
  Drinking, lying, swearing, play.

Such were his fellow servants; thus
  His virtue, like our own, was built
Too much on that indignant fuss
Hypocrite Pride stirs up in us
  To bully out another's guilt.

He had a mind which was somehow
  At once circumference and centre
Of all he might or feel or know;
Nothing went ever out, although
  Something did ever enter.

He had as much imagination
  As a pint-pot:—he never could
Fancy another situation
From which to dart his contemplation,
  Than that wherein he stood.

Yet his was individual mind,
  And new created all he saw
In a new manner, and refined
Those new creations, and combined
  Them, by a master-spirit's law.

Thus—though unimaginative,
  An apprehension clear, intense,
Of his mind's work, had made alive
The things it wrought on; I believe
  Wakening a sort of thought in sense.

But from the first 'twas Peter's drift
    To be a kind of moral eunuch.
He touched the hem of Nature's shift,
Felt faint—and never dared uplift
    The closest, all-concealing tunic.

She laughed the while, with an arch smile,
    And kissed him with a sister's kiss,
And said—'My best Diogenes,°
I love you well—but, if you please,
    Tempt not again my deepest bliss.

''Tis you are cold—for I, not coy,
    Yield love for love, frank, warm and true;
And Burns, a Scottish Peasant boy,—
His errors prove it—knew my joy
    More, learned friend, than you.

'*Bocca baciata non perde ventura*
    Anzi rinnuova come fa la luna:—°
So thought Boccaccio, whose sweet words might cure a
Male prude like you from what you now endure, a
    Low-tide in soul, like a stagnant laguna.'

Then Peter rubbed his eyes severe,
    And smoothed his spacious forehead down
With his broad palm;—'twixt love and fear,
He looked, as he no doubt felt, queer,
    And in his dream sate down.

The Devil was no uncommon creature;
    A leaden-witted thief—just huddled
Out of the dross and scum of nature;
A toadlike lump of limb and feature,°
    With mind, and heart, and fancy muddled.

He was that heavy, dull, cold thing
    The Spirit of Evil well may be:
A drone too base to have a sting,
Who gluts, and grimes his lazy wing,
    And calls lust, luxury.

Now he was quite the kind of wight°
  Round whom collect, at a fixed era,
Venison, turtle, hock and claret,—
Good cheer—and those who come to share it—
  And best East Indian madeira!

It was his fancy to invite
  Men of science, wit and learning
Who came to lend each other light:—
He proudly thought that his gold's might
  Had set those spirits burning.

And men of learning, science, wit,
  Considered him as you and I
Think of some rotten tree, and sit
Lounging and dining under it,
  Exposed to the wide sky.

And all the while, with loose fat smile
  The willing wretch sat winking there,
Believing 'twas his power that made
That jovial scene—and that all paid
  Homage to his unnoticed chair.

Though to be sure this place was Hell;
  He was the Devil—and all they—
What though the claret circled well,
And wit, like ocean, rose and fell?—
  Were damned eternally.

Part Fifth

GRACE

Among the guests who often stayed
  Till the Devil's petits soupers,°
A man there came, fair as a maid,°
And Peter noted what he said,
  Standing behind his master's chair.

He was a mighty poet—and
  A subtle-souled Psychologist;

All things he seemed to understand
Of old or new—of sea or land—
  But his own mind—which was a mist.

This was a man who might have turned
  Hell into Heaven—and so in gladness
A Heaven unto himself have earned;
But he in shadows undiscerned
  Trusted,—and damned himself to madness.

He spoke of poetry, and how
  'Divine it was—a light—a love—
A spirit which like wind doth blow
As it listeth, to and fro;
  A dew rained down from God above;

'A power which comes and goes like dream,
  And which none can ever trace—
Heaven's light on Earth—Truth's brightest beam.'
And when he ceased there lay the gleam
  Of those words upon his face.

Now Peter, when he heard such talk
  Would, heedless of a broken pate
Stand like a man asleep, or baulk
Some wishing guest of knife or fork,
  Or drop and break his master's plate.

At night he oft would start and wake
  Like a lover, and began
In a wild measure songs to make
On moor, and glen, and rocky lake,
  And on the heart of man;°

And on the universal sky—
  And the wide earth's bosom green;—
And the sweet, strange mystery
Of what beyond these things may lie°
  And yet remain unseen.

For in his thought he visited
  The spots in which, ere dead and damned,

He his wayward life had led;
Yet knew not whence the thoughts were fed
Which thus his fancy crammed.

And these obscure remembrances
Stirred such harmony in Peter,
That, whensoever he should please,
He could speak of rocks and trees°
In poetic metre.

For though it was without a sense
Of memory, yet he remembered well
Many a ditch and quickset fence;
Of lakes he had intelligence,
He knew something of heath and fell.

He had also dim recollections
Of pedlars tramping on their rounds,°
Milk pans and pails, and odd collections
Of saws, and proverbs, and reflections
Old parsons make in burying-grounds.

But Peter's verse was clear, and came
Announcing from the frozen hearth
Of a cold age, that none might tame
The soul of that diviner flame
It augured to the Earth:

Like gentle rains, on the dry plains,
Making that green which late was grey,
Or like the sudden moon, that stains
Some gloomy chamber's window panes
With a broad light like day.

For language was in Peter's hand
Like clay while he was yet a potter;
And he made songs for all the land
Sweet both to feel and understand
As pipkins late to mountain Cotter.°

And Mr ——, the Bookseller,
Gave twenty pounds for some:—then scorning°

A footman's yellow coat to wear,
Peter, too proud of heart I fear,
   Instantly gave the Devil warning.

Whereat the Devil took offence,
   And swore in his soul a great oath then,
'That for his damned impertinence,
He'd bring him to a proper sense
   Of what was due to gentlemen!'

Part Sixth

DAMNATION

'O, that mine enemy had written
   A book!'—cried Job:—A fearful curse!°
If to the Arab, as the Briton,
'Twas galling to be critic-bitten:—
   The Devil to Peter wished no worse.

When Peter's next new book found vent,°
   The Devil to all the first Reviews
A copy of it slyly sent
With five-pound note as compliment,
   And this short notice—'Pray abuse.'

Then *seriatim*, month and quarter,°
   Appeared such mad tirades.—One said—
'Peter seduced Mrs Foy's daughter,°
Then drowned the Mother in Ullswater,
   The last thing as he went to bed.'

Another—'Let him shave his head!
   Where's Dr Willis?—Or is he joking?°
What does the rascal mean or hope,
No longer imitating Pope,
   In that barbarian Shakespeare poking?'

One more,—'Is incest not enough,
   And must there be adultery too?

Grace after meat? Miscreant and liar!
Thief! Blackguard! Scoundrel! Fool! Hellfire
   Is twenty times too good for you.

'By that last book of yours WE think
   You've double damned yourself to scorn:
We warned you whilst yet on the brink
You stood. From your black name will shrink
   The babe that is unborn.'

All these Reviews the Devil made
   Up in a parcel, which he had
Safely to Peter's house conveyed.
For carriage ten-pence Peter paid—
   United them—read them—went half mad.

'What!'—Cried he, 'this is my reward
   For nights of thought, and days of toil?
Do poets, but to be abhorred
By men of whom they never heard,
   Consume their spirits' oil?

'What have I done to them?—and who
   Is Mrs. Foy? 'Tis very cruel
To speak of me and Emma so!°
Adultery! God defend me! Oh!
   I've half a mind to fight a duel.

'Or,' cried he, a grave look collecting,
   'Is it my genius, like the moon,
Sets those who stand her face inspecting
(That face within their brain reflecting)
   Like a crazed bell chime, out of tune?'°

For Peter did not know the town,
   But thought, as country readers do,
For half a guinea or a crown,
He bought oblivion or renown
   From God's own voice in a review.°

All Peter did on this occasion
  Was, writing some sad stuff in prose.
It is a dangerous invasion
When Poets criticise: their station
  Is to delight, not pose.

The Devil then sent to Leipsic fair,
  For Born's translation of Kant's book;°
A world of words, tail foremost, where
Right—wrong—false—true—and foul and fair
  As in a lottery wheel are shook.

Five thousand crammed octavo pages
  Of German psychologics,—he
Who his *furor verborum* assuages°
Thereon, deserves just seven months' wages
  More than will e'er be due to me.

I looked on them nine several days,
  And then I saw that they were bad;
A friend, too, spoke in their dispraise,—
He never read them;—with amaze
  I found Sir William Drummond had.°

When the book came, the Devil sent
  It to P. Verbovale Esquire,°
With a brief note of compliment,
By that night's Carlisle mail. It went
  And set his soul on fire.

Fire, which *ex luce praebens fumum*,°
  Made him beyond the bottom see
Of truth's clear well—when I and you, Ma'am,
Go, as we shall do, *subter humum*,°
  We may know more than he.

Now Peter ran to seed in soul
  Into a walking paradox;—
For he was neither part nor whole,
Nor good, nor bad—nor knave, nor fool,
  —Among the woods and rocks

Furious he rode, where late he ran,
 Lashing and spurring his lame hobby;
Turned to a formal Puritan,
A solemn and unsexual man,—
 He half believed *White Obi*!

This steed in vision he would ride,
 High trotting over nine-inch bridges,
With Flibbertigibbet, imp of pride,°
Mocking and mowing by his side—
A mad-brained goblin for a guide—
 Over cornfields, gates and hedges.

After these ghastly rides, he came
 Home to his heart, and found from thence
Much stolen of its accustomed flame;
His thoughts grew weak, drowsy, and lame
 Of their intelligence.

To Peter's view, all seemed one hue;
 He was no Whig, he was no Tory:
No Deist and no Christian he,—°
He got so subtle, that to be
 Nothing, was all his glory.

One single point in his belief
 From his organization sprung,
The heart-enrooted faith, the chief
Ear in his doctrine's blighted sheaf,
 That 'happiness is wrong,'

So thought Calvin and Dominic;°
 So think their fierce successors, who
Even now would neither stint nor stick
Our flesh from off our bones to pick,
 If they might 'do their do.'

His morals thus were undermined:—
 The old Peter—the hard, old Potter—
Was born anew within his mind:
He grew dull, harsh, sly, unrefined,
 As when he tramped beside the Otter.°

In the death hues of agony
    Lambently flashing from a fish,
Now Peter felt amused to see
Shades, like a rainbow's, rise and flee,
    Mixed with a certain hungry wish.°

So in his Country's dying face
    He looked—and, lovely as she lay,
Seeking in vain his last embrace,
Wailing her own abandoned case,
    With hardened sneer he turned away:

And coolly to his own Soul said;—
    'Do you not think that we might make
A poem on her when she's dead?—
Or, no—a thought is in my head—
    Her shroud for a new sheet I'll take:

'My wife wants one.—Let who will bury
This mangled corpse!—And I and you,
My dearest Soul, will then make merry,
As the Prince Regent did with Sherry,—'°
    'Aye—and at last desert me too.'

And so his Soul would not be gay,
    But moaned within him; like a fawn,
Moaning within a cave, it lay
Wounded and wasting, day by day,
    Till all its life of life was gone.

As troubled skies stain waters clear,
    The storm in Peter's heart and mind,
Now made his verses dark and queer;
They were the ghosts of what they were,
    Shaking dim grave clothes in the wind.

For he now raved enormous folly
    Of Baptisms, Sunday-schools and Graves;
'Twould make George Colman melancholy°
To have heard him, like a male Molly,°
    Chanting those stupid staves.

Yet the Reviews, who heaped abuse
   On Peter, while he wrote for freedom,
So soon as in his song they spy
The folly which soothes Tyranny,
   Praise him, for those who feed 'em.

'He was a man, too great to scan;—
   A planet lost in truth's keen rays;—
His virtue, awful and prodigious;—
He was the most sublime, religious,
   Pure-minded Poet of these days.'

As soon as he read that—cried Peter,
   'Eureka! I have found the way
To make a better thing of metre
Than e'er was made by living creature
   Up to this blessed day.'

Then Peter wrote odes to the Devil;—
   In one of which he meekly said:—
'May Carnage and Slaughter,
Thy niece and thy daughter,°
May Rapine and Famine,
Thy gorge ever cramming,
   Glut thee with living and dead!

   'May death and Damnation,
   And Consternation,
Flit up from Hell with pure intent!
   Slash them at Manchester,°
   Glasgow, Leeds and Chester;
Drench all with blood from Avon to Trent.

   'Let thy body-guard yeomen
   Hew down babes and women,
And laugh with bold triumph till Heaven be rent!
   When Moloch in Jewry°
   Munched children with fury
It was thou, Devil, dining with pure intent.'°

Part Seventh

DOUBLE DAMNATION

The Devil now knew his proper cue,—
    Soon as he read the ode, he drove
To his friend Lord MacMurderchouse's,°
A man of interest in both houses,
    And said:—'For money or for love

'Pray find some cure or sinecure,
    To feed from the superfluous taxes
A friend of ours—a Poet—fewer
Have fluttered tamer to the lure
    Than he.'—His Lordship stands and racks his

Stupid brains, while one might count
    As many beads as he had boroughs,—
At length replies;—from his mean front,
Like one who rubs out an account,
    Smoothing away the unmeaning furrows:—

'It happens fortunately, dear Sir,
    I can. I hope I need require
No pledge from you, that he will stir
In our affairs;—like Oliver,°
    That he'll be worthy of his hire.'

These words exchanged, the news sent off
    To Peter:—home the Devil hied;
Took to his bed; he had no cough,
No doctor,—meat and drink enough,—
    Yet that same night he died.

The Devil's corpse was leaded down.—
    His decent heirs enjoyed his pelf;°
Mourning-coaches, many a one,
Followed his hearse along the town:—
    Where was the Devil himself?

When Peter heard of his promotion
    His eyes grew like two stars for bliss:

There was a bow of sleek devotion
Engendering in his back; each motion
  Seemed a Lord's shoe to kiss.

He hired a house, bought plate, and made°
  A genteel drive up to his door,
With sifted gravel neatly laid,—
As if defying all who said
  Peter was ever poor.

But a disease soon struck into
  The very life and soul of Peter—
He walked about—slept—had the hue
Of health upon his cheeks—and few
  Dug better—none a heartier eater.

And yet, a strange and horrid curse°
  Clung upon Peter, night and day—
Month after month the thing grew worse,
And deadlier than in this my verse
  I can find strength to say.

Peter was dull—he was at first
  Dull—O, so dull—so very dull!
Whether he talked, wrote, or rehearsed—
Still with this dullness was he cursed—
  Dull—beyond all conception—dull.—

No one could read his books—no mortal,
  But a few natural friends, would hear him:—
The parson came not near his portal;—
His state was like that of the immortal
  Described by Swift—no man could bear him.°

His sister, wife, and children yawned,
  With a long, slow and drear ennui,
All human patience far beyond;
Their hopes of Heaven each would have pawned,
  Anywhere else to be.

But in his verse, and in his prose,
  The essence of his dullness was

Concentred and compressed so close,—
'Twould have made Guatimozin doze
On his red gridiron of brass.°

A printer's boy, folding those pages,
Fell slumbrously upon one side;
Like those famed seven who slept three ages.°
To wakeful frenzy's vigil rages
As opiates were the same applied.

Even the Reviewers who were hired
To do the work of his reviewing,
With adamantine nerves, grew tired;—
Gaping and torpid they retired,
To dream of what they should be doing.

And worse and worse, the drowsy curse°
Yawned in him—till it grew a pest—
A wide contagious atmosphere,
Creeping like cold through all things near;
A power to infect, and to infest.

His servant maids and dogs grew dull;
His kitten, late a sportive elf;
The woods and lakes, so beautiful,
Of dim stupidity were full;
All grew dull as Peter's self.

The earth under his feet—the springs,
Which lived within it a quick life—
The Air, the Winds of many wings—
That fan it with new murmurings—
Were dead to their harmonious strife.

The birds and beasts within the wood,
The insects, and each creeping thing,
Were now a silent multitude;
Love's work was left unwrought—no brood
Near Peter's house took wing.

And every neighbouring Cottager
Stupidly yawned upon the other;

No jackass brayed;—no little cur
Cocked up his ears;—no man would stir
To save a dying mother.

Yet all from that charmed district went
But some half idiot and half knave,
Who, rather than pay any rent,
Would live, with marvellous content,
Over his father's grave.

No bailiff dared within that space,
For fear of the dull charm, to enter:
A man would bear upon his face,
For fifteen months, in any case,
The yawn of such a venture.

Seven miles above—below—around—
This pest of dullness holds its sway:
A ghastly life without a sound;
To Peter's soul the spell is bound—
How should it ever pass away?

Men of England: A Song

Men of England, wherefore plough
For the lords who lay ye low?
Wherefore weave with toil and care
The rich robes your tyrants wear?

Wherefore feed and clothe and save
From the cradle to the grave,
Those ungrateful drones who would
Drain your sweat—nay, drink your blood?

Wherefore, Bees of England, forge
Many a weapon, chain and scourge
That these stingless drones may spoil
The forced produce of your toil?

Have ye leisure, comfort, calm,
Shelter, food, love's gentle balm?
Or what is it ye buy so dear
With your pain and with your fear?

The seed ye sow, another reaps:
The wealth ye find, another keeps:
The robes ye weave, another wears:
The arms ye forge, another bears.

Sow seed—but let no tyrant reap:
Find wealth—let no impostor heap:
Weave robes—let not the idle wear:
Forge arms—in your defence to bear.

Shrink to your cellars, holes, and cells—
In halls ye deck, another dwells.
Why shake the chains ye wrought? Ye see
The steel ye tempered glance on ye.

With plough and spade and hoe and loom
Trace your grave and build your tomb
And weave your winding-sheet—till fair
England be your Sepulchre.

Lines Written during the Castlereagh Administration

Corpses are cold in the tomb—
Stones on the pavement are dumb—
Abortions are dead in the womb
And their mothers look pale, like the death-white shore
Of Albion, free no more.

Her sons are as stones in the way—
They are masses of senseless clay—
They are trodden and move not away—
The abortion with which she travaileth
Is Liberty, smitten to death.

Then trample and dance, thou Oppressor!
For thy victim is no redressor;
Thou art sole lord and possessor
Of the corpses and clods and abortions—they pave
Thy path to the grave.

Hearest thou the festival din
Of Death and Destruction and Sin,
And Wealth crying 'Havoc!' within?
'Tis the Bacchanal triumph which makes truth dumb,
Thine Epithalamium—

Aye, marry thy ghastly wife!
Let Fear and Disquiet and Strife
Spread thy couch in the chamber of life.
Marry Ruin, thou Tyrant, and Hell be thy guide°
To the bed of the bride.

To S. and C.°

As from their ancestral oak°
Two empty ravens wind their clarion,°
Yell by yell, and croak for croak;

When they scent the noonday smoke
  Of fresh human carrion:—

As two gibbering night-birds flit
  From their homes of deadly yew°
Through the night to frighten it—
When the moon is in a fit,°
  And the stars are none or few:—

As a shark and dogfish wait
  Under an Atlantic isle
For the Negroship whose freight
Is the theme of their debate,
  Wrinkling their red gills the while:—

Are ye—two vultures sick for battle,
  Two scorpions under one wet stone,
Two bloodless wolves whose dry throats rattle,
Two crows perched on the murrained cattle,
  Two vipers tangled into one.°

'What men gain fairly'

What men gain fairly, that should they possess
And children may inherit idleness
From him who earns it . . . this is understood—
Private injustice may be general good.
But he who gains by base and armèd wrong
Or guilty fraud, or base compliances
With those whom force or falsehood has made strong,°
May be despoiled; even as a stolen dress
Is stripped from a convicted thief and he
Left in the nakedness of infamy.

A New National Anthem

God prosper, speed, and save,
God raise from England's grave

Her murdered Queen!
Pave with swift victory
The steps of Liberty,
Whom Britons own to be
Immortal Queen!

See, she comes throned on high.
On swift Eternity!
God save the Queen!
Millions on millions wait
Firm, rapid, and elate,
On her majestic state!°
God save the Queen!

She is thine own pure soul
Moulding the mighty whole
God save our Queen!
She is thine own deep love
Rained down from Heaven above,
Wherever she rest or move
God save our Queen!

'Wilder her enemies
In their own dark disguise
God save our Queen!
All earthly things that dare
Her sacred name to wear,
Strip them, as kings are, bare
God save our Queen!

Be her eternal throne
Built in our hearts alone,
God save our Queen!
Let the oppressor hold
Canopied seats of gold;
She sits enthroned of old
O'er our hearts, Queen!

Lips touched by Seraphim
Breathe out the choral hymn
God save the Queen!

Sweet as if Angels sang,
Loud as that clarion's clang
Wakening the world's dead gang,
God save the Queen!°

Sonnet: England in 1819

An old, mad, blind, despised, and dying King;°
Princes, the dregs of their dull race, who flow°
Through public scorn,—mud from a muddy spring;
Rulers who neither see nor feel nor know,
But leechlike to their fainting country cling
Till they drop, blind in blood, without a blow.
A people starved and stabbed in th'untilled field;°
An army whom liberticide and prey°
Makes as a two-edged sword to all who wield;
Golden and sanguine laws which tempt and slay;°
Religion Christless, Godless, a book sealed;
A senate, Time's worst statute, unrepealed—°
Are graves from which a glorious Phantom may
Burst, to illumine our tempestuous day.

Love's Philosophy

The Fountains mingle with the River
And the Rivers with the Ocean,
The winds of Heaven mix forever
With a sweet emotion;
Nothing in the world is single,
All things by a law divine
In one spirit meet and mingle.°
Why not I with thine?—

See the mountains kiss high Heaven
And the waves clasp one another;
No sister-flower would be forgiven
If it disdained its brother,

And the sunlight clasps the earth
    And the moonbeams kiss the sea;—
What is all this sweet work worth°
    If thou kiss not me?

Ode to Heaven

Chorus of Spirits

First Spirit°

Palace-roof of cloudless nights!
Paradise of golden lights!
    Deep, immeasurable, vast,
Which art now, and which wert then;
    Of the present and the past,
Of the eternal where and when,
    Presence-chamber, temple, home,
    Ever-canopying dome
    Of acts and ages yet to come!

Glorious shapes have life in thee,
Earth, and all earth's company;
    Living globes which ever throng
Thy deep chasms and wildernesses;
    And green worlds that glide along;
And swift stars with flashing tresses;
    And icy moons most cold and bright,
    And mighty suns beyond the night,
    Atoms of intensest light!

Even thy name is as a God,
Heaven! for thou art the abode
    Of that Power which is the glass
Wherein man his nature sees.
    Generations as they pass
Worship thee with bended knees.
    Their unremaining Gods and they
    Like a river roll away:
    Thou remainest such—alway!°

Second Spirit°

Thou art but the mind's first chamber,
Round which its young fancies clamber,
Like weak insects in a cave
Lighted up by stalactites;
But the portal of the grave,
Where a world of new delights
Will make thy best glories seem
But a dim and noonday gleam
From the shadow of a dream!°

Third Spirit°

Peace! the abyss is wreathed with scorn
At your presumption, atom-born!
What is Heaven? and what are ye
Who its brief expanse inherit?
What are suns and spheres which flee
With the instinct of that spirit
Of which ye are but a part?
Drops which Nature's mighty heart
Drives through thinnest veins. Depart!

What is Heaven? a globe of dew,
Filling in the morning new
Some eyed flower whose young leaves waken
On an unimagined world.
Constellated suns unshaken,
Orbits measureless, are furled
In that frail and fading sphere,
With ten millions gathered there,°
To tremble, gleam, and disappear!°

To the Lord Chancellor

Thy country's curse is on thee, darkest Crest
Of that foul, knotted, many-headed worm
Which rends our mother's bosom!—Priestly Pest!
Masked Resurrection of a buried form!°

Thy country's curse is on thee—Justice sold,
  Truth trampled, Nature's landmarks overthrown,
And heaps of fraud-accumulated gold
  Plead, loud as thunder, at destruction's throne.

And whilst that sure, slow Fate which ever stands
  Watching the beck of Mutability
Delays to execute her high commands
  And, though a nation weeps, spares thine and thee—

O let a father's curse be on thy soul,
  And let a daughter's hope be on thy tomb;
Be both, on thy grey head, a leaden cowl
  To weigh thee down to thine approaching doom.

I curse thee! By a parent's outraged love,—
  By hopes long cherished and too lately lost,—
By gentle feelings thou couldst never prove,
  By griefs which thy stern nature never crossed;

By those infantine smiles of happy light,
  Which were a fire within a stranger's hearth,
Quenched even when kindled, in untimely night,
  Hiding the promise of a lovely birth—°

By those unpractised accents of young speech
  Which he who is a father thought to frame
To gentlest lore, such as the wisest teach—
  Thou strike the lyre of mind!—oh, grief and shame!

By all the happy see in children's growth,
  That undeveloped flower of budding years—
Sweetness and sadness interwoven both,
  Source of the sweetest hopes, the saddest fears.

By all the days under a hireling's care
  Of dull constraint and bitter heaviness—
Oh, wretched ye, if any ever were—
  Sadder than orphans—why not fatherless?°

By the false cant which on their innocent lips
  Must hang like poison on an opening bloom,

By the dark creeds which cover with eclipse
  Their pathway from the cradle to the tomb—°

By thy complicity with lust and hate:
  Thy thirst for tears—thy hunger after gold—
The ready frauds which ever on thee wait—
  The servile arts in which thou hast grown old.—

By thy most killing sneer, and by thy smile—
  By all the snares and nets of thy black den;
And—(for thou canst outweep the crocodile)—
  By thy false tears—those millstones braining men—°

By all the hate which checks a father's love,
  By all the scorn which kills a father's care,
By those most impious hands, which dared remove
  Nature's high bounds—by thee—and by despair—

Yes—the despair which bids a father groan
  And cry—'My children are no longer mine—
The blood within those veins may be mine own,
  But, Tyrant, their polluted souls are thine;—'

I curse thee, though I hate thee not.—O, slave!
  If thou couldst quench that earth-consuming Hell
Of which thou art a daemon, on thy grave
  This curse should be a blessing—Fare thee well!

The Sensitive Plant

Part First

A Sensitive Plant in a garden grew,
And the young winds fed it with silver dew,
And it opened its fan-like leaves to the light,
And closed them beneath the kisses of night.°

And the Spring arose on the garden fair,
Like the Spirit of Love felt everywhere;
And each flower and herb on Earth's dark breast
Rose from the dreams of its wintry rest.

But none ever trembled and panted with bliss
In the garden, the field, or the wilderness,
Like a doe in the noontide with love's sweet want,
As the companionless Sensitive Plant.°

The snowdrop, and then the violet,
Arose from the ground with warm rain wet,
And their breath was mixed with fresh odour, sent
From the turf, like the voice and the instrument.

Then the pied wind-flowers and the tulip tall,°
And narcissi, the fairest among them all,
Who gaze on their eyes in the stream's recess,
Till they die of their own dear loveliness;

And the Naiad-like lily of the vale,°
Whom youth makes so fair and passion so pale,
That the light of its tremulous bells is seen
Through their pavilions of tender green;

And the hyacinth purple, and white, and blue,
Which flung from its bells a sweet peal anew
Of music so delicate, soft, and intense,
It was felt like an odour within the sense;°

And the rose like a nymph to the bath addressed,°
Which unveiled the depth of her glowing breast,
Till, fold after fold, to the fainting air
The soul of her beauty and love lay bare:

And the wand-like lily, which lifted up,
As a Maenad, its moonlight-coloured cup,
Till the fiery star, which is its eye,
Gazed through clear dew on the tender sky;

And the jessamine faint, and the sweet tuberose,
The sweetest flower for scent that blows;°
And all rare blossoms from every clime
Grew in that garden in perfect prime.

And on the stream whose inconstant bosom
Was pranked under boughs of embowering blossom°

With golden and green light, slanting through
Their heaven of many a tangled hue,

Broad water lilies lay tremulously,
And starry river-buds glimmered by,
And around them the soft stream did glide and dance
With a motion of sweet sound and radiance.

And the sinuous paths of lawn and of moss,
Which led through the garden along and across—
Some open at once to the sun and the breeze,
Some lost among bowers of blossoming trees—

Were all paved with daisies and delicate bells
As fair as the fabulous asphodels,°
And flow'rets which drooping as day drooped too
Fell into pavilions, white, purple, and blue,
To roof the glow-worm from the evening dew.

And from this undefilèd Paradise°
The flowers (as an infant's awakening eyes
Smile on its mother, whose singing sweet
Can first lull, and at last must awaken it),

When Heaven's blithe winds had unfolded them,
As mine-lamps enkindle a hidden gem,°
Shone smiling to Heaven, and every one
Shared joy in the light of the gentle sun;

For each one was interpenetrated
With the light and the odour its neighbour shed,
Like young lovers whom youth and love make dear
Wrapped and filled by their mutual atmosphere.

But the Sensitive Plant, which could give small fruit
Of the love which it felt from the leaf to the root,
Received more than all, it loved more than ever,
Where none wanted but it, could belong to the giver,

For the Sensitive Plant has no bright flower;
Radiance and odour are not its dower;

It loves, even like Love, its deep heart is full,
It desires what it has not, the beautiful!°

The light winds which from unsustaining wings
Shed the music of many murmurings;
The beams which dart from many a star
Of the flowers whose hues they bear afar;

The plumèd insects swift and free,
Like golden boats on a sunny sea,
Laden with light and odour, which pass
Over the gleam of the living grass;

The unseen clouds of the dew, which lie
Like fire in the flowers till the sun rides high,
Then wander like spirits among the spheres,
Each cloud faint with the fragrance it bears;

The quivering vapours of dim noontide,
Which like a sea o'er the warm earth glide,
In which every sound, and odour, and beam,
Move, as reeds in a single stream;

Each and all like ministering angels were
For the Sensitive Plant sweet joy to bear,
Whilst the lagging hours of the day went by
Like windless clouds o'er a tender sky.

And when evening descended from Heaven above,
And the Earth was all rest, and the air was all love,
And delight, though less bright, was far more deep,
And the day's veil fell from the world of sleep,

And the beasts, and the birds, and the insects were drowned
In an ocean of dreams without a sound,
Whose waves never mark, though they ever impress
The light sand which paves it, consciousness;

(Only overhead the sweet nightingale
Ever sang more sweet as the day might fail,

And snatches of its Elysian chant
Were mixed with the dreams of the Sensitive Plant.)°

The Sensitive Plant was the earliest
Up-gathered into the bosom of rest;
A sweet child weary of its delight,
The feeblest and yet the favourite,
Cradled within the embrace of night.

Part Second

There was a Power in this sweet place,°
An Eve in this Eden; a ruling grace
Which to the flowers did they waken or dream,
Was as God is to the starry scheme.

A Lady, the wonder of her kind,
Whose form was upborne by a lovely mind
Which, dilating, had moulded her mien and motion
Like a sea-flower unfolded beneath the ocean,

Tended the garden from morn to even:
And the meteors of that sublunar Heaven,
Like the lamps of the air when night walks forth,
Laughed round her footsteps up from the Earth!

She had no companion of mortal race,
But her tremulous breath and her flushing face
Told, whilst the morn kissed the sleep from her eyes,
That her dreams were less slumber than Paradise:

As if some bright Spirit for her sweet sake
Had deserted heaven while the stars were awake,
As if yet around her he lingering were,
Though the veil of daylight concealed him from her.

Her step seemed to pity the grass it pressed;
You might hear by the heaving of her breast,
That the coming and going of the wind
Brought pleasure there and left passion behind.

And wherever her airy footstep trod,
Her trailing hair from the grassy sod
Erased its light vestige, with shadowy sweep,
Like a sunny storm o'er the dark green deep.

I doubt not the flowers of that garden sweet
Rejoiced in the sound of her gentle feet;
I doubt not they felt the spirit that came
From her glowing fingers through all their frame.

She sprinkled bright water from the stream
On those that were faint with the sunny beam;
And out of the cups of the heavy flowers
She emptied the rain of the thunder showers.

She lifted their heads with her tender hands,
And sustained them with rods and osier bands;°
If the flowers had been her own infants she
Could never have nursed them more tenderly.

And all killing insects and gnawing worms,
And things of obscene and unlovely forms,
She bore in a basket of Indian woof,°
Into the rough woods far aloof,

In a basket, of grasses and wild flowers full,
The freshest her gentle hands could pull
For the poor banished insects, whose intent,
Although they did ill, was innocent.

But the bee and the beamlike ephemeris°
Whose path is the lightning's, and soft moths that kiss
The sweet lips of the flowers, and harm not, did she°
Make her attendant angels be.

And many an antenatal tomb,°
Where butterflies dream of the life to come,
She left clinging round the smooth and dark
Edge of the odorous cedar bark.

This fairest creature from earliest spring
Thus moved through the garden ministering

All the sweet season of summertide,
And ere the first leaf looked brown—she died!

Part Third

Three days the flowers of the garden fair,
Like stars when the moon is awakened, were,
Or the waves of Baiae, ere luminous°
She floats up through the smoke of Vesuvius.°

And on the fourth, the Sensitive Plant
Felt the sound of the funeral chant,
And the steps of the bearers, heavy and slow,
And the sobs of the mourners deep and low;

The weary sound and the heavy breath,
And the silent motions of passing death,
And the smell, cold, oppressive, and dank,
Sent through the pores of the coffin plank;

The dark grass, and the flowers among the grass,
Were bright with tears as the crowd did pass;
From their sighs the wind caught a mournful tone,
And sate in the pines, and gave groan for groan.

The garden, once fair, became cold and foul,
Like the corpse of her who had been its soul,
Which at first was lovely as if in sleep,
Then slowly changed, till it grew a heap
To make men tremble who never weep.

Swift summer into the autumn flowed,
And frost in the mist of the morning rode,
Though the noonday sun looked clear and bright,
Mocking the spoil of the secret night.

The rose leaves, like flakes of crimson snow,
Paved the turf and the moss below.
The lilies were drooping, and white, and wan,
Like the head and the skin of a dying man.

And Indian plants, of scent and hue
The sweetest that ever were fed on dew,
Leaf by leaf, day after day,
Were massed into the common clay.

And the leaves, brown, yellow, and grey, and red,
And white with the whiteness of what is dead,
Like troops of ghosts on the dry wind passed;
Their whistling noise made the birds aghast.

And the gusty winds waked the wingèd seeds,
Out of their birthplace of ugly weeds,
Till they clung round many a sweet flower's stem,
Which rotted into the earth with them.

The water-blooms under the rivulet
Fell from the stalks on which they were set;
And the eddies drove them here and there,
As the winds did those of the upper air.

Then the rain came down, and the broken stalks,
Were bent and tangled across the walks;
And the leafless net-work of parasite bowers
Massed into ruin; and all sweet flowers.

Between the time of the wind and the snow,
All loathliest weeds began to grow,
Whose coarse leaves were splashed with many a speck,
Like the water-snake's belly and the toad's back.

And thistles, and nettles, and darnels rank,°
And the dock, and henbane; and hemlock dank°
Stretched out its long and hollow shank,°
And stifled the air, till the dead wind stank.

And plants, at whose names the verse feels loath,
Filled the place with a monstrous undergrowth,
Prickly, and pulpous, and blistering, and blue,°
Livid, and starred with a lurid dew.°

And agarics and fungi with mildew and mould°
Started like mists from the wet ground cold;
Pale, fleshy,—as if the decaying dead
With a spirit of growth had been animated!

Their moss rotted off them, flake by flake,
Till the thick stalk stuck like a murderer's stake,
Where rags of loose flesh yet tremble on high,
Infecting the winds that wander by.°

Spawn, weeds, and filth, a leprous scum,°
Made the running rivulet thick and dumb
And at its outlet flags huge as stakes°
Dammed it up with roots knotted like water-snakes.

And hour by hour, when the air was still,
The vapours arose which have strength to kill:
At morn they were seen, at noon they were felt,
At night they were darkness no star could melt.

And unctuous meteors from spray to spray°
Crept and flitted in broad noonday
Unseen; every branch on which they alit
By a venomous blight was burned and bit.

The Sensitive Plant like one forbid°
Wept, and the tears within each lid
Of its folded leaves which together grew
Were changed to a blight of frozen glue.

For the leaves soon fell, and the branches soon
By the heavy axe of the blast were hewn;
The sap shrank to the root through every pore
As blood to a heart that will beat no more.

For Winter came—the wind was his whip—
One choppy finger was on his lip:°
He had torn the cataracts from the hills
And they clanked at his girdle like manacles;

His breath was a chain which without a sound
The earth, and the air, and the water bound;

He came, fiercely driven, in his chariot-throne
By the tenfold blasts of the arctic zone.

Then the weeds which were forms of living death
Fled from the frost to the earth beneath.
Their decay and sudden flight from frost
Was but like the vanishing of a ghost!

And under the roots of the Sensitive Plant
The moles and the dormice died for want.°
The birds dropped stiff from the frozen air
And were caught in the branches naked and bare.

First there came down a thawing rain
And its dull drops froze on the boughs again,
Then there steamed up a freezing dew
Which to the drops of the thaw-rain grew;

And a northern whirlwind, wandering about
Like a wolf that had smelt a dead child out,
Shook the boughs thus laden, and heavy and stiff,
And snapped them off with his rigid griff.°

When winter had gone and spring came back
The Sensitive Plant was a leafless wreck;
But the mandrakes, and toadstools, and docks, and darnels,°
Rose like the dead from their ruined charnels.

Conclusion

Whether the Sensitive Plant, or that
Which within its boughs like a spirit sat
Ere its outward form had known decay,
Now felt this change, I cannot say.

Whether that lady's gentle mind,
No longer with the form combined
Which scattered love, as stars do light,
Found sadness, where it left delight,

I dare not guess; but in this life
Of error, ignorance, and strife,
Where nothing is, but all things seem,
And we the shadows of the dream,°

It is a modest creed, and yet
Pleasant if one considers it,
To own that death itself must be,°
Like all the rest, a mockery.

That garden sweet, that lady fair,
And all sweet shapes and odours there,
In truth have never passed away:
'Tis we, 'tis ours, are changed; not they.

For love, and beauty, and delight,
There is no death nor change: their might
Exceeds our organs, which endure
No light, being themselves obscure.°

An Exhortation

Chameleons feed on light and air:
    Poets' food is love and fame:°
If in this wide world of care
    Poets could but find the same
With as little toil as they,
    Would they ever change their hue
    As the light chameleons do,
Suiting it to every ray
Twenty times a day?

Poets are on this cold earth,
    As chameleons might be,
Hidden from their early birth
    In a cave beneath the sea;
Where light is, chameleons change:
    Where love is not, poets do:
    Fame is love disguised: if few

Find either, never think it strange
That poets range.

Yet dare not stain with wealth or power
A poet's free and heavenly mind:
If bright chameleons should devour
Any food but beams and wind,
They would grow as earthly soon
As their brother lizards are.
Children of a sunnier star,
Spirits from beyond the moon,
O, refuse the boon!°

The Cloud

I bring fresh showers for the thirsting flowers,
From the seas and the streams;
I bear light shade for the leaves when laid
In their noon-day dreams.
From my wings are shaken the dews that waken
The sweet buds every one,
When rocked to rest on their mother's breast,°
As she dances about the sun.
I wield the flail of the lashing hail,
And whiten the green plains under,
And then again I dissolve it in rain,
And laugh as I pass in thunder.

I sift the snow on the mountains below,
And their great pines groan aghast;
And all the night 'tis my pillow white,
While I sleep in the arms of the blast.
Sublime on the towers of my skiey bowers,
Lightning my pilot sits,°
In a cavern under is fettered the thunder,
It struggles and howls at fits;°
Over earth and ocean, with gentle motion,
This pilot is guiding me,
Lured by the love of the genii that move°
In the depths of the purple sea;

Over the rills, and the crags, and the hills,
Over the lakes and the plains,
Wherever he dream, under mountain or stream,
The Spirit he loves remains;
And I all the while bask in Heaven's blue smile,
Whilst he is dissolving in rains.

The sanguine sunrise, with his meteor eyes,
And his burning plumes outspread,
Leaps on the back of my sailing rack,°
When the morning star shines dead;°
As on the jag of a mountain crag,
Which an earthquake rocks and swings,
An eagle alit one moment may sit
In the light of its golden wings;
And when sunset may breathe, from the lit sea beneath,
Its ardours of rest and of love,
And the crimson pall of eve may fall
From the depths of Heaven above,°
With wings folded I rest, on mine airy nest,°
As still as a brooding dove.°

That orbèd maiden with white fire laden,
Whom mortals call the moon,
Glides glimmering o'er my fleece-like floor,
By the midnight breezes strewn;
And wherever the beat of her unseen feet,
Which only the angels hear,
May have broken the woof of my tent's thin roof,
The stars peep behind her and peer;
And I laugh to see them whirl and flee,
Like a swarm of golden bees,
When I widen the rent in my wind-built tent,
Till the calm rivers, lakes, and seas,
Like strips of the sky fallen through me on high,
Are each paved with the moon and these.°

I bind the sun's throne with a burning zone,°
And the moon's with a girdle of pearl;
The volcanos are dim, and the stars reel and swim,
When the whirlwinds my banner unfurl.
From cape to cape, with a bridge-like shape,

Over a torrent sea,
Sunbeam-proof, I hang like a roof,
The mountains its columns be.
The triumphal arch through which I march
With hurricane, fire, and snow,
When the powers of the air are chained to my chair,
Is the million-coloured bow;
The sphere-fire above its soft colours wove,°
While the moist earth was laughing below.

I am the daughter of Earth and Water,
And the nursling of the sky;
I pass through the pores of the oceans and shores;°
I change, but I cannot die—
For after the rain, when with never a stain,
The pavilion of Heaven is bare,
And the winds and sunbeams, with their convex gleams,°
Build up the blue dome of air,
I silently laugh at my own cenotaph,°
And out of the caverns of rain,
Like a child from the womb, like a ghost from the tomb,
I arise, and unbuild it again.

To a Skylark

Hail to thee, blithe Spirit!
Bird thou never wert,
That from Heaven, or near it,
Pourest thy full heart
In profuse strains of unpremeditated art.

Higher still and higher
From the earth thou springest
Like a cloud of fire;°
The blue deep thou wingest,
And singing still dost soar, and soaring ever singest.

In the golden lightning
Of the sunken sun,

O'er which clouds are bright'ning,
Thou dost float and run;
Like an unbodied joy whose race is just begun.

The pale purple even
Melts around thy flight;
Like a star of Heaven,
In the broad daylight
Thou art unseen,—but yet I hear thy shrill delight,

Keen as are the arrows
Of that silver sphere,°
Whose intense lamp narrows
In the white dawn clear,
Until we hardly see—we feel that it is there.

All the earth and air
With thy voice is loud,
As, when night is bare,
From one lonely cloud
The moon rains out her beams—and Heaven is overflowed.

What thou art we know not;
What is most like thee?
From rainbow clouds there flow not
Drops so bright to see,
As from thy presence showers a rain of melody.

Like a poet hidden
In the light of thought,
Singing hymns unbidden,
Till the world is wrought
To sympathy with hopes and fears it heeded not:

Like a high-born maiden
In a palace tower,
Soothing her love-laden
Soul in secret hour
With music sweet as love, which overflows her bower:

Like a glow-worm golden
In a dell of dew,

Scattering unbeholden
Its aerial hue
Among the flowers and grass, which screen it from the view:

Like a rose embowered
In its own green leaves,
By warm winds deflowered,
Till the scent it gives
Makes faint with too much sweet those heavy-wingèd thieves:

Sound of vernal showers
On the twinkling grass,
Rain-awakened flowers,
All that ever was
Joyous, and clear, and fresh, thy music doth surpass.

Teach us, Sprite or Bird,
What sweet thoughts are thine;
I have never heard
Praise of love or wine
That panted forth a flood of rapture so divine.

Chorus Hymenaeal,°
Or triumphal chant,
Matched with thine would be all
But an empty vaunt,
A thing wherein we feel there is some hidden want.

What objects are the fountains
Of thy happy strain?
What fields, or waves, or mountains?
What shapes of sky or plain?
What love of thine own kind? what ignorance of pain?

With thy clear keen joyance
Langour cannot be:
Shadow of annoyance
Never came near thee:
Thou lovest—but ne'er knew love's sad satiety.

Waking or asleep,
Thou of death must deem

Things more true and deep
Than we mortals dream,
Or how could thy notes flow in such a crystal stream?

We look before and after,
And pine for what is not:°
Our sincerest laughter
With some pain is fraught;
Our sweetest songs are those that tell of saddest thought.

Yet if we could scorn
Hate, and pride, and fear;
If we were things born
Not to shed a tear,
I know not how thy joy we ever should come near.

Better than all measures
Of delightful sound,
Better than all treasures
That in books are found,
Thy skill to poet were, thou scorner of the ground!

Teach me half the gladness
That thy brain must know,
Such harmonious madness°
From my lips would flow,
The world should listen then—as I am listening now.

Ode to Liberty

Yet, Freedom, yet thy banner torn but flying,
Streams like a thunder-storm against the wind.

Byron°

I

A glorious people vibrated again°
The lightning of the nations: Liberty
From heart to heart, from tower to tower, o'er Spain,
Scattering contagious fire into the sky,

Gleamed. My soul spurned the chains of its dismay,
And, in the rapid plumes of song,
Clothed itself, sublime and strong;
As a young eagle soars the morning clouds among,
Hovering in verse o'er its accustomed prey;
Till from its station in the Heaven of fame
The Spirit's whirlwind rapt it, and the ray°
Of the remotest sphere of living flame
Which paves the void was from behind it flung,
As foam from a ship's swiftness, when there came
A voice out of the deep: I will record the same.°

2

The Sun and the serenest Moon sprang forth:
The burning stars of the abyss were hurled
Into the depths of Heaven. The daedal earth,°
That island in the ocean of the world,
Hung in its cloud of all-sustaining air:
But this divinest universe
Was yet a chaos and a curse,
For thou wert not: but, power from worst producing worse,°
The spirit of the beasts was kindled there,
And of the birds, and of the watery forms,
And there was war among them, and despair
Within them, raging without truce or terms:
The bosom of their violated nurse
Groaned, for beasts warred on beasts, and worms on worms,
And men on men; each heart was as a hell of storms.

3

Man, the imperial shape, then multiplied
His generations under the pavilion
Of the Sun's throne: palace and pyramid,
Temple and prison, to many a swarming million,
Were as to mountain-wolves their ragged caves.
This human living multitude
Was savage, cunning, blind, and rude,
For thou wert not; but o'er the populous solitude,
Like one fierce cloud over a waste of waves
Hung tyranny; beneath, sate deified

The sister-pest, congregator of slaves;°
  Into the shadow of her pinions wide°
Anarchs and priests, who feed on gold and blood°
  Till with the stain their inmost souls are dyed,
  Drove the astonished herds of men from every side.

4

The nodding promontories, and blue isles,
  And cloud-like mountains, and dividuous waves°
Of Greece, basked glorious in the open smiles
  Of favouring Heaven: from their enchanted caves
Prophetic echoes flung dim melody
      On the unapprehensive wild.
      The vine, the corn, the olive mild,
Grew savage yet, to human use unreconciled;
  And, like unfolded flowers beneath the sea,
    Like the man's thought dark in the infant's brain,
  Like aught that is which wraps what is to be,
    Art's deathless dreams lay veiled by many a vein
Of Parian stone; and, yet a speechless child,°
  Verse murmured, and Philosophy did strain
  Her lidless eyes for thee; when o'er the Aegean main

5

Athens arose: a city such as vision
  Builds from the purple crags and silver towers
Of battlemented cloud, as in derision
  Of kingliest masonry: the ocean-floors
Pave it; the evening sky pavilions it;°
      Its portals are inhabited
      By thunder-zonèd winds, each head
Within its cloudy wings with sunfire garlanded—
  A divine work! Athens, diviner yet,
    Gleamed with its crest of columns, on the will
  Of man, as on a mount of diamond, set;
    For thou wert, and thine all-creative skill
Peopled, with forms that mock the eternal dead
  In marble immortality, that hill°
  Which was thine earliest throne and latest oracle.

6

Within the surface of Time's fleeting river
Its wrinkled image lies, as then it lay
Immovably unquiet, and forever
It trembles, but it cannot pass away!
The voices of its bards and sages thunder
With an earth-awakening blast
Through the caverns of the past
(Religion veils her eyes; Oppression shrinks aghast);
A wingèd sound of joy, and love, and wonder,
Which soars where Expectation never flew,
Rending the veil of space and time asunder!
One ocean feeds the clouds, and streams, and dew;
One sun illumines Heaven; one spirit vast
With life and love makes chaos ever new,
As Athens doth the world with thy delight renew.

7

Then Rome was, and from thy deep bosom fairest,
Like a wolf-cub from a Cadmaean Maenad,°
She drew the milk of greatness, though thy dearest
From that Elysian food was yet unweanèd;°
And many a deed of terrible uprightness
By thy sweet love was sanctified;
And in thy smile, and by thy side,
Saintly Camillus lived, and firm Atilius died.°
But when tears stained thy robe of vestal whiteness,
And gold prophaned thy Capitolian throne,°
Thou didst desert, with spirit-wingèd lightness,
The senate of the tyrants: they sunk prone,
Slaves of one tyrant: Palatinus sighed
Faint echoes of Ionian song; that tone°
Thou didst delay to hear, lamenting to disown.°

8

From what Hyrcanian glen or frozen hill,°
Or piny promontory of the Arctic main,
Or utmost islet inaccessible,
Didst thou lament the ruin of thy reign,
Teaching the woods and waves, and desert rocks,

And every Naiad's ice-cold urn,
To talk in echoes sad and stern,
Of that sublimest lore which man had dared unlearn?
For neither didst thou watch the wizard flocks
Of the Scald's dreams, nor haunt the Druid's sleep.°
What if the tears rained through thy scattered locks
Were quickly dried? for thou didst groan, not weep,
When from its sea of death, to kill and burn,
The Galilean serpent forth did creep,°
And made thy world an undistinguishable heap.

9

A thousand years the Earth cried, 'Where art thou?'
And then the shadow of thy coming fell
On Saxon Alfred's olive-cinctured brow:°
And many a warrior-peopled citadel,
Like rocks which fire lifts out of the flat deep,
Arose in sacred Italy,
Frowning o'er the tempestuous sea
Of kings, and priests, and slaves, in tower-crowned majesty;
That multitudinous anarchy did sweep
And burst around their walls, like idle foam,
Whilst from the human spirit's deepest deep
Strange melody with love and awe struck dumb
Dissonant arms; and Art, which cannot die,
With divine wand traced on our earthly home
Fit imagery to pave Heaven's everlasting dome.°

10

Thou huntress swifter than the Moon! thou terror°
Of the world's wolves! thou bearer of the quiver,
Whose sunlike shafts pierce tempest-wingèd Error,
As light may pierce the clouds when they dissever
In the calm regions of the orient day!
Luther caught thy wakening glance—°
Like lightning, from his leaden lance
Reflected, it dissolved the visions of the trance
In which, as in a tomb, the nations lay;
And England's prophets hailed thee as their queen,°
In songs whose music cannot pass away,
Though it must flow forever: not unseen

Before the spirit-sighted countenance
  Of Milton didst thou pass, from the sad scene°
  Beyond whose night he saw, with a dejected mien.

11

The eager hours and unreluctant years
  As on a dawn-illumined mountain stood,
Trampling to silence their loud hopes and fears,
  Darkening each other with their multitude,
And cried aloud, 'Liberty!' Indignation
    Answered Pity from her cave;
    Death grew pale within the grave,
And Desolation howled to the destroyer, 'Save!'°
  When, like Heaven's sun girt by the exhalation
   Of its own glorious light, thou didst arise,
  Chasing thy foes from nation unto nation
   Like shadows: as if day had cloven the skies
At dreaming midnight o'er the western wave,
  Men started, staggering with a glad surprise,
  Under the lightnings of thine unfamiliar eyes.°

12

Thou heaven of earth! what spells could pall thee then
  In ominous eclipse? A thousand years
Bred from the slime of deep oppression's den,
  Dyed all thy liquid light with blood and tears,
Till thy sweet stars could weep the stain away;
    How like Bacchanals of blood°
    Round France, the ghastly vintage, stood
Destruction's sceptred slaves, and Folly's mitred brood!°
  When one, like them, but mightier far than they,°
   The Anarch of thine own bewildered powers,
  Rose: armies mingled in obscure array,
   Like clouds with clouds, darkening the sacred bowers
Of serene Heaven. He, by the past pursued,
  Rests with those dead but unforgotten hours,
  Whose ghosts scare victor kings in their ancestral towers.

13

England yet sleeps: was she not called of old?
  Spain calls her now, as with its thrilling thunder

Vesuvius wakens Etna, and the cold°
    Snow-crags by its reply are cloven in sunder:
O'er the lit waves every Aeolian isle
        From Pithecusa to Pelorus°
        Howls, and leaps, and glares in chorus:
They cry, 'Be dim; ye lamps of heaven suspended o'er us.'
    Her chains are threads of gold,—she need but smile°
      And they dissolve; but Spain's were links of steel,
    Till bit to dust by virtue's keenest file.
      Twins of a single destiny! appeal
To the eternal years enthroned before us,
    In the dim West; impress, as from a seal,
    All ye have thought and done! Time cannot dare conceal.

14

Tomb of Arminius! render up thy dead,°
    Till, like a standard from a watch-tower's staff,
His soul may stream over the tyrant's head;
    Thy victory shall be his epitaph,
Wild Bacchanal of truth's mysterious wine;
        King-deluded Germany,
        His dead spirit lives in thee.
Why do we fear or hope? thou art already free!
    And thou, lost Paradise of this divine°
      And glorious world! thou flowery wilderness!
    Thou island of eternity! thou shrine
      Where desolation, clothed with loveliness,
Worships the thing thou wert! O Italy,
    Gather thy blood into thy heart; repress
    The beasts who make their dens thy sacred palaces.

15

O that the free would stamp the impious name
    Of KING into the dust! or write it there,
So that this blot upon the page of fame
    Were as a serpent's path, which the light air
Erases, and the flat sands close behind!
      Ye the oracle have heard:°
      Lift the victory-flashing sword,
And cut the snaky knots of this foul gordian word,°
    Which, weak itself as stubble, yet can bind

Into a mass, irrefragably firm,
The axes and the rods which awe mankind;°
The sound has poison in it, 'tis the sperm
Of what makes life foul, cankerous, and abhorred;
Disdain not thou, at thine appointed term,°
To set thine armèd heel on this reluctant worm.

16

O that the wise from their bright minds would kindle
Such lamps within the dome of this dim world,
That the pale name of PRIEST might shrink and dwindle
Into the hell from which it first was hurled,
A scoff of impious pride from fiends impure;
Till human thoughts might kneel alone,
Each before the judgement-throne
Of its own aweless soul, or of the Power unknown!°
O that the words which make the thoughts obscure
From which they spring, as clouds of glimmering dew
From a white lake blot Heaven's blue portraiture,
Were stripped of their thin masks and various hue
And frowns and smiles and splendours not their own,
Till in the nakedness of false and true
They stand before their Lord, each to receive its due.

17

He who taught man to vanquish whatsoever°
Can be between the cradle and the grave
Crowned him the King of Life. O vain endeavour!—
If on his own high will, a willing slave,
He has enthroned the oppression and the oppressor.
What if earth can clothe and feed
Amplest millions at their need,
And power in thought be as the tree within the seed?
Or what if Art, an ardent intercessor,
Diving on fiery wings to Nature's throne,
Checks the great mother stooping to caress her,
And cries: 'Give me, thy child, dominion°
Over all height and depth'?—if Life can breed
New wants, and wealth from those who toil and groan
Rend, of thy gifts and hers, a thousandfold for one.°

18

Come Thou, but lead out of the inmost cave
Of man's deep spirit, as the morning-star
Beckons the Sun from the Eoan wave,°
Wisdom. I hear the pennons of her car
Self-moving, like cloud charioted by flame;
Comes she not, and come ye not,
Rulers of eternal thought,
To judge, with solemn truth, life's ill-apportioned lot?
Blind Love, and equal Justice, and the Fame
Of what has been, the Hope of what will be?
O Liberty! if such could be thy name
Wert thou disjoined from these, or they from thee:
If thine or theirs were treasures to be bought
By blood or tears, have not the wise and free
Wept tears, and blood like tears?—The solemn harmony

19

Paused, and the Spirit of that mighty singing
To its abyss was suddenly withdrawn;
Then, as a wild swan, when sublimely winging
Its path athwart the thunder-smoke of dawn,
Sinks headlong through the aerial golden light
On the heavy-sounding plain,
When the bolt has pierced its brain;
As summer clouds dissolve, unburdened of their rain;
As a far taper fades with fading night,
As a brief insect dies with dying day,—
My song, its pinions disarrayed of might,
Drooped; o'er it closed the echoes far away
Of the great voice which did its flight sustain,
As waves which lately paved his watery way
Hiss round a drowner's head in their tempestuous play.

Sonnet ('Ye hasten to the grave!')

Ye hasten to the grave! What seek ye there,°
Ye restless thoughts and busy purposes

Of the idle brain, which the world's livery wear?
O thou quick Heart, which pantest to possess°
All that pale Expectation feigneth fair!°
Thou vainly curious mind which wouldest guess
Whence thou didst come and whither thou must go,
And all, that never yet was known, wouldst know,
O whither hasten ye, that thus ye press
With such swift feet life's green and pleasant path,
Seeking alike from happiness and woe
A refuge in the cavern of grey death?
O Heart and Mind, and Thoughts, what thing do you
Hope to inherit in the grave below?

Song ('Rarely, rarely comest thou')

Rarely, rarely comest thou,
  Spirit of Delight!
Wherefore hast thou left me now
  Many a day and night?
Many a weary night and day
'Tis since thou art fled away.

How shall ever one like me
  Win thee back again?
With the joyous and the free
  Thou wilt scoff at pain.
Spirit false! thou hast forgot
All but those who need thee not.

As a lizard with the shade
  Of a trembling leaf,
Thou with sorrow art dismayed;
  Even the sighs of grief
Reproach thee, that thou art not near
And reproach thou wilt not hear.

Let me set my mournful ditty
  To a merry measure.
Thou wilt never come for pity—
  Thou wilt come for pleasure.

Pity then will cut away
Those cruel wings, and thou wilt stay.—

I love all that thou lovest,
Spirit of Delight!
The fresh Earth in new leaves dressed,
And the starry night,
Autumn evening, and the morn
When the golden mists are born.

I love snow, and all the forms
Of the radiant frost;
I love waves and winds and storms—
Everything almost
Which is nature's and may be
Untainted by man's misery.

I love tranquil solitude,
And such society
As is quiet, wise and good;
Between thee and me
What difference? but thou dost possess
The things I seek—not love them less.

I love Love—though he has wings
And like light can flee—
But above all things,
Spirit, I love thee—
Thou art Love and Life! O come,
Make once more my heart thy home.

Letter to Maria Gisborne

The spider spreads her webs, whether she be°
In poet's tower, cellar, or barn, or tree;
The silkworm in the dark green mulberry leaves
His winding sheet and cradle ever weaves;
So I, a thing whom moralists call worm,°
Sit spinning still round this decaying form,
From the fine threads of verse and subtle thought—°

No net of words in garish colours wrought
To catch the idle buzzers of the day—
But a soft cell, where when that fades away,°
Memory may clothe in wings my living name
And feed it with the asphodels of fame,
Which in those hearts that must remember me
Grow, making love an immortality.

Whoever should behold me now, I wist,°
Would think I were a mighty mechanist,°
Bent with sublime Archimedean art°
To breathe a soul into the iron heart
Of some machine portentous, or strange gin,°
Which by the force of figured spells might win°
Its way over the sea, and sport therein;°
For round the walls are hung dread engines, such
As Vulcan never wrought for Jove to clutch
Ixion or the Titans:—or the quick°
Wit of that man of God, St Dominic,°
To convince Atheist, Turk, or Heretic,
Or those in philanthropic council met,°
Who thought to pay some interest for the debt
They owed to Jesus Christ for their salvation,
By giving a faint foretaste of damnation
To Shakespeare, Sidney, Spenser and the rest
Who made our land an island of the blest,
When lamp-like Spain, who now relumes her fire
On Freedom's hearth, grew dim with Empire—°
With thumbscrews, wheels, with tooth and spike and jag,
Which fishers found under the utmost crag
Of Cornwall and the storm-encompassed isles,°
Where to the sky the rude sea rarely smiles
Unless in treacherous wrath, as on the morn
When the exulting elements in scorn
Satiated with destroyed destruction, lay
Sleeping in beauty on their mangled prey,
As panthers sleep;—and other strange and dread
Magical forms the brick floor overspread——
Proteus transformed to metal did not make°
More figures, or more strange; nor did he take
Such shapes of unintelligible brass,

Or heap himself in such a horrid mass
Of tin and iron not to be understood;
And forms of unimaginable wood
To puzzle Tubal Cain and all his brood:°
Great screws, and cones, and wheels, and groovèd blocks,
The elements of what will stand the shocks
Of wave and wind and time.—Upon the table
More knacks and quips there be than I am able°
To catalogize in this verse of mine:—°
A pretty bowl of wood, not full of wine,
But quicksilver; that dew which the gnomes drink
When at their subterranean toil they swink,°
Pledging the daemons of the earthquake, who
Reply to them in lava, cry halloo!
And call out to the cities o'er their head,—
Roofs, towers and shrines, the dying and the dead,
Crash through the chinks of earth—and then all quaff
Another rouse, and hold their sides and laugh.°
This quicksilver no gnome has drunk—within
The walnut bowl it lies, veinèd and thin,
In colour like the wake of light that stains
The Tuscan deep, when from the moist moon rains
The inmost shower of its white fire—the breeze
Is still—blue heaven smiles over the pale seas.
And in this bowl of quicksilver—for I
Yield to the impulse of an infancy
Outlasting manhood—I have made to float
A rude idealism of a paper boat:°
A hollow screw with cogs—Henry will know
The thing I mean and laugh at me—if so
He fears not I should do more mischief—next
Lie bills and calculations much perplexed,
With steamboats, frigates and machinery quaint
Traced over them in blue and yellow paint.
Then comes a range of mathematical
Instruments, for plans nautical and statical;°
A heap of rosin, a queer broken glass°
With ink in it, a china cup that was
What it will never be again, I think,
A thing from which sweet lips were wont to drink
The liquor doctors rail at—and which I

Will quaff in spite of them—and when we die
We'll toss up who died first of drinking tea,
And cry out, 'Heads or tails?' where'er we be.
Near that a dusty paint box, some odd hooks,
A half-burnt match, an ivory block, three books
Where conic sections, spherics, logarithms,
To great Laplace, from Saunderson and Sims,°
Lie heaped in their harmonious disarray
Of figures—disentangle them who may.
Baron de Tott's Memoirs beside them lie,°
And some odd volumes of old chemistry.
Near those a most inexplicable thing,
With lead in the middle—I'm conjecturing
How to make Henry understand—but, no—
I'll leave, as Spenser says, with many mo,°
This secret in the pregnant womb of time,°
Too vast a matter for so weak a rhyme.

And here like some weird Archimage sit I,°
Plotting dark spells and devilish enginery,
The self-impelling steam-wheels of the mind
Which pump up oaths from clergymen, and grind
The gentle spirit of our meek reviews
Into a powdery foam of salt abuse,
Ruffling the dull wave of their self-content.
I sit, and smile or sigh as is my bent,
But not for them—Libeccio rushes round°
With an inconstant and an idle sound,
I heed him more than them—the thundersmoke
Is gathering on the mountains, like a cloak
Folded athwart their shoulders broad and bare;
The ripe corn under the undulating air
Undulates like an ocean—and the vines
Are trembling wide in all their trellised lines—
The murmur of the awakening sea doth fill
The empty pauses of the blast—the hill
Looks hoary through the white electric rain—
And from the glens beyond, in sullen strain,
The interrupted thunder howls; above
One chasm of heaven smiles, like the eye of love
On the unquiet world—while such things are,

How could one worth your friendship heed this war
Of worms? the shriek of the world's carrion jays,
Their censure, or their wonder, or their praise?

You are not here . . . the quaint witch Memory sees°
In vacant chairs your absent images,
And points where once you sat, and now should be
But are not.—I demand if ever we
Shall meet as then we met—and she replies,
Veiling in awe her second-sighted eyes;°
'I know the past alone—but summon home
My sister Hope,—she speaks of all to come.'
But I, an old diviner, who know well
Every false verse of that sweet oracle,
Turned to the sad enchantress once again,°
And sought a respite from my gentle pain
In citing every passage o'er and o'er
Of our communion—how on the seashore
We watched the ocean and the sky together
Under the roof of blue Italian weather;
How I ran home through last year's thunderstorm,
And felt the transverse lightning linger warm°
Upon my cheek—and how we often made
Feasts for each other, where good will outweighed
The frugal luxury of our country cheer,
As well it might, were it less firm and clear
Than ours must ever be;—and how we spun
A shroud of talk to hide us from the sun
Of this familiar life, which seems to be
But is not,—or is but quaint mockery
Of all we would believe; or sadly blame
The jarring and inexplicable frame
Of this wrong world; and then anatomize
The purposes and thoughts of men whose eyes
Were closed in distant years—or widely guess
The issue of the earth's great business,
When we shall be as we no longer are—
Like babbling gossips safe, who hear the war
Of winds, and sigh, but tremble not—or how
You listened to some interrupted flow
Of visionary rhyme, in joy and pain°

Struck from the inmost fountains of my brain,
With little skill perhaps—or how we sought
Those deepest wells of passion and of thought
Wrought by wise poets in the waste of years,
Staining their sacred waters with our tears,
Quenching a thirst ever to be renewed!
Or how I, wisest lady! then indued°
The language of a land which now is free°
And winged with thoughts of truth and majesty
Flits round the tyrant's sceptre like a cloud,
And bursts the peopled prisons, and cries aloud,
'My name is Legion!'—that majestic tongue°
Which Calderon over the desert flung°
Of ages and of nations; and which found
An echo in our hearts, and with the sound
Startled oblivion—thou wert then to me
As is a nurse when inarticulately°
A child would talk as its grown parents do.
If living winds the rapid clouds pursue,
If hawks chase doves through the etherial way,
Huntsmen the innocent deer, and beasts their prey,
Why should not we rouse with the spirit's blast
Out of the forest of the pathless past
These recollected pleasures?
You are now
In London, that great sea, whose ebb and flow
At once is deaf and loud, and on the shore
Vomits its wrecks, and still howls on for more.°
Yet in its depth what treasures! You will see
That which was Godwin,—greater none than he
Though fallen—and fallen on evil times—to stand
Among the spirits of our age and land
Before the dread tribunal of *to come*
The foremost—while Rebuke cowers pale and dumb.°
You will see Coleridge—he who sits obscure
In the exceeding lustre, and the pure
Intense irradiation of a mind,
Which, with its own internal lightning blind,
Flags wearily through darkness and despair—
A cloud-encircled meteor of the air,
A hooded eagle among blinking owls.——

You will see Hunt, one of those happy souls
Who are the salt of the earth, and without whom°
This world would smell like what it is—a tomb;
Who is, what others seem; his room no doubt
Is still adorned by many a cast from Shout,°
With graceful flowers tastefully placed about,
And coronals of bay from ribbons hung,
And brighter wreaths in neat disorder flung;
The gifts of the most learn'd among some dozens
Of female friends, sisters-in-law and cousins.
And there is he with his eternal puns
Which beat the dullest brain for smiles, like duns°
Thundering for money at a poet's door;
Alas! it is no use to say, 'I'm poor!'
Or oft in graver mood, when he will look
Things wiser than were ever read in book,
Except in Shakespeare's wisest tenderness.—°
You will see Hogg—and I cannot express
His virtues—though I know that they are great,
Because he locks, then barricades the gate
Within which they inhabit—of his wit
And wisdom, you'll cry out when you are bit.
He is a pearl within an oyster shell,
One of the richest of the deep;—and there°
Is English Peacock with his mountain fair
Turned into a Flamingo, that shy bird
That gleams i' the Indian air—have you not heard
When a man marries, dies, or turns Hindoo,
His best friends hear no more of him?—but you
Will see him, and will like him too, I hope,
With the milk-white Snowdonian antelope
Matched with this camelopard—his fine wit°
Makes such a wound, the knife is lost in it;
A strain too learned for a shallow age,
Too wise for selfish bigots; let his page
Which charms the chosen spirits of the time,
Fold itself up for the serener clime
Of years to come, and find its recompense
In that just expectation.—Wit and sense,°
Virtue and human knowledge, all that might
Make this dull world a business of delight,

Are all combined in Horace Smith.—And these,°
With some exceptions which I need not tease
Your patience by descanting on, are all
You and I know in London.
                                        I recall
My thoughts, and bid you look upon the night.
As water does a sponge, so the moonlight
Fills the void, hollow, universal air—
What see you?—unpavilioned heaven is fair
Whether the moon, into her chamber gone,
Leaves midnight to the golden stars, or wan
Climbs with diminished beams the azure steep;
Or whether clouds sail o'er the inverse deep,
Piloted by the many-wandering blast,
And the rare stars rush through them dim and fast:—
All this is beautiful in every land.—
But what see you beside?—a shabby stand
Of Hackney coaches—a brick house or wall°
Fencing some lordly court, white with the scrawl°
Of our unhappy politics, or worse—
A wretched woman reeling by, whose curse
Mixed with the watchman's, partner of her trade,
You must accept in place of serenade—
Or yellow-haired Pollonia murmuring°
To Henry some unutterable thing.°
I see a chaos of green leaves and fruit
Built round dark caverns, even to the root
Of the living stems that feed them—in whose bowers
There sleep in their dark dew the folded flowers;
Beyond, the surface of the unsickled corn
Trembles not in the slumbering air, and borne
In circles quaint, and ever-changing dance,
Like wingèd stars the fire-flies flash and glance,
Pale in the open moonshine, but each one
Under the dark trees seems a little sun,
A meteor tamed, a fixed star gone astray
From the silver regions of the milky way;—
Afar the contadino's song is heard,°
Rude, but made sweet by distance—and a bird
Which cannot be the nightingale, and yet
I know none else that sings so sweet as it

At this late hour—and then all is still——
Now Italy or London, which you will!

Next winter you must pass with me; I'll have
My house by that time turned into a grave
Of dead despondence and low-thoughted care,°
And all the dreams which our tormentors are;
Oh! that Hunt, Hogg, Peacock and Smith were there,
With everything belonging to them fair!
We will have books, Spanish, Italian, Greek;
And ask one week to make another week
As like his father, as I'm unlike mine,
Which is not his fault, as you may divine.
Though we eat little flesh and drink no wine,
Yet let's be merry: we'll have tea and toast,
Custards for supper, and an endless host
Of syllabubs and jellies and mince-pies,°
And other such lady-like luxuries—
Feasting on which we will philosophize!
And we'll have fires out of the Grand Duke's wood°
To thaw the six weeks' winter in our blood.
And then we'll talk—what shall we talk about?
Oh! there are themes enough for many a bout
Of thought-entangled descant;—as to nerves,
With cones and parallelograms and curves
I've sworn to strangle them if once they dare
To bother me—when you are with me there—
And they shall never more sip laudanum,°
From Helicon or Himeros;—well, come,°
And in despite of God and of the devil,
We'll make our friendly philosophic revel
Outlast the leafless time—till buds and flowers
Warn the obscure inevitable hours
Sweet meeting by sad parting to renew—
'Tomorrow to fresh woods and pastures new.'°

To —— (Lines to a Reviewer)

Alas, good friend, what profit can you see
In hating such a hateless thing as me?

There is no sport in hate when all the rage
Is on one side. In vain would you assuage
Your frowns upon an unresisting smile
In which not even contempt lurks to beguile
Your heart, by some faint sympathy of hate.
O conquer what you cannot satiate!
For to your passion I am far more coy
Than ever yet was coldest maid or boy
In winter noon. Of your antipathy,
If I am the Narcissus, you are free,°
To pine into a sound with hating me.

To ——— (Lines to a Critic)

1

Honey from silkworms who can gather,
  Or silk from the yellow bee?
The grass may grow in winter weather
  As soon as hate in me.

2

Hate men who cant, and men who pray,
  And men who rail, like thee;
An equal passion to repay
  They are not coy—like me.—

3

Or seek some slave of power and gold,
  To be thy dear heart's mate—
Thy love will move that bigot cold
  Sooner than me, thy hate.

4

A passion like the one I prove°
  Cannot divided be—
I hate thy want of truth and love—
  How should I then hate thee?

THE WITCH OF ATLAS

To Mary

(ON HER OBJECTING TO THE FOLLOWING POEM,
UPON THE SCORE OF ITS CONTAINING
NO HUMAN INTEREST)°

1

How, my dear Mary, are you critic-bitten
(For vipers kill, though dead) by some review,
That you condemn these verses I have written
Because they tell no story, false or true?
What, though no mice are caught by a young kitten,
May it not leap and play as grown cats do,
Till its claws come? Prithee, for this one time,
Content thee with a visionary rhyme.

2

What hand would crush the silken-wingèd fly,°
The youngest of inconstant April's minions,
Because it cannot climb the purest sky
Where the swan sings, amid the sun's dominions?°
Not thine. Thou knowest 'tis its doom to die
When day shall hide within her twilight pinions
The lucent eyes, and the eternal smile,
Serene as thine, which lent it life awhile.

3

To thy fair feet a wingèd Vision came°
Whose date should have been longer than a day,
And o'er thy head did beat its wings for fame,
And in thy sight its fading plumes display;
The watery bow burned in the evening flame,
But the shower fell, the swift Sun went his way—
And that is dead.—O, let me not believe
That anything of mine is fit to live!

4

Wordsworth informs us he was nineteen years
  Considering and retouching Peter Bell;°
Watering his laurels with the killing tears
  Of slow, dull care, so that their roots to hell
Might pierce, and their wide branches blot the spheres
  Of Heaven, with dewy leaves and flowers; this well
May be, for Heaven and Earth conspire to foil
The over-busy gardener's blundering toil.

5

My Witch indeed is not so sweet a creature
  As Ruth or Lucy, whom his graceful praise°
Clothes for our grandsons—but she matches Peter,
  Though he took nineteen years, and she three days
In dressing. Light the vest of flowing metre
  She wears; he, proud as dandy with his stays,
Has hung upon his wiry limbs a dress
Like King Lear's 'looped and windowed raggedness.'°

6

If you strip Peter, you will see a fellow,
  Scorched by Hell's hyperequatorial climate°
Into a kind of a sulphureous yellow:
  A lean mark, hardly fit to fling a rhyme at;
In shape a Scaramouch, in hue Othello.°
  If you unveil my Witch, no Priest or Primate°
Can shrive you of that sin, if sin there be°
In love, when it becomes idolatry.

I

Before those cruel Twins, whom at one birth°
  Incestuous Change bore to her father Time,
Error and Truth, had hunted from the earth
  All those bright natures which adorned its prime,
And left us nothing to believe in, worth
  The pains of putting into learned rhyme,
A lady-witch there lived on Atlas' mountain°
Within a cavern, by a secret fountain.°

2

Her mother was one of the Atlantides:°
  The all-beholding Sun had ne'er beholden
In his wide voyage o'er continents and seas
  So fair a creature, as she lay enfolden
In the warm shadow of her loveliness;—
  He kissed her with his beams, and made all golden
The chamber of grey rock in which she lay—
She, in that dream of joy, dissolved away.°

3

'Tis said, she first was changed into a vapour,
  And then into a cloud, such clouds as flit,
Like splendour-wingèd moths about a taper,
  Round the red west when the sun dies in it:
And then into a meteor, such as caper
  On hill-tops when the moon is in a fit:°
Then, into one of those mysterious stars
Which hide themselves between the Earth and Mars.

4

Ten times the Mother of the Months had bent°
  Her bow beside the folding-star, and bidden,°
With that bright sign the billows to indent
  The sea-deserted sand—like children chidden,
At her command they ever came and went—
  Since in that cave a dewy splendour hidden
Took shape and motion: with the living form
Of this embodied Power, the cave grew warm.

5

A lovely lady garmented in light
  From her own beauty—deep her eyes, as are
Two openings of unfathomable night
  Seen through a Temple's cloven roof—her hair
Dark—the dim brain whirls dizzy with delight,
  Picturing her form; her soft smiles shone afar,
And her low voice was heard like love, and drew
All living things towards this wonder new.

6

And first the spotted camelopard came,°
  And then the wise and fearless elephant;
Then the sly serpent, in the golden flame
  Of his own volumes intervolved;—all gaunt
And sanguine beasts her gentle looks made tame.
  They drank before her at her sacred fount;
And every beast of beating heart grew bold,
Such gentleness and power even to behold.

7

The brinded lioness led forth her young,°
  That she might teach them how they should forgo
Their inborn thirst of death; the pard unstrung°
  His sinews at her feet, and sought to know
With looks whose motions spoke without a tongue
  How he might be as gentle as the doe.
The magic circle of her voice and eyes
All savage natures did imparadise.

8

And old Silenus, shaking a green stick°
  Of lilies, and the wood-gods in a crew°
Came, blithe, as in the olive copses thick
  Cicadae are, drunk with the noonday dew:°
And Driope and Faunus followed quick,°
  Teasing the God to sing them something new,
Till in this cave they found the lady lone,
Sitting upon a seat of emerald stone.

9

And Universal Pan, 'tis said, was there,°
  And though none saw him,—through the adamant
Of the deep mountains, through the trackless air,
  And through those living spirits, like a want°
He passed out of his everlasting lair
  Where the quick heart of the great world doth pant,
And felt that wondrous lady all alone—
And she felt him upon her emerald throne.

10

And every nymph of stream and spreading tree,
  And every shepherdess of Ocean's flocks,
Who drives her white waves over the green sea;
  And Ocean, with the brine on his grey locks,
And quaint Priapus with his company°
  All came, much wondering how the enwombèd rocks
Could have brought forth so beautiful a birth;—
Her love subdued their wonder and their mirth.

11

The herdsmen and the mountain maidens came,
  And the rude kings of pastoral Garamant—°
These spirits shook within them, as a flame
  Stirred by the air under a cavern gaunt:
Pigmies, and Polyphemes, by many a name,°
  Centaurs and Satyrs, and such shapes as haunt°
Wet clefts,—and lumps neither alive nor dead,
Dog-headed, bosom-eyed and bird-footed.°

12

For she was beautiful—her beauty made
  The bright world dim, and everything beside
Seemed like the fleeting image of a shade:
  No thought of living spirit could abide,
Which to her looks had ever been betrayed,
  On any object in the world so wide,
On any hope within the circling skies,
But on her form, and in her inmost eyes.

13

Which when the lady knew, she took her spindle
  And twined three threads of fleecy mist, and three
Long lines of light, such as the dawn may kindle°
  The clouds and waves and mountains with, and she
As many star-beams, ere their lamps could dwindle
  In the belated moon, wound skilfully;°
And with these threads a subtle veil she wove—
A shadow for the splendour of her love.

14

The deep recesses of her odorous dwelling
  Were stored with magic treasures—sounds of air,
Which had the power all spirits of compelling,
  Folded in cells of crystal silence there;°
Such as we hear in youth, and think the feeling
  Will never die—yet ere we are aware,
The feeling and the sound are fled and gone,
And the regret they leave remains alone.

15

And there lay Visions swift, and sweet, and quaint,
  Each in its thin sheath like a chrysalis;
Some eager to burst forth, some weak and faint
  With the soft burden of intensest bliss;
It was its work to bear to many a saint
  Whose heart adores the shrine which holiest is,
Even Love's—and others white, green, grey and black,
And of all shapes—and each was at her beck.

16

And odours in a kind of aviary°
  Of ever-blooming Eden-trees she kept,
Clipped in a floating net, a love-sick Fairy
  Had woven from dew-beams while the moon yet slept;
As bats at the wired window of a dairy,
  They beat their vans; and each was an adept,°
When loosed and missioned, making wings of winds,
To stir sweet thoughts or sad in destined minds.

17

And liquors clear and sweet, whose healthful might
  Could medicine the sick soul to happy sleep,
And change eternal death into a night
  Of glorious dreams—or if eyes needs must weep,
Could make their tears all wonder and delight—
  She in her crystal vials did closely keep:
If men could drink of those clear vials, 'tis said
The living were not envied of the dead.

18

Her cave was stored with scrolls of strange device,
  The works of some Saturnian Archimage,
Which taught the expiations at whose price
  Men from the Gods might win that happy age
Too lightly lost, redeeming native vice;
  And which might quench the earth-consuming rage
Of gold and blood—till men should live and move
Harmonious as the sacred stars above.°

19

And how all things that seem untameable,
  Not to be checked and not to be confined,
Obey the spells of wisdom's wizard skill;°
  Time, Earth and Fire—the Ocean and the Wind,
And all their shapes—and man's imperial will;
  And other scrolls whose writings did unbind
The inmost lore of Love—let the profane
Tremble to ask what secrets they contain.

20

And wondrous works of substances unknown,
  To which the enchantment of her father's power
Had changed those ragged blocks of savage stone,
  Were heaped in the recesses of her bower;
Carved lamps and chalices, and phials which shone
  In their own golden beams—each like a flower,
Out of whose depth a fire-fly shakes his light
Under a cypress in a starless night.

21

At first she lived alone in this wild home,
  And her own thoughts were each a minister,
Clothing themselves or with the ocean-foam,
  Or with the wind, or with the speed of fire,
To work whatever purposes might come
  Into her mind; such power her mighty Sire
Had girt them with, whether to fly or run,
Through all the regions which he shines upon.

22

The Ocean-nymphs and Hamadryades,°
   Oreads and Naiads with long weedy locks,°
Offered to do her bidding through the seas,
   Under the earth, and in the hollow rocks,°
And far beneath the matted roots of trees,
   And in the gnarlèd heart of stubborn oaks,
So they might live forever in the light
Of her sweet presence—each a satellite.

23

'This may not be,' the wizard maid replied;
   'The fountains where the Naiades bedew°
Their shining hair, at length are drained and dried;
   The solid oaks forget their strength, and strew
Their latest leaf upon the mountains wide;
   The boundless ocean like a drop of dew
Will be consumed—the stubborn centre must
Be scattered, like a cloud of summer dust.°

24

'And ye with them will perish one by one:
   If I must sigh to think that this shall be,
If I must weep when the surviving Sun
   Shall smile on your decay—Oh, ask not me
To love you till your little race is run;
   I cannot die as ye must—over me
Your leaves shall glance—the streams in which ye dwell
Shall be my paths henceforth, and so, farewell!'

25

She spoke and wept: the dark and azure well
   Sparkled beneath the shower of her bright tears,
And every little circlet where they fell,
   Flung to the cavern-roof inconstant spheres
And intertangled lines of light:—a knell
   Of sobbing voices came upon her ears
From those departing Forms, o'er the serene
Of the white streams and of the forest green.

26

All day the wizard lady sat aloof,
  Spelling out scrolls of dread antiquity,
Under the cavern's fountain-lighted roof;
  Or broidering the pictured poesy
Of some high tale upon her growing woof,°
  Which the sweet splendour of her smiles could dye
In hues outshining heaven—and ever she
Added some grace to the wrought poesy.

27

While on her hearth lay blazing many a piece
  Of sandalwood, rare gums and cinnamon;
Men scarcely know how beautiful fire is—
  Each flame of it is as a precious stone
Dissolved in ever-moving light, and this
  Belongs to each and all who gaze upon.
The Witch beheld it not, for in her hand
She held a woof that dimmed the burning brand.

28

This lady never slept, but lay in trance
  All night within the fountain—as in sleep.
Its emerald crags glowed in her beauty's glance:
  Through the green splendour of the water deep
She saw the constellations reel and dance
  Like fire-flies—and withal did ever keep°
The tenour of her contemplations calm,°
With open eyes, closed feet and folded palm.

29

And when the whirlwinds and the clouds descended
  From the white pinnacles of that cold hill,
She passed at dewfall to a space extended,
  Where in a lawn of flowering asphodel°
Amid a wood of pines and cedars blended,
  There yawned an inextinguishable well
Of crimson fire, full even to the brim
And overflowing all the margin trim.

30

Within the which she lay when the fierce war
Of wintry winds shook that innocuous liquor
In many a mimic moon and bearded star°
O'er woods and lawns—the serpent heard it flicker
In sleep, and dreaming still, he crept afar—
And when the windless snow descended thicker
Than autumn leaves, she watched it as it came
Melt on the surface of the level flame.

31

She had a Boat which some say Vulcan wrought°
For Venus, as the chariot of her star;
But it was found too feeble to be fraught
With all the ardours in that sphere which are,°
And so she sold it, and Apollo bought,
And gave it to this daughter: from a car
Changed to the fairest and the lightest boat
Which ever upon mortal stream did float.

32

And others say, that when but three hours old,
The first-born Love out of his cradle leapt,
And clove dun Chaos with his wings of gold,
And like an horticultural adept,
Stole a strange seed, and wrapped it up in mould,
And sowed it in his mother's star, and kept
Watering it all the summer with sweet dew,
And with his wings fanning it as it grew.

33

The plant grew strong and green—the snowy flower
Fell, and the long and gourd-like fruit began
To turn the light and dew by inward power
To its own substance; woven tracery ran
Of light firm texture, ribbed and branching, o'er
The solid rind, like a leaf's veinèd fan,
Of which Love scooped this boat, and with soft motion
Piloted it round the circumfluous ocean.°

34

This boat she moored upon her fount, and lit
  A living spirit within all its frame,
Breathing the soul of swiftness into it.
  Couched on the fountain like a panther tame,
One of the twain at Evan's feet that sit;°
  Or as on Vesta's sceptre a swift flame,°
Or on blind Homer's heart a wingèd thought—
In joyous expectation lay the boat.

35

Then by strange art she kneaded fire and snow
  Together, tempering the repugnant mass
With liquid love—all things together grow°
  Through which the harmony of love can pass;
And a fair Shape out of her hands did flow—
  A living Image, which did far surpass
In beauty that bright shape of vital stone
Which drew the heart out of Pygmalion.°

36

A sexless thing it was, and in its growth
  It seemed to have developed no defect
Of either sex, yet all the grace of both—°
  In gentleness and strength its limbs were decked;
The bosom swelled lightly with its full youth—
  The countenance was such as might select
Some artist that his skill should never die,
Imaging forth such perfect purity.

37

From its smooth shoulders hung two rapid wings,
  Fit to have borne it to the seventh sphere,°
Tipped with the speed of liquid lightnings,°
  Dyed in the ardours of the atmosphere:
She led her creature to the boiling springs
  Where the light boat was moored, and said—'Sit here!'
And pointed to the prow, and took her seat
Beside the rudder with opposing feet.

38

And down the streams which clove those mountains vast°
  Around their inland islets, and amid
The panther-peopled forests, whose shade cast
  Darkness and odours, and a pleasure hid
In melancholy gloom, the pinnace passed;°
  By many a star-surrounded pyramid
Of icy crag cleaving the purple sky,
And caverns yawning round unfathomably.

39

The silver noon into that winding dell,
  With slanted gleam athwart the forest tops,
Tempered like golden evening, feebly fell;
  A green and glowing light, like that which drops
From folded lilies in which glow-worms dwell,
  When earth over her face night's mantle wraps;
Between the severed mountains lay on high
Over the stream, a narrow rift of sky.

40

And ever as she went, the Image lay
  With folded wings and unawakened eyes;
And o'er its gentle countenance did play
  The busy dreams, as thick as summer flies,
Chasing the rapid smiles that would not stay,
  And drinking the warm tears, and the sweet sighs
Inhaling, which, with busy murmur vain,
They had aroused from that full heart and brain.

41

And ever down the prone vale, like a cloud°
  Upon a stream of wind, the pinnace went:
Now lingering on the pools, in which abode
  The calm and darkness of the deep content
In which they paused; now o'er the shallow road
  Of white and dancing waters all besprent°
With sand and polished pebbles:—mortal boat
In such a shallow rapid could not float.

42

And down the earthquaking cataracts which shiver°
  Their snow-like waters into golden air,
Or under chasms unfathomable ever
  Sepulchre them, till in their rage they tear
A subterranean portal for the river,
  It fled—the circling sunbows did upbear°
Its fall down the hoar precipice of spray,
Lighting it far upon its lampless way.

43

And when the wizard lady would ascend
  The labyrinths of some many-winding vale,
Which to the inmost mountain upward tend—
  She called 'Hermaphroditus!' and the pale
And heavy hue which slumber could extend
  Over its lips and eyes, as on the gale
A rapid shadow from a slope of grass,
Into the darkness of the stream did pass.

44

And it unfurled its heaven-coloured pinions,
  With stars of fire spotting the stream below;
And from above into the Sun's dominions
  Flinging a glory, like the golden glow
In which Spring clothes her emerald-wingèd minions,
  All interwoven with fine feathery snow
And moonlight splendour of intensest rime,°
With which frost paints the pines in winter time.

45

And then it winnowed the Elysian air
  Which ever hung about that lady bright,
With its ethereal vans—and speeding there,
  Like a star up the torrent of the night,
Or a swift eagle in the morning glare
  Breasting the whirlwind with impetuous flight,
The pinnace, oared by those enchanted wings,
Clove the fierce streams towards their upper springs.

46

The water flashed like sunlight by the prow
  Of a noon-wandering meteor flung to Heaven;
The still air seemed as if its waves did flow
  In tempest down the mountains—loosely driven
The lady's radiant hair streamed to and fro:
  Beneath, the billows having vainly striven
Indignant and impetuous, roared to feel
The swift and steady motion of the keel.

47

Or, when the weary moon was in the wane,
  Or in the noon of interlunar night,
The lady-witch in visions could not chain
  Her spirit; but sailed forth under the light
Of shooting stars, and bade extend amain°
  Its storm-outspeeding wings, th' Hermaphrodite;
She to the Austral waters took her way,°
Beyond the fabulous Thamondocana,°

48

Where, like a meadow which no scythe has shaven,
  Which rain could never bend, or whirl-blast shake
With the Antarctic constellations paven,
  Canopus and his crew, lay th' Austral lake—°
There she would build herself a windless haven
  Out of the clouds whose moving turrets make
The bastions of the storm, when through the sky
The spirits of the tempest thundered by.

49

A haven beneath whose translucent floor
  The tremulous stars sparkled unfathomably,
And around which, the solid vapours hoar,
  Based on the level waters, to the sky
Lifted their dreadful crags; and like a shore
  Of wintry mountains, inaccessibly
Hemmed in with rifts and precipices grey,
  And hanging crags, many a cove and bay.

50

And whilst the outer lake, beneath the lash
  Of the wind's scourge, foamed like a wounded thing,
And the incessant hail with stony clash
  Ploughed up the waters, and the flagging wing
Of the roused cormorant in the lightning flash
  Looked like the wreck of some wind-wandering
Fragment of inky thundersmoke—this haven
Was as a gem to copy Heaven engraven.

51

On which that lady played her many pranks,
  Circling the image of a shooting star,
Even as a tiger on Hydaspes' banks°
  Outspeeds the antelopes which speediest are,
In her light boat; and many quips and cranks°
  She played upon the water, till the car
Of the late moon, like a sick matron wan,
To journey from the misty east began.

52

And then she called out of the hollow turrets
  Of those high clouds, white, golden and vermilion,
The armies of her ministering spirits—
  In mighty legions million after million
They came, each troop emblazoning its merits
  On meteor flags; and many a proud pavilion°
Of the intertexture of the atmosphere
They pitched upon the plain of the calm mere.°

53

They framed the imperial tent of their great Queen
  Of woven exhalations, underlaid°
With lambent lightning-fire, as may be seen°
  A dome of thin and open ivory inlaid
With crimson silk—cressets from the serene°
  Hung there, and on the water for her tread
A tapestry of fleece-like mist was strewn,
Dyed in the beams of the ascending moon.

54

And on a throne o'erlaid with starlight, caught
  Upon those wandering isles of aery dew,
Which highest shoals of mountain shipwreck not,
  She sate, and heard all that had happened new
Between the earth and moon, since they had brought
  The last intelligence—and now she grew
Pale as that moon lost in the watery night—
  And now she wept, and now she laughed outright.

55

These were tame pleasures.—She would often climb
  The steepest ladder of the crudded rack°
Up to some beakèd cape of cloud sublime,
  And like Arion on the dolphin's back°
Ride singing through the shoreless air. Oft time
  Following the serpent lightning's winding track,
She ran upon the platforms of the wind,
And laughed to hear the fire-balls roar behind.°

56

And sometimes to those streams of upper air,
  Which whirl the earth in its diurnal round,
She would ascend, and win the spirits there
  To let her join their chorus. Mortals found
That on those days the sky was calm and fair,
  And mystic snatches of harmonious sound
Wandered upon the earth where'er she passed,
And happy thoughts of hope, too sweet to last.

57

But her choice sport was, in the hours of sleep,
  To glide adown old Nilus, where he threads°
Egypt and Ethiopia, from the steep
  Of utmost Axumè, until he spreads,°
Like a calm flock of silver-fleecèd sheep,
  His waters on the plain: and crested heads
Of cities and proud temples gleam amid
And many a vapour-belted pyramid.

58

By Moeris and the Mareotid lakes,°
   Strewn with faint blooms like bridal chamber floors,
Where naked boys bridling tame water-snakes,
   Or charioteering ghastly alligators,
Had left on the sweet waters mighty wakes
   Of those huge forms—within the brazen doors
Of the great Labyrinth slept both boy and beast,°
Tired with the pomp of their Osirian feast.°

59

And where within the surface of the river
   The shadows of the massy temples lie,
And never are erased—but tremble ever°
   Like things which every cloud can doom to die,
Through lotus-pav'n canals, and wheresoever
   The works of man pierced that serenest sky
With tombs, and towers, and fanes, 'twas her delight°
To wander in the shadow of the night.

60

With motion like the spirit of that wind
   Whose soft step deepens slumber, her light feet
Passed through the peopled haunts of human kind,
   Scattering sweet visions from her presence sweet,
Through fane and palace-court and labyrinth mined
   With many a dark and subterranean street
Under the Nile; through chambers high and deep
She passed, observing mortals in their sleep.

61

A pleasure sweet doubtless it was to see
   Mortals subdued in all the shapes of sleep.
Here lay two sister-twins in infancy;
   There, a lone youth who in his dreams did weep;
Within, two lovers linked innocently
   In their loose locks which over both did creep
Like ivy from one stem—and there lay calm
Old age with snow-bright hair and folded palm.

62

But other troubled forms of sleep she saw,
Not to be mirrored in a holy song—
Distortions foul of supernatural awe,
And pale imaginings of visioned wrong,
And all the code of custom's lawless law
Written upon the brows of old and young:
'This,' said the wizard maiden, 'is the strife
Which stirs the liquid surface of man's life.'

63

And little did the sight disturb her soul—
We, the weak mariners of that wide lake
Where'er its shores extend or billows roll,
Our course unpiloted and starless make
O'er its wild surface to an unknown goal—
But she in the calm depths her way could take,
Where in bright bowers immortal forms abide,
Beneath the weltering of the restless tide.°

64

And she saw princes couched under the glow
Of sunlike gems: and round each temple-court
In dormitories ranged, row after row,
She saw the priests asleep—all of one sort,
For all were educated to be so.—
The peasants in their huts, and in the port
The sailors she saw cradled on the waves,
And the dead lulled within their dreamless graves.

65

And all the forms in which those spirits lay
Were to her sight like the diaphanous
Veils, in which those sweet ladies oft array
Their delicate limbs, who would conceal from us
Only their scorn of all concealment: they
Move in the light of their own beauty thus.
But these and all now lay with sleep upon them,
And little thought a Witch was looking on them.

66

She all those human figures breathing there
Beheld as living spirits—to her eyes
The naked beauty of the soul lay bare,
And often through a rude and worn disguise
She saw the inner form most bright and fair—
And then, she had a charm of strange device,
Which murmured on mute lips with tender tone,
Could make that spirit mingle with her own.

67

Alas, Aurora! what wouldst thou have given
For such a charm when Tithon became grey?°
Or how much, Venus, of thy silver Heaven
Wouldst thou have yielded, ere Proserpina
Had half (oh! why not all?) the debt forgiven
Which dear Adonis had been doomed to pay,°
To any witch who would have taught you it?
The Heliad doth not know its value yet.°

68

'Tis said in after times her spirit free
Knew what love was, and felt itself alone—
But holy Dian could not chaster be
Before she stooped to kiss Endymion,°
Than now this lady—like a sexless bee
Tasting all blossoms, and confined to none—
Among those mortal forms, the wizard-maiden
Passed with an eye serene and heart unladen.

69

To those she saw most beautiful, she gave
Strange panacea in a crystal bowl.
They drank in their deep sleep of that sweet wave,
And lived thenceforward as if some control,
Mightier than life, were in them; and the grave
Of such, when death oppressed the weary soul,
Was as a green and overarching bower
Lit by the gems of many a starry flower.

70

For on the night that they were buried, she
  Restored the embalmer's ruining, and shook
The light out of the funeral lamps, to be°
  A mimic day within that deathy nook;
And she unwound the woven imagery
  Of second childhood's swaddling bands, and took
The coffin, its last cradle, from its niche,
And threw it with contempt into a ditch.

71

And there the body lay, age after age,
  Mute, breathing, beating, warm, and undecaying
Like one asleep in a green hermitage,
  With gentle smiles about its eyelids playing,
And living in its dreams beyond the rage
  Of death or life; while they were still arraying
In liveries ever new the rapid, blind
And fleeting generations of mankind.

72

And she would write strange dreams upon the brain
  Of those who were less beautiful, and make
All harsh and crooked purposes more vain
  Than in the desert is the serpent's wake
Which the sand covers—all his evil gain
  The miser in such dreams would rise and shake
Into a beggar's lap;—the lying scribe
Would his own lies betray without a bribe.

73

The priests would write an explanation full,
  Translating hieroglyphics into Greek,°
How the god Apis really was a bull,°
  And nothing more; and bid the herald stick
The same against the temple doors, and pull
  The old cant down; they licensed all to speak
Whate'er they thought of hawks, and cats, and geese,°
By pastoral letters to each diocese.

74

The king would dress an ape up in his crown
And robes, and seat him on his glorious seat,
And on the right hand of the sunlike throne
Would place a gaudy mock-bird to repeat
The chatterings of the monkey.—Every one
Of the prone courtiers crawled to kiss the feet
Of their great Emperor when the morning came;
And kissed—alas, how many kiss the same!°

75

The soldiers dreamed that they were blacksmiths, and
Walked out of quarters in somnambulism;°
Round the red anvils you might see them stand
Like Cyclopses in Vulcan's sooty abysm,°
Beating their swords to ploughshares—in a band°
The jailors sent those of the liberal schism
Free through the streets of Memphis; much, I wis,°
To the annoyance of king Amasis.°

76

And timid lovers who had been so coy
They hardly knew whether they loved or not,
Would rise out of their rest, and take sweet joy,
To the fulfilment of their inmost thought;
And when next day the maiden and the boy
Met one another, both, like sinners caught,
Blushed at the thing which each believed was done
Only in fancy—till the tenth moon shone;

77

And then the Witch would let them take no ill:
Of many thousand schemes which lovers find
The Witch found one,—and so they took their fill
Of happiness in marriage warm and kind.
Friends who by practice of some envious skill
Were torn apart, a wide wound, mind from mind!
She did unite again with visions clear
Of deep affection and of truth sincere.

78

These were the pranks she played among the cities
   Of mortal men, and what she did to sprites
And Gods, entangling them in her sweet ditties
   To do her will, and show their subtle slights,
I will declare another time; for it is
   A tale more fit for the weird winter nights°
Than for these garish summer days, when we°
Scarcely believe much more than we can see.

Song of Apollo

The sleepless Hours who watch me as I lie
   Curtained with star-enwoven tapestries
From the broad moonlight of the sky,
   Fanning the busy dreams from my dim eyes,
Waken me when their mother, the grey Dawn,
Tells them that Dreams and that the moon is gone.

Then I arise; and climbing Heaven's blue dome,
   I walk over the mountains and the waves,
Leaving my robe upon the Ocean foam.
   My footsteps pave the clouds with fire; the caves
Are filled with my bright presence, and the air
Leaves the green earth to my embraces bare.

The sunbeams are my shafts with which I kill
   Deceit, that loves the night and fears the day.
All men who do, or even imagine ill
   Fly me; and from the glory of my ray
Good minds and open actions take new might
Until diminished by the reign of night.

I feed the clouds, the rainbows and the flowers
   With their etherial colours; the moon's globe
And the pure stars in their eternal bowers
   Are cinctured with my power as with a robe;°
Whatever lamps on Earth or Heaven may shine
Are portions of one spirit; which is mine.

I stand at noon upon the peak of Heaven;
   Then with unwilling steps, I wander down
Into the clouds of the Atlantic even;
   For grief that I depart they weep and frown—
What look is more delightful, than the smile
With which I soothe them from the Western isle?

I am the eye with which the Universe
   Beholds itself, and knows it is divine;
All harmony of instrument and verse,

All prophecy and medicine are mine;
All light of art or nature;—to my song
Victory and praise, in its own right, belong.°

Song of Pan

From the forests and highlands
We come, we come,
From the river-girt islands
Where loud waves were dumb
Listening my sweet pipings.
The wind in the reeds and the rushes,
The bees in the bells of thyme,
The birds on the myrtle bushes,
The cicadae above in the lime,
And the lizards below in the grass,
Were silent as even old Tmolus was,°
Listening my sweet pipings.

Liquid Peneus was flowing—°
And all dark Tempe lay
In Pelion's shadow, outgrowing°
The light of the dying day,
Speeded with my sweet pipings.
The sileni and sylvans and fauns
And the nymphs of the woods and the waves
To the edge of the moist river-lawns
And the brink of the dewy caves,
And all that did then attend and follow,
Were as silent for love, as you now, Apollo,
For envy of my sweet pipings.

I sang of the dancing stars,
I sang of the daedal Earth,
And of Heaven, and the giant wars,°
And Love, and Death, and Birth
And then I changed my pipings,
Singing how down the vales of Maenalus°
I pursued a maiden and clasped a reed.°

Gods and men, we are all deluded thus!—
It breaks on our bosom and then we bleed;
They wept as, I think, both ye now would,°
If envy or age had not frozen your blood,
At the sorrow of my sweet pipings.

Sonnet: Political Greatness

Nor happiness, nor majesty nor fame,°
Nor peace nor strength, nor skill in arms or arts
Shepherd those herds whom Tyranny makes tame.
Verse echoes not one beating of their hearts;
History is but the shadow of their shame;
Art veils her glass, or from the pageant starts
As to oblivion their blind millions fleet,°
Staining that Heaven with obscene imagery
Of their own likeness. What are numbers, knit
By force or custom? Man, who man would be,
Must rule the empire of himself; in it
Must be supreme, establishing his throne
On vanquished will; quelling the anarchy
Of hopes and fears; being himself alone.

The Indian Girl's Song

I arise from dreams of thee
In the first sleep of night—
The winds are breathing low
And the stars are burning bright.
I arise from dreams of thee—
And a spirit in my feet
Has borne me—Who knows how?
To thy chamber window, sweet!—

The wandering airs they faint
On the dark silent stream—
The champak odours fail°

Like sweet thoughts in a dream;
The nightingale's complaint—
It dies upon her heart—
As I must die on thine
O beloved as thou art!

O lift me from the grass!
I die, I faint, I fail!
Let thy love in kisses rain
On my lips and eyelids pale.
My cheek is cold and white, alas!
My heart beats loud and fast.
Oh press it close to thine again
Where it will break at last.

EPIPSYCHIDION

VERSES ADDRESSED TO THE NOBLE AND UNFORTUNATE LADY

EMILIA V——

NOW IMPRISONED IN THE CONVENT OF ——

L'anima amante si slancia fuori del creato, e si crea nel infinito un Mondo tutto per essa, diverso assai da questo oscuro e pauroso baratro.

Her own words°

ADVERTISEMENT

The Writer of the following Lines died at Florence, as he was preparing for a voyage to one of the wildest of the Sporades,° which he had bought, and where he had fitted up the ruins of an old building, and where it was his hope to have realized a scheme of life, suited perhaps to that happier and better world of which he is now an inhabitant, but hardly practicable in this. His life was singular; less on account of the romantic vicissitudes which diversified it, than the ideal tinge which it received from his own character and feelings. The present Poem, like the *Vita Nuova*° of Dante, is sufficiently intelligible to a certain class of readers without a matter-of-fact history of the circumstances to which it relates; and to a certain other class it must ever remain incomprehensible, from a defect of a common organ of perception for the ideas of which it treats. Not but that, *gran vergogna sarebbe a colui, che rimasse cosa sotto veste di figura, o di colore rettorico: e domandato non sapesse denudare le sue parole da cotal veste, in guisa che avessero verace intendimento.*°

The present poem appears to have been intended by the Writer as the dedication to some longer one. The stanza on the opposite page is almost a literal translation from Dante's famous Canzone

Voi, ch'intendendo, il terzo ciel movete, &c.°

The presumptuous application of the concluding lines to his own composition will raise a smile at the expense of my unfortunate friend: be it a smile not of contempt, but pity.

S.

My Song, I fear that thou wilt find but few
Who fitly shall conceive thy reasoning,
Of such hard matter dost thou entertain;
Whence, if by misadventure, chance should bring
Thee to base company (as chance may do)
Quite unaware of what thou dost contain,
I prithee, comfort thy sweet self again,
My last delight! tell them that they are dull,
And bid them own that thou art beautiful.°

Sweet Spirit! Sister of that orphan one,°
Whose empire is the name thou weepest on,°
In my heart's temple I suspend to thee
These votive wreaths of withered memory.

Poor captive bird! who, from thy narrow cage,
Pourest such music, that it might assuage
The rugged hearts of those who prisoned thee,
Were they not deaf to all sweet melody;
This song shall be thy rose: its petals pale
Are dead, indeed, my adored Nightingale!
But soft and fragrant is the faded blossom,
And it has no thorn left to wound thy bosom.

High, spirit-wingèd Heart! who dost forever
Beat thine unfeeling bars with vain endeavour,
Till those bright plumes of thought, in which arrayed
It oversoared this low and worldly shade,
Lie shattered; and thy panting, wounded breast
Stains with dear blood its unmaternal nest!
I weep vain tears: blood would less bitter be,
Yet poured forth gladlier, could it profit thee.

Seraph of Heaven! too gentle to be human,
Veiling beneath that radiant form of Woman
All that is insupportable in thee
Of light, and love, and immortality!
Sweet Benediction in the eternal Curse!
Veiled Glory of this lampless Universe!
Thou Moon beyond the clouds! Thou living Form
Among the Dead! Thou Star above the Storm!
Thou Wonder, and thou Beauty, and thou Terror!

Thou Harmony of Nature's art! Thou Mirror
In whom, as in the splendour of the Sun,
All shapes look glorious which thou gazest on!
Ay, even the dim words which obscure thee now
Flash, lightning-like, with unaccustomed glow;
I pray thee that thou blot from this sad song
All of its much mortality and wrong,
With those clear drops, which start like sacred dew
From the twin lights thy sweet soul darkens through,
Weeping, till sorrow becomes ecstasy:
Then smile on it, so that it may not die.

I never thought before my death to see
Youth's vision thus made perfect. Emily,
I love thee; though the world by no thin name
Will hide that love from its unvalued shame.°
Would we two had been twins of the same mother!°
Or, that the name my heart lent to another
Could be a sister's bond for her and thee,
Blending two beams of one eternity!
Yet were one lawful and the other true,
These names, though dear, could paint not, as is due,
How beyond refuge I am thine. Ah me!
I am not thine: I am a part of *thee*.

Sweet Lamp! my moth-like Muse has burnt its wings;
Or, like a dying swan who soars and sings,
Young Love should teach Time, in his own grey style,°
All that thou art. Art thou not void of guile,
A lovely soul formed to be blessed and bless?
A well of sealed and secret happiness,°
Whose waters like blithe light and music are,
Vanquishing dissonance and gloom? A Star°
Which moves not in the moving Heavens, alone?
A smile amid dark frowns? a gentle tone
Amid rude voices? a beloved light?
A Solitude, a Refuge, a Delight?
A lute, which those whom love has taught to play
Make music on, to soothe the roughest day
And lull fond grief asleep? a buried treasure?
A cradle of young thoughts of wingless pleasure?

A violet-shrouded grave of Woe?—I measure
The world of fancies, seeking one like thee,
And find—alas! mine own infirmity.

She met me, Stranger, upon life's rough way,°
And lured me towards sweet Death; as Night by Day,
Winter by Spring, or Sorrow by swift Hope,
Led into light, life, peace. An antelope,
In the suspended impulse of its lightness,
Were less ethereally light: the brightness
Of her divinest presence trembles through
Her limbs, as underneath a cloud of dew
Embodied in the windless Heaven of June
Amid the splendour-wingèd stars, the Moon
Burns, inextinguishably beautiful:
And from her lips, as from a hyacinth full
Of honey-dew, a liquid murmur drops,
Killing the sense with passion; sweet as stops°
Of planetary music heard in trance.
In her mild lights the starry spirits dance,
The sunbeams of those wells which ever leap
Under the lightnings of the soul—too deep
For the brief fathom-line of thought or sense.
The glory of her being, issuing thence,
Stains the dead, blank, cold air with a warm shade
Of unentangled intermixture, made
By Love, of light and motion: one intense
Diffusion, one serene Omnipresence,
Whose flowing outlines mingle in their flowing
Around her cheeks and utmost fingers glowing
With the unintermitted blood, which there
Quivers (as in a fleece of snow-like air
The crimson pulse of living morning quiver),°
Continuously prolonged, and ending never,
Till they are lost, and in that Beauty furled
Which penetrates and clasps and fills the world;
Scarce visible from extreme loveliness.
Warm fragrance seems to fall from her light dress,
And her loose hair; and where some heavy tress
The air of her own speed has disentwined,
The sweetness seems to satiate the faint wind;

And in the soul a wild odour is felt,
Beyond the sense, like fiery dews that melt
Into the bosom of a frozen bud.—
See where she stands! a mortal shape indued
With love and life and light and deity,
And motion which may change but cannot die;
An image of some bright Eternity;
A shadow of some golden dream; a Splendour
Leaving the third sphere pilotless; a tender°
Reflection of the eternal Moon of Love
Under whose motions life's dull billows move;
A Metaphor of Spring and Youth and Morning;
A Vision like incarnate April, warning,
With smiles and tears, Frost the Anatomy°
Into his summer grave.

Ah, woe is me!
What have I dared? where am I lifted? how
Shall I descend, and perish not? I know
That Love makes all things equal: I have heard
By mine own heart this joyous truth averred:
The spirit of the worm beneath the sod,
In love and worship, blends itself with God.

Spouse! Sister! Angel! Pilot of the Fate
Whose course has been so starless! O too late
Beloved! O too soon adored, by me!
For in the fields of immortality
My spirit should at first have worshipped thine,
A divine presence in a place divine;
Or should have moved beside it on this earth,
A shadow of that substance, from its birth;
But not as now:—I love thee; yes, I feel
That on the fountain of my heart a seal
Is set, to keep its waters pure and bright
For thee, since in those *tears* thou hast delight.
We—are we not formed, as notes of music are,
For one another, though dissimilar;
Such difference without discord, as can make
Those sweetest sounds, in which all spirits shake
As trembling leaves in a continuous air?

Thy wisdom speaks in me, and bids me dare
Beacon the rocks on which high hearts are wrecked.
I never was attached to that great sect,
Whose doctrine is, that each one should select
Out of the crowd a mistress or a friend,
And all the rest, though fair and wise, commend
To cold oblivion, though it is in the code
Of modern morals, and the beaten road
Which those poor slaves with weary footsteps tread,
Who travel to their home among the dead
By the broad highway of the world, and so
With one chained friend, perhaps a jealous foe,
The dreariest and the longest journey go.

True Love in this differs from gold and clay,
That to divide is not to take away.
Love is like understanding, that grows bright.
Gazing on many truths; 'tis like thy light.
Imagination! which from earth and sky,
And from the depths of human fantasy,
As from a thousand prisms and mirrors, fills
The Universe with glorious beams, and kills
Error, the worm, with many a sun-like arrow
Of its reverberated lightning. Narrow
The heart that loves, the brain that contemplates,
The life that wears, the spirit that creates
One object, and one form, and builds thereby
A sepulchre for its eternity.°

Mind from its object differs most in this:
Evil from good; misery from happiness;
The baser from the nobler; the impure
And frail, from what is clear and must endure.
If you divide suffering and dross, you may
Diminish till it is consumed away;
If you divide pleasure and love and thought,
Each part exceeds the whole; and we know not
How much, while any yet remains unshared,
Of pleasure may be gained, of sorrow spared:
This truth is that deep well, whence sages draw
The unenvied light of hope; the eternal law°
By which those live, to whom this world of life

Is as a garden ravaged, and whose strife
Tills for the promise of a later birth
The wilderness of this Elysian earth.

There was a Being whom my spirit oft
Met on its visioned wanderings, far aloft,
In the clear golden prime of my youth's dawn,
Upon the fairy isles of sunny lawn,
Amid the enchanted mountains, and the caves
Of divine sleep, and on the air-like waves
Of wonder-level dream, whose tremulous floor
Paved her light steps;—on an imagined shore.
Under the grey beak of some promontory
She met me, robed in such exceeding glory,
That I beheld her not. In solitudes
Her voice came to me through the whispering woods,
And from the fountains, and the odours deep
Of flowers, which, like lips murmuring in their sleep
Of the sweet kisses which had lulled them there,
Breathed but of *her* to the enamoured air;
And from the breezes whether low or loud,
And from the rain of every passing cloud,
And from the singing of the summer-birds,
And from all sounds, all silence. In the words
Of antique verse and high romance,—in form
Sound, colour—in whatever checks that Storm
Which with the shattered present chokes the past;
And in that best philosophy, whose taste°
Makes this cold common hell, our life, a doom
As glorious as a fiery martyrdom;
Her Spirit was the harmony of truth.—

Then, from the caverns of my dreamy youth
I sprang, as one sandalled with plumes of fire,
And towards the lodestar of my one desire,
I flitted, like a dizzy moth, whose flight
Is as a dead leaf's in the owlet light,
When it would seek in Hesper's setting sphere°
A radiant death, a fiery sepulchre,
As if it were a lamp of earthly flame.—
But She, whom prayers or tears then could not tame,

Passed, like a God throned on a wingèd planet,
Whose burning plumes to tenfold swiftness fan it,
Into the dreary cone of our life's shade;
And as a man with mighty loss dismayed,
I would have followed, though the grave between
Yawned like a gulf whose spectres are unseen:
When a voice said:—'O Thou of hearts the weakest,
The phantom is beside thee whom thou seekest.'
Then I—'Where?'—the world's echo answered 'where!'
And in that silence, and in my despair,
I questioned every tongueless wind that flew
Over my tower of mourning, if it knew
Whither 'twas fled, this soul out of my soul;
And murmured names and spells which have control
Over the sightless tyrants of our fate;
But neither prayer nor verse could dissipate
The night which closed on her; nor uncreate
That world within this Chaos, mine and me,
Of which she was the veiled Divinity,
The world I say of thoughts that worshipped her:
And therefore I went forth, with hope and fear
And every gentle passion sick to death,
Feeding my course with expectation's breath,
Into the wintry forest of our life;°
And struggling through its error with vain strife,
And stumbling in my weakness and my haste,
And half bewildered by new forms, I passed
Seeking among those untaught foresters
If I could find one form resembling hers,
In which she might have masked herself from me.
There,—One, whose voice was venomed melody
Sate by a well, under blue nightshade bowers;
The breath of her false mouth was like faint flowers,
Her touch was as electric poison,—flame
Out of her looks into my vitals came,
And from her living cheeks and bosom flew
A killing air, which pierced like honey-dew
Into the core of my green heart, and lay
Upon its leaves; until, as hair grown grey
O'er a young brow, they hid its unblown prime
With ruins of unseasonable time.

In many mortal forms I rashly sought
The shadow of that idol of my thought.°
And some were fair—but beauty dies away:
Others were wise—but honeyed words betray:
And One was true—oh! why not true to me?
Then, as a hunted deer that could not flee,
I turned upon my thoughts, and stood at bay,
Wounded and weak and panting; the cold day
Trembled, for pity of my strife and pain.
When, like a noon-day dawn, there shone again
Deliverance. One stood on my path who seemed°
As like the glorious shape which I had dreamed,
As is the Moon, whose changes ever run
Into themselves, to the eternal Sun;
The cold chaste Moon, the Queen of Heaven's bright isles,
Who makes all beautiful on which she smiles,
That wandering shrine of soft yet icy flame
Which ever is transformed, yet still the same,
And warms not but illumines. Young and fair
As the descended Spirit of that sphere,
She hid me, as the Moon may hide the night
From its own darkness, until all was bright
Between the Heaven and Earth of my calm mind,
And, as a cloud charioted by the wind,
She led me to a cave in that wild place,
And sate beside me, with her downward face
Illumining my slumbers, like the Moon
Waxing and waning o'er Endymion.
And I was laid asleep, spirit and limb,°
And all my being became bright or dim
As the Moon's image in a summer sea,
According as she smiled or frowned on me;
And there I lay, within a chaste cold bed:
Alas, I then was nor alive nor dead:—
For at her silver voice came Death and Life,
Unmindful each of their accustomed strife,
Masked like twin babes, a sister and a brother,
The wandering hopes of one abandoned mother,°
And through the cavern without wings they flew,
And cried 'Away, he is not of our crew.'
I wept, and though it be a dream, I weep.

What storms then shook the ocean of my sleep,
Blotting that Moon, whose pale and waning lips
Then shrank as in the sickness of eclipse;—
And how my soul was as a lampless sea,
And who was then its Tempest;° and when She,°
The Planet of that hour, was quenched, what frost
Crept o'er those waters, till from coast to coast
The moving billows of my being fell
Into a death of ice, immoveable;—
And then—what earthquakes made it gape and split,
The white Moon smiling all the while on it,
These words conceal:—If not, each word would be°
The key of staunchless tears. Weep not for me!

At length, into the obscure Forest came
The Vision I had sought through grief and shame.
Athwart that wintry wilderness of thorns
Flashed from her motion splendour like the Morn's,
And from her presence life was radiated
Through the grey earth and branches bare and dead;
So that her way was paved, and roofed above
With flowers as soft as thoughts of budding love;
And music from her respiration spread
Like light,—all other sounds were penetrated
By the small, still, sweet spirit of that sound,
So that the savage winds hung mute around;
And odours warm and fresh fell from her hair
Dissolving the dull cold in the froze air:
Soft as an Incarnation of the Sun,
When light is changed to love, this glorious One
Floated into the cavern where I lay,
And called my Spirit, and the dreaming clay
Was lifted by the thing that dreamed below
As smoke by fire, and in her beauty's glow
I stood, and felt the dawn of my long night
Was penetrating me with living light:
I knew it was the Vision veiled from me
So many years—that it was Emily.

Twin Spheres of light who rule this passive Earth,°
This world of love, this *me*; and into birth

Awaken all its fruits and flowers, and dart
Magnetic might into its central heart;
And lift its billows and its mists, and guide
By everlasting laws, each wind and tide
To its fit cloud, and its appointed cave;
And lull its storms, each in the craggy grave
Which was its cradle, luring to faint bowers
The armies of the rainbow-wingèd showers;
And, as those married lights, which from the towers
Of Heaven look forth and fold the wandering globe
In liquid sleep and splendour, as a robe;
And all their many-mingled influence blend,
If equal, yet unlike, to one sweet end;—
So ye, bright regents, with alternate sway
Govern my sphere of being, night and day!
Thou, not disdaining even a borrowed might;
Thou, not eclipsing a remoter light;
And, through the shadow of the seasons three,
From Spring to Autumn's sere maturity,
Light it into the Winter of the tomb,
Where it may ripen to a brighter bloom.
Thou too, O Comet beautiful and fierce,
Who drew the heart of this frail Universe
Towards thine own; till, wrecked in that convulsion,
Alternating attraction and repulsion.
Thine went astray and that was rent in twain;
Oh, float into our azure heaven again!°
Be there love's folding-star at thy return;
The living Sun will feed thee from its urn
Of golden fire; the Moon will veil her horn
In thy last smiles; adoring Even and Morn
Will worship thee with incense of calm breath
And lights and shadows; as the star of Death
And Birth is worshipped by those sisters wild
Called Hope and Fear—upon the heart are piled
Their offerings,—of this sacrifice divine
A World shall be the altar.

Lady mine,
Scorn not these flowers of thought, the fading birth
Which from its heart of hearts that plant puts forth

Whose fruit, made perfect by thy sunny eyes,
Will be as of the trees of Paradise.

The day is come, and thou wilt fly with me.
To whatsoe'er of dull mortality
Is mine, remain a vestal sister still;
To the intense, the deep, the imperishable,
Not mine but me, henceforth be thou united
Even as a bride, delighting and delighted.
The hour is come:—the destined Star has risen
Which shall descend upon a vacant prison.
The walls are high, the gates are strong, thick set
The sentinels—but true love never yet
Was thus constrained: it overleaps all fence:
Like lightning, with invisible violence
Piercing its continents; like Heaven's free breath,
Which he who grasps can hold not; liker Death,
Who rides upon a thought, and makes his way
Through temple, tower, and palace, and the array
Of arms: more strength has Love than he or they;
For it can burst his charnel, and make free
The limbs in chains, the heart in agony,
The soul in dust and chaos.

Emily,
A ship is floating in the harbour now,
A wind is hovering o'er the mountain's brow;
There is a path on the sea's azure floor,
No keel has ever ploughed that path before;
The halcyons brood around the foamless isles;°
The treacherous Ocean has forsworn its wiles;
The merry mariners are bold and free:
Say, my heart's sister, wilt thou sail with me?
Our bark is as an albatross, whose nest
Is a far Eden of the purple East;
And we between her wings will sit, while Night
And Day, and Storm, and Calm, pursue their flight,
Our ministers, along the boundless Sea,
Treading each other's heels, unheededly.
It is an isle under Ionian skies,°
Beautiful as a wreck of Paradise,

And, for the harbours are not safe and good,
This land would have remained a solitude
But for some pastoral people native there,
Who from the Elysian, clear, and golden air
Draw the last spirit of the age of gold,
Simple and spirited; innocent and bold.
The blue Aegean girds this chosen home,
With ever-changing sound and light and foam,
Kissing the sifted sands, and caverns hoar;
And all the winds wandering along the shore
Undulate with the undulating tide:
There are thick woods where sylvan forms abide;
And many a fountain, rivulet, and pond,
As clear as elemental diamond,
Or serene morning air; and far beyond,
The mossy tracks made by the goats and deer
(Which the rough shepherd treads but once a year),
Pierce into glades, caverns, and bowers, and halls
Built round with ivy, which the waterfalls
Illumining, with sound that never fails
Accompany the noon-day nightingales;
And all the place is peopled with sweet airs;°
The light clear element which the isle wears
Is heavy with the scent of lemon-flowers,
Which floats like mist laden with unseen showers,
And falls upon the eyelids like faint sleep;
And from the moss violets and jonquils peep,
And dart their arrowy odour through the brain
Till you might faint with that delicious pain.
And every motion, odour, beam, and tone,
With that deep music is in unison:
Which is a soul within the soul—they seem
Like echoes of an antenatal dream.—
It is an isle 'twixt Heaven, Air, Earth, and Sea,
Cradled, and hung in clear tranquillity;
Bright as that wandering Eden Lucifer,°
Washed by the soft blue Oceans of young air.
It is a favoured place. Famine or Blight,
Pestilence, War and Earthquake, never light
Upon its mountain-peaks; blind vultures, they
Sail onward far upon their fatal way:

The wingèd storms, chanting their thunder-psalm
To other lands, leave azure chasms of calm
Over this isle, or weep themselves in dew,
From which its fields and woods ever renew
Their green and golden immortality.
And from the sea there rise, and from the sky
There fall, clear exhalations, soft and bright,
Veil after veil, each hiding some delight,
Which Sun or Moon or zephyr draw aside,
Till the isle's beauty, like a naked bride
Glowing at once with love and loveliness,
Blushes and trembles at its own excess:
Yet, like a buried lamp, a Soul no less
Burns in the heart of this delicious isle,
An atom of th' Eternal, whose own smile
Unfolds itself, and may be felt not seen
O'er the grey rocks, blue waves, and forests green,
Filling their bare and void interstices.—
But the chief marvel of the wilderness
Is a lone dwelling, built by whom or how
None of the rustic island-people know:
'Tis not a tower of strength, though with its height
It overtops the woods; but, for delight,
Some wise and tender Ocean-King, ere crime
Had been invented, in the world's young prime,
Reared it, a wonder of that simple time,
An envy of the isles, a pleasure-house
Made sacred to his sister and his spouse.°
It scarce seems now a wreck of human art,
But, as it were Titanic; in the heart
Of Earth having assumed its form, then grown
Out of the mountains, from the living stone,
Lifting itself in caverns light and high:
For all the antique and learned imagery
Has been erased, and in the place of it
The ivy and the wild-vine interknit
The volumes of their many twining stems;
Parasite flowers illume with dewy gems
The lampless halls, and when they fade, the sky
Peeps through their winter-woof of tracery
With moonlight patches, or star atoms keen,

Or fragments of the day's intense serene;—
Working mosaic on their Parian floors.°
And, day and night, aloof, from the high towers
And terraces, the Earth and Ocean seem
To sleep in one another's arms, and dream
Of waves, flowers, clouds, woods, rocks, and all that we
Read in their smiles, and call reality.

This isle and house are mine, and I have vowed
Thee to be lady of the solitude.—
And I have fitted up some chambers there
Looking towards the golden Eastern air,
And level with the living winds, which flow
Like waves above the living waves below.—
I have sent books and music there, and all
Those instruments with which high spirits call
The future from its cradle, and the past
Out of its grave, and make the present last
In thoughts and joys which sleep, but cannot die,
Folded within their own eternity.
Our simple life wants little, and true taste
Hires not the pale drudge Luxury, to waste
The scene it would adorn, and therefore still,
Nature, with all her children, haunts the hill.
The ring-dove, in the embowering ivy, yet
Keeps up her love-lament, and the owls flit
Round the evening tower, and the young stars glance
Between the quick bats in their twilight dance;
The spotted deer bask in the fresh moonlight
Before our gate, and the slow, silent night
Is measured by the pants of their calm sleep.
Be this our home in life, and when years heap
Their withered hours, like leaves, on our decay,
Let us become the overhanging day,
The living soul of this Elysian isle,
Conscious, inseparable, one. Meanwhile°
We two will rise, and sit, and walk together,
Under the roof of blue Ionian weather,
And wander in the meadows, or ascend
The mossy mountains, where the blue heavens bend
With lightest winds, to touch their paramour;

Or linger, where the pebble-paven shore,
Under the quick, faint kisses of the sea
Trembles and sparkles as with ecstasy,—
Possessing and possessed by all that is
Within that calm circumference of bliss,
And by each other, till to love and live
Be one:—or, at the noontide hour, arrive
Where some old cavern hoar seems yet to keep
The moonlight of the expired night asleep,
Through which the awakened day can never peep;
A veil for our seclusion, close as Night's,
Where secure sleep may kill thine innocent lights;
Sleep, the fresh dew of languid love, the rain
Whose drops quench kisses till they burn again.
And we will talk, until thought's melody
Become too sweet for utterance, and it die
In words, to live again in looks, which dart
With thrilling tone into the voiceless heart,
Harmonizing silence without a sound.
Our breath shall intermix, our bosoms bound.
And our veins beat together; and our lips
With other eloquence than words, eclipse
The soul that burns between them, and the wells
Which boil under our being's inmost cells,
The fountains of our deepest life, shall be
Confused in passion's golden purity,
As mountain-springs under the morning Sun.
We shall become the same, we shall be one
Spirit within two frames, oh! wherefore two?
One passion in twin-hearts, which grows and grew,
Till, like two meteors of expanding flame,
Those spheres instinct with it become the same,
Touch, mingle, are transfigured; ever still
Burning, yet ever inconsumable:
In one another's substance finding food,
Like flames too pure and light and unimbued
To nourish their bright lives with baser prey,
Which point to Heaven and cannot pass away:
One hope within two wills, one will beneath
Two overshadowing minds, one life, one death,
One Heaven, one Hell, one immortality,

And one annihilation. Woe is me!
The wingèd words on which my soul would pierce
Into the height of love's rare Universe,
Are chains of lead around its flight of fire.—
I pant, I sink, I tremble, I expire!

Weak Verses, go, kneel at your Sovereign's feet,
And say:—'We are the masters of thy slave;
What wouldest thou with us and ours and thine?'
Then call your sisters from Oblivion's cave,
All singing loud: 'Love's very pain is sweet,
But its reward is in the world divine
Which, if not here, it builds beyond the grave.'
So shall ye live when I am there. Then haste
Over the hearts of men, until ye meet
Marina, Vanna, Primus, and the rest,°
And bid them love each other and be blessed:
And leave the troop which errs, and which reproves,
And come and be my guest,—for I am Love's.°

ADONAIS

AN ELEGY ON THE DEATH OF JOHN KEATS, AUTHOR OF 'ENDYMION', 'HYPERION' ETC.

Αστήρ πρὶν μέν ἔλαμπες ενι ζώοισιν εῶος.
Νυν δε θανῶν, λαμπεις ἕσπερος εν φθίμενοις.

Plato°

PREFACE°

Φάρμακον ἦλθε, Βίων, ποτι σον στομα, φάρμακον ἔιδες
Πῶς τευ τοῖς χέιλεσσι ποτεδραμε, κοὐκ εγλυκανθη;
Τις δὲ Θροτος τοσσοῦτον ἀνάμερος, ἢ κερκσαι τοι,
Ἠ δοῦναι λσλέοντι το φάρμακον; ἔκφυγεν ὠδαν.

Moschus, *Epitaph. Bion.*°

It is my intention to subjoin to the London edition of this poem a criticism upon the claims of its lamented object to be classed among the writers of the highest genius who have adorned our age. My known repugnance to the narrow principles of taste on which several of his earlier compositions were modelled prove° at least that I am an impartial judge. I consider the fragment of *Hyperion*,° as second to nothing that was ever produced by a writer of the same years.

John Keats, died at Rome of a consumption, in his twenty-fourth year, on the —— of —— 1821;° and was buried in the romantic and lonely cemetery of the protestants° in that city, under the pyramid which is the tomb of Cestius, and the massy walls and towers, now mouldering and desolate, which formed the circuit of ancient Rome. The cemetery is an open space among the ruins, covered in winter with violets and daisies. It might make one in love with death,° to think that one should be buried in so sweet a place.

The genius of the lamented person to whose memory I have dedicated these unworthy verses, was not less delicate and fragile than it was beautiful; and where canker-worms abound, what wonder, if its young flower was blighted in the bud? The savage criticism on his *Endymion*, which appeared in the *Quarterly Review*, produced the most violent effect on his susceptible mind; the agitation thus originated ended in the rupture of a blood-vessel in the lungs; a rapid consumption ensued, and the succeeding acknowledgements from more candid critics, of the true greatness of his powers, were ineffectual to heal the wound thus wantonly inflicted.

It may be well said, that these wretched men know not what they do.° They scatter their insults and their slanders without heed as to whether the poisoned shaft lights on a heart made callous by many blows, or one like Keats's composed of more penetrable stuff.° One of their associates is, to my knowledge, a most base and unprincipled calumniator.° As to *Endymion*; was it a poem, whatever might be its defects, to be treated contemptuously by those who had celebrated with various degrees of complacency and panegyric, *Paris*, and *Woman*, and a *Syrian Tale*, and Mrs Lefanu, and Mr Barrett, and Mr Howard Payne,° and a long list of the illustrious obscure? Are these the men, who in their venal good nature, presumed to draw a parallel between the Rev. Mr Milman° and Lord Byron? What gnat did they strain at here, after having swallowed all those camels?° Against what woman taken in adultery dares the foremost of these literary prostitutes to cast his opprobrious stone?° Miserable man! you, one of the meanest, have wantonly defaced one of the noblest specimens of the workmanship of God. Nor shall it be your excuse, that, murderer as you are, you have spoken daggers, but used none.°

The circumstances of the closing scene of poor Keats's life were not made known to me until the Elegy was ready for the press.° I am given to understand that the wound which his sensitive spirit had received from the criticism of *Endymion* was exasperated by the bitter sense of unrequited benefits; the poor fellow seems to have been hooted from the stage of life, no less by those on whom he had wasted the promise of his genius, than those on whom he had lavished his fortune and his care. He was accompanied to Rome, and attended in his last illness by Mr Severn,° a young artist of the highest promise, who, I have been informed, 'almost risked his own life, and sacrificed every prospect to unwearied attendance upon his dying friend.' Had I known these circumstances before the completion of my poem, I should have been tempted to add my feeble tribute of applause to the more solid recompense which the virtuous man finds in the recollection of his own motives. Mr Severn can dispense with a reward from 'such stuff as dreams are made of.'° His conduct is a golden augury of the success of his future career—may the unextinguished Spirit of his illustrious friend animate the creations of his pencil, and plead against Oblivion for his name!

I

I weep for Adonais—he is dead!
O, weep for Adonais! though our tears°
Thaw not the frost which binds so dear a head!
And thou, sad Hour, selected from all years
To mourn our loss, rouse thy obscure compeers,°
And teach them thine own sorrow, say: with me
Died Adonais; till the Future dares
Forget the Past, his fate and fame shall be
An echo and a light unto eternity!

2

Where wert thou mighty Mother, when he lay,°
When thy Son lay, pierced by the shaft which flies
In darkness? where was lorn Urania°
When Adonais died? With veilèd eyes,
'Mid listening Echoes, in her Paradise
She sate, while one, with soft enamoured breath,
Rekindled all the fading melodies,
With which, like flowers that mock the corse beneath,°
He had adorned and hid the coming bulk of death.

3

O, weep for Adonais—he is dead!
Wake, melancholy Mother, wake and weep!
Yet wherefore? Quench within their burning bed
Thy fiery tears, and let thy loud heart keep
Like his, a mute and uncomplaining sleep;
For he is gone, where all things wise and fair
Descend;—oh, dream not that the amorous Deep°
Will yet restore him to the vital air;
Death feeds on his mute voice, and laughs at our despair.

4

Most musical of mourners, weep again!
Lament anew, Urania!—He died,
Who was the Sire of an immortal strain,
Blind, old, and lonely, when his country's pride
The priest, the slave, and the liberticide
Trampled and mocked with many a loathèd rite

Of lust and blood; he went, unterrified,
Into the gulf of death; but his clear Sprite
Yet reigns o'er earth; the third among the sons of light.°

5

Most musical of mourners, weep anew!
Not all to that bright station dared to climb;
And happier they their happiness who knew,
Whose tapers yet burn through that night of time
In which suns perished; others more sublime,°
Struck by the envious wrath of man or God,
Have sunk, extinct in their refulgent prime;
And some yet live, treading the thorny road,
Which leads, through toil and hate, to Fame's serene abode.

6

But now, thy youngest, dearest one, has perished,
The nursling of thy widowhood, who grew,
Like a pale flower by some sad maiden cherished,
And fed with true love tears, instead of dew;°
Most musical of mourners, weep anew!
Thy extreme hope, the loveliest and the last,°
The bloom, whose petals nipped before they blew
Died on the promise of the fruit, is waste;
The broken lily lies—the storm is overpast.

7

To that high Capital, where kingly Death°
Keeps his pale court in beauty and decay,
He came; and bought, with price of purest breath,
A grave among the eternal.—Come away!
Haste, while the vault of blue Italian day
Is yet his fitting charnel-roof! while still
He lies, as if in dewy sleep he lay;
Awake him not! surely he takes his fill
Of deep and liquid rest, forgetful of all ill.°

8

He will awake no more, oh, never more!—
Within the twilight chamber spreads apace

The shadow of white Death, and at the door
Invisible Corruption waits to trace
His extreme way to her dim dwelling-place;
The eternal Hunger sits, but pity and awe
Soothe her pale rage, nor dares she to deface
So fair a prey, till darkness, and the law
Of change, shall o'er his sleep the mortal curtain draw.°

9

O, weep for Adonais!—The quick Dreams,
The passion-wingèd Ministers of thought,
Who were his flocks, whom near the living streams°
Of his young spirit he fed, and whom he taught
The love which was its music, wander not,—
Wander no more, from kindling brain to brain,
But droop there, whence they sprung; and mourn their lot
Round the cold heart, where, after their sweet pain,°
They ne'er will gather strength, or find a home again.

10

And one with trembling hands clasps his cold head,
And fans him with her moonlight wings, and cries;
'Our love, our hope, our sorrow, is not dead;°
See, on the silken fringe of his faint eyes,
Like dew upon a sleeping flower, there lies
A tear some Dream has loosened from his brain.'
Lost Angel of a ruined Paradise!
She knew not 'twas her own; as with no stain
She faded, like a cloud which had outwept its rain.

11

One from a lucid urn of starry dew
Washed his light limbs as if embalming them;
Another clipped her profuse locks, and threw
The wreath upon him, like an anadem,°
Which frozen tears instead of pearls begem;
Another in her wilful grief would break
Her bow and wingèd reeds, as if to stem
A greater loss with one which was more weak;
And dull the barbèd fire against his frozen cheek.

12

Another Splendour on his mouth alit,°
That mouth, whence it was wont to draw the breath
Which gave it strength to pierce the guarded wit,
And pass into the panting heart beneath
With lightning and with music: the damp death
Quenched its caress upon his icy lips;
And, as a dying meteor stains a wreath
Of moonlight vapour, which the cold night clips,°
It flushed through his pale limbs, and passed to its eclipse.

13

And others came . . . Desires and Adorations,
Wingèd Persuasions and veiled Destinies,
Splendours, and Glooms, and glimmering Incarnations
Of hopes and fears, and twilight Fantasies;
And Sorrow, with her family of Sighs,
And Pleasure, blind with tears, led by the gleam
Of her own dying smile instead of eyes,
Came in slow pomp;—the moving pomp might seem
Like pageantry of mist on an autumnal stream.

14

All he had loved, and moulded into thought,
From shape, and hue, and odour, and sweet sound,
Lamented Adonais. Morning sought
Her eastern watchtower, and her hair unbound,
Wet with the tears which should adorn the ground,
Dimmed the aerial eyes that kindle day;
Afar the melancholy thunder moaned,
Pale Ocean in unquiet slumber lay,
And the wild winds flew round, sobbing in their dismay.

15

Lost Echo sits amid the voiceless mountains,
And feeds her grief with his remembered lay,
And will no more reply to winds or fountains,
Or amorous birds perched on the young green spray,
Or herdsman's horn, or bell at closing day;
Since she can mimic not his lips, more dear

Than those for whose disdain she pined away
Into a shadow of all sounds:—a dear
Murmur, between their songs, is all the woodmen hear.°

16

Grief made the young Spring wild, and she threw down
Her kindling buds, as if she Autumn were,
Or they dead leaves; since her delight is flown
For whom should she have waked the sullen year?
To Phoebus was not Hyacinth so dear
Nor to himself Narcissus, as to both
Thou Adonais: wan they stand and sere
Amid the drooping comrades of their youth,
With dew all turned to tears; odour, to sighing ruth.

17

Thy spirit's sister, the lorn nightingale
Mourns not her mate with such melodious pain;°
Not so the eagle, who like thee could scale
Heaven, and could nourish in the sun's domain
Her mighty youth with morning, doth complain,
Soaring and screaming round her empty nest,
As Albion wails for thee: the curse of Cain°
Light on his head who pierced thy innocent breast,
And scared the angel soul that was its earthly guest!

18

Ah woe is me! Winter is come and gone,
But grief returns with the revolving year;
The airs and streams renew their joyous tone;
The ants, the bees, the swallows reappear;
Fresh leaves and flowers deck the dead Seasons' bier;
The amorous birds now pair in every brake,
And build their mossy homes in field and brere;°
And the green lizard, and the golden snake,
Like unimprisoned flames, out of their trance awake.

19

Through wood and stream and field and hill and Ocean
A quickening life from the Earth's heart has burst

As it has ever done, with change and motion,
From the great morning of the world when first
God dawned on Chaos; in its steam immersed
The lamps of Heaven flash with a softer light;
All baser things pant with life's sacred thirst;
Diffuse themselves; and spend in love's delight,
The beauty and the joy of their renewèd might.

20

The leprous corpse touched by this spirit tender
Exhales itself in flowers of gentle breath;
Like incarnations of the stars, when splendour
Is changed to fragrance, they illumine death
And mock the merry worm that wakes beneath;
Nought we know, dies. Shall that alone which knows°
Be as a sword consumed before the sheath
By sightless lightning?—th' intense atom glows°
A moment, then is quenched in a most cold repose.

21

Alas! that all we loved of him should be,
But for our grief, as if it had not been,
And grief itself be mortal! Woe is me!
Whence are we, and why are we? of what scene
The actors or spectators? Great and mean
Meet massed in death, who lends what life must borrow.
As long as skies are blue, and fields are green,
Evening must usher night, night urge the morrow,
Month follow month with woe, and year wake year to sorrow.

22

He will awake no more, oh, never more!
'Wake thou,' cried Misery, 'childless Mother, rise
Out of thy sleep, and slake, in thy heart's core,
A wound more fierce than his with tears and sighs.'
And all the Dreams that watched Urania's eyes,
And all the Echoes whom their sister's song°
Had held in holy silence, cried: 'Arise!'
Swift as a Thought by the snake Memory stung,
From her ambrosial rest the fading Splendour sprung.°

23

She rose like an autumnal Night, that springs
Out of the East, and follows wild and drear
The golden Day, which, on eternal wings,
Even as a ghost abandoning a bier,
Had left the Earth a corpse. Sorrow and fear
So struck, so roused, so rapt Urania;
So saddened round her like an atmosphere
Of stormy mist; so swept her on her way
Even to the mournful place where Adonais lay.

24

Out of her secret Paradise she sped,°
Through camps and cities rough with stone, and steel,
And human hearts, which to her aery tread
Yielding not, wounded the invisible
Palms of her tender feet where'er they fell:°
And barbèd tongues, and thoughts more sharp than they
Rent the soft Form they never could repel,
Whose sacred blood, like the young tears of May,
Paved with eternal flowers that undeserving way.

25

In the death chamber for a moment Death,
Shamed by the presence of that living Might,
Blushed to annihilation, and the breath
Revisited those lips, and life's pale light
Flashed through those limbs, so late her dear delight.
'Leave me not wild and drear and comfortless,
As silent lightning leaves the starless night!
Leave me not!' cried Urania: her distress
Roused Death: Death rose and smiled, and met her vain caress.

26

'Stay yet awhile! speak to me once again;
Kiss me, so long but as a kiss may live;°
And in my heartless breast and burning brain°
That word, that kiss shall all thoughts else survive,
With food of saddest memory kept alive,
Now thou art dead, as if it were a part

Of thee, my Adonais! I would give
All that I am to be as thou now art!
But I am chained to Time, and cannot thence depart!

27

'Oh gentle child, beautiful as thou wert,
Why didst thou leave the trodden paths of men
Too soon, and with weak hands though mighty heart
Dare the unpastured dragon in his den?°
Defenceless as thou wert, oh where was then
Wisdom the mirrored shield, or scorn the spear?°
Or hadst thou waited the full cycle, when
Thy spirit should have filled its crescent sphere,
The monsters of life's waste had fled from thee like deer.

28

'The herded wolves, bold only to pursue;
The obscene ravens, clamorous o'er the dead;
The vultures to the conqueror's banner true
Who feed where Desolation first has fed,
And whose wings rain contagion;—how they fled,
When like Apollo, from his golden bow,
The Pythian of the age one arrow sped°
And smiled!—The spoilers tempt no second blow,
They fawn on the proud feet that spurn them lying low.

29

'The sun comes forth, and many reptiles spawn;
He sets, and each ephemeral insect then
Is gathered into death without a dawn,
And the immortal stars awake again;
So is it in the world of living men:
A godlike mind soars forth, in its delight
Making earth bare and veiling heaven, and when
It sinks, the swarms that dimmed or shared its light
Leave to its kindred lamps the spirit's awful night.'°

30

Thus ceased she: and the mountain shepherds came°
Their garlands sere, their magic mantles rent;

The Pilgrim of Eternity, whose fame°
Over his living head like Heaven is bent,
An early but enduring monument,
Came, veiling all the lightnings of his song
In sorrow; from her wilds Ierne sent°
The sweetest lyrist of her saddest wrong,°
And love taught grief to fall like music from his tongue.

31

Midst others of less note, came one frail Form,°
A phantom among men; companionless
As the last cloud of an expiring storm
Whose thunder is its knell; he, as I guess,
Had gazed on Nature's naked loveliness,
Actaeon-like, and now he fled astray°
With feeble steps o'er the world's wilderness,
And his own thoughts, along that rugged way,
Pursued, like raging hounds, their father and their prey.

32

A pardlike Spirit beautiful and swift—°
A Love in desolation masked;—a Power
Girt round with weakness;—it can scarce uplift
The weight of the superincumbent hour;°
It is a dying lamp, a falling shower,
A breaking billow;—even whilst we speak
Is it not broken? On the withering flower
The killing sun smiles brightly: on a cheek
The life can burn in blood, even while the heart may break.

33

His head was bound with pansies overblown,°
And faded violets, white, and pied, and blue;
And a light spear topped with a cypress cone,
Round whose rude shaft dark ivy tresses grew°
Yet dripping with the forest's noonday dew,
Vibrated, as the ever-beating heart
Shook the weak hand that grasped it; of that crew
He came the last, neglected and apart;
A herd-abandoned deer struck by the hunter's dart.°

34

All stood aloof, and at his partial moan°
Smiled through their tears; well knew that gentle band
Who in another's fate now wept his own;
As in the accents of an unknown land,
He sung new sorrow; sad Urania scanned
The Stranger's mien, and murmured: 'who art thou?'
He answered not, but with a sudden hand
Made bare his branded and ensanguined brow,
Which was like Cain's or Christ's—Oh! that it should be so!°

35

What softer voice is hushed over the dead?
Athwart what brow is that dark mantle thrown?
What form leans sadly o'er the white death-bed,
In mockery of monumental stone,
The heavy heart heaving without a moan?
If it be He, who, gentlest of the wise,°
Taught, soothed, loved, honoured the departed one;
Let me not vex, with inharmonious sighs
The silence of that heart's accepted sacrifice.

36

Our Adonais has drunk poison—oh!
What deaf and viperous murderer could crown
Life's early cup with such a draught of woe?
The nameless worm would now itself disown:°
It felt, yet could escape the magic tone
Whose prelude held all envy, hate, and wrong,
But what was howling in one breast alone,
Silent with expectation of the song,
Whose master's hand is cold, whose silver lyre unstrung.

37

Live thou, whose infamy is not thy fame!
Live! fear no heavier chastisement from me,
Thou noteless blot on a remembered name!°
But be thyself, and know thyself to be!
And ever at thy season be thou free
To spill the venom when thy fangs o'erflow:

Remorse and Self-contempt shall cling to thee;
Hot Shame shall burn upon thy secret brow,
And like a beaten hound tremble thou shalt—as now.

38

Nor let us weep that our delight is fled
Far from these carrion kites that scream below;
He wakes or sleeps with the enduring dead;°
Thou canst not soar where he is sitting now.—°
Dust to the dust! but the pure spirit shall flow°
Back to the burning fountain whence it came,°
A portion of the Eternal, which must glow
Through time and change, unquenchably the same,
Whilst thy cold embers choke the sordid hearth of shame.

39

Peace, peace! he is not dead, he doth not sleep—
He hath awakened from the dream of life—
'Tis we, who lost in stormy visions, keep
With phantoms an unprofitable strife,
And in mad trance, strike with our spirit's knife
Invulnerable nothings.—*We* decay
Like corpses in a charnel; fear and grief
Convulse us and consume us day by day,
And cold hopes swarm like worms within our living clay.

40

He has outsoared the shadow of our night;
Envy and calumny and hate and pain,
And that unrest which men miscall delight,
Can touch him not and torture not again;
From the contagion of the world's slow stain
He is secure, and now can never mourn
A heart grown cold, a head grown grey in vain;
Nor, when the spirit's self has ceased to burn,
With sparkless ashes load an unlamented urn.

41

He lives, he wakes—'tis Death is dead, not he;
Mourn not for Adonais.—Thou young Dawn°

Turn all thy dew to splendour, for from thee
The spirit thou lamentest is not gone;
Ye caverns and ye forests, cease to moan!
Cease ye faint flowers and fountains, and thou Air
Which like a mourning veil thy scarf hadst thrown
O'er the abandoned Earth, now leave it bare
Even to the joyous stars which smile on its despair!

42

He is made one with Nature: there is heard
His voice in all her music, from the moan
Of thunder, to the song of night's sweet bird;°
He is a presence to be felt and known
In darkness and in light, from herb and stone,
Spreading itself where'er that Power may move
Which has withdrawn his being to its own;
Which wields the world with never wearied love,
Sustains it from beneath, and kindles it above.

43

He is a portion of the loveliness
Which once he made more lovely: he doth bear
His part, while the one Spirit's plastic stress°
Sweeps through the dull dense world, compelling there
All new successions to the forms they wear;°
Torturing th'unwilling dross that checks its flight
To its own likeness, as each mass may bear;
And bursting in its beauty and its might
From trees and beasts and men into the Heaven's light.

44

The splendours of the firmament of time
May be eclipsed, but are extinguished not;
Like stars to their appointed height they climb
And death is a low mist which cannot blot
The brightness it may veil. When lofty thought
Lifts a young heart above its mortal lair,
And love and life contend in it, for what
Shall be its earthly doom, the dead live there
And move like winds of light on dark and stormy air.

45

The inheritors of unfulfilled renown°
Rose from their thrones, built beyond mortal thought,
Far in the Unapparent. Chatterton°
Rose pale, his solemn agony had not
Yet faded from him; Sidney, as he fought°
And as he fell and as he lived and loved
Sublimely mild, a Spirit without spot,
Arose; and Lucan, by his death approved:°
Oblivion as they rose shrank like a thing reproved.

46

And many more, whose names on Earth are dark
But whose transmitted effluence cannot die°
So long as fire outlives the parent spark,
Rose, robed in dazzling immortality.
'Thou art become as one of us,' they cry,
'It was for thee yon kingless sphere has long
Swung blind in unascended majesty,
Silent alone amid an Heaven of song.°
Assume thy wingèd throne, thou Vesper of our throng!'°

47

Who mourns for Adonais? oh come forth
Fond wretch! and know thyself and him aright.
Clasp with thy panting soul the pendulous Earth;°
As from a centre, dart thy spirit's light
Beyond all worlds, until its spacious might
Satiate the void circumference: then shrink
Even to a point within our day and night;
And keep thy heart light lest it make thee sink
When hope has kindled hope, and lured thee to the brink.°

48

Or go to Rome, which is the sepulchre°
O, not of him, but of our joy: 'tis nought
That ages, empires, and religions there
Lie buried in the ravage they have wrought;
For such as he can lend,—they borrow not
Glory from those who made the world their prey;

And he is gathered to the kings of thought
Who waged contention with their time's decay,
And of the past are all that cannot pass away.

49

Go thou to Rome,—at once the Paradise,
The grave, the city, and the wilderness;
And where its wrecks like shattered mountains rise,
And flowering weeds, and fragrant copses dress
The bones of Desolation's nakedness
Pass, till the Spirit of the spot shall lead
Thy footsteps to a slope of green access°
Where, like an infant's smile, over the dead,
A light of laughing flowers along the grass is spread.

50

And grey walls moulder round, on which dull Time°
Feeds, like slow fire upon a hoary brand;
And one keen pyramid with wedge sublime,°
Pavilioning the dust of him who planned
This refuge for his memory, doth stand
Like flame transformed to marble; and beneath,
A field is spread, on which a newer band
Have pitched in Heaven's smile their camp of death,
Welcoming him we lose with scarce extinguished breath.

51

Here pause: these graves are all too young as yet
To have outgrown the sorrow which consigned
Its charge to each; and if the seal is set,
Here, on one fountain of a mourning mind,
Break it not thou! too surely shalt thou find
Thine own well full, if thou returnest home,
Of tears and gall. From the world's bitter wind
Seek shelter in the shadow of the tomb.
What Adonais is, why fear we to become?

52

The One remains, the many change and pass;
Heaven's light forever shines, Earth's shadows fly;

Life, like a dome of many-coloured glass,
Stains the white radiance of Eternity,°
Until Death tramples it to fragments.—Die,°
If thou wouldst be with that which thou dost seek!
Follow where all is fled!—Rome's azure sky,
Flowers, ruins, statues, music, words, are weak
The glory they transfuse with fitting truth to speak.

53

Why linger, why turn back, why shrink, my Heart?
Thy hopes are gone before: from all things here
They have departed; thou shouldst now depart!
A light is passed from the revolving year,
And man, and woman; and what still is dear
Attracts to crush, repels to make thee wither.
The soft sky smiles,—the low wind whispers near:
'Tis Adonais calls! oh, hasten thither,
No more let Life divide what Death can join together.°

54

That Light whose smile kindles the Universe,°
That Beauty in which all things work and move,
That Benediction which the eclipsing Curse
Of birth can quench not, that sustaining Love
Which through the web of being blindly wove
By man and beast and earth and air and sea,
Burns bright or dim, as each are mirrors of
The fire for which all thirst, now beams on me,
Consuming the last clouds of cold mortality.°

55

The breath whose might I have invoked in song°
Descends on me; my spirit's bark is driven
Far from the shore, far from the trembling throng
Whose sails were never to the tempest given;°
The massy earth and spherèd skies are riven!
I am borne darkly, fearfully, afar;
Whilst burning through the inmost veil of Heaven,
The soul of Adonais, like a star,
Beacons from the abode where the Eternal are.

To Night

Swiftly walk o'er the western wave,
 Spirit of Night!
Out of the misty eastern cave
Where, all the long and lone daylight
Thou wovest dreams of joy and fear,
Which make thee terrible and dear,—
 Swift be thy flight!

Wrap thy form in a mantle grey,
 Star-inwrought!
Blind with thine hair the eyes of day,
Kiss her until she be wearied out—
Then wander o'er city and sea and land,
Touching all with thine opiate wand—
 Come, long-sought!

When I arose and saw the dawn
 I sighed for thee;
When Light rode high, and the dew was gone,
And noon lay heavy on flower and tree,
And the weary day turned to his rest,
Lingering like an unloved guest,
 I sighed for thee.

Thy brother Death came, and cried,
 'Wouldst thou me?'
Thy sweet child Sleep, the filmy-eyed,
Murmured like a noontide bee,
'Shall I nestle near thy side?
Wouldst thou me?' and I replied,
 'No, not thee!'

Death will come when thou art dead,
 Soon, too soon—
Sleep will come when thou art fled;
Of neither would I ask the boon
I ask of thee, beloved Night—
Swift be thine approaching flight,
 Come soon, soon!

The Aziola

'Do you not hear the Aziola cry?
Methinks she must be nigh—'
Said Mary as we sate
In dusk, ere stars were lit or candles brought—
And I who thought
This Aziola was some tedious woman
Asked, 'Who is Aziola?' How elate
I felt to know that it was nothing human,
No mockery of myself to fear or hate!—
And Mary saw my soul,
And laughed and said—'Disquiet yourself not,
'Tis nothing but a little downy owl.'

Sad Aziola, many an eventide
Thy music I had heard
By wood and stream, meadow and mountainside,
And fields and marshes wide,
Such as nor voice, nor lute, nor wind, nor bird
The soul ever stirred—
Unlike and far sweeter than them all.
Sad Aziola, from that moment, I
Loved thee and thy sad cry.

HELLAS

A LYRICAL DRAMA

Μάντις εἰμ' ἐσθλῶν ἀγώνων°

Oedip. Colon.

TO

HIS EXCELLENCY

PRINCE ALEXANDER MAVROCORDATO

LATE SECRETARY FOR FOREIGN AFFAIRS

TO THE HOSPODAR° OF WALLACHIA,

THE DRAMA OF HELLAS

IS INSCRIBED

AS AN IMPERFECT TOKEN

OF THE ADMIRATION, SYMPATHY, AND FRIENDSHIP

OF

THE AUTHOR.

PISA,
November 1st, 1821.

PREFACE

The poem of *Hellas*, written at the suggestion of the events of the moment, is a mere improvise; and derives its interest (should it be found to possess any) solely from the intense sympathy which the Author feels with the cause he would celebrate.

The subject, in its present state, is insusceptible of being treated otherwise than lyrically, and if I have called this poem a drama from the circumstance of its being composed in dialogue, the licence is not greater than that which has been assumed by other poets who have called their productions epics, only because they have been divided into twelve or twenty-four books.

The *Persae* of Aeschylus afforded me the first model of my conception, although the decision of the glorious contest now waging in Greece being yet suspended forbids a catastrophe parallel to the return of Xerxes and the desolation of the Persians. I have, therefore, contented myself with exhibiting a series of lyric pictures, and with having wrought upon the curtain of futurity, which falls upon the unfinished scene, such figures of indistinct and visionary delineation as suggest the final triumph of the Greek cause as a portion of the cause of civilization and social improvement.

The drama (if drama it must be called) is, however, so inartificial that I doubt whether, if recited on the Thespian waggon to an Athenian village at the Dionysiaca, it would have obtained the prize of the goat.° I shall bear with equanimity any punishment greater than the loss of such a reward which the Aristarchi of the hour° may think fit to inflict.

The only *goat-song* which I have yet attempted° has, I confess, in spite of the unfavourable nature of the subject, received a greater and a more valuable portion of applause than I expected or than it deserved.

Common fame is the only authority which I can allege for the details which form the basis of the poem, and I must trespass upon the forgiveness of my readers for the display of newspaper erudition° to which I have been reduced. Undoubtedly, until the conclusion of the war, it will be impossible to obtain an account of it sufficiently authentic for historical materials; but poets have their privilege, and it is unquestionable that actions of the most exalted courage have been performed by the Greeks, that they have gained more than one naval victory, and that their defeat in Wallachia° was signalized by circumstances of heroism more glorious even than victory.

The apathy of the rulers of the civilized world to the astonishing circumstance of the descendants of that nation to which they owe their civilization, rising as it were from the ashes of their ruin, is something perfectly inexplicable to a mere spectator of the shows of this mortal scene. We are all Greeks. Our laws, our literature, our religion, our arts, have their root in Greece. But for Greece, Rome, the instructor, the conqueror, or the metropolis of our ancestors, would have spread no illumination with her arms, and we might still have been savages and idolaters; or, what is worse, might have arrived at such a stagnant and miserable state of social institution as China and Japan possess.

The human form and the human mind attained to a perfection in Greece which has impressed its image on those faultless productions, whose very fragments are the despair of modern art, and has propagated impulses which cannot cease, through a thousand channels of manifest or imperceptible operation, to ennoble and delight mankind until the extinction of the race.

The modern Greek is the descendant of those glorious beings whom the imagination almost refuses to figure to itself as belonging to our kind, and he inherits much of their sensibility, their rapidity of conception, their enthusiasm, and their courage. If in many instances he is degraded, by moral and political slavery to the practice of the basest vices it engenders, and that below the level of ordinary degradation; let us reflect that the corruption of the best produces the worst, and that habits which subsist only in relation to a peculiar state of social institution may be expected to cease so soon as that relation is dissolved. In fact the Greeks, since the admirable novel of *Anastasius*° could have been a faithful picture of their manners, have undergone most important changes; the flower of their youth returning to their country from the universities of Italy, Germany, and France, have communicated to their fellow-citizens the latest results of that social perfection of which their ancestors were the original source. The university of Chios contained before the breaking out of the Revolution eight hundred students, and among them several Germans and Americans. The munificence and energy of many of the Greek princes and merchants, directed to the renovation of their country with a spirit and a wisdom which has few examples, is above all praise.

The English permit their own oppressors to act according to their natural sympathy with the Turkish tyrant, and to brand upon their name the indelible blot of an alliance with the enemies of domestic happiness, of Christianity and civilization.

Russia desires to possess, not to liberate Greece; and is contented to see the Turks, its natural enemies, and the Greeks, its intended slaves, enfeeble each other until one or both fall into its net. The wise and generous policy of England would have consisted in establishing the independence of Greece, and in maintaining it both against Russia and the Turk;—but when was the oppressor generous or just?

Should the English people ever become free they will reflect upon the part which those who presume to represent their will, have played in the great drama of the revival of liberty, with feelings which it would become them to anticipate. This is the age of the war of the oppressed against the oppressors, and every one of those ringleaders of the privileged gangs of murderers and swindlers, called Sovereigns, look to each other for aid against the common enemy and suspend their mutual jealousies in the presence of a mightier fear. Of this holy alliance all the despots of the earth are virtual members. But a new race has arisen throughout Europe, nursed in the abhorrence of the opinions which are its chains, and she will continue to produce fresh generations to accomplish that destiny which tyrants foresee and dread.°

The Spanish Peninsula is already free. France is tranquil in the enjoyment of a partial exemption from the abuses which its unnatural and feeble government are vainly attempting to revive. The seed of blood and misery has been sown in Italy, and a more vigorous race is arising to go forth to the harvest. The world waits only the news of a revolution of Germany to see the tyrants who have pinnacled themselves on its supineness precipitated into the ruin from which they shall never arise. Well do these destroyers of mankind know their enemy, when they impute the insurrection in Greece to the same spirit before which they tremble throughout the rest of Europe, and that enemy well knows the power and the cunning of its opponents, and watches the moment of their approaching weakness and inevitable division to wrest the bloody sceptres from their grasp.

DRAMATIS PERSONAE

Mahmud.
Hassan.
Daood.
Ahasuerus, *a Jew*.
Chorus of Greek Captive Women.
Messengers, Slaves and Attendants.
Phantom of Mahomet the Second.

Scene, *Constantinople*.
Time, *Sunset*.

scene.—*A Terrace on the Seraglio*.°

Mahmud (*sleeping*), *an Indian Slave sitting beside his Couch*.

Chorus of Greek Captive Women°

We strew these opiate flowers
On thy restless pillow,—
They were stripped from Orient bowers,
By the Indian billow.
Be thy sleep
Calm and deep,
Like theirs who fell, not ours who weep!

Indian

Away, unlovely dreams!
Away, false shapes of sleep!
Be his, as Heaven seems,
Clear, and bright, and deep!
Soft as love, and calm as death,
Sweet as a summer night without a breath.

Chorus

Sleep, sleep! our song is laden
With the soul of slumber;
It was sung by a Samian maiden,°
Whose lover was of the number
Who now keep
That calm sleep
Whence none may wake, where none shall weep.

Indian

I touch thy temples pale!
I breathe my soul on thee!
And could my prayers avail,
All my joy should be
Dead, and I would live to weep,
So thou mightst win one hour of quiet sleep.

Chorus

Breathe low, low
The spell of the mighty mistress now!
When Conscience lulls her sated snake,
And Tyrants sleep, let Freedom wake.
Breathe low—low
The words which, like secret fire, shall flow
Through the veins of the frozen earth—low, low!

Semichorus 1

Life may change, but it may fly not;
Hope may vanish, but can die not;
Truth be veiled, but still it burneth;
Love repulsed,—but it returneth

Semichorus 2

Yet were life a charnel where
Hope lay coffined with Despair;
Yet were truth a sacred lie,
Love were lust—

Semichorus 1

If Liberty
Lent not life its soul of light,
Hope its iris of delight,
Truth its prophet's robe to wear,
Love its power to give and bear.

Chorus

In the great morning of the world,
The spirit of God with might unfurled
The flag of Freedom over Chaos,
  And all its banded anarchs fled
Like vultures frighted from Imaus°
  Before an earthquake's tread.—
So from Time's tempestuous dawn
Freedom's splendour burst and shone:—
Thermopylae and Marathon°
Caught, like mountains beacon-lighted,
  The springing Fire.—The wingèd glory
On Philippi half-alighted,°
  Like an eagle on a promontory.
Its unwearied wings could fan
The quenchless ashes of Milan.°
From age to age, from man to man,
  It lived; and lit from land to land,
  Florence, Albion, Switzerland.—

Then night fell; and, as from night,
Re-assuming fiery flight,
From the West swift Freedom came,
  Against the course of Heaven and doom,
A second sun arrayed in flame,
  To burn, to kindle, to illume.
From far Atlantis its young beams.°
Chased the shadows and the dreams.
France, with all her sanguine steams,°

Hid, but quenched it not; again
Through clouds its shafts of glory rain
From utmost Germany to Spain.—

As an eagle fed with morning
Scorns the embattled tempest's warning,
When she seeks her eyrie hanging
In the mountain-cedar's hair,
And her brood expect the clanging
Of her wings through the wild air,
Sick with famine:—Freedom, so
To what of Greece remaineth now
Returns; her hoary ruins glow
Like Orient mountains lost in day;
Beneath the safety of her wings
Her renovated nurslings prey,
And in the naked lightnings°
Of truth they purge their dazzled eyes.
Let Freedom leave, where'er she flies,
A Desert or a Paradise:
Let the beautiful and the brave
Share her glory, or a grave.

Semichorus 1

With the gifts of gladness
Greece did thy cradle strew;

Semichorus 2

With the tears of sadness
Greece did thy shroud bedew!

Semichorus 1

With an orphan's affection
She followed thy bier through Time;

Semichorus 2

And at thy resurrection
Reappeareth, like thou, sublime!

Semichorus 1

If Heaven should resume thee,
To Heaven shall her spirit ascend;

Semichorus 2

If Hell should entomb thee,
    To Hell shall her high hearts bend.

Semichorus 1

If Annihilation——

Semichorus 2

Dust let her glories be!
And a name and a nation
    Be forgotten, Freedom, with thee!

Indian

His brow grows darker—breathe not—move not!
He starts—he shudders—ye that love not,
With your panting loud and fast,
Have awakened him at last.

Mahmud (*starting from his sleep*).
Man the Seraglio-guard! make fast the gate.
What! from a cannonade of three short hours?
'Tis false! that breach towards the Bosphorus°
Cannot be practicable yet—who stirs?
Stand to the match; that when the foe prevails
One spark may mix in reconciling ruin
The conqueror and the conquered! Heave the tower
Into the gap—wrench off the roof!
(*Enter* HASSAN.)
Ha! what!
The truth of day lightens upon my dream
And I am Mahmud still.°

Hassan. Your Sublime Highness
Is strangely moved.

Mahmud. The times do cast strange shadows
On those who watch and who must rule their course,
Lest they, being first in peril as in glory,
Be whelmed in the fierce ebb:—and these are of them.
Thrice has a gloomy vision hunted me
As thus from sleep into the troubled day;

It shakes me as the tempest shakes the sea,
Leaving no figure upon memory's glass.
Would that—no matter. Thou didst say thou knewest
A Jew, whose spirit is a chronicle
Of strange and secret and forgotten things.
I bade thee summon him:—'tis said his tribe
Dream, and are wise interpreters of dreams.

Hassan. The Jew of whom I spake is old,—so old
He seems to have outlived a world's decay;
The hoary mountains and the wrinkled ocean
Seem younger still than he;—his hair and beard
Are whiter than the tempest-sifted snow;
His cold pale limbs and pulseless arteries
Are like the fibres of a cloud instinct
With light, and to the soul that quickens them
Are as the atoms of the mountain-drift
To the winter wind:—but from his eye looks forth
A life of unconsumèd thought which pierces
The present, and the past, and the to-come.
Some say that this is he whom the great prophet
Jesus, the son of Joseph, for his mockery
Mocked with the curse of immortality.°
Some feign that he is Enoch: others dream°
He was pre-adamite and has survived
Cycles of generation and of ruin.
The sage, in truth, by dreadful abstinence
And conquering penance of the mutinous flesh,
Deep contemplation, and unwearied study,
In years outstretched beyond the date of man,
May have attained to sovereignty and science
Over those strong and secret things and thoughts
Which others fear and know not.

Mahmud. I would talk
With this old Jew.

Hassan. Thy will is even now
Made known to him, where he dwells in a sea-cavern
'Mid the Demonesi, less accessible°
Than thou or God! He who would question him

Must sail alone at sunset, where the stream
Of Ocean sleeps around those foamless isles,
When the young moon is westering as now,
And evening airs wander upon the wave;
And when the pines of that bee-pasturing isle,
Green Erebinthus, quench the fiery shadow
Of his gilt prow within the sapphire water,
Then must the lonely helmsman cry aloud
'Ahasuerus!' and the caverns round
Will answer 'Ahasuerus!' If his prayer
Be granted, a faint meteor will arise
Lighting him over Marmora, and a wind°
Will rush out of the sighing pine-forest,
And with the wind a storm of harmony
Unutterably sweet, and pilot him
Through the soft twilight to the Bosphorus:
Thence at the hour and place and circumstance
Fit for the matter of their conference
The Jew appears. Few dare, and few who dare
Win the desired communion—but that shout
Bodes—— [*A shout within*

Mahmud. Evil, doubtless; like all human sounds.
Let me converse with spirits.

Hassan. That shout again.

Mahmud. This Jew whom thou hast summoned—

Hassan. Will be here—

Mahmud. When the omnipotent hour to which are yoked
He, I, and all things shall compel—enough.
Silence those mutineers—that drunken crew,
That crowd about the pilot in the storm.
Ay! strike the foremost shorter by a head!
They weary me, and I have need of rest.
Kings are like stars—they rise and set, they have
The worship of the world, but no repose.

[*Exeunt severally*.

Chorus°

Worlds on worlds are rolling ever
From creation to decay,
Like the bubbles on a river
Sparkling, bursting, borne away.
But they are still immortal
Who, through birth's orient portal
And death's dark chasm hurrying to and fro,
Clothe their unceasing flight
In the brief dust and light
Gathered around their chariots as they go;
New shapes they still may weave,
New gods, new laws receive,
Bright or dim are they as the robes they last
On Death's bare ribs had cast.°

A power from the unknown God,°
A Promethean conqueror came;
Like a triumphal path he trod
The thorns of death and shame.
A mortal shape to him
Was like the vapour dim
Which the orient planet animates with light;
Hell, Sin and Slavery came,
Like bloodhounds mild and tame,
Nor preyed, until their Lord had taken flight;
The moon of Mahomet°
Arose, and it shall set:
While blazoned as on Heaven's immortal noon
The cross leads generations on.

Swift as the radiant shapes of sleep
From one whose dreams are Paradise
Fly, when the fond wretch wakes to weep,
And day peers forth with her blank eyes;
So fleet, so faint, so fair,
The Powers of earth and air
Fled from the folding star of Bethlehem:
Apollo, Pan, and Love,
And even Olympian Jove

Grew weak, for killing Truth had glared on them;
Our hills and seas and streams
Dispeopled of their dreams,
Their waters turned to blood, their dew to tears,
Wailed for the golden years.°

Enter MAHMUD, HASSAN, DAOOD, *and others.*

Mahmud. More gold? our ancestors bought gold with victory,
And shall I sell it for defeat?

Daood. The Janizars°
Clamour for pay.

Mahmud. Go! bid them pay themselves
With Christian blood! Are there no Grecian virgins
Whose shrieks and spasms and tears they may enjoy?
No infidel children to impale on spears?
No hoary priests after that Patriarch°
Who bent the curse against his country's heart,°
Which clove his own at last? Go! bid them kill,
Blood is the seed of gold.

Daood. It has been sown,
And yet the harvest to the sicklemen
Is as a grain to each.

Mahmud. Then, take this signet,
Unlock the seventh chamber in which lie
The treasures of victorious Solyman.°
An empire's spoil stored for a day of ruin.
O spirit of my sires! is it not come?
The prey-birds and the wolves are gorged and sleep;
But these, who spread their feast on the red earth,
Hunger for gold, which fills not.—See them fed;
Then, lead them to the rivers of fresh death.

[*Exit* DAOOD.

O! miserable dawn, after a night
More glorious than the day which it usurped!
O, faith in God! O, power on earth! O, word
Of the great prophet, whose o'ershadowing wings

Darkened the thrones and idols of the West,
Now bright!—For thy sake cursèd be the hour,
Even as a father by an evil child,
When the orient moon of Islam rolled in triumph
From Caucasus to White Ceraunia!°
Ruin above, and anarchy below;
Terror without, and treachery within;
The chalice of destruction full, and all
Thirsting to drink; and who among us dares
To dash it from his lips? and where is Hope?

Hassan. The lamp of our dominion still rides high;
One God is God—Mahomet is his prophet.
Four hundred thousand Moslems, from the limits
Of utmost Asia, irresistibly
Throng, like full clouds at the Sirocco's cry;°
But not like them to weep their strength in tears:
They bear destroying lightning, and their step
Wakes earthquake to consume and overwhelm,
And reign in ruin. Phrygian Olympus,
Tmolus, and Latmos, and Mycale, roughen°
With horrent arms; and lofty ships even now,
Like vapours anchored to a mountain's edge,
Freighted with fire and whirlwind, wait at Scala°
The convoy of the ever-veering wind.
Samos is drunk with blood;—the Greek has paid.
Brief victory with swift loss and long despair.
The false Moldavian serfs fled fast and far,°
When the fierce shout of 'Allah-illa-Allah!'°
Rose like the war-cry of the northern wind
Which kills the sluggish clouds, and leaves a flock
Of wild swans struggling with the naked storm.
So were the lost Greeks on the Danube's day!°
If night is mute, yet the returning sun
Kindles the voices of the morning birds;
Nor at thy bidding less exultingly
Than birds rejoicing in the golden day,
The Anarchies of Africa unleash°
Their tempest-wingèd cities of the sea,
To speak in thunder to the rebel world.
Like sulphurous clouds, half-shattered by the storm,

They sweep the pale Aegean, while the Queen
Of Ocean, bound upon her island-throne,°
Far in the West sits mourning that her sons
Who frown on Freedom spare a smile for thee:
Russia still hovers, as an eagle might
Within a cloud, near which a kite and crane
Hang tangled in inextricable fight,
To stoop upon the victor;—for she fears
The name of Freedom, even as she hates thine.
But recreant Austria loves thee as the Grave°
Loves Pestilence, and her slow dogs of war,
Fleshed with the chase, come up from Italy,
And howl upon their limits; for they see
The panther, Freedom, fled to her old cover,
'Mid seas and mountains, and a mightier brood
Crouch round. What Anarch wears a crown or mitre,
Or bears the sword, or grasps the key of gold,
Whose friends are not thy friends, whose foes thy foes?
Our arsenals and our armories are full;
Our forts defy assault; ten thousand cannon
Lie ranged upon the beach, and hour by hour
Their earth-convulsing wheels affright the city;
The galloping of fiery steeds makes pale
The Christian merchant; and the yellow Jew
Hides his hoard deeper in the faithless earth.
Like clouds, and like the shadows of the clouds,
Over the hills of Anatolia,°
Swift in wide troops the Tartar chivalry
Sweep;—the far flashing of their starry lances
Reverberates the dying light of day.
We have one God, one King, one Hope, one Law;°
But many-headed Insurrection stands
Divided in itself, and soon must fall.

Mahmud. Proud words, when deeds come short, are seasonable:
Look, Hassan, on yon crescent moon, emblazoned
Upon that shattered flag of fiery cloud
Which leads the rear of the departing day;
Wan emblem of an empire fading now!
See how it trembles in the blood-red air,
And like a mighty lamp whose oil is spent

Shrinks on the horizon's edge, while, from above,
One star with insolent and victorious light
Hovers above its fall, and with keen beams,
Like arrows through a fainting antelope,
Strikes its weak form to death.

Hassan. Even as that moon
Renews itself——

Mahmud. Shall we be not renewed!
Far other bark than ours were needed now
To stem the torrent of descending time:
The spirit that lifts the slave before his lord
Stalks through the capitals of armèd kings,
And spreads his ensign in the wilderness:
Exults in chains; and, when the rebel falls,
Cries like the blood of Abel from the dust;
And the inheritors of the earth, like beasts
When earthquake is unleashed, with idiot fear
Cower in their kingly dens—as I do now.
What were Defeat when Victory must appal?
Or Danger, when Security looks pale?—
How said the messenger—who, from the fort
Islanded in the Danube, saw the battle
Of Bucharest?—that—°

Hassan. Ibrahim's scimitar
Drew with its gleam swift victory from heaven,
To burn before him in the night of battle—
A light and a destruction.

Mahmud. Ay! the day
Was ours: but how?——

Hassan. The light Wallachians,
The Arnaut, Servian, and Albanian allies
Fled from the glance of our artillery
Almost before the thunderstone alit.
One half the Grecian army made a bridge
Of safe and slow retreat, with Moslem dead;
The other—

Mahmud. Speak—tremble not.—

Hassan. Islanded
By victor myriads, formed in hollow square
With rough and steadfast front, and thrice flung back
The deluge of our foaming cavalry;
Thrice their keen wedge of battle pierced our lines.
Our baffled army trembled like one man
Before a host, and gave them space; but soon,
From the surrounding hills, the batteries blazed,
Kneading them down with fire and iron rain;
Yet none approached; till, like a field of corn
Under the hook of the swart sickleman,
The band, intrenched in mounds of Turkish dead,
Grew weak and few.—Then said the Pacha, 'Slaves,°
Render yourselves—they have abandoned you—
What hope of refuge, or retreat, or aid?
We grant your lives.' 'Grant that which is thine own!'
Cried one, and fell upon his sword and died!
Another—'God, and man, and hope abandon me;
But I to them, and to myself, remain
Constant:'—he bowed his head, and his heart burst.
A third exclaimed, 'There is a refuge, tyrant,
Where thou darest not pursue, and canst not harm,
Shouldst thou pursue; there we shall meet again.'
Then held his breath, and, after a brief spasm,
The indignant spirit cast its mortal garment
Among the slain—dead earth upon the earth!
So these survivors, each by different ways,
Some strange, all sudden, none dishonourable,
Met in triumphant death; and when our army
Closed in, while yet wonder, and awe, and shame,
Held back the base hyenas of the battle
That feed upon the dead and fly the living,
One rose out of the chaos of the slain:
And if it were a corpse which some dread spirit
Of the old saviours of the land we rule
Had lifted in its anger wandering by;—
Or if there burned within the dying man
Unquenchable disdain of death, and faith
Creating what it feigned;—I cannot tell—

But he cried, 'Phantoms of the free, we come!
Armies of the Eternal, ye who strike
To dust the citadels of sanguine kings,
And shake the souls throned on their stony hearts,
And thaw their frostwork diadems like dew;—
O ye who float around this clime, and weave
The garment of the glory which it wears,
Whose fame, though earth betray the dust it clasped,
Lies sepulchred in monumental thought;—
Progenitors of all that yet is great,
Ascribe to your bright senate, O accept°
In your high ministrations, us, your sons—
Us first, and the more glorious yet to come!
And ye, weak conquerors! giants who look pale
When the crushed worm rebels beneath your tread,
The vultures and the dogs, your pensioners tame,
Are overgorged; but, like oppressors, still
They crave the relic of Destruction's feast.
The exhalations and the thirsty winds
Are sick with blood; the dew is foul with death;
Heaven's light is quenched in slaughter: thus, where'er
Upon your camps, cities, or towers, or fleets,
The obscene birds the reeking remnants cast
Of these dead limbs,—upon your streams and mountains,
Upon your fields, your gardens, and your housetops,
Where'er the winds shall creep, or the clouds fly,
Or the dews fall, or the angry sun look down
With poisoned light—Famine and Pestilence,
And Panic, shall wage war upon our side!
Nature from all her boundaries is moved
Against ye: Time has found ye light as foam.
The Earth rebels; and Good and Evil stake
Their empire o'er the unborn world of men
On this one cast;—but ere the die be thrown,
The renovated genius of our race,
Proud umpire of the impious game, descends
A seraph-wingèd Victory, bestriding
The tempest of the Omnipotence of God,
Which sweeps all things to their appointed doom,
And you to oblivion!'—More he would have said,
But—

Mahmud. Died—as thou shouldst ere thy lips had painted
Their ruin in the hues of our success.
A rebel's crime gilt with a rebel's tongue!
Your heart is Greek, Hassan.

Hassan. It may be so:
A spirit not my own wrenched me within,
And I have spoken words I fear and hate;
Yet would I die for—

Mahmud. Live! O live! outlive
Me and this sinking empire. But the fleet—

Hassan. Alas!——

Mahmud. The fleet which, like a flock of clouds
Chased by the wind, flies the insurgent banner.
Our wingèd castles from their merchant ships!
Our myriads before their weak pirate bands!
Our arms before their chains! our years of empire
Before their centuries of servile fear!
Death is awake! Repulse is on the waters!
They own no more the thunder-bearing banner
Of Mahmud; but, like hounds of a base breed,
Gorge from a stranger's hand, and rend their master.

Hassan. Latmos, and Ampelos, and Phanae, saw
The wreck—

Mahmud. The caves of the Icarian isles°
Told each to the other in loud mockery,
And with the tongue as of a thousand echoes,
First of the sea-convulsing fight—and, then,—
Thou darest to speak—senseless are the mountains;
Interpret thou their voice!

Hassan. My presence bore
A part in that day's shame. The Grecian fleet
Bore down at day-break from the North, and hung
As multitudinous on the ocean line,
As cranes upon the cloudless Thracian wind.

Our squadron, convoying ten thousand men,
Was stretching towards Nauplia when the battle°
Was kindled.—
First through the hail of our artillery
The agile Hydriote barks with press of sail°
Dashed:—ship to ship, cannon to cannon, man
To man were grappled in the embrace of war,
Inextricable but by death or victory.
The tempest of the raging fight convulsed
To its crystalline depths that stainless sea,
And shook Heaven's roof of golden morning clouds,
Poised on an hundred azure mountain-isles.
In the brief trances of the artillery
One cry from the destroyed and the destroyer
Rose, and a cloud of desolation wrapped
The unforeseen event, till the north wind
Sprung from the sea, lifting the heavy veil
Of battle-smoke—then victory—victory!
For, as we thought, three frigates from Algiers
Bore down from Naxos to our aid, but soon°
The abhorrèd cross glimmered behind, before,
Among, around us; and that fatal sign
Dried with its beams the strength in Moslem hearts,
As the sun drinks the dew.—What more? We fled!—
Our noonday path over the sanguine foam
Was beaconed—and the glare struck the sun pale—
By our consuming transports: the fierce light
Made all the shadows of our sails blood-red,
And every countenance blank. Some ships lay feeding
The ravening fire, even to the water's level;
Some were blown up; some, settling heavily,
Sunk; and the shrieks of our companions died
Upon the wind, that bore us fast and far,
Even after they were dead. Nine thousand perished!
We met the vultures legioned in the air
Stemming the torrent of the tainted wind;
They, screaming from their cloudy mountain peaks,
Stooped through the sulphurous battle-smoke and perched
Each on the weltering carcase that we loved,
Like its ill angel or its damnèd soul,
Riding upon the bosom of the sea.

We saw the dog-fish hastening to their feast.
Joy waked the voiceless people of the sea,
And ravening Famine left his ocean cave
To dwell with war, with us, and with despair.
We met night three hours to the west of Patmos°
And with night, tempest——°

Mahmud. Cease!
(*Enter a Messenger.*)

Messenger. Your Sublime Highness,
That Christian hound, the Muscovite Ambassador,
Has left the city.—If the rebel fleet°
Had anchored in the port, had victory
Crowned the Greek legions in the Hippodrome,°
Panic were tamer.—Obedience and Mutiny,
Like giants in contention planet-struck,°
Stand gazing on each other.—There is peace
In Stamboul.—

Mahmud. Is the grave not calmer still?
Its ruins shall be mine.

Hassan. Fear not the Russian:
The tiger leagues not with the stag at bay
Against the hunter.—Cunning, base, and cruel,
He crouches, watching till the spoil be won,
And must be paid for his reserve in blood.
After the war is fought, yield the sleek Russian
That which thou canst not keep, his deserved portion
Of blood, which shall not flow through streets and fields,
Rivers and seas, like that which we may win,
But stagnate in the veins of Christian slaves!
(*Enter second Messenger.*)

Second Messenger. Nauplia, Tripolizza, Mothon, Athens,
Navarin, Artas, Monembasia,°
Corinth and Thebes are carried by assault,
And every Islamite who made his dogs
Fat with the flesh of Galilean slaves
Passed at the edge of the sword: the lust of blood

Which made our warriors drunk, is quenched in death;
But like a fiery plague breaks out anew
In deeds which make the Christian cause look pale
In its own light. The garrison of Patras°
Has store but for ten days, nor is there hope
But from the Briton: at once slave and tyrant
His wishes still are weaker than his fears,
Or he would sell what faith may yet remain
From the oaths broke in Genoa and in Norway;°
And if you buy him not, your treasury
Is empty even of promises—his own coin.
The freedman of a western poet chief°
Holds Attica with seven thousand rebels,°
And has beat back the Pacha of Negropont:°
The aged Ali sits in Yanina°
A crownless metaphor of empire:
His name, that shadow of his withered might,
Holds our besieging army like a spell
In prey to famine, pest, and mutiny;
He, bastioned in his citadel, looks forth
Joyless upon the sapphire lake that mirrors
The ruins of the city where he reigned
Childless and sceptreless. The Greek has reaped
The costly harvest his own blood matured,
Not the sower, Ali—who has bought a truce
From Ypsilanti with ten camel loads°
Of Indian gold.

(*Enter a third Messenger.*)

Mahmud. What more?

Third Messenger. The Christian tribes
Of Lebanon and the Syrian wilderness
Are in revolt;—Damascus, Hems, Aleppo
Tremble;—the Arab menaces Medina,
The Ethiop has intrenched himself in Sennaar,°
And keeps the Egyptian rebel well employed,
Who denies homage, claims investiture
As price of tardy aid. Persia demands
The cities on the Tigris, and the Georgians
Refuse their living tribute. Crete and Cyprus,°

Like mountain-twins that from each other's veins
Catch the volcano-fire and earthquake spasm,
Shake in the general fever. Through the city,
Like birds before a storm, the Santons shriek,°
And prophesyings horrible and new°
Are heard among the crowd: that sea of men
Sleeps on the wrecks it made, breathless and still.
A Dervise, learned in the Koran, preaches°
That it is written how the sins of Islam
Must raise up a destroyer even now.
The Greeks expect a Saviour from the west,
Who shall not come, men say, in clouds and glory,°
But in the omnipresence of that spirit
In which all live and are. Ominous signs
Are blazoned broadly on the noonday sky:
One saw a red cross stamped upon the sun;
It has rained blood; and monstrous births declare
The secret wrath of Nature and her Lord.
The army encamped upon the Cydaris,°
Was roused last night by the alarm of battle,
And saw two hosts conflicting in the air,
The shadows doubtless of the unborn time
Cast on the mirror of the night. While yet
The fight hung balanced, there arose a storm
Which swept the phantoms from among the stars.
At the third watch the spirit of the plague
Was heard abroad flapping among the tents;
Those who relieved watch found the sentinels dead.
The last news from the camp is that a thousand
Have sickened, and——

(*Enter a fourth Messenger.*)

Mahmud. And thou, pale ghost, dim shadow
Of some untimely rumour, speak!

Fourth Messenger. One comes
Fainting with toil, covered with foam and blood:
He stood, he says, on Chelonites'°
Promontory, which o'erlooks the isles that groan°
Under the Briton's frown, and all their waters
Then trembling in the splendour of the moon,

When as the wandering clouds unveiled or hid
Her boundless light, he saw two adverse fleets
Stalk through the night in the horizon's glimmer,
Mingling fierce thunders and sulphureous gleams,°
And smoke which strangled every infant wind
That soothed the silver clouds through the deep air.
At length the battle slept, but the Sirocco
Awoke, and drove his flock of thunder-clouds
Over the sea-horizon, blotting out
All objects—save that in the faint moon-glimpse
He saw, or dreamed he saw, the Turkish admiral
And two the loftiest of our ships of war,
With the bright image of that Queen of Heaven
Who hid, perhaps, her face for grief, reversed;
And the abhorrèd cross—

(*Enter an Attendant.*)

Attendant. Your Sublime Highness,
The Jew, who——

Mahmud. Could not come more seasonably:
Bid him attend. I'll hear no more! too long
We gaze on danger through the mist of fear,
And multiply upon our shattered hopes
The images of ruin. Come what will!
Tomorrow and tomorrow are as lamps°
Set in our path to light us to the edge
Through rough and smooth, nor can we suffer aught
Which he inflicts not in whose hand we are.

[*Exeunt.*

Semichorus I

Would I were the wingèd cloud
Of a tempest swift and loud,
I would scorn
The smile of morn
And the wave where the moonrise is born!
I would leave
The spirits of eve
A shroud for the corpse of the day to weave
From other threads than mine!

Bask in the deep blue noon divine
Who would, not I.

Semichorus 2

Whither to fly?

Semichorus 1

Where the rocks that gird th' Aegean
Echo to the battle paean
Of the free—
I would flee,
A tempestuous herald of victory!
My golden rain
For the Grecian slain
Should mingle in tears with the bloody main,
And my solemn thunder-knell
Should ring to the world the passing bell
Of tyranny!

Semichorus 2

Ha king! wilt thou chain
The rack and the rain?
Wilt thou fetter the lightning and hurricane?
The storms are free,
But we?

Chorus

O Slavery! thou frost of the world's prime,
Killing its flowers and leaving its thorns bare!
Thy touch has stamped these limbs with crime,
These brows thy branding garland bear,
But the free heart, the impassive soul
Scorn thy control!

Semichorus 1

Let there be light! said Liberty,
And like sunrise from the sea,
Athens arose!—Around her born,
Shone like mountains in the morn
Glorious states;—and are they now
Ashes, wrecks, oblivion?

Semichorus 2

Go,
Where Thermae and Asopus swallowed°
Persia, as the sand does foam.
Deluge upon deluge followed,
Discord, Macedon, and Rome:
And lastly thou!

Semichorus 1

Temples and towers,
Citadels and marts, and they
Who live and die there, have been ours,
And may be thine, and must decay;
But Greece and her foundations are
Built below the tide of war,
Based on the crystalline sea
Of thought and its eternity;
Her citizens, imperial spirits,
Rule the present from the past,
On all this world of men inherits
Their seal is set.

Semichorus 2

Hear ye the blast,
Whose Orphic thunder thrilling calls
From ruin her Titanian walls?
Whose spirit shakes the sapless bones
Of Slavery? Argos, Corinth, Crete
Hear, and from their mountain thrones
The daemons and the nymphs repeat
The harmony.

Semichorus 1

I hear! I hear!

Semichorus 2

The world's eyeless charioteer,
Destiny, is hurrying by!
What faith is crushed, what empire bleeds
Beneath her earthquake-footed steeds?
What eagle-wingèd victory sits

At her right hand? what shadow flits
Before? what splendour rolls behind?
Ruin and renovation cry
'Who but we?'

Semichorus I

I hear! I hear!
The hiss as of a rushing wind,
The roar as of an ocean foaming,
The thunder as of earthquake coming.
I hear! I hear!
The crash as of an empire falling,
The shrieks as of a people calling
'Mercy! mercy!' How they thrill!
Then a shout of 'kill! kill! kill!'
And then a small still voice, thus—

Semichorus 2

For°
Revenge and wrong bring forth their kind,
The foul cubs like their parents are,
Their den is in the guilty mind,
And Conscience feeds them with despair.

Semichorus I

In sacred Athens, near the fane
Of Wisdom, Pity's altar stood:
Serve not the unknown God in vain,°
But pay that broken shrine again,
Love for hate and tears for blood.
(*Enter* MAHMUD *and* AHASUERUS.)

Mahmud. Thou art a man thou sayest even as we.

Ahasuerus. No more!

Mahmud. But raised above thy fellow men
By thought, as I by power.

Ahasuerus. Thou sayest so.

Mahmud. Thou art an adept in the difficult lore
Of Greek and Frank philosophy; thou numberest°
The flowers, and thou measurest the stars;
Thou severest element from element;
Thy spirit is present in the past, and sees
The birth of this old world through all its cycles
Of desolation and of loveliness,
And when man was not, and how man became
The monarch and the slave of this low sphere,
And all its narrow circles—it is much—
I honour thee, and would be what thou art
Were I not what I am; but the unborn hour,
Cradled in fear and hope, conflicting storms,
Who shall unveil? Nor thou, nor I, nor any
Mighty or wise. I apprehended not
What thou hast taught me, but I now perceive
That thou art no interpreter of dreams;
Thou dost not own that art, device, or God,
Can make the future present—let it come!
Moreover thou disdainest us and ours;
Thou art as God, whom thou contemplatest.

Ahasuerus. Disdain thee?—not the worm beneath thy feet!
The Fathomless has care for meaner things
Than thou canst dream, and has made pride for those
Who would be what they may not, or would seem
That which they are not. Sultan! talk no more
Of thee and me, the future and the past;
But look on that which cannot change—the One,
The unborn and the undying. Earth and ocean,
Space, and the isles of life or light that gem
The sapphire floods of interstellar air,
This firmament pavilioned upon chaos,
With all its cressets of immortal fire,
Whose outwall, bastioned impregnably
Against the escape of boldest thoughts, repels them
As Calpe the Atlantic clouds—this Whole°
Of suns, and worlds, and men, and beasts, and flowers,
With all the silent or tempestuous workings
By which they have been, are, or cease to be,
Is but a vision;—all that it inherits°

Are motes of a sick eye, bubbles and dreams;°
Thought is its cradle and its grave, nor less
The future and the past are idle shadows
Of thought's eternal flight—they have no being:
Nought is but that which feels itself to be.°

Mahmud. What meanest thou? Thy words stream like a tempest
Of dazzling mist within my brain—they shake
The earth on which I stand, and hang like night
On Heaven above me. What can they avail?
They cast on all things surest, brightest, best,
Doubt, insecurity, astonishment.

Ahasuerus. Mistake me not! All is contained in each.
Dodona's forest to an acorn's cup°
Is that which has been, or will be, to that
Which is—the absent to the present. Thought
Alone, and its quick elements, Will, Passion,
Reason, Imagination, cannot die;
They are, what that which they regard appears,
The stuff whence mutability can weave
All that it hath dominion o'er, worlds, worms,
Empires, and superstitions. What has thought
To do with time, or place, or circumstance?
Wouldst thou behold the future?—ask and have!
Knock and it shall be opened—look and, lo!°
The coming age is shadowed on the past
As on a glass.

Mahmud. Wild, wilder thoughts convulse
My spirit—Did not Mahomet the Second
Win Stamboul?°

Ahasuerus. Thou wouldst ask that giant spirit
The written fortunes of thy house and faith.
Thou wouldst cite one out of the grave to tell
How what was born in blood must die.

Mahmud. Thy words
Have power on me! I see——

Ahasuerus. What hearest thou?

Mahmud. A far whisper——
Terrible silence.

Ahasuerus. What succeeds?

Mahmud. The sound
As of the assault of an imperial city,
The hiss of inextinguishable fire,
The roar of giant cannon; the earthquaking
Fall of vast bastions and precipitous towers,
The shock of crags shot from strange engin'ry,
The clash of wheels, and clang of armèd hoofs,
And crash of brazen mail as of the wreck
Of adamantine mountains—the mad blast
Of trumpets, and the neigh of raging steeds,
And shrieks of women whose thrill jars the blood,
And one sweet laugh, most horrible to hear,
As of a joyous infant waked and playing
With its dead mother's breast, and now more loud
The mingled battle-cry,—ha! hear I not
'*Εν τούτῳ νικη!*' 'Allah, Illah, Allah!'°

Ahasuerus. The sulphurous mist is raised—thou seest—

Mahmud. A chasm,
As of two mountains in the wall of Stamboul;
And in that ghastly breach the Islamites,
Like giants on the ruins of a world,
Stand in the light of sunrise. In the dust
Glimmers a kingless diadem, and one
Of regal port has cast himself beneath
The stream of war. Another proudly clad
In golden arms spurs a Tartarian barb°
Into the gap, and with his iron mace
Directs the torrent of that tide of men,
And seems—he is—Mahomet!

Ahasuerus. What thou seest
Is but the ghost of thy forgotten dream.

A dream itself, yet less, perhaps, than that
Thou call'st reality. Thou mayst behold
How cities, on which Empire sleeps enthroned,
Bow their towered crests to mutability.
Poised by the flood, e'en on the height thou holdest,
Thou mayst now learn how the full tide of power
Ebbs to its depths.—Inheritor of glory,
Conceived in darkness, born in blood, and nourished
With tears and toil, thou seest the mortal throes
Of that whose birth was but the same. The Past
Now stands before thee like an Incarnation
Of the To-come; yet wouldst thou commune with
That portion of thyself which was ere thou
Didst start for this brief race whose crown is death.
Dissolve with that strong faith and fervent passion
Which called it from the uncreated deep,
Yon cloud of war, with its tempestuous phantoms
Of raging death; and draw with mighty will
The imperial shade hither.

[*Exit* AHASUERUS.

Mahmud. Approach!

Phantom. I come
Thence whither thou must go! The grave is fitter
To take the living than give up the dead;
Yet has thy faith prevailed, and I am here.
The heavy fragments of the power which fell
When I arose, like shapeless crags and clouds,
Hang round my throne on the abyss, and voices
Of strange lament soothe my supreme repose,
Wailing for glory never to return.—
A later Empire nods in its decay:
The autumn of a greener faith is come,
And wolfish change, like winter, howls to strip
The foliage in which Fame, the eagle, built
Her eyrie, while Dominion whelped below.
The storm is in its branches, and the frost
Is on its leaves, and the blank deep expects
Oblivion on oblivion, spoil on spoil,
Ruin on ruin:—Thou art slow, my son;

The Anarchs of the world of darkness keep
A throne for thee, round which thine empire lies
Boundless and mute; and for thy subjects thou,
Like us, shalt rule the ghosts of murdered life,
The phantoms of the powers who rule thee now—
Mutinous passions, and conflicting fears,
And hopes that sate themselves on dust and die!—
Stripped of their mortal strength, as thou of thine.
Islam must fall, but we will reign together
Over its ruins in the world of death:—
And if the trunk be dry, yet shall the seed
Unfold itself even in the shape of that
Which gathers birth in its decay. Woe! woe!
To the weak people tangled in the grasp
Of its last spasms.

Mahmud. Spirit, woe to all!
Woe to the wronged and the avenger! Woe
To the destroyer, woe to the destroyed!
Woe to the dupe, and woe to the deceiver!
Woe to the oppressed, and woe to the oppressor!
Woe both to those that suffer and inflict;
Those who are born and those who die! but say,
Imperial shadow of the thing I am,
When, how, by whom, Destruction must accomplish
Her consummation?

Phantom. Ask the cold pale Hour,
Rich in reversion of impending death,°
When *he* shall fall upon whose ripe grey hairs
Sit Care, and Sorrow, and Infirmity—
The weight which Crime, whose wings are plumed with years,
Leaves in his flight from ravaged heart to heart
Over the heads of men, under which burden
They bow themselves unto the grave: fond wretch!
He leans upon his crutch, and talks of years
To come, and how in hours of youth renewed
He will renew lost joys, and——

Voice without

Victory! Victory!

[*The Phantom vanishes.*

Mahmud. What sound of the importunate earth has broken
My mighty trance?

Voice without

Victory! Victory!

Mahmud. Weak lightning before darkness! poor faint smile
Of dying Islam! Voice which art the response
Of hollow weakness! Do I wake and live?
Were there such things, or may the unquiet brain,
Vexed by the wise mad talk of the old Jew,
Have shaped itself these shadows of its fear?°
It matters not!—for nought we see or dream,
Possess, or lose, or grasp at, can be worth
More than it gives or teaches. Come what may,
The future must become the past, and I
As they were to whom once this present hour,
This gloomy crag of time to which I cling,
Seemed an Elysian isle of peace and joy
Never to be attained.—I must rebuke
This drunkenness of triumph ere it die,
And dying, bring despair. Victory! poor slaves!

[*Exit Mahmud.*

Voice without

Shout in the jubilee of death! The Greeks
Are as a brood of lions in the net
Round which the kingly hunters of the earth
Stand smiling. Anarchs, ye whose daily food
Are curses, groans, and gold, the fruit of death
From Thule to the girdle of the world,°
Come, feast! the board groans with the flesh of men;
The cup is foaming with a nation's blood,
Famine and Thirst await! eat, drink, and die!

Semichorus I

Victorious Wrong, with vulture scream,
Salutes the risen sun, pursues the flying day!
I saw her, ghastly as a tyrant's dream,
Perch on the trembling pyramid of night,
Beneath which earth and all her realms pavilioned lay
In visions of the dawning undelight:

Who shall impede her flight?
Who rob her of her prey?

Voice without.

Victory! Victory! Russia's famished eagles°
Dare not to prey beneath the crescent's light.
Impale the remnant of the Greeks! despoil!
Violate! make their flesh cheaper than dust!

Semichorus 2

Thou voice which art
The herald of the ill in splendour hid!
Thou echo of the hollow heart
Of monarchy, bear me to thine abode
When desolation flashes o'er a world destroyed:
Oh, bear me to those isles of jagged cloud
Which float like mountains on the earthquake, mid
The momentary oceans of the lightning,°
Or to some toppling promontory proud
Of solid tempest whose black pyramid,
Riven, overhangs the founts intensely bright'ning
Of those dawn-tinted deluges of fire
Before their waves expire,
When heaven and earth are light, and only light
In the thunder night!

Voice without

Victory! Victory! Austria, Russia, England,
And that tame serpent, that poor shadow, France,
Cry peace, and that means death when monarchs speak.
Ho, there! bring torches, sharpen those red stakes,
These chains are light, fitter for slaves and poisoners
Than Greeks. Kill! plunder! burn! let none remain.

Semichorus 1

Alas! for Liberty!
If numbers, wealth, or unfulfilling years,
Or fate, can quell the free!
Alas! for Virtue, when
Torments, or contumely, or the sneers.°
Of erring judging men
Can break the heart where it abides.

Alas! if Love, whose smile makes this obscure world splendid,
Can change with its false times and tides,
Like hope and terror,—
Alas for Love!
And Truth, who wanderest lone and unbefriended,
If thou canst veil thy lie-consuming mirror
Before the dazzled eyes of Error,
Alas for thee! Image of the Above.°

Semichorus 2

Repulse, with plumes from conquest torn,
Led the ten thousand from the limits of the morn
Through many an hostile Anarchy!
At length they wept aloud, and cried, 'The Sea! The Sea!'°
Through exile, persecution, and despair,
Rome was, and young Atlantis shall become°
The wonder, or the terror, or the tomb
Of all whose step wakes power lulled in her savage lair:
But Greece was as a hermit-child,
Whose fairest thoughts and limbs were built
To woman's growth, by dreams so mild,
She knew not pain or guilt;
And now, O Victory, blush! and Empire tremble
When ye desert the free—
If Greece must be
A wreck, yet shall its fragments reassemble,
And build themselves again impregnably
In a diviner clime
To Amphionic music on some Cape sublime,°
Which frowns above the idle foam of Time.

Semichorus 1

Let the tyrants rule the desert they have made;
Let the free possess the paradise they claim;
Be the fortune of our fierce oppressors weighed
With our ruin, our resistance, and our name!

Semichorus 2

Our dead shall be the seed of their decay,
Our survivors be the shadow of their pride,
Our adversity a dream to pass away—
Their dishonour a remembrance to abide!

Voice without

Victory! Victory! The bought Briton sends
The keys of ocean to the Islamite.—°
Now shall the blazon of the cross be veiled,
And British skill directing Othman might,°
Thunderstrike rebel victory. O keep holy
This jubilee of unrevengèd blood—
Kill! crush! despoil! Let not a Greek escape!

Semichorus 1

Darkness has dawned in the East
On the noon of time:
The death-birds descend to their feast,
From the hungry clime.
Let Freedom and Peace flee far
To a sunnier strand,
And follow Love's folding star
To the Evening land!°

Semichorus 2

The young moon has fed
Her exhausted horn,
With the sunset's fire:
The weak day is dead,
But the night is not born;
And, like loveliness panting with wild desire
While it trembles with fear and delight,
Hesperus flies from awakening night,
And pants in its beauty and speed with light
Fast flashing, soft, and bright.
Thou beacon of love! thou lamp of the free!
Guide us far, far away,
To climes where now veiled by the ardour of day
Thou art hidden
From waves on which weary noon,
Faints in her summer swoon,
Between Kingless continents sinless as Eden,
Around mountains and islands inviolably
Pranked on the sapphire sea.°

Semichorus I

Through the sunset of hope,
Like the shapes of a dream,
What Paradise islands of glory gleam!
  Beneath Heaven's cope,
Their shadows more clear float by—
The sound of their oceans, the light of their sky,
The music and fragrance their solitudes breathe
Burst, like morning on dream, or like Heaven on death,
  Through the walls of our prison;
And Greece, which was dead, is arisen!

Chorus°

The world's great age begins anew,
  The golden years return,°
The earth doth like a snake renew
  Her winter weeds outworn:°
Heaven smiles, and faiths and empires gleam,
Like wrecks of a dissolving dream.

A brighter Hellas rears its mountains
  From waves serener far;
A new Peneus rolls his fountains°
  Against the morning-star.
Where fairer Tempes bloom, there sleep
Young Cyclads on a sunnier deep.°

A loftier Argo cleaves the main,°
  Fraught with a later prize;
Another Orpheus sings again,
  And loves, and weeps, and dies.°
A new Ulysses leaves once more
Calypso for his native shore.°

O, write no more the tale of Troy,
  If earth Death's scroll must be!
Nor mix with Laian rage the joy°
  Which dawns upon the free:
Although a subtler Sphinx renew°
Riddles of death Thebes never knew.

Another Athens shall arise,
  And to remoter time
Bequeath, like sunset to the skies,
  The splendour of its prime,
And leave, if nought so bright may live,
All earth can take or Heaven can give.

Saturn and Love their long repose
  Shall burst, more bright and good
Than all who fell, than One who rose,°
  Than many unsubdued:
Not gold, not blood, their altar dowers°
But votive tears and symbol flowers.

O cease! must hate and death return?
  Cease! must men kill and die?
Cease! drain not to its dregs the urn
  Of bitter prophecy.
The world is weary of the past,
O might it die or rest at last!

NOTES TO 'HELLAS'°

Line 60

The quenchless ashes of Milan.

Milan was the centre of the resistance of the Lombard league against the Austrian tyrant. Frederic Barbarossa burnt the city to the ground, but liberty lived in its ashes, and it rose like an exhalation from its ruin. See Sismondi's *Histoire des Républiques Italiennes*, a book which has done much towards awakening the Italians to an imitation of their great ancestors.

Line 197

The Chorus.

The popular notions of Christianity are represented in this chorus as true in their relation to the worship they superseded, and that which in all probability they will supersede, without considering their merits in a relation more universal. The first stanza contrasts the immortality of the living and thinking beings which inhabit the planets, and to use a common and inadequate phrase, *clothe themselves in matter* with the transience of the noblest manifestations of the external world.

The concluding verses indicate a progressive state of more or less exalted existence, according to the degree of perfection which every distinct intelligence may have attained. Let it not be supposed that I mean to dogmatize upon a subject, concerning which all men are equally ignorant, or that I think the Gordian knot of the origin of evil can be disentangled by that or any similar assertions. The received hypothesis of a Being resembling men in the moral attributes of his nature, having called us out of non-existence, and after inflicting on us the misery of the commission of error, should superadd that of the punishment and the privations consequent upon it, still would remain inexplicable and incredible. That there is a true solution of the riddle, and that in our present state that solution is unattainable by us, are propositions which may be regarded as equally certain: meanwhile, as it is the province of the poet to attach himself to those ideas which exalt and ennoble humanity, let him be permitted to have conjectured the condition of that futurity towards which we are all impelled by an inextinguishable thirst for immortality. Until better arguments can be produced than sophisms which disgrace the cause, this desire itself must remain the strongest and the only presumption that eternity is the inheritance of every thinking being.

Line 245

No hoary priests after that Patriarch.

The Greek Patriarch after having been compelled to fulminate an anathema against the insurgents was put to death by the Turks.

Fortunately the Greeks have been taught that they cannot buy security by degradation, and the Turks, though equally cruel, are less cunning than the smooth-faced tyrants of Europe. As to the anathema, his Holiness might as well have thrown his mitre at Mount Athos for any effect that it produced. The chiefs of the Greeks are almost all men of comprehension and enlightened views on religion and politics.

Line 563

The freedman of a western poet chief.

A Greek who had been Lord Byron's servant commands the insurgents in Attica. This Greek, Lord Byron informs me, though a poet and an enthusiastic patriot, gave him rather the idea of a timid and unenterprising person. It appears that circumstances make men what they are, and that we all contain the germ of a degree of degradation or of greatness whose connexion with our character is determined by events.

Line 598

The Greeks expect a Saviour from the west.

It is reported that this Messiah had arrived at a sea-port near Lacedaemon in an American brig. The association of names and ideas is irresistibly ludicrous, but the prevalence of such a rumour strongly marks the state of popular enthusiasm in Greece.

Lines 814–15

The sound
As of the assault of an imperial city.

For the vision of Mahmud of the taking of Constantinople in 1453,° see Gibbon's *Decline and Fall of the Roman Empire*, vol. xii. p. 223.

The manner of the invocation of the spirit of Mahomet the Second will be censured as over subtle. I could easily have made the Jew a regular conjuror, and the Phantom° an ordinary ghost. I have preferred to represent the Jew as disclaiming all pretension, or even belief, in supernatural agency, and as tempting Mahmud to that state of mind in which ideas may be supposed to assume the force of sensations through the confusion of thought with the objects of thought, and the excess of passion animating the creations of imagination.

It is a sort of natural magic, susceptible of being exercised in a degree by any one who should have made himself master of° the secret associations of another's thoughts.

Line 1060

The Chorus

The final chorus is indistinct and obscure, as the event of the living drama whose arrival it foretells. Prophecies of wars, and rumours of wars, &c. may safely be made by poet or prophet in any age, but to anticipate however darkly a period of regeneration and happiness is a more hazardous exercise of the faculty which bards possess or feign. It will remind the reader 'magno *nec* proximus intervallo'° of Isaiah and Virgil, whose ardent spirits overleaping the actual reign of evil which we endure and bewail, already saw the possible and perhaps approaching state of society in which the '*lion shall lie down with the lamb*,' and 'omnis feret omnia tellus.'° Let these great names be my authority and my excuse.

Lines 1090–1

Saturn and Love their long repose
Shall burst.

Saturn and Love were among the deities of a real or imaginary state of innocence and happiness. *All* those *who fell*, or the Gods of Greece, Asia, and Egypt; *the One who rose*, or Jesus Christ, at whose appearance the idols of the Pagan World were amerced° of their worship,° and *the many unsubdued*, or the monstrous objects of the idolatry of China, India, the Antarctic islands, and the native tribes of America, certainly have reigned over the understandings of men in conjunction or in succession, during periods in which all we know of evil has been in a state of portentous, and, until the revival of learning and the arts, perpetually increasing activity. The Grecian gods seem indeed to have been personally more innocent, although it cannot be said that as far as temperance and chastity are concerned, they gave so edifying an example as their successor. The sublime human character of Jesus Christ was deformed by an imputed identification with a Demon,° who tempted, betrayed, and punished the innocent beings who were called into existence by his sole will; and for the period of a thousand years, the spirit of this, the most just, wise and benevolent of men, has been propitiated with myriads of hecatombs° of those who approached the nearest to his innocence and his wisdom, sacrificed under every aggravation of atrocity and variety of torture.° The horrors of the Mexican, the Peruvian, and the Indian superstitions are well known.

Written on Hearing the News of the Death of Napoleon

1

What! alive and so bold, oh Earth?
  Art thou not overbold?
  What! leapest thou forth as of old
In the light of thy morning mirth,
The last of the flock of the starry fold?
Ha! leapest thou forth as of old?
Are not the limbs still when the ghost is fled,
And canst thou move, Napoleon being dead?

2

How! is not thy quick heart cold?
  What spark is alive on thy hearth?°
How! is not *his* death-knell knolled?
  And livest *thou* still, Mother Earth?
Thou wert warming thy fingers old
O'er the embers covered and cold
Of that most fiery spirit, when it fled—
What, Mother, do you laugh now he is dead?

3

'Who has known me of old,' replied Earth,
  'Or who has my story told?
  It is thou who art overbold.'
And the lightning of scorn laughed forth
As she sung, 'To my bosom I fold
All my sons when their knell is knolled,
And so with living motion all are fed
And the quick spring like weeds out of the dead.

4

'Still alive and still bold,' shouted Earth,
  'I grow bolder and still more bold.
  The dead fill me ten thousand fold
Fuller of speed and splendour and mirth.

I was cloudy, and sullen, and cold,
Like a frozen chaos uprolled,
Till by the spirit of the mighty dead
My heart grew warm. I feed on whom I fed.

5

'Aye, alive and still bold,' muttered Earth,
  'Napoleon's fierce spirit rolled,
  In terror and blood and gold,
A torrent of ruin to death from his birth.
Leave the millions who follow to mould
The metal before it be cold,
And weave into his shame, which like the dead
Shrouds me, the hopes that from his glory fled.'

'The flower that smiles today'

The flower that smiles today
  Tomorrow dies;
All that we wish to stay
  Tempts and then flies;
What is this world's delight?
Lightning, that mocks the night,
  Brief even as bright.—°

Virtue, how frail it is!—
  Friendship, how rare!—
Love, how it sells poor bliss
  For proud despair!
But these, though soon they fall,°
Survive their joy, and all°
  Which ours we call.—

Whilst skies are blue and bright,
  Whilst flowers are gay,
Whilst eyes that change ere night
  Make glad the day;
Whilst yet the calm hours creep

Dream thou—and from thy sleep
Then wake to weep.

To —— ('One word is too often profaned')

One word is too often profaned
For me to profane it,
One feeling too falsely disdained
For thee to disdain it.
One hope is too like despair
For prudence to smother,
And Pity from thee more dear
Than that from another.

I can give not what men call love,
But wilt thou accept not
The worship the heart lifts above
And the Heavens reject not,
The desire of the moth for the star,
Of the night for the morrow,
The devotion to something afar
From the sphere of our sorrow?

'When the lamp is shattered'

When the lamp is shattered
The light in the dust lies dead—°
When the cloud is scattered
The rainbow's glory is shed—
When the lute is broken
Sweet tones are remembered not—
When the lips have spoken
Loved accents are soon forgot.

As music and splendour
Survive not the lamp and the lute,
The heart's echoes render

No song when the spirit is mute—
  No song—but sad dirges
Like the wind through a ruined cell
  Or the mournful surges
That ring the dead seaman's knell.°

  When hearts have once mingled°
Love first leaves the well-built nest—
  The weak one is singled
To endure what it once possessed.
  O Love! who bewailest
The frailty of all things here
  Why choose you the frailest
For your cradle, your home and your bier?

  Its passions will rock thee°
As the storms rock the ravens on high—
  Bright Reason will mock thee
Like the Sun from a wintry sky—
  From thy nest every rafter
Will rot, and thine eagle home
  Leave thee naked to laughter
When leaves fall and cold winds come.°

To —— ('The serpent is shut out from Paradise')

1

The serpent is shut out from Paradise—
The wounded deer must seek the herb no more
In which its heart's cure lies—
The widowed dove must cease to haunt a bower
Like that from which its mate, with feignèd sighs,
Fled in the April hour—
I, too, must seldom seek again
Near happy friends a mitigated pain.

2

Of hatred I am proud,—with scorn content;
Indifference, which once hurt me, is now grown

Itself indifferent.
But not to speak of love, Pity alone
Can break a spirit already more than bent.
The miserable one
Turns the mind's poison into food:
Its medicine is tears, its evil, good.°

3

Therefore, if now I see you seldomer,
Dear friends, dear *friend*, know that I only fly°
Your looks, because they stir
Griefs that should sleep, and hopes that cannot die.
The very comfort which they minister
I scarce can bear; yet I
(So deeply is the arrow gone)
Should quickly perish if it were withdrawn.

4

When I return to my cold home, you ask
Why I am not as I have lately been?
You spoil me for the task
Of acting a forced part in life's dull scene.°
Of wearing on my brow the idle mask
Of author, great or mean,
In the world's carnival. I sought
Peace thus, and but in you I found it not.

5

Full half an hour today I tried my lot
With various flowers, and every one still said,
'She loves me, loves me not.'
And if this meant a Vision long since fled—
If it meant Fortune, Fame, or Peace of thought—
If it meant—(but I dread
To speak what you may know too well)—
Still there was truth in the sad oracle.

6

The crane o'er seas and forests seeks her home.
No bird so wild, but has its quiet nest°

When it no more would roam.
The sleepless billows on the Ocean's breast
Break like a bursting heart, and die in foam
And thus, at length, find rest.
Doubtless there is a place of peace
Where *my* weak heart and all its throbs will cease.

7

I asked her yesterday if she believed
That I had resolution. One who *had*
Would ne'er have thus relieved
His heart with words, but what his judgement bade
Would do, and leave the scorner unrelieved.—
These verses were too sad
To send to you, but that I know,
Happy yourself, you feel another's woe.

To Jane. The Invitation

Best and brightest, come away—
Fairer far than this fair day
Which like thee to those in sorrow
Comes to bid a sweet good-morrow
To the rough year just awake
In its cradle on the brake.—°
The brightest hour of unborn spring
Through the winter wandering
Found it seems this halcyon morn
To hoar February born;
Bending from Heaven in azure mirth
It kissed the forehead of the earth
And smiled upon the silent sea,
And bade the frozen streams be free
And waked to music all their fountains
And breathed upon the frozen mountains
And like a prophetess of May
Strewed flowers upon the barren way,
Making the wintry world appear
Like one on whom thou smilest, dear.

Away, away from men and towns
To the wild wood and the downs,
To the silent wilderness
Where the soul need not repress
Its music lest it should not find
An echo in another's mind,
While the touch of Nature's art
Harmonizes heart to heart.—
'I leave this notice on my door
For each accustomed visitor—
I am gone into the fields
To take what this sweet hour yields—
Reflection, you may come tomorrow,
Sit by the fireside with Sorrow—
You, with the unpaid bill, Despair,
You, tiresome verse-reciter Care,
I will pay you in the grave
Death will listen to your stave—
Expectation too, be off!
Today is for itself enough—
Hope, in pity mock not woe
With smiles, nor follow where I go;
Long having lived on thy sweet food
At length I find one moment's good
After long pain—with all your love
This you never told me of.'

Radiant Sister of the day,
Awake, arise and come away°
To the wild woods and the plains
And the pools where winter-rains
Image all their roof of leaves,
Where the pine its garland weaves
Of sapless green and ivy dun
Round stems that never kiss the Sun—
Where the lawns and pastures be
And the sand hills of the sea—
Where the melting hoar-frost wets
The daisy-star that never sets,°
And wind-flowers, and violets
Which yet join not scent to hue

Crown the pale year weak and new
When the night is left behind
In the deep east dun and blind
And the blue noon is over us,
And the multitudinous
Billows murmur at our feet
Where the earth and ocean meet
And all things seem only one°
In the universal Sun.—

To Jane—The Recollection

Feb. 2. 1822

Now the last day of many days,
All beautiful and bright as thou,
The loveliest and the last, is dead.
Rise Memory, and write its praise!
Up to thy wonted work! come, trace
The epitaph of glory fled;°
For now the Earth has changed its face,
A frown is on the Heaven's brow.

1

We wandered to the pine forest
That skirts the Ocean foam;
The lightest wind was in its nest,
The Tempest in its home;
The whispering waves were half asleep,
The clouds were gone to play,
And on the bosom of the deep
The smile of Heaven lay;
It seemed as if the hour were one
Sent from beyond the skies,
Which scattered from above the sun
A light of Paradise.

2

We paused amid the pines that stood
The giants of the waste,

Tortured by storms to shapes as rude
As serpents interlaced,
And soothed by every azure breath
That under Heaven is blown
To harmonies and hues beneath,
As tender as its own;
Now all the tree-tops lay asleep
Like green waves on the sea,
As still as in the silent deep
The Ocean woods may be.

3

How calm it was! the silence there
By such a chain was bound
That even the busy woodpecker
Made stiller with her sound
The inviolable quietness;
The breath of peace we drew
With its soft motion made not less
The calm that round us grew.—
There seemed from the remotest seat
Of the white mountain-waste,
To the soft flower beneath our feet
A magic circle traced,
A spirit interfused around°
A thrilling silent life.
To momentary peace it bound
Our mortal nature's strife;—
And still I felt the centre of
The magic circle there
Was *one* fair form that filled with love
The lifeless atmosphere.

4

We paused beside the pools that lie
Under the forest bough—
Each seemed as 'twere, a little sky
Gulfed in a world below;
A firmament of purple light
Which in the dark earth lay

More boundless than the depth of night
And purer than the day,
In which the lovely forests grew
As in the upper air
More perfect, both in shape and hue,
Than any spreading there;
There lay the glade, the neighbouring lawn,
And through the dark green wood
The white sun twinkling like the dawn
Out of a speckled cloud.

5

Sweet views, which in our world above
Can never well be seen,
Were imaged in the water's love
Of that fair forest green;
And all was interfused beneath
With an Elysian glow,
An atmosphere without a breath,
A softer day below—
Like one beloved, the scene had lent
To the dark water's breast
Its every leaf and lineament
With more than truth expressed;
Until an envious wind crept by,
Like an unwelcome thought
Which from the mind's too faithful eye
Blots one dear image out.—
Though thou art ever fair and kind
And forests ever green,
Less oft is peace in ——'s mind°
Than calm in water seen.

The Magnetic Lady to Her Patient

'Sleep, sleep on, forget thy pain—
My hand is on thy brow,
My spirit on thy brain

My pity on thy heart, poor friend;
And from my fingers flow
The powers of life, and like a sign°
Seal thee from thine hour of woe,
And brood on thee, but may not blend
With thine.

'Sleep, sleep, sleep on—I love thee not—
Yet when I think that *he*°
Who made and makes my lot
As full of flowers, as thine of weeds,
Might have been lost like thee,—
And that a hand which was not mine
Might then have charmed his agony
As I another's . . . my heart bleeds
For thine.

'Sleep, sleep, and with the slumber of
The dead and the unborn . . .
Forget thy life and love;
Forget that thou must wake;—forever
Forget the world's dull scorn.—
Forget lost health, and the divine
Feelings which died in youth's brief morn;
And forget me, for I can never
Be thine.—

'Like a cloud big with a May shower
My soul weeps healing rain
On thee, thou withered flower.—
It breathes mute music on thy sleep—
Its odour calms thy brain—
Its light within thy gloomy breast
Spreads, like a second youth again—
By mine thy being is to its deep
Possessed.

'The spell is done—how feel you now?'
'Better, quite well' replied
The sleeper—'What would do

You good when suffering and awake,
What cure your head and side?'
'What would cure that would kill me, Jane,
And as I must on earth abide
Awhile yet, tempt me not to break
My chain.'

With a Guitar. To Jane

Ariel to *Miranda*;—Take
This slave of music for the sake
Of him who is the slave of thee;
And teach it all the harmony,
In which thou canst, and only thou,
Make the delighted spirit glow,
Till joy denies itself again
And too intense is turned to pain;
For by permission and command
Of thine own *prince Ferdinand*
Poor Ariel sends this silent token
Of more than ever can be spoken;
Your guardian spirit Ariel, who
From life to life must still pursue
Your happiness, for thus alone
Can Ariel ever find his own;
From Prospero's enchanted cell,
As the mighty verses tell,°
To the throne of Naples he
Lit you o'er the trackless sea,
Flitting on, your prow before,
Like a living meteor.
When you die, the silent Moon
In her interlunar swoon
Is not sadder in her cell
Than deserted Ariel;
When you live again on Earth°
Like an unseen Star of birth
Ariel guides you o'er the sea
Of life from your nativity;

Many changes have been run
Since Ferdinand and you begun
Your course of love, and Ariel still
Has tracked your steps and served your will.
Now, in humbler, happier lot
This is all remembered not;
And now, alas! the poor sprite is
Imprisoned for some fault of his
In a body like a grave.—
From you, he only dares to crave
For his service and his sorrow
A smile today, a song tomorrow.

The artist who this idol wrought
To echo all harmonious thought
Felled a tree, while on the steep
The woods were in their winter sleep
Rocked in that repose divine
On the wind-swept Apennine;
And dreaming, some of autumn past
And some of spring approaching fast,
And some of April buds and showers
And some of songs in July bowers
And all of love,—and so this tree—
O that such our death may be—
Died in sleep and felt no pain
To live in happier form again,
From which, beneath Heaven's fairest star,
The artist wrought this loved guitar,
And taught it justly to reply
To all who question skilfully
In language gentle as thine own;
Whispering in enamoured tone
Sweet oracles of woods and dells
And summer winds in sylvan cells.
For it had learnt all harmonies
Of the plains and of the skies,
Of the forests and the mountains,
And the many-voicèd fountains,
The clearest echoes of the hills,
The softest notes of falling rills,

The melodies of birds and bees,
The murmuring of summer seas,
And pattering rain and breathing dew
And airs of evening;—and it knew
That seldom heard mysterious sound,
Which, driven on its diurnal round
As it floats through boundless day
Our world enkindles on its way—
All this it knows, but will not tell
To those who cannot question well
The spirit that inhabits it:
It talks according to the wit
Of its companions, and no more
Is heard than has been felt before
By those who tempt it to betray
These secrets of an elder day.—
But, sweetly as its answers will
Flatter hands of perfect skill,
It keeps its highest holiest tone
For our beloved Jane alone.—

To Jane ('The keen stars were twinkling')

The keen stars were twinkling
And the fair moon was rising among them,
Dear Jane.
The guitar was tinkling
But the notes were not sweet 'till you sung them
Again.—
As the moon's soft splendour
O'er the faint cold starlight of Heaven
Is thrown—
So your voice most tender
To the strings without soul had then given
Its own.

The stars will awaken,
Though the moon sleep a full hour later,
Tonight;

No leaf will be shaken
While the dews of your melody scatter
Delight.
Though the sound overpowers
Sing again, with your dear voice revealing
A tone
Of some world far from ours,
Where music and moonlight and feeling
Are one.°

Lines Written in the Bay of Lerici

Bright wanderer, fair coquette of Heaven,
To whom alone it has been given
To change and be adored forever. . . .
Envy not this dim world, for never
But once within its shadow grew
One fair as you, but far more true.
She left me at the silent time
When the moon had ceased to climb
The azure dome of Heaven's steep,
And like an albatross asleep,
Balanced on her wings of light,
Hovered in the purple night,
Ere she sought her Ocean nest,
In the chambers of the west.—°
She left me, and I stayed alone
Thinking over every tone,
Which though now silent to the ear
The enchanted heart could hear
Like notes which die when born, but still
Haunt the echoes of the hill:
And feeling ever—O too much—
The soft vibrations of her touch
As if her gentle hand even now
Lightly trembles on my brow;
And thus although she absent were
Memory gave me all of her
That even fancy dares to claim.—

Her presence had made weak and tame
All passions, and I lived alone
In the time which is our own;
The past and future were forgot
As they had been, and would be, not.—°
But soon, the guardian angel gone,
The demon reassumed his throne
In my faint heart . . . I dare not speak
My thoughts; but thus disturbed and weak
I sate and watched the vessels glide
Along the Ocean bright and wide,
Like spirit-wingèd chariots sent
O'er some serenest element
To ministrations strange and far;
As if to some Elysian star
They sailed for drink to medicine
Such sweet and bitter pain as mine.—
And the wind that winged their flight
From the land came fresh and light,
And the scent of sleeping flowers
And the coolness of the hours
Of dew, and the sweet warmth of day
Was scattered o'er the twinkling bay;
And the fisher with his lamp
And spear, about the low rocks damp
Crept, and struck the fish who came
To worship the delusive flame:
Too happy, they whose pleasure sought
Extinguishes all sense and thought
Of the regret that pleasure [ ],°
Seeking life alone, not peace.°

THE TRIUMPH OF LIFE

Swift as a spirit hastening to his task
  Of glory and of good, the Sun sprang forth
Rejoicing in his splendour, and the mask

  Of darkness fell from the awakened Earth.
The smokeless altars of the mountain snows
  Flamed above crimson clouds, and at the birth

Of light, the Ocean's orison arose°
  To which the birds tempered their matin lay.
All flowers in field or forest which unclose

  Their trembling eyelids to the kiss of day,
Swinging their censers in the element,
  With orient incense lit by the new ray

Burned slow and inconsumably, and sent
  Their odorous sighs up to the smiling air,
And in succession due, did Continent,

  Isle, Ocean, and all things that in them wear
The form and character of mortal mould
  Rise as the Sun their father rose, to bear

Their portion of the toil which he of old
  Took as his own and then imposed on them;
But I, whom thoughts which must remain untold

  Had kept as wakeful as the stars that gem
The cone of night, now they were laid asleep,
  Stretched my faint limbs beneath the hoary stem

Which an old chestnut flung athwart the steep
  Of a green Apennine: before me fled
The night; behind me rose the day; the Deep

  Was at my feet, and Heaven above my head°
When a strange trance over my fancy grew
  Which was not slumber, for the shade it spread

Was so transparent that the scene came through
As clear as when a veil of light is drawn
O'er evening hills they glimmer; and I knew

That I had felt the freshness of that dawn,
Bathed in the same cold dew my brow and hair
And sate as thus upon that slope of lawn

Under the self-same bough, and heard as there
The birds, the fountains and the Ocean hold
Sweet talk in music through the enamoured air.
And then a Vision on my brain was rolled. . . .

As in that trance of wondrous thought I lay
This was the tenour of my waking dream.
Methought I sate beside a public way

Thick strewn with summer dust, and a great stream
Of people there was hurrying to and fro°
Numerous as gnats upon the evening gleam,

All hastening onward, yet none seemed to know
Whither he went, or whence he came, or why
He made one of the multitude, yet so

Was borne amid the crowd as through the sky
One of the million leaves of summer's bier.—
Old age and youth, manhood and infancy,

Mixed in one mighty torrent did appear,
Some flying from the thing they feared and some°
Seeking the object of another's fear,

And others as with steps towards the tomb
Pored on the trodden worms that crawled beneath,
And others mournfully within the gloom

Of their own shadow walked, and called it death . . .
And some fled from it as it were a ghost,
Half fainting in the affliction of vain breath.

But more with motions which each other crossed
Pursued or shunned the shadows the clouds threw
Or birds within the noonday ether lost,

Upon that path where flowers never grew;
And weary with vain toil and faint for thirst
Heard not the fountains whose melodious dew

Out of their mossy cells forever burst,
Nor felt the breeze which from the forest told
Of grassy paths, and wood lawns interspersed

With overarching elms and caverns cold,
And violet banks where sweet dreams brood, but they
Pursued their serious folly as of old . . .

And as I gazed methought that in the way
The throng grew wilder, as the woods of June
When the South wind shakes the extinguished day.—

And a cold glare, intenser than the noon
But icy cold, obscured with [ ] light°
The Sun as he the stars. Like the young moon

When on the sunlit limits of the night
Her white shell trembles amid crimson air,
And whilst the sleeping tempest gathers might

Doth, as a herald of its coming, bear
The ghost of her dead mother, whose dim form°
Bends in dark ether from her infant's chair,

So came a chariot on the silent storm°
Of its own rushing splendour, and a Shape
So sate within as one whom years deform

Beneath a dusky hood and double cape
Crouching within the shadow of a tomb,
And o'er what seemed the head a cloud like crape°

Was bent, a dun and faint etherial gloom
Tempering the light; upon the chariot's beam
A Janus-visaged Shadow did assume°

The guidance of that wonder-wingèd team.
The Shapes which drew it in thick lightnings
Were lost: I heard alone on the air's soft stream

The music of their ever-moving wings.
All the four faces of that charioteer
Had their eyes banded . . . little profit brings

Speed in the van and blindness in the rear,
Nor then avail the beams that quench the Sun
Or that his banded eyes could pierce the sphere

Of all that is, has been, or will be done.—
So ill was the car guided, but it passed
With solemn speed majestically on . . .

The crowd gave way, and I arose aghast
Or seemed to rise, so mighty was the trance,
And saw like clouds upon the thunder-blast

The million with fierce song and maniac dance
Raging around; such seemed the jubilee
As when to greet some conqueror's advance

Imperial Rome poured forth her living sea
From senate-house and prison and theatre,
When Freedom left those who upon the free

Had bound a yoke which soon they stooped to bear.°
Nor wanted here the true similitude
Of a triumphal pageant, for where'er

The chariot rolled a captive multitude
Was driven; all those who had grown old in power
Or misery,—all who have their age subdued

By action or by suffering, and whose hour
Was drained to its last sand in weal or woe,
So that the trunk survived both fruit and flower;

All those whose fame or infamy must grow
Till the great winter lay the form and name°
Of their green earth with them forever low—

All but the sacred few who could not tame°
Their spirits to the Conqueror, but as soon
As they had touched the world with living flame

Fled back like eagles to their native noon,
Or those who put aside the diadem
Of earthly thrones or gems, till the last one

Were there; for they of Athens and Jerusalem
Were neither mid the mighty captives seen
Nor mid the ribald crowd that followed them

Or fled before . . . Now swift, fierce and obscene,
The wild dance maddens in the van, and those
Who lead it, fleet as shadows on the green,

Outspeed the chariot and without repose
Mix with each other in tempestuous measure
To savage music. . . . Wilder as it grows,

They, tortured by the agonizing pleasure,
Convulsed and on the rapid whirlwinds spun
Of that fierce spirit, whose unholy leisure

Was soothed by mischief since the world begun,
Throw back their heads and loose their streaming hair,
And in their dance round her who dims the Sun°

Maidens and youths fling their wild arms in air
As their feet twinkle; they recede, and now
Bending within each other's atmosphere

Kindle invisibly; and as they glow
Like moths by light attracted and repelled,
Oft to new bright destruction come and go,

Till like two clouds into one vale impelled
That shake the mountains when their lightnings mingle
And die in rain—the fiery band which held

Their natures, snaps . . . ere the shock cease to tingle
One falls and then another in the path
Senseless, nor is the desolation single,

Yet ere I can say *where* the chariot hath
Passed over them; nor other trace I find
But as of foam after the Ocean's wrath

Is spent upon the desert shore.—Behind,
Old men, and women foully disarrayed
Shake their grey hair in the insulting wind,

Limp in the dance and strain with limbs decayed
To reach the car of light which leaves them still
Farther behind and deeper in the shade.

But not the less with impotence of will
They wheel, though ghastly shadows interpose
Round them and round each other, and fulfil

Their work and to the dust whence they arose
Sink, and corruption veils them as they lie,
And frost in these performs what fire in those.°

Struck to the heart by this sad pageantry,
Half to myself I said, 'And what is this?
Whose shape is that within the car? and why'—

I would have added—'is all here amiss?'
But a voice answered . . . 'Life' . . . I turned and knew
(O Heaven have mercy on such wretchedness!)

That what I thought was an old root which grew
To strange distortion out of the hillside
Was indeed one of that deluded crew,

And that the grass which methought hung so wide
And white, was but his thin discoloured hair,
And that the holes it vainly sought to hide

Were or had been eyes.—'If thou canst forbear
To join the dance, which I had well forborne,'
Said the grim Feature, of my thought aware,°

'I will now tell that which to this deep scorn
Led me and my companions, and relate
The progress of the pageant since the morn.

'If thirst of knowledge doth not thus abate,
Follow it even to the night, but I
Am weary' . . . Then like one who with the weight

Of his own words is staggered, wearily
He paused, and ere he could resume, I cried,
'First who art thou?' . . . 'Before thy memory

'I feared, loved, hated, suffered, did, and died,
And if the spark with which Heaven lit my spirit
Earth had with purer nutriment supplied

'Corruption would not now thus much inherit
Of what was once Rousseau—nor this disguise
Stained that within which still disdains to wear it.—

'If I have been extinguished, yet there rise
A thousand beacons from the spark I bore.'°
'And who are those chained to the car?' 'The wise,

'The great, the unforgotten: they who wore
Mitres and helms and crowns, or wreaths of light,
Signs of thought's empire over thought; their lore

'Taught them not this—to know themselves; their might
Could not repress the mutiny within,
And for the morn of truth they feigned, deep night

'Caught them ere evening.' 'Who is he with chin°
Upon his breast and hands crossed on his chain?'
'The Child of a fierce hour; he sought to win

'The world, and lost all it did contain
Of greatness, in its hope destroyed; and more
Of fame and peace than Virtue's self can gain

'Without the opportunity which bore
Him on its eagle's pinion to the peak
From which a thousand climbers have before

'Fall'n as Napoleon fell.'—I felt my cheek
Alter to see the great form pass away
Whose grasp had left the giant world so weak

That every pigmy kicked it as it lay—
And much I grieved to think how power and will
In opposition rule our mortal day—

And why God made irreconcilable
Good and the means of good; and for despair
I half disdained mine eye's desire to fill

With the spent vision of the times that were
And scarce have ceased to be . . . 'Dost thou behold,'
Said then my guide, 'those spoilers spoiled, Voltaire,

'Frederick and Kant, Catherine and Leopold,°
Chained hoary anarch, demagogue and sage°
Whose name the fresh world thinks already old,

'For in the battle Life and they did wage
She remained conqueror—I was overcome
By my own heart alone, which neither age

'Nor tears nor infamy nor now the tomb
Could temper to its object.' 'Let them pass',°
I cried, '—the world and its mysterious doom

'Is not so much more glorious than it was
That I desire to worship those who drew
New figures on its false and fragile glass

'As the old faded.'—'Figures ever new
Rise on the bubble, paint them how you may;
We have but thrown, as those before us threw,

'Our shadows on it as it passed away.
But mark, how chained to the triumphal chair
The mighty phantoms of an elder day—

'All that is mortal of great Plato there
Expiates the joy and woe his master knew not;°
That star that ruled his doom was far too fair—°

'And Life, where long that flower of Heaven grew not,
Conquered the heart by love which gold or pain
Or age or sloth or slavery could subdue not—

'And near [ ] walk the [ ] twain,
The tutor and his pupil, whom Dominion°
Followed as tame as vulture in a chain.—

'The world was darkened beneath either pinion
Of him whom from the flock of conquerors
Fame singled as her thunder-bearing minion;

'The other long outlived both woes and wars,
Throned in new thoughts of men, and still had kept
The jealous keys of truth's eternal doors

'If Bacon's spirit had not leapt
Like lightning out of darkness; he compelled
The Proteus shape of Nature's as it slept

'To wake and to unbar the caves that held
The treasure of the secrets of its reign.—
See the great bards of old who inly quelled°

'The passions which they sung, as by their strain
May well be known: their living melody
Tempers its own contagion to the vein

'Of those who are infected with it—I
Have suffered what I wrote, or viler pain!

'And so my words were seeds of misery—°
Even as the deeds of others.'—'Not as theirs,'
I said—he pointed to a company

In which I recognized amid the heirs
Of Caesar's crime from him to Constantine°
The Anarchs old whose force and murderous snares

Had founded many a sceptre-bearing line,
And spread the plague of blood and gold abroad,
And Gregory and John and men divine°

Who rose like shadows between Man and god°
Till that eclipse, still hanging under Heaven,
Was worshipped by the world o'er which they strode

For the true Sun it quenched.—'Their power was given
But to destroy,' replied the leader—'I
Am one of those who have created, even

'If it be but a world of agony.'—
'Whence camest thou and whither goest thou?
How did thy course begin,' I said, 'and why?

'Mine eyes are sick of this perpetual flow
Of people, and my heart of one sad thought.—
Speak.'—'Whence I came, partly I seem to know,

'And how and by what paths I have been brought
To this dread pass, methinks even thou mayst guess;
Why this should be my mind can compass not,

'Whither the conqueror hurries me still less.
But follow thou, and from spectator turn
Actor or victim in this wretchedness,

'And what thou wouldst be taught I then may learn
From thee.—Now listen . . . In the April prime
When all the forest tops began to burn

'With kindling green, touched by the azure clime
Of the young year, I found myself asleep
Under a mountain which from unknown time

'Had yawned into a cavern high and deep,
And from it came a gentle rivulet
Whose water like clear air in its calm sweep

'Bent the soft grass and kept forever wet
The stems of the sweet flowers, and filled the grove
With sound which all who hear must needs forget

'All pleasure and all pain, all hate and love,
Which they had known before that hour of rest:
A sleeping mother then would dream not of

'The only child who died upon her breast
At eventide, a king would mourn no more
The crown of which his brow was dispossessed

'When the sun lingered o'er the Ocean floor
To gild his rival's new prosperity.—
Thou wouldst forget thus vainly to deplore

'Ills, which if ills, can find no cure from thee,
The thought of which no other sleep will quell
Nor other music blot from memory—

'So sweet and deep is the oblivious spell.—
Whether my life had been before that sleep
The Heaven which I imagine, or a Hell

'Like this harsh world in which I wake to weep,
I know not. I arose and for a space
The scene of woods and waters seemed to keep,

'Though it was now broad day, a gentle trace
  Of light diviner than the common Sun°
Sheds on the common Earth, but all the place

  'Was filled with many sounds woven into one
Oblivious melody, confusing sense
  Amid the gliding waves and shadows dun;

'And as I looked the bright omnipresence
  Of morning through the orient cavern flowed,
And the Sun's image radiantly intense

  'Burned on the waters of the well that glowed
Like gold, and threaded all the forest maze
  With winding paths of emerald fire—there stood

'Amid the Sun, as he amid the blaze
  Of his own glory, on the vibrating
Floor of the fountain, paving with flashing rays,

  'A shape all light, which with one hand did fling°
Dew on the earth, as if she were the Dawn
  Whose invisible rain forever seemed to sing

'A silver music on the mossy lawn,
  And still before her on the dusky grass
Iris her many-coloured scarf had drawn.—°

  'In her right hand she bore a crystal glass
Mantling with bright Nepenthe;—the fierce splendour°
  Fell from her as she moved under the mass

'Of the deep cavern, and with palms so tender°
  Their tread broke not the mirror of its billow,
Glided along the river, and did bend her

  'Head under the dark boughs, till like a willow
Her fair hair swept the bosom of the stream
  That whispered with delight to be their pillow.—

'As one enamoured is upborne in dream
O'er lily-paven lakes mid silver mist
To wondrous music, so this shape might seem

'Partly to tread the waves with feet which kissed
The dancing foam, partly to glide along
The airs that roughened the moist amethyst,

'Or the slant morning beams that fell among
The trees, or the soft shadows of the trees;
And her feet ever to the ceaseless song

'Of leaves and winds and waves and birds and bees
And falling drops moved in a measure new
Yet sweet, as on the summer evening breeze

'Up from the lake a shape of golden dew
Between two rocks, athwart the rising moon,
Dances i' the wind where eagle never flew.—

'And still her feet, no less than the sweet tune
To which they moved, seemed as they moved, to blot
The thoughts of him who gazed on them, and soon

'All that was seemed as if it had been not,
As if the gazer's mind was strewn beneath
Her feet like embers, and she, thought by thought,

'Trampled its fires into the dust of death,
As Day upon the threshold of the east
Treads out the lamps of night, until the breath

'Of darkness re-illumines even the least
Of heaven's living eyes—like day she came,
Making the night a dream; and ere she ceased

'To move, as one between desire and shame
Suspended, I said—"If, as it doth seem,
Thou comest from the realm without a name

'"Into this valley of perpetual dream,
Show whence I came, and where I am, and why—
Pass not away upon the passing stream."

'"Arise and quench thy thirst," was her reply.
And as a shut lily, stricken by the wand
Of dewy morning's vital alchemy,

'I rose; and, bending at her sweet command,
Touched with faint lips the cup she raised,
And suddenly my brain became as sand

'Where the first wave had more than half erased
The track of deer in desert Labrador,
Whilst the fierce wolf from which they fled amazed

'Leaves his stamp visibly upon the shore
Until the second bursts—so on my sight
Burst a new Vision never seen before.—

'And the fair shape waned in the coming light
As veil by veil the silent splendour drops
From Lucifer, amid the chrysolite

'Of sunrise ere it strikes the mountain tops—
And as the presence of that fairest planet,
Although unseen, is felt by one who hopes

'That his day's path may end as he began it
In that star's smile, whose light is like the scent
Of a jonquil when evening breezes fan it,

'Or the soft note in which his dear lament
The Brescian shepherd breathes, or the caress°
That turned his weary slumber to content—

'So knew I in that light's severe excess°
The presence of that shape which on the stream
Moved, as I moved along the wilderness,

'More dimly than a day-appearing dream,
The ghost of a forgotten form of sleep,
A light from Heaven whose half-extinguished beam

'Through the sick day in which we wake to weep
Glimmers, forever sought, forever lost.—
So did that shape its obscure tenour keep

'Beside my path, as silent as a ghost;
    But the new Vision, and its cold bright car,
With savage music, stunning music, crossed

    'The forest, and as if from some dread war
Triumphantly returning, the loud million
    Fiercely extolled the fortune of her star.—

'A moving arch of victory the vermilion
    And green and azure plumes of Iris had
Built high over her wind-wingèd pavilion,

    'And underneath etherial glory clad
The wilderness, and far before her flew
    The tempest of the splendour which forbade

'Shadow to fall from leaf or stone;—the crew
    Seemed in that light like atomies that dance°
Within a sunbeam.—Some upon the new

    'Embroidery of flowers that did enhance
The grassy vesture of the desert, played,
    Forgetful of the chariot's swift advance;

'Others stood gazing till within the shade
    Of the great mountain its light left them dim.—
Others outspeeded it, and others made

    'Circles around it like the clouds that swim
Round the high moon in a bright sea of air,
    And more did follow, with exulting hymn,

'The chariot and the captives fettered there,
    But all like bubbles on an eddying flood
Fell into the same track at last and were

    'Borne onward.—I among the multitude
Was swept; me sweetest flowers delayed not long,
    Me not the shadow nor the solitude,

'Me not the falling stream's Lethean song,°
Me, not the phantom of that early form
Which moved upon its motion,—but among

'The thickest billows of the living storm
I plunged, and bared my bosom to the clime
Of that cold light, whose airs too soon deform.—

'Before the chariot had begun to climb
The opposing steep of that mysterious dell,
Behold a wonder worthy of the rhyme°

'Of him who from the lowest depths of Hell°
Through every Paradise and through all glory
Love led serene, and who returned to tell

'In words of hate and awe the wondrous story
How all things are transfigured, except Love;
For deaf as is a sea which wrath makes hoary

'The world can hear not the sweet notes that move
The sphere whose light is melody to lovers—°
A wonder worthy of his rhyme—the grove

'Grew dense with shadows to its inmost covers,
The earth was grey with phantoms, and the air
Was peopled with dim forms, as when there hovers

'A flock of vampire-bats before the glare
Of the tropic sun, bringing ere evening
Strange night upon some Indian isle,—thus were

'Phantoms diffused around, and some did fling
Shadows of shadows, yet unlike themselves,°
Behind them, some like eaglets on the wing

'Were lost in the white blaze, others like elves
Danced in a thousand unimagined shapes
Upon the sunny streams and grassy shelves;

'And others sate chattering like restless apes
On vulgar hands and over shoulders leapt;
Some made a cradle of the ermined capes

'Of kingly mantles, some upon the tiar
Of pontiffs sate like vultures, others played
Within the crown which girt with empire

'A baby's or an idiot's brow, and made
Their nests in it; the old anatomies°
Sate hatching their bare brood under the shade

'Of demon wings, and laughed from their dead eyes
To reassume the delegated power
Arrayed in which these worms did monarchize

'Who make this earth their charnel.—Others more
Humble, like falcons sate upon the fist
Of common men, and round their heads did soar

'Or like small gnats and flies as thick as mist
On evening marshes thronged about the brow
Of lawyer, statesman, priest and theorist,

'And others like discoloured flakes of snow
On fairest bosoms and the sunniest hair
Fell, and were melted by the youthful glow

'Which they extinguished; for like tears, they were
A veil to those from whose faint lids they rained
In drops of sorrow.—I became aware

'Of whence those forms proceeded which thus stained
The track in which we moved; after brief space
From every form the beauty slowly waned,

'From every firmest limb and fairest face
The strength and freshness fell like dust, and left
The action and the shape without the grace

'Of life; the marble brow of youth was cleft
With care, and in the eyes where once hope shone
Desire like a lioness bereft

'Of its last cub, glared ere it died; each one
Of that great crowd sent forth incessantly
These shadows, numerous as the dead leaves blown

'In Autumn evening from a poplar tree—
Each, like himself and like each other were,
At first, but soon distorted, seemed to be

'Obscure clouds moulded by the casual air;
And of this stuff the car's creative ray°
Wrought all the busy phantoms fluttering there

'As the sun shapes the clouds—thus, on the way,
Mask after mask fell from the countenance
And form of all, and long before the day

'Was old, the joy which waked like Heaven's glance
The sleepers in the oblivious valley, died,
And some grew weary of the ghastly dance

'And fell, as I have fallen by the wayside,
Those soonest, from whose forms most shadows passed
And least of strength and beauty did abide.'—

'Then, what is Life?' I said . . . the cripple cast°
His eye upon the car which now had rolled
Onward, as if that look must be the last,

And answered . . . 'Happy those for whom the fold
Of°

PROSE

An Address to the People on the Death of the Princess Charlotte

BY THE HERMIT OF MARLOW°

'We pity the plumage, but forget the dying bird.'°

I. The Princess Charlotte is dead. She no longer moves, nor thinks, nor feels. She is as inanimate as the clay with which she is about to mingle. It is a dreadful thing to know that she is a putrid corpse, who but a few days since was full of life and hope; a woman young, innocent, and beautiful, snatched from the bosom of domestic peace, and leaving that single vacancy which none can die and leave not.

II. Thus much the death of the Princess Charlotte has in common with the death of thousands. How many women die in childbed and leave their families of motherless children and their husbands to live on, blighted by the remembrance of that heavy loss? How many women of active and energetic virtues; mild, affectionate, and wise, whose life is as a chain of happiness and union, which once being broken, leaves those whom it bound to perish, have died, and have been deplored with bitterness, which is too deep for words?° Some have perished in penury or shame, and their orphan baby has survived, a prey to the scorn and neglect of strangers. Men have watched by the bedside of their expiring wives, and have gone mad when the hideous death-rattle was heard within the throat, regardless of the rosy child sleeping in the lap of the unobservant nurse. The countenance of the physician had been read by the stare of this distracted husband, till the legible despair sunk into his heart. All this has been and is. You walk with a merry heart through the streets of this great city, and think not that such are the scenes acting all around you. You do not number in your thought the mothers who die in childbed. It is the most horrible of ruins:—In sickness, in old age, in battle, death comes as to his own home; but in the season of joy and hope, when life should succeed to life, and the assembled family expects one more, the youngest and the best beloved, that the wife, the mother—she for whom each member of the family was so dear to one another, should die!—Yet thousands of the poorest poor, whose misery is aggravated by what cannot be spoken now, suffer this. And have they no affections?° Do not their hearts beat in their bosoms, and the tears gush from their eyes? Are they not human flesh and blood? Yet none weep for them—none mourn for them—none when their coffins are carried to the grave (if indeed the parish furnishes a coffin for all) turn aside and moralize upon the sadness they have left behind.

III. The Athenians did well to celebrate, with public mourning, the death of those who had guided the republic with their valour and their understanding, or illustrated° it with their genius. Men do well to mourn for the dead: it proves that we love something beside ourselves; and he must have a hard heart who can see his friend depart to rottenness and dust, and speed him without emotion on his voyage to 'that bourne whence no traveller returns.'° To lament for those who have benefited the state, is a habit of piety yet more favourable to the cultivation of our best affections. When Milton died it had been well that the universal English nation had been clothed in solemn black, and that the muffled bells had tolled from town to town. The French nation should have enjoined a public mourning at the deaths of Rousseau and Voltaire. We cannot truly grieve for every one who dies beyond the circle of those especially dear to us; yet in the extinction of the objects of public love and admiration, and gratitude, there is something, if we enjoy a liberal mind, which has departed from within that circle. It were well done also, that men should mourn for any public calamity which has befallen their country or the world, though it be not death. This helps to maintain that connection between one man and another, and all men considered as a whole, which is the bond of social life. There should be public mourning when those events take place which make all good men mourn in their hearts,—the rule of foreign or domestic tyrants, the abuse of public faith, the wresting of old and venerable laws to the murder of the innocent, the established insecurity of all those, the flower of the nation, who cherish an unconquerable enthusiasm for public good. Thus, if Horne Tooke and Hardy° had been convicted of high treason, it had been good that there had been not only the sorrow and the indignation which would have filled all hearts, but the external symbols of grief. When the French Republic was extinguished, the world ought to have mourned.

IV. But this appeal to the feelings of men should not be made lightly, or in any manner that tends to waste, on inadequate objects, those fertilizing streams of sympathy which a public mourning should be the occasion of pouring forth. This solemnity should be used only to express a wide and intelligible calamity, and one which is felt to be such by those who feel for their country and for mankind; its character ought to be universal, not particular.

V. The news of the death of the Princess Charlotte, and of the execution of Brandreth, Ludlam, and Turner,° arrived nearly at the same time. If beauty, youth, innocence, amiable manners, and the exercise of the domestic virtues could alone justify public sorrow when they are extinguished forever, this interesting Lady would well deserve that exhibition. She was the last and the best of her race. But there were thousands of others equally distinguished as she, for private excellencies, who have been cut off in youth and hope. The accident of her birth neither made her life more virtuous nor her death more worthy of grief. For the public she had done nothing either good or evil; her education had rendered her incapable of either in a large and comprehensive sense. She was born a Princess; and those who are destined to rule mankind are dispensed with acquiring that wisdom and that experience which is necessary even to rule themselves. She was not like Lady Jane Grey, or Queen Elizabeth, a woman of profound and various learning. She had accomplished nothing,° and aspired to nothing, and could understand nothing respecting those great political questions which involve the happiness of those over whom she was destined to rule. Yet this should not be said in blame, but in compassion: let us speak no evil of the dead. Such is the misery, such the impotence of royalty.—Princes are prevented from the cradle from becoming any thing which may deserve that greatest of all rewards next to a good conscience, public admiration and regret.

VI. The execution of Brandreth, Ludlam, and Turner, is an event of quite a different character from the death of the Princess Charlotte. These men were shut up in a horrible dungeon, for many months, with the fear of a hideous death and of everlasting hell thrust before their eyes; and at last were brought to the scaffold and hung. They too had domestic affections, and were remarkable for the exercise of private virtues. Perhaps their low station permitted the growth of those affections in a degree not consistent with a more exalted rank. They had sons, and brothers, and sisters, and fathers, who loved them, it should seem, more than the Princess Charlotte could be loved by those whom the regulations of her rank had held in perpetual estrangement from her. Her husband° was to her as father, mother, and brethren. Ludlam and Turner were men of mature years, and the affections were ripened and strengthened within them. What these sufferers felt shall not be said. But what must have been the long and various agony of their kindred may be inferred from Edward Turner, who, when he saw his brother dragged along upon the hurdle,° shrieked horribly and fell in a fit, and was carried away like a corpse by two men. How fearful must have been their agony, sitting in solitude on that day when the tempestuous voice of horror from the crowd told them that the head so dear to them was severed from the body! Yes—they listened to the maddening shriek which burst from the multitude; they heard the rush of ten thousand terror-stricken feet, the groans and the hootings which told them that the mangled and distorted head was then lifted into the air. The sufferers were dead. What is death? Who dares to say that which will come after the grave?° Brandreth was calm, and evidently believed that the consequences of our errors were limited by that tremendous barrier. Ludlam and Turner were full of fears, lest God should plunge them in everlasting fire. Mr Pickering, the clergyman, was evidently anxious that Brandreth should not by a false confidence lose the single opportunity of reconciling himself with the Ruler of the future world. None knew what death was, or could know. Yet these men were presumptuously thrust into that unfathomable gulf, by other men, who knew as little and who reckoned not the present or the future sufferings of their victims. Nothing is more horrible than that man should for any cause shed the life of man. For all other calamities there is a remedy or a consolation. When that Power through which we live ceases to maintain the life which it has conferred, then is grief and agony, and the burden which must be borne: such sorrow improves the heart. But when man sheds the blood of man, revenge, and hatred, and a long train of executions, and assassinations, and proscriptions, is perpetuated to remotest time.

VII. Such are the particular, and some of the general considerations depending on° the death of these men. But however deplorable, if it were a mere private or customary grief, the public, as the public, should not mourn. But it is more than this. The events which led to the death of those unfortunate men are a public calamity. I will not impute blame to the jury who pronounced them guilty of high treason, perhaps the law requires that such should be the denomination of their offence. Some restraint ought indeed to be imposed on those thoughtless men who imagine they can find in violence a remedy for violence, even if their oppressors had tempted them to this occasion of their ruin. They are instruments of evil, not so guilty as the hands that wielded them, but fit to inspire caution. But their death, by hanging and beheading, and the circumstances° of which it is the characteristic and the consequence, constitute a calamity such as the English nation ought to mourn with an unassuageable grief.

VIII. Kings and their ministers have in every age been distinguished from other men by a thirst for expenditure and bloodshed. There existed in this country, until the American war, a check,° sufficiently feeble and pliant indeed, to this desolating propensity. Until America proclaimed itself a republic, England was perhaps the freest and most glorious nation subsisting on the surface of the earth. It was not what is to the full desirable that a nation should be, but all that it can be, when it does not govern itself. The consequences however of that fundamental defect° soon became evident. The government which the imperfect constitution of our representative assembly threw into the hands of a few aristocrats, improved the method of anticipating the taxes by loans, invented by the ministers of William III, until an enormous debt had been created. In the war against the republic of France, this policy was followed up, until now, the *mere interest* of the public debt amounts to more than twice as much as the lavish expenditure of the public treasure, for maintaining the standing army, and the royal family, and the pensioners, and the placemen. The effect of this debt is to produce such an unequal distribution of the means of living, as saps the foundation of social union and civilized life. It creates a double aristocracy, instead of one which was sufficiently burdensome before, and gives twice as many people the liberty of living in luxury and idleness, on the produce of the industrious and the poor. And it does not give them this because they are more wise and meritorious than the rest, or because their leisure is spent in schemes of public good, or in those exercises of the intellect and the imagination, whose creations ennoble or adorn a country. They are not like the old aristocracy men of pride and honour, *sans peur et sans tache*,° but petty piddling slaves who have gained a right to the title of public creditors, either by gambling in the funds,° or by subserviency to government, or some other villainous trade. They are not the 'Corinthian capital of polished society,'° but the petty and creeping weeds which deface the rich tracery of its sculpture. The effect of this system is, that the day labourer gains no more now by working sixteen hours a day than he gained before by working eight. I put the thing in its simplest and most intelligible shape. The labourer, he that tills the ground and manufactures cloth, is the man who has to provide, out of what he would bring home to his wife and children, for the luxuries and comforts of those, whose claims are represented by an annuity of forty-four millions a year levied upon the English nation. Before, he supported the army and the pensioners, and the royal family, and the landholders; and this is a hard necessity to which it was well that he should submit. Many and various are the mischiefs flowing from oppression, but this is the representative of them all; namely, that one man is forced to labour for another in a degree not only not necessary to the support of the subsisting distinctions among mankind, but so as by the excess of the injustice to endanger the very foundations of all that is valuable in social order, and to provoke that anarchy which is at once the enemy of freedom, and the child and the chastiser of misrule. The nation, tottering on the brink of two chasms,° began to be weary of a continuance of such dangers and degradations, and the miseries which are the consequence of them; the public voice loudly demanded a free representation of the people. It began to be felt that no other constituted body of men could meet the difficulties which impend. Nothing but the nation itself dares to touch the question as to whether there is any remedy or no to the annual payment of forty-four millions a year, beyond the necessary expenses of state, forever and forever. A nobler spirit also went abroad, and the love of liberty, and patriotism, and the self-respect attendant on those glorious emotions, revived in the bosoms of men. The government had a desperate game to play.

IX. In the manufacturing districts of England discontent and disaffection had prevailed for many years; this was the consequence of that system of double aristocracy produced by the causes before mentioned. The manufacturers,° the helots° of our luxury, are left by this system famished, without affections, without health, without leisure or opportunity for such instruction as might counteract those habits of turbulence and dissipation, produced by the precariousness and insecurity of poverty. Here was a ready field for any adventurer who should wish for whatever purpose to incite a few ignorant men to acts of illegal outrage. So soon as it was plainly seen that the demands of the people for a free representation must be conceded if some intimidation and prejudice were not conjured up, a conspiracy of the most horrible atrocity was laid in train. It is impossible to know how far the higher members of the government are involved in the guilt of their infernal agents. It is impossible to know how numerous or how active they have been, or by what false hopes they are yet inflaming the untutored multitude to put their necks under the axe and into the halter. But thus much is known, that so soon as the whole nation lifted up its voice for parliamentary reform, spies were sent forth.° These were selected from the most worthless and infamous of mankind, and dispersed among the multitude of famished and illiterate labourers. It was their business if they found no discontent to create it. It was their business to find victims, no matter whether right or wrong. It was their business to produce upon the public an impression, that if any attempt to attain national freedom, or to diminish the burdens of debt and taxation under which we groan, were successful, the starving multitude would rush in, and confound all orders and distinctions, and institutions and laws, in common ruin. The inference with which they were required to arm the ministers was, that despotic power ought to be eternal. To produce this salutary impression, they betrayed some innocent and unsuspecting rustics° into a crime whose penalty is a hideous death. A few hungry and ignorant manufacturers seduced by the splendid promises of these remorseless blood-conspirators, collected together in what is called rebellion against the state. All was prepared, and the eighteen dragoons assembled in readiness, no doubt, conducted their astonished victims to that dungeon which they left only to be mangled by the executioner's hand. The cruel instigators of their ruin retired to enjoy the great revenues which they had earned by a life of villainy. The public voice was overpowered by the timid and the selfish, who threw the weight of fear into the scale of public opinion, and parliament confided anew to the executive government those extraordinary powers° which may never be laid down, or which may be laid down in blood, or which the regularly constituted assembly of the nation must wrest out of their hands. Our alternatives are a despotism, a revolution, or reform.

X. On the 7th of November, Brandreth, Turner, and Ludlam ascended the scaffold. We feel for Brandreth the less, because it seems he killed a man. But recollect who instigated him to the proceedings which led to murder. On the word of a dying man, Brandreth tells us, that 'OLIVER *brought him to this*'°—that, '*but for* OLIVER, *he would not have been there*.' See, too, Ludlam and Turner, with their sons and brothers, and sisters, how they kneel together in a dreadful agony of prayer. Hell is before their eyes, and they shudder and feel sick with fear, lest some unrepented or some wilful sin should seal their doom in everlasting fire. With that dreadful penalty before their eyes—with that tremendous sanction for the truth of all he spoke, Turner exclaimed loudly and distinctly, *while the executioner was putting the rope round his neck*, 'THIS IS ALL OLIVER AND THE GOVERNMENT.' What more he might have said we know not, because the chaplain prevented° any further observations. Troops of horse, with keen and glittering swords, hemmed in the multitudes collected to witness this abominable exhibition. 'When the stroke of the axe was heard, there was a burst of horror from the crowd. The instant the head was exhibited, there was a tremendous shriek set up, and the multitude ran violently in all directions, as if under the impulse of sudden frenzy. Those who resumed their stations, groaned and hooted.' It is a national calamity, that we endure men to rule over us, who sanction for whatever ends a conspiracy which is to arrive at its purpose through such a frightful pouring forth of human blood and agony. But when that purpose is to trample upon our rights and liberties forever, to present to us the alternatives of anarchy and oppression, and triumph when the astonished nation accepts the latter at their hands, to maintain a vast standing army, and add, year by year, to a public debt, which, already, they know, cannot be discharged; and which, when the delusion that supports it fails, will produce as much misery and confusion through all classes of society as it has continued to produce of famine and degradation to the undefended poor; to imprison and calumniate those who may offend them, at will; when this, if not the purpose, is the effect of that conspiracy, how ought we not to mourn?

XI. Mourn then People of England. Clothe yourselves in solemn black. Let the bells be tolled. Think of mortality and change. Shroud yourselves in solitude and the gloom of sacred sorrow. Spare no symbol of universal grief. Weep—mourn—lament. Fill the great City—fill the boundless fields, with lamentation and the echo of groans. A beautiful Princess is dead:—she who should have been the Queen of her beloved nation, and whose posterity should have ruled it forever. She loved the domestic affections, and cherished arts which adorn, and valour which defends. She was amiable and would have become wise, but she was young, and in the flower of youth the despoiler came. LIBERTY is dead. Slave! I charge thee disturb not the depth and solemnity of our grief by any meaner sorrow. If One has died who was like her that should have ruled over this land, like Liberty, young, innocent, and lovely, know that the power through which that one perished was God, and that it was a private grief. But *man* has murdered Liberty, and whilst the life was ebbing from its wound, there descended on the heads and on the hearts of every human thing, the sympathy of an universal blast and curse. Fetters heavier than iron weigh upon us, because they bind our souls. We move about in a dungeon more pestilential than damp and narrow walls, because the earth is its floor and the heavens are its roof. Let us follow the corpse of British Liberty slowly and reverentially to its tomb: and if some glorious Phantom° should appear, and make its throne of broken swords and sceptres and royal crowns trampled in the dust, let us say that the Spirit of Liberty has arisen from its grave and left all that was gross and mortal there, and kneel down and worship it as our Queen.

On Love

What is Love? Ask him who lives what is life; ask him who adores what is God.

I know not the internal constitution of other men, or even of thine whom I now address. I see that in some external attributes they resemble me, but when misled by that appearance I have thought to appeal to something in common and unburden my inmost soul to them, I have found my language misunderstood like one in a distant and savage land. The more opportunities they have afforded me for experience, the wider has appeared the interval between us, and to a greater distance have the points of sympathy been withdrawn. With a spirit ill fitted to sustain such proof, trembling and feeble through its tenderness, I have everywhere sought,° and have found only repulse and disappointment.

Thou demandest what is Love.° It is that powerful attraction towards all that we conceive or fear or hope beyond ourselves when we find within our own thoughts the chasm of an insufficient void and seek to awaken in all things that are a community with what we experience within ourselves. If we reason, we would be understood; if we imagine, we would that the airy children of our brain° were born anew within another's; if we feel, we would that another's nerves should vibrate to our own, that the beams of their eyes should kindle at once and mix and melt into our own, that lips of motionless ice should not reply to lips quivering and burning with the heart's best blood. This is Love. This is the bond and the sanction which connects not only man with man, but with everything which exists. We are born into the world, and there is something within us which from the instant that we live and move thirsts after its likeness. It is probably in correspondence with this law that the infant drains milk from the bosom of its mother. This propensity develops itself with the development of our nature. We dimly see° within our intellectual nature a miniature as it were of our entire self, yet deprived of all that we condemn or despise, the ideal prototype° of everything excellent or lovely that we are capable of conceiving as belonging to the nature of man. Not only the portrait of our external being, but an assemblage of the minutest particles of which our nature is composed: a mirror whose surface reflects only the forms of purity and brightness: a soul within our soul° that describes a circle around its proper Paradise which pain and sorrow and evil dare not overleap. To this eagerly we refer all sensations, thirsting that they should resemble or correspond with it. The discovery of its antitype:° the meeting with an understanding capable of clearly estimating the deductions of our own, an imagination which should enter into and seize upon the subtle and delicate peculiarities which we have delighted to cherish and unfold in secret, with a frame whose nerves, like the chords of two exquisite lyres strung to the accompaniment of one delightful voice, vibrate with the vibrations of our own; and a combination of all these in such proportion as the type within demands: this is the invisible and unattainable point to which Love tends; and to attain which it urges forth the powers of man to arrest the faintest shadow of that without the possession of which there is no rest or respite to the heart over which it rules. Hence in solitude, or in that deserted state when we are surrounded by human beings and yet they sympathize not with us, we love the flowers, the grass and the waters and the sky. In the motion of the very leaves of spring, in the blue air, there is then found a secret correspondence with our heart. There is eloquence in the tongueless wind, and a melody in the flowing brooks and the rustling of the reeds beside them, which by their inconceivable relation to something within the soul awaken the spirits to a dance of breathless rapture, and bring tears of mysterious tenderness to the eyes like the enthusiasm of patriotic success or the voice of one beloved singing to you alone. Sterne says that if he were in a desert he would love some cypress° . . . So soon as this want or power is dead, man becomes a living sepulchre of himself, and what yet survives is the mere husk of what once he was.

On Life

Life, and the world, or whatever we call that which we are and feel, is an astonishing thing. The mist of familiarity obscures from us the wonder of our being. We are struck with admiration at some of its transient modifications; but it is itself the great miracle. What are changes of empire, the wreck of dynasties with the opinions which supported them; what is the birth and the extinction of religions and political systems to life? What are the revolutions of the globe which we inhabit, and the operations of which it is composed, compared with life? What is the universe of stars and suns [of]° which this inhabited earth is one and their motions and their destiny compared with life? Life, the great miracle, we admire not, because it is so miraculous. It is well that we are thus shielded by the familiarity of what is at once so certain and so unfathomable from an astonishment which would otherwise absorb and overawe the functions of that which is [its]° object.

If any artist (I do not say had executed) but had merely conceived in his mind the system of the sun and stars and planets, they not existing, and had painted to us in words or upon canvas, the spectacle now afforded by the nightly cope of Heaven and illustrated it by the wisdom of astronomy, how great would be our admiration. Or had he imagined the scenery of this earth, the mountains, the seas and the rivers, and the grass and the flowers and the variety of the forms and masses of the leaves of the woods and the colours which attend the setting and the rising sun, and the hues of the atmosphere, turbid or serene, these things not before existing, truly we should have been astonished and it would have been more than a vain boast to have said of such a man, 'Non merita nome di creatore, sennon Iddio ed il Poeta.'° But now these things are looked on with little wonder and to be conscious of them with intense delight is esteemed to be the distinguishing mark of character of a refined and extraordinary person. The multitude of those men care not for them. It is thus with Life—that which includes all.

What is life? Thoughts and feelings arise, with or without our will, and we employ words to express them. We are born, and our birth is unremembered and our infancy remembered only in fragments. We live on, and in living we lose the apprehension of life. How vain it is to think that words can penetrate the mystery of our being. Rightly used they may make evident our ignorance to ourselves, and this is much.

For what are we? Whence do we come, and whither do we go? Is birth the commencement, is death the conclusion of our being? What is birth and death?

The most refined abstractions of logic conduct to a view of life which, though startling to the apprehension, is in fact that which the habitual sense of its repeated combinations has extinguished in us. It strips, as it were, the painted curtain from this scene of things. I confess that I am one of those who am unable to refuse my assent to the conclusions of those philosophers, who assert that nothing exists but as it is perceived.°

It is a decision against which all our persuasions struggle, and we must be long convicted, before we can be convinced that the solid universe of external things is 'such stuff as dreams are made of.'°—The shocking absurdities of the popular philosophy of mind and matter, and its fatal consequences in morals, their violent dogmatism concerning the source of all things, had early conducted me to materialism. This materialism is a seducing system to young and superficial minds. It allows its disciples to talk and dispenses them from thinking. But I was discontented with such a view of things as it afforded; man is a being of high aspirations 'looking both before and after,'° with° 'thoughts that wander through eternity,'° disclaiming alliance with transience and decay, incapable of imagining to himself annihilation, existing but in the future and the past, being, not what he is, but what he has been, and shall be. Whatever may be his true and final destination, there is a spirit within him at enmity with nothingness and dissolution, change and extinction.° This is the character of all life and being.—Each is at once the centre and the circumference; the point to which all things are referred, and the line within which all things are contained.—Such contemplations as these materialism and the popular philosophy of mind and matter, alike forbid; they are consistent only with the intellectual system.

It is absurd to enter into a long recapitulation of arguments sufficiently familiar to those enquiring minds whom alone a writer on abstruse subjects can be conceived to address. Perhaps the most clear and vigorous statement of the intellectual system is to be found in Sir W. Drummond's *Academical Questions*. After such an exposition it would be idle to translate into other words what could only lose its energy and fitness by the change. Examined point by point and word by word, the most discriminating intellects have been able to discover no train of thoughts in the process of its reasoning, which does not conduct inevitably to the conclusion which has been stated.

What follows from the admission? It establishes no new truth, it gives us no additional insight into our hidden nature, neither its action, nor itself. Philosophy, impatient as it may be to build, has much work yet remaining as pioneer for the overgrowth of ages. It makes one step towards this object; it destroys error, and the roots of error. It leaves, what is too often the duty of the reformer in political and ethical questions to leave, a vacancy. It reduces the mind to that freedom in which it would have acted, but for the misuse of words and signs,° the instruments of its own creation.—By signs, I would be understood in a wide sense, including what is properly meant by that term, and what I peculiarly mean. In this latter sense almost all familiar objects are signs, standing not for themselves but for others, in their capacity of suggesting one thought, which shall lead to a train of thoughts.—Our whole life is thus an education of error.

Let us recollect our sensations as children. What a distinct and intense apprehension had we of the world and of ourselves. Many of the circumstances of social life were then important to us, which are now no longer so. But that is not the point of comparison on which I mean to insist. We less habitually distinguished all that we saw and felt from ourselves. They seemed as it were to constitute one mass. There are some persons who in this respect are always children. Those who are subject to the state called reverie feel as if their nature were dissolved into the surrounding universe, or as if the surrounding universe were absorbed into their being. They are conscious of no distinction. And these are states which precede or accompany or follow an unusually intense and vivid apprehension of life. As men grow up, this power commonly decays, and they become mechanical and habitual agents. Their feelings and their reasonings are the combined result of a multitude of entangled thoughts, of a series of what are called impressions, planted by reiteration.

The view of life presented by the most refined deductions of the intellectual philosophy, is that of unity. Nothing exists but as it is perceived. The difference is merely nominal between those two classes of thought which are vulgarly distinguished by the names of ideas and of external objects. Pursuing the same thread of reasoning, the existence of distinct individual minds similar to that which is employed in now questioning its own nature, is likewise found to be a delusion. The words, *I*, *you*, *they*, are not signs of any actual difference subsisting between the assemblage of thoughts thus indicated, but are merely marks employed to denote the different modifications of the one mind. Let it not be supposed that this doctrine conducts to the monstrous presumption, that I, the person who now write and speak, am that one mind. I am but a portion of it. The words *I*, and *you* and *they* are grammatical devices invented simply for arrangement and totally devoid of the intense and exclusive sense usually attributed to them. It is difficult to find terms adequately to express so subtle a conception as that to which the intellectual philosophy has conducted us. We are on that verge where words abandon us, and what wonder if we grow dizzy to look down the dark abyss of—how little we know.

The relations of *things* remain unchanged by whatever system. By the word *things* is to be understood any object of thought, that is, any thought upon which any other thought is employed, with an apprehension of distinction. The relations of these remain unchanged; and such is the material of our knowledge.

What is the cause of life?—that is, how was it preceded,° or what agencies distinct from life, have acted or act upon life? All recorded generations of mankind have wearily busied themselves in inventing answers to this question. And the result has been . . . Religion. Yet, that the basis° of all things cannot be, as the popular philosophy alleges, mind is sufficiently evident. Mind, as far as we have any experience of its properties, and beyond that experience how vain is argument, cannot create, it can only perceive. It is said also to be the Cause. But cause is only a word expressing a certain state of the human mind with regard to the manner in which two thoughts° are apprehended to be related to each other.—If any one desires to know how unsatisfactorily the popular philosophy employs itself upon this great question, they need only impartially reflect upon the manner in which thoughts develop themselves in their minds.—It is infinitely improbable that the cause of mind, that is, of existence, is similar to mind. It is said that mind produces motion and it might as well have been said that motion produces mind.

From *A Philosophical View of Reform*

1st. Sentiment of the Necessity of change.
2nd. Practicability and Utility of such change.
3rd. State of Parties as regards it.
4th. Probable mode—Desirable mode.°

> Let us believe not only that is necessary because it is just and ought to be, but necessary because it is inevitable and must be.°

Those who imagine that their personal interest is directly or indirectly concerned in maintaining the power in which they are clothed by the existing institutions of English Government do not acknowledge the necessity of a material change in those institutions. With this exception, there is no inhabitant of the British Empire of mature age and perfect understanding not fully persuaded of the necessity of Reform.

Introduction

From the dissolution of the Roman empire, that vast and successful scheme for enslaving the most civilized portion of mankind, to the epoch of two recent wars° have succeeded a series of schemes on a smaller scale, operating to the same effect. Sacred names borrowed from the life and opinions of Jesus Christ were employed as symbols of domination and imposture; and a system of liberty and equality, for such was the system preached by that great Reformer, was perverted to support oppression—. Not his doctrines, for they are too simple and direct to be susceptible of such perversion—but the mere names. Such was the origin of the Catholic Church, which, together with the several dynasties then beginning to consolidate themselves in Europe, means, being interpreted, a plan according to which the cunning and selfish few have employed the fears and hopes of the ignorant many to the establishment of their own power and the destruction of the real interest of all.

The Republics and municipal governments of Italy° opposed for some time a systematic and effectual resistance to the all-surrounding tyranny. The Lombard League defeated the armies of the despot in open field, and until Florence was betrayed to those flattered traitors [and] polished tyrants, the Medici, Freedom had one citadel wherein it could find refuge from a world which was its enemy. Florence long balanced, divided, and weakened the strength of the Empire and the Popedom. To this cause, if to anything, was due the undisputed superiority of Italy in literature and the arts over all its contemporary nations, that union of energy and of beauty which distinguish from all other poets the writings of Dante, that restlessness of fervid power which expressed itself in painting and sculpture and in rude but daring architectural forms, and from which, conjointly from the creations of Athens, its predecessor and its image, Raphael and Michelangelo drew the inspiration which created those forms and colours of what is now the astonishment of the world. The father of our own literature, Chaucer, wrought from the simple and powerful language of a nursling of this Republic the basis of our own literature. And thus we owe, among other causes, the exact condition belonging to our own intellectual existence to the generous disdain of submission which burned in the bosoms of men who filled a distant generation and inhabited another land.

When this resistance was overpowered (as what resistance to fraud and [tyranny] has not been overpowered?) another was even then maturing. The progress of philosophy and civilization which ended in that imperfect emancipation of mankind from the yoke of priests and Kings called the Reformation had already commenced. Exasperated by their long sufferings, inflamed by the sparks of that superstition from the flames of which they were emerging, the poor rose° against their natural enemies, the rich, and repaid with bloody interest the tyranny of ages. One of the signs of the times was that the oppressed peasantry rose like the negro slaves of West Indian plantations and murdered their tyrants when they were unaware. For so dear is power that the tyrants themselves neither then nor now nor ever left or leave a path to freedom but through their own blood. The contest then waged under the names of religion, which have seldom been any more [than] only the popular and visible symbols which express the degree of power in some shape or other asserted by one party and disclaimed by the other, ended; and the result, though partial and imperfect, is perhaps the most animating that the philanthropist can contemplate in the history of man. The republic of Holland, which has been so long an armoury of the arrows of learning by which superstition has been wounded even to death,° was established by this contest. What though the name of Republic—and by whom but by conscience-stricken tyrants could it be extinguished—is no more? The Republics of Switzerland derived from this event their consolidation and their union. From England then first began to pass away the strain of conquest.° The exposition° of a certain portion of religious imposture drew with it an inquiry into political imposture, and was attended with an extraordinary exertion of the energies of intellectual power. Shakespeare and Lord Bacon and the great writers of the age of Elizabeth and James I were at once the effects of this new spirit in men's minds, and the causes of its more complete development. By rapid gradation the nation was conducted to the temporary abolition of aristocracy and episcopacy, and the mighty example which, 'in teaching nations how to live,' England afforded to the world of bringing to public justice one of those chiefs° of a conspiracy of privileged murderers and robbers whose impunity has been the consecration of crime.

After the selfish passions and compromising interests of men had enlisted themselves to produce and establish the Restoration of Charles II the unequal combat was renewed under the reign of his successor, and that compromise between the unextinguishable spirit of Liberty, and the ever-watchful spirit of fraud and tyranny, called the Revolution,° had place. On this occasion Monarchy and Aristocracy and Episcopacy were at once established and limited by law. Unfortunately they lost no more in extent of power than they gained in security of possession. Meanwhile, those by whom they were established acknowledged and declared that the will of the People was the source from which these powers, in that instance, derived the right to subsist. A man has no right to be a King or Lord or a Bishop but so long as it is for the benefit of the People and so long as the People judge that it is for their benefit, that he should impersonate that character. The solemn establishment of this maxim, as the basis of our constitutional law, more than any beneficial and energetic application of it to the circumstances of this era of its promulgation, was the fruit of that vaunted event. Correlative with this series of events in England was the commencement of a new epoch in the history of the progress of civilization and society.

That superstition which has disguised itself under the name of Jesus subsisted under all its forms, even where it had been separated from those things especially considered as abuses by the multitude, in the shape of intolerant and oppressive hierarchies. Catholics massacred Protestants and Protestants proscribed Catholics, and extermination was the sanction of each faith within the limits of the power of its professors. The New Testament is in everyone's hand, and the few who ever read it with the simple sincerity of an unbiased judgement may perceive how distinct from the opinions of any of those professing themselves established° were the doctrines and the actions of Jesus Christ. At the period of the Reformation this test was applied and this judgement formed° of the then existing hierarchy, and the same compromise was then made between the spirit of truth and the spirit of imposture after [the] struggle which ploughed up the area of the human mind as was made in the particular instance of England between the spirit of freedom and the spirit of tyranny at that event called the Revolution. In both instances the maxims so solemnly recorded remain as trophies of our difficult and incomplete victory, planted on the enemies' land. *The will of the People to change their government is an acknowledged right in the Constitution of England*. The protesting against regular and graduated systems of alternate slavery and tyranny by which all except the lowest and the largest class were to be gainers in the materials of subsistence and ostentation at the expense of that class, the means being fraud or force established in the shape of feudal monarchies upon the ruins of religious dogmas which present themselves to his mind as false is the inalienable prerogative of every human being.

This new epoch was marked by the commencement of deeper enquiries into the forms of human nature than are compatible with an unreserved belief in any of those popular mistakes upon which popular systems of faith with respect to the agencies of the universe, with all their superstructure of political and religious tyranny, are built. Lord Bacon, Spinoza, Hobbes, Bayle,° Montaigne regulated the reasoning powers, criticized the past history, exposed the errors by illustrating their causes and their connection, and anatomized the inmost nature of social man. Then with a less interval of time than of genius followed Locke° and the philosophers of his exact and intelligible but superficial school. Their illustrations of some of the minor consequences of the doctrines established by the sublime genius of their predecessors were correct, popular, simple and energetic. Above all, they indicated inferences the most incompatible with the popular religions and the established governments of Europe.° Berkeley and Hume [and] Hartley°, in a later age, following the traces of these inductions, have clearly established the certainty of our ignorance with respect to those obscure questions which under the name of religious truths have been the watchwords of con[tention] and the symbols of unjust power ever since they were distorted by the narrow passions of the immediate followers of Jesus from that meaning to which philosophers are even now restoring them.—A crowd of writers in France° seized upon the most popular topics of these doctrines, and developing those particular portions of the new philosophy which conducted to inferences at war with the dreadful oppressions under which the country groaned, made familiar to mankind the falsehood of the pretences of their religious mediators and political oppressors. Considered as philosophers their error seems to have consisted chiefly of a limitedness of view; they told the truth, but not the whole truth. This might have arisen from the terrible sufferings of their countrymen inciting them rather to apply a portion of what had already been discovered to their immediate relief, than to pursue the abstractions of thought, as the great philosophers who preceded them had done, for the sake of a future and more universal advantage. Whilst that philosophy which, burying itself in the obscure parts of our nature, regards the truth and falsehood of dogmas relating to the cause of the universe, and the nature and manner of man's relation with it, was thus stripping Power of its darkest mask, Political philosophy, or that which considers the relations of Man as a social being, was assuming a precise form. This philosophy indeed sprang from and maintained a connection with that other, as its parent. What would Swift and Bolingbroke° and Sidney and Locke and Montesquieu, or even Rousseau, not to speak of political philosophers of our own age, Godwin and Bentham, have been but for Lord Bacon, Montaigne, and Spinoza, and the other great luminaries of the preceding epoch? Something excellent and eminent, no doubt, the least of these would have been, but something different from and inferior to what they are. A series of these writers illustrated with more or less success the principles of human nature as applied to man in political society. A thirst for accommodating the existing forms according to which mankind are found divided to those rules of freedom and equality which thus have been discovered as being the elementary principles according to which the happiness resulting from the social union ought to be produced and distributed, was kindled by these inquiries. Contemporary with this condition of the intell[ect] all the powers of man seemed, though in most cases under forms highly inauspicious, to develop themselves with uncommon energy. The mechanical sciences attained to a degree of perfection which, though obscurely foreseen by Lord Bacon, it had been accounted madness to have prophesied in a preceding age. Commerce was pursued with a perpetually increasing vigour, and the same area of the Earth was perpetually compelled to furnish more and more subsistence. The means and sources of knowledge were thus increased together with knowledge itself, and the instruments of knowledge. The benefit of this increase of the powers of man became, in consequence of the inartificial forms into which society continues to be distributed, an instrument of his additional evil. The capabilities of happiness were increased and applied to the augmentation of misery. Modern European society is thus an engine assumed to be for useful purposes, whose force is by a system of subtle mechanism augmented to the highest pitch, but which, instead of grinding corn or raising water, acts against itself and is perpetually wearing away and breaking to pieces the wheels of which it is composed.

The result of the labours of the political philosophers has been the establishment of the principle of Utility° as the substance, and liberty and equality as the forms, according to which the concerns of human life ought to be administered. By this test the various institutions regulating political society have been tried and, as the undigested growth of the private passions, errors, and interests of barbarians and oppressors, have been condemned. And many new theories, more or less perfect, but all superior to the mass of evil which they would supplant, have been given to the world.

The system of Government in the United States of America was the first practical illustration of the new philosophy. Sufficiently remote, it will be confessed, from the accuracy of ideal excellence is that representative system which will soon cover the extent of that vast Continent. But it is scarcely less remote from the insolent and contaminating tyrannies under which, with some limitation of these terms as regards England, Europe groaned at the period of the successful rebellion of America. America holds forth the victorious example of an immensely populous and, as far as the external arts of life are concerned, a highly civilized community administered according to republican forms. It has no King, that is, it has no officer to whom wealth and from whom corruption flows. It has no hereditary oligarchy, that is, it acknowledges no order of men privileged to cheat and insult the rest of the members of the state, and who inherit a right of legislating and judging which the principles of human nature compel them to exercise to their own profit and to the detriment of those not included within their peculiar class. It has no established Church, that is, it has no system of opinions respecting the abstrusest questions which can be topics of human thought, founded in an age of error and fanaticism, and opposed by law to all other opinions, defended by prosecutions sanctioned by enormous bounties given to idle priests and forced through the unwilling hands of those who have an interest in the cultivation and improvement of the soil, whose consequences are captivity, confiscation, infamy and ruin. It has no false representation, but a true representation. The will of the many is represented by the few in the assemblies of legislation, and by the officers of the executive entrusted with the administration of the executive power almost as directly as the will of one person can be represented by the will of another. Lastly, it has an institution by which it is honourably distinguished from all other government which ever existed. It constitutionally acknowledges the progress of human improvement, and is framed under the limitation of the probability of more simple views of political science being rendered applicable to human life. There is a law by which the Constitution is reserved for revision every ten years. Every other set of men who have assumed the office of legislating and framing institutions for future ages, with far less right to such an assumption than the founders of the American Republic, assumed that their work was the wisest and the best that could possibly have been produced; these illustrious men° looked upon the past history of their species and saw that it was the history of his mistakes, and his sufferings arising from his mistakes; they observed the superiority of their own work to all the works which had preceded it, and they judged it probable that other political institutions would be discovered bearing the same relation to those they had established which they bear to those which have preceded them. They provided therefore for the application of these contingent discoveries to the social state without the violence and misery attendant upon such change in less modest and more imperfect governments. The United States, as would have been expected from theoretical deduction, affords an example, compared with the old governments of Europe and Asia, of a free, happy and strong people. Nor let it be said that they owe their superiority rather to the situation than to their government. Give them a King, and let that King waste in luxury, riot, and bribery the same sum which now serves for the entire expenses of their government. Give them an aristocracy, and let that aristocracy legislate for the people. Give them a priesthood, and let them bribe with a tenth of the produce of the soil a certain set of men to say a certain set of words. Pledge the larger portion of them by financial subterfuges to pay the half of their property or earnings to another portion, and let the proportion of those who enjoy the fruits of the toil of others without toiling themselves be three instead of one. Give them, as you must if you give them these things, a great standing army to cut down the people if they murmur. If any American should see these words, his blood would run cold at the imagination of such a change. He well knows that the prosperity and happiness of the United States, if subjected to such institutions, [would] be no more. Give them a Court of Chancery,° and let the property, the liberty, and the interests, in the dearest concerns of life, the exercise of the most sacred rights of a social being, depend upon the will of one of the most servile creature[s] of the kingly and oligarchical and priestly power to which every man, in proportion as he is of an inquiring and philosophical mind and of a sincere and honourable disposition, is a natural and necessary enemy.

The just and successful Revolt of America corresponded with a state of public opinion in Europe of which it was the first result. The French Revolution was the second. The oppressors of mankind had enjoyed (O that we could say suffered) a long and an undisturbed reign in France, and to the pining famine, the shelterless destitution of the inhabitants of that country, had been added, and heaped up, insult harder to endure than misery. For the feudal system (the immediate causes and conditions of its institution having become obliterated) had degenerated into an instrument not only of oppression but of contumely; and both were unsparingly inflicted. Blind in the possession of strength, drunken as with the intoxication of ancestral greatness, the rulers perceived not that increase of knowledge in their subjects which made its exercise insecure. They called soldiers to hew down the people when their power was already past. The tyrants were, as usual, the aggressors. Then the oppressed, having been rendered brutal, ignorant, servile, and bloody by long slavery, having had the intellectual thirst excited in them by the progress of civilization, satiated from fountains of literature poisoned by the spirit and the form of monarchy, arose and took a dreadful revenge on their oppressors. Their desire to wreak revenge to this extent, in itself a mistake, a crime, a calamity, arose from the same source as their other miseries and errors, and affords an additional proof of the necessity of that long-delayed change which it accompanied and disgraced. If a just and necessary revolution could have been accomplished with as little expense of happiness and order in a country governed by despotic as [in] one governed by free laws, equal liberty and justice would lose their chief recommendations, and tyranny be divested of its most revolting attributes. Tyranny entrenches itself within the existing interests of that great mass of the most refined citizens of a nation and says, 'If you dare trample upon these, be free.' Though this terrible condition shall not be evaded, the world is no longer in a temper to decline the challenge.

The French were what their literature is (excluding Montaigne and Rousseau), weak, superficial, vain, with little imagination, and with passions as well as judgements cleaving to the external form of things. Not that [they] are organically different from the inhabitants of the nations who have become [. . .]° or rather not that their organical differences, whatever they may amount to, incapacitate them from arriving at the exercise of the highest powers to be attained by man. Their institutions made them what they were. Slavery and superstition, contumely and the tame endurance of contumely, and the habits engendered from generation to generation out of this transmitted inheritance of wrong, created this thing which has extinguished what has been called the likeness of God in man. The Revolution in France overthrew the hierarchy, the aristocracy, and the monarchy, and the whole of that peculiarly insolent and oppressive system on which they were based. But as it only partially extinguished those passions which are the spirit of these forms a reaction took place which has restored in a certain limited degree the old system—in a degree, indeed, exceedingly limited, and stripped of all its ancient terrors. The lion of the Monarchy of France, with his teeth drawn and his claws pared, now sits maintaining the formal likeness of a most imperfect and insecure dominion. The usurpation of Bonaparte, and then the Restoration of the Bourbons were the shapes in which this reaction clothed itself, and the heart of every lover of liberty was struck as with palsy by the succession of these events. But reversing the proverbial expression of Shakespeare, it may be the good which the Revolutionists did lives after them, their 'ills are interred with their bones.'° But the military project of government of the great tyrant having failed, and there being even no attempt, and, if there were any attempt, there being not the remotest possibility of re-establishing the enormous system of tyranny abolished by the Revolution, France is, as it were, regenerated. Its legislative assemblies are in a certain limited degree representations of the popular will, and the executive power is hemmed in by jealous laws. France occupies in this respect the same situation as was occupied by England at the restoration of Charles II. It has undergone a revolution (unlike in the violence and calamities which attended it, because unlike in the abuses which it was excited to put down) which may be paralleled with that in our own country which ended in the death of Charles I. The Authors of both revolutions proposed a greater and more glorious object than the degraded passions of their countrymen permitted them to attain. But in both cases abuses were abolished which never since have dared to show their face. There remains in the natural order of human things that the tyranny and perfidy of the reigns of Charles II and James II (for these were less the result of the disposition of particular men, than the vices which would have been engendered in any but an extraordinary man by the natural necessities of their situation), perhaps under a milder form and within a shorter period, should produce the institution of a government in France which may bear the same relation to the state of political knowledge existing at the present day, as the Revolution under

William III bore to the state of political knowledge existing at that period . . .°

Lastly, in the West Indian islands, first from the disinterested yet necessarily cautious measures of the English Nation, and then from the infection of the Spirit of Liberty in France, the deepest stain upon civilized man is fading away. Two nations° of free negroes are already established; one, in pernicious mockery of the usurpation over France, an empire, the other a republic; both animating yet terrific spectacles to those who inherit around them the degradation of slavery and the peril of dominion.

Such is a slight sketch of the general condition of the hopes and aspirations of the human race to which they have been conducted, after the obliteration of the Greek republics by the successful external tyranny of Rome—its internal liberty having been first abolished—and by those miseries and superstitions which consequent upon that event ha[ve] compelled the human race to begin anew its difficult and obscure career of producing, according to the forms of society, the greatest portion of good.

Meanwhile England, the particular object for the sake of which these general considerations have been stated on the present occasion, has arrived, like the nations which surround it, at a crisis in its destiny.

The literature of England, an energetic development of which has ever followed or preceded a great and free development of the national will, has arisen, as it were, from a new birth. In spite of that low-thoughted envy which would undervalue, through a fear of comparison with its own insignificance, the eminence of contemporary merit, ours is in intellectual achievements a memorable age, and we live among such philosophers and poets as surpass beyond comparison any who have appeared in our nation since its last struggle for liberty.° For the most unfailing herald, or companion, or follower, of an universal employment of the sentiments of a nation to the production of beneficial change is poetry, meaning by poetry an intense and impassioned power of communicating intense and impassioned impressions respecting man and nature.° The persons in whom this power takes its abode may often, as far as regards many portions of their nature, have little correspondence with the spirit of good of which it is the minister.° But although they may deny and abjure, they are yet compelled to serve, that which is seated on the throne of their own soul.° And whatever systems they may professedly support, they actually advance the interests of Liberty. It is impossible to read the productions of our most celebrated writers, whatever may be their system relating to thought or expression, without being startled by the electric life which there is in their words. They measure the circumference or sound the depths of human nature with a comprehensive and all-penetrating spirit, at which they are themselves perhaps most sincerely astonished, for it [is] less their own spirit than the spirit of their age. They are the priests of an unapprehended inspiration, the mirrors of gigantic forms which futurity casts upon the present, the words which express what they conceive not, the trumpet which sings to battle and feels not what it inspires, the influence which is moved not but moves. Poets and philosophers are the unacknowledged legislators of the world.

But, omitting these more abstracted considerations, has there not been and is there not in England a desire of change arising from the profound sentiment of the exceeding inefficiency of the existing institutions to provide for the physical and intellectual happiness of the people? It is proposed in this work (1) to state and examine the present condition of this desire, (2) to elucidate its causes and its object, (3) to the[n] show the practicability and utility, nay the necessity of change, (4) to examine the state of parties as regards it, and (5) to state the probable, the possible, and the desirable mode in which it should be accomplished.

On the Sentiment of the Necessity of Change°

Two circumstances arrest the attention of those who turn their regard to the present political condition of the English nation; first, that there is an almost universal sentiment of the approach of some change to be wrought in the institutions of the government, and secondly, the necessity and desirableness of such a change. From the first of these propositions, it being matter of fact, no person addressing the public can dissent. The latter, from a general belief in which the former flows and on which it depends, is matter of opinion, but [one] which to the mind of all excepting those interested in maintaining the contrary is a doctrine so clearly established that even they, admitting that great abuses exist, are compelled to impugn it by insisting upon the specious topic that popular violence, by which they alone could be remedied, would be more injurious than the continuance of these abuses. But as those who argue thus derive for the most part great advantage and convenience from the continuance of these abuses, their estimation of the mischiefs of temporary popular violence as compared with the mischiefs of permanent tyrannical and fraudulent forms of government is likely, from the known principles of human nature, to be exaggerated. Such an estimate comes too with a worse grace from them who, if they would in opposition to their own unjust advantage take the lead in reform, might spare the nation from the inconveniences of the temporary dominion of the poor, who by means of that very degraded condition which their insurrection would be designed to ameliorate are sufficiently incapable of discerning their own genuine and permanent advantage, though surely less incapable than those whose interests consist in proposing to themselves an object perfectly opposite [to] and wholly incompatible with that advantage. These persons (I mean the government party) propose to us the dilemma of submitting to a despotism which is notoriously gathering like an avalanche year by year; or taking the risk of something which it must be confessed bears the aspect of revolution. To this alternative we are reduced by the selfishness of those who taunt us with it. And the history of the world teaches us not to hesitate an instant in the decision, if indeed the power of decision be not already past.

The establishment of King William III on the throne of England has already been referred to as a compromise between liberty and despotism. The Parliament of which that event was the act had ceased to be, in an emphatic sense, a representation of the people.° The Long Parliament, questionless, was the organ of the will of all classes of people in England since it effected the complete revolution in a tyranny consecrated by time. But since its meeting, and since its dissolution, a great change had taken place in England. Feudal manners and institutions having become obliterated, monopolies and patents having been abolished, property and personal liberty having been rendered secure, the nation advanced rapidly towards the acquirement of the elements of national prosperity. But for want of just regulations in the distribution of these elements—which is indeed the great problem of government,—the elements of prosperity and power became, when combined, the sources of despotism and misery. Population increased, a greater number of hands were employed in the labours of agriculture and commerce, towns arose where villages had been, and the proportion borne by those whose labour produces the materials of subsistence and enjoyment to those who claim for themselves a superfluity of these materials began to increase indefinitely. A fourth class therefore appeared in the nation, the unrepresented multitude. Nor was it so much that villages which sent no members to Parliament became great cities, and that towns which had been considerable enough to send members dwindled from local circumstances into villages. This cause no doubt contributed to the general effect of rendering the Commons House a less complete representation of the people. Yet had this been all, though it had ceased to be a legal and actual, it might still have been a virtual Representation of the People. But the nation universally became multiplied into a denomination which had no constitutional presence in the state. This denomination had not existed before, or had existed only to a degree in which its interests were sensibly interwoven with that of those who enjoyed a constitutional presence. Thus, the proportion borne by the Englishmen who possessed [the] faculty of suffrage to those who were excluded from that faculty at the several periods of 1641 and 1688 had changed by the operation of these causes from 1 to 5 to 1 to 20. The rapid and effectual progress by which it changed from 1 to 20 to one to many hundreds in the interval between 1688 and 1819 is a process, to those familiar with the history of the political economy of that period, which is rendered by these principles sufficiently intelligible. The number therefore of those who have influence on the government, even if numerically the same as at the former period, was relatively different. And a sufficiently just measure is afforded of the degree in which a country is enslaved or free, by the consideration of the relative number of individuals who are admitted to the exercise of political rights. Meanwhile another cause was operating of a deeper and more extensive nature. Those who compose the Lords must, by the advantage of their situation as the great landed proprietors, possess a considerable influence over nomination to the Commons.° This influence from an original imperfection in the equal distribution of suffrage was always enormous, but it is only since it has been combined with the cause before stated that it has appeared to be fraught with consequences incompatible with public liberty. In 1641 this influence was almost wholly inoperative to pervert the counsels of the nation from its own advantage. But at that epoch the enormous tyranny of the agents of the royal power weighed equally upon all denominations of men, and united all counsels to extinguish it; add to which, the nation was in a very considerable degree as stated before fairly represented in Parliament. The common danger which was the bond of union between the aristocracy and the people having been destroyed, the former systematized their influence through the permanence of hereditary right, whilst the latter were losing power by the inflexibility of the institutions which forbade a just accommodation to their numerical increase. After the operations of these causes had commenced, the accession of William III placed a seal upon forty years of Revolution.

The Government of this country at the period of 1688 was regal, tempered by aristocracy, for what conditions of democracy attach to an assembly one portion of which [was] imperfectly nominated by less than a twentieth part of the people, and another perfectly nominated by the nobles? For the nobility, having by the assistance of the people imposed close limitations upon the royal power, finding that power to be its natural ally and the people (for the people from the increase of their numbers acquired greater and more important rights whilst the organ through which those rights might be asserted grew feebler in proportion to the increase of the cause of those rights and of their importance) its natural enemy, made the Crown the mask and pretence of their own authority.

At this period began that despotism of the oligarchy of party, and under colour of administering the executive power lodged in the King, represented in truth the interests of the rich. When it is said by political reasoners, speaking of the interval between 1688 and the present time, that the royal power progressively increased, they use an expression which suggests a very imperfect and partial idea. The power which has increased is that entrusted with the administration of affairs, composed of men responsible to the aristocratical assemblies, or to the reigning party in those assemblies which represents those orders of the nation which are privileged, and will retain power as long as it pleases them and must be divested of power as soon as it ceases to please them. The power which has increased therefore is the power of the rich. The name and the office of King is merely the mask of this power and is a kind of stalking-horse used to conceal these 'catchers of men'° whilst they lay their nets.—Monarchy is only the string which ties the robber's bundle. Though less contumelious and abhorrent from the dignity of human nature than an absolute monarchy, an oligarchy of this nature exacts more of suffering from the people because it reigns both by the opinion generated by imposture and the force which that opinion places within its grasp.

At the epoch adverted to, the device of public credit° was first systematically applied as an instrument of government. It was employed at the accession of William III less as a resource for meeting the financial exigencies of the state, than as a bond to connect those in the possession of property with those who had, by taking advantage of an accident of party, acceded to power. In the interval elapsed since that period it has accurately fulfilled the intention of its establishment and has continued to add strength to the government, even until the present crisis. Now this device is one of those execrable contrivances of misrule which overbalance the material of common advantage produced by the progress of civilization and increase the number of those who are idle in proportion to those who work, whilst it increases, through the factitious wants of those indolent, privileged persons, the quantity of work to be done. The rich, no longer being able to rule by force, have invented this scheme, that they may rule by fraud. [. . .]°

The existing Government of England in substituting a currency of paper to one of Gold has had no need to depreciate the currency by alloying the coin of the country; they have merely fabricated pieces of paper on which they promise to pay a certain sum. The holders of these papers came for payment in some representation of property universally exchangeable. They then declared that the persons who held the office for that payment could not be forced by law to pay. They declared subsequently that these pieces of paper were the legal coin of the country. Of this nature are all such transactions of companies and banks as consist in the circulation of promissory notes to a greater amount than the actual property possessed by those whose names they bear. They have the effect of augmenting the prices of provision, and of benefiting at the expense of the community the speculators in this traffic.—One of the vaunted effects of this system is to increase the national industry. That is, to increase the labours of the poor and those luxuries of the rich which they supply. To make a manufacturer work sixteen hours where he only worked eight. To turn children into lifeless and bloodless machines at an age when otherwise they would be at play before the cottage doors of their parents. To augment indefinitely the proportion of those who enjoy the profit of the labour of others as compared with those who exercise this labour. [. . .]°

The consequences of this transaction have been the establishment of a new aristocracy, which has its basis in fraud as the old one has its basis in force. The hereditary land-owners in England derived their title from royal grants—they are fiefs bestowed by conquerors, or church lands, or they have been bought by bankers and merchants from those persons. [. . .]

Since usage has consecrated a distortion of the word aristocracy from its primitive meaning, let me be allowed to employ the word aristocracy in that ordinary sense which signifies that class of persons who possess a right to the produce of the labour of others, without dedicating to the common service any labour in return.—This class of persons, whose existence is a prodigious anomaly in the social system, has ever constituted an inseparable portion of it, and there has never been an approach in practice towards any plan of political society modelled on equal justice, at least in the complicated mechanism of modern life. Mankind seem to acquiesce, as in a necessary condition of the imbecility of their own will and reason, in the existence of an aristocracy. With reference to this imbecility, it has doubtless been the instrument of great social advantage, although the advantage would have been greater which might have been produced according to the forms of a just distribution of the goods and evils of life. The object therefore of all enlightened legislation, and administration, is to enclose within the narrowest practicable limits this order of drones. The effect of the financial impostures of the modern rulers of England has been to increase the number of the drones. Instead of one aristocracy the condition which, in the present state of human affairs, the friends of justice and liberty are willing to subscribe as to an inevitable evil, they have supplied us with two aristocracies: the one, consisting [of] the great land proprietors and merchants who receive and interchange the produce of this country with the produce of other countries; in this, because all other great communities have as yet acquiesced in it, we acquiesce. Connected with the members of [this aristocracy] is a certain generosity and refinement of manners and opinion which, although neither philosophy nor virtue has been that acknowledged substitute for them, at least is a religion which makes respected those venerable names. The [other] is an aristocracy of attorneys and excisemen, and directors, and government pensioners, usurers, stock jobbers, country bankers, with their dependents and descendants. These are a set of pelting wretches in whose employment there is nothing to exercise, even to their distortion, the more majestic faculties of the soul. Though at the bottom it is all trick, there is something magnificent in the chivalrous disdain of infamy connected with a gentleman. There is something to which—until you see through the base falsehood upon which all inequality is founded—it is difficult for the imagination to refuse its respect in the faithful and direct dealings of the substantial merchant.° But in the habits and lives of this new aristocracy created out of an increase [in] the public calamities, and whose existence must be determined by their termination, there is nothing to qualify our disapprobation. They eat and drink and sleep and, in the intervals of those things performed with most ridiculous ceremony and accompaniments, they cringe and lie. They poison the literature of the age in which they live, by requiring either the antitype of their own mediocrity in books, or such stupid and distorted and inharmonious idealisms as alone have the power to stir their torpid imaginations. Their hopes and fears are of the narrowest description. Their domestic affections are feeble and they have no others. They think of any commerce with their species but as a means, never as an end, and as a means to the basest forms of personal advantage.

If this aristocracy had arisen from a false and depreciated currency to the exclusion of the other, its existence would have been a moral calamity and a disgrace, but it would not have constituted an oppression. But the hereditary aristocracy who held the political administration of affairs took the measures which created this other, for purposes peculiarly its own. Those measures were so contrived as in no manner to diminish the wealth and power of the contrivers. The lord does not spare himself one luxury, but the peasant and artisan are amerced° of many needful things. To support the system of social order according to its supposed unavoidable constitution, those from whose labour all those external accommodations which distinguish a civilized being from a savage arise, worked, before the institution of this double aristocracy, eight hours. And of these only the healthy were compelled to labour, the efforts of the old, the sick and the immature being dispensed with, and they maintained by the labour of the sane, for such is the plain English of the poor-rates.° That labour procured a competent share of the decencies of life, and society seemed to extend the benefits of its institution even to its most unvalued instruments. Although deprived of those resources of sentiment and knowledge which might have been their lot could the wisdom of the institutors of social forms have established a system of strict justice, yet they earned by their labour a competency in those external materials of life which, and not the loss of moral and intellectual excellence, is supposed to be the legitimate object of the desires and murmurs of the poor. Since the institution of this double aristocracy, however, they have worked not ten but twenty hours a day. Not that all the poor have rigidly worked twenty hours, but that the worth of the labour of twenty hours now, in food and clothing, is equivalent to the worth of ten hours then. And because twenty hours' labour cannot, from the nature of the human frame, be exacted from those who before performed ten, the aged and the sickly are compelled either to work or starve. Children who were exempted from labour are put in requisition, and the vigorous promise of the coming generation blighted by premature exertion. For fourteen hours' labour which they do perform, they receive—no matter in what nominal amount—the price of seven. They eat less bread, wear worse clothes, are more ignorant, immoral, miserable and desperate. This, then, is the condition of the lowest and the largest class, from whose labour the whole materials of life are wrought, of which the others are only the receivers or the consumers. They are more superstitious, for misery on earth begets a diseased expectation and panic-stricken faith in miseries beyond the grave. 'God,' they argue, 'rules this world as well as that; and assuredly since his nature is immutable, and his powerful will unchangeable, he rules them by the same laws.' The gleams of hope which speak of Paradise seem like the flames in Milton's hell only to make darkness visible, and all things take [their] colour from what surrounds them. They become revengeful [. . .].

But the condition of all other classes of society, excepting those within the privileged pale, is singularly unprosperous, and even they experience the reaction of their own short-sighted tyranny, in all those sufferings and deprivations which are not of a distinctly physical nature, in the loss of dignity, simplicity and energy, and in the possession of all those qualities which distinguish a slave-driver from a proprietor. Right Government being an institution for the purpose of securing such a moderate degree of happiness to men as has been experimentally practicable, the sure character of misgovernment is misery, and first discontent and, if that be despised, then insurrection, as the legitimate expression of that misery. The public ought to demand happiness. By a fortunate law of nature the labouring classes, when they cannot get food for their labour, are [certain] to take it by force. Laws and assemblies and courts of justice and delegated powers placed in balance or in opposition are the means and the form, but public happiness is the substance and the end of political institution. Whenever this is attainted in a nation, not from external force, but from the internal arrangement and divisions of the common burdens of defence and maintenance, then there is oppression. And then arises an alternative between Reform and the institution of a military Despotism, or a Revolution in which various parties, one striving after ill-digested systems of democracy, and the other clinging to the outworn abuses of power, leave the few who aspire to more than the former and who would overthrow the latter at whatever expense, to wait until that modified advantage which results from [this conflict] produces a small portion of that [social improvement] which, with the temperance and the toleration which both regard as a crime, might have resulted from the occasion which they let pass in a far more signal manner.

The propositions which are the consequences or the corollaries to which the preceding reasoning seems to have conducted us are—

That the majority [of the] people of England are destitute and miserable, ill-clothed, ill-fed, ill-educated.

That they know this, and that they are impatient to procure a reform of the cause of their abject and wretched state.

That a cause of this peculiar misery is the unequal distribution which, under the form of the national debt, has been surreptitiously made of the products of their labour and the products of the labour of their ancestors; for all property is the produce of labour.

That the cause of that cause is a defect in the government.

That if they knew nothing of their condition, but believed that all they endured and all [they] were deprived of arose from the unavoidable condition of human life, this belief being an error, the endurance of [which] enforces an injustice, every enlightened and honourable person, whatever may be the imagined interests of his peculiar class, ought to excite them to the discovery of the true state of the case and to the temperate but irresistible vindication of their rights.

A Reform in England is most just and necessary. What ought to be that reform?

A writer of the present day (a priest, of course, for his doctrines are those of a eunuch and of a tyrant) has stated that the evils of the poor arise from an excess of population,° and that after they have been stripped naked by the tax gatherer and reduced to bread and tea and fourteen hours of hard labour by their masters, and after the frost has bitten their defenceless limbs, and the cramp has wrung like a disease within their bones, and hunger, and the suppressed revenge of hunger, has stamped the ferocity of want like the mark of Cain upon their countenance, that the last tie by which Nature holds them to [a] benignant earth whose plenty is garnered up in the strongholds of their tyrants, is to be divided; that the single alleviation of their sufferings and their scorns, the one thing which made it impossible to degrade them below the beasts, which amid all their crimes and miseries yet separated a cynical and unmanly contamination, an anti-social cruelty, from all the soothing, elevating and harmonious gentlenesses of the sexual intercourse, and the humanizing charities of domestic life which are its appendages,—that this is to be obliterated. They are required to abstain from marrying under penalty of starvation. And it is threatened to deprive them of that property which is as strictly their birthright as a gentleman's land is his birthright, without giving them any compensation but the insulting advice to conquer, with minds undisciplined in the habits of higher gratification, a propensity which persons of the most consummate wisdom have been unable to resist, and which it is difficult to admire a person for having resisted. The doctrine of this writer is that the principle of population, when under no dominion of moral restraint, outstripping the sustenance produced by the labour of man, and that not in proportion to the number of inhabitants, but operating equally in a thinly peopled community as in one where the population is enormous, [is] not a prevention but a check. So far a man might have been conducted by a train of reasoning which, though it may be shown to be defective, would argue in the reasoner no selfish and slavish feelings. But he has the hardened insolence to propose as a remedy that the poor should be compelled (for what except compulsion is a threat of the confiscation of those funds which by the institutions of their country had been set apart for their sustenance in sickness or destitution?) to abstain from sexual intercourse, whilst the rich are to be permitted to add as many mouths to consume the products of the labour of the poor as they please.° If any new disadvantages are found to attach to the condition of social existence, those disadvantages ought not to be borne exclusively by one class of men, nor especially by that class whose ignorance leads them to exaggerate the advantages of sensual enjoyment, whose callous habits render domestic endearments more important to dispose them to resist the suggestions to violence and cruelty by which their situation ever exposes them to be tempted, and all whose other enjoyments are limited and few, whilst their sufferings are various and many. In this sense I cannot imagine how the advocates of equality could so readily have conceded [that] the unlimited operation of the principle of population affects the truth of their theories. On the contrary, the more heavy and certain are the evils of life, the more injustice is there [in] casting the burden of them exclusively on one order in the community. They seem to have conceded it merely because their opponents have insolently assumed it. Surely it is enough that the rich should possess to the exclusion of the poor all other luxuries and comforts, and wisdom, and refinement, the least envied but the most deserving of envy among all their privileges.

What is the Reform that We Desire?

Before we aspire after theoretical perfection in the amelioration of our political state, it is necessary that we possess those advantages which we have been cheated of, and [to] which the experience of modern times has proved that nations even under the present [conditions] are susceptible: first, we would regain these; second, we would establish some form of government which might secure us against such a series of events as have conducted us to a persuasion that the forms according to which it is now administered are inadequate to that purpose.

We would abolish the national debt.

We would disband the standing army.

We would, with every possible regard to the existing interests of the holders, abolish sinecures.

We would, with every possible regard to the existing interests of the holders, abolish tithes. And make all religions, all forms of opinion respecting the origin and government of the Universe, equal in the eye of the law.

We would make justice cheap, certain and speedy, and extend the institution of juries to every possible occasion of jurisprudence.

The national debt was chiefly contracted in two liberticide wars, undertaken by the privileged classes of the country°—the first, for the ineffectual purpose of tyrannizing over one portion of their subjects; the second, in order to extinguish the resolute spirit of obtaining their rights in another.

The labour which this money represents, and that which is represented by the money wrung for purposes of the same detestable character out of the people since the commencement of the American war, would, if properly employed, have covered our land with monuments of architecture exceeding the sumptuousness and the beauty of Egypt and Athens; it might have made every peasant's cottage, surrounded with its garden, a little paradise of comfort, with every convenience desirable in civilized life; neat tables and chairs, and good beds, and a nice collection of useful books; and our ships manned by sailors well-paid and well-clothed might have kept watch round this glorious island against the less enlightened nations which assuredly would have envied, until they could have imitated, its prosperity. But the labour which is expressed by these sums has been diverted from these purposes of human happiness to the promotion of slavery, or the attempt at dominion, and a great portion of the sum in question is debt and must be paid.° Is it to remain unpaid forever, an eternal rent-charge upon the land from which the inhabitants of these islands draw their subsistence? This were to pronounce the perpetual institution of two orders of aristocracy, and men are in a temper to endure one with some reluctance. Is it to be paid now? If so what are the funds, or when and how is it to be paid? The fact is that the national debt is a debt, not contracted by the whole nation towards a portion of it, but a debt contracted by the whole mass of the privileged classes towards one particular portion of those classes. If the principal were paid, the whole property of those who possess property must be valued and the public creditor, whose property would have been included in this estimate, satisfied out of the proceeds. It has been said that all the land in the nation is mortgaged for the amount of the national debt. This is a partial statement. Not only all the land in the nation but all the property of whatever denomination, all the houses and the furniture and the goods and every article of merchandise, and the property which is represented by the very money lent by the fund-holder, who is bound to pay a certain portion as debtor, whilst he is to receive another certain portion as creditor. The property of the rich is mortgaged: to use the language of the law, let the mortgagee foreclose.

If the principal of this debt were paid, after such reductions had been made so as to make an equal value, taking corn for the standard, [. . .] it would be the rich who alone could, as justly they ought to, pay it. It would be a mere transfer among persons of property.° As it is, the interest is chiefly paid by those who had no hand in the borrowing and who are sufferers in other respects from the consequences of those transactions in which the money was spent.

The payment of the principal of what is called the National debt, which it is pretended is so difficult a problem, is only difficult to those who do not see who is the creditor and who the debtor, and who the wretched sufferers from whom they both wring the taxes which under the form of interest are given by the former° [latter] and accepted by the latter [former]. It is from the labour of those who have no property that all the persons who possess property think to extort the perpetual interest of a debt, the whole of them to the part, which the latter [former] know they could not persuade the former [latter] to pay, but by conspiring with them in an imposture which makes the third class pay what the first [second] neither received by their sanction nor spent for their benefit, and what the second [first] never lent to them. They would both shift to the labour of the present and of all succeeding generations the payment of the interest of their own debt, from themselves and their posterity, because the payment of the principal would be no more than a compromise and transfer of property between each other, by which the nation would be spared forty-four millions a year, which now is paid to maintain in luxury and indolence the public debtors and to protect them from the demand of their creditors upon them, who, being part of the same body, and owing as debtors whilst they possess a claim as creditors, agree to abstain from demanding the principal which they must all unite to pay, for the sake of receiving an enormous interest which is principally wrung out of those who had no concern whatever in the transaction. One of the first acts of a reformed government would undoubtedly be an effectual scheme for compelling these to compromise their debt between themselves.

When I speak of persons of property, I mean not every man who possesses any degree of property; I mean the rich. Every man whose scope in society has a plebeian and intelligible utility, whose personal exertions are more valuable to him than his capital; every tradesman who is not a monopolist, all surgeons and physicians, and those mechanics and editors and literary men and artists, and farmers, all those persons whose profits spring from honourably and honestly exerting their own skill and wisdom or strength in greater abundance than from the employment of money to take advantage of the necessity of the starvation of their fellow citizens for their profit, are those who pay, as well as those more obviously understood by the labouring classes, the interest of the national debt. It is the interest of all these persons as well as that of the poor to insist upon the payment of the principal.

For this purpose the form ought to be as simple and succinct as possible. The operations of deciding who was to pay, at what time, and how much, and to whom, are divested of financial chicanery, problems readily to be determined. The common tribunals may possess a legal jurisdiction to award the proportion due upon the several claims of each.

There are two descriptions of property which, without entering into the subtleties of a more refined moral theory as applicable to the existing forms of society, are entitled to two very different measures of forbearance and regard. And this forbearance and regard have by political institution usually been accorded in an inverse reason from what is just and natural. Labour, industry, economy, skill, genius, or any similar powers honourably and innocently exerted are the foundations of one description of property, and all true political institution ought to defend every man in the exercise of his discretion with respect to property so acquired. Of this kind is the principal part of the property enjoyed by those who are but one degree removed from the class which subsists by daily labour. Yet there are instances of persons in this class who have procured their property by fraudulent and violent means, as there are instances in the other of persons who have acquired their property by innocent or honorable exertion. All political science abounds with limitations and exceptions. Property thus acquired men leave to their children. The absolute right becomes weakened by descent, first because it is only to avoid the greater evil of arbitrarily interfering with the discretion [of any man] in matters of property that the great evil of acknowledging any person to have an exclusive right to property who has not created it by his skill or labour is admitted, and secondly because the mode of its having been originally acquired is forgotten, and it is confounded with the property acquired in a very different manner, and the principle upon which all property justly rests, after the great principle of the general advantage, becomes thus disregarded and misunderstood. Yet the privilege of disposing of property by will is one necessarily connected with the existing forms of domestic life, and exerted merely by those who have acquired property by industry or who have preserved it by economy, would never produce any great and invidious inequality of fortune. A thousand accidents would perpetually tend to level the accidental elevation, and the signs of property would perpetually recur to those whose deserving skill might attract, or whose labour might create it.

But there is another species of property, which has its foundation in usurpation, or imposture, or violence, without which, by the nature of things, immense aggregations of possessions of gold or land could never have been accumulated. Of this nature is the principal part of the property enjoyed by the aristocracy and by the great fund-holders, the great majority of whose ancestors never either deserved it by their skill and talents or acquired and created it by their personal labour. It could not be that they deserved it, for if the honourable exertion of the most glorious imperial faculties of our nature had been the criterion of the possession of property, the posterity of Shakespeare, of Milton, of Hampden, of Lor[d Bacon]° would be the wealthiest proprietors in England. It could not be that they acquired it by legitimate industry,—for besides that the real mode of acquisition is matter of history, no honourable profession or honest trade, nor the hereditary exercise of it, ever in such numerous instances accumulated masses of property so vast as those enjoyed by the ruling orders in England. They were either grants from the feudal sovereigns whose right to what they granted was founded upon conquest or oppression, both a denial of all right; or they were the lands of the ancient Catholic clergy which, according to the most acknowledged principles of public justice, reverted to the nation at their suppression, or they were the products of patents and monopolies, an exercise of sovereignty more pernicious than direct violence to the interests of a commercial nation; or in later times such property has been accumulated by dishonourable cunning and the taking advantage of a fictitious paper currency to obtain an unfair power over labour and the fruits of labour.

Property thus accumulated being transmitted from father to son acquires, as property of the more legitimate kind loses, force and sanction, but in a more limited manner. For not only on an examination and recurrence to first principles is it seen to have been founded on a violation of all that to which the latter owes its sacredness, but it is felt in its existence and perpetuation as a public burden, and known as a rallying point to the ministers of tyranny, having the property of a snowball, gathering as it rolls, and rolling until it bursts.

Labour and skill and the immediate wages of labour and skill is a property of the most sacred and indisputable right, and the foundation of all other property. And the right [of a man] to property in the exertion of his own bodily and mental faculties, or to the undoubted produce and free reward of that exertion is the most [inalienable of rights]. If, however, he takes by violence or appropriates to himself through fraudulent cunning, or receives from another property so acquired, his claim to that property is of a far inferior force. We may acquiesce, if we evidently perceive an overbalance of public advantage in submission, under this claim; but if any public emergency should arise, at which it might be necessary as at present to satisfy by a tax on capital the claims of a part of the nation by a contribution from such national resources as may with the least injustice be appropriated to that purpose, assuredly it would not be on labour and skill, the foundation of all property, nor on the profits and savings of labour and skill, which are property itself, but on such possessions which can only be called property in a modified sense, as have from their magnitude and their nature an evident origin in violence or imposture.

The national debt, as has been stated, is a debt contracted by the whole of a particular class in the nation towards a portion of that class. It is sufficiently clear that this debt was not contracted for the purpose of the public advantage. Besides there was no authority in the nation competent to a measure of this nature. The usual vindication of national debts is that, [since] they are contracted in an overwhelming measure for the purpose of defence against a common danger, for the vindication of the rights and liberties of posterity, it is just that posterity should bear the burden of payment. This reasoning is most fallacious. The history of nations presents us with a succession of extraordinary emergencies; their existence is perpetually threatened by new and unexpected combinations and developments of foreign or internal force. Imagine a situation of equal emergency to occur to

England as that which the ruling party assume to have occurred as their excuse for burdening the nation with the perpetual payment of £45,000,000 annually. Suppose France and Russia and Austria were to enter into a league against England, the first to revenge its injuries, the second to satisfy its ambition, the third to soothe its jealousy. Could the nation bear £90,000,000 of yearly interest, must there be twice as many luxurious and idle persons, must the labourer receive for twenty-eight hours' work what he now receives for fourteen, as he now receives for fourteen what he once received for seven? But this argument [. . .]°

What is meant by a Reform of parliament? If England were a Republic governed by one assembly; if there were no chamber of hereditary aristocracy which is at once an actual and a virtual representation of all who claim through rank or wealth superiority over their countrymen; if there were no King who is as the rallying point of those whose tendency is at once to [gather] and to confer that power which is consolidated at the expense of the nation, then [. . .]°

The advocates of universal suffrage have reasoned correctly that no individual who is governed can be denied a direct share in the government of his country without supreme injustice. If we pursue the train of reasonings which have conducted to the conclusion, we discover that systems of social order still more incompatible than universal suffrage with any reasonable hope of instant accomplishment appear to be that which should result from a just combination of the elements of social life. I do not understand why those reasoners who propose at any price an immediate appeal to universal suffrage, because it is that which it is injustice to withhold, do not insist on the same ground on the immediate abolition, for instance, of monarchy and aristocracy, and the levelling of inordinate wealth, and an agrarian distribution, including the Parks and Chases of the rich, of the uncultivated districts of the country. No doubt the institution of universal suffrage would by necessary consequence tend to the abolition of these forms; because it is impossible that the people, having attained power, should fail to see what the demagogues now conceal from them [as] the legitimate consequence of the doctrines through which they had attained it. A Republic, however just in its principle and glorious in its object, would, through [the] violence and sudden change which must attend it, incur a great risk of being as rapid in its decline as in its growth.

A civil war, which might be engendered by the passions attending on this mode of reform, would confirm in the mass of the nation those military habits which have been already introduced by our tyrants, and with which liberty is incompatible. From the moment that a man is a soldier, he becomes a slave. He is taught obedience; his will is no longer, which is the most sacred prerogative of man, guided by his own judgement. He is taught to despise human life and human suffering; this is the universal distinction of slaves. He is more degraded than a murderer; he is like the bloody knife, which has stabbed, and feels not; a murderer we may abhor and despise; a soldier is by profession beyond abhorrence and below contempt.

It is better that [the people°] should be instructed in the whole truth, that they should see the clear grounds of their rights, the objects to which they ought to tend; and be impressed with the just persuasion that patience and reason and endurance [are the means of] a calm yet irresistible progress.

Probable Means

That the House of Commons should reform itself, uninfluenced by any fear that the people would, on their refusal, assume to itself that office, seems a contradiction. What need of Reform if it expresses the will, and watches over the interests of the public? And if, as is sufficiently evident, it despises that will and neglects that interest, what motives would incite it to institute a reform which the aspect of the times renders indeed sufficiently perilous, but without which there will speedily be no longer anything in England to distinguish it from the basest and most abject community of slaves that ever existed.

The great principle of Reform consists in every individual of mature age and perfect understanding giving his consent to the institution and the continued existence of the social system, which is instituted for his advantage and for the advantage of others in his situation. As in a great nation this is practically impossible, masses of individuals consent to qualify other individuals, whom they delegate to superintend their concerns. These delegates have constitutional authority to exercise the functions of sovereignty; they unite in the highest degree the legislative and executive functions. A government that is founded on any other basis is a government of fraud or force, and ought on the first convenient occasion to be overthrown. The grand principle of political reform is the natural equality of men; not with relation to their property but to their rights. That equality in possessions which Jesus Christ° so passionately taught is a moral rather than political truth,° and is such as social institutions cannot, without mischief, inflexibly secure. Morals and politics can only be considered as portions of the same science, with relation to a system of such absolute perfection as Christ and Plato and Rousseau and other reasoners have asserted, and as Godwin has, with irresistible eloquence, systematized and developed. Equality in possessions must be the last result of the utmost refinements of civilization; it is one of the conditions of that system of society towards which, with whatever hope of ultimate success, it is our duty to tend. We may and ought to advert to it, as to the elementary principle, as to the goal, unattainable perhaps by us, but which, as it were, we revive in our posterity to pursue. We derive tranquillity and courage and grandeur of soul from contemplating an object which is, because we will it, and may be, because we hope and desire it, and must be, if succeeding generations of the enlightened sincerely and earnestly seek it. [. . .]

But our present business is with the difficult and unbending realities of actual life, and when we have drawn inspiration from the great object of our hope it becomes us with patience and resolution to apply ourselves to accommodating our theories to immediate practice.

That Representative Assembly called the House of Commons ought questionless to be *immediately* nominated by the great mass of the people. The aristocracy and those who unite in their own persons the vast privileges conferred by the possession of inordinate wealth is sufficiently represented by the House of Peers and by the King. Those theorists who admire and would put into action the mechanism of what is called the British Constitution would acquiesce in this view of the question. For if the House of Peers be a permanent representative of the privileged classes, if the regal power be no more than another form, and a form still more jealously to be regarded, of the same representation; whilst the House of Commons be not chosen by the mass of the population, what becomes of that democratic element, upon the presence of which it has been supposed that the waning superiority of England over the surrounding nations has depended?

Any sudden attempt at Universal suffrage would produce an immature attempt at a Republic; it [is better] that [an] object so inexpressibly great and sacred should never have been attempted than that it should be attempted and fail. It is no prejudice to the ultimate establishment of the boldest political innovations that we temporize so as, when they shall be accomplished, they may be rendered permanent.

Considering the population of Great Britain and Ireland as twenty millions and the representative assembly as five hundred, each member ought to be the expression of the will of 40,000 persons; of these two-thirds would be women and children and persons under age; the actual number of voters therefore for each member would be 13,300. The whole extent of the empire might be divided into five hundred electoral departments or parishes, and the inhabitants assemble on a certain day to exercise their right of suffrage.

Mr Bentham and other writers have urged the admission of females to the right of suffrage; this attempt seems somewhat immature. Should my opinion be the result of despondency, the writer of these pages would be the last to withhold his vote from any system which might tend to an equal and full development of the capacities of all living beings.

The system of voting by ballot,° which some reasoners have recommended, is attended with obvious inconveniences. It withdraws the elector from the regard of his country and his neighbours, and permits him to conceal the motives of his vote, which, if concealed, cannot but be dishonourable; when, if he had known that he had to render a public account of his conduct, he would have never permitted them° to guide him.—There is in this system of voting by ballot and of electing a member of the Representative Assembly as a church-warden is elected something too mechanical. The elector and the elected ought to meet one another face to face and interchange the meanings by actual presence and share some common impulses and, in a degree, understand each other. There ought to be the common sympathy of the excitements of a popular assembly among the electors themselves. The imagination would thus be strongly excited, and a mass of generous and enlarged and popular sentiments be awakened, which would give the vitality of [. . .]°

That republican boldness of censuring and judging one another, which [is] indeed exerted in England under the title of 'public opinion', though perverted from its true uses into an instrument of prejudice and calumny, would then be applied to its genuine purposes. Year by year the people would become more susceptible of assuming forms of government more simple and beneficial. [. . .]

If the existing government shall compel the Nation to take the task of reform into its own hands, one of the most obvious consequences of such a circumstance would be the abolition of monarchy and aristocracy. Why, it will then be argued, if the subsisting condition of social forms is to be thrown into confusion, should these things be endured? Why do we now endure them? Is it because we think that an hereditary King is cheaper and wiser than an elected President, or a

House of Lords and a Bench of Bishops are institutions modelled by the wisdom of the most refined and civilized periods, beyond which the wit of mortal man can furnish nothing more perfect? In case the subsisting Government should compel the people to revolt to establish a representative assembly in defiance of them, and to assume in the defence of that assembly an attitude of resistance and defence, this question would probably be answered in a very summary manner: no friend of mankind and of his country can desire that such a crisis should suddenly arrive; but still less, once having arrived, can he hesitate under what banner to array his person and his power. At the peace, the people would have been contented with strict economy and severe retrenchment, and some direct and intelligible plan for producing that equilibrium between the capitalists and the landholders which is delusively styled the payment of the national debt. Had this system been adopted, they probably would have refrained from exacting Parliamentary Reform, the only secure guarantee that it would have been pursued.—Two years ago it might still have been possible to have commenced a system of gradual reform. The people were then insulted, tempted and betrayed,° and the petitions of a million of men rejected with disdain. Now they are more miserable, more hopeless, more impatient of their misery. Above all, they have become more universally aware of the true sources of their misery. It is possible that the period of conciliation is past, and that after having played with the confidence and cheated the expectations of the people, their passions will be too little under discipline to allow them to wait the slow, gradual and certain operation of such a Reform as we can imagine the constituted authorities to concede.

Upon the issue of this question depends the species of reform which a philosophical mind should regard with approbation. If Reform shall be begun by the existing Government, let us be contented with a limited [beginning], with any whatsoever opening; let the rotten boroughs be disfranchised, and their rights transferred to the unrepresented cities and districts of the Nation; it is no matter how slow, gradual and cautious be the change; we shall demand more and more with firmness and moderation, never anticipating, but never deferring the moment of successful opposition, so that the people may become habituated [to] exercising the functions of sovereignty, in proportion as they acquire the possession of it.

If reform could begin from within the Houses of Parliament, as constituted at present, it appears to me that what is called moderate reform, that is a suffrage whose qualification should be the possession of a certain small property, and triennial parliaments,° would be principles—a system in which, for the sake of obtaining without bloodshed or confusion ulterior° improvements of a more important character, all reformers ought to acquiesce. Not that such are first principles, or that they would produce a system of perfect social institution or one approaching to [such a system]. But nothing is more idle than to reject a limited benefit because we cannot without great sacrifices obtain an unlimited one. We might thus reject a Representative Republic, if it were attainable, on the plea that the imagination of man can conceive of something more absolutely perfect. Towards whatsoever we regard as perfect, undoubtedly it is no less our duty than it is our nature to press forward; this is the generous enthusiasm which accomplishes not indeed the consummation after which it aspires, but one which approaches it in a degree far nearer than if the whole powers had not been developed by a delusion. It is in politics rather than in religion that faith is meritorious.

If the Houses of Parliament obstinately and perpetually refuse to concede any reform to the people, my vote is for universal suffrage and equal representation.

It is asked, how shall this be accomplished, in defiance of and in opposition to the constituted authorities of the Nation, they who possess whether with or without its consent the command of a standing army and of a legion of spies and police officers and hold all the strings of that complicated mechanism with which the hopes and fears of men are moved like puppets? They would disperse any assembly really chosen by the people; they would shoot and hew down any multitude without regard to sex or age (as the Jews did the Canaanites) which might be collected in its defence; they would calumniate, imprison, starve, ruin and expatriate every person who wrote or acted, or thought, or might be suspected to think against them; misery and extermination would fill the country from one end to another.

This question I would answer by another.

Will you endure to pay the half of your earnings to maintain in luxury and idleness the confederation of your tyrants as the reward of a successful conspiracy to defraud and oppress you? Will you make your tame cowardice and the branding record of it the everlasting inheritance of your degraded posterity? Not only this: will you render by your torpid endurance this condition of things as permanent as the system of castes in India by which the same horrible injustice is perpetrated under another form?

Assuredly no Englishmen by whom these propositions are understood will answer in the affirmative; and the opposite side of the alternative remains.

When the majority in any nation arrive at a conviction that it is their duty and their interest to divest the minority of a power employed to their disadvantage, and the minority are sufficiently mistaken as to believe that their superiority is tenable, a struggle must ensue.

If the majority are enlightened, united, impelled by a uniform enthusiasm, and animated by a distinct and powerful apprehension of their object,—and full confidence in their undoubted power—the struggle is merely nominal. The minority perceive the approaches of the development of an irresistible force, by the influence of the public opinion of their weakness on those political forms of which no government but an absolute despotism is devoid. They divest themselves of their usurped distinctions; the public tranquillity is not disturbed by the revolution.

But these conditions may only be imperfectly fulfilled by the state of a people grossly oppressed and impotent to cast off the load. Their enthusiasm may have been subdued by the killing weight of toil and suffering; they may be panic-stricken and disunited by their oppressors and the demagogues; the influence of fraud may have been sufficient to weaken the union of classes which compose them by suggesting jealousies; and the position of the conspirators, although it is to be forced by repeated assaults, may be tenable until the siege can be vigorously urged. The true patriot will endeavour to enlighten and to unite the nation and animate it with enthusiasm and confidence. For this purpose he will be indefatigable in promulgating political truth. He will endeavour to rally round one standard the divided friends of liberty, and make them forget the subordinate objects with regard to which they differ, by appealing to that respecting which they are all agreed. He will promote such open confederations among men of principle and spirit as may tend to make their intentions and their efforts converge to a common centre. He will discourage all secret associations which have a tendency, by making national will develop itself in a partial and premature manner, to cause tumult and confusion. He will urge the necessity of exciting the people frequently to exercise their right of assembling, in such limited numbers as that all present may be actual parties to the proceedings of the day. Lastly, if circumstances had collected a more considerable number as at Manchester on the memorable 16th of August,° if the tyrants command their troops to fire upon them or cut them down unless they disperse, he will exhort them peaceably to risk the danger, and to expect without resistance the onset of the cavalry, and wait with folded arms the event of the fire of the artillery and receive with unshrinking bosoms the bayonets of the charging battalions. Men are every day persuaded to incur greater perils for a less manifest advantage. And this, not because active resistance is not justifiable when all other means shall have failed, but because in this instance temperance and courage would produce greater advantages than the most decisive victory. In the first place, the soldiers are men and Englishmen, and it is not to be believed that they would massacre an unresisting multitude of their countrymen drawn up in unarmed array before them and bearing in their looks a calm and deliberate resolution to perish rather than abandon the assertion of their rights. In the confusion of flight the ideas of the soldier become confused, and he massacres those who fly from him by the instinct of his trade. In the struggle of conflict and resistance he is irritated by a sense of his own danger; he is flattered by an apprehension of his magnanimity in incurring it; he considers the blood of his countrymen at once the price of his valour, the pledge of his security. He applauds himself by reflecting that these base and dishonorable motives will gain him credit among his comrades and his officers who are animated by the same, as if they were the same. But if he should observe neither resistance nor flight he would be suddenly reduced to impotence and indecision. Thus far, his ideas were governed by the same law as those of a dog who chases a flock of sheep to the corner of a field, and keeps aloof when they make the firm parade of resistance.—But the soldier is a man and an Englishman. This unexpected reception would probably throw him back upon a recollection of the true nature of the measures of which he was made the instrument, and the enemy might be converted into the ally.

The true patriot will be foremost to publish the boldest truths in the most fearless manner, yet without the slightest tincture of personal malignity. He would encourage all others to the same efforts and assist them to the utmost of his power with the resources both of his intellect and fortune. He would call upon them to despise imprisonment and persecution and lose no opportunity of bringing the public opinions and the power of the tyrants into circumstances of perpetual contest and opposition.

All might, however, be ineffectual to produce so uniform an impulse of the national will as to preclude a further struggle. The strongest argument, perhaps, for the necessity of Reform is the inoperative and unconscious abjectness to which the purposes of a considerable mass of the people are reduced. They neither know nor care. They are sinking into a resemblance with the Hindoos and the Chinese, who were once men as they are. Unless the cause which renders them passive subjects instead of active citizens be removed, they will sink with accelerated gradations into that barbaric and unnatural civilization which destroys all the differences among men. It is in vain to exhort us to wait until all men shall desire Freedom whose real interest will consist in its establishment. It is in vain to hope to enlighten them whilst their tyrants employ the utmost artifices of all their complicated engine to perpetuate the infection of every species of fanaticism and error from generation to generation. The advocates of Reform ought indeed to leave no effort unexerted, and they ought to be indefatigable in exciting all men to examine [. . .]°

But if they wait until those neutral politicians whose opinions represent the actions of this class are persuaded that [some] effectual reform is necessary, the occasion will have passed or will never arrive, and the people will have exhausted their strength in ineffectual expectation and will have sunk into incurable supineness. It was principally [through] a similar quietism that the populous and extensive nations of Asia have fallen into their existing decrepitude; and that anarchy, insecurity, ignorance and barbarism, the symptoms of the confirmed disease of monarchy, have reduced nations of the most delicate physical and intellectual organization and under the most fortunate climates of the globe to a blank in the history of man. The manufacturers° to a man are persuaded of the necessity of reform; an immense majority of the inhabitants of London [. . .]°

The reasoners who incline to the opinion that it is not sufficient that the innovators should produce a majority in the nation, but that we ought to expect such an unanimity as would preclude anything amounting to a serious dispute, are prompted to this view of the question by the dread of anarchy and massacre. Infinite and inestimable calamities belong to oppression, but the most fatal of them all is that mine of unexploded mischief which it has practised beneath the foundation of society, and with which, 'pernicious to one touch'° it [threatens] to involve the ruin of the entire building together with its own. But delay merely renders these mischief[s] more tremendous, not the less inevitable. For the utmost may now be the crisis of the social disease [which] is rendered thus periodical, chronic and incurable.

The savage brutality of the populace is proportioned to the arbitrary character of the government, and tumults and insurrections soon, as in Constantinople, become consistent with the permanence of the causing evil, of which they might have been the critical determination.

The public opinion in England ought first to [be] excited to action, and the durability of those forms within which the oppressors intrench themselves brought perpetually to the test of its operation. No law or institution can last if this opinion be distinctly pronounced against it. For this purpose government ought to be defied, in cases of questionable result, to prosecute for political libel. All questions relating to the jurisdiction of magistrates and courts of law respecting which any doubt could be raised ought to be agitated with indefatigable pertinacity. Some two or three of the popular leaders have shown the best spirit in this regard; they only want system and co-operation. The tax-gatherer ought to be compelled in every practicable instance to distrain, whilst the right to impose taxes, as was the case in the beginning of the resistance to the tyranny of Charles I, is formally contested by an overwhelming multitude of defendants before the courts of common law. Confound the subtlety of lawyers with the subtlety of the law. All of the nation would thus be excited to develop itself, and to declare whether it acquiesced in the existing forms of government.—The manner in which all questions of this nature might be decided would develop the occasions, and afford a prognostic as to the success, of more decisive measures. Simultaneously with this active and vigilant system of opposition means ought to be taken of solemnly conveying the sense of large bodies and various denominations of the people in a manner the most explicit to the existing depositaries of power. Petitions, couched in the actual language of the petitioners, and emanating from distinct assemblies, ought to load the tables of the House of Commons. The poets, philosophers and artists ought to remonstrate, and the memorials entitled their petitions might show the diverse convictions they entertain of the inevitable connection between national prosperity and freedom, and the cultivation of the imagination and the cultivation of scientific truth, and the profound development of moral and metaphysical enquiry. Suppose these memorials to be severally written by Godwin and Hazlitt and Bentham and Hunt,° they would be worthy of the age and of the cause; radiant and irresistible like the meridian Sun [they] would strike all but the eagles who dared to gaze upon its beam, with blindness and confusion. These appeals of solemn and emphatic argument from those who have already a predestined existence among posterity, would appal the enemies of mankind by their echoes from every corner of the world in which the majestic literature of England is cultivated; it would be like a voice from beyond the dead of those who will live in the memories of men, when they must be forgotten; it would be Eternity warning Time.

Let us hope that at this stage of the progress of Reform, the oppressors would feel their impotence and reluctantly and imperfectly concede some limited portion of the Rights of the people; and disgorge some morsels of their undigested prey. In this case the people ought to be exhorted by everything ultimately dear to them to pause until by the exercise of those rights which they have regained they become fitted to demand more. It is better that we gain what we demand by a process of negotiation which would occupy twenty years, than that by communicating a sudden shock to the interests of those who are the depositaries and dependents of power we should incur the calamity which their revenge might inflict upon us by giving the signal of civil war.—If, after all, they consider the chance personal ruin and the infamy of figuring on the page of history as the promoters of civil war preferable to resigning any portion how small soever of their usurped authority, we are to recollect that we possess a right beyond remonstrance. It has been acknowledged by the most approved writers on the English constitution (which is in this instance merely declaratory of the superior decisions of eternal justice) that we possess a right of resistance. The claim of the reigning family° is founded upon a memorable exertion of this solemnly recorded right.

The last resort of resistance is undoubtedly insurrection.—The right of insurrection is derived from the employment of armed force to counteract the will of the nation. Let the government disband the standing army, and the purpose of resistance would be sufficiently fulfilled by the incessant agitation of the points of dispute before the courts of common law and by an unwarlike display of the irresistible numbers and union of the people.

Before we enter into a consideration of the measures which might terminate in civil war, let us for a moment consider the nature and the consequences of war. This is the alternative which the unprincipled cunning of the tyrants has presented to us, from which we must not sh[rink]. There is secret sympathy between Destruction and Power, between Monarchy and War; and the long experience of the history of all recorded time teaches us with what success they have played into each other's hands. War is a kind of superstition; the pageantry of arms and badges corrupts the imagination of men. How far more appropriate would be the symbols of an inconsolable grief—muffled drums, and melancholy music, and arms reversed, and the livery of sorrow rather than of blood. When men mourn at funerals, for what do they mourn in comparison with the calamities which they hasten with every circumstance of festivity to suffer and to inflict. Visit in imagination the scene of a field of battle, or a city taken by assault, collect into one group the groans and the distortions of the innumerable dying, the inconsolable grief and horror of their surviving friends, the hellish exultation, and unnatural drunkenness of destruction of the conquerors, the burning of the harvests and the obliteration of the traces of cultivation.—To this, in civil war is to be added the sudden disruption of the bonds of social life, and 'father against son.'

If there had never been war, there could never have been tyranny in the world; tyrants take advantage of the mechanical organization of armies to establish and defend their encroachments.—It is thus that the mighty advantages of the French Revolution have been almost compensated by a succession of tyrants (for demagogues, oligarchies, usurpers and legitimate Kings are merely varieties of the same class) from Robespierre to Louis XVIII. War, waged from whatever motive, extinguishes the sentiment of reason and justice in the mind. The motive is forgotten, or only adverted to in a mechanical and habitual manner. A sentiment of confidence in brute force and in a contempt of death and danger is considered as the highest virtue, when in truth, however indispensable, they are merely the means and the instruments, highly capable of being perverted to destroy the cause they were assumed to promote. It is as a foppery the most intolerable to an amiable and philosophical mind.—It is like what some reasoners have observed of religious faith; no fallacious and indirect motive to action can subsist in the mind without weakening the effect of those which are genuine and true. The person who [may] think it virtuous to believe, will think a less degree of virtue attaches to good actions than if he had considered it as indifferent. The person who has been accustomed to subdue men by force will be less inclined to the trouble of convincing or persuading them.

These brief considerations suffice to show that the true friend of mankind and of his country would hesitate before he recommended measures which tend to bring down so heavy a calamity as war.

I imagine, however, that before the English Nation shall arrive at that point of moral and political degradation now occupied by the Chinese, it will be necessary to appeal to an exertion of physical strength. If the madness of parties admits no other mode of determining the question at issue [. . .]°

When the people shall have obtained, by whatever means, the victory over their oppressors and when persons appointed by them shall have taken their seats in the Representative assembly of the nation, and assumed the control of public affairs according to constitutional rules, there will remain the great task of accommodating all that can be preserved of ancient forms with the improvements of the knowledge of a more enlightened age in legislation, jurisprudence, government, and religious and academical institution. The settlement of the national debt is, on the principles before elucidated, merely circumstance of form, and however necessary and important is an affair of mere arithmetical proportions readily determined; nor can I see how those, who being deprived of their unjust advantages will probably inwardly murmur, can oppose one word of open expostulation to a measure of such irrefragable justice.—There is one thing which certain vulgar agitators endeavour to flatter the most uneducated part of the people by assiduously proposing, which they ought not to do nor to require: and that is, Retribution. Men having been injured desire to injure in return. This is falsely called an universal law of human nature; it is a law from which many are exempt, and all in proportion to their virtue and cultivation.—The savage is more revengeful than the civilized man, the ignorant and uneducated than the person of a refined and cultivated intellect; the generous and [. . .]°

A Defence of Poetry

According to one mode of regarding those two classes of mental action which are called Reason and Imagination,° the former may be considered as mind contemplating the relations borne by one thought to another, however produced; and the latter as mind, acting upon those thoughts so as to colour them with its own light, and composing from them as from elements, other thoughts, each containing within itself the principle of its own integrity. The one is the *τὸ ποιειν* or the principle of synthesis; and has for its objects those forms which are common to universal nature and existence itself; the other is the *τὸ λογιζειν*,° or principle of analysis and its action regards the relations of things, simply as relations; considering thoughts, not in their integral unity, but as the algebraical representations which conduct to certain general results. Reason is the enumeration of quantities already known; Imagination the perception of the value of those quantities, both separately and as a whole. Reason respects the differences, and Imagination the similitudes of things. Reason is to Imagination as the instrument to the agent, as the body to the spirit, as the shadow to the substance.

Poetry, in a general sense, may be defined to be 'the expression of the Imagination':° and Poetry is connate° with the origin of man. Man is an instrument over which a series of external and internal impressions are driven, like the alternations of an ever-changing wind over an Aeolian lyre; which move it, by their motion, to ever-changing melody. But there is a principle within the human being, and perhaps within all sentient beings, which acts otherwise than in the lyre, and produces not melody alone, but harmony, by an internal adjustment of the sounds or motions thus excited to the impressions which excite them. It is as if the lyre could accommodate its chords to the motions of that which strikes them, in a determined proportion of sound; even as the musician can accommodate his voice to the sound of the lyre. A child at play by itself will express its delight by its voice and motions; and every inflexion of tone and every gesture will bear exact relation to a corresponding antitype in the pleasurable impressions which awakened it; it will be the reflected image of that impression; and as the lyre trembles and sounds after the wind has died away, so the child seeks, by prolonging in its voice and motions the duration of the effect, to prolong also a consciousness of the cause. In relation to the objects which delight a child, these expressions are, what Poetry is to higher objects. The savage (for the savage is to ages what the child is to years) expresses the emotions produced in him by surrounding objects in a similar manner; and language and gesture, together with plastic or pictorial imitation, become the image of the combined effect of those objects and of his apprehension of them. Man in society, with all his passions and his pleasures, next becomes the object of the passions and pleasures of man; an additional class of emotions produces an augmented treasure of expressions, and language, gesture and the imitative arts become at once the representation and the medium, the pencil and the picture, the chisel and the statue, the chord and the harmony. The social sympathies, or those laws from which as from its elements society results, begin to develop themselves from the moment that two human beings co-exist; the future is contained within the present as the plant within the seed; and equality, diversity, unity, contrast, mutual dependence become the principles alone capable of affording the motives according to which the will of a social being is determined to action, inasmuch as he is social; and constitute pleasure in sensation, virtue in sentiment, beauty in art, truth in reasoning, and love in the intercourse of kind. Hence men, even in the infancy of society, observe a certain order in their words and actions, distinct from that of the objects and the impressions represented by them, all expression being subject to the laws of that from which it proceeds. But let us dismiss those more general considerations which might involve an enquiry into the principles of society itself, and restrict our view to the manner in which the imagination is expressed upon its forms.

In the youth of the world, men dance and sing and imitate natural objects, observing in these actions, as in all others, a certain rhythm or order. And, although all men observe a similar, they observe not the same order in the motions of the dance, in the melody of the song, in the combinations of language, in the series of their imitations of natural objects. For there is a certain order or rhythm belonging to each of these classes of mimetic representation, from which the hearer and the spectator receive an intenser and a purer pleasure than from any other: the sense of an approximation to this order has been called taste by modern writers. Every man, in the infancy of art, observes an order which approximates more or less closely to that from which this highest delight results: but the diversity is not sufficiently marked, as that its gradations should be sensible, except in those instances where the predominance of this faculty of approximation to the beautiful (for so we may be permitted to name the relation between this highest pleasure and its cause) is very great. Those in whom it exists in excess are poets, in the most universal sense of the word; and the pleasure resulting from the manner in which they express the influence of society or nature upon their own minds, communicates itself to others, and gathers a sort of reduplication from that community. Their language is vitally metaphorical;° that is, it marks the before unapprehended relations of things, and perpetuates their apprehension, until the words which represent them become through time signs for portions and classes of thoughts, instead of pictures of integral thoughts; and then, if no new poets should arise to create afresh the associations which have been thus disorganized, language will be dead to all the nobler purposes of human intercourse. These similitudes or relations are finely said by Lord Bacon to be 'the same footsteps of nature impressed upon the various subjects of the world'°—and he considers the faculty which perceives them as the storehouse of axioms common to all knowledge. In the infancy of society every author is necessarily a poet, because language itself is poetry; and to be a poet is to apprehend the true and the beautiful, in a word the good which exists in the relation, subsisting, first between existence and perception, and secondly between perception and expression. Every original language near to its source is in itself the chaos of a cyclic poem:° the copiousness of lexicography and the distinctions of grammar are the works of a later age, and are merely the catalogue and the form of the creations of Poetry.

But Poets, or those who imagine and express this indestructible order, are not only the authors of language and of music, of the dance and architecture and statuary and painting; they are the institutors of laws and the founders of civil society and the inventors of the arts of life and the teachers, who draw into a certain propinquity with the beautiful and the true that partial apprehension of the agencies of the invisible world which is called religion. Hence all original religions are allegorical or susceptible of allegory, and like Janus have a double face of false and true. Poets, according to the circumstances of the age and nation in which they appeared, were called in the earlier epochs of the world legislators or prophets:° a poet essentially comprises and unites both these characters. For he not only beholds intensely the present as it is, and discovers those laws according to which present things ought to be ordered, but he beholds the future in the present, and his thoughts are the germs of the flower and the fruit of latest time. Not that I assert poets to be prophets in the gross sense of the word, or that they can foretell the form as surely as they foreknow the spirit of events: such is the pretence of superstition which would make poetry an attribute of prophecy, rather than prophecy an attribute of poetry. A Poet participates in the eternal, the infinite and the one; as far as relates to his conceptions, time and place and number are not. The grammatical forms which express the moods of time, and the difference of persons and the distinction of place are convertible with respect to the highest poetry without injuring it as poetry, and the choruses of Aeschylus, and the Book of Job,° and Dante's *Paradise* would afford more than any other writings examples of this fact, if the limits of this paper did not forbid citation. The creations of sculpture, painting and music are illustrations still more decisive.

Language, colour, form, and religious and civil habits of action are all the instruments and the materials of poetry; they may all be called poetry by that figure of speech which considers the effect as a synonym of the cause. But poetry in a more restricted sense expresses those arrangements of language, and especially metrical language, which are created by that imperial faculty whose throne is curtained within the invisible nature of man. And this springs from the nature itself of language, which is a more direct representation of the actions and passions of our internal being, and is susceptible of more various and delicate combinations than colour, form or motion, and is more plastic and obedient to the control of that faculty of which it is the creation. For language is arbitrarily produced by the Imagination and has relation to thoughts alone; but all other materials, instruments and conditions of art have relations among each other, which limit and interpose between conception and expression. The former is as a mirror which reflects, the latter as a cloud which enfeebles, the light of which both are mediums of communication. Hence the fame of sculptors, painters and musicians, although the intrinsic powers of the great masters of these arts may yield in no degree to that of those who have employed language as the hieroglyphic° of their thoughts, has never equalled that of poets in the restricted sense of the term; as two performers of equal skill will produce unequal effects from a guitar and a harp. The fame of legislators and founders of religions, so long as their institutions last, alone seems to exceed that of poets in the restricted sense: but it can scarcely be a question whether if we deduct the celebrity which their flattery of the gross opinions of the vulgar usually conciliates, together with that which belonged to them in their higher character of poets, any excess will remain.

We have thus circumscribed the word Poetry within the limits of that art which is the most familiar and the most perfect expression of the faculty itself. It is necessary however to make the circle still narrower, and to determine the distinction between measured and unmeasured language; for the popular division into prose and verse is inadmissible in accurate philosophy.

Sounds as well as thoughts have relation both between each other and towards that which they represent, and a perception of the order of those relations, has always been found connected with a perception of the order of the relations of thoughts. Hence the language of poets has ever affected a certain uniform and harmonious recurrence of sound, without which it were not poetry, and which is scarcely less indispensable to the communication of its influence, than the words themselves without reference to that peculiar order. Hence the vanity of translation; it were as wise to cast a violet into a crucible that you might discover the formal principle of its colour and odour, as seek to transfuse from one language into another the creations of a poet. The plant must spring again from its seed or it will bear no flower—and this is the burden of the curse of Babel.

An observation of the regular mode of the occurrence of this harmony, in the language of poetical minds, together with its relation to music, produced metre, or a certain system of traditional forms of harmony and language. Yet it is by no means essential that a poet should accommodate his language to this traditional form, so that the harmony which is its spirit be observed. The practice is indeed convenient and popular and to be preferred, especially in such composition as includes much action: but every great poet must inevitably innovate upon the example of his predecessors in the exact structure of his peculiar versification. The distinction between poets and prose-writers is a vulgar error. The distinction between philosophers and poets has been anticipated. Plato was essentially a poet°—the truth and splendour of his imagery and the melody of his language is the most intense that it is possible to conceive. He rejected the measure of the epic, dramatic and lyrical forms, because he sought to kindle a harmony in thoughts divested of shape and action, and he forebore to invent any regular plan of rhythm which would include, under determinate forms, the varied pauses of his style. Cicero° sought to imitate the cadence of his periods but with little success. Lord Bacon was a poet.°—His language has a sweet and majestic rhythm which satisfies the sense no less than the almost superhuman wisdom of his philosophy satisfies the intellect; it is a strain which distends, and then bursts the circumference of the reader's mind, and pours itself forth together with it into the universal element with which it has perpetual sympathy. All the authors of revolutions in opinion are not only necessarily poets as they are inventors, nor even as their words unveil the permanent analogy of things by images which participate in the life of truth; but as their periods are harmonious and rhythmical and contain in themselves the elements of verse; being the echo of the eternal music. Nor are those supreme poets, who have employed traditional forms of rhythm on account of the form and action of their subjects, less incapable of perceiving and teaching the truth of things, than those who have omitted that form. Shakespeare, Dante and Milton (to confine ourselves to modern writers) are philosophers of the very loftiest powers.

A poem is the very image of life expressed in its eternal truth. There is this difference between a story and a poem,° that a story is a catalogue of detached facts, which have no other bond of connection than time, place, circumstance, cause and effect; the other is the creation of actions according to the unchangeable forms of human nature, as existing in the mind of the creator, which is itself the image of all other minds. The one is partial, and applies only to a definite period of time, and a certain combination of events which can never again recur; the other is universal, and contains within itself the germ of a relation to whatever motives or actions have place in the possible varieties of human nature. Time, which destroys the beauty and the use of the story of particular facts, stripped of the poetry which should invest them, augments that of Poetry; and forever develops new and wonderful applications of the eternal truth which it contains. Hence epitomes° have been called the moths of just history;° they eat out the poetry of it. The story of particular facts is as a mirror which obscures and distorts that which should be beautiful: Poetry is a mirror which makes beautiful that which is distorted.

The parts of a composition may be poetical, without the composition as a whole being a poem. A single sentence may be considered as a whole though it may be found in the midst of a series of unassimilated portions; a single word even may be a spark of inextinguishable thought. And thus all the great historians, Herodotus,° Plutarch,° Livy,° were poets; and although the plan of these writers, especially that of Livy, restrained them from developing this faculty in its highest degree, they make copious and ample amends for their subjection, by filling all the interstices of their subject with living images.

Having determined what is poetry, and who are poets, let us proceed to estimate its effects upon society.

Poetry is ever accompanied with pleasure:° all spirits on which it falls, open themselves to receive the wisdom which is mingled with its delight. In the infancy of the world, neither poets themselves nor their auditors are fully aware of the excellence of poetry: for it acts in a divine and unapprehended manner, beyond and above consciousness: and it is reserved for future generations to contemplate and measure the mighty cause and effect in all the strength and splendour of their union. Even in modern times, no living poet ever arrived at the fullness of his fame; the jury which sits in judgement upon a poet, belonging as he does to all time, must be composed of his peers: it must be impanelled° by Time from the selectest of the wise of many generations. A Poet is a nightingale who sits in darkness, and sings to cheer its own solitude with sweet sounds; his auditors are as men entranced by the melody of an unseen musician, who feel that they are moved and softened, yet know not whence or why. The poems of Homer and his contemporaries were the delight of infant Greece; they were the elements of that social system which is the column upon which all succeeding civilization has reposed. Homer embodied the ideal perfection of his age in human character; nor can we doubt that those who read his verses were awakened to an ambition of becoming like to Achilles, Hector and Ulysses: the truth and beauty of friendship, patriotism and persevering devotion to an object, were unveiled to the depths in these immortal creations: the sentiments of the auditors must have been refined and enlarged by a sympathy with such great and lovely impersonations; until from admiring they imitated, and from imitation they identified themselves with the objects of their admiration. Nor let it be objected that these characters are remote from moral perfection, and that they can by no means be considered as edifying patterns for general imitation. Every epoch under names more or less specious has deified its peculiar errors; Revenge is the naked Idol of the worship of a semi-barbarous age; and self-deceit is the veiled Image of unknown evil before which luxury and satiety lie prostrate. But a poet considers the vices of his contemporaries as the temporary dress in which his creations must be arrayed, and which cover without concealing the eternal proportions of their beauty. An epic or dramatic personage is understood to wear them around his soul, as he may the ancient armour or the modern uniform around his body; whilst it is easy to conceive a dress more graceful than either. The beauty of the internal nature cannot be so far concealed by its accidental vesture, but that the spirit of its form shall communicate itself to the very disguise; and indicate the shape it hides from the manner in which it is worn. A majestic form and graceful motions will express themselves through the most barbarous and tasteless costume. Few poets of the highest class have chosen to exhibit the beauty of their conceptions in its naked truth and splendour; and it is doubtful whether the alloy of costume, habit &c. be not necessary to temper this planetary music° for mortal ears.

The whole objection however of the immorality of poetry° rests upon a misconception of the manner in which poetry acts to produce the moral improvement of man. Ethical science arranges the elements which poetry has created, and propounds schemes and proposes examples of civil and domestic life: nor is it for want of admirable doctrines that men hate, and despise, and censure, and deceive, and subjugate one another. But poetry acts in another and a diviner manner. It awakens and enlarges the mind itself by rendering it the receptacle of a thousand unapprehended combinations of thought. Poetry lifts the veil from the hidden beauty of the world; and makes familiar objects be as if they were not familiar; it reproduces all that it represents, and the impersonations clothed in its Elysian light stand thenceforward in the minds of those who have once contemplated them, as memorials of that gentle and exalted content which extends itself over all thoughts and actions with which it co-exists. The great secret of morals is Love; or a going out of our own nature, and an identification of ourselves with the beautiful which exists in thought, action or person, not our own. A man to be greatly good, must imagine intensely and comprehensively; he must put himself in the place of another and of many others; the pains and pleasures of his species must become his own. The great instrument of moral good is the imagination: and poetry administers to the effect by acting upon the cause. Poetry enlarges the circumference of the imagination by replenishing it with thoughts of ever new delight, which have the power of attracting and assimilating to their own nature all other thoughts, and which form new intervals and interstices whose void forever craves fresh food. Poetry strengthens the faculty which is the organ of the moral nature of man in the same manner as exercise strengthens a limb. A Poet, therefore, would do ill to embody his own conceptions of right and wrong,° which are usually those of his place and time, in his poetical creations, which participate in neither. By this assumption of the inferior office of interpreting the effect, in which perhaps after all he might acquit himself but imperfectly, he would resign a glory in a participation in the cause. There was little danger that Homer or any of the eternal poets, should have so far misunderstood themselves as to have abdicated this throne of their widest dominion. Those in whom the poetical faculty, though great, is less intense as Euripides, Lucan, Tasso, Spenser, have frequently affected a moral aim; and the effect of their poetry is diminished in exact proportion to the degree in which they compel us to advert to this purpose.

Homer and the cyclic poets were followed at a certain interval by the dramatic and lyrical Poets of Athens, who flourished contemporaneously with all that is most perfect in the kindred expressions of the poetical faculty; architecture, painting, music, the dance, sculpture, philosophy, and, we may add, the forms of civil life. For although the scheme of Athenian society was deformed by many imperfections° which the poetry existing in Chivalry and Christianity have erased from the habits and institutions of modern Europe; yet never at any other period has so much energy, beauty and virtue been developed; never was blind strength and stubborn form so disciplined and rendered subject to the will of man, or that will less repugnant to the dictates of the beautiful and the true, as during the century which preceded the death of Socrates. Of no other epoch in the history of our species have we records and fragments stamped so visibly with the image of the divinity in man. But it is Poetry alone, in form, in action or in language, which has rendered this epoch memorable above all others, and the storehouse of examples to everlasting time. For written poetry existed at that epoch simultaneously with the other arts, and it is an idle enquiry to demand which gave and which received the light, which all as from a common focus have scattered over the darkest periods of succeeding time. We know no more of cause and effect than a constant conjunction of events:° Poetry is ever found to co-exist with whatever other arts contribute to the happiness and perfection of man. I appeal to what has already been established to distinguish between the cause and the effect.

It was at the period here adverted to, that the Drama had its birth; and however a succeeding writer may have equalled or surpassed those few great specimens of the Athenian drama which have been preserved to us, it is indisputable that the art itself never was understood or practised according to the true philosophy of it, as at Athens. For the Athenians employed language, action, music, painting, the dance, and religious institution to produce a common effect in the representation of the highest idealisms° of passion and of power; each division in the art was made perfect in its kind by artists of the most consummate skill, and was disciplined into a beautiful proportion and unity one towards the other. On the modern stage a few only of the elements capable of expressing the image of the poet's conception are employed at once. We have tragedy without music and dancing; and music and dancing without the highest impersonation of which they are the fit accompaniment, and both without religion and solemnity. Religious institution has indeed been usually banished from the stage. Our system of divesting the actor's face of a mask, on which the many expressions appropriated to his dramatic character might be moulded into one permanent and unchanging expression, is favourable only to a partial and inharmonious effect; it is fit for nothing but a monologue where all the attention may be directed to some great master of ideal mimicry. The modern practice of blending comedy with tragedy, though liable to great abuse in point of practice, is undoubtedly an extension of the dramatic circle; but the comedy should be as in *King Lear*, universal, ideal° and sublime. It is perhaps the intervention of this principle which determines the balance in favour of *King Lear* against the *Oedipus Tyrannus* or the *Agamemnon*, or, if you will, the trilogies° with which they are connected; unless the intense power of the choral poetry, especially that of the latter, should be considered as restoring the equilibrium. *King Lear*, if it can sustain this comparison, may be judged to be the most perfect specimen of the dramatic art existing in the world; in spite of the narrow conditions to which the poet was subjected by the ignorance of the philosophy of the Drama which has prevailed in modern Europe. Calderon in his religious Autos° has attempted to fulfil some of the high conditions of dramatic representation neglected by Shakespeare; such as the establishing a relation between the drama and religion, and the accommodating them to music and dancing, but he omits the observation of conditions still more important, and more is lost than gained by a substitution of the rigidly defined and ever-repeated idealisms of a distorted superstition for the living impersonations of the truth of human passion.

But we digress.—The Author of the *Four Ages of Poetry* has prudently omitted to dispute on the effect of the Drama upon life and manners. For, if I know the knight by the device of his shield, I have only to inscribe *Philoctetes*,° or *Agamemnon*, or *Othello* upon mine to put to flight the giant sophisms° which have enchanted him, as the mirror of intolerable light, though on the arm of one of the weakest of the Paladins,° could blind and scatter whole armies of necromancers° and pagans. The connection of scenic exhibitions with the improvement or corruption of the manners of men has been universally recognized: in other words, the presence or absence of poetry in its most perfect and universal form has been found to be connected with good and evil in conduct or habit. The corruption which has been imputed to the drama as an effect begins, when the poetry employed in its constitution ends: I appeal to the history of manners whether the periods of the growth of the one and the decline of the other have not corresponded with an exactness equal to any other example of moral cause and effect.

The drama at Athens, or wheresoever else it may have approached to its perfection, ever co-existed with the moral and intellectual greatness of the age. The tragedies of the Athenian poets are as mirrors in which the spectator beholds himself, under a thin disguise of circumstance, stripped of all, but that ideal perfection and energy which every one feels to be the internal type of all that he loves, admires and would become. The imagination is enlarged by a sympathy with pains and passions so mighty that they distend in their conception the capacity of that by which they are conceived; the good affections are strengthened by pity, indignation, terror and sorrow; and an exalted calm is prolonged from the satiety of this high exercise of them into the tumult of familiar life; even crime is disarmed of half its horror and all its contagion by being represented as the fatal consequence of the unfathomable agencies of nature; error is thus divested of its wilfulness; men can no longer cherish it as the creation of their choice. In a drama of the highest order there is little food for censure or hatred: it teaches rather self-knowledge and self-respect. Neither the eye or the mind can see itself unless reflected upon that which it resembles. The drama, so long as it continues to express poetry, is as a prismatic and many-sided mirror,° which collects the brightest rays of human nature and divides and reproduces them from the simplicity of these elementary forms; and touches them with majesty and beauty, and multiplies all that it reflects, and endows it with the power of propagating its like wherever it may fall.

But in periods of the decay of social life, the drama sympathizes with that decay. Tragedy becomes a cold imitation of the form of the great masterpieces of antiquity, divested of all harmonious accompaniment of the kindred arts; and often the very form misunderstood: or a weak attempt to teach certain doctrines, which the writer considers as moral truths; and which are usually no more than specious flatteries of some gross vice or weakness with which the author in common with his auditors are infected. Hence what has been called the classical and the domestic drama. Addison's *Cato*° is a specimen of the one, and would it were not superfluous to cite examples of the other! To such purposes Poetry cannot be made subservient. Poetry is a sword of lightning ever unsheathed,° which consumes the scabbard that would contain it. And thus we observe that all dramatic writings of this nature are unimaginative in a singular degree; they affect sentiment and passion which divested of imagination are other names for caprice and appetite. The period in our own history of the grossest degradation of the drama is the reign of Charles II when all forms in which poetry had been accustomed to be expressed became hymns to the triumph of kingly power over liberty and virtue. Milton stood alone illuminating an age unworthy of him. At such periods the calculating principle pervades all the forms of dramatic exhibition, and poetry ceases to be expressed upon them. Comedy loses its ideal universality: wit succeeds to humour; we laugh from self-complacency and triumph instead of pleasure; malignity, sarcasm and contempt succeed to sympathetic merriment; we hardly laugh, but we smile. Obscenity, which is ever blasphemy against the divine beauty in life, becomes, from the very veil which it assumes, more active if less disgusting: it is a monster for which the corruption of society forever brings forth new food, which it devours in secret.

The Drama being that form under which a greater number of modes of expression of poetry are susceptible of being combined than any other, the connection of beauty and social good is more observable in the drama than in whatever other form: and it is indisputable that the highest perfection of human society has ever corresponded with the highest dramatic excellence: and that the corruption or the extinction of the drama in a nation where it has once flourished is a mark of a corruption of manners, and an extinction of the energies which sustain the soul of social life. But, as Machiavelli° says of political institutions, that life may be preserved and renewed, if men should arise capable of bringing back the drama to its principles. And this is true with respect to poetry in its most extended sense: all language, institution and form require not only to be produced but to be sustained: the office and character of a poet participates in the divine nature as regards providence no less than as regards creation.

Civil war, the spoils of Asia, and the fatal predominance first of the Macedonian, and then of the Roman arms were so many symbols of the extinction or suspension of the creative faculty in Greece. The bucolic writers° who found patronage under the lettered tyrants of Sicily and Egypt were the latest representatives of its most glorious reign. Their poetry is intensely melodious; like the odour of the tuberose it overcomes and sickens the spirit with excess of sweetness; whilst the poetry of the preceding age was as a meadow-gale of June which mingles the fragrance of all the flowers of the field and adds a quickening and harmonizing spirit of its own which endows the sense with a power of sustaining its extreme delight. The bucolic and erotic delicacy in written poetry is correlative with that softness in statuary, music and the kindred arts, and even in manners and institutions which distinguished the epoch to which we now refer. Nor is it the poetical faculty itself, or any misapplication of it, to which this want of harmony is to be imputed. An equal sensibility to the influence of the senses and the affections is to be found in the writings of Homer and Sophocles: the former especially has clothed sensual and pathetic images with irresistible attractions. Their superiority over these succeeding writers consists in the presence of those thoughts which belong to the inner faculties of our nature, not in the absence of those which are connected with the external: their incomparable perfection consists in a harmony of the union of all. It is not what the erotic poets have, but what they have not, in which their imperfection consists. It is not inasmuch as they were Poets, but inasmuch as they were not Poets, that they can be considered with any plausibility as connected with the corruption of their age. Had that corruption availed so as to extinguish in them the sensibility to pleasure, passion and natural scenery, which is imputed to them as an imperfection, the last triumph of evil would have been achieved. For the end of social corruption is to destroy all sensibility to pleasure; and therefore it is corruption. It begins at the imagination and the intellect as at the core, and distributes itself thence as a paralysing venom, through the affections into the very appetites, until all become a torpid° mass in which sense hardly survives. At the approach of such a period, Poetry ever addresses itself to those faculties which are the last to be destroyed, and its voice is heard, like the footsteps of Astraea,° departing from the world. Poetry ever communicates all the pleasure which men are capable of receiving: it is ever still the light of life; the source of whatever beautiful, or generous, or true can have place in an evil time. It will readily be confessed that those among the luxurious° citizens of Syracuse and Alexandria who were delighted with the poems of Theocritus were less cold, cruel and sensual than the remnant of their tribe. But corruption must utterly have destroyed the fabric of human society before Poetry can ever cease. The sacred links of that chain have never been entirely disjoined, which descending through the minds of many men is attached to those great minds whence as from a magnet the invisible effluence is sent forth which at once connects, animates and sustains the life of all.° It is the faculty which contains within itself the seeds at once of its own and of social renovation. And let us not circumscribe the effects of the bucolic and erotic poetry within the limits of the sensibility of those to whom it was addressed. They may have perceived the beauty of these immortal compositions, simply as fragments and isolated portions: those who are more finely organized, or born in a happier age may recognize them as episodes of that great poem, which all poets like the co-operating thoughts of one great mind have built up since the beginning of the world.

The same revolutions within a narrower sphere had place in ancient Rome: but the actions and forms of its social life never seem to have been perfectly saturated with the poetical element. The Romans appear to have considered the Greeks as the selectest treasuries of the selectest forms of manners and of nature and to have abstained from creating in measured language, sculpture, music or architecture anything which might bear a particular relation to their own condition whilst it should bear a general one to the universal constitution of the world. But we judge from partial evidence, and we judge perhaps partially. Ennius,° Varro,° Pacuvius° and Accius,° all great poets, have been lost. Lucretius is in the highest, and Virgil in a very high sense, a creator. The chosen delicacy of the expressions of the latter are as a mist of light which conceal from us the intense and exceeding truth of his conceptions of nature. Livy is instinct with poetry. Yet Horace, Catullus, Ovid, and generally the other great writers of the Virgilian age, saw man and nature in the mirror of Greece. The institutions also and the religion of Rome were less poetical than those of Greece, as the shadow is less vivid than the substance. Hence Poetry in Rome seemed to follow rather than accompany the perfection of political and domestic society. The true Poetry of Rome lived in its institutions; for whatever of beautiful, true and majestic they contained could have sprung only from the faculty which creates the order in which they consist. The life of Camillus;° the death of Regulus;° the expectation of the senators in their godlike state of the victorious Gauls;° the refusal of the republic to make peace with Hannibal after the battle of Cannae,° were not the consequences of a refined calculation of the probable personal advantage to result from such a rhythm and order in the shows of life, to those who were at once the poets and the actors of these immortal dramas. The imagination beholding the beauty of this order, created it out of itself according to its own idea: the consequence was empire, and the reward everliving fame. These things are not the less poetry *quia carent vate sacro*.° They are the episodes of that cyclic poem written by Time upon the memories of men. The Past, like an inspired rhapsodist,° fills the theatre of everlasting generations with their harmony.

At length the ancient system of religion and manners had fulfilled the circle of its revolutions. And the world would have fallen into utter anarchy and darkness, but that there were found poets among the authors of the Christian and Chivalric systems of manners and religion, who created forms of opinion and action never before conceived; which, copied into the imaginations of men, became as generals to the bewildered armies of their thoughts. It is foreign to the present purpose to touch upon the evil produced by these systems: except that we protest, on the ground of the principles already established, that no portion of it can be attributed to the poetry they contain.

It is probable that the poetry of Moses, Job, David, Solomon and Isaiah° had produced a great effect upon the mind of Jesus and his disciples. The scattered fragments preserved to us by the biographers of this extraordinary person are all instinct with the most vivid poetry. But his doctrines seem to have been quickly distorted. At a certain period after the prevalence of a system of opinions founded upon those promulgated by him, the three forms into which Plato had distributed the faculties of mind° underwent a sort of apotheosis, and became the object of the worship of the civilized world. Here it is to be confessed that 'Light seems to thicken', and

> the crow makes wing to the rooky wood,
> Good things of day begin to droop and drowze
> And night's black agents to their preys do rouse.°

But mark how beautiful an order has sprung from the dust and blood of this fierce chaos! how the World, as from a resurrection, balancing itself on the golden wings of knowledge and of hope, has reassumed its yet unwearied flight into the Heaven of time! Listen to the music, unheard by outward ears, which is as a ceaseless and invisible wind nourishing its everlasting course with strength and swiftness.

The poetry in the doctrines of Jesus Christ, and the mythology and institutions of the Celtic conquerors° of the Roman Empire, outlived the darkness and the convulsions connected with their growth and victory, and blended themselves into a new fabric of manners and opinion. It is an error to impute the ignorance of the dark ages to the Christian doctrines or to the predominance of the Celtic nations. Whatever of evil their agencies may have contained sprung from the extinction of the poetical principle, connected with the progress of despotism and superstition. Men, from causes too intricate to be here discussed, had become insensible and selfish: their own will had become feeble, and yet they were its slaves, and thence the slaves of the will of others: lust, fear, avarice, cruelty and fraud characterized a race amongst whom no one was to be found capable of *creating* in form, language or institution. The moral anomalies of such a state of society are not justly to be charged upon any class of events immediately connected with them, and those events are most entitled to our approbation which could dissolve it most expeditiously. It is unfortunate for those who cannot distinguish words from thoughts that many of these anomalies have been incorporated into our popular religion.

It was not until the eleventh century that the effects of the poetry of the Christian and the Chivalric systems began to manifest themselves. The principle of equality had been discovered and applied by Plato in his *Republic*, as the theoretical rule of the mode in which the materials of pleasure and of power produced by the common skill and labour of human beings ought to be distributed among them.° The limitations of this rule were asserted by him to be determined only by the sensibility of each, or the utility to result to all. Plato, following the doctrines of Timaeus and Pythagoras, taught also a moral and intellectual system of doctrine comprehending at once the past, the present and the future condition of man. Jesus Christ divulged the sacred and eternal truths contained in these views to mankind, and Christianity, in its abstract purity, became the exoteric° expression of the esoteric° doctrines of the poetry and wisdom of antiquity. The incorporation of the Celtic nations with the exhausted population of the South, impressed upon it the figure of the poetry existing in their mythology and institutions. The result was a sum of the action and reaction of all the causes included in it; for it may be assumed as a maxim that no nation or religion can supersede any other without incorporating into itself a portion of that which it supersedes. The abolition of personal and domestic slavery, and the emancipation of women from a great part of the degrading restraints of antiquity were among the consequences of these events.

The abolition of personal slavery is the basis of the highest political hope that it can enter into the mind of man to conceive. The freedom of women produced the poetry of sexual love. Love became a religion, the idols of whose worship were ever present. It was as if the statues of Apollo and the muses had been endowed with life and motion and had walked forth among their worshippers; so that earth became peopled by the inhabitants of a diviner world. The familiar appearances and proceedings of life became wonderful and heavenly; and a paradise was created as out of the wrecks of Eden. And as this creation itself is poetry, so its creators were poets; and language was the instrument of their art; 'Galeotto fu il libro, e chi lo scrisse'.° The Provençal Trouveurs,° or inventors, preceded Petrarch,° whose verses are as spells which unseal the inmost enchanted fountains of the delight which is in the grief of Love. It is impossible to feel them without becoming a portion of that beauty which we contemplate: it were superfluous to explain how the gentleness and the elevation of mind connected with these sacred emotions can render men more amiable, and generous, and wise, and lift them out of the dull vapours of the little world of self. Dante understood the secret things of love even more than Petrarch. His *Vita Nuova* is an inexhaustible fountain of purity of sentiment and language: it is the idealized history of that period, and those intervals of his life which were dedicated to love. His apotheosis of Beatrice in Paradise and the gradations of his own love and her loveliness, by which as by steps he feigns himself to have ascended to the throne of the Supreme Cause, is the most glorious imagination of modern poetry. The acutest critics have justly reversed the judgement of the vulgar and the order of the great acts of the 'Divine Drama'° in the measure of the admiration which they accord to the Hell, Purgatory and Paradise. The latter is a perpetual hymn to everlasting love. Love, which found a worthy poet in Plato° alone of all the ancients, has been celebrated by a chorus of the greatest writers of the renovated world; and the music has penetrated the caverns of society, and its echoes still drown the dissonance of arms, and superstition. At successive intervals Ariosto, Tasso, Shakespeare, Spenser, Calderon, Rousseau and the great writers of our own age have celebrated the dominion of love; planting as it were trophies in the human mind of that sublimest victory over sensuality and force. The true relation borne to each other by the sexes into which human kind is distributed has become less misunderstood; and if the error which confounded diversity with inequality of the powers of the two sexes has been partially recognized in the opinions and institutions of modern Europe, we owe this great benefit to the worship of which Chivalry was the law, and poets the prophets.

The poetry of Dante may be considered as the bridge thrown over the stream of time which unites the modern and the ancient world. The distorted notions of invisible things which Dante and his rival Milton have idealized are merely the mask and the mantle in which these great poets walk through eternity enveloped and disguised. It is a difficult question to determine how far they were conscious of the distinction which must have subsisted in their minds between their own creeds and that of the people. Dante at least appears to wish to mark the full extent of it by placing Riphaeus whom Virgil calls *justissimus unus* in Paradise,° and observing a most heretical caprice in his distribution of rewards and punishments. And Milton's poem contains within itself a philosophical refutation of that system of which, by a strange but natural antithesis, it has been a chief popular support. Nothing can exceed the energy and magnificence of the character of Satan as expressed in *Paradise Lost*. It is a mistake to suppose that he could ever have been intended for the popular personification of evil. Implacable hate, patient cunning, and a sleepless refinement of device to inflict the extremest anguish on an enemy: these things are evil; and although venial in a slave are not to be forgiven in a tyrant; although redeemed by much that ennobles his defeat in one subdued, are marked by all that dishonours his conquest in the victor. Milton's

Devil as a moral being is as far superior to his God as one who perseveres in some purpose which he has conceived to be excellent in spite of adversity and torture, is to one who in the cold security of undoubted triumph inflicts the most horrible revenge upon his enemy—not from any mistaken notion of inducing him to repent of a perseverance in enmity, but with the alleged design of exasperating him to deserve new torments.° Milton has so far violated the popular creed (if this shall be judged to be a violation) as to have alleged no superiority of moral virtue to his God over his Devil. And this bold neglect of a direct moral purpose is the most decisive proof of the supremacy of Milton's genius. He mingled as it were the elements of human nature, as colours upon a single pallet, and arranged them into the composition of his great picture according to the laws of epic truth: that is, according to the laws of that principle by which a series of actions of the external universe, and of intelligent and ethical beings is calculated to excite the sympathy of succeeding generations of mankind. The *Divina Commedia* and *Paradise Lost* have conferred upon modern mythology° a systematic form; and when change and time shall have added one more superstition to the mass of those which have arisen and decayed upon the earth, commentators will be learnedly employed in elucidating the religion of ancestral Europe, only not utterly forgotten because it will have been stamped with the eternity of genius.°

Homer was the first, and Dante the second epic poet: that is, the second poet the series of whose creations bore a defined and intelligible relation to the knowledge, and sentiment, and religion, and political condition of the age in which he lived, and of the ages which followed it: developing itself in correspondence with their development. For Lucretius had limed the wings of his swift spirit in the dregs of the sensible world:° and Virgil, with a modesty that ill became his genius, had affected the fame of an imitator even whilst he created anew all that he copied;° and none among the flock of mock-birds,° though their notes were sweet, Apollonius Rhodius,° Quintus Calaber Smyrnaeus,° Nonnus,° Lucan,° Statius° or Claudian° have sought even to fulfil a single condition of epic truth. Milton was the third epic poet: for if the title of epic in its highest sense be refused to the *Aeneid* still less can it be conceded to the *Orlando Furioso*, the *Gerusalemme Liberata*, the *Lusiad* or the *Fairy Queen*.°

Dante and Milton were both deeply penetrated with the ancient religion of the civilized world; and its spirit exists in their poetry, probably in the same proportion as its forms survived in the unreformed worship of modern Europe. The one preceded and the other followed the Reformation at almost equal intervals. Dante was the first religious reformer, and Luther° surpassed him rather in the rudeness and acrimony than in the boldness of his censures of papal usurpation. Dante was the first awakener of entranced Europe; he created a language in itself music and persuasion out of a chaos of inharmonious barbarisms.° He was the congregator of those great spirits who presided over the resurrection of learning; the Lucifer° of that starry flock which in the thirteenth century shone forth from republican Italy, as from a heaven, into the darkness of the benighted world. His very words are instinct with spirit;° each is as a spark, a burning atom of inextinguishable thought; and many yet lie covered in the ashes of their birth, and pregnant with a lightning which has yet found no conductor. All high poetry is infinite; it is as the first acorn which contained all oaks potentially. Veil after veil may be undrawn and the inmost naked beauty of the meaning never exposed. A great Poem is a fountain forever overflowing with the waters of wisdom and delight; and after one person and one age has exhausted all its divine effluence° which their peculiar relations enable them to share, another and yet another succeeds, and new relations are ever developed, the source of an unforeseen and an unconceived delight.

The age immediately succeeding to that of Dante, Petrarch and Boccaccio was characterized by a revival of painting, sculpture, music and architecture. Chaucer caught the sacred inspiration, and the superstructure of English literature is based upon the materials of Italian invention.°

But let us not be betrayed from a defence into a critical history of poetry and its influence on society. Be it enough to have pointed out the effects of poets in the large and true sense of the word upon their own and all succeeding times, and to revert to the partial instances cited as illustrations of an opinion the reverse of that attempted to be established in the *Four Ages of Poetry*.

But Poets have been challenged to resign the civic crown to reasoners and mechanists° on another plea. It is admitted that the exercise of the imagination is more delightful, but it is alleged that that of reason is more useful. Let us examine as the ground of this distinction what is meant by Utility. Pleasure or good in a general sense, is that which the consciousness of a sensitive and intelligent being seeks, and in which when found it acquiesces. There are two kinds of pleasure, one durable, universal and permanent; the other transitory and particular. Utility may either express the means of producing the former, or the latter. In the former sense, whatever strengthens and purifies the affections, enlarges the imagination, and adds a spirit to sense, is useful. But the meaning in which the author of the *Four Ages of Poetry* seems to have employed the word utility is the narrower one of banishing the importunity of the wants of our animal nature, the surrounding men with security of life, the dispersing the grosser delusions of superstition, and the conciliating such a degree of mutual forbearance among men as may consist with the motives of personal advantage.

Undoubtedly the promoters of utility in this limited sense, have their appointed office in society. They follow the footsteps of poets, and copy the sketches of their creations into the book of common life. They make space and give time. Their exertions are of the highest value so long as they confine their administration of the concerns of the inferior powers of our own nature within the limits of what is due to the superior ones. But whilst the sceptic destroys gross superstitions, let him spare to deface, as some of the French writers° have defaced, the eternal truths charactered upon the imaginations of men. Whilst the mechanist° abridges, and the political economist combines, labour,° let them beware that their speculations, for want of a correspondence with those first principles which belong to the imagination, do not tend, as they have in modern England, to exasperate at once the extremes of luxury and want. They have exemplified the saying, 'To him that hath, more shall be given; and from him that hath not the little that he hath shall be taken away.'° The rich have become richer, and the poor have become poorer; and the vessel of the state is driven between the Scylla and Charybdis° of anarchy and despotism.° Such are the effects which must ever flow from an unmitigated exercise of the calculating faculty.

It is difficult to define pleasure in its highest sense; the definition involving a number of apparent paradoxes. For, from an inexplicable defect of harmony in the constitution of human nature, the pain of the inferior is frequently connected with the pleasures of the superior portions of our being. Sorrow, terror, anguish, despair itself are often the chosen expressions of an approximation to the highest good. Our sympathy in tragic fiction depends on this principle: tragedy delights by affording a shadow of the pleasure which exists in pain. This is the source also of the melancholy which is inseparable from the sweetest melody. The pleasure that is in sorrow is sweeter than the pleasure of pleasure itself. And hence the saying, 'It is better to go to the house of mourning, than to the house of mirth.'° Not that this highest species of pleasure is necessarily linked with pain. The delight of love and friendship, the ecstasy of the admiration of nature, the joy of the perception, and still more of the creation of poetry is often wholly unalloyed.

The production and assurance of pleasure in this highest sense is true utility. Those who produce and preserve this pleasure are poets or poetical philosophers. The exertions of Locke, Hume, Gibbon, Voltaire, Rousseau° and their disciples in favour of oppressed and deluded humanity are entitled to the gratitude of mankind. Yet it is easy to calculate the degree of moral and intellectual improvement which the world would have exhibited, had they never lived. A little more nonsense would have been talked for a century or two; and perhaps a few more men, women and children burnt as heretics. We might not at this moment have been congratulating each other on the abolition of the Inquisition in Spain.° But it exceeds all imagination to conceive what would have been the moral condition of the world, if neither Dante, Petrarch, Boccaccio, Chaucer, Shakespeare, Calderon, Lord Bacon, nor Milton had ever existed: if Raphael and Michelangelo had never been born; if the Hebrew poetry had never been translated; if a revival of a study of Greek Literature had never taken place; if no monuments of ancient sculpture had been handed down to us; and if the poetry of the religion of the ancient world had been extinguished together with its belief. The human mind could never, except by the intervention of these excitements, have been awakened to the invention of those grosser sciences, and that application of analytical reasoning to the aberrations of society, which it is now attempted to exalt over the direct expression of the inventive and creative faculty itself.

We have more moral, political and historical wisdom than we know how to reduce into practice: we have more scientific and economical knowledge than can be accommodated to the just distribution of the produce which it multiplies. The poetry, in these systems of thought, is concealed by the accumulation of facts and calculating processes. There is no want of knowledge respecting what is wisest and best in morals, government and political economy, or at least what is wiser and better than what men now practise and endure. But we 'let *I dare not* wait upon *I would*, like the poor cat in the adage'.° We want the creative faculty to imagine that which we know; we want the generous impulse to act that which we imagine; we want the poetry of life; our calculations have outrun conception; we have eaten more than we can digest. The cultivation of those sciences which have enlarged the limits of the empire of man over the external world, has, for want of the poetical faculty, proportionally circumscribed those of the internal world, and man, having enslaved the elements, remains himself a slave. To what but a cultivation of the mechanical arts in a degree disproportioned to the presence of the creative faculty which is the basis of all knowledge is to be attributed the abuse of all invention for abridging and combining labour, to the exasperation of the inequality of mankind? From what other cause has it arisen that the discoveries which should have lightened, have added a weight to, the curse imposed on Adam?° Poetry, and the principle of Self, of which money is the visible incarnation, are the God and the Mammon° of the world.

The functions of the poetical faculty are twofold: by one it creates new materials of knowledge, and power, and pleasure; by the other it engenders in the mind a desire to reproduce and arrange them according to a certain rhythm and order, which may be called the beautiful and the good. The cultivation of poetry is never more to be desired than at periods when from an excess of the selfish and calculating principle, the accumulation of the materials of external life exceed the quantity of the power of assimilating them to the internal laws of human nature. The body has then become too unwieldy for that which animates it.

Poetry is indeed something divine. It is at once the centre and circumference of knowledge;° it is that which comprehends all science, and that to which all science must be referred. It is at the same time the root and the blossom of all other systems of thought: it is that from which all spring, and that which adorns all; and that which if blighted denies the fruit and the seed, and withholds from the barren world the nourishment and the succession of the scions of the tree of life. It is the perfect and consummate surface and bloom of things; it is as the odour and the colour of the rose to the texture of the elements which compose it, as the form and splendour of unfaded beauty to the secrets of anatomy and corruption. What were Virtue, Love, Patriotism, Friendship—what were the scenery of this beautiful universe which we inhabit, what were our consolations on this side of the grave, and what were our aspirations beyond it, if Poetry did not ascend to bring light and fire from those eternal regions where the owl-winged faculty of calculation dare not ever soar? Poetry is not like reasoning, a power to be exerted according to the determination of the will. A man cannot say, 'I will compose poetry.' The greatest poet even cannot say it: for the mind in creation is as a fading coal which some invisible influence, like an inconstant wind, awakens to transitory brightness: this power arises from within like the colour of a flower which fades and changes as it is developed, and the conscious portions of our nature are unprophetic either of its approach or its departure. Could this influence be durable in its original purity and force, it is impossible to predict the greatness of the results: but when composition begins, inspiration is already on the decline, and the most glorious poetry that has ever been communicated to the world is probably a feeble shadow of the original conceptions of the poet. I appeal to the greatest Poets of the present day, whether it be not an error to assert that the finest passages of poetry are produced by labour and study. The toil and the delay recommended by critics can be justly interpreted to mean no more than a careful observation of the inspired moments, and an artificial connection of the spaces between their suggestions by the intertexture° of conventional expressions; a necessity only imposed by a limitedness of the poetical faculty itself. For Milton conceived the *Paradise Lost* as a whole before he executed it in portions. We have his own authority also for the Muse having 'dictated' to him 'the unpremeditated song'.° And let this be an answer to those who would allege the fifty-six various readings of the first line of the *Orlando Furioso*. Compositions so produced are to poetry what mosaic is to painting. This instinct and intuition of the poetical faculty is still more observable in the plastic and pictorial arts: a great statue or picture grows under the power of the artist as a child in the mother's womb, and the very mind which directs the hands in formation is incapable of accounting to itself for the origin, the gradations, or the media of the process.

Poetry is the record of the happiest and best moments of the happiest and best minds. We are aware of evanescent visitations of thought and feeling sometimes associated with place or person, sometimes regarding our own mind alone, and always arising unforeseen and departing unbidden, but elevating and delightful beyond all expression: so that even in the desire and the regret they leave there cannot but be pleasure, participating as it does in the nature of its object. It is as it were the interpenetration of a diviner nature through our own,° but its footsteps are like those of a wind over the sea, which the coming calm erases, and whose traces remain only as on the wrinkled sand which paves it. These and corresponding conditions of being are experienced principally by those of the most delicate sensibility and the most enlarged imagination. And the state of mind produced by them is at war with every base desire. The enthusiasm of virtue, love, patriotism and friendship is essentially linked with such emotions; and whilst they last self appears as what it is, an atom to an Universe. Poets are not only subject to these experiences as spirits of the most refined organization, but they can colour all that they combine with the evanescent hues of this ethereal world; a word, a trait in the representation of a scene or a passion will touch the enchanted chord, and reanimate in those who have ever experienced these emotions the sleeping, the cold, the buried image of the past. Poetry thus makes immortal all that is best and most beautiful in the world; it arrests the vanishing apparitions which haunt the interlunations° of life, and veiling them or in language or in form sends them forth among mankind bearing sweet news of kindred joy to those with whom their sisters abide—abide, because there is no portal of expression from the caverns of the spirit which they inhabit into the universe of things. Poetry redeems from decay the visitations of the divinity in man.

Poetry turns all things to loveliness: it exalts the beauty of that which is most beautiful, and it adds beauty to that which is most deformed: it marries exultation and horror, grief and pleasure, eternity and change; it subdues to union under its light yoke all irreconcilable things. It transmutes all that it touches, and every form moving within the radiance of its presence is changed by wondrous sympathy to an incarnation of the spirit which it breathes: its secret alchemy turns to potable° gold the poisonous waters which flow from death through life; it strips the veil of familiarity from the world, and lays bare the naked and sleeping beauty which is the spirit of its forms.

All things exist as they are perceived; at least in relation to the percipient—'The mind is its own place, and of itself can make a Heaven of Hell, a Hell of Heaven.'° But Poetry defeats the curse which binds us to be subjected to the accident of surrounding impressions. And whether it spreads its own figured curtain or withdraws life's dark veil from before the scene of things, it equally creates for us a being within our being. It makes us the inhabitants of a world to which the familiar world is as a chaos. It reproduces the common Universe of which we are portions and percipients, and it purges from our inward sight the film of familiarity° which obscures from us the wonder of our being. It compels us to feel that which we perceive, and to imagine that which we know. It creates anew the universe after it has been annihilated in our minds by the recurrence of impressions blunted by reiteration. It justifies that bold and true word of Tasso: *Non merita nome di creatore se non Iddio ed il Poeta.*°

A Poet, as he is the author to others of the highest wisdom, pleasure, virtue and glory, so he ought personally to be the happiest, the best, the wisest and the most illustrious of men. As to his glory, let Time be challenged to declare whether the fame of any other institutor of human life be comparable to that of a poet. That he is the wisest, the happiest and the best, inasmuch as he is a poet, is equally incontrovertible: the greatest Poets have been men of the most spotless virtue, of the most consummate prudence, and, if we would look into the interior of their lives, the most fortunate of men: and the exceptions, as they regard those who possessed the poetic faculty in a high yet inferior degree, will be found on consideration to confine rather than destroy the rule. Let us for a moment stoop to the arbitration of popular breath, and usurping and uniting in our own persons the incompatible characters of accuser, witness, judge and executioner, let us decide without trial, testimony or form that certain motives of those who are 'there sitting where we dare not soar'° are reprehensible. Let us assume that Homer was a drunkard, that Virgil was a flatterer, that Horace was a coward, that Tasso was a madman, that Lord Bacon was a peculator, that Raphael was a libertine, that Spenser was a poet laureate.° It is inconsistent with this division of our subject to cite living poets, but Posterity has done ample justice to the great names now referred to. Their errors have been weighed and found to have been dust in the balance; if their sins were as scarlet they are now as white as snow: they have been washed in the blood of the mediator and the redeemer Time. Observe in what a ludicrous chaos the imputations of real and of fictitious crime have been confused in the contemporary calumnies against poetry and poets; consider how little is as it appears, or appears as it is; look to your own motives, and judge not, lest ye be judged.°

Poetry, as has been said, differs in this respect from logic that it is not subject to the control of the active powers of the mind, and that its birth and recurrence has no necessary connection with consciousness or will. It is presumptuous to determine that these are the necessary conditions of all mental causation when mental effects are experienced insusceptible of being referred to them. The frequent recurrence of the poetical power, it is obvious to suppose, may produce in the mind an habit of order and harmony correlative with its own nature and with its effects upon other minds. But in the intervals of inspiration, and they may be frequent without being durable, a Poet becomes a man and is abandoned to the sudden reflux of the influences under which others habitually live. But as he is more delicately organized than other men, and sensible to pain and pleasure both his own and that of others in a degree unknown to them, he will avoid the one and pursue the other with an ardour proportioned to this difference. And he renders himself obnoxious° to calumny, when he neglects to observe the circumstances under which these objects of universal pursuit and flight have disguised themselves in one another's garments. But there is nothing necessarily evil in this error, and thus cruelty, envy, revenge, avarice, and the passions purely evil, have never formed any portion of the popular imputations on the lives of poets.

I have thought it most favourable to the cause of truth to set down these remarks according to the order in which they were suggested to my mind by a consideration of the subject itself, instead of following that of the treatise which excited me to make them public. Thus, although devoid of the formality of a polemical reply, if the view which they contain be just, they will be found to involve a refutation of the *Four Ages of Poetry*, so far at least as regards the first division of the subject. I can readily conjecture what should have moved the gall of the learned and intelligent author of that paper. I confess myself like him unwilling to be stunned by the *Theseids* of the hoarse Codri° of the day: Bavius and Maevius° undoubtedly are, as they ever were, insufferable persons. But it belongs to a philosophical critic to distinguish rather than confound.

The first part of these remarks has related to poetry in its elements and principles; and it has been shown, as well as the narrow limits assigned them would permit, that what is called poetry in a restricted sense has a common source with all other forms of order and of beauty according to which the materials of human life are susceptible of being arranged; and which is Poetry in an universal sense.

The second part will have for its object an application of these principles to the present state of the cultivation of Poetry, and a defence of the attempt to idealize the modern forms of manners and opinion, and compel them into a subordination to the imaginative and creative faculty. For the literature of England, an energetic development of which has ever preceded or accompanied a great and free development of the national will, has arisen as it were from a new birth. In spite of the low-thoughted envy° which would undervalue contemporary merit, our own will be a memorable age in intellectual achievements, and we live among such philosophers and poets as surpass beyond comparison any who have appeared since the last national struggle for civil and religious liberty. The most unfailing herald, companion and follower of the awakening of a great people to work a beneficial change in opinion or institution, is Poetry. At such periods there is an accumulation of the power of communicating and receiving intense and impassioned conceptions respecting man and nature. The persons in whom this power resides, may often as far as regards many portions of their nature, have little apparent correspondence with that spirit of good of which they are the ministers. But even whilst they deny and abjure, they are yet compelled to serve, the Power which is seated on the throne of their own soul. It is impossible to read the compositions of the most celebrated writers of the present day without being startled with the electric life which burns within their words. They measure the circumference and sound the depths of human nature with a comprehensive and all-penetrating spirit, and they are themselves perhaps the most sincerely astonished at its manifestations, for it is less their spirit than the spirit of the age. Poets are the hierophants° of an unapprehended inspiration, the mirrors of the gigantic shadows which futurity casts upon the present, the words which express what they understand not, the trumpets which sing to battle and feel not what they inspire: the influence which is moved not, but moves. Poets are the unacknowledged legislators of the World.°

NOTES

ABBREVIATIONS

Bonca Teddi Chichester Bonca, *Shelley's Mirrors of Love: Narcissism, Sacrifice, and Sorority* (Albany, NY, 1999)

Brett-Smith H. F. B. Brett-Smith (ed.), *Peacock's Four Ages of Poetry, Shelley's Defence of Poetry and Browning's Essay on Shelley* (Oxford, 1921)

BSM Donald H. Reiman (gen. ed.), *The Bodleian Shelley Manuscripts* (23 vols., New York, 1986–2002): vol. 1: *'Peter Bell the Third' . . . Bodleian MS. Shelley adds. c. 5 . . . and 'The Triumph of Life' . . . Bodleian MS. Shelley adds. c. 4, folios 18–58*, ed. Donald H. Reiman (1986); vol. 2: *Bodleian MS. Shelley adds. d. 7*, ed. Irving Massey (1987); vol. 3: *Bodleian MS. Shelley e. 4*, ed. P. M. S. Dawson (1988); vol. 4: *Bodleian MS. Shelley d. 1*, ed. E. B. Murray, 2 parts (1988); vol. 5: *The 'Witch of Atlas' Notebook . . . Bodleian MS. Shelley adds. e. 6*, ed. Carlene Adamson (1997); vol. 6: *Shelley's Pisan Winter Notebook (1820–1821) . . . Bodleian MS. Shelley adds. e. 8*, ed. Carlene Adamson (1992); vol. 7: *Shelley's Last Notebook . . . Bodleian MS. Shelley adds. e. 20 . . . with Bodleian MS. Shelley adds. e. 15 . . . and Bodleian MS. Shelley adds. c. 4, folios 212–246*, ed. Donald H. Reiman and Hélène Dworzan Reiman (1990); vol. 8: *Bodleian MS. Shelley d. 3*, ed. Tatsuo Tokoo (1988); vol. 9: *The 'Prometheus Unbound' Fair Copies . . . Bodleian MSS. Shelley e. 1, e. 2, and e. 3*, ed. Neil Fraistat (1991); vol. 10: *Mythological Dramas . . . Bodleian MS. Shelley d. 2 . . . with 'Relation of the Death of the Family of the Cenci' . . . Bodleian MS. Shelley adds. e. 13*, ed. Betty T. Bennett and Charles E. Robinson (1992); vol. 11: *The Geneva Notebook of . . . Shelley . . . Bodleian MSS. Shelley adds. e. 16 and adds. c. 4, folios 63, 65, 71, and 72*, ed. Michael Erkelenz (1992); vol. 12: *Shelley's 'Charles the First' Draft Notebook . . . Bodleian MS. Shelley adds. e. 17*, ed. Nora Crook (1991); vol. 13: *Drafts for 'Laon and Cythna' . . . Bodleian MSS. Shelley adds. e. 14 and adds. e. 19*, ed. Tatsuo Tokoo (1992); vol. 14: *Shelley's 'Devils' Notebook . . . Bodleian MS. Shelley adds. e. 9*, ed. P. M. S. Dawson and Timothy Webb (1993); vol. 15: *The 'Julian and Maddalo' Draft Notebook . . . Bodleian MS. Shelley adds. e. 11*, ed. Steven E. Jones (1990); vol. 16: *The 'Hellas' Notebook . . . Bodleian MS. Shelley adds. e. 7*, ed. Donald H. Reiman and Michael C. Neth (1994); vol. 17: *Drafts for 'Laon and Cythna'*

. . . *Bodleian MS. Shelley adds. e. 10*, ed. Steven E. Jones (1994); vol. 18: *The Homeric Hymns and 'Prometheus' Draft Notebook . . . Bodleian MS. Shelley adds. e. 12*, ed. Nancy Moore Goslee (1996); vol. 19: *The Faust Draft Notebook . . . Bodleian MS. Shelley adds. e. 18*, ed. Nora Crook and Timothy Webb (1997); vol. 20: *The 'Defence of Poetry' Fair Copies . . . Bodleian MSS. Shelley e. 6 and adds. e. 8*, ed. Michael O'Neill (1994); vol. 21: *Miscellaneous Poetry, Prose and Translations . . . Bodleian MS. Shelley adds. c. 4, etc*, ed. E. B. Murray (1995); vol. 22, Part One: *Bodleian MS. Shelley adds. d. 6 . . .*; vol. 22, Part Two: *Bodleian MS. Shelley adds. c. 5 . . .*, ed. Alan M. Weinberg (1997); vol. 23: *Indexes to the Bodleian Shelley Manuscripts . . .*, ed. B. C. Barker-Benfield and Tatsuo Tokoo (2001)

Butter — P. H. Butter (ed.), *Percy Bysshe Shelley: Alastor and Other Poems; Prometheus Unbound with Other Poems; Adonais* (London, 1970)

Chernaik — Judith Chernaik, *The Lyrics of Shelley* (Cleveland and London, 1972)

Clark — David Lee Clark (ed.), *Shelley's Prose; Or, The Trumpet of a Prophecy* (corr. edn., Albuquerque, N. Mex., 1966)

Conc. — F. S. Ellis (ed.), *A Lexical Concordance of the Poetical Works of Shelley* (London, 1892)

FQ — Edmund Spenser, *The Faerie Queene*, ed. A. C. Hamilton (London, 1977)

Hogg — Thomas Jefferson Hogg, *The Life of Shelley* (1858), in Humbert Wolfe (intro.), *The Life of Percy Bysshe Shelley* (2 vols., London, 1933)

Inf. — *Inferno*

L — Frederick L. Jones (ed.), *The Letters of Percy Bysshe Shelley* (2 vols., Oxford, 1964)

Locock — C. D. Locock (ed.), *The Poems of Percy Bysshe Shelley* (2 vols., London, 1912)

Longman — Kelvin Everest and G. M. Matthews (eds.), *The Poems of Shelley, 1804–1819* (2 vols. to date, Harlow, 1989, 2000)

Mary Jnl. — Paula R. Feldman and Diana Scott-Kilvert (eds.), *The Journals of Mary Shelley 1814–1844* (2 vols., Oxford, 1987)

Massey — Irving Massey (ed.), *Posthumous Poems of Shelley, Mary Shelley's Fair Copy Book, Bodleian MS. Shelley adds. d. 9* (Montreal, 1969)

Met. — *Metamorphoses*; quotations are taken from A. D. Melville's Oxford World's Classics translation (Oxford, 1987)

Murray — E. B. Murray (ed.), *The Prose Works of Percy Bysshe Shelley, Volume One* (Oxford, 1993)

MWSL	Betty T. Bennett (ed.), *The Letters of Mary Wollstonecraft Shelley* (3 vols., Baltimore, 1980–8)
MWS (1)	Mary Wollstonecraft Shelley (ed.), *The Poetical Works of Percy Bysshe Shelley* (4 vols., London, 1839)
MWS (2)	Mary Wollstonecraft Shelley (ed.), *The Poetical Works of Percy Bysshe Shelley* (1 vol., London, 1839)
MWS: Prose	Mary Wollstonecraft Shelley (ed.), *Essays, Letters from Abroad, Translations and Fragments by Percy Bysshe Shelley* (2 vols., London, 1840 [1839])
MYR: Shelley	Donald H. Reiman (gen. ed.), *Manuscripts of the Younger Romantics: Shelley* (9 vols., 1985–97). Relevant volumes: vol. 1: *The Esdaile Notebook*, ed. Donald H. Reiman (1985); vol. 2: *The Mask of Anarchy* (1985), ed. Donald H. Reiman; vol. 3: *Hellas: a Lyrical Drama* (1985), ed. Donald H. Reiman; vol. 4: *The Mask of Anarchy Draft Notebook . . . Huntington MS. HM 2177*, ed. Mary A. Quinn (1990); vol. 5: *The Harvard Shelley Poetic Manuscripts*, ed. Donald H. Reiman (1991); vol. 6: *Shelley's 1819–1821 Huntington Notebook . . . Huntington MS. HM 2176*, ed. Mary A. Quinn (1994); vol. 7: *Shelley's 1821–1822 Huntington Notebook . . . MS. HM 2111*, ed. Mary A. Quinn (1996); vol. 8: *Fair-Copy Manuscripts of Shelley's Poems in European and American Libraries*, ed. Donald H. Reiman and Michael O'Neill (1997)
Norton	Donald H. Reiman and Sharon B. Powers (eds.), *Shelley's Poetry and Prose*, Norton Critical Edition (New York, 1977)
Norton²	Donald H. Reiman and Neil Fraistat (eds.), *Shelley's Poetry and Prose*, Norton Critical Edition, 2nd edn. (New York, 2002)
Notopoulos	James A. Notopoulos, *The Platonism of Shelley: A Study of Platonism and the Poetic Mind* (Durham, NC, 1949)
Par.	*Paradiso*
PL	John Milton, *Paradise Lost* (Oxford Authors edition)
PP	Mary Wollstonecraft Shelley (ed.), *Posthumous Poems of Percy Bysshe Shelley* (London, 1824)
Purg.	*Purgatorio*
Rognoni	Francesco Rognoni (ed.), *Shelley: Opere* (Turin, 1995)
Rossetti	William Michael Rossetti (ed.), *The Poetical Works of Percy Bysshe Shelley* (2 vols., London, 1870)
SC	Kenneth Neill Cameron and Donald H. Reiman (eds.), *Shelley and His Circle 1773–1822* (Cambridge, Mass., 10 vols. to date, 1961–)
Sperry	Stuart M. Sperry, *Shelley's Major Verse: The Narrative and Dramatic Poetry* (Cambridge, Mass., 1988)
Webb	Timothy Webb (ed.), *Percy Bysshe Shelley: Poems and Prose*, with a critical selection by George E. Donaldson (London, 1995)

Aeschylus' *Prometheus Bound* and *The Persians* are quoted from Philip Vellacott's Penguin translation (1961); Ovid's *Metamophoses* are quoted from A. D. Melville's World's Classics translation (Oxford, 1987; 1986). Other Latin and Greek texts are cited from the relevant Loeb editions, unless indicated otherwise in the Notes. Dante is quoted from the Temple Classics series, Petrarch from E. H. Wilkins (trans.), *The Triumphs of Petrarch* (Chicago, 1962), Spenser from *FQ* and the Oxford Standard Authors edition, Shakespeare from *The Norton Shakespeare, Based on the Oxford Edition*, ed. Stephen Greenblatt (New York, 1997), and the Bible from the Authorized Version. Where possible, other writers are cited from the relevant Oxford Authors editions. Wordsworth's *Peter Bell* is quoted from the first edition (1819), as edited by John E. Jordan for the Cornell Wordsworth (1985). Shelfmarks for manuscripts in the Bodleian can be found by referring to the relevant volume in *BSM*; shelfmarks for other manuscripts are provided with the relevant facsimile volume.

1 *'A Cat in distress'*. Variously dated *c.*1802–11. First published *Hogg*. Text from an unpunctuated transcript by S.'s sister Elizabeth, photofacsimile in *SC* 4. 813–19. Perhaps S.'s earliest recorded poem, even if composed as late as 1810.

2 *To the Emperors of Russia and Austria Who Eyed the Battle of Austerlitz from the Heights whilst Buonaparte was Active in the Thickest of the Fight*. Composed 1810–13(?). Text from the unpublished *Esdaile Notebook*, transcript in *SC* 4. 937–9 (see *MYR: Shelley* 1). Napoleon defeated the combined Russian and Austrian armies at Austerlitz, in the Czech province of Moravia, on 2 Dec. 1805.

l. 26. *Exalt the high, abase the low. Longman* 1 thinks this line a slip on S.'s part, and prints instead 'Abase the high, exalt the low'.

3 l. 42. *Thou Northern chief.* The Russian Tsar, Alexander I (1777–1825).

l. 43. *Pale Austria*. Francis I, emperor of Austria (1768–1835).

l. 44. *The tyrant*. Napoleon, himself an emperor since 1804.

Zeinab and Kathema. Composed 1810–11(?). Text from *Esdaile Notebook*, transcript in *SC* 4. 1040–47 (see *MYR: Shelley* 1). The name 'Zeinab' derives from Southey's *Thalaba the Destroyer* (1801); 'Kathema' may have been suggested by 'Kehama' in Southey's *The Curse of Kehama* (1810). As *Longman* 1 points out, Sydney Owenson's (Lady Morgan's) anti-imperialist novel *The Missionary: an Indian Tale* (1811) is a probable source for the Cashmire setting, and Charlotte Dacre's (Mrs Byrne's) 'The Poor Negro Sadi' in *Hours of Solitude* (1805), I. 117–22 is a probable source for the plot. The poem anticipates themes and images from *Laon and Cythna*.

l. 8. *where yonder Sun now speeds*. That is, to England.

6 l. 90. *motes*. Particles or specks of dust.

7 l. 132. *gibbet*. A gallows with an extended wooden arm from which the

bodies of executed criminals were hung in chains. There was a gibbet on Hounslow Heath, in Middlesex, near Shelley's first school, Syon House. 'Gibbeting' was legal in England until 1834.

7 l. 150. *turns to life*. That is, as the food of worms.

8 l. 164. *shriven*. 'Removed', as in Byron's 'To shrive from man his weight of mortal sin' (*Childe Harold* 2. 78, cited in *OED* 8b), which also makes play (though not ironic play, as here) with 'confessed' or 'absolved'.

l. 172. *matin prime*. Morning prayers.

Sonnet: On Launching Some Bottles Filled with Knowledge *into the Bristol Channel*. Composed mid-August 1812 in Lynmouth in Devon, at a time when S. was disseminating revolutionary writings in a variety of ways (see the following poem), to the consternation of the Home Office. Text from *Esdaile Notebook*, transcript in *SC* 4. 977 (see *MYR: Shelley* 1).

Title. 'Knowledge' refers to such propaganda pieces as 'The Devil's Walk: A Ballad' (1811–12), an attack on the Prince Regent in the manner of similar verses by Southey and Coleridge, and the prose broadsheet 'Declaration of Rights' (1812), modelled on comparable declarations adopted by the French National Assembly (1789). A copy of the latter was discovered in a bottle floating near the entrance of Milford Haven in Wales, presumably having crossed the Bristol Channel from Lynmouth.

l. 3. *stern*. Steer through or pass by (see *OED* 4), though *Longman* 1 calls this sense 'an improbable archaism' and, like some earlier editors, prints 'stem' instead.

9 l. 8. *west*. Because Liberty resides in the United States, without need of crown or elevated throne.

Sonnet: To a Balloon, Laden with Knowledge. See headnote to previous sonnet. Text from *Esdaile Notebook*, transcript in *SC* 4. 976–7 (see *MYR: Shelley* 1). No record survives of the sighting of one of these balloons.

Title. For 'Knowledge' see headnote to previous sonnet.

10 *Queen Mab; A Philosophical Poem with Notes*. Composed 1812–13, although conceived in December 1811. Printed in 1813 in an edition of 250 copies, but not published because of fears of prosecution (although S. distributed 70 copies to friends and fellow radicals, carefully removing his own name and address from the title-page). Our text is from the 1813 printing. A pirated edition of the poem was published in 1821 by William Clark, to S.'s disapproval. The poem influenced early trade union and Chartist movements; also, more generally, nineteenth- and twentieth-century radical working-class and British Marxist thinkers and activists. It draws on phrases, images, themes, and ideas from a range of radical sources, in particular Paine, Holbach, and Rousseau. For 'Queen Mab' herself see Mercutio's speech in *Romeo and Juliet* (1. 4. 55–94).

Epigraph 1. 'Crush superstition!' A frequent phrase in the correspondence of Voltaire (1694–1778); 'L'Infâme' might also signify 'fanaticism', 'religion', 'infamy', 'the infamous wretch', 'the demon'.

Epigraph 2. From *De Rerum Natura* ('On the Nature of Things'), a philosophical poem by the Roman Epicurean poet and philosopher Lucretius (*c*.99–*c*.55 BC). The epigraph comes from the beginning of book 4 (1–7; S. omits l. 4): 'A pathless country of the Pierides I traverse, where no other foot has ever trod. I love to approach virgin springs, and there to drink; I love to pluck new flowers [and to seek an illustrious chaplet for my head from fields] whence before this the Muses have crowned the brows of none: first because my teaching is of high matters, and I proceed to set free the mind from the close knots of superstition.'

Epigraph 3. 'Give me a place to stand, and I will move the earth', attributed to the Greek mathematician and scientist Archimedes (287–212 BC). *Longman* 1 cites the use of this saying by Paine and other radical writers of the Romantic period.

To Harriet *****. Harriet Westbrook, S.'s first wife.

11 *Canto 1*. l. 27. *Ianthe*. The name of S.'s and Harriet's first child, born 23 June 1813.

12 l. 52. *that strange lyre*. An Aeolian harp or lyre, placed in a window or on a porch and played on by the wind (hence 'Aeolian', from Aeolus, Greek god of winds). Repeatedly alluded to in poetry of the Romantic period.

l. 53. *genii*. Attendant gods or spirits.

l. 61. *pennons*. Wings.

13 l. 94. *fibrous*. Formed of fibres or fibre-like; thus 'cirrus' (*Longman* 1).

ll. 98–9. *fair star . . . of morn*. The planet Venus, as the morning star.

l. 102. *purpureal*. Purple; though *Longman* 1 conjectures 'bright, beautiful', from Latin *purpureus*.

l. 108. *amaranth*. Mythic unfading flower, from the Greek word for 'unfading' or 'incorruptible'.

14 l. 140. *Wrapt*. We have retained the original spelling because of a possible pun on 'rapt'.

l. 149. *sempiternal*. Eternal, everlasting.

17 l. 235. *a belt*. 'The Milky Way' (*Longman* 1).

ll. 242–3. *The sun's . . . black concave*. See S.'s note (p. 71).

ll. 252–3. *Whilst . . . rolled*. See S.'s note (pp. 71–2).

l. 259. *Hesperus*. The planet Venus, as the evening star.

l. 260. *Some . . . with trains of flame*. Comets, with their fiery tails.

19 *Canto 2*. l. 21. *fane*. Temple.

l. 52. *for*. For all, despite.

20 l. 59. *meed*. Reward.

21 l. 110. *Palmyra's ruined palaces.* The city of Palmyra, in present-day Syria, grew powerful enough, under the princess Zenobia (*c.* AD 266), to challenge Rome, its protector. This challenge failed and Palmyra was totally destroyed in AD 273 by the Roman emperor Aurelian, although its impressive ruins are still visible today. Thomas Love Peacock, S.'s friend, had commemorated the city's lost glory in the poem *Palmyra* (1806), as had Constantin François Chassebœuf, Comte de Volney, in *Ruins of Empire* (1791), which influenced both Peacock and S.

22 l. 137. *Salem's haughty fane.* The Temple at Jerusalem, built by King Solomon ('Salem') in the ninth century BC, sacked by the Roman emperor Vespasian and his son Titus in AD 70. For the building of the Temple see 1 Kings 5–8 and 2 Chronicles 3–4.

l. 148. *dotard's.* King Solomon's.

l. 153. *Promiscuous.* Indiscriminately.

l. 155. *he.* Moses.

ll. 158–60. *tales . . . till terror credits.* The Old Testament stories retailed by priests (collectively 'imposture') to the Hebrews (collectively 'terror', presumably because terrorized, and thus 'crediting' out of fear).

23 l. 176. *tyrant's slave.* Since the current rulers of Greece are obedient to Turkish overlords.

ll. 179–81. *Where . . . deceives.* Rome, where worthy men like Cicero and Antoninus once lived, is now ruled by the Papacy. Cicero (106–43 BC) was a republican orator and sceptic. Antoninus is either the emperor and stoic philosopher Marcus Aurelius Antoninus (AD 121–80, who reigned AD 161–80), or the emperor Antoninus Pius (AD 86–161, who reigned AD 138–61).

l. 187. *a stately city. Longman* 1 conjectures Tenochtitlan (today's Mexico City), the capital of the Aztec empire, famed for botanical gardens, and built on islands in Lake Texococo (hence the 'ships' of l. 201). S., the same edition also conjectures, might have read of the city in D. F. S. Clavigero's *History of Mexico* (1787; 2nd edn. 1807), though he may also have been thinking of Southey's fictional 'Aztlan' in *Madoc* (1805), where the titular hero does battle with 'Aztecas'.

25 *Canto 3.* l. 17. *imbecility.* Feebleness, weakness, impotence.

26 l. 46. *palled.* Enfeebled.

28 l. 110. *mechanic's.* Manual labourer's. *hind.* Farm worker.

l. 111. *glebe.* Soil or earth.

29 l. 157. *impassive.* Invulnerable, unyielding, immovable.

30 l. 182. *lowered.* Frowned, looked darkly over.

l. 217. *aye.* Ever.

31 *Canto 4.* l. 10. *depend.* Hang down.

33 l. 66. *outsallying.* From the verb 'sally': 'to issue suddenly from a place of defence or retreat in order to make an attack' (*OED* 1).

l. 83. *poison-tree*. *Longman* 1 suggests a reference to the fabulous upas tree, alleged to have existed in Java, and so poisonous as to destroy all animal and vegetable life within 15 or 16 miles. An account of the tree appeared in the *London Magazine* in 1783, from which Erasmus Darwin drew in 'Loves of the Plants', book 2 of the *Botanic Garden* (1789), where its serpent-like and bleaching properties are reported.

34 l. 102. *But* ... *glare*. That is, 'serving to highlight the terrible gulf between man and happiness, happiness being out of grasp, elusive, like a "meteor"'.

l. 122. *tenement*. The body, which houses the 'stranger-soul' or new-born child.

35 ll. 132–6. *The untainting* ... *defencelessness*. An allusion in part to the exploitation of young children in factories, shut away from the 'untainting light of day'.

ll. 151–3. *Soul* ... *arise*. That is, the soul is pure, like the beams of the sun, 'heaven's pure orb', at least until clouded over or 'tainted' (polluted?) by the earth's 'atmospheres'.

36 l. 174. *participate*. Participate in, share.

ll. 178–9. *These* ... *throne*. See S.'s note (pp. 72–5).

37 ll. 203–20. *Then grave* ... *power*. These lines were omitted by Mary S. from *MWS (1)*.

l. 240. *master*. Jesus.

38 l. 252. *unripe*. Premature.

ll. 260–5. *When* ... *die?* Another reference to the upas tree (see note to 4. 83 above).

Canto 5. ll. 1–2. *Thus* ... *the womb*. See S.'s note (p. 75).

ll. 4–6. *Even* ... *soil*. See S's note (p. 75).

39 l. 34. *impassive*. 'Not susceptible of physical impression' (*OED* 2); hence 'by'.

40 l. 58. *The mob* ... *kings*. See S's note (p. 75).

l. 80. *wealth of nations*. Alludes to Adam Smith's defence of *laissez-faire* capitalism in *An Inquiry into the Nature and Causes of the Wealth of Nations* (1776).

ll. 93–4. *And statesmen* ... *wealth!* See S.'s note (p. 76).

41 ll. 112–13. *Or religion* ... *mad*. See S.'s note (p. 76).

l. 135. *plastic*. Mouldable.

42 l. 140. *Cato*. The Roman senator Marcus Porcius Cato (234–149 BC), long-lived upholder of the Republic and its civic and moral virtues. *Longman* 1 quotes Cicero on Cato's active old age: 'The senate and the popular assembly never find my vigour wanting, nor do my friends, my dependants, or my guests' (*De Senectute*, 10. 32).

42 ll. 137–46. *How many . . . town!* This passage alludes to Gray's *Elegy Written in a Country Church Yard* (first publ. 1751), ll. 45–60, with its reference to 'some mute inglorious Milton' (l. 59) (quoted from David Fairer and Christine Gerrard (eds.), *Eighteenth-Century Poetry*, Oxford, 1999).

43 l. 189. *Even love is sold.* See S.'s note (pp. 76–8).

l. 194. *pestilence.* Venereal disease, though perhaps not exclusively.

44 l. 220. *his.* This pronoun should be 'its', referring to 'virtue' (l. 217); as it stands, it might refer to an implied 'that man' (*Longman* 1) or 'that virtuous man'.

l. 231. *commerce.* Selling (i.e. of virtue for material reward or 'human weal').

45 *Canto* 6. l. 4. *periods.* Sentences.

46 ll. 35–8. *The truths . . . death. Norton* cites 'Pliny and other natural historians of antiquity' for the belief that scorpions commit suicide if surrounded by fire.

l. 41. *Symphonious . . . spheres.* An allusion to the classical and Renaissance theory of the music produced by the spheres (the seven immortal planets) as they move through their revolutions. From this cosmic harmony earth is (though will not always be, S. is suggesting) excluded, being 'motionless at the centre or bottom of the universe . . . alone silent and corruptible' (*Longman* 1).

ll. 45–6. *To the red . . . there.* See S.'s note (p. 79).

47 l. 72. *Thou.* 'Religion' personified.

48 l. 111. *Earth . . . trembled.* An ironic allusion to *PL* 2. 787–9 ('I fled, and cried out Death; | Hell trembled at the hideous name, and sighed | From all her caves, and back resounded Death') and 9. 782–4 ('Earth felt the wound, and nature from her seat | Sighing through all her works gave signs of woe, | That all was lost').

l. 132. *horrent.* Shuddering.

49 l. 154. *sublunary.* Mortal, because subject to change or decay, like all things beneath the moon (e.g. Earth, as in the note to 6. 41).

ll. 171–3. *No atom . . . act.* See S.'s note (p. 79).

50 ll. 192–6. *Of all . . . see.* An allusion to Plato's allegory of the cave in *Republic*, 514a–521b.

l. 198. *Necessity . . . world!* See S.'s note (p. 79).

51 l. 231. *sensitive extension.* The meaning is uncertain, perhaps 'moral consciousness'.

ll. 54–238. *Now . . . strength.* Omitted by Mary S. from *MWS (1)*.

Canto 7. The whole of Canto 7 was omitted by Mary S. from *MWS (1)*.

l. 13. *There is no God!* See S.'s note (pp. 79–81).

52 l. 30. *Seeva . . . Lord.* Seeva is Shiva, the Hindu name for God as destroyer or transmuter (in the Hindu Trinity with Brahma and Vishnu); Buddh is Buddha; Foh, according to *Norton*, is the name used in England in S.'s day for Fu Hsi, the legendary or quasi-historical 'first king of China, who is said to have founded this empire soon after the deluge' (George Crabb, *Universal Historical Dictionary*, London, 1833), whilst *Longman* 1 cites Volney, *Ruins*, ch. 20, on 'one God, who under various names, is acknowledged by the nations of the East. The Chinese worship him under the name of *Fot*'; Jehovah is the Hebrew God ('Yahweh'); Lord (in Hebrew 'Adonai') is another name for Yahweh, used most frequently in invocations, suggesting authority, command, kingship.

ll. 33–6. *hosts . . . groans.* An allusion to the car of the Hindu god Vishnu (also called 'Jagannath', hence 'juggernaut') under which devotees are reputed to have thrown themselves to be crushed; *Brahmins* are the highest caste of Hindu.

l. 43. *religion's iron age.* The present, which in classical thought is the last and least noble of the four traditional ages of man: Golden, Silver, Bronze, and Iron.

l. 53. *Tablets.* Imagined as the Spirit's inner 'memoranda-book' (see *OED* 1c), on which are written eternal truths.

53 l. 65. *purblind.* Produced by defective vision; figuratively, 'obtuse', 'stupid'.

l. 66. *Ahasuerus.* The Wandering Jew. See S.'s note (p. 82).

l. 67. *wight.* Person.

54 l. 100. *A murderer.* Moses; see Exodus 2: 11–12.

55 ll. 135–6. *I will . . . world.* See S.'s note (p. 82).

56 l. 192. *ghastily.* Cited in *OED* as a rare form of 'ghastlily' or 'ghastly'.

l. 195. *Hell's freedom . . . heaven.* An allusion to Satan in *PL* 1. 263: 'Better to reign in hell, than serve in heaven.'

l. 208. *So.* That is, 'so also' or 'just so'.

57 l. 218. *winepress . . . wrath.* The image of the apocalyptic winepress comes from Revelation 14: 19–20.

58 *Canto 8.* l. 5. *half-devoured babes.* A reference to Cronus, Greek god commonly associated with time, who devoured his sons as soon as they were born.

60 l. 86. *basilisk.* A legendary reptile hatched by a snake from a cock's egg (also called a cockatrice, as in Isaiah 9: 8). Its breath and look killed.

61 l. 97. *vocal to.* Sounding of, resounding with.

l. 108. *consentaneous.* Mutual, agreeing.

ll. 124–6. *The lion . . . dreadless kid.* From Isaiah 11: 6–7 and Virgil's *Eclogues*, 4. 22. See our note on p. 811, on Shelley's Note on the final chorus in *Hellas*.

62 ll. 127–8. *custom's force*. As the lion grows accustomed to a meatless diet (having forgotten 'to thirst for blood') he grows pacific.

63 l. 183. *led to legal butchery*. *Longman* 1 thinks this a reference to being induced into the Egyptian campaigns of the Napoleonic War, 1798–1807.

ll. 184–6. *that burning sun . . . name of God*. Egypt is here conceived of as the birthplace of the linked tyrannies of priesthood and monarchy.

64 ll. 203–7. *Him . . . eternity*. See S.'s note (pp. 82–3), which begins with an alternative version of the lines in question: 'Him, (still from hope to hope the bliss pursuing, | Which, from the exhaustless lore of human weal | Dawns on the virtuous mind,) the thoughts that rise | In time-destroying infiniteness, gift | With self-enshrined eternity, &c.' This version is no clearer than that of the text. The subject of the sentence contained in either version is 'thoughts' (i.e. 'that rise | In self-destroying infiniteness'), the verb or predicate is 'gift', and the object is 'him' (i.e. 'the human being').

ll. 211–12. *no longer . . . face*. See S.'s note (pp. 83–8).

l. 222. *prune*. Preen.

Canto 9. l. 1. *'O . . . Heaven*. The Fairy continues to speak.

65 ll. 23–37. *Even Time . . . fall*. See S.'s letter to Elizabeth Hitchener of 14 February 1812 (*L* 1. 251–2), which, though written in prose, contains a strikingly similar passage (see *MYR* 8).

66 l. 48. *Nor . . . God*. This line was omitted by Mary S. from *MWS (1)* and, unlike other censored passages, was not restored in *MWS (2)*.

l. 76. *that sweet bondage*. Sexual love.

67 l. 86. *senselessness*. Absence of feeling.

68 l. 130. *wreck*. Trace, vestige; one meaning of 'wrack'.

71 *Notes to 'Queen Mab'*. S.'s Notes to *QM* are longer than the poem itself. They combine untranslated extracts from French, Latin, and Greek authors, and extended treatises on astronomy, religion, marriage, atheism, necessity, and vegetarianism, some of which are redactions of earlier printed texts, others of which were later published separately. When S. quotes directly and at length from another writer the reference alone will be given.

Note, 1. 242–3. Here, as in the Note to 1. 252–3, S.'s science is 'without serious error' (D. King-Hele, *Shelley: His Thought and Work* (London, 1960), 39).

72 *Note*. 1. 252–3. S.'s footnote to his Note here reads 'See Nicholson's Encyclopedia, art. Light', a reference to William Nicholson, *The British Encyclopedia*, 6 vols. (1807–9).

Note, 4. 178–9. *a little poem*. *Locock* suggests Coleridge's 'Fire, Famine, and Slaughter' (1798) as a model for 'Falsehood and Vice: A Dialogue', since both poems are written in the same octosyllabic metre and attack government abuse. *Longman* 1 identifies the second witches' scene in *Macbeth* (1. 3. 1–37) as the ultimate archetype of all such contemporary dialogues. Probably composed between December 1811 and March 1812.

76 *Note*, 5. 112–13. *Lucretius*. From *De Rerum Natura*, 3. 85–6: 'for often before now men have betrayed fatherland or beloved parents in seeking to avoid the regions of Acheron.'

77 *Note*, 5. 189. S.'s footnote to his Note here reads: 'The first Christian emperor made a law by which seduction was punished by death: if the female pleaded her own consent, she also was punished by death; if the parents endeavoured to screen the criminals, they were banished and their estates were confiscated; the slaves who might be accessory were burned alive, or forced to swallow melted lead. The very offspring of an illegal love were involved in the consequences of the sentence.' He cites as source Gibbon's *Decline and Fall of the Roman Empire* (1776–81), ch. 14, and refers also, 'for the hatred of the primitive Christians to love and even marriage', to Gibbon's ch. 15.

79 *Note*, 6. 198. S.'s lemma has a comma after 'Necessity'; the text has an exclamation mark.

Note, 7. 13. *A close examination.* From here to the paragraph ending 'no proof of the existence of a Deity' (p. 81), S. reproduces (with minor emendations and expansions) *The Necessity of Atheism*, published in 1811 by S. and his friend Thomas Jefferson Hogg at Oxford. This pamphlet eventually caused S.'s expulsion from the university. The differences between the Note and the pamphlet (mostly a matter of additions or expansions) are bracketed in our text. The Note ends with quotations from Bacon, Holbach (an extended selection of passages from the *Système de la Nature*), Pliny, and Spinoza.

80 *least*. 'Less' in the pamphlet.

But our idea of causation . . . reasoning experimentally. 'But what does this prove?' in the pamphlet.

81 *omnipotent being*. 'Almighty Being' in the pamphlet.

Hypotheses non fingo . . . non habent. From Newton's *Philosophiae Naturalis Principia Mathematica* (1687; 3rd edn. 1726), 3. 530): 'I do not make hypotheses, for whatever is not deduced from the phenomena must be called a hypothesis, and hypotheses, whether in metaphysics or physics, or occult qualities, or mechanics, have no place in philosophy.'

occult qualities . . . of Herschel. Peripatetics are followers of Aristotle's philosophical school. The chemist Robert Boyle (1627–91), who promoted a corpuscular or atomistic view of matter, applied the word 'effluvia' to material particles. The astronomer Sir Frederick William Herschel (1792–1871) used the words 'crinities' and 'nebulae' to refer to comets and distant star clusters.

praedicate in non. Negative proposition.

82 *Pour dire . . . lui-même*. The quotation comes from Holbach's *Système de*

la Nature (1781), where its author is unidentified. Also from Holbach is the following passage from Bacon's *Moral Essays* (1625), which S. translates back into English, and a further long passage in French, omitted here, consisting of selections from 2. 16–18, 27, 319–26. This is followed by comparably atheistic quotations in Latin from Pliny (*Naturalis Historia*, 2. 4. 14, 27, published after Pliny's death in AD 79), an assertion that 'The consistent Newtonian is necessarily an atheist' followed by refutation of Sir William Drummond (in *Academical Questions*, book 2, ch. 3) for apparently regarding the atheistic implications of Newton's 'system of gravitation' (S.'s phrase) as proof of the system's falsity, and a Latin passage from ch. 1 of Spinoza's *Tractatus Theologico-Politicus* (1670), arguing the indistinguishability of God and nature. These passages are also omitted.

82 *Note*, 8. 203–7. *Him, (still from hope . . .)* See note to the text of 8. 203–7, which S. has altered here in several respects.

83 *Dark flood of time! . . . unredeemed.* ll. 58–69 of 'To Harriet' ('It is not blasphemy to hope'), a poem of uncertain date of composition (*Longman* 1 conjectures late 1812), from the unpublished *Esdaile Notebook*. At the end of the Note, S. cites Godwin's *Political Justice* and Condorcet's *Esquisse d'un Tableau Historique des Progrès de l'Esprit Humain* (1793–4).

Note, 8. 211–12. This Note in its entirety varies only slightly from S.'s 1813 pamphlet *A Vindication of Natural Diet*. S. became a vegetarian in 1812, and for the most part remained one throughout his life. Probable sources for the Note include Joseph Ritson, *An Essay on Abstinence from Animal Food as a Moral Duty* (1802), William Lambe, *Reports on the effect of a peculiar regimen on scirrhous tumours and cancerous ulcers* (1811), from which are drawn 'all [S.'s] citations of Cuvier's *Leçons d'Anatomie Comparée*' (*Longman* 1), and John Frank Newton, *The Return to Nature; or, a Defence of the Vegetable Regimen* (1811). The note concludes with a lengthy quotation from Plutarch, *Moralia*, 'On the Eating of Flesh', omitted here.

Milton. PL 11. 477–88, where the speaker is Michael not Raphael.

84 *Horace. Odes*, 1. 3. 25–33: 'Bold to endure all things, mankind rushes even through forbidden wrong. Iapetus' daring son [Prometheus] by impious craft brought fire to the tribes of men. After fire was stolen from its home in heaven, wasting disease and a new throng of fevers fell upon the earth, and the doom of death, that before had been slow and distant, quickened its pace.'

mouflon. Wild sheep. This paragraph does not appear in the 1813 pamphlet.

85 *It is true . . . human evil.* This paragraph does not appear in the 1813 pamphlet.

if remote from . . . his inventions. S.'s footnote to his Note reads: 'The necessity of resorting to some means of purifying water, and the disease which arises from its adulteration in civilized countries, is sufficiently apparent—see Dr Lambe's Reports on Cancer. I do not assert that the use of water is in itself unnatural, but that the unperverted palate would swallow no liquid capable of occasioning disease.'

86 *Muley Ismael's.* Sultan of Morocco (1672–1727), surnamed 'the Bloodthirsty'.

88 *The labour . . . far lighter.* S.'s footnote to his Note reads: 'It has come under the author's experience, that some of the workmen on an embankment in North Wales, who, in consequence of the inability of the proprietor to pay them, seldom received their wages, have supported large families by cultivating small spots of sterile ground by moonlight. In the notes to Pratt's Poem, "Bread, or the Poor," is an account of an industrious labourer, who, by working in a small garden, before and after his day's task, attained to an enviable state of independence.' 'Pratt's Poem' is Samuel Jackson Pratt's *Bread; or, The Poor* (1802).

natural playfulness. S.'s footnote to his Note reads: 'See Mr Newton's book. His children are the most beautiful and healthy creatures it is possible to conceive; the girls are perfect models for a sculptor; their dispositions are also the most gentle and conciliating; the judicious treatment, which they experience in other points, may be a correlative cause of this. In the first five years of their life, of 18,000 children that are born, 7,500 die of various diseases; and how many more of those that survive are not rendered miserable by maladies not immediately mortal? The quality and quantity of a woman's milk are materially injured by the use of dead flesh. In an island near Iceland, where no vegetables are to be got, the children invariably die of tetanus, before they are three weeks old, and the population is supplied from the main land.—Sir G. Mackenzie's Hist. of Iceland.' S. also refers to Rousseau's *Émile* (1762), ch. i.

Stanzas.—April, 1814. Composed in April 1814 at Bracknell, the Berkshire village S. moved to in July 1813. Copy-text from *Alastor; or The Spirit of Solitude: And Other Poems* (1816) (henceforth *Alastor* (1816)). Though himself married (to Harriet Westbrook, since 1811), S. fell in love at Bracknell with the married Cornelia Turner, daughter of Harriet Collins de Boinville, the 'friend' of l. 6.

l. 8. *dereliction.* Presumably on the part of daughter and mother.

89 *'O! there are spirits of the air'.* Date of composition unknown, probably 1815. Published in *Alastor* (1816) under the Greek heading of the epigraph only (the text in this volume supplies our copy-text). According to Mary Shelley, who published the poem in *MWS (1)* under the heading 'To ****', 'The poem beginning "Oh, there are spirits in the air [*sic*]," was addressed in idea to Coleridge, whom he never knew; and at whose character he could only guess imperfectly, through his writings, and accounts he heard of him from some who knew him well. He regarded his change of opinions as rather an act of will than conviction, and believed

that in his inner heart he would be haunted by what Shelley considered the better and holier aspirations of his youth.' The poem explores the tensions between spiritual or ideal and earthly realms and the dangers of living purely 'in thine own mind', themes explored also in *Alastor*.

89 *Epigraph*. 'still my eyes shall be wet with tears | for your heartless doom' (trans. by David Grene, in *The Complete Greek Tragedies*, ed. David Grene and Richard Lattimore, 9 vols, Chicago, 1967, vol. 4). From Euripides, *Hippolytus* (1143–4), spoken by the Chorus about Hippolytus, who has been exiled by his father, Theseus, after his stepmother Phaedra's false accusations of rape.

90 *To Wordsworth*. Written in 1814 or 1815, published in *Alastor* (1816). S. never met Wordsworth, whose poetry he admired, but whose gathering political and religious conservatism he consistently deplored. He visited Keswick in the Lake District from November 1811 to January 1812, where he met Robert Southey. Subsequently, he suspected Southey (wrongly) of attacking his morality in an anonymous article in the *Quarterly Review*. The sonnet to Wordsworth may have been occasioned by a first reading of *The Excursion* in September 1814, or by a later reading in 1815, or after reading Wordsworth's *Poems* soon after their publication (in April 1815). It echoes Wordsworth's sonnet 'London, 1802', with its famous invocation: 'Milton! thou should'st be living at this hour' (e.g. in l. 7, 'Thou wert as a lone star', which recalls l. 9 of Wordsworth's sonnet: 'Thy soul was like a Star and dwelt apart').

92 *Alastor; or, The Spirit of Solitude*. Composed in the autumn and early winter of 1815, in a cottage in Bishopsgate (in Windsor Park), where S. and Mary had been living since August. Published in *Alastor*, from which our text is taken. The title, suggested by Thomas Love Peacock, comes from the Greek word *alastor* meaning 'evil genius' (also, according to *Longman* 1, 'avenging spirit or, more rarely, the victim of such a spirit'). Peacock explains in his *Memoirs of Shelley*: 'The poem treated the spirit of solitude as a spirit of evil' (*The Works of Thomas Love Peacock*, ed. H. F. B. Brett-Smith and C. E. Jones, 10 vols. (London, 1924–34), 8. 100), and the destructiveness of such a spirit is clear whether conceived of as supernatural agent (Peacock's view, supported, for example, in ll. 285 ff.) or imaginary creation (that is, of the poet-protagonist, as suggested, for example, in ll. 149 ff). The poet-protagonist has been variously associated with Wordsworth (to whose poetry S.'s Preface and poem explicitly allude on a number of occasions), Coleridge and S. himself. Mary S. and others attribute the poem's preoccupation with death to S.'s illness in the spring of 1815, when his doctor told him he was dying of consumption. The poem surrounds its account of the Poet's fate with opening and closing passages concerning the speaker. Much critical debate has taken place about the relation between the Narrator and the Poet, and between the poem and its Preface, and about the poem's view of the Poet, who has been seen as embodying the dangers of 'self-centred seclusion' (Preface) or as an admired if tragic questor after ideals.

93 *Preface. All else.* In complete contrast.

'The good . . . socket!'. From Wordsworth, *The Excursion*, 1. 500–2, slightly misquoted.

Epigraph. 'I was not in love as yet, yet I loved to be in love, I sought about for something to love, loving still to be in love' (Augustine, *Confessions*, 3. 1). S. omits from the original, between 'amare amabam' and 'quaerebam', words which translate thus: 'and with a more secret kind of want, I hated myself having little want.'

l. 3. *natural piety.* See Wordsworth, 'My heart leaps up,' ll. 8–9: 'And I could wish my days to be | Bound each to each by natural piety.'

94 l. 26. *obstinate questionings.* See Wordsworth, 'Ode: Intimations of Immortality,' ll. 144–5: '. . . those obstinate questionings | Of sense and outward things.'

ll. 45–9. *I wait . . . man.* See Wordsworth, 'Tintern Abbey', ll. 96–103: 'a sense sublime | Of something far more deeply interfused, | Whose dwelling is the light of setting suns, | And the round ocean, and the living air, | And the blue sky, and in the mind of man, | A motion and a spirit, that impels | All thinking things, all objects of all thought, | And rolls through all things.'

l. 56. *cypress wreath.* Offered to the gods by mourners on behalf of the dead; see Ovid, *Met.* 10.

95 l. 85. *bitumen lakes.* Lakes of molten lava; as *Norton* points out, the exact phrase is found in Southey, *Thalaba*, 6. 15; 'bituminous' appears in *PL* 10. 562 and 12. 41, in descriptions of Hell.

l. 94. *chrysolite.* A greenish semi-precious gem.

96 l. 118. *daemons.* 'Intermediate spirits' (*Norton*) or minor deities capable of communicating between gods and men, from Greek mythology and Plato.

l. 120. *on the mute walls around.* Perhaps alluding to the temple of Isis at Dendera in Egypt, decorated (on the ceiling not the walls) with images of gods 'arranged within the pattern of the Zodiac' (*Norton*).

ll. 106–28. *His wandering step . . . birth of time.* The Poet's journey in search of knowledge takes him round the eastern Mediterranean and up the Nile; he travels back in time from the Greeks (Athens) to the Phoenicians (Tyre, Balbec), to the Jews (Jerusalem), the Babylonians (Babylon), the Egyptians (Memphis, Thebes), to Ethiopia, described by Volney, *Ruins*, ch. 19, as the 'cradle of the sciences'.

97 l. 139. *Wildered.* Bewildered, lost.

ll. 140–5. *The Poet wandering . . . vale of Cashmire.* A journey eastward through Arabia, Persia (including the Desert of Karmin, in the south-east), the Hindu Kush Mountains (setting of *Prometheus Unbound*, 1, and source of the rivers Indus and Oxus), to the vale of Kashmir in north-west India (in which *Prometheus Unbound*, 2. 1 is set).

97 l. 163. *numbers.* Verses.

99 l. 229. *precipitates.* Hastens.

l. 232. *aery.* Lofty.

l. 233. *shadow.* Image.

l. 240. *Till vast Aornos . . . Petra's steep.* Aornos was a mountain fortress on the Indus river; Petra is probably the Sogdian Rock, a steep summit above the Oxus river in Uzbekistan.

l. 242. *Balk.* An ancient Persian province south of the River Oxus, later the site of an independent Parthian kingdom; now Balkh, in Afghanistan.

100 l. 272. *Chorasmian.* The land between the Caspian and Aral Seas (about 175 miles) in what is now modern Russia; 'the lone Chorasmian shore' is either the eastern shore of the Caspian or the western shore of the Aral.

l. 299. *shallop.* Light open boat for shallow water.

101 l. 327. *ruining. Longman* 1 cites Latin *ruere*, 'to fall in disorder'. *MWS (1)* and *(2)* read 'running'; we have stayed with our copy-text.

102 l. 352. *etherial.* Here, high in the air.

103 l. 406. *yellow flowers.* Narcissi, recalling Narcissus, the youth in Greek mythology (Ovid, *Met.* 3), who pines away out of self-love, unresponsive to the love of others.

104 l. 425. *Mocking its moans.* Imitating the moans of the forest (l. 421) as the wind blows through it.

l. 426. *implicated.* Interwoven.

105 l. 490. *Two starry eyes.* These eyes recall the earlier 'beamy bending eyes' (l. 179).

106 l. 526. *lightsome.* Luminous.

l. 528. *windlestrae.* 'A dry thin withered stalk of grass, such as is left standing after the flower or seed is shed' (*OED*).

107 l. 546. *its precipice. Norton* explains this phrase as meaning the dell's 'headlong descent—*its* refers to *dell*, l.541'. 'Precipice' as 'headlong fall or descent' is the first definition offered in *OED*, but was already obsolete in S.'s time; nor does it help much in explaining ll. 547–8. If 'its' refers to 'stream' (l. 540) 'obscuring the ravine' makes more sense, but how a 'headlong descent' (whether of stream or dell) can 'disclos[e] above' 'toppling stones,' 'gulfs,' and 'caves,' remains unclear.

108 l. 585. *Red, yellow, or etherially pale.* See 'Ode to the West Wind': 'Yellow, and black, and pale, and hectic red' (l. 4).

109 l. 651. *meteor.* The moon; at this time the word 'meteor' applied to any phenomenon within the earth's atmosphere, including the moon (thought to be at the atmosphere's outer limit).

l. 654. *two lessening points of light.* Suggesting either the eyes of the dream-maid (ll. 179, 489–92) or the tips of a crescent moon.

110 l. 672. *Medea's wondrous alchemy.* Medea brewed a magic potion to revivify the aged Aeson, Jason's father; when she spilled some on the ground flowers and grass sprang up (see Ovid, *Met.* 7).

l. 677. *one living man.* Ahasuerus, the Wandering Jew; according to medieval legend he insulted Christ on the way to his crucifixion and was condemned to wander the earth as an outcast until the second coming. He appears as a character in *Queen Mab*, 7. 64–275.

l. 705. *senseless.* Unfeeling.

111 l. 713. *too 'deep for tears'.* See the last line of Wordsworth, 'Ode: Intimations of Immortality': 'Thoughts that do often lie too deep for tears.'

112 *Mutability.* Date of composition unknown, published in *Alastor* (1816), our copy-text.

1.5. *dissonant.* 'variously-sounding' (*Longman* 1); the wind lyre or Aeolian harp was repeatedly alluded to in the poetry of the period, frequently serving as an image for the mind, either in perception or creation; it is found also in *Alastor* (ll. 41–9, 663–8) and 'Ode to the West Wind'.

Verses Written on Receiving a Celandine in a Letter from England. Our copy-text is Mary S.'s transcription in the Smaller Silsbee Account Book at Harvard (MS Eng. 258.3; *MYR: Shelley*, 5). The poem was written in June/July 1816, and was not published until 1925. It expresses disenchantment with Wordsworth's growing conservatism. S. turns against Wordsworth the latter's own use of the celandine as an emblem of 'an altered Form' ('The Small Celandine', l. 10).

l. 2. *aery blue.* The celandine is yellow.

113 l. 29. *changed and withered.* See Wordsworth, 'The Small Celandine', ll. 18–19, where the poet says of the flower, 'It cannot help itself in its decay; | Stiff in its members, withered, changed of hue'.

l. 30. *Fallen . . . time.* See *PL* 7. 26: 'On evil days though fallen, and evil tongues.'

ll. 45–8. *That blood . . . celebrate.* Alludes to Wordsworth's poems celebrating the victory at Waterloo.

114 l. 59. *divine and simple song.* Poems such as those contained in *Lyrical Ballads.*

Hymn to Intellectual Beauty. Composed in the summer of 1816, the poem was first published by Leigh Hunt in the *Examiner*, 19 January 1817, and then in the *Rosalind and Helen* volume (1819). There is an intermediate fair copy in the Bodleian (*BSM* 11). Like 'Mont Blanc', the 'Hymn' also exists in a fair-copied version (in Mary S.'s hand) in the Scrope Davies Notebook, now in the British Library (*MYR: Shelley*, 8). S. probably lent this notebook, which came to light in 1976, to Byron in Switzerland. Byron, in turn, probably gave it to Scrope Davies for safe return to S. Since Davies did not return the notebook to S., the latter was obliged to finish both poems again, in all likelihood after returning to his drafts. We print both completed versions of the 'Hymn' and 'Mont

Blanc'; in each case copy-text for version B is the Scrope Davies fair copy, which we reproduce from the manuscript versions with some editorial intervention (some punctuation is added and spellings are modernized). Copy-text for version A of the 'Hymn' is based on the *Examiner* text, with corrections in S.'s hand (now at Harvard: see *MYR: Shelley* 5). 'Intellectual beauty' is a phrase S. could have met in writings by various authors, including William Godwin and Mary Wollstonecraft, and suggests a beauty of the mind or spirit; it is also used by him in his translation of Plato's *Symposium*. The 'Hymn' adapts the genre of the hymn to unorthodox ends. It responds to and reworks Spenser's 'An Hymne of Heavenly Beautie', Wordsworth's 'Ode: Intimations of Immortality', and Rousseau's epistolary novel *Julie; ou, La Nouvelle Héloïse* (with its emphasis on the protagonist's journey towards universal benevolence). It has affinities with passages in the poet's 'On Christianity' (1817) and the seven and a half stanzas beginning 'Frail clouds arrayed in sunlight lose their glory' (in *Longman* 2). The notes are keyed to version A of the poem.

114 l. 2. *some unseen Power.* See 'On Christianity' (1817): 'There is a power by which we are surrounded, like the atmosphere in which some motionless lyre is suspended, which visits with its breath our silent chords, at will' (*Murray*, p. 251).

l. 5. *shower.* A verb governed by 'moonbeams'.

115 l. 17. *vale of tears.* Phrase in the Catholic prayer, 'Salve Regina'. See Keats in a letter of 1819: 'The common cognomen of this world among the misguided and superstitious is "a vale of tears"', *Letters*, ed. Hyder E. Rollins (2 vols., Cambridge, Mass., 1958), 2. 101.

l. 36. *grace and truth.* See John 1: 17: 'but grace and truth came by Jesus Christ.'

l. 37. *Love, Hope, and Self-esteem.* 'Self-esteem', by which S. means proper regard for one's human value, replaces 'faith' in St Paul's trinity of faith, hope, and charity (1 Corinthians 13: 13).

116 l. 45. *darkness . . . flame!* Though *Longman* 1 suggests that, in S.'s day, 'Strong light was believed to stifle a flame', the image is paradoxical and doubt-ridden.

l. 52. *Hopes . . . dead.* See James Thomson, 'Winter' (1746), ll. 431–2: 'There studious let me sit, | And hold high converse with the mighty dead'; quoted from *The Seasons*, ed. James Sambrook (Oxford, 1981).

ll. 53–4. *I called . . . I was not heard.* See the more direct attack on 'that false name' and 'the false name' in version B and the draft, respectively.

117 l. 84. *To fear himself.* To have due respect for his worth. *Longman* 1 cites Ecclesiastes 12: 13: 'Fear God, and keep his commandments: for this is the whole duty of man.'

120 *Mont Blanc.* Composed in July 1816 after S., Mary, and Claire Clairmont visited Chamonix and its Alpine environs (see S.'s account in

L 1. 495–502). Version B of the poem (copy-text supplied by the version in S.'s hand in the Scrope Davies Notebook) was completed by the time S. and his party left Geneva on 29 August. The text in *History of a Six Weeks' Tour* by Mary and P. B. Shelley (1817) provides the copy-text for version A. There is a draft in the Bodleian (*BSM* 11). In the Preface to *History* we are told that 'Mont Blanc' 'was composed under the immediate impression of the deep and powerful feelings excited by the objects which it attempts to describe' and that it is 'an undisciplined overflowing of the soul' which 'rests its claim to approbation on an attempt to imitate the untameable wildness and inaccessible solemnity from which those feelings sprang'. The poem's irregular rhyme-scheme, modelled on that of Milton's *Lycidas*, mimics the effort to give verbal form to these feelings. 'Mont Blanc' reads the Alpine landscape as sublime, but the sublimity it finds does not prove the existence of God, as it does in Coleridge's 'Hymn before Sun-Rise, in the Vale of Chamouni'. When Coleridge's poem was first printed (1802), it was accompanied by a note which included the exclamation, 'Who *would* be, who *could* be an Atheist in this valley of wonders!' In 'Mont Blanc' S., who had described himself (in Greek) in a number of Swiss hotel registers as a lover of mankind, democrat, and atheist, appears to respond to Coleridge's challenge, yet he is prepared (as in the 'Hymn') to invoke a heterodox 'power' (l. 127) or 'secret strength of things' (l. 139), possibly identifiable with the idea of Necessity. The poem begins with an emphasis on the power of the 'universe of things' (l. 1); it ends by pointing up (albeit in a question) the significance of 'the human mind's imaginings' (l. 143). The notes are keyed to version A.

l. 2. *the mind.* Has been read as the 'Universal Mind as distinct from the individual mind' (*Longman* 1), but S. is less explicit here than he is in 'The Daemon of the World' (a reworking, published in the *Alastor* volume, of parts of *Queen Mab*), 2. 248–51: 'For birth but wakes the universal Mind | Whose mighty streams might else in silence flow | Through the vast world, to individual sense | Of outward shows'. *rolls . . . waves.* See Wordsworth, 'Tintern Abbey', l. 103: 'And rolls through all things'.

l. 6. *half its own.* See Wordsworth, 'Tintern Abbey', ll. 106–8: 'the mighty world | Of eye and ear, both what they half-create, | And what perceive'; the referent of 'its' is more likely to be 'The source of human thought' (l. 5) than the 'universe of things' (l. 1).

ll. 1–11. *The everlasting . . . raves.* The poem begins with a meditation on 'things' and 'thought' before it moves, in the second section, to the Alpine scene, read as illustrative ('Thus', l. 12) of the opening propositions.

l. 12. *Ravine of Arve.* The Arve flows through Chamouni into Lake Geneva.

l. 27. *unsculptured.* Both not sculptured (because natural) and still to be sculptured (awaiting the human mind's imaginings).

121 l. 43. *that or thou.* Throughout this part of section 2, the referents of S.'s pronouns are elusive as he struggles to render 'an unremitting interchange' (l. 39). Here, 'that' may refer back to 'My own, my human mind' (l. 37); 'thou' refers to the Ravine.

l. 45. *Seeking.* The likely subject is 'One legion of wild thoughts' (l. 41) or 'my human mind' (l. 37).

l. 47. *the breast.* Either the poet's or some supra-human source, such as the 'Power' (l. 16).

l. 53. *unfurled.* The usual sense of the word is 'unrolled', but some commentators agree with *Locock* that the intended meaning is 'drawn aside'.

122 l. 69. *tracks her there.* Version B has the more likely 'watches her'.

ll. 71–4. *Is this . . . silent snow?* Possible geological explanations for the Alpine scenery; ll. 73–4 refer to the theory proposed by the Comte de Buffon (1707–88) that the earth had begun as fluid heat and subsequently cooled. For S.'s awareness at this time of Buffon's ideas, see *L* 1. 499.

l. 77. *awful doubt, or faith so mild.* Awe-inducing scepticism about the existence of a benevolent creative deity, or trust in the existence of a 'Power' that differs from the Christian God by being indifferent to human existence and thus not exploitable by those who wish to find a divine sanction for oppressive forms of human authority ('Large codes of fraud and woe', l. 81).

l. 79. *But for such faith.* In version B, S. writes 'In such a faith', which makes more obvious sense. 'But for' may mean 'Only through'.

l. 86. *daedal.* Intricately wrought, after Daedalus, mythical inventor who built the Cretan labyrinth.

ll. 96–7. *Power . . . inaccessible.* See the Note to *Queen Mab*, 7. 13, where S. rejects the idea of 'a creative Deity' but not of 'a pervading Spirit coeternal with the universe' (p. 79). S.'s sense of 'Power' dwelling apart owes something to the Lucretian stricture against the belief 'that any holy abode of the gods exists in any part of the world' (*De Rerum Natura*, 5. 146–7).

l. 100. *adverting.* Attentive.

123 l. 105. *distinct.* Decorated (*OED* 4).

l. 120. *their place is not known.* See Job 7: 10: 'He shall return no more to his house, neither shall his place know him any more.'

ll. 120–2. *vast caves . . . welling.* There are echoes of Coleridge's 'Kubla Khan' here (see that poem's 'caverns measureless to man' (l. 4), 'deep romantic chasm' (l. 12), and river that 'sank in tumult to a lifeless ocean' (l. 28)): although S. did not receive his copy of Coleridge's *Christabel* volume (containing 'Kubla Khan') until late August 1816, he evidently knew 'Kubla Khan', possibly via Southey or Byron.

l. 123. *one majestic River*. The Rhône, fed by Lake Geneva into which the Arve flows.

l. 135. *Silently*. See Coleridge, 'Hymn before Sun-rise', ll. 6–7, describing how Mont Blanc 'Risest from forth thy silent sea of pines, | How silently!'

124 ll. 142–4. *And what . . . vacancy?* See S.'s comment in his journal-letter (22 June 1816) about visiting the Alps: 'All was as much our own as if we had been the creators of such impressions in the minds of others, as now occupied our own' (*L* 1. 497).

128 *To Constantia*. Composed between April 1817 and January 1818. First published in *Oxford University and City Herald*, 31 January 1818, which supplies our copy-text, though we have also consulted S.'s rough draft in the Bodleian (*BSM* 3) and his fair copy in the Smaller Silsbee Account Book at Harvard (MS Eng. 258.3; *MYR: Shelley* 5). Its first publication was under the pseudonym 'Pleyel', the name both of a contemporary pianist and composer, Ignaz Pleyel, Handel's pupil, and a character in the novel *Wieland, or the Transformation* (1798), by the American novelist Charles Brockden Brown. 'Constantia', S.'s name for Claire Clairmont, also comes from a novel by Brown, *Ormond; or the Secret Witness* (1799) about which Peacock wrote: 'The heroine of this novel, Constantia Dudley, held one of the highest places, if not the very highest, in Shelley's idealities of female character' (*Works*, ed. Brett-Smith and Jones, 8. 77).

l. 27. *cope of Heaven*. The roof or vault of Heaven, which the singing of St Cecilia, patron saint of music, was said to have the power of opening.

l. 32. *Nature's utmost sphere*. The orbit of the moon, thought to mark the atmosphere's outer limit (or 'verge'); all things below (that is, 'sublunary') belonged to the realm of nature.

129 l. 38. *Even . . . were*. This awkward line makes sense if the phrase 'its voice that were' is understood as appositional, describing the sounds which constitute the voice of the 'power' of l. 27; hence the surrounding commas, an editorial addition. S.'s first thought, in a notebook draft (though not the later fair copy), was: 'Even tho' the sounds which were its voice.'

130 From *Laon and Cythna; Or, The Revolution of the Golden City: A Vision of the Nineteenth Century. In the Stanza of Spenser*. The longest of S.'s poems (4,818 lines), composed in Great Marlow, Buckinghamshire, in spring, summer, and autumn 1817. Published by Charles Ollier in early December 1817 (though dated 1818), then immediately withdrawn and revised at Ollier's insistence, after protests from customers over its attacks on religion and the incestuous love of its title-characters. Republished in revised form in January as *The Revolt of Islam; A Poem, In Twelve Cantos*. Because S. agreed to revisions only as a last resort, our copy-text is the original published version, supplemented by surviving fair-copy manuscripts (of the Preface, Dedication, and 200 lines of Canto

9, in *BSM* 8) and notebook drafts of the poem as a whole (in *BSM* 8, 13, 17). *Laon and Cythna* derives from a period of intense political controversy and personal unhappiness (over the Lord Chancellor's decision in March to deny S. custody of his and Harriet's two children, S.'s own recurring fears of illness, and the recent suicides, in autumn 1817, of S.'s first wife Harriet and Mary's half-sister Fanny). Though S. identified the poem's 'Golden City' as Constantinople, its 'Revolution' is of a sort that 'might be supposed to take place in an European nation'. The poem is visionary, a '*beau ideal*' (*L* I. 564) of the French Revolution, 'the master theme of the epoch' (*L* I. 504). Its aim in part is to counter the disillusion of contemporaries such as Wordsworth, Coleridge, and Southey with the Revolution's failings. Though these failings are acknowledged and anatomized in *Laon and Cythna*, they are also seen from a wider and more optimistic perspective. As for the work's literary influences, these include the major poems of the heroic tradition, including those of Homer, Virgil, Lucan, Tasso, Spenser, and Milton, as well as contemporary works such as Volney's *Ruins* (1791); Peacock's *Ahrimanes* (1813), also written in Spenserian stanzas; Southey's Eastern narrative poems, *Thalaba the Destroyer* (1801) and *The Curse of Kehama* (1810); and Byron's *Childe Harold's Pilgrimage* (1812–18), which combines Eastern settings, the theme of political revolution, and romance motifs.

130 *Title*. 'Laon', the name of the poem's hero, comes from the Greek word for 'the people'; 'Cythna', his sister, may derive her name either from Cytherea, Aphrodite's surname (after the island Cythera), or from another Greek island, 'Cythnos', near Argolis, perhaps Laon and Cythna's original home (see l. 676; see *Longman* 2). The 'Stanza of Spenser' of the subtitle is the nine-line stanza of *FQ* (1590–6).

Epigraph. 'Give me a place to stand and I will move the earth' (see our note to third epigraph to *Queen Mab*, p. 707).

Preface. experiment. See Advertisement to Wordsworth and Coleridge's *Lyrical Ballads* (1798): 'The majority of the following poems are to be considered as experiments.'

enlightened and refined. The poem's intended audience, like that of *Queen Mab*, seems to have been chosen in part to avoid government prosecution, the fate of writers and publishers of comparably radical works written in a more popular idiom.

131 *'all . . . sun'*. See Ecclesiastes 4: 1: 'So I returned, and considered all the oppressions that are done under the sun: and behold the tears of such as were oppressed, and they had no comforter; and on the side of their oppressors there was power; but they had no comforter.'

confederacy . . . by foreign arms. Alludes to the restoration of the French monarchy in 1814 by the anti-revolutionary coalition of Austria, Great Britain, Prussia, and Russia.

scope. Intention.

132 *atrocities*. In subsequent sentences these atrocities are seen as con-

sequences of the oppressions and inequalities of pre-revolutionary France, an argument familiar from Paine's *Rights of Man* (1791). (See *Longman* 2.)

133 *Metaphysics*. S. adds a note: 'I ought to except Sir W. Drummond's "Academical Questions," a volume of very acute and powerful metaphysical criticism.' Sir William Drummond (1770–1828) was the author of *Academical Questions* (1805), a work of philosophical idealism which criticizes Kant's ideas and much influenced S.

like those. S. adds a note: 'It is remarkable, as a symptom of the revival of public hope, that Mr Malthus has assigned, in the later editions of his work, an indefinite dominion to moral restraint over the principle of population. This concession answers all the inferences from his doctrine unfavourable to human improvement, and reduces the "Essay on Population" to a commentary illustrative of the unanswerableness of "Political Justice."' Thomas Robert Malthus (1736–1834), an Anglican priest as well as a political economist, was the author of *Essay on the Principles of Population* (1798). In second and subsequent editions of the *Essay*, Malthus admitted 'moral restraint' (bk. IV, ch. 1) as a possible check to population growth.

infectious gloom. Such as is expressed, for example, in Byron's writings, notably *Manfred* (1817), which made S. feel 'dreadfully melancholy. . . . Why do you indulge such despondency?' (*L* 1. 547).

accidental education. That is, by experience, including not only the sorts of travels recounted in the next few sentences, which allude to S.'s expeditions with Mary and Claire Clairmont to the Vale of Chamonix in 1816 and through France, Switzerland and Germany two years previously, but S.'s personal relations with such 'men of genius' as Byron and Godwin.

134 *the Metaphysicians*. S. adds a note: 'In this sense there may be such a thing as perfectibility in works of fiction, notwithstanding the concession often made by the advocates of human improvement, that perfectibility is a term applicable only to science.' This Note alludes to contemporary controversies about improvement or perfectibility, including of the arts, sparked by Godwin's *Enquiry Concerning Political Justice* (1793).

age of Pericles. Pericles (*c*.495–429 BC) ruled Athens at the height of its prosperity and cultural achievement.

. . . *and Lord Bacon*. S. adds a note: 'Milton stands alone in the age which he illumined.'

Ford. John Ford (1586–?1639), dramatist, most famous for *'Tis Pity She's a Whore* and *The Broken Heart* (both 1633).

135 *alexandrine . . . in the middle of a stanza*. An alexandrine is a twelve-syllable line; there are at least two such lines in the poem, both in the fifth or middle lines of their respective stanzas (in Canto 4, stanza 27—not in this selection—and Canto 10, stanza 36).

system of criticism. S. is probably alluding to the influential rule-bound criticism of French neo-classicist critics such as Nicholas Boileau (1636–1711), also deplored by Keats in 'Sleep and Poetry' (1817).

135 *Longinus*. Supposed author of the literary treatise *On the Sublime* (first century AD), translated by Boileau in 1674.

anonymous censure. Most reviews in contemporary periodicals were unsigned.

my first serious appeal to the Public. A claim that S. might also have made for *Queen Mab* (1813) and the *Alastor* volume (1816) (see *Longman* 2).

136 *Lucretius*. For Lucretius and his poem *De Rerum Natura* see our note to epigraph 2 of *Queen Mab* (p. 707).

Ashtaroth. The Syrian moon-goddess Ashtoreth, or Astarte; the obscene behaviour of her priests was alluded to by S. in a review of Peacock's *Rhododaphne* (1818) (quoted in *Longman* 2).

unworthy successors of Socrates and Zeno. The Greek successors of Socrates (469–399 BC) and the Stoic philosopher Zeno (*c*.333–262 BC) were considered 'unworthy' because of their background as slaves of Rome and subjects of despotic rule in Asia; S. follows Lucan and other Roman writers in seeing their teachings as tainted by habits of subservience and submission (see *Longman* 2).

The latest . . . footsteps. That is, S. himself.

as many years. That is, in the six years since S.'s expulsion from Oxford on 25 March 1811.

express in the cruelty and malevolence of God. Replaced in *The Revolt of Islam* by 'entertain of the Deity, as injurious to the character of his benevolence', a revision signed by the printer Buchanan McMillan.

137 *The circumstance of which I speak . . . to promote*. S. adds a note: 'The sentiments connected with and characteristic of this circumstance, have no personal reference to the Writer.' This Note alludes to rumours concerning the supposed sexual entanglement of Byron, Claire Clairmont, Mary S. and S.

In the personal conduct of my Hero and Heroine . . . of the multitude. The entire concluding paragraph excised in *The Revolt of Islam*.

Dedication.

Epigraph. From *The Conspiracy of Charles Duke of Byron* (1608), a tragedy by George Chapman (?1599–1634).

Mary —— ——. 'Mary Wollstonecraft Shelley', as originally written, then cancelled (and replaced with dashes), in the notebook draft (*BSM* 8).

l. 3. *Knight of Faery*. One of Mary S.'s pet names for S. was 'Elfin Knight' (*Mary Jnl*. I. 80).

138 l. 9. *thou Child of love and light*. A reference to Mary S.'s parents, Mary Wollstonecraft and William Godwin.

l. 16. *my lone boat*. See Mary S.'s 'Note on the Revolt of Islam,' in *MWS (1)*: 'The poem was written in his boat, as it floated under the beech-groves of Bisham, or during wanderings in the neighbouring country.'

l. 27. *of tyrants and of foes*. S.'s unhappiness at Eton, which he attended from 1804 to 1810, both with the masters ('tyrants') and with the fagging system (administered by older students, hence 'foes'), was attested to by all who knew him.

l. 38. *forbidden mines of lore*. Such as Godwin's *Political Justice*, first read while at Eton.

139 l. 47. *one*. That is, one person, the beloved.

l. 54. *clog*. Impediment, encumbrance, hindrance.

ll. 58–9. *In thy young wisdom . . . rend in twain*. Mary S. was 16 when she took the initiative and declared her love for the married S.

l. 61. *which . . . breathed*. 'Which' refers to the clouds (of detraction) 'breathed' (in the sense of 'breathed forth') by 'envious slaves', before Mary broke through them like a ray of 'light'.

l. 69. *Poverty*. In part a product of S.'s extravagance and generosity, among others to Godwin, Hunt, and Peacock.

l. 70. *Infamy*. Occasioned in part by the ruling of the Lord Chancellor in March 1817 depriving S. of custody of his two children by Harriet, on grounds of immorality, atheism, and political radicalism.

140 l. 77. *two gentle babes*. William S., born 24 January 1816, and Clara Evelina S., born 2 September 1817. S. omits a first child, a girl, born 22 February 1815 (died 6 March 1815).

l. 86. *Anarch*. Ruler over darkness and chaos (as in *PL* 2. 988 and Pope's *Dunciad* 4. 653), identified here with 'Custom'.

l. 88. *Amphion's*. That is, Amphion's lyre. Amphion, the son of Zeus and Antiope, was a poet and the father of music; his lyre was a gift from Hermes.

l. 90. *Death*. S. had twice been diagnosed with consumption and feared for his life during the time of the poem's composition.

l. 99. *vestal fire*. Vesta was the Roman goddess of the hearth; her flame was thought to bring prosperity to the state.

l. 102. *One*. Mary Wollstonecraft, who died on 10 September 1797, eleven days after giving birth to Mary S.

141 l. 108. *Sire*. William Godwin.

Epigraph. From the tenth Pythian Ode of the Greek lyric poet Pindar (*c*.522–443 BC): 'but among those glories that we of mortality attain to he goes | the whole way. Never on foot or ship could you explore | the marvelous road to the feast of the Hyperboreans' (*The Odes of Pindar*, trans. Richmond Lattimore, Chicago, 1976). The Hyperboreans were a mythic northern people, devoted to Apollo, who lived in a state of blessedness and harmony.

141 *Canto First*. l. 127. *trampled France*. After the defeat at Waterloo and the restoration of the Bourbon monarchy.

142 l. 135. *last wreck*. The Apocalypse (see Revelation 6.12–14).

l. 140. *complicating*. Intimately or intricately combining. *steep*. Bathe, envelop like a flood.

l. 142. *keep*. Pervade, hold possession of (*Conc.*).

l. 146. *yawn*. A difficult image to visualize; the lightnings emerge from the sky like open or gaping mouths.

l. 156. *Fretted*. Both 'worn away' and 'agitated' (as by a storm or gust of wind).

143 l. 164. *rack*. Clouds, or a mass of cloud, driven before the wind in the upper air.

l. 172. *I could not choose but gaze*. Echoing 'He cannot choose but hear', from Coleridge, 'The Rime of the Ancient Mariner' (l. 18), the source also of 'A speck, a cloud, a shape' (l. 178), describing the distant 'bark' (l. 180), as in the Mariner's first glimpse of the spectre-ship: 'A speck, a mist, a shape, I wist' (l. 153).

l. 193. *An Eagle and a Serpent*. For S.'s use of snake–eagle imagery see *Alastor*, ll. 227–37; classical sources include *Iliad*, 12. 200–7, *Aeneid*, 11. 751–6, and *Met*. 4. 361–4, 714–17 (see *Longman* 2).

144 l. 207. *steadfast eye*. Alone among creatures, according to legend, the eagle is able to look directly into the sun.

l. 209. *clang*. As of armed combatants, but also, as *Longman* 2 points out, drawing on 'clang' as 'the loud harsh resonant cry or scream of certain birds' (*OED* 2).

l. 213. *eager*. Sharp, fierce, keen.

l. 224. *they*. Either 'talons' (l. 223) or 'foes' (l. 219).

145 l. 245. *unprevailing*. Without victor. *event*. Outcome.

l. 246. *portentous*. Monstrous, ominous, prophetic (a portent or prophecy of the narrative to come, with its visionary rendering or '*beau ideal*' of the French Revolution).

l. 248. *lifeless*. Exhausted (since the serpent is alive at l. 280), taking 'stark,' the next word, as 'motionless' or 'desolate,' rather than 'rigid, stiff (in death)' (*OED* 4).

146 l. 269. *sea-mark*. Mark made by the tide.

l. 283. *immovable*. Fixed (on the Serpent) (*Longman* 2).

l. 290. *alone*. Only.

147 l. 304. *marmoreal*. Marble-like.

l. 325. *A boat of rare device*. 'It was a miracle of rare device, | A sunny pleasure-dome with caves of ice!', Coleridge, 'Kubla Khan', ll. 35–6.

148 ll. 331–3. *the mountains hang . . . we go*. It is hard to see how the mountains can 'hang and frown over' the 'starry deep that gleams below' unless by 'deep' S. means 'sea' (with reflected stars), making the phrase 'A vast and dim expanse' appositional; hence our comma after 'below', an editorial insertion.

l. 345. *urn*. 'Water-vessel, used figuratively for the source of a river or stream' (*Longman* 2).

l. 350. *Genii*. Plural of 'genius,' meaning tutelary spirit of a place, institution, etc.

l. 351. *Nought*. The 'chaos' of l. 353, taking chaos as 'formless void' (*OED* 2), as *Longman* 2 suggests.

l. 355. *jar*. Dissension or strife; also harsh sound, concussion, physical shock.

l. 356. *A blood-red Comet*. *Longman* 2 suggests an allusion to the red planet, Mars.

l. 359. *flood*. The chaos of the sublunary world.

149 l. 362. *which none may know*. Either 'none may know Power itself, only its "shapes" or manifestations', or 'none may know all Power's "shapes" or manifestations'.

l.368. *He*. The 'Fiend' of l. 363, our 'immortal foe' (l. 367).

l. 377. *In mockery*. Mocking the fact that the names of Good and Evil were misapplied.

l. 378. *own*. 'Yield obedience or submission to' (*OED* 6c).

150 l. 395. *beneath nether skies*. The skies of the underworld or 'hell' (l. 394).

l. 396. *blasting*. Infecting, blighting, as by a curse.

l. 405. *sanguine*. Bloody.

l. 413. *save*. Both preserve (in 'combat') and bring eternal happiness (presumably in contrast to the false 'Paradise' of religion promised after death).

l. 419. *hydra brood*. The Hydra was a mythical snake with poisonous breath and blood and numerous heads (hence 'brood').

151 l. 427. *garbage*. 'Offal of an animal used for food' (*OED* 1) (*Longman* 2).

l. 441. *unnatural*. Since infant sleep is meant to be untroubled by dream (as in line 261). (See *Longman* 2.)

l. 454. *A dying poet*. Recalls the youthful, dying poet of *Alastor*.

152 l. 466. *Hope's deep source*. Conceived of as an 'immortal urn' from which pours 'fresh light' in l. 647 (hence 'flows forth' here).

l. 485. *Morning Star*. The planet Venus.

153 l. 497. *speechless*. Defeating speech (too beautiful to be described).

153 l. 514. *that vast and peopled city*. Recalling Revolutionary Paris, where Mary Wollstonecraft—a spiritual guide for S., like the 'mortal maiden' (l. 505) whose 'strange and awful tale' (l. 334) is being recounted here—lived from late 1792 to 1795.

l. 522. *ruth*. Compassion.

154 l. 525. *others*. For example, as *Longman* 2 suggests, Coleridge and Wordsworth, both of whose poems echo in the following lines; Coleridge's 'France: An Ode' (1798) (stanza 1) in ll. 527–8, and Wordsworth's 'Ode: Intimations of Immortality', ll. 12–15, and 'Tintern Abbey', ll. 5–6, in ll. 530–1 and 533–4, respectively.

155 ll. 550–8. *And swift and swifter . . . far away*. See 'Rime of the Ancient Mariner', part 5, for several resemblances in this stanza, though 'the pole' of l. 553 is more likely the North than the South Pole, given the northern location of the temperate realm of the Hyperboreans (see our note to epigraph, Canto First, p. 727).

l. 568. *vast dome*. Of the heavens.

l. 578. *blosmy*. Blossomy, blooming.

l. 581. *aerial*. Elevated, but also etherial, ideal, imaginary.

156 l. 607. *mild, beautiful, and blind*. Identified in *Longman* 2 as the sightless poets Homer and Milton, indubitably 'Great' (l. 605) and 'beautiful' (as poets).

l. 621. *spherèd stars*. That is, the stars set in the 'hollow hemisphere' (l. 594) of the sky, the 'glorious roof' (l. 586) of the temple.

157 l. 625. *meteors*. Any atmospheric phenomenon, including, as suggested here, marsh gas, the *ignis fatuus* or will-o'-the-wisp.

l. 632. *a Form*. See Leigh Hunt's paraphrase of this episode in his review in the *Examiner* (1 February 1818): 'A magic and obscure circumstance then takes place, the result of which is, that the woman and serpent are seen no more, but that a cloud opens asunder, and a bright and beautiful shape, which seems compounded of both, is beheld sitting on a throne,—a circumstance apparently imitated from Milton' (a reference to *PL* 10. 441–584).

l. 635. *inform*. 'Pervade as a spirit, inspire, animate' (*OED* 2 3b).

l. 649. *one*. Laon, though not named until l. 791.

158 l. 659. *One*. Cythna, though not named until l. 855.

l. 662. *lines*. Rays of light.

Canto Second. l. 676. *Argolis*. A mountainous region in the north-eastern Peloponnesus.

159 ll. 691–2. *had given . . . in the grave*. 'Had given the state's priests, or ministers, power over them by accepting their authority in matters of divine judgement (about the afterlife, the life beyond the grave).'

l. 694. *bane*. Curse, poison.

l. 710. *the light which shows its worth.* Presumably an inner light, given the prevailing darkness; 'its' is 'Earth's' (from 'Earth', l. 703).

l. 716. *A deeper prison and heavier chains.* The constraints and fears of religion.

160 l. 718. *a stern Ruler.* Presumably a figure like Satan.

l. 719. *Terror and Time conflicting.* 'The contending fears of passing time and of punishment after death' (*Longman* 2).

l. 722. *a dark dwelling.* Like Hell.

l. 737. *fanes.* Temples.

l. 744. *polluted.* Sexually ('violated' in cancelled notebook draft: *BSM* 19).

l. 749. *even.* Evening.

161 l. 776. *glorious dead.* The ancient Greeks.

l. 778. *wingèd child.* Hope.

l. 783. *impious trust.* Ironic, since trust in the idol would have been pious before the called-for awakening.

163 l. 822. *his friend.* The most likely real-life model is Thomas Jefferson Hogg (1793–1862), co-author with S. of *The Necessity of Atheism* (1811), for which both were expelled from Oxford. Hogg was 'false' to S. by making advances to his first wife Harriet (in November 1811); the two friends reconciled in 1812, as will Laon and his friend (in Canto 5, stanzas 3–4).

l. 828. *had bled.* Either 'would have bled', taking 'for' as 'in place of,' or 'had bled' (i.e. in sympathy with the false friend), taking 'his own' as the friend's heart.

ll. 835–7. *but I betrayed it not . . . its wisdom blind.* A difficult passage. If 'it' refers to the 'great aim,' as opposed to 'sorrow' (both l. 829), and 'its' means 'sorrow's', then the meaning is something like: 'I did not betray the great aim, but selflessly, out of a love that needed no reciprocation, sought to disperse the clouds that blind, and thus falsify, the supposed wisdom of sorrow.'

l. 847. *I had . . . fair eyes.* Altered in *Revolt of Islam* to 'An orphan with my parents lived, whose eyes'.

l. 848. *lodestars.* Guiding-stars, especially the pole star.

165 l. 884. *sister.* In *Revolt of Islam* 'playmate'.

l. 885. *twelve years old.* Since the main public events in the poem are said (in Canto 4, l. 1509) to take place in seven years' time, Cythna will become a revolutionary at age 19, Mary S.'s age at the time of the poem's composition (see *Longman* 2).

l. 888. *cells.* Caves.

ll. 895–6. *It had . . . my toil.* 'The time spent with Cythna was not wasted, since it left me with a memory ("memorial") which braced ("strung") me to my struggle ("toil").'

165 l. 904. *pauses.* Cadences.

l. 912. *secret bird.* The nightingale (often heard but not seen, as in Keats's 'Ode to a Nightingale').

166 ll. 915–6. *strong . . . to be.* The meaning seems to be: '[the hymns are] more than capable of rousing a passion for freedom in others, the very passion that inspired me to compose them in the first place.'

ll. 937–45. *And this beloved child . . . had learned to trace.* 'One is reminded . . . of the atmosphere of Shelley's childhood at Field Place, the community of sympathy the poet sought to create for himself and his imaginative creations in the audience composed of his four younger sisters, especially Elizabeth, his intimate companion and poetical collaborator' (*Sperry*, p. 48).

168 l. 982. *coldly felt.* That is, by me (Laon).

l. 986. *mewed.* Shut up, confined, enclosed.

l. 992. *flushed o'er her.* Suffused her mind as a blush suffuses the cheek.

l. 1006. *The Golden City.* See note on the poem's title.

170 ll. 1048–52. *Can they . . . of woman.* 'Can men who oppress their wives ever be bold enough to overcome their own oppressors? The wives of such men will blight the home and the lives of their children, generating all the old crimes and religious frauds.'

171 l. 1081. *dare nor tremble.* 'Dare without trembling' (*Longman* 2).

From *Canto Sixth.* ll. 2578–9. *The autumnal winds . . . that recess.* After a prolonged and painful separation, and the revolution's seeming defeat, Laon and Cythna are reunited in a scene of sexual consummation. The transcendent as well as earthly nature of this consummation is signalled by the timeless character of its removed and paradisial mountain setting, in a hidden bower or 'recess | Which seasons none disturbed', a prefiguring of the bliss that awaits them after death.

172 l. 2581. *parasites.* Climbing plants, like ivy (mentioned in stanza 27).

l. 2585. *Whose.* Refers less to the 'blooms' of the 'flowering parasites' of l. 2581 (Longman 2) than to 'The wandering wind' of l. 2584.

l. 2596. *To the pure all things are pure!* A quotation from St Paul's Epistle to Titus, 1: 15.

l. 2610. *common blood.* In *Revolt of Islam* 'blood itself'.

l. 2612. *our very names.* In honour of her lost brother, Cythna adopted the name 'Laone' when she became a revolutionary.

173 l. 2617. *A wandering Meteor.* See note to l. 625.

l. 2620. *its blue hair.* That of the 'Meteor', as light from a flickering blue flame.

l. 2624. *ties.* 'Bands, plaits' (*Conc.*).

ll. 2633–4. *one interval | Made still.* Stopped for a moment.

174 l. 2649. *below.* On earth.

l. 2659. *It is the shadow.* Of the spirit. See the opening lines of 'Hymn to Intellectual Beauty': 'The awful shadow of some unseen Power | Floats though unseen amongst us.'

From *Canto Seventh.* l. 3091. *We live in our own world.* Cythna has been recounting her sufferings to Laon, which parallel Laon's own sufferings in the first half of the poem. Now she turns to the hopes that led her back to sanity and the renewed fight for liberty.

l. 3093. *Aye.* Ever, always.

l. 3095. *Such power.* The power to 'cast a lustre on' or illuminate departed hopes (thus gathering courage from them), rather than be cast down by ('darkened with') them (see *Longman* 2).

175 l. 3104. *One mind.* Revealed to Cythna by the exploration of her own mind; for ll. 3104–5 as a whole, see Coleridge, 'The Eolian Harp' (1795): 'O the one life within us and abroad, | Which meets all motion and becomes its soul' (ll. 26–7), lines added in a revised version of 1817.

ll. 3113–14. *truths which once . . . in old Crotona.* Perhaps alluding to the Pythagorean belief that number lay at the heart of material reality. Pythagoras lived and taught in Croton, in southern Italy, in the sixth century BC.

176 l. 3147. *Even.* Namely.

l. 3156. *there.* In the sea-cave, a sort of prison, to which Cythna was transported (see ll. 2929–30) after the most distressing of the experiences she recounts in this Canto, her rape (and impregnation) by the tyrant Othman.

l. 3160. *Scythian.* Scythia was an ancient region extending over most of European and Asiatic Russia.

177 From *Canto Eighth.* l. 3226. *What dream ye?* Cythna recalls how, as she sailed back to the City of Gold, she addressed the mariners who rescued her from imprisonment in the sea-cave at the end of Canto Seventh.

l. 3234. *that God.* In *Revolt of Islam* 'some Power', just as the next line's 'What then is God?' becomes 'What is that Power?'

178 l. 3251. *God has appointed Death.* 'That Power has chosen death' in *Revolt of Islam*; in next line 'his will' becomes 'it's [*sic*] laws.'

ll. 3253–5. *Men say . . . a rod.* 'Men say that they themselves have heard and seen, | Or known from others who have known such things, | A Shade, a Form, which Earth and Heaven between | Wields an invisible rod', in *Revolt of Islam*.

l. 3262. *that God.* In *Revolt of Islam* 'this Power'.

l. 3264. *And his red hell's undying snakes among.* 'And deepest hell, and deathless snakes among' in *Revolt of Islam*; where, in the next line, 'he' becomes 'is'.

179 l. 3275. *rests thereon.* That is, on opinion.

l. 3297. *To weep for crime.* But not to seek revenge, even for the blood of one's dearest friend.

180 ll. 3309–10. *For it is said . . . is made.* 'And as one Power rules both high and low, | So man is made . . .' in *Revolt of Islam*.

ll. 3330–3. *well ye know . . . to the oppressors flow.* 'You understand women because in oppressing them you also feel woe, the woe any oppressor feels when faced with the suffering of one he oppresses' (see also gloss in *Longman* 2).

181 l. 3361. *one human heart.* See Wordsworth, 'The Old Cumberland Beggar' (1800): 'That we have all of us one human heart' (l. 146).

l. 3368. *they.* Humankind (from l. 3366).

182 l. 3386. *Amphisbaena.* A mythic serpent, with a head at either end.

From *Canto Ninth.* l. 3649. *The blasts of autumn.* Cythna, addressing Laon, prophesies change and renewal, despite the collapse of the Revolution in the immediately preceding stanzas.

183 l. 3670. *germs.* Seeds.

l. 3674. *sanguine.* Bloody.

184 ll. 3688–91. *Spring comes, though we must pass . . . a broad sunrise.* 'Though we will not live to see the renewal of liberty for which we fought, our deaths presage that renewal, like mountain shadow dispersed by the coming sun' (see also gloss in *Longman* 2).

l. 3698. *thine own heart . . . a paradise.* Cythna advises Laon to look within, to the paradise of his own renovated consciousness, for a vision of the external spring or new age they may not live to see.

ll. 3708–11. *Necessity . . . divided never!* For S.'s views on the doctrine of necessity see *Queen Mab* 6. 146–238. In his lengthy Note on this passage (omitted in our edition), S. discusses the relation of necessity to liberty, morality and divinity, drawing on the writings of Hume, Holbach and Godwin. The Note does not, as here, suggest that good inevitably begets good (or bad bad), a view *Locock* and others trace to Aeschylus' *Agamemnon*, which S. was reading in late July 1817 (see *Longman* 2).

l. 3714. *prevailing Sages.* Those whose ideas have prevailed.

187 ll. 3788–91. *Fair star . . . its thousand eyes.* A loose translation of an epigram from Plato which Mary S. and S. cite as derived from the *Apologia* of Apuleius, a second-century AD rhetorician; also found in a passage marked by S. in *Lives of the Philosophers* by Diogenes Laertius, who lived in the third century AD. The epigram exists in a slightly different form in a fair-copy transcript by Mary S. (see *Longman* 1, pp. 581–2).

From *Canto Tenth.* l. 3937. *Day after day.* The Revolution has collapsed and in this extract the City of Gold and its environs suffer terribly under the renewed tyranny.

l. 3945. *Lethe's.* Lethe is the river of forgetfulness in Hades.

188 l. 3964. *blue Plague.* A reference to the blue spots commonly associated with plague.

l. 3980. *blains.* Blisters, pustules, swellings.

l. 3990. *Almighty God.* In *Revolt of Islam* 'the avenging Power'.

189 l. 3999. *Like forms . . . to agony.* An allusion to the Pygmalion story (see Ovid, *Met.* 10. 243–97).

ll. 4003–8. *Famine can smile . . . her prey.* A difficult passage, the main thrust of which seems to be that Plague, likened to a winged wolf, cannot be evaded by the rich or titled ('the throne'), whereas famine, likened to a house-dog (also a grey-haired courtier), can be, by being 'fed'. That Plague is winged and feeds on garbage ('offal', see note to l. 427) conforms to the theory that the disease originates from rotting meat and is carried on the wind.

l. 4010. *dight.* Clothed.

l. 4024. *Of their Amighty God, the armies wind.* 'The many-tongued and endless armies wind' in *Revolt of Islam.*

190 l. 4036. *O God Almighty!* 'O King of Glory' in *Revolt of Islam.*

l. 4055. *their own hearts' image.* A projection of their fears and inadequacies, like the 'Form' worshipped by the 'sophist' of ll. 3244–5, 'from his own soul upthrown.'

l. 4062. *God.* Lower-case 'god' in *Revolt of Islam.*

191 ll. 4063–4. *And Oromaze . . . and Foh.* Oromaze is the principle of Good in the dualistic theology of the Zoroastrians; 'Christ' becomes 'Joshua' (the Hebrew for Jesus, the learned would know) in *Revolt of Islam*; Brahm is Brahma, creator of the universe in the Hindu religion; Zerdusht is Zoroaster, founder of Zoroastrianism. For 'Foh' see our note to *Queen Mab*, 7. 30 (p. 711).

l. 4072. *He was a Christian Priest.* ''Twas an Iberian Priest' in *Revolt of Islam*; as, later, 'rebel Atheists' (l. 4075) and 'God' (l. 4080) become 'unbelievers' and 'Heaven'.

ll. 4094–5. *His cradled . . . creed.* 'The expiation, and the sacrifice, | That, though detested, Islam's kindred creed' in *Revolt of Islam.*

192 l. 4107. *And thrones . . . in God.* 'And kingly thrones, which rest on faith' in *Revolt of Islam.*

l. 4115. *the twain.* Laon and Cythna.

193 l. 4138. *God.* 'Heaven' in *Revolt of Islam.*

l. 4142. *speechless.* Unexpressed (his pride, that is, as opposed to his curses).

193 From *Canto Twelfth.* l. 4666. *When the consuming flames . . . round.* The speaker is Cythna's child, offspring of her rape by Othman, the tyrant ruler of the Golden City. She is recounting to Laon and Cythna (in the present of the poem, where they have been reunited in the Temple of the Spirit) what happened to her after their immolation.

l. 4674. *death-mark.* A blain or mark of plague (see l. 3980 and note).

194 l. 4705. *Atheists.* Laon and Cythna, whose calm death has helped to banish fear of tyranny, both political and religious; changed to 'unbelievers' ('In pain and fire have unbelievers gone') in *Revolt of Islam.*

l. 4714. *How Atheists . . . can die.* 'How those who love, yet fear not, dare to die' in *Revolt of Islam.*

195 l. 4739. *Between a chasm . . . riven.* See Coleridge, 'Kubla Khan', ll. 12–13: 'But oh! that deep romantic chasm which slanted | Down the green hill athwart a cedarn cover!'

196 l. 4762. *Cyclopean piles.* Huge buildings constructed by the Cyclops, giant figures famed as workmen of Hephaestus, the Greek god of fire and crafts.

ll. 4783–4. *Three days and nights . . . delightful hours.* The passage of days is calculated subjectively, since in their journey through celestial realms clock and calendar time do not apply.

197 l. 4799. *sunbows.* Rainbows formed by sun on spray or mist.

l. 4805. *on a line.* 'On one line' in both printed versions; frequently altered, as here, on grounds of meaning and metrical consistency (with the previous line).

l. 4813. *sphere.* See note to line 621.

l. 4818. *The charmèd boat . . . found.* Alludes to *FQ* 1.12.1, in which the poem is likened to a 'feeble barke'. The Canto opens: 'Behold I see the haven nigh at hand.' (This and subsequent references to *FQ* cite book, canto, and stanza.)

198 *Ozymandias.* Composed late 1817, as S.'s contribution to a competition with Horace Smith (see note to l. 250 of 'Letter to Maria Gisborne', p. 786). Smith visited S. in Marlow for two nights after Christmas 1817. First published in the *Examiner*, 11 January 1818, under the pseudonymn 'Glirastes', a jokey Latin and Greek compound meaning 'Dormouse lover' ('Dormouse' being one of S.'s pet names for Mary S.). 'Ozymandias' is the Greek name for Pharaoh Ramses II (reigned 1279–1213 BC), renowned as a model ruler, and for erecting many buildings and statues during his reign. No single source inspires the poem, though behind a range of possible sources lies the description of a monument to 'Osymandias' (the conventional spelling) quoted in the *Library of History* (*c.*60 BC to 30 BC), a forty-volume world history by the Greek Sicilian historian Diodorus Siculus. Our text is from *Rosalind and Helen* (1819), supplemented in places by S.'s pointing and capitalization in a careful fair copy in the Bodleian (*BSM* 3).

l. 8. *The hand.* The sculptor's. *mocked.* Imitated, perhaps also derided. *heart.* Ozymandias'.

Lines Written among the Euganean Hills. Begun in October 1818 while S. was staying in Byron's summer villa, 'I Cappucini', in the medieval fortress town of Este in the Euganean Hills, 40 miles south-west of Venice. Posted to Charles Ollier in December 1818 or January 1819 for inclusion in *Rosalind and Helen* (May 1819). 'Euganean' is pronounced in the English rather than Italian manner, with a stress on the third syllable. Our copy-text is *Rosalind and Helen* (1819) corrected, for ll. 56–112, from Huntington Library MS HM331 (*MYR: Shelley* 3) and, for ll. 165–205, from Tinker Library MS, Yale University (*MYR: Shelley* 8).

l. 2. *In the deep wide sea of Misery.* A condensed echo, the first of several, of Coleridge's 'Rime of the Ancient Mariner' (ll. 233–5); see also ll. 100–3, 238–40.

199 l. 34. *wreak.* Cause or effect.

l. 54. *sea-mews.* Seagulls.

200 ll. 45–65. *On the beach . . . nor murmurs not.* This passage, with its disturbing metaphor of the 'mariner, worn and wan' (l. 3) drifting towards 'the haven of the grave' (l. 26), has a suggestive power, but eludes biographical elucidation (though see *Norton*, pp. 582–4 for an allegorical interpretation). *Chernaik* quotes Sophocles' *Oedipus at Colonus* as a possible source: 'Think of some shore in the north the | Concussive waves make stream | This way and that in the gales of winter: | It is like that with him: | The wild wrack breaking over him | From head to foot, and coming on forever' (ll. 1239–44); *Chernaik* quotes from *The Complete Greek Tragedies*, ed. Grene and Lattimore, vol. 3.

l. 97. *Amphitrite's.* The daughter of Oceanus (the 'sire' of the next line) and wife of Poseidon, from Greek mythology.

201 ll. 111–14. *As the flames . . . Apollo spoke of old.* A reference to the Temple of Delphi, where there were sacrifices to the oracle of Apollo, god of light, prophecy, and art.

l. 117. *a darker day.* Once-conquering Venice had itself been conquered by Napoleonic France (1797); then ceded by France to Austria (1798); then retaken by France after the Battle of Austerlitz (1806); then returned to Austrian rule after Waterloo (1815).

l. 123. *slave of slaves.* S. means that Austria is the very epitome of tyranny, hence enslaved by its need to dominate. The reversal, whereby 'slave' is used of the 'tyrant', accords with S.'s sense that tyranny is a form of slavery.

202 l. 152. *Celtic Anarch's hold.* Refers to Austria's rule over Venice; 'Celtic' (pronounced 'Keltic') means northern or non-Mediterranean in this context; 'Anarch' means an author or agent of chaos (see *PL* 2. 988).

l. 174. *Swan.* Lord Byron, who had lived in and around Venice since 1816; swans were sacred to Apollo, associated with art and prophecy.

202 l. 177. *evil dreams.* The prurient rumour and scandal that drove Byron from England after his separation from his wife.

203 ll. 178–83. *and Ocean . . . terror.* Alludes to Byron's concluding apostrophe to the ocean in *Childe Harold*, canto 4, stanzas 179–84 (1817).

l. 195. *Scamander's.* Chief river of the Trojan plain, personified as a god in Homer's *Iliad*, where it fights and discomforts Achilles.

l. 200. *Petrarch's urn.* The tomb and remains of Francesco Petrarch (1304–74) were located in the village of Arqua, near Este, in the Euganean Hills, where the poet and humanist spent his last years.

204 l. 219. *In the garner of his foe.* The peasant's harvest is gathered for the Austrian overlord (the 'Celt' of l. 223); a 'garner' is a granary or storehouse.

l. 228. *foison.* Plentiful harvest.

ll. 238–48. *Son and Mother . . . Austrian.* For Sin and Death see *PL* 2; their dice game recalls Coleridge's 'Rime of the Ancient Mariner' (ll. 196–7); 'Ezzelin' is Ezzelino da Romano, tyrannical ruler ('Vice-Emperor' is partly a pun) of Padua, 'won' by death in 1259, after the death of his own protector, Emperor Frederick II ('the Mighty Austrian').

l. 257. *Padua.* Seat of one of Europe's oldest universities, founded in the eleventh century.

205 l. 258. *meteor.* Here with the properties of both shooting star and *ignis fatuus* or will-o'-the-wisp.

ll. 269–79. *As the Norway woodman . . . down in fear. Longman* 2 cites Letter 15 of Mary Wollstonecraft's *Letters Written . . . in Sweden, Norway, and Denmark* (1796) which describes a raging forest fire near Christiania (Oslo) begun after a sudden rising of the wind spread sparks from smaller fires set by farmers burning off 'roots of trees, stalks of beans, &c.'.

206 l. 323. *that one star.* Hesperus, the evening star (Venus).

207 l. 356. *The polluting multitude.* Those who 'must reap the things they sow' (l. 231).

l. 361. *heaves;. Longman* 2 substitute a comma for a semi-colon after 'heaves', to ensure that 'And the love' (l. 366) is understood to depend on 'subdued' (l. 357) rather than 'supplies' (l. 364), arguing that the latter reading 'would make the all-embracing love merely intermittent'. But love can be understood as implicit in the subduing influence of clime, winds, and leaves.

l. 371. *sprite.* Spirit or being.

ll. 352–73. *We may live . . . again.* The 'Paradise' S. imagines in the poem's concluding lines recalls Prospero's island in *The Tempest*.

208 *The Two Spirits—An Allegory*. Probably written in 1818, first published in *PP*. The only authoritative manuscript for this lyric is a rough draft in the Bodleian (*BSM* 18) (a later transcription by Mary S. in the Bodleian (*BSM* 2) is based on this manuscript), and the poem, an open-ended debate between an ardent, hopeful perspective and one that is fearful and admonitory, cannot be regarded as finished. Above and below the title S. wrote and cancelled the lines: 'Two genii stood before me in a dream | Seest [?] thou not the shades of even'; above those cancelled lines are the words: 'The good die first', the opening of the lines from Wordsworth's *Excursion* used as an epigraph for *Alastor*.

l. 1. *O*. Cancelled in the draft. We have kept for the metre; *Longman* 2 discards.

l. 3. *A*. Cancelled in the draft. 'Shadow' without an article is distinctly unusual; the 's' is not capitalized.

l. 6. *winds and beams*. No verb follows the phrase in the draft.

ll. 9–10. *The . . . night.—*. Punctuation as in draft; other editors point after l. 9, setting it off as a separate unit of sense. S.'s meaning includes: 'There is light—the light of the stars—should I venture into the night.'

l. 18. *Eclipse*. Written above 'The hail' (cancelled) and 'Hail' (uncancelled) in the draft.

l. 21. *And swift*. The start of this line is hard to decipher; the reading adopted is speculative.

209 l. 37. *languid*. Mary S.'s reading, and adopted here, but see *Longman* 2 which reads 'leagued'; in the draft the word seems to begin 'lea'.

Stanzas Written in Dejection—December 1818, near Naples. Composed in 1818, first published in *PP*. There is a rough draft in the Bodleian (*BSM* 15) and two fair copies in S.'s hand, one in the Pierpont Morgan Library (MA 406; *MYR: Shelley* 5) and one in the Bodleian (*BSM* 21). Our copy-text is the Bodleian fair copy, part of a booklet of S.'s 'saddest verses' (*L* 2. 246) sent to Ollier in November 1820. The poem emerges from a period of personal unhappiness for S. ('I have neither good health or spirits just now', he wrote to Leigh Hunt in December 1818; *L* 2. 68). Clara, his and Mary S.'s daughter, had died in September 1818. A further and possibly related cause of unhappiness was the mysterious case of S.'s 'Neapolitan charge' (*L* 2. 211), Elena Adelaide (who died in June 1820, not in the Shelleys' care). The baby, entered as S.'s and Mary's in the city's records, was not their child; it seems unlikely that S. was the father, and the child may have been adopted by him to comfort Mary in her loss. S. was also depressed by an attack on him (that did not name him) in a review in the *Quarterly Review* of Hunt's *Foliage* (see *L* 2. 66). The poem is written in modified Spenserian stanzas, and is influenced by Wordsworth's 'Resolution and Independence' and 'Ode: Intimations of Immortality' and Coleridge's 'Dejection: An Ode'.

ll. 10, 12. *I see*. See Coleridge, 'Dejection: An Ode', l. 38: 'I see, not feel, how beautiful they are!'

209 l. 10. *untrampled*. Cannot be walked upon (*Conc*.).

210 l. 22. *The sage*. S. is unspecific, but he may have Socrates in mind.

l. 27. *that cup*. A biblical metaphor for experience, often of suffering, as in Matthew 26: 39: 'O my Father, if it be possible, let this cup pass from me.'

l. 40. *this untimely moan*. In the draft S. replaced 'this' with 'such', but he returned to 'this' in both fair copies.

Sonnet ('Lift not the painted veil'). The poem's date of composition is uncertain, though likely to be between 1818 and 1819, possibly with later revisions (Mary S. includes it among 'Poems Written in 1818'). There is a draft in the Bodleian (*BSM* 18) and a fair copy (in S.'s hand) in the Pierpont Morgan Library (MA 406; *MYR: Shelley* 5). This fair copy differs verbally from the text of the poem's first publication, in *PP* (1824). In turn, the text in *PP* differs from that in *MWS (1)*. Our copy-text is based on *MWS (1)* since, as *Longman* 2 argues, 'this text probably derives from S.'s own best revised version'. Some punctuation has been modified in the light of the Morgan text. The poem inverts the usual pattern of the Petrarchan sonnet by placing the sestet before the octave.

l. 1. *painted veil*. The veil image suggests Plato, but no ideal world of forms rewards the questor.

211 l. 6. *Their . . . drear*. In *PP*, the line reads: 'The shadows, which the world calls substance, there.'

l. 13. *Upon . . . strove*. In the fair copy, the line reads: 'Cast on this gloomy world—a thing which strove'.

l. 14. *the Preacher*. The speaker in Ecclesiastes, who asserts that all is vanity.

212 *Julian and Maddalo*. Probably begun in September 1818 when S. was staying at Este and finished in 1819: a fair copy in S.'s hand in the Pierpont Morgan Library (MA 974; *MYR: Shelley* 8), our copy-text, was sent on 15 August 1819 to Hunt to give to Ollier for publication. In the event, the poem was not published until its appearance in *PP*. A draft exists in the Bodleian (*BSM* 15), which does not include 150 lines of the final version. The missing lines are from the Maniac's soliloquy. The poem was sparked into being by S.'s meeting with Byron in Venice in late August 1818 (see *L* 2. 36–7). Claire Clairmont wished to see Allegra, her daughter by Byron, and S. was negotiating with Byron on Claire's behalf. The two poets rode together on the Lido, discussing personal matters and literary topics, including the fourth canto of *Childe Harold*, stanzas of which Byron recited. S. would a few months later deplore the pessimistic tone of the canto, but he singled out the address to the Ocean at the close as proof that Byron was 'a great poet' (*L* 2. 58). Aspects of the Maniac's soliloquy may draw on S.'s and Mary's marital difficulties following the deaths of their children, Clara (in September 1818) and

William (in June 1819). The poem bears the impress of S.'s interest in the Italian poet, Torquato Tasso (1544–95), whose prison in Ferrara he visited in November 1818 and whose handwriting he analysed as 'the symbol of an intense & earnest mind exceeding at times its own depth' (*L* 2. 47); earlier in 1818 he told Peacock that he intended to write 'a tragedy on the subject of Tasso's madness' (*L* 2. 8). S. was conscious of *Julian and Maddalo* as written in a style 'quite opposed to the idealism' (*L* 2. 196) of *Prometheus Unbound*, and felt that it had something in common with Leigh Hunt's post-Wordsworthian attempts to 'express', in S.'s words to Hunt about *Julian and Maddalo*, 'the actual way in which people talk with each other whom education and a certain refinement of sentiment have placed above the use of vulgar idioms' (*L* 2. 108). S. goes on in the same letter to point out that vulgarity is not class-specific.

Epigraph. From Virgil's *Eclogues*, 10, translated at greater length (including these lines) by S. in June 1818 (see *Longman* 2 for a text).

[Preface]. *concentered*. Packed closely as round a centre (*OED* 2). See Byron, *Prometheus*, l. 57: 'Its own concentered recompense'.

Count Maddalo . . . countries. Maddalo (stress on the first syllable) is modelled on Byron; S.'s description can be paralleled with comments he makes in letters about Byron.

213 *Julian . . . serious*. Julian is based on S. himself. The name may allude, given Julian's 'heterodox opinions', to Julian the Apostate; Byron wrote an unfinished poem entitled 'Julian'.

the Maniac. The word 'Maniac' suggests mental derangement. S., who had written to Hunt that 'two of the characters [in the poem] you will recognize', remarked in the same letter that the third character (evidently the Maniac) was 'also in some degree a painting from nature, but, with respect to time and place, ideal' (*L* 2. 108).

l. 2. *bank of land*. The Lido.

l. 3. *Adria*. The Adriatic.

l. 17. *boundless*. A word that would suggest for S.'s contemporaries experence of the sublime: see Hugh Blair: 'Remove all bounds from any object, and you presently render it sublime,' quoted from Andrew Ashfield and Peter de Bolla (eds.), *The Sublime: A Reader in British Eighteenth-Century Aesthetic Theory* (Cambridge, 1996), 214.

l. 23. *the blue heavens were bare*. See Wordsworth, 'Ode: Intimations of Immortality', ll. 12–13: 'The moon doth with delight | Look round her when the heavens are bare'.

l. 25. *sound like delight*. See Coleridge, 'The Eolian Harp', l. 28: 'A light in sound, a sound-like power in light'.

214 ll. 39–45. *'twas forlorn . . . achieve*. See *PL* 2. 555–61, where the fallen angels' debate, though 'sweet', leaves them 'in wandering mazes lost'.

214 l. 46. *descanted.* Talked lengthily and freely.

ll. 63–4. *As those . . . pilgrimage.* See *PL* 12. 1–2: 'As one who in his journey bates at noon, | Though bent on speed': a simile used of the Archangel Michael.

l. 67. *hoar.* Greyish-white.

215 l. 92. *Like fabrics . . . Heaven.* See *The Tempest*, 4. 1. 151: 'And like the baseless fabric of this vision'.

l. 95. *gondolieri.* Rowers of the gondola.

ll. 102–4. *hung . . . swung . . . tongue.* A triplet, reinforcing the impact of the bell's sound.

l. 107. *Shall be.* Maddalo is not simply pointing out a madhouse; he is also suggesting that what they observe might be interpreted as if it were a madhouse.

216 ll. 117–18. *if you can't swim . . . Providence.* S. could not swim, as Byron knew from their boat-trip round Lake Geneva in 1816: Byron admired S.'s composure and refusal to accept help when their boat was in danger of being capsized.

l. 143. *his child.* Based on Byron's daughter, Allegra, who died in 1822 at the age of 5.

217 l. 162. *saws.* Proverbial sayings, maxims.

l. 164. *a teachless nature.* A nature that cannot be taught the 'faith' (l. 165) on which Julian prides himself.

ll. 188–9. *those kings . . . blind.* Julian alludes to philosophers, such as Plato, Aristotle, and Socrates, who lived and thought before Christianity imposed, as he sees it, fetters on free thought.

ll. 190–1. *And those . . . religion.* Either 'Those who explain their compassion for others in religious terms', or 'Those whose capacity to feel for others is "as religion"' (quoted phrase is from the draft).

218 l. 204. *"soul of goodness".* Julian quotes from *Henry V*, 4. 1. 4–5: 'There is some soul of goodness in things evil, | Would men observingly distil it out.'

l. 211. *spoke.* The only unrhymed line in the poem.

219 l. 244. *humourist.* Both 'subject to humours' and 'capable of humour' (see *Longman* 2).

ll. 263–5. *None . . . reverse.* Maddalo says that the Maniac has the same claim on him that he would have on 'all mankind', were he reduced to the Maniac's condition.

220 l. 282. *apart—.* The dash (the copy-text punctuation) connects the simile in ll. 283–4 to the account of the Maniac's grief-stricken smiling in ll. 281–2, even as that simile looks ahead to ll. 284–6 (see *Longman* 2).

l. 301. *jade.* Inferior or worn-out horse.

221 l. 337. *my spirit's mate.* There has been debate about whether this woman is the same as the figure addressed in ll. 384–5.

l. 350. *subdued.* See Shakespeare's Sonnet 111, ll. 6–7: 'And almost thence my nature is subdued | To what it works in, like the dyer's hand'.

222 l. 375. *red scaffold . . . bends.* The line alludes to execution and suggests the Maniac's fear of state punishment.

l. 384. *death's dedicated bride.* The draft identifies this figure as Laura, Tasso's beloved (see *BSM* 15).

223 l. 397. *I am left alone—.* The series of asterisks (*x*'s in the manuscript) following this line here and elsewhere serves to point up the 'unconnected' nature of the Maniac's 'exclamations' (Preface).

l. 405. *I loved . . . overthrow.* See Byron, '[Epistle to Augusta]', ll. 23–4: 'I have been cunning in mine overthrow | The careful pilot of my proper woe'.

ll. 416–18. *As the slow . . . ever-moving.* See *Othello*, 4. 2. 55–7: 'to make me | The fixed figure for the time of scorn | To point his slow and moving finger at'.

224 l. 433. *ceareds*t. Embalmed; shut up. (We have kept S.'s spelling, rather than alter it to 'ceredst', because of the play on 'sear' it accommodates.)

l. 450. *The else unfelt oppressions of this earth.* See Ecclesiastes 4: 1: 'all the oppressions that are done under the sun'.

225 l. 476. *And from my pen.* The Maniac depicts himself as writing.

l. 499. *that sweet sleep.* Death.

228 l. 597. *'That.* We follow the copy-text in placing the opening quotation-mark at this point; the 'my' of the next line refers to Julian and not the speaker (Maddalo's daughter).

l. 614. *ceared.* See note to l. 433.

229 *Prometheus Unbound.* Composed at intervals between August or September 1818 and mid-1820; published by Charles Ollier in 1820, probably in August, as the title-poem of *Prometheus Unbound, with Other Poems.* S., who had not, despite his wishes, been sent proofs, regretted that 'the errors of the press' were 'so numerous' (*L* 2. 246). In the absence of Mary S.'s press transcript, we have taken the printed edition of 1820 as our copy-text, but have departed from it on numerous occasions after consulting Mary S.'s 1839 editions (incorporating some of S.'s 'errata' (*L* 2. 246)), the poet's fair copy in the Bodleian (*BSM* 9), and drafts in the Bodleian (*BSM* 18). The poem remodels genres and traditions to articulate S.'s most original and sublime imagining of freedom. Act 1 contains allusions to Aeschylus' *Prometheus Bound* and Milton's *PL*, as it depicts Prometheus overcoming his hatred for Jupiter while resisting the Furies' temptations to despair; subsequently the Spirits of the Human Mind offer visions of a more hopeful kind. Act 2 is

full of intimations of a world heading towards desired transformation. To help activate this change, Asia (the partner of Prometheus) and Panthea, her sister, descend into the Cave of Demogorgon. Demogorgon answers Asia's questions about the origin of evil and the nature of Jupiter in enigmatic ways, which serve to liberate her from needing explanations about ultimate reality. The 'destined hour' (2. 4. 128) arrives, and the act concludes with lyrics that depict Asia as an indefinable principle of beauty embarking on a voyage 'to a diviner day' (2. 5. 103). Act 3 depicts the overthrow of Jupiter, the freeing of Prometheus, the reuniting of the hero and Asia, and, often by descriptions that negate the negations of things as they are, change for the better among human beings. Act 4 evokes the cosmic dimension of the alteration imagined by the poem and builds on the analogy between love and forms of energy which S. articulates throughout.

229 *Lyrical Drama*. Suggests the work's mixture and reworking of genres.

Epigraph. 'Do you hear this, Amphiaraus, in your home under the earth?': a line from a lost play by Aeschylus (*Epigoni*) extant in Cicero's *Tusculan Disputations*. In a notebook (*BSM* 15) S. quotes the line below the words 'To the Ghost of Aeschylus'.

Preface. The 'Prometheus Unbound' . . . Hercules. S. alludes to a lost play of Aeschylus.

230 *One word is due*. The five paragraphs beginning here were added after S. read in October 1819 an adverse review of *The Revolt of Islam* (*Laon and Cythna*) in the *Quarterly Review*, attacking him for his heterodox 'system' and accusing him of being 'an unsparing imitator' who 'draws largely on the rich stores' of Wordsworth's poetry.

232 *a Scotch Philosopher*. Robert Forsyth, quoted from his *The Principles of Moral Science* (1805).

'a passion . . . world'. See Thomas Love Peacock's humorous portrait of S. as Scythrop Glowry in *Nightmare Abbey* (1818); Scythrop 'became troubled with the passion for reforming the world' (ch. 2).

Paley. William Paley (1743–1805), author of *The Principles of Moral and Political Philosophy*, a book disliked by S. (see *L* 1. 200).

Malthus. Thomas Malthus (1766–1834) argued, against Godwin and other advocates of human perfectibility, that population increase outstripped food supply and that, therefore, it needed checks.

233 *Act 1. Stage direction*. S. shifts the scene from the Caucasus mountains in Georgia to the Indian Caucasus, supposedly the place where civilization originated.

PROMETHEUS. In Greek mythology, one of the Titans, who gave men fire and was punished by Jupiter for withholding from him a secret (that the offspring of any marriage between Jupiter and Thetis would lead to a son who would be greater than his father).

l. 1. *Monarch.* Jupiter. *Daemons.* In Plato's *Symposium*, beings intermediary between the divine and the mortal.

l. 2. *One.* Prometheus. *Longman* 2 offers Demogorgon as another possibility.

l. 6. *knee-worship.* See *PL* 5. 782 ('Knee-tribute').

l. 7. *hecatombs.* Large sacrifices.

l. 9. *eyeless in hate.* See Milton's *Samson Agonistes*, l. 41: 'Eyeless in Gaza'. That the phrase goes with 'thou' (l. 10), but might also refer backwards to 'me' (l. 9), has a psychological and thematic appropriateness.

l. 20. *wall . . . mountain.* See *Prometheus Bound*, l. 15: 'this bitter, bleak ravine'.

234 ll. 44–7. *And yet to me . . . east.* See *Prometheus Bound*, ll. 23–5: 'Glad you will be to see the night | Cloaking the day with her dark spangled robe; and glad | Again when the sun's warmth scatters the frost at dawn.' S. departs from Aeschylus by having Prometheus voice his trust in an eventual overthrow of tyranny.

ll. 53–9. *Disdain? . . . recall.* Records a pivotal change in the hero, from hatred of Jupiter to pity for him.

l. 59. *recall.* The verb brings into play two meanings, 'remember' and 'revoke'.

235 ll. 82–3. *I had clothed . . . not their own.* Colour is produced by light; it is not an inherent property of material objects.

236 ll. 99–102. *By such dread words . . . blood.* Suggestive of the Crucifixion. See Luke 23: 44–6.

l. 121. *frore.* Frozen.

237 l. 135. *inorganic.* 'Not furnished with or acting by bodily or material organs' (*OED* 2, which cites this usage). Prometheus cannot trace the voice he hears to a bodily source.

l. 137. *And love.* 'And lovest'.

l. 141. *wheel of pain.* Both Ixion's wheel and the earth's axis.

238 l. 170. *Blue thistles.* Blue is often linked with disease in S. (See 'Blue Plague' in *Laon and Cythna*, 10. 20.)

l. 178. *contagion.* Here 'communication of disease', but the word can have good as well as bad connotations in S. (see 2. 3. 10 below).

l. 192. *Zoroaster.* Persian founder (also known as Zarathustra) of religion based on the idea of conflict between the spirit of good and light (Ormuzd) and the spirit of evil and darkness (Ahriman).

239 l. 202. *Terrible . . . shapes.* See Edmund Burke on Milton's description of Death in *PL*: 'all is dark, uncertain, confused, terrible, and sublime to the last degree' (*Philosophical Enquiry into the Origin of Our Ideas of the Sublime and Beautiful* (1757), ed. Adam Phillips (Oxford, 1990), 55).

239 l. 207. *Demogorgon.* A figure who resists allegorical translation; often connected by critics with Necessity, and sometimes with the people (his name might be read as meaning 'people [*Demos*] monster [*gorgon*]').

l. 221. *Phantasm of Jupiter.* Phantom, called up to utter Prometheus' former curse. There is a resemblance (see especially ll. 258–61) between the Phantasm and Prometheus before he expressed pity for Jupiter.

240 ll. 222, 231. *Ione . . . Panthea.* Younger sisters of Asia, who perform a choric role and act as intermediaries between Prometheus and Asia while they are separated.

241 ll. 292–3. *Heap . . . beholding good.* See *PL* 1. 209–20, where Satan is allowed to rise from 'the burning lake' (l. 210) only so as to 'Heap on himself damnation' (l. 215) and permit the workings of 'Infinite goodness' (l. 218): Milton's explanation is attacked by S. in 'On the Devil, and Devils' in a passage reworked in *A Defence of Poetry* (p. 692).

243 l. 325. *Mercury.* Messenger of the gods.

l. 331. *Jove's tempest-walking hounds.* The Furies. In Greek mythology, they are figures who torment someone guilty of crime (such as Orestes); S. builds on the Greek conception by making his Furies embody Prometheus' temptations to despair. They bring visions of physical pain (ll. 475–91); and then of war, the doomed fate of idealism (symbolized by the bloody outcome of the French Revolution and the perversion by institutionalized Christianity of the teachings of Christ), and the failure of nerve and will in the present generation (ll. 495–631).

l. 345. *streams of fire and wail.* Refers ('wail' is probably a noun) to two rivers in Hades, Phlegethon and Cocytus.

l. 346. *Geryon.* In Virgil (*Aeneid*, 6. 289) a monster with three heads. *Gorgon.* Medusa, killed by Perseus; her gaze turned the onlooker to stone.

l. 347. *Chimaera.* A monster with lion's head, goat's body, and serpent's tail. *Sphinx.* Winged monster of Thebes with woman's head and lion's body.

l. 348. *Unnatural love . . . hate.* Oedipus solved a riddle put by the Sphinx; this led ('Unnatural love') to his marriage with Jocasta, his mother (though not known by Oedipus to be so) and to his cursing his two sons to kill one another ('unnatural hate').

245 l. 387. *thought-executing.* See the 'sulphurous and thought-executing fires' in *King Lear* (in the third or Conflated Text printed in *Norton Shakespeare*), 3. 2. 4. Here S. may mean both 'as speedy as thought' and 'putting a stop to thought'.

l. 398. *the Sicilian's . . . sword.* Damocles was made by Dionysius I of Syracuse to dine under a sword hanging by a single horse-hair, so that he might experience the insecurity of being a ruler.

249 l. 530. *Kingly conclaves.* Alludes to the Congress of Vienna (1814–15),

when arrangements were made for the post-Napoleonic rule of Europe, arrangements which S. saw as reactionary.

250 l. 546. *One came forth.* Christ, whose 'words' (l. 548) have been used to justify actions at odds with the spirit of his teaching.

l. 563. *pillow of thorns.* Alludes to Christ's crown of thorns (Matthew 27: 29).

l. 567. *disenchanted nation.* France at the outset of the French Revolution, freed from an evil spell. For the same phrase, see Coleridge, 'France: An Ode', l. 28.

251 ll. 573–7. *See how . . . win.* Alludes to the Reign of Terror, the Revolutionary and Napoleonic wars, and the ultimate victory of the forces of reaction with the restoration of Bourbon monarchies in France and Spain after the Battle of Waterloo (1815).

252 l. 609. *ounces.* Leopards.

l. 631. *they know not what they do.* Christ's words on the cross (Luke 23: 34).

253 l. 658. *subtle and fair spirits.* Contrasting with the classical Furies, these 'spirits'—to be found within individual minds ('dim caves of human thought', l. 659) and the Zeitgeist ('world-surrounding ether', l. 660)—bear a resemblance to the angels who minister to Christ after he has been tempted by Satan (Matthew 4: 11).

255 ll. 718–22. *I alit . . . die.* S. sets this example of self-sacrifice against the malevolence of the 'Second Voice' in Byron's *Manfred* (1817) who describes causing a shipwreck and saving 'A traitor . . . and pirate' only so that he can 'wreak further havoc' (2. 3. 32, 33).

256 l. 765. *planet-crested.* Love, linked with 'lightning', wears the crest of Venus.

257 ll. 772–9. *Desolation . . . greet.* Draws on Plato's *Symposium*, 195, in which Love is described as 'the most delicate of all things, who touches lightly with his feet only the softest parts of those things which are the softest of all' (S.'s translation in *Notopoulos*, p. 435).

258 l. 825. *eastern star.* Venus.

259 *Act 2, Scene 1. Stage direction.* There has been debate about whether the action of the lyrical drama is simultaneous or sequential. As *Longman* 2 observes, support is given for the sequential view by the entrance of Panthea at this point; see also ll. 107–8 later in this scene.

260 l. 43. *erewhile.* A time before Prometheus' 'fall' (l. 40).

l. 44. *glaucous.* Dull greyish-green or blue.

262 l. 127. *shape.* Panthea's second dream (l. 61).

l. 135. *almond-tree.* An emblem of hope and expectation: see Jeremiah 1: 11–12. The Hebrew word for 'almond' also means 'hasten'.

l. 136. *Scythian wilderness.* The setting for *Prometheus Bound*.

262 l. 140. *Hyacinth.* A youth loved by Apollo and killed by Zephyrus out of jealousy; from Hyacinth's blood sprang up a flower whose petals were marked 'ai ai' (Greek for 'alas').

265 *Act 2, Scene 2.* l. 2. *cedar . . . yew.* See the wood in *PL* 4 surrounding Eden, 'A sylvan scene' made up of 'Cedar, and pine, and fir, and branching palm' (ll. 140, 139).

l. 10. *Hangs . . . flowers.* See *A Midsummer Night's Dream*, 2. 1. 14–15: 'I must go seek some dewdrops here, | And hang a pearl in every cowslip's ear'.

266 l. 50. *the destined.* Those who, wakened from 'talk or slumber' (l. 49) as a result of 'Demogorgon's mighty law' (l. 43), have a destiny to fulfil as harbingers of the coming revolutionary change; they believe that they 'obey' 'The sweet desires within' (l. 56). S. fuses notions of free-will and necessity.

l. 52. *breathing earth.* Vapours issuing out of the earth, especially as a result of volcanic activity: the volcano, a crucial image in the work, is associated by S. with revolution.

267 ll. 70–82. *I have heard . . . again.* Describes the hydrogen cycle, whereby hydrogen is released from plants in ponds, rises into the air and there ignites as 'meteors' (l. 79).

l. 90. *Silenus.* Aged, satyr-like tutor to Dionysus. His song is at the centre of Virgil, *Eclogues*, 6. *thwart.* crossed, frustrated. *undrawn.* Unmilked.

268 *Act 2, Scene 3.* l. 3. *Like . . . chasm.* Alludes to exhalations from a volcano.

l. 4. *oracular vapour.* Vapour from a cleft in the earth inspired the priestess at the Delphic oracle to prophecy; Asia detects a comparable power at work here.

l. 9. *Maenads.* Female followers of Dionysus, driven to frenzy by their worship of the god. *Evoe.* The cry associated with Maenads.

l. 10. *The voice . . . world.* Either 'the voice which conventional-minded people disapprove of as a kind of disease' or 'the voice which spreads enthusiasm throughout humanity'.

269 ll. 28–42. *And far . . . now.* Above a rough draft of these lines (*BSM* 21) S. wrote: 'This was suggested by the Xterly Review.' S.'s lines counter the attack on him in the *Quarterly Review*'s notice of Leigh Hunt's *Foliage*, by showing that it is possible to respond to sublime scenery in a different spirit (here of revolutionary hope) than that of Christian reverence. See Timothy Webb, '"The Avalanche of Ages": Shelley's Defence of Atheism and *Prometheus Unbound*', *Keats–Shelley Memorial Bulletin*, 35 (1984), 1–39.

ll. 59–60. *Through . . . are.* Plato's distinction between shadows and reality is remodelled here: Asia and Panthea are 'descending into a cave . . ., whereas in Plato's myth [in the *Republic* 514a-521b]' what would be involved would be 'the ascent from the cave into the light of the sun' (*Butter*).

l. 70. *stone*. Lodestone.

270 l. 95. *the Eternal, the Immortal*. Demogorgon.

l. 97. *snake-like Doom*. Doom is 'fate' or 'destiny' (*OED* 4), imaged as a coiled snake waiting to be unloosed 'through life's portal' (l. 96). The unloosing of this 'Doom' will prove beneficial partly because of the hopes and 'sweet desires' of Asia and Panthea. *throne*. A word associated with tyranny, but here given a positive meaning, implying an alternative rule to that of Jupiter.

Act 2, Scene 4. ll. 2–5. *I see . . . shapeless*. See the account of Death in *PL* 2. 666–70: 'The other shape, | If shape it might be called that shape had none | Distinguishable in member, joint, or limb, | Or substance might be called that shadow seemed, | For each seemed either; black it stood as night.' *Webb* suggests an accompanying allusion to God as 'Dark with excessive bright' (*PL* 3. 380).

271 ll. 20–2. *Which . . . heavily*. See S.'s description of '300 fettered criminals' with legs 'heavily ironed' in the square of St Peter's in Rome (*L* 2. 93).

272 l. 32. *Heaven and Earth*. Uranus and Gaia, parents of the Titans, including Saturn.

l. 52. *unseasonable seasons*. In the golden age preceding Jove's rule there was supposed to be perpetual spring.

l. 61. *Nepenthe*. A drug that dispelled care. *Moly*. Plant given by Hermes to Odysseus to nullify Circe's potion. *Amaranth*. Unfading flower.

273 ll. 77–9. *And music . . . sound*. The lines imply a Christ-like ability to walk on water: see Matthew 14: 25–6.

l. 80. *mimicked*. Imitated.

ll. 83–4. *And mothers . . . race*. Pregnant women gazing on beautiful statues absorb a beauty which shows in their children.

l. 87. *implicated*. Entangled.

l. 88. *wide-wandering stars*. Planets or comets.

l. 89. *Changes his lair*. The sun seems to change its position with regard to the constellations.

l. 91. *interlunar*. The dark between the old and new moons.

l. 101. *immedicable*. Unhealable.

ll. 102–3. *Man . . . glorious*. Gives to human beings the power traditionally associated with God (see Genesis 1: 31: 'And God saw every thing that he had made, and behold, it was very good').

l. 107. *adamantine*. Unbreakable.

275 l. 142. *A spirit with a dreadful countenance*. Represents the element of potentially violent overthrow involved in revolution. It contrasts with the 'young spirit' at l. 159.

275 l. 157. *ivory shell.* Links Asia with Aphrodite (see below, 2. 5. 20–30).

276 *Act 2, Scene 5.* l. 2. *respire.* To breathe; here, to 'take a breather'.

l. 7. *Alas! it could not.* The arrival of the 'destined hour' cannot be speeded up by Asia.

ll. 11–14. *the light . . . sister.* Asia is the source of light.

l. 20. *Nereids.* Daughters of Nereus, the old sea-god.

l. 21. *hyaline.* Glass-like sea.

277 ll. 20–30. *The Nereids . . . within them.* Asia is associated with Aphrodite, carried on a shell to the island of Cythera after her birth from sea-foam; See Botticelli's *The Birth of Venus*, which S. may have seen in the Uffizi Gallery in Florence.

ll. 26–30. *love . . . them.* See Wordsworth's 'Tintern Abbey', ll. 94–103.

278 l. 70. *as I am failing.* The 'failing' of inspiration is a frequently dramatized event in S.'s poetry.

279 ll. 98–103. *We . . . day.* Whereas Wordsworth in 'Ode: Intimations of Immortality' describes the soul as moving from a pre-existent state to its earthly condition, Shelley reverses the process.

ll. 109–110. *And rest . . . melodiously!* 'We' (Asia and Prometheus) 'rest'; the 'shapes' which 'walk' and 'chant' are 'somewhat like thee' (Prometheus).

280 *Act 3, Scene 1.* l. 11. *pendulous air.* See *King Lear*, 3. 4. 64–5: 'Now, all the plagues that in the pendulous air | Hang fated o'er men's faults light on thy daughters!'

l. 12. *flake by flake.* Recalls with dramatic irony Asia's image for the coming of revolutionary change: see 2. 3. 39.

ll. 18–19. *Even now . . . child.* See *PL* 5. 603–4: 'This day I have begot whom I declare | My only son'.

l. 19. *That fatal child.* C. E. Pulos suggests that the 'child' might be the doctrines of Malthus (*PMLA* 67 (1952), 113–24).

l. 25. *Idaean Ganymede.* Ganymede was a youth taken from Mount Ida by Jupiter because of his beauty; he became the cup-bearer to the gods.

281 l. 36. *Thetis.* A sea-nymph who became the mother of Achilles and wife of Peleus.

ll. 37–9. *Insufferable . . . presence.* See the fate of Semele, destroyed in the act of love-making with Jupiter: Ovid, *Met.* 3: 'her mortal frame | Could not endure the tumult of the heavens; | That gift of love consumed her.'

ll. 40–1. *Like him . . . poison.* The allusion is to Lucan, *Pharsalia*, 9. 762–88; Sabellus, bitten by a fabled poisonous snake (seps) in the Numidian desert, 'dissolved' (l. 41).

l. 48. *Griding*. Cutting with a grating or strident sound. See *PL* 6. 329: 'The griding sword'.

l. 62. *Titanian*. Alludes to the imprisonment of the Titans underground in Tartarus after their defeat by Jupiter and the gods.

282 l. 79. *Ai! Ai!* A Greek cry of lament.

Act 3, Scene 2. Stage direction. Atlantis. Mythical island, scene of ideal commonwealth in Plato's *Critias*.

Ocean. The god of the sea and source of all rivers (hence the stage direction, 'The mouth of a great river').

Apollo. Greek god of the sun, poetry, medicine, and prophecy.

283 l. 19. *unstained with blood*. Wars at sea will be no more; S. may also allude to the end of the slave-trade (see l. 31).

l. 27. *sightless*. Invisible.

l. 49. *unpastured*. Unfed.

284 *Act 3, Scene 3*. l. 10. *a Cave*. Whereas in Plato (*Republic*, 514 ff) the image of a cave allegorizes the condition of ignorance, here it suggests a superior vantage-point from which Prometheus and his companions can 'sit and talk of time and change' (l. 23).

ll. 23–4. *Where . . . unchanged*. See *King Lear*, 5. 3. 8–19, where Lear describes to Cordelia how they might spend their time in prison.

285 l. 42. *Enna*. A meadow in Sicily from where Proserpina was taken by Dis (see Ovid, *Met*. 5).

l. 43. *Himera*. A town in Sicily.

ll. 49–53. *And lovely . . . reality*. See Diotima's explanation to Socrates in the *Symposium* of how the mind is nourished by 'contemplation of the beautiful' (S.'s translation in *Notopoulos*, p. 450).

l. 65. *Proteus*. Sea-god famous for shape-changing and prophecy; associated with elemental matter.

287 l. 124. *a Cavern*. Possibly the same as that described by Prometheus earlier in the scene (l. 10). In the past it has been a place of menacing oracle, its fumes inhaled by those who were thenceforward 'oracular' (l. 128) in misguided ways. Now its 'breath' (l. 131) is benign.

l. 136. *ivy*. Sacred to Dionysus (see later reference at l. 154).

288 l. 154. *Bacchic Nysa*. S.'s possible source, Arrian, *The Life of Alexander the Great*, trans. de Selincourt, 1958, mentions in book 5 'the city of Nysa, supposed to have been founded by Dionysus'.

l. 155. *beyond Indus . . . rivers*. Arrian (book 5) recounts Alexander's arrival at the Indus, then describes its tribute rivers.

l. 165. *Praxitelean*. Praxiteles was a Greek sculptor who lived in the fourth century BC.

ll. 168–70. *there the emulous . . . emblem*. The allusion is to the Lampadephoria, a race run in ancient Athens by young men carrying torches in remembrance of Prometheus' gift of fire to human beings. See Plato, *Republic*, 328a, and Lucretius, *De Rerum Natura*, 2. 78–9.

288 *Act 3, Scene 4. Stage direction. The* SPIRIT OF THE EARTH. Identified by various critics with electricity, the force which animates the physical universe in a way analogous to the operation of love in the moral universe.

l. 3. *A light . . . star.* Image may be borrowed from a Leyden jar, an early version of a battery, which gives off a green light.

289 l. 19. *dipsas.* A snake causing thirst though its bite.

290 ll. 65–7. *Those ugly . . . air.* Alludes to the Lucretian idea of *simulacra*, images that float off from the surfaces of things into the air. See *De Rerum Natura*, 4. 30–7.

l. 80. *halcyons.* Kingfishers, now vegetarian.

291 l. 112. *Phidian.* Phidias (fifth century BC) was the most famous sculptor in classical Greece.

292 l. 119. *amphisbaenic.* See note to *Laon and Cythna*, l. 3386 (p. 734).

l. 120. *mock.* Imitate as well as deride.

ll. 111–21. *And where . . . repose.* Based on S.'s sight in the Vatican Museum of a *biga* or chariot drawn by two horses yoked together by a two-headed snake.

l. 136. *'All . . . here'.* Quotation is from Dante, *Inf.* 3. 9, trans. by Henry Cary, *The Vision of Dante* (1814) exactly as in S.'s line.

l. 151. *unmeant hypocrisy.* See Coleridge, *Christabel*, l. 665: 'words of unmeant bitterness'.

293 l. 187. *unreclaiming tears.* Love's fate induces pity but no practical effort to 'reclaim' it.

294 l. 204. *inane.* A noun, meaning empty space.

295 *Act 4.* l. 14. *We . . . eternity.* S. implies not a complete escape from 'Time', but the burial of the past.

296 l. 34. *One.* Prometheus.

297 l. 58. *figured.* Embellished with patterns.

299 l. 110. *Delaying.* Time can be slowed down through the effort of acquiring 'Wisdom' (l. 109).

l. 116. *his.* The fair-copy reading appears to be 'her'.

300 l. 140. *clips.* Embraces.

301 l. 169. *gathering sphere.* Might allude to the theory of various scientists of the day that new planets are formed from clouds of dust and gases.

302 l. 213. *Regard like.* Look like (a rare usage).

ll. 219–24. *Within it . . . white light.* See Revelation 1: 14: 'His head and his hairs were white like wool, as white as snow; and his eyes were as a flame of fire.'

303 l. 230. *fire . . . brightness.* May refer to infra-red radiation discovered by Herschel and described by Humphry Davy.

ll. 236–7. *And . . . harmony.* See *PL* 6. 749: 'forth rushed with whirlwind sound'.

l. 246. *inter-transpicuous.* Visible through or between each other.

ll. 236–61. *And from . . . sense.* Influences on Panthea's vision of the Spirit of the Earth include the account of the 'living creatures' in Ezekiel 1: 5: 'the exalted wheels, . . . where the one movement smiteth on the other', Dante, *Par.* 10. 7–9; and the 'chariot of paternal deity' in *PL* 6. 750.

l. 261. *drowns the sense.* Overwhelms the capacity for sensuous response.

304 l. 269. *mocking.* Imitating, but possibly with a suggestion of lightly teasing.

l. 272. *tyrant-quelling myrtle.* The Greeks crowned triumphant soldiers with myrtle. The compound adjective, drawn from Coleridge's 'France: An Ode', l. 37, may refer to Harmodius and Aristogeiton who killed Hipparchus the Tyrant in 514 BC.

l. 281. *Valueless.* Cannot be valued.

305 ll. 270–318. *And from . . . no more.* This account of an uncovering of the earth's geology, history and prehistory is influenced by Keats, *Endymion*, 3. 119–41, part of which was singled out for praise by S. (see *L* 2. 252). It also shows the influence of contemporary geological theories, both evolutionary (as argued by James Hutton, who believed that change took place in long, gradual cycles, obedient to natural laws) and catastrophic (as argued by George Cuvier, who thought that successive phases of earth's prehistory bore witness to disasters such as floods). S. is also indebted to James Parkinson, *Organic Remains of a Former World* (1804–11), which he read in 1812.

ll. 314–18. *till . . . no more.* Two causes of extinction are suggested here: a flood or a comet.

307 ll. 388–93. *Leave . . . restored.* Alludes to the story of King Bladud, the mythical founder of Bath.

308 l. 415. *Orphic.* Orpheus was the archetypal poet, able to entrance all listeners, living, dead, animal, or inanimate.

309 ll. 444. *pyramid of night.* The conical shadow of the earth cast by the sun.

l. 474. *Agave.* Mother of Pentheus and daughter of Cadmus; in her unknowing frenzy she kills Pentheus in Euripides' *Bacchae.*

l. 475. *Cadmaean.* Pertaining to Cadmus, founder of Thebes.

310 l. 493. *And . . . weeps.* The Earth completes the Moon's lines, answering her for the first time.

311 l. 522. *The love . . . skies.* S.'s reworking of 'the Love that moves the sun and the other stars', in Dante, *Par.* 33. 145.

312 l. 539. *elemental Genii.* Personifications of the elements.

l. 555. *Earth-born's.* Prometheus'.

l. 556. *And Conquest . . . deep.* See Ephesians 4: 8: 'he led captivity captive'.

313 l. 575. *nor repent.* See *PL* 1. 94–6: 'yet not for those . . . do I repent or change'.

314 *The Cenci.* Written between May and August 1819; by late September 1819, 250 copies had been printed by the Italian firm of Glauco Masi to be shipped to England. S. hoped that the play would be performed in a London theatre, with Edmund Kean as the Count and Eliza O'Neill as Beatrice (*L* 2. 102–3). In the event, it was not accepted at Covent Garden (and possibly Drury Lane) 'on a plea', as S. put it wryly, 'of the story being too horrible', adding, '*I* believe it singularly fitted for the stage' (*L* 2. 178). The play also appeared in an authorized second edition (1821) incorporating errata in Mary S.'s hand (now pasted into a copy of the first edition in the Bodleian), presumably the same list as that mentioned by S. in a letter to Ollier (*L* 2. 188). We have taken the 1819 text as our copy-text, making corrections as warranted by the list of errata and by comparison with the second edition; we have also consulted the text in *Longman* 2 for its detailing of corrections made in a presentation copy of the 1819 edition given by S. to John Taaffe (see *Longman* 2, p. 724). Though *The Cenci* represents a conscious attempt on S.'s part to write for a popular audience, it broaches topics also addressed in *Prometheus Unbound*, including the theme of revenge, and has political resonances. S. drew on the translation in Mary S.'s hand of the Cenci story. Transcribed in *BSM* 10, this translation was first published in *MWS (2)*. The play explores Beatrice's response to the tyranny of her father, who subjects her to incestuous rape. Her decision to take revenge on her father gives rise in the audience, as S. notes, to a 'restless and anatomizing casuistry', an attempt to excuse what is felt to need excusing. In shaping his tragedy, S. made use of a wide range of models and analogues, including classical tragedy, Dante, various works by Byron, Coleridge's play *Remorse*, and (especially) Shakespeare's tragedies. The play was first produced by the Shelley Society in 1886; its first public staging in England took place in 1922, with Sybil Thorndike as Beatrice.

Dedication. sad reality. See S.'s letter of 15 December 1819 in which he speaks of poems whose subjects (like that of *Julian and Maddalo*) 'will all be drawn from dreadful or beautiful realities' (*L* 2. 164).

315 *Preface. Clement VIII.* Pope from 1592 until his death in 1605.

revenue. The errata say that the following sentence, in the main body of the Preface in the first edition, should be printed as a note: 'The Papal Government formerly took the most extraordinary precautions against the publicity of facts which offer so tragical a demonstration of its own wickedness and weakness; so that the communication of the MS had become, until, very lately, a matter of some difficulty.'

316 *Guido's picture . . . La Cenci.* S. alludes to a portrait of Beatrice Cenci by Guido Reni; it is now believed that the painting was not of Beatrice nor by Guido Reni.

317 *restless and anatomizing casuistry.* See the discussion in the Preface to *Prometheus Unbound* of the 'pernicious casuistry' provoked by the presentation of Satan in *PL*.

318 *nature.* S. keyed the following note: 'An idea in this speech was suggested by a most sublime passage in *El Purgatorio de San Patricio* of Calderon: the only plagiarism which I have intentionally committed in the whole piece.' (See this edition's note to 3. 1. 241–65.)

those modern critics. Principally Wordsworth and Coleridge in the Preface to *Lyrical Ballads* (1800).

the real language of men. The phrase is used in the Preface to *Lyrical Ballads* (1800). S.'s reservations about the Preface's programme are apparent in this sentence.

320 *Act 1, Scene 1.* l. 1. *matter of the murder.* Alludes to l. 23.

l. 3. *the Pincian gate.* Gate at the north end of the Via Veneto in Rome (*Norton*).

l. 16. *the nephew of the Pope.* 'Nephew' may be a euphemism for an ecclesiastic's illegitimate child; the word also suggests the Pope's network of nepotism (see *Longman* 2).

321 l. 57. *Aldobrandino.* Either the Pope, referred to by his family name (*Norton*), or the Pope's 'nephew' (l. 16) (*Longman* 2).

323 ll. 113. *bloody sweat of Christ.* Alludes to Christ in Gethsemane: see Luke 22: 44.

324 ll. 141–4. *Thou . . . intent!* See *Macbeth*, 2. 1. 56–8: 'Thou sure and firm-set earth, | Hear not my steps which way they walk, for fear | Thy very stones prate of my whereabout'.

326 *Act 1, Scene 2.* l. 85. *anatomize.* Analyse minutely.

327 *Act 1, Scene 3.* l. 4. *Anchorite.* Hermit.

328 l. 34. *dreadful ill.* See *Julian and Maddalo*, l. 525.

ll. 40–1. *God! | I thank thee.* An odd, possibly sardonic echo of Malvolio in *Twelfth Night*, 2. 5. 154: 'Jove, I thank thee.' See also note to 5. 3. 123–7.

ll. 58–61. *Rocco . . . Cristofano.* Cenci's sons.

329 l. 68. *the twenty-seventh of December.* The eve of the Feast of the Holy Innocents: the date points up Cenci's Herod-like conduct towards his children.

l. 73. *Infanta.* Daughter of the king of Spain.

l. 74. *El Dorado.* Fictitious city of gold.

l. 82. *like a sacrament.* Suggests Cenci's blasphemous mimicry of the Eucharist.

330 l. 109. *prone.* 'Ready in mind . . . eager' (for 'love' and 'reverence'): cited, as *Longman* 2 points out, in *OED* (a. 7).

l. 110. *it thus vanquish shame and fear.* As *Longman* 2 comments, 'shame and fear' govern the verb of which 'it' (that is, 'love' (l. 109)) is the object.

331 l. 126. *Prince Colonna.* The Colonna were a famous noble Roman family.

l. 151. *ill must come of ill.* A tragic topos at the play's thematic heart.

332 ll. 177–8. *The charm . . . done.* See *Macbeth*, 1. 3. 35 ('The charm's wound up') and several uses of 'done' in the same play (1. 4. 53; 1. 7. 1–2; 2. 1. 62).

334 *Act 2, Scene 1.* ll. 46–7. *Until . . . wrath.* See Lear to Kent in *King Lear*, 1. 1. 122: 'Come not between the dragon and his wrath.'

335 l. 86. *coil.* Turmoil.

336 l. 111. *that the earth would gape.* See Marlowe, *Doctor Faustus* ('Gape earth' in Faustus's last soliloquy; quoted from Charles Lamb, *Specimens of English Dramatic Poets* (1808)).

338 l. 177. garish. See *Romeo and Juliet*, 3. 2. 25: 'the garish sun'.

l. 181. *Come, darkness!* See *Macbeth*, 1. 5. 48: 'Come, thick night'.

ll. 184–5. *a bewildering mist | Of horror.* See John Webster, *The Duchess of Malfi* (quoted from Lamb, *Specimens*): 'Their life, a general mist of error; | Their death, a hideous storm of terror'.

339 *Act 2, Scene 2.* l. 14. *thrice-driven beds of down.* See *Othello*, 1. 3. 229: 'My thrice-driven bed of down'.

340 l. 49. *Visconti, Borgia, Ezzelin.* Three famous tyrants whom S. would have read about in Sismondi, *History of the Italian Republics in the Middle Ages* (1818). Galeazzo Visconti (1351–1402), leader of a well-known family in Milan; Cesare Borgia (1475–1507), the son of Pope Alexander VI; Ezzelino da Romano (1194–1259), leader of the Ghibelline faction in Lombardy (see *Norton*).

341 ll. 70–1. *And . . . death.* See Byron, *The Giaour*, ll. 422–38: 'The Mind, that broods o'er guilty woes, | Is like the Scorpion girt by fire . . .'.

342 l. 120. *fee.* Bribe.

343 l. 147. *I see . . . all.* See *Richard III*, 2. 4. 53: 'I see, as in a map, the end of all.'

344 *Act 3, Scene 1.* l. 13. *The beautiful . . . blood.* See Marlowe, *Doctor Faustus*: 'See [*sic*] where Christ's blood streams in the firmament' (quoted from *Specimens*).

345 ll. 36–7. *Like . . . father.* Beatrice's misery is so great it has 'killed' its 'father', that is, awareness of its cause.

l. 44. *hales.* Drags.

346 ll. 86–7. *something . . . not.* See *King Lear*, 2. 4. 275–7: 'I will do such things— | What they are, yet I know not; but they shall be | The terrors of the earth!' S. quoted Beatrice's words in a letter responding to news of the Peterloo massacre (*L* 2. 117).

348 ll. 132–4. *Self-murder . . . it.* See *Hamlet*, 1. 2. 131–2, where the hero wishes that 'the Everlasting had not fixed | His canon 'gainst self-slaughter'.

352 ll. 241–65. *But . . . night.* The passage mentioned by S. in the Preface as the only possible exception to his avoidance of 'mere poetry'. In fact, the passage bears on Cenci's moral wretchedness and, possibly, Beatrice's, too. In a footnote to the Preface S. suggests the influence on these lines of Calderón's *El Purgatorio de San Patricio*: the relevant passage occurs in Act 2, ll. 2019–26.

357 *Act 3, Scene 2.* ll. 8–18. *O . . . flesh.* Clearly modelled on *Othello*, 5. 2. 7–15.

358 l. 51. *relume.* See *Othello*, 5. 2. 12–13: 'I know not where is that Promethean heat | That can thy light relume'.

l. 62. *castellan.* Governor of a castle.

361 *Act 4, Scene 1.* l. 10. *her stubborn will.* Cenci seeks to make Beatrice will her own degradation, but see ll. 44–5 later in the scene when he appears to give up the wish 'To poison and corrupt her soul' (l. 45).

363 l. 83. *blazoned.* Proclaimed.

ll. 85–8. *She . . . others.* See Byron, *Manfred*, 2. 2. 204–5 ('But I can act even what I most abhor, | And champion human fears').

364 l. 115. *specious.* Fair or right on the surface but not in reality.

365 l. 131. *the Maremma's dew.* The Maremma is a low marshy area on the Tuscan coast from which pestilential vapours were supposed to rise.

l. 140. *That if she have a child.* As close as the play gets to describing explicitly Cenci's incestuous rape of Beatrice.

366 ll. 114–59. *God! . . . heaven.* Cenci curses the absent Beatrice in words that recall Lear's cursing of Goneril in *King Lear*, 1. 4. 252–66 and 2. 4. 155–7, 158–61. S. described Cenci's curse as 'a particular favourite with me' (*L* 2. 219).

ll. 187–9. *All good . . . quickened.* See *Macbeth*, 3. 2. 53–4: 'Good things of day begin to droop and drowse, | Whiles night's black agents to their preys do rouse'.

367 *Act 4, Scene 2.* l. 11. *recking.* Taking account of.

368 l. 33. *the Hell within him.* See *PL* 4. 20: 'The hell within him'.

370 *Act 4, Scene 3.* l. 8. *Did you not call? | When? | Now.* A strong reminiscence of *Macbeth*, 2. 2. 17.

370 l. 28. *equivocation.* A central theme in *Macbeth*; see 2. 3. 8–11.

371 l. 42. *light of life.* See *Prometheus Unbound*, 3. 3. 6; the phrase occurs in John 8: 12.

l. 43. *jellied.* Congealed.

373 *Act 4, Scene 4.* l. 23. *unappealable.* Cannot be appealed against.

l. 28. *warrant for his instant death.* S.'s ironic addition to the source-plot.

l. 49. *Free as . . . air.* See *Macbeth*, 3. 4. 22: 'As broad and general as the casing air'.

375 l. 76. *effortless.* Lifeless; with no sign of struggle.

380 *Act 5, Scene 1.* ll. 19–24. *O . . . desire.* See Coleridge, *Remorse*, 3. 2: 'O that I ne'er had yielded | To your entreaties'; quoted from *The Complete Poetical Works of Samuel Taylor Coleridge*, ed. E. H. Coleridge (2 vols., Oxford, 1912).

381 l. 56. *Put up your weapon.* See Jesus to Peter: 'Put up thy sword into the sheath' (John 18: 11).

382 l. 87. *misdeeming.* Misjudging.

l. 92. *that within.* See *Hamlet*, 1. 2. 85: 'But I have that within which passeth show.'

383 l. 99. *A word?* Another example of the play's obsession with the power and limits of language.

385 *Act 5, Scene 2.* ll. 49–54. *that fair . . . grief.* Mary S. remarks in her editorial note (*MWS (1)*) that these lines reflect the feelings which 'haunted' S. after the death of their son, William, in June 1819.

387 ll. 124–5. *that peace . . . heart.* See *Hamlet*, 3. 2. 65–6: 'I will wear him | In my heart's core, ay, in my heart of heart.'

388 l. 164. *pain.* The second edition reads 'pang'.

l. 169. *strain.* Sift.

389 ll. 172–5. *Who . . . one?* See Vittoria in Webster, *The White Devil* ('The arraignment of Vittoria', as Lamb calls the scene in question in *Specimens*): 'if you be my accuser | Pray cease to be my judge.' S., who could have read Lamb's account in *Specimens* of Vittoria's 'innocence-resembling boldness', may suggest likeness and unlikeness between his heroine and Webster's.

392 *Act 5, Scene 3.* l. 89. *No . . . word.* See Iago in *Othello*, 5. 2. 310: 'From this time forth I never will speak word.'

394 ll. 123–7. *Come . . . live.* See *Twelfth Night*, 2. 4. 42–5: there is an ironic contrast between Beatrice's situation (facing death) and that of Orsino and Viola (Cesario) (preoccupied with love).

395 *Act 5, Scene 4.* l. 13. *deprecation.* Disapproval.

396 ll. 47–9. *Oh . . . suddenly?* See Mary's translation of the Cenci story, where Beatrice says, 'How is it possible—oh my God—that I must so suddenly die!'

l. 56. *Let me not go mad!* See *King Lear*, 1. 5. 38: 'O, let me not be mad, not mad, sweet heaven!'

ll. 72–3. *Who . . . realm?* See *Hamlet*, 3. 1. 80–2: 'death, | The undiscovered country from whose bourn | No traveller returns.'

ll. 47–75. *Oh . . . whither.* See Claudio's speech beginning 'Ay, but to die, and go we know not where' in Shakespeare, *Measure for Measure*, 3. 1. 118–32.

ll. 77–8. *ere . . . Paradise!* Alludes to Christ's words on the Cross to the 'good thief' in Luke 23: 43: 'Today shalt thou be with me in paradise.'

397 l. 80. *How tedious . . . things.* See *Hamlet*, 1. 2. 133–4: 'How weary, stale, flat, and unprofitable | Seem to me all the uses of this world!'

l. 100. *narrow.* Brief.

398 l. 136. *Whose . . . loves.* This line lacks a syllable: *Rossetti* emended by inserting 'as' before 'a bond'.

400 *The Mask of Anarchy.* Composed at Leghorn (Livorno) in September 1819 and sent on the 23rd to Leigh Hunt for publication in the *Examiner*, though it never appeared there (partly out of Hunt's fear of prosecution); published posthumously in an edition by Leigh Hunt (1832) and in *MWS (1)*. The poem is S.'s response, intended for a wide public audience, to the 'Peterloo Massacre' of 16 August 1819. 'Peterloo' (an ironic allusion to the defeat of the French at Waterloo) took place at St Peter's Fields, Manchester. Its occasion was a peaceful mass political protest in support of parliamentary reform. As the radical 'Orator' Henry Hunt was about to address a crowd of 60,000–80,000 men, women, and children, the assembly was brutally broken up, on orders from local magistrates, by regular cavalry and the Manchester Yeomanry (mounted militia, some of them drunk, mostly drawn from the city's industrial middle class). The militia panicked and charged the crowd, fifteen people were killed and 500 injured (by some estimates), and public revulsion at the unprovoked violence of the authorities provided opponents of the government with a powerful image of the cruelty of state repression. That this image also frightened the forces of established order, would lead, ironically, to increased repression: the 'Six Acts' of December 1819, limiting the right of assembly, reinforcing laws against 'Blasphemous and Seditious Libels', tightening the Press laws. The excuse for this new stringency was the threat of anarchy, which S.'s poem turns on its head. 'Mask' in the title means both masquerade, or allegorical pageant, and disguise or covering. The most important of the poem's political sources were Leigh Hunt's editorials about Peterloo in the issues of the *Examiner* for 22 and 29 August, the first of which pours scorn on 'these Men in the Brazen Masks of power'. Its literary models derive from poetical dream vision, a tradition stretching back to Chaucer, and popular ballad. Our copy-text is Mary S.'s press copy, with S.'s additions and corrections, in the Library of Congress (MMC 1399;

MYR: Shelley 2), though we have also consulted S.'s intermediate fair copy in the British Library (Ashley MS 4086; also in *MYR: Shelley* 2).

400 l. 1. *asleep in Italy*. Perhaps figurative and self-critical, implying S.'s lack of awareness of the political situation in England.

l. 6. *Castlereagh*. Robert Stewart, Viscount Castlereagh (1769–1822), Foreign Secretary (since 1812) and leader of the Tories in the House of Commons. Associated with suppression in Ireland and at home; also with support of the Napoleonic wars and the reactionary Holy Alliance.

l. 8. *seven bloodhounds*. *Norton* thinks this refers to the seven other nations (Austria, France, Russia, Prussia, Portugal, Spain, and Sweden) Britain allied itself with in 1815 when it agreed 'to postpone final abolition of the slave trade', and also points out that politicians who supported the war were frequently called 'bloodhounds' by its opponents.

l. 15. *Eldon*. John Scott, Baron Eldon (1751–1838), Lord Chancellor; in 1817 he had refused S. custody of his children by Harriet. His 'erminèd gown' marks his legal authority (and supposed 'purity', ermine being a symbol of purity). Though famous for public tears he also often separated parents from children in his Chancery judgements.

ll. 18–21. *And the little . . . by them*. See Luke 17: 2: 'It were better for him that a millstone were hanged about his neck, and he cast into the sea, than that he should offend one of these little ones.' Among the dead and wounded at Peterloo were several children.

l. 24. *Sidmouth*. Henry Addington, Viscount Sidmouth (1757–1844), Home Secretary (since 1812), and thus in charge of internal spying (a realm of 'shadows' and 'disguise'). In 1818 Sidmouth lobbied for a million pounds to be spent on churches for the poor in the new industrial towns, in hopes of quieting disorder among the labouring classes.

l. 25. *a crocodile*. Suggestive of hypocrisy.

401 l. 30. *Anarchy*. S.'s use of anarchy as a symbol of ultimate evil may derive from *PL* 2. 988, where Satan encounters Chaos, the 'anarch old,' ruler of the abyss. For details of Anarchy's personification see Revelation 6: 8: 'And I looked, and behold a pale horse; and his name that sat on him was Death, and Hell followed with him. And power was given unto them over the fourth part of the earth, to kill with sword, and with hunger, and with death, and with the beasts of the earth.' See also Benjamin West's painting *Death on the Pale Horse* (1783), in which Death, wearing a crown, and surrounded by sword-bearing followers, tramples a crowd.

402 l. 80. *globe*. The orb, along with sceptre and crown, a symbol of sovereignty.

l. 83. *Tower*. In addition to being a place of imprisonment, the Tower of London is the repository of the crown jewels; hence its coupling with the Bank of England.

l. 85. *pensioned*. Bribed or corrupted (as in the awarding of state pensions).

l. 97. *Misery, oh, Misery! Webb* cites Wordsworth's 'The Thorn' (1798): 'And to herself she cries, | "Oh misery! oh misery! | Oh woe is me! oh misery!"' (ll. 64–6).

403 l. 110. *a Shape*. The Shape's sudden materialization anticipates that of the 'glorious Phantom' in 'England in 1819'. Its association with a snake anticipates the imagery of ll. 227–9 (see note).

l. 115. *the Morning's*. The planet Venus, as the morning star.

404 l. 145. *accent*. Utterance.

l. 155. *Ye*. Here, as in the poem's final line, S. implies a gap, at once social and geographical, between himself and the audience he is addressing.

405 l. 169. *peak*. Droop, waste away, look sickly.

l. 176. *the Ghost of Gold*. Paper money, seen by S. as an imposture, a way of tricking the poor out of proper recompense for their labour. S. was influenced in this regard by the radical journalist William Cobbett (1763–1835), in *Paper Against Gold* (1815) and elsewhere.

406 l. 200. *When . . . air*. After this line, the following stanza is found in S.'s intermediate fair copy of the poem (and in Leigh Hunt's posthumous publication of it in 1832) but not in Mary S.'s press copy (which S. himself corrected): 'Horses, oxen, have a home, | When from daily toil they come; | Household dogs, when the wind roars, | Find a home within warm doors.' Either Mary S. forgot to transcribe the stanza or she convinced S. (or S. convinced her, on second thoughts) to omit it.

ll. 201–4. *Asses . . . hast none*. See Matthew 8: 20: 'The foxes have holes, and the birds of the air have nests; but the Son of man hath not where to lay his head.'

l. 216. *Fame*. Rumour.

l. 229. *That . . . snake*. 'This image had been used by the American Revolutionists in their "Don't Tread on Me" flag picturing a coiled rattlesnake' (*Norton*).

407 l. 241. *Gaul*. France, leagued against in 1793 by Britain, Austria, Prussia, Holland, Spain, and Sardinia.

ll. 246–7. *the rich . . . free*. Perhaps alluding to Mary Magdalen ('him' notwithstanding), whose kiss signalled repentence and submission (Luke 7: 45).

l. 257. *So . . . not*. S.'s intermediate holograph revised this line to read 'Such, they curse their Maker not.' What is not clear is whether this revision occurred after Mary S. had completed the press copy (which would make it the preferred reading), or whether Mary S. persuaded him against preferring the revision while she was making the press copy.

408 l. 282. *tares*. Weeds.

409 l. 301. *targes.* Shields.

l. 315. *scimitars.* Curved swords, especially associated with tyrannical 'Oriental' peoples (especially Turks and Persians).

l. 316. *sphereless stars.* That is, meteors, stars shooting from their fixed spheres in the heavens.

410 ll. 340–7. *And if then . . . away.* That S.'s advocacy of passive resistance could succeed as a political strategy is attested to by the examples of Gandhi, who was directly influenced by S.'s writings, and Martin Luther King.

411 l. 363. *A volcano . . . afar.* Volcanoes as images of rebellion against tyranny frequently occur in S.'s poetry.

412 *Ode to the West Wind.* Begun in Florence in October 1819; published in the 1820 volume, *Prometheus Unbound, with Other Poems*, which supplies our copy-text. There are drafts of different parts of the poem in the Bodleian (including drafts of stanzas 1–4 in *BSM* 18 and drafts of stanzas 4 and 5 in *BSM* 5) and the Huntington (MS HM 2176; *MYR: Shelley* 6). Each of the poem's five sections is a sonnet in *terza rima*, with a concluding couplet. The Ode is concerned with rebirth and regeneration in the personal and political spheres. Throughout, the wind is addressed as though it were a god-like force, but at the close it is the poet who asserts his poetic power. S. scrawled a line in Greek from Euripides, *Heracles*, l. 342, at the end of his draft in *BSM* 5; translated, it reads, 'In goodness I, though mortal, surpass you, a mighty god'. In 1820 the title is keyed to a note which reads: 'This poem was conceived and chiefly written in a wood that skirts the Arno, near Florence, and on a day when that tempestuous wind, whose temperature is at once mild and animating, was collecting the vapours which pour down the autumnal rains. They began, as I foresaw, at sunset with a violent tempest of hail and rain, attended by that magnificent thunder and lightning peculiar to the Cisalpine regions. The phenomenon alluded to at the conclusion of the third stanza is well known to naturalists. The vegetation at the bottom of the sea, of rivers, and of lakes, sympathizes with that of the land in the change of seasons, and is consequently influenced by the winds which announce it.'

ll. 2–3. *the leaves . . . | Are driven.* Fallen autumnal leaves are a traditional image for death or defeat: see Dante, *Inf.* 3. 112–17, and *PL* 1. 302–4.

l. 5. *Pestilence-stricken multitudes.* Throughout, S. treats the leaves figuratively as well as literally; here, they suggest crowds of people suffering from plague.

l. 9. *azure sister.* The warm west wind in spring, traditionally masculine in Greek and Latin mythology; S. makes it feminine.

l. 14. *Destroyer and Preserver.* Titles for the Hindu gods, Shiva (the Destroyer) and Vishnu (the Preserver); S.'s poem both revises Christian imagery and draws on Indian religion. *hear . . . hear!* See Psalm 61: 1: 'Hear my cry, O God: attend unto my prayer.'

l. 16. *Loose clouds.* Wispy, cirrus clouds.

l. 17. *tangled boughs.* S.'s metaphor is based on the exchange of water and vapour between sky and sea.

l. 18. *Angels.* Messengers.

l. 23. *locks . . . storm.* Dense clouds that run before the coming storm.

413 l. 32. *pumice isle.* Island formed from porous lava. *Baiae's bay.* Bay to the west of Naples, visited by the Shelleys in December 1818.

ll. 33–4. *And saw . . . day.* When S. visited the Bay of Baiae, he was able to see 'the ruins of its ancient grandeur standing like rocks in the transparent sea under our boat' (*L.* 2. 61).

ll. 51–2. *I would . . . sore need.* S. comes close to the posture and accents of biblical poetry here, a secular Psalmist or latter-day Job.

l. 54. *the thorns of life.* Possible sources include Keats, 'Sleep and Poetry', where he attacks poetry that merely 'feeds upon the burrs, | And thorns of life' (ll. 244–5).

414 l. 64. *new birth.* The phrase has a personal resonance since Mary S. was pregnant; Percy Florence Shelley was born on 12 November 1819.

ll. 69–70. *O . . . behind?* In a draft (*BSM* 5), S. finished with a statement: 'o Wind | When Winter comes Spring lags not far behind.'

415 *Peter Bell the Third.* Written sometime between July and 24 October 1819 in Leghorn (Livorno) and/or Florence (where S. moved on 2 October), inspired in part by reading (in the previous June) three pieces from Leigh Hunt's *Examiner*: Hunt's review of 2 May of Wordsworth's poem *Peter Bell* (published on 22 April 1819); a parody of the poem by John Hamilton Reynolds, entitled *Peter Bell; A Lyrical Ballad*, which appeared on 15 April (before Wordsworth's original had been published, but after rumours of its theme of sin and religious redemption had begun to circulate); and Keats's anonymous review of the Reynolds parody, which appeared on 25 April. Whether S. had read the Wordsworth poem itself in its entirety (as opposed to the excerpts in Hunt's review) is uncertain. The title of S.'s poem alludes to its place in a sequence: the Reynolds parody comes first (which is why S. calls it 'the antenatal Peter, | Wrapped in weeds of the same metre', ll. 3–4, Prologue); Wordsworth's poem is 'the second Peter' (l. 7, Prologue), because published after the parody; and S.'s poem is therefore 'Peter Bell the Third'. S.'s Peter is a Methodist (in Wordsworth's poem the sinful Peter's redemption is connected to his having overheard 'a pious Methodist' (l. 1134) urging sinners to repent) and a poet (whose career satirizes that of Wordsworth himself); in Wordsworth's poem Peter was an itinerant potter. S.'s poem takes as its starting point Hunt's

description of Wordsworth's poem as 'a didactic little horror', the moral of which was 'founded on the bewitching principles of fear, bigotry, and diseased impulse' (quoted in *Norton*). It opens with Peter's repentence, taking as the objects of its satire religion in general (and the political quietism, asceticism, and sexual guilt cultivated by Methodism in particular); the deficiencies of Wordsworth's perceptual imagination (ll. 268–82, 293–312, though these lines also acknowledge Wordsworth's characteristic strengths); Wordsworth's gathering conservatism (S. had recently deplored the poet's intervention on behalf of the Lowthers, his patrons and benefactors, against the reformer Henry Brougham in the Westmorland election of 1818); and the highly politicized culture of literary London and its reviews (S. having recently suffered at the hands of the conservative *Quarterly Review*, which not only abused *The Revolt of Islam*, in the issue of *c.*15 October, but accused S. of imitating Wordsworth). In its attack on literary culture the poem recalls Pope's *Dunciad* (1743), which it echoes in several ways. Its five-line iambic tetrameter stanzas are rhymed like the first five lines of a Spenserian stanza (though *abaab* rather than *ababb*); they also recall the knockabout *ottava rima* of Byron's *Don Juan* and *Beppo*. The radical nature of the poem's satire links it with S.'s political poems of autumn 1819, whose fate it shared: though sent to Hunt on 2 November 1819 to be passed on to Ollier and published anonymously, it only appeared posthumously, in *MWS (2)*. Our text for the poem is Mary S.'s press copy in the Bodleian (*BSM* 1), with headings, some notes, and corrections in S.'s hand.

415 *By Miching Mallecho, Esq.* See note to second epigraph.

First Epigraph. The fourth stanza from the end of Part First in the 1819 version of Wordsworth's poem, beginning after l. 515, a conjectured hallucination of Peter's, omitted in subsequent editions ('so as not to offend the pious', Wordsworth explained in a letter of 24 October 1828 to Barron Field (in *Letters of William and Dorothy Wordsworth: The Later Years 1821–1853*, ed. E. De Selincourt, rev. Alan G. Hill, 4 vols. (Oxford, 1978–88), 1. 312)).

Second Epigraph. From *Hamlet*, 3. 2. 123–5. The 'this' of Ophelia's question is the dumb-show, mounted by Hamlet to catch out Claudius; '*miching*' is sneaking, stealthy, secret, truant; '*mallecho*' (S. uses the Folio spelling) from the Spanish for misdeed or mischief.

Dedication. 'Thomas Brown, the Younger', was a pseudonym used by the popular Irish poet Thomas Moore (1779–1852) for a series of doggerel satires, including *The Fudge Family in Paris* (1818); 'H.F.' ('Historian of Fudges', according to *Norton*; '*Hibernicae Filius*', or 'Son of Ireland,' according to *Rossetti*) plays on Wordsworth's dedication of *Peter Bell* to 'Robert Southey, Esq., P.L.' (that is, 'Poet Laureate').

the Rat and the Apostate. The 'Rat' is Reynolds's Peter; Wordsworth's Peter, like his progenitor, was for S. a political apostate.

eleutherophobia. Fear of liberty (*eleutheros* is Greek for 'free').

Mr Murray's upper room. The *Quarterly Review*, the Tory rival of Hunt's *Examiner*, was edited in an upper room of the publishing house of John Murray ('our great friend') in Albemarle Street.

this monkey. Hunt.

two of the Mr Bells. Those of Reynolds's parody and Hunt's review of Wordsworth's poem.

416 *Proteus*. Greek god who could change shape at will.

ultra-legitimate. ultra-respectable.

White Obi. 'Obi' is a West Indian term for magic; 'White Obi' is Christianity or religion. The indented quotation immediately following is from Wordsworth's 'The French Revolution as It Appeared to Enthusiasts at Its Commencement' (1809), reprinted in *Poems* (1815).

six or seven days. Wordsworth had worked hard on *Peter Bell*, from 1798 to 1819, defiantly declaring (given its determinedly unelevated subject-matter and style) his aim, to quote from the poem's Dedication, 'to make the production less unworthy of a favourable reception; or, rather, to fit it for filling *permanently* a station however humble, in the Literature of my Country.' When S. sent his own poem to Hunt he claimed, in contrast, to 'have only expended a few days on this party squib' (*L* 2. 135).

417 *bitterns*. Marshland birds.

P.S. Pray excuse the date of place. 'Miching Mallecho' is ashamed to offer his address, as had been 'Tom Brown' in *The Fudge Family in Paris* (written from '245, Piccadilly'), because the street where he lodges is not 'respectable' or fashionable.

Prologue. l. 3. *antenatal Peter*. See headnote.

l. 10. *Aldric's themes*. Henry Aldrich (1647–1710) was the author of a standard school logic text, *Artis Logicae Compendium* (1691), from which come terms like 'proposition', 'mean of two extremes', and 'syllogism'.

l. 16. *his*. That is, the first or antenatal Peter's (whose 'antitype' is Wordsworth's Peter, a 'substantial' character, unlike Reynolds's Peter, who is only a 'shadow' or 'reflection').

418 l. 32. *predevote*. Predestined.

l. 35. *Cotter*. A peasant who lives in a cottage.

l. 36. *polygamic Potter*. Wordsworth's Peter was an itinerant potter, a maker and seller of pots; called 'polygamic' because, as Wordsworth tells us, 'He had a dozen wedded wives' (l. 256). S. adds a note of cod scholarship (in the manner of Pope's notes to *The Dunciad*): 'The oldest scholiasts read—A *dodecagamic* Potter. This is at once descriptive and more megalophonous—but the alliteration of the text had captivated the vulgar ears of the herd of later commentators.' ('Dodecagamic' here means married twelve times, from the Greek prefix 'dodeca-' (twelve); 'megalophonous' means great-sounding or high-sounding, from Greek 'mega-' (great)).

418 *Poem*. l. 8. *oiled his hair*. S.'s note reads: 'To those who have not duly appreciated the distinction between *whale* and *Russia* oil this attribute might rather seem to belong to the Dandy than the Evangelic. The effect, when to the windward, is indeed so similar, that it requires a subtle Naturalist to discriminate the animals. They belong however to distinct genera.' 'Russia oil', made from birch trees imported from Russia, was more expensive than whale oil, 'the common man's cheap substitute' (*Norton*).

419 l. 15. *the gravel*. A disease associated with pain and difficulty in passing urine, produced by 'an aggregation of urinary crystals which can be recognised as masses by the naked eye' (*OED* 4).

l. 25. *The other . . . with you*. 'The other' is Peter's 'skin . . . of a brimstone hue' (which rhymes with 'you').

l. 32. *Windermere*. The first of several Lake District sites, familiar from Wordsworth's life and writing, mentioned in the poem (see also ll. 56 and 60).

420 l. 66. *The Devil 'was' in it*. The devil's arrival in 'a black storm' (l. 61) echoes God's arrival to Job in a whirlwind (Job 38: 1) (Job is alluded to again in l. 459).

421 l. 81. *He is—what we are*. The devil exists only in the devilish behaviour of men, a theme reiterated throughout the poem.

l. 84. *for sack*. The Poet Laureate (Robert Southey in 1819) was paid in sack, a type of wine; Wordsworth succeeded Southey as Poet Laureate in 1843.

l. 86. *A thief . . . night*. An ironic allusion to Christ's second coming (1 Thess. 5:2).

l. 92. *slop-merchant from Wapping*. A seller of cheap sailor's clothing; 'Wapping', located on the Thames in the East End of London, was a poor seamen's district.

l. 94. *perk*. 'To assume . . . a lively, self-assertive, or self-conceited attitude or air' (*OED* 1).

l. 96. *an upper Benjamin*. A short overcoat.

ll. 108–10. *Each had . . . well*. Here and elsewhere S. deplores airy or fanciful abstraction ('an upper stream of thought'); l. 110 is ironic.

422 l. 116. *phiz*. Face (from 'physiognomy').

l. 118. *clomb*. Climbed.

l. 127. *Grosvenor square*. London's largest square, completed in 1837, 'inhabited by the *nouveaux riches*, including John Westbrook, the wealthy coffee-house owner who was Shelley's first father-in-law, and William Gifford, editor of the *Quarterly Review*' (*Norton*).

423 ll. 152–3. *There is . . . Castlereagh*. Hell's or London's inhabitants come from all political persuasions: John Castle ('Castles' in the press copy) was a government informer; George Canning (1770–1827) a liberal Tory

minister and polemicist; William Cobbett (1763–1835) a radical journalist; and Castlereagh (for whom see note to *Mask of Anarchy*, l. 6) the much-hated Foreign Secretary.

l. 154. *cozening*. Cheating. *trepanning*. Catching in a trap, swindling.

l. 157. *There is a* * * *. In the press-copy, the asterisks are inserted above 'S–th–y', evidently a reference to Robert Southey.

l. 163. *Chancery Court*. Presided over in 1819 by Lord Eldon, the Lord Chancellor (see *Mask of Anarchy*, l. 15 and note).

l. 167. *Paper money*. For S.'s attack on paper money see *Mask of Anarchy*, l. 176 and note.

l. 174. *German soldiers*. Rumoured to be brought in by George III, Elector of Hanover as well as King of England, to put down radical dissent. *Webb* quotes S. to Leigh Hunt: 'The tremendous question is now agitating, whether a military & judicial despotism is to be established by our present rulers, or some form of government less unfavourable to the real & permanent interests of all men is to arise from the conflict of passions now gathering to overturn them' (*L* 2. 148).

l. 176. *methodism*. Methodism belongs with suicide because both, for S., as for Leigh Hunt in his review of Wordsworth's *Peter Bell*, grow from despair.

424 l. 183. *amant misere*. Love miserably (they screech or 'caterwaul' when in heat). S. adds a note: 'One of the attributes in Linnaeus's description of the Cat. To a similar cause the caterwauling of more than one species of this genus is to be referred;—except indeed that the poor quadruped is compelled to quarrel with its own pleasures, whilst the biped is supposed only to quarrel with those of others.'

l. 186. *chastity*. S. adds a note: 'What would this husk and excuse for a Virtue be without its kernal prostitution, or the kernal prostitution without this husk of a Virtue? I wonder the Women of the Town do not form an association, like the Society for the Suppression of Vice, for the support of what may be considered the "King, church, and Constitution" of their order. But this subject is almost too horrible for a joke.' The Society for the Suppression of Vice, founded in 1787 by the Evangelicals William Wilberforce and Dr John Bowdler, discouraged brothels, pornography, and Sunday games.

l. 187. *hobnobbers*. Those who drink together, or to each other, or are on familiar terms.

l. 190. *stock-jobbers*. Stockbrokers, speculators.

l. 197. *moiling*. Drudging, in dirt, mud, mire.

l. 202. *levees*. Assemblies held in the early afternoon, originally at court and for men only; more generally, for and by persons of distinction.

l. 209. *Cretan-tonguèd*. Cretans were proverbial liars.

424 l. 210. *Alemannic.* German.

425 l. 212. *conversazioni.* Social gatherings at which art, literature, science, and culture are discussed.

l. 213. *Conventicles.* Meetings (or meeting-houses) of Dissenters or Nonconformists. More generally, 'a meeting (*esp.* a religious meeting) of a private, clandestine, or illegal kind' (*OED*).

ll. 220–3. *They are damned . . . 'God damns!'.* As the devil exists only in the devilish behaviour of men (l. 81), and Hell is 'a city much like London' (l. 147), so damnation is an exclusively human not divine punishment. The stanza of which ll. 220–22 are a part alludes to the poem's first epigraph, from Wordsworth's *Peter Bell*. S. adds the following note to l. 223: 'This libel on our national oath, and this accusation of all our countrymen of being in the daily practice of solemnly asseverating the most enormous falsehood I fear deserves the notice of a more active Attorney General than that here alluded to.'

l. 224. *flams.* Humbugs, deceptions.

l. 236. *stripe.* Stroke or lash-mark, of a whip or scourge.

l. 239. *Cobbett's snuff, revenge.* Cobbett's *Weekly Political Register* (1802–1835) could be accused of seeking to stir the poor to revenge against the ruling classes.

l. 242. *like we know who.* S. himself, and other like-minded reformers.

426 ll. 273–7. *All things . . . him.* An early allusion to what, after Keats, is often referred to as the Wordsworthian 'egotistical sublime'. Though S. himself could at times be accused of a comparable 'self-absorption', in the recently completed *Julian and Maddalo* and *The Cenci* he showed an ability to imagine situations from different points of view.

427 l. 285. *trim.* Character.

428 l. 320. *Diogenes.* The Cynic philosopher (*c.*400–325 BC), known for his espousal of asceticism, contempt for the body, and self-sufficiency.

ll. 328–9. *Bocca . . . luna.* 'A mouth kissed doesn't lose its freshness, for like the moon it always renews itself' (Boccaccio, *Decameron*, 2. 7, trans. G. H. McWilliam, Harmondsworth, 1972).

l. 341. *A toadlike lump.* An allusion to Satan 'Squat like a toad', *PL* 4. 800; Pope alludes to the same passage in his description of Sporus in 'Epistle to Dr Arbuthnot' (1735), l. 319.

429 l. 348. *wight.* Person.

l. 374. *petits soupers.* Intimate, informal suppers.

l.375. *A man.* Based on Coleridge.

430 l. 407. *And . . . man.* A conflation of ll. 96–100 of Wordsworth's 'Tintern Abbey' and l. 203 of 'Ode: Intimations of Immortality' ('the human heart by which we live').

l. 411. *lie*. In the press copy, Mary S. wrote 'lie' and 'be', as though offering S. a choice (see *BSM* 1, p. 107 for commentary).

431 l. 421. *of rocks and trees*. See the concluding lines of Wordsworth's 'A Slumber Did My Spirit Seal': 'Rolled round in earth's diurnal course | With rocks and stones and trees.'

l. 429. *pedlars*. The Pedlar figures prominently in Wordsworth's *Excursion* (1814).

l. 447. *pipkins*. Small earthenware pots or pans.

ll. 448–9. *And Mr ——, the Bookseller, | Gave twenty pounds*. An allusion to Joseph Cottle, publisher of the *Lyrical Ballads* (who paid thirty guineas, not £20, for the copyright).

432 l. 459. *'O, that . . . book!'*. See Job 31: 35: 'Oh that one would hear me! behold, my desire is, that the Almighty would answer me, and that mine adversary had written a book.'

l. 463. *Peter's next new book*. Wordsworth's *Poems: In Two Volumes* (1807), much abused by the reviewers, famously by Francis Jeffrey in the *Edinburgh Review*.

l. 468. *seriatim*. In succession.

l. 470. *Mrs Foy's daughter*. Betty Foy is the mother of Wordsworth's 'Idiot Boy,' from *Lyrical Ballads*; she has no daughter in the poem. In the fair copy this stanza is followed by a crossed stanza reading: 'Another—"Impious Libertine! | That commits i——t with his sister. | In ruined Abbies—mighty fine | To write odes on *it*!"—I opine.'

l. 474. *Dr Willis*. Either Francis Willis (1718–1807) or his sons John (1751–1835) and Robert Darling Willis (1760–1821), all of whom treated George III for mental illness.

433 l. 500. *Emma*. The press-copy reading; S. asked Ollier to change 'Emma' to 'Betty' because, mistakenly, he thought that 'Emma' was 'the real name of the sister of a great poet who might be mistaken for Peter [i.e. Wordsworth]' (*L* 2. 196). *MWS (2)* reads 'Emma'.

l. 507. *Like . . . tune*. See *Hamlet*, 3. 1. 156–7: 'Now see that most noble and sovereign reason | Like sweet bells jangled out of tune and harsh.'

l. 512. *God's own voice*. S. adds a note: '*Vox populi, vox dei* [the voice of the people is the voice of God]. As Mr Godwin truly observes of a more famous saying, of *some merit as a popular maxim, but totally destitute of philosophical accuracy*.'

434 l. 519. *Born's . . . Kant's book*. F. G. Born's four-volume Latin translation of Kant, *Opera ad philosophiam criticam pertinentia* (1796–8). Immanuel Kant (1724–1824), German philosopher, was an influential opponent (for Coleridge in particular) of the empirical philosophy and atheistic tendencies of the eighteenth century.

l. 525. *furor verborum*. Inspired frenzy (especially of poets and prophets).

434 l. 532. *Sir William Drummond*. Author (1770–1828) of *Academical Questions* (1805), hereafter *AQ*, a book which criticizes Kant's ideas and much influenced S.

l. 534. *P. Verbovale Esquire*. S.'s note reads: 'Quasi, *Qui valet verba*:—*i.e.* all the words which have been, are, or may be expended by, for, against, with, or on him. A sufficient proof of the utility of this History. Peter's progenitor who selected this name seems to have possessed *a pure anticipated cognition* of the nature and modesty of this ornament of his posterity.' 'Pure anticipated cognition' is a phrase used jokily elsewhere by S. (see *L* 2. 438); Peacock pokes fun at Scythrop in *Nightmare Abbey* (1818) for his '*pure anticipated cognitions*' of female beauty (ch. 3), and the shared joke seems to have its origins in Sir William Drummond's attack on the 'admirers' of the 'Kantian system' 'who deduce truth from *anticipated cognitions*' (*AQ* 351, 352).

l. 538. *ex luce praebens fumum*. 'From light he then gives smoke', an inversion of ll. 143–4 of Horace's *Ars Poetica* (*c*.19 BC): 'His [a post-Homeric cyclic poet's] aim is not to have smoke after a flash, but light | emerging from smoke' (*Horace: Satires and Epistles; Persius: Satires*, trans. Niall Rudd (Harmondsworth, 1979)).

l. 541. *subter humum*. Underground.

435 l. 555. *Flibbertigibbet*. The name of a devil ('the foul fiend Flibbertigibbet', *King Lear*, 3. 4. 106).

l. 566. *Deist*. A believer in 'natural religion'; one who rejects revelation, the divinity of Jesus, and the supernatural doctrines of Christianity.

l. 574. *Calvin and Dominic*. Calvin (1509–64), French theologian and reformer, and St Dominic (1170–1221), Spanish Catholic, founder of the Dominican order.

l. 583. *the Otter*. 'A famous river in the new Atlantis of the Dynastophylic Pantisocratists' (S.'s note). The River Otter passed by Coleridge's boyhood home and figures in his poetry; Pantisocracy was the name Coleridge, Southey, and their wives gave to the utopian movement they hoped to found on the banks of the Susquehanna River in Pennsylvania. According to *Norton*, '*Dynastophylic* refers to Southey's and Coleridge's later support of the established dynasties of Europe'.

436 ll. 584–8. *In the death hues . . . wish*. S.'s note reads: 'See the description of the beautiful colours produced during the agonizing death of a number of trout, in the fourth part of a long poem in blank verse [*The Excursion*, 8. 568–71], published within a few years. That Poem contains curious evidence of the gradual hardening of a strong but circumscribed sensibility, of the perversion of a penetrating but panic-stricken understanding. The Author might have derived a lesson which he had probably forgotten from these sweet and sublime verses [the concluding lines of 'Hart-Leap Well', from the 1800 edition of *Lyrical Ballads*]: "This lesson, Shepherd, let us two divide, | Taught both by what She (Nature)

shews and what conceals, | Never to blend our measure or our pride | With sorrow of the meanest thing that feels."'

l. 603. *Sherry*. Richard Brinsley Sheridan (1751–1816), dramatist, wit, and Liberal MP; although a friend of George IV in George's days as Prince Regent, Sheridan was later shunned by him for his liberal political views.

l. 616. *George Colman*. George Colman, the Younger (1762–1836), dramatist and writer of farces, noted for his wit and bawdy good-humour.

l. 617. *male Molly*. Effeminate man.

437 ll. 636–7. *'May Carnage . . . daughter*. These lines allude to a notorious passage (ll. 106–9) in the first edition of Wordsworth's 'Ode, 1815', celebrating victory over Napoleon at Waterloo: 'But Thy most dreaded instrument, | In working out a pure intent, | Is Man—arrayed for mutual slaughter, | —Yea, Carnage is thy daughter.'

l. 644. *Slash . . . Manchester*. An allusion to the Peterloo Massacre.

l. 650. *Moloch*. A Canaanite god to whom children were sacrificed (see Leviticus 18: 21); also one of Milton's devils in *PL* 2. 43.

l. 652. *intent*. S.'s note reads: 'It is curious to observe how often extremes meet. Cobbett and Peter use the same language for a different purpose: Peter is indeed a sort of metrical Cobbett. Cobbett is however more mischievous than Peter because he pollutes a holy and now unconquerable cause with the principles of legitimate murder; while the other only makes a bad one ridiculous and odious. If either Peter or Cobbett should see this note, each will feel more indignation at being compared to the other than at any censure implied in the moral perversion laid to their charge.'

438 l. 655. *Lord MacMurderchouse's*. 'Chouse' means to cheat or swindle; as a noun, a cheat or swindler. Wordsworth received his government post in 1813, as Distributor of Stamps for Westmorland and Cumberland counties, a post in the revenue service, from William Lowther, Earl of Lonsdale.

l. 671. *Oliver*. A government spy (like Castle, l. 152), known as 'Oliver', thought by S. and other liberals to have worked as an *agent provocateur* in the Pentridge Rising of 1817; see S.'s *Address to the People on the Death of the Princess Charlotte*.

l. 679. *pelf*. Riches.

439 l. 688. *a house*. An allusion to Rydal Mount, the house Wordsworth purchased in 1813, after receiving his government post. The house was larger and more imposing than his previous house in Grasmere, Allan Bank; he lived there until his death in 1850.

l. 698. *curse*. Like the curse that visits Harry Gill in Wordsworth's 'Goody Blake and Harry Gill', in *Lyrical Ballads* (1798).

ll. 711–12. *the immortal . . . Swift*. An allusion to one of the Struldbrugs, who are endowed with immortality (which they find a misery), in Swift's *Gulliver's Travels* (1726), pt. 3, ch. 10.

440 l. 721–2 *Guatimozan . . . brass.* The successor of his uncle, the Aztec leader Montezuma; he led the failed Aztec attack against the Spaniards; after his capture he was tortured on a hot metal grid.

l. 725. *those famed seven.* Christian youths of Ephesus, sealed in a cave during the Decian persecution of AD 250, said to have awoken after a sleep of 187 years (according to Gibbon's calculation in *The History of the Decline and Fall of the Roman Empire*, ch. 33).

l. 733. *the drowsy curse.* Like the all-encompassing 'cosmic yawn' that settles over London at the end of Pope's *Dunciad*, resulting in that poem's final line: 'And universal darkness buries all.'

442 *Men of England: A Song.* Composed in Florence in late 1819 or early 1820, published posthumously in *MSW (1)*, this poem is probably one of a series of popular political verses referred to in a letter S. wrote to Leigh Hunt on 1 May 1820: 'I wish to ask you if you know of any bookseller who would like to publish a little volume of *popular songs* wholly political, & destined to awaken & direct the imagination of the reformers' (*L* 2. 191). Though this volume was never published, in a note to *MSW (1)* Mary S. refers to it: 'He had an idea of publishing a series of poems adapted expressly to commemorate . . . [the people's] circumstances and wrongs—he wrote a few, but in those days of prosecution for libel they could not be printed.' Three such poems, most scholars agree, are printed directly after *The Mask of Anarchy* in *MWS (1)*: 'Song, to the Men of England' (Mary S.'s retitling of the notebook version, 'Men of England: A Song'), 'Lines Written During the Castlereagh Administration' (titled 'England' in S.'s draft), and 'Similes' (a retitling of the notebook draft 'To S. and C.' (i.e. Sidmouth and Castlereagh), later expanded by Mary S. to 'Similes for Two Political Characters of 1819'). Among other poems subsequently associated with the series we print 'A New National Anthem', 'England in 1819', and 'What men gain fairly'. Our copy-text for 'Men of England: A Song' is S.'s fair copy in the Bodleian, originally part of the Larger Silsbee Notebook at Harvard (MS Eng. 258. 2; *MYR: Shelley* 5), supplemented by Mary S.'s text in *MSW(1)*.

443 *Lines Written during the Castlereagh Administration.* Composed in late 1819 or early 1820, published posthumously by Thomas Medwin, S.'s cousin, in the *Athenaeum*, 8 December 1832, where it first received this title, and by Mary S. in *MSW(1)*. For background see headnote to 'Men of England: A Song'. Our copy-text is taken from S.'s very lightly punctuated fair copy, titled 'To —', in Harvard fMS Eng. 822, folio 1b (*MYR: Shelley* 5), with some accidentals from S.'s intermediate fair copy, titled 'England', in Harvard MS Eng. 258.2 (*MYR: Shelley* 5) and *MSW (1)*. The poem is known by the Medwin title, which we have retained, despite Michael Scrivener's contention that it 'distances the political meaning for the 1832 audience' (*Radical Shelley* (Princeton, 1982), 227). For Castlereagh see note to *Mask of Anarchy*, l. 6.

l. 24. *Hell*. 'God' in the earlier Harvard MS (Eng. 258.2) and *MSW (1)*.

To S. and C. Composed late 1819 or early 1820, published posthumously in the *Athenaeum*, 25 August 1832 (where it was titled 'Similes') and in Mary S.'s 1839 editions. For background see headnote to 'Men of England: A Song'. Our copy-text is S.'s lightly punctuated draft in the Bodleian (*BSM* 18), supplemented by punctuation from Mary S.'s text in *MWS (2)*, which expands Medwin's title to 'Similes for Two Political Characters of 1819'. In the Harvard safe-keeping notebook the title is 'To Sxxxxxth and Cxxxxxxxxgh' (MS Eng. 258. 2; *MYR: Shelley* 5).

l. 1. *their*. Mary S.'s 1839 editions read 'an'.

l. 2. *wind*. Mary S.'s 1839 editions read 'sound'.

444 l. 7. *yew*. Mary S.'s 1839 editions read 'hue'.

l. 9. *moon*. Mary S.'s 1839 editions read 'morn'.

l. 20. *Two . . . one*. In another draft of stanza 4 of the poem in the Bodleian (*BSM* 7), its final line reads 'Two tangled snakes which are but one.'

'What men gain fairly'. Composed late 1819 or early 1820, published posthumously in *MWS (2)*; probably a fragment. For background see headnote to 'Men of England: A Song'. Our copy-text is S.'s holograph in the Huntington (MS. HM 2177; *MYR: Shelley* 4).

l. 7. *With those . . . strong*. This line omitted by Mary S.

A New National Anthem. Composed late 1819 or early 1820, published posthumously in the 'Note on Poems of 1819' (see headnote to 'Men of England: A Song') in *MWS (2)*. Our copy-text is S.'s draft in the Bodleian (*BSM* 5), which is not a fair copy; we have also consulted *MWS (2)*, especially for punctuation.

445 l. 13. *majestic*. Thus *MWS (2)*; the word in the draft is all but indecipherable; the transcription in *BSM* 5 reads '<approvative>'.

446 l. 42. *Queen*. After this word, two incomplete stanzas in the draft, one very difficult to decipher, have been omitted here, as in *MWS (2)*.

Sonnet: England in 1819. Composed in Florence in late 1819, sent to Leigh Hunt for publication on 23 December 1819, but only published posthumously, in *MWS (1)*. The poem may have been considered for the volume of 'popular songs' S. hoped to publish in 1820 (see headnote to 'Men of England: A Song'). *Webb* quotes the Westminster MP and parliamentary reformer Francis Burdett (1770–1844), in an Election Address of 11 October 1812, published in Hunt's *Examiner*: 'an army of spies and informers . . . a Phantom for a king; a degraded aristocracy; an oppressed people . . . vague and sanguinary laws.' Our copy-text is S.'s fair copy in the Bodleian (*BSM* 18).

l. 1. *King*. George III had reigned since 1760, had been insane since 1811, and was soon to die, aged 81, on 29 January 1820; his 'blindness' was metaphorical, Lear's rather than Gloucester's.

446 l. 2. *Princes.* George III's sons were notoriously dissolute.

l. 7. *A people . . . field.* An allusion to the Peterloo Massacre (see headnote to *Mask of Anarchy*).

l. 8. *liberticide.* The killing of liberty (S.'s coinage).

l. 10. *Golden and sanguine.* Gold and blood ('sanguine' here means bloody rather than hopeful or confident) recurrently symbolize the twin origins and underpinnings of tyranny in S.'s poetry: money and violence.

l. 12. *A senate . . . unrepealed.* The 'senate' here is the unreformed Parliament. 'Time's worst statute, unrepealed' refers to the Test and Corporations Acts which imposed disabilities upon Dissenters and Roman Catholics (and survived several attempts at repeal and modification).

Love's Philosophy. Published by Leigh Hunt in the *Indicator* in December 1819 and in *PP*; transcribed by S. in Harvard MS Eng. 258. 2 (*MYR: Shelley* 5) where it is entitled (possibly by Mary S.) 'An Anacreontic' and by S. for Sophia Stacey in a copy of the *Literary Pocket-Book for 1819* in Eton College Library (*MYR: Shelley* 8). This last manuscript supplies our copy-text (title added from *PP*). Sophia Stacey, a ward of S.'s uncle, shared the same boarding-house as the Shelleys in Florence, 1819; S. wrote a number of lyrics for her.

l. 7. *In . . . mingle.* 'In one another's being mingle', *PP*; Harvard.

447 l. 18. *What . . . worth.* 'What were these examples worth', Harvard; 'What are all these kissings worth,', *PP*.

Ode to Heaven. Composed in December 1819 and published in *Prometheus Unbound, with Other Poems*, which supplies our copy-text; we have also consulted the fair copy in the Bodleian (*BSM* 9) and the fair copy (by Mary S.) in the Larger Silsbee Notebook at Harvard (MS Eng. 258. 2; *MYR: Shelley* 5). In the Preface to *MWS: Prose*, Mary S. links the poem to the following account of S.'s metaphysical outlook: 'The creation, such as it was perceived by his mind—a unit in immensity, was slight and narrow compared with the interminable forms of thought that might exist beyond, to be perceived perhaps hereafter by his own mind; or which are perceptible to other minds that fill the universe, not of space in the material sense, but of infinity in the immaterial one'. The poem, written in trochaic tetrameters, shows S.'s interest in dialectic and perspective as its sections work through and set against each other different views of the idea of heaven.

First Spirit. 'Chorus of Spirits' in *BSM* 9.

ll. 1–27. *Palace-roof . . . alway!.* The First Spirit describes heaven in terms influenced by eighteenth-century astronomy and Deist theology; it equivocates about the existence of a 'Power' (l. 21), which may be only a human projection (ll. 21–2).

448 *Second Spirit.* 'A Remoter Voice' in *BSM* 9.

ll. 28–36. *Thou art . . . dream.* The Second Spirit suggests that the human notion of heaven is an imperfect sketch of 'delights' (l. 33) that exceed conception.

Third Spirit. 'A Louder and Still Remoter Voice' in *BSM* 9.

l. 53. *millions. BSM* 9 has 'million'.

ll. 37–54. *Peace! . . . disappear!* The Third Spirit asserts that heaven and humans alike are insignificant in the scheme of things, yet that seemingly insignificant things can offer a glimpse of heaven, here 'an unimagined world' (l. 49).

To the Lord Chancellor. Dated 1819 by Mary S. but probably composed in 1820 (see *BSM* 14, pp. xviii–xix), 'To the Lord Chancellor' was published in part in Mary S.'s first 1839 edition and was published in full in her second 1839 edition. There is a draft in the Bodleian (*BSM* 14) and a later draft in Harvard MS Eng. 258. 2 (*MYR: Shelley* 5). A subsequent transcription by Mary S., with corrections by S., in Harvard fMS. Eng 822 (*MYR: Shelley* 5) provides our copy-text. After the death of his first wife, Harriet, S. had been refused custody of their children, Ianthe and Charles, in a Chancery case presided over by Lord Eldon, the Lord Chancellor. On 27 March 1817 Eldon decided against S. on the grounds that the latter's 'principles' would lead to the recommendation of 'conduct' that was 'immoral and vicious'. In her 'Note on Poems of 1819' Mary S. writes: 'No words can express the anguish he felt when his elder children were torn from him.' S. was also concerned that his children by Mary would be taken from him. For the idea of a curse and the poem's concluding twist, S. may be indebted to Byron's *Childe Harold*, 4. 132–5.

Title. The copy text has 'To Lxxd Exxxn', cancelled, presumably for prudential reasons, in favour of 'To ——'; the intermediate Harvard draft has 'To the Lord Chancellor', with the last two words cancelled. We have adopted the title in this intermediate draft before the cancellations, as did Mary S. and subsequent editors.

l. 4. *a buried form.* 'The Star-chamber' (Mary S. in her second 1839 edition).

449 ll. 21–4. *By . . . birth.* Cancelled in copy-text; S. then wrote in the right-hand margin 'Insert this'.

l. 36. *why not fatherless?* S. altered Mary S.'s transcription from 'yet not fatherless'.

450 l. 40. *tomb.* After this stanza, the copy-text has the following stanza cancelled with the instruction 'dele' (delete): 'By thy most impious Hell, and all its terror, | By all the grief, the madness, and the guilt | Which [*for* Of] thine impostures, which must be their error, | That sand on which thy crumbling Power is built'. The stanza is usually printed by editors (though not *Longman* 1) as part of the poem.

ll. 47–8. *And . . . men.* For Eldon's notorious weeping in court, see *Mask of Anarchy*, ll. 16–17.

450 *The Sensitive Plant.* Written in Pisa in the spring of 1820, *The Sensitive Plant* was included in the volume *Prometheus Unbound, with Other Poems* (1820). This text supplies our copy-text, though we have also consulted the fair copy in Mary S.'s hand in the Larger Silsbee Notebook at Harvard (MS Eng. 258. 2; *MYR: Shelley* 5); there is draft material in the Bodleian (*BSM* 18) and the Huntington (MS HM 2176; *MYR: Shelley* 6). Employing anapaestic tetrameters for its three Parts, before switching to octosyllabic iambics for its coda-like Conclusion, the poem questions whether our senses play us false in reporting that 'love, and beauty, and delight' are subject to decay. The poem may obliquely articulate S.'s political hopes and fears following the Cato Street Conspiracy of February 1820 in which an attempted assassination of ministers of the crown was foiled; S. regretted the attempted assassination as working against the cause of reform. S. draws on a variety of poems, most notably the account of the Garden of Adonis in Spenser's *FQ* 3. 6, and Milton's description of Eden in *PL*; he also returns to Erasmus Darwin's *The Loves of the Plants*, an early favourite. The sensitive plant, or *mimosa pudica*, was of interest in the period as occupying an ambiguous border between the vegetable and animal worlds, and had been made use of by William Cowper in his poem 'The Poet, the Oyster, and the Sensitive Plant' (1782). S. refers to himself in a letter of December 1821 as an 'Exotic . . . unfortunately belonging to the order of mimosa' (*L* 2. 368).

Part First. ll. 3–4. *And it opened . . . light.* See Erasmus Darwin, *The Loves of the Plants*, where the 'chaste MIMOSA' 'Shuts her sweet eye-lids to approaching night, | And hails with freshen'd charms the rising light' (1. 247, 253–4; quoted from Woodstock Books facsimile, 1991).

451 l. 12. *companionless.* The sensitive plant is an annual; all the other flowers in Part First are perennials.

l. 17. *pied.* Varied in colour.

l. 21. *Naiad-like.* Naiads were water nymphs, who incarnated the divinity of the springs and streams which they inhabited.

l. 25. *the hyacinth . . . sense.* The synaesthetic mingling of sound and odour here and elsewhere in Part First evokes a sense of harmony and interchange.

l. 29. *addressed.* Made ready.

l. 38. *blows.* Blooms; blossoms.

l. 42. *pranked.* Decked out; spangled.

452 l. 54. *fabulous asphodels.* Asphodels were flowers fabled to grow in the Elysian fields.

l. 58. *undefilèd Paradise.* In the draft S. wrote and cancelled 'this Republic of odours & hues'.

l. 63. *mine-lamps.* Humphry Davy had invented his safety-lamp for miners in 1815 (*Webb*).

453 ll. 76–7. *It loves . . . the beautiful!* See S.'s translation of Plato's *Symposium*: '"It is conceded, then, that Love loves that which he wants but possesses not?"—"Yes, certainly."—"But Love wants and does not possess beauty?"—"Indeed it must necessarily follow"' (*Notopoulos*, p. 440).

454 ll. 98–109. *And when evening . . . Sensitive Plant.* See *PL* 4. 598–604, which describes how when 'came still evening on' (l. 598) all beasts and birds went to sleep to the accompaniment of 'Silence' (l. 600)—'all but the wakeful nightingale; | She all night long her amorous descant sung' (ll. 602–3).

Part Second. l. 1. *a Power . . . place.* See Milton, *Arcades*, where the Genius of the Wood describes himself as 'the power | Of this fair wood' (ll. 44–5) and asserts that 'all my plants I save from nightly ill' (l. 48).

455 ll. 37–8. *lifted . . . bands.* See *PL* 9. 424–31, where Satan spies on Eve 'stooping to support | Each flower of slender stalk' (ll. 427–8).

l. 38. *osier.* Made of willow.

l. 43. *woof.* Woven fabric.

l. 49. *beam-like ephemeris.* Mayfly that sparkles like a line of light.

l. 51. *and harm not.* See *The Tempest*, 3. 2. 131, where Caliban describes 'sweet airs, that give delight and hurt not'.

l. 53. *antenatal.* Before birth. The idea of life before birth is central to the Platonic doctrine of reminiscence articulated in the *Phaedo*.

456 *Part Third.* l. 3. *Baiae.* A bay in the Gulf of Naples from which Mt. Vesuvius can be seen.

l. 4. *She.* The moon.

457 l. 54. *darnels.* Grass that can grow as a weed.

l. 55. *dock . . . hemlock.* 'Dock' is a coarse weed; 'henbane' and 'hemlock' are poisonous plants.

l. 56. *shank.* Lower part of leg, used metaphorically.

l. 60. *pulpous.* Pulpy.

l. 61. *Livid.* Of bluish leaden colour; discoloured as by bruise. *lurid.* Dingy yellowish brown.

458 l. 62. *agarics.* Gill mushrooms. *mildew.* Destructive growth of minute fungi on plants.

ll. 66–9. *Their moss . . . by.* Cancelled in Mary S.'s transcription in *MYR: Shelley* 5 and omitted in her collected editions.

l. 70. *Spawn.* White fibrous matter from which mushrooms are produced.

l. 72. *flags.* Plant with bladed leaf growing on moist ground.

l. 78. *unctuous.* Greasy.

458 l. 82. *forbid.* Cursed. See *Macbeth*, 1. 3. 20: 'He shall live a man forbid.'

l. 91. *One . . . lip.* See *Macbeth*, 1. 3. 42–3: 'each at once her choppy finger laying | Upon her skinny lips.'

459 l. 103. *want.* Typical of this Part's ironic echoes of earlier Parts: here of 'love's sweet want' (1. 11).

l. 113. *griff.* Claw.

l. 116. *mandrakes.* Poisonous plant with white or purple flowers and large yellow fruit; once thought to resemble human form and to shriek when plucked.

460 *Conclusion.* l. 12. *shadows of the dream.* Plato and Calderón (*Life is a Dream*) are likely influences.

l. 15. *own.* To admit; to concede something is the case. In drafts S. wrote 'think' and 'say'.

ll. 21–4. *For love . . . obscure.* The death and decay of love, beauty and delight are apparent, but not real: the result of failure on the part of our organs of perception and understanding.

An Exhortation. Composed in Pisa, April 1820 (place and date given in the fair copy in Mary S.'s hand in the Larger Silsbee Notebook at Harvard (MS Eng. 258. 2; *MYR: Shelley* 5)), sent to Maria Gisborne on 8 May 1820 ('a little thing about Poets . . . a kind of an excuse for Wordsworth' (*L* 2. 195)), and published in *Prometheus Unbound, with Other Poems* (1820). The 1820 published text supplies our copy-text. The poem represents a further stage in S.'s reflections on Wordsworth and, more generally, on the question that Wordsworth himself raises in the Preface to *Lyrical Ballads* (1802), 'What is a Poet?'

ll. 1–2. *Chameleons . . . fame.* Comparison and contrast between the shape-changing of chameleons and poets run through the poem.

461 l. 27. *the boon!* Possibly an ironic allusion to Wordsworth's sonnet, 'The world is too much with us', l. 4: 'We have given our hearts away, a sordid boon!'

The Cloud. Composed 1820 and published in *Prometheus Unbound, with Other Poems* (1820), which supplies our copy-text, though we have also consulted a draft in the Bodleian and fair copy of ll. 35–84 (both in *BSM* 5). *Norton* cites a work S. knew and admired, the song of the Nepheliads in part 2 of Leigh Hunt's 'The Nymphs', published in *Foliage* (1818), as the poem's most likely literary source; for a scientific source see the note to l. 18 below.

l. 7. *mother's.* The earth's.

l. 18. *pilot.* The positively charged electricity in the cloud, which reacts with the negatively charged electricity of 'Earth and Ocean', producing rain and thunderstorms. As the cloud is guided by the 'pilot', so 'Earth and Ocean' are guided by 'genii' (l. 23), 'the Spirit' (l. 28). *Norton* and

Webb cite Adam Walker's *A System of Familiar Philosophy*, 2 vols. (1799): 'water rises through the air, flying on the wings of electricity'. Walker had lectured both at Syon House Academy and Eton during S.'s years there.

l. 20. *at fits*. At intervals, randomly.

l. 23. *Lured by the love of the genii*. The attraction of 'pilot' and 'genii' is mutual, as suggested by this phrase, which refers both to the pilot's and the genii's love.

462 l. 33. *sailing rack*. Mass of clouds.

l. 34. *morning star*. The planet Venus (known as Hesperus, the evening star, at night).

l. 42. *depths*. The reading in the Bodleian fair copy; the copy-text has 'depth'.

l. 43. *airy nest*. A pun, the nest being both high in the air and made of air.

l. 44. *brooding dove*. An echo of the opening of *PL*, in which Milton invokes the 'Heavenly Muse' (identified with the Holy Spirit) which 'Dove-like sat'st brooding on the vast abyss | And mad'st it pregnant' (1. 21–2).

ll. 45–58. *That orbèd . . . moon and these*. See Wordsworth's 'A Night-Piece' in *Poems* (1815) for a comparable (and contrasting) scene of moon, stars, thinly textured cloud, and revelation.

l. 58. *paved with the moon and these*. The reflections of moon and stars ('these'), shining through 'rents' in the cloud, 'pave' the 'calm rivers, lakes, and seas'.

l. 59. *zone*. Belt or encircling band (like 'girdle' in next line).

463 l. 71. *sphere-fire*. The sun, a fiery sphere. The Bodleian fair copy and draft have 'sphere-fires', so there is a case for emendation.

l. 75. *pores*. Cloud-forming moisture (like 'sweat') is drawn from the earth's 'oceans and shores', as from the 'pores' of a body. *oceans*. The reading in the fair copy. The copy-text has 'ocean'.

l. 79. *convex gleams*. From the cloud's perspective the rays of the sun ('gleams') would look curved ('convex') as they spread over the earth, since the earth's atmosphere bends or refracts them as they enter it.

l. 81. *cenotaph*. An empty tomb, the previous line's 'dome of blue air', 'unbuilt' in the last line by the cloud's return.

To a Skylark. Composed near Leghorn in summer 1820, published with *Prometheus Unbound, with Other Poems* (1820), which supplies our copy-text, though we have also consulted S.'s fair copy in the Larger Silsbee Notebook at Harvard (MS. Eng. 258. 2; *MYR: Shelley* 5). Skylarks sing only in flight, often when too high to be seen.

l. 8. *cloud of fire*. A cloud illuminated by the sun, fiery.

464 l. 22. *silver sphere*. The morning star (Venus).

465 l. 66. *Hymenaeal.* Pertaining to a wedding; Hymen is the Greek god of marriage.

466 ll. 86–7. *We look . . . what is not.* S. may be alluding to a comparable distinction between humans and animals in *Hamlet*, 4. 4. 23–9.

l. 103. *harmonious madness.* S. may have taken this view of the poet from Plato's *Phaedrus*, which he had read in May 1819.

Ode to Liberty. Composed between March and July 1820, published in *Prometheus Unbound, with Other Poems* (1820), as the final poem in the volume; this volume supplies our copy-text, though we have also consulted a rough draft in the Bodleian (*BSM* 5), a transcript of ll. 1–21 by Mary S. in the Larger Silsbee Notebook at Harvard (MS Eng. 258. 2; *MYR: Shelley* 5), and S.'s translation into Italian of stanzas 1–13 and 19 in the Bodleian (*BSM* 21). The poem's occasion was the success of the Spanish Revolution begun on 1 January and issuing in a string of liberal reforms, including suffrage to all literate males, biennial parliaments, freedom of the press, and abolition of the Inquisition. The poem follows the progress of Liberty through history in the manner of Thomas Gray's tracing of 'The Progress of Poetry,' in his Pindaric Ode of 1754.

Epigraph. Taken from Canto 4, stanza 98 of Byron's *Childe Harold* (1818), the last of 21 stanzas tracing the struggle of liberty against tyranny.

l. 1. *vibrated.* Made animate; more specifically, 'emitted the electric charge of revolution whose current links nation with nation' (*Webb*). *again.* Perhaps referring to the earlier resistance of the Spanish people against the French in 1807–8.

467 l. 11. *Rapt it.* Made S.'s 'soul' (l. 5) rapt or awestruck.

ll. 5–15. *My soul . . . the same.* In these lines S.'s 'soul' is inspired in phrases drawn from both classical and biblical visionary poetry. *Webb* cites analogues from Pindar (*Nemeans*, 3. 80–82), Dante, and Revelation 16–17.

l. 18. *daedal.* Artfully constructed and adorned, like the work of Daedalus, master-craftsman of Greek mythology.

ll. 16–23. *The Sun . . . wert not.* A description of the Creation, described as 'a chaos and a curse' (l. 22) until redeemed by Liberty ('thou', l. 23).

468 l. 41. *sister-pest.* Religion; 'Pest' means pestilence, plague, curse.

l. 42. *pinions.* Wings.

l. 43. *Anarchs.* Tyrants, authors or agents of chaos, anarchy.

l. 47. *dividuous.* Broken up, or separated, one from the other, individual.

l. 58. *Parian stone.* The fine white marble favoured by Greek sculptors, quarried from the island of Paros.

l. 65. *Pave it . . . pavilions it.* The imagined city built by 'vision' (l. 61), likened to Athens.

l. 74. *that hill.* The Acropolis, site of the Parthenon and other public buildings decorated with sculptures of heroes and gods ('forms that mock the eternal dead | In marble immortality', ll. 73–4).

469 l. 92. *Maenad.* S.'s note, keyed to the end of this line, reads, 'See the Bacchae of Euripides'.

ll. 91–4. *Then Rome . . . unweanèd.* Though Athens ('thy dearest') was still devoted to Liberty ('From that Elysian food was yet unweaned'), Rome, too, drew inspiration ('the milk of greatness') from her, like one of the wolf cubs (the wolf was a symbol of Rome) suckled by Agave, Cadmus' daughter (hence 'Cadmaean'), and other ecstatic or possessed female followers of Dionysus ('Maenads') in Euripides' *Bacchae*.

l. 98. *Saintly Camillus . . . firm Atilius.* The general and statesman Marcus Furius Camillus, 'saviour of his country and second founder of Rome' (Livy, 5. 2), returned from voluntary exile to lead resistance to Rome's occupation by Gauls (*c.*390 BC); called 'saintly' because he refused an offer to use schoolchildren as hostages. 'Atilius' was Marcus Atilius Regulus (third century BC), Roman consul and a commander of the Roman expedition to Africa in the First Punic War; called 'firm' because, after he was captured by the Carthaginians and paroled to Rome to negotiate a peace, he kept his word and returned to them, despite advising the Romans to continue fighting and knowing his return meant certain death.

l. 100. *Capitolian throne.* The Capitoline hill in Rome, associated with the Republic.

ll. 103–4. *Palatinus sighed . . . Ionian song.* The Palatine hill, associated here with Empire, sighs in songs which echo those of Greek poets (as do the songs of Virgil and Horace, first poets of the Empire).

ll. 99–105. *But when tears . . . disown.* These lines trace Liberty's reluctant desertion of Rome as it grows from Republic to Empire.

l. 106. *Hyrcanian.* Refers to an area of Persia just south of the Caspian (Hyrcanian) Sea.

470 l. 115. *Scald's dreams . . . Druid's sleep.* Scalds (or 'skalds') were Norwegian and Icelandic poets; Druids were Celtic priests. Liberty plays no part in their dreams.

l. 119. *Galilean serpent.* The Christian religion.

l. 123. *Alfred's olive-cinctured brow.* King Alfred (848–99), king of the West Saxons from 871 to his death, poet and scholar; his brow is circled ('cinctured') with olive leaves, in ancient Greece the highest distinction of a citizen who deserved well of his country.

ll. 124–35. *And many . . . dome.* 'The rise of the communes, independent city-state republics in medieval Italy, led to the revival of the arts' (*Norton*). Presumably the 'warrior-peopled citadel[s]' of l. 124, likened to volcanoes rising out of the sea, are the republics of medieval Italy that fostered the arts.

470 l. 136. *Thou huntress . . . the Moon!* Liberty is swifter than Diana, goddess of the moon and of hunting.

l. 141. *Luther.* Martin Luther (1483–1546), leader of the Reformation in Germany, was partly a disciple of Liberty, helping to waken the nations from 'trance' (l. 143), but his lance, though capable of reflecting Liberty's 'lightning,' was 'leaden' (l. 142).

l. 145. *England's prophets.* See *A Philosophical View of Reform*: 'Shakespeare and Lord Bacon and the great writers of the age of Elizabeth and James I were at once the effects of this new spirit in men's minds, and the cause of its more complete development' (p. 638).

471 l. 149. *the sad scene.* The restoration of the Stuart monarchy.

l. 158. *the destroyer.* Death.

ll. 159–65. *When . . . eyes.* Liberty's rise, likened to that of the sun, is depicted in these lines as 'the Enlightenment and subsequent reform and revolutionary movements of the eighteenth century' (*Norton*).

l. 171. *Bacchanals of blood.* The excesses of the French Revolution, likened to those of the followers of Dionysus in Euripides' *Bacchae.*

l. 173. *Destruction's . . . brood!* The anti-revolutionary forces of Europe, both political ('sceptred slaves') and religious ('mitred brood').

l. 174. *one.* Napoleon.

472 l. 183. *Vesuvius wakens Etna.* 'The interconnection of the volcanic regions of the globe (which was first fully expounded by John Michell in 1760) provides a scientific basis for this image of a sympathetic network of revolutionary activity' (*Webb*).

ll. 185–6. *every Aeolian isle . . . Pelorus.* The islands from the Bay of Naples to Sicily. 'Aeolian' means wind-swept (from the Greek god of the winds, Aeolus). 'Pithecusa' is Ischia, west of Naples and Cumae; 'Pelorus' is Cape Faro, the north-east point in Sicily.

l. 189. *Her chains.* England's, 'threads' (in comparison to Spain's 'links of steel') because of her less tyrannical history.

l. 196. *Tomb of Arminius.* Germany; Arminius (18 BC–AD 19) was the Germanic tribal leader who freed Germany from Roman rule in AD 6.

l. 204. *thou.* Italy.

l. 216. *Ye.* 'The free' of l. 211.

l. 218. *gordian word.* 'KING' (l. 212); 'gordian' because difficult to undo, like the complicated knot of King Gordius of Phrygia; by cutting through it with his sword Alexander became emperor of Asia, as prophesied by an oracle (like the one heard by Liberty in l. 216).

473 l. 221. *The axes and the rods.* The *fasces* ('bundles', Lat.), a bundle of rods tied round with a red thong from which an axe projected, were assigned to the higher magistrates in ancient Rome as symbols of authority.

l. 224. *thou.* Liberty.

l. 233. *Power*. The nature of this power, a potential source of inspiration, is unspecified, though it is distinguished here from the 'aweless soul', an internal or human divinity.

l. 241. *He*. Either the 'aweless soul' or the 'Power unknown' of l. 233.

l. 252. *thy*. Art refers to itself as Nature's child; 'thy' means 'Nature's'.

l. 255. *thy gifts and hers*. Liberty's and Art's gifts.

474 l. 258. *Eoan*. Eastern, from Eos, the Greek name for Aurora, goddess of the dawn.

Sonnet ('Ye hasten to the grave!') Mary S. dates the poem to 1820. First published in *The Literary Pocket-Book for 1823* (1822). There is a transcription by S. in the Larger Silsbee Notebook at Harvard (MS Eng. 258. 2; *MYR: Shelley* 5) and one by S. in the Pierpont Morgan Library (MA 3223; *MYR: Shelley* 8). This latter transcription supplies our copy-text. The sonnet reverses the order of octave and sestet, and sustains its *b* rhyme from sestet to octave.

l. 1. *grave*. In Harvard MS, 'dead'; in copy-text, 'dead' and 'grave' are both cancelled.

475 l. 4. *Heart*. S.'s first thought was 'Sense'.

l. 5. *pale Expectation*. In Harvard, 'anticipation'.

Song ('Rarely, rarely comest thou'). Composed in Pisa, May 1820, according to S.'s note at the end of his transcription in the Larger Silsbee Notebook at Harvard (MS Eng. 258. 2; *MYR: Shelley* 5), which supplies our copy-text. The poem was first published in *PP*.

476 *Letter to Maria Gisborne*. The poem, written in June and posted in July 1820, was first published in incomplete form in *PP*. S.'s draft in the Bodleian can be consulted in *BSM* 14; there is also a transcription by Mary S. in the Huntington Library (HM 12338; *MYR: Shelley* 3), probably made in 1823, and a fair copy by John Gisborne in the Bodleian (Abinger Deposit d. 475), made in 1831, presumably from the copy sent by S. This last text serves as our copy-text, though we have also consulted the draft and Mary S.'s fair copy. *Letter to Maria Gisborne* was composed when the Shelleys were staying in the Leghorn house of their friends, John and Maria Gisborne, while the latter were visiting London. Maria had rejected a proposal of marriage by William Godwin after the death of Mary Wollstonecraft; she taught S. Spanish, principally so that the poet could read Calderón. Her son by an earlier marriage, Henry Reveley, was a nautical engineer. Helped by S., he had been designing a steamboat (which never materialized), and it is his workshop which S. describes in the poem. The poem only hints at the unhappiness that S. and Mary were experiencing in 1820. Mary was upset by Godwin's dire financial problems and attempts to borrow money. In a letter to the Gisbornes of 26 May 1820 S. describes Godwin as 'the only sincere enemy I have in the world' but asserts his 'admiration' for his father-in-law's 'intellectual powers, & even the moral

resources of his character' (*L* 2. 202, 203). Throughout, the poem asserts, through its very manner (which includes playful allusions to Spenserian romance), the improvisatory power of the creative imagination.

476 l. 1. *spider*. Jonathan Swift uses the spider as an emblem of the modern writer who spins meanings out of his own entrails (*The Battle of the Books*); S. reverses Swift's derogatory view of this activity.

l. 5. *whom . . . worm*. See Job 25: 6: 'How much less man, that is a worm? and the son of man, which is a worm?'

l. 7. *verse*. The reading in the draft and Gisborne fair copy; previous printed editions follow Mary S.'s 'rare' in the Huntington fair copy.

477 l. 10. *soft cell*. Cocoon from which S.'s winged 'living name' (l. 11) will emerge. *that*. 'This decaying form' (l. 6).

l. 15. *I wist*. I know.

l. 16. *mechanist*. One skilled in mechanics.

l. 17. *Archimedean*. The adjective is formed from Archimedes (*c*.287–212 BC), the Greek scientist and inventor.

l. 19. *gin*. Mechanical contrivance or trap.

l. 20. *figured spells*. Draft has 'written spells'.

l. 21. *Its way . . . sea*. Alludes to the steamboat which Henry Reveley had been planning with S.'s financial support; it was planned that the steamboat should ply between Leghorn and Marseilles.

ll. 23–4. *Vulcan . . . the Titans*. At Jove's command Vulcan had made an ever-turning wheel on which Ixion was bound, as well as the chains that tied Prometheus (one of the Titans) to his mountain.

l. 25. *St Dominic*. Dominic (1170–1221) was the founder of the Dominicans and associated with the Inquisition.

l. 27. *philanthropic council*. Ironic allusion to councils of the Catholic Church, particularly the Council of Trent (1545–63) which launched the Counter-Reformation.

ll. 33–4. *lamp-like Spain . . . hearth*. Alludes to the virtually bloodless Spanish Revolution in 1820, when, in response to widespread revolt, King Ferdinand re-established the Constitution (see headnote to 'Ode to Liberty', p. 780).

ll. 36–7. *utmost crag . . . Cornwall*. Alludes to the defeat of the Spanish Armada (1588) when many ships were wrecked off the coast of Cornwall and off coasts as far north as the Orkneys.

l. 37. *the storm-encompassed isles*. Either islands off the Cornish coast or islands further north, such as the Orkneys. In the Bodleian draft S. cancelled 'the' in favour of 'its'.

l. 45. *Proteus*. Greek god who could change his shape at will.

478 l. 51. *Tubal Cain.* See Genesis 4: 22: 'an instructer of every artificer in brass and iron'.

l. 55. *knacks.* Ingenious contrivances.

l. 56. *catalogize.* Make a catalogue of.

l. 59. *swink.* Labour. A term found in Spenser (see 'Prosopopoia: or Mother Hubberds Tale', l. 163: 'For they doo swinke and sweate to feed the other').

l. 65. *rouse.* Draught of drink; drinking-bout. See *Hamlet*, 1. 2. 127: 'the King's rouse'.

l. 75. *a rude idealism.* A rough notion or version.

l. 83. *statical.* Concerned with statics, bodies at rest or in equilibrium.

l. 84. *rosin.* Resin.

479 l. 95. *Laplace.* Marquis Pierre Simon de Laplace (1749–1827). French mathematician and astronomer. S. alludes to him in a note to section 6 of *Queen Mab* (not included here). *Saunderson.* Nicholas Saunderson (1682–1739), Cambridge mathematician, early teacher of Newtonian science, author of books on algebra and mathematical physics (see *Norton*). *Sims. Norton* suggests either Thomas Simpson (1710–61), author of books on algebra, geometry, and trigonometry, or Robert Simson (1687–1768), author of books on geometry and conic sections.

l. 98. *Baron . . . Memoirs.* Baron François de Tott's *Memoirs sur les Turcs et les Tartares* (1784).

l. 103. *as . . . mo.* Mo (or moe) means more. See Spenser, *FQ* 4. 1. 24: 'And eke of private persons many moe'.

l. 104. *womb of time.* See *Othello*, 1. 3. 358–9: 'There are many events in the womb of time.'

l. 106. *Archimage.* Alludes ironically to Archimago, the evil enchanter in *FQ*.

l. 114. *Libeccio.* The south-west wind.

480 l. 132. *quaint.* Delicately odd, with something of the older meanings of the word, 'wise, knowing' (*OED* 1).

l. 137. *second-sighted.* Able to perceive future or distant occurrences.

l. 142. *sad enchantress.* Memory.

l. 149. *transverse.* In crosswise direction.

l. 168. *visionary rhyme.* See *The Witch of Atlas*, l. 8.

481 l. 175. *indued.* Put on; learned.

l. 176. *a land . . . free.* See note to ll. 33–4 above.

l. 180. *My name is Legion.* The words of an 'unclean spirit' in Mark 5: 9; legion means numberless.

481 l. 181. *Calderon*. Pedro Calderón de la Barca (1600–81), the Spanish dramatist, and author of many *autos sacramentales* (religious plays), was much admired by S., who translated scenes from *El mágico prodigioso*, and comments in a letter of November 1820, 'I am bathing myself in the light & odour of the flowery & starry Autos' (*L* 2. 250).

ll. 184–5. *thou . . . nurse*. S. learned Spanish with Maria Gisborne.

ll. 193–5. *that great sea . . . more*. The shipwreck imagery picks up that in ll. 36–7.

ll. 196–201. *That which . . . dumb*. S.'s portrait of William Godwin, his father-in-law, alludes to Milton's self-portrait in *PL* 7. 24–6 as singing 'with mortal voice, unchanged | To hoarse or mute, though fallen on evil days, | On evil days though fallen'.

482 l. 210. *salt of the earth*. Alludes to Matthew 5: 13: 'Ye are the salt of the earth.'

l. 213. *Shout*. Robert Shout was a London maker of plaster copies of antique statues. See Keats's 'Sleep and Poetry', ll. 354–91, for an 'inventory of the art garniture', as Charles Cowden Clarke called it, in Hunt's Hampstead cottage.

l. 220. *duns*. Debt-collectors.

ll. 209–25. *You will see Hunt . . . tenderness*. Leigh Hunt (1784–1859), dedicatee of *The Cenci*, was a poet, journalist, and editor: his familiar style is an influence on S.'s poem.

ll. 226–32. *You will see Hogg . . . deep*. Thomas Jefferson Hogg (1792–1862) was S.'s closest friend at Oxford, from where he was expelled with S. Hogg lived with Jane Williams after her return from Italy and wrote an entertaining but unreliable biography of the poet.

l. 240. *camelopard*. Giraffe.

ll. 232–47. *And there . . . expectation*. Thomas Love Peacock (1785–1866), a close friend of S., was a comic novelist, who worked for the East India Company (hence 'the Indian air', l. 235) and on 22 March 1822 had married Jane Gryffydh, who came from Snowdonia in Wales (hence l. 239).

483 l. 250. *Horace Smith*. (1779–1849), poet, parodist (the author, with his brother James, of *Rejected Addresses* (1812)), and stockbroker. Smith was admired by S., who, according to Hunt in his *Autobiography*, ed. J. E. Morpurgo, London, 1949, said of him, 'he writes poetry and pastoral dramas, and yet knows how to make money, and does make it, and is still generous!' (p. 190).

l. 266. *Hackney coaches*. Horse-drawn carriages for hire.

l. 267. *lordly*. The draft reading; copy-text and Huntington manuscript read 'lonely'.

l. 272. *Pollonia*. Alludes to Apollonia Ricci, one of the daughters of the Gisbornes' landlord at Leghorn; Mary S. teasingly refers to Apollonia's (and her sister Carlotta's) supposed fondness for Henry Reveley: 'the Miss Riccis . . . greatly lament the Caro Giovane' (*MWSL*, I. 153).

ll. 272–3. *Or yellow-haired . . . thing*. This couplet is written in the margin of S.'s draft (*BSM* 14), and is not included in the Huntington manuscript; it was omitted from *PP* and Mary S.'s first 1839 edition.

l. 286. *contadino*. Italian peasant.

484 l. 294. *low-thoughted care*. See Milton, *Comus*, l. 6.

l. 305. *syllabubs*. A dish made of cream or milk flavoured, sweetened, and whipped to thicken it.

l. 308. *the Grand Duke's*. Belonging to Ferdinand III, Grand Duke of Tuscany.

l. 316. *they*. S.'s 'nerves' (l. 312). *laudanum*. Preparation of opium in liquid form.

l. 317. *Helicon*. A mountain which contained a spring sacred to the Muses. *Himeros*. 'A synonym of Love' (S.'s note).

l. 323. *'Tomorrow . . . new.'* S. quotes the last line (l. 193) of Milton's *Lycidas*.

To —— (Lines to a Reviewer). Published posthumously, under the signature [Σ], in *The Literary Pocket-Book* (1823), ed. Leigh Hunt (where it was titled 'To ——'); the poem is related to 'To —— (Lines to a Critic)' and the fragmentary 'Satire on Satire', both of which also reject hatred, and was probably composed in 1820 after S. exchanged letters with Southey, whom he suspected (incorrectly) of attacks on him in the *Quarterly Review*. Our copy-text is S.'s fair copy in the Bodleian on sheets torn—probably by Mary S. or Leigh Hunt—out of the Larger Silsbee Notebook at Harvard (see *MYR: Shelley* 5 for a photofacsimile). This fair copy is entitled 'To ——'. We have adopted this title, but appended to it in parentheses the title, 'Lines to a Reviewer', by which the poem is better known.

485 l. 12. *Narcissus*. S. is as unresponsive to the critic's hate as Narcissus was to Echo's love.

To —— (Lines to a Critic). Published posthumously in Hunt's *The Liberal*, No. 3, 1823 and in *PP*, where Mary Shelley dates it December 1817 (though recent editors date it rather later; it may have been composed in the wake of S.'s 1820 dispute with Southey; see headnote to 'To —— (Lines to a Reviewer)', above). There is a draft of the poem in the Bodleian (*BSM* 14), where it is entitled 'A Hate-Song'. Our copy-text is a fair copy in Mary S.'s hand, now in the Bodleian on sheets torn—probably by Mary S. or Leigh Hunt—from the Larger Silsbee Notebook at Harvard (see *MYR: Shelley* 5 for a photofacsimile of the manuscript). This fair copy is entitled 'To ——', the title we use, though we also append in parentheses the title of its first posthumous printing, by which it is better known. The poem was probably addressed to Southey, mentioned by name in 'Satire on Satire'.

485 l. 13. *prove*. S.'s draft has 'move'.

486 *The Witch of Atlas*. Written from 14 to 16 August 1820 after S. had visited a shrine at the top of Monte San Pellegrino in the previous three days. Sent to Ollier on 20 January 1821, with instructions that the poem should be published. Ollier did not publish the poem, which appeared in print for the first time in *PP* (without the introductory stanzas to Mary S.). The text in *PP* supplies our copy-text for the main part of the poem; the text in Mary S.'s 1839 editions supplies the copy-text for the introductory stanzas. Draft material survives in the Bodleian (*BSM* 5); there is also an intermediate fair copy in S.'s hand in the Bodleian (*BSM* 4). *The Witch of Atlas* is a comic epyllion (miniature epic poem). Its heroine can be interpreted as 'a personification of the imaginative faculty in its most airy abstractions' (Leigh Hunt, review of *PP*), but, as Hunt points out, the poem is highly aware of 'reality'; moreover, S.'s playful, metaphorical mode is at war with allegorical fixities of interpretation. If the poem's synthesis of classical, Egyptian, and mythological materials (drawn from Herodotus, Diodorus Siculus, Virgil, Ovid, Spenser, Milton, and others) makes it a *tour de force*, its suggestion that it is holding at arm's length 'the strife | Which stirs the liquid surface of man's life' (ll. 543–4) gives it a latent pathos. The poem's humour and use of *ottava rima* derive (and deviate) from two principal influences: the Italian poet Niccolo Fortiguerri, whose *Ricciardetto* had been read by S. and Mary in June and July 1820, and the Byron of *Beppo* (1818) and *Don Juan*, cantos 1 and 2 (1819). Just before writing *The Witch of Atlas*, S. composed his high-spirited *ottava rima* translation of Homer's 'Hymn to Mercury'.

ON . . . INTEREST. See Samuel Johnson (in *Lives of the Poets*) on *PL*: 'The want of human interest is always felt.'

l. 9. *the silken-wingèd fly*. See Spenser, *Muiopotmos*, l. 17, where the ill-fated Clarion (a butterfly trapped by a spider) is said to be the most 'favourable' and 'fair' (l. 20) 'Of all the race of silver-winged Flies' (l. 17).

l. 12. *the swan . . . dominions*. In classical mythology, the swan is sacred to Apollo, god of the sun.

l. 17. *a wingèd Vision*. May allude to *Laon and Cythna* (*The Revolt of Islam*) by whose reception S. had been disappointed.

487 l. 26. *Peter Bell*. See the notes to *Peter Bell the Third* (above).

l. 34. *Ruth or Lucy*. Female figures in Wordsworth's contributions to *Lyrical Ballads* (1800).

l. 40. *'looped . . . raggedness.'* S. quotes from *King Lear*, 3. 4. 32.

l. 42. *hyperequatorial*. Extremely equatorial, that is, very hot.

l. 44. *Scaramouch*. In Italian farce, a boastful coward who is constantly cudgelled by Harlequin. *in hue Othello*. Black, like Othello.

l. 46. *Primate*. Archbishop.

l. 47. *shrive.* Perform the office of a confessor.

l. 49. *at one birth.* See Milton, 'L'Allegro', l. 14: 'at a birth'.

l. 55. *lady-witch.* S. uses 'witch' primarily to mean a fascinating figure capable of magic. *Atlas' mountain.* Atlas, descended from the Titans, was forced by Zeus to bear the earth and heavens on his shoulders. He was changed into stone (and thus a mountain) by Perseus who showed him Medusa's head after Atlas had refused to give him shelter.

ll. 55–6. *A lady-witch . . . fountain.* Cf. the Massylian priestess, said by Dido to live 'where mightiest Atlas on his shoulders turns the sphere' (*Aeneid*, 4. 481–2) and to claim that 'her spells' can 'set free the hearts of whom she wills' or bring 'cruel love-pains' (4. 487–8).

488 l. 57. *Atlantides.* Daughters of Atlas and Hesperus, also known as the Hesperides, the Atlantides lived in a beautiful garden near Mt. Atlas.

ll. 58–64. *The all-beholding . . . away.* Modelled on the description in *FQ* 3. 6. 4–9 of how Chrysogonee was impregnated by the sun and gave birth to Belphoebe and Amoretta.

l. 70. *fit.* Capricious mood.

l. 73. *the Mother of the Months.* The moon.

ll. 73–4. *bent | Her bow.* Extended the curvature of its rim as it filled out from a crescent.

l. 74. *folding-star.* The evening star (Venus).

489 l. 89. *spotted camelopard.* A 'camelopard' is a giraffe. See Milton, *Comus*, l. 444, where Dian is said to tame 'the spotted mountain pard'.

l. 97. *The brinded lioness.* See Milton, *Comus*, l. 443 ('the brinded lioness'). 'Brinded' is an alternative of 'brindled', that is, brownish or tawny with streaks of other colour.

l. 99. *pard.* Leopard.

l. 105. *Silenus.* See note to *Prometheus Unbound*, 2. 2. 90 (p. 748).

l. 106. *wood-gods.* See *FQ* 1. 6. 9, where the 'wyld woodgods' pity Una; the episode is drawn on by S. elsewhere in this section of his poem.

l. 108. *Cicadae.* Transparent-winged, shrill-sounding insects.

l. 109. *Driope.* The consort of Faunus and beloved by Pan; see *FQ* 1. 6. 15. *Faunus.* Ancient and legendary king of Italy; worshipped as a god.

l. 113. *Universal Pan.* God of the woods and shepherds; The phrase occurs in *PL* 4. 266.

l. 116. *want.* *Norton* suggests 'mole' (*OED*, sb1); in context, though, a more usual sense—'desire for thing held necessary'—seems appropriate.

490 l. 125. *Priapus.* God of procreation and fertility, gardens, and vineyards.

490 l. 130. *pastoral Garamant*. The Garamantes are an African people (north central Libya), described by Herodotus in his *Histories*, 4, as 'having no weapons of war' and living a twenty-day journey from the foot of Atlas.

l. 133. *Polyphemes*. One-eyed giants, after Polyphemus in Homer, *Odyssey*, 9.

l. 134. *Centaurs*. Fabled creatures, half-horse, half-man, born from Ixion and Juno in the form of a cloud: hence described by Ovid, *Met*. 12 as 'half-man centaurs' and 'cloud-born centaurs'. *Satyrs*. Mythological woodland figures in human form with (in Roman accounts) goat's ears, tail, legs, and budding horns; associated with lechery.

ll. 135–6. *lumps . . . bird-footed*. See Herodotus' account of 'the dog-headed men and the headless that have their eyes in their breasts' (book 4).

ll. 145–7. *spindle . . . Long lines of light*. Possibly making playful use of a passage in Plato, *Republic*, 616b–c, where, in an account of the afterlife, there is mention of 'a straight shaft of light' and 'the spindle of Necessity' (see Robin Waterfield, trans. (Oxford, 1994), 454–6 for commentary).

l. 150. *belated*. Late-coming; tardy.

491 l. 156. *cells*. Small containers.

l. 169. *aviary*. Large cage or building for keeping birds.

l. 174. *vans*. Wings.

492 ll. 185–92. *Her cave . . . above*. These 'scrolls' were the work of a benevolent magician (the reverse of Spenser's malevolent Archimago in *FQ* 1), who lived in the Golden Age of Saturn, the loss of which led to the emergence of 'native vice', that is, evil that seems innate in human beings.

l. 195. *wizard*. Marvellous; magical.

493 l. 217. *Hamadryades*. Wood-nymphs.

l. 218. *Oreads*. Mountain-nymphs. *Naiads*. Nymphs of fountains and streams.

ll. 217–20. *The Ocean-nymphs . . . rocks*. See *FQ* 1. 6. 18: 'The wooddy Nymphes, fair Hamadryades, | Her to behold do thither runne apace; | And all the troupe of light-foot Naiades | Flocke all about to see her lovely face.'

l. 226. *Naiades*. Alternative spelling of 'Naiads' (for metre).

ll. 225–32. *This . . . dust*. According to Plutarch, nymphs enjoyed unfading youth for 9,720 years.

494 l. 253. *woof*. The weft, transverse threads woven into the warp to make a web (*OED*).

l. 270. *withal*. In addition; moreover.

l. 271. *tenour*. Settled or prevailing course.

l. 276. *asphodel*. Immortal flower in Elysium.

495 l. 283. *bearded star*. Comet.

l. 289. *Boat*. Compare this boat with the narrator's 'little Boat' in Wordsworth's *Peter Bell* (l. 4); Wordsworth thinks of sporting 'amid the boreal morning' (l. 97), but his boat flies off, indignant at the poet's mock-reproof for forgetting 'What on the earth is doing' (l. 125), and Wordsworth proceeds to tell his earth-bound story. *Vulcan*. Blacksmith god, husband of Venus.

l. 292. *sphere*. 'Spheres' were revolving globe-shaped shells in which, according to the Ptolemaic system, heavenly bodies were supposed to be set.

l. 312. *circumfluous*. Flowing around; Ocean was thought in ancient times to be a stream flowing round the world.

496 l. 317. *Evan's feet*. Bacchus' feet.

l. 318. *Vesta's sceptre*. Vesta was a Roman goddess of the hearth, represented as holding a sceptre in her left hand.

ll. 321–3. *by strange art . . . love*. See the account in *FQ* 3. 8. 6 of the creation of the false Florimell by a malevolent Witch from 'purest snow in massie mould congeald'; S.'s Witch adds 'fire' (l. 321) and 'liquid love' (l. 323).

l. 328. *Pygmalion*. Pygmalion fell in love with a sculpture of a young woman he had made, and prayed to Venus that his bride should be its 'living likeness'. Venus granted his prayer by making the statue come to life (Ovid, *Met*. 10); hence, 'vital stone' (l. 327).

l. 329–31. *A sexless thing . . . sex*. The Witch's creation is a hermaphrodite (see l. 422). In classical myth Hermaphroditus was the son of Hermes (Mercury) and Aphrodite (Venus); his body was joined to that of a nymph, Salmacis, who lusted passionately after him (Ovid, *Met*. 4). Presented as 'both super- and non-human' (Michael O'Neill, *Human Mind's Imaginings* (Oxford, 1989), 154), the hermaphrodite suggests art's possibilities and limits.

l. 338. *seventh sphere*. Sphere to which the planet Saturn is fixed; see note to l. 292.

l. 339. *lightnings*. Here the word is trisyllabic (for the metre); in l. 445 'lightning' is disyllabic.

497 l. 345. *And down the streams*. The Witch's journey involves a descent from the head of the Nile, finally ending up in human habitation.

l. 349. *pinnace*. Small boat.

l. 369. *prone*. With downward slope.

l. 374. *besprent*. Sprinkled.

498 l. 377. *cataracts*. Waterfalls.

l. 382. *sunbows*. Produced by the rainbow-like effect given by sunlight on spray.

498 l. 399. *rime*. Frost formed from fog or cloud.

499 l. 421. *amain*. Vehemently; in haste.

l. 423. *the Austral waters*. Waters to the south.

l. 424. *Thamondocana*. The old name of Timbuctoo, an 'African El Dorado' (Frederick S. Colwell, *Rivermen* (Kingston, 1989), 177).

l. 428. *Canopus*. A brilliant star in the Carina (Keel) part of the constellation Argo Navis.

500 l. 451. *Hydaspes' banks*. Hydaspes, a river in what is now north-east Pakistan, gives its name to a famous victory of Alexander the Great.

l. 453. *quips and cranks*. See Milton, 'L'Allegro', l. 27: 'Quips and cranks, and wanton smiles'. By the phrase Milton means 'witty remarks' and 'verbal tricks' (Oxford Authors edn., p. 745); S. suggests non-verbal capers and games.

l. 462. *meteor flags*. See Satan's 'ensign' which 'Shone like a meteor streaming to the wind' (*PL* 1. 536, 537).

l. 464. *mere*. Lake.

ll. 465–6. *tent . . . exhalations*. See Milton's account of Pandaemonium: 'a fabric huge | Rose like an exhalation' (*PL* 1. 710–11).

l. 467. *lambent*. Softly radiant.

l. 469. *cressets*. Metal vessels for holding oil or coal, usually mounted on a pole. There are 'blazing cressets' in *PL* 1. 728.

501 l. 482. *crudded rack*. A rack of clouds that looks as though coagulated like curd.

l. 484. *like Arion . . . back*. In Herodotus (book 1) Arion was a Greek musician and poet who, about to be killed by the sailors of his ship, sang a song and threw himself into the sea; a dolphin bore him away to safety on its back. See *Twelfth Night*, 1. 2. 14: 'like Arion on the dolphin's back'.

l. 488. *fire-balls*. Balls of lightning.

l. 498. *Nilus*. The river Nile.

l. 500. *Axumè*. Mountain in north-east Ethiopia.

502 l. 505. *Moeris . . . lakes*. Lake Moeris is above the city of Memphis; Lake Mareotis is located in the lower Nile Delta.

l. 511. *the great Labyrinth*. See Diodorus Siculus, 1. 61 and 66 for an account of this intricate, huge, and beautiful Egyptian tomb.

l. 512. *Osirian feast*. According to Diodorus Siculus, Osiris, the son of Zeus and Hera and husband of the moon-goddess Isis, was a sun-god who became a wise Egyptian king, making 'mankind give up cannibalism'. Killed by Typhon, his dismembered body was recovered by Isis and honoured in 'rites and sacrifices' that anticipate, in their emphasis on fertility, the Greek 'festivals connected with Dionysus' (1. 14, 22).

l. 515. *And . . . ever.* See Wordsworth, 'Elegiac Stanzas, Suggested by a Picture of Peele Castle', l. 8: 'It trembled, but it never passed away.'

l. 519. *fanes.* Temples.

503 l. 552. *weltering.* Tossing and tumbling. See Milton, *Lycidas*, l. 13: 'and welter to the parching wind'.

504 ll. 577–8. *Aurora . . . grey.* Aurora, goddess of the dawn, fell in love with Tithonus, and asked Zeus to grant him immortality (which Zeus did), but she forgot to ask for eternal youth for him as well.

ll. 579–82. *Or how . . . pay.* Adonis, loved by Venus, was killed while hunting; Proserpina, queen of the underworld and wife of Hades, gave him back life on the condition that he spend half the year with her and half with Venus.

l. 584. *The Heliad.* The Witch of Atlas herself, daughter of the sun, or Helios.

ll. 587–8. *holy Dian . . . Endymion.* Diana, goddess of the moon, fell in love with the shepherd Endymion as he lay asleep on Mount Latmos: the theme of Keats's *Endymion*.

505 ll. 602–3. *shook . . . of.* Borrowed the light from.

l. 626. *Translating . . . Greek.* For S., Greek is the language of enlightened thought.

l. 627. *god . . . bull.* The holy bull or bull-god of Memphis, Apis was supposed to be the living manifestation of Osiris. S. may pun on 'bull' meaning 'expression containing contradiction in terms' (*OED*).

l. 631. *hawks . . . geese.* Diodorus Siculus comments that 'the Egyptians venerate certain animals exceedingly' (1. 83). The hawk was sacred to the Egyptian god, Horus. The Egyptian goddess, Bastet (equated by the Greeks with Diana), was cat-headed. As *Norton* suggests, the geese seem to be included for an effect of deliberate bathos.

506 ll. 633–40. *The king . . . same.* In Spenser, *Prosopopoia*, the Ape puts on the Lion's crown and is worshipped (with the support of the Fox) by the other animals: the two in turn govern corruptly (see ll. 967 ff).

l. 642. *somnambulism.* Sleep-walking.

l. 644. *Like . . . abysm.* Vulcan made arms for the gods and heroes, with the help of the Cyclopes, in his forge under Mt. Etna.

l. 645. *Beating . . . ploughshares.* Isaiah 2: 4: 'and they shall beat their swords into ploughshares.'

l. 647. *I wis.* I think or know. S. plays on 'iwis' (one word) meaning 'surely' and having nothing to do with 'I'.

l. 648. *Amasis* (570–526 BC). Diodorus Siculus remarks that 'Amasis . . . ruled the masses of the people with great harshness' (1. 60).

507 l. 670. *weird.* Uncanny, unearthly.

507 l. 671. *garish.* Obtrusively bright.

508 *Song of Apollo.* Composed in 1820 as part of Mary S.'s unpublished blank-verse drama *Midas*, which, like its source, Ovid's *Met.* 11, tells of a singing contest between Pan and Apollo. This contest is judged by Tmolus, god of the mountain of the same name, who decides in Apollo's favour; when Midas, King of Phrygia, questions Tmolus' verdict, Apollo turns the king's ears into those of an ass. In Ovid, Pan sings first and Apollo has the last word; in Mary S.'s play, order and outcome are reversed. The songs were first published in *PP*. Our copy-texts for this poem and for the 'Song of Pan' are supplied by S.'s drafts in the Bodleian (*BSM* 5).

l. 22. *cinctured.* Girdled, encircled.

509 ll. 31–6. *I am the eye . . . belong.* Apollo describes himself as the god of light, music, poetry, prophecy, and medicine; his haughty, self-satisfied manner is traditional.

Song of Pan. See previous headnote. Pan, a late god in the Olympian pantheon, is associated with universal nature ('pan' is the Greek word for 'all'); the fertility of flocks; mountains, caves, and lonely places; and music, especially piping (whereas Apollo is associated with the lyre, as in Ovid, *Met.* 11: 'Old Tmolus bade the reed bow to the lyre').

l .11. See headnote to *Song of Apollo*; 'even old Tmolus', because Tmolus will champion Apollo.

l. 13. *Peneus.* A river in Thessaly that flows through the valley of Tempe, which lies between Mt. Olympus to the north-west and Mt. Ossa to the south-east.

l. 15. *Pelion's.* A wooded mountain in Thessaly; in their attempt to scale the heavens and overthrow the Olympians the Giants (see note to l. 27) piled Mt. Pelion on Mt. Ossa and Mt. Ossa on Mt. Olympus. We have retained this reading ('Pelion'), which is in *PP*, but see *BSM* 5, p. 373 for a discussion of the difficulty of deciphering the word in question in the copy-text.

l. 27. *giant wars.* The giants were sons of Gaia (Earth) and in post-Homeric legend were involved in several battles with the Olympians, first as allies (against the Titans) than as enemies; they were ultimately defeated by the Olympians with the aid of Heracles (Hercules), a mortal.

l. 30. *Maenalus.* A mountain sacred to Pan, in Arcadia, a mountainous region in the centre of the Peloponnese.

l. 31. *a maiden.* Syrinx, a nymph, was the maiden; when the gods turned her into a reed to escape Pan's pursuit, he used the reed to construct an elaborate musical pipe, which he named after her.

510 l. 34. *ye.* Apollo and Tmolus.

Sonnet: Political Greatness. Date of composition uncertain, probably sometime after July 1820; first published in *PP*, under the title 'Political Greatness'. There is draft material in the Bodleian (*BSM* 6). Our copy-text is a fair copy in S.'s hand in the Bodleian (*BSM* 22), with the title 'Political Greatness'. An earlier fair copy in the Larger Silsbee Notebook at Harvard in S.'s hand, entitled 'To the Republic of Benevento' (MS Eng. 258. 2; *MYR: Shelley* 5), provides a clue to the poem's context. Benevento, a town north-east of Naples, briefly established itself as a 'republic' in the wake of a popular revolt in July 1820 against the despotic Bourbon Ferdinand, King of Naples. This revolt was crushed by Austria in the spring of 1821, as was the republic.

l. 1. *Nor . . . nor.* Neither . . . nor.

l. 7. *fleet.* Hurry or hasten.

The Indian Girl's Song. Our copy-text for this version of the poem, making clear that the speaker is not the poet, is based on a manuscript in S.'s hand in the Bibliotheca Bodmeriana, Cologny-Genève (see *MYR: Shelley* 8), a manuscript probably written in 1820–1. Under the title 'The Indian Serenade' different versions of the poem can be found in the Larger Silsbee Notebook at Harvard (MS Eng. 258. 2; *MYR: Shelley* 5) and the Pierpont Morgan Library (MA 814; *MYR: Shelley* 8). A version of the poem appears to have been given to Sophia Stacey in 1819. The poem was first published in the *Liberal* (1823) as 'Song. Written for an Indian Air' and in *PP* as 'Lines to an Indian Air'.

l. 11. *champak.* Highly fragrant species of magnolia.

512 *Epipsychidion.* Finished by 16 February 1821 when S. sent Ollier the poem with instructions that it should be published anonymously, as it was later in the year: this first edition supplies our copy-text. The poem was inspired by the predicament of Teresa Viviani (known as Emilia by the Shelleys). The daughter of the Governor of Pisa, she was confined to a convent while awaiting the outcome of marriage arrangements made on her behalf. Though some material had already been drafted in late 1819 to early 1820 (see *BSM* 6 and 18), the poem was brought to completion after S. met Viviani towards the end of 1820 and developed an intense friendship with her, involving the exchange on both sides of writings in Italian: Shelley translated parts of *Prometheus Unbound* and 'Ode on Liberty'; Viviani gave Shelley her essay *Il vero amore*, quoted in the epigraph. The poem's riddling title is modelled, ironically, given the attack on marriage in ll. 148–59, on 'Epithalamion' ('a song about a wedding'); by analogy, S.'s title means 'a song about a little soul' or 'little soul song'. Mary S., who did not comment on the poem in her 1839 Notes, summed up S.'s relationship with Viviani as 'Italian platonics' (*MWSL* 1. 223). S. called *Epipsychidion* 'an idealized history of my life and feelings' (*L* 2. 434). The description anticipates S.'s description in *A Defence of Poetry* of Dante's *Vita Nuova*, a major influence on the poem, as 'the idealized history of that period, and those intervals of [Dante's] life which were dedicated to love' (p. 690). S. asserted to John Gisborne that 'The Epipsychidion is a mystery—As to real flesh & blood, you know that I do not deal in those articles'; that the poem was being reduced to a tale of 'a servant girl & her sweetheart'; and that he intended

'to write a Symposium of my own to set all this right' (*L* 2. 363). This 'Symposium'—akin to Dante's *Convivio*—was never composed and S. soon grew disillusioned with the poem and its object (see *L* 2. 434), instructing Ollier to withdraw from circulation any remaining copies.

512 *Epigraph*. Quoted from Teresa Viviani, *Il vero amore*: 'The loving soul launches itself outside creation, and creates for itself in the infinite a world all its own, very different from this dark and frightening abyss' (editors' trans.).

Advertisement. the Sporades. Islands grouped together in the Aegean Sea; there are four main islands; round these, and mostly uninhabited, are many small islands and rocky outcrops.

Vita Nuova. S. read Dante's poem to Mary S. on 31 January 1821.

gran vergogna . . . intendimento. Quoted from *Vita Nuova*, section 25: 'deep shame were it to him who should rhyme under cover of a figure or of a rhetorical colour and, afterwards, being asked, knew not how to strip such vesture from his words, in such wise that they should have a real meaning.'

Voi . . . movete. The first line of the Canzone at the head of Dante's *Convivio*, 2: S. translated the Canzone, rendering the first line thus: 'Ye who intelligent the third Heaven move'.

513 *My Song . . . beautiful*. S.'s translation of the last stanza of 'Ye who intelligent the third Heaven move'. S.'s major change is the addition of the words 'tell them that they are dull'.

l. 1. *that orphan one*. Either S.'s or Mary S.'s spirit.

l. 2. *Whose . . . on*. Either (if the 'orphan one' refers to S.) the 'empire' of his name ('Percy' in Italian (*persi*) means 'lost') that provokes her compassionate tears. Or (if the 'orphan one' refers to Mary) the 'empire' of Mary's title as wife or Mrs Shelley, a title that provokes envious tears.

514 l. 44. *unvalued*. Both great and unmerited.

l. 45. *Would . . . mother!* See the Song of Solomon 8: 1: 'O that thou wert as my brother, that sucked the breasts of my mother!'

l. 55. *grey style*. The manner of traditional love-poetry.

l. 58. *A well . . . happiness*. See the Song of Solomon 4: 12, where the 'sister' is a 'spring shut up, a fountain sealed'.

l. 60. *A Star*. The pole star.

515 l. 72. *Stranger*. Shelley's draft has 'Reader'.

l. 85. *the sense*. The means by which sensation is experienced. See also l. 91.

l. 100. *quiver*. In the process of redrafting, Shelley failed to notice the lack of agreement between singular noun and plural verb.

516 l. 117. *the third sphere*. That of Venus.

l. 122. *Anatomy*. Skeleton.

517 l. 162–73. *Love . . . eternity*. With heterodox wit, the passage reworks Dante, *Purg*. 15. 46–75, where Virgil explains that in heaven love is unexclusive and infinite.

l. 185. *the eternal law*. See Keats's 'Hyperion', 2. 228–9: ''tis the eternal law | That first in beauty should be first in might.'

518 l. 213. *that best philosophy*. Refers to the ability to wrest value out of 'this cold common hell, our life' (l. 214) rather than to any philosopher's system of ideas.

l. 222. *Hesper's setting sphere*. The evening star.

519 l. 249. *wintry forest*. See the *selva oscura* (dark wood) in Dante, *Inf*. 1. 2.

520 l. 268. *idol of my thought*. 'Ideal image produced by and nurtured in my mind'. See S.'s 'On Christianity': 'Every human mind has, what Lord Bacon calls its *idola specus*, peculiar images which reside in the inner cave of thought' (*Murray*, p. 261).

l. 277. *One*. Usually identified with Mary S.

l. 295. *I was laid asleep*. An echo, ironic in effect, of Wordsworth's 'Tintern Abbey', ll. 46–7 ('we are laid asleep | In body, and become a living soul').

l. 304. *The wandering . . . mother*. Alludes to S.'s first wife Harriet Westbrook, whom he left for Mary S. in 1814, and by whom S. had two children, Ianthe and Charles; he was denied custody of the children after Harriet's suicide in 1816.

521 l. 312. *Tempest*. This may allude to Eliza Westbrook, older sister of Harriet S.; Shelley viewed her as hostile. *She*. Probably alludes to Harriet Shelley.

ll. 308–19. *What . . . conceal*. This passage probably alludes, in a highly metaphorical way, to events in S.'s life in 1816 and 1817.

l. 345. *Twin Spheres*. Emily (the sun) and Mary (the moon).

522 ll. 368–73. *Thou . . . again!* Alludes to Claire Clairmont, Mary S.'s half-sister; she had a daughter, Allegra, by Byron, after a brief affair with him. Her presence in the Shelley household was the source of difficulty between her and Mary; as a result, she was living in Florence when the poem was being written. S. was close to Claire and negotiated on her behalf with Byron.

523 l. 412. *halcyons*. Seabirds mythically supposed to have the power to calm waves and winds.

l. 422. *Ionian*. Ionia was the name of the colony in western Asia Minor and neighbouring islands occupied by Hellenic settlers from Attica and the northern coast of the Peloponnesus.

524 l. 445. *peopled with sweet airs*. See *The Tempest*, 3. 2. 130–1, 'The isle is full of noises, | Sounds, and sweet airs, that give delight and hurt not.'

524 l. 459. *that wandering Eden Lucifer*. 'Lucifer' is Venus as the morning star, described with a flicker of irony (given Lucifer's other identity as the leader of the fallen angels), as 'that wandering Eden'.

525 l. 492. *sister and his spouse*. See the Song of Solomon 4: 9: 'Thou hast ravished my heart, my sister, my spouse.'

526 l. 507. *Parian*. Of the island of Paros in the Aegean, famed for white marble.

l. 540. *Conscious*. Aware, but also 'co-knowing', knowing as though they were one person.

528 l. 601. *Marina, Vanna, Primus*. Mary S.; Jane Williams; Edward Williams. Alludes to a sonnet from Dante to Cavalcanti, translated by S. (and included in the *Alastor* volume), in which Dante appeals to 'Vanna and Bice and my gentle love' (l. 10).

ll. 592–604. *Weak Verses . . . Love's*. This envoi is modelled on Dante's addresses to the poems of the *Vita Nuova*.

529 *Adonais*. Written between April 1821 and June 1821, *Adonais*, an elegy for John Keats, who had died in Rome in February 1821, was published in Pisa in July 1821. S. was pleased with the first edition (see *L* 2. 311), which, with a few emendations from *MWS (1)*, supplies our copy-text. There is a good deal of relevant manuscript material in the Bodleian (see *BSM* 7 and 14). S. saw Keats as persecuted and driven to an untimely death by hostile reviews, especially the review of *Endymion* in the *Quarterly Review* (April 1818), where the anonymous reviewer (John Wilson Croker) stigmatized Keats as 'a disciple of the new school . . . of Cockney Poetry' and asserts that 'our author . . . has no meaning'. Feeling himself to be similarly ill-used, S.'s anger at Keats's treatment duplicates the anger he felt on his own behalf. Yet the 'interposed stabs on the assassins of [Keats's] peace and of his fame' (*L* 2. 297) are only part of a poem described by S. as 'a highly wrought *piece of art*' (*L* 2. 294): this artistry shows in the original way that the poem (written in Spenserian stanzas) fulfils elegy's traditional task of supplying consolation in the last movement (stanzas 39–55) in which the idea of an afterlife for Adonais is evoked in language that reworks Platonic and Christian images and ideas, but locates permanence in the enduring significance of great poetry. The poem's title, as Earl Wasserman suggests in *Shelley: A Critical Reading* (Baltimore, 1971), probably conflates the Greek 'Adonis' with the Hebrew 'Adonai', meaning 'Lord'. Other influences include pastoral elegies by Bion and Moschus, Milton's *Lycidas*, and Spenser's *Astrophel*. Dante's *Paradiso* comes to the fore in the poem's closing stanzas. Extensive commentary is provided in Anthony D. Knerr (ed.), *Shelley's 'Adonais': A Critical Edition* (New York, 1984) (hereafter *Knerr*).

Epigraph. S. translated these lines as follows: 'Thou wert the morning star among the living, | Ere thy fair light had fled;— | Now, having died, thou art as Hesperus, giving | New splendour to the dead.'

Preface. The Greek is from Moschus' *Lament for Bion*, which translates: 'Poison, Bion, poison came to your lips, | and you took it. How could it touch | such lips without becoming nectar? | And what man on earth could be so vicious | as to mix poison and give it you | when you asked? He has poisoned music' (*Greek Pastoral Poetry*, trans. Anthony Holden (Harmondsworth, 1974)).

prove. Seemingly another instance of lack of agreement between noun and verb in S., but it is possible that an ellipsis ('should prove') is to be understood.

Hyperion. Published in Keats's *Lamia, Isabella, and Other Poems* (1820) and admired by S. as being 'in the very highest style of poetry' (*L* 2. 252–3).

on the —— of —— 1821. S. omits the precise date of Keats's death (23 February), presumably because he was not certain of it.

cemetery . . . protestants. The Cimitero Acattolico in Rome; S.'s son William was buried there (a fact alluded to in stanzas 49 and 51).

in love with death. See Keats's 'Ode to a Nightingale', l. 52: 'I have been half in love with easeful Death'.

530 *know not what they do*. See Luke 23: 34. One of a number of biblical allusions in the Preface turned ironically against those who disliked Keats's poetry, according to a cancelled draft of the Preface, solely because the poet was associated with Leigh Hunt, William Hazlitt, and 'other enemies of despotism & superstition'.

penetrable stuff. Ultimately *Hamlet*, 3. 4. 35; also quoted by Byron in his *English Bards and Scotch Reviewers* (l. 393; line number from Oxford Authors edn.) in a passage relevant to *Adonais*.

One . . . calumniator. Alludes to Robert Southey; S. mistakenly thought Southey was the author of a hostile review of *The Revolt of Islam* for the *Quarterly Review* in 1819.

Paris . . . Mr Howard Payne. *Paris in 1815* (1817) by George Croly (who gave *Adonais* a bad review in *Blackwood's*); *Woman*, a poem (1810) by Eaton Stannard Barrett; *Ilderim: A Syrian Tale*, part of *Eastern Sketches in Verse* (1816) by H. Galley Knight; *Mrs Lefanu*: possibly Alicia Lefanu (1753–1817), author of romances (see *Knerr*); *John Howard Payne*, an American dramatist who courted Mary S. after S.'s death.

the Rev. Mr Milman. Henry Hart Milman, author and contemporary of S. at Eton and Oxford; S. thought (incorrectly) that he might have written the review in the *Quarterly Review* mentioned above, after his suspicions had moved away from Southey (see *L* 2. 298–9).

What gnat . . . camels? See Matthew 23: 24: 'Ye blind guides, which strain at a gnat, and swallow a camel.'

Against . . . stone. See John 8: 7: 'He that is without sin among you, let him first cast a stone at her.'

530 *you have spoken . . . none.* See *Hamlet*, 3. 2. 366: 'I will speak daggers to her, but use none.'

The circumstances . . . press. S. refers to a letter from the Revd Robert Finch to John Gisborne, who passed it on to him.

Mr Severn. Joseph Severn (1793–1879), a painter and Keats's companion throughout his final months.

'such . . . of.' See *The Tempest*, 4. 1. 156–7: 'We are such stuff | As dreams are made on'.

531 ll. 1–2. *I weep . . . Adonais!* See Bion's *Lament for Adonis*, ll. 1–2: 'I mourn Adonis dead—loveliest Adonis— | Dead, dead Adonis'; S.'s translation (*MYR: Shelley* 8).

l. 5. *compeers.* Equals, peers. They are 'obscure' because, unlike the 'sad Hour', they have not been singled out ('selected', l. 3) for such duties of mourning.

l. 10. *mighty Mother.* Urania.

ll. 10–12. *Where . . . darkness?* See *Lycidas*, ll. 50–1: 'Where were ye nymphs when the remorseless deep | Closed o'er the head of your loved Lycidas?'

l. 12. *Urania.* Classical muse of astronomy, and also, more relevantly, the muse of sublime poetry for Dante and Milton (see *Purg*. 29. 41–2 and *PL* 7. 1–12). She assumes the place of Venus/Aphrodite in S.'s reworking of the original myth of Adonis.

l. 17. *corse.* Corpse.

l. 26. *Deep.* Abyss or pit—in effect, grave.

532 ll. 29–36. *He died . . . light.* These lines describe and praise Milton, isolated yet 'unterrified' after the Restoration. He is the 'third among the sons of light' because he is, for S., the greatest epic poet after Homer and Dante.

ll. 38–41. *happier they . . . perished.* Lesser poets whose 'tapers' still 'burn', unlike greater poets whose works have been lost.

ll. 48–9. *Like a pale flower . . . dew.* Alludes to the close of Keats's *Isabella* (1820).

l. 51. *extreme.* Utmost.

l. 55. *high Capital.* Rome, where Keats died. Milton (*PL* 1. 756) uses the phrase to describe Pandaemonium.

l. 63. *liquid.* Clear, undisturbed.

533 l. 72. *o'er . . . draw.* In the first printing, the relevant text read 'o'er his sleep the mortal curtain draw'.

l. 75. *flocks.* That is, the 'quick [living] Dreams' of l. 73, who take the place of the 'Loves' that mourn Adonis in Bion.

l. 80. *sweet pain.* The 'pain' is 'sweet' because the 'Dreams' have been imbued by Adonais with poetic 'music' (l. 77).

l. 84. *Our love . . . dead.* See *Lycidas*, l. 166: 'For Lycidas your sorrow is not dead'.

l. 94. *anadem.* Garland worn as a headband.

534 l. 100. *Splendour.* See Dante's 'splendori', in *Par.* (e.g. 9. 13) and discussed in the *Convivio*, 3. 14. 29–50, where 'splendour' is defined as reflected light.

l. 107. *clips.* 'Embraces' is the dominant sense, though 'cuts off' is another possible meaning.

535 ll. 132–5. *Since she . . . hear.* Alludes to the myth of Echo and Narcissus: Echo was a nymph who fell in love with Narcissus; when her love was not returned by Narcissus, who was in love with his reflection, she wasted away until she became merely a voice (see Ovid, *Met.* 3).

ll. 145–6. *Thy spirit's sister . . . pain.* Alludes to Keats's 'Ode to a Nightingale'; 'lorn' may allude to 'forlorn' in Keats's poem, ll. 70, 71.

l. 151. *Albion.* England. *the curse of Cain.* Cain, the first murderer, was condemned by God to be 'a fugitive and a vagabond' (Genesis 4: 12).

l. 160. *brere.* Archaic form of 'briar'.

536 l. 177. *that alone which knows.* Consciousness, the mind.

ll. 178–9. *as a sword . . . lightning.* See Byron's *Childe Harold*, 3. 97, and his 'So, we'll go no more a roving'.

l. 179. *sightless.* Invisible, but also blind.

l. 195. *sister's song.* The Echo (ll. 15–18) repeating Adonais's 'melodies' (l. 16).

l. 198. *fading Splendour.* Urania.

537 l. 208. *Out of . . . Paradise.* Urania's journey to Adonais is modelled on Venus' journey to Adonis in Bion.

l. 212. *Palms.* Soles of the feet.

ll. 226–7. *Stay . . . live.* Like the whole stanza, these lines are close to Bion ('Wait yet a while, Adonis—oh, but once, | That I may kiss thee now for the last time'; S.'s translation).

l. 228. *heartless.* Having lost heart.

538 l. 238. *the unpastured dragon.* The hostile critic, responsible, in Shelley's view, for Keats's premature death; 'unpastured' means 'unfed'.

l. 240. *mirrored shield.* Alludes to Perseus' defence against Medusa, whose looks turned the beholder to stone.

l. 250. *The Pythian of the age.* Byron, who confronted the adverse reviewers of his *Hours of Idleness* volume in his satire *English Bards and Scotch Reviewers* in a way that is compared to the slaying by Apollo of the serpent Python (Apollo 'known | As Pythian from that serpent overthrown', Ovid, *Met.* 1). Apollo shot 'a thousand arrows'; Byron only needed 'one' (l. 250).

538 ll. 253–61. *'The sun . . . night.'* The 'sun' is a 'godlike mind' or great poet; the 'swarms' are lesser poets and critics who 'dimmed or shared its light' (l. 260); they vanish when the sun sinks and joins the 'immortal stars' (l. 261) (other great writers).

l. 262. *mountain shepherds.* Fellow-poets, as in other pastoral elegies, such as *Lycidas* with its 'woeful shepherds' (l. 165).

539 l. 264. *Pilgrim of Eternity.* Byron, who speaks in *Childe Harold*, 3. 70 of 'wanderers o'er Eternity | Whose bark drives on and on' (an image recalled in the final stanza of *Adonais*).

l. 268. *Ierne.* Ireland.

l. 269. *The sweetest lyrist.* Thomas Moore, author of *Irish Melodies*, a collection of lyrical poems (hence 'lyrist').

l. 271. *one frail Form.* Shelley himself.

l. 276. *Actaeon-like.* Actaeon, out hunting, saw the goddess Diana naked; she punished him by turning him into a stag, after which he was chased and killed by his own hounds (Ovid, *Met.* 3).

l. 280. *pardlike.* A 'pard' is a leopard, sacred to Dionysus.

l. 283. *superincumbent.* Lying on, pressing down upon.

l. 289. *pansies.* Associated with thoughts, as in *Hamlet*, 4. 5. 174.

ll. 291–2. *a light spear . . . grew.* Suggests the 'thyrsus', or staff carried by Dionysus and his followers.

l. 297. *A herd-abandoned . . . dart.* See William Cowper's self-portrait: 'I was a stricken deer, that left the herd | Long since' (*The Task*, 3. 108–9; quoted from *The Complete Poetical Works*, ed. H. S. Milford (London, 1905)).

540 l. 298. *partial.* Prejudiced. The 'frail Form' takes Adonais' part against the hostile reviewers; his doing so is motivated by fellow-feeling (see l. 300).

l. 306. *Cain's or Christ.* In a letter to John Taaffe, S. commented: 'The introduction of the name of *Christ* as an antithesis to *Cain* is surely any thing but irreverence or sarcasm' (*L* 2. 306).

l. 312. *He.* Leigh Hunt, who encouraged Keats and promoted his poetry.

l. 319. *nameless worm.* The anonymous reviewer of Keats's *Endymion* for the *Quarterly Review*.

l. 327. *noteless.* Without distinction.

541 l. 336. *wakes or sleeps.* S. takes a more unequivocal position in l. 343.

l. 337. *Thou . . . now.* See *PL* 4. 828–9: 'Know ye not me? Ye knew me once no mate | For you, there sitting where ye durst not soar'.

l. 338. *Dust to the dust!* The phrase occurs in the service for the Burial of the Dead in the Book of Common Prayer.

l. 339. *the burning fountain.* The image of spirit as fire derives from Plotinus and the Platonic tradition. See S.'s reference in 'On Christianity' to 'The unobscured irradiations from the fountain fire of all goodness' (*Murray*, p. 255).

l. 362. *Mourn not for Adonais.* Reverses the injunction in l. 2.

542 l. 372. *night's sweet bird.* The nightingale.

l. 381. *the one Spirit's plastic stress.* See Coleridge's 'The Eolian Harp', l. 47: 'Plastic and vast, one intellectual breeze'; 'plastic' means 'shaping' or 'moulding'.

ll. 381–3. *while . . . wear.* See S.'s essay 'On the Devil, and Devils': 'But the Greek philosophers . . . accounted for evil by supposing that . . . God in making the world . . . moulded the reluctant and stubborn materials ready to his hand into the nearest arrangement possible to the perfect archetype existing in his contemplation' (*Clark*, p. 266).

543 l. 397. *inheritors of unfulfilled renown.* Those who inherit the condition of incomplete fame, either because they died before receiving due recognition, or because they died before realizing their creative potential.

l. 399. *the Unapparent.* S. may have shaped his noun from *PL* 7. 103 ('the unapparent deep') or Wordsworth's *The Excursion*, 9. 605 ('the unapparent fount of glory'). *Chatterton.* Thomas Chatterton (1753–1770), to whose memory Keats dedicated *Endymion*, died at the age of 17; he was, until recently, supposed to have committed suicide.

l. 401. *Sidney.* Sir Philip Sidney (1554–86), poet, soldier, and courtier.

l. 404. *Lucan.* Roman poet (AD 39–65) and author of the *Pharsalia*; he committed suicide when his part in a conspiracy against Nero was discovered. *by his death approved.* The phrase probably distances S. from the view of Suetonius who accuses Lucan of having falsely incriminated his mother Attilla in a cowardly attempt to save himself.

l. 407. *effluence.* Literally 'flowing out'; influence.

l. 413. *an Heaven of song.* Alludes to and adapts the Ptolemaic system, used by Dante, according to which there are a series of heavens.

l. 414. *Vesper.* Hesperus. See the poem's epigraph.

l. 417. *pendulous.* Suspended, oscillating.

ll. 422–3. *And keep . . . brink.* Shelley urges the 'Fond wretch' (l. 416) to keep his heart light (remain light-hearted, cheerful) lest his hopes (probably of immortality, a world better than this) lure him dangerously towards 'the brink' (tempt him towards self-destruction).

l. 424. *Rome.* See S.'s letter (in December 1818): 'Rome is a city as it were of the dead, or rather of those who cannot die' (*L* 2. 59).

544 l. 439. *a slope of green access.* See S.'s acccount of the Protestant Cemetery as 'a green slope near the walls, under the pyramidal tomb of Cestius . . . the most beautiful & solemn cemetery I ever beheld' (*L* 2. 59–60).

544 l. 442. *grey walls.* Of Rome.

l. 444. *one keen pyramid.* The tomb of Caius Cestius, a Roman tribune during the first century BC (see Preface, second paragraph).

545 l. 463. *Stains.* Enriches or disfigures.

ll. 460–4. *The One remains . . . fragments.* See *Par.* 29. 142–5: 'See now the height and breadth of the eternal worth, since it hath made itself so many mirrors wherein it breaketh, remaining in itself one as before', and Southey's *Thalaba*, 5: 'The many-coloured domes | Yet wore one dusky hue'.

l. 477. *No more . . . together.* See Matthew 19: 6: 'What therefore God hath joined together, let not man put asunder.'

l. 478. *That Light . . . Universe.* See *Par.* 1. 1–2 ('The All-mover's glory penetrates through the universe').

l. 486. *Consuming . . . mortality.* See *Par.* 33. 31–3, where St Bernard prays to Mary on Dante's behalf that 'thou do scatter for him every cloud of his mortality with prayers of thine, so that the joy supreme may be unfolded to him'.

l. 487. *The breath . . . song.* Possibly alludes to the 'Ode to the West Wind'.

ll. 488–90. *my spirit's bark . . . given.* See *Par.* 2. 1–6: 'O ye who in your little skiff, longing to hear, have followed on my keel that singeth on its way, turn to revisit your own shores; commit you not to the open sea; for perchance, losing me, ye would be left astray.'

546 *To Night.* Composed 1821, first published in *PP*. Our copy-text is S.'s fair copy in the Larger Silsbee Notebook at Harvard (MS Eng. 258. 2; *MYR: Shelley* 5).

547 *The Aziola.* Probably composed in 1821, first published in *The Keepsake for 1829* (1828). There is a draft in S.'s hand of the first stanza and the last two lines in the Bodleian (*BSM* 21) and complete transcriptions by Mary S. in the Bodleian (*Massey*) and in the Pierpont Morgan Library (MS PM; *MYR: Shelley* 8), and an incomplete transcription by Mary S. in the Bodleian (*BSM* 2). Our copy-text is based on the Pierpont Morgan transcription; we have also consulted the draft. The title refers to the 'assiolo' or small owl.

548 *Hellas.* 'I am just finishing a dramatic poem called *Hellas* upon the contest now waging in Greece—a sort of imitation of the Persae of Aeschylus' (*L* 2. 363–4); so S. wrote to John Gisborne from Pisa on 22 October 1821. Sent to Ollier on 11 November, the poem was published in 1822, with some prudential cuts made by the publisher (S. had indicated that cuts to the Notes were permissible: see *L* 2. 365). S. received his copy in April and wrote to Gisborne that the poem was 'prettily printed, & with fewer mistakes than any poem I ever published' (*L* 2.

406); his short list of errata, sent to Ollier on 11 April, and the press copy manuscript are now in the Huntington Library (HM 329 and HM 20152; *MYR: Shelley* 3). The Bodleian holds drafts of the poem (*BSM* 16) and of some of the Notes and the title-page (*BSM* 21). We have taken the first edition as our copy-text, restoring suppressed material and consulting the drafts and the press copy manuscript. *Hellas* is dedicated to Prince Alexandros Mavrokordatos (Alexander Mavrokordato), the central figure of a group of Greeks exiled in Pisa; S. met him in December 1820. Mavrokordatos, who went in June 1821 to fight in the War of Greek Independence that broke out earlier that year, would later become prime minister of Greece after it had achieved independence. One of the purposes of *Hellas* was to mobilize British opinion on the side of the Greeks; at the outset of the war, the British were neutral. It is apparent from the finally discarded but extensive 'Prologue' (see Thomas Hutchinson (ed.), G. M. Matthews (corr.), *Shelley: Poetical Works* (London, 1970), for a text and *BSM* 16 for relevant draft material) that a point of departure for S. in conceiving *Hellas* was Goethe's *Faust*, part 1. But, as S. indicates, the structure of the published version (his second 'lyrical drama') is based on Aeschylus' *Persians*, in which the central figure is the Persian commander, Xerxes, who learns of the present and future defeats of his army through a series of messengers and the ghost of his predecessor, Darius. Like *Persians*, *Hellas* obeys the unities of time, action, and place, and explores the overthrow of tyranny from the perspective of the tyrant. The work sees history as a cycle of destruction and renewal, and offers a more favourable if strictly qualified view of Christianity than one finds elsewhere in S.'s poetry. Valuable information about the War of Greek Independence is provided in William St Clair, *That Greece Might Still Be Free* (London, 1972).

Epigraph. 'This day shall victory bring', Sophocles, *Oedipus at Colonus*, 1078.

Dedication. Hospodar. A word meaning 'lord', used for the governors of Wallachia and Moldavia.

549 *Preface. the prize . . . goat*. A goat is thought to have been the prize for the best tragedy (whose etymology has been traced to 'goat-song') at dramatic festivals in honour of Dionysus.

the Aristarchi . . . of the hour. Aristarchus of Samothrace (*c*.220–143 BC) was a notoriously harsh critic of Greek literature.

The only 'goat-song' . . . attempted. S. alludes to *The Cenci*.

display of newspaper erudition. In particular, S. relied on the *Examiner*, which was strongly pro-Greek and opposed to Britain's non-interventionist policy.

their defeat in Wallachia. At the battle of Dragashan ('battle | Of Bucharest', ll. 362–3); see ll. 373–457. Wallachia was a Turkish province north of the Danube, now part of Romania.

550 *Anastasius*. A novel by Thomas Hope, published anonymously in 1819: 'a faithful picture they say of modern Greek manners' (S. in *L* 2. 332).

551 *Should the English . . . foresee and dread*. This paragraph was left out of the first edition by Ollier.

Scene. Seraglio. The part of the Sultan's palace in which the women were secluded.

Chorus of Greek Captive Women. This chorus allows S. to voice 'lyrics of affirmation' (Carl Woodring, in *Norton*, p. 676). Aeschylus' chorus (by contrast) is Persian.

552 l. 16. *Samian*. From the island of Samos in the Aegean.

553 l. 50. *Imaus*. The Himalayas. In *PL* 3. 431, Satan is compared to 'a vulture on Imaus bred'.

l. 54. *Thermopylae*. Site of a heroic last stand (480 BC) by Leonidas of Sparta and his allies against the Persian army. *Marathon*. A plain where the Greeks won a famous victory (490 BC) against a much larger Persian army.

l. 57. *Philippi*. Site of battle (42 BC) where Brutus and Cassius were defeated by Mark Antony and Caesar. Hence freedom only 'half-alighted' (l. 57).

l. 60. *Milan*. See S.'s Note, p. 584.

l. 70. *far Atlantis*. America.

l. 72. *sanguine streams*. The bloody excesses of the French Revolution.

554 l. 88. *lightnings*. Trisyllabic for the metre.

555 l. 116. *the Bosphorus*. The strait that links the Black Sea to the Sea of Marmara.

l. 123. *I am Mahmud still*. See Webster, *The Duchess of Malfi*, 4. 2. 134: 'I am Duchess of Malfi still'; the scene is in Lamb, *Specimens*.

556 ll. 149–51. *Some say . . . immortality*. Alludes to the Wandering Jew, the subject of an early long poem by S., and a figure in *Queen Mab*.

l. 152. *Enoch*. A biblical figure who did not die but was taken directly to heaven. See Genesis 5: 24: 'And Enoch walked with God: and he was not; for God took him.'

l. 164. *the Demonesi*. A group of nine islands in the Sea of Marmara, a few miles south-east of Constantinople (Istanbul).

557 l. 177. *Marmora*. Alternative spelling of Marmara.

558 l. 197. *Chorus*. See S.'s note (p. 584).

ll. 201–10. *But they . . . had cast*. *Notopoulos* finds an echo of an argument in Plato's *Phaedo*, 87–8: 'that the soul may pass through many bodies, just as the weaver may outlive many coats' (p. 304).

l. 211. *A power*. Jesus Christ.

l. 221. *The moon . . . of Mahomet.* The crescent moon, an emblem of Islam.

559 ll. 225–38. *Swift . . . golden years.* Alludes to Milton's account in 'On the Morning of Christ's Nativity' of the conquering of pagan gods by Christ; S.'s Chorus is overtly sympathetic to the victims of 'killing Truth' (l. 234).

l. 240. *The Janizars.* The janizaries were a body of Turkish infantry, forming the Sultan's guard and the chief part of the army (*OED*).

l. 245. *No hoary priests after that Patriarch.* See S.'s note (p. 585).

ll. 245–6. *that Patriarch . . . heart.* Gregorios, Patriarch of Constantinople, hanged by the Turks on 22 April 1821 in reprisal for the Greek revolt, even though he excommunicated the Greek rebels (l. 246). See S.'s Note, p. 585.

l. 252. *Solyman.* Suleiman I, the Magnificent, was Sultan 1520–66, and presided over Turkish victories and cultural achievements.

560 l. 266. *From . . . Ceraunia.* Mountain ranges that bounded the limits of the Turkish Empire: the Caucasus Mountains lie between the Black Sea and the Caspian Sea; the Ceraunian (or Acroceraunian) Mountains are in north-west Greece.

l. 277. *Sirocco's.* South-east wind from Africa, associated with fierce storms.

l. 281–2. *Phrygian . . . Mycale.* Mountains in Asia Minor.

l. 285. *Scala.* Scala Tyriorum, a promontory south of Tyre on the southern coast of Lebanon.

l. 289. *Moldavian.* Moldavia lies between Romania and Russia.

l. 290. *Allah-illa-Allah!.* A cry meaning 'There is no god but God!'

l. 294. *So were . . . the Danube's day!* Alludes to the defeat of Alexandros Ypsilantis in June 1821; Ypsilantis began the War of Greek Independence by crossing from Russia into Moldavia in March 1821; he fled to Austria, but the Austrians were allies of the Turks and imprisoned him until 1827.

l. 299. *The Anarchies of Africa.* Piratical states in North Africa: Algiers, Tunis, and Tripoli (*Norton*).

561 ll. 303–4. *the Queen | of Ocean.* Great Britain.

l. 312. *recreant.* Cowardly.

l. 329. *Anatolia.* The part of Turkey in Asia equivalent to the peninsula between the Black Sea and the Mediterranean.

l. 333. *One God . . . one Law.* See, to gauge S.'s irony here, *Mask of Anarchy*, l. 37.

562 l. 362–3. *battle . . . Bucharest.* A Turkish victory in a battle in June 1821 to the north-west of Bucharest; S. had read and been told how a group of Greek youths (the 'Sacred Legion') defended their standard bravely (see ll. 385–451).

563 l. 385. *the Pacha*. A title given to Turkish officers of high rank: here the army commander.

564 l. 422. *Ascribe to*. Enrol among.

565 ll. 470–1. *Latmos . . . Icarian isles*. Latmos and Ampelos are mountains in Asia Minor; Phanae is a promontory in Asia Minor. The Icarian isles are to the east of the island of Icaria.

566 l. 482. *Nauplia*. Nauplia lies on the east of the Peloponnesus (the peninsula to the south of mainland Greece and the Gulf of Corinth) at the head of the Gulf of Argolis; it fell to the Greeks in December 1822.

l. 485. *Hydriote*. Relating to the island of Hydra off the east coast of the Peloponnesus. Hydra joined the Greek rebels in April 1821, just after the War began.

l. 500. *Naxos*. Largest island of the Cyclades in the Aegean Sea.

567 l. 526. *Patmos*. An island to the east-north-east of Naxos.

ll. 476–527. *My presence . . . tempest*. This description is based on the destruction by the Greeks of a Turkish battleship. S., influenced by the Messenger's account of the battle of Salamis in *Persians*, aggrandizes the scale of the Turkish defeat.

ll. 528–9. *That Christian . . . the city*. The Russian Ambassador left Constantinople on 31 July 1821.

l. 531. *Hippodrome*. Course for chariot races.

l. 533. *planet-struck*. See *Coriolanus*, 2. 2. 109–110: 'struck | Corioles like a planet'. Planets were supposed to induce bewilderment or terror.

ll. 546–7. *Tripolizza . . . Monembasia*. Tripolis, in the Peloponnesus, fell to the Greeks on 5 October 1821; some ten thousand Turks were killed in the ensuing massacre. *Mothon* (Methoni), *Navarin* (Pilos), which fell to the Greeks in August 1821, and *Monembasia* (Monemvasia), which fell to the Greeks in the same month, are also in the Peloponnesus. *Artas* (Arta) is in mainland Greece (Epirus).

568 ll. 554–5. *In deeds . . . light*. The 'deeds' appear to be those of the Greeks.

l. 555. *Patras*. On the north coast of the Peloponnesus (also called Patrai). Mavrocordato took part in the siege of Patras in August 1821.

l. 560. *oaths . . . Norway*. The British promised to restore the Genovese Republic, encouraging the Genovese to rebel against Napoleon, but the city was given to the kingdom of Sardinia. Norway, given to Sweden in 1814, rebelled and established a constitutional monarchy; but Britain, along with Austria, Russia, and Prussia, allowed Norway to be invaded by Sweden in 1818.

l. 563. *The freedman*. See S.'s Note, p. 585.

l. 564. *Attica*. The territory of Athens, bordering Boeotia and Megaris.

l. 565. *Negropont*. Euboea, an island off the coast of Attica.

l. 566. *Ali.* Ali (1741–1822) was a governor in Albania; *Yanina* (Ioannina) was the capital of his virtually autonomous state. His conflict with Mahmud, by whose army he was finally defeated, was among the catalysts of the War of Greek Independence.

l. 577. *Ypsilanti.* See note to l. 294.

l. 582. *Sennaar.* Sennaar (Sennar) is in the Sudan.

l. 587. *tribute.* Of females for the Sultan's harem.

569 l. 591. *Santons.* Islamic holy men, who pass their lives in fasting, meditation, and prayer.

l. 592. *prophesyings horrible.* See *Macbeth*, 2. 3. 53: 'prophesying with accents terrible'.

l. 595. *Dervise.* Muslim religious man devoted to poverty and austerity (*OED*).

ll. 598–9. *The Greeks . . . glory.* See Mark 13: 26: 'And then shall they see the Son of man coming in the clouds with great power and glory.'

l. 606. *Cydaris.* A small stream (now called Ali Bey Souyou), a northern tributary of the Golden Horn (a bay of water to the north of Constantinople).

l. 620. *Chelonites.* Westernmost point on the mainland of the Peloponnesus (*Norton*).

l. 621. *isles that groan.* The Ionian Islands, seven small islands in the Ionan Sea, became a British protectorate in 1815.

570 l. 627. *sulphureous.* S. uses this form of 'sulphurous' (see l. 829) for the metre.

l. 644. *Tomorrow and tomorrow.* Mahmud echoes Macbeth's 'Tomorrow, and tomorrow, and tomorrow' (5. 5. 18).

572 l. 688. *Thermae . . . Asopus.* Rivers close to which the Persians under Xerxes suffered defeats at Thermopylae (480 BC) and Plataea (479 BC) (*Norton*).

573 l. 728. *a small still voice.* See 1 Kings 19: 12: 'but the Lord was not in the fire: and after the fire a still small voice'. *For.* Some editors have conjectured 'Fear', but there is no warrant for this in the press-copy manuscript or the draft.

l. 735. *the unknown God.* See Paul's rebuke to the Athenians for being 'too superstitious. For as I passed by, and beheld your devotions, I found an altar with this inscription, TO THE UNKNOWN GOD. Whom therefore ye ignorantly worship, him declare I unto you' (Acts 17: 22–3). Paul can identify God; S.'s Chorus suggests that God remains 'unknown'.

574 l. 742. *Frank.* Of western nationality.

l. 776. *Calpe.* Rock of Gibraltar.

l. 780. *all that it inherits.* See *The Tempest*, 4. 1. 154: 'all which it inherit'. Prospero's sense of life as illusion is re-articulated by Ahasuerus.

575 l. 781. *motes of a sick eye*. See *Hamlet*, 1. 1. 106.5: 'A mote it is to trouble the mind's eye.' Motes are small particles of dust.

l. 785. *Nought is . . . be*. See 'On Life', p. 635: 'nothing exists but as it is perceived.'

l. 793. *Dodona's forest*. Dodona was the location in Epirus (north-west Greece) of an oak grove containing an oracle sacred to Jupiter.

l. 804. *Knock . . . opened*. See Matthew 7: 7: 'knock, and it shall be opened unto you.'

ll. 807–8. *Mahomet . . . Stamboul*. Sultan Mahomet the Second conquered Constantinople (Stamboul or Istanbul) in 1453.

576 l. 829. *Εν τούτῳ νίκη*. 'In this [sign], victory': the Greek war-cry, set beside that of the Turks (see note to l. 290).

l. 838. *Tartarian barb*. Horse from Tartary (region in central Asia, peopled by Turks and Mongols, among others).

578 l. 903. *reversion*. The Hour will be enriched by what reverts to it on Mahmud's death.

579 ll. 918–20. *Were there such . . . fear?* See *Macbeth*, 1. 3. 81–3: 'Were such things here . . . Or have we eaten on the insane root | That takes the reason prisoner?'

l. 936. *Thule*. In ancient times, the northernmost part of the inhabitable world. *the girdle of the world*. The Equator.

580 l. 948. *Russia's famished eagles*. 'The flag of Russia under the Romanov czars featured a double-headed eagle' (*Norton*).

l. 959. *lightning*. Trisyllabic for the metre.

l. 977. *contumely*. Scornful insolence.

581 l. 987. *Image of the Above*. The 'Image' is Liberty, the phrasing Platonic.

l. 991. *'The Sea! the Sea!'*. The cry is that of Greek troops retreating from Persia as described by Xenophon in *Anabasis*, 4. 7.

l. 993. *young Atlantis*. America.

l. 1006. *Amphionic music*. Amphion, legendary son of Zeus and Antiope, charmed the walls of Thebes into position through his music.

582 ll. 1016–17. *bought Briton . . . Islamite*. The British would not intervene with their navy.

l. 1019. *Othman*. Ottoman; Turkish.

l. 1030. *Evening land*. The West; specifically, America.

l. 1049. *Pranked*. Set, displayed.

583 l. 1059. *Chorus*. See S.'s note (p. 586).

ll. 1060–1. *The world's . . . return*. See Virgil, *Eclogues*, 4. 5–6: 'the great Sequence of the Ages starts afresh . . . and the rule of Saturn is restored' (E. V. Rieu, trans., Virgil, *The Pastoral Poems* (Harmondsworth, 1954)).

l. 1063. *winter weeds.* Garments; here snake-skin.

l. 1068. *Peneus.* River in Thessaly (north-central Greece) flowing through Tempe (l. 1070), a beautiful valley.

l. 1071. *Cyclads.* The Cyclades, a cluster of islands in the Aegean.

l. 1072. *Argo.* The ship in which Jason and the Argonauts sailed in their quest for the Golden Fleece.

ll. 1074–5. *Another Orpheus . . . dies.* Alludes to Orpheus' power of song, his love for Eurydice, his grief both at her loss and his failure to bring her out of the underworld (he looked back against Hades' order), and his death, torn to pieces by Maenads.

ll. 1075–6. *A new Ulysses . . . shore.* Alludes to the *Odyssey*, and to Odysseus' leaving of Calypso, the goddess-nymph with whom he stayed for seven years, for his home (in Ithaca) and wife (Penelope).

ll. 1072–7. *A loftier . . . shore.* Modelled on Virgil, *Eclogues*, 4. 34–6: 'a second Argo will set out . . . Wars even will repeat themselves, and the great Achilles will be despatched to Troy once more'. Virgil's words about repeated wars contribute to the sombre colouring of S.'s last two stanzas.

l. 1080. *Laian rage.* Warned by an oracle that he would be killed by his child, King Laius of Thebes ordered that his new-born son, Oedipus, should be exposed on a mountain. In Sophocles' version, *Oedipus the King*, the servant commanded to expose the baby gave it to shepherds. Oedipus grew up to fulfil the oracle, albeit unwittingly.

l. 1082. *Sphinx.* A monster with the face of a woman, the chest and feet of a lion, and wings like a bird of prey, who lived outside Thebes and posed riddles to passers-by, whom she devoured if they could not provide the right answer. Oedipus solved the riddles, and the Sphinx killed herself.

584 l. 1092. *One who rose.* See S.'s Note, p. 586.

l. 1094. *dowers.* A verb, meaning endows. In the draft it replaces the verbs 'wears' and 'vests'.

586 *Notes to 'Hellas'. Note*, ll. 814–15. *1453.* Corrected by editors since *Rossetti* from S.'s '1445'.

Phantom. S.'s draft has 'phantasm'.

master of. S.'s draft has 'master'.

Note, l. 1060. *magno nec proximus intervallo.* S. reworks a phrase from Virgil, *Aeneid*, 5. 320, *longo sed proximus intervallo* ('but next by a long distance'): S.'s meaning is 'and not next by a great distance', which appears to be assertive rather than deprecatory (but see *BSM* 21, where S.'s phrase is translated 'not near <but> at a great interval').

the 'lion shall lie down with the lamb'. A common misquotation of Isaiah 11: 6: 'The wolf also shall dwell with the lamb, and the leopard shall lie down with the kid.'

586 *omnis feret omnia tellus*. Virgil, *Eclogues*, 4. 39: 'each land makes all it needs' (editors' trans.).

Note, ll. 1090–1. *amerced*. Here, 'punished by being deprived'.

'the One who rose' . . . worship. Omitted from the first edition.

587 *Demon*. The press copy reading.

hecatombs. Sacrifices of many victims. S. refers to the slaughter committed in the name of the Christian religion.

The sublime . . . torture. Omitted from the first edition.

588 *Written on Hearing the News of the Death of Napoleon*. Composed sometime between the death of Napoleon, on 5 May 1821 (though news of the death would not have reached S. for several weeks), and 11 November 1821, the date he sent it, along with the manuscript of *Hellas*, to his publisher, Charles Ollier, with instructions to print it 'at the end' of the *Hellas* volume (1822), our copy-text, though we have also consulted the fair copy in the Huntington (HM 330; *MYR: Shelley* 3). For S. on Napoleon see also 'Ode to Liberty', *The Triumph of Life*, and 'Feelings of a Republican on the Fall of Buonaparte' (not included in this selection).

l. 10. *Hearth*. One of the names the Romans worshipped the earth under was Vesta; she was also the goddess of the hearth.

589 *'The flower that smiles today'*. Composed 1821–2. There are drafts and a fair copy in the Bodleian (*BSM* 16); the fair copy supplies our copy-text. G. M. Matthews argued that the lyric, drafted in the same notebook as *Hellas*, 'was evidently written for the opening of *Hellas*' (*Norton*, p. 690). But the manuscript evidence is inconclusive (see *BSM* 16, pp. liv–lv). The poem, first published in *PP* under the title 'Mutability', shares the concern of other late lyrics (such as 'When the lamp is shattered') with the brevity of 'delight' (l. 5) and with enduring after such delight has gone.

ll. 6–7. *Lightning . . . bright*. See *Romeo and Juliet*, 2. 1. 161–2: 'Too like the lightning which doth cease to be | Ere one can say it lightens'.

l. 12. *these*. Virtue, friendship, and love.

l. 13. *Survive their joy*. 'These' (see note to l. 12) persist but without joy once they have 'fallen' (see l. 12) from their original state.

590 *To —— ('One word is too often profaned')*. Dated 1821 by Mary S. who published it in *PP*, under the title 'To ——', to which we have added in parentheses the first-line title by which the poem is often known. PP supplies our copy-text; there is also a transcription by Mary S. in the Bodleian (*BSM* 2).

'When the lamp is shattered'. Composed 1821–2, first published in full in *PP*. There is a draft in the Bodleian (*BSM* 19), a fair copy of the first three stanzas in Glasgow University Library (MS Gen. 505/34; *MYR: Shelley* 8), and a fair copy of the whole poem in the British Library (Add. MS 37232, f. 75; *MYR: Shelley* 8). The British Library manuscript

supplies our copy-text. The poem depends for its power on great rhythmic skill (mixing iambs and anapaests) and the movement from argument by analogy to the concentrated metaphoric force of the last stanza.

l. 2. *The light . . . dead.* As *Chernaik* notes, 'the "light in the dust" has not disappeared, but rather "lies dead"'.

591 l. 16. *That ring . . . knell.* See *The Tempest*, I. 2. 406: 'Sea-nymphs hourly ring his knell' (*Rognoni*).

l. 17. *When . . . mingled.* Above this line in the Glasgow fair copy are the words 'second part'; S. may have thought of the poem at one stage as a debate, chorus-like lyric or part of a drama.

l. 25. *thee.* 'Love' (l. 21).

l. 32. *When . . . come.* The rhythm slows expressively (the result of stressed monosyllables).

To —— ('The serpent is shut out from Paradise'). Composed in January 1822, and a fair copy sent (our copy-text) to Edward Williams with an accompanying letter (referring to the 'dismal' (that is, 'sombre') nature of the verse); first published by Medwin (in corrupted form) in *Fraser's Magazine* (Nov. 1832). The fair copy and letter are now in the University of Edinburgh Library (Dc. I. 100^{4}; *MYR: Shelley* 8). The poem is written in *ottava rima*, with modified line-lengths, a possible gesture towards Byron whose nickname for S. ('The Snake') is adopted by the poet. If there is such a gesture, its purpose is to underscore Byron's far greater popularity: in the poem, S. refers not only to marital problems (see esp. l. 25) but also to the struggles of authorship (ll. 29–31).

592 l. 16. *its evil, good.* See Satan in *PL* 4. 110: 'Evil be thou my good.'

l. 18. *Dear friends, dear 'friend'.* Whether the 'friend' is Edward Williams or Jane Williams is left unclear.

l. 28. *scene.* We have retained the copy-text's full stop at the end of this line because it is expressive of the speaker's momentary, wearied halting.

l. 42. *No bird . . . nest.* See Matthew 8: 20: 'The foxes have holes, and the birds of the air have nests; but the Son of man hath not where to lay his head.'

593 *To Jane. The Invitation.* Composed in 1822 after S. had walked through a forest near Pisa to the sea with Mary S. and Jane Williams; first published (with 'To Jane—The Recollection') in *PP* as 'The Pine Forest of the Cascine, near Pisa'. This first publication was based on a transcription by Mary S. in the Bodleian (*BSM* 2). Mary must have copied from a draft in which the two poems were one. S. evidently decided to divide the poem into two. Our copy-text is supplied by his fair copy in the University Library, Cambridge (MS Add. 4444; *MYR: Shelley* 8). 'To Jane. The Invitation' was first published as a separate complete poem in *MWS (2)*.

The poem is written in tetrameters, mainly trochaic but occasionally iambic.

593 l. 6. *brake*. Thicket.

594 l. 48. *Awake . . . away*. See Satan in *PL* 1. 330: 'Awake, arise, or be forever fallen'.

l. 58. *daisy-star*. Marguerite (ox-eye daisy).

595 l. 68. *seem*. The verb's cautiousness (S. could have written 'are') is appropriate for a poem that celebrates 'one moment's good' (l. 44).

To Jane—The Recollection. (See the above headnote.) Composed 1822, first published as a separate complete poem in *MWS (2)*. Our copy-text is supplied by S.'s fair copy in the British Library (Add. MS 37538, ff. 40–1; *MYR: Shelley* 8), which contains below the title the date ('Feb. 2, 1822') of the walk through the pine forest mentioned in 'To Jane. The Invitation'. There is a draft of ll. 29–32 in the Bodleian (*BSM* 21).

l. 6. *fled*. The reading in *BSM* 2 and *PP*; 'dead' in the fair copy is presumably a slip.

596 l. 45. *A spirit interfused*. See Wordsworth, 'Tintern Abbey', l. 97: 'something far more deeply interfused'.

597 l. 87. ——*'s mind*. The gap asks to be filled by 'Shelley'.

The Magnetic Lady to Her Patient. Probably composed in 1822, first published (in corrupted form) by Medwin in 1832. Mary S. published an improved text in *MWS (2)*. S sent a fair copy to Jane and Edward Williams with the following notes: 'For Jane & Williams alone to see' (at the top of the page) and 'To Jane. Not to be opened unless you are alone, or with Williams' (on the outer wrapping). This fair copy, in the University Library, King's College, Aberdeen, supplies our copy-text (MS 937; *MYR: Shelley* 8). Given the personal nature of the poem (the 'chain' of the last line appears to refer to S.'s marriage), S. did not wish Mary S. to see it. Jane is a 'magnetic lady' because she has been mesmerizing the poet to alleviate the pain probably caused by a kidney stone.

598 l. 6. *like a sign*. Compare (and contrast) the 'Incantation' in Byron's *Manfred*, esp. 1. 201: 'With a power and with a sign'.

l. 11. *he*. Edward Williams.

599 *With a Guitar. To Jane*. Composed 1822; ll. 43–90 first published by Medwin in the *Athanaeum*, 20 October 1832, and *The Shelley Papers* (1833); ll. 1–42 first published in *Fraser's Magazine* (1833). First complete corrected text published in *MWS (2)*. There is a draft of the first twelve lines (*BSM* 19) and a fair copy (*BSM* 21) in the Bodleian: the fair copy supplies our copy-text. S. had tried to buy a harp for Jane Williams; when that attempt failed, he gave her a Pisan guitar, now in the Bodleian. The poem, written in octosyllabic couplets and recalling seventeenth-

century lyrics by poets such as Robert Herrick, is spoken by S. in the guise of Ariel, the spirit in Shakespeare's *The Tempest* who was freed from a pine-tree by Prospero; Jane Williams is addressed as Miranda and Edward Williams as Ferdinand, from the same play. Covertly the poem reflects on the artist, art, and its audience.

l. 18. *As . . . tell.* See *The Tempest*, 5. 1. 317–21, where Ariel is charged by Prospero with the safe return to Naples of those on the island.

l. 27. *live again.* Alludes playfully to the notion of reincarnation.

601 *To Jane ('The keen stars were twinkling').* Our copy-text is the fair copy (now in the John Rylands University Library of Manchester: *MYR: Shelley* 8) sent by S. to Jane Williams in June 1822 with a note: 'I sate down to write some words for an ariette which might be profane. . . . I commit them to your secrecy & your mercy & will try & do better another time' (see *MYR: Shelley* 8). The poem was first published in truncated form by Medwin in the *Athenaeum*, 17 November 1832; it was first published in complete form in *MWS (2)*. There is a draft in the Bodleian (*BSM* 1). The poem's virtuoso rhythms and sound-patterns are attuned to the musicality of Jane Williams's singing, and to S.'s desire for 'some world far from ours'.

602 l. 24. *Are one.* The draft reads 'Are won'.

Lines Written in the Bay of Lerici. Composed in June 1822, first published by Richard Garnett in 1862. The only textual authority is a rough draft in the Bodleian (*BSM* 1), which supplies our copy-text. The poem typifies the psychological inwardness to be found in the late poems to Jane Williams.

ll. 1–14. *Bright . . . west.* Added (see *BSM* 1) after the main body of the poem had been drafted.

603 ll. 31–2. *The past . . . not.* S. means that past and present were forgotten as if the former had never been and the latter would never come to be.

l. 57. *pleasure.* There is no word after 'pleasure' in the draft.

l. 58. *Seeking . . . peace.* Any reading of the line is bound to be conjectural because of its unfinished state. *Chernaik* reads: 'Seeking life not peace'. *Norton* reads 'Destroying life alone not peace'. In the MS, 'Seeking' is written below '~~Destroying~~'.

604 *The Triumph of Life.* Composed between May and July 1822, in the last months of S.'s life, and left uncompleted at his death, *The Triumph of Life* was first published from S.'s draft in the Bodleian (see *BSM* 1) by Mary S. in *PP*. This draft, in places very rough, supplies our copy-text. The title is ironic: 'Life' triumphs because it devastates those who live. The poem owes much to S.'s reading of Dante and Petrarch, and is written in the same verse form, *terza rima*, as Dante's *Commedia* and Petrarch's *Trionfi*; Dante's use of Virgil as a guide is echoed by S.'s use of Rousseau, while the central image of a Roman triumph recalls Petrarch's *Trionfi*, which is made up of successive triumphs, culminating in the triumph of Eternity. However, where Dante's quest is ordered, S.'s is

bewildering, and whether his poem would have followed a similar sequence to Petrarch's is doubtful. *The Triumph of Life* sees Rousseau as a figure associated with ideas that led to the French Revolution and as a precursor of Romanticism. Other texts drawn on by the poem include Lucretius' *De Rerum Natura*; *PL*; Goethe's *Faust* (parts of which S. translated in his final year); plays by Calderón (especially *La vida es sueño* [*Life is a Dream*]); Byron's *Childe Harold's Pilgrimage*, canto 3 (with its portraits of Napoleon, Voltaire, and Rousseau); and Wordsworth's 'Ode: Intimations of Immortality'. A further influence was probably the painting of the *Triumph of Death* in the Campo Santo in Pisa. *The Triumph of Life* re-explores the public themes of S.'s earlier work, but it lays emphasis on the apparent refusal of history to fulfil the hopes and desires of the revolutionary imagination.

604 l. 7. *orison*. Prayer.

ll. 26–8. *before . . . head*. The lines echo Goethe's *Faust*, part 1, ll. 1087–8: 'The day ahead, behind my back the night, | The sky above me and the waves below . . .' (trans. David Luke, Oxford, 1987). By contrast with Faust, S.'s narrator has his back to the day.

605 ll. 44–5. *a great stream | Of people*. Dante, *Inf.* 3. 55–7: 'behind it came so long a train of people, that I should never have believed death had undone so many.'

l. 54. *Some . . . feared*. See 'Tintern Abbey', ll. 71–2: 'more like a man | Flying from something that he dreads'.

606 l. 78. *light*. There is a blank space before 'light'; S.'s original thought (cancelled) was 'fascinating'; Mary S. inserted 'blinding' in *PP*.

l. 84. *The ghost . . . mother*. See Coleridge, 'Dejection: An Ode', first two lines of the epigraph ('Ballad of Sir Patrick Spens'): 'Late, late yestreen I saw the new Moon, | With the old Moon in her arms'.

l. 86. *a chariot*. Recalls and ironizes chariots in Ezekiel, esp. chs. 1 and 10; Dante, *Purg.* 29 (the car of the Church); and *PL* ('The chariot of paternal deity', 6. 750).

l. 91. *o'er . . . the head*. See *PL* 2. 672–3, where the phrase is used to describe Death; 'cloud', in our text, is the subject of 'Was bent' (l. 92), though the manuscript is difficult at this point, and other syntactical arrangements are possible.

607 l. 94. *Janus-visaged Shadow*. Refers, as l. 99 confirms, to 'Janus Quadrifrons', a figure with four faces.

ll. 111–16. *such seemed . . . bear*. The comparison is with a 'triumph' in 'Imperial Rome' (l. 113), marking the successful return of a military leader from war.

608 l. 126. *the great winter*. The conclusion of time.

l. 128. *the sacred few*. Principally 'they of Athens and Jerusalem' (l. 134), in particular Socrates and Jesus, both admired by S. as exemplary human beings.

l. 148. *her*. Establishes the gender of the Shape within the chariot.

609 l. 175. *And frost . . . those*. See *PL* 2. 594–5: 'the parching air | Burns frore, and cold performs the effect of fire.'

610 l. 190. *grim Feature*. See *PL* 10. 279, where the phrase is used of Death.

ll. 207. *A thousand . . . bore*. See Dante, *Purg*. 21. 94–6, where Statius speaks of the influence of Virgil's *Aeneid*: 'The sparks, which warmed me, from the divine flame whence more than a thousand have been kindled, were the seeds of my poetic fire.'

611 ll. 214–15. *And . . . evening*. See Petrarch, *Trionfo della Morte*, 1. 38–9: 'deaf and blind, night falls upon you ere 'tis eventide' (Death is speaking). Rousseau, speaking metaphorically, sees the victims of Life as undone by their inner chaos ('the mutiny within', l. 213) and their feigning of 'truth'; 'night' (the damage done to them by Life) occurs before their illusory 'morn of truth' can ripen into any resulting 'evening'.

ll. 235–6. *Voltaire . . . Leopold*. Figures from the Enlightenment, including so-called benevolent despots, Frederick the Great of Prussia (1712–86), Catherine the Great of Russia (1729–96), and Leopold II of Austria (1747–92), and intellectuals, Voltaire (1694–1778) and Immanuel Kant (1724–1804).

l. 237. *anarch*. A ruler who does not rule properly, because he governs despotically, and therefore gives rise to a state of 'anarchy'.

612 l. 243. *its object*. The object, in turn, of age, tears, infamy, and the tomb; to none of the objects of these things could Rousseau's heart be tempered.

l. 255. *his master*. Socrates, who did not succumb to sexual temptation, refusing the advances of Alcibiades (see the last section of Plato's *Symposium*).

l. 256. *That star . . . fair*. Alludes to the youth Aster, the Greek word for 'star', with whom Plato was believed to have fallen in love.

l. 261. *The tutor and his pupil*. Aristotle and Alexander the Great.

613 l. 274. *the great bards of old*. In the manuscript S. substitutes this phrase for the cancelled 'Homer & his brethren'.

ll. 276–80. *Their living . . . misery*. Rousseau contrasts the contained effect of poetry written by classical authors with the less controllable 'infection' spread by his own more confessional work.

l. 284. *Caesar's crime*. The building-up of state power under Julius Caesar. *Constantine*. The Emperor who made Christianity the official state religion.

l. 288. *Gregory and John*. Possibly Pope Gregory VII (1073–85) and Pope John XXII (1316–34), but as likely to be used as generic names for successions of Popes.

613 l. 289. *Man and god.* The manuscript capital and lower-case reinforce S.'s heterodox meaning.

615 l. 338. *common Sun.* As Rousseau wakes from the 'oblivious spell' (l. 331), his language echoes that of Wordsworth's 'Ode: Intimations of Immortality', especially its reference to 'the light of common day' (l. 76) into which the 'vision splendid' (l. 73) is fated to 'die away' (l. 75).

l. 352. *shape all light.* The last and most enigmatic of S.'s female figures. The focus is on Rousseau's shifting apprehensions of her. For a complex analogue, see Dante's encounter with Matilda (*Purg.* 28) in the Earthly Paradise, a passage which S. translated.

l. 357. *Iris.* The goddess of the rainbow.

l. 359. *Nepenthe.* In Homer, *Odyssey*, 4, Helen of Troy give Menelaus the grief-dispelling drug, nepenthes, also alluded to in Milton's *Comus*, ll. 675–6.

l. 361. *palms.* Soles of the feet, as in *Adonais*, l. 212.

617 l. 422. *The Brescian shepherd.* In *PP*, Mary S. adds this footnote to the line: 'The favorite [*sic*] song, "Stanco di pascolar le peccorelle ['I am weary of pasturing my sheep']," is a Brescian national air.' Brescia is a city in northern Italy.

l. 424. *So knew I.* See the narrator's 'I knew | That I had felt' (ll. 33–4): one of several links between the narrator's and Rousseau's experiences.

618 l. 446. *atomies.* Tiny motes of dust.

619 l. 463. *Lethean.* Having the power to induce forgetfulness, a power attributed to the mythological river Lethe.

l. 471. *Behold a wonder.* See *PL* 1. 777.

l. 472. *him.* Dante.

l. 479. *The sphere.* The Third Heaven of Dante's *Paradiso*, the sphere of Venus.

ll. 488. *Shadows of shadows.* See the depiction in Lucretius, *De Rerum Natura*, 4. 30 ff. of *simulacra*, 'films' thrown off the surfaces of things.

620 l. 500. *anatomies.* Skeletons.

621 l. 533. *the car's creative ray.* Ironic; the car's ray is miscreative and distorting.

l. 544. *I said.* Revised from 'I cried' in the manuscript.

ll. 547–8. *'Happy . . . | Of.* Compare (and contrast) Petrarch's *Trionfi dell'Eternità*, ll. 46–8, 82–4, which employs the 'Happy' ('felice') formula to imagine the condition of those souls heading towards 'the final goal' (l. 83) (see Alan M. Weinberg, *Shelley's Italian Experience* (Basingstoke,1991), 241–2).

623 *An Address to the People on the Death of the Princess Charlotte.* Composed 11–12 November 1817, in response to the death in childbirth on 6 November of Princess Charlotte (b. 1796), daughter of the Prince

Regent, and the hanging and quartering on 7 November of Jeremiah Brandreth, Isaac Ludlam, and William Turner, three working men accused of treasonable utterances and actions as leaders of the 'Derbyshire Insurrection' or 'Pentridge Rising'. The death of Princess Charlotte, known to have liberal or reformist sympathies, was much lamented in pamphlets, poems (including canto IV of Byron's *Childe Harold's Pilgrimage*, stanzas 169–70) and the public press. The execution of the 'Pentridge Three' was controversial in part because of the leading role played by the government spy, 'William Oliver', who seems to have acted as an *agent provocateur*. S. argues that public mourning for the Princess ought more properly to be directed at the executed working men, entrapped by a government bent on suppressing liberty itself. Our copy-text is the only extant source of the pamphlet, an 1843 reprint, reproduced in *Murray*, pp. 229–39; we have used a copy of the reprint in Durham University Library. No copies of Ollier's original 1817 printing survive, in part because fear of prosecution seems to have limited their number to twenty (according to the publisher of the 1843 reprint), nor is there a surviving holograph or draft material. We follow our copy-text in leaving a line between each of the essay's numbered paragraphs.

The Hermit of Marlow. A pseudonym used also for the pamphlet *A Proposal for Putting Reform to the Vote* (1817); Marlow, in Buckinghamshire, had been S.'s residence since March 1817, though he actually wrote the *Address* in London.

Epigraph. A quotation from part 1 of Paine's *Rights of Man* (1791), in which Paine criticizes Burke's *Reflections* (1790) for pitying Marie Antoinette and the French aristocracy while wholly ignoring the plight of the people.

too deep for words. See the last line of Wordsworth, 'Ode: Intimations of Immortality': 'Thoughts that do often lie too deep for tears.'

624 *And have they no affections?* This question and the questions that follow recall *The Merchant of Venice*, 3.1. 49–56 ('Hath not a Jew eyes?' etc.).

illustrated. Shed lustre upon; made illustrious (see *OED* 4).

'that bourne . . . returns'. See *Hamlet*, 3. 1. 81–2: 'The undiscovered country from whose bourn | No traveller returns.'

Horne Took and Hardy. John Horne Tooke (1736–1812) and Thomas Hardy (1752–1832), radical reformers, acquitted of high treason in a notorious trial of 1794.

625 *Brandreth, Ludlam, and Turner*. The 'Pentridge Three'. Brandreth, a framework-knitter, was the most clearly culpable (he had killed a man, the only fatality of the uprising); Ludlam, part-owner of a stone quarry near Derby and a Methodist preacher, and Turner, a stone-mason, 'might well have been accused only of riot' (E. P. Thompson, *The Making of the English Working Class* (1963; repr. Harmondsworth, 1977), 727; and more generally pp. 723–34).

625 *She had accomplished nothing*. See *Murray*, pp. 452–3, for the 'rhetorical and relatively invidious' nature of S.'s criticism of the Princess.

626 *Her husband . . . brethren*. Charlotte had married Prince Leopold of Saxe-Coburg in May 1816; she was estranged from both her parents.

hurdle. A kind of sledge, on which convicted traitors would be carried to execution.

Who dares . . . grave? S. appends a note: '"Your death has eyes in his head—mine is not painted so." Cymbeline.' S. quotes from *Cymbeline*, 5. 5. 268–9 (omitting 'then' after 'head' and substituting 'painted' for 'pictured').

depending on. Resulting from.

627 *circumstances*. Political and economic oppression (as detailed in the next section).

a check. 'S. probably refers to the institution of the Sinking Fund in 1786, which seemed to provide a mechanism for retiring the national debt but in fact provided an excuse for raising it' (*Murray*, p. 453).

fundamental defect. A limited or restricted suffrage.

sans . . . tache. Without fear and without stain.

gambling in the funds. Lending money to government.

'Corinthian . . . society'. Burke's description of the aristocracy in *Reflections* (singled out for censure in part 2 of Paine's *Rights of Man*).

628 *two chasms*. Anarchy (here meaning 'lawlessness') and misrule.

manufacturers. Factory workers.

helots. Slaves or serfs.

629 *spies were sent forth*. See Luke 20: 20: 'And they watched him, and sent forth spies'.

innocent and unsuspecting rustics. An inaccurate (perhaps 'rhetorical') characterization, according to Thompson, *The Making of the English Working Class*, 723–34.

extraordinary powers. In March 1817 Parliament passed the Seditious Meetings Act and suspended Habeas Corpus.

'OLIVER brought him to this'. S. appends a footnote here: 'These expressions are taken from the Examiner, Sunday, Nov. 9'; the italicized words three sentences later (*'while the executioner . . .'*) are also taken from the *Examiner*, as is the passage from 'when the stroke' to 'hosted'.

630 *the chaplain prevented*. For fear of what would be revealed about Oliver's role, according to liberal sentiment, thus denying the accused their right of last words.

631 *Phantom*. See 'England in 1819', 'A New National Anthem', ll. 110ff. of *The Mask of Anarchy*, and *Laon and Cythna*, all of which imagine a rebirth of hope and liberty.

On Love. Composed at Bagni di Lucca in July 1818, probably between 20 and 25 July, after S. had finished his translation of Plato's *Symposium* (between 7 and 20 July) and before he began *A Discourse on the Manners of the Ancient Greeks Relative to the Subject of Love*, an essay that explores the difference between the ancient Greeks and modern Europeans 'in the regulations and the sentiments respecting sexual intercourse' (*Notopoulos*, p. 407). First published in the *Keepsake for 1829* (1828). In 'On Love' S., influenced by Plato's impassioned rhetoric in the *Symposium*, explores love in a psychological analysis that recalls *Alastor* and looks ahead to *Epipsychidion*. Our copy-text for the essay, unpublished in S.'s lifetime, is his draft in the Bodleian (*BSM* 15).

sought. *MWS: Prose* reads 'sought sympathy', but there is no warrant for this addition in our copy-text. We have added a comma after 'sought'.

demandest what is Love. This is followed in the draft by the cancelled sentence: 'It is the sweet chalice of life whose dregs are bitterer than wormwood.'

airy children of our brain. S.'s cancelled alternative in his draft was 'creations of our mind'.

632 *We dimly see*. S. inserted an 'x' to key the following footnote (usually keyed to 'composed' in the next sentence): 'These words inefficient and metaphorical—Most words so—No help—'.

prototype. An original thing or person in relation to a copy, imitation, representation, later specimen, improved form (*OED*).

a soul within our soul. See *Epipsychidion*, l. 238 ('this soul out of my soul') and contrast the more other-centred account of love in *A Defence of Poetry* as 'a going out of our own nature' (p. 682).

antitype. That which a type or symbol represents (*OED*): here, 'not the person herself but rather the "soul within [her] soul"' (*Bonca*, p. 273 n. 31).

Sterne . . . cypress. See Laurence Sterne's *A Sentimental Journey through France and Italy* (1768): 'was I in a desert, I would find out wherewith in it to call forth my affections—If I could not do better, I would fasten them upon some sweet myrtle, or seek some melancholy cypress to connect myself to', ed. Graham Petrie (Harmondsworth, 1967), 51.

633 *On Life*. Written around late 1819 in the notebook in which S. drafted *A Philosophical View of Reform*; subsequently torn out of the notebook (in 1916); the manuscript is currently in the Pierpont Morgan Library (MA 408) and supplies our copy-text. A draft with cancellations, it presents some editorial problems, but it is the sole authority for a text unpublished in S.'s lifetime (it was first published by Medwin in 1832 and 1833, and, in a more accurate form, by Mary S. in *MWS: Prose*). Occasionally we follow Mary S.'s emendations. The work offers a short but important overview of S.'s metaphysical beliefs and allegiances, tracking his movement from materialism to the 'intellectual philosophy'. This philosophy

seems close in certain respects to the idealism of George Berkeley and his tenet, *esse est percipi aut percipere* (to be is to be perceived or to perceive); indeed, Mary S. writes in her Preface to her 1840 edition of Shelley's prose writings that 'Shelley was a disciple of the Immaterial Philosophy of Berkeley' (p. xii). But S. departs from Berkeley's belief in the mind of God as ultimately guaranteeing reality. The major influence on 'On Life' is *Academical Questions* (1805) (hereafter *AQ*) by Sir William Drummond, described by S. in a letter of November 1819 as 'the most acute metaphysical critic of the age' (*L* 2. 142). Drummond draws on David Hume's sceptical arguments about causality to reject the materialist argument that mind is subject to matter, and, indeed, to cast doubt upon the assumption 'that the objects of sense are different from the sensations, feelings, or perceptions, which exist in our own minds' (*AQ* 91). Out of this series of counter-intuitive doubts emerges 'the ideal system' (*AQ* 383), by which Drummond means acceptance of the view that we know only our ideas about things; we do not have direct knowledge of the world itself. Where S. differs from Drummond is his emphasis on 'unity' and the implicit trust he places in imagination as an escape from sceptical doubt: Drummond is quietly scornful of the way 'A poet saves himself by a metaphor' (*AQ* 96); S. is determined to heed 'high aspirations'.

633 *[of]*. The manuscript has 'by'.

[its]. Not in manuscript.

'Non merita . . . Poeta'. See note to *A Defence of Poetry*, p. 835.

634 *those philosophers . . . perceived*. Such as David Hume, quoted approvingly by Drummond as questioning the supposition that there is 'an external universe, which depends not on our perception' (*AQ* 397).

'such stuff . . . made of'. See *The Tempest*, 4. 1. 156–7: 'We are such stuff | As dreams are made on'.

'looking . . . after'. See *Hamlet*, 4. 4. 26–7 'Sure, he that made us with such large discourse, | Looking before and after'.

with. Cancelled in favour of 'whose' in the manuscript, but restored here, to make sense of the subsequent 'disclaiming', which is ungrammatical if 'whose' is kept.

'thoughts . . . eternity'. See Belial in *PL* 2. 146–8: 'for who would lose, | Though full of pain, this intellectual being, | Those thoughts that wander through eternity.'

change and extinction. Written above 'nothingness and dissolution' in the manuscript; neither pair of nouns is cancelled. We have included both pairs.

635 *misuse of . . . signs*. See *AQ* 407: 'the inaccuracies into which we are often betrayed in our habits of thinking from our habits of speaking.'

636 *preceded*. Other editors (though not *Norton*[2]) follow Mary S.'s 'produced'.

the basis. Written above 'the cause' in the manuscript; neither term is cancelled.

the manner in which two thoughts. In the manuscript S. seems to have written 'things' first, then to have written 'thoughts' above it. Neither word is cancelled; we have chosen what appears to have been S.'s latest choice.

A Philosophical View of Reform. Composition began towards the end of 1819 and continued into 1820. Described in a letter of 15 December 1819 to Charles Ollier as 'an octavo on reform. . . . I intend it to be an instructive and readable book, appealing from the passions to the reason of men' (*L* 2. 164). The original manuscript, unfinished and with many gaps and problematic insertions and alterations, was not published until 1920, though Mary S. transcribed a version, now in the Bodleian (*BSM* 22), with a view to its being 'published when [Shelley's] works assume a complete shape' (*MWS: Prose* 1, p. xviii). Our copy-text is the original manuscript, now in the Carl H. Pforzheimer Library, as transcribed in *SC* 6. All ellipses in square brackets are editorial; some omit incomplete sentences or passages, or sentences or passages which do not follow; in the case of more extended omissions or omissions of interest in themselves but disruptive of local arguments, we have paraphrased or quoted the omitted material in our endnotes.

1st. Sentiment . . . Desirable mode. These numbered headings are set out on the verso of the first page of the manuscript and may constitute an outline for the work as a whole; in l. 2, S. has written 'Probability' above 'Practicability' and 'Necessity' above 'Utility', without cancelling the originals.

637 *Epigraph.* Probably of S.'s devising; *MWS* and others add 'it' after 'that'.

two recent wars. Presumably the American and French Revolutions; Mary S.'s copy reads 'the French Revolution'.

The Republics and municipal governments of Italy. In 1176 the Lombard League of northern Italian communes overthrew the tyrannical rule of Frederick Barbarossa, leading to the Peace of Constance (1183) and greater autonomy for the Italian city-states. In later wars, between the popes and Holy Roman (German) emperors, Florence played a balancing role, preventing the dominance of either religious or political authority.

638 *The poor rose.* A reference to the Peasants' War (1522–5) in Germany.

The republic of Holland . . . even to death. According to Reiman, 'S. was thinking not only of Spinoza's writings but also of the numerous publications by French *philosophes* that were published (or purported to be published) in Holland during the seventeenth and eighteenth centuries' (*SC* 6. 966).

the strain of conquest. S. must be thinking only of Europe; by 1558, the date of the fall of Calais, at the time the last English stronghold on the continent, England no longer sought the conquest of France.

638 *exposition.* expulsion (*OED* 1), exposure (*OED* 2).

639 *one of those chiefs.* Charles I, about whom S. would later attempt to write a drama.

Revolution. The Glorious Revolution of 1688, in which James II was replaced by Mary and William III (of Orange).

those professing themselves established. 'The Pope, Luther, Calvin and others' (*Clark*).

this test was applied . . . this judgement formed. By measuring the doctrines and actions of Christ against those of religious authorities and interpreters (i.e. the 'established').

640 *Bayle.* Pierre Bayle (1647–1706), author of *Dictionaire historique et critique* (1695–97), a key influence on eighteenth-century French scepticism, also on S. and Byron.

Locke. John Locke (1632–1704), English philosopher and political theorist.

governments of Europe. Followed in the manuscript by a sentence S. subsequently brackets for exclusion, probably because he lifted it for use in the unfinished essay 'On Life', which he drafted in the back of this notebook at roughly the same time. The sentence reads: 'Philosophy went forth into the enchanted forest of the daemons of worldly power, as the pioneer of the overgrowth of ages.'

Berkeley and Hume and Hartley. George Berkeley, Bishop of Cloyne (1685–1755), David Hume (1711–76), and David Hartley (1705–57), English philosophers.

A crowd of writers in France. Preceded in the manuscript by a cancelled passage listing three philosophers, only the first of whom, Montesquieu, is French (the other two are the English philosophers Sidney and Harrington). Charles Louis de Secondat, Baron de la Brede et de Montesquieu (1689–1755) was the author of *L'Esprit des lois* (1748), the most influential political study of its time. Algernon Sidney (1622–83) was the author of the posthumously published *Discourses concerning Government* (1698), James Harrington (1611–77) of a comparably influential work of political theory, *The Commonwealth of Oceana* (1656).

641 *Bolingbroke.* Henry St John, Viscount Bolingbroke (1678–1751), Tory politician, political theorist, and friend of Pope, who versifies his ideas in *An Essay on Man* (1733–4).

642 *Utility.* The belief that society should be ordered to promote the 'happiness' of the greatest number of men, a view traced in Hume's *Enquiry concerning the Principles of Morals* (1751), Bentham's *Introduction to the Principles of Morals and Legislation* (1789), and Godwin's *Political Justice* (1793).

643 *These illustrious men.* The framers of the Constitution.

Court of Chancery. The institution which in March 1817 deprived S. of the care of his children, Ianthe and Charles, after the death of their mother, Harriet Westbrook Shelley.

644 *who have become*. S. appears to have missed out a word after 'become'; perhaps 'free' or 'freer'.

645 *their 'ills are interred with their bones'*. See *Julius Caesar*, 3. 2. 73: 'The good is oft interred with their bones.'

646 *at that period. [. . .].* We have here omitted several pages detailing the political histories of Germany, Spain, South America, Asia, India, and the Middle East.

Two nations. In 1819 there were two black nations in Haiti: an 'empire' in the north under Henri Cristophe and a 'republic' in the south under General Jean Pierre Boyer. The 'cautious measures' alluded to in the previous sentence were the Parliamentary acts of 1807 and 1811, the first abolishing the slave trade in British colonies (though not slavery itself), the second making slave-trading a felony; the phrase 'infection of the Spirit of Liberty' alludes to the efforts of Toussaint L'Ouverture (1743–1803), leader of the revolt of Haitian blacks, and other French West Indian revolutionaries.

since its last struggle for liberty. See the last paragraph of *A Defence of Poetry* for a revised version of this sentence; 'since its last struggle for liberty' means since the Renaissance and the religious turmoil which followed.

man and nature. We have omitted the following interpolated sentence (a later addition, crosswritten in darker ink) which Mary S. prints as a note: 'In this sense, Religion may be called Poetry, though distorted from the beautiful simplicity of its truth—Coleridge has said that every poet was religious, the converse, that every religious man must be a poet was more true—'.

of which it is the minister. 'It' refers to 'power' earlier in the sentence.

But although . . . their own soul. This sentence appears in the peroration to *A Defence of Poetry*, along with the more famous sentence beginning 'Poets and philosophers . . .', which appears twice in the paragraph in manuscript: in the sentence after next, and also as the final sentence of the paragraph (we include only the latter instance).

647 *On the Sentiment of the Necessity of Change*. This subtitle recalls point 2 from S.'s 'outline' at the beginning of the manuscript: '2nd. Practicability and Utility of such change.'

648 *The Parliament . . . of the people*. William and Mary were made sovereigns, 'with the acquiescence of a large part of the English public' (Reiman, *SC* 6. 998), by a 'Convention Parliament' that assembled on 22 January 1689, was declared a regular Parliament on 20 March 1689, and was not dissolved until October 1695; the 'Long Parliament', to which it is compared by S. in the next sentence, met from 3 November 1640 to late in 1648, when most of its members were expelled, leaving the

'Rump Parliament'. The Long Parliament was revived in 1659, after Cromwell's death, and dissolved itself to bring in new elections in a 'Convention Parliament'. This is the Parliament that recalled Charles II from Holland.

649 *the Commons.* 'In *The Black Book; or, Corruption Unmasked* (London, 1820), John Wade calculated (p. 423) that, of 658 members of the House of Commons, 300 were nominated by peers, 187 by rich commoners or by the government itself, and only 171 were returned by popular elections of any sort (many of which were also influenced by the same rich and powerful individuals)' (Reiman, *SC*, 6. 999).

650 *catchers of men.* See Luke 5: 10: 'from henceforth thou shalt catch men.'

public credit. The national debt came to prominence as an issue of public concern at the time of the chartering of the Bank of England in 1693, rose steadily over the next 125 years, and after Waterloo was calculated at '£885 million, with an annual interest of £32 million' (Reiman, *SC* 6. 1003).

651 *that they may rule by fraud [. . .].* We here omit several paragraphs on the history of public credit as a device of policy.

labour. [. . .]. At this point in the manuscript S. brackets the following passage, perhaps for use as a footnote: 'In a treatise devoted to general considerations it would be superfluous to enter into the *mode* in which this has been done; those who desire to see a full elucidation of that mode, may read Cobbett's *Paper Against Gold*. Our present business is with consequences. I would awaken, from a consideration that the present miseries of our country are nothing necessarily inherent of the stage of civilization at which we have arrived, foresight and hope.' William Cobbett's *Paper Against Gold* (1815, 2 vols.) reprints letters that had appeared in 1810–12 in the *Political Register*.

652 *There is something . . . merchant.* A bracketed sentence lower down on this page of the manuscript may be intended as a footnote to this sentence (or to follow it in the main text): 'As usual the first persons deceived are those who are the instruments of the fraud, and the merchant and the country gentleman may be excused for believing that their existence is connected with the permanence of the best practicable forms of social order.'

653 *amerced.* Punished by exacting an arbitrary fine.

poor-rates. Paid by working members of the community to support the poor, including widows, orphans, the aged, and the infirm. The Poor Laws were in effect from 1601. By 1819 they were under attack from merchants, industrialists, and urban taxpayers, in part because they were subject to abuse, in part because of pressures on the system caused by the rise of industrial cities (and resulting periods of mass unemployment) and an increase in the number of agricultural day-labourers (many of whom were often unemployed in the post-war period, after the return of foreign competition). In 1834 the Poor Laws were amended by

Parliament; the basic system was maintained but its administration was reformed and the conditions of the workhouses themselves were made as dehumanizing as possible, to encourage the poor to find employment.

655 *A writer of the present day . . . excess of population.* Thomas Robert Malthus (1736–1834), author of *An Essay on the Principles of Population* (1798), was an Anglican priest as well as an economist.

656 *please.* The following sentence in the manuscript is bracketed by S.: 'The rights of all men are intrinsically and originally equal and they forgo the assertion of all of them only that they may the more securely enjoy a portion.'

657 *The national debt . . . of the country.* See Godwin's *Political Justice*, book 5, ch. 16, for a similar analysis.

must be paid. These words are followed in the manuscript by an incomplete sentence bracketed by S., perhaps for use as a footnote: 'This sum cannot have amounted to less than two thousand millions; it would be a curious problem in political economy to calculate the precise degree of comfort and of ornament—'.

658 *persons of property.* These words are followed in the manuscript by a sentence bracketed by S., perhaps for use as a footnote: 'Such a gentleman must lose a third of his estate, such a citizen the fourth of his money in the funds; the persons who borrowed would have paid, and the juggling and complicated system of paper finance be suddenly at an end.'

former. 'latter' (i.e. the debtor) subsequent 'formers' and 'latters', and 'firsts' and 'seconds', are also confused; correct forms are given in square brackets.

660 *Lor[d Bacon].* The manuscript is blank here, and left so in Mary S.'s transcription; 'Lord Bacon' is Peck's editorial conjecture in the Julian edition of the *Complete Works* (1926–30), followed by *Clark*.

662 *argument [. . .].* The sentence is left incomplete in the manuscript.

then [. . .]. The sentence is left incomplete in the manuscript.

663 *[the people].* 'they' in the manuscript, those whose interests 'the advocates of universal suffrage' (at the beginning of the preceding paragraph) would advance.

Jesus Christ. This reading is preferred as more appropriate to the context than 'Moses', which in *SC* is described as a 'possible reading'.

a moral rather than political truth. This distinction was a familiar feature of contemporary political economy.

665 *voting by ballot.* S. means by secret ballot.

them. Motives.

vitality of [. . .]. S.'s sentence is incomplete in the manuscript.

666 *tempted, and betrayed.* By government spies and informers, presumably.

667 *triennial parliaments.* England had elected annual Parliaments (excepting numerous abridgements) from 1330 to 1676, when elections were made triennial; in 1715 Parliaments could be extended to seven years. S.'s proposal is to return to the middle position of triennial elections.

ulterior. Further (*OED* 1).

668 *16th of August.* Alludes to the Peterloo Massacre. See headnote to *Mask of Anarchy*.

670 *to examine [. . .].* S.'s sentence is incomplete in the manuscript.

manufacturers. Factory workers.

inhabitants of London [. . .]. S.'s sentence is incomplete in the manuscript.

'pernicious to one touch'. A quotation from *PL* 6. 520 describing the Devil's invention of cannon.

671 *Godwin and Hazlitt and Bentham and Hunt.* Byron's name is cancelled in the manuscript. S.'s list 'may simply have been an attempt to name eloquent spokesmen for four reformist viewpoints. Note the absence of William Cobbett, whom he feared at this time as an incendiary influence upon ignorant people' (Reiman, *SC* 6. 1060).

672 *the reigning family.* A reference to the Act of Settlement of 1701, which brought in the House of Hanover.

673 *question at issue [. . .].* S.'s sentence is incomplete in the manuscript.

674 *generous and [. . .].* S.'s sentence is incomplete in the manuscript.

A Defence of Poetry. Composed in February and March 1821. A press copy in the Bodleian (*BSM* 20) transcribed by Mary S., with corrections in S.'s hand, was sent by S. to Charles Ollier on 20 March 1821; this press copy supplies our copy-text, though we have also consulted S.'s intermediate fair copy (*BSM* 7) and his draft (*BSM* 4). S. had intended to publish the essay in Ollier's *Literary Miscellany*, the first number of which appeared in 1820, containing Thomas Love Peacock's 'The Four Ages of Poetry'. This witty attack on the poet as 'a semi-barbarian in a civilized community' and on poetry as merely 'the mental rattle that awakened the attention of intellect in the infancy of civil society' (quoted from *Brett-Smith*) 'excited' S., as he put it in a letter to Peacock, 'to a sacred rage' and desire to vindicate 'the insulted Muses' (*L* 2. 261). However, Ollier's *Miscellany* folded after one issue. Subsequent attempts after S.'s death to publish his essay came to nothing, until it appeared (minus the references to Peacock) in *MWS: Prose*. On the last blank page of the press copy (a home-made notebook), S. gives as the full title: *A Defence of Poetry. Or Remarks Suggested by an Essay Entitled 'The Four Ages of Poetry'. Part 1*. In the text he states that the 'second part' (never written) will address 'the present state of the cultivation of Poetry' (p. 700). S. draws on a range of sources, including Plato's *Ion*, which he had translated in 1819–21, and Sir Philip Sidney's *The Defence of Poesy* (1595) (hereafter *Defence*), and recycles material from his other prose writings (the peroration is taken, with some revision, from *A Philosophical View of Reform*). What is original about the essay is inseparable from its 'vitally metaphorical' (p. 676) eloquence. It is at once aesthetic treatise and prose poem. S. turns Peacock's utilitarian arguments on their head; nothing is more useful than poetry because poetry, defined in both a 'general' and a 'restricted' way (pp. 675, 700), is the ordering principle at work in human creativity. S. also suggests that poetry is not left behind by the advance of civilization; rather, it is 'The most unfailing herald, companion and follower of the awakening of a great people to work a beneficial change in opinion or institution' (pp. 700–1).

Reason and Imagination. See S.'s draft letter to Ollier in which he says that Peacock 'would extinguish Imagination, which is the Sun of life, & grope his way by the cold & uncertain & borrowed light of [*that which is called*] the Moon which he calls Reason' (*L* 2. 273).

τὸ ποιειν . . . τὸ λογιζειν. The Greek words, transliterated, are *poiein* (making) and *logizein* (reasoning). For *poiein*, see Sidney, *Defence*, when he points out that the word 'poet' 'cometh of this word *poiein*, which is, to make'.

675 *'the . . . Imagination'*. The phrase seems to be S.'s own.

connate. Born at the same time.

676 *vitally metaphorical*. See S.'s comment to Leigh Hunt, 'Strong passion expresses itself in metaphor borrowed from objects alike remote or near, and casts over all the shadow of its own greatness' (*L* 2. 108).

'the same . . . world'. S.'s footnote to this quotation refers to Francis Bacon, *De Dignitate et Augmentis Scientiarum* (1623), 3. 1. In English translation, Bacon says that the connections he has drawn between different branches of knowledge are not 'only similitudes' but 'the same footsteps of nature, treading or printing upon several subjects or matters'; quoted from *The Works of Francis Bacon*, ed. J. Spedding and D. D. Heath (7 vols., London, 1857–9).

677 *the chaos . . . poem*. The material from which a 'cyclic poem', or series of epics, is made; these epics are probably those written by the 'cyclic poets' who followed Homer (p. 682).

Poets . . . prophets. See Sidney, *Defence*: 'Among the Romans a poet was called *vates*, which is as much as a diviner, foreseer, or prophet.'

the Book of Job. See S.'s account in 'On Christianity' of the way in which 'The sublime dramatic poem entitled *Job*, had familiarized his [Christ's] imagination with the boldest imagery afforded by the human mind' (*Murray*, p. 249).

678 *hieroglyphic*. Symbol.

679 *Plato . . . poet*. See S.'s 'On the *Symposium*, or Preface to the *Banquet* of Plato', where he finds in Plato 'the rare union of close and subtle logic, with the Pythian enthusiasm of poetry' (text from *Notopoulos*, p. 402);

see, too, Sidney, *Defence*: 'of all philosophers he [Plato] is the most poetical.'

679 *Cicero.* Roman statesman and author (106–43 BC), famous for his eloquent speeches in law-courts and senate.

Lord Bacon . . . poet. S. keys the following footnote to 'poet': 'See the Filum Labyrinthi, and the Essay on Death particularly'. *Filum Labyrinthi* (1607) is a fragment in which Bacon, referring to himself in the third person, describes his empirical view of human knowledge. The essay *On Death* (1612) is a typical example of Bacon's memorably aphoristic style.

a story . . . poem. Sidney, *Defence*, argues that for Aristotle (*Poetics*, 9) 'poetry' 'is more philosophical . . . than history', since it 'dealeth with . . . the universal consideration' and history with 'the particular'.

680 *epitomes.* Summaries.

have been called . . . history. Alludes to Bacon, *The Advancement of Learning* (1605), 2: 'As for the corruptions and moths of history, which are Epitomes, the use of them deserveth to be banished.'

Herodotus. Greek historian (*c.*484–425 BC), known as 'the father of history' and author of the first Greek history in nine books.

Plutarch. Greek author (*c.*AD46–120) of the *Parallel Lives* of Roman and Greek figures.

Livy. Roman historian (*c.*59 BC–AD 17), author of a history of Rome in 142 books, 35 of which survive.

Poetry . . . pleasure. See Coleridge, *Biographia Literaria*, ch. 14, where he defines a poem as 'proposing for its immediate object pleasure, not truth'.

impanelled. Be enrolled (for a jury).

681 *planetary music.* See Sidney, *Defence*: 'the planet-like music of poetry'.

the immorality of poetry. S. probably has in mind Plato's objections to 'representational poetry', such as the view that 'It has a terrifying capacity for deforming even good people' (*Republic*, 605c).

682 *his own conceptions . . . wrong.* In his intermediate fair copy, S. pencilled the following comment: 'This was Mr Shelley's error in the Revolt of Islam [*Laon and Cythna*]. He has attempted to cure himself in subsequent publications but, except in the tragedy of the Cenci, with little success.'

many imperfections. Especially what S. in *A Discourse on the Manners of the Ancient Greeks* calls 'personal slavery and the inferiority of women' (*Clark*, p. 220).

683 *We know . . . events.* Derives from David Hume's scepticism about causation; see S.'s direct reference to Hume in this context in *A Refutation of Deism* (*Murray*, p. 121).

idealisms. Here, representations informed by an idea and an ideal.

comedy . . . ideal. Comedy should be in keeping with the main 'idea' of the tragedy.

trilogies. Respectively, *Antigone*, *Oedipus the King*, and *Oedipus at Colonus* by Sophocles (though not strictly a trilogy), and *Agamemnon*, *Libation Bearers*, and *Eumenides* by Aeschylus.

684 *Calderon . . . Autos.* See the note to *Letter to Maria Gisborne*, l. 181, p. 786.

Philoctetes. A play by Sophocles, whose hero, like Agamemnon and Othello, is a warrior; S.'s metaphor humorously casts his debate with Peacock as a chivalric joust.

sophisms. Clever but fallacious arguments.

Paladins. The twelve peers of Charlemagne, alluded to by Peacock in 'The Four Ages of Poetry' as among 'the heroes of the iron age of chivalrous poetry'.

necromancers. Practitioners of black magic.

685 *The drama . . . mirror.* See *Hamlet*, 3. 2. 19–20: 'the purpose of playing, whose end . . . was and is to hold as 'twere the mirror up to nature.'

Cato. Tragedy (1713) by Joseph Addison; criticized by Samuel Johnson in his *Preface to Shakespeare* as containing 'nothing that acquaints us with human sentiments or human actions'.

Poetry . . . unsheathed. See Byron, *Childe Harold*, 3. 97: 'With a most voiceless thought, sheathing it as a sword' and his 'So, we'll go no more a roving', l. 5: 'For the sword outwears the sheath'.

686 *Machiavelli.* Niccolò Machiavelli (1469–1527), Florentine writer, author of *The Prince*, to which S. probably alludes here.

bucolic writers. These include Theocritus, Bion, and Moschus (S. translated from the last two of these poets).

687 *torpid.* Benumbed.

Astraea. Mythological goddess of justice; in Ovid, *Met.* 1, the last of the gods to leave the earth ('Justice, virgin divine, | The last of the immortals fled away').

luxurious. Sensually indulgent and wealthy.

The sacred links . . . all. This image derives from Plato's *Ion* (see *Notopoulos*, p. 472).

688 *Ennius.* Considered the father of Latin literature (*c.*239–170 BC); author of an influential epic, *Annales*.

Varro. Latin writer (*c.*116–27 BC); author of a great variety of works, and renowned for his learning.

Pacuvius. Tragic poet (*c.*220–130 BC) and nephew of Ennius.

Accius. Tragic poet (b. 170 BC).

Camillus. Defended Rome against the Gauls in the fourth century BC.

688 *Regulus*. See note to 'Ode to Liberty', l. 98 (p. 781).

the senators . . . Gauls. When the Gauls entered Rome in 390 BC they were met by senators so calm in their demeanour that they might have been mistaken for 'statues in some holy place' (Livy, *The Early History of Rome*, trans. Aubrey de Selincourt (Harmondsworth, 1960)). S. does not mention the fact that all the senators 'were butchered where they sat'.

battle of Cannae. In 216 BC, when the Roman army was destroyed by Hannibal.

quia . . . sacro. 'because they lack a sacred poet' (Horace, *Odes*, 4. 9. 28).

rhapsodist. One who declaims the works of poets, such as Ion in Plato's dialogue (while Socrates is probably ironic about the rhapsodist's 'inspired' state, S. appears not to be).

Moses . . . Isaiah. See Sidney, *Defence*, when he lists 'the poetical part of the Scripture' as including 'David in his Psalms; Solomon in his Song of Songs, in his Ecclesiastes, and Proverbs; Moses and Deborah in their Hymns; and the writer of Job'.

689 *the three . . . mind*. Plato distinguished between 'a ruling immortal soul, seated in the brain; a higher mortal soul, seated in the heart; and a lower appetitive soul, also ruled by the immortal but directly commanded by the higher mortal soul' (*Brett-Smith*, p. 95).

Light . . . rouse. *Macbeth*, 3. 2. 51–4. For S.'s 'And night's', Shakespeare has 'Whiles night's'. S. is agreeing with Peacock's ironical account of 'the dark ages' as a time 'in which the light of the Gospel began to spread over Europe, and in which, by a mysterious and inscrutable dispensation, the darkness thickened with the progress of light'.

Celtic conquerors. S. uses 'Celtic' to mean northern European.

690 *The principle . . . among them*. See Plato, *Republic*, 369, a passage translated by S.

exoteric. Intelligible to all. See S.'s description of *The Mask of Anarchy* 'as of the exoteric species' (*L* 2. 152).

esoteric. Intended only for the initiated. See S.'s comment that *Epipsychidion* 'is to be published simply for the esoteric few' (*L* 2. 263).

'Galeotto . . . scrisse'. 'Galeotto was the book, and he who wrote it' (editors' trans), Dante, *Inf*. 5. 137. The allusion is to the book which catalysed the illicit love of Paolo and Francesca, and to the name of the character who acted as messenger between Lancelot and Guinevere.

Trouveurs. The Troubadours, lyric poets (between the eleventh and thirteeenth centuries), writing mainly of love.

Petrarch. Italian poet (1304–74), admired by S. for his 'tender & solemn enthusiasm' (*L* 2. 20).

691 *Divine Drama*. Dante's *Divine Comedy*.

Love . . . Plato. See Agathon's speech about love in the *Symposium* (*Notopoulos*, pp. 434–7).

Dante . . . 'justissimus unus' in Paradise. Refers to Dante, *Par*. 20. 67–9 ('Who would believe, down in the erring world, the Trojan Ripheus in this circle to be the fifth of the holy lights') and Virgil, *Aeneid*, 2. 426 ('foremost in justice among the Trojans').

692 *alleged design . . . new torments*. See *PL* 1. 209–20.

modern mythology. Christianity.

And Milton's . . . eternity of genius. Much of this material, with variations, is taken from S.'s 'On the Devil, and Devils' (for a text see *Webb*, pp. 185–6). The earlier essay is more outspoken in its antagonism to 'the popular creed' (*Webb*, p. 185).

Lucretius . . . sensible world. Alludes to Lucretius' interest in atomic materialism. S. rejects a vision of reality as consisting only of that which is 'sensible' (that is, perceptible by the senses).

Virgil . . . copied. See Peacock, 'The Four Ages of Poetry': 'The imitative consists in recasting, and giving an exquisite polish to, the poetry of the age of gold: of this Virgil is the most obvious and striking example.'

mock-birds. Mocking-birds, that is, birds that mimic the notes of other birds.

Apollonius Rhodius. Alexandrian epic poet (b. 295 BC), author of *Argonautica*, read by S. in August 1820.

Quintus Calaber Smyrnaeus. Quintus Smyrnaeus wrote *Posthomerica*, a continuation in Greek of Homer in fourteen books; he was known as 'Calaber' because the manuscript of *Posthomerica* was found in Calabria (*Norton*).

Nonnus. Member of an epic school founded in Upper Egypt in the fifth century BC; author of *Dionysiaca*, a Greek epic in forty-eight books, ordered by S. in 1817 (see *L* 1. 575, 585) and praised by Peacock in 'The Four Ages of Poetry' as containing 'many passages of exceeding beauty in the midst of masses of amplification and repetition'.

Lucan. See note to *Adonais*, l. 404 (p. 803).

Statius. Epic poet (AD 45–96), author of the *Thebaid*.

Claudian. Latin poet (*c*.AD 370–404), author of a mythological epic on the rape of Proserpine (*Norton*).

Orlando Furioso . . . Fairy Queen. Epics written, respectively, by the Italian poets Ariosto (1474–1533) and Tasso (1544–95), the Portuguese poet Camões (1525–80), and the English poet Spenser.

693 *Luther*. See note to 'Ode to Liberty', l. 141 (p. 782).

Dante . . . barbarisms. In *De Vulgari Eloquentia* Dante argued in favour of an Italian (rather than Latin) literary language.

Lucifer. 'Bearer of light'; Venus as the morning star; Satan's name before he fell. S. alludes to *PL* 5. 708–10: 'His countenance, as the morning star that guides | The starry flock, allured them, and with lies | Drew after him the third part of heaven's host.'

693 *instinct with spirit*. See *PL* 6. 752: 'Itself instinct with spirit'.

effluence. Flowing out.

The age . . . invention. See Sidney, *Defence*, where he argues that poets are 'fathers in learning', refers to 'the poets Dante, Boccacio, and Petrarch' as the first 'in the Italian language . . . that made it aspire to be a treasure-house of science', and claims for 'Gower and Chaucer' a comparable distinction.

mechanists. Not merely makers of machines, unlike the use of 'mechanist' a little later in the essay (see below), but also those whose view of usefulness is narrowly mechanical.

694 *some of the French writers*. S. appears to have in mind writers such as Helvetius and Condorcet, and to be quarrelling with their intransigent materialism.

mechanist. Machine-maker.

combines, labour. Oversees organization of labour.

'To him . . . away.' S. quotes imprecisely from Mark 4: 25: 'For he that hath, to him shall be given; and he that hath not, from him shall be taken even that which he hath.'

Scylla and Charybdis. Sea-monster and whirlpool in Greek mythology, so positioned in the Straits of Messina that to avoid one was to risk the other.

anarchy and despotism. See S.'s comment in August 1819: 'But the change should commence among the higher orders, or anarchy will be only the last flash before despotism' (*L* 2. 115).

'It . . . mirth'. S. quotes inexactly from Ecclesiastes 7: 2: 'It is better to go to the house of mourning, than to go to the house of feasting.'

695 *Rousseau*. S. keys the following footnote: 'I follow the classification adopted by the author of the Four Ages of Poetry. But Rousseau was essentially a poet. The others, even Voltaire, were mere reasoners.' In 'The Four Ages of Poetry' Peacock speaks of Hume, Gibbon, Rousseau, and Voltaire as 'four extraordinary minds' that shook 'every portion of the reign of authority'.

Inquisition in Spain. The Inquisition was suppressed in 1820.

'I dare . . . adage'. Quoted from *Macbeth*, 1. 7. 44–5.

696 *the curse . . . Adam*. See Genesis 3: 17–19, where Adam is cursed to 'eat bread' 'In the sweat of thy face'.

Mammon. See Matthew 6: 24 and Luke 16: 13: 'Ye cannot serve God and mammon.'

the centre . . . knowledge. See Wordsworth, Preface to *Lyrical Ballads*: 'Poetry is the breath and finer spirit of all knowledge.'

697 *intertexture*. Matter that is woven in.

'dictated . . . song'. See *PL* 9. 23–4, where the poet's 'celestial patroness' (l. 21) 'inspires | Easy my unpremeditated verse'.

It is . . . own. See S.'s translation of Plato's *Ion*: 'For the authors of those great poems which we admire do not attain to excellence through the rules of any art but they utter their beautiful melodies of verse in a state of inspiration and, as it were, *possessed* by a spirit not their own' (*Notopoulos*, p. 472).

698 *interlunations*. Periods between the appearance of the moon.

potable. Drinkable.

'The mind . . . Heaven'. S. quotes from *PL* 1. 254–5, which reads 'in itself', not, as S. has it, 'of itself'.

film of familiarity. See Coleridge's 'film of familiarity' in *Biographia Literaria*, ch. 14.

Tasso: 'Non merita . . . Poeta'. The quotation comes from Tasso's *Discorsi del poema eroico* (S. may have met it in Pietro Serassi, *La vita di Torquato Tasso* (1785)) and translates as 'None merits the name of creator except God and the poet'.

699 *'there . . . soar'*. Adapted from *PL* 4. 829–30.

Homer . . . laureate. In S.'s ironic catalogue of poets' supposed moral failings, Homer might be described as a 'drunkard' because in the *Ion* poets are said to become 'like the Bacchantes' (S.'s translation, *Notopoulos*, p. 472); Virgil as a 'flatterer' because of his deference to the Emperor Augustus; Horace as a 'coward' because of his account of his retreat from the battle of Philippi (*Odes*, 2. 7); Tasso as a 'madman' because of his mental problems and imprisonment (see headnote to *Julian and Maddalo*, p. 741); Bacon as a 'peculator' (or embezzler) because he was convicted of receiving gifts from suitors in the court of Chancery; Raphael as a 'libertine' because of some remarks in Vasari's *Lives*; and Spenser as a 'poet laureate' because in *FQ* he extolled the virtues of Queen Elizabeth I.

Their errors . . . judged. Various biblical references occur here: they include Daniel 5: 27: 'Thou art weighed in the balances, and art found wanting'; Isaiah 1: 18: 'though your sins be as scarlet, they shall be as white as snow'; Revelation 7: 14: 'washed their robes, and made them white in the blood of the Lamb'; and Matthew 7: 1: 'Judge not, that ye be not judged.'

700 *obnoxious*. Liable.

Theseids . . . Codri. Juvenal (*Satires*, 1) refers to his being 'so often bored by the Theseid of the ranting Cordus'.

Bavius and Maevius. Types of the bad poet in Virgil, *Eclogues*, 3. 90: 'Maevius, I hope that anyone who can put up with Bavius's verse may fall for yours.'

700 *low-thoughted envy*. See Milton, *Comus*, l. 6: 'low-thoughted care'.

701 *hierophants*. Initiating priests; expounders of sacred mysteries. S. wrote 'priests' in the version of this passage in *A Philosophical View of Reform*.

Poets . . . World. In *A Philosophical View of Reform* S. wrote 'Poets and philosophers' (p. 647). In Samuel Johnson's *Rasselas* Imlac asserts that the poet 'must write as the interpreter of nature, and the legislator of mankind'.

FURTHER READING

Where an abbreviated title is used in the Notes, it is repeated here; see the head of the Notes for a full list of abbreviations.

EDITIONS

Stephen C. Behrendt (ed.), *Zastrozzi and St. Irvyne* (Oxford, 1986).

Betty T. Bennett (ed.), *The Letters of Mary Wollstonecraft Shelley* (3 vols., Baltimore, 1980–8) [*MWSL*].

H. F. B. Brett-Smith (ed.), *Peacock's Four Ages of Poetry, Shelley's Defence of Poetry and Browning's Essay on Shelley* (Oxford, 1921) [*Brett-Smith*].

P. H. Butter (ed.), *Percy Bysshe Shelley: Alastor and Other Poems; Prometheus Unbound with Other Poems; Adonais* (London, 1970) [*Butter*].

Kenneth Neill Cameron and Donald H. Reiman (eds.), *Shelley and His Circle 1773–1822* (Cambridge, Mass., 1961– ; 10 vols. to date) [*SC*]. Contains important critical and biographical essays.

Judith Chernaik, *The Lyrics of Shelley* (Cleveland and London, 1972) [*Chernaik*]. Contains newly edited texts of shorter poems by Shelley as well as critical commentary.

David Lee Clark (ed.), *Shelley's Prose; Or, The Trumpet of a Prophecy* (corr. edn., Albuquerque, N. Mex., 1966) [*Clark*].

Kelvin Everest and G. M. Matthews (eds.), *The Poems of Shelley, 1804–1819* (2 vols. to date, Harlow, 1989, 2000) [*Longman* 1 and 2].

Paula R. Feldman and Diana Scott-Kilvert (eds.), *The Journals of Mary Shelley 1814–1844* (2 vols., Oxford, 1987) [*Mary Jnl.*].

H. Buxton Forman (ed.), *The Poetical Works of Percy Bysshe Shelley* (2nd edn., 2 vols., London, 1886).

Thomas Hutchinson (ed.), G. M. Matthews (corr.), *Shelley: Poetical Works* (London, 1970).

Roger Ingpen and Walter E. Peck (eds.), *The Complete Works of Percy Bysshe Shelley* (10 vols., London, 1926–30).

Frederick L. Jones (ed.), *The Letters of Percy Bysshe Shelley* (2 vols., Oxford, 1964) [*L*].

C. D. Locock (ed.), *The Poems of Percy Bysshe Shelley* (2 vols., London, 1912) [*Locock*].

E. B. Murray (ed.), *The Prose Works of Percy Bysshe Shelley, Volume One* (Oxford, 1993) [*Murray*].

James A. Notopoulos, *The Platonism of Shelley: A Study of Platonism and the Poetic Mind* (Durham, NC, 1949) [*Notopoulos*]. Contains texts of Shelley's translations from Plato as well as commentary.

Donald H. Reiman (gen. ed.), *Manuscripts of the Younger Romantics: Shelley* (9 vols., 1985–97) [*MYR: Shelley*].

Donald H. Reiman (gen. ed.), *The Bodleian Shelley Manuscripts* (23 vols., New York, 1986–2001) [*BSM*].

—— and Neil Fraistat (eds.), *The Complete Poetry of Percy Bysshe Shelley* (1 vol. to date, Baltimore, 2000).

—— and Sharon B. Powers (eds.), *Shelley's Poetry and Prose*, Norton Critical Edition (New York, 1977) [*Norton*].

—— and Neil Fraistat (eds.), *Shelley's Poetry and Prose*, Norton Critical Edition, 2nd edition (New York, 2002) [*Norton*[2]].

Francesco Rognoni (ed.), *Shelley: Opere* (Turin, 1995) [*Rognoni*].

William Michael Rossetti (ed.), *The Poetical Works of Percy Bysshe Shelley* (2 vols., London, 1870) [*Rossetti*].

Mary Wollstonecraft Shelley (ed.), *Posthumous Poems of Percy Bysshe Shelley* (London, 1824) [*PP*].

—— (ed.), *The Poetical Works of Percy Bysshe Shelley* (4 vols., London, 1839) [*MWS (1)*].

—— (ed.), *The Poetical Works of Percy Bysshe Shelley* (1 vol., London, 1839) [*MWS (2)*].

—— (ed.), *Essays, Letters from Abroad, Translations and Fragments by Percy Bysshe Shelley* (2 vols., London, 1840 [1839]) [*MWS: Prose*].

Timothy Webb (ed.), *Percy Bysshe Shelley: Poems and Prose*, with a critical selection by George E. Donaldson (London, 1995) [*Webb*].

BIOGRAPHY, REFERENCE, AND 'LITERARY LIVES'

B. C. Barker-Benfield, *Shelley's Guitar* (Oxford, 1992).

Edmund Blunden, *Shelley: A Life Story* (1946; repr. London, 1965).

Kenneth Neill Cameron, *The Young Shelley: Genesis of a Radical* (New York, 1950).

—— *Shelley: The Golden Years* (Cambridge, Mass., 1974).

Richard Holmes, *Shelley: The Pursuit* (London, 1974).

Sylva Norman, *Flight of the Skylark: The Development of Shelley's Reputation* (London, 1954).

Michael O'Neill, *Percy Bysshe Shelley: A Literary Life* (Basingstoke, 1989).

—— 'Shelley', forthcoming in *New Dictionary of National Biography* (Oxford, 2004).

Donald H. Reiman, *Percy Bysshe Shelley: Updated Edition* (Boston, 1990).

Norman Ivey White, *Shelley* (2 vols., London, 1947).

Humbert Wolfe (intro.), *The Life of Percy Bysshe Shelley, as Comprised in 'The Life of Shelley' by Thomas Jefferson Hogg, 'The Recollections of Shelley and Byron' by Edward John Trelawny, 'Memoirs of Shelley' by Thomas Love Peacock* (London, 1933).

CRITICISM

Stephen C. Behrendt, *Shelley and His Audiences* (Lincoln, Nebr., 1989).

G. Kim Blank (ed.), *The New Shelley: Later Twentieth-Century Views* (Basingstoke, 1991).

Harold Bloom, *Shelley's Mythmaking* (Ithaca, NY, 1959).

Teddi Chichester Bonca, *Shelley's Mirrors of Love: Narcissism, Sacrifice, and Sorority* (Albany, NY, 1999) [*Bonca*].

Timothy Clark, *Embodying Revolution: The Figure of the Poet in Shelley* (Oxford, 1989).

Timothy Clark and Jerrold E. Hogle (eds.), *Evaluating Shelley* (Edinburgh, 1996).

Richard Cronin, *Shelley's Poetic Thoughts* (London, 1981).

Stuart Curran, *Shelley's Annus Mirabilis: The Maturing of an Epic Vision* (San Marino, Calif., 1975).

P. M. S. Dawson, *The Unacknowledged Legislator: Shelley and Politics* (Oxford, 1980).

David Duff, *Romance and Revolution: Shelley and the Politics of a Genre* (Cambridge, 1994).

Kelvin Everest (ed.), *Shelley Revalued: Essays from the Gregynog Conference* (Leicester, 1983).

—— (ed.), *Percy Bysshe Shelley: Bicentenary Essays: Essays and Studies 1992* (Cambridge, 1992).

Michael Ferber, *The Poetry of Shelley* (Harmondsworth, 1993).

Barbara Charlesworth Gelpi, *Shelley's Goddess: Maternity, Language, Subjectivity* (New York, 1992).

Paul Hamilton, *Percy Bysshe Shelley* (Tavistock, 2000).

Jerrold E. Hogle, *Shelley's Process: Radical Transference and the Development of His Major Works* (New York, 1988).

Steven E. Jones, *Shelley's Satire: Violence, Exhortation, and Authority* (DeKalb, Ill., 1994).

William Keach, *Shelley's Style* (New York, 1984).

Angela Leighton, *Shelley and the Sublime: An Interpretation of the Major Poems* (Cambridge, 1984).

Timothy Morton, *Shelley and the Revolution in Taste: The Body and the Natural World* (Cambridge, 1994).

Michael O'Neill, *The Human Mind's Imaginings: Conflict and Achievement in Shelley's Poetry* (Oxford, 1989).

—— (ed.), *Shelley*, Longman Critical Readers (London, 1993).

—— *Romanticism and the Self-Conscious Poem* (Oxford, 1997).

C. E. Pulos, *The Deep Truth: A Study of Shelley's Scepticism* (Lincoln, Nebr., 1954).

Tilottama Rajan, *Dark Interpreter: The Discourse of Romanticism* (Ithaca, NY, 1980).

Hugh Roberts, *Shelley and the Chaos of History: A New Politics of Poetry* (University Park, Pa. 1997).

Bryan Shelley, *Shelley and Scripture: The Interpreting Angel* (Oxford, 1994).

Stuart M. Sperry, *Shelley's Major Verse: The Narrative and Dramatic Poetry* (Cambridge, Mass., 1988) [*Sperry*].

Patrick Swinden (ed.), *Shelley: Shorter Poems and Lyrics, A Casebook* (London, 1976).

Ronald Tetreault, *The Poetry of Life: Shelley and Literary Form* (Toronto, 1987).

William A. Ulmer, *Shelleyan Eros: The Rhetoric of Romantic Love* (Princeton, 1990).

Earl R. Wasserman, *Shelley: A Critical Reading* (Baltimore, 1971).

Timothy Webb, *The Violet in the Crucible: Shelley and Translation* (Oxford, 1976).

—— *Shelley: A Voice Not Understood* (Manchester, 1977).

Alan M. Weinberg, *Shelley's Italian Experience* (Basingstoke, 1991).

Susan J. Wolfson, *Formal Charges: The Shaping of Poetry in British Romanticism* (Stanford, Calif., 1997).

ORDERING OF POEMS IN VOLUMES PUBLISHED BY SHELLEY FROM 1816 TO 1822

(This list excludes volumes publishing only one poem and lists some poems not included in this selection.)

Alastor . . . and Other Poems *(1816)*

Alastor; or, the Spirit of Solitude
'O! there are spirits of the air'
Stanzas.—April, 1814
Mutability
'The pale, the cold, and the moony smile'
A Summer-Evening Churchyard
To Wordsworth
Feelings of a Republican on the Fall of Bonaparte
Superstition
Sonnet. From the Italian of Dante
Translated from the Greek of Moschus
The Daemon of the World

Rosalind and Helen: A Modern Eclogue; with Other Poems *(1819)*

Rosalind and Helen
Lines Written among the Euganean Hills
Hymn to Intellectual Beauty
Ozymandias

Prometheus Unbound . . . with Other Poems *(1820)*

Prometheus Unbound
The Sensitive Plant
A Vision of the Sea
Ode to Heaven
An Exhortation
Ode to the West Wind
An Ode, Written, October, 1819, before the Spaniards Had
Recovered Their Liberty
The Cloud
To a Skylark
Ode to Liberty

Hellas *(1822)*

INDEX OF TITLES OF POEMS AND PROSE WORKS

INDEX OF FIRST LINES OF POEMS

MORE ABOUT **OXFORD WORLD'S CLASSICS**

American Literature

British and Irish Literature

Children's Literature

Classics and Ancient Literature

Colonial Literature

Eastern Literature

European Literature

Gothic Literature

History

Medieval Literature

Oxford English Drama

Poetry

Philosophy

Politics

Religion

The Oxford Shakespeare

A SELECTION OF OXFORD WORLD'S CLASSICS

JANE AUSTEN	**Emma** **Mansfield Park** **Persuasion** **Pride and Prejudice** **Sense and Sensibility**
MRS BEETON	**Book of Household Management**
LADY ELIZABETH BRADDON	**Lady Audley's Secret**
ANNE BRONTË	**The Tenant of Wildfell Hall**
CHARLOTTE BRONTË	**Jane Eyre** **Shirley** **Villette**
EMILY BRONTË	**Wuthering Heights**
SAMUEL TAYLOR COLERIDGE	**The Major Works**
WILKIE COLLINS	**The Moonstone** **No Name** **The Woman in White**
CHARLES DARWIN	**The Origin of Species**
CHARLES DICKENS	**The Adventures of Oliver Twist** **Bleak House** **David Copperfield** **Great Expectations** **Nicholas Nickleby** **The Old Curiosity Shop** **Our Mutual Friend** **The Pickwick Papers** **A Tale of Two Cities**
GEORGE DU MAURIER	**Trilby**
MARIA EDGEWORTH	**Castle Rackrent**

A SELECTION OF OXFORD WORLD'S CLASSICS

George Eliot	Daniel Deronda The Lifted Veil and Brother Jacob Middlemarch The Mill on the Floss Silas Marner
Susan Ferrier	Marriage
Elizabeth Gaskell	Cranford The Life of Charlotte Brontë Mary Barton North and South Wives and Daughters
George Gissing	New Grub Street The Odd Woman
Thomas Hardy	Far from the Madding Crowd Jude the Obscure The Mayor of Casterbridge The Return of the Native Tess of the d'Urbervilles The Woodlanders
William Hazlitt	Selected Writings
James Hogg	The Private Memoirs and Confessions of a Justified Sinner
John Keats	The Major Works Selected Letters
Charles Maturin	Melmoth the Wanderer
Walter Scott	The Antiquary Ivanhoe Rob Roy
Mary Shelley	Frankenstein The Last Man

A SELECTION OF OXFORD WORLD'S CLASSICS

Robert Louis Stevenson	Kidnapped and Catriona The Strange Case of Dr Jekyll and Mr Hyde and Weir of Hermiston Treasure Island
Bram Stoker	Dracula
William Makepeace Thackeray	Vanity Fair
Oscar Wilde	Complete Shorter Fiction The Major Works The Picture of Dorian Gray
Dorothy Wordsworth	The Grasmere and Alfoxden Journals
William Wordsworth	The Major Works

TROLLOPE IN OXFORD WORLD'S CLASSICS

ANTHONY TROLLOPE

An Autobiography
The American Senator
Barchester Towers
Can You Forgive Her?
The Claverings
Cousin Henry
Doctor Thorne
The Duke's Children
The Eustace Diamonds
Framley Parsonage
He Knew He Was Right
Lady Anna
The Last Chronicle of Barset
Orley Farm
Phineas Finn
Phineas Redux
The Prime Minister
Rachel Ray
The Small House at Allington
The Warden
The Way We Live Now

A SELECTION OF **OXFORD WORLD'S CLASSICS**

HANS CHRISTIAN ANDERSEN	**Fairy Tales**
J. M. BARRIE	**Peter Pan in Kensington Gardens** and **Peter and Wendy**
L. FRANK BAUM	**The Wonderful Wizard of Oz**
FRANCES HODGSON BURNETT	**The Secret Garden**
LEWIS CARROLL	**Alice's Adventures in Wonderland** and **Through the Looking-Glass**
CARLO COLLODI	**The Adventures of Pinocchio**
KENNETH GRAHAME	**The Wind in the Willows**
ANTHONY HOPE	**The Prisoner of Zenda**
THOMAS HUGHES	**Tom Brown's Schooldays**